Who's Who in the South and Southwest®

Published by Marquis Who's Who®

Titles in Print

Who's Who in America®
Who's Who in America Junior & Senior High School Version
Who Was Who in America®
  Historical Volume (1607–1896)
  Volume I (1897–1942)
  Volume II (1943–1950)
  Volume III (1951–1960)
  Volume IV (1961–1968)
  Volume V (1969–1973)
  Volume VI (1974–1976)
  Volume VII (1977–1981)
  Volume VIII (1982–1985)
  Volume IX (1985–1989)
  Volume X (1989–1993)
  Volume XI (1993–1996)
  Index Volume (1607–1996)
Who's Who in the World®
Who's Who in the East®
Who's Who in the Midwest®
Who's Who in the South and Southwest®
Who's Who in the West®
Who's Who in American Art™
Who's Who in American Education®
Who's Who in American Law®
Who's Who in American Nursing®
Who's Who in American Politics™
Who's Who in Entertainment®
Who's Who in Finance and Industry®
Who's Who in Medicine and Healthcare™
Who's Who in Religion®
Who's Who in Science and Engineering®
Who's Who in the Media and Communications™
Who's Who of American Women®
Who's Who of Emerging Leaders in America®
Index to Marquis Who's Who® Publications
The *Official* ABMS Directory of Board Certified Medical Specialists®

Available on CD-ROM

The Complete Marquis Who's Who® on CD-ROM
ABMS Medical Specialists *PLUS*™

Who's Who in the South and Southwest®

1997~1998

Including Alabama, Arkansas, Florida, Georgia, Kentucky, Louisiana, Mississippi, North Carolina, Oklahoma, South Carolina, Tennessee, Texas, Virginia, West Virginia, Puerto Rico, the Virgin Islands, and Mexico.

121 Chanlon Road
New Providence, NJ 07974 U.S.A.

Who's Who in the South and Southwest®

Marquis Who's Who®

Published by Marquis Who's Who, a division of Reed Elsevier Inc.

Library of Congress Catalog Card Number 50-58231
International Standard Book Number 0-8379-0827-2 (Classic Edition)
0-8379-0828-0 (Deluxe Edition)
International Standard Serial Number 0083-9809

Manufactured in the United States of America

Table of Contents

Preface vi

Board of Advisors vii

Standards of Admission viii

Key to Information ix

Table of Abbreviations x

Alphabetical Practices xvii

***Who's Who in the South and Southwest* Biographies** 1

Professional Area Index 1037
- Agriculture 1037
- Architecture and Design 1037
- Arts
  - Literary 1038
  - Performing 1040
  - Visual 1042
- Associations and Organizations 1044
- Athletics 1046
- Communications Media 1047
- Education 1050
- Engineering 1060
- Finance
  - Banking Services 1065
  - Financial Services 1066
  - Insurance 1069
  - Investment Services 1070
  - Real Estate 1072
- Government
  - Agency Administration 1073
  - Executive Administration 1075
  - Legislative Administration 1076
- Healthcare
  - Dentistry 1077
  - Health Services 1078
  - Medicine 1087
- Humanities
  - Liberal Studies 1094
  - Libraries 1098
  - Museums 1100
- Industry
  - Manufacturing 1101
  - Service 1105
  - Trade 1112
  - Transportation 1113
  - Utilities, Energy, Resources 1114
- Law
  - Judicial Administration 1116
  - Law Practice and Administration 1117
- Military 1124
- Religion 1125
- Science
  - Life Science 1128
  - Mathematics and Computer Science 1131
  - Physical Science 1133
- Social Science 1135

Preface

The Silver 25th Edition of *Who's Who in the South and Southwest* is our most recent compilation of biographical information on men and women of distinction whose influence is concentrated in the southern and southwestern sectors of North America. Such individuals are of reference interest regionally, and to an increasing degree, nationally.

The volume contains approximately 24,000 names from the region embracing Alabama, Arkansas, Florida, Georgia, Kentucky, Louisiana, Mississippi, North Carolina, Oklahoma, South Carolina, Tennessee, Texas, Virginia, West Virginia, Puerto Rico, and the Virgin Islands. Because of its importance and its contiguity to the southwestern United States, Mexico is also covered in this volume. In some instances, persons who do not reside in the southern or southwestern region of the U.S. have also been included as Biographees. They appear in this edition because they have made significant professional or civic contributions to the South and Southwest. Reviewed and revised, the Silver 25th Edition offers current coverage of a broad range of individuals based on position or individual achievement.

The persons sketched in this volume represent virtually every important field of endeavor. Included are executives and officials in government, business, education, medicine, religion, the press, law, and other fields. This edition also includes significant contributors in such areas as contemporary art, music, and science.

In most cases, Biographees have furnished their own data, thus ensuring a high degree of accuracy. In some cases where individuals failed to supply information, Marquis staff members compiled the data through careful, independent research. Sketches compiled in this manner are denoted by an asterisk. As in previous editions, Biographees were given the opportunity to review prepublication proofs of their sketches to make sure they were correct.

The question is often asked, "How do people get into a Marquis Who's Who volume?" Name selection is based on one fundamental principle: reference value. Biographees of *Who's Who in the South and Southwest* can be classified in two basic categories: (1) Persons who are of regional reference importance to colleagues, librarians, researchers, scholars, the media, historians, biographers, participants in business and civic affairs, and others with specific or general inquiry needs; (2) individuals of national reference interest who are also of such regional or local importance that their inclusion in the book is essential.

In the editorial evaluation that resulted in the ultimate selection of the names appearing in this directory, an individual's desire to be listed was not sufficient reason for inclusion; rather it was the person's achievement that ruled. Similarly, neither wealth nor social position was a criterion; only occupational stature or achievement in a field within the southern or southwestern region of North America determined selection.

Also included in the Silver 25th Edition is a Professional Index, which groups Biographees professionally, and within profession, geographically. This reference tool will make it easy for interested readers to find Biographees in any given profession or region.

Marquis Who's Who editors exercise the utmost care in preparing each biographical sketch for publication; occasionally, however, errors occur. Users of this directory are requested to draw the attention of the publisher to any errors found so that corrections can be made in a subsequent edition.

The Silver 25th Edition of *Who's Who in the South and Southwest* carries on the tradition of excellence established in 1899 with the publication of the first edition of *Who's Who in America.* The essence of that tradition is reflected in our continuing effort to produce reference works that are responsive to the needs of their users.

Board of Advisors

Marquis Who's Who gratefully acknowledges the following distinguished individuals who have made themselves available for review, evaluation, and general comment with regard to the publication of the Silver 25th Edition of *Who's Who in the South and Southwest.* The advisors have enhanced the reference value of this edition by the nomination of outstanding individuals for inclusion. However, the Board of Advisors, either collectively or individually, is in no way responsible for the final selection of names appearing in this volume, nor does the Board of Advisors bear responsibility for the accuracy or comprehensiveness of the biographical information or other material contained herein.

Hector L. Acevedo
Mayor
San Juan, Puerto Rico

Edward J. Boling
President Emeritus and University Professor
The University of Tennessee
Knoxville, Tennessee

J. Douglas Donehue
Vice President Corporate Communications
The Evening Post Publishing Company
Charleston, South Carolina

Meredith Emmett
Executive Director
North Carolina Community Shares
Durham, North Carolina

Joseph M. Jadlow
Secretary-Treasurer
Southern Economic Association
Stillwater, Oklahoma

Joseph D. Jamail
Partner
Jamail & Kolius
Houston, Texas

Joseph B. Johnson
President
Talladega College
Talladega, Alabama

Standards of Admission

The foremost consideration in selecting Biographees for *Who's Who in the South and Southwest* is the extent of an individual's reference interest. Such reference interest is judged on either of two factors: (1) the position of responsibility held, or (2) the level of achievement attained by the individual.

Admissions based on the factor of position include:

Members of the U.S. Congress

Federal judges

Governors of states covered by this volume

State attorneys general

Judges of state and territorial courts of highest appellate jurisdiction

Mayors of major cities

Heads of major universities and colleges

Heads of leading philanthropic, educational, cultural, and scientific institutions and associations

Chief ecclesiastics of the principal religious denominations

Principal officers of national and international business

Admission for individual achievement is based on qualitative criteria. To be selected, a person must have attained conspicuous achievement.

Key to Information

[1] ASHTON, HARDY AMES, [2] lawyer; **[3]** b. Topeka, Aug. 3, 1944; **[4]** s. Samuel Taylor and Barbara (Hanson) A.; **[5]** m. Nancy Richardson, June 20, 1965; **[6]** children: Marilyn Ashton Heim, Barbara Anne, William Marc. **[7]** BA, Pa. State U., 1965; JD, Syracuse U., 1970. **[8]** Bar: Ark. 1970, U.S. Supreme Ct. 1978. **[9]** Assoc. Prine, Belden and Coates, Little Rock, Ark., 1970-77; mem. Johnson, Sikes and Bord, Little Rock, 1977—, ptnr., 1979-84, sr. ptnr., 1984-94, of counsel, 1994—; **[10]** legal cons. Little Rock Urban League. **[11]** Author: Urban Renewal and the Law, 1975; contbr. articles to profl. jours. **[12]** Commr. Monroe County Park Dist., 1981-88; mem. planning com. Crossroads Redevel. Project, Little Rock, 1990—; bd. dirs. Hargrave Inst. **[13]** Served with U.S. Army, 1966-67. **[14]** Named Man of the Yr., Little Rock C. of C., 1986. **[15]** Mem. ABA, Ark. Bar Assn., Little Rock Bar Assn., Am. Judicature Soc., Order of Coif., Little Rock Country, Tuesday Luncheon, Lions. **[16]** Democrat. **[17]** Episcopalian. **[18]** Home 3080 Grant St Little Rock AR 72216 **[19]** Office: Johnson Sikes & Bord 10 Saint Paul St Little Rock AR 72201

KEY

[1] Name
[2] Occupation
[3] Vital statistics
[4] Parents
[5] Marriage
[6] Children
[7] Education
[8] Professional certifications
[9] Career
[10] Career-related
[11] Writings and creative works
[12] Civic and political activities
[13] Military
[14] Awards and fellowships
[15] Professional and association memberships, clubs and lodges
[16] Political affiliation
[17] Religion
[18] Home address
[19] Office address

Table of Abbreviations

The following abbreviations and symbols are frequently used in this book.

*An asterisk following a sketch indicates that it was researched by the Marquis Who's Who editorial staff and has not been verified by the Biographee.
A Associate (used with academic degrees only)
AA, A.A. Associate in Arts, Associate of Arts
AAAL American Academy of Arts and Letters
AAAS American Association for the Advancement of Science
AACD American Association for Counseling and Development
AACN American Association of Critical Care Nurses
AAHA American Academy of Health Administrators
AAHP American Association of Hospital Planners
AAHPERD American Alliance for Health, Physical Education, Recreation, and Dance
AAS Associate of Applied Science
AASL American Association of School Librarians
AASPA American Association of School Personnel Administrators
AAU Amateur Athletic Union
AAUP American Association of University Professors
AAUW American Association of University Women
AB, A.B. Arts, Bachelor of
AB Alberta
ABA American Bar Association
ABC American Broadcasting Company
AC Air Corps
acad. academy, academic
acct. accountant
acctg. accounting
ACDA Arms Control and Disarmament Agency
ACHA American College of Hospital Administrators
ACLS Advanced Cardiac Life Support
ACLU American Civil Liberties Union
ACOG American College of Ob-Gyn
ACP American College of Physicians
ACS American College of Surgeons
ADA American Dental Association
a.d.c. aide-de-camp
adj. adjunct, adjutant
adj. gen. adjutant general
adm. admiral
adminstr. administrator
adminstrn. administration
adminstrv. administrative
ADN Associate's Degree in Nursing
ADP Automatic Data Processing
adv. advocate, advisory
advt. advertising
AE, A.E. Agricultural Engineer
A.E. and P. Ambassador Extraordinary and Plenipotentiary
AEC Atomic Energy Commission
aero. aeronautical, aeronautic
aerodyn. aerodynamic
AFB Air Force Base
AFL-CIO American Federation of Labor and Congress of Industrial Organizations
AFTRA American Federation of TV and Radio Artists
AFSCME American Federation of State, County and Municipal Employees
agr. agriculture
agrl. agricultural
agt. agent
AGVA American Guild of Variety Artists
agy. agency
A&I Agricultural and Industrial
AIA American Institute of Architects
AIAA American Institute of Aeronautics and Astronautics
AIChE American Institute of Chemical Engineers
AICPA American Institute of Certified Public Accountants
AID Agency for International Development
AIDS Acquired Immune Deficiency Syndrome
AIEE American Institute of Electrical Engineers
AIM American Institute of Management
AIME American Institute of Mining, Metallurgy, and Petroleum Engineers
AK Alaska
AL Alabama
ALA American Library Association
Ala. Alabama
alt. alternate
Alta. Alberta
A&M Agricultural and Mechanical
AM, A.M. Arts, Master of
Am. American, America
AMA American Medical Association
amb. ambassador
A.M.E. African Methodist Episcopal
Amtrak National Railroad Passenger Corporation
AMVETS American Veterans of World War II, Korea, Vietnam
ANA American Nurses Association
anat. anatomical
ANCC American Nurses Credentialing Center
ann. annual
ANTA American National Theatre and Academy
anthrop. anthropological
AP Associated Press
APA American Psychological Association
APGA American Personnel Guidance Association
APHA American Public Health Association
APO Army Post Office
apptd. appointed
Apr. April
apt. apartment
AR Arkansas
ARC American Red Cross
arch. architect
archeol. archeological
archtl. architectural
Ariz. Arizona
Ark. Arkansas
ArtsD, ArtsD. Arts, Doctor of
arty. artillery
AS American Samoa
AS Associate in Science
ASCAP American Society of Composers, Authors and Publishers
ASCD Association for Supervision and Curriculum Development
ASCE American Society of Civil Engineers
ASHRAE American Society of Heating, Refrigeration, and Air Conditioning Engineers
ASME American Society of Mechanical Engineers
ASNSA American Society for Nursing Service Administrators
ASPA American Society for Public Administration
ASPCA American Society for the Prevention of Cruelty to Animals
assn. association
assoc. associate
asst. assistant
ASTD American Society for Training and Development
ASTM American Society for Testing and Materials
astron. astronomical
astrophys. astrophysical
ATLA Association of Trial Lawyers of America
ATSC Air Technical Service Command
AT&T American Telephone & Telegraph Company
atty. attorney
Aug. August
AUS Army of the United States
aux. auxiliary
Ave. Avenue
AVMA American Veterinary Medical Association
AZ Arizona
AWHONN Association of Women's Health Obstetric and Neonatal Nurses

B. Bachelor
b. born
BA, B.A. Bachelor of Arts
BAgr, B.Agr. Bachelor of Agriculture
Balt. Baltimore
Bapt. Baptist
BArch, B.Arch. Bachelor of Architecture
BAS, B.A.S. Bachelor of Agricultural Science
BBA, B.B.A. Bachelor of Business Administration
BBB Better Business Bureau
BBC British Broadcasting Corporation

BC, B.C. British Columbia
BCE, B.C.E. Bachelor of Civil Engineering
BChir, B.Chir. Bachelor of Surgery
BCL, B.C.L. Bachelor of Civil Law
BCLS Basic Cardiac Life Support
BCS, B.C.S. Bachelor of Commercial Science
BD, B.D. Bachelor of Divinity
bd. board
BE, B.E. Bachelor of Education
BEE, B.E.E. Bachelor of Electrical Engineering
BFA, B.F.A. Bachelor of Fine Arts
bibl. biblical
bibliog. bibliographical
biog. biographical
biol. biological
BJ, B.J. Bachelor of Journalism
Bklyn. Brooklyn
BL, B.L. Bachelor of Letters
bldg. building
BLS, B.L.S. Bachelor of Library Science
BLS Basic Life Support
Blvd. Boulevard
BMI Broadcast Music, Inc.
BMW Bavarian Motor Works (Bayerische Motoren Werke)
bn. battalion
B.&O.R.R. Baltimore & Ohio Railroad
bot. botanical
BPE, B.P.E. Bachelor of Physical Education
BPhil, B.Phil. Bachelor of Philosophy
br. branch
BRE, B.R.E. Bachelor of Religious Education
brig. gen. brigadier general
Brit. British, Brittanica
Bros. Brothers
BS, B.S. Bachelor of Science
BSA, B.S.A. Bachelor of Agricultural Science
BSBA Bachelor of Science in Business Administration
BSChemE Bachelor of Science in Chemical Engineering
BSD, B.S.D. Bachelor of Didactic Science
BSEE Bachelor of Science in Electrical Engineering
BSN Bachelor of Science in Nursing
BST, B.S.T. Bachelor of Sacred Theology
BTh, B.Th. Bachelor of Theology
bull. bulletin
bur. bureau
bus. business
B.W.I. British West Indies

CA California
CAA Civil Aeronautics Administration
CAB Civil Aeronautics Board
CAD-CAM Computer Aided Design–Computer Aided Model
Calif. California
C.Am. Central America
Can. Canada, Canadian
CAP Civil Air Patrol
capt. captain
cardiol. cardiological
cardiovasc. cardiovascular
CARE Cooperative American Relief Everywhere
Cath. Catholic
cav. cavalry
CBC Canadian Broadcasting Company
CBI China, Burma, India Theatre of Operations
CBS Columbia Broadcasting Company
C.C. Community College
CCC Commodity Credit Corporation
CCNY City College of New York
CCRN Critical Care Registered Nurse
CCU Cardiac Care Unit
CD Civil Defense
CE, C.E. Corps of Engineers, Civil Engineer
CEN Certified Emergency Nurse
CENTO Central Treaty Organization
CEO chief executive officer
CERN European Organization of Nuclear Research
cert. certificate, certification, certified
CETA Comprehensive Employment Training Act
CFA Chartered Financial Analyst
CFL Canadian Football League
CFO chief financial officer
CFP Certified Financial Planner
ch. church
ChD, Ch.D. Doctor of Chemistry
chem. chemical
ChemE, Chem.E. Chemical Engineer
ChFC Chartered Financial Consultant
Chgo. Chicago
chirurg. chirurgical
chmn. chairman
chpt. chapter
CIA Central Intelligence Agency
Cin. Cincinnati
cir. circle, circuit
CLE Continuing Legal Education
Cleve. Cleveland
climatol. climatological
clin. clinical
clk. clerk
C.L.U. Chartered Life Underwriter
CM, C.M. Master in Surgery
CM Northern Mariana Islands
CMA Certified Medical Assistant
cmty. community
CNA Certified Nurse's Aide
CNOR Certified Nurse (Operating Room)
C.&N.W.Ry. Chicago & North Western Railway
CO Colorado
Co. Company
COF Catholic Order of Foresters
C. of C. Chamber of Commerce
col. colonel
coll. college
Colo. Colorado
com. committee
comd. commanded
comdg. commanding
comdr. commander
comdt. commandant
comm. communications
commd. commissioned
comml. commercial
commn. commission
commr. commissioner
compt. comptroller
condr. conductor
Conf. Conference
Congl. Congregational, Congressional
Conglist. Congregationalist
Conn. Connecticut
cons. consultant, consulting
consol. consolidated
constl. constitutional
constn. constitution
constrn. construction
contbd. contributed
contbg. contributing
contbn. contribution
contbr. contributor
contr. controller
Conv. Convention
COO chief operating officer
coop. cooperative
coord. coordinator
CORDS Civil Operations and Revolutionary Development Support
CORE Congress of Racial Equality
corp. corporation, corporate
corr. correspondent, corresponding, correspondence
C.&O.Ry. Chesapeake & Ohio Railway
coun. council
CPA Certified Public Accountant
CPCU Chartered Property and Casualty Underwriter
CPH, C.P.H. Certificate of Public Health
cpl. corporal
CPR Cardio-Pulmonary Resuscitation
C.P.Ry. Canadian Pacific Railway
CRT Cathode Ray Terminal
C.S. Christian Science
CSB, C.S.B. Bachelor of Christian Science
C.S.C. Civil Service Commission
CT Connecticut
ct. court
ctr. center
ctrl. central
CWS Chemical Warfare Service
C.Z. Canal Zone

D. Doctor
d. daughter
DAgr, D.Agr. Doctor of Agriculture
DAR Daughters of the American Revolution
dau. daughter
DAV Disabled American Veterans
DC, D.C. District of Columbia
DCL, D.C.L. Doctor of Civil Law
DCS, D.C.S. Doctor of Commercial Science
DD, D.D. Doctor of Divinity
DDS, D.D.S. Doctor of Dental Surgery
DE Delaware
Dec. December
dec. deceased
def. defense
Del. Delaware
del. delegate, delegation
Dem. Democrat, Democratic
DEng, D.Eng. Doctor of Engineering
denom. denomination, denominational
dep. deputy
dept. department
dermatol. dermatological
desc. descendant
devel. development, developmental
DFA, D.F.A. Doctor of Fine Arts
D.F.C. Distinguished Flying Cross
DHL, D.H.L. Doctor of Hebrew Literature
dir. director
dist. district
distbg. distributing
distbn. distribution
distbr. distributor
disting. distinguished
div. division, divinity, divorce
divsn. division
DLitt, D.Litt. Doctor of Literature
DMD, D.M.D. Doctor of Dental Medicine
DMS, D.M.S. Doctor of Medical Science
DO, D.O. Doctor of Osteopathy
docs. documents
DON Director of Nursing
DPH, D.P.H. Diploma in Public Health
DPhil, D.Phil. Doctor of Philosophy
D.R. Daughters of the Revolution
Dr. Drive, Doctor
DRE, D.R.E. Doctor of Religious Education
DrPH, Dr.P.H. Doctor of Public Health, Doctor of Public Hygiene
D.S.C. Distinguished Service Cross

DSc, D.Sc. Doctor of Science
DSChemE Doctor of Science in Chemical Engineering
D.S.M. Distinguished Service Medal
DST, D.S.T. Doctor of Sacred Theology
DTM, D.T.M. Doctor of Tropical Medicine
DVM, D.V.M. Doctor of Veterinary Medicine
DVS, D.V.S. Doctor of Veterinary Surgery

E, E. East
ea. eastern
E. and P. Extraordinary and Plenipotentiary
Eccles. Ecclesiastical
ecol. ecological
econ. economic
ECOSOC Economic and Social Council (of the UN)
ED, E.D. Doctor of Engineering
ed. educated
EdB, Ed.B. Bachelor of Education
EdD, Ed.D. Doctor of Education
edit. edition
editl. editorial
EdM, Ed.M. Master of Education
edn. education
ednl. educational
EDP Electronic Data Processing
EdS, Ed.S. Specialist in Education
EE, E.E. Electrical Engineer
E.E. and M.P. Envoy Extraordinary and Minister Plenipotentiary
EEC European Economic Community
EEG Electroencephalogram
EEO Equal Employment Opportunity
EEOC Equal Employment Opportunity Commission
E.Ger. German Democratic Republic
EKG Electrocardiogram
elec. electrical
electrochem. electrochemical
electrophys. electrophysical
elem. elementary
EM, E.M. Engineer of Mines
EMT Emergency Medical Technician
ency. encyclopedia
Eng. England
engr. engineer
engring. engineering
entomol. entomological
environ. environmental
EPA Environmental Protection Agency
epidemiol. epidemiological
Episc. Episcopalian
ERA Equal Rights Amendment
ERDA Energy Research and Development Administration
ESEA Elementary and Secondary Education Act
ESL English as Second Language
ESPN Entertainment and Sports Programming Network
ESSA Environmental Science Services Administration
ethnol. ethnological
ETO European Theatre of Operations
Evang. Evangelical
exam. examination, examining
Exch. Exchange
exec. executive
exhbn. exhibition
expdn. expedition
expn. exposition
expt. experiment
exptl. experimental
Expy. Expressway
Ext. Extension

F.A. Field Artillery
FAA Federal Aviation Administration
FAO Food and Agriculture Organization (of the UN)
FBA Federal Bar Association
FBI Federal Bureau of Investigation
FCA Farm Credit Administration
FCC Federal Communications Commission
FCDA Federal Civil Defense Administration
FDA Food and Drug Administration
FDIA Federal Deposit Insurance Administration
FDIC Federal Deposit Insurance Corporation
FE, F.E. Forest Engineer
FEA Federal Energy Administration
Feb. February
fed. federal
fedn. federation
FERC Federal Energy Regulatory Commission
fgn. foreign
FHA Federal Housing Administration
fin. financial, finance
FL Florida
Fl. Floor
Fla. Florida
FMC Federal Maritime Commission
FNP Family Nurse Practitioner
FOA Foreign Operations Administration
found. foundation
FPC Federal Power Commission
FPO Fleet Post Office
frat. fraternity
FRS Federal Reserve System
FSA Federal Security Agency
Ft. Fort
FTC Federal Trade Commission
Fwy. Freeway

G-1 (or other number) Division of General Staff
GA, Ga. Georgia
GAO General Accounting Office
gastroent. gastroenterological
GATE Gifted and Talented Educators
GATT General Agreement on Tariffs and Trade
GE General Electric Company
gen. general
geneal. genealogical
geod. geodetic
geog. geographic, geographical
geol. geological
geophys. geophysical
geriat. geriatrics
gerontol. gerontological
G.H.Q. General Headquarters
GM General Motors Corporation
GMAC General Motors Acceptance Corporation
G.N.Ry. Great Northern Railway
gov. governor
govt. government
govtl. governmental
GPO Government Printing Office
grad. graduate, graduated
GSA General Services Administration
Gt. Great
GTE General Telephone and ElectricCompany
GU Guam
gynecol. gynecological

HBO Home Box Office
hdqs. headquarters
HEW Department of Health, Education and Welfare
HHD, H.H.D. Doctor of Humanities
HHFA Housing and Home Finance Agency
HHS Department of Health and Human Services
HI Hawaii
hist. historical, historic
HM, H.M. Master of Humanities
HMO Health Maintenance Organization
homeo. homeopathic
hon. honorary, honorable
Ho. of Dels. House of Delegates
Ho. of Reps. House of Representatives
hort. horticultural
hosp. hospital
H.S. High School
HUD Department of Housing and Urban Development
Hwy. Highway
hydrog. hydrographic

IA Iowa
IAEA International Atomic Energy Agency
IATSE International Alliance of Theatrical and Stage Employees and Moving Picture Operators of the United States and Canada
IBM International Business Machines Corporation
IBRD International Bank for Reconstruction and Development
ICA International Cooperation Administration
ICC Interstate Commerce Commission
ICCE International Council for Computers in Education
ICU Intensive Care Unit
ID Idaho
IEEE Institute of Electrical and Electronics Engineers
IFC International Finance Corporation
IGY International Geophysical Year
IL Illinois
Ill. Illinois
illus. illustrated
ILO International Labor Organization
IMF International Monetary Fund
IN Indiana
Inc. Incorporated
Ind. Indiana
ind. independent
Indpls. Indianapolis
indsl. industrial
inf. infantry
info. information
ins. insurance
insp. inspector
insp. gen. inspector general
inst. institute
instl. institutional
instn. institution
instr. instructor
instrn. instruction
instrnl. instructional
internat. international
intro. introduction
IRE Institute of Radio Engineers
IRS Internal Revenue Service
ITT International Telephone & Telegraph Corporation

JAG Judge Advocate General
JAGC Judge Advocate General Corps
Jan. January
Jaycees Junior Chamber of Commerce
JB, J.B. Jurum Baccalaureus

JCB, J.C.B. Juris Canoni Baccalaureus
JCD, J.C.D. Juris Canonici Doctor, Juris Civilis Doctor
JCL, J.C.L. Juris Canonici Licentiatus
JD, J.D. Juris Doctor
jg. junior grade
jour. journal
jr. junior
JSD, J.S.D. Juris Scientiae Doctor
JUD, J.U.D. Juris Utriusque Doctor
jud. judicial

Kans. Kansas
K.C. Knights of Columbus
K.P. Knights of Pythias
KS Kansas
K.T. Knight Templar
KY, Ky. Kentucky

LA, La. Louisiana
L.A. Los Angeles
lab. laboratory
L.Am. Latin America
lang. language
laryngol. laryngological
LB Labrador
LDS Latter Day Saints
LDS Church Church of Jesus Christ of Latter Day Saints
lectr. lecturer
legis. legislation, legislative
LHD, L.H.D. Doctor of Humane Letters
L.I. Long Island
libr. librarian, library
lic. licensed, license
L.I.R.R. Long Island Railroad
lit. literature
litig. litigation
LittB, Litt.B. Bachelor of Letters
LittD, Litt.D. Doctor of Letters
LLB, LL.B. Bachelor of Laws
LLD, L.L.D. Doctor of Laws
LLM, L.L.M. Master of Laws
Ln. Lane
L.&N.R.R. Louisville & Nashville Railroad
LPGA Ladies Professional Golf Association
LPN Licensed Practical Nurse
LS, L.S. Library Science (in degree)
lt. lieutenant
Ltd. Limited
Luth. Lutheran
LWV League of Women Voters

M. Master
m. married
MA, M.A. Master of Arts
MA Massachusetts
MADD Mothers Against Drunk Driving
mag. magazine
MAgr, M.Agr. Master of Agriculture
maj. major
Man. Manitoba
Mar. March
MArch, M.Arch. Master in Architecture
Mass. Massachusetts
math. mathematics, mathematical
MATS Military Air Transport Service
MB, M.B. Bachelor of Medicine
MB Manitoba
MBA, M.B.A. Master of Business Administration
MBS Mutual Broadcasting System
M.C. Medical Corps
MCE, M.C.E. Master of Civil Engineering
mcht. merchant
mcpl. municipal
MCS, M.C.S. Master of Commercial Science
MD, M.D. Doctor of Medicine
MD, Md. Maryland
MDiv Master of Divinity
MDip, M.Dip. Master in Diplomacy
mdse. merchandise
MDV, M.D.V. Doctor of Veterinary Medicine
ME, M.E. Mechanical Engineer
ME Maine
M.E.Ch. Methodist Episcopal Church
mech. mechanical
MEd., M.Ed. Master of Education
med. medical
MEE, M.E.E. Master of Electrical Engineering
mem. member
meml. memorial
merc. mercantile
met. metropolitan
metall. metallurgical
MetE, Met.E. Metallurgical Engineer
meteorol. meteorological
Meth. Methodist
Mex. Mexico
MF, M.F. Master of Forestry
MFA, M.F.A. Master of Fine Arts
mfg. manufacturing
mfr. manufacturer
mgmt. management
mgr. manager
MHA, M.H.A. Master of Hospital Administration
M.I. Military Intelligence
MI Michigan
Mich. Michigan
micros. microscopic, microscopical
mid. middle
mil. military
Milw. Milwaukee
Min. Minister
mineral. mineralogical
Minn. Minnesota
MIS Management Information Systems
Miss. Mississippi
MIT Massachusetts Institute of Technology
mktg. marketing
ML, M.L. Master of Laws
MLA Modern Language Association
M.L.D. Magister Legnum Diplomatic
MLitt, M.Litt. Master of Literature, Master of Letters
MLS, M.L.S. Master of Library Science
MME, M.M.E. Master of Mechanical Engineering
MN Minnesota
mng. managing
MO, Mo. Missouri
moblzn. mobilization
Mont. Montana
MP Northern Mariana Islands
M.P. Member of Parliament
MPA Master of Public Administration
MPE, M.P.E. Master of Physical Education
MPH, M.P.H. Master of Public Health
MPhil, M.Phil. Master of Philosophy
MPL, M.P.L. Master of Patent Law
Mpls. Minneapolis
MRE, M.R.E. Master of Religious Education
MRI Magnetic Resonance Imaging
MS, M.S. Master of Science
MS, Ms. Mississippi
MSc, M.Sc. Master of Science
MSChemE Master of Science in Chemical Engineering
MSEE Master of Science in Electrical Engineering
MSF, M.S.F. Master of Science of Forestry
MSN Master of Science in Nursing
MST, M.S.T. Master of Sacred Theology
MSW, M.S.W. Master of Social Work
MT Montana
Mt. Mount
MTO Mediterranean Theatre of Operation
MTV Music Television
mus. museum, musical
MusB, Mus.B. Bachelor of Music
MusD, Mus.D. Doctor of Music
MusM, Mus.M. Master of Music
mut. mutual
MVP Most Valuable Player
mycol. mycological

N. North
NAACOG Nurses Association of the American College of Obstetricians and Gynecologists
NAACP National Association for the Advancement of Colored People
NACA National Advisory Committee for Aeronautics
NACDL National Association of Criminal Defense Lawyers
NACU National Association of Colleges and Universities
NAD National Academy of Design
NAE National Academy of Engineering, National Association of Educators
NAESP National Association of Elementary School Principals
NAFE National Association of Female Executives
N.Am. North America
NAM National Association of Manufacturers
NAMH National Association for Mental Health
NAPA National Association of Performing Artists
NARAS National Academy of Recording Arts and Sciences
NAREB National Association of Real Estate Boards
NARS National Archives and Record Service
NAS National Academy of Sciences
NASA National Aeronautics and Space Administration
NASP National Association of School Psychologists
NASW National Association of Social Workers
nat. national
NATAS National Academy of Television Arts and Sciences
NATO North Atlantic Treaty Organization
NATOUSA North African Theatre of Operations, United States Army
nav. navigation
NB, N.B. New Brunswick
NBA National Basketball Association
NBC National Broadcasting Company
NC, N.C. North Carolina
NCAA National College Athletic Association
NCCJ National Conference of Christians and Jews
ND, N.D. North Dakota
NDEA National Defense Education Act
NE Nebraska
NE, N.E. Northeast
NEA National Education Association
Nebr. Nebraska
NEH National Endowment for Humanities
neurol. neurological
Nev. Nevada
NF Newfoundland

NFL National Football League
Nfld. Newfoundland
NG National Guard
NH, N.H. New Hampshire
NHL National Hockey League
NIH National Institutes of Health
NIMH National Institute of Mental Health
NJ, N.J. New Jersey
NLRB National Labor Relations Board
NM New Mexico
N.Mex. New Mexico
No. Northern
NOAA National Oceanographic and Atmospheric Administration
NORAD North America Air Defense
Nov. November
NOW National Organization for Women
N.P.Ry. Northern Pacific Railway
nr. near
NRA National Rifle Association
NRC National Research Council
NS, N.S. Nova Scotia
NSC National Security Council
NSF National Science Foundation
NSTA National Science Teachers Association
NSW New South Wales
N.T. New Testament
NT Northwest Territories
nuc. nuclear
numis. numismatic
NV Nevada
NW, N.W. Northwest
N.W.T. Northwest Territories
NY, N.Y. New York
N.Y.C. New York City
NYU New York University
N.Z. New Zealand

OAS Organization of American States
ob-gyn obstetrics-gynecology
obs. observatory
obstet. obstetrical
occupl. occupational
oceanog. oceanographic
Oct. October
OD, O.D. Doctor of Optometry
OECD Organization for Economic Cooperation and Development
OEEC Organization of European Economic Cooperation
OEO Office of Economic Opportunity
ofcl. official
OH Ohio
OK Oklahoma
Okla. Oklahoma
ON Ontario
Ont. Ontario
oper. operating
ophthal. ophthalmological
ops. operations
OR Oregon
orch. orchestra
Oreg. Oregon
orgn. organization
orgnl. organizational
ornithol. ornithological
orthop. orthopedic
OSHA Occupational Safety and Health Administration
OSRD Office of Scientific Research and Development
OSS Office of Strategic Services
osteo. osteopathic
otol. otological
otolaryn. otolaryngological

PA, Pa. Pennsylvania
P.A. Professional Association
paleontol. paleontological
path. pathological
PBS Public Broadcasting System
P.C. Professional Corporation
PE Prince Edward Island
pediat. pediatrics
P.E.I. Prince Edward Island
PEN Poets, Playwrights, Editors, Essayists and Novelists (international association)
penol. penological
P.E.O. women's organization (full name not disclosed)
pers. personnel
pfc. private first class
PGA Professional Golfers' Association of America
PHA Public Housing Administration
pharm. pharmaceutical
PharmD, Pharm.D. Doctor of Pharmacy
PharmM, Pharm.M. Master of Pharmacy
PhB, Ph.B. Bachelor of Philosophy
PhD, Ph.D. Doctor of Philosophy
PhDChemE Doctor of Science in Chemical Engineering
PhM, Ph.M. Master of Philosophy
Phila. Philadelphia
philharm. philharmonic
philol. philological
philos. philosophical
photog. photographic
phys. physical
physiol. physiological
Pitts. Pittsburgh
Pk. Park
Pky. Parkway
Pl. Place
P.&L.E.R.R. Pittsburgh & Lake Erie Railroad
Plz. Plaza
PNP Pediatric Nurse Practitioner
P.O. Post Office
PO Box Post Office Box
polit. political
poly. polytechnic, polytechnical
PQ Province of Quebec
PR, P.R. Puerto Rico
prep. preparatory
pres. president
Presbyn. Presbyterian
presdl. presidential
prin. principal
procs. proceedings
prod. produced (play production)
prodn. production
prodr. producer
prof. professor
profl. professional
prog. progressive
propr. proprietor
pros. atty. prosecuting attorney
pro tem. pro tempore
PSRO Professional Services Review Organization
psychiat. psychiatric
psychol. psychological
PTA Parent-Teachers Association
ptnr. partner
PTO Pacific Theatre of Operations, Parent Teacher Organization
pub. publisher, publishing, published
pub. public
publ. publication
pvt. private

quar. quarterly
qm. quartermaster
Q.M.C. Quartermaster Corps
Que. Quebec

radiol. radiological
RAF Royal Air Force
RCA Radio Corporation of America
RCAF Royal Canadian Air Force
RD Rural Delivery
Rd. Road
R&D Research & Development
REA Rural Electrification Administration
rec. recording
ref. reformed
regt. regiment
regtl. regimental
rehab. rehabilitation
rels. relations
Rep. Republican
rep. representative
Res. Reserve
ret. retired
Rev. Reverend
rev. review, revised
RFC Reconstruction Finance Corporation
RFD Rural Free Delivery
rhinol. rhinological
RI, R.I. Rhode Island
RISD Rhode Island School of Design
Rlwy. Railway
Rm. Room
RN, R.N. Registered Nurse
roentgenol. roentgenological
ROTC Reserve Officers Training Corps
RR Rural Route
R.R. Railroad
rsch. research
rschr. researcher
Rt. Route

S. South
s. son
SAC Strategic Air Command
SAG Screen Actors Guild
SALT Strategic Arms Limitation Talks
S.Am. South America
san. sanitary
SAR Sons of the American Revolution
Sask. Saskatchewan
savs. savings
SB, S.B. Bachelor of Science
SBA Small Business Administration
SC, S.C. South Carolina
SCAP Supreme Command Allies Pacific
ScB, Sc.B. Bachelor of Science
SCD, S.C.D. Doctor of Commercial Science
ScD, Sc.D. Doctor of Science
sch. school
sci. science, scientific
SCLC Southern Christian Leadership Conference
SCV Sons of Confederate Veterans
SD, S.D. South Dakota
SE, S.E. Southeast
SEATO Southeast Asia Treaty Organization
SEC Securities and Exchange Commission
sec. secretary
sect. section
seismol. seismological
sem. seminary
Sept. September
s.g. senior grade
sgt. sergeant
SHAEF Supreme Headquarters Allied Expeditionary Forces
SHAPE Supreme Headquarters Allied Powers in Europe
S.I. Staten Island

S.J. Society of Jesus (Jesuit)
SJD Scientiae Juridicae Doctor
SK Saskatchewan
SM, S.M. Master of Science
SNP Society of Nursing Professionals
So. Southern
soc. society
sociol. sociological
S.P.Co. Southern Pacific Company
spkr. speaker
spl. special
splty. specialty
Sq. Square
S.R. Sons of the Revolution
sr. senior
SS Steamship
SSS Selective Service System
St. Saint, Street
sta. station
stats. statistics
statis. statistical
STB, S.T.B. Bachelor of Sacred Theology
stblzn. stabilization
STD, S.T.D. Doctor of Sacred Theology
std. standard
Ste. Suite
subs. subsidiary
SUNY State University of New York
supr. supervisor
supt. superintendent
surg. surgical
svc. service
SW, S.W. Southwest
sys. system

TAPPI Technical Association of the Pulp and Paper Industry
tb. tuberculosis
tchg. teaching
tchr. teacher
tech. technical, technology
technol. technological
tel. telephone
Tel. & Tel. Telephone & Telegraph
telecom. telecommunications
temp. temporary
Tenn. Tennessee
Ter. Territory
Ter. Terrace
TESOL Teachers of English to Speakers of Other Languages
Tex. Texas
ThD, Th.D. Doctor of Theology
theol. theological
ThM, Th.M. Master of Theology
TN Tennessee
tng. training
topog. topographical
trans. transaction, transferred
transl. translation, translated
transp. transportation
treas. treasurer
TT Trust Territory
TV television
TVA Tennessee Valley Authority
TWA Trans World Airlines
twp. township
TX Texas
typog. typographical

U. University
UAW United Auto Workers
UCLA University of California at Los Angeles
UDC United Daughters of the Confederacy
U.K. United Kingdom
UN United Nations
UNESCO United Nations Educational, Scientific and Cultural Organization
UNICEF United Nations International Children's Emergency Fund
univ. university
UNRRA United Nations Relief and Rehabilitation Administration
UPI United Press International
U.P.R.R. United Pacific Railroad
urol. urological
U.S. United States
U.S.A. United States of America
USAAF United States Army Air Force
USAF United States Air Force
USAFR United States Air Force Reserve
USAR United States Army Reserve
USCG United States Coast Guard
USCGR United States Coast Guard Reserve
USES United States Employment Service
USIA United States Information Agency
USMC United States Marine Corps
USMCR United States Marine Corps Reserve
USN United States Navy
USNG United States National Guard
USNR United States Naval Reserve
USO United Service Organizations
USPHS United States Public Health Service
USS United States Ship
USSR Union of the Soviet Socialist Republics
USTA United States Tennis Association
USV United States Volunteers
UT Utah

VA Veterans Administration
VA, Va. Virginia
vet. veteran, veterinary
VFW Veterans of Foreign Wars
VI, V.I. Virgin Islands
vice pres. vice president
vis. visiting
VISTA Volunteers in Service to America
VITA Volunteers in Technical Assistance
vocat. vocational
vol. volunteer, volume
v.p. vice president
vs. versus
VT, Vt. Vermont

W, W. West
WA Washington (state)
WAC Women's Army Corps
Wash. Washington (state)
WATS Wide Area Telecommunications Service
WAVES Women's Reserve, US Naval Reserve
WCTU Women's Christian Temperance Union
we. western
W. Ger. Germany, Federal Republic of
WHO World Health Organization
WI Wisconsin
W.I. West Indies
Wis. Wisconsin
WSB Wage Stabilization Board
WV West Virginia
W.Va. West Virginia
WWI World War I
WWII World War II
WY Wyoming
Wyo. Wyoming

YK Yukon Territory
YMCA Young Men's Christian Association
YMHA Young Men's Hebrew Association
YM & YWHA Young Men's and Young Women's Hebrew Association
yr. year
YT, Y.T. Yukon Territory
YWCA Young Women's Christian Association

zool. zoological

Alphabetical Practices

Names are arranged alphabetically according to the surnames, and under identical surnames according to the first given name. If both surname and first given name are identical, names are arranged alphabetically according to the second given name.

Surnames beginning with De, Des, Du, however capitalized or spaced, are recorded with the prefix preceding the surname and arranged alphabetically under the letter D.

Surnames beginning with Mac and Mc are arranged alphabetically under M.

Surnames beginning with Saint or St. appear after names that begin Sains, and are arranged according to the second part of the name, e.g. St. Clair before Saint Dennis.

Surnames beginning with Van, Von, or von are arranged alphabetically under the letter V.

Compound surnames are arranged according to the first member of the compound.

Many hyphenated Arabic names begin Al-, El-, or al-. These names are alphabetized according to each Biographee's designation of last name. Thus Al-Bahar, Neta may be listed either under Al- or under Bahar, depending on the preference of the listee.

Also, Arabic names have a variety of possible spellings when transposed to English. Spelling of these names is always based on the practice of the Biographee. Some Biographees use a Western form of word order, while others prefer the Arabic word sequence.

Similarly, Asian names may have no comma between family and given names, but some Biographees have chosen to add the comma. In each case, punctuation follows the preference of the Biographee.

Parentheses used in connection with a name indicate which part of the full name is usually deleted in common usage. Hence Chambers, E(lizabeth) Anne indicates that the usual form of the given name is E. Anne. In such a case, the parentheses are ignored in alphabetizing and the name would be arranged as Chambers, Elizabeth Anne. However, if the name is recorded Chambers, (Elizabeth) Anne, signifying that the entire name Elizabeth is not commonly used, the alphabetizing would be arranged as though the name were Chambers, Anne. If an entire middle or last name is enclosed in parentheses, that portion of the name is used in the alphabetical arrangement. Hence Chambers, Elizabeth (Anne) would be arranged as Chambers, Elizabeth Anne.

Where more than one spelling, word order, or name of an individual is frequently encountered, the sketch has been entered under the form preferred by the Biographee, with cross-references under alternate forms.

Who'sWho in the South and Southwest®

Biographies

AALUND, PEGGY MACHELL, nurse, educator; b. Quonset Point, R.I., Nov. 4, 1951; d. Reginald Montague and Nancy (Heberton) Machell; m. Tony Ray Aalund; children: Robert, Rebecca, Rex, Troy. BSN with honors, U. Tex. Sch. Nursing, Galveston, 1974, MSN with highest honors, 1975. RN, Tex.; cert. childbirth educator. Pediatric nurse John Sealy Hosp., Galveston, 1974; nurse educator U. Tex. Sch. Nursing, 1976-77; pediatric nurse Humble (Tex.) Pediatric Assn., 1977-80; childbirth educator N.E. Med. Ctr., Humble, 1981-83; owner, childbirth educator Prepared Childbirth: A Shared Beginning, Humble, 1983-85; nurse educator North Harris Coll., Houston, 1985-95; program dir. ADN program North Harris Montgomery C.C. dist., 1995—; mother and baby nurse Northeast Med. Ctr. Hosp., Humble, Tex., 1992-95. Vol. 3H Community Ctr., Humble, 1981; Sunday sch. tchr. St. Martha's Cath. Ch., Kingwood, Tex., 1988-92; speaker to health classes Humble Ind. Sch. Dist., 1980—. Winner Tchr. Excellence award, 1994; recipient Nat. Inst. Staff Orgnl. Devel. award, 1995, Excellence award. Mem. Sigma Theta Tau. Home: 3431 Tree Ln Humble TX 77339-2643

AANSTOOS, CHRISTOPHER MICHAEL, psychology educator; b. Saipan Island, U.S. Trust Ter., Apr. 4, 1952; s. Anthony Matthew and Frances Henrietta (Jambrick) A.; children: Megan Elizabeth, Lucas Mathew. BA, Mich. State U., 1974; MA, Duquesne U., 1976, PhD., 1982. Instr. Pa. State U., McKeesport, 1979-82; asst. prof. psychology State U. West Ga., Carrollton, 1982-87; assoc. prof., 1987-92, prof., 1992—, chmn., 1995-96; contracted rschr. Pitts. Sch. Dist., 1979; manuscript reviewer Harcourt, Brace, Jovanovich, N.Y., 1983, New Ideas in Psychology, 1984-85, Saybrook Inst., 1986, Metaphor and Symbolic Activity, 1985-88, Sage, 1989, Guilford, 1990. Editor Exploring the Lived World, 1984, The World of the Infant, 1987, Human Growth and Development, 1990; Studies in Humanistic Psychology, 1991; Jour. The Humanistic Psychologist, 1984—; assoc. editor Jour. Theoretical and Philosophical Psychology, 1986-89; cons. editor Jour. Phenomenological Psychology, 1982—; contbr. over 60 articles to profl. jours., books. Coord. Fund Drive Am. Heart Assn., State U. West Ga., 1985; vol. West Ga. Coll. Speakers Bur., 1983—. Faculty Rsch. grantee State U. West Ga., 1983-85, 89-90, 92-93. Mem. APA (exec. bd. divs. 24, 32, program chmn. div. 24 1991, pres. divsn. 32 1996-97), AAUP, Human Sci. Research Assn. (program chmn. 1984), Southeastern Psychol. Assn., Assn. Qualitative Research Psychology (chmn. program com. 1987), Chess Fedn. (West Ga.), Phi Beta Kappa. Home: 2175 Hog Liver Rd Carrollton GA 30117-9308 Office: State U West Ga Psychology Dept Carrollton GA 30118

AARON, BERTRAM DONALD, corporation executive; b. Newport News, Va., Jan. 10, 1922; s. Harry and Lillian (Blackman) A.; BS in Elec. Engring., Va. Poly. Inst., 1943; children: Harry, Cynthia, Jill; m. Marcia Kurke, 1952 (dec. Nov. 1974); m. Judith Goldstein, Dec. 28, 1985 (dec. May 1993). Aero. rsch. scientist Nat. Adv. Com. for Aeros., Langley AFB, Va., 1946-50; pres. Aaron Investors, Inc., 1948-90; elec. engr. Signal Corps Supply Agy., Phila., 1950-53; propr. Bertram D. Aaron and Co., L.A., 1953-58, pres., Plainview, N.Y., 1958-91, Aaron Tech. Cons., 1990—; pres. Microwave Instrumentation Labs., 1959-80, HAL Antenna Products, Inc., Aaron Tech. Market, Inc. Dir. devel. Va. Breast Cancer Found., 1993, organizer, chmn. symposium Primary Care Perspectives, 1995. Served to capt., Signal Corps, U.S. Army, 1943-46. Registered profl. engr., N.Y., Pa., Va. Mem. IEEE (various offices), Electronic Reps. Assn. (pres., chmn. bd., nat. del. MY chpt.), Assn. of Old Crows (pres. Tidewater, Va. chpt. 1993-95). Jewish. Author: Hydrogen Thyratron Circuitry Considerations, 1953; Surveillance Under Low Light Level Conditions, 1971; editor Procs. of Integration Com. on Hydrogen Thyratrons, 1951-53; patentee antenna. Home and Office: Aaron Tech Cons Inc 212 Burtcher Ct Williamsburg VA 23185-8905

AARON, DONNIE RAY, carpenter, poet; b. El Dorado, Ark., June 13, 1954; s. Donnie and Dora Jean (Redding) A.; children: Donna Michell, April, Donnie Ray Jr. Grad., El Dorado H.S. Author: (poetry) Mistake, 1995, This Feeling Called Love, 1995, A Doubtful Minded Person, 1995. Sgt. U.S. Army, 1972-76. Home: 1110 Ross St El Dorado AR 71730

AARON, HENRY L. (HANK AARON), professional baseball team executive; b. Mobile, Ala., Feb. 5, 1934; s. Herbert and Estella A.; children: Gail, Hank, Lary, Gary (dec.), Dorinda; m. Billye Suber, Nov. 1973; 1 child, Ceci. Ed. pub. schs. Former semi-pro baseball player; baseball player Milw. Braves (became Atlanta Braves 1966), 1954-74, v.p. player devel., 1976-89, sr. v.p., asst. to pres., 1989—, also bd. dirs.; player Milw. Brewers, 1974-76; bd. dirs. Turner Broadcasting. Author: (autobiography) I Had A Hammer: The Hank Aaron Story, 1991. Pres. No Greater Love, 1974; state chmn. Wis. Easter Seal Soc., 1975; nat. sports chmn. Nat. Easter Seal Soc., 1974; nat. chmn. Friends of Fisk for Athletics; organizer Hank Aaron Scholarship Fund, 1974; sponsor Hank Aaron Celebrity Bowling Tournament for Sickle Cell Anemia, 1972; mem. exec. bd. PUSH; mem. nat. bd. Big Bros./Big Sisters Am., NAACP; mem. Atlanta bd. Am. Cancer Soc.; mem. sterling com. Morehouse Coll.; active Leukemia Soc. Atlanta. Mem. Nat. League All-Star Team, 1955-74, Am. League All-Star Team, 1975, World Series Championship Team, 1957; Most Valuable Player, Nat. League, 1957; named Player of Yr. Sporting News, 1956, 63; inducted into Baseball Hall of Fame, 1982; broke Babe Ruth's career home run record with 715th home run, April 8, 1974; holder major league record for most home runs, most runs batted in. Office: care Atlanta Braves PO Box 4064 Atlanta GA 30302-4064

AARON, SHIRLEY MAE, tax consultant; b. Covington, La., Feb. 28, 1935; d. Morgan and Pearl (Jenkins) King; m. Richard L. King, Feb. 16, 1952 (div. Feb. 1965); children: Deborah, Richard, Roberta, Keely; m. Michael A. Aaron, Nov. 27, 1976 (dec. July 1987). Adminstrv. asst. South Central Bell, Covington, La., 1954-62; acct. Brown & Root, Inc., Houston, 1962-75; timekeeper Alyeska Pipeline Co., Fairbanks, Alaska, 1975-77; adminstrv. asst. Boeing Co., Seattle, 1979-93; pres. Aaron Enterprises, Seattle, 1977—; owner Gabriel's Dinner Club, La., 1993—. Contbr.: Who's Cooking What in America by Phyllis Hanes, 1993. Bd. dirs. Burien 146 Homeowners Assn., Seattle, 1979—, pres., 1980-83, 92. Mem. NAFE. Avocation: singing, art. Home: 131 Gerard St Mandeville LA 70448-5808

AARONS-HOLDER, CHARMAINE MICHELE, lawyer; b. Kingston, Jamaica, Jan. 24, 1959; came to U.S., 1982; d. Alan and Berly-Mae Aarons; m. Lisle Anthony Holder, 1982. LLB honors, U. W.I., Barbados, 1980; Cert. Legal Edn., Norman Manley Law Sch., Kingston, 1982; JD cum laude, U. Houston, 1987. Bar: Barbados 1982, Tex. 1987, U.S. Dist. Ct. (so. dist.) Tex. 1988, U.S. Ct. Appeals (5th cir.) 1996. Participating assoc. Fulbright & Jaworski, Houston, 1987-94; atty. Wickliff & Hall, Houston, 1994—. Co-editor, co-author: The Texas Environmental Law Handbook, 1989, 2nd edit., 1990, 3rd edit., 1993. Mem. ABA, Tex. Bar Assn., Houston Bar Assn. (chair campaign for homeless com. 1996-97), Houston Young Lawyers Assn. (chair hunger relief com. 1994-95), Tex. Young Lawyers Assn., Order of Coif, Order of Barons. Democrat. Office: Wickliff & Hall 1000 Louisiana St Houston TX 77002

AARONSON, JOYCE ROSALIND, elementary school educator; b. Balt., Aug. 22, 1948; d. Lewis and Lillian (Entin) Levin; m. Allen Edward Aaronson, Dec. 22, 1968; children: Adam, Laurie, Jeremy. BS, Temple U., 1969; MA, Shippensburg (Pa.) U., 1972. Cert. reading, Va. Tchr. Richboro (Pa.) Elem. Sch., 1969-70, Tri-Cmty. Elem. Sch., Harrisburg, Pa., 1970-74, Bryant Elem. Sch., Phila., 1974-77; reading tchr. Courtland Elem. Sch., Spotsylvania, Va., 1988—. Bylaws chmn. Rappabannock Reading Coun., Fredericksburg, Va., 1990—; edn. chmn. Beth Sholom Temple, Fredericksburg, 1991-95, Mitzvah chmn., 1995-96. Republican. Home: 4 Cobblestone Ct Fredericksburg VA 22407 Office: Courtland Elementary School 6601 Smith Station Rd Spotsylvania VA 22553

AARS, RALLIN JAMES, management and marketing communications executive; b. Clifton, Tex., Sept. 28, 1941; s. C. Pernell and Rosalie (Rueter) A.; m. Barbara Ann Zuehlke, June 13, 1964; children: Christian, James, Michael. BA, Baylor U., 1964; MA, Mich. State U., 1970; Grad. with honors, Indsl. Coll. of the Armed Forces, 1980. Commd. USAF, 1964, advanced through grades to col., 1980; ops. officer HQ USAF Armed Forces Radio and TV Svc.-Europe, Wiesbaden, Germany, 1964-66; comdr. Am. Forces TV, Berlin, 1966-69; chief of pub. affairs Bergstrom AFB Austin, Tex., 1970-72; chief of info. and liaison Armed Forces Radio and TV, L.A., 1972-76; exec. officer Joint Casualty Resolution Ctr., U'Tapao, Thailand, 1976-77; dir. pub. affairs Electronic Security Command USAF, San Antonio, Tex., 1977-80; dir. plans and resources, office of pub. affairs, sec. of the Air Force Washington, 1980-82; dir. pub. affairs UN Command Seoul, Korea, 1982-84; ret. USAF, 1984; v.p. Gurasich, Spence, Darilek & McClure, Dallas, 1984-86, The Oakley Co., Dallas, 1986-87; v.p. comm. PARTNERS Nat. Health Plans, Irving, Tex., 1987-90, Aetna Health Plans, Irving, Tex., 1990-93; v.p. mktg. and communications Aetna Profl. Mgmt. Corp., Irving, Tex., 1993-94; health plan mgr., exec. dir. bus. devel. Kaiser Found. Health Plan of Tex., Dallas, 1994—. Producer (TV documentary) Berlin: Freedom's Island, 1968 (George Washington honor medal 1968), Airlift Anniversary, 1969 (George Washington honor medal 1969), Money Box (Golden Tops award 1988), Healthwise Today Newsletter (Dallas Press Club KATIE award 1988), Perfect Health Plan (Silver Tops award 1989, Bronze Tops award 1989), Super Dave Ad Campaign (Golden Tops award 1990), Preventive Health Care Campaign (four gold and two silver awards Health Mgmt. Rev. 1992). Pres. Internat. Luth. Ch., Seoul, 1983; v.p. New Life In Christ Luth. Ch., Dallas, 1986-88. Decorated Legion of Merit; Nat. Order Mil. Merit (Republic of Korea); recipient 3 gold and 2 silver awards for significant achievement in healthcare advt. Health Mgmt. Rev. mag., 1992. Mem. VFW, Am. Legion, Nat. Assn. Govt. Communicators, Am. Managed Care and Rev. Assn. (chmn. pub. affairs com.), Am. Mktg. Assn., Pub. Rels. Soc. Am. (v.p. San Antonio chpt. 1979-80), Tex. Pub. Rels. Assn., Aviation and Space Writers Assn., Armed Forces Broadcasters Assn. (golden anniversary com), Air Force Assn., Assn. U.S. Army, Ret. Officers Assn., Air Force Pub. Affairs Alumni Assn. (charter life mem.), LaCima Club. Home: 1254 Whispering Oaks Dr De Soto TX 75115-7439 Office: Kaiser Found Health Plan Tex Ste 600 12720 Hillcrest Rd Dallas TX 75230

ABALO, TOMAS CONFESOR, physician; b. Roxas City, The Philippines, Sept. 25, 1961; s. Eduardo Aldea and Jeanette (Confesor) A.; m. Anna Isabel Resurreccion, May 9, 1991; children: Alexandra Maria, Theresa Isabella, Gabriela Mara. BS in Zoology, U. of the Philippines, Quezon City, 1983; MD, U. of the Philippines, Manila, 1987. Resident in internal medicine Sinai Hosp. Balt., 1989-92; fellow in infectious diseases Brown U., Providence, 1992-94; staff physician Morgan County ARH Hosp., West Liberty, Ky., 1995—. Mem. AMA, ACP, Infectious Diseases Soc. Am. Roman Catholic. Home: 60 Townhouse Ln Apt #6 West Liberty KY 41472 Office: ARH Salyersville Clinic Maple St Salyersville KY 41465

ABAUNZA, DONALD RICHARD, lawyer; b. New Orleans, Oct. 25, 1945; s. Alfred E. and Virginia (White) A.; m. Carolyn Thompson; 1 child, Richard. BA, Vanderbilt U., 1966; JD, Tulane U., 1969. Bar: La. 1969, U.S. Dist. Ct. (ea. dist.) La. 1969, U.S. Dist. Ct. (we. dist.) La. 1980, U.S. Supreme Ct. 1986. Assoc. Lemle, Kelleher, Kohlmeyer, Dennery, Hunley, Moss & Frilot, New Orleans, 1969-76; mng. ptnr. Liskow & Lewis, New Orleans, 1977—; adj. faculty Tulane Sch. Law, 1981-89. Fellow Am. Coll. Trial Lawyers; mem. La. Bar Assn. (Pres.'s award 1988). Office: Liskow & Lewis 1 Shell Sq 50th Fl 701 Poydras St New Orleans LA 70139-6001

ABBASCHIAN, REZA, materials science and engineering educator; b. Zanjan, Iran, Jan. 23, 1944; came to U.S., 1966; s. Ebrahim and Motahreh Abbaschian; m. Janette S. Johnson, Sept. 6, 1973; children: Lara S., Cyrus E. BS, U. Tehran, Iran, 1965; MS, Mich. Tech. U., 1968; PhD, U. Calif., Berkeley, 1971. Rsch. analyst U.S. Steel Corp., Gary, Ind., 1967; rsch. asst. U. Calif., 1968-71; asst. prof. Shiraz (Iran) U., 1972-74, assoc. prof., 1974-80; with U. Fla., Gainesville, 1980—, acting chmn., 1986-87, chmn., prof., 1987—; vis. assoc. prof. dept. metallurgy and mining engring. U. Ill., Urbana, 1976-78; vis. scientist MIT, Cambridge, 1980, NASA Space Processing Lab., Marshall Space Flight Ctr., Huntsville, Ala., 1981; chmn. Shiraz U., 1974-76; mem. Nat. Materials Adv. Bd., 1996—. Co-author: Physical Metallurgy Principles, 1992; editor: Grain Refinement in Castings and Welds, 1983, Solidification Processing of Eutectic Alloys, 1988, Modeling and Control of Casting, 1988. Grantee NSF, NASA, 1984—. Office: U Fla Dept Materials Sci and Engring PO Box 116400, 132 Rhines Gainesville FL 32611

ABBIT, BEN, food products executive; b. 1950. With Fla. Agrl. Rsch. Inst., Gainesville, 1974-85; gen. mgr. Haines City (Fla.) Citrus Growers Assn., 1985—. Office: Haines City Citrus Growers Assn US Hwy 17 92 Haines City FL 33844

ABBOTT, CRIS PYE, apparel executive; b. Dallas, Sept. 29, 1951; d. Jimmie Edwin and Maie Marie (Fountain) F.; m. Kenneth G. Abbott, Nov. 12, 1988. Student, U. Tex., Arlington, 1969-71, cert., 1984. V.p. sales and mktg. Eidelberg & Assocs., Inc., Dallas, 1974-82; regional v.p. Uniforms to You & Co., Chgo., 1982—. Mem. Amarillo Symphony Guild, Lone Star Ballet, Art Alliance; bd. dirs. Airport Assistance Ctr., Dallas/Ft. Worth Airport, 1986—; social v.p. Amarillo Art Alliance, 1990-92; chmn. Discover '91; bd. dirs. Am. Cancer Soc., 1990—. Named one of Outstanding Young Women of Am., 1985. Mem. NAFE, Nat. Assn. Accts., Sales and Mktg. Execs., Dallas Bapt. Univ. Women (exec. bd. 1986—), Jr. Women's Club (chmn. and dir. 1981-83), Delta Delta Delta (advisor). Home and Office: 5800 Royal Oak Dr NE Albuquerque NM 87111

ABBOTT, CYNTHIA ALLEN, nurse administrator; b. Ponca City, Okla., Dec. 15, 1954; d. Thomas J. and Peggy Joan (Fugate) Allen; children: Michael Charles, Caroline Alyssa Allen. BSN, Okla. U., 1978; MSN, U. Tex., Austin, 1987, PhD, 1993. RN, Okla.; cert. perioperative nursing. Commd. 2d lt. U.S. Army, 1978, advanced through grades to lt. col., 1993; charge nurse Eisenhower Army Med. Ctr., Ft. Gordon, Ga., 1978-79, head nurse neurol. surg. svcs., 1979-80; oper. room staff devel. coord. 98th Gen. Hosp., Nuremberg, Germany, 1980-81; head nurse ctrl. material supply 98th Gen. Hosp., Nuremberg, 1981-83; head nurse oper. rm. gen. surgery svcs. Darnall Army Community Hosp., Ft. Hood, Tex., 1983-84; mem. assoc. faculty U. Tex. Sch. Nursing, San Antonio, 1988-90; sr. instr. operating rm. br., nursing sci. divsn. Acad. Health Scis., U.S. Army, Ft. Sam Houston, Tex., 1987-90; dir. perioperative nursing svcs. Ireland Army Cmty. Hosp., Ft. Knox, Ky., 1993-94, dir. patient care svcs. of surg. svcs. team, 1994; sr. nurse rschr. Ctr. for Health and Edn. Studies, Acad. Health Scis., Ft. Sam Houston, Tex., 1995—; chmn. patient/home health nursing Healthcare 2020 Futures Trisvc. Initiative, 1995—; presenter in field. Mem. editorial bd.: Seminars in Perioperative Nursing, 1992-93, Pathways, 1992-93; contbr. articles to profl. jours. Lt. col. U.S. Army, 1978—. Named ROTC Disting. Mil. Grad., U. Okla., 1978; decorated Expert Field Med. badge, Army Commendation medal with 4 oakleaf clusters, Meritorious Svc. medal with oakleaf cluster, 1995, Dr. Anita Newcomb McGee award Daughters of the Am. Revolution, 1995; named Army Surg. Gen. Nurse of Yr., 1995. Mem. ANA, Assn. Operating Rm. Nurses, Inc. (nat. com. on edn., rep. region VI, del. 36th Congress, Anaheim, Calif., 1989, chmn. nat. com. on edn., del. 37th Congress, Houston, 1990, chmn. nat. com. on edn., del. 38th Congress, Atlanta, 1991, nursing rsch. com., del. 39th Congress, Dallas, 1992, nursing rsch. com., chair-elect, del. 40th Congress, Anaheim, 1993, chmn. program com. San Antonio AORN chpt. 1987, mem. task force on data elements and unlicensed assistive personnel 1993-94, co-chair rsch. and legis coms., 28th annual symposium planning com. 1988, chmn. rsch. com., newsletter com. 1989-90, moderator/chmn. 29th annual symposium, sec. 1988-90, pres.-elect., chmn. bylaws com. 1990-91, pres. 1991-92, bd. dirs. nominating com. 1992-93), Tex. Nurses Assn., Sigma Theta Tau (Delta Alpha chpt. policy and bylaws com. 1988-90), Phi Kappa Phi. Methodist. Home: 6903 S Jamestown Tulsa OK 74136 Office: Ctr for Health Edn Studies CHES MCCS-HR AMEDD Ctr/Sch Acad Health Scis Fort Sam Houston TX 78234

ABBOTT, FRANCES ELIZABETH DOWDLE, journalist, civic worker; b. Rome, Ga., Mar. 21, 1924; d. John Wesley and Lucille Elizabeth (Field) Dowdle; m. Jackson Miles Abbott, May 15, 1948; children: Medora Frances, David Field, Elizabeth Stockton, Robert Jackson; m. Archibald W. Lyon, Oct. 15, 1993. Student, Draughon's Bus. Coll., Columbia, S.C.. Feature writer Mt. Vernon corr. Alexandria Gazette, Va., 1967-75; libr., rsch. assoc. Gadsby's Tavern Mus., Alexandria, 1977—. Chmn. ann. George Washington Birthnight Ball, Mt. Vernon, 1974-82; sec. George Washington 250th Birthday Celebration Commn., 1979-82; mem. steering com. Neighborhood Friends Hist. Mt. Vernon, 1988-92; chmn. publicity Waynewood Woman's Club, Waynewood Citizens Assn.; treas. Mt. Vernon Citizens Assn., 1967-82; dist. chmn. Mt. Vernon March of Dimes, 1960-62; sec. Waynewood Sch. PTA, 1962-64; tchr. 1st aid Girl Scouts U.S., 1964-65; den mother Cub Scouts, 1966; registrar DAR, 1968-77; chmn. publicity Mt. Vernon Women's Rep. Club, 1955. Named Mrs. Waynewood by Community Vote, 1969. Mem. Audubon Naturalist Soc., Nat. Trust Hist. Preservation. Episcopalian. Home: 9110 Belvoir Woods Pky # J-414 Fort Belvoir VA 22060-2716 Office: 134 N Royal St Alexandria VA 22314-3226

ABBOTT, GAYLE ELIZABETH, human resources consultant; b. Cleve., July 7, 1954; d. Olcott Rutherford and Eleanor Francis (Norley) A.; 1 child, Elizabeth Laura. BA, Am. U., 1976; MBA, Loyola Coll., Balt., 1983. Cert. sr. profl. in human resources, compensation profl. Personnel mgmt. specialist Food and Drug Adminstrn., Washington, 1975-77; personnel mgr. Computer Network Corp., Washington, 1977-78; dir. human resources STSC, Inc., Rockville, Md., 1978-84; compensation cons. Comm. Satellite Corp., Washington, 1984-85; pres., founder HURECO, Inc. (formerly Human Resource Solutions), Fairfax, Va., 1985—; lectr., adj. faculty Marymount U., Arlington, Va., 1990-95, Am. U., Washington; spkr. profl. assns. and confs. Co-author: Deflecting Workplace Violence, 1994; contbr. articles to profl. jours. Chmn. pers. com. Lewinsville Presbyn. Ch., 1987-91. Recipient Lodestar award Am. U., 1992. Mem. AAUW (bd. rec. sec. 1987, v.p. membership 1988-89), Soc. for Human Resource Mgmt. (dir. Va. state coun. 1991), No. Va. Soc. for Human Resource Mgmt. (legis. rep. 1987-88, v.p. programs 1988, pres. 1989-90, dir. 1991-93, Disting. Leadership award 1991), Am. U. Alumni Assn. (v.p. 1988-90, pres. 1990-92, bd. dirs. 1993—). Presbyterian. Office: HURECO Inc 3603 Chain Bridge Rd Ste B Fairfax VA 22030-3244

ABBOTT, GREG WAYNE, lawyer; b. Wichita Falls, Tex., Nov. 13, 1957; s. Calivn Roger and Doris Lacristia (Jacks) Rowley A.; m. Cecilia Therese Phalen, Aug. 15, 1981. BBA, U. Tex., 1981; JD, Vanderbilt U., 1984. Bar: Tex. 1985, U.S. Dist. Ct. (so. dist.) Tex. 1985. Atty. Butler & Binion, Houston, 1984—; elected judge, appointed to Supreme ct. 129th State Dist. Ct.Houston, 1992; judge Texas Supreme Ct., 1996—. Dir. Houston Ctr. for Barrier Free Living, 1986-87; capt. March of Dimes Team Walk, Houston, 1986-87. Named Disabled Person of the Yr., Harris County Com. on Employment of Disabled Persons, 1986; recipient Am. Jurisprudence award Am. Jur, 1983, Named Outstanding Trial Judge, Texas Assn. of Civil Trial and Appellate Specialists, 1995. Mem. State Bar Tex. (com. on legal advt. 1988), Houston Bar Assn., houston Young Lawyers Assn. Republican. Roman Catholic. Home: 5573 Bordley Dr Houston TX 77056-2327 Office: Butler & Binion 1500 1st Interstate Bank Plz Houston TX 77002•

ABBOTT, LINDA JOY, stained glass artisan, educator; b. Hemstead, N.Y., Oct. 10, 1943; d. Edward Morton Brandstatter and Evalyne Manchik; divorced 1971; children: David Edward Black, Adam Michael Black. AAS in Design, SUNY at FIT, N.Y.C., 1963; Cert. paralegal, Tarrant County C.C., Fort Worth, Tex., 1983. Fashion designer Alyssa/Little Craft, N.Y.C., 1963-65; bus. owner Virgin Islands Diving Sch., St. Thomas, V.I., 1972-76; stained glass artisan Creative Glass, Salt Lake City, 1978-81, Linda Abbott Glass Art, Willow Park, Tex., 1981-86; stained glass artisan, instr. Crystal Rainbow Glass Studio, Dania, Fla., 1986—; freelance calligrapher various colls., Covina, Calif., 1968-71; freelance artist, Lancaster, Calif., 1976-78; cons. various stained glass cos., 1989—; product cons. various stained glass equipment mfrs., 1994—. Co-author: (books) Hot & Wired, 1993, Some Things Fishy, 1993, Rainforest, 1994, Stargazing, 1995, Image is Everything, 1996; contbr. articles to mags. in field. Recipient Best in Show award Calif. City Art Assn., 1978, Glass Expo, Salt Lake City, 1982. Mem. So. Fla. Ferret Club, Internat. Art Glass Suppliers Assn. (com. chair 1996—), Internat. Stained Glass Designers Assn. (pres. 1995—), Art Glass Guild Artisans (dir. 1996—). Jewish. Office: Crystal Rainbow Glass Studio # 2B 1300 Stirling Rd # 28 Dania FL 33004-3537

ABBOTT, PAUL SCOTT, writer, public relations executive, consultant; b. Chgo., Nov. 15, 1956; s. Thomas Charles and Shirley May (Schuette) A.; 1 child: Ashleigh Danielle. BS in Journalism, Northwestern U., Evanston, Ill., 1978. Bus. reporter The Cin. Enquirer, 1978; staff writer The Richmond (Va.) News Leader, 1978-84; editor, pub. The County Line, Richmond, 1984-86; bus. writer Albuquerque Jour., 1986-87; mng. editor Carlsbad (N.Mex.) Current Argus, 1987; bur. mgr. PR Newswire, Miami, Fla., 1987-89; exec. v.p. Stuart Newman Assocs., Miami, 1989-93; independent writer, cons. Paul Scott Abbott Pub. Rels./Comm., Miramar, Fla., 1993—; cons. Nat. Assn. Chiefs of Police, Miami, 1989—, Port of Miami, 1993—. Author: Hot Pursuit, 1996; contbr. numerous articles to Ft. Lauderdale Sun-Sentinel, 1996; contbr. numerous articles, contbg. editor World Wide Shipping, 1993-96; conbr. articles, weekly columnist Fla. Shipper Mag., 1993-96. Founder Miramar Tower Power Com., 1994—; wildlife rescuer Duck Haven, Margate, Fla., 1994—. Recipient Cert. of Merit Va. Press Assn., Richmond, 1983, Red Ribbon award Informed Families of Dade County, Miami, 1990. Mem. Propeller Club of U.S. (pres. Port of Miami chpt. 1996—), Soc. Prof. Journalists (pres. South Fla. chpt. 1994-95), Fla. Pub. Rels. Assn. (accredited pub. rels. profl., pres. Greater Miami chpt. 1993-95). Republican. Lutheran. Home: 7130 Granada Blvd Miramar FL 33023 Office: Paul Scott Abbott Pub Rels/ Comm 7130 W Granada Blvd Miramar FL 33023-5922

ABBOTT, REGINA A., neurodiagnostic technologist, consultant, business owner; b. Haverhill, Mass., Mar. 5, 1950; d. Frank A. and Ann (Drelick) A. Student, Pierce Bus. Sch., Boston, 1967-70, Seizure Unit Children's Hosp. Med. Ctr. Sch. EEG Tech., Boston, 1970-71. Registered technologist. Tech. dir. electrodiagnostic labs. Salem Hosp., 1972-76; lab. dir. clin. neurophysiology Tufts U. New Eng. Med. Ctr., Boston, 1976-78; clin. instr. EEG program Laboure Coll., Boston, 1977-81; adminstrv. dir. dept.

Neurology Mt. Auburn Hosp., Cambridge, Mass., 1978-81; tech. dir. clin. neurophysiology Drs. Diagnostic Service, Virginia Beach, Va.; tech. dir. neurodiagnostic ctr. Portsmouth Psychiatric Ctr., 1981-87; founder, pres., owner Commonwealth Neurodiagnostic Services, Inc., 1986—; co-dir. continuing edn. program EEG Tech., Boston, 1977-78; mem. adv. com. sch. neurodiagnostic tech. Laboure Coll., 1977-81, Sch. EEG Tech. Children's Hosp. Med. Ctr., Boston, 1980-81; assoc. examiner Am. Bd. Registration of Electroencephalographic Technologists, 1977-83; mem. guest faculty Oxford Medilog Co., 1986; cons. Nihon Kohden Am., 1981-83; cons., educator Teca Corp., Pleasantville, N.Y., 1981-87; allied health profl. staff mem. Virginia Beach Gen. Hosp., Humana Hosp. Bayside, Virginia Beach; clin. evaluator Calif. Coll. for Health Scis., 1995—. Contbr. articles to profl. jours. EIL scholar, Poland/USSR, 1970; recipient Internat. Woman of Yr. award in bus. and sci. Internat. Biographical Ctr., London, 1993-94, Woman of Yr. award Am. Biographical Inst., 1993. Mem. NAFE, Am. Soc. Electroneurodiagnostic Technologists, New Eng. Soc. EEG Technologists (bd. dirs., sec., tng. and edn. com., faculty tng. and edn.), Am. Assn. Electrodiagnostic Technologists, Epilepsy Soc. Mass. Office: Commonwealth Neurodiagnostic Svcs Inc 400 Biltmore Ct Virginia Beach VA 23454-3459

ABBOTT, VICKY LYNN, educational administrator; b. Evansville, Ind., Aug. 27, 1951; d. Irl Raymond and Juanita Joyce (Becker) Hicks; m. Bill David Abbott, Aug. 4, 1973. BS in Elem. Edn., Ind. State U., 1972; MA in Elem. Edn., U. S.C., 1979, postgrad., 1988. Cert. elem. tchr., mid. sch. sci. tchr., S.C. Tchr. math. Dade Christian Sch., Hialeah, Fla., 1972-73, Alice Drive Mid. Sch., Sumter, S.C., 1973-84; staff developer Sumter Sch. Dist. 17, Sumter, 1984-89, coord. instrn., 1989—; condr. insvc. workshops. Mem. sch. bd. Sumter Christian Sch., 1983-85; treas. Alice Dr. Mid. Sch. PTA, 1983-84; chmn. Sumter County Clemson Extension Adv. Coun., 1989; bd. dirs. Sumter YMCA. Named mem. 1992 Citizen Amb. Program to Russia and Estonia; honoree Tribute to Women in Industry, 1990. Mem. ASCD (assoc.), Nat. Coun. Tchrs. Math., Nat. Sci. Tchrs. Assn., S.C. Coun. Tchrs. Math., S.C. Coun. Suprs. Math. (sec.), S.C. Assn. for Supervision and Curriculum Devel., S.C. Sci. Coun., S.C. Sci. Suprs. Assn., S.C. Assn. Chemistry Tchrs., Sumter County Hist. Soc., U.S.C. Alumni Assn., Ind. State U. Alumni Assn., Phi Delta Kappa (newsletter editor 1991-93, rsch. rep. 1994, pres. 1995), Delta Kappa Gamma (treas.). Republican. Baptist. Home: 709 White Pine Way Sumter SC 29154-6210 Office: Sumter Sch Dist 17 PO Box 1180 Sumter SC 29151-1180

ABBOTT, WILLIAM THOMAS, claim specialist; b. Guthrie, Okla., Jan. 6, 1938; s. Benjamin Franklin and Eva Mae (Lattin) A.; m. Jerri Evelyn Stacy, Apr. 20, 1974. BS, Cen. State U., Okla., 1960; Casualty Claim Law Assoc., Am. Ednl. Inst., 1975. Cert. Fraud Examiner, Assn. Cert. Fraud Examiners, 1996. Claim adjuster Crawford and Co., Lubbock, Tex., 1964-67, Tulsa, 1967-70; sr. claim specialist State Farm Ins. Co., Tulsa, 1970—; bd. dirs. Okla. Arson Adv. Coun., chmn., 1996—. Mem. Young Reps., 1967, Tulsa Met. Ministries, 1971-75, Tulsa Mental Health Hotline, 1971-73, Okla. Hist. Soc. With USMC, 1960-64. Mem. Am. Legion, Internat. Assn. Arson Investigators (bd. dirs. Okla. chpt. 1985-93, pres. 1991), Assn. Cert. Fraud Examiners, Tulsa Claims Assn. (pres. 1981, Claimsman of Yr. 1979), pres. Mt Carmel Cemetry Assn., Noble Co., Okla., Internat. Assn. Spl. Investigation Units, Profls. Against Confidence Crime (assoc.), Investigative Reporters and Editors (assoc.), Santa Fe Trail Assn., Blue Goose, Fire Marshale Assn. Okla. (assoc.), Tulsa Pond, League Am. Bicyclists (life), Adventure Cyclists, Tulsa Bicycle Club, Nat. Off-Road Bicycle Assn. Republican. Methodist. Office: State Farm Ins Co 12222 State Farm Blvd Tulsa OK 74146-5400

ABDEL-RAHMAN, MOHAMED, agribusiness consultant; b. Cairo, Egypt, July 3, 1941; came to U.S., 1965; m. Janine Neerdaels, Dec. 21, 1967 (div. 1989); children: Magda, Susan; m. NaimaA.K. Abdel-Ghany, May 8, 1994. BS, Ain-Shams U., 1962, MS in Plant Pathology, 1964; PhD in Hort., U. Fla., 1970; postgrad., Cornell U., 1971-72. Instr. Ain-Shams Coll. Agr., 1962-65; rsch. assoc. U. Fla. Coll. Agrl., Gainesville, 1968-70; product devel. mgr., planning & devel. mgr., bus. mgr. Agway Inc., Syracuse, N.Y., 1972-82; v.p. rsch. devel. Food Source Inc., Larkspur, Calif., 1982-83; dir. Agri-Intelligence Doane Inc., Princeton, N.J., 1983-85; pres. I.A-M Corp., Trenton, N.J., 1985-89; mktg. product mgr. fungicides and herbicides BASF, Inc., Rsch. Triangle Park, N.C., 1989-95; v.p. HAAN Internat., Chapel Hill, N.C., 1995—; sec. gen. PGRWG, 1977-79; pres. I.A.M. Corp., Trenton, N.J., 1985-89. Author: Agway Chemical and CropProtection Guides, 1972-82; contbr. over 240 articles to profl. jours. Vol. Flood Relief Orgn., N.Y., 1972. Recipient Nat. award Excellence, Egyptian Govt., 1962. Mem. Am. Soc. Hort. Sci. (program chmn. 1970-76), Am. Phytopathological Soc. (numerous exec. positions 1971—), Plant Growth Regulator Soc. Am. (numerous exec. positions 1973—). Muslim. Home: 23 Beechtree Ct Durham NC 27713-1942

ABEL, FRANCIS LEE, physiology educator; b. Iowa City, Apr. 12, 1931; s. Earl Lester A.; m. Evelyn Joyce Reischauer, Sept. 11, 1954 (div. Mar. 1974); children: Wanda, Donna, Carolyn; m. Anne Elizabeth Sutherland, June 9, 1974; 1 child, Jonathan. AA, Creston Jr. Coll., 1950; BA in Physics, U. Kans., 1952; MD, Harvard U., 1957; PhD in Physiology, U. Wis., 1960. Postdoctoral fellow, postdoctoral trainee Wis. Heart Assn. USPHS, Madison, 1958-60; intern in pediatrics Children's Hosp., L.A., 1960-61; from asst. prof. to prof. dept. physiology Sch. Medicine Ind. U., Indpls., 1962-75; prof., chmn. dept. physiology Sch. Medicine U. S.C., Columbia, 1975—; interim dean Sch Medicine U. S.C., Columbia, 1976, assoc. dean basic sci. affairs, 1976-78; vis. prof. dept. biomed. engring. U. So. Calif., L.A., 1970; vis. prof. dept. kinesiology Simon Fraser U., Burnaby, B.C., Can., 1982; vis. prof. dept. physiology U. Limburg, Maastricht, The Netherlands, 1989-90; cons. Eli Lilly & Co., Indpls., 1965-68, VA Hosp., Columbia, 1976-80. Co-author: Basic Physiology for the Health Sciences, 1975, Cardiovascular Function, Principles and Applications, 1979, Functional Aspects of the Normal Hypertrophied and Failing Heart, 1984. Recipient Career Devel. award NIH, 1968-73, Nat. Rsch. Svc. award NIH, 1989-90. Fellow Cardiovascular sect. Am. Physiol. Soc.; mem. Am. Physiol. Soc., Am. Heart Assn., Biomed. Engring. Soc. (sr.), Shock Soc. (councillor 1980-82). Office: USC Dept Physiology Columbia SC 29208

ABEL, HOWARD RICHARD, oncologist, hematologist; b. N.Y.C., May 4, 1938; s. Joseph and Eleanor (Freedman) A.; m. Grace Gorfin; children: Alexander, Elaine. BA, Cornell U., 1958; MD, Harvard U., 1962. Intern, resident in medicine U. Hosps. of Cleve., 1962-64; resident in medicine Bronx Mcpl. Hosp. Ctr., 1966-67; fellow in hematology Albert Einstein Coll. Medicine, N.Y.C., 1967-68, assoc. in medicine, 1968-69; pvt. practice Ft. Lauderdale, Fla., 1969—. Lt. comdr. USPHS, 1964-66. Mem. AMA, ACP, Am. Soc. Clin. Oncology, Am. Soc. Hematology, Fla. Med. Assn., Broward County Med. Assn. Office: 4800 NE 20th Ter Ste 211 Fort Lauderdale FL 33308-4510

ABELL, JOHN DAVIS, economics educator. BS in Econs. and Mgmt., Centre Coll. Ky., 1976; MS in Econs., U. Ky., 1982, PhD in Econs., 1985. Lectr. U. Ky., 1984-85; asst. prof. econs. U. N.C., Charlotte, 1985-91; assoc. prof. econs., chair econs. Randolph-Macon Woman's Coll., Lynchburg, Va., 1991—. Contbr. numerous articles to profl. jours. Office: Randolph-Macon Womans Coll Dept Econs Lynchburg VA 24503

ABELL, THOMAS LYMAN, physician; b. Vermillion, S.D., Mar. 9, 1948; married; 2 children. BA, Yale U., 1971; BSM, U. S.D., 1975, MD, 1977. Diplomate Am. Bd. Family Practice, Am. Bd. Internal Medicine. Intern So. Ill. U. Affiliated Hosps., Springfield, 1977-78; resident in family medicine Ohio State U. Hosp., Columbus, 1978-80, instr., 1978-80; preceptor in family medicine Mayor Med. Sch., Rochester, Minn., 1981-84, instr. family medicine, 1985-86; internal medicine coord. U. Tenn. HealthPlex Family Medicine Residency/Bapt. Hosp., Memphis, 1986-87; asst. prof. dept. medicine U. Tenn., Memphis, 1988—, asst. prof. dept. family medicine, 1989—, asst. prof. dept. pharmacology, 1991—, assoc. prof. dept. medicine, 1992—; vis. scientist in gastroenterology dept. medicine Mayor Clinic, Rochester, 1982-86; staff Olmsted Cmty. Hosp., Rochester, 1980-86, Rochester Health Care Ctr., 1980-86, U. Tenn. Med. Ctr. (Bowld Hosp.), 1988—, Regional Med. Ctr., VA Med. Ctr., 1988—, Bapt. Meml. Hosp., 1988—, LeBonheur Children's Hosp., Memphis, 1988—; mem. behavioral medicine study sect. NIH, 1989-90; med. staff U. Tenn. Med. Group, Memphis, 1988—; mem. clin. rsch. ctr. renewal com., 1992. Cons. editor Behavioral Medicine Abstracts, 1983-86; abstract reviewer Soc. Behavioral Medicine Ann. Meeting, 1985, Soc. Tchrs. Family Medicine Ann. Meeting, 1986; reviewer Diabetes Care, 1985-86, Gastroenterology, 1988—, Am. Jour. Gastroenterology, 1988—, Dig Dis Sci, 1988—, Am. Jour. Physiology, 1988—; book reviewer Psychosomatics, 1986; contbr. numerous articles to profl. jours. Grantee Olmsted Med. Group, 1982-83, Mayo Found., 1984-85, Janssen Pharmeceutica, 1985-92, Ross Labs., 1988, CRC, 1989-91, NIH, 1992, Glaxo Pharms., 1993, TAP Pharms., 1993-96. Mem. ACP, AMA, Tenn. Acad. Family Practice, Am. Acad. Family Practice, Med. Assn. Soc. of Psychophysiologic Rsch., Soc. for Behavioral Medicine, Am. Gastroenterol. Assn., Am. Fedn. for Clin. Rsch., Janssen Rsch. Coun., Am. Soc. Internal Medicine, Am. Motility Soc., Gastroenterology Rsch. Group. Office: Univ of Tenn Med Group Inc 920 Madison Ave Ste 300 Memphis TN 38103-3438

ABELLA, MARISELA CARLOTA, business executive; b. Havana, Cuba, Feb. 5, 1943; d. Carlos and Angela (Acosta) A.; m. Alberto Herrera Nogueira, Apr. 6, 1968 (div. Apr. 1986); 1 child, Carlos Alberto Herrera Abella. Asst. to v.p. and gen. mgr. bonding dept. Manuel San Juan (P.R.) Co. Inc., 1962-64; asst. corp. sec. and exec. sec. to pres. and stockholder Interstate Gen. Corp., Hato Rey, P.R., 1964-72, corp. sec. and pvt. sec. to corp. pres., 1972-79; sec.-treas., dir. A. H. Enterprises Inc., Caparra Heights, P.R., 1979-86; v.p., sec., bd. dirs. El Viajero Inc.; bd. dirs. A. H. Enterprises Inc., San Juan; pres. Marisela Abella Mktg. and Selling Promotional Items and Ideas, Caparra Heights, 1986—. Roman Catholic. Clubs: Caribe Hilton Swimming and Tennis, Barry U. Alumnae Assn. Home: 909 Borinquen Towers 2 Caparra Heights PR 00920 Office: PO Box 10510 Caparra Heights San Juan PR 00922-0510

ABERCIA, RALPH, lawyer, financial advisor; b. Houston, Aug. 24, 1923; s. Tofie and Libbie (Faour) A.; m. Mary Adelene Shawhean, Apr. 27, 1952; children: Sharon, Sandra, Mary Kathryn, Ralph F. BA, U. Houston, 1949; LLB, South Tex. Coll., 1951. Bar: Tex. 1951; lic. real estate broker. Founder, advising dir. E.E. Properties, Inc., Houston, 1948—; pvt. practice law Houston, 1951—; owner, founder Sylvian Enterprise, Inc., 1976—; pres., owner Ralph Abercia Investments, Houston, 1984—. Chmn., pres., bd. trustees St. George Orthodox Ch., 1968-74, others; mem. nat. bd. trustees Antiochian Christian Archdiocese of N.Am., 1974—, others; pres. So. Fedn. Syrian Lebanese Am. Clubs, 1966, chmn. bd. dirs., 1979-82, others; dr. chmn. Aid Leukemia Stricken Children, Houston, 1986; co-chmn. Kalil Gibran Found., Houston, 1991; mem. host com. GOP Conv., Houston, 1992; conv. chmn. St. Jude Childrens Rsch. Hosp., Houston, 1993; others. With USAF, 1942-45. Recipient Key to the City, Houston City Coun., 1980, Nigata, Japan, 1981, Antonio award Antiochian Orthodox Christian Archdiocese, N.Y.C., 1988. Mem. State Bar Assn. Tex., Houston Bar Assn., Houston Trial Lawyers Assn., Nat. Assn. Realtors, So. Fedn. SLAC (pres. 1966-67, chmn. bd. 1972-76, Man of Yr. 1972), Houston Realtor Assn., Order St. Ignatius (sec., bd. dirs. 1980, 2d vice-chmn., bd. dirs. 1986-87, 1st vice-chmn., bd. dirs. 1987-90, chmn. 1991—), Masons (32 degree), Shriners. Home: 314 Gentilly Pl Houston TX 77024-6315 Office: Ralph Abercia Investments 12438 Memorial Dr Houston TX 77024-6100

ABERCROMBIE, CHARLOTTE MANNING, reading specialist, supervisor; b. Swampscott, Mass., Oct. 25, 1915; d. Fredric Wilbur and Mary Sayer (Delano) Manning; m. Alexander Vaughan Abercrombie, Oct. 17, 1937; children: Lois A. Street, Paul M., David M., Lucia A. Harvilchuck. BA, Marietta Coll., 1937; MA, Columbia U., 1974, EdD, 1976. Cert. tchr. R.I., Wash., Wis., N.J.; cert. reading specialist, supr. N.J. Tchr. elem. schs. Tacoma (Wash.) Pub. Schs., 1958-62, Warwick (R.I.) Pub. Schs., 1957; tchr., reading specialist Milw. Pub. Schs., 1966-69; elem. tchr. and reading specialist, supr. East Orange (N.J.) Pub. Schs., 1969-79; dir. Fla. Ctr. for Philosophy for Children, Pensacola, 1994—. Mem. Nat. Assn. Congregational Chs. (exec. com. 1980-84). Mem. AAUW (v.p. Marco Island, Fla. chpt. 1988-89, bd. dirs. State of Fla. 1990, bd. dirs. Pensacola br. Coll. Univ., 1992). Repulican. Home: 10100 Hillview Rd Apt 616 Pensacola FL 32514-5460

ABERCROMBIE, FREDA A., secondary education educator. Tchr. Thomas E. Weightman Mid. Sch., Zephyrhills, Fla. Recipient Sallie Mae First Yr. Tchr. award, 1992. Office: Thomas E Weightman Mid Sch 30649 Wells Rd Zephyrhills FL 33544-3903

ABERCROMBIE, STONEY ALTON, family physician; b. Six Mile, S.C., Dec. 9, 1949; s. William Morris and Mildred Marette (Ellenburg) A.; m. Donna Gay Underwood, June 17, 1973; children: Jonathan Edward, Kristina Katherine. BS, Clemson U., 1972; MD, Med. U. S.C., 1976. Diplomate Am. Bd. Family Practice; lic. physician, S.C. Family practice intern Greenville (S.C.) Hosp. System, 1976, family practice resident, 1979-80; pvt. practice Seneca (S.C.) Med. Assocs., 1981-88; asst. residency dir. Self Meml. Hosp., Greenwood, 1989-90; residency dir. and dir. med. edn. Med. U. S.C., Charleston, 1990—; prof. family medicine MUSC, 1995—; staff physician Oconee Meml. Hosp., Seneca, 1981-88, chief of staff, 1988, bd. trustees, 1987-88; mem. utilization rev. com. Oconee Geriatric Ctr., 1981-87; asst. med. dir. Greenwood Health Care Ctr., 1990—, chmn. utilization rev. com., 1990—; med. dir. Greenbrook Manor Nursing Home, 1989-93; lectr. in field. Contbr. articles to profl. jours. Founder Oconee County Prenatal Clinic for Indigent OB Patients, 1983; mem. Upstate S.C. Emergency Svcs. Coun., 1981-84, Upstate S.C. Perinatal Adv. Com., 1981-84, Teen Pregnancy Prevention Coun., Oconee, 1988; mem. Gov.'s Task Force on Primary Health Care in Oconee County, 1984, Med.-Industry Com. for Health Care in Oconee County, 1984-85; bd. visitors Lander U., Greenwood, 1991-93; bd. advisors Vocat. Rehab. Ctr., Greenwood, 1991-94; bd. trustees Greenwood Literacy Coun., 1994-97, chmn. 1996, mem. century club Clemson U., 1981—, mem. IPTAY, 1981—, alumni loyalty fund vol., 1984; active Gideon's Internat., 1984—. Recipient disting. svc. to mankind award Rotary, 1995, Halford award excellence in human medicine S.C. AHEC, 1996. Fellow Am. Bd. Family Practice; mem. AMA, Am. Acad. Family Physicians (reviewer Huffington Libr. 1991—, pub. com. 1994-96), S.C. Acad. Family Physicians (bd. trustees 1987—, editor S.C. Family Physician, v.p. 1995, pres. 1996, 97), Soc. of Tchrs. Family Practice, S.C. Med. Assn. (liability case reviewer 1990—, assoc. chmn. CME com. 1995—), Greenwood Med. Soc. (pres. 1992-93), Clemson Alumni Physicians Soc. (charter), Med. U.S.C. Alumni Assn. (Alumni Assn. centennial Recognition List 1992), Assn. of Family Practice Residency Dirs. (charter, S.C. chpt. chmn. 1994—), Emerald City Rotary Club (bd. dirs. 1989-96, pres. 1992-93). Republican. Ch. of God. Office: Self Meml Hosp Family Practice Residency 160 Academy Ave Greenwood SC 29646-3808

ABERNATHY, BARBARA EUBANKS, counselor; b. Mobile, Ala., Aug. 28, 1963; d. Hardy Millard and Sarah Louise (Pate) Eubanks; m. James Abernathy Jr., Dec. 15, 1984. BS, Northwestern U., 1984; MS, U. South Ala., 1986; MS in Biol. Sci., Fla. Atlantic U., 1995. Mental health worker 11 Charter Southland Hosp., Mobile, 1985-86; counselor Indian River Community Mental Health, Ft. Pierce, Fla., 1986-87; family counselor Youth Svc. Bur., Palm Beach County, Fla., 1987-93; owenr Wet Dreams Scuba, Inc., Palm Beach Gardens, Fla., 1988—; behavior mgmt. cons. Okeechobee (Fla.) Sch. Sys., 1987; cons. Palm Beach County Sch. Bd., 1989—; instr., adj. prof. Palm Beach C.C., Palm Beach Gardens, 1990—; case mgmt. supr. Parent-Child Ctr., West Palm Beach, 1993-95; therapy cons. Alternative Family Care, Jupiter, Fla., 1995—, Comprehensive AIDS Program, West Palm Beach, 1995—. Counselor Rape Crisis Ctr., Mobile, 1985-86, Contact Mobile, 1985-86; troop leader Girl Scouts Chgo., 1982-84; dir. marine mammal rsch. South Fla. Sci. Mus., West Palm Beach, 1995—. Mem. APA, ACA, Kappa Delta Pi. Office: Parent Child Ctr 2500 Metrocentre Blvd Ste 3 West Palm Beach FL 33407-3107

ABERNATHY, JERRY DON, clergy member, educator; b. Red Oak, Okla., July 31, 1938; s. Woodford Donald and Pearl Palestine (Deere) A.; m. Ann Jaxie Farrell, Nov. 16, 1958; children: Jaxie Laniece, Jerry Don Jr., Steven Wayne. BA, Northeastern State U., 1960; MA in Religious Edn., Southwestern Bapt. Theol. Sem., 1962; D in Theology, Luther Rice Sem., 1969. Dir. Bapt. student ctr. Northeastern State U., Tahlequah, Okla., 1958-59; pastor First Bapt. Sherwood, North Little Rock, Ark., 1962-64; pastor First Bapt. Ch., Crossett, Ark., 1966-1970, McAllen, Tex., 1970-74; pastor Immanuel Bapt. Ch., Tulsa, 1974-80, Sunnylane So. Bapt. Ch., Oklahoma City, 1987—; assoc. religion edn. dir. Ark. Bapt. State Conv., Little Rock, 1964-66; dir. evangelism Bapt. Gen. Conv. Okla., Oklahoma City, 1980-87; pres. Ark. Bapt. Pastors Conf., Little Rock, 1968-69, Bapt. Gen. Conv., Okla. City, 1977-79; mem. Fgn. Mission Bd., So. Bapt. Conv., 1985-86. Author: Roadblocks to Backsliding, 1973, Living in God's Promises, 1984; contbr.articles to profl. jours. Mem. Del City (Okla.) C. of C. Republican. Home: 10900 Quail Run Rd Oklahoma City OK 73150 Office: 3900 S Epperly Del City OK 73115

ABERNATHY, MARGARET DENNY, elementary school educator; b. Durham, N.C., Aug. 23, 1948; d. John Howard and Myrtle Ruth (Lunsford) Denny; divorced; children: Guenevere Anjanette, Chadwick Sean. BS in Spanish, Appalachian State U., 1970; BS in Early Childhood Edn., Brenau Coll., 1976; postgrad., N.C. Cen. U., 1981-83. Cert. tchr. Spanish, 7-12, early childhood edn., K-4, N.C. Tchr. Spanish/English North Wilkes High Sch., Hays, N.C., 1970-71; tchr. coll.-level basic English Army Edn. Ctr. Lang. Sch., Fort Bragg, N.C., 1972; tchr. Spanish/English North Hall High Sch., Gainesville, Ga., 1976-77; Title 1 1st-grade tchr. Hall County Schs., Gainesville, 1978-79; tchr. asst. Durham (N.C.) County Schs., 1979-86, tchr. third grade, 1986—, team leader 3d grade, 1991-93, sch. sci. liaison, 1995—. Mem. PTA, Durham, 1979—; pianist, Sunday Sch. tchr., mem. adminstrv. bd. Rougemont (N.C.) United Meth. ch., 1979—, v.p. Rougemont United Meth. Women; helper, den mother Boy Scouts Am., Durham, 1984-85, 87-94. Mem. NEA, N.C. Assn. Educators, Durham Assn. Educators, Christian Bus. and Profl. Women (Stonecroft Durham chpt.). Democrat. Home: 12507 Roxboro Rd Rougemont NC 27572 Office: Easley Elem Sch/Durham Pub Schs 302 Lebanon Cir Durham NC 27712-2644

ABERNATHY, SUE EURY, physical education educator; b. Washington, N.C., July 28, 1947; d. Craig Stanford and Lelia Frances (McHarney) Eury; m. Dean Judson Abernathy Jr., Dec. 27, 1970; children: Kristan Joanna, Dean Judson III. BS in Health and Phys. Edn., Campbell U., 1969; MA in Tchg., U. N.C., 1970; DA in Phys. Edn., Middle Tenn. State U., 1995. Cert. tchr. Tchr. Lee County Schs., Lemon Springs, N.C., 1970-71, Weatherford County Schs., Reno, Tex., 1971-73, Prince George's County Schs., Suitland, Md., 1973-75, Duval County Schs., Jacksonville, Fla., 1975-84, Akiva Sch., Nashville, 1984-92, Metro Nashville (Tenn.) Schs., Lakeview Elem Sch., 1992—; 4th degree black belt World Tae Kwon Do Fedn., Seoul, Korea, 1987—; writer Tenn. Elem. Tae Kwon Do curriculum, 1993; mem. adv. team Lakeview Elem. Sch., 1993-94; presenter in field. Youth dir., tchr. Brentwood (Tenn.) Bapt. Sunday Sch., 1984—; active tchg. mission trip Brentwood Bapt. Ch., Scotland, 1990, 92. Recipient Mayor's Acts of Excellence award Mayor of Nashville, 1994, 95, Tchr. award grant Hosp. Corp. Am., 1994, Eskind Ednl. grant, 1995, 96, Am. South Excellence in Edn. grant, 1995, Letter of Commendation, World Tae Kwon Do Fedn., 1994. Mem. AAHPERD (presenter so. dist. 1994-95, sec. hist. coun. 1995-96), Tenn. AHPERD (presenter 1994, 95, 96), N.Am. Assn. Sport History, All-Am. Scholar, Phi Epsilon Kappa, Kappa Delta Pi, Phi Kappa Phi. Home: 1020 Highland Rd Brentwood TN 37027-5528

ABERNETHY, FRANCIS EDWARD, English educator; b. Altus, Okla., Dec. 3, 1925; s. Talbot and Aileen (Cherry) A.; m. Hazel Marian Shelton, June 12, 1948; children: Luanna Cole, Robert, Sarah Blackley, Margaret Duffin, Benjamin. BA, Stephen F. Austin State U., 1949; postgrad., U. Neuchatel, Switzerland, 1949; MA, La. State U., 1951, PhD, 1956. Tchr. Woodville (Tex.) H.S., 1951-53; grad. instr. La. State U., Baton Rouge, 1953-56; assoc. prof. Lamar State Coll., Beaumont, Tex., 1956-65; prof. English Stephen F. Austin State U., Nacogdoches, Tex., 1965—; editl. bd. UNT Press, Denton, Tex. Co-author: How to Write a Theme, 1961; author: J. Frank Dobie, 1967, How the Critters Created Texas, 1982, Singin' Texas, 1983 (San Antonio Conservation Soc. award 1984), Legends of Texas' Heroic Age, 1984, The Epic Adventure - Texas!, 1985, Introduction to Folklore, 1985, The Texas Folklore Society: 1909-1943, Vol. I, 1992 (San Antonio Conservation Society award 1993), The Texas Folklore Society: 1943-1971, Vol. II, 1994; editor: Tales from the Big Thicket, 1966, Observations and Reflections on Texas Folklore, 1972, The Folklore of Texan Cultures, 1974, Some Still Do: Essays on Texas Customs, 1975, What's Going On? (In Modern Texas Folklore), 1976, Paisanos: A Folklore Miscellany, 1978, Built in Texas, 1979, Legendary Ladies of Texas, 1981, T For Texas, 1982, Folk Art in Texas, 1985, Sonovagun Stew, 1985, Hoein' the Short Rows, 1987, Texas Toys and Games, 1989, The Bounty of Texas, 1990, Corners of Texas, 1993; co-editor: Juneteenth Texas: Essays in African-American Folklore, 1996; records/tapes include: East Texas String Ensemble Live! at the Texas Folklife Festival, 1974, East Texas String Ensemble from Nacogdoches, 1983, Singin' Texas, 1983, Texas: The Epic Adventure, 1985, How the Critters Created Texas, 1986; films include: Big Thicket in Texas, 1960, Buffalo, Canebrakes and Old Texas Love Songs, 1983, Texas Myths and Texas Writers, 1987. Bd. dirs. Tex. Com. for Humanities, Austin, Tex. Com. for the Arts, Austin, Big Thicket Assn., Beaumont, Tex.; chmn. LaNana Creek Trail Com., Nacogdoches, 1976—; actor Lamp Lite Theatre Prodns., Nacogdoches; bass fiddle player East Tex. String Ensemble, Nacogdoches. With USN, 1943-46. Named Stephen F. Austin Alumni Disting. Profl., 1982. Mem. Tex. Folklore Soc. (sec.-editor 1971—), Tex. Inst. Letters, Tex. State Hist. Assn., Tex. Humanities Alliance, Big Thicket Conservation Assn., East Tex. Hist. Assn. Office: Texas Folklore Society PO Box 13007 SFASU Nacogdoches TX 75962

ABERNETHY, KATHRYN GRANT, mental health nurse, rehabilitation nurse; b. Atlanta, Sept. 6, 1964; d. William Glen Jr. and Kathryn Mecham (Byrd) G. BSN, U. N.C., Charlotte, 1986. RN, N.C.; cert. Wickersty aggression control trainer. Primary nurse, therapy group facilitator Presbyn. Hosp., Charlotte, 1986-90, prim. nurse, quality assurance nurse, 1986-90; neuro trauma rehab. nurse Mercy Hosp., Charlotte, 1990; with Profl. Health Svcs., 1984-85; asst. head nurse Adolescent Unit Ctr. for Mental Health, Charlotte, 1990-91; adult unit mgr. CPC Cedar Springs Hosp., 1991—, nurse mgr. adult and adolescent program, 1992-93; RN clin. coord. partial hospitalization Rapha Svc., 1993-94; pvt. practice with Bret Burquest MD Charlotte, 1994—. Contbr. articles to Quality Assurance Journal of Nursing vol. 5, 1990. Mem. NAFE.

ABERSON, LESLIE DONALD, lawyer; b. St. Louis, May 30, 1936; s. Hillard and Adele (Wenneker) A.; m. Regene Jo Lowenstein, Oct. 16, 1960; children—Karen, Angie, Leslie. BS, U. Ky., 1957, JD, 1960. Bar: Ky. 1960, U.S. Dist. Ct. (we. dist.) Ky. 1964, U.S. Tax Ct. 1968, U.S. Supreme Ct. 1975. Assoc. Washer, Kaplan, Rothschild, Aberson & Miller, Louisville, 1963-65, ptnr., 1965—; dir. Bank of Louisville. Bd. dirs. Ky. Athletic Hall of Fame, 1965—, Jewish Hosp. Louisville, 1978—, Louisville Med. Rsch. Found., 1975—, NCCJ; bd. dirs., past pres. B'rith Sholom Temple; bd. dirs., past v.p. Jewish Community Fedn. Louisville; bd. dir. Louisville Free Pub. Libr. Found. Recipient Louis Cole Young Leadership award Louisville C. of C. Mem. Ky. Bar Assn., Louisville Bar Assn., Ky. Trial Lawyers Assn., Am. Trial Lawyers Assn., Louisville C. of C. (instl. rev. com.), U. Ky. Law Sch. Alumni Assn. (bd. dirs.). Home: 2306 Merrick Rd Louisville KY 40207-1255 Office: Washer Kaplan Rothschild Aberson & Miller Ky Home Life Bldg 239 S 5th St Fl 17 Louisville KY 40202-3213

ABLE, LUKE WILLIAM, retired pediatric surgeon, consultant; b. Pt. Arthur, Tex.; s. James Levert and Minnie Maude (Branson) A.; m. Mary Beth Able, June 7, 1937 (div. Dec. 1984); children: Luke William, Stephen Smith; m. Margaret Galloway, Dec. 29, 1984 (dec. Dec. 1993); m. Hester Finke, July 14, 1995. BA, U. Tex., 1933, MD, 1940. Diplomate Am. Bd. Surgery and Pediat. Surgery. Extern So. Pacific Hosp., 1939; intern, surg. resident Hermann Hosp., Houston, 1940-43; resident in gen. and cardiovasc. surgery Boston Children's Hosp., 1946-48; pvt. practice Tex., 1948; clin. prof. surgery Baylor Med. Coll., Houston, 1950—; surgeon-in-chief, head dept. surgery Tex. Children's Hosp., Houston, 1954-87, surgeon-in-chief, head dept. surgery emeritus, 1987—; active staff/cons. St. Luke's Episcopal Hosp., Meml. Sys., Meth. Hosp., Hermann Hosp., Tex. Children's Hosp.; teaching assoc. U. Tex., Houston. Author: Siamese Twins, 1968; contbr. numerous articles to surg. and med. jours., chpts. to med. and surg. books. Lt. USNR, 1943-46, PTO. Decorated Purple Heart, Silver Star. Mem. ACS (Outstanding Presentation award), AMA, Am. Med. Soc., Am. Acad. Pediats. (surg. sect. 1949—, Outstanding Presentation award), Am. Pediats. Surg. Assn. (charter), Am. Trauma Assn., Tex. Med. Soc., Tex. Pediat. Soc., Tex. Surg. Soc. (v.p. 1953—, pres. 1987, Comty. Svc. award), Tex. Assn. Pediat. Surgeons (past pres.), Houston Pediat. Soc., Houston Surg. Soc. (pres. 1969-70, Outstanding Surgeon of Yr. 1991, Comty. Svc. award). Harris County

Med. Soc. (sec. 1958). Republican. Baptist. Home: 18734 Murrell Rd Hockley TX 77447-9781 Office: Pediat Surgery Cons 6624 Fannin Ste 1590 Houston TX 77002-7616

ABLES, NANCY BUMSTEAD, sales executive; b. Galesburg, Ill., Mar. 9, 1948; d. Charles Heath Bumstead and Thelma Delta (Hughes) McDonald; m. Laurence Clifton Greenwold, June 4, 1966 (div. Feb. 1987); children: Laurie J. Greenwold Campos, Charles Howard Greenwold; m. David Stephen Ables, Mar. 15, 1987. With, Knox Coll., 1965-69. Assembler printed circuit bd. Astro Internat. Corp., League City, Tex., 1987, spare parts sales mgr., 1987-95, parts cons., 1995-96; edn. coord. Astro Internat. Corp., League City, 1996—; printed cir. bd. assembler Gadget Electronics, Pasadena, Tex., 1986—; v.p. Gadget Electronics, Pasadena, 1987—; cons. parts bus., Houston, 1995-96; environ. edn. advisor. Chmn. Environ. Commn., Park Forest South, Ill., 1971-74; v.p. Balmoral Elem. P.T.O., Crete, Ill., 1980-81, pres., 1981-83; campaign mgr. J. Gustafson Sch. Bd. mem., Crete, 1980. Home: 9800 Hollock St Apt 1009 Houston TX 77075-1833 Office: Earth Found 5151 Mitchelldale Houston TX 77092

ABLORDEPPEY, SETH Y., medicinal chemistry educator; b. Agordome, Ghana, July 16, 1953; came to U.S., 1985; s. Sam H. and Adzoyo (Kuotsrowo) A.; m. Joy H. Amemornu, Sept. 19, 1979; children: Enyo, Edem, Sroda, Kafui, Suboe, Aseye. BSc, U. Cape Coast, 1977; MSc, U. Sci. & Tech. Ghana, 1980; PhD, U. Miss., 1990. Lectr. U. Lagos, Nigeria, 1981-85; rsch. fellow Va. Commonwealth U., Richmond, 1991-93; asst. prof. Fla. A&M U., Tallahassee, 1993—. Mem. Am. Assn. Colls. Pharmacy, Am. Chem. Soc. Baptist. Home: 3526 Limerick Dr Tallahassee FL 32308 Office: Fla A&M Univ Coll Pharmacy Tallahassee FL 32307

ABRAHAM, JOHN EDWARD, environmental health scientist; b. Hartford, Conn., Aug. 9, 1951; s. Walter B. and Lucy R. (Eshoo) A.; m. Corrine A. Bowers, Aug. 22, 1981; children: David, Rachel, Michael. BA, U. Denver, 1973; MA, U. Hartford, 1976; PhD, U. Iowa, 1981; MPH, Tulane U., 1986; MBA, Ga. State U., 1990. Environ. health scientist/epidemiologist Ctr. for Environ. Health, CDC, Atlanta, 1985-87; environ. health scientist Agy. for Toxic Substances and Disease Registry, Atlanta, 1987-90, supr. fed. facilities activity divsn. health assessment and consultation, 1990-91, chief def. facilities assessment sect. fed. programs br., 1991-93, chief exposure investigations sect., 1994—; coord. environ. topics course Sch. Pub. Health, Emory U., Atlanta, 1985; adj. prof. Sch. Pub. Health and Tropical Medicine, Tulane U., New Orleans, 1986—, Coll. Bus. Adminstrn., Ga. State U., Atlanta; tech. cons. Evaluating Hazardous Waste Grad. Curriculums, 1986, Evaluating Environ. Health Workforce, Airlie Ho., Warrenton, Va., 1987, Faculty/Employer Environ. Health Forum, U. Mich., Ann Arbor, 1988, Evaluating Hazardous Waste Continuing Edn. Courses, 1989. Capt. U.S. Army, 1982-85; capt. USPHS, 1985—. NIH cancer fellow, 1977-81; recipient Svc. Commendation, USPHS, 1991, Achievement medal, 1989. Mem. Nat. Environ. Health Assn. (cert. hazardous waste specialist, Am. Indsl. Hygiene Assn. (mem. occupational epidemiology com. 1982-85, mem. pub. policy com. 1982-85). Home: 1660 Pinefield Way Marietta GA 30066-1253 Office: ASTDR MS E-32 1600 Clifton Rd NE Atlanta GA 30329-4018

ABRAHAMS, LAWRENCE MICHAEL, psychiatrist; s. Rolland Schwartz and Johanna Muriel (Lichtenfels) A.; m. Hanna Elizabeth Den Hartog, July 5, 1969. AB in Econs. cum laude, Harvard U., 1956; MD, Vanderbilt U., 1961. Diplomate Am. Bd. Psychiatry and Neurology. Rotating intern Lankenau Hosp., Phila., 1961-62; resident psychiatry N.Y. Hosp. Westchester Divsn., White Plains, 1962-63, Grasslands Hosp., Valhalla, N.Y., 1964-65; rsch. fellow in psychiatry, resident Peter Bent Brigham Hosp. and Harvard Med. Sch., Boston, 1965-66; from sr. psychitrist to dir. psychiatry Taunton (Mass.) State Hosp., 1967-73; clin. asst. prof. of psychiatry LSU Med. Sch., New Orleans, 1973—; psychiatrist New Orleans Mental Health Ctr., 1973-82, Ctrl. City Mental Health Ctr., New Orleans, 1973-91; from psychiatrist to acting chief, chief drug dependence treatment unit, staff psychiatrist VA Med. Ctr., New Orleans, 1974—; v.p. med. staff Taunton State Hosp., 1971-72; treas. Mass. State Employed Physicians Soc., 1972-73; dir. Touro Mental Health Ctr., New Orleans, 1973; cons. psychiatrist Social Security Disability Determination Unit, New Orleans, 1973-81. Served to col. M.C., USAR, 1961-94. Mem. Am. Psychiat. Assn., La. Psychiat. Assn, Orleas Parish Med. Soc. Republican. Home: 5320 Bellaire Dr New Orleans LA 70124-1033 Office: VA Med Ctr 1601 Perdido St New Orleans LA 70112-1207

ABRAHAMSON, A. CRAIG, lawyer; b. Washington, May 24, 1954; s. Joseph Labe and Helen Dorothy (Selis) A.; m. Mary Ellen Bernard, Dec. 29, 1979; children: Nicholas Eric, Amy Nicole. BA, U. Minn., 1976; JD, U. Tulsa, 1979. Bar: Minn. 1979, U.S. Dist. Ct. Minn. 1979, Okla. 1982, U.S. Dist. Ct. (no. and ea. dists.) Okla. 1983, Mo. 1991. Assoc. Law Office of Joseph L. Abrahamson, Mpls., 1979-82, Freese & March, Tulsa, 1982-83, Barlow & Cox, Tulsa, 1983-86; sole practice Tulsa, 1986-95; ptnr. Levinson, Smith & Abrahamson, Tulsa, 1995—. V.p. program com. Youth Svcs., Tulsa, Inc., Leadership Tulsa Class XVII, 1989-92. Recipient Am. Jurisprudence Evidence award Lawyers Co-operative Pub. Co. Bancroft-Whitney Co., 1978. Mem. ABA (litigation sect.), Okla. Bar Assn. (family law sect.), Assn. Trial Lawyers Am., Okla. Trial Lawyers Assn., Tulsa County Bar Assn. (profl. responsibility com.). Democrat. Jewish. Lodge: Masons. Home: 7518 S 107th East Ave Tulsa OK 74133-2530 Office: 35 E 18th St Tulsa OK 74119 also: PO Box 3366 Tulsa OK 74101-3366

ABRAHAMSON, MICHAEL WILLIAM, process engineering technician; b. Long Beach, Calif., Jan. 30, 1956; s. Jack Gordon and Diana Joan (Majors) A.; children: Diana Alisha, Jack William. BS in Biology, Coll. of the Ozarks, 1978. Asst. mgr. Valmac, Russellville, Ark., 1978-80; derrickman, leadman Miller Drilling Co., Ft. Smith, Ark., 1981-84; quality control technician Magentics-Divsn. of Spang, Booneville, Ark., 1984-87, process technician engring., 1987—; security capt. Concert Tech. Assn., Ft. Smith, 1986—. Com. chair Cub Scouts Am., Magazine, Ark., 1991-94; com. mem. Boy Scouts Am., Magazine, 1992—. Mem. Ark. Archaeology Soc. (state bd. advisors, pres. River Valley Chpt. 1996). Home: PO Box 493 Magazine AR 72943-0493

ABRAMOWITZ, JERROLD, lawyer; b. Bklyn., July 15, 1953; s. Harry and Zelda (Underberg) A.; m. Tina Hope Cohen, Aug. 26, 1973; children: David B., Daniel R. BA, U. Conn., 1974; MS in Judicial Adminstrn., U. Denver, 1976; JD, U. Toledo, 1981. Bar: Ohio 1982, Okla. 1990. Staff assoc. Nat. Ctr. for State Courts, Denver, 1976; mgmt. analyst U.S. Ct. Appeals (6th cir.), Cin., 1976-79; court adminstr. Toledo Mcpl. Ct., 1979-86; adminstrv. dir. Pierce, Couch, Hendrickson, Baysinger & Green, Oklahoma City, 1986-95; adminstr. Best, Sharp, Holden, Sheridan, Best & Sullivan, Tulsa, Okla., 1995—; lectr. 22d Ann. Inst. on Law Firm Mgmt., 1993. Author: Partner Productivity: Measure of the 90's, 1993, Electronic Imaging Systems, 1993, Loose Lips Sink Ships and Firms, 1995. Bd. dirs. Court Diagnostic and Treatment Ctr., Toledo, 1982-86, Toledo/Lucas County Criminal Justice Bd., Toledo, 1979-86. Mem. ABA, Okla. Bar Assn., Tulsa County Bar Assn., Assn. for Legal Adminstrs. (treas. Oklahoma City chpt. 1989—, v.p. 1992, pres. 1993, treas. Tulsa chpt. 1996), Ohio Assn. Ct. Adminstrs. (treas. 1984, v.p. 1985, pres. 1986). Office: Best Sharp Holden Sheridan Best & Sullivan 100 W 5th St Ste 808 Tulsa OK 74103-4225

ABRAMS, BRENDA M., lawyer; b. N.Y.C., July 13, 1942; d. Nathan N. and Frances (Margulies) Greenberg; m. Ira Abrams, Mar. 1, 1962; 1 child, Jennifer. AB cum laude, U. Miami, 1964, JD cum laude, 1971. Bar: Fla. 1971, U.S. Ct. Appeals (5th cir.) 1971, U.S. Supreme Ct. 1976. Law clk. to chief judge U.S. Dist. Ct. Fla., Miami, 1971-72; sole practice Miami, 1972-74; ptnr. Abrams, Abrams, & Etter PA, Miami, 1974—; faculty U. Miami Law Sch., 1974-88, Nova Law Sch., 1982-83. Author: 6 vols. Florida Family Law; editor Family Law Reporter, 1986—; contbr. articles to profl. jours. Named one of the Best Lawyers of Am. Woodward/White, Inc., 1987-90, 91-93, 93-94, 95. Fellow Am. Acad. Matrimonial Lawyers (mgr. 1983—, cert., bd. dirs.); mem. Am. Law Inst., Fla. Bar Assn. (chmn. family law sect. 1984-86, sec./treas. 1983-84, exec. council, Award Merit 1985). Office: Abrams, Abrams & Etter PA 3341 Cornelia Dr Miami FL 33133-5313

ABRAMSON, ELAINE SANDRA, graphic designer, crafts artist; b. Cleve., Aug. 27, 1942; d. Norman Morris and Ruth Leah (Glassman) Splaver; m. Martin Stanley Abramson, May 27, 1977; children: Deborah Sue, Mitchell Lee. Hebrew tchr. cert. Hyam Greenberg Inst., Jerusalem, 1960-61; cert. in appraising fine and decorative arts NYU, 1990, Cleve. Inst. Art, 1954-64, 90, NYU, 1990; BS in Edn., Kent State U., 1964. Illustrator Ednl. Research Council, Cleve., 1964-65; tchr. art Cleve. Bd. Edn., 1965-67; pres., owner A & A (formerly Create-A-Craft), Ft. Worth, 1967—; author, spkr. affects of copyright law and politics on the artist, 1991—; founding artist, publicity designer Sassy Cat, Chagrin Falls, Ohio, 1967-71; adviser Women's Am. ORT Collection, Houston, 1983-84; designer Golden Gourmet dolls, Hobby Industries Am., Dallas, 1981, 85; intern, columnist Appraisers Assn. Am., 1990; cons. appraising and decorative arts for copyright law. Group shows of illustration, soft crafts, toys, enamelling include: Cleve. Mus. Art, 1964, Cleve. Inst. Art, 1964-71, Towson Courthouse Art Exhibit, Md., 1972-77; one-woman shows include: Kent State U., 1963-64, Central Nat. Bank Cleve., 1961-66; Md. Pub. TV Arts Exhibits, 1972-77, Tex. State Artist Competition. Designer, inventor, creator craft kits, toys, games, 1967—; author: (syndicated column) Appraisals by Abramson, (cartoons) Rojo the Red Lobster, The Golden Gourmets, Those Characters From Cowtown, 1991; editor, art dir. Art Forum, 1991—; creator, lic. Those Characters from Cowtown (recipient citation Tex. Ho. Reps. 1987, Tex. Senate Proclamation, 3 Mayor of Fort Worth Proclamations incl. Proclamation First Woman State Artist of Tex., 1993, numerous letters, used to stimulate Tex. tourism 1988-91, used in Richards for Gov. campaign 1990, used in state artist competition and other art work). Advisor Jr. Achievement, Fort Worth. Named Internat. Woman of the Yr. England, 1994; nominee First Woman State Artist, 1988-91, now State Artist Tex., 1993-94, Tex. Women Hall of Fame, 1989-91, Guinness Book of Records, 1991, Practicing Law Inst. scholar, 1992, Internat. Woman of Yr. Art, 1994 Mem. Soc. Craft Designers (in Dallas Showcase of Designers 1985), Md. Art League (bd. dirs., workshop chmn.), Graphic Artists Guild (bd. dirs. 1991-94, editor Art Forum 1990-94), Cartoonists Guild, Am. Crafts Coun., Nat. Enamelists Guild, Am. Mus. Natural History, Nat. Geographic Soc., Smithsonian Instn., Nat. Assn. Self-Employed, Orgn. for Enforcement of Child Support, Internat. Historic Preservation Soc., Composers, Authors and Artists in Am., Tex. Accts., Lawyers for Arts, Graphic Artists Guild (founder Tex. chpt. 1991), Authors & Artists of Am., Nat. League Advt. Agys., Am. Film Inst., Nat. Writers Club, Nat. Mus. Women in the Arts, Tex. Accts. and Lawyers for the Arts (cons. for lawyers on copyrights and appraising fine and decorative arts, 1991—), Bus. Profl. Women's Found., Delegation for Friendship among Women Writers' Workshop, Dallas Soc. Illustrators, Soc. Children's Book Writers and Illustrators, Nat. League of Am. Pen Women, Advt. Club Ft. Worth, Am. Advt. Fedn., Graphic Artists Guild (founder Tex. -at-large chpt. 1991, first chpt. dir., sr. adv.), Zonta. Jewish. Avocations: sewing, painting, reading, travel. Office: A & A PO Box 330008 Fort Worth TX 76163-0008

ABRAMSON, HYMAN NORMAN, engineering and science research executive; b. San Antonio, Mar. 4, 1926; s. Nathan and Pearl (Westerman) A.; m. Idelle Rebecca Ringel, Apr. 20, 1947; children—Phillip David, Mark Donald. B.S.M.E., Stanford U., 1950, M.S. in Engring. Mechanics, 1951; Ph.D. in Engring. Mechanics (So. Fellowship Fund fellow), U. Tex., Austin, 1956. Engr. U.S. Naval Air Missile Test Center, Point Mugu, Calif., 1947-48; project engr. Chance Vought Aircraft Co., Dallas, 1951-52; assoc. prof. aero. engring. Tex. A&M U., 1952-55; sect. mgr., dept. dir. S.W. Research Inst., San Antonio, 1956-72, v.p. div. engring. scis., 1972-85, exec. v.p., 1985-91, also bd. dirs.; mem. many research adv. coms. U.S. Govt.; bd. dirs. Broadway Nat. Bank. Author: An Introduction to the Dynamics of Airplanes, 1958, reprinted, 1971; contbr. numerous articles to profl. publs.; editor: (with others) Applied Mechanics Surveys, 1966, The Dynamic Behavior of Liquids in Moving Containers, 1966; assoc. editor: (with others) Applied Mechanics Revs, 1954-85; editorial adv. bd.: (with others) Jour. Computers and Structures, 1970—, Aeros. and Astronautics, 1975-80. Mem. Greater San Antonio C. of C., and City of San Antonio Market Sq. Adv. Com., 1973-77; mem. U.S. Bicentennial Com. of San Antonio, 1975-76; mem. adv. bd. dirs. U.S. Alamo, Inc., 1985—. Served with USN, 1943-45. Fellow AIAA (Disting. Service award 1973, dir., Structures, Structural Dynamics and Materials award 1991), ASME (v.p., gov., hon. mem.); mem. Nat. Acad. Engring., Soc. Naval Architects and Marine Engrs., Nat. Acad. Engring. Mexico, AAAS, Sigma Xi. Republican. Jewish. Home: 1511 Spanish Oaks San Antonio TX 78213-1635 Office: SW Research Inst 6220 Culebra Rd PO Drawer 28510 San Antonio TX 78228-0510

ABRIL, MARCIA, author; b. Jesus Maria, Santander, Colombia, Mar. 21, 1928; came to U.S., 1985; d. Jorge Benjamin and Ana Isabel (Valenzuela) Telles; m. Rafael A. Cardenas, Mar. 12, 1959; children: Willyam, Harold, Alix, Ela, Rafael, Katiana. BA in Edn. and Psychology, Normal Superior A. Narino, Malaga, Santander, 1950. Prodr. Continental Network Channel 14 TV, Miami, Fla., 1989; participant/writer Mcpl. Matanzas en el Exilio, Miami, Fla., 1986. Author: Para ti Cartagena, 1982, Aguilas e Ilusiones, 1986, Insolito, 1990, 2d edit., 1995, Viento y Sol, 1995; author/composer: Colombia Aqui Esta tu Gente, Miami, 1986. Vol. Empresa Promotora de Turismo, Cartagena, 1982-83; benefactor Biblioteca Nacional, Bogota, Colombia, 1982, U. Nacional de Colombia, Bogota, 1982; guest/participant Primer Encuentro de la Cultura Hispanoamericana, Bogota, 1983. Recipient Honorary award Municipio de Matanzas en el Exilio, Miami, 1986, Meritory award Eva Am. Prodns., 1995, Cert. of Recognition, Libr. of Congress, 1995. Roman Catholic. Office: 815 SW 8th St Miami FL 33130

ABSHIRE, MARY YOUNG, dietitian, small business owner; b. El Campo, Tex., Jan. 10, 1952; d. Robert Joshua and Virginia Berniece (Braden) Young; m. Russell John Abshire, June 22, 1978; children: Russell Braden, Marissa Michelle, Ryan Ross. BS in Foods and Nutrition, U. Tex., 1973. Lic. dietitian, Tex. Dietetic trainee U. Tex. Sys. Cancer Ctr.-M.D. Anderson Hosp., Houston, 1974-75; regional dietary cons. Nat. Living Ctrs. Inc., Victoria, Tex., 1975-77; quality assurance dietitian Nat. Living Ctrs. Inc., Houston, 1977-78, corp. dietitian, dietary coord., 1978-81; restaurant owner, operator Virginia Young, Inc., El Campo, Tex., 1980-86; ind. cons. El Campo, 1981-88; v.p. nutrition and dietary svcs. The Arboretum Group, Inc., Victoria, 1988-94; owner, pres. Abshire & Assocs., Inc., El Campo, 1994—. Author: Dietary Forms for Long Term Care, 1994, Dietary Inservices for Long Term Care, 1994. Mem. Am. Dietetic Assn. (registered dietitian), Houston Area Dietetic Assn., Tex. Cons. Gerontol. Dietitians Practice Group (chair-elect/chair 1996—), Gerontol. Nutritionists Practice Group, Cons. Dietitians in Health-Care Facilities, Tex. Cons. Dietitians in Healthcare Facilities (chair-elect/chair 1990-91), Tex. Health Care Assn. (certs. and stds. com., peer rev. com. 1978-81), Beta Sigma Phi (sec.), Omicron Nu. Home and Office: Abshire & Associates Inc 2409 Hutchins Ln El Campo TX 77437

ABSTEIN, WILLIAM ROBERT, II, minister; b. Jacksonville, Fla., Aug. 21, 1940; s. William Russell and Edith Virginia (Sanders) A.; m. Roberta Joy Warren, July 1, 1966; children: William Robert III, Roberta Chandler. BA, Fla. State U., 1962; MDiv, U. of the South, 1965, D Ministry, 1978. Ordained to ministry Episcopal Ch., as deacon, 1965, priest, 1966. Vicar St. Cyprian's Ch., Pensacola, Fla., 1965-67, St. Monica's Ch., Cantonment, Fla., 1965-67; asst. rector Holy Trinity Episcopal Ch., Decatur, Ga., 1967-70; rector St. Jude's Episcopal Ch., Smyrna, Ga., 1970-84, St. John's Episcopal Ch., Tallahassee, Fla., 1984-94, St. George's Episcopal Ch., Nashville, 1994—; bd. dirs. St. George's Kindergarten, St. George's Episcopal Trust Fund; mem. Commn. on Ministry, Diocese of Tenn., 1995—; mem. vis. com. Sch. Theology, Sewanee, 1996—; del. Gen. Conf. Episcopal Ch., Detroit, 1988, Phoenix, 1991; chmn. Episcopal Found. of Tallahassee, 1984-94; rep. Ecumenical Dialogue with Lutherans., Diocese of Fla., 1990-94, chmn. Divsn. Social Ministries, 1991-94. Bd. dirs. Friends of Leon County Libr., Tallahassee, 1989-91, Nashville Health Mgmt. Found., 1996—, Covenant Group, Nashville; pres., treas. Literacy Vols. of Leon County, Tallahassee, 1989-93; mem. adv. bd. for religious news Tallahassee Democrat newspaper, Tallahassee, 1988-94; mem. adv. bd. Ctr. for Profl. Devel., Fla. State U., Tallahassee, 1990-93. Recipient Outstanding Alumnus award Sch. Theology, Sewanee, Tenn., 1993. Mem. Associated Parishes for Liturgy and Mission, Downtown Episcopal Rectors of New South, Rotary. Office: St George's Episcopal Ch 4715 Harding Rd Nashville TN 37205-2809

ABURAHMA, ALI F., surgeon, educator; b. Jordan, Apr. 22, 1946; U.S. citizen; Grad., Alexandria U., 1965, MB ChB summa cum laude, 1970. Diplomate Am. Bd. Surgery, sub-bd. gen. vascular surgery; lic. physician, W.Va., Mich., Ariz. Intern Alexandria (Egypt) U. Hosps., 1970-71; house officer Dhahran Health Ctr., Saudi Arabia, 1971-73; resident in surgery SUNY, Syracuse, 1973-74; fellow in vascular surgery Ariz. Heart Inst., Phoenix, 1977-78; resident in surgery W.Va. U. Med. Ctr., Charleson, 1974-77; from clin. instr. surgery to clin. prof. surgery W.Va. U. Health Scis. Ctr., Charleston, 1978-90, prof., chief vascular surgery, 1991—, dir. surgery rsch.; med. dir. Vascular Lab., active staff Charleston Area Med. Ctr., 1978—; vis. prof. and invited speaker. Editor: Current Noninvasive Vascular Diagnosis, 1988; contbr. numerous articles to profl. jours.; reviewer Archives of Surgery, Am. Jour. Surgery, others. Recipient State prize of Egypt for 1st standing among all med. grads. in Egypt, 1970; Vincent Von Kern award W.Va. U., 1986. Fellow ACS, Royal Coll. Surgeons (Can.), Am. Coll. Angiology, Internat. Coll. Surgeons; mem. Soc. for Vascular Surgery, Ctrl. Surg. Assn., Internat. Soc. Cardiovascular Surgery, So. Assn. for Vascular Surgery, Am. Venous Forum, Soc. for Clin. Vascular Surgery, Ea. Vascular Soc., Allegheny Vascular Soc., Southeastern Surg. Congress, W.Va. Med. Assn., Kanawha Valley Med. Soc., others. Office: Robert C Byrd Health Scis Ctr of W Va Univ 3100 Maccorkle Ave SE Ste 603 Charleston WV 25304-1215

ABUZAAKOUK, ALY RAMADAN, publishing executive; b. Misurata, Libya, Sept. 12, 1942; came to U.S., 1977; s. Ramadan Khalil and Umm Khatirha A. (Balam) A.; m. Fawzia Faraj Al Nahly, July 17, 1972; children: Asmaa, Ahmad, Anas, Aalaa. BA in Journalism, U. Cairo, 1968; MA in Comm., Stanford U., 1971; MA in Middle East Studies, U. Mich., 1980, postgrad., 1977-81. Lectr. Faculty Arts, U. Benghazi, Libya, 1972-76; dir. Internat. Muslim House, Ann Arbor, Mich., 1977-80; pres. New Era Publs., Ann Arbor, 1980-81; dir. info. NSFL, Chgo., 1981-87; dir. publs. Internat. Inst. Islamic Thought, Herndon, Va., 1987-93; publs. mgr. amana publ., Beltsville, Md., 1994—; elected mem. Faculty Arts Acad. Coun., Libya, 1973-75, U. Benghazi Acad. Coun., Libya, 1974-75; chmn. 1st Congress of the Libyan Students in N.Am., 1980; founding mem. Nat. Front for the Salvation of Libya, 1981; pres. N.Am. News Media, Fairfax, Va., 1993. Editor-in-chief: AL INQATH, 1981-86. Mem., founder Nat. Front for the Salvation of Libya, 1980, Libyan League for Human Rights, Geneva, 1990; founder, bd. dirs. Libyan Studies Ctr., Oxford, Eng., Ctr. for Devel. of Mughrib, Montreal, 1994; mem. Amnesty Internat., 1983, Am. Muslim Coun., Washington, 1990; bd. dirs., v.p. Minaret of Freedm Inst., Bethesda, Md. Mem. Assn. Muslim Social Scientists, Fgn. Press Ctr., bd. dirs. The Minaret of Freedom Inst. Republican. Office: North Am News Media PO Box 7148 Fairfax Station VA 22039

ABZUG, ROBERT HENRY, historian, educator; b. N.Y.C., May 2, 1945; s. F. Seymour William and Frances (Wolff) A.; m. Penne Lee Restad, Nov. 16, 1980; children: Benjamin Cameron, Johanna Wolff. BA magna cum laude, Harvard U., 1967; PhD, U. Calif., Berkeley, 1977. Lectr. UCLA, 1977-78; from asst. prof. to prof. U. Tex., Austin, 1978—, dir. religious studies program, 1989-90, dir. Am. studies program, 1990—; Eric Voegelin vis. prof. U. Munich, Germany, 1990-91. Author: Passionate Liberator: Theodore Dwight Weld and the Dilemma of Reform, 1980, Inside the Vicious Heart: Americans and the Liberation of Nazi Concentration Camps, 1985, Cosmos Crumbling: American Reform and the Religious Imagination, 1994; co-editor: New Perspectives on Race and Slavery in America: Essays in Honor of Kenneth M. Stampp, 1986; contbr. articles and revs. to profl. jours. Trustee George Washington Carver Mus. African-Am. History, Austin, 1980-83. Recipient Detur prize Harvard U., 1966, numerous tchg. fellowships; Harvard Coll. scholar, 1964-65, John Harvard scholar, 1965-66, Knox Travelling fellow Harvard U., 1967-68, Danforth Grad. fellow, 1967-72, Ford Found. fellow, 1967-72, Fred Crawford Meml. rsch. assoc. Emory U., 1983, NEH fellow, 1983-84, ACLS grantee, 1984, NEH Travel grantee, 1989, Frederick Binkard Artz rsch. grantee Oberlin Coll., 1993, others. Mem. Am. Hist. Assn., Orgn. Am. Historians, Am. Studies Assn. Tex. (pres. 1996), Internet on the Holocaust and Denocide, Soc. Historians of the Early Republic, Phi Beta Kappa, Omicron Delta Kappa, Beta Alpha Phi. Democrat. Jewish. Home: 3504 Cactus Wren Way Austin TX 78746-6637 Office: U Tex Am Studies Program Austin TX 78712

ACEREDA, ALBERTO, Spanish language and literature educator; b. Calahorra, Spain, Jan. 1, 1965; came to U.S., 1988; s. Alberto Acereda and María J. Extremiana. BA in Hispanic Philology, U. Barcelona, Spain, 1988; MA in Spanish Lit., U. Ga., 1990, PhD in Romance Langs. and Lit., 1994. Grad. tchg. asst. U. Ga., Athens, 1988-94; asst. prof. Spanish Radford (Va.) U., 1994—. Author books on Hispanic lit.; editor poetry works and anthols.; contbr. articles to lit. jours. Mem. socs. dealing with Hispanic studies and lit. Office: Radford U PO Box 6937 Radford VA 24142

ACERS, PATSY PIERCE, financial seminars company executive; b. Muskogee, Okla., Mar. 10, 1933; d. Claude James and Clara B. (Chaney) Pierce; m. Thomas Edward Acers, Apr. 9, 1955 (div. Feb. 1980); children: Alison Ann, Angela Lynn, Ann Pierce, Ashley French. BA, U. Okla., 1955. Tchr. Oklahoma City Pub. Schs., 1955-58; dir. spl. events Am. Cancer Soc., 1980-86, dir. legacies and planned giving, 1983-86; ins. agt. life and health Conn. Mut., Oklahoma City, 1986-90; pres., owner Bag Lady Fin. Svcs., Inc., Oklahoma City, 1987—. Developer slide seminars: Do You Really Want to Be a Bag Lady, 1987, The Bag Lady Returns With Who Do You Trust, 1991, There Is Financial Life for Singles, 1989. Mem. Women Life Underwriters (pres. 1989-90), High Noon Profl. Women (pres. 1990-91), Women's Exec. Network (pres. 1988-89), Million Dollar Round Table, Am. Bus. Women's Assn., Okla. Spkrs. Assn., Nat. Spkrs. Assn., Nat. Leaders Club. Methodist. Home: 1413 Sims Ave Edmond OK 73013-6355 Office: Bag Lady Fin Seminars Inc PO Box 20213 Oklahoma City OK 73156-0213

ACEVEDO, HÉCTOR LUIS, mayor; b. Rio Piedras, P.R., Nov. 8, 1947; m. Carmen Roca, 1972; children: David Miguel, Jasmine, Luis Manuel. BA magna cum laude, Univ. P.R., 1969, JD; lawyers instrn. program, Harvard Univ., 1978. With legal adv. Office of P.R., Washington, 1973, asst. to sec. justice, 1973-75; asst. to the Governor of Puerto Rico, 1975-76; electoral commr. Popular Dem. Party, 1976-84; sec. of state P.R., 1985-88; mayor San Juan, 1989—. Pres. Pan Am. AIDS Found.; chmn. task force on AIDS; mem. bd. trustees U.S. Conf. Mayors; chmn. Task Force on Violence, Nat. League Cities; pres. bd. dirs. Interamerican Cities Found.; pres. Popular Dem. Party. Lt. col. USAR. Mem. P.R. Bar Assn., Am. Soc. Internat. Law, Alpha Phi Omega.

ACHAMPONG, FRANCIS KOFI, law educator, consultant; b. Kumasi, Ghana, Feb. 18, 1955; came to U.S., 1981; s. John Wilberforce and Salome (Mensa) A. LLB, U. Ghana, 1976; LLM, U. London, 1977, PhD, 1981; LLM, Georgetown U., 1985. Bar: N.Y. 1986, Va. 1988, U.S. Dist. Ct. (ea. dist.) Va. 1988, U.S. Ct. Appeals (4th cir.) 1988, U.S. Supreme Ct. 1990. Adj. lectr. George Washington U., Washington, 1981-82; asst. prof. Howard U., Washington, 1981-85; prof. Norfolk (Va.) State U., 1985—; cons. Aetna Life & Casualty, Hartford, Conn., 1981-82, Profl. Ins. Assn. of Md., Pa., 1986, Shapiro, Meiselman & Greene, P.C., Rockville, Md., 1987, Crowell & Moring, Washington, 1988, Clark & Stant, Virginia Beach, Va., 1988. Contbr. articles to profl. jours. Mem. ABA, Am. Risk and Ins. Assn., Am. Bus. Law Assn. Home: 1509 Colebrook Dr Virginia Beach VA 23464-7206 Office: Norfolk State U 2401 Corprew Ave Norfolk VA 23504-3907

ACKER, VIRGINIA MARGARET, nursing educator; b. Madison, Wis., Aug. 11, 1946; d. Paul Peter and Lucille (Klein) A. Diploma in Nursing, St. Mary's Med. Ctr., Madison, 1972; BS in Nursing, Incarnate Work Coll., San Antonio, 1976; MS in Health Professions, S.W. Tex. State U., 1980; postgrad., U. Tex., 1992-93. RN, Wis., Tex. Staff nurse St. Mary's Hosp., Milw., 1972-73, Kenosha Meml. Hosp., Wis., 1973-74, S.W. Tex. Meth. Hosp., San Antonio, 1974-75, Met. Gen. Hosp., San Antonio, 1975-76; instr. Bapt. Meml. Hosp. System Sch. Nursing, San Antonio, 1976-83; dir. nursing Meml. Hosp., Gonzales, Tex., 1983-84; instr., dir. nursing Victoria Coll., Cuero, Tex., 1984-86; dir. nursing Rocky Knoll Health Care Facility, Plymouth, Wis., 1986-87, Unicare Health Facilities, Milw., 1987-88; coord. nursing edn. St. Nicholas Hosp., Sheboygan, Wis., 1989-90; instr. U. Wis., Oshkosh, 1990-92, St. David's Hosp., Austin, Tex., 1992-95, Bailey Sq. Surg. Ctr., 1995—. Roman Catholic. Avocations: cross-stiching, reading, camping, fishing. Home: 2103 Four Oaks Ln Austin TX 78704-4624

ACKER, WILLIAM MARSH, JR., federal judge; b. Birmingham, Ala., Oct. 25, 1927; s. William Marsh and Estelle (Lampkin) A.; m. Martha Walters, 1957; children—William Marsh III, Stacey Reed. BA, Birmingham So. Coll., 1949; LLB, Yale U., 1952. Bar: Ala. 1952. Assoc. Graham, Bibb, Wingo & Foster, Birmingham, Ala., 1952-57, Smyer, White, Reid & Acker, 1957-72, Dominick, Fletcher, Yeilding, Acker, Wood & Lloyd, Birmingham, 1972-82; judge U.S. Dist. Ct. (no. dist.) Ala., 1982—. Mem. Ala. Republican Exec. Com.; del. to Repub. Nat. Convention, 1972, 76, 80. Mem. Birmingham Bar Assn. Office: 481 Hugo L Black Courthouse 1729 5th Ave N Birmingham AL 35203-2000

ACKER, WOODROW LOUIS (LOU ACKER), security and protection professional; b. Amarillo, Tex., Mar. 24, 1937; s. Doyle and Jewel (Talley) A.; m. Peggy Ann Thompson, Jan. 1, 1959, 1 child, Kelly Michael Kennedy. Cert. protection profl., lic. peace officer, Tex. BS in Police Sci., Sam Houston State U., 1974; BA in History, U. Tex., Dallas, 1985; grad. U.S. Army Command & Gen. Staff Coll., 1989. Dir. adminstrv. services bur. Dallas County Sheriffs Dept., 1965-76; chief campus police dept. North Lake Coll., Irving, Tex., 1977-84; ops. mgr. for security cos., Dallas, 1984-87; pvt. investigator, acad. dir. Dear & Assoc., DeSoto, Tex., 1987-90; acad. dir., co-owner Acker and Acker Tng. Acad., Mesquite, Tex., 1990-91; chief police, Cockrell Hill, Tex., 1992; chief instr. Lakeside Tng. Acad., Dallas, 1994—. Scoutleader Boy Scouts Am., Dallas; mem. CAP, Mesquite; chmn. bd. Shekinah Messianic Ministries; planter, pastor Seventh Day Bapt. Ch., Mesquite. With AUS, 1955-57; maj. Tex. State Guard. South Found. fellow. Fellow Confederate Hist. Inst.; mem. Internat. Police Assn. (Tex. div.), Am. Soc. Indsl. Security (North Tex. chpt.), NRA (life), Tex. Rifle Assn. (life), Am. Legion, Sons Am. Revolution, Sons of Confederate Vets. (life), Milt. Order Stars and Bars (life), Soc. Order of So. Cross (life), Confederate Meml. Assn., Clan Sutherland Soc. Home: 3502 Palm Dr Mesquite TX 75150-3433

ACKERMAN, BRUCE AINSLIE, public relations professional; b. Cleve., May 17, 1948; s. William Houston Ackerman and Margaret Ackerman (Ainslie) Post; m. Kathy Elaine Morra Ackerman, Aug. 17, 1974. BA in Journalism, Ohio Wesleyan U., Delaware, 1971; MEd (hon.), Boston U., Heidelberg, Germany, 1972. Publs. editor Okla. State U., Stillwater, 1981-90; mem. svcs. rep. Okla. Mcpl. Power Authority, Edmond, 1990—; part time tech. writer Okla. Dept. Vo-Tech Edn., Stillwater, 1990. Contbr. articles to profl. jours. Deacon Ctrl. Presbyn. Ch., Massillon, Ohio, 1980. With U.S. Army, 1971-74. Mem. Pub. Rels. Soc. Am. Home: 1408 NW 183rd Ter Edmond OK 73003-4066

ACKERMAN, PAUL ADAM, pharmacist; b. Cleve., Oct. 6, 1945; s. Kenneth Edwin and Jane (Hand) A.; m. Charity Reba Schierhorst, June 5, 1971; 1 child, Adam. BS, U. Fla., 1969. Lic. pharmacist, Fla., Ga. Pharmacist Robalo Pharmacy, Lake Park, Fla., 1969-73, Tru Valu Drugs, Lake Worth, 1973-77, Village Pharmacy, Tequesta, Fla., 1977-79, Shoppers Drug Mart, Palm Beach Garden, Fla., 1979-86; pharmacy mgr. Walgreen's, Palm Beach Garden, 1986—. Member Airports and Aviation Adv. Com., Palm Beach County, Fla., 1985—; mem. adv. bd. Coll. of Pharmacy, U. Fla., 1986—; bd. dirs. Am. Cancer Soc., Palm Beach County, 1983-89. Recipient Pharmacy Disting. Svc. Alumnus award U. Fla., 1991. Mem. Am. Pharmacy Assn., Fla. Pharmacy Assn. (exec. com. Tallahassee chpt. 1984-85, 88, chmn. Acad. Pharmacy Practice 1987-88, bd. dirs. ho. of dels. 1988-90, vice-speaker 1991, speaker 1992, pres.-elect 1996-97, Practitioner Merit award 1990), Palm Beach County Pharmacy Assn. (pres. West Palm Beach, Fla. chpt. 1983-85, Joe Price Pharmacist of Yr. 1985), Fla. Aero Club, Jupiter Elks, Palm Beach Gardens Moose, Masons, Shriners, Phi Lambda Sigma. Republican. Home: 12931 Inshore Dr West Palm Beach FL 33410-2005 Office: Walgreens 7170 Fairway Dr West Palm Beach FL 33418-3763

ACLIN, KEITH ANDREW, radar meteorologist; b. Meridan, Conn., May 9, 1960; s. John Joseph and Anne (Barr) A.; m. Jean Anne Taylor, May 28, 1983. BA in Psychology, Rutgers U., 1983; MS in Meteorology, Tex. A&M U., 1995. Navigator tng. USAF, Mather AFB, Calif., 1983-86; navigator USAF, Carswell AFB, Tex., 1986-88, radar navigator, 1988-91; radar navigator USAF, K.I. Sawyer AFB, Mich., 1991-92; radar meteorologist TVR Comms., Oklahoma City, 1995-96. Aerospace officer Aux. USAF CAP, 1995. NSF grantee, 1993-95. Mem. Am. Meteorol. Soc., DAV, Maysons. Home: 604 Harrier Hawk Edmond OK 73003 Office: TVR Comms Inc 500 N Meridian Ste 100 Oklahoma City OK 73107

ACOMB, ROBERT BAILEY, JR., lawyer, educator; b. New Orleans, July 28, 1930; s. Robert Bailey and Catherine (Ryan) A.; m. Greta LeBlanc, Apr. 25, 1953; children: Robert III, Dwight J., Greta, William Ryan, John. BBA, Tulane U., 1951, JD, 1953. Bar: La. 1953, U.S. Dist. Ct. (ea. and mid. dist.) La. 1953, U.S. Ct. Appeals (5th cir.) 1955, U.S. Supreme Ct. 1967, U.S. Ct. Appeals (7th cir.) 1976, U.S. Ct. Appeals (11th cir.) 1981, U.S. Dist. Ct. (we. dist.) La. 1989. Assoc. Jones, Walker, Waechter, Poitevent, Carrere & Denegre, New Orleans, 1953-56, ptnr., 1956, sr. ptnr., 1968—; adj. prof. law Tulane U., New Orleans, 1969—; bd. dirs. Attys. Liability Assurance Soc. Ltd., Hamilton, Bermuda, 1979—; pres. bd. dirs. Christian Bros. Found., Inc., New Orleans, 1976-78; trustee Christian Bros. Retirement Fund, New Orleans, 1989—. Author: Maritime Personal Injury & Death, 4th edit., 1993; editor: Damages Recovered, 1984; contbr. articles to profl. jours.; chmn. adv. editors: Tulane Maritime Law Jour., 1976-93. Chmn. Archbishop's Community Appeal, New Orleans, 1993; pres. Tulane U. Assocs., New Orleans, 1990-92. Decorated knight cmdr. Equestrian Order of Holy Sepulchre of Jerusalem. Fellow Am. Coll. Trial Lawyers (state chair 1972—), Am. Bar Found.; mem. ABA (mem. standing com. on admiralty, chmn. 1979-83), Tulane Maritime Law Ctr. (chmn. 1982—), Maritime Law Assn. U.S. (proctor, mem. exec. com. 1981-84), Tulane Maritime Law Inst. (chmn. 1991—), Tulane U. Alumni Assn. (pres. 1989-90, Vol. of Yr. 1992), Navy League U.S. (pres. New Orleans chpt. 1987-88, state pres. 1994), Assn. Average Adjusters U.S. (chmn. 1992-93), New Orleans Country Club, Boston Club, Pickwick Club, Stratford Club, Order of St. Louis. Roman Catholic. Home: 3450 Vincennes Pl New Orleans LA 70125-4350 Office: Jones Walker Waechter Poitevent Carrere & Denegre 201 Saint Charles Ave New Orleans LA 70170-1000

ACOSTA, NAHYR MERCEDES, editor-in-chief; b. Ponce, P.R., Mar. 21, 1959; came to U.S., 1982; d. Francisco and Providencia (Albizu) A.; m. Luis M. Guardia, Apr. 24, 1993. B in Pub. Comm., U. P.R., San Juan. Staff writer Editorial Am., Miami, Fla., 1982-88, exec. writer, 1988-90, editor in chief Coqueta, 1990-92, editor in chief spl. issues, 1992-93, editor in chief TU mag., 1993-95; editor in chief Showbiz Mag., 1996—. Roman Catholic. Office: Showbiz News Mag 6070 NW 167th St Ste C-14 Hialeah FL 33014-6142

ACOSTA, RAYMOND LUIS, federal judge; b. N.Y.C., May 31, 1925; s. Ramon J. and Carmen J. (Acha-Jimenez) Acosta-Colon; m. Marie Hatcher, Nov. 2, 1957; children: Regina, Gregory, Ann Marie. Student, Princeton U., 1948; J.D., Rutgers U., 1951. Bar: N.J. 1953, U.S. Supreme Ct. 1956, P.R. 1959. Sole practice Hackensack, N.J., 1953-54; spl. agt. FBI, San Diego, Washington, Miami, Fla., 1954-58; asst. U.S. atty. San Juan, P.R., 1958-61; sole practice San Juan, 1961-67; trust officer Banco Credito y Ahorro Ponceno, San Juan, 1967-80; U.S. atty. Dist. P.R., Hato Rey, 1980-82; judge U.S. Dist. Ct. P.R., San Juan, 1982—; Alt. del. U.S.-P.R. Commn. on Status, 1962-63; mem. Gov.'s Spl. Com. to Study Structure and Orgn. Police Dept., P.R., 1969. Contbr. articles to profl. jours. Pres. United Fund, P.R., 1979. Served with USN, 1943-46. Recipient Merit cert. Mayor of San Juan, 1973. Mem. Fed. Bar Assn. (pres., P.R. 1967), P.R. Bankers Assn. (chmn. trust div. 1971, 75, 77), P.R. Bar Assn., Soc. Former Spl. Agts. FBI. Office: US Dist Ct Chase Manhattan Bldg 1200C 254 Munoz Rivera Ave Hato Rey PR 00918-1909

ACOSTA, URSULA, psychologist; b. Hannover, Germany, Jan. 14, 1933; came to U.S., 1954, naturalized, 1958; d. Johannes Karl and Irma (Ulrich) Schmidt; B.A., U. P.R., 1971, M.E., 1973; Ph.D. in Psychology, Gutenberg U., Mainz, Ger., 1979; m. Sebastian Acosta-Ronda, June 12, 1954; children: Johann, Dennis, Peter. Various occupations, 1954-66; from instr. to asst. prof., assoc. prof. then prof. psychology U. P.R., Mayagüez, 1973-95, ret. 1995. Chairperson appeal bd. SSS. Mem. LWV (unit chair 1977-78, 86-88), Puerto Rican Geneal. Soc. (editor jour.). Active Puerto Rican Statehood Movement. Co-author: Familias de Cabo Rojo (History prize Ateneo Puertorriqueno de New York 1983); author: Quien era Cofresí?, 1984, New Voices of Old: Five Centuries of Puerto Rican Cultural History, 1987, Cofresi y Ducoudray: Dos Hombres Al Margen de la Historia, 1991; co-author: Cabo Rojo: Notas para su historia, 1985; editor: Boletín de la Sociedad Puertorriquén a de Genealogía, 1994—; contbr. articles to various jours. and newspapers. Republican. Office: U PR Box 8 Hormigueros PR 00660

ACUFF, JOHN EDGAR, lawyer; b. Chattanooga, Tenn., July 20, 1940; s. White Hollis and Estelle (Johnson) A; m. Carolyn Howell, Sept. 6, 1963; children: John E. Jr. (dec.), William Ira Howell, Karl David. BA, David Lipscomb U., Nashville, 1962; JD, Vanderbilt U., 1969. Bar: Tenn. 1969, U.S. Dist. Ct. (mid. dist.) Tenn. 1970, U.S. Ct. Appeals (6th cir.) 1970, U.S. Supreme Ct. 1982, U.S. Ct. Claims 1986. Assoc. Cable, McDaniel, Bowie & Bond (now McGuire Battle), Balt., 1969; law clk. to chief judge Harry Phillips U.S. Ct. Appeals, Nashville, Cin., 1969-70; assoc. Crawford & Barnes, Cookeville, Tenn., 1970-71; ptnr. Barnes & Acuff, Cookeville, 1971—; mem. disciplinary hearing bd. Tenn. Supreme Ct., 1978-84. Dir. Law Students Nixon Agnew, 1968; mem. citizens com. Gov.'s Prayer Breakfast, 1980-93, chmn., 1991; elder Christ's Fellowship, Cookeville, 1981-91; bd. dirs. Dismas House, Habitat of cumberlands, Lazrus House Hospice; active Leadership Putnam '97. Lt. USNR, 1962-66. Mem. ATLA, Tenn. Bar Assn. (ho. of dels. 1980—, speaker 1995-97, bd. govs. 1995-97) Tenn. Trial Lawyers Assn., Am. Judicature Soc., Christian Legal Soc., Tenn. Christian Legal Soc. (pres. 1993—), Putnam County Bar Assn. (pres. 1984-85), Putnam County C. of C., White County C. of C., Phi Alpha Delta, Alpha Kappa Psi. Home: Crossroads Farm 542 Almyra Rd Sparta TN 38583-5139 Office: Acuff & Acuff 101 S Jefferson Ave Cookeville TN 38501-3424

ADAIR, JAMES HANSELL, materials science and engineering educator; b. Indpls., Aug. 3, 1952; s. John William and Ann Walton (Ellis) A.; m. Susan Bailey, May 20, 1975 (div. Aug. 1989); children: Kathleen Ann, Elizabeth Carol; m. Bernadette McMahon, July 20, 1990; children: Brian James, Patrick Benjamin. BS in Chemistry, U. Fla., 1975, MS in Materials Sci. and Engring., 1979, PhD in Materials Sci. and Engring., 1981. Rsch. assoc. materials sci. and engring. dept. U. Fla., Gainesville, 1975-81, assoc. prof., 1990—; J. William Fulbright postdoctoral fellow U. Western Australia, Perth, Australia, 1981-82; mem. rsch. staff Battelle Columbus (Ohio) Labs., 1982-86; mem. rsch. staff materials rsch. lab. Pa. State U., University Park, 1986-90, dir. consortium on chemically bonded ceramics, 1988-90. Contbr. over 70 articles, chpts. to profl. publs. Recipient Cabot Inventor award Cabot Corp., 1996. Mem. Am. Ceramic Soc. (sec. basic sci. divsn. 1996, symposium organizer, chair 1976—), Materials Rsch. Soc., Am. Chem. Soc. (symposium organizer, chair meetings), Internat. Soc. Hybrid Microelectronics, N.Y. Acad. Scis., Keramos, Alpha Sigma Mu (nat. bd. trustees 1989-91), Epsilon Lambda Chi, Omicron Delta. Roman Catholic. Office: U Fla 207 Materials Bldg Gainesville FL 32605

ADAIR, LILA MCGAHEE, secondary education physics educator; b. Griffin, Ga., Jan. 8, 1947; d. Henry Grady and Lila (Smith) McGahee; m. Terry Wayne Adair, July 21, 1973; 1 child, James. BS in Biology, Oglethorpe U., 1967; MAT in Physics, Ga. State U., 1978; Diploma for Advanced Study of Teaching in Ednl. Leadership, Emory U., 1990. Cert. tchr. physics, leadership/supervision, Ga. Tchr., sci. dept. chmn. Lindley Jr. High, Mableton, Ga., 1967-72; tchr. Hohenwald (Tenn.) Elem. Sch., 1972-74; tchr. physics, chemistry South Gwinnett High, Snellville, Ga., 1974-79; tchr., physics, sci. dept. chmn. Cen. Gwinnett High, Lawrenceville, Ga., 1979—; instr. NSF Inst., Emory U., Atlanta, 1985; sci. demonstrator in field. Inventor/dir. Gwinnett County Sci. Bowl, 1980-92. Adv. bd. SciTrek, Atlanta, 1988-91; tchr. Boy Scouts Am., Snellville, Ga., 1990—; instr. Summerscape, Ga. Tech, Atlanta, 1990—; mag. evaluator Coun. for Agrl. Sci. and Tech., Athens, Ga., 1984. Recipient Presdl. award for Excellence in Sci. Teaching, Pres. Reagan, Washington, 1985, Tchr. Hall of Fame awards Gwinnett County Schs., Lawrenceville, 1984, STAR Tchr. award Gwinnett County Schs., 1980, 82, 85, 87, 93; named Tchr. of Yr. Gwinnett County Schs., 1985, 88. Mem. Am. Assn. Physics Tchrs. (sect. v.p. 1991, pres. 1992, exec. bd. 1988-90, physics teaching resource agt. 1986—, planning com., internat. com. 1989-91), Ga. Jr. Acad. Sci. (state dir. 1985), Ga. Sci. Tchrs. Assn. (dist. bd. dirs. 1981-82, sec. 1979-80, Ga. Sci. Tchr. of Yr. 1985), Am. Phys. Soc. (co-chmn. local physics alliance conf. 1991), Ga. Acad. Sci. (symposium speaker 1990), Sigma Pi Sigma, Alpha Delta Kappa. Democrat. Baptist. Home: 1994 Skyland Glen Dr Snellville GA 30278-3862 Office: Ctrl Gwinnett High School 564 W Crogan St Lawrenceville GA 30245-4725

ADAIR, TOBY WARREN, JR., minister; b. Beaumont, Tex., Sept. 8, 1922; s. Toby Warren and Mildred Lee (Muldrow) A.; m. Ann Ivareese Redden, May 8, 1943; 1 child, Robin Lee Adair. BS, Centenary Coll., 1947; MDiv, Golden Gate Bapt. Theol. Sem., 1973, MA, 1974; ThD, Internat. Sem., 1990. Ordained to ministry So. Bapt. Conv., 1973. Commd. 2d lt. USAF, 1944, advanced through grades to maj., 1959, command pilot, 1967-70, ret., 1967; founding pastor South Reno (Nev.) Bapt. Ch., 1973-77; pastor Bancroft Bapt. Ch., Spring Valley, Calif., 1977-81, Mt. Zion Bapt. Ch., Praireville, La., 1982-85, Forrest Park Bapt. Ch., Pine Bluff, Ark., 1986-93; pres. pastor's conf. San Diego (Calif.) So. Bapt. Assn., 1981, Ascension So. Bapt. Assn., Prairieville, 1984, Harmony So. Bapt. Assn., Pine Bluff, 1988. Prayer-time host Radio Sta. KNIS, Reno-Carson City, Nev., 1974-76. Bd. dirs. Pine Bluff-Jefferson County Hist. Mus. Guild, 1991-92, mem. adminstrv. bd. trustees 1992—, chmn. 1995—. Decorated Army Commendation medal USAF, Japan, 1950, DFC Air Medal with 2 oak leaf clusters USAF, Korea, 1951, USAF Commendation medal, USAF, USA, 1959. Named Boss of the Yr., Am. Bus. Women Assn., Reno, 1975. Mem. Jefferson County Clergy Conf. (treas.), Confedn. Air Forces (chaplain Razor Base wing), Kemper Mil. Sch. and Coll. Alumni Assn. (bd. dirs. 1991—, trustee 1993—), Rotary (Pine Bluff, bd. dirs. 1988-91, pres. 1991-92, dist. gov.'s rep. 1992-93, dist. gov. 1995-96). Republican. Home: 803 W 12th Ave Pine Bluff AR 71601-5631

ADAMCZYK, EDMOND DAVID, metallurgical engineer; b. Weirton, W.Va., June 16, 1957; s. Edmond and Elizabeth Marie (Kelchak) A. BS in Engring. and Econs., Carnegie-Mellon U., 1979, MS, 1980. Metall. engr., rsch. engr Nat. Steel Corp., Weirton, 1980-85; rsch. and devel. engr. Weirton Steel Corp., 1985-89, sr. product specialist, 1989-95, rsch. assoc., 1995—. Mem. Nat. Coil Ctrs. Assn. (mktg. sect. container task force 1987-90, sec. 1987-90, chmn. mem. com. 1987-90, tech. sect. container task force 1987-90, chmn. statis. process control com. 1987-90), Minerals, Metals and Materials Soc. (chmn. Three Rivers sect. program com. 1984-85, treas. 1986, vice chmn. 1987, chmn. 1988, exec. com. 1984-89, Outstanding Young Mem. award 1986, mem. devel. com. 1989-92), Am. Soc. for Metals, Am. Welding Soc., Soc. Automotive Engrs., Soc. Mfg. Engrs., Inst. Packaging Profls., Soc. Vacuum Coaters. Office: 3006 Birch Dr Weirton WV 26062-5133

ADAMKIN, DAVID HOWARD, pediatric medicine educator; b. N.Y.C., Apr. 4, 1948; s. Joseph and Julie (Termin) A.; m. Carol Ann Seyfferth, Aug. 18, 1979; children: Stephanie Merete, Michelle Rachel, Matthew David. BS in cum laude, Ohio State U., 1970; MD, Upstate Med. Coll., 1974. Diplomate Am. Bd. Pediatrics; diplomate Sub-Bd. Neonatal-Perinatal Medicine, Am. Bd. Pediatrics. Pediatric resident Upstate Med. Ctr., Syracuse, N.Y., 1974-76; neonatalology fellow U. Louisville (Ky.) Sch. Med., 1976-78, asst. prof. pediatrics, asst. prof. obstetrics, 1978-85, assoc. prof. pediatrics, assoc. prof. obstetrics, 1985—, prof. pediatrics, 1992—; vis. prof. U. Ill., Chgo., 1984, Ind. U., Riley-Children's Hosp. and the Ind. Perinatal Assn., Indpls., 1985, La. State U., Baton Rouge, 1987; mem. adv. com. Gov.'s Conf. on Infant Mortality, Frankfort, Ky., 1989; dir. Divsn. Neonatal Medicine, U. Louisville, 1994—; dir. nurseries Kosair Children's Hosp., Louisville, Women's Pavilion, The Norton Hosp., Louisville, 1994—; staff mem. U. Louisville (Ky.) Hosp.; various coms. and adv. positions Kosair Children's Hosp., 1980—; presenter in field. Contbr. chpts. to books and textbooks and articles to profl. jours; manuscript reviewer Jour. of Perin, Ped Rsch., Jour. of Am. Coll. of Nutrition. Active March of Dimes State Coun., Mid-Am. Region for Maternal and Child Health, 1989—, rev. panel for Phys. and Devel. Environ. of High Risk Inf.; bd. dirs. Ronald McDonald House, 1996. Grantee Abbott Labs., 1978, 79, 80, 81, 82, 83, 85, 87, 91, WHAS Crusade for Children, 1979, 82, 87, 88, 90, 92, 93, 94, 95, 96, Travenol Labs., 1981, Mead Johnson, 1982, 91, 92, 93, Ross Labs., 1984, 85, 87, 90, 96, Nat. Eye Inst. NIH, 1989, Alliant Cmty. Trust, 1990, 93, Wyeth-Ayerst, 1995. Fellow Am. Coll. Nutrition; mem. Am. Pediatric Soc., Am. Acad. Pediatrics, Subsection Neonatal/Perinatal Medicine-Am. Acad. Pediatrics, Am. Soc. for Parenteral and Enteral Nutrition (Pediatric planninc com. 1989), Nat. Perinatal Assn. (coun. 1989-91), So. Soc. for Pediatric Rsch. (instn. rep. 1982—), Ky. Perinatal Assn. (organizer 1988, first pres. 1988-91, Disting. Leadership award 1991, Outstanding Leadership and Founder award 1993), Ky. Sect. Acad. Pediatrics, Ky. Med. Assn., Jefferson County Med. Soc. Jewish. Home: 9109 Brookwood Path Louisville KY 40241-2417 Office: 571 S Floyd St Ste 300 Louisville KY 40202-3830

ADAMO, DEBRA ORVIS, nurse research specialist; b. Pasadena, Calif., Nov. 13, 1952; d. Ernest and Estelene Ruth (Preusch) Orvis; m. Martin Louis Adamo, Sept. 16, 1989; children: Ernest Michael, Amy Victoria, Paul Martin. BSN, U. Nev., 1980; AA in Fgn. Language, Pasadena City Coll., 1972; BA in Math., U. Calif., Santa Barbara, 1975; MSN, Catholic U. Am., 1988. Clin. nurse Johns Hopkins Hosp., Balt., NIH, Bethesda, Md.; nurse specialist rsch. Nat. Cancer Inst., Bethesda, Md., Cancer Therapy and Rsch. Ctr., San Antonio. Mem. ANA (cert.), Md. Nurses Assn., Am. Heart Assn.

ADAMS, ALFRED BERNARD, JR., environmental engineer; b. Asbury Pk., N.J., Oct. 15, 1920; s. Alfred Bishop and Julia Ruth (Wiseman) A.; m. Claudia Neff, Dec. 28, 1942; children: Alfred B. III, Tamara Adams Dohn, Carla Adams York. BSChemE, Ga. Inst. Technol., 1943; postgrad., Wayne State U., 1946-48, U. Ala., Birmingham, 1986-88, Jefferson State C.C., 1989-95. Registered profl. engr., Ala., Mich., Fla., Ga., N.C.; Diplomate in Am. Acad. Environ. Engrs. Project engr. Pennwalt, Wyandotte, Mich., 1946-50; sales mgr., design engr. Goslin-Birmingham Div., Birmingham, Ala., 1950-61; field engr. & Sales Elmco Corp., Birmingham, Ala., 1961-62; prin. engr. Morton-Thiokol Corp., Brunswick, Ga., 1962-64; tech. mgr. Rust Internat., Birmingham, 1964-86; pres., owner Adams Cons. & Engring. Svcs., Birmingham, 1986—; cons. in field. Contbr. tech. papers to profl. publs. Pres. Woodhaven Lakes Property Owners Assn., Pinson, Ala., 1980-82; mem. Pub. Health Com., Birmingham, 1975-78. 2d lt. U.S. Army Chem. Corps, 1943-53. Mem. Air & Waste Mgmt. Assn., Tech. Assn. Pulp & Paper Industries. Presbyterian. Home: 1824 Lake Park Ln Birmingham AL 35215-5748 Office: Adams Cons & Engring Svcs 1824 Lake Park Ln Birmingham AL 35215-5748

ADAMS, ALFRED GRAY, lawyer; b. Winston-Salem, N.C., Feb. 28, 1946; s. Carlton Noble and Elizabeth (Walker) A.; m. Elizabeth Lark; children: Alfred Gray Jr., Amanda Laing. BA, Wake Forest U., 1968, JD, 1973. Bar: N.C. 1973; cert. specialist residential, bus., comml., and indsl. real property transactions. Ptnr. Van Winkle, Buck, Wall, Starnes & Davis, P.A., Asheville, N.C., 1973-94, Petree Stockton L.L.P, Winston-Salem, N.C., 1994—; adj. prof. law Wake Forest U., 1996—. Assoc. editor Wake Forest Law Rev., 1972. Chmn. Buncombe County Tax Adv. Com., Asheville, 1983. James Mason scholar Wake Forest U., 1972. Mem. ABA, N.C. Bar Assn. (bd. govs. 1987-90, real property sect. vice chmn. 1982-83, chmn. 1983-84, writer, lectr. real property and future interests bar rev. course 1981-83, mem. real property curriculum adv. com. 1984-91, chmn. 1988-91, seminar planner and lectr. real property 1987-96, chmn. continuing legal edn. com. 1991-93), Am. Coll. Real Estate Lawyers, Am. Coll. Mortgage Attys. (state chair 1995—, bd. regents 1996—), Biltmore Forest Country Club (bd. govs. 1993-94), Forsyth Country Club, Rhododendron Royal Brigade Guards Club (capt. Ensign Class 1986). Democrat. Methodist. Home: 1033 Cross Gate Rd Winston Salem NC 27106-6324 Office: 1001 W 4th St Winston Salem NC 27101-2410

ADAMS, BELINDA JEANETTE SPAIN, nursing administrator; b. Rome, Ga., Dec. 5; d. Oscar Joe and Eleanor (Camacho) Spain. Diploma, Ga. Bapt. Hosp. Sch. Nursing, Atlanta, 1974; BS in Nursing, Med. Coll. Ga., Augusta, 1976; MS in Nursing, Ga. State U., Atlanta, 1980, postgrad., 1990—. Cert. clin. specialist in med.-surg. nursing, intravenous nurse. Critical care flight nurse Critical Care Medflight, Inc., Atlanta, 1984-88; intravenous therapy coord. DeKalb Gen. Hosp., Atlanta, 1974-81; asst. prof. Mercer U., Atlanta, 1981-87; corp. dir. infusion/high tech. svcs. Kimberly Quality Care, Atlanta, 1988-92; cons. Profl. Learning Systems, 1992—; asst. prof. Clayton State Coll., Morrow, Ga., 1992-94, Ga. Bapt. Coll. Nursing, Atlanta, 1994-95. Mem. ANA, Intravenous Nurses Soc. (rsch. com.), Ga. Nurses Assn. Home: 5979 Eton Ct Norcross GA 30071-2030

ADAMS, BETH FORD, interior designer; b. Montgomery, Ala., Oct. 23, 1959; d. Schuyler Colfax and Nancy Joe Eubank; m. Steve Adams; children: Jennifer Marie, Melanie Virginia. B. of Interior Design, Auburn U., 1983. Registered interior designer. Comml. interior designer PH & J Archs., Montgomery, Ala., 1986—. Mem. NCIDQ, IIDA, Am. Soc. Interior Designers. Home: 4033 Meredith Dr Montgomery AL 36109 Office: PH&J Architects Inc 807 S Mcdonough St Montgomery AL 36104-5054

ADAMS, BRENDA KAY, publisher, advertising/management consultant; b. Chickasha, Okla., Dec. 5, 1954; d. William Opal and Frances Mahota (Greer) Pettigrew; m. Phillip Wayne Haney, May 29, 1976 (div. Feb. 1995); children: Kristin Lea, Phillip Kollin, Kasey Kay; m. Warren Lynn Adams, Feb. 3, 1996; stepchildren: Lindsay Nichelle, London Reed. BA, U. Sci. and Arts of Okla., 1976. Photographer, reporter Chickasha Daily Express, 1974, lifestyles editor, 1974-78, advt. dir., 1978-88, pub., 1992-95; pub. Pauls Valley (Okla.) Democrat, 1988-92, Real Estate Exec., Chickasha, 1996—, Builder/Architect, Chickasha, 1996—; pub. cons. Adams Assocs., Ninnekah, Okla., 1995—. Contbr. articles to profl. jours. Bd. dirs. Grady County Family YMCA, Chickasha, 1993-96, United Way of Grady County, Chickasha, 1993-96; v.p., treas. Cmty. Edn. Adv. Coun., Pauls Valley, 1990-92; bd. dirs. (alumni) U. Sci. and Arts of Okla., Chickasha, 1993-96, bd. dirs. (found.), 1993-96; founding bd. dirs. Festival of Light, Chickasha, 1993-96. Mem. Okla. Press Assn. (better newspaper contest com. chair 1992-95, newspaper in edn. com. chmn. 1992-95, advt. com. chmn. 1993-95, conv. com. 1993-95, 1st place in sales promotion 1991-92, 1st place in cmty. leadership 1991-92), Pauls Valley C. of C. (bd. dirs. 1988-92). Democrat. Christian Ch. Home: Route 2 Box 6 Ninnekah OK 73067 Office: Builder/Architect PO Box 1191 Chickasha OK 73023

ADAMS, C. LEE, marketing executive; b. Houston, Dec. 5, 1940; s. Carl Adams and Ruth (Carroll) Adams McGraw; BBA, Tex. A&M U., 1963; m. Betty Leatherwood, June 1, 1963; children: Diana, Carroll Ann. Export sales service asst. Comet Rice Mills, Inc., Houston, 1963-64, asst. export sales mgr., 1964-67, export sales mgr., 1967-68; gen. mgr. Country Cupboard Foods Divsn., Comet Rice Mills, 1968-71; sales mgr. Childers Mfg. Co., Houston, 1971-75; export sales mgr. Am. Rice, Inc., Houston, 1975-76, v.p. internat. mktg., 1976-80, group v.p. mktg., 1980-85, group v.p. internat. mktg., 1986-93, sr. v.p., 1993—; bd. dirs. USA Rice Fedn., mem. rice com. New Orleans Commodity Exchange, 1981-84. Bd. dirs. Harris County Water Control and Improvement Dist. 93, 1974-76; mem. Chelford One Mcpl. Utility Dist. Appraisal Rev. Bd., 1982-85. Served with USMCR, 1960-66. Mem. Am. Arab C. of C. (dir. 1978-81), TAMU 12th Man Found. (bd. dirs. 1987—), USA Rice Coun. (bd. dirs. 1995—), Rice Millers Assn. (dir. 1983-95, pres. 1986-87), Assn. Former Students Tex. A&M U. Roman Catholic. Clubs: Elsik High Sch. Ram Rods (pres. 1984-85), Sweetwater Country. Lodge: K.C., Am. Legion. Office: Am Rice Inc PO Box 2587 Houston TX 77252-2587

ADAMS, CAROLINE JEANETTE H., writer; b. Dallas, June 15, 1951; d. Bill Gene and Anita N. (Murrah) Hickey. BFA, So. Meth. U., 1973. Media buyer Jim Leslie & Assocs., Dallas, 1973; continuity dir. Sta. KZEW-FM, Dallas, 1973-75; adminstrv. asst. Neiman-Marcus Co., Dallas, 1975-77; exec. sec. Harris Data Communications, Dallas, 1978-80; mgr. classified sales ADWEEK/Southwest mag., Dallas, 1980-91; freelance copywriter, editor, proofreader, 1992-95; exec. asst. to pres., gen. mgr. KDFW-TV, 1995—. Editor, writer Dallas Advt. League newsletter, 1987-89. Mem. Press Club Dallas (editor bulletin 1993). Methodist. Avocations: travel, antiques, collecting soundtrack and rare record albums, restoring classic automobiles.

ADAMS, CAROLYN BETHA, minister; b. Sandersville, Ga., Oct. 18, 1955; d. George Eddie Betha and Sallie Kate Betha Butler Walls; children: Sylvia Melinda Betha, Felica Tamekin. Paramedic Baldwin Area Vocat. Sch., Milledgeville, 1971-73; nurse asst. Americo Tech. Int Career, Macon, Ga., 1988-89; preacher, songwriter Lighthouse Ministries, Covington, Ga., 1994-96. Office: Lighthouse Ministries PO Box 3974 Eatonton GA 31024

ADAMS, CHARLES, company executive; b. 1935. With Hale Williams Ins., Atlanta, 1967-85; pres. Adams Land Co., Leachville, Ark., 1985—. Office: Adams Land Co N Main St Leachville AR 72438

ADAMS, CORLYN HOLBROOK, nursing facility administrator; b. Beloit, Kans., Sept. 28, 1926; d. Charles Benjamin and Hazel Marian (Brokaw) Holbrook; m. Henry Robert Adams, Oct. 28, 1961; 1 child, Charles Paul. Student, U. Kans., 1944-45. Lic. nursing facility adminstr. Clk. bd. edn. Beloit (Kans.) City Schs., 1945-48; adminstr. Stanford Conv. Ctrs., Fort Worth, 1973-79; adminstr., owner Four Nursing Homes, Fort Worth, 1979-84. Author, editor: The Jose Family, 1994. Mem. Order of Ea. Star, DAR, Nat. Soc. New England Women (sec. 1975), Nat. Hugenot Soc., Gen. Soc. Mayflower Descendents, Daus. of Utah Pioneers. Republican.

ADAMS, DANIEL FENTON, law educator; b. Reading, Pa., July 29, 1922; s. Daniel Snyder and Carrie Betsy (Vought) A.; m. Eloise Williams, Sept. 6, 1968. A.B., Dickinson Coll., 1947; LL.B., Dickinson Sch. Law, 1949. Bar: Pa. 1951, Ark. 1984. Prof. law Dickinson Sch. Law, Carlisle, Pa., 1949-65, asst. to dean, 1952-54, 56-60, acting dean, 1954-56, asst. dean, 1960-65; prof. U. Ark. Sch. Law, Little Rock, 1965-70, 77-93, prof. emeritus, 1993—, asst. dean, 1966-70, acting dean, 1981-82, interim dean, 1989-91; prof. U. Miss. Sch. Law, Oxford, 1970-77; vis. prof. Stetson U. Sch. Law, St. Petersburg, Fla., 1976-77, U. Tenn. Coll. Law, 1993. Contbr. articles to profl. jours. Served with U.S. Army, 1943-44. Mem. ABA, Pa. Bar Assn., Ark. Bar Assn. Home: 32571 River Rd Orange Beach AL 36561-5713

ADAMS, DARLENE AGNES, secondary education educator; b. Prague, Okla., Aug. 23, 1952; d. Carney and Bertha Ellen (Capps) A. AS, Murray State Coll., 1972; BA, East Ctrl. State Coll., 1974, MEd, 1978. Tchr., libr. Carney Pub. Schs., 1974-75, Paden (Okla.) Pub. Schs., 1975—; staff devel com. Paden Pub. Schs., 1985-90, curriculum guidelines com., 1985—, career counseling com., 1990—, gifted and talented com., 1993—, sponsor jr. and sr. class plays and proms. Pres. The Chem. People, Paden, 1983—; sponsor Beta Club, 1990-91, 95-96. Mem. ALA, NEA, Okla. Library Asnn., Okla. Edn. Assn., Smithsonian, Phi Theta Kappa. Republican. Pentacostal. Home: RR 1 Box 82 Paden OK 74860-9766 Office: Paden Pub Schs PO Box 370 Paden OK 74860-0370

ADAMS, DAVID GRAY, lawyer; b. Tyler, Tex., Feb. 18, 1961; s. Ralph Judson and Laura (George) A. BBA, U. Tex., 1983; M in Taxation, Baylor U., 1987; JD, U. Houston, 1995. CPA, Tex. Acct. Grant Thornton, Dallas, 1983-85; tax mgr. Ernst & Young, Dallas, 1987-91; jud. law clk. to Hon. Joe J. Fisher U.S. Dist. Ct. (ea. dist.) Tex., 1995-96; jud. law clk. to Hon. Robert M. Parker U.S. Ct. Appeals (5th cir.), 1996-97; mem. Tex. Bd. Pub. Acctg. Mem. AICPA, ABA, State Bar Tex. Episcopalian.

ADAMS, DAVID HUNTINGTON, judge; b. Cleve., May 30, 1942; s. Donald Croxton and Nancy (Downer) A.; m. Ann Arendell Rawls, Oct. 2, 1965 (div. 1982); children: Ann Arendell, David Huntington, Susannna Camp; m. Mary Watson, Dec. 4, 1982. AB, Washington and Lee U., 1965, JD, 1968. Bar: Va. 1968, U.S. Dist. Ct. (ea. dist.) Va. 1968, U.S. Ct. Appeals (4th cir.) 1968, U.S. Supreme Ct. 1973. Law clk. U.s. dist. Ct., Norfolk, Va., 1968-69; assoc. law firm Willcox, Savage, Norfolk, Va., 1969-72; ptnr. law firm Agelasto, Bernard & Adams, Norfolk, Va., 1972-74, Taylor, Walker Bernard & Adams, Norfolk, 1974-78, Taylor, Walker & Adams, Norfolk, 1974-87, Clark & Stant, P.C., 1987-93; judge U.S. Bankruptcy Ct. (ea. dist. Va.), 1993—; master of the bench James Kent Am. Inn of Ct., 1994—, pres., 1995—; lectr. bankruptcy practice joint com. on continuing legal edn. Va. Bar Found., 1981, 89. Adminstrv. hearing officer Commonwealth of Va., 1974-89. Author: Virginia Landlord and Tenant Law, 1980. Bd. dirs. Heritage Mus., Norfolk, 1991-94; pres. Bay Colony Civic League, Virginia Beach, 1978, Princess Anne Hills Civic League, Virginia Beach, 1988; mem. 4th Cir. Jud. Conf., 1974—; mem. 2d dist. ethics com. Va. State Bar, 1983-84. Mem. ABA, Am. Bankruptcy Inst., Nat. Conf. Bankruptcy Judges (bd. govs. 1996—), Norfolk-Portsmouth Bar Assn., Virginia Beach Bar Assn., Va. Bar Assn. (bd. dirs. bankruptcy sect. 1990-93, mem. coun. jud. sect. 1995—) Episcopalian. Clubs: Princess Anne Country (sec. 1981-92), Cavalier Golf and Yacht (commodore 1994, bd. dirs. 1993—), Pyramid. Avocations: yachting, swimming, cycling. Home: 1533 Quail Point Rd Virginia Beach VA 23454-3115 Office: United States Bankruptcy Ct Walter E Hoffman US Courthouse 600 Granby St Norfolk VA 23510-1915

ADAMS, DONALD EDWARD, biotechnology patent examiner; b. Pitts., June 4, 1964; s. George Oliver and Norma Shirley (Whetton) A.; m. Daria Ann Novekosky, Oct. 21, 1989. BS in Chemistry and Biology, Geneva Coll., 1986; PhD in Microbiology, U. Ala., Birmingham, 1991; postgrad., George Mason U., 1994—. Lic. radioactive materials mgr., Ala. Teaching asst. Geneva Coll., Beaver Falls, Pa., 1985-86; rsch. scientist Sch. Medicine, U. Ala., Birmingham, 1986-91; patent examiner U.S. Dept. Commerce, Patent & Trademark Office, Arlington, Va., 1991—; adj. prof. sci. Marymount U., 1991-93; judge Patent and Trademark Office Regional Sci. Fair. Contbr. articles to scholarly and profl. jours. NIH grantee, 1986; U. Ala. fellow, 1987. Mem. AAAS, N.Y. Acad. Scis., Patent and Trademark Office Soc., Am. Soc. for Microbiology, Phi Sigma (grad. student advisor). Office: US Dept Commerce Patent and Trademark Office Crystal Mall Rm 9a01 Arlington VA 22202

ADAMS, EDDIE, company executive; b. 1958. With Greater Atlanta Printing, 1979-85; pres. Adams Land Co., Leachville, Ark., 1985—. Office: Adams Land Co N Main St Leachville AR 72438*

ADAMS, ELAINE PARKER, college president. BA in Spanish Edn., Xavier U., 1961; MS in Libr. Sci., La. State U., 1966; PhD in Libr. Sci., U. So. Calif., 1973. Cert. learning resources specialist. Dist. catalog libr. Grossmont Union High Sch. Dist., La Mesa, Calif., 1971; mid. sch. libr. Upper St. Clair (Pa.) Sch. Dist., 1972-73; vis. asst. prof. U. Md., College Park, 1973; media specialist U. So. Calif., L.A., 1974-75; coord. Learning Resources Ctr. Tex. So. U., Houston, 1976-80; supr. libr. svcs. and tech. tng. Getty Oil Rsch. Ctr., Houston, 1980-83; assoc. v.p. acad. svcs. and planning Prairie View (Tex.) A&M U., 1983-85, v.p. student affairs, 1985-89; asst. commr. Edn. Opportunity Planning Tex. Higher Edn. Coordinating Bd., Austin, 1989-91; pres. N.E. Coll. Houston C.C. System, 1991—; lectr. Sch. Profl. Edn. U. Houston-Clear Lake, summers 1977-79; planner Honors Coll. Prairie View A&M U., 1983-84, user coord. bldg. cons. libr., 1984-88; cons. Libr./Pharmacy Addition Xavier U., New Orleans, 1988-93; evaluator Mid States Assn. Commn. on Higher Edn., Phila., 1988—, So. Assn. Colls. and Schs., 1991—. Co-editor: Media and the Young Adult, 1981; contbr. articles to profl. jours. Trustee Xavier U., 1990-95, Lon Morris Coll., 1993-94, Houston Pl. Preservation, 1993—; mem. ACE Commn. on Leadersip Devel., 1994-96. Fellow U. So.. Calif., 1968-71; scholar Xavier U., 1957-61, AT&T scholar Harvard U. Inst. for Edn. Mgmt., Cambridge, Mass., 1989. Mem. ALA, Am. Assn. C.C.s, Nat. Assn. Student Pers. Adminstrs. (editl. bd. 1988-90), Am. Assn. for Higher Edn. (Black Caucus exec. bd. 1990—), Nat. Assn. Women in Edn., Nat. Coalition of 100 Black Women (bd. dirs. Houston chpt., Makeda award 1993), Xavier Univ. Alumni Assn. (nat. pres. 1990-91, Alumna of Yr.). Office: NE Coll Houston C C Sys PO Box 7849 Houston TX 77270-7849

ADAMS, FRANCES GRANT, II, lawyer; b. Wheeling, W.Va., Nov. 30, 1955; d. Jack Richard and Frances Irene (Grant) A. BA, W.Va. U., 1976, JD, 1979; MA, Webster U., 1983. Bar: W.Va. 1979, U.S. Dist. Ct. (so. dist.) W.Va. 1979, U.S. Ct. Mil. Appeals 1979, U.S. Supreme Ct. 1988, D.C. 1989. Asst. staff judge advocate armament div. USAF, Eglin AFB, Fla., 1979-82; dep. staff judge advocate USAF, Keflavik, Iceland, 1982-83; staff judge advocate 71st Air Base Group USAF, Vance AFB, Okla., 1984-86; chief gen. torts sect. claims and tort litigation staff hdqrs. USAF, Washington, 1986-88; chief mgmt. and analysis br. claims and tort litigation div. Air Force Legal Svcs. Agy., Washington, 1988-92, sr. tort atty. tort claims and litigation div., 1992—; atty. USAFR, USAF Environ. Law and Litig. Divsn., USAF Legal Svcs. Agy., Washington, 1992—. Program chmn. Pentagon chpt. Fed. Bar Assn., 1989-90. Mem. DAR (chmn. procedures manual W.Va. chpt. 1989-92), Magna Carta Dames, Ancient and Honorable Arty. Co., Air Force Assn. (life), Ret. Officers Assn. (life).

ADAMS, GARY LEE, engineering manager; b. Clearfield, Pa., May 23, 1947; s. William Ellsworth and Ethel Mae (Ling) A.; m. Rebecca Estelle Peppers, Dec. 29, 1967; children: William Matthew, Preston Lee. BSEE, Tulane U., 1969; Grad. of Theology, Bapt. Bible Coll., 1974. Assoc. engr. Westinghouse Electric Corp., Balt., 1969-71; asst. prin., dean edn. Hollywood (Fla.) Christian Sch., 1974-79; assoc. engr. Martin Marietta Corp., Orlando, Fla., 1979-80, engr., 1980-82, sr. engr., 1982-84, group engr., 1984-85; sr. lead engr. Harris Corp., Orlando, Fla., 1985, engring. sect. head, 1985-89; engring. br. mgr. Pentastar Electronics, Inc., Huntsville, Ala., 1989—; vice chmn. Nat. Indsl. Assn. MATE Users Group Test Program Set Com., Washington, 1986-88. Deaf interpreter First Bapt. Ch., Hollywood, 1974-79, Tabernacle Bapt. Ch., Orlando, 1979-89, Triana Village Bapt. Ch., Huntsville, 1989-93; deacon Granite Bapt. Ch., Glen Burnie, Md., 1970-71, Friendship Bapt. Ch., Huntsville, 1995—. Recipient Jung scholarship Tulane U., 1965-68. Mem. Assn. U.S. Army. Republican. Baptist. Home: 95 Indian Creek Rd NW Apt 104 Huntsville AL 35806-2613

ADAMS, HAROLD DALE, food company executive; b. Sampson AFB, N.Y., May 8, 1953; s. Harley DeMille and Teresa Anita (Furano) A.; m. Shirley Ann Flaherty, May 7, 1978. BA, Tenn. Temple U., 1983. Pres. Dee's Candies, Inc., Dallas, 1984-89, Falherty's Fine Confections, Inc., Midlothian, Tex., 1989—. Republican. Baptist. Office: Flahertys Fine Confections PO Box 848 Midlothian TX 76065-0848

ADAMS, JAMES MILTON, biomedical engineering educator; b. Roanoke, Va., Sept. 22, 1949. BSEE, Va. Tech., 1971; PhD in Biomed. Engring., U. Va., 1976. Fellow, instr. Albany (N.Y.) Med. Coll., 1976-78; asst. prof. biomed. engring. U. Va., Charlottesville, 1978-84, assoc. prof., 1984-92, prof., 1992—, asst. dean for grad. programs Sch. Engring. and Applied Sci., 1996—. Office: U Va Dept Biomed Engring Box 377 Charlottesville VA 22908

ADAMS, JOHN CARTER, JR., insurance executive; b. Williston, Fla., June 13, 1936; s. John Carter and Katharine Anna (Beall) A.; m. Leila Nora Johnson, Nov. 28, 1958; children: Julia Katharine, Ruth Anne. BSBA, U. Fla., 1958. Agt. Pan Am. Ins. Co. 1958-59; acct. exec. Guy B. Odum & Co., Inc. 1959-63, v.p. 1963-66, exec. v.p. 1966-71, pres. 1971-76; pres. Jay Adams & Assocs., Inc. Daytona Beach, 1976-85, pres. Hilb Rogal & Hamilton Co., Daytona Beach, 1986-89, chmn., chief exec. officer, 1989-93, bd. dirs., 1987-95; mem. exec. com. Hilb Rogal & Hamilton Co., Richmond, Va., 1988-95, chmn. operating com., 1987-93, sr. v.p. ops., 1989-90, exec. v.p. sales & mktg., 1991-93, exec. v.p., COO, 1993-94, exec. v.p. ops., 1994—. bd. dirs. Westside Atlantic Bank, 1972-76, First Atlantic Nat. Bank, 1976-81, Heritage Fed. Savings & Loan, 1981-85, Daytona Beach, 1985-90, Am. Pioneer Savings Bank, Fla., 1985-90, Consol. Tomoka Land Co., 1976—; chmn. adv. bd. Datona Beach region Am. Pioneer Savs. Bank, Orlando, Fla., 1986-90; chmn. compensation com., Consol.-Tomoka Land Co., 1990—. Mem. bd. visitors Embry-Riddle Aero. U., Daytona Beach, 1967-69, trustee, 1969—, mem. exec. com., 1972—, vice chmn. bd., 1981—, chmn. exec. com., 1983—, devel. coun. chmn. fund drive Hunt Meml. Libr. Embry-Riddle Aero U., 1985; chmn. Committment 2000 Fund Drive Embry-Riddle Aero U.; campaign chmn. Easter Seal Soc. 1969, trustee 1970-73, pres. 1972-73; bd. dirs. YMCA, Daytona Beach 1968-76, 1978—, treas. 1970, v.p. 1971-82, pres., 1983; mem. Metro Bd. Daytona Beach YMCA, 1992—; dir. Futures, Inc., 1985-93, Nat. Intercollegiate Sports Festival, 1985-87; gen. campaign chmn. United Way of Volusia County, Fla. 1977, pres. 1979, dir. 1976-82, trustee, 1985—; chmn. Civic League of Halifax Area, 1983-84, exec. com., 1977-92, chmn., 1981-82; chmn. Fla. Internat. Festivals, Inc., 1990-91, bd. dir. 1987—; mem. Tourist Devel. Council Volusia County, 1983-85, Halifax Advt. Authority, 1985; bd. dirs. Volusia County Bus. Devel. Council, 1984-92; bd. dirs. Daytona Beach Community Found., 1984-87, Fla. State C. of C., 1985-86. Served with USNR 1953-61. Recipient Disting. Service award Bd. visitors Embry-Riddle Aero. U. 1975, Champion Higher Ind. Edn. in Fla. award Ind. Colls. and Univs. of Fla., 1973, 1st Ann. Herbert M. Davidson Community Svc. award United Way of Volusia County, 1992; established John C. Adams Community Svc. award Embry Riddle Aero. U., U., 1990. Mem. Daytona Beach C. of C. (bd. govs. 1968-70, v.p. bus. and govt. 1970, pres. 1975, gen. campaign chmn. devel. fund drive 1984, Louis Fuchs Man of Yr. award, 1985), Volusia County Insurors Assn. (pres. 1971-72), Fla. Assn. Ins. Agts. (bd. dirs. 1978-81), Coun. Ins. Agents and Brokers (bd. dirs. 1989-93, bd. dirs. coun. of ins. agents and brokers, 1993—, co-chmn. exec. liasion com., mem. fin. and audit com. 1993-94, sec. 1994-95, treas. 1995-96, vice chmn. 1996—), Rotary Club (bd. dirs. 1989-91. Republican. Episcopalian. Home: 1616 S Peninsula Dr Daytona Beach FL 32118-4948 Office: 115 N Ridgewood Ave Daytona Beach FL 32114

ADAMS, JOHN WHITE, investment company executive, engineer; b. Houston, Mar. 1, 1948; s. Clifton A. and Lois W. Adams; m. Cathy Gail Hillard; children: Ryan, Vincent, Katherine. BSChemE, Tex. A&M U., 1970; MBA, Harvard U., 1976; postgrad., Northwestern U., 1984, Tex. Engring. Ext. Svc., 1991. Registered profl. engr., Tex. Owner, operator Cir. A Ranch, North Zulch, Tex., 1976—; project engr. Continental Pipeline Co., Ponca City, Okla., 1970; from sr. analyst corp. office to sr. engr. Deer Park Mfg. Shell Oil Co., Houston, 1976-80; sr. planning analyst processing and mktg. Tenneco, Houston, 1980, bus. devel. supr., 1981-84, planning mgr. corp. planning and devel., 1984-89; pres., founder Phase I Environ., Inc., Conroe, 1991—; pres., bd. dirs. BanChem Fin. Svcs., Inc. (formerly Windham Capital, Inc.), Conroe, 1989—; bd. dirs. Holston Energy, Chattanooga, Focused Energy Texh., Austin, Tex.; instr. San Jacinto Coll. N., North Shore, Tex. Contbr. articles to profl. publs. Bd. dirs. Lee Coll. Found., 1981—, bd. regents, 1978-90; mem. adminstrn. bd. dirs. Grace Meth. Ch., 1986-88; bd. dirs. Bay Area Rehab. Ctr., 1987—; mem. adv. bd. East Harris County ARC, 1986—; asst. scoutmaster Troop 105 Boy Scouts Am.; mem. Baytown Area Devel. Coun. With USAF, 1971-74. Decorated Bronze Star. Mem. AICE, Tex. and Southwestern Cattleraisers Assn., Sons Rep. of Tex., Am. Chem. Soc., Nat. Assn. Accts. Home: 4818 Saint Andrews Dr Baytown TX 77521-3016 Office: BanChem Fin Svcs Inc 409 N Loop 336 Ste 6 Conroe TX 77301

ADAMS, JOHN WILSON, JR., healthcare executive; b. Houston, July 31, 1953; s. John Wilson Sr. and Leota Georgene (Roundey) A.; m. Anne Margaret Darrah, Mar. 29, 1986; children: John Wilson III, Benjamin Darrah. BBA in Mgmt., U. Tex., 1975; MS in Health Care Adminstrn., U. Houston, 1981. Bus. office dir. Med. Ctr. Del Oro Hosp., Houston, 1976; bus. office mgr. Westbury Hosp., Am. Med. Internat., Houston, 1977; medicaid provider rels. rep. Nat. Heritage Ins. Houston, 1979; adminstrv. resident Meth. Hosp., Houston, 1980; asst. v.p. patient svcs. divsn. Meth. Hosp., 1981, asst. v.p. Sid W. Richardson Inst. for Preventive Medicine, 1983, v.p., adminstrv. dir., 1981-83, v.p. patient svcs. divsn., 1981-88, 89-90, v.p. support svcs. divsn., 1988; sr. v.p. Tex. Children's Hosp., Houston, 1990—; speaker, presenter in field; guest lectr. U. Houston, Clear Lake City, 1983. Chmn. recycling and resource recovery task force Greater Houston Hosp. Coun., 1992, chmn. waste mgmt. task force, 1989; deacon, Sunday sch. dir., fin. com. Second Bapt. Ch., Houston; bd. dirs. Houston Area Parkinsonism Soc., 1986-88, The Shoulder, 1994—; coord. United Way campaign, 1980; mem. Briargrove Park Civic Assn. Mem. Am. Coll. Healthcare Execs. (chmn. bylaws com. Houston chpt. 1992—), Am. Hosp. Assn., Healthcare Forum, Tex. Hosp. Assn., Greater Houston Hosp. Coun., Assn. of Am. Med. Colls. (group on pub. affairs), Woodmark Forum, U. Houston Alumni Assn. Adminstrn. of Health Svcs. Program (pres. 1984-85), Forum Club Houston. Republican. Office: Tex Children's Hosp 6621 Fannin St Houston TX 77030-2303

ADAMS, KELLY LYNN, emergency physician; b. High Point, N.C., Oct. 17, 1959; d. Roger Lee and Kathryn Maxine (Floyd) A. AA in Gen. Studies, U. Md., 1979; BA in Biology, Va. Intermont Coll., 1980; DO, Southeastern Coll. Osteo. Med., 1988. Cert. Am. Coll. Osteopathic Family Physicians. Emergency physician Humana South Broward, Hollywood, Fla., 1989-91; family practice physician Adams and Herzog, DO, PA, Plantation, Fla., 1990-91; emergency physician Homestead (Fla.) AFB, 1991-92, Mariners Hosp., Tavernier, Fla., 1991-93, Meml. Hosp., Pembroke Pines, Fla., 1992-96, Comp Health, Salt Lake City, 1996—. Recipient Cert. of Merit, State of Fla. and Fla. N.G., 1992. Mem. AMA, Am. Osteo. Assn., Fla. Osteo. Med. Assn., Broward County Osteo. Med. Assn., Assn. Emergency Physicians, Mensa. Republican. Home and Office: 5722 S Flamingo Rd # 273 Fort Lauderdale FL 33330-3206

ADAMS, LAURA ANN, critical care nurse; b. Thibodaux, La., Mar. 17, 1960; d. John Anthony Sr. and M. Elma Theresa (Dufrene) A. AD, Nicholls State U., Thibodaux, 1981, BSN, 1988. RNC, La.; cert. neonatal intensive care. Staff nurse TravCorps Nursing Agy., Malden, Mass., 1991-93, South La. Med. Ctr. (now Leonard J. Chabert Med. Ctr.), Houma, 1981-89, 90-94, Earl K. Long Med. Ctr., Baton Rouge, 1992—. Mem. Assn. Women's Health, Obstetric and Neonatal Nurses, Nat. Assn. Neonatal Nurses, Nat. League of Nurses. Home: PO Box 356 Cut Off LA 70345-0356

ADAMS, LINAS JONAS, gastroenterologist; b. Akron, Ohio, May 2, 1955; s. Vladas and Veronika (Somkaite) A.; m. Elaine Kay Bulchik, Aug. 30, 1980; children: Jillian, Jonas, Nikolas, Madeline. MD, U. Autonoma of Guadalajara, Mex., 1978. Diplomate Am. Bd. Internal Medicine with subspecialty in gastroenterology; lic. physician, Tenn., Ky. Rotating intern St. Thomas Hosp. Med. Ctr., Akron, 1978-79; intern in internal medicine Tijuana BC Mex./Mexican Social Svc., 1979-80; resident Akron City Hosp., 1980-83; fellow in gastroenterology U. Ky. Med. Ctr., Lexington, 1983-86, clin. scholar, 1985-86; staff physician VA Hosp., Lexington, 1985-88; asst. prof. medicine U. Ky. Med. Ctr., Lexington, 1986-88; clin. asst. prof. medicine U. Tenn. Med. Ctr., Knoxville, 1988-89, asst. prof. medicine, 1989-94, assoc. prof. medicine, 1994—; physician dir. nutritional support team VA Med. Ctr., Lexington, 1984-86, fellowship dir. divsn. digestive diseases and nutrition, 1985-86, dir. therapeutic endoscopy, 1985-88, med. supr. D.R.G. allocations, 1985-88; co-dir. drug studies divsn. digestive diseases and nutrition U. Ky., 1985-88; dir. gastroenterology clinic U. Tenn. Med. Ctr., Knoxville, 1988—, dir. gastro-intestinal endoscopic, diagnostic and therapeutic lab., 1989—, chief divsn. gastroenterology and nutrition, 1989—; med. cons. Contbr. numerous articles to profl. jours., chpts. to books. Grantee U. Tenn. Physicians Med. Edn. and Rsch. Found., 1993—, Karl Storz Endoscopy-Am., Inc., 1990-91, VA, 1987-88, Smith, Kline and French, 1986-88, VA Coop. Studies Program, 1986-90, Upjohn Co., 1986-87, Eli Lilly and Co., 1985-87. Fellow Am. Coll. Gastroenterology; mem. ACP, Nat. Assn. Residents and Interns, Am. Gastroenterology Assn., Am. Soc. Parenteral and Enteral Nutrition, Am. Soc. Gastrointestinal Endoscopy, Ky. Soc. Gastrointestinal Endoscopy, Knoxville Acad. Medicine, Tenn. Med. Assn., tenn. Soc. Gastrointestinal Endoscopy, Crohn's Colitis Found. Am., Am. Soc. Internal Medicine, So. Med. Assn., Internat. Assn. Pancreatology, Am. Lithotripsy Soc., Am. Endosonography Club. Office: University Gastroenterology Physicians Office Bldg 1924 Alcoa Hwy # 100 Knoxville TN 37920-1511

ADAMS, LISA ANN, public administrator; b. Port Arthur, Tex., Nov. 6, 1962; d. John Prentice and Margaret Elizabeth (Grantham) A.; m. Michael Prestarri, Sept. 30, 1988 (div. Apr. 1994). AA, Okaloosa-Walton Jr. Coll., 1983; BA, U. Fla., 1985; MPA, U. West Fla., 1991. Substitute tchr. Okaloosa County Sch. Sys., Okaloosa City, Fla., 1985-86; mgmt. support Wal-Mart Stores, Inc., Ft. Walton Beach, Fla., 1986-87; tech. editor Sverdrup Technology, Inc., Eglin AFB, Fla., 1987-90; contract mgr., security officer Orlando Technology, Inc., Shalimar, Fla., 1990-94; contract adminstr. Metric Sys. Corp., Ft. Walton Beach, 1994-95; acting exec. dir. Nat. Coun. on Qualirications for the Lighting Professions, Ft. Walton Beach, 1995-96; contract mgr. Orlando Tech., Inc., Shalimar, Fla., 1996; publicity chair, grants Highsteppers, Inc., Ft. Walton Beach, 1993-96. Songwriter. Mem. Nat. Contract Mgmt. Assn. (membership chair 1994, sec. 1993, scholarship chair 1992), NAFE. Office: NCQLP 11A 3148 SW Miracle Strip Pkwy Fort Walton Beach FL 32548

ADAMS, MAERITA ELAINE OWEN, early childhood educator; b. Asheville, N.C., Aug. 11, 1946; d. Troy Everette and Ethel Melinda (Rhodes) Owen; m. Charles Ronald Adams, Mar. 4, 1967; 1 child, Charles Ronald II. Diploma T-4 Early Childhood Edn., Valdosta State Coll., 1968, Diploma T-5 Early Childhood Edn., 1976, T-6 Specialist in Early Childhood Edn., 1980. Tchr. Lowndes County Sch. System, 1969-70, W.G. Nunn Elem., Valdosta, Ga., 1971-93, J.L. Newbern Mid. Sch.; edn. fair chmn. W.G. Nunn Elem., 1989-91. Poll worker Charles Hatcher Campaign, Valdosta, 1988. Mem. Ga. Assn. Educators, NEA, Valdosta Assn. Educators (legis. chmn. 1989-91), Internat. Reading Assn., Phi Delta Kappa (historian 1989-91). Republican. Baptist. Office: WG Nunn Elementary 2201 N Forrest St Valdosta GA 31602-2003

ADAMS, MARY ELISSA, English language educator, consultant; b. Louisville, Ky., Nov. 24, 1919; d. Walter Terry and Mary Elizabeth (Eberenz) A. BA, Ursiline Coll. now Bellarmine, Lousiville, 1854; MA, Xavier U, Cin., 1962; MEd, U. Louisville, 1973, PhD, 1985. Cert. secondary sch. English tchr. (life), supr. cert., guidance counseling cert., Ky. Tchr. Jr. H.S. St. Peter Elem. Sch., Columbia, S.C., 1949-50, Jr. H.S. Holy Spirit Sch., Louisville, 1950-56; English tchr., home rm. St. Patrick H.S., North Platte, Nebr., 1956-57; 6th grade home rm. St. Helen Elem. Sch., Louisville, 1957-58; jr. h.s, home rm. St. Rita Elem. Sch., Louisville, 1958-63; English tchr., chair English dept. Angela Merici H.S., Louisville, 1963-69; English tchr. Sacred Heart Acad., Louisville, Ky., 1969-72; lectr. on English Watterson Coll., Louisville, 1972-79, Univ. Louisville, 1979—; cons. Ednl. Testing Svc., Princeton, N.J., 1986-96. Contbr. articles to Ednl. and Regligious Mags. Vol. Women's State Prison, Louisville, 1970's, Suburban Hosp., 1980's, Ky. Ctr. for Arts., 1993—. Grantee Drake U., 1980's. Mem. Nat. Coun. Tchrs. of English (Recognition Svc. award 1994), Ky. Coun. Tchrs. of English (bd. dirs.), Greater Louisville English Tchrs. Coun. Republican. Roman Catholic. Home: 3175 Lexington Rd Louisville KY 40206 Office: U Louisville Belknap Campus Louisville KY 40292

ADAMS, MARY RAPRICH, retired nursing education administrator; b. Lonoke, Ark., July 25, 1918; d. Fred A. and Katie (Kittler) Raprich; children: Richard, Dorothy A. Grad., St. Vincent Infirmary, Little Rock; BSN, Case Western Res. U., 1951, MSN, 1953. Sr. asst. nurse officer USPHS, 1944-48; head nurse, supr. Ohio USPHS, Ohio, 1954-58; instr. nursing edn. Akron (Ohio) City Hosp. Sch. Nursing, 1954-58, Akron Gen. Hosp. Sch. Nursing, 1958-60; dir. nursing edn. affiliate program pediatrics Children's Hosp., Akron, 1961-83, ret. Sr. asst. nurse officer USPHS, 1944-48. Mem. Nat. League for Nursing, Sigma Theta Tau. Home: 1146 Raprich Rd Lonoke AR 72086-9271

ADAMS, MENDLE EUGENE, minister; b. Bath County, Va., July 1, 1938; s. Earl and Margaret M. (Godsey) A.; m. N. Ruth Williams, Feb. 2, 1957; children: David Mendle, Brian Richard, Josef Wayne, Vicki Ruth. AB, Ind. Wesleyan U., 1967; MA in Religion, Christian Theol. Sem., 1969; postgrad., Aquinas Coll., 1977, Harvard U., 1978. Ordained to ministry Meth. Ch. as deacon, 1968, as min., United Ch. of Christ, 1981; orders accepted The Old Cath. Order, 1993. Pastor Windfall (Ind.) Pilgrim Ch., 1960-63, Mt. Olive Meth. Ch., Marion, Ind., 1963-67, Mt. Comfort United Meth. Ch., Indpls., 1967-69, United Meth. Cir., Donnybrook, Maxbass, Lansford, N.D., 1979, Hope Congl. United Ch. of Christ, Granville, N.D., 1980-82, 1st Congl. United Ch. of Christ, McPherson, Kans., 1982-87; chaplain ecumenical campus Okla. State U., Stillwater, 1987-91; interim pastor Peace United Ch. of Christ, Loyal, Okla., 1988, 1st Christian Ch. (Disciples of Christ), Stillwater, 1990, Bethel Congl. Ch., Edmond, Okla., 1991; organizing min. High Point United Ch. of Christ, Boone County, Ky., 1991—; ednl. trips to Israel-Palestine, 1980, Nicaragua, 1983, The Philippines, 1985. Co-author: Touching Center Adventures in Christ Consciousness, 1990. Mem. Ind. Ho. of Reps., 1975-76, Ind. Solid Waste Com., 1976; mem. Ind. and Okla. group for Equal Rights Ammendment to U.S. Constn., 1977, 81; bd. dirs. McPherson Family Life Ctr., 1983-84; chmn. com. McPherson Community Nursing Home, 1984; mem. Gov.'s Task Force on AIDS, Okla., 1987-88, Gov.'s Cabinet on Children's Issues, 1988-91, Ecumenical Coun. on Maternal and Infant Health, So. Gov.'s Leadership Coun., 1989-91; cert. mediator Okla. Dispute Resolution, Supreme Ct. Okla., 1991; mem. Chs. Uniting in Global Mission, 1992—. Recipient Honored Legislator citation Ind. Coun. Chs., 1976. Democrat. Home: 11176 Us Highway 42 Union KY 41091-9480

ADAMS, NANCY ANN, school system administrator; b. Syracuse, N.Y., Mar. 20, 1932; d. Percival William Normand and Marion Vivian (Arnold) Taylor; m. Walter Adams, June 19, 1959 (div. 1970); children: Norman, Laurie. BEd, U. Miami, Coral Gables, 1957; MEd, Fla. Atlantic U., 1969; PhD, U. Wyoming, 1981. Cert. tchr., Fla. Tchr. Broward County Schs., Ft. Lauderdale, Fla., 1957-62, rsch. asst., 1969-73, counselor high sch. srs., 1973-79, counselor adults, 1980-81, coord. adult program, 1981-93. Mem. Fla.

Adminstrs. Adult Edn. (vice chmn. 1984-86), Adult and Cmty. Educators of Fla. (bd. dirs. 1988-96), Am. Assn. Adult and Continuing Edn., Fla. Sch. Counselor Assn. (v.p. 1987), Adult and Cmty. Educators of Fla. (chmn. adminstr.'s affiliate). Democrat. Home: 800 NW 6th Ter Boca Raton FL 33486-3506 Office: 700 NE 56th Ste Oakland Park FL 33334

ADAMS, NANCY R., nurse, military officer. BSN, Cornell U., N.Y. Hosp. Sch. Nursing; MSN, Cath. U. Am.; grad., Command and Gen. Staff Coll., U.S. Army War Coll. Commd. Nurse Corps, U.S. Army, 1968, advanced through grades to brig. gen., 1991; chief nurse Army Regional Med. Ctr., Frankfurt, Germany, 1987-89; nursing adminstr. various locations; nurse cons. to U.S. Surgeon Gen., 1989-91; chief Nurse Corps Ctr. for Health Promotion and Preventive Medicine, U.S. Army, 1991—, asst. surgeon gen., comdr., 1993—; now Army Nurse Corps Office of Chief, Surgeon Gen. U.S. Army, 1994—. Author textbooks; contbr. articles to profl. jours. Fellow Am. Acad. Nursing; mem. ANA, Assn. Mil. Surgeons of U.S., Am. Orgn. Nurse Execs., Sigma Theta Tau. Office: SW Health Svc Support Area 5005 N Piedras St El Paso TX 79920

ADAMS, PAMELA JEANNE, nurse, flight nurse; b. West Palm Beach, Fla., Aug. 7, 1959; d. Walter Maxim and Dorothy Althea (Mitchell) Carlisle; m. Timothy Weldon Adams, July 1, 1978; children: Rebecca Jeanne, Brian Peter, Holly Suzanne. ASN, Palm Beach C.C., 1981. Cert. paramedic, Fla. Vol. Good Samaritan Med. Ctr., West Palm Beach, Fla., 1973-75, RN LORP and antepartum unit, 1983-95, maternal transport coord., 1992-95; emergency med. technician Atlantic P.B. Ambulance, West Palm Beach, Fla., 1979-82; RN emergency dept. Bethesda Meml. Hosp., Boynton Beach, Fla., 1981-83; asst. childbirth educator Palm Beach Med. Group, West Palm Beach, Fla., 1985-88; clin. instr. paramedics Palm Beach C.C., Lake Worth, Fla., 1986-91; RN labor and delivery Meml. Mission Hosp., Asheville, N.C., 1995—; cons., expert witness for def. Obstetric Malpractice cases, Fla., 1995—; adv. com. for merger Good Samaritan Med. Ctr. and St. Mary's Hosp., 1995. Author: O.B. STAT Maternal Transport Manual, 1992; co-author: Flight Nurse Association Core Curriculum, 1996. Mem. Nat. Flight Nurses Assn., Nat. Flight Spl. Interest Group for Maternal Transports. Prebyterian. Home: 23 Turnberry Dr Arden NC 28704

ADAMS, PHYLLIS CURL, nursing educator; b. Houston, Sept. 15, 1947; d. Kenneth H. and Helen (Phillips) Curl; m. Todd E. Adams, Aug. 28, 1982. BSN, Dillard U., 1969; MSN, Ohio State U., 1972; EdD, Tex. Southern U., 1989; FNP, Tex. U. Woman's U., 1995. Charge nurse The Methodist Hosp., Houston, 1969-71; faculty coord. Columbus (Ohio) Tech. Inst., 1973-81; practitioner, asst. mgr. The Methodist Hosp., 1981-90; coord., asst. prof. Sch. Nursing U. Tex. Health Sci. Ctr., Houston, 1990-95; spl. asst. to pres. for Office of Campus Diversity U. Tex. Health Sci. Ctr., 1993-95; staff nurse The Meth. Hosp., 1990-95; asst. prof. Sch. Nursing U. Tex., Arlington, 1995—. contbr. articles to profl. jours. Mem. ANA, Tex. Nurses Assn. (bd. dirs. 1994-95, mem. dist. 4), Minority Faculty Assn., Profl. Women's Breakfast Club, Sigma Theta Tau, Phi Delta Kappa. Home: 1225 Chinkapin Pl Flower Mound TX 75028 Office: U Tex-Arlington Sch Nursing PO Box 19407 411 S Nedderman Dr Arlington TX 76019-0407

ADAMS, RICHARD PAUL, healthcare management executive; b. Boston, Dec. 25, 1945. Cert. med. record tech., Rindge Tech. Inst., Cambridge, Mass., 1969; BS in Health Info. Mgmt., U. Tex., Galveston, 1989; MPH, U. Tex., Houston, 1992. Registered record adminstr. Asst. supr. med. record dept. Childrens Hosp. Med. Ctr., Boston, 1967-69; dir. inpatient med. records Boston City Hosp., 1969-71; ann. meeting coord., asst. continuing edn. divsn. Am. Health Info. Mgmt. Assn., 1971-75; dir. med. records Miami Valley Hosp., Dayton, Ohio, 1975-76; asst. dir., dir. med. record svcs. Med. Dimensions, Inc., Houston, 1976-78, dir. med. record svcs., 1977-78; cons., dir. health info. svcs. Contemporary Health, Inc., Houston, 1978-84, Cambridge Internat., Inc., Houston; adminstrv. assoc. Orchard Creek Hosp., Houston, 1984-89; dir. health info. svcs. IntraCare Hosp. Cambridge Internat., Inc., Houston, 1989-90, corp. dir. quality assessment risk mgmt., 1990—; cons. NASA/Lyndon Baines Johnson Space Ctr., Houston, 1992; med. record cons. Yale Clinic and Hosp., Houston, 1983-92, nursing homes in Chgo., 1971-75; instr. med. terminology Thornton C.C., South Holland, Ill., 1973-74. Bd. trustees IntraCare Hosp., Houston, 1988—; chmn. Mayor's Task Force on AIDS, Houston, 1984-87; bd. dirs. The Montrose Clinic, Inc., Houston, 1980-87, mem. planning com., 1980-82, corp. sec., 1982-83, chmn., 1984-85, 87, vice chmn., 1986; mem. substance abuse svcs. panel The United Way of Tex. Gulf Coast, Houston, 1989-90. Recipient Mayoral Proclamation City of Houston, 1985; State of Fla. grantee, 1975-76. Mem. Am. Health Info. Mgmt. Assn. (mem. mental health record sect. 1985—), Tex. Health Info. Mgmt. Assn. (chmn. publs. com. 1979-81, ad hoc com. 1977-78), Houston Area Health Info. Mgmt. Assn. Home: 13526 Clarewood Dr Houston TX 77083-2622 Office: Cambridge Internat Inc 7505 Fannin St Ste 600 Houston TX 77054-1913

ADAMS, ROBERT WAUGH, state agency administrator, economics educator; b. Johnstown, Pa., Oct. 26, 1936; s. Robert Waugh and Mary Louise (Pyle) A.; m. Karen Day, June 13, 1964; children: Robert W. and Tara Anne Adams Mason. BS in Acctg., Pa. State U., 1958; MBA, U. Louisville, 1967. Acct., comptroller, v.p. lending Citizens Fidelity Bank, Louisville, Ky., 1959-77; dir. fin., planning, and from dep. exec. dir. to exec. dir. Ky. Housing Corp., Frankfort, 1977-96; owner Adams Consulting Co., Louisville, 1996—; past pres. Bank Adminstrv. Inst., 1966, Planning Exec. Inst., 1970, Fin. Exec. Inst., 1974. Capt. U.S. Army Infantry, 1958-62. Mem. Louisville Boat Club (bd. dirs.). Republican. Roman Catholic. Home: 4410 Deepwood Dr Louisville KY 40241-1047

ADAMS, ROSE ANN, management consultant; b. McHenry, Ill., Apr. 4, 1952; d. Clemens Jacob and Marguerite Elizabeth (Freund) A. BS in Edn., Ill. State U., 1974; MEd, U. Ark., 1979. Supt., exec. dir. Clinton County Children's Services, Wilmington, Ohio, 1979-81; dir. ednl. and adult svcs. Bost Human Devel. Svcs., Ft. Smith, Ark., 1981-87; adminstrv. officer Cen. Ark. Devel. Coun., Benton, 1987; adminstrv. officer, interim Head Start dir., dir. resource devel. Community Orgn. Poverty Elimination Pulaski, Lonoke Counties, Little Rock, 1987-93; exec. dir. So. Early Childhood Assn., 1993-94; sr. cons. Earl Moore and Assocs., Little Rock, 1994—. Active Welfare Adv. Bd., Clinton County, 1979-81, Home Econs. Extension Svcs. Adv. Com., 1979-81, adv. bd. U. Ark. Women's Ctr., 1979; coord. White House Conf. on Families, 1980; mem. Task Force Child Abuse, 1985; trustee Multiple Sclerosis Soc., Ark.; bd. dirs. Morris Found.; chair Ark. Health Promotion Coalition; vice-chair Pulaski County Local Planning Group; chair Ark. Com. on Women's Concerns; charter mem. Am. Lung Assn. of Ark. Aux.; adv. com. Ark. Mentors; pres., v.p. Ark. Single Parent Scholarship Fund. Named one of Outstanding Young Women of Am., 1982. Mem. Am. Bus. Women's Assn. (Woman of Yr. Avant Garde chpt. 1992). Home: Sonata Trl # 1 Little Rock AR 72205-1632 Office: Earl Moore and Assocs 300 S Spring St Ste 612 Little Rock AR 72201-2422

ADAMS, SALVATORE CHARLES, lawyer, speaker, financial consultant, radio and television commentator; b. Bklyn., July 10, 1934; s. Charles Joseph and Rose (Scala) A.; m. Ann Shepherdson, Aug. 3, 1957 (div. Feb. 1973); children: Mark, Scott, David, Christopher; m. Mary Jo Comstock, Dec. 8, 1990. BCE, Rensselaer Poly. Inst., 1955; MS, U. Conn., 1961; JD, U. Miami, 1968. Bar: Fla 1968, U.S. Dist. Ct. (so. dist.) Fla. 1969, U.S. Tax Ct. 1990, U.S. Ct. Appeals (11th cir.) 1974, U.S. Supreme Ct., 1974; registered profl. engr., N.Y., Conn. Pres. Motivation Cons., Miami, Fla., 1965-68; v.p. Exposition Corp., Miami, 1968-72; gen. counsel City of Pompano Beach, Fla., 1972-76; mcpl. judge Broward County, Fla., 1974-76; corp. counsel Five Star Industries, Hialeah, Fla., 1976-80; gen. counsel Good Steward Ministries, 1992—; chmn., CEO Atlantic Svcs. Group, Ft. Lauderdale, Fla., 1977-86; prin. S. Charles Adams & Assocs., Ft. Lauderdale, 1986—; dir. Minute Man Found., 1994—, In God We Trust, 1994—; investment advisor U.S. SEC; gen. coun. Planned Giving Found., 1993—, Morgan, Howen & Co., 1993—; dir. Planned Giving Roundtable, 1994—. Author: Your Fiscal Fitness; creator radio commentary Your Fiscal Fitness; host talk show The Bus. Round Table; pub. Timely Tax and Money Strategies Newsletter. Bd. dirs., pres. Planned Giving Coun., 1993-96, Fla. Bar Mgmt. Sect.; del. White House Conf. on Small Bus., Washington, 1986; apptd. to joint Presdl.-Congl. Com. by Pres. Reagan, 1984; pres. Broward Planned Giving Coun., 1994-95, Broward Estate Planning Coun., endowment com. Broward Performing Arts Ctr., planned giving com. United Way, 1992—, fin. com. Honda Classic, 1988—; bd. dirs. Minute Man Found., 1995—, In God We Trust Ministries. Recipient Pres.'s award Broward County Bar Assn., 1975. Mem. Nat. Soc. Fundraising Execs. (bd. dirs. 1991—), North Broward County Bar Assn. (treas., bd. dirs.), Broward County Mcpl. Judges Assn. (pres. 1976), Nat. Inst. Mcpl. Law Officers (chmn. ethics com.), Rensselaer Poly. Inst. Alumni Assn. (pres. South Fla. chpt.), Christian Stewardship Assn., Christian Legal Soc. Republican. Office: Adams & Assocs PO Box 30488 Fort Lauderdale FL 33303-0488

ADAMS, SAM, newspaper journalist; b. Hazard, Ky., Oct. 22, 1963; s. Charles Lee and Helen (Minor) A.; m. Legina Caudill, May 11, 1991; 1 child, Ian Jeffery. AS, Hazard C.C., 1983; BA, U. Ky., Lexington, 1985. Reporter The Mountain Eagle, Whitesburg, Ky., 1986-93; disc jockey/programmer WMMT-FM, Whitesburg, 1987-89; environ. reporter The Daily Ind., Ashland, Ky., 1993—. Mgmt. devel. v.p. Letcher (Ky.) Area Jaycees, 1992. Recipient 3rd pl. award investigative reporting Ky. Press Assn., 1994, honorable mention story series, 1995. Office: The Daily Ind 226 17th St PO Box 311 Ashland KY 41105

ADAMS, SAMUEL FRANKLIN, lawyer; b. Jacksonville, Fla., Jan. 9, 1958; s. Samuel Eugene and Lucille (Quinn) A.; m. Beverly June Walls, Sept. 27, 1986 (div. 1996); m. Ronda Jean Pence, Sept. 7, 1996. BA in Polit. Sci., Stetson U., 1980; JD, Samford U., 1983. Bar: Fla. 1983, S.C. 1987, U.S. Dist. Ct. S.C. 1988. Assoc. Phil Trovillo, P.A., Ocala, Fla., 1983-86; v.p.adminstrn. Good Shepherd Meml. Pk., Spartanburg, S.C., 1986-88, C & C Properties, Spartanburg, 1988—; pvt. practice law Spartanburg, 1988-95; assoc. Dallis Law Firm, PA, 1995—; atty. for City of Chesnee, S.C., 1991-92; magistrate Spartanburg County, 1992—; city judge Pallot Mills, 1992—. Pres. Boiling Springs Jaycees, 1996—. Mem. ABA, Fla. Bar Assn., Am. Assn. Trial Lawyers, Jaycees (v.p. enrollment and growth Spartanburg 1988, legal counsel Boiling Springs 1991-92, 96, pres. 1996-97), Optimists (sec., treas. Ocala chpt. 1984-85). Democrat. Baptist. Office: PO Box 16243 Spartanburg SC 29316-6243

ADAMS, SCOTT LESLIE, accountant; b. Seattle, Nov. 23, 1955; s. Brock and Mary Elizabeth (Scott) A.; m. Crystal Hood, Aug. 7, 1978; children: Brock, Justin, Betsy, Brooke. BS in Acctg. magna cum laude, Jones Coll., 1984. CPA. Dist. dir. The Scott Co., Washington, 1972-75; pres. Slade Corp., Greenbelt, Md., 1977-80; shift supr. U.S. Ho. Reps., Washington, 1977-82; acct. Comprehensive Bus. Svcs., Jacksonville, Fla., 1984-85; prin. Contemporary Bus. Svcs., Jacksonville, 1985—, Tax Consultants, P.A., 1991—; pres. Scott Investment Inc., Jacksonville; v.p. Adams Mgmt. Svcs. Chmn. fin. com., deacon chmn. St. John's Park Bapt. Ch., Jacksonville, 1987—; v.p. Jacksonville West Camp, Gideons U.S.A., 1987—. Mem. AICPA, Nat. Soc. Pub. Accts., Nat. Soc. Tax Practitioners, Fla. Inst. CPA's, Nat. Assn. Accts., Small Bus. Network, Jacksonville C. of C. Republican. Home: 4984 Ortega Forest Dr Jacksonville FL 32210 Office: Contemporary Bus Svcs 4070 Herschel St Jacksonville FL 32210-2239

ADAMS, THURMAN LEON, JR., minister; b. Jackson, Miss., Dec. 21, 1945; s. Thurman Leon Adams Sr. and Erma Frances (Evans) Lemser; m. Mary Eloise Hardwick, Nov. 24, 1965; children: Stephanie Renee, Lori Marie. BA, Miss. Coll., 1969; postgrad., New Orleans Bapt. Theol. Sem., 1977-79, 81-82. Ordained to ministry So. Bapt. Conv., 1968. Pastor Salem Bapt. Ch., Preston, Miss., 1970-72, Mashulaville Bapt. Ch., Macon, Miss., 1972-73, Macedonia Bapt. Ch., Louisville, Miss., 1973-76, Arkadelphia Bapt. Ch., Bailey, Miss., 1976-80, Oak Grove Bapt. Ch., Meridian, Miss., 1980-95; East Highland Bapt. Ch., Hartselle, Ala., 1995—; chaplain Meridian Police Dept., 1981-95, Hartselle Police Dept., 1996—, Ala. Dept. Pub. Safety, 1996—; mem. Meridian/Lauderdale County ACTS Bd., 1983—, chmn., 1986-88; assoc. moderator Lauderdale Bapt. Assn., Meridian, 1989-90. Recipient Citation for meritorious svc. Meridian Police Dept., 1994. Mem. Internat. Conf. Police Chaplains (cert. sr. chaplain, regional dir., bd. dirs. 1990—), Miss. Bapt. Chaplains Assn. (pres. 1987). Home: 804 Cindy St NE Hartselle AL 35640-1656 Office: East Highland Bapt Ch PO Box 888 Hartselle AL 35640-0888

ADAMS, TODD PORTER, financial and investment advisor; b. Nyack, N.Y., Oct. 11, 1955; s. Edmond Robert and Georgina (Porter) A.; m. Catherine Elizabeth Jarboe, Dec. 26, 1982 (div. Dec. 1985); 1 child, Danielle Elyce; m. Janine Marilyn Leduc, Jan. 29, 1994. BS, St. Thomas Aquinas Coll., 1977; MBA, SUNY, Buffalo, 1981. CFP. Acct. trainee Allied Chem., Syracuse, N.Y., 1977-78; from acct. to supr. of acctg. %, Buffalo, 1978-80; pvt. practice fin. cons. Buffalo, 1980-81; account exec. Dean Witter Reynolds, Cape Coral, Fla., 1981-82, E.F. Hutton & Co., Cape Coral, 1982-85; v.p. investments Advest, Inc., Ft. Myers, Fla., 1985-90; rep. Linsco/Pvt. Ledger, Ft. Myers, 1990—; fin. and investment advisor Mills-Price & Assoc., Inc., Ft. Myers, 1990—; investment and inf. commentator WINK-TV, 1989—. Chmn. Jr. Olympic Torch Run, Lee County, Fla., 1990. Mem. Inst. CFPs, Nat. Assn. Investors Corp., Am. Assn. Ind. Investors, Assn. MBA Execs., Kiwanis (life, v.p. house South Ft. Myers chpt. 1984—, Kiwanian of Yr. award 1983, 95). Republican. Presbyterian. Office: Mills-Price & Assoc Inc 6700 Winkler Rd Ste 3 Fort Myers FL 33919-7235

ADAMS, VICTORIA ELEANOR, retired realty company executive; b. San Francisco, Feb. 8, 1941; d. George Mulford and Sarah Louise (Dearborn) A.; m. Gene M. Richardson, 1965 (div. 1972); 1 child, Raymond; m. Franklin Carlisle Boosman, 1972 (div. 1990); 1 child, Eric; m. Harold Glen Kirchner, Mar. 14, 1992. AA, Palomar Coll., 1976; BBA summa cum laude, Nat. U., 1978. Sales adminstr. Evergreen Internat. Airlines, McMinnville, Oreg., 1983; corp. adminstr. N.N. Jaeschke, Inc., San Diego, 1984—; adminstrv. mgr. Tomlinson Agy., Inc., Spokane, Wash., 1980-86; v.p. Champion Realty Inc., Spokane, 1987-93; pub. dir. Champion Pubs., 1987-93; ret., 1993. Editor: Bravura, 1976; (text) Science Among Us, 1965, Principles in Action Newsletter, 1992—; author: No More than 4 Ingredients Cookbook, 1994; designer Astrology game, 1974. Contbr. articles to profl. jours. Solicitor, Am. Heart Assn., 1985. Recipient Cert. Real Estate Sales Achievment, 1978, 1982, 85, 86, 88, 89, 91; Cert. Outstanding Contbn. to Real Estate Edn., 1980. Avocations: writing, ednl. rsch., fishing, camping, traveling. Home and Office: Apt 3433 6110 Pleasant Ridge Rd Arlington TX 76016-4307

ADAMS, WARREN LYNN, publisher, business consultant; b. Clarksville, Ark., Jan. 11, 1955; s. Warren Earnest Adams and Doris Anita (Reed) Crandall; m. Pamela Jo Sullivan, Sept. 9, 1978 (div. 1995); children: Lindsay Nichelle, London Reed; m. Brenda Kay Pettigrew, Feb. 3, 1996; children: Kristin Lea Haney, Phillip Kollin Haney, Kasey Kay Haney. BA, U. Ctrl. Okla., 1978, BS, 1994; MBA, Oklahoma City U., 1996. Dir. pub. rels. Oklahoma City Zoo, 1979-80; dir. sports info. Oklahoma City U., 1980-82; chief operating officer Fite-Davis & Assocs., Oklahoma City, 1982-84; pres., CEO Lynn Adams & Assocs., Oklahoma City, 1984-88; pub. rels. technician Runkle-Moroch Advertising, Oklahoma City, 1988-89; chief operating officer Jim Fite Mktg. and Mgmt. Resources, Edmond, Okla., 1989-92; administrator Okla. Ctr. for Alcohol and Drug-Related Studies, Oklahoma City, 1992—; publ. cons. First Baptist Ch., Oklahoma City, 1984-95; bus. cons. Adams Assocs., Ninnekah, Okla., 1995—; pub., bus. mgr. Real Estate Exec. Mag., Chickasha, Okla., 1996—, Builder/Architect Mag., Chickasha, 1996—. Contbr. articles to profl. jours. Master mason Ancient, Free & Accepted Masons, Oklahoma City, 1981—; 32 Mason Okla. Scottish Rite, Guthrie, 1982—; recreation coord. First Baptist Ch., 1984-95; sec., bd. deacons 1988-90. Named Gov.'s Non-Profit Corp. of Yr., Okla. Fedn. of Parents for Drug-Free Youth, Oklahoma City, 1994. Mem. Outstanding Young Men of Am. (named Outstanding Young Men of Am. 1987, 88, 89, 92; mem. nat. nom. com.), U. Okla. Health Scis. Ctr. (OUHSC) Staff Senate. Democrat. First Christian. Home: Rte 2 Box 6 Ninnekah OK 73067 Office: Okla Ctr for Alcohol & Drug-Related Studies 800 NE 15th St Ste 410 Oklahoma City OK 73104

ADAMS-ALLEN, JUNE EVELYN, real estate broker; b. Houston, Feb. 14, 1956; d. S.G. and Martilla (Traylor) Adams; m. Larry Craig Strickland, June 19, 1982 (div. May 1984); m. Theodore Allen Jr., Aug. 16, 1985; 1 child, Jesselyn Evette Allen. BBA in Acctg., U. Houston, 1978. Lic. real estate broker, Tex. Receptionist State Rep. Craig Washington, Houston, 1976-80; revenue acct. Chevron U.S.A., Houston, 1980-85; acct. Gulf Interstate Engring. Co., Houston, 1978; auditor, acct. Dwight Staes CPA, Houston, 1979-70; broker, owner J.E.A. Unltd. Realty, Houston, 1987—; broker assoc. ERA Classic Properties, Spring, Tex., 1989-92; apt. locator Tex. Apt. Locators, Houston, 1984-85; substitute tchr., Aldine Ind. Sch., Houston, 1988-93; real estate instr. George Leonard Real Estate Sch., Houston, 1995—; owner J.E.A. Unltd. Locators, Houston, 1994—, J.E.A. Unltd. Svcs., Houston, 1987—. Author: JEA Way-Apartment Locating and the Real Estate Transaction, 1994. Mem. Houston Assn. Realtors and Credit Union. Office: JEA Unltd Realty/Locators 5511 Austin Houston TX 77004

ADAMSON, JAMES B., business executive; b. 1948. Various positions The Gap, 1975-84; exec. v.p. mktg. Revco Inc., 1984-91; various positions, CEO Burger King Corp., 1991-95; pres., CEO Flagstar Corp., Spartanburg, S.C., 1995—. Office: Flagstar Corp 203 E Main St Spartanburg SC 29319

ADAMSON, JANE NAN, elementary school educator; b. Amarillo, Tex., Feb. 5, 1931; d. Carl W. and Lydie O. (Martin) Ray; 1 child, Dave R. Student, Amarillo Coll., Richland Coll. Univ. Dallas, U. North Tex.; BS, West Tex. A&M U., Canyon, 1953; MEd, Tex. A&M U., Commerce, 1975; diploma, Inst. Children's Lit., 1991; cert., Bur. Edn. and Rsch., 1995. Cert. elem. tchr., Tex.; lic. real estate salesman. Tchr. Dallas Ind. Sch. Dist. Mem. Alliance of Dallas Educators, Navy League U.S.

ADAMSON, WALTER LUIZ, history educator; b. Washington, Feb. 28, 1946; s. Walter and Mariza (de Faro) A.; m. Lauren Nash Bernstein, June 11, 1972; children: Daniel, Thomas. BA, Swarthmore Coll., 1968; MA, U. Calif., Berkeley, 1969; PhD, Brandeis U., 1976. Asst. prof. polit. sci. Whitman Coll., Walla Walla, Wash., 1975-77; Mellon fellowship in history Harvard U., Cambridge, Mass., 1977-78; asst. prof. history Emory U., Atlanta, 1978-82, assoc. prof. history, 1982-86, prof. history, 1986—, Samuel C. Dobbs prof. of intellectual history, 1987—. Author: Hegemony and Revolution, 1980 (Best Book in Italian History 1981), Marx and the Disillusionment of Marxism, 1985, Avant-garde Florence, 1993 (Best Book in Italian History 1994). Recipient Sr. fellowship Am. Coun. Learned Socs., 1991-92, fellowship Howard Found., Brown U., 1984-85. Mem. Am. Hist. Assn., Am. Assn. Italian Studies, Assn. for Study of Modern Italy. Democrat. Office: Emory Univ Dept History Atlanta GA 30322

ADCOCK, BETTY S., poet, humanities educator; b. San Augustine, Tex., Sept. 16, 1938; d. Ralph Lafayette and Sylvia (Hudgins) Sharp; m. Donald Brandt Adcock, June 24, 1957; 1 child, Sylvia Elizabeth. Student, Tex. Tech. U., 1956-57, N.C. State U., 1965-66, Goddard Coll., 1966-68. Copywriter Ralph Johnson Assocs., Raleigh, N.C., 1969-73; creative dir. Percivall Advt. and Mktg., Raleigh, 1973-79; writer in residence Kalamazoo (Mich.) Coll., 1983; Kenan writer in residence Meredith Coll., Raleigh, 1983—; vis. lectr. Duke Univ., Durham, N.C., 1977; writer in residence Lenoir Rhyne Coll., Hickory, N.C. Author: Walking Out, 1975, Nettles, 1983, Beholdings, 1988, The Difficult Wheel, 1995; assoc. editor So. Poetry Rev., 1966-76. Recipient award Great Lakes Coll. Assn., 1975, Roanoke-Chowan award N.C. Literary and Hist. Assn., 1983, Natalie Ornish Poetry prize Tex. Inst. Letters, 1996, James Boatwright Poetry prize Shenandoah Mag., 1994; fellow Nat. Endowment Arts, 1984, N.C. award for Lit., 1996. Mem. Poetry Soc. Am., Associated Writing Programs, N.C. Writers Network. Office: Meredith Coll English Dept 3800 Hillsborough St Raleigh NC 27607

ADCOCK, SCOTTY WILSON, elementary education educator; b. Monroe, N.C., Sept. 9, 1969; s. James Wilson and Barbara Jean (Furr) A.; m. Teresa Dawn Lowdermilk, Apr. 27, 1996. BA, U. N.C. Charlotte, 1992. Cert. tchr., N.C. Tchr. elem. Statesville Rd. Elem. Sch., Charlotte, N.C., 1992-93, Albemarle Rd. Elem. Sch., Charlotte, 1993—. Baptist. Home: 1272 Midlake Ave Kannapolis NC 28083 Office: Albemarle Rd Elem Sch 7800 Riding Trail Rd Charlotte NC 28212

ADDERLEY, CHRISTOPHER MARK, English educator; b. Crewe, Cheshire, Eng., Mar. 29, 1965; came to the U.S., 1989; s. Christopher James and Kathleen Vera (Davies) A.; m. Adrianne Marie Suarez, Jan. 13, 1990; children: Kit, Jack. BA in English and History, N.E. Wales Inst. Higher Edn., Wrexham, Clwyd, U.K., 1987; MA in English, U. Wales, Bangor, Gwynedd, U.K., 1990; PhD in English, U. South Fla., 1996. Cert. tchr. ESL. V.p. N.E. Wales Inst. Students' Union, Wrexham, 1985-86; history tchr. N.E. Wales Inst. Higher Edn., Wrexham, 1989; ESL tchr. English Lang. Inst., U. South Fla., Tampa, 1990-91; mng. editor Lang. Quarterly, U. South Fla., Tampa, 1991-96; English tchr. St. Petersburg (Fla.) Jr. Coll., 1993—. Mng. editor Lang. Quarterly, 1991-96; contbr. articles and revs. to profl. publs., 1991—. Instr. Elderhostel, Eckerd Coll., St. Petersburg, 1993-95. Recipient Tchg. Excellence cert. Eckerd Coll. Elderhostel, 1995. Mem. Internat. Arthurian Soc., New Chaucer Soc. Roman Catholic. Office: Divsn Lang Univ South Fla Tampa FL 33620

ADDIS, GARY WAYNE, freelance writer; b. Athens, Ga., June 5, 1948; s. Jay Hovie and Lydia Ruth (Crumley) A.; m. Sandra Burke, Nov. 2, 1975 (div. Nov. 1988); children: Brandy, Gary W. II, Tacha; m. Rebecca Izell, Dec. 23, 1988. Assoc. in Journalism, Internat. Corr. Schs., Scranton, Pa., 1972; AS in Bus. Adminstrn., Bond Coll., 1977. Owner, operator Pro Gym, El Paso, Tex., 1972-79; owner, mgr. Brandy's Liquors, El Paso, Tex., 1979-84; mgr., acct. Ibero-Am. Imports, Cochabamba, Bolivia, 1984-87; editor Sunbelt gazette Sunbelt Transp., Waco, Ga., 1987-89; contbg. editor, journalist Truckers/USA, Tuscaloosa, Ala., 1988—; mem. organizing com. Teamsters Local 63, Rialto, Calif., 1993. Author: Blood Oath, 1991, Cochabamba Connection, 1993; contbg. editor Truckers News, 1993—. Vol. Dem. Com., Lownder County, Ga., 1992. With U.S. Army, 1968-70. Named Mr. Southeastern Am., AAU, 1985, Mr. Ga., 1985, Masters Mr. S.Am., 1986. Mem. Mystery Writers Am., Authors Guild, Authors League. Democrat. Baptist. Office: Truckers/USA PO Box 3168 Tuscaloosa AL 35403-3168

ADDISON, LINDA LEUCHTER, lawyer; b. Allentown, Pa., Nov. 25, 1951; d. Marcus and Sophie Theresa (Tisch) Leuchter; m. Max M. Addison, Sept. 10, 1977; 1 child, Alexandra Leuchter Addison. BA with honors, U. Tex., 1973, JD, 1976. Bar: Tex. 1976, U.S. Dist. Ct. (so. dist.) Tex. 1977, U.S. Ct. Appeals (5th cir.) 1981. Assoc. Fulbright & Jaworski L.L.P., Houston, 1976-83, ptnr., 1984—; expert on fed. and Tex. evidence; mem. personal injury trial law cert. commn. Tex. Bd. Legal Specialization, 1986-91. Author: Texas Civil Evidence, 1995; mng. editor Tex. Law Rev. 1975-76; contbr. articles to profl. jours. Vice-chmn. Mission Task Force of The Centennial Commn. of U. Tex., Austin, 1981-83; mem. bd. advisors Books for Texans, 1982-84; mem. Pres.'s Assocs., U. Tex., 1982-84; mem. adv. council Tex. Union Found., U. Tex., 1984-86; trustee U. Tex. Law Sch. Found., 1994—. Named one of Outstanding Young Women of Am.; named Outstanding Young Lawyer of Houston, 1984-85; named one of Outstanding Young Houstonians, 1986. Fellow Am. Bar Found., Tex. Bar Found. (life), Houston Bar Found.; mem. State Bar Tex. (mem. bar conv. com. 1980-81, mem. bar jour. com. 1981-82, chmn. bar jour. com. 1988-90, 91—, chmn. adminstrn. rules evidence com. 1988—, mem. evidence inst. planning com. 1983-84), Houston Bar Assn. (mem. continuing legal edn. com. 1979-80, chmn. continuing legal edn. com. 1981-82, mem. jud. evaluations com. 1982-83, Pres.'s award), Tex. Young Lawyers Assn. (bd. dirs. 1981-83), Tex. Law Rev. Ex-Editors Assn., Friar Soc. (steering com. Houston chpt. 1985—), Houston Young Lawyers Assn. (chmn. continuing legal edn. com. 1977-78, bd. dirs. 1978-81, Outstanding Chmn. award), Anti-Defamation League (bd. dirs. S.W. Region 1992—), Am. Arbitration Assn. (panel of neutrals 1992—), Omicron Delta Kappa. Office: Fulbright & Jaworski LLP 1301 Mckinney St Ste 5100 Houston TX 77010

ADDISON, RANDOLPH, biochemistry educator; b. Bentonia, Miss., July 10, 1950; s. Montgomery and Ella D. A. BS, Jackson State U., 1972; PhD, Cornell U., 1977. Asst. prof. U. N.C., Chapel Hill, 1983-84, Rockefeller U., N.Y.C., 1984-88, U. Tenn., Memphis, 1988-95; program office molecular and cell biology NSF, Arlington, Va., 1995—; assoc. prof. cell biology Rockefeller U., N.Y.C., 1995—; panelist Nat. Rsch. Coun., Washington, 1985-88, Howard Hughes Med. Inst., Washington, 1992-93, NSF, 1995—. Contbr. articles to profl. jours. Grantee NSF, 1990-92. Mem. Am. Soc. Biochemistry and Molecular Biology. Office: NSF MCB Rm #655 4201 Wilson Blvd Arlington VA 22230

ADELSON, GLORIA ANN, financial executive; b. Savannah, Ga., Aug. 3, 1944; d. Lee Roy and Edith Thelma (Horovitz) Schraibman; m. Joseph Harvey Adelson, Mar. 19, 1967 (dec.). BA in Polit. Sci., U. Fla., 1965; MA in Bus., Webster U., 1991. Budget analyst U.S. Dept. Labor, Silver Spring, Md., 1967; mgmt. analyst U.S. Naval Supply Ctr., Charleston, S.C., 1967-69, budget analyst, 1969-70, head fin. mgmt. staff, 1970-73, head. ops. and maintenance br., 1973-75; mgmt. coord. officer So. Divsn. Naval Facilities Engrng. Commd., Charleston, 1975-80, dir. budget br., 1980-85, dir. budget and programs divsn., 1985-88, dep. dir. programs and comptroller dept., 1988—. Fin. sec., treas. Synagogue Emanu-El, Charleston, 1982-88; pres. Sisterhood Emanu-El, Charleston, 1993-94, 95-96; active patron com. Am. Cancer Soc., Charleston, 1989, 91, 95; mem. fed. sector com. United Way, Charleston, 1991. Mem. Am. Soc. Mil. Comptrollers (Charleston chpt., chair coms. 1987—, v.p. Navy, 1990-91, pres., 1991-92), Trident Area Cmty. Excellence Comm. Team. Home: 4 Berwick Cir Charleston SC 29407 Office: So Divsn Naval Facilities Engrng Commd 2155 Eagle Dr Charleston SC 29406-4804

ADER, JOSEPH DANIEL, stockbroker; b. Greensboro, N.C., Jan. 4, 1947; s. Edward Arthur and Mary Sue (Rogers) A.; m. Beth Lynn Anderson, Aug. 2, 1969; children: Jadee Lynn, Joseph Daniel Jr. BS, The Citadel, 1969. Asst. v.p. Bankers Trust S.C., Columbia, 1972-80; account exec. E.F. Hutton, Columbia, 1980-87; assoc. v.p. Prudential Securities, Inc., Columbia, 1987—. Treas. Joseph Keels PTA, Columbia, 1986-87; mem. Joseph Keels Found., 1990—, sec., 1991-92; mem. fin. com. Richland Sch. Dist. II Referendum campaign, 1987, 90, 93. 1st lt. U.S. Army, 1969-72. Mem. Columbia Jaycees (bd. dirs. 1975-80), Forest Acres Rotary (treas. 1987-88, pres. 1988-89, dist. conf. chmn. 1991-92, dist. interact com. 1993, 94). Home: 309 Wood Duck Rd Columbia SC 29223-3120 Office: Prudential Securities Inc 1330 Lady St Ste 205 Columbia SC 29201-3300

ADIELE, NKWACHUKWU MOSES, state official; b. Umuahia, Abia, Nigeria, June 22, 1951; came to U.S. 1973; s. Robert O. and Virginia A. Adiele; m. Vickie I. Eseonu, July 7, 1984; children: Elizabeth, Robert, Casey. BS, Ga. Inst. Tech., 1976; MD, Howard U., 1980; MPH, Johns Hopkins U., 1981. Diplomate Nat. Bd. Med. Examiners, Fed. Licensure Examiners Med. B. Internship family practice Howard U. Hosp., Washington, 1981-82, residence family practice, 1982-84; pub. health clinician Balt. City Health Dept., 1980-81; med. ho. officer Howard U. Hosp., Washington, 1981-84; internship in family practice N000, 1981-82, residency in family practice, 1982-84; asst. dir. pub. health Va. State Health Dept., Richmond, 1984-86; dist. health dir. Va. State Health Dept., Boydton, 1986-87; pub. health officer, clinician Va. State Health Dept., Richmond, 1987-90; cons., dir. med. support svcs. Va. State Dept. Med. Asst. Svcs., Richmond, 1990—; cons. Internat. United Black Fund, Washington, 1984-90. Role model youth edn. Richmond Redevel. and Housing Authority, 1984; vol. physician Richmond Area High Blood Pressure Ctr., 1985-90. Lt. col. USAR, 1996—. Named Outstanding Resident Physician, Howard U. Hosp., Washington, 1982. Fellow Am. Acad. Family Physicians (recognition award 1991), Am. Coll. Med. Quality (recognition award 1992); mem. AMA (physician recognition award 1984, 89, 91), Assn. African Physicians in N.Am. (pres. 1982-84, recognition award 1991), Va. Pub. Health Assn. Home: 1305 Cedar Crossing Trl Midlothian VA 23113-3148 Office: Va State Dept Med Asst Svcs 600 E Broad St Ste 1300 Richmond VA 23219-1800

ADKINS, BARBARA L., mediator; b. Sugarland, Tex., Oct. 26, 1946; d. Thomas H. and Patricia M. Adkins. MBA, U. Dallas, 1982. With Pier 1 Imports, 1967-83, dir. European fin., 1973-76, mgr. mdse. stats., 1977, asst. to exec. v.p., 1977-78, merchandising systems analyst, 1979, real estate property mgr., 1980, real estate mgr. eastern U.S., 1981-83; v.p. Bright Banc, Tex., 1984-88; pres. Adkins and Assocs., Tex., 1988—. Mem. Soc. Profls. in Dispute Resolution, Tex. Assn. Fed. Mediators, Irving Women's C. of C., Sigma Iota Epsilon.

ADKINS, FREDRICK EARL, III, financial consultant, educator; b. Florence, Ala., Oct. 12, 1952; s. Frederick Earl and E. Virginia (Beavers) A.; m. Maureen Blackburn, Aug. 10, 1974; children: Sarah C., Laura E. BS in Mgmt., Harding Coll., 1975; MBA, U. Miss., 1976; cert. in Fin. Planning, Coll. for Fin. Planning, Denver, 1986. CLU, ChFC, CFP; admitted to Registry of Fin. Planning Practitioners, 1987. Mgmt. trainee Met. Life, Little Rock, 1976-79; tng. supr. Conn. Mutual Life Ins., Little Rock, 1979-82, gen. agt., 1982-84; pres. Ark. Fin. Group, Inc., Little Rock, 1984—; adjunct prof. fin. U. Ark., Little Rock, 1990—. Pres. Little Rock Founders Lions Club, 1986-87, Ctrl. Ark. Life Underwriters, 1984-85; bd. dirs. Ark. Eye Bank and Lab., Inc., Little Rock, 1986-95, pres., 1989-90, Jones Eye Inst., U. Ark. Med. Scis. Campus, 1993—; Whitbeck Beyer chair Ins. and Fin. Svcs. Adv. Bd., 1994—. Melvin Jones fellow, 1996. Mem. Am. Soc. CLU and ChFC (pres. Ark. chpt. 1989-90), Internat. Assn. Fin. Planning (pres. Ark. chpt. 1991-92), Beta Gamma Sigma, Omicron Delta Epsilon. Mem. Ch. of Christ. Home: 95 White Oak Ln Little Rock AR 72207-2549 Office: Ark Fin Group Inc 225 E Markham St Ste 375 Little Rock AR 72201-1635

ADKINS, ROSANNE BROWN, speech and language pathologist, myofunctional therapist; b. Norfolk, Va., Jan. 10, 1944; d. Melvin Dillard and Mattye Marie (Cox) Brown; BS, U. Ga., 1968, MEd, 1971; m. Steve Bunker, Aug. 24, 1962 (div.); children: Steve, Amy Bunker Patterson; m. Jon Adkins, May 27, 1988. Speech pathologist Barrow County Schs., Winder, Ga., 1968-69, Madison County Schs., Danielsville, Ga., 1969-70, Hall County Schs., Gainesville, Ga., 1971-72, Hope Haven Sch. for Retarded Children, Athens, Ga., 1972-73, Buford (Ga.) City Schs., 1973-75, Duval County Bd. Pub. Instrn., Jacksonville, Fla., 1975-79, Orange County Pub. Schs., Orlando, Fla., 1979—. Sallie Maude Jones scholar, U. Ga., 1966-68; USPHS grad. fellow, 1970-71. Mem. Am. Speech-Lang.-Hearing Assn. (cert. of clin. competence), Fla. Lang. Speech and Hearing Assn. Delta Zeta, Zeta Phi Eta, Kappa Delta Pi, Phi Kappa Phi. Mem. Disciples of Christ. Clubs: Order Amaranth (past Royal Matron). Editor, Speakeasy, Speech and Language Newsletter, 1982—. Home: 2997 Carlsbad Ct Oviedo FL 32765-8438 Office: Orange County Sch System 434 N Tampa Ave Orlando FL 32805-1220

ADKINS, SUSAN IRENE, pediatric orthopedic nurse; b. Miami, Fla., Aug. 28, 1953; d. Robert Count Adkins and Mary Louise Craig. Student, Tex. Women's U., 1976. Cert. Am. Oper. Rm. Staff nurse St. Luke's Hosp., Houston, 1976-80; ICU/PACU dialysis nurse Med. Plz. Hosp., Ft. Worth, 1980-81; OR nurse spl. project St. Luke's Hosp., Houston, 1982-89; customer support rep. Enterprise Sys., Inc., Bannockburn, Ill., 1989-90; mgr. surgical support scheduling St. Lukes Hosp., Houston, 1990-91; nurse Fondren Orthopedic Group, Houston, 1991—. Mem. Am. Oper. Rm. Nurses. Republican. Roman Catholic. Home: 3310 Sansford Cir Katy TX 77449-6639

ADKISON, LINDA RUSSELL, geneticist, consultant; b. Columbia, S.C., Apr. 28, 1951; d. George Palmer Russell, Jr. and Annie Frances (Ingram) White; m. Daniel Lee Adkison, Jan. 28, 1978; children: Emily Kathleen, Seth Adams Russell. BS, Ga. So. U., 1973, MS, 1977; PhD, Tex. A&M U., 1986. Lab. tech. VA Hosp., Gainesville, 1973-75, Shands Teaching Hosp., Gainesville, Fla., 1973-75; grad. teaching asst. Ga. So. U., Statesboro, 1975-77; rsch. assoc. U. South Ala. Med. Sch., Mobile, 1978-80; instr. St. Mary's Dominican Coll., New Orleans, 1980-81; grad. rsch. asst. Tulane Med. Sch., New Orleans, 1980-82, Tex. A&M U., College Station, 1982-86; postdoctoral fellow Jackson Lab., Bar Harbor, Maine, 1986-89; asst. prof. genetics Mercer U. Sch. Medicine, Macon, Ga., 1989-94, assoc. prof. genetics, 1994, assoc. prof. ob-gyn., 1995—, asst. prof. ob-gyn., 1991-95, assoc. prof. ob-gyn., 1995—. contbr. more than 40 articles to profl. jours. Vol. Girl Scouts Mid. Ga., Macon, 1990—, Abnaki Girl Scout Coun., Bar Harbor, 1986-89, Ctrl. Ga. Boy Scouts, Macon, 1993—. Mem. AAAS, Am. Soc. Human Genetics, Grad. Women in Sci., Internat. Mammalian Genome Soc., S.E. Regional Genetics Group, Genetics Soc. Ga. (bd. dirs. 1990—), Ga. Acad. Sci., Am. Men and Women in Sci., Sigma Xi. Home: 1699 Wesleyan Bowman Rd Macon GA 31210-1037 Office: Mercer Univ Sch Medicine 1550 College St Macon GA 31201-1554

ADKISON, RONNIE DARRELL, metal company executive, sales executive; b. Russellville, Ark., Aug. 19, 1958; s. Reece Thomas and Ouida (Hipps) A.; m. Terri Lynne Stubbs, Aug. 15, 1981; children: Ashton Lauren, Jordan Reece. BSBA, Ark. Tech. U., 1980. Mgr. trainee Peoples Bank & Trust, Russellville, 1980-81; salesman, bus. mgr. Hopkins Oldsmobile-Toyota, Inc., Russellville, 1981-84; sales mgr. Wicks Lumber Co., Russellville, 1984-85; salesman, product mgr., sales mgr. Afco Metals, Inc., Little Rock, 1985—. Mem. Little Rock Metro Rotary, Kappa Alpha (Epsilon Zeta chpt.). Home: 251 Willow Ln Brandon MS 39042-8084 Office: Afco Metals Inc PO Box 720070 1065 Mendell Davis Dr Jackson MS 39272

ADKISSON, PERRY LEE, university system chancellor; b. Hickman, Ark., Mar. 11, 1929; s. Robert Louis and Imogene (Perry) A.; m. Frances Rozelle, Dec. 29, 1956; 1 dau., Jean Amanda. B.S., U. Ark., 1950, M.S., 1954; Ph.D. in Entomology, Kans. State U., 1956. Asst. prof. entomology U. Mo., 1956-58; assoc. prof. Tex. A&M U., 1958-63, prof., 1963-67, Disting. prof. entomology, 1967—, head dept. entomology, 1967-78, v.p. for agr. and renewable resources, 1978-80, dep. chancellor for agr., 1980-83, dep. chancellor, 1983-86, chancellor, 1986-91, regent's prof., 1991—; cons. Internat. AEC, Vienna, 1969-74; chmn. sci. adv. panel Gov. Tex. on Agrl. Chems., 1970-72; chmn. Tex. Pesticide Adv. Com., 1972; mem. panel experts on integrated pest control UN/FAO, Rome, 1971-78, chmn., 1992—; mem. Structural Pest Control Bd., Tex., 1972-78, NRC World Food and Nutrition Study Team, 1977; chmn. com. biology pest species NRC, 1974; mem. environ. studies bd., study group problems pest control NAS-NRC, 1973-75; mem. U.S. directorate UNESCO Man and the Biosphere Program, 1975-77; mem. bd. on agr. NRC, 1985-87, mem. Nat. Sci. Bd., 1985—; mem. governing bd. Internat. Crops Rsch. Inst. for Semi-Arid Tropics, 1982-88; mem. rsch. adv. com. Agr. for Internat. Devel., 1986; mem. com. on life scis. NRC, 1985-85; mem. Tex. Sci. and Tech. Coun., 1986-88; mem. Standing Com. for Internat. Plant Protection Congresses, 1984—, adv. dir. Export-Import Bank U.S., 1987. Mem. editorial com. Ann. Rev. Entomology, 1973-78; contbr. articles to profl. jours. Exec. dir. G.H.W. Bush Presdl. Libr. Ctr. and Bush Libr. Found., 1991-93. With M.C., U.S. Army, 1951-53. Recipient Faculty Disting. Achievement award for rsch. Tex. A&M U., 1965, Alexander Von Humboldt award, 1980; Disting. Svc. award Am. Registry Prof. Entomology, 1979, Disting. Scientist of Yr. award Tex. Acad. Scis., 1982, Disting. Alumnus Svc. award Kans. State U., 1980, Disting. Svc. award Am. Inst. Biol. Sci., 1987, Nat. 4-H Alumni award, 1988, Outstanding Alumnus award Coll. of Agr. and Home Econs., U. Ark., 1990, Disting. Alumni award U. Ark., 1990, Disting. Svc. award Am. Agricultural Editors Assn., 1992, Wolfe Prize in Agriculture, 1994-95; USPHS postdoctoral fellow Harvard U., 1963-64. Fellow AAAS, Entomol. Soc. Am. (governing bd. 1971-75, pres. 1974, Bussart Meml. award 1967, Founders Meml. lectr. 1985); mem. Am. Acad. Arts and Scis., Kans. Entomol. Soc., Internat. Orgn. Biol. Control, Am. Registry Profl. Entomologists (governing council 1976-78, pres. 1977), Nat. Acad. Scis., Phi Kappa Phi, Sigma Xi. Office: Tex A&M U Dept Entomology College Station TX 77843-2475

ADKISSON, RANDALL LYNN, minister; b. Atlanta, May 28, 1957; s. John Earl and Mearl (Cox) A.; m. Salee Robin Smith, Nov. 7, 1981; children: Katheryn Lynsey, Keith Alan. BA in Journalism, U. Ga., 1979; MDiv, Southwestern Bapt. Theol. Sem., Ft. Worth, 1985; PhD, New Orleans Bapt. Theol. Sem., 1990. Licensed to ministry So. Bapt. Conv., 1974; ordained, 1979. Min. of youth Bethel Bapt. Ch., Good Hope, Ga., 1976-79; assoc. pastor Orange Hill Bapt. Ch., Austell, Ga., 1979-82; pastor Shifalo Bapt. Ch., Kiln, Miss., 1985-88, Foxworth (Miss.) 1st Bapt. Ch., 1988-91, 1st Bapt. Ch., Monroeville, Ala., 1991—; teaching fellow New Orleans Bapt. Theol. Sem., 1985-86. Bd. govs. Judson Coll., 1994—. Mem. Marion Bapt. Assn. (pastoral ministries dir. 1990-91, pres. min.'s conf. 1990-91), Nat. Assn. Bapt. Profs. Religion, Soc. Bibl. Lit., Alumni Assn. New Orleans Bapt. Theol. Seminary (v.p. to pres.-elect Ala. chpt., 1993, pres. 1994), Am. Assn. Christian Counselors. Office: 1st Bapt Ch 420 Pineville Rd Monroeville AL 36460-1334

ADLER, BRIAN UNGAR, English language educator, program director; b. El Paso, Tex., May 28, 1957; s. Bernard Abraham and Helene Selma (Ungar) A.; m. Felicia Mitchell, Oct. 13, 1978 (div. Oct. 22, 1981); m. Annette Louise Vaigneur, Sept. 6, 1988; children: Sarah, Noah. BA, U. S.C., 1978; MA, U. Ga., Athens, 1984; PhD, U. Tenn., Knoxville, 1988. Tchr. Allendale (S.C.) Mid. Sch., 1979-80; rsch. asst. U. Tenn., Knoxville, 1982-86, vis. asst. prof., 1986-89; asst. prof. English Marian Coll., Indpls., 1989-92, assoc. prof. English, head dept. English, 1992-94; assoc. prof. English, dir. honors program Valdosta (Ga.) State U., 1994—; evaluator Ford Found., Knoxville, 1985-88; cons. Ednl. Testing Svc., Princeton, N.J., 1989-93. Reviewer (evaluations) CHOICE, 1989—; contbr. poems to New Arts Rev., The Sun, 1982—. Leader Elderhostel/Geneva Bay Ctr., Lake Geneva, Wis., 1990—. Ind. Humanities Coun. grantee, 1990, Lilly Endowment Devel. grantee, 1992. Mem. MLA (sec. N.E. chpt. 1990—, chair psychology sect. N.E. chpt. 1995), Bernard Malamud Soc., Nat. Collegiate Honors Coun. Jewish. Office: Honors Program Valdosta State U Valdosta GA 31698

ADLER, MICHAEL M., real estate developer, construction executive; s. Samuel I. and Bernyce Adler; m. Judith C. Selling; children: Matthew Lawrence, David Scott, Rachel Ann. BBA, U. Miami, 1973. Lic. gen. contractor. Pres., chief exec. officer Adler Group, Inc., Miami, 1973—; pres. Adler Group Israel Inc.; major developments include Miami Internat. Commerce Ctr., Boca Commerce Ctr., Vista Ctr.; ptnr. Skyway Assocs., So. Warehouse Assocs., Ives Dairy Assocs., Gables I Tower; v.p. So. Gen. Builders, Inc., Standard Concrete Corp., Standard Rock Pit Corp. Mem. Beacon Coun., Brickell Area Assn., Nat. Realty Com., United Way Dade County, U. Miami Founder, Citizens Bd., Hurricane Club; bd. govs. South Dade Jewish Community Ctr.; bd. dirs. Greater Miami Jewish Fedn.; chmn. bd. Jewish Fedn. Housing Inc., bd. dirs. Jewish Fedn. Cable TV, Inc.; v.p. Am. Israel Pub. Affairs Com. Named Outstanding Young Leaders United Jewish Appeal, 1986; recipient Stanley C. Myers Young Leadership award, Anti Defamation League Young Leadership award, David Ben-Gurion Centennial medal, 1987. Democrat. Office: Adler Group Inc 8181 NW 14th St Miami FL 33126-1603*

ADREON, BEATRICE MARIE RICE, pharmacist; b. Huntington, W.Va., July 23, 1929; d. Lloyd Emerson and Beatrice (Odell) Rice; student Mary Washington Coll., 1947-49; B.S. in Pharmacy, Med. Coll. Va., 1952; M.A. in Spl. Studies and Women's Studies, George Washington U., 1976; m. Harry Barnes Adreon, Jr., Dec. 27, 1952. Summer vol. worker pharmacies De Paul Hosp., Norfolk, Va., 1949, U.S. Marine Hosp., Norfolk, 1950; pharmacist Washington Clinic, 1954-71; counselor George Washington U., 1976-77, cons. gerontology health scis. dept., 1977—; cons. medicine control traffic patterns nursing homes Cross & Adreon, Washington, 1962-87; founder, pres. Pharmacy Counseling Services, Inc., 1978—. Instr. advanced first aid ARC, 1952—, civil def. instr., 1952—; vol. Spanish Edn. Devel. Center, Washington, 1972; mem. Arlington (Va.) Community Services Bd., 1980-83; chmn. com. substance abuse. Recipient Arnold and Marie Schwartz award in pharmacy, 1980. Mem. Acad. Pharmacy Practice and Mgmt., Am. Pharm. Assn., Va. Pharm. Assn., Potomac Pharmacists Assn., Am. Inst. History of Pharmacy, Nat. Council Patient Info. and Edn. (task force pub. info.), Panhellenic Assn., Kappa Epsilon. Episcopalian (mem. bishop's com. neighborhood services 1967-69, chmn. services for aged div. 1967-69). Contbr. articles in field to profl. jours. Home: 4524 19th Rd N Arlington VA 22207-2352 Office: Pharmacy Counseling Svcs Inc 950 N Glebe Rd # 140 Arlington VA 22203-1824

ADY, LAURENCE IRVIN, academic administrator; b. Washington, Mar. 15, 1932; s. Laurence E. and Georgiana C. (Covington) A.; m. Jan. 10. 1959; children: Marc S., Lori L. BA, U. Md., 1956; MA in Tchg., Rollins Coll., 1964, Ednl. Specialist, 1974. Cert. ednl. adminstrn. & supervision, elem. edn., early childhood edn., drivers edn., history, adult edn.; lic. police officer. Police officer Orlando Police Dept., 1958-59, Ocoee (Fla.) Police Dept., 1959-64; constable Dist. #3, Orange County, Fla., 1964-66; tchr. H.S. Sch. Bd. Orange Ct., Fla., 1967-68; from supervisor adult basic edn. to sch. adminstr. Sch. Bd. Orange Ct., 1968—; dep. sheriff Orange County, 1971-80; elem. sch. tchr. Sch. Bd. Orange Ct., 1959-67; pres. Commn. on Adult Basic Edn., 1984-85, treas. 1979—. Commr. City of Belle Isle, Fla., 1977—; treas. Dem. exec. com., Orange County, 1982—. Named to Fla. Adult Edn. Hall of Fame Fla. Adult Edn. Assn., Cocoa Beach, 1985. Mem. Am. Assn. for Adult/Continuing Edn. (treas. 1987-91), Tiger Bay Orlando, Kiwanis (treas., dir. 1972—). Methodist. Home: 2495 Trentwood Blvd Orlando FL 32812-4833 Office: COABE PO Box 592053 Orlando FL 32859-2053

AERTS, CINDY SUE, nurse; b. Green Bay, Wis., Oct. 18, 1946; d. John and Winon (Kazilek) A. RN, St. Mary's Sch. Nursing, 1967; BSN, U. Wis., 1985; MSN in Critical Care Nursing, Med. Coll. Wis., 1987. CCRN; cert. ACLS instr.; CEN. Dir. coronary care unit St. Vincent Hosp., Green Bay, Wis., 1970-85; dir. critical care nursing Mary Washington Hosp., Fredericksburg, Va., 1986, L.W. Blake Hosp., Brodenton, Fla., 1988; RN Sarasota Mem. Hosp. Health Care Pers., Sarasota, Fla., Manatee Meml. ECC. Recipient Linda Daniels Award 1985, Vol. of Year Am. Health Assn., Green Bay 1978. Mem. AACN (Northeastern Wis. chpt. pres. 1976, 77, manasota chpt. pres. 1991, 92), ENA. Home: 4513 Park Lake Ter S Bradenton FL 34209-6221

AFFLICK, CLIVE HENRY, minister, guidance counselor; b. Kingston, Jamaica, Oct. 26, 1933; came to U.S., 1977; s. Jabez Gilbert and Hattie Laura (Kennedy) A.; m. Deta Pauline Burrowes, June 11, 1960; 1 child, Clive Henry Jr. BS, Phila. Coll. Bible, 1959; MA, Temple U., 1965; DA, U. Miami, 1989; DDiv, Internat. Sem., 1982. Adminstrv. asst. Chase Manhattan Bank, N.Y.C., 1969-71; prin. Dunrobin High Sch., Kingston, Jamaica, 1971-79; head dept. history, guidance coord. Univ. Christian Sch., Jacksonville, Fla., 1979-82, dir. guidance, acad. advisor, counselor, 1990—; pres. Jamaica Theol. Sem., Kingston, 1983-90; pres. Caribbean Evangel. Theol. Assn., Kingston, 1988-90. min., teacher Bapt. Ch., Jacksonville, 1990—. Mem. Am. Assn. Christian Counselors, Orgn. Am. Historians, Fla. Christian Counselors Assn. Baptist. Office: Univ Christian Sch 5520 University Blvd W Jacksonville FL 32216-5557

AFTUCK, RODNEY D., food products executive; b. Corning, N.Y., Aug. 27, 1955; s. Benjamin Albert and Mary Ellenor (Chesonis) A.; 1 child, Philip Maxwell. BS in Acctg., St. John Fisher Coll., 1977; postgrad., Rochester Inst. Tech., 1977-78. Registered investment advisor. Sr. ter. mgr. Internat. Paper Co., Buffalo, 1977-81; pres. MBA, Inc., Buffalo, 1982-84; fin. cons. Shearson Lehman/Am. Express, Buffalo, 1984-86; v.p. Oppenheimer & Co., Atlanta, 1986-87; sr. account exec. Dean Witter Reynolds, Atlanta, 1987-92; sales mgr. 4M Mfg. Group of Ga., Inc., Atlanta, 1992-94; founder Ace Packaging, Atlanta, 1994—; S.E. regional mgr., nat. accts. mgr. Wilton Connor Packinging - Pop Specialists, Charlotte, N.C., 1995—; v.p. Am. Wealth Mgmt., Inc.; instr. Options Inst., Chgo. Bd. Exch., 1985—; founder The Merritt Group, Atlanta. Active High Mus., Atlanta, Atlanta Botanical Gardens Soc., Atlanta Area Boy Scout Coun., Rep. Found. of Ga.; sec. fin. com.; mem. Rep. Com. Mem. Am. Assn. Ind. Corrugated Converters, Am. Stock Exch. Club, Atlanta C. of C., Ducks Unltd., Atlanta Saltwater Sportsman Club, Nat. Account Sr. Mgrs. Home: PO Box 420216 Atlanta GA 30342-0216 Office: Ste 520 485 Valley Ln NE Atlanta GA 30328

AGALIOTIS, DIMITRIOS PHILIPPOS, hematologist, oncologist; b. Athens, Greece, Dec. 28, 1957; came to U.S., 1989; s. Philippos Marinos and Aikaterini (Sotiropoulos) A. MD, U. Athens, 1981. Lic. physician Belgium, Ala., Fla.; bd. cert. in internal medicine Kingdom of Belgium, Am. Bd. Internal Medicine. Intern Nat. and Capodistrian U. of Athens, 1982-85; resident in internal medicine Cath. U. Louvain, Brussels, Belgium, 1985-86; resident internal medicine Cath. U. Louvain, Haine-St. Paul, Belgium, 1986-87; clin. fellow med. oncology/hematology U. Fla., Gainesville, 1989-92; clin. fellow divsn. bone marrow transplantation Coll. of Medicine, U. South Fla., Tampa, 1992-93, clin. instr. divsn. bone marrow transplantation, 1993-94; faculty dept. internal medicine U. South Ala., 1995—. Contbr. articles to profl. jours. Pres. parish coun. Greek Orthodox Ch., Gainesville, 1991. Med. officer Greek Navy, 1988-89. Nat. Grants scholar, 1975-81, Greek Nat. Found. of Grants scholar, 1982, St. Luc U. Hosp., Brussels fellow, 1985, Internat. Sci. and Technol. Coop. of Greek Ministry of Rsch. and Tech. fellow, 1986, Commn. of European Communities grantee, 1987, Coll. de Medecine des Hopitaux de Paris grantee, 1989. Mem. AMA, ACP, Am. Soc. Hematology, Med. Assn. Brussels, Med. Assn. Athens. Home: 251 Montclair Loop Daphne AL 36526 Office: Univ of South Ala USA Campus USA Cancer Ctr Rm 414 Mobile AL 36688-0002

AGEE, BOB R., university president, educator, minister; b. Brownsville, Tenn., Sept. 30, 1938; s. Edwin L. and Katie L. (Stewart) A.; m. Nelle Rose; children—Nancy Denise, Robyn Janelle. B.A., Union U., Tenn., 1960; M.Div., So. Bapt. Theol. Sem., 1964, D.Min., 1974; Ph.D., Vanderbilt U., 1986. Ordained to ministry Baptist Ch. Pastor Shively Heights Bapt. Ch., Louisville, 1964-70; pastor Ardmore Bapt. Ch., Memphis, 1970-75; dean, v.p. religious affairs Union U., Jackson, Tenn., 1975-82; pres. Okla. Bapt. U., Shawnee, 1982—; mem. edn. commn. So. Bapt. Conv., 1985-93, chmn., 1987-90; bd. dirs. Co-op Svcs. Internat. Edn. Consortium, chmn., 1988-90; cons. evaluator North Ctrl. Assn. Colls. and Univs., 1987—; bd. dirs. Nat. Assn. Ind. Colls. and Univs., 1986-90, 93—. Author Bibl. study materials and articles. Mem. human relations com. Memphis Bd. Edn., 1972-74; mem. Memphis Mayor's Crime Commn., 1973-75; mem. Okla. Ind. Coll. Found., 1982—, chmn., 1985-87. Mem. Soc. Coll. and Univ. Planning, Shawnee C. of C. (bd. dirs. 1983—), So. Bapt. Theol. Sem. Alumni Assn. (nat. pres. 1985-86), AAUP, Am. Assn. Univ. Adminstrs., Nat. Assn. Ind. Colls. and Univs. (bd. dirs. 1988—). Republican. Office: Okla Bapt U 500 W University St Shawnee OK 74801-2558

AGEE, NELLE HULME, art history educator; b. Memphis, May 22, 1940; d. John Eulice and Nelle (Ray) Hulme; m. Bob R. Agee, June 7, 1958; children: Denise, Robyn. Student Memphis State U., 1971-72; BA, Union U., Jackson, Tenn., 1978; postgrad. Seminole Okla. Coll., 1982, Okla. Bapt. U., 1984; MEd Cen. State U., Edmond, Okla., 1989. Cert. tchr. art, history, Ky., Tenn., Okla. Offices services supr. So. Bapt. Theol. Sem., Louisville, 1961-64; kindergarten tchr. Shively Heights Bapt. Ch., Louisville, 1965-70; editorial asst. Little Publs., agrl. mags., Memphis, 1973-75; tchr. art Humboldt High Sch., Tenn., 1978-82; vis. artist-in-schs. Tenn. Arts Commn., Nashville, 1978, 81, 82; adj. prof. art history Seminole Coll., Okla., 1985-86, 87, 89; instr. art Okla. Baptist U., 1989, asst. prof. art and edn., 1989—; frequent speaker art orgns., ch. groups; tchr. art workshops Humboldt City Sch. system; tchr. Cultural Arts Day Camp, Jackson, Tenn., 1982; nat. pres. ministers' wives conf. So. Bapt. Conv., 1987-88; vol. Mabee-Gerrer Mus., Shawnee. Exhibited art in various shows. Bd. dirs. Robert Dotson Found., Mabee-Gerrer Mus., Family Resource Ctr. 1993—; active Salvation Army Aux., Shawnee; v.p. Union U. Woman's Club, 1976-77, pres., 1978. Recipient Disting. Classroom Tchr. award Tenn. Edn. Assn., 1982. Mem. Univ. Alliance, Okla Bapt. U., Goals 2000, Delta Kappa Gamma, Alpha Delta Kappa. Democrat. Baptist. Avocations: stained glass, pottery making, travel. Home: 616 University Pky Shawnee OK 74801-1711

AGEE, WARREN KENDALL, journalism educator; b. Sherman, Tex., Oct. 23, 1916; s. Frederic M. and Minnie E. (Logsdon) A.; m. Edda Robbins, June 1, 1941; children: Kim Kendall Schmidman, Robyn Kendall Ansley. BA cum laude, Tex. Christian U., 1937; MA, U. Minn., 1949, PhD, 1955. Mem. editorial staff Ft. Worth Star-Telegram, 1937-48; instr. journalism Tex. Christian U., 1948-50, asst. prof., 1950-55, asso. prof., 1955-57, prof., 1957-58, chmn. dept., 1950-58, faculty adviser student publs., 1949-58; prof. journalism, dean sch. journalism W.Va U., 1958-60; mem. ednl. adv. com. WJPB-TV, Fairmont and Weston, W.Va., 1959-60; nat. exec. officer Soc. Profl. Journalists, Sigma Delta Chi, 1960-62; prof. journalism, dean Evening Coll., Tex. Christian U., Ft. Worth, 1962-65; dean William Allen White Sch. Journalism, U. Kans., Lawrence, 1965-69; dean Henry W. Grady Coll. Journalism and Mass Communication U. Ga., 1969-75, prof. journalism, 1975-87, dean and prof. emeritus, 1987—; vis. scholar U. Tex., fall 1975; copy editor Atlanta Constn., summer 1977; combat corr. USCG Res., 1941-44; pub. info. specialist USCG Res. Hdqrs., 1944-45; mem. adv. screening com. journalism, com. internat. exchange of persons Conf. Bd. Assn. Rsch. Couns., Washington, 1958-62; mem. Am. Coun. Edn. for Journalism and Mass Communication, 1958-60, 65-67, mem. accrediting com., 1969-76, vice chmn., 1973-74, chmn., 1974-76, chmn. appeals bd., 1977, 79, 81, 83; mng. dir. William Allen White Found., 1965-69, trustee, 1970—; mng. dir. George Foster Peabody Radio and TV awards, 1969-75, Sigma Delta Chi Nat. Journalism Awards, 1960-62; assoc. James M. Cox Jr. Ctr. Internat. Mass Comm. Tng. and Research, U. Ga., 1985—. Author: (with Edwin Emery and Phillip H. Ault) Introduction to Mass Communications, 1960, 11th rev. edit., 1994, Reporting and Writing the News, 1983, (with Dennis L. Wilcox, Ault) Public Relations Strategies and Tactics, 1986, rev. edit., 1989, 3d edit., 1992, 4th edit., 1995, (with Nelson Traquina) O Quarto Poder Frustrado: Os Meios de Comunicação Social No Portugal Pós-Revolucionário, 1988; also articles.; editor: The Press and the Public Interest,

1968, Mass Media In A Free Society, 1969, (with Emery and Ault) Perspectives on Mass Communications, 1982, Maincurrents in Mass Communications, 1986, rev. edit., 1989; assoc. editor, bus. mgr.: The Quill, 1960-62; press rev. columnist, contbg. editor, 1977-82; adv. editorial bd.: Journalism Quar, 1955-60. Mem. Athens (Ga.) Internat. Rels. Cmty. Coun., pres., 1980-82; pres. Friends of Mus. Art U. Ga., 1974-75; mem. Howard Blakeslee Media Awards judging com. Am. Heart Assn., 1976-94, chmn. judging com., 1980-94. Recipient Journalism award Fort Worth Press, 1936; Outstanding News Writing award Ft. Worth Profl. chpt. Sigma Delta Chi, 1946; Carl Towley award Journalism Edn. Assn., 1969; Outstanding Achievement award U. Minn., 1973; Wells Meml. key Sigma Delta Chi, 1978, Disting. Teaching award Soc. Profl. Journalists, 1987; Fulbright grantee to Portugal, 1982, 85. Mem. Assn. Edn. in Journalism and Mass Communication (pres. 1958), Am. Soc. Journalism Sch. Adminstrs. (pres. 1956), Am. Studies Assn., Southwestern Journalism Congress (sec. 1957-58), Soc. Profl. Journalists, Sigma Delta Chi (pres. Fort Worth profl. chpt. 1954-55, sec. Tex. 1957-58, nat. v.p. campus chpt. affairs 1966-69, leader council 1982—, v.p. N.E. Ga. profl. chpt. 1978-79, pres. 1979-80), Kappa Tau Alpha (50 yr. journalism edn. service award 1987), Alpha Chi, Phi Kappa Sigma, Alpha Sigma Lambda, Phi Beta Delta. Presbyterian. Club: Gridiron (Ft. Worth). Lodge: Rotary. Home: 130 Highland Dr Athens GA 30606-3212 Office: U Ga Henry W Grady Coll Journalism and Mass Communication Athens GA 30602

AGERS, BOBBY LEE, middle school educator, coach; b. Glasgow, Ky., Jan. 21, 1955; s. Cecil William and Ruth Barbara (Sherfey) A.; m. Linda Louise Gund, Mar. 22, 1991. AS, Kilgore (Tex.) Jr. Coll., 1979; BS, East Tex. State U., 1980, MS, 1984. Cert. history, health, phys. edn., and drivers edn., Tex. Tchr., coach Mt. Vernon (Tex.) Ind. Sch. Dist., 1980, North Hopkins Ind. Sch. Dist., Sulphur Springs, Tex., 1980-83, Armstrong Mid. Sch., Plano, Tex., 1983—. Sgt. U.S. Army, 1973-77. Named Tchr. of Yr., Armstrong Mid. Sch., 1988; recipient cert. Armstrong Parents-Tchrs.-Students Assn., 1988. Democrat. Baptist. Home: 1129 Canoe Ln Plano TX 75023-2000 Office: Armstrong Mid Sch 3805 Timberline Dr Plano TX 75074-4001

AGRAZ, FRANCISCO JAVIER, lawyer, public affairs representative; b. Laredo, Tex., Aug. 21, 1947; s. Jose Jesus and Irene (Garcia-Gomez) A.; m. Rosalinda Varela, Aug. 23, 1969 (div. Feb. 1980); children: Francisco Javier Jr., Raquel Jeanne; m. Ruth Urquidi, Jan. 1, 1984. BA in Journalism, U. Tex. at El Paso, 1970; JD, U. Houston, 1987. Bar: Tex. 1988, U.S. Dist. Ct. (so. dist.) Tex. 1988. Anchor reporter KENS-TV, San Antonio, 1970; corr. ABC Capital Cities Comms., Chgo., Houston, N.Y., 1970-77; pub. affairs analyst Exxon Corp., Houston and Memphis, 1977-83; assoc. Wood, Burney, Cohn & Bradley, Corpus Christi, Tex., 1987-89, Redford, Wray & Woolsey, P.C., Corpus Christi, 1989-91; pres., atty. at law Francisco J. Agraz P.C., Houston, 1991—. Bd. govs. United Way of Coastal Bend, Corpus Christi, Tex., 1987-91. Mem. State Bar of Tex. (grievance com., pub. rels. com.), Houston Hispanic Bar Assn., Tex. Assn. Def. Counsel, Houston Rotary Club. Roman Catholic. Office: Francisco J Agraz PC 2472 Bolsover Ste 442 Houston TX 77005

AGRESTI, ALAN, statistics educator; b. Syracuse, N.Y., Feb. 6, 1947; m. Jacalyn Levine. BA, U. Rochester, 1968; PhD, U. Wis., 1972. Prof. U. Fla., Gainesville, 1972—. Author: Categorical Data Analysis, 1990, Statistical Methods for the Social Sciences, Analysis of Ordinal Categorical Data, 1984, Introduction to Categorical Data Analysis, 1996. Fellow Am. Statis. Assn.; mem. Royal Statis. Soc., Internat. Statis. Inst., Biometric Soc., Inst. Math. Stats. Office: U Fla Griffin-Floyd Hall Gainesville FL 32611

AGUINALDO, JORGE TANSINGCO, chemical engineer, water treatment consultant; b. Paniqui, Tarlac, The Philippines, Feb. 22, 1952; s. Andres Pagaduan and Lydia Obcena (Tansingco) A.; m. Juliet Sibal, May 10, 1978; children: Janice, Jeremy. BSChemE, Adamson U., Manila, 1973; postgrad., De La Salle U., Manila, 1977-82, Calif. State U., Sacramento, 1990-91. Registered chem. engr., Philippines. Supr. Paniqui (Tarlac) Sugar Corp, 1973-77; product mgr. water treatment and pollution control Alpha Machinery & Engring. Corp., Manila, 1977-83; sr. project engr. Metito Saudi Arabia Ltd., Riyadh, 1983-85, Metito Engring., Ltd., Nicosia, Cyprus, 1985-86; sr. project engr. Metito Arabia Industries Ltd., Riyadh, 1986-89, project mgr., 1989-90; proposals mgr. Am. Engring. Svcs., Inc., Tampa, Fla., 1991—; bd. dirs. Bios Trading & Mgmt. Svcs. Corp., Manila; cons. J.M. Templa & Assocs., Manila, 1980—. Mem. Am. Inst. Chem. Engrs., Am. Chem. Soc., Instrument Soc. Am. (sr.), Am. Water Works Assn., Water Environ. Fedn., Philippine Inst. Chem. Engrs., Indsl. Computing Soc., Knights of Columbus, Tampa Bay Cross Fit Club. Roman Catholic. Office: 5912 Breckenridge Pky Ste F Tampa FL 33610-4200

AGUIRRE, MIRTHA GUERRA, accountant; b. Habana, Cuba, Mar. 11, 1946; came to U.S., 1961; d. José Guerra and Mirtha Regalado; m. Horacio Stuart Aguirre, Oct. 29, 1988; children: Alessandra, Horacio Stuart Jr. BBA in Acctg., U. Miami, 1972; MS in Taxation, Fla. Internat. U., 1982. CPA. Sr. tax. mgr. Ernst & Young CPA, Miami, 1972-82; mgr. in charge tax dept. Grant Thorton CPA, Miami, 1982-84; with Grau & Co. CPA, Miami, 1984-85; pvt. practice acct. Miami, 1985—; adj. prof. taxes Fla. Internat. U., 1982; mem. Hispanic coun. South Fla. Water Mgmt. Dist.; mem. worker's compensation adv. coun. Office Gov. Treas. YMCA Jose Marti, Coalition for Integration of Disabled; mem. finance com. YMCA Metro; bd. dirs., mem. steering com. Marian Ctr. for Devel. Handicapped; sec. Kensington Park Elem. Mem. AICPA, Am. Soc. Women Accts. (past pres.), Nat. Orgn. Bus. Owners (bd. dirs.), Cuban-Am. CPAs, Fla. Inst. CPAs (Dade County chpt.), Internat. Tax Group, Greater Miami Tax Inst. (past pres.), Estate Planning Coun., Latin Bus. and Profl. Women's Club. (past pres.), Coconut Grove Sailing Club (past treas.). Office: 1000 Brickell Ave Ste 620 Miami FL 33131-3047

AGUIRRE, SAMUEL HONORATO, electrical engineer; b. Manila, Philippines, Mar. 4, 1938; came to U.S., 1961; s. Abundio and Petra (Mendoza) A.; m. Erlina S. Manuel, Apr. 10, 1965; children: Evelyn, Emerald, Emmeline. BSEE, Mapua Inst. Tech., Manila, 1960. Design engr. Allis-Chalmers Corp., Gadsden, Ala., 1965-75, TOCCO-Ala., Inc., Boaz, 1975-77, GE Co., Hickory, N.C., 1977-80; sr. devel. engr. Siemens Energy & Automation, Bradento, Fla., 1980-87; sr. engr. Cooper Industries, Nacogdoches, Tex., 1987-88, Magnetek, Bradento, 1988-90, S.W. Electric Co., Oklahoma City, 1990-96; transformer cons. Oklahoma City, 1996—; mem.-at-large Dist. Com. on Superintendency; chmn. Adminstrv. Coun. V.p. Philippine-Am. Civic Orgn., Oklahoma City, 1993; mem. Okla. Conf. on Christian Unity and Inter-religious Concern, Oklahoma City, 1992-96; bd. dirs. Evangelism, Oklahoma City, 1996—. Mem. IEEE (mem. performance characteristics sub-com. Transformers Stds. Com.), Asia Soc. Okla. (bd. dirs.). Republican. Methodist. Home: 2516 SW 124th St Oklahoma City OK 73170-4835

AHL, JANYCE BARNWELL, historian, writer, speaker, retired educator; b. St. Augustine, Fla., Oct. 13, 1911; d. Carlos Drew and Martha Rebecca (Adams) A. BS in English and Biology, Fla. Southern Coll., Lakeland, Fla., 1939. Tchr., sci. Lake Wales Jr. High, Fla. Author: Early History of Lake Wales Woman's Club, 1989, Crown Jewel of the Highlands: Lake Wales, Florida, 1983 (donated proceeds from book to Lake Wales Libr. Assn.), Early History of the Lake Wales Cemetery, 1984; co-author Late History of the First Presbyterian Church of Lake Wales Florida, 1989. Mem. Prayer and Care Group, Sunday Afternoon Circle (life mem.), Lakes Wales Hist. Soc. (life mem.), Lake Wales Mus. and Culture Ctr. (charter mem.), Polk County Hist. Soc., Friends of Bok Tower, Polk County Hist. Commn., 1992—; campaigned for Gov. Lawton Chiles; guest spkr. various schs., civic and social orgns. Named Pioneer of the Yr. City of Lake Wales, 1979, citizen of the Yr. Lake Wales Masonic Lodge, 1990; recipient key to the City of Lake Wales, 1979, Gold pin Woman's Soc., 1982, Lifetime Achievement award Polk County Sch. Bd., 1992, Disting. svc. to Humanity award Fla. So. Coll. Ann. Alumni Awards, 1996. Mem. Am. Legion Aux. (pres. 1988, 89, past pres. pin), Polk County Ret. Tchrs. Assn., Fla. Ret. Educators Assn., Nat. Edn. Assn., Lake Wales Dem. Club. Democrat. Presbyterian.

AHL, MARIAN ANTOINETTE, government investigator; b. Louisville, Ky., Sept. 18, 1952; d. Marion William and Anna (Self) A.; m. Timothy J. Vrana, Aug. 20, 1976 (div. 1980); Richard Allen Link, Oct. 10, 1981 (div. Apr. 1993); children: Tamara Ann, Kenneth Allen. BA, U. Louisville, 1974. Service rep. Soc. Security Adminstrn., Louisville, 1975-76, Asheville, N.C., 1976-77, Muncie, Ind., 1977; claims rep. Soc. Security Adminstrn., Indpls., 1977-79; tax auditor IRS, New Albany, Ind., 1979-84; investigator Equal Employment Oppurtunity Commn., Louisville, 1984—. Mem. Mortar Bd., Federally Employed Women, Pi Beta Phi. Democrat. Roman Catholic. Home: 1615 Dundee Rd Louisville KY 40205 Office: EEOC Ste 458 600 Dr Martin Luther King Pl # 68 Louisville KY 40202-2239

AHLGREN, DENISE MARY, nursing consultant; b. Rockford, Ill., Jan. 21, 1950; d. John R. and Mary Ann (Astikis) Ahlgren; m. Robert A. Hester, May 12, 1989. BS in Nursing, U. Md., Balt., 1972; MA in Bus. Adminstrn., Cen. Mich. U., 1982. Commd. 1st lt. U.S. Army, 1972, advanced through grades to maj., 1982; indsl. nurse Furst Temp., Rockford; clin. head nurse emergency rm., quality assurance nurse U.S. Army, Ft. Rucker, Ala.; orthoneuro head nurse U.S. Army, Aurora, Colo.; ret. U.S. Army, 1988; med.-legal cons. Home Care Cons. divsn. Specialized Care for Children-UIC. Served Operation Desert Shield Storm, 1990. Decorated Expert Field Med. badge, Army Commendation medal. Mem. Am. Assn. Legal Nurse Cons., Ret. Officers Assn.

AHLSTROM, MICHAEL JOSEPH, lawyer; b. N.Y.C., June 1, 1953; s. Albert Warren and Bernadette Patricia (Flynn) A.; m. Mary Lou Donnelly, Apr. 19, 1980; 1 child, Courtney Leigh. BS, St. Francis Coll., 1975; JD, U. San Francisco, 1978. Bar: N.Y. 1980, U.S. Dist. Ct. (so. and ea. dists.) N.Y. 1980, Ga. 1982, U.S. Dist. Ct. (no. dist.) Ga. 1983, U.S. Ct. Appeals (11th cir.) 1984, U.S. Supreme Ct. 1987. Counsel Gear Design, Inc., N.Y.C., 1979-80; ptnr. Ahlstrom & Ahlstrom, N.Y.C., 1981-83; gen. counsel Network Rental, Inc., Atlanta, 1984-87; assoc. John Marshall and Assocs., P.C., Atlanta, 1987; ptnr. Marshall & Ahlstrom, P.C., Atlanta, 1987-88; pvt. practice Marietta, Ga., 1988-92; mng. atty. United Auto Workers-Gen. Motors-Ford Chrysler Legal Plan Ga., Atlanta, 1993-96; arbitrator NASD. Arbitrator Superior Ct. Fulton County, Ga., 1987—, Ga. Lemon Law, 1991—; panel atty. Cobb County Cir. Defender; spl. master Cobb County Superior Ct. Named one of Outstanding Young Men Am. U.S. Jaycees, 1986. Mem. ABA, N.Y. Bar Assn., Ga. Bar Assn. (pub. rels. com. 1989-91), Atlanta Bar Assn., Cobb County Bar Assn., Am. Corp.Counsel Assn. (program chmn. 1986-87), Am. Arbitration Assn. (comml. panel 1987—), Ga. Assn. Criminal Def. Lawyers, KC, Phi Delta Phi, Alpha Kappa Psi. Republican. Roman Catholic. Home: 613 Fairway Ct Marietta GA 30068-4159

AHMAD, SALAHUDDIN, nuclear scientist; b. Sylhet, Bangladesh, Nov. 25, 1954; arrived in Can., 1978; came to U.S., 1990; s. Jalal and Momtaz (Begum) A.; m. Munawar Sultana, June 1, 1978; 1 child, Nahid Rubaba. MSc, Dhaka U., Bangladesh, 1975; PhD, U. Victoria, B.C., Can., 1981. Lectr. Dhaka U., 1978; postdoctoral rsch. assoc. U. Victoria, 1981; rsch. scientist U. Paris South, Orsay, France, 1982-83; profl. rsch. assoc. U. Sask., Saskatoon, Can., 1983-84; rsch. assoc. Triumf Nat. Lab., Vancouver, 1984-86, U. B.C., Vancouver, 1987-89; faculty fellow Rice U., Houston, 1990—; sci. assoc. Brookhaven Nat. Lab., 1990—; mem. Solenoidal Tracker at Relativistic Heavy Ion Collider, Continuous Electron Beam Accelerator Facility, Large Acceptance Spectrometer Collaboration. Contbr. more than 110 articles to sci. jours. and conf. procs., including Physics Letters, Phys. Rev., Phys. Rev. Letters. Bangladeshi rep. World Muslim Youth Conf., Abha, Saudi Arabia, 1977; founder, pres. Bangladesh-Can. Cultural Assn. B.C., Vancouver, 1988-89, Bangladesh-Am. Lit., Art and Cultural Assn., Houston, 1992-95. Raja Kalinarayan scholar U. Dhaka, 1974-75; fellow Can. Commonwealth Fellowship Com., 1978-81. Mem. Am. Phys. Soc. Office: Rice U Bonner Lab Houston TX 77251

AHMED, JEFFREY JALIL, neurologist; b. Alexandria, Va., Aug. 13, 1961; s. Shafaat and Carol Marilyn (Holeski) A. BA, Stetson U., 1986; MD, Chgo. Med. Sch., 1990. Intern in internal medicine U. Hosp., U. Fla., Jacksonville, Fla., 1990-91; resident in neurology U. N.Mex., Albuquerque, 1991-94; neurologist Daytona Neurol. Assocs., Daytona Beach, Fla., 1994—. Mem. AAAS, AMA, Am. Acad. Neurologists. Republican. Roman Catholic. Office: Daytona Neurol Assocs 1430 Mason Ave Daytona Beach FL 32117-4551

AHMED, M. BASHEER, psychiatrist, educator; b. Hyderbad, India, June 7, 1935; came to U.S., 1968; s. M. Quameruddin and Aziz Fatima Ahmed; m. Shakila Khatoon, Dec. 7, 1967; children: Sameer, Araj. Osmania U., Hyderabad, 1954; MD, Dow Med. Coll., 1960. Diplomate Am. Bd. Psychiatry and Neurology, Am. Bd. Geriatric Psychiatry. Dir. psychiat. dept. St. Louis County Gen. Hosp., Clayton, Mo., 1969-71; dir. sound view Throngs Neck Community Mental Health Ctr., Bronx, N.Y., 1971-76; chief psychiatry VA Hosp., Dayton, Ohio, 1976-78; dir. psychiat. dept. John Peter Smith Hosp., Ft. Worth, 1978-82; pvt. practice, Ft. Worth, 1984—; dir. dept. psychiatry St. Joseph Hosp., Ft. Worth, 1985-89; chief staff Care Unit Hosp., Ft. Worth, 1989-94; dir. psych. geriatric unit Med. Plaza Hosp., Ft. Worth, 1992—; asst. prof. Albert Einstein Coll. Medicine, N.Y.C., 1971-76; prof. Wright State U. Med. Sch., Dayton, 1976-78, U. Tex. Southwestern Med. Sch., Dallas, 1978-88, U. Tex. Health Sci. Ctr., Ft. Worth, 1982—; chmn. dept. psychiatry Plaza Med. Ctr. East, 1995—. Contbg. author: Group Counseling and Psychotherapy, 1976, Administration of Mental Health, 1980. Life mem. Rep. Presdl. Task Force, Washington, 1986—. Hogg Found. grantee, 1980-81, U. Tex. Health Sci. Ctr. grantee, 1981. Fellow Am. Psychiat. Assn.; mem. AMA (Physician's Recognition award 1971—), Tex. Med. Assn., Tex., Soc. Psychiat. Physicians (pres. Tarrant County chpt. 1989-90), Tarrant County Med. Soc. (task force for homeless 1989-90), Islamic Med. Assn. (pres. 1978-79), Internat. Inst. Islamic Medicine. Home: 10 Home Place Ct Arlington TX 76016-3913 Office: 1015 S Henderson St Fort Worth TX 76104-2924

AHMED, SYED MAHTAB, physician, immunologist, nutritionist; b. Brahman Baria, Bangladesh, July 10, 1953; s. Syed Muslehuddin and Ayesha Akhtar (Khatoon) A.; m. Syeda Shamima Mahmood, Jan. 6, 1984; children: Syed Rashdi, Syed Sunan. MBBS, U. Chittagong, Bangladesh, 1982; PhD, Kyoto (Japan) U., 1989. In svc. tng. Sylhet (Bangladesh) Med. Coll. Hosp., 1982-83; med. officer Ministry of Health, Dhaka, Bangladesh, 1983-84; rsch. student Kyoto U., 1984-85; postdoctoral fellow Nat. Inst. Health and Nutrition, Tokyo, 1989-92; rsch. officer Fuji Sangyo Kaisha, Marugame, Japan, 1992-94; rsch. fellow Kyoto U., 1992-95; med. rsch. assoc. Riverside Med. Ctr., Bellevue, Ky., 1995—; mem. Human Scis. Found., Tokyo, 1989-92; tech. advisor 2d meeting of Internat. Soc. for Trace Elements Rsch., Tokyo, 1989; gen. sec. (acting) Fedn. Asian Nutrition Socs., Kuala Lumpur, Malaysia, 1991. Contbr. articles to profl. jours.; patentee in field. Monbusho scholar Ministry of Edn., Japan, 1984-89. Mem. AAAS, Asia and Pacific Pub. Health Nutrition Assn., Japanese Soc. Allergology, Japanese Biochem. Soc. Islam. Home: 419 W Side Dr Apt 201 Gaithersburg MD 20878-3124 Office: Riverside Med Ctr 200 Fairfield Ave Bellevue KY 41073-1041

AHMED, SYED Z., anthropologist; b. Meerut, India, Aug. 19, 1923; s. Syed Riazuddin and Shah Jehan Begum; m. Susan Ahmed, Feb. 20, 1944; 1 child, Suraiya. PhD, Eng. Leader Sahara Recon Expdn., North Africa; producer scientific documentary films for TV, Europe; pres., exec. prodr. Xploration Internat.; rschr., traveler numerous expdns. worldwide. Author: Twilight of an Empire in India, Twilight of an Empire in China, Twilight on the Silk Road, Ruwenzori: A Land Journey Through Europe to Central Africa, Twilight on Caucasus; publisher: Exploration mag., London. Islamic. Office: Pres Office Xploration Internat Houston TX 77062

AHRENDSEN, BRUCE LOUIS, economist, educator; b. Oxford Junction, Iowa, Dec. 21, 1959; s. Gayle Henry and Donna Lou (Christensen) A.; m. Jolene Rae Schnoor, May 9, 1987; children: Blake Roy, Connor Bruce. BS, Iowa State U., 1983; M in Econs., N.C. State U., 1987, PhD in Econs., 1990. Mem. cast Up With People Corp., Broomfield, Colo., 1979-80; agrl. mgmt. specialist Farmers Home Adminstrn. USDA, Maquoketa, Iowa, 1983-85; teaching asst. N.C. State U., Raleigh, 1985-86, rsch. asst., 1986-90; asst. prof. agrl. econs. U. Ark., Fayetteville, 1990-96, assoc. prof., 1996—; prin. Ctr. for Farm and Rural Bus. Fin.; cons. in fie.d. Contbr. articles and abstracts to profl. jours. Rep. United Way, Fayetteville, 1992-93. Recipient Am. Citizenship award Iowa State Bar Assn. Mem. Am. Agrl. Econs. Assn., Am. Econ. Assn., So. Agrl. Econs. Assn., Western Agrl. Econs. Assn., Gamma Sigma Delta. Office: U Ark 221 Agriculture Bldg Fayetteville AR 72701

AHYSEN, HARRY JULES, artist, educator; b. Pt. Arthur, Tex., Sept. 6, 1928. BFA in Art, U. Houston, 1955; MFA in Art, U. Tex., 1962; pvt. study in art, dance and music. Organizer, operator Prep. Sch. Ballet, Houston, 1956; mgr. Hotel Buccaneer, Galveston, Tex., 1957-59; supr. art Orleans Parish Sch. Bd., New Orleans, 1961-62; designer Man from the Sea Gallery, 1969; establisher Hex House Antiques, Huntsville, Tex., 1976; v.p. Ahysen Marine Trans., Inc., 1980; artist-in-residence Bankers Land Corp. and MacArthur Found., West Palm Beach, Fla., summer 1983; mem. faculty dept. art Sam Houston State U., Huntsville, 1963-94, prof. emeritus, 1996—; cons. art Frankel Group, Boca Raton, Fla., 1983, Finley Devel. Corp., Jupiter Island, Fla., Fayette County Mus., Washington Courthouse, Ohio, 1987; juror many exhbns., including La. Fest. of Arts, Sulphur, 1980, Brazos Valley Art League, Bryan, Tex., 1982, 86, 87, 92-93, Worlds Fair, New Orleans; lectr./presenter profl. confs. and workshops, instns. including Galveston (Tex.) Are League, 1965, Sta. KJAC-TV, Pt. Arthur, 1974, Allen Acad., 1985, Conroe Art League, 1987, 90, several others; curator art shows, 1989; mem. faculty So. State C.C., Willimington, Ohio, 1994. One-man shows include Drawing Rm., Houston, 1985, Hearnwood Gallery, Hearne, Tex., 1985, Allen Acad., Bryan, 1985, Zanesville (Ohio) Mus., 1988, Lowman Student Ctr., Sam Houston State U., 1984, 87, 89, 93; exhibited in group shows, most recently Cmty. Ctr., Temple, Tex., 1990, Wabash Gallery, Cin., 1990, Hillsboro Art Guild, 1989-93 (1st prize/best of show); represented in permanent collections Am. Bank, Huntsville, City of Huntsville, Brown & Root, Houston, Gulf Oil Corp., Dallas, IBM, San Antonio, Sam. Houston State U., others; prin. commd. works include design of omnibus City of Galveston, 1974, murals restoration Flagship Hotel, 1982, mural City of Wash. Court House, 1994, pelican sculpture City of Huntsville, Tex., 1994, various murals, publ. covers; choreographer numerous ballets; arranger, performer music Taft Hotel Orch., Harry James Orch., USN Band, others. Charter mem. bd. dirs. Houston Youth Ballet, 1959. Lt. (j.g.) USN, 1950-54. Recipient key to city, merit award City of New Orleans, 1962, Internat. Tomaso Campenelle Silver medal, Rome, 1972, Gold Medal painting Ohio Art Guide, 1994, numerous art exhbn. awards; honoree City of Huntsville, 1985; designated State Artist of Tex., Tex. State Legislature, 1980-81; selected one of 12 nat. artists Franklin Mint Gallery Am. Art Competition, 1974; grantee Kraisner Pollock Found., N.Y., 1986. Mem. Am. Soc. Marine Painters, Tex. Artist Mus. Soc., Ohio Watercolor Soc. Office: Dept Art PO Box 2089 Huntsville TX 77341-2089

AIDA, YUKIE, psychological educator, researcher; b. Warabi, Saitama, Japan, Oct. 30, 1953; came to U.S., 1978; d. Eizaburo and Kimi (Inada) A.; m. Brendan Earl Hussey, Dec. 26, 1988. AA, Bunkyo U. Women's Coll., Tokyo, 1974; BEd magna cum laude, Seattle U., 1981; BA, U. Wash., 1982; MA, U. Tex., 1986, PhD, 1988. Cert. middle sch. English tchr. English instr. New Ednl. Media Inst., Tokyo, 1975-78; teaching asst. U. Tex., Austin, 1984-88, rsch. assoc., 1987-88; psychology instr. Austin Community Coll., 1986—; lectr. in Japanese U. Tex., 1989—. Recipient Benjamin and Dorothy Fruchter Ann. prize for excellence in edn. psychology rsch. U. Tex., 1988; U. Tex. Austin Computation Ctr. Project Quest awardee; Statira Biggs scholar U. Wash., 1982; Tex. Pub. Edn. grantee U. Tex., 1985-88. Mem. APA, Am. Coun. on Teaching Fgn. Langs., Assn. Asian Studies, Assn. Tchrs. of Japanese, Japanese Soc. Social Psychology, Japanese Psychol. Assn., Phi Kappa Phi, Kappa Delta Pi. Office: Dept Asian Studies U Tex at Austin WCH 4-134 G9300 Austin TX 78712

AIDMAN, BARTON TERRY, accountant; b. Cleve., Aug. 14, 1947; s. Samuel Mayor and Freda (Grossman) A.; m. Leslie Hope Fleischer, Aug. 2, 1970; children: Todd Sidney, Ashley Dean. Student, So. Meth. U., 1967; BA in Acctg., U. S. Fla., 1969. CPA, Fla. Tax cons. Peat Marwick & Mitchell, Tampa, Fla., 1969-73; ptnr. B. Terry Aidman, CPA, Tampa, 1973-77; tax ptnr. Laventhol & Horwath, Tampa, 1977-90; mem., ptnr. Aidman, Piser & Co., Tampa, 1991—; mem. membership com. Adv. Bd. of Sch. of Accountancy at U. So. Fla. Editorial advisor Jour. Accountancy; weekly tax columnist local newspaper; monthly tax tip for regional TV; monthly video presentation nat. continuing edn. tax program. Active Big Bros. of Tampa, United Way, St. Joseph's Devel. Coun., Fgn. Trade Zone, Jr. Achievement, Berkeley Prep. Sch., Menorah Manor Nursing Home, Muscular Dystrophy Assn., Jewish Nat. Fund, Fla. Gulf Coast Orch. and Tampa Performing Arts Ctr., Bayshore Little League; pres. Cong. of Schaarai Zedek, Tampa Conv. Facilities Bd., Tampa Hillsborough County Tourist and Vis. Bur., Tampa Jewish Family Svc. Co-recipient Freedom award Israel Bonds; recipient Up and Comers award Price Waterhouse, 3 Citations of Honor, Jewish Nat. Fund. Mem. AICPA (various coms.), Fla. Inst. CPAs (various coms., Pub. Svc. Awards 1988, 89), Nat. Assn. Lawyers and CPAs, Am. Inst. CPAs, Nat. Assn. Accts., Tampa Bay Investment Coun. (pres., co-founder), Estate Planning Coun., Tampa World Trade Coun., Planned Philanthropy Coun. of Suncoast (charter), C. of C. (various coms.), Com. of 100. Home: 4925 St Croix Dr Tampa FL 33629-4830 Office: Aidman Piser & Co 101 E Kennedy Blvd Ste 1960 Tampa FL 33602-5148

AIGNER, EMILY BURKE, lay worker; b. Henrico, Va., Oct. 28, 1920; d. William Lyne and Susie Emily (Willson) Burke; m. Louis Cottrell Aigner, Nov. 27, 1936; children: Lyne, Betty, D. Muriel (dec.), Willson, Norman, William, Randolph, Dorothy. Cert. in Bible, U. Richmond, 1969; postgrad., So. Bapt. Sem. Extension, Nashville, 1987, Va. Commonwealth U., 1981; diploma in Bible, Liberty Home Bible Inst., 1992. Deacon Four Mile Creek Bapt. Ch., Richmond, Va., 1972—, trustee, 1991, dir. Woman's Missionary Union, 1986-94, treas., 1984-89, dir. Sunday sch., 1993—; chaplain Richmond Meml. Hosp., 1996—; spl. edn. tchr.; acctg. tech., 1959-80. Prodr. Dial-A-Devotion for pub. by telephone, 1978-85. Solicitor ARC, Henrico County, 1947-49, induction ctr. vol., 1994—; solicitor, United Givers' Fund, Henrico County, 1945-48; sec.-treas. soliciting funds Bible Edn. in Varina Sch., 1946-49; singer Bellwood Choir, Chesterfield County, Va., 1965-70; telephone counselor Richmond Contact, 1980-82, Am. Cancer Soc., Richmond, 1980-82; program chmn. Varina (Va.) Home Demonstration Club, 1950-53; worker Vol. Visitor Program Westport Convalescent Home, 1983—; vol. patient rep. Richmond Meml. Hosp., 1994—; vol. Crisis Pregnancy Ctr., 1995—; jail min. Richmond City Jail, 1973—; chaplain Richmond Meml. Hosp., 1996—. Named Woman of Yr., Henrico Farm Bur., 1996. Mem. Gideons Internat. (sec. Va. aux. 1977-80, 82-84, new mem. plan rep. 1981, 85, 91, 94, zone leader 1988-89, 90-91, state cabinet rep. 1989-90, pres. Richmond N.E. Camp 1976-78, sec.-treas. 1980-82, 93, scripture sec. 1973-75, 87-89, chmn. Va. state widows com. 1993—), Henrico Farm Bur. (women's com. 1994—), Farm Bur. Fedn. (Henrico Farm Woman of Yr. 1996), Alpha Phi Sigma. Home: 9717 Varina Rd Richmond VA 23231-8428

AIKEN, WALTER JEFF, III, chemical company executive; b. Columbia, S.C., Feb. 8, 1961; s. Walter Jeff Jr. and Flora Jane (Elliott) A.; m. Jacqueline Dawn Jackson, Mar. 30, 1986; 1 child, Alexandra Dawn. BA, St. Andrews Presbyn. Coll., 1983. Chemist Solene Lubricants divsn. Elf Lubricants N.A., Inc., Rockingham, N.C., 1987-94, tech. svcs. dir., health and safety dir., 1995—. Author: (manual) Lubrication Fundamentals: Technical Training Series, 1993. Treas., emergency coord. Richmond County (N.C.) Amateur Radio Emergency Svc., Rockingham, 1990—. Recipient Good Citizenship award Jr. Women's Club, 1978. Mem. Am. Soc. Safety Engrs., Richmond County Safety Dirs. Assn., Soc. Tribologists and Lubrication Engrs., Richmond County Amateur Radio Club (treas. 1990—). Office: Elf Lubricants NAm PO Box 1058 709 Airport Rd Rockingham NC 28380

AIKMAN, ALBERT EDWARD, lawyer; b. Norman, Okla., Mar. 11, 1922; s. Albert Edwin and Thelma Annette (Brooke) A.; m. Shirley Barnes, June 24, 1944; children: Anita Gayle, Priscilla June, Rebecca Brooke. B.S., Tex. A&M U., 1947; J.D. cum laude, So. Meth. U., 1948, LL.M., 1954. Bar: Tex. 1948, U.S. Supreme Ct. 1956. Staff atty. Phillips Petroleum Co., Amarillo, Tex., 1948-49; sole practice, Amarillo, 1949-53; tax counsel Magnolia Petroleum Co., Dallas, 1953-56; ptnr. Locke, Purnell, Boren, Laney & Neely, Dallas, 1956-71; sole practice, Dallas, 1973-81; of counsel Pickens Energy Corp., Dallas, 1981—. Served with inf. U.S. Army, 1943-45. Mem. ABA, Tex. Bar Assn., Dallas Bar Assn. Methodist. Contbr. articles in field to profl. jours.

AILES, MARILYN CAROL, ecologist; b. Spirit Lake, Iowa, Aug. 16, 1946; d. Norman Bradford and Velma Ruth (Roberts) Stevens; m. Irvin Winfield, Aug. 3, 1968; children: Charsa Loretta McPherson, Clinton Lorne Ailes. BA in Environ. Biology, U. Calif., 1968; MS in Marine/Estuarine Environ. Sci., U. Md., 1993, PhD, 1996. Word processor U.S. Army, Anchorage, 1968-69; word processor/lab. tech. U. Alaska, Fairbanks, 1969-73; word processor Sentry Ins., Stevens Point, Wis., 1974-76; ecologist AEGIS Combat Systems Ctr., Wallops Island, Va., 1984—. Author/dir.: (play) Time and the Constitution, 1981. Leader, trainer Girl Scouts U.S., Chesapeake Bay, 1979—; instr. ARC, Accomack County, 1981—. Office: AEGIS Combat Systems Ctr Pub Works Office Wallops Island VA 23337

AILOR, EARL STARNES, lawyer; b. Newport, Tenn., Jan. 27, 1920; s. Thurman and Lena Belle (Starnes) A.; m. Margaret Aileen Nelson, June 3, 1947; children: Annabell, Albert Earl (dec.), Margaret Pauline, William Thurman. BA, U. Tenn., 1941, JD, 1947. Bar: Tenn. 1946, U.S. Supreme Ct. 1960. Pvt. practice Knoxville, Tenn., 1947-60, 87—; ptnr. Asquith, Ailor & Jones, Knoxville, 1961-87; solicitor Knox County, Knoxville, 1954-68. Mem. devel. bd. U. Tenn.; trustee, Sunday sch. tchr. Ch. St. United Meth. Ch., 1978-80, chancellor Holston conf., 1981-95, del. Southea. Jurisdictional Conf. 1988, 92, Gen. Conf., 1988—. With U.S. Army, 1941-46, NATOUSA, MTO, ETO, JAGC, 1951-52. Decorated Bronze Star with oak leaf cluster, Normandy Jubilee of Liberty medal. Mem. ABA, ATLA, Tenn. Trial Lawyers Assn., Am. Judicature Soc., Tenn. Bar Assn., Knoxville Bar Assn., U. Tenn. Alumni Assn. (pres. 1963), Lions (life), Masons, Omicron Delta Kappa, Phi Delta Phi (life). Democrat. Home: 3905 Kenilworth Dr Knoxville TN 37919-6640 Office: 707 Medical Arts Bldg 603 W Main Ave # 707 Knoxville TN 37902-2603

AINSA, FRANCIS SWINBURNE, lawyer; b. El Paso, Tex., Jan. 7, 1915; s. Frank S. and Roselle (McNamee) A.; m. Evelyn Fraser, Jan. 14, 1941; children: Dorothy, Francis Jr., Michael, Mary, Kathleen, Richard, Barbara, Stephen. AB, Georgetown U., 1936; LLB, Harvard U., 1940; postgrad., U.S. Army Sch. Mil. Govt.; postgrad ethnology, archaeology, U. Tex., El Paso. Legal officer sup. hq. AEF Mission to Luxembourg, 1944-45; atty. pvt. practice El Paso, Tex., 1947—. Bd. chmn. Mary L. Peyton Found., El Paso, 1955—; mem. zoning bd. of adjustment, El Paso, 1960. Maj. U.S. Army Cavalry, 1942-46 ETO. Decorated Bronze Star, 1946, Croix de Guerre (Luxembourg), 1946; named Officer Order of Couronne de Chene (Luxembourg), Officer Order of Leopold II (Belgium), 1946, Knight of St Gregory, Holy See, 1965, Knight Grand Comdr. Equestrian Order of Holy Sepulchre Jerusalem, 1985. Roman Catholic. Home and Office: 525 Corto Way El Paso TX 79902-3817

AIRST, MALCOLM JEFFREY, electronics engineer; b. Toronto, Jan. 12, 1957; s. Herman and Faye (Stulberg) A.; m. Victoria Kessler, Feb. 27, 1981. EET, DeVry Inst., Toronto, 1977-80; BSEE, George Mason U., 1987; M Engring. Mgmt., Old Dominion U., 1994. Assoc. engr. Satellite Bus. Systems, McLean, Va., 1983-84; lead engr. COMSAT, Fairfax, Va., 1984-87, MITRE Corp., McLean, 1987—; mem. tech. lead Internat. Trade and Tech. Directorate; mem. VME Internat. Trade Assn., Stds. Orgn., Space and Naval Warfare com. USN, fixed and mobile stds. com. Ballistic Missile Def. Orgn. Pres. McLean Greens Homeowners Assn., 1990—. Mem. IEEE, Armed Forces Communications and Electronics Assn. Office: MITRE Corp 7525 Colshire Dr Mc Lean VA 22102-7500

AITKEN, THOMAS DEAN, lawyer; b. Coffeyville, Kans., July 9, 1939; s. Arthur E. and Kathleen Lucille (Bressie) A.; m. Molly Alexandrea Coston, Dec. 17, 1960; children: Molly Kym Aitken Wright, Michele Bressie Aitken McKinney. BBA, U. Okla., 1961, LLB, 1964; LLM in Taxation, NYU, 1965. Bar: Okla. 1964, Fla. 1966. Assoc. Carlton, Fields, Ward, Emmanuel, Smith & Cutler, P.A., Tampa, Fla., 1965-70, ptnr., 1971-96; of counsel Trenam, Kemker, Scharf, Barkin, Frye, O'Neill & Mullis, P.A., Tampa, Fla., 1996—. Contbr. articles, speaker NYU Tax Inst., 1972; editor NYU Intramural Law Rev., 1964-65; mng. editor Okla. Law Rev., 1963-64; articles editor ABA jour. The Tax Lawyer, 1987. Bd. dirs. ARC, Tampa, 1984-87; pres., bd. dirs. Met. Ministries, Tampa, 1979-80. Fellow Am. Coll. Trust and Estate Counsel; mem. Fla. Bar (tax sect. exec. coun. 1970-82), Tampa Bay Estate Planning Coun. (pres. 1975-76), Beta Gamma Sigma, Phi Eta Sigma. Democrat. Methodist. Office: Trenam Kemker Scharf Barkin Frye ONeill & Mullis PA 2700 Barnett Plz 101 E Kennedy Blvd Tampa FL 33602

AKERS, OTTIE CLAY, lawyer, publisher; b. Huntsville, Ala., Sept. 4, 1949; s. Merrideth Townsend and Mary Lois (Reed) A.; m. Marcia Bradley Ligon, Mar. 21, 1971; 1 child, Katie Virginia. BA, U. Alabama, Birmingham, 1972, MA, 1976; JD, Samford U., Birmingham, 1985. Bar: Ala. 1985. Assoc. Haskell, Slaughter, Young & Lewis, Birmingham, 1985-86; pub., chief exec. officer Clay-Bradley, Washington, 1986-90; prin. Ottie Akers Law Offices, Birmingham, 1986—. Mem. adminstrv. bd., fin. com. East Lake United Meth. Ch., 1996—; bd. dirs. Bankhead Trail Trust, 1996—. Mem. ABA, Am. Judicature Soc., Assn. Trial Lawyers Am., Ala. Bar Assn., Exch. Club (bd. dirs. Birmingham chpt. 1986, child abuse prevention ctr. 1985-86, 94—, v.p. fin. 1995—), Friends of Ala. Sch. Fine Arts Theatre (pres. 1989-90). Home: 1244 Stonehenge Dr Birmingham AL 35235-2739 Office: Ottie Akers Law Offices 2121 8th Ave N Ste 1614 Birmingham AL 35203-2321

AKERS, SAMUEL LEE, lawyer; b. Chattanooga, Oct. 20, 1943; s. Shelby Russell and Helen Louise (Crumley) A.; m. Mercedes Lilia Vuksanovic, Mar. 13, 1967; children: Bradford Lee, Camby Leigh. BA, Berry Coll., 1966; JD, Memphis State U., 1974. Bar: Tenn. 1974, U.S. Dist. Ct. (ea. dist.) Tenn. 1976, U.S. Ct. Appeals (6th cir.) 1985, U.S. Supreme Ct. 1987, U.S. Dist. Ct. (mid. dist.) Tenn. 1989. Trust examiner Office of the Compt. of the Currency, Memphis, 1975-76; assoc. Luther, Anderson, Cleary & Ruth, Chattanooga, 1976-78, 81-84, ptnr., 1985-93; ptnr. Hatfield Van Cleave & Akers, Chattanooga, 1994, Hatfield Van Cleave Akers & Adams, P.L.C., Chattanooga, 1995—; spl. agt. FBI, Orlando, Fla., 1978-81; mem. comml. panel Am. Arbitration Assn., N.Y.C., 1986—. Lt. comdr. USNR, 1967-71. Named Outstanding Young Man of Am. Jaycees, 1977. Mem. Tenn. Bar Assn., Chattanooga Bar Assn. (bd. govs. 1995—), Soc. Former Spl. Agts. of the FBI (chmn. Chattanooga chpt. 1987-88, 95-96). Republican. Roman Catholic. Home: Williams Island Ferry Rd PO Box 1337 Chattanooga TN 37401 Office: Hatfield Van Cleave 428 Mccallie Ave Chattanooga TN 37402-2009

AKINS, KENNETH MAUNEY, historic park manager; b. Blairsville, Ga., July 26, 1956; s. James K. and Joan M. (Dyer) A. BA magna cum laude, Piedmont Coll., 1978. Tchr. Union County Bd. Edn., Blairsville, Ga., 1979-82; interpretive park ranger Ga. Dept. Natural Resources, Darien, Ga., 1982-84; asst. park supt. Ga. Dept. Natural Resources, Crawfordville, Ga., 1984-86; historic park mgr. Ga. Dept. Natural Resources, Darien, 1986—; bd. dirs. Lower Altamaha Hist. Soc., Darien, Ashantilly Found., Darien. Chmn., organizer 200th Birthday Celebration McIntosh C. of C., 1993, pres. Coastal Ga. Wilderness Soc., 1996. Home and Office: GA Dept Natural Resources Ft King George Dr Darien GA 31305

AKMAKJIAN, ALAN PAUL, English language, literature and creative writing educator; b. Highland Park, Mich., July 18, 1948; s. Kizer and Mary Elizabeth (Goshgarian) A. BA, MA, Ea. Mich. U., 1974; PhD, Wayne State U., 1979; MFA, Calif. State U., San Francisco, 1991; PhD, St. John's U., Jamaica, N.Y., 1995. Instr./area coord. Poets in the Schs., Santa Clara, Calif., 1984-91; asst. prof. English and creative writing St. John's U., 1994—; appointed amb. in linguistics, language and culture to India, 1996. Author: (books of poetry) Treading Pages of Water, 1992, Grounded Angels, 1993, Let the Sun Go, 1993, California Picnic, 1993, Breaking the Silence, 1993, California Picnic and Other Poems, 1996; contbr. articles to profl. jours. Recipient award Cranbrook Art Acad., Mich., 1979, NEA/Calif. Arts Coun., 1984; univ. fellow U. Tex., Dallas, 1994, 96, 97, St. John's U., 1995, Jordan fellow for the Arts, 1995, 96, 97; grantee Alex Manoogian Cultural Fund, Mich., 1992, Tex. Pub. Ednl. grantee, 1996, 97. Mem. MLA, PEN, Acad. Am. Poets, Nat. Women's Book Club, PEN West (liaison officer), Poetry Soc. Am., Writer's Garret. Home: 2200 Waterview Pky Apt 2134 Richardson TX 75080-2268

AKUJUOBI, CAJETAN MADUABUCHUKWU, research engineer, electrical engineering educator; b. Umuahia, Abia, Nigeria, Apr. 18, 1950; came to U.S., 1977; s. John Ohiri and Roseline (Amadi) A.; m. Caroline Chioma Njoku, May 8, 1982; children: Obinna Chukwuemeka, Chijoke Eze. BSEE, So. Univ., 1980; MSEE, Tuskegee (Ala.) Inst., 1983; MBA, Hampton U., 1987; PhD, George Mason U., 1995. Asst. prof. elec. engr. Norfolk State U., Va., 1983-96; R&D engr. Austin Product Ctr., Schlumberger Inc., 1996—; adj. assoc. prof. U. D.C., 1989-90; rsch. fellow NASA, Langley, Va., 1987; tech. staff AT&T Bell Labs., Holmdel, N.J., 1986, 88, 90, 91; prin. engr. Spectrum Engring. & Tech., Washington, 1991-92; rschr. George Mason U., Fairfax, Va., 1991-94; engr. Intelsat, Washington, 1993; session chmn. Modeling and Simulation Conf., Pitts., 1986-90; judge Tidewater Sci. Fair, Southampton H.S., Courtland, Va., 1994; chief judge sr. engring. design projects Tidewater Sci. Fair, 1996, head jusge, 1995; faculty rsch. participant Argonne Nat. Lab., 1995-96. Mem. SPIE, IEEE (award 1982, 83, counselor 1977—, judge 1986), Instrument Soc. Am. (chmn. digital sys. 1986, session organizer 1986—), Am. Soc. Engring. Edn. (campus rep. 1983—), Soc. Indsl. and Applied Math., Sigma Xi, Alpha Kappa Mu. Roman Catholic. Home: 10507 Wendts Way Austin TX 78750 Office: Schlumberger Inc PO Box 200015 8311 N FM 620 Rd Austin TX 78726

ALAIMO, ANTHONY A., federal judge; b. 1920. AB, Ohio No. U.; JD, Emory U. Bar: Ga. 1948, Ohio 1948. Assoc. Reuben A. Garland, 1949-51, 53-56; pvt. practice, Atlanta, 1967-63; ptnr. Highsmith, Highsmith, Alaimo & Knox, Brunswick, Ga., 1963-67, Cowart, Sapp, Alaimo & Gale, Brunswick, 1963-67, Alaimo, Taylor & Bishop, Brunswick, 1967-71; judge U.S. Dist. Ct. (so. dist.) Ga., Brunswick, 1971—, now sr. judge. Office: US Dist Ct PO Box 944 Brunswick GA 31521-0944

ALAM, MOHAMMED BADRUL, history and political science educator; b. Cuttack, Orissa, India, Feb. 27, 1954; s. Shelkh and Hedatun (Nesa) Islam; m. Ruhi Alam, Dec. 29, 1987; children: Saira, Zubair, Sadaf. MA, Cornell U., 1988, PhD, 1990. Instr. Cornell U., Ithaca, N.Y., 1987-89; lectr. Elmira (N.Y.) Coll., 1989-90, SUNY, Cortland, 1990-91; prof. Midway (Ky.) Coll., 1991-94; prof. history and polit. sci. Marysville C.C., Cynthiana, Ky., 1996—. Author: Aspects of American Goverment, 1994, India's Nuclear Policy, 1988; editor Essays on Nuclear Proliferation, 1995. Named Ky. Col. Commonwealth of Ky., 1995. Mem. Am. Hist. Assn. Home: Apt 30 1972 Cambridge Dr Lexington KY 40504

ALAN-MOORMAN, TESS, special education educator; b. Niskayuna, N.Y., Nov. 18, 1964; d. James and Helga (Luedtke) Granan; m. Martin J. Moorman, June 19, 1994; children: Casey Lynn Moorman, Seth Alan Moorman. BBA, Webber Coll., 1988; M in Vocat./Tech. Edn., U. West Fla., 1993. Cert. bus. edn. 6-12, spl. edn./emotionally handicapped K-12. Social worker, case mgr. Dept. Health and Rehab. Svcs., Fla., 1989-93; tchr. educable mentally handicapped Bay County Schs., Panama City, Fla., 1993, tchr. severely emotionally disturbed & mentally handicapped, 1993—; cons. Bay County Schs., Panama City, 1994—; bus. ptnr. Applebee's Restaurant, Panama City, 1994—. Author: (curriculum models) Alantown Learning and Living, 1993 (award 1993), C.H.O.I.C.E. Diner, 1994. Grantee Bay Coun. for Children, 1994. Mem. CEC (presenter 1994, grantee 1993-94), CEC Divsn. Career Devel. and Transition (presenter 1994), ASCD, Am. Vocat. Assn. (presenter 1994). Home: 106 Bid-A-Wee Ln Panama City FL 32413 Office: Haney Vocat-Tech Ctr 3016 Hwy 77 N Panama City FL 32405

ALARCON, RENATO DANIEL, psychiatry educator, researcher, medical facility executive; b. Arequipa, Peru, Apr. 11, 1942; came to U.S., 1967; s. Jose Romulo and Rosa Aurea (Guzman) A.; m. Graciela E. Solis, June 8, 1967; children: Patricia, Sylvia, Daniel. MD, Cayetano Heredia U. Med. Sch., Lima, Peru, 1966; MPH, Johns Hopkins U., 1972. Diplomate Am. Bd. Psychiatry and Neurology. Fellow in psychosomatic medicine Johns Hopkins U. Sch. Medicine, Balt., 1967-68, resident in psychiatry, 1968-72; asst. prof. psychiatry U. Peru-Cayetano Heredia, Lima, 1972-76, assoc. prof. psychiatry, 1976-80; prof. psychiatry U. Ala. Sch. Medicine, Birmingham, 1981-83; chief of adult svcs. Univ. Hosp.-U. Ala. Med. Ctr., Birmingham, 1981-92; chief affective disorders program U. Ala. Sch. Medicine, Birmingham, 1991-93; chief psychiatry svc. VA Med. Ctr., Atlanta, 1993—; prof., vice chmn. dept. psychiatry Emory U. Sch. Medicine, Atlanta, 1993—; cons. Pan Am. Health Orgn., Washington, 1974-87; examiner Am. Bd. Psychiatry and Neurology, 1989—. Author: Psicoterapia, 1979, Psiquiatria, 1986, Identidad de la Psiquiatria Latinoamericana, 1990; co-editor: Enciclopedia Iberoam, Psiquiatria, Buenos Aires, 1990-94; assoc. editor Acta Psiq. Am. Latin, 1989-94; contbr. numerous articles to psychiat. jours. Active Physicians for Social Responsibility, 1982, Amnesty Internat., 1986. Rockefeller Found. scholar, 1988; named Exemplary Psychiatrist, Nat. Alliance for the Mentally Ill, 1992. Fellow APA, Am. Soc. Hispanic Psychiatrists (pres. 1994—); mem. Am. Coll. Psychiatrists, Am. Psychopathology Assn. Roman Catholic. Office: Atlanta VA Med Ctr 1670 Clairmont Rd Atlanta GA 30033

ALARCON, TERRY QUENTIN, judge; b. New Orleans, July 6, 1948; s. Frederick Joseph and Ann Marie (Quentin) A.; m. Mollie Ann McCullough, June 2, 1972; children: Joseph McCullough, Joshua Holland. BS, Spring Hill Coll., 1970; MSW, U. Ala., 1974; JD, Loyola U., New Orleans, 1979. Bar: La. 1979. Asst. to criminal sheriff Orleans Parish, New Orleans, 1974-78, asst. dist. atty., 1978-83; asst. dist. atty. Jefferson Parish, Gretna, La., 1983-86; ptnr. Brandt, Alarcon & McDonald, Metairie, La., 1983-86; judge Traffic Ct., City of New Orleans, 1991—; trial adv. lectr. Tulane U. Sch. Law, New Orleans, 1981—; exec. counsel to mayor, New Orleans 1986-90; chief of staff, 1989-90; elected judge Traffic Ct., City of New Orleans, 1990; appointed by Pres. U.S. to Nat. Inst. Justice. Mem. ABA, La. Bar Assn. Democrat. Roman Catholic. Home: 6225 St Bernard Ave New Orleans LA 70122-1327 Office: 2950 Energy Ctr 1100 Poydras St New Orleans LA 70163-1100

ALAUPOVIC, PETAR, biochemist, educator; b. Prague, Czechoslovakia, Aug. 3, 1923; came to U.S., 1957; married, 1947; 1 child. ChemE, U. Zagreb, 1948, PhD in Chemistry, 1956; DHC (hon.), U. Lille, France, 1987, U. Buenos Aires, 1994. Rschr. pharms. rsch. lab. Chem Corp, Prague, 1948-49; rschr. organic lab. Inst. Indsl. Rsch., Yugoslavia, 1949-50; asst. agrl. faculty U. Zagreb, 1951-54, asst. chem. inst. med. faculty, 1954-56; rsch. biochemist U. Ill., 1957-60; with cardiovascular sect. Okla. Med. Rsch. Found., Oklahoma City, 1960—, head lipoprotein lab., 1972-92, also head lipoprotein and atherosclerosis rsch. program; prof. rsch. biochemistry, sch. med. U. Okla., 1960—. Assoc. editor Lipids, 1974-78. Named Disting. Career Scientist Okla. Med. Rsch. Fund, 1990; NIH grantee, 1961-95. Mem. AAAS, Am. Soc. Biol. Chemists, Am. Chem. Soc., Am. Heart Assn. (Spl. Recognition award 1994), Am. Oil Chemistry Soc. Office: OK Med Rsch Found Lipoprotein & Artherosclerosis 825 NE 13th St Oklahoma City OK 73104-5005

ALAWANA See WALDMAN, ALAN I.

ALBAN, GENEVIEVE NOVICKY, city official; b. Youngstown, Ohio, Mar. 7, 1919; d. Joseph and Mary (Istocin) Sofranec; m. H. Edward Novicky (dec.); children: Carolee Monroe, Gen Parm, John, Sally Anstrom, Marita, Mary Sue Clark; m. Russell Alban, Aug 15, 1992. BA, Kent State U., Ohio, 1938. Tchr. Cath. schs. Youngstown, Ohio, 1938-40; tchr. Cath. schs. Youngstown, 1959-65, tchr. pub. schs., 1965-76; clk.-treas. Boardman, Ohio, 1976-82, ret. Author: History of Slovaks of Mahoning Valley, 1976; author booklet: How to Help Children Learn, 1974. Bd. dirs. Reading Ctr., Struthers Sch., Ohio, 1970-76; chmn. Mcpl. Employee Safety Com., Ohio Safety Congress, 1978-79; active various polit. orgns. Honored at Genevieve Novicky Day, City of Boardman, 1982. Mem. DeSoto Artists Guild (sec. 1988-89), Offstage Ladies, Anna Marie Artists (founder). Republican. Roman Catholic. Address: 912 N Shore Dr Box 1212 Anna Maria FL 34216

ALBANI, THOMAS J., manufacturing company executive; b. Hartford, Conn., May 3, 1942; s. Charles A. and Marie F. Albani; m. Suzanne Beardsley, Sept. 3, 1966; children: Karin, Steven. B.A., Amherst Coll., 1964; M.B.A., Wharton Sch. U. Pa., 1967. Asst. product mgr. Gen. Mills, Inc., Mpls., 1967-69; dir. mktg. Am. Can Co., Greenwich, Conn., 1969-73; mgmt. cons. McKinsey and Co., Inc., N.Y.C., 1973-78; gen. mgr. Gen. Electric Corp., Bridgeport, Conn., 1978-84; group v.p. Black & Decker, Inc., Bridgeport, 1984; pres. Sunbeam No. Am. Appliance Div. Allegheny Internat., Oak Brook, Ill., 1984-86; pres. appliance bus. Allegheny Internat. Inc., Pitts., 1986, exec. v.p., chief operating officer, 1986-89; prin. New England Cons. Group, Westport, Conn., 1990-91; pres., chief exec. officer Electrolux Corp., Marietta, Ga., 1991—. Mem. Nat. Housewares Mfrs. Assn. (bd. dirs. 1985-90), Assn. Home Appliance Mfrs. (bd. dirs. 1985-87), Chgo. Assn. Commerce and Industry (bd. dirs. 1986). Office: Electrolux Corp 2300 Windy Ridge Pky Ste 900 Marietta GA 30067-5202*

ALBANO, ROBERT A., English language educator; b. Springfield, Mass., June 5, 1956; s. Michael J. and Helen A. (Hadenchuk) A. BA, Calif. State U., Northridge, 1978; MA, Calif. State U., Sacramento, 1982; PhD, Purdue U., 1992. Tchr. Valley Profl. Sch., Van Nuys, Calif., 1978-79, Our Lady of Loretto H.S., L.A., 1979-80, Robert Frost Jr. H.S., Granada Hills, Calif., 1982, Chaminade Prep. Sch., Canoga Park, Calif., 1982-83, Granada Hills H.S., 1984-86; instr. Purdue U., West Lafayette, Ind., 1987-92; lectr. U. Nev., Las Vegas, 1992-93; asst. prof. English Troy State U., Dothan, Ala., 1994—. Author: Middle English Historiography, 1993. Mem. Internat. Soc. Anglo-Saxonists, Medieval Assn. of Pacific. Office: Troy State U Dept English 501 University Dr Dothan AL 36304

ALBERGA, ALTA WHEAT, artist; b. Ala.; d. James Richard and Leila Savannah (Sullivan) Wheat; BA, MA, Wichita State U., 1954; BFA, Washington U., St. Louis, 1961; MFA, U. Ill., 1964; m. Alvyn Clyde Alberga, Dec. 3, 1930. Mem. faculty Wichita (Kans.) State U., 1955-56, Webster Coll., St. Louis, 1969. art tchr. Ossining (N.Y.) High Sch., 1968; asst. prof., head visual arts Presbyn. Coll., Clinton, S.C., 1969-74; pvt. art tchr., Greenville, S.C., 1972—; substitute tchr. Greenville County Schs.; tchr. painting Tempo Gallery Sch., Greenville, 1974—, Greenville County Mus. Sch., 1975—, Tryon (N.C.) Fine Arts Ctr., 1986 (merit award 1987); tchr. Tri-County Tech. Coll., Pendleton, S.C., 1975. One-woman shows include Greenville County Mus., 1979, Greenville Artists Guild Gallery, 1979, 83, Wichita State U., 1954, St. Louis Artists Guild, 1956, N.C. State U., 1965, 66, Met. Arts Council, Greenville, 1980, 83, 85, Tryon Fine Arts Ctr., 1988, S.C. State U., 1992, 93; exhibited in group shows at Pickens County Mus., 1979, 88-89, Internation, Washington, 1981-82, Greenville Artists Guild, 1982, 88, Art/7, Washington, 1983, N.C. Univ., Charlotte invitational, 1989, Furman U. Women's Show, 1989, S.C. State U., 1992, Upstate Visual Arts, 1993, S.C. State U., 1993, Rolling Green Gallery, 1993, Internationale Grafiek Biennale, Maastricht, the Netherlands, 1993, S.C. Watercolor Soc., 1994 (award), Greenville County Mus. Art, 1995; represented in permanent collections S.C. State Mus., Columbia, S.C. Arts Commn., Pickens County Mus.; represented in pvt. collections; bd. dirs. Greenville Artists Guild, 1977-79, pres., 1985; bd. dirs. Guild Gallery, 1978, Guild Greenville Symphony, 1989-90. Recipient Richard K. Weil award St. Louis Mus., 1957; Purchase prize S.C. Arts Commn., 1972; Merritt award Greenville Mus., 1986, Pickens County Mus., 1987, 88; Cash award S.C. Water Color Assn. Mem. Artists Equity (pres. St. Louis chpt. 1962), Internat. Platform Assn. (life), Art Students League (life), Guild Greenville Artists (pres. 1984-85), S.C. Artists Guild, Southeastern Council Printmakers, Greenville Symphony Guild, Mus. Assn. (invited Greenville County Mus. 1993), Kappa Pi, Kappa Delta Pi. Democrat. Home: 11 Overton Ave Greenville SC 29617

ALBERS, EDWARD JAMES, SR., social studies educator; b. Centralia, Wash., July 6, 1922; s. Otto Johnson and Nell Genevieve Albers; m. Caroline Constance Cochran, July 30, 1944; 1 child, Edward James Jr. Student, Wash. State Coll., 1942, U. Ariz., 1949-51; BA, U. Nebr., Omaha, 1959; MA, Rollins Coll., 1966. Cert. tchr., Fla. Commd. 2d lt. USAF, 1944, advanced through grades to maj., 1961, pilot, 1944-65, served command pilot SAC, ret., 1965. Tchr. social studies Winter Park (Fla.) High Sch., 1966-96, chmn. dept. social studies, 1973-88. Decorated Yun-Hui medal, Chinese pilot wings. Mem. Nat. Geog. Soc., Air Force Assn., Burma Star (England), Mil. Order of the World Wars, Exptl. Aircraft Assn., Ret. Officers' Assn., China Assn., Burma Assn., India Assn., Santa Ana Calif. AAF Alumni, Sigma Phi Epsilon. Democrat. Episcopalian. Clubs: Train Collectors Assn., Lionel Collectors Assn., Officers' Club, Navy Base (Orlando), Hump Pilots' Assn., Corvette Club Cen. Fla., Daedalians. Avocation: antique toy train collecting, golf, scuba diving, snow and water skiing, flying. Office: 2100 Summerfield Rd Winter Park FL 32792-5037

ALBERT, PHILLIP, filmmaker and videographer; b. Oklahoma City. MA in Journalism, Radio-TV-Film, U. Okla., 1987. Film and video projects include My Trip to China, 1988, Tomorrow's In Our Pocket, 1989, Okla. Inner Views, 1990, Juneteenth on Greenwood, 1991, Mazareunner: The Life and Art of T.C. Cannon, 1993; exhibited for pub. screening Palace of Fine Arts, San Francisco, 1993, Arts Festival Atlanta, 1993, New Orleans Film and Video Festival, 1993, Dallas Video Festival, 1993, Met. Mus. Art, N.Y.C., 1994, Am. Film Inst. 13th Nat. Video Festival, L.A., 1994, Breckenridge (Colo.) Festival of Film, 1995, others; represented in permanent collections Smithsonian Instn's. Nat. mus. Am. Indian, Heard Mus., Phoenix; broadcast of Mazerunner, Bravo Cable Channel and Ind. Film Channel, 1995, KQED's Living Rm. Festival, San Francisco, 1996. Recipient Cert. Merit for spl. Achievement in Editing 27th Chgo. Internat. Film Festival, 1991, awards and honors from Best Exptl. Video award N.C. Internat. Film and Video Festival, 1993, Spl. Commendation, Can. Internat. Ann. Film Festival, Barrie, Ont., Can., 1993, CINE Eagle award Coun. Internat. Nontheatrical Events, 1993, 1st pl. Best short Exptl. Documentary award 20th Athens Internat. Film Video Festival, 1993, Bronze plaque 41st Ann. Columbus Internat. Film Video Festival, 1993, Juror's Choice award 1993 Charlotte Film and Video Festival, 1993, 1st pl. award 28th Bklyn. Arts Coun. Film and Video Festival, 1994, Best Made in Okla. Prodn. award, Best Exptl. Work award Am. Indian Film and Video Competition, 1994, Best Exptl. Video award 18th Atlanta Film and Video Festival, 1994, Worldfest Silver award 27th Worldfest-Houston Internat. Film and Video Festival, Worldfest Silver award 2d Worldfest-Charleston Internat. Film and Video Festival, 1994, Gold Seal award IAC Movie '94 Internat. Film Festival, Manchester, Eng., 1994, Bronze Cineman award, 27th Melbourne Internat. Film and Video Festival, 1994, Best Exptl. Work 23rd Festival of Nations Internat. Festival for Non-Comml. Film and Video, Ebensee, Austria, 1995. Mem. Kappa Tau Alpha. Home: 3230 NW 50th St Oklahoma City OK 73112-5325

ALBERTHAL, LESTER M., JR., information processing services executive; b. Corpus Christi, Tex., Feb. 27, 1944; married. BBA, U. Tex., 1967. With EDS, Plano, Tex., 1968—; v.p. ins. group Electronic Data Systems Corp., Plano, 1979-84; v.p. bus. ops. Electronic Data Systems Corp., Dallas, from 1984, pres., 1986-96, CEO, 1987—, also dir., chmn., 1989—. Office: Electronic Data Systems H2-7W-40 5400 Legacy Dr Plano TX 75024-3199

ALBERTO, PAUL A., special education educator; b. N.Y.C., May 1, 1947; s. Paul J. and Catherine (Pastorino) A. BA, CUNY, 1971; MS, Fordham U., 1973; PhD, Ga. State U., 1976. Tchr. spl. edn. N.Y.C. Bd. Edn.; prof. spl. edn. Ga. State U., Atlanta. Author: (with A. Troutman) Applied Behavior Analysis for Teachers, 4th edit., 1995, (with K. Heller, P.Forney and M. Schwartzman) Understanding Physical, Sensory and Health Impairments, 1996. With U.S. Army, 1967-69. Recipient Disting. Profl. award Ga. State U., 1986. Mem. Assn. for Persons with Severe Handicaps, Am. Assn. on Mental Retardation, Coun. for Exceptional Children.

ALBERTS, HAROLD, lawyer; b. San Antonio, Tex., Apr. 3, 1920; s. Bernard H. and Rose Alberts; m. Rose M. Gaskin, Mar. 25, 1945; children—Linda Rae, Barry Lawrence. LL.B., U. Tex.-Austin, 1942. Bar: Tex. 1943, U.S. Supreme Ct. 1950, U.S. Ct. Mil. Apls. 1959. Tchr., U. Tex. 1942; legal officer Chase Field, 1944; sole practice, Corpus Christi, Tex. Pres. Jewish Welfare Fund, Corpus Christi, 1948; chmn. Southwest Regional Anti-Defamation League, Tex. and Okla., 1970-71, chmn., 1969-72, chmn. Brotherhood Week, 1957; chmn. Nueces County (Tex.) Red Cross, 1959-61; mem. campaign exec. com., chmn. meetings United Community Services, 1961; v.p. Little Theatre, Corpus Christi, 1964; chmn. Corpus Christi NCCJ, 1967-69, nat. dir., 1974-76; bd. dirs. Tex. State Assn. Mental Health; pres. Combined Jewish Apl., Corpus Christi, 1974-76; moderator Friday Morning Group, 1975, 96. Served to lt. (sr. grade) USNR, 1942-46. Mem. ABA, Tex. Bar Assn., Corpus Christi Bar Assn. Clubs: Kiwanis (pres. 1962), B'nai B'rith (pres. 1955), Mason (32d degree). Home: 5314 Hulen Dr Corpus Christi TX 78413-2247 Office: PO Box 271477 Corpus Christi TX 78427-1477

ALBIN, LESLIE OWENS, biology educator; b. Spur, Tex., Jan. 8, 1940; s. John Leslie and Ottie Maude (Lassetter) A.; m. Monta Kay Gragg, Sept. 3,

1961 (div. 1982); children: Leslie Susan Albin Gann, Kimberly Ann Albin. BA, McMurry Coll., Abilene, 1962; MA, N. Tex. State U., 1969. Instr. biology E. Cen. State U., Ada, Okla., 1969-71; rsch. assoc. M.D. Andrson Hosp. & Tumor Inst., Houston, 1971; asst. prof. biology Western Tex. Coll., Snyder, 1971-74, assoc. prof. biology, 1974-77; prof., head dept. biology Austin (Tex.) C.C., 1977-78, 95—, chmn. divsn. natural scis., 1978-95. NDEA fellow, 1968. Mem. Am. Inst. Biol. Scis., Faculty Assn. Western Tex. Coll. (pres. 1973-74), Faculty Assn. Austin C.C. (pres. 1987-88), Faculty Senate Austin C.C. nity Coll, Tex. C.C.. Coll. Tchrs. Assn., Tex. Acad. Sci., Nat. Sci. Tchrs. Assn., Alpha Chi. Office: Austin Community Coll 1212 Rio Grande St Austin TX 78701-1710

ALBRECHT, ARTHUR JOHN, advertising agency executive; b. Woodhaven, N.Y., June 11, 1931; s. Charles Arthur and Anna (Klingner) A.; m. Sandi Edith Roberson, May 14, 1952; 1 child, Sherylyn. BA cum laude, Fla. State U., 1957. Salesman, sales promotion mgr., product mgr. Vick Chem. Co., N.Y.C., 1958-63; group product mgr. Whitehall Labs., N.Y.C., 1963-65; v.p. mktg. J.B. Williams Inc., N.Y.C., 1965-66; sr. v.p. mktg. Mitchum-Thayer div. Revlon, N.Y.C., 1966-71; sr. v.p., mgmt. supr. William Esty Co. Inc., N.Y.C., 1971-81; pres. Petersen Albrecht Co., N.Y.C., 1981-85, Albrecht Advt., Inc., Boca Raton, Fla., 1985—; adj. asst. prof. Pace U., 1976-85; bd. dirs. Brand Acceleration, Inc., N.Y.C., Damon Therepeutics, Inc., N.Y.C., Advanced Response Corp., Del.; cons./lectr., 1985—. Author: Magic Town, U.S.A, 1978; contbr.: articles to profl. jours. Ency. Advt. Pres. Villard Hill Assn., 1973-74. With USMC, 1950-55. Mem. Pharm. Advt. Club, Nat. Writers Club, Fla. State U. Alumni Assn., Internat. Platform Assn., Phi Beta Kappa, Phi Kappa Phi, Phi Eta Sigma, Alpha Delta Sigma (past chpt. pres., Outstanding Service award 1957), Indian Spring Country Club, Century Club. Republican. Unitarian. Home: 1148 Parkside Cir N Boca Raton FL 33486-8505

ALBRECHT, CAROL HEATH, artist, educator; b. Lafayette, Ind., May 26, 1921; d. Donald Leroy and Zula Elpha (Whicker) Heath; m. Edward Mathews Albrecht, May 25, 1944; children: Lynn, Catherine. Grad. high sch., Lafayette, Ind. Sec. U.S. Maritime Commn., San Francisco, 1941-44; mem. faculty art dept. Pensacola (Fla.) Jr. Coll., 1984-86, Eastern Shore Fine Arts Acad., Fairhope, Ala., 1986-91; presenter workshops in field, including oriental brush painting workshop/seminar, Sarasota, Fla., Clearwater, Fla., Pensacola. One-woman shows include Maison Le Cel, Ft. Walton Beach, Fla., 1976, 77, Whiting Gallery, Fairhope, 1989, Estate Gallery, Pensacola, 1991, Elliott Mus., Stuart, Fla., 1983; group shows include Fla. Watercolor Soc., Tallahassee, 1982, Pensacola Mus. Art, 1983-93, Sumi-e Soc. Am., Washington, 1982-94, Fla. Gulf Coast Art Ctr., Belleair, 1983, Asheville (N.C.) Mus. Art, 1983, Yosemite (Calif.) Renaissance Nat. Art Exhibit, 1987. Recipient purchase award Elliot Mus., 1983. Mem. Sumi-e Soc. Am. (pres. White Lotus chpt., Best in Show award 1990, Grumbacher gold medal 1991, Winsor-Newton award 1992, Sarasota chpt. award 1993, Shaffer award for brush mastery 1994, Reba Dickerson Hill Meml. award 1994). Home and Studio: 2026 Copley Dr Pensacola FL 32503-3349

ALBRECHT, URS EMANUEL, biochemist; b. Mexico City, Feb. 3, 1962; came to U.S., 1993; s. Theodor Ernst and Maria Theresia (Lötscher) A. Dipl. phil II, U. Zurich, 1988; Dr.phil.nat., U. Bern, Switzerland, 1993. Asst. in basic math. U. Zurich, 1985-86, asst. in biochemistry, 1987-88; asst. in zoology U. Bern, 1989-92, lectr., 1990-92; rsch. assoc., postdoctoral fellow Baylor Coll. Medicine, Houston, 1993—. Contbr. articles to profl. jours. Swiss Nat. Sci. Found. fellow, 1995. Mem. AAAS, Union Swiss Socs. for Exptl. Biology, Soc. for Developmental Biology, Soc. for Neurosci., Houston Football Assn.

ALBRIGHT, JOSEPH P., judge; b. Parkersburg, W.Va., Nov. 8, 1938; s. M.P. and Catherine (Rathbone) A.; m. Patricia Ann Deem, 1958 (dec. 1993); children: Terri Albright Cavi, Lettie Albright Elder, Joseph P. Jr., John Patrick (dec.); m. Nancie Gensert Divvens; stepchildren: Susan Divvens Bowman, Debbie Divvens Holcomb, Sandy Divvens Fox. BBA cum laude, U. Notre Dame, JD, 1962. Bar: W.Va. 1962, U.S. Dist. Ct. W.Va. 1962. Pvt. practice Parkersburg, 1964-95; asst. prosecuting atty. Wood County, 1965-68; city atty. City of Parkersburg, W.Va., 1968-70; judge W.Va. Supreme Ct. of Appeals, Charleston, 1995—; mem. W.Va. State Ethics Commn.; bd. dirs. Belpre (Ohio) Inc. Former clk. Charter Bd. of Parkerburg; mem. W.Va. Ho. of Dels., 1970-86, freshman mem. of jud. com., chmn. of ho. com. on edn., chmn. ho. com. on judiciary, 52nd spkr. of Ho. of Dels., 1984-86; mem., chmn. Blennerhassett Hist. Park Commn.; co-chmn. Blennerhassett Hist. Commn.; mem. St. Francis Xavier Ch., Parkersburg, past pres. parish adv. coun. Named Freshman Legislator of Yr., Charleston Gazette, 1970. Office: WVa Supreme Ct Appeals E 317 State Capital Charleston WV 25305*

ALBRINK, MARGARET JORALEMON, medical educator; b. Warren, Ariz., Jan. 6, 1920; d. Ira Beaman and Dorothy (Rieber) Joralemon; m. Wilhelm Stockman Albrink, Sept. 16, 1944 (dec. July 1991); children: Frederick Henry, Jonathan Wilhelm, Peter Varick. MA in Psychology cum laude, Radcliffe Coll., 1941; MS in Physiol. Chemistry, Yale U., 1943, MD, 1946, MPH, 1951. Diplomate Am. Bd. Med. Examiners, Am. Bd. Nutrition; lic. physician and surgeon, W.Va., Calif. Intern New Haven (Conn.) Hosp., 1946-47; NIH postdoctoral fellow Yale U., New Haven, 1947-49, fellow pub. health, 1950-51, instr. medicine, 1952-58, asst. prof. medicine, 1958-61; assoc. prof. W.Va. U., Morgantown, 1961-66, prof. medicine, 1966-90, prof. emeritus, 1990—, mem. grad. faculty, 1977-92; mem. med. and dental staff W.Va. U. Hosp., Morgantown, 1961—; vis. scientist Donner Lab., U. Calif., Berkeley, 1993-96; assoc. physician Grace-New Haven Cmty. Hosp., 1952-61; cons. nutrition study sect. NIH; vis. scholar U. Calif., Berkeley, 1977-78; established investigator Am. Heart Assn., 1958-63. Guest editor: Clinics in Endocrinology and Metabolism, 1976; guest editor Am. Jour. Clin. Nutrition, 1968, mem. editorial bd., 1963-68; mem. editorial adv. bd. Jour. Am. Coll. Nutrition, 1988-89; reviewer jours.; contbr. articles, chpts. and abstracts to profl. jours. Recipient Rsch. Career award Nat. Heart, Lung and Blood Inst., 1963-90. Fellow ACP, Am. Coll. Nutrition; mem. Am. Fedn. Clin. Rsch., Am. Soc. Clin. Investigation, Am. Soc. Clin. Nutrition, Am. Heart Assn. (fellow arteriosclerosis coun., fellow coun. epidemiology), Am. Diabetes Assn. (epidemiology coun.), Alpha Omega Alpha, Sigma Xi, Phi Beta Kappa. Democrat. Home: 817 Augusta Ave Morgantown WV 26505-6237 Office: WVa U Dept Medicine Box 9159 Morgantown WV 26506-9159

ALBRITTON, DEBORAH LYNN, health administrator; b. Greenville, N.C., July 15, 1963; d. Quill and Joyce (Jolly) A. BS, East Carolina U., 1986, MPA, 1990; postgrad., Penn State U., 1990. Registered health educator. Tchr. inter D.H. Conley High Sch., 1985; pub. involvement coord., health edn. intern, planner Eastern Carolina Health Systems Agy., 1986; adminstrv. intern Pitt County Meml. Hosp., 1987; grad. rsch. asst. dept. community health East Carolina U., 1986-90; asst. editor PNG Publs., 1990-91, mng. editor, 1991-92, edn., promotion, 1990-92; rsch. asst., tobacco policy specialist, patient counselor W.Va. U., 1990-91; health policy cons., community devel. specialist Eastern N.C. Poverty Ctr., 1990—, 92-93; health dir. Kinston (N.C.) Community Health Ctr., Inc., 1993-94; cons. Pitt-Greenville Wellness Coun., 1987, rep. to Am. Exec. Dirs. Meeting, Omaha, 1988. Contbr. articles to profl. jours. Vol. dept. phys. therapy Regional Rehab. Ctr., 1982-84, Eastern Carolina Vocat. Ctr., 1983-84, Remedial Edn. Activity Program, 1984; mem. Pitt County Young Dems., N.C. Equity's Women's Resource Ctr. Named Pitt County Meml. Hosp. Outstanding Vol., 1985; recipient Most Outstanding Sr. award in Dept. of Health, Phys. Edn., Recreation and Safety/Sch. and Community Health Edn., East Carolina U., 1986, First Place, Grad. Student Paper award N.C. Chpt. Soc. for Pub. Health Edn., 1988. Mem. ASPA, N.C. Pub. Health Assn., N.C. Chpt. Soc. for Pub. Health Edn., Inc., N.C. AHPERD, The Acad. Polit. Sci., Phi Alpha Alpha, Phi Sigma Pi, Gamma Beta Phi, Eta Sigma Gamma. Home: 105 Woodside Cir Snow Hill NC 28580-1546

ALBRITTON, WILLIAM HAROLD, III, federal judge; b. Andalusia, Ala., Dec. 19, 1936; s. Robert Bynum and Carrie (Veal) A.; m. Jane Rollins Howard, June 2, 1958; children: William Harold IV, Benjamin Howard, Thomas Bynum. A.B., U. Ala., 1959, LL.B., 1960. Bar: Ala. 1960. Assoc. firm Albrittons & Rankin, Andalusia, 1962-66, ptnr., 1966-76; ptnr. firm Albrittons & Givhan, Andalusia, 1976-86; ptnr. Albrittons, Givhan & Clifton, Andalusia, 1986-91; judge U.S. Dist. Ct. (mid. dist.) Ala., Montgomery, 1991—. Pres. Ala. Law Sch. Found., 1988-91, Ala. Law Inst. Fellow Am. Coll. Trial Lawyers, Am. Bar Found.; mem. ABA, Ala. State Bar (commr. 1981-89, disciplinary commn. 1981-84, v.p. 1985-86, pres.-elect 1989-90, pres. 1990-91), Am. Judicature Soc., Am. Inns of Ct., Bluewater Bay Sailing Club, Bluewater Bay Country Club, Phi Beta Kappa, Phi Delta Phi, Omicron Delta Kappa, Alpha Tau Omega. Office: US Dist Ct S Court St Rm 311 Montgomery AL 36104-4009

ALBURY, CHARLIE POWELL, school psychologist; b. West Palm Beach, Fla.; d. Charlie B. Powell and Retha Mae (Byrd) Phillips; m. Thomas Leo Albury, Jr., July 8, 1978. AA, Roosevelt Jr. Coll., 1962; BA, Fisk U., 1964; MA, Atlanta U., 1973; D Psychology, Fla. Inst. Tech., 1986. Nat. cert. sch. psychol. Tchr. Dade County Pub. Schs., Miami, Fla., 1964-73, sch. psychol., 1973—; mem, Dade Monroe Alcohol, Drug Abuse, Mental Health Planning Coun., 1988-91. Mem. adv. bd. McKnight Ctr. of Excellence, 1990-91; life mem. NAACP; mem. Nat. Urban League, Nat. Coun. Negro Women, Nat. Coalition 100 Black Women; bd. dirs. Women Involved in Serving Humanity, 1992—; trustee Ch. of Open Door, United Ch. of Christ. Recipient cert. commendation Mental Health Assn. Dade County, 1986, Charlie Albury Day award Met. Dade County, 1988, Outstanding Cmty. Svc. award Algonquin Club, 1993, Outstanding Fraternal Leadership award So. Fla. Nat. Negro Bus. and Profl. Women's Club, 1995. Mem. Fla. Assn. Sch. Psychologists, South Eastern Psychol. Assn., Dade Assn. Sch. Psychologists (sec. 1983-85, pres. 88-89, Sch. Psycholgist of Yr. 1990), Order of Eastern Star (Prince Hall affiliated, past worthy matron T.A. Rolle chpt. #137), Heroines of Jericho (sr. matron St. Maria Ct. #50, 1990—), Order of Golden Circle (1.1 ruler Deborah Assembly #10), Phylaxis Soc. (life mem. Phyllis chpt.), Crusaders (grand registrar Hattie C. Dandridge Grand Guild 1988—), Daus. of Isis (imperial oriental guide, imperial ct.), Alpha Kappa Alpha (life), Psi Chi, Phi Delta Kappa. Democrat. Office: Dade County Public Schs 1080 La Baron Dr Miami FL 33166-6064

ALCALA, JOSE RAMON, anatomy educator; b. Ponce, P.R., May 1, 1940; s. Jose Antonio and Aurea Estela (Ruiz) A.; m. Susan Elizabeth Vesper, Aug. 7, 1964; 1 child, Omar Dante. BA, U. Mo., 1964, MA, 1966; PhD, U. Ill., Chgo., 1972. Instr. biology Mt. Union Coll., Alliance, Ohio, 1967-69; prof. Wayne State U. Sch. Medicine, Detroit, 1972-92; prof., chair dept. anatomy Ponce Sch. Medicine, 1992-95. Contbr. numerous articles and abstracts to sci. jours., chpts. to books. Rsch. grantee Nat. Eye Inst., 1984-89, 90—. Mem. AAAS, AAUP, Am. Assn. Anatomists, Assn. for Rsch. in Vision and Ophthalmology, Internat. Soc. for Eye Rsch., Am. Assn. Clin. Anatomists, Sigma Xi. Office: Ponce Sch Medicine Dept Anatomy PO Box 7004 Ponce PR 00732-7004

ALCANTARA, FELICISIMA GARCIA, dietitian, nutrition consultant; b. Manila, Oct. 26, 1938; came to U.S., 1971; d. Pascual Cruz and Matilde Castro Garcia; m. Filemon Ocampo Alcantara, May 22, 1966; children: Philip, Manny. BS with honors in Food and Nutrition, Centro Escolar U., Manila, 1960; MS in Food and Nutrition, U. Ill., 1965. Lic. dietitian, Fla.; registered Am. Dietetic Assn. Dietetic intern Ind. U. Med. Ctr., Indpls., 1960-61; staff dietitian St. Elizabeth Med. Ctr., Dayton, 1962-63; rsch. asst. U. Ill., Urbana, 1963-65; assoc. prof. St. Paul Coll., Manila, 1965-68; community nutritionist Cleve. Met. Gen. Hosp., 1973-76; cons. nutritionist various midwestern extended care facilities, 1977-83; dir. dietary svcs. Gainesville (Fla.) Nursing Ctr., 1983-84; clin. dietitian Tacachale Community of Excellence, Gainesville, 1985—. Mem. Am. Dietetic Assn., Fla. Dietetic Assn. Roman Catholic.

ALDAVE, BARBARA BADER, law educator, lawyer; b. Tacoma, Dec. 28, 1938; d. Fred A. and Patricia W. (Burns) Bader; m. Ralph Theodore Aldave, Apr. 2, 1966; children—Anna Marie, Anthony John. B.S., Stanford U., 1960; J.D., U. Calif.-Berkeley, 1966. Bar: Oreg. 1966, Tex. 1982. Assoc. law firm Eugene, Oreg., 1967-70; asst. prof. U. Oreg., 1970-73; vis. prof. U. Calif., Berkeley, 1973-74; from vis. prof. to prof. U. Tex., Austin, 1974-89, co-holder James R. Dougherty chair for faculty excellence, 1981-82, Piper prof., 1982, Joe A. Worsham centennial prof., 1984-89, Liddell, Sapp, Zivley, Hill and LaBoon prof. banking financial and comml. law, 1989; dean sch. law St. Mary's U., San Antonio, 1989—; vis. prof. Northeastern U., 1985-88; ABA rep. to Coun. Inter-ABA, 1995—; NAFTA chpt. 19 panelist, 1994—. Pres. NETWORK, 1985-89; chair Gender Bias Task Force of Supreme Ct. Tex., 1991-94; bd. dirs. Partnership for Hope, Tex. Resource Ctr., Assn. Religiously Affiliated Law Schs., Lawyer's com. for Civil Rights Under Law of Tex., Mex. Am. Legal Def. and Ednl. Fund. Recipient Tchg. Excellence award U. Tex. Student Bar Assn., 1976, Appreciation awards Thurgood Marshall Legal Soc. of U. Tex., 1979, 81, 85, 87, Tchg. Excellence award Chicano Law Students Assn. of U. Tex., 1984, Hermine Tobolowsky award Women's Law Caucus of U. Tex., 1985, Ethics award Kugle, Stewart, Dent & Frederick, 1988, Leadership award Women's Law Assn. St. Mary's U., 1989, Ann. Inspirational award Women's Advocacy Project, 1989, Appreciation award San Antonio Black Lawyers Assn., 1990, Spl. Recognition award Nat. Conv. Nat. Lawyers Guild, 1990, Spirit of the Am. Woman award J. C. Penney Co., 1992, Sarah T. Hughes award Women and the Law sect. State Bar Tex., 1994, Ann. Tchg. award Soc. Am. Law Tchrs., 1996. Mem. ABA (com. on corp. laws sect., banking and bus. law 1982-88), Bexar County Women's Bar Assn. (Belva Lockwood Outstanding Lawyer award 1991), San Antonio Bar Assn., Nat. Lawyers Guild, William S. Sessions Inn of Ct., World Affairs Coun. San Antonio, Harlan Soc., Tex. Women's Forum, Stanford U. Alumni Assn., Order of Coif, Phi Delta Phi, Iota Sigma Pi, Omicron Delta Kappa, Delta Theta Phi (Outstanding Law Prof. award St. Mary's U. chpt. 1990, 91). Roman Catholic. Home: 323 W Woodlawn Ave San Antonio TX 78212-3312 Office: St Mary's U 1 Camino Santa Maria St San Antonio TX 78228-5433

ALDERMAN, EUGENE WAYNE, metal products executive, mathematics educator; b. Tampa, Fla., June 13, 1936; s. Wade Hampton and Clyde (Register) A.; m. Patricia Ann Strickland, Aug. 18, 1955 (div. July 1973); children: David, Kimber, Stacey; m. Earlean Fay Gooding, Mar. 10, 1990; stepchildren: Andy, Shannon, Jake. BA, Stetson U., 1960; postgrad., Midwestern Bapt. Theol. Sem., Kansas City, Mo., 1960-63; postgrad. U. Ala., Tuscaloosa, 1965; MA, U. South Fla., 1970. Cert. Tchr., Fla.; ordained to ministry Bapt. Ch., 1955. Pastor Calvary Bapt. Ch., Welaka, Fla., 1958-60, Santa Rosa (Mo.) Bapt. Ch., 1960-63; curriculum dir. Hillsborough County Sch. Bd., Tampa, Fla., 1963-68, supr. tchr. corp., 1970-72; teaching asst. U. South Fla., Tampa, 1969-70; dist. mgr. edn. div. Reader's Digest, Pleasantville, N.Y., 1973-74; dir. talent devel. project Little Tenn. Valley Edn. Coop., Maryville, 1975-78; ptnr. Alderman's Spray Co., Tampa, 1979-81; pres. Dura-Static, Inc., Tampa, 1982-94; prof. math. Tri-County C.C., Murphy, N.C. Editor: (manual) Meeting the Challenge, 1978. Vice chmn. Hillsborough County I.D.E.A.L.S. Com., Tampa, 1968-69; mem. Tampa City Code Enforcement Bd., 1986-88. Named Fla. Star Tchr., Brevard County C. of C., 1968; fellow NSF, 1964, 65, U. South Fla., 1969-70. Mem. Phi Delta Kappa. Home and Office: PO Box 99 Morganton GA 30560-0099

ALDERSON, CREED FLANARY, JR., financial services executive; b. Norton, Va., Nov. 21, 1933; s. Creed Flanary and Mary (Ford) A.; BS in Commerce, U. Va., 1959; m. Nicola DeChurch, July 16, 1983; children: Robert Barney, Mary Anne. Vice pres., resident mgr. Dean Witter Reynolds, Ft. Lauderdale, Fla., 1974-79; sr. v.p., resident mgr. Smith Barney, Ft. Lauderdale, 1979-91; now sr. v.p. and regional mgr. Interstate/Johnson Lane, Asheville, N.C. 1st lt. C.E., U.S. Army, 1952-55. Mem. Biltmore Forest Country Club, Grove Park Inn and Country Club. Home: 3 Charlyn Dr Asheville NC 28803-2074 Office: Interstate/Johnson Lane Boston Way Fl 12 Asheville NC 28803-2657

ALDERSON, GLORIA FRANCES DALE, rehabilitation specialist; b. Rainelle, W.Va., May 11, 1945; d. Orval Rupert and Juanita Rose (Nelson) Dale; m. Grayson Raines Alderson, June 3, 1964; children: John Grayson, James Leslie, Kathy LeDawn. ADN, U. Charleston; BS, W.Va. U. DON Charleston Area Med. Ctr., Charleston, 1977-84; head nurse Eye & Ear Clinic, Charleston, 1981-84; owner, operator ABZ Nursing, Kanawha County, W.Va., 1983-87; rehab. specialist W.Va., 1983—; bd. dirs. Profl. and Social Com. on Nursing. Bd. dirs. Urban Politics Symposium, Charleston, 1978; election campaign mgr. Rep. Party, Charleston. Scholarship Bd. Regents, 1974-77. Mem. AAUW, Am. Rehab. Profls., Internat. Platform Assn., Order Ea. Star. Home and Office: 1089 Highland Dr Saint Albans WV 25177-3675

ALDRETE, JOAQUIN SALCEDO, surgeon, educator, researcher; b. Mexico City, Mar. 2, 1936; came to U.S., 1960; s. Joaquin M. and Maria Refugio (Salcedo) A.; m. Melinda Luz Santoyo, June 5, 1960; 1 child, Gregory Scott. BS in Biology, Centro U. Mex., Mexico City, 1952; MD, Nat. U., Mexico City, 1959; MS in Surgery, U. Minn., 1968. Diplomate Am. Bd. Surgery. Intern Rochester (N.Y.) Gen. Hosp., 1960-61, resident in surgery, 1961-62; resident in surgery Mayo Clinic, Rochester, Minn., 1962-67; asst. prof. surgery U. Ala., Birmingham, 1969-71, assoc. prof. surgery, 1971-75, prof. surgery, 1975—, vice chmn. dept. surgery, 1986—, dir. gastrointestinal surgery sect., 1975—; dir. Surgeon's Asst. Program, U. Ala., Birmingham, 1984—. Contbr. 10 chpts. to books, 120 papers to med. jours. Capt. U.S. Army, 1967-69. Howard K. Gray fellow, 1966; recipient Spl. Recognition, Guadalajara (Mex.) chpt., ACS, 1984. Mem. Columbian Soc. Gastroent. (corr. mem.), Collegium Internat. Chriurgiae Digestivae (U.S. chpt. bd. trustees 1977), So. Med. Assn. (sec. 1975-78, chmn. 1978-79, sect. of surgery, assoc. councilor 1979-81, councilor 1982-87), Colombian Soc. Critical Care (corr. mem.), Nat. Acad. Medicine Mex. (corr. mem.), Mex. Acad. Surgery (corr. mem.), Assn. Mil. Surgeons, Am. Gastroent. Assn., Am. Surg. Assn., So. Surg. Assn., Assn. Acad. Surgery, ACS, Soc. Univ. Surgeons, Sigma Xi, and others. Republican. Office: Univ of Ala Dept of Surgery University Sta Birmingham AL 35205

ALDRICH, C. ELBERT, real estate broker; b. Rosebud, Tex., Sept. 12, 1923; s. Murdock Collins and Mamie (Mock) A.; m. Dorothy Ann Cox, June 30, 1947; children: Ann Aldrich Dunn, Amy Aldrich Thomas. Student, Temple Jr. Coll., 1946-47. Co-owner M.C. Aldrich & Son, Temple, Tex., 1946-65; pres. Elbert Aldrich Realtor, Inc., Temple, 1965—; bd. dirs. 1st Fed. Savs. & Loan, Temple, Temple Indsl. Found. Served with USN, 1942-46, PTO. Decorated D.F.C.; named Realtor of Yr., Temple Bd. Realtors, 1971, 73, 77, Farm and Land Broker of Yr., Tex. chpt. Farm and Land Inst., 1979. Mem. Realtors Land Inst. (regional v.p. 1977-79, pres. Tex. chpt. 1978), Soc. Indsl. Realtors (pres. South Cen. Tex. chpt. 1989-90), Realtors Nat. Mktg. Inst. (cert.), Tex. Assn. Realtors (bd. dirs. 1965), Nat. Assn. Realtors, Temple C. of C. (v.p. 1973-75). Baptist. Lodges: Rotary, Masons, Shriners, Descendents of San Jacinto. Home: 2410 Birdcreek Dr Temple TX 76502-1242 Office: 18 N 3rd St Temple TX 76501-7617

ALDRICH, DAVID ALAN, accountant; b. West Haven, Conn., Jan. 14, 1958; s. Harold and Janet (Candia) A. BS in Fin. Acctg., U. New Haven, 1980; BS in Profl. Acctg., Tampa Coll., 1990. CPA, Fla. Acct. State Nat. Bank of Conn., Bridgeport, 1981-82, Coordinated Benefit Plans Inc., Tampa, Fla., 1984-85, N.Am. Telephone, Tampa, 1986; acctg. mgr. Coordinated Benefit Plans Inc., Tampa, 1987-90; acct. Payroll Transfers, Inc., Tampa, 1991—. Mem. AICPA, Fla. Inst. CPAs. Home: 11261 Riddle Dr Spring Hill FL 34609-3439

ALDRICH, LOVELL W(ELD), lawyer; b. Port Chester, N.Y., Dec. 21, 1942; s. Laurence Weld and Leota (Burton) A.; m. Sharon King, Aug. 20, 1966; children: Molly Colleen, Abigail Elizabeth. BBA in Fin., Tex. A&M U., 1965; JD, St. Mary's U., San Antonio, 1968. Bar: Tex. 1968, U.S. Dist. Ct. (so. dist.) Tex. 1971, U.S. Dist. Ct. (ea. dist.) Tex. 1980, U.S. Ct. Appeals (5th cir.) 1981. Assoc. Law Office of Fred Parks, Houston, 1970-72, Lloyd & Hoppess, Houston, 1972-75; sole practice Houston, 1975-78; ptnr. Aldrich & Buttrill, Houston, 1978-81, Aldrich, Buttrill & Kuhn, Houston, 1981-87, Lovell W. Aldrich & Assocs., A Profl. Legal Corp., Houston, 1987—. Served to capt. U.S. Army, 1968-70, Vietnam. Mem. ATLA, ABA, Tex. Trial Lawyers Assn., Tex. Bar Assn. (cert. personal injury trial law, bd. cert. legal specialization personal injury trial law), Am. Bd. Trial Advs. Episcopalian. Home: 1007 Horseshoe Dr Sugar Land TX 77478-3460 Office: Lovell W Aldrich & Assocs PC 1201 Louisiana St Ste 3180 Houston TX 77002-5608

ALDRIDGE, ADRIENNE YINGLING, accountant, consultant; b. Hershey, Pa., June 10, 1959; d. Richard Terry Yingling and Dolores Jean (Ott) Brown. BA in Acctg. summa cum laude, N.C. State U., 1989. CPA, FLMI. Asst. mgr. Fast Fare, Raleigh, 1979-80; statis. analyst S.P.A.R., Elmsford, N.Y., 1980-81; relocation dir., sales assoc. Realty World, Cary, N.C., 1981-83; product mgr. Southeastern Electronics, Raleigh, 1983-84; results acct. No. Telecom, Rsch. Triangle Park, N.C., 1984-88; sr. auditor Deloitte & Touche, 1989-93; group contr. SPAR Mktg., Bloomington, Minn., 1994; pvt. practice, 1995; acctg. mgr. U. N.C. Physicians & Assocs., Chapel Hill, 1996—. Mem. AICPA, NCACPA, Phi Kappa Phi, Omicron Delta Epsilon. Avocations: photography, painting, physical fitness, travel, music. Home: 6116 River Landings Dr Raleigh NC 27604 Office: 143 W Franklin St Ste 600 Chapel Hill NC 27516

ALEWINE, JAMES WILLIAM, financial executive; b. Williamston, S.C., Apr. 26, 1930; s. David Andrew and Ruby Mae (Moore) A.; B.A., Carolina Sch. Commerce, 1961; m. Bobbie Sue Crawford, June 18, 1949; children—David, Susan. With Daniel Internat. Corp., 1947-92, mgr. internal audit, Greenville, S.C., 1970-72, adminstrv. mgr. M & M div., 1972-73, fin. adminstr., Jenkinsville, S.C., 1973-77, mgr. accounting M-E-T Group, Greenville, 1977-78, asst. treas., 1978-92. Served with USN, 1952-55; maj. S.C. State Guard, 1993—. Cert. internal auditor, S.C. Mem. Inst. Internal Auditors (pres. Palmetto chpt. 1975-76), Masons (past grand high priest, knight York grand cross of honour, 32d degree), Scottish Rite, Elks. Baptist. Home: 2 Broad St Williamston SC 29697-1808

ALEXANDER, ANDREW LAMAR (LAMAR ALEXANDER), lawyer, former secretary of education, former governor; b. Maryville, Tenn., July 3, 1940; s. Andrew Lamar and Genevra Floreine (Rankin) A.; m. Leslee Kathryn Buhler, Jan. 4, 1969; children: Andrew, Leslee, Kathryn, Will. B.A., Vanderbilt U., 1962; J.D., NYU, 1965. Bar: Tenn. 1965. Law clk. to Hon. John Wisdom U.S. Ct. Appeals (5th cir.), New Orleans; assoc. Fowler, Rountree, Fowler & Robertson, Knoxville, 1965; legis. asst. to Senator Howard Baker, 1967-68; exec. asst. to Bryce Harlow, White House Congl. Liaison Office, 1969-70; ptnr. Dearborn and Ewing, Nashville, 1970-76; gov. State of Tenn., Nashville, 1979-87; chmn. Leadership Inst. Belmont Coll., Nashville, 1987-88; pres. U. Tenn., 1988-91; sec. Dept. Edn., Washington, 1991-93; counsel Baker, Donelson, Bearman & Caldwell, Nashville, 1993—; mem. Pres.'s Task Force on Federalism; chmn. Nat. Govs. Assn., 1985-86, Pres.'s Commn. on Ams. Outdoors, 1985-87; co-director Empower Am., 1994-95. Author: Steps Along the Way, 1986, Six Months Off, 1988, We Know What To Do, 1995; co-editor: The New Promise of American Life, 1995. Mgr. Winfield Dunn for Gov. Campaign, 1970, chief transition, 1970-71; Rep. nominee for Gov. of Tenn., 1974; chmn. Rep. Exch. Satellite Network, 1993-95; Rep. Presdl. candidate, 1995-96. Recipient Nat. Disting. Svc. to Edn. award Burger King, 1988, James B. Conant award Edn. Commn. of the States, 1988, Disting. State Leadership award Am. Assn. State Colls. and Univs., 1989, Teddy Roosevelt award Nat. Coll. Athletic Assn., 1993, honored as Silver Anniversary scholar-athlete, 1987; NYU Law Sch. Root-Tilden scholar. Fellow (sr.) Hudson Inst.; mem. Phi Beta Kappa. Republican. Presbyterian. Office: Baker Donelson 511 Union St Nashville TN 37219-1733

ALEXANDER, ARTHUR FRANK, sales executive; b. Anderson, S.C., July 29, 1948; s. Linnaeus Garnett and Dorothy Frances (Clement) A.; m. Kathleen Gramling, July 17, 1971. BS, Cen. (S.C.) Wesleyan Coll., 1971. Sch. tchr. Crescent High Sch., Iva, S.C., 1971-72; sales rep. Armour-Dial div. Dial Corp., 1972—. Named Jaycee of Quarter, dist. 6 Anderson Jaycees, 1982 (2), Outstanding Program Mgr., Anderson Jaycees, 1982-83, Outstanding Bd. Mem., Anderson Jaycees, 1982-83. Republican. Baptist. Lodge: Lions (bd. dirs. 1986—, Lion of Yr. 1986). Home: 308 Holly Ridge Dr Anderson SC 29621-2069

ALEXANDER, BEVERLY MOORE, mechanical engineer; b. Portsmouth, Va., Apr. 11, 1947; d. Julian Morgan and Ezefferlee (Griffin) Moore; m. Ronald Lee Rutherford, Dec. 21, 1969 (div. Dec. 1977); m. Larry Ray Alexander, Mar. 4, 1978. BS, Aero. Engring., Va. Poly. Inst. and State U., 1969; postgrad., U. New Orleans. Registered profl. engr., La. Assoc. engr. McDonnell Douglas Corp., St. Louis, 1969-74; design engr. Bell Aerospace Textron, New Orleans, 1974-81; supr. systems integration, New Orleans, 1981-83, chief interface activities, 1983-84; chief engr. Bell Aerospace Textron, New Orleans, 1984-85, dir. engring. planning and control, 1985-86, chief engr. engring. svcs., 1986-88, asst. chief engr., supr. of shipbuilding USN, New Orleans, 1988—. Mem. La. Engring. Soc., NAFE, ASNE (sect.

chmn. 1992, vice chmn. 1993), SNAME. Republican. Presbyterian. Office: PO Box 6401 New Orleans LA 70174-6401

ALEXANDER, BURT EDWARD, quality improvement consultant, management consultant; b. Warren, Pa., June 21, 1946; s. Robert Henry and Margaret (Beckenbach) A.; m. Patricia Alene Wolfe, Mar. 15, 1969 (div.); 1 child, Jeffrey Robert; m. Lida Frances Greene, May 29, 1971; children: William Andrew, Christopher Edward. BS in Phys. Edn., W.Va. Wesleyan Coll., 1968; MA in Human Resource Mgmt., Pepperdine U., 1981; postgrad., Va. Poly. Inst. and State U., 1983-84. Mgmt. cons. Achievements in Mgmt., Unltd., Knoxville, Tenn., 1989-90; quality improvement cons. QualPro, Knoxville, 1990—. Pres. San Onofre PTO, Camp Pendleton, Calif., 1979-81; chmn. San Onofre Parents Action Com., Camp Pendleton, 1980-82; mem. U.S. English, Inc., Washignton, 1986—; mem. Fedn. for Am. Immigration Reform, Washington, 1986—; bd. dirs. Setenga chpt. Nat. Multiple Sclerosis Soc., 1994-96. Lt. col. USMC, 1968-89. Mem. Am. Soc. Quality Control, Retired Officers Assn., Kiwanis of West Knoxville (v.p, pres. elect 1991-93). Republican. Methodist. Office: QualPro 3117 Pellissippi Pky Knoxville TN 37931-3036

ALEXANDER, CHARLES, housing authority executive; b. Ft. Pierce, Fla., Dec. 10, 1942; s. George and Chris (Butler) A.; m. Ola M. Shelton, July 6, 1968; 1 child, Carlos David. BS, Troy State U., 1979, MS, 1987; MS, Troy State U., 1989. Enlisted U.S. Army, 1961, advanced through grades to master sgt., 1982; ret., 1984; from north area cluster mgr. to mgr. Columbus (Ga.) Housing Authority; exec. dir. Warner Robins (Ga.) Housing Authority, 1990; dir. youth counselors Elizabeth Canty, Warren Williams Apts., Columbus, 1988-90. Vol. worker Sta. FOXY-FM, Columbus, 1989-90; telephone operator United Negro Coll. Fund Campaign, Columbus, 1990; Omega chmn. membership A.J. McClung YMCA, Columbus, 1990. Mem. Nat. Assn. Housing R.O., Am. Assn. Ret. Persons, Omega Psi Phi (vice basileus 1987-89, basileus 1990). Methodist. Office: Warner Robins Housing Auth PO Box 2048 Warner Robins GA 31099-2048

ALEXANDER, CONSTANCE JOY (CONNIE ALEXANDER), stone sculptor; b. Hillsboro, Ohio, Oct. 13, 1939; d. Laurence Adair and Martha Ellen (Hill-Overman) Lucas; m. Anfred Agee Alexander, June 6, 1959; children: Troy Arthur, Andrea Ellen. Grad., Cin. Art Acad., 1961, postgrad., 1962; postgrad., Atlanta Coll. of Art, 1977. represented by Miller Gallery Cin., also various galleries in Ga. and Fla. Exhibited in group exhibitions at Southeastern Artists Ga. Jubilee Festival (1st in sculpture award 1974), Southeastern Arts & Crafts Festival, Macon (Ga.) Colisuem, 1977 (1st in sculpture), World's Fair, Knoxville, Tenn., 1982, David Schaeffer Gallery, Alpharetta, Ga., 1988-93, Ga. Marble Festival, Jasper, 1989 (1st place award), Ariel Gallery, Soho, N.Y., 1989 (award of excellence), 90, 45th Ann. Pen & Brush Sculpture Exhbn., Soho, N.Y., 1991 (Excalibur Bronze Sculpture Foundry award), Ariel Gallery, Soho, 1989-91, Tim Verstegen's The Dutch Framer Gallery, Canton, Ga., 1989-93, Artistic Frames & Gallery, Jasper, Ga., 1991-93, Buckhead Trinity Arts Group, Atlanta, Ga., 1994, Gallery 300, Atlanta, 1994; represented in permanent collections Cin. Pub. Libr., Ga. Inst. Tech., Atlanta, Hartsfield Internat. Airport, North Dekalb Coll., Coca-Cola Internat. Hdqs. Mem. Soc. of Friends. Home: PO Box 67 Canton GA 30114-0067 Office: Trinity Arts Gallery 315 E Paces Ferry Rd NE Atlanta GA 30305-2307

ALEXANDER, DEBORAH RADFORD, elementary education administrator; b. Knoxville, Tenn., July 29, 1953; d. Frank Stanley and Elizabeth Anne (Poer) Radford; m. Bobby Davis, Jan. 3, 1992. BA in Religious Studies, U. Tenn., 1973, MS in Spl. Edn., 1975, EdS in Curriculum and Instrn., 1979, EdD in Curriculum and Instrn., 1982, postdoctoral. Cert. spl. edn. tchr., K-12 adminstr. and supr., career level III tchr., Tenn. Head Start Mideast Community Action Agy., Kingston, Tenn., 1975-77; resource tchr. Roane County Schs., Kingston, 1978-94, designated prin., 1992-94, asst. prin., 1994-96, prin., 1996—. Contbr. articles to profl. jours. Mem. NEA, ASCD, NAESP, Nat. Assn. Secondary Sch. Prins., Coun. for Exceptional Children, Am. Ednl. Rsch. Assn., Assn. for Children With Learning Disabilities, Tenn. Edn. Assn., Roane County Edn. Assn. (pres. 1986-87), Am. Contract Bridge League (pres. Tennessee Valley unit 1986-87), Oak Ridge Bridge Assn. (pres. 1983-84), Am. Belgian Malinois Club (sec. 1984-90, pres. 1991-95, bd. dirs. 1995—), Coun. Adminstrs. Spl. Edn., Phi Kappa Phi. Home: PO Box 5747 Oak Ridge TN 37831-5747 Office: Kingston Elem Sch 2009 Kingston Hwy Kingston TN 37763-4831

ALEXANDER, EDNA M. DEVEAUX, elementary education educator; d. Richard and Eva (Musgrove) DeVeaux. BBA, Fla. A & M U., 1943; BS in Elem. Edn., Fla. A&M U., 1948; MS in Supervision and Adminstrn., U. Pa., 1954; cert., U. Madrid, 1961; postgrad., Dade Jr. Coll., U. Miami. Sec. Dunbar Elem. Sch., 1943-46, tchr., 194-55; tchr. Orchard Villa Elem., 1959-66; prin. A. L. Lewis Elem. Sch., 1955-57; reading specialist North Cen. Dist., 1966-69; tchr. L. C. Evans Elem. Sch., 1969-71; first black woman newscaster in Miami, Sta. WBAY, 1948. V.p. Fla. Council on Human Relations Dade County, Coun. for Internat. Visitors Greater Miami; past pres. Episcopal Churchwomen of Christ Ch., Miami; bd. dirs. YWCA; vice chmn. Community Action Agy. Dade County; chmn. Dade County Minimum Housing Appeals Bd.; active Vol. Unltd. Project Nat. Coun. Negro Women; sponosr Am. Jr. Red Cross, Girl Scouts U.S.; trustee Fla. Internat. U. Found., 1974-79; mem. Jacksonville Symphony Assn. Guild. Named to Miami Centennial Women's Hall of Fame, 1996. Mem. AAUW (life, Edna M. DeVeaux Alexander fellowship named in her honor Miami br.), NEA (life), LWV, Fla. Edn. Assn., Classroom Tchrs. Assn., Dade County Edn. Assn. (chmn. pub. rels. com.), Dade County Reading Assn., Assn. for Childhood Edn., Internat. Reading Tchr. Assn., U. Pa. Alumni Assn., Alpha Kappa Alpha. Home: 805 Blue Gill Rd PO Box 26063 Jacksonville FL 32226

ALEXANDER, ELIZABETH FAYE TUTOR, nursing educator; b. Pontotoc, Miss., Oct. 27, 1940; d. Vearl Arlis and Rozelle Lavonia (Walls) Tutor; m. Kenneth Barber Alexander, Aug. 9, 1959; children: Kenneth Barber, Sherrie Alexander Williams. ADN, John C. Calhoun Community Coll., 1976. Cert. Red Cross instr. Dir. nursing asst. course Nash Community Coll., Rocky Mount, N.C.; supr. newborn nursery Florence (S.C.) Gen. Hosp.; dialysis nurse VA, Salem, Va.; instr. Nash Community Coll., Rocky Mt., N.C.

ALEXANDER, HAROLD CAMPBELL, insurance consultant; b. Houston, Dec. 11, 1920; s. Henry Campbell and Essie Mae (Gilbert) A.; m. Dorothy Emma Schraub, Aug. 21, 1925; children: Linda Carol, Beverly Lynn Whitworth, Daniel James Alexander, William Campbell. BS, Miss. State U., 1938-42; postgrad., South Tex. Sch. Law, 1954-56, Harvard U., 1943, Navy Fin. and Supply Sch., 1942-43. Asst. div. credit mgr. Continental Emsco Co., Houston, 1953-56; gen. agt. and mgr. United Founders Life Ins. Co., 1956-69; mgr. Holt & Bridges Ins., Houston, 1960-69; owner, pres. Holt & Alexander Ins. Agy., Inc., Houston, 1969-85; ins. cons. Lawrence Ilfrey & Co., Houston, 1985—. Mem. Houston Adv. Council Bd., 1985; bd. dirs. 500 Club Ltd., Houston, 1984—. Served as lt. commdr. USN, 1942-46, 1950-52. Mem. Profl. Ins. Agts. Tex. (state bd. dirs. 1973-74), Soc. Cert. Ins. Counselors. Republican. Presbyterian. Club: Pine Forest Country, Club of Houston. Home and Office: 8727 Manhattan Dr Houston TX 77096-1318

ALEXANDER, JAMES PATRICK, lawyer; b. Glendale, Calif., Oct. 14, 1944; s. Victor Elwin and Thelma Elizabeth (O'Donnell) A.; m. Jeanne Elizabeth Bannerman, June 10, 1967; children: Rene Leigh, Amy Lynne. AB, Duke U., 1966, JD, 1969. Bar: Ala. 1969. Assoc. Bradley, Arant, Rose & White, Birmingham, Ala., 1969-75, ptnr., 1975—; adj. lectr. employment discrimination law U. Ala. Sch. of Law, 1981—; mem. exec. adv. com. spl. studies program U. Ala., Birmingham, 1991-93. Trustee Ala. chpt. Nat. Multiple Sclerosis Soc. (vice chmn. 1987-89, chmn. 1990-91). Mem. Birmingham Bar Assn., Ala. State Bar, ABA, Am. Arbitration Assn. (comml. arbitrator), Indsl. Rels. Rsch. Assn. (Ala. chpt.), Sigma Nu, Duke Law Alumni Assn. (pres. Ala. chpt. 1989-90). Home: 4309 Altamont Rd Birmingham AL 35213-2407 Office: Bradley Arant Rose & White 1400 Park Pl Tower 2001 Park Pl Birmingham AL 35203-2735

ALEXANDER, JOHN ROBERT, hospital administrator, internist; b. Tulsa, July 28, 1936; s. Hiram Marshall and Roberta Alice (Greene) A.; m. Marjorie Louise Okeson, Aug., 1958; children: Stephanie Maine, Paul Fulton, James Marshall, Cynthia Ann, Karen Louise, Robert Thomas. BS, U. Okla., 1958; MD, U. Okla., Oklahoma City, 1961. Intern St. John's Hosp., Tulsa, 1961-62, 1961-62; resident Meth. Hosp. of Dallas, Tex., 1962-65; resident in internal medicine Methodist Hosp. of Dallas, 1962-65; pres. Tulsa Internists, Ltd., 1974-89, Wheeling Med. Group, Inc., Tulsa, 1989-90; mem. staff St. John Med. Ctr., Tulsa, chief of staff, 1977-78, v.p. med. affairs, 1991—; vice chmn., bd. dirs. Physicians Liability Ins. Co., Oklahoma City; bd. dirs., mem. adv. coun. Okla. Bd. Nurse Registration and Nursing Edn., Oklahoma City; clin. prof. U. Okla. Coll. Medicine, 1974; mem. Okla. Bd. Med. Licensure and Supervision, Tulsa, 1993—, pres., 1995-96. Editor (report) Med. Edn. in Tulsa County, 1981. Pres. Tulsa County Heart Assn., 1970-71; elder Kirk of the Hills Presbyn. Ch., Tulsa, 1970—; med. dir. Wright City (Okla.) Free Health Clinic, 1975-80; chmn. bd. dirs. Tulsa County Health Dept., 1982; pres. bd. dirs. Tulsa Med. Edn., 1994—. Recipient Disting. Medical Svc. award U. Okla. Alumni Assn., 1995, Disting Svc. award Am. Heart Assn., 1971; named Friends of Nursing, Okla. Nurses Assn., 1990. Fellow ACP; mem. AMA (del. 1985—), Okla. State Med. Assn. (pres. 1989-90), Tulsa County Med. Soc. (pres. 1983), Tulsa Internists Soc.(pres. 1972), U. Okla. Alumni Assn. (pres. 1982-83), Rotary Club Will Rogers (pres. 1973-74), Alpha Omega Alpha. Republican. Home: 6733 S Gary Ave Tulsa OK 74136-4515 Office: St John Med Ctr 1923 S Utica Ave Tulsa OK 74104-6520

ALEXANDER, JUDD HARRIS, retired paper company executive; b. Owatonna, Minn., Mar. 23, 1925; s. Mark Hastings and Veta Enola (Harris) A.; m. Theo Mary Paltzer, May 19, 1956; children: Morah Lee, Duncan McIndoe, Todd Stewart. B.A., Carleton Coll., 1949; postgrad. in bus, Harvard U., 1967. Co-founder Nu-Bilt Co., Owatonna; dir. Nu-Bilt Co., 1942-71; sec. in pres.'s office, salesman Marathon Corp., Rothschild, Wis., 1949-57; with Am. Can Co., Greenwich, Conn., 1957-82, v.p., gen. mgr. spl. products packaging, 1972-73, sr. v.p. group exec. packaging, 1974-75, sr. v.p. office of chmn., 1975-81, exec. v.p. paper sector, 1981-82; exec. v.p. James River Corp., Norwalk, Conn., 1982-89, ret., 1989; chmn. Paperboard Packaging Council, 1976-78, Can Mfrs. Inst., 1978-80, Solid Waste Coun. of Paper Industry, 1977-88; bd. dirs. encore Paper Co., Inc., 1992-95; adj. prof. environ. sci. SUNY, Syracuse, 1979-84. Author: In Defense of Garbage, 1993; contbr. articles to profl. and bus. jours., including Wall Street Jour., N.Y. Times, Industry Week. Trustee Carleton Coll., 1973—, Am. Shakespeare Theater, 1980-82; bd. dirs. New Eng. Legal Found., 1979-82, Norwalk (Conn.) Hosp., 1985-88, Ctr. for Advanced Studies U. Va., 1988—; chmn. bd. trustees Keep Am. Beautiful (bd. dirs. 1979-90), 1986-88. Decorated Bronze Star medal; Woodrow Wilson vis. fellow, 1975-82. Mem. Conn. Bus. Industry Assn. (bd. dirs. 1976-80, 85-89), Quechee Club, Isleworth Club. Republican. Congregationalist. Home: 9844 Lake Louise Dr Windermere FL 34786-8905

ALEXANDER, KATHLEEN DENISE, medical/surgical nurse; b. Kansas City, Mo., Feb. 2, 1963; d. Irwin Eugene and Carolyn Sue (Fortune) A. Diploma, Bapt. Sch. Nursing, Memphis, 1985. Cert. BLS. Staff RN Bapt. Meml. Hosp., Memphis, 1985-87; contract RN Largo (Fla.) Med. Hosp., 1988, New Hanover, Wilmington, N.C., 1988; PRN Bapt. Mem. Hosp., Memphis, 1988; contract RN Mother Francis, Tyler, Tex., 1989, Burdette Tomlin Hosp., Sea Isle City, N.J., 1989, Dominquez Hosp., Compton, Calif., 1990, St. Vincent Hosp., L.A., 1990; staff RN Bapt. Meml. Desoto, Southaven, Miss., 1990—. Home: 6365 Riverbirch Rd Walls MS 38680-9476

ALEXANDER, LAMAR See ALEXANDER, ANDREW LAMAR

ALEXANDER, LINDA BALDWIN, library skills educator; b. Chatham County, N.C., June 3, 1948; d. Thomas Fleet and Ruby Baldwin; divorced; children: Robert L. Shoffner III, Elizabeth Shoffner; m. John Christopher, 1990. BA in Sociology, East Carolina U., 1970, MAEd in Spl. Edn., 1973, MLS, 1986, MAEd in Adult Edn., 1993. Cert. tchr., N.C. Tchr. spl. edn. Edgecombe County Schs., Tarboro, N.C., 1970-72; social worker foster care and protective svcs. Pitt County Dept. Social Svcs., Greenville, N.C., 1977-79; instr. Librs. 1000 East Carolina U., Greenville, 1984-93; coord. libr. media edn. 101 Western Ky. U., Bowling Green, 1993—. Contbr. articles to profl. jours. Recipient N.C. Meml. scholarship N.C. Libr. Assn., 1986. Mem. Kappa Delta Pi (hon.). Office: Western Ky U Helm Libr Rm 6 Bowling Green KY 42101

ALEXANDER, MICHAEL C., interior designer, business owner; b. Miami, Fla., Jan. 19, 1951; s. Waddie A. and Carmen Alexander Printup. AA, Bauder Fashion Coll., 1982; BA, Fla. Internat. U., 1986. Design asst. Edith Irma Siegal Interiors, Bay Harbour, Fla., 1982-84; owner, pres. M.C.A. Interiors and Assocs., Bal Harbour, 1985—. Exhibits designer South Fla. Home Shows, 1992, Hist. Soc. Palm Beach, 1994. Mem. ball com. Moon Over Miami, 1993—, Miami Design Preservation League for Art Deco, 1991—; com. mem. Miami chpt. Cystic Fibrosis Assn., 1991-96, gala chairperson, 1996, Palm Beach chpt., 1994, 95. Mem. Am. Soc. Interior Designers (allied, admissions com. 1992-94), Interior Design Guild (historian, admissions com. 1991-93, v.p. admissions 1994, Designer of Yr. 1991), Internat. Interior Design Assn. (regional dir. 1995, bd. dirs. 1992-94), Internat. Furnishings and Design Assn. (bd. dirs. 1993-94, pres. 1995-96), Greater Biscayne Blvd. C. of C. (bd. dirs.), Men's Opera Build Greater Miami, Internat. Soc. Palm Beach, Greater Miami, Internat. Soc. Palm Beach, Surf Club, Bal Harbour Club, Govs. Club, Williams Island Country Club. Republican. Roman Catholic. Home and Office: 118 Camden Dr Bal Harbour FL 33154-1329

ALEXANDER, MICHAEL EDWARD, systems engineer; b. Council Bluffs, Iowa, May 13, 1949; s. Clarence E. A.; m. Nidia E., June 15, 1973; children: Michael Christian, Nicole Renee. BS in Math., Tex. A&M, 1971, MS in Computing Sci., 1974. Various positions in field to systems mgr. Cellstar Devel., Harris-Rochester, N.Y., 1982-83; staff cons. Connect 1100 Design Sperry, BlueBell, Pa., 1983-84, staff cons. Advanced DataBase Systems, 1984, profl. cons. EMX Devel., 1984-85; mgr. ops. Atlanta Devel. Ctr. Sperry, Atlanta, 1985-87; tech. program mgr. HUD/UNISYS, McLean, Va., 1987; dir. preprocessor, compiler and database planning Nat. Advanced Systems, Atlanta, 1987-88; mgr. systems engring. GSD-Unisys, Atlanta, 1988-91, Systems Integration Ops./U.S. Comml. Mktg., McLean, Va., 1991-96; solution architect AT&T Solutions, Chantilly, Va., 1996—. Office: AT&T Solutions 15000 Conference Center Dr Chantilly VA 20151-3823

ALEXANDER, PATRICIA ROSS, administrative assistant; b. Blue Ridge, Ga., May 19, 1955; d. Ernest B. and Sara P. (Williams) Ross; m. Robert W. Alexander, Jr., June 24, 1978; children: Sarah E., Robert R. AA, Young Harris (Ga.) Coll., 1975; BA, North Ga. Coll., 1978, postgrad.; postgrad., Emory U. Fiber artist Morganton, Ga.; clk., postmaster relief U.S. Postal Svc., Mineral Bluff, Ga., 1987-96; adminstrv. asst. Indsl. Strength Art, Morganton. Contbr. articles to publs. Recipient cert. of Appreciation and Pride in Performance Gold medal, U.S. Postal Svc., 1992; grantee Ga. Coun. for Arts, 1984, NSF, 1979. Mem. NAPUS, So. Highlands Handicraft Guild, Ga. Mountain Crafts (bd. dirs. 1981-84), Copper Basin/Fannin C. of C., Blue Ridge Mountains Arts Assn. (v.p. 1979-80, coord. 1980-81, bd. dirs. 1993-96), Basket Weavers Guild Ga., Fannin County Heritage Found., Fannin County Tree League (bd. dirs. 1993-95), Ga. Pub. TV Leadership Cir. Baptist. Home: PO Box 599 Morganton GA 30560-0599 Office: US Post Office Mineral Bluff GA 30559

ALEXANDER, PAULETTE S., computer information systems educator; b. Birmingham, Ala., May 24, 1947; d. Norman and Mary Evelyn W. Shirley; m. James Guy Alexander, Aug. 22, 1970; children: Michael Guy Shirley, Richard Norman. BS in Math. and Physics, U. Ala., 1969, MA in Bus. Statistics, 1970; MPA, U. Tex., 1973; postgrad., U. Memphis, 1992—. Cert. data processer. Cons. Lyndon B. Johnson Sch. Pub. Affairs U. Tex., Austin, 1972; program assoc. Tex. Adv. Commn. on Intergovtl. Rels., Austin, 1972-74; sr. program assoc. State of Tex. Legis. Budget Bd., Austin, 1974-80; assoc. prof. computer info. systems U. North Ala., Florence, 1981—; dir. distance learning U. North Ala., 1995—; cons. Crown Imports, Inc., Haleyville, Ala., 1987, Reynolds Metals, Inc., Muscle Shoals, Ala., 1989, William Byrd Press, Inc., Richmond, Va., 1991; rschr. Bur. Bus. and Econ. Rsch. U. Memphis, 1994-96. Co-author: (monograph series) NASA's ASRM Plant Impact Study, 1989-90; contbr. articles to profl. jours. Bd. dirs. Shoals Entrpreneurial Ctr., Florence, 1989—, chmn., 1993; bd. dirs. Shoals Indsl. Devel. Auth., Florence, 1992-95, chair com., 1992; mem., forum organizer A statewide edn. reform effort, Ala., 1993—; bd. dirs., chair com. ARC Lauderdale County chpt., Florence, 1995—; pres., bd. dirs. LWV of the Shoals. Named to Leadership Am., Found. for Women's Resources, 1991; named Vol. of Quar., ARC, Lauderdale County chpt., Florence, 1988. Mem. Assn. for Info. Systems, Decision Scis. Inst., So. Mgmt. Info. Systems Assn., Ala. Acad. Sci., C of C. of the Shoals (chair edn. com.), Phi Kappa Phi, Kappa Delta Pi. Office: U North Ala UNA Box 5124 Florence AL 35632

ALEXANDER, ROBERT EARL, university chancellor, educator; b. Kinston, N.C., Oct. 21, 1939; s. Joseph Culbreath and Pauline (Fussell) A.; m. Leslie Johnson, Mar. 11, 1971; children—Lara, Robert. B.A. in Polit. Sci., Duke U., 1962, M.Div., 1966; D. in Higher Edn., U. S.C., 1977. Ordained to ministry United Methodist Ch., 1967. Assoc. chaplain N.C. State U., Raleigh, 1965-66; assoc. chaplain U. S.C., Columbia, 1966-68, dir. vol. services, 1969-70, adminstrv. asst. to v.p. student affairs, 1970-71, dean student activities, 1971-75, dean students, asst. v.p. student affairs, 1975-78, assoc. prof., 1981-83, assoc. v.p. for 2-year campuses and continuing edn., 1978-83; chancellor U. S.C., Aiken, 1983—; chmn. systems rev. panel U. S.C., 1981-83; bd. dirs. Security Fed. Savs. Bank S.C. Contbr. articles to profl. jours. Nat. observer White House Conf. on Youth, Denver, 1971; bd. dirs. United Way, Aiken, S.C., Bus. Tech. Ctr. of N. Augusta, S.C., 1984-89, Strom Thurmond Found., Inc., Aiken, 1985—, now sec. Econ. Devel. Partnership, 1984—, sec., 1989—; mem. Commn. on Future S.C., 1987—, Commn. on Future of Aiken County, 1987-89, chmn., 1989-90; trustee Hopeland Gardens, Aiken, 1984—; mem. S.C. Coun. Econ. Edn., 1988—; chmn. Peach Belt Athletic Conf., 1989-91; mem. regional adv. bd. SCANA, 1990—; mem. nat. adv. com. on Student Fin. Assistance, 1991—, chair 1996—; bd. trustees Aiken Regional Med. Ctrs., 1992—; vice chmn., chmn. exec. com. Savannah River Regional Diversification Initiative, 1993—. Named Man of Yr., Greater Aiken C. of C., 1985; Kellog grantee, 1981; NEH grantee, 1982, 85—. Mem. S.C. Assn. Higher Continuing Edn. (pres. 1980-81, Outstanding Pres.'s award 1987), S.C. Assn. for Comty. Edn., Nat. Comty. Edn. Assn., Assn. Higher Continuing Edn., Nat. Entertainment and Campus Activities Assn. (bd. dirs. 1973-79), Inst. for Continuing Edn. Nat. Univ. Continuing Edn. Assn. (bd. dirs. 1981-83), S.C. Coun. Pub. Coll. and Univ. Pres. (chmn. 1996—), S.C. 2000 (bd. dirs. 1989—), Greater Aiken C. of C. (pres. 1987), Am. Assn. State Colls. and Univs. (com. on sci. and tech. 1987-90, state rep. 1990-95, fins. in higher edn. 1991—, fed./state rels. com. 1984—), Rotary (Aiken bd. dirs. 1984—, scholarship com. Internat. chpt. 1993—), Houndslake Country Club, Woodside Plantation Country Club, Green Boundary Country Club, Phi Delta Kappa, Alpha Kappa Psi, Gamma Beta Phi, Omicron Delta Kappa. Methodist. Office: Univ SC 171 University Pky Aiken SC 29801-6309

ALEXANDER, ROBERT HAROLD, clinical psychologist; b. Alton, Ill., Sept. 18, 1918; s. Harold Chartis and Florence Marie (Steiner) A.; m. Helen Louise Snyder, Nov. 17. 1962 (dec. Feb. 1975); 1 child, Richard Robert. AB, Washington U., 1940, MA, 1948, PhD, 1953. Psychotherapist VA, St. Louis, 1947-48; instr. Washington U., St. Louis, 1948-49; chief area psychologist Ill. Dept. Pub. Inst., Jacksonville, 1949-55; chmn. dept. psychology MacMurray Coll., Jacksonville, 1955-57; pvt. practice Springfield, Ill., 1957-69, Jacksonville, Fla., 1969-85; cons. Jacksonville, 1985—. Author: It Never Rains in Africa, 1989, By Command, 1990. Mem. Recycles Sr. Citizen Band, Morocco Shrine Temple Band, 1982—; bd. dirs. New Life Mission, 1984—, Dem. Exec. Com., Duval County, Fla., 1985—. Capt. U.S. Army, 1942-44. Fellow Am. Psychol. Assn.; mem. Am. Soc. Clin. Hypnosis, VFW, DAV. Episcopalian.

ALEXANDER, STEVEN ALBERT, physics researcher; b. Natchez, Miss., June 11, 1957; s. Michael and Barbara Jean (Wilkins) A.; m. Catherine Sikora, June 15, 1996. BS in Math., U. Tex., 1978, PhD in Physics, 1982. Asst. rsch. scientist dept. physics U. Fla., Gainesville, 1992-93; rsch. scientist Constellation Tech. Corp., St. Petersburg, Fla., 1993-95; vis. asst. prof. dept. physics Univ. Tex. Arlington, 1995-96; physics instr. El Centro Coll., Dallas, 1996—. Mem. Am. Phys. Soc., Phi Beta Kappa.

ALEXANDRATOS, SPIRO DIONISIOS, chemistry educator; b. N.Y.C., Dec. 11, 1951; m. Olga Pantos; 1 child, Jonathan. BS, Manhattan Coll., 1973; PhD, U. Calif., Berkeley, 1977. Sr. rsch. chemist Rohm and Haas Co., Phila., 1977-81; from asst. prof. to assoc. prof. U. Tenn., Knoxville, 1981-92, prof. chemistry, 1993—; bd. dirs. Eichrom Industries, Darien, Ill. Holder 7 patents in field; mem. editorial adv. bd. Reactive and Functional Polymers, Separation Science and Technology, Solvent Extraction and Ion Exchange. Recipient Hoechst-Celanese Rsch. award, 1993, R & D 100 award R & D Mag., 1994. Mem. Am. Chem. Soc. (chmn. divsn. indsl. engring. chemistry 1993-94, chmn. subdivsn. separation sci. 1991-92; assoc. editor Jour. of Indsl. and Engring. Chemistry Rsch.), Sigma Xi, Phi Beta Kappa (cert. merit 1993). Home: 2137 Cherokee Blvd Knoxville TN 37919-8342 Office: U Tenn Dept Chemistry Knoxville TN 37996

ALEXIOU, NICHOLAS G., health facility administrator, consultant; b. Manchester, N.H., Jan. 2, 1926; s. George and Mary (Kakou) A.; m. Anthie Gatzoulis, Sept. 2, 1951; children: Vicki Maria, George N. AB, St. Anselms Coll., 1950; MD, U. Vt., Burlington, 1955; MPH, Yale U., 1961. Asst. prof. maternal and child health Sch. Hygiene and Pub. Health, Johns Hopkins U., Balt., 1962-67; assoc. dir. divn. Preventive Health Svc. N.Y. State Health Dept., Albany, 1967-73; med. dir. Employee Health Svc. N.Y. State Dept. Civil Svc., Albany, 1973-78; dir. Children's Med. Svcs. Fla. Dept. Health and Rehab. Svc., Tallahassee, 1978-79; asst. prof. Medicine U. South Fla., Tampa, 1979-88; dir. Occupational Medicine Eastern Airlines, Miami, Fla., 1988-89; dir. Occupational Med. Clinics, Clearwater, Fla., 1989—; intern in Medicine George Washington U., Washington, 1955-56; resident in Pediatrics Children's Hosp. of D.C., Washington, 1956-57, Grace New Haven (Conn.) Comm. Hosp., 1957-58; fellow in cystic fibrosis Yale U., New Haven, 1958-59; cons. Fla. State Health Dept., Jacksonville, 1959-62. Contbr. articles to book and profl. jours. Mem. bd. dirs. local emergency planning coun., St. Petersburg, Fla.; bd. dirs. U. South Fla. Inst. for Environ. Studies, Tampa, 1981—; mem. Dem. Exec. Com. Pinellas County, 1988—. Served with USN, 1943-45. Conn. Cystic Fibrosis fellow, 1958, Sister Cities Internat. grantee, 1980, Am. Coll. Preventive Medicine fellow, 1973. Mem. Hellenic Profl. and Cultural Soc. (pres. 1993-94), Fla. Assn. Occupational and Environ. Medicine, North Pinellas Dem. Club (pres. 1991-94). Greek Orthodox. Home: 400 Island Way Ph 202 Clearwater FL 34630-2132

ALFORD, DOLORES IDA M., nursing consultant; b. New Orleans, Sept. 13, 1928; d. Theodore Henry and Dolores Marie (Guerrero) Marsh; m. John Herbert Alford, Apr. 4, 1958. Diploma, Charity Hosp. Sch. Nursing, 1951; BS in Nursing Edn., La. State U., 1957; MSN, U. Tex., 1961; PhD, Columbia Pacific U., 1989. Cons. Tex. Dept. of Health, Austin, 1969-70; ind. cons. gerontic nursing Dallas, 1970—. Contbr. articles to profl. jours. Mem. ANA (site visitor accreditation unit), Tex. Nurses Assn. (vice chmn. gerontol. conf. group, coord. manpower project), Sigma Theta Tau. Home: 3184 Lockmoor Ln Dallas TX 75220-1630

ALFORD, LINDA CONERLY, elementary education educator; b. Tylertown, Miss., Apr. 6, 1939; d. James Lamkin and Mary Vesta (Fornea) Conerly; m. Billy E. Alford, Dec. 23, 1961; children: Cynthia A. Polk, Shari A. McCullough. BS, U. So. Miss., 1960. Cert. elem. and bus. edn. Bus. edn. and elem. tchr. Walthall County Schs., Tylertown, 1960-70, elem. tchr., 1980—; elem. tchr. Washington Parish Schs., Franklinton, La., 1970-80; ret., 1995. Mem. NEA, Miss. Edn. Assn., Walthall Assn. Edn., Miss. Coun. for Tchrs. of Math., Miss. Ret. Tchrs. Assn. Baptist. Home: 28 Alford Rd Tylertown MS 39667-6229

ALFORD, ROBERT WILFRID, JR., elementary school educator; b. Langley, Va., Nov. 8, 1955; s. Robert Wilfrid and Ella Ramona (Coker) A.; m. Cynthia Marie Avery, Dec. 23, 1978; children: Deborah Louise, Phillip Glenn. BS, Appalachian State U., 1978. Cert. social sci. tchr. Tchr. Wren Mid. Sch. Anderson Sch. Dist., Piedmont, S.C., 1978-81, Tanglewood Mid. Sch. Greenville (S.C.) County Sch. Dist., 1984—; cons. Student Svcs., Greenville, 1985-91. Scoutmaster Troop 749, 1989-93, 95—, asst. scoutmaster 1993-94; deacon Fourth Presbyn. Ch. Named Boy Scouter of Yr., Reed Falls dist. Boy Scouts Am., 1994. Mem. Greenville County Edn. Assn. (bd. dirs. 1986-88, sec. 1988-89), S.C. Council Social Studies Tchrs., S.C. Council

Middle Schs., S.C. Edn. Assn. (educator rights com. 1987-88), Kappa Delta Pi, Phi Alpha Theta, Alpha Phi Omega (pres. Tau Beta chpt. 1976-77). Democrat. Presbyterian. Office: Tanglewood Mid Sch 44 Merriwoods Dr Greenville SC 29611-7111

ALFRED, BOB, business executive; b. 1948. With Jenkins Brick Co., Montgomery, Ala.; CFO South Eastern Boll Weevil ERA, Montgomery, Ala., 1988—. Office: South Eastern Boll Weevil ERA 2424 E South Blvd Montgomery AL 36116-2506

ALFRED, DEWITT CLINTON, JR., university dean, psychiatrist; b. Chattanooga, Oct. 12, 1937; s. Dewitt Clinton and O'Teele Eloise (Nichols) A.; m. Marion Leticia Bottoms, Aug. 22, 1959; children: Leticia O'Teele Alfred Garrick, Dewitt Clinton Alfred III. BS cum laude, Morehouse Coll., 1956; MD, Howard U., 1960. Diplomate Am. Bd. Psychiatry and Neurology. Commd. USAFR, 1962, advanced through grades to col., 1979; intern H.G. Philips Gen. Hosp., St. Louis, 1961; residency in psychiatry Walter Reed Gen. Hosp., Washington, 1967; gen. med. officer Regional Hosp. USAF, Rantoul, Ill., 1962-64; resident psyhiatrist Walter Reed Gen. Hosp., Washington, 1964-67; asst. chief psychiatry USAF Area Med. Ctr., Andrews AFB, Washington, 1967-68; chief psychiatrist USAF Regional Hosp. Sheppard AFB USAFR, Wichita Falls, Tex., 1968-71; prof. psychiatry, chief of svc., Grady Meml. Hosp. Emory U., Atlanta, 1971-84; ret. USAFR, 1982; founding chmn. psychiatry dept. Morehouse Sch. Medicine, Atlanta, 1984—; regional cons. Hdqrs. USAF Surgeon Gen., Washington, 1968-71, res. cons., 1971-82; cons. psychiatrist Atlanta Univ. Ctr., Inc., 1972—; cons. NIMH, Rockville, Md., 1977-85, North Ga. Hlth Sys. Agy., Atlanta, 1979-82; dir. Morehouse Med. Assocs., Inc., 1985-93. Co-author: (textbook chpts.) Social Psychiatry, 1974, Psychosomatic Disorders, 1979, Schizophrenia, 1983, 88, 92, 95, Paranoia, 1992, 95. Active Ga. Bd. of Human Resources, 1984-94, chmn., 1989-91; founding mem. Regional Leadership Inst. Atlanta Regional Commn. and Metro-Atlanta Bus. Forum, 1991; mem. Nat. Mental Health Coun., 1992—. Early Entrance scholar Ford Found., 1952-56; Named Young M.D. of the Yr., Atlanta Med. Assn., 1976; recipient Pub. Svc. award Mental Health Assn., Metro-Atlanta, 1989. Mem. APA (sec. 1981-85 Ga. dist. br., pres.-elect 1985-86, pres. 1986-87, named Psychiatrist of Yr. 1993-94 Ga. Psychiat. Physicians Assn. dist. br. APA, Solomon Carter Fuller award 1994, Solomon Carter Fuller lectr. 1994), AMA, Soc. USAF Psychiatrists, So. Psychiatric Assn.,. Presbyterian. Office: Morehouse Sch of Medicine 720 Westview Dr SW Atlanta GA 30310-1458

ALGILANI, KAMRAN CAMERON, physician, surgeon, researcher; b. Uromia, Kurdistan, Iran, July 17, 1951; came to U.S., 1979; s. Fosch Pousho and Asma (Mohammadi-Nari) A.; m. Chilé Saleh Taha, Nov. 2, 1993; 1 child, Daniel Kamiar. BSc in Biology, Mashad (Iran) U., 1975; MSc in Microbiology, East Tenn. State U., 1982; DO, Okla. State U., 1990. Rschr. Tehran (Iran) Rehab. Ctr., 1977-79, Oral Roberts U., Tulsa, 1983-85, Okla. State U., Tulsa, 1985-86; intern Dallas Meml. Hosp., 1990-91; family practice resident N.E. Community Hosp., Bedford, Tex., 1991-93; pvt. practice Dallas, 1993—. Contbr. rsch. articles to profl. jours. Active with Kurdish-U.S. Orgn., Dallas, 1992—. 2d lt. Iranian Army, 1975-77. Mem. AMA, Am. Osteo. Assn., Terrant County Med. Assn., Okla. Osteo. Assn., Tex. Osteo. Med. Assn., Osteo. Physicians and Surgeons Calif. Office: PO Box 202438 Arlington TX 76006-8438

AL-HASHIMI, IBTISAM, oral scientist, educator; b. Karbala, Iraq; d. Hadi A. and Rabab H. Al-H. B Dental Sci., Sch. Dentistry, Baghdad, 1973; MS, SUNY, Buffalo, 1985, PhD, 1989. Diplomate in Oral Surgery. Registrar Sch. Dentistry, Baghdad, 1975-81; postdoctoral assoc. SUNY, Buffalo, 1984-88, asst. prof., 1988-89; asst. prof. U. Pacific, San Francisco, 1989-90; dir. stomatology lab. Baylor Coll. Dentistry, Dallas, 1991—, dir. salivery dysfunction clinic, 1992—; clin. asst. prof. surgery U. Tex. Southwestern Med. Ctr., Dallas, 1996—; adv. com. mem. SS Found. (we. N.Y. chpt.) Buffalo, 1985-89, Dallas-Ft. Worth chpt., 1992—; mem. med. adv. bd., organizer Sjogren's Multispecialty Referral Ctr., 1996. Author: Proceeding of the Second Dows Symposium, 1987; contbr. articles to profl. jours. Mem. med. adv. bd. SS Found., 1995. Mem. AAAS, Am. Assn. Dental Schs., N.Y. Acad. Sci., Internat. Platform Assn., Internat. Assn. Dental Rsch., Libr. Congress Assn., Salivary Rsch. Group, Sigma Xi. Office: Baylor Coll Dentistry 3302 Gaston Ave Dallas TX 75246-2013

ALI, ODEH SAID, petroleum geologist; b. Elbireh, Palestine, May 31, 1939; s. Said Ibrahim and Sabha Ahmed (Abu Ras) A.; m. Linda Lee King, Feb. 5, 1968; children: Karawan, Kareem, Feriel. BA Geology, Simpson Coll., 1964; MS Geology, U. Iowa, 1966, PhD Geology, 1969. Geologic engr. Sonatrach Oil Co., Algiers, Algeria, 1967-69, dist. geologist, 1969-70; asst. prof. Guilford Coll., Greensboro, N.C., 1970-72; chief geologist Alcore Cons., Algier, 1972-74; sr. staff geologist Mobil Oil Co., Dallas, 1975-86; sr. v.p. Christian Internat. Ltd., London, 1987—; cons. Petroleum Geology of the Mid. East, 1990. Mem. Am. Assn. Petroleum Geologists (assoc. editor 1983-86). Home: 1618 Walker Dr Carrollton TX 75007

ALICH, JOHN ARTHUR, JR., manufacturing company executive; b. Cleve., Dec. 2, 1942; s. John Arthur and Jeanette Marie (Kusa) A.; m. Susan Jane Moras, May 8, 1965; children: Michelle Monet, Amy Catherine. BS in Engring., U.S. Naval Acad., 1964; MBA, U. Del., 1971. Sr. cons./dir. Stanford Rsch. Inst., Menlo Park, Calif., 1973-77; mgr. devel. Baker Hughes Inc./Envirotech Corp., Menlo Park, 1977-80; v.p. devel. Baker Hughes Inc./Eimco Mining Machinery Internat., Menlo Park, 1980-82; v.p. mktg. Baker Hughes Inc./Eimco Mining Machinery Internat., Salt Lake City, 1982-85; group v.p., gen. mgr. Baker Hughes Inc./Eimco Secoma, Lyon, France, 1985-87; exec. v.p. ops. Baker Hughes Inc./Eimco Jarvis Clark, Toronto, Can., 1987-88; pres. Baker Hughes Inc./Baker Hughes Mining Tools, Grand Prairie, Tex., 1988-92, Baker Hughes Inc/Envirotech Measurements and Controls, Austin, Tex., 1992-94, Thermo Instrument Controls Inc., Austin, 1994-95; bus. devel. dir. Thermo Instrument Sys. Inc.,, Austin, 1995—. Bd. dirs. Serra H.S. Bd. Regents, San Mateo, Calif., 1975-77, Boys and Girls Club, Grand Prairie, 1988-92. Lt. USN, 1964-70. DuPont fellow U. Del., 1970-71. Mem. Soc. Mining Engrs., Inst. Soc. Am., Am. Nuclear Soc., Beta Gamma Sigma. Office: Thermo Instrument Sys Inc 2215 Grand Ave Pkwy Austin TX 78728-3812

ALIZY, NOURI, reliability engineer; b. Tehran, Iran, Apr. 28, 1954; came to U.S., 1976; s. Kochak and Hosnien N. (Loyah) A.; m. Christina, Sept. 30, 1993. BS in Elec. Engring., U. Tex., 1982. Registered profl. engr., Tex. Engring. tech. Automation Products Co., 1982-83; water fab processor Motorola Semiconductor Product Sector, Austin, Tex., 1983-84, staff reliability engr., 1984—. Office: Motorola 3501 Ed Bluestein Blvd Austin TX 78721-2903

ALLAMEH, ELINOR JOY, English language educator; b. Winchester, Tenn., Jan. 17, 1940; d. Dempsie Pharus and Inez Elinor (Hamilton) Goode; m. Ahmad Eddie Allameh, Sept. 12, 1970; 1 child, Catherine Jaleh. BS in English, Mid. Tenn. State U., 1962; MA in English, U. Ark., 1964; EdD in Policy Studies and Evaluation, U. Ky., 1990. Double grad. assistantships U. Ark., Fayetteville, 1962-63; 8th grade tchr. Estill Springs (Tenn.) Sch., 1964; tchr. of English Murray State U., Ky., 1964-71, Jundi Shapur U., Ahwaz, Iran, 1971-75, Oscar Rose Jr. Coll., Midwest City, Okla., 1975-78; tchr. of English Eastern Ky. U., Richmond, 1978—, dir. English lang. instrn. program, 1990—. Presenter in field. Regional coord. EF Found., Cambridge, Mass., 1981—. Mem. TESOL, Nat. Assn. Fgn. Student Affairs, Ky. Coun. Internat. Edn., Ky. Coun. Tchrs.of English, Ky. TESOL, S.E. TESOL. Democrat. Office: Eastern Ky U Case Annex 467-3140 Richmond KY 40475

ALLAN, YVONNE LETICIA, medical illustrator, computer graphics designer; b. Buenos Aires, Argentina, Sept. 14, 1927; came to U.S., 1949; d. Miguel Angel Marino and Maria Dominica (Baumgartner) de Marino; m. Laurence Ralph Allan, May 8, 1948; children: Richard Keneth, Edwin Hobbs, Mary Elizabeth. Art teaching degree, Sch. Fine Arts Manuel Belgrano, Buenos Aires, 1945; postgrad., Coll. Fine Arts, Buenos Aires, 1945-49; BFA, U. Cen. Fla., 1976, postgrad. in Biology, 1985-86. Archtl. model maker James A. Britton AIA, Greenfield, Mass., 1950-55; biology illustrator U. Cen. Fla., Orlando, 1974-76; free lance artist, medical illustrator Yvonne L. Allan Studios, Winter Park, Fla., 1976—. Illustrator: Mitral Valve Reconstruction, 1987, (posters) New Method of Ear Cropping, 1977, Light Reflection in Eye, 1978, Chinese Exercises, black and white ink drawings, 1985, Chiropractic Educational Charts, 1984-85, The Human Heart, 1986, Ten Consecutive Cases of Mitral Valve Repair, 1986-87, Transseptal Technique, a Workbook, 1988-89, Debriment of Annular Abscesses of the Heart and Repair, 1989, Aneurysms of the Aorta, 1990. Active Parents of Hard of Hearing Children, Orlando, 1962—; coord. Parent to Parent Program Seminole County Ct. House, 1982-84, group facilitator, 1984-86; counselor, trainer Cen. Fla. Helpline, Winter Pk., 1987—. Mem. Nat. League Am. Pen Women (past sec.), Assn. Med. Illustrators. Republican. Baptist.

ALLAND, LAWRENCE MARTIN, pastoral counselor, marriage and family therapist; b. Ft. Worth, Sept. 29, 1931; s. Alvin Henry and Mary Estelle (Belew) A.; m. Rosemary Evans, Dec. 29, 1953; children: Mary Margaret, John Mark, James Michael, Timothy Kirk. BA, Tex. Christian U., 1953, MDiv, 1957, ThM, 1972; postgrad., Mich. State U., 1980-82. Lic. profl. counselor, Tex.; lic. marriage counselor, Mich., lic. marriage and family therapist, Tex.; ordained to ministry Christian Ch. (Disciples of Christ), 1957. Missionary tchr. United Christian Missionary Soc., Indpls., 1957-60; assoc. min. Country Club Christian Ch., Kansas City, Mo., 1960-63; resident in psychiatry and religion Menninger Found., Topeka, 1963-64; min. Highlands Christian Ch., Dallas, 1964-67; min. counseling Park Congl. Ch., Grand Rapids, Mich., 1967-71; exec. dir. Community Counseling Ministry, Grand Rapids, 1971-77; ptnr. Kooistra, Alland, Jansma and Elders, Grand Rapids, 1977-82; exec. dir. Samaritan Counseling Ctr., Ft. Worth, 1982-84; ptnr. Counseling and Consulting Assocs., Ft. Worth, 1984-95; ret., 1995; mem. adj. faculty Mich. State U. Med. Sch., Lansing, 1972-82, Brite Div. Sch., Tex. Christian U., Ft. Worth, 1985-94. Bd. dirs. Project Rehab. Drug Treatment Ctr., Grand Rapids, 1968-74; pres. bd. dirs. Grand Rapids Child Guidance Clinic, 1970-72; chmn. gen. bd. Univ. Christian Ch., Ft. Worth, 1990-92. Alumni scholar Tex. Christian U., 1953; fellow NIMH, 1963-64. Mem. Am. Assn. Pastoral Counselors (diplomate, pres. Midwest region 1977-79, nat. bd. govs. 1978-79), Am. Assn. Marriage and Family Therapy (clin.), Tarrant County Assn. Marriage and Family Therapy (pres. 1989-90). Democrat. Home: 4701 Shady Ridge Ct Fort Worth TX 76109-1803

ALLBRIGHT, KARAN ELIZABETH, psychologist, consultant; b. Oklahoma City, Okla., Jan. 28, 1948; d. Jack Gahnal and Irma Lolene (Keesee) A. BA, Oklahoma City U., 1970, MAT, 1972; PhD, U. So. Miss., 1981. Cert. sch. psychologist, psychometrist; lic. psychologist, Okla., Ark. Psychol. technician Donald J. Bertoch, Ph.D., Oklahoma City, 1973-76; asst. adminstr. Parents' Assistance Ctr., Oklahoma City, 1976-77; psychology intern Burwell Psycho-ednl. Ctr., Carrollton, Ga., 1980-81; staff psychologist Griffin Area Psychoednl. Ctr., Ga., 1981-85; clinic dir. Sequoyah County Guidance Clinic, Sallisaw, Okla., 1985-88; psychologist Baker Psychiatric Clinic, Ft. Smith, Ark., 1988-90; cons. Harbor View Mercy Hosp., 1988-90, Columbia Med. Ctr., 1992—; pvt. practice, Oklahoma City, 1990—; lectr. various orgns.; bd. dirs. workshops. Mem. Task Force to Prevent Child Abuse, Fayette County, Ga., 1984-85, Task Force on Family Violence, Spalding County, Ga., 1983-85; cons. Family Alliance (Parents Anonymous) Sequoyah County, Okla., 1985-88; assoc. bd. dirs. Lyric Theatre. Named Outstanding Young Women in Am., 1980. Mem. APA, Southeastern Psychol. Assn., Nat. Assn. Sch. Psychologists (cert. sch. psychologist), Okla. Psychol. Assn., Play Therapy Assn., Nat. Assn. Health Svc. Providers in Psychology, Psi Chi, Delta Zeta (chpt. dir. 1970-72). Democrat. Presbyterian. Home: 3941 NW 44th St Oklahoma City OK 73112-2517 Office: Northwest Mental Health Assocs 3832 N Meridian Ave Oklahoma City OK 73112-2820

ALLBRITTON, JOE LEWIS, diversified holding company executive; b. D'Lo, Miss., Dec. 29, 1924; s. Lewis A. and Ada (Carpenter) A.; m. Barbara Jean Balfanz, Feb. 23, 1967; 1 son, Robert Lewis. LLB, Baylor U., 1949, LLD (hon.), 1964, JD, 1969; LHD, Calif. Bapt. Coll., 1973. Bar: Tex. 1949. Dir. Perpetual Corp., Houston, 1958—; pres. Perpetual Corp., 1965-76, 78-81, chmn. bd., 1973—; bd. dirs. Pierce Nat. Life Ins. Co., L.A., chmn., 1958-82, 75-92; chmn. Univ. Bancshares, Inc., Houston, 1975—, Allbritton Comms. Co., 1974—, Houston Fin. Svcs., Ltd., London, 1977—, Riggs Bank, NA, Washington, 1981—, Riggs Nat. Bank, Washington, 1983—; dep. chmn. Riggs AP Bank, Ltd., London, 1986-92, chmn., 1992—; mem. Greater Washington Bd. Trade, 1983-88, 92—; trustee The Mitre Corp., Bedford, Mass., 1987-93. Trustee Fed. City Coun., Washington, 1975—, John F. Kennedy Ctr. for Performing Arts, Washington, 1985-90, Nat. Geog. Soc., 1986—, The Ronald Reagan Presdl. Found., Washington, 1990, George Bush Presdl. Found., College Station, Tex., 1993—; bd. dirs. Nat. Fund for U.S. Bot. Garden, 1992-95, The Lyndon Baines Johnson Found., 1989—, Georgetown U., Washington, 1990-96. With USN, 1943-46. Mem. State Bar Tex., Assn. Res. City Bankers. Office: Perpetual Corp 808 17th St NW Washington DC 20006-3903

ALLDAY, MARTIN LEWIS, lawyer; b. El Dorado, Ark., May 30, 1926; s. Martin L. Sr. and Bess (Kavanaugh) A.; m. Patricia Pryor, May 1, 1954; children: Katherine, Elizabeth, Martin III. JD, U. Tex., Austin, 1951. Bar: Tex. 1951. Examiner oil and gas div. R.R. Commn. of Tex., Austin, 1951-53; legal dept. Superior Oil Co., Midland, Tex., 1953-57, Houston, 1957-59; ptnr. Lynch, Chappell, Allday and Alsup, Midland, Austin & Dallas, 1959-89; past solicitor Dept. of Interior, Washington, 1989; chmn. Fed. Energy Regulatory Commn., Washington, 1989-93; of counsel Scott, Douglass, Luton and McConnico, Austin, Houston, Dallas, Tex., 1993—; bd. dirs. N.Am. Royalties, Inc. Past pres. Midland Jaycees, C. of C., Indsl. Found.; past trustee, gov. Midland Meml. Hosp.; bd. dirs. Petroleum Mus. Hall of Fame. With Inf. U.S. Army, 1944-46. Decorated Purple Heart, Bronze Star. Mem. ABA, Tex. Bar Assn. (chmn. oil, gas and mineral sect. 1970), D.C. Bar Assn., Tex. Bar Found., Midland County Bar Assn. (pres. 1972-73), Midland Country Club (pres.), Petroleum Club (bd. dirs.). Republican. Episcopalian. Office: 600 Congress Ave Ste 1500 Austin TX 78701-3234

ALLEN, BARRY MORGAN, corporate communications consultant; b. N.Y.C., June 3, 1939; s. Robert Mitchell and Edna B. (Feldman) A.; m. Carol Joyce Applestein, Sept. 20, 1961 (div. June 1974); 1 child, Sheri; m. Rena Susan Garfinkle, June 16, 1974; children: Linda Krasno Gicca, David Krasno. BS in Journalism, U. Md., 1961. Mng. editor Diamondback, 1959; assoc. editor Old Line, 1959; reporter Radio News Assocs., 1960, Hearst Metrotone News/ABC-TV, 1961; account mgr. Burson-Marsteller, Washington, 1967-71; dir. communications Archon Pure Products Corp., Beverly Hills, Calif., 1971-73; v.p. communications Glass Packaging Inst., Washington, 1973-77; 1st v.p., corp. communications Bank of Boston, 1977-86; sr. v.p. corp. affairs Hartford (Conn.) Nat. Corp., 1986-88; sr. v.p., exec. dir. corp. and internat. affairs Manning, Selvage & Lee, N.Y.C., 1988-94, also mem. exec com.; pres. Barry Allen & Assocs., Inc., Boca Raton, Fla., 1994—; sr. ptnr. Emerald Ptnrs., N.Y.C., 1994—; charter mem. Evanston Group, 1985-87. Mem. Gov.'s Alliance Against Drugs, Mass., 1985-86; bd. dirs. Morgan Meml. Good Will, Boston, 1986, Bay State Games, Mass., 1986. Lt. USNR, 1961-67, Vietnam. Scholar Montgomery County, Md., 1960. Mem. Pub. Rels. Soc. Am., Union League Club N.Y.C., Boca Raton Resort and Club, Pi Delta Epsilon. Home: 3752 Gorham Way Boca Raton FL 33487-1017 Office: 3752 Gorham Way Boca Raton FL 33487-1017

ALLEN, BERTHA LEE, social worker, family counselor; b. Bexley, Miss., Mar. 28, 1908; d. Charles H. and Winnie (McLeod) A. Student, Maryville Coll., 1928-29; BA, Miss. U. for Women, 1932; postgrad., U. Ala., 1936, La. State U., 1937, Miss. State U., 1939, U. Miss., 1940; MSW, Tulane U., 1949. Cert. tchr. life, Miss., social worker, La., Ala., Miss., first aid instr.; bd. cert. diplomate clin. social work. Tchr. high sch. English and Latin, Rocky Creek Sch., Lucedale, Miss., 1932-33, Agricola, Miss., 1933-36, Tchula, Miss., 1936-44; child welfare worker Miss. Dept. Pub. Welfare, Jackson, Columbus, Pascagoula, 1944-48; caseworker Columbia (Miss.) Tng. Sch., 1949-50; case work supr., chief social worker Osawatomie (Kans.) State Hosp., 1950-51; dir. casework Miss. Children's Home Soc., Jackson, 1952-54; casework supr. Child and Family Svc., Mobile, Ala., 1954-58; supr. casework practice Family Counseling Ctr., Mobile, 1958-65; caseworker ARC Disaster Svcs., Hurricane Betsy, New Orleans, 1965, Family Svc. Soc., New Orleans, 1965-66, Jewish Family and Children's Svc., New Orleans, 1966-71, Willow Wood, New Orleans Home for Jewish Aged, 1971-73; pvt. practice individual, marital and family counseling, New Orleans, Mobile, Lucedale, 1969—; cons. Wilmer Hall, Protestant Children's Home, YWCA, Mobile, 1954-65, Providence Nursing Home, New Orleans, 1972-77, Willow Wood, New Orleans Home for Jewish Aged, 1974-75. Bd. dirs. Mulherin Home for Spastic Children, Mobile, 1958-59; charter mem., sec. Miss. Mental Health Assn., 1953-54; mem. casework com. Mobile Coun. Social Agys., 1954-58, mem. interagy. planning com., 1958-62, mem. in-svc. tng. com., 1963-65; mem. program com. Southeastern Inst., Family Svc. Assn. Am., 1960; mem. planning com. Mobile County Mental Health Assn., 1964-65; sec. Assn. Maternity and Adoption Agys., New Orleans, 1969-70. Nat. Assn. Social Workers (diplomate), Acad. Cert. Social Workers, La. Soc. Clin. Social Work, Miss. Conf. Social Welfare, Ala. Conf. Social Work, Internat. Platform Assn., Oakliegh Garden Soc., Eta Sigma Phi. Presbyterian. Home and Office: 1050 Palmetto St Mobile AL 36604-3041 also: RR 9 Box 796 Lucedale MS 39452-8630

ALLEN, BESSIE MALVINA, music educator, church organist; b. LaKemp, Okla., Oct. 14, 1918; d. Percy J. and Mary Allen (Hagler) Gheen; m. Edgar Charles Allen, Aug. 29, 1940 (dec. May 1981); children: Stanley Charles, Stephen Wayne. BA in English, Tex. Woman's U., 1939; MA in Music, W. Tex. State U., 1970. Cert. secondary edn. Tchr. English Balko (Okla.) High Sch. and Jr. High Sch., 1939-40; pvt. practice Phillips, Tex., 1950-85; tchr. music Frank Phillips Coll., Borger, Tex., 1960-63, 65-73, 76-85; pvt. practice Borger, 1986—; organist First Bapt. Ch., Borger, 1947-65, Faith Covenant Ch.-Ind., Borger, 1970-81, First Christian Ch., Borger, 1981-82, Faith Covenant Ch., Borger, 1982—. Active Nat. Rep. Senatorial Com., Washington, 1988-91. Recipient Presdl. Order of Merit, Nat. Rep. Senatorial Com., 1991; McCulley Organ scholar, W. Tex. State U., Canyon, 1969. Mem. Music Tchrs. Nat. Assn., Tex. Fedn. Music Clubs, Amarillo Music Tchrs. Assn., Borger Music Club. Home and Office: 221 Inverness St Borger TX 79007-8215

ALLEN, BONNIE MARIE, reporter; b. Biloxi, Miss., May 2, 1972; d. Robert John and Susan Lynn (Howell) A. AA, Miss. Gulf Coast C.C., Gautier, 1993; BS, Miss. State U., 1996. Libr. page St. Martin Pub. Libr., Biloxi, Miss., 1990-94; news reporter intern Miss. Press, Pascagoula, 1994; news reporter The Reflector, Starkville, Miss., 1994-95, The Comml. Dispatch, Columbus, Miss., 1995—. mem. publicity com. United Way of Oktibbeha County, Starkville, Miss., 1996. Recipient Sr. award Phi Kappa Phi, 1995. Republican. Baptist.

ALLEN, CHARLES MENGEL, federal judge; b. Louisville, Nov. 22, 1916; s. Arthur Dwight and Jane (Mengel) A.; m. Betty Anne Cardwell, June 25, 1949; children: Charles Dwight, Angela M. BA, Yale U., 1941; LLB, U. Louisville, 1943. Bar: Ky. 1944. Assoc. Doolin, Helm, Stites and Wood, 1944-45; pvt. practice Louisville, 1946-47; assoc. Farnsley, Hottell and Stephenson, 1947-53; pvt. practice, 1953-55; asst. U.S. atty. Western Dist. Ky., Dept. Justice, 1955-59; ptnr. Booth, Walker & Allen, Louisville, 1959-61; circuit judge Jefferson Cir. Ct., 4th Chancery Br. Jefferson County, 1961-71; dist. judge U.S. Dist. Ct. (we. dist.) Ky., Louisville, 1971-77, chief judge, 1977-85, sr. judge, 1985—. Named Outstanding Alumnus U. Louisville, 1984; recipient Brandeis award U. Louisville Law Sch., 1985, Thomas Hogan Meml. Found award Ky. Civil Liberties Union, 1986, Grauman award U. Louisville, 1986. Mem. ABA, Fed. Bar Assn., Ky. Bar Assn. (Judge of Yr. award 1996), Louisville Bar Assn., Nat. Ry. Hist. Soc. Office: US Dist Ct 252 US Courthouse 601 W Broadway Louisville KY 40202-2238

ALLEN, CHARLES NORMAN, television, film and video producer; b. Miami, July 13, 1944; s. Claude Braswell and Virginia Lucille (Gravitt) A.; m. Susan Carole Dorn, May 1, 1970; children: Jennifer, Brian. BS, U. Miami, 1967. V.p. Tel-Air Interests Inc., Miami, 1967-79; pres. Cinema East Corp., Miami, 1979—, World Studios Corp., Atlanta, 1987—, ADR Internat., Miami, 1991—; bd. dirs. World Studios Corp., ADR Internat. Representer prodns. U.S. internat. film events CINE-Washington, 1974, 75, 80, 81, 87, 88, 89, 92. Trustee Dade County Pub. Health Trust; commr. Biscayne Park, Fla., 1974-76; active Dade County Dem. Exec. Commn., 1976-80, Dade Dem. Treas., 1976-79. Mem. Am. Advt. Fed., South Fla. Film & Tape Producers Assn., Assn. Indep. Comml. Producers, Nat. Advt. Fraternity, Greater Miami Advt. Fed., Advt. Miami, Greater Miami C. of C., Sigma Chi Frat., Iron Arrow Honor Soc., Alpha Delta Sigma. Democrat. Methodist. Office: Cinema East Corp 5859 Biscayne Blvd Miami FL 33137-2638

ALLEN, CYNTHIA LYNN, elementary education educator; b. Indpls., Apr. 22, 1960; d. Byron Albert and Cora (Looper) A. BA, Oakwood Coll., 1977-81; MEd, Clark Atlanta U., 1992-94. Lic. real estate agent, Ind. Respiratory technician Ind. U. Hosp., Indpls., 1982-88; sr. rsch. technician Ind. U., Indpls., 1987-88; case mgr. Social Svcs., Key West, Fla., 1988-89; rsch. technician III Morehouse Sch. of Medicine, Atlanta, 1989-91; tchr. DeKalb County Schs., Atlanta, 1991—; educational tech. adv. Kennesaw State Coll., Atlanta, 1994-95; cons. math book adoption DeKalb County Schs., Atlanta, 1994-95. Founder Black History Museum, DeKalb County Sch., 1996; women ministry Decatur Seventh Day Advent Ch., 1996—; cook Homeless Feeding, Decatur, 1994—. Mem. Nat. Edn. Assn., Nat. Alliance of Black Sch. Educators, Ga. Tchrs. Assn. Adventist. Home: 3807 Tree Mtn Pkwy Stone Mountain GA 30083

ALLEN, DAVID ROGER, theatre educator; b. N.Y.C., Oct. 20, 1952; s. Merton and Barbara Ann (Goldstein) A.; m. Katherine G. Horchler, Aug. 5, 1995. BFA, Ithaca Coll., 1974; MA in Theatre, U. Conn., 1978; postgrad., Southwest Tex. State U., 1991; PhD of Fine Arts, Tex. Tech. U., 1994. Instr. speech Phillips Sch. Bus., Austin, Tex., 1990; instr. theatre Austin CC., 1990-91; instr. English and math. Grad. Record Exam Prep. Svcs., Lubbock, Tex., 1991-95; asst. prof. theatre Palm Beach C.C., Lake Worth, Fla., 1995—; tchg. asst. dept dance and theatre Tex. Tech. U., Lubbock, 1992-94, vis. asst. prof. theatre, 1994-95. Editor Mgmt. Matters jour., 1989—; assoc. editor Indsl. Health and Hazards Update jour., 1988—; presenter of papers and workshops in field; numerous directing and acting performances. Named Outstanding Young Man of Yr. Jaycees, 1979, Best Actor Hon. Mention Lubbock Avalanche-Jour., 1994. Mem. Assn. Theatre in Higher Edn., Southeast Theatre Conf., Theatre Comm. Group, Speech Comm. Assn., Fla. Theatre Conf., Phi Kappa Phi, Alpha Psi Omega.

ALLEN, DENNY, energy company executive; b. Wichita Falls, Tex., Nov. 16, 1939; s. Herman S. Allen and Fay Glenn (Heasley) Kuykendahl; m. Martha Carolyn Newton, Apr. 5, 1958 (div. 1977); children: Lita Louise Allen, Lori Lea Allen; m. Marylinda Breeckner, Jan. 30, 1986; 1 child, Marie Denise. Grad. high sch., San Angelo, Tex. Rodeo clown, bull fighter Rodeo Cowboy's Assn., various locations throughout U.S., 1956-68; pres. Sweet River Inc., Dallas and Goias, Brazil, 1968-71; cattle specialist E.F. Hutton & Co., Houston, 1971-73; pres. Larry Mahan Boot Co., El Paso, Tex., 1973-82; pres. Club Nautico Adventurent, Ft. Lauderdale, Fla., 1983-86, chmn., 1986-87; ptnr. Sierra Oil Co., Keller, Tex., 1987-90; pres. Allen Energy Co., 1990—; chmn. Handler/Fenton Shirt Co., Denver, 1981-82, 1st Nat. Bank Cripple Creek, Colo., 1970, 1st Nat. Bank Milltown, Ind., 1970, 1st Nat. Bank Wilcox, Ariz., 1970. Served with USN, 1958-62. Republican. Home: 3940 Glenwick Ln Dallas TX 75205-1238 Office: Allen Energy Co 3419 Westminster Ave # 310G Dallas TX 75205-1387

ALLEN, DIANA D., insurance agent, author; b. Dallas, Nov. 26, 1945; d. William S. and Pearl P. (Sessions) Dandridge; m. Edwin Richard Allen, Dec. 23, 1966; children: Reagan, Ryan. BS, U. Ark., 1967. Tchr. elem. sch. Lincoln/McKinley Sch., Enid, Okla., 1967-72; real estate agent House of Hough Agy., Enid, 1972-75; ins. agent Dick Allen Ins. Co., Inc., Enid, 1990—. Author: Gourmet: The Quick and Easy Way, 1992. Asst. pack master, den leader Boy Scouts Am., Glenwood Sch., Enid, 1981-85; sustaining chmn. Jr. Welfare League, Enid, 1979, 94; head Parent of Okla. Tiger Football Parents Orgn., Columbia, Mo., 1994—; bd. dirs. Arts and Humanities Coun., Enid, 1994—; mem. Rep. Women's Club; tchr. Bible and Sunday Sch.; sponsor Bravettes Pep Club, 1993-95; pres. Enid High Sch. Parent Tchr. Student Assn., 1993-94, parliamentarian, 1994-95. Mem. PEO (pres. 1987-88), DAR, Ladies Shrine (v.p. 1970), Oakwood Ladies Golf Assn. (v.p. 1992-93), Bravettes Pep Club (sponsor 1994—), PTA (pres. 1993-94), Circle Two (nurturing com.), Kappa Alpha Theta (alumni pres. 1969, 85). Presbyterian. Home: 1614 Quailwood Dr Enid OK 73703-2047

ALLEN, DOROTHY JEAN, librarian; b. McComb, Miss., Oct. 4, 1952; d. John Lee and Mary Louise (Wells) A.; children: Gregory, Demetrious. BA, Southern U., Baton Rouge, 1978; MLS, U. Pitts., 1979. Reference libr.

W.Va. U., Morgantown, 1980-81; sch. libr. Eva Gordon Elem. Sch., Magnolia, Miss., 1981-82, 85-86; libr. East La. State Hosp., Jackson, 1982-85; reference libr. Jackson (Miss.) Hinds Libr. Sys., 1986-88; circulation libr. Rowland Med. Libr., Jackson, 1988-94; acquisitions libr. Southern Univ. Law Ctr. Libr., 1994—. Mem. Am. Assn. Law Librs. Democrat. Baptist. Office: Southern U Law Ctr Libr 2 Swan Ave Baton Rouge LA 70813

ALLEN, EDISON BRENT, journalist, columnist; b. Greensboro, N.C., Apr. 7, 1927; s. William Brent and Lula (Osborne) A.; m. Gladys Herring, Dec. 22, 1969 (dec. July 1984); children: Donna A. James, Joy A. Currin. Student, U. N.C., 1945-47, Tulane U., 1958-60. Staff writer, columnist The Charlotte (N.C.) Observer, 1942-52; asst. dir. athletics Tulane U., New Orleans, 1952-57, dir. alumni fund, 1957-64, dir. devel., 1964-68; v.p. U. Ala., Tuscaloosa, 1968-69; v.p., vice chmn. C.W. Shaver & Co., Inc., N.Y.C., 1969-88; exec. counsel Ketchum, Inc., Pitts., 1989-92; columnist Scripps Howard News Svc., Washington, 1995—. Author: Of Time and Chase, 1969; author, editor: Fundamentals of Educational Fundraising, 1968. Mem. nat. bd. dirs. Am. Alumni Coun., 1965-69. Mem. Pi Kappa Alpha, Omicron Delta Kappa, Mensa. Office: 1260 Brookforest Dr NE Atlanta GA 30324

ALLEN, ELIZABETH MARESCA, marketing executive; b. Red Bank, N.J., Jan. 4, 1958; d. Paul William Michael and Roberta Gertrude (Abbes) Maresca; m. David D. Allen; 1 son, Brandon D. Student, Brookdale Community Coll., 1976-77; A Bus. Adminstrn., Tidewater C.C., 1988; student, Va. Wesleyan Coll., 1994—. Systems analyst Methods Research Corp., Farmingdale, N.J., 1977-79; div. mgr. Abacus Bus. Svcs., Inc., Virginia Beach, Va., 1979—. Bd. dirs. Arthritis Found., Norfolk, Va., 1986-90; v.p. Charlestowne Civic League, Virginia Beach, 1983-84, Plantation Lakes Homeowners Assn., Chesapeake, Va., 1992—; advisor Commonwealth Coll., Norfolk, 1984-91; del. Va. Rep. Conv., 1993—. Mem. Women's Network Hampton Roads (publicity chmn. 1988-91, chmn. publicity for Job Fair 1989), Hampton Roads C. of C. (com. chmn. 1985, 88), Williamsburg Area C. of C. (exhibit chmn. 1987). Republican. Roman Catholic. Office: Abacus Bus Svcs Inc 5620 Virginia Beach Blvd Virginia Beach VA 23462-5631

ALLEN, EUGENE R., construction executive; b. 1926. With Herman Weber Inc., Beaumont, Tex., 1947-54, 62-64, Chris Smith Constrn., Beaumont, Tex., 1954-62, Bella Constrn., Beaumont, Tex., 1964-85; pres., CEO Allco Inc., Beaumont, Tex., 1985—.

ALLEN, FRANCES NORMAN, dental association adminstrator; b. Shelby, N.C., Feb. 28, 1935; d. Walter B. and Frances Irene (Keener) Norman; m. Dewey L. Allen, Jr., July 2, 1952; children: Roger L., Gregory W. Student, Hinds Jr. Coll., Raymond, Miss., 1966-68, Durham C.C. Rsch. sec. Rsch. Triangle Inst., Research Triangle Park, N.C., 1967; asst. to dept. head U. N.C. Sch. Medicine, Chapel Hill, 1968-69; continuing edn. dir. N.C. Assn. CPAs, 1969-73; adminstrv. asst. Miss. Dental Assn., Jackson, 1973-76; exec. dir. So. Acad. Periodontology, Clinton, Miss., 1975—; project dir. Health Edn. and Welfare, Jackson, Miss., 1974-78. Asst. editor newsletters So. Acad. Periodontology, 1973—. Mem. NAFE, Am. Soc. Assn. Execs., Miss. Soc. Assn. Execs. Baptist. Office: Southern Acad of Periodontology PO Box 1300 Clinton MS 39060

ALLEN, FRANK, retail executive, entrepreneur, writer; b. Alexandria, La., Feb. 25, 1966; s. Fred Allen and Gloria Mae (Richard) Johnson; m. Wanda A. Allen; children: Adrian, Aundrea. BA in Bus., Northwestern State Coll., Natchitoches, La., 1988. Ops. mgr. RPM Corporate, Livonia, Miss., 1989-91; owner, operator Allen's Clothing, Alexandria, 1992-94; owner Unique Fashions, Pineville, La., 1992-94, Allen's Fine Art Studio, Alexandria, 1994-96, The Tie Shop Inc (8 stores), Alexandria, 1995—; pres. T.I.E. Inc., Alexandria, 1995—. Author: The Real Problem, 1995, True Guidance, 1995; pub.: (jour.) Testimonies, 1995. Chmn. bd. dirs. African Expo, Alexandria, 1995-96; red coat amb. The C. of C., Alexandria, 1992-94. Named New Artist of Yr. Black Heritage Com., Natchitoches, 1995, New Upcoming Entrepreneur, Alexandria Daily Town Talk, 1995. Mem. Nat. Entrepreneur Assn., Kappa Alpha Psi (pres. Natchitoches chpt. 1987-88). Office: The Tie Shop 3437 Masonic Dr Ste 1190 Alexandria LA 71301

ALLEN, G. CHRISTY L., elementary schoool educator; b. Ft. Scott, Kans., Dec. 1, 1968; d. Stanley N. and Margaret G. (Steele) A. BS in Phys. Edn. and Biology, McPherson Coll., 1991; MS in Biomechanics, Kans. State U., 1994. Cert. tchr., Tex. Grad. tchg. asst. Kans. State U., Manhattan, 1991-94; tchr., coach Peaster (Tex.) Ind. Sch. Dist., 1993-94, Rains Ind. Sch. Dist., Emory, Tex., 1994—; counselor Heart of Am. Camps, Salina, Kans., 1990-93; volleyball dir. Rains-Alba Volleyball Camps, Emory, 1994; health curriculum cons. Rains H.S., Emory, 1994-95; biology curriculum cons. Rains Ind. Sch. Dist., 1994-95. Cons. Rains Youth Sports Assn., Emory, 1994-95. Kans. State rsch. grantee, 1993. Mem. Women's Basketball Coaches Assn., Tex. Girl's Coaches Assn., Nat. Softball Coaches Assn., Sci. Tchrs. Assn. Tex., Classroom Tchrs., Fellow Christian Athletes (asst. dir. Rains chpt. 1994-95). Republican. Nazarene. Office: Rains Ind Sch Dist PO Box 247 Emory TX 75440

ALLEN, GEORGE FELIX, governor; b. Whittier, Calif., Mar. 8, 1952; s. George H. and Henrietta Lumbroso A.; m. Susan M. Brown; children: Tyler, Forrest. BA cum laude in History, U. Va., 1974, JD, 1977. Mem. Va. Ho. of Dels., Richmond, 1983-91, 102d Congress from 7th Dist. Va., 1991-93; gov. State of Va., 1994—. Vol. Earlysville Vol. Fire Dept., Earlysville, Va., 1980-91; advisor Pres. Coun. Phys. Fitness and Sports, 1981-91. Presbyterian. Office: State Capitol 3rd Fl Gov Office Richmond VA 23219*

ALLEN, GILBERT BRUCE, English language educator, poet; b. Rockville Centre, N.Y., Jan. 1, 1951; s. Joseph Aloysius and Marie Dawn (Skocik) A.; m. Barbara Jean Szigeti, Aug. 17, 1974. BA, Cornell U., 1972, MFA, 1974, PhD, 1977. Tchr. English Odessa-Montour Cen. Sch., Odessa, N.Y., 1974-75; instr. English Cornell U., Ithaca, N.Y., 1975-77; asst. prof. English Furman U., Greenville, S.C., 1977-83, assoc. prof., 1983-89, prof., 1989—. Author: In Everything: Poems 1972-1979, 1982, Second Chances, 1991, Commandments at Eleven, 1994; editor Furman Studies, 1981-90. Recipient various poetry and fiction awards. Mem. South Atlantic MLA, Poetry Soc. Am., Nat. Coun. Tchrs. English, Philological Assn. of the Carolinas. Office: Furman U Box 30891 English Dept Greenville SC 29613

ALLEN, JAMES HARMON, JR., civil engineer; b. Pratt, Kans., Apr. 8, 1948; s. James Harmon and Glenda Rosena (Hackenberg) A.; m. Betty June Schlegel, July 11, 1970; children: James III, Christine, Benjamin. BCE, Kans. State U., 1971. Registered profl. engr., Kans., Okla.; lic. surface mining blaster, Okla. Asst. supt. Richards spur Dolese Bros. Co., Elgin, Okla., 1980-82, supt., 1982-84; asst. gen. supt. Dolese Bros. Co., Oklahoma City, 1984, chief engr., 1984-87, asst. aggregate ops. mgr., 1987-88, gen. mgr. aggregate and prestress ops., 1988-91, gen. mgr. ops., 1991—; chmn. surface mining adv. coun. Dept. of Mines, Oklahoma City, 1988-92; mem. asphalt task force Okla. Dept. Transp., Oklahoma City, 1988. 1st lt. U.S. Army, 1971-74. Mem. NSPE, Nat. Stone Assn. (chmn. com. 1990-92, vice chmn. ops. divsn. 1993-94, chmn. ops. divsn. 1995—, chmn. plant cert. com.), Okla. Soc. Profl. Engrs., Okla. Air Quality Task Force, Audubon Soc. Republican. Presbyterian. Home: 12717 Saint Andrews Dr Oklahoma City OK 73120-8812 Office: Dolese Bros Co PO Box 677 20 NW 13th Oklahoma City OK 73101

ALLEN, JAMES HENRY, magistrate; b. Memphis, May 10, 1935; s. Henry L. and Hazel V. A.; m. Charlene Anne Jayroe, July 29, 1961; children—James Henry, Elizabeth Hazel, Luanne Mae. A.B., Memphis State U., 1957; LL.B., Tulane U., 1960. Bar: La. 1960, Tenn. 1961, U.S. Dist. Ct. (we. dist.) Tenn. 1961, U.S. Ct. Appeals (6th cir.) 1973, U.S. Supreme Ct. 1969. Assoc. Tual, Allan, Keltner, and Lee, Memphis, 1960; assoc. Nelson, Norvell & Floyd, Memphis, 1961; claims adjuster State Farm Mut. Automobile Ins. Co., Memphis, 1961-65; adminstrv. asst. law clk. Bankruptcy Ct., Memphis, 1965-67; assoc. Charles G. Black, Memphis, 1967-69; asst. atty. gen. Shelby County (Tenn.), 1969-79; U.S. magistrate, Memphis, 1979—; lectr. on criminal law, recruit class Shelby County Sheriff's Dept., Memphis, 1976; lectr. on fed. rules civil procedure Continuing Legal Edn., Memphis, 1981. Served with USMCR, 1957-65. Tulane U. scholar, 1957-60. Mem. La. State Bar Assn., Memphis and Shelby County Bar Assn., Nat. Council U.S. Magistrates, Phi Alpha Delta. Baptist. Office: US Dist Ct 317 Fed Bldg 167 N Main St Memphis TN 38103-1816

ALLEN, JAMES MADISON, family practice physician, lawyer, consultant; b. Columbus, Ohio, Nov. 14, 1944; s. D.C. Allen and Edith Melvin; m. Elizabeth Wolfe, Dec. 30, 1972, children: Elaine, Michelle, Katherine, James Jr. BA, U. Ga., 1969, MA, 1970; BS in Medicine, U. N.D., Grand Forks, 1977; MD, U. Ala., Birmingham, 1980; JD, Birmingham Sch. Law, Birmingham, 1994. Resident in pathology Bapt. Med. Ctrs., Birmingham, Ala., 1980-81; resident in internal medicine Bapt. Med. Ctrs., Birmingham, 1985-86; med. officer U.S. Indian Health Svc., Phila., Miss., 1981-82; clinic dir. Rush Hosp. Clinics, Phila., 1983-85; v.p., bd. dirs. Am. Family Care, Birmingham, 1986-88; pvt. practice AMI Brookwood Family Med. Ctr., Birmingham, 1988—; cons. Riverchase Clin. Rsch., Birmingham, 1990—; pres. U.S. Physicians Inc., Birmingham, 1982—; cons. DiGiorno Foods divsn. Kraft Foods, Birmingham, 1988—, So. Nuclear Oper. Co., 1993—, So. Drug Rsch., Birmingham. Commr. Boy Scouts Am., Birmingham, 1988—. With USMC, 1962-66, Viet Nam. Recipient award of merit B'nai B'rith, 1970, Eagle Scout award, Scouter's award, Wood Badge Boy Scouts Am. Mem. Am. Acad. Family Physicians, Med. Assn. Ala., Assn. Am. Indian Physicians, Shriners (Noble 1988), Masons (Master 1966, 32nd degree 1978), Riverchase Country Club, Phi Gamma Delta (Ga. chpt. pres. 1967-68), Sigma Delta Kappa. Home: 857 Tulip Poplar Dr Birmingham AL 35244-1639 Office: Riverchase Convenient Care 4515 Southlake Pkwy Ste 104 Birmingham AL 35244-3318

ALLEN, JEFFREY RODGERS, lawyer; b. West Point, N.Y., Aug. 15, 1953; s. James R. and Kathryn (Lewis) A.; m. Cynthia Lynn Colyer, Aug. 10, 1975; children: Emily Rodgers, Elizabeth Colyer, Richard Byrd. BA in History, U. Va., 1975; JD, U. Richmond, 1978. Bar: Va. 1978, U.S. Ct. Mil. Appeals 1981, U.S. Ct. Appeals (4th cir.) 1982, U.S. Supreme Ct. 1982. Trial atty. Michie, Hamlett, Donato & Lowry, Charlottesville, Va., 1982-86; chief counsel Va. Dept. Mil. Affairs, Richmond, 1986—; atty., advisor U.S. Army Mobile Air Surg. Transport Team, Savannah, Ga., 1980-82; mem. steering com. X-Car Litigation Group, 1983-85; lectr., organizer Law Everyone Should Know series Piedmont (Va.) C.C., Charlottesville, 1984-86; trial atty., of counsel Thorsen, Marchant & Scher Richmond, 1986—; mem. legal adv. com. Va. Gov.'s Mil. Adv. Commn., 1987—, judge advocate adv. coun. N.G. Bur., 1993-96. Pres. Regency Woods Condominium Assn., Richmond, 1976-78, Ashcroft Neighborhood Assn., Charlottesville, 1983-86; treas. Va. N.G. Found., 1986—; mem. Tuckahoe YMCA Indian Programs, 1991—. Capt. U.S. Army, 1978-82, lt. col. JAGC, Va. Air N.G., 1982—. Mem. Assn. Trial Lawyers Am., Va. Trial Lawyers Assn., Richmond Bar Assn. Republican. Methodist. Home: 2700 Cottage Cove Dr Richmond VA 23233-3318 Office: Va Dept Mil Affairs 600 E Broad St Richmond VA 23219-1800

ALLEN, JOHN THOMAS, JR., lawyer; b. St. Petersburg, Fla., Aug. 23, 1935; s. John Thomas and Mary Lita (Shields) A.; m. Joyce Ann Lindsey, June 16, 1958 (div. 1985); children: John Thomas, III, Linda Joyce, Catherine Lee (dec.); m. Janice Dearmin Hudson, Mar. 16, 1987. BS in Bus. Adminstrn. with honors, U. Fla., 1958; JD, Stetson U., 1961. Bar: Fla. 1961, U.S. Dist. Ct. (mid. dist.) Fla. 1962, U.S. Ct. Appeals (5th cir.) 1963, U.S. Ct. Appeals (11th cir.) 1983, U.S. Supreme Ct. 1970. Assoc. Mann, Harrison, Mann & Rowe and successor Greene, Mann, Rowe, Davenport & Stanton, St. Petersburg, 1961-74, ptnr., 1967-74; sole practice, St. Petersburg, 1974-95; pvt. practice Allen & Maller, P.A., 1996—; counsel Pinellas County Legis. Del., 1974-75; counsel for Pinellas County as spl. counsel on water matters, 1975—. Mem. Com. of 100, St. Petersburg, 1975—. Mem. ABA, Fla. Bar Assn., St. Petersburg Bar Assn., St. Petersburg C. of C., Beta Gamma Sigma. Democrat. Methodist. Club: Lions (St. Petersburg). Office: County of Pinellas 4508 Central Ave Saint Petersburg FL 33711-1041

ALLEN, JOHN TIMOTHY, mechanical engineer; b. Columbus, Tex., Sept. 25, 1954; s. Jack Kenneth and Genola Marie (Gardner) A.; m. Nancy Marie Choate, Dec. 18, 1982; children: John Timothy II, Elizabeth Suzanne. BS Mech. Engring., Tex. A&M U., 1976. Sr. project engr. Halliburton Energy Svcs., Duncan, Okla., 1976-94; mgr. ops. CECO Equipment/Div. Nowsco, Kilgore, Tex., 1994-95; mgr. prodn. and tech. JM Clipper Corp., Nacogdoches, Tex., 1995—. Patentee in field. Precinct chmn. Stephens County Rep. Party, Okla., 1993; county campaign co-chmn. Nichols for U.S. Senate Com., 1980. Mem. Am. Soc. Mech. Engrs., Energy Rubber Group, Wafer jet Technology Assn. Mem. Disciples of Christ. Office: JM Clipper Corp PO Drawer 632340 Nacogdoches TX 75963-2340

ALLEN, MARILYN MYERS POOL, theater director, video producer; b. Fresno, Calif., Nov. 2, 1934; d. Laurence B. and Asa (Griggs) Myers; BA, Stanford U., 1955, postgrad., 1955-56; postgrad. U. Tex., 1957-60, West Tex. State U. summers 1962, 63, Odessa Coll., 1987-88; m. Joseph Harold Pool, Dec. 28, 1955; children: Pamela Elizabeth, Victoria Anne, Catherine Marcia; m. Neal R. Allen, Apr. 1982. Pvt. tchr. drama, speech, acting, directing, speech correction, Amarillo, Tex., 1960-82, Midland, Tex., 1982—; free-lance radio and TV actress; asst. mng. dir. Amarillo Little Theatre, 1964-66, mng. dir., 1966-68; mng. dir. Horseshoe Players, touring profl. theater, 1969-73; actress, multi-media prodn. Palo Duro Canyon, 1971; dir. touring children's theatre, 1978-79 guest actress in Medea, Amarillo Coll., 1981; guest reciter Amarillo Symphony, 1972, Midland-Odessa Symphony, 1984. Pres. Tex. Non-Profit Theatres, 1972-74, 75-77, bd. dirs., 1988-91; 1st v.p. High Plains Center for Performing Arts, 1969-73; adv. mem. dept. fine arts Amarillo Coll., 1980-82. Adv. mem. Tex. Constnl. Revision Commn., 1973-75; mem. adv. coun. U. Tex. Coll. Fine Arts, 1969-72; cmty. adv. com. for women Amarillo Coll., 1975-79; conv. program com. Am. Theatre Assn., 1978, program participant 1978-80, bd. dirs., 1980-83; bd. dirs. Amarillo Found. Health and Sci. Edn., 1976-82, program v.p., 1979-81; bd. dirs. Domestic Violence Coun., 1979-82, March of Dimes, 1979-81, Tex. Panhandle Heritage Found., 1964-82, Friends of Fine Arts, W. Tex. State U. (now West Tex. A&M U.), 1980-82, Amarillo Pub. Libr., 1980-82, Amarillo Symphony, 1981-82; publicity chmn. Midland Cmty. Theatre, 1984-87, bd. govs., 1986-92, sec., 1987-88, v.p., 1988-92; mem. Mus. of S.W., Midland Arts Assembly; bd. dirs. Midland County Rep. Women, Ways and Means Ch., 1991, 1st v.p., 1992, publicity chair, 1994; mem. Midland County Redistricting com., 1991; cultural exchange del. from Midland, Tex., to Dong Ying, China, 1993; Tex. UIL one act play adjudicator, 1974—. Recipient cert. of appreciation Woman of Year, Amarillo Bus. and Profl. Women's Club, 1966; Best Actress award for Hedda Gabler role Amarillo Little Theatre 1965, Best Dir. award for Rashomon, 1967, 1st Pl. award for video spl. Tex. Press Conf., 1988, 1st Pl. award for news Tex. Press Conf., 1989, Disting. Svc. award Tex. Non-Profit Theatres, 1992; named Amarillo Woman of Yr., Beta Sigma Phi, 1980, Broadcaster of the Yr., Rocky Mountain Press Conf., 1988, Hamhock of Yr., Midland Cmty. Theatre, 1992, Outstanding Svc. award Midland Arts Assembly, 1992; Travel fellow AAUW, 1973, 78. Fellow Am. Assn. Cmty. Theatre (dir. 1979-82, 82-84, v.p. planning and devel. 1985-87, co-chair AACT/Fest '95); mem. USTA (sr. women's team sect. winner 1993, 94), S.W. Theatre Conf. (assoc.dir., 1973-76, 82-84, exec. com. 1982-84, Disting. Svc. award 1985), Tex. Theatre Council (dir. 1974-78, exec. com., pres. 1975-76), AAUW (br. pres. 1973-75, state chmn. cultural interests 1975-77, 86-88, state program v.p. 1977-79, state bd. dirs. 1984-88, program v.p. Midland 1988-89), Episc. Ch. Women (program v.p. Midland 1988-89, outreach chair 1996), DAR (chpt. chaplain 1971-75, historian 1975-77), C. of C. (fine arts coun.), U.S. Judo Assn., Symphony Guild, Amarillo Art Assn., Midland Symphony Guild (arrangements chmn. 1983-84), Act IX, Shakespeare As We Like It, Amarillo Law Wives Club (pres. 1976-77), Midland Law Wives, Hamhocks (v.p. 1985-86).

ALLEN, MARJORIE JOAN, librarian; b. Austin, Tex., Feb. 11, 1931; d. Dwight Edward Sr. and Marguerite Faye (Jackson) Farr; m. Frank Morrell Jr., June 25, 1955; children: Edward, Debra, David (dec.), Faye. BFA in Theatre, U. Tex., 1951; MLS, 1977, postgrad 1976-78. Technician Tex. Touring Theatre, Austin, 1951-52; sec. to econs. dir. UN, Beirut, 1953-54; elem. and secondary tchr. Smithville (Tex.) Ind. Sch. Dist., 1954-74, theatre dir., 1962-74; tchr. San Marcos (Tex.) Consol. Sch. Dist., 1974-75; tchr., theatre dir. Wiemar (Tex.) Ind. Sch. Dist., 1975-76; tchr., theatre dir., libr. Tex. Sch. for Blind, Austin, 1976-82; theatre dir., libr. Smithville Ind. Sch. Dist., 1982-92, secondary libr., 1992—; cons. in field. Author: Hope Made A Window, 1991; author poems. Del. to state conv. Rep. Com., Houston, Tex., 1988, Ft.Worth, 1990, San Antonio, 1996, precinct chmn. 1995, 96, alt. state conv., Dallas, 1992. Mem. ALA (Tex. del. legis. day 1992), Tex. Ednl. Theatre Assn. (sec. 1974-76, bd. dirs. 1976-78, achievement award 1980), Tex. Libr. Assn. (sec.-treas. 1978-80), Tex. Assn. Secondary Librs. (bd. dirs. 1980-82), Tex. Ednl. Theatre Assn. Adjudicators Orgn. (critic judge 1992—), Univ. Interscholastic League (critic judge 1992—), Romance Writers Am. (editor newsletter 1993—), PEO (various offices 1987-92, pres. 1992-94). Republican. Methodist. Home: PO Box 660 Smithville TX 78957-0660 Office: Smithville Ind Sch Dist PO Box 479 Smithville TX 78957-0479

ALLEN, MARYON PITTMAN, former senator, journalist, lecturer, interior and clothing designer; b. Meridian, Miss., Nov. 30, 1925; d. John D. and Tellie (Chism) Pittman; m. Joshua Sanford Mullins, Jr., Oct. 17, 1946 (div. Jan. 1959); children: Joshua Sanford III, John Pittman, Maryon Foster; m. James Browning Allen, Aug. 7, 1964 (dec. June 1978). Student, U. Ala., 1944-47, Internat. Inst. Interior Design, 1970. Office mgr. for Dr. Alston Callahan, Birmingham, Ala., 1959-60; bus. mgr. psychiat. clinic U. Ala. Med. Center, Birmingham, 1960-61; life underwriter Protective Life Ins. Co., Birmingham, 1961-62; women's editor Sun Newspapers, Birmingham, 1962-64; v.p., ptnr. Pittman family cos., J.D. Pittman Partnership Co., J.D. Pittman Tractor Co., Emerald Valley Corp., Mountain Lake Farms, Inc., Birmingham; mem. U.S. Senate (succeeding late husband James B. Allen), 1978; dir. pub. rels. and advt. C.G. Sloan & Co. Auction House, Washington, 1981; feature writer Birmingham News, 1964; writer syndicated column Reflections of a News Hen, Washington, 1969-78; feature writer, columnist Maryon Allen's Washington, Washington Post, 1979-81; columnist McCall's Needlework Mag., 1993—; owner The Maryon Allen Co. Cliff House (Restoration/Design), Birmingham. Contbg. editor So. Accents Mag., 1976-78. Mem. Ladies of U.S. Senate unit ARC, Former Mems. of Congress, Ala. Hist. Commn., Blair House Fine Arts Commn.; charter mem. Birmingham Com. of 100 for Women; trustee Children's Fresh Air Farm; trustee, deacon, elder Ind. Presbyn. Ch., Birmingham; Democratic Presdl. elector, Ala., 1968. Recipient 1st place award for best original column Ala. Press Assn., 1962, 63, also various press state and nat. awards for typography, fashion writing, food pages, also several awards during Senate service; sponsor, U.S. Navy Nuclear submarine, U.S.S. Birmingham, S.S.N. 695, launched Newport News, Va., 1977, commissioned 1978. Mem. Nat. Press Club, 1925 F Street Club, 91st Congress Club, Congl. Club, Birmingham Country Club. Home: Cliff House 3215 Cliff Rd S Birmingham AL 35205-1405

ALLEN, NANCY BATES, medical educator; b. Phila., May 26, 1952; d. Paul Bassett and Mary Jean (Ford) Bates; m. Barry Worth Allen, June 7, 1974; children: Dorothy Jean, Peter Woodward. BA, Wellesley Coll., 1974; student, Med. Coll. Va., Richmond, 1974-75; MD, Tufts U., 1978. Diplomate Am. Bd. Internal Med. Rheumatology. Intern then resident Duke U. Med. Ctr., Durham, N.C., 1978-81, fellow in rheumatology, 1980-82, assoc. medicine, 1982-83; asst. prof. medicine Duke U. Med. Ctr., Durham, 1984-92, assoc. prof. medicine, 1992—. Reviewer jours.; contbr. articles to profl. jours. and books chpts. Elected mem. Exec. Com. Acad. Coun. Duke U., 1993-95, pres. Clin. Scis. Faculty Coun. Acad. Affairs, 1993-95; pres. Duke Park Neighborhood Assn., Durham, 1985-91; mem. Inter-Neighborhood Coun. Durham, 1985-86; cons. Wegeners Granulomatosis Internat. Support Group, 1992—. Fellow Am. Coll. Rheumatology; mem. N.C. Rheumatology Assn., Internat. Network for Study Vasculitis, Alpha Omega Alpha. Democrat. Office: Duke U Med Ctr PO Box 3440 Durham NC 27710

ALLEN, NINA STRÖMGREN, biology educator; b. Copenhagen, Denmark, Sept. 17, 1935; came to U.S. 1951; d. Bengt G.D. and Sigrid C.S. (Hartz) Strömgren; m. Robert Jackson Williams, July 18, 1958 (div. 1970); children: Erik Robert, Harriet Hopf; m. Robert Day Allen, Sept. 11, 1970 (dec.); 1 child, Barbara Sigrid. BS, U. Wis., 1957; MS, U. Md., 1970, PhD, 1973. Teaching asst. botany U. Wis., 1957-58; teaching asst. botany U. Md., 1964-67, NIH predoctoral fellow, 1967-70; rsch. asst. SUNY, Albany, 1970-73, postdoctoral fellow, 1973-95; summer rschr. Marine Biol. Lab., Woods Hole, Mass., 1970-94; vis. asst. prof., rsch. assoc. Dartmouth Coll., Hanover, N.H., 1975-76, asst. prof., 1976-83; assoc. prof. biology Wake Forest U., Winston-Salem, 1984-92, prof. biology, 1993—; prof. botany N.C. State U., Raleigh, 1995—; NSF vis. prof. for women Stanford U., 1990-91; lectr. in field; ad hoc reviewer NIH Biomed. Rsch. Tech. Rev. Com., 1988, study sect. mem., 1989-94; trustee, mem. exec. com. Marine Biol. Labs.; mem. NSF Instrumentation Panel. Editl. bd. Cell Motility, 1980-85, BioTechniques, 1989-96, Jour. Eukaryotic Micorbiology, 1995—, Jour. Microscopic and Microtechnique, 1995—; series editor, founder Plant Biology, Wiley-Liss, 1985—; contbr. articles to profl. jours.; prodr. sci. films and videos. Fellow AAAS; mem. Am. Soc. Cell Biology, Am. Soc. Plant Physiologists, N.E. Algal Soc. (founding mem.), Phycol. Soc. Am., N.C. Acad. Sci., Am. Soc. for Gravitational and Space Biology, Electron Microscopical Soc. Am., Royal Microscopical Soc. (fellow 1985), Phi Beta Kappa, Sigma Xi. Democrat. Unitarian Universalist. Home: 4920 Richland Dr Raleigh NC 27612 Office: NC State U Dept Botany Raleigh NC 27695

ALLEN, NOREEN JEANNE, secondary school educator; b. Holyoke, Mass., July 1, 1943; d. Paul Robert and Claire (Willett) Boucher; m. Robert N. Allen Jr., Apr. 15, 1967; children: Kevin, Ray, Michelle. BA in Math., Our Lady of the Elms, 1965. Cert. tchr., Mass., W.Va. Tchr. math Ludlow (Mass.) High Sch., 1965-72; adminstr. Webster (N.Y.) Montessori Sch., 1973-75; tchr. math South Charleston (W.Va.) County Schs., South Charleston Jr. High Sch., 1979-86; tchr. math. George Washington High Sch., Charleston, 1987—; chair math. dept. George Washington High Sch., 1987—; adminstr. SAT, 1987—; math. software reviewer Kanawha County schs., 1995—. Contbg. author math curriculum Kanawha City Schs. Coord. ushers and greeters Blessed Sacrament Ch., So. Charleston, 1990—. Named Tchr. of Yr., South Charleston, 1984; NASA grantee Wheeling Jesuit Coll., 1990; selected to W.Va. Tchrs. Acad., 1992. Mem. Nat. Coun. Tchrs. Math., W.Va. Tchrs. Math. (presider regional math. conf. 1994), Kanawha County Tchrs. Math. Roman Catholic. Home: 766 Echo Rd Charleston WV 25303-2709

ALLEN, PATRICIA J., library director; b. McLean County, Ky., Nov. 10, 1941; d. Richard Louis and Helen (Hancock) Jones; m. Jerry M. Mize, Mar. 19, 1960 (div. 1978); children: Martin P., Elizabeth M. Atherton; m. Lawrence A. Allen, Nov. 24, 1983 (div. 1985). Student, Murray (Ky.) State U., 1959-60; BA, Ky. Wesleyan Coll., 1962; MA, Western Ky. U., 1974; MLS, U. Ky., 1982; postgrad., U. N.C., 1983-84. Libr. pub. elem. schs. Daviess County, Ky., 1963-70; media specialist pub. elem., mid. and high schs. McLean County, Ky., 1970-78; head pub. svcs., assoc. prof. libr. sci. Ky. Wesleyan Coll., Owensboro, 1978-83; asst. dir. Evansville (Ind.) Vanderburgh County Pub. Libr., 1985-89; dir. Carmel (Ind.) Clay Pub. Libr., 1989-91, Sanibel (Fla.) Pub. Libr., 1991—; mem. adj. faculty Western Ky. U., Bowling Green, 1977-78, Ind. U., Bloomington, 1988; workshop presenter Nursing Home Activities Dirs. Assn., Owensboro, Ky., 1981; cons. Ky. Dept. Librs. and Archives, Frankfort, 1982, Purchase (Ky.) Regional Libr. Sys., Murray, 1983, Henderson (Ky.) C.C. Libr., 1988. Editor: Emergency Handbook, 1987, Circulation Policies and Procedures, 1988, Sanibel Public Library Building Program Statement, 1992; contbr. article to profl. jours. Pres. Ret. Sr. Vol. Program Adv. Coun., Evansville, 1986-88; bd. dirs. Evansville Goodwill Industries, 1987-89. Named Outstanding Citizen of the Yr., Sanibel-Captiva Islands C. of C., 1995; Caroline M. Hewins scholar U. Ky., 1982, Margaret Ellen Kalp scholar U. N.C., 1983-84; hon. Ky. Col., 1981. Mem. ALA, Ky. Libr. Assn., Fla. Libr. Assn. (Transformer award 1996), Pub. Libr. Assn., Libr. Adminstrs. and Mgrs. Assn., P.E.O., Altrusa Club (bd. dirs. Evansville chpt. 1988, treas. Hamilton County chpt. 1990-91), Tales and Scales (pres. Evansville chpt. 1986), Beta Phi Mu. Democrat. Baptist. Office: Sanibel Pub Libr 770 Dunlop Rd Sanibel FL 33957-4016

ALLEN, PEGGY GRAFFIGNIA, data processing consultant; b. New Orleans, Dec. 4, 1948; d. Corleh Jr. and Dora Ann Graffignia; m. William Weeks Allen, Jr., Sept. 9, 1967; 1 child, William Weeks III. BS in Math., La. State U., 1969; postgrad. in Math., Tulane U., 1969-70; postgrad. in Acctg., U. New Orleans, 1970-72. Cert. data processer. Adminstrv. ptnr. Software Cons., Metairie, La., 1976—. Contbr. articles to tech. jours., 1984—. Recipient NSF fellowship, 1969-70. Mem. Richard III Soc., Inc. (treas. 1993-96, membership sec. 1996—), Am. Contract Bridge League. Office: 1421 Wisteria Dr Metairie LA 70005-1061

ALLEN, ROBERT DEE, lawyer; b. Tulsa, Oct. 13, 1928; s. Harve and Olive Jean (Brown) A.; m. Mary Latimer Conner, May 18, 1957; children: Scott, Randy, Blake. BA, U. Okla., 1951, LLB, 1955, JD, 1970. Bar: Okla. 1955, Ill. 1979, U.S. Dist. Ct. (we., no. and ea. dists.) Okla. 1955, U.S. Dist. Ct. (no. dist.) Ill. 1979, U.S. Ct. Appeals (10th cir.) 1956. Assoc. Abernathy & Abernathy, Shawnee, Okla., 1955; law clk. to judge 10th U.S. Ct. Appeals, Denver, 1956; to judge Western Dist. Okla., 1956-57; asst. ins. commr., counsel Okla. Ins. Dept., 1957-63; partner firm Quinlan, Allen & Batchelor, Oklahoma City, 1963-65, DeBois & Allen, 1965-66; counsel AT&T, Washington, 1966-67; gen. atty. Southwestern Bell Telephone Co., Okla., 1967-79; v.p., gen. counsel Ill. Bell Telephone Co., Chgo., 1979-83; sole practice law Chgo. and Oklahoma City, 1983—; mcpl. counselor Oklahoma City, 1984-89; of counsel Hartzog, Conger, Cason & Hargis, 1983-90, Kimball, Wilson, Walker and Ferguson, 1990-93, Berry & Durland, 1993-94, Durland & Durland, 1994-96, White, Coffey, Galt & Fite P.C., 1996—; spl. counsel Okla. Mcpl. Power Authority, 1990-94, City of Altus, Okla., 1990—; mem. Gov.'s Ad Valorem Tax Structure and Sch. Fin. Commn., 1972; bd. dirs. Taxpayers Fedn. Ill., 1980-83; adv. bd. dirs. Southwestern Legal Found., 1985—; rsch. fellow Southwestern Legal Found., 1994—; adj. prof. ins. law Oklahoma City U. Coll. Law, 1985—, agy. and partnership law, U. Okla. Coll. Law, 1989—; Okla. State chmn. Nat. Inst. Mcpl. Law Officers, 1984-89; apptd. mem. Legis Task Force on Okla. Adminstrv. Code, 1987. Bd. dirs. Oklahoma County Legal Aid Soc., 1973—. Served to 1st lt. U.S. Army, 1946-48, 51-53; lt. col. USAR. Fellow Am. Bar Found.; mem. ABA, Fed. Bar Assn. (v.p. Okla. Chpt. 1977—), Okla. Bar Assn., Okla. County Bar Assn., Chgo. Bar Assn., Am. Judicature Soc., Okla. Assn. Mcpl. Attys. (bd. dirs. 1984-89), Order of Coif, Phi Delta Phi, Sigma Phi Epsilon (dir.). Presbyterian. Clubs: Chicago, Oklahoma City Golf and Country, Sunset Ridge Country (Northfield, Ill.). Home: 8101 Glenwood Ave Oklahoma City OK 73114-1107

ALLEN, ROBERT ENGLISH, business development executive, consultant; b. Mt. Pleasant, Tenn., Mar. 31, 1945; s. Robert English and Ruth Faye (Hill) A.; m. Patricia Ann Gifford, June 12, 1968 (div. 1982); children: George Clayton, Paedra Thais; m. Robin Ann Enscore, May 26, 1984 (div. 1990); m. Judith Ann Coble (Nee Lilly), Jan. 1, 1993; stepchildren: Matthew Coble, Stephanie Coble. BS in Chemistry, U. Tenn., 1968; PhD, Iowa State U., 1974. Rsch. scientist Celanese Fibers Co., Charlotte, N.C., 1974-78; tech. mgr. Celanese Fibers Mktg. Co., Charlotte, 1978-82; mgr. new bus. devel. Celanese Fibers Ops. Co., Charlotte, 1982-85; dir. ops. Chardon Labs, Charlotte, 1985; pres., CEO, Allen Cons. Group Inc., Charlotte, 1985-90; mgr. bus. devel. separations divsn. Hoechst Celanese, Charlotte, 1990-94; dir. mktg. Rexham Custom, Matthews, N.C., 1994—; cons. Jordan Constrn. Co., Charlotte, 1984-90, Oro Mfg. Co., Monroe, N.C., 1986-90; CEO, Allen-Marshall Inc., Charlotte, 1987-88; pres. Rosegate Internat. Inc., Charlotte, 1988-89; arbitrator N.Y. Stock Exch., 1993-94. Contbr. articles to profl. jours. Bd. dirs. Drug Edn. Ctr., 1992-94; bd. dirs. Jr. Achievement, Charlotte, 1986—, mem. pub. rels. and strategic planning coms. 1986-93. Mem. Charlotte C. of C. (small bus. action coun. 1987-88, pub. affairs com. 1988-92), Execs. Club (v.p. 1987-88, pres. 1988-89), Tips Club (v.p. 1986-88), Phi Kappa Phi, Phi Lambda Upsilon, Alpha Chi Sigma. Republican. Home: 16 Red Fox Trl Fort Mill SC 29715-9754 Office: Rexham Custom Products Divsn PO Box 368 Matthews NC 28106-7003

ALLEN, ROLAND EMERY, physicist; b. Houston, Sept. 3, 1941; s. Nollie Emery and Lounetta Evelyn (Wimberley) A.; m. Susan Jinx Milliken, July 21, 1983; 1 child, Ethan James. BA, Rice U., 1963; PhD, U. Tex., 1968. Rsch. assoc. U. Tex., Austin, 1969-70; resident assoc. Argonne Nat. Lab., Chgo., 1969; asst. prof. Tex. A&M U., College Station, 1970-76, assoc. prof., 1976-83; sabbatical scientist Solar Energy Rsch. Inst., Golden, Colo., 1979-80; prof. Tex. A&M U., College Station, 1983—; vis. assoc. prof. U. Ill., Urbana, 1980-81; cons. Allied/Signal Corp., Des Plaines, Ill., 1985-86. Mem. editorial bd. Superlattices and Microstructures, 1989—; editor: Theory, Modeling and Instrumentation for Materials by Design, 1989; contbr. more than 170 sci. articles to profl. jours. Grantee Robert A. Welch Found., 1982—, Office Naval Rsch., 1982—, U.S. Dept. Energy, 1983-85. Fellow Am. Vacuum Soc.; mem. AAAS, Am. Phys. Soc. Office: Tex A&M U Dept Physics College Station TX 77843-4242

ALLEN, RONALD WESLEY, financial executive; b. Jacksonville, Fla., Sept. 7, 1948; s. John Wesley and Frances Alida (Hadler) A.; m. Bonnie June Smith, Aug. 31, 1968; children: Donna Laurie, Marguerite Theresa. Student, Tulane U., 1966-67; AA with high honors, Fla. Jr. Coll., Jacksonville, 1972; BA with honors, U. North Fla., 1974; MS, U. Fla., 1976. Salesman, electronic technician J.W. Allen & Assocs., Inc., Jacksonville, 1971-74, exec. v.p., 1976-88, chief exec. officer, 1988—; pres. Steamchem Products, Inc., Gainesville, 1975, A&B Carpet Cleaning, Inc., Gainesville, Fla., 1974-75; chief exec. officer Allen Wholesale Supply div. J.W. Allen & Assocs., Inc., Jacksonville, 1979-88; regional v.p. Primerica Fin. Svcs., Jacksonville, 1989-97; dir., sec., treas. Madcem Inc., Jacksonville, 1985-87, Madcem of Fla., Inc., 1987-96; bd. dirs. Beaches Acad., Inc., Jacksonville, Crown Offshore Products, Inc., 1985-92, Forest Hills Meml. Park, Palm City, Fla., 1987-96, Forest Hills Funeral Home, Palm City, 1987-96, Crown Coast Mgmt. Inc., Jacksonville, 1983-94; gen. ptnr. First Coast Investments, Ltd., Jacksonville, 1984-92, J&R Products, Jacksonville, 1991-94. Vestry mem. Christ Ch., Ponte Verda Beach, Fla., 1988-91; v.p. exec. bd. Towers of Love, Inc., St. Augustine, Fla., 1984-95; vol. ann. fund Bolles Sch., Jacksonville, 1976—, Ronald McDonald Ho., Jacksonville, 1991; exec. bd. Living Waters Ministries, St. Augustine, Fla., 1991-93; lay min. Espiscopal Diocese of Fla., 1991—. Sgt. USAF, 1968-72. Mem. Jacksonville C. of C. (com. of 100, 1976-79, armed forces com. 1976-79), Northside Bus. Club, Beaches Bus. Assn. (bd. dirs. 1991-93), Alumni Coun. Bolles Sch., North Fla. Cruising Club (bd. dirs. 1979-86, Yachtsman of Yr. 1983), Navy Jacksonville Yacht Club, Performance Racing Handicap Circuit (bd. dirs. 1982-86, chmn. 1986, Yachtsman of Yr. 1983), Ponte Vedra Country Club, U. North Fla. Alumni Assn. Episcopalian. Office: Corp Offices PO Box 3805 Jacksonville FL 32206-0805

ALLEN, TED TIPTON, biology educator; b. McKenzie, Tenn., Mar. 22, 1932; s. Cornell Tipton and Lenora Anne (Wynns) A.; m. Suzan M. O'Brien, Sept. 5, 1958; children: Jeffrey Brian (dec.), David Craig. BA in Biology, Murray State Coll., 1954; MS in Zoology, U. Wis., 1958; PhD in Biology, U. Fla., 1962. From instr. to prof. Jacksonville (Fla.) U., 1961—. Foreman Duval County Grand Jury, Jacksonville, Fla., 1990; founder Tree Hill Nature Ctr., Preservation Assn. for Tree Hill, 1971-92. With U.S. Army, 1954-56. Recipient N.S.F. Summer fellowship, 1961, Adams Environ. award, Adams Com. Jacksonville, Fla., 1979, Sears Teaching award, 1991; named Prof. of Yr., Jacksonville U., 1970-71. Home: 5647 Saint Isabel Dr Jacksonville FL 32277-1759 Office: Jacksonville U Dept Math & Sci 2800 University Blvd N Jacksonville FL 32211-3321

ALLEN, TIMOTHY LELAND, critical care nurse; b. Mobile, Ala., Apr. 30, 1961; s. Frank Bettis and Margaret Carol (Scott) A.; m. Katrina Lynn Davis, June 2, 1984 (div.); 1 child, Kristin Danielle; m. Renee Buxton, Sept. 24, 1994. LPN, S.W. State Tech. Coll., Mobile, 1982; RN, Bishop State Community Coll., Mobile, 1986. Cert. ACLS, CCRN. LPN Mobile Infirmary Med. Ctr., 1982-86, staff nurse, 1986-88, charge nurse, 1988-90, 1991—, preceptor new employees, 1989—, nurse mgr., 1990-91; staff nurse USA Med. Ctr., Mobile, 1991; speaker on cleft lip and palate to nursing profls. neonatal workshops, Mobile, 1990—. Counselor parents with cleft lip/palate babies Mobile Infirmary Med. Ctr., 1990—; youth counselor Chickasaw United Meth. Ch., 1990—, Pleasant Valley Ch. of Christ, 1990-93, Pleasant Valley Ch. of Christ. Mem. AACN. Home: 4601-A Bush Ln Mobile AL 36619 Office: Mobile Infirmary Med Ctr PO Box 2144 Mobile AL 36652-2144

ALLEN, TIMOTHY MICHAEL, secondary education educator; b. Chgo., Oct. 28, 1950; s. Frederick Earl and Colleen Mae (Smirl) A.; m. Anita Sue Greenway, March 19, 1983; children: Christopher Sean, Samuel Blake DeSpain, Brady J. DeSpain. BS in edn., S.W. Okla. State U., 1987. Cert. tchr., Okla. Curriculum coord., aircraft loadmaster USAF, Altus, Okla., 1970-81, Travis, Calif., 1970-81; lectr. NASA/Aerospace Edn. Svcs. Project Okla. State U., Stillwater, 1986-89; tchr. Stillwater Pub. Schs., 1989—; cons. Okla. 4H, Stillwater, 1992—, Mo. 4H, Carthage, 1995—, Frontier City, Okla., 1993—; challenge course instr. Okla. State U. Challenge Course, Stillwater, 1991—, Tulsa County C.C., 1996—. Author: Physics Day Handbook for Frontier City, 1994; editor: (newsletter) SEA Newsline, 1995-96. Mem. Nat. Edn. Assn., Okla. Acad. of Scis., Okla. Edn. Assn., Stillwater Edn. Assn., Lacrosse Found. Home: 2030 W Sherwood Stillwater OK 74074

ALLEN, VIVIEN GORE, agronomist, researcher; b. Nashville, Mar. 31, 1940; d. Lacy Lawton and Sara Azilee (Parks) Gore; m. Harry Evans Allen Jr., Aug. 14, 1962; children: Harry Evans III, Warren Lawton, Stephen Henry. BS, U. Tenn., 1962; MS, La. State U., Baton Rouge, 1973, PhD, 1979. Owner, mgr. Forage Beef Cattle Farm, Huntland, Tenn., 1970—; rsch. asst. La. State U., Baton Rouge, 1978-79, postdoctoral fellow, 1980; asst. prof. agronomy Va. Polytech. Inst. & State U., Blacksburg, 1980-86, assoc. prof. agronomy, 1986-93; prof. crop and soil environ. scis., 1993-95; Thornton Disting. prof. Texas Tex. U., Lubbock, 1995—; supt. Va. Agr. Exptl. Sta., Middleburg, 1984-88. Mem. Am. Forage and Grassland Coun. (pres. 1992-93), Am. Soc. Agronomy, Am. Soc. Animal Sci., Soc. for Range Mgmt., Coll. Agr. and Life Sci. Faculty Assn. (pres. 1989-91), Sigma Xi, Gamma Sigma Delta (chpt. pres. 1990-91). Episcopalian. Office: Texas Tech U Bpx 42122 Dept Plant and Soil Scis Lubbock TX 79409-2122

ALLEN, W. WAYNE, oil industry executive; b. 1936. BS, Okla. State U., 1959, MME, 1969. With Phillips Petroleum Co., 1961-84, regional mgr. U.K., 1984-85, gen. mgr. exploration and prodn. western divsn., 1986-89, sr. v.p. exploration and prodn., 1989-91, pres., COO, 1991-94, chmn. bd., CEO, 1994—. Capt. U.S. Army, 1959-61. Office: Phillips Petroleum Co 18 Phillips Bldg Bartlesville OK 74004

ALLEN, WANDA RUTH, secondary school educator; b. Savannah, Tenn., Sept. 16, 1957; d. Curtis Eugene and Vada Ruth (Gilham) Waller; m. Ricky Lee Allen, May 25, 1980; 1 child, Tyler Lee. BA in English, U. Tenn., Martin, 1979, BA in History, 1979; MA in History, Murray State U., 1992. Cert. secondary history, English, polit. sci. and psychology tchr., Tenn. Tchr. Big Sandy (Tenn.) H.S., Benton County Bd. Edn., 1980-81, Briarwood Jr. H.S., Benton County Bd. Edn., 1981-83; tchr., chair social studies dept. Camden (Tenn.) Ctrl. H.S., Benton County Bd. Edn., 1984—. Author: (booklet) Benton County's Sesquicentennial, 1986. Pres. Cumberland Presbyn. Women, 1990—; mem. Benton County Arts Coun., Camden, 1992—. Named Outstanding History Tchr., DAR, 1992. Mem. NEA, Nat. Coun. Social Studies (com. on nat. conv.), Tenn. Edn. Assn., Tenn. Coun. Social Studies, Benton County Geneal. Assn., Lions (sec. Camden 1985—, Lioness of the Decade 1995), Phi Kappa Phi. Republican. Home: Rt 4 Box 86 Camden TN 38320

ALLEN, WILLIAM DEAN, financial consultant; b. Lake Charles, La., Dec. 1, 1950; s. William Edward and Hazel Dorothy (Reese) A.; m. Sandra Patricia Stroud; children: William Dean, Robert E. Lee. Student, N.Mex. State U., 1972, Coll. of Mainland, 1974-76; BA in Polit. Sci., Franklin U., 1977. Recognized as expert on fed. income tax law. Infantry, mil. police U.S. Army, 1968-72; process operator Oil Refinery, Houston, 1976-81; author, writer Houston, 1982-84; lectr., cons. fin. seminars U.S., Latin Am., 1984-88; v.p. Winner's Circle Internat., Houston, 1989; exec. dir. Constl. Rights Found., Spindale, N.C., 1990; pub., editor Internat. Fin. Jour., Rutherfordton, N.C., 1992, We The People, Forest City, N.C., 1990—; dir. Constl. Rights Found., Houston, 1990-93; cons. Tax Haven Reporter, Nassau, Bahamas, 1991-93; pres. Am. Dream Mktg. Co., Spindale, N.C., 1992-93; dir. Rsch. Found., Honolulu, 1993. Author: The American Dream, 1991, International Financial Privacy, 1990, Unjust Taxation In America, 1978. Candidate N.C. Ho. of Reps., Dist. 48, 1992, 94; del. Rep. State Convs., N.C., Tex., 1975-93; office mgr. Ronald Reagan Campaign Hdqs., Galveston County, Tex., 1980; hon. mem. Cleve. County Rep. Women's Club, Shelby, N.C., 1992. With U.S. Army, 1968-72, Vietnam. Recipient Combat Infantryman's badge U.S. Army, Air medal, Gallantry Cross, Vietnam Svc. medal, Vietnam Campaign medal, Nat Def. Svc. medal. Mem. NRA, VFW (jr. vice comdr. 1977-78), DAV, Am. Legion, Rutherford County Vietnam Vets., Sons of Confederate Vets., Young Reps. Club, Moose (sgt.-at-arms 1994, past gov. 1995-96). Republican. Office: We The People 135 Thomas St Forest City NC 28043-3031

ALLEN, WILLIAM RILEY, lawyer; b. Coral Gables, Fla., Oct. 24, 1953; s. William George and Winnie (Woodall) A.; m. Mary Faith Ford, June 3, 1989. BA with honors, U. Cen. Fla., 1977; JD with honors, Fla. State U., 1981. Bar: Fla. 1982, U.S. Dist. Ct. (mid. dist.) Fla. 1982, U.S. Ct. Appeals (11th cir.) 1982, U.S. Ct. Appeals (4th cir.) 1988, U.S. Supreme Ct., 1992. With Pitts, Eubank & Ross, P.A., Orlando, 1981-85; prin. W. Riley Allen P.A., Orlando, 1985—. Author: Do Students Know Their Rights?, 1978, Bad Faith Litigation, 1984, Insurance Litigation in Florida, 1992. Recipient Am. Jurisprudence award in criminal law. Mem. ABA (tort and ins. practice com.), ATLA (sustaining, trial lawyer sect.), Fla. Bar Assn. (trial laywers sect.), Acad. Fla. Trial Lawyers (EAGLE, trial lawyers sect.), Orange County Bar Assn. (law and edn., lawyer advt. com., guardian ad litem coms. 1981—), Def. Rsch. Inst., Am. Judicature Soc., Cen. Fla. Trial Lawyers (founding dir.), Phi Delta Phi. Republican. Anglican Catholic. Office: 228 Annie St Orlando FL 32806-1208

ALLENDER, JOHN ROLAND, lawyer; b. Boone, Iowa, Oct. 22, 1950; s. John S. and C. Corinne (Hayes) A.; children: Susan A., Andrew J. BS, Iowa State U., 1972; JD, U. San Diego, 1975; LLM in Taxation, NYU, 1976. Bar: Calif. 1976, Tex. 1977, U.S. Ct. Claims 1977, U.S. Tax. Ct. 1977, U.S. Dist. Ct. (so. dist.) Tex. 1977. Assoc. Fulbright & Jaworski, Houston, 1976-83, ptnr., 1983—; mem. adv. commn. Tex. Bd. Legal Specialization, 1986—. Bd. dirs. Ronald McDonald House, Houston, 1990—. Mem. State Bar of Tex. (chmn. sect. taxation 1990), Houston Bar Assn. (chmn. sect. taxation 1979). Office: Fulbright & Jaworski 1301 Mckinney St Houston TX 77010

ALLERTON, WILLIAM, III, public relations executive; b. New Orleans, June 20, 1951; s. William Jr. and Marion (Helmstetter) A.; m. Constance Rose Driscoll, Dec. 18, 1971; children: Amy Elizabeth, Timothy Daniel, Sean Patrick, Colleen Rose. Student, U. New Orleans, 1969-73; fellow, Loyola U. Inst. Politics, 1980-81. Pres. Capitol Pub. Rels., 1978-86; chmn., CEO Capitol Comm., New Orleans, 1986—; with office presdl. advance White House, 1990-93; dir. Advertisers Legis. Action Council, Baton Rouge, 1985-86; bus. ptnr. Benjamin Franklin High Sch. New Orleans Pub. Schs., 1987—; bd. dirs. Inst. Politics Loyola U.; del. White House Conf. on Bus., Washington, 1995. Participant Met. Area Com. Tulane U., 1978; apptd. mem. nat. adv. com. U.S. SBA, 1989-93; mem. La. State Bd. Elem. and Secondary Edn. Non-Pub. Sch. Commn., 1986—, Nat. Coun. Trustees Freedoms Found. at Valley Forge, 1989—, La. Commn. on the Bicentennial of U.S. Constn., 1986-91; vice-chmn. Marine Corps Scholarship Fund Leatherneck Ball, 1986; vice chmn. 83d Anniversary Dinner of Navy League of U.S., 1987; mem. exec. com. Archbishops Cmty. Appeal, 1975-85; mem. U.S. adv. coun. SBA dist., La., 1973-76; mem. Mayor's Coun. Youth Opportunity, New Orleans, 1969-70; dist. chmn. New Orleans coun. Boy Scouts Am., 1992-93, mem. exec. bd., 1990—, chmn. centennial pledge of allegiance salute, 1992, coun. activities chmn., 1992—, mem. exec. com., 1992—, mem. nat. coun., 1994—, New Orleans coun. commr., 1995—; bd. dirs. La. State Mus., 1988-94; participant Columbia U. Am. Assembly, 1989. Recipient Addy award Am. Advt. Fedn., 1983, Tops award Dallas Advt. League, 1983, Geroge Washington Honor medal Freedoms Found. at Valley Forge, 1989, Friends of Edn. award La. Fedn. Tchrs., 1989, Presdl. Recognition Office Nat. Svc., Points of Light Found., 1992, Silver Beaver award Boy Scouts Am., 1992; James E. West Fellowship award, 1994, Cathedral award Archdiocese of New Orleans Cath. Com. on Scouting, 1995. Mem. Am. Assn. Polit. Cons. (Media Excellence awards 1984, 86, 88), So. Polit. Sci. Assn., Acad. Polit. Sci., Soc. for U.S. Constn., U.S. Capitol Hist. Soc., Ctr. for Study of the Presidency, Assn. Descendants Isaac Allerton Mayflower, Order of Arrow (Chilantakoba lodge). Office: Capitol Comm PO Box 791348 New Orleans LA 70179-1348

ALLES, RODNEY NEAL, SR., information management executive; b. Orleans, Nebr., Aug. 24, 1950; s. Neal Stanley and Evelyn Dorothy (Zelske) A.; m. Diana Kay Koenig, Nov. 25, 1978; children: Rodney Neal Jr., Jennifer E., Victoria E. BS in Indsl. Engring., U. Okla., 1973, MBA, 1977. Asst. to the pres. Skytop Brewster Co., Inc., Houston, 1978-79, mgr. planning and mfg., 1979-83; v.p. adminstrn. Internat. Meter Co. Inc., Arkansas City, Kans., 1983-84, v.p., 1984-85; dir. info. mgmt. McAlester (Okla.) Army Ammunition Plant, 1987-96; chief info. sys. divsn. S.E. Regional Civilian Pers. Ops. Ctr., Ft. Benning, Ga., 1996—. Lt. USN, 1973-76. Mem. Am. Inst. Indsl. Engrs., Fed. Info. Processing Coun., Fed. Mgrs. Assn., U.S. Golf Assn., Okla. Golf Assn., Loyal Knight of Old Trusty, U. Okla. Alumni Assn. (alumni coun. Coll. Bus. Adminstrn.), Rotary Internat., McAlester Country Club, Omicron Delta Kappa, Tau Beta Pi, Sigma Tau, Alpha Pi Mu. Democrat. Lutheran. Office: SE Regional Civilian Pers Ops Ctr Attn: SF-CP-SE-A Meloy Hall Bldg 6 Fort Benning GA 31905 also: Army Info Sys Commd ATTN: SIOMC-IM 1 C Tree Road Mcalester OK 74501-9002

ALLEY, MARCUS M., agronomy educator. BS, Berea Coll., 1969; MS in Agronomy, Va. Poly. Inst. and State U., 1971, PhD in Agronomy, 1975. Agronomist Park Forest Farms, Inc., Baskerville, Va., 1975; rsch. rep. Ohio and Ky. divsns. Ciba-Geigy Corp., 1975-77; asst. prof. soil and crop mgmt. Va. Poly. Inst. and State U., 1977-83, assoc. prof., 1983-89, prof., 1989—; advisor to exec. bd. Va. Agrl. Chem. and Soil Fertility Assn., 1989—; mem. project com. Best Mgmt. Practices Manual for Wheat Growers, 1993—; invited participant ARS-CSRS Soil Nitrate Workshop, Washington, 1991; mem. nitrogen, phosphorus, waste and metals work com. So. Region review USDA Funded Projects, 1992. Contbr. over 30 papers and abstracts to profl. and refereed jours., 3 chpts. to books. Recipient Werner L. Nelson award Fluid Fertilizer Found., 1986, Robert E. Wagner award Potash and Phosphate Inst./Am. Soc. Agronomy, 1990, Rsch. award Va. Small Grains Assn. Fellow Soil Sci. Soc. Am.; mem. Am. Soc. Agonomy (aronomic achievement awards com. 1989-90, Agronomic Achievement award 1988), Soil Sci. Soc. Am. (assoc. editor jour. 1990-93, chair divsn. S-4, 1994). Office: Virginia Polytechnic I Blacksburg VA 24061

ALLEY, THOMAS ROBERTSON, psychology educator; b. Bryn Mawr, Pa., Oct. 20, 1953; s. Thomas R. and Ann (Higbee) A.; m. Pamela R. Pollack, July 31, 1977; children: Rebecca, Jennifer. BA, BS, Pa. State U., 1975; MA, U. Conn., 1979, PhD, 1981. Lectr. U. Conn., Storrs and Hartford, 1980-83; postdoctoral fellow U. Conn. Health Ctr., Farmington, 1981-84; asst. prof. psychology Clemson (S.C.) U., 1984-89, assoc. prof., 1989-92, prof. psychology, 1992—; vis. scholar Emory U., 1991-92. Editor: Social and Applied Aspects of Perceiving Faces, 1988; contbr. articles to profl. jours., chpts. to books. Mem. Am. Psychol. Soc., Ea. Psychol. Assn., Psychonomic Soc., Internat. Soc. for Ecol. Psychology. Office: Clemson U Dept Psychology Clemson SC 29634-1511

ALLEY, WAYNE EDWARD, federal judge, retired army officer; b. Portland, Oreg., May 16, 1932; s. Leonard David and Hilda Myrtle (Blum) A.; m. Marie Winkelmann Dommer, Jan. 28, 1978; children: Elizabeth, David, John; stepchildren: Mark Dommer, Eric Dommer. A.B., Stanford U., 1952, J.D., 1957. Bar: Calif. 1957, Oreg. 1957, Okla. 1985. Ptnr. Williams & Alley, Portland, 1957-59; commd. officer JAGC, U.S. Army, advanced through grades to brig. gen., ret., 1981; dean Coll. Law, dir. Law Ctr. U. Okla., Norman, 1981-85; judge U.S. Dist. Ct. Western Dist. Okla., Oklahoma City, 1985—. Decorated D.S.M., Legion of Merit, Bronze Star. Mem. Fed. Bar Assn., Oreg. Bar Assn., Okla. Bar Assn., Order of Coif, Phi Beta Kappa. Office: US Dist Ct 3102 US Courthouse 200 NW 4th St Oklahoma City OK 73102-3003

ALLGOOD, JOHN FRANKLIN, lawyer; b. Atlanta, May 1, 1946; s. George N. and Dollie (Lowe) A.; m. Patricia Louise McCusker, Aug. 11, 1973; children: Sara Elizabeth, John F. G., Margaret Barrett. BBA, Ga. State U., 1968; JD, U. Ga., 1973. Bar: Ga. 1973, U.S. Dist. Ct. (no. dist.) Ga. 1973. Assoc. Fisher & Phillips, Atlanta, 1973-74; atty. Union Camp Corp., Savannah, Ga., 1975-78; labor counsel Union Camp Corp., Wayne, N.J., 1979-80; regional counsel Container Corp. Am., Atlanta, 1980-86, Container Corp. Am.-Jefferson Smurfit Corp., Atlanta, 1987—. Exec. editor Ga. Jour. Internat. and Comparative Law, 1972-73; contbr. articles to profl. jours. V.p. bd. dirs. Rsch. Atlanta, 1993—; mem. Leadership Savannah, 1976; mem. Planning Commn., Tybee Island, Ga., 1976-77, maj. gifts com. Woodruff Arts Ctr., Atlanta, 1986—. 1st lt. Signal Corps, U.S. Army, 1968-70, Vietnam. Mem. Ga. Bar Assn. (chair S.E. corp. counsel seminar 1982-83, chair corp. sect. 1986-87, chair edn. and admission to bar com. 1989-90), Atlanta Bar Assn. (chair corp. counsel assocs. 1986-87), Am. Corp. Counsel Assn., Am. Arbitration Assn. (arbitrator), Ga. Forestry Assn. (bd. dirs. 1992), Atlanta Legal Aid Soc. (steering com. 1986—), Lawyers Club Atlanta (chair planning com. 1990-91), Order of Barristers, Phi Eta Sigma. Home: 1925 Castleway Ln NE Atlanta GA 30345-4017 Office: Container Corp Am Jefferson Smurfit Corp 5853 E Ponce De Leon Ave Stone Mountain GA 30083-1503

ALLIGOOD, MARY SALE, special education educator; b. Richmond, Va., Oct. 28, 1942; d. Charles Latané and Virginia Carter (Elmer) Sale; m. Frederick Marvin Alligood, Jr., June 12, 1965; children: Anne Hassell Alligood Tadlock, Frederick Carter. BA in Psychology, Mary Washington Coll., 1965; MEd in Spl. Edn./Learning Disabilities, Va. Commonwealth U., 1982. 2d grade tchr. West Columbia-Cayce Schs., Columbia, S.C., 1965-67; 3d/4th grade tchr. Riverside Sch., Richmond, Va., 1972-79; 1st/2d grade tchr. Steward Sch., Richmond, Va., 1979-83; learning disabilities tchr. Chesterfield County Schs., Richmond, Va., 1983-85; spl. edn. educator Powhatan (Va.) County Schs., 1985-96. Bd. dirs., sec., chair Redeemer Episcopal Day Sch., Midlothian, Va., 1992—; mem., treas. Episcopal Ch. Women, Richmond, 1967—; mem. vestry Episcopal Ch. of Redeemer, Midlothian, 1975-78, 81-83, mem. search com., 1994, stewardship co-chair, 1996—. Mem. ASCD, Coun. for Learning Disabilities, Assn. for Children/Adults with Learning Disabilities, Powhattan County Edn. Assn. (pres. 1989-91), Delta Kappa Gamma (membership com., programs 1989-92, pres. 1996-98). Home: 2841 River Oaks Dr Midlothian VA 23113-2226 Office: Powhatan Elem Sch 4111 Old Buckingham Rd Powhatan VA 23139

ALLIN, JOHN MAURY, bishop; b. Helena, Ark., Apr. 22, 1921; s. Richard and Dora (Harper) A.; m. Frances Ann Kelly, Oct. 18, 1949; children: Martha May, Kelly Ann and John Maury (twins), Frances Elizabeth. BA, U. of South, 1943, MDiv, 1945, DD, 1962; MEd, Miss. Coll., 1960. Ordained to ministry Episcopal Ch., 1944; vicar St. Peter's Ch., Conway, Ark., 1945-49; curate St. Andrew's Ch., New Orleans, 1950-51; chaplain to Episcopal students and insts. New Orleans, 1950-52; rector Grace Ch., Monroe, La., 1952-58; rector, pres. All Saints Jr. Coll., Vicksburg, Miss., 1958-61; bishop coadjutor Diocese of Miss., P.E. Ch., Jackson, 1961-66; bishop Diocese of Miss., P.E. Ch., 1966-73; 23d presiding bishop Episcopal Ch. in U.S.A., 1974-86; chaplain Christ Meml. Chapel, Hobe Sound, Fla., 1984-94; chaplin St. Ann's Summer Chapel, Kennebunkport, Maine, 1991—; mem. Joint Commn. on Ecumenical Rels., 1964-73; mem. Anglican-Roman Cath.Consultation, 1967-73; mem. exec. coun. Episcopal Ch., 1970-85; mem. Miss. Religious Leadership Conf., 1969-73, chmn., 1972-73. Trustee All Saints Episcopal Sch., Vicksburg, 1961—; trustee U. of South, 1961—, bd. regents, 1965-71, 79-85, chancellor, 1973-79. Home: 2015 Douglas Dr Jackson MS 39211-6606

ALLIN, LAWRENCE CARROLL, historian, educator; b. Independence, Mo., July 17, 1932; s. John Marshall and Josephine Vivian (Luther) A.; m. Roswitha Bresinsky, Aug. 28, 1988; children by previous marriage: L. Kirk, L. Kyle, L. Kevin, Lisa. AB, Coll. of Pacific, 1954; MA, Syracuse U., 1967; Diplomate, Frank C. Munson Inst., 1971; PhD, U. Maine, 1976; postgrad., Air Univ., 1991, U. Okla., 1993. Tchr. Cucamonga (Calif.) Jr. High Sch., 1958-69; instr. history U. Maine, Orono, 1970-79; dist. historian Omaha Dist. U.S. Army C.E., 1979-82; Maine historian U. Maine, 1982-88; vis. prof. history Bangor Theol. Sem., 1983-87; columnist Naval Inst. Proceedings, 1987; chief historian 28th Air Div. USAF, 1988-92; historian Tinker Mgmt. Assn., 1991-92, Tinker AFB, Tinker AFB, 1992—, Tuskegee Airmen, 1994—. Author: U.S. Naval Institute: Intellectual Forum of the New Navy, 1971; America's Maritime Legacy, 1979; Searsport Master Builders, 1980; Maine in Print, 1983; A Maine Maritime Miscellany, 1984; Little Long and Mud Ponds: An Environmental History, 1986; Ships, Seafaring and Society, 1987, New Dimensions in Maritime History, 1987, History of Tinker Air Force Base, 1993, Central Oklahoma Aviation in World War II, 1993, Index to Tinker AFB in Okla., 1995; Maine: The Pine Tree State: Prehistory to the Present, 1995; contbr. articles to profl. jours. Bd. overseers Marine Maritime Mus., 1971-88. Served with USN, 1955-57. Recipient Neal Allen award Maine Hist. Soc., 1995; Fulbright-Hays fellow Brown U., Am. U., Beirut, 1967; grantee Price Found., 1964, 69, U. Maine, 1976, 79, NEH, 1977. Mem. Soc. Am. Mil. Engrs., U.S. Naval Inst., Orgn. Am. Historians, N.Am. Soc. Oceanic Historians, Okla. Orgn. Profl. Historians, Univ. Club, Tuskegee

Airmen, Okla. Hist. Soc., Fulbright Assn., Phi Alpha Theta. Office: Ste 319 380 A Ave Tinker AFB OK 73145-9101

ALLING, CHARLES CALVIN, III, oral-maxillofacial surgeon, educator, writer; b. Guthrie, Okla., Dec. 27, 1923; s. Charles Calvin Jr. and Bessie Palmer (Keller) A.; m. Laura Esther Freeland, May 10, 1947; children: Elaine Sue (Mrs. Andrew W. Lilliston Jr.), Rocklin David, Robert Freeland. AB, Ind. U., 1943, DDS, 1946; MS, U. Mich., 1954; DSc (hon.), Georgetown U., 1987. Diplomate Am. Bd. Oral and Maxillofacial Surgery (pres. 1983-84). Prof., chmn. dept. oral surgery U. Ala., Birmingham, 1969-81; oral-maxillofacial surgeon Drs. Alling & Alling, 1981—; adj. prof. Coll. Dentistry, U. Iowa; cons. ADA, U.S. Army Med. R & D Command, Surgeon Gen., VA; vis. prof. and lectr. Howard U., Georgetown U., Seoul U. Editor, author: Maxillofacial Trauma, 1988, Facial Pain, 3d edit., 1991, Oral Maxillofacial Surgery Clinics North America, 1973, 93, Impacted Teeth, 1993; mem. editorial bd. Oral Surgery, Oral Medicine, Oral Pathology; contbr. chpts. to books, articles to profl. jours. Bd. dirs. Kwang Myung Orphanage and Sch. for Blind, Inchon, Republic of Korea. With U.S. Army, 1943-69. Decorated Legion of Merit; Medaslha Le Rene Forte (Brazil); recipient U.S. Army Outstanding Civilian Svc. award, W.F. Harrigan award Bellevue Hosp., Sadi Fountaine award Alameda Med. Instns., Fauchard Disting. Svc. award, W.J. Gies Disting. Svc. award. Fellow Am. Coll. Dentists; mem. ADA, Am. Soc. Oral Surgeons (bd. dirs.), Am., Southeastern, Ala. Internat. Assn. Oral-Maxillofacial Surgeons, Chalmer Lyons Acad. Oral Surgery, 38th Parallel Dental Soc. (charter pres.), Greater Washington Soc. Oral Surgeons (charter pres.), Internat. Assn. Dental Rsch., Pan Pacific Implant Assn., Masons, Shriners, Phi Kappa Phi. Home: 1509 Panorama Dr Birmingham AL 35216-3316 Office: Drs Alling & Alling 1957 Hoover Ct Ste 206 Birmingham AL 35226-3618

ALLINGTON, GLORIA JEAN HAM, medical education administrator; b. Northwood, N.D., May 21, 1945; d. John Henry Ham and Selma Tina (Haabak) Thorson; m. Gary Francis Allington, June 6, 1966 (div. May 1986). Student, U. N.D., 1963-66; ADN, Miami Dade Community Coll., 1968; BCS, U. Miami, 1976, MS in Edn., 1987. RN, Fla.; cert. meeting profl. Staff nurse Jackson Meml. Hosp., Miami, Fla., 1969-71, asst. head nurse, 1971-73; nurse educator U. Miami Sch. Medicine, 1973-75, adminstrv. asst., 1975-81, asst. dir. div. continuing med. edn., 1981, dir. div. continuing med. edn., 1981—. Contbr. articles to profl. jours. Exec. bd. dirs. Project Newborn, Miami, 1977-86; bd. dirs. Ronald McDonald House of So. Fla., Miami, 1977-82; mem. Zool. Soc. of South Fla., Miami, 1986—. Recipient James W. Colbert, Jr., M.D. award, Health Edn. Media Assn., 1977. Mem. Soc. Med. Coll. Dirs. of Continuing Med. Edn. (cert. of achievement 1991, sec. 1992-93, v.p. 1993, pres.-elect 1994, pres. 1995-96), Alliance for Continuing Med. Edn., Meeting Planners Internat. (internat. dir. 1986-88). Democrat. Roman Catholic. Office: U Miami Sch Medicine PO Box 016960 Miami FL 33101-6960

ALLIO, ROBERT JOHN, management consultant, educator; b. N.Y.C., Sept. 1, 1931; s. Albert Joseph and Helen (Gerbereux) A.; m. Barbara Maria Littauer, Oct. 3, 1953; children: Mark, Paul, David, Michael. BAMetE, Rensselaer Poly. Inst., 1952, PhD, 1957; MS, Ohio State U., 1954. Mgr. advanced materials Gen. Electric Co., Schenectady, 1957-60; sr. staff AEC, Washington, 1962; engring. mgr. atomic power div. Westinghouse Corp., Pitts., 1962-68; dir. corp. planning Babcock & Wilcox, N.Y., 1968-75; v.p. Can. Wire Co., Toronto, Ont., 1975-78; pres. Canstar Communications, Toronto, 1976-78; sr. staff mem. Arthur D. Little Co., Cambridge, Mass., 1978-79; dean Rensselaer Poly. Inst. Sch. Mgmt., Troy, N.Y., 1981-83; pres. Robert J. Allio and Assoc., Atlanta, 1979—; prof. mgmt. Babson Coll, Wellesley, Mass., 1979—; bd. dirs. TBS Funding Corp.; chmn. Trac Rac Inc., NICON, Inc., Atlanta. Author: Corporate Planning: Techniques and Applications, 1979, Corporate Planning, 1985, The Practical Strategist, 1988; editor: Planning Rev. Jour. Mem. Planning Forum (pres. 1976-77), Union League Club (N.Y.C.). Office: Atlanta Fin Ctr East Tower 3343 Peachtree Rd NE # 920 Atlanta GA 30326-1022

ALLISON, CHRISTOPHER FITZSIMONS, bishop; b. Columbia, S.C., Mar. 5, 1927; s. James Richard and Susan Milliken (FitzSimons) A.; m. Martha Allston Parker, June 10, 1950. B.A., U. of South, 1949, D.D., 1978; M.Div., Va. Theol. Sem., 1952, D.D., 1981; D.Phil., Oxford U., 1956; D.D., Episcopal Theol. Sem. Ky., 1981. Asst. Trinity, Columbia, 1952-54; assoc. prof. ch. history U. of South, Sewanee, Tenn., 1956-67; prof. ch. history Va. Theol. Sem., Alexandria, 1967-75; rector Grace Ch., N.Y.C., 1975-80; bishop of S.C. Episcopal Ch., Charleston, S.C., 1980-90, ret., 1990. Author: Fear, Love & Worship, 1962, Rise of Moralism, 1966, Guilt, Anger & God, 1972, The Cruelty of Heresy: An Affirmation of Christian Orthodoxy, 1994. Served as sgt. U.S. Army, 1945-47. Home: 1081 Indigo Ave Georgetown SC 29440-2875

ALLISON, DAVID LAWRENCE (DAVID LAWRENCE SCREWS), graphic designer; b. Craig Field, Ala., June 13, 1945; s. Charles Beverly and Marguerite (Allison) Screws; m. Betty Kay Kelley; step son Joshua Wesley Cochran. BA in Polit. Sci., Tex. A&M U., 1981. Spl. hazards fire protection engr. Grinnell Corp., Dallas and Providence, 1969-71; planning technician dept. planning & devel. City of Dallas, Tex., 1971-91; mgr. tech. svcs., graphic designer dept. planning & devel. City of Dallas, 1991—; owner Allison Photo-Graphics, Carrollton, Tex., 1983-86. Appeared in: (tv and movies) Walker-Texas Ranger, Dallas-The Early Years, Thompson's Last Run, When Dreams Come True, Dallas, The Magic Dirt Bike, Peyton Place-The Next Generation, Stormin' Home, Jessie Owens' Story, others. Lectr. in history. Named Ky. Col. Mem. Am. Rifle Assn., SCV (past comdr. Gen. W.L. Cabell Camp 1313, adjutant, chaplain, past comdr. Gen. de Polignac Camp 1648, past comdr. North Tex. Brigade, corps. comdr. Army of Trans-Miss.), Sons Union Vets. of the Civil War (comdr. Lone Star Camp; chaplain, sec., treas. Dept. of S.W.), SAR (pres. Arlington chpt.), M.O.S.B. (head aide-de-camp Army of Trans-Miss.), Tex. Pub. Workers Assn. (CWA/6100 AFL-CIO). Home: 117 Oram St Arlington TX 76010-2835 Office: Dept Planning & Devel 5CN Dallas City Hall Dallas TX 75201

ALLISON, JOAN KELLY, music educator, pianist; b. Denison, Iowa, Jan. 25, 1935; d. Ivan Martin and Esther Cecelia (Newborg) K.; m. Guy Hendrick Allison, July 25, 1954 (div. Apr. 1973); children: David, Dana, Douglas, Diane. MusB, St. Louis Inst. of Music, 1955; MusM, So. Meth. U., 1976. Korrepetitor Corpus Christi (Tex.) Symphony, 1963-85; staff pianist Am. Inst. Mus. Studies, Graz, Austria, 1974-89; prof. Del Mar Coll., Corpus Christi, 1976—; adj. prof. Del Mar Coll., 1959-75, Corpus Christi State U., 1978-93, Tex. A&M U., Corpus Christi, 1993—; program dir. Corpus Christi Chamber Music Soc., 1986—; piano chmn. Corpus Christi Young Artists' Competition, 1987—; chmn. Del Mar Coll. Student Programs Com., 1986-88, 91-92, 94-95; chmn. radio com., S.Tex. Pub. Broadcasting Svc., Corpus Christi, 1987-88; asst. mus. dir. Little Theater, Corpus Christi, 1970-74; judge, Houston Symphony Auditions, 1988, S.C. Young Artist Competition, Columbia, 1990; freelance accompanist, 1955—, adjudicator, 1960—; v.p. united fac., Del Mar Coll., 1986-88; pianist with Del Mar Trio, 1965-95, Young Audiences, Inc., 1975-83; recital tours in U.S., Mex., Austria, 1954-88. Piano soloist, St. Louis Symphony, 1956, 57, Bach Festival Orch., St. Louis, 1955, Corpus Christi Symphony; recipient Artist Presentation award, Artist Presentation Soc., St. Louis, 1956. Co-chmn. Mayor's Com. on Recycling, Corpus Christi, 1989-91; bd. dirs. Corpus Christi Symphony; adv. bd. Corpus Christi Concert Ballet; mem. steering com. cultural devel. plan City of Corpus Christi, 1995-96. Mem. Music Tchrs. Nat. Assn., Tex. Music Tchrs. Assn., Corpus Christi Music Tchrs. Assn., Liszt Soc. (contbr. to jour.). Home: 4709 Curtis Clark Dr Corpus Christi TX 78411-4801 Office: Del Mar Coll Baldwin & Ayers Corpus Christi TX 78404

ALLISON, STEPHEN GALENDER, broadcast executive; b. Springfield, Mo., Dec. 11, 1952; s. Edgebert Allcorn and Naomi Louise (Chamless) A.; children: Julie Ann, Jennifer Erin; m. Tara Rae Foster, Aug. 20, 1986 (div. Aug. 1994). Cert. radio mktg. cons. Radio Advt. Bur. On-air personality Sta. WSBB, New Smyrna, Fla., 1971-72, Sta. WMFJ-AM-FM, Daytona Beach, Fla., 1972-75, Sta. KADI-FM, St. Louis, 1975-76, Sta. KAUM-FM, Houston, 1976-79, Sta. WKYS-FM, Washington, 1979-81; gen mgr. Sta. KSTM-FM, Phoenix, 1981-85; pres. Allison Broadcasting Co., Inc., Phoenix, 1985—, Allison Broadcast Group, Inc., Dallas, Del Mar, Calif., 1987—; owner Stas. KGRX-FM/KIKO, Phoenix, 1986-91, Sta. KDGE-FM, Dallas, 1989-94, WLVX-FM, Gainesville, Fla., 1994-95; mgr. news, talk, business prgmg. ABC Radio Networks, Dallas, 1996—; mktg. cons. St. Louis Post-Dispatch, 1975-76, Houston Chronicle, 1976-79, Washington Star, 1980-81; advt. cons. Celebrity Theatre, Phoenix, 1985-86; pres. JFM Branson (Mo.) Inc., 1993—; owner Doc Severinsen Theater. Bd. dirs. Desert-Mt. Foothills Assn., Scottsdale, Ariz., 1981-91, Alwun House Cultural Ctr., Phoenix, 1982—, Film in Ariz., Phoenix, 1985-93, Ariz. Commn. on the Arts, Phoenix, 1986-89; active Nat. Rep. Congl. Com., 1988-94, No. Tex. Commn. Mem. Nat. Assn. Broadcasters, Ariz. Broadcasters Assn., Tex. Assn. Broadcasters, Phoenix Active 20-30 Club, Internat. Platform Assn., Las Colinas Sports Club, Pointe Royale Country Club, Preston Trails Country Club, The Heritage Club. Office: ABC Radio Networks 13725 Montfort Dr Dallas TX 75240

ALLISON, WILLIAM B., lawyer; b. Austin, Tex., Nov. 23, 1952; s. Robert S. and Martha Ann (Greenwood) A.; m. Pat East, Sept. 8, 1984; children: Lauren Faulkner, Courtney Faulkner, Megan Allison. BA, Rice U., 1975; JD, U. Tex., 1979. Bar: Tex. 1980, U.S. Ct. Appeals (5th cir.) 1981, U.S. Supreme Ct. 1984. Law clk. U.S. Ct. Appeals, Montgomery, Ala., 1979-80; assoc. Sewell & Riggs, Houston, 1980-86, ptnr., shareholder, 1986-95; ptnr. Gardere, Wynne, Sewell & Riggs, Houston, 1995—; counsel mem. consumer law sect. Tex. State Bar, 1986-92; program com. mem. PetroSafe '95, Houston, 1994-95; spkr. in field. Youth soccer coach YMCA, Houston, 1990-95. Fellow Houston Bar Found.; mem. ABA, Nat. Inst. Mcpl. Law Officers, Greater Houston Partnership (environ. com.), Houston Bar Assn. (chair environ. law 1994-95), Am. Inns Ct. Office: Gardere Wynne Sewell & Riggs 333 Clay St Ste 800 Houston TX 77002-4000

ALLMAN, MARK C., engineer, physicist; b. Rochester, Pa., Aug. 4, 1958; s. Crawford Marcus and Darl Terresa (Hazenstab) A.; m. Mary Beth Decker, Apr. 30, 1983 (div. 1987); m. Janice Kay Hempleman, Dec. 8, 1989. BSBA, Robert Morris Coll., 1980; MS in Phys. Sci., U. Houston Clear Lake, 1991. Programmer/analyst Transcomm Data Systems, Inc., Pitts., 1980-81; ind. cons. Pitts., 1981-82; programmer/analyst, cons. ComTech Systems, Inc., Columbus, Ohio, 1982-83; systems programmer, mgr., project leader DataCom, Inc., Columbus, 1983-86; systems engr. R&D Discovery Systems, Dublin, Ohio, 1986-88; systems analyst On-Line Computer Libr. Ctr., Dublin, 1988-89; engr., physicist Rockwell Space Ops. Co., Houston, 1989-95; sr. engr. McDonnell Douglas Aerospace, 1995—; mem. data collection team Allegheny Obs., U. Pitts., 1981-82; presenter at profl. confs. Author: Introduction to the C Programming Language, 1994; co-author: Modern Astrodynamics, 1996. Mem. campaign coun. Rep. Nat. Com., Washington, 1991—, Rep. Presdl. Task Force; pres. Haw Rang Do Kung-Fu Martial Arts Team, 1991-93. Mem. AIAA, AAAS, Am. Astron. Soc. (assoc.), Coun. Fgn. Rels., Wu Shu Kung Fu Fedn. (2d deg. black belt), Greater Houston Deming Alliance. Republican. Roman Catholic. Home: 2912 Hamm Rd Pearland TX 77581 Office: McDonnell Douglas Aerospace 13100 Space Center Blvd Houston TX 77059

ALLMAN, RICHARD MARK, physician, gerontologist; b. Columbus, Ohio, Feb. 23, 1955; m. Connie Lou Allman; children: Justin Mark, Philip Randolph. BA in Biology magna cum laude, W.Va. U., 1977, MD, 1980. Diplomate Am. Bd. Internal Medicine, sub.-bd. Geriatric Medicine; diplomate Nat. Bd. Med. Examiners. Internal medicine intern W.Va. U. Sch. Medicine, 1980-81, resident in internal medicine, 1981-83; fellow in internal medicine Johns Hopkins U., Balt., 1983-85; asst. in medicine, staff physician Johns Hopkins U./Hosp., Balt., 1985-86; staff physician U. Ala. Hosp., VA Med. Ctr., Birmingham, 1986—; asst. prof. medicine U. Ala., Birmingham, 1986-90, assoc. prof. medicine, dir. div. gerontology/geriatric med., 1990-96, dir. Ctr. for Aging, 1992—, dir. Geriatric Edn. Ctr., 1993—, prof. medicine, 1996—; prin. clin. coord. Ala. Quality Assurance Found., Birmingham, 1995—; chief geriatrics sect. Birmingham VA Med. Ctr., 1990—. Assoc. editor Am. Jour. Medicine, 1988-92; mem. editorial bd. Advances in Wound Healing, 1989—, Jour. Am. Geriatrics Soc., 1994—; ad hoc reviewer for jours.; contbr. numerous articles to profl. jours. Recipient Lange Book award, 1977, Mosby Book award, 1978, John A. Hartford Found. award, 1991, others. Mem. ACP, Am. Fedn. for Aging Rsch., Assn. Dirs. Geriatric Acad. Programs (nat. coun. 1993—), Wound Healing Soc., Ala. Gerontol. Soc., So. Soc. for Clin. Investigation, Gerontol. Soc. Am., Am. Heart Assn. (coun. on epidemiology), Am. Geriatrics Soc., Am. Fedn. for Clin. Rsch. (Henry Christian Meml. award 1993), Soc. Gen. Internal Medicine, Phi Beta Kappa, Alpha Omega Alpha. Office: U Ala Ctr for Aging 933 19th St S Ste 201 Birmingham AL 35205-3703

ALLMAND, LINDA F(AITH), library director; b. Port Arthur, Tex., Jan. 31, 1937; d. Clifton James and Jewel Etoile (Smith) A. BA, North Tex. State U., 1960; MA, U. Denver, 1962. Clerical asst. Gates Meml. Libr., 1953-55; libr. asst. Houston Pub. Libr., 1955-58; children's libr. Denver Pub. Libr., 1960-63; children's coord. Anaheim Pub. Libr., Calif., 1963-65; br. mgr. Dallas Pub. Libr., 1965-71, chief br. svcs., 1971-81; dir. Ft. Worth Pub. Libr., 1981—; instr. North Tex. State U., Denton, 1967—; instr. Dallas County C.C., 1981; bldg. cons. Dallas Pub. Libr., 1974-80, Hurst Pub. Libr., 1977-78, Jacksonville (Tex.) Pub. Libr., 1976-79, Carrollton Pub. Libr., 1979-81, Haltom (Tex.) City Pub. Libr., 1984, Iowa Park (Tex.) Pub. Libr., 1985, S.W. Regional Libr., Ft. Worth, 1987. Author: 1981-2000, Ft. Worth Public Library—Facilities and Long-Range Planning Study, 1982; contbr. chpts. to books, articles to profl. jours. Bd. dirs. City of Dallas Credit Union, 1973-81, Sr. Citizen's Ctrs., Inc., 1982; com. chmn. Goals for Dallas, 1967-69; mem. Forum Ft. Worth, 1983. Pilot Club of Port Arthur scholar, 1954, Libr. Binding Inst. scholar, 1958; recipient Disting. Alumnus award North Tex. State U., 1983, Leadership Ft. Worth, 1982-83; named Tarrant County Newsmaker of the Yr., 1984, Outstanding Leader, Ft. Worth Star Telegram, 1989, Outstanding Woman of the Yr., Mayor's Commn. on Status of Women, 1989, North Tex. Pub. Adminstr. of the Yr., 1990. Mem. ALA, AAUP, AAUW, Tex. Libr. Assn. (pres. pub. libr. divsn. 1980-81, chmn. planning com. 1982-84, pres.-elect 1985-86, pres. 1986-87, Libr. of Yr. award 1985, North Tex. Pub. Adminstr. of Yr. award 1990), Tarrant Regional Librs. Assn., Am. Mgmt. Assn., Dallas County Librs. Assn. (pres. 1968-69), Downtown Ft. Worth (mem. edn. info. task force 1992-93), Freedom to Read Found., Ft. Worth C. of C. (bd. dirs. 1993—), Rotary, Sister Cities, Inc., Ft. Worth Pub. Libr. Found. Home: 701 Timberview Ct N Fort Worth TX 76112-1715 Office: Fort Worth Pub Libr 300 Taylor St Fort Worth TX 76102-7309

ALLRED, RITA REED, artist; b. Davenport, Iowa, Apr. 12, 1935; d. Edward Platt and Delia Marie (Quinn) Reed; m. Glenn Charles Scott, June 9, 1956 (div. Nov. 1977); children: Sheryl Marie, Laura Ann; m. Robert Yates Allred, Dec. 9, 1977. Student Marycrest Coll., Davenport, 1953-56; BS in Art Edn., Drake U., 1958; MFA in Painting, Winthrop U., 1995. Art tchr. Fayetteville City Schs., N.C., 1961-64, Charlotte-Mecklenburg Schs., N.C., 1967-71; cons., project dir. PCA Internat., Matthews, N.C., 1981; artist, art cons., dir. workshops, 1976—; civilian artist USCG, 1981—; instr. portrait painting Cen. Piedmont Community Coll., 1986—; instr. drawing and painting Mint Mus. Art, 1991—; courtroom sketch artist WBTV, 1991-92; adj. prof. art Gardner-Webb U., Boiling Springs, N.C., 1993—; painter in oils; recent commns. include paintings for U.S. Army, USCG, portraits for ABCO Industries, U.S. Naval Inst. Service Head Portrait Series, NASA Art Team; pres. Willow Reed Studios, 1986-90. Bd. dirs. Internat. House, Charlotte, 1985-86; mem. Sister Cities Com., Charlotte, 1984-85. Recipient George Gray award USCG, 1983. Democrat. Mem. Cedarwood Country Club. Avocation: golf. Home and Studio: 7217 Quail Meadow Ln Charlotte NC 28210-5124 Office: Willow Reed Studios 7217 Quail Meadow Ln Charlotte NC 28210-5124

ALLS, GARY LEE, municipal official; b. Paducah, Ky., Dec. 3, 1947; s. Howard and Evelyn (Driggers) A.; m. Lissa Anne Young, Dec. 4, 1971; children: Angela Beth, Oma Rebeccah. Student, Paducah Jr. Coll., 1965-66, Bowling Green Bus. Coll., 1982-84. Engring. tech. Ky. Dept. Transp., Leitchfield, 1992-76; supt., estimator Qualified Paving and Constrn., Leitchfield, 1976-78; supt. Scotty's Constrn., Bowling Green, Ky., 1978-80; labor foreman Bell Constrn., Frankfort, Ky., 1980-81; supt. S.B. Owen Constrn., Bowling Green, 1981-82; carpenter D. Kessinger Bldg. Contractor, Bowling Green, 1982-83; foreman, estimator Ervin Sorrell Contracting, Bowling Green, 1983-84; from asst. supt. to supt. City of Owensboro, Ky., 1984—. Vol. ARC, Owensboro, 1989—. Mem. Am. Pub. Works Assn. (v.p. Ky. so. br. 1991, pres. 1994). Democrat. Home: 4239 Buckland Sq Apt 1 Owensboro KY 42301 Office: City of Owensboro 1426 W 5th St Owensboro KY 42301-1942

ALLSBROOK, OGDEN OLMSTEAD, JR., economics educator; b. Wilmington, N.C., July 1, 1940; s. Ogden Olmstead Sr. and Elizabeth Barringer (Warren) A. BA, Wake Forest U., 1962; PhD, U. Va., 1966. Ops. rsch. analyst Dep. Def., Washington, 1966-68; asst. prof. econs. U. Ga., Athens, 1968-73, dir. grad. studies econs., 1971-81, assoc. prof., 1974-96, ret., 1996. Author: Utilization of Military Resources, 1969; contbr. articles to profl. jours. Capt. U.S. Army, 1966-68. Mem. AAUP, Nat. Soc. SAR (pres. Athens chpt. 1992-94), Cape Fear Club, Atlanta Econ. Club, So. Econ. Assn. Lutheran. Home: 115 Tillman Ln Athens GA 30606-4115

ALM, JOHN RICHARD, beverage company executive; b. Jamestown, N.Y., Feb. 25, 1946; s. Carl Raymond and Erma Grace (Williams) A.; m. Cheryl D. Van Marter; Apr. 26, 1969; children: Lara, Richard. BS in Acctg., SUNY, Buffalo, 1972. Sr. auditor Price Waterhouse, N.Y.C. and Los Angeles, 1974-77; sr. v.p. fin., controller Johnston Coca-Cola Bottling Group, Inc., 1977—; v.p., CFO Johnston Coca-Cola Bottling Group, Inc., Atlanta; CPA, Minn. Served with USAF, 1969-72. Mem. Fin. Execs. Inst., Am. Inst. CPA's, Minn. Soc. CPA's.

ALMEIDA, JOSÉ AGUSTÍN, romance languages educator; b. Waco, Tex., Aug. 28, 1933; s. Jesse M. and Teodora (Mancillas) A.; m. Maritza Barros, Sept. 5, 1964; 1 son, José Rodolfo. BA, Baylor U., 1961; MA, U. Mo., 1964, PhD, 1967. Teaching asst. U. Mo., Columbia, 1961-66; instr. Baylor U., Waco, 1962-63; asst. prof. dept. Romance langs. U. N.C., Greensboro, 1966-77, assoc. prof., 1977—, chmn. Latin Am. studies, 1979-81; vis. prof. Elmira (N.Y.) Coll., summer 1967; asst. prof. Inst. in Mid. Am., summers 1968-69, Cali, Colombia, summer 1973; assoc. prof. study abroad program U. N.C.-Greensboro-Guilford Coll., Madrid, 1980, dir. grad. studies in Spanish, 1991-95; cons. verbal-active teaching method Hampton Inst., 1976, 77, U. N.C.-Charlotte, 1984; lectr. 1st Internat. Conf. Picaresque Lit., Madrid, 1976, 6th Conf. Internat. Assn. Hispanists, 1977, 1st Internat. Conf. on Lope de Vega, 1980. Author: (with Stephen C. Mohler and Robert R. Stinson) Descubrir y crear, 1976, 3d edit., 1986; La crítica literaria de Fernando de Herrera, 1976. With USAF, 1953-57. Nat. Endowment for Humanities fellow, 1970. Mem. MLA, S. Atlantic MLA, Am. Assn. Tchrs. Spanish and Portuguese, Internat. Assn. Hispanists, Cervantes Soc. Am., Asociación de Cervantistas, Sigma Delta Pi (faculty sponsor 1989—). Democrat. Roman Catholic. Home: 1410 Valleymede Rd Greensboro NC 27410-3938

ALMON, RENEAU PEARSON, state supreme court justice; b. Moulton, Ala., July 8, 1937; s. Nathaniel Lee and Mary (Johnson) A.; m. Deborah Pearson Preer, June 27, 1974; children by previous marriage: Jonathan, Jason, Nathaniel; 1 stepson: Tommy Preer. B.S., U. Ala., 1959; LL.B., Cumberland Sch. Law Samford U., 1964. Bar: Ala. 1964. Price analyst NASA; law clk. to justice Ala. Supreme Ct.; sole practice Moulton; judge 36th Jud. Circuit Ala., 1966-69, Ala. Ct. Criminal Appeals, 1969-75; justice Ala. Supreme Ct., Montgomery, 1974—. Served with U.S. Army. Named one of Outstanding Young Men in Am., 1971. Mem. ABA, Ala. Bar Assn., Lawrence County Bar Assn., Montgomery County Bar Assn., Kappa Alpha, Phi Alpha Delta, Omicron Delta Kappa. Methodist. Office: Ala Supreme Ct 300 Dexter Ave Montgomery AL 36104-3741

ALMON, TERRY MICHELLE, banker; b. San Rafael, Calif., Nov. 25, 1955; d. Robert Richard and Barbara Jean (Walker) Kelley; m. John S. Almon, Mar. 12, 1977; children: Matthew Steven, Laura Michelle. BA, Tex. Christian U., 1977; postgrad., U. Tex., San Antonio. Tchr. Ft. Worth, San Antonio and Klein (Tex.) pub. schs., 1977-86; continuing edn. coord. Soc. of Exploration Geophysicists, Tulsa, 1988-89; sr. v.p., mktg. dir., loan officer Stillwater Nat. Bank and Trust Co., Tulsa, 1990—. Author: San Antonio Tour Guide; editor North San Antonio Rotary newsletter. Mem. bd. edn. Jenks Sch. Bd., Tulsa, 1993-96; bd. dirs. Southwestern Ednl. Devel. Lab., Tulsa, 1994—, Am. Lung Asn., 1993-95, Magic Empire Coun. Girl Scouts U.S., Tulsa, 1990-95; chmn. Okla. Commn. for Tchr. Preparation, 1992—, chmn. subcom. on cultivating talent, human devel. and tchg. skills, 1992-95; auction chmn. Jenks Pub. Schs. Found. Ann. Auction, 1994; chmn. Tulsa Women's Found., 1993-94, mem. ann. Pinnacle Awards Dinner com., 1994; active numerous other civic orgns. Recipient Friend of Edn. award Okla. Edn. Assn., 1992. Mem. Juliette Low Leadership Soc. (charter founding mem.), LWV, Okla. Acad. State Goals, Tulsa Rotary. Democrat. Disciples of Christ. Home: 7627 S Quebec Ave Tulsa OK 74136-8102 Office: Stillwater Nat Bank & Trust 2431 E 61st St Ste 170 Tulsa OK 74136-1229

ALMOND, DAVID R., lawyer. BS, U. Va., 1962, LLB, 1967; postgrad. in Exec. Program, MIT, 1981. Assoc. Reid & Priest, N.Y.C., 1967-71; asst. gen. counsel Boise Cascade Corp., Idaho, 1971-77, assoc. gen. counsel and asst. sec., 1977-84; sr. v.p. Wilson Foods Corp., Oklahoma City, 1985-89; sr. v.p., gen. counsel, sec. Fleming Cos. Inc., Oklahoma City, 1989—. Office: Fleming Cos Inc 6301 Waterford Blvd Oklahoma City OK 73118-1103

ALMOND, GILES KEVIN, accountant, financial planner; b. Albemarle, N.C., June 16, 1956; s. Horace David and Helen Ruth (Hauser) A.; m. Anita Elizabeth Lanier, Oct. 21, 1978; children: Cassandra, Kevin, Alice. BS in Acctg., U. N.C., Wilmington, 1978. CPA, N.C., S.C.; CFP; PFS. Revenue agt. IRS, Dothan, Ala., 1978-82; acct. Brittain, Almond & Simpson, P.A., Charlotte, N.C., 1982-87; sr. tax mgr. Nasekos, Ryan and Co. CPAs, Charlotte, 1987-90; pres. Matrix Fin. Mgmt. Cons., Charlotte, 1990—; mem. N.C. Bd. CPA Examiners, Raleigh, 1986-89; mem. steering com. Queens Coll. Estate Planners Day; chmn. ednl. needs analysis task force Internat. Bd. Standards and Practices for Cert. Fin. Planners, 1992-94. Mem. council Cen. Ch. God, Charlotte, 1986—. Fellow N.C. Assn. CPA; mem. AICPA, Nat. Assn. Personal Fin. Advisors, Fellowship Christian Fin. Advisors, Inst. CFPs, Charlotte Estate Planning Coun. Republican. Office: Ste 270 4500 Cameron Valley Pky Charlotte NC 28211-3552

ALMOND, JOAN, retired chemist; b. Bklyn., May 19, 1934; d. Harry Christian Nintzel and Helen Pauline (Diviak) Levesen; m. Randall Leroy Field Sr., Nov. 15, 1952 (div. Feb. 1972); children: Randall Leroy Jr., Roland, Gary, Brian, Lorraine, Thomas; m. Bransford Wayne Almond, Dec. 9, 1986. Grad. high sch., Bklyn. Sec. Fulton Savs. Bank, Bklyn., 1952-53; mgr. reprodn. Air Pre-heater Corp., Wellsville, N.Y., 1958; chemistry technician fibers div. Allied Chem., Hopewell, Va., 1963-76; chemistry technician Va. Power Co.-North Anna Power Sta., Mineral, 1976-86, assoc. instr., 1987-92, sr. chemistry technician, 1992-94, sr. chemistry technician shift leader, 1992-94; ret., 1994; craft shop owner Stuffed Stuff and Other Stuff, Bumpass, Va., 1994—. Recipient cert. of achievement Nat. Acad. for Nuclear Tng., 1988. Mem. Women of Moose (com. chmn. Moosehart Hopewell 1971). Roman Catholic.

ALMY, MARION MARABLE, archaeologist; b. Sarasota, Fla., Dec. 5, 1946; d. Marshall Edward and Ethel Virginia (Yentner) Marable; m. Richard Ernest Almy, June 22, 1968; children: Maranda Marable Almy, Rachael Elaine Almy. BA in Anthropology, Fla. State U., 1968; postgrad., U. Mo., 1969-71; MA in Anthropology, U. South Fla., 1976. Cert. in field archaeology Soc. Profl. Archaeologists. Archaeologist, cultural resource survey coord. Little Salt Spring Rsch. Facility, North Port, Fla., 1974-75; sr. site archaeologist Fla. Dept. of State, 1975-76; pres. Archaeological Consultants, Inc., Sarasota, Fla., 1976—; instr. archaeology Manatee C.C., Manatee and Sarasota Counties, Fla., 1987-90; mem. Fla. Hist. Preservation Adv. Coun., 1987-93, chmn., 1989-90. Contbr. articles to Fla. Anthropologist, 1976-89; co-author pamphlet on archeol. laws in Fla., 1989, pamphlets on archeol. preservation, 1991. Mem. City of Sarasota Planning Bd., 1990-95, chmn., 1991; mem. County of Sarasota Planning Commn., 1993—, Sarasota County Hist. Commn., 1984-92, chmn., 1988-90; supr. Sarasota Soil and Water Conservation Dist., 1987-91; sustainer Jr. League Sarasota, 1989—; mem. citizens adv. com. Sarasota Bay Project, Nat. Estuary Program, 1989-91, LWV, Sarasota, 1990—; bd. dirs. South Fla. Mus., Bradenton, 1989—; dir. Gulf Coast Heritage Assn., 1993—, sec., 1994—. Recipient Disting. Alumna award U. South Fla., 1991, Crystal Heart award Gulf Coast coun. Girl Scouts U.S., 1992; Project RENEW grantee Sarasota br. AAUW, 1975. Mem. Fla. Women's Alliance, Fla. Anthropol. Soc. (pres. 1982-83, Outstanding Svc. award 1988, 92), Fla. Trust for Hist. Preservation (bd. dirs. 1994—), Fla. Archaeol. Coun. (pres. 1990-92), Time Sifters

Archaeol. Soc. (bd. dirs. 1988-91, v.p. 1991-92). Office: Archaeol Cons 2345 Bee Ridge Rd Ste 6 Sarasota FL 34239-6211

ALONSO, ANTONIO ENRIQUE, lawyer; b. Havana, Cuba, Aug. 31, 1924; came to U.S., 1959; s. Enrique and Inocencia (Avila) A.; m. Daisy Ojeda, July 20, 1949; children: Margarita, Antonio, Enrique, Jorge. JD, U. Habana, Cuba, 1946; PhD, U. Habana, 1952; student, U. Fla., 1974-76. Bar: Fla. 1976. Pub. defendant High Ct. Las Villas, Cuba, 1946-49; atty. Provincial Gov., Cuba, 1950-52; under sec. Treasury, Cuba, 1952-54; mem. House of Reps. Congress of Cuba, 1954-58; sole practice Miami, 1976—. Author: (with others) Violation of Human Rights in Cuba, 1962, History of the Communist Party of Cuba, 1970; weekly columnist on real estate and law Diaros Las Ams. newspaper; contbr. articles to profl. jours. Mem. Fla. Bar Assn. Republican. Roman Catholic. Home: 1900 SW 12th Ave Miami FL 33129-2613 Office: 1699 Coral Way Ste 315 Miami FL 33145-2860

ALPART, NANCY MICHELE, special education educator; b. Phila., Sept. 22, 1953; d. Sam Ross and Harriet Roberta (Helfant) Magedoff; m. Gary Alpart. BA in Elem. Edn., Fairleigh Dickinson U., 1975; MS in Mental Retardation, Barry Coll., 1977. Religious sch. tchr. Temple Israel, Miami, Fla., 1975-76; learning disabilities tchr. Gratigny Elem., Miami, 1976-78; varies exceptionalities tchr. Mae M. Walters Elem., Hialeah, Fla., 1978-87, Ojus and Greynolds Pk. Elem., Miami, 1987-88, Biscayne Gardens Elem., Miami, 1988—; sponsor Future Educators Am., Miami, 1990—; rep. Limited English Proficiency, 1990—. Treas. Scoliosis Assn. Greater Miami, 1984-86, v.p., 1986-88; chairperson Sch. Adv. Coun., Biscayne Gardens Elem. Sch. Named Tchr. of Yr., Biscayne Gardens Elem. Sch., 1995; grantee Impact II, 1991. Mem. Coun. Exceptional Children (treas. 1990-92, pres.-elect 1992-93, pres. 1993-94, Dade County Elem. Spl. Edn. Tchr. of Yr. award 1995), Alpha Delta Kappa (sec. 1984-86, pres. 1988-90). Democrat. Jewish. Home: 481 Ives Dairy Rd Miami FL 33179-5433 Office: Biscayne Gardens Elem Sch 560 NW 151st St Miami FL 33169-6613

ALPERT, BARRY MARK, insurance company and banking executive; b. Chgo., Apr. 17, 1941; s. Isadore Daniel and Betty Shane A.; m. Judith Rae Schwartz, Dec. 24, 1969; children: Daniel Ian, Jason Bradley, Stephanie Ann. Student, Ind. U., 1958-60; BBA, Roosevelt U., 1961; MBA in Banking, U. Wis., 1965. V.p. Exch. Nat. Bank, Chgo., 1961-72; pres., CEO Belleair Bluffs Corp., Largo, Fla., 1973-77; chmn., CEO Orange State Life and Health Ins. Co., Largo, 1977-87, Home Life Fin. Assurance Corp., 1982-88; pres., CEO United Ins. Cos., Inc., Largo, 1988-89; pres. Pioneer Western Corp., Largo, 1989-91; vice chmn. Western Res. Life Assurance Co. of Ohio, Largo, 1989-91, Colony Savs. Bank, Clearwater, 1989-92; chmn. bd., CEO Alpert Fin. Group Inc., 1988; sr. v.p. Robert W. Baird & Co., Inc., Tampa, Fla., 1991—; chmn. bd., founder Life Savs. and Loan Assn., Clearwater, Vla., 1979-83; asst. prof. fin. Roosevelt U., Chgo., 1965-69; host radio program Ask a Banker, Sta. WBBM/CBS, Chgo., 1966-67. Founding dir., treas. Ruth Eckerd Hall-Pact Inc., Clearwater, 1980-86; founder North Suncoast Symphony Guild, Clearwater, 1974; bd. dirs. Fla. Orch., Clearwater, 1974-80, St. Petersburg (Fla.) chpt. United Way, 1975; trustee Fla. House Washington, 1984—, Tampa Bay Rsch. Inst., 1993—. Served with USAFR, 1961-65. Home and Office: Alpert Fin Group Inc 14123 85th Ave Largo FL 34646-2830

ALPERT, JACK NATHANIEL, neurologist; b. Newark, July 20, 1938; s. Louis Seymour Alpert and Ruby Margulis-Alpert; m. Ruth Doris Reich, July 17, 1942; children: Daniel, Richard, Ariela, Jessica. BA, Johns Hopkins U., 1960; MD, Tufts U., 1964. Lic. neurologist. Intern medicine New Eng. Ctr. Hosp., Boston, 1964-65; resident neurology Mt. Sinai Hosp., N.Y.C., 1965-68; pvt. practice Houston, 1971; pvt. practice St. Luke's Hosp., Houston, 1972—, chief dept. neurology, 1986—; clin. assoc. prof. neurology U. Tex. Sch. Medicine, 1986-94, clin. prof. neurology, 1994—. Contbr. articles to med. jours. Capt. USAF, 1968-70. Fellow Am. Acad. Neurology. Office: 6624 Fannin St Houston TX 77030-2312

ALPHER, VICTOR SETH, clinical psychologist, consultant; b. Washington, Oct. 20, 1954; s. Ralph Asher and Louise Ellen (Simons) A. BA, U. Pa., 1976; PhD, Vanderbilt U., 1985. Lic. psychologist, Tex., Tenn.; diplomate in clin. psychology Am. Bd. Profl. Psychology. Grad. fellow Vanderbilt U., Nashville, 1981-85; asst. prof. U. Tex. Health Sci. Ctr., Houston, 1986-88, clin. asst. prof., 1989—; cons. Rsch. Inst. on Addictions, Buffalo, 1990—, Meml. Geriatric Evaluation and Resource Ctr., Houston, 1991-95; bd. cons. Fla. Inst. Psychology, 1994—. Cons. reviewer Jour. Cons. and Clin. Psychology, 1996—; contbr. articles to profl. jours., including Jour. Cons. and Clin. Psychology, Jour. Personality Assessment, Jour. Psychopathology and Behavioral Assessment, Psychotherapy, and Jour. Applied Physiology. Fellow Acad. Clin. Psychology; mem. APA, Soc. Psychotherapy Rsch., Soc. Personality Assessment, Sigma Xi. Office: Weslayan Sta PO Box 270263 Houston TX 77277-0263

ALSCHULER, AL, freelance writer, public relations counselor; b. Gary, Ind., Jan. 27, 1934; s. Harold Morris and Sarah N. Alschuler; m. Joy Van Wye, June 28, 1956 (div. 1986); children: Mari Lynn, David Van, Mark Jonathan. BA in Journalism with honors, U. Okla., 1955. Exec. v.p. Vanleigh Furniture Showrooms, N.Y.C., 1958-71, Miami, Fla., 1971-79; advt. and pub. rels. cons., Miami Beach, Fla., 1979-82; mng. editor Fla. Designer Quar., Miami, 1982-84, Design South, Miami Beach, 1984-87; freelance writer, pub. rels. counsel, Miami, 1987—; cons. interior design adv. bd. Fla. Internat. U., Miami, 1988—, Art Inst. Ft. Lauderdale. Editor I.D.E.A.S., 1994-95; contbg. editor South Florida, 1996—; contbr. numerous articles to N.Y. Times, San Francisco Chronicle, Orlando-Ft. Lauderdale Sun-Sentinel, Miami Today, Fla. Home and Garden, Fla. Architecture, Fla. Travel and Life, Design South, Palm Beach Life, Inside Miami, Haut Decor, A View on Design, Selecta, Casa & Estilo Internat., El Herald, Caribbean Network, Country Life, others; guest expert on design WFOR-TV. Committeeman East Rockaway (N.Y.) Dem. Com., 1968-69; founding chmn. Players State Theatre Conservatory, Coconut Grove, Fla., 1975; mem. Metro Dade Performing Arts Dist. Commn., 1976-77, Miami Com. on Beautification, 1977; bd. dirs. Miami's For Me, Skyline Theatre Co.; trustee Miami Design Preservation League, 1988—. Recipient Rachline Comms. award, 1996. Fellow Interior Design Guild (Comms. award 1996, past pres.); mem. Am. Soc. Interior Designers, Internat. Interior Design Assn., Soc. Profl. Journalists, Miami Internat. Press Club (pres. 1994), Mensa, Phi Beta Kappa. Home and Office: 2449 S Bayshore Dr Coconut Grove FL 33133

ALSCHULER, ALFRED SAMUEL, psychology educator; b. Chgo., Aug. 14, 1939; s. Alfred Samuel and Helen Nancy (Adler) A.; m. Irene Ultika Hystrom, June 21, 1964 (div. Aug. 1976); children: Lisa, Brigette, Alfred; m. Cathryn Fishman, Aug.,21, 1981; 1 child, Elena. BA, Amherst Coll., 1961; MA, Harvard U., 1963, PhD, 1966; LHD (hon.), John F. Kennedy U., 1978; DPsych. (hon.), Rosebridge Grad. Sch., 1989. Diplomate N.Y. Bd. Psychology. Asst. prof. Harvard Grad. Sch. Edn., Cambridge, Mass., 1966-69; assoc. prof. SUNY, Albany, 1969-71; prof. U. Mass., Amherst, Mass., 1971-89; pres. John F. Kennedy U., Orinda, Calif., 1989-90, Inst. Transpersonal Psychology, Menlo Park, Calif., 1990-92; dean Appalachian State U., Boone, N.C., 1992-94; prof. Appalachian State U., Boone, 1992—; pres. Devel. Rsch. Assocs., Cambride, 1966-69; bd. trustees Traveling Sch. Internat., Santa Cruz, Calif., 1989—; and many other bds. Author: (books) Teaching Achievement Motivation, 1970, School Discipline. 1980, Teacher Burnout, 1982, Weapons of Construction, 1989,. Recipient 3 pre-doctoral grants, NIMH, 1960-66; 2 Fulbright fellowships, Holland, Norway, T. Scott Rogo award Parapsychology Found., N.Y.C., 1994. Home: 500 Circle Dr E Boone NC 28607 Office: Appalachian State U. Duncan Hall/RCOE Boone NC 28608

ALSTON, EUGENE BENSON, communications company executive; b. Halifax County, N.C., Sept. 12, 1934; s. Eugene Johnston and Zelma Ruby (Benson) A.; m. Geraldine Coleman, (div. Oct. 1990); children: Ruby Lynn, MIchial Claude, Carl Branch; m. Linda Sue Wiley, Jan. 22, 1991. Student, Wake Forest (N.C.) U., 1955. Lineman Carolina Telephone Co., New Bern, N.C., 1957-61; installer Carolina Telephone Co., Jacksonville, N.C., 1961-66; plant instr. Carolina Telephone Co., Rocky Mount, N.C., 1966-68; plant instr. GTE South, Durham, N.C., 1968-70, tng. mgr., 1970-74; dist. mgr. GTE South, Richlands, Va., 1974-78; outside plant adminstr. GTE South, Durham, 1978-84, div. constrn. mgr., 1984-87; gen. market mgr. Micro Computer Systems, Greensboro, N.C., 1987-89; ops. mgr. Globe Comm., Durham, 1989-92, Lucent Technologies Svcs. Co., Durham, 1992—; with Lucent Techs. Svcs. Co., Durham. Mem. coun. City of Creedmoor, N.C., 1979-87. With U.S. Army, 1953-55. Recipient Svc. award Gov. James Holshouser, 1973. Mem. Creedmoor Lions Club (pres. 1991), Butner Lions Club (Key 1973). Republican. Methodist.

ALTALIB, OMAR HISHAM, sociologist; b. Kirkuk, Mosul, Iraq, May 16, 1967; s. Hisham Yahya and Ilham (Ismail) A.; m. Nina Junaina Al-Batati, Dec. 31, 1991. Shahada, Manarat al-Riyadh, 1982; BA, George Mason U., 1989; MA, U. Chgo., 1993, PhD, 1996. Rsch. asst. Nat. Opinion Rsch. Ctr., 1992—; vis. scholar Internat. Islamic U., Malaysia. Advisor Muslim Youth Coun., Chgo., 1990; mem. Citizens Utility Bd., Chgo., 1992; explorer scout Fairfax County Police Dept. Fellow Inst. for Humane Studies; scholar Minaret of Freedom Inst. Mem. Am. Sociol. Assn., Nat. Assn. Grad. and Profl. Students, Mid. Ea. Studies Ctr. (affiliate), Econs. Honor Soc., Soc. Social Rsch., Internat. Studies Assn., Soc. Advancement of Socio-Econs., Free Market Soc./Chgo., Electronic Frontier Found., Co-Op Am., Golden Key, Assn. Muslim Social Scientists, Am. Hist. Assn., All Dulles Area Muslim Soc., Alpha Chi. Libertarian. Islam. Office: 555 Grove St Herndon VA 22070

ALTAN, M(USTAFA) CENGIZ, mechanical engineering educator; b. Ankara, Turkey, Dec. 26, 1963; s. A. Rifki and Nursel Altan; m. Betul S. Marmara, July 4, 1992. BSME, Mid. East Tech. U., Ankara, 1985; PhD in Mech. Engring., U. Del., 1989. Tchg. asst. U. Del., Newark, 1985-86, rsch. asst., 1986-89; asst. prof. mech. engring. U. Okla., Norman, 1989-95, assoc. prof., 1995—. Editor: (conf. procs.) Developments in Non-Newtonian Fluid Mechanics, 1993, Intelligent Manufacturing and Material Processing, 1995; contbr. articles to profl. jours. Recipient rsch. initiation award Soc. Mfg. Engrs., 1990; rsch. grantee Okla. Ctr. for Advancement Sci. and Tech., 1991, NASA, 1996. Mem. ASME (assoc., chmn. materials processing com. materials div. 1994—), Soc. Rheology, Internat. Polymer Processing Soc., Am. Soc. Engring. Edn., Pi Tau Sigma (hon.). Office: U Okla Sch Aero-Mech Eng 865 Asp Ave Rm 212 Norman OK 73019-1050

ALTENBURGER, KARL MARION, allergist, immunologist; b. Coral Gables, Fla., Nov. 13, 1949; s. Karl and Carol Altenburger; m. Carol Bauer, May 25, 1974; children: Laura Alyson, Ashley Carolyn, Elizabeth Ann, Allison Nicole. BA in Zoology, U. South Fla., 1971, MD, 1974. Diplomate Am. Bd. Pediatrics, Am. Bd. Allergy and Immunology, Nat. Bd. Med. Examiners. Intern in pediatrics U. Colo. Med. Ctr., Denver, 1975-76, resident, 1976-78, fellow in allergy and immunology, 1978-81; fellow in allergy and immunology Nat. Jewish Hosp. and Rsch. Ctr.-Nat. Asthma Ctr., Denver, 1978-81; pvt. practice, Ocala, Fla., 1981—; instr. dept. pediatrics U. Colo. Sch. Medicine, 1980-81; bd. dirs. Fla. Med. Polit. Action Com., 1991—. Contbr. articles to med. jours. Trustee Am. Lung Assn. Ctrl. Fla., 1985-93. Fellow Am. Acad. Allergy, Asthma and Immunology, Am. Coll. Allergy Asthma and Immunology, Am. Acad. Pediatrics; mem. AMA, Southeastern Allergy Assn., Am. Assn. for History Medicine, Fla. Med. Assn. (Marion County del. 1990—), Fla. Allergy Asthma and Immunology Soc. (exec. com. 1990—, pres. 1993-94, cons. editorial staff FMA Jour. 1986-92), Marion County Med. Soc. (bd. dirs. 1983-88, pres. 1985-86, editor Bull. 1986-89), U. South Fla. Coll. Medicine Alumni Assn. (pres. 1983-87), Alpha Omega Alpha. Roman Catholic. Office: 1800 SE 17th St # 300 Ocala FL 34474-4446

ALTER, NELSON TOBIAS, jewelry retailer and wholesaler; b. San Antonio, July 14, 1926; s. William and Celia (Tobias) A.; m. Shirley Ann Jacobs, June 12, 1949; children: Dennis Ira, Keith Alan, Brian Reid, Wendy Ilene. BBA in Acctg., U. Tex., 1948, JD, 1950. Mgr. 9 coin-operated washeterias, 1960-67; mgr. Sta. KOGT radio, Orange, Tex., 1950-65; ptnr. Calder Properties, 1977—; mng. ptnr. Crow Road Devel. Co., Beaumont, Tex., 1976-77, Normandy Townhomes, Beaumont, 1978—, Griffing Devel. Co., Beaumont, 1978—, Griffing Realty Joint Venture, Beaumont, 1983—; comptroller Gem Jewelry Cos., Beaumont, 1950-58; pres. Gem Jewelry Co. of Beaumont, Inc., 1958—, chmn. of bd., 1991—; mng. ptnr. Gem Distbg. Co. Wholesale Jewelry, Beaumont, 1958—; also pres., chmn. of bd. Gem Jewelry Co. of Port Artur, Inc., 1991—, Gem Jewelry C. of Orange, Inc., 1991—, Gem. Jewelry C. of Alexandria (La.), Inc., 1991—, Gem. Jewelry C. of Rapides (La.) Inc., 1991, Gem Jewelry Distbg. Co. Inc., 1991—; U.S. rep. Tex. region Habsbourg-Feldman Fine Art Auctioneers, Geneva, 1986, 87, 88, 89; real estate developer Normandy Townhomes, Griffing Devel. Co., Joint Venture, Griffing Realty Joint Venture, Partner Calder Properties. Past pres. Downtown Beaumont Unltd.; co-chmn. Beaumont Urban Renewal; drive chmn. United Jewish Appeal, Beaumont, 1954, 67; v.p. Temple Emanuel, 1974-75, pres., 1981; mem. Beaumont Heritage Soc., Beaumont Music Commn., Beaumont Symphony Soc., Am. Cancer Soc.; co-founder, mem. BBB S.E. Tex.; bd. dirs. A.W. Schlesinger Geriatric Ctr., 1996-98. Mem. Tex. Retail Jewelers Assn. (v.p. 1974-75), Jefferson County Bar Assn., Tex. Bar Assn., Edna Gladney Aux., Beaumont Jewish Fedn., Buckner Benevolences, Tower Club, Masons, B'nai Brith, Phi Eta Sigma, Beta Gamma Sigma, Phi Alpha Delta, Sigma Alpah Mu. Jewish. Office: Gem Jewelry Co 795 N 11th St Beaumont TX 77702-1501

ALTHAUS, DAVID STEVEN, chemicals executive, controller; b. Massilon, Ohio, Dec. 25, 1945; s. James Horace and Mary Jane (Horan) A.; m. Joan Elizabeth Wrenn, Aug. 4, 1973; children: D. Steven Jr., Matthew, Beth Anne. BA, Miami U., Oxford, Ohio, 1967; cert., Def. Lang. Inst., Monterey, Calif., 1969; MBA, Miami U., Oxford, Ohio, 1976. CPA, N.C., Ohio; Cert. profl. in human resources. Internal auditor Harris Corp., Cleve., 1976-77; sr. staff acct. Harris Corp., Rochester, N.Y., 1977-78; acctg. supr. Imperial Group Ltd., Wilson, N.C., 1978-80; dir. planning Am. Mortgage Ins. Cos., Raleigh, N.C., 1980-83; asst. v.p., budget mgr. Gen. Electric Mortgage Ins. Cos., Raleigh, 1983-84; contr., asst. treas. Chem. Industry Inst. Toxicology, Research Triangle Park, N.C., 1984—, mgr. human resources, 1984-90, asst. sec., 1989—. Cubmaster Boy Scouts Am., 1986-90, asst. scoutmaster, 1990-95; bd. dirs., treas. Vol. Families for Children of N.C. Capt. USMC, 1968-74, Vietnam. Decorated Cross of Galantry, Rep. of Vietnam, Da Nang, 1970. Mem. AICPA, Inst. Mgmt. Accts., Am. Compensation Assn., Contr.'s Coun., Soc. for Human Resources Mgmt., U.S. Naval Inst. Baptist. Office: Chem Industry Inst Toxicology PO Box 12137 Durham NC 27709-2137

ALTIERI, PABLO IVAN, cardiologist; b. P.R., May 16, 1943; s. Pablo Altieri and Monsita Nieto; M.D., U. P.R., 1967; m. Emma, June 2, 1967; children—Pablo Ivan, II, Mariemma. Intern, Univ. Hosp.-U. P.R. Med. Sch., 1967-68, resident, 1968-71; research fellow, clin. instr. Ohio State U., 1972-73; dir. cardiovascular lab. U. P.R. Med. Sch., 1975—, prof. medicine, 1975—, assoc. dir. physiology, also faculty pres. Served with M.C., USAF, 1973-75; dir. cardiovascular labs. P.R. Heart Ctr., The Caribbean Heart Ctr.; bd. dirs. Orental Fed. Savs. Bank, Humacao, P.R. Fellow Am. Coll. Cardiology; mem. AMA, Internat. Soc. Heart Rsch., Am. Fedn. Clin. Research, Am. Heart Assn. (dir. P.R. chpt. 1975, Disting. Mem. 1975), Am. Soc. Electrophysiology. Roman Catholic. Club: Rotary (Humacao). Office: PO Box 23134 U PR Sta Rio Piedras PR 00931

ALTMAN, DAVID WAYNE, geneticist; b. Portsmouth, Va., June 6, 1951; s. Ivan Stuart and Elaine Louise (Koll) A.; m. Kathleen Mary Healy, Dec. 16, 1972; children: Erin Healy, Regan Lewisia, Devin Armand. BA, Vanderbilt U., 1972; BS, Oreg. State U., 1978, MS, 1981; PhD, U. Minn., 1983. Cert. secondary sch. tchr. Vol. prof. Peace Corps, Chott Mariem, Tunisia, 1974-75; curriculum developer dept. crop sci. Oreg. State U., Corvallis, 1977-78, rsch. asst. dept. crop sci., 1978-80; rsch. asst. dept. agronomy and plant genetics U. Minn., St. Paul, 1980-83, postdoctoral specialist dept. agronomy and plant genetics, 1983; rsch. geneticist USDA Agrl. Rsch. Svc., College Station, Tex., 1983-92; prof. dept. plant breeding & biometry Cornell U., Ithaca, N.Y., 1992-95; dir. agrl. biotech. UST Inc., Nashville, 1995—; vice chair faculty of genetics Tex. A&M U., College Station, 1989-91, adj. assoc. prof., 1989; faculty Met. State U., Mpls., 1981-83; pres. Internat. Svc. for Acquisition of Agri-Biotech Applications, 1992-94. Assoc. editor: In Vitro Cellular and Developmental Biology, 1990—; editl. adv. bd. CAB Internat., AgBiotech News and Information; editor: Plant Biotechnology Transfer to Developing Countries, 1995; contbr. articles to Jour. Heredity, Genome, Plant Cell Reports, Crop Science, others, chpts. in books. Pres. Unitarian Fellowship, College Station, 1988; v.p. Aggie Swim Club, College Station, 1987; v.p. Falcon Heights Elem. Sch. PTA, St. Paul, 1979. Oreg. Seed Trade Commn. scholar, 1978, DuPont Corp. fellow, 1979, 80; State of Tex. grantee, 1987, 89, USDA grantee, 1990, 91. Mem. Soc. for In Vitro Biology (mem. exec. coun. 1990-94, pres. plant divsn. 1996—), Crop Sci. Soc. Am., Am. Genetic Assn., Sigma Xi (coord. task force 1989-91). Office: UST Inc/R&D 800 Harrison St Nashville TN 37203-3336

ALTMAN, IDA, history educator; b. Washington, Apr. 30, 1950; d. Ralph and Jeanne (Weinberger) A. BA in Latin Am. Studies, U. Mich., 1971; MA in Latin Am. Studies, U. Tex., 1972; MA in History, Johns Hopkins U., 1978, PhD in History, 1982. Postdoctoral fellow dept. Latin Am. studies Hebrew U., Jerusalem, 1981-82; asst. prof. history dept. U. New Orleans, 1982-88, assoc. prof., 1988-93, prof., 1993—; cons. Xavier de Salas Found., Trujillo, Spain, 1983-85; mem. NEH Preservation Panel, 1990; guest curator Libr. of Congress Quincentenary Exhibit, 1992-93; cons. Libr. of Congress Quincentenary Program, 1989-92. Author: Emigrants and Society: Extremadura and Spanish America in the Sixteenth Century, 1989; contbr. articles to profl. jours. Nat. Def. Fgn. Lang. fellow U. Tex. Inst. Latin Am. Studies, 1971-72, Johns Hopkins U. fellow, 1976-78, 79-81, NEH Summer Inst. fellow, Madison, Wis., 1989, Austin & Puebla, 1992; Fulbright-Hays scholar, Spain, 1978-79, NEH fellow for Coll. Teaching, 1994-95; U. New Orleans faculty rsch. grantee, 1983, 84, 87, 92, postdoctoral grantee Treaty for Friendship, Coop. and Def. Between Spain & U.S., 1985, NEH grantee, Seville, Spain, 1989-90; recipient award U. New Orleans Alumni Assn., 1989, prize Spain & Am. Quincentennial Discovery, 1991. Mem. Am. Hist. Assn. (premio del rey prize com. 1994—), Assn. Caribbean Historians, Conf. Latin Am. History (program com. 1994, gen. com. 1995—, Herbert E. Bolton Meml. prize 1990), Sixteenth Century Studies Assn., Soc. Spanish and Portuguese Hist. Studies. Home: 2125 Mirabeau Ave New Orleans LA 70122-3919 Office: U New Orleans Dept History New Orleans LA 70148

ALTMAN, ROY DAVIS, rheumatologist, medical educator; b. Astoria, N.Y., May 16, 1937; s. Carl and Evelyn (Lachman) A.; m. Linda Roberta Tyler, June 24, 1963; children: Evelyn, Sarah, Aaron, Ruth. MD, U. Miami, 1962. Rsch. assoc. VA Med. Ctr., Miami, Fla., 1969-72, chief arthritis sect., 1972—; from asst. prof. medicine to assoc. prof. medicine U. Miami, 1971-81, prof. medicine, 1981—, chief (acting) arthritis, 1994—; staff physician Jackson Meml. Hosp., Miami, 1969—; dir. clin. rsch. Geriatric Rsch. Edn. and Clin. Ctr., Miami, 1993—. Editor-in-chief Osteoarthritis and Cartilage, 1993; editor Seminars in Arthritis and Rheumatism. Trustee Pagets Disease Found., N.Y.C., 1990—. Fellow Am. Coll. Rheumatology (del. AMA 1987—); mem. AMA Splty. Svc. Soc. (Recognition award 1979, 82, 85, 88), AMA Coun. on Scientific Affairs, Osteoarthritis Rsch. Soc. (pres.-elect 1990-94, pres. 1994-96), Orthopaedic Rsch. Soc., Am. Soc. Bone and Mineral Rsch., Czech Republic Soc. Rheumatology, Italian Soc. Rheumatology, Alpha Omega Alpha. Jewish. Office: VA Med Ctr 1201 NW 16th St Miami FL 33125-1624

ALTMAN, WILLIAM CARL, investment manager, consultant; b. La Grange, Tex., Nov. 11, 1957; s. Lester Arthur and Goldie Bertha (Kretzschmar) A.; m. Danguole Julia Spakevicius, Sept. 2, 1989. BS, Tex. A&M U., 1979; BA, Oxford U., Eng., 1982; MBA, Harvard U., 1984. Project dir. Trammell Crow Co., Houston, 1984-85; cons. McKinsey & Co., Inc., Houston, N.Y.C., 1985-89; v.p. Capital Guidance Corp., Houston, 1989-93, sr. v.p., 1993-94; COO Obstet. and Gynecol. Assocs., PA, Houston, 1994—; bd. dirs. Tredex Tile Corp., Houston, 1991-94, pres., 1993-94. Devel. bd. dirs. Tex. A&M U. Coll. Liberal Arts, College Station, 1987—; bd. dirs. U.S.-Baltic Found., Washington, 1990—, chmn., 1993—; mem. Houston com. Coun. on Fgn. Rels., 1990—; co-chair Houston com. Campaign for Oxford, 1990-91. Recipient Rhodes scholarship Rhodes Scholarship Trustees, Oxford, Eng., 1980. Mem. Houston Club. Republican. Office: Obstet & Gynecol Assocs PA 7550 Fannin St Houston TX 77054-1911

ALTMAN, WILLIAM KEAN, lawyer; b. San Antonio, Feb. 18, 1944; s. Marion K. and Ruth (Nunnelee) A.; m. Doris E. Johnson, May 29, 1964; children: Brian, Brad, Blake. BBA, Tex. A&M U., 1965, MBA, 1967; JD, U. Tex., 1979. Bar: Tex. 1970, Okla. 1993, U.S. Dist. Ct. (no. and ea. dists.) Tex., U.S. Ct. Appeals (5th and 11th cirs.), U.S. Supreme Ct. Pres. Altman & Nix, Wichita Falls, Tex., 1970—. Mem. ABA, Tex. Bar Assn., Assn. Trial Lawyers Am. (life) (bd. of govs. 1980-83, active coms. and sects.), Tex. Trial Lawyers Assn. (assoc. bd. dirs. 1977-78, bd. dirs. 1978—, active various coms. and sect.). Democrat. Baptist. Office: PO Box 500 Wichita Falls TX 76307-0500

ALTSHULER, LANNY STEPHEN, retail executive; b. Rockville Centre, N.Y., Jan. 7, 1948; s. Morris and Laura Estelle (Eisenberg) A.; m. Linda Susan Schillinger; children: Sean David, Sara Danielle. BS, U. R.I., 1970; MBA, U. Mich., 1972. Pres. Mr. Pottery of Fla., Inc., Miami, 1972—; pres. L & LRetail Group, Inc. Office: Mr Pottery 1983 Tigertail Blvd Dania FL 33004-2104

ALVARADO, ALFREDO, surgeon; b. Bogotá, Colombia, May 9, 1931; came to U.S., 1964; s. Ciro A. and Maria J. (Barrera) A.; m. Aura S. Burbano, July 3, 1964; children: Ciro, Lorena, Salesia, Natalia. Bachelor degree, Camilo Torres, Bogotá, 1950; MD, Nat. U. Bogotá, 1957. Diplomate Am. Bd. Surgery, Am. Bd. Emergency Medicine. Med. officer Colombian Navy, 1957-64; intern Charleston (W.Va.) Gen. Hosp., 1964; house physician Laird Meml. Hosp., Montgomery, W.Va., 1964; resident in gen. surgery Good Samaritan Hosp., Cin., 1965-66, Orange Meml. Hosp., Orlando, Fla., 1966-67, Nazareth Hosp., Phila., 1967-68; resident in thoracic surgery Temple U. Hosp., Phila., 1968-69, Episcopal Hosp., Phila., 1969-70; pvt. practice, surgeon Phila., 1970-84, Plantation, Fla., 1984—; attending physician Plantation (Fla.) Gen. Hosp., 1984—, Westside Regional Med. Ctr., Plantation, 1984—, Fla. Med. Ctr., Ft. Lauderdale, 1988—; clin. instr. surgery Temple U., Phila., 1973-80. Contbr. articles to profl. jours.; patentee in field. Recipient Safety Devices award Inventors Soc. South Fla., 1993. Fellow Internat. Coll. Surgeons; mem. Soc. Laparoendoscopic Surgeons. Roman Catholic. Office: Alfredo Alvarado MD 4101 NW 4th St Ste 407 Plantation FL 33317-2836

ALVAREZ, JOSE ARMANDO, accountant; b. Guanabacoa, Havana, Cuba, Mar. 3, 1949; s. Jose and Gladys Eugenia (Garcia) A.; m. Janet Lee Gleason, Mar. 21, 1970; children: Steven Michael, Kevin Joseph, Ryan Vincent. BA in Acctg., U. S. Fla., 1971. CPA, Fla. Internal auditor Maas Bros., Inc., Tampa, Fla., 1971-73, Dwight Drby& Co., Tampa, 1973-75; shareholder, pres. Alvarez & Co. and Predecessors, Tampa, 1975—; exec. v.p., CFO Annicott Worldwide Enterprises, Inc., Phoenix, 1995—, Great Wisdom Books, Inc., L.A., 1996—; asst. acctg. prof. Hillsborough Community Coll., Tampa/Brandon, 1975-81; founder Hillsborough County Mgmt. of An Acctg. Practice Roundtable, 1985—; cons. in field; lectr. in field. Contbr. articles to profl. jours. Soccer coach Brandon Area Youth Soccer League, 1978—, pres., 1983-84, 87-88, bd. dirs. 1980-89, pres. Assoc. Soccer Clubs West Fla., 1986-88; bd. dirs., v.p. Nativity Cath. Sch. Bd., 1985-88; coach Little League Baseball; active in past various charitable orgns.; sec., treas. St. Leo Coll. Parent's Coun., 1991-92. Mem. AICPA, Fla. Inst. CPAs, Inst. Bus. Appraisers, Tampa Bay Estate Planning Coun., Ybor City C. of C., Greater Tampa C. of C., Kiwanis Club of Ybor City (Chpt. pres.), Kiwanis (divsn. treas., chpt. pres.), Roughriders Club, KC. Republican. Roman Catholic.

ALVAREZ, JOSE FLORENCIO, food products executive, mechanical engineer; b. Camagüey, Cuba, June 25, 1948; came to U.S. 1962; s. Orlando L. and Angela (Portilla) A.; m. Patricia V. Suarez, Aug. 7, 1971; children: Andres, Carlos, Nicolas, Patrick. BSME, La. State U., 1972, MBA in Fin., 1980. Registered profl. engr., Fla. Applications engr. Ingersoll Rand, Phillipsberg, N.J., 1972-73; project engr. IPS Engrs., Baton Rouge, 1973-77; sr. mech. engr. Kaiser Aluminum and Chems., Gramercy, La., 1977-80; project mgr. Georgia-Pacific, Plaquemine, La., 1980-81; v.p., gen. mgr. Atlantic Sugar Assn., Belle Glade, Fla., 1981-89; v.p. planning and plant ops. Sugar Cane Grower Coop of Fla., 1989—; bd. dirs. Fla. Molasses Exch., Inc.; v.p., gen. mgr. Atlantic Sugar Assn., 1981-89. Recipient George Samuels award Inter-Am. Sugar Cane Seminar, 1987. Mem. Am. Soc. Sugar Cane Tech. (exec. com. 1982-87, pres. 1986), ASME, Fla. Sugar Cane League (environ. quality com. 1983-89). Republican. Roman Catholic. Office: Sugar Cane Growers Coop Fla Airport Rd PO Box 666 Belle Glade FL 33430-0666

ALVIS, JOEL LAWRENCE, JR., minister; b. Memphis, Nov. 12, 1955; s. Joel Lawrence Sr. and Martha Jean (Lowe) A.; m. Vicki Lynn Welch, Aug. 12, 1978; children: Joel Lawrence III, Mark Thomas. BA, Samford U., 1977; MA, U. Miss., 1980; PhD, Auburn U., 1985; MDiv, Louisville Presbyn. Theol. Sem, 1989. Ordained to ministry Presbyn. Ch. (U.S.A.), 1989. Local ch. history and records adminstr. Presbyn. Hist. Found., Montreat, N.C., 1982-86; rsch. assoc. Louisville Presbyn. Sem., 1986-89; pastor St. Pauls (N.C.) Presbyn. Ch., 1989—; mem. com. on ministry Coastal Carolina Presbytery, 1990-93. Author: (with others) Diversity of Discipleship, 1991, Religion and Race: Southern Presbyterians, 1946-1983, 1994. Mem. Com. on Disabled, St. Pauls, 1991, John Walker Meml. Fund, St. Pauls, 1990; treas. Robeson County Ch. and Cmty. Ctr., 1992-95. Recipient Nelson R. Burr prize Hist. Soc. of Episcopal Ch., 1981, Book award N.C. Presbyn. Hist. Soc., 1995; Univ. fellow U. Miss., 1977-78, Anderson fellow Louisville Presbyn. Theol. Sem., 1991. Office: St Pauls Presbyn Ch PO Box 283 Saint Pauls NC 28384-0283

ALWINE, LINDA MAE, pediatrics nurse; b. Lewistown, Pa., Nov. 8, 1955; d. Jack Mizell and Betty Jane (Hoffman) Musselman; m. Jeffrey Lynn Alwine, Apr. 27, 1974; children: Michael Jeffrey, Mark Allan. BSN, Austin Peay State U., 1987. RN, Tenn., S.C.; cert. BLS, PALS, Am. Heart Assn. Staff nurse med./surg. dept. Vanderbilt U., Nashville, 1987; staff nurse obstetrics dept. Clarksville (Tenn.) Meml. Hosp., 1987-88; staff nurse pediatric ICU Spartanburg (S.C.) Regional Hosp., 1988-89, staff nurse pediatrics emergency rm., 1989—; staff nurse neonatal ICU Mary Black Meml. Hosp., Spartanburg, 1989. Vol. nurse St. Luke's Free Clinic, Spartanburg; v.p. Children of Attention Deficit Disorder, Spartanburg, 1994. mem. ANA, Sigma Theta Tau, Phi Kappa Phi. Republican. Presbyterian. Home: 140 Willowood Dr Inman SC 29349-7530

AMADOR, JOSE MANUEL, plant pathologist, research center administrator; b. Calimete, Matanzas, Cuba, Mar. 3, 1938; came to U.S., 1957; s. Luis Felipe and Blanca Rosa (Muñiz) A.; m. Silvia G. Garcia, Nov. 25, 1965; children: Silvia G. Amador Bibb, Marian L., Daniel J. BS in Agronomy and Soil Chemistry, U. Havana, Cuba, 1960; MS in Botany, Plant Pathology and Breeding, La. State U., 1962, PhD in Plant Pathology and Biochemistry. Rsch. asst. in plant pathology La. State U., Baton Rouge, 1960-65; extension plant pathologist Tex. A&M U. Extension, Weslaco, 1965-91, dir. agrl. rsch. and extension ctr., 1991—; mem. extension futures task force Tex. A&M U. Extension, 1988, internat. task force agrl. complex, 1989; cons. Rio Grande Sugar Growers, Inc., Santa Rosa, Tex., Big-B Ranch, Belle Glade, Fla., US/AID/U. Fla.-El Salvador, Internat. Planning Svcs., Inc., US/AID Mission, Panama, Citrus Devel. Corp., Chiquita Brands Internat., XAFRA, Inc., Veracruz, Mex. Contbr. articles to profl. and sci. publs. Recipient Svc. to Agriculture award Hidalgo Farm Bur., 1993. Mem. Am. Phytopathological Soc. (long standing, adv. bd. office internat. programs 1989, rep. to Internat. Soc. Plant Pathology 1989, immediate past chmn. tropical plant pathology com. 1989, past chmn. internat. cooperation com. 1980-90, mem. coun., past mem. extension com., counselor Carribean divsn. 1980-89, Excellence in Extension award 1990), Tex. Vegetable Assn. (bd. dirs.), Tex. Assn. Plant Pathologists and Nematologists, Lower Rio Grande Valley Hort. Soc. (past treas.), Gamma Sigma Delta, Epsilon Sigma Phi. Roman Catholic. Home: 100 Cardinal Ave Mcallen TX 78504-2217 Office: Texas A & M Univ Agricultural Rsch & Extension Ctr 2415 E Us Highway 83 Weslaco TX 78596-8344

AMBER, LAURIE KAUFMAN, lawyer; b. N.Y.C., Apr. 15, 1954; d. Martin and Barbara (Schiffman) Kaufman; m. Henry Michael Amber, June 18, 1977; children: Ian, Kyle. BS, Cornell U., 1974, MBA, 1975; JD, U. Miami, 1978. Bar: Fla. 1978, U.S. Dist. Ct. (so. dist.) Fla. 1978, U.S. Tax Ct. 1978, U.S. Ct. Appeals (5th cir.) 1979, U.S. Ct. Customs and Patent Appeals 1979, U.S. Customs Ct. 1979, U.S. Ct. Appeals (11th cir.) 1981, U.S. Ct. Internat. Trade 1981, U.S. Supreme Ct. 1982, U.S. Claims Ct. 1985. Staff mgr. Proctor & Gamble Mfg. Co., Staten Island, N.Y., 1975; adj. asst. prof. Nova U., Fort Lauderdale, Fla., 1976-77; atty., labor arbitrator Amber & Amber, P.A., South Miami, Fla., 1978—; arbitrator nat. labor panel Am. Arbitration Assn., Miami, 1982—, Grievance Arbitration Panel of Fla. PERC, Tallahassee, 1979—; hearing examiner pers. appeals County of Dade, Miami, 1985-91. Pres. Office Village Condominium Assn., South Miami, 1994. Named Woman of Yr. ABWA, 1983. Mem. ABA, Zonta (bd. dirs. Coral Gables, Fla. club 1988). Office: 7731 SW 62nd Ave Ste 202 Miami FL 33143-4908

AMBLER, JOYCE ANNE, psychotherapist; b. Detroit, Mar. 20, 1936; d. Stuart William and Janet Francis (Howell) Hill; m. John Stewart Ambler, June 19, 1959; children: Lorraine, Deborah, Mark. BA, Willamete U., 1958; MSW, U. Calif., Berkeley, 1960. Cert. social worker; diplomate clin. social work. Social worker Adoptions Conta Costa County, Martinex, Calif., 1960-63; psychotherapist, social worker Hedgecroft Hosp., Houston, 1963-66; Catholic Charities Hedcraft Hosp., 1966-69, Trims, Houston, 1969-85; pvt. practice Houston, 1975—; psychotherapist West Oaks Hosp., Houston, 1985-88, acting dir. social work, 1988, coord., 1988—; cons. nursing homes, Houston, 1971-75. Bd. dirs. Step-family Assn. Am., Washington, 1983-86. Recipient Rsch. award Kepner Found., 1983. Fellow Am. Orthopsychiatric Assn.; mem. NASW, Am. Group Psychotherapy, ACLU, A.K. Rice Group Rels. Unitarian. Home: 2242 Dryden Rd Houston TX 77030-1102 Office: Greenbriar Psychiat Assoc 2211 Norfolk St Ste 140 Houston TX 77098-4044

AMBROSE, CHARLES STUART, sales executive; b. Jacksonville, NC, Nov. 28, 1951; s. Samuel Sheridan and Elizabeth (Stansbury) A. BBA, Emory U., 1974. Asst. mgr. Fifth Quarter Restaurant Shoney's, Birmingham, Ala., 1975; asst. chemist Mackay Paint Co., Birmingham, 1975-76; salesman, sales mgr. Francis & Lusky Co., Nashville, 1976-85; pres. SST Sales Co., Inc., Nashville, 1982—. Republican. Presbyterian. Home: 5018 Franklin Rd Nashville TN 37220-1520 Office: SST Sales Co Inc PO Box 41188 Nashville TN 37204-1188

AMBROSE, SAMUEL SHERIDAN, JR., urologist; b. Jacksonville, N.C., Oct. 2, 1923; s. Samuel Sheridan and Beatrice (Collins) A.; m. Betty Stuart Stansbury, Oct. 7, 1950; children: Charles Stuart, Ann Collins, Samuel Bruce. A.B. in Chemistry, Duke U., 1943, M.D., 1947. Diplomate: Am. Bd. Urology, Nat. Bd. Med. Examiners. Intern in surgery, then asst. resident in urology Duke U. Hosp., 1947-50, resident in urology, 1953; instr. physiology Duke U. Med. Sch., 1947, instr. urology, 1953; mem. faculty Emory U. Med. Sch., 1954—, prof. urology, 1972-92, prof. urology surgery emeritus, 1992—, chmn. div. urology, 1985-89; mem. staff Emory U. Hosp., 1972-92, chief urology, 1972-91; pvt. practice medicine specializing in urology Atlanta, 1954-71; mem. staff Piedmont Hosp., 1954-72, chief urology, 1960; mem. staff Grady Meml. Hosp., 1954-92, Henrietta Egleston Hosp. for Children, 1956-92; retired, 1992. Contbr. numerous articles to med. jours. Served as officer M.C. USNR, 1950-52. Fellow Royal Soc. Medicine; mem. AMA, ACS, Am. Urol. Assn. (hon. mem. S.E. chpt., pres. Southeastern sect. 1974-75, chmn. nat. sci. exhibits com. 1974-83, mem. exec. com. 1983-90, Disting. Svc. award 1990, Gold Cane award 1995, hon. mem. 1996—), Soc. Pediatric Urology (pres. 1971-72), Am. Assn. Clin. Urologists, Am. Acad. Pediat., Am. Assn. Genito-Urinary Surgeons, Soc. Internat. D'Urologie, Pan-Pacific Surg. Assn., Med. Assn. Ga., Ga. Urol. Assn. (pres. 1967), So. Med. Soc. (chmn. urology sect. 1970-71), Fulton County Med. Soc., Atlanta Clin. Soc. (v.p. 1964), Soc. Univ. Urologists, Piedmont Driving Club, Cherokee Town and Country Club (pres. 1968-69), Univ. Yacht Club (commodore 1973), Homosassa Fishing Club (v.p. 1980-81, 92-94). Presbyterian. Home: 1014 Nawench Dr NW Atlanta GA 30327-1340

AMBRUSKO, JOHN STEPHEN, retired surgeon, county official; b. North Tonawanda, N.Y., May 3, 1913; s. Joseph and Magdalena (Isky) A.; m. Phyllis Eusterman, Sept. 21, 1946; children: Therese Ambrusko Carlson, Gretchen Ambrusko Schaeffer, Mary Ambrusko Bennett, Sara Ambrusko Tokars (dec.), Joni Ambrusko Crane, Karen Ambrusko Wilcox, Krissy. MD, SUNY, Buffalo, 1937. Diplomate Am. Bd. Surgery, FACS. Intern Buffalo Gen. Hosp., 1937-38; asst. resident surgeon Buffalo Gen. Hosp., Buffalo Children's Hosp., 1938-39, resident pathology, 1939-40; fellow in gen. surgery Mayo Found., Rochester, Minn., 1940-42, 46-47; asst. surgeon Mayo Clinic, Rochester, 1947-48; instr. surgery SUNY, Buffalo, 1948-56; chief surgery, chmn. dept. surgery Kenmore (N.Y.) Mercy Hosp., 1950-70, chief cons. surgeon, 1970-90; med. exec. dir. Manatee County Pub. Health Dept., Bradenton, Fla., 1977-90; ret., 1990; clin. asst. prof. U. South Fla. Med. Sch., Tampa, 1979-89; surg. cons. quality assurance program Manatee Meml. Hosp., Bradenton, 1991; assoc. med. examiner State of Fla., 1977-95. Mem. Erie County (N.Y.) Alcoholic Beverage Control Commn., 1965-75; trustee Rosary Hill Coll., Buffalo, 1965-75; bd. visitors Roswell Park Cancer Rsch. Hosp., Buffalo, 1965-75. Lt. comdr. USN, 1942-46, PTO. Doctor John Ambrusko Pub. Health Ctr. named in his honor Mannatee County Bd. of County Commrs., 1988; recipient Outstanding Achievement award Western N.Y. Jr. C. of C., 1949, Sci. Achievement award N.Y. State Med. Soc., 1952, Cancer Rsch. award Roswell Park Cancer Rsch. Hosp., 1974, Outstanding Achievement award Nat. Assn. Counties, 1989. Fellow ACS, Plaza Club (bd. dirs. 1985-89), Buffalo Club. Republican. Roman Catholic. Home: 3804 Bayside Dr Bradenton FL 34210-4109 Office: Dr John Ambrusko Pub Health Ctr 410 6th Ave E Bradenton FL 34208-1928

AMEDEO, RALPH MICHAEL, physician; b. Waco, Tex., June 7, 1953; s. Ralph Frank and Hope Emmaline (James) A.; m. Donna Mary Valis, June 22, 1980; children: Elizabeth Hana, Sean Michael Sae-Yoon. BS, Duke U., 1975; MD, Georgetown U., 1979. Diplomate Am. Bd. Internal Medicine. Intern Georgetown U. Hosp., Washington, 1979-80, resident, 1980-82; physician internal medicine pvt. practice, Arlington, Va., 1984—; chmn. bd. Va. Integrated Physicians, 1995—. With USPHS, 1982-84. Mem. AMA, ACP, Am. Soc. Internal Medicine. Republican. Roman Catholic. Office: 1715 N George Mason Dr Ste 306 Arlington VA 22205-3609

AMEND, EUGENE MICHAEL, art advisor, appraiser; b. Jefferson City, Mo., Oct. 31, 1950; s. Paris James and Mary Catherine (Grant) A.; m. Brenda Kay Pemberton, July 2, 1977; children: Michael, Matthew, Bryan. BA, U. Mo., 1975, MA, 1977. Art cons. S.W. Art Ctr., Dallas, 1977-78; curator, art historian Stewart Gallery, Dallas, 1978-80; instr. Richland Coll., Dallas, 1980-93; pres. E.M. Amend & Assoc., Dallas, 1980—, Omni Art, Inc., Dallas, 1983—; curator Norman Lloyd Estate, Dallas, 1983—. Leader troop 21 Boy Scouts Am., Carrolton, Tex., 1993—. Mem. Am. Soc. Appraisers (candidate 1993—), Artist Coalition of Tex., Tex. Assn. Art Dealers, Internat. Soc. Appraisers (assoc. 1989-91). Home: 3130 Chatsworth Farmers Branch TX 75234 Office: EM Amend & Assoc 13616 Gamma Rd #101 Dallas TX 75244

AMES, ALFRED CAMPBELL, journalist, educator; b. Spokane, Wash., July 21, 1916; s. William Porter and Anna (Campbell) A.; m. Eleanor Alice Holliday, Feb. 4, 1951. A.B., U. Kans., 1936; A.M., U. Ill., 1937, Ph.D., 1943. Asst. English U. Ill., 1937-43, instr., 1943-44; instr. English Ill. Inst. Tech., 1944-46, asst. prof., 1946-51; asso. editor book sect. Chgo. Tribune, 1951-56, editorial writer, 1956-81; lectr. bus. English Northwestern U., 1945-64, lectr. journalism, 1964-81; adj. prof. English Brevard (N.C.) Coll., 1981-83. Mem. Modern Lang. Assn., Phi Beta Kappa. Quaker. Home: Sherwood Forest 9 Warbler Way Brevard NC 28712-9783

AMICK, WILLIAM WALKER, golf course architect; b. Scipio, Ind., June 16, 1932; s. George Ellsworth Sr. and Myrtle (Walker) A.; m. Sara Dell Rogers, Apr. 6, 1957; 1 child, David Walker. BA, Ohio Wesleyan U., 1954. Registered landscape architect, Fla. Golf course architectural asst. William H. Diddle, GCA, Carmel, Ind., 1954-55, Charles Adams, GCA, Atlanta, 1957-58; golf course architect Daytona Beach, Fla., 1959—. Capt. USAF, 1955-57. Mem. Am. Soc. of Golf Course Architects (treas., v.p., pres. 1975-77). Office: PO Box 1984 Daytona Beach FL 32115-1984

AMIOT, DAVID BRUCE, information officer; b. Hartford, Conn., Sept. 28, 1947; m. Carolyn Engel; 1 child, David Engel Amiot. JD, George Washington U., 1969, MS in Adminstrn., 1972; BS, Stetson U., 1981. CPA, Washington. Cons. Touche Ross & Co., Washington, 1974-77, dir. office ops., 1977-89; dir. office ops. Deloitte & Touche, Washington, 1989-94; dir. info. sys. div. Deloite & Touche, Hermitage, Tenn., 1994—, dep. chief info. officer, 1995—. Capt. U.S. Army, 1969-74, Korea. Mem. Met. Club, Chevy Chase Club, Rotary Club of Washington. Office: Deloitte & Touche 4022 Sells Dr Hermitage TN 37076-2903

AMITRANO, SHIRLEY ANN, research associate; b. Colorado Springs, Colo., Oct. 1, 1963; d. Francis A. and shirley (Castaldo) Filardi; m. Robert Amitrano, June 15, 1986; 1 child, Nicholas Robert. BA in Psychology, SUNY, Fredonia, 1985; MPA, U. Memphis, 1994. Paralegal Va. Dept. Transp., Richmond, 1986-89; regional employment specialist Nutri-Sys., Birmingham, Ala., 1989-91; employment counselor Stonewall Ins., Birmingham, Ala., 1990-91, Blue Cross/Blue Shield Ala., Birmingham, 1991-92; rsch. assoc. U. Memphis, 1993—; quality reviewer Tenn. quality award, Memphis, 1995-96. Fundraiser U. Memphis, 1992-96, Meth. Hosp., Memphis, 1995-96. Mem. Am. Mgmt. Assn., Assn. Hosp. Mgmt., Assn. Pub. Adminstrn. Home: 1606 Wood Farm Cordova TN 38018

AMMANN, LILLIAN ANN NICHOLSON, interior landscape executive; b. Pearsall, Tex., June 20, 1946; d. Harvey Franklin and Annie Laura (Matthews) Nicholson; m. Jack Jordan Ammann Jr., May 31, 1967; 1 child, William Erik. BA magna cum laude, Southwestern U., 1968. Mgr. inventory Kelly AFB, San Antonio, 1967-70; employment counselor Tex. Employment Commn., San Antonio, 1970-75; owner, operator Lillie's Lovely Little Gardens, San Antonio, 1975-77; owner, operator Lillie's Interior Landscapes, San Antonio, 1980-82, pres., 1983—; sec. Jack Ammann Inc., 1983-87; pres. Lillie's & Sherry's Plants & Pottery, San Antonio, 1977-80. Author: Lillie's Lovely Little Gardening Book, 1976. Mem. Women in Bus. (past pres.), San Antonio Interior Landscape Assn. (founder, 1st pres.), cert. interior landscape profl., North San Antonio C. of C, San Antonio Bldg. Owners & Mgrs. Assn. Episcopalian. Home: 603 Mauze Dr San Antonio TX 78216-3711 Office: Lillie's Interior Landscapes 17585 Blanco Rd Ste 16-1 San Antonio TX 78232-1037

AMONETT, RANDALL THAYNE, dentist; b. Vernon, Tex., Apr. 22, 1954; s. Derward Thayne and Dorothy Maxine (Johnson) A.; m. Donna Marie Maurer, June 24, 1989; 1 child, James Ashley. BA with honors, Tex. Tech. U., 1976, MEd in Higher Edn., 1994; DDS, U. Tex. Health Sci. Ctr., San Antonio, 1981. Registered microbiologist; cert. tchr., Tex. Ambulance driver, emergency care attendant Collingsworth County Ambulance Svc., Wellington, Tex., 1972-74; sci. tchr., athletic coach Hutchinson Jr. H.S., Lubbock, Tex., 1977; substitute tchr. Lubbock Pub. Schs., 1976-78; Lab. tech. asst. dept. physiology U. Tex. Health Sci. Ctr., San Antonio, Tex., 1978-81; dentist pvt. practice, Lubbock, Tex., 1981-83, Mineral Wells, Tex., 1983-84; clin. asst. prof. dept. surgery Tex. Tech. U. Health Scis. Ctr. Sch. Medicine, Lubbock, 1986—; clin. staff dentist, gen. practice dept. Vets. Affairs Med. Ctr., Big Spring, Tex.; adj. asst. prof. dept. microbiology and immunology Tex. Tech. U. Health Scis. Ctr. Sch. Medicine, 1989—; adj. faculty dept. dental hygiene Howard Coll., Big Spring, Tex., 1984—; presenter and spkr. in field. Contbr. articles to dental jours. Acad. recruiter Tex. Tech. U., 1992—; host family Rotary Group Study Exch. and Youth Exch. Programs, 1991—, Rotary Com. for Internat. Svc., 1994—; host family Cmty. Friends of Internat. Students, Tex. Tech. U., 1981-83; bd. dirs. Am. Heart Assn., Big Spring, 1986-88, Am. Cancer Soc., Lubbock, 1982-84; mem. Dental Recruitment Ptnr. SELECT Program, 1991—. Tex. Legis. Merit scholar, 1981. Mem. ADA, Am. Assn. Dental Schs., Am. Profl. Practice Assn. (life), Am. Soc. Forensic Odontology, Permian Basin Dist. Dental Soc., Tex. Dental Assn., Nat. Assn. VA Physicians and Dentists, Nat. Registry Microbiologists, Ex-Students Assn. Tex. Tech. U., Am. Radio Relay League (amateur radio emergency svc. team mem. 1996—), Rotary, Tex. Tech. Lettermen's Assn., Student Alumni Assn. U. Tex. Dental Sch. (life), Big Spring Amateur Radio Club, Xi Psi Phi, Phi Kappa Phi, Phi Eta Sigma. Home: 403 Hillside Dr Big Spring TX 79720-5338

AMORNMARN, RUMPA, physician; b. Rangoon, Burma, Oct. 2, 1946; came to U.S., 1972; s. Che Peng and Me Cho (Che) Moy; m. Surachai Sutha, July 19, 1980; one child, Ken. MD, Chulalongkorn U., Bangkok, 1967, Mahidol U., Bangkok, 1971. Diplomate Am. Bd. Radiology. Rotating internship Siriraj Hosp., Bangkok, 1971-72; internship VA Hosp., Washington, 1972-73; resident, fellow therapeutic radiology Johns Hopkins Cancer Ctr., Balt., 1973-77; staff mem. VA Med. Ctr., East Orange, N.J., 1977-81; asst. prof. radiation N.J. Med. Sch., Newark, 1978-81; asst. prof. dept. radiation oncology U. Md. Hosp., Balt., 1981-83; physician Univ. Hosp. of Jacksonville, Fla., 1983—; assoc. prof. radiology U. Fla., Jacksonville, 1983—; cons. Balt. City Hosp., 1976-77. Author numerous presentations; contbr. over 25 articles to profl. jours. Mem. Am. Soc. Therapeutic Radiologists, Am. Coll. Radiology, Duval County Med. Soc. Office: Radiation Oncology Ctr 655 W 8th St Jacksonville FL 32209-6511

AMORY, DAVID WILLIAM, anesthesiologist, educator; b. Newark, Jan. 27, 1928; s. David Buchanan and Rose Regina (Schaeffer) A.; m. Margaret Anne Malo Lynch, Aug. 26, 1960; children: David William Jr., John Kenneth. BS in Biology, St. Johns U., 1952, MS in Physiology, 1955; PhD in Pharmacology, U. Wash., 1961; MD, U. B.C., Vancouver, Can., 1967. Diplomate Nat. Bd. Med. Examiners, Am. Bd. Anesthesiology. Pharmacologist CIBA Pharm. Co., Inc., Summit, N.J., 1955-57; intern Virginia Mason Hosp., Seattle, 1967-68; USPHS postdoctoral scholar U. Calif., San Francisco, 1968-69; resident in anesthesiology U. Wash. Sch. Medicine, Seattle, 1969-71; from asst. prof. to prof. U. Wash., Seattle, 1971-88; prof. biomed. engring. Rutgers U., Piscataway, N.J., 1995—; prof. Robert Wood Johnson Med. Sch., New Brunswick, N.J., 1988-95; rsch. prof. Duke U. Med. Ctr., Durham, N.C., 1995—; chief divsn. cardiac anesthesia R.W. Johnson Univ. Hosp., N.J., 1988-95, dir. rsch. dept. anesthesia, 1988-95; cons. in field. Co-author: (with others) Noninvasive Cardiovascular Dynamics, 1995; contbr. articles to profl. jours. With U.S. Army, 1946-48, Japan. Rsch. grantee Nat. Heart Lung Inst., 1972-75, 79-82, Nat. Heart, Lung and Blood Inst., 1983-86, Cardiovascular Inst., 1988-91, 93-94, Am. Paralysis Assn., 1990-93, Am. Heart Assn., 1992-94, Abbott Labs., 1992-93; recipient Mt. Sinai prize in anesthesiology CUNY, 1971. Fellow Am. Coll. Anesthesiologists; mem. AAUP, Am. Soc. Anesthesiologists (rsch. com. 1982-85, subcom. on exptl. circulation 1994-95), Assn. Univ. Anesthesiologists, Soc. Cardiovascular Anesthesiologists (edn. and rsch. com. 1981), Internat. Anesthesia Rsch. Soc., World Assn. Cardiac, Thoracic and Vascular Anesthesia, Internat. Soc. on Oxygen Transport to Tissue, Sigma Xi. Home: 4613 D Hope Valley Rd Durham NC 27707 Office: Duke Univ Med Ctr Dept Anesthesiology Box 3094 Durham NC 27707

AMOS, BETTY GILES, restaurant company executive, accountant; b. Lebanon, Mo., July 18, 1941; d. Clarence Edgar and Clara Mae (Gann) Giles; m. E.L. Amos, Sept. 18, 1959 (div. Oct. 1965); 1 child, Jeffrey Lee; m. Thomas R. Righetti, Jan. 2, 1983. BBA magna cum laude, U. Miami, Coral Gables, Fla., 1973, MBA, 1976; D of Bus. Adminstrn. honoris causa, Johnson & Wales U., 1990. CPA, Fla. Sec. City of Lebanon, 1959-63; dept. head Empire Gas Co., Lebanon, 1963-68; fin. analyst asst. Biscayne Assocs., Ltd., Miami, Fla., 1968-73; investment mgr. Universal Restaurants Inc., Miami, 1973-77; pvt. practice accountant, investment mgr. Miami, 1977-83; pres. The Abkey Cos., Miami, 1983—; founder, Mega Bank, Miami, 1983-94; adv. com. Fuddruckers, Inc., Boston. Trustee Miami Project, 1986-89, United Fund of Dade County, 1992—; pres. Humane Soc. Greater Miami, 1994—, bd. dirs., 1993—; mem. pres. coun. U. Miami, 1994—, mem. founder's soc., 1994—. Recipient Philip J. Romano Founders award, 1988. Mem. AICPA, Fla. Inst. CPAs, Am. Women's Soc. CPAs, Coconut Grove C. of C. (trustee 1988—), Nat. Assn. Women Bus. Owners. Republican. Roman Catholic. Home: 13724 SW 92nd Ct Miami FL 33176-6858 Office: The Abkey Cos 3444 48 Main Hwy 3d Floor PO Box 330927 Coconut Grove FL 33233-0927

AMOS, DANIEL PAUL, insurance executive; b. Pensacola, Fla., Aug. 13, 1951; s. Paul Shelby and Mary Jean (Roberts) A.; m. Mary Shannon Landing, Sept. 12, 1972; children—Paul Shelby, Lauren Alyse. B.S. in Risk and Ins. Mgmt., U. Ga., 1973. Co-state mgr. Am. Family Life Assurance Co., Columbus, Ga., 1973-78, state mgr., 1978-83, pres., 1983—; now also dep. chief exec. officer Am. Family Corp., Columbus, Ga., vice chmn., pres., CEO; dir. Columbus Bank & Trust Co. Methodist. Office: Am Family Life Assurance 1932 Wynnton Rd Columbus GA 31999-0001

AMOSCATO, GUY THOMAS, retired air force officer, information analyst; b. N.Y.C., June 5, 1936; s. Gasper and Rose (Botti) A.; m. Sharon Joan Jostedt, Nov. 30, 1968; children: Carl John, Laura Elizabeth. BS, Syracuse U., 1961, MBA, 1969; M of Libr. Info. Sci., U. Tex., 1989. Commd. 2nd lt. USAF, 1962; advanced through grades to lt. col. N000, 1978; logistics officer various sites and locations including Viet Nam., 1961-80; ops. mgr. Rockford Bus. Interiors, Austin, 1981-84; ref. libr. Corpus Christi (Tex.) State U., 1990-92; info. analyst Tex. Rsch. Instn., Austin, 1992—; indexer, abstractor Oral History Project, LBJ Libr., Austin, 1984-90. Sec.-treas. CE-Bar Vol. Fire Dept., Austin, 1986-88. Decorated Bronze Star, 1970, Air Force Commendation medal, 1971, Meritorious Svc. medal, 1975, 78. Mem. Spl. Librs. Assn., Austin Civil War Round Table, Am. Soc. for Nondestructive Testing. Democrat. Roman Catholic. Home: 9608 Southward Cv Austin TX 78733-3220 Office: Tex Rsch Instn Austin Inc 415 Crystal Creek Dr Austin TX 78746-4725

AMOSS, W. JAMES, JR., shipping company executive; b. 1924; married. BBA, Tulane U., 1947. With Lykes Bros. Steamship Co. Inc., New Orleans, 1947-93, v.p. traffic, 1963-70, exec. v.p., 1970-73, pres., 1973-86, chief exec. officer, dir., 1981—, chmn., 1986-93; chmn. Interocean Steamship Corp, Tampa, Fla.; pres. Marine Logistics, Inc., New Orleans, 1993—; dir. Hibernia Nat. Bank. With USN, 1942-46, 50-52. Office: Marine Logistics Inc 2 Canal St New Orleans LA 70130-1408

AMSTUTZ, DANIEL GORDON, international trade association administrator, former grain dealer, government and intergovernment official; b. Cleve., Nov. 8, 1932; s. Gordon M. and Elizabeth (Kiss) A. B.S., Ohio State U., 1954. Trainee Cargill, Inc., Mpls., 1954-55; grain mcht. Tradax Can., Ltd., Montreal, Que., Can., 1955-56, Tradax Geneva, S.A., Geneva, 1956-57; mgr. Deutsche Tradax Gmbh, Hamburg, Germany, 1957-58; grain mcht. Cargill, Inc., Fort Worth, 1959, sr. grain merchant, Mpls., 1960-72; pres. Cargill Investor Services, Inc., Chgo., 1973-78; ptnr. Goldman, Sachs & Co., N.Y.C., 1978-82; undersec. for internat. affairs and commodity programs Dept. Agr., Washington, 1983-87; pres. Commodity Credit Corp., Washington, 1983-87; ambassador, chief trade negotiator for agr. USDA, Washington, 1987-89; exec. dir. Internat. Wheat Coun., London, 1992-95; pres./CEO North Am. Export Grain Assn., Inc., Washington, 1995—; mem. com. agri-bus. U.S.-Russian Joint Commn. on Econ. and Tech. Coop., 1996—. Mem. U.S. Feed Grains Council (dir. 1967-72), Nat. Grain and Feed Assn. (dir. 1973-82), Ohio State U. Alumni Assn. (v.p. 1989, co-chair fund-raising campaign 1990—). Republican.

AMTOFT-NIELSEN, JOAN THERESA, physician, educator, researcher; b. Reading, Pa., Jan. 31, 1940; children: Andre Christian, Nikolaj Johan, Anja. BS, Kutztown (Pa.) State U., 1960; MD, Ansalt U. Munchen, Fed. Republic Germany, 1965; DC, Nat. Coll., 1968; MD, U. Copenhagen, 1978; postgrad., Harvard U., 1989-90, 91. Regional dir. Pa. Acad. Sci., Reading, 1961; intern Cook County Hosp., Chgo., 1966-68; clin. instr. U. Copenhagen, 1975-80; proctor N.C. Coalition Health, Durham, 1985-87; founder, cons. Triangle PMS Ctr., Cary, N.C., 1987—, also bd. dirs. Contbr. articles to profl. jours. Bd. dirs. shelter St. Francis Ho., Chapel Hill, N.C., 1989—; bd. dirs., grant coordinator N.C. Coalition Chs., Raleigh; v.p. Danish Red Cross, 1975-80; cons. physician Handicapped Encounter in Christ, Raleigh, 1984-87. NSF grantee, 1961; recipient award Sardoni Found., 1964, Walter Morris Found., 1957, Community Svc. award K.C., 1989. Mem. Am. Acad. Holistic Physicians, European Acad. Preventative Medicine, AAUW (v.p. Raleigh chpt. 1987—), NAFE, Scandinavian Club. Republican. Roman Catholic. Home: 218 Rosebrooks Dr Cary NC 27513-3609

AMY, JAMES BORDEN, mechanical engineer; b. Lafayette, Ind., Sept. 16, 1951; s. Jonathan Weekes and Ruthanna (Borden) A.; m. Janet Sue St. John, Aug. 17, 1974; children: David Jeffrey, Kristen Elizabeth. BSME, Purdue U., 1974, MSME, 1976. Registered profl. engr., Ill. Co-op. engr. Pontiac motor divsn. GM, Pontiac, Mich., 1971-73; rsch. engr. Caterpillar, Inc., Peoria, Ill., 1975-83, sr. test engr., 1983-91; project engr. Caterpillar, Inc., Clayton, N.C., 1991-93, sr. project engr., 1994—, chmn. fin. com., 1997. Chmn. adminstrv. bd. St. Francis United Meth. Ch., Cary, N.C., 1995-96; vice-chair-trustee 1st United Meth. Ch., Peoria, 1990. Mem. ASME, Soc. Automotive Engrs. (assoc., sec. 1994-95, Outstanding Session Organizer earth moving industry conf. 1982). Home: 110 Clubstone Ln Cary NC 27511 Office: Caterpillar Inc 2500 NC 42 E Clayton NC 27520

ANANDAN, JEEVA SATCHITH, physics educator; b. Sri Lanka, June 10, 1948; came to U.S., 1972; BSc, U. Ceylon, Colombo, 1970; MS, U. Pitts., 1973, PhD, 1978. Asst. lectr. U. Ceylon, Colombo, 1970-72; postdoctoral fellow U. Md., 1978-80, U. Calif., Berkeley, 1980-82, Max Planck-Inst. for Physics and Astrophysics, Munich, Germany, 1982-85; assoc. prof. U. S.C., Columbia, 1986-90, prof., 1990—; pres. Math. Soc., U. Ceylon, 1969; vis. scholar Inst. for Advanced Study, Princeton, 1978, Lawrence Berkeley Lab., 1978, U. Tex., Austin, 1980, Oersted Inst., Copenhagen, 1981, Harvard U., 1984, Inst. Henri Poincare, Paris, 1985, Rijksuniversiteit Utrecht, The Netherlands, 1986, NYU, 1987-88, U. Calif., Berkeley, 1987, 88, Max Planck-Inst. for Physics and Astrophysics, Munich, 1989-90, Cambridge (Eng.) U., 1989, Wolfson Coll., Oxford (Eng.) U., 1990. Recipient 1st prize Gravity Rsch. Found., 1983, Russell Rsch. award, 1992; A.W. Mellon fellow, 1973-76, Centre Nat. de la Recherche Scientifique fellow, France, 1985, Alexander von Humboldt Rsch. fellow, 1989. Fellow Am. Phys. Soc. Home: 7500 Yorkhouse Rd Columbia SC 29223-1827 Office: Dept Physics & Astronomy Univ SC Columbia SC 29208

ANANTHANARAYANAN, VENKATARAMAN, physics educator; b. Madras, India, Oct. 22, 1936; came to U.S., 1963; s. S. Venkataraman and V. Valambal; m. A. Jayalakshmi, Aug. 27, 1967; 1 child, Radha. MA, Annamalai U., Madras, 1957, MSc, 1958; PhD, Indian Inst. Sci., Bangalore, 1961. Jr. and sr. fellow Indian Inst. Sci., 1958-62; rsch. fellow Mellon Inst., Pitts., 1963, Tex. A&M U., College Station, 1964; prof. physics Savannah (Ga.) State Coll., 1965—; faculty rsch. participant Oak Ridge (Tenn.) Nat. Lab., 1970—, summer fellow, 1987, 89, 90, 91, 92, 93, 94, 96; faculty rsch. participant Bruceton Rsch. Lab., Pitts., 1985—, summer fellow, 1985, 86, 88. Discovered new formula for focal length of lenses and curved mirrors; contbr. articles to internat. sci. jours. Mem. AAUP, Am. Assn. Physics Tchrs., Soc. Applied Spectroscopy. Home: 12350 Mercy Blvd Savannah GA 31419-3401 Office: Savannah State Coll PO Box 20473 Savannah GA 31404-9716

ANASTASI, RICHARD JOSEPH, computer software consultant; b. N.Y.C., Aug. 30, 1951; s. Alfred J. and Mary T. (Lo Cicero) A. Student, Boston Coll., 1973, U. Pa., 1975. Staff cons. Arthur Andersen & Co., N.Y.C., 1975-76; customer svc. rep. Compu Serve, West Caldwell, N.J., 1976-77, Turnkey Systems Internat., Norwalk, Conn., 1977-79; tech. svcs. rep. Applied Data Rsch., Paramus, N.J., 1980-84, regional tech. mgr., 1985-86; mgr. tactical svcs. Applied Data Rsch., Princeton, N.J., 1986-88; tech. dir. Computer Assocs. Internat., Irving, Tex., 1988-91, product cons., 1991-93; mgr. tech. resources Integris, Phoenix, 1993; pres., CEO InfoVantage, Dallas, 1993-94; sr. product specialist Open Vision Techs., Inc., Dallas, Tex., 1994—, sr. systems engr. Roman Catholic. Home: 302 Old York Rd Irving TX 75063-4246 Office: 222 W Colinas Rd Irving TX 75039

ANASTASIOU, VAN E., lawyer; b. Ft. Lauderdale, Fla., Oct. 2, 1953; s. Vasilios and Aphrodite (Zophres) A.; m. Stephanie Ayvas, July 21, 1979; 1 child, William John. BA in Polit. Sci. magna cum laude, U. Miami, 1975, JD cum laude, 1978. Bar: Bar: Fla. 1978. Assoc. Carey, Dwyer, Cole, Selwood & Bernard, PA, Ft. Lauderdale, 1978-83; pvt. practice, Ft. Lauderdale, 1983—; litigation atty. City of Deerfield Beach, Fla., 1985—. Mem. Acad. Fla. Trial Lawyers, Broward County Trial Lawyers Assn., Am. Hellenic Ednl. Progressive Assn. (treas. 1984-87). Republican. Greek Orthodox. Home: 301 Tropic Dr Fort Lauderdale FL 33308-5429 Office: 305 SE 18th Ct Fort Lauderdale FL 33316-2829

ANDELSON, ROBERT VERNON, social philosopher, educator; b. Los Angeles, Feb. 19, 1931; s. Abraham and Ada (Markson) A.; m. Bonny Orange Johnson, June 7, 1964. A.A., Los Angeles City Coll., 1950; A.B. equivalent, U. Chgo., 1952; A.M., U. So. Calif., 1954, Ph.D., 1960. Exec. dir. Henry George Sch. Social Sci., San Diego Extension, Calif., 1959-62; instr. philosophy and religion Northland Coll., Wis., 1962-63; asst. prof. govt. and philosophy Northwestern State U., La., 1963-65; mem. faculty Auburn (Ala.) U., 1965—; prof. philosophy Auburn U., 1973-92, prof. emeritus, 1992—, mem. grad. faculty, 1969-92; mem., dir. Robert Schalkenbach Found., 1986—; v.p. Internat. Union Land Value Taxation and Free Trade, 1986-88; inaugural lectr. philosophy lecture series U. Ala. at Birmingham, 1975; mem. acad. staff Ludwig von Mises Inst., 1983—; ordained to ministry Congregational Ch., 1959; reviewer instl. grant applications NEH, 1987; fac. assoc. Lincoln Inst. Land Policy, 1993—. Author: Imputed Rights: An Essay in Christian Social Theory, 1971; editor, co-author: Critics of Henry George, 1979, Commons Without Tragedy, 1991; joint author (with J.M. Dawsey) From Wasteland to Promised Land: Liberation Theology for a Post-Marxist World, 1992; mem. editl. bd. Am. Jour. Econs. and Sociology, 1969—. The Personalist, 1975-80; contbr. articles to scholarly jours. Asst. sgt. at arms Republican Nat. Conv., 1952; mem. Lee County Rep. Exec. Com., 1967-79; trustee Henry George Found. Am., 1971-75, mem. adv. commn., 1975—. Recipient Rsch. awards Found. Social Rsch., 1959, Relm Found., 1967, 2 George Washington Honor medals Freedom Found., 1970, 72; Disting. rsch. fellow Am. Inst. for Econ. Rsch., 1993—. Mem. AAUP (pres. Auburn chpt. 1975-76), So. Soc. Philosophy and Psychology, Ala. Philos. Soc. (pres. 1968-69, 78-79). Home: 534 Cary Dr Auburn AL 36830-2502 Office: Auburn U Dept Philosophy Auburn AL 36849

ANDEREGG, M. L., education educator; b. Wilmington, N.C., Mar. 24, 1943; d. George Keilly Duncan and Tenae Lee Gossage; m. David L. Anderegg; 1 child, Joshua D. BS, Ga. State U., 1980, MS, 1986, PhD, 1989. Supr., audit trainer Rome (Ga.) Bank & Trust Co., 1963-67; trainer Citizens Fed. S&L, Rome, 1967-76; tchr., chair Hiram (Ga.) Elem. Sch., 1976-78; researcher Ga. State U., Atlanta, 1984-88; instr. Kennesaw State Coll., Marietta, Ga., 1988-90, asst. prof. curriculum, 1990-91, exec. dir. Cobb edn. consortium, asst. prof., 1992—; cons. metro pvt. edn., Atlanta, 1986—; mem. Leadership Kennesaw, Kennesaw State Coll., Atlanta, 1993—. Co-author: (book) Curriculum Guide, 1982; field editor: Teacher Education and Special Education, Gainesville, Fla., 1991-94, Exceptional Children, Pitts., 1992-95, Jour. Teacher Edn., Washington, 1994-95; contbr. articles to profl. jours. Mem. Give Our Schs. A Hand com., Cobb County, Ga., 1990—, spl. edn. adv. panel, Cobb County, 1992-93; del. 47th Del. Assembly of Children, San Antonio, 1993; mem. grant rev. bd., 1993. Recipient Ga. Econ. Developers award, 1994. Mem. NEA, Coun. for Exceptional Children (chair 1993-94), Ga. Assn. of Educators, Phi Delta Kappa, Kappa Delta Pi. Republican. Home: 9251 N White Pines Dr Dallas GA 30132-7453 Office: Kennesaw State Coll 3455 Steve Frey Rd Kennesaw GA 30144

ANDERS, CAMILLE SHEPHARD, director of adult and family ministries; b. Meridian, Miss., Dec. 28, 1938; m. Dan Raney Anders, Sept. 3, 1994; children: Christel Camille Funk, Lisa Leah Funk Nied, Melanie Maria Funk Futch, Wendi Wanita Funk. BA, U. Miss., 1960; Lang. Cert., Yale Inst. Far Ea. Langs., 1962. Speech pathologist Quincy (Mass.) City Schs., 1960-61; lay ednl. missionary Gen. Bd. Global Ministries, Un. Meth. Ch., Kapit and Sibu, Sarawak, Malaysia, 1962-71; sec. Gen. Bd. Global Ministries, Un. Meth. Ch., Atlanta, 1976-84, mission educator, 1985, southeastern mission devel. field rep., 1986-94; gen. sec. Global Mission Ptnrs., 1994—; mem., organizer U.S.-China Peoples Friendship Assn., Atlanta, 1974—; leader mission edn. workshops. Author (study book guide) 10 Sessions for 3d-4th Grade, 1989, (study book guide) Winds Across China, 1985 (study program) God, Our World, and Me, 1989, Leader's Guide to The Enduring Church, an ecumenical Mission study on China/Hong Kong, 1996; contbr. articles to publs. Democrat. Home: 3216 Prince William Dr Fairfax VA 22031-3020

ANDERS, ELIZABETH RAMBO, physical education educator, athletic coach; b. Norristown, Pa., Nov. 13, 1951; d. Stanley and Alice Anders. BS in Health and Phys. Edn., Ursinus Coll., Collegeville, Pa., 1973. Cert. health and phys. edn. tchr., Pa. Tchr. phys. edn. Perkiomen (Pa.) Valley High Sch., 1973-80; instr. phys. edn., lacrosse coach Old Dominion U., Norfolk, Va., 1980-84, instr., head coach athletics, 1987-89, field hockey coach, 1990—; head clinician U.S. Coaches Clinic, U.S. Field Hockey Assn., Atlantic City, 1991-93, coach, 1985, 90-93; U.S. nat. women's head coach, 1990-93; mem. U.S. Nat. Field Hockey Team, 14 yrs., team capt., 1 yr. Author: (manual) USA Junior Field Hockey, 1985, On the Rebound-The Hit, 1988, Summer Training for Field Hockey, 1989, The Coaches, 1992, Fitness Training for Field Hockey, 1995, (book) Lessons in Field Hockey, 1996, also pamphlet. Recipient Bronze medal Internat. Olympics, 1984; named Sportswoman of Yr., U.S. Olympic Com., 1980, Sportswoman of Yr. for field hockey, 1981, Amateur Olympic Athlete of Yr., 1984, Amateur Athlete of Yr., Phila. Sportswriters, 1984, Va. Coach of Yr., 1985, Coach of Yr., Virginia Beach Club, 1984, Portsmouth Sports Club, 1984, 88, 90, Colonial Athletic Assn., 1991, 92, Norfolk Sports Club, 1993; named to Ursinus Coll. Hall of Fame, 1988, U.S. Field Hockey Assn., 1989; numerous others. Mem. AAHPERD, Nat. Strength and Conditioning Assn., Golden Key, Omicron Delta Kappa. Office: Old Dominion U Health Phys Edn Bldg Hampton Blvd Norfolk VA 23529

ANDERS, WALTER CHARLES, human resources administrator; b. Mar. 12, 1929; s. James W. Sr. and Nettie R. (Staley) A.; m. Erslyn Louise Ferguson, Dec. 21, 1958; children: Walter Jr., Nina Elayne. BA, Huston Tillotson Coll., 1951; MA, U. Mich., 1957; MPA, D of Pub. Adminstrn., Nova U., 1977. Tchr., counselor Mays Jr. and Sr. H.S., Miami, Fla., 1958-68; supt. Kendall Children's Home, Miami, 1968-72; corrections planner Dade County Criminal Justice, Miami, 1972-74; adminstr. dept. human resources Perdue Med. Ctr., Miami, 1974-82, dir. dept. human resources Office of Comty. Svcs., 1982-93; asst. dir. Dept. Human Resources, Miami, 1993—; instr. Nova U., Ft. Lauderdale, Fla., 1980-85, U. Miami, Coral Gables, Fla., 1991-94. Co-author: Corrections and Rehabilitation in Dade County, 1972. Bd. dirs. South Fla. coun. Boy Scouts Am., Miami, 1980—, Miami Coalition for Homeless, Miami, 1986—, Counseling Ministry of South Fla., 1984—, Prevent Blindness of Fla., Miami, 1993—; coun. commr. Boy Scouts Am., 1991; bd. dirs., chmn. budget com. Office of Ch. Life and Leadership United Ch. of Christ, 1989-91. Staff sgt. USAF, 1951-55. Mem. Am. Soc. Pub. Adminstrn. (chpt. pres., nat. coun. mem., Glassman-Donaldson award South Fla. chpt. 1988), Sigma Pi Phi (pres. 1992-94), Kappa Alpha Psi (pres. 1976-79). Home: 78 NE 156th St Miami FL 33162-4255 Office: Dept Human Resources 111 NW 1st St Miami FL 33128-1902

ANDERSEN, MELVIN ERNEST, toxicologist, consultant; b. Providence, Dec. 13, 1945; s. Magnus and Mildred Elaine (Petersen) A.; m. Christine Ann Jaeger, Aug. 3, 1968; children: Kathryn Louise, Heidi Lynn, Rebecca Arline. BSc in Chemistry, Brown U., 1967; PhD in Biochemistry, Cornell U., 1971. Diplomate Am. Bd. Indsl. Hygiene, Am. Bd. Toxicology. Civil svc. staff Dept. of Def., Dayton, Ohio, 1979-88; dept. head, sr. scientist Chem. Ind. Inst. Toxicology, Research Triangle Park, N.C., 1989-92; rsch. prof. Duke U., Durham, N.C., 1992-93; sr. scientist U.S. EPA, Research Triangle Park, 1993-94; v.p. KS Crump divsn. ICF Kaiser Engrs., Research Triangle Park, N.C., 1994—; sci. adv. panel Chem. Industry Inst. Toxicology, Research Triangle Park, 1984-88; adj. prof. Wright State U., Dayton, 1979-89; adj. prof. medicine Duke U., 1994-95; adj. assoc. prof. U. N.C., Chapel Hill, 1993-95. Contbr. articles to profl. jours., chpts. to books. Lt. comdr. USN, 1971-78. Recipient Kenneth Morgareidge award Internat. Life Scis. Inst., 1989, George Scott award Toxicology Forum, 1993, Harry G. Armstrong award Aerospace Med. Rsch. Lab., 1982, Outstanding Profl. Achievement award Engring./Sci. Found. of Dayton, 1985. Mem. Soc. Toxicology (Frank Blood award 1982, Achievement award 1984), Soc. Risk Analysis, Am. Bd. Toxicology (bd. dirs. 1991-94), Am. Conf. Govtl. Indsl. Hygienists (Herbert Stokinger award 1988). Methodist. Home: 8701 Drew Ln Chapel Hill NC 27516-9495

ANDERSEN, STEPHEN PERRY, art educator, art gallery director; b. Chgo., Oct. 21, 1942; s. George Olaf and Kathryne Lillian (Larsen) A.; m. Janet Graham Diss, Mar. 29, 1968; children: Tor, Leif, Soren. BA in Art, So. Ill. U., 1964; MFA in Ceramics, U. Colo., 1974. Art tchr. Base Line Jr. H.S., Boulder, Colo., 1964-70; art tchr., coach Colo. Rocky Mt. Sch., Carbondale, 1970-72; art tchr. Blatchley Jr. H.S., Sitka, Alaska, 1973-74; art tchr., coach Homer (Alaska) H.S., 1974-78; art tchr. Black Hills State U., Spearfish, S.D., 1978-84; art tchr., chmn. Sul Ross State U., Alpine, Tex., 1984-88; art tchr., gallery dir. Valdosta (Ga.) State U., 1988—; part-time tchr. U. Colo., Boulder, 1969-70, Sheldon Jackson Coll., Sitka, Alaska, 1973-74, U. Alaska, Sitka, 1973-74, Homer, 1974-78; studio potter Virginia City (Mont.) Pottery, 1972-73. Exhibited art work in region, in nation and in fgn. countries; contbr. articles to profl. jours. and mags. Pres. Valdosta Internat. Club, 1991-92, Black Hills State U. Faculty Senate, Spearfish; v.p. Valdosta Unitarian Ch., 1991-92. Fulbright Teaching fellow Wakefield Coll., Eng., 1982-83; recipient Internat. Tchg. Exch. fellowship Casterton Sch., Victoria, Australia, 1977, numerous awards for art work in regional and nat. juried. Mem. AAUP (treas. 1992-93), Nat. Conf. for Edn. in Ceramic Arts, Nat. Art Edn. Assn., Internat. Soc. for Edn. Through Art, Ga. Assn. of Mus. and Galleries. Democrat. Unitarian. Office: Valdosta State Univ Dept Art Brookwood St Valdosta GA 31698

ANDERSON, ALBERT SEVERIN, allergist, nutritionist; b. Bridgeport, Conn., July 29, 1929; s. Albert Sigfred and Deborah Pernella (Didriksen) A.; m. Anne J. Denisevich, June 26, 1953; children: Christopher Bradford, Timothy Albert, Paul Hilary Parrish. AB, Johns Hopkins U., 1951; MD, N.Y. Med. Coll., 1955; postgrad., Northwestern U., Chgo., 1963. Diplomate Am. Bd. Med. Examiners. Rotating gen. intern Greenwich (Conn.) Hosp. Assn., 1955-56; resident in internal medicine U. Mich. Med. Ctr., Ann Arbor, 1956-59; chief med. svcs. USAF Hosp., Loring AFB, Limestone, Maine, 1959-63; mem. staff, pvt. practice R.I. Hosp., Roger Williams Gen. Hosp., Providence, 1963-69; coll. physician, chmn. sci. dept. Shelton Coll., Cape May, N.J., 1969-71; mem. staff, pvt. practice Burbank Hosp., Fitchburg, Mass., 1971-72, Sturdy Meml. Hosp., Attleboro, Mass., 1972-73; pvt. practice, pres. Creation Health Found., Taylors, S.C., 1973—; guest lectr. Greenville (S.C.) Presbyn. Theol. Sem., 1992—; bd. dirs. Creation Study Group, Greenville, 1991—, v.p., 1995—. Author: (booklets) WARNING: Evolution is Hazardous to Your Health, 1980, Creation Health: Forgotten Medical Science, 1980, Optimal Nutrition for Creation Health Fitness, 1982, Magnificent Miracle: The Virgin Conception of Jesus Christ, 1992. Lectr., past v.p., bd. dirs. Bible-Sci. Assn., Mpls., 1968-89; pres. PTA, Caribou, Maine, 1961; ruling elder 2d Presbyn. Ch., Greenville, 1991—. Capt. USAF, 1956-63. Mem. Greenville County Med. Soc. (emeritus), Assn. Am. Physicians and Surgeons (emeritus, lobbyist 1995), Am. Acad. Allergy, Asthma and Immunology (emeritus), Price-Pottenger Nutrition Found., Internat. Acad. Preventive Medicine (emeritus), Northfield Mt. Hermon Christian Concern Fellowship (bd. dirs., pres. 1982-84). Republican. Office: Creation Health Found 19 Gallery Ctr Taylors SC 29687

ANDERSON, ALBERT SYDNEY, III, lawyer; b. Atlanta, July 7, 1940; s. Albert S. Jr. and Constance S. (Spalding) A.; m. Isabel Morrison, Nov. 25, 1984; children: Judith, William, Margaret. BA in Math., Emory U., 1962; MS in Physics, Stanford (Calif.) U., 1964, PhD in Physics, 1968, JD, 1977. Bar: Ga. 1978, U.S. Patent and Trademark Office 1980, U.S. Supreme Ct. 1981. Assoc. Stokes & Shapiro, Atlanta, 1978-81, Kutak, Rock & Huie, Atlanta, 1981-84; ptnr. Jones & Askew, Atlanta, 1984-96; pvt. practice Norcross, Ga., 1996—; asst. atty. gen. State of Ga., Atlanta, 1984-88. Elder Trinity Presbyn. Ch., Atlanta, 1978-81; chmn. bd. trustees Trinity Sch., Atlanta, 1971-74. Mem. Am. Phys. Soc., Kiwanis. Office: Patent Law Offices 35 Technology Pky S Ste 170 Norcross GA 30092

ANDERSON, AMY KINSEY, sales executive, bridal consultant; b. Rome, Ga., Oct. 20, 1969; d. Alford Warren and Lavonia Gwendolyn (Litton) Kinsey; m. Sean G. Anderson. BA in Mass Communication, West Ga. Coll., 1991. Broadcasting intern WJSU-TV, Anniston, Ala., 1991; radio personality Sta. WTSH-FM, Rome, 1992; sales rep. Photo Fashion Internat., Tucker, Ga., 1992-94, Air Touch Paging, Tucker, Ga., 1995, Lewis Paging, Cartersville, Ga., 1995—; owner Elegant Events; ins. svc. rep. Tillman Ins., Rome, 1992. Congrl. intern G. Buddy Darden Campaign, Rome, 1992; poll monitor 7th Dist. Dem. Ctrl. Com., Rome, 1992. Mem. West Ga. Coll. Alumni Assn., Pilot Club Internat., Kappa Delta (alumni adv. bd. Delta Psi chpt.). Baptist. Home: 4318 Roland Hayes Pkwy Calhoun GA 30701-9999 Office: Elegant Events 4318 Roalnd Hayes Pkwy Calhoun GA 30701

ANDERSON, ANN DAVIS, curriculum and staff development specialist; b. Washington, Mar. 24, 1946; d. George Perry and Irene Delores (Stewart) Davis; m. Ronald Clifford Anderson, Oct. 13, 1973; 1 child, Tahira Mali. BS in Edn., Bucknell U., Lewisburg, Pa., 1968; MA in Edn., George Washington U., 1972. Cert. reading specialist, Va. Tchr. grades 2-5 D.C. Pub. Schs., 1968-73; reading specialist Alexandria (Va.) City Pub. Schs., 1973-93, curriculum/staff devel. specialist, 1993—; cons. NEA, Washington, 1986-88; reviewer of grants Nat. Found. for Improvement of Edn., Washington, 1993—; mem. nat. rev. panel for blue ribbon schs. U.S. Dept. Edn., Washington, 1992—; staff devel. presenter Alexandria City Pub. Schs., 1989—. Co-author: A Research Framework for the Middle Grades. Recipient Award of Excellence in Edn., Alexandria C. of C., 1986, Am. Tchr. award Walt Disney Corp., L.A., 1990; Washington Post grantee, 1987, Readers Choices 1000 Women for the Nineties, 1994, Reader's Choices 1000 Women for the Nineties, Mirabella mag., 1994. Mem. ASCD, NEA, Internat. Reading Assn., Nat. Coun. for Social Studies, Nat. Coun. Negro Women, Nat. Tots and Teens Inc. (v.p., youth coord. Prince Georges County chpt. 1991-93), Va. Edn. Assn., Edn. Assn. Alexandria, Phi Delta Kappa, Kappa Pi. Home: 12802 Berwick Cir Fort Washington MD 20744-6409 Office: Alexandria City Pub Schs 2000 N Beauregard St Alexandria VA 22311-1712

ANDERSON, BARBARA, elementary school educator; b. Nashville, Oct. 26, 1946; d. John Elgin and Frances (Pitts) Watts; m. Paul Clifford Anderson, Feb. 17, 1968; children: Jake, Jody. BS, Middle Tenn. State U., 1968; MEd, U. Southern Miss., 1988. Cert. elem. tchr., Fla. Tchr. Phippsburg (Maine) Elem. Sch., 1969; tchr. 4th grade Mirror Lake Elem., Ft. Lauderdale, Fla., 1970-73; tchr. kindergarten Floral City (Fla.) Elem. Sch., 1982-90; curriculum resource specialist Pleasant Grove Elem. Sch., Inverness, Fla., 1990—. Mem. Assn. for Childhood Edn. Internat., Fla. Assn. Children under Six, Phi Delta Kappa. Office: Pleasant Grove Elem Sch 630 Pleasant Grove Rd Inverness FL 34452-5747

ANDERSON, CHARLES HILL, lawyer; b. Chattanooga, June 16, 1930; s. Ray N. and Lois M. (Entrekin) A.; div.; children: Eric S., Alicia L., Burton H.; m. Shirley Roach, May 17, 1996. JD, U. Tenn., 1953. Bar: Tenn. 1953, U.S. Dist. Ct. Tenn. 1953, U.S. Ct. Appeals (6th cir.) 1956, U.S. Supreme Ct. 1956, U.S. Ct. Mil. 1964. Pvt. practice Chattanooga, 1953-59; assoc. gen. counsel Life & Casualty Ins. Co. Tenn., Nashville, 1960-69; U.S. dist. atty. U.S. Dept. Justice, Nashville, 1969-77; pvt. practice Nashville, 1977-79, 87—; asst. adj. gen. State of Tenn., Nashville, 1979-87;. Mem. U.S. Atty. Gen. Adv. Com., Washington, 1973-77; del. Tenn. Constl. Conv., Nashville, 1965-66. Brig. gen. USAR, ret., 1987. Mem. ABA, Tenn. Bar Assn., Nashville Bar Assn., Fed. Bar Assn. (pres. Nashville chpt. 1972), Am. Arbitration Assn. (arbitrator), Assn. Life Ins. Counsel, Am. Soc. Corp. Secs., Nat. Fedn. Ind. Bus., Cumberland Club (pres. 1981-82). Presbyterian. Home: 221 Diane Dr Madison TN 37115-2565 Office: 2323 Crestmoor Rd Nashville TN 37215-2003

ANDERSON, DALE, film production executive; b. Houston, Aug. 15, 1933; s. Elwin Dale Sr. and Thelma Ilene (Phillips) A.; m. Patricia Ann Lawrence, Aug. 29, 1952; children: Roxann, Ross, Eleceann. Student, Welch Sch. Music, Houston, 1952-57, U. Houston, 1956-59. Owner Dale Anderson Prodns. Internat., Houston, 1963—. Producer over 500 films for world's largest corps., 15 internat. TV spls. in numerous langs.; over 300 guest appearances TV, travel, music and other programs, (album) A Program of Beautiful Music, 1989, Home TV Entertainment, California Highlights (1992 Nat. Telly award winner in entertainment), Tex. Hill, Country Treasures, Ceacar's Palace Forum Shops and Festival Fountain Show, 1994, Ctrl. Fla. space Coast (TV program) The Golden Road to Music, 1995; tenor concert series. Office: Dale Anderson Prodns Internat PO Box 8905 The Woodlands TX 77387-8905 also: Los Angeles CA 90000

ANDERSON, DAVID PREWITT, university dean; b. Twin Falls, Idaho, Sept. 14, 1934; m. Janice Gale Schmied, Dec. 21, 1962; children: Kathryn Lynn, Christopher Kyle. Student, U. Idaho, 1952-54; BS, Wash. State U., 1959, DVM, 1961; MS, U. Wis., 1964, PhD, 1965. NIH trainee U. Wis., 1961-62, asst. prof. vet. sci., asst. dir. biotron, 1965-69; prof. med. microbiology, dir. Poultry Disease Research Center, U. Ga., 1969-71, asso. dean research and grad. affairs Coll. Vet. Medicine, 1971-73, dean, 1975-96; retired; animal health com. NAS, 1977-80; animal health sci. rsch. adv. bd. USDA, 1978-85, nat. adv. com. on meat and poultry inspection, 1990-92; adv. com. Ctr. for Vet. Medicine/FDA, 1984-88; tech. analysis group Food Safety Inspection Svc./USDA, 1994-95. Editor Avian Diseases, 1973-93. Mem. AVMA, Am. Coll. Vet. Microbiologists (diplomate), Am. Coll. Poultry Vets. (diplomate), Am. Assn. Avian Pathologists (pres. 1988-89), Nat. Acads. Practice. Home: 190 Harris St Winterville GA 30683-9710

ANDERSON, DAVID WALTER, physics educator, consultant; b. Heron Lake, Minn., June 18, 1937; s. Walter Olaf and Martha Gladys (Bonnell) A.; m. Jane Louise Friedlund, Dec. 17, 1960; children: Bonnie Jean, Brian David. BS in Physics summa cum laude, Hamline U., 1959; PhD in Nuclear Physics, Iowa State U., 1965. Diplomate Am. Bd. Radiology. Postdoctoral fellow in physics Iowa State U., Ames, 1965-66; prof. U. Okla., Norman, 1966-82; prof. radiation physics U. Okla. Health Ctr., Oklahoma City, 1966-82; prof., dir. radiol. physics City of Faith Med. Ctr., Tulsa, 1982-88, Tulsa Regional Med. Ctr., 1988—; presenter in field; advisor MS and PhD students, 1970-83. Author: Absorption of Ionizing Radiation, 1984; referee articles in profl. jours. Chmn. coun. ministry McFarlin Meth. Ch., 1979, chmn. adminstrv. bd., 1978. Grantee Rsch. Corp., Am. Cancer Soc., Radiation Measurement Inc. Fellow Am. Coll. Radiology; mem. Am. Assn. Physicists in Medicine (physics com. on profl. activities 1986-90), Am. Bd. Radiology (physics examiner 1986-90), Am. Coll. Radiology, Soc. Nuclear Medicine, Phi Kappa Phi. Democrat. Home: 3617 Guilford Ln Norman OK 73072-3037 Office: Tulsa Regional Med Ctr 744 W 9th St Tulsa OK 74127-9028

ANDERSON, DOLORES MAY, music educator; b. Mpls., Aug. 25, 1924; d. Henry John Wepplo and Mary Elsie Lillian Maynard; m. Clayton Lavern Anderson, Aug. 24, 1954; children: Michael Henry, Mary Louise. Cert. music tchr., Trafficante Accordion Sch., Mpls., 1942; cosmetologist, Robinsons Beauty Sch., St. Paul, Minn., 1957; real estate agt., Anthony's Sch. of Realty, La Mesa, Calif., 1972. Clk., typist Minn. Farmers Mutual Ins. Co., Mpls., 1942-43; accordion tchr. Trafficante Accordion Sch., Mpls., 1943-51; bookkeeping/billing clk. Northwestern Hosp., Mpls., 1952-54; co-owner Charm House Beauty Salon, Mpls., 1957-70; sec. to dir. nurses El Cajon (Calif.) Valley Hosp., 1973-74; piano tchr. Anderson Ednl. Svcs., El Cajon, 1975—. Author: Piano Improvisation Made Easy, Level I, 1992, Piano Improvisation Made Easy, Level II, 1992. Congrl. candidate, Mpls., 1968; city coun. candidate, Mpls., 1969, 71. Republican. Presbyterian. Home: 246 Oxford St Sistersville WV 26175-1029

ANDERSON, DONALD NORTON, JR., retired electrical engineer; b. Chgo., Aug. 15, 1928; s. Donald Norton and Helen Dorothy (Lehmann) A. BS, Purdue U., 1950, MS, 1952. With Hughes Aircraft Co., Culver City and El Segundo, Calif., 1952-84, sect. head, sr. project engr., 1960-65, tech. mgr. Apollo program, 1965-66, mgr. visible systems dept., 1966-69, 70-73, project mgr., 1969-70, mgr. space sensors lab., 1973-79, mgr. space electro-optical systems labs., 1979-80, mgr. space electro-optical systems labs., 1980-84, ret., 1984. Recipient Apollo Achievement award, 1970; Robert J. Collier Landsat award, 1974. Mem. Research Soc. Am., Nat. Speleological Soc., Am. Theatre Organ Soc., Sigma Xi (sec. Hughes Labs. br. 1974-75), Eta Kappa Nu, Sierra Club. Home: 1885 Craig's Store Rd Afton VA 22920-9634

ANDERSON, DONALD ROGER, cardiologist; b. Mpls., June 27, 1946; s. Bennie Lester and Dorothy Catherine (Golden) A.; m. Marie J. Seaman, June 1, 1968 (div. 1985); children: David J, Karin J.; m. Cecilia B. Kempton, June 2, 1985. BS, Creighton U., 1968, MD, 1972. Resident internal medicine Creighton U. Affiliated Hosps., Omaha, Neb., 1972-75; staff physician Bartron Clinic, Watertown, S.D., 1975-79; commd. M.C. U.S. Army, 1973, advanced through grades to lt. col., 1985, resigned to active reserve, 1986; chief internal med. clinic Brooke Army Med. Ctr. Ft. Sam Houston, San Antonio, 1979-82, cardiology fellow, 1982-84; dir. CCU, staff William Beaumont Army Med. Ctr., El Paso, Tex., 1984-86; dir. Cardiology Assocs. Summit, N.J., 1986-91; pres. Camden County Med. Soc., 1996-97; clin. asst. prof. N.J. Med. Sch., Newark, 1986-91; chmn. ambulance com., Watertown, S.D., 1977-79; chief staff St. Ann's Hosp., Meml. Med. Ctr. Watertown, 1979. Fellow Am. Coll. Cardiology, Am. Coll. Chest Physicians; mem. AMA, Am. Heart Assn. Republican. Congregationalist. Club: Golf Club of Amelia Island. Office: 2040 Dan Proctor Dr Ste 170 Saint Marys GA 31558 also: 3212 Shrine Rd Brunswick GA 31520

ANDERSON, DONNA ELAINE, elementary and secondary school educator; b. Lone Wolf, Okla., Mar. 26, 1935; d. William Herbert and Lois Alta (Montgomery) Tolleson; m. Frank D. Anderson, Sept. 3, 1955; 1 child, Valerie Elaine. BA cum laude, U. North Tex., 1957, MEd, 1960. Cert. edn. diagnostician, elem. tchr., bus. tchr.; registered profl. ednl. diagnostician. Tchr. White Deer (Tex.) Ind. Sch. Dist., 1957-62; tchr. Pampa (Tex.) Ind. Sch. Dist., 1962-70, ednl. diagnostician, 1973—. Missionette dir. First Assembly God Ch., Pampa, 1973—; mem. Pampa Fine Arts Assn., 1978—, Community Concert Assn., Pampa, 1965—. Mem. NEA (life), Tex. Ednl. Diagnosticians Assn., Tex. State Tchrs. Assn. (life), Ednl. Diagnosticians Golden Spread, Coun. Exceptional Children, Knife and Fork Club, Delta Kappa Gamma. Democrat. Mem. Assemby of God Ch. Office: Pampa Ind Sch Dist 321 W Albert St Pampa TX 79065-7801

ANDERSON, DUWAYNE MARLO, earth and polar scientist, university administrator; b. Lehi, Utah, Sept. 9, 1927; s. Duwayne LeRoy and Fern Francell (Fagan) A.; m. June B. Hodgin, Apr. 2, 1980; children by previous marriage: Lynna Nadine, Christopher Kent, Lesleigh Leigh. B.S., Brigham Young U., 1954; Ph.D. (Purdue Research Found. fellow), Purdue U., 1958. Prof. soil physics U. Ariz., Tucson, 1958-63; rsch. scientist, chief earth scis. br. (Cold Regions Research and Engring. Lab.), Hanover, N.H., 1963-76; chief scientist divsn. polar programs NSF, Washington, 1976-78; mem. Viking sci. team NASA, 1969-76; dean faculty natural scis. and math. SUNY Buffalo, 1978-84; assoc. provost for rsch. and grad. studies Tex. A&M U., College Station, 1984-92, prof. Coll. Geoscis., 1992—; also councilor Tex. A&M Rsch. Found., 1984-93; Pegrum lectr. SUNY, 1980; v.p. Assn. Tex. Grad. Schs., 1990-91, pres., 1991-92; cons. NASA, 1964, NSF, 1979-81, U.S. Army Cold Regions Rsch. and Engring. Lab., Hanover, N.H.; sr. U.S. rep., Antarctica, 1976, 77; bd. dirs., exec. com. Houston Area Rsch. Ctr., 1984-89; vis. prof., lectr., cons. numerous univs. Editor: (with O.B. Andersland) Geotechnical Engineering for Cold Regions, 1978; cons. editor Soil Sci, 1965—, Cold Regions Sci. and Tech., 1978-82; contbr. numerous sci. and tech. articles to profl. jours. Bd. dirs. Ford K. Sayre Meml. Ski Coun., Hanover, 1969-71; bd. dirs. Grafton County Fish and Game Assn., 1965-76, pres., 1968-70; bd. dirs. Hanover Conservation Coun., 1970-76, v.p., 1970-73. Served in USAF, 1946-49. Recipient Sci. Achievement award Cold Regions Research and Engring. Lab., 1968; co-recipient Newcomb Cleveland award AAAS, 1976; Sec. of Army Research fellow, 1966. Fellow Geol. Soc. Am., Am. Soc. Agronomy, Soil Soc. Am.; mem. AAAS, Internat. Glaciological Soc., Am. Polar Soc., Am. Geophys. Union (spl. task force on cold regions hydrology 1974-84), Soil Sci. Soc. Am., Niagara Frontier Assn. R&D Dirs. (pres. 1983-84), Licensing Execs. Soc., NASA Teams (Viking, Skylab and Planetary Geology and Geophys. Working Group), Comet Rendevous/Asteroid Flyby Mission Team, Arctic Rsch. Consortium U.S. (exec. com.), Sigma Xi, Sigma Gamma Epsilon, Phi Kappa Phi. Home: 8720 Bent Tree Dr College Station TX 77845-5558 Office: Tex A&M U Dept Geology and Geophysics 267 Halbouty Bldg College Station TX 77843-3115

ANDERSON, EDWARD RILEY, state supreme court justice; b. Chattanooga, Aug. 10, 1932. BS, U. Tenn., 1955, JD, 1957. Bar: Tenn. 1958, U.S. Dist. Ct. (ea. dist.) Tenn. 1965, U.S. Ct. Appeals (4th cir.) 1985, U.S. Ct. Appeals (6th cir.), U.S. Supreme Ct. 1988. Assoc. Joyce & Wilson, Oak Ridge, Tenn., 1957-61; ptnr. Joyce, Anderson & Meredith, Oak Ridge, 1961-87; judge Tenn. Ct. Appeals, Knoxville, 1987-90; justice Tenn. Supreme Ct., Knoxville, 1990—, now chief justice; mem. Tenn. Jud. Conf., 1987—; chmn. Tenn. Jud. Coun., 1990—, Select Senate/House Com. on Ct. Automation, 1990—. Past commr. Oak Ridge City Charter. Fellow Am. Bar Found., Tenn. Bar Found.; mem. ABA, Am. Bd. Trial Advocates (pres. Tenn. chpt. 1987-88), Tenn. Bar Assn., Anderson County Bar Assn. (pres. 1961), Tenn. Def. Lawyers Assn. (pres. 1980-81), Am. Inns of Ct. (pres. Tenn. chpt. 1988-90). Office: Tenn Supreme Ct 719 Locust St Knoxville TN 37902-2512*

ANDERSON, ELSIE MINERS, mathematics educator; b. Harare, Zimbabwe, July 4, 1931; came to U.S., 1961; d. William James and Winifred Ethel (Lowe) Miners; m. Larry Vance Anderson, Dec. 22, 1961; children: Winifred Jean Whitmore, Margaret Elizabeth Daly. BS, Rhodes U., Grahamstown, South Africa, 1951, EdD, 1952; MLS, East Tex. State U., 1966. Tchr. geography and math. Govt. Cen. African Fedn., Salisbury, 1953-61; tchr. math. Desdemona (Tex.) Ind. Sch. Dist., 1962-64; head libr. Holding Inst., Laredo, Tex., 1971-72; instr. math. Western Tex. Coll., Snyder, 1973-74, prof. math., 1974—; exchange tchr. in geography Mill Hill, North London, Eng., 1957. Active Girl Scouts U.S., Abilene, Tex., 1972—. Recipient Theater Patron award Western Tex. Coll. Drama Dept., Snyder, 1986. Mem. Tex. Jr. Coll. Tchrs. Assn., Tex. Math. Assn. 2-Yr. Colls., Am. Math. Assn. 2-Yr. Colls., Math. Assn. Am., Order of Eastern Star. Baptist. Home: 600 29th St Snyder TX 79549-3614 Office: Western Tex Coll Mathematics Dept Snyder TX 79549

ANDERSON, ERIC SEVERIN, lawyer; b. N.Y.C., Dec. 16, 1943; s. Edward Severin and Dorothy Elvira (Ekbloom) A. BA in History summa cum laude, St. Mary's U., San Antonio, 1968; JD cum laude, Harvard U., 1971. Bar: Tex. 1971. From assoc. to ptnr. Fulbright & Jaworski, L.L.P., Houston, 1971—. Served with USAF, 1961-65. Mem. ABA, State Bar Tex., Houston Bar Assn. Democrat. Clubs: Houston Ctr., Houston City. Home: 14 E Greenway Plz Apt 21-o Houston TX 77046-1400 Office: Fulbright & Jaworski LLP 1301 McKinney St Houston TX 77010-3049

ANDERSON, ETHEL AVARA, retired retail executive; b. Meridian, Miss.; d. Thomas Franklin and Annie Ethel (Jones) Avara.; m. Theron Young Anderson, Aug. 2, 1940 (dec. Aug. 1964); 1 child, Brenda Anderson Jackson. Grad. high sch., Meridian. Mem. exec. bd., sec. United Way of Meridian, Industries for Developmentally Disabled, Meridian, 1984-93, Lauderdale Assn. Retarded Children, Meridian, 1983-91; mem. exec. bd. Lauderdale County Mental Health, 1991, 92, 93, v.p., 1993-94; bd. dirs. 1st Ladies Civitan of Meridian, 1980-93. Mem. Meridian C. of C. (liaison 1985-87), Xi Gamma, Beta Sigma Phi (life). Methodist. Home: 3400 20th St Meridian MS 39301-2834

ANDERSON, FREDERICK JARRARD, historian; b. Albany, Ga., Dec. 26, 1944; m. Nancy Simmons, June 24, 1967; children: Christopher, Matthew. BS, Berry Coll., 1966; MEd, West Ga. Coll., 1973; MLS, Peabody Coll., 1974. Divsn. head English & social studies Cherokee High Sch., Canton, Ga., 1966-73; adminstrv. asst. Henrico Pub. Libr., Richmond, Va., 1974-79; exec. dir. Va. Bapt. Hist. Soc., Richmond, 1979—; clk. Bapt. Gen. Assn. Va., Richmond, 1982—; sec. Va. Bapt. Gen. Bd., Richmond, 1982—; columnist Religious Herald, Richmond, 1983—. Author: A People Called Northminster, 1978, The Third Jubilee, 1983, Hearts and Hands, 1990, Land of Goshen, 1992. Archivist U. Richmond, 1982—; historian Richmond Bapt. Assn., 1979—; pres. So. Bapt. Hist. Soc., Nashville, 1992-93. Office: Va Bapt Hist Soc PO Box 34 Richmond VA 23173

ANDERSON, GEORGE ROSS, JR., federal judge; b. Anderson, S.C., Jan. 29, 1929; s. George Ross and Eva Mae (Pooler) A.; m. Dorothy M. Downie, Dec. 2, 1951; 1 son, G. Ross. B.Comml. Sci., Southeastern U., 1949; postgrad., George Washington U., 1949-51; LL.B., U. S.C., 1954, LLD (hon.), 1984. Bar: S.C. 1954. Mem. identification div. FBI, Washington, 1945-47; clk. to U.S. Senator Olin D. Johnston, Washington, 1947-51, Columbia, S.C., 1953-54; individual practice law Anderson, S.C., 1954-79; U.S. dist. judge Dist. Ct. of S.C., Anderson, 1980—. Asst. editor: U. S.C. Law Rev, 1953-54. Bd. dirs. Salvation Army, 1968, YMCA, 1968-79, Anderson Youth Assn., 1978-80. Served with USAF, 1951-52. Recipient War Horse award So. Trial Lawyers Assn., 1990. Fellow Internat. Acad. Trial Lawyers (dir. 1979-81), Internat. Soc. Barristers; mem. S.C. Bar Assn. (dir. 1977-80, past cir. v.p.), Assn. Trial Lawyers Am. (bd. govs. 1969-71), S.C. Trial Lawyers Assn. (v.p. 1970-71, pres. 1971-72, Outstanding Trial Judge of Yr. 1984), hon. doctor of Laws, U. SC, 1984, bd. dirs.,Federal Judges Assn., 1993-97. Democrat. Baptist. Office: US Dist Ct PO Box 2147 Anderson SC 29622-2147

ANDERSON, GERALD M(ICHEL), electronics marketing executive; b. Dallas, Sept. 22, 1944; s. James T. and Margaret Mary (O'Grady) A.; m. Claire Knox, Dec. 20, 1969; children: Claire, Michael. BA, Baylor U., 1966; MBA, Pepperdine U., 1979. Dir. mktg. Tex. Instruments, Dallas, 1966-85; dir., sales Honeywell, Colorado Springs, 1985-87; pres. Anderson Mktg., Colorado Springs, 1987-90; v.p. Compu Route, Garland, Tex., 1990—; pres. Anderson Mktg., Plano, Tex., 1990—; v.p. Tronix Corp., Phoenix, Ariz., 1996; cons. Diamond Materials, Inc., State College, Pa., 1987-88, Origin Systems, Colorado Springs, ESH, Tempe, Ariz., Lone Star, Rockwell, Tex., Quality for Am. Communities, Richardson, Tex., SCM Industries, Richardson, Silicon Hills Design, Austin, AIC Quality, Houston, ECS, Richardson, Sony Microelectronics, San Antonio, Stark Advertising, Dallas. Mem. Jaycees. Office: Anderson Mgt PO Box 940686 Plano TX 75094-0686

ANDERSON, HELEN SHARP, civic worker; b. Ennis, Tex., June 10, 1916; d. John H. and Eula (King) Sharp; A.B., U. Tex., 1937; m. Thomas Dunaway Anderson, Feb. 21, 1938; children—John Sharp, Helen Shaw, Lucille Streeter. Mem. Mt. Vernon Ladies Assn. of the Union, vice regent, 1967-91, regent, 1982-86, vice regent for Tex. (emerita) 1991—; bd. dirs. Nat. Cathedral Assn., Washington, 1971-75, also mem. various spl. coms.; mem. Garden Club Am., 1945—, zone vice-chmn., 1959-62, nat. dir., 1975-77, nat. v.p., 1977-79, nat. chmn. long-range planning, 1979-80; bd. dirs. Japan Am. Soc. Houston, 1974-78; hon. mem. fine arts adv. com. U. Tex., Austin, 1963—; Bayou Bend adv. com., 1988—; chmn. Jr. Gallery, Mus. Fine Arts, Houston, 1953-54, docent, 1964-70; bd. dirs. Houston and Harris County council Girl Scouts U.S.A., 1966-67, Sheltering Arms, 1964-67; bd. trustees Winedale Hist. Ctr., 1987—; bd0 dirs. Harris County Heritage Soc., 1963-65, v.p., 1965-66; mem. River Oaks Garden Club, Houston, 1945—, pres., 1958, 59; vol. Vols. for Endowment for Patient Support, M.D. Anderson Cancer Ctr., 1995—; mem. St. John the Divine Episcopal Ch., Houston; mem. Houston Jr. League. Recipient Achievement medal Garden Club Am., 1988. Mem. Assembly Bolero Clubs (Houston, Sulgrave, Washington, Colony, N.Y.), Pi Beta Phi. Republican. Episcopalian. Address: 3925 Del Monte Dr Houston TX 77019-1001

ANDERSON, HENRY WARREN, petroleum company executive; b. Atlanta, Feb. 14, 1956; s. James Oscar and Jane (Greer) A.; m. Sheri Bolton. BA in Hist. and Polit. Sci., Emory U., 1984. Gen. mgr. Anderson Oil Co., Covington, Ga., 1978-82; v.p., gen. mgr. Jones Petroleum, Jackson, Ga., 1982-86, v.p., 1986—; pres. Starrsville Properties, Covington, Ga., 1986-90, Knight Petroleum Co. Inc., 1994—. Recipient State Bus. Clerical award, Nat. TV Commls. award Future Bus. Leaders of Am., 1974. Mem. Ga. Oilman's Assn., Ga. Wildlife Fedn., Safari Club Internat. Republican. Methodist. Home: PO Box 947 Covington GA 30210-0947 Office: Jones Petroleum 407 E 2nd St Jackson GA 30233-2035

ANDERSON, IVAN VERNER, JR., newspaper publisher; b. Columbus, Ohio, Dec. 6, 1939; m. Josephine Blackwell; children: Thomas, Charlotte. BA, U. N.C., 1961; MBA, U. S.C., 1970. Sr. v.p. for loan adminstrn., regional mgr. Wachovia Bank and Trust Co., Winston-Salem, N.C., 1980-84; sr. v.p., regional exec. S.C. Nat. Bank, Charleston, 1984; exec. v.p. Evening Post Pub. Co., Charleston, 1984, pres., 1987—; asst. pub. The News and Courier, The Evening Post, Charleston, 1984; pub. The Post and Courier, 1987—. Bd. dirs. Trident United Way, S.C. Hist. Soc., Charleston Symphony Orch., Ashley Hall Sch., Enston Home, Ind. Colls. and Univs.; bd. visitors U. N.C., Chapel Hill; mem. city bd. Wachovia Bank S.C.; active U. S.C. Coll. Bus. Adminstrn. Bus. Partnership Found., Nature Conservancy. With USN, 1961-64. Mem. So. Newspaper Pub. Assn., Beta Gamma Sigma. Episcopalian. Home: 133 Tradd St Charleston SC 29401-2419

ANDERSON, JAMES EDWARD, physical education educator; b. Jackson, Miss., Aug. 5, 1953; s. Artis Edwards and Annie Bell (Anderson) Jones; m. Rhonda Marie Teaque, May 13, 1983; children: Jessica Hope, James Edward II. BS in Edn., Paul Quinn Coll., 1977; MS in Edn., Jackson State U., 1979. Cert. health-history and phys. edn. tchr., Tex. With Jackson Hilton Hotel, 1978-79; substitute tchr. Houston Ind. Sch. Dist., 1980-84; with Air Dyne Inc., Houston, 1984-85; tchr. Paul Quinn Coll., Waco, Tex., 1985-90; spl. assignment tchr. Waco Ind. Sch. Dist., 1990-91; security officer Hawks Security Svc., Hewitt, Tex., 1993-94; social svc. technician Tex. Dept. Human Svcs., 1994; belman, houseman, airport driver, host Quality Inn of Waco, 1993-95; substitute tchr. Lavega Ind. Sch. Dist., 1993-95, Aldine (Tex.) Ind. Sch. Dist., 1995—; security officer Advance Security, Inc., Houston, 1996—; bar, dining rm. attendent Houston Marriott, Houston, 1995—; supr. undergraduate workstudy Students' Health, Phys. Edn. and Recreation Dept., Jackson (Miss.) State U., 1977-78, instr. health, phys. edn. and recreation, 1985-90; women's volleyball coach Paul Quinn Coll., Waco, 1985-89, supr. undergrad. workstudy, supr. women's volleyball recruitment, 1985-90, coach men's and women's track and field team, 1986; part-time dining room, bar attendant Houston Marriott Hotel North, Greenspoint, 1995; subst. tchr. Aldine Ind. Sch. Dist., Houston, 1995-96. Fundraiser United Negro Coll. Funds, Waco, 1974-85; cmty. worker Omega Psi Phi, Waco, 1977-85, Jackson/Hinds Detention Ctr., 1978; vol. Vol. Alive Program, Waco, 1985-88. Mem. NEA, ASCD, Tex. State Tchrs. Assn., Waco Classroom Tchrs. Assn., AAHPERD, Tex. Health, Phys. Edn., Recreation and Dance, Internat. Platform Assn., Am. Volleyball Coaches Assn., Nat. Assn. Intercollegiate Athletics. Democrat. A.M.E. Home: 8042 Sharon Dale St Houston TX 77033

ANDERSON, JAMES L., history educator, business developer; b. Colorado Springs, Colo., Mar. 25, 1940; s. George L. and Caroline M. Anderson; m. Geraldine M McMurry, Dec. 4, 1968; children: Robert J, William T. AB with honors, U. Kans., 1958-62, MA, 1962-64; PhD, U. Va., 1964-67. Asst. prof. U. Ga., Athens, 1967-75; assoc. prof. U. Ga., 1975-80; acting assoc. prof. U. Conn., Storrs, 1970; prof. constitutional history U. Ga., 1980—; pres., CEO Anderson & Assocs., Winterville, Ga., 1980—; motivational lectr., 1980—. Author: The Gun in America, 1975, The History of Georgia, 1979. V.p. Boy Scouts of Am. N.E. Ga., Athens, 1972-84. Mem. Orgn. of Am. Historians, Raven Soc, Phi Delta Phi, Omicron Delta Kappa. Republican. Lutheran. Home: 1525 Robert Hardeman Rd Winterville GA 30683-9721 also: 390 Gulfpines Dr Port Saint Joe FL 32456-6817 Office: U Ga Dept History La Conte Hall Athens GA 30609

ANDERSON, JANICE GWENDOLYN, quality control professional; b. Dalton, Ga., Feb. 24, 1955; d. Ernest B. and Evelyn Irene (DuVall) A. Cert., Sears Extension Inst., 1984; student, Fgn. Svc. Inst., 1987—; AS in BA cum laude, Dalton Coll., 1993. Customer svc. rep., cashier Sears, Roebuck & Co., Dalton, 1984; acctg. mgr. Southeastern Coatings, Dalton, 1986-87; accounts receivable clk. Aladdin Mills, Inc., Dalton, 1988-90; head bookkeeper Skinner Furniture Co., Dalton, 1990-94; quality control mgr. The Andersen Co., Dalton, 1996—. Contbr. short stories to profl. publs. Mem. Acad. Polit. Sci., N.Y.C., 1993-94; Ctr. for Study of the Presidency, N.Y.C., 1993-94. Mem. NAFE, Am. Inst. Profl. Bookkeepers, Assn. Interactive Mgmt. (v.p. 1993, treas. Collegiate chpt. 1993, Leadership award 1993), Phi Theta Kappa. Home: PO Box 1713 Dalton GA 30722-1713

ANDERSON, JANICE LINN, real estate brokerage professional; b. Paris, Tenn., Sept. 2, 1943; d. Orel Vernon and Rosie Elizabeth (Brockwell) L.; m. David James Anderson, June 11, 1965 (div. Oct. 1973). Entertainer, recording artist 4-Sons Record Co., Paris, Tenn., 1958-73; med. transcriptionist The Paris Clinic, 1965-73; computer operator, asst. to v.p. Medicare Adminstrn./Equitable, Nashville, 1973-74; property mgmt. asst. Dobson & Johnson, Inc., Nashville, 1974-76; dir. leasing and mgmt. Fortune-Nashville Co., 1976-78; real estate brokerage asst. J.G. Martin, Jr./Caudill Properties, Inc., Nashville, 1978—; pvt. practice med. ins. filing and collection, 1995—; pvt. practice resume preparation, Nashville, 1982—; pvt. practice med. ins. filing svc., 1995—. Bd. govs. Interant. Biog. Ctr., Cambridge, Eng.; active Girls Scouts U.S., Paris, 1967-69; mem. ARC, Nashville, 1978, Christian Appalachian Project, Lancaster, Ky., 1986; mem. citizen's adv. coun. Am. Inst. Cancer Rsch., Washington, 1985. Mem. NAFE, Bus. and Profl. Womens Club (pres. 1965-73), Profl. Musicians Union, Womens Missionary Union (bd. dirs. Paris chpt. 1970-71), Internat. Platform Assn., Realtors Secs. Assn., Am. Biog. Inst. Inc. (rsch. bd. advisors), Internat. Biographical Centre of Cambridge,Eng. (bd. govs.). Baptist. Home: 812 Elissa Dr Nashville TN 37217-1323 Office: JG Martin Jr 208 3rd Ave N Fl 4 Nashville TN 37201-1617

ANDERSON, JIM See BERTELS, FRANK

ANDERSON, JOAN WELLIN FREED, communications executive, consultant, freelance journalist, writer; b. Shreveport, La., Aug. 18, 1945; d. Cyril and Rose (Friedman) F.; m. J. Warren Anderson, July 21, 1984 (div. 1991). BA in Gen. Studies, Tex. Christian U. Freelance reporter Sta. KERA-TV, Dallas, 1979-80, Fort Worth Star-Telegram, 1980-83, Fort Worth bur. Dallas Morning News, 1980-82; pub. rels. coord. Amon Carter Mus., Fort Worth, 1982; med. writer Tex. Coll. Osteo. Medicine, Fort Worth, 1982-85; freelance writer, 1985-87; producer video programs for pub. access cable channel, Ft. Worth, 1987-90; cmty. programming coord. cable TV channel City of Ft. Worth, 1988-90, chair; v.p. corp. comms. & health svcs. Comm. Osteo. Health System of Tex., 1990—; co-owner, playwright, actress Catered Theater, Character Acts. Bd. dirs. Am. Cancer Soc., 1982-84, Am. Heart Assn. 1993-94, Leadership Texas Class 1993, active Cancer Hotline, Cmty. Programming Adv. Coun.; facilitator for fair housing edn. and info. for Cmty. Housing Resource Bd., Ft. Worth; bd. dirs. Women's Haven of Tarrant County (Tex.) Inc., 1987-88, chmn. cmty. rels. com., 1988, Dispute Resolutions Svcs. Tarrant County (bd. dirs., chmn. cmty. rels. 1989-90); mem. Court Apptd. Spl. Adv. for Foster Children, 1986-88. Mem. Women in Comm., Inc. (past dir.), Internat. Assn. Bus. Communicators, Soc. for Theatrical Artists' Guidance and Enhancement, Advt. Club, Sigma Delta Chi. Author: (juvenile) Diggy Armadillo Goes to the Rodeo, Arnie Armadillo Goes to Cowtown; playwright: 1-800-4ADVICE, 1994; contbr. articles to popular mags. Office: Osteopathic Health System of Tex 3715 Camp Bowie Blvd Fort Worth TX 76107-3353

ANDERSON, JOHN KERBY, communications executive, radio talk show host; b. Berkeley, Calif., Dec. 7, 1951; s. John Albert and Mary Lorraine (Allen) A.; m. Susanne Elise Pardey, Aug. 3, 1974; children: Amy, Jonathan, Catherine. BS, Oreg. State U., 1974; MFS, Yale U., 1976; MA, Georgetown U., 1981. V.p. Probe Ministries, Richardson, Tex., 1976—; host syndicated radio program Probe, 1983—; host The Kerby Anderson Show Salem Radio Network, 1995-96; host NewsTalk satellite radio talk show Criswell Radio Network, 1989-93; adj. prof. Dallas Theol. Sem., 1986—; guest host Point of View satellite radio talk show, USA Radio Network. Author: Life, Death and Beyond, 1980, Genetic Engineering, 1982, Origin Science, 1987, Living Ethically in the 90s, 1990, Signs of Warning, Signs of Hope, 1994; contbg. author: Ency. Bibl. and Christian Ethics, 1987, Integrity of Heart, Skillfulness of Hands, 1994, Vital Contemporary Issues, 1994. Evangelical Christian. Office: Probe 1900 Firman Dr Richardson TX 75081-1869

ANDERSON, JOHN QUENTIN, rail transportation executive; b. Portland, Oreg., July 30, 1951; s. Vernon G. and Loretta (Bezdek) A.; m. Wendy Sargent, June 23, 1973; children: Mark, Karen, Benjamin, Meredith. BS in Mech. Engring., Stanford U., 1973; MBA, Harvard U., 1977. Ptnr. McKinsey & Co., L.A., 1977-90; exec. v.p. Burlington No. R.R., Ft. Worth, 1990-95; sr. v.p. Burlington No. Santa Fe corp., Ft. Worth, 1995-96; exec. v.p. CSX Transp., Jacksonville, Fla., 1996—; fed. appointee Nat. Coal Coun., Washington, 1992—. Dir. Joffrey Ballet, N.Y.C., L.A., 1987-90, Constl. Rights Found., L.A., 1988-90, Ft. Worth Ballet, 1994-96. Mem. Phi Beta Kappa. Office: CSXT 500 Water St Jacksonville FL 32202-4422

ANDERSON, JOHN ROY, grouting engineer; b. Culberson, N.C., June 22, 1919; s. Oscar Garfield and Lula Adeline (Russell) A.; m. Rheba Ulma Nichols, Dec. 31, 1951 (dec. Oct. 1989); children: Richard Allen, John Steven, Mark Garfield. Student, Berea Coll., 1950. From clk. to field inspector, then constrn. engr. Govt. Agys., 1941-51; project engr., mgr. Intrusion Prepakt, Cleve., 1951-58, 64-65; regional mgr./project mgr. Lee Turzillo Contracting Co., Breaksville, Ohio, 1957-60; engr. foundations, ops. mgr. Harza Engring. Co., Chgo., 1960-61, 65-68, 1972-86; foundations engr. Tippetts Abbett McCarthy Stratton, N.Y.C., 1961-64, 68-72. Mem. ASCE. Baptist. Home and Office: 7770 Skipper Ln Tallahassee FL 32311-4530

ANDERSON, KAREN SUZANNE SIGMON, elementary educator; b. Stone Mountain, Ga., Feb. 7, 1972; d. Powell Floyd and Virginia Diane (Clay) Sigmon; m. Aldred Charles Anderson Jr., Jan. 1, 1994. BA in Interdisciplinary English, Emory & Henry Coll., 1994. Cert. elem. and mid. sch. tchr., Va. 6th grade tchr. Cumberland (Va.) Mid. Sch., 1994—. Paul Douglass tchr. scholar, 1993-94. Mem. NEA, Va. Edn. Assn., Cumberland Edn. Assn. Republican. Home: Rt 2 Box 120 B Cumberland VA 23040

ANDERSON, KENNETH EDWIN, writer, educator; b. N.Y.C., Sept. 7, 1931; s. Murray Simon and Louise Merchant; m. Therese Catherine Tully, Apr. 18, 1955; children: Karen A. Dow, Kim A. Payne, Deborah A. Doggett, Barbara A. Stuehm. BS with honors, U. Fla., 1969, MA, 1970; PhD, Okla. State U., 1975. Instr. Eastern Ill. U., Charleston, 1970-71; editor engring. publs. Okla. State U., Stillwater, 1971-74, founder, dir. Native Am. program in engring., tech. and architecture, 1974-78; pres. Anderson Petroleum Svcs., Stillwater, 1978-87; tech. program designer TAD Tech. Svcs., Norman, Okla., 1987-89; instrnl. systems designer U. Okla., Norman, Okla., 1989-92; project dir., instrnl. sys. designer Redlands C.C., El Reno, Okla., 1995—; ptnr. Berger & Anderson Consultants, Yale, Okla., 1977—, Anderson-Baldwin Consultants, Tulsa, 1986—; cons. to energy cos. and Indian tribes on energy and environ. matters; presenter numerous seminars and tng. events for industry and govt. Co-author: Modern Petroleum, 1st edit., 1978, 3rd edit., 1992, Basic Processing Knowledge, 1979, Refinery Operations, 1979, Gas Handling and Field Processing, 1980, Tales From The Oil Patch, 1994; editor: Manual of Practical Pipeline Construction, 1982; contbr. more than 100 articles to profl. jours. Active Rock Knoll Homeowners Assn., Oklahoma City, 1991—, Marine Corps League, 1987—. With USMC, 1950, Sgt. Corps of Engrs., 1957. Named Most Disting. Grad., Coll. of Journalism, 1969, master presenter Nat. Inst. Staff and Orgn. Devel., U. Tex., 1996; recipient Grad. fellowship Poynter Found., 1970, Okla. Heritage Assn., 1974; recipient Citation for Excellence FAA, 1992. Mem. Internat. Platform Assn., Soc. Profl. Journalists, Marine Corps League, Am. Legion, Okla. Hist. Soc., Phi Kappa Phi, Omicron Delta Kappa, Phi Alpha Theta, Kappa Tau Alpha. Republican. Home and Office: 6505 Eastbourne Ln Oklahoma City OK 73132-2006

ANDERSON, KENNETH LEVERNE, military officer; b. Lumberton, N.C., Apr. 18, 1953; s. Everette Leverne Anderson and Treva Rose (Rogers) Taylor; m. Marinda Sue Woodard, July 11, 1987. BS in Social Sci., Campbell U., 1991; MS in Aero. Sci., Embry-Riddle Aero. U., 1995. Enlisted USMC, 1977, advanced through grades to gunnery sgt., 1992; aircraft mechanic HMLA-269 USMC, Jacksonville, N.C., 1978-80; helicopter crew chief in A flying status HMLA-167 USMC, Jacksonville, 1980-83; recruiter USMC, Charleston, W.Va., 1983-86; aviation student tng. monitor USMC, Jacksonville, 1986-92, aircraft maintenance supr. HMLA-167, 1992-95, tng. and ops. supr. H&HS MCAS New River, 1995—. Voting registration officer Hdqrs., MCAS New River, Jacksonville, 1996. Decorated Commendation medal, Achievement medals. Republican. Baptist. Home: 437 Candlewood Dr Jacksonville NC 28540

ANDERSON, KENNETH NORMAN, retired magazine editor, author; b. Omaha, July 10, 1921; s. Duncan McDonald and Letitia Jane (Steed) A.; m. Lois Elaine Harmon, Jan. 12, 1945; children: Eric Stephen, Randi Laine, Jani Jill, Douglas Duncan. Student, U. Omaha, 1939-41, Oreg. State Coll., 1943-44, Stanford U., 1944-45, Northwestern U. Coll. Medicine, 1945-46, U. Chgo., 1958-60. With U.S. Army Fin. Office, Nebr. and Mont., 1941-42; engring. aid U.S. Army C.E., Omaha, 1946; radio news editor Sta. KOIL, Omaha, 1946-47; bur. mgr. Internat. News Service, Omaha, 1947-56, Kansas City, Mo., 1947-56; spl. features editor Better Homes and Garden mag., 1956-57; assoc. editor Popular Mechanics mag., 1957-59; editor Today's Health mag., pub. by AMA, Chgo., 1959-65, Holt, Rinehart & Winston, N.Y.C., 1965-70; exec. dir. Coffee Info. Inst., N.Y.C., 1970-81; pres. Pubs. Editorial Svcs., Inc., Katonah, N.Y., 1981-90, The Editorial Guild, Inc., Katonah, N.Y., 1981-90; lectr. mag. writing New Sch. Social Research, 1959, NYU, 1960, Omaha U., 1961, Rensselaer Poly. Inst., 1964; cons. med. editor Ferguson Pub. Co., 1971-76. Author: (with others) Lawyers' Medical Cyclopedia, 1962, The Family Physician, 1963, Today's Health Guide, 1965, Pictorial Medical Guide, 1967, Field and Stream Guide to Physical Fitness, 1969, New Concise Family Medical and Health Guide, 1971, Complete Illustrated Book of Better Health, 1973, The New Complete Medical and Health Ency., 4 vols., 1977, The Sterno Guide to the Outdoors, 1977, Eagle Claw Fish Cookbook, 1978, Guide to Weight Control and Fitness, 1978, Newsweek Ency. of Family Health, 1980, Urdang Dictionary of Current Medical Terms, 1981, Pocket Guide to Coffee and Teas, 1982, Bantam Medical Dictionary, 1982, Mosby's Medical and Nursing Dictionary, 1982, Longman's Dictionary of Psychology and Psychiatry, 1983; editor: Hudson Health Newsletter, 1982—, Orphan Drugs, 1983, Gourmet Guide to Fish and Shellfish, 1984, Prentice-Hall Dictionary of Nutrition and Health, 1984, U.S. Military Operations, 1945-84, 1984, Mosby's Medical Encyclopedia, 1985, The Language of Sex, 1986, Industrial Medicine Desk Reference, 1986, New Pediatric Guide to Drugs & Vitamins, 1987, Symptoms after 40, 1987, Signet/Mosby Medical Encyclopedia, 1987, Consumer Guide Illustrated Medical Dictionary, 1988, Sex A to Z, 1989, Mosby's Medical, Nursing and Allied Health Dictionary, 4th edit., 1994, New York Public Library Desk Reference, 1989, Mosby's Pocket Dictionary of Medicine, Nursing and Allied Health, 1990, 2d edit., 1994, History of U.S. Military Operations Since World War , 1992, History of the U.S. Marines, 1992, Internat. Menu Speller, 1993, Internat. Dictionary of Food and Nutrition, 1993, Mosby's Medical, Nursing & Allied Health Dictionary, 4th Edition, 1994, Mosby's Pocket Medical Dictionary of Medicine, Nursing and Allied Health, 2d Edition, 1994, Wordsworth Dictionary of Sex, 1994; contbr. Grolier, Funk & Wagnalls Encys.; adv. editor Nutrition Today, 1965-75. Home and Office: 1278 Kingswood Blvd Mountain Home AR 72653-8083

ANDERSON, LARRY ARNOLD, mathematician, educator; b. Ames, Iowa, Nov. 2, 1945; s. Arnold J. and Jean (Borthwick) A.; m. Barbara J. Krohn, Aug. 12, 1972; children: Ginger, Jonathan. BS, Wheaton Coll., 1967; MS, Purdue U., 1969, PhD, 1974. Instr. Wheaton (Ill.) Coll., 1969-72; teaching asst. Purdue U., West Lafayette, Ind., 1972-74; asst. prof. math. Le Tourneau U., Longview, Tex., 1974-77, prof., chmn. math. and computer sci. divsn., 1977—. Mem. Assn. Computing Machinery, Math. Assn. Am. Office: LeTourneau U PO Box 7001 Longview TX 75607-7001

ANDERSON, LEE STRATTON, newspaper publisher, editor; b. Trenton, Ky., Dec. 15, 1925; s. Herbert Love and Corinne (Kirkpatrick) A.; m. Elizabeth McDonald, June 10, 1950; children: Corinne Elizabeth Anderson Adams, Mary Stewart. AB, U. Chattanooga, 1948. Reporter Chattanooga Free Press, 1942-48, assoc. editor, 1948-58, editor, 1958—, pub., 1990—. Author: Battles of Chickamauga and Chattanooga-1863, 1959, Israel: I Looked Over Jordan, 1996. Pres. Chattanooga Conv. and Visitor's Bur., 1958; chmn. Chattanooga chpt. ARC, 1968-70, United Way Campaign, 1979. With USAAF, World War II, maj. USAR. Recipient numerous awards for editls., lectrs. and civic svcs. Freedoms Found. Mem. Sigma Chi, Rotary (pres. Chattanooga 1964-65). Presbyterian (elder). Home: 220 N Crest Rd Chattanooga TN 37404-1018 Office: Chattanooga Free Press 400 E 11th St PO Box 1447 Chattanooga TN 37401-1447

ANDERSON, MARGERY LAWRENCE, computer programmer, consultant; b. Summit, N.J., Dec. 28, 1949; d. John R. and Margaret (Wiley) A. B of Music, Coll. Wooster, 1971; MEd, Xavier U., 1976. Analyst Cin. Bell, 1977-87; sr. cons. Circorp, Pitts., 1987-94; sr. programmer analyst Blue Cross and Blue Shield N.C., Durham, 1994—. Pres. Parkview Condo West Assn., Pitts., 1988-91; chmn. Sunday divsn. Tuesday Mus. Club, Pitts., 1992-94. Mem. Data Processing Mgmt. Assn. (chair auditing com. Ctrl. Carolina chpt. 1995), Chapel Hill Music Tchrs. Assn., Raleigh Music Club, Toastmasters (v.p. edn. 1995-96). Presbyterian. Office: PO Box 2291 Durham NC 27702-2291

ANDERSON, MARK STEPHEN, recovery company executive; b. Rochester, N.Y., Oct. 9, 1948; s. Ernest T. and Wanda E. (Blake) A.; m. Donna M. Heinold, June 14, 1969 (div. Feb. 1989); children: Eric S., Dana M.; m. Karen Ann Demers, Aug. 6, 1992. BA in Sociology/Psychology, Houghton Coll., 1970; MTh in Bibl. Study, Inst. Bibl. Studies, San Bernardino, Calif., 1974. Bus. mgr. Athletes in Action, Indpls., 1970-74; v.p. sales Kinman of Indpls., 1974-81; pres. Internat. Recovery Assocs., Inc., Riviera Beach, Fla., 1982—; owner, CEO Air Cushions U.S.A. Inc., Lake Park, Fla., 1989—, Sea-Air-Land Recovery Inc., Lake Park, Fla., 1991—; founder Eagle Prodns. Internat., 1994. Author: Recovery Operations Update, 1984, 85; editor: We the Professionals, Book 2, 1986, Principles of Towing and Recovery, 1989, 90; author, compiler: Towing and Recovery - Heavy Duty Manual, 1991. Mem. Towing and Recovery Assn. Am. (Network instr. 1987—, Presdl. award for excellence 1992, 94). Home: 313 Lake Cir No Palm Beach FL 33408-5235 Office: Air Cushions USA Inc 1401 Old Dixie Hwy Ste 6 Lake Park FL 33403-1933

ANDERSON, MARK WENDELL, gastroenterologist; b. Berwyn, Ill., Feb. 20, 1964; s. Wendell Carl and Joyce Mae (Henn) A.; m. Michelle Gay Kreiner, May 9, 1992. BS in Biology, Hardin-Simmons U., Abilene, Tex., 1986; MD, Southwestern Med. Sch., Dallas, 1990. Cert. bd. internal medicine. Resident, intern in internal medicine U. Iowa, Iowa City, 1990-93; fellow in gasteroenterology U. Okla. Hosp., Oklahoma City, 1993—. Mem. Alpha Omega Alpha. Office: Carolina Gastroenterology 30 Memorial Medical Dr Greenville SC 29605

ANDERSON, MARTHA JEAN, media specialist; b. Greenville, S.C., May 15, 1946; d. Benjamin Mason and Gladys (Harling) A. BS, Appalachian State U., Boone, N.C., 1968; M.Librarianship, Emory U., Atlanta, 1974, Diploma Advanced Study in Librarianship, 1983. Libr. Arlington Schs., Atlanta, 1968-70, Archer Public High Sch., Atlanta, 1970-74; media specialist Woodmont High Sch. Greenville County Sch. Dist., Piedmont, S.C., 1974-76; media specialist Berea High Sch. Greenville County Sch. Dist., Greenville, S.C., 1976-80; media specialist Hillcrest High Sch. Greenville County Sch. Dist., Simpsonville, S.C., 1980—. Recipient Citation award S.C. Occupational Info. Coord. Com., 1988. Mem. NEA, S.C. Assn. Sch. Librs., S.C. Edn. Assn., Greenville County Edn. Assn., Riedville (S.C.) Hist. Soc. (charter mem., historian), Rotary, Iota Alpha Delta Kappa (historian 1978-80, 88-90, 92-94, v.p. 1980-82, pres. 1982-84, 94-96, sgt.-at-arms 1990-92). Methodist. Home: 537 Harrison Bridge Rd Simpsonville SC 29680-7004 Office: Hillcrest High Sch 3665 S Industrial Dr Simpsonville SC 29681-3238

ANDERSON, MICHAEL CURTIS, computer industry analyst; b. Belton, Tex., Nov. 19, 1953; s. Curtis Raymond Anderson and Joan Evelyn (Sievers) Bleuer; m. Debra Beth Shlaes, June 7, 1975; children: Sara Joyce, John Michael. BA cum laude, Augustana Coll., 1975; postgrad., U. Iowa, 1982—. Mgmt. sci. analyst Deere & Co., Moline, Ill., 1975-80, mgr. office automation, 1980-88; sr. planner office systems IBM, Roanoke, Tex., 1988-89, mgr. strategy and requirements, planning-office systems, 1989-90; program dir. office info. systems Gartner Group, Stamford, Conn., 1990-93; dir. mkt. rsch. & competitive analysis Ameritech, Chgo., 1993-94; v.p., rsch. dir. adv. techs. Gartner Group, Stamford, Conn., 1994—. Ill. State scholar, 1971, I.B. McGladrey Accountancy award McGladrey-Hendrickson, 1974. Home: 2109 Reynolds Dr Colleyville TX 76034-5790 Office: Gartner Group 222 Las Colinas Blvd W Ste 1650 Irving TX 75039-5436

ANDERSON, NANCY, musuem administrator; married; 3 children. BA in History, Wellesley Coll., 1962; MA in History, Coll. William and Mary, 1968. Tchr. history high sch., 1963-65; newspaper columnist, freelance writer, 1974-82; exec. dir. Mus. Arts and Scis., Macon, Ga., 1982—; grant reviewer Inst. Mus. Svcs., 1986-88. Bd. dirs. Ga. Humanities Coun., 1991-96; bd. dirs., mem. exec. com. Ga. Citizens for Arts, 1991-96; mem. visual art adv. panel Ga. Coun. for Arts, 1987-90; vol. Ga. Hist. Soc.; com. chmn. Assn. Jr. Leagues; a developer Rent-A-Teen, 1970, Mid. Ga. Coun. on Drugs, 1971, Vol. Macon, 1973, Ga. Jubilee, 1974, Hay House, 1979, Celebratiton-at-Sta., 1980; pres., trustee Ga. Women Achievement; mem. Macon-Bibb County Interracial Coun., Macon Progress. mem. Lamar lectr. com. Mercer U.; mem. Leadership Ga., 1975. Recipient Vol. on Yr. award Vol. Macon, 1977, Sta. WMAZ, 1978, spl. award Macon Heritage Found., 1978, cultural award Macon Arts Alliance, 1993. Mem. Am. Assn. Mus. (panelist 1990, 92, ethics commn. 1992-94, Nancy Hanks Meml. award for profl. excellence 1989), Ga. Assn. Mus. and Galleries (bd. dirs. 1983-85, presenter 1985, 92, Profl. of Yr. award 1986), Southeastern Mus. Conf. (panelist 1988, 90-95, Ga. rep. 1985-87, sec. coun. 1990-94), Am. Assn. Mus. Vols. (S.E. regional chmn. 1989—), Career Women's Network, Rotary. Office: Mus Arts and Scis 4182 Forsyth Rd Macon GA 31210-4806

ANDERSON, NANCY DIXON, librarian; b. Clarkesville, Ga., Oct. 7, 1938; d. Sherman Allen and Willie Mae (Black) Dixon; m. David Morris Anderson, Nov. 23, 1958 (div. June 1978); children: Wendy, Laurie, David Jr. BS in Mid. Grades Edn., Brenau Coll., 1981; MEd in Ednl. Media, U. Ga., 1985. Asst. prof. humanities, libr. Brenau Coll., Gainesville, Ga., 1979-87; also acad. tutor Learning Disability Ctr., 1985-87; head libr. Hightower Libr. Gordon Coll., Barnesville, Ga., 1987—. Children's ch. dir. 1st Presbyn. Ch., Gainesville, 1983-87; v.p. Friends of Libr., Barnesville/Lamar County, 1991; pres. Newcomers Club, Gainesville, 1974, Phoenix Soc., Ga. Fedn. Women's Club, Gainesville, 1978; pub. chmn. Barnesville Women's League, 1992-94; pres. Barnesville Garden Club, 1992; mem. Community Svcs. Bd., Barnesville, 1994—. Mem. Ga. Libr. Assn., Ctr. Ga. Associated Librs. Consortium (pres. 1992-93). Home: 236 Harrell Cir Barnesville GA 30204-1751 Office: Gordon Coll Hightower Libr 419 College Dr Barnesville GA 30204-1746

ANDERSON, NANCY FIX, history educator; b. Dallas, Tex, Aug. 23, 1941; d. George Joseph and Frances Bartlett Fix; m. Clifford Hamilton Anderson; children: Michael, Kathryn. BA, Stanford U., 1965; MA, U. Calif., Irvine, 1967; PhD, Tulane U., 1973. Asst. prof. history U. New Orleans, 1979-87; assoc. prof. history Loyola U., New Orleans, La., 1987--. Author: Woman Against Women in Victorian England, 1987; contbr. articles to profl. jours. Recipient Walter Graddock prize, Southwestern Hist. Assn, 1989, William Langer prize, Psychohistory Review, 1983, fellow Am. Inst. Indian Studies, 1990. Mem. Am. Hist. Assn., So. Assn. Women Historians, North Am. Conf. on British Studies, Conf. Group Women's History. Office: Loyola U 6363 St Charles Ave New Orleans LA 70118-6143

ANDERSON, NILS, JR., former government official, retired business executive, industrial historian; b. Plainfield, N.J., Jan. 28, 1914; s. Nils and Marguerite (Stephens) A.; m. Jean Derby Ferris, July 30, 1938; children: Nils III (dec.), Derby Ferris, Stephens Massie, Ward Reynolds. Grad., Lawrenceville and Loomis Schs.; BA, Williams Coll., 1937; postgrad., Colo. Sch. Mines, George Washington U. Law Sch., Alexander Hamilton Inst. With Debevoise-Anderson Co., summers 1927-28; cadet engr. S.S. Iron Ranger Isthmian Steamship Co., summer 1930; cadet engr., chemist Koppers Co., Pitts., summers 1932-37; sales engr. Bakelite Corp., 1937-41; chemicals adminstr. War Prodn. Bd., 1941-45, chief adhesives sect., 1942, chief plastics branch, 1944; ptnr. Trand Plastics, 1955-56; bd. dirs. Am. Plastics Co.; pres. Debevoise-Anderson Co. Inc., 1950-60, chmn., 1965-87, also bd. dirs.; pres. Port Ore Processing Co., 1965-87, Fairfield Sales Corp. and Cia Minera Dominica C por A, 1960-65; bd. dirs. Sturm-Ruger Co., Inc.; adv. chemical divsn. U.S. Dept. Agr. stockpile and shipping br., adhesive and plastic, textile, paper and pulp, plywood and furniture industry adv. coms., 1941-44; mem. 1st U.S. trade mission to Ea. Europe, 1965. Author: North American Coke Today, Chemicals, Metals and Men; contbr. tech. articles on plastics and adhesives to profl. jours. and encyclopedias. Trustee, pres. U.S. Naval War Coll. Found., 1988-89; trustee Wakeman Meml. Assn. Southport, Conn.; past pres. Sasquanaug Assn., Southport; founder, past chmn. Southport Conservancy. Mem. ASME, Coke Oven Mgrs. Assn. (England), Am. Chem. Soc., Iron and Steel Engrs. Assn., Am. Coke and Coal Chemicals Inst. (hon.), Newcomen Soc. in N. Am., Gen. Soc. Colonial Wars, Soc. of War of 1812, Pilgrim Soc., Pa. Soc., Pequot Yacht Club (Southport), Fairfield (Conn.) Country Club, Univ. Club (N.Y.C.), Links Club (N.Y.C.), Alpha Delta Phi. Republican. Episcopalian.

ANDERSON, PAUL MILTON, steel company executive; b. Richland, Wash., Apr. 1, 1945; s. Paul Milton and Elfrieda (Blehm) A.; m. Kathleen Sue Kinzel, Feb. 25, 1984; children: Wendy Christine, Heather Colleen. BSME, U. Wash., 1967; MBA, Stanford U., 1969. Mgr. product planning Ford Motor Co., Dearborn, 1969-77; various positions Tex. Eastern Corp., Houston, 1977-85, v.p., 1985-87, sr. v.p., 1987-89; v.p. fin., chief fin. officer Inland Steel Industries, Chgo., 1990-91; exec. v.p. Panhandle Eastern Corp., 1991-94, pres., 1994—; pres. Panhandle Eastern Pipe Line Co., 1991—; pres., CEO Panenergy, Houston. Mem. Interstate Natural Gas Assn. Am., Inst. Gas Tech. *

ANDERSON, PETER JOSEPH, lawyer; b. Camden, N.J., Mar. 15, 1951; s. Lester Ryan and Rose Helen; m. Sheila K.; children: Elizabeth Rose, Hannah Louise. BA, Dickinson Coll., 1972; JD, Dickinson Sch. of Law, 1975. Bar: Pa. 1975, Ga. 1978, U.S. Dist. Ct. (ea. dist.) Pa. 1978, U.S. Dist. Ct. (no. dist.) Ga. 1978, U.S. Ct. Appeals (11th cir.) 1978, U.S. Tax Ct. 1986, U.S. Supreme Ct. 1989. Dep. dist. atty. Dist. Attys. Office, Harrisburg, Pa., 1974-77; ptnr. Peterson, Dillard, Young, Self & Asselin, Atlanta, 1977-92, Sutherland, Asbill & Brennan, Atlanta, 1992—. Mem. ABA (subcom. securities litigation 1978—), Ga. Bar Assn., Pa. Bar Assn., Atlanta Bar Assn., Assn. Trial Lawyers Am. Republican. Roman Catholic. Home: 1503 Emory Rd NE Atlanta GA 30306-2429 Office: Sutherland Asbill & Brennan 999 Peachtree St NE Ste 2300 Atlanta GA 30309-3964

ANDERSON, RICHARD EDMUND, city manager, management consultant; b. Ferndale, Mich., Dec. 23, 1938; s. Richard H. and Carolyn Jeanne (Figg) A.; children: Pam, Mark, Linda. B.A., Mich. State U., 1962; postgrad. in advanced mgmt., Harvard U., 1979. Aide to mgr. City of St. Petersburg, Fla., 1962-64; adminstrv. asst. City of Ft. Lauderdale, Fla., 1964-67, dep. mgr., 1967-75, city mgr., 1975-80; v.p. Fla. Innovation Group, Tampa, 1980-81; pres. Integrated Systems Assocs., Inc., Ft. Lauderdale, 1981-90; city mgr. City of Florida City, Fla., 1990-94, City of Brooksville, Fla., 1995—. Contbr. articles to profl. jours. Mem. Internat. City Mgmt. Assn. Office: 26 S Brooksville Ave Brooksville FL 34601-2904

ANDERSON, RICHARD MCLEMORE, internist; b. Gainesville, Fla., Mar. 3, 1930; s. Montgomery Drummond and Myrtle (McLemore) A.; m. Leewood Shaw, Mar. 21, 1959; children: Richard McLemore Jr., Bruce Dexter. BS, U. Fla., 1951; MD, Emory U., 1958. Diplomate Am. Bd. Internal Medicine. Chief of staff Alachua Gen. Hosp., Gainesville, Fla., 1973-75; internist Gainesville, Fla., 1962—; Chmn. of bd. Santa Fe Health Care, Gainesville, 1984-91; bd. dirs. AV Med. Santa Fe. Pres. Rotary Club of Gainesville, 1980-81. Capt. USAF, 1951-54. Mem. AMA, Alachua County Med. Soc. (v.p. 1972), Fla. Med. Assn., Am. Soc. Internal Medicine. Presbyterian. Office: 106 SW 10th St Gainesville FL 32601-6201

ANDERSON, ROBIN YOUNG, pharmacist; b. Columbia, S.C., Sept. 10, 1959; d. Samuel James Jr. and Mary Ann (Tyler) Y.; m. David Allen Anderson Sept. 2, 1989; 1 child, Samuel Warren. BS in Biology, Coll. Charleston, S.C., 1981; BS in Pharmacy, Med. U. S.C., Charleston, 1985. Rep. pharm. products, territory mgr. Roche Labs., Greenville, S.C., 1985-89; sr. territory mgr. Roche Labs., Columbia, S.C., 1992—; prof. rep. Park-Davis, Daleville, Ala., 1989-91. Contbr. articles to profl. jours. Mem. S.C. Soc. Health Sys. Pharmacy, S.C. Pharm. Assn. Methodist. Home: 3423 Duncan St Columbia SC 29205-2705

ANDERSON, RON JOE, hospital administrator, physician, educator; b. Chickasha, Okla., Sept. 6, 1946; s. Ted J. and Ruby (Harston) Anderson Benjamin; m. Sue Ann Blakely, Apr. 12, 1975; children: Sarah Elizabeth, Daniel Jerrod, John Charles. B.S. in Pharmacy, Southwest U. Okla., 1969; M.D., U. Okla., 1973. Diplomate Am. Bd. Internal Medicine, Am. Bd. Geriatrics. Intern U. Tex. Southwestern Med. Sch., Parkland Meml. Hosp., VA Hosp., Dallas, 1973-74, resident and chief resident in internal medicine, 1974-76; asst. prof. internal medicine U. Tex. Health Sci. Ctr., Dallas, 1976-81, asst. dean clin. affairs, 1979-82, prof. internal medicine, 1981—; med. dir. ambulatory-emergency services Dallas County Hosp. Dist., 1979-82, acting. med. dir., 1981-82, CEO, 1982—; chmn. Tex. Bd. Health, 1991-93; mem. task force on teaching hosps. Tex. Hosp. Assn., 1982—, task force on indigent health care, 1983-86; cons. on high blood pressure Am. Heart Assn., 1981-83; advisor Tex. Assn. Physician Assts.; chmn. Neighborhood Clinic Cooperating Com., Dallas, 1980-82; bd. dirs. Children's Oncology Services Tex., Dallas, 1982-86, Addison, Carrollton, Coppell, Farmers Branch chpt. Am. Heart Assn., 1978-80; mem. Tex. Gov.'s Task Force on Indigent Health Care, 1983-86, Tex. Health and Human Services Coordinating Council, 1983-86, Tex. Cancer Council, 1985-87, Spl. Task Force on Future of Long-Term Health Care for Tex., Mayor's Task Force on Internat. Devel., Dallas AIDS Planning Commn.; mem. Tex. Bd. Health, 1983—, chmn., 1983-87, 91—; mem. Dallas Council on Alcoholism and Drug Abuse, 1982, bd. dirs., 1982—, v.p., 1986, pres., 1987-88; mem. adv. com. program to improve maternal and infant care in South Robert Wood Johnson Found. Contbr. articles to profl. jours. Bd. dirs. Project Independence, Greater Dallas Ahead, 1985—, Kaiser Found. Health Plan Tex., 1991, Interfaith Housing Coalition; preceptor Dallas Ind. Sch. Dist. Talented and Gifted Program, 1977; mem. Dallas Commrs. Ct. Task Force on Mental Patients, 1979, Dallas Alliance, 1986—, Dallas Assembly, 1984—, Hogg Found. for Mental Health Commn. on Community Care of Mentally Ill, 1987—; adv. bd. Dallas Challenge, 19846; co-chmn. Tex. Response, 1985—; chmn. mission bd. 1st Bapt. Ch. of Oak Cliff, and others. Recipient Tex. Aging Leadership award, 1987, Community Service award Community and Migrant Health Ctrs. Tex., 1986, Tex. Leadership in Aging award Tex. 6th Annual Joint Conf. on Aging, 1987, Disting. Alumnus award S.W. U. Okla., 1987, James E. Peavy Meml. award Tex. Pub. Health Assn., 1988, Dallas Hist. Soc. award, Headliner award Dallas Press Club, Health Care Profl. of Yr. award Tex. Nurses Assn., 1990; named to Disting. Alumni Hall of Fame Southwestern Okla. State U., 1987. Fellow ACP; mem. AMA, Nat. Assn. Pub. Hosps. (bd. dirs., exec. com., chmn.-elect 1991, Safety Net awrd 1990), Nat. Pub. Health and Hosp. Inst. (bd. dirs., chmn. devel. com., chmn. 1991), Tex. Med. Assn., Dallas County Med. Soc., Am. Soc. Internat. Medicine, Soc. Gen. Internal Medicine, Dallas-Ft. Worth Hosp. Coun. (chmn.-elect 1991), Salesmanship Dallas Club. Democrat. Baptist. Home: 1022 Wind Ridge St Duncanville TX 75137 Office: Dallas County Hosp Dist Parkland Meml Hosp 5201 Harry Hines Blvd Dallas TX 75235-7708

ANDERSON, RONALD EARL, precision machining company executive; b. Highland Park, Mich., Apr. 21, 1948; s. Ernest Sigfried and Edith Mae (Hall) A.; m. Janet Ellen Lee, Sept. 26, 1987. Student, Brevard Community Coll., 1966-68. Owner, mgr. Fla. TV Sales & Svcs., Cape Canaveral, 1969-71; sales rep. Lykes Electronics, Cocoa, Fla., 1972-74; v.p. Armorflite Southeast, Inc., Cocoa, 1974-81; owner, pres., chief exec. officer Flite Technology, Inc., Cocoa, 1981—; CEO, pres. Internat. Trade Ctr. Ctrl. Fla., Inc., Cocoa; cons. Shear Precision, Inc., Cocoa Beach, Fla., 1977-85; dir. ops. U.S. Fgn. Free Trade Sub-Zone 136-A; pres. Fla. Leasing Svcs., Cocoa, 1978-81. Patentee micrometer devices. Reservist Fla. Game and Fish Commn., Ocala, 1988-93; aux. officer Cocoa Police Dept., 1988-90; vol. Guardian Ad Littem Program 18th Cir. Ct., 1990—; mem. health and human svcs., vice chair bd. dirs. State of Fla. Health and Rehab. Svcs., 1993—; bd. dirs. Leadership Brevard, 1995—, Space Coast World Trade Coun., Brevard Workforce Devel., 1996—; mem. East Coast Zool. Soc. Fla., Founders Cir.; exec. dir. Fla. Bus. Fedn., Inc.; float host Cape Canaveral Hosp. Found. Mardi Gras, 1994—. Mem. ASME, Am. Chem. Soc., Soc. Plastics Engrs., Fla. Ctr. for Children and Youth, Internat. Platform Assn., Brevard County Mfg. Assn. (bd. mem. elect 1993-94), Soc. Plastics Industry (mem. internat. trade adv. com. 1993-95, dir. ea. divsn.), Cocoa Beach Area C. of C. (bd. dirs. 1996—, chair govt. and ednl. affairs com. 1996—). Republican. Episcopalian. Office: Flite Tech Inc 411 Shearer Blvd Cocoa FL 32922-7249

ANDERSON, RUSSELL LEE, family medicine educator; b. Lincoln County, Ky., June 14, 1936; s. Russell Craig and Mary Louise (Chevillet) A.; m. Mary Carolyn Hamilton, Dec. 31, 1954; children: R. Scott, Sherryl Lynn Beatty, James Walker, Mary Elizabeth Cherry. BSc in pharmacy, Univ. Cin., 1959; MD, Univ. Ky., 1969. Diplomate Am. Bd. Family Practice. Pharmacist Elsmere Drugs, Elsmere, Ky., 1960-65; physician Page Medical Clinic, Luray, Va., 1970-76; asst. prof. Univ. Ala. Sch. Medicine, Tuscaloosa, 1976-78, residency program dir., 1979-81, chair dept. family medicine, 1981-89, assoc. dean academic affairs, 1991-93, dir. occupational medicine, 1993-95; prof., head family medicine La. State Univ. Sch. Medicine, New Orleans, 1995—; cons. Family Practice R.A.P., Kansas City, Mo., 1982—; pres. Capstone Health Svcs., Tuscaloosa, 1993-95, v.p., 1987-93. Author (book chpt.): Primary Care of Families, 1995; contbr. articles to profl. jours. Fellow Am. Acad. Family Physicians; mem. Ala. Acad. Family Practice (bd. dirs. 1988-95), Am. Medical Assn., Soc. Tchrs. Family Medicine, Am. Coll. Occupational & Environ. Medicine. Home: 78270 Highway 1081 Covington LA 70435 Office: La State U Sch Medicine Dept Family Medicine 1542 Tulane Ave New Orleans LA 70112-2822

ANDERSON, SHARON RICE, special education educator; b. Nagoya, Japan, Aug. 6, 1948; d. Marvin E. and Oma (Brown) Rice; m. Michael Anderson, Nov. 19, 1990 (div. June 1993). AA, Ctrl. Tex. Coll.; BS in Social Scis., Mary Hardin Coll.; MS in Spl. Edn., Jacksonville State U. Tchr. U.S history & govt. Cobb Jr. H.S., Anniston, Ala., 1973-85; tchr. spl. edn. Talladega (Ala.) H.S., 1986—. Vol. Coosa Valley Juvenile Ctr., Anniston, 1973-74; tchr. CCD Cath. Ch., Anniston, 1984—; mem. Greater Talladega Multicultural Concerns com., 1994—. Mem. AAUW, NEA (conv. del. 1983), Ala. Edn. Assn. (conv. del. 1978-85, pres. Anniston chpt. 1983-84, v.p. 1982-83), Nat. Mus. Women in Arts. Republican. Roman Catholic. Office: Talladega HS 1177 Mcmillan St E Talladega AL 35160-3128

ANDERSON, STEVEN HUNTER, media relations professional; b. Washington, Feb. 3, 1962; s. Alfred Joseph and Frances Helen (Harrison) Mendez; m. Nancy Louise Sowders, July 29, 1989. BA in Organizational Communications, James Madison U., 1985. Pub. affairs asst. Gannett Co., Inc., Arlington, Va., 1984-85, corp. writer, 1985-88; account exec. Jaffe Assocs., Washington, 1988; promotion ops. specialist USA Today, Arlington, 1988-89, pub. rels. coord., 1989-90, mgr. pub. rels., 1990-91, mgr. media rels., 1991-95, dir. media rels., 1995—. Mem. Internat. Assn. Bus. Communicators. Republican. Roman Catholic. Office: USA Today 1000 Wilson Blvd Arlington VA 22209-3901

ANDERSON, THOMAS JEFFERSON, publisher, rancher, public speaker, syndicated columnist; b. Nashville, Nov. 7, 1910; s. William J. and Nancy Lucas (Joseph) A.; m. Carolyn Montague Jennings, Dec. 24, 1936; 1 child, Carolyn A. Porter. BA, Vanderbilt U., 1934; LLB (hon.), Bob Jones U., 1967. Securities salesman Gray-Shillinglaw & Co., Nashville, 1934-36; salesman Nunn-Schwab Securities Co., 1936-39; mgr. unlisted securities dept. J.C. Bradford Co., 1939-43; So. sales mgr. So. Agriculturist, Nashville, 1943-47; owner, pub. So. Farm Publs., 1947-71, Farm and Ranch mag., 1953-63, Am. Way Features (nat. newspaper syndicate), Straight Talk (weekly newsletter Anderson Enterprises); radio commentator, world traveler. Author: Straight Talk, 1967, Silence Is Not Golden It's Yellow, 1973. Vice presdl. candidate Am. Party, 1972, nat. chmn., 1976-78, presdl. nominee, 1976; mem. coun. John Birch Soc., 1959-76; nat. chmn. We-the-People, 1966-72. Lt. USN, 1943-46. Recipient Liberty awards Congress of Freedom, 1964—, Pub. Address award Freedoms Found. Valley Forge, 1959, 60; named Man of Yr. God and Country Rally, 1966. Mem. Am. Agrl. Editors Assn. (pres. 1954), Phi Delta Theta (pres. Tenn. Alpha chpt. 1934, province pres. 1936-39), Omicron Delta Kappa. Baptist. Office: Jupiter Inlet Colony 128 Lighthouse Dr Jupiter FL 33469-3511

ANDERSON, VIOLET HENSON, artist, educator; b. June 8, 1931; m. Charles A. Anderson, 1953. Grad., U. Tenn., Knoxville. Tchr. art Oak Ridge (Tenn.) Sch. System, 1953-54, Andrew Jackson Elem. Sch., Nashville, 1969-79; originator, dir. Andrew Jackson Art Show, Old Hickory, Tenn., 1972-79. One-woman shows include Nashville Bd. Edn., 1972, Cookeville (Tenn.) Art Ctr., 1972, Tenn. Art Gallery, 1983, 88, Brentwood (Tenn.) Libr., 1991; exhibited in group shows at Falls Creek Falls State Park, Tenn., 1984, 86, Castner Knott Art Festival, Nashville, 1983-89, 90, Downtown Arts Gallery, Nashville, 1989, Dogwood Art Festival, Knoxville, 1993, 94, 95, Summer Lights Art Festival, Nashville, 1989, 92, 93, 94; also 1928 paintings and prints in pvt. and pub. collections in 38 states and 9 fgn. countries; work featured in Nashville Banner, Chattanooga Free Press, Knoxville News Sentinel, others. Named Golden Poet, World of Poetry, 1989-92; included in Best Poems of 90s and Disting. Poets of Am., 1993 Nat. Libr. Poetry, Best Poems of 95, Nat. Libr. Poetry, 1996 Best Poems. Mem. Tenn. Watercolor Soc., Tenn. Art League (past officer), Friends of Tenn. Art League (bd. dirs., 1st v.p.), Cumberland Art Soc., Tenn. Artists Assn., Artists Guild, Hendersonville, Nat. Women's Caucus for Art, Mid. Tenn. Com., Nat. Mus. of Women in the Arts (charter mem., slides and photos in libr. archives), Knoxville Arts Coun., Donelson-Hermitage C. of C., Stones River Woman's Club, Internat. Soc. Poets (charter mem.), Delta Zeta (past province alumnae dir.), Alpha Delta Kappa.

ANDERSON, WILLIAM HARVEY, JR., secondary education educator; b. Greenwood, S.C., Aug. 22, 1951; s. William Harvey, Sr. and Margaret Jean (Long) A.; m. Brenda Mae Sharp, Apr. 13, 1974; children: Sarah Elizabeth, Grace Rebecca. BS in Oceanography, U.S. Naval Acad., 1973. Commd. ensign USN, 1973, advanced through grades to comdr., 1988; flt. instr. USN, various cities, 1973-83; spl. weapons ofcr. USS John F. Kennedy USN, Norfolk, Va., 1983-85; ops. ofcr., Patrol Squad. 49 USN, Jacksonville, Fla., 1985-88; dir. Joint Reconnaisse Ctr., U.S. Atlantic Command USN, Norfolk, 1988-91, commanding ofcr. Nuclear Weapons Tng. Group, Atlantic, 1991-95; ret. USN, 1995; tchr. secondary sch. Sullivan County Dept. of Edn., Blountville, Tenn., 1995-96. Decorated Def. Meritorious Svc. medals, Navy Achievement medal, Navy Commendation medal. Republican. Baptist. Home: 120 Charlton Ct Bluff City TN 37618 Office: Sullivan E High Sch 4180 Weaver Pike Bluff City TN 37618-2031

ANDERSON, YASMIN LYNN MULLIS, educational consultant, small business owner; b. Roanoke, Va., Oct. 5, 1953; d. Lonnie Cecil Jr. and Sarah Frances (Cunningham) Mullis; m. Jerry Doyle Anderson, Mar. 1, 1991; 1 child from previous marriage, R. Allen. BS in Edn., U Tenn., 1975, postgrad., 1989-90, 93. Employment counselor State Dept. Employment Security, Knoxville, Tenn., 1975-79; GED instr. Loudon (Tenn.) County Schs., 1979-81; edn. specialist Tenn. Valley Authority, Knoxville, 1979-94; pvt. practice Knoxville, 1991—; ednl. cons. Acad. Innovations, Santa Barbara, Calif., 1991—; edn. specialist Inclusion for All Children Task Force, Nashville, 1992—; advisor tech./Prep. Consortium, Tenn., 1993—; presenter in field; sr. cons. Mary Kay Cosmetics. Mem. ASCD, AAUW, Am. Vocat. Assn. (presenter). Baptist. Home and Office: 1236 Lovell View Dr Knoxville TN 37932-2591

ANDERSON-CERMIN, CHERYL KAY, orthodontics educator; b. Osceola, Wis., Aug. 28, 1956; d. Darrell Duane and Barbara Carolyn (Paulson) Peterson; m. Paul Bradley Anderson, Aug. 12, 1978 (div. June 1986); m. Jonathan A. Cermin, Dec. 31, 1995; 1 child, Hayley Kristine. AA, Normandale C.C., Bloomington, Minn., 1977; BS, U. Minn., 1985, DDS, 1986; cert. in advanced grad. studies, Boston U., 1990. Intern Sch. Dental Medicine Harvard U., Boston, 1986-87; pvt. practice, Boston, 1988-90; rsch. fellow U. Tex. S.W. Med. Sch., Dallas, 1990-91, asst. prof. orthodontics, dir. orthodontics, 1991—. Bd. dirs. Life Enhancement for People, Dallas, 1993-94; sec. ch. coun. Shepherd of Life Luth. Ch., Arlington, Tex., 1993-94. Mem. ADA, Am. Assn. Orthodontists, Am. Cleft Palate Assn.

ANDERSON-MANN, SHELLEY N., institutional review specialist; b. Cleve., Jan. 21, 1964; d. William Henry and Frances Louise (Anderson) Mann. AS in Computer Sci., El Centro, 1990, AA in Acctg., 1990; BS in Sociology, Paul Quinn Coll., 1992, BSBA, 1992; MSI in Interdisciplinary Study, Dallas Bapt. U.-U. Tex., Arlington, 1993. Youth supr. City of Dallas Park and Recreation, 1979-87; instnl. rev. officer U.S. Dept. Edn., 1979-87; acct. asst. Dallas County Sheriff Adult Probation Dept., Dallas, 1984-89; claims asst. Social Security Adminstrn., Dallas, 1989—; founder Shelley Anderson-Mann Computer Ctr., Paul Quinn Coll., 1992; exec. dir. Shelley's Enterprises, Inc.; founder, pres. Grant Me the Freedom Domestic Violence Rape Recovery Tng. Unit, Let's Make it Safe, In my Brother's House, Helping Hands Found., Lancaster, Tex. Author: DQB Procedural Manual, 1991 (Yes award 1991), EPA Archive Manual, 1991 (Promotion award 1991). Mem. exec. bd., vol. City of Dallas Parks and Recreation; vol. Youth Village Criminal Justice, Dallas Ind. Sch. Dist., Dallas County Juvenile Assn., Youth in Action, Dallas; founder Grant Me the Freedom, 1996. Recipient commendation Dallas Police Dept., 1988, Dept. of Treasury, 1988, award City of Dallas Vol. of the Dallas, 1989, Am. Disting. Women, 1990, Bronze medal for gymnastics, Admired Women of Decade award, 1996-97. Mem. NAFE, NOW, Am. Mgmt. Assn. (1st place 1991), Nat. Coun. Colored Women, Nat. Assn. Negro Women, Liberty U. Charter, Student Free Enterprise (1st place 1991), Distributive Edn. Club (1st place 1991), Internat. Platform Assn., Grant Me the Freedom Let's Make It Safe in My Brother's Place Helping Hand Found. (founder). Democrat. Baptist. Home: PO Box 41247 Dallas TX 75241-0247

ANDERT-SCHMIDT, DARLENE, management consultant and trainer. BA in Bus. Mgmt. and Communications, Alverno Coll., Milw., 1983; M in Adminstrn., Cen. Mich. U., 1993. Cert. fin. mgr.; cert. mgmt. cons. Pres., owner Dance in Exercise, Inc., Milw., 1980-85; security sales Prudential Bache and The Equitable, Milw., 1985-86; stockbroker Merrill Lynch, Ft. Myers, Fla., 1986-89; trainer, cons. Bus. & Industry Svcs., Ft. Myers, 1989; pres. mgmt. Concepts Mgmt., Cape Coral, Fla., 1989—; pres. mgmt. Concepts Mgmt., Cape Coral, Fla. Author: Diversity at Work, 1994. Trustee Lee County Electric Coop., Inc., 1994—. Mem. ASTD, Inst. Mgmt. Cons. (cert.). Office: PO Box 150904 Cape Coral FL 33915-0904

ANDES, JOAN KEENEN, tax specialist, executive; b. Clarksburg, W.Va., Apr. 23, 1930; d. Ree Martin and Mary Ruth (Pyle) Groghan; m. William Anderson Keenen, Oct. 15, 1949 (div. 1969, dec. 1992); children: Paula Annette Keenen Skelton, William Ree Keenen; 1 foster child, Donald Monroe Dreyer; m. Ralph Paul Andes, Sept. 29, 1976. Pvt. sec. State Capitol, Charleston, W.Va., 1948-49; statis. typist various acctg. offices, Beaumont, Tex., 1949-60; owner Machine Acctg. and Computing, Beaumont, 1960-70, Automated Enterprises Keypunch Sch., 1962-72; pres. Applied Data Processing, Beaumont, 1970-83; owner Applied Info. Processing, Beaumont, 1983-90, APEX-Bookeeping, Tax Svc., 1991-95; ret. Active Democratic Party, Westgate Youth Group, 1984-90; vol. Mexican Mission Ch. of Christ, 1984—. Mem. Data Processing Mgmt. Assn. (pres. 1972-73, 80, awards chmn. 1985-86), Nat. Fedn. Ind. Bus. Republican. Mem. Ch. of Christ. Avocations: counted cross stitch, collecting Coke memorabilia, coin collecting. Home: 1410 Marshall Place Dr Beaumont TX 77706-3221

ANDRAKO, JOHN, health sciences educator; b. Perth Amboy, N.J., Jan. 19, 1924; s. Charles and Helen (Turjanitsa) A.; m. Ruth Augusta Whitt, June 26, 1948 (dec. Oct. 19, 1973); children: John David, Diane Carol Shasky, Susan Elizabeth Heiligman; m. Wanda Jean Schutt Barth, Nov. 22, 1978. BS, Rutgers U., 1947, MS, 1949; PhD, U. N.C., 1953. Lic. pharmacist, Va. Teaching fellow in chemistry Rutgers U. Coll. Pharmacy, New Brunswick, N.J., 1947-49; instr. Sch. of Pharmacy U. N.C., Chapel Hill, 1949-53, asst. prof. Sch. of Pharmacy, 1953-55, assoc. prof. Sch. of Pharmacy, 1955-56; assoc. prof. Sch. of Pharmacy Med. Coll. of Va., Va. Commonwealth U., Richmond, 1956-62, prof. medicinal chemistry, 1962-91, asst. dean Sch. of Pharmacy, asst. v.p. for health scis., 1965-73, 73-75, asst. provost for acad. and profl. affairs, acad. planning, 1975-78, asst. v.p., assoc. v.p. for health scis., 1978-82, 82-92, interim v.p. for health scis., 1988-91; prof. emeritus Sch. Pharmacy, 1991. Contbr. articles to profl. jours. Sun. sch. tchr. St. Matthew's Episcopal Ch., 1960-69, mem. vestry 1963-67, 75-78). Recipient Ciba Teaching fellowship Rutgers U., 1947-49, Presdl. medallion Va. Commonwealth U., 1992; named Am. Found. for Pharm. Edn. Summer fellow U. N.C., 1949-50, vis. scientist Am. Assn. Colls. of Pharmacy and NSF, 1963-64; grantee NIH, 1962-66, 67-72, NIGMS, 1962-66, 67-72, Bur. of Health Manpower, 1979-82, 85-88, 88-91, Statewide Va. Health Edn. Ctr., 1990-91. Mem. Am. Pharm. Assn., Am. Pharm. Assn. Acad. Pharm. Scis., Am. Chem. Soc. (medicinal chemistry divsn.), Va. Pharm. Assn., Am. Assn. Colls. Pharmacy Coun. Faculties and Coun. Sects., Va. Orchid Soc. (pres. 1984-86, newsletter editor 1993-96), Rotary (med. svc. com. Richmond 1972-78, chmn. 1973-74), Rho Chi Soc., Sigma Xi, Alpha Sigma Chi, Kappa Psi Pharm. Frat. Episcopalian. Home: 1970 Albion Rd Midlothian VA 23113-4147

ANDRAU, MAYA HEDDA, physical therapist; b. Digboi, Assam, India, Apr. 15, 1936; came to U.S., 1946; d. William Henry and Klara Irén Judit (Sima) Andrau; married, Sept. 1971 (div. July 1989); children: Francis Meher Traver, Darwin Meher Traver. BS in Phys. Therapy, Columbia U., 1958; MA in Social Anthropology, NYU, 1966. Lamaze cert. childbirth educator; lic. and registered phys. therapist. Phy. therapist Beekman-Downtown Hosp., N.Y.C., 1959-60; physiotherapist Stamford (Conn.) Hosp., 1963-64, Benedictine Hosp., Kingston, N.Y., 1966-69; pvt. practice in phys. therapy and lamaze Woodstock, N.Y., 1968-71; chief phy. therapist No. Duchess Hosp., Rhinebeck, N.Y., 1970-71; phy. therapist Waccamaw Pub. Health Dist., S.C. Dept. Health, Myrtle Beach, 1982-84; pain clinic specialist Pain Therapy Ctr. of Columbia (S.C.), Richland Meml. Hosp., 1986-87; phy. therapist Comprehensive Med. Rehab. Ctr., Conway, S.C., 1988-92; phys. therapist, instr. conditioning program Pawleys Island (S.C.) Wellness Inst., 1993; phys. therapist Total Care, Inc., 1993—; instr. phys. conditioning and therapeutic exercise courses, 1980—. Instr. Conditioning Program, Health Focus Brief for TV, 1990. Mem. Meher Spiritual Ctr., Inc., Alpha Kappa Delta. Follower of Avatar Meher Baba.

ANDREASON, GEORGE EDWARD, university administrator; b. Seattle, July 4, 1932; s. Alfred M. Andreason and Alberta (Brewer) Andreason Thompson; B.S. in Bus. Adminstrn., Tex. Wesleyan U., Ft. Worth, 1960; M.P.A. (Ford. Found. scholar), Ind. U., 1966; Ph.D., Clayton U., St. Louis, 1979; m. Carolyn A. McKown, June 30, 1973; 1 son, Paul Edward. Program analyst U.S. Army, Washington, 1963-64; asst. chief mgmt. analysis div. FAA, Ft. Worth, 1964-67, chief mgmt. analysis div., Oklahoma City, 1968-70, exec. officer, 1970-71; mgmt. cons. Dept. Transpo., 1966-67; asst. dir. IRS, Denver, 1971-72, asst. regional commr. adminstrn., Dallas, 1972-74, dist. dir., Denver, 1974, asst. dir., St. Louis, 1974-76; dir. adminstrv. services McLennan Community Coll., Waco, Tex., 1976-77; v.p. bus. and adminstrn. U. Mary Hardin-Baylor, Belton, Tex., 1977-80, exec. v.p., 1980—; partner McGregor Assos., bus. and mgmt. cons., McGregor, Tex.; pres., CEO, A&A Consulting Co., 1989—. Served with USN, 1951-55. Recipient Career Edn. award FAA and Nat. Inst. Public Affairs, 1965. Fellow Nat. Inst. Public Affairs; mem. Am. Soc. Public Adminstrn., Personnel and Mgmt. Assn., Nat. Coll. and Univ. Bus. Officers, So. Assn. Coll. and Univ. Bus. Officers, Belton C. of C. Baptist. Clubs: Rotary (Belton); Masons (master McGregor 1977, Tex. dist. dep. grand master 1980) (McGregor and Ft. Worth). Home: PO Box 181 Mc Gregor TX 76657-0181 Office: U Mary Hardin-Baylor Sta Belton TX 76513

ANDREWS, AARON R., army officer; b. July 27, 1951; s. William J. and Lina J. (James) A.; m. Connie Valda Dennis, Oct. 7, 1974; children: Raven, Aaron II. BS, Morgan State U., 1974; MBA, Fla. Inst. Tech., 1980; MS, Indsl. Coll. Armed Forces, Washington, 1996. Commd. U.S. Army, 1978—, advanced through grades; comdr. 4th 2M Brigade, Ft. Lee, Va., 1978-81; WWMCCS staff officer Forces Command, Ft. McPherson, Ga., 1982-85; mem. battalion S-3 10th Divsn., Ft. Drum, N.Y., 1985-87; automation staff officer US Forces Korea, Yongsan, 1987-89; project officer Devel. Ctr., Ft. Lee, 1989-92; product mgr. PEO Stanis, Ft. Belvoir, Va., 1992-95. Coach Girls Softball, Yongsan, 1988, Boys Basketball, Yongsan, 1987, Ft. Lee, 1991. Decorated Def. Medal, Dept. of Def., 1989, Meritorious Svc. medal with 3 oak leaf clusters, 1995. Mem. Indsl. Coll. Armed Forces. Baptist. Home: 3953 Pearlberry Ct Woodbridge VA 22193 Office: Industrial College of Armed Forces Fort McNair VA 22060

ANDREWS, ANTHONY PARSHALL, anthropology educator, archaeologist; b. Washington, Aug. 23, 1949; s. Edward Wyllys and Ann (Wheeler) A.; m. Mary K. Janis; children: Julian, Katherine. BA in Anthropology magna cum laude, Harvard U., 1973; MA, U. Ariz., 1976, PhD, 1980. Asst. prof. anthropology Hamilton Coll., Clinton, N.Y., 1980-81; asst. prof. anthropology New Coll. of U. South Fla., Sarasota, 1981-85, assoc. prof., 1985-89, prof., 1989—, chair divsn. social scis., 1989-95; archaeology rschr. Mex., Central Am. Research grantee Nat. Geog. Soc., Instituto Nacional de Antropología e Historia (Mex.), U. South Fla. Research Council. Mem. Am. Anthrop. Assn., Soc. Am. Archaeology, Sociedad Española de Estudios Mayas, Sociedad Mexicana de Antropologia. Author: (with E.W. Andrews IV) A Preliminary Study of the Ruins of Xcaret, Quintana Roo, Mexico, 1975; (with Antonio Benavides) Ecab. Poblado y Provincia del Siglo XVI en Yucatán, 1979; Maya Salt Production and Trade, 1983; editor (with Antonio Benavides) Arqueología Histórica en el Area Maya, 1985; author, editor (with Fernando Robles) Excavaciones Arqueologicas en El Meco, Quintana Roo, 1986; author: The First Cities, 1995; contbr. articles to profl. jours. Home: 6964 Country Lakes Cir Sarasota FL 34243-1839 Office: New Coll of U South Fla Divsn Social Scis Sarasota FL 34243

ANDREWS, BETHLEHEM KOTTES, research chemist; b. New Orleans, Sept. 18, 1936; d. George Leonidas and Anna Mercedes (Russell) Kottes; B.A. with honors in Chemistry, Newcomb Coll., Tulane U., 1957; m. William Edward Andrews, May 9, 1959 (dec.); children—Sharon Leslie, Keith Edward. Chemist wash wear investigation, So. Regional Research Center, Sci. and Edn. Adminstrn., Dept. Agr., New Orleans, 1958-63, research chemist wash wear investigation, cotton textile chemistry lab., 1968-70, research chemist spl. products research, cotton textile chemistry lab., 1976-83, sr. research chemist cotton chem. reactions research, 1983-85, lead scientist textile finishing chemistry research, 1985—; scientist-supr. Grace King High Sch. Lab. Tech. Tng. Program; mem. U.S. del. meeting on textiles Internat. Stds. Orgn., 1984—, head U.S. del., 1992, chmn. TC38/SC-2, 1995—. Recipient outstanding professionalism citation New Orleans Fedn. Businessman's Assn., 1977, Disting. Service award in med./sci. category, 1983, named Women of Yr. award in profl. category, 1978; recipient Profl. Excellence award Ita Sigma Pi, 1990, Miles award Cotton Found., 1991, Tech. Transfer award USDA-ARS, 1992; La. Heart Assn. grantee, 1957. Mem. Am. Chem. Soc., Am. Assn. Textile Chemists and Colorists (v.p. 1990, 91, exec. com. on research, Olney medal 1992), Fiber Soc., Phi Beta Kappa, Sigma Xi, Phi Mu. Democrat. Greek Orthodox. Clubs: P.E.O., Southern Yacht. Contbr. chpts. to books, articles to sci. jours.; patentee. Office: So Regional Rsch Ctr 1100 Robert E Lee Blvd New Orleans LA 70124-4305

ANDREWS, CHRISTINA, lawyer; b. Temple, Tex., Jan. 17, 1944; d. Catherine Andrews. BA, Baylor U., 1966, JD, 1973. Bar: Tex. 1973. Atty. Union Pacific Resources, Ft. Worth, 1973-76, 1976-78, staff atty., 1978-79, sr. staff atty., 1979-81, gen. atty., 1981-83, sr. gen. atty., asst. gen. counsel, 1984—. Pres. Am. Petroleum Labor Lawyers Assn., 1988-89. Recipient Letter of Commendation U.S. Pres. Ronald Reagan, 1982, UPRC Culture award, 1996, Visions 2020 Visionary Leadership award, 1996; named Disting. Alumna, Hill Coll., 1987, Catalyst, 1995. Mem. ABA, Tex. Bar Assn., Petroleum Club Ft. Worth (sec. 1989-90, 1st v.p. 1990-91, bd. dirs. 1991-94). Republican. Greek Orthodox. Office: Union Pacific Resources Corp PO Box 7 Mail St 4010 801 Cherry St Fort Worth TX 76101-0007

ANDREWS, DIANE RANDALL, nursing administrator, critical care nurse; b. Clinton, Iowa, Dec. 30, 1953; d. Eugene E. and Carol Lee (Walker) Randall; m. Thomas Wescott Andrews, Oct. 2, 1982; children: Christine, Charles. BSN, U. Iowa, 1976; MS, U. Ill., Chgo., 1981. RN, Fla., Ill. Unit leader/instr. Rush Presbyn. St. Lukes Med. Ctr., Chgo., 1976-84; cons. Longwood, Fla., 1990—; trustee, mem. adv. com. Fla. Hosp. Coll. of Health Scis., 1993—; mem. adv. com. Fla. Hosp., 1992—; chair endowment oversight com. Fla. Hosp./Univ. of Ctrl. Fla., 1996-98. Author: After Anesthesia; former editor jour. Kaleidoscope; contbg. editor Jour. of the Fla. Med. Assn.; contbr. articles to profl. publs. Bd. dirs. Orange County Med. Soc. Alliance, Fla. Hosp. Golden Cir. of Friends, Fla. Hosp. Found., Fla. Med. Assn. Alliance, Jewish Family Svcs., Walt Disney Meml. Cancer Inst. State of Iowa scholar. Mem. Am. Soc. Post Anesthesia Nursing, Sigma Theta Tau. Home and Office: 1821 Alaqua Dr Longwood FL 32779-3105

ANDREWS, EDSON JAMES, JR., radiologist; b. Tallahassee, Fla., Apr. 30, 1940; s. Edson James and Lola Irene (French) A.; m. Winifred Lynn Keller, Nov. 22, 1961; children: Michael Scott, James Brian. BA, U. Colo., 1962; MD, U. Fla., 1966. Diplomate Am. Bd. Radiology. Intern Charlotte (N.C.) Meml. Hosp., 1966-67; resident in radiology Barnes Hosp. of Washington U., Mallinckrodt Inst. Radiology, St. Louis, 1969-71; NIH postdoctoral fellow in cardiovascular radiology U. Fla., Gainesville, 1971-72; ptnr. Gadsden (Ala.) Radiology Assocs., 1972-77; staff radiologist West Fla. Hosp. Med. Ctr., Pensacola, 1977—, co-chair dept. nuclear cardiology, 1979—, chief nuclear medicine, 1982—, chmn. dept. radiology, 1993-95; bd. dirs. Med. Edn. and Rsch. Found. West Fla.; adj. assoc. prof. U. Fla. Coll. Med., 1985—; assoc. clin. prof. radiology U. South Ala., 1993—. Co-editor: (text) Color Atlas of First Pass Functional Imaging of the Heart, 1985; contbr. articles to profl. jours. Served with USPHS, 1967-69. Fellow Am. Coll. Radiology (councilor 1994—), Am. Coll. Cardiology; mem. Am. Soc. Nuclear Cardiology (founding mem.), Soc. Nuclear Medicine, Radiol. Soc. N.Am., Am. Roentgen Ray Soc. Republican. Home: 2713 Del Mar Dr Gulf Breeze FL 32561-3015 Office: 8333 N Davis Hwy Pensacola FL 32514-6048

ANDREWS, GEORGE ANDREAS, cardiologist; b. Asha, Cyprus, Oct. 14, 1950; came to U.S., 1970; s. Andreas A. and Eleni A. (Antoniou) Vassiliades; m. Diane G. Weisman, July 11, 1976; children: Brian, Nicole. BA magna cum laude, Columbia U., 1974; MD, Mt. Sinai Sch. Medicine, 1978. Diplomate Nat. Bd. Med. Examiners, Am. Bd. Internal Medicine, cardiovascular disease and internal medicine; lic. physician, N.Y., Fla. Intern, resident Columbia Presbyn. Hosp., N.Y.C., 1978-81; cardiology fellow U. Miami, Jackson Meml. Hosp., 1981-83; chmn. dept. medicine, mem. exec. com. U. Hosp., Tamarac, Fla., 1991-93; pvt. practice Coral Springs (Fla.) Cardiology Assocs., 1983—; chmn. credentials/qualifications com. Coral Springs Med. Ctr., 1991-93, chmn. dept. medicine, mem. exec. com., 1993-95, vice chief of staff, 1995—; expert witness Dept. Profl. Regulation, Bd. Medicine, Fla., 1992-96; mem. State Com. on Peer Med. Utilization Rev., Fla., 1992-95. Fulbright Commn. scholar Columbia U., 1970-74; grantee Inst. Internat. Edn., N.Y.C., 1970-74. Fellow ACP, Am. Coll. Cardiology, Am. Coll. Chest Physicians, Am. Coll. Angiology, Coun. Clin. Cardiology, Am. Heart Assn.; mem. Phi Beta Kappa, Phi Lambda Upsilon. Republican. Christian Orthodox. Office: Coral Springs Cardiology 9800 W Sample Rd Ste A Coral Springs FL 33065-4039

ANDREWS, GROVER JENE, adult education educator, administrator; b. Batesville, Ark., June 1, 1930; s. Grover Jones and Ruth Burlie (Ruble) A. BA, Vanderbilt U., 1963, MA, 1964; EdD, N.C. State U., 1972. Dir. univ. rels. Baylor U., Waco, Tex., 1955-61; asst. to pres. Peabody Coll. Vanderbilt U., Nashville, 1961-64; asst. prof. English, asst. acad. dean U. Ark., Little Rock, 1964-66; dir. of devel. Meredith Coll., Raleigh, N.C., 1966-67; asst. to dean of extension N.C. State U., Raleigh, 1967-68, assoc. vice chancellor for extension, assoc. prof. adult edn, 1979-89; assoc. exec. dir. commn. on colls. Southern Assn. of Colls. and Schs., Atlanta, 1968-79; assoc. dir. for instrn. U. Ga. Ctr. for Continuing Edn., 1989—, sr. pub. svc. assoc., chair sr. pub. svc. faculty, 1989—, adj. assoc. prof. adult edn., 1989—; bd. dirs. Am. Tech. Inst., Memphis, 1985—; bd. trustees Coun. for Adult and Exptl. Learning, Chgo., 1985-91; dir. of rsch. Internat. Assn. for Continuing Edn. and Tng., Washington, 1987-92, pres., 1992-96. Member Raleigh Lions, 1967-68, 79-89; chair Christmas pageant Waco Jaycees, 1956-60; patron Atlanta Arts Ctr., 1968-79. With USN, 1948-50. Named Educator of the Yr., Fedn. of Women's Clubs, 1966; recipient Nat. Leadership award Assn. for Continuing Higher Edn., 1984, Gruman award N.C. Adult Edn. Assn., 1985, Pinnacle award for outstanding leadership Internat. Assn. for Continuing Edn. and Tng., 1996; named to Internat. Hall of Fame for Adult and Continuing Edn., 1996; Grover J. Andrews Rsch. Endowment established by Internat. Assn., for Continuing Edn. and Tng., 1996. Mem. Nat. Univ. Continuing Edn. Assn. (Julius M. Nolte award 1995), Ga. Adult Edn. Assn., So. Assn. Colls. and Schs. (chair accrediting comms. 1980—), Internat. Hall of Fame for Adult and Lifelong Edn., 1996, Phi Delta Kappa, Sigma Tau Delta, Pi Kappa Alpha. Democrat. Baptist. Home: 243 Ashbrook Dr Athens GA 30605-3956 Office: U Ga Ctr for Continuing Edn Athens GA 30602

ANDREWS, HOLDT, investment banker; b. N.Y.C., May 2, 1946; s. William Lloyd and Edna (Faulconer) A.; m. Nina Lawrence, Sept. 16, 1982; 1 child, Kelli. BS, U. Fla., 1968; MBA, Fla. Atlantic U., 1971. Asst. to v.p. mktg. Eltra Corp., Wilmington, Mass., 1972-74; v.p. Bank of Am., N.Y.C., 1974-81; group v.p. Amrobank, N.Y.C., 1981-84; exec. v.p. CenTrust Savs. Bank, Miami, Fla., 1984, KMC Group, Miami, 1985-86; sr. mng. dir. J.W. Charles Capital Corp.-Bush Securities, Boca Raton, Fla., 1986-89; v.p. corp. fin. dept. Internationale Nederlanden Bank N.V., N.Y.C., 1989-94; sr. v.p. S.N. Phelps and Co., Greenwich, Conn., 1994; chief oper. officer VHC, Ltd., West Palm Beach, Fla., 1994—; mem. adv. bd. Tucker State Bank, Jacksonville, Fla., 1987-88; bd. dirs. Qilu-Maul, Shandong, Peoples Republic China. 1st lt. U.S. Army, 1968-70. Mem. Blue Key. Office: VHC Ltd 50 Cocoanut Row Ste 119 Palm Beach FL 33480-4026

ANDREWS, JEAN, artist, writer; b. Kingsville, Tex., Dec. 23, 1923; d. Herbert and Katharine Keith (Smith) A.; divorced; children: Robert Fleming Wasson Jr., Jean Andrews Wasson (dec.). BS in Home Economics, U. Tex., 1944; MS in Edn., Tex. A & I Univ., 1966; PhD in Fine Arts, U. North Tex., 1976. Cert. home economist. Artist, writer Austin, Tex.; vis. scholar dept. botany U. Tex., Austin, also mem. adv. coun. Coll. Natural Sci., mem. exec. com., 1986—, chmn. botany dept. vis. com.; presenter to seminars and confs. in field. Author: Sea Shells of the Texas Coast, 1971, Shells and Shores of Texas, 1977, Tesax Shells: A Field Guide, 1981, Peppers: The Domesticated Capsicums, 1984, rev. edit., 1995, The Texas Bluebonnet, 1985, rev. edit., 1993, An American Wildflower: Florilegium, 1992, Texas Monthly Field Guide to Shells of the Texas Coast, 1992, Red Hot Peppers, 1993, Texas Monthly Field Guide to the Shells of the Florida Coast, 1994; also articles; one-woman shows include RGK Found. Gallery, Austin, 1993, numerous others. Nat. adv. bd. Leadership Am., 1988-95; trustee Laguna Gloria Art Mus., 1985-91, Nat. Wildflower Rsch. Ctr., 1987-94, adv. coun. 1995—; past trustee Art Mus. of S. Tex.; past bd. dirs. Planned Parenthood; mem. Austin Symphony Soc., Friends of Huntington Gallery/Univ. Tex., others. Recipient Disting. Alumna award U.North Tex., 1991, Hall of Honor award U. Tex. Coll. Natural Sci., 1991; endowments include Jean Andrews vis. professorship in human nutrition U. Tex., vis. professorship in tropical and econ. botany, endowed scholar Tex. Found. for Women's Resources, also others; named Tex. Inst. Letters. Mem. DAR, Am. Malacol. Union, Tex. Pepper Found. (life), Tex. State Tchrs. Assn. (life), U. Tex. Alumni Assn. (life), U. North Tex. Alumni Assn. (life), Colonial Dames of 17th Century, Nat. Soc. Ams. of Royal Descent, Nat. Soc. Colonial Dames in Am., Nat. Soc. Magna Charta Dames, Daus. of Cin., Huguenot Soc., Order of Descendants of Ancient Planters, Daus. of the Confederacy.

ANDREWS, JO BONEY, corporate communications manager; b. Burlington, N.C., Apr. 20, 1966; d. Thomas Evans and Sarah Jean (Sandifer) Boney; m. Neal Coleman Andrews, Apr. 13, 1991. BA in Journalism, U. N.C., 1988. Reporter The Alamance News, Graham, N.C., 1983-88; adminstrv. asst. Nat. Newspaper Assn., Washington, 1988-89; news editor The Alamance News, Graham, 1989-92; corp. comms. mgr. Oakwood Homes Corp., Greenboro, N.C., 1992-96, mgr. corp. comms., 1996—. Recipient 3d pl. news enterprise N.C. Press Assn., 1991, Agrl. Reporting award Farm Bur., 1992, 1st pl. investigative reporting N.C. Press Assn., 1993, Award of Merit one-person pubs. Internat. Assn. Bus. Communicators Triangle chpt. N.C., 1994. Mem. Pub. Rels. Soc. Am. (officer). Republican. Home: 3500 NC Hwy 150 East Greensboro NC 27455 Office: Oakwood Homes Corp 7800 McCloud Rd Greensboro NC 27409

ANDREWS, JOHN SCOTT, JR., public health administrator, educator; b. Tifton, Ga., Dec. 23, 1946; s. John Scott and Ella Selina (Fraser) A.; m. Linda Ann Laurel, June 23, 1979; children: Anne, Jane, Jeffrey. BA, Wesleyan U., Middletown, Conn., 1969; MD, Case Western Res., 1973; MPH, Johns Hopkins U., 1985. Cert. Am. Bd. Internal Medicine, cert. occupational medicine, gen. preventive medicine and pub. health Am. Bd. Preventive Medicine. Intern Boston (Mass.) City Hosp., 1973-74, resident, 1974-75; epidemic intelligence officer Ctrs. for Disease Control, Atlanta, 1975-77; sr. med. resident U. Hosps. of Cleve., Ohio, 1977-78; geographic medicine fellow U. Hosps. of Cleve., 1978-80; med. epidemiologist Ctrs. for Disease Control, Port of Spain, Trinidad, 1980-82; asst. divsn. dir. Ctrs. for Disease Control, Atlanta, 1982-84, br. chief, 1985-89; assoc. adminstr. for sci. Agy. for Toxic Substances and Disease Registry, Atlanta, 1989—; clin. asst. prof. Emory U., Atlanta, 1988—, Mercer U., Macon, Ga., 1990—. Editor: Proceedings of 4th National Environmental Health Conference, 1990, Proceedings International Congress on Health Effects of Hazardous Waste, 1994. Fin. com. Neely Farm Homeowners Assn., Norcross, Ga., 1988-90; local sch. adv. bcom. Peachtree Elem. Norcross, 1990-94, Pinkneyville Mid. Sch., Norcross, 1993-95. Decorated Hazardous Duty Svc. ribbon USPHS, 1991, Commendation medal, U.S. Army, 1991, Nat. Def. Svc. medal, U.S. Army, 1991, Surgeon Gen.'s Exemplary Svc. medal USPHS, 1992. Fellow Am. Coll. Preventive Medicine, Royal Soc. Tropical Medicine and Hygiene, Collegium Ramazzini. Home: 4210 Quail Ridge Way Norcross GA 30092-1317

ANDREWS, KAREN ELIZABETH, town manager; b. Rutherfordton, N.C., Jan. 31; d. Charles S. and Margie L. (Bailey) A. BA, Gardner-Webb U., Boiling Springs, N.C., 1978. Town mgr. Town of Rutherfordton, 1993—. Mem. N.C. City-County Mgmt. Assn., Rutherfordton Kiwanis Club. Office: Town of Rutherfordton 110 N Washington St Rutherfordton NC 28139

ANDREWS, MARGARET LOVE, nurse, educator; b. Alamo, Tenn., Jan. 20, 1955; d. Elzie and Ada Mai (Smith) Love; m. Samuel Andrews Jr., Dec. 28, 1992; children: William Anthony, Marcus Anthony. BSN, Howard U., 1979; MA, Webster U., St. Louis, 1982; MSN, San Jose (Calif.) State U., 1994. Head nurse USAF, San Antonio, 1980-82; dir. nursing Eskaton Glenwood, Sacramento, 1988-90; commd. capt. U.S. Army, 1989, promoted to major, 1992; nursing adminstr. U.S. Army, Ft. Ord, Calif., 1990-92; head nurse U.S. Army, Ft. Gordon, Ga., 1994—; staff nurse Hospice, Augusta, Ga., 1994—; home care nurse Hospice, Monterey, Calif., 1992-94. Served to maj. U.S. Army, 1989—. Decorated Army Commendation medal. Mem. Nat. Black Nurses Assn., NAFE, The Rock, Inc. (Most Notable Women of Tex. 1982), Chi Eta Phi (pres. 1977-79). Home: 558 Waterford Dr Evans GA 30809-8516

ANDREWS, MARIE STAYLOR, special education educator; b. Farmville, Va., Oct. 29, 1959; d. Luther Presley and Betty Jean (Strum) Staylor; m. Gary Hilton Andrews, Dec. 22, 1990; children: Brian Edward, Forrest Presley. BM, Mars Hill Coll., 1982; postgrad., So. Bapt. Theol. Sem., 1982-89, Longwood Coll., 1989-90. Cert. music tchr., Va. Spl. edn. tchr. Bacon Dist. Elem. Sch., Charlotte County Pub. Schs., Charlotte Court House, Va., 1990—. Leader, receptionist Weight Watchers, Southside, Va., 1988-91;

mem. choir, choir dir., pianist Crewe (Va.) Bapt. Ch., 1988-90. Republican. Home: Rt 1 Box 424-C Keysville VA 23947-0723 Office: Bacon Dist Sch RR 1 Box 134 Saxe VA 23967-9533

ANDREWS, MASON COOKE, mayor, obstetrician, gynecologist, educator; b. Norfolk, Va., Apr. 20, 1919; s. Charles James and Jean (Cooke) A.; m. Sabine Goodman, Sept. 24, 1949; c.Jean, Mason. B.A., Princeton U., 1940; M.D., Johns Hopkins U., 1943; Doctor of Laws (hon.), Eastern Virginia Med. School, 1987. Diplomate: Am. Bd. Ob-Gyn. Intern ob-gyn Johns Hopkins U., Balt., 1944, resident ob-gyn, 1946-50; pvt. practice ob-gyn Norfolk, Va., 1950-70; lectr. Johns Hopkins U. Sch. Medicine, Balt., 1971-72; prof. dept. ob-gyn. Eastern Va. Med. Sch., Norfolk, 1974—, chmn. dept. ob-gyn., 1974-90; mayor City of Norfolk, 1992-94; bd. dirs. First Va. Bank of Tidewater, Chesapeake and Potomac Telephone Co.; mem., dir. Norfolk City Planning Commn., 1963-65, twice chmn., commr., exec. com. mem. Hampton Rds. Planning Dist. Commn., pres. (1971) Planning Coun. of United Communities, Norfolk City Coun., 1974—; chmn. Ea. Va. Med. Authority, 1964-70; pres. Am. Assn. Obstetricians Found., 1986-89. Contbr. (numerous articles to sci. jours.). Councilman City of Norfolk, 1974—, vice mayor, 1978-82, mayor, 1992-94. Recipient First Citizen citation Norfolk Cosmopolitan Club, 1968, Norfolk citation for outstanding svc., 1964, award for cmty. svc. Med. Soc. Va., AMA, Nat. Brotherhood award Norfolk Conf. Christians and Jews. Fellow Am. Gynecol. and Obstet. Soc. (v.p. 1982-83, pres. 1992-93); mem. South Atlantic Assn. (pres. 1972), Va. Obstet. and Gynecol. Soc. (pres. 1975), Norfolk Acad. Medicine (pres. 1961), Johns Hopkins Soc. Scholars, Harbor Club, Norfolk Yacht and Country Club. Presbyterian. Home: 1011 N Shore Rd Norfolk VA 23505-3119 Office: Eastern Va Med Sch Dept Ob-Gyn 601 Colley Ave Norfolk VA 23507-1627

ANDREWS, MELINDA WILSON, human development researcher; b. N.Y.C., Aug. 12, 1956; d. William Maurice and Natalie Maxine (Amos) Wilson; m. James Robert Andrews, Dec. 3, 1977; children: Christopher Wilson Andrews, William James Andrews. BBA in Mgmt./Mktg., Abilene (Tex.) Christian U., 1977; MS in Human Devel., U. Tex., Dallas, 1988; PhD, ABD in Human Devel., U. Tex., 1994. Logics adminstr. Texas Instruments, Dallas, 1977-79, contract adminstr., 1979-81, 82-83; grocery mgr.; co-asst. store dir. Tom Thumb, Dallas, 1981-82; teaching asst. U. Tex. at Dallas, Richardson, Tex., 1988-91; rsch. asst. U. Tex. at Dallas, 1991—; presenter in field. Mem. Richardson Symphony Orch., 1977-79, Canyon Creek Elem. PTA, 5th v.p., 1994-95, libr. rep., 1992-94. Mem. Soc. for Rsch. in Child Devel. (co-author paper-poster session 1991, 93 confs.), Southwest Soc. for Rsch. in Child Devel., Psi Chi. Mem. Ch. of Christ. Home and Office: 2109 Flat Creek Dr Richardson TX 75080

ANDREWS, MICHAEL FRANK, education educator; b. Cairnbrook, Pa., Mar. 4, 1916; s. Frank and Libra (Testa) A.; widowed May 14, 1992; children: Judi Lynn, Connee Jean, Michael Curtis. BFA in Art Edn., U. Kans., 1940, MS in Edn., 1948; PhD in Fine Arts, Psychology, Philosophy, Ohio State U., 1952. Tchr. Lawrence (Kans.) Pub. Sch., 1940-41, Hayes (Kans.) Pub. Sch., 1941-42; prof. U. Kans., 1945-48, Ohio State U., 1948-50, U. So. Calif., 1950-52, U. Wis., 1952-59, U. Hawaii; prof. Sch. Edn., Coll. Visual and Performing Arts Syracuse U., 1955-82; chmn. dept. synaesthetic edn. Syracuse U., bd. dirs. Syracuse Symposia on Creative Arts Edn., mem. numerous coms. Sch. of Art, Sch. of Edn.; mem. creative leadership coun. Creative Edn. Found., Buffalo U.; mem. adv. coun. Marcy State Hosp. Occupational Therapy Program; mem. Nat. Rsch. Labs. for Early Childhood Edn.; lectr. in field. Author, editor: Aesthetic Form and Education, 1958, Creativity and Psychological Health, 1961; author: Creative Printmaking, 1964, Creative Education: The Liberation of Man, 1965, Sculpture and Ideas, 1965, Pine Cone: Sensory Awareness Module, 1977; author numerous book chpts. and newsletters; co-author: Synaesthetic Education, 1971; co-author: (series of textbooks) Growing with Art, 1950, 2d edit., 1960; consulting editor Jour. Creative Behavior; contbr. articles to profl. jours.; works exhibited at U. Kans., Lawrence, U. Wis. Madison, U. So. Calif., L.A., Wichita (Kans.) Mus. Art, Baker U., Baldwin, Kans., Ohio State U., Columbus, Mus. Modern Art, N.Y.C., Syracuse (N.Y.) U., Skidmore Coll., Saratoga, N.Y., Nelson Art Gallery, Kansas City, Mo., U. Hawaii, Honolulu. Chmn. activity com., bd. dirs. Lake Towers, Sun City Center, Fla., 1993—. 1st lt. USAF, 1942-45. Recipient 1st place sculpture Ohio State Fair, 1949, Hon. mention Nat. Decorative Arts and Ceramic Exhbn., 1949, Columbus Art League Sculpture award, 1950, Sculpture House award, 1953, Wis. Salon of Art award, 1954, Hon. mention Design Hall of Edn., N.Y. World's Fair, 1962, award Nat. Libr. Poetry, 1993. Mem. NEA, AAUP, Nat. Art Edn. Assn. (past sec., v.p., pres. ea. regional), Internat. Soc. Edn. Trough Art, Kans. State Art Tchrs. Assn. (past pres.), Pacific Arts Assn. (past treas., v.p.). Home: PO Box 223 101 Trinity Lakes Dr Sun City Center FL 33573-5736

ANDREWS, ROBERT LLOYD, insurance company executive; b. Clovis, N.Mex., Dec. 13, 1937; s. John Marion and Helen Lucille (Johnston) A.; children: Erin Allison, Maura Peyton, Jennifer Regan; m. Nancy Mason, Nov. 22, 1981. BA, N.Mex. State U., 1960. Agent Western Am. Life Ins. Co., Albuquerque, 1960-64; area mgr. Franklin Life Ins. Co., 1964-68; v.p. mktg. Am. Bankers Life Assurance, Miami, Fla., 1968-70; regional mgr. Coastal States Life Ins. Co., Atlanta, 1970-73; regional dir. Gen. Life Ins. Co. of Wis., Atlanta, 1973-77; gen. agt. Am. Gen. Life Ins. Co., Atlanta, 1977-86; gen. agt. Ky. Ctrl. Life Ins. Co., Atlanta, 1986-89, regional gen. agt., 1989-91; divsn. mgr., so. divsn. Ohio State Life Ins. Co., Columbus, 1992—; pres. DeKalb Gen. Agt. and Mgr. Assn., Atlanta, 1982-83; instr. Life Underwriter Tng. Coun., Atlanta, 1979, 1982-83. Contbr. articles to profl. jours. Founder Young Am. Football League, Albuquerque, 1965; Pres. Sandy Springs Youth Football League, Atlanta, 1985-88, coach, 1971-89; tchr. Sunday sch. Mt. Vernon Presbyn. Ch., Atlanta, 1982. Named Life Member Life Ins. Leaders of Ga., Atlanta, 1982. Mem. Gen. Agts. and Mgrs. Assn. (life mem. nat. mgmt. award, 1985), Million Dollar Roundtable (life mem. 1989), DeKalb Assn. Life Underwriters, Masons, Shriners, N.Mex. State U. Aggie Sports Assn. Republican. Presbyterian. Home: 4534 Mount Paran Pky NW Atlanta GA 30327-3724 Office: The Best Insurance Corp 6650 Powers Ferry Rd NW # 120 Atlanta GA 30339-2914

ANDREWS, STEVEN JAMES, aerospace company executive; b. Cedar Rapids, Iowa, Oct. 5, 1940; s. Dale Brewer and Esther Louise (Reed) A.; m. Mariel Laurene Carter, Sept. 9, 1961; children: James, Kristin. BS in Bus., BS in Engring., U. Colo., 1963; MBA, So. Meth. U., 1969. Registered profl. engr., Tex.; lic. real estate broker. 747 facilities mgr. Vought Corp., Dallas, 1967-68, cost control supr., 1969-70; sr. bus. planner LTV Aerospace Corp., Dallas, 1971-76; prin. cost estimator Gen. Dynamics, Ft. Worth, 1977-78, F-16 fin. mgr., 1979-85, dir. cost proposals, 1986-88; dir. bus. acquisition Lockheed Ft. Worth Co., 1989-94; mng. dir. Lockheed Investment Holding Co., Ankara, Turkey, 1995—; adj. prof. Tex. Christian U., Ft. Worth, 1972-73; lect. U. Tex., Arlington, 1989-93. Treas. Grand Prairie (Tex.) C. of C., 1976. Served to lt. USN, 1963-69, Vietnam. Recipient Achievement medal for professionalism USN, 1966. Office: Lockheed Yatirim Holding Anonim Sirketi, 211 Ataturk Bulvari 11th Fl, 06680 Ankara Turkey

ANDREWS, WILLIAM FREDERICK, manufacturing executive; b. Easton, Pa., Oct. 7, 1931; s. William Frederick and Lydia Nielson (Cross) A.; m. Carol Beaman, Feb. 8, 1962; children: William Frederick III, Whitney, Carter, Clayton, Sloane. BS, U. Md., 1953; MBA, Seton Hall U., 1961. Product mgr. Scovill Mfg. Co., Waterbury, Conn., 1965-68; v.p., gen. mgr. Scovill Mfg. Co., Raleigh, N.C., 1968-73; group v.p. Scovill Mfg. Co., Nashville, 1973-79; pres. Scovill Mfg. Co., Waterbury, 1979-81; chmn., pres., chief exec. Scovill Mfg. Co., 1981-86; chmn., pres., CEO Singer Sewing Machine Co., 1986-89; pres. Massey Investment Co., 1989-90; pres., chief exec. officer UNR Industries Inc., 1990-92; CEO, chmn. bd. Amdura Corp., Conn., 1992-94; chmn. bd. Utica Corp., Utica, N.Y., 1992-94; chmn. Schrader Inc., Monroe, N.C., 1995—, Scovill Fasteners, 1995—; chmn. Scovill Fasteners Inc., 1995—; bd. dirs. Northwestern Steel & Wire Co., So. New Eng. Tel. Co., Corrections Corp., Navistar Internat. Co., Harley Davidson Co., Johnson Controls, Katy Industries, Black Box, Inc., MC Comm., Process Techs. Inc. Chmn. Waterbury chpt. ARC. Capt. USAF, 1953-56. Recipient Silver Beaver award Boys Scouts Am., 1979, Significant Sig award Sigma Chi, 1992. Mem. Bellemeade Country Club (Nashville), Highfield Country Club, Waterbury (Conn.) Country Club, Teton Pines Country Club (Jackson, Wyo.), Chgo. Club, Univ. Club (N.Y.C.). Republican. Episcopalian.

ANDRISANI, JOHN ANTHONY, editor, author, golf consultant; b. Bayshore, N.Y., Sept. 24, 1949; s. Pat and Gwendoline Mary (Rose) A. Student, SUNY, Stony Brook, 1968-71. Instr. golf in country club N.Y., 1971-78; freelance writer golf mags., 1977—; asst. editor Golf Illustrated mag., London, 1980-82; sr. editor instrn. Golf mag., N.Y.C., 1982—. Co-author: (with Sandy Lyle) Learning Golf: The Lyle Way, 1986, (with Seve Ballesteros) Natural Golf, 1987 (Book of Month Club 1987), (with Chi Chi Rodriguez) 101 Supershots, 1990, (with Robin McMillan) The Golf Doctor, 1990 (Brentanos bestseller 1990), (with Mike Dunaway) Hit It Hard!, 1991, (with Phil Ritson) Golf Your Way, 1992, (with John Daly) Grip It, and Rip It!, 1992, (with Fred Couples) Total Shotmaking, 1994, (with Craig Stadler) I Am The Walrus, 1995, (with Claude "Butch" Harmon Jr.), The Four Cornerstones of Winning Golf, 1996, (with Jim McLean) The X-Factor Swing, 1996 ; contbr. articles to jours. and mags. Mem. Golf Writer's Assn. (assn. champion 1985), Ballybunion Golf Club (life, Ireland), Lake Nona Golf Club (Orlando Fla.).

ANDRUS, SUSAN JOYCE, librarian; b. Dover, N.J., July 10, 1964; d. James Ellsworth and Jean Lucille (Dahler) A. BS in Edn., Clarion U. of Pa., 1986, MLS, 1988. Cert. libr., S.C. Automation coord. Oconee County Pub. Libr., Walhalla, S.C., 1989, system mgr., 1991—; office mgr. Wildwater Ltd., Long Creek, S.C., 1990-91. Mem. Piedmont Libr. Assn., S.C. Libr. Assn., Foothills Mopar Club. Office: Oconee County Libr 501 W S Broad St Walhalla SC 29691

ANDRUZZI, ELLEN ADAMSON, nurse, marital and family therapist; b. Colon, Panama, Dec. 15, 1917; d. Charles and Annie Isabel (Grinder) Adamson; m. Francis Victor Andruzzi, May 28, 1941; children: Barbara F., Francis C., Judith E., Antonette T., John J. BS in Pub. Health Nursing, Cath. U. Am., 1947, MS in Nursing, 1951. Cert. clin. specialist, psychiat. nurse. Pub. health nurse Washington Health Dept., 1942-44; instr. psychiat. nursing St. Elizabeth's Hosp., Washington, 1948-57; dir. nursing Glenn Dale Hosp., Md., 1961-67; chief mental health nurse dept. human resources D.C. Govt., 1967-73; cons. NIMH, HHS, Rockville, Md., 1973-81; marital and family therapist TA Assocs., Camp Springs, Md., 1973-94; assoc. GWITA, Rockville, 1975-79; instr. Charles County C.C., LaPlata, Md., 1976-78, Prince George Community Coll., Largo, Md., 1973-81; assoc. Ctr. for Study of Human Systems, Chevy Chase, Md., 1976-94; nurse, psychotherapist pvt. practice. Author chpts. in books. Dist. co-capt. Prince Georgians for Glendening, Prince George County, Md., 1985-86; chmn. plan devel. com. So. Md. Health Systems Agy., Clinton, 1984-89, sec. governing body, 1978-80; chmn. Mental Health Adv. Com. Prince George County, Cheverly, Md., 1983-85; mem. Blue Ribbon Commn. on Health, Prince George's County, 1991-92; mem. Commn. Health, Prince George's County, 1992-94; mem. health com. and voter reporter League Women Voters. Recipient Disting. Nurse award St. Elizabeths Hosp., 1985, Paula Hamburger Vol. award Mental Health Assn. Md., 1985, Recognition of Service award Md. Nurses Assn., 1983, Prince Georgian of the Yr. award, 1994, Vol. award Prince George's County, 1995. Fellow Am. Acad. Nursing, Am. Orthopsychiat. Assn.; mem. Internat. Transactional Analysis Assn. (clin.), Am. Nurses Assn., World Fedn. for Mental Health, Am. Assn. for Marriage and Family Therapy (clin.), Nat. Mental Health Assn. (v.p. 1984-87, bd. dirs. 1982-87), Mental Health Assn. Prince George County (pres. 1974-76, 87-88, Vol. of Yr. award 1993), Sigma Theta Tau (Kappa chpt., Excellence in Nursing award 1984). Democrat. Roman Catholic. Avocations: theatre, ballet, swimming, foreign travel.

ANGEL, STEVEN MICHAEL, lawyer; b. Frederick, Md., Sept. 19, 1950; s. Charles Robert and Laura Emily (Holland) A.; children: Michael Sean, James Curtis; m. Peggy Whitten, May 4, 1996. BS, U. Md., 1972; JD, Oklahoma City U., 1976; LL.M., George Washington U., 1979. Bar: Okla. 1976, U.S. Dist. Ct. Md. 1977, U.S. Dist. Ct. (no. dist.) Tex. 1979, Tex. 1981, U.S. Dist. Ct. (we. dist.) Okla. 1981, U.S. Dist. Ct. (we. dist.) Tex 1981, U.S. Ct. Claims 1981, U.S. Ct. Appeals (5th, 10th, and 11th cirs.) 1981, U.S. Ct. Appeals (D.C. cir.) 1983, U.S. Supreme Ct. 1984, D.C. 1986. Field atty. NLRB, Balt., 1976-79; supervising trial atty. Fed. Labor Rels. Authority, Dallas, 1979-80; mem. Hughes & Nelson, Oklahoma City and San Antonio, 1980-89. Articles editor Oklahoma City U. Law Rev., 1976, 77; contbr. articles to profl. jours. Recipient cert. Spl. Competence in Labor, Law Tex. Bd. Legal Specialization, 1982; various awards Oklahoma City U., 1975, 76; Spl. Achievement cert. Fed. Labor Rels. Authority, 1980. Mem. ABA, Okla. Bar Assn., State Bar Tex., Phi Delta Phi. Democrat. Baptist. Home: 2313 Silverfield Ln Edmond OK 73003-1501 Office: 6488 Avondale # 359 Oklahoma City OK 73116-6438

ANGELIDES, DEMOSTHENES CONSTANTINOS, civil engineer; b. Thessaloniki, Greece, June 18, 1947; came to U.S., 1973; s. Constantinos D. and Chrysavgi (Papatsa) A.; m. Chryssanthi Koutsandrea, Dec. 25, 1991; 1 child, Constantine. Diplom. ingenieur, Aristoteles U., Greece, 1970; MSCE, MIT, 1975, PhD, 1978. Registered profl. engr., Tex. Rsch. asst. MIT, Cambridge, 1973-78; supervising structural engr. Brian Watt Assocs., Inc., Houston, 1978-80; sr. cons. structural engr. McDermott, Inc., New Orleans, 1980-83, Hudson Engring./McDermott, Inc., Houston, 1983-85; sr. cons. engr. McDermott, Inc., New Orleans, 1985-90, mgr. total quality, 1990-93, dir. bus. process improvement, 1993—; mem. tech. com. Am. Petroleum Inst., New Orleans, 1983-85; McDermott rep. Indsl. Liaison program MIT, New Orleans, 1981-89. Co-author: Offshore Structures, 1991; contbr. articles to Earthquake Engring. and Structural Dynamics, Jour. Engring. Mechanics, Jour. Structural Div., Jour. Offshore Mechanics and Arctic Engring. Mem. La. Fin. com. Dukakis for Pres., 1988; pres. Hellenic Arts Soc., New Orleans, 1986-88; bd. dirs. Trustees of Holy Trinity Greek Orthodox Ch., New Orleans, 1989-90; 2d lt. corps. engrs. Hellenic Army, Greece, 1971-73. Postdoctoral fellowship Coun. for Sci. and Indsl. Rsch., 1978; Govtl. scholar Aristoteles U., Thessaloniki, 1965-70. Mem. ASCE, ASME (chmn. computer tech. comm. of offshore mechanics and arctic engring. div. 1985-88), Am. Assn. Artificial Intelligence, Am. Geophys. Union, Sigma Xi. Home: 3915 Saint Charles Ave Apt 606 New Orleans LA 70115-4662 Office: McDermott Internat Inc 1450 Poydras St New Orleans LA 70112-6010

ANGEL-JUNGUITO, ANTONIO, writer; b. Bogota, Colombia, Dec. 9, 1946; s. Alberto and Maria (Junguito) Angel-Montoya; children: Javier, Ana Maria. Bachillerato, Colegio San Carlos, Bogota, Colombia, 1965; BA, U. Bogota, Colombia, 1970; MA, U. Ga., 1972. Tchr. Colegio San Carlos, Bogota, Colombia, 1969-70; chess prof. U. Ga. Ctr. for Continuing Edn., Athens, 1972; editor Ga. Chess Assn., Athens, 1975-76; writer, journalist Newspaper El Tiempo, Bogota, 1977; prof. polit. sci. U. Bogota, Bogota, 1977; prof. history U. El Rosario, Bogota, 1977; art, gem dealer various orgns., Colombia, U.S.A., Europe, 1979—; prof. history, polit. sci., chess various schs., 1972-90. Author: A Cry of Innocence-In Defense of Colombians, 1993; contbr. articles to profl. jours. Recipient various chess titles in field. Mem. Pi Sigma Alpha. Home: PO Box 1968 Miami Beach FL 33119

ANGLEA, JOY SHARON, family practice physician; b. Eatonton, Ga., Aug. 6, 1955; d. Raymond Gant and Marilyn (Bratton) A. BS, Bob Jones U., 1977; MD, U. Va., 1981. Intern Greenville (S.C.) Hosp. System, 1981-82, resident in family practice, 1984; pvt. practice Greenville, 1984—. Mem. editl. bd. Postgrad. Medicine, 1995—. Chmn. Insights, Greenville, 1992-93; mem. adv. bd. S.C. Citizens for Life, Columbia, 1989—, Piedmont Women's Ctr., Greenville, 1992—; bd. dirs. Joyful Woman, Chattanooga, 1992—. Mem. Am. Acad. Family Physicians, AMA, So. Med. Assn., S.C. Med. Assn., Am. Acad. Med. Ethics, S.C. Acad. Family Physicians (chmn. bd. 1992, bd. dirs. 1987-92). Republican. Baptist. Office: 2323 E North St Greenville SC 29607-1238

ANGLIKER, COLIN C.J., forensic psychiatrist; b. Belfast, No. Ireland, Sept. 5, 1937; came to U.S., 1977; s. H. William and Mary McClurg (Scott) A.; m. Lucy Angliker; children: Susan G., Kimberley M., Nicole L., Keri A. MB,BCh,BAO, Queen's U. Belfast, 1962; DipPsych, McGill U., 1967. Lic. Med. Coun. Can.; lic. physician and surgeon, Conn., Va. Intern Belfast City Hosp., 1962-63; resident in adult and child psychiatry Kingston (Ont.) Gen. Hosp., 1963-65; resident in adult psychiatry Douglas Hosp./McGill U., Montreal, 1965; sr. asst. resident in psychiatry Allan Meml Inst., Royal Victoria Hosp./McGill U., Montreal, 1966; sr. resident in child psychiatry Montreal Children's Hosp./McGill U., 1966-67; clin. fellow dept. psychiatry Royal Victoria Hosp., 1968-69, mem. staff, 1970-77; asst. dir. McGill Clinic in Forensic Psychiatry, 1968-74; dir. Miriam Kennedy Child & Family Clinic, Montreal, 1974-77, Whiting Forensic Inst., Middletown, Conn., 1977-86; clin. dir. Feliciana Forensic Facility, Jackson, La., 1986-88; med. dir. Marion (Va.) Correctional Centre, 1988—; from lectr. to asst. prof. dept. psychiatry McGill U., 1969-77; assoc. clin. prof. Sch. Medicine, Yale U., New Haven, 1977-86; assoc. prof. dept. psychiat. medicine U. Va., 1991-94, assoc. clin. prof., 1994—; psychiat. cons. Cmty. Correctional Ctr., New Haven, 1981-82, Cmty. Correctional Ctr., Hartford, Conn., 1981-82, Mass. Rehab. Commn., 1982-86, Dept. Corrections, Topeka, 1989. Contbr. numerous chpts. to books, articles to profl. jours. Fellow Royal Coll. Physicians and Surgeons Can., Am. Psychiat. Assn.; mem. Can. Acad. Child Psychiatry (founding 1980), Am. Acad. Psychiatry and the Law, Can. Psychiat. Assn. Home: 19378 Hunt Club Rd Abingdon VA 24211-6762 Office: Marion Correctional Treatment Ctr PO Box 1027 Marion VA 24354-1027

ANGLIN, BETTY LOCKHART, artist, educator; b. Greenwood, S.C., Apr. 23, 1937; d. Malcolm Mabry and Dorothy (Roessler) Lockhart; m. Ernie LaRue Anglin, June 10, 1957; children—Nancy Louise, Malcolm Lawrence. B.A., Coll. William and Mary, 1972. Instr., Hampton Arts and Humanities, Va., 1967-73, Cecil Rawls Mus., Courtland, Va., 1973-84; tchr. Trinity Lutheran Sch., Newport News, Va., 1972-86; part time prof. Christopher Newport U., Newport News, 1975—. One woman shows include Va. Wesleyan Coll., 1972, Peninsula Arts Assn., Newport News, 1972, Arts Internat. Gallery Ltd., Norfolk, Va., 1973, 74, Virginia Beach Arts Ctr., 1973, 74, Kirn Meml. Library, Norfolk, 1976, Jr. League of Hampton Rds. Hdqrs., 1981, Coliseum Mall, Hampton, Va., 1982, Mary Immaculate Hosp., 1983, Jr. League Offices, Newport News, 1983, Village Gallery, Newport News 1983, Hampton (Va.) Arts and Humanities, 1986; exhibited in numerous group shows including Va. Mus., Richmond, Chrysler Mus., Norfolk, Parthenon, Nashville, High Mus., Atlanta, Portsmouth (Va.) Mus., Cecil Rawls Mus., Suffolk (Va.) Mus.; represented in permanent collections Hampton Sch. System, City of Hampton, Tenneco, Va. State Fair Collection, Cecil Rawls Mus., Peninsula Arts Assn., Riverside Hosp., City of Stoney Creek, Va., Corning Glass, Anderson, S.C., Eastman Kodak, Phila., Hosp. of Kings Daus., Virginia Beach, Va., others. Work appears in numerous publs. Active Hidenwood Presbyn. Ch., Newport News. Recipient numerous awards and prizes; grantee Va. Endowment Arts, Va. Mus. artist-in-residence 1991-92. Mem. Peninsula Arts Assn., Hampton Arts and Humanities, Va. Mus., Chrysler Mus., Virginia Beach Arts Assn., Tidewater Artists, Va. Watercolor Soc., P.E.O., On The Hill Arts and Crafts Co-op. Home: 213 Parkway Dr Newport News VA 23606-3651 Office: Christopher Newport Coll 50 Shoe Ln Newport News VA 23606-2949

ANGLIN, LINDA MCCLUNEY, elementary school educator; b. Turrell, Ark., Apr. 20, 1929; d. Denton Sims and Helen Louise (Davis) McCluney; m. Joe Van Anglin, Aug. 30, 1952; children: Van, Cheryl, Dent, George. BA magna cum laude, Millsaps Coll., 1951; MEd, Miss. Coll., 1970; Edn. Specialist, Miss. State U., 1974. Cert. tchr., Miss. Tchr. St. Andrew's Sch., Jackson, Miss., 1952-53, Carthage (Miss.) Elem. Sch., 1956-57, Jackson Pub. Schs., 1957-94; founder Miss. Profl. Educators, 1979, pres., 1979-82; dir. Pub. Edn. Forum Miss., Jackson, 1989-93; classroom cons. Scholastic Tchr. Lobbyist for edn. and children's issues State of Miss., 1980—; charter mem. Jackson Assn. for Children with Learning Disabilities, bd. dirs., historian, mem. adv. bd. Miss. chpt.; active many civic groups. Recipient Book of Golden Deeds award Exch. Club North Jackson, 1989; active PTA. Mem. Jackson Profl. Educators (pres. 1988-90), Jackson Area Reading Coun. (pres. 1975-76, Outstanding Svc. award 1987), Sigma Lambda, Kappa Delta Pi, Phi Kappa Phi, Delta Kappa Gamma (workshop presenter 1985, pres. Tau chpt. 1986-88, Woman of Distinction 1990, Disting. Svc. to Edn. award 1984). Methodist. Home: 785 Cedarhurst Rd Jackson MS 39206-4954

ANGLIN, MICHAEL WILLIAMS, lawyer; b. Chelsea, Mass., Dec. 3, 1946; s. John M. and Lillian Rogene (Williams) A. BS, E. Tex. State U., 1969; JD, U. Tex., 1976. Bar: Tex. 1976, U.S. Dist. Ct. (no. dist.) Tex. 1979, U.S. Dist. Ct. (we. and ea. dists.) Tex. 1987, U.S. Dist. Ct. Ariz. 1992, U.S. Ct. Appeals (5th and 11th cirs.) 1981, U.S. Supreme Ct. 1986. With Passman & Jones, Dallas, 1976-87; ptnr. Fulbright & Jaworski, LLP, Dallas, 1987—; trustee Official Panel Bankruptcy Trustees for No. Dist. Tex., 1980—. Corp. mem. Dallas Mus. Fine Arts, 1984; ct. apptd. spl. advocate, 1990—; bd. dirs. Dallas Opera, 1992—; mem. Greater Dallas Planning Coun., 1994—; mem. Greater Dallas Crime Commn., 1994—; mem. Youth Crime Coun., 1994—. Mem. ABA, Tex. Bar Assn., Dallas Bar Assn., Am. Bankruptcy Inst. Office: Fulbright & Jaworski LLP 2200 Ross Ave Ste 2800 Dallas TX 75201-6766

ANGLIN, WALTER MICHAEL, evangelist, minister, law enforcement professional; b. Cheverly, Md., Jan. 10, 1958; s. Lawrence Tilmon and Margaret Lorraine (Thrash) A.; m. Meloene Alene Williams, Mar. 1, 1980; children: Walter Michael Jr., Mary Elizabeth. A in Practical Theology, Christ For The Nations Inst., 1979; BA in Pastoral Ministry, S.W. Assemblies of God Coll., 1991. Ordained to ministry Am. Bapt. Assn., 1978; lic. to ministry Assemblies of God, 1980. Evangelist Assemblies of God, Duncanville, Tex., 1980-92; police officer Duncanville Police Dept., 1986-92, chaplain, 1990-92, high sch. liaison officer, 1990-92; pastor Immanuel Word Ctr., Homer, La., 1996—; youth sponsor Meml. Assembly of God, Duncanville, 1989-91; youth care leader Ch. on the Rock S., Duncanville, 1991-92; youth evangelist SWAT Youth Ministries, Duncanville, 1989-92; del. South Dallas sect. coun. Assemblies of God, Dallas, 1989, 90, Am. Bapt. Assn., Plain Dealing, La., 1974; youth pastor Word of Faith Joaquin, Tex., 1992-96. Exec. advisor local post Duncanville Law Enforcement Post, 1990-91; asst. coach Best S.W. Soccer Assn., Duncanville, 1989-91, YMCA Youth Baseball, Dallas, 1990; assoc. coord. Duncanville Citizen's Police Acad., 1990-91; head umpire Toledo Bend Dixie League, Joaquin, Tex., 1994-95. Fellow FOP (chaplain local chpt. 1989—); mem. Tex. Peace Officers Assn. (cert. advanced peace officer), Duncanville Youth Pastor's Assn., Tex. Sch. Resource Officer's Assn. (pres., founder 1992). Office: Immanuel Word Center 401 E 5th St Homer LA 71040

ANGST, KAREN K., mental health nurse; b. Houston, Tex., May 16, 1948; d. Conrad Wilbur and Wanda Lee (Sullivan) A. Student, Sacred Heart Dominican Coll., Houston, 1966-68; cert., Houston C.C., 1972; student, U. Houston, 1977-78; ADN, Alvin (Tex.) C.C., 1979. RN, LVN, Tex.; cert. mental health nurse. Staff nurse Gready Clinic, Houston, 1969-71, St. Joseph Hosp., Houston, 1967-68; charge nurse cognitive impaired care unit and psychiat. acute care unit St Joseph Hosp., Houston, 1971—; mem. planning com. Cognitive Impaired Care Unit, St. Joseph Hosp., Houston. Mem. Am. Assn. Ret. Persons, Alzheimer Assn., Houston Gerontol. Soc., Chi Sigma Nu. Lutheran.

ANGSTROM, WAYNE RAYMOND, communications executive; b. Chgo., Mar. 26, 1939; s. Raymond Harry and Dorothy Louise (Dixon) A.; m. Sandra Sue Weber, Oct. 5, 1963; children: Mark, Carl, David, Kristina. AA in Bus. Adminstrn., Chgo. City Coll., 1962; student, Northwestern U., 1963-68. Mfg. mgr. R.R. Donnelley & Sons Co., Chgo., 1962, div. dir., v.p., 1981-87; exec. v.p. Maxwell Communications Corp., St. Paul, 1987-90, Quebecor Printing Inc., Boston, 1990-91; pres., CEO St. Ives Inc., Hollywood, Fla., 1992—. Home: 7082 Valencia Dr Boca Raton FL 33433-7404 Office: St Ives Inc 2025 Mckinley St Hollywood FL 33020-3139

ANKROM, CHARLES FRANKLIN, golf course architect, consultant; b. Parkersburg, W.Va., Nov. 7, 1936; s. Donsel and Elva Dale (Cale) A.; m. Evelyn Kay Smith, 1957 (div. Feb. 1966); children: Beverly Lyn, Jan Ellen; m. Alice Lynell Glass, Aug. 24, 1968; children: Steven Charles, Cheryl Lyn. Student, W.Va. U., 1955, Eli Frank Sch. Design Arts, Tampa, Fla., 1956, Indian River C.C., Stuart, Fla. Exec. dir. golf, corp. golf course architect Gen. Devel. Corp., Miami, Fla., 1964-70; exec. dir. golf, golf course architect Boise Cascade Recreation Communities Group, Palo Alto, Calif., 1970-73; pres. Charles F. Ankrom, Inc., Stuart, Fla., 1973—. Prin. works include Sabal Trace C.C., Sun 'N Lake Country Club, Sebring, Fla., Cocoa Beach Mcpl. Golf Course, Cocoa Beach City, Fla., Ft. Lauderdale (Fla.) Country Club, Boca Raton (Fla.) Mcpl. Golf Course, The Habitat Golf Course, Brevard County, Fla., Aquarina, Melbourne, Fla., Crane Creek C.C., Stuart, Fla., Meadowood C.C., Ft. Pierce, Fla., Indian River Planatation Resort, Jensen Beach, Fla., Metro Country Club, Dominican Republic, numerous others. Donated design & adminstrv. svcs. for Bulldog Sportsturf

Complex, Martin County (Fla.) Schs. Recipient Outstanding Achievement by Ind. in Bus. or Industry award State of Fla. Coun. on Vocat. Edn., 1992, Bus. Ptnr. award Martin County Sch. Dist., 1991. Mem. Am. Soc. Golf Course Architects (bd. dirs., various nat. coms., Presdl. citation 1993), Nat. Golf Found. Home: 1831 SW Crane Creek Ave Palm City FL 34990-2215 Office: Charles F Ankrom Inc PO Box 898 Stuart FL 34995-0898

ANNS, ARLENE EISERMAN, publishing company executive; b. Pearl River, N.Y.; d. Frederick Joel and Anna (Behnke) E.; student Bergen Jr. Coll., 1946-48; BS, Utah State U., 1950; postgrad. Traphagen Sch. Design, 1957, NYU, 1958, Hunter Coll., 1959-60. Rsch. and promotion asst. Archtl. Record, N.Y.C., 1952-56; asst. rsch. dir. Esquire Mag., N.Y.C., 1956-62; rsch. mgr. Am. Machinist, publ. McGraw-Hill, Inc., N.Y.C., 1962-67, mktg. svc. mgr., 1967-69, 1969-71, sales mgr., 1976-77, dir. mktg., 1977-78; v.p. mktg. svcs. Morgan-Gramplan, Inc., N.Y.C., 1971-72; mktg. dir. Family Health & Diversion mag., 1972-74; dist. sales mgr. Postgrad. Medicine, 1974-76; advt. sales mgr. Contemporary Ob/Gyn, 1976-78; dir. profl. devel., 1978-80; pub. graduating engr. and dir. mktg. Aviation Week Group, 1980-90; pub. World Aviation Directory; dir. communications Aviation Week Group, 1990-92; v.p., Phase, Ltd., 1993—. Mem. SCORE Resource for SBA. Mem. Am. Mktg. Assn., Pharm. Advt. Club, Advt. Women N.Y., Advt. Club N.Y., Sales Exec. Club, Employment Mgmt. Assn., Am. Soc. Pers. Adminstrs., Nat. Orgn. Disability (bd. dirs.), Internat. Platform Assn., Coll. Placement Coun., Svc. Corps Ret. Execs., Wings Club, Dir. Assn., Pi Sigma Alpha. Home: Barnahill Farm Rt # 1 Box 162 Stanardsville VA 22973

ANSCHER, BERNARD, manufacturing executive, investor, consultant; b. Bklyn., June 9, 1922; s. Abraham and Esther (Draznin) A.; student Sch. Tech., CCNY, 1939-42; BS in Mech. Engring., NYU, 1948, MBA, 1953, postgrad., 1953-65; children: William, Marlene, Joseph. Cert. mfg. engr. robotics, mfg. engr. Chief, metall. and fabrication devel. reactor materials br. AEC, N.Y.C., 1946-50; devel. mgr., gen. sales mgr. domestic sales, asst. to v.p. Loewy-Hydropress, Inc., N.Y.C., 1950-55; cons., mfrs.' rep. Mercury Engring. Co., N.Y.C., 1955-65; founder, chmn. bd. dirs., pres. Nat. Molding Corp., Farmingdale, N.Y., 1965-87; pres. Anscher Mgmt. Corp. (formally Custom Molds), Opa Locka, Fla., 1975—; founder, pres. Nat. Indsl. Robotic Controls, 1983-90; mfg. cons., 1991—; founder, instr. mktg. program in community coll., N.Y.C., 1962-65; mem. industry adv. group Underwriters Labs., robotics standards com. Robot Inst.; corp. mem. Automotive Industry Action Group, 1984-87. Mem. Met. Opera Guild, Am. Queens County committeeman Rep. Party, 1960-68; mem. Dem. Exec. Com., Dade County, Fla., 1990-92; Dem. Party nominee for Congress, 18th Dist., Fla., 1990; ind. candidate Congress 22d Dist., Fla., 1992; mem. platform com. Dem. Party Presdl. Election, 1992; treas. Temple Emanu-el, 1994-95, Lehrman Day Sch., 1994-95. With AUS, 1943-46; PTO. Recipient Spl. award Manhattan Dist., 1946; cert. mfg. engr. Mem. N.Y. State Mktg. Educators (chmn. curriculum rsch. com. 1964), Soc. Mfg. Engrs., Soc. Plastics Engrs., Robotics Internat., Am. Jewish Congress (commn. law and social action), Pres.'s Club U. Miami, NYU Alumni Assn. Reviewing editor Die Design Handbook, 1954-55; polit. columnist Miami Beach Sunpost, 1991-92; patentee; contbr. publs. in field. Office: Anscher Mgmt Corp PO Box 610157 Miami FL 33261-0157

ANSLEY, CAMPBELL WALLACE, JR., retired veterinary drug distributor; b. Thomasville, Ga., July 4, 1921; s. Campbell Wallace and Jane (Hollenshead) A.; m. Elizabeth Nadeene Darbyshire, Sept. 6, 1946; children: Elizabeth Glen Ansley Dixson, Margaret Jane Ansley Kirbo. BS in Chemistry, Davidson Coll., 1943. Chief textile chemist Munitex Corp.-Tryon (N.C.) Processing, 1946-47; owner, gen. mgr. Moultrie (Ga.) Serum Distbrs., 1947-78, Ansley Nash Motors, Moultrie, 1949-54; credit mgr. Riverside Mfg. Co., Moultrie, 1978-81; inventory control mgr. Riverside Mfg. Co., 1981-83, corp. dir. purchasing, 1983-86; cons. credit and fin. Ansley Cons., Moultrie, 1986-90; genealogy and family history cons. Moultrie, 1987—. Author: Indians in Confederacy, 1958, Confederate Newspapers, 1966, Writing Family History, 1986, Who Am I, 1989, History of William Ansley Family, 1989, Making of the Man-Boyhood of Robert E. Lee, 1988, Piney Woods Child, 1989, Bifocal Souls, 1989, Snowbird, 1990, Next of Kin, 1992, The Snowbird Indian Tribe, 1993, The Making of Britain - 6000 BC-1952, 1993, Highland Kin, 1994, Cousins-Nixon & Carter, 1994, My War, 1995, Vereen Huguenot Family, 1996, Precious Moments, 1996. V.p. United Way, 1954; county chmn. Moultrie area Boy Scouts Am., 1955-59; chmn. bd. dirs. Colquitt-Thomas Regional Libr., Moultrie, 1960-63; clk. of session Moultrie Presbyn. Ch., 1958-87, bd. deacons, 1947-56, bd. elders, 1956-93; bd. dirs. TV-Radio-Audio, Synod of Ga., 1963-68, YMCA, 1979-83; mem. Moultrie Colquitt Devel. Authority; trustee Odom Geneal. Libr. Bd., Ga. History Soc. 1st lt. inf., U.S. Army, 1943-46, Aleutian Islands. Recipient Presdl. Order of Merit, 1991. Mem. Augusta Genealogy Soc., Ga. Hist. Soc., Moultrie C. of C., Kiwanis (bd. dirs., pres. Moultrie chpt. 1956-57). Republican. Office: PO Box 2377 Moultrie GA 31776-2377

ANSLEY, DARLENE H., communications executive; b. Anderson, Ind., Aug. 21, 1942; d. Byron J. and Edith O. (Earlywine) Howell; children: David, Bradley, Lisa. Student, Anderson U., 1960-61; BS in Communications, Fla. State U., 1978. Asst. project Boydston Advt. & Creative Svcs., Tallahassee, 1978; asst. dir. Pub. Broadcasting Svc., Alexandria, Va., 1982-85, assoc. dir., 1985-87, advt. mgr., nat. programming & promotion svcs., 1987-93; prin. Ansley Comms., Inc., 1993—. Office: Ansley Comms Inc 5707 Walnut Wood Ln Burke VA 22015-2710

ANSLEY, SHEPARD BRYAN, lawyer; b. Atlanta, July 31, 1939; s. William Bonneau and Florence Jackson (Bryan) A.; m. Boyce Lineberger, May 9, 1970; children—Anna Rankin, Florence Bryan. BA, U. Ga., 1961; LLB, U. Va., 1964. Bar: Ga. 1967. Assoc. Carter & Ansley and predecessor firm Carter, Ansley, Smith & McLendon, Atlanta, 1967-73, ptnr., 1973-84, of counsel, 1984-91; bd. dirs. Prime Bancshares, Inc., Prime Bank, FSB; chmn. bd. dirs., pres. Sodamaster Co. Am.; exec. v.p. Woodridge Realty, Inc. Sr. v.p., ACA Consulting, Inc., Bd. dirs. Jour. Pub. Law Emory U., 1961-62. Mem. vestry St. Luke's Episcopal Ch., Atlanta, 1971-74; treas., mem. exec. com., bd. dirs. Alliance Theatre Co., Atlanta, 1974-85; trustee Atlanta Music Festival Assn., Inc., 1975—; v.p., bd. dirs. Atlanta Preservation Ctr. Inc., pres., 1988-90; bd. visitors Lineberger Cancer Research Ctr. U. N.C. at Chapel Hill, 1987-92; pres., bd. dirs. The Study Hall at Emmaus House, Inc. Served to capt. U.S. Army, 1965-67. Mem. ABA, Ga. Bar Assn., Atlanta Bar Assn., Atlanta Lawyers Club, Am. Coll. Mortgage Attys., Atlanta Jr. C. of C. (bd. dirs. 1968-72), Piedmont Driving Club.

ANSTEAD, HARRY LEE, judge. Former judge, chief judge U.S. Ct. Appeals. (4th dist.), Fla.; justice Fla. Supreme Ct., Tallahassee, 1994—. Office: Supreme Ct Bldg 500 S Duval St Tallahassee FL 32399-6556*

ANTALFFY, LESLIE PETER, mechanical engineer; b. Budapest, Hungary, Oct. 31, 1942; came to U.S., 1973; s. Vilmos Leslie and Margo (Simay) A.; m. Barbara Ann Clark, Jan. 19, 1970; children: Julie, Michael, Nicole. B in Mech. Engring., U. Adelaide, Australia, 1970; MBA, Sam Houston State U., 1980. Registered profl. engr., Tex.; chartered profl. engr. Instn. Engrs. Australia. Mech. engr. T. O'Connor & Sons, Adelaide, 1968-69; vessel engr. Lummus Co. Can., Toronto, 1970-71, A.G. McKee Co. Can., Toronto, 1972; sr. vessel engr. Lummus Co. Can., Toronto, 1972-73; sr. vessel engr. Fluor Daniel, Houston, 1973-75, prin. engr., 1975-80, supervising mech. engr., 1980-89, mech. engring. dir., 1989-95, sr. mech. engring. dir., 1995—, sr. tech. fellow, 1996—. Contbr. articles to profl. jours. Mem. ASME (spl. working group on high pressure vessels task group chmn. fabrication, examination testing of ASME VIII divsn. 3, 1992—, chmn. high pressure tech.-design 1993—). Republican. Roman Catholic. Home: 11946 Summerdale Dr Houston TX 77077

ANTE, RICHARD LOUIS, civilian military employee; b. Cin., July 26, 1936; s. Louis John and Mildred Cecelia (Timmerding) A.; m. Rosalind Marie Schuppert, June 17, 1961; children: Jonathan, Alison, Brian, Eric, Alex. BA in Acctg., Thomas More Coll., 1958; MBA in Mgmt., Xavier U., Cin., 1965. CPA, Ohio; cert. profl. contract mgr.; cert. internal auditor. Auditor gen. USAF, Cin., 1962; internal auditor Hartford Ins. Co., Cin., 1960-62; indsl. cost auditor USAF Auditor Gen. GE Co., Evendale, Ohio, 1962-65; sr. auditor Def. Contract Audit Agy., Cin., 1965-76; chief Contr. Adminstrn. Branch Air Force Plant Rep. Office GE Co., Cin., 1976-84; chief Contr. Adminstrn. Divsn., 1984-89, chief Subcontract Mgmt., 1989-94; leader Naval Systems Team Def. Logistics Agy. GE Co., 1994—; adminstrv. contracting officer Def. Logistics Agy., Cin., termination contracting officer, mem. def. acquisition corps level III, Boston, 1993. Contbr. articles to profl. jours. With U.S. Army, 1958-64. Fellow Nat. Contract Mgmt. Assn. (1st v.p. 1993, Blanche White Meml. award 1994), Fed. Govt. Accts. Assn. (pres. 1985). Republican. Roman Catholic. Home: 1 Rosemont Ave Fort Thomas KY 41075 Office: DLA/DCMDN care GE Co 1 Neumann Way Evendale OH 45215

ANTHONY, GRETCHEN WILHELMINA HAUSER, architect; b. Mpls., Nov. 13, 1936; d. Theodor Emmanuel and Margrete Alice (Norman) Hauser; m. John Duncan Anthony, June 17, 1961 (div. Jan. 1980); children: Caitlin Anharad, Ian David. Student Pa. State U., 1954-59; BArch, U. Mich., 1961. Registered profl. architect, Pa. Draftswoman, designer Todd & Giroux AIA, Rochester, N.Y., 1961-62, Michaell DeAngelis AIA, Rochester, 1962-63, John M. Puskar AIA, Pitts., 1963-66; ptnr. Puskar & Anthony, Pitts., 1968-70; self-employed architect, 1970—, Fairmont, W.Va., 1974—; cons. Washington County Planning Commn., Pa., 1966-67, 1970-73. Draftswoman, designer and specifications writer on variety of constrn. and remodeling projects. Organizer, past pres. Marion County High Spirit MS Com., Fairmont, W.Va., 1975-90; del. Gov. of W.Va. Conf. on Handicapped Individuals, Charleston, 1976; alt. White House Conf. on Handicapped Individuals, 1976; mem. W.Va. Adv. Council on Edn. of Exceptional Children, Charleston, 1978-81; organizer Handicapped United of W.Va., Fairmont, pres., 1982-92, Govs. Coun. on Pers. with Disabilities, 1992-93; bd. dirs. greater W.Va. chpt. Nat. M.S. Soc., Charleston, 1983-87; past vice chmn. consumer adv. com. Clarksburg Dist. div. W.Va. Vocat. Rehab., 1983-90; trustee Coordinating Council for Ind. Living, Morgantown, W.Va., 1984-90; chairperson consumer adv. com. W.Va. Client Assistance Program, Charleston, 1984—, W.Va. Ind. Living Coun., 1987-93, U. W.Va. Social Justice Coun., 1987-89, U. W.Va. Handicapped Accessibility Com., 1987-89; sec. adv. bd. W.Va. Assistive Tech. Systems, bd. sec., 1992—. Recipient award W.Va Adv. Com on Edn. of Exceptional Children, Merit award W.Va. Rehab. Assn. Avocations: reading; knitting. Home and Office: 6 Diana Dr Fairmont WV 26554-1220

ANTHONY, JACK RAMON, mechanical engineer, retired; b. Hobbs, N.Mex., Dec. 9, 1932; s. Wadie Fowler and Zelma Ray Anthony; m. Peggy Lou Berryhill, July 17, 1953; children; Vera Lynn Anthony Robertson, Michael Ray. BSME, U. N.Mex., 1959; ME, Tex. Tech. U., 1974. Registered profl. engr., Tex. Engr. Chrysler, New Orleans, 1963-65, Eberline Instruments, Santa Fe, 1959-63, Dresser Golf, Houston, 1965-67; project engr. Mason & Hagner co., Amarillo, Tex., 1967-90, Nuclear Fuel Svcs., Erwin, Tenn., 1990-95; retired, 1995—. With U.S. Army, 1953-55. Mem. NSPE (chpt. pres. 1973-74), Pi Tau Sigma. Republican. Methodist. Home: PO Box 308 Buffalo OK 73834

ANTHONY, LAURA G., real estate broker; b. Dallas, June 28, 1958; d. Frank Snider Groseclose and Sandra Jeanne (Hobbs) Gaines; m. Thomas Daniel Anthony, July 19, 1980 (div. June 1995); children: Kaitlin, Alexandra, Daniel. BBA, U. Tex., 1979. Lic. real estate broker, Tex. Loan officer Investors, Inc., Austin, 1979-80, Ellison Industries, San Antonio, Tex., 1980-81; v.p. Gill Savings, San Antonio, Tex., 1981-91; project dir. Westlakes, San Antonio, Tex., 1982—; real estate broker San Antonio, Tex., 1978—; land devel. and mktg. cons. Bd. dirs. St. David's Episcopal Sch., San Antonio, 1992-94. Mem. Network of Women in Comml. Real Estate (pres. 1986-94), Real Estate Coun., Real Estate Breakfast Club (pres.), Real Estate Fin. Soc., San Antonio Bd. Realtors, San Antonio Country Club. Office: Westlakes Tower Life Bldg 10th Fl San Antonio TX 78205

ANTHONY, ROBERT ARMSTRONG, law educator; b. Washington, Dec. 28, 1931; s. Emile Peter and Martha Graham (Armstrong) A.; m. Ruth Grace Barrons, Feb. 7, 1959 (div.); 1 child, Graham Barrons; m. Joan Patricia Caton, Jan 3, 1980; 1 child, Peter Christopher. BA, Yale U., 1953; B.A. in Jurisprudence (Rhodes scholar), Oxford U., 1955; JD, Stanford U., 1957. Bar: Calif. 1957, N.Y. 1971, D.C. 1972. Assoc. Pillsbury, Madison & Sutro, San Francisco, 1957-62, Kelso, Cotton & Ernst, San Francisco, 1962-64; assoc. prof. law Cornell U. Law Sch., 1964-68, prof., 1968-75, dir. internat. legal studies, 1964-74; chief counsel, later dir. Office Fgn. Direct Investments, Dept. Commerce, 1972-73; cons. Adminstrv. Conf. U.S., Washington, 1968-71; chmn. Adminstrv. Conf. U.S., 1974-79; ptnr. McKenna, Conner & Cuneo, Washington, 1979-82; sole practice Washington, 1982-83; prof. law George Mason U., Arlington, Va., 1983—; Fulbright lectr., Slovenia, 1994; lectr. Acad. Am. and Internat. Law, Southwestern Legal Found., Dallas, summers 1967-72, instr. Golden Gate U., 1961. Mem. editorial adv. bd. Jour. Law and Tech., 1986-91; contbr. articles to profl. jours. Active Pres.'s Inflation Program Regulatory Coun., 1978-79, Fairfax County (Va.) Rep. Com., 1984-86; chmn. panel U.S. Dept. Edn. Appeal Bd., 1981-83; cons., chmn. pubs. adv. bd. Internat. Law Inst., 1984—; cons. Inst. Pub. Adminstrn., Slovenia, 1994—; bd. dirs. Marin Shakespeare Festival, San Rafael, Calif., 1961-64, Nat. Ctr. for Adminstrv. Justice, 1974-79, Va. Assn. Scholars, 1990-96; commr. Sausalito (Calif.) City Planning Commn., 1962-64. Mem. ABA (coun., sec. sect. adminstrv. law and regulatory practice 1988-94), Assn. Am. Rhodes Scholars, Am. Law Inst., Stanford U. Law Soc. Washington (pres. 1982), Cosmos Club. Home: 2011 Lorraine Ave Mc Lean VA 22101-5331 Office: George Mason U Sch Law 3401 N Fairfax Dr Arlington VA 22201-4498

ANTHONY, SUSAN MAE, entrepreneur; b. Elmhurst, Ill., Oct. 11, 1959; d. Neil Jack and Shirley Mae (Deckard) A.; m. Mark Stephan Rogers, Jan. 28, 1989 (div. May 1993); 1 child, Ryan James Rogers. Student, Edison C.C., 1977-82; AS, Internat. Corr. Sch., 1982. Clk. Lee County Elec. Coop., North Ft. Myers, Fla., 1975-78, apprentice journeyman, 1978-82; spl. agt. Northwestern Mut. Life, Ft. Myers, Fla., 1982-86; broker rep. Paul Revere Ins. Co., Ft. Myers, 1986-88; owner Anthony Ins. Svcs., Ft. Myers, 1982-92; co-owner Soil Plus, Ft. Myers, 1988-92; pres. Crews Sanitation Co., Ft. Myers, 1993—; owner Anthony Contracting Svcs., Ft. Myers, 1992—. Author: (guidebook) Guide and Checklist for Starting a Small Business, 1993. Founder, organizer New Directions, Am. Cancer Soc., Ft. Myers, 1986-88, crusade chmn., bd. officer, 1986-88; organizer, co-chmn., pres. Interfaith Vol. Caregivers Project, Ft. Myers, 1993—; founder, chmn. Elder Abuse Task Force, Ft. Myers, 1993-95; elder abuse prevention coord. Area Agy. on Aging of S.W. Fla., Ft. Myers, 1993-95; mem. steering com. for minority task force Horizon Coun. on Econ. Devel., Ft. Myers, 1991-93; active Fla. and Nat. Women's Polit. Caucus, 1991-93. Mem. NRA, Fla. Septic Tank Assn., Fla. Restaurant Assn., Ft. Myers Womens Network (steering com., bd. dirs. 1984-92). Republican. Home: PO Box 2031 Fort Myers FL 33902-2031 Office: Crews Sanitation Co PO Box 27 Fort Myers FL 33902-0027

ANTON, S. DAVID, lawyer; b. Tampa, Fla., Nov. 25, 1958; s. Leonard Morton Anton and Joyce (Schonbrun) Hartmann. BS in Econs., U. Fla., 1981, JD, 1984. Cert. mediator. Pvt. practice family law, dept collection and corp. law Tampa. Mem. Fla. Bar Assn., Hillsborough County Bar Assn. Office: Harvey Schonbrun PA 1802 N Morgan St Tampa FL 33602-2328

ANTOUN, MIKHAIL, medicinal chemistry and pharmacognosy educator; b. Khartoum, Sudan, Aug. 20, 1946; came to U.S., 1979; s. Daoud and Badia (Boulos) A.; m. Slavomira Kucerova, Sept. 14, 1973; children: Helena, David Emmanuel, Anna Maria. B in Pharm. with distinction, U. Khartoum, 1968; PhD, U. London, 1974. Asst. prof. pharm. U. Khartoum (Sudan), 1974-78, assoc. prof., 1978-81; sr. rsch. scientist Purdue U., West Lafayette, Ind., 1981-86; assoc. prof. medicinal chemistry U. P.R. Sch. Pharm., San Juan, 1986-92, prof. medicinal chemistry, faculty chairprof., dept. head, 1993—; vis. prof., rsch. assoc. Sch. Pharmacy & Pharm. Sci., West Lafayette, 1979-81. Contbr. articles to profl. jours. Sr. scholar U. Khartoum, 1968-69; teaching fellow U. London, 1969-73. Fellow Linnean Soc.; mem. AAAS, Am. Assn. Pharm. Scientists, Am. Chem. Soc., Am. Assn. Colls. Pharmacy, Am. Soc. Pharmacognosy, Sigma Xi. Home: Calle A #6 La Antillana Trujillo Alto PR 00976

ANTUNEZ DE MAYOLO, JORGE CARLOS, hematologist, oncologist, geriatrician; b. Lima, Peru, Mar. 4, 1958; m. Gigi Antunez de Mayolo; children: Ximena, Adriana, Alonso. Gen. Studies Diploma, Cayetano Heredia Peruvian U., Lima, 1977, MB, 1983, MD Diploma, 1983. Diplomate Am. Bd. Internal Medicine, Subspecialty Bd. Hematology, Subspecialty Bd. Med. Oncology, Subspecialty Bd. Geriatrics; lic. MD, Fla., Md. Osler clerkship in internal medicine Johns Hopkins U., Balt., 1983; internship internal medicine U. Miami/Jackson Meml. Med. Ctr., Miami, Fla., 1984-85, residency internal medicine, 1985-87; fellowship in clin. hematology U. Miami (Fla.) Sch. of Medicine, 1987-89, fellowship in med. oncology, 1989-90; Fogarty vis. assoc. clin. hematology br. Nat. Heart, Lung and Blood Inst., NIH, Bethesda, Md., 1990-92; hematologist, oncologist pvt. practice Miami, 1992—; attending physician hematology and oncology Mercy Hosp., Miami, Victoria Hosp., Miami, Cedars Med. Ctr., Miami. Contbr. articles to profl. jours. Fellow ACP, Am. Coll. Internat. Physicians; mem. AMA, AAAS, Peruvian Coll. Physicians, Am. Soc. Hematology. Office: 3661 S Miami Ave Ste 305 Miami FL 33133-4206

APELIAN, CLOVER B., non-profit management consultant; b. St. Marys, Ohio, Feb. 23, 1937; d. Howard Alois and Jessie Clara (Clover) Werner; m. George Michael Apelian, July 12, 1957; children: Georganne Apelian Shockey, Julia Apelian Green, Michael Werner Apelian. Student, Ohio State U.; BSBA, Barry U., 1980. Cert. fundraising exec., cert. assoc. for healthcare philanthropy. With Hannah Neil Ctr. for Children, Columbus, Ohio, 1970-78; with Papanicolaou Cancer Rsch. Inst. U. Miami Sch. Medicine-St. Francis Hosp., Miami Beach, Fla., 1978-81; with Mailman Ctr. Child Devel. U. Miami Sch. Medicine, 1980-87; v.p. Charitable Fund for Healthcare Excellence North Broward Hosp. Dist./Found. Healthcorp, Inc., 1987-90; pres. and non-profit mgmt. cons. Clover Devel. Strategies, Inc., Boca Raton, Fla., 1990—; assoc. prof. Non-Profit Mgmt. Inst., Nova U., 1990-91. Mem. Nat. Soc. Fund Raising Execs. (pres. Broward chpt.), Nat. Assn. Hosp. Devel. (sec.-treas. multi-hosp. systems sect.). Office: 1699 S Federal Hwy # 3A Boca Raton FL 33432-7410

APINIS, JOHN, chemist; b. Katvari, Latvia, Mar. 20, 1933; came to U.S., 1949, naturalized, 1954; s. Augusts and Marta (Gravelsins) A.;m. Johnnie Verena Burden, Feb. 6, 1960. B.S., Clemson U., 1960. Apprentice, Am. Thread Co., Willimantic, Conn., 1951-52, Leiss Velvet Mfg. Co., Willimantic, 1952-53; asst. plant chemist Burlington Industries, Wake Finishing Co., Raleigh, N.C., 1960-65, plant chemist, 1965-75, mgr. dept. dyeing, 1975-76, tech. coordinator, 1976-94; ret. Served with AUS, 1953-55. Mem. Am. Assn. Textile Chemists and Colorists. Clubs: Elks, Rotary (v.p. 1963-64, pres. 1964-65, dir. 1963-66), Raleigh Music, Questers (v.p. 1977-78, pres. 1978-79), Raleigh Clemson Alumni (pres. 1976-77). Research in textile color computer and chromosorter. Home: 502 Oakmont Dr Anderson SC 29621-3747

APOLINSKY, STEPHEN DOUGLAS, lawyer; b. Birmingham, Ala., Dec. 5, 1961; s. Harold Irwin and Sandra Jean (Rubenstein) A. BA, U. Mich., 1983; JD, Emory U., 1987. Bar: Ga. 1987, U.S. Dist. Ct. (no. dist.) Ga. 1987, D.C. 1989, Ala. 1994. Litigation assoc. Bentley, Karesh & Seacrest, Atlanta, 1987-94; named mem. firm Eastman, Stapleton & Apolinsky, LLC, Atlanta, 1995—. Mem. Assn. Trial Lawyers Am., Ga. Trial Lawyers Assn., Atlanta Bar Assn., Atlanta Claims Assn. Office: Eastman Stapleton Apolinsky 100 Colony Sq Ste 404 1175 Peachtree St NE Atlanta GA 30361

APP, JAMES LEONARD, dean; b. Fairmont, Minn., Jan. 27, 1936; s. Leonard Walter and Lucia Irene (Hellbusch) A.; m. Diane Catherine Conoryea, July 5, 1957; children: Timothy, Lisa, Polly, Peter. BS, U. Minn., 1957; MS, U. Wis., 1960, PhD, 1961. Asst. prof. U. Minn., 1961-63, assoc. prof., 1963-72, prof., asst. dean, 1972-73; county extension dir. Manatee County Coop. Extension, Palmetto, Fla., 1973-75; dist. agt. U. Fla. Coop. Extension, Gainesville, 1975, asst. dean, 1975—; vice chmn. So. Region Extension Agrl. and Natural Resources, 1983-84, chmn., 1984-85, chmn. program planning, 1985-86; sec. So. Region Extension Cmty. Resource Devel. Com., 1986-87. Contbr. articles to profl. jours.; presenter in field. Mem. Community Leaders of Am. Recipient Spl. Accomplishments award Fla. Landscape Maintenance Assn., 1989, Innovative and Aggressive Program Support award U. Fla. Or. Hort. Extension Specialists, 1979; named Hon. Fla. Master Gardener U. Fla. Cooperative Extension Specialists, 1984; Computerized Producers Guides grantee, 1978, 82. Mem. Am. Men of Sci., Gamma Sigma Delta. Office: Univ Fla Agrl Programs PO Box 110210 Gainesville FL 32611-0210

APPEL, JAMES BARRY, psychology educator; b. N.Y.C., Feb. 18, 1934; m. Hope E. Mag, Nov. 24, 1965. AB, Columbia U., 1955; PhD, Ind. U., 1960. Postdoctoral rsch. fellow Inst. Psychiat. Rsch., Ind. U. Sch. Medicine, 1959-60; rsch. asst. dept. psychiatry Yale U. Sch. Medicine, 1960-61, asst. prof. psychology, 1961-66; assoc. prof. psychology dept. psychaitry U. Chgo. Sch. Medicine, 1966-70, assoc. prof., 1970-72; prof. psychology dept. psychology U. S.C., Columbia, 1972-85, Carolina Rsch. prof., 1986-94, dir. grad. programs in gen.-exptl. psychology, 1982-86, Carolina Disting. prof., 1994—; vis. prof. MRC unit on neural mechanisms of behaviour Univ. Coll., London, 1978; vis. rsch. scientist Nat. Inst. on Drug Abuse/Addiction Rsch. Ctr., Balt., 1986; APA vis. scientist George Mason U., 1974, Wofford Coll., 1975; cons. Nat. Inst. Drug Abuse, NIMH, NIH, NSF, Schizophrenia Rsch. Program, Scottish Rite, No. Masonic Jurisdiction, Student Assn. for Study of Hallucinogens. Editorial advisor Animal Learning and Behavior, Archives of Gen. Psychiatry, Life Scis., Nature, Pharmacology, Biochemistry and Behavior, Physiology and Behavior, Sci.; mem. editl. Bd. Jour. Psychoactive Drugs, Behavioral Pharmacology, Psychopharmacology; contbr. articles to profl. jours. Recipient MERIT (Method to Extend Rsch. in Time) award Nat. Inst. Drug Abuse, 1989, award U. S.C. Ednl. Found., 1989; grantee NSF, 1955-56, 67-68, 69-70, State of Ill. Dept. Mental Health, 1970-72, NIMH, 1969-72, 73-79, NIH, 1963-65, 76-77, 79-81, Nat. Inst. Drug Abuse, 1976-79, 88-94. Fellow AAAS, APA, Am. Coll. Neuropsychopharmacology; mem. Behavioral Pharmacology Soc., Collegium Internat. Neuro-Psycopharmacologicum, Ea. Psychol. Assn., Internat. Brian Rsch. Orgn., Soc. Neurosci. (pres. S.C. chpt. 1982-83, 90-91), Soc. for Stimulus Properties of Drugs (pres. 1981-82), Sigma Xi. Office: U SC Dept Psychology Columbia SC 29208

APPEL, TRUMAN FRANK, surgeon; b. St. Louis, Apr. 4, 1936; s. Myron Henry and Ida Doris (Pearline) A.; children: Leslie Carol, Sarah Elizabeth. BS, Tulane U., 1956; MD, St. Louis U., 1960. Diplomate Am. Bd. Surgery, Am. Bd. Colon and Rectal Surgery. treas., bd. dirs. Coastal Bend Health Plan, Corpus Christi, 1984-92. Served to capt. USAF, 1961-64. Fellow AMA, ACS, Am. Soc. Colon and Rectal Surgeons Tex., Tex. Med. Assn., Masons, Shriners. Jewish. Office: 307 Spohn Med Pl 1415 Third St Corpus Christi TX 78404

APPERSON, BERNARD JAMES, lawyer; b. Washington, June 28, 1956; s. Bernard James Jr. and Ann Wentworth (Anderson) A. BA in Polit. Sci., Am. U., 1978; JD, Cumberland Sch. Law, 1981; LLM in Internat. Law, Georgetown U., 1985. Bar: Fla. 1981, Ga. 1981, D.C. 1983, U.S. Supreme Ct. 1985. Atty., U.S. trustee for so. dist. N.Y. U.S. Dept. Justice, N.Y.C., 1981; atty. EPA, Washington, 1981-83; atty. civil rights div. U.S. Dept. Justice, Washington, 1983-84, atty. office legis. affairs, 1986-87; asst. U.S. atty. Ea. Dist. Va., Alexandria, 1987—; counsel to dir. Legal Services Corp., Washington, 1985-86; instr. FBI Tng. Acad., Quantico, Va., 1990; lectr. law U. London and U. Ga., 1990. Assoc. editor Am. Jour. Trial Advocacy Cumberland Sch. Law, 1979-81. County chmn. Paula Hawkins for U.S Senate, Volusia County, Fla., 1974; nat. staff Citizens for Reagan, Fla., Kansas City, Mo., 1976; cons. Reagan for Pres., Detroit, 1980; dep. northeastern regional dir. Reagan-Bush 1984, Washington, 1984. Lewis F. Powell Medal for Excellence in Advocacy Am. Coll Trial Lawyers, 1980. Mem. Federalist Soc. for Law and Pub. Policy Studies, Order of Barristers, St. Andrew's Soc. Republican. Episcopalian. Home: 545 E Braddock Rd Apt 704 Alexandria VA 22314-2171 Office: Office US Atty Ea Dist Va 2100 Jaimison Ave Alexandria VA 22314-2944

APPLEGATE, J. PHILLIP, psychology educator, state official; b. Chickasha, Okla.; s. Clarence Ellsworth and Daisy Eleanor (Pybas) A.; m. Perri Jeanne Brewer, June 14, 1980. BEd, U. Okla., 1979, EdD, 1993; MEd, Ctrl. State U., Edmond, Okla., 1986. Cert. elem., secondary tchr., Okla. Tchr. Velma-Alma Pub. Schs., Velma, Okla., 1980-81; tchr. Chickasha H.S., 1981-95; rsch. asst. U. Okla., Norman, 1988; prof. Rose State Coll., Midwest City, Okla., 1994; counselor Upward Bound Rose State Coll., 1994; adminstr. Dept. Edn., State of Okla., Oklahoma City, 1995-96, dir. instrnl. tech. and telecomms., 1996—; cons. Human Techs., Edmond, 1996—. Editor: (textbook) World History, 1995. City councilman, Chickasha, 1992-95; bd. dirs. Grady County YMCA, Chicasha, 1993-95; mem. Grady County Dem.

Ctrl. Com., 1992-93. Mem. Nat. Coun. for the Social Studies (archives com. 1995—), Okla. Coun. for the Social Studies (bd. dirs. 1995—), Okla. Alliance for Geog. Edn. (bd. dirs. 1995—), Okla. Coun. for Econs. Edn. (bd. dirs. 1995—), Okla. Social Studies Suprs. Assn., Nat. Coun. for History in the Schs. Home: 1225 S 8th St Chickasha OK 73018-4435 Office: Okla State Dept Edn 2500 N Lincoln Blvd Oklahoma City OK 73105

APRIL, JOHN JAMES, sociology educator, clergyman; b. Worcester, South Africa, July 19, 1955; came to U.S., 1977; s. John James and Frances (Arendse) A.; m. Gwendolyn Marie Weathersby, Dec. 21, 1982 (dec. Aug. 1991); m. Yvette April Dixon, July 10, 1993; children: Ashley Nicole, Jonathan Jamal. BA, Paul Quinn Coll., Waco, Tex., 1980; MA in Sociology/Ednl. Psychology, Baylor U., Waco, 1982; MDiv, Guadalupe Coll./Theol. Sem., 1992. Ordained to ministry Methodist Ch., 1992. Grad. tchr. and rsch. asst. Baylor U., Waco, 1980-82; assoc. prof., head dept. social and behavioral scis. Paul Quinn Coll., Waco, 1982-88; prof. sociology Tex. State Tech. Coll., Waco, 1989—; adj. prof. sociology Ctrl. Tex. Coll., Killeen, 1990—; min. Bush Chapel Presbyn. Ch., Elm Mott, Tex., 1984-91, African Meth. Episcopal Ch., Falls County, 1992—; adj. prof. sociology McClennan C.C., Waco, 1988-90; area dir. Youth in Action for Econ. Opportunity Advancement Corp., 1989-91. Contbg. author, editor: (textbook) Sociological Outlook, 1995; editor cmty. newspaper The Bottom Line, 1985; host TV rogram Central Issues, Waco, 1994-95. V.p. NAACP, McClennan County, 1985-89; moderator Tex. Synod, Presbyn., Tex., Elm Mott, 1987-92. Scottish Rite acad. scholar, 1983. Mem. Am. Sociol. Assn., Alpha Phi Alpha. Home: 201 Robin Loop Waco TX 76705 Office: Tex State Tech Coll 3801 Campus Dr Waco TX 76705

ARAICO, ENRIQUE JESUS, insurance executive; b. Havana, Cuba, Dec. 26, 1955; came to U.S., 1963; s. Jesus and Marina (Carrasco) A.; m. Sonja Sheree Nave, Nov. 6, 1988; children: Vanessa Marina, Michael Roman, Steven Andrew. A in Bus., Miami Dade Community Coll., 1977; student, U. Miami, 1977-78, 79. Sales rep. Fed. Employees Benefits Assn., Pembroke Pines, Fla., 1975-84, sales mgr., 1985-91; pres. Araico and Assocs., Stockbridge, Ga., 1990—; sales mgr. Trustmark Ins., 1992—. Organizer George Bush Presdl. Campaign, Atlanta, 1988; pres. Fed. Benefit Planners, 1991—. Roman Catholic. Office: Fed Benefit Planners 3839 4th St N Ste 570 Saint Petersburg FL 33703-6112

ARAN, FERNANDO SANTIAGO, lawyer; b. Havana, Cuba, July 25, 1957; s. Armando and Lidia (Lazcano) A.; m. Marianela Morejon, Aug. 8, 1980; children: Fernando S. Jr., Roberto J., Jacqueline A. BBA, U. Miami, Coral Gables, Fla., 1978; JD, Georgetown U., 1981. Bar: Fla. 1982, U.S. Dist. Ct. (so. dist.) Fla. 1982, U.S. Ct. Appeals (11th cir.) 1983, U.S. Supreme Ct. 1987. Assoc. Kelley, Drye & Warren, Miami, 1981-90; ptnr. Aran, Correa & Guarch, P.A., Miami, Fla., 1990—. Exec. bd. dirs. So. Fla. coun. Boy Scouts Am., 1994—, Miami. Mem. Hispanic Nat. Bar Assn. (pres. S.E. region 1987-89), Cuban Am. Bar Assn. (bd. dirs. 1988-92, v.p. 1992, pres. 1995), U.S. Propeller Club (Miami pres. 1987-89). Office: Aran Correa & Guarch PA 710 S Dixie Hwy Coral Gables FL 33146-2602

ARANAS, NOEL BAUTISTA, systems analyst, consultant; b. Bauan, Batangas, Philippines, Jan. 20, 1962; came to U.S., 1988; naturalized, 1994; s. Jose Liwanag and Mary Azucena (Bautista) A.; m. Rhea Velez, 1994; 1 child, Kenneth Roy Velez-Aranas. BS in Electronics and Communications Engring., Don Bosco Tech. Coll. of Italy, Manila, 1984; postgrad., U. Tex., 1991-92. Lic. electronics and communications engr., Philippines. Systems engr. Applied Systems, Inc., Manila, 1983-84; project planner, cost engr. Sadelmi of GE, Italy, Egypt, USA, 1985-87; systems analyst Intermec Corp., Richardson, Tex., 1988-90; systems mgr. Internat. Claims, Dallas, 1990; cons. Nat. Hole-in-One Assn., Dallas, 1990—; owner, pres. Viper Telecom, Richardson, Tex., 1995—; cons. Ralph Kirkley and Assocs., Dallas, Austin, Tex., 1990-91. Sector leader Don Bosco Civic Assistance Team, Manila, 1980; mem. YMCA, Dallas, Garland, Tex., 1990; donor Salesian Missions Internat., New Rochelle, N.Y., 1990. Mem. Am. Mgmt. Assn., Rotary (dir. internat. affairs Antipolo Hills 1981-82, pres. 1981-82, Youth Leadership award dist. 380, 1982). Roman Catholic. Office: PO Box 831511 Richardson TX 75083-1511 also: Nat Hole-in-One Assn 730 Campbell Ctr I 8350 N Central Expy Dallas TX 75206-1625

ARANGO, ANTHONY GLENN, sales executive; b. Tampa, Fla., Nov. 14, 1945; s. Antonio Louis and Olga (Castro) A.; m. Loretta Dyer, Sept. 10, 1969 (div. 1975); 1 child, Anthony Glenn Jr.; m. Ruth Gordon, June 27, 1981. Student, Hillsboro Community Coll., 1970-74. Owner Diversified Maintenance Co., Tampa, 1970-77; mgr. sales Western-So. Life Ins. Co., Cin., 1978-80; pres. Ins. Planning Systems Inc., Tampa, 1980-84; CEO Dynex Industries Internat. Inc., Tampa, 1984—, also chmn.; cons., agt. Nat. Gen. Corp., Riyadh, Saudi Arabia, 1986—, Oriental Import Co., W.L.L., Safat, Kuwait, 1987—; cons., v.p. Inverstones Cusco Corp., Lima, Peru, 1987—. Mem. Inter-Am. Security Orgn., Washington, 1987, Rep. Nat. Com., Washington, 1987. Served as petty officer 2d class USN, 1966-68. Roman Catholic. Home: 4402 W Beach Park Dr Tampa FL 33609-3731

ARANGO, RICHARD STEVEN, architect, graphic and industrial designer; b. Bogota, Colombia, June 30, 1953; s. Jorge Arango Sanin and Judith (Wolpert) Arango; m. Maria Francesca Violich, Aug. 1977; children: Ruy Rafael, Antonia. AB in Architecture with honors, U. Calif., Berkeley, 1976, MArch, 1980. Registered architect. Prin. Richard Arango Design, Berkeley, 1976-85, Richard Arango Architects, Coral Gables, Fla., 1986-88, Seckinger Arango Architects, Coral Gables, 1988-93, Arango Architects, Coconut Grove, Fla., 1993—; cons. designer Herman Miller Corp., Berkeley, 1984; John K. Branner traveling fellow U. Calif.-Berkeley grad. div., 1980. Designer greeting cards Mus. Modern Art, 1991; contbr. articles to profl. jours. Mem. Bd. Architects, City of Coral Gables, 1988-90. Recipient Commendation for furniture design Progressive Architecture Mag., 1982. Mem. AIA (chair architecture in the schs. 1988-90, editor, chair Miami chpt. Newsletter 1990—). Democrat. Unitarian.

ARANSON, ROBERT, physician; b. Portland, Maine, Dec. 18, 1953; s. Albert and Golde Leah (Rodman) A. BS in Biology, Trinity Coll., 1976; MD, Tufts U., 1980. Diplomate Am. Bd. Internal Medicine-Pulmonary Diseases, Critical Care Medicine. Resident in internal medicine Maine Med. Ctr., Portland, 1980-83; fellow in pulmonary and critical care medicine Albert Einstein Med. Ctr. & Temple U. Hosp., Phila., 1983-85; clin. instr. of medicine Temple U. Sch. of Medicine, Phila., 1983-85, asst. prof. of medicine, 1985-88; asst. prof. of medicine Tufts U. Sch. of Medicine, Boston, 1988-93; asst. prof. medicine Emory U. Sch. Medicine, Atlanta, 1993—; dir. med. ICU and respiratory care dept. Grady Meml. Hosp., Atlanta, 1993—; assoc. prof. cardiopulmonary care scis. Ga. State U., Atlanta, 1993—, med. dir. Sch. Respiratory Therapy, 1993—; dir. med. respiratory ICU Temple U. Hosp., Phila., 1985-88, St. Elizabeth Hosp., Boston, 1988-93, dir. pulmonary fellowship program; med. physician Phila. Seventy-Sixers Profl. Basketball Team, Phila., 1987-88. Contbr. articles to profl. jours. Fellow ACP, Am. Coll. Chest Physicians; mem. Am. Soc. Internal Medicine, Am. Thoracic Soc., Soc. Critical Care Medicine, Nat. Assn. for Med. Direction of Respiratory Care. Jewish. Home: 2619 Danforth Ln Decatur GA 30033-2214 Office: Grady Meml Hosp Box 26034 80 Butler St SE Atlanta GA 30335-3801

ARBIB, JOHN A., home builder, developer; b. Lawrence, N.Y., Sept. 18, 1924; s. Robert Simeon and Edna (Henry) A.; student Pa. State Coll., 1942-43, Ala. Poly. Inst., 1943, Columbia U., 1946-47; m. Leonore Grandlinger, June 5, 1949; children: John Paul, Peter Laurence, Diane Lynn. Partner, Robert S. Arbib & Co., N.Y.C., 1946-57; pres. Arbib Building Corp., Margate, Fla., 1958-62; pres. Custom Craft Homes of So. Fla., Inc., Boca Raton, 1962-65; v.p. VR Corp., Hallandale, Fla., 1965-68; v.p. Royal Palm Beach Colony Inc., Hallandale, 1968-72, St. Petersburg, Fla., 1971-72; v.p., gen. mgr. Pinebrook Bldg. Corp., Pembroke Pines, Fla., 1972-76; v.p. Pasadena Homes, Inc., gen. mgr. Pinebrook div., 1976-86; pres., chief exec. officer Multicon S.E., 1986—; gen. mgr. Pinebrook Bldg. Co., 1986—; pres. Home Owners Warranty Corp. of South Fla., 1974-76, v.p., 1977-81, dir., 1981—; dir. Home Owners Warranty Corp., Washington, 1974-80, mem. exec. com., 1979-80. Pres., Lakeville Estates, N.Y. Civic Assn., 1953-54; mem. Fla. Sec. Edn. Constrn. Industry Adv. Com., 1980-85; mem. Fla. Condominium Commn., 1972—; mem. Gov.'s Econ. Adv. Com., 1980-81. Bd. dirs. Govs. Fla. Philharmonic Orch., Inc. (formerly Philharmonic Orch. Fla.) 1981-96, mem. exec. com., 1983—; v.p. Broward Mktg. and Pub. Rels., 1990-92; v.p. Broward Corp. Devel., 1992—; mem. Ft. Lauderdale Opera Guild, 1988-95 bd. dirs. The Youth Orchestra of Fla., Progress for Dade County, Fla., 1973—, Broward County Urban League, 1980-85; pres., trustee Broward Philharmonic, 1988—; mem. Fla. Housing Fin. Agy., 1980-88, 91—, vice chmn., 1980-82, chmn., 1983; mem. Broward County Bd. Rules and Appeals, 1975-81, mem. exec. com., 1979-81; trustee Fla. House, 1985—; mem. Aurora competition bd. Fla. HomeBuilder Hall of Fame, 1987—, trustee, 1988—; mem. bd. govs. Fame awards, 1990—; judge Greater Tampa Parade of Homes, 1992, ACE Nat. Award Construction Excellence competition. Served with AUS, 1943-46, ETO. Named Builder of Month, Gen. Electric Corp., Oct. 1971. Mem. Builders Assn. S. Fla. (dir. 1966—, pres. 1973; Recipient of the BASF Lifetime Acheivement Award, Pres.'s award 1975, Builder of Year 1976, South Fla. Builders Hall of Fame 1989, Fla. Home Builders Hall of Fame, 1992, judge Mid-Fla. Parade of Homes 1990-91, lectr. S.E. Builders Conf. 1991), Fla. Home Builders Assn. (dir. 1969—, area v.p. 1973, sec. 1977, treas. 1978, pres. 1980, Fla. Builder of Yr. 1984), Nat. Assn. Home Builders (dir. 1970—, chmn. bus. mgmt. com. 1975-76, vice chmn. consumer affairs com. 1977, resolutions com. 1979-81, 85-90, chmn. 90, nat. v.p. 1981-82, planning com. 1982—, mortgage fin. com. 1982—, chmn. state and local housing fin. agys. com. 1983—, chmn. assn. planning com. 1985—, exec. com. 1981, 82, 85, 90, exec. com. Coml. Housing Agy. Chmn. and Commrs. 1983—, vice chmn. 1985), Nat. Inst. Bldg. Scis. (dir. tech. div.), Constrn. Council Fla. (pres. 1975, dir. 1974-82), Lauderdale Yacht Club. Democrat, Tower Club. Unitarian (pres. Ft. Lauderdale ch. 1969, bd. dirs. 1965-70). Home: 7 Poplar Ct Sapphire NC 28774-9614

ARBID, ELIAS JOSEPH, vascular surgeon, researcher, medical educator; b. Beirut, Sept. 10, 1959; came to U.S., 1984; s. Joseph and Roueida (Debbas) A.; m. Rita Hanna Howayeck, May 22, 1987; 1 child, Michelle. BS, Am. U., Beirut, 1982; MD, U. Mass., Norchester, 1987. Cons. surgeon Lawrence Meml. Hosp., New Bedford, Mass., 1993—, Jordan Hosp., Plymouth, Mass., 1993—, VA Med. Ctr., Clarksburg, W.Va., 1995—; asst. prof. surgery W.Va. U., Morgantown, 1995—. Contbr. articles to profl. jours. Recipient Sci. Paper award New Eng. Surg. Soc., 1984. Mem. ACP, AMA, Soc. Clin. Vascular Surgery, Peripheral Vascular Surgery Soc., Mass. Med. Soc., So. Med. Soc. Office: West Virginia University PO Box 9238 Morgantown WV 26506

ARBOLEYA, CARLOS JOAQUIN, lawyer, broker; b. Havana, Cuba, Aug. 16, 1958; came to U.S., 1960; s. Carlos Jose and Marta Aurora (Quintana) A. AA in Bus. Adminstrn., Miami Dade C.C., 1977; BBA in Fin., U. Miami, 1980, MBA in Fin., 1981, JD, 1987. Bar: Fla. 1989, U.S. Ct. Appeals (D.C. cir.) 1990. From teller to br. mgr. North Miami Beach office Barnett Bank South Fla. N.A., 1975-84; realtor, assoc. Cervera Real Estate, 1980—; pres. Owner's Box Promotions, 1993-95; owner Carlos J. Arboleya, Jr., P.A., Coral Gables, 1988—; adv. bd. Exec. Nat. Bank, 1994—, Linda Ray Infant Ctr., 1990—; bd. dirs. Pvt. Industry Coun. Jobs for Miami; Hispanic adv. com. U. Miami Sports Mktg., 1992—. Bd. dirs. Greater Miami Tennis Found., 1995, U. Miami Ear Inst., 1993; planning adv. bd. City of Miami, vice chmn. 1993-95, chmn. 1995-96, code enforcement bd. chmn. 1990-91, vice chmn. 1989-90; asst. scout master Boy Scouts Am.; participant joint civilian orientation conf. U.S. Dept. Def., 1995. Mem. ABA, Nat. Soc. Hispanic MBAs, Nat. Eagle Scout Assn., Cuban Am. Bar Assn., Builders Assn. South Fla., Am. Title Ins. Co., Attys. Title Ins. Fund, Inc., Fla. Bar Assn., Latin Bus. Assn., Latin Builders Assn., Hispanic Law Students Assn., Coral Gables C. of C., Greater Miami C. of C. (sports coun., chmn., homestead motorsports complex com., 1994—, co-chmn. existing events com., 1992-94), Leadership Miami (exec. com. 1990-93, task force 1984-88, Coconut Grove Jaycees, Phi Delta Phi, Delta Sigma Pi (Outstanding Alumni award 1982). Republican. Roman Catholic. Office: Carlos J Arboleya Jr PA 2550 S Dixie Hwy Coconut Grove FL 33133-3137

ARBURY, ANDREW STEPHEN, III, art historian; b. Midland, Mich., Mar. 3, 1953; s. Andrew Stephen and Beryl D. A. BA, Albion Coll., 1975; MA, Rutgers U., 1978; diploma, U. Madrid, Spain., 1982; PhD, Rutgers U., 1992. Cert. Tchr. of English as Foreign Lang. Cataloger Midland County Hist. Soc. Museum, 1979; instr. Rutgers U., New Brunswick, N.J., 1979-80; curatorial asst. Rutgers U. Fine Arts Collection, New Brunswick, N.J., 1980-81; instr. U. Urbino, Italy, 1981; tcher. of English Ponce De Leon Found., Madrid, Spain, 1983-84; instr., slide curator, gallery dir. Roanoke Coll., Salem, Va., 1984-88; assoc. prof. Radford (Va.) U., 1988—. Co-founder, editor Rutgers Art Rev., 1979-81; contbr. articles to profl. jours. Vol. Save the Environment, Albion, Mich., 1975. Named Outstanding Young Men of Am., 1985; recipient Mary Bartlett Cowdrey Fellow, Rutgers U., 1979-80, Louis Bevier Grad. Fellow, 1980-81, Fulbright Commn. Scholarship, 1981-83, Disting. Leadership award, 1986, Men of Achievement award, 1987. Mem. Coll. Art Assn. of Am., Midwest Art History Soc., Am. Soc. for Hispanic Art Studies, Visual Resources Assn., Am. Acad. of Research Historians of Medieval Spain, Sixteenth Century Studies Conf., Southeastern Coll. Art Conf., The Spanish Inst., Phi Beta Kappa. Office: Radford U Powell Hall Radford VA 24142

ARCHAMBEAULT, WILLIAM GEORGE, criminologist, educator, researcher; b. Terre Haute, Ind., May 3, 1947; s. George W. and Birdilyn Jeanette (Watson) A.; m. Betty J. Conaway, Aug. 28, 1968 (div. 1989); children: John William, Marie Jeanette; m. Violet Rose Olson, May 26, 1990. BS in Criminology, Ind. State U., 1969, MA in Criminology, 1973; PhD in Criminology, Fla. State U., 1979. Probation officer Vigo County Cir. Juvenile Ct., Terre Haute, 1968-69, chief probation officer, 1970-71, asst. dir. regional youth ctr., 1971-73; instr. Valencia Cmty. Coll., Orlando, Fla., 1973-79; asst. prof. criminal justice La. State U., Baton Rouge, 1980-83, assoc. prof. criminal justice, 1983-89, prof., Sch. of Social Work, 1989—; cons. UN, Crime Prevention and Criminal Justice Br., 1989; mem. La. Bd. Pardons, Baton Rouge, 1988-92; noted lectr. Co-author: Computers in Criminal Justice Administration and Management, 1984, 1989, Microcomputers in Criminal Justice: Current Issues and Applications, 1987, Correctional Supervisory Management: Principles of Organization, Policy and Law, 1982; co-author two instr.'s manuals; contbr. numerous articles to profl. jours. and book chapters. Major, USAR Mil. Police, 1969-89. Recipient special award for svc., So. Region Acad. Criminal Justice Scis., New Orleans, 1990; recipient numerous rsch. grants. Mem. NASW Rschrs., Acad. Criminal Justice Scis., Am. Soc. Criminology, Am. Correctional Assn., Nat. Coun. on Crime and Delinquency, Am. Criminal Justice Statis. Assn. Roman Catholic. Home: 7878 Tiffany Dr Ethel LA 70730 Office: La State Univ Sch of Social Work Baton Rouge LA 70803

ARCHER, CARL MARION, oil and gas company executive; b. Spearman, Tex., Dec. 16, 1920; s. Robert Barton and Gertrude Lucille (Sheets) A.; student U. Tex., Austin, 1937-39; m. Peggy Garrett, Aug. 22, 1939; children—Mary Frances, Carla Lee. Pres., Anchor Oil Co., Spearman, 1959—, Carl M. Archer Farms, Spearman, 1960—; gen. mgr. Speartex Grain Co., Spearman, 1967—, Speartex Oil & Gas Co., 1974—. Mem. Tex. Grain Dealers Assn., Tex. Grain and Feed Assn., Ind. Royalty Owners and Producers Assn., Nat. Grain Dealers Assn., Am. Petroleum Landmen Assn. Mem. Ch. of Christ. Clubs: Perryton, Borger Country, Amarillo. Home: PO Box 488 Spearman TX 79081-0488 Office: 405 Collard St Spearman TX 79081-2045

ARCHER, GRACE EMILY, obstetrician, gynecologist; b. Dallas, Tex.; d. Richard K. and Ruth Evelyn (Boehning) A.; m. William Curtis Biggs, June 25, 1983; children: Richard, William, Sarah, Grace. AA, Amarillo Coll., 1976; BA, U. Tex., 1978; MD, Southwestern Med Sch., Dallas, 1982. Diplomate Am. Bd. Ob-Gyn. Intern Brigham & Women's Hosp., Boston, 1982-83; ob-gyn. resident Brigham & Women's Hosp., 1983-86; clin. fellow Harvard U. Med. Sch., Boston, 1982-86; pvt. practice Amarillo, 1986—. Fellow Am. Coll. Ob-Gyn; mem. Tex. Med. Assn., Southwestern Med. Sch. Alumni Assn. (life). Office: 1900 Coulter Dr Ste O Amarillo TX 79106-1784

ARCHER, JOSEPH NEALE, industrial designer; b. Sistersville, W.Va., Apr. 14, 1933; s. Oliver William and Netta Lee (Davis) A.; m. Clara Mae Ash, Dec. 25, 1952 (dec. Oct. 1990); children: Kathy, Judith, Mary, William. Grad. H.S., Middlebourne, W.Va. Draftsman Olin Aluminum, Hannibal, Ohio, 1956-67; estimator Ball Electric Co., Belpre, Ohio, 1967-78, Woodhurst Electric Co., Marietta, Ohio, 1978-80; cons. Indsl. Consultants, Sistersville, 1980—; designer GE Plastics, Parkersburg, W.Va., 1985-91, Parsons-SIP, Houston, 1991-93, Apex Engring., Parkersburg, W.Va., 1994—. Mem. Instrument Soc. Am. Home: Rt 2 Box 237 Sistersville WV 26175

ARCHER, SANFORD MITCHELL, otolaryngologist; b. N.Y.C., Nov. 28, 1955; s. Allan Jack and Ruth Beverly (Kleinman) A.; m. Sandra Rouzaglou, June 9, 1984; children: Daniel Jacob, Joshua Nathaniel. BS in Biology, Wake Forest U., 1977; MD, Chgo. Med. Sch., 1983. Diplomate Am. Bd. Otolaryngology. Intern Michael Reese Hosp., Chgo., 1983-85; resident in otolaryngology U. Iowa Hosps., Iowa City, 1985-88; asst. prof. U. Ky. Coll. Medicine, Lexington, 1988—. Fellow ACS, Am. Acad. Facial Plastic and Reconstructive Surgery, Am. Acad. Otolaryngology, Am. Acad. Otolaryngic Allergy; mem. Ky. Soc. Otolaryngology (pres. 1993-94), Assn. VA Otolaryngologists, N.Am. Skull Base Soc. Office: Univ of Ky Med Ctr 800 Rose St C-236 Lexington KY 40536

ARCHER, WILLIAM REYNOLDS, JR. (BILL REYNOLDS), congressman; b. Houston, Tex., Mar. 22, 1928; s. William Reynolds and Eleanor M. (Miller) A.; m. Sharon Sawyer; children: William Reynolds III, Richard M., Sharon, Elizabeth, Barbara. BBA, U. Tex., Austin, LLB with honors. Bar: Tex. Pvt. practice law; pres. Uncle Johnny Mills, Inc.; dir. Heights State Bank, Houston; councilman, mayor pro-tem Village of Hunters Creek, 1955-62; mem. Tex. Ho. of Reps., 1966-70, 92nd-104th Congresses from 7th Tex. dist., Washington, D.C., 1971—; chmn. House ways and means com., 1995—; mem. Joint Com. on Taxation, Rep. Policy Com., Rep. Leaders Task Force on Health. Bd. dirs. Houston Soc. Prevention Cruelty to Animals; past chmn. Rep. Study Com. Task Force on Regulatory Reform, Rep. Leadership's Econ. Task Force; mem. Rep. Leadership Task Force on Health, Nat. Commn. on Social Security Reform, 1982. Served with USAF, 1951-53. Recipient numerous svc. and honor awards, Taxpayer's Best Friend award Nat. Tax Payers Union, Taxpayer's Hero award Citizen Against Govt. Waste; named Most Respected Congressman from Tex., Tex. Bus. mag., Watchdog of the Treasury Nat. Associated Bus. Office: 1236 Longworth Bldg Washington DC 20515-0004

ARCHIE, JOSEPH PATRICK, JR., vascular surgeon, educator; b. Nashville, July 14, 1938; s. Joseph Patrick and Mary Ann (Burns) A.; m. Sarah Ellen White, Sept. 6, 1960; children: Sarah G., Joseph Patrick III, Thomas J.W. BS, N.C. State U., 1960, MS, 1962, PhD, 1968; MD, U. N.C., 1968. Diplomate Am. Bd. Surgery, Am. Bd. Vascular Surgery. Resident in surgery U. Ala. Med. Ctr., Birmingham, 1968-74, asst. prof., 1976-77; fellow U. Calif. Med. Ctr., San Francisco, 1970-71; dir. surg. residency program Carroway Meth. Med. Ctr., Birmingham, 1977-81; pvt. practice, Raleigh, N.C., 1981—; clin. instr. U. Tex. Med. Ctr., San Antonio, 1974-76; clin. asst. prof. U. N.C., Chapel Hill, 1984-87, assoc. prof., 1987-92, prof., 1992—; adj. assoc. prof. N.C. State U., Raleigh, 1985-93, prof., 1993—. Contbr. over 100 articles to med. and engring. jours. Maj. M.C., USAF, 1974-76. Recipient Young Investigator's award Am. Coll. Cardiology. Fellow ACS; mem. Am. Heart Assn. (fellow stroke coun.), Soc. for Vascular Surgery, Internat. Soc. for Cardiovascular Surgery, So. Assn. for Vascular Surgery, Carolina Country Club, Sphinx Club. Episcopalian. Home: 2309 Woodrow Dr Raleigh NC 27609-7626 Office: Carolina Cardiovascular Surg Assocs 3020 New Bern Ave Ste 560 Raleigh NC 27610-1249

ARENS, KATHERINE MARIE, language educator; b. Chgo., Nov. 25, 1953; d. Edward James and Eleanor (Baumgartner) A. BA, Northwestern U., 1975; AM, Stanford U., 1976; PhD, PhD, 1981. Tchg. fellow in German studies and humanities Stanford (Calif.) U., 1976-79; asst. prof. Germanic langs. U. Tex., Austin, 1980-86, assoc. prof. Germanic langs., 1986-93, prof. Germanic langs., 1993—. Author: Functionalism and Fin de Siècle, 1984, Structures of Knowing, 1989; co-author: (with Swaffar and Byrnes) Reading for Meaning, 1991. Fulbright Hays grantee, 1978-79, NEH summer stipend, 1982; C.G. Whiting Found. fellow, 1979-80. Home: 4806 Red River Austin TX 78751 Office: U Tex Dept Germanic Langs Austin TX 78712

ARESKOG, DONALD CLINTON, retired chiropractor; b. Bklyn., Aug. 6, 1926; s. Andrew Albert and Jennie Margaret (Dickson) A.; m. Julia Catherine Koskela, May 15, 1954. D Chiropractic, Logan Coll., St. Louis, 1950; Philosopher of Chiropractic, Atlantic States Chiropractic Coll. Ret., 1989; pvt. practice Bklyn., 1952-56, Wappingers Falls, N.Y., 1956-61, Poughkeepsie, N.Y., 1961-89; retired, 1989; bd. govs. Atlantic States Chiropractic Coll., Bklyn., 1954; research in field. Developer technique for removal of mental aberrations. Mem. Am. Chiropractic Assn. (speakers bur. 1964), Ednl. Rsch. Soc., Internat. Basic Rsch. Inst., Internat. Platform Assn., Wappingers Falls C. of C. (treas. 1959), Toastmasters. Home: 330 SE 20th Ave Apt 514 Deerfield Beach FL 33441-5181

AREY, ROBERT JACKSON, JR., small business owner; b. Shelby, N.C., Apr. 7, 1952; s. Robert Jackson Sr. and Lorraine (Clay) A.; m. Nancy Candace Johnson, Dec. 8, 1973; children: Robert J. III, Mathew Johnson, Julian Clay. Student, Lenoir Rhyne Coll., Hickory, N.C., 1971-74. Driver, maintenance worker Arey Oil Co., Shelby, 1966-71, maintenance supr., 1972-74, v.p., 1975—; v.p. Arey Realty, Inc., Shelby, 1975—; gen. mgr. Robert Arey Oil Co., Shelby, 1975-77, pres., 1978—; founder, pres. One Stop Food Stores, Shelby, 1980—; pres. Arey Cos., Shelby, 1993—; brand chmn. N.C. Exxon Distbrs., 1982; nat. distbr. adv. coun. Exxon Co. U.S.A., Houston, 1984; founder, chmn. S.E. Petro-Food Exposition, Charlotte, N.C., 1983; bd. dirs. BB&T Bank. Lay leader Aldersgate United Meth. Ch., Shelby, 1985. Mem. Young Pres. Orgn., N.C. Petroleum Marketers Assn. (bd. dirs. 1983-85, treas. 1985, v.p. 1986, pres. 1987, Oil Industry Edn. award 1984), N.C. Assn. Convenience Stores (bd. dirs. 1989—, v.p. 1994), Petroleum Marketers Assn. Am. (bd. dirs. 1988), Cleveland Country Club, Rotary (bd. dirs. Shelby 1984, 92). Democrat. Office: Arey Cos 1906 E Dixon Blvd Shelby NC 28152-6943

ARGIBAY, JORGE LUIS, information systems firm executive and founder; b. Montevideo, Uruguay, May 17, 1953; s. Candido Argibay and Blanca Martinez; m. Stella Gonzalez, Feb. 20, 1974 (div. Aug. 1981); children: Laura, Andres; m. M. Ines Sencion, Mar. 22, 1982; 1 child, Nicolas. Ingeniero de Sistemas, U. de la Republica, 1978. Cert. engring. Researcher laser optics Univ. Inst. of Physics, Montevideo, 1971-74; researcher operating systems Univ. Computing Div., Montevideo, 1975-77; prof. automata theory Faculty of Engring., Montevideo, 1977-81, prof. low level langs., 1977-81; pres. Swann S.A., Montevideo, 1980-91, Fla. Swan, Inc., Miami, 1991—; cons. Supreme Ct. of Justice, Montevideo, 1987—. Contbr. articles to profl. jours.; co-inventor DACOL programming lang. Home and Office: 4726 NW 97th Ct Miami FL 33178-1977

ARGO, WILLIAM FRANK, automotive executive; b. Oak Ridge, Tenn., Sept. 23, 1951; s. General Marion and Mary Catherine (Donnell) A.; m. Vicki Roberts Argo. BS, East Tenn. State U., 1974. Sales mgr. Lakeside Ford, Milledgeville, Ga., 1975-77; zone mgr. Ford Motor Co., Atlanta, 1977-82; distbn., merchandising, bus. mgmt. mgr. Ford Motor Co., St. Louis, 1982-84; distbn. mgr. BMW N.Am., Inc., Atlanta, 1984-87; nat. distbn. ops. mgr. BMW N.Am., Inc., Montvale, N.J., 1987-89; area distbn. mgr., ea. area, so. area Lexus-New Luxury Car (div. of Toyota), Parsippany, N.J., 1989-91, bus. mgmt. mgr. so. area, 1991-93; gen. mgr. John Roberts BMW and Lexus of Austin, 1993—. Home: 1400 Rockcliff Rd Austin TX 78746-1207

ARIAS, JUDITH HEPLER, Spanish language educator; b. Reading, Pa., Jan. 1, 1941; d. Marvin Monroe and Leah Naomi (Zimmerly) Hepler; m. Luis Augusto Arias (div. 1981); 1 child, Luis Marvin. BA, Lake Erie Coll., 1962; MA, Middlebury Coll., 1963; PhD, U. N.C., 1987. Vis. lectr. N.C. State U., Raleigh, 1987-88; assoc. prof. Spanish East Carolina U., Greenville, N.C., 1988—; mem. adv. bd. colloquium violence and religion Stanford U., Calif., 1991—. Author: (with others) Modern Myth, 1993; editor Contagion: Jour. of Violence, Mimesis and Culture; contbr. articles to profl. jours. Mem. MLA, Am. Assn. Tchrs. Spanish and Portuguese, South Atlantic Modern Lang. Assn., Philol.Assn. Carolinas, Assn. Internat. Hispanistas, Assn. Hispanic Classical Theater. Unitarian. Office: East Carolina U Dept Fgn Langs & Lits Greenville NC 27858

ARIAS-BOLZMANN, LEOPOLDO, marketing educator; b. Lima, Peru, Nov. 2, 1956; came to U.S., 1984; m. Veronica V. Segovia-Arias, Apr. 12, 1985; children: Veronica, Nicole. BBA, U. Lima, 1980; MBA, U. St.

Thomas, 1986; PhD in Bus. Adminstrn., Okla. State U., 1993. Fin. asst. Cosapi Equipo Uno-Peru, 1979-80; advt. mgr. Eastman Kodak Co.-Peru, 1980-84; instr. U. St. Thomas, 1986-90; grad. teaching assoc. Okla. State U., 1990-93; asst. prof. mktg. Palm Beach Atlantic Coll., West Palm Beach, Fla., 1993—; mktg. cons., 1994—. Contbr. articles to profl. jours. U. Lima Presdl. scholar, 1978-80, ESAN scholar, 1983, U. St. Thomas/U. Lima Presdl. scholar, 1985, 86, Okla. State U. scholar, 1990. Mem. Am. Mktg. Assn., So. Mktg. Assn. Home: 8128 Sedgewick Ct Apt D West Palm Beach FL 33406-8421 Office: Palm Beach Atlantic Coll Dept Marketing 901 S Flagler Dr West Palm Beach FL 33401-6505

ARISON, MICKY, cruise line company executive; b. Tel Aviv, June 29, 1949. Student, U. Miami. Pres., chief exec. officer Carnival Cruise Lines Inc., until 1990, chmn., CEO, 1990—; mng. gen. ptnr., chmn. CEO Carnival Cruises Line Inc.. Office: Carnival Cruise Lines Inc 3655 NW 87th Ave Miami FL 33178-2418

ARKIN, STANLEY HERBERT, construction executive; b. N.Y.C., Aug. 28, 1932; s. Joseph Lawrence and Mildred (Neidenberg) A.; m. Jill Theo Flitman, June 21, 1958; children: Bradley, Robert, Gregory. BBA cum laude, U. Miami, Coral Cables, Fla., 1954. Pres. Arkin Constrn. Co., Inc., Miami Beach, Fla., 1954—. Trustee, mem. exec. com. U. Miami; cons. Greater Miami Jewish Fedn. Housing Corp.; chmn. bd. govs. Bascom Palmer Eye Inst./Ann Bates Leach Eye Hosp.; vice mayor, commr. City of Miami Beach, acting mayor, 1991; mem. Metro Dade County Performing Art Ctr. Trust. Mem. U. Miami Soc. Founders, Miami Beach Devel. Assn. (chmn.), Masons, Mahi Shrine, Iron Arrow, Phi Eta Sigma, Alpha Delta Sigma, Alpha Sigma Upsilon, Omicron Delta Kappa, Alpha Epsilon Pi. Republican. Home: #603 5500 Collins Ave Miami Beach FL 33140-3314 Office: Arkin Constrn Co Inc 1827 Purdy Ave Miami FL 33139-1425

ARLEDGE, DAVID A., business executive; b. 1944. BBA, U. Tex., 1965, JD, 1968. With Touch Ross & Co., CPA's, 1968-72, ptnr., 1975-80; ptnr. Penfold & Arledge, 1972-75; sr. exec. v.p., COO Coastal Corp., West Memphis, Ark., 1980—. Office: Coastal Unilube Inc 310 Mid Continent Plz West Memphis AR 72301-1748*

ARMACOST, MARY-LINDA SORBER MERRIAM, former college president; b. Jeannette, Pa., May 31, 1943; d. Everett Sylvester Calvin and Madeleine (Case) Sorber; m. E. William Merriam, Dec. 13, 1969 (div. 1975); m. Peter H. Armacost, July 10, 1993. Student, Grove City Coll., 1961-63; BA, Pa. State U., 1963-65, MA, 1965-67, PhD, 1967-70; HHD (hon.), Carroll Coll., 1991; LLD (hon.), Wilson Coll., 1994. Rsch. assoc. Pa. State U., University Park, 1970-72; asst. prof. speech Emerson Coll., Boston, 1972-79, dir. continuing edn., 1974-77, spl. asst. to pres., 1977-78, v.p. adminstrn., 1978-79; asst. to pres. Boston U., 1979-81; pres. Wilson Coll., Chambersburg, Pa., 1981-91, Moore Coll. Art and Design, Phila., 1991-93; sr. fellow Office of Women in Higher Edn. Am. Coun. on Edn., 1994—; cons. Govt. Edn. and Secondary Edn. Act Title III, Alameda County, Calif., 1968. Bd. dirs. Sta. WITF, Inc., Harrisburg, Pa., 1982-91, chmn. bd., 1988-91; bd. dirs. Chambersburg Hosp., 1984-89, vice chmn. bd., 1987-89; bd. dirs. Elderhostel, 1997—, Sta. WHYY-FM-TV, Phila., 1992-93, Sta. WEDU-TV, Inc., Tampa, Fla., 1995—, Boston Zool. Soc., 1980-81, Arts Boston, 1979-81, Scotland Sch. Vets. Children, Pa., 1984-90, Fla. Orch., 1993-96; mem. exec. com. Found. for Ind. Colls., 1989-91; pres. Chambersburg Area Coun. Arts, 1988-90; chmn. higher edn. com. Gen. Assembly Presbyn. Ch., 1987-90; elder Falling Spring Presbyn. Ch., 1988-90. Recipient Disting. Alumna award Pa. State U., 1984, Disting. Dau. of Pa., 1986, Athena award Chambersburg C. of C., 1988, Outstanding Alumnae award Sch. Dist. Jeannette, 1991. Mem. NATAS (bd. govs. New Eng. chpt. 1980-81), AAUW, Am. Coun. Edn. (commn. on women 1992-93, commn. on govtl. rels. 1985-89, fellow 1977-78), Speech Comm. Assn., Pa. Assn. Colls. and Univs. (exec. com. 1984-90), Assn. Presbyn. Colls. and Univ. (exec. com. 1983-88, pres. 1986-87), Am. Assn. Higher Edn., Nat. Soc. Arts and Letters, Forum for Exec. Women, Phi Kappa Phi, Rho Tau Sigma, Phi Delta Kappa.

ARMACOST, ROBERT LEO, management educator, former coast guard officer, educator; b. Balt., July 17, 1942; s. Leo Mathias and Margaret Virginia (Ruth) A.; m. Susan Marie Danesi, Jan. 16, 1965 (div.); children: Robert Leo, Andrew Paul, Kathleen Erin. BS with honors, U.S. Coast Guard Acad., 1964; MS, U.S. Naval Postgrad. Sch., 1970; DSc in Ops. Rsch., George Washington U., 1976. Engring. officer USCG Cutter Mendota, Wilmington, N.C., 1964-66; ops. officer USCGC Cook Inlet, Portland, Maine, 1966-68; ops. rsch. analyst, ops. planning staff USCG Hdqrs., Washington, 1970-75; planning officer, aids to navigation divsn., 1976-78; comdr. Coast Guard Group, Milw., 1978-81; comdg. officer USCG Marine Safety Office, Milw., 1981-84, capt. of port, 1981-84, officer in charge of marine inspection, 1981-84; ret., 1984; instr. computer sci. Milw. Area Tech. Coll., 1982-83; asst. prof. mgmt. sci. Marquette U., Milw., 1984-91, assoc. prof. mgmt. sci., 1991; asst. prof. ops. res. U. Ctrl. Fla., 1991-96, assoc. prof. ops. res., 1996—, IE Grad. Program Coord. First v.p. Md. Right to Life, 1976-78; active Wis. Marine Hist. Soc.; mem. Archdiocese Milw. Pastoral Coun., 1984-89, vice chmn., 1986-87, chmn., 1987-88; bd. dirs. Nicolet High Sch. Found., 1986-88. Contbr. articles to profl. jours. Recipient USCG commendation award, 1972, 74, 78, 81, 84; named Outstanding Civic Vol., Bowie, Md., 1976; nat. finalist White House fellow, 1977-78. Mem. Ops Rsch. Soc. Am. (mem. com. 1983-94, chmn. 1990-94, fin. com. 1993-94), Math. Programming Soc., Inst. Mgmt. Sci., Decision Scis. Inst., Acad. of Mgmt., Inst. Ind. Engrs., Inst. Ops. Rsch. and Mgmt. Scis. (chair membership com. 1995—, mem. fin. com. 1995—, dir. at large 1995—, bd. dirs. 1995—). Roman Catholic. Home: 8487 Ridgewood Ave Cape Canaveral FL 32920-2161 Office: U Ctrl Fla Dept IEMS Orlando FL 32816

ARMAN, SANDRA ANN, mathematics educator; b. Great Lakes, Ill., Oct. 12, 1955; d. Albert Alfred and Joyce Violet (Fletcher) Durkee; m. Ehssanollah Farshad, June 19, 1972; children: Ali, Mehdi, Hadi, Hassan, Mohammad-Hossain. AS, Motlow State C.C., 1986; BS, Mid. Tenn. State U., 1988, M of Sci. in Teaching, 1992. Instr. Motlow State C.C., Tullahoma, Tenn., 1988—; adj. instr. Mid. Tenn. State U., Murfreesboro, 1993—. Recipient Recognition of Achievement award State of Tenn., 1987, Outstanding Tchr. award Gamma Beta Phi, 1995. Mem. AAUP, Nat. Coun. Tchrs. Math., Mid. Tenn. Math. Tchrs., Tenn. Math. Tchrs. Assn., Gamma Beta Phi (assoc. adv.). Home: 384 Limbo Dr PO Box 01 Hillsboro TN 37342 Office: Motlow State CC PO Box 88100 Tullahoma TN 37388

ARMANIOS, ERIAN ABDELMESSIH, aerospace engineer, educator; b. Cairo, July 6, 1950; came to the U.S., 1980; s. Abdelmessih Armanios; m. Mahera S. Philobos, May 2, 1980; children: Daniel, Laura. BS in Aero. Engring., Cairo U., 1974, MS in Aero. Engring., 1979; PhD in Aerospace Engring., Ga. Inst. Tech., 1985. Teaching asst. U. Cairo, 1974-79, asst. lectr., 1979-80; grad. rsch. asst. Ga. Inst. Tech., Atlanta, 1980-84, rsch. engr. I, 1985-86, asst. prof., 1986-91, assoc. prof., 1991—; cons. Bell Helicopter Textron Inc., Ft. Worth, 1984-85, Rolls-Royce Inc., Atlanta, 1989-95, Allison Engine Co., Indpls. 1995—, Guided System Techs., 1991-92; judge Ga. Sci. and Engring. Fair, Atlanta, 1987; judge space sci. student program NASA, Atlanta, 1988—; dir. Ga. Space Grant Consortium, 1991—. Editor: Interlaminar Fracture of Composites, 1989, Fracture of Composites, 1996; mem. editl. bd. Jour. Composites Tech. and Rsch., 1992—, Jour. of Nat. Tech. Assn., 1995—; contbr. articles to profl. jours. Recipient Teaching Excellence award Ctr. for Enhancement of Teaching and Learning Amoco Found., 1990, Outstanding Paper award Jour. Aerospace Engring., 1990, Sigma Xi Outstanding PhD Thesis Advisor award, 1991, Jr. Faculty award, 1991, Ga. Inst. Tech. Faculty Rsch. award 1996, Sci. Application Internat. Corp. cert. of award, 1990, 95, Ga. Inst. Tech. Faculty leadership award, 1996. Fellow AIAA (assoc.); mem. ASTM (com. on high modulus fibers and composites 1988); Am. Soc. for Composites, Am. Helicopter Soc. (com. on structures and materials). Office: Sch Aerospace Engring Ga Inst Tech Atlanta GA 30332

ARMENTROUT, DEBRA CATHERINE, neonatal nurse practitioner; b. Grand Forks, N.D., Mar. 26, 1953; d. Howard and Delores (Wilhelmi) Armentrout. BSN, U. N.D., 1975; MSN, U. Tex. Health Ctr., Houston, 1985. RN, Tex. Staff nurse Turner Newborn ICU, Hermann Hosp., Houston, 1975-79, 80-83; staff nurse, charge nurse newborn ICU/pediatrics Rogue Valley Meml. Hosp., Medford, Oreg., 1979-80; neonatal transport nurse Turner Newborn ICU, Hermann Hosp., Houston, 1984-86, 88-90, clin. nurse specialist, 1986-88; staff nurse nurseries and pediatrics Sierra Vista Regional Med. Ctr., San Luis Obispo, Calif., 1988; instr. clin. pediatrics, assoc. coord. neonatal nurse practioner U. Tex. Health Ctr., Houston, 1990-94, asst. prof. pediatrics, 1994—; clin. asst. prof. gen. instrn. Sch. Nursing U. Tex.; presenter in field. Contbr. articles to profl. publs. Mem. Nat. Assn. Neonatal Nurses (corr. mem. spl. interest group advanced practice role com., sec. practice com. 1990-94), Am. Acad. Nurse Practitioners, Houston Area Assn. Neonatal Nurses (sec. 1993-94, pres. 1995), Sigma Theta Tau. Office: 2 NT 9100 2C LBJ 5656 Kelley St Houston TX 77026-1967

ARMEY, RICHARD KEITH (DICK ARMEY), congressman; b. Cando, N.D., July 7, 1940; s. Glen Forest and Marion (Gutschlog) A.; m. Susan Byrd; children: Kathryn, David, Scott A., Chip Scott Oxendine. B.A., Jamestown Coll., N.D., 1963; M.A., U. N.D., 1964; Ph.D., U. Okla., Norman, 1968. Mem. econs. faculty U. Mont., 1964-65; asst. prof. West Tex. State U., 1967-68, Austin Coll., 1968-72; assoc. prof. North Tex. State U., 1972-77, chmn. dept. econs., 1977-84; mem. 99th-104th Congresses from 26th Tex. dist., Washington, D.C., 1985—; former mem. edn. and labor com., chmn. ho. rep. conf. com., 1992-94, former mem. joint economic com., majority leader, 1995—. Author: Price Theory, 1977, The Freedom Revolution, 1995, The Flat Tax-A Citizen's Guide to the Facts on What it Will Do For You, Your Country, and Your Pocketbook, 1996. Disting. fellow, Fisher Inst. Office: Ste 3050 9901 Valley Ranch Pky Irving TX 75063-6707 also: US Ho of Reps 301 Cannon Bldg Washington DC 20515-0003

ARMIGER, GENE GIBBON, telecommunications executive, consultant; b. Balt., Oct. 17, 1931; s. Edward Gibbon and Irene Juliet (Peppler) A.; m. Cynthia Clare Carroll, Feb. 14, 1954 (div. 1971); children: Karen Lee, Scott Andrew; m. Dorothy Sue Looney, Feb. 17, 1979. Archtl. student, U. Md., 1951-52, Md. Inst., 1956-58. Cert. lic. capt. USCG. Project engr. Cook Electric Co., Chgo., 1958-62, U.S. Underseas Cable Corp., Washington, 1962; gen. mgr. sales/mktg. Superior Cable Corp., Hickory, N.C., 1963-74; dir. sales/mktg. No. Telecom Inc., Nashville, 1974-76, Porta Systems Inc., Syosset, N.Y., 1976-78; founder/chief exec. officer Armiger & Assocs. Inc., Ft. Worth, Tex., 1978-86; v.p. Richard Thomas & Assocs., Chgo., 1986-88, Suttle Armiger Telecom, Hector, Minn., 1988-90; cons. Telecom. Cons., Ft. Worth, 1990—; mem. FCC Telecom Industry Ad-hoc com. Washington, 1979-87. Contbr. articles to profl. jours. Bd. dirs. Telecommunications Industry Assocs., Washington, 1985-87. Sgt. U.S. Army, 1951-61, Korea. Mem. Am. Mgmt. Assn., U.S. Power Squadron, USCG Aux. Tel. Pioneer Assn., Ind. Tel. Pioneer Assn. (v.p. 1968-69), Va. Yatch Club, Ridglea Country Club, Moslah Temple. Republican. Episcopalian. Home: 5330 Collinwood Ave Fort Worth TX 76107-3634

ARMSTEAD, TRESSA MADDUX, secondary school educator; b. Pecos, Tex., Apr. 23, 1949; d. Obie Eugene and Nell (Simpson) Maddux; m. Karl Frank Armstead, June 8, 1974; children: Stephen Kristopher, Tiffany Julene. BS, Sul Ross State U., 1970; MA, Eastern New Mex. U., 1977. Cert. secondary tchr., Tex. Educator Boyd (Tex.) Ind. Sch. Dist.; grad. asst. Eastern N.Mex. U., Portales; tchr. Pecos (Tex.)-Barstow-Toyah Ind. Sch. Dist., Midland (Tex.) Ind. Sch. Dist., Ector County Ind. Sch. Dist. Mem. Tex. Classroom Tchrs. Assn., Nat. Coun. Tchrs. English, Tex. Joint Coun. Tchrs. English, Delta Kappa Gamma.

ARMSTRONG, DAVID G., journalist; b. L.A., Mar. 8, 1960; m. Noëlle McAfee, Aug. 8, 1992. BA in English and Creative Writing, UCLA, 1986; MA in Journalism, U. Tex., 1989, postgrad. in Am. Studies. Editorial asst., reporter KPFK Radio, L.A., 1981-82; editorial intern L.A. Weekly, 1983-84; reporter, ops. mgr. Beverly Hills (Calif.) Courier, 1986; reporter KPFK Radio, L.A., summer 1988; editor Random Lengths News, San Pedro, Calif., 1990-91, Texas Observer, Austin, 1991; freelance journalist, 1992; asst. instr. dept. journalism U. Tex., Austin, 1992-93, tchg. asst. Am. Studies program, 1993-95, asst. instr. Am. Studies program, 1996—; lectr. in field; mem. bd. operating trustees Tex. Student Publs., 1994. Mem. editorial bd. Pub. Media Monitor, 1994; contbr. over 40 articles to profl. jours. Bd. dirs. Liberated Learning, Austin, 1992. Recipient Martin Emmet Walter fellowship U. Tex., 1987, 88, 89, Marjorie Kovler fellowship John F. Kennedy Libr. Found., 1993; Kennedy Rsch. grantee, 1994, LBJ Found. Moody grantee, 1994, 96; Pat and Jack Maguire scholar U. Tex. Ex-Students' Assn., 1995-96. Home: 4314 Duval St Austin TX 78751-3916

ARMSTRONG, DEANNA FRANCES, engineer; b. Winchester, Va., July 14, 1962; d. Gerald Francis and Reta Marie (Wyatt) A. AS in Mech. Engring. Tech., W.Va. Inst. Tech., 1982, AS in Elec. Engring. Tech. cum laude, 1983, BS in Electronics Engring. Tech. cum laude, 1984. Student engring. asst. Monongahela Power Co., Elkins, W.Va., summers 1980-83; machine shop lab. asst. W.Va. Inst. Tech., Montgomery, 1982-83, acad. asst., 1983-84; engring. technician Monongahela Power Co., Elkins, 1984-96; rep. customer svcs. Tech. Allegheny Power, Fairmont, W.Va., 1996—; competition judge Vocat. and Indsl. Club. Am., Elkins, 1985—; mem. Partnership in Edn. Com. Corr. Monongahela News, 1993—. Mem. adv. coun. Randolph County Vocat. Tech. Ctr., Partnership in Edn. Com.; vol. Mountain State Forest Festival. Mem. Elkins Jr. C. of C., Alpha Chi Nat. Honor Soc. Republican. Home: 508 Center St Elkins WV 26241-3729 Office: Monongahela Power Co US Rte 215 & 250 Elkins WV 26241

ARMSTRONG, EDWIN ALAN, lawyer; b. Atlanta, June 20, 1950; s. Carl Edwin and Betty (Hawkins) A.; m. Marlene Bryant, Aug. 12, 1978. BA, Berry Coll., 1972; JD, Emory U., 1976. Bar: Ga. 1976, U.S. Dist. Ct. (no. dist.) Ga. 1977, U.S. Ct. Appeals (5th cir.) 1981, U.S. Ct. Appeals (11th cir.) 1982, U.S. Supreme Ct. 1989, U.S. Dist. Ct. (so. dist.) Ga., U.S. Ct. Appeals (4th cir.), U.S. Ct. Appeals (D.C. cir.) 1992, U.S. Ct. Appeals (6th cir.) 1992, U.S. Dist. Ct. (mid. dist.) Ga 1992. Atty. Flynt Jud. Cir. Pub. Defenders Office, McDonough, Ga., 1976-77; assoc. Neely, Neely & Player, Atlanta, 1977; sole practice Atlanta, 1977-79, 81—; assoc. Stolz, Shulman & Loveless, Atlanta, 1979-81. Contbr. articles to profl. jours. mem. ABA (forum com. on air and space law, tort and ins. practice sect.), Atlanta Bar Assn., Decatur-DeKalb Bar Assn., State Bar of Ga., The Assn. of Trial Lawyers of Am., Ga. Trial Lawyers Assn., Nat. Transp. Safety Bd. Bar Assn. (founding, com. legis. and regulatory activity 1989—, editor newsletter 1991-92), Lawyer-Pilots Bar Assn. Episcopalian. Home: 4098 Northlake Creek Cv Tucker GA 30084-3416

ARMSTRONG, IVY CLAUDETTE, nursing administrator; b. Kingston, Jamaica, Feb. 24, 1942; d. Henry Emmanuel and Beatrice Elfleda (Ridgeway) A.; m. Sidney Leslie Cooper, Jan. 11, 1964 (div. June 1971); 1 child, Christine Thomas. Cert. in nursing, Worthing (Eng.) Sch. Nursing, 1969; grad., Southlands Sch. Midwifery, Shoreham, Eng., 1971; diploma in pub. health, W.I. Sch. Pub. Health, Kingston, 1977; BS in Sociology cum laude, Internat. Coll., Grand Cayman Island, 1981; MPH, Glasgow (Scotland) U., 1986. RN, Fla.; cert. psychiatric nurse. Sch. health nurse, educator Cayman Islands Govt., Grand Cayman, B.W.I., 1979-84; nurse Coral Ridge Hosp., Ft. Lauderdale, Fla., 1987-89; nurse supr., cons. Locktowns Community Mental Health Ctr., Miami, Fla., 1981-83; nurse supr. South Fla. State Hosp., Pembroke Pines, Fla., 1989—; sch. health nurse/educator Jamaican Govt., Kingston, 1974-79; nursing supr. Worthing Dist. Hosp., 1971-74. Author: (poems) Share My Precious Stones, 1993, Native Dawta, 1993, Lignumvitae and Leather, 1994, (essays) Strugglers in De Sun, 1993. Actress Cayman Nat. Theater, Grand Cayman, 1982-84; govt. rep. Cayman Islands Govt., London, 1983; minister Bethel Apostolic Ch., 1992—. Recipient Best Supporting Actress award Cayman Nat. Theater, 1983, Actress of Yr. award Cayman Nat. Theater, 1983, 84. Mem. Fla. Nurses Assn. Office: South Fla State Hosp 1000 SW 84th Ave Hollywood FL 33025-1419

ARMSTRONG, JACK GILLILAND, lawyer; b. Pitts., Aug. 10, 1929; s. Hugh Collins and Mary Elizabeth (Gilliland) A.; m. Ellen Lee Gliem, June 10, 1951 (dec.); children: Thomas G., Elizabeth Armstrong Pride; m. Elizabeth Lacewell White, March 27, 1993. AB, U. Mich., 1951, JD, 1956. Bar: Pa. 1956, Mich. 1956, U.S. Supreme Ct. 1968, Fla. 1981. Assoc. Buchanan, Ingersoll, Rodewald, Kyle & Buerger, Pitts., 1956-65; ptnr. Buchanan Ingersoll P.C., 1965-90, counsel 1990-94, of counsel, 1995; of counsel Rothman Gordon P.C., 1996—; dir. Standard Steel Splty. Co., Duncan, S.C. Trustee Union Dale Cemetery, 1972—, pres., 1992-95; elder Southminster Presbyn. Ch. Lt. U.S. Army, 1951-53. Mem. ABA (sects. taxation, real property, probate and trust law), Pa. Bar Assn. (real property, probate and trust law sect., mem. coun. 1981-84, treas. 1985, vice chmn. probate div. 1986-88, chmn. 1988-89, tax law sect.), Fla. Bar (real property, probate and trust law sect., tax sect.), Allegheny County Bar Assn. (taxation, probate and trust law), Estate Planning Coun. Pitts., Am. Coll. Trust and Estate Counsel (Pa. state chmn. 1990-95), Am. Coll. Tax Counsel, U. Mich. Alumni Assn. (Disting. Alumni Svc. award 1981), Am. Arbitration Assn. (nat. panel 1965—), Order of Coif, Duquesne Club, Univ. Club (pres. 1988-89), St. Clair Country Club, Town Club Jamestown, Delray Beach Club, Chautauqua Golf Club, Pine Tree Golf Club, Masons, Shriners, Royal Order Jesters, Phi Alpha Delta, Sigma Nu. Home: 4376 Pine Tree Dr Boynton Beach FL 33436

ARMSTRONG, (ARTHUR) JAMES, minister, religion educator, religious organization executive, consultant; b. Marion, Ind., Sept. 17, 1924; s. Arthur J. and Frances (Green) A.; m. Sue Peterson, Dec. 10, 1988; children: Eve Stoughton, Allison Peterson; children from previous marriage: James, Teresa, John, Rebecca Armstrong Putens, Leslye Armstrong Hope. AB, Fla. So. Coll., 1948; BD, Candler Sch. Theology, Emory U., 1952; DD, Fla. So. U., 1960, DePauw U., 1965; LHD, Ill. Wesleyan U., 1970, Dakota Wesleyan U., 1970, Westmar Coll., 1971, Ind. Ctrl. U., 1982, Emory U., 1982. Ordained to ministry Meth. Ch., 1948; minister in Fla., 1945-58; sr. minister Broadway Meth. Ch., Indpls., 1958-68; bishop United Meth. Ch., Dakotas area, 1968-80, Ind. area, Indpls., 1980-83; exec. v.p. conflict resolution firm, Washington, 1984-87; vis. prof. preaching and social ministries Iliff Sch. Theology, Denver, 1985-91; sr. min. 1st Congl. Ch., Winter Park, Fla., 1991—; exec. dir. Ctr. on Dialogue and Devel., Denver, 1984-96; instr. Christian Theol. Sem., Indpls., 1961-68; del. 4th Gen. Assembly, World Coun. Chs., 1968, 6th Gen. Assembly, 1983; pres. Nat. Coun. Chs., 1982-83; pres. bd. ch. and soc. United Meth. Ch., 1972-76, chmn. com. for peace and self devel. of peoples, 1972-76, pres. Commn. on Religion and Race, 1976-83; exec. v.p. Pagan Internat., 1985-87. Author: The Journey That Men Make, 1969, The Urgent Now, 1970, Mission: Middle America, 1971, The Pastor and the Public Servant, 1972, United Methodist Primer, 1973, 77, Wilderness Voices, 1974, The Nation Yet To Be, 1975, Telling Truth: The Foolishness of Preaching in a Real World, 1977, From the Underside, 1981; contbg. author: The Pulpit Speaks on Race, 1966, War Crimes and the American Conscience, 1970, Rethinking Evangelism, 1971, What's a Nice Church Like You Doing in a Place Like This?, 1972, The Miracle of Easter, 1980, Preaching on Peace, 1982, Ethics and the Multi-National Enterprise, 1986, The Best of the Circuit Rider, 1987. Vice-chmn. Hoosiers for Peace, 1968; mem. Ind. State Platform Com. Democratic Party, 1968, Nat. Coalition for a Responsible Congress, 1970. With USNR, 1942. Recipient distinguished service award Indpls. Jr. C. of C., 1959. Mem. Fla. Coun. Chs. (pres. 1996—), Ctrl. Fla. Interfaith Alliance (co-chair 1994-96). Office: 1st Congl Ch 225 S Interlachen Ave Winter Park FL 32789-4411

ARMSTRONG, JAMES LOUDEN, III, lawyer; b. Miami, Fla., Jan. 7, 1932; s. James Louden and Jean Macrea (Cawley) A.; m. Mary Elizabeth McCall, Aug. 25, 1955; children: Patricia Payan, James L. IV. BA, Yale U., 1955, LLB, 1958. Bar: Fla. 1958, U.S. Dist. Ct. (so. dist.) Fla. 1958, U.S. Dist. Ct. (middle dist.) Fla. 1960, U.S. Dist. Ct. (no. dist.) Fla. 1964, U.S. Ct. Appeals (5th and 11th cir.) 1962, U.S. Supreme Ct. 1962. Assoc. Smathers & Thompson, Miami, 1958-64, ptnr., 1964-87; ptnr. Kelley Drye & Warren, Miami, 1987—. Pres. Orange Bowl Com., Miami, 1976. Fellow Am. Coll. Trial Lawyers, Internat. Acad. Trial Lawyers; mem. Dade County bar Assn.(pres. 1972), Yale Club (pres. 1966). Republican. Presbyterian. Home: 4911 Alhambra Cir Coral Gables FL 33146-1600 Office: Kelley Drye & Warren 2400 Miami Ctr 201 S Biscayne Blvd Miami FL 33131-4332

ARMSTRONG, JAMES P., housing administrator, policy analyst; b. N.Y.C., June 21, 1948; s. John Fisher and Fay (Sappington) A.; m. Susilee Jane Reynolds, Apr. 26, 1969 (div. July 1, 1995); children: John Douglas, Valerie, Fay. BA, Beloit Coll., 1969; MBA, Old Dominion U., 1982; postgrad., Va. Tech., 1995—. Cert. housing counseling adminstr. Admintrv. asst. Hampton (Va.) Cmty. Action Agy., 1970-73, Hampton Youth Opportunity Comm., 1973-76; housing tech. Hampton Red and Housing Auth., 1976-78, housing counseling supr., 1978-80, housing mgmt. supr., 1980-84, dir. mgmt. and program devel., 1984-89, dir. housing, 1989-94; exec. dir. Suffolk (Va.) Red and Housing Auth., 1995; v.p. Va. Assn. Housing and Cmty. Devel. Ofcls., Portsmouth, 1995; treas. Va Peninsula Cmty. Housing Resources Bd., Newport News, 1993-96. Contbr. articles to profl. jours. Mem. Am. Soc. Pub. Adminstrn., Nat. Assn. Housing and Redevel. Ofcls. (cert. pub. housing mgr.). Home: 619 Highland Ave SW Roanoke VA 24016 Office: PO Box 1404 Roanoke VA 24017

ARMSTRONG, JENNIFER JO, adult nurse practitioner; b. Nagoya, Japan, Oct. 25, 1959; came to U.S., 1962; d. John Tiffany and Nancy Lina (Parsons) A. BSN, U. R.I., 1986, MSN, 1995. RN; cert. adult nurse practitioner, ANCC. Enlisted U.S. Army, 1978, commd 2d lt., 1986, advanced through grades to capt., 1990; clin. nurse surg. fl. Dewitt Comty. Hosp. U.S. Army, Ft. Belvoir, Va., 1986-87, clin. nurse med. fl. Dewitt Comty. Hosp., 1987-89; clin. nurse U.S. Army, Soto Cano Airbase, Honduras, 1988-89; head nurse post anesthesia care unit Dewitt Comty. Hosp. U.S. Army, Belvoir, 1989-90; adult nurse practitioner Madigan Med. Ctr. U.S. Army, Tacoma, 1990-92; adult nurse practitioner trauma Operation Desert Storm U.S. Army, Saudi Arabia, 1990-91; adult nurse practitioner, internal medicine Womack Army Med. Ctr., U.S. Army, Ft. Bragg, N.C., 1995—; adjunct faculty LPN course Madigan Med. Ctr., Tacoma, 1991-92. Mem. Uniformed Svcs. Nurse Practitoner Assn., R.I. State Nurses Assn., Scottish Am. Mil. Soc., Sigma Theta Tau (Upsilon chpt.), Phi Kappa Phi. Republican. American Baptist.

ARMSTRONG, JOANNE MARIE, clinical and consulting psychologist, business advisor, mediator; b. Cooperstown, N.Y., Nov. 26, 1956; d. William John and Joan Alice (Larsen) A.; m. Brian Joseph Yore, July 31, 1983; children: Mackensie A., Campbell A. BA, Trinity U., San Antonio, 1978; MA, U. Louisville, 1982, PhD, 1987. Lic. psychologist Wis., S.C. Mgmt. positions in ops., adminstrn. and purchasing Gentec Hosp. Supply Co., San Antonio and Dallas, 1978-79; rsch. asst. U. Louisville, 1980-81; therapist Seven Counties Svcs., Louisville, 1981-82; mental health prof. Head Start, Louisville, 1982-83; psychology intern Dallas VA Med. Ctr./Dallas Ghild Guidance Clinic, 1983-84; dir. Kaufman County Outreach Clinic, Tex. Dept. Mental Health-Mental Retardation, Terrell, 1984-85; clin. psychologist Nicolet Clinic/La Salle Clinic, S.C., Menasha, Wis., 1987-89; pvt. practice, Neenah, Wis., 1989-93; pvt. practice Spartanburg and Greenville, S.C., 1993—; founder Advisors to Bus. and Profls., 1995—; cons. Wellness Counseling Ctr., Appleton, Wis., 1989-93, Fox Valley Hosp., Green Bay, Wis., 1990-91, Brownell Ctr., Greenville, S.C., 1993—, Greenville Hosp. Sys. Mem. bd. Birthing Network, Neenah, 1988-93; mem. Citizens for Better Environ., Neenah, 1989-93. Rsch. fellow U. Louisville, 1985-86. Mem. APA, Nat. Register Health Svc. Providers in Psychology, S.C. Psychol. Assn., S.C. Assn. Profl. Psychologists, Family Firm Inst., Acad. Family Mediators, S.C. Coun. Mediation and Alt. Dispute Resolution, Upstate Mediation Network. Episcopalian. Office: 390 E Henry St Ste 206 Spartanburg SC 29302-2659 also: 330 Pelham Rd Ste 103B Greenville SC 29615-3111

ARMSTRONG, MARTHA SUSAN, accountant, educator; b. Harrisonburg, Va., Dec. 28, 1954; d. Harry Lee and Elizabeth (Roller) Anderson; m. Marvin Edward Armstrong, May 27, 1978; children: Nathaniel Roller, Andrew Michael. BBA cum laude, Bridgewater Coll., 1977; MS in Acctg., U. Va., 1985. CPA, Va. Asst. dir. of fin. aid Bridgewater (Va.) Coll., 1978-81, asst. prof. acctg. and bus. adminstrn., 1981—; staff acct. Morris & Sprinkel CPA's, Harrisonburg, 1985—; cons. acctg. edn. WLR Foods, Hinton, 1990—. Deacon Bridgewater Presbyn. Ch., 1982-85, v.p. Women of the Ch., 1983-85, asst. ch. treas., 1990—; concert bell ringer Harrisonburg 1st Presbyn. Ch., 1987-91, asst. treas., 1990—; treas. Dayton Nursery Sch., 1991-94. Named one of Outstanding Young Women Am., 1986. Mem. AICPA, Va. Soc. CPAs. Home: RR 1 Box 177 Harrisonburg VA 22801-8607 Office: Accounting Dept Bridgewater Coll Bridgewater VA 22812

ARMSTRONG, MICHAEL DAVID, investment banker; b. Bronxville, N.Y., May 7, 1955; s. Frank and Dorothy Armstrong; m. Deborah Jane Lauderdale, 1984. BA, Washington and Lee U., 1977; MBA, Coll. William and Mary, 1982. Prodn. mgr., account exec. Austin Kelley Adv., Atlanta,

1977-80; sr. assoc. 1st San Francisco Corp., Foster City, Calif., 1983-88, Bankers Trust Co., Atlanta, 1988-90; gen. mgr. Gimborn U.S., Atlanta, 1990-93; pres. New Market Beverage Co., Atlanta, 1994—. Mem. Atlanta Hist. Soc., Atlanta Speech Sch., ZooAtlanta, Ga. Pub. TV, Atlanta Bot. Gardens, High Mus. Guild, Washington and Lee Alumni Bd. Mem. Mu Beta Psi.

ARMSTRONG, ROBERT BEALL, physiologist; b. Hastings, Nebr., Nov. 13, 1940; s. Edwin Ollis and Elena (Beall) A.; m. Ingrid Elizabeth Vaiciulenas, Apr. 9, 1966; children: Edwin John, Andrew Niel, Sarah Elizabeth. BA, Hastings Coll., 1962; MS, Wash. State U., 1970, PhD, 1973. Asst. prof. biology Boston U., 1973-78; assoc. prof. physiology Oral Roberts U., Tulsa, Okla., 1978-81, prof. physiology, 1981-85; prof. U. Ga., Athens, 1985-90, rsch. prof., 1990-92; Omar Smith prof., head dept. health and kinesiology Tex. A&M U., College Station, 1992—, Omar Smith chair, 1995—; disting. prof., 1995—; assoc. zoology Harvard U., Cambridge, Mass., 1977-87; external examiner Nat. U. Singapore, 1984-85; rsch. com. Am. Heart Assn., Athens, 1987-89. Assoc. editor Med. Sci. Sports Exercise, Indpls., 1985-87; contbr. articles to Jour. Applied Physiology, Am. Jour. Physiology. NSF fellow, 1970-73; grantee NIH, 1975—, Am. Heart Assn., 1981-89. Fellow Am. Coll. Sports Medicine (trustee 1986-88); mem. Am. Physiol. Soc. Office: Tex A & M U Dept Health & Kinesiology College Station TX 77843

ARMSTRONG, SARAH PRICE, librarian; b. Jackson, Miss., Sept. 27, 1969; d. John Therrell, Jr. and Sarah Price (Wells) A. BA, U. Miss., 1992; MLS, U. Ala., 1993. Ref. libr. U. So. Miss., Hattiesburg, 1993—. Editor: (jour.) Mississippi Libraries, 1994-96. Mem. First Presbyn. Ch., Hazelhurst, Miss. Recipient Past Pres.'s award Miss. Libr. Assn., 1995. Mem. Delta Gamma, Phi Kappa Phi (sec. 1993—). Presbyterian. Home: 114 Westover Dr Hazelhurst MS 39083 Office: Cook Library U So Miss Box 5053 Hattiesburg MS 39406

ARMSTRONG, WARREN BRUCE, university president, historian, educator; b. Tidioute, Pa., Oct. 16, 1933; s. Mead C. and Mary (Griffin) A.; m. Elizabeth Ann Fowler, Aug. 7, 1954 (div. 1973); children: Linda Susan, Heidi Jo; m. Joan Elizabeth Gregory, Apr. 19, 1974; children: Susan Elizabeth, Pamela Anne. Th.B., Bapt. Coll. Pa., 1956; A.M., U. Mich., 1958, Ph.D., 1964. Instr. history Olivet Coll., 1961-63, asst. prof., 1963-65, chmn. dept., 1964-65; asst. prof. U. Wis., Whitewater, 1965-66, assoc. prof., 1966-69, prof., 1969-70, asst. dean Coll. Arts and Scis., 1966-69, assoc. dean, 1969-70; dean St. Cloud (Minn.) State U., 1970-75, prof. history, 1970-75; pres. Ea. N.Mex. U., Portales, 1975-83; pres. Wichita (Kans.) State U., 1983-93, pres. emeritus, 1993, prof. history, 1993, Univ. prof., 1993—; bd. dirs. Bank IV-Wichita, bd. dirs. The Coleman Co., 1985-89. Author: (with Dae Hong Chang) The Prison: Voices from the Inside, 1972; Contbr. articles to profl. jours. Councilman, Whitewater, 1968-70; bd. visitors Air U., Maxwell AFB, Montgomery, Ala., 1986-90. Mem. AAUP, Orgn. Am. Historians, Am. Conf. Acad. Deans., Am. Assn. Higher Edn., Am. Assn. State Colls. and Univs. (bd. dirs., chmn.), Phi Kappa Phi. Democrat.

ARNAUD, SANDRA, financial advisor; b. Arnaudville, La., July 6, 1945; d. Clarence and Nola (Artigue) A.; divorced; children: Andrea, Geralyn. Attended, U. Southwestern La. Cert. fin. planner. Bus. mgr. Schexnaider Farms, Arnaudville, 1969-81; fin. planner Apex Investors Corp., Lafayette, La., 1981-86, IDS Fin. Svcs., Ft. Myers, Fla., 1986; acct. exec. Securicorp., Inc., Ft. Myers, 1986-88; mgmt. cons. Profl. Strategies, Houston, 1988-89; fin. cons. Shearson Lehman Bros., Houston, 1989-93; fin. advisor Investment Mgmt. & Rsch., Inc., Houston, 1993—; developer, producer edn. program on retirement planning and mng. retirement plan distbns.; conductor retirement planning program for various colls. and chem., aerospace and mfg. cos. in Houston area. Contbr. fin. articles to Bay Area Times newspaper, Houston. Featured in Wall Street Transcript. Mem. Internat. Bd. Standards and Practices for Cert. Fin. Planners. Office: Investment Mgmt & Rsch Inc 1560 W Bay Area Blvd Ste 195 Friendswood TX 77546-2668

ARNDT, JOHN CHRISTOPHER, history educator; b. Point Pleasant, N.J., Sept. 29, 1955; s. Rudolf Otto and Norma June (Waller) A.; m. Susan E. McDonald, Dec. 31, 1984 (div. Mar. 1992); m. Andrea Louise Oster, June 17, 1995. BA, Gettysburg Coll., 1977; MA, Auburn U., 1982; PhD, Fla. State U., 1987. Instr. Ga. So. Coll., Statesboro, 1984-85; from instr. to assoc. prof. James Madison U., Harrisonburg, Va., 1985—. Editor: Voices of the American Past, 1995; contbr. articles to profl. jours. Lutheran. Office: Dept History James Madison U Harrisonburg VA 22807

ARNDT, STEVEN ANDREW, nuclear engineer; b. Landcaster, Calif., Mar. 8, 1959; s. Harold Henry and Jacqueline (Pichford) A. BS, Ohio State U., 1981, MS, 1985; EdD, LaSalle U., 1996; PhD, Ohio State U., 1996. Cert. quality engr., quality auditor, reliability engr., quality mgr. Grad. assoc. Ohio State U., Columbus, 1981-85; rsch. intern Battelle Meml. Inst., Columbus, 1985-86; asst. prof. Am. Tech. Inst., Brunswick, Tenn., 1987; sr. fellow Adv. Com. on Reactor Safeguards, Washington, 1988; asst. prof. US Naval Acad., Annapolis, Md., 1988-90; tech. advisor U.S. Nuclear Regulatory Commn., Washington, 1990-92, Chattanooga, Tenn., 1992—; cons. in field; adj. prof. U. Md., College Park, 1990-94, U. Tenn., Chattanooga, 1994—. Author: (book) Encyclopedia of Microcomputer, 1994; editor Simulation, 1993—; contbr. articles to profl. jours. Bd. dirs. Orton Dyslexia Soc., Washington, 1988-95; mem. U.S. Naval Inst., Annapolis, 1989-95; mem. Ohio Acad. Sci., Columbus, 1990-95. Mem. IEEE, Soc. for Computer Simulation, Am. Nuclear Soc. (nat. planning com., publ. steering com. 1981—), Am. Soc. for Quality Control (local award chmn. 1992—). Office: US Nuclear Regulatory Commn 5700 Brainerd Rd Chattanooga TN 37411

ARNEL, CRAIG LEE, poet, lyricist, musician; b. Forest Hills, N.Y., May 23, 1959; s. Harvey and Beatrice Abelowitz. Student, Nassau C.C., Garden City, N.Y., 1977-80. Adminstrv. position Better Bus. Bur., Suffolk, N.Y., 1982; various sales and clerical jobs N.Y., 1983-87; commodities analyst Scott Arnel Inc., N.Y.C., 1988—. Author: Logical Path, 1995, Soft Spoken, 1995, Oppression of Expressions, 1996, Write to Recite, 1996. Recipient various poetry awards including Golden Poet award World of Poetry, 1989, 90, 91. Mem. Poets of the Palm Beaches, South Fla. Poetry Inst. Jewish.

ARNETT, TRACI WENDELL, English language educator; b. Newport News, Va., Sept. 2, 1970; d. Jack Wendell and Peggy Dare (Isley) A. BA in English, James Madison U., 1992, MA in English, 1994. Tchr. Dominion Bus. Sch., 1992—; tchg. asst. English James Madison U., Harrisonburg, Va., 1993-94; English instr. James Madison U., Harrisburg, Va., 1994—; spkr. in field. Mem. AAUP, Nat. Coun. Tchrs. English.

ARNO, RANDAL ERIC, public administrator; b. Woodstock, Va., Sept. 17, 1946; s. Clayton Walter and Jane (Evans) A.; m. Jodi Hicks, Aug. 18, 1967 (div. 1983); children: Stephanie Shawn, C. Evan. BA in Govt./Internat. Affairs, Fla. State U., Tallhassee, 1969. Regional planner Richmond (Va.) Regional Planning Dist. Commn., 1970-73; county adminstr. Fluvanna County, Palmyra, Va., 1973-75; coord. city-county consolidation Lincoln/Lancaster County, Nebr., 1975-77; asst. to mayor, treas. City of Papillion, Nebr., 1977-80; county adminstr. Alleghany County, Covington, Va., 1980-86, Tazewell County, Tazewell, Va., 1986-88, Floyd County, Floyd, Va., 1988-95; dir. Southside office Weldon Cooper Ctr. for Pub. Svc., Danville, Va., 1995—; state coord.-support Va. Local Govt. Mgmt. Assn., 1987—. Methodist. Home: 1008 S Main St Danville VA 24541 Office: Danville CC 1008 S Main St Danville VA 24541

ARNOLD, ANITA LANCE, community health nurse; b. Biltmore, N.C., July 27, 1939; d. Lincoln L. and Bernice (Young) Lance; m. Sam C. Arnold, May 21, 1961; children: Sandra, Michael. BSN, Berea Coll., 1961; cert. in N.P., Ea. Ky. U., 1978; EMT cert., Hazard (Ky.) State Vocat. Sch., 1991. RN, Ky. Family nurse practitioner Ky. River Dist. Health Dept., Hazard; clin. instr. Frontier Sch. Nurse Midwifery and Family Nursing, 1987-89. Mem. ANA (cert. family nurse practitioner). Baptist. Home: PO Box 484 Beattyville KY 41311-0484

ARNOLD, BILL, freelance writer. BBA in Fin., U. Mass., 1964, MFA in Creative Writing, 1967. Teletype operator, comm. ctr. specialist USAF, Tex., Wyo., 1957-63; motion picture projectionist Mass., 1961-84; instr. Mahar Regional High Sch., Orange, Mass., 1967-68; asst. prof. English Massasoit C.C., Brockton, Mass., 1968-75; substitute tchr. Tisbury Schs., Martha's Vineyard, Mass., 1976-79; freelance writer Palm Beach, Fla., 1979—. Recipient 2d prize N.Am. Poetry Contest, 1993, 95. Mem. MLA, Acad. Am. Poets, Poetry Soc. Am., Modern Poetry Assn., Emily Dickinson Internat. Soc., Internat. Soc. Poets, Poets of Palm Beaches, Book Group of South Fla., Fla. State Poets Assn., Found. for Study of Cycles, Mystery Writers of Am. Home: PO Box 6004 West Palm Beach FL 33405-0004

ARNOLD, CECIL BENJAMIN, former small business owner; b. Bryantsville, Ky., Jan. 23, 1927; s. Walter Tribble and Ella Mae (Hagan) A.; m. Billie Jean Watkins, July 25, 1947; children: Mary Adrianne Davis, Cecil Benjamin Jr. Student, Heidelburg (Fed. Republic of Germany), 1945. Farmer Lancaster, Ky., 1947-50, grocery store owner, 1950-54; ins. agt. Commonwealth Life Ins., Lancaster, Ky., 1954-57; pres. Cecil Arnold Real Estate, Lancaster, Ky., 1957—; agt. Arnold & Boone Ins., Lancaster, Ky., 1957-81; owner Arnold's Furniture, Inc., Lancaster, Ky., 1971-90; ret., 1992; chmn. Lancaster-Garrard Indsl. Authority, 1993—. Pres. Lancaster-Garrard Indsl. Devel., 1984-90; mem. Exec. Com. Dem. Orgn., Lancaster, 1965-75; bd. dirs. Ky. Ins. Guaranty Bd., 1972-75; mem. Ky. legis. rsch. com. for revision of Commonwealth of Ky. Ins. Law, 1969-70; Danville Dist. trustee United Meth. Ch., com. property and location supts.; dir. Garrard County Habitat for Humanity. Served with U.S. Army, 1945-47, ETO. Mem. Nat. Assn. Realtors, Ky. Assn. Realtors, Ky. Assn. Profl. Ins. Agts. (pres. 1968-69, bd. dirs. 1963-72, Mr. Chmn. award 1970, Mr. Profl. Agt. 1972, Profl. Agt. of Yr. 1975-76), Nat. Assn. Profl. Ins. Agts. (bd. dirs. 1972-80, v.p. 1979-80, Profl. Agt. of Yr. 1976-77), Dix River Bd. Realtors (pres. 1972), Nat. and Ky. Assn. Auctioneers, Lancaster-Garrard C. of C. (pres. 1966-68), Ky. Ins. Dept. (Ins. Svc. award 1969, 73; Special Recognition award 1975), Rotary (pres. 1966-68). Democrat. United Methodist. Home: 641 Danville Rd Lancaster KY 40444-9327

ARNOLD, ERNEST WOODROW, minister; b. White Springs, Fla., Mar. 20, 1914; s. Turner Benjamin and Francis Essie (Wise) A.; m. Mildred Virginia Thomas, Jan. 26, 1945; children: Ernest Woodrow Jr., Cheryl Ruth Arnold Daves. BA magna cum laude, Furman U., 1943; BD, New Orleans Bapt. Theol. Sem., 1948; ThD, Luther Rice Sem., 1965. Ordained to ministry So. Bapt. Conv., 1942. Pastor East Pk. Bapt. Ch., Greenville, S.C., 1950-54, Brentwood Bapt. Ch., Charleston, S.C., 1955-58, Bethel Bapt. Ch., Shelby, N.C., 1958-72, Catawba Bapt. Ch., Rock Hill, S.C., 1972-75, 1st Bapt. Ch., Bostic, N.C., 1975-81, Lily Meml. Bapt. Ch., Shelby, 1987—; mem. faculty Luther Rice Sem., 1968-76. Author: Truth: Tried and Tested, 1996. With USMC, 1934-38. Recipient commendation USMC, 1935; New Orleans Bapt. Theol. Sem. fellow, 1948-50. Democrat. Home: 117 Ken Daves Rd Box 715 Boiling Springs NC 28017

ARNOLD, FRANCES DEUPREE, early childhood educator; b. Vicksburg, Miss., Oct. 14, 1940; d. Edward Madison and Carolyn Anne (Viverette) Deupree; m. Arthur Wallace Arnold, Dec. 29, 1961; children: Angela Grey Arnold, Louise Arnold Koulermos. BS, Auburn U., 1963; MEd, Auburn U., Montgomery, Ala., 1973, EdS, 1986. Presch. tchr. Sta. Nursery and Kindergarten, Cherry Point, N.C., 1965-66; kindergarten tchr. South YMCA, Montgomery, 1970-73; dir. Westminster Schs., Inc., Montgomery, 1973-74; dir. early childhood ctr. Auburn U., Montgomery, 1974-92; asst. dir. for day care Ala. Dept. Human Resources, Montgomery, 1992—; cons. Selma (Ala.) City Sch. System, 1987—, AUM Day Care and Mgmt. Cert. Tng., Montgomery, 1987—. 1st v.p. South Cen. Ala. Girl Scout Coun., Montgomery, 1980-88; chmn. Ala. Adv. Com. on Children and Youth, Montgomery, 1986; bd. dirs. Montgomery Latchkey Children's Program, 1988—. Mem. Ala. Assn. for Young Children (resource chair 1989—, pres. 1980), So. Assn. for children Under Six (chair membership 1989—), Ala. Assn. Early Childhood Tchr. Educators (mem. at large 1987-89). Methodist. Home: 212 Holly Brook Dr Montgomery AL 36109-4013 Office: Ala Dept Human Resources 50 N Ripley 7300 University Dr Montgomery AL 36117-3531

ARNOLD, GAYLE GARDNER, pediatrician; b. Erlanger, Ky., Oct. 5, 1920; s. Gayle William and Pearl G. A.; m. Elizabeth K. Boyle, Nov. 17, 1945 (dec. Sept. 1963); children: Gayle William II, Roger B., Stacey K.; m. Judith E. Fought, Mar. 2, 1986. AB, Johns Hopkins U., 1942; MD, U. Md., Balt., 1945. Diplomate Am. Bd. Pediatrics. Intern Union Meml. Hosp., Balt., 1945-46; asst. resident Univ. Hosp., Md., 1948-49; asst. resident pediatrics Duke U. Hosp., 1949-50; chief resident Children's Meml. Hosp., Montreal, 1950-51; attending surgeon Langley Field Hosp., Va., 1946-47; active staff Richmond (Va.) Meml. Hosp., St. Mary's Hosp., Henrico Doctor's Hosp.; cons. staff Chippenham Hosp.; active staff RichmondCerebral Palsy Ctr.; med. dir. Richmond Cerebral Palsy Ctr., 1953—. Capt. USAF, 1946-48. Recipient Point of Light #114 award Pres. Bush, 1990. Fellow Am. Acad. for Cerebral Palsy and Devel. Medicine (pres. 1989-90), Am. Acad. Pediatrics. Office: 3603 Grove Ave Richmond VA 23221-2201

ARNOLD, HOLLIS DAVID, financial analyst; b. Mobile, Ala., Sept. 27, 1949; s. Hollis E. and Alleen (Allegri) A.; children: Griffin, Hollis, McCain. BA, Auburn U., 1971; MS, U. So. Calif., 1975; PhD, U. Ala., 1983. Lic. comml. pilot. Commd. USN, 1971, aviator, 1971-85; prin., cons. Arnold & Assocs., Mobile, 1985-92; prof. finance Auburn (Ala.) U., 1985-88, U. South Ala., Mobile, 1988-91; CFO Oil Recovery Co., Mobile, 1991-92; fin. analyst, dir. rsch. evaluation Dept Def., Maxwell AFB, Ala., 1992—; dir. State Regional Inventors Assn., Mobile, 1988-90. Doctoral fellow USN/U. Ala., 1980, rsch. fellow Def. and Fgn. Affairs Group, London, 1994, 95. Mem. Fin. Mgmt. Assn. Home: PO Box 2037 Daphne AL 36526-2037 Office: ACSC/Dr 225 Chennault Cir Maxwell AFB AL 36112-6426

ARNOLD, J(AMES) BARTO, III, marine archaeologist; b. San Antonio, Jan. 9, 1950; s. J. Barto Jr. and Wilnora (Barton) A.; m. Aurora Irene Foreman, Aug. 28, 1970; children: Kathryn, Julia, Jessica. BA cum laude, U. Tex., 1971, MA, 1973. Rsch. asst. Tex. Archeol. Rsch. Lab. U. Tex., Austin, 1970-72; asst. state marine archaeologist Tex. Antiquities Com., Austin, 1972-75; state marine archaeologist Tex. Hist. Com., Austin, 1975—; dir. La Salle Shipwreck Project; cons. NOAA, 1977-91, Nat. Trust Hist. Preservation, Washington, 1979-90, Congl. Office Tech. Assessment, Washington, 1986; mem. Md. Gov.'s Adv. Com. on Marine Archaeology, Annapolis, 1987-90; mem. history area com. nat. park sys. adv. bd. U.S. Dept. Interior, 1994-95. Co-author: Nautical Archaeology of Padre Island, 1978, Documentary Sources for the Wreck of the New Spain Fleet of 1554, 1979 (Presidio La Bahaia 1979), others; contbr. articles to profl. jours. Recipient Achievement award for Hist. Preservation Dept. Interior, 1980. Mem. Soc. Profl. Archaeologists (cert.; sec.-treas. 1987-89, Spl. Achievement award 1990), Soc. Hist. Archaeology (pres. 1993), Tex. Archeol. Soc., Archaeol. Inst. Am., Coun. Tex. Archaeologists, Phi Beta Kappa. Methodist. Office: Tex Historical Com PO Box 12276 Austin TX 78711-2276

ARNOLD, JAMES PHILLIP, religious studies educator, history educator; b. Greenville, S.C.; s. David Lee and Vera Irene (Wilson) A. MA in Am. History, U. Houston, 1979; MA in Religious Studies, Rice U., 1984, PhD in Religious Studies, 1991. Instr. Am. History U. Houston, 1972-76; instr. religion Rice U., Houston, 1976-81; instr. ch. history, biblical studies, homiletics Houston Grad. Sch. Theology, 1984-86; instr. religion and history, exec. dir. The Reunion Inst., Houston, 1986—; pres. Living History Studies, Inc., Houston, 1993—; counselor families divided by religious cult issues; advisor to FBI on Branch Davidian crisis, Waco, Tex., 1993, Freeman crisis, 1996. Dir. Fine Arts Found., Houston, 1987—; founder Religion-Crisis Task Force, 1994. Rice U. fellow, 1980-91, U. Houston fellow, 1972-76; Tex. Com. for Humanities grantee, 1979. Mem. Am. Acad. Religion, Soc. Biblical Lit. Office: Reunion Inst 5508 Chaucer Dr Houston TX 77005-2632

ARNOLD, LESLIE BISGER, educational administrator; b. Cheyenne, Wyo., Aug. 26, 1956; d. Fred Bennett and Natalie Sylvia (Cohen) B.; m. Kevin Durkin Arnold, July 6, 1980. BS in Spl. Edn. cum laude, Old Dominion U., 1978, MS in Edn. cum laude, 1984. Cert. spl. educator, emotionally disturbed, mentally retarded, presch. handicapped, severly and profoundly handicapped. Tchr. multiple handicapped Virginia Beach (Va.) Pub. Schs., 1978-81; tchr. autistic Southeastern Coop. Ednl. Programs, Norfolk, Va., 1981-82; tchr. emotionally disturbed/mentally retarded Norfolk Pub. Schs., 1983-86, tchr. specialist, 1986-89, ednl. diagnostician, 1989-90, liaison program mgr., 1990-95, ednl. adminstr., 1995—, coord. pupil pers., 1995—; mental health worker Tidewater Psychiat. Inst., Virginia Beach, 1985-86; curriculum coord. CHANCE program Old Dominion U., Norfolk, 1986-91; ednl. cons. St. Croix, V.I., 1991; speaker in field. Author: Behavioral Disorders, 1987, Developmental Skills Attainment Sequence Guide, 1989, ERIC-CEC, 1991, Programming for Behaviorally Disordered Adolescents, 1991, CHIME (Clearinghouse for Immigrant Education), 1993. Recipient Sch. Bell award Norfolk Pub. Sch. Bd., 1989, 91, 94; Nat. Found. for Improvement of Edn. grantee, 1992. Mem. ASCD, Assn. Ctrl. Office Adminstrs., Autism Soc. Am., Tidewater Soc. Autistic Children (pres. 1980-82), Nat. Alliance for Mentally Ill, Optimists Internat. Home: 1920 Hunters Trail Norfolk VA 23518-4919

ARNOLD, MORRIS SHEPPARD, judge; b. Texarkana, Tex., Oct. 8, 1941. Student, Yale U., 1959-61; BSEE, U. Ark., 1965, LLB, 1968; LLM, Harvard U., 1969, SJD, 1971; MA (hon.) U. Pa., 1977. JD (hon.), 1986. Bar: Ark. 1968, Pa. 1985. Teaching fellow in law Harvard U., 1969-70; asst. prof. Ind. U. Law Sch., 1971-74, assoc. prof., 1974-76, prof., 1976-77, dean, fall 1985; prof. law and history, U. Pa., 1977-81, prof. law, 1984-85; Ben J. Altheimer disting. prof. law U. Ark., Little Rock, 1981-84; judge U.S. Dist. Ct. (we. dist.) Ark., Ft. Smith, 1985-92; U.S. circuit judge 8th circuit, 1992—; vis. fellow commoner Trinity Coll, Cambridge U., 1978; v.p., dir. Office of Pres., U. Pa., 1980-81; vis. prof. Stanford (Calif.) U. Law Sch., 1985. Author: Old Tenures and Natura Brevium, 1974, Yearbook 2 Richard II, 1378-79, 1975, On the Laws and Customs of England, 1980, Unequal Laws Unto a Savage Race, 1985, Select Cases of Trespass from the King's Courts, 1307-1399, 2 vols., 1985, 87, Arkansas Colonials, 1986, Colonial Arkansas 1686-1804: A Social and Cultural History, 1991. Pres. Am. Soc. for Legal History, 1980-84; Rep. gen. counsel, Ark., 1982, chmn., 1983; bd. dirs. Nature Conservancy of Ark., 1982-87, Ark. Arts Ctr., 1981-84. Decorated Chevalier l'Ordre des Palmes Académiques (France); Frank Knox fellow, Harvard U., U. London, 1970-71; fellow Mus. Sci. and Natural History, Little Rock, 1986; Harvey Levin Teaching award U. Pa. Law Sch., Phila., 1980, 85. Fellow Am. Soc. Legal History (hon.); mem. Chevalier de l'Ordre des Palmes Académiques, Athenaeum Club (London), Union League Club (Phila.), Country Club of Little Rock. Office: US Cir Judge PO Box 2060 Little Rock AR 72203-2060

ARNOLD, NANCY NAKAMURA, mental health therapist; b. Hilo, Hawaii, Dec. 14, 1949; m. Roy Noel Arnold, July 24, 1982. BA with distinction, U. Hawaii, 1972; postgrad., Columbia U., 1973, U. Hawaii, 1974-75; JD, George Washington U., 1985. Tng. cons. Honolulu, 1972-75; program dir., officer, editor APA, Washington, 1975-87; health policy cons. Washington, 1987-88; mediator Fairfax County (Va.) Dept. Consumer Affairs, 1988-92; mental health therapist Fairfax Falls Ch. Community Svcs. Bd., Annandale, Va., 1992—; legal asst. Gallaudet U., Washington, 1984; legal fellow George Washington U., 1985; cons. Nat. AIDS Network, Washington, 1987; symposium panel mem. APA, Washington, 1986. Expert rev. panelist: (book) AIDS Information Resources Directory, 1988. Mem. Am. Soc. on Aging., Phi Beta Kappa. Home: 3954 Mountain Rd Haymarket VA 22069-1716

ARNOLD, P. A., special education educator; b. Toledo; d. Mattie Spear; m. Earl E. Arnold. BA, BS, David Lipscomb Coll., 1960; MA, Wayne State U., 1962; MS, Nova U., 1986. Cert. spl. edn., psychology, speech, mental retardation, emotional disturbance, Bible tchr., Fla. Tchr. dactyology, interpreter for deaf, 1960—; tchr. Hobbs (N.Mex.) Mcpl. Schs., 1981-82; tchr. spl. edn. City Systems, Rockford and Warren, Mich., 1960-67; dir. Four-County Ctr. Handicapped, Ark., 1977-81; dir. model project ACTION; Project TREE Tech. Resources Exceptional Edn.; instr. Little Red Schoolhouse. Author: Light for Deaf, 1992, Ol' Time Preacher Man, 1995. Bd. dirs., deaf advisor Hearing Soc. Volusia County; mem. project TREE-Tech. Resources in Exceptional Edn.-SY 2000, Dept. Edn., Fla. State U. Ctr. Ednl. Tech. Grantee Pub. Welfare, Nat. Gardening Assn., FUTURES, Newspapers in Edn. Mem. NEA, ARC, ASCD, VEA, Fla. Edn. Assn., Coun. for Exceptional Children, Am. Assn. on Mental Deficiency, Nat. Assn. Deaf.

ARNOLD, RONALD LEE, financial planner; b. Knoxville, Tenn., July 9, 1952; s. Berle Lois and Mollie Louise (Ingram) A.; m. Cindy Lou Kendrick, Oct. 4, 1980. BS in Physics with honors, U. Md. Extension, Frankfurt, Dem. Republic of Germany, 1978; BA in Math. with honors, U. Md. Extension, Frankfurt, German Dem. Republic, 1978. Registered broker/dealer; registered rep. Gen. mgr. The Original Hot Tub Co., Knoxville, 1981-85; regional v.p. Catalina Waterbeds, Bristol, Va., 1986-89; gen. mgr. Bedroom City, Johnson City, Tenn., 1989-90; account exec. Equicomp Trust Corp., Panama City, Fla., 1991; acct. exec. Michelson & Assocs., Atlanta, 1991; fin. planning rep. The Ins. Specialists Group, Kingsport, Tenn., 1990-92; v.p., mng. gen. agt. Toohey, Jordan and Stewart, Inc., Kingsport, Tenn., 1992-95; with The Ins. Specialist, Mount Carmel, Tenn., 1995—. With USAF, 1971-80. Home: 1017 Independence Ave Mount Carmel TN 37645-3304 Office: PO Box 1810 Mount Carmel TN 37645-1810

ARNOLD, STEPHEN PAUL, investment professional; b. San Antonio, Mar. 26, 1957; s. Francis Andrew and Charlene (Tyler) A.; m. Kenzie Lou Box, Dec. 16, 1978; children: Stephen Kameron, Kalen Lou. BS in Agrl. Econs., Tex. A&M U., 1979. Rsch. specialist Employee's Retirement System of Tex., Austin, 1982-84, adminstr. of spl. programs, 1984-85, dir. of spl. programs, 1985-87, asst. investment officer, 1987-91, investment portfolio mgr., 1991-94; strategist and portfolio mgr. Bluestone Investments, 1994—; mem. Tex. Econ. Forum, Austin, 1989-92; adv. bd. Internat. Bus. Forum, N.Y.C. Del. Tex. Rep. Party, Austin, 1980-86. Named to Outstanding Young Men of Am., 1983. Mem. Austin Investment Assn., Fin. Analyst Assn., Capitol City A&M Club, Former Student Assn./Tex. A&M. Baptist. Home: 7903 Palacios Dr Austin TX 78749-3840 Office: Bluestone Investments 7903 Palacios Dr Austin TX 78749

ARNOLD, STEVE, state legislator, state commissioner; s. Gordon and Rosalie A. BA in Polit. Sci., U. N.C., 1984. With High Point (N.C.) City Coun., 1985-87; rep. N.C. House of Reps., 1988—; commr. Guilford County (N.C.) Bd. Commrs., 1990—, chmn., 1990-91; owner Arcon, Inc. Active Green Street Bapt. Ch., High Point. Office: 1610 Bridges Dr High Point NC 27262

ARNOLD, SUSAN BIRD, safety education training, consulting and products company executive; b. Reading, Pa., Feb. 28, 1951; d. Frank Edward and Esther (Savidge) Bird; B.A., Mercer U., Macon, Ga., 1972; m. Robert Melvin Arnold, Jr., Mar. 18, 1972; children—Jennifer Michelle, Amelia Michelle, Stephanie Michelle, Elizabeth Michelle. Audio-video technician Internat. Safety Acad., 1971; with Internat. Loss Control Inst., 1974—, mgr. ednl. products div., 1978-82, v.p. adminstrv. services, v.p. press div., Loganville, Ga., 1982-85, exec. dir., gen. mgr., 1985-91, v.p. customer svc., sales, 1991-92, comml. dir., v.p., 1992-94, mgr. mktg. and product sales, 1992-96; pres. AEI Loss Control Svcs., 1996—. Contbr. to Risk Control Rev. Mem. adv. com. Inst. Safety, Health and Rehab. for the Exceptional, 1978-84; bd. dirs. Bluesprings Day Camp for Handicapped (chmn. lang. plan com.); mem. nat. trust U. Macon; chmn. Long Range Planning Com. UMC, 1991. Mem. AVMA Aux., Zool. Soc. Methodist. Home: PO Box 609 Loganville GA 30249-0609 Office: Internat Loss Control Inst Hwy 78 Loganville GA 30249

ARNOLD, TIMOTHY JAY, therapist, educator; b. Chattanooga, Tenn., Mar. 18, 1954; s. Frederick Wright and Ethelwyn Marie (Sylar) A.; div. Sept., 1981; m. Zoila Georgia Leon, Aug. 5, 1990; stepchildren: Cristina Renae Chambers, Wesley Philip Chambers. BS in Psychology, U. Tenn., 1979; AS in Respiratory Therapy, Chattanooga State, 1984. Licensed respiratory therapist. Psychiatric tech. Valley Psychiatric Hosp., Chattanooga, Tenn., 1977-82; respiratory therapist Erlanger Med. Ctr., Chattanooga, Tenn., 1982—; mem. locatl emergency planning com., Chattanooga, Tenn., 1995-96. Disaster vol. ARC, Chattanooga, Tenn., 1995-96; olympic vol. Atlanta Com. for Olympic Games, Ocoee, Tenn., 1996; assoc. mem. Civil Air Patrol, Chattanooga, 1995-96. Lt. USPHS, 1991-96. Mem. Am. Assn. Respiratory Care, Am. Lung Assn. (mem. adv. coun. S.E. region 1993-96), Tenn. Acad. Sci., State Guard Assn. of U.S., Tenn. Thoracic Soc., Psi Chi. Methodist. Home: 4811 Montcrest Cir Chattanooga TN 37416 Office: Erlanger Med Ctr 975 E 3rd St Chattanooga TN 37403-2112

ARNOLD-NOBBMAN, MILDRED MAXINE BERRY, association executive; b. Pocahontas, Ark., Feb. 5, 1936; d. John Ephriam and Rubye Pearl (Tyler) Berry; m. Jimmie Lee Arnold, July 30, 1955 (div. 1973); children: Janet E. Arnold Brown, Douglas Lee; m. Donald L. Nobbman, Mar. 28, 1992. BS in Edn., U. Tex., El Paso, 1967, MEd, 1971. Cert. tchr., Tex. Tchr. Ysleta Ind. Sch. System, El Paso, 1966-68; program dir. N.E. YMCA, El Paso, 1968-70, mem. youth ct., 1968-76; met. program dir. Cen. Br. YMCA, El Paso, 1970-76; exec. dir. Belleville (Ill.) Family YMCA, 1976-80, Met. YMCA Dallas, Grand Prairie, Tex., 1980—; dist. exec. Met. YMCA Dallas, Dallas, 1988-89; instr. phys. edn. U. So. Ill., Edwardsville, 1979-80; bd. dirs. Mid-Am. region YMCA, 1985-88, chmn. youth devel. com.; participant YMCA of U.S. and U.K. exch. program, London and Cardiff, Wales, 1986. Contbr. articles to profl. jours. Mem. El Paso Mayor's Com. on Drug Abuse, 1974-76; chmn. Child Care Task Team, 1985-90; del. world alliance meeting and woman's forum YMCA, Seoul, Korea, 1991. Mem. Assn. Profl. Dirs. (pres. 1984-87, v.p. south cen. dist. 1990—, Adminstrv. Excellence award Red River chpt. 1985, Outstanding Svc. award 1986), Grand Prairie C. of C., Grand Prairie Bus. and Profl. Women's Club (pres. 1992—, outstanding mem. 1991), Soroptomists. Methodist. Home: 1009 Bert Dr Arlington TX 76012-4136 Office: Grand Prairie YMCA 333 NE 5th St Grand Prairie TX 75050-5742

ARNOTT, ELLEN MARIE, medical case management and occupational health executive; b. Berwyn, Ill., Apr. 28, 1945; d. Howard Thomas and Catherine Marie (Stauber) Simon; m. John Michael Arnott, Dec. 16, 1967; children: John Michael II, Michelle Marie. BSN, Seton Hall U., 1981; MA, Tex. Woman's U., 1991. Cert. occupational health nurse, case mgr. Staff nurse oncology, med.-surgery, ICU, CCU, recovery, 1981-83, community health nurse, 1982-83; disability health nurse AT&T, 1983-84; mgr. health svcs. Lone Star Gas Co., 1985-86, Abbott Labs., 1986-88; corp. nursing supr. J.C. Penney, 1988-89; pres. Arnott & Assocs., Grapevine, Tex., 1989—, New Vision Nursecare, 1996—; wellness cons.; cons. health fair; occupl. health mgmt. cons.; workers compensation case mgmt. cons.; spkr. in field. CPR instr. trainer Am. Heart Assn.; vol. and facilitator SBE and smoking cessation Am. Cancer Soc., edn. com., skin cancer com.; CPR instr. to cmty.; first aid vol.; local rescue squad vol.; bd. dirs. Ctr. for Computer Assistance to the Disabled. Recipient Tex. State Achievement award for excellence in occupational health, 1990; named one of the Great One-Hundred Nurses of 1991, Dallas/Ft. Worth. Mem. Am. Assn. Occupational Health Nurses, Nat. Assn. Women Bus. Owners, Case Mgmt. Soc. Am., Tex. Assn. Occupational Health Nurses (fin. com. 1989-90, v.p. 1989-91), Dallas Tex. Assn. Occupational Health Nurses (hospitality com. 1985, edn. com. 1986-87, dir.-newsletter editor 1987, v.p. 1988-90, pres. 1991-93), ANA, Tex. Nurses Assn., Ctr. Computer Assistance to the Disabled (bd. dirs.), Omicron Delta Epsilon. Roman Catholic. Office: New Vision NurseCare PO Box 923 Grapevine TX 76099

ARNOW, PAT, editor; b. Chgo., Jan. 31, 1949; d. Robert D. and Edna L. Arnow; m. Steven L. Giles, Nov. 25, 1978. BA, Marshall U., 1981. Pub. info. officer Woodland Ctr., Gallipolis, Ohio, 1979-84; editor Now & Then Mag. East Tenn. State U., Ctr. for Appalachian Studies and Svcs., Johnson City, 1986-94; editor So. Exposure Mag. Inst. for So. Studies, Durham, N.C., 1994—; chair Independent Press Assn., 1996—, chair pubs. com. Appalachian Consortium Press, Boone, N.C., 1990-91. Mng. editor Jour. of Appalachian Studies Assn., 1990-94; co-playwright Cancell'd Destiny, 1990. Home: 305 Clark St Durham NC 27701-1602 Office: So Exposure Mag Inst for So Studies PO Box 531 Durham NC 27702

AROCKIASAMY, MADASAMY, engineering educator; b. Kodiankulam, Tamilnadu, India, Oct. 9, 1936; came to U.S., 1967; s. Madasamy and Sudalaimadi Sivaraman; m. Thayammal, May 11, 1961; children: Mohan, Subha. BS in Engring. with honors, Guindy Engring. Coll, U. Madras, India, 1960, MS in Engring., 1963; PhD in Engring., U. Wis., 1970. Assoc. lectr. Gruindy Coll. Engring., U. Madras, India, 1960-63; lectr., asst. prof. U. Madras Guindy Coll. Engring., 1963-76, prof., 1976-81; assoc. prof. Meml. U. of Newfoundland, St. John's, Newfoundland, Can., 1981-84; assoc. prof., dept. ocean engring. Fla. Atlantic U., Boca Raton, 1984-87, prof., dir. Ctr. Infrastsructure and Constructed Facilities, 1987—; v.p. Structural Synthesis Inc., Boca Raton, 1987—. Author: Prestressed Concrete Structures, 1972, Offshore Structures, 1991, Expert Systems Applications to Structural, Construction, Transportation and Environmental Engineering, 1991; contbr. over 200 articles on civil and ocean engring. to profl. jours. Mem. ASCE, Am. Concrete Inst. Office: Fla Atlantic U 500 NW 20th St Boca Raton FL 33431-6415

AROMIN, MERCEDES FUNG, portfolio manager, investment advisor, consultant; b. Kowloon, Hong Kong, Dec. 1, 1956; came to U.S., 1974; d. Remigio N. and Josephine (Fung) A. BS in Bus. Adminstrn., U. Tenn., Knoxville, 1978; MBA, Ga. State U., 1989. Mgr. Ramada Inn, Scottsburg, Ind., 1978; asst. mgr. York Steak House, Nashville, 1978-80; asst. terminal mgr. Greyhound Lines Inc., Atlanta, 1980-84; staff asst. The Coca-Cola Co., Atlanta, 1985-87; staff asst. Coca-Cola Enterprises Inc., Atlanta, 1987-89, shareholder rels. mgr., 1989-92; pres., CEO MFA Fin. Asset Mgmt., Atlanta, 1992—; sec.-treas. Coca-Cola Enterprises Inc. Employee Nonpartisan Com. for Good Govt., Atlanta, 1989-91. William Way scholar, 1976, Alcoa Found. scholar, 1977. Mem. Atlanta Investment Group (founder, chief investment officer 1990, exec. com., adv. com.), Ga. State U. MBA Alumni Group (charter). Roman Catholic. Office: 2040 Bascomb Carmel Rd Woodstock GA 30189-3545

ARON, MARK G., transportation executive, lawyer; b. Hartford, Conn., Jan. 27, 1943; s. Samuel H. and Florence A.; m. Cindy Sondik, June 1, 1966; 1 child, Samantha. B.A. summa cum laude, Trinity Coll., 1965; LL.B., Harvard U., 1968. Bar: Va., Mass., D.C. Asst. prof. law Osgood Hall Law Sch., York U., Toronto, 1968-70; assoc. Goulston & Storrs, Boston, 1970-71; atty., asst. gen. counsel then dep. gen. counsel U.S. Dept. Transp., Washington, 1971-81; asst. gen. counsel CSX, Richmond, Va., 1981-83, gen. counsel spl. projects, 1983-85; sr. v.p. corp. svcs. Chessie System R.R., Balt., 1985-86; sr. v.p. law and pub. affairs CSX Corp., Richmond, 1986-95, exec. v.p. law and pub. affairs, 1995—. Trustee Va. Union U.; mem. Richmond Leadership Metro; bd. dirs. Va. Literacy Found., Theatre IV; mem. Or Ami Cong. Mem. Va. Bar Assn., Mass. Bar Assn., D.C. Bar Assn., Country Club Va. Office: CSX Corp Box 85629 901 E Cary St Richmond VA 23219

ARONOWITZ, JACK LEON, biotechnology and diagnostic manufacturing company executive, consultant; b. Bklyn., Feb. 29, 1940; s. Harry and Evelyn (Kaftal) A.; m. Jeanette T. Sofia, Nov. 9, 1963; children—Eric Scott, Francine Marie. B.S., Poly. Inst. Bklyn., 1960, M.S., 1962, Pres. Hall Labs, Plainview, N.Y., 1960-67; v.p. Internat. Hosp. Supply Corp., N.Y.C., 1967-68; dir. labs. Sigma Chem. Co., St. Louis, 1968-70; v.p., tech. dir. Reliable Chem. Co., St. Louis, 1970-74; pres., tech. dir. Leon Industries Inc., St. Charles, Mo., 1974-83; pres., chief exec. officer Techimed Corp., St. Charles, 1983-91; founder, pres., CEO, chmn. Technical Chems. & Products Inc., 1992—; instr. analytical chemistry C.W. Post U., Greenvale, N.Y., 1964-65; panel mem., lectr. Tissue Culture Soc., Lake Placid, N.Y., 1978-80; lectr. clin. and biochem. procedures, 1972-80. Author: (with others) Growth Requirements of Vertebrate Cells in Vitro, 1982. Patentee multi purpose mixer, 1960. Scoutmaster St. Louis Boy Scouts Am., 1974, 77. Fellow Am. Inst. Chemists; mem. Empire State Soc. Med. Tech., Am. Assn. Exfoliative Cytologists, Am. Assn. Clin. Chemists, Am. Chem. Soc., Registry Med. Technologists Internat., Fla. Inst. Chemists (pres. 1994—). Republican. Jewish. Clubs: Bellerose Rod and Gun, Angel Flight USA (exec. v.p.). Avocations: pilot; outdoor sports; hunting; fishing.

ARONSON, MARK THEODORE, chemical engineer; b. Mpls., Jan. 10, 1961; s. Arthur L. and Marilyn (Lundeen) A.; m. Marianne S. Sarsfield, June 21, 1988; children: Matthew, Julia. BS, U. Va., 1983; MS, U. Pa., 1984, PhD, 1987. Divsn. engr. DuPont, Buffalo, 1987-91; rsch. engr. DuPont Ctrl. R&D, Wilmington, Del., 1991-94; sr. rsch. engr. DuPont Ctrl. R&D, Waynesboro, Va., 1994—. Contbr. articles to profl. jours. Lutheran. Home: 136 Berkeley Dr Waynesboro VA 22980 Office: DuPont Lycra 400 DuPont Blvd Waynesboro VA 22980

ARORA, SRI NATH, internist, hematologist; b. Kanpur, India, Mar. 1, 1940; came to U.S., 1964; s. Ram Nath and Jamuna Devi Arora; m. Geeta Mehrotra, June 17, 1967; children: Vinita, Nitin. BS, Agra U., Kanpur, 1957; MD, Lucknow U., Kanpur, 1962. Diplomate Am. Bd. Internal Medicine. House physician in internal medicine L.L.R. and Associated Hosps., Kanpur, 1962-63; registrar in internal medicine M.L.N. Med. Coll., Allahabad, India, 1963-64; intern New Britain (Conn.) Gen. Hosp., 1964-65, resident in internal medicine, 1965-68, resident in pathology, 1968-69; fellow in hematology U. Miami (Fla.) Sch. Medicine, 1969-70; chief resident hematology dept. lab. medicine U. Conn. Sch. Medicine, 1970-72; staff physician, hematologist VA Hosp., Columbia, S.C., 1972-73, cons. hematology and internal medicine, 1973-75; pvt. practice West Columbia, S.C., 1973—. Office: Dr SN Arora MD 2317 Sunset Blvd West Columbia SC 29169-4715

AROVA, SONIA, artistic director, ballet educator; b. Sofia, Bulgaria; came to U.S., 1954; d. Albert and Rene (Melamedoff) Errio; m. Thor Sutowski, Mar. 11, 1965; 1 child, Ariane. Grad. Fine Arts Sch., Paris, 1940, Eng., 1944. Ballerina Internat. Ballet, London, 1944-47, Rambert Ballet, London, 1947-50, Royal Ballet, London, 1962-63, Festival Ballet, London, 1950-54, Ballet deChamps-Elysees, Paris, 1958-60, Am. Ballet Theater, N.Y.C., 1954-58, Ballet Russe, 1960-62; artistic dir. Nat. Ballet, Oslo, 1964-70, Hamburg Ballet, Fed. Republic Germany, 1970-71; co-dir. San Diego Ballet, 1971-75; dir. State of Ala. Ballet, Ballet South, Birmingham, 1981—, instr. Sch. Fine Arts, 1975—; guest tchr. Australian Ballet, 1993, 94, Bayerische Staatsballet, Munich, Germany, 1994. Recipient World Championship of Dance award Ballet Jury, Paris, 1939; decorated knight of First Order, King Olav of Norway, 1971.

ARP, ROBERT KELLEY, clergyman; b. Bremen, Ga., Dec. 23, 1962; s. George Marion Arp and Janelle (Robinson) Benton; m. Robbin Carole Patterson, May 9, 1984; children: Emily Elizabeth, Robert Charles. BA in Theology, Lee Coll., 1984; MDiv, Columbia Sem., 1988; D Ministry, Erskine Theol. Sem., 1994. Ordained to ministry, Living Faith Fellowship, 1988. Chaplain Alpha Gamma Chi, Cleveland, Tenn., 1983-84; youth pastor Hairston Rd. Ch. of God, Stone Mountain, Ga., 1984-86; missionary St. John, V.I., 1986-87; pastor to single adults Living Faith Fellowship, Athens, Ga., 1987-92; family ministries pastor Mt. Paran Ch. of God, Atlanta, 1992-96; sr. min. Newberry (S.C.) Christian Ministries, 1996—. Staff writer Charisma Life Pubs.; contbg. author: Single to Single, 1991. Mem. Nat. Single Adult Leaders, Nat. Christian Counselors Assn. (assoc.), Campus Ministry Assn. (assoc.), Alpha Gamma Chi (chaplain 1983-84), Sigma Nu Sigma (Big Bro. 1983-84). Home: 1400 Main St Newberry SC 29108 Office: Newberry Christian Ministries PO Box 1037 Newberry SC 29108

ARP LOTTER, DONNA, investor, venture capitalist; b. Henrietta, Tex., Dec. 17, 1950; d. T.S. Jr. and Coy Lee (Howard) Grimsley; m. Bruce D. Lotter, Feb. 18, 1984; children: Brandon, Collin. BS, Midwestern State U., 1975, M in Counseling, 1979. Sales rep. Burroughs-Wellcome Co., Fort Worth, Tex., 1978-79; sales mgr. Procter & Gamble Co., Dallas, 1979-84; pres. Arp-Lotter Investments, Colleyville, Tex., 1984—; prin. DBL Investments, Inc.; sec., officer KCB Corp., Inc.; bd. dirs. Landmark Bank. Chmn., trustee Baylor Hosp., Grapevine, Tex., 1991; bd. dirs. Am. Cancer Soc.; bd. govs. N.E. Arts Coun.; bd. dirs. North Tex. Commn. Hardin scholar Midwestern State U., 1975; named Alumnus of Yr. Midwestern State U., 1995. Mem. Bus. Profl. Womens Club, Nat. Assn. Women Bus. Owners, Colleyville C. of C. (pres. 1995), Am. Heart Assn. (bd. dirs., Legacy of Women award 1995, Vol. of Yr. award Colleyville 1996). Republican. Methodist.

ARRINGTON, DOROTHY ANITA COLLINS, retired real estate broker; b. Laurel, Miss., Sept. 9, 1922; d. Jeff Clay and Maude Eula (Sudduth) Collins; m. Robert Newton Arrington, Oct. 27, 1956; children: Robert William, Cynthia Anne Arrington Morris. AA, Jones County Jr. Coll., 1941; student, U. Ala., 1942-43. Assoc. realtor Town & Country Village Realtors, Houston, 1970-72, McGuirt & Co., Realtors, Houston, 1974-77, 79-81, Duffy & LaRoe, Realtors, Houston, 1978-79; owner-broker Dotty Arrington, Realtors, Houston, 1972-74; asst. sales mgr. Realmco, Inc., Houston, 1977-78; pres. Dotty Arrington, Inc., Houston, 1981-89, ret., 1989; adult tchr. Bethel Bible Series. Mem. Daus of the King, Delphians. Republican. Episcopalian.

ARRINGTON, RICHARD, JR., mayor; b. Livingston, Ala., Oct. 19, 1934. A.B., Miles Coll., 1955; M.S., U. Detroit, 1957; Ph.D. in Zoology, U. Okla., 1966. Asst. prof. Miles Coll., 1957-63, prof., 1966-70; exec. dir. Ala. Ctr. for Higher Edn., 1970-79; mayor City of Birmingham, Ala., 1979—; counselor Miles Coll., 1962-63, dir. summer sch., acting dean, 1966-67, dean, 1967-70. Mem. Birmingham City Council, 1971-79. Office: Office of Mayor 710 20th St N Birmingham AL 35203-2216

ARRINGTON, TERESA ROSS, religion educator, language educator; b. Detroit, July 2, 1949; d. Arthur Peter and Mary Stella (McRae) Ross; m. Melvin Slay Arrington, Jr., Aug. 10, 1973; children: Linda Diane, Debra Anne. AB, U. Detroit, 1971; MA, U. Ky., 1973, PhD, 1977. Cert. secondary tchr., Mich., Miss. Tchr. confrat. Christian doctrine St. John Cath. Ch., Oxford, Miss., 1983-87, coord., 1982-95; asst. prof. modern langs. U. Miss., University, 1982-95; asst. prof. Spanish Ctr. Coll., Danville, Ky., 1995-96; adj. prof. Millsaps Coll., Jackson, Miss., 1996—. Contbg. author: Escitoras hispanoamericanas, 1991, Dictionary Mexican Literature, 1991. Troop leader Girl Scouts U.S.A., Knoxville, Tenn., 1981-82, Oxford, 1984-88, com. mem., Oxford, 1982-84, chmn., 1985-90. Grad. fellow NDEA, 1972-74, U. Ky., 1974-75; scholar Ford Motor Co. Fund, 1967-71. Mem. MLA, Am. Assn. Tchrs. Spanish and Portuguese, Southeastern Coun. on L.Am. Studies, Miss. Fgn. Lang. Assn. (exec. dir. 1988-95). Office: Millsaps Coll PO Box 151566 Jackson MS 39210

ARROWSMITH, MARIAN CAMPBELL, secondary education educator; b. St. Louis, Nov. 12, 1943; d. William Rankin and Elizabeth (Mitchell) Arrowsmith; m. William Earl Schroyer, July 23, 1983; stepchildren: Carey Jo, Amy Lynn. BS, La. State U., 1961; MEd, Southeastern La. U., 1978. Lic. tchr., La.; cert. practicum supr. Inst. for Reality Therapy. Tchr. 1st grade McDonough #26, Jefferson Parish Sch. Bd., Gretna, La., 1966; 2nd grade tchr. Woodlawn High Sch., Baton Rouge, 1966-67; kindergarten tchr. Univ. Terrace Elem. Sch., Baton Rouge, summer 1967; 1st grade tchr. Westminster Elem. Sch., Baton Rouge, 1967-72, Elm Grove Elem. Sch., Harvey, La., 1972-73; kindergarden tchr. Westminster Elem. Sch., Baton Rouge, summers 1968, 69, 70, 71, Elm Grove Elem. Sch., summer 1973; 1st grade tchr. St. Andrews Episcopal Sch., New Orleans, 1973-74; kindergarten tchr. St. Tammany Parish Sch. Bd., Folsom, La., 1974-77; early childhood specialist St. Tammany Parish Sch. Bd., Covington, La., 1977-87; prin. Woodlake Elementary Sch., 1987—; off-campus coordinating asst. St. Tammany Parish for Dept. Continuing Edn., Southeastern La. U., 1985-87; condr. workshops in field; selected ofcl. pres. Sunbelt Region of Reality Therapists, 1983; regional dir. La. and Miss. Reality Therapists, Sunbelt Bd. of Reality Therapists, 1983. Author: Helping Your Child at Home, 1982-83; Handbook for Early Childhood Tutorial Program, 1983-84. Mem. AAUW, La. Assn. Sch. Execs., La. Assn. Prins., Nat. Assn. Elem. Sch. Prins., St. Tammeny Humane Soc., Sunbelt Assn. Reality Therapists (regional bd. 1982-88, pres. and internat. bd. dirs. 1986-88), Internat. Assn. Reality Therapists, Assn. Tchr. Educators, St. Tammany Assn. Prins., Pontchartrain Yacht Club, Delta Kappa Gamma (v.p. 1986), Alpha Delta Kappa, Kappa Alpha Theta, Phi Delta Kappa. Democrat. Presbyterian. Avocations: horticulture, reading, fishing, dancing. Home: 1000 Montgomery St Mandeville LA 70448-5517

ARSAN, JANICE HOLT, university administrator; b. Washington, May 15, 1944; d. Fred Edward and Helen Louise (Brett) H.; m. Noyan Arsan; children: Tanju, N. Yasemin. AB, Colby Coll., 1970; MPA, Ga. State U., 1987. From adminstrv. asst. to dir. libraries SUNY, Binghamton, 1970-72, asst. registrar, 1973; alumni adminstrv. supr. Ga. State U., Atlanta, 1981-86, asst. dir. alumni, 1986-88, dir. devel. and alumni support svcs., 1988—. Office: Ga State U Devel & Alumni Support Svcs 33 Gilmer St SE Atlanta GA 30303-3083

ARTEMOV, VLADIMIR NIKOLAEVICH, gymnastics coach; b. Vladimir City, Russia, Dec. 7, 1964; came to U.S., 1990; s. Nikolai Filippovich and Maria vasilievna (Mileshnikova) A.; m. Susan Ann Wallace, July 28, 1991; children: Glenn Vladimirovich, Alexander Vladimirovich. Phys. conditioning instr. USSR Mil., 1987-88; staff mem. South Tex. Gymnastics Acad., 1991-92, Team USA Gynmastics Camp, 1991; head coach Kips Gymnastics, 1993—; coach Pan Am. Tng. Camp, 1994; mem. U.S.A. Nat. Coaching staff, 1990—; cons. Elios Gynmastic Tng. Ctr., Mex., 1995—; spkr. in field. Contbr. articles to profl. jours. Recipient Master of Sport Internat. Class, 1981, 83, 88. Address: 520 N 38th Ave #65 Hattiesburg MS 39401

ARTHUR, GUY, farming executive; b. 1946. Farmer Trenton, N.C., 1967—; v.p. Jones County Cotton Gin, Inc., Trenton. Office: Jones County Cotton Gin Inc 888 Nobles Ln Trenton NC 28585

ARTIGLIERE, RALPH, lawyer, educator; b. Morristown, N.J., Mar. 1, 1947; s. Fiore Joseph and Mary (Bolcar) A.; m. Gale Anderson, June 14, 1969; children: William Michael, Adam Robert. BS in Engring., U.S. Mil. Acad., 1969; JD, U. Fla., 1977. Bar: Fla. 1977, U.S. Dist. Ct. (mid. dist.) Fla. 1978, U.S. Ct. Appeals (11th cir.) 1981, U.S. Dist. Ct. (no. dist.) Fla. 1984. Project mgr. Ryder System, Inc., Miami, Fla., 1974-75; cons. Ryder System, Inc., Gainesville, Fla., 1975-77; atty. Holland & Knight, Lakeland, Fla., 1977-81, Lane, Trohn, Clarke, Bertrand & Williams, Lakeland, Fla., 1981-91, Anderson & Artigliere, P.A., Lakeland, Fla., 1991—; mem. jury instrn. com. Fla. Supreme Ct., Tallahassee, 1990—; aj. prof. U. South Fla., Tampa, 1991-92; instr. legal writing U. Fla. Law Sch., Gainesville, 1976-77. Author: (chpt.) Florida Forms of Jury Instruction, 1990. Pres. Santa Fe High Sch. Bd., Lakeland, 1985; chmn. 10th Cir. Jud. Nominating Commn., Polk County, Fla., 1985-86; bd. dirs. Polk Pub. Mus., Lakeland, 1987-89, United Cerebral Palsy of Polk County, Lakeland, 1980-82. Capt. U.S. Army, 1969-74, Vietnam. Decorated Bronze Star, Air medal with "V"; recipient Fla. Bar Pro Bono award Fla. Supreme Ct., 1982. Mem. ABA, FBA, Fla. Bar (cert. civil trial lawyer 1993—, chmn. CLE comm.), Fedn. Ins. and Corp. Counsel, Def. Rsch. Inst., Polk County Trial Lawyers Assn. (pres. 1995—), Phi Kappa Phi, Order of Coif. Republican. Home: 1142 Waterfall Ln Lakeland FL 33803-3011 Office: Anderson & Artigliere PA 4927 Southfork Dr Lakeland FL 33813-2043

ARTLEY, NATHAN MONROE, music educator; b. Burlington, N.C., June 27, 1959; s. Malvin Newton and Joan (Brown) A. BS, Elon Coll., 1981; MA, Ohio State U., 1988. Dir. of orch. Salisbury (N.C.) City Schs., 1981-86; dir. of orchs. Cumberland County Schs., Fayetteville, N.C., 1988—; adj. faculty of music Pfeiffer Coll., Misenheimer, N.C., 1982-84, Elon (N.C.) Coll., 1984-85. Mem. NEA, N.C. Music Educators Assn. (chair N.C. orch. divsn. 1992-94, chair Ea. N.C. orch. contest 1993—, chair N.C. honors orch. 1990-92), Nat. Sch. Orch. Assn. (pres. N.C. nat. sch. orch., 1991-93, creator N.C. orch. retreat 1992-93), Am. Strings Tchr. Assn., Am. Viola Soc., Omicron Delta Kappa. Home: 150 Homeplace Dr Fayetteville NC 28311

ARUFFO, HENRY ANTHONY, geographer, educator; b. Phila., Nov. 3, 1949. AA, U. South Fla., 1991, BA cum laude, 1992, MA, 1993. Lic. ships capt. U.S. Coast Guard. Owner Mid Am. Constrn. Supply, Oklahoma City, 1973-83; ship capt. Dream Weaver Adventures, British West Indies, 1983-86; dir. pub. rels. Suntech Corp., St. Petersburg, Fla., 1986-89; prof. geography U. South Fla., Tampa, 1993—. Author, editor: Geography of Current Events, 1994, 95, 96. With USMC, 1967-71. Fellow Royal Geog. Soc., Royal Inst. Navigation; mem. Am. Assn. Geogs., Union Concerned Scientists (lectr.), Fla. Geog. Assn., Bayboro Geog. Soc. (pres. 1991-92, editor, pub. newsletter 1991-92). Home: 5849 B Lynn Lake Dr S St Petersburg FL 33712-6258 Office: Univ South Fla 4202 E Fowler Ave Tampa FL 33620-9900

ARVIEW, KATHLEEN YVONNE, geriatrics nurse; b. Tucson, Dec. 31, 1957; d. Merwin Lawrence and Betty Alice (Damrau) Saxe; m. Arthur Ray Arview, Mar. 18, 1986 (dec. Feb. 1992); 1 child, Bettina Raye. Lic. vocat. nurse, Howard County Jr. Coll., 1989. Cert. BLS instr.; cert. nurse aide instr. Nurse Scenic Mountain Med. Ctr. Hosp., Big Spring, Tex., 1989-91, Mt. View Lodge, Big Spring, 1991-92; staff devel. coord. Manor Park, Midland, Tex., 1993; treatment nurse Stanton (Tex.) Care Ctr., 1993-94; coord. infection control, quality assurance com. Mt. View Lodge, Big Spring, 1991-92; instr. BSL. Comdr. DAV Aux., Big Spring, 1986-87; asst. leader Girl Scout U.S. Home: 4610 Thomason Dr Midland TX 79703

ARYA, SATYA PAL, meteorology educator; b. Mavi Kalan, Dist Meerut, India, Aug. 24, 1939; came to U.S., 1965.; BE (Civil), U. Roorkee (India), 1961, ME (Civil), 1964; PhD, Colo. State U., 1968. Asst. engr. Irrigation Dept., Lucknow, India, 1961-62; lectr. U. Roorkee, 1963-65; rsch. asst. Colo. State U., Ft. Collins, 1965-68, rsch. assoc., 1968-69; rsch. asst., assoc. prof. U. Wash., Seattle, 1969-76; assoc. prof. N.C. State U., Raleigh, 1976-81, prof. meteorology, 1981—, acting head MEAS dept., 1982-83; vis. prof. Indian Inst. Tech., Delhi, 1983-84. Author: Introduction to Micrometeorology, 1988; contbr. sci. articles to jours. of atmospheric scis., applied meteorology, fluid mechanics, others. Fellow AAAS, Am. Meteorol. Soc.; mem. Am. Geophys. Union, Sigma Xi. Office: NC State U Dept Marine Earth & Atmospheric Sci Raleigh NC 27695-8208

ASENCIO, DIEGO C., state agency administrator, former federal commission administrator, consultant, business executive; b. Nijar, Spain, July 15, 1931; m. Nancy Rodriguez Asencio; children—Manuel, Diego, Anne, Maria, Frank. BS, Georgetown U., 1952. Underwriter Prudential Ins. Co., Newark, 1952-55; fgn. svc. officer Prudential Ins. Co., 1957-86; spl. asst. to asst. sec. for Inter-Am. affairs U.S. Dept. State, 1965-67; counselor polit. affairs, then deputy chief of mission U.S. Dept. State, Lisbon, Portugal, 1967-72; counselor polit. affairs U.S. Dept. State, Brasilia, Brazil, 1972-75; dep. chief U.S. Dept. State, Caracas, Venezuela, 1975-77; ambassador U.S. Dept. State, Colombia, 1977-80; asst. sec. for consular affairs U.S. Dept. State, 1980-83; U.S. ambassador Brazil, 1983-86; exec. dir. Una Chapman Cox Found., Washington, 1986-87, pres. adv. coun., 1988-91; chmn. Commn. for Study Internat. Migration and Cooperative Econ. Devel., Washington, 1987-90; exec. dir. Fla. Internat. Affairs Commn., 1991-93; cons. to Becker & Poliakoff, Miami, 1994—. Co-author: Our Man Is Inside. Served with AUS, 1955-57. Office: Diego C Asencio & Assocs Inc 328 Australian Ave Palm Beach FL 33480-4628 also: Becker & Poliakoff PA 500 Australian Ave S Ste 900 West Palm Beach FL 33401

ASH, DOROTHY MATTHEWS, civic worker; b. Dresden, Germany, Nov. 10, 1918; came to U.S., 1924; d. Kurt Horst and Ana (Sekes) Matthesius; m. Harry A. Ash, Apr. 13, 1941 (dec. June 1981); children: Fredrick Curtis, Dorothea Ash Linklater. Dancer, 1933-40; treas. Inheritance Abstractors Inc., Chgo., 1949-70; reporter Miami (Fla.) Sun Post, 1983; reporter, columnist Social Mag., Miami, 1984—; chmn. Miss Universe Pageant, 1983-85; cruise chmn. Miami U., 1984, mem. Pres.'s Club, 1983. Pres. Big Bros. and Big Sisters, 1982-83; founding mem. World Sch. of Arts, 1985—; founding Notable Douglas Gardens 1988: Pres.'s Club U. of Miami, 1989; founding and bd. mem. Cancer Link Rsch., 1990; mem. Bd. Animal Welfare; active Project: Newborn, Am. Cancer Soc., March of Dimes, chmn. quest for the best, 1988-92, winner gourmet gala, 1988, Children's Resource, Erase Diabetes, founding and bd. mem. 1990, Cerebral Palsy Found., Theatre Arts League, Linda Ray Infant Ctr., Miami City Ballet, Am. Ballet; bd. dirs. Greater Miami Opera, 1975—; pub. rels. vol. Miami Heart Inst., 1988—; com. mem. Miami Beach (Fla.) Beautification Program, 1984; mem. bd. Miami Mayor's Ad Hoc Com., 1984; mem. com. Challenger Seven Meml., 1988; active Cousteau Coun.; numerous others. Named Woman of Yr., Big Bros. and Big Sisters, Miami, 1981, Best Dressed, Am. Cancer Soc., 1981, Outstanding Humanitarian and Civic Leader, Mayor City of Miami, 1985, Woman of the Yr., Project: New Born, 1985, Miss Charity, Biscayne Bay Hosp., 1986, Queen of Hearts, Miami Children's Hosp., 1988; recipient Shining Star award Bon Secours Hosp., 1993, Patron Recognition award Mia Heart Rsch. Inst., 1993, Goddess of Love award Villa Maria Hosp., 1995. Mem. Miami Internat. Press Club. Home: 10245 Collins Ave Bal Harbour FL 33154-1406 also (summer): 330 W Diversey Pky Chicago IL 60657-6229

ASH, MARY KAY, cosmetics company executive; b. Hot Wells, Tex., May 12; d. Edward Alexander and Lula Vember (Hastings) Wagner; m. Melville Jerome Ash, Jan. 6, 1966 (dec.); children: Marylyn Theard (dec.), Ben Rogers, Richard Rogers. Student, U. Houston, 1942-43. Mgr. Stanley Home Products, Houston, 1939-52; nat. tng. dir. World Gift Co., Dallas, 1952-63; founder, chmn. emeritus Mary Kay Cosmetics, Inc., Dallas, 1963—; speaker to various orgns. Bd. dirs. Horatio Alger Assn.; hon. chmn. Tex. Breast Screening Project. Office: Mary Kay Inc 16251 N Dallas Pkwy Dallas TX 75248-2696

ASHBOURNE, WILLIAM H., lawyer; b. N.Y.C., Mar. 10, 1957; s. David George Ashbourne and Carrie (Johnson) Rhudes; m. Karen Wyatt, March 20, 1993; children: Kaseama-Joy, Kareem William, Andre, Hahnaha. BBA, Howard U., 1975-80; JD, Brklyn. Law Sch., 1981-84. Sr. tax examiner Spicer & Oppenheim CPA, N.Y.C., 1984-88; tax counsel City of N.Y., 1988-90; pres. Kaseam Artist Mgmt. Co., Atlanta, 1994—; adv. counsel NAACP, Atlanta, 1993-94; legal advisor/educator Urban Jam Network, Tampa, Fla., 1994-95; moderator A & R Music Seminars, Atlanta, 1996. Editor: Music Industry Profiles Mag., 1996. Basketball coach YMCA, Atlanta, 1995—. Mem. Prince Hall Masons (32nd degree), W.C. Thomas Masonk Lodge (Master Mason, Golden Certificate award, 1995). Office: Kaseam Artist Mgmt Co Inc PO Box 110070 Atlanta GA 30311

ASHCRAFT, JAMES HAROLD, JR., engineer; b. Tuscaloosa, Ala., May 1, 1957; s. James Harold and Frances (Norwood) A.; m. Julie Doyle, Sept. 20, 1986; children: James W., Mary Frances, Beth Anne, John. BSEE cum laude, U. Ala., 1979; MS in Engring., U. Ala., Huntsville, 1994. Registered profl. engr., Ala. Test engr. Electronics div. Avco Corp., Huntsville, Ala., 1979-81, project engr., 1981-86, mfg. engr., 1986-87; sr. engr. Thiokol Corp., Huntsville, 1987-93, Intergraph Corp., Huntsville, 1994—. Vol. leader Young Life, Huntsville, 1980-86, mem. Young Life Com., 1986-90. Mem. IEEE, Tau Beta Pi, Eta Kappa Nu. Baptist. Home: 813 Eldorado Ave SE Huntsville AL 35802-3209 Office: Intergraph Corp CR2904 Huntsville AL 35894

ASHDOWN, PAUL GEORGE, journalist, educator; b. N.Y.C., July 26, 1944; s. Cecil Spencer and Annabelle (Marrone) A.; m. Ellen Kay Abernethy, Apr. 24, 1966 (div. Feb. 1969); 1 child, Lance Spencer; m. Barbara Ann Green, Apr. 18, 1975; m. Joanne Wagstrom, Dec. 9, 1970 (div. Nov. 1973). BS, U. Fla., 1966, MA, 1969; PhD, Bowling Green State U., 1975. Reporter Gainesville (Fla.) Sun, 1966-67; pub. info. officer Fla. Dept. of Agr., Gainesville, 1967-68; corr. UPI, Miami, Fla., 1969-70; instr. U. So. Colo., Pueblo, 1970-71, U. Toledo, 1971-75; asst. prof. mass comm. Western Ky. U., Bowling Green, 1975-77; prof. journalism U. Tenn., Knoxville, 1977—; vis. prof. journalism Dutch Sch. of Journalism, Utrecht, The Netherlands, 1993-94; vis. prof. N.Am. studies U. Bonn, Germany, 1994-95. Editor: James Agee: Selected Journalism, 1985; contbr. articles to books and profl. jours. Mem. Assn. for Edn. in Journalism and Mass Comm., Kappa Tau Alpha. Episcopalian. Home: 4033 Sequoyah Ave Knoxville TN 37919 Office: Univ Tenn 330 Communications Bldg Knoxville TN 37996

ASHE, BETTY L., nursing educator; b. Vicksburg, Miss., July 9, 1955; d. Harvey Kinzey and Martha (Louis) Bell. BSN, U. Miss. Med. Ctr. Sch. Nursing, 1977, MSN, 1985. Cert. pediatric nurse. Staff nurse U. Miss. Med. Ctr., Jackson; home health nurse South Miss. Home Health, Long Beach; instr. Miss. Gulf Coast Community Coll., Gulfport, Miss. Elder 1st Presbyn. Ch. Bay St. Louis. Mem. Miss. Nurse's Assn.

ASHER, INNESS, college educator, author; b. Detroit, Apr. 28, 1962; m. Lynn Ann Parvin, May 28, 1989; children: Kaitlyn Emily, Alexandria Leigh, William Ian. BA, Ea. Ky. U., 1989, MA, 1992; PhD, U. Southwest La., 1997. Writing cons. Ea. Ky. U., Richmond, 1989-92; tutor Ea. Ky. U., Richmond and Auburn, Ala., 1989-93; editl. cons., ind. Richmond, Auburn and Lafayette, La., 1989—; spkr. Deep South Writer's Conf., Lafayette, 1995-96; judge. Ala. State Poetry Soc., Montgomery, 1995-96. Author: (short fiction) Appalachian Heritage, 1989, Borderlands IV, 1992. With USMC, 1980-84, Japan. Mem. MLA. Office: U SW Louisiana Griffin Hall Lafayette LA 70504

ASHER, KATHLEEN ANN, small business owner; b. St. Louis, Sept. 6, 1948; d. Roy and Anna Mae (Proctor) A.; m. George Arthur Loucks, July 6, 1968 (div. 1969); m. Devery Rhodes, July 4, 1971 (div. Apr. 1975). Student, SE Mo. State Coll., 1966-67. Order writer Southwestern Bell Telephone, St. Louis, 1967-68; controller Carp's Super Stores, Inc., St. Louis, 1968-71; bookkeeper Ingram Ocean Systems, Inc., New Orleans, 1971-72; med. sec. LeNoir, Licciardi & Russo, New Orleans, 1972-74; office mgr. Sandra, Inc. Real Estate, New Orleans, 1975-77, Columns Three, Inc., New Orleans, 1978-79; pres. Asher & Assocs., Inc., Metairie, La., 1983—; instr. Delgado Community Coll., New Orleans, 1984-85. Mem. Nat. Shorthand Reporters Assn., La. Shorthand Reporters Assns. Republican. Methodist. Office: Asher & Assocs Inc PO Box 7218 Metairie LA 70010-7218

ASHINGTON-PICKETT, MICHAEL DEREK, construction company executive, journalist; b. London, Oct. 11, 1931; s. Edward Robert and Mary Dorothy (Trewhella) Ashington-Pickett; came to U.S., 1965, naturalized, 1971; Civil and Structural Engring. degrees London U., 1956; m. Sandra Helen Smart, Nov. 20, 1976; children: Michael Derek II, Claire Amanda. Constrn. mgr. various firms in Eng., 1956-63; pres. So. Precast Holdings, London, Eng., 1963-65, The Ashington-Pickett Group of Cos., 1965—; chmn. Ashington-Pickett Found., Inc., 1986—, Orlando Constrn. and Licensing Bd., 1974-78, 82-88, bd. dirs., 1978-80; lectr. for Brit. Council, 1963-65; chmn. Mid-Pac, 1982-88. Editor, pub. The Ashington-Pickett Airlines & Travel Report, 1982—, The Ashington-Pickett Wine Rev., 1992—. Served as officer Brit. Army, 1950-52; Korea. Recipient Disting. Svc. award Orange County Bicentennial Commn., 1976; cert. of merit ComitéNational des Vins de France; decorated Chaine De Rotisseurs, Order de Mondial, Campanion Order of Beaujolais, Chevalier Ordre des Chevaliers Bretvins. Mem. Home Builders Assns. Am. (pres., dir. Mid-Fla. chpt.; Disting. Svc. award 1973, life dir. Fla. chpt., Builder of Yr. award 1981), Econs. Club (dir. 1986-96, pres. 1992-93), Orlando C. of C. (dir., v.p. 1981-83), Orlando Jaycees, Kiwanis, Citrus Club. Presbyterian. Home: 1307 Montcalm St Orlando FL 32806-7055 Office: PO Box 149044 Orlando FL 32814-9044

ASHLEY, JAMES MACGREGOR, management consultant; b. Little Falls, N.Y., July 29, 1941; s. Robert Cudworth and Vivien Arlene (McCaughan) A.; m. Jane Stazewski, Apr. 20, 1995; children: Christopher Robert, Kimberly Dawn. BA, U. Miami, 1964. Program dir. Sta. VUNC Radio, Okinawa, Japan, 1965-67; photographer Sta. WOKR-TV, Rochester, N.Y., 1968-70; film dir. Sta. WVNY-TV, Burlington, Vt., 1969-71; mng. dir. Champlain Coun. Holiday Magic Dist., Burlington, 1971-72; sales mgr. MAICO Hearing Aid Ctr., Burlington, 1972-77; buyer IBM, Burlington, 1978-83; internat. contract cons. IBM, Boca Raton, Fla., 1983-87, mgr., 1987—; pres. Procurement Arts Internat., Boca Raton, 1988—. Co-author: Handbook of Buying and Purchasing Management, 1992. Capt. U.S. Army, 1964-67. Mem. ASTD (past pres.), Am. Mgmt. Assn. (faculty), Am. Purchasing Soc. (exec. bd.), Nat. Speakers Assn., Inst. Mgmt. Cons. (v.p.), Fla. Freelance Writers Assn., Japan Soc., Am. Soc. for Quality Control. Episcopalian. Home and Office: 744-2 NE 12th Terr Boynton Beach FL 33435-3252

ASHLEY, JOHN BRYAN, software executive, management consultant; b. Lake Charles, La., Dec. 1, 1955; s. John Nathaniel and Anne Lee (Baker) A.; m. Peggy Anne Daly, Mar. 21, 1988; children: John B. Jr., Robert Lee. BS, La. Tech. U., 1977, MS in Econs., 1977. Mktg. rep. IBM, Shreveport, La., 1978-81, acct. mgr., 1981-84; product mgr. IBM, Rochester, Minn., 1984-88; product cons. IBM, Atlanta, 1988-93; v.p. mktg., sr. ptnr. Distbr. Solutions Internat., Alpharetta, Ga., 1993-95; dir. strategic alliances Software 2000, Hyannis, Mass., 1995—, also London, Paris, Singapore; mng. dir. Software 2000, Europe, Middle East, Africa, 1996—; cons. to IBM Corp., USA, 1993, IBM Europe, Paris, 1994, 95, Russian Fedn., 1995; market cons. to European Software Vendors, 1994, 95. Fund raiser United Way of Mcpl. Atlanta, 1990; del. Ga. State Rep. Party, 1992-93, Cobb Rep. Party, 1992-93. Mem. Sons of Confederate Vets., Colonial Williamsburg Found., Ravinia Club Atlanta, Kappa Sigma (pres.). Presbyn. Home: 1214 Saddle Ridge Ct Kennesaw GA 30144 Office: Software 2000 # 2 Ravinia Dr Atlanta GA 30346 also: Crosby House Meadow Bank, Bourne End, Bucks England also: Tour Arago La Defense, Paris France

ASHLEY, PERRY JONATHAN, journalism educator; b. West Lebanon, Ind., May 1, 1928; s. Terrell Garner and Viola Ethel (Whitmer) A.; m. Lita Grey Cochran, Nov. 29, 1952; children: Jonathan Edward, Richard Douglas. AB in Journalism, U. Ky., 1956, MA in Polit. Sci., 1966; PhD in Journalism, So. Ill. U., 1968. Instr. Sch. Journalism U. Ky., Lexington, 1956-65; teaching assoc. Sch. Journalism So. Ill. U., Carbondale, 1965-67; prof. Coll. Journalism and Mass Comm. U. S.C., Columbia, 1967-93, interim dean Coll. Journalism, 1985-86, assoc. dean, 1986-92, disting. prof. emeritus, 1993—; dir. Ky. Scholastic Press Assn., U. Ky., 1956-65; dir. media rsch. Coll. Journalism, U. S.C., 1970-90; dir. S.C. Scholastic Press Assn., U. S.C., 1971-74; cons.on audience analysis S.C. Ednl. TV System, 1969-72. Editor: Newspaper Publishing in South Carolina, 1980, American Newspaper Journalists, 1873-1900, 1983, American Newspaper Journalists, 1901-1925, 1984, American Newspaper Journalists, 1926-1950, 1984, American Newspaper Journalists, 1690-1872, 1985, American Newspaper Publishers, 1951-1990, 1993. Mem. Gov.'s Safety Coun., Commonwealth of Ky.; mem. East Richland Pub. Svc. Commn., Columbia, 1972-79, chmn., 1973-77; trustee Richland County Sch. Dist. 2, Columbia, 1981-87, chmn., 1985. Cpl. U.S. Army, 1950-52, Germany. Named Nation's Outstanding Yearbook Adviser Nat. Coun. Coll. Publs. Advisers, 1964. Mem. Am. Journalism Historians Assn. (program chmn., bd. dirs. 1988-91), Assn. Edn. in Journalism and Mass Comm., Soc. Profl. Journalists (Disting. Campus Chpt. Adviser 1982), Alpha Delta Sigma, Kappa Tau Alpha, Alpha Epsilon Rho, Phi Alpha Theta, Psi Sigma Alpha, Omicron Delta Kappa. Independent. Presbyterian. Home: 3747 Greenleaf Rd Columbia SC 29206-3362

ASHLEY-CANTER, CHRISTIE, municipal administrator; b. Roxboro, N.C., July 19, 1969; d. Stephen Timothy Ashley and Bonnie Sharon (Oakley) Briggs; m. Dennis Wayne Canter, Jr., June 27, 1992; children: Dalton Scott. BA, Catawba Coll., 1991. Sec. Organon Teknika, Durham, N.C., 1992-93; cultural arts coord. Person County, Roxboro, 1993—; asst. dir. summer theatre Person County, 1989, dir., 1990; chmn. fair com. Week of Young Child, Roxboro, 1995-96; permanent exec. dir. Person Co Arts Coun., 1996, Reorganized Arts Coun., 1996. Asst. dir. Village Players Theatre, Roxboro, 1994, 95; storytime reader Person County Libr., 1996. Mem. Person County Writer's Group. Democrat. Baptist. Home: 160 Indian Tr Rd Timberlake NC 27583

ASHTON, RONALD IRVING, army officer; b. Nanticoke, Pa., May 7, 1948; s. Irving Washington and Irene Emily (Burgham) A.; m. Paulette Marie Erwine, July 17, 1971; children: Heidi Ann, Christopher Michael, Heather Rene. BA in Psychology, Wilkes U., 1970; MPA, U. Okla., Lawton, 1988. Commd. 2d lt. U.S. Army, 1971, advanced through grades to lt. col., 1988; platoon leader A Co. 11th AD Signal Bn. U.S. Army, Kaiserslautern, Germany, 1973-75; project officer Tobyhanna (Pa.) Army Depot, 1975-79; adminstrv. and svcs. mgr. Commonwealth Telephone Co., Dallas, 1979-82; asst. divsn. signal officer 5th Inf. Divsn., Fort Polk, La., 1982-84; exec. officer 5th Signal Battalion, Fort Polk, 1984-85; info. mgmt. officer 500th MI Brigade, Camp Zama, Japan, 1985-88; systems engr. U.S. Army Intel & Security Co., Ft. Belvoir, Va., 1988-91; commdr. 5th and 142d signal bns. U.S. Army, Ft. Polk and Ft. Hood, La., Tex., 1991-93; dep. dir. U.S. Army Intel Material Mgmt. Ctr., Warrenton, Va., 1993—. Author: Productivity Improvement, 1981. Chmn. Boy Scouts Am., Camp Zama, Japan, 1985-87; vol. fireman Pocono Lake (Pa.) Fire Dept., 1975-79; vol. med. technician Pocono Lake Ambulance Corps, 1975-79. Mem. Soc. Logistics Engrs., U.S. Ind. Telephone Assn. (ops. com. 1979-82), Assn. U.S. Army. Home: 9 Old Ridge Rd Fredericksburg VA 22407 Office: US Army CECOM Intel Material Mgmt Ctr Vint Hill Farms Sta Warrenton VA 22186

ASHTON, THOMAS WALSH, investment banker; b. Rochester, N.Y., May 11, 1929; s. Charles Edward and Marie Margaret (Walsh) A.; m. Frances E. Hickey, May 16, 1953 (div. 1977); children: Lucy M. Van Atta, Mary B. Ashton Anders, Monica H., William T; m. Mary K Joy, Dec. 20, 1978. B.S., U.S. Mil. Acad., 1952; M.B.A., Harvard U., 1957. Assoc. corp. fin. Eastman Dillon Union Securities, N.Y.C, 1957-61, gen. ptnr., 1967-69; asst. v.p. Harris Upham & Co., N.Y.C., 1961-67; v.p. duPont Glore Forgan, Inc., N.Y.C., 1971-73; sr. v.p. ABD Securities Corp., N.Y.C., 1973-75; fin. cons. Am. Cancer Soc. of N.Y.C., East West Group Inc.; chmn. Peninsular Investments, Treasure Island, Fla., 1977-87; cons. Dept. Commerce, 1971; chmn. Ashton Investments, Inc., 1987—. Chmn. parents's coun. Smith Coll., 1974-76. With AUS, 1946-48, 52-55. Mem. Soc. Harvard Engrs. & Scientists (gov. 1974-75), West Point Soc. N.Y. (dir. 1971-75), Army and Navy Club (Washington), Treasure Island Yacht Club. Republican. Office: 153d Ave Madeira Beach FL 33708

ASHWORTH, DENISE MARCHANT, landscape architect; b. Langrick, Eng., Apr. 6, 1917; came to U.S., 1946; d. Gerald Marchant and Ella (Brand) Davis; divorced; children: Ella Marchant Ashworth Ingraham, Sarah Elizabeth Marchant Ashworth Flavell. MS summa cum laude, U. Conn., 1975, MS, 1977; MLA, U. Ga., 1978. Asst. landscape architect U.S. Forest Svc., Cleveland, Tenn., 1979-84; zone landscape architect U.S. Forest Svc., Greeneville, Tenn., 1984-86; other resources asst. forest landscape architect U.S. Forest Svc., Jackson, Miss., 1986-90; owner, operator Hilltop House Bed & Breakfast, Greeneville, 1990—. Pres. Magnolia Garden Club, Cleveland, 1985-86. Recipient Outstanding Job Performance award U.S. Forest Svc., 1988, Sustained Outstanding Job Performance award, 1989. Mem. Am. Soc. Landscape Archs., Soc. Am. Foresters, U. Tenn. Arboretum Soc., Tenn. Native Plant Soc., Audubon Soc., Westside Garden Club, Meadow Rose Garden Club (pres. 1989-90), Toastmasters (pres. Jackson 1988-89, area bd. govs. dist. 43 1989, dist. 63 1990-91). Democrat. Episcopalian. Home and Office: Hilltop House Bed/Breakfast 6 Sanford Cir Greeneville TN 37743-4022

ASHWORTH, EDWARD, lawyer, legal association administrator. Exec. dir. So. Poverty Law Ctr., Montgomery, Ala. Office: So Poverty Law Ctr PO Box 2087 Montgomery AL 36102

ASHWORTH, HELEN JOHNSON, nurse educator; b. Portsmouth, Ohio, June 18, 1924; d. Mitchell and Maymie Elizabeth (Warner) Johnson; m. John S. Ashworth, Nov. 29, 1947; children: Lynn, Robert Warner. Grad., Johns Hopkins Sch. Nursing, Balt., 1947; postgrad., Columbia U., 1951; BS in Zoology, Marshall U., 1976; postgrad., U. Ky., 1983-86. RN, Md. Nurse cadet USPHS, 1944-47; instr. Sch. Nursing St. Mary's Hosp., Huntington, W.Va., 1947-48; dir. nursing edn. Ky. Bapt. Hosp., Louisville, 1948-50; instr. psychiat. nursing Ctrl. State Hosp., Louisville, 1950-52; dir. nurses Eastern State Hosp., Lexington, Ky., 1952-53; instr. Coll. Arts and Scis., U. Louisville, 1958-62; cons. Ky. Dept. Mental Health, 1966-76. Author: Anatomy and Physiology for Nurses, 1948, (manual) Nursing Procedures and Practices, 1948, 53, The Learning Disabled Child-Parents' Rights and Responsibilities, 1995; author mag. article for Their World, 1994. Pres. Ky. Regional Mental health Bd., 1966-68, Ky. Med. Aux., 1970-72; mem. Ky. State Health Planning Coun., 1970; chmn. Gov.'s Mental Health Task Force, 1972. Recipient Disting. Svc. award Ky. Psychol. Assn., 1976, Ky. Assn. Regional Mental Health Programs, 1981, Ky. Mental Health Assn., 1991, Award for Outstanding Cmty. Svc. Pathways, Inc., 1993; fellow U. Ky., 1991. Mem. Learning Disabilities Assn. Ky. (pres. 1992-93, Disting. Svc. award 1995). Home: 608 Pine Grove Ct Ashland KY 41101-2156

ASHWORTH, KENNETH HAYDEN, state educational commissioner; b. Abilene, Tex., Feb. 24, 1932; s. Harold Laverne and Mae Beatrice (Grote) A.; m. Emily Yaung; children: Rodney Brian, Karen Grace Saulsberry. B.A., U. Tex., 1958, Ph.D., 1969; M. Pub. Adminstrn., Syracuse U., 1959. Asst. commr. Tex. Higher Edn. Coordinating Bd., Austin, 1965-69; commr. higher edn. Tex. Higher Edn. Coordinating Bd., 1976—; vice chancellor for acad. affairs U. Tex. System, Austin, 1969-73; exec. v.p. U. Tex. at San Antonio, 1973-76. Author: Scholars and Statesmen, 1972, American Higher Education in Decline, 1979, (with Norman Hackerman) Conversations on the Use of Science and Technology, 1996. Served with USN, 1951-55. Mem. Philos. Soc. Tex., Sembradores de Amistad, Phi Beta Kappa, Phi Delta Kappa, Phi Kappa Phi, Pi Sigma Alpha. Democrat. Unitarian. Club: Town and Gown. Home: 7616 Rustling Rd Austin TX 78731-1365 Office: Tex Higher Edn Coordinating Bd PO Box 12788 Austin TX 78711-2788

ASHWORTH, LAWRENCE NELSON, bank executive; b. Richmondd, Va., Mar. 17, 1942; s. Durwood Ormond and Lillian Annie (Thomas) A.; m. Sandra Miller, Aug. 3, 1962; children: Christopher Sean, Matthew Todd. BBA, Marshall U., 1964; MBA, U. Richmond, 1980. Buyer Houdaille Industries, Huntington, W.Va., 1964-65; factory acct. Houdaille Industries, Huntington, 1965-68; asst. div. contr. Houdaille Industries, Frankenmuth, Mich., 1968-70; dir. fin. planning Carlton Industries, Richmond, 1970-72; v.p. fin., co-founder TransAm Co., Richmond, 1972-76; asst. v.p. Signet Bank, Richmond, 1976-78, v.p., div. v.p., 1978-90, sr. v.p., unit mgr., 1990-91, sr. v.p., div. mgr., 1991—. Author: (with others) Handbook of Bank Accounting and Finance, 1989. Pres. Tuckahoe Little League, Richmond, 1981, bd. dirs., 1976-83, coach, mgr., 1976-80; bd. dirs. Tuckahoe Sports, Inc., Richmond, 1984-94. Mem. Nat. Comml. Fin. Assn. (dir., mem. exec. com.), Hermitage Country Club, Downtown Club, Am. Inst. Bankers. Office: Signet Bank 7 N 8th St Richmond VA 23219-3301

ASHWORTH, ROBERT VINCENT, data processing executive; b. Kingsport, Tenn., Sept. 3, 1952; s. Ivan Henry and Mary Ann (Greene) A.; m. Nancy Marie Fricke, Oct. 15, 1983; children: Rachael, Sarah. BS in Tourism, Food and Lodging, U. Tenn., 1978; AS in Computer Sci., State Tech. Inst., Knoxville, Tenn., 1981. Cert. info. systems auditor, 1995. Computer programmer City of Knoxville, 1981-87; systems analyst Knoxville Utilities Bd., 1987-88; data processing auditor Piedmont Bank-Group, Inc., Martinsville, Va., 1988-95; quality assurance analyst Shaw Industries, Inc., Dalton, Ga., 1995—. Mem. Big Bros./Big Sisters, Knoxville, 1987, 88. Mem. Electronic Data Processing Auditors Assn., KC. Home: 804 Piedmont Ln Dalton GA 30720 Office: Shaw Industries Inc Mail Drop 072-29 PO Drawer 2128 Dalton GA 30722-2128

ASKEW, PENNY SUE, choreographer, artistic director, ballet instructor; b. Fairview, Okla., Oct. 8, 1967; d. Donald Lee and Susan Lea (Johnson) A. BS in Psychology, Southwestern Okla. U., 1989, MS in Applied Psychology, 1996. Ballet tchr. Western Okla. Ballet Acad., Clinton, 1986-88, owner, dir., 1988—; artistic dir. Western Okla. Ballet Theatre, Clinton, 1988—. Choreographer: (musical theater) Oklahoma!, 1990, Kiss Me Kate, 1992, Quilters, 1993, Nunsense, 1993, Annie Get Your Gun, 1993, Guys and Dolls, 1994, Nunsense II, 1995, over 40 dance works. Named Outstanding Choreographer of 1996 RDA Nat. Performance/Choreography Conf., 1996. Mem. Southwestern Regional Ballet Assn.-Regional Dance Am. (sec. 1991—), Okla. Arts Inst. Alumni Coun., Clinton C. of C. (Art in the Park com. 1990—). Democrat. Office: Western Okla Ballet Theatre PO Box 1602 512 Frisco Ave Clinton OK 73601-3442

ASKINS, ARTHUR JAMES, accountant, finance management and auditing executive; b. Phila., Dec. 12, 1944; s. William J. and Rita M. (O'Brian) A.; m. Nancy E. Paulsen, Apr. 28, 1979. BS, LaSalle U., 1967; MA, Rider Coll., 1971; cert. of specialization Hospitality Acctg. and Mgmt., Am. Hotel and Motel Assn., 1989. CPA, Pa., N.J.; cert. fraud examiner, hotel adminstr. Tchr. Cardinal Dougherty H.S., Phila., 1967-70; pvt. practice acctg., 1967—; staff acct. Gross Master & Co., Jenkintown, Pa., 1970-74; asst. contr. Hankin Trustee, Willow Grove, Pa., 1974-79; mgr. internal audit Resorts Internat. Hotel Casino, Atlantic City, N.J., 1979-87, dir. revenue acctg., 1987-89, hotel contr., 1989; dir. internal audit Divi Resorts, 1989-91, Steamboat Devel., Corp., Bettendorf, Iowa, 1991-92; dir. internal audit, Casino Am., Inc, 1992-93; v.p. fin. Sea Escape Cruises, Inc., 1993-94; dir. fin., CFO Castle Beach Casino Hotel, Biloxi, Miss., 1994-95; dir. internal audit Lady Luck Gaming Corp., Las Vegas, Nev., 1995—. Recipient cert. of Commendation Twp. of Abington (Pa.), 1967, Disting. Service award Cmty. Accts., Phila., 1982, Superstar award Resorts Internat. Casino-Hotel, 1982, Brotherhood award NCCJ, Atlantic City, 1983, Mgmt. award Resorts Internat. Casino Hotel, 1986, 1st Mgrs. award Resort Internat. Casino-Hotel, 1986, Outstanding Vol. Service award Big Bros./Big Sisters, 1987. Mem. Nat. Assn. Accts. (nat. bd. dirs. 1983-85), pres. South Jersey Shore chpt. 1979-81, Community Affairs award Suburban Northeast Phila. 1978), Inst. Internal Auditors (bd. dirs. 1984-89), AICPA, N.J. Soc. CPAs, Pa. Inst. CPAs, Greater Mainland C. of C., Nat. Assoc. Cert. Internat. Fraud Examiners (audit com. 1979-83), Internat. Assn. Hosp. Accts. Republican. Roman Catholic. Home: PO Box 3148 Gulfport MS 39505-3148 Office: Lady Luck Gaming Corp 1848 Beach Blvd Biloxi MS 39531-5208

ASLAM, MUHAMMED JAVED, physician; b. Shillong, India, June 27, 1938; came to U.S., 1963; m. Tasnim Qadir, Feb. 5, 1967; children: Anissa, Shaazia, Sohail. MBBS, King Edward Med. Coll., Lahore, Pakistan, 1962. Diplomate Am. Bd. Internal Medicine, Am. Bd. Hematology; Fellow Royal Coll. Physicians/Can. Hematologist Winnipeg (Can.) Clinic, 1971-77; pvt. practice, hematologist Houston, 1977—; pres. Tess Data Systems, Houston, 1985—. Author: (computer software) Dietician, 1980, Tess System One, 1985, Tess System Two, 1987, Tess System Three, 1990; co-author: (computer software) Dietician Dietwae, 1984. Mem. Tex. Med. Assn., Harris County Med. Soc., N.Y. Acad. Scis. Office: Tess Data Systems Inc Ste 280 14340 Torrey Chase Blvd Houston TX 77014-1021

ASSOUAD, MARIO, internist, nephrologist; b. Aleppo, Syria, Oct. 2, 1967; came to U.S., 1990; s. Jean and Saloua Denise (Akel) A. MD, U. Aleppo, 1990. Diplomate Am. Bd. Internal Medicine. Intern U. Nev. Sch. Medicine, Reno, 1992-93, resident in internal medicine, 1993-95; fellow in nephrology Baylor Coll. Medicine, Houston, 1995-97; presenter 5th Internat. Congress Cancer Chemotherapy, Paris, 1995. Contbr. articles to med. jours. Mem. AMA, ACP (assoc.), Am. Soc. Nephrology, Renal Physicians Assn. Roman Catholic. Home: 6540 Bellows Ln Apt 405 Houston TX 77030 Office: Baylor Coll Medicine 6550 Fannin St Rm 1277 Houston TX 77030

ASSUNTO, RICHARD ANTHONY, payroll executive; b. New Haven, Conn., Nov. 15, 1942; s. Joseph and Anne Maude (Tull) Martin. BA, Biola U., 1970; MBA, U. Hartford, 1987. Mgr. life issue Aetna Life Ins., Hartford, Conn., 1973-81, mgr. payroll, 1981-89, mgr. purchasing, 1989-92; mgr. payroll Allied Signal, Tempe, Ariz., 1992-94; dir. payroll Norrell Corp., Atlanta, 1994—. Chmn. United Way Aetna Life Ins., 1983; treas. Hill Ctr., Hartford, 1983-85. With USAF, 1961-65. Mem. Am. Payroll Assn. (pres. 1983-85, v.p. 1993-94, Communications award 1989, Speakers award 1989), Am. Soc. Payroll Mgrs. Office: Norrell Corp 3535 Piedmont Rd NE Atlanta GA 30305-4535

ASTERN, LAURIE, psychotherapist; b. N.Y.C., Nov. 13, 1952; d. Seymour and Hilda (Weintraub) A. BA in Psychology, Fla. Atlantic U., 1983; MS in Counseling Psychology, Nova U., 1992; postgrad., Fielding Inst., 1996—. Lic. MHC, Fla.; cert. family mediator, clin. assoc. Am. Bd. Med. Psychotherapists. Mem. crisis intervention and sexual assault staff Broward County, Ft. Lauderdale, Fla., 1984-86, victim advocate, 1986-88, substance abuse counselor, 1990-94; pvt. practice in psychotherapy Pompano, Fla., 1987—; facilitator HIV AIDS support groups, Pompano, Fla., 1990—; founder PIC, Inc., Hollywood, Fla., 1980-85. Founder, dir. Ctr. for Victims of Crime, Pompano, 1987—. Recipient Innovation and Creativity award Broward County Bd. of Commrs., 1987. Mem. Nat. Assn. Drugs and Alcohol Counselors, Nova Southeastern U. Alumni Assn. Office: Profl Psychotherapy Group Ste 420 1600 S Federal Hwy Pompano Beach FL 33062-7517

ASTLER, VERNON BENSON, surgeon; b. Wyoming, Ohio, Sept. 5, 1925; s. Vernon Wolfert and Blanche (Benson) A.; m. Louise Menge, Aug. 9, 1949 (div.); children: Kim Louise, Kristy Lee, Douglas Vernon; m. Diane Rosacker, Dec. 31, 1969 (div.); m. Frances Croft, Mar. 21, 1991. Student, Miami U., Oxford, Ohio, 1943-45; MD, Temple U., 1949; MS, U. Mich., 1953. Diplomate Am. Bd. Surgery. Intern Univ. Hosp., Ann Arbor, Mich., 1949-50, resident, 1950-57; practice medicine specializing in surgery, Boynton Beach, Fla., 1958-90; mem. hon. staff Bethesda Hosp., Boca Raton Hosp.; past mem. Fla. Bd. Med. Examiners, pres., 1971-73; past mem. Fla. Council of 100. Served with M.C., AUS, 1953-55. Fellow ACS (life mem.), Coll. Physicians of Phila., Southeastern Surg. Congress; mem. AMA, Am. Hosp. Assn. (com. on physicians 1974-76), Am. Soc. Bariatric Physicians, Fla. Med. Assn. (life, gov. 1971-84, pres. 1975-76), Frederick A. Coller Surg. Soc., Delray Beach C. of C., Am. Legion, Sigma Nu, Phi Chi. Clubs: Sapphire Valley Country (N.C.). Lodges: Masons, Shriners, Kiwanis. Office: 1220 Hendersonville Rd Asheville NC 28803

ATA, MUHAMMAD EJAZ, internist; b. Sargodha, Punjab, Pakistan, Dec. 5, 1962; s. Muhammad Ata; m. Nabila Asghar, Mar. 19, 1990; 1 child, Muhammad Omair-Ahsan. M.B.B.S., Dow Med. Coll., Karachi, Pakistan, 1987. Diplomate Am. Bd. Internal Medicine. Resident house officer internal medicine/gen. surgery Civil Hosp., Karachi, 1987-88; resident in internal medicine Aga Khan Hosp., Karachi, 1988-90, Wright State U., Dayton, Ohio, 1990-92; internist, chief of medicine Jackson County Hosp., Scottsboro, Ala., 1992—; pvt. practice internal medicine Pisgah (Ala.) Med. Clinic, 1992—. Mem. AMA, So. Med. Assn. Office: Pisgah Medical Clinic 100 Main St Pisgah AL 35765

ATCHISON, ARTHUR MARK, industrial, research and development engineer; b. Cleve., Aug. 22, 1944; s. James Edward and Zella Katherine (Beecher) A.; m. Lora Suzanne Ferlet (div.); 1 child, Tiara Lynne; m. Patricia Fay Jones, July 9, 1983; 1 child, James Edward II. AA, Cuyahoga C.C., Parma, Ohio, 1971; BS in Indsl. Mgmt., U. Akron, 1973; MS in Indsl. Engring. and Ops. Rsch., Va. Poly. Inst. and State U., 1980; PhD in Indsl. Engring., Kennedy-Western U., 1992. Supr. indsl. engring. Firestone Tire and Rubber Co., Akron, Ohio, 1973-76; divisional indsl. engr. Firestone Internat. Co., Akron, 1976-77; regional ops. engr. Reynolds Aluminum Co., Richmond, Va., 1981-82; plant engr. AMP, Inc., Harrisonburg, Va., 1982-83; supr. engring. lab. E.R. Carpenter Co., Richmond, 1977-81; mgr. corp. devel. engring. E.R. Carpenter Co., Elkhart, Ind., 1983-94; sr. tech. cons. Carpenter Co., Richmond, Va., 1994—; co. advisor Jr. Achievement, Akron, 1976. Vol. for emergency communications, Kodak Liberty Bike-a-thon, Richmond, 1986. Vol. lic. examiner FCC. With USN, 1964-70, Vietnam. Mem. Am. Inst. Indsl. Engrs. (sr.), Am. Soc. Quality Control, Amateur Radio Relay League, Richmond Amateur Telecom. Soc., Internat. Amateur Radio Soc., Greater Richmond Sailing Assn., Delta Sigma Pi (life). Republican. Episcopalian. Office: Carpenter Co 5016 Monument Ave Richmond VA 23230-3620

ATCHISON, MICHAEL DAVID, financial and management consultant, investor, investment bank executive; b. Gallup, N.Mex., Oct. 31, 1938; s. Thomas Wesely and Grace Dixon A.; m. Margrit G. Koch, Feb. 18, 1961; children: Christina, Stephanie. BA in English, U. Tex., 1965, MBA in Fin., 1971. Mgr. bus. office Southwestern Bell, Dallas, 1965-70; v.p. 1st Nat. Bank Dallas, 1971-73; v.p., mgr. internat. div. Interfirst Bank-Houston, 1974-75; v.p. fin. and adminstrn. W.W. Young Interests Inc., Houston, 1975-82; founder, CEO M.D. Atchison Co., Atlanta, 1992—, Houston, 1982-91. Contbr. articles to profl. jours. With U.S. Army, 1958-60, ETO. Mem. Fin. Execs. Inst., Internat. Transp. Mgmt. Assn. (bd. dirs. 1976-79), Rotary. Republican. Presbyterian. Home and Office: 24215 Plantation Dr NE Atlanta GA 30324-2944

ATCHLEY, CURTIS LEON, mechanical engineer; b. Lexington, Okla., June 3, 1940; s. Curtis Marvin and Hazel (Franks) A.; m. Barbara Ann Bryant, Feb. 14, 1976; children: Jeffrey Allen, Eric Andrew. BSME, U. Okla., 1970. Engr. Halliburton Oil Svc. Co., Enid, Okla., 1970-71, Tinker AFB, Midwest City, Okla., 1971-79; supervisory gen. engr. Lajes AFB, Azores, Portugal, 1979-80; gen. engr. Hdqrs. USAFE, Ramstein AFB, Fed. Republic Germany, 1980-82, Hdqrs. Air-Edn. and Tng. Command, Randolph AFB, 1985—; mem. staff Air Force Civilian Pers. Ctr., Randolph AFB, Universal City, Tex., 1983-85. U.S. and fgn. patentee in solar tech., U.S. patentee for light intensifying device for cameras and telescopes. Mem. Dem. Nat. Com., 1996. Sgt. USAF, 1964-68. Mem. Amnesty Internat. (freedom writer), Internat. Soc. Poets (life, charter), Nashville Song Writers Assn., Broadcast Music Inc. Home: 7531 Oriental Trl San Antonio TX 78244-2400 Office: Hdqrs AETC Randolph Afb Universal City TX 78150

ATCHLEY, DANIEL GENE, business executive; b. Ft. Worth, Oct. 29, 1942; s. Emory and Edith Blanch (Stanley) A.; m. Susan Marie Gosciej; children: John Chandler, Natalie Gayle, David Franklin II, Katherine Marie, Pamela Ann, Adrianne Edith. D. Comml. Sci., London Inst., 1974; D.Comml.Sci., SUNY, 1978; postgrad., U. Houston, 1984; command officer diploma, Air Univ., USAF, 1979; honor grad. in Electronic Warfare System, Avionics Inertial & Radar, Biloxi, Miss., 1976. Cert. data educator, data processor, sys. profl., computer profl. Computing dir. Pace Consultants, Houston, 1967-71; real estate developer G/A Intervests, Houston, 1971-72; exec. producer 20th Century Fox, Century City, Calif., 1973-74; movie producer Media Trend Prodns., Hollywood, Calif., 1972-75; computer scientist Atmore Systems, Houston, 1975-80; regional tech. mgr. Univ. Computing Co., Houston, 1980-82; pres., bd. chmn., CEO TEXLA Enterprises, Inc., Katy, Tex., 1982—; project mgr., sr. cons., field mgr. CIBER, Houston, Tex., 1995—. Patentee in field; author Programming Standards and Conventions, 1985. Pres. Avalon River Oaks Area Civic Assn., Houston, 1967-71; v.p. Lions Club, Houston, 1970; com. mem. Houston Livestock Show, 1977-82; v.p. Mcpl. Utility Dist., Harris County, Tex., 1983—, Optimist Club, 1986; Rep. Presdl. Task Force, 1980—; mem. Meth. Ch. Adminstrv. Bd., 1984-86. With USAF, Tex. Air N.G., 1975-81. Recipient Faithful Svc. medal The State of Tex., 1980, Cert. of Attainment Assn. Water Bd. Dirs., 1986; decorated D.S.M., Tex. Air Nat. Guard Longevity medal, 1981, Automation Dedicated Svc. award AMOCO, 1994. Mem. Adminstrv. Mgmt. Soc., Project Mgmt. Inst., ANSI, DPMA, Assn. Computer Programmers & Analysts, Assn. for Systems Mgmt., Soc. Data Educators, Inst. Cert. Computer Profls., Digital Equipment Users Group, Oracle Developers Alliance, Desktop Publishers Assn., NaSpa, Sons. of Confederate Vets., SAR, SCV, Tex. Hist. Soc., Nat. Geneal. Soc., Toastmasters Soc. Republican. Methodist. Home: 22506 Coriander Dr Katy TX 77450-1522 Office: TEXLA Enterprises Inc PO Box 74 Barker TX 77413-0074

ATCHLEY, ROGER KENT, marketing and management consultant; b. Cin., Aug. 12, 1942; s. Shurley Moreton and Sherie Marcella (Purdue) A.; m. Patricia Ann Ford, Apr. 8, 1967; children: Tambre Annelle, Jennifer Danelle. Student, U. Louisville, 1971; grad. in banking, La. State U., 1979. Lic. ins. agt., Fla. Asst. v.p., mktg. dir. Louisville Trust Bank, 1969-77; asst. vp., mgr. product devel. First Nat. Bank Denver, 1977-79; v.p., mgr. product devel. Columbia Savs., Denver, 1979-80, First Fed. Chgo., 1980-83; v.p., mgr. corp. mktg. Moore Fin. Group, Boise, Idaho, 1983-86; sr. v.p., regional mgr. First Am. Bank, North Palm Beach, Fla., 1986-88; pres., CEO, dir. Roger K. Atchley, Inc., Boca Raton, Fla., 1988—. Contbr. articles to profl. jours. With USN, 1961-65, PTO. Named Outstanding Vol. Firefighter, Louisville Jaycees, 1972, Ky. Col., Gov. of Ky., 1979. Mem. Am. Mktg. Assn. (exec.), Bank Mktg. Assn. Republican. Presbyterian. Home and Office: 10792 Avenida Santa Ana Boca Raton FL 33498-6715

ATHANAS, EMANUEL STYLIANOS, journalist, educator, radio program director; b. Rhodes Island, Greece, Jan. 17, 1907; came to U.S., 1926; s. Stylianos and Maria Z. (Papazacharias) Athanasiades; m. Maria P. Paleogos; children: Daphne, Joan. BS, Worcester (Mass.) Poly. Inst., 1932; MS, Trinity Coll., Hartford, Conn., 1933; postgrad., Columbia U., 1933-36. Prof. modern Greek lang. and lit. Columbia U., N.Y.C., 1936-54; radio broadcaster, commentator, writer, program dir. U.S. Info. Svc.-Voice of Am., Washington, 1942-46, 48-77; translator Fgn. Broadcast Info. Svc., Washington, 1965—; Washington corr. Athens Politika Themata. Author: (in Greek) Rhodians in U.S., 1982, The Liberation of the Dodecanese Islands, 1984; editor Rodos mag., Washington, 1950—. Decorated Grand Cross of Order of Phoenix (Greece), Archon Ekdikos of Orthodox Ecumenical Patriarchate, Gold medal Dodecanesian Fedn. Am., Silver medal City of Rhodes (Greece); named Hon. Citizen of City of Rhodes, Greece. Mem. Am. Hellenic Inst., Pan Rhodian Soc., Am. Friends of Greece, Am. Translators Assn., Am. Hellenic Ednl. Progressive Assn. Greek Orthodox. Home: 401 S Garfield St Arlington VA 22204-2051

ATHANSON, MARY CATHERYNE, elementary school principal. Prin. Marjorie Kinnan Rawlings Elem. Sch., Pinellas Park, Fla. Office: Marjorie Kinnan Rawlings Elem Sch 6505 68th St Pinellas Park FL 33781-4946

ATHY, LAWRENCE FERDINAND, JR., historian; b. Ponca City, Okla., Oct. 6, 1927; s. Lawrence Ferdinand and Helen Elizabeth (Thiel) A.; m. Martha Jane Anthony, May 3, 1952; 1 child, Gayle Lynn. BSME, Rice U., 1950. Registered profl. engr. (ret.), Tex. Roustabout Warren Oil Corp., McLean, Tex., 1950; asst. chief draftsman Wyatt Industries, Houston, 1950-55; mgr. engring. and mfg. Polymer Engring. Corp., Hitchcock, Tex., 1955-57; sr. v.p. Southwestern Mfg. Co., Houston, 1957-79; owner Fluid Power Cons., Houston, 1979-87; historian and epigrapher, Houston, 1987—; chpt. pres. Fluid Power Soc., Houston, 1970. Author: Captain George Athy of Galway and Maryland and his Descendants, 1987; contbr. articles to profl. jours.; patentee in field. Precinct chmn. Rep. Party, Houston, 1978-84; election judge Harris County, Houston, 1993-94. With USN, 1945-46. Mem. ASME, The Epigraphic Soc. (ogam archivist 1990—), Archaeol. Inst. Am., Inst. for the Study Ancient Am. Culture, Archaeol. Conservancy, Victorian Owners Assn. (bd. dirs. 1990), The Briar Club (com. chair 1960). Home and Office: 3834 Overbrook Ln Houston TX 77027-4038

ATKEISON, BARBARA JEAN GARRISON, university administrator; b. Moscow, Tenn.; d. Samuel Garrison and Mavis Marie (Hoskins) Jones; m. Ernest Chevis Atkeison, Sept. 29, 1956 (dec. Jan. 1992); children: Ernest Chevis Jr., Edwin Spencer. BA in Bus. Adminstrn./Acctg., Antioch Coll., 1982; MS in Edn. Adminstrn. and Supr., U. Memphis, 1991. Chief acct. Fayette County Pub. Sch. System, Somerville, Tenn., 1969-76, bus. mgr., 1976-86; coop. edn. coord., coll. placement asst. dir. State Tech. Inst. at Memphis, 1986-90, asst. dir. bus. and industry and govt. tng. divsn., 1990-92, asst. dir. institutional devel, 1992-95, dir. institutional devel. and alumni affairs, 1995—; Fayette County assessor of property Fayette County Govt., Somerville; chairperson Nat. Coun. for Resource Devel., fed. funding task force coms., 1994-95; mem. State Tech. Adminstrv. Coun., 1996; mem. state tech. campus adv. com., 1992-95, state tech. facilities com., 1995-96, acad. awards program com., 1995-96, state tech baldridge total quality assessment team, 1995. Past chair Fayette County Dem. Party, 1994-95. Recipient Woman of Yr. award Fayette County C. of C., 1983, Fayette County Bus. and Profl. Women's Club, 1983, Disting. Svc. award Fayette County Governing Body of Commrs., 1979. Mem. Nat. Soc. of Fund Raising Execs., Women in Higher Edn. Assn., Nat. Coun. for Resource Devel. Assn. Home: 7651 Dexter Park Dr Cordova TN 38018

ATKINS, CANDI, management consultant, small business owner; b. Chgo., Aug. 19, 1946; d. Norman R. and Catherine Kay (Coughlin) Wolfe; children: James N., Amanda Kate. Assoc. in Edn., Thornton C.C., 1968. Chief exec. officer Candi Atkins & Assocs., Phoenix, 1992-95, Largo, Fla., 1995—; faculty Diablo Valley Community Coll., Pleasant Hill, Calif., 1982-85; nat. trainer HUD Occupancy Issues, 1984—. Author: Shopping for Big Wonderful Me, 1988, Management Forms for HUD Assisted Housing, 1991. Candi Atkins Day named in her honor Mayor of San Francisco, 1984; named to hon. Order Ky. Col. Mem. NAFE, Inst. Real Estate Mgmt. (exec. com. San Francisco chpt. 1980-84, instr. 1981-91, accredited resident mgr., cert. property mgr. Accredited Resident Mgmt. of Yr. 1980), Nat. Speakers Assn. Roman Catholic. Home and Office: 10093 86th St N Ste 100 Largo FL 33777-1818

ATKINS, C(ARL) CLYDE, federal judge; b. Washington, Nov. 23, 1914; s. C. C. and Marguerite (Criste) A.; m. Esther Castillo, Jan 18, 1937; children: Julie A. Landrigan, Carla A. Schulte (dec.), Carl Clyde (dec.). Student, U. Miami, Fla., 1931-32; LLB, U. Fla., 1936, JD, 1967; LLD, Barry Coll. (now Barry U.), Miami Shores, 1966, St. Thomas of Villanova U. (formerly Biscayne Coll.), Miami, 1970. Bar: Fla. 1936. Practice in Stuart, 1936-41; pvt. practice law Miami, 1941-66; ptnr. firm Walton, Lantaff, Schroeder, Atkins, Carson & Wahl (and predecessors), 1941-66; judge U.S. Dist. Ct. (so. dist.) Fla., 1966—, chief judge, 1977-82, sr. judge, 1983—; founder-trustee Lawyers Title Guaranty Fund, 1948-66, treas., 1963-66. Contbr. articles to profl. jours. Pres. St. Augustine Diocesan Union of Holy Name Societies, 1950-51, Miami Archdiocesan Coun. Cath. Men, 1959-70. Recipient Outstanding Cath. award NCCJ, 1959. Fellow Am. Coll. Trial Lawyers; mem. ABA, jud. adminstrv. divsn. (ho. of dels. 1960-66, 79-80), Dade County Bar Assn. (pres. 1953-54), The Fla. Bar (bd. govs. 1954-59, pres. 1960-61), Nat. Conf. Fed. Trial Judges (chmn. exec. com. 1975-77, del. Jud. Adminstrn. Coun. 1979-82), Nat. Conf. Christians and Jews (chmn. Miami region 1989-95), Tau Kappa Alpha, Phi Kappa Tau, Phi Alpha Delta, Miami Kiwanis Club (past dir.), Coral Gables Country Club, Century Club of Coral Gables (past dir.), Serra Club (pres. 1965-66, 91-92). Office: US Dist Ct 301 N Miami Ave Miami FL 33128-7702

ATKINS, CHESTER BURTON, record company executive, guitarist, publisher; b. Luttrell, Tenn., June 20, 1924; s. James J. and Ida (Sharp) A.; m. Leona Johnson, June 3, 1947; 1 child, Merle. Student pub. schos., Hamilton, Ga. Cons. Gretsch Guitar Co., Bklyn.; former div. v.p. country music RCA Records; chmn. bd. dirs. Famous Am. Musicians and Educators, Inc.; dir. Aurora Pub. Co.; bd. dirs. Nashville Symphony; bd. dirs. Atkins Video Soc., 1985—. Profl. debut (radio show) The Midday Merry-Go-Round, Sta. WNOX, Knoxville, Tenn., 1941; performer with The Old Dominion Barn Dance, Richmond, Va., Radio Ozark, Springfield, Mo.; albums include: Stay Tuned, 1985, Sweet Dreams, 1986, Tennessee Guitar Man, 1986, C.G.P., 1988, Neck & Neck, 1990, Sneakin' Around, 1992, Read My Licks, 1994; TV appearances include The Tonight Show, Austin City Limits, A Session with Chet Atkins: Certified Guitar Player. Recipient Grammy award, 1967, 86, 90, 91, 92, Grammy Lifetime Achievement award, 1993, Humanitarian Svc. award NCCJ, 1970; named Instrumentalist of Yr. Country music Assn., 1969, 81-84, Most Outstanding Guitarist Guitar Player mag., 1970, Instrumentalist of Yr. Playboy, 1969. Mem. NARAS, AFTRA, Am. Fedn. Musicians, Country Music Assn., Nashville C. of C. (bd. govs.). Office: CGP Entertainment 1013 17th Ave S Nashville TN 37212-2201

ATKINS, DIXIE LEE, critical care nurse; b. Elkin, N.C., Oct. 8, 1953; d. Charles Lee and Betty Lou (Southard) Cook; m. Ronnie Steven Atkins, Aug. 30, 1984; children: Sarah Kathryn, Carl Steven, William Shane. AD in Applied Sci., Surry C.C., Dobson, 1973; student, St. Joseph's Coll., North Windham, Maine, 1990—. Cert. provider ACLS, NRP, Am. Heart Assn. Indsl. nurse Brown-Wooten Mills Inc., Mount Airy, N.C.; relief charge nurse pediatrics Forsyth Meml. Hosp., Winston-Salem, N.C., 1973-78; charge nurse emergency rm. No. Hosp. Surry County, Mount Airy, 1979—; nursing supr. No. Hosp. of Surry County, Mount Airy, 1995—; instr., CEN, basic trauma life support, CPR; mobile intensive care nurse; provider advanced cardiac life support, PALS; provider NRP; neonatal recussitation provider; part-time instr. Surry C.C.; profl. photographer Images Studio, Dobson, N.C. Mem. Surry County chpt. MADD; bd. dirs. Dobson Rescue Squad; chairperson Surry Nursing Domiciliary Home Cmty. Adv. Com.; vol. ARC. Mem. Emergency Nurses Assn. Home: PO Box 992 407 Marion St Dobson NC 27017-8430

ATKINSON, BARBARA ANN, internist; b. Grand Rapids, Mich., Mar. 22, 1942; d. Kenneth Wendell and Marion (Burton) Atkinson. BS, Mich. State U., 1964; degree in med. tech., St. Luke's Hosp. Sch. Med. Tech., Saginaw, Mich., 1965; MA in Health Care Edn., Cen. Mich. U., 1978; D Osteopathic Medicine, Mich. State U., 1988. Diplomate Am. Bd. Osteopathy. From med. tech. to microbiology supr. tech. St. Luke's Hosp., Saginaw, 1965-73; from rsch. microbiologist to assoc. microbiologist Bronx (N.Y.) Lebanon Hosp. Ctr., 1973-83; intern Flint (Mich.) Osteopathic Hosp., 1988-89, resident internal medicine, 1989-91; fellow in infectious diseases U. Tex. Health Sci. Ctr., San Antonio, 1991-94; asst. prof. dept. medicine U. North Tex. Health Sci. Ctr., Ft. Worth, 1994—. Mem. DAR, Am. Soc. Microbiology, Am. Osteo. Assn., Infectious Diseases Soc. Am., Nat. Registry Microbiologists, Beta Siga Phi (v.p. Chi chpt. Saginaw, Mich. 1971-72, pres. 1972-73, treas. Xi Gamma chpt. N.Y.C. 1975-76, v.p. 1976-77, pres. 1978-79, v.p. Xi Phi Theta chpt. San Antonio 1993-94). Home: 3409 Riveroad Ct Apt 2005 Fort Worth TX 76116-1193 Office: U North Tex Health Sci Ctr Dept Medicine 3500 Camp Bowie Blvd Fort Worth TX 76107-2644

ATKINSON, DIANE LEE, environmental resource planner. BS in Psychology, Kans. State U., 1983, M in Regional and Cmty. Planning, 1991. Cmty. devel. planner Big Lakes Regional Coun., Manhattan, Kans., 1989-92; environ. resource planner Ark-Tex. Coun. of Govts., Texarkana, 1993—; coord. solid waste planning Tex. Watch Citizens Monitoring, Texarkana, Tex., 1993-94. Fundraiser United Way, 1989-91; active fundraising activities Big Bros./Big Sisters, Manhattan, 1990-91. Mem. Am. Planning Assn., Am. Soc. Govt. Indsl. Hygienists. Office: PO Box 5307 Texarkana TX 75505-5307

ATKINSON, HAROLD WITHERSPOON, utilities consultant, real estate broker; b. Lake City, S.C., June 12, 1914; s. Leland G. and Kathleen (Dunlap) A.; BS in Elec. Engring., Duke, 1934; MS in Engring., Harvard U., 1935; m. Pickett Rancke, Oct. 6, 1946; children: Henry Leland, Harold Witherspoon. Various positions in sales, engring. Cambridge Electric Light Co. (Mass.), 1935-39, 46-73, asst. mgr. power sales dept., 1946-49, gen. mgr., 1957-73, dir., 1959-84, exec. v.p., 1972-73; mgr. Pee Dee Electric Membership Corp., Wadesboro, N.C., 1939-46; gen. mgr. Cambridge Steam Corp., 1951-73, v.p., 1959-73, dir. 1955-84. Chmn., Cambridge Traffic Bd., 1962-73; pres. Cambridge Ctr. Adult Edn., 1962-64; v.p. Cambridge Mental Health Assn.; chmn. allocations com. Greater Boston United Community Svcs., 1971-72; chmn. Cambridge Commn. Svcs., 1955-56; adv. bd. Cambridge Coun. Boy Scouts Am.; mem. corp., chmn. camping com. Cambridge YMCA, 1964-71; chmn. Cambridge chpt. ARC, 1969-71; trustee of trust funds Town of Harrisville, N.H., 1976-83; treas. North Myrtle Beach Citizens Assn., 1982-84. Served from pvt. to capt. AUS, 1942-45. Registered profl. engr., Mass. Mem. IEEE (sr.), Mass. Soc. Profl. Engrs., Elec. Inst. (pres. 1971), Harvard Engring. Soc., Cambridge C. of C. (pres. 1957-58). Newcomen Soc. N.Am., Phi Beta Kappa, Tau Beta Pi, Pi Mu Epsilon. Clubs: Cambridge Boat (treas. 1962-65), Cambridge (pres. 1972-73), Bay Tree Golf; Plantation; Civitan (pres. Wadesboro 1940-41); Rotary (pres. Cambridge club 1959-60, former v.p. North Myrtle Beach, S.C. club) Home: 705 Holloway Cir N North Myrtle Beach SC 29582-2613 Office: 710 17th Ave S North Myrtle Beach SC 29582-4011

ATKINSON, MICHAEL PEARCE, lawyer; b. Ft. Worth, Feb. 19, 1946; s. Charles Pearce and Nancy Lou (Thompson) A.; m. Melissa Jan Potter, July 17, 1976; children: Charles Travis, Kellen Elizabeth. BA, U. Okla., 1968, JD, 1971; MS, U. Tex., 1975. Bar: Okla. 1972, U.S. Dist. Ct. (we. and ea. dists.) Okla. 1972, U.S. Dist. Ct. (no. dist.) Okla. 1975, U.S. Ct. Appeals (10th cir.) 1981. Ptnr. Jones, Atkinson, Williams, Bane & Klingenberg, Enid, Okla., 1972, Best Sharp Thomas Glass & Atkinson, Tulsa, 1980-87, Thomas Glass Atkinson Haskins Nellis & Bondreaux, Tulsa, 1980-93, Aktinson, Haskins, Nellis, Boudreaux, Holeman, Phipps & Brittingham, Tulsa, 1994—; asst. pub. defender Office of Oklahoma County Pub. Defender, Oklahoma City, 1973; asst. dist. atty. Office of Oklahoma County Dist. Atty., Oklahoma City, 1974; asst. adj. prof. Coll. of Law U. Tulsa, 1976-77. With USAR, 1970-72. Master Am. Inns of Ct. (emeritus); fellow Am. Coll. Trial Lawyers; mem. Internat. Assn. Def. Counsel (faculty trial acad. 1986), Am. Bd. Trial Advocates (pres. Okla. chpt. 1995, diplomate). Presbyterian. Home: 2440 E 28th St Tulsa OK 74114 Office: Atkinson Haskins Nellis 525 S Main Tulsa OK 74103

ATKINSON, REGINA ELIZABETH, medical social worker; b. New Haven, May 13, 1952; d. Samuel and Virginia Louise Griffin. BA, U. Conn., Storrs, 1974; MSW, Atlanta U., 1978. Social work intern Atlanta Residential Manpower Center, 1976-77, Grady Meml. Hosp., Atlanta, 1977-78; med. social worker, hosp. coordinator USPHS, Atlanta, Palm Beach County (Fla.) Health Dept., West Palm Beach, 1978-81; dir. social services Glades Gen. Hosp., Belle Glade, Fla., 1981-95; case mgr. divsn. sr. svcs. Palm Beach County Cmty. Svcs., West Palm Beach, Fla., 1996—; instr. Palm Beach Jr. Coll.; participant various work shops, task forces. Vice pres. Community Action Council South Bay, 1978-79. Whitney Young fellow, 1977; USPHS scholar, 1977. Mem. NAFE, NAACP, Am. Hosp. Assn. (soc. for social work adminstrn. in health care), Soc. Hosp. Social Work Dirs., Assn. State and Territorial Pub. Health Social Workers, Nat. Assn. Black Social Workers, Nat. Assn. Social Workers, Fla. Soc. for Hosp. Social Work Dirs. (adminstrn. in health care), Glades Area Assn. for Retarded Citizens. Home: 525 1/2 SW 10th St Belle Glade FL 33430-3712 Office: 810 Datura St Ste 100 West Palm Beach FL 33401-5204

ATKINSON, SCOTT ESTES, economics educator; b. El Paso, Tex., July 27, 1944; s. John Allen and Emma Elizabeth (Estes) A.; m. Mable (Scottie) Frieda Frascati, Oct. 21, 1968; children: Kirk, Beth. BA in Am. History and Lit., Williams Coll., Williamstown, Mass., 1966; MA in Econs., No. Colo. U., 1969; PhD in Econs., U. Colo., Boulder, 1972. Adj. prof. econs. Va. Poly. Inst. and State U., Reston, 1979-81; assoc. prof. dept. econs. U. Wyo., 1981-85, dir. Inst. Policy Rsch., 1984-86, prof. dept. econs., adj. prof. dept. stats., 1985-86; prof. dept. econs. U. Ga., Athens, 1986—; instr. econs. and history Colo. Acad., Englewood, 1968-69; teaching assoc. dept. econs. U. Col., 1969-72, teaching asst., 1969-72; environ. economist EPA, Office Rsch. and Devel., Washington, 1972-73; sr. economist Dept. Energy, Washington, 1973-79, Am. Petroleum Inst., Washington, 1979-81; Selig rsch. fellow, U. Ga., 1990-92; econ. cons. Natural Gas Pipeline Co. Am. and MIDCON Corp., Am. Smelting and Refining Co., Am. Petroleum Inst., Mountain Bell, EPA; dir. grad. studies U. Wyo., 1982-84. Mem. editl. coun. Journ. Environ. Econs. and Mgmt., 1990-92, assoc. editor, 1993—; reviewer manuscripts various jours.; contbr. 42 articles to profl. jours., 9 chpts. to books. Recipient Spl. Achievement award Fed. Energy Adminstrn., 1975, Disting. Rsch. award Terry Coll., 1992, Kamerschen/Hampton Outstanding Rsch. award, 1990; grantee U. Wyo. Dept. Econs., 1981-82, 82-83, 83-84, Wyo. Indsl. Fund, 1982-83, 83-84, NSF Rsch. grantee, 1984-85, U. Wyo. and U. Ga. Dept. Econs., 1987-88. Mem. Beta Gamma Sigma. Home: 345 Red Fox Run Athens GA 30605-4408 Office: U Ga Dept Econs Athens GA 30601

ATKINSON, WILLIAM JAMES, JR., retired cardiologist; b. Mobile, Ala., July 4, 1917; s. William J. and Gertrude (Smith) A.; m. Glenda E. Street, Oct. 29, 1949; children: Glenda Street, Regina Creswell, William James III. BA, Amherst Coll., 1939; MD, U. Pa., 1943; MS in Internal Medicine, St. Louis U., 1949. Intern, Phila. Gen. Hosp., 1943-44; resident in medicine St. Louis City Hosp., 1946-48; resident in cardiology St. Louis U., 1948-49; practice medicine specializing in internal medicine and cardiology, Mobile, Ala., 1949—; chief cardiac clinic Mobile City Hosp., 1950-60; electrocardiographer Mobile Infirmary, 1949-92, Providence Hosp., 1949-75; cardiologist Diagnostic and Med. Clinic, 1949-92; mem. staff U. South Ala. Med. Ctr. Hosp., Mobile Infirmary, Providence Hosp.; chmn. bd. Diagnostic and Med. Clinic P.A., 1973-92; clin. assoc. prof. medicine U. Ala., 1964-89; clin. assoc. prof. medicine U. South Ala., 1973-92; ret. Served as capt. M.C., AUS, 1944-46. Decorated Bronze Star. Diplomate Am. Bd. Internat. Medicine, Am. Bd. Cardiovascular Disease. Fellow ACP, Am. Coll. Cardiology, Am. Coll. Chest Physicians; mem. Am. Heart Assn., Ala. Heart Assn. (chmn. bd. 1956), AMA, Am. Soc. Clin. Pharmacology and Therapeutics, Mobile C. of C. Republican. Episcopalian. Clubs: Rotary, Mobile Country, Mobile Yacht. Home: 3965 Byronell Ct Mobile AL 36693-5502

ATTAL, GENE (FRED EUGENE ATTAL), hospital executive; b. Austin, Tex., Oct. 6, 1947; s. Sam Arthur and Olga (Johns) A.; B.J. with spl. honors (NDEA fellow in langs. 1968-69), U. Tex., 1970; M.S. (Internat. fellow 1972), Columbia U., 1972; m. Marsha Ablah, July 26, 1970; children—Christopher, Allison, Anne. Public relations exec. Westinghouse Electric Corp., 1972-75; v.p. pub. affairs Seton Med. Center, Austin, 1975—; pres. The Seton Fund; mem. faculty U. Tex. Recipient Telstar Excellence in Communication award, annually 1978-81, Arthur W. Page award U. Tex., 1986. Mem. Am. Soc. Hosp. Public Relations (regional dir.), Assn. Healthcare Philanthropy (internat. bd. dirs.), Tex. Soc. Hosp. Public Relations (pres. 1981), Barton Creek Country Club. Greek Orthodox. Home: 1201 Constant Springs Dr Austin TX 78746-6615 Office: 1201 W 38th St Austin TX 78705-1006

ATTANASI, EMIL DONALD, economist, municipal official; b. Newark, July 5, 1947; s. Dominick Joseph and Katherine (Cavitch) A.; m. Diana Elizabeth Frank, Aug. 29, 1969; children: Jennifer, Katherine, Marie. BA in Math. magna cum laude, Evangel Coll., 1969; MA in Econs., U. Mo., 1971, PhD, 1972. Economist, U.S. Geol. Survey, Reston, Va., 1972—; mem. faculty George Mason U., Fairfax, Va., 1979-80; commr. Vienna Town Planning Commn., 1983—, vice chmn., 1989-90, chmn., 1991-92; lectr. U.S. Congl. Fellows, Washington, 1982. Contbr. articles to profl. jours.; co-editor spl. jour. issues of procs. of Mineral Economics Symposium, 1980-83. Trustee Fairfax Assembly of God, 1980-84; trustee, bd. dirs. Key to Life Assembly of God, McLean, Va., 1977-78. Recipient Community Builders award Masonic Lodge, 1993, Meritorious Svc. award U.S. Dept. Interior, 1994; U. Mo. fellow, 1969-72. Mem. So. Econ. Assn. (jour. referee), Am. Econ. Assn., Am. Inst. Mining Engrs (sec. local minerals econs. subsect. 1985-86), Omicron Delta Epsilon (treas. 1971-72). Office: US Geol Survey Nat Ctr MS 956 Reston VA 22092

ATTARDO, LEWIS CHARLES, business and technology development consultant; b. Wilkes-Barre, Pa., Dec. 3, 1950; s. Charles J. and Gertrude (Volpe) A.; children: Aimee, Jessica, Jill, L. Antonio. AS, Luzerne Community Coll., 1970; BA in Econs., Bloomsburg U., 1972. Pres., chief exec. officer Attardo Enterprises, Augusta, Ga., 1976—; dir. Ben Franklin Tech. Ctr., Pa. State U. at Harrisburg, Middletown, 1984-90; cons. Orgn. for Econ. Co-operation and Devel., Paris, 1990—; Informest, Gorizia, Italy, 1993—; program coord. Small Bus. Devel. Ctr. St. Petersburg (Fla.) Jr. Coll., St. Petersburg (Fla.) Jr. Coll., 1993; exec. dir. Savannah River Regional Diversification Initiative, Aiken, S.C., 1995—; cons. Enterprise Corp., Tampa Bay, Fla., 1993-94, v.p., dir. def. transition programs; evaluator, panelist role of flexible automation in Pa. project Commonwealth of Pa., 1987-88; mem. tech. adv. coun. Pa. State U., York, 1985—, adj. instr., 1992—, bd. advisors Small Bus. Devel. Ctr. Pa. State U., Harrisburg, 1984-90; charter mem. Venture Investment Forum Ctrl. Pa., Inc., 1986-91, v.p., 1988-89; bd. advisors WITF-TV Netsource, 1985-89. Dir. Tampa Bay Def. Transition Task Force, 1993-94. Mem. AAAS (voting sect. K), Ea. Econ. Assn. (charter), Air and Space Smithsonian (charter), Ctrl. Pa. Internat. Bus. Assn. (sec., bd. dirs. 1986-91), Ctrl. Pa. Tech. Coun. (bd. dirs. 1990-91), Nat. Coun. Urban Econ. Devel. Roman Catholic. Office: Savannah River Regional Diversification Initiative Aiken Tech Coll PO Box 696 Aiken SC 29802 also: 2617 Edison Pl Holiday FL 34691

ATTEBERRY-LUCKINBILL, CLARA DEANN, interior designer; b. Jefferson, Iowa, Dec. 22, 1937; d. Byron George and Verna Mae (Hutchinson) Safley; m. John B. Atteberry, Aug. 17, 1956 (dec.); children: John B. III, Scott M. (dec.), Kristin Lee, Kathryn Marie (dec.); m. Merle Ervin Luckinbill, Oct. 28, 1983 (div. Jan. 1996). Student, Delgado, New Orleans, 1978-79. Interior cons. Montgomery Ward's, Des Moines, 1975-76; interior designer Drapery House & Interiors, New Orleans, 1978-82; interior designer, owner Custom Interiors, New Orleans, 1983-95; cons. Home Depot, New Orleans, 1992-94; owner, operator, pres. Fire Extinguisher Co. of La., Harvey, 1993—. Pub. rels. dir. Faithwalk, New Orleans, 1988; fellowship group leader, bus. com. Believer's Life Assembly, Harvey, 1986-93, area deaconess spl. ministries, 1988-93, promotions dir., mem. follow up steering com. We Are Possessing Campaign, prayer ministry dir., stewardship com.; counselor Good Samaritan Food Bank, 1988-93; historian Iowa Dem. Party, 1958-60; mime team mem. Praise Fellowship Ch.; officer, agt. Greater Harvey Civic Assn., 1994—; mem. Rep. Nat. Comm., 1993, 96—. Recipient Rep. Legion of Merit, 1994. Mem. Interior Design Soc. (assoc.), Internat. Soc. Poets (life). Office: Firex Inc 1215 Lochlomand Dr Harvey LA 70058-3827

ATTEBURY, WILLIAM HUGH, construction company executive; b. Amarillo, Tex., Jan. 8, 1929; s. Arnold Gentry and Lula Vivian (Dunn) A.; student Iowa State Coll., 1947-49; B.A., Okla. U., 1951; m. Joyce B. Kallin, June 7, 1951; children: Julie Anne, William Arnold, Nancy Ellen, Elizabeth Grace, Edward Anton. Vice pres. Attebury Elevators, Inc., Amarillo, 1954—; pres. Bison Devel. Co., 1960—, A & S Steel Bldgs Inc., Amarillo, 1961—, El Poso Oil Co., Amarillo, 1969—, Bison Chem. Co., Port Neches, Tex., 1969-77, ptnr. Tex. Beef Producers Group, 1978—; dir. Western Data, Inc., Boatman's 1st Nat. Bank Amarillo, Master Films Co. Dir. Amarillo Bd. City Devel., 1969-73; adv. bd. Salvation Army, 1973-77; bd. mgrs. Amarillo Hosp. Dist., 1978-79; bd. dirs. Amarillo Children's Home, 1978-82; chmn. bd. dirs. Harrington Cancer Ctr; bd. dirs. Village of Hope, 1972-74; elder Westminster Presbyterian Ch., 1970—. Served with USNR, 1951-54; Korea. Mem. Panhandle Producers and Royalty Owners, Tex. Cattle Feeders Assn. (bd. dirs. 1981-83, 90-94), Nat. Cattleman's Assn. (bd. dirs. 1990-94), Amarillo Club, Amarillo Country Club. Home: 3202 S Lipscomb St Amarillo TX 79109-3536 Office: PO Box 7446 Amarillo TX 79114-7446

ATTERMEIER, FREDRIC JOSEPH, lawyer; b. Milw., Mar. 27, 1946; s. Fredric J. and Olga B. (Uldrian) A. BA, Rice U., 1968; MS, U. Houston, 1976; JD, South Tex. Coll. Law, 1975; LLM in Taxation, DePaul U., 1987. Bar: Tex. 1975, U.S. Tax Ct. 1975, U.S. Ct. Appeals (5th, 7th, 10th and 11th cirs.) 1975, U.S. Ct. Claims 1976, U.S. Ct. Internat. Trade 1976, U.S. Supreme Ct. 1979, Ill. 1984; CPA, Ill., Tex.; cert. in taxation law Tex. Bd. of Legal Specialization. Pvt. practice Houston, 1975-78; tax supr. Grant Thornton & Co., Houston, 1978-79; tax atty. Texaco Inc., Houston, 1979—; gen. counsel Internat. Congress on Cyclosporine, 1993—. Contbr. articles to profl. jours. lectr. continuing edn. programs bar and acctg. groups, Nationwide, 1978—; cooperating atty. Houston Vol. Lawyers Program, 1986—. Mem. State Bar Tex. (mem. tax sect. continuing edn. com. 1983—), Houston Bar Assn. (former tax sect. chmn.). Home: 4007 Levonshire Houston TX 77025-3912 Office: Texaco Inc PO Box 4696 Houston TX 77210-4696

ATTOH-OKINE, NII OTOKUNOR, civil engineer, educator; b. Accra, Ghana, Oct. 10, 1958; came to U.S., 1990; s. Richard Ayi and Georgina Charkor (Quaynor) Attoh-O.; m. Rebecca Bamfo. MS in Civil Engring., Rostov Inst. of Civil Engring., 1986; PhD, U. Kans., 1993. Lectr. U. Sci. and Tech., Kumasi, Ghana, 1987-90; rsch. engr. Transp. Ctr. U. Kans., Lawrence, 1992-93; asst. prof. Fla. Internat. U., Miami, 1993—. Contbr. chpts. in books and articles to profl. jours. D.D. Eisenhower fellow U.S. Dept. Transp., 1994, 95. Home: 12201 SW 91st Ter # 804 Miami FL 33186 Office: Fla Internat Univ University Pk VH-160 Miami FL 33199

ATWATER, MARY MONROE, science educator; b. Roswell, N.Mex., July 26, 1947; d. John C. and Helen (Wallace) Monroe; children: Helena A., Jonathen A. BS magna cum laude, Meth. Coll., 1969; MA, U. N.C., 1972; PhD, N.C. State U., 1980. Nat. sci. coord. Fayetteville (N.C.) State U., 1975-77; teaching asst. dept. maths. and sci. N.C. State U., Raleigh, 1977-79, rsch. asst., 1977-79; assoc. dir. N.Mex. State U., Las Cruces, 1980-83; asst. prof., program dir. sci., maths., tech. edn. Atlanta U., 1984-87, assoc. prof. and program dir. sci., math., tech. edn., 1987; asst. prof. dept. sci. edn. U. Ga., 1987-92, assoc. prof. dept. sci. edn., 1993—; vis. assoc. prof. Cornell U., 1993; adj. prof. Atlanta U., 1987-88; mem. rev. com. NSF, 1993, cons., 1994, Harvard-Smithsonian Ctr. Astrophysics, 1993, N.Y. Biology Network Workship, 1993, ABT Assocs., Inc., 1993; mem. adv. com. World Book Publ., 1993; presenter at numerous convs., speaker in field. Co-editor Multicultural Edn.: Inclusion of All, 1994; contbr. chpts. to books; contbr. numerous articles to profl. jours. Cons. Sci. Edn. in Mich. Schs., 1990-91; elem. sci. curriculum guide project Ga. Dept. Edn., 1988-90; judge numerous internat., state, local sci. fairs, 1978-96. Recipient Herbert Lehman Edn. Fund award, 1965, NSTA OHAUS award for innovations in four-yr. coll. tchg., 1990, Coll. Edn. and Psychology Disting. Alumnus award N.C. State U., 1996; numerous rsch. grants; Lily Tchg. fellow, 1989. Fellow AAAS; mem. ASCD, Am. Chem. Soc., Am. Edn. Rsch. Assn., Assn. Edn. Tchrs. in Sci., Assn. Tchr. Edn., Ga. Sci. Tchrs. Assn., Nat. Assn. Multicultural Edn., Nat. Assn. Rsch. in Sci. Tchg., Southeastern Assn. Edn. Tchrs. in Sci., Phi Delta Kappa (Warren Finley Rsch. award 1996). Office: U Ga 212 Alderhold Hall Athens GA 30602-7126

ATWILL, WILLIAM HENRY, physician; b. Jackson, N.C., July 10, 1932; s. Charles Bailey and Mary Frances (Beaman) A.; m. Agnes Craighead Pierce, June 10, 1955; children: William H. Atwill Jr., E. Bennett Atwill, Charles B. Atwill II. BS, Va. Mil. Inst., 1953; MD, U. Va., 1960. Diplomate Am. Bd. Urology. Surg. intern, then asst. resident U. Fla. Med. Ctr., Gainesville, 1960-62; rsch. fellow in urology Duke U. Med. Ctr., Durham, N.C., 1964; asst. resident, chief resident, instr. urology Duke U. Med. Ctr., 1965-68; pvt. practice urology Richmond, Va., 1968—; pres. Urology Inc., Richmond, 1989-95, 1989-95; pres. Urology, Inc., Richmond, 1989—; clin. prof. surgery Med. Coll. Va. and Va. Commonwealth U., Richmond, 1986—. Contbr. articles to profl. jours. Capt. USAF, 1953-56. Fellow ACS, Country Club of Va. Republican. Episcopalian. Office: Urology Inc 5224 Monument Ave Richmond VA 23226-1405

AUBREY, SHERILYN SUE, elementary school educator; b. Louisville, Nov. 7, 1951; d. Sheridan and Alice (Rivera) A. BA in Edn., U. Ky., 1974; MA in Edn., Murray State U., 1979. Cert. elem. tchr., Ky. Primary tchr. Hopkins County Bd. Edn., Madisonville, Ky., 1975—; mem. coun. site-base com. Grapevine Sch., Madisonville, 1991—. Mem. NEA, Ky. Edn. Assn., Hopkins County Edn. Assn. (rep. 1986-90), Alpha Delta Kappa (chair altruistic com. Omicron chpt. 1988-91). Baptist. Home: 501 E Morehead St Central City KY 42330-1238 Office: Grapevine Sch Hayes Ave Madisonville KY 42431-3296

AUCHMUTY, GILES, applied mathematics educator; b. Dublin, Ireland, June 1, 1945; s. James J. and Margaret (Walters) A. BSc, Australian Nat. U., Canberra, 1966; MS, U. Chgo., 1968, PhD, 1970. Rsch. instr. SUNY, Stony Brook, 1970-72; from asst. prof. to assoc. prof. Ind. U., Bloomington, 1972-81; prof. U. Houston, 1982—; vis. mem. Inst. for Advanced Study, Princeton, N.J., 1989. Editor publs. in applied math. for Am. Math. Soc., 1987-90; mng. editor Houston Jour. Math., 1993-96, editor, 1996—; contbr. more than 50 articles to profl. jours. Fellow Brit. Sci. Rsch. Coun., 1975-76; rsch. grantee NSF, 1971—; recipient rsch. award Robert A. Welch Found., 1984-90. Office: U Houston Dept Math Houston TX 77204-3476

AUCHTER, EDMUND LOUIS, economist, consultant; b. Cin., May 27, 1932; s. Alois Thadeus and Hedwig Marie (Anselment) A.; m. Edith Anne Catherine McLennan, Jan. 25, 1959; children: James Grant, Robert Alois. BS, Xavier U., Cin., 1957; MA, Johns Hopkins U., 1959; PhD, MA, Claremont Coll., 1968. Economist Dept. Commerce, Washington, 1959-60; fgn. svc. officer Dept. State, Saigon, 1961-64, Washington and worldwide, 1967-87; asst. prof. econs. Fresno (Calif.) State U., 1964-69; ind. cons. Washington, 1987—; cons. team leader USAID, UN, IBRD, Indonesia, Bangladesh. With U.S. Army, 1951-53.

AUCKLAND, JAMES CRAIG, mechanical engineer; b. Wellsville, N.Y., Nov. 20, 1948; s. Harold Claude and Nancy Jane (Snyder) A.; m. Alice Theresa Gilbert, Aug. 14, 1971; children: Allison Marie, Adam James. BSME, Clarkson U., 1970. Registered profl. engr., Va., Calif.; cert. plant engr.; cert. energy mgr. Nuclear engr. Norfolk Naval Shipyard, Portsmouth, Va., 1970-74; gen. engr. Newport News Shipbuilding, 1974-78; project engr. Riddleberger Bros. Inc., Harrisonburg, Va., 1978-79; plant engr. James Madison U., Harrisonburg, 1979-86; chief engr., asst. dir. physical plant James Madison U., 1986-92, dir. facilities mgmt. ops., 1992-93; dir. facilities mgmt. 1993—; county rep. Va. Air Pollution Control Bd., Norfolk, 1976-78. With Army N.G., 1971-77. Mem. Assn. Phys. Plant Adminstrs., Assn. Facility Engrs. Republican. Presbyterian. Office: James Madison U Faculties Mgmt Dept Harrisonburg VA 22807

AUER, RUDOLPH GERHART, small business owner; b. N.Y.C., Apr. 4, 1940; s. Albert and Johanna Erna (Rode) A.; m. Elisabeth Ashley Johnson, July 13, 1974 (div. Jan. 1977); 1 child, Katharina Johanna Auer. Owner, mgr. Atlantic Ave. Hair Stylist, Daytona Beach Shores, Fla., 1968-84; pres. Way to Play, Inc., Daytona Beach Shores, 1988—. Author, designer gameboard Monarch, 1988; inventor indoor ball game Rampball. Youth motivator Volusia County schs., 1992-93; nominating bd. City of Daytona Beach Shores, 1991-92; mem. civil svc. bd. City of Daytona Beach Shores, 1992-93; city coun. candidate, 1992. Mem. Hon. Order Ky. Cols., Elks. Democrat. Home and Office: 3516 Cardinal Blvd Daytona Beach FL 32127-4683

AUERBACH, ERNEST SIGMUND, lawyer, company executive, writer; b. Berlin, Dec. 22, 1936; s. Frank L. and Gertrude A.; m. Jeanette Taylor, 1990; 1 child, Hans Kevin. AB, George Washington U., 1958, JD, 1961. Bar: D.C. 1962, Pa. 1978. Atty. So. Ry. Co., Washington, 1961-62; commd 1st lt. U.S. Army, 1962, advanced through grades to col.; served in Germany, Vietnam, Pentagon; div. counsel Xerox Corp., Stamford, Conn., 1970-75; mng. atty. NL Industries, Inc., N.Y.C., 1975-77; from asst. to assoc. gen. counsel, staff v.p. INA Corp., Phila., 1977-79; sr. v.p. INA Svc. Co., 1979-82, INA Internat., 1982-83; pres. internat. life and group ops. CIGNA Worldwide Corp. div. CIGNA Corp., Phila., 1984-89; mng. dir. Crusader Life Ins. PLC, Reigate, Eng., 1984-86, chmn., 1986-89; pres., COO N.Y. Life Worldwide Holding, Inc., N.Y.C., 1989-90; pres., CEO Paperless Claims, Inc., N.Y.C., 1991-92; dir. gen. Seguros Azteca Ins. Co., Mexico City, 1992-93; sr. cons. Anderson Consulting, Mexico City, 1993-95; ptnr. Law Firm of Soules & Wallace, San Antonio, Tex., 1995; sr. v.p. United Ins. Cos., Inc., Irving, Tex., 1995—, also pres., CEO student ins. divsn., 1996—. Author: Joining the Inner Circle—How To Make It As A Senior Executive, 1990; contbg. author: The Wall St. Jour. on Mng., 1990; contbr. articles to legal, fin., news, and def. jours. Mem. Am. Coun. on Germany; computer sys. tech. adv. com. Dept. Commerce. Ret. col. USAR, 1985. Decorated Legion of Merit with oak leaf cluster, Bronze Star. Mem. ABA, Westchester-Fairfield Corp. Counsel Assn. (founding officer), Univ. Club, Nat. Arts Club (N.Y.C.). Home: 625 Cambridge Manor Ln Coppell TX 75019 Office: UICI 5125 N O'Connor Blvd Irving TX 75039

AUGUR, MARILYN HUSSMAN, distribution executive; b. Texarkana, Ark., Aug. 23, 1938; d. Walter E. and Betty (Palmer) H.; m. James M. Augur, Dec. 29, 1962; children: Margaret M. Hancock, Elizabeth H. Taylor, Ann Louise. BA, U. N.C., 1960; MBA, So. Meth. U., 1989. Pres. North Tex. Mountain Valley Water, Dallas, 1989—; bd. dirs. Camden News Pub. Co., Little Rock. Trustee Hussman Found., Little Rock, 1991—, U. Tex. Southwestern Med. Found., 1993—, Nat. Jewish Hosp., 1993—, Marilyn Augur Found., Dallas, 1991—; bd. dirs. Baylor Health Sys. Found., 1992—, chmn., 1995; bd. dirs. Dallas Summer Musicals, 1992-95, mem. exec. com., 1992-94; bd. dirs. Tate Lectr. Series, 1994—, Salvation Army, 1996, adv. bd.; mem. Tex. Bus. Hall of Fame, 1992—, exec. com., 1994; exec. com. Dallas Citizens Coun., 1994-95, Dallas County C.C., Dist. Found., 1995, Dallas Helps, 1995, Charter 100. Mem. Dallas Country Club, Crescent Club, Dallas Women's Club, Beta Gamma Sigma. Episcopalian. Office: North Tex Mountain Valley Water 3131 Turtle Creek Blvd Dallas TX 75219

AUGUST, A. T., III, publishing executive. Pres., gen. mgr. Richmond (Va.) Times Dispatch. OFfice: Richmond Newspapers Inc PO Box 85333 333 E Grace St Richmond VA 23293*

AULBACH, GEORGE LOUIS, property investment company executive; b. York, Pa., July 9, 1925; s. George A. and Mary N. (Goulden) A.; m. Gertrude Frisby, June 24, 1949; children—Jeanne, Cynthia, Patricia, Kathleen, Barbara. B.S. in Civil Engring., Villanova U., 1945. Registered profl. engr., Pa., Ga. Successively field engr., estimator, chief engr., project mgr., exec. v.p., pres. R.S. Noonan, Inc., York, Pa., 1946-63, pres., chief exec. officer R.S. Noonan, Inc. and Noonan Engring. Corp., York, 1963-72; pres. systems building div. McCrory-Sumwalt, Columbia, S.C., 1972-76; pres., chief exec. officer Laing Properties, Inc., Atlanta, 1976-90; ret. bd. dirs. Laing Properties plc, London, Eng., 1990; adv. bd. dirs. Bank South, Atlanta; bd. dirs. Ga. Tech. Rsch. Inst., Northside Hosp. Found., Cath. Housing Initiative; trustee So. Tech. Found. Served to lt. (j.g.) USN, 1943-46. Mem. NSPE, Ga. Soc. Profl. Engrs., Soc. Internat. Bus. Fellows, York area C. of C. (pres. 1965), Pa. Keystone Chpt. AGC Bldg. Contractors Assn. (pres. 1969-70), Urban Land Inst., Roman Catholic. Clubs: Cherokee Town and Country.

AULETTA, JOAN MIGLORISI, construction company executive, mortgage and insurance broker; b. N.Y.C., July 23, 1940; d. Angelo George and Ann (Passa) Miglorisi; ABS, Bklyn. C.C., 1957; m. E.V. Auletta, Oct. 5, 1958; children—Ann, Vincent, George, Jeanne. Owner-mgr. Auletta Realty, also owner-mgr. E&J Pancake House, L.I., N.Y., 1947-76; office and fin. mgr. Larchwood Constrn. Co., Farmingville, N.Y., 1976-77; prodn. mgr. Lawlor Industries, Holtsville, N.Y., 1977-79; real estate and fin. adv. Family Home Improvement Corp., Queens Village, N.Y., 1979-81; co-owner Total Home Constrn. Co., N.Y.C., 1981-86; owner-mgr. Century 21, Echo Hills Realtors Inc., Miller Place, N.Y., 1987-92 , Auletta Realty, 1989—, Tone-O-Matic, 1988-89; owner-mgr. comml. property, 1970—; bd. dirs. Multiple Listing Svc. of L.I., 1986-91, L.I. Bd. Realtors, 1986-92, Fin. Dept. Waste Industry, 1992—. Mem. Miller Pl.-Mt. Sinai C. of C. (pres. 1988-90). Roman Catholic. Home: 6715 NW 71st Ct Tamarac FL 33321-5447

AULL, JAMES STROUD, retired bishop; b. Winnsboro, S.C., Mar. 3, 1931; s. Luther Bachman and Ruth (Bull) A.; m. Virginia Kloeppel, Aug. 9, 1958; children: Diane, James Jr. (dec.), Virginia Ruth. AB magna cum laude, Newberry Coll., 1953; MDiv cum laude, Luth. Theol. So. Sem., Columbia, S.C., 1960; M in Systematic Theology, Luth. Sch. Theology, Chgo., 1970; PhD, Duke U., 1971; DD (hon.), Newberry Coll., 1988. Ordained to ministry United Luth. Ch. in Am., 1961. Pastor St. Timothy Luth. Ch., Camden, S.C., 1961-62; instr., staff mem. Luth. Theol. So. Sem., Columbia, S.C., 1962-79; sec. S.C. Synod, Luth. Ch. in Am., Columbia, 1979-87, bishop, 1988-96; ret., 1996. Author: Obey My Voice: a Form Critical Study of Selected Prose in the Book of Jeremiah", 1971. Trustee Newberry Coll., 1972-96, sec., 1977-82; trustee Luth. Home, White Rock, S.C.; bd. dirs. Div. for Edn., Evang. Luth. Ch. Am., Chgo., 1988-91; mem. ch. coun. Evang. Luth. Ch. Am., Chgo., 1991-96. Mem. Soc. Bibl. Lit., Rotary (bd. dirs. 1987-90, pres. 1996-97). Home: 413 Challedon Dr Columbia SC 29212-3210

AULL, SUSAN, physician; b. N.Y.C., Nov. 6, 1959; d. Eugene and Ines Aull. BA, Vassar Coll., 1981; MD, N.Y. Med. Coll., 1986. Diplomate Am. Acad. Phys. Medicine and Rehab., Am. Acad. Pain Mgmt. Intern internal medicine L.I. Coll. Hosp., Bklyn., 1986-87; phys. medicine and rehab. PGY II, III Westchester County Med. Ctr., Valhalla, N.Y., 1987-89; phys. medicine and rehab. PGY IV Lincoln Hosp., Bronx, N.Y., 1989-90; med. dir. dept. phys. medicine and rehab. Halifax Med. Ctr., Daytona Beach, Fla., 1992—; med. dir. 21st Century Rehab. and Wound Mgmt. Ctr., Maitland, Fla., 1992; mem. staff dept. internal medicine Winter Park (Fla.) Meml. Hosp., 1991—; pvt. practice Winter Park, 1991—; multi-specialty group practice, dir. phys. medicine and rehab. Ctrl. Fla. Physicians Rehab., Orlando, 1990-91; electrodiagnostic cons. SEA Med. Svcs., P.A., Goldenrod, Fla., 1990—; adj. clin. prof. U. Ctrl. Fla., Orlando, 1991—. Author: (with others) Strength Conditioning for Preventive Medicine, 1992, ISC Control Points - New Generation of Pressure Points, 1993. Recipient Leadership award Defensive Tactics Newsletter, 1993; grantee PPCT Mgmt. Systems, Inc., 1992. Fellow Am. Acad. Phys. Medicine and Rehab.; mem. AMA, Am. Congress Rehab., Am. Coll. Sports Medicine, Fla. State Med. Soc., Orange County Med. Soc. Office: Winter Woods Physical Medicine PO Box 32 Sarasota FL 34230

AULT, ETHYL LORITA, special education educator, consultant; b. Bklyn., May 30, 1939; d. Albert Nichols Fadden and Marion Cecil (Corrigan) Snow; (div.); children: Debra Marie Ault Butenko, Milinda Lei Jones, Timothy Scott. BS, Ga. State U., MEd, 1976, cert. in spl. edn. 6th yr., 1984. Tchr. spl. edn. Butts County Sch. System, Jackson, Ga., 1972-73; tchr. spl. edn. Rockdale County Sch. System, Conyers, Ga., 1973-75, lead tchr., 1975-77; cons. spl. edn. Newton County Sch. System, Covington, Ga., 1977-79; curriculum specialist spl. edn. La Grange (Ga.) Sch. System, 1979-83, dir. spl. edn., 1983-94, dir. accredited studies curriculum, 1994—, dir. student svcs., 1995—; collaboration process trainer State of Ga., 1990—, dir. student svcs./spl. program, 1996—; instr. La Grange Coll., 1984—; mem. Tchr. Competency Testing Commn., Atlanta, 1988—, Task Force Documentation and Decision Making, Atlanta, 1988—. Contbg. editor: (manual) Mainstream Modification Handbook, 1989. Chairperson Jud. Adv. Panel, LaGrange, 1988; bd. dirs. Crawford Tng. Ctr. Adv. Panel, La Grange, 1985—; pres. West Ga. Youth Coun. Bd., La Grange, 1980—; mem. State Adv. Panel for Spl. Edn. Mem. Coun. Exceptional Children, Ga. Assn. Edn. Leaders, Ga. Assn. Curriculum and Instrn. Supervision, Ga. Coun. Adminstrs. Spl. Edn. (v.p. 1988—, pres.-elect 1989, pres. 1992—, Gifted State Task Force 1994—), La Grange Women's Club (v.p. 1989—), Profl. Assn. Ga. Spl. Educators (Adminstr. of Yr. 1993), Ga. Supporters of the Gifted, Nat. Assn. for Gifted Edn. Democrat. Episcopalian. Home: 441 Gordon Cir Lagrange GA 30240 Office: 200 Mooty Bridge Rd Lagrange GA 30240

AULT, JEFFREY MICHAEL, investment banker; b. Norfolk, Va., Jan. 20, 1947; s. Frank Willis and Helen Blake (Hamner) A.; m. Lizbeth Anne Berulis, Aug. 6, 1994; 1 child, Jeffrey Franklin. BS, U. Calif., San Diego, 1974; postgrad., U. San Diego, 1975-84, Word of Faith Bible Inst., Dallas. Ordained to ministry Fedn. Gen. Assemblies Internat., 1988. Dir. nat. bus. devel. Mayflower, San Diego, 1970-75; dir. new accounts Aero-Mayflower Transit Co., Alexandria, Va., 1976-78; v.p. Mchts. Mgmt. Co., Washington, 1976-78; v.p. mktg. Stevens Van Lines, various states, 1978-80; exec. v.p. Fla. Am. Van Lines Inc., Tampa, 1980-84; pres. Victory World Trade Corp., Washington, 1984-85; chmn., CEO Maranatha Van Lines, Inc., Tampa, 1984-90; exec. dir. Maranatha Vision Ministries Inc., Tampa, Swords Into Plowshares, France, Russia, Vietnam, U.S.; pres. Eastern Star Trading Co., Minsk, Belarus; pres. JRW Corp., S.A., Santiago, Tampa, Seattle, Moscow, Bangkok, Mpls., Buenos Aires, Miami; v.p., st. ptnr. Noord Prince Mcths. Bank, Curacao; trustee Gold-Lyon Trust. Mem. U.S. Senate Trust, Hillsborough County Republican Party; sustaining mem. Rep. Nat. Com. Sgt. USMC, 1966-72, Vietnam. Mem. Aircraft Owners and Pilots Assn., U. Calif. at San Diego Alumni Assn., First U.S. Marine Div. Assn., USMC Combat Corrs. Assn., Mensa. Home: PO Box 811 Odessa FL 33556-0811 Office: JRW Corp SA Swords Into Plowshares Intn PO Box 391 Odessa FL 33556-0391 also: Samarkandsky Bulvar 15/1, Flat 142, Moscow Russia

AULTHOUSE, AMY LYNN, anatomist and educator; b. Lancaster, Pa., July 15, 1958; d. Harry David and Dolores Lucille (Delafield) A. BS in Botany, Shippensburg (Pa.) U., 1980; PhD in Anatomy, U. S.D., 1984. Postdoctoral rsch. fellow, NIH molecular biology tumor grant trainee U. Iowa, Iowa City, 1984-86; postdoctoral rsch. fellow U. Tex. Health Sci. Ctr., Houston, 1986-88; asst. prof. anatomical scis. U. Okla. Health Sci. Ctr., Oklahoma City, 1988—; cons. faculty devel. grant U.S.D. Med. Sch. Alumni Found., Vermillion, 1988, NASA, Ames Rsch. Ctr., Moffett Field, Calif., 1988; ad hoc grant reviewer NSF-EPSCOR, Vermillion, 1994; internat. vis. scientist Deutscher Akademischer Austausch Dienst, Mainz, Germany, 1992. Contbr. articles to profl. jours. Bd. dirs. Okla. Literacy Coun., Oklahoma City, 1991—; pres. German Am. Heritage Assn. Okla., Oklahoma City, 1993-94; sci. fair judge Regional and Elem. Exposition, Oklahoma City, 1991-93. Mem. Am. Assn. Anatomists, Am. Soc. Cell Biology, Sigma Xi (nat. meeting election ofcl. 1994, exec. com. 1993—, chpt. pres. 1994—). Office: Univ of Okla Health Sci Ctr Coll of Medicine BMSB553 940 Stanton L Young Blvd Oklahoma City OK 73104-5020

AURBACH, MICHAEL LAWRENCE, art educator, sculptor; b. Wichita, Kans., Dec. 13, 1952; s. Frederick Aurbach and Gertrude Berkowitz. BA, U. Kans., 1974, BS in Journalism, 1976, MA, 1979, BFA, 1981; MFA, So. Meth. U., 1983. Instr. U. Kans., Lawrence, 1978-81; vis. asst. prof. art Hamilton Coll., Clinton, N.Y., 1983-84; asst. prof. Ea. Ill. U., Charleston, 1984-86; asst. prof. Vanderbilt U., Nashville, 1986-91, assoc. prof., 1991—. Fellow Art Matters, Inc., 1989, 92; NEA/So. Arts Fedn. grantee, 1987, Tenn. Arts Commn. grantee, 1990, NEA/Art in Pub. Places grantee, 1993; recipient Southea. Coll. Art Conf. award for Outstanding Artistic Achievement, 1995. Mem. College Art Assn., Internat. Sculpture Ctr., Kans. Grassroots Art Assn., S.E. Coll. Art Assn. Democrat. Office: Vanderbilt U PO Box 1801B Nashville TN 37202-1801

AUSBAND, JERRY C., newspaper editor; b. Conway, S.C., Nov. 13, 1937; s. Joe Hill and Viven Leola (Cox) A.; m. Ruth Pluma Martin, July 6, 1963 (div. Mar. 1981); children: Joseph Ward, Sarah Elizabeth; m. Lorna LaVaughan Brown Lucas, Dec. 23, 1981; stepchildren: Dylan Sean Lucas, Melissa Lucas. BA, Clemson U., 1959. Reporter The Greenville (S.C.) News, 1959-61, bur. chief, 1961-63; bur. chief The State, Florence, S.C., 1963-64; state news editor The State, Columbia, S.C., 1964-66, night city editor, 1966-67; editor The Daily Star, Shelby, N.C., 1967-79; editor The Sun News, Myrtle Beach, S.C., 1979-86, editl. page editor, 1986—. Tchr. various churches and civic orgns.; pres. Crime Stoppers, Conway, S.C., 1986-87; chair Cleve. Orgn./Drug Abuse Prevention, Shelby, N.C., 1974. Mem. Surfside Moose Lodge, Nat. Conf. of Editl. Writers, N.C. AP News Coun. (pres. 1977), S.C. AP News Coun. (pres. 1987). Methodist. Home: 405 Old South Cir Garden City Beach SC 29576 Office: The Sun News PO box 406 Myrtle Beach SC 29578

AUSTERMAN, DONNA LYNNE, Spanish language educator; b. Colorado Springs, Colo., Aug. 5, 1947; d. Herman Raymond Ogg and Shirley (Cooper) Price; m. Thomas Lanham Brown, Jan. 26, 1966 (div. Jan. 1972); 1 child, Thomas Roy; m. Randy Lynn Austerman, Nov. 25, 1972; 1 child, Michael Neil. Student, Washburn U., 1965-67; BS, Pittsburg State U., 1970, MS, 1971; postgrad., U. Kans., 1980, U. Okla., 1983, Okla. State U., 1990. Cert. tchr. (life), Mo., std. tchr., Okla. Tchr. Spanish, English Liberal (Mo.) R-2 Schs., 1970-72, Unified Sch. Dist. 346, Mound City, Kans., 1972-74, Nowata (Okla.) Pub. Schs., 1983-86; tchr. Spanish Bartlesville (Okla) Sch. Dist. # 30, 1986—. Steering com. mem. North Ctrl. Assn., 1993—. Mem. NEA, ASCD, Am. Assn. Tchrs. Spanish and Portuguese, Nat. Staff Devel. Coun., Okla. Edn. Assn., Okla. Fgn. Lang. Tchrs. Assn., Bartlesville Edn. Assn., Bartlesville Fgn. Lang. Coun., Bartlesville Profl. Improvement Com. (chmn. mid-h.s. staff devel. com.). Home: 5648 Steeper Dr Bartlesville OK 74006-9116 Office: Bartlesville Mid/HS 5900 Baylor Dr Bartlesville OK 74006-8909

AUSTIN, ANN SHEREE, lawyer; b. Tyler, Tex., Aug. 25, 1960; d. George Patrick and Mary Jean (Brookshire) A. BA cum laude, U. Houston, 1983; JD, South Tex. Coll., 1987. Bar: Tex. 1987, U.S. Dist. Ct. (no. dist.) Tex. 1988, U.S. Ct. Appeals (5th cir.) 1989, U.S. Dist. Ct. (we. dist.) Tex. 1990, U.S. Ct. Appeals (D.C. cir.) 1992, U.S. Supreme Ct. 1992, U.S. Dist Ct. (ea. dist.) Tex. 1993. With First City Ops. Ctr., Houston, 1980-85; law clk. Lipstet, Singer, Hirsch & Wagner, Houston, 1985-86, Pizzitola, Hinton & Sussman, Houston, 1986-87; briefing atty. Hon. Hal M. Lattimore Ct. Appeals, 2d Jud. Dist., Ft. Worth, 1987-88; assoc. Cantey & Hanger, Ft. Worth and Dallas, 1988-93, Smith, Ralston & Russell, Dallas, 1993-94, Russell, Austin & Henschel, Dallas, 1994-95; prin. Ann S. Austin, Atty. at Law, Arlington, 1995—; tchr. Project Outreach State Bar of Tex., 1992. Chpt. editor: Cases and Materials on Civil Procedure, 1987. Mem. Ft. Worth Hist. Preservation Soc., com. mem., 1992; fundraiser Nat. Com. Prevention Child

Abuse, 1988—, Women's Haven. Mem. Tex. Young Lawyers Assn. (women in the profession com. 1992-94, profl. ethics and grievance awareness com. 1992-94, jud. rev. com. 1990), Dallas Bar Assn. (jud. com. 1993-94), Dallas Assn. Young Lawyers, Dallas Women's Bar Assn., Ft. Worth Tarrant County Young Lawyers Assn. (treas. 1989-90, dir. 1989, judge Teen Ct., co-chair Adopt-A-Sch. program), Tarrant County Women's Bar Assn., 5th Cir. Fed. Bar Assn., Am. Inns. of Ct. Methodist. Office: Landau Omahana & Kopka Three Lincoln Ctr 5430 LBJ Pkwy Ste 980 Dallas TX 75240

AUSTIN, BILL RAY, mathematician, mathematics educator; b. Atkins, Ark., July 25, 1940; s. O. C. and Beatrice (Coffman) A.; m. Julia Ellis, Sept. 9, 1962 (div. 1985); children: William Andrew, Shelly Diane, Bradley Ellis; m. Dianne Miller, Jan. 1, 1990. BA, Ark. Coll., 1962; MS, La. State U., Baton Rouge, 1964; PhD, U. Miss., Oxford, 1976. Instr. Christian Bros. Coll., Memphis, 1964-65; instr. math. U. Tenn., Martin, 1965-69, asst. prof. math., 1969-76, assoc. prof. math., 1976-83, prof., chmn. math., 1983--. Mem. Am. Math. Soc., Math. Assn. Am., Nat. Coun. Tchrs. Math., Kiwanis (pres. 1980), Masons (master 1975), Sigma Xi (pres. 1991). Presbyterian. Home: 217 Redbud Cir Martin TN 38237-3615 Office: Univ Tenn Dept of Math Martin TN 38238

AUSTIN, CHARLES PERRY, law enforcement administrator; b. Greenville, S.C., Sept. 30, 1950; s. Furman Jr. and Mary Alton (Dawson) A.; m. Ava Francine Frederick, Dec. 23, 1972; children: Charles P. Jr., Charnequa, Chandra. BS, S.C. State U., 1976; MA in Criminal Justice, U. S.C., 1985. Patrolman Greenville Police Dept., S.C., 1973, Easley Police Dept., S.C., 1973-75; spl. agent S.C. Law Enforcement Divsn., Columbia, 1975-86; chief of pub. safety S.C. State U., Orangeburg, 1986-88; major Chatham County Ga. Police Dept., Savannah, 1988-89; dep. chief Columbia Police Dept., 1989-90, chief of police, 1990—; instr. Midlands Tech. Coll., Columbia, 1989—, U. S.C., 1990—; cons. Bur. Justice Assistance, Washington, 1994. hon. mem. Rotary Internat., 1993; mem. bd. trustees Epworth Children's Home, 1992—, Eisenhower Found., 1994; mem. bd. dirs. Cities in Schs. of Columbia, 1991—. Recipient Pub. Svc. award Columbia Urban League, 1990, Svc. to Mankind award State Sertoma Club, 1990, Law Enforcement of the Yr. S.C. Vets. of Fgn. Wars, 1993, Walker E. Solomon award S.C. Edn. Assn., 1991. Mem. S.C. Law Enforcement Officer's Assn. (dist. rep. 1993), S.C. Juvenile Justice Reform Task Force, Atty. Gen's. Task Force on Crime and Violence (vice chmn. 1994), Omega Psi Phi Fraternity, Inc. (Basileus 1986-88, Named Man of the Yr. 1988). Methodist. Home: 180 King Charles Rd Columbia SC 29209-2240 Office: Columbia Police Dept 1409 Lincoln St Columbia SC 29201-3109

AUSTIN, DAN, retired dean; b. DeKalb County, Ala., Aug. 24, 1929; s. William J. and Edwina (Murphy) A.; m. Myra Sue Emmett, Jan. 14, 1951; 1 child, Deborah Elaine Austin Land. B.S. in Edn., Jacksonville U., 1964, M.S. in Edn., 1971. Tchr., Etowah County Bd. Edn., Gadsden, Ala., 1964-65, Anniston City Bd. Edn., Ala., 1965-66; faculty Ayers State Tech. Coll., Anniston, 1966-67, dean of instrn., 1967-88; ret 1988. Bd. dirs. Jacksonville Hosp.; mem. Jacksonville City Bd. Edn.; adv. bd. Ayers State Tech. Coll. Served as sgt. U.S. Army, 1951-53. Mem. Dean's Assn. Ala. (pres. 1969-70, treas. 1972-74). Democrat. Baptist. Avocations: photography, camping, gardening. Home: 600 11th St NE Jacksonville AL 36265-1129

AUSTIN, JEAN PHILIPPE, medical educator, radiologist. BA, NYU, 1980; MD, SUNY, N.Y.C., 1985. Diplomate Am. Bd. Radiology. Intern in internal medicine Orlando (Fla.) Regional Med. Ctr., 1985-86; chief resident, resident in radiation oncology SUNY Health Sci. Ctr., 1986-89; clin. fellow in radiation oncology Harvard U. Med. Sch., Boston, 1989-90; mem. jr. staff in radiation oncology Mass. Gen. Hosp., Boston, 1989-90; asst. prof. radiation oncology La. State U. Med. Ctr.-Tulane U. Med. Ctr., New Orleans, 1990—; papers presented at New Eng. Cancer Soc., 1989, Am. Radium Soc. Proceedings, 1990, A.S.T.R.O. Ann. Meeting, 1990, La. Soc. Radiologic Technologists Acadian Soc., 1991, Internat. Conf. of Hematology and Oncology, Cali, Colombia, 1992, 74th Ann. Meeting of the Am. Radium Soc., Orlando, 1992, La. Med. Assn. and Pelican State Dental Assn., Lafayette, 1992, New Orleans Med. Assns., 1992, Physician Assn. La., 1993, Am. Coll. Chest Physicians, New Orleans, 1993; with cancer com. Children's Hosp. La. State U. Med. Ctr.; affiliated physician VA Hosp., Mercy Hosp., Med. Ctr. La. New Orleans, United Med. Ctr., Univ. Hosp., Children's Hosp., Tulane U. Med. Ctr. Contbr. articles to profl. jours. Mem. Am. Soc. for Therapeutic Radiology and Oncology, Am. Radium Soc., Nat. Med. Assn., Orleans Parish Med. Soc., Physicians Assn. La., New Orleans Med. Assn., Radiation Therapy Oncology Group, S.W. Oncology Group. Office: Covenant Med Ctr 1400 W Park St Urbana IL 61801

AUSTIN, JOE DAN, mathematics educator, researcher; b. Hot Springs, Ark., Feb. 13, 1944; s. James Charles and Edmonia Nadine A.; m. Kathleen Ann Kabat, Aug. 9, 1969; children: Michael, Jonathan, Cheryl. BS in Applied Math., Ga. Inst. Tech., 1966; MS in Statistics, Purdue U., 1968, PhD in Math. Edn., 1972. Cert. tchr. math., learning disabled, Tex. Edn. Agy. Asst. prof. math. edn. Gothe U., Frankfurt, Germany, 1972-73; asst. prof. math. Emory U., Atlanta, 1973-78; assoc. prof. edn. and statistics Rice U., Houston, 1978-84, 85—; secondary sch. math. tchr. Houston Ind. Sch. Dist., 1984-85; vis. assoc. rsch. prof. Mont. State U., Bozeman, 1992-93; mem. adv. bd. Investigations in Math Edn., Ohio, 1980-93; external evaluator NSF grant to Houston Ind. Sch. Dist., 1996—. Author: Mathematics of Money, 1992, 2nd edit., 1994; editor: Texas Mathematics Teacher, 1991; mem. editl. bd. Undergraduate Math and Application, 1987; contbr. articles to profl. jours. Grantee Tex. title II higher edn. grant program, 1987, Exxon, 1988, NSF, 1991. Mem. Nat. Coun. Tchr. of Math., Tex. Coun. Tchrs. Math., Sch. Sci. and Math. Office: Rice U Dept Edn PO Box 1892 Houston TX 77251

AUSTIN, JOHN RILEY, surgeon, educator; b. St. Louis, Feb. 19, 1960; s. Thomas L. and Barbara (Riley) A.; m. Sara Beth Goehringer, May 16, 1987; children: Claire Frances, Emily Grace, John Michael. BS with highest honors, U. Wyo., 1982; MD, U. Utah, 1986. Diplomate Am. Bd. Facial Plastic and Reconstructive Surgery, Am. Bd. Otolaryngology. Surg. intern U. So. Calif., L.A. County Med. Ctr., L.A., 1986-87, resident otolaryngology, head and neck surgery dept., 1987-91; fellow in head and neck surg. oncology M.D. Anderson Cancer Ctr. M.D. Anderson Cancer Ctr. U. Tex., Houston, 1991-92; asst. surgeon, clin. instr. U. Tex., Houston, 1992-93; asst. prof., asst. surgeon M.D. Anderson Cancer Ctr. U. Tex., Houston, 1993-95, clin. asst. prof., 1995—; adj. asst. prof. dept. otorhinolaryngology/comm. disorders Baylor Coll. Medicine, 1993-95; otolaryngologic cons. dept. infectious diseases U. So. Calif., 1988-91; mem. utilization com. M.D. Anderson Cancer Ctr., U.Tex., 1993-95, mem. laser com., 1993-95; presenter in field. Cons. editor Head and Neck, Laryngoscope, Otolaryngology-Head and Neck Surgery, Cancer, 1993—, Archives of Otolaryngology; contbr. articles to profl. jours. Mem. Graduate Edn. com. U. Tex., 1994. Fellow ACS, Am. Acad. Otolaryngology (human resource com.), AMA, Am. Acad. Facial Plastic and Reconstructive Surgery (mem. publs. com.), Tex. Med. Assn. (mem. physician oncology edn. program 1993—, mem. com. cancer 1993—), M.D. Anderson Assocs., Soc. Univ. Otolaryngologists, N.Am. Skull Base Soc., Tex. Assn. Otolaryngology, Sir Charles Bell Soc. (founding), Travis County Med. Soc. (jour. com.), Salerni Colegium, Phi Kappa Phi, Phi Beta Kappa, Sigma Nu. Methodist. Home: 3507 Cactus Wren Way Austin TX 78746 Office: 3705 Medical Pkwy Ste 310 Austin TX 78705

AUSTIN, JUDY ESSARY, scriptwriter; b. Jackson, Tenn., Apr. 7, 1948; d. Hershel Dee and Elizabeth Sue (Rhodes) Essary; m. James Michael Austin, July 4, 1965; children: James Allan Austin, Julia Ann Austin Patterson. AS, DeKalb Coll., 1988; BA in Communications and Journalism, Mercer U., 1989. Retail mgr. Bankers Note, Atlanta, 1980-84, Le Chocolat Elegant, Atlanta, 1984-85; student asst. student affairs DeKalb Coll., Dunwoody, Ga., 1987-88; asst. art dir. Sportime, Atlanta, 1990-92; writer, prodr. CAMA, Atlanta, 1993-94; freelance scriptwriter Atlanta, 1994-96; bd. dirs. Second Wind Orgn., Dekalb Coll., Dunwoody, 1987-88. Scholar Am. Bus. Womens Assn., 1987. Mem. Women in Communications, NAFE, Phi Kappa Phi. Home: 3133 Raymond Dr Atlanta GA 30340-1826

AUSTIN, MARGARET CULLY, school administrator; b. St. Louis, July 18, 1930; d. Ben Allen and Rosalie Ada (Mersman) Cully; m. June 19, 1954; children: Steven W., Katherine E., Andrea C. AA in Music, Motlow State C.C., Tullahoma, Tenn., 1973; BS in Elem. Edn., Mid. Tenn. State U., 1975, MEd in Reading, 1979; Cert. in Adminstrn., Trevecca Coll., Nashville, 1989. Elem. music tchr. St. Paul the Apostle Sch., Tullahoma, Tenn., 1969-73; teaching prin. Normandy Sch., Bedford County, Tenn., 1975-76; reading specialist Bedford County Schs., 1976-88, Chpt. I cons. tchr., 1989-94, supr. title I/fed. projects, 1994—, testing coord., 1994—, reading cons. spl. edn., 1994—, migrant edn. coord., 1996—. Mem. NEA, Tenn. Edn. Assn., Bedford County Edn. Assn., Internat. Reading Assn., Tenn. Supr. of Edn. Assn. Home: 601 Crestwood Dr Tullahoma TN 37388-2929 Office: Bedford County Bd of Edn 500 Madison St Shelbyville TN 37160-3341

AUSTIN, PHILIP EDWARD, university chancellor; b. Fargo, N.D., 1942; s. William and Angelyn A.; m. Susan Gates; children: Patrick William, Philip James. B.S., N.D. State U., 1964, M.S., 1966; M.A., Mich. State U., 1968, Ph.D., 1969; hon. doctorate, Autonomous U. Guadalajara, Mexico. Economist U.S. Office of Mgmt. and Budget, Washington, 1971-74; dep. asst. sec. HEW, Washington, 1974-77; acting asst. sec. HEW, 1977; dir. doctoral program in pub. policy George Washington U., Washington, 1977-78; v.p. for acad. affairs, prof. econs. and fin. Bernard Baruch Coll., N.Y.C., 1978-84; pres., prof. econs. Colo. State U., Fort Collins, 1984-89; chancellor U. Ala. System, Tuscaloosa, 1989-96; pres. U. Conn., Storrs, 1996—; bd. dirs. Ala. Power Co., Am. Cast Iron Pipe Co. Served with U.S. Army, 1969-71. Decorated Bronze Star. Office: U Ala System Gulley Hall 352 Mansfield Rd Storrs CT 06269-2048

AUSTIN, PHYLIS ANN, medical writer, editor; b. Logansport, Ind., Oct. 14, 1943; d. Donald Paul and Ollie Ann (Cunningham) A. BS in Comty. Svcs., So. Coll., Collegedale, Tenn., 1965. Prin., tchr. elem. sch. Brooksville, Fla., 1965-66; med. social worker Fla. Hosp., Orlando, 1967-69; med. transcriber Hialeah (Fla.) Hosp., 1969-72; founder Outdoor Living Libr., 1972; med. transcriber, med. libr. Madison (Tenn.) Hosp., 1972-76; med. sec., editl. asst. Emory U. Sch. Medicine, Atlanta, 1988—. Author: Natural Remedies, 1982, More Natural Remedies, 1982, Food Allergies Made Simple, 1985, Fatigue: Causes, Treatment and Prevention, 1986, Natural Healthcare for Your Child, 1990; co-author: (quar. publ.) Come Out!, 1974; publ. Science/Health Abstracts, 1980. Mem. Am. Med. Writer's Assn. Office: Science/Health Abstracts PO Box 553 Georgetown GA 31754-0553

AUSTIN, ROBERT EUGENE, JR., lawyer; b. Jacksonville, Fla., Oct. 10, 1937; s. Robert Eugene and Leta Fitch A.; div. Feb. 86; children: Robert Eugene, George Harry Talley. B.A., Davidson Coll., 1959; J.D., U. Fla., 1964. Bar: Fla. 1965, D.C. 1983, U.S. Supreme Ct. 1970; cert. in civil trial law Nat. Bd. Trial Advocacy, Fla. Bar. Legal asst. Fla. Ho. Reps., 1965; assoc. firm Jones & Sims, Pensacola, Fla., 1965-66; ptnr. firm Warren, Warren & Austin, Leesburg, Fla., 1966-68, McLin, Burnsed, Austin & Cyrus, Leesburg, 1968-77, Austin & Burleigh, Leesburg, 1977-81; sole practice Leesburg, 1981-83, Leesburg and Orlando, Fla., 1984-86; ptnr. firm Austin & Lockett P.A., 1983-84; ptnr. Austin, Lawrence & Landis, Leesburg and Orlando, 1986-92, Austin & Pepperman, Leesburg, 1992—; asst. state atty., 1972; mem. Jud. Nominating Commn. and Grievance Com. 5th Dist. Fla.; gov. Fla. Bar, 1983. Chmn. Lae Dist. Boy Scouts Am.; asst. dean Leesburg Deanery Diocese Cen. Fla.; trustee Fla. House, Washington, U. Fla. Law Ctr., 1983—, chmn., 1988-90. Mem. Acad. Fla. Trial Lawyers, Am. Arbitration Assn., ABA, Am. Judicature Soc., Am. Law Inst., Assn. Trial Lawyers Am., Nat. Inst. Trial Advocacy, Def. Research Inst., Fed. Bar Assn., Lake County Bar Assn., Roscoe Pound Am. Trial Found., Timuquana Country Club (Jacksonville), Kappa Alpha, Phi Delta Phi. Democrat. Episcopalian. Home: PO Box 490200 Leesburg FL 34749-0200 Office: Austin & Pepperman 1321 C Citizens Blvd Leesburg FL 34748-3985

AUSTIN, ROBERT JAMES, archaeologist; b. Berea, Ohio, May 31, 1949; s. Jonathan Weaver and Jane Lucy (Dittrick) A.; m. Rebecca Ileen Means, Mar. 25, 1972 (div. 1980); m. Karen Marie Davis, Mar. 21, 1987. BA in English, U. South Fla., 1973, BA in Anthropology, 1979, MA in Anthropology, 1983; postgrad., U. Fla., 1992—. Field archaeologist Nat. Park Svc., Tallahassee, Fla., 1979; field archaeologist, rsch. analyst Fla. Divsn. Hist. Resources, Tallahassee, 1979-81; grad. asst., project archaeologist U. South Fla., Tampa, 1981-82; staff archaeologist Armac Engrs., Inc., Tampa, 1983-84, Archaeol. Cons., Inc., Worland, Wyo., 1984; sr. archaeologist Piper Archaeol. Rsch., Inc., St. Petersburg, Fla., 1985, v.p. archaeol. rsch., 1986-92; exec. v.p. Janus Rsch., St. Petersburg, 1992—. Editor jour. Fla. Anthropologist, 1995—; contbr. articles to profl. jours. Mem. exec. bd. Mus. Fla. Art and Culture, Sebring, 1995—. Recipient Meritorious Achievement award Fla. Trust for Hist. Preservation, 1996. Mem. Soc. Profl. Archaeologists, Fla. Archaeol. Coun. (v.p. 1990-91, bd. dirs. 1992-94), Fla. Anthrop. Soc. (bd. dirs. 1988-90, Ripley P. Bullen award 1993), Fla. Acad. Scis. (chair anthropol. scis. sect. 1994-95), Phi Kappa Phi. Democrat. Office: Janus Rsch 2935 1st Ave N Saint Petersburg FL 33713

AUSTIN, ROGER QUARLES, III, political consultant, lawyer; b. Ft. Walton Beach, Fla., Dec. 1, 1956; s. Roger Q. Jr. and Sally Powell (Rippey) A. BA in History, U. Fla., 1979, JD, 1982. Bar: Fla. 1983. Atty. Padgett, Teasley, Niles & Shaw, Coral Gables, Fla., 1984-86, Fowler & Clark, Jacksonville, Fla., 1986-87; pvt. practice law, polit. cons., Jacksonville, 1987-89; polit. dir. Reps. of Fla., Tallahassee, 1989-92; polit. cons. Data Targeting, Gainesville, Fla., 1992-96; cons. Gainesville, 1996—. Home and Office: 4511 NW 18th Pl Gainesville FL 32605-3494

AUSTIN, SIGRID LINNEVOLD, counselor; b. Madison, Wis., Aug. 15, 1939; d. Bernhard Olaf Johann and Agnes Elizabeth (Spiva) Linnevold; m. William Jerome Austin, May 16, 1962; children: Christopher Peter, Douglas Patrick, Colin Michael. BA, Barnard Coll., 1961; MS, Va. Commonwealth U., 1986. Lic. profl. counselor. Sr. counselor Peninsula Hosp., Hampton, Va., 1986-88; counselor Williamsburg (Va.) Ctr. for Therapy, 1988—; counselor outreach program Williamsburg Hosp., 1988—; counselor eating disorder program Williamsburg Hosp. Outreach, 1993; crisis counselor William & Mary Police Dept., 1993—; adj. faculty Va. Commonwealth U., Richmond, 1988-90. Asst. editor: (newsletter) The Addiction Letter, 1986-89; contbr. articles to profl. jours. Bd. dirs. Surry County Soc. Prevention of Cruelty to Animals, Surry, Va., 1993; active Nat. Trust Hist. Preservation, Washington, 1992-93, Nat. Conservancy, 1992-93. Scholar Sch. Pub. Affairs, Va. Commonwealth U., 1986. Mem. Internat. Assn. Eating Disorders, Nat. Assn. Alcohol and Drug Abuse, Va. Assn. Alcohol and Drug Abuse, Va. Mental Health Assn., Va. Assn. Clin. Counselors, Obsessive Compulsive Found., Phi Kappa Phi. Democrat. Lutheran. Office: Williamsburg Ctr Therapy 217 Mclaws Cir Ste 2 Williamsburg VA 23185-5649

AUSTIN-LONG, JEAN AUDREY, nurse supervisor; b. Stoughton, Mass., Apr. 23, 1940; d. James Webster and Helen Audrey (Foster) Austin; m. Thomas Alan White I, Sept. 28, 1958 (div. Sept. 1974); children: Thomas Alan White II, Sherri Lee Austin; m. Gary Francis Long, Dec. 28, 1985. BSN, U. Mass., 1984; MEd in Psychiat. Counseling, U. Louisville, 1992. RN, Mass. Staff/charge nurse med.-surg. Morton Hosp., Taunton, Mass., 1984-85; staff/charge nurse spinal cord injury VA Hosp., Brockton, Mass., 1985-86; staff/charge nurse med.-surg. VA Hosp., Louisville, 1986-87; staff nurse obstetrics/labor & delivery Tri-County Hosp., La Grange, Ky., 1987-88; staff supr. adolescent dual diagnosis unit Charter Hosp. of Louisville, 1988-91; staff nurse med.-surg. Tri-County Hosp., La Grange, 1991-93; nurse supr. Correctional Med. Sys. Corp. Jefferson County Youth Ctr. Med. Unit, Louisville, 1993-95; nursing mgr. adult psychiatric unit Beaufort (S.C.) Meml. Hosp., 1995-96, dept. dir. adult psychiat. unit, 1996—; award presenter Nurse's Day Recognition, Louisivlle, 1988; instr. basic CPR and first aid ARC, Louisville, 1994. Recipient Nurse's Day Recognition award, Louisville, 1989. Mem. Ky. Nursing Assn., S.C. Nurses Assn., Sigma Theta Tau (mem. S.C. chpt.), Iota Zeta chpt. Soc. Nursing. Home: 703 Winter Trout Rd Saint Helena Island SC 29920

AUTHEMENT, RAY P., college president; b. Chauvin, La., Nov. 19, 1929; s. Elias Lawrence and Elphia (Duplantis) A.; m. Barbara B. Braud, June 1, 1950; children: Kathleen Elizabeth, Julie Ann. B.S., U. Southwestern La., 1950; M.S., La. State U., 1952; Ph.D., 1956. Instr. La. State U., Baton Rouge, 1952-56; asso. prof. McNeese State Coll., Lake Charles, La., 1956-57; asso. prof. U. Southwestern La., 1957-59, prof. math., from, 1959, acad. v.p., 1966-73, pres., 1973—; vis. prof. U. N.C., Chapel Hill, 1962-63. Mem. Downtown Devel. Com. Lafayette, 1972—; commr., mem. exec. com. Lafayette Econ. Devel. Authority, 1988—; mem. La. Bicentennial Commn., 1973, Lafayette Bicentennial Commn., 1973, Econ. Devel. Com., Lafayette, 1973, Sch. Bd. Fatima Parish, Lafayette, 1963-65; bd. dirs. United Way, 1973, U. Southwestern La. Found., 1967, Gulf South Rsch. Inst., 1985-91; trustee Lafayette Gen. Hosp., 1981—; mem. bd. advisers John Gray Inst., 1982-91, St. Joseph Sem., 1967; mem. Commn. Colleges So. Assn. Colls., 1981-83; bd. dirs. Lafayette Health Ventures, Inc., 1989—, Enterprise Ctr. of La., Inc., 1990—, Affiliated Blind of La., Inc., 1991—, La. Partnership for Tech. and Innovation, 1989—, chmn., 1993; chmn. Acadiana Navigation Channel Task Force, 1990—. Named Outstanding Citizen of Acadiana Internat. Rels. Assn. Acadiana, 1991; recipient Lafayette Civic Cup award, 1991. Mem. AAAS, Lafayette C. of C. (dir. 1983—), Blue Key, Phi Kappa Phi, Kappa Mu Epsilon, Sigma Pi Sigma, Phi Kappa Theta. Roman Catholic. Home: PO Drawer 41008 USL Station Lafayette LA 70504 Office: U Southwestern La Office Pres USL Drawer 41008 University Ave Lafayette LA 70504-1008

AUTORINO, ROBERTA CATHERINE, community health nurse; b. Corona, N.Y., June 20, 1938; d. Arthur Robert and Helen Anna (Slater) Helmers; children: Roberta Anne Autorino Stewart, Anthony Michael Autorino. RN, Meth. Hosp., Bklyn., 1958; student, Polk Community Coll., Winter Haven, Fla., 1975, U. S. Fla., Tampa, 1983. Cmty. health nurse HRS-Polk County Health Unit, Lakeland, Fla., 1976-79; sr. cmty. health nurse HRS-Polk County Health Unit, 1979-86; cmty. health nursing supr. communicable disease/AIDS HRS-Polk County Health Unit, Winter Haven, Fla., 1986-96; nursing program specialist communicable disease/AIDS Auburndale, Fla., 1996—. 1st lt. Nurse Corps., USAF, 1960-62. Recipient ARC Award for Svc. to Clients, 1983. Mem. ANA, Fla. Nurses Assn., Fla. Pub. Health Nurse. Home: 317 Santiago Ct Lakeland FL 33809-4201

AUVENSHINE, WILLIAM ROBERT, academic administrator; b. Waco, Tex., June 21, 1937; s. E.H. and Corinne (Clark) A.; m. Anna Banks, Dec. 21, 1963; children: Karen, Lee. AA, Arlington State Jr. Coll., 1957; BS, Tex. Christian U., 1959; MS, West Tex. State U., 1967; EdD, U. No. Colo., 1973. Tchr. music Chico (Tex.) Pub. Schs., 1957-60, Ranger (Tex.) Pub. Schs., 1960-64; mgr., part-owner Megert Music Co., Amarillo, Tex., 1964-70; counselor Loveland (Colo.) Pub. Schs., 1970-72; dean Ranger Jr. Coll., 1972-84; pres. Hill Coll., Hillsboro, Tex., 1984—. Mem. Heritage League, Hillsboro, 1984—; chmn. State Task Force on C.C. Annexation, 1993; chmn. bd. dirs. Eastland County Tax Appraisal Dist., 1979-84; mem. Indsl. Com., Cleburne, 1984—, Hillsboro, 1984—; mem. First United Meth. Ch., Hillsboro; mem. gen. bd. discipleship com. that rewrote Book of Worship for Meth. Ch.; lay leader Ctrl. Tex. Conf., leader del. to gen. conf.; bd. dirs. Nat. Jr. Coll. Atletic Assn., 1993—. Recipient Disting. Alumni award West Tex. State U., Canyon, 1983, Jefferson Davis award United Daus. of Confederacy, 1991; named Man of Yr., Ranger C. of C., 1963. Mem. Tex. Jr. Coll. Assn. (pres. 1991-92), Tex. Pub. Community Jr. Coll. Assn. (sec., treas. 1985-90), Tex. Assn. for C.C. Chief Student Affairs Adminstrs. (pres. 1982-83), Tex. C.C. Ins. Consortium (pres. 1992—), Hillsboro C. of C., Lions (dist. gov. 1977-78, Internat. Press award 1983, Lion of Yr. award Ranger chpt. 1975, Citizen of Yr. award Hillsboro chpt. 1986), Sons of Confederate Vets. (past comdr. 1988-90), Sons of Union Vets. of Civil War (chaplain), Masons (32d degree), Shriners, Hillsboro Country Club (pres. 1993—), Phi Delta Kappa. Home: 412 Corsicana St Hillsboro TX 76645-2230 Office: Hill Coll 111 Lamar Dr Hillsboro TX 76645-2712

AVANT, TRACY WRIGHT, artist; b. Fort Dix, N.J., 1960. Studied with various artists, 1988—. conductor workshops. One-woman shows include Coppini Gallery, 1992, The Longhorn Gallery, 1993, Ceci's Gallery Fine Art, Bryan, Tex., 1994, Briarcrest Country Club, 1994; exhibited in group shows Dilley Civic Ctr., Dilley, Tex, 1987-88, Artbeat, San Antonio, 1992, Coppini Gallery, San Antonio, 1993, Joe Freeman Coliseum, San Antonio, 1988-93, La Villita Assembly Hall, San Antonio, 1993, Richardson (Tex.) Pub. Libr., 1993, 95, Bridge Gallery, N.Y.C., 1993, Irving (Tex.) Art Ctr., 1993, J.R. Mooney Gallery, San Antonio, 1993, 94, St. Edwards U., Austin, Tex., 1993, Palette and Chisel Gallery, Chgo., 1993, 94, Gwendolyn's Gallery, Colo., 1993, 94, D Art Gallery, Dallas, 1994, Scottsdale (Ariz.) Artist's Sch., 1994-96, Ceci's Gallery Fine Art, 1994-95, Carol's at the Hitching Post, 1994, Mae S. Bruce Libr., Santa Fe, Tex., 1994, 95, Deposit Guaranty Salon Internat., Jackson, Miss., 1994, Bosque County Conservatory, Clifton, Tex., 1994, Nanette Richardson Gallery, San Antonio, 1994 (Judge's Choice award 1994), Thomas Gilcrease Mus., 1994, Nat. Soc. Artists, 1994-96, Pasadena (Tex.) Art League, 1995, and numerous others; represented in permanent collections Wyoming Gallery, Jackson, Tex. Trails Gallery, San Antonio, Love Tex. Gallery, San Antonio, Triple C Gallery, Devine, Tex., Phil Isley Inc., Tex., Normangee State Bank, Tex., Ocean Wash USA, Tex., pvt. individuals. Mem. Am. Soc. Classical Realists, Nat. Soc. Artists, Nat. Wildlife Art Mus. Assn., Allied Artists Am., Oil Painters Am., Cowboy Artists Am. Mus. Assn., Tex. Watercolor Soc., Houston Civil Arts Assn., Artists and Craftsmen Assn. Dallas, Palette and Chisel Acad. Fine Art Chgo., Austin Palette Club, Scottsdale Artist Sch., New Braunfels Art League, Coppini Acad. Fine Art, Knickerbocker Artist Assocs., Western Acad. Women Artists. Home and Studio: Box 4 1120 Hwy 81 N Dilley TX 78017

AVELLANO, GEORGE PAUL, academic administrator; b. Chgo., Oct. 2, 1939; m. Deborah Skehan; children: John, Joseph. BS, Eastern Ill. U., 1967; MS, U. Mont., Missoula, 1970; PhD, U. Okla., 1975. Instr., asst. prof. Ctrl. State U., Edmond, Okla., 1970-78, chair mktg. dept., 1978-88; dean rsch./grad. studies U. Ctrl. Okla., Edmond, 1988-96; assoc. v.p. acad. affairs, grad. programs & planning U. Tex.-Pan Am., Edinburg, 1996—; pres. faculty senate, 1986-87, v.p., 1985-86; ofcl. NCAA Track & Field, Edmond, 1988—; faculty rep. NCAA Divsn. II, 1995-96. With U.S. Army, 1961-63. Mem. Conf. So. Grad. Schs. (v.p. 1995-96, pres. 1996—), Coun. Grad. Schs., Midwest Assn. Grad. Schs., Met. Univ. Consortium. Office: Univ Tex-Pan Am 1201 W University Dr Edinburg TX 78539

AVERDICK, MICHAEL ROBERT, librarian; b. Covington, Ky., Nov. 22, 1948; s. Robert Joseph and Mary Esther (Sommerkamp) A. Student, U. Cin., 1966-68, Thomas More Coll., Ft. Mitchell, Ky., 1969; BA in Sociology, U. Ky., 1970, MS in Libr. Sci., 1971. Cert. libr., Ky. Bookmobile libr. Lexington (Ky.) Pub. Libr., 1970-71; coord. spl. svcs. Ky. Dept. for Librs., Frankfort, 1971-73; head adult svcs. Kenton County Pub. Libr., Covington, 1973-86, assoc. dir., 1978—, dir. pub. svcs., 1990—. Compiler: KCPL: Self Evaluation and Transition Plan, 1992; editor: Frank Duveneck: Catalog of Paintings, 1993; editor Jour. Ky. State Libr., 1971-73. Trustee, co-founder Kenton County Hist. Soc., Covington, 1977—; bd. dirs. Covington Cmty. Ctr., 1996—; pres., mem. bd. dirs. Behringer Crawford Mus., Covington, 1979-85; mem. cornerstone com. Covington Police Dept., 1980; co-chair Ret. Sr. Vol. Program, Covington, 1974-76; chair Parish Kitchen, Mother of God Ch., Covington, 1973-74; mem. Greater Cin. Bicentennial Commn. Task Force on No. Ky. History, 1984-88. Recipient Mayor's Citation, City of Covington, 1981, Gov.'s Citation, State of Ky. Pre-White House Conf. on Librs., 1978. Mem. Ky. Libr. Assn. (bd. dirs. 1977-78, pres. pub. libr. sect. 1977-78, v.p. 1976-77, sec.-treas. 1975-76), Greater Cin. Libr. Consortium (bd. dirs. 1983-87), White Villa Country Club, Knights of St. John. Democrat. Home: 829 Willard St Covington KY 41011 Office: 5th and Scott St Covington KY 41011

AVERETT-SHORT, GENEVA EVELYN, college administrator; b. Boston, Mar. 12, 1938; d. William Pinkney and Geneva Zepplyn (Stepp) A.; m. Roger Inman Blackwell, Dec. 19, 1959 (div. 1975); children: Thomas, LaVerne, Constance; m. Floyd J. Short Jr., July 3, 1984. BA in Social Sci., Bennett Coll., Greensboro, N.C., 1958; EdM, SUNY, Buffalo, 1972; paralegal cert., Prince George's C.C., Largo, Md., 1994. Social caseworker Erie County Dept. Pub. Welfare, Buffalo, 1958-59; substitute tchr. Buffalo Bd. Edn., 1959-60; employment inteviewer N.Y. Dept. Labor, Div. Employment, Buffalo, 1967-69; admissions counselor SUNY, Buffalo, 1969-72; assoc. dean students U. Utah, Salt Lake City, 1972-74; coordinator counseling svcs. Ednl. Devel. Prog., SUNY, Fredonia, 1974-77; acting dir. Ednl. Devel. Prog., SUNY, 1976-77; substitute tchr. Greensboro (N.C.) pub. schs., 1977-78; prog. asst. D.C. Dept. Human Svcs. Commn. on Pub. Health, 1978-89; assessment counselor, coord. Prince George's Community Coll., Largo, Md., 1989-94; cons. in field. Active in past various charitable orgns. Mem. Nat. Alumnae Assn. Bennett Coll., S. Fla. Alumnae Assn. (sec. Bennett Coll. chpt., 1996—), Pierians, Inc. (pres. D.C. chpt. 1992-94). Democrat. Episcopalian. Address: 21621 Altamira Ave Boca Raton FL 33433

AVERITT, RICHARD GARLAND, III, securities executive; b. Kearney, Nebr., Jan. 27, 1945; m. Sandra Louise Smith, June 7, 1967; children: Dawn, Rick, Scott. BA, Duke U., 1967. Cert. fin. planner. Account exec. Merrill Lynch, Pierce, Fenner & Smith, Atlanta, 1976-78; v.p. Consol. Planning Co., 1978-84; v.p. mktg. Investment Mgmt. & Rsch., Inc., Atlanta, 1984-87, 1st v.p., dir. mktg., 1987-91, sr. v.p., nat. sales mgr., 1991—, also bd. dirs. Founding chmn. Atlanta Area Marine Corps Coord. Coun. Col. USMCR ret. Mem. Internat. Assn. Fin. Planning (bd. dirs. Ga. chpt. 1978-79), Inst. Cert. Fin. Planners, Mensa. Republican. Office: Investment Mgmt & Rsch Inc 1647 Mount Vernon Rd Ste 200 Atlanta GA 30338-4205

AVERY, REIGH KESSEN, legal assistant; b. Cin., Sept. 16, 1949; d. Henry Charles and Margaret Elizabeth (Dam) Kessen; m. Gerald L. Poe, Oct. 5, 1968 (div. Nov. 1989); children: Amy Kathleen, Michael Lee; m. Melvin L. Avery, May 6, 1996. AAS, El Centro Coll., Dallas, 1988. Legal sec. Victor C. McCrea Jr. & Co., Dallas, 1983-84, legal asst., 1986-90; legal sec. Fanning, Harper & Martinson, Dallas, 1984-86, Thompson & Knight, Dallas, 1986; legal asst. Nacol, Wortham & Assocs., Dallas, 1990-91; sr. legal asst. Snelling and Snelling, Inc., Dallas, 1992-93; free-lance legal asst. Tex., 1993-95; legal asst. Wausau Ins. Cos., 1995—. Chmn. comm. Fox Meadow Farms Homeowners Assn., Loveland, Ohio, 1972-74; pro bono vol. Child Support Clinic, Dallas, 1988, North Ctrl. Tex. Legal Svcs. Found., Inc., Dallas, 1988—; vol. Ramses The Gt. Exhbn. Dallas Mus. Nat. History Assn., 1989. Mem. Nat. Assn. Legal Assts., Nat. Fedn. Paralegal Assns., State Bar Tex. (legal assts. div.), Dallas Assn. Legal Assts. (litigation sect., com. nat. affairs 1988-89), Phi Theta Kappa, Phi Beta Lambda. Home and Office: 725 Pinoak Dr Grand Prairie TX 75052-6522

AVERY, SUSAN ELIZABETH, journalist; b. Northampton, Mass., Aug. 6, 1960; d. James B. Avery and Eleanor G. (Van Pelt) Levall; 1 child, Aaron A. Avery-Speer. BA in Journalism, NYU, 1982. Editorial asst. Railway Age, Simmons-Boardman, N.Y.C., 1981-83, mng. editor, 1983-84; asst. editor Modern Plastics, McGraw-Hill, N.Y.C., 1985-86; freelance journalist Nashville, 1986—.

AVILA, WILLIAM THADDEUS, lawyer, economist; b. San Antonio, Feb. 27, 1954; s. Fernando Jr. and Victoria (Cuellar) A. BA in Econ., U. Notre Dame, 1977, MA in Econ., 1978; JD, George Washington U., 1981. Bar: Tex. 1982. Rsch. asst. S.W. Border Regional Commn., Washington, 1979-80; rsch. economist Nat. Commn. Employment Policy, Washington, 1980-81; law clk. Exec. Office of Pres., Washington, 1981, U.S. Sen. Com. on Banking, Housing and Urban Affairs, Washington, 1981, U.S. Bur. Mint, Dept. Treasury, Washington, 1981; instr. econ. U. Tex., San Antonio, 1981-83; legal counsel Harris Systems Internat., San Antonio, 1982-83; asst. city atty. City of San Antonio, 1983-89; assoc. Kaufman, Becer, Pullen & Reibach, San Antonio, 1989-91; pvt. practice San Antonio, 1991-93; ptnr. McCall, Parkhurst & Horton, L.L.P., San Antonio, 1993—; instr. econs. Trinity U., San Antonio, 1986-87, U. Tex., San Antonio, 1981-83; prof. law San Antonio Sch. Law, 1993—; legal counsel San Antonio YMCA, 1982—, San Antonio Local Devel. Co., 1983—, Mayor's Commn. on Status of Women, San Antonio, 1984-88; rschr. reports on econ. devel. and employment. Mem. task force San Antonio Youth Literacy, 1988; mem. exec. com. San Antonio Sports Found., 1988-91; mem. devel. bd. Incarnate Word Coll., San Antonio, 1988-91; mem. City of San Antonio Small and Minority Bus. Adv. Coun.; mem. community adv bd. Bank One. Ford Found. fellow in econ., 1977. Mem. ABA (vice chmn. bonds and sureties com., pub. contracts law sect.), San Antonio Bar Assn. (law day com. 1985), Mex.-Am. Bar Assn. (elections com. 1987, chmn. bus. law sect. 1991—), Hispanic Nat. Bar Assn., Notre Dame Club San Antonio (treas. 1986-88, pres. 1988-91). Democrat. Roman Catholic. Office: McCall Parkhurst & Horton 1225 One Riverwalk Pl San Antonio TX 78205

AVIRAM, AMITTAI F., English and comparative literature educator; b. Lynn, Mass., Sept. 6, 1957; s. Itamar and Rachel (Newton) A.; 1 child, Blake Aviram Gilson. BA magna cum laude, Columbia U., 1978; MA, Yale U., 1980, MPhil, 1982; PhD in English Lang. and Lit., 1984. Teaching fellow Yale U., New Haven, 1981-83, instr., 1983-84; vis. asst. prof., Mellon fellow Cornell U., Ithaca, N.Y., 1986-87; med. rsch. writer Pfizer, Inc., N.Y.C., 1987-88; asst. prof. English and comparative lit. U. S.C., Columbia, 1984-92, assoc. prof., 1992—; presenter in field. Author: Tender Phrases, Brassy Moans, 1994; Telling Rhythm: Body and Meaning in Poetry, 1994; mem. editorial bd. Genders; contbr. poetry to anthologies, jours. and chapbooks; contbr. scholarly articles to profl. jours. Recipient Creative Writing Contest prize Meridian mag., 1990; Nat. Merit and N.Y. State Regents scholar, 1974; recipient numerous fellowships and grants. Mem. Phi Beta Kappa. Office: U SC English Dept Columbia SC 29208

AVRUCH, KEVIN, anthropologist; b. Bklyn., Feb. 22, 1950; s. Benjamin and Edith (Kramer) A.; m. Sheila K. Smith, Mar. 25, 1977; children: Carla Rachel, Elizabeth Sophia. AB, U. Chgo., 1972; MA, U. Calif., San Diego, 1973; PhD, 1978. Lectr. U. Calif., San Diego, 1978-79; asst. prof. anthropology U. Ill., Chgo., 1979-80; prof. anthropology George Mason U., Fairfax, Va., 1980—. Author: American Immigrants in Israel, 1981; editor: Conflict Resolution: Cross-Cultural Perspectives, 1991, Critical Essays on Israeli Society, Religion and Government, 1996; assoc. editor Jour. Polit. & Mil. Sociology, Chgo., 1991-96; book rev. editor, Anthrop. Quar., Washington, 1986-91. Bd. dirs. Cultural Ctr. for Social Change, Washington, 1992—. Fellow Am. Anthrop. Assn., Mid. East Studies Assn.; mem. Assn. for Israel Studies (sec., treas. 1993—). Office: George Mason U Dept Sociology Anthropology Fairfax VA 22030

AWAD, ELIAS MICHAEL, business educator, computer consultant; b. Latakia, Syria, Oct. 6, 1934; came to U.S., 1954; s. Michael I. and Naifa Awad; m. Sandy Tremaine, Mar. 31, 1970; children: Michael D., E. Bruce, Brenda E. BS, Geneva Coll., 1956; MBA, Tulsa U., 1957; MA, Northwestern U., 1967; PhD, U. Ky., 1975. Asst. prof. Rochester (N.Y.) Inst. Tech., 1960-65; assoc. prof. DePaul U., Chgo., 1967-75; George Ball disting. prof. bus. Ball State U., Muncie, Ind., 1975-77; prof. bus. Fla. Internat. U., Miami, 1977-82; Virginia Bankers assoc. prof. bank mgmt. U. Va., Charlottesville, 1982—; mgmt. cons. Awad and Assocs., Inc., Chgo., 1967—. Author: (textbooks) Business-Data Processing, 5 edits., 1964-80, Systems Analysis, 1977, 2d edit., 1982, Data Base, 1992, Building Expert Systems, 1996; contbr. articles to profl. jours. Mem. Assn. for Computing Machinery (chair 1978-92), Assn. for Artificial Intelligence (conf. chair 1991-93). Republican. Office: Univ Va McIntire Sch Commerce Charlottesville VA 22903

AWALT, MARILENE KAY, principal; b. Mineral Wells, Tex., Mar. 20, 1942; d. Pat O. T. and Mary Lee (Curry) Morse; children: Stacy (dec.), Bradley. BS, Tex. Wesleyan Coll., 1966; MS in Edn., Baylor U., 1972; PhD, George Peabody Coll., Vanderbilt U., 1988. Cert. tchr., prin., supr. Elem. tchr. San Antonio Pub. Schs., 1966, LaVega Pub. Schs., Waco, Tex., 1966-68; with reading clinic Baylor U., Waco, 1969-70; tchr. reading Franklin Spl. Schs. (Tenn.), 1970-71, first grade tchr., 1971-80, asst. prin., 1980-84, prin., 1984-90; prin. Moore Elem. Sch., Franklin, 1990—. Mem. adv. council for tchr. cert. and edn. Tenn. State Sch. Bd., 1977-86; adminstr. career level III State of Tenn., 1987—. Tenn. spl. scholar, 1983-84. Named Tenn. Elem. Prin. of Yr., 1994, Nat. Disting. Prin. Tenn., 1996—. Mem. ASCD (bd. dirs. 1992—, exec. coun. 1995—), Mid. Tenn. Coun. Internat. Reading Assn., Internat. Reading Assn., Tenn. Assn. Supervision and Curriculum Devel. (pres. 1986-87, 92-93, exec. sec. 1993—), Tenn. Bd. of Examiners for State for Approval of Tchr. Edn., Delta Kappa Gamma (pres. Rho chpt.). Baptist. Co-author Religious Christian Day Sch. Curriculum, 1978; author: Study Book for 6-8 Year Olds, 1980; chmn. for revision elem. cert. State of Tenn. Office: Moore Elem Sch 1061 Lewisburg Pike Franklin TN 37064-6727

AWTRY, THOMAS HAROLD, mathematician; b. Shreveport, La., June 14, 1964; s. Ted A. and Cheryl L. (Walton) A.; m. Paula Rushing, Aug. 3, 1991. BS in Math. and Computer Sci., La. State U., Shreveport, 1986; MS in Math., La. State U., Baton Rouge, 1988; PhD in Math. Edn., La. State U., 1993. Mem. Am. Math. Soc., Phi Kappa Phi, Omicron Delta Kappa. Republican. Mem. Ch. of Christ. Home: 5820 Mary Jude Loop Alexandria VA 71303

AXEL, BERNARD, restaurant owner; b. Bklyn., May 23, 1946; s. Joseph and Irene (Rosen) A.; m. Tobie Reznik, Sept. 3, 1995. BS, U. Ala., 1967; grad., Am. Inst. Banking, 1970. Asst. cashier, comptroller Nat. Bank of Commerce (formerly Am. Nat. Bank), Birmingham, Ala., 1967-72; supr. internat. travel Travel Anywhere, Birmingham, 1972; acctg. and purchasing agt. U.S. Dept. Justice, Texarkana, Tex., 1972-74; mgr. Styslinger Realty, Birmingham, 1974-75; pres. Christian's Inc., Birmingham, 1975-92, Christian's Tutwiler, Inc., Birmingham, 1992—; gourmet chef Top of Morning show Sta. WVTM-T-V, Birmingham, 1991—. Contbr. recipes to mags. Judge March of Dimes Gourmet Gala, Birmingham, 1986, Miss Ala.-U.S.A. Pageant, 1990, 91, Miss Teen Ala., 1992; mem. gov.'s staff State of Ala., Montgomery, 1968-70, mem. lt. gov.'s staff, 1980-84; bd. dirs. Temple Beth El, 1969-72; mem. adv. bd. U. Ala. Sch. Restaurant Hospitality Mgmt., 1989—, chmn. adv. bd., 1992—. Awarded Key to City of Birmingham, Ala., 1991. Mem. Nat. Restaurant Assn. (cert. foodsvc. mgmt. profl., mem. adv. bd. polit. action com. 1987—, state chmn. 1993—, bd. dirs. 1996—), Am. Culinary Fedn. (bd. dirs. Birmingham chpt., medal 1986, Appreciation award 1991), Ala. Restaurant and Food Svc. Assn. (pres. 1990-92, trustee self-ins. fund 1994-96, Restaurateur of Yr. 1992, Polit. Eagle award 1994), Birmingham-Jefferson County Restaurant Assn. (bd. dirs. 1981-83, 89—, Restaurant Operator of Yr. 1995), Birmingham-Jefferson Restaurant Assn. (pres. 1995), Chaine des Rotisseurs (L'Order Mondial des Gourmets Degustateurs 1989), Les Disciples d'Auguste Escoffier Assn. Gastronomique, Commanderie des Cordon Bleus France. Republican. Home: 2625 Highland Ave S Birmingham AL 35205-1760 Office: Christian's Tutwiler Inc Park Pl and 21st St N Birmingham AL 35203

AYER, JOHN BUTLER, transportation executive; b. N.Y.C., Apr. 21, 1948; s. Winslow Bartlet and Mary Payson (Clark) A.; m. Pamela Susan Kelley, June 25, 1971 (div. 1988); 1 child, Kelley Camblin; m. Luann Long, Sept. 30, 1989. BS in Bus., U. Conn., 1977. Lic. Merchant Marine Masters. Capt. New England Steamboat Lines, Haddam, Conn., 1974-76; capt. Am. Cruise Line, Haddam, 1976-78, dir. ops., 1979-83; gen. mgr. Midway Marine, Haddam, 1978-79, Williams and Manchester Shipyard, Newport, R.I., 1983-85; capt. Clipper Cruise Line, 1985-86; dir. ops. Clipper Cruise Line, St. Louis, 1986-87, v.p. marine ops., 1987-88, v.p. passenger svcs., 1988-90, capt., 1990-93; dir. marine ops. Delta Queen Steamboat Co., Inc., New Orleans, 1993-95, v.p. marine ops., 1995—; marine cons. City Pennsacola, 1981-82. With USCG, 1970-74. Mem. Am. Mgmt. Assn., Propellor Club. Lutheran.

AYLIN, ELIZABETH TWIST PABST, real estate broker, developer; b. Pueblo, Colo., Aug. 22, 1917; d. Earl Joshua and Mabel Prudence (Benning) Twist; m. Julius Frohne Pabst, Apr. 16, 1944 (dec. Mar. 1984); children: Rachel Pabst Mrvichin, Jane Selkirk Pabst; m. Robert Norman Aylin, May 5, 1990. AB, U. No. Colo., 1939. English lang. teacher high sch., Holyoke, Colo., 1939-40; sec. to chancellor U. Denver, 1940-41; sec. to regional dir. Civil Svc., Denver, 1941-42; pers. dir. Denver Med. Depot, U.S. Quartermaster Corps, 1942; bus. adminstr. Pabst Home Builders and Lumber Co., Houston, 1945-84; owner, pres. Selkirk Island Corp., Houston, 1984—, Selkirk Island Utilities Corp., Houston, 1984—, Pabst Corp., Houston, 1984—. Wave ensign USN, 1942-44. Recipient Alumni Contbn. to Bus. award U. No. Colo., 1991. Mem. Houston Area Ret. Officers Assn. (v.p. 1986-90, 92-93). Home: 3835 Olympia Dr Houston TX 77019-3031 Office: 1 Selkirk Rd Bay City TX 77414-9341

AYNESWORTH, HUGH GRANT, reporter, author; b. Clarksburg, W.Va., Aug. 2, 1931; s. Kenneth and Martha (Fairfield) A.; m. Paula Eby, Apr. 5, 1962 (div. Jan. 1985); children: Allyson, Allysa, H. Grant; m. Paula Butler Stinson, July 20, 1987. Mng. editor The Southwest-Times Record, Ft. Smith, Ark., 1954-57; reporter The Dallas Morning News, 1960-67; S.W. bur. chief Newsweek, Houston, 1967-74; investigative reporter Dallas Times Herald, 1975-78, 84-86; investigative prodr. 20-20 ABC-TV News, N.Y.C., 1979-82; editor-in-chief Parkway Mag., Dallas, 1982-83; investigative reporter The Washington Times, 1986-88; S.W. bur. chief The Washington Times, Dallas, 1988—; Bd. mem. Press Club Dallas Found., 1992—. Coauthor: The Only Living Witness, 1983, If You Love Me, You Will Do My Will, 1990, Murderers Among Us, 1992, Conversations With a Killer-Ted Bundy, 1989; co-prodr.: (TV documentary) Psychic Confession, 1985. Recipient J.B. Marryat award Press Club Dallas, 1974. Mem. Sigma Delta Chi (pres. Tex. chpt. 1983-85). Home and Office: The Washington Times 3828 Townsend Dr Dallas TX 75229

AYRES, EDWIN MICHAEL, librarian; b. Kaufman, Tex., Nov. 2, 1953; s. Edwin Earl and Rubye Virginia (Watt) A.; m. Lisa Jean Arsenault, May 18, 1985; children: David Michael, Paul Freeman. BBA, Abilene Christian U., 1976, BMEd, 1980; MLS, North Tex. State U., 1982. Asst. libr. for cataloging Abilene Christian U., 1982-86; libr. svcs. supr. Irving (Tex.) Pub. Libr., 1986-93, libr. svcs. mgr., 1994—. Mem. ALA, Tex. Libr. Assn. Ch. of Christ. Home: 124 Leslie Ln Irving TX 75060 Office: Irving Public Library System 801 W Irving Blvd Irving TX 75060

AYRES, JAYNE LYNN ANKRUM, community health nurse; b. Reed City, Mich., Oct. 12, 1944; d. Quinten Wayne and Marshia Agetha (Crum) Ankrum; m. Ronald Francis Ayres, Apr. 16, 1977; children: Linda, Michele, Julie. ADN, Manatee C.C., Bradenton, Fla., 1975. RN, Fla., Ga. Staff nurse med.-surg., cardiac, oncology and float team Sarasota (Fla.) Meml. Hosp., 1975-77; nursing supr. Upjohn Healthcare Svcs., Sarasota, 1981-85; staff nurse Devereux Found., Kennesaw, Ga., 1986-89; staff nurse, supr. Vis. Nurse Health Sys., Metro, Atlanta, 1989—. Vol. ARC, M.U.S.T. Ministries Health Clinic for Homeless, Summer Olympics Games, 1996. Mem. Am. Legion (hon.), Fla. Nurses Assn. (hon.), Beta Sigma Phi.

AYRES, JULIA SPENCER, artist, author; b. Havana, Cuba, Aug. 16, 1931; (parents Am. citizens); d. Robert Vaughn and Ruth Mathilda (Meyer) Spencer; m. David Brent Ayres, Mar. 16, 1953; children: Robert, William, Gail, Clark. Student, Mass. Coll. Art, 1949-50, Art Inst., Chgo., 1951-53. Represented in permanent collections Marriott Hotel Internat., Home Savs. of Am., Toyota Corp. Hdqrs., Unocal Corp. Hdqrs., Russell Hunt Lodge, Am. Small Bus. Co.; author: Monotype, 1991, Printmaking Techniques, 1993; contbr. articles to profl. jours. Recipient Winsor Newton award Nat. Watercolor Soc., 1984. Office: Julia Ayres Studio PO Box 667 Chouteau OK 74337-0667

AYRES, MARY JO, professional speaker; b. Aberdeen, Miss., Jan. 27, 1953; d. Walter Stephen and Sarah Louise (Pearson) Peugh; m. William Stanley Ayres, June 28, 1975; children: Elizabeth, Will. BS, Miss. State U., Starkville, 1974; MEd, Delta State U., 1993. Tchr. Greenville (Miss.) Pub. Schs., 1974-75, Leland (Miss.) Acad., 1975-77; tchr. Leland United Meth. Child Devel. Ctr., Leland, 1984-91, chmn. bd. dirs., 1993—; profl. speaker Natural Learning, Leland, 1987—. Author: Happy Teaching and Natural Learning, 1992; prodr. cassette 32 Natural Learning Songs from A-Z; contbr. articles to profl. jours. Mem. Assn. for Childhood Edn. Internat., Miss. Early Childhood Assn., So. Assn. for Children Under Six, So. Early Childhood Assn., Miss. Reading Assn., Internat. Reading Assn. Home and Office: 103 Sycamore St Leland MS 38756-3136

AYSSE, PATRICIA ELAINE, health facility administrator; b. Groton, Conn., Feb. 6, 1959; d. Francis J. Sr. and Margaret E. (Kincaide) LaPlante; m. Jeffrey D. Aysse, May 15, 1982; 1 child, Brittany Elaine Aysse. BS in Nursing, Ball State U., 1981; postgrad., Med. U. S.C. Staff nurse Ball Meml. Hosp., Muncie, Ind., discharge planner; chief nurse neuro intensive care unit Med. U. S.C., Charleston, patient care coord., nurse mgr. orthopaedics/trauma and ophthalmology units., 1990-94, nurse mgr. pre- and post-anesthesia units, 1994—. Mem. Sigma Theta Tau. Home: 1754 Clark Hills Cir Johns Island SC 29455-7605

AZGHANI, ALI OWSAT, biomedical researcher; m. Cynthia Soto; children: Jason S., Jasmine S. BS in Med. Tech., U. Tabriz, Iran, 1972; MS in Microbiology, Tex. Woman's U., 1981, PhD in Radiation Biology, 1986. Med. tech. Ctr. for Cardiovascular Diseases, Tehran, Iran, 1972-76; teaching asst. dept. biology Tex. Woman's Univ., Denton, 1979-85; instr. dept. biochemistry U. Tex. Health Ctr., Tyler, 1989-92, asst. prof. dept. biochemistry, 1992—; lectr. in field. Contbr. articles to profl. jours. Recipient Rsch. grant award Am. Lung Assn., 1989-92, Am. Heart Assn., 1990-95; grantee Carrington Labs., 1991-93, NIH, 1994—. Mem. Am. Thoracic Soc., Am. Soc. for Microbiology, Am. Soc. for Cell Biology, Am. Heart Assn. (coun.). Office: Univ Tex Health Ctr Dept Biochemistry PO Box 2003 Tyler TX 75710-2003

BAAR, JAMES A., public relations and corporate communications executive, author, consultant, software developer; b. N.Y.C., Feb. 9, 1929; s. A.W. and Marguerite R. B.; m. Beverly Hodge, Sept. 2, 1948; 1 son, Theodore Hall. A.B., Union Coll., Schenectady, 1949. Washington corr. UPI, also other wire service burs. and newspapers, 1949-59; sr. editor Missiles and Rockets mag., 1959-62; mgr. various news bur. ops. Gen. Electric Co., 1962-66; mgr. European Mktg. Communications Ops., 1966-70; pres. Gen. Electric subs. Internat. Mktg. Communications Cons., 1970-72; sr. v.p., dir. public relations Lewis & Gilman, Inc., Phila., 1972-74; exec. v.p. Creamer Dickson Basford, Inc., 1974-78; pres. Creamer Dickson Basford-New Eng., 1978-83; sr. v.p./mgr. Northeast region Hill & Knowlton, Inc., Boston, 1983-84; v.p. communications Computervision Corp., 1984-86; sr. v.p. Gray & Co. Pub. Communications and gen. mgr. Gray & Co., N.Y., 1986-87; exec. v.p., worldwide dep. dir. advanced tech. practice Hill & Knowlton, Inc., 1987-90; pres., mng. cons. Omegacom, Inc., Boston, 1990—; corp. comms. and internet software developer and strategic comms. cons., 1990—. Author: Polaris, 1960, Combat Missileman, 1961, Spacecraft and Missiles of the World, 1962; (novel) The Great Free Enterprise Gambit, 1980, The Careful Voters Guide to Language Pollution, 1996; also numerous articles. Bd. overseers New Eng. Conservatory Music. Mem. Nat. Investor Relations Inst., Pub. Relations Soc. Am., Counselors Acad., Internat. Pub. Relations Assn., Chi Psi, Nat. Press Club, Overseas Press Club, English Speaking Union (bd. dirs. Boston), Univ. Club (Providence). Republican. Roman Catholic. Office: PO Box 26369 Christiansted VI 00824-2369

BABAOGLU, REHIM, lawyer; b. Milan, Apr. 16, 1946; came to U.S., 1951; s. Rehim and Tarlan (Nadir) B.; m. Lydia Amelia Zajcew, Nov. 30, 1968; children: Laura, R. Christopher. BA, Rutgers U., Newark, 1969; JD, U. Memphis, 1974. Bar: Tenn. 1974, U.S. Ct. Appeals (6th cir. 1983 and 8th cir. 1980), U.S. Ct. Internat. Trade, U.S. Supreme Ct. 1979. Probation officer Essex County Probation Dept., Newark, 1969-71; ptnr. Crislip, Clausel & Babaoglu, Memphis, 1974-78; assoc. prof. Law Sch. U. Memphis, 1978-80; assoc. Farris, Hancock, Gilman & Hellen, Memphis, 1980-82; ptnr. Byrd, Cobb, Norwood, Lait & Babaoglu, Memphis, 1982—; bd. dirs. Memphis Area Legal Svcs. Inc., 1984—, chmn., 1994—. V.p. Memphis Ballet Co., 1979; treas. Transitional Ctr. for Women, Memphis, 1980-88. Staff sgt. USAR, 1968-75. Mem. ABA, Memphis Bar Assn. (fee dispute com. 1984-88, chmn. lawyer referral svc. com., continuing legal edn. com., bd. dirs. 1990-92), Am. Immigration Lawyers Assn., Amnesty Internat., Greenpeace. Republican. Roman Catholic. Home: 91 Stonewall St Memphis TN 38104-2455 Office: Byrd Cobb Lait & Babaoglu 99 N 3rd St Memphis TN 38103-2306

BABB, ROBERTA J., educational administrator; b. East Chicago, Ill., Jan. 5, 1944; d. Joseph A. and Katherine Phillips; m. Donald L. Babb, July 30, 1966; children: Sasha M., Holly S. BS in Edn., Ind. U., 1966; postgrad., De Paul U. Tchr. East Chicago Pub. Schs., Hammond (Ind.) Pub. Schs.; head tchr. The Lab Sch., Washington; co-founder, dir. Creme de le Creme, Houston. Scholar Ind. U., PTA.

BABCOCK, KEITH MOSS, lawyer; b. Camden, N.J., Aug. 5, 1951; s. William Strong Jr. and Dinah Leslie (Moss) B.; m. Jacquelyn Sue Dickman, Aug. 16, 1975; children: Michael Arthur, Max William. AB, Princeton U., 1973; JD, George Washington U., 1976. Bar: S.C. 1977, U.S. Dist. Ct. S.C. 1977, U.S. Ct. Appeals (4th cir.) 1977, U.S. Supreme Ct. 1980. Staff atty. S.C. Atty. Gen.'s Office, Columbia, 1977-78, state atty., 1978-79, asst. atty. gen., 1979-81; ptnr. Barnes & Austin, Columbia, 1981-82, Austin & Lewis, Columbia, 1982-84, Lewis, Babcock & Hawkins, Columbia, 1984—; mem. civil justice adv. com. for dist. S.C., 1991—. Bd. dirs. Columbia Jewish Community Pre-Sch., 1984, chmn., 1985-86; bd. dirs. Columbia Jewish Community Ctr., 1986-88. Mem. ABA, S.C. Bar Assn. (chmn. prof. resp. com. 1985-86), Richland County Bar Assn., Princeton Alumni Assn. of S.C. (v.p. 1980-86, 88-89, pres. 1990-93, 96—), George Washington U. Law Sch. Alumni Assn. (bd. dirs. 1983-87), Summit Club, Spring Valley Country Club (Columbia). Democrat. Episcopalian. Home: 233 W Springs Rd Columbia SC 29223-6912 Office: Lewis Babcock & Hawkins 1513 Hampton St Columbia SC 29201-2928

BABCOCK, PETER HEARTZ, professional sports executive; b. Bangor, Maine, May 12, 1949; s. Bernard Roland and Jeanne Sargent (Heartz) B.; m. Yolanda Marie Cava; children: Amy, Katherine. BA, Ariz. State U., 1971, MA, 1976. Tchr., coach Glendale Union High Sch. Dist., Phoenix, 1972-80; asst. coach San Diego Clippers, 1980-82, dir. player pers., 1982-83, v.p. basketball ops., 1983-84; dir. player pers. Denver Nuggets, 1984-85, dir. basketball ops., 1985-86, v.p. basketball ops., 1986-87, pres., gen. mgr., 1987-90; exec. v.p., gen. mgr. Atlanta Hawks, 1990—; mem. competition and rules com., dir. Chgo. pre-draft camp NBA, 1985—, mem. steering com., 1995—; mem. USA Basketball Sr. National Team Com., 1995—. Mem. bd. addiction rsch. and treatment svcs. U. Colo. Med. Sch., 1986—, vis. mem. dept. psychiatry, 1989—; mem. bd. Adopt-A-Sch., Denver Pub. Schs., 1985-89; adv. bd. Big Bros., Denver, 1985—, Kops N Kids, 1987—; exec. com. Cmtys. for Drug Free Colo., Denver, 1987—; pres. NET Found./Charitable Fundraising, 1987-90; mem. Mayor's Coun. on Phys. Fitness, 1987-90. Recipient Golden Apple award Atlanta Pub. Schs., 1996; named Outstanding Sports Personality of Ga., Spl. Olympics, 1992. Mem. Denver C. of C. (sports com. 1987—), Atlanta Tip Off Club (mem. nat. adv. bd. 1990—), Yes! Atlanta (bd. dirs. 1990—). Episcopalian. Office: Atlanta Hawks 1 Cnn Ctr NW Ste 405 Atlanta GA 30303-2705

BABER, WILBUR H., JR., lawyer; b. Shelby, N.C., Dec. 18, 1926; s. Wilbur H. and Martha Corinne (Allen) B.; BA, Emory U., 1949; postgrad. U. N.C., 1949-50, U. Houston, 1951-52; JD, Loyola U., New Orleans, 1965. Bar: La. 1965, Tex. 1966. Sole practice, Hallettsville, Tex., 1966—. Trustee Raymond Dickson Found. Served with U.S. Army. Mem. ABA, ASCE, La. Bar Assn., Tex. Bar Assn., La. Engring. Soc., Tex. Surveyors Assn. Methodist. Lodge: Rotary. Office: PO Box 294 Hallettsville TX 77964-0294

BABIN, CLAUDE HUNTER, JR., marketing executive; b. Pensacola, Fla., Aug. 23, 1952; s. Claude Hunter and Barbara Ann Murphy; m. L. Joyce Bradley, Sept. 28, 1988; 1 child, Catherine Joyce. BA, U. Ark., 1975, M. of Pub. Adminstrn., 1979. Acctg. supr. Ark. La. Gas Co., Little Rock, 1975-78, budget analyst, 1978-80; sr. sales rep. Sperry Corp., Little Rock, 1980-84; mktg. rep. Systematics, Inc., Little Rock, 1984; acct. rep. Wang Labs., Little Rock, 1985—, team leader southern region. Moderator local issues TV program, 1983. Bd. dirs. Little Rock Multiple Sclerosis Soc., 1979, Cen. Ark. chpt. March of Dimes, 1980; charter mem. com. for the future Ark. Children's Hosp., 1987—; mem. exec. bd. Quapaw coun. Boy Scouts Am., 1990—. Mem. Ark. Leadership Seminar (founder, bd. dirs. 1980-86), Alpha Kappa Lambda. Democrat. Methodist. Home: 29 Ledgelawn Dr Little Rock AR 72212-2650

BABIN, REGINA-CHAMPAGNE, artist, consultant; b. New Orleans, July 17, 1956; d. Eddie Anthony and Martha Ann (Bergeron) Champagne; m. Terry Lynn Babin, Apr. 25, 1981; children: Jonathan Paul, Michelle Elizabeth. BA, Nicholls State U., 1978, postgrad., 1992-96. Pvt. portraitist Houma, La., 1972—; freelance artist, musician, writer So. Portraits, Plus, Houma, 1981—; bank teller Raceland Bank and Trust, Larose, La., 1979-80; sch. tchr. Lockport (La.) Christian, 1979-80; bank teller Nat. Bank Commerce, Kenner, La., 1980-81; free-lance author Terrebonne Enhancement Commn., Houma, 1985—; artist-in-residence, tour guide Terrebonne Hist. and Cultural Soc., Houma, 1981-85; founding chairperson Houma (La.)-Terrebonne Community Band, 1984-85; gallery dir. Terrebonne Fine Arts Guild, Houma, 1985-86; founding bd. dirs. Houma (La.)-Terrebonne Arts & Humanities Coun., 1985-87. Author, composer: (books with music) Pistoche, 1985, Santa's Prayer, 1991, The J.A.M. Adventure, 1994, (anti-drug packet with music tape) Just Say No To Drugs, 1989 (Nat. Jr. Aux. award 1990, South La. Alcohol and Drug Abuse Coun. 1990). Art/music demonstrater Terrebonne Parish Libr., St. Charles Parish Libr., 1980's; art program designer, instr. Y.M.C.A., Houma, 1981-87; artist, docent musician Southdown Mus., Houma, 1981-87; hurricane aid vol. ARC, Houma, 1986. Recipient Cert. Honor/Svc. award South La. Alcohol and Drug Abuse Coun., Houma, 1989. Mem. ALA, Internat. Reading Assn., Nat. Mus. Women in Arts (charter mem., supporter), Terrebonne Fine Arts Guild,

Terrebonne Hist. and Cultural Soc., Houma Jr. Aux. (life). Republican. Office: So Portraits Plus 107 Willard Ave Houma LA 70360-7554

BABINEAU, ALPHEE ADAM, systems analyst, educator; b. New Bedford, Mass., Dec. 15, 1935; s. Alphee Joseph and Katherine (Praisnar) B. BA in Sociology, U. Conn., 1957; MBA, U. So. Calif., 1967; PhD in Rsch. and Devel. Mgmt., U. Tex., 1973; post doctoral, Air War Coll. of Air U., 1977. Commd. 2d lt. USAF, 1958, advanced through grades to lt. col., various positions with electronic warfare unit, 1958-72, curriculum dir. for edn. and acad. planning, 1972-74, chief edn. and evaluation, 1974-76, dep. dir. acquisition, dir. multiple divs., 1976-78, dir. fin. mgmt., 1978-79, ret., 1979; cons. on electronic warfare systems Alphatech Inc., 1984—; adj. prof. systems analysis, decision making, pub. govt. Troy State U., Fort Walton Beach, Fla., 1984—; adj. prof. U. So. Calif., 1977-79. Bd. dirs. Cmty. Concern Assn., Ft. Walton Beach, 1980; v.p., bd. dirs. Emerald Coast Concert Assn., 1990-94. Fellow Acad. of Mgmt.; mem. Am. Acad. Polit. and Social Scientists, Soc. Logistic Engrs., Am. Arbitration Assn., Beta Gamma Sigma, Sigma Iota Epsilon, Phi KappaPhi, Fort Walton Yacht Club (bd. dirs. 1976-80). Home: 35 Pryor Rd SE Fort Walton Beach FL 32548-5756 Office: Troy State U Beal St Fort Walton Beach FL 32548

BABLER, WAYNE E., retired telephone company executive, lawyer; b. Orangeville, Ill., Dec. 8, 1915; s. Oscar E. and Mary (Bender) B.; m. Mary Blome, Dec. 27, 1940; children: Wayne Elroy Jr., Marilyn Anne Monson, Sally Jane Sperry. BA, Ind. Cen. Coll., 1935; JD, U. Mich., 1938; LLD, Ind. Cen. U., 1966. Bar: Mich. 1938, N.Y. 1949, Mo. 1955, Wis. 1963, U.S. Supreme Ct. 1963. Assoc. Bishop & Bishop, Detroit, 1938-42; ptnr. Bishop & Bishop, 1945-48; atty. AT&T, 1948-55; gen. solicitor Southwestern Bell Tel. Co., St. Louis, 1955-63; v.p., gen. counsel, sec. Southwestern Bell Tel. Co., 1965-80, ret., 1980; v.p., gen. counsel Wis. Tel. Co., Milw., 1963-65. Bd. dirs., chmn. St. Louis Soc. Crippled Children; bd. dirs. St. Louis Symphony Soc. Mem. ABA (chmn. pub. utility sect. 1978-79), Fed. Communications Bar Assn., Wis. Bar Assn., Mo. Bar. Assn., Delray Dunes Country Club, Ocean Club. Home: 11943 Date Palm Dr Boynton Beach FL 33436-5534

BACA, ERNESTO, environmental engineer, consultant; b. Lima, Peru, Mar. 27, 1955; came to U.S., 1974; s. Miguel and Anita (Zapatel) B.; m. Barbara Elizabeth Murray, Feb. 5, 1988. BS, Rensselaer Poly. Inst., 1978; MS, Rice U., 1981. Registered profl. engr., Tex. Rsch. scientist Rice U., Houston, 1980-81; sr. staff engr. Woodward-Clyde Cons., Houston, 1981-85; environ. cons. Bac-Ground, Houston, 1985—. Author Bac-Ground Newsletter, 1989—; aux. editor Nat. Ground Water Assn., 1991—. Mem. Houston Area Next Group. Home and Office: Bac-Ground 3216 Georgetown St Houston TX 77005-2906

BACH, CAROLE ANN, rehabilitation, nursing educator; b. Covington, Ky., Oct. 3, 1944; d. Byron Theodore and Martha Ann (Coleman) B. BSN, Ind. U., Indps., 1966; MSN, Washington U., 1968; PhD, U. Tex. at Austin, 1988. RN, Tex. Staff nurse ICU, neurosurgery Vanderbilt U. Hosp., Nashville, 1966-68; instr. med./surg. dept. Va. Commonwealth U., 1968-72, asst. prof., 1972-79, assoc. prof., 1979-84; asst. prof. U. Mo., Columbia, 1988-95; asst. prof. practice of nursing Vanderbilt U., Tenn., 1995—; assoc. chief nursing rsch. Nashville VA Med. Ctr., 1995; various part-time nursing positions. Contbr. articles to profl. jours. Austin Paralyzed Vets. Am. rsch. grantee, 1986. Mem. ANA, Assn. Rehab. Nurses, U. Tex. Austin Alumni Assn., Sigma Theta Tau Internat. Home: 865 Bellevue Rd Apt E9 Nashville TN 37221

BACH, LINDA WALLINGA, special education educator; b. Rock Rapids, Iowa, Feb. 13, 1953; d. Warren Dale and Beverley (Gardner) Wallinga; m. Daniel Lee Beber, Nov. 2, 1974 (div. Nov. 1980); m. Daniel Louis Bach, June 10, 1981; children: Davin Lane, Thadeous Colin. BEd, U. Nebr., 1975; M Early Childhood Edn., U. S.C., 1989. Substitute tchr. Omaha Pub. Schs., 1975-76; drug mgr. Alan Eber Assocs., Denver, 1976-77; spl. edn. tchr. Winters (Tex.) Elem. Sch., 1978-81; substitute tchr. Dept. Def. Sch., Woodbridge, U.K., 1981-83; spl. edn. tchr. DeLaine Elem. Sch., Sumter, S.C., 1983-85; lead spl. edn. tchr. Oakland Elem. Sch., Sumter, 1985-94; tchr. spl. edn. Oakland Elem. Sch., 1994—; mem. project team to write presch. and kindergarten inclusion program for handicapped children and regular children, 1994; mem. action team for site-based 5 yr. planning Oakland Spl. Olympics Team Coach Elem. Sch., 1994. Chair Oakland Elem. Sch. PTA Haloween Carnival, Sumter, 1989, 90, 92. Basic skills multi-sensory curriculum mini-grantee S.C. Coun. Exceptional Children and Upgrade Systems, 1990, Edn. Improvement Act grantee for improving math. and reading skills, 1995. Mem. NEA, PTA, Coun. Exceptional Children (sec.-treas. 1988-90, membership chmn. 1990-93, pres. elect 1993-94, membership chmn. 1995—). Methodist. Office: Oakland Elem Sch Oakland St Oakland Plantation Sumter SC 29154

BACHMAN, JOHN ANDREW, JR., retired engineer; b. Washington, Apr. 26, 1926; s. John Andrew and Margaret Eleanor (Hauf) B.; m. Mary Irene Dougherty, Dec. 27, 1952; children: Barbara Lee (dec.), Robert J., John D. (dec.), Thomas A., Lisa Marie. B of Aero. Engring., Ga. Inst. Tech., 1951. Jr. engr. Boeing Co., Seattle, 1951-52; aerodynamist Chase Aircraft Co., Trenton, N.J., also Fairchild Aircraft Co., Hagerstown, Md., 1953-54; engring. cons. Washington area, 1955-57; staff engr. Honeywell Inc., Mpls. and Washington, 1957-68; regional mgr. Ground Transp. div. LTV Corp., Washington, 1968-73; with trans. system engring. Mitre Corp., McLean, Va., 1973-77; dept. head RR engring. Unified Industries Inc., Alexandria, Va., 1977-81, Riverside Research Inst., Arlington, Va., 1981-83, 86-89; prin. Bachman Assocs., 1983-92; dir. rail systems engr. Louis Berger Internat. Inc., 1989-91; tech. adv. Seoul-Pusan High-Speed Rail Project, Korea, 1988-90; ret. Author publs. in field. Active Boy Scouts Am., 1938-72. With USNR, 1944-46. Fellow AIAA (assoc., sect. coun. 1976-78); mem. ASME (rail div.), Transp. Research Bd., High Speed Rail Assn. Episcopalian. Home: 6307 Albatross Dr New Bern NC 28560-7143

BACHMANN, BILL, photographer; b. Pitts., Mar. 4, 1946; s. Ernest Edward and Helen May (Himler) B. BS, Roberts Wesleyan Coll., Rochester, N.Y., 1967; MS, SUNY, Brockport, 1971; postgrad., U. London, U. Calif., Berkeley, Rochester Inst. Tech., U. Pitts. Freelance comml. and advt. photographer Miami, Orlando, N.Y.C., 1972—; worked in over 100 countries worldwide; instr. photography Art Inst., Ft. Lauderdale, Fla., 1979-81, Broward C.C., Ft. Lauderdale, 1974-76, Triangle Inst., 1992; guest numerous TV programs, 1978—; lectr. in field. Prin. works include Miami Herald, 1978-80, Fla. Tourism, 1982—, Sheraton Hotels, 1982—, Gen. Mills Restaurants, 1983—, Olive Garden, 1986—, Marriott Hotels, 1992—, Bahamas Tourism, Radisson Hotels, 1986—, Grosvenor Hotels, 1988—, Revlon, 1991—, Harris Corp., 1993—, Sea Escape Cruises, 1988—, Fuji, 1990—, Nickelodeon, 1989—, Merv Griffin's Paradise Island, Bahamas, 1990—, Regal Boats, 1990—, Renaissance Cruises, 1996—, Universal Studios, 1990—, Citibank VISA, 1990—, Delta Airlines, 1991—, Am. Showcase, 1991—, Hilton Hotels Internat., 1992—; dir. TV commls. and videos, 1987—; author: Clicking the Shutters is the Easy Part, 1988, Introspective World, 1996, Welcome Back Berlin, 1990, Shooting Figure Studies, 1990, One Dream Too Many, Images of Women, 1996, Treasures of the Caribbean, 1992; photographer 295-Day Kodak World Photo Tour, 1992-95. Bd. dirs. Big Bros.; active Vols. in Action, 1989—. Named Photographer of Yr. Fla. Peoples Choice Awards, 1987, Photographer of Yr. Asia, 1993; recipient Addy awards, 1976—. Mem. One Club (bd. dirs. 1988—), Sales and Mktg. Execs. (bd. dirs., officer), Am. Soc. Mag. Photographers N.Y., Orlando C. of C. (pres.' club 1983—), Cen. Fla. Photographers Assn. (v.p., bd. dirs. 1983—), Fla. Motion Pictures and TV Guild, Heathrow Club (social dir. 1986—), Rotary. Republican. Methodist. Home and Office: PO Box 950833 Lake Mary FL 32795-0833

BACHMANN, RICHARD ARTHUR, oil company executive; b. Green Bay, Wis., Dec. 6, 1944; s. Richard Arthur and Anita Sidonia (Dohmeyer) B.; children: Richard A., Joseph E., Christina J.; m. Susan Dawn Minney, July 31, 1993. BBA, Wis. State U., 1967; MBA, U. Wis., 1968. Mgr. fgn. fin. Exxon Corp., N.Y.C., 1968-78; v.p., treas. Itel Corp., San Francisco, 1978-81; sr. v.p. fin. and adminstrn., chief fin. officer La. Land and Exploration Co., New Orleans, 1981-85, exec. v.p. fin. and adminstrn., chief fin. officer, 1985—; pres., COO, 1995—; also bd. dir. La. Land and Exploration Co., New Orleans; bd. dirs. Univ. Health Care Sys. Gov. Com. Bd. dirs., mem. exec. com., sustaining membership com. chmn. New Orleans coun. Boy Scouts Am., 1984—, pres., mem. exec. bd., 1988-92, nat. bd. coun. fin. cabinet mem., chmn. supply com., 1990-92; bd. dirs. Audubon Park and Zool. Garden, Audubon Inst.-Aquarium of Ams., Covenant House, 1990—; bd. dirs., chmn. fin. oversight com. met. Arts Fund; bd. govs. Isadore Newman Sch., bd. dirs., 1990—; adv. bd. Summerbridge, 1989—. Office: LA Land & Exploration Co PO Box 60350 909 Poydras St New Orleans LA 70160

BACKELJAUW, PHILIPPE FERDINAND, pediatric endocrinologist, clinical researcher; b. Ghent, Belgium, Apr. 8, 1960; came to U.S., 1987; s. Roger Henri and Fernande Emilienne (De Graeve) B.; m. Ann Marie Griep, Dec. 1, 1985; children: Barynia, Nathalia. BS in Med. Scis., State U. of Ghent, 1982, MD with honors, 1986. Diplomate Am. Bd. Pediatrics, Am. Bd. Pediatric Endocrinology. Resident in pediat. Cleve. Clinic Childrens Hosp., 1988-91; fellow in pediat. endocrinology U. N.C., Chapel Hill, 1991-94, clin. asst. prof., 1994—; pediat. endocrinologist Carolinas Med. Ctr., Charlotte, N.C., 1994—; clin. rschr. U. N.C., 1991—; newborn screening adv. com., State of N.C., Raleigh, 1994—; ethic com. Carolinas Med. Ctr., 1995—. Contbr. articles to profl. jours., chpt. to book. Vol. physician Camp Kudos Diabetes Camp, Charlotte, 1995—. Lt., Med. Svcs. Belgian Army, 1986-87. Mem. Endocrine Soc., , Am. Acad. Pediat. (N.C. chpt.), N.C. Pediat. Soc., Mecklenburg Med. Soc., Lawson Wilkins Pediatric Endocrine Soc. Office: Carolinas Medical Center PO Box 32861 Charlotte NC 28232

BACKMAN, JEAN ADELE, real estate executive; b. N.Y.C., Mar. 3, 1931; d. Seraphin Michael and Helen Elma (Matthews) Millon; m. Frank F. Backman, Sept. 27, 1953; children: Carl Eric, Adam Andrew. BA, Hunter Coll., 1954; degree in real estate mgmt., Am. U., 1980. Sales assoc. Ted Lingo Realty, Potomac, Md., 1970-73; sales mgr. House and Home Real Estate, Potomac, 1973-74; dist. mgr. Panorama Real Estate, Md., 1975-78; v.p., dir. mktg., sales Panorama Real Estate, Tysons Corner, Va., 1978-82; sr. v.p., regional sales mgr. Coldwell Banker Real Estate, Vienna, Va., 1983-88; sr. v.p., regional dir. orgnl. devel. and tng. Coldwell Banker Real Estate, Balt. and Washington, 1988-89; sr. v.p. Coldwell Banker Stevens REaltors, Vienna, Va., 1989-95; mgmt. cons. Coldwell Banker Stevens REaltors, Vienna, 1996—; cons. Reston Pub. Co., Reston, Va., 1979-82, Panorama Condominiums, Tysons Corner, 1979-82. Mem. Realtors for Pol. Action, Falls Church, Va., 1985, profl. stds. com., 1989. Mem. Am. Mgmt. Assn., Nat. Assn. REaltors, Va. Assn. Realtors, No. Va. Bd. Realtors, Va. C. of C., Potomac C. of C., Grad. Realtors Inst., Cert. Residential Brokerage Mgr. Republican. Presbyterian. Office: Coldwell Banker Residential 6858 Old Dominion Dr Mc Lean VA 22101-3832

BACON, JOHN LEE, marine officer; b. Oceanside, Calif., May 22, 1955; s. Franklin Camp and Marjorie Edna (Caldwell) B.; m. Carol Lynn Duncan, Nov. 5, 1977 (div. June 1992); m. Sandra Lois Pierce, July 24, 1993; 1 child, Robyn Dawn. BS, La. State U., 1977; MS, U. So. Calif., 1984; grad., USMC Command & Staff Coll., 1991, Sch. Advanced Warfighting, 1991-92. Commd. USMC, 1977, advanced through grades to lt. col., 1995; forward observer, exec. officer 3d Battalion, 10th Marines, Camp Lejeune, N.C., 1978-81, battery commanding officer, 1985-87; writer sect. OIC Marine Barracks, Washington, 1981-84; co. officer U.S. Naval Acad., Annapolis, Md., 1987-90; target info. officer II Marine Expeditionary Force, Camp Lejeune, 1992-94; tng. officer III Marine Expeditionary Force USMC, Okinawa, 1994-95; inspector, instr. 4th bn. 14th Marines USMC, Bessemer, Ala., 1995—. Decorated Navy Achievement medal, Navy Commendation medal. Home: 5017 Stone Bridge Ln Birmingham AL 35242 Office: I-I Staff 1001 4th Ave SW Bessemer AL 35023-4731

BACON, MARTHA BRANTLEY, small business owner; b. Wrightsville, Ga., Apr. 20, 1938; d. William Riley and Susie Mae (Colston) B.; m. Albert Sidney Bacon, Jr., Aug. 3, 1958; children: Albert Sidney, III, Gregory Riley. BS, Ga. So., Statesboro, 1959; grad., Realtors Inst., 1959; Post Grad., U. Va., Charlottesville, 1978-80, Adrian Hall Interior Design, Savannah, Ga., 1984. Lic. real estate broker, Ga., Va. Tchr. Chatham Bd. Edn., Savannah, Ga., 1961; co-owner mgr. Two Kentucky Fried Chicken Restaurants, Charlottesville, Va., 1967-80; real estate broker Real Estate III, Charlottesville, Va., 1978-83, Landmark Realty, Statesboro, Ga.; tree farmer Johnson Co., Ga., 1980—; mgr., co-owner Restaurant, 1987-92; co-owner Plunderosa Antiques and Collectibles, Statesboro, Ga., 1993—; v.p. Bd. Realtors Statesboro Ga. 1985; regional franchise agt., owner Ice Cream Churn of South Ga. Chmn. Jaycettes Gov. Columbus, Ga., 1962; vol. First Bapt. Ch. Pers. Com., Charlottesville, 1978, U. Va. Hosp., 1980-83; com. mem. Athletic Hall of Fame Ga. So. U.; mem. Ga. Forestry Stewardship, 1991—. Recipient Outstanding Sales award Real Estate III Co. Charlottesville 1980; named Outstanding Jaycette 1961, Jaycettes Gov. Columbus, 1962. Mem. AAUW, Charlottesville Restaurant Assn., Westchester Garden Club, Ga. Restaurant Assn., Ga. So. Univ. Alumni Bd., Ga. So. Symphony Guild, Ga. So. Univ. Athletic Boosters Club, Pilot Club, Evergeen Garden Club, Ga. (v.p.), Optimist (Stateboro essay chmn.),. Baptist. Home: 30 Golf Club Cir Statesboro GA 30458-9163

BACOT, HENRY PARROTT, museum administrator, art historian, consultant; b. Shreveport, La., Dec. 13, 1941; s. Henry Parrott Sr. and Martha Jane (Van Loan) B.; m. Barbara Evelyn SoRelle, Aug. 1, 1970. BA, Baylor U., 1963; MA, SUNY, Oneonta, 1972. Curator Anglo-Am. Art Mus., La. State U., Baton Rouge, 1967—, dir., 1983—; exec. dir. La. State U. Mus. Complex, Baton Rouge, 1983—; prin. H. Parrott Bacot Hist. Interiors, Baton Rouge, 1968—. Author: 19th Century Lighting, 1987, exhbn. catalogues, 1968—; co-author: Crescent City Silver, 1980; contbr. articles to profl. mags. Bd. dirs. Found. Hist. La., Baton Rouge, 1972-73; adv. Am. Friends Attingham, N.Y.C., 1977—; mem. Citizen's Com. Preservation of the Old State Capitol, Baton Rouge, 1977-82; gov.'s mansion commn., 1996—. Recipient Preservation award Found. Hist. La., Baton Rouge, 1978, Rsch. Master award Phi Delta Kappa, Baton Rouge, 1989. Mem. Soc. Archtl. Historians, Decorative Arts Soc. Episcopalian. Home: 1758 Silliman Dr Baton Rouge LA 70808-1359 Office: La State U Mus of Art Memorial Towers Baton Rouge LA 70803

BACOT, MARIE, management consultant, researcher; b. Jackson, Miss., Oct. 2, 1942; d. James Peter and Marie (Moore) B. BA, Millsaps Coll., 1964; MEd, U. New Orleans, 1974, PhD, 1992. Tchr. Houston Ind. Sch. Dist., 1964-68, Jefferson Parish Sch. Bd., Gretna, La., 1968-86; dir. Ednl. Testing Assocs., New Orleans, 1982-86, Marie Bacot Innovation & Creativity Cons., New Orleans, 1987—; presenter Acad. Mgmt., 1989, So. Mgmt. Assn., 1989, Decision Scis. Inst., 1990. Co-author chpt.: Understanding Students with High Incidence Exceptionalities: Categorical and Non-categorical Perspectives, 1991; contbr. articles to profl. jours. Recording sec. The New Orleans City Ballet, 1986-87; publicity chmn. book fair New Orleans Symphony Orch., 1986-87; spl. donor chmn. opera ball New Orleans Opera Assn. 1986-87; soloist, quartet/trio choir mem. Trinity Episcopal Ch., 1981-88. Mem. Ctr. for Rsch. in Applied Creativity, Creative Edn. Found., Acad. Mgmt., Am. Soc. for Quality Control. Republican. Episcopalian. Office: PO Box 15695 New Orleans LA 70175-5695

BADA, HENRIETTA SALVILLA, medical educator; b. The Philippines, July 30, 1945; d. Jose Reyes and Antonia (Salvilla) B.; m. Joel William Ellzey, Dec. 3, 1988. BS, U. Santo Tomas, The Philippines, 1964, MD, 1969. Diplomate Am. Bd. Pediatrics, Am. Bd. Neonatal Medicine. Intern South Side Hosp., Pitts., 1970-71; resident in pediatrics U. Louisville, 1971-73, fellow in neonatal-perinatal medicine, 1973-75; clin. asst. prof. So. Ill. U., Springfield, 1975-76, asst. prof., 1976-80; assoc. prof. U. Tenn., Memphis, 1980-84, prof., 1984—. Mem. AMA, Am. Pediatric Soc., Soc. Pediatric Rsch. Office: U Tenn 853 Jefferson Ave Memphis TN 38103-2807

BADEN, THOMAS JAMES, dermatologist; b. Coral Gables, Fla., Dec. 29, 1951; s. Thomas Benjamin and Helen (Threadgill) B.; m. Sandra Louise Bradley, June 22, 1974; children: Craig, Scott, Michael. AB in Chemistry, Duke U., 1973; MD cum laude, Emory U., 1977. Diplomate Am. Bd. Internal Medicine, Am. Bd. Dermatology. Internal medicine resident N.C. Meml. Hosp., Chapel Hill, 1977-80; dermatology resident N.C. Meml. Hosp., 1983-86; internist Toe Valley Med. Assn., Spruce Pine, N.C., 1980-83; dermatologist West Piedmont Dermatology Assn., Morganton, N.C., 1986—; consulting dermatologist Western Carolina Ctr., Broughton Hosp., Morganton, 1986—; staff dermatologist Grace Hosp., Morganton, 1986—. Contbr. articles to profl. jours. Troop leader Boy Scouts Am.; deacon First Bapt. Ch., Morganton. Fellow ACP, Am. Acad. Dermatology, Am. Soc. Dermatology Surgeons; mem. AMA, Christian Med. Soc. Office: West Piedmont Dermatology 111 Foothills Dr Morganton NC 28655-5152

BADER, CAROL HOPPER, developmental studies educator; b. Navasota, Tex., Sept. 14, 1949; d. Hugh Leo and Virginia Frances (Sibley) Hopper; m. Lawrence Edward Bader, Aug. 4, 1973; 1 child, Joseph Scott. BA, La. Tech. U., 1971; MA, Purdue U., 1973; PhD, La. State U., 1978. Cert. tchr., Ind., La. Title I reading tchr. Ascension Parrish Sch. Bd., Donaldsonville, La., 1973-74; reading tchr., dept. chair Ascension Parrish Sch. Bd., St. Amant, La., 1974-76; cons. Exxon Co., Baton Rouge, La., 1976-78; reading coord. La. State U., Baton Rouge, 1978-87; chair, prof. developmental studies Middle Tenn. State U., Murfreesboro, 1987—; cons. Bader Reading Cons., Baton Rouge, 1976-87; leader scholar Kellogg Inst., Boone, N.C., 1989. Author: Keys to Better College Reading, 1994, Improving Reading Comprehension, 1992; contbr. articles to profl. jours. Scout leader, asst. Cub Scouts, Baton Rouge, Murfreesboro, 1984-87. Mem. Nat. Assn. for Developmental Edn. (chair profl. devel. 1988-90, 95-96, chair election com. 1993-94, chair nat. conf. 1991-92, chair profl. liaison, 1990-91, co-chair membership 1996—), Tenn. Assn. for Developmental Edn. (newsletter editor 1988-90, Outstanding Devel. Educator 1992), La. Assn. for Developmental Edn. (sec. 1985-87, sec. 1982-85, newsletter editor). Methodist. Home: 711 Bradford Pl W Murfreesboro TN 37130-1441 Office: Middle Tenn State Univ PO Box 16 Murfreesboro TN 37132

BADER, LAWSON REECE, university programs director; b. Washington, Aug. 29, 1966; s. William Reece and Jean (McCarty) B.; m. Cynthia Naomi Ellsworth, July 27, 1991; 1 child, Phillip Lawson. BA, Wheaton (Ill.) Coll., 1988; postgrad., Johns Hopkins U. Legis. analyst U.S. Senate Com. on Vets. Affairs, Washington, 1987; policy analyst, rschr. Pierson, Semmes & Finley, Washington, 1988-89; sr. policy analyst SRI Internat., Arlington, Va., 1989-96; dir. fed. programs Ctr. for Market Processes, George Mason U., Fairfax, Va., 1996—. Bd. dirs. Cavalcade Homeowners Assn., Annandale, Va., 1994—; del. Rep. State Conv., 1994. Mem. AAAS, Nat. Security Indsl. Assn. (legis. com. 1990—), Nat. civil War Roundtable Assocs., Va. Hist. Soc. Republican. Presbyterian. Office: George Mason Univ Ctr for Market Processes 4084 University Dr Ste 208 Fairfax VA 22030

BADGER, DAVID PIERSON, journalism educator; b. Evanston, Ill., Nov. 28, 1949; s. Frank Kelly and Margaret Frances (Pierson) B.; m. Sherry Ellen Taggart, May 8, 1982; 1 child, Jeffrey Ross. AB, Duke U., 1971; MS in Journalism, Northwestern U., Evanston, Ill., 1972; PhD, U. Tenn., 1987. Instr. journalism and English Western Ill. U., Macomb, 1972-76; asst. prof. journalism U. Tenn., Nashville, 1976-80; coord. student publs. Mid. Tenn. State U., Murfreesboro, 1980-82, asst., assoc. prof. journalism, 1982—; film critic WPLN Pub. Radio, Nashville, 1977-91; book critic Nashville Tennessean, 1977-93. Editor: At the Water's Edge: Wading Birds of North America, 1993; author: Frogs, 1995. Office: Mid Tenn State U Dept Journalism Murfreesboro TN 37132

BADGER, PHILLIP CHARLES, engineer; b. Lodi, Ohio, Jan. 7, 1948; s. Clifford Russell and Helen Pauline (Fair) B.; m. Cheryl Lynn Baker, Aug. 14, 1971; children: Brian, Scott, Mark. BS in Agrl. Engring., Ohio State U., 1971, MSc in Agrl. Engring., 1973; MBA, Vanderbilt U., 1993. Registered profl. engr., Ohio, Ala. Design engr. Ideanamics, Columbus, Ohio, 1972-74; rsch. assoc., project engr. Ohio State U. and Ohio Agrl. R & D Ctr., Wooster, 1975-78, ext. specialist, rsch. assoc., 1978-79; mgr. waste heat utilization project TVA, Muscle Shoals, Ala., 1979-80; mgr. small scale fuel ethanol project TVA, Muscle Shoals, 1980-82, mgr. fuel ethanol from non-woody cellulose program, 1982-84; mgr. Regional Biomass Energy program U.S. Dept. Energy, Muscle Shoals, 1984—; mem. biomass and waste energy com. Electric Power Rsch. Inst., Palo Alto, Calif., 1990—. Author: Conserving Energy in Ohio Greenhouses, 1979 (Am. Soc. Agr. Engrs. blue ribbon award 1979). Recipient Tech. Achievement award Dept. Energy, 1985, Outstanding Tech. Presentation award WATTec '89, 1989, Cert. of Environ. Achievement, Nat. Awards Coun. for Environ. Sustainability, 1994-96, Industry Leader award Fiber Fuels Inst., 1993. Mem. Am. Soc. Agrl. Engrs. (v.p. energy com. 1990-91, pres. 1991-92), Am. Solar Energy Soc., Internat. Solar Energy Soc., Nat. Mgmt. Assn., Biomass Energy Rsch. Assn. (bd. dirs. 1987—), Coun. of Forest Engring., Coun. for Agrl. Sci. and Tech., Florence Exch. Club (bd. dirs. 1985-86). Home: 104 Creekwood Cir Florence AL 35630-1107 Office: TVA PO Box 1010 Muscle Shoals AL 35662-1010

BAEHR, THEODORE, religious organization administrator, communications executive; b. May 31, 1946; m. Liliana Milani, 1975; children: Thedore Peirce, James Stuart Castiglioni, Robert Gallatin, Evelyn Noelle. Student in French lit. U. Bordeaux and Toulouse, France, 1967; student English lit. Cambridge (Eng.) U., 1967; student German lit. U. Munich, 1968; BA in Comparative Lit. with high distinction, Dartmouth Coll., 1969; JD, NYU, 1972; postgrad. Inst. Theology, Cathedral St. John the Divine, N.Y.C., 1978-80. Rsch. engr. Precision Sci. Co., Chgo., 1964-65; legal cons. firm Dandeub, Fleissig & Assocs., N.Y.C., 1970-71; law student asst. U.S. Atty.'s Office, So. Dist. N.Y., 1971-72; pres. Agape Prodns., N.Y.C., 1972-79, chmn. bd., 1979-82; exec. dir. Good News Comms., Inc., N.Y.C., 1978-80, chmn. bd., 1980—; pres. Episc. Radio-TV Found., Inc., Atlanta, 1981-82, Trinity Concepts, 1982; cons. media; dir. TV Center, CUNY at Bklyn. Coll., 1979-80, 82—; Episc. Communicators, 1981-84; exec. prodr. Ch.'s Presence at World's Fair, Knoxville, Tenn., 1982; dir. Am. Theater Actors, Episc. Comms. Editor, Commentator, NYU Law Sch. newspaper, 1969-72, Contemporary Drug Problems, 1971-72, Atlanta Area Christian News; creator, coord. Communicate Workshops, 1979; creator, writer, editor Episc. Ch. Video Resource Guide and Episcopal Video/TV Newsletter, 1979; prodr., dir., writer various TV and radio programs including Movieguide, Joy of Music, Perspectives, PBS, 1981-82, Religionwise on WGST, CBS, 1981— (Religion in Media award), Searching, 1978-80, others; editor, writer various books, including TV and Reality, Asking the Right Questions, Tangled Christian Communications, Getting the Word Out (Wilbur award), Movie and Video Guide for Christian Families (Religion in Media award), Hollywood's Reel of Fortune, 1991; dir. Runaways (Chgo. Intercom Gold Plaque and Religion in Media award 1989); prodr. In Their Own Words, Was It Love (Religion in Media award). V.p. Ctr. for TV in Humanities, 1982; chmn. bd. Christian Film & TV Commn., 1990—; bd. dirs. Celebrate Life, Christian Conciliation Svc., Dorsey Theatre, SUP, Inc., Coalition on Revival, Habitat for Humanity; mem steering com. Theol. Summit Conf. Mem. Nat. Assn. TV Arts and Scis., Nat. Religious Broadcasters (dir., chmn. TV com.), Bishop in Ind. Christian Chs. Internat., Seawanhaka Corinthian Yacht Club, Nat. Press Club.

BAER, THOMAS STRICKLAND, environmental company executive; b. Huntington, W.Va., May 24, 1942; s. Peter Harrison and Helen Virginia (Strickland) B.; m. Margaret Teresa Durkin, Nov. 21, 1964; children: Kathleen Nancy Baer Stovall, Thomas Holman (dec.). BS in Naval Sci., U.S. Naval Acad., 1964; MS in Nuclear Engring., U. Cin., 1971, PhD in Nuclear Engring., 1973; MA in Nat. Security and Strategic Studies, U.S. Naval War Coll., 1991. Sta. engr. Met. Edison Co., Middletown, Pa., 1973-74; v.p., gen. mgr. Protective Packaging, Inc., Louisville, 1974-76; v.p. U.S. Ecology Inc., Louisville, 1977-81, sr. v.p., dir., 1986-91; project mgr. Bechtel Nat. Inc., Oak Ridge, Tenn., 1981-86; v.p. PAI Corp., Oak Ridge, 1991-93; dir. ops. Automated Scis. Group, Inc., Oak Ridge, 1994-96; v.p. safety and regulatory Nuclear Fuel Svcs., Inc., Erwin, Tenn., 1996—. V.p. Great Smoky Mountain Coun. Boy Scouts Am., Knoxville, 1991-95; bd. dirs. Security on Campus, Inc., Gulph Mills, Pa., 1990—; chmn. legis. com. East Tenn. Victim's Rights Task Force, 1991—. Lt. USN, 1964-69, Vietnam; capt. USNR, 1990-91. Roman Catholic. Home: 621 Summit Lake Ct Knoxville TN 37922-3152 Office: Nuclear Fuel Svds Inc 1205 Banner Hill Rd Erwin TN 37830-6927

BAER, WILLIAM HAROLD, business executive; b. Eatontown, N.J., Dec. 6, 1947; s. Irving and Martha Ann (Ruddy) B.; BS in Bus. Adminstrn., Waynesburg Coll., 1971. Pres., Baldinos, Inc., Fayetteville, N.C., 1976—, Rondout Country Club, Ltd., Accord, N.Y., 1979-81, W.H.B. Cons., Accord, 1979-85, Baldinos Giant Jersey Subs, Inc., Hinesville, Ga., 1982—, chmn., chief exec. officer, 1982—; with Baldinos Mgmt. Group, Ltd.,

Augusta, Ga., 1987—; pres. Baldinos of Atlanta, 1991; pres. Leisure Life Inc., Tinton Falls, N.J., 1980-87, Baldinos of Savannah, 1989—, Pro Active Enterprises, Inc., Savannah, Ga., 1986-89, bd. dirs., 1989; bd. dirs. Triumph Steel, Inc., Birmingham, Ala., 1992, vice chmn. Chmn. campaign March of Dimes, Liberty County, 1986-87; dir. Coastal Ga. March of Dimes, Savannah, 1986-92. Served to 1st lt. USMC, 1971-75. Recipient Navy Achievement medal. Mem. Forward Atlanta, 1992—, Atlanta Sports Coun., 1992—. Mem. Hinvesville-Liberty County, Ga. C. of C. (bd. dirs. 1989-91), Atlanta C. of C., 1992—. Coastal Racquet Club (pres. 1986-87, treas.-sec. Hinesville chpt. 1987—). Home: 708 Robinson Farms Dr Marietta GA 30068-3277 Office: 760 Elaine St Hinesville GA 31313-4825

BAERGA-VAQUER, RAFAEL ANTONIO, insurance agent; b. Ponce, P.R., Oct. 16, 1948; s. Rafael Baerga and Isabel Vaquer; m. Carmen Ortiz-Abreu, Dec. 27, 1969; children: Abel, Amanda, Luis, Vanesa, Maria-Victoria. BA in Econs., U. P.R., 1969. Registered rep., CLU, ChFC. Instr. econs. CUNY-Lehman Coll., N.Y.C., 1970-74; life ins. agt. Equitable Life Assurance Soc. of U.S., Ponce and San Juan, P.R., 1977—; dist. mgr. Equitable Life Assurance Soc. of U.S., Ponce, 1979-82, San Juan, 1982-93. Mem. Fondo de Mejoramiento, 1986—. Mem. Am. Soc. CLU & ChFC (pres. 1993-94). Office: Ste 1700 255 Ponce de Leon Ave Hato Rey PR 00917

BAGBY, DANIEL GORDON, religious studies educator, clergyman; b. Porto Alegre, Brazil, May 30, 1941; (parents Am. citizens); s. Albert Ian and Thelma (Frith) B.; m. Janet Glee Pitman, June 12, 1965; children: Douglas Ian, Meredith Bryn. BA, Baylor U., 1962, MS, 1964; B.D., So. Bapt. Theol. Sem., 1967, PhD, 1973. Ordained to ministry Bapt. Ch., 1968. Chaplain Louisville Detention Ctr., 1964-68; assoc. pastor Ravensworth Bapt. Ch., Annandale, Va., 1968-71; chaplain Ky. Correctional Instn. for Women, Pewee Valley, 1971-74; marriage and family counselor Jeffersonville Personal Counseling Ctr., Clarksville, Ind., 1971-74; instr. psychology of religion So. Bapt. Theol. Sem., Lousiville, 1972-74, state alumni pres., 1975-76; pastor Calvary Bapt. Ch., West Lafayette, Ind., 1973-79, Seventh & James Bapt. Ch., Waco, Tex., 1979-94; prof. pastoral care, marriage and family counseling Bapt. Theol. Sem., Richmond, Va., 1994—; mem. adv. bd. clin. pastoral edn. dept. Med. Coll. Va. Author: Understanding Anger in the Church, Transition and Newness, Before You Marry, The Church: The Power to Help and to Hurt; contbr. articles to religious publs. Pres. Tippecanoe County Ministerial Assn., Waco Conf. Christians and Jews; mem. McLennan County Youth Collaboration Bd., Family Abuse Ctr. Bd.; trustee Midwestern Bapt. Theol. Sem., Kansas City, Mo., Baylor U., 1980-88; active Ind. InterReligious Commn. on Human Equality; chmn. bd. dirs. pres. McLennan County United Way; mem. Food and Emergency Bd., McLennan County. Recipient Disting. Alumnus Men and Women of Merit award. Mem. Am. Assn. Marriage and Family Counselors (clin.), Am. Assn. of Pastoral Counselors, Omicron Delta Kappa (Men of Merit award). Home: 12821 Church Rd Richmond VA 23233-7649 Office: 1204 Palmyra Ave # 9157 Richmond VA 23227-4435

BAGBY, WILLIAM RARDIN, lawyer; b. Grayson, Ky., Feb. 19, 1910; s. John Albert and Nano A. (Rardin) B.; m. Mary Carpenter, Sept. 3, 1939; 1 child, John Robert; m. Elizabeth Hinkel, Nov. 22, 1975. AB, Cornell U., 1933; JD, U. Mich., 1936; postgrad., Northwestern U., 1946-47. Bar: Ky. 1937, Ohio 1952, U.S. Tax Ct. 1948, U.S. Supreme Ct. 1950, U.S. Ct. Appeals (6th cir.) 1952. Pvt. practice Grayson, 1937-43; atty., judge City of Grayson, 1939-43; counsel Treasury Dept., Chgo., Cleve. and Cin., 1946-54; pvt. practice Lexington, Ky., 1954—; prof. U. Ky., 1956-57; gen. counsel Headley-Whitney Mus., 1974-84; mem. Bd. of Adjustment, Lexington-Urban County City Govt., 1965—, chmn. 1981—. Trustee Bagby Found. Musical Arts, N.Y.C., 1963-74; trustee, gen. counsel McDowell Cancer Found., 1979-91, pres., 1988-91. Lt. USN, 1943-46. Mem. ABA (hon. life), Am. Judicature Soc., Ky. Bar Assn. (hon. life), Fayette County Bar Assn., Keeneland Club, Lexington Club, U. Ky. Faculty Club, Rotary. Democrat. Home: 228 Market St Lexington KY 40507-1030 Office: 1107 1st National Bldg Lexington KY 40507

BAGGETT, ALICE DIANE, critical care nurse; b. Louisville, Dec. 27, 1964; d. Stanley Wayne and Pauline (Stearman) B. BSN cum laude, Spalding U., Louisville, 1988. Nurses aide Wesley Manor-Meth. Retirement Homes, Louisville, 1983-88, medication technician; staff nurse, charge nurse TCU, ICU nurse, relief house supr. Humana Hosp.-Suburban, Louisville, 1988—. Home: 177 Wise Ct Louisville KY 40229-3545

BAGGETT, DONNIS GENE, journalist, editor; b. Livingston, Tex., July 16, 1952; s. Sam Jr. and Mavis (Baxley) B.; m. Jean Shaddix, May 18, 1974; children: Valerie Shaddix, David Shaddix. BA, Stephen F. Austin State U., 1973. Reporter, photographer East Tex. Eye, Livingston, Tex., 1973-74, co-editor, 1974; reporter Longview (Tex.) Morning Jour., 1974-75, East Tex. editor, 1975-76; reporter The Dallas Morning News, 1976, asst. night city editor, 1977, asst. state editor, 1977-82, state editor, 1982-94, asst. mng. editor, 1994-95; pub., editor The Eagle, Bryan-College Station, Tex., 1996—. Recipient Sweepstakes award Tex. Press Assn., 1973, News and Feature award AP, 1975, News and Feature award UPI, 1976, Spot News, AP, 1993. Mem. Press Club of Dallas (pres. 1992-94, treas. 1991-92, sec. 1990-91, Katie award for spot news reporting 1983, Katie award for beat reporting 1978). Methodist.

BAGGETT BOOZER, LINDA DIANNE, lawyer; b. Pascagoula, Miss., Jan. 22, 1956; d. Grady Milton and Ruby Constance (Hunter) Baggett; m. John Singleton Boozer, June 14, 1986; children: Constance Elizabeth, Zachary Singleton. Student, Universidad de Filosofia y Letras, Valencia, Spain, 1976; BA in Spanish and Secondary Edn. with highest honors, U. So. Miss., 1978; JD cum laude, U. Miss., 1981. Bar: Miss. 1981, U.S. Dist. Ct. (no. and so. dists. Miss. 1981, U.S. Ct. Appeals (5th cir. 1982), U.S. Ct. Appeals (11th cir.) 1991, U.S. Ct. Appeals (fed. cir.) 1996. Assoc. Megehee, Brown, Williams & Mestayer, Pascagoula, 1981-84; atty. Ingalls Shipbuilding Inc., subs. Litton Industries Inc., Pascagoula and Woodland Hills, Calif., 1984—. Mem. Miss. div. Am. Cancer Soc., pres. Jackson County Unit, 1983-85; participant 1987 Leadership Miss. Program Miss. Econ. Council. Named one of Outstanding Young Women Am., 1983, 84, Outstanding Young Careerist Pascagoula Bus. and Profl. Women's Club, 1985. Mem. ABA, Miss. Bar Assn., Jackson County Bar Assn. (treas. 1984-85, sec. 1985-86), Jackson County Young Lawyers Assn. (treas. 1982-83), Leadership Miss. Alumni Assn., U. Southern Miss. Alumni Assn., Phi Kappa Phi, Phi Delta Phi, Omicron Delta Kappa (sec./treas.), Phi Delta Rho, Pi Tau Chi (pres.), Cwens/Lambda Sigma (pres.), Alpha Lambda Delta, Kappa Delta Pi, Chi Omega (corresponding sec., scholarship award). Baptist. Home: 3019 Northwood Ave Pascagoula MS 39567-7535 Office: Ingalls Shipbldg Inc PO Box 149 Pascagoula MS 39568-0149

BAGLEY, JAMES ROBERT, freelance writer; b. Valdosta, Ga., Dec. 7, 1946; s. Rayford Virdoe and Frances (Cowart) B.; m. Carol Ann Blackman, Dec. 17, 1972; children: James Brennan, Kimberly Ann. BS, Valdosta State U., 1975. Numerous positions including dep. sheriff, probation officer, 1975-85; clerical specialist Fla. Hwy. Safety Dept., Tallahassee, 1985-86; freelance writer, Tallahassee, 1986-89; security officer Mus. Fla. History, Tallahassee, 1989-93; cons. State Bd. Adminstrn., Tallahassee, 1994-95; freelance writer. Author: (poetry) The Star, 1977, The Alchemist, 1980, Soul-Speak from the Matrix, 1985, I Am No River Like Yesterday, 1995, (novel) Lustmords of Bithinsinia, 1995. With U.S. Army, 1966-69, Vietnam. Recipient cert. of appreciation Lions Club, Valdosta, 1977. Mem. Charlie Co. Assn., Author's Guild, Poetry Soc. Am. Home and Office: 2317 Limerick Dr Tallahassee FL 32308

BAGLEY, PHILIP JOSEPH, III, lawyer; b. Richmond, Va., Nov. 24, 1941; s. Philip Joseph Jr. and Louise (Bourne) B.; m. Sally Ann Twedell, Aug. 18, 1967; children: Elizabeth Bourne Faulkner, Anne Tunstall Twedell. BA, U. Richmond, 1963; LLB, U. Va., 1966. Bar: Va. 1966, U.S. Supreme Ct. 1972. Assoc. Mays & Valentine, Richmond, 1970-74, ptnr., 1974—; chmn. state adv. coun. Nat. Legal Svcs. Corp., Richmond, 1977-79; bd. dirs. Legal Svc. Corp. Va., 1978-86. Legal advisor Jr. League Richmond, 1977—; bd. dirs. Richmond Symphony, 1986—, pres. 1992-94; bd. dirs. Richmond Eye and Ear Hosp., 1988—, pres. 1991—; trustee Benedictine H.S., 1994—. Fellow Am. Bar Found., Va. Bar Found.; mem. ABA (lectr. real estate financing com. 1984, title ins. com. 1987, leasing 1992, coun. real property, probate and trust law sect. 1993—), Am. Coll. Real Estate Lawyers (bd. govs. 1988—, treas. 1991-93, v.p. 1993-94, pres. 1995—), Anglo-Am. Real Property Inst. (bd. govs. 1995—), Coun. for Am.'s 1st Freedom (bd. govs. 1994—), Internat. Coun. Shopping Ctrs. (law conf. com.), Va. Bar Assn., Richmond Bar Assn., Carpenter Ctr. (bd. dirs. 1995), Carpenter Ctr. Found. (bd. dirs. 1995—), Country Club Va., Commonwealth Club, Order of Coif, Phi Beta Kappa, Omicron Delta Kappa. Roman Catholic. Office: Mays & Valentine 1111 E Main St Richmond VA 23219-3500

BAGWELL, GERALD E., minister; b. Buford, Ga., Feb. 20, 1936; s. Cecil E. and Ola (Roberts) B.; m. Betty Tanner, Sept. 2, 1955; children: Gregory Charles, Jeffery Gerald, Philip Edward. BS, Piedmont Coll., Demorest, Ga., 1963; MDiv, Southeastern Bapt. Theol. Sem., Wake Forest, N.C., 1966; ThM, Luther Rice Sem., Jacksonville, Fla., 1968, ThD, 1969. Ordained to ministry So. Bapt. Conv., 1961. Pastor Mountain Park 1st Bapt. Ch., Stone Mountain, Ga., 1970-77, 1st Bapt. Ch., Lakeland, Fla., 1978-86, Bethany Bapt. Ch., Snellville, Ga., 1986-92, Celebration Bapt. Worship Ctr., Lakeland, Fla., 1992—; pres. Gwinnett Metro Pastor's Conf., Lawrenceville, Ga., 1970-71; tchr. nationwide seminar on ch. growth, Republic of Korea, 1978; chmn. evangelism South Fla. Bapt. Assn., Lakeland, 1979-80; trustee Fla. Bapt. Theol. Coll., Graceville, 1984-86; speaker Someone Cares program Sta. WONN, Lakeland, 1982-85. Columnist Lakeland Ledger, 1984-86, Lakeland Consumer Shopping News, 1985. Home: 6143 Mountain Lake Dr Lakeland FL 33813

BAGWELL, STEVEN CHARLES, association executive; b. Conroe, Tex., Jan. 10, 1965; s. Billy Charles Bagwell and Martha Jane (Inglet) Mann; m. Jeanetta E. Horne, Aug. 31, 1991. BA, Baylor U., 1987. Sr. legis. corr. The Hon. Phil Gramm, Washington, 1987-88; legis. asst. The Hon. Joe Barton, Washington, 1988-89; mgr. legis. affairs Water Environment Fedn., Alexandria, Va., 1989—. Contbr. articles to profl. jours. Vol. Tom Davis for Congress, Fairfax, 1994; deacon Columbia Bapt. Ch., Falls Church, Va., 1995. Mem. Am. Soc. Assn. Execs. Baptist. Home: 8811 Cromwell Dr Springfield VA 22151 Office: Water Environment Fedn 601 Wythe St Alexandria VA 22314

BAHADUE, GEORGE PAUL, general, family physician; b. Havana, Cuba, June 29, 1954; came to U.S., 1959; s. Teodosio and Carmen (Chabali) B.; m. Lori Dee Stampler, June 11, 1983; children: Felicia Lynn, Suria, George Paul Jr. BS cum laude, U. Miami, Coral Gables, Fla., 1978; DO, Coll. Osteo. Medicine, Kirksville, Mo., 1982. Diplomate Nat. Bd. Examiners, Nat. Bd. Examiners for Osteo. Physicians and Surgeons. Am. Osteo. Assn. rotating intern Southeastern Med. Ctr., North Miami Beach, Fla., 1982-83, resident in internal medicine, 1984; pvt. practice gen. and family medicine North Miami Beach, 1984-92; with pediatric emergency room Parkway Regional Med. Ctr., North Miami Beach, 1993-94; gen. medicine and pediatrics Town & Country Med. Ctr., Miami, 1993—; with Internat. Health Svcs., North Miami Beach, 1994—, Camillus Health Concern, Miami, 1996—; asst. clin. prof. Southeastern U. Coll. Osteo. Medicine, North Miami Beach, 1984—; active dept. family medicine Parkway Hosp., North Miami Beach, 1990—; preceptor Coll. Osteo. Medicine of te Pacific, 1986. Del. annual conv. Student Osteo. Med. Assn., 1980; mem. Republican Senatorial Inner Circle, Washington, 1990; charter mem. U.S. Com. for the Battle of Normandy Mus., Washington, 1990; mem. Republican Presdl. Task Force, Washington, 1990 (Recognition award 1990), Psi Chi; vol. svc. to homeless Family Migrant Pediatric Clinic/Camillus Health Concern, 1994, also to victims of hurricane Andrew, 1993. Honors scholar and Jane P. Simmons Sci. scholar U. Miami, 1976-78; recipient Honors award City of North Miami Beach, 1984-90. Mem. Soc. Critical Care Medicine, Dade County Med. Assn., Delta Theta Mu, Alpha Epsilon Delta (v.p. 1976-77, del. nat. conv. Ala. 1977). Republican. Roman Catholic. Home: 19665 E Saint Andrews Dr Hialeah FL 33015 Office: Camillus Health Concern 726 NE 1st Ave Miami FL 33132-1808

BAHNER, CARL TABB, retired chemistry educator, researcher; b. Conway, Ark., July 14, 1908; s. Gustavus Lonsford and Augusta Thomas (Moore) B.; m. Mary Catharine Garrott, Sept. 17, 1931; children: Thomas Maxfield, Mary Catharine, Frances Jane. BA, Hendrix Coll., Conway, 1927; MS, U. Chgo., 1928; ThM, So. Bapt. Theol. Sem., Louisville, 1931; PhD, Columbia U., 1937. Head physics dept. Union U., Jackson, Tenn., 1936-37; head chemistry dept. Carson-Newman Coll., Jefferson City, Tenn., 1937-67, coord. rsch., 1967-73; assoc. prof. Walters State Community Coll., Morristown, Tenn., 1973-78; prof. chemistry Bluefield (Va.) Coll., 1978-91, ret., 1991; rsch. chemist Roswell Park Meml. Inst. Buffalo, summer 1956, Chester Beatty Rsch. Inst., London, summer 1957; cons. TVA, 1941-46, Oak Ridge (Tenn.) Nat. Labs., 1948-79, Oak Ridge Inst. Nuclear Studies, 1950-56; part-time researcher in field, 1993—. Contbr. over 75 articles to sci. jours.; patentee in field. Chmn. Jefferson City Charter Revision Com. Recipient award for excellence in teaching Mfg. Chemists Assn., 1967, Disting. Alumnus award Hendrix Coll., 1969, Algernon Sydney Sullivan award Carson-Newman Coll., 1969, So. Chemist award 1977, Disting. Svc. award Walters State Community Coll., 1978; numerous rsch. grants Nat. Cancer Inst., Damon Runyon Fund, Am. Cancer Soc., Rsch. Corp., Med. Rsch. Found., also others. Fellow AAAS, Tenn. Acad. Sci. (pres. 1951), Am. Inst. Chemists, Tenn. Inst. Chemists (pres. 1972); mem. Am. Assn. Cancer Rsch., Am. Chem. Soc. (chmn. East Tenn. sect. 1951, award Fla. sect. 1964, Shirley award East Tenn. sect. 1990), Sigma Xi, Phi Lambda Upsilon, Sigma Pi Sigma, Alpha Chi. Baptist. Home: 424 Buckingham Dr Jefferson City TN 37760

BAHR, CARMAN BLOEDOW, internist; b. Middletown, Ohio, Mar. 24, 1931; d. Edwin Louis and Berneice Mae (Bacon) Bloedow; m. Walter Julien Bahr, Aug. 28, 1968 (dec. Sept. 1971). BA cum laude, Miami U., Oxford, Ohio, 1952; MD, Ohio State U., 1956. Cert. diabetes educator, 1992. Intern St. Luke's Hosp., Chgo., 1956-57; resident U. Okla. Health Sci. Ctr., 1971; assoc. prof. medicine Okla. City VA-U. Okla. Health Sci. Ctr., 1971-93, prof. emeritus, 1993—. Fellow ACP; mem. AMA (Physician's Recognition award 1976, 79, 82, 85, 88, 91, 93), Am. Diabetes Assn. (chpt. pres. 1989, Robert Endress award 1985), Am. Assn. Diabetes Educators, Western Okla. Diabetes Educators, Am. Med. Women's Assn. Home: 5609 N Everest Ave Oklahoma City OK 73111-6729 Office: VA Med Ctr 921 NE 13th St Oklahoma City OK 73104-5007

BAICY, JANET KAREN, nursing executive; b. Tulsa, Oct. 2, 1944; d. David Alexander Sr. and Helen Marie (Oliver) Simons; John Williamson Baicy, Jan. 20, 1968 (div. 1974); 1 child, Eric Simons. BSN, U. Md., 1967; M in Nursing, UCLA, 1971. Staff nurse Univ. Hosp., Balt., 1967-68; staff/triage nurse emergency dept. Children's Hosp., Hollywood, Calif., 1968-69; writer, rschr. Career Devel. Corp., Glendale, Calif., 1970-72; asst. clin. dir. Deer Park (U. Calif.-San Diego Dept. Psychiatry Inpatient Narcotic Treatment Program, 1971-72; instr. nursing Idaho State U., Boise, 1972-74; coord. activity therapies Dept. Health and Welfare, Boise, 1975; assoc. prof. nursing program Boise State U., 1975-79; clin. specialist VA Med. Ctr., Boise, 1979, nursing supr., 1979-80, assoc. chief nursing svc. for edn., 1981-84, staff nurse, 1984-86; dir. nursing Intermountain Hosp., Boise, 1986-87; head nurse neuropsychiat. and chem. dependency unit West Valley Med. Ctr., Caldwell, Idaho, 1987-89, chief nursing officer, 1989-93; assoc. adminstr. patient care svcs. Coronado Hosp., Pampa, Tex., 1993-94, chief nursing officer, 1993-94; assoc. adminstr. patient care svcs. McMinneville Cmty. Hosp., Oreg., 1993—; nursing cons. Bd. of Nurse Examiners, Austin, Tex., 1995-96; chief of staff, patient care officer Columbus Bayview Psychiat. Hosp., Corpus Christi, Tex., 1996—; mem. adj. faculty Boise State U., 1991-93, cons., 1994—. Active United Meth. Ch., Caldwell, Idaho, Speakers' Bur., Paint the Town, 1991-92. Mem. ANA, AAUW, Tex. Nurses Assn., Tex. Orgn. Nurse Execs., Idaho Orgn. Nurse Execs., Alpha Phi (Delta Zeta chpt.), Sigma Theta Tau. Democrat. Methodist. Office: Bayview Hosp 6226 Saratoga Blvd Corpus Christi TX 78414

BAIG, EJAZ AHMED, environmental engineer; b. Karachi, Sind, Pakistan, Aug. 1, 1950; came to the U.S., 1982; s. Nazir Ahmed; m. Zubida Khatoon Khan, June 23, 1980; children: Salman, Sania. BS in Mech. Engring., U. Engring. and Tech., Lahore, Pakistan, 1973; MS in Mech. Engring., U. Houston, 1985. Registered profl. engr., Tex., Pakistan. Trainee engr., jr. mech. engr. Nat. Constrn. Co., Islamabad, Pakistan, 1973-74; jr. mech. engr., mech. engr. Tehran (Iran) Joncob Tech. and Constrn. Co., 1975-79; sr. mech. and project engr. Nat. Constrn. Co., Islamabad, 1979-82; engring. asst. III Tex. Natural Resource Conservation Commn., Ft. Worth, 1985-87; engring. specialist II Tex. Air Control Bd., Ft. Worth, 1987-88, engr. III, 1988-93; engring. team leader Tex. Natural Resource Conservation Commn., Ft. Worth, 1993—. Mem. Air & Waste Mgmt. Assn.

BAILEY, AMOS PURNELL, clergyman, syndicated columnist; b. Grotons, Va., May 2, 1918; s. Louis Willian and Evelyn (Charnock) B.; m. Ruth Martin Hill, Aug. 22, 1942 (dec. 1992); children: Eleanor Carol Bailey Harriman, Anne Ruth Bailey Page, Joyce Elizabeth Bailey Richardson, Jeanne Bailey Dodge-Allen; m. Betty Lou Sheffield, Mar. 5, 1994. BA, Randolph-Macon Coll., 1942, DD, 1956; BD, Duke U., 1948; ThM, Union Theol. Sem., 1957; postgrad., Ecumenical Inst., Jerusalem, 1977. Ordained to ministry United Meth. Ch., 1942; pastor Emporia, Va., 1938, Beulah UMC Ch., Richmond, Va., 1938-43, New Kent circuit, 1943-44, Grace United Meth. Ch., Norfolk, 1948-50, Oak Grove United Meth. Ch., Newport News, Va., 1950-54, Centenary Ch., Richmond, 1954-61; supt. Richmond dist. United Meth. Ch., 1961-67; sr. minister Reveille Ch., Richmond, 1967-70; assoc. gen. sec., div. chaplains Bd. Higher Edn. and Ministry United Meth. Ch., Washington, 1970-79; v.p. Nat. Meth. Found., 1979-82; interim minister Herndon Ch., 1985-86; pres., CEO Nat. Temple Ministries, Inc., Arlington, Va., 1982—; pres. S.E.J. and S.C.U. Comms., 1968-76; dir. Reeves-Parvin Co., 1978-85; v.p. Va. Conf. Bd. Missions, 1955-61, Meth. Commn. Town and Country Work, 1956-67; mem. Meth. Commn. on Higher Edn., 1960-70, Meth. Interbd. Coun., 1960-70; del. Southeastern Jurisdictional Conf., 1964, 68, Gen. Conf., 1964, 66, 68, 70, World Meth. Conf., London, 1966, Denver, 1970, Dublin, 1976, Rio de Janeiro, 1996; exec. com. Congress, 1987-88; fin. com. Nat. Ch. Growth Rsch. Ctr., 1986-89; frequent chaplain U.S. Senate, U.S. Ho. of Reps., Va. Gen. Assembly; mem. coun., exec. com., pres. comms. com. Southeastern Jurisdiction, 1968-76; pres. Joint Comms. Com., 1968-76; vice chmn. Ministry to Svc. Pers. in East Asia, 1972-79; mem. Commn. on Interpretation, Va. Conf. Bd. Ordained Ministry, 1974-82; participant Ednl. Study Mission to Eng., 1988. Writer syndicated column Daily Bread, 1945— (50th Anniversary award 1995), syndicated radio devotional, 1945-69; condr. weekly radio counseling program The Night Pastor, 1955-69, Sunshine and Shadows, 1967-70; contbr. articles to profl. jours. Mem. exec. com. Va. Conf. Bd. Edn., 1968-72; mem. World Meth. Coun., Va. Commn. Aging; pres. adv. bd. Richmond Welfare Dept., 1956-68, Va. Conf. Bd. Ministry, Richmond Pub. Assistance Com., Richmond Coun. Alcoholism, Citizen Adv. Bd. Duke U. Comprehensive Cancer Ctr., 1995—; group chmn. industry divsn. Richmond United Givers Fund, 1961; chmn. chaplains adv. coun. VA, Washington; bd. mgrs. Richmond YMCA, 1961-69; bd. dirs. Va. Meth. Advisers; trustee Randolph-Macon Coll., 1960-82, trustee emeritus, 1986; bd. visitors Duke Div. Sch., 1964-70; trustee So. Sem., 1961-76. With Chaplains Corps AUS, 1945-47. Mem. DAV (life), Meth. Hist. Soc., Duke Div. Alumni Assn. (pres.). Club: Kiwanis. Home: 7815 Falstaff Rd Mc Lean VA 22102-2724 Office: 1835 N Nash St Arlington VA 22209-1519

BAILEY, BRIDGET, lawyer; b. Chgo., May 7, 1963; d. Marvin Oscar and Florence Veronica (Kimbrough) B. BA, Grambling State U., 1985, MPA, 1987; JD, U. Tenn., 1994. Bar: Tenn. 1994. Intern WLS Radio, Chgo., 1985; intern talk show host Centel Cable, Matteson, Ill., 1985; TV model, spokesperson Designer Mart, Chgo., 1986-88; computer programmer AMCCOM, Rock Island, Ill., 1987-88; computer programmer/analyst U.S. Railroad Retirement Co., Chgo., 1988-91; law clk. Lewis, King, Krieg & Waldrop, Knoxville, Tenn., 1993-94; assoc. Lewis, King, Krieg, Waldrop & Catron, Knoxville, Tenn., 1994—; mem. continuing legal edn. com., H.S. mock trial competition com., U. Tenn. Coll. of Law mentor program; exec. bd. profl. responsibility Supreme Ct. Tenn. Active Big Bros./Big Sisters, 1983-84. Recipient Cmty. Svc. award YWCA, 1995. Mem. Knoxville Bar Assn., Women and Minorities Com., Barristers (exec. bd. 1994—), Hamilton Burnett Am. Inn of Ct. (exec. bd. dirs.), Knoxville Quarterback Club, Black Achievers, Alpha Kappa Alpha, Alpha Kappa Mu. Democrat. Office: Lewis King Krieg & Waldrop PO Box 2425 Knoxville TN 37901

BAILEY, CAROLYN SUE DODSON, home economics educator, apparel designer; b. Doyle, Tenn., Mar. 11, 1946; d. William Mitchell and Mattie Enzie (Bryant) Dodson; m. David William Bailey, June 21, 1980; 1 child, Matthew Sewell. BS, Middle Tenn. State U., 1967; MS, U. Tenn., 1971; PHD, U. Wis., 1980. Cert. family and consumer scientist, Am. Assn. Family and Consumer Scis. Home economist Agrl. Ext. Svc., Pikeville, Tenn., 1967-70; instr. No. Mich. U., Marquette, 1971-75; rsch. asst. U. Wis., Madison, 1975-78; instr. Tex. Tech. U., Lubbock, 1978-79; asst. prof. James Madison U., Harrisonburg, Va., 1981-84; asst. prof. home econs. Tenn. Tech. U., Cookeville, 1986-90, assoc. prof., 1991-95, prof. home econs., 1996—, dir. Sch. Home Econs., 1996—; faculty fellow Textiles/Clothing Tech. Ctr., Raleigh, N.C., 1991; mem. Van Buren County Vocat. Bd., Spencer, Tenn., 1992—. Contbr. chpts. to books. Designer, coord. "Treasures from the Trunk" for Tenn. Bicentennial Celebration in 1996. Update recipient Am. Textile Mfrs. Inst., Washington, 1994. Mem. AAUP (v.p. Tenn. Tech. U. chpt.), Internat. Fabricare Inst., Am. Assn. Family and Consumer Scis. (mem. coms.), Tenn. Assn. Family and Consumer Scis. (v.p., pres. elect 1996), Internat. Textiles/Apparel Assn. (com. mem.), Costume Soc. Am., Tenn. Home Econs. Assn. (dist. award 1992). Republican. Christian. Home: 1260 River Hill Rd Sparta TN 38583 Office: Tenn Tech Univ PO Box 5035 Cookeville TN 38505

BAILEY, CHARLES DENNIS, school system administrator; b. Nashville, Aug. 18, 1949; s. Charles Blair and Mary Claudia (Lee) B.; m. Linda Kae Willingham, Oct. 21, 1989; children: Melissa K., David J.; stepchildren: Jason Q. Head, Jonathan B. Head. BS in Secondary Edn., Middle Tenn. State U., 1967; MEd in Edn. Adminstrn., Ala. A&M, 1976; advanced studies, ednl. leadership, U. Ala., 1980-84. Cert. tchr., Ala., Tenn., Fla. Indsl. arts tchr., coach Decatur (Ala.) City Schs., 1971-82, asst. prin. middle sch., 1982-86; tchr. phys. edn., coach Gadsen (Ala.) City Schs., 1987-88, asst. prin. middle high sch., 1989-90; asst. prin. h.s. Anniston (Ala.) City Schs., 1990-91, vocat. adminstr., 1992—; coach girls' basketball Brookhaven, Oak Park Middle Schs., Decatur, Ala., 1980-85; coach football, baseball Litchfield H.S., Gadsden, Ala., 1987-88. Columnist Decatur Daily, 1985. Bd. dirs. Com. on Ch. Cooperation, Decatur, Ala., 1982-84, Boys and Girls Clubs, Gadsden, Ala., 1987-91; coach youth sports Anniston, Gadsden, Decatur City Recreation Depts., Ala., 1971—. Mem. Am. Vocat. Assn., Ala. Assn. Vocat. Adminstrn., Ala. Coun. Sch. Adminstrn. and Supervision, Nat. Assn. Secondary Sch. Prins., Ala. Assn. Secondary Sch. Prins., Elks. Baptist. Home: 2317 Dale Ct Oxford AL 36203 Office: Anniston City Schs 1109 Woodstock Ave Anniston AL 36207-4708

BAILEY, CLARK TRAMMELL, II, public relations/public affairs professional; b. Chickasha, Okla., Jan. 28, 1961; s. Clark Trammell and Virginia (Anderson) B. BS with honors, Okla. State U., 1983; MBA with high honors, Okla. City U., 1990. Pub. rels. coord. Sta. KOSU-FM, 1981-83; advt. coord. Dallas Downtown News, 1983-84; voter registration coord. Reagan-Bush '84, Austin, Tex., 1984; campaign mgr. Buechner for Congress, St. Louis, 1986; asst. to gov. Office of the Gov., Oklahoma City, 1986-89; area mgr. pub. affairs Southwestern Bell, Oklahoma City, 1989—. Founding editor newsletter Telecomms.: Advantage Okla., 1993-95. Mem. exec. edn. program Class I Okla. Partnership, 1995; mem. pub. rels. subcom. Oklahoma City Meml. Task Force, 1995—; chmn. Festival of Lights, Downtown Now, 1995-96; co-chmn. opening ceremonies com. Festival of the Arts, 1996—; chmn. Excellent Educator Awards Okla. City Pub. Schs. Found., 1996, 97; mem. steering com. Bush for Pres.-Okla., Oklahoma City, 1988; chmn. pub. rels., co-chmn. adv. and promotions com. Arts Coun. Oklahoma City Opening Night, 1991, ch-chmn. outdoor entertainment and visual, 1992; chmn. pub. rels. Red Earth Auction, 1991, Buffalo Bash, 1991; com. mem. Met. Area Projects; co-chmn. Silent Night Auction, 1993, 94; co-chmn. com. Sports Fest, 1994; mem. Class XIII Leadership Oklahoma City, 1994-96; v.p., bd. dirs. Downtown Now, 1995—. Recipient B.L. Semtner Meml. award of excellence United Way Ctrl. Okla., 1991, award of merit Internat. Assn. Bus. Communicators, 1992, 93, 94, Group Gold Vail award for noteworthy pub. svc. SBC Comms., 1995. Mem. Pub. Rels. Soc. Am. (accredited; bd. dirs. Oklahoma City chpt. 1995, Upper Case award Oklahoma City chpt. 1990, 94, 95), Okla. Acad. for State Goals, Oklahoma City U. Alumni Assn. (bd. dirs. 1995—). Republican. Episcopalian. Office: Southwestern Bell Telephone 800 N Harvey Ave Rm 378 Oklahoma City OK 73102-2813

BAILEY, CYNTHIA ANN, neuropsychologist; b. Hampton, Va., June 19, 1954; d. Charles C. and Eleanor Joyce (Pierce) B. Student, La. State U., 1972-74; BS in Applied Biology, Ferris State Coll., Big Rapids, Mich., 1976; MA in Clin. Neuropsychology, U. Houston, 1984, PhD in Clin. Neuropsychology, 1988. Lic. psychologist, Pa. Supr. neuropsychol. svcs. Pate Rehab., Houston and Dallas, 1982-88; dir. neuropsychol. svcs. Pate Rehab., Sarasota, Fla., 1989-92; dir. outpatient svcs. Larry Pollock & Assocs., Houston, 1988-89; pres. Capriotti & Bailey, PA, Sarasota, 1992—; founding bd. dirs. Suncoast Ctr. for Ind. Living, Sarasota, 1989-93, treas., 1991-93; neuropsychol. cons. Fawcett Meml. Hosp., Port Charlotte, Fla., 1993—. Bd. dirs. Vol. Ctr., Sarasota, 1994. Mem. Fla. Psychol. Assn. Office: 1219 S East Ave Ste 103 Sarasota FL 34239-2351

BAILEY, DONALD WAYNE, financial planner and consultant; b. Richardson, Tex., Apr. 12, 1965; s. Louis Glenn and Billie Joyce (Cooke) B. BSBA in Fin., U. Tulsa, 1987. CFP. Fin. cons. Dean Witter Reynolds, Dallas, 1988-89, Smith Barney, Dallas, 1990—. Host: (radio talk show) Investment Talk, Talk Radio 570, Sta. KLIF, 1994. Mem. Internat. Assn. Fin. Planning, Assn. Lambda Chi Alpha Alumni (treas. 1990, 91). Republican. Methodist. Office: Smith Barney 12377 Merit Dr Dallas TX 75251

BAILEY, EARL EUGENE, religion educator; b. Shreveport, La., Apr. 16, 1927; s. William Henry and Essie Belle (Crowell) B.; m. Doris Josephine Fox, June 1, 1946; children: Marilyn Elizabeth Bailey Lewis, Margaret Cecilia Bailey Neudstatler. BA, La. Coll., Pineville, Ark., 1948; MusM Edn., Ouachita U., 1964; postgrad., U. West Fla., 1972. Min. music and edn. First Bapt. Ch., Hope, Ark., 1953-54, Marshall, Tex., 1955-56; min. music and edn. Sunset Acres Bapt. Ch., Shreveport, 1956-57; min. edn. Cen. Bapt. Ch., Magnolia, Ark., 1958-66, First Bapt. Ch., Panama City, Fla., 1966-71; prof. religion Gulf Coast Community Coll., Panama City, 1971-94, prof. emeritus, 1994—; lectr. Holy Land Tours, 1983—; mem. faculty Ridgecrest Bapt. Assembly, Black Mountain, N.C., 1969; bd. dirs. Bailey Tours, Inc., Panama City. Host, producer weekly TV program This Believing World, Panama City, 1983—; columnist Panama City News Herald, 1970—; contbr. articles to various jours. Pres. Rotary Club, Magnolia, Ark., 1966, program chmn., Panama City, 1970, chaplain, 1972; vice chmn. State Bd. Missions, Jacksonville, Fla., 1969. Named Outstanding Prof. Yr., Gulf Coast Community Coll., 1986; Paul Harris fellow Rotary Club, 1987. Mem. Ark. Bapt. Religious Edn. Assn. (pres.), Bibl. Archael. Soc., Fla. Assn. Community Colls. Democrat. Home: 799 Wood Ave Panama City FL 32401-2359

BAILEY, GEORGE THOMAS, real estate association executive; b. Gulfport, Miss., May 29, 1929; s. Stanley Louis and Estelle (Eisele) B.; m. Annette Charmian Lejeune, Oct. 5, 1957; children: Mark, Richard, David, Patrick. BBA, U. Miss., Oxford, 1951. Commd. ensign USN, 1953, advanced through grades to capt., 1972, ret., 1983; office mgr. Donovan Realty Inc., Pensacola, Fla., 1984-92; exec. officer Pensacola Assn. Realtors, 1992—. Bd. govs. Pensacola Jr. Coll., 1988-93. Mem. Am. Soc. Assn. Execs., Rotary (bd. dirs. 1984-86, Paul Harris fellow 1991). Office: Pensacola Assn Realtors 420 S Alcaniz St Pensacola FL 32501-6015

BAILEY, GRACE DANIEL, retired secondary school educator; b. Wilson, N.C., Dec. 7, 1927; d. James Clenon and Ella Mae (West) Daniel; m. Hubert Jesse Bailey, Apr. 27, 1951; 1 child, Vicky Lynette Bailey Freeman. BS in Bus. Edn. and English, East Carolina U., 1950, MAE in Guidance and Counseling, 1966. Tchr. bus. edn., English Apex (N.C.) H.S., 1950-51; tchr. bus. edn. Atlantic Christian Coll., Wilson, N.C., summer 1951; tchr. bus. edn., English Lucama (N.C.) H.S., 1951-53, 1956-75, tchr. bus. edn., counselor, 1975-77, counselor, 1977-78; counselor Hunt H.S., Wilson, 1978-79, counselor, dept. chair, 1979-86, ret., 1986. Sec. adv. com. Cmty. Manpower and Tng., Wilson, 1973-74; organizer Wilson Cmty. Coun., 1973-74; sec. Wilson County Humane Soc., 1978; mem. edn. com. Am. Cancer Soc., Wilson, 1987-88. Recipient award Am. Legion, Wilson, 1986; grantee Wilson County Mental Health Assn., 1964. Mem. AAUW, N.C. Assn. Educators (treas. Wilson County chpt. 1974-75), Wilson County Guidance Pers. Assn. (organizer, 1st pres. 1966-67), Wilson Women's Club (co-chairperson comm. com. 1993-94), Delta Kappa Gamma (v.p. Gamma Mu chpt. 1986-88, pres. 1988-90). Methodist. Home: 4021 Us Highway 117 Wilson NC 27893-0916

BAILEY, IRVING WIDMER, II, insurance holding company executive; b. Cambridge, Mass., June 8, 1941; s. Harwood and Esther (Hill) B.; m. Nancy Lawrence, Sept. 21, 1963; children: Christopher L., Michele. Grad., Phillips-Exeter Acad., 1959; student, U. Paris, 1961-62; B.A. in French, U. Colo., 1963; M.B.A., NYU, 1968. Investment officer, asst. v.p. Mut. Life Ins. Co., N.Y.C., 1963-71; v.p. bond investment Phoenix Mut. Life Ins. Co., Hartford, Conn., 1971-76, sr. v.p. investments, 1976-81; exec. v.p., chief investment officer Capital Holding Corp./Providian Corp., Louisville, 1981-87, pres., chief operating officer, 1987-88, chmn., pres., chief. exec. officer, 1988—, bd. dirs.; bd. dirs. BellSouth Telecomms., Inc., Computer Scis. Corp. Mem. Leadership Louisville Found., 1989—, Life Span, 1989—; mem. exec. com. Downtown Devel. Corp., 1988, Ky. Econ. Devel. Corp., 1988; bd. dirs., mem. exec. com. Greater Louisville Econ. Devel. Partnership, 1988—. Mem. Am. Coun. Life Ins. (dir., audit, exec., fin. coms., pers. and fiduciary sub. com., steering com. on fed. taxation), N.Y. Soc. Security Analysts, River Valley Club, Jefferson Club. Republican. Presbyterian. Office: Providian Corp 400 W Market St Louisville KY 40202-3346

BAILEY, JAMES ANDREW, middle school educator; b. Jackson, Tenn., Mar. 15, 1957; s. John Truman and Hazel (Cox) B.; m. Lisa McDaniel, June 13, 1992. AS, Jackson (Tenn.) State C.C., 1977; BS, Memphis State U., 1980; MA, Bethel Coll., 1989. Cert. tech. edn. instr., Tenn. Indsl. arts instr. Kirby High Sch., Memphis, 1980-83; tech. edn. instr. Parkway Mid. Sch., Jackson, 1983—; writing team mem. State Tenn. Tech. Edn. Curriculum Project, 1984—; tech. edn. participant People to People/Citizen Amb. Program, People's Republic China, summer 1991. Co-author: Instructor's Guide to Metric 500, 1980; contbg. author: Production Technology, 1991. Chmn. Madison-Chester Assn. Bapt. Singles Coun., Jackson, 1990-91; mem. West Jackson (Tenn.) Bapt. Ch. Named Outstanding Young Man of Am., 1985, Indsl. Arts Advisor of Yr., Tenn. Indsl. Arts Students Assn., 1987, 2000 Notable Am. Men, 1994. Mem. NEA, Tenn. Edn. Assn., Am. Vocat. Assn., Jackson-Madison County Edn. Assn. (exec. bd. 1995-97, chmn. instruction and profl. devel. com. 1995-97, mem. legis. com. 1995-96), Tenn. Vocat. Assn. (Tech. Tchr. of Yr. 1989), Internat. Tech. Edn. Assn. (area rep. 1991-92), Tenn. Tech. Edn. Assn., West Tenn. Tech. Edn. Assn. (bd. mem. 1990—). Home: 20 London Park Pl Jackson TN 38305 Office: Parkway Middle Sch 1341 N Parkway Jackson TN 38305-4626

BAILEY, JAMES (JACK) RICHARD, newspaper editor; b. Charleston, W.Va., Feb. 24, 1970; s. Marshall Seymour and Janie Kathryn (Coffman) B. BA in Journalism, Marshall U., Huntington, W.Va., 1992. Reporter, columnist The Parthenon, Huntington, W.Va., 1989-90; news editor The Parthenon, Huntington, 1991, editor coll., 1992; reporter The Parkersburg (W.Va.) News, 1992-93; asst. editor The State Jour., Charleston, 1993-95, mng. editor, 1995-96, editor, 1996—; legis. writer, columnist W.Va. Press Assn., Charleston, 1995-96; part-time faculty W.Va. State Coll., 1996—. Author: (short stories) Under Distant Suns, 1992, Pablo Lennis, 1996, Lost Worlds, 1996. Poll worker Rep. party, Kanawha County, W.Va., 1995. Recipient Pub. Spkg. award VFW Ripley area, 1988, feature writing award W.Va. Press Assn., 1992. Mem. Soc. Profl. Journalists (award news reporting 1992, award feature writing 1992), W.Va. Writers. Methodist. Home: 2111 Pond Fork Dr Charleston WV 25312 Office: The State Jour 904 Virginia St E Charleston WV 25301

BAILEY, JEFFREY RANDOLPH, librarian; b. Dayton, Ohio, Feb. 26, 1961; s. Randolph and Marjorie Rose (Crisp) B.; m. Deborah Lynn Newman, July 2, 1987; 1 child, Amber Nicole. BA, Morehead State U., 1989; MSLS, Clarion U. Pa., 1990. Libr. tech. asst. II Ark. State U., State University, 1991-92, head circulation libr., 1992—, interim libr. dir., 1996. Home: PO Box 2040 State University AR 72467 Office: Ark State Univ PO Box 2445 State University AR 72467

BAILEY, JOY HAFNER, university program administrator, psychologist, educator; b. Weehawkin, N.J., Aug. 15, 1928; d. Elmar William and Fern (Williams) Hafner; children: Kerry, Jan, Leslie, Liza, Annie Laurie, Kristin. BA, Austin Coll., 1974; MS, East Tex. State U., 1975, EdD, 1977. Lic. marriage and family therapist, profl. counselor; nat. cert. counselor. Counselor, instr. East Tex. State U., 1976-80; dir. student support services acad./counseling program Ga. State U., 1980—, asst. prof. learning support programs, 1980—, asst. prof. counseling and psychol. svcs., 1988—; pvt. practice marriage and family therapy. Mem. APA, Am. Counseling Assn., Am. Assn. Marriage and Family Therapists (approved supr.), Ga. Assn. Marriage and Family Therapists (approved supr.), Atlanta Mallet Club (v.p. 1989-92), Psi Chi. Office: Ga State U 1 Park Place South SE Ste 701 Atlanta GA 30303-2911

BAILEY, KEITH E., petroleum pipeline company executive; b. 1942; married. B.S., Mo. Sch. Mines, 1964. With Continental Pipe Line, 1964-66; with Yellowstone Pipeline, 1966, Continental Pipeline, 1966-73, William Pipe Line Co. Inc., Tulsa, 1973-83; past pres. William Pipe Line Co. Inc.; pres., chief oper. officer N.W. Central Pipeline Corp., Tulsa; past exec. v.p. fin. and adminstrn. The Williams Cos., Tulsa, pres., 1992, now chmn., pres., CEO, dir. Office: Williams Cos Inc 1 Williams Ctr PO Box 74102 Tulsa OK 74102*

BAILEY, KEVIN WILLIAM, educational administrator; b. Phila., July 20, 1964; s. William Samuel and Lenora (Jordan) B. BS, Indiana U. of Pa., 1986, MA, 1990. Dir. grad. residence hall Indiana U. of Pa., 1988-90; residence coord. U. N.C., Charlotte, 1990-92, asst. dir., 1993—; adj. lectr. U. N.C., Charlotte, 1994-95. Editor: (newsletters) N.C. Housing Officers Newsletter, 1994-95, Kappa Alpha Psi Fraternity Newsletter, 1994-95. Mentor 1st Ward Elem. Sch., Charlotte, 1994. Recipient Achievement award Kappa Alpha Psi, 1994, Black Student Union, U. N.C., 1994. Mem. Am. Coll. Pers. Assn. (commn. directorate 1993-95), So. Assn. Coll. Student Affairs (com. chair 1994-95), Assn. for Student Jud. Affairs, Southeastern Assn. Housing Officers (state rep. 1994-95), N.C. Housing Office (newsletter editor 1994-95), N.C. Coll. Pers. Assn. (mem.-at-large 1993-95). Office: U NC Dept Housing Charlotte NC 28223

BAILEY, LARRIE (JOHN), state treasurer; b. Weston, W.Va., Mar. 2, 1934; s. John W. and Carrie Elizabeth (Given) B.; m. Joyce Kennedy, Oct. 15, 1966; children: John Kennedy, David Cleveland, Anne Joyce. AB, U. S.C., 1955; MA in Polit. Sci., W.Va. U., 1966. Registered investment advisor. Tchr. Lost Creek (W.Va.) High Sch., 1960-62; mem. W.Va. Ho. of Dels., 1960-62; stockbroker Parker-Hunter, Inc., Clarksburg, W.Va., 1969-71; pres. Bailey & Assocs., Inc., Fairmont, W.Va., 1971-76; treas. State of W.Va., 1976-85, 96—; investment adviser, 1985-90. Served as officer USN, 1956-59. Recipient Meritorious Svc. medal W.Va. N.G., 1981. Mem. Naval Res. Assn., Res. Officers Assn. (v.p. for navy, marine corps and coast guard 1967-68), Nat. Assn. State Treas. (pres. 1984), S.R. (pres. W.Va. 1982-84, 89-91), Navy League, Elks, Shriners, Rotary, Phi Kappa Sigma. Democrat. Baptist. Home: 5 Jo Harry Rd Fairmont WV 26554-3542 Office: State Capitol Bldg 145 E Wing Charleston WV 25305

BAILEY, LARRY RONALD, elementary school educator; b. Darlington, S.C., Aug. 7, 1944; s. Herbert Clarence and Lois Louise (Bryant) B.; m. Martha Ann Hough, July 11, 1983; children: Jennifer Renee, Melissa Joy. AA in Liberal Arts, Sparttanburg Coll., 1966; BS in Social Scis., Pembroke State Coll., 1968. Cert. tchr. social studies, learning disabilities, N.C. Tchr. Spl. Edn., Halifax, Va., 1968-69; probation officer N.C. Dept. Correction, Raleigh, N.C., 1973-86; tchr. Monroe (N.C.) City Schs., 1987-88, Union County Schs., Monroe, 1988-89, Montgomery County Schs., Troy, N.C., 1989—; coach basketball, baseball Parkwood Middle Sch., Monroe, 1988-89; coach track West Middle Sch., Troy, 1990-91. Mem. NEA, Masons (32 degree), LOM, Rotary. Methodist. Home: 12428 Alberta Dr Norwood NC 28128-8438 Office: Montgomery Schs Troy NC

BAILEY, LOUISE SLAGLE, English language educator; b. Gainesville, Fla., June 26, 1930; d. Dean and Alma (Spencer) Slagle; m. G.A. Bailey Jr., June 10, 1961 (div. 1983); 1 child, Frances L. BA with hons., U. Fla., 1951, MA, 1953; postgrad., U. Tenn., 1955-59. Instr. English U. Tenn., 1959-61; instr. English Marshall U., Huntington, W.Va., 1961-63, asst. prof., 1963-87, ret., 1987—. Contbr. story critiques to Magill Masterplots, poetry to various publs. Mem. AAUP, AAUW, Modern Lang. Assn., W.Va. Writers, Inc., W.Va. Poetry Soc., Guyandotte Poets, Soc. Study Southern Lit., South Atlantic Modern Lang. Assn., Literary Landmarks Assn., Marjorie Kinnan Rawlings Soc., Huntington Panhellenic Assn. (sec.), Phi Beta Kappa, Phi Kappa Phi, Sigma Tau Delta, Delta Delta Delta, Friends of the Cabell County Libr., Marshall U. Libr. Assn., Dem. Women of Claybell County. Democrat. Methodist. Home and Office: 1204 9th Ave Huntington WV 25701

BAILEY, MICHAEL KEITH, lawyer; b. Washington, Feb. 19, 1956; s. Alda Merrill and Joan (Moyers) B.; m. Linda Ann Braswell, Dec. 18, 1982; children: Julia Anne, David Allen. AB in Econs. and Polit. Sci., Coll. William and Mary, 1978; JD, Stetson U., 1981. Bar: Fla. 1981, U.S. Dist. Ct. (mid. dist.) Fla. 1982, U.S. Ct. Appeals (11th cir.) 1982, U.S. Supreme Ct. 1986. Assoc. Pitts, Eubanks, et al, Orlando, Fla., 1981-86; ptnr. Parrish, Bailey & Morsch, P.A., Orlando, 1986—. Mem. ABA, Assn. Trial Lawyers Am. (sustaining mem.), So. Trial Lawyers Assn., Def. Rsch. Inst., Orange County Bar Assn., Acad. Fla. Trial Lawyers (eagle patron), Nat. Bd. Trial Adv. (cert. civil trial advocate), Fla. Bar Bd. Ctr. (civil trial atty.). Republican. Baptist. Home: 701 E Lake Sue Ave Winter Park FL 32789-5804 Office: Parrish Bailey & Morsch PA 116 W America St Orlando FL 32801-3610

BAILEY, PHILLIP DOUGLAS, foreign language educator; b. Carbondale, Ill., Nov. 6, 1962; s. Douglas John and Beatrice Mercedes (Seitz) B.; m. Marion Sheila Salmons, Jan. 13, 1964; 1 child, Emily Katherine. BA in French and Humanities, St. John's U., Collegeville, Minn., 1985; MA in French, U. Va., 1987, PhD in French, 1993. Part-time instr. French U. Va., Charlottesville, 1992; vis. asst. prof. French Union Coll., Schenectady, N.Y., 1992-93; asst. prof. French U. Ctrl. Ark., Conway, 1993—; pvt. practice translator. Author: Proust's Self-Reader: The Pursuit of Literature as Privileged Communications, 1997. Presdl. scholar U. Va., Charlottesville, 1985-88. Fellow Soc. of Fellows U. Va. (jr.); mem. MLA, South Ctrl. MLA, Am. Coun. on the Tchg. Fgn. Lang., Am. Assn. Tchrs. French, Ark. Fgn. Lang. Tchrs. Assn., South Atlantic MLA. Office: Dept Fgn Langs Univ Ctrl Ark Conway AR 72035

BAILEY, ROBERT LESLIE, minister; b. Detroit, May 26, 1945; s. Robert and Dorothy (Hollis) B.; m. Connie J. Gaddy, Nov. 20, 1964; children: Kerissa Michelle, Robert L. Jr. BA, Lee Coll., 1978; grad., Ch. of God Sch. Theology, 1991. Ordained to ministry Ch. of God (Cleveland, Tenn.), 1970. State evangelist Ch. of God, Atlanta, 1964-66, 74-78; pastor Atlanta, 1966-68; sr. pastor Rockmart (Ga.) Ch. of God, 1968-70; pastor Bremen (Ga.) Ch. of God, 1970-72; sr. pastor Ch. of God, Toledo-Sylvania, Ohio, 1972-74; state evangelist Ch. of God, 1974-78; nat. evangelist Ch. of God, Cleveland, Tenn., 1978-81; sr. pastor Woodlawn Hills Ch. of God, Canton, Ohio, 1981-87, South Cleveland (Tenn.) Ch. of God, 1987-92, New Hope Ch. of God, Sevierville, Tenn., 1992-94, Valley View Ch. of God, Sylacauga, Ala., 1994—; chmn. Ordain Ministerial Examining Bd., Chattanooga, Ministerial examining Bd., Birmingham, Ala., Evangelism Bd. Akron, South Youth Bd., Atlanta; dist. overseer Ch. of God, Canton, 1982-87, Cleve., 1987-92, Sevierville, 1992-94, Sylacauga, 1994—; mem. Family and Social Concerns Commn., Ch. of God Internat. Office, 1988-92, state coun., Akron, 1984-87; mem. study com. No. Ohio state office Ch. of God; dist. youth dir. Rome, Ga., 1968-70. Named one of Outstanding Young Men of Am., 1976. Mem. Sylacauga Ministerial Assn. (pres. 1995—). Home: PO Box 2326 Sylacauga AL 35150-5326 Office: Valley View Church of God PO Box 2326 Sylacauga AL 35150-5326

BAILEY, STEVEN SCOTT, operations research analyst; b. Ft. Benning, Ga., Dec. 9, 1948; s. Claude Esmond and Marietta (Tanzola) B.; m. Wendy Cropf, Dec. 10, 1988; 1 child, Michael. BS, U.S. Mil. Acad., 1970; MPA, U. Colo., Denver, 1977, MS, 1981; PhD, Colo. Sch. of Mines, 1989. Cert. prodn. and inventory mgmt. Commd. 2nd lt. U.S. Army, 1970, advanced through grades to lt. col., 1987; asst. prof. U.S. Mil. Acad., West Point, N.Y., 1981-84; ops. rsch. analyst Concepts Analysis Agy. U.S. Army, Bethesda, Md., 1984-86; asst. prof. Park Coll., Denver, 1986-89; ops. rsch. analyst RAND Corp., Santa Monica, Calif., 1989-92; rsch. analyst Ctr. for Naval Analyses, Alexandria, Va., 1992—; dir. analysis COMUSNAVCENT, Bahrain, 1994—; instr. C.W. Post Coll., L.I. (N.Y.) U., 1982-84, Colo. Sch. Mines, Golden, 1988-89, UCLA Extension, 1990-91, CSUN, 1991-92, Amideast, 1996—. Mem. Am. Prodn. and Inventory Control Soc., Inst. Mgmt. Sci., RAND Scuba Club (pres. 1989-92), Phi Kappa Phi. Office: Ctr for Naval Analysis Field Office PO Box 16268 Alexandria VA 22302-8268

BAIMAN, GAIL, real estate broker; b. Bklyn., June 4, 1938; d. Joseph and Anita (Devon) Yalow; m. James F. Becker, Oct. 1970 (div. 1978); children: Steven, Susan, Barbara. Student Bklyn. Coll., 1955-57. Lic. real estate broker, N.Y., Pa., Fla. Personnel-pub. relations dir. I.M.C., Inc., N.Y.C., 1970-72; pres., broker Gayle Baiman Assocs., Inc., N.Y.C., 1972-74; v.p., broker Tuit Mktg. Corp., Mt. Pocono, Pa., 1974-83; pres., broker Ind. Timeshare Sales, Inc., St. Petersburg, Orlando, 1983—. Author: Vacation Timesharing, A Real Estate, 1992. Mem. Am. Resort Developers Assn., Better Bus. Arbitrator Assn., Internat. Resale Brokers Assn. (co-founder), Chmns. League, Better Bus. Bur. Arbitrators. Office: Ind Timeshare Sales Inc 5680 66th St N Saint Petersburg FL 33709-1515

BAIN, DALE WADE, marine officer; b. Waco, Tex., July 28, 1962; s. James Sandlin and Mattie Rose (Smith) B.; m. Suzanne Marie Mraz, July 4, 1992; 1 child, Tyler Philip. BA, U. Colo., 1984; postgrad., So. U. and A&M Coll., 1995—. Commd. 2d lt. USMC, 1984, advanced through grades to capt., 1990; platoon comdr., exec. officer 1st Battalion, 4th Marines, Twentynine Palms, Calif., 1985-87, 3d Light Armored Vehicle Battalion, Twentynine Palms, 1987-88; platoon comdr. 3d Light Armored Infantry Battalion, Okinawa, Japan, 1988-89; tactics instr. The Basic Sch., Quantico, Va., 1989-92; tactical readiness officer 2d Force Svc. Support Group, Camp LeJeune, N.C., 1992-93; co. comdr. hdqr. and svc. co. 3d Battalion, 6th Marines, Camp LeJeune, 1993-94, co. comdr. weapons co., 1994-95; inspector-instr. I-I Staff, Baton Rouge, 1995—. Mem. NRA, Marine Corps Assn., Nat. Eagle Scout Assn., U. Colo. Alumni Assn. Roman Catholic. Office: 8410 Gen Chennault Dr Baton Rouge LA 70807

BAIN, DANIEL ALBERT, educational administrator; b. St. Louis, Jan. 20, 1955; s. Jack Arthur and Ann E. Bain; m. Sandra Lee Ellenwood Burnard, June 9, 1984; 1 child, Erin Ellenwood. Cert. of Merit, Webber Douglas Acad. Dram. Art, London, 1976; BA, U. Iowa, 1977. Lic. residential real estate, Calif. Telecomms. planner L.A. Olympic Organizing Com., Marina del Rey, Calif., 1983-84; dir. mktg. Sigma Sys., West L.A., 1984-86; sr. mktg. rep. Nynex Bus. Ctrs., Encino, Calif., 1986-88; syllabi coord., instr. Inst. Computer Tech., L.A., 1988-93; mgmt. analyst City of L.A., 1990-93; curriculum developer Delaware (Ohio) County Vocat. Sch., 1993-94; distance edn. facilitator Pitt C.C., Greenville, N.C., 1994—; corp. cons. DB Solutions, Winterville, N.C., 1994—; cons. dba DAB, Columbus, Ohio, 1994. Mentor City of L.A. Mayor's Office, 1994; mem. Councilman Bernson's Citizen's Adv. Coun., Northridge, Calif., 1990-94; liaison U. Iowa Cultural Arts Coun., Iowa City, 1977, John Douglas Real Estate Co., Encino, Calif., 1991-92. Telecomm. grantee State of N.C., 1995. Office: Pitt C C PO Drawer 7007 Hwy 11 S Greenville NC 27835-7007

BAIN, WILLIAM DONALD, JR., lawyer, chemical company executive; b. Rochelle, Ill., July 1, 1925; s. William Donald and Gretchen (Kittler) B.; m. Pauline Thomas, Jan. 14, 1950 (dec. Nov. 1991); children: Elizabeth Kittler Zibart, Anne Alexander, Nancy Hemenway Coté; m. Barrie Feighner, Mar. 30, 1996. BS in Econs, U. Pa., 1947; JD, Washington and Lee U., 1949. Bar: S.C. 1952. Mortgage loan field rep. Travelers Ins. Co., Hartford, Conn., Cleve.; Orlando, Fla., 1949-51; with Moreland-McKesson Chem. Co., Spartanburg, S.C., 1951-83, pres., 1965-83, also dir.; v.p., gen. mgr. McKesson Chem. Corp., San Francisco, 1982-84; bd. dirs. Cote Color & Chem. Co., Inc., Spartan Radiocasting Corp., Tietex Corp.; co-founder, bd. dirs. Affiliated Chem. Group, Bermuda; ptnr. Triple B Ptnrs. Mem. Spartanburg Sch. Bd., 1958-72, chmn., 1963-72; trustee Converse Coll., 1968-92, chmn. bd., 1985-92; chmn. alumni bd. Washington and Lee U., 1979-82; trustee Hollins (Va.) Coll., 1992—; bd. dirs. Mary Black Meml. Hosp., 1975—, chmn. 1980-82. With USAAC, 1943-45. Mem. S.C. Bar Assn., Rotary. Republican. Presbyterian.

BAINE, BURTON H., company executive. Pres. Brooks-Baine Golf, Inc. Office: # 707 1320 S University Dr Fort Worth TX 76107

BAINS, LEE EDMUNDSON, state attorney general; b. Birmingham, Ala., June 18, 1912; s. Herman Lipsey and Myrtle (Edmundson) B.; m. Ruel Eneida Burton, Jan. 1, 1938; children: Sandra Anita (Mrs. Henry Barnard Hardegree), Myrtle Lee, Lee Edmundson. Student, Birmingham So. Coll., 1930-31; B.S., U. Ala., 1934, J.D., 1936. Bar: Ala. 1936, U.S. Supreme Ct 1936; diplomate: Nat. Coll. Advocacy. Practiced in Bessemer, 1936-94, city atty., 1950-58; instr. Birmingham Sch. Law, 1937-41; faculty Nat. War Coll., 1960; atty. for Ala. Power Co., South Central Bell Telephone Co., Phillips Petroleum Co., AmSouth Bank; apptd. by gov. as spl. asst. atty. gen. State of Ala., 1980—. Contbr. article to profl. jour.; Author: Basic Legal Skills, 1976. Pres. Bessemer Bd. EDn., 1955-58, Bessemer YMCA, 1961; advisor Bd. Family Ct., Jefferson County, 1966-74; chmn. fin. com. Nat. Vets. Day for Birmingham, 1973; alt. del. Dem. Nat. Conv., 1941; tchr. men's Bible class First United Meth. Ch., 1966-93; tchr. Bible classes Canterbury Meth. Ch., Mountain Brook, 1994—. Rear adm. USNR, 1930-72, WWII. Fellow Am. Coll. Trial Lawyers; mem. ABA (vice chmn. environ. law sect. 1979), ATLA, Ala. Assn. Trial Lawyers, Ala. Bar Assn. (chmn. unauthorized practice com. 1977-79, mem. mil. law com.), Bessemer Bar Assn. (pres. 1983-84), Birmingham Bar Assn., Res. Officers Assn., Naval Res. Assn., Soc. Colonial Wars (state gov. 1972-73, corr. sec. 1976-80), SAR (pres. Ala.), Kiwanis, Birmingham Ski Club, Downtown Club, The Club, Phi Gamma Delta, Beta Gamma Sigma. Home: 2602B Park Lane Ct N Mountain Brook AL 35223-1816 Office: 1813 3rd Ave N Bessemer AL 35020-4963

BAIRD, CHARLES BRUCE, lawyer, consultant; b. DeLand, Fla., Apr. 18, 1935; s. James Turner and Ethelyn Isabelle (Williams) B.; m. Barbara Ann Fabian, June 6, 1959 (div. Dec. 1979); children: C. Bruce Jr., Robert Arthur, Bryan James; m. Byung-Ran Cho, May 23, 1982; children: Merah-Iris, Haerah Violet. BSME, U. Miami, 1958; postgrad UCLA, 1962-64; MBA, Calif. State U., 1966; JD, Am. U., 1971. Bar: Va. 1971, U.S. Dist. Ct. (ea. dist.) Va. 1971, D.C. 1973, U.S. Dist. Ct. D.C. 1973, U.S. Ct. Appeals (4th cir.) 1974, U.S. Supreme Ct. 1975. Rsch. engr. Naval Ordnance Lab., Corona, Calif., 1961-67; aerospace engr. Naval Air Systems Command, Washington, 1967-69; cons. engr. Bird Engring. Rsch. Assts., Vienna, Va., 1969-71; prof. Def. Systems Mgmt. Coll., Ft. Belvoir, Va., 1982; spl. asst. for policy compliance USIA Voice of Am., Washington, 1983-84; cons. Booz, Allen & Hamilton, Inc., Bethesda, 1975-82, IBM, Bethesda, Md., 1984; Logistics Mgmt. Inst., Bethesda, 1986—; adj. prof. Fla. Inst. Tech., 1988. Contbr. articles to profl. jours. Inventor computer-based communications systems for the gravely handicapped. Bd. govs. Sch. Engring. U. Miami, 1957; trustee Galilee United Meth. Ch., Arlington, Va., 1983-87. Mem. ATLA, Internet Soc., Soc. Gen. Systems Rsch., United We Stand Am. (founding mem.), Sigma Alpha Epsilon. Republican. Home and Office: 5396 Gainsborough Dr Fairfax VA 22032-2744

BAIRD, HAYNES WALLACE, pathologist; b. St. Louis, Jan. 28, 1943; s. Harry Haynes and Mary Cornelia (Wallace) B.; m. Phyllis Jean Tipton, June 26, 1965; children: Teresa Lee, Christopher Wallace, Kelly Wallace. BA, U. N.C., 1965, MD, 1969. Diplomate Am. Bd. Pathology. Radio announcer, disc jockey, 1961-63; intern N.C. Meml. Hosp., Chapel Hill, 1969-70, resident in pathology, 1970-72, chief resident in pathology, 1972-73; assoc. pathologist Moses H. Cone Meml. Hosp., Greensboro, N.C., 1973—; practice medicine, specializing in pathology Greensboro, 1973—; adj. asst. prof. U. N.C., Chapel Hill, 1978-96, adj. assoc. prof., 1996—; clin. lectr. chemistry U. N.C., Greensboro, 1973—. Mem. adminstrv. bd. West Market St. United Meth. Ch., 1985-88, usher, 1988—; bd. dirs. Greensboro unit Am. Cancer Soc., 1980-81; mem. com. protection of rights of human subjects (Instl. Rev. Bd.) Moses H. Cone Meml. Hosp., 1989—. Fellow Coll. Am. Pathologists (ho. of dels. 1983-85, insp. commn. on lab. accreditation); mem. AMA, So. Med. Assn., Am. Soc. for Clin. Chemistry, Am. Soc. Cytology, Papanicolaou Soc. of Cytopathology, Am. Soc. Clin. Pathologists, Internat. Acad. Pathology, N.C. Med. Soc., Greater Greensboro Soc. Medicine, N.C. Soc. Pathologists (sec.-treas. 1977-79). Methodist. Home: 2805 New Hanover Dr Greensboro NC 27408-6705 Office: 1200 N Elm St Greensboro NC 27401-1004

BAIRD, LARRY DON, minister, nurse; b. Abilene, Tex., Sept. 23, 1949; s. Delmar Lee baird and Frances Elizabeth Weathers; m. Mary Margaret Ledbetter, Dec. 22, 1970; 1 child, Shannon Kirk; 1 adopted child, Walter Dale. Student, San Diego State U., 1971-72, Cisco Jr. Coll., Clyde, Tex., 1977-78; diploma in nursing, Hendrick Meml. Hosp., Abilene, 1972-73. Ordained to ministry United Pentecostal Ch. Internat., 1973-84, Assemblies of Lord Jesus Christ, 1984. Evangelist United Pentecostal Ch., 1973-78; pastor United Pentecostal Ch., Hamlin, Tex., 1979-82; residential dir. Tupelo (Miss.) Children's Mansion, 1982-84, campus dean, 1983-84; co-pastor 1st Pentecostal Ch., Abilene, 1984; DON Valley View Care Ctr., Anson, Tex., 1990-91; unit dir. Hill Resources Inc., Abilene, Tex., 1992—; asst. choir dir., musician, dir. and interpreter for deaf United Penecostal Ch., Abilene, 1984—; dir. Spirit of Freedom Alcoholic Ministries, 1984—; pvt. nurse coord. Health Care Svcs., Abilene, 1984-85; sr. pastor Abundant Life Apostolic Ministries, Abilene, 1984—; dir. home missions Tex.-N.Mex. Distr. for Assemblies of Lord Christ Jesus Christ, 1986-91; bd. dirs. Blue Mountain (Miss.) Childrens Home. Active various health support groups, Abilene, 1984—; chmn., mem. exec. bd. Abilene Coord. Coun., 1984—; chmn. adv. com. Home Cmty. Svc. Mental Health-Mental Retardation Program, Abilene, 1994—. With USNR, 1970-76. Fellow Ministerial Alliance (pres. 1980-82). Republican. Home: 1918 Sayles Blvd Abilene TX 79605-6036 Office: Abundant Life Apostolic Ministries 741 S 11th St Abilene TX 79602-3852

BAIRD, MARIANNE SAUNORUS, critical care clinical specialist; b. Chgo., Dec. 15, 1953; d. John and Irene (Lameka) Saunorus; m. Thomas W. Baird, Sept. 10, 1983; 1 child, Rachel. BSN, Loyola U., Chgo., 1975; MSN, Emory U., 1982. Critical care RN, cert. advanced cardiac life support affiliate faculty mem., Ga. Supr. surg. nursing Rush-Presbyn. St. Lukes Med. Ctr., Chgo.; staff nurse, clin. mgr. intensive care unit St. Joseph's Hosp., Atlanta, dir. meg.-surg. unit, clin. specialist, case mgr. Author several nursing textbooks; contbr. articles to profl. jours. Recipient Fed. traineeship Emory U., 1980-81; named one of Outstanding Young Women of Am., 1991. Mem. AACN (bd. dirs. Atlanta chpt. 1984-86), Blue Key Nat. Honor Fraternity, Kappa Gamma Pi, Sigma Theta Tau. Home: 3788 Glengarry Way Roswell GA 30075-2615

BAIRD, SCOTT JAMES, English language educator; b. Shelby, Nebr., May 16, 1939; s. Hugh Vance and Faye Maureen (Roberts) B.; m. Jill Renee Smith, June 18, 1966; children: Nicole, Tania Lawson. BA, Midland Coll., 1961; MA, U. Tex., 1968, PhD, 1969. H.s. tchr. Kyushu Gakuin, Kumamoto, Japan, 1961-64; prof. Internat. Christian U., Tokyo, 1969-74, Trinity U., San Antonio, 1974—; lectr. Fulbright Assn., Japan, 1970, 72; mem. English Devel., Coll. Bd., Dallas, 1980-83;; tchr. cons. Ednl. Testing Svc., Princeton, N.J., 1980—; commr. Accrediting Coun. Continuing Edn., Washington, 1991-94. Contbr. revs., articles and columns to popular and profl. publs. Bd. dirs. Tokyo Women's Christian U., 1970-74, Good Samaritan Ctr., San Antonio, 1977-85; co-dir. name booth Tex. Folklife Festival, San Antonio, 1985—; mem. cemetery conservation Alama Area Coun. Govt., San Antonio, 1994—. Rsch. grantee Am. Folklife Ctr., 1982, writing program grantee NEH, 1984-85, equipment grantee Ednl. Tng., Inc., 1992. Mem. TESOL, Am. Dialect Soc. (regional sec. 1981-89, chair Non-English 1969—), Linguistic Soc. Am., Am. Name Soc., Assn. Graveyard Studies, Am. Culture Assn., San Antonio Rd. Runners Assn. (officer). Lutheran. Office: Trinity U 715 Stadium Dr San Antonio TX 78212-7200

BAIRD, THOMAS BRYAN, JR., lawyer; b. Newport News, Va., June 21, 1931; s. Thomas Bryan and Mary Florence (Rieker) B.; m. Mildred Katherine Clark, June 23, 1956; children: Sarah, Thomas Bryan III, William, Laura. BA, U. Va., 1952; LLB, U. Tenn., 1960. Bar: Tenn. 1964, Va. 1969, U.S. Dist. Ct. (we. dist.) 1970. With State Farm Ins., Knoxville, Tenn., 1960-68; asst. commonwealth atty., Wytheville, Va., 1969-71; commonwealth atty. Wythe County, 1972—; prin. Thomas B. Baird, Jr. Trustee, Simmerman Home for the Aged, 1972-83. Served with U.S. Army, 1953-55. Mem. ABA, ATLA, Nat. Dist. Attys. Assn., Va. Bar Assn., Am. Judicature Soc., Va. Trial Lawyers Assn., Phi Alpha Delta. Democrat. Presbyterian. Home: 875 N 18th St Wytheville VA 24382-1022

BAIRSTOW, FRANCES KANEVSKY, labor arbitrator, mediator, educator; b. Racine, Wis., Feb. 19, 1920; d. William and Minnie (DuBow) Kanevsky; m. Irving P. Kaufman, Nov. 14, 1942 (div. 1949); m. David Steele Bairstow, Dec. 17, 1954; children: Dale Owen, David Anthony. Student U. Wis., 1937-42; BS, U. Louisville, 1949; student Oxford U. (Eng.), 1953-54; postgrad. McGill U., Montreal, Que., 1958-59. Rsch. economist U.S. Senate Labor-Mgmt. Subcom., Washington, 1950-51; labor edn. specialist U. P.R., San Juan, 1951-52; chief wage data unit WSB, Washington, 1952-53; labor rsch. economist Canadian Pacific Ry. Co., Montreal, 1956-58; asst. dir. indsl. rels. ctr. McGill U., 1960-66, assoc. dir., 1966-71, dir., 1971-85, lectr., indsl. rels. dept. econs., 1960-72, asst. prof. faculty mgmt., 1972-74, assoc. prof. faculty mgmt., 1974-83, prof., 1983-85; lectr. Stetson Law Sch., Fla. spl. master Fla. Pub. Employees Rels. Commn., 1985—; dep. commr. essential svcs. Province of Que., 1976-81; mediator So. Bell Telephone, 1985—, AT&T and Comm. Workers Am., 1986—; cons. on collective bargaining arbitrator to OECD, Paris, 1979; cons. Nat. Film Bd. of Can., 1965-69; arbitrator Que. Consultative Coun. Panel of Arbitrators, 1968-83, Ministry Labour and Manpower, 1971-83, United Airlines and Assn. Flight Attendants, 1990-95, State U. System of Fla., 1990—; Orlando Utilities Commn., Orlando, 1994, FDA, 1996—, Social Security Adminstrn., 1996—; mediator Canadian Public Svc. Staff Rels. Bd., 1973-85; contbg. columnist Montreal Star, 1971-85. Chmn. Nat. Inquiry Commn. Wider-Based Collective Bargaining, 1978. Fulbright fellow, 1953-54. Mem. Canadian Indsl. Rels. Rsch. Inst. (exec. bd. 1965-68), Indsl. Rels. Rsch. Assn. Am. (mem. exec. bd. 1965-68, chmn. nominating com. 1977), Nat. Acad. Arbitrators (bd. govs. 1977-80, program chmn. 1982-83, v.p. 1986-88, nat. coord. 1987-90), Nat. Treasury Employees Assoc. Home and Office: 1430 Gulf Blvd Apt 507 Clearwater FL 34630-2856

BAISIER, MARIA DAVIS, English language educator, theater director; b. Louisville, Aug. 15, 1947; d. Alvin Joseph and Alice Josephine (Ostertag) Davis; m. Bernard Leon Baisier, May 23, 1970; children: Bernard Paul Leon, Aimée Louise Davis. BA, St. Mary's Dominican Coll., 1969; secondary cert. in English, Tulane U., 1992. Asst. mng. editor So. Ins. Mag., New Orleans, 1979-85; tchr. St. Catherine of Siena Sch., Metairie, La., 1969-75, 85—, chair English dept., 1985—, dir. theatre, 1991—. Creator, dir. Camp Big Foot Summer Camp, Metairie, 1974, 75; v.p. Sacred Heart Sch. PTA, Arabi, La., 1977; vol. worker Sta. WYES-TV Auction, New Orleans, 1978-83; mem. women's com. New Orleans Opera Assn., 1979—, chair Opera Ball, 1984; various com. positions Women's Guild, 1980-84; chair ann. fundraiser fair St. Francis Xavier Ch., 1982-84; mem. hospitality com. Rep. Nat. Conv., 1988. Mem. Nat. Coun. Tchrs. English, Kappa Delta Pi, Phi Beta. Home: 210 Hector Ave Metairie LA 70005-4118

BAJPAI, SANJAY KUMAR, pharmaceutical executive, consultant; b. Indore, India, May 22, 1965; s. Shri Dhar and Kamal Kumari (Tripathi) B. BPharm, Banaras Hindu U., Varanasi, India, 1986; MA in Bus. Adminstrn., Ohio State U., 1991, MS in Pharm. Adminstrn., 1991, PhD, 1992. Prodn. supr. Rusoma Lab. Pvt. Ltd., Indore, India, 1986; resident Cadila Group of Cos., Ahmedabad, India, 1989; sr. rsch. analyst State & Fed. Assoc., Alexandria, Va., 1993-94; dir. health care rsch. G. Bhalla & Assocs., Vienna, Va., 1994—. Grad. fellow Ohio State U., 1987-92; recipient Alumni Rsch. award, 1991. Mem. Am. Assn. Pharm. Scis., Drug Info. Assn., Assn. of Pharmacoeconomy and Outcomes Rsch., Am. Mktg. Assn. Home: 2251 Pimmit Dr # 723 Falls Church VA 22043 Office: G. Bhalla & Assocs 8605 Westwood Ctr Ste 207 Vienna VA 22182

BAKER, AMANDA SIRMON, university dean, nursing educator; b. Daphne, Ala., Apr. 3, 1934; d. Joel Green and Edna Mae (Miller) Sirmon; m. Malcolm Davis Baker, Mar. 30, 1957; children: Leonard Eric, Michael Davis. BSN, U. Ala., Tuscaloosa, 1955; M in Nursing, U. Fla., Gainesville, 1972, PhD, 1974; cert., Bryn Mawr Coll., 1983. Office nurse R.P. Maxon, M.D., Ft. Walton Beach, Fla., 1955-58; pub. health nurse County Health Dept., Clovis, N.Mex., 1963-64; staff nurse, night supr. Pheobe Putney Hosp., Albany, Ga., 1964-67; developer, implementor home svc. nursing program for children and adults with cerebral palsy United Cerebral Palsy, Southwest Ga., 1967-68; instr. in child health, med./surg. and pharmacology Albany (Ga.) Jr. Coll., 1968-69; grad. teaching asst. child health nursing U. Fla., 1972-73, grad. teaching assoc. child health nursing, 1973-74, asst. dean continuing profl. edn. Coll. of Nursing, 1974-76, asst. dean. undergrad. studies, 1976-78, acting dean Coll. of Nursing, 1978-80, asst. dean. undergrad. studies Coll. of Nursing, 1980-81, assoc. dean Coll. of Nursing, 1981-85; dean Sch. of Nursing Troy State U., 1985-89; dean Coll. of Nursing U. South Ala., 1989—; mem. search com. Coll. Medicine, 1990-92, chair search com. VPAA, 1990-91, mem. fin. resources com., 1991-93, chair subcom.; speaker and presenter in field. Contbr. articles to profl. jours. Chair Ala. Nurses Polit. Action Com., 1986-89. Mem. ANA (coun. nurse rschr., S.E. region accrediting com., charter 1974-78), NLN (coun. baccalaureate and higher degree end. 1974-96), Ala. State Nurses Assn. (dist. 8 chpt.), Ala. League for Nursing, Soc. for Rsch. in Nursing Edn., Am. Assn. Colls. Nursing (semi-ann. meetings 1985—, program com. 1990-92, pub. rels. com. 1992-94, govtl. affairs com. 1994-96), So. Coun. on Collegiate Edn. in Nursing, Phi Kappa Phi, Pi Lambda Theta, Sigma Theta Tau. Presbyterian. Office: U South Ala Coll Nursing Springhill Campus Mobile AL 36688

BAKER, ANITA DIANE, lawyer; b. Atlanta, Sept. 4, 1955; d. Byron Garnett and Anita (Swanson) B.; m. Thomas Johnstone Robison III, Sept. 26, 1995. BA summa cum laude, Oglethorpe U., 1977; JD with distinction, Emory U., 1980. Bar: Ga. 1980. Assoc. Hansell & Post, Atlanta, 1980-88, Kitchens, Kelley, Gaynes, Huprich & Shmerling, 1989-90; asst. gen. counsel NationsBank Corp., 1991—. Mem. ABA (com. on savs. and loan instns., com. on consumer fin. svcs.), Atlanta Bar Assn., Ga. Bar Assn., Atlanta Hist. Soc., Pace Acad. Alumni Assn. (bd. dirs.), Oglethorpe Univ. Alumni Assn. (bd. dirs.), Order of Coif, Phi Alpha Delta, Phi Alpha Theta, Alpha Chi, Omicron Delta Kappa. Office: NationsBank Corp 600 Peachtree St NE Fl 5 Atlanta GA 30308-2214

BAKER, BARRY BOYD, librarian; b. Louisville, Sept. 3, 1944; s. Ollie James and Virginia (Warren) B.; m. Lillian Janette Davis, May 29, 1969; 1 child, Terri Lynne. BA in History, La. State U., 1966, MLS, 1967. Trainee La. State U. Library, Baton Rouge, 1966-67, sr. librarian, 1967-68; asst. librarian Macon (Ga.) Jr. Coll. Library, 1968-70; asst. order librarian U. S.C., Columbia, 1970-72, head order dept., 1972-75, asst. dir. libraries, tech. service, 1975-78; assoc. U. librarian for tech. services Appalachian State U., Boone, N.C., 1978-80; asst. dir. for tech. services U. Ga., Athens, 1980—; chmn. bibliographic access com. Univ. Ctr., Ga., Atlanta, 1981-96; SOLINET rep. OCLC Adv. Commn. on Acquisitions, Columbus, Ohio, 1976-82, del. OCLC Users Coun., 1988-92; cons. Nat. Agrl. Library, Beltsville, Md., 1985; mem. editorial bd. Info. Tech. and Libraries, 1988-92; mem. adv. bd. ALA Guide to Tech. Svcs. Resources, 1994; Southeastern Libr. Network bd. dirs., 1993-96, sec. 1995, vice chair 1996; mem. CONSER Policy Com., 1987—; mem. exec. coun. Program for Coop. Cataloging, 1995—. Editor: From Tape to Product, 1985, The USMARC Format, 1987; news editor Technical Services Quarterly, 1987—; editor: Cooperative Cataloging, 1994; advt. mgr. The Georgia Librarian, 1996— (edtl. bd. 1993—); author book reviews and various articles on tech. svcs. Treas. Snapfinger Woods Homeowners Assn., Athens, 1984-92. Mem. ALA (com. on rsch. and stats. 1989-93, chmn. tech. svcs. cost commn. Resources and Tech. Svc. div., 1978-82), Assn. for Libr. Collections and Tech. Svcs. (chmn. membership com. 1991-93, chmn. com. on planning 1995—, bd. dirs. 1995—), Assn. Coll. and Rsch. Librs. (chmn. univ. libr. sect. 1987-88), Libr. and Info. Tech. Assn. (mem. publs com. 1984-89), chmn. video tutorial com. 1985-89), Southeastern Libr. Assn. (chmn. resources and tech. svcs. 1980-82, chmn. univ. and coll. libr. sect. 1984-86, chmn. conf. site selection com. 1989-95, vice-chair resources and tech. svcs., 1994-96, chair resources and tech. svcs. 1996—, handbook com., 1994—), Lions (pres. Classic City club 1984-85, 1st v.p. 1983-84, editor Lion Talk 1988-91). Independent. Episcopalian. Lodge: Lions (pres. Classic City club 1984-85, 1st v.p. 1983-84, editor Lion Talk 1988-92). Home: 285 Millstone Cir Athens GA 30605-4933 Office: U Ga Libraries Athens GA 30602

BAKER, BERNARD ROBERT, II, lawyer; b. Toledo, Nov. 19, 1915; s. Joseph Lee and Grace (Baker) O'Neil; m. Elinor Shutts, Oct. 16, 1943; children—Bernard Robert III, Lynn Agnes. A.B., Kenyon Coll., 1936; J.D., Harvard U., 1941. Bar: Ohio 1946. Practice in Toledo, 1947—; ptnr. Brown, Baker, Schlageter & Craig and predecessor firm, 1950-91, now of counsel; Pres. B.R. Baker Co., 1946-60; dir. emeritus First Nat. Bank Toledo, First Ohio Bankshares; ret. sec., dir. Toledo Blade Co., Blade Communications, Inc. Regional vice chmn. U.S. Com. for UN, 1955-62; past pres. St. Vincent Hosp., Toledo United Apeal, Toledo C. of C.; past trustee Med. Coll. Ohio at Toledo, Salvation Army, Toledo, Goodwill Industries, Toledo, St. Vincent Hosp. Found.; trustee emeritus Rutherford B. Hayes Presdl. Ctr., Fremont, Ohio; past trustee Boys Clubs Toledo; past pres., trustee Med. Coll. Ohio Found., Toledo. Lt. comdr. USNR, 1940-45. Recipient Boys Club Bronze Keystone award, 1965, Disting. Citizen award Toledo Med. Coll., 1986; named Toledo Outstanding Man of Year, 1948. Mem. ABA, Ohio Bar Assn., Chevalier du Tastevin, Harvard Club (N.Y.C.), Belmont Country Club, Carranor Hunt and Polo Club (Toledo), Bath and Tennis Club, Beach Club (Palm Beach), Psi Upsilon. Roman Catholic. Home: 1801 S Flagler Dr Ph 09 West Palm Beach FL 33401-7348

BAKER, BETTY SUE, elementary and secondary education educator; b. Abilene, July 26, 1946; d. D.L. and Bettye Ruth (Harris) Fender; m. Robert Calvin Baker, June 14, 1969; children: Robert Stephen, Jon Michael. MusB, U. Houston, 1968; MSc, U. Houston, Clear Lake, 1986. Cert. music tchr., Tex., reading specialist, English. Orch. tchr. Pasadena (Tex.) Ind. Sch. Dist., 1968-72, 1977-79, 1982-85, reading tchr., 1986—; pvt. violin tchr., Beaumont, Tex., 1973-77, Houston, 1979-82; acad. competition judge Nat. Acad. League, Pasadena, 1993—. Recipient Excellence in Edn. award Rotary, Pasadena, 1996. Mem. Assn. for Supervision and Curriculum Devel. (Nat. and Tex. Divsns.), Assn. of Tex. Profl. Educators. Mem. Ch. of Christ. Office: Pasadena ISD 3003 Dabney Pasadena TX 77502

BAKER, BRINDA ELIZABETH GARRISON, infectious disease nurse; b. Groveland, Ga., May 9, 1946; d. Archie and Nora Lee (Haynes) Garrison; m. Jerome Baker, Feb. 1970 (div. 1972); children: Katrina Lenyse Adams, Kelbert Lenard Adams. Student, Savannah (Ga.) State Coll., 1964-68; LPN, Savannah Tech. Sch., 1968; ADN, Armstrong State Coll., 1984, BSN, 1990. RN, Ga.; cert. provider BLS, Am. Heart Assn. LPN Candler Gen. Hosp., Savannah, 1968-72, staff nurse Cross Country Traveling Corps, 1990; LPN Ga. Regional Hosp., Savannah, 1972-74, sr. staff nurse, 1989-92; LPN St. Joseph Hosp., Savannah, 1974-84, staff nurse, 1984-90; sr. nurse, clinic supr. Chatham County Health Ctr., Savannah, 1992-95, clinic supr., 1995—; part-time clin. instr. Armstrong State Coll., Savannah, 1991—. Mem. ANA, Ga. Nurses Assn., Assn. Nurses in AIDS Care. Democrat. Roman Catholic. Home: 1307 E 71st St Savannah GA 31404-5735 Office: Chatham County Health Dept 2011 Eisenhower Dr Savannah GA 31406-3905

BAKER, CHARLES DOUGLAS, JR., architect; b. Columbia, S.C., Sept. 6, 1948; s. Charles Douglas Sr. and Anna Ruth (Kelehear) B. BArch, Clemson U., 1970. Registered architect, N.C., S.C. Archtl. designer Stanley Smith & Sons, Cayce, S.C., 1971-86; architect, pres., chief exec. officer Archtl. Concepts, Inc., Cayce, 1986—. Recipient Building of the Year award Systems Bldrs. of S.C., 1983,84,85,86,87,88. Mem. AIA (Washington and Columbia, S.C. chpts.), Cons. Specification Inst., Nat. Coun. Archtl. Registration Bds., Jaycees. Republican. Methodist. Home: 524 Patio Pl Columbia SC 29212-2496 Office: Architectural Concepts Inc 1833 Airport Blvd Cayce SC 29033-1814

BAKER, DANIEL RICHARD, computer company executive, consultant; b. Kopenhagen, Denmark, Mar. 19, 1932; came to U.S., 1936, naturalized, 1945; s. Arthur and Molly (Needman) B.; student Tufts Coll., 1949-51; B.A., Bklyn. Coll., 1957; postgrad. Fairleigh Dickinson U., 1961-64; postgrad. Am. U., 1968-69; Grad. U. Va. Grad. Realtors Inst., 1973; m. June Ellin Nebenzahl, Oct. 2, 1960; children—David Charles, Jill Alison. Tchr. math. N.Y.C. Public Schs., 1958-59; computer programmer Systems Devel. Corp., Paramus, N.J., 1959-61; programmer analyst ITT, Paramus, 1961-64; sr. mathematician Melpar Corp., Falls Church, Va., 1964-65; systems analyst Wolf Research & Devel. Corp., Bladensburg, Md., 1965-66, Aries Corp., McLean, Va., 1966-68; sr. systems analyst N.Am. Rockwell Corp., Roslyn, Va., 1968-70; pres. Data Assocs., Fairfax Station, Va., 1970—; real estate broker; permanent group leader Dale Carnegie Sales Courses. Vol. ann. fund campaign Tufts Coll., 1976—. Served with AUS, 1954-55. Mem. No. Va. Assn. Realtors (multilist com., edn. com., pub. rels. com., 5-yr. Million Dollar Sales Club award), Va. Assn. Realtors (dir. 1977-80, 83—, Lifetime award 1992, 94, 95, 96), Nat. Assn. Realtors, Am. Soc. Cybernetics, Silvanus Packard Soc. Club: Washington Tufts (v.p. 1975). Office: Data Assocs 5622-G Ox Rd Ste 310 Fairfax VA 22039-1018

BAKER, DEBORAH ALYSANDE, poet; b. Bartlesville, Okla., Oct. 8, 1949; d. Curtis Lee and Alice Cathrine (Fears) B. BS in Speech, Tex. Woman's U., 1977. Contbr. anthologies Rainbows and Rhapsodies, 1988, Orchids and Daffodils, 1988, Living Jewels, 1993; contbr. to periodicals A Galaxy of Verse, 1988, 89, Gt. Plains Canal and Avalon Dispatch, 1994, Lines 'N Rhymes, 1994, The Apostolic Crusade, 1996. Initiator, leader Mineral Wells (Tex.) Singles, 1988, 90. Mem. Brazos Writers Group (co-founder 1988—). Home: Apt 33 2503 SE 7th St Mineral Wells TX 76067-5710

BAKER, DONALD PARKS, journalist, educator; b. Wheeling, W. Va., Nov. 20, 1932; s. Clarence Parks and Katherine Ruth (Rapp) B.; m. Nancy Cottrell, Aug. 30, 1959; children—Lisa Dawn, Amanda Jean. AB in Journalism, W. Va. Inst. Tech., 1954. Reporter Daily Record, Wooster, Ohio, 1954-57; reporter Courier Press, Evansville, Ind., 1957-60; reporter, editor Indpls. Times, 1960-66, Cleve. Press., 1966-70, Washington Post, Washington, 1970—; adj. prof. Am. U., Washington, 1971-76; part-time faculty Marymount Coll., Arlington, Va., 1984-85, U. Md., College Park, 1980-83, Va. Commonwealth U., 1986-89, 92—. Author: Wilder: Hold Fast to Dreams, 1989. Alicia Patterson fellow, 1995. Office: Washington Post Old City Hall 1001 E Broad St # 420 Richmond VA 23219-1928

BAKER, DREAMA GAIL, psychologist; b. Meadow Bridge, W.Va., June 29, 1948; d. Joseph Robert and Gertrude Ethel (Llewellyn) Baker Goddard. Student, Fgn. Lang. League Schs., Jerusalem, Israel, 1969; BS, Salem-Teikyo U., 1970; M in Psychology, Cen. Mich. U., 1973; postgrad., Saybrook Inst., 1992—. Lic. psychologist, W.Va. Psychology intern Bay-Aranac Mental Health Ctr., Bay City, Mich., 1972-73; psychologist Fayette, Monroe, Raleigh, Summers counties Mental Health Clinic, Beckley, W.Va., 1973-74, Beckley Mental Health Ctr., 1974-76, Beckley Appalachian Hosp., 1977-78; psychologist Raleigh Psychiat. Svcs., Beckley, 1978-83, psychologist contractor, 1983—; cons. Beckley Appalachian Regional Hosp., 1978—, chief divsn. psychology, 1986-90; cons. Beckley Hosp., 1983—, Wyo. Gen. Hosp., Mullins, 1985-87, Raleigh Gen. Hosp., 1986—, Whelan Med. Clinic, Hinton, 1989-90, Beckley, 1990-91; probable cause hearings co-contractor So. Highlands Cmty. Mental Health Ctr., Itmann, W.Va., 1990—. Contbr. articles to profl. jours. Mem. legis. com. W.Va. Human Resources Assn., 1984-85; mem. adv. bd. Cherry Hill Children's Shelter, 1990-91; mem. human rights adv. com. VOCA, 1992—. Mem. Assn. for Applied Psychophysiology and Biofeedback, W.Va. Psychol. Assn., Biofeedback Soc. Am., W.Va. Human Resources Assn., W.Va. Soc. Autistic Children, Am. Assn. for Mental Retardation (religion div. 1990—), Internat. Platform Assn., People for Ethical Treatment of Animals. Democrat. Home: 271 Hoist Rd Beckley WV 25801 Office: Raleigh Psychiat Svcs Inc PO Box 1025 Mallard Ct Beckley WV 25801

BAKER, EDWARD GEORGE, retired mechanical engineer; b. Freeport, N.Y., Oct. 20, 1908; s. Edward George and Mary (Dunham) B.; m. Mary Louise Freer, Feb. 7, 1931; children—Edward Clark, Marna Larson, Ellen Freer (Mrs. George W. Lewis), John Durrin, Bruce Robert. B.A., Columbia Coll., 1930, M.A., 1931, Ed.D., 1938. Assoc. prof. math. Newark Coll. Engring., N.J., 1930-42; mem. tech. staff Am. Bur. Shipping, N.Y.C., 1942-73. Author: First Course in Mathematics, 1942. Contbr. articles on marine engring. to profl. jours. Pres. Nutley (N.J.) Symphony Soc., 1939-41; chmn. zoning bd. of adjustment, Pine Knoll Shores, N.C., 1979-84. Recipient Order of Long Leaf Pine award State of N.C., 1982. Mem. Am. Math. Soc., ASME, Soc. Naval Architects and Marine Engrs., N.Y. Acad. Sci., Phi Beta Kappa. Republican. Episcopalian. Home: 812 Shepard St Morehead City NC 28557-4324

BAKER, GEORGE HAROLD, III, physicist; b. Cheverly, Md., Mar. 23, 1949; s. George Harold Jr. and Betty (Fost) B.; m. Donna Prillaman, Jun 21, 1975; children: Matthew C., Jeffrey P., Virginia E. MS, U. Va., 1974; PhD, USAF Inst. Tech., Dayton, Ohio, 1987. Teaching asst. U. Va., Charlottesville, 1971-73; physicist Harry Diamond Labs., Adelphi, Md., 1973-77; physicist Def. Nuclear Agy., Alexandria, 1977-87, group leader, 1987-89, asst. for program devel., 1989-94; chief innovative concepts divsn., 1994-96; dir. Springfield Rsch. Facility, 1996—; physicist Def. Spl. Weapons Agy., Alexandria, Va., 1996—. Contbr. articles to profl. jours. Tchr. Agape Christian Fellowship, Chantilly, Va., 1974—; music and youth leader New Life Fellowship, Annandale, Va., 1979-83; canvasser Citizens for Sensible County Planning, Fairfax County, Va., 1989—. Fellow Nuclear Electromagnetic Soc. (chmn. program com. 1984); mem. IEEE (session chmn. 1987, 92), N.Y. Acad Sci., Forum for Mil. Application of Directed Energy, Phi Delta Theta. Office: Def Nuclear Agy 6801 Telegraph Rd Alexandria VA 22310-3328

BAKER, JAMES A., justice; b. Evansville, Ind., Mar. 30, 1931. BBA, So. Meth. U., 1953, LLB, 1958. Bar: Tex. 1958, U.S. Dist. Ct. (no. dist.) Tex. 1958, U.S. Ct. Appeals (5th cir.) 1961, U.S. Ct. Appeals (11th cir.) 1981, U.S. Supreme Ct. 1980. Atty. Goldberg, Alexander and Baker, 1958-72, Weber, Baker and Allums, 1972-79; prin. Law Office of James A. Baker, 1979-86; judge U.S. Ct. Appeals (5th cir.), Dallas, 1986-95; justice Supreme Ct. of Tex., Austin, 1995—; lectr. State Bar of Tex. Profl. Devel. Program; guest lectr. So. Meth. U. Sch. Law, Dallas Bar Assn., El Centro Dalls C.C. Contbg. author Tex. Collection Manual, 1980. Fellow Tex. Bar Found., Dallas Bar Found.; mem. ABA (mem. task force on appellate delay reduction 1991-92), State Bar Tex., Dallas Bar Assn. (former chair bankruptcy and comml. law sect. 1974, bd. dirs. 1995), Coll. of State Bar Tex., Am. Judicature Soc., Inst. Judicial Adminstrn., William Mac Taylor Jr. Inn of Ct. Office: Supreme Ct Tex PO Box 12248 Austin TX 78711*

BAKER, JAY MILTON, obstetrician/gynecologist; b. Honolulu, Oct. 2, 1949; s. Robert Leon and Betty Jo (Hill) B.; m. Susan Helen Hitner (div. June 7, 1993); 1 child, Caryn Allysa. BA, BS, U. Mo., 1977, MD, 1981. Diplomate Am. Bd. Obstetrics and Gynecology. Intern, resident in ob/gyn Naval Hosp., Portsmouth, Va., 1981-85, staff physician med. corps, 1985-92; asst. prof. ob/gyn Ea. Va. Med. Sch., Norfolk, 1993—. Fellow Am. Coll. Obstetrics and Gynecology; mem. Phi Kappa Phi, Alpha Omega Alpha. Avocations: camping, cycling, astronomy, chess, geology. Office: Ea Va Med Sch Dept Ob/Gyn 601 Colley Ave Norfolk VA 23507

BAKER, JEAN MARY, cable television executive; b. Laconia, N.H., July 24, 1944; d. Marshall Dwight and Eugenia Mary (O'Mara) Whedon; m. Frank J. Haley, Feb. 3, 1968 (div. Feb. 1978); children: Kathleen A., Colleen E.; m. Frank J. Baker, July 6, 1985 (dec. Sept. 1986). Grad. high sch., Laconia, N.H. Supr. OS & D Willeys Express, Concord, N.H., 1974-80; exec. sec. Perry Cable TV, Riviera Beach, Fla., 1981-84; ops. mgr. Perry Cable TV, Riviera Beach, 1984-86; community devel. mgr. Centel Cable TV of Fla., Palm Beach Gardens, 1986-88, Adelphia Cable Comm., Palm Beach Gardens, 1988-94; gen. mgr. Adelphia Cable Comm., Elizabeth City, N.C., 1994—. Team capt. March of Dimes Walkamerica, West Palm Beach, Fla., 1987-94, steering com., 1990-93. Named Vol. of Yr. No. Palm Beach C. of C., 1989. Mem. Women in Cable (pres. South Fla. chpt. 1988, bd. dirs. 1989-94), Elizabeth City C. of C. (bd. dirs., chmn. tourism com.), Pasquotank County LEPC. Home: 733 Riverside Ave Elizabeth City NC 27909 Office: Adelphia Cable Comm 701 N Hughes Blvd Elizabeth City NC 27909

BAKER, JUDITH J., nurse manager; b. Augusta, Ga., Oct. 30, 1955; D. Glenn and Mattie (Roberson) Beard. AD, U. S.C., Aiken, 1978, BSN, 1988; MS in Nursing Adminstrn., Med. Coll. Ga., 1992. Staff and charge nurse Med. Coll. Ga., Augusta, 1977; sr. nurse Ga. Regional Hosp., Augusta, 1978, lead nurse, 1980, nurse mgr. adult psychiat. unit, 1987, temporary staffing coord., 1992; part-time nurse adminstr., 1994, acting nurse mgr. child and adolescent program, 1996; grad. Dept. Human Resources Leadership Program, 1991.

BAKER, KATHERINE JUNE, elementary school educator, minister; b. Dallas, Feb. 3, 1932; d. Kirk Moses and Katherine Faye (Turner) Sherrill; m. George William Baker, Jan. 30, 1955; children: Kirk Garner, Kathleen Kay. BS, BA, Tex. Women's U., 1953, MEd, 1979; cert. in religious edn.,

Meadville Theol. U., 1970; postgrad., North Tex. State U., 1987—; DD (hon.), Am. Fellowship Ch., 1981. Cert. elem. and secondary tchr., adminstr., Tex.; lic. and ordained min. Kingsway Internat. Ministries, 1991. Mgr. prodn. Woolf Bros., Dallas, 1953-55; display mgr. J.M. Dyer and Co., Corsicana, Tex., 1954; advt. artist Fair Dept. Store, Ft. Worth, 1954-56; artist, instr. Dutch Art Gallery, Dallas, 1960-65; dir. religious edn. 1st Unitarian Ch., Dallas, 1967-69; dir. day care, tchr. Richardson (Tex.) Unitarian Ch., 1971-73; dir. camp Tres Rios YWCA, Glen Rose, Tex., 1975-76; dir. program of extended sch. instrn. Hamilton Park Elem. Sch. Richardson Ind. Sch. Dist., 1975-78, tchr. Dover Elem. Sch., 1979-92, tchr. Jess Harben Elem. Sch., 1979-92; founder ednl., editorial and arts/evang. assn. Submitted Ministries, Richardson, 1992—; dir. Flame Fellowship Internat., 1987—, state rep., 1994—. Contbr. articles to ch. newspaper, 1967-69; exhibited in group show at Tex. Art Assn., 1966; one-woman show Dutch Art Gallery - Northlake Ctr., Dallas, 1965. Advocate day care Unitarian Universalist Women's Fedn., Boston, 1975-76, mem. nominating com., 1976-77. Mem. NEA, ASCD, Nat. Coun. Social Studies, Tex. State Tchrs. Assn. (treas. Richardson chpt. 1984-85), Women's Ctr. Dallas, Sokol Athletic Ctr., Smithsonian Assn., Dallas Mus. Assn., Alpha Chi, Delta Phi Delta (pres. 1952-53), Phi Delta Kappa. Home: 2711 Sherrill Park Dr Richardson TX 75082-3217

BAKER, KERRY ALLEN, executive business recruiter; b. Selmer, Tenn., Sept. 21, 1949; s. Austin Clark and Betty Ann (Brooks) B.; m. Ellen Fleming. BIE, Ga. Inst. Tech., 1971; MBA, Ga. State U., 1973; JD, Memphis State U., 1987. With dept. law State of Ga., 1971-73; div. engr. N.W. Ga. div. Gold Kist Inc., Ellijay, 1977-80; sr. mfg. engr. Plough, Inc., Memphis, 1980-82; mgr. indsl. engring. Plough, Inc., 1983-86, supr. mfg. engr., 1986-90; plant bus. mgr. Clorox Co., Dyersburg, Tenn., 1990-95; ops. mgr. Huish Detergents, Inc., Dyersburg, Tenn., 1995; exec. dir. Mgmt. Recruiters of Dyersburg (Tenn.), 1996—. Bd. dirs. Dyersburg Cmty. Concerts Assn., Adopt-a-Sch. Capt. U.S. Army, 1973-77. Decorated Order of St. Barbara. Mem. Inst. Indsl. Engrs., Am. Prodn. and Inventory Control Soc., Nat. Fire Protection Assn., Scabbard and Blade, Rotary, Masons, Dyer County C. of C. (bd. dirs.). Methodist. Home: 727 N Sampson Ave Dyersburg TN 38024-3961

BAKER, LEE EDWARD, biomedical engineering educator; b. Springfield, Mo., Aug. 31, 1924; s. Edward Fielding and Oneita Geneva (Patton) B.; m. Jeanne Carolyn Ferbrache, June 20, 1948; children: Carson Phillips, Carolyn Patton. BEE, U. Kans., 1945; MEE, Rice U., 1960; PhD in Physiology, Baylor U., 1965. Registered profl. engr., Tex. Asst. prof. electrical engring. Rice U., Houston, 1960-64; asst. prof. physiology Baylor U. Coll. Medicine, Houston, 1965-69, assoc. prof., 1969-75; prof. biomed. engring. U. Tex., 1975-82; Robert L. Parker Sr. Centennial Prof. Engring. U. Tex., Austin, 1982—. Co-author: Principles of Applied Biomedical Engineering, 1968, 3d edit., 1989; author, co-author scientific papers. Served to lt. USN, 1943-46, PTO, 1951-53. Spl. research fellow NIH, 1964-65. Fellow Am. Inst. Med. and Biol. Engring., Royal Soc. Medicine; mem. IEEE (sr.), Biomed. Engring. Soc. (sr.), Assn. for Advancement Med. Instrumentation, Am. Physiol. Soc. Episcopalian. Office: Univ Tex ENS 610 Biomed Engring Program Austin TX 78712

BAKER, LESLIE MAYO, JR., banker; b. Brunswick, Md., May 22, 1942; s. Leslie Mayo Sr. and Betty Jane (Rinker) B.; m. Suzanne Baldwin Borum, Dec. 19, 1964; children: Leslie Roderic, Benjamin Spencer, Leslie Margaret Cecil. BA in English Lit., U. Richmond, 1964; MBA, U. Va., 1969. With Wachovia Bank and Trust Co., Winston-Salem, N.C., 1969—, asst. v.p., 1972-73, v.p. gen. loan adminstrn. office, then v.p. loan adminstrn. office, 1973-74, v.p., mgr. internat. dept., 1974-77, sr. v.p., mgr. internat. dept., 1977-80, exec. v.p. div. exec. adminstrn., 1980-90, pres., chief exec. officer, 1990—. Trustee Southeastern Ctr. Contemporary Art, Winston-Salem, 1988; trustee Colgate Darden Grad. Sch., Charlottesville, 1982—; bd. visitors U. N.C. Grad. Sch., Chapel Hill, 1988; trustee Summit Sch., Winston-Salem, 1988. Capt. USMC, 1964-67, Vietnam. Mem. Robert Morris Assocs. (sr. assoc. Phila. 1980—). Episcopalian. Office: Wachovia Bank and Trust Co PO Box 3099 Winston Salem NC 27150*

BAKER, LINDA LESLIE, social services administrator, consultant; b. Eugene, Oregon, Sept. 15, 1948; d. Charles Andrew and Ashley Estelle (Durrett) Marcum. BS in Psychology, Ft. Hays (Kans.) State U., 1972, MS in Counseling, 1973; MSW, U. Kans., 1984. Lic. Social Worker. Social worker Dept. Social and Rehab. Svcs., Topeka, 1972-79; foster care program specialist Kans. Children's Svc. League, Topeka, 1979-83, dist. dir., 1983-88; dir. programs Kans. Children's Svc. League, 1989-93, assoc. exec. dir., 1993-95; dir. ARCH Nat. Resource Ctr., 1995—; cons. Nat. Directory Foster Care Program and Ednl. Consultant, 1985—; cons., trainer Permanency Planning Resources for Children, 1983—; instr. U. Kans., 1986-95; tech. advisor NASW Communications Network, Inc. Active Kans. Children and Adolescent Svc. System Programs, Topeka, 1985-86, Children's Coalition, Topeka, 1985-86; mem. adv. bd. Family Svc. and Guidance Ctr., Topeka, 1985-86, Family Preservation Project, 1986-95, Kans. Foster Care Task Force, 1988-95, Kans. Adoption Coalition, 1989; mem. Kans. Com. for Prevention Child Abuse. Mem. NASW, Kans. Assn. Social Workers, Kans. Polit. Action for Candidate Election, Coun. on Children and Families (sec. 1979—), Phi Kappa Phi. Democrat. Home: 300 McCauley St Chapel Hill NC 27516 Office: ARCH Nat Resource Ctr 800 Eastowne Chapel Hill NC 27514

BAKER, LORI ANN, physical therapist; b. Detroit, July 16, 1957; d. Richard Gary and Mary Barbara (Vail) Griffith; m. Joseph Kurtyka, Nov. 22, 1980 (div. Sept. 1984); m. William Randall Baker, June 24, 1989; 1 child, Katherine Elisabeth Baker. BS, U. Mich., 1979; MBA, Kennesaw Coll., 1990. Phys. therapist Lansing Sch. Dist., Mich., 1979-81, Mich. Sch. for Blind, 1980-81, Ingham Med. Ctr., 1980-81; pediatric phys. therapist Toledo Hosp., 1981-84, Childrens Ortho Hosp. and Med. Ctr., Seattle, 1984-85; pediatric clin. specialist Kennestone Hosp., Marietta Ga., 1985-89, supr. acute care therapy, 1989-90; phys. therapist Am. Home Health Care, 1987-91; contract phys. therapist, 1990-91; clin. mgr. Atlanta Rehab. Inst., 1991-95; phys. therapist Grandview Health Care Ctr., Atlanta, 1995-96—, Lumpkin County Schs., Atlanta, 1995-96, Global Rehab., 1996—. Comprehensive Therapy, Cons., 1996—. Mem. Am. Phys. Therapy Assn., Neurodevelopmental Treatment Assn. Avocations: stained glass; furniture refinishing, running, biking. Home: 402 Wild Hill Rd Woodstock GA 30188-1972 Office: 340 W Peachtree St NW Ste 250 Atlanta GA 30308-3517

BAKER, MARK BRUCE, lawyer, educator; b. Bridgeport, Conn., Dec. 27, 1946; s. Phillip and Lillian (Islovitz) Bader; m. Sandra Fay Wolf, June 9, 1968 (div. 1982); 1 dau., Rachel Barrett Bader; m. 2d Nora Kay Mandell, Dec. 30, 1984; 1 dau., Lisa Anne Baker. B.B.A., U. Miami, Coral Gables, Fla., 1968; J.D., So. Meth. U., 1974. Bar: Tex. 1974. Assoc. firm Herndon, Girand and Dooley, Dallas, 1974-76; ptnr. firm Pailet and Bader, Dallas, 1976-80; prof. internat. law U. Tex., Austin, 1980—; of counsel firm Bard and Groves, Houston, 1981-83; gen. counsel Embree Constrn. Group, Inc., 1987—; of counsel Goodall, Davison and Goldsmith, Austin, 1991—; chmn. bd. Embree Health Care Group, Inc. Contbr. articles to legal publs. Bd. dirs. Jewish Community Council Austin, 1983-86. Recipient Outstanding Asst. Prof. award U. Tex., 1982, Outstanding Class Lectr. award, 1984; Tex. Excellence Teaching award U. Tex. Alumni Assn., 1983. Mem. ABA, Union Internationale des Avocats, Am. Friends of Wilton Park (sec.-treas. 1982-84), Tex. Bar Assn. (internat. law sect.), Austin Fgn. Trade Coun., Am. Bus. Law Assn. (internat. law sect., pres. 1990-91). Home: 406 Brookhaven Trl Austin TX 78746-5413 Office: 8050 Airport Rd Georgetown TX 78628

BAKER, MICHAEL LEE, librarian; b. Jackson, Tenn., Sept. 3, 1959; s. John William and Grace Alma (Bartman) B. BS, Lambuth Coll., 1981. Reference librarian Jackson-Madison County Libr., 1983, audio-visual librarian, 1983—. Talent coord. Blues Fest '90, Jackson Arts Coun., 1990; talent coord., co-founder Shannon St. Blues Fest, Jackson, 1991-96; mem. folk arts bd. Tenn. Arts Coun., Nashville, 1992-96. Home: 52 Lassiter Rd Jackson TN 38301 Office: Jackson-Madison County Libr 433 E Lafayette St Jackson TN 38301-6340

BAKER, REBECCA LOUISE, musician, music educator, consultant; b. Covina, Calif., Apr. 12, 1951; d. Allen Herman and Hazel Margaret (Maki) Flaten; m. Jerry Wayne Baker, Dec. 22, 1972; children: Jared Wesley, Rachelle LaDawn, Shannon Faith. Grad. high sch., Park River, N.D.; student, Trinity Bible Inst., 1968-69. Sec. Agrl. Stblzn. & Conservation Svc. Office, Park River, N.D., 1969; pianist, singer Paul Clark Singers & Vic Coburn Evangelistic Assn., Portland, Oreg., 1969-72; musician, singer Restoration Ministries Evangelistic Assn., Richland, Wash., 1972-80; musician, pvt. instr. Calvary Temple Ch., Shawnee, Okla., 1980-81; organist, choirmaster St. Francis Episcopal Ch., Tyler, 1984-87; co-founder, owner Psalmist Sch. of Music & Recording Studio, Whitehouse, 1983—; pianist/entertainer Willowbrook Country Club, Tyler, Tex., 1991—; pianist, vocalist Mario's Italian Restaurant, Tyler, 1994—; pianist Garner Ted Armstrong, Tyler, 1986—; pianist, dir. Children's Choir, Calvary Bapt. Ch., Tyler, 1987—; pianist, entertainer Ramada Hotel, Tyler, 1988-90; pianist Whitehouse (Tex.) Sch. Dist. choirs, 1988—; accompanist Tyler Area Children's Chorale, 1988-90, Univ. Interscholastic League; pvt. instr. keyboard and vocal. Composer: Religious Songs (12 on albums), 1979; pianist, arranger, prodr., rec. artist 6 albums; editor, arranger: Texas Women's Aglow Songbook, 1987; editor Shekinah Glory mag., 1989—; developer improvisational piano course; star, prodr. mus. religious spls. nat. syndicated for TV, 1995; played for receptions honoring Gov. George Bush and Congressman John Bryant. Performer, spkr. many charitable, civic and religious orgns., Tex. and U.S. including AAUW, Kiwanis Clubs; co-founder Psalmist Mins. Internat., 1988—; founder, pres. Christian Music Tchr.'s Assn., 1991; worship leader Mayor's Prayer Breakfast, Tyler, 1994. Mem. Women's Aglow Fellowship (music dir., spkr., performer at retreats and tng. seminars including reception honoring Tex. Gov. George W. Bush and Congressman John Bryant; starred in and produced two musical TV religious spls. aired on several Tex. channels 1995). Republican. Full Gospel. Home and Office: Psalmist Music & Recording PO Box 961 Whitehouse TX 75791-0961

BAKER, RICHARD HUGH, congressman; b. New Orleans, LA, May 22, 1948; m. Karen Carpenter; children: Brandon, Julie. BA, La. State U. State rep. La. Dist. 64, former chmn. com. on transp., hwys. and pub. works, 1981-82; mem. La. Ho. of Reps., 100th-103rd Congresses from 6th La. Dist., 1987—; mem. ag. com., chmn. Banking & Fin. Svcs. subcom. on Capital Mkts., Securities and Govt. Sponsored Enterprises, also real estate broker. Methodist.

BAKER, ROBERT WOODWARD, airline executive; b. Bronxville, N.Y., Sept. 3, 1944; s. Richard Woodward and Dorothy Marilyn (Garett) B.; m. Martha Jane Hauschild, June 11, 1966; children: Richard Woodward, Robert Woodward, William Garrett, Suzanne. B.A., Trinity Coll., 1966; M.B.A., U. Pa., 1968. Dir. ramp services Am. Airlines, Inc., N.Y.C., 1973-76; asst. v.p. mktg. adminstrn. Am. Airlines, Inc., 1976-77; v.p. so. div. Am. airlines, Inc., Dallas, 1977-79; v.p. freight mktg. Am. Airlines, Inc., Dallas-Ft. Worth Airport, 1979-80; v.p. sales and advt. Am. Airlines, Inc., 1980-82, v.p. mktg. automation systems, 1982-85, sr. v.p. info. systems, 1985, sr. v.p. ops., 1985-89; sr. v.p. AMR Corp., 1985-89; exec. v.p. ops. Am. Airlines, Inc., 1989—. Office: Am Airlines Inc PO Box 619616 Dallas TX 75261-9616

BAKER, ROGER DALE, city administrator; b. Wikel, W.Va., Sept. 2, 1946; s. Eugene Hunter and Naomi Vienna (Riner) B.; m. Linda Gaye Wilmer, Apr. 2, 1950; 1 child, April Christine. BA, W.Va. Inst. Tech., 1974; MPA, Murray State U., 1978. Evaluation & prodn. supervisor Valley Workshops, Inc., Covington, Va., 1975; adminstrv. asst. to city mgr. Covington, 1975-76; coord. cmty. career ctr/ Dabney S. Lancaster C.C., Clifton Forge, Va., 1978; quality control inspector Daniel Constrn. Co., Warm Springs, Va., 1978-80; dir. spl. projects City of Clifton Forge, 1981-82; town mgr. City of Colonial Beach, Va., 1982-84; city mgr. City of Clifton Forge, 1984-87; asst. city mgr. City of Harrisonburg, Va., 1987—. Bd. dirs. Va. Skyline Girls Scout Coun., Salem, Va., 1989-93, United Way Harrisonburg/Rockingham, 1989-95; bd. dirs., sec.-treas. Upper Valley Regional Park Authority, Harrisonburg, 1987-95; bd. dirs., chmn. Ctrl. Shenandoah Juvenile Detention Home, Staunton, 1992-95, Harrisonburg Rockingham Regional Sewer Authority, 1989-95. Staff sgt. USAF, 1967-71, Europe. Mem. Va. Local Govt. Mgr. Assn. Baptist. Office: City of Harrisonburg 345 S Main St Harrisonburg VA 22801

BAKER, SAMUEL GARRARD, advertising agency executive; b. Austin, Tex., Nov. 20, 1950; s. Norman Linwood and Clara Stuart (Bierbower) B.; m. Nancy Dawn White, Nov. 12, 1988; children: Jamie, Jack, Angela, Christopher. AA in Journalism, De Anza Coll., Cupertino, Calif., 1979; BA in Radio/TV journalism, San Jose State U., 1983. Advt. exec. Sta. KCEN-TV, Killeen, Tex., 1986-95, prodr. TV promotion, 1988; owner Baker Constrn., Killeen; pres., CEO NSB Advt., 1995—. Pres. Ft. Hood area United Way, Killeen, Tex., 1991, Killeen Vol. Fire Dept., 1991; chmn. bd. dirs. Killeen Crimestoppers, 1988; arts commr. City of Killeen, 1990-91; chmn. Arts Commn., 1992-93; bd. dirs. Cen. Tex. Better Bus. Bur., 1993—. Recipient Addy award, 1989, 92, 94, 95, 96. Mem. 1st Cav. Divn. Assn., Ctrl. Tex. Homebuilders Assn. (bd. dirs. 1992—, treas. 1995), Ctrl. Tex. Advt. League (founder, pres. 1988-89, 94-95), Killeen C. of C. (mil. affairs com. 1988—, govt. affairs com. 1987—, chmn. ambs. 1990-91), Exch. Club (pres. 1989-91), Hell on Wheels Assn. Methodist. Home and Office: NSB Advt PO Box 11555 Killeen TX 76547

BAKER, SARA ANN, vocational education educator; b. Dallas, Jan. 21, 1952; d. Edwin Richard and Winifred (Stainbrook) Etgen; m. Billie Dean Baker, Apr. 30, 1983. BA, East Tex. State U., 1974, MS, 1976. Lifetime tchg. cert. Tex. Edn. Agy. Legal sec. Taylor & Mizell, Dallas, 1979-81; instr. Exec. Secretarial Sch., Dallas, 1981-83, Dallas County C.C., Dallas, 1983-89; word processing mgr. Thompson & Knight, Dallas, 1989-91; English instr. Fabens (Tex.) Ind. Sch. Dist., 1992-94, instr. career/tech., 1996—; chmn. career and tech. dept. Fabens H.S., 1996-97; instr. career/tech. Am. Inst. Commerce, Dallas, 1994-96; mem. site base decision making coun. Fabens (Tex.) H.S. Grantee Rio Grande Tech. Prep., El Paso, Tex., 1996. Mem. Nat. Bus. Edn. Assn. Office: Fabens Ind Sch Dist PO Box 697 Fabens TX 79838

BAKER, THOMAS EDWARD, lawyer, accountant; b. Washington, July 24, 1923; s. John Thad and Angelina E. (Rappa) B.; m. Mildred M. Younglove, Dec. 26, 1944; children: Jean Ann Baker Holland, Cindy Baker Goralewicz, Linda Hogan. BS U. Okla., 1950, JD, 1950. Bar: Okla. 1950; CPA, Okla. Pvt. practice, Oklahoma City, 1950; IRS agt., spl. agt., 1951-53; ptnr. Shutler Baker Simpson & Logsdon, Kingfisher, Okla., 1953-79, Baker Logsdon & Schulte, Kingfisher, 1979—. Trustee U. Okla. Found., Inc., 1987-89. Served with AUS, 1943-46. Mem. Am. Legion (past service officer). Democrat. Mem. Christian Ch. (Disciples of Christ). Lodge: Elks, Rotary (pres. Kingfisher club 1957). Home: 903 Park Ln Kingfisher OK 73750-3833 Office: Baker Logsdon & Schulte 302 N Main St Kingfisher OK 73750-2740

BAKER, WINDA LOUISE (WENDY BAKER), social worker; b. Suwannee County, Fla., July 16, 1952; d. Austin Sidney Baker and Jessie Mae (Williams) Baker Jones. BA in Theology, Berkshire Christian Coll., 1974. Clk.-typist State of Fla., Tallahassee, 1974-76; cashier Tallahassee-Eastern Theatres, 1975-76; field rep. Commn. Human Relations, 1976-77; asst. to dir. retirement living, sec., receptionist Advent Christian Village, Dowling Park, Fla., 1977-79, admissions counselor, social worker, after 1979, multi-purpose worker, 1980; geriatric care worker Advent Christian Village, Dowling Park, Fla., 1983-85, med. transcriptionist, 1985, advt. sales staff, 1986-87; processor H&R Block, 1987-1988; legal sec., McAlpin, Fla., 1987—; geriatric care person , Valdosta, Ga., 1989-94, Alpharetta, 1994—. Vol. ARC and Asso. Charities, 1977—; founder Suwannee County Overeaters Anonymous, Live Oak, Fla., 1982; live-in companion for the elderly Serve Care Nursing Svcs. of South Ga., 1988-89, for Ann Mason, 1989-92. Mem. Suwannee County Mental Assn., Assn. Informed Travelers, Christian Fin. Planning, Inc., Cheeks Sch. Gymnastics Alumni. Republican. Advent Christian. Home: 15950 Freemanville Rd Alpharetta GA 30201-2711

BAKER-BRANTON, CAMILLE B., counselor, educator; b. Greenwood, Miss., Aug. 30, 1950; d. Don Otho and Sarah (Goodpasture) Baker; children: Irene, Sarah. BS, MS, Miss. State U., 1972, PhD, 1989; MEd, MS, Delta State U., Cleveland, Miss., 1987. Lic. counselor, Miss.; cer. counselor; Diplomate Am. Bd. Med. Psychotherapists. Assoc. prof. behavioral scis. Delta State U., Cleveland, Miss., 1989—; mem. Job Tng. Placement Act Rev. Bd. Author: Coercive Sexual Behavior among College Students: A Causal Model, Coercive Sexual Behavior Rating Scale. Mem. AACD, DAR, Nat. Bd. Cert. Counselors, Coun. Exceptional Children, Assn. Children Learning Disabilities, Am. Mental Health Counselors Assn., Miss. Counseling Assn., Exch. Club, Phi Delta Kappa, Kappa Delta Pi, Delta Gamma. Home: 305 E Gresham St Indianola MS 38751 Office: Delta State U PO Box 3142 Cleveland MS 38733

BAKER-GARDNER, JEWELLE, business executive, interior designer; b. Ayden, N.C., May 23, 1925; d. Roland Ray and Helen Wingate (Jackson) Cannon; m. Paul Thomas Baker, July 25, 1956 (dec. 1963); children: Paula Jewelle Baker Bryan, Paul Thomas; 1 stepchild, Blanche Baker Miller; m. Fred Calvin Gardner, Apr. 19, 1969 (dec. May 1983); 1 stepchild, Angela Gardner Jones. Student Woods Bus. Sch., New Bern, N.C., 1942-45; BA, Am. Sch. Design, N.Y.C., 1948; BFA, U. N.C., Greensboro, 1950. Dept. head Navy Supply, Cherry Point, N.C., 1941-45; ptnr. Cannons Paint & Wallpaper Co., Ayden, 1945-70; exec. v.p. Baker Furniture Co., Kinston, N.C., 1950-63; operator Cannon Farms, Ayden, 1956—; pres., treas. Baker Furniture Co., Kinston, 1963-69; with consumer program Drexel Co., 1965-66; owner Jewelle Baker Cons., Kinston, 1969—; v.p. Gardner Homes, Elizabeth City, N.C., 1972-81; bus. cons. Gardner Constrn. Co., Kinston, 1975-81; bus. cons. Lenoir Plumbing & Heating Co., Kinston, 1975-81; chief exec. officer Gardner Homes, Elizabeth City, 1982—; chmn. bd., chief exec. officer Lenoir Plumbing & Heating Co., 1982—, Gardner Constrn. Co., 1982—; cons. Carolina Power & Light, 1963-65, N.C. Solar Energy Assn., 1977-79, Nutritional Therapy, Durham, 1979-81; lectr., 1950-63; del. U.S.-China Joint Session on Industry, Trade, and Econ. Devel., Beijing, 1988. Mem. Devel. Auth. of Neuse River Council of Govts., 1984-85. Columnist, Ayden Dispatch and Greenville News Leader, 1940-56; producer Performer Baker's Commls., 1960-69. Mem. C. of C. Kinston (bd. dirs., v.p., chmn. retail mchts. div.), So. Retail Furniture Assn., Nat. Retail Furniture Assn., N.C. Mchts. Assn., N.C. Farm Assn., Assoc. Gen. Contractors Am., Community Council for the Arts, Internat. Platform Assn., N.C. Zool. Assn., N.C. Art Soc., Kinston Country Club, Coral Bay Club, Pinecknoll Golf and Country Club, Sea Water Marina Club. Democrat. Mem. Ch. Disciples of Christ. Home: 1708 Elizabeth Dr Kinston NC 28501-3416 Office: Gardner Constrn Co PO Box 856 Kinston NC 28502-0856

BAKER-WHITE, ROBERT ELLIOTT, drama educator; b. Boston, Feb. 26, 1959; s. George Pierce and Katharine Hale (Elliott) B.; m. Tracy Ann Baker-White, Aug. 17, 1985, Children: Emily, Matthew. BA, Williams Coll., Williamstown, Mass., 1980; MFA in theater directing, U. Washington, Seattle, 1983; PhD in Drama and Humanities, Stanford U., 1990. Literary assoc. Williamstown (Mass.) Theatre Festival, 1980-81, Seattle Reperatory Theatre, 1983, Am. Reperatory Theatre, Cambridge, Mass., 1984-85; literary mgr. Playwright's Platform, Boston, 1985-86; asst. prof. of drama Trinity U., San Antonio, Tex., 1990-96, assoc. prof. drama, 1996—. Mem. editl. bd. Theatre Topics, 1993—; referee (jours.) Text and Performance Quarterly, 1993—, Essays in Theatre/Etudes Théâtrale, 1995—; contbr. articlesto profl. jours. Recipient Whitney Dissertation fellow Stanford U., 1990, Jr. Faculty fellow Trinity U., 1991-94; Gilbert Gabriel award Williams Coll., 1980. Mem. MLA, Am. Soc. Theater Rsch., Theory and Criticism Focus Group, Assn. for Theatre in Higher Edn. (sec. steering. com. 1990-91, 95-96). Home: 501 Abiso Ave San Antonio TX 78209 Office: Trinity U Dept Speech & Drama 715 Stadium Dr San Antonio TX 78212

BALABAN, MURAT OMER, food science educator; b. Ankara, Turkey, Feb. 5, 1952; came to U.S., 1977; s. Faruk Mehmet and Selma (Fetgeri) B.; m. Canan Bayezit, Aug. 10, 1977; 1 child, Denis Tan. BChemE, Mid. East Tech. U., 1976; PhD in Food Sci. & Tech., U. Wash., 1984. Ind. software cons., 1984-85; postdoctoral rsch. assoc. food sci. dept. Rutgers U., New Brunswick, N.J., 1985-86; asst. prof. food processing & engring. U. Fla., Gainesville, 1986-91; assoc. prof. food processing & engring. U. Fla., 1991—; mem. scientific adv. bd. FMC Corp., 1991—; ops. analysis group Singleton Seafood, Tampa, Fla. Assoc. editor Jour. Aquatic Food Product Tech.; editl. bd. Food Tech. in Turkey. Fulbright scholar, 1995. Mem. Nat. Assn. Colls. & Tchrs. Agr., Inst. Food Technologists (exec. com. food engring. group 1989-92, ann. program com., exec. com. seafood divsn. 1995—), Am. Soc. Agrl. Engrs., Inst. Thermal Processing Specialists, Tropical and Subtropical Fisheries Soc. (exec. com. 1994—), Gamma Sigma Delta. Home: 4008 NW 122nd St Gainesville FL 32606-3631 Office: U Fla FSHN 359 Gainesville FL 32611

BALANOFF, HOWARD RICHARD, social sciences educator; b. N.Y.C., Dec. 12, 1942; s. Louis and Freida (Pagawitz) B.; m. Marilyn Kay Ucci, Jan. 27, 1968; children: Emily Kay, Amy Michelle. BA in Polit. Sci. and History, CUNY, 1964; M in Urban Planning, Tex. A&M U., 1972, DEd in Urban Planning, 1974. Planning coord. Tex. Dept. Water Resources, Austin, 1973-76; from asst. to assoc. prof. S.W. Tex. State U., San Marcos, 1976-88, prof. pub. adminstrn. and planning polit. sci. dept., 1988—, dir. community devel. inst., 1976-81, dir. grad. program pub. adminstrn., 1980-83; vis. and adj. prof. LBJ sch. pub. affairs U. Tex., Austin, 1985-88, adj. prof. dept. ednl. adminstrn., 1988—; presenter in field. Editor: Public Administration: Annual Editions, 1991/1992, 1990, 91, 92; contbr. chpts. to books and articles to profl. jours. Missile combat crew comdr., comm. electronics officer USAF, 1964-71, Korea, major Res. ret. Recipient Award for Devel. Young Profls. in Pub. Sector, Austin Soc. Pub. Adminstrn., 1992. Mem. Am. Soc. Pub. Adminstrn. (mem. nat. coun. 1993—, vice chmn. internat. relations com.), Am. Inst. Cert. Planners (cert.), Am. Planning Assn. (Best Class Project award ctrl. Tex. chpt. 1991), Nat. Assn. Schs. Pub. Affairs and Adminstrn. (mem. site accreditation team), Tex. Assn. Schs. Pub. Affairs and Adminstrn. (sec., mem. exec. bd. 1987-89), Tex. City Mgrs.' Assn. (mem. profl. devel. and edn. com. 1988—), Internat. Assn. Provision for Local Democracy Devel. (mem. exec. com. 1993—), Phi Alpha Alpha (chpt. advisor). Baptist. Home: 10910 Sierra Colorado Austin TX 78759-5114 Office: SW Tex State U Polit Sci Dept San Marcos TX 78666 also: U Tex Austin TX 78759

BALÁS, IRENE BARBARA, artist; b. Budapest, Hungary, Feb. 28, 1928; came to U.S., 1973; d. Sandor and Ilona (Udvardy) B.; m. Tom Elliot, July 30, 1974 (dec. May. 1980). Studies with Karl Kaufmann and Hans Hoff, Vienna, Austria; B Degree, Budapest, 1943; MA in Art Therapy and Psychology, KunstAkad./Sigmund Freud Inst., Vienna, 1948. Cert. art therapist, psychoanalyst. Artist, 1974—. One-woman shows in Vienna, Paris, Munich, Madrid, Chile, Bolivia, Peru, Venezuela, Colombia, Haiti, N.Y., San Francisco, Miami and L.A.; represented in permanent collections Vatican, Mus. Atelier, other museums, and pvt. collections of Rockefeller, Henry Ford, Olga, Bruce Walker and others; commd. to paint History of Cuba in 7 paintings, 1990, Hungarian Hang Gliding Expdn. Around the World in 7 paintings for Mil. Mus. in Budapest, 1993; TV show hostess, 1977-78. Recipient Nat. prize of Austrian Painters, 1948. Home and Office: 1621 Collins Ave Apt 907 Miami FL 33139

BALCONIS, ANDREA JO, physician; b. Port Chester, N.Y., June 23, 1946; d. Andrew Theodore and Lucille Eudora (Cluxton) B. BS in Math., Siena Heights Coll., 1971; MA in Theology, Boston Coll., 1980; MD, U. Miami, 1991. Joined Adrian Dominican Sisters, Roman Cath. Ch., 1967; diplomate Am. Bd. Family Practice. Tchr. Aquinas Coll., Nassau, Bahamas, 1967-71, 72-76; tchr. St. Anastasia Sch., Ft. Pierce, Fla., 1971-72; pastoral worker Human Promotion and Devel. Project Nuestra Senora de Guadalupe parish, Callao, Peru, 1976-78; health worker HEW, Blissfield, Mich., summer 1978; tchr., vol., adminstr. Human Promotion and Devel. Project Casa Communal, Managua, Nicaragua, 1980-85; premed. student Barry U., Miami Shores, Fla., 1985-87; intern, resident, chief resident family practice svc. Jackson Meml. Hosp., Miami, 1991-94; asst. med. dir. DePorres Health Ctr., Marks, MS, 1994-95, med. dir., 1995—; overseas mission del., guest speaker Adrian Dominican Sisters gen. chpt. assembly, 1985; musician for liturgies at Barry U., 1986-87. Vol. Martin Luther King Migrant Workers Clinic, 1989. Fla. Keys Health Fair, 1988, 90, sch. phys. exams in Dade County, 1992, in Fla. Keys, 1993. Mem. AMA, Fla. Med. Assn., Dade County Med. Assn., Am. Acad. Family Physicians, Am. Med. Women's Assn., Assn. Sister, Brother and Priest Physicians. Democrat.

BALDERSTON, THOMAS WILLIAM, banker, corporate executive; b. Phila., Feb. 28, 1941; s. Hugh Eastburn and Pauline (Schaaf) B.; BS, Pa. State U., 1963; MBA, U. So. Calif., 1973; m. Louise Talmage, June 5, 1971 (dec. Jan. 1991); children: Kristin Clark, Thomas Talmage, Melissa Fleshman, Amanda Fleshman; m. F. Dee Gregory, Jan. 30, 1993; children: Melisa Dee, Amanda Anne. Mktg. rep. Rohm & Haas Co., Phila., 1966-72; asst. v.p. Warburg Paribas Becker Inc., N.Y.C., 1973-77; sr. v.p. Blyth

Eastman Paine Webber Health Care Funding Inc., N.Y.C., 1977-81, also dir.; chmn. bd., pres., founder Health Care Capital Alliance, Inc., 1981—; pres., founder Retirement Ctrs. Group, Inc., 1983-89; mng. gen. ptnr. Heather Hills Ltd. Partnership, 1984—; co-founder, bd. dirs. Genesis Health Ventures, Inc., Kennett Sq., Pa., 1985-95; CEO Retirement Ctr. Network (joint venture ITD Group, Inc. and Retirement Ctr. Group, Inc.), 1985-89; bd. dirs. Quality Med. and Rehab Svcs., Inc., Linwood, N.J., 1991-92, Blue Star Health and Rehab., Inc, 1992—; pres. Health Care Properties, Inc.. 1st lt. C.E., U.S. Army, 1963-65. Mem. Am. Hosp. Assn., Fedn. Am. Hosps., Am. Health Care Assn., Am. Assn. Homes for the Aging, Nat. Assn. Sr. Living Ind., Pi Kappa Phi. Republican. Clubs: Round Hill (Greenwich, Conn.); Riverside (Conn.) Yacht, Boca West (Boca Raton, Fla.), Royal Palm Yacht and Country Club (Boca Raton), Boca Raton Resort & Club.

BALDOCCHI, DENNIS DAVID, micrometeorologist; b. Antioch, Calif., Apr. 12, 1955; s. Evo Savario and Helen Marie (Marieni) B.; m. Nicole Marie Lepoutre, Nov. 24, 1984; 1 child, Ian McCully. BS, U. Calif., Davis, 1977; MS, N. Nebr., 1979, PhD, 1982. Biometeorologist ORAU, Oak Ridge, Tenn., 1983-86; physical scientist NOAA/ATDD, Oak Ridge, Tenn., 1986—; vis. scientist U. Stockholm, 1990; mem. exec. bd. NASA Boreas Project, 1993—; mem. editorial bd. Agrl. Forest Meteorology, 1993—; mem. sci. panel Internat. Satellite Land-Surface Climatology Project, 1994—; mem. steering com. Trace Gas Network. Author: (12 chpts.) Scaling Physiological Processes: contbr. 45 articles to profl. jours.; editl. bd. Plant, Cell and Environ., 1996—, Boundary Layer Meteoroloyg, 1996—. RAISA fellow U. Tuscia, Viterbo, Italy, 1992-93, postdoctoral fellow ORAU, 1982. Mem. Am. Mateorological Soc. (Biometeorological com. 1990-93), Am. Geophys. Soc. (Editorial citation 1990). Home: 11415 Morgan Overlook Dr Knoxville TN 37931-2816 Office: NOAA/ATDD PO Box 2456 Oak Ridge TN 37831-2456

BALDON, SUZANNE BROWN, anthropologist; b. Kilgore, Tex., Nov. 13, 1948; d. Warren Corder Brown and Betty Sue (Florey) White; m. Phillip Emile Mahfood, June 24, 1968 (div. June 1984); children: John-Phillip, Sebastian, Vincent, Valerie; m. Paul Aaron Baldon, Nov. 24, 1989. AA in Art, Tyler Jr. Coll., 1983; BA in Art/Psychology, U. Tex. at Tyler, 1986; MA in Anthropology, U. Tex. at Arlington, 1994. Artist, art tchr. Tyler, 1976-84; studio supr. Cynthia Jean Originals, Tyler, 1984-86; pvt. investigator Hooper Holmes/Gen. Info. Svc., Dallas, 1986-91; park ranger Tex. Parks & Wildlife Dept., Cedar Hill, Tex., 1991-95; sales rep., bus. office Amon Carter Mus., Ft. Worth, Tex., 1996—. Home: PO Box 1004 Cedar Hill TX 75106 Office: Amon Carter Mus 3501 Camp Bowie Blvd Fort Worth TX 76107-2695

BALDRIDGE, MELISSA ANNE, curator, editor; b. Tulsa, Oct. 10, 1963; d. Edgar Earl Baldridge and Bettie Gay (Burton) Sypniewski. BA, Rice U., 1986; postgrad., Sotheby's Connoisseurship Tng., London, 1986-87; student, Rice U., 1992. Curatorial asst. intern Mus. Fine Arts, Houston, 1985; field participant, rec. keeper Archaeological Excavation, Rome, 1985; para-appraiser Furniture Appraisal Svc. Tex., Houston, 1988-92; contract researcher, editorial intern Houston Met. Mag., 1992; curator of collections, editor Torch Energy Advisors, Houston, 1992—. Freelance writer for various publs. Vol. M.D. Anderson Hosp., Houston, 1990-92. Mem. Am. Asns. Mus., Tex. Assn. Mus., Assn. Corp. Art Curators, Nat. Bit Spur and Saddle Collectors Assn., Daus. Rep. of Tex., Tex. State Hist. Assn., Greater Houston Preservation Alliance. Office: Torch Energy Advisors 1221 Lamar St Ste 1600 Houston TX 77010-3039

BALDWIN, DEANNA LOUISE, dietitian; b. Oklahoma City, Okla., Jan. 14, 1946; d. Jesse Burlin and Celena Mae (Robison) Smith; m. James Stephen Baldwin, Apr. 7, 1989; 1 child, Melissa. BS, Stephen F. Austin, 1985. Dietetic tech. Pasadena (Tex.) Bayshore Hosp., 1969-70; payroll clk. Seismic Computing Corp., Houston, 1971-72; restaurant mgr., mgr. trainer H. Salt Fish n' Chips, Pasadena, 1972-75; asst. food svc. dir. East Tex. Med. Ctr. Hosp., Tyler, 1990-92. Mem. Am. Dietetic Assn.

BALDWIN, JAMES EDWIN, civil engineer, land development executive; b. Naylor, Ga., Jan. 22, 1924; s. Camillus Edwin and I. Elizabeth (Ledford) B.; m. Janet Smith, 1950 (div. 1981); children: Gary E., Janet C. BSCE, Ga. Inst. Tech., 1949. Registered profl. engr., Ga., S.C. Prin. Baldwin Engring. Co., Augusta, Ga., 1953-68; pres. Baldwin & Cranston Assocs., Inc., Cons. Engrs., Augusta, 1968-81, Columbia Land Corp., Augusta, 1964—; arbitrator Am. Arbitration Assn., Charlotte, N.C., 1981—; chmn. Augusta-Richmond County Planning and Zoning Commn., 1968-81. Mem. Richmond County Bd. Equalization, Augusta, 1978. Lt. (j.g.) USN, 1942-45. Mem. ASCE (past chpt. pres.), Ga. Soc. Profl. Engrs. (past state dir.), Augusta Country Club. Presbyterian. Home and Office: 4900 Columbia Rd Grovetown GA 30813-9129

BALDWIN, JOHN CHARLES, surgeon, researcher; b. Ft. Worth, Sept. 23, 1948; s. Charles Leon and Anabel (West) B.; m. Christine Janet Stewart, Mar. 31, 1973; children: Alistair Edward Stewart, John Benjamin West, Andrew Christian William. BA summa cum laude, Harvard U., 1971; MD, Stanford U., 1975; MA Privatim (hon.), Yale U., 1989. Diplomate Am. Bd. Internal Medicine, Am. Bd. Surgery, Am. Bd. Thoracic Surgery. Fellow in medicine Harvard Med. Sch., Boston, 1975-77, fellow in surgery, resident in surgery, 1977-81; resident in surgery Mass. Gen. Hosp., 1977-81; resident in cardiothoracic surgery Stanford (Calif.) U., 1981-82, chief resident cardiothoracic surgery, 1983, asst. prof., 1984-87; dir. heart-lung transplantation, transplant rsch. lab. Stanford U., 1986-87; prof. surgery and chief cardiothoracic surgery Yale U., New Haven, 1988-94; cardiothoracic-surgeon-in chief Yale-New Haven Hosp.; DeBakey/Bard prof., chmn. Baylor Coll. Medicine, Houston, 1994—; sr. attending physician, chief surg. svcs. Meth. Hosp., Houston, 1994—; sr. attending physician, surgeon in chief Ben Taub Gen. Hosp., Houston, 1994; dir. multi-organ transplant ctr. Meth. Hosp./ Baylor U., Houston; dir. thoracic surgery residency program Coll. Medicine Baylor U., Houston; dir. thoracic surgery residency program Yale-New Haven Hosp., 1988-94; vis. lectr. Yale U., bd. permanent officers, 1988-94; cons. gen. thoracic surgery Waterbury (Conn.) Hosp. health Ctr., 1988-94; bd. dirs. United Network Organ Sharing, 1984-87; mem. clin. rsch. com. ad hoc rsch. grant rev. Cystic Fibrosis Found.; trustee New Eng. Organ Bank, 1988; mem. solid organ transplant com. Blue Cross & Blue Shield of Conn., 1990—; mem. sci. adv. bd. Alexion Pharms., Inc., 1991-94; bd. dirs. Baylor Coll. medicine Healthcare, Inc.; mem. adv. bd. Donate Life Found.; mem. exec. faculty Baylor Coll. of Medicine, pres.'s coun.; bd. dirs. New England chpt. Transplant Recipients Internat. Orgn., 1992-94. Co-editor: Thoracic Surgery, Oxford Textbook of Surgery, 1989—; editor: Cardiac Surgery: Principles and Techniques, 1994; assoc. editor Jour. Applied Cardiology, 1985-92; editorial bd. Jour. Thoracic and Cardiovascular Surgery, 1990—, Transplantation, 1990—, Transplantation Sci., 1992—, Andromeda Interactive Ltd., The Cardiovasc. System Interactive Teaching Program, 1993—; contbr. numerous articles and book chpts. in field. Mem. Harvard Club Schs. Com., Harvard Coll. Fund, Harvard U. Undergrad. Admissions Interview Com.; fellow Timothy Dwight Coll. Yale U., Yale U. Art Gallery Assocs.; mem. appointments and promotions com. Sch. Medicine, Yale U., 1991—, clin. scis. bldg. planning com., 1990—; bd. dirs. Neighborhood Music Sch. New Haven., 1989-92; bd. overseers Harvard U., 1995—; bd. permanent officers Yale U., 1988-94. John Harvard scholar, 1969, 70, Wendell scholar Harvard U., 1969, Rhodes scholar Oxford U., Alumni scholar Stanford Sch. Medicine, 1974 ; medalist Gothenburg (Sweden) Thoracic Soc., 1985; recipient Medaille de la Ville de Bordeaux French Thoracic Soc., 1987, travelling lectureship, 1988, Master Tchr. award Cardiovascular Revs. & Reports, 1990; travelling fellow Australia and New Zealand chpt., ACS, 1989; traveling lectureship, 1989. Fellow ACP, ACS, Royal Coll. Surgeons (Eng., traveling lectr. 1989), Am. Coll. Angiology, Am. Coll. Cardiology (mem. transplantation com. 1991—, chmn. task force cardiac donor procurement Bethesda Conf. 1992), Am. Coll. Surgeons (bd. govs. 1993—), Am. Coll. Chest Physicians, Mass. Med. Soc.; mem. AMA, AAAS, Am. Assn. Thoracic Surgery (mem. com. grad. edn. thoracic surgery 1992—, Evarts A. Graham Meml. Traveling Fellowship com. 1993—), Am. Soc. Transplant Surgeons (com. on heart transplantation 1986—, adv. com. in issues 1989—, chmn. subcom. on heart transplantation, physician payment reform commn. 1989—), Nat. Heart, Lung and Blood Inst. (cons. divsn. extramural affairs rev. br. 1990—), Assn. Acad. Surgery, Am. Physiol. Soc., Am. Heart Assn. (mem. rsch. grant peer rev. subcom 1984—, coun. circulation, cert. of appreciation for outstanding svc. 1986), Am. Surg. Assn., Am. Thoracic Soc., Am. Soc. Artificial Internal Organs, Am. Soc. Extracorporeal Tech., Am. Assn. Lab. Animal Sci., Am. Organ Transplant Assn., Am. Venous Forum, Internat. Soc. Heart and Lung Transplantation (chmn. program com. 1988), Internat. Assn. Cardiac Biol. Implants, Internat. Fedn. Surg. Colls., Internat. Soc. Cardiovasc. Surgery, Internat. Soc. Cardio-Thoracic Surgeons, Internat. Soc. for Heart Rsch. (mem. Am. sect.), Internat. Soc. for Artificial Organs, Mediterranean Assn. for Cardiology and Cardiac Surgery, New Century Soc., Thoracic Surgery Found. for Rsch. and Edn., Norman E. Shumway Surg. Soc., New Eng. Surg. Soc., Pan Am. Med. Assn. (coun. on organ transplantation), North Am. Soc. Pacing and Electrophysiology, Societe Internat. de Chirurgie, Royal Soc. Medicine, Soc. Univ. Surgeons, Thoracic Surgery Dirs. Assn. (chmn. curriculum com. transplantation 1993), Transplantation Soc., Assn. Alumni of Magdalen Coll. Oxford U., Assn. Rhodes Scholars, Acad. Surg. Rsch., Assn. Surg. Edn., Assn. Program Dirs. in Surgery, Conn. Thoracic Soc., Harris County Med. Soc., Calif. Med. Assn., Calif. Thoracic Soc., Calif. Thoracic Soc. Respiratory Care Assembly, No. Calif. Cystic Fibrosis Found., So. Calif. Transplant Soc., Conn. Med. Soc., Conn. Soc. Am. Bd. Surgeons, Mass. Med. Soc., N.Y. Soc. Thoracic Surgery, New Haven County Med. Soc., Harvard Med. Alumni Assn. (assoc.), Physicians' Assn. New Haven County, Soc. Crit. Care Medicine, Soc. Thoracic Surgeons, Southeastern Surg. Congress, Southern Surg. Assn., Southwestern Surg. Congress, Tex. Surg. Soc., Halsted Soc., Houston Surg. Soc. Soc. for Organ Sharing, United Network for Organ Sharing, San Francisco Surg. Soc., Santa Clara Med. Soc., Stanford Med. Alumni Assn., Stanford Club Conn., Harvard Clubs San Francisco, Peninsula, N.Y.C., So. Conn., Houston, Boston, Mory's Assn., New Haven Lawn Club, Inner Quad Stanford U., The Hasty Pudding Club - Inst. 1770, Quinnipiack Club, Yale Club New Haven, Forum World Affairs, Ambs. Roundtable, Oxford Soc., Phi Beta Kappa, others. Office: Dept Surgery One Baylor Plz Houston TX 77030

BALDWIN, NANCY GODWIN, program director; b. Fairfax, Okla., Feb. 20, 1935; d. Francis King and Cannie (Sells) Godwin; m. Thomas Lee Baldwin, Dec. 3, 1960 (dec. 1996). AB, Sweet Briar Coll., 1957; postgrad., Bowling Green State U., 1957-58. Asst. to dir. of admission Sweet Briar (Va.) Coll., 1958-60, asst. dir. admission, 1960-65, dir. admission, 1965-80, editor alumnae mag., 1986—, coord. devel. communications, 1990—; mem. alumnae assn. bd. Sweet Briar Coll., 1986—. Episcopalian. Office: Sweet Briar Coll Sweet Briar VA 24595

BALÉE, WILLIAM L., anthropology educator; b. Ft. Lauderdale, Fla., Oct. 12, 1954; s. William Lockert Balée and Lorraine Kathryn Monahan; m. Pamela Van Rees, May 24, 1980 (div. Dec. 1986); m. Maria da Conceição Bezerra, Mar. 9, 1987; children: Nicholas, Isabel. BA with high honors, U. Fla., 1975; MA, Columbia U., 1979, MPhil, 1980, PhD, 1984. Assoc. rschr. ecology Museu Paraense Emílio Goeldi, Belém, Brazil, 1988-91; chair ecology Museu Paraense Emilio Goeldi, Belém, Brazil, 1990-91; assoc. prof. anthropology Tulane U., New Orleans, 1991—; adj. prof. anthropology CUNY, 1983, 84, SUNY, Purchase, 1982; adj. prof. social scis. CUNY, 1983; adj. prof. sociology and anthropology Rutgers U., 1984; vis. assoc. prof. Ctr. for L.Am. Studies, U. Fla., 1990; extensive fieldwork with forest peoples in Amazon of Brazil and Bolivia, 1980-94. Author: Footprints of the Forest: Ka'apor Ethnobotany, 1994; co-editor: Resource Management in Amazonia: Indigenous and Folk Strategies, Advances in Economic Botany, Vol. 7, 1989; mem. editl. bd. Ethnobotany. Decorated officer Order of the Golden Ark (Netherlands); N.Y. Bot. Garden fellow, 1984-88, Fulbright-Hays fellow, 1980-81, Newcomb Coll. fellow, 1992-94, Conselho Nacional de Desenvolvimento Tecnológico e Científico fellow, 1988-91; grantee Ford Found., 1989-90, Jessie Smith Noyes Found., 1990-91, World Wildlife Fund, 1991-92, Tulane U., 1992, Wenner-Gren Found., 1993-94; apptd. to 60th Coll. Disting. Lectrs., Sigma Xi, 1997—. Fellow Am. Anthrop. Assn., Associação Brasileira de Antropologia, Internat. Soc. Ethnobiology, Soc. Ethnobiology, Soc. Ethnobotanists, Phi Beta Kappa, Phi Kappa Phi. Office: Tulane U Dept Anthropology 1021 Audubon St New Orleans LA 70118-5238

BALES, AVARY, nurse; b. Atlanta, July 22, 1940; d. Eugene Carlston and Florence Elizabeth (Cox) B. Diploma, Ga. Bapt. Hosp. Sch. Nursing, Atlanta; BS in Allied Health, Coll. of St. Francis, Joliet, Ill.; M in Health Care Adminstrn, Ctr. Mich. U., 1994. RN, Ga. Asst. dept. head Ga. Bapt. Hosp., Atlanta; house supr. Clayton Gen. Hosp., Riverdale, Ga.; capt. emergency med. svcs. tng. div. Clayton County Fire Dept., Jonesboro, Ga.; dir. info. svcs. West Paces Med. Ctr., Atlanta. Home: 3281 Rock Creek Dr Rex GA 30273-2456

BALES, RICHARD HENRY HORNER, conductor, composer; b. Alexandria, Va., Feb. 3, 1915; s. Henry Ahijah and Henrietta Wyeth (Horner) B.; m. Mary Elizabeth Starley, Nov. 7, 1942; 1 child, Mary Starley Alterman. MusB, Eastman Sch. Music, 1936; postgrad., Juilliard Grad. Sch., 1938-41; studies with, Serge Koussevitzky, 1940; ArtsD (hon.), Shenandoah U. and Conservatory, 1986. Tchr. Mass. State Tchrs. Coll., summer 1941, George Washington U., 1953; lectr. music. Debut as condr. with Nat. Symphony Orch., 1935, condr. Va.-N.C. Symphony, 1936-38, music dir. Nat. Gallery Art and, condr. Nat. Gallery Orch., Washington, 1943-85, Washington Cathedral Choral Soc., 1945-46, music dir. Nat. Symphony Orch., summer 1947, guest condr. orchs. in Phila., N.Y.C., St. Louis, Rochester, San Antonio, N.Mex., Boston, Cleve., Nat. Symphony Orch., Am. Little Symphony, Naumburg Orch., vis. lectr., condr. Eastman Chamber Orch. Eastman Sch. Music, Rochester, N.Y., summers 65, 66, 67, appointed condr. emeritus Nat. Gallery Orch., 1986; composer various works, orchestral, film, instrumental, choral selections. Decorated Officer's Cross Republic of Austria, 1991; recipient 1st prize Arts Club Washington, 1940, award Merit Nat. Assn. Composers and Condrs., 1959, Alice M. Ditson award Columbia U., 1960; 1st ann. arts award Washington Times, 1983; Internat. Inst. Arts and Letters life fellow, 1961. Mem. ASCAP, Am. Fedn. Musicians, Soc. Cin., Civil War Round Table D.C. (Gold medal 1960, pres. 1960-61), USN Band (hon. life), Bruckner Soc. in Am. (hon.), Kindler Found. (pres. 1959-62), S.C.V. (hon. life mem., 1st lt. comdr. 1963-64). Episcopalian. Club: Cosmos (club award 1985). Home and Office: 12178 Clipper Dr Woodbridge VA 22192-2209

BALES, ROBERTA KINTER, critical care nurse; b. Ind., Pa., Nov. 19, 1940; d. Ivan J. and Cevilla (Work) Kinter; divorced; children: Debra Bales Luikens, Garry, Laurie Bales Paige, Linda. AD, N.Mex. State U., Carlsbad, 1986; student, Amarillo Coll., High Plains Hosp. RN, Tex. Staff nurse coronary care High Plains Bapt. Hosp., Amarillo, Tex. Scholar N.Mex. State U., Carlsbad.

BALFANZ, ROBERT DON, automotive executive, investment counselor; b. Evanston, Ill., Nov. 29, 1951; s. William R. and Eunice Nora (McGraw) B. BA, Northeastern Ill. U., 1973. Owner, operator Corvette Clinic, Dallas, 1979—, Corvette Salvage, Dallas, 1982—; prin., investment counselor R. Donald Balfanz, Inc., 1989—; presenter seminars. Columnist, corr. Keepin' Track of Vettes mag., Spring Valley, N.Y., 1976-87. Mem. Nat. Inst. Automotive Service Excellence (cert. master auto technician), Chili Appreciation Soc. Internat. (judge ann. world championship chili cookoff 1980-86). Lodges: Masons, Shriners. Office: Corvette Clinic 10265 Miller Rd Ste 104 Dallas TX 75238-1224

BALINT, DAVID LEE, engineering company executive; b. Cleve., June 27, 1946; s. Robert Stephen and Edna Mae (Alward) S. BBA, Cleve. State U., 1969; grad., U.S. Naval War Coll., 1982; MBA, Temple U., 1986. Cert. purchasing mgr., profl. contracts mgr. Commd. ensign USN, 1970, advanced through grades to lt. comdr., retired, 1990; deputy dir. contract adminstrn. Teledyne Brown Engring., Huntsville, Ala., 1990—, mgr. compliance programs, 1996—; adj. faculty Temple U., Phila., 1986-90, Southeastern Inst. Tech., Huntsville, 1991-94, U. Ala., Huntsville, 1994—. Del. mem. People-to-People Contract Mgmt. Del., Peoples Republic China, 1986, 89. Fellow Nat. Contract Mgmt. Assn. (nat. v.p. N.E. region 1989-90, nat. v.p. membership 1990-91, nat. functional dir. 1991—, Nat. Edn. award 1994, Disting. Svc. award 1995), Soc. Logistics Engrs., Am. Assn. Adult and Continuing Edn. Home: 107 Huntington Ridge Rd Madison AL 35758-9349 Office: Teledyne Brown Engring 300 Sparkman Dr NW Huntsville AL 35805-1912

BALISH, RUTH REITZ, community health nurse, medical technologist; b. Palmerton, Pa., Oct. 1, 1919; d. Chas. B. and Minnie E. Reitz; m. George F. Balish, Nov. 5, 1949; children: Deidre B. Talarico, Vicki B. DelMonte, Lori S. Hedges. Student, Moravian Coll., 1937-38; diploma in nursing, Grandview Hosp. Sch. Nursing, 1942; BSN, Temple U., 1944; cert., New England Hosp. Women, 1943; diploma in med. tech., Sacred Heart Hosp. Sch., 1945. Chief med. tech. Morris County Chest Clinic, Morris Pl., N.J.; public health nurse City of Summit (N.J.); chief rsch. histologist Merck Co., Rahway, N.J.; pvt. duty nurse Boca Raton, Fla., Clearwater, Fla.; vol. nurse ARC Disaster Shelter, Boca Raton, Fla., Waynesville, N.C., Pinellas County, Fla., Lakeland Fla.; co-owner, med. technologist North Summit Med. Lab., Summit, N.J., 1951-64. Vol. nurse Lakeland Regional Ctr., Morton Plant Hosp., Clearwater; adv. bd. J. Haley Vets. Hosp., Tampa, 1991-95, Bay Pines Vets. Hosp., St. Petersburg, Fla., VA Vol. Svc. Mem. DAR (officer 1961—, bd. dirs. 1980—, area chmn. commemorative WWII 50th anniversary Lakeland chpt. 1992-95, Excellence Cmty. Svc. award 1995), Am. Soc. Clin. Pathologists, Am. Chem. Soc., Daus. Am. Colonists, Order Ea. Star. Home: 4747 N Rte 33 # 86 Lakeland FL 33805

BALKCOM, CAROL ANN, insurance agent; b. Newport, R.I., June 20, 1952; d. Robert Terrence and Barbara Ruth (Hilton) Hannaway; m. Richard Roger Balkcom, Oct., 1981; children: Richard Robert, Geoffrey Adam. BA, R.I. Coll., 1974, MA in Teaching, 1981; Cert. Life Underwriter, Am. Coll., 1984, CHFC, 1986. CLU, ChFC. Tchr. Lincoln (R.I.) Jr. High Sch., 1974-78; sales agt. Met. Life Ins. Co., Pawtucket, R.I., 1978-80; mgr., agt. Phoenix Mut. Life Ins. Co., Providence, 1980-94; instr. R.I. Lic. Sch., Providence, 1986-93; dist. mgr. New Eng. Life, New Port Richey, 1994—. Mem. R.I. Life Underwriters (bd. dirs. 1981-84, 90—, 1st v.p. 1983-84). Office: New Eng Life 6313 Adams St New Port Richey FL 34652-2301

BALL, DEBORAH CHEEK, physical education educator; b. Gainesville, Ga., July 2, 1950; d. Frank and Louise Cheek; m. James A. Ball, July 8, 1978; children: William Dusty Perdue, Austin, Alexander. BS in Edn., U. Ga., 1973; MS in Edn., Ga. Southwestern Coll., 1985; EdD, Auburn U., 1995. Cert. health and phys. edn. tchr., Ga. Phys. edn. tchr. Shaw H.S., Columbus, Ga.

BALL, JOSEPH E., association executive; b. Birmingham, Ala., Sept. 15, 1942; s. Joseph Kern and Lou T. (Tilghman) B.; m. Linda Jean Hilton, Sept. 3, 1963; children: Jeffrey, Mark. BS, U. Ark., 1965; MBA, George Washington U., 1969. Housing bus. mgr. U. Fla., Gainesville, 1970-82; adminstrv. v.p. Fla. Gift Fruit Shippers Assn., Orlando, 1982-88, exec. v.p., 1988—. Monthly columnist, Mailer's Review, 1992—. Lt. USN, 1964-69, capt. USNR, 1964-89. Named Mailing Industry Exec. of Yr., U.S. Postal Svc., 1993. Mem. Parcel Shippers Assn. (bd. dirs.). Republican. Protestant. Home: 142 W Magnolia St Groveland FL 34736 Office: Fl Gift Fruit Shippers Assn 521 N Kirkman Rd Orlando FL 32808-7644

BALL, MARGIE BARBER, elementary school educator; b. San Antonio, Tex., June 28, 1943; d. Truman Joseph and Margaret Evelyn (Norman) Barber; m. Flamen Ball Jr., Aug. 20, 1966; children: Michael David, Matthew Joseph, Marissa Anne. BS, U. Houston, 1963; MS, Stephen F. Austin State U., 1985. Texas Tchr. Cert. Spanish tchr. Spring Branch Ind. Sch. Dist., Houston, Tex., 1964-66, tchr., 1966-68; dir. mother's day out Holy Spirit Episcopal, Tex., 1977-78; tchr. Nacogdoches (Tex.) Ind. Sch. Dist., 1979-82; kindergarten tchr. Christ Episc. Sch., 1982-87; early childhood tchr. Hudson Ind. Sch. Dist., Lufkin, Tex., 1987-94; tchr. pre-kindergarten/bilingual Lufkin Ind. Sch. Dist., 1994-95, tchr. pre-kindergarten/multi-age, 1995-96; tchr. kindergarten Hudson ISD, Lufkin, 1996—. Mem. Tex. State Tchr. Assn., East Tex. Assn. Educators Young Children, Nacogdoches, Med. Wives Auxillary, Phi Delta Kappa. Republican. Presbyterian. Office: Hudson ISD Rt 12 Box 8600 Lufkin TX 75901-4118

BALL, MILLICENT JOAN (PENNY BALL), multimedia developer; b. Buffalo, Sept. 15, 1939; m. Neil Baggett, Aug. 9, 1965 (div. Nov. 1991). BS, Antioch Coll., 1961; PhD, U. Md., 1969. Rsch. assoc. Inst. Hochenergiephysik, Heidelberg, Germany, 1969-71; sr. programmer Imperial Coll., London, 1971-73; asst. prof. Purdue U., West Lafayette, Ind., 1973-77; systems analyst Calculon Corp., Germantown, Md., 1978-80; computer analyst Brookhaven Nat. Lab., Upton, N.Y., 1980-90; data mgmt. group leader Super Collider Lab., Dallas, 1990-94; sr. analyst/pres. MJB Cons., DeSoto, Tex., 1994—. Recipient SBIR award Dept. Energy, 1994. Mem. AAUW, Assn. Computing Machinery, Assn. for Women in Sci. Home: 1415 County Ridge Dr De Soto TX 75115-7423 Office: MJB Consulting Ste 304 119 Executive Way De Soto TX 75115

BALL, REX MARTIN, urban designer, architect; b. Oklahoma City, June 14, 1934; s. Ralph Martin and Sarah Mae (Kellner) B. BArch, Okla. State U., 1956; MArch, MIT, 1958. Lic. arch. Nat. Coun. Arch. Registration Bd.; cert. planner Am. Inst. Cert. Planners. With HTB Inc. (archtl., engring., interior planning firm), Oklahoma City, 1958-94, chmn., chief exec. officer, 1981-94; chmn. emeritus HTB Inc. (archtl., engring., interior planning firm), 1994—; presdl. appt. to U.S. Commn. of Fine Arts, 1994—; guest lectr., moderator. Participant joint U.S./USSR exhibit "The Socially Responsible Environment," U.S.A./USSR, 1980-90; contbr. articles to profl. jours. Capt. U.S. Army Corps of Engrs. Recipient Bus. in the Arts award, 1988, 5 Who Care Corp. Humanitarian award, Gannett Found., 1988, Curt Schwartz Bus. in the Arts award, 1989, Phoenix award/Downtown Now, 1992, Cityscape award City of Oklahoma City, 1992, Disting. Alumni award Okla. State U., 1995. Fellow AIA; mem. The Octagon Soc., Am. Archtl. Found., Eastern Okla. AIA (past pres.), Tulsa C. of C. (past bd. dirs.), Urban Land Inst. (retiree assoc.), Oklahoma City C. of C. (former v.p., bd. dirs. 1980-90), Nat. Trust for Hist. Preservation, Nat. Bldg. Mus., Okla. Heritage Assn., Soc. Am. Mil. Engrs., Am. Planning Assn., Am. Soc. Interior Designers (assoc.), Okla. State U. Alumni Assn. (life mem., past bd. dirs., Tulsa and Okla. counties pres.), MIT Alumni Assn. (past Okla. pres.), Air Force Assn. (past pres. Gerrity chpt.), Navy League, Urban League of Greater Oklahoma City (past bd. dirs.), Blue Key Club, Sigma Nu, Alpha Rho Chi. Home: 2203 East 20th St Tulsa OK 74104

BALL, TRAVIS, JR., educational consultant, editor; b. Newport, Tenn., July 13, 1942; s. Travis and Ruth Annette (Duyck) B.; BA, Carson Newman Coll., 1964; MA, Purdue U., 1966. Instr., then asst. prof. English, Ill. Wesleyan U., Bloomington, 1966-69; vis. prof. English edn. Millikin U., 1969; asst. headmaster, chmn. English dept. Brewster Acad., Wolfeboro, N.H., 1969-72; dir. admissions, asst. to headmaster Park Tudor Sch., Indpls., 1972-88; cons. to Selwyn Sch., Denton, Tex., 1988-89; pres. Travis Ball & Assos., 1980-88; dir. comm. Verde Valley Sch., Sedona, Ariz., 1988-91; editor Projects in Enrollment Mgmt., 1992—; mem. commn. on curriculum and grad. requirements Ind. Dept. Public Instrn., 1974-76; mem. adv. council Ednl. Records Bur.; reviewer Nat. Stds. Project in Sci., Civics and Govt., 1994-95; ednl. cons., 1992—. Mem. Indiana Non-Public Edn. Assn. (treas., dir., vice chmn.), Independent Schs. Assn. Central States (conf. chmn.), Nat. Council Tchrs. English, Assn. Supervision and Curriculum Devel., Council Advancement and Support Edn. (adv. com. on ind. schs.), Nat. Assn. Ind. Schs. (workshop faculty 1986, 87), Sigma Tau Delta, Pi Kappa Delta, Phi Delta Kappa. Baptist. Editor, Tchrs. Service Com. Newsletter for English Tchrs., 1977-82; dept. editor English Jour., 1976-82; editor/pub. Contact: Newsletter for Admissions Mgmt., 1980-88. Office: 1739 Log Church Rd Newport TN 37821-5535

BALLANFANT, KATHLEEN GAMBER, newspaper executive, public relations company executive; b. Horton, Kans., July 11, 1945; d. Ralph Hayes and Audrey Lavon (Heryford) G.; m. Sid Roberts; children: Andrea, Benjamin. BA, Trinity U., 1967; postgrad. NYU, 1976, Am. Mgmt. Inst., 1977, Belhaven Coll., 1985. Pub. info. dir. Tex. Dept. Community Affairs, Austin, 1972-74; pub. affairs mgr. Cameron Iron Works, Houston, 1975-77, Assoc. Builders and Contractors, Houston, 1982-84; pres. Ballanfant & Assoc., Houston, 1977-82, 84—; pres. Village Life Inc., 1985—; pres., chief exec. officer Village Life Publs.; owner Village Life newspaper, Southwest News newspaper, Houston Observer/Times newspaper, Village Life Printing & Typesetting, South Post Oak newspaper; mem. adv. council on Construction Edn., Tex. So. U., Houston, 1984—; mem. task force on ednl. excellence Houston Ind. Sch. Dist., 1983—; mem. devel. bd. Inter First Fannin Bank, 1986-88; bd. dirs. Bellaire Hosp., Westbury-Southwest Assn. Author: Something Special-You, 1972, Prevailing Wage History in Houston, 1983;

editor newspaper Bellaire Texan, 1981-82, Austin Times, 1971. Vice pres. West Univ. Republic Women's Club, Houston, 1984—; fgn. vis. chmn. Internat. Inst. Edn., Houston, 1980—; docent Houston Zoo, 1982; bd. dirs. Westland YMCA. Named Tex. Woman of Achievement Tex. Womans Hosp., 1986; recipient Apollo IX Medal of Honor Gov. Preston Smith, 1970, Child Abuse Prevention award Gov. Dolph Briscoe, 1974, Tex. Community Newspaper Assn. (pres. 1988-89, bd. dirs. 1987-96). Mem. Bellaire C. of C. (bd. dirs. 1987-90, sec., treas. 1988), Rotary. Republican. Presbyterian. Avocations: traveling, racquetball, reading. Office: Village Life Inc 5160 Spruce St Bellaire TX 77401-3309

BALLANTINE, TODD H., environmental scientist; b. Washington, Aug. 9, 1946. BA in Econs., Colo. Coll., 1968; MS in Environ. Sci., U. Oxford, Eng., 1981. Pres., environ. scientist Ballantine Environ. Resources, Hilton Head Island, S.C., 1968—; produced prototype concept for San Jose River Watershed trust, Baja, Mex.; created prototype Wetland Evaluation Program, Hilton Head Island; planned and monitor 3 prototype systems for application of advanced-treated wastewater into wetlands, Hilton Head Island; designed and constructed programs for beach and dune stblzn., Hilton Head Island; chmn. Beaufort County Coun. Victoria Bluff Task Force; assessed and delineated more than 75 "404" wetlands in U.S. Author: Woodland Walks, 1978, Tideland Treasure, 1983; writer, illustrator 20 interpretive guides for nature preserves, hist. parks and wildlife refuges. Recipient Harry Hampton Conservation Journalism award S.C. Wildlife Fedn., 1988; faculty fellow Leadership Hilton Head Island. Mem. Southeastern Ecol. Inst. (chmn.). Office: Ballantine Environ Resource PO Box 23032 Hilton Head Island SC 29925-3032

BALLANTYNE, CHRISTIE MITCHELL, medical educator; b. Houston, Sept. 13, 1955; m. Yasmine Attie, June 21, 1980; children: Maria Leyla, Christina, Katina. BA magna cum laude, U. Tex., 1977; postgrad., NYU, Madrid, Spain, 1977; MD cum laude, Baylor Coll. Medicine, 1982. Diplomate Am. Bd. Internal Medicine, Am. Bd. Internal Medicine subspecialty Cardiovascular Disease; cert. ACLS instr. Resident in internal medicine U. Tex. Southwestern Med. Sch., Dallas, 1982-85; fellowship in cardiology Baylor Coll. Medicine, Houston, 1985-87, instr. sect. atherosclerosis and cardiology dept. medicine, 1988-89, asst. prof. atherosclerosis & cardiology dept. medicine, 1989-95, assoc. prof. dept. medicine, 1996—; attending Ben Taub Gen. Hosp. Cardiac Catherterization Lab., Houston, 1988—, Lipid Metabolism and Atherosclerosis Clinic, The Meth. Hosp., Houston, 1988—, Ben Taub Coronary Care Unit, Houston, 1989—; faculty mem. Am. Heart Assn./Squibb Tng. Ctr. for Clin. Mgmt. of Lipid Disorders, Baylor Coll. Medicine, 1990; co-investigator Lipoprotein and Coronary Atherosclerosis Study, 1990; sci. grant rev. com. Am. Heart Assn. Tex. Affiliate, 1991-96; pharmacy and therapeutics com. The Meth. Hosp., 1992-95. Contbr. chpts. to books and articles to profl. jours. Recipient Mosby scholarship award, Grant-in-Aid awards Am. Heart Assn. Tex. Affiliate, 1989, 91, Sanofi-Winthrop Grant-in-Aid award, 1994, Established Investigator award, 1996, Clin. Investigator award Nat. Heart Lung and Blood Inst., NIH, 1990, Caroline Wiess Law award in Molecular Medicine, 1992; named fellow Am. Heart Assn./Bugher Found. Ctr. for Molecular Biology in the Cardiovascular Sys., 1987-89. Fellow ACP, Am. Coll. Cardiology, Coun. on Clin. Cardiology Am. Heart Assn., Coun. on Arteriosclerosis; mem. Am. Fedn. Clin. Rsch. (sch. rep. for Baylor 1992), Tex. Med. Assn., Harris County Med. Soc., Houston Cardiology Soc. (pres. 1996), Phi Kappa Phi, Phi Beta Kappa, Alpha Omega Alpha. Office: Baylor Coll Medicine Sect Atherosclerosis 6565 Fannin Ms # A601 Houston TX 77030

BALLANTYNE, MAREE ANNE CANINE, artist; b. Sydney, NSW, Australia, Oct. 22, 1945; came to U.S., 1946; d. Charles Venice and Yvonne Mavis (McSpeerin) Canine; m. Kent McFarlane Ballantyne, Apr. 22, 1967; children: Christopher Kent, Joel Sokson. AA, Del Mar Coll., 1966; BA in English, U. Tex., 1971; postgrad., U. South Ala., 1974, U. Houston, 1981, Sonoma State U., 1982, 84, 85. Exhibited paintings in Mass., Tex., Ala.; creator logo for Gulf Coast Area Childbirth Edn. Assn., 1972, logo for Calif. Health Resources, 1985; contbr. articles to profl. jours. Charter mem. Gulf Coast Area Childbirth Edn. Assn., Mobile, Ala., 1971-76; mem. Mus. Guild, Corpus Christi, 1978-80, Art Mus., Mobile, 1972-76, Nat. Trust for Hist. Preservation, 1977-80. Recipient Cert. Appreciation, USCG, 1993, Letter of Appreciation USCG, 1993. Mem. Nat. Mus. of Women in the Arts (charter 1987-97), Coast Guard Officers Wives Club. Home: 1920 SW 56th Ave Plantation FL 33317-5938

BALLANTYNE, RICHARD LEE, lawyer; b. Evanston, Ill., Dec. 10, 1939; s. Frank and Grace (Bowles) B.; children: Richard L. Jr., Brant. BS in Engring., U. Conn., 1965, MBA, 1967; JD with honors, George Washington U., 1969. Bar: Mass., 1970, Fla. 1994, U.S. Dist. Ct. Mass. 1976, U.S. Patent Office 1982. Dir. corp. devel. Itek Corp., Lexington, Mass., 1969-73, assoc. counsel, 1973-75; corp. counsel, sec. Goodhope Industries, Springfield, Mass., 1975-77; gen. counsel, asst. treas., sec. Compugraphic Corp., Wilmington, Mass., 1977-82; v.p., gen. counsel, sec. Prime Computer Inc., Natick, Mass., 1982-89, Harris Corp., Melbourne, Fla., 1989—. Served with U.S. Army, 1958-61. Mem. ABA, N.E. Corp. Counsel Assn. Inc. (pres. 1984-86), Licensing Execs. Soc., Am. Soc. Corp. Secs, Computer Law Forum. Republican. Office: Harris Corp 1025 W NASA Blvd Melbourne FL 32919-0001

BALLARD, DAVID JOSEPH, epidemiologist, educator; b. Lexington, Ky., Mar. 2, 1956; m. Michela Caruso; children: Elisa Justine, Alessandro David. AB in Chemistry and Econs. with honors, U. N.C., 1978, MD, 1983, MS in Pub. Health, 1983, PhD in Epidemiology, 1990. Diplomate Am. Bd. Internal Medicine; lic. physician, Va., Minn. Chem. applications software programmer Hewlett-Packard, Palo Alto, Calif., 1976; acad. tutor U. N.C. Athletic Assn., Chapel Hill, 1976-78; dir. student health action com. clinic U. N.C. Sch. Medicine, Chapel Hill, 1979-80; resident dept. internal medicine, rsch. fellow Mayo Clinic, Rochester, Minn., 1983-86, head sect. health svcs. evaluation, 1989-91; asst. prof. epidemiology Mayo Med. Sch., 1986-90, assoc. prof., 1991; assoc. prof. medicine divsn. gen. medicine, dept. medicine U. Va. Sch. Medicine, 1991-94, assoc. prof. epidemiology, 1991-94; sr. scholar, dir. Health Data Ctr. Va. Health Policy Rsch. Ctr., 1991-94; pres. Kerr L. White Inst. for Health Svcs. Rsch., Decatur, Ga., 1991—; prof. dept. medicine Sch. Medicine Emory U., Decatur, 1994—, prof. dept. epidemiology Rollins Sch. Pub. Health, 1994—; dir. Emory U. Ctr. Clin. Evaluation Scis., Decatur, 1994—; USPHS trainee dept. epidemiology U. N.C. Sch. Pub. Health, 1981-82; rsch. asst. med. utilization rev. com. N.C. Meml. Hosp., Chapel Hill, 1977-78; co-investigator Edgecombe County High Blood Pressure Control Program, dept. epidemiology U. N.C. Sch. Pub. Health, Chapel Hill, 1981-83; study coord. chronotherapeutic insulin trial, clin. rsch. unit N.C. Meml. Hosp., Chapel Hill, 1982-83; epidemiologic cons. dept. ophthalmology U. N.C. Sch. Medicine, Chapel Hill, 1982-83; sr. assoc. cons. dept. health scis. rsch. Mayo Clinic, sect. clin. epidemiology, 1986-88, sect. health svcs. evaluation, 1987-88, cons. dept. health scis. rsch., 1988-91; vis. scientist, 1992—; mem. RAND/Acad. Med. Ctr. Consortium Clin. Appropriateness Initiative Working Group, 1988—; mem. AMA Clin. Appropriateness Initiative Ad Hoc Adv. Panel, 1991—; mem. steering com. Stroke Prevention Patient Outcome Rsch. Team, 1991—; assoc. Williamson Inst., Richmond, Va., 1992; cons. regional health care tech. assessment unit Unita Locale Socio Sanitaria, Italy, 1992—; mem. exec. com. Vets. Affairs Coop. Study, The Aneurysm Detection and Mgmt. Trial, 1992—; mem. adv. panel Battelle/Ctrs. for Disease Control and Prevention Diabetic End-Stage Renal Disease Program, 1993—; mem. adv. bd. Canadian Randomized Trial of Propanolol for Mgmt. of Patients with Small Abdominal Aortic Aneurysms, 1994—; rsch. fellow Cecil G. Sheps Ctr. for Health Svcs. Rsch., U. N.C., Chapel Hill, 1995-97; chairperson Adv. Coun. Internat. Soc. Quality in Health Care, 1995-97; external adv. group Morehouse Med. Treatment Effectiveness Ctr., 1995—. Mem. editl. bd. Health Svcs. Rsch., 1994—, Internat. Jour. for Quality in Health Care, 1994-96, Mayo Clinic Procs., 1988-91; peer reviewer Am. Jour. Epidemiology, Am. Jour. Medicine, Annals Internal Medicine, Arthritis and Rheumatism, Clin. Performance and Quality Health Care, Diabetes, Diabetes Care, Gastroenterology, Health Affairs, Internat. Jour. Epidemiology, Jour. Clin. Epidemiology, Jour. Gen. Internal Medicine, Jour. Rural Health, Jour. Rheumatology, Jour. Vascular Surgery, New Eng. Jour. Medicine, Western Jour. Nursing; contbr. articles to profl. jours. John Motley Morehead scholar U. N.C., 1974-78, N.C. fellow U. N.C., 1974-78, Holderness med. fellow U. N.C. Sch. Medicine, 1982-83, Merck/Soc. for Epidemiologic Rsch. Clin. Epidemiology, 1990-93; recipient John Motley Morehead grad. travel fellowship, 1978, U. N.C. Sch. Medicine fgn. travel fellowships Lyme Hosp., Lyme Regis, Dorset, Eng., 1979, Royal Maternity Hosp., Glasgow, Scotland, 1981, Ciba-Geigy Cmty. Svc. award U. N.C. Sch. Medicine, 1980, Clin. Paper Competition award ACP Assocs., 1985, Doctoral Dissertation Rsch. Grant award Nat. Ctr. Health Svcs. Rsch., 1985, Fischbach Found. rsch. fellowship Juvenile Diabetes Found. Internat., 1985-87, Instnl. Acad. Rsch. award U. Va., 1993-94, Young Investigator award Assn. Health Svcs. Rsch., 1995. Fellow ACP, Am. Coll. Angiology; mem. AMA, APHA, Assn. Health Svcs. Rsch., Soc. Med. Decision Making, Internat. Soc. Tech. Assessment in Health Care, Am. Heart Assn. (epidemiology coun.), Soc. Gen. Internal Medicine, Soc. Rsch. and Edn. in Primary Care Internal Medicine, Internat. Epidemiology Assn., Soc. Epidemiologic Rsch. Office: Emory U Sch Medicine Ctr Clin Evaluation Scis 101 W Ponce de Leon Ave Decatur GA 30030-2542 also: Kerr L White Inst Decatur Plaza Ste 610 101 W Ponce de Leon Ave Decatur GA 30030

BALLARD, RONALD DOYLE, theologian, educator; b. Houston, June 25, 1934; s. Brents L. and Irene (Hodges) B.; m. Wanda Tatum, Nov. 15, 1960; children: Rhonda, Kyle, Christa. BS, U. No. Tex., 1956; MDiv, Emory U., 1960; PhD, U. Glasgow, Scotland, 1971. Ordained elder United Meth. Ch., 1960. Instr. religion Oxford (Ga.) Coll. Emory U., 1970-71; from asst. to assoc. prof. religion Tex. Wesleyan U., Ft. Worth, 1971-80, chmn. dept. philosophy, religion, 1978-80, dean, sch. sci., humanities, 1980-89, asst. to pres., 1990-92, prof. religion, 1992—; spkr. Nat. Conf., Creative Mgt. Higher Ed., San Francisco and Washington, 1988-89; reviewer Wadsworth Publ. Co., Ca., 89; pres. Ronald D. Ballard Enterprise, Inc., Ft. Worth, 84-90; cons. S.W. Bell, St. Louis, 88-89. Cons. The Exec. Comm., Dallas, 1987, Gen. Dynamics, Ft. Worth, 1982-83, 88-90; exec. comm. Lydia Patterson Inst., El Paso, Tex., 1990—; pres. bd. dirs. Dallas/Ft. Worth Airport Chaplaincy, 1995—. Recipient Sam Taylor fellowship award, 1982, 83, 88, 90, Mortar Bd. award Nat. Hon. Soc., 94; named Hon. Adm. Tex. Navy, Tex. Governor, 95. Mem. Assn. Higher Edn. (v.p. 1989-90). Home: 313 Charleston Pl Hurst TX 76054 Office: Tex Wesleyan U 1201 Wesleyan St Fort Worth TX 76105

BALLARD, WILEY PERRY III, hematologist, oncologist; b. Atlanta, Mar. 30, 1952; s. Wiley Perry Jr. and Anne Sykes (Equen) B.; m. Jane Elliot Roberts, Aug. 15, 1992; 1 child, Wiley Perry IV. AB with high honors, Dartmouth Coll., 1974; MD, Emory U., 1978. Diplomate Am. Bd. Internal Medicine, Am. Bd. Med. Oncology, Am. Bd. Hematology. Intern in medicine N.Y. Hosp.- Cornell Med. Ctr., N.Y.C., 1978-79, resident in medicine, 1979-81, asst. chief resident in medicine, 1981, fellow in hematology-oncology, 1983-84, chief clin. fellow in hematology-oncology, 1984-85, asst. attending physician, 1985-87; fellow in infectious disease Tufts-New England Med. Ctr., Boston, 1981-82; fellow in gen. internal medicine Cornell U. Sch. of Medicine, N.Y.C., 1982-83; instr. in medicine Cornell U. Med. Coll., N.Y.C., 1984-86, asst. prof. medicine, 1986-87; attending physician Piedmont Hosp., Atlanta, 1987—; pvt. practice Atlanta, 1987—; mem. adv. bd. Am. Cancer Soc., Atlanta, 1990-92, v.p. med. affairs, 1992—, bd. dirs., 1993—, exec. com., 1993—. Contbr. articles to profl. jours. Bd. dirs. CHRIS Homes, 1991—. Clin. fellow Am. Cancer Soc., 1983-85, Kate Rosenberg fellow N.Y. Hosp.- Cornell Med. Ctr. Mem. ACP, Am. Soc. Clin. Oncology, Am. Soc. Hematology, Piedmont Driving Club, Peachtree Golf Club, Phi Beta Kappa, Alpha Omega Alpha. Episcopalian. Home: 562 Arden Oaks Ct NW Atlanta GA 30305-1955 Office: Peachtree Hematology-Oncology Ste 5015 95 Collier Rd Atlanta GA 30309-1710

BALLENGEE, BRUCE VAN, software developing company executive; b. Corpus Christi, Tex., Jan. 22, 1957; s. Buddy Vernon and Catherine Jan (Zymaris) B.; m. Billie Ricks Driver, July 4, 1981; children: Jason, Brooke. BBA in Fin. and Econs., Baylor U., 1979; MBA in Fin., U. Chgo., 1981. Staff Andersen Consulting, Dallas, 1981-85, mgr., 1985-91, assoc. ptnr., 1991; sr. assoc. Booz, Allen & Hamilton, Dallas, 1991-92, prin., 1992-93; dir. Sprint, Dallas, 1993-94; v.p., assoc. ptnr. BancA Enterprise of Andersen Cons., Dallas, 1994-95; COO, chmn. bd. dirs. Dolphin Internat., Inc., Dallas, 1996—. Contbr. articles to profl. jours. Chmn. fin. com. Trinity Presbyn. Ch., Dallas, 1989-91; exec. systems advisor Am. Heart Assn., Dallas, 1993—; bd. dirs. Oasis Housing Corp., Dallas, 1989-91. Mem. IEEE, Thorntree Country Club, City Club.

BALLIET, JAMES LEE, manufacturing company executive; b. St. Louis, July 19, 1930; s. John Jacob Balliet and Alma Carrie Wingerter-Balliet; divorced; children: Diane L., Patricia L., James L. Jr., Mark E., Teri L., William L. Student, Nat. Staff Coll., 1973; postgrad., Southeastern Bible Coll., 1969-70; AA in Fin. Planning, Mo. State U., 1975. Agt. New Eng. Ins. Co., Rome, N.Y., 1961-62; mgr. Munal of N.Y., Huntsville, Ala., 1967-69, Score/Ace, Meridian, Miss., 1987—; owner, bd. dirs. Meridian Saw and Small Engring. Inc., 1988—, Sumter County Saw and Small Engine Inc., York, Ala.; tchr. h.s. Rankin County, 1984-85, Jackson City Schs., 1986, Meridian, 1988; bd. dirs., sec., treas Sumter County Saw & Small Engines, Inc., 1994. State dir. Jaycees, Rome, 1961-62; pres. PTA, Huntsville, Ala., 1963-67; commdr. CAP, 1970-90. With U.S. Army, 1983. Named Squadron Leader of Yr., CAP, 1974, Recruiter of Yr., 1980. Mem. Am. Legion, Rotary, Masons (pres. 1993-94), Shriners (sec. 1995, treas. 1996). Baptist. Home: PO Box 2167 Meridian MS 39302-2167 Office: Meridian Saw & Small Eng 1204 B St Meridian MS 39301-5415

BALLIETT, JOHN WILLIAM, entrepreneur, real estate executive; b. Rochester, N.Y., Sept. 10, 1947; s. Charles Garrison and Burnetta Elizabeth (Purtell) B.; BS in Physics, Grove City Coll., 1969; postgrad. U. Rochester, 1969-71; m. Betsy Jane Van Patten, Jan. 25, 1969; 1 child, Noelle Elizabeth. Devel. engr. Eastman Kodak Co., 1969-70; scientist Tropel Inc., 1970, mgr. applied optics, 1971-72, mktg. mgr., 1972-73; exec. v.p., dir. Quality Measurement Systems Inc., Penfield, N.Y., 1973-77; pres. QMS Internat., Inc., Penfield, 1974-77, Balliett Assocs., Sarasota, Fla., 1978—, Shore Lane Devel. Corp. subs. (merger Sandbar Devel. Corp. 1990), 1981—, pres., 1990—; pres., pub. Suncoast TV Facts, Inc., Sarasota, 1979-81; pres. Charter One, Inc., Sarasota, 1981—, Palma Sola Enterprises, Inc., 1990—; chmn., chief exec. officer Charter One Hotels & Resorts, Inc., 1989—; pres. Alacho Inc., 1992—; speaker at nat. and internat. timesharing confs. Founding dir. Internat. Found. for Timesharing. Mem. U.S. C. of C., Sarasota County C. of C., Am. Land Devel. Assn., Nat. Timeshare Council, Fla. Hotel-Motel Assn. Contbr. articles on timesharing to profl. publs. Patentee optical systems. Home: 1404 Westbrook Dr Sarasota FL 34231-3549 Office: 2032 Hillview St Sarasota FL 34239-2334

BALLOU, HOWARD BURGESS, commercial plumbing designer; b. New Haven, Feb. 12, 1938; s. Raymond Cotton and Edith Yale (Ballou) B.; m. Elizabeth Capacite Flores, June 27, 1987; children from previous marriage: Jeffrey Howard, Scott Raymond, Rachel Cotton. Assocs. in Constrn. Mgmt. with honors, Richland Coll., Dallas, 1979; student in acctg. and econs., U. Tex., Dallas, 1980. Lic. gen. contractor, Va.; cert. sr. engring. tech.; cert. master plumber, Tex. Constrn. trades, draftsman, 1958-68; sr. designer, resident engr. ICI Am., Stamford, Conn., 1968-70; sr. designer Connell Assocs. and J.M. Montgomery, Miami and Ft. Lauderdale, Fla., 1970-74; pvt. practice Va., Tex., 1975-77; project engr. Continental Mech., Dallas, 1977-85; sr. plumbing designer Purdy-McGuire, Dallas, 1977-85; mech. coord. Tech. Constrn. Svc., Nashville, 1986; project mgr. J.K. Johnson Mech. Contractors, Sheffield, Ala., 1987-88; designer Kimberly Clark, Memphis, 1988-94; plumbing designer Shappley Design Cons., Memphis, 1994-95; pvt. practice Memphis, 1995—; instr., head drafting dept. Elkins Inst., Dallas, 1977-85; columnist Contractor Mag., 1984-85. Co-author: Beth Howard Associates Guide Book, 1989, Beth Howard Associates Fiancee Visa Guide, 1990; contbr. articles to profl. jours. Chmn. plumbing and mech. bd. City of Plano, Tex., 1980-84; scoutmaster Boy Scouts Am., Conn., Fla., 1950-69; officer, instr. CAP, New Haven; eucharistic min. Holy Rosary Cath. Ch., Memphis, 1995—. Mem. Am. Soc. Plumbing Engrs. (v.p. tech. 1981-82), Nat. Writers Club (profl., founder, pres. North Tex. chpt. 1984-85), St. Vincent DePaul Soc., Philippine-Am. Club, KC (3d degree). Republican. Home: 503 Chalmers Rd Memphis TN 38120-1516

BALOG, RICHARD THOMAS, management consultant, educator; b. Balt., Sept. 15, 1951; s. Michael Anthony and Viola Ann (Wisniesky) B.; m. Kathleen Robbins, Apr. 11, 1992; 1 child, Richard Thomas Jr. BA in Acctg., Loyola Coll., Balt., 1971. CPA, Md., Fla.; cert. internal auditor, fraud examiner, govtl. fin. mgr. Sr. acct. Main LeFrantz, Balt., 1970-72; mgr. Blue Cross of Md., Inc., Balt., 1972-79, Inst. Internal Auditors Inc., Orlando, Fla., 1979-83; sr. mgr. Peat Marwick Main & Co., N.Y.C., 1983-88; pres., CEO The Audit Resource Ctr., Inc., Jacksonville, Fla., 1988—; chmn. bd. dirs. Resource Ctrs., Inc., Jacksonville, 1989—; on-site assoc. AMA, 1988—, Mgmt. Ctr. Europe, 1991—, Mid. East Mgmt. Ctr., 1995—; gov. Inst. Internal Auditors, Balt., 1974-79; mem. faculty U. Ctrl. Fla., 1980-81, Orlando Coll., 1981-82; mem. adj. faculty Fla. Cmty. Coll., Jacksonville, 1988—, George Mason U., 1994—. Editor: (periodical) Internal Auditing, 1984—; contbr. bus. articles to profl. jours. Scoutmaster Balt. coun. Boy Scouts Am., 1975-79, Orlando, 1980-83, coun. Wilton, Conn., 1984, asst. scoutmaster Passaic County coun., 1987-88. Named Eagle Scout, Balt. council Boy Scouts Am., 1967. Mem. AICPA, Inst. Cert. Fraud Examiners, Inst. Internal Auditors (gov. 1974-79, outstanding profl. of yr. 1981), Md. Assn. CPAs, Nat. Assn. Accts., Inst. Fin. Crime Prevention, Fla. Inst. CPAs, Assn. Govt. Accts. Republican. Roman Catholic. Office: The Audit Resource Ctr 10991-55 San Jose Blvd Jacksonville FL 32223-7229

BALTARO, RICHARD J., pathologist; b. Caracas, Venezuela, June 15, 1950; came to the U.S., 1964; s. Dimitri and Maria Silvana (Vici) B.; m. Laura E. Neece, Sept. 9, 1972; children: Elizabeth B., John C. BA, Earlham Coll., 1972; PhD summa cum laude, U. Rome, Italy, 1977; MD magna cum laude, Cath. U., Rome, 1983. Bd. cert. anatomic and clin. pathology Am. Bd. Pathology, cert. immunopathology Am. Bd. Pathology. Pathology resident Brown U., Providence, 1983-87; clin. pathology fellow George Washington U. Hosp., Washington, 1987-88; asst. in pathology George Washington Med. Sch., Washington, 1987-88; sr. staff fellow NIH Clin. Ctr. Immunology, Bethesda, Md., 1988-90; jr. active staff NIH Clin. Ctr., Bethesda, 1988-90; asst. prof. Marshall U. Sch. Medicine, Huntington, W.Va., 1990-93; dir. pathology residency program Marshall U. Sch. Medicine, Huntington, 1991-93; staff pathologist lab. svc. VA Med. Ctr., Huntington, 1990-93; pathologist Med. Arts Lab., Oklahoma City, 1993—; stockholder Med. Arts Lab., 1994—; ptnr. Med. Arts Pathologists, 1995; adj. assoc. prof. U. Okla. Health Sci., Oklahoma City, 1993—; assoc. dir. Histocompatibility, 1995—; dir. Microbiology Lab., 1993—, Med. Arts Lab, Oklahoma City, 1995—; expert witness, cons. Nat. Med. Adv. Svc., Bethesda, 1990—; bd. trustees John Marshall Med. Svcs., Inc.; residency adv. com., search com., chmn. ob-gyn. Marshall U. Sch. Medicine; spkr. in field. Contbr. articles to profl. jours. Recipient NIH grant, 1991. Fellow Coll. Am. Pathologists (lab. insp. 1985—), Am. Soc. Clin. Pathologists, Internat. Acad. Pathology, Acad. Clin. Lab. Physicians and Scientists, Am. Coll. Internat. Physicians, Assn. Clin. Scientists; mem. AMA, AAAS, Am. Soc. Microbiology, Am. Assn. for Clin. chemistry, Assn. Med. Lab. Immunologists. Office: Med Arts Lab 1111 N Lee Ave Ste 100 Oklahoma City OK 73103-2620

BAMBER, LINDA SMITH, accounting educator; b. Columbus, Ohio, Jan. 4, 1954; d. Charles Randall and Martha Jo (Wise) Smith; m. Edward Michael Bamber, Mar. 13, 1981. BS summa cum laude, Wake Forest U, 1976; MBA, Ariz. State U., 1980; PhD, Ohio State U., 1983. Cost acct. RJ Reynolds, Winston-Salem, N.C., 1975-76, gen. acct., 1976-77; tutor, rsch. asst. Ariz. State U., Tempe, 1977-78; teaching asst. Ohio State U., Columbus, 1978-82; asst. prof. U. Fla., Gainesville, 1983-88, assoc. prof., 1988-90; assoc. prof. U. Ga., Athens, 1990-96, prof., 1996—; vis. assoc. prof. Ind. U., Bloomington, 1989-90. Author: Annotated Instructor's Edition of Cost Accounting: A Managerial Emphasis, 1990, 93, 96, assoc. editor: Acctg. Horizon, 1993—; mem. editl. bd. The Acctg. Rev., 1987-89, 93—, Advances in Acctg., 1992—; contbr. articles to profl. jours. Selig fellow U. Ga., 1991, Terry fellow U. Ga., 1994, 95, 96; recipient Rsch. Devel. award U. Fla., 1985, Tchg. award Ohio State U., U. Fla., U. Ga., 1981-94. Mem. Am. Acctg. Assn. (S.E. dir. fin. reporting sect. 1993-94, group leader, panelist, chmn. New Faculty Consortium 1991-94, rsch. adv. com. 1996-97, wildman medal award com. 1996-97, nominations com. 1996-97), Beta Gamma Sigma (mem. coun. 1995—, mgmt. acctg. sect. chmn. membership outreach com. 1995—), Phi Beta Kappa, Phi Kappa Phi, Beta Gamma Sigma. Office: U Ga JM Tull Sch Acctg Athens GA 30602

BAMBERG, LOUIS MARK, estate planning specialist; b. Miami, Fla., Dec. 1, 1948; s. Harold Sidney and Estelle Grace (Nagorski) B.; m. Virginia Bamberg, Aug. 27, 1987; 1 child, Heather. AA, Miami Dade Jr. Coll., Perrine, Fla., 1968; B Bus., Ga. State U., 1970; JD, John Marshall U., Atlanta, 1977. CLU, ChFC; Bar: Ga. 1977. Salesman, buyer, mgr. Levitz, Inc., 1970-78; atty. SBA, Atlanta, 1976-78; salesman Equitable Life Assurance, Miami, 1978-85; estate planning specialist Merrill Lynch Life Agy., Ft. Lauderdale, Fla., 1985—. Bd. dirs. United HEaring & Deaf Svcs., Ft. Lauderdale, 1990. Mem. ABA, Advanced Assn. Life Underwriters, Estate Planning Coun., Top of Table, 25 Million Dollar Forum, Million Dollar Round Table. Home: 310 N Gordon Rd Fort Lauderdale FL 33301-3775 Office: Merrill Lynch Life Agy Ste 601B 2601 E Oakland Park Blvd Fort Lauderdale FL 33306-1617

BANEGAS, ESTEVAN BROWN, environmental biotechnology executive; b. Hatch, N.Mex., May 10, 1941; s. Estevan Vera Banegas and Josephine (Brown) Crew; m. Amanda Martin, Sept. 5, 1970. BS, N.Mex. U., 1964; MBA, Wake Forest U., 1978. Sales mgr. agr. div. Ciba-Geigy Corp., San Juan, P.R., 1968-73; mktg. mgr. agr. div. Ciba-Geigy Corp., Greensboro, N.C., 1974-80; dir. corp. planning Ciba-Geigy Corp., Ardsley, N.Y., 1980-81; dir. product mgmt. agr. div. Ciba-Geigy Corp., Greensboro, 1981-83, dir. strategic planning agr. div., 1983-85; pres. joint venture Union Carbide Corp. & DNA Plant Tech. Agri-Diagnostics Assocs., Cinnaminson, N.J., 1985-92, bd. dirs., 1985-92; pres. Techshare, Inc, Greensboro, 1992—; pres., CEO Dominion BioScis., Inc., Blacksburg, Va., 1993—; spkr. mktg. biotech. products Agbio Conf., 1989; vis. faculty joint ventures and strategic partnering Internation Rsch. Inst., 1992; bd. advisors U. Minn., St. Paul, 1985-88, N.Mex. State U. Leadership Project, 1993—, Radford Coll. for Global Studies, 1994; bd. dirs. Va. Tech. Intellectual Properties, Inc., 1994—; bd. dirs. agrl. devel. bd. Ohio State U., Columbus, 1987-93. Capt. USMC, 1964-67, Vietnam. Decorated Cross of Gallantry with silver star Govt. of South Vietnam, 1966. Mem. Am. Chem. Soc. (speaker mktg. strategies 1988), Am. Phytopathology Soc., Golf Course Supts. Am., Sedgefield Country Club, Rotary. Republican. Roman Catholic. Office: Techshare Inc 3558 Old Onslow Rd Greensboro NC 27407-7826

BANFIELD, WILLIAM SCOTT, educational fund raising executive; b. Kansas City, Mo., Sept. 4, 1940; s. William S. and Libera (Williams) B.; m. Mary L. Carson, Aug. 11, 1962; children: Rebecca Lynn, W. Scott. BA, Mount Union Coll. Cert. fund raising exec. Alumni dir. Mount Union Coll., Alliance, Ohio, 1964-70; dir. devel. No. Ill. U., DeKalb, 1970-73; account exec. Charles R. Feldstein & Co., Chgo., 1973-74; dir. alumni and annual giving Culver (Ind.) Mil. Acad., 1974-84; v.p. Knox Coll., Galesburg, Ill., 1984-86; pres. Mich. Colls. Found., Southfield, 1986-91; pres. Fla. Ind. Coll. Fund, Lakeland, 1991—, also bd. dirs.; bd. dirs. Found. for Ind. Higher Edn., Chgo. Mem. Nat. Soc. Fund Raising Execs. (bd. dirs. 1987-91, chpt. pres. 1990-91), Rotary. Home: 5862 Windwood Dr Lakeland FL 33813-4802 Office: Fla Ind Coll Fund 106 E College Ave Ste 640 Tallahassee FL 32301-7721

BANGA, AJAY KUMAR, pharmacy educator; b. New Delhi, India, Nov. 1, 1960; came to U.S., 1985; s. Madan L. and Parmesh (Gumbhir) B.; m. Saveta Dube, Dec. 12, 1989. B of Pharm., U. Delhi, 1981, M of Pharm., 1983; MS, U. Okla., 1986; PhD, Rutgers U., 1990. Rsch. scientist Ranbaxy Labs., Ltd., New Delhi, India, 1983-85; formulation scientist Bausch & Lomb, Rochester, N.Y., 1990-91; asst. prof. Auburn (Ala.) U., 1991-96, assoc. prof., 1996—. Author: Therapeutic Peptides and Proteins, 1995; contbr. chpts. to books and articles to profl. jours. Mem. Am. Assn. Pharm. Scientists (chair com. 1994—), Ala. Acad. Scis., Controlled Release Soc., Sigma Xi. Home: 1924 Kerihill Circle Auburn AL 36830 Office: Auburn U Dept Pharm Scis Sch Pharmacy Auburn AL 36849

BANICK, CYRIL JOSEPH, chemist; b. Scranton, Pa., Dec. 11, 1928; s. Simon and Frances (Krupar) B.; m. Nancy Barrett, Nov. 16, 1957; children: Martha B. Wright, Cyril Joseph, James Henley. MS, Ga. Inst. Tech., Atlanta, 1952. Chemist E.I. DuPont, Aiken, S.C., 1953-89, Westinghouse, Aiken, 1989—. Mem. Am. Chem. Soc., KC. Republican. Roman Catholic. Home: 2914 Kipling Dr Augusta GA 30909

BANKS, ALLAN RICHARD, artist, art historian, researcher; b. Dearborn, Mich., Feb. 15, 1948; s. Henry Selman and Lillian Margaret (Radovic) B.;

divorced; children: Christine Marie, Aaron Richard. Ind. pvt. study, Soc. Arts and Crafts, Detroit, 1966-69; student, Atelier Lack, Inc., Mpls., 1970-73, R.H. Ives Gammell Studio, Williamstown, Mass., 1976. Artist, with studio in Newburg, N.Y., 1979-81, Huron, Ohio, 1981-87; portrait artist, with studio in Spring Hill, Fla., 1987-93; dir. Atelier of Plein Air, Safety Harbor, Fla., 1993—; lectr./demonstrator Portraits South, Inc., Raleigh, N.C., 1993, Atelier LeSueur, Mpls., 1995. Exhibited in group shows Guild of Boston Artists, 1996, 20th Century Exhbn., Amarillo Tex.-Springville, Utah, 1982, Butler Inst. Am. Art, Vixseboxse Art Galleries, Cleve., Salmagundi Club, Amarillo (Tex.) Art Ctr., Maryhill Mus. Art, Goldendale, Wash., Historic East-West Russia Exhibit, 1996, others; represented in collections at Wadsworth Athenaeum, Newark Art Mus., Montclair (N.J.) Mus., Hamilton Fish Meml. Libr., Nat. Portrait Gallery/Smithsonian. Trustee Mus. Natural History, Safety Harbor, 1995—; mem. Downtown Bus. Assn., Inc., Safety Harbor, 1994—. Elizabeth T. Greenshields Found. fellow, Montreal, 1972, 73; John and Anna Stacey Found. grantee, N.Mex., 1979, Ohio Arts Coun. grantee. Mem. Am. Soc. Classical Realism, Met. Mus. Art, Appleton Mus. Art (Ocala, Fla.), Salmagundi Club, New Am. Acad. Ard. Lutheran. Home: PO Box 233 Safety Harbor FL 34695

BANKS, BETTIE SHEPPARD, psychologist; b. Birmingham, Ala., June 8, 1933; d. Francis Wilkerson and Bettie Pollard (Woodson) Sheppard; B.A., Ga. State U., 1966, M.A., 1968, Ph.D., 1970; m. Frazer Banks, Jr., Mar. 22, 1952; children: Bettie Banks Daley, Lee Frazer Banks III. Clin. assoc. Lab. for Psychol. Svcs., Ga. State U., 1968-70; intern Ga. State U. Counseling Ctr., 1969-70, Ga. Mental Health Inst., Atlanta, 1970-71, psychologist, 1971-72, chief psychologist, 1973; pvt. practice, Atlanta, 1972—; adj. assoc. prof. clin. psychology Ga. State U.; adj. asst. prof. Dept. Psychiatry, Emory U., 1974-83, 94—; mem. peer rev. panel Ga. Med. Care Found., 1980-86, chmn., 1986-88. Diplomate in clin. psychology Am. Bd. Profl. Psychology; Nat. Register Health Svc. Psychology Providers, 1977—, Nat. Register Cert. Group Psychotherapists, 1994—. Fellow Ga. Psychol. Assn. (chmn. div. E 1980, program chair ann. meeting 1991, treas. divsn. F 1993-95, chair publicity divsn. F 1995—); mem. APA, Am. Acad. Psychotherapists (exec. com. 1980-82, sec. 1982-86, 94—, ann. workshop chair 1979, com. ann. Inst. and Conf. 1975, 86, com. ann. workshop 1984), Am. Group Psychotherapy Assn. (clin. mem., co-chair local host com. 1995 Ann. Inst. and Conf.), Atlanta Group Psychotherapy Soc. (bd. exec. com. 1982-83, 91-92, treas. 1995—), Southeastern Psychol. Assn. Episcopalian. Club: Jr. League. Cons. editor Voices, The Art and Science of Psychotherapy, 1978-84. Office: 18 Lenox Pointe NE Atlanta GA 30324-3171

BANKS, DAVID RUSSELL, health care executive; b. Arcadia, Wis., Feb. 15, 1937; s. J.R. and Cleone B.; married; children: Melissa, Michael. B.A., U. Ark., 1959. Vice pres. Dabbs, Sullivan, Trulock, Ark., 1963-74; chmn., chief exec. officer Leisure Lodges, Ft. Smith, Ark., 1974-77; registered rep. Stephens Inc., Little Rock, 1974-79; pres., CEO Beverly Enterprises, Ft. Smith, Ark., 1979—, now chmn. bd., dir., 1990—; dir. Nat. Council Health Centers, Pulaski Bank, Little Rock. Served with U.S. Army. Office: Beverly Enterprises Inc 1200 S Waldron Rd Fort Smith AR 72903-2569

BANKS, DONALD JACK, plant geneticist, plant biologist; b. Sentinel, Okla., July 11, 1930; s. Jess C. and Grace (Bale) B.; m. Eneth R. Banks, May 22, 1952 (div. 1988); children: Michael D., Sandra K. BS, Okla. State U., 1953, MS, 1958; PhD, U. Ga., 1963. Instr. agronomy Auburn (Ala.) U., 1958-60; asst. prof. biology Stephen F. Austin State Coll., Nacogdoches, Tex., 1963-66; rsch. geneticist USDA, Stillwater, 1966—; chmn. Peanut Crop Adv. Com., USDA, 1988-90; plant explorer Internat. Bd. for Plant Genetic Resources, S. Am., 1977-85. Contbr. over 100 articles to profl. jours. on plant biology, breeding and peanut genetics. 1st Lt. U.S. Army, 1953-57. Named Master Profl. Agronomist, Agronomy Dept., Okla. State U., 1991; recipient Rsch. & Edn. award, Nat. Peanut Coun., 1991. Fellow Am. Peanut Rsch. & Edn. Soc. Home: PO Box 2286 Stillwater OK 74076-2286

BANKS, FRED LEE, JR., state supreme court judge; b. Jackson, Miss., Sept. 1, 1942; s. Fred L. and Violet (Mabry) B.; m. Taunya Lovell, June 5, 1967 (div. 1975); children: Rachel R., Jonathan L.; m. Pamela Gipson, Jan. 28, 1978; 1 child, Gabrielle G. BA, Howard U., 1965, JD cum laude, 1968. Bar: Miss. 1968, U.S. Dist. Ct. (no. and so. dists.) Miss. 1968, U.S. Ct. Appeals (5th cir.) 1968, D.C. 1969, U.S. Supreme Ct. 1971. Ptnr. Banks, Owens & Byrd and predecessor firms Anderson, Banks, Nichols & Stewart; Anderson, Banks, Nichols & Leventhal; Anderson & Banks, Jackson, 1968-85; judge Miss. Cir. Ct., Hinds County and Yazoo County, 1985-91; assoc. justice Miss. Supreme Ct, Jackson, MS, 1991—; mem. Miss. Bd. Bar Admissions, 1978-79; pres. State Mut. Fed. Savs. and Loan, Jackson, 1976-89. Bd. dirs. NAACP, 1981—; mem. Nat. Adv. Com. for the Edn. of Disadvantaged Children, 1978-80; del. Dem. Nat. Conv., 1976, 1980; co-mgr. Miss. Carter-Mondale presidl. campaign, 1976; legislator Miss. Ho. of Reps., Jackson, 1976-85. Mem. ABA, Magnolia Bar Assn., Nat. Bar Assn., Hinds County Bar Assn. Roman Catholic. Home: 976 Metairie Rd Jackson MS 39209-6948 Office: Miss Supreme Ct Carol Gartin Bldg PO Box 117 Jackson MS 39205-0117

BANKS, JOHN ROBERT, JR., lawyer; b. Balt., Mar. 15, 1958; s. John Robert and Ida Carol (Cromer) B. BA, Coll. William and Mary, Williamsburg, Va., 1980; JD, U. Houston, 1983. Bar: Tex. 1983, U.S. Dist. Ct. (so. dist.) Tex. 1983. Assoc. Levin & Kasner, P.C. fka Levin, Roth & Kasner, P.C., Houston, 1983—. Dir. Cmty. Assn. Inst. Greater Houston, 1995—, chmn. amb.'s subcom., 1994—, chmn. legal com., 1995, vice chmn. legal com., 1994. Mem. Fed. Bar Assn. Republican. Methodist. Office: Levin & Kasner PC Eleven Greenway Plz 500 Summit Tower Houston TX 77046

BANKS, LISA JEAN, government official; b. Chelsea, Mass., Dec. 19, 1956; d. Bruce H. and Jean P. (Como) Banks. BS in Bus. Adminstrn., Northeastern U., Boston, 1979. Coop trainee IRS, Boston, 1975-79, revenue officer, Reno, 1979-81, spl. agt., Houston, 1981-84, Anchorage, 1984-90; spl. agt. DVA-OIG Procurement Fraud Task force, Boston, 1990-92, spl. agt. NASA Kennedy Space Ctr., 1992, NASA OIG-Kennedy Space Ctr., 1992—, fed. womens program mgr., 1980-81; pres. Make-A-Wish Found. of Ctrl. Fla., 1994-96, v.p. wish granting, 1996—. Recipient Superior Performance award IRS, 1981, Spl. Achievement award, 1987, 89, Employee Suggestion award, 1990. Mem. Nat. Assn. Treasury Agts., Fed. Law Enforcement Officers Assn. Roman Catholic Office: NASA Office of Inspector Gen PO Box 21066 Kennedy Space Center FL 32815

BANKS, VIRGINIA ANNE (GINGER BANKS), association administrator; b. Dallas, Mar. 19, 1949; d. James Houston and Mary Virginia (Bussey) B. B of Journalism, U. Tex., 1971. Traveling cons. Alpha Omicron Pi Fraternity, Indpls., 1971-73; adminstrv. asst. Alpha Omicron Pi Fraternity, Nashville, 1973-74; pub. info. officer Tex. Dept. of Community Affairs, Austin, 1974-76; asst. dir. of comm. State Bar of Tex., Austin, 1976-78, assoc. editor Tex. Bar Jour., 1977-79, mng. editor Tex. Bar Jour, 1979-91, comm. dir., 1991—, dir. pub. svcs. divsn., 1992—; internat. rush chmn. Alpha Omicron Pi, Nashville, 1976-77, internat. v.p. ops., 1977-81, internat. pres., 1981-85, v.p. found., 1985-90, mem. fraternity devel. com., 1985-89, pres. Pi Kappa Corp., 1991-95, mem. Austin Alumnae chpt., 1973—, alumnae adv. com. network specialist, 1996—, del. nat. panhellenic Conf., 1987-93, chmn. Perry award com., 1992—; com. to devel. relationship statement, Nat. Panhellenic Conf., 1983, del., 1987-93, area advisor coll. Panhellenics com., 1985-88, chmn. liaison com., 1987-88, mem. Project Future collegiate concerns com., 1987-89, field cons. seminar com., 1987, chmn., 1988, resolutions com., 1988, chmn. pub. rels. com., 1991-93, mem. ednl. devel. com., 1991-93. Editor Centennial History Book, 1995-96; contbr. articles to mags. Bd. dirs. Lone Star Girl Scout Coun., Austin, 1973-75, Nat. Interfraternity Found., 1986-89, M.L. Roller scholarship com., 1988-89, nominations com., 1988-89; mem. Humane Soc. Austin, 1981—; chmn. mag. adv. com. Ex-Students Assn., U. Tex., Austin, 1989-95; mem. Tarrytown United Meth. Ch. Recipient presdl. citation State Bar of Tex., 1981, 90, 94, presdl. citation Alpha Omicron Pi, 1988, Rose award Alpha Omicron Pi, 1991. Mem. Am. Soc. Assn. Execs., Assn. Fraternity Advisors, Internat. Assn. Bus. Communicators, Nat. Assn. Bar Execs. (mem. pub. svcs. activities com. 1995—, chair awards com. 1996—, vice chair 1996—, mem. pub. rels. and comms. sect. 1991—, mem. section's comms. audit com., 1994-95, chair sect.'s comms. audit com., 1995—, mem. sect.'s program com., 1995—, co-chair sects. program com. 1996—), Women in Comm., PEO Sisterhood, Alpha Omicron Pi (Austin alumnae chpt.). Home: 3108 W Terrace Dr Austin TX 78757-4332 Office: State Bar of Tex PO Box 12487 Austin TX 78711-2487

BANKS, WILLIAM ASHTON, librarian; b. Beckley, W.Va., Apr. 24, 1943; s. William Smith and Mary Frances (File) B.; m. Grace Wallace Powers, Aug. 9, 1969; children: Michele, Elizabeth, Nancy, Kathryn. BA in Music, Am. U., 1970; ThM in English Bible, Capital Bible Sem., 1980; MA in Music, Am. U., 1988; MLS, Cath. U., 1989. Pvt. music instr., musician Alexandria, Va., 1961—; adj. prof. Religion Washington Bible Coll., Lanham, Md., 1976-85; music libr. Am. U., Washington, 1985-88; libr. Notre Dame Acad., Middleburg, Va., 1988-94, Washington Bible Coll., Lanham, Md., 1994—. Co-author: Old Testament Parsing Guide, vol. 1, 1985, vol. 2, 1990; author: Justin Holland: The Guitar's Black Pioneer, 1989. Mem. Conservative Club, Alexandria, 1987—. Mem. Am. Fedn. Musicians, Va. Cath. Edn. Assn., Phi Mu Alpha Sinfonia. Republican. Presbyterian. Home: 2601 Londonderry Rd Alexandria VA 22308-2334 Office: Washington Bible Coll 6511 Princess Garden Pky Lanham Seabrook MD 20706

BANNARD, WALTER DARBY, artist, art critic; b. New Haven, Sept. 23, 1934; s. Homes and Janet (Darby) B. B.A., Princeton U., 1956. Chmn. dept. art and art history U. Miami, Fla., 1989—; Lectr. in field, 1969—; vis. prof. Princeton (N.J.) U., 1974, also other univs.; mem. grad. faculty Sch. Visual Arts, N.Y.C., 1984-89; curator Hans Hoffman Hirshorn Mus., 1976; mem. internat. exhbn. com., 1976-78; co-chmn. internat. panel for visual arts Nat. Endowment for Arts, 1979-81. Contbr. articles and revs. on modern painting to profl. jours.; contbg. editor: Artforum, 1973-74; 70 one-man shows internat. galleries and mus. include retrospective Balt. Mus. Art, 1973; numerous internat. group shows; represented in permanent collections at Mus. Modern Art, N.Y.C., Whitney Mus. Am. Art, Met. Mus. Art, N.Y.C., Guggenheim Mus., N.Y.C., others; juror numerous competitions, 1969—; sole juror Australian Bi-Centenary Art Competition, 1988. Recipient Nat. Found. Arts award, 1968-69; Francis J. Greenburger Found. award, 1986; John Simon Guggenheim Meml. Found. fellow, 1968; Richard A. Florsheim Art Fund grantee, 1991. Office: 1300 Campo Sano Ave Coral Gables FL 33146-1171

BANNISTER, DENISE H., publishing executive; b. 1950. Asst. contr. Gainesville (Ga.) Times Gannett, Pensacola, Fla., 1983-84; contr. Gannett, 1984, pres., pub., 1986; pres., pub. Gannett, Huntington, 1989; v.p., pub. Pensacola New Jour. Gannett East Regional Group, 1991—. Office: Pensacola News Jour 1 News Journal Plz Pensacola FL 32501-5607*

BANONIS, EDWARD JOSEPH, gas industry executive; b. Phila., Nov. 10, 1945; s. Edward Joseph and Alberta Lillian (Subach) B.; children: Aaron, Beth; m. Sue Ann Shirkey, Dec. 8, 1996. AS in Engring., Pa. State U., 1965; BSME, Drexel U., 1971; AS in Paralegal Studies, U. Charleston, 1989. Draftsman GE, Phila., 1965-66; metal inspector Getty Oil Co., Delaware City, Del., 1971-75; project engr. Columbia LNG Corp., Wilmington, Del., 1975-82; quality assurance engr. N.W. Alaskan Pipeline, Pasadena, Calif., 1980-81; sr. quality engr. Columbia Gas Transmission, Charleston, W.Va., 1982-85, mgr. purchasing and materials, 1985—. Pres. parish coun. Resurrection Cath. Ch., Newark, Del., 1973-74. Mem. ASME (chmn. Phila. sect. piping and pressure vessel com. 1979-80), Am. Soc. Quality Control, Am. Soc. for Metals, Nat. Assn. Purchasing Mgrs., Del. Assn. Profl. Engrs. Home: 49 Reunion Rd # 3 Elkview WV 25071-9346

BANSEMER, RICHARD FREDERICK, bishop; b. Oswego, N.Y., May 26. 1940; s. Reinhold Mathias and Oralee Ann (Brierly) B.; m. Barbara Anne Gallmeier, June 9, 1962 (dec. Feb. 1968); 1 child, John David.; m. Mary Ann Troutman, July 18, 1971; children: Aaron Richard, Andrew Christopher. BA, Newberry (S.C.) Coll., 1962; BD, Luth. Theol. So. Sem., 1966; DD (hon.), Newberry Coll., 1988, Roanoke Coll., 1988. Ordained to ministry Evang. Luth. Ch. in Am., 1966. Assoc. pastor Univ. Luth. Ch., Gainesville, Fla., 1966-68; pastor St. John Luth. Ch., Roanoke, 1968-73, Lord of the Mountains Luth. Ch., Dillon, Colo., 1973-78, Rural Retreat (Va.) Luth. Parish, 1978-87; bishop Va. Synod Evang. Luth. Ch. in Am., Salem, 1988—. Author: People Prayers, 1976, The Chosen and the Changed, 1977, Grace and the Grave, 1981, Risen Indeed, 1982, In Plain Sight, 1982, Day Full of Grace, 1987, O Lord, Teach Me to Pray, 1995. Trustee Roanoke Coll., 1988—, Luth. Theol. So. Sem., 1988-92. Office: Evang Luth Ch in Am Va Synod PO Box 70 Salem VA 24153-0070

BANSEMER, ROGER LEWIS, artist; b. Brockton, Mass., July 25, 1948; children Lauren, Rachel. Student, Ringling Sch. Art, 1966-69. Author/artist: The Art of Hot-Air Ballooning, 1990, Southern Shores, 1991, Rachael's Splendifilious Adventure, 1992, At Waters Edge, 1993, Mountains in the Mist, 1993. Home: 2352 Alligator Creek Rd Clearwater FL 34625-2205

BANTER, MARY JEAN MCKENZIE, gifted educator; b. Marshallville, Ga., July 14, 1955; d. James Norris and Jean (Lancaster) McKenzie; m. Ken Allen Banter, June 28, 1980; children: John Norris, Jean Helena, James Forrest. BA, Asbury Coll., Wilmore, Ky., 1976; MA, Ga. Southwestern Coll., 1978, EdS, 1988. Tchr. Peach County Bd. of Edn., Ft. Valley, Ga., 1976-85, tchr. gifted, 1985—, coach mid. sch. quiz bowl team, 1986-96, coach future problem solving team, 1993-96. Sunday sch. tchr. Ft. Valley United Meth. Ch., 1989-96, pre-teen coord. BEAS, 1994-96; actor, parent vol. Peach Area Cmty. Theater, 1993-96. Recipient Award of Excellence for coaching future problem solving team Torrance Ctr. for Gifted Studies, U. Ga., Athens, 1996. Mem. Profl. Assn. Ga. Educators, Ga. Supporters of the Gifted. Methodist.

BARAB, PATSY LEE, nutritionist, consultant, realtor; b. Indpls., Sept. 24, 1934; BS, Mich. State U., 1956, MA, 1970; 1 child, Gregory; m. John D. Barab Jr., April 8, 1995. Asst. prof. Med. Coll. Ga., Augusta, 1972-82; nutrition cons., 1982—; assoc. Meybohm Realty, Inc., Augusta, 1987—. Mem. program com. Gertrude Herbert Art Inst., 1992—; mem. promotion com. Imperial Theater. Mem. Am. Dietetic Assn., Ga. Dietetic Assn., Augusta Dietetic Assn., Am. Home Econ. Assn., Ga. Heart Assn., Ga. Nutrition Coun., Soc. Nutrition Edn., Nutrition Today Soc. (charter), Nutritionists in Nursing Edn. (nat. chmn. 1983-84), AAUP, AAUW, GRI, CRS, Augusta Opera Club, Ruth Newman Shapiro Guild, Houndslake Country Club, Racquet Club, Million Dollar Club (life), Omicron Nu, Pi Beta Phi (arrowmont chmn. Augusta Alumnae Club 1992—). Home: 3051 Walton Way Augusta GA 30909

BARAGER, WENDY AYRIAN, communications executive; b. Saranac Lake, N.Y., June 21, 1949; d. Robert Lester and Patricia Margaret (O'Brien) B. Student, Wayne State U., 1967-69; AA in Liberal Arts, Valencia Community Coll., 1969; BA in Edn., Fla. Tech. U. (name now U. Cen. Fla.), 1972; BA in English, U. Cen. Fla., 1976. Clk., typist Orlando Pub. Library, Fla., 1969-70; supr. library Orlando (Fla.) Sentinel Newspaper, 1977-80; display advt. salesperson Thrifty Nickel Want Ads Newspaper, Orlando, 1980-83; clk., typist div. motor vehicles State of Fla., Orlando, 1983-84; librarian Fla. Bankers Assn., Orlando, 1984-88, communications specialist, 1988—; dir. communications Fla. Bankers Assn., Tallahassee, 1993—. Editor Fla. Banker Newsletter, Fla. Banking Mag.; contbr. articles to profl. jours. Bd. dirs. Authors in the Park; mem. Friends of the Libr., Orlando, 1983; assoc. mem. Orlando Mus. of Art. Mem. Women in Comm., Internat. Assn. Bus. Comm., Fla. Pub. Rels. Assn. (sec. bd. dirs.), Tallahassee Soc. Assn. Execs. City Coll. Alumni Assn., U. Cen. Fla. Alumni Assn. Republican. Methodist.

BARAT, LAWRENCE M., epidemiologist; b. N.Y.C., Aug. 13, 1960; s. Jerome and Alma R. (Escobedo) B. BA, Boston U., 1982; MD, SUNY Downstate Med. Ctr., 1986; MPH, Harvard Sch. Pub. Health, Boston, 1995. Diplomate Am. Bd. Internal Medicine. From instr. to asst. prof. medicine Boston U., 1991-95; epidemic intelligence svc. fellow U.S. Ctrs. for Disease Control and Prevention, Atlanta, 1995—; AIDS policy advisor to mayor, City of Boston, 1991-93; med. dir. immunodeficiency unit Boston Specialty and Rehab. Hosp., 1993-95. Trustee Mass. AIDS Discrimination Initiative, Boston, 1992-94. Mem. Infectious Disease Soc. Am., Mass. Med. Soc.

BARATTA, RICHARD VICTOR, biomedical engineer; b. N.Y.C., Oct. 18, 1962; s. Vincent Carmine and Luz Selenia (Bahamonde) B.; m. Nilda Alina Iglesias, June 27, 1986; 1 child, Richard Vincent. BS, Tulane U., 1984, MS, 1986, PhD, 1989. Instr. dept. orthopaedics La. State U. Med. Ctr., New Orleans, 1987-92, asst. prof., 1992-96, assoc. prof., 1996—; chmn. orthopaedic rsch. com. La. State U., 1993—; cons. VA Med. Ctr. Prosthetic Svc., New Orleans, 1984—; mem. stimulator subcom. AAMI Neuromusc., Washington, 1994—; invited lectr. in field. Contbr. articles to profl. jours.; reviewer Jour. Electromyography and Kinesiology. Mem. IEEE, Interna. Soc. Electrophysiol. Kinesiology (treasury auditor 1992-94), Orthopaedic Rsch. Soc., La. Orthopaedic Assn. (assoc.), Biomed. Engring. Soc., Alpha Eta Mu Beta, Tau Beta Pi. Office: La State U Med Ctr Dept Orthopaedics 2025 Gravier St Ste 400 New Orleans LA 70112-2254

BARB, CLAUDE RICHARD, research physiologist, research scientist; b. Washington, July 19, 1948; s. Claude Parker and Mary Theresa (Lowe) B.; m. Susan Martha Weber, Mar. 30, 1970; children: Melinda, Michael, Lauren. BS, U. Md., 1975; MS, U. Ga., 1980, PhD, 1985. Biol. lab. technician USDA-Agrl. Rsch. Svc., Beltsville, Md., 1970-76; biol. lab. technician Russell Rsch. Ctr. USDA-Agrl. Rsch. Svc., Athens, Ga., 1976-85; rsch. physiologist USDA-Agrl. Rsch. Svc., Athens, 1985—; mem. sci. exch. Office Internat. Coop. and Devel., Dept. Agr., Mariensee, Germany, 1986. Author: (with others) Regulation of Ovarian and Testicular Function, 1987; contbr. articles to profl. jours. Mem. Am. Soc. Animal Sci., Soc. for Study of Reproduction, Soc. for Neurosci., Soc. for Exptl. Biology and Medicine. Office: USDA-ARS Russell Rsch Ctr Animal Physiol Unit PO Box 5677 Athens GA 30604-5677

BARBA, ROBERTA ASHBURN, retired social worker; b. Morgantown, W.Va., June 23, 1931; d. Robert Russell and Mary Belle (Rogers) Ashburn; m. Harry C. Barba, Jan. 28, 1956 (div. June 1963); 1 child, Gregory Robert; m. Robert Franklin Church, May 10, 1972. BSSW, W.Va. U., 1953; post-grad., U. Conn., Hartford, 1953-54; MSSW, NYU, 1957. Diplomate in Am. Bd. Examiners; lic. N.Y., W.Va. Pvt. practice W.Va., 1968—; evaluator P.A.C.E., Star City, W.Va., 1973-74; social worker Family Svc. Assn., Morgantown, W.Va., 1974-75, 85-87; human resources asst., social worker Sundale Rest Home, Morgantown, 1977-79; cons., residential svcs. specialist Coordinating Coun. for Ind. Living, Morgantown, 1983-88; provider W.Va. Dept. Welfare, Human Svcs., Morgantown, 1980-87; social worker maternity svcs. Monongalia County Health Dept., Morgantown, 1985-87; social worker Hospice of Preston County, Kingwood, W.Va., 1988-89; shelter worker, field work instr. Bartlett House W.Va. Sch. Social Work, Morgantown, 1986-90; case mgr. Region VI Area Agy. on Aging, Fairmont, W.Va., 1990-92; case mgr. geriatric program W.Va. U., Morgantown, 1992-95; ret., 1995. Author: (with others) Working with Terminally Ill, 1990, (short fiction) Kids Know, 1992; freedom writer Amnesty Internat., 1987—. George Davis Bivens Found. grantee, 1953-54. Mem. NASW (charter mem., cert. diplomate), ACLU, NOW, Acad. Cert. Social Workers, W.Va. Human Resources Assn., W.Va. Child Care Assn., Monongalia County Coun. Social Agys, Phi Beta Kappa. Home: 429 Fairmont Rd Morgantown WV 26505-4244

BARBAROSH, MILTON HARVEY, merchant banking executive; b. Montreal, Que., Can., Apr. 22, 1955; came to U.S., 1986; s. William and Ethel (Greenstone) B.; m. Ricki Tucker, June l, 1980; children: Marli, Lori, Liana. BCom with honours in Acctg., Concordia U., Montreal, 1976; Can. Chartered Acct., McGill U., Montreal, 1977; MBA, York U., Toronto, Ont., Can., 1980. Sr. staff acct. Thorne, Ernst & Whinney/KPMG Peat Marwick, Montreal, 1976-79; mgr. merger and acquisitions Clarkson Gordon/Ernst Young, Toronto, 1980-84, Royal Bank of Can., Toronto, 1984-86; pres. JW Charles Group, Inc., Boca Raton, Fla., 1987-88, JW Charles Capital Corp., Boca Raton, 1986-89; pres. Stenton Leigh Capital Corp., Boca Raton, 1989—. Author: (with others) The Acquisition Decision; editor M&A in Canada for Harris-Bentley Ltd. Fellow Can. Inst. Chartered Bankers; mem. The Can. Inst. of Chartered Bus. Valuators, Am. soc. Appraisers (sr.), Inst. Chartered Accts. Ont., Quebec Order Chartered Accts., McGill U. Alumni, U. Toronto Alumni, Concordia U. Alumni, York U. Alumni, Pres.'s Club Fla. Atlantic U., Boca Raton Golf and Country Club. Office: 1900 Corporate Blvd NW Boca Raton FL 33431-8502

BARBATO, JOSEPH ALLEN, writer; b. N.Y.C., Feb. 23, 1944; s. Joseph Michael and Florence (Kelly) B.; m. Augusta Ann DeLait, Oct. 23, 1965; children: Louise, Joseph. BA, NYU, 1964, MA, 1969. Newswriter NYU, N.Y.C., 1964-68, dir. alumni communications, 1969-74, sr. devel. writer, 1974-78; staff writer Shell Oil Co., N.Y.C., 1968-69; ind. writer N.Y.C., 1978-90; editorial dir. The Nature Conservancy, Arlington, Va., 1990—; mem. edit. bd. Small Press mag., N.Y.C., 1984-86; communications cons. univs., hosps., etc., 1978-90. Co-author: You Are What You Drink, 1989; editor: What We Really Know About Mind-Body Health, 1991; co-editor: Heart of the Land, 1995, Patchwork of Dreams, 1996, Patchwork of Dreams; contbg. author: The Book of the Month, 1986; columnist edn., health, lit. numerous mags. and newspapers including Smithsonian, N.Y. Times, Village Voice, Christian Sci. Monitor, others. Mem. Authors Guild, Nat. Book Critics Cir., Soc. Profl. Journalists. Home: 5420 Gary Pl Alexandria VA 22311 Office: The Nature Conservancy 1815 N Lynn St Arlington VA 22209-2003

BARBER, CHARLES EDWARD, newspaper executive, journalist; b. Miami, Fla., Oct. 30, 1939; s. James Plemon and Margaret Katherine (Grimes) B. m. Judith Margaret Tuck, May 28, 1960; children: Janet Lynn Wood, Christopher Edward. AA, Santa Fe Community Coll., 1971. Prodn. mgr. dept. student publs. U. Fla., Gainesville, 1966-68, ops. mgr., 1968-70, asst. dir., 1970-72, dir. div. publs., 1974; prodn. mgr. State Univ. System Press, Gainesville, 1975-76; pres., gen. mgr. Campus Communications, Inc., Gainesville, 1976—; pres. The Herald Pub. Co., Inc., 1990—, Tuck Barber Assocs., 1995—; pub. The High Springs Herald, 1990—; dir. Campus Press; cons. in field. Co-author: (with Judy Barber) screenplay This Small Island, 1989; adv. editor Fla. Quar., 1973-74; contbr. articles to profl. jours. Mem. citizens adv. coun. Stephen Foster Elem. Sch., Gainesville, 1976-77; mem. Friends of Five, 1975-77, Friends of Libr., 1975-77; chmn. book com. Fla. State Prison, 1973-85, 89-94; bd. dirs. Gainesville H.S. Band Boosters, 1978-79, 83-84, treas., 1984; key communicator Alachua County Sch. Bd., 1980-91; spl. registered dep. sheriff Alachua County Sheriff's Dept., 1979-92; mem. gifted students boosters Howard Bishop Mid. Sch., 1980-82; dir. Howard Bishop Band Boosters, 1980-82; mem. pres.'s coun. U. Fla., 1978—; mem. Leadership Gainesville, 1979; pack com. chmn. Cub Scouts Am., 1977-78; dir. The Prevention Partnership, 1992-94, Hippodrome State Theatre, 1992-95. With USCGR, 1957-65. Recipient Nat. 1st pl. for Editl. Writing Hearst Found., 1965, Svc. award Santa Fe C.C., 1982, Cert. of Appreciation Big Bros. and Big Sisters of Gainesville, 1984, Vols. for Internat. Student Affairs, 1986, 88, 89, 90, Fla. Track Club, 1988, U. Fla. Divsn. Housing, 1990, 91, Addy award Gainesville Advt. Fedn., 1986, 87; named to Ind. Fla. Alligator Hall of Fame, 1996. Mem. Am. Collegiate Network (adv. com. 1989-91), Am. Advt. Fedn., Nat. Press Club, Assn. for Edn. in Journalism and Mass Communication, Coll. Newspaper Bus. and Advt. Mgrs. (bd. dirs. 1978-90), Fla. Scholastic Press Assn. (newspaper judge 1981-85), Fla. Newspaper Advt. and Mktg. Execs. (chmn. edn. com. 1984-87), Fla. Press Club, Fla. Press Assn. (bd. dirs. 1992—, award for weekly newspaper advt. 1993, 1st pl. award for editl. writing 1994, 1st pl. award for newspaper promotion 1992, 1st pl. award weekly newspaper advt. 1994, Best of Show award weekly newspaper advt. 1994, 1st pl. award weekly newspaper promotion 1995, 3rd pl. award weekly newspaper advt. 1996), Gainesville Advt. Fedn. (bd. dirs. 1979-80), Internat. Newspaper Fin. Execs., Internat. Newspaper Mktg. Assn., Coll. Media Advisers, Nat. Newspaper Assn., Newspaper Assn. Am., New Media Fedn., Soc. Newspaper Design, So. Univ. Newspapers (bd. dirs. 1980-89), High Springs Hist. Soc., First Amendment Found., Alachua C. of C., Gainesville Area C. of C., High Springs C. of C., Alligator Alumni Assn. (bd. dirs. 1980—, named Mr. Alligator 1986), U. Fla. Nat. Alumni Assn., Soc. Profl. Journalists (treas. No. Fla. chpt. 1972-75, 86-91, pres.'s club 1994-95), Substance Abuse Prevention Partnership (coun. 1992-95), Cmty. Consensus Initiative, Leadership Gainesville Alumni Assn., Red Herring Club, Rotary (sustaining, sec. 1993-94), Alpha Phi Gamma. Office: Campus Comm Inc PO Box 14257 Gainesville FL 32604-2257

BARBER, D.A., pharmacology educator; b. Finley, Ohio, Sept. 21, 1965; married. BS in Pharmacy, U. Ga., 1990, PhD in Pharmacology, 1994. Rsch. intern Harbor Br./Oceanographic Inst., 1988; tchg. asst. pharmacology lab., Coll. of Pharmacy U. Ga., Athens, 1990-94; pharmacist Gilbert Health Ctr. and Revco Drug, Athens, 1990-94; NIH postdoctoral fellow, dept. surgery Mayo Clinic and Found., 1994—; presenter in field. Contbr. articles to profl. jours./publs. Recipient fellowship Am. Found. for Pharm. Edn., 1992-93. Mem. AAAS, Am. Soc. Pharmacology and Exptl. Therapeutics, The Oxygen Soc., Am. Assn. Colls. of Pharmacy, Ga. Pharm. Assn., Golden Key, Rho Chi, Phi Delta Chi, Phi Lambda Sigma.

BARBER, DEBORAH NUNN, psychotherapist; b. Mt. Airy, N.C., July 16, 1958; d. Keith Dayton Nunn and Atha Jean (Inman) Nunn-Collins; divorced; children: Rosemary Angelica, Christopher Charles. AAS, Surry C.C., Dobson, N.C., 1978; BS in Psychology summa cum laude, High Point U., 1993; postgrad., Wake Forest U., 1994—. Cert. family counselor Nat. Acad. Cert. Family Therapists. Family counselor Family Violence divsn. Family Svcs., 1995—, Addiction Recovery Care Assn., 1995—; guest lectr. Guildford Tech. C.C.; instr. Forsyth Tech. C.C. Mem. ACA, N.C. Counseling Assn., Theta Theta Theta, Alpha Sigma Lambda, Alpha Chi, Chi Sigma Iota (pres.). Republican. Roman Catholic. Home: 1900 Franciscan Dr Winston Salem NC 27127

BARBER, JOHN STEVEN, hospital executive; b. Dalhart, Tex., May 3, 1955; s. Clyde Oliver Jr. and Nancy Jo (Cox) B.; m. Sherri Ann Scott, Jan. 1, 1975; children: Serena Annette, Jared Shane. AA in Liberal Arts, York Coll., 1975; BS in Acctg., Harding U., 1978; MBA in Acctg., Valdosta State Coll., 1988. Staff acct. Reames & Son Constrn. Co., Valdosta, Ga., 1978-81; controller Ga. Home Rehab Svcs. Inc., Valdosta, 1981-86, Berrien County Nursing Ctr., Nashville, Ga., 1983-86; chief fin. officer Comprehensive Health Mgmt., Valdosta, 1985-86; asst. controller Healthcare of Berrien County, Nashville, 1986-87; chief fin. officer Healthcare of Dooly County, Vienna, Ga., 1987, Dooly Med. Ctr., Vienna, 1987-89, Dorminy Med. Ctr., Fitzgerald, Ga., 1989-90; co-adminstr. Dorminy Med. Ctr., 1990-93, adminstr., 1993—; mem. adv. bd. Americare Home Health Agy., Brunswick, Ga., 1990—; coun. mem. Ga. Hosp. Assn. Coun. Fin. and Mgmt., Atlanta, 1991—. Asst. scout master Boy Scouts Am., Gruver, Tex., 1972-74; mem. exec. bd. Cities in Schs., 1993—, Ben Hill County Bd. Health, 1993—. Mem. Ga. Rural Health Assn. (Rural Hosp. of Yr. 1990), Southwest Dist. Ga. Hosp. Assn., Woodpecker Trail Hosp. Consortium, Fitzgerald-Ben Hill C. of C. (econ. devel. com. 1993—), Rotary. Republican. Office: Dorminy Med Ctr PO Box 1447 Fitzgerald GA 31750-1447

BARBER, LARRY LEE, manufacturing executive; b. Ashland, Ky., Dec. 1, 1939; s. Allen L. and S. Helen (Finley) B.; m. Susan Carol Sinks, June 25, 1965; children: Larry Todd, Troy Alexander, Trent Jeremy. BSME, U. Ky., 1963; MS, Purdue U., 1971. Registered profl. engr., Ind. Mgr. ops. Allegheny Ludlum, Louisville, 1976-79; mgr. divsn. IE Browning Mfg. div. Emerson Electric, Maysville, Ky., 1979-82; plants mgr. Fed. Pacific Electric, St. Louis, 1982-86; dir. ops. Revere Corp. div. Allied Signal, Wallingford, Conn., 1986-88; pres. Potentiometer div. Litton Industries, Mt. Vernon, N.Y., 1988-91, Aerospace Techs., Inc., Ft. Worth, 1992—. Mem. ASME, IIE. Office: Aerospace Techs Inc 7445 E Lancaster Ave Fort Worth TX 76112-7306

BARBER, THEODORE FRANCIS, aircraft mechanics professional; b. Port Jervis, N.Y., Jan. 29, 1931; s. Theodore and Frances Mary (Gross) B.; m. Beverly Ann Horton, Mar. 15, 1961 (div. Dec. 1965); 1 child, Theodore Francis Barber, Jr. Student, Arlington Sch. Flight & Engring., Tillamook, Oreg., 1951-52; grad., Jet Engine Specialist Sch., Chanute, Ill., 1952. Lic. comml. eel fisherman, Pa. Laborer Erie RR, Port Jervis, N.Y., 1947-49; carpenter Erie R.R., Port Jervis, N.Y., 1950; mail handler Erie R.R., Jersey City, 1950-51; locomotive fireman Erie RR, Port Jervis, N.Y., 1951-59, locomotive engr., 1959-66; miniature golf course owner/operator Matamoras, Pa., 1963-65; lipstick moulder Kohmar Lab., Port Jervis, N.Y., 1965; interior installer Douglas Aircraft Co., Long Beach, Calif., 1966-67; field and svc. aircraft mechanic Douglas and McDonnell Douglas Aircraft Co., Long Beach, 1967-93; structure assembly mechanic Northrop Corp., Anaheim, Calif., 1969-70; exptl. flight test mechanic McDonnell Douglas Aircraft Co., Long Beach, 1971, 77; systems mechanic Airco Cryogenics, Costa Mesa, Calif., 1977; co-owner C&B Sabot Fiberglass Boat Mfrs., 1976; mech. test technician Space Shuttle Arrowhead Products, Los Alamitos, Calif., 1976-77; B-1 bomber tool maker North Am. Rockwell, El Segundo, Calif., 1977; realtor Real Estate Store, Fullerton, Calif., 1976-79; metal fitter toolmaker F-18, Northrop, Hawthorn, Calif., 1978-79; toolmaker satellite and Space Shuttle divsn. North Am. Rockwell, Seal Beach, Calif., 1984; walnut orchard grower C & B Orchard, Fresno, Calif., 1982-83. With USAF, 1951-55. Mem. VFW, Am. Legion, Gold Wing Rd. Riders Assn., Jacksonville Real Estate Investors Assn., Moose, Eagles. Republican. Roman Catholic.

BARBIERI, JOSEPH JAMES, food company executive; b. St. Louis, Nov. 25, 1939; s. Nicholas Joseph and Julia Marie (Bello) B.; m. Elizabeth Ann Bohr, Apr. 28, 1962; children: Jeanette, Nick, Jim, Dan. BS in Chem. Engring., Washington U., St. Louis, 1961; MBA, St. Louis U., 1966; postgrad., NYU, 1966-68. Process engr., fin. analyst, planning assoc. Mobile Oil, Chem. Plastics, various locations, 1963-73; planning analyst, ops. mgr., v.p. fin. and mktg. Carolina Peanut Co. subs. Anheuser Busch, St. Louis, 1973-83; Midwest reg. mgr. York Snacks, St. Louis, 1983-85; pres. Tampa Bay Snacks, St. Petersburg, Fla., 1985—. Campaign mgr. Mayor of Freehold Twp., Freehold, N.J., 1969; pres. Stonehurst Homeowners Assn., Freehold, 1968. 1st lt. U.S. Army, 1961-63. Mem. Snack Food Assn. Home: 13954 Whisperwood Dr Clearwater FL 34622-3348 Office: Tampa Bay Snack Foods 3320 Scherer Dr N Saint Petersburg FL 33716-1011

BARBORIAK, DANIEL PAUL, radiologist; b. Evansville, Ind., June 30, 1959; s. Joseph J. and Gertrude Barboriak. BS, U. Wis., 1981; MD, Harvard Med. Sch., 1986. Diplomate Am. Bd. Radiology with added qualifications in neuroradiology, 1996. With neuroradiology program Mass. Gen. Hosp., Boston, 1991-92; staff neuroradiologist Shields Healthcare, Brockton, Mass., 1992-95, VA Med. Ctr., Durham, N.C., 1995—. Co-author: Radiology: A Clinical Review, 1995; co-author laser disc project Radiolog-Pathologic, 1994. Mem. Am. Soc. Neuroradiology, Am. Coll. Radiology, Am. Soc. Pediat. Neuroradiology, Radiologic Soc. N.Am., Mass. Musculo-Skeletal MRI Soc. Office: Durham VA Med Ctr Dept Radiology 508 Fulton St Durham NC 27705

BARBOSA, JERRY LEVY, pediatric hematologist, oncologist; b. Santa Ana, Beni, Bolivia, Feb. 24, 1943; came to U.S., 1970; s. Amadeo R. and Eloisa (Levy) B.; m. Carol Joan Bernstein, Dec. 10, 1970; children: Julie Nicole, Jennifer Eli, Michael Levy. BS, Colegio La Salle, Cochabamba, bolivia, 1961; MD, U. Madrid, 1969. Asst. prof. pediats. U. Fla., Gainesville, 1976-79; dir. pediat. hematology and oncology All Children's Hosp., St. Petersburg, Fla., 1979—. Pres. Pinellas County unit Am. Cancer Soc., St. Petersburg, 1986-87. Recipient The Surgeon Gen. Medallion award, Washington, 1989. Office: All Childrens Hospital 801 6th St S Saint Petersburg FL 33701-4816

BARBOUR, CHARLENE, management firm executive; b. Smithfield, N.C., Aug. 23, 1949; d. Charles Ray and Charlotte June (Langdon) B.; m. Phil Barbour, Apr. 14, 1968; 1 child, Phillip Shaun. AA in Bus., Hardbarger Jr. Coll., 1968. Adminstrv. asst. N.C. Dept. Human Resources, Raleigh, 1970-80; account exec. Olson Mgmt. Group, Raleigh, 1980-86; pres., CEO Mgmt. Concepts, Inc., Garner, N.C., 1986—. State campaign mgr. Ruby Hooper for Gov., 1992. Mem. NAFE, Am. Assn. Assn. Execs., Assn. Execs. N.C. (CEO conf. chmn. 1992-93, program com. 1992-93, trade show com. 1992-93), Nat. Fedn. Ind. Bus. Owners, Garner C. of C. (comm. chmn. 1989, bd. dirs., vice chmn. membership and comm. 1989-92), Buena Vista Hospitality Group (coun. advisors 1992), Nat. Assn. of RV Parks and Campgrounds (Exec. Dir. of Yr. award 1994), Campground Assn. Mgmt. Profls. (founder), Cardinal Club (founder). Democrat. Baptist. Home: 2320 Amelia Rd Clayton NC 27520-8307 Office: Mgmt Concepts Inc 1418 Aversboro Rd Garner NC 27529-4547

BARBOUR, JACK ROBERT, security and loss prevention generalist, forensic consultant; b. L.A., Nov. 15, 1925; s. Raymond Elery and May Bella (Hunt) B.; m. Lila Jewel Veach, Feb. 15, 1947 (div. 1959); children: Constance Nan, Raymond Richard, Judy Lynn; m. Gloria Ann Freeman, May 25, 1959; children; Robert Arthur, Kathleen Rene, Ronald Allen, Sharon Lee. Lic. pvt. security cons., Tex.; registered pvt. investigator, Tex. V.p., sr. cons. Chgo. region Gor-Buc Security Systems, Inc., L.A., 1963-67; regional v.p., sr. cons. Wackenhut Corp., Chgo., 1967-68; sr. loss prevention cons. Wackenhut Corp., Coral Gables, Fla., 1972-73, dir. ops., 1973-74, corp. v.p., 1974-79; v.p., sr. cons. Denco Security Systems, Inc., Dallas, 1968-70; security and loss prevention cons. Security & Loss Prevention, Inc., Dallas, 1970-72, Loss Prevention Assocs., Houston, 1979; gen. mgr. Ineeda Linen Svc., Houston, 1979-80; security and loss prevention generalist Security & Loss Prevention Assocs., Inc., Manvel, Tex., 1980—. Contbr. articles to profl. jours. With USN, 1943-47, PTO. Mem. Am. Soc. for Indsl. Security. Republican. Roman Catholic. Office: Security Loss Prevention 4718 Sylvia Ln Manvel TX 77578-3106

BARBOUR, WILLIAM H., JR., federal judge; b. 1941. BA, Princeton U., 1963; JD, U. Miss., 1966; postgrad, NYU, 1966. Bar: Miss. Ptnr. Henry, Barbour & DeCell, Yazoo City, Miss., 1966-83; judge U.S. Dist. Ct. (so. dist.) Miss., 1983—, chief judge, 1989—. Youth counselor Yazoo City, 1971-82. Office: US Dist Ct 245 E Capital St Ste 430 Jackson MS 39201*

BARCA, JAMES JOSEPH, fire department administrative services executive; b. New London, Conn., Feb. 20, 1944; s. Mariano and Angeline (Curzio) B.; m. Elizabeth Drake Garrison, Mar. 28, 1969 (div. Jan. 1983); m. Janet Louise Shields, Jan. 14, 1984. BSE in Indsl. Engring., U. Cen. Fla., 1972. Launch tech. IBM Corp., Cape Canaveral, Fla., 1968-69; indsl. engr. Honeywell, Inc., St. Petersburg, Fla., 1972-75, Tampa, Fla., 1975; mgr. mgmt. div., budget & mgmt. dept. City of St. Petersburg, 1975-81; mgr. fire adminstrv. svcs. St. Petersburg Fire and Rescue Dept., 1981—; exec. mem. Pinellas County (Fla.) Disaster Adv. Com., 1981—; mem. ARC Disaster Com., St. Petersburg, 1985-94, adv. coun., Pinellas, 1994—. Author: Disaster Planning for Adult Congregate Living Facilities, 1985, St. Petersburg Disaster Operations Plan, 1986, 93, 94, 95. Guest speaker representing St. Petersburg Fire and Rescue Dept. various civic assn. mtgs., 1981—. With USN, 1962-66. Recipient NASA Apollo Achievement award for Apollo 11 Moon landing participation. Mem. Alpha Pi Mu. Republican. Roman Catholic. Office: Saint Petersburg Fire & Rescue Dept 400 ML King St S Saint Petersburg FL 33701-4472

BARCENAS, JUDE R. L., financial services company executive. BSBA in Mktg., U. San Carlos, Philippines, 1975; MBA in Internat. Mgmt., U. Dallas, 1978; CFP degree, Coll. for Fin. Planning. CFP. Rsch. cons. MARC Mktg. Rsch., Dallas, 1978-79; family security analyst Met. Life, Dallas, 1979-82, sales mgr., 1982-84; br. mgr. Titan Value Equities, 1982-84, 94—; fin. cons. Cigna Fin. Adv., Inc., 1989-94; pres. BFG Fin. Benefits, Inc., Dallas, 1994—; adj. prof. Dallas County C.C., 1986-94; bd. dirs. Fil-Am. Fed. Credit Union, Carrollton, Tex. Pres. Circle K Club, Kiwanis Internat. Cebu, Philippines, 1973-75; chmn. Civil Svc. Commn. and Trial Bd., City of Mesquite, Tex., 1991-93. Fellow Life Underwriter Tng. Coun.; mem. Am. Soc. of CLU and ChFC, Nat. Assn. Life Underwriters, Philippines Cmty. Ctr., Inc. (v.p. 1991-93, bd. dirs. 1995-96, corp. sec. 1996—), Lions (pres. Dallas-Filipino 1992-93, zone chmn. dist. 2X1 1994), Greater Dallas Asian Am. C. of C. (bd. dirs. 1992-95), Dallas Estate Planning Coun., Million Dollar Round Table, Sigma Iota Epsilon.

BARCLAY, LAURIE LYNN, neurologist, consultant; b. Bryn Mawr, Pa., May 19, 1953; d. John Marshall and Eve (Borduk) B.; m. Richard Joseph Collett, Jan. 28, 1989; 1 child, Brendan Travis Collett. BA cum laude, Princeton (N.J.) U., 1974; MD, Cornell U., 1978. Neurology resident N.Y. Hosp.-Cornell, N.Y.C., 1980-82, chief resident and clin. instr. neurology, 1982-83; chief. Spinal Cord Trauma Burke Rehab. Ctr.-Cornell, White Plains, N.Y., 1983-86; clin. dir. Dementia Rsch., White Plains, N.Y., 1984-87; asst. prof. Neurology Cornell U.-N.Y. Hosp., N.Y.C., 1983-87; asst. prof. U. S. Fla. Neurology, Tampa, 1987-92, clin. asst. prof., 1992; cons. pvt. practice, Tampa, Fla., 1992—; guest lectr. Caldwell Labs., 1993—; nat. speaker Parke Davis, 1994—. Author, editor: Clinical Geriatric Neurology, 1992; contbr. articles to profl. jours. Office: Neurological Consulting Svc 12408 N 56th St Tampa FL 33617-1535

BARD, ALLEN JOSEPH, chemist, educator; b. Dec. 18, 1933; m. Fran; children: Eddie, Sara. BSc in Chemistry summa cum laude, CCNY, 1955; MA in Chemistry, Harvard U., 1956, PhD in Chemistry, 1958. Instr. chemistry The U. Tex., Austin, 1958-60, asst. prof., 1960-62, assoc. prof., 1962-67, prof., 1967—, Jack S. Josey Professorship Energy Studies, 1980-82, Norman Hackerman Prof. Chemistry, 1982-85, Hackerman-Welch Regents Chair Chemistry, 1985—; lectr. numerous univs., 1969-96; mem. U.S. nat. com. Internat. Union Pure and Applied Chemistry-Nat. Rsch. Coun., 1983—, chair, 1988-89, bd. energy and environ. sys., 1983-86, 93—, bd. chem. scis. tech., 1982-87, co-chair, 1985-87, nat. materials adv. bd. com. on electrochem. aspects of energy conservation and prodn., 1985, com. on chem. scis. and ad hoc panel on DOE rsch., 1980-84, NAS, NRC liaison com. on high temp. sci. and tech,. 1984; pres. Internat. Union Pure and Applied Chemistry, 1991-93; mem. adv. bd. Dept. Energy and Energy Rsch., panel on Cold Fusion, 1989; chem. adv. com. NSF, 1981-84; mem. external adv. com. Beckman Inst., 1989—; bd. govs. Weizmann Inst., 1995—, sci. & acad. adv. com., 1995—. Author: Chemical Equilibrium, 1966, Integrated Chemical Systems, 1994; co-author: Electrochemical Methods, 1980; editor Electroanalytical Chemistry, 18 vols., 1966—, Encyclopedia of the Electrochemistry of the Elements, 16 vols., 1973—, (with others) Standard Potentials in Aqueous Solution; mem. editl. and adv. bds. Jour. Am. Chem. Soc., editor-in-chief, 1982—; mem. editl. bd. Electrochimica Acta, divsn. editor, 1978-80; mem. editl. and adv. bds. Dictionary of Modern Sci. and Tech., 1989—, Ency. of Sci. Instrumentation, 1990—, Ency. of Phys. Sci. and Tech., 1989—, Ency. of Sci. and Tech., 1992—, Analytical Letters, 1967—, Catalysis Letters, 1988—, Chem. Instrumentation, 1967-77, Chem. Physics Letters, 1992—, Critical Revs. in Analytical Chemistry, 1985-91, Jour. Photoacoustics, 1982-84, New Jour. Chemistry, 1978-93, Jour. Supercritical Fluids, 1988—, Organic Thin Films and Surfaces, 1991—, Heterogeneous Chemistry Revs., 1993—, Accounts of Chem. Rsch., 1993—, Russian Chem. Bull., 1995—. Recipient Outstanding Achievement in Fields of Analytical Chemistry award Eastern Analytical Symposium, 1990, Townsend Harris medal City Coll. N.Y., 1989, Edward Mack award Ohio State U., 1989, Math. and Phys. Scis. award N.Y. Acad. Scis., 1986, Docteur Honoris Causa award U. de Paris-VII, 1986, Bruno Breyer Meml. award Royal Australian Chem. Inst., 1984, Scientific Achievement award City Coll. N.Y., 1983, Sherman Mills Fairchild scholar Calif. Inst. Tech., 1977, Ward Medal in Chemistry, 1955, Luigi Galvani medal Societa Chimica Italiana, 1992. Fellow Electrochem. Soc. (Olin-Palladium medal 1987, Henry Linford award 1986, Carl Wagner Meml. award 1981); mem. AAAS (coun. del. 1992-95, chair-elect chemistry sect. 1996), Am. Chem. Soc. (G.M. Kosolapoff award 1992, Oesper award Cin. sect. 1989, Analytical Chemistry award 1988, Willard Gibbs award Chgo. sect. 1987, Fisher award in Analytical Chemistry 1984, Harrison Howe award Rochester sect. 1980), Nat. Acad. Scis. (chmn. chemistry sect. 1996-99), Am. Acad. Arts and Scis. (award 1990), Internat. Soc. Electrochemists, Assn. Harvard Chemists, Sigma Xi. Office: U Tex Lab Electrochem Dept Chemsitry Austin TX 78712

BARDELAS, JOSE ANTONIO, allergist; b. Havana, Cuba, Feb. 3, 1948; came to U.S., 1961; s. Jose a. and Georgina (Leyva) B.; m. Sallie Young, July 3, 1971; children: Joseph, Mary. BA in Human Biology, Johns Hopkins U., 1970, MD, 1973. Intern, then resident in pediats. Johns Hopkins Hosp., Balt., 1973-75; fellow in allergy and immunology Nat. Jewish Ctr., Denver, 1975-77; pvt. practice Greensboro, N.C., 1977—; asst. clin. prof. pediats. U. N.C., Chapel Hill, 1979—. Fellow Am. Acad. Allergy and Immunology; mem. AMA, N.C. Soc. Allergy and Immunology (pres. 1982), N.C. Med. Soc. (mem. exec. coun. 1990, 91), High Point Med. Soc. (pres. 1989). Roman Catholic. Home: 1113 Rockford Rd High Point NC 27262-3607 Office: 100 Westwood Ave High Point NC 27262-4322

BARDEN, JANICE KINDLER, personnel company executive; b. Cleve.; d. Norman Allen and Bessie G. (Black) Kindler; m. Hal Barden, Nov. 12, 1944 (dec. Jan. 1985) 1 child, Sheryl Andrea Barden Coholan. BBA, Miami U., Oxford, Ohio, 1947; M in Indsl. Psychology, Kent State U., 1948. Asst. dir. admissions Fairleigh Dickinson U., Teaneck, N.J., 1950-53; gen. mgr. Pilots Employment Assocs., Teterboro, N.J., 1953-71; founder, pres. Aviation Pers. Internat., New Orleans, 1971—; commr. jury U.S. Dist. Ct. (ea. dist.) La., New Orleans, 1965—; lectr. in field. Chmn. History of Aviation Collection U. Tex., Dallas, 1980—; served on Pres. Com. Rehab. Vietnam POW Pilots; mem. FAA's Blue Ribbon Panel. Recipient Disting. Alumnus award Kent State U., 1986, Cuyahoga Falls H.S., 1988, Doswell award Nat. Bus. Aircraft Assn., 1994. Mem. AAUW, Nat. Bus. Aircraft Assn. (chmn. conf. 1975, 85, 87, 90, 94), Flight Safety Found. (chmn. corp. seminar), Profl. Aircraft Maint. Assn., Bus. and Profl. Women's Club, Kent State Alumni Assn. (bd. dirs. 1976-82), Order of Rainbow (grand coord. 1973-84), Psi Chi. Republican. Episcopalian. Office: Aviation Pers Internat PO Box 6846 New Orleans LA 70174-6846

BARDIN, ROLLIN EDMOND, electrical engineering executive; b. Greensburg, Ky., Apr. 2, 1932; s. Tolbert Edward and Mary Margaret (Wise) B.; m. Patricia Lou Ott, Dec. 20, 1953 (div. June 1956); 1 child, Rollin Edmond Jr.; m. Lillian Patricia Sweeney, Jan. 20, 1958; 1 child, Susan Lynn. AA in Engring., Miami Dade Jr. Coll., 1963; BSEE, U. Miami, 1965. Cert. master electrician. Stock clk. Margaret Ann Stores, Miami Shores, Fla., 1950-51; meter reader Fla. Power & Light, Miami, Fla., 1951-56, svc. rep., 1956-61; engr. Hughes & Weaver, Miami, 1965-68, E. R. Brownell, Miami, 1968-70; bldg. inspector FHA, Miami, 1970-73; elec. contractor Bison Electric, Inc., Miami, 1973-80; prin. R. E. Bardin Elec. Contractor, Inc., Miami, 1980—. Chief petty officer, USCGR, 1951-92, ret. Recipient presdl. citation John F. Kennedy, 1961, Ronald Regan, 1981. Mem. NRA, Smithsonian Assocs., U.S. Ski Assn., Moose, Miami Dolphin Club, Coral Gables Country Club, PGA Tour Ptnrs., Am. Legion. Democrat.

BARE, JOHN BOWMAN, media consultant, writer; b. Winston-Salem, N.C., Dec. 22, 1964; s. Hubert Wayne and Margaret Anita (Jarratt) B.; m. Elizabeth Jane Ross, Oct. 31, 1992; 1 stepdaughter: Elizabeth Leslie Warren. BA, U. N.C., 1987, MA, 1992, PhD, 1995. Reporter WCHL-AM, Chapel Hill, N.C., 1985-86; reporter, anchor WMAS-AM-FM, Springfield, Mass., 1987; reporter The Daily Reflector, Greenville, N.C., 1988-89; columnist The Herald-Sun, Chapel Hill, N.C., 1990—; pvt. cons., Chapel Hill, 1992—; Contbr. articles to profl. jours. Journalism scholar Freedom Forum, 1993, 94, Vt. Royster-Dow Jones scholar U. N.C., 1994; fellow Washington Ctr. Politics and Journalism, 1991. Mem. Am. Assn. Pub. Opinion Rsch., Investigative Reporters and Editors, Assn. Edn. in Journalism and Mass Comms. Democrat. Baptist. Office: PO Box 1052 Chapel Hill NC 27514

BAREFOOT, HYRAN EUVENE, academic administrator, educator, minister; b. Mantee, Miss., Jan. 14, 1928; s. James Lee and Martha Caroline (Martin) B.; m. Joyce Lynn Camp, Nov. 24, 1949; children—Judy Barefoot Thomas, June Barefoot Dark, Jane Barefoot Hunter. B.A., Miss. Coll., 1949; B.D., New Orleans Bapt. Theol. Sem., 1952, Th.D., 1955; postdoctoral U. N.Mex., 1965-66, Bapt. Theol. Sem., 1971. Asst. prof. religion Union U., Jackson, Tenn., 1957-60; asst. prof. N.T., So. Bapt. Theol. Sem., Louisville, 1960-62; prof. religion Union U., 1962—, chmn. dept. religion, 1966-75, chmn. div. humanities, 1972-75, v.p. acad. affairs, 1975-87, acad. dean; pres. 1987—; pastor Liberty Bapt. Ch., Calhoun, La., 1946-49, Goss Bapt. Ch., Miss., 1949-52, Hebron Bapt. Ch., New Hebron, Miss., 1952-55, First Bapt. Ch., Crowley, La., 1955-57, Woodland Bapt. Ch., Brownsville, Tenn., 1957-60, 66-75. Recipient Tchr. of Yr. award Union U., 1967, Disting. Faculty award, 1973; named Jackson Tenn. Man of the Yr., 1993. Mem. Assn. So. Bapt. Colls. (sec. 1984-85). Club: Jackson Rotary. Avocations: antique furniture refinishing; hunting; fishing. Home: 120 Redfield Dr Jackson TN 38305-8526 Office: Union U Office of the President Jackson TN 38305

BARETSKI, CHARLES ALLAN, political scientist, librarian, educator, historian, municipal official; b. Mt. Carmel, Pa., Nov. 21, 1918; s. Charles Stanley and Mary Ann (Gorzelnik) B.; m. Gladys Edith von Nyitrai Yartin, Aug. 19, 1950 (dec. Oct. 1989). BA cum laude (scholar), Rutgers U., 1945; BSLS, Columbia, 1946, MSLS, 1951; Diploma, Inst. Bibliog. Orgn. of Knowledge U. Chgo., 1950; diplomas in archival adminstrn., Am. U., 1951, 55; MA in Polit. Sci., U. Notre Dame, 1957, PhD, 1958; MA in Govt. and Internat. Rels., NYU, 1965, PhD in Politics, 1969. From reference libr. to sr. libr. Newark Pub. Libr., 1938-54, profl. book reviewer, 1938—; rsch. intern Am. State Dept. Archives, Nat. Archives, 1951, br. libr. Van Buren br., 1954-56, br. dir., 1957-88, dir. fgn. lang. book collection, 1954-88; nat. archivist, historian Am. Coun. For Polish Culture, 1954-91; commr. Mcpl. Commn. on the Elderly, Richmond, 1991-95, sec., 1992-94; dir., chief lectr., rev. seminars on liberal arts courses and libr. sci., mem. staff groups for N.J. state civil svc. libr. exams., 1950-77, elected to N.J. State Gallery of Disting. Citizens, 1962; cons. doctoral candidates in grad. studies, 1957-88, Richmond Mcpl. Coun.; election campaign, 1990; Richmond del. 4th & 5th Nat. Cath. Golden Age Assn. confs., 1990, 91; Va. state rep. Nat. Legis. Advocacy Commn., Nat. Catholic Golden Age Assn., 1991-92; judge Richmond Mcpl. Spelling Bee in conjunction with Richmond Pub. Sch. System & Sr. Citizen Orgns., 1991, 92; rep. and spokesman for Sr. Citizen Population Greater Richmond Area Anti-Violent Crime Crusade, 1992, chmn. Richmond Mcpl. Com. to revise the criteria of selection for honorees, Richmond's Sr. Citizen Hall of Fame, 1991-92, Richmond Mcpl. Transp. Task Force, 1991-94; dir., program chmn. Richmond's Forum on Nat. Comprehensive Health Care System for Am., 1992-93; chmn. Cosco's Com on Med. Rsch. Devel. of Concern to Va. State's Elderly Population, 1994—; mem. Richmond Mcpl. Needs and Assessment Com., Richmond Mcpl. Dept. Human Resources and Employee Rels., 1992-93, Richmond Mcpl. com. compilation svs. directory for Richmond's Sr. Citizens, 1993-94; chief judge award com. Joseph Conrad Lit. Contest, 1968; mem. faculty Univ. Coll., Rutgers U., Newark, 1965-66; coord. Slavic-Am. hist. studies Sr. Citizens' Inst., Essex County Coll., Newark, 1977-78; dir. Baretski Tutoring Svc., 1935-68; Ednl. Cons. Adv. Bd. Essex County, (N.J.) Office on Aging, founder, dir. Ethnic Rsch. Archives, 1971-91, dir. Rsch. Libr.; mcpl. budget analyst cmty watchdog orgns., Newark, 1954-88, Richmond, 1988—; pres. Associated Community Couns. Newark, 1969-88; mcpl. budget analyst Cmty. Watchdog Orgn., Newark, 1954-88, Richmond, 1988—; pres. Ironbound (Newark) Cmty. Coun., 1961-88; lectr., cons. Am. Ethnic Polit. History, 1968—; ednl. cons. adv. bd. Essex County (N.J.) Office on Aging; vol. tutor, South Bend, Ind.; cons. Doctoral Candidates, U. Notre Dame, 1957-58, genealogical rsch., 1987—; mem. adv. coun. North Essex Ednl. Center, Essex County Coll., Belleville, N.J., 1973-88; treas., chmn. N.J. Coalition for Safe Cmtys., Anti-Crime N.J. State-wide Fedn., 1978-80; cons., speaker problems of elderly Va. State Coun. Sr. Citizens, 1993. Author: Our Quarter Century: History of the American Council of Polish Cultural Clubs 1948-1973, 1973, Fond Memories of Ann Street School Newark, N.J.: 1920's to 1950's, 1986, A Decade of Caring and Sharing: The History of Our Lady of Peace Chapter, Catholic Golden Age Association, Richmond, Virginia: 1981-91, 1991, Ten Commandments for Senior Citizens Prescription Use: Informational Outreach Service for Richmond's Elderly, 1993; co-author: The Polish University Club of New Jersey; A Concise History: 1928-88, 1988, Shearings from the Flock, 1995; author taped narrative The Legend of America's Santa Claus, 1987; author (radio play) The Life and Times of Samuel F.B. Morse: The Inventor of the Telegraph, 1936; editor: Higher Horizons Ednl. Program N.Y.C., 1961; editor and pub. Ironbound (N.J.) Counselor, Newark, 1965; profl. book reviewer, 1938—; contbr. Letters-to-the-Editor columns in newspapers and periodicals including N.Y. Times, Newark Star-Ledger, Richmond News Leader, The Christian Science Monitor, Life mag., ALA Bull., Shearings From the Flock by Seasoned Citizens, articles to numerous profl. jours., also chpts. to books, compiler. Rsch. on contbns. Polish and other immigrants to Am. culture and history; contbg. poet, cons. Richmond Publ. Group; editorial advisor After-Glow: Anthology of Poetry, 3d. edit., 1994. Rep. Clean Govt. candidate for U.S. Congress, 10th Dist. N.J., 1962; N.J. chmn. Polish-Am. Citizens for Goldwater, 1964; N.J. liaison dir. Polish Am. Rep. Nat. Coun., 1971-88; rsch. dir., pub. rels. dir. Polish-Am. Rep. Club N.J. Vol., tutor Mt. Carmel, Pa. and Newark Elem. Schs., 1927-32, Newark Pub. High Schs., 1932-35; reporter Newark Sunday Ledger, 1935; mem. Va. Mus. Fine Arts, Richmond, The Poe Found., Inc.; founder, dir. Inst. Polish Culture, Seton Hall U., South Orange, N.J., 1953-54; rsch. historian of inst., 1953-88; nat. gen. sec. Am. Polish Civil War Centennial com., 1961-65; founder, dir., libr. Ctr. Advancement Slavic Studies, 1970-91; chmn. internat. com. 300th Ann. of Founding of Newark, 1965-66; founder, pres. Ind. Polish-Am. Voters of N.J., 1953-88; state del. Polish Hungarian World Fedn., 1977-83; founder, pres. Newark Pub. Libr. Employees Union Local 2298, Am. Fedn. State, County and Municipal Employees, AFL-CIO, 1971-77, del. internat. convs., 1974, 76, 78, 80, 82, trustee N.J. Pub. Employees Council 52, No. N.J. Pub. Employee Unions, 1978-84; mem. exec. bd. Newark Labor Coalition, 1972-77; ofcl. historian N.J. State Polish-Am. Ethnic Group, 1976-78; bd. dirs. N.J. chpt. Confedn. Am. Ethnic Groups; organizer, cons. Newark Ironbound Sr. Citizen's Multi-Purpose Ctr. Satellite Libr., 1986-88; resource scholar N.J. Gov.'s Commn. on Eastern European and Captive Nation History, 1985-88; historian Newark Multi-Ethnic Coun., 1986-88; trustee Cath.

Golden Age Sr. Citizens Club Richmond, 1990-91, historian and v.p., 1991-93; v.p., program chmn. Coun. Sr. Citizens Orgn. Richmond, 1991-93, pres. 1993-94; commr., bd. dirs. Richmond Mcpl. Commn. on Elderly, 1991-95; sec. 1992-94; judge 4th, 5th Ann. Mcpl. Intergenerational Spelling Bee, 1991, 92; chmn. for revising criteria for selection of honoree's for Richmond Municipal Com. for Richmond Sr. Citizen Hall of Fame, 1992; mem. Richmond Mcpl. Com. Real Estate Tax Relief program for Richmond's Elderly, 1993-94; v.p., program chmn. Cosco Coun. 95 Federated Sr. Citizen Orgns. Richmond, 1991-93, pres. 1993-94; chmn. comm. com. Richmond Story League, 1991-92; ethnic rsch. Historian N.J. State Am. Revolution Celebration commn., 1976-77, Richmond COSCO fedns.; chmn. com. med. and health care rsch. for elderly Cosco Fedn., Richmond, 1994—; mem. Richmond Neighborhood Cmty. Devel. task force, 1994-95. Rutgers U. Scholar, 1939-45; Edna Sanderson fellow, Columbia U., 1946, Newark Pub. Libr. Scholar, 1951; rsch. fellow U. Notre Dame, 1956-57; elected to N.J. State Gallery of Dist. Citizens, 1962; recipient Brotherhood award City of Newark, 1962, Presdl. Leadership and Disting. Svc. award Am. Fedn. State, County and Mcpl. Employees, 1972, Founder's Day award N.Y. U., 1970, Svc. awards Newark Pub. Libr., 1972, 74, 76, 85, 88, Nat. Am. Heritage award J.F. Kennedy Library for Minorities, 1972, Outstanding State Labor Leader award N.J. Pub. Employees, AFL-CIO, 1978; Disting. Educator Am. award, 1979; Nat. Founder's award Am. Coun. Polish Culture, 1980; New Internat. award Polish Govt. in exile, London, 30 years Profl. Svc. award Newark's Ironbound Community, 1984, Sixty Five Yrs Dedicated Vol. Tutoring citation, 1927-92, Humanitarian award for Vol. Tutoring recognizing 65 yrs., 1993; named for the outstanding contbns. to the greater Newark community and devoted svcs. to the growth of the Newark Pub. Libr. system, 1988; grantee N.J. League of Women Voters Ednl. Fund seminar for Newark Inter-Group leaders; elected Nat. Role Model for Am. Youth to Hall of Fame U.S. Acad. Achievement, Lexington, Ky., 1983, Disting. Presdl. Svc. award Coun. Sr. Citizen Orgns. Greater Richmond, Va. & Adjoining Counties, 1996, numerous others; decorated Knight's cross Polonia Restituta. Mem. ALA, Polish-Am. Soc. Va., Italian-Am. Cultural Assn. Va., Polish-Am. Unity League, Polish-Am. Hist. Assn. (asst. editor monthly bull. 1959-61, nat. editor-in-chief 1961-65), Nat. Coun. Sr. Citizens, Nat. Polish Coun. (Am. divsn., del. rep. Polish-Ams. of N.J., pub. rels. counselor), Writers Soc. N.J. (exec. dir. 1947-56), Am. Polit. Sci. Assn., Am. Soc. Internat. Law, Am. Sociol. Assn., Soc. Historians Am. Fgn. Rels., Am. Hist. Assn., N.Y. Libr. Club, Polish-Hungarian World Fedn., Immigration History Soc. N.J., Mid. Atlantic States Coun. Social Studies, Am. Coun. for Polish Culture, Newark Pub. Libr. Guild (founder, pres. 1970), Va. State Coun. Sr. Citizens, Libr. Pub. Rels. Coun., N.J. Libr. Assn., Essex County Librs. Assn., Coll. Art Assn., Assn. Historians of Am. Art, Polish U. Club N.J. (pres. 1953-54), Polish Arts Club Newark (pres. 1980-88, historian 1975-91), Nat. Coun. Sr. Citizens, Nat. Assn. Sr. Travel Planners, Va. State Coun. Sr. Citizens, Nat. Assn. of Sr. Travel Planners. Roman Catholic. Home and Office: 2426 W Tremont Ct Richmond VA 23225-1956

BARFIELD, BOURDON REA, investor; b. Amarillo, Tex., Oct. 28, 1926; s. Bourdon Ivy and Oliver Rea (Eakle) B.; BBA, U. Tex., 1951; m. Carolyn Grissom, Jan. 4, 1951; children: Deyanne, Amanda, Bourdon Ivy, John Callaway. Vice pres. Barfield Corp., Amarillo, 1951-57, pres. 1957—; pres. Guaranty Mortgage Corp., 1979-89. Pres. Penbrooke Corp., Amarillo, 1969-72. Mem. Durett Scholarship Com. Amarillo Pub. Schs., 1951-74; area chmn. Crusade for Freedom, 1957; pres. Amarillo Symphony Orch., 1959-61; chmn. Citizens' Action Program, Amarillo, 1961-63; v.p. U. Tex. Dads' Assn., 1975—; mem. exec. com. Panhandle Plains Hist. Soc., 1984, Llano Cemetery Bd, 1984; co-chmn. Amarillo Centennial Com., 1987; gen. chmn. Festival of Lights, Amarillo, 1990-94; co-moderator Human Rels. Coun. Amarillo, 1992-93. Mem. dist. Dem.Congl. Campaign Com., 1962-65, chmn., 1969; bd. dirs. Dallas Civic Opera, 1962, St. Andrew's Day Sch., Amarillo, 1962, Family Service Inc., Amarillo, 1969, Amarillo Art Ctr., 1972—; chmn. bd. dirs. Amarillo Pub. Library, 1963; exec. com. Panhandle Plains Mus., 1984—; co-chmn. Amarillo Centennial, 1987; steering com. U. Tex. Health Sci. Ctr., San Antonio, 1993—; co-moderator Human Rels. Coun. Amarillo. Recipient Young Man of Yr. award Jr. C. of C., 1960, Man of Yr. award Amarillo Globe-News, 1988, award of Honor Downtown Amarillo Unltd. for Redevel. Work., 1966; named 1st Citizen 2d Century of Amarillo City of Amarillo and Amarillo C. of C., 1987. Mem. Amarillo C. of C. (pres. 1961), U.S. C. of C. (dir. Civic Devel. Com. 1960), Jovian, 49ers, Vagabond Club, Masons (32 deg.), Palo Duro, Beta Theta Pi. Presbyterian (elder 1994—). Home: 3201 S Ong St Amarillo TX 79109-3543 Office: 1620 S Tyler St Amarillo TX 79102-3140

BARFIELD, KENNY DALE, Bible school dean; b. Florence, Ala., Nov. 17, 1947; s. Henry Perry and Bernice Elizabeth (Olive) B.; m. Nancy Ann Cordray, Aug.7, 1970; children: Amber Elizabeth, Lora Allyn. BA in Speech Communication, David Lipscomb Coll., 1969; MA in Speech Communication, U. Ala., Tuscaloosa, 1972; EdS in Ednl. Adminstrn., U. North Ala., 1986; EdD in Ednl. Adminstrn., U. Ala., Tuscaloosa, 1989. Dir. debate, instr. Mars Hill Bible Sch., Florence, 1969—, acad. dean, 1986—, prin., 1990-95; minister Highland Park Ch. of Christ, Muscle Shoals, Ala., 1970-74, Jackson Heights Ch. of Christ, Florence, 1974-78, Sherrod Ave Ch. of Christ, Florence, 1978—; instr. speech communication Internat. Bible Coll., 1972-75, U. North Ala., Florence, 1981-83. Author: 50 Golden Years: The N.F.L. Nationals, 1980, Why The Bible Is Number One, 1988, The Prophet Motive, 1995; editor Pacesetter; contbr. articles to profl. jours. Recipient Outstanding Young Religious Leader award Ala. Jaycees, 1976, Ala. Speech Tchr. of Yr. award 1977, Outstanding Speech and Debate Coach award Comml. Appeal, 1977, Key Coach award Barkley Forum for High Schs., Emory U., 1981, High Sch. Debate Coach of Yr. award Bishop's Guild, Samford U., 1983, Disting. Svc. award Nat. Forensic League, 1981, 86, named Triple Diamond Coach, 1993; U. Miss. Faulkner fellow, 1987; named HS Debate Coach of Yr. Carson Newman U., 1992. Mem. ASCD, Am. Forensic Assn. (ednl. practices com. 1984-86, high sch. affairs com. 1988-90, pub. rels. com. 1990-93), Ala. Forensic Educators Assn. (pres. 1976-77, 82-83, 85-86), Nat. Assn. Secondary Sch. Prins., So. Assn. Colls. and Schs. (cen. rev. com. 1991-95), Speech Comm. Assn., Deep South Nat. Forensic League (chmn. 1977-79, 81-85), Nat. Debate Coaches Assn., Journalism Educators Assn., Phi Delta Kappa. Office: Mars Hill Bible Sch 698 Cox Creek Pky Florence AL 35630-6624

BARGA, SANDRA ANNE MILLER, medical/surgical nurse; b. Utica, Mich., Aug. 31, 1948; d. Maurice A. and Jennie C. (Brooks) Miller; children: Teresa, Catherine, Tara. AS in Nursing, Pasco-Hernando C.C., New Port Richey, Fla., 1988. Staff nurse Citrus Meml. Hosp., Inverness, Fla.; case mgr., staff nurse ABC Home Health, Inverness, Fla., Vis. Nurses, New Port Richey, Fla.; intake coord. ABC Home Health, Port Richey, Fla.; patient car coord., nursing supr.; adminstr. ABC Home Health, Bayonet Point, Fla.; adminstr. ABC Home Health, Bayonnet Point, Fla.; case mgr. 1st Am. Homecare, Zephyr Hills, Fla. Mem. West Pasco Community Svc. Coun. Mem. West Pasco C. of C. (health svcs. com.), COECHA of Pasco, Phi Theta Kappa. Home: 11534 Fox Run Port Richey FL 34668-1209

BARGER, TIMOTHY KNOX, writer, researcher; b. Edwards AFB, Calif., Jan. 4, 1958; s. Lyman Tilden and Katherine (Echols) B. BA, Hendrix Coll., 1978; BJ, U. Tex., 1987, M Libr. and Info. Scis., 1994; postgrad., Syracuse U., 1994—. Assoc. editor The Austin (Tex.) Light, 1987-88; legal editor Tex. Legis. Coun., Austin, 1980-89; coord. editor Butterworth Legal Pubs., Austin, 1989-92; writer, rschr. The Reference Press, Inc., Austin, 1992-94. Author: (with others) Hoover's Handbook of American Business, 1993, 94, 95, Hoover's Handbook of World Business, 1993, Hoover's Handbook of Emerging Companies, 1993-94, Hoover's Guide to the Book Business, 1993, Hoover's Guide to Private Companies, 1994-95, The Texas 500, 1994, The Bay Area 500, 1994. Temple Found. scholar, 1993-94; Syracuse U. fellow, 1994-97. Mem. ALA, Austin Writers League (sec., bd. dirs. 1992-93), Soc. Profl. Journalists, Assn. for Edn. in Journalism and Mass Comms., Phi Kappa Phi.

BARGES, DAISY TERESS, special education educator; b. Baton Rouge, July 24, 1955; d. Comie Lee and Irma Louise (Jackson) B. BA in Elem. Edn., So. U., 1977, M in Elem. Edn., 1980; postgrad., Southeastern La. U., 1988, La. State U., No. La. U. Cert. in noncategorical presch., kindergarten and nursery tchr. Elem. tchr. Marksville (La.) Cath. Sch., 1978-79; asst. mgr. Wee World Day Care Ctr., Baton Rouge, 1978-80; tchr. pre-kindergarten St. Francis Xavier Cath. Sch., Baton Rouge, 1980-86; tchr. presch. handicapped Bogalusa (La.) City Schs. System, 1987—. Mem. NEA, La. Assn. Educators, Coun. Exceptional Children (div. early childhood). Democrat. Baptist. Home: 1621 Charlevoix St Bogalusa LA 70427-5201 Office: Bogalusa City Schs System 113 Cumberland St Bogalusa LA 70427-3101

BARGFREDE, JAMES ALLEN, lawyer; b. Seguin, Tex., Sept. 10, 1928; s. Herman Fred and Elsie (Vorpahl) B.; m. Virginia Felts, Nov. 27, 1970; 1 child, Charles Allen. BS, Tex. A&M U., 1950; postgrad. Ohio State U., 1952-53; JD, St. Mary's U., 1957. Bar: Tex. 1957, U.S. Patent and Trademark Office 1961. Registered profl. engr., Tex. Engr., Signal Corps, San Antonio, 1950-52; elec. engr. San Antonio Pub. Svc. Bd., 1953-58; patent counsel Hubbard & Co., Chgo., 1958-59; pvt. practice law, Chgo., 1959-60, Houston, 1960—; assoc. Butler, Binion, Rice, Cook & Knapp, 1960-68; pvt. practice law, 1968-74, 75—; patent and legal counsel HydroTech Internat., Inc., 1977-81; ptnr. Bargfrede & Thompson, 1974-75. With USAF, 1952-53. Sub-com. chmn. dist. com. on admissions Supreme Ct. Tex., 1988—. Mem. Houston Bar Assn. (chmn. automated equipment com. 1971-75), State Bar Tex., Am. Intellectual Property Law Assn., Houston Intellectual Property Law Assn., Assn. Former Students Tex. A&M U., Houston Livestock Show and Rodeo (life), Briarcroft Civic Club (pres. 1979-82), Houston A&M Club (treas. 1990, sec. 1991, v.p. 1992, pres. 1993), Delta Theta Phi. Baptist. Home: 5649 Piping Rock Ln Houston TX 77056-4028 Office: 7500 San Felipe St Ste 600 Houston TX 77063-1709

BARHAM, CHARLES DEWEY, JR., electric utility executive, lawyer; b. Goldsboro, N.C., July 7, 1930; s. Charles Dewey and Helen Wilkinson (Douglass) Barham Hughes; m. Margaret Wright Crow, June 17, 1960; children: Margaret Douglass, Charles Dewey III. B.S., Wake Forest U., 1952, J.D., 1954. Bar: N.C. 1954. Asst. atty. gen. N.C. Dept. Justice, Raleigh, 1958-66; assoc. gen. counsel Carolina Power & Light Co., Raleigh, N.C., 1966-73; ptnr. Douglass & Barham, Raleigh, 1974-80; v.p., sr. counsel Carolina Power & Light Co., Raleigh, 1981-82, sr. v.p., gen. counsel, 1982-87, sr. v.p., 1982-90, exec. v.p, 1990—; chmn. bd., pres. Nuclear Mut., Ltd., Hamilton, Bermuda, 1981-86, now bd. dirs.; bd. dirs. Nuclear Elec. Ins. Ltd., Hamilton; gen. counsel World Nuclear Fuel Mkt., Atlanta, 1974-80; gen. counsel Meredith Coll., Raleigh, 1977-80, trustee, 1984-87, 90-93; mem. regional bd. dirs. Wachovia Bank of N.C. Pres. Raleigh YMCA, 1982-92. Capt. USNR, 1955-77. Mem. ABA, N.C. Bar Assn., Fed. Energy Bar Assn. Democrat. Baptist. Clubs: Raleigh Civitan (dir. 1974-77), Glen Forest (pres. 1977). Office: Carolina Power & Light Co PO Box 1551 Raleigh NC 27602-1551 also: Carolina Power & Light Co 411 Fayetteville St Mall Raleigh NC 27601-1748

BARIK, SAILEN, biomedical scientist, educator; b. Midnapur, India, June 15, 1954; came to U.S., 1982; s. Narayan C. and Promila (Maiti) B.; m. Kumkum Maiti, June 26, 1981; children: Titus, Tiasha. BSc with honors, R.K.M.R. Coll., Calcutta, India, 1972; MSc, Calcutta U., 1975; PhD, Bose Inst., Calcutta, 1982. Rsch. fellow dept. sci. and tech. Govt. India, Calcutta, 1976-81; postdoctoral assoc. U. Conn. Health Ctr., Farmington, 1982-88; project scientist Cleve. Clinic Found., 1989-91, asst. staff, 1992-93; asst. prof. dept. biochemistry and molecular biology U. South Ala., Mobile, 1994—; spl. reviewer NIH, Bethesda, Md., 1994. Contbr. articles to profl. jours.; radio host John Carroll U., Cleve., 1992. Soccer coach South Euclid-Lyndhurst Recreation Club, Cleve., 1991-93. Mem. Am. Soc. Virology, Am. Soc. Microbiology. Home: 7771 Mallard Dr Mobile AL 36695-4239 Office: U South Ala Dept Biochem & Mol Biology 307 University Blvd N Mobile AL 36688-3053

BARKER, CAROLYN SIMS, diaconal minister; b. Atlanta, Aug. 29, 1968; d. James Dailey and Nancy Jane (Bringhurst) B. AB, Duke U., 1990; MDiv, Emory U., 1994. Upper sch. chaplain Holy Innocents' Episcopal Sch., Atlanta, 1994—. Vol. Hand on Atlanta, 1996; diaconal min. Unite Meth. Ch., 1995—. Office: HIES 805 Mt Vernon Hwy Atlanta GA 30327

BARKER, CHRIS A(LLEN), lawyer; b. Sheffield, Ala., July 24, 1965; s. Allen Dean and Martha Carol (Weatherby) B. BA magna cum laude in History, Birmingham-So. U., 1987; JD, U. Ala., 1990. Bar: Ala. 1990, U.S. Dist. Ct. (mid. dist.) 1992, U.S. Dist. Ct. (so. dist.) 1991, Fla. 1991, U.S. Dist. Ct. (no. dist.) 1991, U.S. Dist. Ct. (mid. dist.) 1993, U.S. Ct. Appeals 1991. Assoc. Trimmier, Atchison & Hayley, Birmingham, 1990-93; ptnr. Alpert, Barker & Calcutt, P.A., Tampa, 1993—; approved counsel Nat. Ctr. for Auto Safety, Washington. Co-author: Florida Practice Handbook-Workers' Compensation, 1994, 95; asst. author: Flordia Practice Handbook-Damages, 1993; editor-in-chief (legal newspaper) The Column, 1989-90. Mem. Rep. Nat. Com., Washington, 1993—; sponsor Paralyzed Vets. Am., Tampa, 1993—. Mem. ABA, Fla. Bar Assn. (workers' compensation sect. 1994-96, Hillsborough County Bar Assn., Corporate Counsel of Hillsborough County. Republican. Methodist. Office: Alpert Barker & Calcutt PA 100 S Ashley Dr Ste 2000 Tampa FL 33602-5311

BARKER, CLAYTON ROBERT, III, lawyer; b. Statesville, N.C., Aug. 27, 1957; s. Clayton Robert Jr. and Alta Jo (Ellis) B.; m. Sandra Ann Mills, June 30, 1990. AB with distinction, Stanford U., 1979; postgrad., Tufts. U., 1982; JD, U. Va., 1983. Bar: N.Y. 1984, Ga. 1995. Assoc. Shearman & Sterling, N.Y.C., 1983-85, Skaddan, Arps, Slate, Meagher & Flom, N.Y.C., 1985-91; counsel The Coca-Cola Co., Atlanta, 1991—. Contbr. articles to profl. jours. Mem. Am. Coun. on Germany. Mem. Internat. Bar Assn., Am. Soc. Internat. Law, N.Y. State Bar Assn. (internat. law and practice sect., fgn. investment in U.S. bus. com.), Am. Coun. on Germany (young leader 1992), Assn. for Corp. Growth (dir. Atlanta chpt.), Omicron Delta Kappa. Republican. Baptist. Office: The Coca-Cola Co 1 Coca Cola Plz NW Atlanta GA 30313-2420

BARKER, HEATHER ANN, earth and environmental scientist; b. Ft. Worth, Nov. 21, 1962; d. James Arlon and Alice Marchita (Mauldin) Williams; m. Charles Donald Barker, Oct. 24, 1986; 1 child, Fiona Nicole. BA, U. Tex., Arlington, 1986, BS, 1987, MS, 1993. Phys. sci. technician U.S. Army Corps. Engrs., Dallas, 1987-91; log technician Union Pacific Resources Corp., Ft. Worth, 1992. Author: Geophysical Surveys of Anasazi Ruins, Indian Camp Ranch, Cortez, Colorado, 1994. Vol. Ft. Worth Mus. Sci. and History, 1994. Mem. AAAS, Am. Assn. Petroleum Geologists (jr. mem., energy minerals div.), Assn. Women Geoscientists. Home: 7437 Arbor Park Dr Fort Worth TX 76120-2415

BARKER, JEANNE WILSON, principal, computer educational consultant; b. Columbus, Ohio, Mar. 10, 1939; d. Robert Sydney and Marjorie Helen (McQuillen) Wilson; m. Larry L. Barker, June 11, 1961 (div. June 1974); children: Theodore Allen, Robert Milford. BS in Edn., Ohio U., 1960, MS, 1963. Cert. edn. specialist, Fla. Music tchr. Newark (Ohio) City Schs., 1960-61; elem. tchr. Logan (Ohio) City Schs., 1962-63, asst. prin. East Elem. Sch., 1963-65; supervising tchr. Ohio U., Logan, 1964-65; dir. R&D Dept. Grant, State of Fla., Tallahassee, 1972-74; pre-sch. tchr. Temple Israel, Tallahassee, 1974-75; elem. tchr. Maclay Sch., Tallahassee, 1975-79, prin., 1980—; dir. Fla. Microcomputer project Fla. State U., Tallahassee, 1983-86, adj. instr., 1988—; computer cons. Jefferson/Wakulla County Schs., 1985—. Contbr. articles to profl. jours.; presenter in field. DeWitt Hooker fellow Fla. Coun. Ind. Schs., Tampa, 1987. Mem. Internat. Reading Assn., Alpha Delta Kappa. Democrat. Methodist. Office: Maclay Sch 3737 N Meridian Rd Tallahassee FL 32312-1110

BARKER, LARRY LEE, communications educator; b. Wilmington, Ohio, Nov. 22, 1941; s. Milford and Ruth Maxine (Garringer) B.; children: Theodore Allen, Robert Milford. B.A., Ohio U., 1962, M.A., 1963, Ph. D, 1965. Asst. prof. So. Ill. U., Carbondale, 1965-66, Purdue U., West Lafayette, Ind., 1966-69; assoc. prof. Fla. State U., Tallahassee, 1969-71, prof., 1971-75; prof. emeritus Auburn (Ala.) U., 1976-95; pres. Spectra Inc., New Orleans, 1979—. Author: (with R. Kibler) Conceptual Frontiers in Speech Communication, 1969, Behavioral Objectives and Instruction, 1970, Listening Behavior, 1971, Speech Communication Behavior, 1971, Communication Vibrations, 1974, Speech—Interpersonal Communication, 1974, (with R. Edward) Intrapersonal Communication, 1980, (with R. Kibler) Objectives for Instruction and Evaluation, 1981, Communication, 1982, Communication in the Classroom, 1982, (with others) Effective Listening, 1982, (with L. Malandro) Nonverbal Communication, 1983, (with K. Wahlers) Groups in Process, 1983, (with others) Intrapersonal Communication Processes, 1987, (with K. Watson) Interpersonal and Relational Communications, 1989; contbr. articles to profl. jours. Recipient outstanding award in discussion Tau Kappa Alpha, 1962, outstanding tchr. award Central States Speech Assn., 1969. Mem. APA, ASTD, Speech Comm. Assn. (Robert J. Kibler Meml. award 1986), Internat. Comm. Assn. (v.p. 1972-74), Internat. Listening Assn. (chmn. rsch. com. 1979-82, pres. 1986-87). Methodist. Home: 2319 Audubon St New Orleans LA 70125

BARKER, LISA ANN, aerospace engineer; b. Lompoc, Calif., Feb. 1, 1965; d. Robert Andrew and Donna Jean (Eden) B. BS in Aerospace, Purdue U., 1987. Aerospace engr. NASA Marshall Space Flight Ctr., Huntsville, Ala., 1987—. Mem. AIAA.

BARKER, MICHAEL DEAN, nuclear engineer, internet engineer; b. Lampasas, Tex., Jan. 21, 1960; s. Hughby Frank Barker and Georgia Ann (Bales) Alsbrooks; m. Joy Ann Lively, May 19, 1984; children: Sarah Elizabeth, Michael Austin, Matthew Hamilton, Philip Nathaniel. B in Nuclear Engring., Ga. Inst. Technology, 1983. Coop. engring. student Ga. Power Co., Waynesboro, 1978-83; sr. nuclear engr. Ga. Power Co., Atlanta, 1983-88; sr. engr. SONOPCO, Birmingham, 1988-90; program mgr. Inst. Nuclear Power Ops., Atlanta, 1991—; pres. C4 Internet Consultants, Atlanta, Ga., 1995—; tech. dir. Internet Bus. Incubator. Candidate U.S. Congress, Rep. Party, Ala., 1990; elected mem. Rep. Exec. Com., Shelby County, Ala., 1989-91. Republican. Presbyterian. Office: C4 Internet Cons Ste 250 1000 Mansell Exchange W Alpharetta GA 30202

BARKER, NEWELL KEITH, petroleum engineer, chief branch of minerals; b. Vandalia, Ill., Feb. 7, 1937; s. Bud Arnold and Jennie Loretta B.; m. Pansy Jean LEathers, Apr. 10, 1965; children: Newell Keith II, Kash. BS in Petroleum Engring., Tex. Tech. U., 1961; Cert., Dale Carnegie Inst., Bartlesville, Okla., 1992. Registered profl. engr., Okla., Tex. Dist. mud engr. Permian Mud Svc., Kermit, Tex., 1961-65; sales engr. Magcobar De Venezuela, Anaco, Venezuela, South America, 1965-66; dist. engr. Phillips Petroleum Co., Morichal, Venezuela, South America, 1966-72; dist. supt. Thermo-Dyne, Inc., Carnegie, Okla., 1972-73; sr. engr. Sohio Petroleum Co., Pauls Valley, Okla., 1973-74; chief br. of minerals Osage Indian Agy., B.I.A., Pawhuska, Okla., 1974—; Registered profl. engr., Okla., Tex. Patentee in field; contbr. tech. paper to profl. publs. Recipient Numerous Golf awards Venezuelan Golf Clubs, 1966-72, Drag Racing awards, 1962-74, Boxing awards, 1955-60, Clown awards, 1978-95. Mem. Okla. Profl. Engrs., Tex. Profl. Engrs., Soc. Petroleum Engrs., Wah-Shah-She #110 Masonic Lodge (worshipful master 1979, 92), Tulsa Scottish Rite (wise master of Rose Croix 1992), Osage County Scottish Rite Chpt. (pres. 1982-83), Wasono Shrine Club (pres. 1983), Barlesville Merri-Maker Shrine Clowns (pres. 1982-87, 90-92), Hon. Order Ky. Cols., Clowns of Am. Internat., World Clown Assn., Internat. Shrine Clown Assn., Ctrl. States Shrine Clown Assn. (pres. 1992), Kara Grotto (monarch 1989), Royal Arch Masons (high priest 1994, coun. illustrious master 1995, comdr. 1996, Olympic Torch Bearer 1996). Baptist. Home: 1521 Revard Ave Pawhuska OK 74056-1853 Office: Osage Indian Agy 813 Grandview Ave Pawhuska OK 74056-3203

BARKER, ROBERT OSBORNE (BOB BARKER), mediator, property management and public relations consultant; b. Cleve., June 13, 1932; m. Sharon Ann; children: Debra, Stephen Robert, Dawn, Michael, Colleen. Student Henry Ford C.C., 1950; BA in Communication Arts and Sci., Mich. State U., 1954; student LaSalle U. Law Sch., 1966-68, U. Wis., 1989. Lic. community assn. mgr., real estate agent, notary public. With public relations dept. Ford Motor Co., Dearborn, Mich., 1953; mgr. Kaiser Aluminum Co., Chgo., 1956-58; advt. mgr. Bastian Blessing Co., Chgo., 1958-59; mgr. Sun Co., Ohio and Detroit, 1959-71, Goodyear Tire & Rubber Co., Detroit, 1971-72; mgr., v.p. NAM, Washington, Boston, and Southfield, Mich., 1972-87, registered lobbyist, 1978-87; pres., CEO Barker Cons. Inc., 1987-96; v.p., mgr. seminars and materials dept. Am. Supplier Inst. , 1987-90; nat. merchandising mgr. Costa Del Mar Sunglsses, Ormond Beach, Fla. 1990-91; reporter Police Times, 1989-93; resort mgr. Oceanside 99 Condo., 1992-93, Outrigger Beach Club, 1994-95. V.p. Findlay (Ohio) Jaycees, 1960-64; twp. trustee, Findlay, Ohio, 1962; vestry Episc. Ch., 1981; mem. St. James Episc. Ch.; mem. Volusia County Rep. Exec. Com., 1991—; bd. dirs. Am. Cancer Soc., 1991—, chmn. pub. issues; bd. dirs. Dearborn Civic Theater, 1980-84, Volusia Presdl. Forum, Ormond Beach Rep. Club, Dearborn City Beautiful commr. emeritus, 1970-90; commr. Ormond Beach Quality of Life, Beautification and Planning Bd.; res. police officer, Dearborn, 1968-88; pres. Dearborn High and Lindbergh Elem. PTA; owner, bd. dirs. Dolphin Beach Club Condo., 1981—; bd. dirs. Bldg. Assn. Mgrs., 1993-95, Community Assoc. Inst., Volusia County Pers. Bd., 1991-93; mem. adj. faculty Daytona Beach (Fla.) C.C.; mem. adv. coun. Coun. of Aging; active Fla. Police Benevolent Assn., Daytona Beach Rep. Club (bd. dirs.), Fla. Sheriffs Assn., Ormond Meml. Art Mus. Served with USNR, 1949-58. Mem. Meeting Planners Internat., Assn. Execs., Fla. Pub. Rels. Soc. (vice chmn. Volusia chpt.), Am. Legion (life), Mich. State U. Alumni (past pres., vice chmn. and participant sr. games 1994), Ormond Beach C. of C. (chmn. pub. rels., Beautification, JazzMatazz, social com.), Ormond Shrine Club (pres. 1994-95), Elks, Exch. Club, Rotary (pres. 1987-88), Masons, Moose-Legion, Shriners (dir. pub. relations 1984, provost unit, FEZ on Wheels and Vets. unit), Delta Tau Delta. Home: 19 Riverview Dr Ormond Beach FL 32174-7056

BARKER, SANDRA MILLS, securities analyst; b. Charlotte, N.C., Aug. 21, 1958; d. Parks Smith and Virginia Elizabeth (Morgan) Mills; m. Clayton Robert Barker III, June 30, 1990; 1 child, John Morgan. BA in Econs. magna cum laude, Wake Forest U., Winston-Salem, N.C., 1980. Chartered fin. analyst. Investment rsch. analyst The Duke Endowment, Charlotte, N.C., 1980-83; asst. v.p., rsch. analyst Trust Co. of Ga., Atlanta, 1983-86, 1st Union Nat. Bank, Charlotte, 1986-88; ptnr., rsch. analyst Eagle Capital Mgmt., N.Y.C., 1988-91; v.p., rsch. analyst Interstate/Johnson Lane, Atlanta, 1992-95. Carswell scholar Wake Forest U., 1976-80. Mem. Assn. for Investment Mgmt. and Rsch., Atlanta Soc. Security Analyst, Phi Beta Kappa, Omicron Delta Epsilon. Republican. Baptist. Home: 4139 Brookview Dr NW Atlanta GA 30339-4603

BARKIN, JAMIE STEVEN, gastroenterologist, educator; b. Miami, Fla., June 1, 1943; s. Mazie Barkin; m. Faith Eileen Block; 1 child, Jodie. Grad., U. Miami, 1965, MD, 1970. Diplomate Am. Bd. Internal Medicine, Am. Bd. Gastroenterology. BS magna cum laude U. Miami, Fla., 1970-71, jr. resident in medicine, 1971-72, sr. resident in medicine, 1972-73, jr. fellow in gastroenterology, 1973-74, sr. fellow in gastroenterology, 1974-75, asst. prof. dept. medicine, 1975-80, assoc. prof. dept. medicine, 1980-87, prof. dept. medicine, 1987—; asst. prof. dept. oncology U. Miami, 1978-81, assoc. prof., 1981-86, prof., 1987—, assoc. prof. dept. pediatrics, 1983-87, prof., 1987—; coord. endoscopy Miami VA Hosp., 1975-85; chief divsn. gastroenterology Mt. Sinai Med. Ctr., 1985—; active attending staff Jackson Meml. Hosp., Miami, 1975—, VA Med. Ctr., Miami, 1975-85, U. Miami Hosps. & Clinics, 1975—, Mt. Sinai Med. Ctr., Miami Beach, 1985—; cons. VA Med. Ctr., 1986; mem. coms. U. Miami Hosps. & Clinics, 1977-84, Jackson Meml. Hosp., 1977-80, VA Med. Ctr., 1977-85, U. Miami Sch. of Medicine, 1982-85, Mt. Sinai Med. Ctr., 1985-90; lectr., cons. in field. Editor: (with A.I. Rogers) Difficult Decisions in Digestive Diseases, 1988, 2d edit., 1994, (with C.A. O'Phelan) Advanced Therapeutic Endoscopy, 1990, 2d edit., 1994; mem. editorial bd. Internat. Jour. Pancreatology, 1985-91, Current Concepts in Gastroenterology, 1985—, Endoscopy Around the World, 1987, Postgrad. Medicine, 1989, Am. Jour. Gastroenterology, 1986-93, Cirugia, Gastro & Ginecologia, 1989, Romanian Jour. Gastroenterology, 1993, Digestive Diseases, 1993; mem. bd. assoc. editors Pancreas, 1993—; contbr. articles and revs. to profl. jours, chpts. to books. With U.S. Army Res., Brigadier Gen. Commdr, 322nd Med. Brigrade, Nashville Tenn. Recipient Rorer Pharm. Corp. award Am. Coll. Gastroenterology, 1989; Grantee AGA Clinicians Postgrad. Support Program, 1989, Women's Cancer League of Miami Beach, 1990. Fellow ACP (chmn. pub. rels. com. Fla. chpt. 1988-93, MKSAP adv. com. 1990-92, MKSAP planning sub-com. 1991-93, gov.-elect Fla. chpt. 1995-96, gov. 1996—); mem. AMA, Am. Coll. Gastroent. (pres.-elect 1988-89, pres. 1989-90), Am. Gastroent. Assn. (abstract selection com. 1988-90, tng. and edn. com. 1988-91), Am. Soc. Gastrointestinal Endoscopy (mem. various coms. 1980-87), Am. Pancreatic Assn., Am. Fedn. Clin. Rsch., Am. Assn. History Medicine, Am. Soc. Laser Medicine and Surgery Inc., Assn. Mil. Surgeons of the U.S., Internat. Biliary Assn., Internat. Assn. Pancreatology, Internat. Gastro-Surg. Club, Bockus Internat. Soc. Gastroenterology (fellowship com. 1983-89, constn. and bylaws com. 1987-89, treas.

1985-93, v.p. 1993), So. Med. Assn., Fla. Gastroent. Soc. (pres. elect 1993-94, pres. 1994-95), Gastroenterology Rsch. Group, Alpha Omega Alpha. Office: 4300 Alton Rd Miami FL 33140-2849

BARKLEY, BRONSON LEE, minister; b. Austin, Tex., July 30, 1949; s. Junius Paul and Ellie Montgomery (Neal) B.; m. Darlene Lynette Hickman, July 21, 1972; children: John Paul, Jared Patrick. BA, Lamar U., 1971, MA, 1974. Ordained to ministry Assemblies of God, 1977. Assoc. pastor 1st Assembly of God, Tyler, Tex., 1972-74; pastor Faith Assembly of God, Alvin, Tex., 1974-76, Golden Acres Assembly of God, Pasadena, Tex., 1979-82, Chapel in the Forest Assembly of God, Kingwood, Tex., 1983—; revivalist Assemblies of God, Port Arthur, Tex., 1976-78, 83; founding pres. WZZJ Radio, Pascagoula, Miss., 1991—; bd. dirs. KSBJ Radio, Humble, Tex. Author play: The Lady and the Middle Cross, 1989; composer various songs. Bd. dirs. Spl. Svcs. Resumé, Birthright of Humble (Tex.), 1990—, Leadership Tng. Internat., Inc., Springdale, Ark., 1991—; precinct chmn. Rep. Party of Harris County, 1988-90; state del. Tex. Rep. Party Conv. Mem. Kingwood Area Clergy Assn., Christian Coalition, Phi Eta Sigma. Office: Chapel in the Forest 4032 Northpark Dr Kingwood TX 77345-4935

BARKLEY, HENRY BROCK, JR., research and development executive; b. Raleigh, N.C., Apr. 5, 1927; s. Henry Brock and Thelma Maurine (Dutt) B.; m. Edith Sumner Stowe, June 24, 1950; children: Margaret Susan, Henry Brock III, Jane Stowe. Student U. N.C., 1944-45; BS, U.S. Naval Acad., 1949; BSEE, U.S. Naval Postgrad. Sch., 1954, MSEE, 1955. Supr. space power sect. Bendix, Ann Arbor, Mich., 1962-63; chief reactor div. Lewis Research Center, NASA, Sandusky, Ohio, 1963-73; asst. gen. mgr., dir. power reactors EG&G Idaho, Inc., Idaho Falls, 1973-81; mgr. internat. bus. Babcock & Wilcox Co., Lynchburg, Va., 1981-83, mgr. 205 plant project services, 1983-87, mgr. space power and propulsion, 1987-89, dir. space and def. systems, 1989-92; cons., 1992—; dir. Devel. Workshop, Inc., Idaho Falls., 1977-81; IEEE Disting. lectr. in S.Am. and C.Am., 1984. Bd. dirs. Sandusky (Ohio) Concert Assn., 1965-73; chmn. Huron (Ohio) sch. levy campaigns, 1970. Served to lt. comdr. USN, 1949-61. Mem. IEEE, Am. Nuclear Soc., Am. Guild Organists. Presbyterian. Home: 1216 Norvell House Ct Lynchburg VA 24503-1940

BARKLEY, MARLENE A. NYHUIS, nursing administrator; b. Waupun, Wis., Aug. 31, 1934; d. Fred and Esther Elsie (Leu) Nyhuis; m. Peter Don Barkley, Sept. 1, 1956; children: Peter Scott, John Fredric. Dipl. nursing, Milw. County Hosp., 1955; cert. nurse practitioner, U. Miami, Fla., 1976; AA, Miami Dade C.C., Fla., 1983; BSN cum laude, U. Miami, 1985; MSN, Barry U., 1996. RN, Fla. Nurse Waupun (Wis.) Meml. Hosp., 1956-57; nurse coord. Courtland Med. Ctr., Milw., 1958-61, Planned Parenthood, Bloomington, Ind., 1971-74; nurse practitioner Miami VA Med. Ctr., 1976-83, program dir., 1983—. Mem. ANA (cert.), Advanced Practice Coun., Fla. Nurses Assn., So. Pain Soc., U. Miami Alumni Assn., Sigma Theta Tau. Presbyterian. Home: 14248 SW 97 Ter Miami FL 33186

BARKLEY, MONIKA JOHANNA, quality control professional; b. Lexington, Ky., Feb. 22, 1961; d. Ellis Leon McCollum and Doris Leni (vonderLippe) Hutson; m. Samuel Custer Barkley II, Feb. 14, 1986. Cert. in acctg., Fayette City Vocat.-Tech Coll., 1982. Claims processor Western Ins., Lexington, 1979-82; constrn. sec. Price, Inc.-Neal, Inc., Lexington, 1982-84; quality control adminstr. Jacobs Builders, Inc., Jacksonville, N.C., 1984-90; pres. Unicorn Constrn., Goldsboro, N.C., 1984—; quality control adminstr. Flynn Co., Inc., Dubuque, Iowa, 1988-89; sec. to pres. Wooten Oil Co., Goldsboro, N.C., 1990-91; contract adminstr. Colejon Corp., Cleve., 1991-95; office mgr.-adminstr. JC&B Constrn. Co., Goldsboro, N.C., 1995—; sec., treas. Vet.'s Contracting, Lexington, 1988-92. Rep. dist. chair, Lexington, 1979; county coord. Dole for Pres., Hayes for Gov., Jones for Congress, 1996; alt. del. to Rep. Nat. Conv., 1996; alt. del. Rep. Nat. Conv., 1996. Recipient Contractor Safety award U.S. Army Corp Engrs., Seymour Johnson AFB, N.C., 1988, Contractor of Yr. award, 1988. Fellow VFW Aux. (Outstanding Svc. award 1985), Order of Ea. Star; mem. Vets. United for Strong Am. (nat. sec. 1985-89), Pearl Harbor Commemorative Assn. (nat. sec. 1989—, Wayne County Rep. Women's Club (v.p. 1995), Wayne County Citizens For Better Tax Control (sec. 1995). Baptist. Home and Office: PO Box 10627 Goldsboro NC 27532-0627

BARKOFF, RUPERT MITCHELL, lawyer; b. New Orleans, May 7, 1948; s. Samuel and Martha (Lewis) B.; m. Susan Joyce Levitt, May 31, 1970; children: Stuart, Jeffrey, Lisa. BA in Econs. with high distinction, U. Mich., 1970, JD magna cum laude, 1973. Bar: Ga. 1973. Assoc. Kilpatrick & Cody, Atlanta, 1973-80, ptnr., 1980—. Contbr. articles to profl. jours. Mem. ABA (bus. law sect., antitrust sect., forum on franchising, panelist ann. forums 1980-92, chmn. 1989-92, assoc. editor Franchise Law Jour. 1981-86), Ga. Bar Assn. (corp. and banking sect.), Atlanta Bar Assn., Lawyers Club Am., Phi Beta Kappa. Democrat. Jewish. Home: 5215 Vernon Springs Trl NW Atlanta GA 30327-4511 Office: Kilpatrick & Cody 1100 Peachtree St NE Ste 2800 Atlanta GA 30309-4528

BARKOWSKY, EDWARD RICHARD, English language educator; b. Lamesa, Tex., Jan. 12, 1942; s. Franz Richard and Anna Otillie Barkowsky; m. Judith Katherine Self, May 31, 1964; children: Lesa Ann, Holly Kay. BA in English, Tex. Tech. U., 1964, MA in English, 1968; PhD in English, Ball State U., 1975. Teaching asst. Tex. Tech. U., Lubbock, 1965-67; instr. English South Plains Coll., Levelland, Tex., 1967-69; doctoral fellow Ball State U., Muncie, Ind., 1969-71; prof. English Western Tex. Coll., Snyder, Tex., 1971—; chair divsn. comm./letters Western Tex. Coll., Snyder, 1973—. Officer Scurry County United Way, Snyder, 1975-96; bd. dirs. West Tex. Girl Scouts Coun., Abilene, 1976-96, pres., 1991-96. Mem. Tex. Jr. Coll. Tchrs. Assn. (vice-chair profl. devel. com. 1991-94). Home: 2804 47th St Snyder TX 79549-5810 Office: Western Tex Coll 6200 College Ave Snyder TX 79549-6105

BARKSDALE, RHESA HAWKINS, federal judge; b. Jackson, Miss., Aug. 8, 1944; s. John Woodson Jr. and Mary Bryan (Saunders) B. BS, U.S. Mil. Acad., 1966; JD, U. Miss., 1972. Law clk. to Hon. Byron R. White U.S. Supreme Ct., 1972-73; assoc., then ptnr. Butler, Snow, O'Mara, Stevens & Cannada, Jackson, 1973-90; judge U.S. Ct. Appeals (5th cir.), Jackson, 1990—; instr. U. Miss. Sch. Law, Jackson, 1975-76, Miss. Coll. Sch. Law, Jackson, 1976. Chmn. Miss. Vietnam Vets. Leadership Program, Jackson, 1982-85; del. Rep. Nat. Conv., New Orleans, 1988; elector election of Pres. of U.S., Jackson, 1988. Capt. U.S. Army, 1966-70, Vietnam. Decorated Silver Star, Bronze Star for Valor, Purple Heart; Cross of Gallantry with silver star (Republic of Vietnam). Mem. Am. Inn of Ct. (Charles Clark chpt.), Phi Delta Phi (Nat. Grad. of Yr. 1972). Episcopalian. Office: US Ct Appeals 5th Cir 245 E Capitol St Rm 246 Jackson MS 39201-2409

BARLASCINI, CORNELIUS OTTAVIO, JR., physician; b. Richmond, Va., Oct. 5, 1956; s. Cornelio O. Sr. and Gloria Stella (Massucco) B.; m. Laura Amelia Petrelli, June 22, 1991; 1 child, Louis Ernest. BA, U. Va., 1979, MD, 1983. Intern, resident and fellow Med. Coll. Va., Richmond, 1983-88; assoc. dir. Diabetes Treatment Ctr., Columbus, Ga., 1988-95; chief endocrinology sect. South Ga. Med. Ctr. Contbr.: (textbook) Drug Therapy in Emergency Medicine, 1990; contbr. articles to profl. jours.; inventor in field. Recipient Sandra Tate Russell award Va. chpt. Am. Diabetes Assn., 1988. Fellow ACP; mem. The Endocrine Soc., Phi Beta Kappa.

BARLEY, DORIS FAYE, sales executive; b. Samson, Ala., Dec. 3, 1936; d. Chester and Alma (Cobb) Simmons; m. L.J. Barley, Nov. 10, 1955. Grad. high sch., Samson. With Ansell, Inc., Dothan, Ala., 1966—, product mgr., 1969-71, nat. sales mgr., 1971-74, v.p., 1974-92; sr. v.p. Tilly Balloon, Inc., Fall River, Mass., 1992—; mem. adv. bd. Gen. Mdse. Distributors Council, Colorado Springs, Colo., 1974-78. Recipient Personal Devel. award Ala. Fed. Bus. and Profl. Women's Club, 1969-70; Flying Col. award Delta Airlines, 1986. Republican. Baptist. Home and Office: Tilly Balloon Inc 2494 Enon Rd Webb AL 36376

BARLEY, JOHN ALVIN, lawyer; b. Jacksonville, Fla., Oct. 16, 1940; s. Lewis Alvin Barley and Catherine Alberta (Curran) McKendree; m. Mary Freida Szarowicz, Nov. 30, 1974 (div. Dec. 1991); children: Jared Scott, Jessica Lauren. BS, Fla. State U., 1963; JD, U. Fla., 1968. Bar: Fla. 1969, U.S. Dist. Ct. (mid. and no. dists.) Fla. 1973, U.S. Ct. Appeals (5th and 11th cirs.) 1973, U.S. Supreme Ct. 1973. Law clk. to judge U.S. Dist. Ct. (so. dist.), Miami, Fla., 1968-69; exec. asst. to Hon. Ray C. Osborne Lt. Gov. Fla., Tallahassee, 1969-70; asst. dir. div. of labor Fla. Dept. Commerce, Tallahassee, 1971; assoc. Maquire, Voorhis & Wells, Orlando, Fla., 1972-73; asst. atty. gen. Dept. of Legal Affairs, Tallahassee, 1974-75; gen. counsel Dept. of Gen. Services, Tallahassee, 1976-78; pvt. practice, Tallahassee, 1978—. Mem. ABA, Fla. Bar Assn. (pub. contract law com., bd. govs. young lawyers div. 1974, rules of civil procedure com. 1974-88, 91-92), Tallahassee Bar Assn., Am. Judicature Soc., Phi Delta Phi. Roman Catholic. Home: 4927 Heathe Dr Tallahassee FL 32308-2134 Office: 400 N Meridian St Tallahassee FL 32301-1254 and: PO Box 10166 Tallahassee FL 32302

BARLEY, STEPHEN W., company executive; b. 1950. Grad., Kans. State U., 1972. With Green Valley Country Club, Birmingham, Ala., 1972-78, Colonial Country Club, Ft. Worth, 1978-82; pres. Landscape Resources, Inc., Irving, Tex., 1982—. Office: Landscape Resources Inc 1870 Crown Dr Ste Farmers Branch TX 75234-3523*

BARLOW, JIM B., newspaper columnist; b. Port Arthur, Tex., Aug. 19, 1936; s. Joseph B. and Goldie (Johnson) B.; m. Karleen Ann Smith, Aug. 24, 1968 (div. Jan. 1974); 1 child, Samantha Lynn; m. Susan Ann Bischoff, June 20, 1975. BA, U. North Tex., Denton, 1972. Newsman KPAC-TV, Port Arthur, Tex., 1959-61; news dir. KPNG-Radio, Port Neches, Tex., 1962-63; reporter Beaumont (Tex.) Enterprise, 1963-64, Denton Record-Chronicle, 1964-66; asst. city mgr. City of Denton, 1967; staff writer U. North Tex., Denton, 1968; newsman AP, Dallas-Houston, 1968-75; dir. info. svcs. Houston Ind. Sch. Dist., 1975-77; reporter Houston Chronicle, 1977-87, columnist, 1987—. Co-author: Big Town, Big Money, 1974. With U.S. Army, 1956-59. Mem. Soc. Am. Bus. Editors and Writers. Home: 6407 Schuler St Houston TX 77007-2064 Office: 801 Texas St Houston TX 77002-2906

BARLOW, JOEL WILLIAM, chemical engineering educator; b. Burbank, Calif., May 2, 1942; married; 2 children. BS, U. Wis., 1964, MS, 1965, PhD in Chem. Engring., 1970. Fellow materials and thermodynamics Washington U., 1968-70; research engr. in plastics Union Carbide Corp., Bound Brook, N.J., 1970-73; from asst. prof. to assoc. prof. U. Tex., Austin, 1973-83, prof. chem. engring., 1983-90, Z.D. Bonner prof. chem. engring., Cullen Trust for Higher Edn. Endowed Professorship Number 5, 1984—. Mem. Am. Chem. Soc., Am. Inst. Chem. Engrs., Soc. Plastics Engrs. Office: Univ Tex Dept Chem Engring CPE 3.466 Austin TX 78712-1062

BARLOW, NADINE GAIL, planetary geoscientist; b. La Jolla, Calif., Nov. 9, 1958; d. Nathan Dale and Marcella Isabel (Menken) B.; divorced. BS, U. Ariz., 1980, PhD, 1987. Instr., planetarium lectr. Palomar Coll., San Marcos, Calif., 1982; grad. rsch. asst. U. Ariz., Tucson, 1982-87; postdoctoral fellow Lunar and Planetary Inst., Houston, 1987-89; NRC assoc. NASA/Johnson Space Ctr., Houston, 1989-91, vis. scientist, 1991-92, support scientist exploration programs office, 1992; vis. scientist Lunar and Planetary Inst., Houston, 1992-95; assoc. prof. U. Houston, Clear Lake, 1991-95; pres. Minerva Rsch. Enterprises, 1995—; instr. astronomy, dir. Robinson Obs. U. Ctrl. Fla., Orlando, 1996—; co-dir. intern program Lunar and Planetary Inst., 1988-89. Editor (slide set) A Guide to Martian Impact Craters, 1988; assoc. editor Encyclopedia of Earth Sciences, 1996; contbr. articles to profl. jours. Named among Outstanding Women and Ethnic Minorities Engaged in Sci. and Engring., Lawrence Livermore Nat. Lab., 1991. Mem. AAUW (pres. Clear Lake chpt. 1991-93, program v.p. 1993-95, v.p. interbr. coun. 1990-91, chmn. Tex. task force on women and girls in sci. and math. 1991-92, dir. state pub. policy 1991-94, Tex. Woman of Yr. 1992, mem. pub. policy com. 1994-95, chmn. steering com. Tex. ednl. equity 1994-95), Am. Astron. Soc. (com. on status of women in astronomy 1995—, pres. officer divsn. planetary scis. 1993—, status of women in astronomy com. 1987-90), Astron. Soc. of Pacific, Meteoritical Soc., Am. Geophys. Union, Geol. Soc. Am., Assn. Women in Sci. (Gulf Coast Houston chpt. councilor 1994-95, pres. 1995-96), Assn. Women Geoscientists. Office: U Ctrl Fla Dept Physics Dept of Physics Orlando FL 32816

BARMETTLER, ROBERT STEPHEN, speech educator, writer; b. Stans, Switzerland, Apr. 25, 1924; came to U.S., 1931; s. Emil Frank and Louisa (Waser) B.; m. Caroline Dorothea Stein, Sept. 4, 1949 (div. Mar. 1987); children: Babette Lucinde, Heidi Elizabeth; m. Jeanne Ellison Shaffer, May 22, 1989. BA in Drama, San Jose State U., 1949; MA in English, Tex. Christian U., 1963; postgrad., NYU, 1977-83, Auburn U., 1971. Commd. 2d lt. USAF, 1949-70, advanced through grades to lt. col., 1966, ret., 1970; dir. of theatre Huntingdon Coll., Montgomery, Ala., 1970-87; profl. actor, writer, 1987-93; prof. speech Ala. State U., Montgomery, 1993—; pres., founder Montgomery Sch. of Fine Arts, 1976-87, Montgomery Performing Arts Co., 1977-95; founder Huntingdon Coll. Summer Repertory Theatre, Montgomery, 1976-83; pres. Freelance Arts Assocs., Montgomery, 1987-95. Author: (musical plays), Heart of Dixie, 1980, Balls!, 1984, End of the Line, 1986; contbr. weekly column Comm-Trails to USAF Acad., 1961-63. Pres. USAF Chatouroux (France) Air Base PTA, 1964-66; pres. Civic Ballet, Montgomery, 1972-73, Arts Coun. of Montgomery, 1974-75. Decorated Bronze Star, Air medal. Mem. SAG, AFTRA, Actors Equity Assn., Southeastern Theatre Conf. (life), Ala. Conf. Theatre and Speech (pres. 1981-82), Delta Upsilon. Episcopalian. Home: 1062 Woodley Montgomery AL 36106 Office: Ala State U 915 S Jackson St Montgomery AL 36104-5732

BARNARD, BARBARA BLACKBURN, dietitian; b. Knoxville, Tenn., Jan. 2, 1937; d. William Ernest and Mary Lucile (Douglass) Blackburn; m. Anthony Charles Barnard, June 6, 1964; children: Lisa Ann, Carol Elizabeth. BS, U. Tenn., 1959. Dietetic intern Tex. VA Hosp., Houston, 1960, clinic dietitian, 1961, dir. nutrition clinic and therapeutic units, 1962-67; nutritionist Jefferson County Health Dept., Nutrition Bur., Birmingham, Ala., 1969; clin. instr. dietetic technician program U. Ala., Birmingham, 1975, cons. dept. nutrition scis., 1988; cons. book div. Oxmoor House, Inc., Birmingham, 1989; cons. dept. nutrition sci. U. Ala., Birmingham, 1991-92; cons. So. Living Mag., Birmingham, 1991-93. Contbr. articles to mags. Bd. dirs. women's com. Ala. Symphony, 1972—, pres., 1986-87; bd. dirs. U. Ala. Birmingham Faculty Women's Club, 1969—, pres., 1990-91, treas., 1982-83; bd. dirs. Creative Schs. Inc., 1977-79; vol. U. Ala. Birmingham Ballet and Town and Gown Theatre; mem. Town and Gown Guild, chair guest artist hospitality; bd. dirs. Antiquarian Soc.; host couple Ala. Symphony Cruise, 1988, 89; bd. dirs., sec. Space One Eleven Regional Art Ctr., Birmingham, 1992-96. Mem. AAUW, Am. Dietetic Assn. (registered dietitian), Tex. Dietetic Assn. (pres. 1966-67), Birmingham Dietetic Assn., Houston Dietetic Assn., Omicron Nu. Home: 3037 Westmoreland Dr Birmingham AL 35223-2727

BARNARD, DONALD ROY, medical and veterinary entomologist; b. Santa Ana, Calif., June 7, 1946; s. Alan Whittaker and Ethel Mae (Kennedy) B.; m. Priscilla Margaret Grier, Aug. 12, 1967; children: Jennifer Erin, David Michael. BS in Zoology, Calif. State U., 1969, MA in Biology, 1972; PhD in Entomology, U. Calif.-Riverside, 1977. Postdoctoral fellow Colo. State U., Ft. Collins, 1977-79; rsch. entomologist agrl. rsch. svc. USDA, Poteau, Okla., 1979-85, supervisory rsch. entomologist, 1985-88; rsch. leader agrl. rsch. svc. USDA, Gainesville, Fla., 1988—; adj. prof. entomology Okla. State U., 1988—, U. Fla., 1991—; tech. reviewer NIH Tropical Medicine and Parasitology, 1989—, Ctr. for Disease Control and Prevention, Health and Human Svcs., PHS, 1991—; cons., tech. reviewer WHO/FAO, 1980—, Bay Region Agrl. Devel. Project, AID, Somali Dem. Republic/U.S.A., 1981—, USDA, ARS liaison to Armed Forces Pest Mgmt. Bd., Dept. Def., 1985—, Dept. Agr., Republic South Africa, 1988—, State of Fla., 1992—; active Fla. Coordinating Coun. for Mosquito Control. Contbr. chpts. to books, articles to profl. jours; mem. editl. bd. Jour. of Med. Entomology, Bull. of the Soc. Vector Ecologists. Mem. Am. Mosquito Control Assn., Internat. Orgn. Biol. Control, Internat. Soc. Ecol. Economics, Entomol. Soc. Am., Entomol. Soc. Can., Ecol. Soc. Am., Fla. Mosquito Control Assn. (mem. rsch. adv. com.).

BARNARD, GEORGE SMITH, lawyer, former federal agency official; b. Opelika, Ala.; s. George Smith and Caroline Elizabeth (Dowdell) B.; m. Muriel Elaine Outlaw, July 26, 1945; children: Elizabeth Elaine Barnard Crutcher, Charles Dowling, Beverly Laura Barnard Parker, Andrew Carey. BA, U. Ala., 1948, LLB, 1950. Bar: Fla. 1978, Ala. 1950, U.S. Tax Ct. 1950, U.S. Dist. Ct. Ala. 1950, U.S. Dist. Ct. Fla. 1978, U.S. Dist Ct. (so. dist. trial bar) Fla. 1995, U.S. Supreme Ct. 1965, U.S. Ct. Claims 1979, U.S. Ct. Appeals (Fed. cir.) 1984, U.S. Ct. Appeals (11th cir.) 1985. Pvt. practice, Opelika, 1950-51; with IRS, 1951-78; attache, revenue service rep., Sao Paulo Brazil, 1965-71, Mexico City, 1971-77; ptnr. Barnard, P.A., Miami, Fla., 1978-87, of counsel, 1987-91; lectr. taxation U. Ala., 1958-60. Pres. Rocky Ridge Vol. Fire Dept., 1956-58, Rocky Ridge Civic Club, 1959, Ala. chpt. Nat. Assn. Internal Revenue Employees, 1962; commr. Rocky Ridge Civic Water Works, 1960-62. With USAAF, 1942-46. Recipient Albert Gallatin award U.S. Treasury Dept., 1978; named Hon. Citizen of Tex., 1979, Hon. Admiral in Tex. Navy, 1979. Mem. Fgn. Svc. Retirees Assn. of Fla. (advisor/dir. for S.E. Fla. 1987—), Kappa Sigma. Republican. Home: 2761 SE 9th St Pompano Beach FL 33062-6712 Office: 200 SE 6th St Ste 502 Fort Lauderdale FL 33301-3420

BARNER, JOHN CHARLES, academic administrator; b. Albany, N.Y., Apr. 13, 1944; s. John H. and Mary L. (Walsh) B.; m. Shirley E. Dixon, May 4, 1961; children: Jackie, Mary Jill, Michael. BA in History and Secondary Edn., Siena Coll., 1967; MA in Polit. Sci., Coll. St. Rose, 1972; postgrad., SUNY, Albany, 1976. Tchr. South Colonie (N.Y.) Ctrl. Schs., 1967-85; dir. undergrad. adminstrn. Coll. St. Rose, Albany, 1985-86, dir. devel., 1986-88; assoc. dir. devel., dir. office of annual support Colgate U., Hamilton, N.Y., 1988-92; exec. dir. devel. Winthrop Coll., Rock Hill, S.C., 1992-95; v.p. institutional advancement Elon Coll. (N.C.), 1995—; exec. dir. arts ctr. capital fund drive Marylrose Arts Ctr., Albany, 1970-71. Mem. Albany Ct. Legislature, 1972-76; v.p. Schs. System Credit Union, Albany, 1974-80; bd. dirs. Earlville (N.Y.) Opera House, 1988-90, Greater Albany Friends of Jazz, 1982-84. Mem. Coun. for Advancement and Support of Edn., Rotary Internat., Greensboro C. of C., Lake Norman Yacht Club. Office: Elon Coll 2600 Campus Bx Elon College NC 27244

BARNES, ANDREW EARL, newspaper editor; b. Torrington, Conn., May 15, 1939; s. Joseph and Elizabeth (Brown) B.; m. Marion Otis, Aug. 26, 1960; children: Christopher Joseph, Benjamin Brooks, Elizabeth Cheney. B.A., Harvard U., 1961. Reporter, bur. chief Providence Jour., 1961-63; from reporter to edn. editor Washington Post, 1965-73; met. editor, asst. mng. editor St. Petersburg Times, Fla., 1973-75, mng. editor, 1975-84; editor, pres. St. Petersburg (Fla.) Times, 1984—, chief exec. officer, 1988—; chmn. bd. dirs. Congl. Quar., Times Pub. Co., Poynter Inst.; mem. Pulitzer prize bd. Mem. Fla. Coun. of 100. With USAR, 1963-65. Alicia Patterson fellow, 1969-70. Mem. Newspaper Assn. Am. (bd. dirs.), Am. Soc. Newspaper Editors, Fla. Soc. Newspaper Editors (pres. 1980-81), Internat. Press Inst. (chmn. Am. com.). Home: 15724 Puckett Rd Dade City FL 33525-7066 Office: St Petersburg Times 490 1st Ave S PO Box 1121 Saint Petersburg FL 33731

BARNES, ANTHONY, business executive; b. 1932. Active Upjohn Co., Inc., Kalamazoo, 1962-83; pres. Cobb, Inc., Littleton, Mass., 1983-86, Cobb-Vantress, Inc., Siloam Springs, Ark., 1986—. Office: Cobb-Vantrees Inc US Hwy 412E Siloam Springs AR 72761

BARNES, BEN BLAIR, company executive, electrical engineer; b. Gadsden, Ala., Mar. 7, 1935; s. Newton Eldridge Jr. and Sara Aileen (Roach) B.; m. Pat Harris, June 3, 1956 (div. 1989); 1 child, Douglas Harris; m. Elba Crowe Clarke, Feb. 25, 1991. BEE, Ala. Poly. Inst., 1956; MSEE, U. Ala., 1962; PhD, Auburn U., 1965. Registered profl. engr., Ala., Tenn. Instrument engr. E.I. du Pont de Nemours & Co., Aiken, S.C., 1957-59; computer engr. NASA Marshall Space Flight Ctr., Huntsville, Ala., 1959-63; mem. faculty elec. engring. dept. Va. Poly. Inst. and State U., Blacksburg, 1965-66; dept. mgr. Computer Scis. Corp., Huntsville, 1966-67; asst. dean engring. U. Tenn., Knoxville, 1967-70; dir. Computer Ctr. Auburn (Ala.) U., 1978-80; head computer sci. Calif. State Coll. Stanislaus, Turlock, 1981; prin. Ben Barnes & Assocs., Auburn, 1981-87; chief exec. officer Ala. Supercomputer Authority, Huntsville, 1987—. 2d lt. U.S. Army, 1956-57. Mem. IEEE, Assn. for Computing Machinery. Home: 1622 Sandstone Ct Montgomery AL 36117-1704 Office: Ala Supercomputer Authority 686 Discovery Dr NW Huntsville AL 35806-2802

BARNES, BERNARD ELLIS, small business executive; b. Gary, Ind., May 5, 1931; s. Harry Carl and Alice Marie (Selman) B.; m. Lila Agnes Sherman, Aug. 2, 1951 (div. June 1971); children: Lyn, Candice, Nancy, Robert, Daniel, Timothy. Corp. pres. Big Town Restaurant, Oklahoma City, 1974-83, Hi-Way Grill and Svc. Sta., Oklahoma City, 1973-96, B-Bar-B Ranch, Elk City, Okla., 1985-88; enlisted USAF, 1950, advanced through ranks to master sgt., 1967, retired, 1970. Decorated Bronze Star. Home: RR 2 Box 188A Purcell OK 73080-9659 Office: Hi-Way Grill 3600 SW 104th St Oklahoma City OK 73159-7801

BARNES, BETTY RAE, counselor; b. Wichita, Kans., June 24, 1932; d. Henry Charles and Vivian Augusta (Lamberth) Archer; m. Orland Eugene Barnes, Mar. 18, 1953; children: Terry Lee, Steven Gregory. BA, Our Lady of the Lake, San Antonio, 1986, MS in Counseling Psychology, 1989. Cert. profl. sec.; lic. profl. counselor; lic. marriage and family therapist; Am. Assn. for Marriage and Family Therapy approved supr. Info. specialist S.W. Rsch. Inst., San Antonio, 1975-96; ret., 1996; counselor Community Clinic, Inc., San Antonio, 1989—, counselor/counseling coord., 1991—; counselor Community Counseling Ctr., Our Lady of the Lake U., San Antonio, 1989-91. Recipient Outstanding Achievement award Sch. Bus. and Pub. Adminstrn., Our Lady of the Lake U., 1984. Mem. Am. Assn. Marriage and Family Therapists (clin.), Tex. Counseling Assn., Internat. Assn. for Addictions and Offender Counselors, San Antonio for Marriage and Family Therapy (pres.-elect), San Antonio Mus. Assn., Delta Mu Delta. Office: Community Clinic Inc 210 W Olmos Dr San Antonio TX 78212-1956

BARNES, CRAIG MARTIN, commodity trading advisor, accountant; b. Oak Park, Ill., May 5, 1949; s. Raymond Herbert and Barbara Anne (Barlow) B.; m. Joyce Marie Brainard, Jan. 31, 1971; children: Annette Marie, Walter Martin. BS in Music Edn., U. Ill., 1971; BA in Acctg. and Fin., U. So. Fla., 1976. CPA, Tenn., tax acct., Tenn. Contr. Fore Line Safe Co., Tampa, Fla., 1973-75, Fore Line Bldgs., Largo, Fla., 1973-75; EDP audit mgr. Comptr. of Treasury State of Tenn., Nashville, 1976-88; pvt. practice Cottontown, Tenn., 1986—; owner CMB Capital Mgmt., Cottontown, 1991—; commodity trading advisor CMB Capital Mgmt., 1991—; gen. ptnr. Foxfire Fund, L.P., 1991—. Mem., singer Nashville Symphony Chorus, 1982-86, coach Comptroller Sox Softball Team, Nashville, 1984-86. Ernst and Whinney scholar, 1976. Adventist.

BARNES, CYNTHIA LOU, gifted education educator; b. Yale, Okla., Jan. 14, 1934; d. Ira and Billie (Reed) Canfield; m. Edward M. Barnes, Jr., June 1, 1954; children: Edis, Barbara, Warren, Adrienne. BS, U. Tulsa, 1970; MS, Okla. State U., 1981. Substitute tchr. Tulsa Pub. Schs., 1970-73, kindergarten tchr., 1981-94, gifted edn. tchr., 1994—; pre-sch. tchr. Meml. Drive Meth., Tulsa, 1976-81; curriculum coord. Barnard Elem. Sch., Tulsa, 1992—, site-base co-chmn., 1992-93; bd. dirs. Great Expectations Educators, Inc., Tulsa, 1985-96; cons. kindergarten guide Tulsa Pub. Schs., 1985, mem. writing team for gifted edn. curriculum, 1996; presenter Elem. Educators Conv., 1994. Confirmation class coord. Meml. Drive United Meth., Tulsa, 1988-94. Grantee Tulsa Edn. Fund, 1994. Mem. Tulsa County Reading Coun., Tulsa Classroom Tchrs. Math. (conf. presider 1994). Home: 7824 E 22nd Pl Tulsa OK 74129-2416

BARNES, DAVID BENTON, school psychologist; m. Cheryle Kirkland; children: David, Matthew, Bryan. BSc with honors, Springfield Coll., 1958; MEd, U. Maine, 1962; EdD, Rutgers U., 1970. Cert. tchr., Maine. Asst. football coach Boston U., 1964-66; dir. Counselling Ctr., asst. prof. edn. Acadia U., Wolfville, N.S., Can., 1966-71, acting dean Sch. Edn., 1969-70, assoc. prof., 1970; chief psychologist Fundy Med. Health Ctr., Wolfville, 1971-73; psychologist Atlantic Child Guidance Ctr., 1974-77; supr. spl. svcs. Cape Breton County Sch. Bd., 1977-82, Lunenburg County Dist. Bd., 1982-87; sch. psychologist, spl. edn. adminstr. Bennington-Rutland Supervisory Union, Vt., 1987-90; psychologist N.W. Psycho-Ednl. Program, Rome, Ga., 1990-92, Chattahoochee-Flint RESA, Ellaville, Ga., 1992—; mem. adminstrv. task force for spl. edn. N.S. Dept. Edn.; mem. N.S. Adv. Coun. on Tchr. Edn.; mem. Met. Mental Health Planning Bd.; mem. Aqua Percept Nat. Adv. Bd.; founder Camp Recskill; founder, bd. dirs. Cape Breton Child Guidance Ctr.; adj. faculty mem. U. Coll. of Cape Breton, Acadia U., Walden U. Co-author: Special Educator's Survival Guide: Practical Techniques and Materials for Supervision and Instruction. Grantee Can.

Govt., 1978-87, Province of N.S., 1978-79, N.S. Tchrs. Union, 1980-81, Internat. Youth Yr., 1985, Donner Found., Laidlaw Found., Windsor Found. Mem. Can. Univ. Counselors Assn., Atlantic Inst. Edn. (steering com. for counselor edn.), Assn. Profl. Staffs of Community Mental Ctrs. (sec.-treas.), Can. Assn. for Children With Learning Disabilties (v.p.), Provincial Assn. for Children with Learning Disabilities (bd. dirs.), N.S. Mental Health Assn. (bd. dirs.), Dartmouth Mental Health Assn. (v.p.), Cape Breton Mental Health Assn. (bd. dirs.), Coun. Exceptional Children, Assn. Psychologists N.C., Nat. Assn. Sch. Psychologists. Home: 309 Rigas Rd Americus GA 31709-2717

BARNES, HARRY F., federal judge; b. 1932. Student, Vanderbilt U., 1950-52; BS, U.S. Naval Academy, 1956; LLB, U. Ark., 1964. With Pryor & Barnes, Camden, Ark., 1964-66, Barnes & Roberts, Camden, 1966-68, Gaughan, Laney, Barnes & Roberts, Camden, 1968-78, Gaughan, Laney & Barnes, Camden, 1978-82; mcpl. judge Camden and Ouachita Counties, 1975-82; circuit judge 13th jud. dist. State of Ark., 1982-93; judge U.S. Dist. Ct. (we. dist.) Ark., 1993—; mem. Ark. Jud. Discipline and Disability Commn. With USMC, 1956-86, col. res. ret. Named Outstanding Trial Judge in Ark., Ark. Trial Lawyers Assn., 1986. Mem. ABA, Ark. Bar Assn., Ark. Jud. Coun. (bd. dirs.). Office: PO Box 1735 El Dorado AR 71731-1735

BARNES, JAMES E., energy company executive; b. Ponca City, Okla., 1934; married. Grad., Okla. State U.; grad. advanced mgmt. program, Harvard U. With Continental Pipe Line Co., 1956-62, Cherokee Pipe Line Co., 1962-64; with Conoco, Inc., Stamford, Conn., 1964-83, mgr. gas products div., 1964-65, gen. mgr. natural gas and gas products dept., 1965-70, v.p. purchasing, 1970-75, v.p. supply and trading, 1975-78, exec. v.p. supply and transp., 1978-83; sr. exec. v.p., chief operating officer Mapco, Inc., Tulsa, 1983-84, chief exec. officer, bd. dirs., 1984—, chmn. bd., 1986—. Office: Mapco Inc 1800 S Baltimore Ave Tulsa OK 74119-5210

BARNES, JUDITH P., nursing administrator; b. Hornsby, Tenn., Mar. 2, 1946; d. Jack Clayton and Ethyl (Tate) Parsons; m. Jesse C. Barnes, Sr., Nov. 11, 1967; children: Jessika, Jesse C., Jason, Jennifer, Jeremiah, Janey. Student, Memphis State U., 1964-65; diploma, Bapt. Nursing Sch., Memphis, 1967; AS, Meridian (Miss.) Jr. Coll., 1975; student, Tidewater Community Coll., Chesapeake, Va., 1983-84, 87-88. Cert. CPR instr., first aide instr. Charge nurse Bapt. Meml. Hosp., 1967-68; charge nurse labor and delivery room, supr. Jeff Anderson Meml. Hosp., Meridian, 1973-76; staff nurse, charge nurse Maryview Hosp., Portsmouth, Va., 1985-89; staff devel. supr. insvc. edn. Newport News (Va.) Gen. Hosp., 1989—; mem. alcohol abuse team Kaiser Meml. Found., Honolulu, 1968-70. Capt. U.S. Army, 1968-73, USAR, 1989—. Mem. Res. Officers Assn., Assn. Mil. Surgeons U.S., Tenn. Nurses Assn., Res. Officers Assn., Emergency Nurses Assn. Home: 3654 Gateway Dr Apt 1-d Portsmouth VA 23703-5053

BARNES, JULIA DIANE WALLS, community health, oncology and geriatrics nurse; b. Kennett, Mo., Dec. 25, 1961; d. Julian Ely and Anna Kathleen (Nuckles) Walls; m. Carl Donald Barnes, Mar. 20, 1981; 1 child, Dustyn Zackary. BSN, Ark. State U., 1987, postgrad. BCLS instr. Ob-gyn. staff nurse Lucy Lee Hosp., Poplar Bluff, Mo.; occupational health nurse Emerson Electric Co., Kennett, Mo.; dir. nursing svcs. Bloomfield (Mo.) Nursing Ctr.; home health nurse Dexter (Mo.) Meml. Hosp.; staff nurse J.J. Pershing VA Med. Ctr., Poplar Bluff, Mo. Recipient Teaching Learning Project award, 1987. Mem. Am. Cancer Soc., Am. Heart Assn., Sigma Theta Tau.

BARNES, LARRY GLEN, journalist, editor, educator; b. Louisville, July 10, 1947; s. Roy Glen and Phyllis Jane (Dunn) B.; m. Susan Gayle Morrow, Dec. 27, 1969 (dec. July, 1973); 1 child, Brian; m. Mary Frances Meiman, July 14, 1979. Student, Murray State U., 1965-68, 71-73, Def. Info. Sch., 1968. Journalist, editor various locations Dept. of the Army, 1968-71; staff writer Louisville Courier-Jour., 1972-75, Lexington (Ky.) Herald-Leader, 1975; mng. editor Corydon (Ind.) Harrison County Press, 1976-77; assoc. editor Ky. Sports World, Louisville, 1977-81; editor Publs. Divsn., Ft. Knox, Ky., 1981-82, Inside the Turret, Ft. Knox, 1982—. With U.S. Army, 1968-71. Recipient Naismith citation Atlanta Tipoff Club, 1981, Journalist award Dept. Army, Washington, 1986, 1st pl. commentary writing Tng. & Doctrine Command. Ft. Monroe, Va., 1985, 87, 88, 89, 90, Thomas Jefferson award Dept. Def., Washington, 1982, 86; named Editor of Yr., Army Tng & Doctrine Command, 1982. Mem. Soc. Profl. Journalists, Am. Fedn. Govt. Employees. Democrat. Baptist. Home: 2220 Manchester Rd Louisville KY 40205-3044 Office: Pub Affairs Office PO Box 995 Fort Knox KY 40121-0995

BARNES, MAGGIE LUE SHIFFLETT (MRS. LAWRENCE BARNES), nurse; b. nr. Spur, Tex., Mar. 29, 1931; d. Howard Eldridge and Sadie Adilene (Dunlap) Shifflett; m. T.C. Fagan, Jan. 1950 (dec. Feb. 1952); 1 child, Lawayne; m. Lawrence Barnes, Sept. 2, 1960. Student, Cogdell Sch. Nursing, 1959-60, Western Tex. Coll., 1972-76; postgrad. Meth. Hosp. Sch. Nursing, Lubbock, Tex., 1975; BSN, W. Tex. State U., 1977. RN, Tex.; cert. gerontol. nurse, Am. Nurses Credentialing Ctr. Fl. nurse D.M. Cogdell Meml. Hosp., Snyder, Tex., 1960-64, medication nurse, 1964-76, asst. evening supr., 1976-78, charge nurse, after 1978, evening nursing supr., 1980; nursing supr. Scurry, Borden, Mitchel, Fisher, Howard Counties, West Cen. Home Health Agy., Snyder, 1980-83; emergency rm. evening supr. Root-Meml. Hosp., 1983-89; dir. of nurses Snyder Oak Core Ctr., 1989-91, Mountain View Lodge, Big Spring, Tex., 1991-92, Med. Arts. Hosp. Home Health, 1992-93, Metplex Home Health Svcs., Snyder, 1993-94, ret. 1994; part time nurse 1994—; regional coord. home health svcs. Beverly Enterprises, 1983. Den mother Cub Scouts, Boy Scouts Am., Holliday, Tex., 1960-61; mem. PTA, Snyder, Tex., 1960-69; adv. Sr. Citizens Assn.; mem. Tri-Region Health Systems Agy., 1979—; mem. adv. bd. Scurry County Diabetes Assn., 1982—. Mem. Vocat. Nurses Assn. Tex. (mem. bd. 1963-65, div. pres. 1967-69), Emergency Dept. Nursing Assn. Apostolic Faith Ch. (sec., treas. 1956-58). Home: 8239 CR 473 Hermleigh TX 79526-9704

BARNES, MELVER RAYMOND, retired chemist; b. nr. Salisbury, N.C., Nov. 15, 1917; s. Oscar Lester and Sarah Albertine (Rowe) B. AB in Chemistry, U. N.C., 1947; D of Physics (hon.), World U., 1983; DSc in Chemistry (hon.), Assoc. Univs., 1987, PhD in Chemistry (hon.), 1990; PhD in Chemistry (hon.), Albert Einstein Internat. Acad. Found. and Associated Univs., 1990. Chemist Pitts. Testing Labs., Greensboro, N.C., 1948-49, N.C. State Hwy. and Pub. Works Commn., Raleigh, 1949-51, Edgewood (Md.) Arsenal, 1951-61, Dugway (Utah) Proving Ground, 1961-70. Recipient Albert Einstein Bronze medal, 1988, Alfred Nobel Medal award Albert Einstein Internat. Acad. Found., 1991, Albert Einstein Acad. Found. Cross of Merit, 1992. Mem. AAAS, Am. Statis. Assn., Am. Chem. Soc., Am. Phys. Soc., Am. Math. Soc., Soc. Indsl. and Applied Math, Math. Assn. Am. Home and Office: 1486 Swicegood Rd Linwood NC 27299-9386

BARNES, NORMAN PATRICK, laser scientist; b. Cleve., Apr. 27, 1942; s. Edmund Joseph and Wanda Barnes; m. Barbara Jon Osterman, Dec. 27, 1965; children: Adam Edmund, Matthew Lloyd, Cherie Nichol. BSc in Engring. Physics, Ohio State U., 1965, MSc in Physics, 1967, PhDEE, 1969. Laser devel. staff Tex. Instruments, Dallas, 1969-72, Martin Marietta, Orlando, Fla., 1972-75, Los Alamos (N.Mex.) Nat. Lab., 1975-86, NASA Langley Rsch., Hampton, Va., 1986—. Contbr. articles to profl. jours.; patentee in field. NDEA Title IV fellow Ohio State U., 1965-69. Fellow Optical Soc. Am.

BARNES, ROBERT WEBSTER, medical educator; b. Chgo., Nov. 9, 1936; s. Broda Otto and Charlotte Edna (Webster) B.; m. Kay Ellen Brockway, Sept. 25, 1960; children: David Webster, Judith Kay Barnes Sauer, Kathleen Susan. BA, U. Colo., 1958; MD, U. Ill., 1961. Rotating intern U. of Ill. Rsch. and Edn. Hosp., 1961-62; resident in gen. surgery U. Wash. Affiliated Hosps., 1962-63, 65-69, resident in thoracic surgery, 1970-71, USPHS rsch. fellow in vascular surgery, 1971-72; USPHS clin. assoc. Nat. Heart Inst. Clinic of Surgery/NIH, 1963-65; asst. prof. surgery U. Iowa Coll. Medicine, Iowa City, 1972-75, assoc. prof. surgery, 1976-77; prof. surgery, Hume prof. Med. Coll. Va., Richmond, 1977-83; prof., chmn. dept. surgery U. Ark. Med. Sci., Little Rock, 1983—; cardiology advisory coun. Nat. Heart Inst., NIH, Bethesda, Md.; residency rev. com. for surgery Accreditation Coun. for Grad. Med. Edn., Chgo., 1987-93; advisory coun. for vascular surgery Am. Coll. Surgeons, Chgo., 1989-96, bd. of govs., 1992—; dir. Am. Bd. Surgery, 1996—. Author over 30 books; contbr. over 200 articles to profl. jours. Lt. comdr. USPHS, 1963-65. Recipient Mead Johnson award U. Wash. Sch. Medicine, 1967. Mem. Internat. Soc. Cariovascular Surgery (sec. 1985-89, pres. 1990-91, award 1974), Am. Surg. Assn., Soc. for Vascular Surgery, Soc. Univ. Surgeons, So. Surg. Soc., Assn. Program Dirs. in Surgery (pres. 1996—). Home: 7 Portland Rd Little Rock AR 72212-2728 Office: Univ Ark Med Sci Slot 520 4301 W Markham St Little Rock AR 72205-7101

BARNES, SHEILA KAYE, educator, consultant; b. Arkadelphia, Ark., May 30, 1954; d. Dalton H. and Krysteen E. (Lewis) B.; 1 child, Bradley Barnes Wilson. BS, U. Cen. Okla., 1974, MEd, 1976; PhD, U. Okla., 1991. Cert. mentally handicapped, physically handicapped, learning disabilities, emotionally disturbed, reading specialist, early childhood, elem. edn., Okla. Spl. educator learning disabled and emotionally handicapped Oklahoma City Pub. Schs., 1976-77, spl. educator physically handicapped, 1977-80, devel. therapist birth to 3 yrs., 1980-81; early interventionist SEARCH Shawnee (Okla.) Pub. Schs., 1981-87; grad. asst., adj. prof. U. Okla., Norman, 1987-91; English tchr. for adjudicated youth Cen. Okla. Juvenile Treatment Ctr., Tecumseh, 1989-91; asst. prof. Southeastern Okla. State U., Durant, 1991—; mem. adv. bd. Okla. Commn. on Children and Youth, Region XI, Oklahoma City, 1991—; exec. dir. Southeastern Okla. Assistive Tech. Ctr., Durant, 1991—; mem. Leadership 2000 Action Team, Oklahoma City, 1992—. Author: (computer program) Special Education—Legal Issues, 1981, (study guide) Behavior Management for Special Education, 1992, (handbook) 101 Ideas for Using Technology/Media, 1995, (songs) Musical Math Multiples, 1996. Bd. dirs., mem. Miss Wheelchair Okla., Oklahoma City, 1981-86. Recipient Young Careerist award Bus. and Profl. women, 1980, Exemplary Pre-svc./inservice Am. Coun. for Rural Spl. Edn., 1996; grantee (7) Okla. State Dept. for Edn., 1991-95. Mem. CEC (membership chair, treas. Texoma chpt. 1991—), Student Coun. for Exceptional Child (faculty advisor 1991—), Okla. Tchr. Edn. (founding mem., pres. 1995-96). Office: Southeastern Okla State U Box 4164 Durant OK 74701

BARNETT, DON MARVIN, lawyer; b. N.Y.C., Dec. 11, 1940. Student, N.Mex. State U., 1957-58; BBA, U. Houston, 1963, JD, 1967. Bar: Tex. 1965, U.S. Dist. Ct. (so. dist.) Tex. 1965, U.S. Ct. Appeals (5th cir.) 1966, U.S. Supreme Ct., 1970. Ptnr. Jamail & Gano, Houston, 1966-78, Stradley, Barnett & Stein, P.C., Houston, 1978—; pvt. practice Houston, 1995—. Sgt. Tex. Air Nat. Guard, 1965-71. Mem. ABA, Assn. Trial Lawyers Am., Houston Bar Assn., State Bar Tex., Tex. Trial Lawyers Assn., Am. Bd. Trial Advocates (advocate). Office: One Riverway Ste 1625 Houston TX 77056

BARNETT, ELIZABETH HALE, organizational consultant; b. Nashville, Mar. 17, 1940; d. Robert Baker and Dorothy (McCarthy) Hale; m. Crawford F. Barnett Jr., June 6, 1964; children: Crawford F. III, Robert H. BA, Vanderbilt U., 1962. Receptionist, sec. U.S. Atty. Gen. Robert F. Kennedy, Washington, 1962-64; free-lance cons. Atlanta, 1973-76; pres. E.H. Barnett & Assocs. orgnl. cons., trainers, Atlanta, 1976-86; trustee The Ga. Conservancy, Atlanta, 1978-92, chmn. bd. trustees, 1986-88, chmn. adv. bd., 1994—; legis. asst. to Senator Michael J. Egan Ga. State Senate, Atlanta, 1990-93. Bd. dirs. Jr. League Atlanta, 1973-75, High Mus. Art, Atlanta, 1977—, v.p. bd. adminstrn. & support, 1994—, sec. bd. and exec. com., 1977—, v.p. adminstrn. bd. dirs., United Way Met. Atlanta, 1981-84, ARCS Found., Atlanta chpt.; active Leadership Atlanta, 1976—, White House Fellows Selection Panel, 1995-96; chmn., pres. bd. dirs. Vol. Coms. Art Mus. U.S. and Can., 1976-79; chmn. bd. dirs. Met. Atlanta chpt. ARC, 1978-80, hon. bd. dirs., 1980—; cmty. adv. com. NW Ga. Coun. Girl Scouts Am., 1979-83; coun. mem. USO Ga., 1981—; bd. sponsors Atlanta Women's Network; apptd. to Ga. Clean and Beautiful Citizens Adv. Com., 1990, Ga. Solid Waste Mgmt. Commn., 1990; appt. sec. to Gov.'s Environ. Edn. Coun., 1992—; sci. coun. Ga. Coalition for Sci. Tech. and Math. Edn., 1993—. Named one of Ten Outstanding Young Women of Am., 1977, Outstanding Young Woman of Ga., 1977; honored by Ga. State Legis., Atlanta, 1978. Mem. LWV. Episcopalian. Office: 3250 Howell Mill Rd NW Ste 205 Atlanta GA 30327-4108

BARNETT, HAROLD THOMAS, school system superintendent; b. Pasadena, Tex., Dec. 8, 1948; s. Herbert G. and Nettie Mae (Sanders) B.; m. Erin Lynn McCommon, Dec. 28, 1971; children: Erin Averyl, Benjamin T. MusB in Edn., Baylor U., 1971; MEd, U. Ga., 1974, EdD, 1983. Cert. tchr., adminstr., Ga. Tchr. St. Albans Episc. Elem. Sch., Waco, Tex., 1972-73; tchr. North Clayton Jr. High Sch., College Park, Ga., 1973-75, asst. prin., 1975-82; prin. Griffin (Ga.) High Sch., 1982-90; supt. of schs. Cartersville (Ga.) City Sch. System, 1990—. Trustee Etowah Found., Cartersville; bd. dirs. Cartersville-Bartow County United Way, Christian Counseling Svc., ARC of Bartow County; bd. control Northwest Ga. Regional Edn. Svcs. Agy. Mem. Ga. Sch. Bd. Assn., Ga. Assn. Ednl. Leaders, Profl. Assn. Ga. Educators, Am. Assn. Sch. Adminstrs., Ga. Sch. Supts. Assn., Cartersville-Bartow County C. of C., Cartersville Rotary Club. Baptist. Office: Cartersville City Schs 310 Old Mill Rd Cartersville GA 30120-4027

BARNETT, JANICE ELAINE, critical care nurse; b. Flagstaff, Ariz., Jan. 3, 1951; d. Garland and Evelyn Rose (Benson) Downum; m. Joe Edwin Barnett, Aug. 9, 1972; children: Analie Rose, Daniel Joseph. BA, U. Okla., 1972; BSN summa cum laude, Tex. Woman's U., 1989. Staff nurse in ICU Decatur (Tex.) Community Hosp. Mem. Mortar Board, Phi Beta Kappa, Sigma Theta Tau, Alpha Chi. Home: RR 1 Box 137 Ponder TX 76259-9601

BARNETT, LINDA KAY SMITH, vocational guidance counselor; b. Booneville, Miss., Nov. 20, 1955; d. John Thomas and Clara Vernell (Brown) Smith; m. William Wayne Barnett, June 26, 1982; 1 child, John William. AA, N.E. Miss. C.C., Booneville, 1975; BS, Miss. State U., 1977, MEd, 1978, EdS, 1982. Vocat. guidance counselor, dist. test coord. Iuka (Miss.) City Schs., 1979-91; vocat. guidance counselor Tishomingo County Schs., Iuka, 1991—. Treas. Iuka High Sch. PTA, 1984-85. Mem. Miss. Sch. Counselors Assn. (state v.p. secondary divsn. 1992-94), N.E. Counseling Assn. (pres. 1989-90, pres.-elect 1987-88, 88-89, sec.-treas. 1982-83), Nat. Bd. for Cert. Counselors (nat. cert. counselor, nat. cert. sch. counselor). Ch. of Christ.

BARNETT, MARTHA WALTERS, lawyer; b. Dade City, Fla., June 1, 1947; d. William Haywood and Helen (Hancock) Walters; m. Richard Rawls Barnett, Jan. 4, 1969; children: Richard Rawls, Sarah Walters. BA cum laude, Tulane U., 1969; JD cum laude, U. Fla., 1973. Bar: Fla. 1973, U.S. Dist. Ct. (mid. and so. dists.) Fla. 1973, U.S. Ct. Appeals (3d, 4th and 11th cirs.) 1975, D.C. 1989. Assoc. Holland & Knight, Lakeland, Tampa and Tallahassee, 1973-78, ptnr., 1979—; bd. dirs., v.p. Fla. Lawyers Prepaid Legal Svc. Corp., 1978-80, pres., 1980-82, legis. com., 1983-84, mem. commn. on access to justice, 1984-86, exec. coun. tax sect., 1987-88, exec. coun. pub. interest sect., 1989-91; active Fla. Commn. Ethics, 1984-87, chairperson, 1986-87, Fla. Taxation and Budget Reform Commn., 1989—; Legal adv. bd. Martindale-Hubbell, 1990—; chair Ho. of Dels., 1994-96; lectr. in field. Mem. Fla. Coun. Econ. Edn., Fla. Edn. Found.; bd. dirs. Lawyers Com. Civil Rights Under Law. Fellow Am. Bar Found. (life); mem. ABA (exec. coun. sect. on individual rights and responsibility 1974-86, chmn. 1983-84, ho. of dels. 1984—, bd. govs. 1986-89, task force on minorities in profession 1984-86, commn. on women in profession 1987-90, long range planning com. 1988-91, chair bd. govs. fin. com. 1988-89, bd. editors ABA Jour. 1990-94, exec. coun. sect. legal edn. and admission to bar 1990-94, chairperson commn. on pub. understanding about the law 1990-93, others), Nat. Inst. Dispute Resolution (sec.-treas. 1988-94, bd. dirs. 1988-94), Am. Law Inst., Fla. Bar Assn. (exec. coun. pub. interest law sect. 1989-91, others), Hillsborough County Bar Assn., Tallahassee Bar Assn., Am. Judicature Soc. (bd. dirs.). Office: Holland & Knight PO Drawer 810 Tallahassee FL 32302-0810

BARNETT, PETER RALPH, health science facility administrator, dentist; b. Bklyn., Oct. 21, 1951; s. Seymour and Betty Natalie (Cobbs) B.; m. Susan Clay, Jan. 27, 1990; children: Regina, Alexis, Alana. AB, Colgate U., 1973; DMD, U. Pa., 1977, MBA, 1979. Lic. dentist, Pa., N.J., N.Y. Dir. mgmt. sys. U. Pa. Sch. Dental Med., Phila., 1979-81, asst. dir. clinic mgmt., 1981-84; dir. profl. affairs Pearle Dental, Inc., Dallas, 1984-86, v.p. and dir. dental ops., 1986-87; dir. vision benefits Pearle Health Svcs., Inc., Dallas, 1987-88, v.p. managed vision care, 1988-91, sr. v.p. franchising and sales, 1991-92, sr. v.p. quality and franchising, 1992-93; assoc. Healthcare Venture Assocs., Irving, Tex., 1993-94; exec. dir. Prudential DMO, Atlanta, 1994-95; sr. v.p. and C.O.O. United Dental Care, Dallas, 1995—. Author and co-author several profl. articles on health care mgmt., fin., and mktg. Bd. dirs. PTA Brinker Elementary Sch. Plano, Tex. 1988-89. Mem. ADA, Nat. Assn. of Dental Plans, Beta Beta Beta. Democrat. Jewish. Home: 1304 Chippewa Dr Plano TX 75093 Office: United Dental Care 14755 Preston Rd Ste 300 Dallas TX 75240-7862

BARNETT, ROSALEA, government official; b. Hugo, Okla., Apr. 21, 1946; d. L.V. and Floradean (Mills) Boyett; 1 child, Billy. Student, Rose Coll., Midwest City, Okla., 1979, Dub Stone Real Estate Acad., Oklahoma City, 1980. Lic. real estate broker, Okla. Adminstrv. aid, dir. VA Med. Ctr., Oklahoma City, 1975-77; office adminstr to postmaster U.S. Postal Svc., Oklahoma City, 1980; acting postmaster U.S. Postal Svc., Jennings, Okla., 1988; broker, assoc. Evelyn Hughes Century 21 Real Estate, Tulsa, 1992—; postmaster Leonard, Okla., 1990—; exec. Am. Comms. Network, 1995—; 1992-94. Active Pleasant Valley Home for Abused Girls, Tulsa Boys Home, Feed the Children Orgn. Mem. NAFE, Female Exec. Club, Federally Employed Women, Toastmasters Internat. (best speaker award), C. of C. Methodist. Office: PO Box 9998 Leonard OK 74043-9998

BARNETT, SHIRLEY R., nursing educator; b. Jefferson County, Ohio, Nov. 17, 1949; d. George I. Cronin and Roxie M. Howell; 1 child, Timothy C. Buchanan. ADN, Kent State U., 1975; BS magna cum laude, U. Steubenville, 1985; MSEd magna cum laude, U. Dayton, 1986; BSN magna cum laude, Wheeling Jesuit Coll., 1989. Clin. specialist adult mental health. Indsl. nurse Townsend and Bottum Constrn. Co., Empire, Ohio; nurse/therapist Family Svcs. Assn., Steubenville, Ohio; crisis intervention nurse Community Mental Health/Jefferson County, Steubenville; nurse educator Ohio Valley Hosp., Steubenville; pvt. counselor in field. Mem. Ohio Nurses Assn., ANA.

BARNETTE, CANDICE LEWIS, speech/language pathologist; b. Huntington, W.Va., Sept. 4, 1950; d. Angelo Ted and Amelda Lucille (Lovell) Lewis; m. John Emile Barnette II, June 13, 1987; stepchildren: Jennifer, Jeffrey, Jason. BA, U. Ala., 1972, MA, 1973. Cert. speech pathologist. Speech pathologist Partlow State Sch. and Hosp., Tuscaloosa, Ala., 1973-75; speech/lang. pathologist Children's Hosp., New Orleans, 1975-77; asst. prof. St. Mary's Dominican Coll., New Orleans, 1977-84; pvt. practice speech/lang. pathologist New Orleans, 1977-87; speech pathologist Novacare, Savannah, Ga., 1988-89; pvt. practice speech/lang. pathologist, owner Barnette Speech & Lang. Ctr., Savannah, 1989—; mem. profl. adv. bd. Staff Builders, New Orleans, 1983-84, Healthmasters Home Health Agy., Savannah, 1984-94, Olsten Kimberly Quality Care, Savannah, 1994—; bd. dirs. Rehab. Interest Group, Savannah, 1992—. Bd. dirs. New Orleans Contemporary Dance Ctr., 1978-80; vol. fundraiser Children's Hosp., New Orleans, 1977-82; vol. sailing venue Atlanta Centennial Olympic Games, Savannah, 1996. Mem. Am. Speech, Lang. and Hearing Assn., Ga. Speech and Hearing Assn. Office: Barnette Speech & Lang Ctr 6815 Forest Park Dr Ste 124 Savannah GA 31406-1511

BARNHART, FORREST GREGORY, lawyer; b. Alpine, Tex., Sept. 11, 1951; d. F. Neil and Jody (Ogg) B. AB, Vassar Coll., 1973; JD, Cornell U., 1976. Bar: Fla. 1976, U.S. Dist. Ct. (so. dist.) Fla. 1977, U.S. Cts. Appeals (5th and 11th cirs.) 1977; cert. civil trial lawyer. Assoc. Levy, Plisco, Perry, Shapiro, Kneen & Kincade, West Palm Beach, Fla., 1976-78; assoc. Montgomery Searcy & Denney, P.A., West Palm Beach, 1978-81, ptnr., 1981-89; ptnr. Searcy, Denney, Scarola, Barnhart & Shipley, P.A., 1989—; lectr. in field; moderator TV show Call the Lawyer, 1983-85; dir. WXEL-TV and FM, Pub. Radio and TV, West Palm Beach. Contbr. chpt. to The Advocates Primer, 1991. Speaker and com. mem. Floridians Against Constl. Tampering, 1984. Mem. Jud. Nominating Commn., 1986-90. Fellow Fla. Bar, ABA, Fed. Bar Assn. (treas. 1983-84, sec., v.p. 1984-85, pres. 1986-87), Palm Beach County Bar Assn. (vice chmn. fed. ct. practice com. 1981-82, media law com. 1981-82, bench bar com. 1980-81; chmn. pub. relations com. 1983-84, TV com. 1984—), Palm Beach Trial Lawyers Assn. (founding dir.), Assn. Trial Lawyers Am., Acad. Fla. Trial Lawyers (sec. 1990-91, treas. 1991-92, pres.-elect 1992-93, pres. 1993—, bd. dirs. 1986-90, chmn., key man legis. com. 1986—, mem. coll. of diplomates, steering counsel continuing edn. com., pres. elect 1992-93, pres. 1993-94, Eagle Benefactor, Disting. Lectr. in Jurisprudence 1988, sec. 1990-91), Fla. Lawyers Action Group (chair bd. trustees), Cornell Club, Governor's Club. Home: 236 Miraflores Dr Palm Beach FL 33480-3618 Office: Searcy Denney Scarola Barnhart & Shipley 2139 Palm Beach Lakes Blvd West Palm Beach FL 33409-6601

BARNHILL, CYNTHIA DIANE, accountant; b. Wilmington, N.C., Oct. 15, 1958; d. James Randolph Barnhill and Mildred Butler Nobles. AAS, Cape Fear C.C., Wilmington, N.C., 1979; BS, N.C. Wesleyan Coll., Rocky Mount, 1991; cert. nonprofit mgmt., Duke U., 1994; AAS in Acctg., Durham Tech. Coll., 1996; MBA, City U., Durham, 1996; postgrad., Pa. State U. Cert. employee benefit specialist. Site supr. New Hanover Summer Feeding Program, Wilmington, 1977; clk. III, nursing svc. New Hanover Regional Hosp., Wilmington, 1979-84; prodn. tech. Amhoist, Wilmington, 1985-86; account rep. V U. N.C. Hosps., Chapel Hill, 1987-88; personnel specialists U.N.C., Chapel Hill, 1988-89; acct. Piedmont Health Svcs. Inc., Chapel Hill, N.C., 1989—. Vol. N.C. Rep. Com. Mem. Nat. Assn. Accts., Am. Coll. Healthcare Execs., Carolinas Chpt. CEBS, Phi Beta Lambda. Baptist. Home: 2701 Homestead Rd Apt 1205 Chapel Hill NC 27516 Office: Piedmont Health Svcs Inc PO Box 17179 Chapel Hill NC 27514

BARNHILL, DAVID STAN, lawyer; b. Washington, N.C., May 10, 1949; s. Arthur David and Ida Bea (Cox) B.; m. Katherine C. Felger, July 26, 1975; children: Hannah Katherine, Mary Rachel. BS, Va. Poly. Inst., 1971, MS, 1973; doctoral studies, U. Va., 1976-79; JD magna cum laude, Washington and Lee U., 1983. Bar: Va. 1983, U.S. Ct. Appeals (4th cir.) 1983, U.S. Supreme Ct. 1990, Federal Ct. Claims 1994. Asst. prof. social sci. Va. Intermont Coll., Bristol, Va., 1973-76; soc. sci. researcher U. Va., Charlottesville, Va., 1979-80; assoc. Woods, Rogers & Hazlegrove, Roanoke, Va., 1983-88, ptnr., 1989—. Author of several profl. articles. Bd. dirs. Total Action Against Poverty, Roanoke, 1987-90, DePaul Children's Svcs., Roanoke, 1985-95, Legal Aid Roanoke Valley, 1990-92. Sgt. USNG, 1972-78. Named Lead Articles Editor Washington & Lee Law Review, 1982-83. Mem. ABA (forum on constrn. industry, civil litigation sect.), Va. State Bar (chmn. 6th dist. ethics com. 1990-91, bd. govs. constrn. law sect. 1991—, state bar coun. 1995—, state bar disciplinary bd. 1995—), Va. Bar Assn. (constrn. law coun., civil litigation coun.), Roanoke Bar Assn. (bd. dirs. 1992-94), Va. Assoc. Gen. Contractors (legal affairs and contract documents coms. 1992—), Va. Tech. Alumni Assn., Order of the Coif, Rotary (Roanoke chpt.). Democrat. Baptist. Home: 5145 Falcon Ridge Rd Roanoke VA 24014-5720 Office: Woods Rogers & Hazlegrove 10 S Jefferson St Roanoke VA 24011

BARNHILL, STEPHEN FULLER, advertising executive; b. Houston, July 22, 1948; s. William Travis Jr. and Nina Elizabeth (Collier) B.; m. Linda Lee Partin, Dec. 31, 1971 (div. 1976); 1 child, Jessica Marie; m. Karen Sara Golden, Feb. 2, 1979 (div. 1992); 1 child, Patrick Jeremiah. Student, U. Denver, 1966-67; BA, Ariz. State U., 1970-72; postgrad., Rice U., 1972-73; student, U. St. Thomas, 1992—. Editor Rice U., Houston, 1973-76, assoc. dir. info. svcs., 1976-79; account supr. Bozell & Jacobs, Houston, 1979-81; prin. Steve Barnhill & Co., Inc., Houston, 1981—; founder, exec. creative dir. Taylor Brown & Barnhill, Inc., Houston, 1983-88. Editor (book) Historic Galveston, 1985; co-author: Business and Managerial Communication, 1992; contbr. various articles to mags. and jours. Bd. dirs. St. Andrew's Presbyn. Sch., Houston, 1983-87; trustee Houston Met. Ministries (Nactigal Tally award 1981), 1980-83; adv. Cenikor Foundn., 1977-80; committeeman Gulf Coast Area Red Cross, Houston, 1986—; vol. NF Found. Served with USCG, 1967-69. Named one of Outstanding Young Men in Am., 1979, 81, 85; Recipient Tex. Ad advtg. award Tex. Monthly mag., 1979, Maury Darst Pub. Awareness award Tex. Neurofibromatosis Found., 1990. Mem. Houston Advt. Fedn. (recipient Addy award 1978, 80, 84,-92), Internat. Assn. of Bus. Communicators (bd. dirs. 1981-83; Gold Quill award 1979, 80, 82, 85-88, ARC Gold award 1991-92). Democrat. Presbyterian. Office: Steve Barnhill & Co 3720 Kirby Dr Houston TX 77098-3914

BARNHILL, SUZANNE SCOGGINS, editor, desktop publisher; b. Wilmington, Del., Sept. 5, 1944; d. Thomas Samuel and Virginia Benton

(Vaughan) Scoggins; m. Matthew Talbot Barnhill, Jr., June 24, 1967; children: Matthew Talbot III, Virginia Vaughan. Postgrad., Georgetown U., 1966, Ga. State U., 1968; BA in Latin, Agnes Scott Coll., 1966; MA in Classics, Emory U., 1972. Computer programmer IBM Corp., Washington, 1964; tchr. Latin and French Sherwood High Sch., Sandy Spring, Md., 1966-67; tchr. Latin Lovett Sch., Atlanta, 1967-70; vis. lectr. Roman comedy Emory U., Atlanta, fall 1972, receptionist, clerk-typist devel. office, 1973-74; freelance writer, editor, typist, word processor, desktop pub. Words into Type, Fairhope, Ala., 1975—; columnist Ea. Shore Courier, 1990—; proofreader, editor, typesetter Fairhope Creative, 1992—; copy editor, proofreader Red Bluff Rev., 1995—. Co-author, editor: Study Guide for Supervisory Management: The Art of Empowering and Developing People, 1993, rev. edit. 1996; contbg. author, editor: Successful Small Business Management, 5th edit., 1988; editor: Barron's How to Prepare for Real Estate Licensing Examinations—Salesperson and Broker, 1979, Income Property Appraisal and Analysis, 1981, Personnel Management: A Human Resources Approach, 4th edit., 1981, Texas Real Estate Examinations Guide, 1985, Business, 1985, Supervisory Management: The Art of Working With and Through People, 2d edit., 1988, Management: Concepts and Applications, 2d edit., 1986, Management: Concepts and Applications, 3d edit., 1988, Real Estate...A 60-Second Guide, 1989, Mud on My Shoes: The Story of a Peculiar Preacher, 1990, Keys to Surviving a Tax Audit, 1991, Management: Concepts and Applications, 1992, Dictionary of Real Estate Terms, 3d edit., 1993, Supervisory Management: The Art of Empowering and Developing People, 3d edit., 1993, 4th edit., 1996, Small Business Management: An Entrepreneur's Guide to Success, 1993, 2nd edit., 1996, Come See...Come Stay, 1993, Dictionary of Tax Terms, 1994, Dictionary of Business Terms, 1995, Human Resource Mgmt., 1995. Publicity chmn. Story Theatre Co., Fairhope, 1989—; publicity chmn. Friends Pub. Libr., Fairhope, 1990—, newsletter editor, 1990—, membership chmn., 1991—; circle chmn. Presbyn. Women Govt. Presbyn. Ch., 1981-83, 91-93; corr. sec. Women of Ch. Presbytery Mobile, 1983-84, rec. sec., 1985-87. Recipient Vol. of Yr. award Friends Fairhope Pub. Libr. and Ea. Shore C. of C., 1993. Mem. Rotary Club Fairhope (editor/pub. weekly bull. 1995—). Home and Office: Words into Type 110 Oak St Fairhope AL 36532-2517

BARNHOLDT, TERRY JOSEPH, chemical, industrial, and general engineer; b. Wiota, Iowa, Sept. 22, 1921; s. Claus Edward and Leona (Consaul) B.; m. Martha Francis Cannon, 1946 (dec. 1975); children: Martha Jane, Terry (Ted) Joseph Jr. BChE, Clarkson Coll. Tech., 1943; postgrad. degree in chem. engring. and adminstrn. engring., Cornell U., 1947; MBA (hon.), U. N.C., Charlotte, 1967; JD, Atlanta Law Sch., 1981. Project, process engr. Std. Oil Co., Richmond, Calif., 1947-49; Perth Amboy, N.J., 1949-51; br. mgr. The Clorox Co., Charlotte, N.C., 1949-51; pres., gen. mgr. Allied Prodrs. Supply Co., Charlotte, 1959-66; mgr. mfg. and engring. BASF Wyandotte, Charlotte, 1966-68; sales mgr. Detrex Chem. Industries, Charlotte, 1969-70; chem. mfg. sales rep. Valchem Chem. United Mchts., Charlotte, 1970-74; sales, mfg. rep. Star Chemicals Co., Macon, Ga., 1976-78; mgr. shipping Pepsi-Cola Beverage Corp., Atlanta, 1979; project engr. Metro Atlanta Rapid Transit Authority, 1981-84; comml. real estate specialist Gen. Svc. Adminstrn., Atlanta, 1984-85; gen., indsl. engr. Def. Logistics Agy., Manassas, Alexandria and Ft. Belvoir, Va., 1986—. 1st lt. U.S. Army, 1943-46. Mem. NSPE, AIChE, ATLA, Am. Chem. Soc., Assn. Energy Engrs., Def. Acquisition Corps, Alpha Chi Sigma. Republican. Presbyterian. Home: 12301 Strong Ct Fairfax VA 22033-2846 Office: Def Logistics Agy MMBIR Ste 2533 8725 John J Kingman Rd Fort Belvoir VA 22060

BARNHOLDT, TERRY JOSEPH, JR., lawyer, real estate executive; b. Charlotte, N.C., Nov. 30, 1954; s. Terry Joseph and Martha Frances (Cannon) B. BA, Duke U., 1977; JD, Wake Forest U., 1982. Bar: N.C. 1986. Assoc. Forsyth Legal Assocs., Winston-Salem, N.C., 1986; real estate negotiator JCP Realty, Inc., N.Y.C., 1986-89; sr. asset mgr. N.Y. Life Ins. Co., N.Y.C., 1989-91; v.p., asset mgr. Citicorp Real Estate, Inc., N.Y.C. and Dallas, 1991—. Recipient Am. Jurisprudence award, 1982; William B. McMannis scholar, 1980-82. Mem. ABA, N.C. Bar Assn., Internat. Coun. Shopping Ctrs., Nat. Retail Mchts. Assn., N.Y. Real Estate Salesmen, Urban Land Inst., Internat. Platform Assn., Washington Duke Club, Phi Delta Theta (pres. 1976). Home: Apt 610 750 Kappock St Riverdale NY 10463 Office: Citicorp Corp Realty Svcs One Court Square 8th Fl Long Island City NY 11120

BARNHOUSE, RUTH TIFFANY, priest, psychiatrist; b. La Mur, Isere, France; d. Donald Grey Barnhouse and Ruth W. Tiffany; m. Francis C. Edmonds Jr. (div.); children: Francis, Ruth; m. William F. Beuscher (div. 1968); children: Robert, Wiliam, Christopher, Thomas, John. Student, Vassar Coll.; BA, Barnard Coll., Columbia U.; MD, Columbia U., 1950; postgrad., Boston Psychoanalytic Inst., 1966-67, Episcopal Theological Sch., 1969-70; ThM, Weston Coll. Sch. Theology, 1974. Diplomate Am. Bd. Psychiatry and Neurology; ordained priest Episcopal Ch., 1980. Intern Monmouth Meml. Hosp., Long Branch, N.J., 1950-51; resident in psychiatry McLean Hosp., Waverly, Mass., 1953-55, staff psychiatrist, 1958-78; fellow in psychiatry Mass. Gen. Hosp., Boston, 1955-56; pvt. practice, 1956—; prof. psychiatry and pastoral care Perkins Sch. Theology So. Meth. U., Dallas, 1980-89, prof. emerita, 1989—; staff psychiatrist Mass. Mental Health Ctr., 1958-59; clin. asst. Harvard U., 1959-78; vis. lectr. in pastoral theology Weston Coll. Theology, 1973-75; adj. prof. pastoral theology Va. Theol. Sem., 1978-80, Loyola Coll., Columbia, Md., 1978-80; with courtesy staff Sibley Hosp., 1979-80; lectr., workshop leader in field. Author: Identity, 1984, Clergy and the Sexual Revolution, 1987, A Woman's Identity, 1994; asst. editor Anglican Theol. Rev.; co-editor: Male and Female: Christian Approaches to Sexuality; contbr. numerous articles to profl. jours. Pres. Peacemakers, Inc., 1989-90, Isthmus Inst., 1989-91. Recipient Maura award Women's Ctr. of Dallas, 1987. Fellow Am. Psychiat. Assn. (life, vice chmn. com. on religion 1989-93), Royal Soc. Medicine; mem. AAS, AAUP, Am. Med. Women's Assn., Am. Acad. Psychoanalysis (sci. assoc.), Am. Acad. Religion, Cong. Anglican Theologians (past pres.), Dallas Area Women Psychiatrists, Hermetic Acad., Internat. Physicians for Prevention of Nuclesar War, Mass. Med. Soc., North Tex. Psychiat. Soc., Physicians for Social Responsibility. Office: Ste 350 100B Turtle Creek Village Dallas TX 75219

BARON, PAUL LAWRENCE, surgical oncologist, educator; b. N.Y.C., Jan. 11, 1958; s. Seymour and Florence (Chill) B.; m. Lisa Forrest, May 20, 1984; children: Jessica Michelle, Jason Alexander, Jennifer Forest. BA, Boston U., 1982, MD, 1982. Diplomate Am. Bd. Surgeons. Resident Med. Coll. Va., Richmond, 1988-90; fellow in surg. oncology Meml. Sloan Kettering Cancer Ctr., N.Y.C., 1990; assoc. prof. surgery Med. U. S.C., Charleston, 1990—. Bd. dirs. Charleston unit Am. Cancer Soc., 1990—, pres., 1993-95. Recipient Clin. Cons. of Yr. award Dept. of Family Medicine, Charleston, 1991-92, 94-95, Career Devel. award Am. Cancer Soc., 1992-95. Fellow ACS (commn. on cancer 1993—), Soc. Surg. Oncology; mem. S.C. Med. Assn. (del.), Charleston County Med. Soc., Assn. Academic Surgery. Office: Med U SC 171 Ashley ave Charleston SC 29425

BAROODY, ALBERT JOSEPH, JR., pastoral counselor; b. Columbia, S.C., Sept. 8, 1952; s. Albert Joseph and Hazel (Haskin) B.; m. Nancy Dell Weatherford, Jan. 3, 1976; children: Joseph McKinley, Blakely Adelle. BS in Sociology, U. S.C., 1974; MDiv, S.E. Bapt. Theol. Sem., Wake Forest, N.C., 1978, D of Ministry, 1984. Ordained to ministry Bapt. Ch., 1977; lic. profl. counselor, S.C., 1991. Chaplain intern and resident Bapt. Med. Ctr., Columbia, S.C., 1977-79; dir. pastoral svcs. Easley (S.C.) Bapt. Hosp., 1979-80, McLeod Regional Med. Ctr., Florence, 1980-91; pastoral counselor McLeod Counseling Svcs., Florence, 1991-94, Cmty. Care and Counseling, Florence, 1994—; chaplain Lions Club, Florence, 1980-83; interim pastor various local chs., S.C., 1981—; pastoral cons. Toumey Hosp., Sumter, S.C., 1983, Conway (S.C.) Hosp., 1985-86, 92-94, Williamsburg County Hosp., Kingstree, S.C., 1986-88. Author: (with others) Ministry to Youth in Crisis, 1988; contbr. articles to profl. jours. including The Care Giver Jour., Bereavement mag. Adv. bd. Salvation Army, Florence, 1987-92, Hospice, Florence, 1988-94, chmn., 1993-94; chmn. Devel. Com. of S.E. Region Assn. for Clin. Pastoral Edn., 1986-90. Fellow Coll. Chaplains; mem. Am. Assn. Pastoral Counselors (grantee 1978). Office: Cmty Care & Counseling St John's Episcopal Ch 252 S Dargan St Florence SC 29506-2534

BARR, JAMES HOUSTON, III, lawyer; b. Louisville, Nov. 2, 1941; s. James Houston Jr. and Elizabeth Hamilton (Pope) B.; m. Sara Jane Todd, Apr. 16, 1970; 1 child, Lynn Jamison. Student U. Va., 1960-63, U. Tenn., 1963-64; B.S.L., J.D., U. Louisville, 1966. Bar: Ky. 1966, U.S. Ct. Appeals (6th cir.) 1969, U.S. Supreme Ct. 1971, U.S. Ct. Mil. Appeals 1978. Law clk., Ky. Ct. Appeals, Frankfort, 1966-67; asst. atty. gen. Ky., Frankfort, 1967-71, 1979-82; asst. U.S. atty. U.S. Dept. Justice, Louisville, 1971-79, 83—; 1st asst. U.S. Atty., 1978-79; asst. dist. counsel U.S. Army C.E., Louisville, 1982-83. Served to lt. comdr. USNR, 1967-81, lt. col. USAR, 1981-91. Mem. Fed. Bar Assn. (pres. Louisville chpt. 1975-76, Younger Fed. Lawyer award 1975), Ky. Bar Assn., Louisville Bar Assn., Soc. Colonial Wars, SAR, Soc. Ky. Pioneers, Delta Upsilon. Republican. Episcopalian. Clubs: Pendennis, Louisville Boat, Filson (Louisville). Home: 100 Westwind Rd Louisville KY 40207-1520 Office: US Atty 510 W Broadway St Louisville KY 40202-2237

BARR, MARY JEANETTE, art educator; b. Chgo., Dec. 30, 1928; d. George Leonard and Leonore Loretto (Marsicano) Tompkins; m. David Harper Barr, Aug. 28, 1954; children: Michael, Nadine, Thomas, Ellen. BS, Ill. State U., 1971, MS, 1981, EdD, 1988. Art specialist teaching cert. K-12, Ill. Art specialist K-8 Chester-East Lincoln Sch. Dist. #61, Lincoln, Ill., 1971-74, Lincoln Elem. Sch. Dist. #27, 1974-80; instr. art edn. Ill. State U., Normal, 1980-85; prin. Carroll Elem. Sch., Lincoln, 1985-87; prof. art edn. Wichita (Kans.) State U., 1988-90, West Ga. Coll., Carrollton, 1990—; art tchr. Lincoln Recreation Dept., summers, 1975-79; writer grant Arts in Gen. Edn. program Lincoln Elem. Sch. Dist. 27, 1979-80; presenter tchr. inst. workshops Ill. State Bd. Edn., 1980-83; mem. Ill. Curriculum Coun., Ill. State Bd. Edn., 1982-88, sec., 1987; panelist gen. meeting Ill. Assn. Art Educators State Conf., Peoria, 1984; workshop participant Getty Ctr. Edn. in the Arts, Cin., 1993; judge numerous profl. and amateur art shows. Author: (with Michael Youngblood) Illinois Art Education Association Position Paper on Art Education, 1987; The Illinois Curriculum Council: Visions and Directions, 1988; contbr.: Art Activities for the Handicapped, 1982. Float designer/parade Jr. Women's Club, Lincoln, 1974-80; chmn. mural C. of C., Lincoln, 1980; festival presenter Carrollton Elem. Schs., 1993, 94; judge H.S. art show U.S. Rep. Darden, Carrollton, 1993, Dallas, Ga., 1994. Recipient Ada Bell Clark Welsh Scholarship Ill. State U., 1984, Exemplary Svc. award Ill. State U. Student Elem. Edn. Bd., Ill. State U., 1985. Mem. ASCD, AAUP, Nat. Art Edn. Assn. (Tchr. of Yr. 1984), Assn. Tchr. Educators, Found. Internat. Cooperation (chpt. chair 1963—), Ga. Art Edn. Assn. (bd. mem. student chpts. 1990—, Higher Edn. Tchr. of Yr. 1994). Roman Catholic. Home: 110 Frances Pl Carrollton GA 30117-4332 Office: West Ga Coll 1600 Maple St Carrollton GA 30117-4116

BARR, RICHARD STUART, computer science and engineering management science educator; b. Austin, Tex., Sept. 3, 1943; s. Howard Raymond and Margaret (Pressler) B.; m. Mary Shipp Sanders, Mar. 10, 1990; 1 child, Johnathan Austin. BSEE, U. Tex., 1966, MBA, 1972, PhD, 1978. Assoc. dir. Coll. of Bus. Computer Ctr., U. Tex., Austin, 1968-72; exec. v.p. Analysis, Rsch. & Computation, Inc., 1975-76; asst. prof. mgmt. info. scis. So. Meth. U., Dallas, 1976-80, assoc. prof., 1980-84; assoc. prof. ops. rsch. and engring. mgmt., 1984-89, assoc. prof. computer sci. and engring., 1989—, dir. parallel processing rsch. lab., 1987—; cons. Dept. Treasury, Dept. Agr., Dept. Health and Human Svcs.; vis. fellow Dept. Treas., 1977-78; vis. scholar Princeton U., 1984, U. Colo., Boulder, 1992; bd. dirs. Parallel Processing Lab., So. Meth. U. Sch. Engring. Grantee NSF, 1993—; Assoc. editor Jour. of Heuristics; recipient Research Excellence award So. Meth. U. Sch. Bus., 1980, Outstanding Grad. Instr. award, 1983, Outstanding Instr. Nat. Tech. U., 1991, 92, 93, 94. Mem. Assn. Computing Machinery, Inst. for Ops. Rsch. and Mgmt. Scis., Inst. Electrical and Electronics Engrs. Computer Soc., Math. Programming Soc. Contbr. articles to profl. jours. Home: 6812 Velasco Ave Dallas TX 75214-3763 Office: So Meth U Sch Engring and Applied Scis Dallas TX 75275

BARR, ROBERT EDWARD, computer company executive; b. Neosho, Mo., July 29, 1956; s. Donald A. and Cecilia B.; m. Aileen Conlon, Nov. 10, 1978; children: Stephanie E., Dacia K., Marysia S. BS, U. S.C., 1978; MBA, U. Pa., 1984. Cert. systems profl., cert. in prodn. and inventory mgmt. Analyst Hanes Hosiery, Winston-Salem, N.C., 1978-80; project leader Cryovac div. WR Grace, Duncan, S.C., 1980-82; mktg. dir. Cullinet Software, Westwood, Mass., 1984-86, Online/Database Software, Pearl River, N.Y., 1986-88; info. resource mgmt. mgr. S.C. Tax Commn., Columbia, 1988-92; v.p. govt. programs Intuit Inc., San Diego, 1992—; mem. adj. faculty Midlands Tech. Coll., Columbia, 1989-92; instr. APICS, Westwood, Mass., 1985; mem. IRS Commr.'s Adv. Group, 1994-96, IRS Info. Returns Program Adv. Com., 1995—. Co-author: Employee Relations..., 1987; contbr. articles to profl. jours. Capt. March of Dimes, Columbia, 1989, 90, 91; steering com. Mainstreet Celebrates Edn., Columbia, 1990; mem. PTO, Columbia, 1989, 90, 91; v.p. Hotspurs Soccer Club, 1995—, pres., 1996—; v.p. PTA, 1996—; mem. Cmty. Planning Group, San Diego, 1996—. Mem. Am. Prodn. and Inventory Control Soc. (sec. 1981-82, Svc. award 1982, 85), Am. Payroll Assn. (svc. award 1993, 96), Am. Nat. Stds. Inst. (accredited stds. com. x12, subcom. chair 1991-92), Cert. Electronic Trade Profls. Assn. (chmn. 1991-92), Coun. for Electronic Revenue Comm. Advancement (pres. 1994-96), Columbia Forum, U. S.C. Alumni Assn., Wharton Alumni Assn. Home: 3110 Sunflower Glen Ct Jamul CA 91935-1502 Office: Intuit Inc 6220 Greenwich Dr San Diego CA 92122-5913

BARR, ROBERT LAURENCE, JR., congressman, lawyer; b. Iowa City, Nov. 5, 1948; s. Robert Laurence and Beatrice Emily (Radenhausen) B.; children: Adrian Robert, Derek Ryan; m. Jerilyn Dobbin, Dec. 31, 1986. B.A. in Internat. Relations, U. So. Calif., 1970; M.A. in Internat. Affairs (grad. fellow), George Washington U., 1972; J.D., Georgetown U., 1977. Bar: Ga. 1977, Fla. 1979. Analyst, atty., chief legis. staff CIA, Washington, 1970-78; asso. Law Offices of Edwin Marger, Atlanta, 1979-81; pvt. practice, Marietta, Ga., 1981-85, 91-94; ptnr. Brock & Barr, Marietta, 1985-86; gen. counsel Cobb County Republican Com., 1981-83, 1st vice-chmn., 1983-85, chmn. 85-86; U.S. atty. for No. Georgia, 1986-90; mem. 104th Congress from the 7th Ga. dist., Washington, 1995—; pres. Southeastern Legal Found., Atlanta, 1990-91; bd. dirs. Met. Atlanta Coun. Alcohol and Drugs, 1989-91. Mem. Ga. Bar Assn., Fla. Bar Assn., Cobb County Bar Assn., Atlanta Bar Assn., Phi Alpha Delta, Delta Phi Epsilon. Methodist. Clubs: Kiwanis. Mem. editorial staff Am. Criminal Law Rev., 1974-77. Home: 631 Concord Rd SW Smyrna GA 30082-4409 Office: US Ho of Reps 1607 Longworth Washington DC 20515

BARRACANO, HENRY RALPH, retired oil company executive, consultant; b. Bklyn., Apr. 8, 1926; s. Ralph Henry and Josephine (Chianese) B.; m. Dorothy Sue Bartlow, Aug. 19, 1945; children: Ralph Robert, Susan Jo Barracano Ratterree, Linda Joyce Barracano Swartz. BSEE, Pa. State U., 1948. Registered profl. engr., Okla. Distbn. engr. Pub. Svc. Co. Okla., Tulsa, 1948-51; elec. engr. W.R. Holway & Assocs., Tulsa, 1951-56; from staff engr. to asst. to sr. v.p. engring. and constrn. Arabian Am. Oil Co., 1956-83; ind. cons., 1983-89; sr. project mgr. Hudson Engring. and Project Mgmt. Corp., 1990-91; ind. cons., 1992—; mem. grievance com. State Bar Tex., 1994—; arbitrator NASD, 1994—. Precinct chair Dem. Party, Harris County, Tex., 1984—; precinct judge Harris County, 1984-90. 1st Lt. Signal Corps U.S. Army, 1943-59. Named Outstanding Engring. Alumnus, Pa. State U., 1993. Mem. IEEE (life sr. mem., various offices held), Petroleum Club Houston (resident mem.), Northgate Country Club, Del Lago Club (resident mem.). Home and Office: 7723 Allegro Dr Houston TX 77040-2508

BARRERA, EDUARDO, Spanish language and literature educator; b. Rio Grande City, Tex., May 29, 1921; s. Bonifacio and Antonia (Rodrígues) B.; m. Maria Ninfa Cárdenas, Aug. 13, 1944; children: Maria Elena, Eduardo Ubil, David. BS, Tex. A&I Coll., 1952, MS, 1953; PhD, U. Tex., 1976. Cert. elem. and secondary sch. tchr., Tex. Tchr. grade 5 Ringgold Annex, Rio Grande City, 1952-53; tchr. Spanish Rio Grande H.S., Rio Grande City, 1956-63; cons. Tex. Edn. Agy., Austin, 1964, 65; tchr. Spanish Pan Am. U., Edinburgh, Tex., 1966-83, chmn. dept. fgn. langs., 1983-86; lectr. U. Tex. Pan Am., Edinburgh, 1987—; evaluator in bilingual proficiency Tex. Edn. Agy., Austin and Edinburgh, 1978-86. With U.S. Signal Corps, 1941-45. Mem. Tex. Assn. Coll. Tchrs. (life, pres. local chpt. 1966—), KC (grand knight 1988-89). Roman Catholic. Home: 1007 W Samano St Edinburg TX 78539-4052 Office: Univ Tex Pan Am 1201 University Dr Edinburg TX 78539

BARRERE, CLEM ADOLPH, business brokerage company executive; b. Bradford, Pa., Jan. 5, 1939; s. Clem A. and Ruth Eleanore (Brauner) B.; m. Jamie Elizabeth Newton, Aug. 30, 1969; 1 child, John Coleman Barrere. B Engring., Yale U., 1960; PhD in Chem. Engring., Rice U., 1965; postgrad., Emory U., 1975. Registered profl. engr., Tex., Okla.; bd. cert. broker; cert. bus. intermediary. Group leader rsch. dept. Conoco, Inc., Ponca City, Okla., 1965-69; dir. gas engring. Conoco, Inc., Houston, 1969-72, dir. gas ops., 1972-77, mgr. loss control, 1977-81; mgr. Dupont-Transp. Svc., Houston, 1981-87, Dupont-Safety and Environ., Houston, 1987-89; pres. Barrere & Co. Ventures, Houston, 1989—; dir. Barrere & Co. Realtors, Houston, 1978—. Contbr. articles to profl. jours.; 7 patents in field. Mem. Mus. Fine Arts, Houston, Zool. Soc., Houston, Mus. Natural Sci., Houston, 1970-96. Recipient Citations for Svc., Am. Petroleum Inst., 1988, Gas Processors Assn., 1989; NSF rsch. grantee, 1963-65. Fellow Internat. Bus. Brokers Assn.; mem. Tex. Bus. Brokers Assn., Houston Gas Processors Assn. (pres. 1981-82), Tex. Rolls-Royce Assn. (dir. 1987-96, Spl. award 1991), Houston Gun Collectors (pres. 1964), Houston Area Realtors, Petroleum Club, Lakeside Country Club, Phi Lambda Upsilon. Republican. Methodist. Home: 5430 Lynbrook Dr Houston TX 77056-2007 Office: Barrere & Co Ventures 5850 San Felipe St Ste 125 Houston TX 77057-3012

BARRERE, JAMIE NEWTON, real estate executive; b. Russellville, Ark., June 7, 1946; d. James Edward Jr. and Martha (Spillers) Newton; m. Clement Adolph Barrere Jr., Aug. 30, 1969; 1 child, John Coleman. BA in Math., U. Ark., 1968; graduate, Realtor Inst., 1984. Cert. real estate brokerage mgr.; grad. Realtor Inst.; accredited relocation coord. Asst. programmer, analyst Conoco, Ponca City, Okla., 1968-69; programmer, analyst Bonner & Moore Assocs., Houston, 1969-70; tchr. math. Lamar Consol. High Sch., Rosenberg, Tex., 1970-72; assoc. broker Betty James, Realtors, Houston, 1972-78; pres. Barrere & Co., Realtors, Houston, 1978-96, Barrere & Co. Relocation, Houston, 1996—; mem. adv. bd. Western Bank-Westheimer, Houston, 1986; mem. Employee Relocation Coun. Mem. Harris County Heritage Soc., Houston, 1970—, Houston Jr. Forum, 1980—, Am. Heart Found., Houston Zool. Soc.; guild mem. Mus. Fine Arts, Houston, 1978—; trustee St. Luke's United Meth. Ch.; bd. dirs., children's dept. vol. Moores Sch. Music Soc. U. Houston, 1992—; life mem. Tex. Real Estate Polit. Action Com.; cub scout leader Boy Scouts Am. Mem. Nat. Assn. Realtors (mem. Equal Opportunity Com. 1985), Tex. Assn. Realtors (bd. dirs. 1989—, mem. Multiple Listing Svc. com. 1985-90), Houston Assn. Realtors (bd. dirs. 1986-89, 93-95, v.p. 1993, mem. and chmn. various coms.), Houston C. of C. (amb. 1986), DAR, U. Ark. Alumnae Assn. (life, v.p. Houston chpt. 1985-88), RELO Internat. Relocation Network, Delta Delta Delta Alumnae Assn. (various offices), Lakeside Country Club, Petroleum Club, Tanglewood Garden Club (Houston, bd. dirs. 1973-86, 93-95). Office: Barrere & Co 5850 San Felipe St Ste 125 Houston TX 77057-3012

BARRETT, BERNARD MORRIS, JR., plastic and reconstructive surgeon; b. Pensacola, Fla., May 3, 1944; s. Bernard Morris and Blanche (Lischkoff) B.; BS, Tulane U., 1965; MD, U. Miami, 1969; m. Julia Mae Prokop, Nov. 26, 1972; children: Beverly Frances, Julie Blaine, Audrey Blake, Bernard Joseph. Surg. intern Meth. Hosp. and Ben Taub Hosp., Houston, 1969-70; resident in gen. surgery Baylor Coll. Medicine, Houston, 1970-71, UCLA, 1971-73; resident in plastic surgery U. Miami Affiliated Hosps., Fla., 1973-75, chief resident in plastic surgery, 1975; fellow in plastic surgery Clinica Ivo Pitanguy, Rio de Janeiro, Brazil, 1973; instr. surgery Baylor Coll. Medicine, 1970-71, clin. instr. plastic surgery, 1977-80, clin. asst. prof., 1980-90, clin. assoc. prof., 1991—; instr. surg. emergencies L.A. County Paramedics, 1972-73; plastic surgery coordinator for jr. med. students Sch. Medicine U. Miami, 1975; practice medicine specalizing in plastic and reconstructive surgery, Houston, 1976—; pres., chmn. bd. dirs. Plastic and Reconstructive Surgeons, P.A., Houston, 1978—; chmn. Tex. Inst. Plastic Surgery, Houston; assoc. chief plastic surgery St. Luke's Episcopal Hosp., Houston, 1991—; attending physician Jr. League Clinic, Tex. Children's Hosp., Houston, 1977—; active staff St. Luke's Hosp., Houston, Meth. Hosp., Houston; clin. assoc. in plastic surgery U. Tex. Med. Sch., Houston, 1976—; instr. surg. emergencies Harris County Community Coll.; dir. Am. Physicians Ins. Exchange, Austin, vice chmn. bd. dirs., 1995—; past chief of staff, chief plastic surgery Travis Centre Hosp., Houston, 1985—; dir. Physicians for Pearle, Norfolk, Va., 1991— cons. physician Houston Oilers, 1978—; attending physician Ontario Motor Speedway, Calif., 1972-73. Bd. dirs. Plastic Surgery Ednl. Found., Chgo; mem. Fed. Coun. on Aging, Washington, 1991-93. Served to lt. comdr., M.C., USNR, 1969-74. Surg. exchange scholar to Royal Coll. Surgeons, London, 1968; hon. dep. sheriff Harris County, Tex. (Houston); diplomate Am. Bd. Plastic Surgery. Fellow ACS; mem. Am. Soc. Plastic and Reconstructive Surgeons, Royal Soc. Medicine, Michael E. DeBakey Internat. Cardiovascular Surg. Soc., Am. Soc. for Aesthetic Plastic Surgery, Denton A. Cooley Cardiovascular Surg. Soc., Tex. Med. Assn., Tex. Soc. Plastic Surgery, Harris County Med. Assn., Lipoplasty Soc. N.Am., Houston Soc. Plastic Surgery, D. Ralph Millard Plastic Surg. Soc. (pres. 1993-94, v.p. 1977-79, sec., treas. 1975-77, historian 1980—), U. Miami Sch. Medicine Nat. Alumni Assn. (bd. dirs. 1975-77), Alpha Kappa Kappa (pres., 1968-69). Clubs: Houston City, Houstonian; Royal Biscayne Racquet; Commodore (Key Biscayne, Fla.), Coral Beach and Tennis Club (Bermuda). Author: Patient Care in Plastic Surgery, 1982; Manuel de Ciudados en Cirugia Plastica, 1985. Author: Patient Care in Plastic Surgery, 2d edit., 1996; contbr. articles to med. publs., presentations to profl. confs.; inventor Barrett sterling surgigrip. Office: 6624 Fannin St Ste 2200 Houston TX 77030-2334

BARRETT, BRIAN LEE, minister, evangelist; b. Huntington, W.Va., Mar. 30, 1959; s. Stanford Lee and Elizabeth Jean (Price) B.; m. Nina Lynn Dimitroff, May 8, 1982. BTh, Internat. Sem., Plymouth, Fla., 1988; postgrad., Internat. Sem., 1988-92; MTh, Andersonville Sem., 1997. Ordained to ministry Ch. of Christ, 1981. Evangelist Ch. of Christ, West Hamlin, W.Va., 1978-79, Buffalo, 1980-81; pulpit min., evangelist Ch. of Christ, Hamlin, W.Va., 1981—; officer in charge U.S. P.O., Woodville, W.Va., 1989-91. Editor Sword of the Spirit jour., 1981-86. Vol. fireman Hamlin Fire Dept., 1976-83; emergency med. technician Lincoln Vol. Ambulance Svc., Hamlin, 1978-80; fund raiser Ohio Valley Coll., Parkersburg, W.Va., 1989-90, Lincoln Primary Care Ctr., Hamlin, 1989-90. Home: 516 May St Hamlin WV 25523-1206 Office: Ch of Christ 8041 Vine Ave Hamlin WV 25523-1509

BARRETT, COLLEEN CROTTY, airline executive; b. Bellows Falls, Vt., Sept. 14, 1944; d. Richard Crotty and Barbara (Hennessey) Blanchard; 1 child, Patrick Allen Barrett. A.A. with highest honors, Becker Jr. Coll., 1964. Legal sec. Oppenheimer Rosenberg Kelleher & Wheatley, San Antonio, 1968-72, adminstrv. asst., paralegal, 1972-78; corp. sec. Southwest Airlines, Dallas, 1978—, exec. asst. to pres. and chmn., 1980-85, v.p. adminstrn., corp. sec., 1985-90, exec. v.p. customs, 1990—. Mem. Leadership Tex. Democrat. Roman Catholic. Office: SW Airlines Co PO Box 37611 Dallas TX 75235-1600

BARRETT, DAVID EUGENE, judge; b. Hiawassee, Ga., June 25, 1955; s. Homer and Laura Arispah (Wilson) B.; m. Nell Mills, June 17, 1978; children: Laura Elizabeth, Thomas Jeffrey. BA summa cum laude, U. Ga., 1977, JD cum laude, 1980. Assoc. Erwin, Epting, et al, Athens, Ga., 1980-84, Blasingame, Burch, et al, Athens, 1984; sole practice Hiawassee, 1984-92; judge Recorders Ct., 1986-92, Superior Ct., Enotah Cir., 1992—; counsel Towns County Humane Soc., Hiawassee, 1985-92; counselor Alzheimer Support, Hiawassee, 1985. Mem. ABA, Ga. Bar Assn., Mountain Bar Assn. (sec. 1987-88, v.p. 1988-89, pres. 1989-90), Western Bar Assn. (sec. 1983-84), Trial Lawyers Assn. Am., Towns County C. of C. (bd. dirs. 1986-87, 90-92, pres. 1988), Demosthenian Lit. Soc. (bd. dirs., sec. bd. trustees 1978-89, chmn. bd. 1986-89), Athens Jaycees (v.p. 1983-84). Home: Sequoia Point Hiawassee GA 30546 Office: Ste K 59 S Main St Cleveland GA 30528-4512

BARRETT, LINDA L., real estate executive; b. Hudson, Mich., Aug. 16, 1948; d. David John and Georgia Elizabeth (Spengler) B.; 1 dau., Toni. Student, U. Mich., 1970-73. Cert. residential brokerage mgr. Sales mgr. Collins Real Estate, Hudson, Mich., 1973-79; owner, broker Homeland Real Estate, Lake Leann, Mich., 1979-82; mgr. broker Mid-Mich. Real Estate, Jackson, Mich., 1982-85; exec. v.p. Michael Saunders & Co., Sarasota, Fla., 1986-95, cons., 1995—; mem. adv. bd. Sotheby's Internat. Mem. AAUW, NAFE, Internat. Real Estate Fedn., Nat. Mktg. Inst., Nat. Assn. Realtors, Fla. Assn. Realtors, Sarasota C. of C., Bradenton C. of C., Com. of

100, 2000 Notable Am. Women (profl. stds. com. woman's coun.). Econ. Devel. Coun., CRB, Estates Club.

BARRETT, LYLE EUGENE, retail buyer, designer, artist; b. Evanston, Ill., Dec. 4, 1942; s. John Harold and Vera (Zinkel) B. BA in Bus. Adminstrn., Northeastern Ill. U., 1976. Display designer Marshall Field's, Chgo., 1962-69, asst. mgr. window display, 1969-79, spectacular designer, 1970-79; dir. visual merchandising So. div. Marshall Field's, Houston, 1979-80; dir. store planning Original Christmas Store, Houston, 1980-83; asst. adminstr. visual merchandising Gordon Jewelry Corp., Houston, 1983-84, purchasing dir. store planning, 1984-89; freelance creative dir. Marilyn Miglin Cosmetics, Chgo., 1969-80; owner, designer P.O. Box Rubberstamps, Houston, 1985—; tchr. Leisure Learning, Houston, 1986-89; owner Stampers and Friends, Houston, 1990—; tchr. Leisure Learning, Houston, 1986—; organizer World MailArt Exhibit various Houston galleries, 1986, 87, 89. Editor newsletters Chgo. Men's Gathering, 1976-79, Great Impressions, 1986—; contbr. articles to profl. publs.; two-man show Missouri Street Gallery, Houston, 1986. Pres. Montrose Art Alliance, Houston, 1984-87; chmn. I.H., Inc., cultural fund raising, Houston, 1985-86. With USNR, 1966-68. Recipient Best of Show award Montrose Art Alliance, 1983, 84, best new mail order catalog Rubberstamp Madness, 1985. Mem. Greater Montrose Bus. Guild. Democrat. Lutheran. Home: 740 E 19th St Houston TX 77008-4472 Office: PO Box Rubberstamps 244 W 19th St Houston TX 77008-4010

BARRETT, MICHAEL JOSEPH, priest; b. N.Y.C., Oct. 6, 1952; s. Patrick Joseph and Margaret Mary (Rogan) B. BA, Columbia Coll., 1974; STD, Pontifical Atheneum Holy Cross, Rome, 1987. Ordained priest by Pope John Paul II, Rome, 1985. Sales rep. Gulf Oil Chems. Co., N.Y.C., 1974-76; acct. exec. Merrill Lynch & Co., N.Y.C., 1976-78; dir. devel. The Heights Found., Inc., N.Y.C., 1978-83; asst. prof. Roman Coll. of Holy Cross, Rome, 1985-88; del. vicar for Tex. Opus Dei Prelature, Houston, 1988—; retreat master Featherock Conf. Ctr., Schulenburg, Tex., 1988—; chaplain Southgate Cultural Ctr., Houston, 1988—. Alumnus advisor Columbia U. Secondary Schs. Com., N.Y.C., 1981-83. Roman Catholic. Home: 5505 Chaucer Dr Houston TX 77005-2631 Office: 5505 Chaucer Dr Houston TX 77005-2631

BARRIER, JOHN WAYNE, engineer, management consultant; b. Savannah, Tenn., June 17, 1949; s. John H. and Evelyn (Williams) B.; m. Janet Putnam, Aug. 21, 1969; children: Jennifer, James, Joseph, Jeremy. BS in Chem. Engring., U. Tenn., 1972, MS in Adminstrn., 1975. Chem. engr. Monsanto Co., Decatur, Ala., 1972-76; chem. engr. TVA, Muscle Shoals, Ala., 1976-82, process devel. leader, 1982-85, project mgr., 1985-86, program mgr., 1986—; instr. mgmt. Faulkner U., Florence, Ala., 1980—. Contbr. articles to profl. jours. Officer Community Youth Program, Florence, 1986—. Named one of Outstanding Young Men in Am., 1979; recipient Tech. Achievement award U.S. Dept. Energy, 1985, Jump Meml. award U.S. Dept Commerce, 1986. Mem. Nat. Mgmt. Assn. Home: RR 12 Box 163B Florence AL 35633-9807 Office: TVA 435 CEB Muscle Shoals AL 35633

BARRIOS, ROGER, software company executive. Dir. R&D Am. Software Inc., Atlanta; CFO AmQuest Inc., Atlanta. Office: Am Software Inc 470 E Paces Ferry Rd Atlanta GA 30305

BARRON, GARY A., airline executive; b. 1943. BA, Tex. Luth. Coll.; JD, St. Mary's Coll. of Calif., 1973. With Gen. Dynamics Corp., Ft. Worth, 1968-70; atty. Oppenheimer, Rosenberg, Kelleher & Wheatley, San Antonio, 1973-78; v.p., gen. counsel S.W. Airlines Co., 1978—, exec. v.p. corp. affairs, 1985, COO, 1989, exec. v.p. ops., 1994—. Office: SW Airlines Co PO Box 36611 2702 Love Field Dr Dallas TX 75235-1600*

BARRON, OSCAR NOEL, gas engineer, consultant; b. Burleson County, Tex., Feb. 4, 1929; S. Tom Joe and Lillian (Robinson) B.; m. Billie O'Dell Lewis; children: Noelie, William Lewis, Kaydell. BSChE, Rice U., 1948, postgrad., 1949; postgrad. in bus. adminstrn., Houston U., 1959. Registered profl. engr., Tex., La. Roustabout Exxon Co. U.S.A., Danciger, Tex., 1949-50; gas engr. Exxon Co. U.S.A., Houston, 1950-60; supervising engr. Exxon Co. U.S.A., Kingsville, Tex., 1960-63; sr. supervising engr. Exxon Co. U.S.A., Corpus Christi, Tex., 1963-66; divsn. prodn. engr. Exxon Co. U.S.A., Midland, Tex., 1967-68; sr. tech. advisor Exxon Co. U.S.A., New Orleans, 1969-71; divsn. gas. engr. Exxon Co. U.S.A., Houston, 1971-79; sect. mgr. Exxon Prodn. Rsch. Co., Houston, 1980-92; cons. Conroe, Tex., 1992—; mem. adv. com. Sch. Gas Tech., U. Tex., Kilgore, 1971-90; pres. gas Processors Assn., 1990-91, bd. dirs., 1986-92. Mem. Soc. Petroleum Engrs. Republican. Presbyterian. Home and Office: 133 Jeb Stuart Ln Conroe TX 77302-1149

BARRON, THOMAS WILLIS, real estate broker; b. Newnan, Ga., Apr. 9, 1949; s. Lindsey Hand and Genet Louise (Henry) B.; m. Margaret Rose MacLennan, Aug. 17, 1973; children: Catharine Lindsey, Thomas Willis Jr., John Taliaferro Gaines. BA, Emory U., 1971; JD, Mercer U., 1974. Assoc. Sanders, Mottola, Haugen, Wood, Goodson and Odom, Newnan, 1974-77; real estate broker Lindsey's, Inc., Newnan, 1977—, Coweta Developers, Inc., Newnan, 1977—; dir. Newnan Savs. Bank, Metro Multi-List, Inc., Atlanta. Dir., sec.-treas. Newnan Hosp., 1992—; trustee Mercer U., Macon, Ga., 1990-95; past pres. Newnan-Coweta United Way, 1982—, Newnan Coweta chpt. ARC, 1980—. Mem. Newnan-Coweta Bd. Realtors (past pres. 1984—, Realtor of Yr. 1991, Million Dollar Club 1989—), Newnan Country Club (past dir.), Newnan Kiwanis Club (past pres.), Sigma Chi (life, past consul), Newnan-Coweta C. of C. (chmn. bd. 1994). Baptist. Office: Lindseys Inc Realtors 14 Jackson St Newnan GA 30263

BARROS-SMITH, DEBORAH LYNNE, publishing executive, editor; b. Washington, Jan. 19, 1959; d. Ford Gibson and Carole Lynne Barros; m. Marcellus Drummer Smith III; 1 child, Marcellus Drummer IV. AS, Oakwood Coll., 1980; BA, Temple U., 1983; postgrad., Lansdale Sch. of Bus., 1982-83. News announcer Sta. WOCG, Huntsville, Ala., 1978-79; news announcer, news dir. Sta. WEUP, Huntsville, 1979-80, talk show host, 1992-93; asst. audience coord. Sta. KYW-TV, Phila., 1981-83; freelance writer Phila., 1982-84; writer, prodr. Cable Adnet, Phila., 1983-86; owner Praise Consultants, Spring City, Pa., 1985-89; city editor Speakin Out News, Huntsville, 1990-92; pub., editor The Valley Informer Inc., Huntsville, 1994—. Youth adv. Pottstown, Pa., Phila., Huntsville, 1980—; lobbyist Welfare Rights Orgn., Phila., 1982; active Minority Prevention of AIDS Through Choices and Tng., Huntsville, 1991-93; co-founder North Ala. Youth Congress, Huntsville, 1991—; HIV/AIDS presenter ARC, Huntsville, 1991—; pub. rels. and field worker Heart, Body and Spirit (Health Outreach Project), Huntsville, 1993—; journalism tchr. Girls Inc., Huntsville, 1994; speaker on child abuse, 1994—; mem. Ala. State Bd. Breast and Cervical Cancer Coalition, Montgomery, 1994—; mem. cable access bd. COMPAT, Huntsville, 1994—; mem. bd., media com. Stop The Violence, Eradication Task Force, Huntsville, 1994—; mem. bd. Family Life Ctr., Ala. A&M U., 1995. Recipient Cert. of Appreciation, U.S. Senator John Heinz, 1982, Welfare Rights Orgn., Phila., 1982, U.S. Congressman Bud Cramer, 1993, Madison County Commr. Dr. Prince Preyer, 1993, Best Media award Twenty Disting. Young Men of Huntsville, Ala., 1993; named Citizen of Yr., Omega Psi Phi, 1994; Poynter Inst. Media Studies scholar, 1991. Mem. Nat. Assn. Black Journalists, Nat. Assn. Female Execs., North Ala. African Am. C. of C., Huntsville Press Club (bd. dirs.). Democrat. Seventh-day Adventist. Home: 1635 Carroll Rd Harvest AL 35749 Office: The Valley Informer Inc PO Box 3585 Huntsville AL 35810-0585

BARROW, THOMAS DAVIES, oil and mining company executive; b. San Antonio, Dec. 27, 1924; s. Leonidas Theodore and Laura Editha (Thomson) B.; m. Janice Meredith Hood, Sept. 16, 1950; children: Theodore Hood, Kenneth Thomson, Barbara Loyd, Elizabeth Ann. BS, U. Tex., 1945, MA, 1948; PhD, Stanford U., 1953; grad. advanced mgmt. program, Harvard U., 1963. With Humble Oil & Refining Co., 1951-72; regional exploration mgr. Humble Oil & Refining Co., New Orleans, 1962-64, sr. v.p., 1967-70, pres., 1970-72, also bd. dirs.; exec. v.p. Esso Exploration, Inc., 1964-65; sr. v.p. Exxon Corp., N.Y.C., 1972-78; chmn., CEO Kennecott Corp., Stamford, Conn., 1978-81; vice chmn. Standard Oil Co., 1981-85; investment cons. Houston, 1985-89; chmn. GX Tech., Houston, 1990—; pres. Thomson-Barrow, 1989—; sr. chmn., bd. dirs. GeoQuest Internat. Holdings, Inc., Houston, 1990—; pres. Tecolotita, Inc., 1991—, T-BAR-X, Houston, 1995—; bd. dirs. GPS Tech. Corp., Houston, McDermott Internat., Inc., New Orleans, J. Ray McDermott, Houston; mem. commn. on natural resources NRC, 1973-78, commn. on phys. sci., math. and natural resources, 1984-87, bd. on earth scis., 1982-84; trustee Woods Hole Oceanographic Instn., 20th Century Fund-Task Force on U.S. Energy Policy. Pres. Houston Grand Opera, 1985-87, chmn., 1987-91; trustee Am. Mus. Natural History, Stanford U., 1980-90, Tex. Med. Ctr., 1983—, Geol. Soc. Am. Found., 1982-87; trustee Baylor Coll. Medicine, 1984—, vice chmn bd. trustees, 1991—. Served to ensign USNR, 1943-46. Recipient Disting. Achievement award Offshore Tech. Conf., 1973, Disting. Engring. Grad. award U. Tex., 1970, Disting. Alumnus, 1982, Disting. Geology Grad., 1985, Disting. Natural Sci. Grad., 1990; named Chief Exec. of Yr. in Mining Industry, Fin. World, 1979. Fellow N.Y. Acad. Scis.; mem. Nat. Acad. Engring., Am. Mining Congress (bd. dirs. 1979-85, vice chmn. 1983-85), Am. Assn. Petroleum Geologists, Geol. Soc. Am., Internat. Copper Research Assn. (bd. dirs. 1979-85), Nat. Ocean Industry Assn. (bd. dirs. 1982-85), AAAS, Am. Soc. Oceanography (pres. 1970-71), Am. Geophys. Union, Am. Petroleum Inst., Am. Geog. Soc., Houston Country Club, The Hills Club, Petroleum Club, River Oaks Country Club, Ramada-Tejas Club, Sigma Xi, Tau Beta Pi, Sigma Gamma Epsilon, Phi Eta Sigma, Alpha Tau Omega. Episcopalian. Office: Ste 3830 5847 San Felipe Houston TX 77057

BARROWS, FRANK CLEMENCE, newspaper editor; b. Lewes, Del., Nov. 2, 1946; m. Mary S. Newsom, Nov. 16, 1985; 1 child, Margaret S. BA, St. Andrews Presbyn. Coll., 1968. Reporter, columnist Charlotte Observer, 1969-72, 76-81, asst. sports editor, 1981-82, asst. met. editor, 1982-83, exec. sports editor, 1983-84, 86, dep. features editor, 1985, dep. met. editor, 1986-87, asst. mng. editor, 1987-88, dep. mng. editor, 1988-92, mng. editor, 1992—. Contbr. numerous articles to mags. Bd. vis. St. Andrews Presbyn. Coll. Mem. Am. Soc. Newspaper Editors, Soc. Newspaper Design, Investigative Reporters and Editors. Home: 1810 Shoreham Dr Charlotte NC 28211-2134 Office: Charlotte Observer 600 S Tryon St Charlotte NC 28202-1842

BARROWS, JOHN FREDERICK, mechanical engineer; b. Detroit, Dec. 26, 1928; s. Elon Carey and Bernice (Vorhes) B.; BS in Mech. Engring., U. Mich., 1951, MSE, 1959, PhD, 1962; m. Carol Jane Roser, Mar. 26, 1951; children—John Edward, Peter Scott, Timothy Allan. Project engr. Allison divsn. Gen. Motors Corp., 1951-58; lectr., asst. prof. mech. engring. U. Mich., Dearborn, 1960-62; asst. prof. Cornell U., Ithaca, N.Y., 1962-67; sr. engr. Rsch. divsn. Carrier Corp., Syracuse, N.Y., 1967-70, chief engr., 1970-78, asst. dir. rsch. labs., 1978-85; prof., dir. mfg. engring. L.C. Smith Coll. Engring., Syracuse U., 1985-94. Pres. Cazenovia Civic Club, 1975. Gen. Motors fellow, 1961. Mem. ASME, ASHRAE, AAAS, Sigma Xi, Phi Kappa Phi, Pi Tau Sigma. Contbr. articles to profl. jours. Home: 60 River Club Dr Hilton Head Island SC 29926-2312

BARRUS, PAUL WELLS, priest; b. Winterset, Iowa, June 29, 1902; s. Charles and Daisy May (Clopton) B. BA with honors, Drake U., 1933, MA, 1936; PhD, State U. Iowa, 1949. Ordained priest Roman Catholic Ch., 1978; cert. tchr., Iowa. Tchr. pub. schs., Ia., 1926-36; asst. prof. Drake U., Des Moines, 1937-42; instr. Iowa State U., Ames, 1943-45; prof., chmn. dept. English East Tex. State U., Commerce, 1949-76; priest Commerce, 1978-83, Grand Prairie, Tex., 1983-90, Richardson, Tex., 1990—. Author: Levels of Consciousness, 1988. Served with U.S. Army, 1942-43. Mem. Phi Beta Kappa, Kappa Delta Pi, Eta Sigma Phi, Phi Sigma Iota. Home and Office: 709 James Dr Richardson TX 75080

BARRY, DAVE, columnist, author; b. Armonk, N.Y.; 1 child, Robert. Grad., Haverford Coll., 1969. Reporter, editor Daily Local News, West Chester, Pa., 1971-75; with AP, instr. bus. writing Phila., 1975-83; columnist The Miami (Fla.) Herald, 1983—. Author: Taming of the Screw: Several Million Homeowner's Problems Sidestepped, 1983, Babies and Other Hazards of Sex, 1984, Bad Habits: A One Hundred Percent Fact Free Book, 1985, Stay Fit and Healthy Until You're Dead, 1985, Dave Barry's Guide to Marriage and/or Sex, 1987, Claw Your Way to the Top, 1987, Dave Barry's Greatest Hits, 1988, Dave Barry Slept Here, 1989, Dave Barry Turns 40, 1990, Dave Barry Talks Back, 1991, Dave Barry's Only Travel Guide You'll Ever Need, 1991, Dave Barry Does Japan, 1992, Dave Barry Is Not Making This Up, 1994, Dave Barry's Complete Guide to Guys, 1995, Dave Barry in Cyberspace, 1996. Recipient Disting. Writing award Soc. Newspaper Editors, 1987, Pulitzer prize for Commentary, 1988. Office: care Miami Herald 1 Herald Plz Miami FL 33132-1609

BARRY, DAVID WALTER, infectious diseases physician, researcher; b. Nashua, N.H., July 19, 1943; s. Walter and Claire B.; m. Gracia Chin; children: Christopher, Jennifer. BA in French literature with highest honors magna cum laude, Yale Coll., 1965; student, Sorbonne, Paris, 1963-64; MD, Yale U., 1969. Cert. State of Conn. Med. Examining Bd., State of Md. Med. Examining Bd., State of N.C. Bd. Med. Examiners; diplomate Nat. Bd. Med. Examiners, Am. Bd. Internal Medicine, Am. Bd. Infectious Diseases. Intern, then resident Yale-New Haven Hosp., 1969-72; staff assoc., dir., acting dep. dir. divsn. virology, bur. biologics FDA, 1972-77; head anti-infectives sect., dept. clin. investigation, med. divsn. Burroughs Wellcome Co., Research Triangle Park, N.C., 1977-78, head dept. clin. investigation, med. divsn., 1978-85, head dept. virology, Wellcome rsch. labs., 1983-89, dir. divsn. clin. investigation, 1985-86, v.p. rsch. Wellcome rsch. labs., 1986-89, v.p. rsch., devel. and med. affairs, Wellcome rsch. labs., 1989-95, pres. Wellcom rsch. labs., 1994-95, also bd. dirs.; chmn., CEO Triangle Pharms. Inc., Durham, N.C., 1995—; dir. influenza vaccine task force, bur. biologics FDA, 1976-77, mem. rsch. human subjects com.; adj. prof. sch. medicine Duke U., 1977—; mem. com. pub.-pvt. sector rels. vaccine innovation, inst. medicine NAS, 1983, roundtable drugs and vaccines against AIDS, 1989, industry liaison panel, 1992; mem. AIDS task force NIH, 1986, AIDS program adv. com., 1988; deans coun. Yale Sch. Medicine, 1989—; cons., lectr. in field; bd. dirs., Wellcome Found., Family Health Internat. Mem. editorial bd. AIDS rsch. and Human Retroviruses, AIDS Patient Care; contbr. articles to profl. jours. Active N.C. Indsl. (Vaccine) Commn. Sr. surgeon USPHS, 1972-77. Vis. fellow U. Md., 1975-76. Fellow ACP, Infectious Diseases Soc. Am., Royal Soc. Medicine; mem. AAAS, AMA, Am. Soc. Virology, Am. Soc. Microbiology, Am. Fedn. Clin. Rsch., Pharm. Mfrs. Assn. (med. and sci. sect., com. AIDS 1989, AIDS task force 1989, R & D steering com. 1990, commn. treatment drug dependence and abuse 1990—), N.C. Med. Soc., Durham-Orange Counties Med. Soc., Venezuelan Soc. Internal Medicine (hon.), Alpha Omega Alpha. Office: Triangle Pharms Inc 4 University Pl 4611 University Dr Durham NC 27707

BARRY, FRANCIS JULIAN, JR., lawyer; b. New Orleans, Oct. 7, 1949; s. Francis Julian and Bertha Anna (Lion) B.; m. Janice Leigh Gonzales, May 8, 1976; children: Francis III, Maria. BA, Tulane U., 1970, JD, 1973. Bar: La. 1973, U.S. Dist. Ct. (ea. dist.) La. 1973, U.S. Ct. Appeals (5th cir.) 1973, U.S. Dist. Ct. (we. dist.) La. 1978, U.S. Ct. Appeals (11th cir.) 1982, U.S. Supreme Ct. 1991. Assoc. Deutsch, Kerrigan & Stiles, New Orleans, 1973-78, ptnr., 1978—; Editor Admiralty Law Inst. Symposium Tulane U., New Orleans, 1973. Adv. editor Tulane Maritime Law Jour. (formerly The Maritime Lawyer), 1975—. Served to capt. USAR. Mem. Fed. Bar Assn., La. Bar Assn., New Orleans Bar Assn., Maritime Law Assn. U.S. (proctor, carriage of goods com. 1982-87, transp. hazardous substances com. 1987—), Southeastern Admiralty Law Inst., La. Assn. Def. Counsel, Assn. Average Adjusters London, Am. Legion, Navy League U.S., Army-Navy Club, Bienville Club, Univ. Club, Empire Club, Iris Club, Azalea Club, Lotus Club, Plimsoll Club, Mariners Club, The Round Table Club. Republican. Roman Catholic. Home: 4301 Dumaine St New Orleans LA 70119-3617 Office: Deutsch Kerrigan & Stiles 755 Magazine St New Orleans LA 70130-3629

BARRY, JOYCE ALICE, dietitian; b. Chgo., Apr. 27, 1932; d. Walter Stephen and Ethel Myrtle (Paetow) Barry; student Iowa State Coll., 1950-52, Loyola U., 1952-58; B.S., Mundelein Coll., 1955; postgrad. Simmons Coll., 1963-64, U. Ga., 1979, Calif. Western U., 1980—. Reg. dietician. Prodn. supr. Marshall Field & Co., Chgo., 1955-59; dir. food services Women's Ednl. and Indsl. Union, Boston, 1959-62; dir. food services Wellesley Public Schs., Mass., 1962-70; cons. Stokes Food Services, Newton, Mass., 1960-70; regional dietitian Canteen Corp., Chgo., 1970-83; gen. mgr. bus. devel. Plantation-Sysco, Orlando, Fla., 1983-87; dir. product devel. corp., quality assurance, procurement Mariott Internat. Hdqrs., Washington, 1987-95; owner food svc. consulting svc., 1995—; vis. lectr.; research adv. council Restaurant Bus. Mag.; career adv. council, Am. Dietetics Assn.; treas. Dietitians in Bus. Mem. Am. Home Econs. Assn., Internat. Fedn. Home Economists, Home Economists in Bus., Am. Dietetics Assn., Nat. Assn. Female Execs., Dietitians in Bus., Tex.-Mex. Frozen Food Coun., Internat. Food Technologists, Nat. Frozen Food Coun. Republican. Roman Catholic. Club: La Chaine des Rotisseurs. Home and Office: 175 Heron Bay Cir Lake Mary FL 32746-3423

BARRY, SUSAN BROWN, writer, manufacturer; b. San Antonio, Tex., Sept. 14, 1944; d. Earl A. Jr. and Betty (Galt) Brown; m. Richard Hanley Barry, June 25, 1966 (div. 1973); children: Andrew Earl, Brice Galt. AB, Sweet Briar (Va.) Coll., 1966. Scriptwriter Stas. KUHT-TV, KDOG-TV, KEYT Radio, Houston, 1972-77; originator, adminstr., cons. publ. program Rice U., Houston, 1977-79; liaison book promotion Dell. Publs., Viking Publs., and others, Houston, 1979-85; pres. Savage Designs, Houston, 1985-88; cons. U. Calif., Santa Barbara, 1985; rare book, manuscript cataloguer, writer Randall House Rare Books. Producer hospice-related tng. video and articles; book critic Houston Post; designer greeting cards Neiman-Marcus Dept. Stores; writer Bicentennial Play Houston Pub. Schs. (now in Nat. Archives). Founding coord. Reach to Recovery program Am. Cancer Soc.; rep. Choice in Dying, 1994-96; mem. adv. bd. Hearts for AIDS Found., 1992-94; mem. hospice team Hospice Austin; bd. dirs., com. chair Austin Parks Found., 1995—. Mem. Assn. for Death Edn. and Counseling (chmn. pub. rels. 1992-94), Jr. League (numerous coms. and chairmanships), Asia Soc. (adv. com., fin. chmn. Houston chpt. 1984-85), Austin Coun. on Fgn. Affairs. Republican. Unitarian.

BARSI, LOUIS MICHAEL, college dean; b. Port Reading, N.J., Aug. 26, 1941; s. Louis Joseph and Mary Alice (Remak) B. BA, U. Okla., 1963; MA, Cen. Mich. U., 1966; MA in Edn., U. No. Iowa, 1971; EdS, U. Wis., Stout, 1978; PhD, George Mason U., 1991. Tchr. Searing Sch., N.Y.C., 1963-64, Annunciation H.S., Detroit, 1964-65; dean of students Mount St. Clare Coll., Clinton, Iowa, 1969-76, chmn. social sci. div., 1975-76, athletic dir., 1970-76; coord. fin. aid U. Wis., Waukesha, 1977-80, adminstr. honors program, 1978-80; asst. campus dir., dean of student affairs Pa. State U., DuBois, 1980-87; program assoc. acad. programs and dir. of the ctr. for ednl. opportunity and achievement Am. Assn. State Colls. and Univs., Washington, 1988-90, exec. asst. to the pres., 1990-91; dean student svcs. Del. Tech. and C.C., Terry Campus, Dover, 1991-95, Bluefield (W.Va.) State Coll., 1995—; intern Office Ednl. Rsch. and Improvement U.S. Dept. of Edn., Washington, 1987-88, Coun. on Post-Secondary Accreditation, Washington, 1988; bd. dir. Ctr. for Ednl. Opportunity and Achievement; mem. rev. panel U.S. Dept. Edn.-Regional Tng. Workshop, 1989, rev. panel coun. advancement and support edn. 1988-91; group leader Student Pers. Conf., U. No. Iowa; speaker on student leadership tng. to various high schs., colls. and confs., 1987—. Co-developer of instnl., faculty, and student inventories of good practice in undergrad. edn.; contbr. articles to profl. jours. Bd. dirs. HANDS, Clinton, Iowa, 1970-71; mem. pers. com. Du Bois YMCA, 1982-84; bd. dirs., mem. budget and fin. com. DuBois United Way, 1983-87, chmn. long-range planning com., 1984-86, co-chmn. edn. div. 1985 campaign, sec., 1985-87, v.p. and chmn. campaign com., 1986, pres., 1987, AASCU United Way campaign coord., 1990, 91; adv. Explorer Post, Boy Scouts Am., 1981-83, mem. exec. com. Bucktail coun., 1982-87, bd. dir. career svcs., 1984-87; mem. planning com. Higher Edn. Group, Washington; tchg. asst. Cen. Mich. U., 1965-66; rsch. asst. U. No. Iowa, 1968-69, George Mason U., 1987-88; assistantship U. Wis., Stout, 1976-77; leadership program Mercer-Tazewell C. of C., 1996. Recipient Disting Svc. award for developing career awareness program Boy Scouts Am., 1985, Nat. Quality Dist. award Bucktail Coun., BSA, 1987. Mem. Am. Assn. State Colls. and Univs. (Spl. Achievement award 1990), Nat. Assn. Student Pers. Adminstrs., DuBois C. of C. (bd. dirs. 1981-84, chmn. govtl. affairs com. 1981-83), Pa. State U. DuBois Campus Alumni Soc. (bd. dirs. 1980-87, bd. dirs. DuBois Ednl. Found. 1987-91), W.Va. Assn. of Student Personnel Adminstrs. (mem. exec. bd. 1996—), Greater Washington Soc. Assn. Execs. (vol. career counselor 1989-92), DuBois Area Hist. Soc. (co-founder), Rotary (bd. dirs., 1982-87, v.p. 1983, pres. 1985-86), Phi Delta Kappa, Phi Alpha Theta, Phi Theta Kappa. Home: PO Box 690 Bluefield WV 24701 Office: Office of the Dean Student Svcs Bluefield State Coll Bluefield WV 24701

BARTA, DOROTHY ELAINE, portrait artist; b. Toledo, Ohio, June 23, 1924; d. Ira Aldo and Gladys Josephine (Swantek) Woods; m. Clarence E. Vadala Jr., June 13, 1943 (dec. Jan. 1960); children: John Vadala, Lawrence Vadala, Richard Vadala, Jeanne Vadala, Tom Vadala, Rob Vadala, June Vadala; m. Rudolph J. Barta, Dec. 27, 1961; children: Sharon, Mike; stepchildren: Randy, Rick. Student, Dallas Mus. Fine Arts, 1946-50, Art Students League, N.Y.C., 1979-81. Freelance artist and instr. Dallas, 1946—; master gardener Tex. Agr. Dept., 1991-96; lectr. Master Gardeners, Dallas, 1993—. Painted portrait Judge Sarah T. Hughes, U. North Tex., 1996; one person shows at Plano Cultural Art Ctr., Plano, Tex., 1984, U. Va., Charlottesville, 1985, Irving Ctr. for the Arts, 1987, Sheraton Gallery, Dallas, 1988, Wichita Falls Tex. Art Assn., 1990; group shows include D-ART, Dallas, 1984, 85, ARCO Tower Realism, Dallas, 1989, North Lake Coll., Irving, 1989, Art Focus XC, Dallas, 1994—; work featured in various publs. including The Best of Watercolor, 1995, How to Paint Skin Colors (by James Horton), 1995, PAastel School (by Hazal Harrison), 1996, The Art of Pastel Portraiture (by Madlyn-Ann C. Woolwich), 1996, also mags. Active various wildflower preservation orgns., Dallas, 1993—. Creative Endeavors nominee Sanus 65 Sr. Salute, Dallas, 1995; recipient First Am. Artist Achievement award 1992, First Sr. Hall of Fame award for Creative Endeavors, 1989. Mem. Pastel Soc. Am., Am. Soc. Portrait Artists, Tex. Watercolor Soc., Southwestern Watercolor Soc., Artists and Craftsmen Assn. (bd. dirs. 1960s), Knickerbocker Artist, Pastel Soc. S.W. (founder, pres. 1979-85, 94). Home: 3151 Chapel Downs Dallas TX 75229 Office: Barta Originals 3151 Chapel Downs Dallas TX 75229

BARTEE, TED RAY, commodities trader, rancher; b. Holt, Mo., July 5, 1938; s. Lawrence Wesley and Zetta (Dykes) B.; m. Jennie Wynn Bass, Aug. 26, 1967; children: William Clay, Brandon Sample, Bailey Bass, Clay Dillon. AB in Econs., William Jewell Coll., 1960. Grain mgr. Cen. Soya Co., Chattanooga, Tenn., 1964-70; v.p. Harris-Crane, Inc., Charlotte, N.C., 1970—. Advisor S.C. Jr. Angus Assn., Clover, 1989—; pres. Rep. Precinct Clover II, 1989—; trustee Lincoln Meml. U., 1974-79. Lt. USN, 1960-64. Named Hon. Farmer, State of S.C., 1987, Family of the Yr., Clover Jaycee-ettes, 1982, Advisor of the Yr., Nat. Jr. Angus Assn., 1990. Mem. S.C. Angus Assn. (pres. 1987-89), York County Cattlemen's Assn. (pres. 1984-87), Nat. Block and Bridle Club (hon.), VFW, Masons, Shriners. Methodist. Home: 1717 Saint Paul Church Rd Clover SC 29710-8222 Office: Harris-Crane Inc 6230 Fairview Rd Charlotte NC 28210-3253

BARTEL, JEFFREY SCOTT, lawyer; b. Miami, Fla., Nov. 18, 1965; s. Stanley Jay and Maxine L. (Young) B. BA cum laude, Harvard U., 1988; JD with honors, U. Fla., 1994. Bar: Fla. 1994, U.S. Dist. Ct. (mid. and no. dists.) Fla. 1995, U.S. Ct. of Claims 1995, U.S. Dist. Ct. Appeals (11th cir.) 1995. Sr. adminstrv. asst. Office of Mayor, Miami, Fla., 1988-90; chief of staff, adminstrv. asst. Congressman Lincoln Diaz-Balart, U.S. Ho. of Reps., Washington, 1992-93; atty. Steel Hector & Davis, Miami, 1994—; city atty. City of Biscayne Park, Fla., 1995—. Adv. bd. Jackson Meml. Hosp. Found., Miami, 1995, Camillus House, 1995—; external affairs com. Miami Midnight Basketball League, 1994—; mem. selection com. Congl. Hispanic Cir., Washington, 1993; chmn. cmty. devel. block grant com. City of Miami, 1988-90, chmn. underwriters selection com., 1988-90; bd. dirs. Do the Right Thing of Miami, 1995—; guardian ad litem 11th Jud. Cir. Put Something Back program, 1996—; mem. U. Fla. Coll. Law Alumni Coun., 1994—; S.E. regional chair Leadership Fla. Bd. Regents, 1996—. Named to U. Fla. Hall of Fame, 1992; recipient Up and Comer award Price Waterhouse LLP/South Fla. Bus. Jour., 1995; Darcey A. Davis Meml. scholar, 1992, Harvard Coll. scholar, 1985, 86, 87, 88. Mem. ABA (urban, state and local govt. law sect. 1994—), Fla. Bar Assn. (city, county, local govt. law sect. 1994—), Miami Runners Club, Harvard Club of Miami (exec. com., v.p. 1994—). Home: 2101 Brickell Ave #215A Miami FL 33129 Office: 200 S Biscayne Blvd Miami FL 33131-2310

BARTELSTONE, RONA SUE, gerontologist; b. Bklyn., Jan. 10, 1951; d. Herbert and Hazel (Mittman) Canarick; m. Alan Joel Markowitz. BS in Social Welfare, SUNY, Buffalo, 1972; MSW, Ind. U., 1974. Licensed Clin. Social Worker, Fla. Diplomate of Social Work. Social worker YM-YWHA of Greater N.Y., 1974-75; dist. supr. N.Y.C. Housing Authority, Bklyn., 1975-77; field instr. Barry U. Sch. Social Work, 1980-81; project dir. United Family & Children's Svcs., 1977-81; faculty Miami Dade Community Coll., 1981-82; adult educator Sch. Bd. Dade County, 1981-82; med. social worker Mederi Home Health Agy., 1979-82; mem. adj. faculty Nova U., 1986-88; pvt. practice Rona Bartelstone Assocs., Inc., Ft. Lauderdale, Fla., 1981—; adj. faculty Fla. Internat. U., S.E. Ctr. on Aging, 1996; cons. and trainer in field. Contbr. articles to various mags. d. dirs. Jewish Vocat. Svcs., Miami, 1985-92; mem. funding panel Area Agy. on Aging, Miami, 1985-89; active Friends of the Family Counseling Svcs., Miami, 1983-88; adv. bd., chair internship subcom. Lynn U., 1993—; exec. bd. Fla. Geriatric CAre Mgrs., 1993—; chair tng. com., exec. v.p. Alzheimer's Assn., Miami, 1994-96; co-chair Nat. Acad. Cert. Care Mgrs., 1994—. Recipient Dade County Citizen of the Yr. award, 1982, NASW Social Worker of the Yr. award, 1982-83, Trail Blazer award, 1984, Up & Comers award in health care Price Waterhouse and So. Fla. Bus. Jour., 1990. Mem. NASW (treas. 1987-89), Gerontology Soc. Am., Am. Soc. on Aging, Nat. Coun. on Aging, Assn. Profl. Geriatric Care Mgrs. (pres. 1988-94, chmn. credential com. 1993—), Nat. Acad. Cert. Care Mgrs. (co-chmn. 1994—), Fla. Geriatric Care Mgrs. Assn. (exec. bd. 1993—). Democrat. Jewish. Home: 2365 N 37th Ave Hollywood FL 33021-3645 Office: 2699 Stirling Rd Ste 304C Fort Lauderdale FL 33312-6546

BARTELT, JOHN ERIC, physics researcher and educator; b. Milw., Aug. 11, 1955; s. Robert Louis and Lois Marie (Wallschlaeger) B.; m. Lucy Mary Huntzinger, Oct. 21, 1989. BS, U. Wis., 1977; PhD, U. Minn., 1984. Rsch. assoc. Stanford (Calif.) Linear Accelerator Ctr., 1983-88, exptl. physicist, 1988-89; asst. prof. Vanderbilt U., Nashville, 1990—; conducted seminars and lectrs. in field. Contbr. articles to profl. jours. Mem. Am. Phys. Soc. Office: Vanderbilt U Dept Physics PO Box 1807 Sta B Nashville TN 37235

BARTH, MELISSA ELLEN, English language and women's studies educator; b. Chewelah, Wash., Nov. 24, 1948; d. Harold Walter and Thelma Madge (Braker) B. Student, U. South Wales, Cardiff, 1969-70; BA in English magna cum laude, Wash. State U., 1971, MA in English, 1974; PhD in English, Purdue U., 1981. Advisor for fgn. study Wash. State U., Pullman, 1972-76; asst. prof. English, DePauw U., Greencastle, Ind., 1981-82; asst. prof. English, Appalachian State U., Boone, N.C., 1982-87, assoc. prof., 1987-91, prof., 1991—, dir. Office Women's Concerns and Women's Studies, 1991-96, dir. Equity Office, 1996—; vis. prof. Duke U., Durham, N.C., 1988. Author: Strategies for Writing with the Computer, 1986, Writing for the World of Work, 1991; author, editor: Reading for Difference: Texts on Gender, Race and Class, 1993. Bd. dirs. Catawba Valley coun. Girl Scouts U.S.A., 1993—. David Ross fellow Purdue U., 1979-81. Mem. NOW, Popular Culture Assn., Phi Kappa Phi (sec.). Office: Appalachian State U Office Women's Concerns Boone NC 28608

BARTHEL, WILLIAM FREDERICK, JR., engineer, electronics company executive; b. Washington, July 14, 1940; s. William Frederick and Eva (Buday) B.; m. Barbara Joan Adams, Nov. 18, 1961; 1 son, William Frederick III. BS, McNeese State U., 1972. Shop mgr. Electronic Unlimited, Lake Charles, La., 1968; quality control engr. Rockwell Internat., Cedar Rapids, Iowa, 1974-79, mgr. quality assurance, 1979, sr. engring. scientist, process control devel., 1980-81; engring. mgr. process reliability Digital Equipment Corp., Andover, Mass., 1981-87, engring. mgr. performance assurance, 1987-91; dir. quality Gables Engring., Inc., Coral Gables, Fla., 1991-93, v.p. ops., 1993—. Served with USAF, 1958-62. Mem. Am. Chem. Soc., Am. Inst. Chemists. Republican. Home: 745 SE 25th Ln Homestead FL 33033-5234 Office: Gables Engring Inc 247 Greco Ave Miami FL 33146-1808

BARTHOLOMAY, WILLIAM C., insurance brokerage company executive, professional baseball team executive; b. Evanston, Ill., Aug. 11, 1928; s. Henry C. and Virginia (Graves) B.; m. Sara Taylor, 1950, (div. 1964); children: Virginia, William T., Jamie, Elizabeth, Sara; m. Gail Dillingham, May 1968 (div. Apr. 1980). Student, Oberlin Coll., 1946-49, Northwestern U., 1949-50; BA, Lake Forest Coll., 1955. Ptnr. Bartholomay & Clarkson, Chgo., 1951-63; v.p. Alexander & Alexander, Chgo., 1963-65; pres. Olson & Bartholomay, Chgo. and Atlanta, 1965-69; sr. v.p. Frank B. Hall & Co. Inc., N.Y.C. and Chgo., 1969-72, exec. v.p., 1972-73, pres., 1973-74, vice chmn., 1974-90; chmn. bd., dir. Atlanta Braves, 1966—; pvt. practice cons. Chgo., 1990-91; pres. Near North Nat. Group, 1991—; vice chmn. Turner Broadcasting System, Inc., Atlanta; bd. dirs. WMS Industries Inc., Chgo., Exec. Coun. Maj. League Baseball, Maj. League Baseball Players Pension Plan; bd. govs. Arlington Internat. Racecourse, Ltd. Commr. Chgo. Park Dist., 1980—; mem. Chgo. Pub. Bldg. Commn., 1989—; bd. dirs. Chgo. Maternity Ctr., Lincoln Park Zool. Soc.; trustee Adler Planetarium, Mus. Sci. and Industry; former trustee Lake Forest (Ill.) Coll., Ogelthorpe Coll., Atlanta, Marymount Manhattan Coll., N.Y. With USNR, 1951-54. Mem. Chief Execs. Orgn., World Pres.'s Orgn., Chgo. Pres.'s Orgn., Nat. Assn. CLU, Chgo. Assn. CLU, Chgo. Club, Racquet Club, Saddle and Cycle Club, Econ. Club, Onwentsia Club, Shoreacres Club (Lake Forest), Brook Club, Links Club, Racquet & Tennis Club, Doubles Club (N.Y.C.), Piedmont Driving Club, Atlanta Country Club, Peachtree Golf Club, Commerce Club. Episcopalian. Home: 180 E Pearson St Chicago IL 60611-2130 Office: Near North Nat Group 875 N Michigan Ave Ste 2000 Chicago IL 60611-1802 also: Atlanta Braves PO Box 4064 Atlanta GA 30302-4064

BARTHOLOMEW, ARTHUR PECK, JR., accountant; b. Rochester, N.Y., Nov. 20, 1918; s. Arthur Peck and Abbie West (Dawson) B.; m. Mary Elizabeth Meyer, Oct. 4, 1941(wid. Oct. 1992); children: Susan B. Hall, Arthur Peck III, James M., Virginia B. Keyser. AB, U. Mich., 1939, MBA, 1940. With Ernst & Whinney (name now Ernst & Young), 1940-79, successively jr. accountant, partner charge Eastern dist., Detroit office, 1940-64; nat. office, Cleve. Ernst & Whinney, 1964-65, N.Y. office, 1965-79, also mem. mng. com.; instr. accounting U. Mich., 1940, George Washington U., 1945-46. Mem. Mich. Gov.'s Task Force for Expenditure Mgmt., 1963-64; mem. 2d Regional Plan Commn. N.Y.; Bd. dirs. Detroit League for Handicapped, 1952-64; treas. Grosse Pointe War Meml. Assn., 1961; bd. dirs., v.p. Greater N.Y. council Boy Scouts Am. Served from pvt. to capt. AUS, 1942-46. Mem. AICPA, Inst. Mgmt. Accts. (pres. Detroit 1963-64, nat. pres. 1974-75), The Conf. Bd., Mich. Soc. CPAs, N.Y. Soc. CPAs, Detroit Country Club, Gulf Stream Golf Club (treas.), Wall St. Club (pres. 1976-78), Ocean Club Fla. (pres. 1993-94), Phi Beta Kappa, Phi Kappa Phi, Beta Gamma Sigma, Phi Eta Sigma, Beta Alpha Psi, Phi Kappa Sigma. Republican. Presbyterian. Home: 6665 N Ocean Blvd Boynton Beach FL 33435-3329

BARTLETT, JANET SANFORD (WALZ), school nurse; b. Bryn Mawr, Pa., Aug. 13, 1930; d. Edward Joseph Walz and Anna Downing (Little) Walz Tomlin; m. Joseph Richard Bartlett, May 6, 1952 (div. April 1972); children: Cheryl, Elaine, Karen, Lee, Patrick, Michael. Diploma nursing, Meml. Mission Sch. Nursing, 1953; EMT-I cert., El Paso C.C., 1983. RN, N.C., Tex. Office nurse William F. Hillier, M.D., Asheville, N.C., 1953-55; school nurse Ysleta Ind. Sch. Dist., El Paso, 1973-93. Author: (manual) Sch. Nurse Manual, 1979, Volunteer's Handbook, 1979, (cookbook) Bartlett Heritage Cookbook; editor: (newsletter) Nurses Notes Newsletter, 1983-88; co-creator, copyright, D.K. Buster, 1989. Mem. El Paso Health Issues Forum, 1985-88; co-chair El Paso Oral Health Commn., 1987—; life mem. PTA; pres. El Paso Coun. bd. dirs. Campfire Girls, Inc., 1971-74 (Luther Halsey Gulick award 1972), also Blue Bird leader, Camp Fire guardian; active Boy Scouts Am., Girl Scouts Am.; com. chair El Paso chpt. Am. Cancer Soc.; co-chair Ysleta Sch. Dist. Employee Wellness, 1989-90, compiler manual; sec. Unite El Paso Birth Packet Com., 1993-96, chmn., 1996—. Recipient Outstanding Staff Support award Ysleta Vol. Svcs., 1988-89, Stand Up for El Paso award KDBC TV, 1991, REACH award YWCA/El Paso Healthcare System, 1992; named Woman of Yr. El Paso Parks and Recreation, 1995. Mem. Nat. Assn. Sch. Nurses, Tex. Assn. Sch. Nurses (Pres.'s award 1990, Tex. Sch. Nurse of Yr. 1991), Tex. Assn. Sch. Nurses Region 19 (v.p. 1982, 83, Sch. Nurse of Yr. 1990), Ysleta Sch. Nurses Assn. (pres. 1988, Sch. Nurse of Yr. 1987, World Healer award 1995), Assistance League of El Paso (yearbook chmn. 1994, 95, Sch. Bell. com. 1994—). Home: 10249 Bayo Ave El Paso TX 79925-4347

BARTLETT, RICHARD ADAMS, American history educator, history consultant; b. Boulder, Colo., Nov. 23, 1920; s. John Thomas and Margaret Emily (Abbott) B.; m. Marie Regina Cosgrove, Dec. 26, 1945; children: Richard, Margaret, Thomas, Mary. BA, U. Colo., 1942; MA, U. Chgo., 1947; PhD, U. Colo., 1953. Instr. Tex. A&M U., College Station, 1945-51; asst. prof. Fla. State U., Tallahassee, 1955-63, assoc. prof., 1963-67, prof., 1968-89, prof. emeritus, 1989—. Author: Great Surveys of the American West, 1962, 66, paperback, 1980, 86, 89, 93 (Spur award Western Writers Am. 1962, Desert Mag. award 1962), The Wilderness and the Indians: Challenges in the New World, 1970, Nature's Yellowstone, 1974, paperback, 1989, The New Country: A Social History of the American Frontier, 1776-1890, 1974, paperback, 1976, Freedom's Trail, 1979, 2d edit., 1981, Yellowstone: A Wilderness Besieged, 1985, paperback, 1989, From Cody to the World: The First Seventy-Five Years of the Buffalo Bill Memorial Association, 1992, Troubled Waters: Champion International and the Pigeon River Controversy, 1995; editor: The Gilded Age: America, 1865-1900, 1969, Rolling Rivers: An Encyclopedia of America's Rivers, 1984; assoc. editor Jour. Libr. History, 1964-74; mem. editorial bd. Jour. of the West; mem. editl. rev. bd. Colo. Heritage, 1979—; contbr. articles and book revs. to profl. jours. Huntington Libr. fellow, 1967, Woodrow Wilson fellow Smithsonian Inst., 1979-80; recipient fellowship Am. Philos. Soc., 1967, Rsch. grant Fla. State U., grant Am. Philos. Soc. Mem. Western History Assn. (governing coun. 1976-79, edtl. bd. The Am. West 1980-82), Fla. Coll. Tchrs. History (pres. 1974-75), Phi Alpha Theta. Episcopalian. Home: 2205 Mendoza Ave Tallahassee FL 32304-1319

BARTLETT, ROGER ALAN, attorney; b. Ft. Smith, Ark., June 6, 1944; s. Roger Frost and Dorothy Louise (Loop) B.; m. Susannah Rusk Mills, June 17, 1992. JD, U. Tex., Austin, 1974. Bar: Tex., 1974. Legal editor State Bar of Tex., Austin, 1974-80; atty. Clark, Thomas & Winters, P.C., 1981-92; Hilgers & Watkins, P.C., 1992—. Co-editor: Texas Collections Manual 2d edit., 1987. Mem., bd. dirs. Recording for the Blind and Dyslexic-Tex. Unit, Austin, 1983—. Recipient Sidekick award State Bar of Tex., 1994. Mem. ABA, State Bar of Tex., Travis County Bar Assn., Tex. Assn. Bank Counsel. Home: 2415 Vista Ln Austin TX 78703 Office: Hilgers & Watkins PC 98 San Jacinto Ste 1300 Austin TX 78701

BARTLING, PHYLLIS MCGINNESS, oil company executive; b. Chillicothe, Ohio, Jan. 3, 1927; d. Francis A. McGinness and Gladys A. (Henkelman) Bane; m. Theodore Charles Bartling; children: Pamela, Theodore, Eric C. Student, Ohio State U., 1944-47. Bookkeeper, Bartling & Assocs., Bartling Oil Co., Houston 1974-80; sec.-treas., dir. both cos., 1980—. Co-chmn. ticket sales Tulsa Opera, 1956-61; bd. dirs. Tex. Speech and Hearing Ctr., Houston, 1967-70. Republican. Episcopalian. Avocations: gardening, bicycling, cooking, golf. Home and Office: 11 Inwood Oaks Dr Houston TX 77024-6803

BARTOLO, DONNA MARIE, hospital administrator, nurse; b. Springfield, Ill., Mar. 21, 1941; d. Elmer Ralph Bartolomucci and Zoe (Rose) Cavatorta. Diploma in nursing, St. John's Sch. Nursing, Springfield, Ill., 1962; BS, Milliken U., 1976; MA, Sangamon State U., 1978. Pediatric nurse Springfield Clin., 1962-64, physician's asst., 1972-74; gynecol. nurse Watson Clin., Lakeland, Fla., 1964-66; cons. state sch. nurses Office of Edn. State of Ill., Springfield, 1974-78; assoc. dir. operating rm. svcs. Cedars-Sinai Med. Ctr., L.A., 1978-82, co-dir. div. nursing, 1981-82; surg. nurse Emory U. Hosp., Atlanta, 1966-70, asst. dir. nursing, surg. svcs., 1982-94, dir. surg. svcs., dir. nursing, 1994-95, dir. nursing for surg. scis., 1995—; adj. prof. Nell Hodgson Woodruff Sch. Nursing Emory U. Mem. editorial bd. Perioperative Nursing Quarterly; contbr. articles to nursing jours. Mem. Org. Nurse Execs., Ga. Assn. Nurse Exec. (pres. elect, pres. 1992), Assn. Operating Rm. Nurses, Sigma Theta Tau (sec. 1990—). Home: 1328 Mill Glen Dr Dunwoody GA 30338-2720

BARTON, ALEXANDER JAMES, retired ecologist, educator, naval officer; b. Mt. Pleasant, Pa., May 9, 1924; s. Paul Carnahan and Barbara (Eggers) B.; m. Arlene Florence Arment, Oct. 6, 1945; children: Sandra, Lynne, Alexander James III. BS, Franklin and Marshall Coll., 1946; MS, U. Pitts., 1957. Herpetologist Highland Park Zool. Gardens, Pitts., 1946-52; instr. biology Stony Brook (N.Y.) Sch., 1952-63, dir. admissions and fin. aid, 1957-63; profl. asst. NSF, Washington, 1963-65, profl. assoc., 1965-70, program dir., 1970-88, cons., 1989-95; adj. asst. prof. biology C.W. Post Coll., Brookville, N.Y., 1961-63; chmn. U.S. planning com., mem. U.S. delegation UN Conf. on Environ. Edn., Tbilisi, USSR, 1977; cons. sci. books Doubleday & Co., 1962-64. contbr. numerous articles and papers to profl. publs. Extended mil. furlough serving as capt. U.S. Navy, naval mem. OSD staff revising Res. Officers' Personnel Mgmt. Act, 1981-83; dir. Savannah (Ga.) Natural History Mus., 1957; chmn. Fed. Interagency subcom. Environ. Edn., 1980-81; Scoutmaster Allegheny County coun. Boy Scouts Am., Pitts., 1947-52, mem. nat. adv. com., 1950-54, mem. exec. coun. Suffolk County coun., 1957-63; mem. Internat. Com. on Endangered Reptiles and Amphibians, 1967-74; town councilman, 1989—; chmn. Mayor's Commn. on Youth, 1990—; deacon Presbyn. Ch., 1946—, lay preacher, 1954-65, 89-93, commissioned lay preacher, 1993—, tchr. adult bible class, 1964-68, 88-91, elder, 1990—; mem. adv. com. gifted and talented students Highland County Schs., Va., 1990-94; pastor Presbyn. Chs. of the North Fork, W.Va., 1991—; vice-chmn. Highland County Architecture Rev. Bd., 1995—; adminstr. U.S. Nat. Pk. Svc./Va. Dept. Hist. Resources Project to Survey Hist. Assets Monterey, 1996—. Capt. USNR, 1943-45, 81-83. Fellow Explorers Club; mem. Acad. Ind. Scholars (charter mem.), Arlington Rose Found. (pres. 1970-71), Potomac Rose Soc. (1st v.p. 1972-73, pres. 1974-75, dir. 1976-88, gold medal 1983), Am. Rose Soc. (vice chmn. Colonial dist. 1971-72, chmn. 1985-88, cons. rosarian 1970-95, chmn. nat. long-range planning com. 1973-75; accredited rose show judge 1970-77, life judge 1978-95, gen. chmn. nat. conv. 1981, bd. dirs. 1985-88, outstanding dist. judge award 1983, Silver Honor Medal 1984, dir. 1st nat. judges sch. 1991), Assn. Admissions Officers Ind. Secondary Schs. (pres. 1959-62), Herpetologists' League. Home: The Crow's Nest Box 100 West Main St Monterey VA 24465-0100

BARTON, CHARLES DAVID, religious studies educator, author, researcher, historian; b. Austin, Tex., Jan. 28, 1954; s. Charles Grady and Hilda Rose (Seely) B.; m. Cheryl Edith Little, Mar. 18, 1978; children: Damaris Ann, Timothy David, Stephen Daniel. Degree in religious edn., Oral Roberts U., 1976. Dir. youth Aledo (Tex.) Christian Ctr., 1974-75, dir. Christian edn., dir. youth, 1977-87, dir. Christian edn., elder, 1987—; dir. youth Jenks (Okla.) 1st Assembly, 1975-76; dir. Christian edn., dir. youth Sheridan Christian Ctr., Tulsa, Okla., 1976-77; pres. Splty. Rsch. Assocs., Inc./WallBuilders, Aledo, 1987—. Author: America: To Pray or Not to Pray, 1987, The Myth of Separation, 1988, What Happened in Education?, 1989, The Bulletproof George Washington, 1990, Original Intent, 1995; prodr. (videos) America's Godly Heritage, Keys to Good Government, Edn. and the Founding Fathers, Spirit of the American Revolution, Foundations of American Government. Bd. dirs. Youth Leadership Coun., Cin., 1990, Tex. Christian Coalition, 1993—; mem. bd. advisors Released Time, Sacramento, 1987, Nat. Prayer Embassy, Washington, 1988; mem. coun. Nat. Policy Forum, 1994. Recipient Writing award Amy Found., 1989, 2 Angel awards Excellence in Media, 1995, George Washington medal Freedoms Found. at Valley Forge. Republican. Office: WallBuilders PO Box 397 Aledo TX 76008-0397

BARTON, JAMES CARY, lawyer; b. Raymondville, Tex., Sept. 1, 1940; s. Dewey Albert and Dorothy Marie (Keene) B.; m. Isabel Pattee Critz, Sept. 12, 1964 (div. June 1975); children: Hamilton Keene, James Albert, John Franklin; m. Carolyn Ann Cox, Dec. 20, 1975; stepchildren: Holly Ann Adams, Laura Lee Adams, Jennifer Lynn Adams. BA, Baylor U., 1962; LLB, Harvard U., 1965. Bar: Tex. 1965, U.S. Dist. Ct. (so. dist.) Tex. 1972, U.S. Tax Ct. 1977. Trial atty. FPC, Washington, 1965-67; atty.-advisor U.S. Tax Ct., Washington, 1967-68; assoc. to ptnr. Kleberg, Mobley, Lockett & Weil, Corpus Christi, Tex., 1969-75, Brown, Maroney, Rose, Baker & Barber, Austin, Tex., 1975-82; ptnr. to of counsel Johnson & Swanson, Austin and Dallas, 1982-88; dir. Smith, Barshop, Stoffer & Millsap, Inc., San Antonio, 1988-91; prin. J. Cary Barton, P.C., San Antonio, 1991-93; prin Barton & Schneider, L.L.P., San Antonio, 1993—; speaker in field. Sgt. USAF, 1968-69. Mem. ABA, State Bar Tex. (mem. coun. of real estate probate and trust law sect. 1982-85, mem. real estate forms com. 1986—), Am. Coll. Real Estate Lawyers, Tex. Bd. legal Specialization (cert. in comml. real estate law). Democrat. Episcopalian. Office: One Riverwalk Pl 700 N Saint Marys St Ste 1825 San Antonio TX 78205-3501

BARTON, JOE LINUS, congressman; b. Waco, Tex., Sept. 15, 1949; s. Larry Linus and Bess Wynell (Buice) B.; m. Janet Sue Winslow, Jan. 31, 1970; children—Bradley Linus, Alison Renee, Kristin Elizabeth. BS in Indsl. Engring., Tex. A&M U., 1972; MS in Indsl. Adminstrn., Purdue U., 1973. Asst. to v.p. Ennis (Tex.) Bus. Forms, 1973-81; The White House fellow Washington, 1981-82; cost control cons. ARCO, Dallas, 1982-84; mem. 101st-104th Congresses from 6th Tex. dist., 1985—; dep. whip, mem. energy and commerce com., mem. sci. and tech. com. Mem. Assn. Former Students Tex. A&M U. (councilman at large 1985—). Methodist.

BARTON, JONATHAN MILLER, clergyman; b. Elizabeth, N.J., June 26, 1952; s. Douglas William and Deborah (Gray) B.; m. Elizabeth Dora Rinehart, May 19, 1985 (div. June 1990); 1 child, Katherine Nicole; m. Elizabeth Wood Stark, July 17, 1994; stepchildren: Liza, Archer Blair. Student, Union Coll., 1970-72; BA in Psychology, Kean Coll., 1974; MDiv, Drew U, 1978. Ordained to ministry Presbyn. Ch., 1981. Asst. chaplain Drew U., Madison, N.J., 1976-78, resident dir., 1977-81; hunger action enabler Elizabeth, Newark, Newton presbyteries United Presbyn. Ch. U.S.A., 1978-82; cons. World Hunger Edn. Svc., Washington, 1983; assoc. regional dir. Ch. World Svc., Rocky Hill, N.J., 1983-85; regional dir. Ch. World Svc., Richmond, Va., 1985—; mem. Nat. IMPACT Briefings, Washington, 1978-84; mem. coord. com. N.J. State Food Conf., 1979; spl. asst. to coord. U.S. Nat. Com. for World Food Day, 1981-83; mem. 4th World Food Issues Conf., Cornell U., 1982; testifier Senate Subcom. on edn., ARts and Humanities, 1982; mem. NGO Com. for UN Internat. Conf. on Population Consultation, 1984, UN/NGO Com. on Food and Rural Devel. Food Forum, 1985, UN/NGO Consultation on African Crisis, 1985; mem. Summer Inst. in Devel. Edn., Tao, N.Mex., 1986; mem. prep. com. for visit Dir.-Gen. UN/FAO on FAO's 50th anniversary commemoration, Washington, 1993; attended US AID Conf. Global Edn., Williamsburg, Va., 1989; mem. Gov.'s Conf. Infant Mortality, Richmond, Va., 1986. Regional editor Va. Steps, Ch. World Svc., 1985—; contbr. articles to various publs. in field. Co-chair grant com. Va. Hands Across Am., 1986; co-founder, chair Madison, N.J. chpt. Amnesty Internat., 1976-80; chair program adv. com. Ch. World Svc., 1987-89; chair Divsn. Mission and Svc., Presbytery of James, 1992-93; bd. dirs. Va. Interfaith Ctr. Pub. Policy, 1987-93; bd. dirs. Direct Ministries, Va. Coun. Chs., 1986—, mem. Va. refugee adv. coun., 1992— ; co-founder, convener Va. Congress on Hunger, 1987—; founding mem. bd. dirs. Va. Hunger Found., 1992—. Recipient C.J. Helen svc. award Miquin Lodge #68, 1967, Virgil honor Order of the Arrow, 1968, Lighthouse award Foodbank S.E. Va., 1993. Mem. Internat. Platform Assn. Office: Church World Svc 1627 Monument Ave Richmond VA 23220-2906

BARTON, KATHRYN JEAN, elementary education educator; b. Alexandria, Va., Feb. 28, 1970; d. Robert F. and Beverly Jean (Shafer) B. B of Early Edn., George Mason U., 1993. Cert. NK-4, Va. Presch. tchr. Life in Learning Presch., Alexandria, 1989-94, Children's Internat. Sch., Arlington, Va., 1994—. Mem. ASCD, Va. Edn. Assn. Presbyterian.

BARTON, NANCY SHOVER, nursing administrator; b. Harrisburg, Pa., May 31, 1951; d. Marlin Burd and Zelma Pearl (Schell) Shover; 1 child, Sandra Gehl. Diploma, Ga. Bapt. Hosp. Sch. Nursing, 1972; BSN, Med. Coll. of Ga., 1974, MSN, 1976; cert. in total quality mgmt., Xavier U., 1992. Asst. prof. nursing Hall Sch. of Nursing Brenau Coll., Gainesville, Ga., 1979-83; asst. prof., coord. ADN program Houston Bapt. U., 1984-88; gerontology clin. nurse specialist N.E. Ga. Med. Ctr., Gainesville, 1988-90, nursing quality assurance coord., dir. nursing, profl. practice, 1990-95; dir. clin. mgmt. sys. Med. Ctr. of Ctrl. Ga., Macon, 1995—. Mem. ANA, Ga. Nurses' Assn., Nat. Assn. Healthcare Quality, Nat. Assn. Quality Assurance Profls., Ga. Orgn. Nurse Execs., Sigma Theta Tau.

BARTON, RAYMOND OSCAR, III, concrete company executive; b. Augusta, Ga., Sept. 30, 1949; s. Raymond Oscar Jr. and Anne Wilcox (Claussen) B.; m. Jane Barbara Tilley, Dec. 28, 1972; 1 child, Todd Jeffrey. BS, USAF Acad., 1972; MS, Troy State U., 1984. Commd. instr. pilot USAF, 1973, advanced through grades to capt., 1984; pilot, instr. USAF, Nellis AFB, Nev., 1983-84; exec. v.p. Claussen Concrete Co., Inc., Augusta, Ga., 1985-88; pres. Claussen Concrete Co., Inc., 1988-89, also bd. dirs.; spl. agt. Northwestern Mut. Life Ins. Co., 1989-91; real estate agt. VIP Realty Svcs., Inc., Augusta, 1991-93; pres. Am. Concrete, Inc., Augusta, 1993—; concrete technologist Nat. Ready-Mixed Concrete Assn., 1986. Chmn. troop com. Boy Scouts Am., 1991, den leader Webelo coun., 1988-89. Lt. Col. Ga. Air N.G., until 1995. Decorated Commendation medal, Meritorious Svc. medal. Mem. Augusta Country Club. Republican. Episcopalian. Home: 754 Tripps Ct Augusta GA 30909-1816

BARTON, ROBERT L., JR., judge, educator; b. Ballston Spa, N.Y., June 19, 1943; s. Robert L. Sr. and Bertha (Di Pasquale) B.; m. Jean M. Adamchic, Aug. 14, 1965; children: Robert Joseph, Katherine Anne. BA, U. Pitts., 1965; JD, Boston Coll., 1969. Bar: Mass. 1969, R.I. 1970, D.C. 1972, U.S. Ct. Appeals (1st cir.) 1970, U.S. Ct. Appeals (D.C. cir.) 1973, U.S. Dist. Ct. R.I., 1971, U.S. Dist. Ct. D.C. 1973, U.S. Dist. Ct. Md. 1973. Law clk. U.S. Dist. Ct. R.I., Providence, 1969-70; staff atty. R.I. Legal Svcs., Providence, 1970-71; spl. asst. to solicitor U.S. Dept. Labor, Washington, 1971-72; assoc. Sherman, Dunn, Cohen & Leifer, Washington, 1972-75; trial atty. FTC, Washington, 1975-88; judge Pa. Office of Hearing & Appeals, Pitts., 1988-90; judge Office of Hearings, Washington, 1990-95, judge, chief adminstrv. hearing office, 1995—; trial instr. Nat. Inst. Trial Advocacy, Washington, 1982-86, U.S. Dept. Justice, Washington, 1986—. Chair com. Cath. League for Religious Rights, Milw., 1983-84. Master Am. Inn of Ct.; mem. Am. Judges Assn., Fed. Bar Assn. (co-chair adminstrv. jud. com.), Am. Judicature Assn., Fed. Adminstrn. Law Judges Assn. (mem. exec. com.), Nat. Lawyers Assn.,Nat. Assn. Adminstrn. Law Judges. Roman Catholic. Office: Office of Chief Adminstrv Hearing Officer 5107 Leesburg Pike Ste 2519 Falls Church VA 22041

BARTOS, JERRY GARLAND, corporate executive, mechanical engineer; b. Dallas, Feb. 5, 1933; s. Vladimir Thomas and Ella Marie (Rezek) B; m. Marlene Louise Buehrer, Sept. 25, 1954 (div. 1978); children: Marla Jeanette, Sara Jane, Julie Ann; m. Candye Laverna Gould, Feb. 24, 1979; 1 child, Mary Meghan. BSME, So. Meth. U., 1954. Registered profl. engr., Tex. Sales engr. Trane Co., Dallas, 1957-61; asst. v.p. Trane Co., LaCrosse, Wis., 1961-62; chief engr. Linskie Co., Dallas, 1962-64; pres. Bartos, Inc., Dallas, 1964—; Hon. Consul Czech Republic for North Tex., 1996—. Contbr. articles to profl. jours. Mem. Dallas City Coun., 1987—; chmn. Clean Dallas, Inc., 1974, Greater Dallas Planning Coun., 1986, pres., 1984-86; bd. dirs. Dallas Ind. Sch. Dist., 1979-81; pres. North Dallas C. of C., 1975-76; hon. consul Czech Republic for North Tex., 1995—. Recipient Speakers-Authors award Am. Air Filter Co., 1972, Svc. award Luth. Ch., 1975, Life Mem. award State PTA, 1976, Rotarian award, 1993; Paul Harris fellow, 1993. Mem. Am. Soc. HVAC Engrs. (chair com. Dallas chpt. 1957—), Tex. Soc. Profl. Engrs., U.S. C. of C. (founder, regional chair small bus. orgn. 1978-79), Dallas C. of C. (vice chmn. 1976-77), North Dallas C. of C. (pres. 1975-76, chmn. 1976), Small Businessmen Assn. (Small Businessman of Yr. award 1974). Republican. Office: Bartos Inc 3239 Oradell Ln Dallas TX 75220-6040

BARTSCH, RICHARD ALLEN, chemist, educator; b. Portland, Oreg., June 7, 1940; s. Harold Emil and Myrtle Blanche (Sitz) B.; m. Nadine Laverne Putnam, Aug. 20, 1966; children: Robert Allen, Lisa Jo. BA in Chemistry, Oreg. State U., 1962, MS in Chemistry, 1963; PhD in Chemistry, Brown U., 1967. NATO postdoctoral fellow U. Wurzburg, Germany, 1967-68; asst. prof. Washington State U., Pullman, 1968-73; asst. program adminstr. Petroleum Rsch. Fund, Washington, 1973-74; assoc. prof., prof. Tex. Tech. U., Lubbock, 1974-88, Horn prof., 1988—. Contbr. more than 200 articles to profl. jours. Office: Dept of Chemistry & Biochemistry Tex Tech U Lubbock TX 79409-1061

BASANEZ, EDWARD SAMUEL, management educator; b. New Orleans, Jan. 19, 1930; s. Edward Santiago and Florence Marie (Naquin) B.; m. Jo Anne Heirtzler, Dec. 30, 1950; children: Sidney Lee, Leslie Ann. BS, La. State U., 1951; MBA, Syracuse U., 1962; EdD, La. State U., 1978. Commd. 2d lt. U.S. Army, 1951, advanced through grades to col., 1971; mil. asst. fin. mgmt. Asst. Sec. of the U.S. Army, 1971-72; comdr. 101st ABN Div. Artillery, 1972-73; chief of staff Ft. Campbell, Ky., 1973-75; v.p. Orgnl. Mgmt. Assocs., New Orleans, 1978-85; adj. mgmt. faculty Fla. Inst. Tech., New

Orleans, 1985—; exec. cons. Exxon Refining, U.S.A., Baton Rouge, 1980-85, Gulf Oil Co., Houston, 1983-85, Tenneco Oil Co., Houston, 1981-85, Middle South Utilities Inc., New Orleans, 1981-85, Bank of Am., San Francisco, 1986-87. Author: Model for Educational Television in Higher Education, 1978. J.W. Bateman fellow La. State U., 1977; decorated Legion of Merit, DFC, Bronze Star, Meritorious Svc. medal, Air medal, Army Commendation medal. Mem. U.S. Army War Coll. Alumni Assn., Omicron Delta Kappa. Episcopalian. Home: 8332 Makiki Dr Diamondhead MS 39525-4027

BASCO, JULIE ANN, poet, activist; b. Madison, Wis., Nov. 9, 1961; d. David Reid and Judith Lee (Feher) Basco; m. Robert Dalrymple, July 29, 1989 (div. Feb. 1990); m. Herbert Stanley Dew, Apr. 8, 1996; 1 child, Marcia Ariana Ledbetter. BA with honors, U. Tex., 1983, MA, 1987. Cert. tchr. ESL, 1982. Office asst. U. Tex. Librs., Austin, 1988-89; writing instr. Austin C.C., 1989-90; word processor/youth tutor Broken Chains, Internat./Regent U., Chesapeake, Va., 1991; telephone sec. Hastings Telephone Asnwering Svc., Austin, 1991-93; Montessori, toddler tchr. S.W. Child Devel. Inst., Austin, 1993; clerical staff Adia Pers. Svcs., Virginia Beach, Va., 1994—; lit./history/lang. tchr. Tabernacle of Prayer Christian Sch., Norfolk, Va., Sept. 1995; substitute tchr. Norfolk City Schs., 1995; tchg. asst. Writing Lab., U. Tex., 1985-87. Author: New Age Eve, 1987; author poetry in Austin Chronicle, 1988-89. Mem. citizens adv. bd. Capitol Met. Transp. Authority, Austin, 1993; music tchr., tutor Broken Chains, Internat., Austin, 1991, cmty. activist, 1992-93. Recipient Appreciation award AME Ch., 1992. Mem. Nat. Parks and Wildlife Conservation Assn., Phi Beta Kappa. Home: 6144 Sylvan St Norfolk VA 23508

BASHORE, ROBERT LEROY, college administrator; b. Lebanon County, Pa., Feb. 18, 1936; s. LeRoy W. and Mae M. (Weidner) B.; m. Joy Kittredge Wackerbarth, June 27, 1964; children—Scott W., Robert S. A.A., York Coll. of Pa., 1959; B.A., Defiance Coll., 1962; M.S., Radford U., 1971; Ed.D., Va. Poly. Inst. and State U., 1979. Dist. exec. Blue Ridge Council Boy Scouts Am., Roanoke, Va., 1962-69; counselor Central Va. Community Coll., Lynchburg, 1970-73, fin. aid adminstr., 1974-75, dir. admissions and student services, 1975-80, dean student services, 1980-93. Chmn. Campbell County Sch. Bd., Rustburg, Va., 1981-82, 86-87, mem., 1979-95; mem. Regional Magnet Sch. Bd., math. and sci., Lynchburg, 1985-95, chmn., 1992-93; chmn. Cen. Va. Career Fair, 1975—; chmn. Central Dist. Boy Scouts Am., Lynchburg, 1984-87, mem. exec. bd. Blue Ridge Coun., 1987, budget chmn., 1988, commr., 1991-96; EE chair Presbyn. Ch., 1989-90, elder edn. com. 1989—. Recipient Dist. Award of Merit, Boy Scouts Am., 1985, Silver Beaver award, 1990; mem. Nat. Staff Jamboree, Nat. Council Boy Scouts Am., 1981, 85; Gen. Electric fellow, 1971, Mgmt. Devel. Program, Harvard U., Grad. Sch. Edn., 1996., Berlin Seminar, Bradley U., Mem. Am. Assn. Coll. Admissions and Registrars, Va. Assn. Student Personnel Adminstrs., So. Va. Regional Sch. Bd. Assn. (pres. Charlottesville 1985-86), Assn. Psychol. Type, Phi Delta Kappa (exec. com. 1984—, rep. to Testing Service 1981—, wintergreen ski patrol 1984—, found. rep. 1986-88, v.p. program 1992—). Republican. Avocations: Snow skiing; reading; golf; travel. Home: 138 Sailview Dr Forest VA 24551-1842 Office: Central Va Community Coll 3506 Wards Rd Lynchburg VA 24502

BASHOUR, FOUAD ANIS, cardiology educator; b. Tripoli, Lebanon, Jan. 3, 1924; s. Anis E. and Mariana (Yazigi) B.; m. Val Imm, Sept. 28, 1978. BA, Am. U. of Beirut, Lebanon, 1944, MD, 1949; PhD, U. Minn., 1957. Intern Am. U. of Beirut Hosp., Beirut, 1949-50; med. officer UNRWA, 1950-51; resident in internal medicine U. Minn. Hosps., 1951-54; rsch. fellow U. Minn. Med. Schs., 1954-55; instr. in medicine U. Minn., 1955-57; rsch. assoc. Am. U. Med. Sch., Beirut, 1957, asst. prof. medicine cardiopulmonary lab. sect., 1957-59; instr. internal medicine U. Tex. Southwestern Med. Ctr., Dallas, 1959-60, assoc. prof. internal medicine, 1963-71, dir. Cardiovascular Inst., 1967-78, prof. medicine, 1971-85, prof. medicine and physiology, 1985—; mem. staff Parkland Meml. Hosp., Dallas; prof. emeritus of physiology and internal medicine, 1995—; mem. staff Zale-Lipshy Univ. Hosp., Dallas; cons. in field. Mem. editorial bd. Chest, 1963-69, Lebanese Med. Jour., 1957-59, cited in the Warren Commn. Pub; contbr. more than 200 articles to profl. publs. Elder Christ Luth. Ch., Dallas. Recipient Americanism award DAR, 1970; named Knight Order of Holy Cross Jerusalem; Fouad Bashour ann. lectr. disting. physiologist in his honor, 1974—, Fouad Bashour distinguished chair in physiology in his honor, 1990, eminent scholar, Tex., 1985. Fellow Am. Coll. Chest Physicians (emeritus), Am. Physiol. Soc. (circulation group), Am. Heart Assn. (coun. on basic sci., coun. on circulation); mem. Am. Fedn. Clin. Rsch. (emeritus), Ctrl. Soc. Clin. Rsch. (emeritus), So. Soc. Clin. Investigation (emeritus), Tex. Med. Assn., Dallas County Med. Assn., Am. Soc. Internal Medicine, Tex. Med. Found., Order of Cedars of Lebanon (officer 1971), cons. Tex. Bd. of Med. Examiners. Christian Orthodox. Office: U Tex Southwestern Med Ctr 5323 Harry Hines Blvd Dallas TX 75235

BASKARAN, MAHALINGAM, marine science educator; b. Watrap, India, May 31, 1956; came to U.S., 1987; s. Solaiappan Mahalingam and Mahalingam Seeniammal; m. Inthumathi Balasubramoniam, Apr. 23, 1983; children: Angelin R., Gracelin C. BS, Virudhunagar Hindu Nadars', Senthikumara Nadar Coll., Tamilnadu, 1977; MS, M.K. U., Madurai, Tamilnadu, 1979; PhD, Phys. Rsch. Lab., Ahmedabad, Gujarat, 1985. Postdoctoral fellow Phys. Rsch. Lab., Ahmedabad, Gujarat, 1985-87, U. Alaska, Fairbanks, 1987-88; lectr. Tex. A&M U., Galveston, 1988-92, sr. lectr., 1992—; rsch. scientist, 1995—. Contbr. articles to profl. jours; pub. over 50 peer-reviewed papers. Rsch. grantee Tex. Higher Edn. Coordinating Bd., Austin, 1992, Dept. of Energy, Washington, 1992-95, Office Naval Rsch., Washington, 1993-95. Mem. Am. Geophys. Union, Sigma Xi. Evangelical Christian. Office: Tex A&M U 5007 Avenue U Galveston TX 77551-5926

BASKERVILL, CHARLES THORNTON, lawyer; b. South Boston, Va., May 26, 1953; s. William Nelson and Julia Alice (Moore) B.; m. Pamela Temple Shell, July 17, 1976; children: Ann Cabell, Susannah Thornton. BA, Hampden-Sydney Coll., 1975; JD, U. Richmond, 1978. Bar: a. 1978, U.S. Dist. Ct. (ea. dist.) Va. 1978. Assoc. White, Hamilton, Wyche & Shell, P.C., Petersburg, Va., 1978—; asst. commonwealth's atty Petersburg, 1985-96; assoc. Shell, Johnson, Andrewss, Baskervill & Baskervill, P.C., Petersburg, 1996—; commr. of accts. City of Petersburg, Va., 1996—. Dir. Petersburg Crime Prevention Found. Named to Athletic Hall of Fame, Hampden-Sydney Coll., 1988. Mem. Prince George County Bar Assn. (sec.-treas. 1990-91, pres. 1991-92), Petersburg Bar Assn., Kiwanis Club Petersburg (past dir.). Methodist. Office: Shell Johnson Andrews Baskervill & Baskervill PC 43 Rives Rd Petersburg VA 23805

BASKETT, FRANZ KEITH, creative writing educator; b. Texarkana, Ark., July 21, 1952; s. Edward Keith and Carol June (Brown) B.; m. Nancy Gene Ruppert, May 21, 1975 (div. June 1979); m. Cynthia Dale Wise; children: Sperry, Shana, Keith. BFA in Studio Art and Painting, U. Ark., 1975, MFA in Creative Writing and Poetry, 1990. Lectr. in creative writing U. Miss., Oxford, 1991—; referee Mercher U. Press, Macon, Ga., 1992—; reader Associated Writing Program Benefit Reading Series, 1995—. Author: (poems) The Accident Prone Man, 1993; contbr. more than 60 poems to profl. jours. Reader to blind U. Svcs., U. Ark., 1989-90. Recipient Raymond L. Barnes award U. Ark. Press, 1990, prize Am. Acad. Poets, 1991, Top 10 Finisher award Coast Mag. fiction contest, 1995. Mem. AAUP, Assoc. Writing Programs, U.S. Golf Assn., Rebel Golf Assn., Amnesty Internat., Students for Environ. Awareness. Office: U Miss English Dept Oxford MS 38677

BASKIN, C(HARLES) R(ICHARD), retired civil engineer, physical scientist; b. Houston, Mar. 6, 1926; s. Charles Todd and Bessie Emma (Heilig) B.; B.S. in Civil Engring., La. State U., 1953; m. Peggy June Holden, Dec. 31, 1952; children: Richard Karl, Sheila Frances. Design engr. City-Parish Dept. Pub. Works, Baton Rouge, 1953-57; city engr. City of Plaquemine (La.), 1957-58; sect. head, asst. chief engr. Tex. Bd. Water Engrs., Austin, 1958-62; asst. chief engr. Tex. Water Commn., Austin, 1962-65; asst. chief engr. and chief engr. Tex. Water Devel. Bd., Austin, 1965-77; dir. data and engring. services div. Tex. Dept. Water Resources, Austin, 1977-83; spl. asst. Office of Asst. Dir. Info. Systems, U.S. Geol. Survey, Reston, Va., 1983-92. Chmn., Tex. Mapping Adv. Com., 1968-83, Water Oriented Data Programs sect. Tex. Interagy. Council on Natural Resources and the Environment, 1968-72, Tex. Natural Resources Info. System Task Force, 1972-83; mem. Non-Fed. Adv. Com. on Water Data for Public Use, 1970-83; chmn. Water Data Coordination Task Force, Interstate Conf. on Water Problems, 1975-83. Served with U.S. Army, 1944-47; POW; Commd. Adm. Tex. Navy, 1961; recipient John Wesley Powell award U.S. Geol. Survey, 1972, Combat Inf. badge. Mem. Phi Kappa Phi, Tau Beta Pi (chpt. pres. 1950), Chi Epsilon, Phi Eta Sigma, Sigma Tau Sigma (pres. 1950). Adventist (elder). Avocations: photography, walking. Contbr. articles to profl. jours. Home: 4824 Smallwood Rd # 195 Columbia SC 29223-3238

BASKIN, WILLIAM GRESHAM, counselor, music educator, vocalist; b. Cameron, Tex., July 14, 1933; s. James Dollar and Ruth (McKinney) B.; m. Margaret Lee Williams, Mar. 26, 1959; 1 child, Susan Elizabeth. Student, U. Tex., 1951-54; B of Music Edn., S.W. Tex. State U., 1955; postgrad., Ea. Wash. U., 1956; MEd, S.W. Tex. State U., 1961. Cert. life elem. and secondary tchr., profl. music tchrs., provisional vis. techr., profl. counselor, profl. prin., Tex.; lic. profl. counselor, Tex.; nat. cert. counselor; nat. cert. career counselor; nat. cert. sch. counselor. Choral dir. San Marcos (Tex.) Bapt. Acad., 1957-58, Carrizo Springs (Tex.) Ind. Sch. Dist., 1958-62, Victoria (Tex.) High Sch., 1962-68; counselor Brazosport Ind. Sch. Dist., Freeport, Tex., 1968—; music dir. 1st Bapt. Ch., Carrizo Springs, 1958-62, Bapt. Temple, Victoria, 1962-64; interim music dir. 1st Bapt. ch., Victoria, 1965, Freeport, 1972-73, 87-88, 89, Lake Jackson, Tex., 1978-79, Temple Bapt. Ch., Clute, Tex., 1990; mem. Music Educators Nat. conf., 1958-68; del. Am. Mental Health Counselors Assn. and Citizen Amb. Program People to People Internat. to Chinese Assn. Mental Health and Chinese Assn. for Sci. and Tech. of People's Republic of China in Beijing, Shanghai and Kunming, 1994; del. from Am. Sch. Counselor's Assn. and Citizen Amb. Program of People to People Internat. to 1st U.S./Russia Joint Conf. on Edn., Moscow, 1994. Mem. Victoria Fine Arts Assn. (pres. 1964-66), 1963-68; mem. Brazosport Fine Arts Coun., Lake Jackson, 1970-73, Brazoria County Hist. Mus., Angleton, Tex., 1990—; del. Tex. Gov.'s Conf. on Arts, Austin, 1966-68; del. Dem. Precinct Conv., Lake Jackson, 1976, 77, 93, Brazoria County Dem. Conv., Angleton, 1977, Tex. Dem. Conv., San Antonio, 1977; deacon 1st Bapt. Ch., Lake Jackson, 1989, also youth worker. Scholar PTA, Victoria, 1966. Mem. Music Educator's Nat. Conf., NEA (del. 1977-79), Am. Sch. Counselors Assn., Nat. Career Devel. Assn., Assn. for Specialists in Group Work, Assn. for Measurement and Evaluation in Counseling and Devel., Tex. Assn. for Measurement and Evaluation in Counseling and Devel., Tex. Career Guidance Assn., Tex. Sch. Counselors Assn., Tex. Assn. for Counseling and Devel. (senator 1979-82, legis. com. 1984-87), Tex. Music Educators Assn. (state bd. dirs. 1964-68, dist. choral chmn. 1964-68), Tex. State Schrs. Assn., Brazosport Edn. Assn. (pres. 1977-78), Brazoria County Assn. Counseling and Devel. (legis. chmn. 1984—), Rotary (Brazosport club, Paul Harris fellow 1988). Home: 111 Oyster Bend Ln Lake Jackson TX 77566-3105 Office: Brazosport Ind Sch Dist PO Drawer Z Freeport TX 77541

BASS, CAROL ANN (MITZI), English language educator; b. Dallas, Aug. 29, 1951; d. Charles Eugene and Lucy (Patrick) Watson; m. Harold F. Bass, Jr., Jan. 8, 1972; children: Jessica, Franklin. BA with honors, George Peabody Coll. Tchrs., Nashville, 1973; MA, George Peabody Coll. Tchrs., 1974. Tchr. Battle Ground Acad., Franklin, Tenn., 1974-77; adj. instr. Henderson State U., Arkadelphia, Ark., 1985-94; instr. Henderson State U., 1994—. Deacon 1st Bapt. Ch., Arkadelphia, 1993—; vol. Clark County Election Com., Arkadelphia, 1996, Am. Cancer Soc., Arkadelphia, 1985—; bd. dirs. Group Living, Inc., Arkadelphia, 1995—. Mem. AAUP, Nat. Coun. Tchrs. English, Sigma Tau Delta, Pi Beta Phi. Democrat. Office: Henderson State U 1100 Henderson St Arkadelphia AR 71999

BASS, DANIEL BARRY, lawyer; b. Detroit, Apr. 5, 1944; s. Henry R. and Dorothy P. (Webb) B.; divorced; children: David Alan, Jonathan Brooke. BA, U. Fla., 1965, JD, 1967. Bar: Fla. 1968; cert. mediator in family law and cir. ct. civil; cert. arbitrator. Atty. Broward Legis. Del., Ft. Lauderdale, Fla., 1969, Tallahassee, 1969; city prosecutor City of Sunrise (Fla.)., 1973-76; pvt. practice, pvt. practice, Ft. Lauderdale, 1968-86; with Bench & Bar Mediations, Inc., Ft. Lauderdale, 1994—. Mem. Fla. House Reps., Talahassee, 1972-74. Mem. Oak Tree Country Club, Lifespring. Republican. Baptist. Office: Bench & Bar Mediations Inc 1995 E Oakland Park Blvd Fort Lauderdale FL 33306-1137

BASS, GEORGE FLETCHER, archaeology educator; b. Columbia, S.C., Dec. 9, 1932; s. Robert Duncan and Virginia (Wauchope) B.; m. Ann Singletary, Mar. 19, 1960; children: Gordon Wauchope, Alan Joseph. MA, Johns Hopkins U., 1955; PhD, U. Pa., 1964; PhD (hon.), Bogazici U., Istanbul, Turkey, 1987. Asst. prof. U. Pa., Phila., 1964-68, assoc. prof., 1968-73; prof. archaeology Tex. A&M U., College Sta., 1976-80, Disting. prof., 1980—, George T. and Gladys H. Abell prof. nautical archaeology, 1986—; Yamini Family prof., 1994—; dir. excavations of ancient shipwrecks off Turkish coast, 1960—. Author: Archaeology Under Water, 1966, Cape Gelidonya, 1967, History of Seafaring, 1972, Archaeology Beneath the Sea, 1975, Yassi Ada I, 1982, Ships and Shipwrecks of the Americas, 1988; adv. editor Am. Jour. Archaeology, 1987—, Archaeology, 1987—, Internat. Jour. Nautical Archaeology, 1987—, Nat. Geog. Rsch., 1987-94. Served to lt. U.S. Army, 1957-59, Korea. Recipient Centennial award Nat. Geog. Soc., 1988, La. Gorce Gold medal, 1979, Lowell Thomas award Explorers Club, 1986; named one of Outstanding Young Men of Yr., Jaycees, 1967. Mem. Inst. Nautical Archaeology (pres. 1973-82), Archaeol. Inst. Am. (Gold medal for disting. archaeol. achievement 1986), Soc. for Hist. Archaeology, Nat. Maritime Hist. Soc., Mothers Against Drunk Driving. Presbyterian. Home: 1600 Dominik Dr College Station TX 77840-3623 Office: Tex A&M U Nautical Archaeology College Station TX 77843-4352

BASS, GEORGE HAROLD, religious organization administrator; b. Nashville, Feb. 23, 1936; s. Harold G. and Marjorie (Owens) B.; m. Lorena Johnson, June 7, 1957; children: Patricia Jo Bass Pulley, Janet Gail Bass Drake. BSCE, Tenn. Tech. U., 1958; Cert. Mgmt., U. Tenn., 1979. Profl. engr., Tenn. Youth dir. Waverly Place United Meth. Ch., Nashville, 1961-69, Blakemore United Meth. Ch., Nashville, 1969-77; exec. dir. Mountain Top/Tenn. Outreach Project, Nashville, 1974—; owner, cons. George Bass & Assocs., Nashville, 1987—; dist. youth coord. Tenn. Conf. United Meth. Ch., Nashville, 1971-73; chmn. coun. on ministries, Blakemore United Meth. Ch., Nashville, 1983-85; bd. global ministries, Tenn. Conf. United Meth. Ch., Nashville, 1987—. Bd. dirs. Tenn. Conf. Children's Agy., 1990-94; bd. dirs., vice-chair Opportunity House, 1993—; mem. adv. coun. Trust for the Future, 1994—. 1st lt. artillery U.S. Army, 1958-66. Mem. Am. Soc. Tng. and Devel. (Torch award 1977), Christian Camping Internat. Office: Mountain TOP 2704 12th Ave S Nashville TN 37204-2506

BASS, HAROLD FRANKLIN, JR., political science educator; b. Corpus Christi, Dec. 4, 1948; s. Franklin and Bettye Jane (Sparkman) B.; m. Carol Ann Watson, Jan. 8, 1972; children: Jessica Marie, Franklin Sparkman. BA, Baylor U., 1971; MA, Vanderbilt U., 1974, Ph.D., 1978. Instr. polit. sci. Ouachita Baptist U., Arkadelphia, Ark., 1976-78, asst. prof., 1978-83, assoc. prof., 1983-89, prof., 1989-96, Moody prof. prelaw studies, 1996—, chmn. dept., 1979—, chmn. divsn. social scis., 1990—; exec. dir. Maddox Pub. Affairs Ctr., 1986—. Author: (with others) Presidents and their Parties: Leadership or Neglect, 1984, The End of Realignment: Interpreting American Electoral Eras, 1991, Leadership and the Bush Presidency: Prudence or Drift in an Era of Change, 1992, Building Democracy in One Party Systems Theoretical Perspectives and Cross-National Experiences, 1993; mem. editorial bd. Ark. Polit. Sci. Jour. (now Am. Rev. of Politics), 1983—. Named Outstanding Faculty Mem. student senate Ouachita Bapt. U., 1978-79, 83-84, 87-88, 92-93. Mem. Am. Polit. Sci. Assn., Southwestern Polit. Sci. Assn. (sec.- treas.), Ark. Polit. Sci. Assn., AAUP, Ctr. for Study of Presidency, Alpha Kappa Psi, Sigma Phi Epsilon. Baptist. Club: Arkadelphia Country. Avocation: golf. Home: 828 N Park Dr Arkadelphia AR 71923-3526 Office: Ouachita Baptist U Dept Polit Sci Arkadelphia AR 71998-0001

BASS, MARY CATHERINE, clinical social worker, psychotherapist; b. Magnolia, N.C., Aug. 10, 1941; d. Paul and Louise Katherine (Peterson) B. BA, Wake Forest U., 1963; MDiv, Southeastern Bapt. Theol. Sem., 1967; MSW, U. N.C., 1972; postgrad., Georgetown U., 1978-82. Cert. clin. social worker; cert. marital and family therapist; cert. med. psychotherapist; diplomate Am. Bd. Med. Psychotherapy. Tchr. biology and earth sci. James Kenan High Sch., Warsaw, N.C., 1963-64; social worker Bapt. Children's Home of N.C., 1967-68, 1969-71; unit coord. Meth. Home for Children, Raleigh, N.C., 1972-73; family counselor III and clin. supr. Family Svcs. for Wake County, Inc., 1973-81; contract counselor Life Enrichment Ctr., Raleigh, 1983-84; pvt. practice individual, marital and family psychotherapy Raleigh, 1981—; clin. social worker, clin. supr. social work staff Dorothea Dix Hosp., 1981-86; clin. assoc. individual, marital and family psychotherapy Carolina Psychiatry, Raleigh, 1986-94; dir. Ea. N.C. Family Ctr., 1994—; cons. Med. Staff Health Care Affiliate, Charter Northridge Hosp., 1986—, Holly Hill Hosp., 1991—, Duplin County Coop. Ext. Svcs., Kenansville, N.C., 1994—; clergy cons., counselor Pullem Meml. Bapt. Ch., Raleigh, 1970s; cons., supr. Bowen Family Therapy, 1981—; cons., med. psychotherapist Goshen Med. Ctr., 1994—; field faculty Sch. Social Work ECU, 1995; lectr. in field; condr. workshops in field. Contbr. to book: The Aggressive Adolescent, 1984. Active Friends of the Arboretum, Raleigh, 1985—. Mem. NASW, AAUW, Acad. Cert. Social Workers, N.C. Bd. Marital and Family Therapists, Am. Family Therapy Acad. (clin. mem.), Am. Forestry Assocs., N.C. Forestry Assocs., Carolina Farm Stewardship Assn. Home: 1210 Harwich Ct Raleigh NC 27609-3958 also: PO Box 63 Magnolia NC 28453 Office: 219 E Carron St PO Box 63 Magnolia NC 28453 also: 8404-B Glenwood Ave Raleigh NC 27613

BASS, PERRY RICHARDSON, oil company executive; b. Wichita Falls, Tex., Nov. 11, 1914; s. E. Perry and Annie (Richardson) B.; m. Nancy Lee Muse, June 28, 1941; children: Sid R., Edward P., Robert M., Lee M. B.S. in Geology, Yale U., 1937; D. Humanitarian Service (hon.), Tex. Christian U., 1983; LHD (hon.), Yale U., 1993. Chmn. Sid Richardson Carbon & Gas, Ft. Worth, 1959—; pres. Perry R. Bass, Inc., Ft. Worth, 1941—, also dir.; pres. Sid Richardson Found., Ft. Worth, 1960—, also dir.; dir. Bass Enterprises Prodn. Co., Ft. Worth; mem. ad hoc com. Tex. Energy and Natural Resources Adv. Com.; mem. exec. com. Nat. Petroleum Council, 1961-75, Nat. Oil Policy Commn. on Possible Future Petroleum Problems; designer, builder fireboats for U.S. Navy. Chmn. Tex. Parks and Wildlife Commn., 1977-83, chmn. emeritus, 1988—; mem. adv. com. bd. visitors Univ. Cancer Found. of M.D. Andersen Hosp. and Tumor Inst. Recipient Silver Beaver award Boy Scouts Am., 1965, Silver Antelope award, 1969, Silver Buffalo award, 1976; Golden Deed award Ft. Worth Exchange Club, 1967; Disting. Civic Service award Dallas/Ft. Worth Hosp. Council, 1983, Conservation award Chevron, 1988, Bus. Hall of Fame Tex., 1989, Charles Goodnight award Star-Telegram & Nat. Cutting Horse Assn., 1991, Conservationist of the Yr. Tex. Outdoor Writer's Citizens, 1992, Humanitarian Newsmaker of the Yr. Ft. Worth Chpt. Soc. Profl. Journalist and Tex. Gridiron Club, 1992, Conservationist of the Yr. Sportsmen Conservationists of Tex., 1992. Mem. Am. Assn. Petroleum Geologists, Am. Petroleum Inst. (exec. com.), All Am. Wildcatters, Ind. Petroleum Assn. Am., Tex. Mid-Continent Oil and Gas Assn. (exec. com., City Club of Ft. Worth, Ft. Worth Boat Club, River Crest Country Club (Ft. Worth), Petroleum Club of Ft. Worth, N.Y. Yacht Club, Royal Ocean Racing Club (London). Office: Richardson Sid Carbon & Gas Co 201 Main St Fort Worth TX 76102-3105

BASSETT, LISA JANE, English language educator, author; b. Winter Park, Fla., Jan. 26, 1958; d. Samuel Taylor and Barbara Jane (Crisler) B.; m. J. William Johnston. BA with honors in English, Rollins Coll., 1984; MA in English, U. Tex., 1986, PhD, 1992. Lectr. tech. comm. dept. elec. and computer engring. U. Tex., Austin, 1992-95. Author: A Clock for Beany, 1985, Beany and Scamp, 1987, Very Truly Yours, Charles L. Dodgson, Alias Lewis Carroll, 1987, Beany Wakes Up for Christmas, 1988, Koala Christmas, 1991, Ten Little Bunnies, 1993, The Bunnies' Alphabet Eggs, 1993. Mem. MLA.

BASSFORD, DANIEL JOSEPH, marketing and business planning executive; b. Caro, Mich., Jan. 31, 1949; s. Joseph Daniel and Marcia Faye (Gohs) B.; m. Janet Claire Osgerby, June 20, 1970; children: Christine Anne, Catherine Lynne, Laura Elizabeth. BSME, We. Mich. U., 1972; MBA, Bowling Green State U., 1991. Design engr. Tappan Appliance Co., Mansfield, Ohio, 1972-75, project engr., 1975-76; sales engr. Dana Corp., Cleve., 1976-79; dist. sales mgr. Dana Corp., Cin., 1979-81, regional sales mgr., 1981-82; mgr. distbr. sales Dana Corp., Toledo, 1982-83, dir. corp. planning, 1985-87; mktg. mgr. Dana Corp., Ft. Wayne, Ind., 1983-85; mgr. spl. projects SBI Corp., Ft. Wayne, 1987-88, mktg. mgr., 1988-89; dir. mktg. and bus. planning Sprague Devices, Inc., Michigan City, Ind., 1989-91; dir. mktg. Korody-Colyer, Compton, Calif., 1992-94; dir. mktg. and sales Hurd Corp., 1994-96; field parts sales mgr. Western Star Trucks, Inc., 1996—. Mem. Soc. Automotive Engrs., Planning Forum. Republican. Presbyterian.

BASS-RUBENSTEIN, DEBORAH SUE, social worker, educator, consultant; b. Springfield, Ill., Jan. 21, 1951; d. Ralph and Dorothy Bernice (Feuer) Bass; m. Jeffrey Rubenstein, Oct. 12, 1975; children: Jonathan, Benjamin. BA, MSW, U. Ill., 1973. Social worker Dept. Human Resources, Washington, 1974-75; analyst Asst. Sec. for Planning and Evaluation, Washington, 1975-76, Adminstrn. for Pub. Svcs., Washington, 1976-79, Health Care Financing Adminstrn., Washington, 1979; sr. analyst OHDS, Washington, 1979-83, 84-87, Adminstrn. on Aging, Washington, 1983-84; dir. Office Human Devel. Svcs., Exec. Secretariat, HHS, Washington, 1987-90; cons. and pres. Deborah Bass Assocs., Manassas, Va., 1990—; assoc. faculty Johns Hopkins Sch. Continuing Studies, 1993; sec. U.S. com. Internat. Coun. on Social Welfare, Washington, 1991-93, bd. dirs., 1987-90; convenor Fed. Social Workers Consortium, Washington, 1986-90; participant Dartmouth-Hitchcock Med. Ctr. Project on Family Support, 1993; co-facilitator Unity in the Community, 1995—, chair, 1996—; mem. multi-cultural com. Prince William County Sch. Divsn., 1993—; chair civic affairs com. Congregation Ner Shalom Sisterhood, 1996—. Author: Caring Families, 1990, Helping Vulnerable Youths, 1992; contbr. Ency. Social Work, 1995. Chmn. Congregation Nev Shalom Sisterhood civic affairs com., 1996—; co-pres. Coles Sch. PTO, Manassas, 1987-88; bd. dirs. Mid-County Coalition, Prince William County, Va., 1986; mem. multi-cultural com. Prince William County Sch. Divsn., 1993—; co-facilitator Citizens of Faith/Citizens Concerned About Discrimination in Prince William County, 1994-95; co-facilitator Unity in the Cmty., 1995—, chmn., 1996; mem. polit. affairs com. Jewish Cmty. Ctr. No. Va., 1995—. James scholar U. Ill., 1969-73. Mem. NASW (poetry com. 1988-90). Home and Office: 7092 Kings Arms Dr Manassas VA 20112-3237

BAST, ROBERT CLINTON, JR., medical researcher, medical educator; b. Washington, Dec. 8, 1943; s. Robert Clinton and Ann Christine (Borland) B.; m. Blanche Amy Simpson, Oct. 21, 1972; 1 child, Elizabeth Simpson Bast. BA cum laude, Wesleyan U., Middletown, Conn., 1965; MD magna cum laude, Harvard U., 1971. Diplomate Am. Bd. Internal Medicine, Am. Bd. Med. Oncology, Am. Bd. Hematology. Predoctoral fellow dept. pathology Mass. Gen. Hosp., Boston, 1967-69; intern Johns Hopkins Hosp., Balt., 1971-72; research assoc. biology br. Nat. Cancer Inst., NIH, Bethesda, Md., 1972-74, research scientist biology br., 1974-75; asst. resident Peter Bent Brigham Hosp., Boston, 1975-76; fellow med. oncology Sidney Farber Cancer Inst., Boston, 1976-77; asst. prof. medicine Harvard U. Med. Sch., Boston, 1977-83, assoc. prof., 1983-84; prof. Duke U. Med. Ctr., Durham, N.C., 1984-92, Wellcome clin. prof. medicine in honor of R. Wayne Rundles, 1992-94, co-dir. div. hematology-oncology, 1984-94; dir. clin. research programs Duke U. Comprehensive Cancer Ctr., Durham, 1984-87; dir., 1987-94; Harry Carothers Wiess chair cancer rsch. U. Tex. Cancer Ctr., 1987-94, head med. divsn., 1994—; dir. divsn. med. oncology dept. medicine U. Tex. Health Sci. Ctr., Houston, 1994—; hosp. appointments include asst. in medicine Peter Bent Brigham Hosp., 1976-77; jr. assoc. in medicine Brigham and Women's Hosp., 1977-82; cons. oncologist Boston Hosp. Women, 1978-80; mem. biol. response modifiers decision network com. Nat. Cancer Inst., 1984-87, exptl. immunology study sect., 1983-84, 90-92; mem. grant rev. com. Leukemia Soc. Am., 1985-87, adv. com. oncologic drugs FDA, 1985-89, chmn. 1988-89; bd. dirs. Cancer and Leukemia Group B., 1986-88, Am. Council Transplantation, 1985-87; mem. grant rev. com. Am. Cancer Soc., 1987; numerous other coms.; Edward G. Waters Meml. lectr., 1987; John Ohtani Meml. lectr., 1991; D. Nelson Henderson lectr., 1991; Stolte Meml. lectr., 1992; Arnold O. Beckman Disting. Lectureship, 1993. Contbr. numerous articles on tumor immunology, immunodiagnosis and immunotherapy of cancer and cellular immunology to profl. jours. Served as surgeon USPHS, 1972-75. Recipient Dominus award, 1984, Robert C. Knapp award, 1990, Recognition Outstanding Leadership and Advocacy award Nat. Coalition for Cancer Rsch., 1995; grantee Nat. Cancer Inst., NIH, HHS, 1978—; scholar Leukemia Soc. Am., 1978-83. Fellow ACP; mem. The Reticuloendothelial Soc., Am. Soc. Microbiology, Am. Assn. Cancer Rsch., Am. Assn. Immunologists, Assn. Am. Physicians, Am. Soc. Clin. Oncology, Am. Fedn. Clin. Rsch., Am. Soc. Clin. Investigation, Internat. Soc. Immunopharmacology, Soc. Biol. Therapy (bd. dirs. 1984-86), Am. Soc. Hematology, Soc. Gynecol. Oncology (assoc.). Office: U Tex MD Anderson Cancer Ctr 1515 Holcombe Blvd Box 092 Houston TX 77030-4009

BASTIEN, CAROL LANGFORD, librarian; b. Dothan, Ala., Nov. 4, 1944; d. Earnest L. and Lilie Edna (Davis) Langford; m. Bill T. Bastien, Aug. 21, 1965. BS in Secondary Edn., Troy (Ala.) State U., 1967. Adj. tchr. freshman English lab. Troy (Ala.) State Coll., 1966; tchr. English and social studies Houston County Sch. Sys., Dothan, 1967-79; acquisitions libr. Southwestern Bapt. Theol. Sem., Ft. Worth, 1979—. Mem. So. Bapt. Librs. Assn., Southwestern Assn. Theol. Librs. Office: Roberts Libr PO Box 22000 Fort Worth TX 76122-1490

BASU, SUNANDA, scientific administrator, researcher in space physics; b. Calcutta, West Bengal, India, Dec. 9, 1940; d. Chunilal and Amita Chatterjee Ganguli; m. Santimay Basu, Apr. 5, 1961; 1 child, Susanto. BSc in Physics, Calcutta (India) U., 1960, PhD in Radio Physics, 1972; AM in Physics, Boston U., 1963. Rsch. assoc. Inst. Radio Physics, U. Calcutta, India, 1973-75; NAS resident rsch. assoc. Air Force Geophysics Lab., Hanscom AFB, Mass., 1975-78; sr. physicist Emmanuel Coll., Boston, 1978-89; sr. rsch. physicist Inst. Space Rsch., Boston Coll., 1989-92; program dir. aeronomy, atmospheric scis. divsn. NSF, Arlington, Va., 1992—; mem. com. Solar Terrestrial Rsch. Panel on Jicamarca Radio Obs., Peru, 1980-83; chairperson CEDAR Working Group on High Latitude Plasma Structure, 1987-92, STEP WG3 Project on Global Aspects of Plasma Structures, 1990—, USNC/URSI Commn. G, 1994—, mem. exec. com., 1988-90, vice chairperson, 1991-93; mem. adv. com. atmospheric scis. NSF, 1988-92; organizer CEDAR/HLPS & STEP/GAPS Workshop, Peaceful Valley, Colo., 1992; cons. Ctr. Space Rsch. MIT, Cambridge, Mass., 1991-92; active U.S. Nat. Delegation to Internat. Sci. Radio Union Gen. Assemblies, 1981, 84, 87, 90, 93. Author chpts. to books; contbr. over 60 papers, articles to profl. jours. Mem. AAAS, Am. Geophy. Union, Internat. Sci. Radio Union (mem. commns. G and H), Sigma Xi (pres. Hanscom chpt. 1986-87). Office: NSF 4201 Wilson Blvd Rm 775 Arlington VA 22230-0001

BASZTO, THEODORE FRANCIS, JR., financial planner; b. Rochester, N.Y., Dec. 10, 1954; s. Theodore Francis Sr. and Evelyn Mae (Rogers) B.; m. Maryjoy Burgess, Nov. 16, 1951; children: Theodore Francis III, Barron Arthur, Ashley Victoria. Student, St. John Fisher Coll., 1973-74; AA in Psychology, Manatee Community Coll., 1976; student, U. South Fla., 1976-83. V.p. Warm Mineral Springs (Fla.) Motel, 1975-89; assoc. Sam H. Herron Jr. Realtors, Warm Mineral Springs, 1976-84; real estate instr., regional tnr. Century 21 Acad. Real Estate, Miami, Fla., 1979-92; pvt. practice real estate Warm Mineral Springs, 1984-89. Bd. dirs. Sarasota (Fla.) Com. 100, 1983-84; candidate dist. 71 Fla. Ho. Reps., 1984; exec. com. Sarasota County Rep., 1984-87; founding dir. Triangle Econ. Devel. Authority, 1985-89, pres., 1987-88; co-chmn. Sarasota County Blue Chip Com., 1985; adv. bd. dirs. Englewood Bank, 1988-90. Mem. Punta Gorda-Port Charlotte Bd. Realtors (edn. chmn. 1986), North Port Area C. of C. (founding pres. 1986-87), Manatee C.C. Alumni Assn. (bd. dirs. 1985-87), Kiwanis (pres. North Port chpt. 1983-84). Roman Catholic. Office: 1 Sarasota Tower 2 N Tamiami Trl Ste 604 Sarasota FL 34236-5559

BATA, RUDOLPH ANDREW, JR., lawyer; b. Akron, Ohio, Jan. 9, 1947; s. Rudolph Andrew and Margaret Eleanor (Ellis) B.; m. Genevieve Ruth Brannan, Aug. 25, 1968 (div. May 1985); 1 child, Seth Andrew; m. Linda Lee Waldo, May 7, 1985; 1 child, Sarah Ariel. BS, So. Coll., Collegedale, Tenn., 1969; JD, Emory U., 1972. Bar: D.C. 1973, N.C. 1978, U.S. Dist. Ct. N.C. 1991, U.S. Ct. Appeals (4th cir.) 1991; cert. mediator AOC. Assoc. ICC, Washington, 1972-73; in house counsel B.F. Saul Real Estate Investment Trust, Chevy Chase, Md., 1973-74; staff atty. Martha, Cafferky, Powers & Jordan, Washington, 1974-75; asst. corp. counsel Hardee's Food Systems, Inc., Rocky Mount, N.C., 1975-78; ptnr. Bata & Blomeley, Murphy, N.C., 1978-87, 88-90, Bata & Sumpter, Murphy, 1987-88; sole practice Murphy, 1990—. Bd. dirs. Cherokee County United Fund, Murphy, 1981-83. Mem. ABA, N.C. Bar Assn., D.C. Bar Assn., 30th Jud. Dist. Bar Assn., So. Soc. of Adventist Attys. (pres. 1984-85), Cherokee County C. of C. (bd. dirs. 1980-82). Office: 302 Valley River Ave Murphy NC 28906-2923

BATCH, MARY LOU, guidance counselor, educator; b. McKeesport, Pa.. BS in Edn., Cen. State U., Wilberforce, Ohio, 1970; MS in Spl. Edn., Syracuse U., 1971; PhD in Counselor Edn., U. Pitts., 1982. Cert. in spl. and elem. edn., Ohio; cert. in elem. and mid. sch. edn., secondary guidance, Va.; cert. in NK-8 edn., edn. of mentally retarded, Va. Various edn. and counseling positions Va. schs., military and other insts., 1965-72; tchr. adult edn. Big Bend C.C., Germany. Am. Coll. System Overseas, 1973-75; counselor, coord. U. Pitts., 1975-79; asst. prof. spl. edn. Ind. U. of Pa., 1979-85; testing specialist C.C. of Allegheny County, Braddock Ctr., Pa., 1985-86; guidance counselor Henrico H.S., Henrico County Schs., Richmond, Va., 1987—, John Rolfe Middle Sch., Richmond, 1991-96, Maude Trevett Elem. Sch., 1996—; edn. specialist U.S. Govt. in Germany, 1974-75; cons., workshop conductor, in Pa., N.J., Va. at ednl. facilities, civic orgns. and with parent groups, 1978—; mem. So. States Evaluation Team, Manassas Va., 1988; mem. peer advisor steering com. and student peer advisor supr. Henrico High Sch., 1987-90. extended del. position Citizen Ambassador Program of People to People Internat. to Soviet Union and Hungary, Am. Sch. Counselor Assn., 1991, U.S./China Joint Conf. on Edn., 1992. Bd. dirs. Richmond Residential Svcs., 1989—, sec., 1990-91, chmn. program and planning com., 1991-92, vice chmn., 1992—; group facilitator Henrico County Ct. Alternative; mem. Henrico County Edn. 2000 Commn., mem. action team; active in Head Start movement and teen parenting counseling; mem. Statewide Mid. Sch. Coun., 1994—; mem. tech. pres. steering com. Henrico County Pub. Schs., 1994—; active Nat. Multiple Sclerosis Soc., inductee leadership cir., 1995; mem. steering com. Tech Prep Henrico County, Richmond, Va., 1994-95; mid. sch. state rep. coun. mem., 1995. Inductee, Nat. Leadership Circle. Mem. LWV, ASCD, Am. Fedn. Tchrs., Nat. Coun. of Negro Women, Va. Personnel and Guidance Assn., Va. Sch. Counselors Assn., Richmond Personnel and Guidance Assn., Henrico County Guidance Assn. (pres. 1989-91), Va. Assn. Multicultural Devel., Greater Richmond Involved Parents, Nat. Coun. for Self Esteem, Nat. Coun. Sr. Citizens, Alpha Kappa Mu, Zeta Phi Beta. Home: 5022 W Seminary Ave Richmond VA 23227-3408 Office: John Rolfe Mid Sch 6901 Messer Rd Richmond VA 23231-5507

BATCHELOR, RUBY STEPHENS, retired nurse; b. Rocky Mount, N.C., Sept. 27, 1931; d. Paul Madison and Ruby Leigh (Coggins) Stephens; m. Sherwood H. Batchelor, Nov. 1, 1952; children: Paula S. Liggon, G. Brooks. Diploma, Wilson Sch. Nursing, 1953; student, Atlantic Christian Coll. Cert. med./surg. nurse. Assessment nurse Wilson (N.C.) Meml. Hosp., head nurse pediatrics, primary care nurse ob./gyn. unit, primary care nurse med./surg. unit, primary care nurse psychiat. unit, 1991-93, ret., 1993; organizer Al-A-Non, Wilson, N.C., 1973. Deacon Westview Christian Ch., 1995, 96, 97. cjmn. membership com., 1996. Mem. N.C. Nurse's Assn. (past dist. pres.), Am. Nurses' Assn. Home: 1300 Dogwood Ln NW Wilson NC 27896-1420

BATEMAN, HERBERT HARVELL, congressman; b. Elizabeth City, N.C., Aug. 7, 1928; m. Laura Yacobi; children: Herbert Harvell, Laura Margaret. B.A., Coll. William and Mary, 1949; J.D., Georgetown U., 1956. Bar: Va. 1956. Practice law Newport News, Va., 1957-82; law clk. U.S. Ct. Appeals for D.C. Cir., 1956-57; mem. firm Jones, Blechman, Woltz & Kelly, 1957-82; mem. Va. Senate, 1968-82, chmn. consumer credit study commn., 1970-74, chmn. milk commn. study commn., 1973-75; mem. 98th-104th Congresses from 1st Va. dist., Washington, D.C.; mem. House com. on sci. and tech., 1982-84; mem. House merchant marine com., 1982-94; mem. House armed svcs. com. (name now nat. security com.), 1984—; co-chmn. Congrl. Space Caucus, 1984—; founder Va. Joint Legis. Audit and Rev. Commn.; ranking Rep. Merchant Marine Subcom.; mem. House transp. and infrastructure com., 1995—; chmn. subcom. on mil. readiness, 1995—. Mem. adv. bd. Mary Immaculate Hosp. Newport News; pres. Peninsula United Fund, 1966-67; chmn. Peninsula Arena-Auditorium Authority, 1964-68; pres. Newport News Homeownership Assn., 1969-71; commr. Peninsula Ports Authority Va., 1969-74; bd. dirs. Peninsula Econ. Devel. Council, 1968—; coordinator Citizens for Rev. Constrn., 1970; chmn. Heart Fund campaign, Newport News, 1971. Served to 1st lt. USAF, 1951-53. Mem. Va. Jaycees (past pres.), U.S. Jaycees (gen. legal counsel 1962-63), Hampton Roads Jaycees (hon. pres. 1960-63), Peninsula C. of C. (chmn. legis. com. 1970-72), Newport News Propeller Club, Omicron Delta Kappa, Phi Delta Phi, Pi Kappa Alpha. Republican. Office: US Ho of Reps 2350 Rayburn HOB Washington DC 20515

BATEMAN, JOHN ROGER, investment holding company executive; b. Medford, Oreg., Sept. 21, 1927; s. Joseph Nielson and Bessie Mable (Jackson) B.; children: David, Sally, Susan; m. Freddie Orlean Johnson, 1984; stepchildren: Randy, Kirk. Student, U. Redlands, 1944-45, Mont. Sch. Mines, 1945, Colo. Coll., 1945-46, San Diego State Coll., 1948; BS with honors, U. Calif., Berkeley, 1951, MBA, 1952. CPA, Tex., Calif. Acctg. trainee Standard Oil Co. Calif., San Francisco, 1952; sr. acct. Slavik & Ponder, CPAs, Corpus Christi, Tex., 1953-57; chief acct. Coastal States Corp., Corpus Christi, 1957-59, treas., 1959-66, v.p. fin., 1963-66; mng. ptnr. Bateman Investments, Corpus Christi, 1967—; with Bateman Alamo Group, Ltd., 1971-74, Bateman Meridian Group Ltd., 1972-75; mng. ptnr. Bateman Luxor Group Ltd., 1969-76; pres., chmn. bd. Bay Fabricators, Inc., 1973-78, dir., 1972-78; pres., chmn. bd. Bay Industries, Inc., 1975-78, Bateman Industries, Inc., 1976—, Bay Heat Transfer Corp., 1977-81; v.p., treas., dir. Integral Petroleum Corp., 1973-75; with Integral Energy Corp., 1975-79, Camden Drilling Co., 1974-79, Integral Drilling Co., 1974-79; dir. Guaranty Nat. Bank, 1972-75; ptnr. Jaro Leasing, 1980-85; dir. Summit Geophys. Internat., Inc., 1980-82; ptnr. Act I Properties, 1981-84, First City Tower II, 1981—; chmn. bd. dirs. Bajon Signs Co., 1982; ptnr. Bajon Investments, 1980-87; chmn. bd. Bajon Corp., 1980-87, Bajon Devel. Corp., 1981-83. Bd. dirs., pres., treas. Little Theatre Corpus Christi, 1964-68; ofcl. bd. 1st United Meth. Ch., 1964-67, 70-73, 78-80, 84-85; bd. govs. United Way Coastal Bend, 1964-67, 73-83, campaign chmn., 1977, pres., 1981; mem. exec. coun. USO, 1971-73; mem. YMCA Capital Devel. Camp Com., 1982, YWCA Capital Fund Adv. Com., 1982-85, co-chmn. YWCA Capital Fund Drive, 1985-87; chmn. So. Shore Christian Ch. Bldg. Renewal Camp, 1986, chmn. vision 2010 campaign, 1994—, elder, 1996—; bd. dirs. Camp Fire Girls, 1967-69; Tex. Bd. Mental Health and Mental Retardation, 1981-88, vice chmn., 1985-87, chmn., 1987-88; mem. Tex. Health and Human Svcs. Planning Coun., 1987-88; del. Rep. Party of Tex. Convention, 1972, 76, 84, 90; Tex. mem. Nat. Rep. Senatorial Com., 1978-81, Rep. Eagles, 1980-81; mem. Rep. Govs. Assn., 1980-81; co-chmn. Tex. Rep. Fin. Com., 1980-81.; bd. dirs. Crippled Children's Found. South Tex., 1985-86; chmn. adv. bd. Corpus Christi Salvation Army, 1990-91; bd. mgrs. Meml. Med. Ctr., 1990-94; mem. dist. bd. mgrs. Nueces County Hosp., 1990-94, 96—, vice-chmn., 1991-94; mem. Nueces County Mental Health and Mental Retardation Found. Bd., 1990—, vice-chmn., 1996—; chmn. Nueces County Psychiatric Crisis Svcs., 1992-94; trustee Nueces County Mental Health and Mental Retardation, 1996—. Lt. (j.g.) UNSR, 1945-50. Mem. Tex. Soc. CPAs, Navy League U.S., Confederate Air Force, Pima Air Mus., Nueces Club, Rotary, Phi Beta Kappa, Beta Alpha Psi, Beta Gamma Sigma, Alpha Lambda Nu. Home: 401 Cape Cod Dr Corpus Christi TX 78412-2622

BATEMAN, SANDRA BIZZLE, primary school educator; b. St. Louis, Oct. 12, 1942; d. Ralph David and Jo Murrie (Zarecor) Bizzle; m. Doyne Franklin Bateman, Jr. June 10, 1962 (div. Oct. 1976); children: Johanna Elizabeth Smith, Kirklin Joseph, Jannine Ruth Vaughn. BS in Edn., Ark. State U., 1965; MEd, George Mason U., 1995. Cert. elem. tchr., Va. Classroom tchr. Prince William County, Manassas, Va., 1968—; bookkeeper Summertree, Manassas, 1979-80; comm. supr. Norrell, Inc., Washington, 1981-85; supr. Hecht's, Manassas, 1986-87; tchr. mentor Prince William County, Manassas. Fieldtrip docent Prince William County, Manassas, 1981-83; new mem. orienter Parent's Without Ptnrs., Manassas, 1986-88, v.p. membership, 1988-93, comm. officer, 1995—. Mem. Alpha Delta Kappa. Home: 14543 Stephen St Nokesville VA 20181 Office: Prince William County Sch 8600 Mathis Ave Manassas VA 20110

BATES, CAROLYN R., air transportation executive. V.p. reservations S.W. Airlines Co., Dallas. Office: SW Airlines Co Love Field PO Box 36611 Dallas TX 75235-1611

BATES, HAMPTON ROBERT, JR., pathologist; b. Roanoke, Va., Feb. 1, 1933; s. Hampton Robert and Mary Mildred (Crowder) B.; B.S., Roanoke Coll., 1953; M.D., Med. Coll. Va., 1957; m. Carole Harrison Young, Apr. 12, 1958; children—Hampton Robert III, Catherine Louise. Intern, Med. Coll. Va. Hosp., Richmond, 1957-58, resident in pathology, 1958-63; practice medicine specializing in pathology and nuclear medicine, Richmond, 1963-95, ret., 1995; pathologist Johnston-Willis Hosp., Chippenham Med. Ctr.; v.p. Clin. Lab. Consultants, Inc., Richmond, 1972-95; forensic pathologist Richmond Met. Area, 1959-95. Diplomate Am. Bd. Pathology, Am. Bd. Nuclear Medicine, Nat. Bd. Med. Examiners. Fellow Coll. Am. Pathologists (life); mem. AMA, AAAS, Med. Soc. Va., Richmond Acad. Medicine, Swedish Pathol. Soc. (corr.), Rokitansky Soc. Episcopalian. Club: Diogenes. Contbr. articles on descriptive, exptl. and forensic pathology to med. Jours. Home: 641 Mobrey Dr Richmond VA 23236-4148

BATES, HAROLD MARTIN, lawyer; b. Wise County, Va., Mar. 11, 1928; s. William Jennings and Reba (Williams) B.; m. Audrey Rose Doll, Nov. 1, 1952 (div. Mar. 1978); children—Linda, Carl. m. Judith Lee Farmer, June 23, 1978. B.A. in Econs., Coll. William and Mary, 1952; LL.B., Washington and Lee U., 1961. Bar: Va. 1961, Ky. 1961. Spl. agt. FBI, Newark and N.Y.C., 1952-56; tech. sales rep. Hercules Powder Co., Wilmington, Del., 1956-58; investigator U.S. Def. Dept., Lexington, Va., Louisville, 1959-62; practice law, Louisville, 1961-62; sec.-treas., dir., house counsel Life Ins. Co. of Ky., Louisville, 1962-66; practice law, Roanoke, Va., 1966—; sec., dir. James River Limestone Co., Buchanan, Va., 1970-96; sec. Eastern Ins. Co., Roanoke, 1984-87. Pres., Skil, Inc., orgn. for rehab. Vietnam vets., Salem, Va., 1972-75; freshman football coach Washington and Lee U., 1958-60. Served to cpl. U.S. Army, 1946-47, PTO. Mem. Va. Bar Assn., Roanoke Bar Assn., William and Mary Alumni Assn. (bd. dirs. 1972-76), Soc. Former Spl. Agts. of FBI (chmn. Blue Ridge chpt. 1971-72). Republican. Home: 2165 Laurel Woods Dr Salem VA 24153-1807 Office: 406 Professional Arts Bldg Roanoke VA 24011

BATES, HURL, correctional officer; b. Burkhart, Ky., July 31, 1950; s. Estill Lee and Imagene (Trusty) B.; m. Karen Ann Layne-Spencer, Mar. 8, 1968 (div. June 1974); children: Lisa Marie, Johnny Ray, Linda Gayle, Jennifer Lynn, Crystal Lynn; m. Elizabeth Ann Tandy, Aug. 17, 1992; children: Elizabeth Christine, Kelly Lynne, Kandace Marie. Assoc. in Criminology, St. Leo Coll., 1976; cert. radio broadcasting, Paul Henning Broadcasting, 1976; LPN, Lexington Vocat. Tech., 1982; cert. EMT, Ctrl. Vocat. Tech., 1982. Police officer Newport News (Va.) Ship Bldg., 1977-78, Purcell (Okla.) City Police, 1978-79; security staff Storm Security, Jackson, Ky., 1980-82; EMT John Ford Graves Hosp., Georgetown, Ky., 1982-84; truck driver Oliver and Oliver, Campton, Ky., 1984-87; constrn. worker Sullivan Electric, West Liberty, Ky., 1987-88; correctional officer Ky. State Reformatory, LaGrange, Ky., 1989, Ea. Ky. Correctional Complex, West Liberty, Ky., 1989—. Author: Vanishing Prison, 1991, The Blue Murder, 1993. Active Zag (Ky.) Community Ch., 1991-94; speaker Wrigley (Ky.) Elem., 1993. With U.S. Army, 1969-77. Mem. Ky. Writers Assn., Fraternal Order Police. Democrat. Home: 2327 Highway 976 West Liberty KY 41472-9678

BATES, LURA WHEELER, trade association executive; b. Inboden, Ark., Aug. 28, 1932; d. Carl Clifton and Hester Ray (Pace) Wheeler; m. Allen Carl Bates, Sept. 12, 1954; 1 child, Carla Allene. BSBA, U. Ark., 1954. Cert. constrn. assoc. Sec.-bookkeeper, then officer mgr. Assoc. Gen. Contractors Miss., Inc., Jackson, 1958-77, dir. adminstrv. svcs., 1977—, asst. exec. dir., 1980—; owner, Ditty Bag Supply Co., 1987—; adminstr. Miss. Constrn. Found., 1977—; sec. AIA-Assoc. Gen. Contractors Liaisonship Coms., 1977—; sec. Carpenters Joint Apprenticeship Coms., Jackson and Vicksburg, 1977—. Sec. Marshall Elem. Sch. PTA, Jackson, 1962-64, v.p., 1965; sec.-treas. Inter-Club Coun. Jackson, 1963-64; tchr. adult Sunday sch. dept. Hillcrest Bapt. Ch., Jackson, 1975-82; dir. Bapt. Women WMU, 1987—, sec., 1992—; tchr. adult Sunday sch. dept. 1st Bapt. Ch., Crystal Springs, Miss., 1989—; mem. exec. com. Jackson Christian Bus. and Profl. Women's Coun., 1976-80, sec., 1978-79, pres., 1979-80. Named Outstanding Woman in Constrn. Miss., 1962-63, Outstanding Mem. Nat. Assn. Women in Constrn. Fellow Internat. Platform Assn.; mem. AAUW, NAFE, Nat. Assn. Women in Constrn. (life, chpt. pres. 1963-64, 76-77, 92-93, nat. v.p. 1965-66, 77-78, nat. dir. Region 5, 1967-68, nat. sec. 1970-71, 71-72, pres. 1980-81, coord. cert. constrn. assoc. program 1973-78, 83-84 guardian-contr. Edn. Found. 1981-82, chmn. nat. bylaws com. 1982-83, 85-88, nat. parliamentarian 1983-92), Nat. Assn. Parliamentarians, U. Ark. Alumni Assn. (life, pres. ctrl. Miss. chpt. 1992-93, 93-94, 94-95), Delta Delta Delta. Editor NAWIC Image, 1968-69, Procedures Manual, 1965-66, Public Relations Handbook, 1967-68, Profl. Edn. Guide, 1972-73, Guidelines & Procedures Handbook, 1987-88; author digests in field. Home: 1007 Lee Ave Crystal Springs MS 39059-2546 Office: 2093 Lakeland Dr Jackson MS 39216-5010

BATES, MARK C., cardiologist; b. Huntington, W.Va., June 18, 1960. BS in Chemistry, W.Va. State Coll., 1982; MD, W.Va. U., 1986. Diplomate Nat. Bd. Med. Examiners, Am. Bd. Internal Medicine, Cardiovascular Disease Specialty Bd. Intern, resident Charleston (W.Va.) Area Med. Ctr., 1986-88, chief med. resident, 1988-89, mem. clin. faculty, 1993—; fellow in cardiology U. Ky., Lexington, 1989-91, clin. scholar in interventional cardiology, chief fellow, 1991-92; fellow in interventional cardiology and peripheral vascular disease The William Dorros-Isadore Feuer Interventional Cardiovascular Disease Found. Ltd., U. Wis., Madison, 1992-93; mem. clin. faculty Marshall U. Sch. Med., Huntington, W.Va., 1993—. Contbr. articles to profl. jours. Mem. AMA, Am. Coll. Physicians, Wis. State Med. Assn., Ky. Acad. Physician Assts. (hon. life), W.Va. State Med. Assn., Alpha Omega Alpha. Office: Med Staff Office Bldg 3100 Maccorkle Ave SE Ste 709 Charleston WV 25304-1215

BATES, PATRICIA STAMPER, accountant; b. Baton Rouge, Feb. 13, 1947; d. Ernest Rudolphus and Avis (Patton) Stamper; m. James Rogers, Aug. 11, 1968 (div. 1974); 1 child, Brian James; m. Ronald Dean Bates, Feb. 27, 1976. BS in Math and English Edn., La. State U., 1968, M in Supervision with honors, 1978; postgrad., Texas A & I, 1982-83, Lamar U., 1992—. CPA, La., Tex.; cert. tchr. La., Tex., Va. Tchr. East Baton Rouge Schs., 1968-70, East Baton Rouge and Bishop (Tex.) Ind. Sch. Dist., 1977-81; personnel mgr. La. Dept. Fire and Police Civil Service, Baton Rouge, 1971-76; acct. Womack and Womack, CPAs, Kingsville, Tex., 1982, W. Wayne Rasmussen, CPA, Inc., Corpus Christi, Tex., 1982-83; chief acct., pers. dir. Mueller Engring. and Exploration, Inc., Corpus Christi, 1983-84; dir. acctg. Conoco, Inc., Westlake, La., 1984-89; coord. refining cost, downstream tng. coord. Conoco, Inc., Ponca City, Okla., 1989-91; coord. refining cost RMTA Acctg., 1989-91; sr. acctg. specialist DuPont Sabine River Works, Orange, Tex., 1991—; co-chair women's info. network Conoco Inc., 1990-91, cultural diversity task force, 1989-91, tng. subcom., 1989-91. Mem. Tex. Soc. CPAs, Southwest La. C. of C., La. State U. Alumni Group, St. Joseph's Acad. Alumni Group. Clubs: Hickory Ridge Garden (Baton Rouge) (sec. 1978-79); Continental (Westlake). Office: DuPont Sabine River Works Fm1006 Bldg 720-116 Orange TX 77630

BATES, RHONDA BARBER, financial advisor; b. Augusta, Ga., Feb. 18, 1962; d. Howard Wesley Barber and Thelma Jean (Eller) Brown; m. William Bowers III Bates, May 4, 1985. BBA, Augusta Coll., 1989. Fin. advisor William B. Bates III, M.D., P.C., Augusta, Ga., 1985—; fin. tutor Augusta Coll., 1988—. Mem. Fin. Mgmt. Assn. (named to Nat. Honor Soc.), Children's Med. Ctr. Fundraiser Assn., Ga. Med. Assn. Aux., Faculty Wives Club of Med. Coll. Ga., Phi Kappa Phi. Baptist. Home and Office: 2116 Wrightsboro Rd Augusta GA 30904-4763

BATES, WILLIAM LAWRENCE, civil engineer; b. Leominister, Mass., Dec. 6, 1957; s. William Earl and Imogene (Pope) B.; m. Susan Joy Cook, Aug. 16, 1980; children: Jonathan Edwards, David William, Rebecca Ann. BSCE, Clemson U., 1979. Registered profl. engr., N.C., S.C. Design engr. I Duke Power Co., Charlotte, N.C., 1980-88; structural engr. Republic Contracting Corp., Columbia, S.C., 1989—. Mem. ASCE, Am. Inst. Steel Constrn. (profl. mem.). Republican. Office: Republic Contracting Corp 829 Pepper St # 9167 Columbia SC 29209-2138

BATEY, SHARYN REBECCA, clinical research scientist; b. Nashville, Apr. 19, 1946; d. Robert Thomas and Sue (Alred) B. BS in Pharmacy, U. Tenn., 1969, D of Pharmacy, 1975; MS in Pub. Health, U. S.C., 1984. Registered pharmacist, Tenn. Hosp. pharmacist Vanderbilt Hosp., Nashville, 1969-71, VA Hosp., Beckley, W.Va., 1971-72, Gainesville, Fla., 1972-73, Battle Creek, Mich., 1973-74; hosp. pharmacy resident VA Hosp., Memphis, 1974-76; psychopharmacy resident Menninger Found., Topeka, 1976-77; clin. pharmacist William S. Hall Psychiat. Inst., Columbia, S.C., 1977-82; asst. prof. U. S.C. Coll. Pharmacy, Columbia, 1977-83, asst. prof. Sch. Medicine, 1981-83, assoc. prof. Coll. Pharmacy and Sch. Medicine, 1983-89; prof., 1989; chief clin. pharmacy services and ednl. programs William S. Hall Psychiat. Inst., Columbia, 1982-89; clin. rsch. scientist Burroughs Wellcome Co., Research Triangle Park, N.C., 1989-95; clin. program head, Glaxo Wellcome, Inc., Research Triangle Park, 1995—; clin. drug research/drug devel. fellow U. N.C. and Burroughs Wellcome, Research Triangle Park, 1983-84; pharmacist cons. NIMH, Bethesda, Md., 1983-84, Health Care Fin. Adminstrn., Balt., 1985-89. Author audio visual programs Psychotropic Medication Education Program for Adults, Adolescents and Children, 1978, 84, 88, 89; contbr. articles on psychopharmacology to profl. jours. Recipient Significant Achievement award Am. Psychiat. Assn., 1980, Sci. Exhibit award Am. Psychiat. Assn., 1981. Mem. Am. Coll. Clin. Pharmacy, Am. Soc. Hosp. Pharmacists (chmn. edn. and tng. working group of psychopharmacy spl. interest group 1983-85, chmn. elect 1985-86, chmn. 1986-87, past chmn. 1987-88, project leader psycopharmacy specialty recognition petition 1986-89, psychopharmacy fellow selection com. 1986-88, chmn. psychopharmacy spl. practice group 1989), S.C. Dementia Registry (pres. user policy coun. 1989). Avocations: travel, reading. Home: 4824 Highgate Dr Durham NC 27713-9417 Office: Glaxo Wellcome Inc Research Triangle Park NC 27709

BAT-HAEE, MOHAMMAD ALI, educational administrator, consultant; b. Sanandadj, Iran, June 19, 1935; came to U.S., 1964, naturalized, 1991; s. Mohammad Ameen and Khadeejeh (Esteefaee) B.; m. Aghdas Seyedalshohadaee, Aug. 16, 1961; children: Mohammad Sean, Farshad, Neshat. BS, U. Tehran, Iran, 1962; MS in Edn., So. Ill. U., Carbondale, 1966, PhD, 1968. Cert. tchr. level G, N.C. Asst. prof. U. Mo., St. Louis, 1968-69; dean student Pahlavi U., Shiraz, Iran, 1969-70, chmn. dept. psychology, 1971-73; assoc. prof. psychology, assoc. dean Coll. Art and Scis. Pahlavi U., Shiraj, Iran, 1973-75, prof., 1976-84, dean Coll. Art and Scis., 1976-77; instrnl. supr. Wake Tech. C.C., Raleigh, N.C., 1985-87; tchr. O'Berry Ctr., Goldsboro, N.C., 1988-89, asst. dir. programs, 1990-91, cmty. employment dir. III, 1992—. Author: Education, Aims and Techniques, 1970, Psychology of Management, 1971, Elementary Math for Elementary Statistics, 1972; also articles. Bd. dirs. Cmty. Sch., Shiraz, 1972-73, Kanoon-e-Iranian, Raleigh, 1986-88, 1989-94; mem. Kurdish Nat. Congress, N.Am., 1992-94. Rsch. grantee U. Mo., 1969, U. Shiraz, 1970, AID, 1975. Mem. Am. Assn. on Mental Retardation, Am. Psychol. Soc., N.C. Assn. on Mental Retardation (chmn. staff devel. 1992—, award for svcs. in leadership and rsch. 1996), N.C. Applied Behavior Analysis. Democrat. Home: 919 Hampshire Ct Cary NC 27511

BATISTE, ROBERT JOSEPH, military non-commissioned officer, educator; b. Pineville, La., Apr. 25, 1950; s. Leonard Joseph and Francis (Jacob) B.; m. Okee Hui Kong, July 2, 1982; children: Linden, Leonard, Chrysalis. AA, Los Angeles Coll., 1977; AS, Coll. Air Force, 1981; BS, U. Md., 1983; MA, Webster U., 1986. Enlisted USAF, 1968, advanced through grades to master sgt., 1983; aircraft maintenance engr. USAF, Utapao, Thailand, 1970-71, 71-73, Wirthsmith AFB, Mich., 1971, Carswell AFB, Tex., 1974-76, Kadena AFB, Japan, 1976-78; mgmt. engr. USAF, Plattsburgh AFB, N.Y., 1978-80, Osan Air Base, Republic Korea, 1980-84, 87-88, Scott AFB, Ill., 1984-87; mgmt. engr. Keesler AFB, Miss., 1988—; mgmt. engr. USAF, 1978—; instr. Cen. Tex. Coll., Osan Air Base, 1987-88, Gold Star Electronics, Osan City, Republic of Korea, 1987-88, U. So. Miss., Long Beach. Democrat. Roman Catholic. Home: 869 Lackland Dr Biloxi MS 39532-3226 Office: Ingalls Shipbuilding Pascagoula MS 39567

BATSAKIS, JOHN GEORGE, pathology educator; b. Petoskey, Mich., Aug. 14, 1929; s. George John and Stella (Vlahkis) B.; m. Mary Janet Savage, Dec. 28, 1957; children: Laura, Sharon, George. Student, Va. Mil. Inst., 1947, Albion Coll., Mich., 1948-50; M.D., U. Mich., 1954. Diplomate Am. Bd. Pathology. Intern George Washington Univ. Hosp., Washington, 1954-55; resident in pathology U. Mich. Hosp., Ann Arbor, 1955-59; prof.

pathology U. Mich., Ann Arbor, 1969-79; chmn. dept. pathology M.D. Anderson Hosp. U. Tex., Houston, 1981-96; chm. and prof. emeritus dept pathology M.D. Anderson Hosp. U. Tex., 1996—; Ruth Legett Jones prof. U. Tex., Austin, 1982-96; cons. Armed Forces Inst. Pathology, 1972—, VA Hosp., Ann Arbor, 1968-79; Hayes Martin lectr. Am. Soc. for Head and Neck Surgery, 1994; Gunnar Holmgren lectr. Swedish Nat. Ear, Nose, Throat Meeting, 1994; William Christopherson lectr. U. Louisville Dept. of Pathology, 1995; external examiner U. Hong Kong Dental Sch., 1995—. Author: Tumors of the Head and Neck, 2d edit., 1979; editor Clin. Lab. Ann., 1981-86; co-editor Advances in Anatomic Pathology, 1994—; mem. editorial bd. 13 jours., 1974—; contbr. numerous articles to profl. jours. Trustee George C. Marshall Found., Lexington, Va., 1995—. Capt. U.S. Army, 1959-61. Recipient William H. Rorer award Am. Coll. Gastroenterology, 1972, Disting. Alumnus award Albion Coll., 1987, Reviewer of the Decade award AMA Archives Orolaryngology Head Neck Surgery, 1990, Presdl. award Am. Soc. Head and Neck Surgery, 1991, Harlan Spjut award Houston Soc. Clin. Pathologists, 1992, Honor award Am. Laryngologic Assn., 1995; Spl. Honored Guest of Am. Soc. for Head and Neck Surgery, 1993. Fellow ACP, Am. Soc. Clin. Pathologists, Am. Acad. Otolaryngology (assoc., honor award 1994), Coll. Am. Pathologists (chmn. commn. anatomic pathology), Royal Soc. Medicine. Republican. Episcopalian. Home: 1701 Hermann Dr Apt 3304 Houston TX 77004-7331 Office: MD Anderson Hosp Dept Pathology 1515 Holcombe Blvd Houston TX 77030-4009

BATSON, DAVID WARREN, lawyer; b. Wichita Falls, Tex., Jan. 4, 1956; s. Warren M. Batson and Jacqueline (Latham) Rhone. BBA, Midwestern State U., 1976; JD, U. Tex., 1979. Bar: Tex. 1980, U.S. Dist. Ct. (no. dist.) Tex. 1981, U.S. Tax Ct. 1981, U.S. Ct. Appeals (5th cir.) 1983, U.S. Ct. Appeals (D.C. cir.) 1983, U.S. Ct. Claims 1984, U.S. Supreme Ct. 1984. Atty. Arthur Andersen & Co., Ft. Worth, 1980-81; tax atty. The Western Co. of N.Am., Ft. Worth, 1981-85; sr. tax atty. Alcon Labs., Inc., Ft. Worth, 1985; gen. counsel Data Tailor, Inc., Ft. Worth, 1985-87; sr. tax atty. Arco, 1988-90; atty. pvt. practice, Wichita Falls, Tex., 1990—; lectr. U. of Tex., Arlington, 1984-85; of counsel Means & Means, Corsicana, Tex., 1985-86. Contbr. articles to profl. jours. Speaker A Wish With Wings, Arlington, Tex., 1984-85. Mem. Assn. Trial Lawyers Am., Tex. Bar Assn., Christian Legal Soc., Tex. Trial Lawyers Assn., State Bar at Tex. Coll., Phi Delta Phi.

BATSON, STEPHEN WESLEY, university administrator, consultant; b. Wilmington, N.C., Aug. 20, 1946; s. John Thomas and Mildred (Pritchard) B.; m. Kathleen Lawless, Apr. 11, 1985. BA, Mercer U.; MEd, Ga. Coll., EdS; EdD, U. Ga. H.S. tchr., adminstr. various, Ga., 1970-79; asst. v.p. for acad. affairs, dir. instnl. rsch. Ga. So. U., Statesboro, 1979-82; asst. to pres., dir. planning East Tex. State U., Commerce, 1982-86; v.p. planning and advancement W.Va. State Coll., 1986—, exec. dir. R&D corp. Contbr. articles in field to profl. jours. Bd. dirs. Ga. Jr. Acad. Sci., 1979-81, exec. dir., 1981-82; co-chmn. United Way campaign, Commerce, 1984; bd. dirs. Cen. W.Va. chpt. ARC, 1993—, The Friends of W.Va. Pub. Ratio, 1996-99. Named Bulloch County Leader, Ga. Power Leaders of Tomorrow Program, 1980, Outstanding Young Alumnus, Ga. Coll., 1981. Mem. Am. Assn. Higher Edn., Am. Coun. Edn., Nat. Soc. Fund Raising Execs. (cert., W.Va. chpt. sec. 1991-92, pres. 1993-94, nat. bd. dirs. 1995—), NSTA, Soc. Coll. Sci.Tchrs., Assn. for Instl. Rschrs., Soc. for Coll. and Univ. Planning, Coun. for Advancement and Support of Edn. (Gold award 1993, 95), Nat. Assn. Biology Tchrs., Nat. Assn. Title III Adminstrs., Commerce C. of C. (Disting. Cmty. Svc. award 1984), W.Va. C. of C., Charleston C. of C., So. Assn. for Inst. Rsch. (pres. 1986-87), Leadership Charleston Alumni Assn. (bd. dirs., pres. 1995-96), Nat. Orgn. on Legal Problems of Edn. (bd. dirs. 1985-91, pres. 1992-93), Kiwanis (bd. dirs., disting. pres., disting. lt. gov., accredited rep., cert. trainer), Phi Delta Kappa, Phi Eta Sigma. Office: WVa State Coll Office of Planning Campus 180 Institute WV 25112-1000

BATTAGLIA, ROSEMARIE ANGELA, English language educator; b. Wilmington, Del., Dec. 17, 1936; d. Martin Fortunate and Norma Agnes (Ciaramella) B. BA, U. Del., 1958; MA, Temple U., 1973; PhD, SUNY, Binghamton, 1985. Cert. secondary English and French tchr., Del. Tchr. Dover (Del.) High Sch., 1961-62; grad. asst. U. Del., Newark, 1963-64, SUNY, 1978-81; instr. Rider Coll., Lawrenceville, N.J., 1964-65, Cheyney (Pa.) U., 1965-66, Lincoln U., Lincoln University, Pa., 1974-76; vis. instr. Temple U., Phila., 1982-84; asst. prof. Kutztown (Pa.) U., 1984-86; asst. prof. English Mich. State U., East Lansing, 1987-92, Morehead (Ky.) State U., 1992—; test cons. Am. Coll. Testing, Iowa City, 1976, Ednl. Testing Svc., Princeton, N.J., 1976; editorial cons. Yeats Eliot Rev., Little Rock, 1987—; referee-reader Cornell U. Press, Ithaca, N.Y., 1990—; presenter in field, 1984—. Contbr. articles to profl. jours. Recipient prize Acad. Am. Poets, 1958; Woodrow Wilson fellow, 1958. Mem. Ky. Philos. Assn., Internat. James Joyce Found., Phi Beta Kappa, Phi Kappa Phi. Democrat. Home: 865 Kentucky Highway 519 Morehead KY 40351-8761 Office: English Dept Morehead State U Morehead KY 40351

BATTLE, EMERY ALFORD, JR., sales executive; b. McComb, Miss., May 23, 1947; s. Emery Alford and Torrey Wofford (Copenhaver) B.; m. Martha Lee Kuntz, July 1971 (div. Jan. 29, 1985); children: Emery Alford III, Meredith Lindsay. BS in Pharmacy, U. Miss., 1971. Staff pharmacist Wilson-Quick, Super-X Foxall Pharmacy, Nashville, 1971-74; sales rep. Eli-Lilly and Co., Nashville, 1974-79, Deknatel Suture Co., Nashville, 1979-81, U.S.C.I. Inc., Nashville, 1981-84; mfr. rep. Cardiac Systems, Inc., Nashville, 1984-85; sales rep. Cordis Corp., Nashville, 1985-87, mgr. sales, 1992—; mgr. sales Cordis Corp., Dallas, 1987-91. Sales mgr. Cordis Corp., Dallas, 1987-91; sales mgr. Cordis Corp., Nashville, 1991—; mem. Dallas Symphony Assn., 1990. Recipient Pres.'s Club award U.S.C.I. Inc, 1981-83, Pres.'s award Eli-Lilly, 1975-77. Mem. Dallas C. of C., Mayflower Soc., Pilgrim Soc., Carnton Country. Episcopalian.

BATTLE, JOSEPH LAURIE, circuit court judge; b. Augusta, Ga., Nov. 3, 1943; s. David G. and Josephine T. (Troxell) B.; m. Jane Phillips, Aug. 28, 1965; children: Robert, Katherine, Elizabeth. LLB, U. Ala., 1967; LLM, George Washington U., 1969. Bar: Ala. 1967, U.S. Supreme Ct. 1970. Community lawyer fellow U.S. Office of Econ. Opportunity, Washington, 1973-74; spl. asst. atty. gen. State of Ala., Montgomery, 1973-74; adminstrv. law judge Nat. Labor Rels. Bd., Washington, 1976-77; arbitrator Fed. Mediation and Concilliation Svc., Washington, 1978-88; pub. counsel Tenn. Valley Authority, Huntsville, Ala., 1979; pvt. practice Huntsville, Ala., 1977-88; hearing officer City of Huntsville, 1980; circuit ct. judge State of Ala., Huntsville, 1989—; vice chair bd. dirs. Med. Ctr. Hosp., Huntsville, 1992-94; part-time thcr. Cumberland Sch. Law, Birmingham, 1967, Ala. A&M U., Huntsville, Gadsden (Ala.) State Jr. coll., 1967-76. Mem. adminstrv. bd. First United Meth. Ch., Huntsville, 1990. Staff sgt. USAFR, 1961-67. Recipient Am. Jurisprudence award U. Ala. Sch. Law, 1965-67. Mem. ABA (chair group legal svcs. com. 1986). Democrat. Office: Madison County Courthouse 100 Northside Sq Huntsville AL 35801-4800

BATTON, JOSEPH HOWARD, nursing educator; b. Jackson, Miss., Nov. 5, 1962; s. J.E. and Pauline (Howard) B. BSN, Miss. Coll. Sch. of Nursing, 1987; MSN, U. So. Miss., 1993, postgrad., 1993—. ANCC. Nurse neonatal ICU U. Miss. Med. Ctr., 1987-1988; nurse geropsychiatric unit. Vicksburg Med. Ctr., Jackson, Miss., 1988-93; staff/supr. St. Dominic Hosp., Jackson, 1992-94; mem. faculty Hinds C.C., Jackson, Miss., 1994—; nurse St. Dominic Hosp. Mem. ANA (coun. on psychiat. and mental health nursing), Miss. Nurses Assn., Am. Assembly for Men in Nursing, Nat. Assn. Neonatal Nurses, Am. Psychiat. Nurses Assn., ORTHO, Sigma Theta Tau, Gamma Beta Phi, Phi Kappa Phi. Home: 639 Randall Cir Pearl MS 39208-5743

BATY, DAVID F., student services professional; b. Buffalo, Nov. 4, 1965; s. John A. and Mary V. (Averill) B. AA, St. Petersburg Jr. Coll., 1986; BA Psychology, U. South Fla., 1990; MEd, U. Sarasota, 1996. From sr. clk. to acad. advisor St. Petersburg Jr. Coll., Clearwater, Fla., 1985—; advisor Phi Theta Kappa St. Petersburg Jr. Coll., 1991-95. Mem. Fla. Assn. C.C.s. Office: Saint Petersburg Jr Coll 2465 Drew St Clearwater FL 34625

BAUCH, MARY HOUSEHOLDER, retired secondary education educator; b. Knoxville, Tenn., July 12, 1926; d. Henry Jarvis and Margaret Elizabeth (Moore) Householder; m. Joy Coulter, June 10, 1949; 1 child, Henry Coulter. BS in Edn., U. Tenn., 1947; postgrad., Interam. U., Saltillo, Mex., 1968. Tchr. Latin and Spanish, Knox County Schs., Knoxville, 1947-52, 57-91; ret., 1991; mem. com. evaluation team So. Assn. Secondary Schs., Knoxville, 1980-83. Contbr. poetry to anthologies. Mem. Tenn. Ptnrs. of Ams., Nashville, 1973-90. Named Outstanding Tchr. Humanities Tenn. Coun. Humanities, 1985. Mem. Internat. Soc. Poets, Tenn. Writers Alliance, Knox County Ret. Tchrs. Assn., Knoxville Execs. Club. Evangelical. Home: 3501 Raccoon Valley Dr Powell TN 37849

BAUCUM, JANET MARTIN, nursing administrator; b. Seminary, Miss., Apr. 17, 1937; d. Will A. and Annie Maebell (Lowery) Davis; m. Johnnie Martin, Feb. 21, 1959 (dec. Nov. 1982); children: John Milton Martin, Melody Jane Patrick; m. Hilton Baucum, Mar. 24, 1989. Diploma, Meth. Hosp., Hattiesburg, Miss., 1964; BSN, William Carey Coll., Hattiesburg, 1978; MS, U. So. Miss., Hattiesburg, 1979, EdD in Adult Edn., 1982. ACLS, PALS. Staff nurse Forrest Gen. Hosp., Hattiesburg, 1966-67, 69-77; office nurse Hattiesburg, 1967-69; staff devel. Meth. Hosp., Hattiesburg, 1979-81; instr. nursing Pearl River Community Coll., Poplarville, Miss., 1981-82; sophomore coord. U. Southwestern La., Lafayette, 1982-83; DON Conva Rest, Hattiesburg, 1983-86; staff nurse Northshore Regional Med. Ctr., Slidell, La., 1985-86; staff nurse Forrest Gen. Hosp., Hattiesburg, 1986-88, rsch. chair, coord. organ/tissue donation for transplantation program, leadership edn. and devel., spl. projects/change agt. and data mgmt., 1988—; instr. nursing U. So. Miss., Hattiesburg, 1992. Group leader United Way, Hattiesburg, 1990. Mem. AACN, So. Nursing Rsch. Soc., Sigma Theta Tau. Republican. Methodist. Home: 2911 Williamsburg Rd Hattiesburg MS 39402-2474 Office: Forrest Gen Hosp PO Box 16389 Hwy 49 South Hattiesburg MS 39404-6389

BAUCUM, WILLIAM EMMETT, JR., electrical research engineer; b. Magnolia, Ark., July 8, 1945; s. William Emmett Sr. and Bronis Yvonne (Whittington) B.; m. Paulette Phillips, Mar. 21, 1965; children: William III, Rebecca. BA, David Lipscomb Coll., Nashville, 1966; postgrad., Ga. Inst. Tech., 1967; MS, U. Tenn., Knoxville, 1974; postgrad. space inst., U. Tenn., Tullahoma, 1978—. Physicist Y-12 plant Union Carbide Corp., Oak Ridge, Tenn., 1967-74, elec. engr. nat. lab., 1974-78; research engr. space inst. U. Tenn., Tullahoma, 1978-92; with WEBCOMM; cons. Tech. Engring. Services and Cons. Co., Tullahoma, 1992—; adj. faculty Motlow State C.C., Tullahoma, 1987—. Contbr. chpt. to book, articles to profl. jours. Deacon Ch. of Christ; judge 4-H Club, Franklin County, Tenn., 1985; bd. dirs. Short Mountain Christian Camp, 1987. Mem. Internat. Microwave Power Inst. (v.p. bd. dirs. indsl., sci., med. instrumentation sect. 1987-92, pres. 1987-89, bd. dirs. 1989-92), Sigma Xi, Sigma Pi Sigma. Home and Office: 1402 Harton Blvd Tullahoma TN 37388-5580

BAUDOIN, PETER, family business consultant; b. Breaux Bridge, La., Dec. 23, 1946; s. Roy Paul and Carrie (Broussard) B.; m. Donna Renz, Apr. 17, 1971; 1 child, Jonn Pierre. BS in BA, U. Southwestern La., 1968. CPA; cert. mgmt. acct. Ops. auditor Firestone Tire & Rubber Co., Akron, Ohio, 1969-71; sr. acct. Unishops of Clarkins, Inc., Akron, Ohio, 1972-73; cons. supr. Ernst & Young, Cleve., 1973-78; ptnr. Baudoin & Hamza CPAs, Lafayette, La., 1978-82; pres. Peter Baudoin Cons., Lafayette, La., 1982—; mng. dir. Family Bus. Accts. and Advisors, Lafayette, La., 1990—; mem. various coms. Family Firm Inst., Boston, 1990—, chair 1997 internat. conf. in New Orleans; dir. programming Acadiana Family Bus. Forum, 1992—. Contbr. numerous articles to profl. jours. Founding pres. Rocky River (Ohio) Jaycees, 1976; chmn. adv. bd. Charity Depot, an agy. of Lafayette Cath. Svcs. Ctr., Inc. With USAR, 1968-75. Named hon. Paramount Chief Zokai of Liberia, bestowed by Mandingo Tribe, 1975. Mem. Fin. Execs. Inst., Inst. Mgmt. Accts. (nat. bd. 1993-95, pres. Gulf South Coun. 1996—). Republican. Roman Catholic. Home: 101 Florida Ct Lafayette LA 70503-2005 Office: Family Bus Accts and Advisors 158 Industrial Pky Lafayette LA 70508-8309

BAUER, CHARLES RONALD, medical educator; b. N.Y.C., May 16, 1943; s. Charles Felix and Ann Edna (Kalmar) B.; m. Rita Frieda Ehnes, June 30, 1973; children: Charles Ronald Jr., Kristen LeighAnn, Gabrielle Rose-Marie. BS, Iona Coll., 1965; MD, W.Va. U., 1969. Diplomate Am. Bd. Pediatrics, Am. Bd. Neonatal-Perinatal Medicine. Intern pediatrics St. Louis Children's Hosp., 1969-70, resident in pediatrics, 1970-71; fellow in neonatology Montreal Children's Hosp., 1971-73; asst. prof. pediatrics U. Miami, 1973-78, assoc. prof. pediatrics, 1978-86, prof. pediatrics, 1986-87, prof. pediatrics, ob-gyn., 1987-88, prof. pediatrics ob-gyn. and psychology, 1988—; assoc. dir. U. Miami Sch. of Medicine Divsn. Neonatology, 1980—; dir. Divsn. Devel. Medicine Mailman Ctr. for Child Devel., 1989—, dir. early intervention and follow-up program, 1973—; speaker in field. Contbr. articles to profl. jours. Sec. Dade County-Children's Svcs. Coun., Miami, 1990-93. Fellow Am. Acad. Pediatrics; mem. AMA, Am. Pediatric Soc., Fla. Soc. Neonatal Perinatologists (pres., recognition award 1992), Fla. Perinatal Assn. (pres., recognition award 1991), South Fla. Perinatal Network (pres., recognition award 1990), Soc. for Pediatric Rsch. Roman Catholic. Home: 14650 SW 69th Ave Miami FL 33158-1711 Office: U Miami Dept Pediatrics PO Box 016960 Miami FL 33101

BAUER, JOSEPH GERARD, plastic surgeon; b. Balt., Jan. 13, 1960; m. Tracy Marie Pirlot, June 13, 1987; children: Joseph Matthew, Alexander Gerard. MD, Emory U., 1986. Cert. plastic/ reconstructive surgeon. Owner, solo physician Plastic Surgery Assn. Atlanta, Alpharetta, Ga., 1993—; edn. assessment com. Am. Soc. Plastic & Reconstructive Surgery, 1995. Bd. dirs. Am. Cancer Soc. Emory Med. Sch. scholar, March of Dimes scholar. Mem. AMA, Med. Assn. Ga., Rotary. Office: Plastic Surgery Assocs Atlanta 3400-A Old Milton Pky #550 Alpharetta GA 30202

BAUER, KAREN MARY, accountant, consultant; b. Balt., Nov. 25, 1956; d. Bernard Thomas and Mary Szmajda Sporney; m. Michael Joseph Bauer, Aug. 29, 1987; children: John Henry, Anna Marie. BA, Loyola Coll., 1978; MS, U. Balt., 1983; exec. internat. bus. cert., Georgetown U., 1994. CPA, Md. Corp. sec. Allied Rsch. Corp., Vienna, Va., 1991—, chief acctg. officer, 1994—; prin., sec.-treas. Anchor Loan Co., Ltd., Balt., 1992—; sec.-treas. ARC Svcs., Inc., Vienna, 1993—; prin., pres. Ark Roofing & Sheet Metal, Inc., Gaithersburg, Md., 1994—. Mem. AICPA, Md. Assn. CPAs, Am. Soc. Corp. Secs. Home: 17818 Stoneridge Dr Gaithersburg MD 20878-1020 Office: Allied Rsch Corp 8000 Towers Crescent Dr Ste 750 Vienna VA 22182-2700

BAUGE, CYNTHIA WISE, distributing company executive; b. Ottumwa, Iowa, Sept. 7, 1943; d. Donald Carlyle and Opal Dorthea (Douglas) W.; m. Harry Grant Bauge, May 1, 1965; 1 child, Melissa Anne. Student, Iowa State U., 1962-64, Area XI Community Coll., Ankeny 1974-75. Legal sec. City of Ames, Iowa, 1965-69; acctg. mgr. Vivan Equipment Co., Ames, Iowa, 1969; asst. mgr. Bavarian Motor Lodge, Des Moines, 1969-71; bookkeeper TCP of Iowa, Des Moines, 1971-72, Moffitt Bldg Material co., Des Moines, 1972-73, CS Capital/Mid Am. Growth Corp., West Des Moines, 1973-75; v.p., COO Grant Sales Inc., Plano, Tex., 1976—. Bd. dirs. Power, Allen, Tex., 1985-88, chmn. bd. dirs., 1986-88; bd. dirs. Cultural Arts Coun. of Plano, 1985-88, treas., 1986-87, v.p. classics, 1985-86; bd. dirs. North Tex. Rehab. Svcs., 1987-91; adv. bd. Jr. League of Plano, 1988-91; community bd. Physicians for Plano, 1988; mem. found. bd. Collin County Community Coll. Found., 1989—, vice chair, 1991-92, pres. 1992-94; mem. City of Plano Cultural Affairs Commn., 1991-94; mem. Ryko Distbrs. Assn., 1984—, pres. 1991-92. Mem. Women's Div. C. of C. Plano (treas. 1981-82), Plano C. of C. (budget and fin. com., Athena/Bus. Woman of Yr. award 1986), Beta Sigma Phi. Republican. Lutheran. Avocations: home decorating, gaming. Office: Grant Sales Inc 1701 Capital Ave Plano TX 75074-8156

BAUGHER, KATHRYN HESTER, dean; b. Nashville, Tenn., Jan. 20, 1960; d. Ray W. and Jean (Sallee) Hester; m. William Lance Baugher Sr., June 30, 1984; children: William Lance Jr., James Lucas. BS in Edn., Samford U., 1982; MA in Religious Edn., Southwestern Bapt. Theol. Sem., Ft. Worth, 1984; EdD in Ednl. Leadership, Vanderbilt U., 1992. Admissions/fin. aid counselor Samford U., Birmingham, Ala., 1984-90, dir. recruiting, 1990-92, dir. admissions, 1992-93; dean admissions Belmont U., Nashville, 1993—; mem. selection com. Ala. Sch. for Math. and Sci., Mobile, 1992; cons. numerous ednl. instns., 1992—; examiner Tenn. Quality Award, 1993. Author: LEARN: The Student Quality Team Manual, 1992; contbr. chpt. to: Continuous Quality Improvement: Making the Transition to Education, 1993; case author: Assessment in Practice, 1996. Mem. alumni coun. Brentwood (Tenn.) Acad., 1989-90; mem. dist. com. Boy Scouts Am., Brentwood, 1995, 96. Named one of Outstanding Young Women of Am., 1984, 86, 87. Mem. Nat. Assn. Coll. Admission Counselors, Assn. So. Bapt. Admissions Pers. (pres. 1994-95), Am. Assn. Higher Edn., Zeta Tau Alpha (various local officer 1979—). Republican. Home: 225 Williamsburg Cir Brentwood TN 37027 Office: Belmont Univ 1900 Belmont Blvd Nashville TN 37212-3758

BAUGHMAN, GEORGE WASHINGTON, aeronautical operations research scientist; b. Strasbourg, Can., Feb. 22, 1911; came to U.S., 1923; s. Dr. John Allen, M.D. and Daisy (Lafferty) B.; m. Helen Frances Hille, July 2, 1938; children: Barbara Ann (dec.), Susan Jane (dec.), Charles Allen. BS in Aero. Engring. magna cum laude, Wichita State U., 1931; postgrad., Ga. Tech., 1954-55, Wichita State U., 1933-37. Petroleum geologist Phillips Petroleum Co., Wichita, Kans., 1932-40; project engr. Cessna Aircraft Co., Wichita, 1940-51; staff specialist Lockheed Aircraft Corp., Marietta, Ga., 1951-54, ops. rsch. scientist, 1954-56, asst. project engr., Monticello project, 1956-58; prin. ops. analyst Cornell Aero. Lab., Arlington, Va., 1958-67; head systems environ. group Cornell Aero. Lab., Bangkok, Thailand, 1967-70; cons. future aviation Pres. Aviation Adv. Com., Washington, 1971-72; tech. coord. High Frontier Inc., Arlington, 1990—; mem. task force sr. scientists engrs. AAAS, Washington, 1991—; cons. SST program, Fed. Aviation Agy., Washington, 1965-67. Contbr. over 70 corp. tech. pubs. including aircraft pilot handbooks, maintenance manuals, catalogues, structural repair, aircraft design & performance, noise & sonic boom analysis and others. Bd. dirs. Vis. Nurses Assn. Va., 1976-82, Eldercrafters Inc., Alexandria, 1980-86; v.p. Alexandria Taxpayers Alliance, 1980-93; past chmn., pres. several local or nat. aircraft orgns. Recipient Missildine Chemistry prize, Wichita State U., 1928. Mem. AIAA (chmn. Atlanta chpt. 1953-54, nat. counselman 1954), SAR D.C. Soc., Am. Assn. Petroleum Geologists, Kans. Geol. Soc., Tau Beta Pi. Republican. Home: 316 Crown View Dr Alexandria VA 22314-4802 Office: High Frontier Inc 2800 Shirlington Rd Arlington VA 22206-3601

BAUGHMAN, OTIS LEE, III, family physician; b. Wagener, S.C., Feb. 1, 1951; s. Otis Lee Jr. and Ollie Francis (Wilson) B.; m. Margaret McKee Chambers, Sept. 7, 1990; children: Katie, Jason, Jody Leheup, Robert Leheup, Margey Bolen. BS, U. S.C., 1973; MD, Med. U. S.C., 1977. Diplomate Am. Bd. Family Practice. Pvt. practice, Inman, S.C., 1980-85; dir. family medicine residency, dir. med. edn. Self Meml. Hosp., Greenwood, S.C., 1988-90; resident Spartanburg (S.C.) Family Medicine Residency, 1977-80, asst. prof., 1985-88, dir., 1990—; pres. Upper Savannah Area Health Edn. Ctr., Greenwood, 1988-90; asst. dir. med. edn., dir. family med. residing program Spartanburg Regional Med. Ctr., 1990—; mem. S.C. Deans Coun., 1988—. Contbr. articles to med. jours. speaker on health care issues, 1978—; bd. dirs. Safe Homes, Spartanburg, 1994. Named Most Outstanding Resident, Spartanburg Family Medicine Residency, 1980, Tchr. of Yr., 1987. Mem. Am. Acad. Family Physicians, S.C. Acad. Family Physicians (pres. 1993, immediate past pres. 1994), Am. Soc. Addiction Medicine, Am. Coll. Phys. Execs., Soc. for Tchrs. Family Medicine, Am. Assn. Family Practice Dirs. Office: Spartanburg Family Medicine Residency 210 Catawba St Spartanburg SC 29303-3073

BAUGHN, ROBERT ELROY, microbiology educator; b. Chanute, Kans., Jan. 31, 1940; s. Berryman Thomas and Oella Louise (Smith) B.; BS, The Citadel, 1963; MS (USPHS fellow), U. Tenn., 1966; PhD (NIH fellow), U. Cin., 1975; MBA, Houston Bapt. U., 1980; m. Myra Donell Phillips, Dec. 12, 1965; children—Heather Lynne, Brenna Gayle. Microbiologist, Hutcheson Meml. Tri-County Hosp., Ft. Oglethorpe, Ga., 1969-71, Parkridge Hosp., Chattanooga, 1971; instr. dept. dermatology and dept. microbiology and immunology Baylor Coll. Medicine, 1975-77, asst. prof., 1977-83, assoc. prof., 1983-93, prof., 1993—; with dept. med. tech. Sch. Allied Health Scis. U. Tex., Houston, clin. assoc. prof., 1985—; assoc. career rsch. scientist, VA, 1990—. Mem. sch. bd. St. Mark's Episcopal Day Sch., Houston, 1978-81; vestryman St. Mark's Ch., 1983-85. Served as capt. AUS, 1967-69. Fellow Am. Acad. Microbiology; mem. Am. Soc. Microbiology, Am. Assn. Immunologists, Am. Soc. Clin. Pathology, Undersea Med. Soc., Reticuloendothelial Soc., Sigma Xi. Editorial bd. Infection and Immunity, 1985-87, 88-90, 91-93, 94—. Contbr. articles to profl. jours. Home: 11003 Atwell Dr Houston TX 77096-6129 Office: VA Hosp Bldg Dept Infectious Diseases 2002 Holcombe Blvd Houston TX 77030-4211

BAUM, ALVIN JOHN, JR., professional clown, optometrist; b. Birmingham, Ala., June 25, 1918; s. Alvin John and Mildred (Fox) B.; m. Ruth Virginia Marks, Sept. 4, 1943 (div. 1966); children: Barbara, Joanne; m. Charlene Ballingee Wall, Feb. 26, 1971 (div. Oct. 1992). OD, Pa. Coll. Optometry, 1941. Cert. optometrist, Va. Optometrist specializing in contact lenses, Richmond, Va., 1945—. Contbr. articles to profl. jours. Life mem. Tuckahoe Vol. Rescue Squad, Richmond, 1975; dir. Alvin The Clown (Baum) hosp. shows, Richmond, 1986—; producer/dir. Patroitism Day Richmond Newspapers, Inc., 1988-91. Pres. Parents Without Partners, chpt. 116, 1970, Meadowbrook Estates Civic Assn., 1991-92. With U.S. Army, 1942-45, USCG aux., 1942-78, lt. col. USAF aux. CAP, 1952-80. Named Ofcl. Ambassador of Mirth Commonwealth of Va., 1987, Hon. Clown Ringling Bros. & Barnum and Bailey's Circus, 1978, Sr. Vol. Hall of Fame, Chesterfield County, Va., 1989, Clown Wall of Fame, Delavan, Wis. Mem. Richmond Optometric Soc. (past pres. 1950), Clown Assn. Richmond (dir.). Republican. Jewish. Clubs: Virginia Alley 3 (pres. 1969-72), Va. C.B. Communicators (past pres. 1986-87). Avocations: professional clown. Home: 3802 Lake Hills Rd Richmond VA 23234-3665 Office: Clown Assn Richmond 3802 Lake Hills Rd Richmond VA 23234-3665

BAUM, LAWRENCE STEPHEN, biologist, educator; b. Scranton, Pa., Mar. 3, 1938; married; 3 children. BS, U. Ala., 1960, MS, 1962, PhD in Cell Physiology, 1965. Asst. prof. biology Extension Ctr. U. Ala., 1965-66; asst. prof. N.E. La. U., 1966-69, assoc. prof. biology, 1969—, dir. Cancer Rsch. Ctr., 1981—. Mem. Am. Physiol. Soc., Sigma Xi. Office: Northeast La U Cancer Research Ctr 700 University Ave Monroe LA 71209-9000

BAUM, MICHEL GERARD, pediatrician, educator; b. Sheboygan, Wis., Mar. 7, 1952; s. Alexander and Rachel (Meleliat) B.; m. Barbara Melinda Rich, Aug. 25, 1980; 1 child, Rebecca Lauren. BS summa cum laude, UCLA, 1974, MD, 1978. Diplomate Nat. Bd. Med. Examiners, Am. Bd. Pediatric Nephrology (mem. 1991—), Am. Bd. Pediatrics (assoc. mem. 1991—); lic. physician, Calif., Tex. Intern, then resident in pediatrics Yale-New Haven Hosp., 1978-81; clin. fellow Children's Renal Ctr. U. Calif., San Francisco, 1981-82, rsch. fellow in nephrology and renal physiology Cardiovasc. Rsch. Inst., 1982-84; asst. prof. pediatrics divsn. pediatric nephrology U. Tex. Southwestern Med. Ctr., Dallas, 1984-89, assoc. prof., 1989-94, assoc. prof. pediatrics and internal medicine, 1991-94, dir. divsn. pediatric nephrology, 1991—, prof. pediatrics and internal medicine, 1994—; mem. staff Children's Med. Ctr., Dallas, 1984—; Sarah E. and Charles E. Seay chair pediatric rsch. U. Tex. Southwestern Med. Ctr., Dallas, 1993—; NSF summer fellow 1972, 73; NIH summer fellow, 1974; ad hoc reviewer grants NIH, 1988, 89, 91, VA; mem. drug and formulary com. Children's Med. Ctr., 1987-90, co-dir. postdoctoral fellow tng. course dept. pediatrics, 1990-91. Co-contbr. 7 chpts. to books, most recently: Pediatric Therapy, 1993, Pediatric Nephrology, 1994, Hospital Practice, 1994; contbr. many articles to profl. jours., including New England Jour. Medicine, Pediatrics, Jour. Pediatrics, Am. Jour. Kidney Disease; mem. editorial bd. Am. Jour. Physiology: Renal, Fluid, and Electrolyte Physiology, 1989-95; manuscript reviewer various sci. jours. Mem. fellowship selection com. Nat. Kidney Found., 1987-90, mem. sci. adv. bd., 1988-94, bd. dirs. Tex. affiliate, 1993—. Rsch. grantee NIH, 1986-89, 90-91, 91-95, 91-96, NIH Kidney Rsch. Ctr., 1993—, Am. Heart Assn., 1989-92, Genentech, 1992-94, Scottish Rite Hosp., 1992-94, Tex. affiliate Nat. Kidney Found., 1992-93. Fellow Am. Acad. Pediatrics; mem. Am. Soc. Nephrology (mem. abstract coms. 1985, 88), Am. Fedn. for Clin. Rsch., Am. Soc. Pediatric Nephrology (mem. nominating com. 1989-90, mem. rsch. com. 1991—), Soc. for Pediatric Rsch. (mem. abstract com. 1992), Am. Soc. for Clin. Investigation, Internat. Soc. Nephrology, Phi Beta Kappa, Alpha Omega Alpha. Office: U Tex Southwestern Med Ctr Dept Pediatrics 5323 Harry Hines Blvd Dallas TX 75235-7200

BAUM, STANLEY M., lawyer; b. Bronx, N.Y., Mar. 6, 1944; s. Abraham S. and Mae (Weiner) B.; m. Louise Rae Iteld, Aug. 30, 1970; children: Rachel Jennifer, Lauren Amy. BS in Commerce, Rider Coll., 1966; JD summa cum laude, John Marshall Law Sch., 1969. Bar: Ga. 1970, U.S. Dist. Ct. (no. dist.) Ga. 1970, U.S. Ct. Appeals (5th cir.) 1970, U.S. Supreme Ct. 1973, U.S. Ct. Appeals (11th cir.) 1981, U.S. Tax Ct. 1983. Law clk. to U.S. atty. No. Dist. Ga., 1969; legal aide Ga. Gen. Assembly, 1970-71; asst. U.S. atty. No. Dist. Ga., 1971-74; ptnr. Bates & Baum, 1974—. Mem. Southeast regional bd. Anti-Defamation League; pres. Congregation Shearith Israel, 1976-78; chmn. Rep. Party of DeKalb County, 1983-85, 4th Dist. Rep. Party, 1985-89; pres. Resurgens, Atlanta, 1987-88, Electoral Coll., 1988; del. Rep. Nat. Conv., 1992; mem. DeKalb County Bd. Ethics, 1991—, chair 1993; mem. Met. Atlanta Rapid Transit Authority Bd. Ethics, 1993—. Mem. ABA (criminal justice sect. white collar com.), Ga. Bar Assn., Atlanta Bar Assn. (chmn. criminal law sect. 1985-86, bd. dirs. 1986-87), Fed. Bar Assn. (pres. Atlanta chpt. 1976-77, nat. council 1974-77), Dekalb Bar Assn. (pres. 1989-90), Am. Judicature Soc., Nat. Dist. Attys. Assn. Clubs: Atlanta Lawyers. Lodge: Masons. Office: 3151 Maple Dr NE Atlanta GA 30305-2500

BAUM, SUSAN DIANE, mathematics educator; b. Balt., Feb. 22, 1949; d. Harry and Evelyn (Freeman) Polansky; m. Larry A. Baum, Aug. 10, 1971 (div. July 1990); children: Allison Lynn, Meredith Dara. BA in Psychology, Am. U., 1970, MEd, 1971; PhD, U. Md., 1982. Jr. high math. tchr. Prince George's County Sch. Bd., Md., 1971-77; grad. asst. U. Md., College Park, 1979; math. tchr. North Shore H.S., West Palm Beach, Fla., 1983-84; math tchr., guidance coord. Loggers' Run Mid. Sch., Boca Raton, Fla., 1984-90; math. tchr. Internat. Baccalaureate program Atlantic H.S., Delray Beach, Fla., 1990—. Mem. MENSA, Psi Chi, Phi Kappa Phi. Jewish.

BAUMAN, SANDRA SPIEGEL, nurse practitioner, mental health counselor; b. N.Y.C., June 30, 1949; d. Siegmund and Ruth (Josias) S.; student Boston U., 1967-70; B.S. in Nursing, Adelphi U., 1971, postgrad., 1973-74; M.S. in Community Counseling, Barry Coll., 1981; postgrad. Fla. Atlantic U./Fla. Internat. U., 1982—, Gestalt Inst. Miami, 1982—; clin. specialist psychiat./mental health; m. H. Lee Bauman, Nov. 3, 1978 (div.); 1 child, Brandon Spiegel; m. P.McGrath, 1991. Staff nurse educator obstetrics Albert Einstein Hosp., N.Y.C., 1971-72, head nurse newborn nurseries, 1973-74; asst. instr. maternity nursing St. Johns Riverside Hosp., 1972-73; head nurse obstetrics and nurseries, high risk nursery Mt. Sinai Hosp., Miami Beach, Fla., 1974-78; clin. nursing supr., div. pediatrics Jackson Meml. Hosp., Miami, 1978, coordinator div. clin. edn., 1978-81, quality assurance coordinator Maternal-Child Hosp. Center, 1979-81, perinatal coordinator, 1980-81, also core nursing mem. child protection team, 1979-81, asst. adminstr. ob-gyn, 1981-82; adminstr. Meadowbrook Med. Center, Inc., Dania, Fla., 1982—; pvt. practice Psychotherapy, 1983—; asst. adminstr. nursing Miami Gen. Hosp., 1985, assoc. adminstr. pvt. care services, 1985—; asst. prof. Sch. Nursing, Fla. Internat. U., North Miami, 1982-84, coordinator child bearing and child rearing courses, 1982-84; mem. Fla. Bd. Nursing, 1979-85, vice chmn., 1981-82, chmn., 1982-85; CPR instr., 1978; dir. nursing HCA Grant Ctr. Hosp., Miami, 1986-89, asst. adminstr. Dr's. Hosp., 1990-91; pvt. practice, 1991—; cons. State Fla., 1992-95; interim dir. nursing Charter Hosp., Miami, 1995-96; surveyor Fla. Correctional Med. Authority, 1996. Mem. Am. Nurses Assn. (regional editor 1980—), Fla. Nurses Assn., Fla. Soc. Nurse Execs., Fla. Nursing Adminstrn. Assn., Fla. Hosp. Assn., Fla. Nursing Adminstrn. Soc., Sigma Theta Tau. Contbr. articles to RN mag., Fla. Nursing News, Fla. Nurses Assn. Newsletter and Nursing Mgmt. Office: 7600 SW 57th Ct # 309 Miami FL 33143-5404

BAUMBACH, LISA LORRAINE, research scientist; b. Miami, May 22, 1958; d. Robert William and Elly (Hering) Decker. BA with honors, U. Fla., 1980, PhD in Biochemistry, 1986. Postdoctoral fellow Baylor Coll. Medicine, Houston, 1986-89; clin. fellow U. Colo. Sch. Medicine, Denver, 1989-90; asst. prof. U. Miami Sch. Medicine, 1991—; sci. bd. South Fla. Huntington's Disease Assn., Fla. NFS Assn., UM Brain Endowment Bank, South Fla. Muscular Dystrophy Assn. Contbr. articles to profl. jours. and contbr. book chpts. Vol. student health svc. U. Fla., Gainesville, 1976-86, Shand's Hosp., U. Fla., Gainesville, 1977-78, South Broward Community Hosp., Hollywood, Fla., ARC, Hollywood Meml. Hosp. Emergency Rm., 1975-76, Hosp. Aux. Svc., Hollywood Meml. Hosp., 1974-76, ACORN Rural Health Clinic, Gainesville, 1979-80. Paula Ellis scholarship U. Fla. Coll. Medicine, 1983. Mem. AAAS, Am. Soc. Human Genetics, Am. Acad. Neurology, Am. Cancer Soc., N.Y. Acad. Scis. Office: U Miami Sch Medicine Mailman Ctr PO Box 016820 Miami FL 33101

BAUMBERGER, CHARLES HENRY, lawyer; b. Port Huron, Mich., Sept. 13, 1941; s. Peter Julius and Evelyn Margaret (Jackson) B.; m. Martha Carolyn Megathlin, Aug. 8, 1969; children: Peter Scott, Charles Henry Jr. BA, Vanderbilt U., 1963; JD, U. Fla., 1966. Bar: Fla. 1966, U.S. Dist. Ct. (so. dist.) Fla. 1967; cert. civil trial lawyer. Atty. Stephens, Demos & Magill, Miami, Fla., 1967-68; ptnr. Hastings, Goldman & Baumberger, Miami, 1969-74; founding ptnr. Rossman & Baumberger P.A., Miami, 1974—; lectr. various continuing legal edn. programs; guest on numerous radio, TV talk shows, 1987—. Contbr. articles to profl. jours. Mem. Gov's. Task Force on Emergency Room and Trauma Care, 1987; So. Fla. Health Action Coalition, Inc., 1984; task force on trauma and trauma systems Dept. Transp., 1987—. Served to 1st lt. U.S. Army Res., 1966-72. Mem. ABA, ATLA, Fed. Bar Assn., Dade County Bar Assn. (bd. dirs. 1977-88, pres. 1989-90), Fla. Bar (exec. coun. trial lawyers sect. 1983-89, chmn. 1990-91), Acad. Fla. Trial Lawyers (bd. dirs. 1980-89), Dade County Trial Lawyers Assn. (founding mem. bd. dirs. 1981-84), Am. Bd. Trial Advocates (Miami chpt., treas. 1992-93, sec. 1993-94, pres. 1995—), Fla. Lawyers Action Group, So. Trial Lawyers Assn., Trial Lawyers for Pub. Justice (founding mem. 1982—), Am. Coll. Trial Lawyers, Coral Reef Yacht Club, Univ. Club. Democrat. Methodist. Home: 5755 Suncrest Dr Miami FL 33156-5704 Office: Rossman Baumberger & Reboso 44 W Flagler St Fl 23 Miami FL 33130

BAUMGARDNER, KAREN THORNTON, retired newspaper executive; b. Dallas, July 31, 1953; d. Thomas James and Lola Ruth (Russell) Thornton; m. J.W. Baumgardner Jr. BA, U. Tex., Arlington, 1976. Adminstrv. asst. City of LaPorte, Fire Marshal's, Tex., 1977-78; adminstrv. asst., sec. credit/collections/fin. The Houston Post Co., 1978-83; adminstrv. asst., acct. H&C Communications, Inc., Houston, 1983-85, employee benefits mgr., 1985-92; ret., 1992; Mem. Employers Coun. Flexible Compensation, Washington, 1987-92. Precinct del. Tex. Rep. Conv., San Antonio, 1980. Mem. S.W. Benefits Assn., Am. Payroll Assn. Republican. Baptist.

BAUMGARDNER, THEODORE ROGERS, lawyer; b. Cleve., Apr. 28, 1935; s. Harold Koppes and Florence (Secrest) B.; m. Mary Elizabeth Bumiller, June 25, 1959 (div. Aug. 1965); 1 child, Laurie Roberts; m. Mary Ann Esa, Dec. 7, 1969; 1 child, Carol Ann. BA in Philosophy, Williams Coll., 1957; postgrad., Columbia U., 1958-59; MA in Teaching, Johns Hopkins U., 1960; LLB, U. Md., 1963. Bar: Md. 1963, U.S. Supreme Ct. 1971, U.S. Ct. Claims 1971, Fla. 1986. Tchr. french St. Paul's Episcopal Sch. for Boys, Brooklandville, Md., 1959-63; staff atty. bureau supplies and accounts Dept. Navy, Washington, 1963-65; chief counsel Navy Tng. Systems Ctr. Dept. Navy, Port Washington, N.Y., 1965; chief counsel Navy Tng. Systems Ctr. Dept. Navy, Orlando, Fla., 1965-87, so. area counsel Naval Supply Systems Command, 1982-86. Author: GAO's Bid Protest Procedures: A Handbook for the Navy Attorney, 1981, Conducting a Competitive Negotiated Procurement: Fundamental Principles and Special Rules, 1986. Fellow Ford Found., Johns Hopkins U., Balt., 1959-60. Mem. Fed. Bar Assn., ABA, Nat. Contract Mgmt. Assn., Nat. Security Indsl. Assn., E. Cen. Fla. Space Bus. Roundtable, Citrus Club. Republican. Presbyterian. Office: Baker & Hostetler 1300 Barnett Pla PO Box 112 Orlando FL 32802-0112

BAUMGARTEN, DIANA VIRGINIA, gerontological nurse; b. Bklyn., May 24, 1943; d. Francis and Leah (Cuoghi) DeMarco; married; children: Elizabeth Salonia, Matthew, Edward. AS, Broward C.C., 1991. RN, Fla. Pediats. staff nurse North Broward Med. Ctr., Pompano Beach, Fla., 1991; staff nurse Tamarac (Fla.) Convalescent Ctr., 1992; nursing supr. Tamarac (Fla.) Convalescent Ctr., Ft. Lauderdale, Fla., 1992-93; corp. nurse cons. HBA Health Mgmt. Corp., Ft. Lauderdale, Fla., 1993-94; acting DON Broward Convalescent Home, Ft. Lauderdale, 1994; acting asst. DON Springtree Walk Nursing Ctr., Sunrise, Fla., 1994; resident assessment coord., infection control officer Broward Convalescent Home, Ft. Lauderdale, 1994-95; asst. dir. nursing Adon Hillhaven Convalescent Ctr., Fla., 1995—. Mem. ANA, Fla. Nurses' Assn., Phi Theta Kappa. Home: 11417 Little Bear Dr Boca Raton FL 33428

BAUR, ISOLDE NACKE, translator, freelance writer, public speaker; b. Dresden, Saxonia, Germany, May 27, 1923; came to U.S., 1954; d. Otto Ernst and Anna Louise (Liebscher) Nacke; m. Karl Baur, Oct. 23, 1943 (dec. Oct. 1963); children: Ulrich, Marieluise Baur-Kailing. Student, Draughton's Bus. Coll., Dallas, 1964, U. Tex., Arlington, 1974. Milliner Cohn Co., Dresden, Fed. Republic Germany, 1937-39; drill press operator Zeiss-Ikon Corp., Dresden, 1939-41; engring. aid Messerschmitt Aircraft Corp., Augsburg, Fed. Republic Germany, 1941-43; blue print collaborator Ling-Temco-Vought Aerospace Corp., Dallas, 1963-64; office clk. Barnes Group Inc., Grand Prairie, Tex., 1964-69; freelance translator, writer, pub. speaker, 1969-71; manpower analyst Xerox Corp., Dallas and Ft. Worth, 1971-76; owner Baur Translation Svc., 1972—. Contbr. articles to jours. Mem. coun. German Day in Tex. Coun., Dallas, 1964—, awards chmn., 1978-88, hon. chmn., 1981; bd. dirs. Dallas Goethe Ctr., 1964-74, 2d v.p., membership chmn., 1970-72, 1st v.p./program chmn., 1973-75; sec. Unitarian Universalist Ch. Arlington, 1968-70; vol. guardian Tarrant County, Ft. Worth, 1988—; co-leader Girl Scouts Am., 1955-63. Mem. Soaring Soc. Am., Am. Translators Assn. (exec. com. conv. 1981), Tex. Soaring Assn. (hon. life, treas. 1964-66, sec. 1976-78, editor Spirals newsletter 1978-80), Acad. Flying Club U. Tech./Stuttgart (hon. sr.).

BAUSCH, RICHARD CARL, writer, educator; b. Ft. Benning, Ga., Apr. 18, 1945; s. Robert Carl and Helen (Simmons) B.; m. Karen Miller, May 3, 1969; children: Wesley, Emily, Paul, Maggie, Amanda. BA, George Mason U., 1973; MFA, U. Iowa, 1975. Instr. No. Va. C.C., Annandale, Va., 1975-80; prof., Heritage chair of creative writing George Mason U., Fairfax, Va., 1980—; vis. prof. U. Va., Charlottesville, 1985, 88, Wesleyan U., Middletown, Conn., 1986, 90, 92, 93; lectr., reader in field. Author: (stories) Spirits and Other Stories, 1987 (PEN/Faulkner award nomination 1988), The Fireman's Wife & Other Stories, 1990, Rare & Endangered Species, 1994; (novels) Real Presence, 1980, Take Me Back, 1981 (PEN/Faulkner award nomination 1982), The Last Good Time, 1984, Mrs. Field's Daughter, 1989, Violence, 1992, Rebel Powers, 1993. Recipient Lila Wallace Reader's Best Writer's award Lila Wallace Fund, 1992, Acad. award in Lit. AAAL, 1993; grantee Nat. Endowment for the Arts, 1982; Guggenheim fellow John Simon Guggenheim Found., 1984. Mem. PEN Am. Democrat. Roman Catholic. Office: George Mason U English Dept 4400 University Dr Fairfax VA 22030-4443

BAUTISTA, ABRAHAM PARANA, immunologist; b. Davao, Philippines, Mar. 15, 1952; s. Eufronio Bernardo and Loreto (Parana) B. BS in Biology, Far Eastern U., Manila, Philippines, 1972; Diploma in Microbiology, U. Tokyo, 1978; MS, Aberdeen (Scotland) U., 1981, PhD in Immunology, 1984. Sr. rschr. lectr. U. Santo Tomas, Manila, 1976-81; rsch. scholar U. Aberdeen, 1979-84; rsch. assoc. East Carolina U., Greenville, N.C., 1984-89; asst. prof. La. State U. Med. Ctr., New Orleans, 1989-93, assoc. prof., 1993—. Guest editor, reviewer Jour. Leukocyte Biology, 1988—, Circulatory Shock, 1991—, Am. Jour. Physiology, 1991—, Alcohol, 1992—, Alcoholism Clin. and Exptl. Rsch., 1992—, Hepatology, 1993—, Gastroenterology, 1994—, Biochem. Pharmacol, 1995—, Internat. Jour. Cancer, 1995—; contbr. articles to over 60 sci. articles to profl. jours. NIH-NIAAA grantee, 1995—; travel fellow Am. Assn. for Study Liver Disease, 1990; Internat. scholar Brit. Coun., 1979; recipient Rsch. award in Medicine, U. Aberdeen, 1981-84, F.I.R.S.T. award/Rsch. grantee NIH, 1991—; named Internat. UNESCO, 1978. Mem. AAAS, Am. Assn. Immunology, N.Y. Acad. Scis., Inst. of Biology, Soc. for Leukocyte Biology, Rsch. Soc. of Alcoholism, Sigma Xi. Home: 103 Hollow Rock Ct Slidell LA 70461-3422 Office: La State U Med Ctr 1901 Perdido St New Orleans LA 70112-1328

BAVINGER, EUGENE ALLEN, artist, educator; b. Sapulpa, Okla., Dec. 21, 1919. BFA, U. Okla.; MFA, Inst. Allende, Mex. Represented by Addison Gallery Am. Art, Andover, Mass., Nelson Gallery; prof. art. U. Okla., 1947—. One man exhbns. include Philbrook Art Ctr., Tulsa, Okla., 1965, Sheldon Art Gallery, Lincoln, Nebr., 1967, Joslyn Art Mus., Omaha, 1969, Contemporary Arts Found., Oklahoma City, 1972, Kans. State U., Manhattan, 1973, Tibor de Nagy Gallery, Houston, 1975, Tex. Christian U., Ft. Worth, 1976, Razor Gallery, N.Y., 1978, 500 Exposition Gallery, Dallas, 1982, Fred Jones Jr. Mus. Art. U. Okla., Norman, 1986, Kauffman Gallery, Houston, 1987, Dubins Gallery, L.A., 1988, C/G Rein Gallery, Santa Fe, N. Mex., 1992, Pickard Gallery, Oklahoma City, 1994. Recipient First award 22nd Ann Exhib., Ft. Smith Art Ctr., Ark., 1972, Purchase award 19th ann., Ark. Art Ctr., Little Rock, 1976. Address: 730 NE 60th St Norman OK 73071-0710

BAVIS, KAREN ANN, accountant; b. Bklyn., Nov. 9, 1962; d. John Jacob and Janet Mary (Flood) Zerrenner; m. Robert Charles Bavis, Apr. 16, 1988; children: Christopher Robert, Daniel James. BBA in Acctg., Coll. of William and Mary, Williamsburg, Va., 1985; MBA in Fin., The Am. U., 1995. CPA, Va. Acct. Ernst & Young, Washington, 1985-89; contr. Front Royal Group, Inc. and subsidiaries, McLean, Va., 1989-91; corp. sec., treas. Front Royal Ins. Co. and Environ. Ins. Mgmt., 1991-93; ind. practice, 1993—; cons. Sm. Bus. Adminstrn., 1993-95. Bd. dirs., treas. Keene Mill Oaks Homeowners Assn., Springfield, 1990-92; mem. Wolfe Trap Assocs., Vienna, Va., 1989—; resident assoc. Smithsonian Instn., 1991-95. Mem. AICPAs, Smithsonian Inst.

BAXLEY, ELIZABETH DAWN, pharmacist; b. Florence, S.C., May 21, 1963; d. Thomas Orin and Etta Mae (Lundy) B. BS in Biology, Furman U., 1984; BS in Pharmacy, Med. U. S.C., 1988. Registered pharmacist, S.C. Staff pharmacist Anderson (S.C.) Meml. Hosp., 1988-89, Self Meml. Hosp., Greenwood, S.C., 1989-90, 91—; asst. dir. pharmacy ops. Am. Therapeutic Cons., Inc., Spartanburg, S.C., 1990—; cons. Abbott Labs. HPD, Chgo., 1994—; cons. Nat. Data Corp., Atlanta, 1989; relief pharmacist Abbeville County Meml. Hosp., 1989—, Abbeville, S.C., Wal-Mart, Greenwood, 1989—; panel presenter Substance Abuse Prevention A.H.E.A.D. Conf., 1989. Course coord., tchr. vol. Roper Mountain Sci. Ctr. Health Edn. Dept., Greenville, S.C., 1988—; cons., tchr. Anderson/Oconee Drug & Alcohol Abuse Commn., 1988—, leader family group, 1989, vol. medical missions. Mem. Am. Pharm. Assn., Am. Soc. Hosp. Pharmacists, S.C. Pharm. Assn. (Disting. Young Pharmacist of Yr. 1990), S.C. Soc. Hosp. Pharmacists, S.C. Recovery and Intervention Pharmacists' Team (charter, treas. 1988—, del. U. Utah 1988), APhA Pharmacists Recovery Network, Soc. Profl. Well-Being, Christian Pharmacists Fellowship Internat., Phi Delta Chi. Home: PO Box 13895 Anderson SC 29624-0895 Office: Self Meml Hosp Spring St Greenwood SC 29646

BAXLEY, LUCY, state treasurer. Treas. State of Ala., Montgomery, 1996. Office: State Treas Office State Capitol Rm 106 11 S Union St Montgomery AL 36104-3760

BAXTER, BARBARA MORGAN, plastics manufacturing company executive, educator; b. Cleve., Apr. 14, 1939; d. James Clifford and Mildred Elizabeth (Button) Baxter; m. David S. Unkefer, Dec. 28, 1956 (div.); children: Rachel, Clifford David, Elizabeth, Monica, Todd James. BSBA in MIS, Bowling Green State U., 1977, MBA, 1979, postgrad. in psychology, 1984; postgrad. in psychology, Wright State U., 1984-85. Clk. J.C. Baxter Co., Minerva, Ohio, 1962-66; v.p., co-founder Sherwood Plastics, Inc., Fostoria, Ohio, 1966-75, pres., chief exec. officer, 1975-89; mem. adj. faculty Tiffin (Ohio) U., 1984-90; MIS cons. to small bus., 1984-90; adj. continuing edn. faculty Sandhills C.C., Pinehurst, N.C., 1992-93; adj. faculty St. Andrews Coll., Lauringburg, N.C., 1993; CEO, co-founder CompuTutor, Inc., Southern Pines, N.C., 1994—. V.p. Carroll County Young Reps., 1960-61; mem. Carroll County Rep. Cen. and Exec. Com., 1961-65, Wood County Rep. Com., 1967-70; troop leader, troop organizer, badge cons. Girl Scouts U.S., 1967-81; vestrywoman, sr. warden Trinity Episcopal Ch., Fostoria, 1972-75; therapist Community Hospice Care Seneca County, Tiffin, 1987-89; del. U.S.-China Trade Talks People to People, Spokane, Wash., 1988; adv. bd. Tiffin U. Students in Free Enterprise, 1986-87; tchr. applied econs. Jr. Achievement, 1988-89. Mem. Order Eastern Star, Ladies Oriental Shrine N.Am., Fostoria Shrine Club (pres. 1982-83), DAR, Alpha Lambda Delta. Office: 175 E New Hampshire Ave Southern Pines NC 28387

BAXTER, GREGORY WAYNE, human resources consultant; b. Columbus, Ohio, Sept. 27, 1948; s. Aaron and Mary Lou (Long) B.; m. Lucinda Jo Kerley, May 25, 1974. BA in English, Texas A&M U., 1970, MS in Mgmt., 1974; PhD in Bus. Adminstrn., Nova U., 1988. Asst. supr. employment Armco Houston Works, Houston, 1975-76; corp. personnel mgr. Molenco, Inc., Houston, 1976-79; area personnel mgr. Sperry Univac, Houston, 1979-83; founder R.E.S. Inc., Houston, 1983-86; human resources supr. Ericsson Network Systems, Richardson, Tex., 1986; cons. to electronics firms and small businesses, 1987—; asst. prof. mgmt. Southeastern Okla. State U., 1990-94. Contbr. articles to profl. and mil. jours. Lt. col. USAR. Mem. Nat. Acad. Mgmt., Assn. U.S. Army, Reserve Officers Assn., DAV, Mensa. Avocation: comml. air and instrument piloting. Home: 5118 Vanderbilt Ave Dallas TX 75206-6018

BAXTER, RICHARD DAVID, lawyer, minister; b. N.Y.C., Mar. 18, 1947; s. George Leorphan and Evelyn Carolyn (Kollmar) B. BA in Polit. Sci., The Am. U., 1968; JD, Columbia U., 1971, MBA, 1971; MS in Counseling Psychology, Nova Southeastern U., 1991. Bar: N.Y. 1972, U.S. Dist. Ct. (so. and ea. dists.) N.Y. 1978, U.S. Ct. Appeals (2d dir.) 1978, U.S. Tax Ct. 1978, U.S. Supreme Ct. 1978, Fla. 1979, U.S. Dist. Ct. (so. dist.) Fla. 1979; lic. minister, Religious Sci. Internat. Assoc. LeBoeuf, Lamb, Leiby & MacRae, N.Y.C., 1972-79; tax counsel Ruden, Barnett, McClosky, Schuster & Russell, P.A., Ft. Lauderdale, Fla., 1979-81; prof. law N.Y. Law Sch., N.Y.C., 1980-81; assoc. Capp, Reinstein, Kopelowitz & Atlas, P.A., Ft. Lauderdale, 1982-85, Greenberg, Traurig, Askew, Hoffman, Lipoff, Rosen & Quentel, P.A., Ft. Lauderdale, 1985-87; pvt. practice Ft. Lauderdale and Orlando, 1987—; pres., dir., minister New Beginnings Ctr., Toledo, Ohio, 1991-95; pres., of counsel Ctr. for Profl. Legal Svcs., Orlando, 1996—; bus. counselor, lectr. Small Bus. Devel. Ctr. Coll. Bus. U. Ctrl. Fla., Orlando, 1996. Author: The Taxation of Ministers-Blessings in Disguise, 1996. Mem. Winterfest, Ft. Lauderdale, 1985-91, 2d Century Broward, Ft. Lauderdale, 1985-91, Greater Ft. Lauderdale Film Festival, 1988-91, Young Reps., Orlando, 1995—, New Directions-Am. Cancer Soc., 1995—; founding trustee Ohio-Mich. Networking Inst., Toledo, 1992-93. Mem. ABA, Ctrl. Fla. Computer Soc., Greater Orlando C. of C., Outdoors & Active. Office: 5405 Diplomat Cir Ste 201 Orlando FL 32810

BAXTER, SUZANNE DOMEL, nutrition researcher; b. Dallas, Dec. 18, 1958; d. Edwin A. and LaVerne Helen (Hobratsch) D.; m. David Woodrow Baxter, Nov. 16, 1996. BS in Home Economics, Tex. Christian U., 1981; MS in Nutrition, Tex. Women's U., 1987, PhD in Nutrition, 1990. Lic. dietitian, Ga. Nutritionist U. Tex. Med. Br., Galveston, 1981-83; supr.tng. and quality control Grand Prairie (Tex.) Ind. Sch. Dist., 1983-84; supr. WIC Ft. Worth Pub. Health Dept., 1984-86; grad. asst. Tex. Women's U., Denton, 1986-90; postdoctoral fellow Med. Coll. Ga., Augusta, 1991-93, asst. prof. nutrition, 1993—. Contbr. articles, revs. to profl. jours. V.p. Luth. Women's Missionary League Beautiful Savior Luth. Ch., Arlington, Tex., 1989-90; mem. Congl. Missions Com. 1st Presbyn. Ch., Augusta, Ga., 1994—, chmn. Koinonia Adminstrn., 1992, chmn. Koinonia Hospitality, 1993-94. Recipient FIRST award Nat. Cancer Inst./NIH, 1993—; named Young Dietitian of Yr. Dallas Dietetic Assn., 1987. Fellow Am. Dietetic Assn. (registered dietitian, Kraft-Gen. Foods fellow 1988-90), Soc. Nutrition Edn. (Ann. Meeting grantee 1990), Soc. Behavioral Medicine, Soc. Applied Rsch. in Memory and Cognition. Presbyterian. Office: Med Coll Ga Ga Prevention Inst HS-1640 Augusta GA 30912

BAXTER, TURNER BUTLER, independent oil operator; b. Dermott, Ark., Mar. 13, 1922; s. Robert Wiley and Sallie Hollis (Murphy) B.; BBA, U. Tex., 1947; MBA, Pepperdine U., L.A., 1976; m. Pauline Taylor Bond, June 7, 1947; children: David Bond, Paula Taylor. With Rio Grande Nat. Life Ins. Co., Dallas, 1947-67, sr. v.p., 1963-67; engaged in investments, 1967-75, 79—; ind. oil operator, 1979—; pres. Shelby Office Supply Inc., Dallas, 1975-79. Pres. Dallas Health and Sci. Mus., 1953-56; adv. bd. Dallas Community Chest Trust Fund, 1976—; v.p. Circle Ten coun. Boy Scouts Am., 1970-74. With USAAF, 1943-46. Recipient Silver Beaver award Boy Scouts Am., 1968. Mem. Salesmanship Club Dallas. Methodist. Clubs: Kiwanis (pres. 1966), Dallas Country, Petroleum (Dallas). Home: PO Box 620 Kaufman TX 75142-0620 Office: PO Box 620 Kaufman TX 75142-0620

BAYES, RONALD HOMER, English language educator; b. Freewater, Oreg., July 19, 1932; s. Floyd Edgar and Mildred Florence (Cochran) B. BS, East Oreg. State Coll., 1955, MS, 1956; postgrad., U. Pa., 1959-60; DDM, U. Delle Arti, Termi, Italy, 1982. Asst. prof. English Ea. Oreg. State Coll., LaGrande, 1955-56, assoc. prof. English, 1960-68; lectr. English U. Md., College Park, 1958-59, 66-67; prof. St. Andrews Presbyn. Coll., Laurinburg, N.C., 1968—; founder, exec. bd. St. Andrews Rev. & Press, Laurinburg, 1970-95; mem. N.C. State Arts Coun., Raleigh, 1987-89; master poet Atlantic Ctr. for Arts, New Smyrna Beach, Fla., 1988; cons. Nat. Coun. for Arts, Washington, 1969-71. Author: (poetry) Dust & Desire, 1961, Cages & Journeys, 1964, Child Outside My Window, 1965, History of the Turtle, 1970, The Casketmaker, 1972, Porpoise, 1974, Tokyo Annex, 1977, King of August, 1979, Fram, 1979, Beast in View, 1985, Guises, 1992; (fiction) Sister City, 1971. Chmn. Rep. Ctrl. Com., Union County, Oreg., 1967-68, Scotland County, N.C., 1980-81; active Oreg. del. Rep. Nat. Conv., San Francisco, 1956; bd. dirs. Scotland County Humane Soc., Laurinburg, 1993—. With U.S. Army, 1956-58. Woodrow Wilson Nat. fellow, 1959-60; named one of Outstanding Young Men of Am., 1960; recipient Outstanding Alumni award Ea. Oreg. State Coll., 1973; Roanoke-Chowan prize for poetry, 1973, N.C. Writers' Conf. award, 1987, master poet Atlana Ctr. for the Arts, 1988, N.C. arts grantee, 1988, N.C. award for Literature, 1989, cert. honor Poetry Coun. N.C., 1994. Mem. Danforth Found. (assoc.), Internat. House Japan, Japan Soc., N.C. Poetry Soc. (life), Oregon Poetry Soc. Republican. Episcopalian. Home: PO Box 206 Laurinburg NC 28352

BAYLIS, WILLIAM THOMAS, senior systems logistics engineer; b. Bay Shore, N.Y., Oct. 21, 1952; s. William Wood and Viola Elaine (Burtis) B.; m. Milagros Marfisi, July 3, 1988; children: Christopher Thomas, Justin William Andrew. BSBA, U. Tenn., 1981; MBA in Mgmt., Dowling Coll., Oakdale, N.Y., 1984; PhD in Mgmt., Columbia Pacific U., San Raefel, Calif., 1986; postgrad., N.Y. Inst. Tech., 1987—. Asst. mgr. AIL div. Eaton Corp., Deer Park, N.Y., 1984-86, group leader, 1986-88; program mgr. Gen. Instrument Corp., Hicksville, N.Y., 1988-89, mgr. logistics engring., 1988-89; sr. logistics engr., logistics support analysis engring. lead McDonnell Douglas Space Systems Co., Kennedy Space Center, Fla., 1989-94; sys. engr. Avionics Rsch. Corp., Orlando, Fla., 1994—, systems engr., 1994—; Level II Integrated Database adminstr., security coord. for Space Sta. Freedom Program; pres. WTB Enterprises, Melbourne, Fla., 1990—; cons. in logistics and systems engring., systems devel. computer-based tng.; part-time instr. space logistics tech. Brevard C.C. (adv. com. logistics systems tech. program), tchr. various logistics engring. courses; panel spkr. on space sta. group ops./logistics integration, Cocoa Beach, Fla., 1991, logistics support analysis spkr. 27th ann. Internat. Conf. and Tech. Exposition, Indpls., 1992; chmn. tech. adv. bd. SOLE Logistics Engring., 1992-94; mem. tech. adv. bd. chmn. BCC's Multimedia Devel., 1994; guest spkr. ninth annual ILS/LSA Govt./Industry Exchange Conf., 1996. Author, editor: Starting a Retail Business, 1988, Trainer's Guide to Task Analysis, 1989, Logistics Engineer's Desk Reference, 1991, 92, LSA/LSAR Manual, 1992-94, Excel Manual, 1992-94, Word/Windows Manual, 1992-94; author: Training Requirements for Defense Contracts: A Practitioner's Desk Reference, 1989, Developing, Designing and Delivering Productive and Efficient Training, 1992; editor Training Issues column in Soletter, 1994; developer software course Lotus 123, 1989. With USN, 1974-78. Recipient Chmn. award SOLE chpt., 1992, Guest Speaker award SOLE, 1992, Space Congress Achievement award 30th Space Congress, 1992, Speaker award Fla. 1994 Conf. and Workshop, 1994, Cert. of Appreciation Air Force Jour. of Logistics, 1995, Brevard C.C. Outstanding Adjunct of Yr. award, 1994-95, Cert. Appreciation Air Force Jour. Logistics, 1995; named Coord. of Yr. Total Quolets, 1994—, Total Quality Facilitation of Yr., 1995. Mem. AIAA, Am. Mgmt. Assn., Soc. Logistics Engrs. (Splty. award in logistics support analysis 1991, 92, 93), Internat. Soc. Philos. Enquiry, Assn. MBA Execs., Mensa, Intertel, Am. Legion, Phi Eta Sigma. Home: 1988 Trevino Cir Melbourne FL 32935-2136 Office: Northip Grumman Corp Melbourne FL 32935

BAYLISS, GEOFFREY S., chemical company executive. Pres. GeoChem Rsch., Inc., Houston. Office: GeoChem Rsch Inc 1143-C Brittmore Rd Ste C Houston TX 77000

BAYNE, JAMES ELWOOD, oil company executive; b. Detroit, May 6, 1940; s. John David and Alice Angie (Davis) B.; m. Mary Lee Skinner, May 4, 1963; children: James E. Jr., Laura Lee Poe. BA, Yale U., 1962; MBA, Columbia U., 1967. Investment adminstr. Bankers Trust, N.Y.C., 1962-65; fin analyst Standard Oil, N.Y.C., 1967; sr. fin. analyst Esso Internat., N.Y.C., 1967-70; asst. treas. Esso S.A.P.A., Buenos Aires, 1970-71; treas. Intercol, Bogota, Colombia, 1971-74; asst. treas. Esso InterAm., Coral Gables, Fla., 1974-77; asst. gen. mgr. Esso Cen. Am., Coral Gables, Fla., 1977-80; mgr. Mexican Bus. Opportunity, Coral Gables, 1980-81; treas. Exxon Chem. Europe, Brussels, 1981-86; mgr., benefits fin. and investment Exxon, Dallas, 1986—; mem. CIEBA, Washington, 1986—; vice chmn. CIEBA, Washington, 1995-96, exec. com., 1994—, chmn. 1996—; pension adv. com. N.Y. Stock Exch., 1995—; bd. dirs. N.Y. Client Adv. Com.; mem. adv. bd. Wharton Trading Sys., 1993—. Steering com. Interforum; mem. Fin. Execs. Inst.; pres. secretariat Dallas-Ft. Worth Cursillo Movement; dir. Episcopal Renewal Ctr., dir. Dallas-Ft. Worth Episcopal Renewal Ctr.; mem. bd. councillors U. Dallas. Fellow George H. Gallup Internat. Inst.; mem. Pension 21 Club (N.Y.C.), Yale Club Dallas, Harbor Club (gov. Seal Harbor, Maine), Beta Gamma Sigma. Episcopalian. Home: 3204 Saint Johns Dr Dallas TX 75205-2919 Office: Exxon 5959 Las Colinas Blvd Irving TX 75039-2248

BAYRAK, COSKUN, computer scientist, researcher, educator; b. Gümüshane, Torul, Turkey, Mar. 1, 1959; came to U.S., 1982; s. Celal and Sebahat (Karsan) B.; m. Isil Colakoglu, Feb. 28, 1987; children: Sinehan Burcu, Ecehan Didem. BA, Slippery Rock U., 1985; MS, Tex. Tech. U., 1989; PhD, So. Meth. U., 1994. Lectr. Karadeniz Tech. U., Trabzon, Turkey, 1986-90; engring. mgr. Rutishauser, Inc., Dallas, 1990-91; design engr. D. F. Benn & Assocs., Dallas, 1991-92; rschr. Halff & Assocs., Inc., Dallas, 1992-93; system analyst Net Computers Internat., Dallas, 1991—; lab. supr., teaching asst. So. Meth. U., Dallas, 1992—; prof. U. Tex. at Dallas, 1994-95; prof. dept. math. and computer sci. Benedict Coll., 1995—. Contbr. papers to profl. jours. Mem. IEEE, ASME, SDPS, IIGSS, Assn. Computing Machinery, Sigma Xi. Republican. Home: 50-G Paisley Ln Columbia SC 29210

BAYSAL, FATIH DOGAN, trading company executive; b. Diyarbakir, Turkey, Nov. 12, 1955; came to U.S., 1977; s. Selim and Servet (Oztekin) B.; m. Dilsat, Sept. 14, 1990; 1 child, Mirel. BSCE, Bogazici U., Istanbul, Turkey, 1977; MSCE, La. State U., 1979. EIT, La. Rsch. asst. La. State U., Baton Rouge, 1977-79; regional mktg. mgr. Fugro Gulf, Inc., Houston, 1979-82; mktg. mgr. Syminex, Inc., Houston, 1982-83; pres. Seba Internat., Inc., Houston, 1982—; also bd. dirs. Co-author: (tech. book) Thermal and Loading Effects on Soil Parameters, 1979. Mem. Rep. presdl. task force, Washington, 1982—; permanent mem. Nat. Rep. Senatorial Com., Washington, 1984—. Mem. Am. Soc. Civil Engrs., Turkish Chamber of Civil Engrs., C. of C., Am. Turkish Assn. Republican. Office: Seba Internat Inc 9801 Westheimer Rd Ste 203 Houston TX 77042-3900

BAZZELL, JUDY GUNNELL, nursing educator; b. Paintsville, Ky., Dec. 10, 1956; d. Adrian Ghlen and Anna (Hall) Gunnell; m. Samuel Mark Bazzell, June 25, 1976; children: Christopher, Nicholas, Adrianne. AAS, Gulf Coast Community Coll., 1977; BSN, Troy State U., 1982, MSN, 1990. Supr. pediatrics nursing Charles Henderson Child Health Ctr., Troy, Ala., 1982-89; lab. coord. Troy State U., 1989-92, asst. prof. pediatrics, 1992—. Mem. ANA, Ala. Nurses Assn., Pike County Nurses Assn., Sigma Theta Tau, Iota Theta Tau (treas.). Home: 105 Woodley Ave Troy AL 36081-4535

BEACH, BARBARA PURSE, lawyer; b. Washington, June 12, 1947; d. Clifford John and Lillian (Natarus) B. BA, U. Ky., 1968; MSW, U. Md., 1972; JD, Am. U., 1980. Bar: D.C. 1980, Va. 1980. Law clk. to presiding justice benefit rev. bd. U.S. Dept. Labor, Washington, 1980; asst. city atty. City of Alexandria, Va., 1981-85; atty. Ross, Marsh, Foster, Myers & Quiggle, Alexandria, 1985-90, Beach, Butt & Assocs., P.C., Alexandria, 1990-92; prin. Beach & Assocs., Alexandria, 1992—; town atty. Town of Herndon (Va.), 1992-94. Vice chmn. Va. Health Svcs. Cost Rev. Coun., 1989-92; mem. Va. Commn. on Women and Minorities, 1990-92. Mem. Va. Trial Lawyers Assn., Alexandria Bar Assn. (pres. 1987-88). Office: Beach & Assocs 416 Prince St Alexandria VA 22314

BEACH, HAZEL ELIZABETH, nurse; b. Oakdale, Tenn., June 27, 1929; d. Michael Thomas and Susie Margaret (Babinchak) Semanick; m. Edward Junior Beach, Oct. 7, 1961; children: Monica Ann, Edward Michael. RN La., Tenn. Staff nurse Meml. Hosp., Chattanooga, 1952-61, head nurse, 1961-66; evening supr. Downtown Hosp., Chattanooga, 1977-83; staff nurse East Ridge Hosp., Chattanooga, 1983-91, charge nurse, 1991-95; ret., 1996—. Profl. artist. Vol. ARC, Washington, 1960—. Mem. ANA, Cath. Nurses Assn. Roman Catholic. Home: 8419 Oak Dr Chattanooga TN 37421-4342

BEACHUM, SHARON GARRISON, graphic designer and educator; b. Oklahoma City, Dec. 1, 1953; d. Troy S. and Madelene L. (Ball) Swift; m. Brian E. Beachum, Aug. 5, 1989. BFA with honors magna cum laude, U. Okla., 1975; MFA summa cum laude, Old Dominion U./Norfolk State, 1986. Tchr. art Bur. Indian Affairs and Shawnee (Okla.) Pub. Schs., 1976; grad. asst. screenprint Old Dominion U., Norfolk, Va., 1985; instr. design, figure drawing, comml. art Gov.'s Magnet Sch. for the Arts, Norfolk, 1985-88; asst. prof. art Hampton (Va.) U., 1988—, interim chair dept. art, 1990-91, chair dept. art, 1991-94, curator dept. of art gallery, 1990-94; instr. photo workshop Ghent Venture Sr. Citizens Programs, Norfolk, 1987; instr. arts and crafts Norfolk Acad. Summer Art Camp, 1986-89; instr. photography d'Art Ctr., Norfolk, 1986-87; instr. advanced graphic design Norfolk State U., 1987; instr. advt. design Tidewater C.C., Chesapeake, Va., 1987; instr. photography Peninsula Fine Arts Ctr., Newport News, 1990; exchange faculty Internat. Coll. Academics and Bus., Kanuma, Tochigi-Ken, Japan, summer 1993; owner Swift Graphics, 1977-92. Tech. illustrator Telemedia, Inc., Norfolk, 1980-82; lead tech. artist Med. Illustration Dept., U. Okla. Health Scis. Ctr., Oklahoma City, 1977-80; artist U. Okla. Press, Norman, 1975-77; illustrator dept. zoology U. Okla., 1973-75; exhbns. include Okla. Bapt. U., Shawnee, 1976, Okla. Mus. Art, Oklahoma City, 1976, Grover Cleveland Art Ctr., 1978, OMNIPLEX Mus., 1979, 80, Stewart Wilson Gallery, N.Y.C., 1981, Franklin Furnace, 1983, Peninsula Fine Arts Assn., Newport News, Va., 1983, 88, Chrysler Mus., Norfolk, 1984, 86, 87, 90, 91 (Merit award 1986, Purchase award 1986), Artists Against Hunger Show and Auction, 1985, Bodyworks, Norfolk, 1985, 87, d'Art Ctr., Norfolk, 86, 87, 91, 93, Peninsula Fine Arts Ctr., Newport News, 1986, 88, 92 (Photography award 1986), TAG Gallery, Norfolk, 1987, 88, Cafe 21 Town Point Ctr., 1987, Va. Soc. Photographic Arts Exhibit, Richmond, 1987, Hermitage Found. Mus., Norfolk, 1987, Am. Diabetes Show and Auction, Virginia Beach, 1987, 88, On the Hill, Yorktown, Va., 1987, Virginia Beach Pavilion, 1988, Old Dominion U. Gallery, Norfolk, 1988, Washington Ctr. Photography, 1988, 89, Virginia Beach Arts Ctr., 1988, James Madison U., Harrisonburg, Va., 1989, FX Gallery, 1989, Armstrong-Slater Gallery, Hampton, 1992, Birke Gallery of Art, Huntington, W.Va., 1992, Hill Gallery, Yorktown, Va., 1992, d'Art Ctr., Norfolk, 1993, Armstrong-Slate Gallery, Hampton, 1994, Cornell Coll., Mount Vernon, Iowa, 1995, CHristopher Newport U., Newport News, 1995, Peninsula Fine Art Ctr., 1996, Greater Reston (Va.) Art Ctr., 1996; represented in permanent collections Franklin Furnace, Chrysler Mus., various pvt. collections; photographs reproduced in numerous publs. Chmn. Treasures Great and Small, TAG Gallery d'Art Ctr., Norfolk, 1987; co-curator nat. screenprint show Old Dominion U. Gallery, Norfolk, 1985-87. Recipient Clara Barton award ARC, 1986, merit-purchase awards Chrysler Mus., 1986, photography award Peninsula Fine Arts Ctr., 1986, design award Va. Soc. Hosp. Pub. Rels., 1983, Comms. Excellence award ARC, 1990, d'Art Photo award, 1994; fellow Old Dominion U., 1983-86; grantee CopyData Group and Chrysler Mus., 1987, Hampton U., 1990, Nat. Inst. Leadership Devel. Workshop, 1993, Apple Ptnrs. in Edn. grantee Apple Computer Inc., 1994; Guthrie Scottish Rite scholar, S.W. Water Works Assn. scholar, alumni devel. scholar Okla. Bapt. U., Prichard scholar. Mem. AAUW, Chrysler Mus., Coll. Art Assn., Graphic Design Educators Assn., Nat. Assn. Schs. of Art and Design, Soc. of Photographic Educators, Southeastern Coll. Art Assn., Tidewater Artists Assn. (bd. dirs. exhbn. com., gallery guidelines com. 1986-88, publicity chmn. 1986-87), Va. Mus. Fine Arts, Va. Beach Art Ctr., Va. Soc. Photographic Artists, Phi Kappa Phi. Office: Hampton U Dept Fine-Performing Arts Hampton VA 23668

BEAGLE, DONALD ROBERT, library director; b. Jackson, Mich., July 24, 1953; s. Donald Kenneth and Doris Helen (Bryan) B.; m. Susan Elizabeth Dinwiddie, May 1, 1976 (div. June, 1993); 1 child, Lucy Elizabeth. BA, Oakland U., Rochester, Mich., 1975; MLS, U. Mich., 1977; Cert. Pub. Adminstrn., U. N.C., 1985. Reference libr. Aurora (Ill.) Pub. Libr., 1977-78; gen. svcs. libr. Robeson County Pub. Libr., Lumberton, N.C., 1978-79; head of access info. svc. Cumberland County Libr., Fayetteville, N.C., 1980-81; dir. Lee County Libr. System, Sanford, N.C., 1982-89; regional br. head Charleston (S.C.) County Libr., 1990-94, main libr. head, 1995—; libr. coord. Duke U. Ind. Scholars Project, Durham, N.C., 1987-89; mem. state libr. standards commn. N.C. State Libr., Raleigh, 1988-89; libr. panel spkr., Nat. Cmty. Networking, Taos, N. Mex., 1996. Editor, author World-wide Web site Charleston, Multimedia Project, Charleston, S.C., 1995 (Apple grant 1995); also articles profl. jours. Info., libr. advisor Unitarian Ch., 1993-94; info. cons. Mepkin Abbey, Charleston, S.C., 1996; world-wide web cons. Hist. Charleston Found., 1995-96, Charleston Symphony League, 1996. Recipient Doralynn Hickey award N.C. Libr. Assn., Raleigh, 1987. Mem. Am. Libr. Assn., Charleston Symphony League, S.C. Libr. Assn., S.C. Hist. Assn., Gibbes Mus. of Art Assn. Democrat. Unitarian. Home: 1249 Old Ivy Way Mount Pleasant SC 29464 Office: Charleston County Libr 404 King St Charleston SC 29403

BEAHM, EMILY BARCLAY, interior designer; b. Mpls., Jan. 7, 1962; d. H. Hunter and Martha (Karvonen) B. BS in Bus. Adminstrn., U. N.C., 1984; BA in Interior Design, Mt. Vernon Coll., 1990. Owner Barclay Design Group, Alexandria, Va., 1991-94; Owner From Start to Finish Interior Design, Raleigh, N.C., 1994—. Mem.-at-large Jr. League Washington, 1986-94, bd. mem., 1993, Jr. League Raleigh, 1994—, bd. mem. 1995—. Mem. Am. Soc. Interior Designers (profl. mem.).

BEAKLEY, GROVER JAHUE, JR., investor; b. Brownwood, Tex., Sept. 28, 1937; s. Grover J. and Leota Jewel (Baize) B.; m. Jenelle Peoples, June 27, 1958; children: Brent Douglas, Julie Simone O'Neal. BS, Abilene Christian U., 1959; MS, U. Denver, 1961. Sect. head Tex. Instruments, Dallas, 1962-65; tech. dir. 3M Co., Brownwood, 1965-72; self-employed investor Brownwood, 1973—. Dir. United Way, Brown County, Tex., 1969, Youth Fair, Brown County, 1971. Mem. Nat. Assn. Royalty Owners (amb.), Brownwood C. of C. Office: Beakley Royalty PO Box 1264 Brownwood TX 76804-1264

BEAL, WINONA ROARK, retired church administrator; b. Birchwood, Tenn., Aug. 11, 1924; d. Thomas Jefferson and Minnie Belle (Price) Roark; m. Charles Hugh Beal, Aug. 6, 1949; children: Jeremy Lawrence, Eric David. BSBA, Tenn. Tech. U., 1948; postgrad., So. Bapt. Theol. Sem., 1950-54, U. Louisville, 1951-53, Manatee C.C., 1958-60. Tchr. Washington (Ga.) H.S., 1948-50; asst. to treas. So. Bapt. Theol. Sem., Louisville, Ky., 1951-54; asst. to bus. mgr. Agnes Scott Coll., Decatur, Ga., 1968-71; religious edn. dir. Bay Haven Bapt. Ch., Sarasota, Fla., 1976-84, office program dir., 1985-89; ret., 1989; spiritual guide, dir. Bay Haven Elem. Sch., Sarasota, 1965-68; mem. Sapphire Stores-Indian Beach Assn., Sarasota, 1985-96, State Bd. Missions, Fla. Bapt. Conv., 1993-95, re-elected 96-99, mem. program com., 1993-94. 94-95. loans com. 1995-98. Mem. S.W. Fla. Bapt. Assn. (exec. com. 1976-96, dir. Vacation Bible Sch. 1976-89, student work 1976-80, clerk 1994—), S.W. Manatee Assn. (pres. of Metochai), Pastors Wives of S.W. Fla. Assn. (pres. 1972, 80, 84-89), Fla. Pastors' Wives Conf. (v.p. 1975, program chair 1979, sec.-treas. 1983, conf. historian 1983). Democrat. Home: 638 Beverly Dr Sarasota FL 34234-2706

BEALE, DAVID ANTHONY, structural engineering consultant; b. Washington, Oct. 13, 1937; married; 3 children. BCE, George Washington U., 1963, MEA, 1966. Registered engr., Va., W.Va., N.J., Pa., N.C., Md., D.C., Colo., Fla., Del., Conn., Mass., Ind. Ill., Tex., Ohio. Project engr. Wright Contracting Co., Odenton, Md., 1961-63; structural steel draftsman So. Iron Works, Inc., Springfield, Va., 1963-65, asst. chief engr., 1965-68, chief engr., 1968-70; v.p. Profl. Engrs. Inc., Alexandria, Va., 1970-75; owner Advance Engrs., Ltd., Springfield, Va., 1975—. Mem. Fairfax County Bldg. Bd. Appeals, 1989—; exec. vice chmn. SEA/CASE-MW, 1990—, mem. coms.; mem. Nat. Coun. Examiners for Engring. & Surveying, 1992—. Mem. NSPE, Am. Welding Soc., Am. Concrete Inst., Am. Cons. Engrs. Coun., Va. Soc. Profl. Engrs., Internat. Assn. Concrete Repair Specialists, Assn. for Preservation Tech. Internat., Cons. Engrs. Coun., Inst. Timber Constrn., Post-Tesioning Isnt., Masonry Soc., Concrete Reinforcing Steel Inst., Prestressed Concrete Inst. Home: 6834 Tuttle Rd Springfield VA 22152 Office: 6800 Backlick Rd Ste 300 Springfield VA 22150-3008

BEALEY, LAURA ANN, artist, educator; b. Spencer, W.Va., Dec. 19, 1934; d. William Howard and Virginia Stone (Smith) Miller; m. Mike Bealey, Aug. 18, 1956; children: Virginia, Michael, Julie. BS, Mary Washington U., Fredericksburg, Va., 1956; AA in Fine Arts with honors, No. Va. Community Coll., Annandale, 1981; MA in Studio Art, Art Edn., Art History, George Mason U., 1990. Chemist Univ. Hosp. Western Res., Cleve., 1956-57; spl. art instr. Fairfax County (Va.) Sch. System, 1986-87; pvt. tchr. drawing and painting in oil and watercolor; lectr. in field; conductor workshops in field. One woman show at George Mason U., 1988, 1993; exhibited in group shows at George Mason U., 1988, Springfield Art Guild, 1977, 80, 84, 86, 87, Vienna Art Soc., 1979, 80, 81, 83, 85, Seventh Ann. Manassas Exhbn. of Fine Art, 1983, No. Va. Community Coll., 1978, 81, Art League of Alexandria, Va., 1980, Twentieth Century Gallery, Williamsburg, Va., Island Inn Gallery, Ocracoke, N.C., Hayloft Theater Art Gallery, Manassas, Va., Fairfax Hosp. Galleries; represented in permanent collections No. Va. Community Coll., Nat. Com. Creative Nonviolence, Mullaly 128 Studio and Gallery, Elk Rapids, Mich., Fishscale and Mousetoothe Gallery, Manassas, Va. Methodist. Home: 12010 Wayland St Oakton VA 22124-2236

BEALL, GRACE CARTER, business educator; b. Birmingham, Ala., Sept. 12, 1928; d. Edgar T. and Kate (Eubank) Carter; m. Vernon D. Beall, Aug. 27, 1948; children: Robert, Timothy. BS, La. Coll., 1949; MEd, La. State U., 1955; postgrad., U. Wis., East Tex. State U., Temple U., Southwestern Bapt. Theol. Sem., U. Ga. Tchr., asst. prin. Franklin Parish Sch. Bd., Crowville, La., 1949-54; tchr. Grant Parish Sch. Bd., Dry Prong, La., 1954-55; tchr., coord. Rapides Parish Sch. Bd., Pineville, La., 1955-73; assoc. prof. La. Coll., Pineville, 1974-93; past vice chair of faculty, prof. emeritus, 1993—; cons. in field; sec.-treas. Gulf Coast Athletic Conf., 1983—, Nat. Assn. Intercollegiate Athletics Dist. 30, 1983—. Vice chair Civil Svc. Bd., Pineville, 1975--. Recipient Outstanding Svc. award La. Vocat. Assn., 1971, Outstanding Secondary Educators Am., 1973. Mem. AAUP (past sec.), La. Bapt. Hist. Assn. (pres., bd. dirs.), Phi Delta Kappa (historian), Delta Kappa Gamma (past pres.), Kappa Kappa Iota. Republican. Baptist. Home: 3232 Crestview Dr Pineville LA 71360-5804

BEALL, KENNETH SUTTER, JR., lawyer; b. Evanston, Ill., Aug. 9, 1938; s. Kenneth Sutter and Helen Cantlon (Koenig) B.; m. Blair Hamilton Bissett, May 25, 1975; children: Kevina Anne, Hunter Bissett, Baret Bissett. BA, Washington and Lee U., 1961, LLB, 1963. Bar: Fla. 1964. With Gunster, Valdes-Fauli, Yoakley & Stewart, P.A., West Palm Beach, Fla., 1964—, ptnr., 1970—, pres., 1994—. Bd. dirs. The Whitehall Found., The Wells Family Found.; chmn. Palm Beach County Environ. Control Hearing Bd., 1970-1992. Served with USMCR, 1963-68. Mem. ABA, Fla. Bar (Pres. Pro Bono Svc. award 1982), Palm Beach County Bar Assn., Fed. Bar Assn. (pres. Palm Beach County chpt. 1981), Bath and Tennis Club, Everglades Club, Sailfish Club (Palm Beach). Democrat. Roman Catholic. Office: 777 S Flagler Dr Ste 500 West Palm Beach FL 33401-6161

BEALS, BETSY JONES, elementary school educator; b. Durham, N.C., Mar. 6, 1946; d. Robert Monroe and Pauline Mae (Lawrence) Jones; m. Allen Mason Beals Jr., June 19, 1966; 1 child, Aric. Student, Elon Coll., 1964-66, N.C. State U., 1966-67; BA in Edn., U. N.C., 1969. Cert. mentor tchr. Coord. elem. phys. edn. Chapel Hill (N.C.) Pub. Schs., 1968-69; instr. phys. edn. Ravenscroft Sch., Raleigh, N.C., 1979-82; dir. Camp Adventure, Raleigh, 1976-78, Ravenscroft Camp, Raleigh, 1978-82; elem. phys. edn. specialist Lincoln Heights Gifted and Talented Magnet Sch., Fuquay-Varina, N.C., 1982-83, Northwoods Elem. Sch., Cary, N.C., 1983—; mentor Wake County Pub. Sch., Raleigh, 1985—; workshop cons., Cary, 1977—; historian Phys. Edn. Leadership Tng., Reidsville, N.C., 1985—, bd. dirs. and fall inspirational leader, 1988—. Author: Simple Soccer, 1989, Fabulous Fitness Fun, 1990; editor (newspaper) N.C. Pepi-gram, 1989-91. Sec. Reedy Creek Community, Cary, 1985-89; vice-chmn. Cedar Fork Twp., Morrisville, N.C.; chair com. Cary Clean Keep Am. Beautiful, 1986-89; dir. events Wake County Spl. Olympics; vol. Sr. Games. Recipient Tchr. of Yr. awards Lincoln Heights Elem., 1982, Northwood Elem., 1983 and 1987, N.C. Gov.'s Fitness award, 1989, 91. Mem. ASCD, AAHPERD, N.C. Alliance Health, Phys. Edn., Recreation and Dance (coord. PEPI, sec. 1987-89, 91-92), Raleigh Boychoir (chair com. 1985-88). Republican. Mem. United Ch. of Christ. Home: 2335 Old Reedy Creek Rd Cary NC 27513-2113 Office: Northwoods Elem Sch 8850 Old Chapel Hill Rd Cary NC 27513-3705

BEAMAN, MARGARINE GAYNELL, scrap metal broker; b. Feb. 26; d. Margaret Lena Geisweidt; m. Robert W. Beaman; children: Richard Beaman, Ronald Beaman, Lorene Barrera, Jessica Barrera. Student, U. Houston, U. Mich. V.p. Beaman Metal Co., Inc., Austin, 1972—; pres. Beaman Acctg. and Cons., Austin, 1975—. Chair Capital Area Workforce Devel. Bd., 1996; vol. RIF; mem. bd. Austin Crime Stoppers Edn., Austin C. of C., Homeless Com., Cmty. Action Network; vice chair Trans County Hist. Commn.; chair Capital Area Workforce Devel. Bd. Recipient Gov.'s Vol. of Yr. award, 1982, Mayor's Meritorious award, 1982, Svc. awards Sertoma Club, N.Y. Am. Coun. of Blind, Nat. Community Schs. award, Citizen Leadership award Freedom Found. at Valley Forge, 1986, Migel Medal award Am. Found. for Blind N.Y.C., 1992, Outstanding Contrbn. award Blinded Vets. Assn., 1995; inducted into Tex. Assn. Pvt. Colls. Hall of Fame, Austin Women's Hall of Fame; named Outstanding Blind Worker of Tex., 1982, Most Worthy Citizen of Austin, 1989, Austin's Most Worthy Citizen, 1989. Mem. Tex. Fedn. Bus. and Profl. Women's Clubs (Outstanding Dist. Businesswoman 1996), Exec. Women Internat. (past state pres.), Internat. Cert. Consumer Credit Execs., Nat. Assn. Fin. Aid Adminstrs., Austin C. of C., Austin Women's C. of C., Gen. Fedn. Women's Club, Pvt. Industry Coun., Am. Coun. of Blind, Zonta Internat., Rotary (pres. East Austin chpt. 1995-96). Home: 1406 Wilshire Blvd Austin TX 78722-1129 Office: 3409 E 5th St Austin TX 78702-4911

BEAMER, BETSY DAVIS, state official; b. Charleston, W.Va., Feb. 6, 1959; d. Donald Dallas and Laura (Steward) Davis; m. James William Beamer; Aug. 1, 1992. BA in Journalism, Radford U., 1981. News reporter Va. Leader, Pearlsburg, 1980-81, News Gazette, Lexington, Va., 1982; program coord. Muscular Dystrophy Assn., Roanoke, Va., 1983; fin. dir. Stafford for Congress, Pearlsburg, 1984, Chichester for Lt. Gov., Richmond, 1985, Nat. Rep. Congress Commn., Washington, 1985, Epperson for Congress, Winston-Salem, N.C., 1986-90, Rep. Party Va., Richmond, 1990-92; sec. of commonwealth State of Va., Richmond, 1992—. Mem. Nat. Assn. Secs. State, Herrico GOP Women. Republican. Baptist. Home: 1503 Old Compton Rd Richmond VA 23233-4055 Office: Secretary of Commonwealth PO Box 2454 Old Finance Bldg Capitol Sq Richmond VA 23218*

BEAN, GEORGE J., airport executive. Dir. of aviation Hillsborough County Aviation Authority, Tampa, Fla., Tampa Internat. Airport, Fla. Office: Tampa Internat Airport PO Box 22287 Tampa FL 33622-2287

BEAN, GLENNA MAUREEN, city official; b. San Antonio, Feb. 21, 1938; d. J.C. and Frances Elizabeth (Finch) Mayfield; m. M.E. (Bill) Bean, Aug. 1, 1958; children: Kristy Lee Giese, Tracy Lyn DeRossi. Student in bus. adminstrn., Tex. Tech. U., 1956-59. Tchr.'s aid Lake Highlands Jr. H.S., Dallas, 1972-73; bookkeeper/teller First State Bank, Rockwall, Tex., 1973-75; real estate agt. Century 21, Rowlett, Tex., 1979-82; sec. City of Rowlett, 1982—. Recipient Award of Merit, Libr. and Archives Commn., State of Tex., 1991. Mem. Tex. Mcpl. Clks. Assn., Internat. Inst. Mcpl. Clks., Rowlett C. of C. (Outstanding Svc. award 1991), People to People Internat. (Dallas chpt. hon.). Methodist. Home: 5513 Flamingo Rowlett TX 75088 Office: City of Rowlett PO Box 99 4000 Main St Rowlett TX 75030-0099

BEAN, JACK VAUGHAN, author, publisher; b. Ft. Worth, June 30, 1957; s. Charles Jack Bean and Nan (Vaughan) Kennemer. BBA, BBA in Bus. and Mktg., Tex. Christian U., 1979; postgrad., Southwestern Paralegal Inst., 1988. Owner Ft. Worth (Tex.) Sound Studios, 1980-88; paralegal various law firms, Dallas and Ft. Worth, 1988-92; author, pub. Holographic Books, Ft. Worth, 1992—. Author: The Dream Diary, 1992, The ABC's of Meditation and More..., 1994. Office: Holographic Books PO Box 101862 Fort Worth TX 76185-1862

BEAN, SAMUEL FRANKLIN, dermatologist; b. Waco, Tex., Feb. 25, 1937; s. James Allen and Luella Elizabeth (Moore) B.; m. Camille Ione Cheesman, Aug. 27, 1983 (dec. Nov. 1992); children: Allen, Matthew, Scott. BS, Baylor U., 1958; MD, U. Tex., 1962. Diplomat Am. Bd. Dermatology. Rotating intern Madigan Gen. Hosp., Tacoma, Wash., 1962-63; fellow in dermatology U. Minn., 1965-68, clin. instr. dermatology, 1968-69, clin. asst. prof. dermatology, 1969-70; clin. asst. prof. dermatology Baylor Coll. Medicine, 1970-71, asst. prof. dermatology, 1972-78, clin. assoc. prof. dermatology, 1978—; clin. asst. prof. dermatology U. Tex. Med. Sch., Houston, 1972-79, clin. assoc. prof. dermatology, 1979-84, clin. prof. dermatology, 1985—. Contbr. articles to profl. jours. Capt. U.S. Army, 1963-65. Fellow Am. Acad. Dermatology, Am. Soc. Dermatopathology; mem. AMA, Am. Dermatol. Assn., Dermatology Found., Tex. Med. Assn., Tex. Dermatol. Soc., Houston Dermatol. Soc. (pres. 1979), Harris County Med. Assn. Methodist. Office: 1200 Binz St Ste 990 Houston TX 77004-6900

BEANE, JUDITH MAE, psychologist; b. Durham, N.C., Mar. 28, 1944; d. Joseph William Sr. and Antoinette Gwathmey (Dew) B. BA, Campbell U., 1967; MRE, Golden Gate Bapt. Theol. Sem., Mill Valley, Calif., 1972; PhD, Profl. Sch. of Psychology, San Francisco, 1988. Lic. psychologist, Calif.; mental health therapist II, Northern Neck-Middle Peninsula Cmty. Svcs. Bd.; cert. rehab. provider. Home missionary So. Bapt. Home Mission Bd., Atlanta, 1967-69; loan officer Coop Credit Union, Corte Madera, Calif., 1969-70; emergency svcs. specialist Community Action Marin, San Rafael, 1976-78; program coord. Marin Treatment Ctr., San Rafael, Calif., 1980-85; church sec. St. Paul's Episcopal Church, San Rafael, 1979-81; psychol. intern Raleigh Hills Hosp., Redwood City, Calif., 1984; psychol. asst. Lic. Psychologists, San Anselmo, Calif., 1985-92; bd. dirs. The Open Door Ministries, Inc., Sausalito, Calif., 1971—; psychologist Mill Valley, Calif., 1992-93; cons. Ross (Calif.) Hosp., 1991. Guest speaker for Turn on Marin, San Rafael, Calif., 1985. Recipient award Marin County People Speaking, 1985. Mem. Am. Psychol. Assn. (assoc.), Calif. State Psychol. Assn., Marin County Psychol. Assn., Am. Counseling Assn. Baptist. Home: PO Box 172 Lancaster VA 22503-0172

BEANE, KENNETH MARK, designer, scientist, engineering researcher; b. Murray, Ky., Sept. 2, 1959; s. Halford B. and Georgia Nadine (Hutchens) B.; m. Anna Ruth Holland, Aug. 21, 1981; children: Nathaniel Omar, Andrea Caresse. BS in Engring. Geology, Murray State U., 1990; student, Miss. Sch. Arch., 1989-90; MET in Tech. Comm., Miss. State U., 1992, MS in Indsl. Design, 1994; postgrad., Syracuse U., 1996, So. Ill. U., 1996. Registered geologist. Tchg. asst. Miss. State (Miss.) U., 1991-92, rsch. asst., 1992-95; profl. cons. Internat. Soc. for Responsible Tech., Murray, 1995—; adj. faculty engring. Murray State U., 1996. Author: Architectural Design Specifications, 1989, Structural Mechanics and Design, 1994. Mem. ASTM, Assn. Engring. Geologists, Soc. Engring. Sci., Nat. Registry Environ. Profls. (registered), Indsl. Designers Soc. Am. (cert.), Tenn. Acad. Sci., Soc. Wood Sci. and Tech., Assn. Conservation Engrs. Republican. Southern Baptist. Office: 2383 University Sta Murray KY 42071-3301

BEAR, JOSEPH WOLFE, III, personnel administrator; b. Roanoke, Va., Aug. 2, 1955; s. Joseph Wolfe Jr. and Frances Gemble (Nininger) B.; m. Catherine Anne Carpenter, May 12, 1978; children: Joseph Wolfe IV, Michael R., Brian P., Robert M. BA in Psychology and Econs., Hampden-Sydney Coll., 1977; MA in Psychology, George Mason U., 1979. Cert. profl. in human resources. Sales rep. Double Envelope Corp., Roanoke, 1979-81, asst. v.p., gen. mgr. Rotagraphics div., 1981-86; v.p., sec.-treas. Ackley, Perrott & Assocs., Inc., Roanoke, 1986-89; pers. mgr. Va. Transformer Corp., Roanoke, 1989—. Mem. ASTD, Soc. Human Resource Mgmt. Pers. Assn. Roanoke (past pres.), Kiwanis (mem. bd. Roanoke chpt. 1989-90, 91—), Phi Beta Kappa. Methodist. Home: 2510 Nottingham Rd SE Roanoke VA 24014-3410 Office: Va Transformer Corp 220 Glade View Dr Roanoke VA 24012-6470

BEARD, THOMAS LEROY, chemical engineer; b. Conneaut, Ohio, Dec. 8, 1946; s. Horace L. and Laura R. (Litchfield) B.; m. Dana L. Waddell, Sept. 9, 1967; children: Tyler L., Timothy L., Jeffrey T. BS in Chem. Engring., Tex. Tech. U., 1969. Registered profl. engr., Tex.; diplomate Am. Bd. Forensic Examiners. Sr. engr. Shell Oil Co., Houston, 1969-75; engr. Compression Svcs., Inc., Odessa, Tex., 1985-86; pres., cons. engr. Beard Engring., Inc., Houston, Tex., 1975-82, Midland, Tex., 1983—. Mem. AIChE, NSPE, Nat. Acad. Forensic Engrs. (cert. diplomate forensic engr.), Tex. Soc. Profl. Engrs. Republican. Office: Beard Engring Inc 6 Desta Dr Ste 2500 Midland TX 79705-5515

BEARDEN, FRED B(URNETTE), JR., marketing executive; b. McKinney, Tex., July 25, 1923; s. Fred Burnette and Gladys (Chaddick) B.; m. Elizabeth Emery Jackman, Dec. 6, 1947 (div. Nov. 21, 1994); children: Devon Elizabeth Bearden Godenzi, Fred Burnette III. BBA, So. Meth. U., 1946. Cert. practitioner Neuro Linguistic Programming NLP Ctr. for Counseling and Tng. Bus. mgr. Tom Galligan Prodns., Dallas, 1943-47; mfrs. rep. F.B. Bearden Co., Dallas, 1948-53; regional mgr. Waste-King Corp., Dallas, 1955-61; pres. Fred Bearden Co., Dallas, 1961—; founder, chmn. Inst. for Human Achievement/Self Realization; cons., speaker in field. Patentee; contbr. articles to profl. publs. Mem. Mktg. Agts. Food Svc. Industry (dir., pres. 1976-81), Richardson Jaycees (co-founder, pres. 1951), Mensa. Office: 400 Thompson Dr Richardson TX 75080-5523

BEARDSLEY, BRUCE ANTHONY, diplomat; b. L.A., Nov. 17, 1942; s. Samuel F. and Florence E. B. BA, U. Nev., 1964; MPA, Harvard U., 1981. Joined Fgn. Svc., Dept. State, 1969; dist. sr. advisor CORDS/MACV, Tay Ninh, Vietnam, 1970-72; 2nd sec. Am. Embassy, Beirut, Lebanon, 1972-74; consul Am. Embassy, Kabul, Afghanistan, 1974-76, Copenhagen, 1977-80; dep. consul gen. Am. Embassy, Seoul, Korea, 1981-85; dir. U.S. orderly departure program Am. Embassy, Bangkok, 1985-87, counselor for refugee and migration affairs, 1987-89; consul gen. Am. Embassy, Manila, The Philippines, 1989-93; min. counselor for consular affairs Am. Embassy, Mexico City, 1994—. 1st lt. U.S. Army, 1964-66, Vietnam. Decorated Bronze Star. Mem. Am. Fgn. Svc. Assn. (rep.), Consular Officers' Assn., Hash House Harriers (grand master 1984-85, 91-93). Office: Am Embassy Mexico City PO Box 3087 Laredo TX 78044-3087

BEARDSLEY, CHARLES MITCHELL, retired insurance company executive; b. Chgo., Jan. 13, 1921; s. Richard Stanley and Maude Clarice (Mitchell) B.; m. Marjorie Helen Gahan, Feb. 27, 1943; children: Helen Charlene, Karen Jeannette. AB, Depauw U., 1942; MA, U. Wis., 1947. From actuarial student to assoc. actuary Paul Revere Life Ins. Co., Worcester, Mass., 1947-55; from actuary to v.p. Security Life and Trust Co., Winston-Salem, N.C., 1955-63; actuary sr. v.p. H.W. Satchwell & Co., Columbus, Ohio, 1963-67; actuary chmn., chief exec. officer Charles M. Beardsley & Assocs., Columbus, 1967-68; from exec. v.p. to chmn. Booke and Co., Winston-Salem, 1968-85, vice chmn., 1985-91; bd. dirs. Chestatee Minerals, Inc. Author: Life Company Annual Statement Handbook and New Items in the Annual Statement for Life Insurance Companies, 1959-96; contbr. articles to actuarial jours. Pres. Wachovia Hist. Soc., Winston-Salem, 1981, Huguenot Soc. N.C., 1987-89; bd. dirs. Moravian Music Found., Winston-Salem. Served to lt. (j.g.) USN, 1943-46. Fellow Conf. of Cons. Actuaries (v.p. 1980-82), Soc. Actuaries (dir. 1983-86); mem. Am. Acad. Actuaries, Internat. Actuarial Assn., Internat. Assn. cons. Actuaries (bd. dirs. 1980-89). Democratic. Clubs: Forsyth Country, Twin City, Piedmont (Winston-Salem). Lodges: Masons, Kiwanis (local pres.). Home: 341 Muirfield Dr Winston Salem NC 27104

BEARSKIN, LEAFORD, chief Wyandotte Nation; b. Wyandotte, Okla., Sept. 11, 1921; s. John and Myrtle B.; children: Nancy, Ronald; m. Barbara Cannon, May 10, 1975. Student, Omaha U. Pilot-staff officer USAF, 1939-60; staff officer USAF (Fed. Civil Svc.), 1960-79; chief Wyandotte Nation, 1983—; pres. Inter-Tribal Coun., Inc.; exec. bd. dirs. Northeast Counties of Okla.; bd. dirs. Food Coalition Programs, Miami, Okla.; mem. exec. com. United Indian Nations of Okla. Decorated DFC, Air medal; recipient Indian Achievement award Indian Coun. Fire, 1986; named Outstanding Alumnus, Wyandotte Alumni Assn., 1985. Mem. Retired Officer's Assn. Home: PO Box 450 Wyandotte OK 74370-0450 Office: Wyandotte Tribe of Okla PO Box 250 Wyandotte OK 74370-0250

BEASLEY, DAVID BEACH, agricultural engineering educator, administrator; b. Ithaca, N.Y., Apr. 11, 1948; s. Harry Emerson and Eleanor Alice (Beach) B.; m. Jan Marilyn Peacock, Jan. 17, 1976; children: Jessica, Camille. BS, Miss. State U., 1971, MS, 1973; PhD, Purdue U., 1977. Registered profl. engr. Asst. prof. U. Ark. Agrl. Engring. Dept., Fayetteville, 1977-78, Purdue U. Agrl. Engring. Dept., W. Lafayette, 1978-84; assoc. prof. Purdue U. Agrl. Engring. Dept., 1984-88; prof., dept. head U. Ga. Agrl. Engring. Dept., Tifton, 1988-91; prof., head Biol. and Agrl. Engring. Dept. N.C. State U., Raleigh, 1991—; adv. bd. Aral Sea Exch., Atlanta, 1989—. Contbr. articles to profl. jours. and books. Mem. Am. Soc. Agrl. Engrs. (found. trustee 1993-96, Paper award 1981, 87, Hon. Mention Paper award 1990), Am. Soc. Engring. Educators, Soil Water Conservation Soc., Coun. for Agrl. Sci. and Tech., Sigma Xi, Phi Kappa Phi, Tau Beta Pi, Gamma Sigma Delta, Alpha Epsilon, Alpha Zeta. Home: 3701 Stonecrest Ct Raleigh NC 27612-5220 Office: NC State U Box 7625 Raleigh NC 27695-7625

BEASLEY, DAVID MULDROW, governor; b. Lamar, S.C., Feb. 26, 1957; s. Richard Lee and Jacqueline Adele (Blackwell) B.; m. Mary Wood Payne. Student, Clemson U., 1976-78; BA, U. S.C., 1979; JD, U. So. Calif. Mem. Dist. 56 S.C. Ho. Reps., 1979-92, majority leader, 1987, mem. joint legis. com. on edn., vice chmn. joint legis. ccom. children, 1987-88; atty., 1992-94; gov. State of S.C., 1995—. Office: Office Gov PO Box 11369 Columbia SC 29211-1369*

BEASLEY, ERNEST WILLIAM, JR., endocrinologist; b. Atlanta, May 7, 1924; s. Ernest William and Arrinda Elizabeth (Eidson) B.; M.D., Georgetown U., 1949; m. Ann Lee Jeffreys, July 1, 1950; children—Janet Ann, Ernest William III, Mary Elizabeth, Barbara Elaine. Intern, Walter Reed Hosp., Washington, 1949-50; resident in internal medicine VA Hosp.-Grady Meml. Hosp.-Emory U. Hosp., Atlanta; practice medicine specializing in family practice, Atlanta, 1955-65, in internal medicine, Atlanta, 1966-75, in endocrinology, Atlanta, 1975—; chief endocrinology and metabolism Ga. Bapt. Med. Center; assoc. dept. internal medicine Emory U.; cons. Ga. Assn. Retarded Children, 1955-65; dir. Diabetes Assn. Atlanta, 1976. Served with AUS, 1943-45, M.C., U.S. Army, 50-52. Diplomate Am. Bd. Internal Medicine, Sub-Bd. Endocrinology, Am. Bd. Family Practice Geriatrics. Fellow Am. Coll. Endocrinology; mem. AMA, Am. Assn. Clin. Endocrinologists, Med. Assn. Atlanta, Med. Assn. Ga., Am. Soc. Internal Medicine, Am. Diabetes Assn. Methodist. Club: Cherokee Country. Address: 960 Johnson Ferry Rd NE Ste 340 Atlanta GA 30342-1601

BEASLEY, GEORGE GARLAND, broadcasting executive; b. Patrick County, Va., Apr. 9, 1932; s. Murray H. and Mary H. (Epperson) B.; m. Shirley Ann Weathers, July 20, 1954; children: Robert, Bruce, Brian, Bradley, Caroline. BS cum laude, Appalachian State U., 1958, MA, 1959. Asst. prin. Dan River High Sch., Danville, Va., 1959-62; founder, owner, pres. Sta. WPYB, Benson, 1961-66; prin. Meadow High Sch., Benson, N.C., 1962-69; became pres. Beasley Broadcast Group, Goldsboro, N.C., 1967; now chmn., CEO Beasley Broadcast Group, Naples, FL. Chmn. Wayne County (N.C.) Bd. Edn., 1976—; bd. dirs. budget com. United Way, 1979. With Army Security Agy., U.S. Army, 1953-55. Recipient Disting. Alumni award Appalachian State U., 1990, Patrick County H.S., Va., 1994. Mem. Nat. Assn. Broadcasters, N.C. Assn. Broadcasters (bd. dirs. 1977-79, v.p. 1990-91, pres. 1991-92), Ga. Assn. Broadcasters, Ala. Assn. Broadcasters, Goldsboro C. of C. (mil. affairs com. 1979), Shriners, Kiwanis, Phi Delta Kappa. Republican. Office: Beasley Broadcast Group 3033 Riviera Dr Ste 200 Naples FL 34103-2750

BEASLEY, JAMES RONALD, television, video scriptwriter, producer; b. Jackson, Miss., Jan. 5, 1942; s. Jesse James Beasley and Dorothy (Keen) Tushbant. BA, Univ. Miami, 1967. Copy boy and jr. sports writer Miami (Fla.) Herald, 1964-66, bus. writer, 1966-67; t.v. reporter, producer WTVJ News, Miami, 1967-77; pres. JRB and Assocs., Miami, 1977-83; freelance t.v. writer, producer ABC News, Cable Health Net, ET, San Francisco, L.A., 1983-87; ptnr., v.p. World Video Projects, Inc., Miami, 1988—. Producer, writer N. Am. Ski Resort video travel guide series, 1993; contbr. articles to profl. jours. With USNR, 1960-67. Recipient Addy award, 1981. Mem. Spl. Interest Video Assn., Video Software Dealers Assn. (assoc.), South Fla. Sports Car Assn. (founding pres. 1962), Sigma Delta Chi. Home: 4740 SW 83rd Ave Miami FL 33155-5441 Office: World Video Projects 7820 SW 112th St Miami FL 33156-3719

BEASLEY, MARY CATHERINE, home economics educator, administrator, researcher; b. Portersville, Ala., Nov. 29, 1922; d. Albert Otis and Beulah Green (Killian) Reed; m. Percy Wells Beasley, Dec. 15, 1956 (dec. Dec. 1958). BS in Home Econs., Bob Jones U., 1944; MS, Pa. State U., State College, 1954, EdD, 1968. Tchr. Geraldine and Collinsville (Ala.) High Sch., 1944-45; vocat. home econs. tchr. Glencoe (Ala.) High Sch., 1945-48, Washington County High Sch., Chatom, Ala., 1948-51; home econs. tchr. Homewood Jr. High Sch., Birmingham, Ala., 1958-60; asst. supr. and subject matter specialist Ala. Dept. Edn., Montgomery, 1951-57; asst. prof. Samford U., Birmingham, 1960-62; instr. U. Ala., Tuscaloosa, 1951, asst. prof. then assoc. prof., 1962-68, dir. continuing edn. in home econs., 1968-84, prof., 1984-87, prof. emeritus consumer sci. Coll. Human Environ. Sci., 1988—. Author: (with others) Human Ecological Studies, 1986. Pres. Joint Legis. Coun. of Ala., 1973-75; dir. On Your Own Program, 1970-80. Recipient Creative Programming award Nat. U. Extension Assn., 1979. Mem. Am. Home Econs. Assn. (chmn. rehab. com. 1973, 75, leader 1986), Southeastern Coun. on Family Rels. (pres. 1982-84, Disting. Svc. award 1988), Ala. Home Econs. Assn. (pres. 1961-63, leader 1985), Ala. Coun. on Family Rels. (pres. 1981-83, Disting. Svc. award 1987), Altrusa Club of Tuscaloosa (pres. 1988-89, exec. bd. Ft. Payne/DeKalb 1989-93, corr. sec. 1995-96), Collinsville Study Club (v.p. 1992-93, pres. 1996-98), Alpha Delta Kappa (treas. Tuscaloosa chpt. 1973-75), Phi Upsilon Omicron, Kappa Omicron Nu. Republican. Baptist. Home: 12860 US Hwy 11 Collinsville AL 35961-9171

BEASLEY-CARLISLE, LOIS RENÉ, lawyer, educator, nurse; b. Alma, Mich., Aug. 27, 1960; d. Orville Lee and Rosemary Bertha (Van Meer) Lippert; m. Russell Joe Beasley, Feb. 21, 1981 (div. June 1989); children: Rachel Michelle, Ryan Michael, Stephanie Rene, Jessica, Joshua; m. Terry Lee Carlisle, Aug. 22, 1991. ADN, AS, AA and ADPS, Wallace State Community Coll., Hanceville, Ala., 1980; BSN, U. Ala., 1985, MPH, 1988; JD, Samford U., 1989. Bar: Ala. 1989, Fla. 1989, U.S. Dist. Ct. (no. dist.) Ala. 1989. RN Carraway Meth. Med. Ctr., Birmingham, Ala., 1980-87; assoc. Cherry, Givens, Tarver & Aldridge, Birmingham, 1989—, Veigaa & Cox, Birmingham, 1990-93; prin. Terry Carlisle & Assoc. P.C., Fultondale, Ala., 1993—; RN, U. Ala., Birmingham, 1987—, adj. prof. criminal justice, 1990—; guest speaker Auburn U., Montgomery, Ala., 1989, 90. Legal editor Fla. health rsch. publ. Instr. in CPR, Am. Heawrt Assn., Cullman, Ala., 1977-87; music dir. children's choir 1st Bapt. Ch., Warrior, Ala., 1988—; den mother Tiger Cubs, Boy Scouts Am., 1991-92. Mem. ABA, Ala. Bar Assn. (editor newsletter 1990-92), Birmingham Bar Assn. (spkr. young lawyers sect.), Ala. Trial Lawyers Assn. Office: Carlisle & Carlisle PC PO Box 170766 Birmingham AL 35217-0766

BEASLEY-MURRAY, JON, English language educator; b. Wrexham, Wales, Aug. 9, 1969; came to U.S., 1992; s. Paul and Caroline Wynne (Griffiths) B.-M. BA in English, Cambridge (Eng.) U., 1992; MA in English and Comparative Lit., U. Wis., Milw., 1994; postgrad., Duke U, 1994—. Instr. English, U. Wis., 1993-94; rsch. asst., instr. Spanish, Duke U., Durham, N.C., 1995-96, instr. English, 1996—. Uihlein fellow U. Wis., Milw., 1992-93, lit. fellow Duke U., 1994-95. Mem. MLA, L.Am. Studies Assn. Office: Duke U Grad Program in Lit Box 90670 Durham NC 27708

BEATTY, ROBERT CLINTON, religious studies educator; b. Needham, Mass., May 19, 1935; s. Henry Russell and Alice Cornelia (van Schagen) B.; m. Carolyn Phyllis Caton, Oct. 5, 1957; children: Robert Russell, Daniel Clinton, Melissa Lynn, Alicia Felicity. AB in Econs., Northeastern U., 1957; MBA in Mgmt., Fairleigh Dickinson U., 1973; MDiv, Columbia Internat. U., 1983, MA in Bible, 1985; DMin in Orgn. Devel., Fuller Theol. Sem., 1993. Ordained to ministry Harmony Ch., 1984. Commd. 2d lt. U.S. Army, 1957, advanced through grades to lt. col., ret., 1980; dir. U.S. extension ctrs. Columbia (S.C.) Internat. U., 1983-89; assoc. prof., chmn. bus. mgmt. Miami Christian Coll., 1989-92, Trinity Internat. U., Miami, 1992—; coord. South Fla. extension Trinity Evangelical Div. Sch., 1994—; adj. prof. Embry Riddle Aeronautical U., Mannheim, Germany, 1976-77, City Colls. of Chgo., Mannheim, 1976-77; bible study tchr. Prison Fellowship, Columbia, 1981-89; ch./ministry bd. cons., 1987—. Author: Extension Coordinator's Handbook, 1984, 85, 87, 89, (student manual) Practical Applications of Biblical Hermeneutics, 1992-94, Human Resource Management, 1992, (manual) Business Ethics, 1991, Organization Behavior, 1991, Acts: A Sociological and Cross Cultural Communications Perspective, 1991; editor: Adjunct-Extension Faculty Handbook, 1984, 85, 89. Active AARP. Decorated Legion of Merit, Bronze Star with oak leaf cluster, Air medal, Meritorious Svc. medal, Gallantry Cross with Silver Star; recipient Vol. of Yr. award Goodman Correctional Instn., 1985, Broad River Correctional Instn., 1989. Mem. AARP, Ret. Officers Assn., Disabled Am. Vets., Coalition of Prison Evangelists. Republican. Home: 10500 NW 21st Ct Sunrise FL 33322-3509 Office: Trinity Internat U Miami 500 NE 1st Ave Miami FL 33132-1916

BEATY, GILBERT R., private investigator; b. Patagonia, Ariz., Aug. 29, 1933; s. Clarence L. and Rita (Rodriquez) B.; m. Dora Verdugo, Aug. 24, 1959; children: Diana G., Patricia G. B in Police Photography, Nova Coll., Calgary, Alta., Can., 1989; JD, LaSalle U., Mandeville, La., 1989. Lic. pvt. investigator. Police ident officer #22 South Tucson (Ariz.) Police Dept., 1966-75; police ident technician Tucson Police Dept., 1970-71; security police guard Dept. of Def. Police MP, Ft. Huachuca, Ariz., 1960-92; pvt. investigator, 1989; procurement clk. Dir. of Contracting, Ft. Huachuca, 1992-95. With U.S. Army, 1953-58, Korea. Mem. Internat. Assn. Identification (life). Home: 1801 W San Juan Trail Tucson AZ 85713

BEATY, SUSAN BALLARD, nursing educator; b. Chattanooga, Dec. 22, 1956; d. James F. and Gloria Ann (Clark) Ballard; m. Steven L. Beaty, May 30, 1987; 1 child, Steven L. Jr. BSN magna cum laude, U. Tenn., 1985. RN, Tenn. Staff nurse Erlanger Hosp., Chattanooga; oncology clinician Dr. Sylvia Krueger, Chattanooga. Mem. Nat. Oncology Nursing Soc., Chattanooga Regional Oncology Soc. (adv. bd.), Sigma Theta Tau.

BEATY, THOMAS A., business executive; b. 1935. Grad., Auburn U., 1962. With Stevens Industries, Dawson, Ga., 1962-78; chmn. bd. Universal Blanchers Inc., Blakely, Ga., 1978—. Office: Universal Blanchers Inc Hwy 62 Industrial Park Blakely GA 31723

BEAUCHAMP, JEFFERY OLIVER, mechanical engineer; b. Alice, Tex., Jan. 19, 1943; s. Charles Kirkland and Lila Arminda (Calk) B.; m. Toni Ramona Nobler, Sept. 7, 1963. BSME, U. Houston, 1969, MSME, 1973. Registered profl. engr., Tex. Mech. designer Great Lakes Petroleum Service, Houston, 1963-64; mech. engr. Elliott Co. div. Carrier Corp., Houston, 1964-68; research asst. U. Houston, 1968-70; chief engr. Mallay Corp., Houston, 1970-74; project mgr. Fluor Engrs. & Constructors, Houston, 1974-78; chmn., CEO INTERMAT Internat. Materials Mgmt. Engrs., Houston, 1978—; cons. in field; speaker, lectr., founding bd. dirs. Westheimer Nat. Bank, 1983-84. Bd. dirs. Houston Dist. Export Council, Dept. Commerce, 1985-87; pres. Leadership Houston Assn., 1985-86, Sci. Engring. Fair of Houston, Inc., 1983-84, Engrs. Council of Houston, 1982-83. Mem. ASME, NSPE, Tex. Soc. Profl. Engrs. (Outstanding Young Engr., Sam Houston chpt. 1974); pres. bd., CEO Utility Supply Mgmt. Alliance, 1996-97; mem. Constrn. Industry Action Group, Petroleum Industry Data Exch., Cons. Engrs. Coun. Tex., Greater Houston Partnership (CEO Roundtable), Am. Nat. Stds. Inst. (mem. Pan Am. EDIFACT bd., Utility Industry Action Group 1993—), Sigma Xi, Phi Kappa Phi, Pi Tau Sigma. Contbr. articles to profl. jours. Home: 9 Pinehill Ln Houston TX 77019-1111 Office: 9 E Greenway Plz Ste 2400 Houston TX 77046-0904

BEAUDET, PETER ANTHONY, publishing executive; b. Garden City, N.Y., Sept. 9, 1961; s. Victor Gerard and Rose Mary (Gallagher) B.; m. Megan Louise Gibson, July 3, 1993. BA, U. Dayton, 1983. Supr. circulation USA Today, N.Y.C., 1984; auditor BPA Internat., N.Y.C., 1985, asst. mgr. ea. divsn., 1986, mgr. ea. divsn., 1987-89; mgr. so. region BPA Internat., Tampa, Fla., 1989-91; v.p. dir. controlled circulation Palm Coast (Fla.) Data, 1991-92, v.p., dir. consumer mktg., 1992—. Editor Dayton Chamber of Commerce Newsletter, 1983. Mem. Nat. Bus. Circulation Assn., Fla. Mag. Assn. (bd. dirs. 1992-93), Fulfillment Mgmt. Assn., Direct Mktg. Assn. Home: 5 Crescent Lake Way Ormond Beach FL 32174-6798 Office: Palm Coast Data 11 Commerce Blvd Palm Coast FL 32164-7961

BEAVER, BONNIE VERYLE, veterinarian, educator; b. Mpls., Oct. 26, 1944; d. Crawford F. and Gladys I. Gustafson; m. Larry J. Beaver, Nov. 25, 1972 (dec. Nov. 1995). B.S., U. Minn., 1966, D.V.M., 1968; M.S., Tex. A&M U., 1972. Instr. vet. surgery and radiology U. Minn., 1968-69; instr. vet. anatomy Tex. A&M U., College Station, 1969-72, asst. prof., 1972-76, assoc. prof., 1976-82; prof. Tex A&M U., College Station, 1982-86; prof. vet. small animal medicine and surgery Tex A&M U., 1986—, chief medicine, 1990—; mem. vet. medicine adv. com. HEW, 1972-74, nat. adv. food and drug com., HEW, 1975, com. on animal models and genetic stocks NAS, 1984-86, 87-89, panel on microlivestock NRC, 1986-87, task force on animal use study Inst. Lab. Animal Resources, 1986, adv. com. for Pew Nat. Vet. Edn. Program, Pew Charitable Trusts, 1987-92, 10th symposium on Vet. Med. Edn. Com., 1988-89, NASA task force to review the Bion Missions, 1996. Mem. editl. bd. Applied Animal Ethology, 1981-82, 83-84, VM/SAC, 1982-85, Applied Animal Behavior Sci., 1982-84, 84-86, 86-88, 88—, Bull. on Vet. Clin. Ethology, 1994—, Jour. Am. Animal Hosp. Assn., 1995—; contbr. articles to profl. jours. Vice pres. Brazos Valley Regional Sci. and Engring. Fair, 1974—83, dir., 1983-85; bd. dirs. Brazos Valley unit Am. Cancer Soc., 1976-83, v.p., 1976-83. Named Citizen of Week, The Press, 1981, Outstanding Woman Veterinarian of 1982, Disting. Practitioner, Nat. Acads. Practice. mem. AAAS, AVMA, Tex. Vet. Med. Assn. (3d v.p. 1990, 2d v.p. 1991, 1st v.p. 1992, pres.-elect 1993, pres. 1994), Brazos Valley Vet. Med. Assn., Am. Animal Hosp. Assn., Am. Vet. Soc. Animal Behavior (pres. 1975-80), Am. Assn. Vet. Clinicians, Am. Assn. Equine Practitioners, Am. Vet. Neurology Assn., Animal Behavior Soc., Am. Coll. Vet. Behaviorists (chair organizing com. 1976-91, pres. 1991-96, exec. dir. 1996—), charter diplomat 1993—), Nat. Acad. Practice, Palomino Horse Breeders Am. (v.p. 1983-88, treas. 1984-85, pres.-elect 1988-89, pres. 1989-90), Tex. Palomino Exhibitors Assn., Alamo Palomino Exhibitors Assn., Houston Area Palomino Exhibitors, Am. Quarter Horse Assn., Am. Horse Coun., Phi Sigma, Sigma Epsilon Sigma, Phi Zeta (nat. pres. 1979-81), Phi Delta Gamma (pres. 1974-75). Office: Tex A&M Univ Coll Vet Medicine Vet Small Animal Medicine & Surgery College Station TX 77843-4474

BEAVERS, WILLIAM ROBERT, psychiatrist, educator; b. Temple, Tex., Sept. 27, 1929; s. Leighton W. and Marie Esther (Hughes) B.; m. Jeanette Ann Spier, Nov. 23, 1954 (dec. Mar. 1987); children: Bruce Robert, Bonnie Ann Beavers Anderson; m. Donna Marie McMahon, Nov. 23, 1990. MD, U. Tex., 1953. Diplomate Am. Bd. Psychiatry. Intern Wayne County Gen. Hosp., Eloise, Mich., 1953-54; resident in internal medicine St. Paul Hosp., Dallas, 1959-60; fellow in pharmacology U. Tex. Southwestern, Dallas, 1954-55, asst. prof. pharmacology, 1957-60, resident in psychiatry, 1960-63, from asst. prof. to assoc. prof. psychiatry, 1963-79, clin. prof. psychiatry, 1979—; cons. Planned Behavioral Health, Dallas, 1989-91, Health Econs., Corp., Dallas, 1992-95; pres. Human Solutions Assn., Dallas, 1995—. Author: Psychotherapy and Growth, 1977, Successful Marriage, 1986, Successful Families, 1990. Leader China del. People to People, 1988; Tex. del. Dem. Party, Houston, 1993. Maj. USAF, 1955-57. Mem. Am. Assn. for Marriage and Family Therapy (pres. 1987-89). Unitarian.

BEBER, ROBERT H., lawyer, financial services executive; b. N.Y.C., Aug. 17, 1933; s. Morris and Martha (Pollock) B.; m. Joan Parsons, June 14, 1957; children: Andrea, Judith, Deborah. A.B. in Econs, Duke U., 1955, J.D., 1957. Bar: N.Y., N.C. With Everett, Everett & Everett, N.C., 1957-58; atty. SBA, Washington, 1961-63; with RCA, 1963-81; sr. v.p., gen. counsel, sec. GAF Corp., N.Y.C., 1981-83, exec. v.p., dir., 1983-84, dir. subs.; sr. v.p., gen. counsel, sec. Phlcorp, Inc. (formerly Baldwin United Corp.), Phila., 1984-88; asst. gen. counsel litigation W.R. Grace & Co., N.Y.C., 1988-89, v.p., dir. litigation, 1989-91, sr. v.p., gen. counsel, 1991-93, exec. v.p., 1993—. Bd. vis. Sch. Law, Duke U., 1996—; chmn. bd. Health Care Plan N.J., 1975-78; v.p. South Jersey C. of C., 1974-77. Served with U.S. Army, 1958-61. Mem. ABA. Republican. Jewish. Home: 7228 Queenferry Cir Boca Raton FL 33496-5953 Office: WR Grace & Co 1 Town Center Rd Boca Raton FL 33486-1010

BEBON, ROBERT E., insurance executive; b. N.Y.C., May 23, 1943; s. Ernest G. and Dorothy R. (McNally) B. B.Engring.Adminstrn., U. Del., 1966; MBA, Fairleigh Dickinson U., 1981. Registered profl. engr., Conn., N.C. Field engr. Factory Mutual Engring. Assocs., Phila., 1966-75; mgr. ops. Factory Mutual Engring. Assocs., Florham Park, N.J., 1975-85; asst. v.p. loss control svcs. CIGNA Worldwide Inc., Phila., 1985-91; sr. staff engr. ISO Comml. Risk Svcs. Inc., Parsippany, N.J., 1991-92; v.p. engring. IRM Svcs. Inc., Charlotte, N.C., 1992—. Mem. Nat. Fire Protection Assn., Am. Soc. Safety Engrs., Soc. Fire Protection Engrs. Republican. Office: IRM Svcs Inc 4401 Barclay Downs Dr Charlotte NC 28209-4604

BECATTI, LANCE NORMAN, finance company executive; b. Roseland, Ill., Feb. 11, 1959; s. Leroy J. Sr. and Shirley Ann Becatti. CFP, Fla. Dist. adminstr. Lanier Bus. Products, Inc., Sarasota and Ft. Myers, Fla., 1976-79; pres. Alpha I Inc. ADC, Ft. Myers, 1979-84; sr. fin. advisor Am. Express Fin. Advisors, Tampa, Fla., 1984—. Mem. adv. bd. Tampa's Downtown Spl. Svcs. Dist., 1993-96; campaign chmn. March of Dimes, Ft. Myers, 1978-79. Mem. Internat. Assn. for Fin. Planning (practitioners divsn. 1992—), Tampa Bay Bus. Coun. Home: 201 W Laurel St Apt 203 Tampa FL 33602-2935 Office: Am Express Fin Advisors 304 S Plant Ave Tampa FL 33606

BECHAM, GERALD CHARLES, library director; b. Thomaston, Ga., July 20, 1938; s. George Charles and Cecil Eugenia (Pasley) B. BA, LaGrange Coll., 1960; M of Librarianship, Emory U., 1963. Cert. libr., Ga. Tech. libr. Thiokol Chem. Corp., Huntsville, Ala., 1963-64, ARO, Inc., Arnold AFS, Tenn., 1964-70; asst. dir. Ga. Coll. Libr., Milledgeville, 1970-82; dir. Troup-Harris-Coweta Regional Libr., LaGrange, Ga., 1982—. Pres. Troup County Literacy Vols., LaGrange, 1986-87. Barker fellow Emory U., 1962. Mem. ALA, Southeastern Libr. Assn., Ga. Libr. Assn. (treas. 1985-87), Lions (sec. 1990-91). Methodist. Home: 126 Coll Ave Lagrange GA 30240 Office: Troup-Harris-Coweta Reg Lib 115 Alford St Lagrange GA 30240

BECHER, ANDREW CLIFFORD, lawyer; b. Evanston, Ill., Jan. 24, 1946; s. Clifford C. and Ardeth M. (Johnson) B.; m. Deborah M. Bell, Jan. 18, 1969; children: Cory, Megan, Adam J. BS, Purdue U., 1968; JD, U. Ill., 1971. Bar: Ill. 1971, Minn. 1977. Assoc. McDermott, Will & Emery, Chgo., 1972-76; stockholder Briggs & Morgan, Mpls., 1976-87; sr. v.p. Dain Bosworth, Inc., Mpls., 1987-89; ptnr. Robins, Kaplan, Miller & Ciresi, Mpls., 1989-96; sr. v.p., gen. counsel Cal Dive Internat., Houston, 1996—; bd. dirs. Fantasy Flight, Inc., Minn., Tri-Point Ptnrs., L.C., Tex., Hour Glass Golf, Inc., S.C.; lectr. in law Chgo. Kent Coll. Law-Ill. Inst. Tech., 1973-75; assoc. prof. Hamline U., St. Paul, 1978-80. Chair local and state govt. com. St. Paul C. of C., 1978-80. Capt. U.S. Army, 1971-79, USAR. Mem. ABA, Minn. Bar Assn., Ill. Bar Assn., Assn. for Corp. Growth, North Oaks Country Club, Tex. Bar Assn. Presbyterian. Office: Cal Dive Internat Inc Ste 350 13430 NW Freeway Houston TX 77040

BECHTEL, SHERRELL JEAN, psychotherapist; b. Birmingham, Ala., Sept. 23, 1961; d. Lewis Eugene and Sarah Rozelle (Sherrell) B. BS in Social Work, U. Ala., Birmingham, 1989; MSW, U. Ala., Tuscaloosa, 1990. Cert. addiction specialist; cert. group psychotherapist; lic. clin. social worker, Tenn., Ga. Vol. counselor Planned Parenthood, Birmingham, 1986-88; intern Bradford Adult Chem. Dependency, Birmingham, 1989; rsch. staff asst. U. Ala., Tuscaloosa, 1989-90; intern counselor Bradford Adolescent Chem. Dependency, Birmingham, 1990; primary counselor The Crossroads, Chattanooga, 1990-92; owner S. J. Bechtel LCSW, CAS, Chattanooga, 1991—; rschr. Ala. Commn. Youth, Montgomery, 1989-90; trainer Legal and Jud. Aspects Child Welfare, Decatur, Ala., 1989; presenter Ala. Victim Compensation, Mobile, 1990; speaker Limestone Correctional Facility, Huntsville, 1990; lectr. Grad. Sch. Social Wk., Tuscaloosa, 1990, U. Tenn., Chattanooga. Subcom. mem. Atty. Gen. Alliance Against Drug Abuse, Birmingham, 1989; speaker Victims of Crime and Leniency, Tuscaloosa, 1990; planning com. Holistic Health Retreat, Birmingham, 1988; mem. Tenn. Coun. on Children and Youth-Legis./Policy; vol. ARC Disaster Mental Health/Direct

Svcs. Mem. NASW (pres. student orgn. 1986-89), Tenn. Alcohol Drug Assn., Jewish Community Ctr., Phi Kappa Phi. Office: 7405 Shallowford Rd Ste 280 Chattanooga TN 37421-2662

BECHTEL-HOOPES, BRENDA JEAN, educator English, biology, environmental chemistry; b. Feb. 9, 1955. BS in Edn. and English magna cum laude, Millersville U., 1977, MA in English, 1982; cert. in Biology, Wake Forest U. Instr. AP English and English Manheim Twp. High Sch., Lancaster, Pa., 1977-82; instr. AP biology and biology Forsyth Country Day Sch., Lewisville, N.C., 1983-88; chmn. sci dept. Forsyth Country Day Sch., Lewisville, 1987-88; instr. English Grey Culbreth Jr. High Sch., Chapel Hill, N.C., 1988-89; instr. math. and environ. sci. Camelot Acad., Durham, N.C., 1989-90; instr. English and environ. chemistry, advisor lit. mag. Jordan High Sch., Durham, 1990—; tutor English and math. for learning disabled Camelot Acad., Durham, summer 1989; editor, item/specification writer Measurement Inc. Testing Svc., Durham, summer 1990; instr. Young Writers' Camp, Duke U., Durham, summers 1991-96. Swimming coach, lifeguard, ARC instr. Skyline Swim Club, Lancaster, 1974-78 (summers); coach field hockey, swimming, diving, cross country Manheim Twp H.S., Pa., archeol. site, 1980 (summer); naturalist U.S. Forest Svc., 1983 (summer); vol. Soup Kitchen, Winston Salem, N.C., 1984-85; riding instr. N.C. Equestrian Ctr., Winston-Salem, 1984-88, N.C. Outward Bound Sch., Pisgah Nat. Forest, 1984. Home: 1120 Quail Roost Farm Rd Rougemont NC 27572 Office: Jordan HS 6808 Garrett Rd Durham NC 27707-5634

BECHTOLD, SUSAN HATFIELD, legal assistant; b. Enid, Okla., Nov. 4, 1948; d. Jack Kenton and Dorothy Ann (Keltner) H.; divorced; children: Jennifer Rebecca, Casey Wade. BS in Pre-law, Okla. State U., 1976; cert., Tex. Paralegal Sch., Houston, 1983. Legal asst. Atkinson & Assocs., Houston, 1984-86, Brown, Sims, Wise & White, Houston, 1986; assoc. legal asst. Conoco Inc., Houston, 1985-95, legal asst., 1987—, environ. legal asst., 1993—; legal asst. King and Spalding, Houston, 1996; contract legal asst. Houston, 1996—. Mem. State Bar Tex. (legal asst. div.), Nat. Assn. Legal Assts. (cert. legal asst., civil litigation specialist). Republican. Methodist.

BECK, BARBARA NELL, elementary school educator; b. Corpus Christi, Tex., Oct. 25, 1940; d. Marshall Joseph and Madie Ann (Spence) Robertson; m. Joel J. Beck, June 23, 1973. BA, Baylor U., 1964. Tchr. Killeen (Tex.) Ind. Sch. Dist., 1964—. Mem. NEA, Tex. State Tchrs. Assn., Tex. Assn. for the Gifted and Talented, Killeen Edn. Assn. (treas., past pres., bd. dirs.), Clifton Park PTA (past treas.). Office: Clifton Park Elem Sch 2200 Trimmier Rd Killeen TX 76541-8503

BECK, CHARLES EDWARD, psychiatrist, lawyer; b. Jacksonville, Ill., June 14, 1921; s. Jesse Orien and Ruth Eileen (Randall) B.; m. Dora White Kirby, Oct. 4, 1941 (div. July 1958); children: Janice Ruth Beck Burnett, Nancy Lynn Beck Smedley, Donald Wayne; m. Ea Pio, Aug. 15, 1970. AB, Ill. Coll., 1943; student, U. Chgo., 1942-43; MD, U. Okla., Oklahoma City, 1952; JD, Oklahoma City U., 1975. Diplomate Am. Bd. Psychiatry and neurology; bar: Okla. 1976. Intern Wesley Hosp., Oklahoma City, 1953; pvt. practice family medicine, Lindsay, Okla., 1953-60; resident in psychiatry Ctrl. State Hosp., Norman, Okla., 1960-61, VA Med. Ctr., Topeka, 1961-63; dir. zone V, acting supt. Ill. Dept. Mental Health, 1967-70; pvt. practice clin. and forensic psychiatry Oklahoma City, 1970-80; staff physician mental hygiene clinic VA Med. Ctr., Charleston, S.C., 1980-84; med.-legal specialist to ACMD for clin. affairs VA Ctrl. Office, Washington, 1984-88; chief Key West outpatient clinic Miami (Fla.) DVA Med. Ctr., 1988-93; pvt. practice St. Simons Island, Ga., 1993—; chief unit IV VA Med. Ctr., Danville, Ill., 1963-65; med. dir. Ea. Ill. Mental Health Clinics, 1964-67; staff psychiatrist VA Med. Ctr., Oklahoma City, 1971-80; clin. asst. prof. dept. behavioral scis. Okla. U. Health Scis. Ctr., 1971-79, clin. assoc. prof., 1979-80; asst. prof. dept. psychiatry and behavioral scis. Med. U. S.C., 1980-84; lectr. in field; aviation medicine exam., 1971-84; asst. dist. atty. juvenile div., Oklahoma City, 1978; radio and TV appearances, Ill., Okla., 1967-80. Contbr. numerous articles to newsletters and local periodicals. Bd. dirs. Willowview Psychiat. Found., Oklahoma City, 1975-80, Gatewood Pastoral Counseling Ctr., 1978-80, Charleston (S.C.) Mental Health Ctr., 1982-84; sec. Key West Power Squadron, 1991-92. Capt., pilot USAAF, 1942-46. Fellow Am. Psychiat. Assn. (life, parlaimentarian, exec. coun. Okla. dist. br. 1975-80, mem. social security sequential evaluation study 1986), Am. Coll. Legal Medicine; mem. Okla. Bar Assn. (sr.). Home: 136 Saint Clair Dr Saint Simons GA 31522-1035

BECK, DAVID EDWARD, surgeon; b. Geneva, Ill., May 1, 1953; s. George R. and Gloria M. (Zesch) B.; m. Sharon Mieir, Aug. 30, 1983; children: Allison, Lauren, John. BS, USAF Acad., 1975; MD, U. Miami, Fla., 1979; postgrad., USAF Aerospace Medicine Primary Course, Brooks AFB, Tex., 1978, Combat Casualty Care Course, Ft. Sam Houston, Tex., 1980, Hyperbaric Oxygen CourseB, Brooks AFB, 1982, ATLS Instr. Course, Ft. Sam Houston, 1986, Squadon Officers Sch., 1987-88, Mgmt. for Chief of Hosp. Svcs., Sheppard AFB, Tex., 1988, Sch. Pub. Health, Harvard U., 1990. Diplomate Am. Bd. Colon and Rectal Surgery. Lt. Col. USAF, 1975-93; resident in gen. surgery Wilford Hall USAF Med. Ctr., Lackland AFB, Tex., 1979-84, chief colorectal surgery, 1986-92; staff surgeon, chief colorectal surgery svc. Wilford Hall USAF Med. Ctr., Lackland AFB, 1986-92, asst. chmn. dept. gen. surgery, 1988, chmn. dept. gen. surgery, residency program dir., 1988-92; staff gen. surgeon Patrick AFB (Fla.) Hosp., 1984-85; fellow in colorectal surgery Cleve. Clinic Found., 1985-86; residency program dir. gen. surgery Joint Mil. Med. Command, San Antonio, 1989-91; clin. assoc. prof. surgery U. Tex. Health Sci. Ctr., San Antonio, 1990-92, F. Edward Herbert Sch. Medicine, U. Health Scis., Bethesda, Md., 1992—; chief surgery 870 USAF Contingency Hosp., RAF Little Rissington, U.K., 1993; staff colorectal surgeon Ochsner Clinic, New Orleans, 1993—, chmn. dept. colon and rectal surgery, 1994—; cons. USAF Surgeon Gen., Washington, 1986-92. Author chpts. to books; co-editor (textbooks); (with David R. Welling) Patient Care in Colorectal Surgery, 1991, (with Steven D. Wexner) Fundamentals of Anorectal Surgery, 1992, (with T.C. Hicks, F.E. Opelka, A.E., Timmcke) Complications of Colon and Rectal Surgery, 1996; editor: Handbook of Colorectol Surgery, 1997; mem. editl. bd. Current Surgery, 1990—; reviewer Diseases of the Colon and Rectum, 1990—, mem. editl. bd., 1992—, So. Me. Jour., 1988-92; contbr. articles to profl. jours. Decorated Air Force Achievement medal with oak leaf cluster, Air Force Meritorious Svc. medal with oak leaf cluster. Fellow ACS; mem. AMA, Am. Soc. Colon and Rectal Surgeons (mem. socioecon./legis. com. 1991-94, pub. rels. com. 1993—, chmn. 1996—, Outstanding Young Investigator award, 1992), Assn. Mil. Surgeons U.S., La. State Med. Soc., Soc. Air Force Clin. Surgeons (treas. 1989-90, v.p. 1990-92, pres. 1992-93, Excalibur award 1992), Soc. Surgery of Alimentary Tract, So. Med. Assn. (mem. colon and rectal sect., sec. 1988-91, v.p. 1990-91, pres. 1991-92), Soc. Med. Cons. to Armed forces, St. Tamminy Parish Med. Soc., Tex. Soc. Colon and Rectal Surgeons (sec. 1991-93), Air force Assn., USAF Acad. Assn. Grads. Home: 127 Deloaks Rd Madisonville LA 70447-9597 Office: Oschner Clin 1514 Jefferson Hwy New Orleans LA 70121-2429

BECK, DONALD JAMES, veterinarian, educator; b. N.Y.C., Aug. 17, 1957; s. Donald Spence and Margaret Eugene (Moan) B.; m. Julie Anne Hayes, June 14, 1986 (div. Aug. 1995). BS in Animal Sci., U. Fla., 1980, DVM, 1986. Pvt. practice Largo, Fla., 1986-88, 90—; instr. St. Petersburg (Fla.) Jr. Coll., 1988-90; track veterinarian Derby Lanes, St. Petersburg, 1988-89; show veterinarian Cen. Fla. Hunter & Jumper Assn., St. Petersburg, 1987; veterinarian surgeon Pinellas County Animal Control, Clearwater, Fla., 1990—. Dir., v.p., pres. Somerset Village Condominium Assn., Gainesville, Fla., 1983-86; events judge 4-H, Largo, 1989. Mem. AVMA, Fla. Vet. Med. Assn., Sigma Phi Epsilon. Democrat. Roman Catholic. Home: 9374 117th Ave Largo FL 33773-4343 Office: 9374 117th Ave Largo FL 33773-4343

BECK, ESTHER ANN, psychologist; b. Providence, May 23, 1940; d. William Tillinghast and Esther (DeWitt) Broomhead; m. Edward Rubin Beck, Aug. 14, 1958; children: Edward R. Jr., Larry Wayne. BS, Troy State U., 1970; MS, Auburn U., 1971, PhD, 1973. Asst. prof. Auburn U., Montgomery, Ala., 1973-77, assoc. prof., 1977-80; pvt. practice Montgomery, 1975-81; v.p. Aviation Support for Christian Missions Inc., 1986-95; counselor East Brent Bapt. Ch., Pensacola, Fla., 1991-95; bd. dirs. Aviation Support for Christian Missions; speaker on mental health, 1986—; advisor Bay Bapt. Assn., Pensacola, 1992—. Contbr. articles to profl. jours. Home: 912 Largo Dr Pensacola Beach FL 32561

BECK, GEORGE PRESTON, anesthesiologist, educator; b. Wichita Falls, Tex., Oct. 21, 1930; s. George P. and Amanda (Wilbanks) B.; m. Constance Carolyn Krog, Dec. 22, 1953; children: Carla Elizabeth, George P., Howard W. BS, Midwestern U., 1951; MD, U. Tex., 1955. Diplomate Am. Bd. Anesthesiology. Intern John Sealy Hosp., 1955-56; resident anesthesiology Parkland Meml. Hosp., Dallas, 1959-62, vis. staff, 1964—; practice medicine specializing in anesthesiology, Lubbock, Tex., 1964—; chief staff Meth. Hosp., Lubbock, 1967-68; asst. prof. anesthesiology Southwestern Med. Sch., Dallas, 1962-64, asst. clin. prof., 1964-71, prof. 1996—, assoc. clin. prof. anesthesiology U. Tex. Med. Br. at Galveston, 1971— assoc clin prof., 1980-95, clin prof. 1996—; pres. Gt. Plain Ballistics Corp., 1967—; clin. prof. Tex. Tech. U. Sch. Medicine, 1986—, pres. found. bd., 1972-73. Author: The Ideal Anesthesiologist, 1960, Mnemonics as an Aid to the Anesthesiologist, 1961, Anterior Approach to Sciatic Nerve Block, 1962; inventor Beck Airway Airflow Monitor. Pres. Luth. Ch. council, pres. congregation, 1965-66. With USAF, 1956-59. Fellow Am. Coll. Anesthesiologists; mem. Am. Soc. Anesthesiologists, Tex. Soc. Anesthesiologists (pres. 1974) Tex. Med. Soc., Lubbock County Med. Soc., Lubbock Surg. Soc. (pres. 1969); Named Asabel Smith disting. Alumnus award, 1994. Home: 4601 18th St Lubbock TX 79416-5713 Office: PO Box 16385 Lubbock TX 79490-6385

BECK, LUKE FERRELL WILSON, insurance specialist; b. Granbury, Tex., Feb. 2, 1948; s. Don Elder and Georgia Ferrell (Wilson) B.; m. Susan Villars, Nov. 14, 1970 (div. Feb. 1974). BA in Psychology, U. Tex., 1970. CPCU. Claims rep. Employers Ins. Tex., Beaumont, 1975-86; home office supr. Employers Ins. Tex., Dallas, 1986-89; litigation specialist CNA Ins. Co., Dallas, 1989-93, litigation supv., 1993—. 1st lt. U.S. Army, 1971-75. Mem. Soc. of CPCU. Presbyterian. Home: 2108 Barton Dr Arlington TX 76010-4750 Office: CNA Ins PO Box 219046 Dallas TX 75221-9046

BECK, MARY SLATER, administrator; b. Chillicothe, Ohio, Oct. 22, 1946; d. Surrey Winfred and Mary Elizabeth (Murphey) Slater; m. Barry Nathan Beck, Oct. 7, 1967; children: Keith Macaulay, Alexis Elizabeth. Student, U. of Tex., 1963-66, 68-70; cert. non-profit mgmt., Tex. Tech. U., 1993. Clk. The White House, Washington, 1966-68; adminstrv. asst. Navy Publs. and Printing Svcs., Washington, 1968; congrl. liaison Office of Econ. Opportunity, Austin, 1968-77; cmty. vol. various orgns., Midland, Tex., 1975-89; exec. dir. Midland Teen Court, Inc., Midland, Tex., 1989—; adv. bd. mem. Juvenile Adv. Bd., Midland, 1989—. Chmn. nat. young artists competition Midland Odessa Symphony, Midland, 1990; vis. com. U. Tex. Dept. of Psychology, Austin, 1989-95; life mem. Tex. PTA, Midland. Recipient Liberty Bell award Midland Young Lawyers Assn., 1991; named Women of Distinction Permian Basin Girl Scout Coun., 1992. Mem. Nat. Assn. Fund Raising Execs., Midland Health and Welfare Assn., Exec. Women of Midland, Tex. Teen Ct. Assn. (pres. 1995-96), Zeta Tau Alpha (Cert. of Merit 1979). Episcopalian. Office: Midland Teen Court Inc 615 W Missouri # 226 Midland TX 79707

BECK, MORRIS, allergist; b. Miami, Fla., Oct. 12, 1927; s. Max and Anna (Luks) B.; m. Hollis Schwartz, Aug. 6, 1960; children: Gayle Beck Finan, Anne Lin. BA, UCLA, 1949; MD, U. Zurich, Switzerland, 1957. Diplomate Am. Bd. Allergy and Immunology, Am. Bd. Pediatrics. Intern Queens Hosp. Ctr., 1958, resident in pediatrics, 1959-60; preceptor in allergy U. Miami (Fla.) Med. Sch., 1961-77; pvt. practice pediatrician Miami, 1961-77, pvt. practice allergist, 1978—; chief dept. allergy Miami Children's Hosp., 1986—, Miami VA Hosp., 1994—. With U.S. Army, 1950-52. Fellow Am. Coll. Allergy & Immunology, Am. Acad. Pediatrics, Am. Assn. Cert. Allergists; mem. Am. Acad. Allergy & Immunology, Am. Coll. Chest Physicians. Republican. Jewish. Home: 12015 SW 68th Ave Miami FL 33156-5406 Office: Ste B 240 7800 SW 87th Ave Miami FL 33173-3570

BECK, ROBERT BERYL, real estate executive; b. Dalton, Ga., Feb. 25, 1935; s. Carson W. and Gladys (Gray) B.; m. Martha Lucinda Cone, June 14, 1957; children: Perkie Cone Beck Cannon, Robert B. Jr., Carson W. Student, Vanderbilt U., 1953-57; LLB, JD, Nashville Sch. Law, 1964. Salesman Southeastern Inc., Nashville, 1957-64; purchasing agt. Nashville Bd. Edn., 1965-66; pres. Beck & Beck Realty, Nashville, 1967—; pres. Beck & Beck Ins. Co., Nashville, 1967-78, v.p., 1978—; pres. Tri-County Builders, Nashville, 1974—. Editor Grace Bapt. Monthly, 1985, real estate newsletter, 1986-87. Mem. Nashville Bd. Realtors, Profl. Ins. Assn. Democrat. Lodge: Masons. Home: 3500 Brick Church Pike Nashville TN 37207-2002 Office: Beck & Beck 4205 Gallatin Rd Nashville TN 37216-2111

BECK, ROBERT JAMES, editor, energy economist, author, consultant; b. Milw., Nov. 21, 1938; s. Walter John and Evelyn Barbara (Bigus) B.; m. Mary Ellen Drew, Jan. 20, 1968 (div. Aug. 1978); m. Connie Sue Sparling, Apr. 2, 1988 (div. May 1994). BS in Econs. with honors, U. Wis., Milw., 1961; MS in Internat. Econs., U. Wis., 1965; postgrad., Wharton Sch., U. Pa., 1967, U. Okla., 1981. Actuarial asst. Milliman & Robertson, Milw., 1963-64; rsch. asst. U. Wis., Milw., 1964-65; economist, statistician Wis. Telephone Co., Milw., 1965-68; dir. econ. rsch. Mackay Shields Econs., N.Y.C., 1968-69; head oper. planning Oil Svc. Co. Iran, Ahwaz, 1969-79; econs. editor Oil & Gas Jour., Tulsa, 1979—; developer, mgr. Oil & Gas Jour. Energy Database, Tulsa, 1984—; cons. Oil and Gas Jour. On-Line Bull. Bd. for the Oil and Gas Industryy, 1994—, Altec Energy, Centralia, Ill., 1986-90, Rainbow Petroleum, N.Y.C., 1986, Farrar and Assocs., Tulsa, 1985-86. Author: Oil Industry Outlook, 14 edits., 1983—; developer and cons. Energy Statistics Sourcebook, 12 edits., 1986—; editor: International Energy Statistics Sourcebook, 7 edits., 1991—, Natural Gas Statistics Sourcebook, 5 edits., 1993—, Refining Statistics Sourcebook, 5 edits., 1993—, Price Statistics Sourcebook, 3 edits., Company Performance Statistics Sourcebook, 2 edits., 1966—; contbr. articles to mags. and newspapers. Mem. Philbrook Mus. Art, Tulsa, 1989—, Nature Conservancy, Tulsa, 1988—, Tulsa Zoo, 1991—; pres. Young Dems., West Allis, Wis., 1960-62; mem. Wis. Gov.'s Comn. on Econ. Indicators, 1967. Mem. Internat. Assn. Energy Econs., Nat. Assn. Bus. Econs., Assn. Petroleum Writers, Ind. Petroleum Assn. Am. (mem. supply and demand com., cost study com.). Office: Oil & Gas Jour 3050 Post Oak Blvd Ste 200 Houston TX 77056

BECK, WILLIAM HAROLD, JR., lawyer; b. Clarksdale, Miss., Aug. 18, 1928; s. William Harold and Mary (McGaha) B.; m. Nancy Cassity House, Jan. 30, 1954; children—Mary, Nancy, Katherine. BA, Vanderbilt U., 1950; JD, U. Miss., 1954. Bar: Miss. 1954, La. 1960. Atty., Clarksdale, Miss., 1954-57; asst. prof. Tulane U., 1957-59; ptnr. Foley & Judell, New Orleans, 1959-88; of counsel, 1988—. Served to capt., AUS, 1951-53. Mem. La. Bar Assn., Miss. Bar Assn., SAR, Soc. Colonial Wars, S.R., Mil. and Hospitaller Order of St. Lazarus of Jerusalem, Huguenot Soc., Mil. Order Fgn. Wars. Office: Foley & Judell 1 Canal Pl 365 Canal St Ste 2600 New Orleans LA 70130-1138

BECKELHEIMER, CHRISTINE ELIZABETH CAMPBELL, nurse; b. Oak Hill, W.Va., Sept. 6, 1916; d. Charles Earl and Macie Avis (Boothe) Campbell; diploma in nursing Somerset Hosp., Somerville, N.J., 1938; B.S. in Nursing Edn., Hunter Coll., 1954; M.A. in Nursing Service Adminstrn., Tchrs. Coll. Columbia U., 1959, profl. diploma, 1961, postgrad, 1961-65; m. Joseph Howard, June 6, 1941 (dec.); 1 child, Mary Elizabeth (dec.); m. 2d, Harry Abrahamsen, Oct. 10, 1943; 1 dau., Cherri Georgette; m. 3d, Robert Ernest Beckelheimer, Jan. 18, 1980. Staff nurse obstetrics Somerset Hosp., 1939; staff nurse Goldwater Meml. Hosp., Welfare Island, N.Y.C., 1939-40, rsch. nurse, 1940-41; staff nurse St. Vincent's Hosp., N.Y.C., 1941-43; lab. asst. Am. Cyanamid Co., Bound Brook, N.J., 1943; charge nurse Paul Kimball Hosp., Lakewood, N.J., 1943-44; staff nurse to head nurse Pinewald Hosp., Bayville, N.J., 1944-46; staff nurse Morrisania City Hosp., Bronx, N.Y., 1946-49, head nurse, 1949-50, clin. instr., 1950-54; instl. insp. Dept. Hosps. City of N.Y., 1954-58; supr. edn. City Hosp., Elmhurst, N.Y., 1958-60, rsch. asst. Fedn. of the Handicapped, 1962-63; rsch. asso. Yeshiva U. Lincoln Hosp., N.Y.C., 1963-64; asst. coord. exchange grad. nurse program St. Luke's Hosp., N.Y.C., 1964-65, asst. dir. nursing svc. inservice edn., 1966-67; cons. rsch. and hosp. nursing service Nat. League Nursing, N.Y.C., 1968-70, acting dir. rsch. (cons.), 1970-71; assoc. prof. nursing W.Va. Inst. Tech., 1971-73, chmn. dept. nursing, 1973-75; coord. patient care Raleigh Gen. Hosp., Beckley, W.Va., 1975-78, dir. hosp. inservice, 1978-79. USPHS Nurse Research fellow, 1961-63; USPHS grantee, 1965-66. Mem. Am., W.Va. Nurses Assns., Tchrs. Coll. Nurses Alumni Assn., Hunter Coll. Alumni Assn., Nurses Alumni Assn. Somerset Hosp., Sci. Fiction Writers of Am., Pi Lambda Theta, Kappa Delta Pi, Am. Legion Aux., DAR, UDC (past pres. W.Va. div.), Fayette County Hist. Soc., Genealogy Soc. Fayette and Raleigh Counties, Fayette County Hist. Landmark Commn., Wittenfort Long Rifles, Rosicrucian Order. Author: Cristabel Manalacor of Veltakin, 1970; The Cruachan and the Killane, 1970; The Mortal Immortals, 1971; The Golden Olive, 1972; (with Kathleen Westcott) The Bride of Kilkerran, 1972; The Pettus Family of England and Virginia, 1989; editor: newsletter, 1985-89, 1991-94; editorial asst. various jours. Home: 213 Washington Ave Oak Hill WV 25901-3047

BECKEMEYER, NANCY SCOTT, landscape architect; b. Atlanta, Apr. 1, 1953; d. Delmont Emil and Frances Rentz (Howell) B. B in Landscape Architecture, U. Ga., 1977. Registered landscape architect, Ga. Owner So. Landscape Designs, Hattiesburg, Miss., 1977-81; instr. DeKalb Coll., Atlanta, 1990, 91; pres. Autumn Ridge Inc. Landscape Architecture & Constrn. Firm, Atlanta, 1981—; instr. Clayton State Coll., Morrow, Ga., 1981—, Kennesaw (Ga.) Coll., 1985—, Sutton Community Sch., Atlanta, 1986—; instr. Landscape Architecture Uniform Nat. Exam. Rev., 1990, 91, 92, 93, 94. Past pres. appointed to Cen. Atlanta Progress Adv. Coun. Named Outstanding Young Woman of Am., 1981, 83; recipient Award of Merit Sch. Environ. Design, 1977. Mem. Am. Soc. Landscape Architects (awards program chmn. 1985, sec. Ga. chpt. 1986, pres. 1990, nat. nominating com. 1991—), Am. Bus. Women's Assn. (pres. So. Miss. chpt., Woman of Yr. 1981), U. Ga. Alumni Assn. (sch. environ. design, steering com. 1983-86, pres. 1992-94, 1st Quar. Club, SEDAA pres. 1993-94).

BECKER, CHARLES MCVEY, economics and finance educator; b. Cleve., Nov. 13, 1937; s. William Nevison and Helen (McVey) B.; m. Natalie Sage Slaughter, July 25, 1964; children: William Nevison II, James Pahl. BA cum laude, U. Ariz., 1960, MA, 1962, PhD, 1966. Chartered fin. analyst. Asst. prof. fin., econs. Nev. So. U., Las Vegas, 1965-67; asst. prof. Tex. Christian U., Ft. Worth, 1967-70, assoc. prof., 1970—; Asst. dir. Am. Free Enterprise Inst. Contbr. articles to profl. jours. Mem. Southwestern Econs. Assn. (pres. 1990-91), Southwestern Soc. Economists (pres. 1992-93), N.Am. Econs. and Fin. Assn. (adv. bd.), Assn. for Investment Mgmt. and Rsch., Am. Econ. Assn. (life), Ridgelea Country Club, Alpha Kappa Psi, Beta Gamma Sigma, Phi Alpha Theta, Alpha Sigma Phi, Omicron Delta Epsilon. Office: Tex Christian U Dept Economics TCU Campus Fort Worth TX 76129

BECKER, FREDERICK FENIMORE, cancer center administrator, pathologist; b. N.Y.C., July 23, 1931; s. Louis I. and Ruth (Shurr) B.; m. Mary Ellen Terry, Nov. 23, 1971; 1 child, Bronwyn Elizabeth. BA, Columbia U., 1952; MD, NYU, 1956. Intern Harvard svc. Harvard service Boston City Hosp., 1956-57; resident Bellevue Hosp., N.Y.C.; pathology trainee NYU Sch. Medicine, N.Y.C., 1957-60, prof., dir. pathology, 1962-75; chmn. dept. pathology U. Tex. Cancer Center, M.D. Anderson Hosp. and Tumor Inst., Houston, 1976-79; v.p. research U. Tex. M.D. Anderson Cancer Ctr., 1979—. Contbr. numerous articles to various publs. Served with USN, 1960-62. Mem. Am. Assn. Pathologists (pres. 1980-81), Am. Assn. Cancer Research, Am. Soc. Cell Biology, Tex. Med. Assn. Club: Athenaeum (London). Office: U Tex MD Anderson Cancer Ctr 1515 Holcombe Blvd Houston TX 77030-4009

BECKER, HERBERT LAWRENCE, writer, accountant; b. Hollywood, Fla., Aug. 12, 1956; s. Jack and Lorraine (Abrams) B.; m. Malka Gasner, Jan. 1, 1977 (div. Jan. 1990); children: Randi, Adam, Brian; m. Shelly Basser, Nov. 8, 1992; children: Gillah, Dovid. BBA, Roosevelt U., Belgium, 1983, MBA, 1984. CPA, Belgium; cert. mgmt. acct., Soc. Pub. Accts. Dist. mgr. Coles Book Stores, U.S. and Can., 1976-83; pub. acct., U.S. and Can., 1983-87; sr. fin. mgr. Video One, Can., 1987-90; pres. Postal Plus Svcs., Can., 1990-93. Author: All the Secrets of Magic, 1994, Magic Secrets, 1996,, So That's How They Do It, 1996. Democrat. Home: 2607 S Woodland Blvd Deland FL 32720

BECKER, HERMAN ELI, retired pharmacist; b. N.Y.C., Mar. 27, 1910; s. Abraham Jacob and Esther (Sabin) B.; m. Mina Leah Schuchat, Sept. 13, 1936; children: Jerome David, Stanley Harold. Degree in pharmacy, Med. Coll. Va., 1931. RPh, Va. Pharmacist, asst. mgr. Peoples Drug Stores, Richmond, Va., 1931-38; pharmacist Grant Drug Store, Richmond, 1938-40; co-owner, mgr. Blvd. Grant Drug Co., Richmond, 1940-48; pharmacist, asst. mgr. Meadowbridge Pharmacy, Richmond, 1948-67; pharmacist, asst. drug buyer Gem Drug Co., Richmond, 1967-69; pharmacist St. Mary's Hosp., Richmond, 1969-71; pharmacist, asst. mgr. various pharmacies, Richmond, 1971-89. Mem. Henrico County, Va. adv. com. to Va. Ho. of Reps.; adv. com. Congressman Thomas J. Bliley Jr., 3d Congl. Dist. Va.; v.p., chmn. bd. Temple Beth El, Richmond, 1963-64, lay reader evening svcs.; bd. dirs. Beth Sholom Home for Aged, Richmond, 1979-84; active Richmond Jewish Ctr., 1990. Recipient Disting. Worker award Temple Beth El, 1965, Samuel Gerson award, 1978, Methuselah award Beth Sholom Home for Aged, 1984. Mem. Richmond Pharm. Assn. (pres. 1957-58, dist. pres. svc. award 1957, human rels. award 1962), Va. Pharm. Assn., Am. Acad. Gen. Pharmacy Practice, B'nai Brith, Masons, Omega Chi. Republican. Home: 5108 Downy Ln # 101 Richmond VA 23228-3950

BECKER, JAMES RICHARD, lawyer; b. San Juan, P.R., Sept. 25, 1954; s. John Joseph and Patricia (Doherty) B.; m. Mary E. McGurk; children: Colette Anne, Robert Charles II. BA in English, Va. Tech., 1977; JD, George Mason Law Sch., 1982. Bar: Va. 1982, U.S. Dist. Ct. (ea. and we. dists.) Va. 1982, U.S. Ct. Appeals (4th cir.) 1982. Atty. James R. Becker, Esquire, Middleburg and Chantilly, Va., 1982-93; assoc. atty. Nichols, Bergere & Zauzig, P.C., Woodbridge, Va., 1993-94, Joel Atlas Skirble and Assocs., Falls Church, Va., 1994—. Editor Law Rev., 1980-82. Mem. Fairfax Bar Assn. Home: 4515 Fillingame Dr Chantilly VA 20151-2820 Office: Joel Atlas Skirble & Assocs 6316 Castle Pl Ste 300 Falls Church VA 22044-1906

BECKER, JIM, small business owner; b. Sault Sainte Marie, Mich., Apr. 28, 1953; s. Wade Moore and Mary Bonnie (Law) B. BA, U. Ctrl. Fla., 1977; grad., Gemological Inst., 1991. Assoc. Zales Jewelers, Jensen Beach, Fla., 1987-88, Mayor's Jewelers, Jensen Beach, 1988-91; pres., owner Gem Advice Co., Stuart, Fla., 1991—; gem historian Christie's Auction House, Geneva, 1988—, Smithsonian Inst., 1994—; head American Jewelry Co., Vero Beach, Fla.; lectr. and conductor of workshops Sotheby's. Tracer of jewels to major owners, including Catherine the Great, Empress Eugenie, Czarina Alexandra, Maharanee of Baroda, Enid Annenberg Haupt, Queen Mary, Lady Cullinan, others; presented Cullinan Blue Diamond Necklace to Smithsonian Inst., 1994; assisted Smithsonian Inst. to obtain their first Black Pearls for the Gem and Mineral Hall; contbr. articles to profl. jours. Promoter Am. Heart Assn., Stuart, 1991—; mem., sponsor Vero Beach (Fla.) Ctr. for Arts, 1991. Mem. Jewelers of Am., C. of C. Chmn.'s Club Ctr. for Arts, Rotary Internat. Office: Gem Advice Co 3905 12th St Sebastian FL 32976-2829 also: Am Jewelry Co 2855 Ocean Dr Vero Beach FL 32963

BECKER, JOHN LIONEL, JR., insurance company executive, marketing company executive; b. Staten Island, N.Y., Aug. 10, 1956; s. John L. and Marianne (Ziti) B.; m. Patricia Delaney, Nov. 12, 1977; children: Bridget, Benjamin, Robert, Bernadette. BS in Bus. Adminstrn., Portland State U., 1980. Field underwriter N.Y. Life, Portland, Oreg., 1980-86; v.p., sales mgr. Far West Ins. Svcs., Portland, 1986-87; mktg. v.p. United Pacific Life, Portland, 1987-93; exec. v.p., chief mktg. officer CDA Am., Palm Beach, Fla., 1993—, mem. estate income option program, 1996—. Co-creator (sr. life ins. program) Generational TaxSaver; creator Estate Income Option Program, 1996. Pres. student body Portland State U., 1977-78; fin. chmn. Oreg. Rep. Orgn., 1980-81; chmn. bd. Counseling Intervention Programs, Portland, 1984-86; co-chmn. Oreg. prayer com. Nat. Day of Prayer, 1984; fundraiser St. Theresa Cath. Sch., Portland, 1992; chmn. bd. Worldwide Seminarian Support, 1992—; active Nat. Right to Life, Am. Life Lobby; mem. adv. bd. Holy Name of Jesus Sch., 1995—. Recipient Outstanding Man award Oreg. Young Reps., 1980, 81, New Bus. Devel. award United Pacific Life, 1988. Mem. NALU (Million Dollar Roundtable 1985), Assn. Banks-in-Ins., Oreg. Bankers Assn. (assoc.), N.W. Assn. Affiliated Agys. (assoc.), Portland States Pres.' Club, Portland State U. Alumni Assn., 1620 Club (sec.-treas. 1992), Nat. Eagle Scout Assn., KC, 1620 Club, Kappa Sigma. Home: 719 Daffodil Dr West Palm Beach FL 33414-8278 Office: CDA Am 2875 S Ocean Blvd # 2109 Palm Beach FL 33480-5591

BECKER, MAGDALENE NEUENSCHWANDER, English language educator; b. Beaverdam, Ohio, Sept. 5, 1915; d. Walter and Viola Etta (Gratz) Neuenschwander; m. Homer Gerald Becker, Aug. 18, 1935; 1 child, Rachel Etta. BA, Westminster Coll., New Wilmington, Pa., 1954, MEd in Guidance and Counseling, 1971; postgrad. in English, U. Pitts., 1962-65. Cert. tchr. Tchr. pub. speaking New Castle (Pa.) Sr. High Sch., 1954-61; tchr. advanced English Butler (Pa.) Area Sr. High Sch., 1961-77; with Learning Ctr. Sheldon Jackson Coll., Sitka, Alaska, 1977-79; cataloger, reference librarian Lees Coll., Jackson, Ky., 1979-83; coordinator conf. ctr. Cook Christian Tng. Sch., Tempe, Ariz., 1983-85; tutor Armstrong-Ind. County Intermediate Unit, Indiana, Pa., 1985-92; tutor ESL Lakeland, Fla., 1992-94; evaluator Mid-Atlantic Sch. Examiners, 1966; examiner Nat. Coun. Tchrs. of English, 1964-76. Author 11 computer discs of GED programs, 1987-88. Tchr. Sunday Sch., Presbyn. Ch., 1940—, deacon, elder, 1985—, vice moderator women's gathering, 1993-95; bd. dirs. Group Homes, Indiana, 1986-89; vol. in nursing home, 1985-92; sec. Lake Hunter Fellowship. Mem. NEA, Pa. State Edn. Assn., Indiana County Edn. Assn., AAUW (pres. Indiana br. 1988-90, exec. v.p. 1986-88). Republican. Home: A303 16 Lake Hunter Dr Lakeland FL 33803-1280

BECKER, RICHARD CHARLES, retired college president; b. Chgo., Mar. 1, 1931; s. Charles Beno and Rose Mildred (Zak) B.; m. Magdalene Marie Kypry, June 19, 1954; children: Richard J., Daniel P., Douglas F., Steven G., Pamela J. BS in Elec. Engring, Fournier Inst. Tech., 1953; MS in Elec. Engring, U. Ill., 1954, MS in Math. (Arthur J. Schmitt fellow), 1956, PhD in Elec. Engring, 1959. Engr. Ill. Bell Tel. Co., Chgo., 1952, Andrew Corp., Chgo., 1953; rsch. asst. U. Ill., Urbana, 1954-58, asst. prof., 1959; sr. staff engr. Amphenol Corp., Chgo., 1959-60; sr. rsch. scientist Amphenol Corp., 1961-64, dir. program mgmt., 1965-67; dir. Amphenol Corp. (Far Eastern ops.), 1968; group v.p., corporate dir. adminstrn. Bunker Ramo Corp., Oak Brook, Ill., 1968-73; chief exec. officer and chmn. bd. Fortune Internat. Enterprises, Inc., Oak Brook, 1973-76; pres. Benedictine Univ. (formerly Ill. Benedictine Coll.), Lisle, 1976-95; pres. emeritus Ill. Benedictine Univ. (formerly Ill. Benedictine Coll.), Lisle, 1995—; Trustee, prof. Midwest Coll. Engring., Lombard, Ill., 1968-86; trustee Ill. Benectine Coll., Lisle, 1973-76; bd. dir. Amphenol Tyree Proprietary, Ltd., Australia, Amphetronix, Ltd., India, Oxbow Resources, Ltd., Can. Contbr. articles and chpts. to profl. jours. and books. Gov. Brook Forest Community Assn., 1971-74; del. Oak Brook Caucus, 1970; trustee, pres. Arthur J. Schmitt Found., Ill. Benedictine Coll.; chmn. Coun. West Suburban Colls., Chgo. Met. Higher Edn. Coun., officer Fedn. Ind. Ill. Colls. and Univs.; chmn. Associated Colls. of Ill., West Suburban Regional Acad. Consortium. Named Disting. Eagle Scout, 1989, Regent Nat. Eagles Scout Assn. Mem. Am. Phys. Soc., Nat. Assn. Ind. Colls. and Univs. (bd. dirs.), Albertus Magnus Guild, Rotary, Equestrian Order of the Holy Sepulchre of Jerusalem, Sigma Xi, Eta Kappa Nu, Tau Beta Pi.

BECKER, ROBERT STEPHEN, digital multimedia producer; b. Yonkers, N.Y., June 12, 1950; s. Alfred and Maria B.; m. Jody Rae Schwartz, June 1, 1985; children: Samuel Harrison, Elayne Audrey. BA, NYU, 1972, MA, 1975; PhD, U. Reading, Eng., 1980. A.W. Mellon postdoctoral fellow U. Pitts., 1981-82; asst. prof. English Emory U., Atlanta, 1982-85; mgr. multimedia Crawford Comm. Inc., Atlanta, 1987-92; dir. multimedia TW Design, Atlanta, 1992-94; pres. Becker Multimedia, 1994—. Designer and producer bus. and ednl. programs, CD-ROM titles, interactive TV programming. Grantee numerous orgns. Democrat. Jewish. Office: 2353 Massey Ln Decatur GA 30033

BECKER, TERESA ANN, neonatal nurse practitioner; b. Bangor, Maine, Apr. 22, 1957; d. George Robert and Marlene Ellen (Mueller) B. BSN, East Tenn. State U., 1980; cert. nurse practitioner, Georgetown U., 1988; MSN, U. Tenn., 1995. RN, Tenn.; cert. nurse practitioner, physician asst., PNP, regional instr. neonatal resuscitation, pediatric advanced life support instr. Charge nurse newborn Johnson City (Tenn.) Med. Ctr., 1980-82, staff nurse SCN, 1982-84, staff nurse NICU, 1984-85, charge nurse NICU, 1985-88, neonatal nurse practitioner, 1989—; regional instr. neonatal resuscitation AAP, Johnson City, 1989—; instr. PALS Am. Heart Assn., Johnson City, 1991—. Bd. dirs. March of Dimes, Johnson City, 1992-93; chmn. Health Profl. Adv. Com. Mem. Assn. Women's Health, Obstetrics and Neonatal Nurses, Perinatal and Neonatal Assn., Nat. Assn. Neonatal Nurses, Nat. Assn. Pediatric Nurse Assocs. and Practitioners, Sigma Theta Tau. Roman Catholic. Home: 4117 Aztec Dr Johnson City TN 37604-1144 Office: Johnson City Med Ctr 400 N State Of Franklin Rd Johnson City TN 37604-6035

BECKERMAN, MILTON BERNARD, media broker; b. Bronx, N.Y., Sept. 3, 1917; s. Harris and Rachel (Barnett) B.; m. Bernice Smith, Aug. 29, 1937; children: Jay Harry, Dorothy Ann, Dana Charles (dec.), Susan Joyce. Student, NYU, 1935-37. Publicity, pub. rels. and advt. staff Lewis A. Jacobs, Buffalo, 1937-39; salesman Bennett Bros., Waycross, Ga., 1939-40; editor Lyons (Ga.) Progress, 1940-41; assoc. editor Swainsboro (Ga.) Forest-Blade, 1940-41, editor/pub., 1946-49; editor/pub. Claxton (Ga.) Enterprise, 1949-55, Natchitoches (La.) Enterprise, 1955-59; bus./fin. editor, columnist St. Petersburg (Fla.) Times, 1959-63; asst. to pres. Greenbaum & Assocs., St. Petersburg, 1963-68; v.p. EBS Tax Svc., St. Petersburg, 1968-70; co-owner Beckerman Assocs., Inc., Madeira Beach, Fla., 1970—. Corres./stringer 35 trade jours., 1959-69; contbr. articles to profl. jours.; contbg. author: The Last Linotype, 1985. Vice pres. bd. dirs. Fla. Philharmonic Soc., St. Petersburg, 1960-62; bd. dirs. Am. Cancer Soc., Claxton, 1953-55; chmn. Citizens Adv. Com. Elimination Slums/Blight, St. Petersburg, 1961-63; chmn. bd. trustees Gulf Beaches Pub. Libr., Madeira Beach, 1966-67; publicity chmn. Pinellas County Dem. Party, St. Petersburg, 1965; active boy Scouts Am. With U.S. Army, 1945-46. Mem. Soc. Profl. Journalists (chpt. pres. 1960-62), Fla. Advt. Pubs. Assn. (life), Southeastern Advt. Pubs. Assn. (Herb Campbell award 1992), Ind. Free Papers of Am., Assn. Free Cmty. Papers, Fla. Press Assn., Ga. Press Assn. (W. Trox Bankston Trophy 1947, Theron S. Shope Trophy 1947, Sam W. Wilkes Trophy 1952-53), Assn. of Free Newspapers (London), Syndicat National des Éditeurs de Periodiques Gratuits (Paris). Home and Office: 14001 Miramar Ave Madeira Beach FL 33708-2214

BECKINGHAM, KATHLEEN MARY, education educator, researcher; b. Sheffield, Yorkshire, Eng., May 8, 1946; came to U.S., 1976; d. Philip and Mary Ellen (Flint) B.; m. Alan Edward Smith, Oct. 7, 1967 (div. Oct. 1978); m. Robert Bruce Weisman, July 25, 1986; 1 child, Caroline Mary Weisman. BA, U. Cambridge, Eng., 1967, MA, 1968, PhD, 1972. Grad. student Strangeways Rsch. Lab., Cambridge, 1967-70; postdoctoral Inst. Molecular Biology, Aarhus, Denmark, 1970-72; rsch. assoc. Nat. Inst. Med. Rsch., London, 1972-76; rsch. assoc., instr. U. Mass. Med. Sch., Worcester, 1976-80; asst. prof. Rice U., Houston, 1980-85, assoc. prof. biochemistry, cell biology, molecular biology, 1985-92, prof., 1992—. Recipient award Camille and Henry Dreyfus Found., 1979. Office: Rice U PO Box 1892 6100 South Main St Houston TX 77251

BECKMAN, GAIL MCKNIGHT, law educator; b. N.Y.C., Apr. 8, 1938; d. Irland McKnight and Elizabeth B. (Hurlock) B. A.B., Bryn Mawr Coll., 1959; M.A., U. Pa., 1966; J.D., Yale U., 1963, Hague (Netherlands) Acad. Internat. Law, 1977, Brit. Inst. for Comparative Law, 1975; Ph.D., Ga. State U., 1988. Bar: Pa. 1964, D.C. 1964, Ga. 1971. Counselor Legal Aid Soc., Phila., 1961; legal research asst. U. Pa. Law Sch., 1963; assoc. firm Morgan, Lewis & Bockius, Phila., 1963-66; lectr. Faculty Law, U. Glasgow, Scotland, 1967-71; assoc. prof. Ga. State U., Atlanta, 1971-75; prof. Ga. State U., 1976—; Fulbright scholar U. Tuebingen, W. Germany, 1960, guest prof. law faculty, 1988; mem. Fulbright screening com. Inst. Internat. Edn., 1980, 88; vis. scholar Inst. East Asian and Comparative Law, Harvard U. Law Sch., 1980, U. Tuebingen Law Faculty, Germany, 1988. Author: Statutes at Large of Pennsylvania, 1680-1700, 1976, Law for Business and Management, 1975, also articles, revs.; editor: Am. Bus. Law Jour, 1972-79. Bd. dirs. Northside Shepherds Ctr., Atlanta, 1980-83, chmn. bd., 1982-83; active Atlanta Coun. Internat. Visitors, 1975-77; bd. dirs. N.W. Ga. coun. Girl Scouts U.S.A., 1976-78, United Way, 1979. Colonial Williamsburg, grantee, 1965; Ga. State U. grantee, 1980; Fulbright scholar, 1959-60. Mem. ABA (chmn., vice chmn. coms.), Internat. Law Assn. (chmn. intercountry adoption and protection of family, exec. bd. 1995—, rep. to Hague Conf. on Pvt. Internat. Law 1995—), Internat. Bar Assn., Am. Arbitration Assn. (cert.), Ga. Bar Assn., Nat. Assn. Women Lawyers (exec. bd. 1984-92, pres. 1980-81), Juristic Soc. Phila., Nat. Soc. Colonial Dames in Am., DAR, St. Andrews Soc. Atlanta (founder), Commerce Club. Presbyterian. Home: 3747 Peachtree Rd NE Apt 319 Atlanta GA 30319-1360 Office: Ga State U PO Box 106 Atlanta GA 30301-0106

BECKMAN, JAMES WALLACE BIM, economist, marketing executive; b. Mpls., May 2, 1936; s. Wallace Gerald and Mary Louise (Frissell) B. BA, Princeton U., 1958; PhD, U. Calif., 1973. Pvt. practice econ. cons., Berkeley, Calif. 1962-67; cons. Calif. State Assembly, Sacramento, 1967-68; pvt. practice market rsch. and econs. cons., Laguna Beach, Calif., 1969-77; cons. Calif. State Gov.'s Office, Sacramento 1977-80; pvt. practice real estate cons., L.A. 1980-83; v.p. mktg. Gold-Well Investments, Inc., L.A. 1982-83; pres. Beckman Analytics Internat., econ. cons. to bus. and govt., L.A. and Lake Arrowhead, Calif., 1983—, East European/Middle East Bus. and Govt., 1992—; adj. prof. Calif. State U. Sch. Bus., San Bernardino, 1989—, U. Redlands, 1992—; cons. E European, environmental issues. Contbr. articles on regional & internat. econ. devel. & social change to profl. jours. Maj. USMC 1958-67. NIMH fellow 1971-72. Fellow Soc. Applied Anthropology; mem. Am. Econs. Assn., Am. Statis. Assn., Am. Mktg. Assn. (officer), Nat. Assn. Bus. Economists (officer). Democrat. Presbyterian.

BECKNER, DIANA ROBERTS, clinical nurse specialist; b. Knoxville, Tenn., Nov. 22, 1952; d. Jack Thomas and Beulah Lillard (Cummings) Roberts; m. John Morton Beckner, May 6, 1978; 1 child, Jonathan Roberts. BSN, U. Tenn., 1976, MSN, 1982. RN, Tenn.; cert. CPR instr.; cert. med.-surg. clin. specialist ANCC; cert. orthopaedic nurse; cert. wound care nurse. Primary nurse Ft. Sanders Hosp., Knoxville, 1976; staff nurse, asst. head nurse U. Tenn. Meml. Hosp., Knoxville, 1976-80; insvc. dir, head nurse Shannondale Health Care Ctr., Knoxville, 1980-81; tchr. pharmacology Knoxville City Schs., 1980; instr. nursing Lincoln Meml. U., Harrogate, Tenn., 1981-83; clin. mgr. Methodist Med. Ctr., Oak Ridge, Tenn., 1984-89, clin. nurse specialist, 1989—. Mem. Karns Cmty. Club, Karns-Knoxville, 1974—; vol. March of Dimes, Knoxville, 1974—, Am. Cancer Soc., Knoxville, 1974—, Am. Heart Assn., Knoxville, 1974—; liaison nurse, cons. Arthritis Found., Oak Ridge, 1990—, Chrohns Colitis Ostomy Club, Oak Ridge, 1992—. Recognized for Clin. Excellence in Nursing, Knoxville Area Hosps., 1996; Edn. Opportunity grantee Knoxville Edn. Assn., 1970; Ross scholar. Mem. ANA, Nat. Assn. Orthopaedic Nurses, Am. Bus. Women's Assn., Wound, Ostomy and Continent Nurses Soc., United Meth. Women, Sigma Theta Tau. Home: 1708 Gray Oaks Ln Knoxville TN 37932-1600

BEDARD, ROY RAYMOND, law enforcement official, consultant; b. Torrington, Conn., June 11, 1966; s. Leon Ernest and Monika Helga (Plienes) B. Degree in Law Enforcement Standards, Lively Law Enforcement Acad., 1986; AA in Polit. Sci., Fla. State U., 1990. Law enforcement officer Fla. State Univ. Police Dept., Tallahassee, 1987-90; law enforcement officer, trainer Tallahassee Police Dept., 1990—; instr. defense tactics Lively Law Enforcement Acad., Tallahassee, 1987—; instr. Fla. Inst. Martial Arts, Tallahassee, 1980—, dir., 1986—; cons. profl. police svcs., Tallahassee, 1989—. Inventor Rapid Rotation Baton, 1987. Mem. U.S. World Karate Team, 1994. Recipient Recognition of Heroism award Big Bend Law Enforcement Assn., Tallahassee, 1988. Mem. Police Benevolent Assn. (dir.), U.S. Nat. Karate Team (state champion 8 times, blackbelt), Am. Soc. Law Enforcement Trainers, Omega Kappa Alpha (pres. 1985-87), USA Karate Fedn. (dir. N. Fla.), Tallahassee Sports Authority (karate chmn. 1992). Home: 3057 Tipperary Dr Tallahassee FL 32308-3326 Office: Tallahassee Police Dept 234 E 7th Ave Tallahassee FL 32303-5519

BEDDINGFIELD, CAROL ANNE, secondary school educator; b. Dallas, Apr. 14, 1947; d. Rex and Anna Belle (Mathews) Sanders; m. Charles R. Beddingfield, Jan. 28, 1966 (dec. Oct. 1993); children: Jay L., Jody S., Jana L. BA in Teaching, Sam Houston State U., 1970, MEd, 1973. Tchr. math., biology Leon High Sch., Jewett, Tex., 1968—; part-time math. instr. Navarro Coll., Corsicana, Tex., 1990—; trainer Tex. Math. Tchrs. Tng. Modules; mem. curriculum rev. com. State Bd. Edn., 1987—; presenter Conf. for Advancement of Math. Teaching, 1987-90. Tchr. Sunday sch. Sardis Bapt. Ch., Jewett, 1968—; bd. dirs., sec. Jewett Pub. Libr., 1984—. Mem. Nat. Coun. Tchrs. Math., Tex. Coun. Tchrs. Math., Trinity Brazos River Valley Coun. Tchrs. Math. (bd. dirs. 1987-90, v.p. 1988-90, 94-96), Jewett Area C. of C. (charter), Order of Ea. Star (Worthy Matron 1985-86, treas. 1986—), Pi Mu Epsilon. Home: PO Box 308 Jewett TX 75846-0308 Office: Leon Ind Sch Dist PO Box 157 Jewett TX 75846-0157

BEDENBAUGH, ANGELA LEA OWEN, chemistry educator, researcher; b. Seguin, Tex., Oct. 6, 1939; d. Wintford Henry and Nelia Melanie (Fischer) Owen; m. John Holcombe Bedenbaugh, Dec. 27, 1961; 1 child, Melanie Celeste. BS cum laude, U. Tex., 1961; PhD in Organic Chemistry, U. S.C., 1967. Geol. mapping asst. Roland Blumberg Assocs., Seguin, summer 1958, 59; chemistry lab. instr. U. Tex., Austin, 1960-61; rsch. assoc. chemistry U. So. Miss., Hattiesburg, 1966-80, rsch. assoc. prof. chemistry, 1980—. Author: (with John H. Bedenbaugh) Handbook for High School Chemistry Teachers, 1985, (with John H. Bedenbaugh) Teaching First Year Chemistry, 1988, 4th edit., 1993. Mem. adminstrv. bd. Parkway Heights United Meth. Ch., 1974-75, women's unit leader, 1973-75, women's unit treas., 1977, Wesleyan Svc. Guild v.p., 1970, Sunday Sch. tchr., 1973-74; bd. dirs. Forrest Stone Area Opportunity Inc., 1970-72, bd. dirs. exec. com., 1972, mem. com. to rewrite pers. policies and procedures, 1971, mem. Headstart monitoring com., 1971-72, mem. pers. screening com., 1971; mem. nat. Women's Polit. Caucus, 1976—; mem. Toastmasters Internat., 1986—, club. pres., 1993, area gov., 1994. Prin. investigator rsch. grant U.S. Dept. Energy, U. So. Miss., 1980; co-prin. investigator rsch. grant NSF, U. So. Miss., 1985, adminstrv. dir. rsch. grant, 1988-92, 93—, others. Mem. NSTA (mem. nat. resource rev. panel for rev. of instrnl. materials), Am. Chem. Soc. (chairperson 1984-85, program chairperson 1983-84, Chemist of Yr. 1991), Miss. Sci. Tchrs. Assn. (Disting. Sci. Tchr. award 1994, exec. bd. 1994—), Delta Kappa Gamma (pres. Miss. state br. 1989-91, chairperson internat. rsch. com. 1980-82, chairperson internat. computer share fair at internat. conv. 1994), Sigma Xi (charter, sec.-treas. 1967-69, treas. 1970, pres. 1973-74, program chairperson 1972-73). Democrat. Methodist. Home: 63 Suggs Rd Hattiesburg MS 39402-9642 Office: Univ So Miss PO Box 8466 Hattiesburg MS 39406-8466

BEDFORD, CHARLES B., higher education consortium executive; b. Pikeville, N.C., Sept. 20, 1933; s. William and Bettie (Smith) B.; m. Nancy Lee Espey, June 22, 1963. BA, East Carolina U., 1955, MA, 1958, postgrad., 1958-62; postgrad., Ind. U., 1958-62. Classroom tchr. New Hanover County Schs., Wilmington, N.C., 1955-57; tchr., counselor Arlington (Va.) County Schs., 1957-63; asst. dir. admissions Lake Forest (Ill.) Coll., 1963-65; dean of admissions Hanover (Ind.) Coll., 1965-70; program officer The Coll. Bd., Evanston, Ill., 1970-77, N.Y.C., 1977-79, Atlanta, 1979-83; exec. dir. The Univ. Ctr. in Ga., Atlanta, 1983—. Bd. dirs. Boys and Girls Clubs of Metro Atlanta; bd. dirs. Nat. Families in Action; amb. Friendship Force. Mem. Am. Coun. Edn., Am. Assn. Higher Edn., Coun. of Instnl. Leadership (nat. pres. 1991-92), Ansley Golf Club, Rotary Club of Atlanta, Commerce Club, English-Speaking Union, Phi Kappa Delta. Presbyterian. Office: Univ Ctr in Ga Ste 465 50 Aunt Plaza Atlanta GA 30303

BEDINGER, GEORGE MICHAEL, psychologist; b. May 8, 1939. PhD, U. Fla., 1983. Instr. U. Fla., Gainesville; sr. psychologist Fla. Dept. Health and Rehabilitative Svcs. Author: Peer Counseling. Named Professional of Yr., Fla. Assn. for Retarded Citizens, 1992. Mem. Am. Psychol. Assn., Fla. Assn. Behavior Analysis. Home: 8411 SW 43rd Ter Gainesville FL 32608-5116

BEDNAR, SUSAN MARIE, art director; b. Houston, Dec. 24, 1968; d. Eugene David and Julia Marie (Hueske) B. BA, Loyola U., 1991. Cons. Planview, Inc., Austin, 1991-94, mktg., 1994-96; graphic designer Origin Systems, Inc., Austin, 1996, art dir., 1996—; freelance graphic designer, Austin, 1995—. Home: 4423 Marathon Blvd Austin TX 78756-3428 Office: Origin Syss Inc 5918 W Courtyard Austin TX 78730

BEDNARZ, JAMES C., wildlife ecologist educator. BS in Wildlife and Fishery Biology, N.Mex. State U., 1976; MS in Animal Ecology, Iowa State U., 1979; PhD in Biology, U. N.Mex., 1986. Wildlife biologist U.S. Fish and Wildlife Svc., 1977-78; wildlife cons., 1979-80, 91—; rsch. assoc. U. N.Mex., 1985-91; dir. higher edn. and rsch. Hawk Mountain Sanctuary Assn., 1987-90; prin. investigator Greenfalk Cons., 1990-91; asst. prof. wildlife ecology Ark. State U., State Univ., 1993—; rsch. asst. part-time Iowa State U., 1977-78; invited mem. Eastside Forests Scientific Panel; bd. dirs., chair conservation com. Raptor Rsch.; referee Science, Ecology, Auk, Jour. Mammalogy, Wilson Bull., Raptor Rsch. NSF, and others. Contbr. articles to profl. jours. Recipient Rsch. award Hawk Mountain, Marcia Brady Tucker Travel award; Ding Darling scholar. Am. Ornithologists' Union, Animal Behavior Soc., Wildlife Soc., Cooper Ornithological Soc., Wilson Ornithological Soc., Raptor Rsch. Found., Acad. Nat. Scis. Phila. (assoc. in ornithology), Hawk Watch Internat. (rsch. adv. com.). Office: Ark State U PO Box 599 Dept Biological Scis State University AR 72467-0599

BEDNARZYK, MICHELE SMITH, family nurse practitioner, educator; b. Alton, Ill., Dec. 9, 1958; d. William H.C. and Rosalie Anne (Low) Smith; m. Paul Anthony Bednarzyk, Aug. 18, 1990. BSN, Avila Coll., 1980; MN, U. S.C., 1991. Cert. FNP, ANCC. Commd. 2d lt. USAF, 1980, advanced through grades to capt., 1983; staff nurse USAF, Alamogordo, N.Mex., 1980-83; staff nurse, asst. charge nurse USAF, Upper Heyford, Eng., 1983-86; adminstrv. family clinic nurse Shaw AFB USAF, Sumter, S.C., 1986-90; FNP Family Medicine Assocs., Augusta, Ga., 1991-94; asst. prof. U. S.C., Aiken, 1991-94; vis. faculty U. North Fla., Jacksonville, 1994—; nurse practitioner Orange Park Pediatrics, Orange Park, Fla., 1995—; mem. adv. bd. Nat. Health Care, North Augusta, S.C., 1992-94, Keysville (Ga.) Convalescent Health Ctr., 1992-94. Vol. Am. Heart Assn., Augusta, 1992, 93, Am. Cancer Assn., Augusta, 1992, 93. Mem. ANA, AAUP, Am. Assn. Nurse Practitioners. Republican. Roman Catholic. Office: Orange Park Pediatrics 2140 South St Orange Park FL 32073

BEDNER, MARK A., banker; b. Emporia, Kans., Nov. 26, 1948; s. Jerry L. and Marjorie (Dabbs) D.; divorced; 1 child, Elizabeth. BA, U. Kans., 1970, MS, 1975; MA, Fletcher Sch., Medford, Mass., 1976. Writer, reporter Congl. Quar. Mag., Washington, 1972-75; comml. banker Citibank N.A., Citicorp, N.Y.C., Internat., 1976-82, Bank of Am., Atlanta, 1982-83; investment banker Prudential Capital Corp., Atlanta, 1983-86; founder, chmn., CEO The Mcht. Bank of Atlanta, 1987-94; with Cottonwood Capital Corp., Sea Island, 1994—. Bd. dirs. Brain Tumor Found. for Children, Emory U., Atlanta, 1985-87, Children's Mus., Atlanta, 1989-94, Arts Festival of Atlanta, Midtown Bus. Assn., Plum Orchard Found., Cumberland Island, Ga.; founder, pres. The Atlanta Forum, 1985. Named to internship U.S. Senate, 1969, The White House, 1969-70. Mem. Capital City Club, Ocean Forest Golf Club. Office: Cottonwood Capital Corp PO Box 30809 Sea Island GA 31561

BEDWELL, RANDALL JEROME, publisher; b. Paris, Tenn., Nov. 19, 1959; s. Kenneth Gene and Sandra (Clayton) B.; m. Amanda, Sept. 4, 1993. BS cum laude, Lambuth U., 1980; M of History, U. Miss., 1991. Asst. officer United Am. Bank, Nashville, N.Y., 1981-83; acct. exec. Dean Witter Reynolds, Manhattan, N.Y., 1983-85; pres., owner Guild Bindery Press, Inc., Germantown, Tenn., 1986—; mem. publs. com. West Tenn. Hist. Soc., 1990-92; v.p. Henry County Hist. Soc., Paris, Tenn., 1988. Editor, publisher Southern Reader Mag., 1987-91. Charter mem., dir. Brentwood (Tenn.) Kiwanis, 1985. Recipient Cert. of Merit Tenn. Hist. Com., 1988. Mem. Successful Mag. Publ. Group, Publishers Mktg. Assn. Methodist. Office: Guild Bindery Press Inc PO Box 38099 Memphis TN 38183-0099

BEEBE, LARRY EUGENE, quality engineering educator, management consultant; b. Zanesville, Ohio, Feb. 9, 1947; s. George Franklin and Pauline Betty (White) B.; m. Donna Kaye Miles, Apr. 20, 1964 (div.); children: Troy William, Todd Eugene; m. Danna Darlene Smith, Dec. 12, 1986. Diploma in gen. indsl. engring., Granton Inst. Tech., 1987; MBA, City U., Bellevue, Wash., 1989; postgrad., U. Pa., 1990; PhD in Computer Info. Sys., Nova Southeastern U., 1994. Buyer, quality analyst, mgmt. trainee Continental Can Co., Columbus, Ohio, 1966-70; gen. foreman Ohio Malleable Iron, Columbus, Ohio, 1970-74; foreman Ford Motor Co., L.A., 1974-76; ops. mgr. Vallee Machine Works, Houston, 1976-79, Gt. Lakes Engring., Houston, 1979-84; v.p. info. tech. human resources Atlantic Computer Tech., Melbourne, Fla., 1984—, dir. info. tech.; cons. info. sys., Melbourne, 1985—; mem. adj. faculty Webster U., 1992—. Contbr. articles to profl. jours. Mem. Weson Park Townhome Assn., Melbourne, 1985-89; sponsor Spl. Olympics, 1991-92. Fellow Am. Soc. Quality Control, Am. Soc. Non Destructive Test; mem. Am. Welding Soc., Am. Purchasing Assn., Am. Mgmt. Assn., Assn. Info. Profls., Assn. Computer Machinery.

BEEBE, ROBERT DANIEL (DAN), sports association administrator; b. Marceline, Mo., Feb. 27, 1957; s. James Preston and Judith Ann (Rooks) Harwood; m. Jennifer Ann Frisbie, July 28, 1984 (div. Apr. 1993); children: Jessie, Matt, Elaine. AA, Walla Walla C.C., 1977; BS in Social Scis., Calif. Polytech., 1979; JD, U. Calif., Hastings, 1982. Enforcement rep. Nat. Collegiate Athletic Assn., Overland Park, Kans., 1982-85; asst. dir. athletics Wichita (Kans.) State U., 1986; dir. enforcement Nat. Collegiate Athletic Assn., Overland Park, 1987-89; commr. Ohio Valley Conf., Nashville, 1989—; com. NCAA Athletics Cert. com., 1993—, NCAA Pro Sports liaison com., 1992—, NCAA nominating com., 1990-92. Ethics fellowship Inst. for Internat. Sports, 1995. Mem. Wash. State Bar Assn., BRAVONashville. Office: Ohio Valley Conf 278 Franklin Rd Ste 103 Brentwood TN 37027-5224

BEECH, JOHNNY GALE, lawyer; b. Chickasha, Okla., Sept. 18, 1954; s. Lovell Gale and Lucille L. (Phillips) B.; m. Judy Carol Schroeder, Dec. 31, 1977. BS, Southwestern Okla. State U., 1977; JD, U. Ark., Little Rock, 1980; LLM in Energy-Environment, Tulane U., 1985. Bar: Okla. 1980, U.S. Dist. Ct. (we. dist.) Okla. 1982, U.S. Dist. Ct. (no. dist.) Tex. 1983, U.S. Dist. Ct. (no. dist.) Okla. 1986. Assoc. Meacham, Meacham and Meacham, Clinton, Okla., 1980-84, Ford & Brown, Enid, Okla., 1985-86, Wright & Sawyer, Enid, Okla., 1986-88, Phillips, McFall, McCaffrey, McVay, Sheets and Lovelace, Oklahoma City, 1988-90; ptnr., mng. dir. Lester & Bryant, Oklahoma City, 1990-96; mgr. Wright Bryant Beech & Edwards, Pllc, Oklahoma City, 1996&; mcpl. judge Town of Arapaho, Okla., 1982-84. Bd. dirs. Jr. Achievement Garfield County, Enid, 1986-88. Mem. ABA (real property, probate and trusts sect.), ATLA, Okla. Bar Assn. (law sch. com. 1989-91, chmn. desk manual com. young lawyers div., uniform laws com. 1994—), Okla. Assn. Def. Counsel, Garfield County Bar Assn. (treas. 1988-89), Am. Bus. Club, Southwestern Okla. State U. Alumni Assn. (pres. 1983-86, parliamentarian 1992, exec. counsel 1986—), Southwestern Sch. Bus. Alumni Assn. (v.p. 1980-92, pres. 1992—), Jaycees, Am. Bus. Club, Phi Alpha Delta (sec. 1979). Democrat. Methodist. Home: 702 N Cook St Cordell OK 73632-3002 Office: Wright Bryant Beech & Edwards Pllc 119 N Robinson Ave Ste 820 Oklahoma City OK 73102-4613

BEELER, B. DIANE, executive, writer; b. Maryville, Tenn., Mar. 10, 1953; d. Peggy Ann (DeHart) B.; m. James McRay Cormani, June 12, 1975 (div. Sept. 1985); children: Julie Ann Cormani, Valerie Marie Cormani. BA in Music, Agnes Scott Coll., 1974; postgrad., U. Tenn., 1974-75; MS in Bus., U. Tex. at Dallas, Richardson, 1984. Grad. teaching asst. U. Tex. at Dallas, Richardson, 1983-84; knowledge engr., tech. spokesperson Texas Instruments, Austin, 1985-86, product mktg. engr., 1987-88; sr. product mgr. Novell, Austin, 1988-90, mgr. mktg. programs, 1990-91; pvt. cons. Austin, 1992; pres. Beeler Enterprises, Oak Ridge, Tenn., 1993—; gen. mgr. Oak Ridge Civic Music Assn., 1995—; affiliate Speakers USA, Pigeon Forge, Tenn., 1993; gen. mgr. Oak Ridge Civic Music Assn., 1995-96. Columnist: (bus. column) The Oak Ridger, 1993-94; contbr. articles to profl. jours. Mem. Class Leadership, Austin, 1990-91, Leadership Oak Ridge, 1994; mem. steering com. Employees Support Parenting Program, Austin, 1990-92; music dir. Unity Ch., Knoxville, Tenn., 1993-95; bd. dirs. Oak Ridge Civic Music Assn., 1993-94. Mem. Am. Mktg. Assn. (exec. mem.), Nat. Assn. for Self-Employed, Ridge C. of C. Office: 145 High Point Ln Oak Ridge TN 37830-7971

BEELER, BULAH RAY, medical/surgical nurse; b. San Saba, Apr. 8, 1929; d. Noah Bassett and Cora Estelle (Lawrence) Gillentine; m. Waddie O.J. Beeler, June 1, 1948; 1 child, Hubert Dale. Diploma, Lubbock Voct. Sch. Nursing, 1972. Lic. vocat. nurse, Tex.; cert. in CPR. Staff nurse Crosbyton (Tex.) Clinic Hosp., 1957—; dept. mgr. pharmacy, 1992—. Named Lic. Vocat. Nurse of Yr. Lubbock div., 1987. Home: 402 S Durham PO Box # 353 Crosbyton TX 79322

BEELER, WARREN JENNINGS, retired engineering consultant; b. Washburn, Tenn., Apr. 17, 1932; s. Silas Estal and Nola Victoria (Campbell) B.; m. Peggy Ann DeHart, Nov. 10, 1951 (div. 1981); children: Barbara Diane, Lisa Lynn, James Edward, Jonathan Curtis; m. Betty Jane Lawson Martin, Jan. 29, 1982 (div. 1993); m. Ruth McIntosh, Apr. 1, 1995; step-children: Sherman McIntosh, Grace McIntosh Dyrek, David McIntosh, Steve McIntosh, Andrew McIntosh. ABS in Indsl. Engring., Chgo. Inst. Tech., 1951; student, U. Tenn., 1950-52. Trainee Sears, Roebuck & Co., Knoxville, 1952-57; new store tng. mgr. Sears, Roebuck & Co., Maryville and Knoxville, 1958-61; home improvement mgr. Sears, Roebuck & Co., Knoxville, 1962-72; pres. PTSA, Maryville, Tenn., 1968-70; new store design/home improvement mgr. Sears, Roebuck & Co., 1973, group inst. sales mgr., 1974-83; ret.; owner Beeler Appliance, Parts & Repair, Maryville, 1952-55; engring. cons., ins. and fin. cons. Beeler Enterprises, Cleveland, Tenn., 1983—; sales engr. Chancey & Reynolds, Inc., Knoxville, 1983-93, ret., 1993; ptnr. Jacksonville Group 220MH Rapid Comm., 1995—; ptnr. L.A. Group 220MH Rapid Comm. Contbr. articles to profl. jours. Chmn. bldg. com., pres. bd. trustees Beech Grove Bapt. Ch., Louisville, 1991-93, Sunday sch. tchr., 1955-81, 89-93, chmn. budget and fin. com., 1990-93; cons. engr. Midway Rehab. Ctr., Knoxville, 1985-93; bd. dirs. Dismas House, 1992-93, Knox Devel. Coun., 1974-79; tng. dir. Chilhowee Bapt. Assn., 1969-73; chmn. bd. deacons 1st Bapt. Ch., Maryville, 1973-74; mem. Rep. Nat. Com., Presdl. Task Force; active 1st Bapt. Ch., Cleveland, Tenn. Engring. scholar, 1950; named Div. Mgr. of the Yr., Sears, Roebuck & Co., 1970, 71, 72, Nat. Inst. Sales Mgr., 1979. Mem. Order Ea. Star (assoc. patron 1992), Masons (master mason 1988—). Home: 541 Knob Hill Dr NW Cleveland TN 37312

BEEMAN, BOB JOE, minister; b. Billings, Mont., Nov. 3, 1952; s. Marvin Joe and Bonnie Berteen (Boegler) B. CE, Mont. Inst. of the Bible, 1972. Ordained to ministry, 1980. Dir. Acts Alive! Ministries, Billings, 1976-80, Bob Beeman Evangelistic Assn., Calif., 1980-85; pastor, founder Sanctuary Chs. Inc., Redondo Beach, Calif., 1985-94; exec. dir. Sanctuary International, Nashville, 1994—. Office: Sanctuary International PO Box 23945 Nashville TN 37202-3945

BEER, PETER HILL, federal judge; b. New Orleans, Apr. 12, 1928; s. Mose Haas and Henret (Lowenburg) B.; children: Kimberly Beer Bailes, Kenneth, Dana Beer Long-Innes; m. Marjorie Barry, July 14, 1985. BBA, Tulane U., 1949, LLB, 1952; LLM, U. Va., 1986. Bar: La. 1952. Successively assoc., ptnr., sr. ptnr. Montgomery, Barnett, Brown & Read, New Orleans, 1955-74; judge La. Ct. Appeal, 1974-79, U.S. Dist. Ct. (ea. dist.) La., New Orleans, 1979—; vice chmn. La. Appellate Judges Conf.; apptd. by chief justice of U.S. to state-fed. com. Jud. Conf. U.S., 1985-89; apptd. by chief justice of U.S. to Nat. Jud. Coun. State and Fed. Cts., 1993—. Mem. bd. mgrs. Touro Infirmary, New Orleans, 1969-74; mem. exec. com. Bur. Govtl. Rsch., 1965-69; chmn. profl. divsn. United Fund New Orleans, 1966-69; mem. New Orleans City Coun., 1969-74, v.p., 1972-74. Capt. USAF, 1952-55. Decorated AF Commendation medal, Bronze Star. Mem. ABA (mem. ho. dels.), Am. Judicature Soc., Fed. Bar Assn., La. State Bar Assn., Fed. Judges Assn. U.S. (bd. dirs. 1985, 5th cir. rep. bd. govs.), Nat. Lawyers Club, So. Yacht Club, St. John Golf Club. Jewish. Home: 133 Bellaire Dr New Orleans LA 70124-1008 Office: US Dist Ct C-206 US Courthouse 500 Camp St New Orleans LA 70130-3313

BEERS, FREDERICK GORDON, writer, retired corporate communications official; b. Perry, Okla., Aug. 19, 1924; s. Frederick William and Ivy Isabel (Bucklin) B.; m. Laura Belle Thomas, May 2, 1954; children: Kathleen Faye Beers Lindsey, Susan Gail Beers Bieberdorf. Student, St. Bonaventure U., 1943-44. City editor Perry Daily Jour., 1941-43; copy editor Mid-Pacific edit. Stars & Stripes, 1945; mng. editor, columnist Perry Daily Jour., 1946-69; mem. advt. and pub. rels. staff Charles Machine Works, Inc., Perry, 1969-90, cons. in corp. graphics, 1990—; freelance writer, Perry, 1990—; lab. instr. Journalism Sch., Okla. State U., 1968. Author: The First Generation, 1991, History of the Paul W. Cress Family, 1993, Perry Tales, 1995; freelance columnist Perry Daily Jour., 1994—; contbr. numerous hist. articles to newspaper. Sec. Noble County Rep. Com., Perry, 1950-52; pres., mem. Perry Bd. Edn., 1973-83, Stagecoach Community Theatre, Perry, 1975—; bd. dirs. Perry Hist. Preservation Com., 1992—; ruling elder 1st Presbyn. Ch., Perry, 1949—; mem. Perry Libr. Bd. Staff sgt. AUS, 1943-46, PTO. Mem. Soc. Profl. Journalists, Perry C. of C. (pres. 1959, Outstanding Citizen award 1992), Rotary (pres. Perry 1949, Paul Harris fellow). Home: 1715 Parklane St Perry OK 73077-1213

BEERY, DONALD THOMAS, business development executive; b. Washington, Nov. 5, 1960; s. Edmund Joseph Jr. and Mildred Francis (Thompson) B.; m. Jill Marie Johnson, June 28, 1986; 1 child, Jonathan Thomas. AS, Ferrum (Va.) Coll., 1981; BS in Fin., George Mason U., 1990. Field engr. Best Engring. Svcs., Arlington, Va., 1977-82; sales rep. Eastman Kodak Co., Roslyn, Va., 1988-90; fin. analyst Electronic Data Systems, Springfield, Va., 1989-92, account exec., 1992—. Editor jour. Mgmt. Monthly, 1989. Vol. Am. Heart Assn., Fairfax, Va., 1990; group leader walkathon March of Dimes, Arlington, 1990. With USN, 1982-88. Mem. Soc. Advancement of Mgmt. (pres. Fairfax 1989-90, 3d place in internat. competition 1990), Golden Key, Omicron Delta Epsilon. Republican. Roman Catholic. Home: 5124 Winding Woods Dr Centreville VA 20220-4108 Office: EDS A6S-B46 13600 EDS Dr Herndon VA 22071

BEERY, ROGER LEWIS, II, risk management consultant; b. San Antonio, Apr. 9, 1957; s. Roger Lewis Sr. and Margaret (Dorrill) B.; m. Donna M. Hodgkinson. BBA, U. Tex., 1979, MBA, 1981. Founder, pres. Austin (Tex.) Cons. Group, Inc., Breckenridge, Colo., 1980—; lectr. U. Tex., Austin, 1979-87, Rice U., Houston, 1986-88; expert witness in ins. related lawsuits; speaker in field; guest cons. Rice U. Entrepeneur's Conf., 1986-88; speaker Nat. Automobile Dealers Assn. Conv., 1990. Author: Dealership Risk Mgmt. Newsletter; contbr. articles to profl. jours. including Automotive Exec., Ward's Auto Dealer. Founder Exec. Level Mgmt., Ltd., Bermuda, 1991—. Republican. Office: Austin Cons Group Inc 130 Ski Hill Rd #140 Breckinridge CO 80424

BEESLEY, BERNARD FRANKLIN, English language educator; b. Soldier, Kans., Dec. 13, 1933; s. Russell William and Dahlia Margaret (White) B.; m. Hazel Etta Myers, June 13, 1954; children: Aaron Brent, Bruce Allen. BA, Hardin-Simmons U., 1983, MA, 1985; PhD, U. Nebr., 1991. Installation supr. Western Electric Co., Inc., 1951-82; grad. asst. Hardin-Simmons U., Abilene, Tex., 1983-86; instr. English McMurry Coll., Abilene, Tex., 1986; teaching asst. U. Nebr., Lincoln, 1986-89, English instr., 1990-91, English lectr., 1992-93; asst. prof. English Dalton (Ga.) Coll., 1993—. Vol. Centro Latino, Dalton, 1994-96. With U.S. Army, 1954-56. Recipient Harrell scholarship Hardin-Simmons U., 1984. Mem. MLA, Nat. Coun. Tchrs. English, Associated Writing Programs. Office: Dalton Coll 213 College Dr Dalton GA 30720-3745

BEESON, VIRGINIA REED, naval officer, nurse; b. Franklin, N.J., Mar. 14, 1951; d. Colin Reed and Marion (Dailey) B. BSN magna cum laude, U. Vt., Burlington, 1973; MS in Nursing Adminstrn., Boston U., 1987. RN, Vt.; cert. in nursing adminstrn.; cert. ATLS. Commd. ensign USN, 19, advanced through grades to capt., 1994; staff and charge nurse various locations, 1973-85; charge nurse gen. surgery ward Nat. Naval Med. Ctr., Bethesda, Md., 1987-89; Nurse Corps assignment officer U.S. Navy Annex, Washington, 1989-91; head leadership tng. div. Naval Sch. Health Scis., Bethesda, 1991; dir. Nursing Svcs. Naval Hosp., Jacksonville, Fla.; speaker in field. Decorated Naval Commendation medal (3), Navy Achievement medal, Meritorious Svc. medal. Mem. ANA, Fla. Nurses Assn., Women Officers Profl. Assn., Am. Coll. Healthcare Exec., Am. Orgn. of Nurse Exec., Sigma Theta Tau. Home: 91 San Juan Dr F-4 Ponte Vedra Beach FL 32082 Office: Naval Hosp Jacksonville FL 32214

BEETH, PAMELA WILLIAMS, educational diagnostician; b. Tuscaloosa, Ala., Dec. 4, 1938; d. Clanton Ware and Claudine (Payne) Williams; m. Donald Richard Beeth, June 28, 1960; children: Clanton Donald, Rebecca Beeth Lowe. BA magna cum laude, U. Houston, 1960, MEd, 1974. Registered profl. edn. diagnostician, Tex. Presch. tchr. Waxahachie/Dallas, 1961-66; kindergarten tchr. Clear Creek Ind. Sch. Dist., League City, Tex., 1966-73; spl. edn. tchr. Pearland (Tex.) Ind. Sch. Dist., 1974-75, ednl. diagnostician, 1975-79; ednl. diagnostician Santa Fe (Tex.) Ind. Sch. Dist., 1979-95; pvt. cons., Irlen syndrome screener, adj. faculty U. Houston-Clear Lake, Houston, Tex., 1987—; charter bd. dirs., officer Bd. of Registry, Tex. Profl. Ednl. Diagnosticians, 1980-87, cons., 1987-89; cons. in field. Contbr. articles to profl. jours. Active various civic orgns. Mem. Coun. for Exceptional Children, Coun. for Learning Disabilities, Tex. Ednl. Diagnosticians Assn. (chpt. pres.), Learning Disabilities Assn., Mortar Bd., Phi Kappa Phi.

BEEVER, JAMES WILLIAM, III, biologist; b. Balt., Aug. 17, 1955; s. James William Jr. and Virginia Irene (Ruhlmann) B.; m. Lisa Britt Dodd, May 26, 1990. BS, Fla. State U., 1977, MS, 1979; postgrad., U. Calif., Davis, 1991. Environ. specialist Fla. Dept. of Environ. Regulation, Ft. Myers, 1984-88; resource mgmt. and rsch. coord. South West Fla. Aquatic Preserves, Bokeelia, Fla., 1988-90; biol. scientist III Fla. Game and Fresh Water Fish Commn., Punta Gorda, 1990—; adj. faculty biology Edison C.C., Charlotte County; bd. dirs. Environ. Confederation of S.W. Fla., Agy. on Bay Mgmt., Tampa, Fla.; mem. tech. adv. bd. Sarasota Bay and Tampa Bay Nat. Estuary Program, Sarasota, 1989—, mem. policy com. and tech. adv. com. Charlotte Harbor Nat. Estuary Program; chair sci. com. on Mangrove Tech. Adv. Com. Fla. Dept. Environ. Protection, 1994-95; chair Fla. com. on rare and endangered plants and animals, 1994-96; expert witness in field, 1986—; coord. Conservation Plan for the Hillsborough River Greenway Area, 1995. Author: Lemon Bay Aquatic Preserve Management Plan, 1988, The Cedar Point Study, 1992, Hydric Pine Flatwoods of Southwest Florida, 1994, (computer database) Resource Inventory of Species in S.W. Fla.; contbr. articles to profl. jours. Chair Grad. Student Assn., Davis, 1981-83. Regents fellowship U. Calif, 1983-84; recipient Grad. Rsch. award, 1982-83, Outstanding Profl. Achievements award Fla. DNR, 1988. Mem. Fla. Acad. Sci., Estuarine Rsch. Fedn., Soc. Wetland Scientists, Soc. for Conservation Biology, Ecol. Soc. Am., Phi Beta Kappa, Sigma Xi. Office: Fla Game & Freshwater Fish 29200 Tuckers Grade Punta Gorda FL 33955-2207

BEGAYE, HELEN CHRISTINE, editor, religious organization official; b. Ardmore, Okla., Oct. 24, 1943; d. Winston Coleman and Delia (Cooper) Shoemaker; m. Russell Begaye, Aug. 14, 1975; 1 child, Karis Nizhoni. BA, Dallas Bapt. U., 1970; MRE, Southwestern Bapt. Theol. Sem., Ft. Worth, 1972. Missionary So. Bapt. Conv., Albuquerque, 1973-75; co-dir. Bapt. Indian Ctr., Santa Fe, 1978-80; editor Bapt. Sunday Sch. Bd., Nashville, 1988—; mem. adv. bd. Women in Evangelism, Atlanta, 1982-88; mission chmn. Fielder Road Bapt. Ch., Arlington, Tex., 1987-89; mission chmn. Woman's Missionary Union, Tarrant Bapt. Sch., 1989—; trustee Am. Bible Soc., N.Y.C., 1990—. Editor Am. Indian Bible Study quar. jours., 1988-91. Home and Office: 4915 Hyde Ct Cumming GA 30130

BEGGS, SYBLE MARIE, program coordinator; b. Oklahoma City, Aug. 24, 1953; d. Frank V. and Rosetta Pairlee (Floyd) Kirby; m. Ernie Dale Beggs, Oct. 1, 1985; children: Wanda, Dawn. Diploma, Kiamichi VoTech, McAlester, Okla., 1978; BSN, East Cen. U., Ada, Okla., 1989. Staff nurse in critical care McAlester Regional Hosp., nurse mgr. Rehab. unit, adminstr., dir. skilled nursing facility, program coord., concurrent case mgmt.-utilization rev. Home: 416 E Osage Ave Mcalester OK 74501

BEHLMAR, CINDY LEE, business manager, consultant; b. Smyrna, Tenn., July 4, 1959; d. James Wallace and Barbara Ann (Behlmar) Gribble. BBA, Coll. William and Mary, 1981; MBA, Old Dominion U., 1995. Adminstrv. extern Hampton (Va.) Gen. Hosp., 1981-82; mktg. rep., then supr. mktg. svcs. PruCare of Richmond, Va., 1983-85; exec. dir. PhysicianCare, Inc., Newport News, Va., 1986-89; provider rels. cons. Va. Health Network, Richmond, 1989-91; ind. cons. Tidewater Health Care, Virginia Beach, Va., 1991-92; chief ops. officer Tidewater Phys. Therapy, Inc., Newport News, 1993-95; ind. cons. Yorktown, Va., 1996—; sec., bd. dirs. Greater Peninsula Area Med.-Bus. Coalition, Newport News, 1987-89; symposium faculty mem. Am. Hosp. Assn., Orlando, Fla., 1987, Washington, 1988. Mem. ch. coun. St. Mark Luth. Ch., Yorktown, Va., 1988-91. Fin. Exec. Inst. scholar, 1993. Mem. Inst. Mgmt. Accts., Peninsula Toastmasters, Phi Kappa Phi, Beta Gamma Sigma. Home: 103 Jean Pl Yorktown VA 23693-3007

BEHRENS, WILLIAM BLADE, television program syndication executive; b. Burlington, Vt., Oct. 17, 1956; s. Robert Allen and Elizabeth (Husk) B. BA, Emory U., 1978. Video/audio tech. WXII-TV, Winston-Salem, 1979-80; v.p. sales Behrens Co.-Behrens Prodns., Miami, Fla., 1980-87; S.E. sales mgr. Access Syndication, Studio City, Calif., 1987-88, The Great Entertainment Co., N.Y.C., 1988-90; dir. syndication World Sports Syndication, Atlanta, 1988-91; S.E. sales mgr. Colbert TV Sales, L.A., 1988—; v.p. Litton TV Syndications, Balt., 1989-94; pres. Show Bus., Inc., Atlanta, 1989—; dir. southeast sales ITC Entertainment, Beverly Hills, Calif., 1994—. Music editor Emory Wheel, 1977-78; contbr. articles to profl. jours. Mem. Am. Film Inst., Nat. Assn. TV Arts and Scis. Home: PO Box 941787 Atlanta GA 31141-0787 Office: Show Bus Inc 3238-7 Henderson Mill Rd Atlanta GA 30341-4531

BEHRMAN, ROBIN LESLIE, primary education educator; b. Queens, N.Y., Nov. 20, 1953; d. Eli and Lila Norma (Blitz) Pollak; m. Andre Roy Behrman, June 23, 1973; children: Jennifer, Allison. AA, U. Fla., 1973; BS, Fla. Interna. Univ., 1975; MS, Nova Univ., 1982. Cert. elem. tchr., Fla. Tchr. Toras Emes Acad., Miami, Fla., 1979-83, Skyway Elem., Miami, 1983-92, Palm Springs North Elem., Hialeah, Fla., 1992-96; temp. asst. prin. Palm Springs North Elem., Hialeah, 1996—; curriculum revision com. Dade City Pub. Schs., Miami, 1991, USI tchr. cons., 1994-96. Vol., past pres. Muscular Dystrophy Assn., Dade, Broward, Fla., 1974-90; mem. Broward County Gator Boosters, 1992-96. Mem. Assn. Supervision Curriculum Devel., Dade County Coun. Tchrs. Math., Dade County Sci. Tchrs. Assn. Jewish. Home: 16421 Ontario Pl Davie FL 33331 Office: Palm Springs North Elem 17615 NW 82nd Ave Hialeah FL 33015-3606

BEIRNE, MARTIN DOUGLAS, lawyer; b. N.Y.C., Oct. 24, 1944; s. Martin Douglas and Catherine Anne (Rooney) B.; m. Kathleen Harrington; children—Martin, Shannon, Kelley. B.S., Spring Hill Coll., 1966; J.D. summa cum laude, St. Mary's Sch. Law, 1969. Bar: Tex. 1969, U.S. Dist. Ct. (ea. dist.) Tex. 1972, U.S. Dist. Ct. (so. dist.) Tex. 1971, U.S. Ct. Appeals (5th and 11th cirs.) 1974, U.S. Dist. Ct. (ea. dist.) Calif., U.S. Supreme Ct. 1975, U.S. Dist. Ct. (no. dist.) Tex., U.S. Dist. Ct. (we. dist.) Tex. Ptnr. Fulbright & Jaworski, Houston, 1971-85; mng. ptnr. Beirne, Maynard & Parsons, Houston, 1985—. Editor in chief St. Mary's Law Rev. Bd. dirs. St. Thomas U., Houston Law Review. Served to capt. Signal Corps, U.S. Army, 1969-71. Fellow Tex. Bar Found.; mem. ABA, Tex. Bar Assn., Houston Bar Assn., Coronado Club, The Houstonian Club, Legatus-U. Houston Law Sch. Found. Roman Catholic. Office: First Interstate Tower 1300 Post Oak Blvd Fl 24 Houston TX 77056-3010

BEISNER, ERNEST CALVIN, theology and social ethics educator; b. Tuscaloosa, Ala., Dec. 6, 1955; s. Ernest Bronwin and Mary Louise (Ball) B.; m. Deborah Jean Melvin, Nov. 12, 1983; children: David, Susan, Kilby, Rebekah, Peter, Arthur John, Grace. BA in Interdisciplinary studies, U. So. Calif., L.A., 1978; MA in Soc., Internat. Coll., L.A., 1983; postgrad., U. St. Andrews, Scotland. Rsch. assoc. Christian Rsch. Inst., Anaheim, Calif., 1976-78; rsch. cons. Christian Apologetics: Rsch. and Info. Svc., Costa Mesa, Calif., 1978-80; asst. pub. The Times of N.E. Benton County, Ark., 1980-83, 86-88; editor Discipleship Jour., Colorado Springs, 1983-85; author, editor, spkr. Pea Ridge, Ark., 1987-92; vis. lectr. Covenant Coll., Lookout Mountain, Ga., 1992-94; assoc. prof. Covenant Coll., Lookout Mountain, 1994—. Author: The Teachings of Witness Lee and the Local Church, 1977, Is Baptism Necessary for Salvation: A Critical Analysis, 1980, 85, God in Three Persons, 1984, Answers for Atheists, Agnostics, and Other Thoughtful Skeptics: Dialogues About Christian Faith and Life, Russian edit., 1986, 1st English edit. 1988, 2d rev. edit., 1993, Prosperity and Poverty: The Compassionate Use of Resources in a World of Scarcity, 1986, Psalms of Promise: Exploring the Majesty and Faithfulness of God, 1st edit., 1988, 2d edit., 1994, Prospects for Growth: A Biblical View of Population, Resources, and the Future, 1990, Man, Economy, and the Environment in Biblical Perspective, 1994, "Jesus Only" Churches, 1996, False God, False Gospel: The Legacy of Moral Government Theology, 1996, (with others) The New Cults, 1980, Biblical Principles and Economics: Foundations, 1989, Christian Perspectives on Economies, 1989, The World Economy After the Cold War: A Symposium, 1991, Proceedings from the Seminar on Ecology and Religion, 1993, The Word in Life Study Bible, 1993, Where Do We Go From Here? An Agenda for Conservatives During Cultural Captivity, 1993, Christianity and Economics in the Post-Cold War Era: The Oxford Declaration and Beyond, 1994, The Christian Vision: Morality and the Marketplace, 1994, others; contbr. articles to profl. jours.; contbg. editor The Freeman Found. for Econ. Edn., Irvington-on-Hudson, N.Y., 1994—, Christian Rsch. Jour., San Juan Capistrano, Calif., 1995—, Crosswinds: The Reformation Digest, Sunnyvale, Calif., 1992—. Mem. Nat. Assn. of Scholars, Assn. of Christian Economists, Evangelical Theol. Soc., Evangelical Philos. Soc., Coalition on Revival. Republican. Home: 4409 Alabama Ave Chattanooga TN 37409 Office: Covenant Coll Scenic Hwy Lookout Mountain GA 30750

BEITZ, ALEXANDRA GRIGG, political activist; b. Cin., Oct. 15, 1960; d. Kenneth Andrew and Betty Ann (Carpenter) Grigg; m. Charles Arthur Beitz III, Oct. 17, 1987; 1 child, Madeleine Grigg Beitz. BA, Vassar Coll., 1982; MBA, Wake Forest U., 1985. Asst. buyer Bloomingdale's, N.Y.C., 1982-83; dept. mgr. Bloomingdale's, Stamford, Conn., 1983; intern Ciba-Geigy Corp., Greensboro, N.C., 1984; retail sales promotion mgr. Hanes Hosiery, N.Y.C., 1985-86; market rep. May Co., N.Y.C., 1986-87; freelance polit. cons. Winston-Salem, N.C., 1990—. Vol. Planned Parenthood, Winston-Salem, N.C., 1988—, Southeastern Ctr. for Contemporary Art, Winston-Salem, 1992—, exec. bd. dirs. Friends, 1983, v.p.-pres. elect, 1994, pres., 1995, exec. bd. dirs., 1995—; vol. Am. Cancer Soc., Winston-Salem, 1992-94; bd. dirs. Planned Parenthood of the Triad, Winston-Salem, 1995—.

BELATÈCHE, LYDIA, language educator; b. Rabat, Morocco, Sept. 27, 1962; d. Messaoud and Rita (Kelsh) B.; m. John Marshall Graham, May 15, 1990. BA in French, Vassar Coll., 1984; MA in French, Yale U., 1986, MPhil in French, 1988, PhD in French, 1993. Acting instr. dept. French Yale U., New Haven, Conn., 1987-88, 89-90; tchg. asst. English lang. and lit. Lycee Fenelon, Paris, 1988-89; vis. lectr. dept. Romance langs. U. Mich., Ann Arbor, 1991-94; asst. prof. French dept. fgn. langs. Miss. State U., Starkville, 1994—. Contbr. articles, reviews to profl. jours. Mem. Am. Assn. Tchrs. French, Internat. Assn. Multidisciplinary Approaches and Comparative Studies, MLA, Midwest Modern Lang. Assn. Office: Dept Fgn Langs Miss State U PO Drawer FL Mississippi State MS 39762

BELCHER, RONALD ANTHONY, nuclear energy educator; b. Mt. Clemens, Mich., Mar. 12, 1950; s. Earnest W. and Helen S. (Schinkai) B.; m. Janice Rose Bathurst Belcher, Aug. 4, 1973; children: Andrew R., Stefanie Lynn. BS, Cen. Mich. U., 1973; MA, Saginaw Valley State U., 1977; BS in Nuclear Engring., Am. Tech. Inst., 1995. Tchr. Swan Valley High Sch., Saginaw, Mich., 1973-81; gen. nuclear instr. Midland (Mich.) Nuclear Plant, 1981-84; simulator instr. tng. dept. Plant E. I. Hatch, Baxley, Ga., 1984-86, sr. simulator instr., 1986-89, plant nuclear instr., 1989—. Named Nat. Outstanding Tchr. Ednl. Publs. Am., 1975. Mem. Am. Nuclear Soc. Home: 219 Amberwood Dr E Vidalia GA 30474-3079 Office: Plant EI Hatch Tng Dept PO Box 439 Baxley GA 31513-0439

BELCHER, WILLIAM ALVIS, rancher, veterinarian; b. Del Rio, Tex., Aug. 25, 1918; s. Clifton C. and Willie (Cochran) B.; DVM, Tex. A. and M. U., 1943; postgrad. Mich. State U., Colo. State U.; m. Hazel Arledge, Sept. 8, 1937; children: Willie Ellen Langham, Madge Elizabeth Belcher Keys. Gen. practice vet. medicine, Crystal City, Tex., 1943-46; rancher, Brackettsville, Tex., 1946—; owner, operator Shirley Commn. Co.-Ft. Worth Stockyard, 1956-59; area veterinarian Tex. Animal Health Commn., 1965—; 1st v.p. Del Rio Wool and Mohair Co., 1950—; chmn. bd. dirs. San Antonio br. Dallas Fed. Res. Bank. County chmn. Screw Worm Eradication Program, 1961—; veterinarian in charge Tex. Screw Worm Program; Mem. AVMA, Tex. S.W. cattle raisers assn., Tex. Sheep and Goat Raisers Assn. (dir.), Tex. Angus Assn. (dir.). Address: PO Box 588 Brackettville TX 78832-0588

BELEFSKI, MICHAEL EDWARD, secondary education educator, business owner; b. Englewood, N.J., Nov. 27, 1949; s. Edward Carl and Josephine (Kane) B.; m. Alice Sattler, July 24, 1976; children: Carolyn Alice, Brian Michael. BA in History and Govt., Walsh U., 1971; MA in World History, Georgetown U., 1974. Pres. CPC Corp., Fairfax Station, Va., 1975—; tchr. Alexandria City (Va.) Pub. Schs., 1975—; rsch. asst. Va. Gen. Assembly, Richmond, 1978—; mem. Va. Cun. on Info. Mgmt., 1996—. Commr. Fairfax County Park Authority, 1992-96, sec., 1994, treas., 1995; bd. dirs. Fairfax County Airports Adv. Com., 1992-95, Fairfax County Census Com., 1992, Coun. on Govt. Land Use Com., Alexandria, 1976-77; alt. del. Rep. Nat. Conv., Houston, 1992, San Diego, 1996; active Fairfax County Rep. Com., 1977—; treas. 11th Congl. Dist. Rep. Com., 1996—. Sgt. U.S. ANG, 1972-78. Named one of Outstanding Young Men Am., 1981; recipient Cert. of Recognition ARC, 1974-75, Cert. of Appreciation Fairfax County Bd. Suprs., 1992, 95. Mem. Fairfax County C. of C., Nat. Recreation and Parks Assn., Va. Recreation and Park Soc., Inc., Am. Legion, K.C., PTA. Roman Catholic. Home and Office: 9824 S Park Cir Fairfax Station VA 22039-2906

BELEW, DAVID OWEN, JR., judge; b. Ft. Worth, Mar. 27, 1920; s. David Owen and Mazie Desporд (Erskine) B.; m. Joetta Sewell; children: Marjorie Dale Belew Cordray, Susan Elizabeth Belew Arnoult, David Mitchell. BA, U. Tex., 1946, LLB, 1948. Bar: Tex. 1948. Practice with father Ft. Worth, 1948-49; asst. atty. U.S. Dist. Ct. (no. dist.) Tex., 1949-52, judge, 1979—; ptnr. Cantey, Hanger, Gooch, Munn & Collins, Ft. Worth, 1952-79. Served with AUS, 1942-45. Decorated Silver Star, Purple Heart (3). Mem. ABA, Fed. Bar Assn., State Bar Tex., Ft. Worth-Tarrant County Bar Assn. (pres. 1970). Office: US Courthouse 501 W 10th St Ste 402 Fort Worth TX 76102-3642

BELEW, KATHY D., social services researcher; b. Florence, S.C., June 21, 1951; d. Aubrey Laurue and Doris Mae (Weaver) DeWitt; m. Jack Landon Belew, Jan. 1, 1984. BS in Sociology and Psychology, Francis Marion U., 1993; postgrad., U. S.C., 1995—. Social rschr., social svc. dir. II S.C. State Dept. Social Svcs., Columbia, 1972—; exec. tax svcs. H&R Block, Florence, S.C., 1975—; steering com. coun. on Child Abuse and Neglect, Columbia, 1995; vol., student intern Pee Dee Mental Health Ctr., Florence and Hartsville, S.C., 1996; com. mem. S.C. State DSS & HHS, Columbia, S.C., 1995-96. Author: (legislative booklets) Child Welfare overview, 1994, 1995, (booklets) Eau Claire Community Needs Assessment for Health Families of America, 1996, Fetal Abuse, 1995. Vol. Pee Dee Coalition, Florence, 1994-96, Durant Children's Ctr., Florence, 1995-96, Coun. on Child Abuse and Neglect, Columbia, S.C., 1995-96, Inst. for Families and Soc. and U.S.C., Columbia, 1995-96, Children and Family Svcs., U. S.C., Columbia, 1995-96. Recipient Sociology of Yr. award Faculty of Francis Marion U., 1992-93. Mem. Nat. Assn. for Welfare Rsch. and Stats., Healthy Families of Am., Population Assn. of Am., Pi Gamma Mu (pres. 1992-93), Psi Chi, Alpha Kappa Delta. Office: SC State DSS Family Pres/Child Welfare PO Box 1520 Columbia SC 29202

BELFIGLIO, VALENTINE JOHN, political science educator, pharmacist; b. Troy, N.Y., May 28, 1934; s. Edmond Liberato and Mildred Elizabeth (Sherwood) B.; BS, Union U., 1956; MA, U. Okla., Norman, 1967, PhD, 1970; 1 child, by previous marriage, Valentine Edmond. Grad. asst., instr. U. Okla., 1967-70; prof. polit. sci. Tex. Woman's U., Denton, 1970—. Reviewer textbooks in internat. politics Holbrook Press, Boston, 1973-75. Served with USAF, 1959-67. Tex. Woman's U. Instl. Research grantee, 1973-74, 76-77; postdoctoral fellow Republic of South Africa, 1976; NEH grantee, 1978; decorated knight Order of Merit, Republic of Italy; recipient Guido Dorso prize U. Naples, 1985, C.K. Chamberlain award East Tex. Hist. Assn., 1990. Mem. Internat. Studies Assn. (sec.-treas. region 1974-76), Am. Polit. Sci. Assn., Am. Italian Hist. Assn., AAUP, MENSA, Kappa Psi. Republican. Roman Catholic. Avocations: chess, dancing, gourmet cookery. Author: The United States and World Peace, 1971; American Foreign Policy, 1979; The Italian Experience in Texas, 1983; The Best of Italian Cooking, 1985, Alliances, 1986, Go For Orbit, 1987, Pride of the Southwest, 1991, Italian Experience in Texas: A Closer Look, 1994, Honor, Pride, Duty: A History of the State Guard, 1995. Contbr. numerous articles on internat. relations, Asian politics to profl. jours. Home: 704 Camilla Ln Garland TX 75040-4622 Office: Tex Woman's U PO Box 23974 Denton TX 76204-1974

BELGER, PEGGY CORAM, psychiatric clinical nurse specialist; b. Montgomery, Ala., Mar. 7, 1933; d. Henry Hart and Carrie Bell (Weston) Coram; m. Clarence Albert Belger Sr., Mar. 7, 1952; children: Clarence Albert Jr., Candy LeJean Belger Padgett. AA, Augusta Coll., 1975; BSN cum laude, Med. Coll. of Ga., 1977, MSN, 1978. Cert. paralegal, bd. cert. psychiat. clin. nurse specialist, gerongol. nurse, nat. cert. bereavement facilitator. Therapist Augusta (Ga.) Area Mental Health Ctr.; tng. specialist, prin. Ga. Regional Hosp., Augusta; health svcs. supr. Gracewood and State Sch. and Hosp., Gracewood, Ga.; psychiat. clin. nurse specialist Ga. Regional Hosp., Augusta, 1991—; pvt. practice, 1991—; paralegal, med. con., Augusta, 1988—; nurse, paralegal Fulcher, Hagler, Reed, Obenshain, Hanks & Harper, Augusta, 1988-91; clin. specialist, mental health cons., Augusta, 1988—. Mem. ARC Nat. Disaster Response Team, coord. Cmty. Crisis Response Team; bd. dirs. Sr. Citizen's Coun., 1994—. Profl. Nurse Traineeship grantee Med. Coll. Ga., 1977-78; recipient ARC Vol. Svc. award, 1994, Humanitarian award The Spiritual Assembly of The Bahais of Richmond County and The Interracial Family Alliance of Augusta, 1996. Mem. ANA, Ga. Nurses Assn. (10th Dist. award, past chair impaired nurse com., bd. dirs. 1992, bd. dirs. The Sr. Citizens Coun. 1994—), Nat. League Nursing, Ga. League Nursing, ASTD (bd. dirs. Augusta chpt.), Nat. Nurses Soc. Addictions, Nat. Consortium Chemically Dependent Nurses, Alzheimer and Related Disorders, Med. Coll. Ga. Alumni (bd. dirs. Augusta chpt.). Home: 3756 Old Waynesboro Rd Augusta GA 30906-9677

BELGIN, HARVEY HARRY, photojournalist; b. LacDuBonnet, Man., Can., Dec. 7, 1912; came to U.S. 1918, naturalized, 1943; s. Jacob and Ludmilla Lidia (Strungstein) B.; m. Lucile Orr Caskey, Jan. 14, 1946; 1 child, Cathryn Caskey Johnson. Farmer, lumberjack Maine, 1932-36; painter Boston, 1937-41; war photographer Army Signal Corps - Pentagon, 1942-46; sr. photographer San Antonio Light, 1946-81; ret.; free lance photographer San Antonio, 1950—; judge Nat. Amateur Snapshots and Armed Svcs. Photo Exhibits San Antonio, 1964-70. Author: (booklet) Peace in War, 1948; photography exhibited numerous one-man invitationals, 1949-54, including first one-man show held at Smithsonian Inst.; photos in numerous pubs. including Master Detective Mag., The People, London Daily Herald, Quick weekly mag., Look mag., Guidepost mag., Good Housekeeping mag., Guns mag., Readers Digest, others. Photographer Beautify San Antonio Assn., 1970—. With U.S. Army, 1942-46. Recipient Presdl. Unit citation, 1945, Pulitzer Prize nomination, 1952, George Washington Medal, Freedoms Found., 1952, Hearst Newspapers Nat. Photography Contest citations and awards, 1948-50, 60's, 70's, UPI award, 1951, AP nat. awards, 1951, 61, San Antonio Conservation Soc. citation, 1963, San Antonio Press Club Gridiron Pres. award, 1964, inclusion in book: The Instant it Happened, 1972, many others. Mem. Nat. Press Photographers, Friends of Photography. Republican. Episcopalian. Home: 816 Terrell Rd San Antonio TX 78209-6118

BELIN, JACOB CHAPMAN, paper company executive; b. DeFuniak Springs, Fla., Oct. 28, 1914; s. William Jacob and Addie (Leonard) B.; m. Myrle Fillingim, Nov. 28, 1940; children: Jacob Chapman, Stephen Andrew. Student, George Washington U., 1935-38. Dir. sales St. St. Joe Paper Co., Fla., 1949-56; v.p. St. Joe Paper Co., 1956-68, pres., dir., 1968—, chmn. bd., chief exec. officer, 1982-91; dir. St. Joseph Land & Devel. Co. Bd. dirs. Nemours Found., Alfred I. duPont Found.; trustee Estate of Alfred I. DuPont. Mem. Elks, Rotary, Kappa Alpha. Baptist. Office: St Joe Paper Co 1650 Prudential Dr Jacksonville FL 32207-8147

BELISSARY, KAREN, interior designer; b. Columbia, S.C., May 20, 1959; d. James Charles and Linda Gail (Bouknight) B. BFA in Design, N.Y. Sch. Interior Design, 1989; grad., Nat. Ctr. Paralegal Studies, Atlanta, 1991. Pvt. practice interior design, Florence, S.C., 1989—; dir. Pee Dee region Am. Intercultural Exch., Florence, 1989—. Sec. Soc. for Autistic Children, Florence, 1983; v.p. Florence County Dem. Com., 1985; group leader Friends Florence Mus., 1986; bd. dirs. Heart Fund, Florence, 1987, Internat. Women's Club Florence, 1988-89, Florence Area Arts Coun., 1986-87; mem. Friends of Libr., Florence. Named Outstanding Mem., Soc. for Autistic Children, 1983; grantee Young Adult League, 1987. Mem. NOW, Am. Soc. Interior Designers, Amnesty Internat., Greenpeace, Cosmoplitan Book Club (pres.), The Door (pres.), Colonial Heights Garden Club. Greek Orthodox. Home: 3719 Gentry Dr Florence SC 29501-7717 Office: Am Intercultural Exch 804 Loop Rd # 2D Florence SC 29501

BELK, THOMAS MILBURN, apparel executive; b. Charlotte, N.C., Feb. 6, 1925; s. William Henry and Mary Leonora (Irwin) B.; m. Katherine McKay, May 19, 1953; children: Katherine Belk Morris, Thomas Milburn, Jr., Hamilton McKay, John Robert. BS in Mktg., U. N.C., 1948; DHL, St. Andrews Presbyn. Coll., 1978; D of Pub. Svc., U. N.C.C., 1987. With Belk Stores Services, Inc., 1948—, pres., 1980—; also pres. of most Belk Stores throughout S.E.; bd. dirs. exec. com. Nations Bank Corp.; bd. dirs. Bus. Devel. Corp. of N.C., Jefferson-Pilot Corp., Ruddick Corp. (group of supermarkets, textile and paper cos.). Bd. dirs. Mecklenburg County council Boy Scouts Am., U. N.C. at Charlotte Found., Inc.; bd. dirs. YMCA, pres., 1978-79; gen. chmn. Shrine Bowl of Carolinas, 1963-64, United Appeal, 1959; past pres. United Community Services; past chmn., trustee Montreat-Anderson Coll., 1964-68, St. Andrews Presbyn. Coll., Laurinburg, N.C., 1967-71; trustee Crossnore (N.C.) Sch., Inc., Davidson (N.C.) Coll., 1974—, Endowment Fund, 1975-78, Presbyn. Hosp., Charlotte; trustee U. N.C., Charlotte, 1975-84, chmn. 1982-84; mem. bd. visitors Wake Forest U. Lt. (j.g.), USN, 1943-46. Recipient Green Thumb award Apparel Found. of Am. Apparel Mfrs. Assn., 1989; named Young Man of Yr., Jr. C. of C., 1960, Man of Yr., Charlotte News, 1962, Tarheel of Week, Raleigh News & Observer, 1964, Man of Yr., Delta Sigma Pi, 1962. Mem. Charlotte C. of C. (chmn. 1977), N.C. Citizens for Bus. and Industry (past pres.), Cen. Charlotte Assn. (pres. 1965-66), Mountain Retreat Assn. (past chmn. bd. trustees). Democrat. Clubs: Charlotte Country, Quail Hollow Country, Country of N.C., Biltmore Forest, Grandfather Golf and Country (Linville, N.C.), DeBordieu Club (Georgetown, S.C.). Lodges: Rotary, Masons, Shriners (Charlotte bd. dirs.). Home: 2441 Lemon Tree Ln Charlotte NC 28211-3639 Office: Belk Stores Svcs 2801 W Tyvola Rd Charlotte NC 28217-4525

BELL, BRYAN, real estate, oil investment executive, educator; b. New Orleans, Dec. 15, 1918; s. Bryan and Sarah (Perry) B.; m. Rubie S. Crosby, July 15, 1950; children: Rubie Perry Gosnell, Helen Elizabeth, Bryan, Beverly Saunders, Barbara Crosby. BA, Princeton U., 1941; MA, Tulane U., 1962. Pres., Tasso Plantation Foods, Inc., New Orleans, 1945-66; ptnr. Bell Oil Cos., New Orleans, 1962—; gen. ptnr. 26 ltd. partnerships in oil, real estate and venture capital, 1962—; instr. econs. of real estate devel. Sch. Architecture, Tulane U., New Orleans, 1967—; instr. entrepreneurship, Univ. Coll. Mem. Garden Dist. Assn., 1964—. Bd. dirs. United Fund for Greater New Orleans Area, 1964-71, pres., 1968-69; chmn. Human Talent Bank Com., New Orleans, 1969—; mem. City Planning Commn., New Orleans, 1956-58; mem. bd. Met. Area Com., 1968—, pres., 1971—; bd. dirs. Bur. Govtl. Rsch., 1966—, pres., 1971—; chmn. com. Met. Leadership Forum, 1969—; mem. bd. New Orleans Area Health Coun., 1966-70; bd. dirs. Tulane-Lyceum, 1947-51, Family Svc. Soc., 1951-58, pres., 1956-58; bd. dirs. St. Martin's Protestant Episc. Sch., 1964-68, Metairie Park Country Day Sch., 1967-71; bd. dirs. Trinity Episc. Sch., chmn., 1958-68; chmn. Trinity Christian Cmty., 1975—; bd. dirs. Christ Spirit of 76 Com., Fedn. Chs., 1975—, pres., 1984; bd. dirs. aux. Lighthouse for Blind; bd. dirs. Alton Ochsner Med. Found., 1983—. Served to 1st lt. AUS, World War II. Recipient Benemerenti Papal honor from Pope John Paul II, Weiss Brotherhood award NCCJ, 1983, Times Picayune Loving Cup City of New Orleans, 1985. Author: Lessons in Lifemanship. Mem. New Orleans C. of C., Princeton Alumni Assn. La. (pres. 1962-63), Fgn. Rels. Assn., Boston Club, New Orleans Lawn Tennis Club, Wyvern Club, Pickwick Club, New Orleans Country Club. Republican. Episcopalian (vestry 1960—, jr. warden 1968-70, sr. warden 1970-72). Address: 1331 3rd St New Orleans LA 70130-5743

BELL, CRAIG STEVEN, lawyer; b. Benton, Ky., Sept. 30, 1958; s. James Robert and Ona (Freeman) B. BS in Polit. Sci. and History, Murray State U., 1978; JD, U. Louisville, 1980. Bar: N.D. 1981, Ky. 1984, U.S. Dist. Ct. (ea. dist.) Ky. 1986, U.S. Dist. Ct. (we. dist.) Ky. 1987, U.S. Ct. Appeals (6th cir.) 1987. Practicing atty. Commonwealth of Ky., Hickory, 1984—; asst. county atty. County of Magoffin, Ky., 1985-87. Assoc. editor: Louisville Law Examiner, 1978-80. Chmn. Murray (Ky.) State U. Coll. Reps., 1976-78; exec. v.p. U. Louisville Coll. Reps., 1978-80; state vice chmn. Ky. Coll. Rep. Fedn., Frankfort, 1980-81. Mem. Ky. Bar Assn. (Recognition award 1994), State Bar Assn. N.D., Pi Sigma Alpha. Home: 1418 State Rt 534 Hickory KY 42051

BELL, DEBORAH MARIE, social services administrator; b. Syracuse, N.Y., Dec. 3, 1955; d. William Samuel and Helen (Kaminski) Spoto; m. Todd Kevin Bell, Aug. 19, 1989 (dec. Dec. 1993). AS in Adm. Justice, Onondaga Comm. Coll., Syracuse, N.Y., 1976; BS in Pub. Justice, SUNY, Oswego, 1978; MA, Northwestern State U., 1994. Cert. tchr., Fla., 1990. Sch. social worker City of Syracuse, 1978-79; program dir. Rape Crisis Ctr., Syracuse, 1979-85; case mgr. supr. Charlotte County, Port Charlotte, Fla., 1986-87; family resource specialist Charlotte Mental Health, Port Charlotte, 1987-90; parent involvement/social svcs. coord. Charlotte County Head Start, Punta Gorda, Fla., 1990-94; early intervention specialist Charlotte County Pub. Schs., 1994—; bd. dirs. Exch. Ctr. for Child Abuse Prevention, Pt. Charlotte, 1987—, Children Action Network, 1987—, Time Out Respite, Pregnancy Care Line, Sch. Improvement Planning Team-Blueprint 2000. Co-Author: Book, Rape Awareness for Educators 1982, Rape Resource Book. Mem. adv. coun. Health Dept. Indigent Care com., Port Charlotte, 1988, YMCA Youth Enrichment Coun., H.R.S. dist. 8 Abuse Task Force, PreSchool Interagency; mem. Charlotte County Children's Svc. Coun., 1990—. Recipient Outstanding Svc. in Field of Child Abuse Prevention award Fla. Com. for Prevention Child Abuse, 1988. Mem. LWV, Nat. Coalition Against Sexual Abuse, Assn. Sexual Abuse Prevention, Kappa Delta Pi. Roman Catholic. Office: Children and Families First 3131 Lake View Blvd Port Charlotte FL 33948

BELL, HENRY MARSH, JR., banking executive; b. Tyler, Tex., Jan. 23, 1928; s. Henry Marsh and Elizabeth (Loftin) B.; m. Dorothy Nell Allen, Dec. 8, 1951; children: Henry Marsh III, John Allen. Student, The Citadel, 1944-46; BS in Indsl. Adminstrn., Yale U., 1948; LHD (hon.), Tex. Coll., 1992. Various operational positions 1st City Tex.-Tyler (formerly known as 1st City Nat. Bank Tyler), 1948-50, asst. v.p., 1950-52, asst. v.p., dir., 1952-55, v.p., trust officer, 1955-62, sr. v.p., 1962-64, exec. v.p., 1964-67, pres., 1967-70, chmn. bd. dirs., pres., 1970-81, chmn. bd. dirs., chief exec. officer, 1981-87, chief exec. officer, 1987-88, sr. chmn. bd., 1988-93; cons., 1988—; bd. dirs., cons. Tyler Bank & Trust Co., N.A., 1993—; bd. dirs. Indsl. Devel. Corp. Tex., Smith County Indsl. Corp.; chmn. bd. dirs. Tyler Health Facilities Corp. Trustee Tchr. Retirement Sys. Tex., Tex. Chest Found.; pres., bd. dirs. East Tex. Mental Health, Inc.; mem. exec. com., chmn. bd. dirs. East Tex. Hosp. Found., Inc., Tyler Indsl. Found.; treas., chmn. bd. dirs. Better Bus. Bur. Cen. East Tex.; bd. dirs. Tex. Rose Festival Assn., United Way Greater Tyler, Tyler Health Ctr., East Tex. Cancer Ctr., Tex. Coll., Tyler Salvation Army; mem. devel. bd. U. Tex.; vestry, sr. warden Episc. Ch. Named one of Men of Achievement in Tex., 1974; recipient W.C. Windsor award, 1961, T.B. Butler award, 1971. Mem. Philos. Soc. Tex., Tyler Petroleum Club, Willow Brook Country Club, Masons. Office: 816 First Place 100 E Ferguson St Tyler TX 75702-7253

BELL, HOLLEY MACK, retired foreign service officer, writer; b. Windsor, N.C., May 9, 1922; s. John Cartwright and Minnie Turner (Bond) B.; m. Clara Murphy Bond, Apr. 11, 1953; children: Elisabeth Turner Bell Loncella, Clara Bond Bell Guess, Mack III. AB in Journalism, U. N.C., 1943; diploma, Grad. Inst. Internat. Studies, Geneva, 1948; MA, Fletcher Sch. Law & Diplomacy, 1970. Historian U.S. War Dept., Bad Nauheim, Germany, 1947-48; reporter Charlotte (N.C.) News, 1948-52; editor-mgr. Bertie Ledger-Advance, Windsor, 1952-55; editl. writer Greensboro (N.C.) Daily News, 1956-61; press attaché, info. officer U.S. Embassy, Santiago, Chile, 1961-66, Bogotá, Colombia, 1966-69; pub. affairs officer U.S. Embassy, Quito, Ecuador, 1972-77, Santo Domingo, Dominican Republic, 1977-80; desk officer U.S. Info. Agy., Washington, 1970-72, chief media reaction staff, 1980-87; ret., 1987. Mem. Episcopal Found., Kinston, N.C., 1990-93; mem. N.C. Task Force on Cultural Resources, Raleigh, 1991—, Historic Murfreesboro (N.C.) Commn., 1995—; chmn. pub. affairs com. Hist. Hope Plantation, Windsor, 1980—; historiographer Episcopal Diocese of East Carolina, Kinston, N.C., 1992—. 1st lt. U.S. Army, 1943-46, ETO. Recipient Nat. Order Al Mérito, Govt. of Ecuador, 1977. Mem. Nat. Episcopal Historians and Archivists, Coun. of Fgn. Rels., N.C. Art Soc. (chmn. outreach com. 1991-95, co-chmn. 50th anniversary com. 1995—), Rotary. Democrat. Home: 407 S King St Windsor NC 27983 Office: Bertie Ledger-Advance 124 S King St Windsor NC 27983

BELL, JOHN ALTON, lawyer; b. Greer, S.C., Dec. 1, 1958; s. Dallas Frank Sr. and Una Merle (Gay) B.; m. Vida Ivy, June 30, 1984; 1 child, Luke. BA, Carson-Newman Coll., 1980; JD, Memphis State U., 1982. Bar: Tenn. 1983, U.S. Dist. Ct. (we. dist.) Tenn. 1983, U.S. Army Ct. Mil. Rev. 1984, U.S. Ct. Mil. Appeals 1987, U.S. Dist. (ea. dist.) Tenn. 1988. Assoc. Litigation Support, Inc., Memphis, 1983; officer ops. and tng. U.S. Army, Ft. Knox, Ky., 1983-84; legal assistance atty. U.S. Army, Ft. Knox, 1984-86, defense counsel, 1986-87; assoc. King & King, Greeneville, Tenn., 1987-89; ptnr. King, King & Bell, Greeneville and Newport, Tenn., 1989-90, Bell & Bell P.C., Newport, 1990—; instr. bus. law Sullivan Jr. Coll., Ft. Knox, 1986-87; adj. prof. bus. law Walter State C.C., 1989-90. Columnist It's The Law, Newport Plain Talk, 1984-85, 89—. Bd. dirs. Extended Sch. Program, Greeneville, 1988; co-vice chmn. Rep. Com. Cocke County, Tenn., 1989-95. Named Ky. Col., Gov. Ky., 1986. Mem. ABA, Fed. Bar Assn., Tenn. Bar Assn., Assn. Trial Lawyers Am., Judge Advocate Gen.'s Assn. Republican. Baptist. Office: Bell & Bell P C 305 E Broadway St # B Newport TN 37821-3105

BELL, KAREN JUNE, critical care nurse; b. Forsyth County, N.C., Aug. 28, 1954; d. James Cecil and Margaret (Vaughn) B. Student, Rex Hosp. Sch. Nursing, Raleigh, N.C.; BSN, East Carolina U., 1983. Cert. BCLS, ACLS; instr. Am. Heart Assn.; cert. CCRN. Asst. clin. mgr., staff RN med. ICU Rex Hosp., Raleigh, 1977-91; staff nurse ICU Western Wake Med. Ctr., Cary, 1992-93; nurse cons. Divsn. of Facility Svc., State of N.C., 1993-94; staff RN ICU Moses H. Cone Meml. Hosp., 1994-95; med. policy analyst, Medicare adminstr. CIGNA Healthcare, 1995—. Recipient Great 100 Nurse Excellence award, N.C., 1990. Mem. AACN (past treas., speaker, com. mem. Raleigh chpt.).

BELL, MARGARET SHEARIN, English language educator; b. High Point, N.C., Nov. 22, 1939; d. Vern Mark and Elma Beatris Shearin; m. Alonzo Randolph Bell, June 23, 1962; children: Alonzo, Jr., Steven Hamilton. BS, Hampton Inst., 1960, MA, 1971; PhD, Old Dominion Univ., Norfolk, Va., 1990. Tchr. Newport News (Va.) Pub. Schs., 1960-87; asst. prin. Dist. Magnet Sch., Newport News, 1987-88, Denbigh H.S., Newport News, 1988-91; asst. prof. Hampton U., Newport News, 1991—; dir. Dropout Prevention Ctr., 1987-88, U. Writing Ctr. Hampton U., 1994—. Editor: Companion Guide to Freshman Composition, 1994, 3d edit. 1995. Mem. cmty. rel. com. People to People, Newport News, 1993—. Mem. AAUW, Newport News Ret. Tchrs. Assn. (pres. 1995—), Delta Sigma Theta, Delta Kappa Gamma (sec. 1994-96), Sigma Tau Delta, Phi Kappa Phi. Office: Hampton Univ English Dept Hampton VA 23668

BELL, MARY E. BENITEAU, accountant; b. San Antonio, Dec. 20, 1937; d. Thomas Alfred and Mary Elizabeth (McMurrain) Beniteau; BBA, Baylor U., 1959; MBA, U. Tex., 1960; m. William Woodward Bell, May 31, 1969; children: Susan Elizabeth, Carol Ann. Teaching asst. U. Tex., Austin, 1959-60; prin. Deloitte & Touche CPAs, Dallas, 1960-69; county auditor Brown County, Tex., 1972-78; pvt. practice acctg., Brownwood, Tex., 1969-95; ptnr. Bell & Isbell, LLP, CPAs, 1996—; acct. Brownwood Regional Med. Ctr. Aux., 1969—. Mem. bus. and audit com. Bapt. Gen. Conv. Tex., 1985-90, vice chmn., 1987-88, chmn., 1988-89; bd. dirs., sec. Brownwood Civic Improvement Found., Inc., 1991—, pres., 1993-95. Recipient W.R. White Meritorious Svc. award Baylor U., 1996; named Outstanding 4-H Leader, Dist. 8, Tex., 1992, Outstanding Woman Over 35, Brownwood Jaycees, 1986, Outstanding Com. Chmn., Dallas chpt. CPA's, 1968-69; CPA, Tex. Mem. Brownwood C. of C. (dir. 1979-82, sec.-treas. 1981-82), Tex. Soc. CPA's (dir. 1979-82, chair rels. with AICPA com. 1988-89, trustee found. 1981-89, sec.-treas. 1982-84, pres. 1984-86, Kenneth W. Hurst fellow 1990, peer rev. com. 1993-96, CPA's helping Schs. Com., 1994-95), AICPA's, Nat. Soc. Daughters of Am. Revolution (Mary Garland chpt., vice-regent 1994—), Abilene Chpt. CPA's (dir. 1984-85, 87-88, CPA of Yr. 1984-85), Brownwood Com. CPA's (pres. 1987-88), Pi Beta Phi, Baylor U. Alumni Assn. (dir. 1979-82). Baptist. Clubs: Brownwood Woman's (pres. 1980-81), Rotary Ann of Brownwood (pres. 1983-84. Home: PO Box 1564 Brownwood TX 76804-1564 Office: 109 N Fisk Ave Brownwood TX 76801-8207

BELL, MELVIN, management consultant; b. East Chicago, Ind., Jan. 3, 1915; s. Abram and Lillian (Goldenson) B.; m. Lillian Bodnar, 1949 (div. 1969); children: Douglas, Janet; m. Kathy Naylor, 1971. BSME, Purdue U., 1939; MS in Pub. Adminstrn., George Washington U., 1956; PhD in Pub. Adminstrn., Am. U., 1960. With Office of the U.S. Sec. of Def., Washington, 1949-70, dir. Office of Ordnance and Guided Missiles (R&E), ret. 1970; pvt. cons. Lake Worth, Fla., 1970—; exec. v.p. Rhodes Lewis Co., L.A. Contbr. articles to profl. jours. Mem. staff R & D bd. Pentagon, Washington. Lt. comdr. USN, 1942-46, col. USAR, 1958-75, ret. Mem. ASME (life), Retired Officers Assn. (life). Home and Office: 894A Worcester Ln Lake Worth FL 33467-2726

BELL, MILDRED BAILEY, lawyer, educator; b. Sanford, Fla., June 28, 1928; d. William F. and Frances E. (Williford) Bailey; m. J. Thomas Bell, Jr., Sept. 18, 1948 (div.); children: Tom, Elizabeth, Ansley. AB, U. Ga., 1950, JD cum laude, 1969; LLM in Taxation, N.Y. U., 1977. Bar: Ga. 1969. Law clk. U.S. Dist. Ct. No. Dist. Ga., 1969-70; prof. law Mercer U., Macon, Ga., 1970-94, prof. emeritus, 1994—; mem. Ga. Com. Constl. Revision, 1978-79; bd. dirs. Arrowhead Travel, Inc. Bd. editors Ga. State Bar Jour., 1974-76; contbr. articles to profl. jours., chpts. in books. Mem. ABA, Ga. Bar Assn., Phi Beta Kappa, Phi Kappa Phi. Republican. Episcopalian. Home: 14226 Foliage Ct Midlothian VA 23112

BELL, ROBERT MORRALL, lawyer; b. Graniteville, S.C., Feb. 15, 1936; s. Jonathan F. and Ruby Lee (Carpenter) B.; m. Cecelia Richardson Coker, June 11, 1965 (dec.). AB, U. S.C., 1958, LLB, 1965. Bar: S.C. 1965, U.S. Dist. Ct. S.C. 1965, U.S. Ct. Appeals (4th cir.) 1970. With Watkins, Vandiver, Kirven & Long, Anderson, S.C., 1965-67; sr. law clk. to chief judge U.S. Dist. Ct. S.C., Greenville, 1967-69; mem. Abram, Bowen & Townes, Greenville, 1969-71, Bell & Surasky, Langley, S.C., 1971-76, sr. ptnr., 1976—; county atty. Aiken County (S.C.), 1982—. Mem. S.C. Hwy. Commn., 1982-86; state exec. committeeman S.C. Dem. Com., 1980-86; mem. S.C. Bd. Chiropractic Examiners, 1978-80; mem. Svc. Coun. of Aiken County, 1976-82, Aiken County Planning Commn., 1976-80, Chmn. Aiken County Transportation Com., 1993-96; bd. dirs. Aiken County Crippled Children's Soc., 1976-82, Gregg-Graniteville Found., 1984—. With USAR, 1959-60. Mem. ABA, ATLA, Aiken County Bar Assn., S.C. Bar Assn., S.C. Trial Lawyers Assn., Masons, Shriners, Kappa Sigma Kappa, Tau Kappa Alpha, Phi Delta Phi, Chi Psi. Democrat. Methodist. Office: PO Box 1890 2625 Jefferson Davis Hwy Langley SC 29834

BELL, RONALD MACK, university foundation administrator; b. Atlanta, Mar. 4, 1937; m. Deborah Jean Slaton, Dec. 28, 1989. BS in Indsl. Mgmt., Ga. Inst. Tech., 1959; MBA, U. Mich., 1965; attended, Cornell U., 1980. Commd. USN, 1959, advanced through grades to capt., 1979, ret., 1985; assoc. dir. rsch. contracts Ga. Inst. Tech., Atlanta, 1985-88; v.p., gen. mgr. Ga. Tech. Rsch. Corp., Atlanta, 1988—; bd. dirs., past pres., now dir. emeritus Nat. Supply Corps. Assn.; cons. Wesvaco/Post, Buckley, others, 1985—; expert witness ELSCO, U. Tenn., others, 1987-90; nat. chmn. Univ. Connected Rsch. Found., 1990-91. Past chmn., dir. emeritus Naval Supply Corps. Sch. Mus. Com., Athens, mem., 1983—; mem. Exec. Roundtable, Atlanta, 1985—; resource staff Gov.'s Com. Tech. & Devel., Atlanta, 1992—. Decorated Legion of Merit (2), Meritorious Svc. medal (2). Mem. Soc. Rsch. Adminstrs. (nat. coms., chair regional com. 1985—), Licensing Execs. Soc., Nat. Coun. Univ. Rsch. Adminstrs. (chair regional com., nat. panelist 1985—), Coun. Rsch. and Tech. (dir. workshop, tax com. 1986-92), Ga. Tech. Nat. Alumni Assn. (various coms.), Nat. Conf. on the Advancement of Rsch., Theta Chi (past chpt. pres.), Phi Kappa Phi. Home: 1005 Shady Valley Pl NE Atlanta GA 30324-2772 Office: Ga Tech Rsch Corp 400 10th St NW Atlanta GA 30318-5712

BELL, STEVEN MICHAEL, foreign language educator; b. Lawrence, Kans., Nov. 3, 1956; s. W. Fletcher and Mona J. (Slack) B.; m. Rosario Nolasco, Aug. 17, 1985; children: Christopher William, Joseph Anthony. BA, U. Kans., 1977; MA, U. Ky., 1979; PhD, U. Kans., 1984. English instr. Centro Colombo-Americano, Bogota, Colombia, 1980; asst. prof. dept. romance langs. U. Notre Dame, South Bend, Ind., 1984-92; asst. prof. fgn. langs. U. Ark., Fayetteville, 1992-96, assoc. prof. Spanish and L.Am. studies, 1996—. Co-author, editor: Critical Theory, Cultural Politics and Latin American Narrative, 1993. Fulbright grantee, 1987-88; Fulbright fellow, 1983-84. Mem. MLA, Latin Am. Studies Assn., Phi Beta Kappa. Home: 2327 Mockingbird Ln Fayetteville AR 72703-4113 Office: U Ark Dept Fgn Langs Fayetteville AR 72701

BELL, THOMAS EUGENE, psychologist, educational administrator; b. Okmulgee, Okla., Feb. 20, 1945; s. Wilmer Ordell and Betty Jean (Good) Bell; m. Ramona Kay Ashlock, Aug. 26, 1965; 1 child, Stacie Lane. BA, Cen. State U., Edmond, Okla., 1972, MEd, 1975; postgrad., Okla. State U., 1986-88. Lic. profl. counselor, Okla. Psychometrist Guthrie (Okla.) Pub. Schs., 1975-79, sch. psychologist, 1979-89, dir. counseling, 1989-94; pvt. practice Edmond, 1994—. Developer Teen Buddies, 1990. With USAF, 1965-67. Recipient Parent Edn. award Okla. Juvenile Justice, Oklahoma City, 1991. Mem. Mensa Internat. (proctor 1979-86), Okla. Psychol. Assn. (rep. 1986-87), Okla. Sch. Psychology Assn. (area rep. 1987-88), Nat. Assn. Sch. Psychologists, Youth Suicide Prevention Assn. (v.p. 1991—). Democrat. Mem. Ch. of Christ. Home: 1101 Apollo Cir Edmond OK 73003-6013 Office: Meridian Med Tower Bldg 400 Ste A Ste 304 Oklahoma City OK 73120

BELL, WILLIAM WOODWARD, lawyer; b. Brownwood, Tex., May 15, 1938; s. Charles Smith and Janie Mae (Woodward) B.; m. Mary Elizabeth Beniteau, May 31, 1969; children—Susan Elizabeth, Carol Ann. B.B.A., Baylor U., 1960, J.D., 1965. Bar: U.S. Dist. Ct. (we. dist.) Tex. 1967, U.S. Supreme Ct. 1971. Ptnr. Sleeper, Boynton, Burleson, Williams & Johnson, Waco, Tex., 1965-68, Holloway, Slagle & Bell, Brownwood, 1968-71; ptnr. Johnson, Slagle & Bell, Brownwood, 1971-74; sole practice, Brownwood, 1974-80; atty. City of Brownwood, 1980—; ptnr. Bell and Ellis, Brownwood, 1980-89; ptnr. Bell, Franklin & Morelock, Brownwood, 1989-94; v.p. Bell Mortgage and Investment Co., Brownwood, 1962-86. Served to capt. USMC, 1960-63. Fellow Tex. Bar Found.; named Vol. 1991, Developer of Yr. Tex. Industrial Devel. Coun.; mem. Tex. Bar Assn. (chmn. dist. 15B grievance com. 1986-87), Brown County Bar Assn., Am. Judicature Soc., Assn. Trial Lawyers Am., Rotary, Phi Alpha Delta. Baptist. Home: PO Box 1564 Brownwood TX 76804-1564 Office: 115 S Broadway PO Box 1726 Brownwood TX 76804-1726

BELLACK, JANIS PEACOCK, university official; b. Ohio, July 10, 1947; m. Daniel R. Bellack, 1973; 2 children. Diploma, U. Va. Hosp., 1968; BS in Nursing, U. Va., 1970; M in Nursing, U. Fla., 1971; PhD, U. Ky., 1987. Asst. prof. U. Va., Charlottesville, 1971-73, Old Dominion U., Norfolk, Va., 1973-76; assoc. prof. U. Ky., Lexington, 1976-87; assoc. prof., asst. dean Med. U. S.C. Coll. Nursing, Charleston, 1987-92, dir. univ. ednl. planning, 1993-95; assoc. provost for ednl. programs Med. U. S.C., Charleston, 1995—; mem. spl. initiatives nat. grant rev. panel Area Health Edn. Ctrs., 1991; mem. grant rev. panel Divsn. of Nursing Spl. Projects, 1993-95. Author: (with B.J. Edlund) Nursing Assessment and Diagnosis, 2d edit., 1992; manuscript reviewer Jour. Pediatric Nursing, Pub. Health Nursing, Nursing Outlook; editl. bd. Jour. Nursing Edn. Sr. fellow Ctr. for the Health Professions, U. Calif., San Francisco, 1996—; grantee Helene Fuld Found., 1989-91, Teagle Found., 1990-93, HHS, 1990-93, Pew Health Professions Commn., 1993-96, Nat. Network of Librs. of Medicine, 1994-95. Fellow Am. Acad. Nursing; mem. ANA, Nat. League Nursing (program evaluator, mem. bd. rev., mem. exec. com., mem. coun. on baccalaureate and higher degree programs), S.C. Nurses Assn. (chmn, edn. com. 1988-90, chmn. editl. bd. S.C. Nurse 1994-96), S.C. League Nursing (program chmn. 1988-89, pres.-elect 1995-96, pres. 1996—), Sigma Theta Tau. Home: 1159 Shilling Pl Mount Pleasant SC 29464-9251 Office: Med Univ SC Rm 200H Adminstrn Bldg 171 Ashley Ave Charleston SC 29425-1020

BELLANCA, JOSEPH PAUL, engineering/construction executive; b. Rochester, N.Y., Nov. 25, 1936; s. Sam and Anna (Cani) B.; m. Joy Eleanor Gaston, Dec. 5, 1964; children: Joseph Jr., Victoria Ann Gordon, Lizabeth Ann Wilbur, Lorraine Bellanca. BS in Civil Engring., Purdue U., 1958. Registered profl. engr., D.C. and 10 states. Assoc./project mgr. TAMS Consultants, Dallas/Ft. Worth, 1968-73; assoc./resident mgr. TAMS Consultants, Washington, 1973-77; pres. Bellanca Engring. Consultants, Atlanta, others, 1977-85; dir. Schal Assocs., Chgo., 1985-86; v.p. Greiner, Inc., Orlando (Fla.), Denver, 1986-88, Bechtel Internat. Inc., Vienna, Va., 1988-92, Turner Constrn. Co., Atlanta, 1992—; lobbyist Airport Consultants Coun.

Author/editor: (jour.) Airports--Challenges of the Future, 1973, (design compendium) World Travel Center--Detroit Met. Airport (won design competition for $1 billion new air terminal complex. Named Young Engr. Yr. Mid-Cities chpt. Tex. Soc. Profl. Engrs., 1971. Mem. ASCE (sec. 1973, vice chmn. 1979, exec. com., air transport divsn.), NSPE (pres. Mid-Cities chpt. Tex. Soc. Profl. Engrs. 1972-73). Home: 9295 Heatherton Walk Duluth GA 30155 Office: Turner Constrn Co 7000 Central Pkwy #650 Atlanta GA 30328

BELLANTONI, MAUREEN BLANCHFIELD, manufacturing executive; b. Warren, Pa., Mar. 18, 1949; d. John Joseph and Patricia Anne (Southard) Blanchfield; m. Michael Charles Bellantoni, Aug. 12, 1972; children: Mark Christopher, Melissa Catherine. BS in Fin., U. Bridgeport, 1976; MBA, U. Conn., Stamford, 1979. Fin. analyst Dictaphone Corp., Rye, N.Y., 1970-73, Gen. Telephone & Electronics, Stamford, 1973-74, Smith Kline Ultrasonic Products, now Branson, Danbury, Conn., 1974-77; fin. mgr. Gen. Foods, White Plains, N.Y., 1977-80; contr. Branson Ultrasonics Corp. div. Emerson Electric, Danbury, Conn., 1980-88; v.p. fin. Branson Ultrasonics Corp. div. Emerson Electric, Danbury, 1988-90; v.p. fin., CFO Automatic Switch Co. divsn. Emerson Electric, Florham Park, N.J., 1990-93, PYA/Monarch, Inc. divsn. Sara Lee Corp., Greenville, S.C., 1993-94; v.p. fin. CFO Meat Group Sara Lee Corp., Cordova, Tenn., 1994—; bd. dirs. Michael Foods, Inc. Vice chair Nat. Legacy Campaign Cancer Fund, Franciscan Sister of Poor Found. Mem. Fin. Execs. Inst., S.C. C. of C., Danbury C. of C. (leadership program 1989), Beta Gamma Sigma. Home: 3407 Lake Pointe Cove Memphis TN 38125-8842 Office: 8000 Centerview Pkwy Ste 300 Cordova TN 38018-4239

BELLARE, NAGENDRANATH, physician; b. Bangalore, Karnataka, India, June 29, 1944; s. Bhavanishankar Rao and Revathi Bai (Basrur) B.; m. Beatriz Acob Bautista, may 1, 1968 (div. Jan. 1982); children: Nita Bautista, Sanjiv Jayanth; m. Patricia Marie Lopes, Sept. 11, 1982; children: Nicole Marie Priya, Maureen Shanthi. Diploma in Pre-Profl. Medicine, Bangalore U. Med. Sch., India, 1960, MBBS, 1965. Diplomate Am. Bd. Internal Medicine, Am. Bd. Med. Oncology. Intern Cook County Hosp., Chgo., 1967-68; fellow hematology and oncology Cook County Hosp., 1970-72; resident, internal medicine Northwestern U., Chgo., 1968-70; pvt. practice Downers Grove, Ill., 1972-78, Visalia, Calif., 1978-91; pvt. practice Kaweah Sierra Med. Group, Visalia, 1991-93; fellow bone marrow and blood stem cell transplantation M.D. Anderson Cancer Ctr., Houston, 1993-94; med. dir. peripheral blood stem cell transplantation program Forrest Gen. Hosp., Hattiesburg, Miss., 1996—; pvt. practice med. oncology Hattiesburg Clin. P.A., 1994—; med. dir. Hospice of Tulare County, Visalia, 1979-89; chmn. dept. medicine Kaweah Delia Dist. Hosp., 1989-92. Bd. dirs. Am. Cancer Soc., Visalia, 1980-92. Fellow ACP, Internat. Coll. Physicians; mem. AMA, Miss. State Med. Soc.. Republican. Baptist. Office: Hattiesburg Clin PA 415 S 28th Ave Hattiesburg MS 39401-7246

BELLAS, MARC ANDREW, sales and marketing specialist; b. Oakland, Calif., Dec. 10, 1962; s. Edward Mark and Leanore Agnus (Gerheart) B. AAS in Automotive Engrng., U. Ariz., Phoenix, 1983; postgrad., Calif. Coast U., 1992—. Div. mgr. Sears, Roebuck & Co., Phoenix, 1982-85; regional trainer Winston Tire Co., No. Calif., 1985-86; dist. mgr. Assix Inc., Dallas, 1986-88; regional mgr. Assix Inc., Chgo., 1988-89; nat. tng. dir. Assix Inc., Tampa, Fla., 1989-91; internat. tng. dir. Assix Inc., Tampa, 1991-93, chief oper. officer BesTec subs., 1991—, exec. dir., 1993—; chmn. bd. Studio One Graphics, Inc., Tampa. Author, dir. sales tng. and motivational tapes BesTapes. Vol. Am. Cancer Soc., Tampa, 1991. Mem. ASTD, Am. Mgmt. Assn., Automotive Tng. Mgrs. Coun. (cons. 1990—), Nat. Soc. Automotive Svc. (cert.), Toastmasters Internat. Republican. Office: Assix Inc 505 E Jackson St Tampa FL 33602-4935

BELLAVANCE, MARIA ISABEL, librarian; b. Lisboa, Portugal, July 24, 1946; came to U.S., 1966; d. Adriao Garcia and Maria de Lourdes (Serrao) B.; m. David Walter Bellavance, Sept. 28, 1969; 1 child, Angela Maria Bellavance. BS in Elec. Engrng., Brown U., Providence, R.I., 1969; MLS, North Tex. U., Denton, 1985. Tech. staff Bell Lab., Murray Hill, N.J., 1970-72; parish libr. All Saints Cath. Ch., Dallas, 1985—; libr. specialist Southern Meth. Univ., 1996—. Mem. Ch. and Synagogue Libr. Assn. (Outstanding Congl. Libr. award 1993), Tau Beta Pi. Roman Catholic. Home: 7410 La Cosa Dr Dallas TX 75248-5228 Office: All Saints Parish Res Libr 5231 Meadowcreek Dr Dallas TX 75248-4046

BELLEN, HUGO JOSEF, genetics educator; b. Brussels, Apr. 21, 1953; came to U.S., 1983; s. Henri Josef and Josee (Jugters) B.; m. Catherine Tasnier. MBA magna cum laude, Free U. Brussels, 1976; degree prevet. medicine magna cum laude, U. Antwerp, 1980; DVM magna cum laude, U. Ghent, Belgium, 1983; PhD in Genetics, U. Calif., Davis, 1986. Rschr. in econometrics U. Antwerp, 1977-80; postdoctoral rschr. Biozentrum Dept. Cell Biology U. Basel, Switzerland, 1987-89; asst. investigator Howard Hughes Med. Inst., Baylor Coll. Medicine, Houston, 1989—; asst. prof. dept. cell biology, divsn. neurosci. Inst. Molecular Genetics, Baylor Coll. Medicine, Houston, 1989-94, assoc. prof., 1994—; assoc. investigator Howard Hughes Med. Inst. Baylor Coll. Medicine, Houston, 1995—; lectr. in field. Author: Social Welfare in Belgium, 1979, A Course of Genetics, 1980; contbr. articles to profl. publs. Recipient Fulbright award, 1983, NATO fellow, 1986, 87, M. Debakey award for excellence in rsch. Home: 3411 Mount Vernon St Houston TX 77006-3830 Office: Howard Hughes Med Inst One Baylor Plz Houston TX 77030

BELLES, ANITA LOUISE, health care researcher, consultant; b. San Angelo, Tex., Aug. 30, 1948; d. Curtis Lee and Margaret Louise (Perry) B.; m. John Arvel Willey, Jul. 13, 1969 (div. Aug. 1978); children: Suzan Heather, Kenneth Alan; m. John W. Portfield, Dec. 22, 1992. BA, U. Tex., 1972; MS in Health Care Adminstrn., Trinity U., 1984. dir. family planning Bexar County Hosp. Dist., Tex., 1987; mgmt. engr. Inpatient Support Applications, 1987-88; instr. grad. sch. health care adminstrn. S.W. Tex. State U.; researcher on cardiovascular rsch. on artificial heart and heart transplantation, San Antonio Regional Heart Inst., 1993. Regional emergency med. service tng. coordinator Bur. Emergency Med. Service, Lake Charles, La., 1978-79; exec. dir. Southwest La. Emergency Med. Service Council, Lake Charles, 1979-83; project coordinator Tulane U. Med. Sch., New Orleans, 1982-83; dir. La. Bur. of Emergency Med. Service, Baton Rouge, 1982; pres. Computype, Inc., San Antonio, 1983-86, Emergency Med. and Safety Assocs., La. and Tex., 1982—; dir. family planning Bexar County Hosp. Dist., Tex., 1987; mgmt. engr. Inpatient Support Applications, 1987-88; instr. grad. sch. health care adminstrn. S.W. Tex. State U. Editor A.L.E.R.T., 1980-83, San Antonio Executive News, 1987—, Family Living, 1987-88; feature writer Bright Scrawl, 1985-86; contbr. numerous articles on emergency med. services to profl. jours. Bd. dirs. Thousand Oaks Homeowner's Assn., sec., treas., 1985; active Trinity U. Health Care Alumni Assn., Jr. League San Antonio, The Parenting Ctr., Baton Rouge, 1982-83, Jr. League Lake Charles, 1982, Campfire Council Pub. Relations Com., Lake Charles, 1982; newsletter editor Community Food Co-Op, Newsletter Editor, 1979; vol. Lake Charles Mental Health Ctr., 1974. Recipient Outstanding Service award La. Assn Registered Emergency Med. Technicians, 1983, Southwest La. Assn. Emergency Med. Technicians, 1983; named Community Leader KPLC TV, Lake Charles, 1981, regional winner Assn U. Programs in Health Adminstrn., HHS Sec's. Competitions for Innovations in Health, 1982. Mem. Nat. Assn. Emergency Med. Technicians., Tex. Assn. Emergency Med. Technicians, Am. Coll. Health Care Execs., Am. Assn. Automotive Medicine, Southwest La. Assn. Emergency Med. Technicians (founding mem., v.p. 1979-80, CPR com. chmn. 1980-81, pub. relations com. chmn. 1981-82, bd. dirs. 1980-82), Am. Mgmt. Assn., Nat. Soc. Emergency Med. Service Adminstrs., Nat. Coalition Emergency Med. Services, Am. Composition Assn. Methodist.

BELLES, MARTIN RUSSEL, manufacturing engineer; b. Ft. Wayne, Ind., Sept. 4, 1952; s. Russel Elwin and Irene (Crossley) B. Student, U. Calif., Berkeley, Armstrong State Coll., Savannah, Ga. Aircraft assembler Rockwell Internat., Bethany, Okla., 1974-83; process planner Gulfstream Aerospace, Bethany, 1984-85; mfg. engr. Gulfstream Aerospace, Savannah, 1985—. Contbg. author: Stupid Windows Tricks, 1992. Mem. Ga. Hist. Soc., Historic Savannah Found., Telfair Acad. of Arts and Scis. Mem. IEEE, Assn. Computing Machinery, Epsilon Data Pi, Upsilon Pi Epsilon. Office: Gulfstream Aerospace 500 Gulfstream Rd Savannah GA 31407-9643

BELLI, VAHIT M., cardiologist, nephrologist; b. Merzifon, Turkey, Mar. 21, 1927; came to U.S., 1960; s. Abdullah and Habibe B.; m. Jacalyn Lee Almand, Mar. 3, 1979; children: Randy Vahit, Erol Vahit, Yener Vahit. Student, Haydarpasa Coll., Istanbul, Turkey, 1943-48, U. Istanbul Sch. Pharmacy, 1948-53. chief cardiology Brandon Hosp., 1991—. Chief pharmacist Ataturk Sanatorium, Kecioren-Ankara, Turkey, 1953-59; rotating intern Franklin Sq. Hosp., Balt., 1960, resident in internal medicine, 1961-63; fellow in collagen disease St. Barnabas Hosp., Bronx, N.Y., 1963-64; chief resident in internal medicine N.Y. Polyclinic Med. Sch. and Hosp., N.Y.C., 1964-65; fellow in cardiopulmonary Long Island Jewish Med. Ctr., New Hyde Park, N.Y., 1965-66; fellow in cardiology VA Hosp., Bronx, 1966-67, Rsch. fellow in nephrology, 1967-68; fellow in transplant surgery and immunology NYU Med. Ctr., N.Y.C., 1968-73; fellow in hemodialysis and kidney transplantation NYU/Bellevue Hosp. Ctr., N.Y.C., 1971-72; pvt. practice Tampa, Fla., 1973-77, Brandon (Fla.) Med. Ctr., 1975-76, Brandon Cardiology Ctr., 1976—; instr. biochemistry and pharmacology Ankara Sch. Nursing, 1957-59; clin. instr. transplantation surgery NYU Sch. Medicine, N.Y.C., 1968-73, instr. clin. urology (nephrology), 1972-73; assoc. rsch. scientist in transplantation and immunology div. surgery NYU Med. Ctr., N.Y.C., 1968-72, organ transplantation team cardiology and nephrology, 1968-73; vice-chief medicine Humana Hosp. Brandon, 1983-84, chief medicine, 1984-85, chief cardiology, 1988-89, 91—, legis. com. 1988—, spl. care com. 1983-84, 91—. Mem. AMA (Physicians Recognition award 1969, 72, 78, 81, 85, 92-93, Continuing Edn. award 1988-92), Fla. Med. Assn. (Continuing Med. Edn. award 1979, 82, 85). Republican. Moslem. Home: 2300 Green Lawn St Brandon FL 33511-7224 Office: Brandon Cardiology Ctr 107 N Carver St Brandon FL 33510-4526

BELLINGHAM, PAUL HASTY, II, manufacturers' representative; b. Englewood, N.J., May 26, 1944; s. Paul H. and Jemima (Walker) B.; m. Bonnie Marie Atienla, May 17, 1975 (div. Feb. 1988); m. Laura Joyce Alewine, May 26, 1990. Student, Montclair State Coll., 1966-67, City Coll. San Francisco, 1968, 77-78, Diablo Valley Coll., 1970-71. Pres. Bellingham Landscaping, San Francisco, 1968-72; mgr. Nasser Bros. Theatres, San Francisco, 1972-75; pres. Profl. Door Cutting Co., San Francisco, 1973-76, Home Plate Distbg. Co., San Francisco, 1976-80; sales rep. The Newcombs, Pacific Palisades, Calif., 1980-82; sales mgr. Willits Designs, Petaluma, Calif., 1982-86; cons. field sales Talbot House, St. Michaels, Md., 1986-89; pres. Toute Cute, Inc, LaCombe, La., 1989—; cons. Coppersource Inc., Hayward, Calif., 1987-88. Chmn. Santa on the Bayou, Lacombe, 1990-93; active Amnesty Internat., Sonny Boy Blues Soc. With USN, 1962-66. Mem. ACLU, Gulf Coast Conservation Assn., Lacombe C. of C. (bd. dirs. 1990-94, pres. 1992-93, Outstanding Contbn. award 1990), Friends of Earth, Greenpeace, Sierra Club. Democrat. Home: 59505 Bayou Dr Lacombe LA 70445-3623 Office: Toute Cute Inc PO Box 1005 Lacombe LA 70445-1005

BELLO-REUSS, ELSA NOEMI, physician, educator; b. Buenos Aires, Argentina, May 1, 1939; came to U.S., 1972; naturalized, 1989; d. Jose F. and Julia M. (Hiriart) Bello; B.S., U. Chile, 1957, M.D., 1964; m. Luis Reuss, Apr. 15, 1965; children: Luis F., Alejandro E. Intern J.J. Aguirre Hosp., Chile, 1963-64; intern, then resident in internal medicine U. Chile, Santiago, 1964-66; pvt. practice medicine specializing in nephrology Santiago, 1967-72; prof. pathophysiology Sch. Nutrition U. Chile, 1970-72; Internat. NIH fellow U. N.C., Chapel Hill, 1972-74; vis. asst. prof. physiology U. N.C., Chapel Hill, 1974-75; Louis Welt fellow U. N.C.-Duke U. Med. Ctr., 1975-76; mem. faculty Jewish Hosp. St. Louis, 1976-83, asst. prof. medicine, physiology and biophysics Washington U. Sch. Medicine, St. Louis, 1976-86, assoc. prof. physiology dept. cell biology and physiology, 1986; assoc. prof. medicine U. Tex. Med. Br., Galveston, 1986-94, prof. dept. internal medicine and dept. phys. and biophys. medicine, 1994—, dir. Renal Clin, 1995—; mem. reviewers res. study sect. NIH, 1991-95; chair Women's Coun. Internat. Medicine U. Tex. Med. Bd. chpt., 1993—, mem. rsch. coun. Author: (with others) The Kidney and Body Fluids in Health and Disease, 1983; contbr. articles on nephrology and epithelial electrophysiology to med. and physiology jours. Mem. Internat., Am. Socs. Nephrology, Royal Soc. Medicine, Nat. Kidney Found. of S.E. Tex. (med. adv. bd., chairperson med. adv. bd., bd. dirs. 1994-95)), Coun. of Women in Nephrology, Tex. Med. Assn., Am. Fedn. Clin. Rsch., Am. Soc. Renal Biochemistry and Metabolism, Internat. Soc. Renal Nutrition and Metabolism, Am. Physiology Soc., Am. Heart Assn., Kidney Coun., Soc. Gen. Physiologists, Math. Assn. Am., Gt. Houston and Gulf Coast Nephrology Assn., NIH Gen. Medicine B Study Sect. (mem. 1987-91), Reserve reviewer 1991-95, VA grant reviewer, Sigma Xi. Office: U Tex Med Br Dept Medicine Nephrology OJS 4 200 Galveston TX 77555-0562

BELLSTEDT, OLAF, senior software engineer; b. Munich, Oct. 23, 1966; came to U.S., 1984; s. Karl-Heinz and Ria (Filsinger) B.; m. Jessica Mae Patterson, Dec. 16, 1989. BS in Space Sci., Fla. Inst. Tech., 1990. Mgr. product devel., support Varimetrix Corp., Palm Bay, Fla., 1990—. Ambulance driver, attendant Harbor City Vol. Ambulance Squad, Melbourne, Fla., 1988-89. Mem. AIAA (vice chmn. 1988-89), Profl. Assn. Diving Instrs. (dive master), Tau Beta Pi. Office: Varimetrix Corp 2350 Commerce Park Dr NE Ste 4 Palm Bay FL 32905-7722

BELL-TOLLIVER, LAVERNE, social worker; b. Little Rock, Feb. 28, 1949; d. Louis Anthony and Ruby Jewell (Fleming) Bell; 1 child, Stephen Anthony Bell; m. Johnny Marvin Tolliver, Dec. 20, 1970 (div. Apr. 1975); 1 child, Amani Malaika. BA in Sociology and Spanish, Drury Coll., 1971; MSW, U. Ark., 1973; MA in Biblical Counseling with honors, Dallas Theol. Sem., 1996. Lic. master social work, Tex. Clin. social worker Ctrl. Counties Mental Health Mental Retardation, Temple, Tex., 1973-75; worker, supr., trainer Tex. Dept. Human Svcs., Dallas, 1975-91; owner, dir. Empowerment Svcs., Dallas, 1991—; satellite dir. Child Guidance Clinic of Dallas, 1991—; adj. faculty Dallas County C.C., Mesquite, Tex., 1987-91; contract therapist Family Place, Dallas, 1991-94; contract facilitator Tex. Dept. Protective and Regulatory Svcs., Arlington, Tex., 1991—. Author, pub. My Very Own Parent's Training Manual, 1994, also trainers guide, 1994; contbr. Thomas Nelson Women's Study Bible, 1995. Youth dir. Cmty. Bapt. Ch., Dallas, 1979-87, Bexar St. Bapt. Ch., Dallas, 1987—; choir mem. St. Luke Cmty. United Meth. Ch., Dallas, 1991—; adj. mem. Oak Cliff Child Guidance Bd., Dallas, 1993—; mem. edn l. task force Dallas Pub. Schs., 1995—; mem. health fair task force Dallas Urban League, 1995—. Named Master Trainer, Tex. Dept. Human Svcs., Austin, 1983; recipient award of excellence Assn. for Retarded Citizens, Dallas, 1990, scholastic recognition N.Am. Profs. of Christian Edn., 1995. Mem. Am. Assn. Marriage and Family Therapists (clin. mem.), Nat. Assn. Black Social Workers, Assn. Play Therapists (registered play therapist), Tex. Assn. Play Therapists, Oak Cliff C. of C. (edn. adv. bd. 1993—). Democrat. Home: 5729 Arlington Park Dr Dallas TX 75235 Office: Child Guidance Clinic Dallas 8915 Harry Hines Dallas TX 75235

BELSKY, MARTIN HENRY, law educator, lawyer; b. Phila., May 29, 1944; s. Abraham and Fannie (Turnoff) B.; m. Kathleen Waits, Mar. 9, 1985; children: Allen Frederick, Marcia Elizabeth. BA cum laude, Temple U., 1965; JD cum laude, Columbia U., 1968; cert. of study Hague (Netherlands) Acad. Internat. Law, 1968; diploma in criminology Cambridge (Eng.) U., 1969. Bar: Pa. 1969, Fla. 1983, N.Y., 1987, U.S. dist. ct. (ea. dist.) Pa. 1969, U.S. Ct. Appeals (3d cir.) 1970, U.S. Supreme Ct. 1973. Chief asst. dist. atty. Phila. Dist. Atty.'s Office, 1969-74; assoc. Blank, Rome, Klaus & Comisky, Phila., 1975; chief counsel U.S. Ho. of Reps., Washington, 1975-78; asst. adminstr. NOAA, Washington, 1979-82; dir. Ctr. for Govtl. Responsibility, assoc. prof. law U. Fla. Holand Law Ctr., 1982-86; dean Albany Law Sch., 1986-91, dean emeritus, prof. law, 1991-95; dean U. Tulsa Coll. of Law, 1995—; chair Select Commn. on Disabilities, N.Y., Spl. Commn. on Fire Svcs.; bd. advs. Ctr. Oceans Law and Policy; mem. corrections task force Pa. Gov.'s Justice Commn., 1971-75; adv. task force on cts. Nat. Adv. Commn. on Criminal Justice Standards and Goals, 1972-74; mem. com. on proposed standard jury instrns. Pa. Supreme Ct., 1974-81; lectr. in law Temple U., 1971-75; mem. faculty Pa. Coll. Judiciary, 1975-77; adj. prof. law Georgetown U., 1977-81. Chmn. Phila. council Anti-Defamation League, 1975, N.Y. region, mem. D.C. bd., 1977-78, chair N.Y. region, mem. nat. leadership Coun.; exec. v.p. Urban League Northeastern N.Y.; bd. dirs. Coun. on Aging & Disability. Stone scholar and Internat. fellow Columbia U. Law Sch. Mem. N.Y. State Bar Assn., Albany County Bar Assn., Phila. Bar Assn. (chmn. young lawyers sect. 1974-75), Pa. Bar Assn. (exec. com. young lawyers sect. 1973-75), ABA (del. young lawyers sect. exec. bd. 1973-75), Fla. Bar Assn., Fed. Bar Assn., Am. Judicature Soc., Nat. Dist. Attys. Assn., Am. Soc. Internat. Law, Am. Arbitration Assn. (referee N.Y. State Commn. on Jud. Discipline), Temple U. Liberal Arts Alumni Assn. (v.p. 1971-75), Am. Law Inst., Fund for Modern Cts. (bd. dirs.), Hudson-Mohawk Assn. Colls. and Univs. (v.p.), Sword Soc. Jewish. Club: B'nai B'rith (v.p. lodge 1973-75), Cardoto Soc., United Jewish Fedn. Northeastern N.Y. (v.p., pres. elect). Author: (with Steven H. Goldblatt) Analysis and Commentary to the Pennsylvania Crimes Codes, 1973; Handbook for Trial Judges, 1976, Oceans and Capital Law and Policy, 1994; contbr. articles to legal publs.; editor in chief Jour. Transnat. Law, Columbia Law Sch., 1968; mem. bd. advisors Territorial Sea Jour. Office: U Tulsa Coll Law 3120 E 4th Pl Tulsa OK 74104

BELT, JEAN RAINER, art gallery owner; b. Selma, Ala., Sept. 12, 1942; d. Sterling Price and Saidee (Crook) Rainer; m. Kemplin C. Belt, Aug. 31, 1963; children: Keven Curtis, Kelly B. Jones. BS in Math., U. Ala., 1964. Founder, ptnr. Corp. Art Source, Montgomery, Ala., 1983-92, owner, 1992—; owner CAS Gallery & Frames, Montgomery, Ala., 1994; juror Jubilee Galleria Art Show, Montgomery, 1987, Riofest, Harlingen, Tex., 1989-90, BCA on My Own Time, Montgomery, 1990; guest lectr. Riofest, 1990; dir. Armory Gallery Arts Coun. Montgomery, 1989-91; advisor Montgomery Bus. Com. Arts, 1990-94 (Bus. in Arts award 1989); curator Armory Gallery, Montgomery, 1989. Bd. dirs Arts Coun. Montgomery, 1990-94, pres., 1985-87, 92-93; mem. adv. bd. Montgomery Symphony Assn., 1993—; pres. Jr. League Montgomery, 1984, treas., 1981; Stephen min. 1st United Meth. Ch., Montgomery, 1992-94. Named Vol. Action Ctr. Vol. of Yr., 1989; recipient Bus. in the Arts award Montgomery Bus. Com. for the Arts, 1989, Disting. Vol. in the Arts award Art Coun. Montgomery, 1996. Mem. Nat. Assn. Corp. Art Mgrs., Montgomery C. of C., U. Ala. Alumni Assn. Office: Corp Art Source 2960 Zelda Rd # F Montgomery AL 36106-2649

BELTON, DEBORAH CAROLYN KNOX, state agency administrator, accountant; b. Manchester, Tenn., Mar. 31, 1962; d. Eugene Clarke and Myrtle Carolyn (Bell) Knox; m. Joseph Burton Belton, May 23, 1992. BBA in Acctg., Middle Tenn. State U., 1984. CPA, Tenn. Sr. fin. planner Lincoln Fin. Group, Brentwood, Tenn., 1986; staff CPA Charles Tharp & Assocs., Nashville, 1987; staff acct. Dept. Treasury State of Tenn., Nashville, 1984-85, supr. pension payroll Dept. Treasury, 1987, compliance analyst, policy planner, 1988, dir. program acctg. Dept. Fin., Adminstrn., 1988-93; data adminstr. Dept. of Fin. and Adminstrn., Nashville, 1993-95; mgr. distributed bus. info. svc., 1996—. Mem. Assn. Govt. Accts., Nat. Assn. CPAs (John Lewis award 1984).

BELTON, WILLIAM, ornithologist, retired foreign service officer; b. Portland, Oreg., May 22, 1914; s. F. Hugh Belton and Mary Jane Sheehy; m. Julia Hyslop, June 12, 1939; children: Barbara Belton Yngvesson, Hugh, Timothy. AB in Polit. Sci., Stanford U., 1935; grad., Nat. War Coll., 1959. Fgn. svc. officer, 1938-70; rsch. collaborator Smithsonian Instn., Washington, 1970—; mem. exec. com. Internat. Coun. for Bird Preservation, Cambridge, Eng., 1978-86, hon. v.p., 1986-94, bd. dirs. Pan Am. sect., Washington, 1979-80, vice chmn., 1979-80, chmn., 1980-86; bd. dirs. Rare Ctr. for Tropical Conservation, Phila., 1986-93; mem. of honour Birdlife Internat., Cambridge, 1994—. Author: Birds of Rio Grande do Sul, Brazil, 1984-85, Aves Silvestres do Rio Grande do Sul, 1983, 93, 94; translator: Birds in Brazil, 1993. Chmn. Potomac Headwater Resources Devel. and Conservation Com., Romney, W.Va., 1989; mem. Morgan County Fire Bd., Berkeley Springs, W.Va., 1987-89. Recipient Jean Delacour medal Internat. Coun. Bird Preservation, Ottawa, Ont., Can., 1986. Mem. Am. Ornithologists Union (elected), Assn. Field Ornithologists, Assn. Ornitologica del Plata, Brazilian Soc. Ornithology (corr.), Am. Fgn. Svc. Assn., Rotary. Democrat. Home and Office: Rocky Hollow HCR 62 Box 162B Great Cacapon WV 25422

BELYEW, PHILIP A., holding company executive; b. 1948. With Long Transp., Detroit, 1969-72, TOFC divsn. Freuhauf Corp., Chgo., 1972-78; with Courier Dispatch Group Inc. (merged into CDG Holding Corp.ú, Atlanta, 1978—, pres.; with CDG Holding Corp., Roswell, Ga., 1991—, pres. Office: CDG Holding Corp 1080 Holcomb Rd Roswell GA 30076

BELZUNG, PAUL EDWARD, engineering executive; b. San Antonio, Oct. 27, 1934; s. Oscar Albert and Melinda Wilimina (Keller) B.; m. Dylece LaNore Sherbondy, Sept. 19, 1952 (div. Sept. 1969); children: Brenda Belzung Holder, Gary Wayne Belzung, Wanda Belzung Sheetz; m. Teresa Galvan, Aug. 26, 1983; stepchildren: DiAnna VanNess Chavez, Dominic A. VanNess, Jaki VanNess Frost. Student, U. Tex., San Antonio, San Antonio Coll. Various positions Dept. Def.-USAF, Kelly AFB, Tex., 1952-90, gen. mgr. San Antonio Air Logistics Ctr., 1990; ret., gen. mgr. Dept. Def.; officer, pres. Kelly Mgmt. Assoc., San Antonio, 1975-76; v.p. Sunset Resources, Inc., San Antonio, 1992-94; dir. govt. svcs. Karta Tech. Inc., San Antonio, 1995—. Dir. Medina Lake Betterment Assn., Lakehills, Tex., 1988-91, pres. 1991-93; dir. Lakewood Owners Assn., v.p. 1994—; cert. lay spkr. Meth. Ch. Kerrville dist., Tex., 1992—. Mem. Soc. Logistics Engrs. (committeeperson 1992-94), Masons (jr./sr. warden San Antonio lodge 1964-65), Shriners. Republican. Home: 597 Lakepark Dr Lakehills TX 78063 Office: Karta Tech Inc 1892 Grandstand San Antonio TX 78238

BEMIS, ROYCE EDWIN, publishing executive; b. Atlanta, July 31, 1941; s. Edwin O. and Frances Louise (Webb) B.; m. Sandra Jean Goldstein, May 30, 1965; 1 child, David Michael. Student, Western Carlina U., 1959-63. Buyer Rich's Inc., Atlanta, 1964-68; rep. Viking Press, N.Y.C., 1968-77, Houghton Mifflin Co., Boston, 1977-88; dir. sales & mktg. Oxmoor House, Birmingham, Ala., 1987-90; advisor spl. collections Western Carolina U., 1986—. Bd. chmn. Arbor Acad. Spl. Edn., Atlanta, 1979-81; founding dir. Atlanta Group Home for Handicapped, Atlanta, 1979-85; active polit. affairs commn. Retarded Citizens Atlanta, 1986-89. Mem. Southeast Booksellers Assn. (bd. dirs. 1979-86, cons. 1986), So. Book Travellers Assn. (pres. 1986-87), Pubs. Assn. South (exec. com., chmn. mktg. com. 1988-89). Democrat. Jewish. Home: 4303 Ivywood Dr Marietta GA 30062-6432

BENAGE-MYERS, MARGARET ANNA, pediatrics nurse; b. Independence, Mo., Feb. 3, 1957; d. William F. and Agnes Catherine (Hudiburgh) Benage; m. Richard W. Myers, Dec. 28, 1985; children: Nicole, Lesley, Kelly, Samantha. ADN, Hutchinson Cmty. Jr. Coll., Hutchinson, Kans., 1986; BSN, Kans. Newman Coll., 1996. RN, Tex., Kans.; cert. instr. BLS, pediat. advanced life support. Staff nurse St. Francis Regional Med. Ctr., Wichita, Kans., 1986-87, Halstead (Kans.) Hosp., 1987; staff nurse pediat. ICU St. Joseph Med. Ctr., Wichita, 1987-95; pediat. nurse mgr. Coronado Hosp., Pampa, Tex., 1995-96; staff nurse pediat. ICU Via Christi Regional Med. Ctr., Wichita, Kans., 1996—. Mem. ARC (spkrs. bur.). Home: 114 W 17th Hutchinson KS 67501

BENARROCH REINFELD, MARY, music and holistic human development educator; b. Caracas, Venezuela, Sept. 24, 1951; d. Elias and Cecilia (Serebriany) B.; m. Michel Katz, Aug. 15, 1970 (div. Jan. 1976); children: Vanessa, Galia; m. Leo Reinfeld, July 17, 1979; children: Kilay, Ishai. Student, Instituto Psicologia Humanista, Caracas, 1970, Instituto Aveluz, Caracas, 1974, Montessori Sch., Caracas, 1973, Inst. for Children's Lit., West Ridge, Conn., 1992. Asst. to music therapist Exceptional Children Sch., Caracas, 1968-71; founder, dir. Tempo Dance Sch., Caracas, 1975-79; asst. of group therapies Humanistic Inst., Caracas, 1976-79; co-founder, tchr. Maria Montessori Active Ednl. Ctr., Caracas, 1973-78; founder, dir., tchr. Reinfeld Arts Sch., Netherland, Antilles, 1982-85; tchr. theatre and music Miami, Fla., 1993—; coord. ednl. commn. C.E.A.M.M., Caracas, 1987-89; artistic dir. dance group, Netherland Antilles, 1982-85; coord. 1st Congress Human Resources, Venezuela, Caribbean, 1978.

BENAVENTE, JAVIER EDGAR, engineering company executive; b. Chgo., July 20, 1959; s. Javier and Rebecca (Davis) B.; m. Theresa Lucille Augsback, July 28, 1984; children: Javier Christopher, Alexandria Joann. B Aero./Astron.Engrng., Purdue U., 1986, M in Astron. Engrng., 1987; M Engrng. Mgmt., Fla. Inst. Tech., 1989, MBA, 1990. Restaurant mgr. Orlando (Fla.) Marriott Inn, 1980, 81; asst. food and beverage dir. Holiday Inn Fannies, Richmond, Va., 1981; innkeeper Holiday Inn Beachside, Panama City Beach, Fla., 1981-82; mem. tech. staff Hughes Space and Comms., El Segundo, Calif., 1986-87; engr., proposal mgr. Dynacs Engring. Co., Inc., Clearwater, Fla., 1988-92, sr. engr., mgr. bus. devel., 1992-93, v.p., gen. mgr.,

1993—; program mgr./tech. lead on numerous engring. projects inluding the devel. of systems engring. analysis tools, docking and berthing dynamics, multi-body dynamic simulation software, neural network techs., computer animation, multi-media technologies and telecomms. technologies. Contbr. papers, revs. to profl. jours. and mags. Mentor Pinellas County Intership, Clearwater, 1993; coach Countryside Little League, Clearwater, 1993, 94, Countryside Soccer Assn., Clearwater, 1993, 94; mem. Pinellas County Urban League, St. Petersburg, Fla., 1994. Fellow Hughes Aircraft, 1986-87, Ford Found., 1988. Mem. AIAA, IEEE. Methodist. Home: 2738 Poppyseed Ct Clearwater FL 34621-1221 Office: Dynacs Engring 28870 Us Highway 19 N Ste 405 Clearwater FL 34621-2593

BENAVIDES, ADAN, JR., historian; b. Mission, Tex., Dec. 19, 1947; s. Adan and Pilar (Cavazos) B. BA, Loyola U., 1970; MA, U. Tex., 1983. Libr. asst. Benson Latin Am. collection U. Tex., Austin, 1972-74; rsch. historian Tex. Hist. Commn., Austin, 1974; self-employed Austin, 1980—. Compiler, editor: The Bexar Archives: A Name Guide, 1989; contbr. articles to profl. jours. Mem. cmty. adv. bd. Sta. KLRN-TV, San Antonio, 1988-92, pres., 1991-92. U.S. Dept. of Edn. fellow, 1992-94, A.D. Hutchinson fellow, 1994-95, E.D. Farmer fellow, 1994-95. Fellow Tex. Hist. Assn.; mem. Soc. Am. Archivists, Nat. Coalition Ind. Scholars, Soc. Am. Archivists, Southwestern Conf. Latin Am. Studies, Conf. on Latin Am. History. Democrat. Office: U Tex SZB 564 Grad Sch Libr & Info Sci Austin TX 78712-1276

BENAVIDES, FORTUNATO PEDRO (PETE BENAVIDES), federal judge; b. 1947. BBA, U. Houston, 1968, JD, 1972. Atty. Rankin, Kern & Martinez, McAllen, Tex., 1972-74, Cisneros, Beery & Benavides, McAllen, 1974, Cisneros, Brown & Benavides, McAllen, 1975, Cisneros & Benavides, McAllen, 1976; pvt. practice McAllen, 1977; judge Hidalgo County Ct.-at-Law # 2, Edinburg, Tex., 1977-79; prin. Law Offices of Fortunato P. Benavides, McAllen, 1980-81; judge 92nd Dist. Ct. of Hidalgo County, Tex., 1981-84, 13th Ct. Appeals, Corpus Christi, Tex., 1984-91, Tex. Ct. Criminal Appeals, Austin, 1991-92; atty. Atlas & Hall, McAllen, 1993-94; judge U.S. Ct. Appeals (5th cir.), Austin, 1994—; commr. Tex. Juvenile Probation Commn., 1983-89; vis. judge to cts. in Tex., 1993. Active Mex.-Am. Dems. of Tex., 1990-92, Mustangs of Corpus Christi, 1990-91, hon. mem., 1992, St. Michael Episc. Ch., Austin, 1992—. Mem. ABA, State Bar Tex., Hidalgo County Bar Assn. Office: US Ct Appeals 5th cir 903 San Jacinto Blvd Rm 450 Austin TX 78701-2450

BENAVIDES, JAIME MIGUEL, orthopedist; b. Chuquicamata, Chile, Oct. 20, 1923; came to U.S., 1926; s. Jaime and Elena (Spikula) B.; m. Nela Julieta Montejo, May 14, 1947; children: Suzanne Benavides Egle, Maria, Jaime Manuel. AB, Duke U., 1943; MD, U. Pa., 1947. Diplomate Am. Bd. Orthopedic Surgeons. Intern Luth. Hosp., Cleve., 1947-48, resident in surgery, 1948-49; resident in orthopedic surgery U.S. Naval Hosp., Phila., 1953-55; asst. chief orthopedics U.S. Naval Hosp., Newport, R.I., 1955-56; resident in orthopedic surgery Newington (Conn.) Childrens' Hosp., 1957; asst. chief orthopedics U.S. Naval Hosp., Phila., 1958-61; chief of orthopedics, surg. services U.S. Naval Hosp., Key West, Fla., 1961-66; chief of staff Monroe Gen. Hosp., Key West, 1966-70, Fla. Keys Meml. Hosp., Key West, 1971-78; staff physician DePoo Hosp., Key West, 1971-78; staff physician, vice chmn. med. staff Glades Gen. Hosp., Belle Glade, Fla., 1982-83, sec.-treas. med. staff, 1983-84; med. dir. Woodrow Wilson Rehab. Ctr., Fishersville, Va., 1984-86, staff physician, 1986-89; pvt. practice Key West, 1989—; chmn. bd. Lower Fla. Keys Hosp. Tax Dist., 1970-71; bd. dirs. Monroe County Comprehensive Health Planning Council, 1969-75; profl. advisor Easter Seal Soc., Ctr. of Hope in Key West, 1980; profl. adv. com. Fla. Easter Seal Soc.; mem. adv. com. Health Related Occupation Programs Fla. Keys Community Coll., 1972; team physician Key West High Sch., 1966-80, Mary Immaculate High Sch., 1972-80, Key West Conchs Profl. Baseball Team, 1977-80; mem. med. adv. com. Fla. State Dept. Vocat. Rehab., 1980, chmn. med. subcouncil, 1977-78; chmn. regional adv. council Emory U. Research and Tng. Ctr., 1978-84. Bd. dirs., pres. Beachwood Villas Condominium Assn., Stuart, Fla., 1981-84; mem. Mil. Affairs Com. City of Key West, 1980, spl. population adv. bd. Waynesboro (Va.) Dept. Parks and Recreation; lector St. John's Ch., Waynesboro, 1985-87. Named Advisor of Yr. Fla. Easter Seal Soc., 1972. Fellow ACS, Am. Acad. Orthopedic Surgeons; mem. AMA (numerous Recognition awards), Am. Fracture Assn., Am. Coll. Sports Medicine, Soc. Internat. de Chirurgie Orthopedique et Traumatologie, Soc. Latinoam. de Orthopedia y Traumatologia, Physicians for Automotive Safety, Am. Orthopedic Soc. Sports Medicine, Nat. Rehab. Adminstrn. Assn., Am. Congress Rehab. Medicine (Roy Hoover Physician of the Yr. award 1985), So. Orthopedic Assn., Fla. Orthopedic Soc. (program chmn. 1974-75), So. Med. Soc., Navy League (life, pres. Key West council 1979), U.S. Power Squadron, Internat. Oceanographic Found., U.S. Naval Inst., Am. Mgmt. Assn., Va. Rehab. Assn. (bd. dirs. 1985-88). Republican. Roman Catholic. Lodge: Rotary.

BENCINI, SARA HALTIWANGER, concert pianist; b. Winston Salem, N.C., Sept. 2, 1926; d. Robert Sydney and Janie Love (Couch) Haltiwanger; m. Robert Emery Bencini, June 26, 1954; children: Robert Emery, III, Constance Bencini Waller, John McGregor. Mus. B., Salem Coll., 1947; postgrad. grad. Juilliard Sch. Music, 1948-50; M.A., Smith Coll., 1951; D In Mus. Arts, U. N.C., Greensboro, 1989. Head piano dept. Mary Burnham Sch. for Girls, Northampton, Mass., 1949-51; pianist, composer dance and drama dept. Smith Coll., 1951-52; head music dept. Walnut Hill Sch. for Girls, Natick, Mass., 1952-54; pvt. piano tchr., High Point, N.C., 1954-66; concert pianist appearing in Am. and Europe, 1948—; duo-piano performances with PBS-TV, Columbia, S.C., 1967, Winston Salem Symphony, N.C., 1964-68, Ea. Mus. Festival, Greensboro, N.C., 1969. Democrat. Presbyterian.

BENDER, JOHN HENRY, JR. (JACK BENDER), editor, cartoonist; b. Waterloo, Iowa, Mar. 28, 1931; s. John Henry and Wilma (Lowe) B.; divorced; children: Thereza, John Henry IV, Anthony; m. Carole R. Humphrey, 1995. BA, U. Iowa, 1953; MA, U. Mo., 1962; postgrad., Art. Inst. Chgo., 1956, Washington U., St. Louis., 1957. Art dir., asst. editor Commerce Pub. Co., St. Louis, 1953-54, 56-58; editor Florissant Reporter, 1958-61; edit. cartoonist Waterloo Courier, 1962-84, assoc. editor, 1975-83; art. dir., editor Alpha VII Corp., Tulsa, 1984-87; head dept. prodn. art Platt Coll., Tulsa, 1987-92; cartoonist Don Martin Studio, Miami, Fla., 1989-92; cartoonist Alley Oop comic strip United Media Syndicate, N.Y.C., 1991—; sports cartoonist Basketball Weekly, Baseball Digest Mag., U. Iowa, others. Author: Pocket Guide to Judging Springboard Diving, (with Dick Smith) Inside Diving, (with Ed Gagnier) Inside Gymnastics. With USAF, 1954-56, col. USAFR, ret. Recipient Best Editl. award Mo. Press Assn., 1960, Grenville Clark Editl. Page award, 1968, Freedoms Found. award, 1969, 71, 75, Ignatz award Orlandocon, 1992; named to Hall of Fame East H.S., Waterloo, Iowa, 1972. Mem. Assn. Am. Editl. Cartoonists, Nat. Cartoonists Soc., Comic Art Profl. Soc., Sigma Chi. Home: RR 1 Box 540 Terlton OK 74081-9740 Office: 3279 S Cincinnati Rm 472 Tulsa OK 74105

BENDER, JOYCE JACKSON, university English educator; b. Cherokee, Okla., May 28, 1941; d. Erval Earl and Vernon Gertrude (Tullis) Jackson; m. Royce R. Bender, July 24, 1960; children: Lee Ronald Bender, Todd Alan Bender. BA in English Edn., Northwestern Okla. State U., 1973, MEd, 1977; PhD in English, Okla. State U., 1994. Secondary tchr. South Haven (Kans.) H.S., 1973-74, Cherokee (Okla.) H.S., 1974-87; tchg. assoc. Okla. State U., Stillwater, 1989-90; instr. USAO, Chickasha, Okla., 1991-92; asst. prof. Okla. Panhandle State U., Goodwell, Okla., 1993—; adj. instr. Northwestern Okla. State U., Alva, 1990-91, No. Okla. Coll., Tonkawa, 1990-93; faculty cons. Ednl. Testing Svcs., Princeton, 1995—; cons. Okla. Writing Project, Norman, 1983—. Contbr. articles to profl. jours. Speaker Okla. Found. for the Humanities, 1995—. Recipient summer profl. devel. grant Okla. Panhandle State U., Goodwell, 1995. Mem. Nat. Coun. Tchrs. English, MLA, South Ctrl. MLA, Delta Kappa Gamma. Office: Oklahoma Panhandle State U PO Box 430 Goodwell OK 73939

BENDER, NATHAN EDWARD, librarian, archivist; b. Amherst, Ohio, Sept. 29, 1957; s. George Edward and Pauline Ella (Pike) B. BA with distinction in Anthropology, Ohio State U., 1980; MA in Anthropology, U. Wash., 1983; MLS, Kent State U., 1986. Libr. western history collections U. Okla. Librs., Norman, 1986-89; head spl. collections Mont. State U. Librs., Bozeman, 1989-94; head spl. collections, curator W.Va. and regional history collection W.Va. U. Librs., Morgantown, 1994—; dir. Piatt Park Archaeol. Project, Woodsfield, Ohio, 1984-85; mem. W.Va. State Hist. Records, Charleston, 1995—, Mont. Hist. Records Adv. Coun., Helena, 1992-94; reviewer NEH, Washington, 1995. Contbr. articles to profl. jours., chpts. to book. Historian Sweet Pea Festival of the Arts, Bozeman, Mont., 1992-94; advisor Riverfront Mus., Inc., Morgantown, W.Va., 1995—. Grantee US Dept. Edn., 1992-93. Mem. ALA, Soc. Am. Archivists (W.Va. key contact rep. 1996—). Office: WVa U Librs Colson Hall PO Box 6464 Morgantown WV 26506-6464

BENDICKSON, MARCUS J., company executive. Pres. Dynetics, Inc., Ala. Address: Dynetics Inc 1000 Explorer Blvd NW Huntsville AL 35806*

BENEDICT, BARRY ARDEN, dean; b. Wauchula, Fla., Feb. 7, 1942; s. Clifford Allen and Caroline Mae (Watzke) B.; m. Sharon Gail Parker; children: Erin, Beau, Brooke, Mark. BCE, U. Fla., 1965, MS in Engring., 1967, PhD in Civil Engring., 1968. Rsch. assoc. U. Fla., Gainesville, 1968-69, prof., 1980-86; asst. prof. Vanderbilt U., Nashville, 1969-72, assoc. prof., program dir., 1972-75; assoc. prof. Tulane U., New Orleans, 1975-77, U. S.C., Columbia, 1978-80; prof., dept. head La. Tech. U., Ruston, 1986-88, dean., Jack Thigpen prof., 1988—; project dir. La. NSF-EPSCoR, 1989-94; cons. to numerous industries. Contbr. articles to profl. jours. and chpts. to books. Mem. NSPE (gov.-at-large profl. engrs. in edn. divsn.), La. Dept. Econ. Devel., La. Transp. Rsch. Ctr. (vice chair 1993—). Methodist. Home: 2504 Lovers Ln Ruston LA 71270 Office: La Tech U 600 W Arizona BH 201 Ruston LA 71272

BENEDICT, DOROTHY JONES, genealogist, researcher; b. Bronxville, N.Y., Mar. 23, 1916; d. Harry Edwin and Katherine Jones; m. Mark Charles Benedict; children: Ann Benedict Johnson, Sharon Benedict Bash, Gail Benedict Bain, Faye. BA, Goucher Coll., 1938. Statistician E.W. Axe Co., N.Y.C., 1938; with Nat. Labor Rels. Bd., N.Y.C., 1938-39. Leader Girl Scouts of Am., Glastonbury, Conn., 1957-64; creator convalescent homes Sunday mini-svc. Asbury Ch., Glastonbury, 1960-70. Mem. Nat. Soc. Magna Carta Dames, Arts Soc. Orlando Mus., DAR, Delta Delta Delta, Phi Beta Kappa. Methodist. Home: 100 S Interlachen Ave Winter Park FL 32789

BENEPE, VIRGINIA LYNN, medical/surgical and oncological nurse; b. Oak Park, Ill., Mar. 30, 1964; d. Irvin Guy and Marilyn Sherwood (Warner) Goodman; m. John Gregory Benepe, Aug. 30, 1986; 1 child, David Irvin. BSN, Tex. Christian U., 1986. RN, Tex.; cert. chemotherapy therapist, nurse med.-surg. nursing, cert. diabetes educator, gerontology nurse. Staff nurse Breckenridge Hosp., Austin, Tex., 1986-87; staff nurse, relief charge nurse Harris Hosp. Ft. Worth, 1987—. Mem. Am. Diabetes Assn. (bd. dirs. Greater Tarrant County chpt.), Am. Assn. Diabetes Educators (cert.), Tex. Nurses Assn. Home: 3600 Alton Rd Fort Worth TX 76109-2830

BENGE, RAYMOND DOYLE, JR., astronomy educator; b. Houston, Oct. 10, 1961; s. Raymond Doyle and Gladys Jean (Patrick) B. BS, Duke U., 1983; MS, Tex. A&M U., 1988. Teaching asst. Tex. A&M U., College Station, 1984-88; teaching fellow U. N. Tex., Denton, 1988-94; part-time faculty mem. Tarrant County Jr. Coll., Ft. Worth, Tex., 1994—; assoc. faculty mem. Collin County C.C., Plano, Tex., 1994—; adj. faculty mem. Richland Coll., Dallas, 1994—; astronomy lab. coord. Tex. A&M U., College Station, 1986-88; observatory dir. U. N. Tex., Denton, 1991-94; SPICA agt. Harvard-Smithsonian Ctr. for Astrophysics, Cambridge, 1993-95. Author, editor: (lab. manual) Experiments on Stars and the Universe, 1994; contbr. articles to profl. jours. Dorm rep. Baldwin Fedn., Duke U., 1985; organizer pub. observation nights U. N. Tex., Denton, 1991-94. Mem. Am. Astron. Soc., Royal Astron. Soc. Can., Am. Assn. Variable Star Observers. Republican. Office: Richland Coll Evening Divsn Dallas TX 75243-2199

BENHAM, ROBERT, state supreme court justice; m. Nell (Dodson) B.; children: Corey Brevard, Austin Tyler. BS in Polit. Sci. with honors, Tuskegee U.; JD, U. Ga.; LLM, U. Va. Judge Ga. Ct. Appeals, Ga., 1984-89; justice Supreme Ct., State of Ga., Atlanta, 1989—, presiding justice, chief justice; mem. adv. bd. 1st So. Bank. Chmn. Gov.'s Commn. on Drug Awareness and Prevention, State of Ga.; mem. Ga. Hist. Soc.; trustee Fa. Legal Hist. Found.; bd. dirs. Cartersville (Ga.) Devel. Authority, Cartersville-Bartow C. of C.; deacon, former Sunday Sch. supt. The Greater Mt. Olive Bapt. Ch.; notably one of first black individuals elected to a statewide position in the history of Ga. Mem Atlanta Bar Assn. (bd. dirs. jud. sect.), Ga. Bar Found., Lawyers Club Atlanta, Masons, Shriners, Elks. Office: Ga Supreme Ct 507 State Jud Bldg Atlanta GA 30334

BENINI, LORRAINE FRANCIS, fine arts foundation executive, writer; b. Columbus, Ohio, Dec. 25, 1947; d. William Francis and Zuelean (Jeffers) Link; m. Ronald W. Harris, July 17, 1965 (div. 1969); m. Benini, Feb. 14, 1984. BA in Anthropology and Creative Writing, U. South Fla., 1975; MA in Journalism and Communication, U. Fla., 1983. Pres. THEARTFOUNDATION, Hot Springs, Ark., 1986—. Contbr. numerous articles to mags. and newspapers. Dir. Hot Springs Documentary Film Festival, 1993, 94. Recipient John Paul Jones award U. Fla. and Sigma Delta Chi, 1977. Home and Office: 520 Central Ave Hot Springs National Park AR 71901-3556

BENJAMIN, ADELAIDE WISDOM, community volunteer and activist; b. New Orleans, Aug. 23, 1932; d. William Bell and Mary (Freeman) Wisdom; m. Edward Bernard Benjamin Jr., May 11, 1957; children: Edward Wisdom, Mary Dabney, Ann Leith, Stuart Minor. Student, Hollins Coll., 1950-52; BA in English, Newcomb Coll., 1954; JD, Tulane U., 1956; student, Loyola U., New Orleans, 1980-81; grad. extension program Sewanee Theol. Sch., U. South, 1982. Assoc. Wisdom, Stone, Pigman and Benjamin, New Orleans, 1956-58; tchr. ext. courses Tulane U., 1984—; postgrad.; speaker, panelist on school issues various local and nat. groups. Mem. Tulane Law Rev., 1954-56. Pres. bd. New Orleans Symphony, 1984-89; trustee, Mary Freeman Wisdom Charitable Found., sec., 1987-92, pres., 1990-94, treas., 1994—; pres. E&A Charitable Found., New Orleans, 1983—; bd. dirs. Nat. Symphony Orch., Washington, 1992—, RosaMary Charitable Found., New Orleans, 1978—, Loyola Univ., New Orleans, 1989—, mem. exec. com., 1996—, La. Mus. Found. Bd., New Orleans, 1989—, exec. com., 1991—, Children's Hosp., New Orleans, 1976-79, Southeast La. Girl Scouts Coun., New Orleans, 1989—, Louise S. McGehee Sch., New Orleans, 1990—, v.p., 1991—, La. Nature and Sci. Ctr., New Orleans, 1992—, Newcomb Children's Ctr., New Orleans, 1991-94, New Orleans Mus. Art Fellows Forum, 1991—; mem. adv. bd. dept. psychiatry LSU Med. Ctr., 1992—; active Trinity Episc. Ch., New Orleans, sec. parish coun., 1973-75, sec. vestry, 1975-79, leader Trinity Quartet, 1979-84; local YWCA, 1967-75, 76-79, sec. bd. dirs., 1967-68, 1st v.p., 1968-69; trustee Metairie Park Country Day Sch., 1971-79, sec., 1976-79, pres. PTA, 1975-76; mem. Loving Cup selection com. New Orleans Times Picayune, 1985, Bur. Govtl. Rsch.; adv. bd. Pub. Radio Sta. WWNO, 1980—; bd. dirs Parenting Ctr., 1981—, chmn. by-laws com., 1983-84, chmn. pers. com., 1982-83; adv. bd Tulane Summer Lyric Theatre, Tulane U., 1972—, pres. adv. bd., 1977-79. Recipient Weiss Brotherhood award Nat. Conf. Christians and Jews, 1986, Outstanding Philanthropist, Nat. Soc. Fundraising Execs., 1986, Volunteer Activist Award, St. Elizabeth Guild, 1986, Jr. League Sustainer award, 1987, Disting. Alumna award McGehee Sch., 1987, George Washington Honor Medal for Individual Achievement, Freedom Found. at Valley Forge, 1988, Living and Giving award Juvenile Diabetes Found. 1991, Outstanding Citizen New Orleans award La. Colonials, 1994, Jacques Yenni award Outstanding Community Svc. Sch. Bus. Adminstrn. Loyola Univ., 1994, Integritas Vita award for outstanding cmty. svc. Loyola U., 1994; named Goodwill Ambassador for Louisiana Gov.'s Commn. Internat. Trade, Industry and Tourism, 1987, Sweet Art, Contemporary Arts Ctr., 1988, Significant Role Model, Young Leadership Coun., 1988, Woman of Distinction S.E. La. Girl Scout Coun., 1992. Mem. ABA, LWV, La. Bar Assn., New Orleans Bar Assn., Jr. League New Orleans (exec. com. 1971-72, bd. dirs. 1967-72), Ind. Women's Orgn., Com. 21, Am. Symphony Orch. League, Quarante Club (2d v.p. 1978-79), Sybarites Club, Debutante Club, Le Debut des Jeunes Filles Club, New Orleans Town Gardners (pres. 1979-80), Thomas Wolfe Soc. (life mem.). Home: 1837 Palmer Ave New Orleans LA 70118-6215

BENJAMIN, EDWARD BERNARD, JR., lawyer; b. New Orleans, Feb. 11, 1923; s. Edward Bernard and Blanche (Sternberger) B.; m. Adelaide Wisdom, May 11, 1957; children: Edward Wisdom, Mary Dabney, Ann Leith, Stuart Minor. BS, Yale U., 1944; JD, Tulane U., 1952. Bar: La. 1952. Practiced in New Orleans, since 1952; ptnr. Jones, Walker, Waechter, Poitevent, Carrere & Denegre, New Orleans; pres. Am. Coll. Probate Counsel, 1986-87, Internat. Acad. Estate and Trust Law, 1976-78; vice chmn. bd. trustees Southwestern Legal Found., 1986-88, bd. dirs., 1988-90; chmn. bd. Starmount Co., Greensboro, N.C., 1968-88, chmn. emeritus, 1988—. Editor-in-chief Tulane U. Law Rev., 1951-52; mem. editorial bd. Community Property Jour., 1974-89. Trustee Hollins Coll., 1966-87; chancellor Episcopal Diocese of La., 1984—, Trinity Episcopal Ch., New Orleans, 1974-92; mem. adv. bd. CCH Estate & Fin. Planning Svc., 1982-88; chmn. Salavation Army City Commd. Adv. Bd., 1965-68; pres. New Orleans Jr. C. of C., 1953. 1st lt., F.A. pilot, U.S. Army, 1943-46. Mem. Am. Coll. Tax Counsel, Am. Law Inst., ABA (sec. taxation sect. 1967-68, coun. 1976-79, coun. real property, probate and trust law sect. 1978-81), La. Bar Assn. (chmn. taxation sect. 1959-60), La. Law Inst., New Orleans Country Club, Southern Yacht Club, New Orleans Lawn Tennis Club. Home: 1837 Palmer Ave New Orleans LA 70118-6215 Office: Jones Walker Waechter Poitevent Carrere & Denegre 201 Saint Charles Ave Ste 51 New Orleans LA 70170-5100

BENJAMIN, SHEILA PAULETTA, secondary education educator; b. Sept. 28, 1948. AA, Montreat-Anderson Coll., 1966; BA in History, Belhaven Coll., 1968; MEd in History, U. Tampa, 1979. Cert. gifted, social studies and bible tchr. Tchr. Hillsborough H.S., Tampa, Fla., 1980-93; now tchr. Bloomingdale H.S., Valrico, Fla.; clinician tchr. Suncoast Area Tchr. Tng. Honors Program; supervising tchr. Fla. Beginning Tchr. Program; dir. workshops in field. Aviation educator USAF-CAP; vol. Nat. Pks. Svc. 99s-Internat. Women's Pilot Assn. Recipient Photography awards Fla. Strawberry Festival and Hillsborough County Fair; Latin Am. Studies grantee NEH, 1983, African Studies, 1985; Fulbright-Hays scholar in Egypt, 1986, Honduras, 1993. Mem. ASCD, DAR, Nat. Space Soc., Nat. Coun. Social Studies, World Aerospace Edn. Orgn. (U.S. del., Amman, Jordan), Gulf Coast Archeol. Soc., Fla. Alliance for Geography, Fla. Aerospace Edn. Assn. (founding pres.), Fla. Anthrop. Soc. (bd. dirs., Appreciation award, Preservation award), Men of Menendez (Historic Fla. Militia Inc.), Mid. East Educators Network, Hillsborough Classroom Tchr. Assn. (NEA), Hillsborough County/Fla. Social Studies Coun., Young Astronauts, Bibl. Archeol. Soc., Challenger Ctr. Found. (founding sponsor), Fulbright Alumni Asns., Sun-N-Fun EAA, Phi Delta Kappa. Home: 605 Fieldstone Dr Brandon FL 33511-7936 Office: Bloomingdale High Sch 1700 E Bloomingdale Ave Valrico FL 33594

BENN, DOUGLAS FRANK, information technology, computer science executive; b. Detroit, May 8, 1936; s. Frank E. and Madeline (Pond) B.; m. Shirley M. Flanery, July 16, 1955; children—Christopher, Susan, Kathy. BS in Math., Mich. State U., 1960, MA, 1962; cert. data processing (NSF scholar), Milw. Inst. Tech., 1965; postgrad., U. Wis., 1965-66; Ed.Adminstrn., Washington U., 1972; MS in Computer Sci., So. Meth. U., 1982, D of Engring. in Computer Sci., 1990. Tchr. math. and sci. Lansing (Mich.) Public Schs., 1960-64; chmn. computer sci. dept. Kenosha (Wis.) Area Tech. Inst., 1964-67, mgr. data processing, 1965-67; sr. project leader Abbott Labs., North Chicago, Ill., 1967-68, sr. IT cons., 1968-69; dir. data processing div. St. Louis Public Schs., 1969-74; dir. info. systems div. mental health State of Ill., Springfield, 1974-78; dir. data processing div. Med. Computer Systems, Inc., Dallas, 1978; dir. bus. adminstrn. Dallas County Mental Health Center, 1979-80; prof. computer sci. So. Meth. U., Dallas, 1979-82, 89-96; sr. dir. corp. research and devel. Blue Cross & Blue Shield of Tex., Dallas, 1980-83; v.p. mgmt. info. services Western States Adminstrs., Fresno, Calif., 1984-88; pres. D.F. Benn & Assocs. Inc., 1989—; chief info. officer Tex. Natural Resource Conservation Commn., 1996—; prof. Info. Tech. U. Tex., Dallas, 1990-92; lectr. and adv. coun. Great Cities Pub. Sch. Sys., 1969-74; cons. Ill. Med. Soc., 1976-78, Wis. Bd. Vocat. Tech. and Adult Edn., 1964-67; co-dir. mgmt. adv. group Ill. Dept. Mental Health, 1974-78; mem. adv. group Tex. Gov.'s Task on Mental Health, 1980; adj. prof. computer info. sys. Wash. U., 1972-74; expert witness/software appraisal svcs. U.S. Tax Ct., 1995. Contbr. articles on info. techs., engring. mgmt., and software valuation to profl. jours. Arbitrator computer and bus. contract cases, 1976—. Mem. Data Processing Mgmt. Assn., Assn. for Sys. Mgmt. (Disting. Svc. award 1980, Merit award 1976, Achievement award 1978, chpt. pres. 1976-77, dist. dir. 1976-78), Am. Arbitration Assn., Data Processing Mgmt. Assn. (bd. dirs. 1987-89), Am. Soc. Engring. Mgmt. Presbyterian. Home and Office: 6723 Rolling Vista Dr Dallas TX 75248-5436

BENNER, RANDALL RAY, dentist; b. Evansville, Ind., Mar. 3, 1952; s. Melvin Eugene and Joyce Ann (Korb) B.; m. Margaret Austin Moss, June 1, 1974; children: Abby Rae, Ashley Austin. BA in Biol. Scis., Ind. U., 1974; DDS, Ind. U., Indpls., 1978. Gen. practice dentistry Moultrie, Ga., 1978—; mem. governing bd. S.W. Ga. Health Sys. Agy., Albany, 1979-92; pres. hygiene adv. bd. Darton Jr. Coll., 1982; cons. in field. Pres. Camilla C. of C., Ga., 1982. Named Citizen of Yr., Carmilla C. of C., 1981. Fellow Pierre Fauchard Acad., Acad. Gen. Dentistry; mem. ADA, Ga. Dental Assn., Rotary (bd. dirs. Camilla 1978-85), Kiwanis. Office: 1940 S Main St Moultrie GA 31768-6524

BENNETT, BOBBIE JEAN, state commissioner; b. Gwinnett County, Ga., July 13, 1940; d. William Claude and Clara Maude (Nichols) Holcome; BBA magna cum laude, Ga. State U., 1973; 1 child, Terri Lynne. With Ga. State Merit System, Atlanta, 1960—, sr. acct., 1967, asst. div. dir., 1968-70, fiscal officer, 1970-74, div. dir., 1975-78, asst. dep. commr., 1978—, asst. commr., 1985—, dep. commr., 1992, commr 1992. Mem. Ga. Fiscal Mgmt. Coun., Ga. Coun. Pers. Adminstrn., Employers Coun. Flexible Compensation (bd. dirs.), Nat. Assn. Deferred Compensation Adminstrs. (sec., past pres.), Nat. Assn. State Pers. Execs. (past pres.), Ga. Govt. Benefit Assn., Atlanta Govt. Benefit Assn., Atlanta Health Care Alliance, State and Local Govt. Benefit Assn. (past pres.), Internat. Pers. Mgmt. Assn. (past pres. Atlanta chpt.), Internat. Found. on Employee Benefits (past com. mem.), Beta Gamma Sigma, Phi Kappa Phi, Beta Alpha Psi. Democrat. Home: 2072 Malabar Dr NE Atlanta GA 30345-1624 Office: State Merit System 200 Piedmont Ave SE Atlanta GA 30334-9010

BENNETT, CAROLYN L., journalist, writer; b. Augusta, Ga., Feb. 11, 1943; d. Thomas Judson and Laura Lou (Pickett) B. BS in Music Edn., Knoxville Coll., 1964; MMus in Music Edn., DePauw U., 1969; PhD in Curriculum Tchr. Edn., Mich. State U., 1976; MA in Journalism and Pub. Affairs, Am. U., Washington, 1996. Peace corps tchr. Annie Walsh Secondary Sch., Freetown, Sierra Leone, 1964-66; tchr. French and English Boggs Acad. Secondary Sch., Keysville, Ga., 1966-67; tchr., counselor St. Cyril Sch., Detroit, 1969-71; grad. asst., instr. Mich. State U., East Lansing, 1973-76; asst. prof., asst. curriculum reviewer Paine Coll., Augusta, Ga., 1976-77; asst. prof., acad. affairs adminstr. Fayetteville State U., N.C., 1977-79; founding pub., editor Network of N.C. Women, Fayetteville, 1979-81; copyright examiner Libr. of Congress, Washington, 1982—; freelance columnist, Washington corr., 1985—. Author: (books) You Can Struggle Without Hating, 1990, Come Home America, 1991, America's Human Connection, 1992, 94; author, compiler: (manuscript) Writings of Mary McLeod Bethune, 1983. Mem. Nat. Writers Guild, Women's Inst. for Freedom of the Press (assoc.), Internat. Women's Writing Guild, Assn. for Edn. in Journalism and Mass Comm., Washington Ind. Writers, Phi Kappa Phi. Home: 5865 Jacksons Oak Ct Burke VA 22015-2304 Office: Libr of Congress 101 Independence Ave SE Washington DC 20559

BENNETT, CATHERINE JUNE, data processing manager, educator, consultant; b. Augusta, Ga., June 19, 1950; d. Robert Stogner and Catherine Sue (Jordan) Robinson; m. Danny Marvin Bennett, Sept. 5, 1971; children: Timothy Jordan, Robert Daniel. BS in Stats., U. Ga., 1971, MA in Bus., 1973. Programmer William M. Shenkel & Assocs., Athens, Ga., 1971-73; sys. analyst U. Ga., Athens, 1973-76; product cons. ISA/SUNGARD, Atlanta, 1976-78, project leader, 1978-80, mgr. product support, 1980-85, hotline mgr., sr. fin. specialist, 1986-88; mem. edn. staff Investment Client Support, 1988-90, mgr. investment reporting, 1990-91, mgr. reporting, 1991-93, mgr. devel., 1993-95, dir. acctg. products svcs., 1996—. Den leader pack # 419 Cub Scouts, 1989-90, treas., 1990-95; head ofcl. Duluth Thunderbolts,

1994; mem. Gwinnett Swim League (sec. 1995—). Avocations: bridge, swimming, travel. Home: 3604 Berkeley Lake Rd Duluth GA 30136-3008 Office: ISA/SUNGARD 500 Northridge Rd Atlanta GA 30350-3315

BENNETT, CHARLES EDWARD, former congressman, educator; b. Canton, N.Y., Dec. 2, 1910; s. Walter James and Roberta Augusta (Broadhurst) B.; m. Jean Bennett; children: Bruce, James, Lucinda. JD, U. Fla., 1934; HHD (hon.), U. Tampa, 1950; LLD (hon.), Jacksonville U., 1972, Edward Waters Coll., 1988, U. North Fla., 1990; DSc (hon.), Maine Maritime Acad., 1989; LLD (hon.), St. Lawrence U., 1992, U. Fla., 1994. Bar: Fla. 1934. Practiced Jacksonville; mem. Fla. Ho. of Reps., 1941-42; mem. 81st-102d Congresses, 3d Fla. Dist., chair ethics com., mem. armed svcs. com., chmn. seapower subcom.; prof. Jacksonville (Fla.) U., 1992—. Author: Laudonniere and Fort Caroline, 1964, Settlement of Florida, 1968, Southernmost Battlefields of the Revolution, 1970, Three Voyages, 1974, Florida's French Revolution, 1981, Twelve on the River St. Johns, 1989; co-author: Congress and Conscience, 1970, A Quest for Glory, 1991. Capt. AUS, 1942-47; overseas in New Guinea andthe Philippines, including guerrilla fighting in Luzon. Decorated Silver Star, Bronze Star, Philippine Legion of Honor and Gold Cross, 1968, French Legion of Honor, 1976; recipient Disting. Service award Pres.'s Com. on Employment of Handicapped, 1969. Mem. DAV, Am. Legion, VFW, Fla. Bar Assn., Jacksonville Bar Assn., Jacksonville Jr. C. of C. (pres. 1939), U. Fla. Alumni Assn. (pres.). Democrat. Mem. Disciples of Christ Ch. Clubs: Masons, Lions, Rotary. Office: Jacksonville U Dept History Jacksonville FL 32211

BENNETT, ELIZABETH SUSAN, music educator; b. Greenville, S.C., Aug. 24, 1950; d. Clyde Eston and Mae Beatrice (McCrary) B. MusB, Furman U., 1972; M in Ch. Music, So. Bapt. Theol. Seminary, 1974, postgrad., 1975-76. Asst. min. music, organist Pritchard Meml. Bapt. Ch., Charlotte, N.C., 1974-76; tchr. piano and organ Gardner-Webb U., Boiling Springs, N.C., 1976—; organist Pendleton St. Bapt. Ch., Greenville, S.C., 1976, Taylors (S.C.) First Bapt. Ch., 1996—; pvt. practice, 1976—; office and data processing mgr. Cline Co., Greenville, 1977-93; cons. in organ, N.C., S.C., 1976—; soloist and accompanist for various schs. and chs., N.C., S.C., 1974—; travel cons. Linda Long Travel, 1994—. Mem. Am. Guild Organists (sponsor student chpt. 1976—). Home: 126 Sunset Dr Greenville SC 29605-1913 Office: Gardner Webb Univ Music Dept Boiling Springs NC 28017

BENNETT, GERARD PAUL, computer scientist; b. Windsor, Ont., Can., Oct. 31, 1937; came to U.S., 1955; s. Onias and Yvonne (Barnier) B.; m. Patricia Flach, Aug. 30, 1969; 1 child, Douglas Paul. BA in Bus. Mgmt./BA in Computer Info., U. North Tex., 1974. Computer systems programmer The Banks of N.Y., N.Y.C., 1961-67, LTV Electrosystems, Greenville, Tex., 1967-70; software devel. mgr. Cybertek Data Systems, Dallas, 1970-75, Data Gen. Corp., Dallas, 1975-76; computer systems engr. Datapoint Corp., San Antonio, 1976-85; computer rsch. analyst USAA, San Antonio, 1985—. Bd. dirs. Boerne (Tex.) Fine Arts Found., 1985-90; exec. dir. Lordel Inst., Fair Oaks, Tex., 1989-93; sci. fair judge Boerne Ind. Sch. Dist., 1986—; tech. cons. Boerne Pub. Libr., 1989—. Mem. NRA, The Planetary Soc., Nat. Space Soc., Kiwanis of Boerne (v.p., pres. 1978-87, Pres.'s award 1984). Republican. Episcopalian. Home: 146 Steel Valley Dr Boerne TX 78006-7018 Office: USAA Advanced Tech Group 9800 Fredericksburg Rd San Antonio TX 78288-0001

BENNETT, HARRIET COOK, social worker, educator; b. Telfair County, Ga., Aug. 3, 1945; d. Harry A. and Amy H. Cook; B.A., LaGrange (Ga.) Coll., 1967; M.S.W., U. Ga., Athens, 1969; postgrad. Tulane U., 1970; m. Fredrick E. Bennett, Jr., June 6, 1971; children—Amy, Andrew. Med. social reviewer state rev. team, Dept. Family and Children Services, Atlanta, 1969-71; social worker/instr. U. Mo. Med. Center, Columbia, 1971-73; social worker Easter Seal Rehab. Center, Tampa, Fla., 1978-79, Children's Home Society Fla., St. Petersburg, 1984-95; dir. LaPetite Acad., Tampa, 1980, tchr. kindergarten, 1981-84; social worker Hillsborough County Pub. Sch. Sys., 1995—. Vol. cons. Desenzano, Italy, 1976-78; vol. fundraiser Nat. Kidney Found., Arthritis Found. Lic. clin. social worker. Mem. Northdale Civic Assn., Nat. Assn. Social Workers, Acad. Cert. Social Workers, Hillsborough County PTA. Methodist. Home: 16006 Honeysuckle Pl Tampa FL 33624-1723

BENNETT, IVAN STANLEY, school administrator; b. Harrisburg, Pa., Jan. 27, 1949; s. Ivan Frank and Audrey (Poley) B.; student Butler U., 1967-69; BA, Thomas More Coll., 1972; MEd, Xavier U., 1974; m. Susan Lee Elliott, Aug. 3, 1974; children: Jonathan Lee, Jason Charles, Joseph Wesley. Tchr., Covington (Ky.) Ind. Sch. Dist., Job Preparation Ctr., 1973-75; coord. Scott St. Job Preparation Ctr., Covington, 1975-76; mgr.-coord. Greenup St. Job Preparation Ctr., Covington, 1976-77; mgr. Greenup St. Job Preparation Sch., 1977-78; dir. admissions and release No. Ky. State Vocat. Tech. Sch., Covington, 1978-80; sr. counselor Holmes High Sch., Covington, 1980-84; dir. pupil pers./coord. spl. programs Walton-Verona Sch. Dist. (Ky.), 1984-85, asst. prin., 1985-89, dir. pupil pers./coord. spl. programs/dir. spl. edn/svc. dir., 1989-93; br. mgr. chpt. I and II divsn. program resources Office Instrnl. Svcs., Ky. Dept. Edn., Frankfort, 1993-95, branch mgr. sch. of constrn. divsn. facilities mgmt. office dist. support svcs., 1995-96, program cons. I assessment implementation divsn. office of assessment and curriculum svcs., 1996—; mem. tchr. adv. com. Dist. Speakers Bur. Chmn., Com. for Sch. Dropouts, 1974-75; chmn. Alternative Sch. Adv. Com., 1975-76; mem. Juvenile Delinquency Task Force, Ky. Adv. Commn., 1975-76, Regional Council on Substance Abuse, 1975-76, Kenton County Manpower Adv. Com., 1976-77, No. Ky. Adv. and Resources Council for Teenage Parents, 1975-78; den leader Dan Beard council Cub Scouts, 1986-87, cubmaster 1987-88. Cert. tchr. and guidance counselor, Ky., Ohio. Mem. Am. (So. region br. assembly, dir. 1981-84), Ky. (cert. of appreciation; pres. 1980), No. Ky. (cert. of appreciation) personnel and guidance assns., Ky. Assn. Sch. Adminstrs., Ky. Assn. Secondary Sch. Prins. (bd. dirs., vice prin. rep. for Ky. 1988-89, pres. 1992, dir. spl. edn. no. Ky. chpt. 1992), Lambda Chi Alpha. Republican. Lutheran (ch. council 1984-87, 91-92). Home: 6766 Mcville Rd Burlington KY 41005-9675 Office: 500 Mero St Frankfort KY 40601-1957

BENNETT, JAMES PATRICK, healthcare executive, accountant; b. Huntsville, Ala., Oct. 20, 1957; s. Raymond Arthur and Shirley Marie (Breach) B.; m. Marcella Joanne Lakebrink, Sept. 28, 1979; children: Stephanie Erin, James Patrick Jr. BS, U. North Ala., 1979. CPA, Ala. With Ernst & Whinney, Birmingham, Ala., 1979-87, supr., 1983-86, sr. mgr., 1986-87; v.p. fin. Russ Pharms., Inc., Birmingham, 1987-89, v.p. ops., bd. dirs., 1989-91; group v.p. inpatient rehab. ops. HealthSouth Rehab. Corp., Birmingham, 1991-92, pres. inpatient ops., bd. dirs., 1992-95; pres. HealthSouth Rehab. Hosp., 1992-95; pres., COO Healthsouth Corp., Birmingham, 1995—; bd. dirs. Arthritis Found. Ala. chpt. Treas. Shelby Com. of 100, Birmingham, 1987-89; chmn. U. North Ala. Ann. Fund Drive, 1995; chmn. rehab. com. Fedn. Am. Hosps., 1995-96; hon. chmn. Birmingham Multiple Sclerosis Soc., 1996; bd. dirs. Birmingham chpt. Am. Cancer Soc., 1996, Am. Sports Medicine Inst., 1995—. Nominee Leadership Birmingham, 1994, 95; recipient Cmty. Leadership award Multiple Sclerosis Soc., 1994. Mem. AICPA, Ala. Soc. CPAs, Am. Mgmt. Assn., Healthcare Fin. Mgmt. Assn. (regional v.p. 1987-88, Outstanding Mem. 1987), Nat. Assn. Accts., Secession Golf Club, Greystone Golf Club, Shoal Creek Golf Club, Elks. Roman Catholic. Home: 3732 Shady Cove Dr Birmingham AL 35243-2448 Office: Healthsouth Corp Two Perimeter Park S Birmingham AL 35243

BENNETT, JAMES RONALD, secretary of state; b. Red Oak, Iowa, Jan. 3, 1940; s. George T. and Florence B. (Olson) B.; m. Luan Adkins, June 11, 1989; children: Donald B., Tara L.; 1 stepchild, Megan L. Scott. BS, Jacksonville State U., 1961; MA, U. Ala., 1979. Dir. Tannehill Ironworks Hist. State Park, 1990-93; mem. Ala. Ho. of Reps., 1978-83; senator State of Ala., 1983-93, sec. of state, 1993—. Bd. trustees Jacksonville State U. Home: 1600 Shades Park Cove Birmingham AL 35209-5400 Office: PO Box 5616 Montgomery AL 36103-5616

BENNETT, JANET SANDHOFF, physical education educator; b. Goodrich, Mich., Apr. 19, 1951; d. William John and Lucille Marie (Bates) Sandhoff; m. Gerald Alan Bennett; children: Richard Jay Permuy, Julie Lauren Huber, Kaycee Lynn Huber. AA, Manatee Jr. Coll., Bradenton, Fla., 1971; BA in Phys. Edn., U. South Fla., 1973, MA in Adaptive Phys. Edn., 1986. Dir. presch., tchr. Bayshore Reform Ch., Bradenton, 1983-86; tchr. gifted Bradenton Christian Sch., 1985-86; tchr. phys. edn. Harlee Mid. Sch., Bradenton, 1986-87; perceptual motor specialist Snitz Products, Bradenton, 1875-89; owner, dir., tchr. Jungle Gym, Mt. Pleasant, S.C., 1987-90; instr. Parent Workshops, Charleston, S.C., 1987—; owner, tchr. Jumpnastics, Charleston, 1987—, also bd. dirs., 1990—. Author: (book and tape) 5 and 10 You Can Do It Again, 1986; producer movement edn. movie, 1974. Mem. Nat. Phys. Edn. Assn., Nat. Assn. Parents and Tchrs. Children Under Six. Republican. Home: 2047 Hallahan Ct Mount Pleasant SC 29464-6250

BENNETT, JAY BRETT, medical equipment company executive; b. Durham, N.C., Dec. 13, 1961; s. James Leonard Jr. and Yoalder Kathleen (Brunson) B.; m. Trisha Helen Folds, Feb. 3, 1990; children: Lydia Helen, William Chisholm. BA in Econs., Wake Forest U., 1984; M Health Adminstrn., Duke U., 1986. Sr. cons. Ernst and Whinney (now Ernst and Young), Charlotte, N.C., 1986-89; assoc. dir. strategic planning SSI Med. Svcs., Inc., Charleston, S.C., 1989-92, dir. strategic planning, 1992-94; dir. planning and bus. devel. Hill-Rom, Inc., Charleston, S.C., 1994-96, dir. therapeutic products & svcs., 1996—; adj. prof. bus. and econs. Coll. Charleston, 1995—. Mem. alumni coun. Fuqua Sch. Bus., Duke U. Mem. Am. Coll. Healthcare Execs., Nat. Trust for Historic Preservation, Am. Hosp. Assn., Soc. for Healthcare Planning and Mktg., Nat. Soc. SAR, Ducks Unltd., Quail Unltd., Trout Unltd.

BENNETT, JOAN WENNSTROM, biology educator; b. Bklyn., Sept. 15, 1942; d. John Anton and Kerttu L. (Jonnson) Wennstrom; m. David L. Peterson; 3 children. BS, Upsala Coll., 1963; MS, U. Chgo., 1964, PhD, 1967; Litt.D (hon.), Upsala Coll., 1990. NSF postdoctoral rsch. assoc. U. Chgo., 1967-68; NRC rsch. assoc. So. Reg. Rsch. Labs., New Orleans, 1968-70; NSF postdoctoral rsch. assoc. Tulane U., New Orleans, 1970-71, asst. prof. biology, 1971-76, assoc. prof. biology, 1976-81, prof. biology, 1981-89, prof. cell and molecular biology, 1991—; adj. prof. pathology Tunlane U., 1982—; bd. dirs. Nat. Found. Infectious Disease, 1991-95; vis. scientist dept. plant molecular biology Leiden (The Netherlands) U., 1991-92; NRC postdoctoral fellow So. Regional Rsch. Lab., 1968-70, collaborator, 1982—. Editor: (with K.I. Abroms) Genetics and Exceptional Children, 1981, (with A. Giegler) Differentiation and Secondary Metabolism in Fungi, 1983, (with L. Lasure) Gene Manipulations in Fungi, 1985, More Gene Manipulations in Fungi, 1991; editl. bd. Mycol. Rsch., 1991-94, Applied and Environ. Microbiolgoy, 1978-85, Proceedings of the VIth Internat. Fermentation Symposium, 1980, Jour. Indsl. Microbiology, 1985-89, Mycopathologia, 1984-94, Applied Microbiology and Biotechnology, 1985-94, Ann. Rev. Microbiology, 1996—; contbr. articles to profl. jours. Bd. dirs. Newcomb Found., 1988-89. Recipient Mortar Board award of excellence in Teaching, 1974-75, Cert. of award Greater New Orleans Assn. Retarded Citizens, 1980, others; named Honors Prof. of Yr., Tulane U., 1991; Danforth Assoc. fellow, 1977-83; Hutchinson fellow U. Chgo., 1963-64. Fellow Soc. for Indsl. Microbiology (bd. dirs. 1986-89); mem. AAAS, Am. Soc. Microbiology (pres. 1990-91, lectr., vice-chmn. conf. on biotech. 1986, chmn. 1987), Brit. Mycol. Soc. (v.p. 1988-89), La. Acad. Sci., Mycol. Soc. Am., Soc. for Gen. Microbiology, Czech Microbiology Soc. (hon.), Torrey Bot. Club, Sigma Xi (pres. Tulane chpt. 1986-89). Office: Tulane Univ Dept Cell Molecular Biology New Orleans LA 70118

BENNETT, LOIS, real estate broker; b. N.Y.C., Dec. 23, 1933; d. Richard and Fern (Steinberg) B.; m. Barry Silverstein, June 8, 1958 (div. May 1978); children: Mark Shale, Susan Beth, Thomas Benjamin. BA, Smith Coll., 1955. Cert. residential specialist, broker/salesman, Fla. Counselor Women's Health Ctr., Sarasota, Fla., 1977-78; investment counselor, stockbroker Pvt. Bourse Inc., Sarasota, 1978-79; realtor-assoc. Harrison Properties, Inc., Sarasota, 1984-86; broker/salesman Mt. Vernon Realty Co., Inc., Sarasota, 1986-91; broker-salesman Re/Max Properties, Sarasota, 1991-96. Bd. dirs. Planned Parenthood S.W. Fla., Sarasota, 1978-84, fundraising chmn., 1982-84; bd. dirs. Family Counseling Ctr., Sarasota, 1978-81, 90, Sarasota County Arts Coun.; mem. exec. com., bd. dirs. Fla. West Coast Symphony, Sarasota, 1982-88; chmn. spl. events 1st ann. Sarasota French Film Festival, 1989, co-chmn. spl. events, 1990; bd. dirs. Asolo Performing Arts Ctr., Sarasota, 1990-95; bd. dirs. Sarasota French Film Festival, 1989-94; mem. film commn. Com. of 100, 1989-92; chmn. Sarasota County Arts Day, 1994-95. Mem. Women's Coun. Realtors, Realtors Inst. (grad.), Re/Max 100% Club, Sarasota C. of C. Office: Michael Saunders & Co 1801 Main St Sarasota FL 34236

BENNETT, MARSHALL GOODLOE, JR., state official, lawyer; b. Lexington, Miss., Dec. 25, 1943; s. Marshall G. and Tavia (Childress) B.; m. Shirley Shelton, July 15, 1963; children—Steven, Elizabeth, Russell. B.A., U. Miss., 1965, J.D., 1967. Bar: Miss. 1967, U.S. Supreme Ct. 1971. Exec. dir. Miss. Crime Commn., Jackson, 1967-68; asst. atty. gen. State of Miss., Jackson, 1970-72, 74-79; asst. dist. atty. 7th Dist., State of Miss., Jackson, 1972-74; adminstrv. asst. to gov. State of Miss., Jackson, 1980-81; chmn., commr. Miss. Workmen's Compensation Commn., Jackson, 1981-87, elected state treas., 1987—; ptnr. Peters, Royals, Bennett, & Jackson, 1972-74. Chmn. Miss. Spl. Task Force on Econ. Devel.; chmn. bd. trustees Pub. Employees Ret. System; Pres. Nat. Soc. Prevent Blindness, Jackson, 1984-85, So. Workers Compensation Adminstrs., Atlanta, 1984; treas., bd. dirs. State YMCA, Jackson, 1980; bd. dirs. Community Trust Found. Miss., Jackson, 1985. Served to capt. U.S. Army, 1968-70. Mem. Miss. State Bar Assn., So. Treas.'s Assn. (chmn. 1990), Nat. Assn. State Auditors, Comptrs., Treas. (exec. com. 1989-90, v.p.), Jackson Young Lawyers Assn. (sec. 1972), N.J. Assn. State Treas. (pres.). Democrat. United Methodist. Home: PO Box 421 Jackson MS 39205-0421 Office: Treasury Dept PO Box 138 Jackson MS 39205-0138

BENNETT, MARY See THOMPSON, DIDI CASTLE

BENNETT, MICHELE MARGULIS, women's health nurse; b. Oakland, Calif., Mar. 16, 1962; d. Frank and Rosalyn Barbara (Danneman) Margulis; m. Dennis Kerry Bennett, Jan. 1, 1991 (div. Jan. 12, 1995); 1 child, Caitlyn Anne. BA, U. Fla., 1984; BSN, Fla. Internat. U., 1990. Cert. childbirth educator. Staff nurse maternity Lyster Army Cmty. Hosp., Ft. Rucker, Ala., 1991-94; clin. staff nurse maternity Darnall Army Cmty. Hosp., Ft. Hood, Tex., 1994-96; clinical staff nurse WOMACK Med. Ctr., Ft. Bragg, N.C., 1996—; mem. jr. officer coun. Ft. Hood, 1994-96. Capt. U.S. Army, 1984—. Mem. AWHONN. Republican. Jewish.

BENNETT, PAUL HENRY, business consultant; b. Cleve., Oct. 4, 1915; s. Arthur H. and Minnie M. (Rudolph) B.; m. Sarah I. Neff, Nov. 1, 1947. BA, Ohio Wesleyan U., 1938; postgrad., Northeastern U., 1942-43, Cleve. State U., 1945-46. Salesman Dobeckmun Co., Cleve., 1938-41, Phila., 1946-52; div. sales mgr. Dobeckmun Co., Atlanta, 1952-56; dir. sales tng. and selection Dow Chem. Co., Cleve., 1956-60, asst. gen. sales mgr., 1960-63, indsl. rels. mgr., 1964-75, div. mgr. employee rels., 1975-79; pvt. bus. cons. Bennett Assocs., Palm Beach, Fla., 1979—. Capt. United Appeal, Cleve., 1970-78; mem. Rocky River (Ohio) Mayor's Cabinet on Downtown Reconstrn., 1968-69; active mem. town of Palm Beach pub. employees rels. commn.; active Boy Scouts Am., YMCA; docent Henry Flagler Mus., Palm Beach; past pres. Henry Flagler Guides Assn. With USCG, 1942-46, ETO. Mem. Am. Assn. Pers. Mgrs., Greater Cleve. Growth Assn., Am. Assn. Ret. Persons, Hist. Soc. Cleve., Preservation Soc. Palm Beach, Palm Beach Civic Opera, VFW (life), Flagler Museum (life), Cleve. Yachting Club, Masons (32d degree), Shriners (past pres. Boynton Beach Shrine Club), Phi Delta Theta (past pres.), Alumni Club Palm Beach, Poinciana Club of Palm Beach. Republican. Mem. United Ch. of Christ. Home: 2778 S Ocean Blvd Apt S-305 Palm Beach FL 33480

BENNETT, RODNEY DEE, music educator; b. Wichita Falls, Tex., Mar. 7, 1958; s. Vernon Clifton and Beulah Lee (Johnson) B.; m. Marilyn K. Spencer, Aug. 15, 1980; 1 child, Ronald David. MusB, Midwestern State U., 1982, B of Music Edn., 1982. All-level music cert., Tex. Field musician USMC, Camp Pendleton, Calif., 1976-78; equipment mgr. Midwestern State Univ. Band, Wichita Falls, Tex., 1978-82; dir. bands Munday (Tex.) Ind. Sch. Dist., 1983—; pvt. music tchr., Wichita Falls, 1980—; music adjudicator Tex. Music Adjudication Assn., Pleasanton, Tex., 1991—. Named Citizen of Yr., Munday C. of C., 1993. Mem. Assn. Tex. Small Bands, Tex. Music Educators Assn. (region II band chmn. 1994—, Leadership and Achievement award 1994, Honor Condr.-Honor Band 1994), Nat. Band Assn. (Citation of Excellence 1993), Am. Sch. Band Dirs. Assn., Phi Beta Mu. Baptist. Home: PO Box 776 Munday TX 76371-0776 Office: Munday Ind Sch Dist PO Box 300 Munday TX 76371-0300

BENNETT, TANYA ULANDA, bank officer; b. Bronx, N.Y., June 2, 1968; d. Charles Alfred and Evelyn (Prater) B. BA, U. S. Fla., 1990. Merchant rels. rep. Telecredit, Tampa, Fl., 1990-91; acct. rep. Chase Bankcard Svcs., Tampa, Fl., 1991-93, Chase Manhattan Mortgage, Tampa, 1993-94; office asst. U. S. Fla., Tampa, 1994-95; team leader, supr. First Am. Bank, Nashville, Tenn., 1995—; vol. Time Warner, Tampa, 1994; vol., mentor Vanderbilt U., Nashville, 1996. Vol. March of Dimes. Mem. Zeta Phi Beta (grammateurs 1994, undergrad. adv. asst. 1995, treas. 1996—). Baptist. Home: 233 River Oak Cove Nashville TN 37214 Office: First Am Bank 550 Metroplex Dr Nashville TN 37211-3133

BENNETT, TONI ZIMMER, special education educator; b. Rochester, N.Y., Feb. 25, 1945; d. Joseph Austin and Gladys Lucille (Wood) Zimmer; m. cArlton Neil Bennett, Dec. 14, 1963; children: Shannon Dale, Neil Lee. BA, Northwestern U., 1966, MEd, 1971, EdS, 1984. Cert. elem. educator, spl. educator, adminstr., supr., assessor. Asst. adminstr. Natchitoches (La.) Head Start, 1966; spl. edn. tchr. Parish Sch. System, Natchitoches, 1966-72; spl. edn. tchr. Northwestern State U., Natchitoches, 1972-79, adj. faculty, 1972—; pupil appraisal supr. La. Dept. Edn., Baton Rouge, 1979-82; pupil appraisal coord. Parish Sch. System, Natchitoches, 1982-88, prin., 1988-90; spl. edn. coord. La. Dept. Edn., Baton Rouge, 1990—; ednl. assessment diagnostician Parish Sch. Sys., Sabine, 1992-93; project dir., inclusive edn. tchr. tng. grant Northwestern State U., Natchitocles, 1993-94; personnel evaluation/prof. accountability regional coord. L.A. Dept Edn., Baton Rouge, 1994—; cons. in field. Author: Programming Basic Curriculum Skills, 1987; field test cons. (test) Inventory of BAsic Arthmetic Skills, 1983, Individual Evaluation Procedures in Reading, 1983. Named Edn. Assessment Pilot Program Participant, La. Dept. Edn., 1979, La. Ednl. Assessment Tchr. of Yr., 1992. Mem. Natchitoches Assn. Retarded Citizens (bd. dirs. 1986-90, v.p. 1987-88, pres. 1988-90), La. Ednl. Diagnosticians (state treas. 1983-90), La. Coun. for Mental Retardation (state treas. 1982-84), La. Ednl. Assessment Tchrs., Coun. for Exceptional Children (La. Fedn. chair Yes I Can), Phi Delta Kappa. Baptist. Home: 528 Stephens Ave Natchitoches LA 71457-6033 Office: La Dept Edn Baton Rouge LA 70804

BENNETT, VALERIE WELCH, museum curator; b. Sioux City, Iowa, Nov. 12, 1952; d. John and Dorothy (Newell) Welch; m. Barry Lee Bennett, Mar. 24, 1990; children: Meredith, Laurel. BA in Applied Design and Visual Art, U. Houston, 1989; ed. Winedale Mus. Seminar, U. Tex. Hist. Commn., 1990. Registrar archives The Battleship Tex., Tex. Pks. and Wildlife Dept., LaPorte, Tex., 1987-89; curator O. Henry Mus., City of Austin, Tex., 1989—; com. mem. Sixth St. Restoration, Austin, 1991-93; speaker Tex. Hist. Comm. Preservation, Austin, 1993. Judge for Tex. Jr. Historians, Tex. State Hist. Assn., Austin, 1992, 93, Violet Crown Book Award-Austin Writers League, 1994. Grantee Tex. Com. for the Humanities, 1992, Austin Hist. Landmark Commn., 1992, 93; recipient Tex. Hist. Commn. award for mus. excellence in edn. programs, 1993. Mem. AAUW, Am. Assn. State and Local History, Tex. Assn. Mus. (Wilder Graphic Design award 1993, 94), Nat. Trust for Hist. Preservation, Freedoms Found. (pres. 1994-96), PEO Philanthropic Edn. Orgn. Methodist. Home: 8500 Dorotha Ct Austin TX 78759-8111

BENNETT, VERNA GREEN, employee relations executive; b. Memphis, Oct. 4, 1942; d. Agee and Philistine Louvenia (Jackson) Green; m. John Paul Bennett, Sept. 24, 1966 (div. Dec. 3, 1978). BS in Bus. Edn., Knoxville Coll., 1965. Tchr. Stevens Lee High Sch., Asheville, N.C., 1965-66; adminstr. external affairs Youth in Action, Bklyn., 1966-67; adminstr. cmty. rels., pub. rels. Pepsi Cola Co., N.Y.C., 1967-70; staff asst., coll. rels. coord., hdqrs. recruiter Mobil Corp., N.Y.C., 1970-80; western region recruiter Mobil Corp., L.A., 1980-87; EEO rels. mgr. Mobil Corp., Fairfax, Va., 1987-96; head ednl. non-profit orgn. CCDM Inc., Dallas, 1996—; mem. corp. adv. bd. Nat. Assn. Minority Engr. Adminstrs., Fla., 1980-96, Am. Indian Sci. and Engring., Boulder, 1990-96, NAACP ACTSO, Balt., 1989-96; motivational spkr., lectr. on recruitment. Pres. New Dominion chpt. Nat. Coalition of 100 Black Women, 1992-96, chmn. chpt. devel. com., nat. bd. dirs., 1993-96; commr. Nat. Com. Working Women, Washington, 1990-94; chmn. bd. Coun. on Career Devel. for Minorities, Dallas, 1986-96, exec. dir. elect, 1997—; mem. No. Va. Urban League, Alexandria, 1990-96. Recipient Presdl. Achievement and Nat. Amigo of Yr. awards SER-Jobs for Progress, Dallas, 1988, 89, 90, 94, Donald H. McGannon award Nat. Urban League, N.Y.C., 1992, youth award Delta Sigma Theta, 1992. Mem. NAACP (life), Bus. and Profl. Women (corp. adv. resource devel. 1992-96). Home: 8017 N MacArthur Blvd #1063 Irving TX 75063 Office: CCDM Inc Ste 710E 1341 W Mockingbird Ln Dallas TX 75247

BENNETT, WILLIAM LEO, JR., management consultant; b. Bklyn., Nov. 7, 1921; s. William L. and Anna Christine (Lawless) B.; m. Mary Louise Short, Aug. 18, 1948 (div. 1971); children: Mary Christine Bennett Cooke, Elizabeth Nancy Bennett Payne (dec.), Susan Laura Bennett Smith, William Leo III; m. Mary-Louise Aspinwall, Nov. 23, 1972; children: Lucy Knapp Richardson, Molly Knapp Gloss, John F. Knapp, Jr. BS in Naval Sci., U.S. Navl Acad., 1943; postgrad., Test Pilot Sch., 1950, Armed Forces Staff Coll., 1954. Commd. ensign USN, 1943, advanced through grades to capt., ret., 1972; project mgr. ENSCO, Inc., Springfield, Va., 1972-76; dir. quality div. Nat. R.R. Passenger Corp., Washington, 1976-81; v.p. ops. Intertek Svcs. Corp., Fairfax, Va., 1981-88; pvt. practice cons. Falls Church, Va., 1988-94. Mem. Fairfax County Rep. Com., 1981-84. Decorated Legion of Merit. Mem. Early and Pioneer Naval Aviators Assn., Am. Soc. Quality Control, Am. Helicopter Soc., The Retired Officers Assn., Am. Assn. Ret. Persons, U.S. Naval Acad. Alumni Assn., U.S. Naval Acad. Athletic Assn., USS Yorktown Assn. and Found. (v.p., bd. dirs.), Army-Navy Country Club. Episcopalian. Home: 46910 Grissom St Sterling VA 20165

BENNINGER, CHARLES OLIN, nurse, healthcare administrator; b. Meshoppen, Pa., Dec. 30, 1952; s. Harold J. and E. Virginia (Rosengrant) B.; m. L. Jeanne Horton, May 30, 1975; children: Michael, Nathaniel, Joshua. AA, Pa. State U., Wilkes Barre, 1972; ASN, Memphis State U., 1979; BSN, U. South Ala., 1981; MSN, U. S.C., 1983; MHA, Baylor U., 1993. Staff RN emergency Mobile (Ala.) Infirmary; instr. staff devel. div. of nursing Bob Jones U.; head RN staff edn. command edn. and tng. dept. Naval Hosp., Beaufort, S.C.; asst. charge nurse med.-surg. ward Naval Hosp. Guam, FPO San Francisco, charge nurse alcohol rehab. unit; div. officer internal medicine Primary Care Clinic; Baylor U. adminstrn. resident Nat. Naval Med. Ctr., Bethesda, Md., 1992-93; nursing svc. adminstr. Naval Hosp., Charleston, S.C., 1993-94, head alt. healthcare dept., 1994—. Lt. comdr. Nurse Corps, USN, 1992—. Mem. Am. Coll. Health Care Exec. (assoc.). Home: 201 Shaftesburg Ln Summerville SC 29485-8522

BENNINGER, EDWARD C., JR., petroleum and natural gas company executive; b. 1942. BBA, Tex. Tech U., 1965. Mgmt. trainee West Tex. Utilities, 1965-66; sr. auditor Haskins & Sells, 1969-75; asst. v.p. internat. audit Lo Vaca Gathering Co., 1975-77, v.p. treasury svcs., 1977-79; treas. Valero Energy Corp., San Antonio, 1979-83, v.p. corp. financing, 1983-85, v.p., treas., 1985-86, sr. v.p., treas., 1986-92, bd. dirs., 1990—, exec. v.p., CFO, 1992—; exec. v.p. Valero Energy Co., 1992—; pres. Valero Natural Gas, L.P. Cos., 1992—, exec. v.p., COO, bd. dirs., 1992—, exec. v.p. fin. and adminstrn., 1995-96; exec. v.p., CFO Valero Energy Corp., San Antonio, Tex., 1996—. Served to lt. (j.g.) USN, 1966-69. Office: Valero Energy Corp 530 McCullough Ave San Antonio TX 78215

BENNISON, ALLAN PARNELL, geological consultant; b. Stockton, Calif., Mar. 8, 1918; s. Ellis Norman Lambly and Cora Mae (Parnell) B.; m. DeLeo Smith, Sept. 4, 1941; children: Victor, Christina, Mary. BA, U. Calif., Berkeley, 1940. Cert. petroleum geologist, cert. profl. geologist. Geology fellow Antioch Coll., Yellow Springs, Ohio, 1940-42; photogrammetrist U.S. Geol. Survey, Arlington, Va., 1942-45; stratigrapher, asst. chief geologist Companias Unidas de Petroleos, Cartagena, Colombia, 1945-49; staff stratigrapher Sinclair Oil & Gas Co., Tulsa, 1949-69; geol. cons. Tulsa, 1969—; cons. in field. Editor: Tulsa's Physical Environment, 1973; compiler maps; contbr. articles to profl. jours. Fellow AAAS, Geol. Soc. Am., Explorers Club; mem. Am. Assn. Petroleum Geologists (trustee assoc., Disting. Svc. award 1986), Soc. Econ. Paleontologists and Mineralogists (Disting. Svc. award 1990), Tulsa Geol. Soc. (pres. 1965), Tulsa Astronomy Club (v.p. 1965), Sigma Xi. Republican. Episcopalian. Home: 1410 Terrace Dr Tulsa OK 74104-4626 Office: 125 W 15th St # 401 Tulsa OK 74119-3810

BENOIT, JOYCE DIFFORD, school system administrator; b. Warren, Ohio, July 16, 1945; d. Alfred S. and Cleda J. (Shepherd) Difford; m. Thomas J. Adams, Aug. 9, 1969 (div. 1987); m. Patrick L. Benoit, Mar. 25, 1989. BS, Kent State U., 1966; MEd, U. Md., 1974; PhD, N.Mex. State U., 1990. Registered profl. ednl. diagnostician. Tchr. Warren (Ohio) City Schs., 1966-68, Dept. of Def. Schs., Dexheim, Fed. Republic Germany, 1968-69, Town and Country Day Sch., Wheaton, Md., 1969-70; spl. edn. tchr. Anne Arundel Pub. Schs., Annapolis, Md., 1970-72, Fairfax (Va.) County Pub. Schs., 1972-73, El Paso (Tex.) Ind. Sch. Dist., 1973-76, 1976-82, ednl. diagnostician, systemwide testing coord., 1982-91; evaluation specialist Dallas Ind. Sch. Dist., 1991-93; pres., CEO Info Insights Cons., Inc., 1991-94; dir. systemwide testing Dallas Ind. Sch. Dist., 1993—; cons., owner Future Thoughts, 1990-91. Mem. NEA, ASCD, Nat. Assn. Test Dirs., Nat. Coun. on Measurement in Edn., Tex. Assn. Ednl. Diagnosticians. Home: 10554 Cox Ln Dallas TX 75229-5209 Office: Dallas Ind Sch Dist 3801 Herschel Ave Dallas TX 75219-2927

BENOIT, PAUL HARLAND, geologist; b. Blacksburg, Va., Sept. 13, 1964; s. Robert Edward and Jeannine Rita (Lebeau) B.; m. Janice Marie Balog, Apr. 9, 1994. BS, Va. Poly. Inst. and State U., 1985; MS, Lehigh U., 1987, PhD, 1990. Rsch. asst. Lehigh U., Bethlehem, Pa., 1985-87, teaching asst., 1987-90; rsch. assoc. U. Ark., Fayetteville, 1990-95, asst. rsch. prof., 1996—. Contbr. articles to profl. jours. Grantee NSF, 1991. Mem. Am. Geophys. Soc., Mineralogical Soc. of Am., Meteoritical Soc. Office: U Arkansas Dept of Chemistry and Biochemistry Fayetteville AR 72701

BENSMAN, CHARLES J., academic administrator; b. Celina, Ohio, Sept. 4, 1933; s. Ralph Louis and Mary Alice (Athey) B.; m. Virginia Lee Schulte, May 2, 1959; children: Andy, Julie, Joseph. BS, U. Dayton, 1959, MS, 1962; DEd, Ball State U., 1969. Asst. dir. admissions U. Dayton, Ohio, 1962-64; supt. Auglaize-Mercer Joint Vocat. Schs. and Marion Local Sch. Dist., Ohio, 1964-70; dean. acad. student services West Shore Community Coll., Scottville, Mich., 1970-74; pres. Nebr. Western Coll., Scottsbluff, 1974-76; v.p. mktg. The Speicher Corp., Celina, Ohio, 1976-77; pres. Briar Cliff Coll., Sioux City, Iowa, 1977-86, Thomas More Coll., Crestview Hills, Ky., 1976—. Bd. dirs. Bicentennial Commn., Cin., 1987—; Nat. Cath. Com. on Scouting, 1987—. Served to staff sgt. U.S. Army, 1951-55. Scholar Cin. Archidocese, 1957-59; fellow Ball State U. Mem. Assn. Cathl. Colls. and Univs., Council of Ind. Colls. (bd. dirs.), Ky. Ind. Coll. Fund (bd. dirs.), Council of Ind. Ky. Colls. and Univs. (bd. dirs.), No. Ky. C. of C. (bd. dirs. 1987). Republican. Roman Catholic. Clubs: Summit Hills Country (Crestview Hills; Bankers (Cin.). Lodge: Rotary. Office: Thomas More Coll Office of President Covington KY 41017

BENSON, BETTY JONES, school system administrator; b. Barrow County, Ga., Jan. 11, 1928; d. George C. and Bertha (Mobley) Jones; m. George T. Benson; children: George Steven, Elizabeth Gayle, James Claud, Robert Benjamin. BS in Edn., N. Ga. U., Dahlonega, 1958; MEd in Curriculum and Supervision, U. Ga., Athens, 1968, edn. specialist in Curriculum and Supervision, 1970. Tchr. Forsyth County (Ga.) Bd. Edn., Cumming, 1956-66, curriculum dir., 1966—; asst. supt. for instrn. Forsyth County Schs., 1981—. Active Alpine Ctr. for Disturbed Children; chmn. Ga. Lake Lanier Island Authority; mem. North Ga. Coll. Edn. Adv. Com., Ga. Textbook Com.; adv. Boy Scouts; Sunday sch. tchr. 1st Baptist Ch. Cumming; active Forsyth County Substance Abuse Commn., Forsyth County Drug Task Force, Forsyth County Vision 20/20 Com., Forsyth County Drug Commn., Forsyth County Interagency Council for Children and Youth, Forsyth County Health Bd., local coord. council Family and Children Svcs., Blue Ridge Cir. Ct.-Cherokee/Forsyth County Domestic Violence Task Force. Mem. NEA, Ga. Assn. Educators (bd. dir.), ASCD, Ga. Assn. Supervision and Curriculum Devel. (pres.), Assn. Childhood Edn. Internat., Bus. and Profl. Women's Club, Internat. Platform Assn., Ga. Future Tchrs. Adv. Assn. (pres.), Profl. Assn. Ga. Educators, Ga. Assn. Ednl. Leaders (dir.), HeadStart Dirs. Assn., Forsyth County Hist. Soc., Sawnee Mountain Community Ctr. Assn., Ga. Cumming/Forsyth County C. of C. (mem. edn. com.), Mountain Local Coord. Coun. Home: 1235 Dahlonega Hwy Cumming GA 30130-4525 Office: 101 School St Cumming GA 30130-2427

BENSON, BRIAN JOSEPH, English language educator, author; b. San Diego, Calif., Aug. 6, 1941; s. Harry Land and Maude Frances (Walker) B.; m. Heli Koppel, 1993; 1 child, Eleanor Blair. BA, Guilford Coll., 1964; MA, U. N.C., Greensboro, 1967; PhD, U. S.C., 1972. Tchr. English Page High Sch., Greensboro, 1966-67; instr. English A&T State U., Greensboro, 1968-69, assoc. prof., 1972-76, prof., 1977—; writing cons. Magic Gardens Landscape Co., Greensboro, 1988-91. Co-author: Jean Toomer, 1980; asst. (Keneth Kinnamon, editor) A Richard Wright Bibliography, 1990; contbr. articles to profl. jours. Bd. dirs. Creative Renewal Inc., Greensboro, 1986-89. NDEA fellow, 1969; grantee NEH, 1974, N.C. Humanities Coun., 1982, 83. Mem. N.C. Writers Network. Home: 607 Northridge St Greensboro NC 27403-2106 Office: A&T State U 1601 E Market St Greensboro NC 27401-3209

BENSON, KAARON, physician, pathology educator; b. Phila., June 5, 1958; d. Bernard Edward and Doris Lee (Gordon) B.; m. Dan Carl Petrick, May 10, 1986; children: Sara, Marisa. BS, Ursinus Coll., 1979; MD, Med. Coll. Pa., 1983. Diplomate clin. pathology blood banking/transfusion medicine Am. Bd. Pathology. Asst. med. dir. Blood Svcs. of ARC, L.A., 1988-89; asst. prof. Coll. of Medicine U. South Fla., Tampa, 1989-96, assoc. prof., 1996—; asst. med. dir. Fla. Blood Svcs. Inc., Tampa, 1993—; expert witness Fla. Dept. Profl. Regulation, Tallahassee, 1992—; inspector Am. Assn. Blood Banks, Bethesda, Md., 1991—. Recipient Patterson Rsch. award James Patterson Rsch. Fund, Tampa, 1992. Mem. Am. Assn. Blood Banks, Fla. Assn. Blood Banks (bd. dirs. 1992—). Office: H Lee Moffitt Cancer Ctr 12902 Magnolia Dr Tampa FL 33612-9416

BENSON, KIMBERLY LEGGETT, elementary education educator; b. Fayetteville, N.C., May 17, 1960; d. Jerry DeWitt and Helen Carthage (Henson) Leggett; m. Raymond Benjamin Benson Jr., Sept. 28, 1991; children: Tammy Rénee Benson Jett, Kimberly Dawn, Christopher Shannon, Matthew Ray. B of Music Edn., Meredith Coll., 1982; MA in Edn., Coll. William and Mary, 1994. Cert. reading specialist, music K-12. Tchr. K5, 1st grade Lighthouse Christian Acad., Wicomico Church, Va., 1994—; office mgr. Ednl. Svcs., White Stone, Va., 1991-93. Mus. dir., accompanist various arts groups and local theaters including Lancaster Players, Ctr. for Arts, Lancaster, Va., Raleigh, N.C., 1976—. Mem. Kappa Delta Pi. Republican. Baptist. Home: PO Box 1056 White Stone VA 22578

BENSTOCK, SHARI, English language educator; b. San Diego, Dec. 2, 1944; d. Dan and Myrl (Barth) Gabrielson; m. Melvin Shivvers (div.); 1 child, Eric Shivvers; m. Bernard Benstock, May 6, 1973. BA, Drake U., 1967, MA, 1970; PhD, Kent State U., 1975. Adminstrv. asst. U. Ill., Urbana, 1975-77, adminstrv. dir., 1978-81; assoc. prof. U. Tulsa, 1983-86, U. Miami, Coral Gables, Fla., 1986-87; prof. U. Miami, Coral Gables, 1987—. Author: Women of the Left Bank: PAris, 1986, Texualizing the Feminine, 1991, No gifts from Chance: A Biography of Edith Wharton, 1994. AAUW fellow France, 1981-82, Rockefeller Found. fellow Bellagio, Italy, 1990, Donald C. Gallup fellow Yale U., 1991, NEH fellow, 1993-94. Mem. MLA, Internat James Joyce Found. (trustee), Phi Kappa Phil. Office: U Miami PO Box 248145 Coral Gables FL 33124-8145

BENTCH, H(ERMAN) LEONARD, internist, gastroenterologist; b. Houston, Apr. 18, 1946. BA, U. Tex., 1968, MD, 1972. Diplomate Am. Bd. Internal Medicine, Am. Bd. Gastroenterology. Internal medicine intern Emory U., Atlanta, 1972-73, resident in internal medicine, 1973-74, resident internal medicine, 1975-76; fellow gastroenterology U. Tex., San Antonio, 1975-77; gastroenterologist Gastroent. Clinic of San Antonio, 1977—. Fellow Am. Coll. Physicians, Am. Coll. Gastroenterology. Office: 7940 Floyd San Antonio TX 78229

BENTLEY, EARL WILSON, JR., construction executive; b. Oklahoma City, June 27, 1920; s. Earl Wilson and Bessie Claire (Westcott) B.; m. Carolyn Elizabeth Nichols, Feb. 16, 1943; children: Cynthia Ann Bentley Campbell, Steven James, Susan Elizabeth Bentley Erickson, Barbara Lou Bentley Philbin. Student, Okla. U., 1938-41. Ptnr. Earl W. Bentley Operating Co., Oklahoma City, 1947-66, pres., 1966—. Mem. Oklahoma City Better Bus. Bur.; bd. dirs. ARC, Oklahoma City, 1970. Served to 1st lt. USAAF, 1943-46. Mem. Okla. C. of C., Oklahoma City C. of C., Beacon Club, Petroleum Club, Oklahoma City Golf and Country Club, U. Okla. "O" Club. Democrat. Presbyterian. Home: 2508 Lancaster Ln Oklahoma City OK 73116-4413 Office: Bentleys Carpet & Floorin PO Box 290 512 N Broadway Oklahoma City OK 73101

BENTLEY, FRED DOUGLAS, SR., lawyer; b. Marietta, Ga., Oct. 15, 1926; s. Oscar Andrew and Ima Irene (Prather) B.; m. Sara Tom Moss, Dec. 26, 1953; children: Fred Douglas, Robert Randall. BA, Presbyn. Coll., 1949; JD, Emory U., 1948. Bar: Ga. 1948. Sr. mem. Bentley & Dew, Marietta, 1948-51; ptnr. Bentley, Awtrey & Bartlett, Marietta, 1951-56, Edwards, Bentley, Awtrey & Parker, Marietta, 1956-75, Bentley & Schindelar, Marietta, 1975-80, Bentley, Bentley & Bentley, Marietta, 1975-80, 1980—; pres. Beneficial Investment Co., Newmarket, Inc., Happy Valley, Inc., Bentley & Sons, Inc.; chmn. bd. Charter Bank and Trust Co.; trustees Kennesaw Coll. Mem. Ga. Ho. Reps., 1951-57, Ga. Senate, 1958; past pres. Cobb County (Ga.) C. of C.; hon. curator Bentley Rare Book Gallery-Brenau U.; mem., past chmn. Ga. Coun. Arts, 1976-89; mem. Gov.'s Fine Arts Com., 1990-92; attache Ghana Olympic Com. Served with USN. Recipient Blue Key Cmty. Svc. award, Founder's award, 1992, Clarisse Baquell award for outstanding svc., Spl. Svc. award Kennesaw State Coll.; named Citizen of Yr., C. of C., 1951, Leader of Tomorrow, Time mag., 1953, Vol. Citizen of Yr., Atlanta Jour./Constn., 1981, Kennesaw Historical Soc. Man of Yr., 1996, Brenau Univ. Man of Yr., 1996; fellow J. Pierpont Morgan Libr.; Oct. 15 Fred Bentley Day City & Coun. Mem. ABA, Ga. Bar Assn., Ga. Mus. Art (bd. advisors, hon. life mem.), Rotary (hon. life), Georgian Club (bd. dirs.), The Grolier Club (hon.). Republican. Methodist. Home: 1441 Beaumont Dr Kennesaw GA 30144-3201 Office: 260 Washington Ave Marietta GA 30060-1959

BENTLEY, JAMES ROBERT, association curator, historian, genealogist; b. Louisville, Feb. 14, 1942; s. Francis Getty and Katharine Elizabeth (Wescott) B; BA, Centre Coll. Ky., 1964; MA, Coll. William and Mary, 1971. Research asst. Colonial Williamsburg (Va.), 1966-68; asst. to curator Filson Club, Louisville, 1964-65, curator, 1968-83, sec., 1972-84, acting dir., 1983-84, dir., 1984-92; dir. G.R. Clark Press, Louisville, 1974—; mem. adv. com. to photograph archives U. Louisville, 1971-72; mem. Hist. Zoning Task Force Louisville and Jefferson County, 1971-73; mem. hist. protection and preservation com. Bd. Aldermen Louisville, 1972-73; mem. Mayor's Com. Public Amenities, 1991—; mem. Jefferson County Comm. Ky. Bicentennial Comn., 1991-92; commr. Hist. Landmarks and Preservation Dists. Commn., Louisville, 1973-79. Mem. SAR (registrar 1970-93, library com.), Ky. Soc. Mayflower Descs. (historian, librarian 1970-78, gov. 1978-84, dep. gov. gen. 1981-87 , 5 generation project com. 1979-80), Ky. Soc. Colonial Wars (councillor 1971-76, registrar 1976—), Jeffersontown Hist. Soc. (dir. 1972-73, v.p. 1974-76, pres. 1976-78), Soc. Am. Archivists, Manuscript Soc., Nat. Trust Hist. Preservation, Hist. Homes Found. Louisville, Vt. Hist. Soc. (life), New Eng. Hist. Geneal. Soc., English Speaking Union, Nat. Geneal. Soc. (life), Vt. Geneal. Soc., Ind. Hist. Soc., Vt. Old Cemetery Assn., Louisville Hist. League, Alden Kindred Am., Soc. Stukely Westcott Descs., Edmund Rice 1638 Assn., Soc. Descs. Robert Bartlett of Plymouth Colony, Harleian Soc., Order Ky. Cols., Sigma Chi. Episcopalian. Clubs: Pendennis (Louisville), Filson (life). Editor, pub. Ky. Genealogist, 1979-86. Home: 1048 Cherokee Rd Louisville KY 40204-1231

BENTLEY, TIM, editor, journalist, association director; b. Atlanta, July 9, 1953; s. James Asbury and Mary Jane (Hays) B. Mem. staff Ga. Ho. of Reps., Atlanta, 1971-73; staff youth coord. Mayor of Atlanta, 1973-74; job analyst, then ops. supr. Trust Co. Bank, Atlanta, 1975—; dir. communications Dem. Party Ga., Atlanta, 1977; state campaign mgr., then asst. press sec. Ga. Sec. of State, Atlanta, 1981-83, dir. publs., 1984-87, speechwriter, 1988-89, dir. rsch. and pub. svcs., 1989—, press sec., 1990-92; asst. to chmn. Primerica Fin. Svcs., Atlanta, 1992-93; corp. comm. staff The Travelers, N.Y.C., 1993; dir. outreach comm. United Way Met. Atlanta, 1994; editor The Ga. Times, 1994—; mem. Ga. Charitable Contbns. Bd., Atlanta, 1984—; rep. to Stone Mountain (Ga.) Authority, 1988-89, Lake Lanier Islands Authority, Buford, Ga., 1989, Jekyll Island (Ga.) Authority, 1989. Contbg. writer Creative Loafing, 1993—; editor, creator, designer books, pamphlets. Mem. DeKalb County Community Rels. Commn., 1972; alt. del. Dem. Nat. Conv., N.Y.C., 1976; del. Dem. Nat. Mid-term Conf., Memphis, 1978; rep. Gov.'s Growth Strategies Commn., Ga. Agrirama Devel. Authority. Mem. Pub. Rels. Soc. Am., Internat. Assn. Bus. Communicators, Nat. Assn. Govt. Communicators, Am. Polit. Items Collectors. Home: PO Box 15285 Atlanta GA 30333-0285

BENTLEY, WILLIAM ANTERO, manufacturing company executive; b. Ayer, Mass., Aug. 14, 1944; s. Antero D. and Mildred E. (Ruppel) Coelho; m. Joyce Marie Bentley, May 1, 1971; children: Brandon K. and Trevor S. BEE, Rensselear Poly. Inst., 1966, MSEE, 1968. Engr. Procter & Gamble Co., Cinn., 1968-77; group leader Procter & Gamble, Cinn., 1977-80; section mgr. Frito-Lay Inc. subs. PepsiCo Inc., Dallas, 1980-85; dir. Nabisco Brands, Parsippany, N.J., 1985-89; cons. Allen-Bradley subs. Rockwell Internat., Milw., 1989-92; Graseby STI, Ft. Smith, Ark., 1993—. Served to capt. U.S. Army, 1969-71. Mem. IEEE, Instrument Soc. Am. (sr.). Office: 45 Fir St Waldron AR 72958

BENTLEY-SHAW, KATHLEEN, violist; b. Richmond, Va., Nov. 10, 1962; d. Gilliam and Carolyn (Hargrave) Bentley; m. Roderick Kirkpatrick Shaw III, Jan. 11, 1992. Performer's cert., U. Fla., 1986, MusB, 1986; MusM, Fla. State U., 1989, MusD, 1994. Tchg. asst. Fla. State U., Tallahassee, 1988-94; co-chair region I Fla. Am. String Tchrs. Assn., Pensacola and Tallahassee, Fla., 1993—, chair spl. projects, 1993—; coord. chamber strings Fla. State U., Tallahassee, 1993; adminstr. Shelfer Emminent , scholar chair Fla. State U., Tallahassee, chairwoman seminar Playing Well Music Medicine Seminar for String Players, 1994; vis. artist U. N.C.-Greensboro, 1995; dir. music Madison (Fla.) Presbyn. Ch., 1995—. Violist Tallahassee Symphony Orch., 1988—; author: The Sonata for Viola and Piano, 1994; performer over 50 concerts in Leon County Elem. Schs., Tallahassee, 1989-90; performer Madison (Fla.) Hist. Soc., 1995-97. Dir. arts Madison Women's Club, 1995-96; dir. Arts Festival by Madison Women's Club. Travel grantee Fla. State U., Aspen, Colo., 1990, Carmel, Calif., 1994; nat. finalist Chamber Music Competition, Carmel, 1994. Mem. Am. String Tchrs. Assn. (bd. mem. Fla. unit 1993—). Presbyterian. Home: 529 W Base St Madison FL 32340

BENTON, FAYE LOUISE, child care administrator; b. Mecklenburg County, N.C., Feb. 18, 1939; d. Johny Mack and Myrtle Reid (Brown) B.; m. Marshall Durwood Parrish, Nov. 20, 1959 (div. 1966); children: Marty, Tamra, Jeff; m. William A. Soiset, Nov. 24, 1967 (div. 1982); children: Chris, Tiffany. AAS, U. N.C., 1959. RN, N.C., Calif. Staff nurse Moses Cone Hosp., Greensboro, N.C., 1959-60, High Point (N.C.) Meml. Hosp., 1960-61, Presbyn. Hosp., Charlotte, N.C., 1961, 65; office nurse Dr. Kenneth Downs, Charlotte, 1962; intensive care staff nurse Long Beach (Calif.) Meml. Hosp., 1963; intensive care charge nurse Dominquez Valley Hosp., Long Beach, 1964; office nurse Charlotte Youth Clinic, Charlotte, 1965-67; founder, pres., CEO Matthews (N.C.) Country Day Sch. and (After Sch. Club, Inc.), 1967—. Sunday sch. tchr. Matthews Presbyn. Ch., 1969-72; den mother Matthews area Boy Scouts Am., 1979, merit badge counelor, 1975-80, pack rep.; mem. human rights com. N.C. Broughton Hosp., 1988-90; v.p. Alliance for Mentally Ill, Metrolina, Charlotte, 1985-86, pres. 1989-92; mem. Mecklenburg County SPMI Citizens Adv. Coun. Named Adv. of Yr., N.C. Alliance for Mentally Ill, 1989, Entrepreneur of Yr., Bus. Newsletter, Charlotte, 1991, Child Care Adv. of Month, Kids & Teens mag., 1991. Mem. Matthews C. of C. (Small Bus. Owner of Yr. for Svc. award 1984), Mental Health Assn. (task force on goals), Apple Club, Boppers Shag Club, Nat. Honor Soc., Charlotte Singles Golf Assn. Republican. Home: 9820 Mclendon Ct Matthews NC 28105-5508 Office: Matthews Country Day Sch 1373 W John St Matthews NC 28105-5391

BENTON, NICHOLAS FREDERICK, publisher; b. Ross, Calif., Feb. 9, 1944; s. Frederick C. H. and Jeanne Emma (Brun) B.; m. Donna Carley, Apr. 15, 1979 (div. Oct. 1984); m. Janine Schollnick, Oct. 20, 1985. AA, Santa Barbara City Coll., Calif., 1963; BA, Westmont Coll., 1965; MDiv cum laude, Pacific Sch. Religion, Berkeley, Calif., 1969. Reporter Santa Barbara News Press, 1961-66; dir. Christian edn. Plymouth Ch., Oakland, Calif., 1966-69; chief corr. Berkeley Barb, 1970-72; dir. advt. display Syufy Enterprises, San Francisco, 1973-76; regional dir. Fusion Energy Found., Washington, 1976-87; chief Washington corr. Century News Svc., Falls Church, Va., 1987—; chmn., chief exec. officer Century News Svc., Falls Church, 1987—; pub., editor Falls Church News Press, 1991—, chmn., chief exec. officer, 1991—. Pres. Falls Church Baseball, Inc., 1991—; clk. Emmaus Ch., 1989-92; bd. dirs. Arlington (Va.) Symphony, 1992-93. Mem. Greater Falls Church C. of C. (bd. dirs. 1991—, pres. 1993-94, Pillar of Cmty. award 1993), League of Women Voters of Falls Church, Optimists Club of Falls Church, White Ho. Corrs. Assn. Mem. United Ch. Christ. Office: Falls Church News Press 929 W Broad St Ste 200 Falls Church VA 22046-3121

BENTSEN, KENNETH E., JR., congressman; b. Houston, June 3, 1959; m. Tamra Bentsen; children: Louise, Meredith. BA, U. St. Thomas, Houston, 1982; M in Pub. Adminstrn., Am. U., 1985. Mem. staff Congressman Ronald D. Coleman, 1983-87; assoc. staff U.S. House Appropriations Com., 1985-87; chair Harris County Dem. Party, 1990-93; 1st v.p., investment banker Houston, 1987-94; mem. 104th Congress from 25th Tex. dist., 1995—. Presbyterian. Office: US House Reps 128 Cannon House Office Bldg Washington DC 20515-4325

BENTSEN, LLOYD, former government official, former senator; b. Mission, TX, Feb. 11, 1921; s. Lloyd M. and Edna Ruth (Colbath) B.; m. Beryl Ann Longino, Nov. 27, 1943; children: Lloyd M. III, Lan, Tina. J.D., U. Tex., 1942. Bar: Tex. 1942. Practice law McAllen, Tex., 1945-48; judge Hidalgo County, Tex., (hdqs. Edinburg), 1946-48; mem. 80th-83d congresses from 15th Tex. Dist.; pres. Lincoln Consol., Houston, 1955-70; U.S. Senator from Tex., 1971-93, chmn. senate fin. com.; mem. senate commerce, sci., transp. and joint com. on taxation and congl. joint econ. com.; sec. Dept. Treasury, Washington, 1993-94; ret., 1994; Democratic nominee for Vice Pres. U.S., 1988. Served to maj. USAAF, 1942-45. Decorated D.F.C., Air Medal with 3 oak leaf clusters.

BENZ, TODD DAVID, English Latin and history educator; b. Pitts., June 5, 1968; s. David Joseph and Maryann (Kavchak) B. BA cum laude, Dickinson Coll., 1990; MEd, U. Pitts., 1994. Devel. rep. Direct Advantage Mktg., Pitts., 1993-94; dean's office U. Pitts., 1994-95; English and Latin instr. Griffin (Ga.) H.S., 1994—. Mem. ASCD, Am. Classical League, Ga. State Educators, U. Pitts. Alumni Assn., So. Polit. Sci. Assn. Democrat. Roman Catholic.

BEOHM, RICHARD THOMAS, senior loss control engineer; b. Youngstown, Ohio, Nov. 15, 1943; s. John and Eleanor (Leverence) B.; m. Rose Elizabeth Ralston, Oct. 25, 1968; children: Michael F., Eric R. B.E.E.T., Devry Inst. Tech., Chgo., 1969. Registered profl. engr., Ga., Mass.; assoc. in risk mgmt. Asst. engr. North Electric Co. (ITT), Galion, Ohio, 1966-69; engr. Gen. Dynamics, Ft. Worth, Tex., 1969-71; fire protection engr. State of Ga. Self Ins. Program, Atlanta, 1971-80; acting dep. dir. State of Ga. Self Ins. Program, 1980; fire protection cons. State of Ga. Risk Mgmt. Svc., Atlanta, 1981-87, acting field support supr., 1987-88, sr. loss control engring. cons., 1988—. Cartoonist Upson Home Jour., 1986-88; contbr. articles to profl. jours. Mem. Fire Safe Ga. Commn.; vol. safety engr. Olympics, 1996; games risk mgr., Ga. Mem. NSPE, Am. Soc. Safety Engrs. (past pres. Ga. chpt., cert. safety profl., chair com. safety engring. tech. group engring. divsn., asst. adminstrv. engring. divsn., Engrs. Divsn. Safety Profl. of Yr. 1996), Fed. Criminal Investigation Assn. (sec. Atlanta chpt. 1989), Soc. Fire Protection Engrs. (S.E. chpt. Person of Yr. 1992, Nat. Hats Off award, chpt. v.p.). Democrat. Home: 981 Waymanville Rd Thomaston GA 30286-9350 Office: State of Ga Risk Mgmt Svcs 200 Piedmont Ave SE Atlanta GA 30334-5529

BERBARY, MAURICE SHEHADEH, physician, military officer, hospital administrator, educator; b. Beirut, Lebanon, Jan. 14, 1923; came to U.S., 1945, naturalized, 1952; s. Shehadeh M. and Marie K. Berbary; children: Geoffrey Maurice, Laura Marie. BA, Am. U., Beirut, 1943; MD, U. Tex., Dallas, 1948; MA in Hosp. Adminstrn., Baylor U., 1970; diploma, Army Command and Gen. Staff Coll., Leavenworth, Kan., 1963, Air Force Sch. Aerospace Medicine, San Antonio, 1964, Army War Coll., Carlisle, Pa., 1969. Diplomate Am. Bd. Ob-Gyn. Intern Parkland Meml. Hosp., Dallas, 1948-49, resident in ob-gyn., gen. surgery and urology, 1949-53; resident in ob-gyn. Walter Reed Army Hosp., Washington, 1955-57; fellow in obstetric and gynecologic pathology Armed Forces Inst. Pathology, Washington, 1959-60; practice clin. medicine in ob-gyn., 1953—; capt. MC U.S. Army, 1952, advanced through grades to col., 1968, sr. flight surgeon, 1970; chief dept. ob-gyn. U.S. Army Hosp., Ft. Polk, La., 1957-59, Womack Army Hosp., Ft. Bragg, N.C., 1960-62; div. surgeon 1st. inf. div., Ft. Riley, Kans., 1963-64, 3d. Armored div., Germany, 1964-65; corps surgeon V. Corps, Germany, 1965-67, 24th Army Corps, S. Vietnam Theater of Operation, 1970; comdr., hosp. adminstr. U.S. Army Hosp., Teheran, Iran, 1954-55; comdr. 43d Hosp. Group Complex, Vietnam, 1969-70; command surgeon U.S. Armed Forces Command and U.S. Army South, U.S. C.Z., Panama, 1970-73; comdr. 5th Gen. Hosp., Stuttgart, West Germany, 1973-77, Munson Army Hosp., Ft. Leavenworth, Kans., 1977-81; sr. staff officer dept. ob-gyn William Beaumont Army Med. Ctr., Ft. Bliss, Tex., 1981-83; ret., 1983, cons. health care adminstrn. and med.-legal affairs, 1984—; vis. lectr. ob-gyn. pathology Duke U. Med. Ctr., Durham, N.C., 1960-62; clin. instr. dept. ob-gyn. U. Kans. Coll. Medicine, Kansas City, 1963-80, advanced to clin. asst. prof., 1980—; instr. 5th Army NCO Acad., Fort Riley, Kans., 1963-64. Decorated Legion of Merit with three oak leaf clusters, Bronze Star medal, Meritorious Svc. medal, Army Commendation medal, Combat Air medal, Sr. Flight Surgeon's badge, Expert Field Med. badge. Fellow ACS, Am. Coll. Ob-Gyn., Am. Coll. Health Care Execs.; mem. AMA, Assn. Mil. Surgeons, Am. Occupational Med. Assn., Soc. U.S. Army Flight Surgeons, Am. Hosp. Assn., N.Y. Acad. Scis., Tex. State Med. Assn., Dallas County Med. Soc., Internat. Platform Assn., Masons (32 deg.). Home and Office: 7923 Abramshire Ave Dallas TX 75231-4712

BERCHELMANN, D. KEVIN, management consultant; b. San Antonio, Oct. 27, 1958; s. Stephen Ernest and Patricia (Falloure) B.; m. Traci A. Garrison, June 25, 1989; children: Stephen D., Stephanie P. AAS, C.C. of the Air Force, 1986; BS, Park Coll., 1988; MS, Troy State U., 1991. Mgmt. cons. Birchtree Comm., Houston, Tex., 1991; tng. mgr. Bio Three Industries, Houston, 1991-92; employment mgr. Big Three Industries, Houston, 1992-93; pres. Birchtree Comm., Houston, 1993-94; mgr. training and devel. U.S. Zinc, Houston, 1993—; dir. Birchtree Comm., 1993—; bus. faculty Houston C.C., Houston 1992—, Le Toureau U., 1993—. Author: (book) The Resume, 1992, The Job Search, 1993; contbg. editor: Computing Concepts, 1993. Chmn., Special Olympics, Del Rio, Tex., 1988; chmn. Voter Registration Air Force Sgts. Assn., Germany, 1989-90. 1st. Sgt. USAF, 1977-91. Recipient Air Force Commendation medal U.S. Air Force, 1984, Nat. Defense medal U.S. Air Force, 1990. Mem. Mensa, Am. Soc. for Tng. and Devel. (v.p. 1992-93), Air Force Sgts. Assn. (pres. 1988-91, lifetime trustee 1990), Assn. Free and Accepted Masons. Republican. Baptist. Home: 1223 Camino Village Dr Houston TX 77058-3023 Office: US Zinc 6020 Navigation Blvd Houston TX 77011-1132

BERCHTOLD, GLADYS, business executive. Chmn. Std. Labs., South Charleston, W.Va. Office: Std Labs Ste 100 147 11th Ave South Charleston WV 25303

BERDENSEY, HAROLD KENNETH, real estate broker; b. Deep River, Conn., Feb. 10, 1924; s. Arthur and Effie (Dickerson) B.; m. Charlotte Belle Smith, May 30, 1946. Student bus. adminstrn., Coll. William and Mary; student adult edn. sys., Warwick H.S., Newport News, Va.; student real estate bus., Christopher Newport Coll.; grad. Am. Inst. Real Estate Appraisers, U. N.C. Commd. U.S. Army, 1945, advanced through grades to lt. col., ret., 1972; sr. amphibious adv. Trans. Sch. U.S. Army, Ft. Eustis, Va., 1954; tng. adminstr. dept. aviation trades Trans. Sch. U.S. Army; owner, founder Realty World-H.K. Berdensey Realty, Newport News, Va., 1957—;

commn. lt. col. U.S Army, 1969. Trustee Menchville (Va.) Bapt. Ch., Sunday sch. dir., chmn. personnel com., chmn. deacon. Mem. Va. Rental Assn. Realtors (chmn. grievance com., mem. profl. stds. com.), Masons, Shriners. Baptist. Home: 169 Cabell Dr Newport News VA 23602 Office: Realty World Berdensey 15631 Warwick Blvd Newport News VA 23608

BERECKA, ALAN MICHAEL, librarian; b. New Hartford, N.Y., July 22, 1959; s. Albert Joseph and Stella Jane (Puch) B.; m. Alice Ruth Adams, Nov. 23, 1985; children: Rachael Ann, Aaron Michael. BA, U. Dallas, 1981; MA, U. North Tex., 1987; MLS, Tex. Woman's U., 1989. Reference/ bibliographic instrn. libr. North Adams (Mass.) State Coll., 1989-90; circulation reference libr. McLennan Cmty. Coll., Waco, Tex., 1990—. Mem. St. Jeromes Roman Cath. Ch., Waco, 1990—, Cameron Park Zoo, Waco, 1994—. Regents scholarship N.Y. State, 1977. Mem. Tex. Jr. Coll. Tchrs. Assn. (pres. learning resources sect. 1996—, v.p. 1995-96, sect. 1994-95). Office: McLennan Cmty Coll Libr 1400 College Dr Waco TX 76708

BERENTSEN, KURTIS GEORGE, music educator, choral conductor; b. North Hollywood, Calif., Apr. 22, 1953; s. George O. and Eleanor J. (Johnson) B.; m. Jeanette M. Sacco, Aug., 1975 (div. 1977); m. Floy I. Griffiths, March 17, 1984; 1 child, Kendra Irene. MusB, Utah State U., 1975; MA in Music, U. Calif., Santa Barbara, 1986. Cert. cmty. coll. tchr., Calif., pub. tchr., Calif.; commd. minister Luth. Ch., Mo. Synod, 1996. Dir. music Hope Luth. Ch., Daly City, Calif., 1975-81; gen. mgr. Ostara Press, Inc., Daly City, Calif., 1975-78; condr. U. Calif., Santa Barbara, 1981-86; dir., condr. Santa Barbara oratorio Chorale, 1983-85; dir. music 1st Presbyn. Ch., Santa Barbara, 1983-84, Goleta (Calif.) Presbyn. Ch., 1984-85; minister music Trinity Luth. Ch., Ventura, 1985-92, Christ Luth. Ch. & Sch., Little Rock, Ark., 1992—; instr. Ventura Coll., 1987-88; music dir., condr. Gold Coast Community Chorus, Ventura, 1988-92; choir dir. Temple Beth Torah Jewish Community, Ventura, 1982-87; adj. prof. Pepperdine U., Malibu, Calif., 1988; chorus master Ventura Symphony Orch., 1987; owner Music and Ch. Discount Suppliers, 1989-92. Condr. oratorios Christus Am Oelberg, 1983, Elijah, 1984, Hymn of Praise, 1988, cantata Seven Last Words, 1979, 84, Paukenmesse, 1989, Mozart's Requiem, 1990, Requiem-Fauré, 1991, Judas Maccabaeus-Handel, 1992; soloist 15 major oratorio and opera roles, 1971-92, Nat. Anthem, L.A. Dodgers, 1989; dir. (with John Rutter) Gold Coast Community Chorus, Carnegie Hall, N.Y.C., 1991, Tribute to America, Lincoln Ctr. Concert, N.Y.C., 1991. Min. music, tchr. Christ Luth. Ch. and Sch., Little Rock, 1992—. First place winner baritone vocalist Idaho Fedn. Music Clubs, 1971, recital winner Utah Fedn. Music Clubs, 1974. Mem. Choral Condrs. Guild, Assn. Luth. Ch. Musicians, Am. Guild of English Handbell Ringers, Sigma Nu (sec., song leader 1973-75). Home and Office: 4300 Bear Tree Dr Little Rock AR 72212-1952

BERESFORD, WILMA, secondary school educator, gifted education educator; b. Kensett, Ark., Nov. 3, 1931; d. Newton A. and Anna Lucille Murray (Bedair) Graham; m. Robert B. Beresford, Aug. 5, 1949; children: Anna C. Walker, Angela D. Thomas, Robert L. BS, Lamar State Coll., 1963; MEd, McNeese State U., 1971; postgrad., Lamar U. Cert. tchr., Tex. Tchr. Groves (Tex.) Pub. Schs.; spl. assignment tchr. Port Neches Ind. Sch. Dist., Groves, 1963—; Chpt. I tchr., tchr. ESL and computer literacy Port Neches Groves Ind. Sch. Dist.; cons., presenter workshops in field. Mem. ASCD, Tex. Tchrs. Assn., Tex. Gifted and Talented Assn. (cert.), Tex. Computer Edn. Ass., Future Problem Solvers Tex. (cert. evaluator), Tex. States Tchr. Assn., Am. Bus. Women's Assn., Tex. Classroom Tchrs. Assn., Phi Delta Kappa.

BERFIELD, SUE ANN, city commissioner, legal assistant; b. Fremont, Ohio, Nov. 20, 1940; d. William J. and Mary L. (Fetter) Mautz; m. James L. Berfield, Dec. 29, 1962; children: Kimberly, Kristine. Student, Ill. State Normal U., 1959. Bd. dirs. Jolley Trolley Corp., Clearwater, Fla., Clearwater Marine Sci. Ctr.; chairperson Pinellas Planning Coun., Clearwater. Mem. bd. Performing Arts Ctr., Clearwater; commr. City of Clearwater, vice chairperson Cmty. Redevel. Agy.; vice mayor City of Clearwater, 1991-92; Rep. precinct committeewoman, Clearwater; mem. Pinellas County Rep. Exec. Com. Mem. Leadership Pinellas, Clearwater Cmty. Womens' Club,. Baptist. Home: 1466 Flora Rd Clearwater FL 34615-1514 Office: City of Clearwater 112 S Osceola Ave Clearwater FL 34616-5103

BERG, BERND ALBERT, physics educator; b. Delmenhorst, Germany, Aug. 23, 1949; came to U.S., 1985; s. Max and Irmgard (Tetzlaff) B.; m. Ursula A. Schroder, Mar. 26, 1975; 1 child, Felix. Dr rer Nat., Free U., Berlin, 1977. Postdoctoral fellow Free U., Berlin, 1977-78; postdoctoral fellow Univ. Hamburg, Germany, 1978-80, asst. prof., 1982-85; fellow CERN, Geneva, 1980-82; assoc. prof. Fla. State U., Tallahassee, 1985-88, prof., 1988—; vis. prof. U. Bielefeld, Germany, 1990-91; fellow Inst. for Advanced Study, Berlin, 1992-93. Contbr. articles to profl. jours. Mem. Am. Phys. Soc. Office: Fla State U Physics Tallahassee FL 32306

BERG, LILLIAN DOUGLAS, retired chemistry educator; b. Birmingham, Ala., July 9, 1925; d. Gilbert Franklin and Mary Rachel (Griffin) Douglas; m. Joseph Wilbur Berg, June 26, 1950; children: Anne Berg Jenkins, Joseph Wilbur III, Frederick Douglas. BS in Chemistry, Birmingham So. Coll., 1946; MS in Chemistry, Emory U., 1948. Instr. chemistry Armstrong Jr. Coll., Savannah, Ga., 1948-50; rsch. asst. chemistry Pa. State U., University Park, 1950-54; instr. chemistry U. Utah, Salt Lake City, 1955-56; prof. chemistry No. Va. C.C., Annandale, 1974-96. Mem. Am. Chem. Soc., Am. Women in Sci., Mortar Bd. Soc., Iota Sigma Pi, Sigma Delta Epsilon, Phi Beta Kappa. Home: 3319 Dauphine Dr Falls Church VA 22042-3724

BERG, LORINE MCCOMIS, retired guidance counselor; b. Ashland, Ky., Mar. 28, 1919; d. Oliver Botner and Emma Elizabeth (Eastham) McComis; m. Leslie Thomas Berg, Apr. 27, 1946; children: James Michael, Leslie Jane. BA in Edn., U. Ky., 1965; MA, Xavier U., 1969. Tchr. A.D. Owens Elem. Sch., Newport, Ky., 1963-64, 6th dist. Elementary Schs., Covington, Ky., 1965-69; guidance counselor Twenhofel Jr. H.S., Independence, Ky., 1969-78, Scott H.S., Taylor Mill, Ky., 1978-84. Bd. dirs. Mental Health Assn., Covington, Ky, 1970-76, v.p., 1973 (valuable svc. award 1973); mem. Lakeside Christian Ch., Ft. Mitchell, Ky. Named to Honorable Order of Ky. Colonels, Hon. Admissions Counselor U.S. Naval Acad.; cited by USN Recruiting Command for Valuable Assistance to USN, 1981. Mem. Am. Assn. of Univ. Women, Covington Art Club, Retired Tchrs. Assn., Kappa Delta Pi, Delta Kappa Gamma, Phi Delta Kappa. Democrat. Home: 11 Idaho Ave Covington KY 41017-2925

BERG, SISTER MARIE MAJELLA, university chancellor; b. Bklyn., July 7, 1916; d. Peter Gustav and Mary Josephine (McAuliff) B. BA, Marymount Coll., 1938; MA, Fordham U., 1948; DHL (hon.), Georgetown U., 1970, Marymount Manhattan Coll., 1983. Registrar Marymount Sch., N.Y.C., 1943-48; prof. classics, registrar Marymount Coll., N.Y.C., 1949-57; registrar Marymount Coll. of Va., Arlington, 1957-58, Marymount Coll., Tarrytown, N.Y., 1958-60; pres. Marymount U., Arlington, Va., 1960-93, chancellor, 1993—; pres. Consortium for Continuing Higher Edn. in Va., 1987-88; mem. com. Consortium of Univs. in Washington Met. Area, 1987-93, chmn., 1992-93. Contbr. five biographies to One Hundred Great Thinkers, 1965; editor Otherwords column of N.Va. Sun newspaper, Arlington. Bd. dirs. Internat. Hospice, 1984-96, HOPE, 1983—, SOAR, 1993—, 10th Dist. Congl. Award Coun., No. Va.; vice chmn. bd. Va. Found. Ind. Colls., 1992-93; cmty. advisor Jr. League No. Va., 1992—; mem. Friends of TACTS, 1994—. Recipient commendation Va. Gen. Assembly, Richmond, 1990, 93, Elizabeth Ann Seton award, 1991, Arlington Notable Women award Arlington Commn. on Status of Women, 1992, Voice and Vision award Arlington Cmty. TV Channel 33, 1993, Pro Ecclesia et Pontifice medal Holy See, 1993; elected to Va. Women's Hall of Fame, 1992; named Washingtonian of Yr., Washingtonian mag., 1990. Roman Catholic. Home and Office: Marymount U Office of Chancellor 2807 N Glebe Rd Arlington VA 22207-4224

BERG, ROBERT RAYMOND, geologist, educator; b. St. Paul, May 28, 1924; s. Raymond F. and Jennie (Swanson) B.; m. Josephine Finck, Dec. 22, 1946; children: James R., (dec.), Charles R., William R. B.A., U. Minn., 1948, Ph.D., 1951. Geologist, Calif. Co., Denver, 1951-56; cons. Berg and Wasson, Denver, 1957-66; prof. geology, head dept. Tex. A&M U., 1967—, Michel T. Halbouty prof. geology, 1982—; dir. univ. research Tex. A & M U., 1972—; cons. petroleum geology, 1959—. Contbr. papers in field. Served with AUS, 1943-46. Recipient Disting. Achievement award U. Minn., 1992. Fellow Geol. Soc. Am.; mem. Am. Assn. Petroleum Geologists (disting. lectr. 1972, hon. mem. 1985, Sidney Powers Meml. award 1993), Am. Inst. Profl. Geologists (pres. 1971, hon. mem. 1988), Nat. Acad. Engring. Home: 414 Brookside Bryan TX 77801 Office: Texas A&M Univ Geology Dept College Station TX 77843

BERGAL, JENNI, journalist; b. Chgo., Oct. 20, 1957; d. Milton Bergal and Avra (Kanief) Miller. BA, Boston U., 1978; MA in Polit. Sci., Fla. Atlantic U., 1993. Staff writer Danbury (Conn.) News-Times, 1978-81; staff writer Sun-Sentinel, Ft. Lauderdale, Fla., 1981-88, sr. writer, 1988-91, editorial writer, columnist, 1991-94, sr. writer, investigations, 1994—; instr. prof. Fla. Atlantic U., Ft. Lauderdale, 1996—. Recipient Worth Bingham award, 1989, 95, 1st place pub. svc. award Fla. Soc. Newspaper Editors, 1995, Unity award in media, 1995, Green Eyeshade award 1st pl. bus. writing award Sigma Delta Chi, 1995, Pulitzer prize finalist for beat reporting, 1996. Mem. Investigative Reporters and Editors. Office: Sun-Sentinel 200 E Las Olas Blvd Fort Lauderdale FL 33301-2248

BERGAU, FRANK CONRAD, real estate, commercial and investment properties executive; b. N.Y.C., Sept. 17, 1926; s. Frank Conrad and Mary Elizabeth (Davie) B.; BA in English, St. Francis Coll., Loretto, Pa., 1950; MS in Edn. and English, Potsdam (N.Y.) State U., 1969; m. Rita I. Korotkin; children: Mary, Rita, Francis, Theresa, Veronica. Tchr. English Gouverneur (N.Y.) Schs., 1962-81, dir. continuing edn., 1968-81, summer prin., 1974-80; project dir. St. Lawrence County (N.Y.) Bd. Co-op. Ednl. Services, Canton, 1974; pres. Irenicon Assos. Bd. dirs. St. Lawrence County Assn. Retarded Children, 1965—; pres. bd. dirs. Gouverneur Library. Mem. Gouverneur C. of C. (dir. 1963-66), Nat. Assn. Realtors, Lake County Bd. Realtors, NEA, South Lake County Devel. Coun. (pres.), N.Y. Assn. Continuing Edn. (dir.). Certified as tchr., supr., adminstr., N.Y.; cert. coml. investment mem. Club: Gouverneur Luncheon. Lodge: Kiwanis (charter mem. Clermont).

BERGEMAN, GEORGE WILLIAM, mathematics educator, software author; b. Ft. Dodge, Iowa, July 16, 1946; s. Harold Levi and Hilda Carolyn (Nuhn) B.; m. Clarissa Elaine Hellman, Oct. 24, 1968; 1 child, Jessica Ann. BA, U. Iowa, 1970, MS, 1972; postgrad., Va. Inst. Tech., 1978-83. Teaching asst. U. Iowa, Iowa City, 1970-72; coll. instr. Peace Corps, Liberia, 1972-75; asst. prof. math. No. Va. C.C., Sterling, 1975—; software author George W. Bergeman Software, Round Hill, Va., 1984—; cons. Excel Corp., Reston, Va., 1983-84; developer software including graphics and expert systems. Author: (software, book) 20/20 Statistics, 1985, 2nd edit., 1988 (software) MathCue, 1987, 2nd edit., 1991, Graph 2D/3D, 1990, 93, MathCue Solution Finder, 1991, 2nd edit., 1992, F/C Graph, 1993, F/C.P Graph, 1995-96, MathCue Practice, 1994, 95, 96. Cmty. worker VISTA, Ctrl. Fla., 1968-69. Named Outstanding Educator Phi Theta Kappa, 1987. Mem. Math. Assn. Am., Am. Math. Soc., Am. Math. Assn. Two-Yr. Colls., Phi Kappa Phi. Home: 35441 Williams Gap Rd Round Hill VA 22141 Office: No Va CC 1000 Byrd Hwy Sterling VA 22170

BERGEMANN, VERNA ELMYRA, education educator; b. Ransomville, N.Y., Mar. 22, 1921; d. George John and Minnie Christina (Radloff) B. BE, State U. Coll., Brockport, 1943; MS, State U. Coll., Buffalo, 1955; EdD, U. Md., 1969. Cert. elem. tchr., N.Y., N.Mex., adminstr. N.Y., N.C. 2d grade, kindergarten tchr. Niagara St. Sch., Niagara Falls, N.Y., 1943-52; kindergarten tchr. Mesa Sch., Los Alamos, N.Mex., 1952-53; helping tchr. Niagara Falls Pub. Schs., 1953-56; 1st grade supr. Campus Sch. State U. Coll., Oswego, 1956-59, assoc. prof., 1959-68, prof. edn., 1968-69; dir. instrn. McDowell County Schs., Marion, N.C., 1969-71; state curriculum specialist Dept. Pub. Instrn. State of N.C., Raleigh, 1971-73; prof. U. N.C., Asheville, 1973-85, chair Dept. Edn., 1973-85; lang. arts, early childhood, right to read cons. U. N.C., 1969—; adult literacy cons. Buncombe County Literacy Assn., Asheville, 1980—. Co-author, rschr.: In the Classroom: an Introduction to Education, 1992, (guidebook) A Guide to Observation and Participation, 1992. Literacy tutor Buncombe County Literacy Assn., 1980-91; mem. Competency Test Commn., Raleigh, 1976-84; arbitrator Better Bus. Bur., Asheville, 1975—; precinct chmn. Western N.C. Dem. com., Asheville, 1992. Named Woman of Distinction Women's Civic Clubs, Asheville, 1986, Woman Yr. Asheville/Buncombe Community Rels. Coun., 1987. Fellow Nat. Assn. Edn. Young Children, Assn. for Early Childhood Internat., Emmanuel Luth. Ch. and Sch. (chmn. bd. edn. 1980-85), Friends of Libr., Altrusa Club Asheville (pres. 1985-86). Democrat. Lutheran. Office: Rte 4 Box 911 McKinney Rd Marion NC 28752

BERGER, ARTHUR SEYMOUR, author, vice-mayor, lawyer, cultural organization executive; b. N.Y.C., Sept. 19, 1920; m. Joyce Berger. JD cum laude, N.Y.U. Bar: N.Y. 1949. Mcpl. atty. State of N.Y., 1963-71; pres. Survival Rsch. Found., Miami, Fla., 1981—; dir. Internat. Inst. for Study of Death, 1985—; adj. prof. Broward Coll., 1989-94, Union Inst., 1990-92, Fla. Internat. U. Elders Inst., 1996—; cons. Readers Digest. Author: Liberation of the Person, 1964, Aristocracy of the Dead, 1987, Lives and Letters in American Parapsychology, 1988 (outstanding acad. book list), Evidence of Life After Death: Casebook for Tough-Minded, 1988, Dying and Death in Law and Medicine, 1993, When Life Ends, 1995; co-author: The Encyclopedia of Parapsychology and Physical Research, 1991, Fear of the Unknown, 1995; co-editor: Religion and Parapsychology, 1989, Perspectives in Death and Dying, 1989, To Die or Not to Die?, 1990. Vice-mayor City of Aventura, Fla.; mem. ethics com. Broward Gen. Med. Ctr., Columbia-Aventura Med. Ctr.; mem. Barry U. Instnl. Rev. Bd.; mem. Cmty. Hospice Coun.; narrator reading program for the blind Libr. of Congress. 1st lt. U.S. Army, 1942-46, 50-52. Recipient Ashby Meml. award Acad. Religion, grantee, 1985, Phys. Rsch. Found., 1984, Fla. Endowment of the Arts, 1989. Mem. DAV (life), Soc. for Sci. Exploration, Am. Soc. for Psychical Rsch., Soc. for Psychical Rsch., Parapsychol. Assn., Book Group of South Fla. Office: Internat Inst Study Death PO Box 63-0026 Miami FL 33163-0026

BERGER, BARBARA PAULL, social worker, marriage and family therapist; b. St. Louis, June 18, 1955; d. Ted and Florence Ann (Vines) Paull; m. Allan Berger, Dec. 27, 1980; children: Melissa Dawn, Tammi Alyse, Jessica Lauren. BS, U. Tex., 1977; MSSW, U. Wis., 1978. Diplomate Am. Bd. Clin. Social Work; lic. social worker, Tex., Miss., Ky.; cert. marriage and family therapist. Clin. social worker Child and Family Svcs., Buffalo, 1980-81, United Cerebral Palsy Assn., St. Louis, 1982-83; clin. social worker/ coord. Jewish Family Life Edn. Jewish Family Svc., Dallas, 1984-85, 88-90; instr. Miss. Delta C. C., Greenville, 1991; child and adolescent therapist United Behavioral Systems, Louisville, 1993-94; therapist CMG Health-Inpsych, Louisville, 1994—. Mem. NASW, Acad. Cert. Social Workers, Am. Assn. Marriage and Family Therapy, Phi Kappa Phi, Pi Lambda Theta, Omicron Nu. Home: 2719 Avenue Of The Woods Louisville KY 40241-6281

BERGER, BILLIE DAVID, corrosion engineer; b. Yale, Okla., May 30, 1919; s. Edward James Berger and Ada Lucy Botts Berger Roam; m. Twylla I. Briggs, Oct. 11, 1942; children: Nancy Berger Rano, Kay Berger Fritchman, Boise David. AA, Okla. State U., 1951; B.Indsl. Arts, Oklahoma City U., 1960. Cert. corrosion engr., Tex. Elec. contr. Okla., 1945-49; engr. Cities Svc. Gas Co., Oklahoma City, 1951-55, supt. comms. dept., 1956-66; elec. engr. Point Four Program, Ethiopia, 1955-56; supt. comms. Am. Ind. Oil Co., Kuwait, 1966-70; dept. head Occidental of Libya, Inc., Tripoli, 1970-74; instr., acting dept. head Okla. State U., Stillwater, 1974-79; cons., corrosion engr. Berger Cons. Svcs., 1979-94; engr. Municipality of Yale, 1994—. Author: Refinery Operations, 1979, Gas Handling and Field Processing, 1980, Basic Processing Knowledge, 1979, Modern Petroleum, 3d edit., 1992. With USN, 1940-45. Recipient Cert. of Spl. Congl. Recognition, Bill K. Brewster, Mem. of Congress, Washington, 1991, Award for Outstanding Achievement in Writing "Lest We Forget", VFW, Post 1118, Cushing, Okla., 1991, Gov.'s Commendation, State of Okla., 1991. Mem. VFW (jr. vice comdr. 1994-95), Am. Legion, Pearl Harbor Survivors Assn. (Medal), Yale C. of C., Jim Thorpe Meml. Found. (co-chmn. 1987-93). Democrat. Christian Ch. Home: Rt 2 Box 39 Yale OK 74085

BERGER, FRAN BLAKE, speech professional; b. N.Y.C., Dec. 6, 1946; d. Carlton and Mildred (Schwartz) Blake; m. Steven R. Berger, Aug. 21, 1966; children: Amy Judith Berger Chafetz, Charles David Berger. BEd, U. Ala., Tuscaloosa, 1968; MA in Rhetoric and Pub. Address, 1969, MA in Speech Therapy, 1969. Tchr. Math. Augusta Ran Sch., Tallahassee, Fla., 1970; polit. sci. Lively Vocat./Tech. Schs., 1970-71; polit. sci./history Dade Co. Schs., 1970-71; adult edn. specialist Drug Rehab. Ctrs. Dade Co. Schs., 1971-73; GED specialist N. Miami Adult, 1973-76; math specialist S. Dade Hebrew Acad., Miami, Fla., 1979-80; spring exceptionalities Dade Co. Pub. Schs., Miami, Fla., 1979-80; dir. Forensics, 1980-96; chair Nat. Forensic League, 1985-96; pres. Dade Co. Speech Assn., Miami, Fla., 1987-95; chair Nat. Forensic League, S. Fla. Dist., 1995-97; co-chair Coordinating Coun. Miami Palmetto H.S., 1995-96. Home: 10221 SW 129 St Miami FL 33076 Office: Miami Palmetto HS 7462 SW 118th St Miami FL 33156-4572

BERGER, JOYCE MURIEL, foundation executive, author, editor; b. N.Y.C., Oct. 20, 1924; d. Samuel and Daisy (Lichtenstein) Zeitlin; m. Arthur Seymour Berger, Feb. 11, 1946. BA magna cum laude, N.Y. U., 1944, MA, 1946. Editor Theta Psychical Rsch. Found., Durham, N.C., 1978-80; sec.-treas., libr. Survival Rsch. Found., administr. Internat. Inst. for Study of Death, Miami, Fla., 1980—; convener confs. Internat. Inst. Study of Death, Miami, 1985, 87, Survival Rsch. Found., Miami, 1986. Co-author: Reincarnation Fact or Fable, 1991, Encyclopedia of Parapsychology, 1991, Fear of the Unknown, 1995; co-editor: To Die or Not to Die, 1990, Perspectives on Death and Dying, 1989; lectr. and seminar coord. in field. Right to Die conf. grantee Fla. Endowment of the Humanities, Tampa, 1987. Mem. Am. Soc. for Psychical Rsch., Soc. for Psychical Rsch., The Book Group of South Fla., Phi Beta Kappa. Office: Survival Rsch Found PO Box 630026 Miami FL 33163-0026

BERGER, KENNETH WALTER, librarian; b. N.Y.C., Nov. 1, 1949; s. Lewis Joseph and Belle (Burden) B.; m. Katherine Hawes Tyler, Aug. 18, 1973; children: Karen Tyler, Kristen Tyler. BA, Fla. Presbyn./Eckerd Coll., 1972; MA, Fla. State U., 1974, MSLS, 1977. Reference libr. and manuscript cataloger Duke U. Libr., Durham, N.C., 1977-80, reference libr. and bibliographer, 1980-93, head of reference, 1993—; libr. resources cons. Appalachian State U., Boone, N.C., 1988-90; pre-pub. cons. Gale Rsch., Detroit, 1991—. Editor: Annals of the Southeast Conf. of the Assn. for Asian Studies, 1989-93, others; contbr. articles to profl. jours. Recipient Higher Edn. Act Title II-B fellowship Fla. State U., 1976-77, competitive grad. fellow, 1973-74. Mem. ALA, Assn. for Asian Studies, Assn. for Bibliography of History, Southeast Conf. of the Assn. for Asian Studies (chmn. editl. com. 1989-93, archivist 1985—), Beta Phi Mu. Office: Perkins Libr Reference Dept Duke Univ Durham NC 27708-0175

BERGER, LINDA FAY, writer; b. Ft. Worth, Mar. 12, 1943; d. Walter Bob and Bertha Fay (Christensen) B. AA, Tarrant County Jr. Coll., Ft. Worth, 1976; BBA, U. Tex., Arlington, 1981; MBA, North Tex. U., 1987. With Tex. Refinery Corp., Ft. Worth, 1961-91, file clk., telex operator, departmental sec., exec. sec., asst. pers. dir., pers. dir. Co-author: A Joyful Journey, 1995. Mem. Nat. Secs. Assn. (cert. sec. 1975, sec. 1969-79), Tex. Assn. Bus. (sec. 1990), Order of the Eastern Star (Riverside chpt. 834). Republican. Mem. Unity Ch.

BERGER, STEVEN R., lawyer; b. Miami, Fla., Aug. 23, 1945; s. Jerome J. and Jeanne B. B.; m. Francine Blake, Aug. 20, 1966; children: Amy, Charlie. BS, U. Ala., 1967, JD, 1969. Bar: Fla. 1969, U.S. Dist. Ct. (no. dist.) Fla. 1969, U.S. Dist. Ct. (so. dist.) Fla. 1971, U.S. Ct. Appeals (5th cir.) 1971, U.S. Supreme Ct. 1972, U.S. Ct. Claims 1977, U.S. Ct. Appeals (11th cir.) 1981, U.S. Dist. Ct. (mid. dist.) Fla. 1989, N.Y. 1990, U.S. Ct. Appeals (2d and 9th cirs.) 1991, Nev. 1991, U.S. Dist. Ct. Nev. 1991. Assoc., W. Dexter Douglass, Tallahassee, Fla., 1969-71, William R. Dawes, Miami, 1971; ptnr. Carey, Dwyer, Cole Selwood & Bernard, Miami, 1971-81, Steven R. Berger, P.A., Miami, 1981-89, Wolpe, Leibowitz, Berger & Brotman, Miami, 1989-94, Berger & Chafetz, Miami, 1994—; pvt. practice, Miami, 1981-89; mem. faculty Nat. Appellate Advocacy Inst., Washington, 1980; vice chmn. bench and bar adv. com. Ct. Appeals. 4th Dist., 1986-92. Chmn. City Miramar Planning Bd., 1975-76. Mem. ABA (vice chmn. app. practice com. litigation sect. 1981-83, chmn. 5th cir. subcom. appellate practice com. 1978-81), Tallahassee Bar Assn., Kendall-South Miami Dist. Bar Assn., Am. Judicature Soc., Dade County Def. Bar Assn., Fla. Def. Lawyers Assn. (vice chmn. appellate rules com. 1989), Def. Rsch. Inst., Rep. Nat. Lawyers Assn., Am. Arbitration Assn., Internat. Assn. Def. Counsel, N.Y. State Bar Assn., N.Y. State Trial Lawyers Assn., State Bar Nev. Mem. editorial bd. Trial Adv. Quar.; contbr. articles to legal jours. Office: Berger & Chafetz 9350 S Dixie Hwy Ph I Miami FL 33156-2945

BERGERON, WILTON LEE, physician; b. Scott, La., Feb. 13, 1933; s. Lee and Ida (Duhon) B.; m. Juanita Marie Landry, Aug. 3, 1957; children: David, Marcel, René, Jeanne. BS, U. South La., 1956; MD, La. State U., 1958. Diplomate Am. Bd. Allergy and Immunology. Intern Confederate Meml. Med. Ctr. (now La. State U. Med. Sch.), Shreveport, 1958-59; resident Lafayette (La.) Charity Hosp., 1959-60; fellow in allergy Tulane U. Med. Sch., New Orleans, 1968-70; pvt. practice Lafayette and Scott, La., 1960—, allergist, 1970—. Pres. Secular Franciscan Order, 1990-93. Mem. La. Allergy Soc. (former pres.). Republican. Roman Catholic. Home and Office: PO Box 98 # 90 Scott LA 70583-0098

BERGFELD, RUDOLPH PETERS, financial company executive; b. Peoria, Ill., Aug. 5, 1935; s. Rudolph J.H. and Florence Maria (Peters), B.; m. Carolina De Montigne Rawls, June 18, 1966; children: Lisa Kathryn, Karen Maria. BA, Capital U., Columbus, Ohio, 1956; grad. courses in marine engring., U.S. Navy, Calif., 1961. Commd. ensign USN, 1956, advanced through grades to lt. comdr., resigned, 1971; v.p. program devel. Computer Sci. Corp., Falls Ch., Va., 1974-77; v.p. mktg. and spl. programs Systems Control Inc., Palo Alto, Calif., 1977-82; pres. Liberty Bell Comm., Detroit, 1983-84, Duval Marble, Jacksonville, Fla., 1984-87, Internat. Fin. Investments, Jacksonville, 1987—; Founder World Trade Orgn., Jacksonville, Fla., 1986; keynote spkr. Internat. Trade Orgn., Washington. Author: Dollars & Sense, 1990, Employ Your Education, 1992, Passport to Carefree Travel, 1993. Mem. St. John's Episcopal Cathedral, 1983. Decorated by govts. Viet Nam, Korea, Japan; decorated with Bronze Star, U.S. Navy. Republican. Episcopalian. Home: 7829 La Sierra Ct Jacksonville FL 32256 Office: Internat Fin Investments 10991 San Jose Blvd Jacksonville FL 32223-6655

BERGFIELD, GENE RAYMOND, engineering educator; b. Granite City, Ill., July 11, 1951; s. Walter Irvin Bergfield and Venie Edith (Sanders) Bennett; m. Juanita Pauline Kapp, Sept. 19, 1970; children: Gene Raymond Jr., Timothy Shawn. BA in Applied Behavioral Scis., Nat. Coll. Edn., Chgo., 1988. Field engr. Westinghouse PGSD, St. Louis, 1979-81; instr. Westinghouse PGSD, Phila., 1982-84; asst. resource mgr. Westinghouse PGSD, Chgo., 1984-89; power plant instr. Westinghouse PGPD, Orlando, Fla., 1989-93; plant tech. supr. Edison Mission O&M Inc., Auburndale, Fla., 1993—. With USN, 1971-79.

BERGHEL, HAL L., computer science educator, columnist, author; b. Mpls., May 10, 1946; s. Oscar H. and Edna M. (Muller) B.; m. Margi Millard, May 7, 1983; children: David, Steven, Kevin. BA, U. Nebr., 1971, MA, 1973; MA, U. Nebr., 1976, PhD, 1977. Asst. prof. mgmt. U. Nebr., Lincoln, 1979-80, asst. prof. computer sci., 1981-86; prof. computer sci. U. Ark., Fayetteville, 1986—; bd. dirs. The Rosebush Co., N.Y.C.; pres. Fourth Generation Cons., Lincoln, Nebr., 1980-84. Contbr. numerous articles to profl. jours. Mem. IEEE (Disting. visitor 1994—), Ark. Soc. for Computer and Info. Tech. (chair, bd. dirs. 1988—), Assn. for Computing Machinery (nat. lectr. 1991-93, 95-97, publs. bd. 1992—, local activities bd. 1993—, Disting. Svc. award 1996),. Office: U Ark Dept Computer Sci SCEN 230 Fayetteville AR 72701

BERGMAN, ANDREW JAMES, quality control consultant; b. Rockford, Ill., Oct. 11, 1966; s. Donald E. and Liesare E. (Stebner) B.; m. Patricia Lynn Watson, Nov. 28, 1992. BS, Purdue Univ., 1988. Cert. quality engr. Mfg. engr. Saginaw Tonawanda Forge, Tonawanda, N.Y., 1985-89; gen supr. quality assurance & tech. North Star Steel, Houston, 1989-92; quality engr. Oil Tech. Svcs., Inc., Houston, 1992; mgr. of certification OTS Quality Registrars, Inc., Houston, 1992-94; v.p. QSI, Houston, 1994—; participant in numerous confs.; selected as evaluator for 1993 Tex. Quality award. Contbr. articles to profl. jours. Mem. Am. Soc. Quality Control, Am. Mktg. Assn. (assoc.). Home: 20807 Redbud Tr Kingwood TX 77346 Office: QSI Ste 455 363 North Belt Ste 630 Houston TX 77060-2413

BERGMAN, ANNE NEWBERRY, foundation administrator, civic activist; b. Weatherford, Tex., Mar. 12, 1925; d. William Douglas and Mary (Hunter) Newberry; m. Robert David Bergman, Aug. 17, 1947; children: Elizabeth Anne Bozzell, John David, William Robert. BA, Trinity U., San Antonio, 1945; postgrad., UCLA, 1946-47. Councilperson City Weatherford (Tex.), 1986-91, mayor pro tem, 1990-91; pres. Weatherford Libr. Found., 1989—; mem. Heritage Gallery Com., Weatherford Pub. Libr. (Mary Martin Collection), 1993—; bd. dirs. Manna Store House, Inc., 1990—. Founder Hist. Home Tour, Weatherford, 1972; co-chairperson Spring Festival Bd., 1976, Weatherford Planning and Zoning Commn., 1980-85; fundraising chairperson Weatherford Libr. Found., 1985-86; chairperson Tex. State Rev. Com. Cmty. Devel. Block Grants, 1987-91; pres. Tex. Fedn. Rep. Women, 1975-77; regional coord. George Bush for Pres. campaign, 1980, 88; co-chairperson Congl. Dist. 12 Bush-Quayle campaign, 1992, Tex. Women Support Pres., 1983-84; del. Nat. Rep. Conv., 1988; mem. Episcopal Churchwomen's Cabinet, Diocese of Ft. Worth, sec., 1995, 96, del. ECW Triennial, Episcopal Ch. U.S.A., 1997. Named Outstanding Rep. Woman, Tex. Fedn. Rep. Women, 1981. Mem. Parker County Rep. Women, DAR (Weatherford chpt.), Weatherford C. of C. (Outstanding Citizen of the Yr. 1988), Friends of Weatherford Pub. Libr. (life, charter pres. 1959-61, pres. 1973-74). Home: 609 W Josephine St Weatherford TX 76086-4055

BERGMANN, WARREN CLARENCE, mechanical engineer; b. Lyndhurst, N.J., May 21, 1921; s. Frank A. and Matoria C. (Tribout) B.; m. Phyllis E. Rule, Sept. 10, 1949; 1 child, Brian P. BSME, Newark Coll. Engring., 1950. Registered profl. engr., N.J. Devel. engr. Walter Kidde & Co., Belleville, N.J., 1951-55; chief engr. Pneu-Hydro Valve Corp., Cedar Knolls, N.J., 1956-69; sr. design engr. Curtiss-Wright Corp., Caldwell, N.J., 1970; sr. project engr. Valcor Engring. Corp., Kenilworth, N.J., 1970-73; chief engr. Angar Sci. Controls, Cedar Knolls, 1973-82; chief applications engr. sci. div. Valcor Engring. Corp., Springfield, N.J., 1982-87, cons., 1987—. With U.S. Army, 1942-46, MTO. Recipient Tech. Achievement Recognition award Brunswick Corp., Skokie, Ill., 1978. Mem. NSPE, S.C. Soc. Profl. Engrs., N.J. Inst. Tech. Alumni Assn. (pres. 1974-75). Presbyterian. Home: 309 Green Hill Dr Anderson SC 29621-2433

BERGONZI, AL, company executive. Dir. rsch. HBO & Co. Office: 301 Perimeter Ctr N Atlanta GA 30346*

BERGQUIST, SANDRA LEE, medical and legal consultant, nurse; b. Carlton, Minn., Oct. 13, 1944; d. Arthur Vincent and Avis Lorene Portz; m. David Edward Bergquist, June 11, 1966; children: Rion Eric, Taun Erin. BS in Nursing, Barry U., 1966; MA in Mgmt., Central Mich. U., 1975; student U. So. Calif., 1980-82. R.N., registered advanced nurse practitioner; cert. physician asst. Commd. 2d lt. U.S. Air Force, 1968, advanced through grades to lt. col., 1985; staff and charge nurse U.S. Air Force, 1968-76, primary care nurse practitioner, McConnell AFB, Kans., 1976-79, officer in charge Wheeler Med. Facility, Wheeler AFB, Hawaii, 1979-83, supr. ambulatory care services, Elgin AFB, Fla., 1983-84; med.-legal cons., Pensacola, Fla., 1985—; risk mgr., quality assurance coordinator HCA-Twin Cities Hosp., Niceville, 1986-88. Bd. dirs. Okaloosa County (Fla.) Coun. on Aging, 1984—; adv. bd. Advanced Home Health, 1990—; chairperson Niceville/Valparaiso Task Force on Child Abuse Prevention, Fla., 1985-88; chmn. home and family life com. Twin Cities Women's Club, Niceville, 1985-88; chmn. advancement com. Gulf Coast coun. Boy Scouts Am., 1985-87; instr. advanced and basic cardiac life support Hawaii Heart Assn. and Tripler Armaii Heart Assn. and Tripler Army Med. Ctr., 1981-83. Decorated Commendation medal with 1 oak leaf cluster, USAF Meritorious Service medal, Air Force Commendation medal. Mem. Am. Assn. Critical-Care Nurses, Am. Assn. Physician Assts., Assn. Mil. Surgeons U.S., Soc. Ret. Air Force Nurses, Soc. Air Force Physician Assts., Twin Cities Women's Club. Lutheran. Avocations: computer programming, reading, handicrafts.

BERGSTROM, TRUDY SONDEREGGER, elementary school educator; b. N.Y.C., July 10, 1937; d. Ernest and Gunda (Seidl) Sonderegger; m. James Edward Bergstrom, Jan. 2, 1970; 1 child, Carin Sue. Student, Baldwin-Wallace Coll., 1954-57; AB, Rollins Coll., 1960, MA in Tchg., 1964, postgrad., 1973-76. Cert. early childhood edn., elem. edn., adminstrn. and supervision. Sec. to pres. Rollins Coll., Winter Park, Fla., 1958-60; elem. tchr. Orange County Pub. Schs., Orlando, Fla., 1960-74, early childhood resource tchr., 1974-76, basic skills resource tchr., 1977-80; curriculum resource tchr. Durrance Elem. Sch., Orlando, 1980-90, Apopka (Fla.) Elem. Sch., 1990—; cons., workshop presenter in field. Contbr. articles to newspapers and profl. publs. Active Apopka Woman's Club. Recipient Outstanding Golden Apple Coord. award ADDitions Program, Orlando, 1993. Mem. ASCD, NEA, Fla. Tchg. Profession, Orange County Classroom Tchrs. Assn., Errol Country Club, Apopka C. of C. (mem. edn. com. 1990—), Phi Delta Kappa, Pi Gamma Mu, Delta Kappa Gamma, Pi Kappa Delta, Zeta Tau Alpha, Delta Phi Alpha. Home: 1547 Belfast Ct Apopka FL 32712-2025 Office: Apopka Elem Sch 675 Old Dixie Hwy Apopka FL 32712-3421

BERGWALL, EVAN HAROLD, JR., psychologist and minister; b. Bklyn., Mar. 21, 1943; s. Evan Harold and Jean Mitchel (Francis) B.; m. Jacqueline F. Bergwall, Nov. 22, 1974; children: Drew Crawford, Evan Harold III. BA, Taylor U., Upland, Ind., 1964; MDiv, Vanderbilt U., 1969; MA, U. Notre Dame, 1972, PhD, 1975. Lic. psychologist, Fla.; ordained to ministry Meth. Ch., 1965. Clin. intern Oaklawn Psychiat. Ctr., Elkhart, Ind., 1974-75; psychologist Karitas Cmty., Crystal Springs, Miss., 1975; assoc. dir. Montanari Clin. Sch., Hialeah, Fla., 1975-76; cons. Career Mgmt. of Atlanta, Inc., 1977-78; pres. EHB Cons., Roswell, Ga., 1978-91, Humanagerial Sys., Roswell, 1977-88; dir. counseling ctr. Roswell United Meth. Ch., 1978-91; v.p. human resources City Pride Bakery, Pitts., 1991-92; psychologist Bergwall & Assocs., Destin, Fla., 1993—. Exec. dir. Youth Svcs. Bur., South Bend, Ind., 1972-73; counselor Youth Advocacy Program, South Bend, 1971-72; minister of youth Gallatin (Tenn.) Meth. Ch., 1966-69, First United Meth. Ch., South Bend, 1969-71; adv. bd. Drug Free North Fulton, Roswell, 1989-90; bd. dirs. Heart Assn., Roswell, 1987-88; youth del. World Meth. Conf., Oslo, 1961. U. Notre Dame scholar, 1970-74, Vanderbilt U. scholar, 1967. Mem. APA, Soc. Indsl. and Orgnl. Psychology, Rotary (fellow). Office: Bergwall & Associates 3757 Misty Way Destin FL 32541-2104

BERGWERK, JACK EDWARD, retired sales executive consultant; b. N.Y.C., Nov. 27, 1930; s. Louis and Mildred; m. Corinne Finklestein, June 24, 1956. BS, N.Y.U., 1952. Sales Stein Hall & Co., N.Y.C., 1953-60; sales mgr. Steve Hill & Co., N.Y.C., 1960-77; sales mgr., product devel. mgr. Celanece Corp., Louisville, 1977-80; sales mgr. Hoechst Celance, Louisville, 1980-87, Portsmouth, Va., 1987-92; cons., Louisville, 1992-93. Counselor Svc. Corps Ret. Execs., Louisville, 1992-93; mem. Louisville Rep. Com. 1st lt. USAF, 1952-53. Jewish. Home: 2417 Hayward Rd Louisville KY 40242-6427

BERK, JAMES LAWRENCE, II, entertainment executive, producer, songwriter; b. Akron, Ohio, Aug. 2, 1960; s. James L. and Cheryl B. BA cum laude, Yale U., 1982; MBA, Duke U., 1984. Asst. to pres. Multimedia Entertainment, N.Y.C., 1984-86, asst. to v.p. program mktg., 1986; pres., CEO, Platinum Entertainment, Inc., 1986-93; pres. First Media Comms., Inc., 1993—. Writer, prodr.: Digging Up Scotland, Blind Justice, Cellarful of Dreams, Open Season; prodr., composer: (album compilations) The Light of Love, Prison of the Senses, Promised Land, Desert Bloom; exec. prodr. The Possible, The Guthrie Bros., Stranger Things Have Happened; author: There's a Moosh in My Shoe, Boola, Boola.

BERKE, SARAH BALLARD, geriatrics nurse, mental health nurse; b. Bethesda, Md., Feb. 21, 1951; d. Edward B. and Pauline C. (Lowery) Ballard; divorced; children: Nathan M., Adam B. Diploma in nursing, Forsyth Hosp., 1974. RN, N.Mex., Tex. Acting unit dir. N.Mex. State Hosp., Las Vegas, 1976-78; head nurse adult unit U. N.Mex. Mental Health Ctr., Albuquerque, 1986-87; day charge nurse Americare Rio Rancho, N.Mex., 1987-89, St. Joseph West Mesa Hosp., Albuquerque, 1989-90; traveling nurse Rio Rancho, 1990-92; dir. clin. svcs. Kimberly Quality Care, Midland, Tex., 1992-93; DON Glenwood Psychiat. Hosp., Midland, 1993-95, Terrace West Nursing Ctr., Midland, 1995—.

BERKEBILE, CHARLES ALAN, geology educator, hydrogeology researcher; b. Queens, N.Y., Mar. 4, 1938; s. Charles Dean and Bernice (Manlove) B.; m. Jeanne Marie Kleypas, Oct. 21, 1994; children: Patricia Berlowe, Gregory Martin. BS, Allegheny Coll., 1960; MA, Boston U., 1961, PhD, 1964. Mem. rsch. staff MIT, Cambridge, 1963-64; asst. prof. Southampton (N.Y.) Coll. L.I. U., 1964-67, assoc. prof., dept. chair Southampton (N.Y.) Coll., 1969-75, prof., assoc. dir. Southampton (N.Y.) Coll., 1975-81; rsch. mineralogist Corning (N.Y.) Glass Works, 1967-69; prof., dept. chair Corpus Christi (Tex.) State U., 1981-91; prof., dir. Tex. A&M U., Corpus Christi, 1991-94, prof., asst. dean, 1994—; vis. assoc. chemist Brookhaven Nat. Lab., Upton, N.Y., 1966-67; vis. sr. rsch. geologist Princeton (N.J.) U., 1979-80. Contbr. articles to profl. jours. Mem. Regional Stormwater Master Plan Adv. Com., Corpus Christi, 1989-90, Mayor's Adv. Com. on Water Issues, Corpus Christi, 1991-92; treas., bd. dirs. Rockport (Tex.) Country Club Estates Homeowners Assn., 1991-94. Fellow Geol. Soc. Am.; mem. Assn. Ground Water Scientists and Engrs., Nat. Ground Water Assn., Nat. Assn. Geology Tchrs., Tex. Ground Water Assn. (bd. dirs. 1990—, v.p. ground water sci. 1994, pres. 1995-96), Corpus Christi Geol. Soc. Home: 314 Champions Dr Rockport TX 78382 Office: Tex A&M U 6300 Ocean Dr Corpus Christi TX 78412

BERKELEY, BETTY LIFE, college educator; b. St. Louis, May 25, 1924; d. James Alfred and Anna Laura (Voltmer) Life; m. Marvin Harold Berkeley, Feb. 7, 1947; children: Kathryn Elizabeth, Barbara Ellen, Brian Harrison, Janet Lynn. AB, Harris Tchrs. Coll., 1947; MA in Ednl. Adminstrn., Washington U., St. Louis, 1951; PhD, U. North Tex., 1980. Tchr. St. Louis pub. schs., 1946-48, Clayton pub. schs., Mo., 1948-49, Lamplighter Pvt. Sch., Dallas, 1964-67; program devel. specialist Richland Coll., Dallas, 1980-84, instr., 1981—; adj. prof. U. North Tex., Denton, 1981—, cons. Sch. Cmty. Svcs. Ctr. for Studies on Aging, 1981—; pres. Retirement Planning Svcs., Dallas, 1984—. Contbr. articles to profl. jours. Named Outstanding Alumna Coll. of Edn. U. of North Tex., 1992. Mem. Dallas Commn. on Status of Women, 1975-79; bd. dirs. Dallas Municipal Library, 1979-83, Sr. Citizen Greater Dallas, 1986-92, Council on Adult Ministry Lovers Lane United Meth. Ch., 1982; charter mem. bd. dirs., life mem. Friends of U. North Tex. Libr.; mem. Pres.'s Coun. U. North Tex., mem. vol. mgmt. edn. task force, 1978-82. Mem. AAUW (pres. 1973-75; Outstanding Woman of Tex. 1981). Club: Women's Council of Dallas County (v.p. 1977-79). Avocations: travel, cooking, gardening, needlework. Home and Office: 13958 Hughes Ln Dallas TX 75240-3510

BERKELEY, FRANCIS LEWIS, JR., retired archivist; b. Albemarle County, Va., Apr. 9, 1911; s. Francis Lewis and Ethel (Crissey) B.; B.S., U. Va., 1934, M.A., 1940; m. Helen Wayland Sutherland, June 12, 1937. Tchr. Va. pub. schs., 1934-38; curator manuscripts U. Va. Library, Charlottesville, 1938-41, curator and univ. archivist, 1946-63, asso. librarian, 1957-63, sec. of Rector and Visitors, 1953-58, exec. asst. to pres., 1963-74, archivist emeritus, prof. emeritus, 1974—; council Inst. Early Am. History and Culture. Fulbright research fellow U. Edinburgh, 1952-53; Guggenheim fellow U. London, 1961-62; sec. of navy adv. com. on naval history, 1958-74. Trustee Thomas Jefferson Meml. Found.; mem. adv. com. Papers of Thomas Jefferson, Papers of James Madison, Papers of George Washington; mem. Va. Com. on Colonial Records, 1955-71, Va. Commn. on Hist. Records, 1976—. Served with USNR, 1942-46; capt. ret. Fellow Soc. Am. Archivists; mem. Am. Antiquarian Soc., Mass., Va., (v.p. 1970-78, trustee 1979—), other hist. socs., Colonial Soc. Mass., Walpole Soc., Raven Soc., Phi Beta Kappa, Omicron Delta Kappa. Democrat. Episcopalian. Clubs: Colonnade (Charlottesville); Century (N.Y.). Editor and compiler: Dunmore's Proclamation of Emancipation, 1941; Annual Reports on Historical Collections, University of Virginia Library, 1945-50, with cumulative indexes, 1945, 50; Jefferson Papers of the University of Virginia, 1950; Papers of John Randolph of Roanoke, 1950; John Rolfe's True Relation. 1951; Introduction to Thomas Jefferson's Farm Book, 1953. Editorial bd. Va. Quar. Rev., 1961-74. Contbr. to Dictionary of Biography, Ency. Brit., Collier's Nat. Am. Cyclopedia; other reference works. Home: 2600 Barracks Rd Apt 248 Charlottesville VA 22901-2192

BERKING, MAX, retired advertising company executive; b. N.Y.C., July 27, 1917; s. Max and Rhoda (Jones) B.; m. Dorothy Quincy Noyes, Jan. 6, 1951 (dec. Apr. 1962); children: Charles, Peter, Laurence, Charlotte; m. Frances Coner Bauman, Sept. 10, 1979. AB, Williams Coll., 1939. Media analyst McCann-Erickson Advt., N.Y.C., 1939-42; pub. opinion analyst Office of War Info., N.Y.C., 1942-44; asst. to chmn. Fair Employment Practice Com., Washington, 1944-45; campaign dir. Internat. Rescue Com., N.Y.C., 1946-48; pres. Max Berking Advt., N.Y.C., 1958-83. Co-author: Strengthening the Wisconsin Legislature, 1968; columnist: Northport Sun-Herald & Sun, 1991—. State Sen. N.Y., 1965; chmn. Westchester County (N.Y.) Dem. Com., 1971-75. Democrat. Congregationalist. Home: 12120 Hernando North Port FL 34287

BERKOWITZ, GERALD PHILLIP, physician; b. Trenton, N.J., Apr. 18, 1948; m. Allison Davis; children: Joshua Michael, Jacob Franklin, Cathrine Lellie, Martin Ross, Cameron Lee. AB, Franklin and Marshall Coll., 1970; MD, U. Tenn. Coll., 1974. Diplomate Am. Bd. Pediatrics, Neonatal-Perinatal Medicine. Pediatric resident Medical Coll. Va., Richmond, 1974-77; chief resident Medical Coll. Va., 1976; fellow neonatal-perinatel medicine U. Ala., Birmingham, 1977-79; co-dir. Richland Meml. Hosp. Newborn Intensive Care Unit, Columbia, S.C.; asst. dir. div. neonatology Richland Meml. Hosp., Columbia, S.C.; asst. prof. dept. pediatrics U. S. C., 1984-92; neonatologist Presbyterian Hosp., Charlotte, N.C., 1993—; pres. Southside Neonatology Assocs., Charlotte; dir. level II intensive care nursery Mercy Hosp. South, Charlotte. Contbr. articles to profl. jours. Fellow Am. Acad. Pediatrics; mem. AMA, Mecklenburg County Med. Soc., N.C. Med. Assn., Am. Acad. Pediatrics. Office: Southside Neonatology Assoc 10628 Park Rd Charlotte NC 28210-8407

BERKOWITZ, RALPH STEVEN, business executive; b. Atlanta, Mar. 3, 1949; s. Frank Louis Berkowitz and Gerda Dora (Imbach) Naviera; m. Kathy Berkowitz, Jan. 26, 1975; children: Matthew, Rebecca. BA, Rutgers U., 1970, MS, 1973; PhD, Columbia U., 1992; postgrad., Mich. U., 1985-86. Mgr. C.B.S., Inc., N.Y.C., 1970-73; cons. Behavioral Systems, Inc., Atlanta, 1973-75, Alexander Proudfoot Co., Chgo., 1975-79; tng. dir. Domino's Pizza, Inc., Ann Arbor, Mich., 1979-87, Alcoa Fujikura Ltd., Brentwood, Tenn., 1987-92; mng. dir. Resource Mgmt. Systems, Franklin, Tenn., 1992—; advisor Cambridge (Mass.) Ctr. for Behavioral Study, 1990, Nat. Safety Coun., Chgo., 1984-86, Exec. Edn. Forum, Palatine, Ill., 1989. Author: Moving to the Next Generation of Quality, 1993; editor Guidelines to Training Excellence, 1985, Behavioral Training for Line Employees, 1974; contbr. articles to profl. jours.; patentee in field. Mem. Civitan Internat., Ann Arbor, 1984-87. Named All Am. Honorable Mention Football News, 1969, All Am. Baseball Today, 1968; recipient Golden Cassette award Internat. TV Assn., 1984-85, Safety Tng. Excellence award Nat. Safety Coun., 1985. Mem. Am. Mgmt. Assn., Internat. Platform Assn., Cambridge Ctr. Behavioral Study. Home: PO Box 681045 Franklin TN 37068-1045 Office: 109 Holiday Ct Bldg D-9 Franklin TN 37067-3000

BERLAND, LINCOLN LEWIS, radiologist; b. Milw., Apr. 2, 1949; s. Jack Abraham and Helen (Lipshitz) B.; m. Nancy Winnik, June 12, 1971; children: Matthew, Nicole. Student, MIT, 1967-70; BS in Physics, U. Wis., 1971; MD, Washington U., St. Louis, 1975. Cert. diagnostic radiology Am. Bd. Radiology; lic. medicine and surgery, Wis.; lic. medicine, Ala. Clin. intern Med. Coll. Wis. Affiliated Hosps., Milw., 1975-76, resident radiology, 1976-79, fellow in body computed tomography and ultrasound, 1979-80; asst. prof. radiology Med. Coll. Wis., Milw., 1981-82; assoc. prof. radiology, chief sect. U. Ala., Birmingham, 1983-89, prof. radiology, chief body computed tomography, 1989-91, prof. radiology, chief sect., 1991-92, prof. dept. radiology, vice-chmn. planning and adminstrn., 1992—; vis. prof., faculty mem. various colls. and hosps. including Ctrl. Hosp., U. Sherbrooke, Que., 1980, Gunderson Clinic, LaCrosse, Wis., 1981, Madison (Wis.) Gen. Hosp., 1982, Vanderbilt U., 1983, 89, Tulane U., New Orleans, 1987, NYU Med. ctr., 1990; mem. CT med. adv. bd. GE, 1986—; mem. Commn. on Ultrasound Am. Coll. Radiology, 1988—; mem. U. Ala. Hosp. Clin. Coun. Com., 1989—; mem. rsch./sci. com. Soc. Computed Body Tomography, 1991—. Author: Practical CT: Technology and Techniques, 1987; contbr. articles to profl. jours., chpts. to books; reviewer Jour. Clin. Ultrasound, 1982-89, Radiology, 1988—, Gastrointestinal Radiology, 1989—. Chmn. edn. com. Temple Emanuel, Birmingham, 1990-93; mem. steering com. Parent Partnership, Mountain Brook, Ala., 1990-92; sch. supt. selection com. Mountain Brook Sch. System, 1993. Mem. Radiol. Soc. N.Am., Am. Inst. Ultrasound in Medicine, Assn. Univ. Radiologists, Soc. Body Computed Tomography, Soc. Radiologists in Ultrasound (mem. profl. practice and stds. com. 1992—). Jewish. Home: 3421 Brookwood Trce Birmingham AL 35223-2879 Office: U Ala Hosp Dept Radiology 619 19th St S Birmingham AL 35233-1924

BERLER, BEATRICE ADELE, translator, author; b. Bklyn., May 10, 1915; d. Max and Clara (Bichman) Goldenblank; m. Albert Berler, May 15, 1945. BA, Trinity U., 1960, MA in Fgn. Langs. and History, 1961. Author: Azuela y La Veracidad Histórica, 1966; translator: Latin American and the World (Leopoldo Zea), La Revolucion de la Iglesia en America Latina (Hugo La Torre Cabal), Hispanic America and its Civilizations (Edmund S. Urbanski), The Conquest of Mexico, 2d edit., 1988, Ellos Vienen...La Conquista de Mexico (Jose Lopez Portillo), Ellos Vienen...La Conquista de Mèxico, 1992; editor: El Epistalario y Archivo de Mariano Azueula, 1969, 2d edit., 1993; editor, compiler Las Tribulaciones de Una Familia Decente, 1966, El Epistolario y Archivo de Mariano Azuela, 1969, 2d edit., 1993, El Epistolario y Archivo de Mariano Azuela: Documentos Adicionales, 1996; co-translator: (novels by Mariano Azuela) The Underdogs, 1964, Trials of a Respectable Family, The Firefly, 1964, La Luciérnaga, 1964, La Revolución de la Iglesia en Amèrica Latina, 1967, Hispanic America and its Civilizations, 1967, Spanish-Latina America y el Mundo; abbreviator, editor La Coquista de Mèxico, 1996, The Conquest of Mexico, 1988. Pres. Nat. Women's Com. Brandeis U., 1971-73, trustee, 1971-73, fellow. Recipient Brotherhood award Nat. Coun. Christians and Jews, 1988, Outstanding Svc. to Librs. award Tex. Libr. Assn., 1987, Outstanding Cmty. Svc. award Fed. Bar Assn. San Antonio, 1975, Spl award N.Y. Pub. Libr., 1992; named Benefactor City of San Antonio San Antonio City Coun., 1987, Best and the Brightest Univ. Round Table, 1980.

BERLIN, STEVEN RITT, oil company financial official; b. Pitts., July 1, 1944; s. Sidney D. and Pauline (Ritt) B.; student Carnegie Mellon U., 1964-67; BBA, Duquesne U., 1967; MBA, U. Wis., 1969; m. Vera Y. Leffman, June 9, 1968; children—Leslie, Jessica, Loren. CPA. Prof., U. Houston, 1970-72; various fin. positions Cities Svc. Co., Tulsa, 1973-83; v.p. fin. Citgo Petroleum, Tulsa, 1983-85, gen. mgr., 1985-86, chief fin. officer, 1986—; speaker various industry, profl. seminars; instr. U. Tulsa; mem. Acctg. Edn. change Commn. Mem. bd. visitors U. Wis.; sec., treas. Green T Club of Tulsa, Am. Assembly of Collegiate Schs. of Bus. Mem. AICPA, Am. Acctg. Assn., Okla. Soc. CPAs, Stanford U. Alumni Assn., Beta Gamma Sigma. Jewish. Avocations: jogging, reading. Home: 230 E 19th St Tulsa OK 74119-5212 Office: Citgo Petroleum Corp PO Box 3758 Tulsa OK 74102-3758

BERLINGHIERI, JOEL CARL, physicist, educator, consultant; b. Boston, Dec. 18, 1942; s. Joseph and Rose Berlinghieri (DeMarco); m. Susan E. Eden, Aug. 8, 1971; 1 child, Joel C. BS, Boston Coll., 1964; PhD, U. Rochester, 1970. Asst. prof. physics Colgate U., Hamilton, N.Y., 1969-71; prof. physics The Citadel, Charleston, S.C., 1971—, head dept. physics, 1991—; pvt. cons., Charleston, 1990—. Contbr. articles to Jour. Acoustical Soc. Am., Phys. Rev. Letters. Mem. IEEE, Optical Soc. Am., Acoustical Soc. Am. Office: The Citadel 171 Moultrie St Charleston SC 29409

BERMAN, BRUCE JUDSON, lawyer; b. Roslyn, N.Y., Oct. 9, 1946; s. Howard M. Berman and Soosha T. (Draizen) Marks; children: Daniel H., Ann N., Andrew J., Josie A.; m. Susan Leigh Readinger, Dec. 29, 1991. BA, Williams Coll., 1968; MBA, Columbia U., 1972; JD, Boston U., 1972. Bar: Mass. 1972, Fla. 1973, U.S. Dist. Ct. (so. dist.) Fla. 1980, U.S. Dist. Ct. (mid. dist.) Fla. 1990, U.S. Ct. Appeals (5th cir.) 1980, U.S. Ct. Appeals (11th cir.) 1981, U.S. Supreme Ct. 1976. Assoc. Guggenheimer & Untermyer, N.Y.C., 1973-79; from assoc. to ptnr. Myers, Kenin, Levinson, Frank & Richards, Miami, Fla., 1979-85; ptnr. Weil, Gotshal & Manges, Miami, 1985—; mem. spl. ad hoc trial com. to Dade County (Fla.) Cir. Ct., 1988—. Mem. New World Symphony Cmty. Bd., Miami Beach, Fla., 1991—. Mem. Fla. Bar (chmn. civil procedure rules com. 1988-90, chmn. jud. adminstrn. rules com. 1993-94), Dade County Bar, Am. Arbitration Assn. (arbitrator), Nat. Assn. Securities Dealers (arbitrator). Office: Weil Gotshal & Manges 701 Brickell Ave Ste 2100 Miami FL 33131-2861

BERMAN, LARRY F., physician, health facility administrator; b. L.A., Sept. 9, 1959; s. Wallace and Dania Berman; m. Cynthia Redmond, July 26, 1986; children: Ashley Elisabeth, Alexis Sarah, Alyssa Redmond. BS in Psychobiology, UCLA, 1981; MSPH, U. N.C., 1983; MD, Tel Aviv U., Tel Aviv, 1987. Diplomate Am. Bd. Internal Medicine. Intern, resident internal medicine SUNY, Stony Brook, 1987-90; pvt. practice Charlotte, 1991-94; chmn. dept. medicine Mercy Hosp., Charlotte, 1993-94; med. dir. Lakeview Living Ctr., Charlotte, 1993—; mem. exec. bd. Juvenile Diabetes Found., N.C./S.C., 1992—; chief of staff Mercy Hosp. South, Charlotte; med. dir. Sardis Nursing Home, 1996—, Carriage Club of Charlotte, 1996—. Mem. AMA, Am. Coll. Physicians, Mecklenburg County Med. Soc., Am. Soc. Internal Medicine. Republican. Jewish. Office: 10620 Park Rd Ste 128 Charlotte NC 28210-8472

BERMAN, MONA S., actress, playwright, theatrical director and producer; b. Jersey City; d. Edward and Mary (Auster) Solomon; m. Carroll Z. Berman; children: Marcie S. Berman Ries, Laura Jane. BA, Beaver Coll., postgrad. Columbia U., MFA, Boston U. Tchr. English, drama Jersey City High Schs.; actress indsl., stage, TV, Valley Players, Holyoke, Mass., The Millbrook Playhouse, Mill Hall, Pa., 1991; owner, dir. The Theatre Sch. and Producing Co., Maplewood, N.J.; chmn. drama edn. YM-YWHA of Met. N.J. Cons., Clark Ctr. for Performing Arts, N.Y.C., 1965-66; instr. South Orange, Maplewood Adult Sch., 1967; artistic dir. Children's Theatre Co. Inc., Maplewood, 1968-70; cons. The Whole Theater Co.; dir. pub. relations Co. 3 by 2. Playwright: Hello Joe, That Ring in the Center, The Big Show, Interim, Who Can Belong?, Sudden Changes, Without Malice, Interim 2; producer, dir. A Night of Stars; guest theatre reviewer El Paso Herald Post, 1980-82. Active Boston United Fund, 1955-59, chmn. Boston residential area, 1957; bd. dirs. Greater Boston Girl Scouts Am., 1956-58, Tufts Med. Faculty Wives, 1956-58; active S. Fla. Theatre League. Mem. Dramatist Guild, Actors Equity Assn., Profl. Actor's Assn. Fla. Address: 8925 Collins Ave Surfside FL 33154

BERMAN, RICHARD BRUCE, lawyer; b. Freeport, N.Y., Sept. 26, 1951; s. Nathan and Helen Dorothy (Raiden) B.; m. Laurie Michael, Nov. 2, 1985. BA in Speech Communication, Am. U., 1973; JD, U. Miami, 1976. Bar: Fla. 1976, U.S. Dist. Ct. (so. dist.) Fla. 1976, D.C. 1978. Atty. Travelers Ins. Co., Ft. Lauderdale, Fla., 1977-84; assoc. Frank & Flaster P.A., Sunrise, Fla., 1984-88, DeCasare & Salerno, Ft. Lauderdale, Fla., 1988-89; pvt. practice, 1989—; bd. dirs. Frosch Health Care Cons., Inc., Landerhill; mem. worker's compensation rules com. Fla. Bar, 1991-94, Fla. Workers Advs., 1991—. Mem. panel health care Dem. Legis. Task Force, Ft. Lauderdale, 1985-87; mem. adv. bd. Reflex Sympathetic Dystrophy Syndrome Assn. Fla., 1992—. Mem. ABA, ATLA, D.C. Bar, Fla. Bar Assn., Broward County Trial Lawyers Assn. Lodge: B'nai B'rith Justice.

BERNAL, NANCY ELLEN, medical librarian; b. Atlanta, Jan. 14, 1948; d. George Anthony and Edna (Friend) Bayne; m. Ian Christopher Van Buskirk, Mar. 26, 1973 (div. July 1980); children: Ian Christopher Van Buskirk Jr., Nathan Brown Van Buskirk; m. Jose Ruiz Bernal, Aug. 4, 1980; 1 child, Kai Victor. BA with honors, U. South Fla., 1969, MA, 1976. Cert. med. libr., 1976-86. Libr. trainee James A. Haley Vets. Hosp., Tampa, 1974-75, libr. technician, 1976-77, med. libr., 1978-90, chief libr. svc., 1991—; adj. instr. div. lifelong learning U. South Fla., Tampa, 1993. Contbr. articles to profl. jours. H.W. Wilson Co. scholar, 1975; AIDS/HIV Ednl. Demonstration Project grantee VA, 1992. Mem. Fla. Health Scis. Libr. Assn., Tampa Bay Area Med. Libr. Network. Office: James A Haley Vets Hosp 13000 Bruce B Downs Blvd Tampa FL 33612-4745

BERNARD, DAVID A., investment advisor; b. Toronto, Ont., Can., Dec. 19, 1945; s. Seymour and Evelyn (Gensior) B.; m. Francine Claire Gouvin, Oct. 24, 1981; children: Claire Rose, Maximilian David. Student, Columbia U. Pres. D.A. Bernard & Co., N.Y.C., 1967-74, Tower Funding, Inc., N.Y.C., 1974-79; v.p. MCANY, Inc., N.Y.C., 1979-81; dir. Concord Assets Group, Inc., Boca Raton, Fla., 1981-93; COO Milestone Properties, Inc., Boca Raton, 1991-93; pres. June Fourth Corp., Boca Raton, 1993—; pres. Indpls. Securities, Inc., Boca Raton, 1995—. Dir. Com. for a Rep. Assembly, Albany, N.Y., 1983—. Mem. The Sky Club. Home: 234 Park Ave Palm Beach FL 33480-3809

BERNARD, LOUIS JOSEPH, surgeon, educator; b. Laplace, La., Aug. 19, 1925; s. Edward and Jeanne (Vinet) B.; m. Lois Jeannette McDonald, Feb. 1, 1976; children: Marie Antonia, Phyllis Elaine. BA magna cum laude, Dillard U., New Orleans, 1946; MD, Meharry Med. Coll., 1950. Diplomate: Am. Bd. Surgery. Instr. surgery Sch. Medicine, Meharry Med. Coll., Nashville, 1958-59, prof., 1973-90, chmn. dept. surgery, 1973-87, dean, 1987-90, v.p. for health svcs., 1988-90; practice medicine specializing in surgery, 1959-69; mem. clin. faculty U. Okla., 1959-69, assoc. prof., vice chmn. dept. surgery, 1969-73, chmn. dept. surgery, 1973-87, disting. prof. emeritus, 1990—; dir. Drew-Meharry Morehouse Consortium Cancer Ctr., 1990—. Contbr. articles in field to profl. jours. Mem. Okla. State Bd. Corrections, 1968-69. With M.C. U.S. Army, 1951-53. USPHS research fellow NCI, U. Rochester, 1953-54. Fellow A.C.S., Southeastern Surg. Congress; mem. Soc. Surg. Oncology, Internat. Surg. Soc., Am. Assn. Cancer Edn., Sigma Pi Phi, Alpha Omega Alpha. Democrat. Roman Catholic. Home: 156 Queens Ln Nashville TN 37218-1826 Office: Drew-Meharry-Morehouse Consortium Cancer Ctr 1005 Dr Db Todd Jr Blvd Nashville TN 37208-3501

BERNATH, MARY THERESE, special education educator; b. Trenton, N.J., Mar. 15, 1960; d. Joseph Michael and Nellie E. Bernath. BS in Edn., Trenton State Coll., 1983; MEd, U. Cen. Fla., 1989. Tchr. homebound/profoundly mentally handicapped Osceola County Sch. Bd., Kissimmee, Fla., 1983-84; tchr. educable mentally handicapped St. Cloud (Fla.) Middle Sch., 1983-85, tchr. behavior disordered, 1985-86; tchr. educable mentally handicapped Highlands Elem. Sch., Kissimmee, 1986-87; tchr. trainable mentally handicapped Michigan Ave. Elem. Sch., St. Cloud, 1987-88, Ventura Elem. Sch., Kissimmee, 1989-90; tchr. profoundly and trainable mentally handicapped Sidney Lanier Ctr., Gainesville, Fla., 1990—. Vol. Osceola County Spl. Olympics, Kissimmee, 1983-89, chmn. publicity com., 1984-87. Mem. Coun. for Exceptional Children, Kappa Delta Pi. Republican. Roman Catholic.

BERNAY, BETTI, artist; b. 1926; d. David Michael and Anna Gaynia (Bernay) Woolin; m. J. Bernard Goldfarb, Apr. 19, 1947; children: Manette Deitsch, Karen Lynn. Grad. costume design, Pratt Inst., 1946; student, Nat. Acad. Design, N.Y.C., 1947-49, Art Students League, N.Y.C., 1950-51. Exhibited one man shows at Galerie Raymond Duncan, Paris, France, Salas Municipales, San Sebastian, Spain, Circulo de Bellas Artes, Madrid, Spain, Bacardi Gallery, Miami, Fla., Columbia (S.C.) Mus., Columbus (Ga.) Mus., Galerie Andre Weil, Paris, Galerie Hermitage, Monte Carlo, Monaco, Casino de San Remo, Italy, Galerie de Arte de la Caja de Ahorros de Ronda, Malaga, Spain, Centro Artistico, Granada, Spain, Circulo de la Amistad, Cordoba, Spain, Studio H Gallery, N.Y.C., Walter Wallace Gallery, Palm Beach, Fla., Mus. Bellas Artes, Malaga, Harbor House Gallery, Crystal House Gallery, Internat. Gallery, Jordan Marsh, Fontainebleau Gallery, Miami Beach, Carriage House Gallery, Galerie 99, Pageant Gallery, Carriage House, Miami Beach, Rosenbaum Galleries, Palm Beach; exhibited group shows at Painters and Sculptors Soc., Jersey City Mus., Salon de Invierno, Mus. Malaga, Salon des Beaux Arts, Cannes, France, Guggenheim Gallery, Nat. Acad. Gallery, Salmagundi Club, Lever House, Lord & Taylor Art Gallery, Nat. Arts Gallery, Knickerbocker Artists, N.Y.C., Salon des Artistes Independants, Salon des Artistes Francais, Salon Populiste, Paris, Salon de Otono, Nat. Assn. Painters and Sculptors Spain, Madrid, Phipps Gallery, Palm Beach, Artists Equity, Hollywood (Fla.) Mus., Gault Gallery Cheltenham, Phila., Springfield (Mass.) Mus., Met. Mus. and Art Center, Miami, Fla., Planet Ocean Mus., Charter Club, Trade Fair Ams., Guggenheim Gallery, N.Y.C.; represented in permanent collections including Jockey Club Art Gallery, Miami, Mus. Malaga, Circulo de la Amistad, I.O.S. Found., Geneva, Switzerland, others. Bd. dirs. Men's Opera Guild; mem. adv. bd. Jackson Meml. Hosp. Project Newborn; mem. women's com. Bascom Palmer Eye Inst.; mem. working com. Greater Miami Heart Assn., Am. Heart Assn., Am. Cancer Soc., Alzheimer Grand Notable, 2d Generation Miami Heart Inst., Sunrisers Mentally Retarded, Orchid Ball Com., Newborn Neonatal Intensive Care Unit, U. Miami, Jackson Meml. Hosp. Recipient medal City N.Y., medal Sch. Art Leagues, N.Y.C., Prix de Paris Raymond Duncan, 1958, others. Mem. Nat. Assn. Painters and Sculptors Spain, Nat. Assn. Women Artists, Société des Artistes Français, Société des Artistes Independants, Fedn. Francais des Sociétés d'Art Graphique et Plastique, Artists Equity, Am. Artists Profl. League, Am. Fedn. Art, Nat. Soc. Lit. and Arts, Met. Mus. and Arts Center Miami, Pres.'s Club U. Miami. Clubs: Palm Bay, Jockey, Turnberry, Club of Clubs Internat., Miami Shores Country. Address: 10155 Collins Ave Apt 1705 Bal Harbour FL 33154-1629

BERNER, NANCY JANE, biology educator and researcher; b. Hackensack, N.J., Sept. 20, 1962; d. William Gilbert Jr. and Joan Helen (McCullough) B.; m. David Bartels Coe, May 26, 1991; 1 child, Alexis Jordan Berner-Coe. BS, U. Idaho, 1986, MS, 1988; PhD, Stanford U., 1992. Asst. prof. biology U. of the South, Sewanee, Tenn., 1992—. Contbr. articles to Jour. Exptl. Biology. NSF grantee, 1995. Mem. AAAS, Am. Physiol. Soc., Am. Soc. for Integrative and Comp Bio, Am. Soc. Mammalogists, Am. Assn. Women in Sci. Office: U of the South 735 University Ave Sewanee TN 37383-0001

BERNFIELD, LYNNE, psychotherapist; b. N.Y.C., Mar. 16, 1943; d. Meyer and Lilian Claire (Pastel) B.; m. Arthur Dawson Richards, June 16, 1982. BA, Hofstra U., 1964; MA, Azusa Pacific U., 1981. Lic. marriage, family, and child therapist, Calif., Fla. Founder, dir. Writers & Artists Inst., L.A., 1984—. Author: When You Can You Will, 1993. Mem. ASCAP, Calif. Assn. Marriage and Family Therapists, Am. Assn. Marriage and Family Therapists.

BERNHARD, HARRY BARNETT, management consultant, educator; b. N.Y.C., Jan. 5, 1933; s. Walter Sidney and Ruth Francis (Harris) B.; m. Ruthe Fran Korostoff, June 19, 1955; children: Michael Howard, Nancy Ellen. BS in Econs., U. Pa., Phila., 1954; MS in Econs., Columbia U., 1957. Cert. long-term care ombudsman. Mktg. rep., br. mgr. IBM Corp., N.Y.C., 1957-71; human resource exec. IBM Corp., White Plains, N.Y., 1972-80; dir. exec. devel. IBM Corp., Armonk, N.Y., 1981-85; Harvard/IBM fellow Harvard Bus. Sch., Boston, 1985-87; mgmt. cons., 1987—; exec. in residence U. So. Calif. Bus. Sch., L.A., 1987-89, assoc. dean, 1989-90; assoc. dean Emory Bus. Sch., Atlanta, 1990-92; mgmt. cons., 1987—; bd. dirs. Atlanta Industry Liaison Group. Bd. dirs. N.Y. Fedn. Reform Synagogues, N.Y.C., 1984, Shelter for Homeless, Stamford, Conn., 1982; fin. chmn. S.E. Conn. Coun. Chs. and Synagogues, Stamford, 1981; pres. Temple Sinai, Stamford, 1980-82; bd. dirs. Bus. Ethics Found., Boston. 1st lt. USAR, 1955-57. Named Person of Yr., S.E. Conn. Coun. Chs. and Synagogues, Stamford, 1982. Mem. Acad. of Mgmt., Nat. Acad. Nuclear Tng. (mem. nat. accreditation bd. 1991—), N.Y. Acad. Scis., Beta Gamma Sigma. Jewish. Home and Office: 782 Kings Way NW Atlanta GA 30327-2634

BERNHARDT, MARCIA BRENDA, mental health counselor; b. Jersey, N.J., Aug. 22, 1938; d. Jerome and Mitzie (Cohen) B. BA, Fairleigh Dickinson U., 1960; MA, Columbia U., 1960-63, postgrad., 1968-70; postgrad., Hunter Coll., 1973-74. Nat. cert. counselor. Rsch. asst. Tchrs. Coll., Columbia U., N.Y.C., 1963-64; counselor JOIN, N.Y.C., 1965-66; project assoc. Bd. Higher Edn. N.Y., N.Y.C., 1966-68, Tchrs. Coll, Columbia U., N.Y.C., 1968-70; counselor Nassau Community Coll., Garden City, N.Y., 1970-72; rsch. scientist Div. for Youth, N.Y.C., 1972-73; rsch. assoc. Family Svc. Assn., N.Y.C., 1974-76; counselor Div. Blind Svcs., West Palm Beach, Fla., 1984-96; sec., chairperson adv. bd. com. Lighthouse for the Blind, West Palm Beach, 1984-90. Mem. AAUW, ACA, Fla. Counseling Assn., Mental Health Counselor Assn. Greater Palm Beach County, Internat. Platform Assn., Guild for Internat. Piano Competition, Edna Hibel Soc., Smithsonian Instn. Democrat. Jewish. Home: Chatham B # 40 Cv West Palm Beach FL 33417-1807

BERNHARDT, RANDY JOHN, association executive; b. Pigeon, Mich., Mar. 17, 1962; s. John Gerald and Doris Mae (Shapow) B. BS in Agr. Edn., Mich. State U., 1984; MS in Agr. Edn., U. Ill., 1991. Cert. tchr., Ill., Ind., Mich. Cashier NBD Commerce Bank, Lansing, Mich., 1982-84; agr. tchr. Washington High Sch., South Bend, Ind., 1984-86, Chgo. High Sch. for Agrl. Scis., 1986-92; regional dir. Nat. Future Farmers Am. Found., Madison, Wis., 1992-94; team leader, dir. Nat. Future Farmers Am. Orgn., Alexandria, Va., 1995—; curriculum cons. U. Ill., Urbana, 1988-89, Grundy Area Vocat. Ctr., Morris, Ill., 1990-92. Contbr. articles to profl. jours.; editor jour. FFA Advisors Making a Difference. Active mem. Hyde Park Coop. Soc., Chgo., 1986-92; treas. Hampton House Condominium Assn., Chgo., 1991-92. Recipient various awards Ill. Agr. Tchrs. Assn., 1989, 90, 91. Mem. Am. Vocat. Assn., Nat. AgriMktg. Assn., Nat. Assn. Vocat. Agr. Tchrs., Nat. Assn. Parliamentarians, Nat. Assn. State Suprs. of Agrl. Edn. Home: 5921E Coverdale Way Alexandria VA 22310 Office: Nat FFA Orgn 5632 Mt Vernon Memorial Hwy Alexandria VA 22309-0160

BERNHARDT, ROGER, psychoanalyst. MA in Psychology, U. Mich., 1951, PhD in Clin. Psychology, 1954. Staff psychologist VA Hosp., Buffalo, N.Y., 1953-55; chief psychologist Marlboro State Hosp., N.J., 1955-56; psychoanalyst pvt. practice pvt. practice, Naples, Fla., 1956—. Author: (with David Martin) Self-Mastery through Self-Hypnosis, 1977, Self-Mastery English Language book, 1978, Self-Mastery Italian Language book, 1980, Self-mastery Portuguese Language book, 1983, Self-Mastery Dutch Language book, 1985. Home: 1440 Nautilus Rd Naples FL 34102-5152

BERNHEIM, MARY JOSEPHINE, nurse anesthetist; b. Cocoa Beach, Fla., Nov. 10, 1958; d. Edward Stanley and Margaret Yvonne (Latimer) Wickerson; m. David Mayer, May 14, 1983; children: Heather Brianna, Rebekah Rose. BSN, U. N.C., Charlotte, 1984; MSN, U. N.C., Greensboro, 1990. RN, Tenn. Staff nurse U.S. Army, Ft. Polk, La., 1984-87; nurse anesthetist N.C. Bapt. Hosp., Winston-Salem, 1987-91, Bapt. Meml. Hosp., Memphis, 1991-92; staff nurse Meth. Hosp., Memphis, 1992-93, East Tenn. Bapt. Hosp., Knoxville, 1993—. Capt. USAR. Mem. AACN, Am. Assn. Nurse Anesthetists (cert.), Sigma Theta Tau.

BERNSTEIN, DAVID ERIC, gastroenterologist, educator; b. N.Y.C., Apr. 17, 1962; s. Jerome Walter and Barbara (Brown) B.; m. Helen Kim, May 31, 1992. BA, The Johns Hopkins U., 1984; MD, SUNY, StonyBrook, 1988. Diplomate Nat. Bd. Med. Examiners, Am. Bd. Internal Medicine; MD, N.Y., Fla. Intern, resident in internal medicine Montefiore Med. Ctr., Bronx, N.Y., 1988-91; gastroenterology fellowship U. Miami (Fla.) Affiliated Hosps., 1991-93, hepatology fellowship, 1993; asst. prof. U. Miami (Fla.) Sch. of Medicine, 1994—. Contbr. numerous articles to profl. jours., chpts. to books. Mem. AMA, ACP, Fla. Med. Assn., Dade County Med. Assn., Fla. Gastrointestinal Soc., Am. Coll. Gastroenterology, Am. Soc. for Gastrointestinal Endoscopy (trainee), Am. Assn. for Study of Liver Disease (trainee).

BERNSTEIN, JANNA S. BERNHEIM, art educator; b. Memphis, July 21, 1951; d. Berthol Moise and Aline Joy (Kahn) Bernheim; m. Eugene Bernstein Jr., Aug. 12, 1978 (div. Apr. 1992); children: Rachel, Claire, Ruth. BFA, Washington U., 1973; MFA, Memphis State U., 1979, MAT, 1991. Graphic artist Cleo Wrap, Inc., Memphis, 1978-80, Memphis Bd. of Edn., 1980-81; art instr. Memphis Arts Coun., 1983-86, Memphis Brooks Mus., 1985-88; art tchr. St. Agnes Acad./St. Dominic Sch. for Boys, Memphis, 1991—; chmn. cultural arts Richland Elem. Sch., Memphis, 1988-90. Co-author: (lesson packets) Ancient Egypt: An Educator's Guide, 1991, Imprint on the World, 1993; exhibited in group shows at Memphis Brooks Mus., 1976, Memphis May Banner Competition, 1981. Curator docent edn. Temple Israel Judaica Mus., Memphis, 1994; mem. gifts and arts com. Temple Israel, Memphis, 1994—; docent Wonders Internat. Cultural Svcs., Memphis, 1986, 92, 93; worker Temple Israel Habitat for Humanity, Memphis. Shakespeare Festival grantee Tenn. Arts Commn., 1994. Mem. Tenn. Art Edn. Assn., West Tenn. Art Edn. Assn. (exhbn. coord. 1993-95), Memphis Artists Crafts Mem. Assn. (bd. dirs. 1993-95). Home: 319 Fernway Cv Memphis TN 38117-2012 Office: St Dominic Sch for Boys 30 Avon Rd Memphis TN 38117-2502

BERNSTEIN, JOSEPH, lawyer; b. New Orleans, Feb. 12, 1930; s. Eugene Julian and Lola (Schlemoff) B.; m. Phyllis Maxine Askanase, Sept. 4, 1955; children: Jill, Barbara, Elizabeth R, Jonathan Joseph. BS, U. Ala., 1952, LLB, Tulane U., 1957. Bar: La., 1957. Clk. to Justice E. Howard McCaleb of La. Supreme Ct., 1957; assoc. Jones, Walker, Waechter, Poitevent, Carrere & Denegre, 1957-60, ptnr., 1960-65; pvt. practice New Orleans, 1965—; former gen. counsel Alliance for Affordable Energy. Past pres. New Orleans Jewish Community Ctr., Met. New Orleans chpt. March of Dimes. Trustee New Orleans Symphony Soc.; past mem. adv. council New Orleans Mus. Art; past nat. exec. com. Am. Jewish Com. 2d lt. AUS, 1952-54. Mem. ABA, La. Bar Assn., New Orleans Bar Assn., Phi Delta Phi, Zeta Beta Tau. Republican. Jewish. Home: 3119 Prytania St New Orleans LA 70115-3414

BERNSTEIN, MICHAEL JOEL, retail corporation executive; b. Jamaica, N.Y., July 29, 1938; s. Abraham Lazarus and Ida (Siegel) B.; m. Diane Nancy Schneider, June 16, 1968; children: Avron, David. Student in mktg., NYU, 1961; BA in Econs., CUNY, Flushing, 1962; postgrad. in bus. adminstrn., Calif. State U., Los Angeles, 1964. With store mgmt. Thrifty Drug Store, Los Angeles, 1962-68; dist. mgr. House of Nine, Inc., Mid-Atlantic area, 1968-69; real estate mgr. House of Nine, Inc., Eastern U.S., 1969-70; mgr. can. ops. House of Nine, Inc., Montreal, 1971-72; mgr. U.S. ops. House of Nine, Inc., Los Angeles, 1971-72; dir. mktg. Dentsply Internat., York, Pa., 1972-77; founder optical div. Shopko Stores, Inc., Green Bay, Wis., 1977-79; dir. optical services Jack Eckerd Corp., Clearwater, Fla., 1979-84, v.p. optical svcs., 1984-91; pres. ProActive Bus. Svcs., Clearwater, 1992-95, OnSight Optical Inc., Clearwater, 1995—; consumer rep. Am. Nat. Standards Inst., N.Y.C., 1973-78. Bd. dirs. Ohev Shalom Synagogue, York, 1972-75, pres. 1975-77; bd. dirs. Cnesses Israel Synagogue, Green Bay, 1977-79, Beth Shalom Synagogue, Clearwater, 1979-85. Served with U.S. Army, 1957-59. Mem. Nat. Assn. Optometrists and Opticians (v.p. 1975-87, legis. rep. 1973-75). Home: 2226 Buena Vista Dr Clearwater FL 34624-6632

BERNSTEIN, STEPHEN ADAM, physician, career officer; b. Chgo., July 6, 1964; s. Stanley J. and Elyse E. (Glustoff) B.; m. Audrey D. Myers, May 20, 1990; 1 child, Victoria Stephanie. BA, BA, Tex. Christian U., 1986; MD, Uniformed Svcs. U. Health Sci., 1990. Commd. med. officer U.S. Army, 1990, advanced through grades to flight surgeon, 1991; family practice resident Womack Army Med. Ctr., Ft. Bragg, N.C., 1994-96; with US Navy Health Clinic Mannheim, 1996—; med. examiner U.S. Army, Ft. Bragg, 1991—; presenter in field. Recipient George C. Marshall award Dept. Army, 1986. Mem. AMA, Am. Acad. Family Physicians, Assn. Mil. Surgeons U.S., Soc. Mil. Flight Surgeons, Am. Diabetes Assn. Jewish. Office: US Army Health Clinic Mannheim Unit 29920 APO AE 09086

BERRIGAN, HELEN GINGER, federal judge; b. 1948. BA, U. Wis., 1969; MA, Am. U., 1971; JD, La. State U., 1977. Staff rschr. Senator Harold E. Hughes, 1971-72; legis. aide Senator Joseph E. Biden, 1972-73; asst. to mayor City of Fayette, Miss., 1973-74; law clk. La. Dept. Corrections, 1975-77; staff atty. Gov. Pardon, Parole and Rehab. Commn., 1977-78; prin. Gravel Brady & Berrigan, New Orleans, 1978-94, Berrigan, Litchfield, Schonekas, Mann & Clement, New Orleans, 1984-94; judge U.S. Dist. Ct. (ea. dist.) La., New Orleans, 1994—; active La. Sentencing Commn., 1987. Active Com. of 21, 1989, pres., 1990-92, ACLU of La., 1989-94, Forum for Equality, 1990-94, Amistad Rsch. Ctr. Tulane U., 1990-95. Mem. La. State Bar Assn. (mem. fed. 5th cir. 1986—), La. Assn. Criminal Def. Lawyers, New Orleans Assn. Women Attys. Office: US Dist Ct 500 Camp St Rm 556 New Orleans LA 70130-3313

BERRY, CHARLES ROSS, sales/marketing executive; b. Charleston, S.C., Nov. 18, 1961; s. Charles McLees and Mary Flack (Ross) B.; m. Julie Alyson Merritt, Jan. 19, 1991; children: Alyson Latha, Rachel McLees. BS, Francis Marion U., Florence, S.C., 1987; postgrad., Kennesaw State U., 1996—. Store mgr. Sherwin Williams, Aiken, S.C., 1987-90; sales mgr. Rose Talbert, Columbia, S.C., 1990-91; dir. ednl. svcs. ARC, Atlanta, 1991-93; dir. ops. & bus. devel. Columbia/HCA, Atlanta, 1993-95; bus. mgr. The Emory Clinic, Inc., 1995—; co-owner Shandon Enterprises, 1994—. Pres. Chandler Creek Homeowners Assn., Lawrenceville, Ga., 1993—. Mem. Am. Mktg. Assn. Republican. Methodist. Office: The Emory Clinic Emory Primary Care Ctrs 101 W Ponce de Leon Ave Decatur GA 30030

BERRY, CLARE GEBERT, real estate broker; b. Carlisle, Pa., Oct. 4, 1955; d. George Robert and Helen (Davis) Gebert; m. James Isaac Vance Berry Jr., June 16, 1977; 1 child, James Isaac Vance Berry III. BA, Auburn U., 1977. Advt. assoc., circulation mgr. The News-Gazette, Lexington, Va., 1977-79; sales and editorial asst. Ponte Vedra (Fla.) Recorder Newspaper, 1979-81; co-founder, bus. mgr. The Sun-Times Newspaper, Jacksonville Beach, Fla., 1981-82; mgr. Arvida-Clearview Cable TV, Ponte Vedra Beach, 1982-85; broker, agt. Watson Realty Corp., Ponte Vedra Beach, 1985-90, Marsh Landing Realty, Ponte Vedra Beach, 1990-93; founder, broker, owner Berry & Co. Real Estate Sales & Mktg., Ponte Vedra Beach, 1993—. Com. chmn. The Players Championship/TPC Charities, Ponte Vedra Beach, 1982-96; cmty. chmn. United Way Campaign, Ponte Vedra Beach; dir. Marsh Landing Homeowners Assn. Bd., Ponte Vedra Beach, 1989-90. Mem. N.E. Fla. Assn. Realtors, N.E. Fla. Builders Assn. Sales and Mktg. Coun., Ponte Vedra Assn. of Realtors (edn. com. chmn. 1991, dir. 1992-94, pres. 1994), Ponte Vedra Assn. Realtors (Realtor of the Yr. 1992). Home: 113 Linkside Cir Ponte Vedra Beach FL 32082-2032 Office: Berry & Co Real Estate 330 Hwy AIA Ste 200 Ponte Vedra Beach FL 32082

BERRY, DAVID VAL, newspaper editor; b. Hoisington, Kans., May 20, 1948; s. Lester Maxwell and Neva Ethel Grace (Bridenstine) B.; m. Martha Katheryn York, Dec. 24, 1972; children: Christina, Karen. BS in journalism, Kans. State U., 1970. News editor Manhattan (Kans.) Mercury, 1970; combat corr. U.S. Army, Vietnam, 1971-72; copy editor Tulsa (Okla.) Tribune, 1972-77; mng. editor Brazosport Facts, Lake Jackson, Tex., 1977-82; v.p., exec. editor Dallas-Ft. Worth Suburban Newspapers, Arlington, Tex., 1982-90; editor Messenger-Inquirer, Owensboro, Ky., 1991-93; mng. editor Tyler (Tex.) Morning Telegraph, 1994—; cons. Westward Comms., Dallas, 1991; pres., owner Tex. Ink Editorial Svcs., Arlington, 1990-91; mem. profl. adv. bd. We. Ky. U., Bowling Green, 1993. Grad. Leadership Arlington, 1984-85, Leadership Owensboro, 1992-93. Decorated Bronze Star medal U.S. Army, 1972; recipient Best Daily Newspaper award Dallas Press Club, 1982. Mem. AP Mng. Editors, Soc. Newspaper Design, Soc. Profl. Journalists, Rotary Club (sec. Arlington North 1991). Office: Tyler Morning Telegraph 410 W Erwin St Tyler TX 75710

BERRY, DONALD LEE, accountant; b. Ft. Dodge, Iowa, Nov. 8, 1940; s. John Donald and Margaret Ann (Lichter) B.; m. Barbara B. Beyer, Aug. 11, 1962; children: Patrick Curtis, Dawn Marie. AA, Edison Community Coll., 1965; BS in Acctg., Fla. Atlantic U., 1967. CPA, Fla. Sr. acct. Haskins & Sells, CPAs, Ft. Lauderdale, Fla., 1967-71; corp. controller King Motor Ctr., Ft. Lauderdale, 1971-73, Krehling Industries, Naples, Fla., 1973-74; stockholder Wentzel, Berry, et. al., Naples, 1974-89; mng. prin. Wentzel, Berry & Alvarez PA, Naples, 1989—. active Mornings Park, Inc., Mother of God, House of Prayer. Recipient Outstanding Citizen award Naples Daily News, 1990. Mem. AICPA, Fla. Inst. CPAs (exec. com. 1989-91, bd. govs. 1984, pres. S.W. Fla. chpt. 1978-79, pres. PAC 1993-94, Pub. Svc. award 1993), Naples Area C. of C. (former pres., bd. govs.), Fellowship of Christian Athletes (former pres.), Fla. Inst. CPAs Ednl. Found., Inc. (v.p., past pres.), KC (past pres.), Pelican Bay Bus. Assn. (past pres.), Leadership S.W. Fla., Naples H.S. Quarterback Club (former pres.), Pelican Bay Rotary (former pres.). Republican. Roman Catholic. Office: Wentzel Berry & Alvarez 801 Laurel Oak Dr Naples FL 34108-2748

BERRY, FRED CLIFTON, JR., author, magazine editor, book packager; b. Neponset, Ill., May 11, 1931; s. Fred C. and Dorothy (Benedict) B.; m. Irene Semcho, Nov. 10, 1958; children—Jeffrey, Thomas. B.S., George Washington U., 1961; M.A., Stanford U., 1967. Commd. 2d. lt. U.S. Army, 1955, advanced through grades to col. (select), 1975; editor-in-chief Air Force Mag., Washington, 1980-83; chief U.S. editor, exec. v.p. Interavia Pub. Group, Washington, 1983-86; pres. FCB Assocs., Arlington, Va., 1986—; exec. v.p. Pathfinder Assocs., Fairfax, VA, 1978-79. Author: Sky Soldiers, 1987, Strike Aircraft, 1987, Chargers, 1988, Gadget Warfare, 1988, Air Cav, 1988, Inventing the Future, 1993; co-author: CNN: War in the Gulf, 1991, Flights, 1994; editor: Avon Books illustrated series on near future warfare 1990, Air Traffic Control, 1990; editor Air Power History mag., 1989-91; contbr. articles to profl. jours. Trustee Air Force Hist. Found. Mem. Aviation/Space Writers Assn., Authors Guild Am., Nat. Press Club (Washington). Office: FCB Assocs 2111 Wilson Blvd Ste 700 Arlington VA 22201-3001

BERRY, JACK, JR., business executive; b. 1957. Pres. Jack M. Berry Inc., La Belle, Fla., 1977—. Office: Jack M Berry Inc Hwy 80 Labelle FL 33935

BERRY, JACK M., business executive; b. 1920. Chmn. Jack M. Berry Inc., La Belle, Fla., 1940—.

BERRY, JANET CLAIRE, librarian; b. Jonesboro, Ark., Dec. 1, 1948; d. Troy Berry and Olivia Rosetta (Irwin) Thompson; m. Julius Jerome Mitcham, Mar. 27, 1970 (div. 1981); m. Gary Neville Hays, Nov. 10, 1987 (div. 1989). BSE, U. Cen. Ark., 1970; MLS, Vanderbilt/Peabody U., 1981. Libr./tchr. Greenbrier (Ark.) High Sch., 1970-72; employment counselor Dixie Employment Agy., Little Rock, 1973-76; sr. libr. asst. U. Ark. for Med. Sci., Little Rock, 1976-85; coord. cataloging svc. Ark. State Libr., Little Rock, 1985—; Instr. U. Ark., Little Rock, 1986-88. Editor La Docere for Am. Bus. Women's Assn. newsletter (regional top 5 award 1991, 92). Mem. ALA, Ark. Libr. Assn. (pres. 1983-84), Ark. Region Sports Car Club of Am. (editor 1988—), Am. Bus. Women's Assn. (La Petite Roche chpt., editor 1990-92, 1992 Woman of Yr.). Democrat. Methodist. Office: Ark State Libr One Capitol Mall Little Rock AR 72201

BERRY, JONI INGRAM, hospice pharmacist, educator; b. Charlotte, N.C., June 6, 1953; d. James Clifford and Patricia Ann (Ebener) Ingram; m. William Rosser Berry, May 29, 1976; children: Erin Blair, Rachel Anne, James Rosser. BS in Pharmacy, U. N.C., 1976, MS in Pharmacy, 1979. Lic. pharmacist, N.C. Resident in pharmacy Sch. Pharmacy, U. N.C., Chapel Hill, 1977-79, adj. asst. prof., 1985—; pharmacist Durham County Gen. Hosp., Durham, N.C., 1977-79; coord. clin. pharm. Wake Med. Ctr., Raleigh, N.C., 1979-80; co-dir. pharmacy edn. Wake Area Health Edn. Ctr., Raleigh, 1980-85; pharmacist cons. Hospice of Wake County, Raleigh, 1980—; co-owner Integrated Pharm. Care Systems, Inc., 1995—. Mem. editorial adv. bd. Hospice Jour., 1985-91, 94—, Jour. Pharm. Care in Pain and Symptom Mgmt., 1992—; reviewer Am. Jour. Hospice Care, 1986—; editor pharmacy sect. news NHO Coun. Hospice Profls.; contbr. articles to profl. jours. Troop leader Girl Scouts U.S.A., Raleigh, 1987—, trainer, 1989-91, mgr. svc. unit, 1990-94; Sunday sch. tchr. St. Phillips Luth. Ch., Raleigh, 1990-92, 94-95, asst. min., 1995—. Recipient Silver Pinecone award Girl Scouts U.S., 1991, Golden Rule award J.C. Penney Co., 1991. Mem. Am. Pharm. Assn. (hospice pharmacist steering com. 1990—), Acad. of Pharmacy Practice and Mgmt. (mem.-at-large 1996—), Am. Soc. Hosp. Pharmacists, Nat. Hospice Orgn., Am. Pain Soc., N.C. Pharm. Assn. (Don Blanton award 1985, mem. continuing edn. com. 1986-87, com. chair 1981-84), N.C. Soc. Hosp. Pharmacists (bd. dirs. 1984-86, program com. 1988-91), Wake County Pharm. Assn. (sec. 1982-85), Rho Chi. Democrat. Office: Hospice Wake County 4513 Creedmoor Rd Fl 4 Raleigh NC 27612-3815

BERRY, LINDA TOMLINSON, international communications corporation executive; b. Smithville, Mo., Jan. 22, 1946; d. Fleet Terrell and Ruth (Baine) Tomlinson; children: Sean A. Sudduth, Juliet Sudduth George. BA, Millsaps, 1971; MA, U. Miss., 1972. Field agt. Miss. Region Assocs., Jackson, Miss., 1976-78; mgr. Ball Assocs., Ltd., Blackhawk, Colo., 1979-80; asst. to pres. Inst. for Tech. Devel., Jackson, 1985-86; pres., chief exec. officer LBA Internat., Jackson, 1989—; founder The Embassy Internat. Networking Group. Polit. cons. pub. speaking, 1989—; lobbyist pro-life movement Miss. legis., Jackson, 1989—; vice chmn. Women's Polit. Network, 1991-92; state convener N.O.E.L., Miss., 1991—; acquisitions com. Miss. Mus. Art, Thombai Auction, 1990—; vol. Miss. Opera Assn., Jackson, 1990—. Mem. Internat. Trade Club, Safari Club, New Orleans World Trade Ctr., Memphis World Trade Club. Republican. Episcopalian. Home and Office: LBA Internat 4326 Robin Dr Jackson MS 39206

BERRY, MICHAEL CODY, educational administrator; b. Covington, Ky., July 10, 1951; s. Harvey Wells and Dorothy Helen (Cody) B.; m. Melanie Ann Klotter Garner, July 6, 1985; stepchildren: Erin K. Garner, Shannon C. Garner, Sean B. Garner. AA, BA, No. Ky. U., Highland Heights, 1973; MA, U. Cin., 1978. Cert. secondary tchr., Ky. Tchr. 7th and 8th grade English Ockerman Jr. H.S., Florence, Ky., 1973-76; adj. instr. English U. Cin., 1978-81; adj. instr. English No. Ky. U., Highland Heights, 1979-81, spl. lectr. English, 1981-84, cooperating lectr. English, 1984—, admissions counselor, 1984-87, acting dir. student support svcs., 1995, distance learning adv. bd., dir. ednl. talent search, 1987—, dental hygiene adv. bd., 1991-95, acting dir. Upward Bound, 1996, rsch. grants and contracts adv. bd., 1996; mem. futures adv. bd. Ky. Coun. on Higher Edn., Frankfort, 1994-95; mem. No. Ky. Local Labor Market's Sch.-to-Work Commn., 1995—. Author short stories. Mem. No. Ky. Youth Collaborative in Edn., No. Ky. U., 1988-89, mem. alumni coun., 1988-94; vol. mentor Project Continued Success, Aiken H.S., Cin., 1985-87. Recipient Award for Outstanding Leadership, Coca Cola, 1995, Disting. Svc. award No. Ky. U. Alumni Assn., 1995; named to Outstanding Young Men of Am.; U.S. Dept. Edn. grantee, 1987—. Mem. No. Ky. Counseling Assn., Southeastern Assn. Ednl. Opportunity Program Pers. (Pres.'s award 1996, bd. dirs. 1994-95, editor regional newsletter The Sentinel 1995-96, conf. co-chair 1997), Ky. Assn. Ednl. Opportunity Program Pers. (v.p. 1992-93, pres. 1994-95), No. Ky. C. of C. (participant No. Ky. Edn. alliance 1992—). Home: 3727 Middlebrook Ave Cincinnati OH 45208-1118 Office: Northern Kentucky Univ Ednl Talent Search Nunn Dr Highland Heights KY 41099

BERRY, MICHAEL WAITSEL, computer science educator; b. Atlanta, Nov. 17, 1960; s. Charles Waitsel and Lenora Elizabeth (Wingo) B.; m. Teresa Ann Underwood, June 18, 1983; children: Amanda Jane, Rebecca Gene. BS in Math. magna cum laude, U. Ga., 1981; MS in Applied Math., N.C. State U., 1983; PhD in Computer Sci., U. Ill., 1990. Summer intern, then assoc. programmer computer products div. IBM, Research Triangle Park, N.C., 1983, 83-84; computing cons. Triangle Univs. Computation Ctr., Research Triangle Park, 1984; grad. teaching asst. dept. math. N.C. State U., Raleigh, 1981-85, grad. rsch. asst. dept. math., 1983-85; computer scientist Ctr. for Supercomputing R&D U. Ill., Urbana, 1985-90; asst. prof. computer and info. scis. U. Ala., Birmingham, 1990-91; rsch. prof. computer sci., Ctr. Rsch. Parallel Computation U. Tenn., Knoxville, 1991, asst. prof. computer sci., 1991—. Contbr. articles to profl. publs. Grantee Apple Computer, Inc., 1992-93, Grad. Sch., U. Tenn., 1992-93, So. Appalachian Man and the Biosphere Program, 1993—, NSF, 1992—. Mem. IEEE Computer Soc., Assn. Computing Machinery, Soc. Indsl. and Applied Math. Methodist. Home: 1226 Harrington Dr Knoxville TN 37922 Office: U Tenn Dept Computer Sci 107 Ayres Hall Knoxville TN 37996-1301

BERRY, PETER DUPRE, real estate executive; b. Augusta, Ga., July 25, 1943; s. James A. and Carrie A. (Dupre) B.; children: Daniel D., David E., Katherine M. AB, Wofford Coll., Spartanburg, S.C., 1965; MBA, U. S.C., 1966. Treas. Landmarks Group, Inc., Atlanta, 1968-72; ptnr. Berry & Freyer Land Co., Atlanta, 1972-75; project developer Cochran Properties, Atlanta, 1975-77; pres. Berry Bros. Enterprises, Inc., Union, S.C., 1977—; bd. dirs. S.C. Nat. Bank, Union, S.C.; permanent mem. adv. com. S.C. State Devel. Bd., 1986—, downtown revitalization bd., 1984-92; mem., permanent adv. bd. S.C. State Devel. Bd., 1980-90; gov.'s health care adv. com., 1994; pvt. industry coun., 1993—. 1st lt. U.S. Army, 1966-68. Named to Outstanding Young Men Am., 1970. Mem. Carolina Lumber Dealers Assn. (bd. dirs. 1979-84), Young Carolinians Assn., Union C. of C. (bd. dirs. 1980-82), Downtown Merchants Assn., Union Country Club (pres.), Debordieu Beach Club (Georgetown, S.C.). Methodist. Office: Berry Builder Mart 109 Lakeside Dr Union SC 29379-1927

BERRY, RITA KAY, medical technologist; b. Borger, Tex., July 2, 1958; d. Thomas Vickers, Floy (Martin) Livingston; m. James William Berry, Feb. 20, 1982; children: Matthew Tyler, Rachael Breanne. AAS, Amarillo Coll., 1978; BS, West Tex. State U., 1980. Cert. med. technologist, blood bank technologist, specialist in blood banking. Phlebotomist Coffee Meml. Blood Ctr., Amarillo, 1977-78; med. lab. tech. Northwest Tex. Hosp., Amarillo, 1978-80, med. technologist, 1980-82; med. technologist St. Anthony's Hosp., Amarillo, 1982-84, program dir. Sch. of Med. Technology, 1984-88; med. technologist VAMC, Amarillo, 1988-90, High Plains Bapt. Hosp., Amarillo, 1990—; mem. bone marrow transplant team, High Plains Bapt. Hosp., Amarillo, 1996; inspector lab. accreditation program Coll. of Am. Pathologists, Northfield, Ill., 1991—. Designer greeting card/Rubber Stamper's World Mag., 1995 (2nd place award 1995); author poetry. Coach Odyssey of the Mind Amarillo Ind. Sch. Dist., 1995-96; coach cheerleading Kids Inc., Amarillo, 1993. Mem. Am. Assn. Blood Banks, Am. Soc. Clin. Pathologists, Internat. Soc. Poets (chmn. student poetry contest com. Hi-Plains chpt.), Poetry Soc. of Tex., Inspirational Writers-Alive. Republican. Baptist. Home: 2914 Trigg St Amarillo TX 79103

BERRY, ROBERT BASS, construction executive; b. Tulsa, Jan. 29, 1948; s. Guy Leonard and Barbara (Bass) B.; m. Catherine Cowles, Jan. 16, 1971; children: Matthew Knipe, Eli Banjamin. BA in Fin., Okla. U., 1970. Ops. mgr. D.C. Bass & Sons Constrn., Inc., Enid, Okla., 1971-73, chief exec. officer, exec. v.p., 1973-75, pres., 1975—; chief exec. officer, pres. Mosher Devel. Co., Enid, 1975—; pres. Bobsfarm, Inc., Enid, 1975—. Mem. Okla. Acad. State Goals, Oklahoma City, 1985—, Gov.'s Internat. Trade Team, 1986-88; trustee Okla. chpt. The Nature Conservancy; active Leadership Okla., Oklahoma City, 1991, Habitat for Humanity, Enid, 1984; chmn. State Alcohol Beverage Law Enforcement Commn., Oklahoma City, 1984-88, State Tort and Liability Task Force, 1986-87; bd. dirs. Enid Wellness Ctr., 1985-87, Enid Joint Indsl. Found., 1984—. Capt. C.E. U.S. Army, 1971. Named Exec. of Yr., Profl. Secs. Internat., 1981; recipient Pres.'s Coun. award Phillips U., 1984, Developer's award Heritage League Enid, 1985. Mem. Okla. State C. of C. (bd. dirs. 1986—, chmn. 1989), Enid C. of C. (bd. dirs. 1975-78, 81-84, Vol. of Yr.), Associated Gen. Contractors (legis. team 1985-87), Young Pres.' Orgn., Okla. Futures, Grand Nat. Quail Hunt Club. Republican. Presbyterian. Office: DC Bass & Sons Constrn Co 205 E Maine Ave Enid OK 73701-5743

BERRY, STEPHEN JOSEPH, reporter; b. Ft. Jackson, S.C., May 2, 1948; s. Charles Berry and Marjorie (Sheehan) B.; m. Cheryl C. Berry, Nov. 24, 1973; 1 child, Stephen Richard. BA in Polit. Sci., U. Montevallo, 1970; MA, U. N.C. at Greensboro, 1984. Mem. city staff Dothan (Ala.) Eagle, 1970-71; reporter Greensboro (N.C.) News & Record, 1972-81, copy editor, 1981-84, reporter, 1984-89; reporter The Orlando (Fla.) Sentinel, 1989—. Recipient 3d pl. Spot News award N.C. Press Assn., 1978, Benjamin Fine award, 1985, N.C. Sch. Bell award, 1986, 2d pl. Spot News award N.C. Press Assn., 1987, 3d pl. Lead Reporter award Fla. Soc. Newspaper Editors, 1992, Pulitzer Prize for investigative reporting, 1993, 1st place Soc. Profl. Journalism's Excellence award in sports reporting, 1994. Mem. Phi Alpha Theta. Home: 241 Stevenage Dr Longwood FL 32779-4558 Office: The Orlando Sentinel 633 N Orange Ave Orlando FL 32801-1300

BERRY, THOMAS EUGENE, lawyer; b. San Antonio, July 26, 1923; s. Kearie Lee and Alice Celeste (Fleming) B.; m. Joan Jester, June 30, 1951; children: James Buchanan, Janet, Alice. BBA, Southwestern U., Georgetown, Tex., 1944, U. Tex., 1949; LLB, U. Tex., 1951. Bar: Tex. 1951, U.S. Dist. Ct. (so. dist.) Tex. 1951, U.S. Ct. Appeals (5th cir.) 1953, U.S. Supreme Ct. 1960. V.p. Goodrich Oper. Co., Inc., Houston, 1962—; ptnr. Baker & Botts, Houston, 1963-90; pvt. practice, Houston, 1990—. Trustee R.H. and E.F. Goodrich Found., Houston, 1963—, M.B. Flake Home for Old Ladies, Houston, 1965—, Hermann Eye Fund, Houston, 1996—, Turner Charitable Found., Houston, 1975—, Isla Carroll Turner Friendship Trust, Houston, 1975—, Hope Ctr. for Youth and Family Svcs., 1976—; bd. dirs. Student Aid Found., Houston, 1975—, Houston area Parkinsonism Soc., 1991-92. With USMC, 1942-48, lt. col. Tex. N.G. ret. Fellow Am. Coll. Trust and Estate Counsel, Am. Coll. Tax Counsel; mem. ABA (past com. chair taxation sect., real property, probate and trust law sect.), Tex. Acad. Probate and Trust Lawyers, State Bar Tex., Houston Bar Assn., N.G. Assn. Tex. (Minuteman award 1967), Phi Delta Phi, Delta Kappa Epsilon. Democrat. Episcopalian. Office: 811 Rusk St Ste 225 Houston TX 77002-2811

BERRY, WILLIAM DALE, insurance agent; b. Hot Springs, Ark., Sept. 15, 1948; s. Claude and Marylan (Doyle) B.; m. Pamela Jean Woodruff; children: Erin L., Traci S., Brett W. Student, Hendrix Coll., 1966-68; BS, U. Ctrl. Ark., 1970. Tchr. Carlisle (Ark.) H.s., 1971-76; state bank examiner Ark. Banking Dept., Little Rock, 1976-79; owner, mgr. Carlisle Ins. Agy., 1979—. Deacon 1st Bapt. Ch., Carlisle, 1980—; mem. City of Carlisle Zoning Bd., 1980—, Lonke County Libr. Bd., 1994—. With U.S. Army, 1970-76. Mem. Ind. Ins. Agts. Ark. (mem. small and rural agts. com. 1992—, mem. agy. svcs. com. 1990—), Lions Club (pres. Carlisle 1986-87, sec. 1980-81), Carlisle C. of C. (bd. dirs. 1991—). Baptist. Home: PO Box 29 Carlisle AR 72024-0029

BERRY, WILLIAM WILLIS, retired utility executive; b. Norfolk, Va., May 18, 1932; s. Joel Halbert and Julia Lee (Godwin) B.; m. Elizabeth Mangum, Aug. 23, 1958; children: Preston Blackburn, John Willis, William Godwin. BSEE, Va. Mil. Inst., 1954; MS in Commerce, U. Richmond, 1964. Registered profl. engr., Va. Engr. Gen. Electric Co., 1954-55; with Va. Power, Richmond, 1957-92, v.p. div. ops., then sr. v.p. comml. ops., 1976-78, exec. v.p., 1978-80, pres., chief oper. officer, 1980-83, pres. chief exec. officer, 1983-85, chmn., chief exec. officer, 1985-86; chmn., chief exec. officer Dominion Resources Inc., 1986-90; chmn. Dominion Resources Inc., Richmond, 1990-92; bd. dirs. Ethyl Corp., Richmond, Universal Corp., Richmond, Scott and Stringfellow Fin. Corp., Richmond. Trustee Union Theol. Sem., Richmond, Va.; pres. bd. visitors Va. Mil. Inst., Lexington. Mem. Commonwealth Club, Country Club of Va., Norfolk Yacht and Country Club. Republican. Office: Three James Ctr 1051 E Cary St Ste 1201 Richmond VA 23219-4029

BERSCHEIDT, JOANNE MARIE, lawyer; b. Ventura, Calif., Apr. 13, 1944; d. Nicholas Melvin and Gretchen Elizabeth (Klein) B. BA cum laude, U. Santa Clara, Calif., 1966; MA, Calif. Polytech. U., San Luis Obispo, 1970; JD, St. Mary's U., San Antonio, 1983. Bar: Tex. 1984, U.S. Dist. Ct. (we., so. and ea. dists.) Tex. 1985. Assoc. Branton & Hall, San Antonio, 1983-90; sr. assoc. Brock & Person, San Antonio, 1990-93; ptnr. Brock & Person, P.C., San Antonio, 1993—. Mem. com. Boy Scouts Am., San Antonio, 1989-90. Mem. San Antonio Bar Assn. (bd. dirs.), Bexar County Women's Bar Assn., San Antonio Trial Lawyers Assn. (bd. dirs. 1988-90), Women Trial Lawyers Caucus, Phi Delta Phi. Repubclcan. Roman Catholic. Home: 140 Deer Hollow Dr Boerne TX 78006-1908 Office: Brock & Person PC 10101 Reunion Pl Ste 1000 San Antonio TX 78216-4157

BERT, CHARLES WESLEY, mechanical and aerospace engineer, educator; b. Chambersburg, Pa., Nov. 11, 1929; s. Charles Wesley and Gladys Adelle (Raff) B.; m. Charlotte Elizabeth Davis (June 29, 1957); children: Charles Wesley IV, David Raff. B.S. in Mech. Engring, Pa. State U., 1951, M.S., 1956; Ph.D. in Engring. Mechanics, Ohio State U., 1961. Registered profl. engr., Pa., Okla. Jr. design engr. Am. Flexible Coupling Co., State Coll., Pa., 1951-52; aero. design engr. Fairchild Aircraft div. Fairchild Engine and Airplane Corp., Hagerstown, Md., 1954-56; prin. M.E. Battelle Inst., Columbus, Ohio, 1956-61; sr. research engr., 1961-62, program dir., solid and structural mechanics research, 1962-63, cons., 1964-65; assoc. prof. U. Okla., 1963-66, prof., 1966—; dir. Sch. Aerospace and Mech. Engring., 1972-77, 90-95, Benjamin H. Perkinson Chair prof. engring., 1978—; instr. engring. mechanics Ohio State U., Columbus, 1959-61; vis. scholar U. Calif., San Diego, 1996; cons. various indsl. firms; chmn. Midwestern Mechanics Conf., 1973-75; Honor lectr. Mid-Am. State Univs. Assn., 1983-84; seminar lectr. Midwest Mechanics, 1983-84; Plenary lectr. 4th Internl Conf. on Composite Structures, Paisley, Scotland, 1987. Mem. editl. bd.: Composite Structures Jour., 1982—, Jour. Sound & Vibration, 1988—, Advanced Composite Materials, 1991—, Composites Engring., 1991-95, Mechanics of Composite Materials and Structures, 1993—, Applied Mechanics Revs., 1993—, Composites, 1996—; assoc. editor: Exptl. Mechanics, 1982-87, Applied Mechanics Revs., 1984-87; contbr. chpts. to books and articles to profl. jours. Served from 2d lt. to 1st lt. USAF, 1952-54. Sr. rsch. scholar U. Calif., San Diego, 1996; recipient Disting. Alumnus award Ohio State U. Coll. engring., 1985. Fellow AAAS, AIAA (nat. tech. com. structures 1969-72, chmn. Ctrl. Okla. sect. 1966-67) ASME (Ctrl. Okla. sect. exec. com. 1973-78, 90-95, sec. 1990-91, region X mech. engring. dept. heads com. 1972-77, 90-95, chmn. 1975-77), Am. Acad. Mechs. (bd. dirs. 1978-82), Soc. Exptl. Mechanics (monograph com. 1978-82, chmn. 1980-82, sec. Mid-Ohio chpt. 1958-59, chmn. 1959-60, adv. bd. 1960-63), Soc. Engring. Sci. (bd. dirs. 1982-88); mem. NSPE, Am. Soc. Composites, Okla. Acad. Sci., Okla. Soc. Profl. Engrs., Scabbard and Blade, Pa. State Alumni Assn. (Oustanding Engring. Alumnus award 1992), Sigma Xi, Sigma Tau, Ph Tau Sigma, Sigma Gamma Tau (Disting. Engr. award), Tau Beta Pi (Disting. Engr. award). Home: 2516 Butler Dr Norman OK 73069-5059 Office: U Okla Sch Aerospace and Mech Engring 865 Asp Ave Norman OK 73019-0601

BERT, CLARA VIRGINIA, home economics educator, administrator; b. Quincy, Fla., Jan. 29, 1929; d. Harold C. and Ella J. (McDavid) B. BS, Fla. State U., 1950, MS, 1963, PhD, 1967. Cert. tchr., Fla.; cert. home economist; cert. pub. mgr. Tchr. Union County High Sch., Lake Butler, Fla., 1950-53, Havana High Sch., Fla., 1953-65; cons. rsch. and devel. Fla. Dept. Edn., Tallahassee, 1967-75, sect. dir. rsch. and devel., 1975-85, program dir. home econs. edn., 1985-92, program specialist resource devel., 1992-96, program specialist, spl. projects, 1996—; cons. Nat. Ctr. Rsch. in Vocat. Edn., Ohio State U., 1978; field reader U.S. Dept. Edn., 1974-75. Author, editor booklets. Mem. devel. bd., adv. bd. Family Inst., 1994—. U.S. Office Edn. grantee, 1976, 77, 78; recipient Dean's award Coll. Human Scis., Fla. State U., 1995; named Disting Alumna Coll. Human Scis., Fla. State U., 1994. Mem. Am. Home Econs. Assn. (state treas. 1969-71), Am. Vocat. Assn., Fla. Vocat. Assn., Fla. Vocat. Home Econs., Fla. Home Econs., Am. Vocat. Edn. Rsch. Assn. (nat. treas. 1970-71), Nat. Coun. Family Rels., Am. Ednl. Rsch. Assn., Fla. State U. Alumni Assn. (bd. dirs. home econs. sect.), Havana Golf and Country Club, Fla. State U. Ctr. Club, Kappa Delta Pi, Kappa Omicron Nu (chpt. pres. 1965-66), Delta Kappa Gamma (pres. 1974-76), Sigma Kappa (pres. corp. bd. 1985-91), Phi Delta Kappa. Office: Fla Dept Edn FEC Tallahassee FL 32399

BERTELS, FRANK (JIM ANDERSON), male rights activist, foundation administrator; b. St. Louis, July 29, 1926; s. James W. Anderson and Cecelia Bertels; m. Andree Juliette Brun (dec. 1989); m. Linda Kuechler Rollins Anderson. BS, St. Louis U., 1950. Mktg. assoc. Philip Morris/Westinghouse, St. Louis, 1950-54; account exec., v.p. sales MetroMedia and ABC TV Network, N.Y.C., 1955-70; ptnr. Tacono Anderson Advt. Co., Miami, Fla., 1970-72; investor, writer Miami, 1972—; lectr. numerous univs., 1993—. Pub., editor: Male Lib News, 1972—; author: 1st Book on Male Liberation Sex Equality, 1975, (video) Make Love Not Gender War, 1993, (as Jim Anderson) How to Live Rent-Free; contbr. numerous papers on male perspective, audiotapes to maj. news confs. Founder, dir. Organized Proud Property Owners of Am., 1980—. Congregational. Home and Office: Male Liberation Found Inc 701 NE 67th St Miami FL 33138

BERTELSMAN, WILLIAM ODIS, federal judge; b. Cincinnati, Ohio, Jan. 31, 1936; s. Odis William and Dorothy (Gegan) B.; m. Margaret Ann Martin, June 13, 1959; children: Kathy, Terri, Nancy. B.A., Xavier U., 1958; J.D., U. Cin., 1961. Bar: Ky. 1961, Ohio 1962. Law clk. firm Taft, Stettinius & Hollister, Cin., 1960-61; mem. firm Bertelsman & Bertelsman, Newport, Ky., 1962-79; judge U.S. Dist. Ct. (ea. dist.) Ky., Covington, 1979—, chief judge, 1991—; instr. Coll. Law U. Cin., 1965-72; city atty., prosecutor Highland Heights, Ky., 1962-69; adj. prof. Chase Coll. of Law, 1989—. Contbr. articles to profl. jours. Served to capt. AUS, 1963-64. Mem. ABA, Ky. Bar Assn. (bd. govs. 1978-79), U.S. Jud. Conf. (standing com. on practices and procedure 1989-95, liaison mem. adv. com. on civil rules 1989-95), No. Ky. C. of C. (pres. 1974, bd. dirs. 1969-77). Republican. Roman Catholic. Club: Optimist.

BERTI, MARGARET ANN, early childhood education educator; b. Jersey City, Oct. 1, 1961; d. John Albert and Jane Matilda (McNair) Condon; m. Douglas Anthony Berti, Aug. 4, 1990; children: Matthew Douglas, Allison Nicole. BA, William Paterson Coll., Wayne, N.J., 1983, MEd, 1985. Tchr. 1st grade Paterson (N.J.) Pub. Schs., 1984-85; tchr pre-kindergarten and ESL Dallas Ind. Sch. Dist., 1985-92; tchr. kindergarten Pearland (Tex.) Ind. Sch. Dist., 1992—. Named Tchr. of Yr., George W. Truett Elem. Sch., 1988, Rustic Oak Elem. Sch., Pearland, 1994; named to Outstanding Young Women of Am., 1991; Title VII grantee Tex. Woman's U., 1987. Mem. Nat. Assn. Edn. Young Children, Classroom Tchrs. Dallas (bldg. rep. 1991), Dallas-Internat. Reading Assn. (corr. sec. 1992), Pearland Edn. Assn. (bldg. rep. 1993-95), Delta Kappa Gamma (Delta Rho chpt.). Roman Catholic. Home: 1526 Saxony Ln Houston TX 77058-3442

BERTINO, SHEILA ELAINE, college relations and marketing director; b. Erin, Tenn., Sept. 1, 1949; d. Claude Preston and Dorothea Marie (Roberts) Brooks; m. James J. Bertino Sr., Oct. 18, 1980; 1 child, Matthew Brooks. BS, U. Tenn., 1970, MS, 1975; postgrad., Union Coll., 1976-77; cert., Fla. Atlantic U., 1986. Cert. elem., secondary sch. tchr. Tenn., Ky. Secondary edn. tchr. Knox County Schs., Knoxville, Tenn., 1971-77; extension agt. County of Fayette, Lexington, Ky., 1978-79; state program specialist U. Ky., Lexington, 1979-80; info. svcs. specialist Seattle City Light, 1981-83; pub. info. officer Palm Beach County Govt., West Palm Beach, Fla., 1984-87; dir. coll. rels. Palm Beach C.C., Lake Worth, Fla., 1987—. Campaign coord. United Way, Seattle, 1982, West Palm Beach, 1985, Lake Worth, 1987; mem. com. Airport 88, West Palm Beach, 1985-88. Recipient Model Program award Tenn. PTA, 1976. Mem. Nat. Coun. Mktg. and Pub. Rels. (state bd. dirs. 1989, dist. II bd. dirs.), Fla. Assn. Cmty. Colls., Kappa Omicron Nu, Alpha Delta Pi. Republican. Methodist. Office: Palm Beach CC 4200 S Congress Ave Lake Worth FL 33461-4705

BERTLES, JAMES BILLET, lawyer; b. New Rochelle, N.Y., May 16, 1955; s. William Matthew and Eileen (Billet) B.; m. Lisa Conger Preston, Aug. 15, 1981; children: Katherine Conger, Preston Elizabeth, Alexander Harrison. BA, Amherst Coll., 1977; JD, Fordham U., 1981. Bar: Conn. 1981, Fla. 1982; bd. cert. in wills, trusts and estate law, Fla. Assoc. Cummings & Lockwood, Stamford, Conn., 1981-85, Palm Beach, Fla., 1985-89; assoc. Cadwalader, Wickersham & Taft, Palm Beach, Fla., 1989-90, ptnr., 1990-94; ptnr. Gunster, Yoakley, Valdes-Fauli & Stewart, P.A., West Palm Beach, Fla., 1994—; bd. dirs. Wilmar Corp. Bd. dirs. Palm Beach Civic Assn., Palm Beach Fellowship of Christian & Jews, Inc., Beach Club; chmn. planned giving com., bd. dirs. Norton Mus. Art; mem. Town of Palm Beach Zoning Commn.; chancellor, mem. vestry Bethesda By-the-Sea Episcopal Ch., Palm Beach, Fla.; chmn. Probate and Guardianship Com.; dir., pres. East Coast Estate Planning Coun. Mem. ABA, Fla. Bar Assn., Palm Beach County Bar Assn., The Beach Club (bd. dirs.). Republican. Home: 226 Eden Rd Palm Beach FL 33480-3316 Office: 777 S Flagler Dr West Palm Beach FL 33401-6161

BERTOLET, CRAIG EUGENE, English language educator; b. Pottstown, Pa., Jan. 27, 1965; s. Warren Eugene and Joyce Arlene (Eschbach) B. BA, Millersville State U., 1986; M in English, Pa. State U., 1989, PhD, 1995. Teaching asst. Pa. State U., University Park, 1988-91, rsch. asst., 1991-92, predoctoral lectr., 1992-93, NEH fellow dept. English, 1993-95; asst. prof. English James Madison U., Harisonburg, Va., 1995—. Organizer, dir. Medieval Luncheon Series, University Par, 1993-94; PhD rep. English Grad. Orgn., University Park, 1991-92, chair, 1992-93. Grantee Pa. State U. Grad. Sch., 1993, Pa. State U. Liberal Arts Coll., 1993. Mem. MLA, Northeastern MLA, Dante Soc., John Gower Soc., New Chaucer Soc., Medieval Acad. Am. Mem. United Ch. of Christ. Office: James Madison U Dept English Harrisonburg VA 22807

BERTOLETT, CRAIG RANDOLPH, mechanical engineer consultant; b. Richmond, Va., Oct. 16, 1936; s. Arthur Disbrow and Marget (Richardson) B.; m. Sarah G. Swaim, June 27, 1959 (div. July, 1978); children: Craig R. Jr., Christopher Robert, Margo Elizabeth; m. Barbara Frances Bertolett, Dec. 9, 1978. BS, U.S. Military Acad., 1959; MS in Mech. Engring., New Mex. State U., 1965; MBA, Loyola Coll., Balt., 1974. Registered profl. engr., Tex.; cert. product safety engr.; cert. hazard control mgr. Internat. Cert. Bd. Commd. 2nd lt. U.S. Army, 1959, advanced through grades to major, 1970, resigned, 1970; dir. test and evaluation Black & Decker Mfg. Co., Towson, Md., 1970-76; v.p. engring. spl. products divsn. Emerson Elect. Co., St. Louis, 1976-80; pres., prin. CR Bertolett Assocs., Inc., San Antonio, 1980—; mem. Am. Nat. Standards Inst. Z535.4 Com. Mem. Mayor's Blue Ribbon Com., Castle Hills, Tex., 1989-94; vestry St. Luke's Epsic. Ch., 1989-92; mem. Castle Hill Water Policy Com., 1992. Col. USAR, 1970-86; ret., 1986. Fellow Nat. Acad. Forensic Engrs.; mem. ASME, NSPE, Am. Nat. Standards Inst., Human Factors Soc., Nat. Safety Coun., Profl. Engrs. in Pvt. Practice, Soc. Automotive Engrs., Tex. Soc. Profl. Engrs., Illuminating Engring. Soc. (security lighting com. 1995—), The Ordnance Corps Assn.

BERTRAND, ANNABEL HODGES, civic worker, artist, calligrapher; b. Birmingham, Ala., Jan. 4, 1915; d. Thomas Edmund and Mae (Crawford) Hodges; m. John Raney Bertrand, Oct. 23, 1942; children: John Thomas, Diana Bertrand Williams, Karen Bertrand Wilson, J'May Bertrand Rivara. BS, Tex. Woman's U., 1935, MA, 1936; postgrad., Columbia U., 1938. Tchr. White Deer (Tex.) Consol. Sch., 1936-37, Tyler (Tex.) Pub. Sch. System, 1938-39; instr. Sam Houston State U., Huntsville, Tex., 1939-42; interim tchr. Portsmouth (N.H.) Pub. Sch., 1943. Bd. dirs. Rome Area Coun. for the Arts, 1980—, Ga. Coun. for Arts and Humanities, Atlanta, 1979-83, Mental Health Assn. Floyd County, Rome, Ga., 1980—; active High Mus. Art, Atlanta, 1979—, Rome Symphony Guild, 1980—, Friends of Rome/Floyd County Libr., 1985—, Christian Personhood Book Discussion Group of First United Meth. Ch., 1980—. Mem. AAUW, United Meth. Women, Rome Music Lovers Club, Sigma Alpha Iota (patroness). Republican. Home: 18 Rosewood Rd Rome GA 30165-4269

BERTRAND, SCOTT RICHARD, chiropractic physician; b. Dayton, Ohio, May 13, 1954; s. Richard Earl and Eleanor Catherine (Swanson) B.; m. Theresa Jean Bertrand, Feb. 9, 1974 (div. 1977); m. Vicki Lynn Buckner, July 11, 1980; children: Stephanie Marie, Lucas Scott. BS, Wright State U., Fairborn, Ohio, 1978; postgrad., Ohio State U., 1980; DC, Life Chiropractic Coll., Marietta, Ga., 1984. Mgr. Holiday Health Spa, Dayton, Ohio, 1975-77; dir., chief of staff Arrowhead Clinics of Am., Jonesboro, Ga., 1984-90; pres. Diversified Tech., Marietta, 1980—; pres. The Fitness Concept. Inventor in field. With U.S. Army, 1973-76. Mem. Am. Chiropractic Assn., Mensa. Republican. Roman Catholic. Home: 1460 Sweet Bottom Cir Marietta GA 30064-5223 Office: Bertrand Chiropractic Ctr 3433 Main St Atlanta GA 30337-1911

BESHEAR, STEVEN L., lawyer; b. Dawson Springs, Ky., Sept. 21, 1944. A.B., U. Ky., Lexington, 1966, J.D., 1968. Bar: N.Y. 1969, Ky. 1971. Assoc. White and Case, N.Y.C., 1968-70; later ptnr. Beshear, Meng and Green, Lexington; mem. Ky. Ho. of Reps., 1974-79; atty. gen. State of Ky., Frankfort, 1979-83, lt. gov., 1983-87; ptnr. Stites & Harbison, Lexington, 1987—. Bd. editors, Ky. Law Jour., (1967-68.). Mem. Fayette County Bar Assn., Ky. Bar Assn., ABA, Order of Coif, Phi Beta Kappa, Phi Delta Phi, Omicron Delta Kappa. Office: Stites & Harbison 2300 Lexington Fin Ctr 250 W Main St Lexington KY 40507-1738

BESHEARS, BETTY WILLIAMS, nurse; b. Lenoir, N.C., Aug. 21, 1954; d. Milton Franklin and Irene Mantha (Mask) Williams; m. Robert Ross Beshears, Sept. 2, 1986. ADN, Western Piedmont Coll., 1979; BSN, Lenoir Rhyne Coll., 1995. RN, N.C.; cert. EMT, BLS, ACLS, advanced trauma life support, mobile intensive care nurse, cert. emergency nurse preceptor, laser operator, cell saver operator/coord., PALS. Health care tech. Broughton Hosp., Morganton, N.C., 1972-79, deaf interpretor, rsch. tech., 1978-79, staff nurse, 1979-80; RN, staff nurse Caldwell Meml. Hosp., Lenoir, 1979-89, asst. supr. emergency dept., 1981-89, EMT, 1980-89, mobile intensive care nurse, cert. emergency room nurse, 1982-89; BLS nurse Caldwell Meml. Hosp. and Catawba Meml. Hosp., Lenoir and Hickory, N.C., 1979—; preceptor Catawba Meml. Hosp., Hickory, 1991-95, coord. autotransfusion, 1991-94, team leader vascular surgery, laser operator, 1992—. Active Mt. Hermon Meth. Ch., Hudson, N.C., 1954—. Western Piedmont/N.C. Bd. Nursing grantee, 1978-79. Mem. Assn. Operating Rm. Nurses (capt. 1989-90), Mu Sigma Epsilon, Sigma Theta Tau. Home: 6204 Vandresser Point Hickory NC 28601

BESSER, LAWRENCE WAYNE, corporate accountant; b. Louisville, Feb. 28, 1948; s. Norman George and Dorothy Catherine (Biegert) B.; m. Mary Pamela McAdam, Nov. 22, 1970 (div. Apr. 1985); 1 child, Lawrence W. Jr. BS in Acctg., U. Louisville, 1977. Acct. Kelley Tech. Coatings Inc., Louisville, 1982—, adminstrv. staff, 1983—; head computer dept. Kelley Tech. Coatins Inc., Louisville, 1984—, head benefits dept., 1985—, EEOC rep., 1987—; documentor Aries Software Co., Louisville, 1986-87. Co. campaign coord. Metro United Way, Louisville, 1985. Fellow Am. Mgmt. Assn., Am. Inst. Profl. Bookkeepers, Common, Ky. Small Systems Assn., mem. investment panel for KTC Profit-Sharing Trust. Democrat. Roman Catholic. Office: Kelley Tech Coatings Inc 1445 S 15th St Louisville KY 40210-1837

BESSINGER, COLONEL DONIVAN, JR., surgeon, writer; b. Louisville, Oct. 15, 1936. BS, Carson-Newman Coll., 1958; MD, U. N.C., Chapel Hill, 1961; MS in Surgery, U. Va., 1968. Diplomate Am. Bd. Surgery. Intern

Queen's Hosp., Honolulu, 1961-62; resident in surgery Greenville (S.C.) Gen. Hosp., 1964-66, 67-68, chief resident in surgery, 1968-69; surg. rsch. fellow U. Va. Hosp., Charlottesville, 1966-67; pvt. practice Greenville, S.C., 1969—; med. staff Greenville Meml. Hosp. and St. Francis Hosp., 1969—. Author: Religion Confronting Science: And There Was Light, 1991, Milk of Dreams: Cosmic Hymn. Quest, Ekklesia, 1992, Emerging from Chaos: Wholeness Ethic and New World Order, 1993; bull. editor Greenville County Med. Soc., 1978-85; contbr. articles to profl. jours. Lt. USMC, 1962-64. Fellow ACS; mem. AMA, Greenville County Med. Soc., S.C. Med. Assn., S.C. Surg. Soc. Office: 10 Enterprise Blvd Ste 210 Greenville SC 29615-3554

BEST, FREDERICK NAPIER, artist, designer, educator; b. Macon, Ga., Jan. 17, 1943; s. John Frederick and Sara (Napier) B.; m. Rebecca Alice Freeman, Apr. 6, 1974; children: Eric Jonathan, Emily Anne. Student, Auburn U., 1961-64; BA, Birmingham So. Coll., 1969; MA U. Ala., Birmingham, 1994. Artist Birmingham News, 1969; design dept. mgr. Dampier-Harris, Alabaster, Ala., 1970-78; model designer Rust Engring., Birmingham, 1978-81; owner, mgr. Best Finesse Studio, Trussville, Ala., 1981-96; design instr. Jefferson State Coll., Birmingham, 1981-96; instr. Erwin H.S., Birmingham, 1994-95; edn. supr. ITT Tech. Inst., Birmingham, 1996—. Contbr. articles to profl. jours. Recipient award of honor Birmingham Advt. Club, 1982; Artist Fellowship grantee Ala. State Coun. on the Arts, 1993, 94. Mem. AIA, Nat. Art Edn. Assn., Am. Inst. Graphic Arts, Am. Engring. Model Soc. Methodist. Avocations: writing, reading. Home: 209 Wildwood Dr Trussville AL 35173-1961

BEST, ROBERT GLEN, geneticist; b. Springfield, Ohio, Jan. 27, 1958; s. Richard Alexander and Ella Marie (Buss) B.; m. Sara Felicia Newton, June 2, 1984; children: Cami DeNeil, Heidi Amber, Adrian Alexander, Joshua Ellis. BS in Biochemistry, Lehigh U., 1981; MS in Toxicology, N.C. State U., 1983, PhD in Genetics/Toxicology, 1987. Diplomate Am. Bd. Med. Genetics. Med. geneticist, clin. cytogeneticist Richland Mem. Hosp., Columbia, S.C., 1986-89; from acting dir. to assoc. dir. clin. genetics U. S.C., Columbia, 1989-91, dir. clin. genetics, 1991—; assoc. prof. ob-gyn., dir. divsn. clin. genetics; cons. Hybritech Inc., San Diego, 1989—. Grantee March of Dimes, 1990, Ctrs. for Disease Control, 1993-96. Mem. Am. Soc. Human Genetics, Am. Soc. Hematology, European Soc. Human Genetics, Genotoxicity and Environ. Mutagenesis Soc. Home: 101 White Falls Cir Columbia SC 29212-1241 Office: U SC Dept Ob-Gyn Two Med Park # 301 Columbia SC 29203

BETANCOURT, OSCAR, pediatrician; b. Havana, Cuba, May 8, 1940; came to U.S., 1963; s. Temistocles and Margarita (Alcalde) B.; m. Lourdes Martinez, June 24, 1961; children: Laura, Michel. MD, U. Ill., Chgo., 1970. Diplomate Am. Bd. Pediatrics. Intern in pediatrics U. Fla.-Shands Hosp., Gainesville, 1970-71; resident U. Miami (Fla.)-Jackson Meml. Hosp., 1971-73; pvt. practice, Plantation, Fla., 1973—; chmn. dept. pediatrics Bennett Community Hosp., Plantation, 1974-76, Broward Gen. Med. Ctr., Ft. Lauderdale, Fla., 1985-89, Plantation Gen. Hosp., 1989-91. Fellow Am. Acad. Pediatrics; mem. Fla. Pediatric Soc., Broward County Med. Assn., Children's Med. Assn. (pres.). Republican. Roman Catholic. Office: Children's Med Assocs 201 N University Dr Plantation FL 33324-2039

BETHEA, EDWARD EVANS, public relations executive; b. Mullins, S.C., Nov. 23, 1956; s. Eugene Strobel and Helen (Currie) B.; m. Marcia McRae Hall, Apr. 11, 1987. BS in BA, Francis Marian U., Florence, S.C., 1980; MA in English, Wake Forest U., 1988. Editor/reporter Dillon (S.C.) Herald, 1980-83; tchr. English Thomas Hart Acad., Hartsville, S.C., 1984-85, J.V. Martin Jr. H.S., Dillon, 1986-87; dir. pub. rels. St. Eugene Cmty. Hosp., Dillon, 1987-89, Florence-Parlington Tech. Coll., Florence, 1989—. Recipient Wallie award (1st pl.) Carolinas Hosp. Mktg. and Pub. rels. Soc., 1989, Wallie award (2d pl.), 1989. Mem. Masons (master). Home: 116 Dew St Latta SC 29565 Office: Florence-Darlington Tech Coll 2715 W Lucas St Florence SC 29501

BETHUNE, GORDON, airline executive; married; 3 children. BS, Abilene Christian U., Dallas; AMP, Harvard U., 1992. Lic. comml. pilot, lic. airframe and power plant mechanic. V.p. engring. and maintenance Braniff and Western Airlines; sr. v.p. ops. Piedmont Airlines; v.p., gen. mgr. Renton div. Boeing Comml. Airplane Group, 1988-94; pres., CEO Continental Airlines, Inc., Houston, 1994—. Served with USN. Office: Continental Airlines Inc PO Box 4607 Houston TX 77210-4607*

BETTMAN, JAMES ROSS, management educator; b. Laurinburg, N.C., Sept. 15, 1943; s. Roland David and Virginia Gertrude (Hare) B.; m. Joan Carol Scribner, Dec. 16, 1967; 1 child, David James. BA, Yale U., 1965, MPhil, 1969, PhD, 1969. Prof. mgmt. Grad. Sch. Mgmt., UCLA, 1969-82; IBM rsch. prof. Fuqua Sch. Bus., Duke U., Durham, N.C., 1982-83, Burlington Industries prof., 1983—. Author: An Information Processing Theory of Consumer Choice, 1979, The Adaptive Decision Maker, 1993; co-editor Jour. of Consumer Research, 1981-87; contbr. chpts. to books, articles to profl. jours. Named Scholar/Tchr. of Year Duke U., 1988. Fellow APA, Am. Psychol. Soc.; mem. Assn. Consumer Rsch. (bd. dirs. 1976-79, pres. 1987, fellow in consumer behavior 1992), Inst. Ops. Rsch. and Mgmt. Sci., Am. Mktg. Assn. (Harold M. Maynard award 1979, Paul D. Converse award 1992). Democrat. Episcopalian. Home: 213 Huntington Dr Chapel Hill NC 27514-2419 Office: Duke U Fuqua Sch of Bus Durham NC 27708-0120

BETTS, DIANNE CONNALLY, economist, educator; b. Tyler, Tex., Sept. 23, 1948; d. William Isaac and Martine (Underwood) Connally; m. Floyd Galloway Betts Jr., Feb. 14, 1973. BA in History, So. Meth. U., 1976, MA in History, 1980; MA in Econ., U. Chgo., 1986; PhD in Econ., U. Tex., 1991. Affiliated scholar Inst. for Rsch. on Women and Gender/Stanford U., 1993—; economist, tech. analyst, fin. cons. Smith Barney, Dallas, 1994—; mem. women studies coun. So. Meth. U., 1993-94, Fulbright campus interviewing com. mem. 1992-93, pub. rels. and devel. liaison dept. econ., 1990-92, faculty mentor U. honors first year mentoring program,adj. asst. prof. dept. econ. and history So. Meth. U., 1992—, vis. asst. prof. 1990-92, faculty, Oxford, summer 1991-93, adj. instr. dept. history, 1989-90, adj. instr. dept. econ., 1985-89, teaching asst. dept. history, spring 1980; lectr. dept. polit. economy U. Tex., Dallas, summer 1988. Author: Crisis on the Rio Grande: Poverty, Unemployment, and Economic Development on the Texas-Mexico Border, 1994, Historical Perspectives on the American Economy: Selected Reading, 1995; contbr. articles to profl. jours. Rsch. Planning grant NSF, 1992; recipient Marguereta Deschner Teaching award, 1991; Humanities and Scis. Merit scholar, 1978. Mem. Am. Econ. Assn., Am. History Assn., Econ. History Assn., Cliometric Soc., Social Sci. History Assn., N.Am. Conf. on British Studies, Nat. Coun. for Rsch. on Women (affiliate), Omicron Delta Epsilon, Phi Alpha Theta. Home: 6267 Revere Pl Dallas TX 75214-3099 Office: Smith Barney 500 N Akard St Ste 3900 Dallas TX 75201-6604

BETZER, ROY JAMES, national park service administrator; b. Rapid City, S.D., June 9, 1936; s. Bruce and Virginia Rose (Coppo) B.; m. Jeanette Menegas, Dec. 23, 1962 (div.). BS, Black Hills State Coll., 1959, BS in Edn., 1961; MA, U. S.D., 1966. Radio announcer Sta. KOZY; night club singer, tchr., coll. instr.; acting coach San Antonio Performing Arts, Barbizon; promotion specialist City of San Antonio; mus. tech. living history interpreter U.S. Dept. Army. With USN. Home: PO Box 840 Stonewall TX 78671-0840

BEU, MARJORIE JANET, music director; b. Elgin, Ill., Nov. 22, 1921; d. Herman Henry and Hattie Belle (Beverly) B. MusB, Am. Conservatory Music, 1949; B Musical Ed, 1949, M in Musical Ed., 1953; advanced cert. No. Ill. U., 1969; DEd, U. Sarasota, 1979. Music tchr. Sch. Dist. 21, Wheeling, Ill., 1961-64; music and fine arts coord., 1964-68, asst. supt. instrn., 1968-79; min. of music United Meth. Ch., Sun City Center, Fla., 1980—; dir. Sun City Ctr. Kings Point Community Chorus, 1984-89; pres. Council Study and Devel. Ednl. Resources, 1971-79. Pres., Wheeling Community Concerts Assn.; dir. Community Chorus; pres. Sun City Center Concert Series. Mem. NEA, Am. Guild Organists and Choir Dirs., Music Educators Nat. Conf., Assn. Supervision and Curriculum Devel., Ill. Edn. Assn., Ill. Council Gifted, No. Ill. Assn. Ednl. Research, Evaluation and Devel. (pres.), Mu Phi Epsilon, Phi Delta Kappa (sec. N.W. Suburban Cook County chpt.), Kappa Delta Pi (pres. also counselor alumni com.). Home: 610 Fort Duquesna Dr Sun City Center FL 33573-5156

BEUTTENMULLER, RUDOLF WILLIAM, lawyer; b. St. Louis, Dec. 20, 1953; s. Paul A. and Doris R. (Henle) B.; m. Ragina Lee Winters, July 14, 1984. AB cum laude, Princeton U., 1976; JD with distinction, Duke U., 1980. Bar: Tex. 1980, U.S. Dist. Ct. (no. dist.) Tex. 1980. Assoc. Jenkens & Gilchrist, Dallas, 1980-83; ptnr. Gregory, Self & Beuttenmuller, Dallas, 1983-88, Bradley, Bradley & Beuttenmuller, Irving, Tex., 1988-93; dir. Thomas & Self, Dallas, 1994—. Articles editor Duke Law Jour., Durham, 1979-80. Mem. Rep. Nat. Com., Washington, 1984. Mem. ABA, Dallas Bar Assn., Duke Law Alumni Assn., Princeton Alumni Assn. Home: 4417 Amherst Ave Dallas TX 75225-6907 Office: Thomas & Self 5339 Spring Valley Rd Dallas TX 75240-3009

BEVERLAND, WANDA LOU, textile executive, consultant; b. Rising Sun, Ind., Mar. 17, 1941; d. Leslie Lyle and Hazel Marie (Welch) Silvers; m. Jerald Banks Beverland, Mar. 12, 1956; children: Robyn, Hope, Jeri Shaine, Shawn. Grad. high sch., Tampa, Fla. Sec. Beverland Enterprises, Inc., Oldsmar, Fla., 1968—; v.p. Beverland Enterprises, Inc., Oldsmar, 1987—; owner Wanda's Quilts, Oldsmar, 1980—; cons. and purchasing agt. in field. Author: Quilts-A Southern Legacy, 1989, Black American Folk Art Quilts, 1990. Mem. Better Bus. Bur. W. Fla., Inc., Greater Suncoast C. of C., Oldmar C. of C. Republican. Home: PO Box 250 Oldsmar FL 34677-0005

BEVERLY, BETTY MOORE, counselor; b. Clarksville, Va., Oct. 4, 1939; d. Junius Chappell and Edna (Burton) Moore; m. Aubrey S. DesPortes, Aug. 31, 1962 (div. Oct. 1973); children: Aubrey S. DesPortes Jr., Betty Layne DesPortes; m. Elton R. Beverly, Apr. 7, 1975; 1 stepchild, Roberta B. Eddy. BA in Psychology, U. S.C., 1962; MS in Rehab. Counseling, Va. Commonwealth U., 1987. Lic. counselor, Va.; cert. substance abuse counselor. Order libr. U. S.C., Columbia, 1962-63; tchr. spl. edn. Chesterfield (Va.) Pub. Schs., 1973-75; coord. outpatient treatment HCA Poplar Springs Hosp., Petersburg, Va., 1988-90; pvt. practice Chesterfield, Va., 1990—. Author: History of Buckhead, 1976. mem. Chesterfield Cmty. Svc. Bd., 1988-93, chmn., 1990-92; mem. state coun. Mental Health Planning Coun., Richmond, Va., 1989-94; mem. Chesterfield Comprehensive Svcs. Policy and Mgmt. Team, 1994—; mem. Chesterfield County Cmty. Mobilization. Pathfinder scholar U.S. Govt., 1986. Mem. ACA, Mental Health Assn. Va., Chesterfield Mental Health Assn., Chester Garden Club (past pres.), Chester Rotary Club Internat. Republican. Methodist. Home: PO Box 967 4740 Crossgate Rd Chester VA 23831 Office: 9842 Lori Rd Ste 102 Chesterfield VA 23832

BEVERLY, LAURA ELIZABETH, special education educator; b. Glen Jean, W.Va., Nov. 26; d. Sidney and Alma Logan. BA in Elem. Edn., W.Va. State Coll., 1960; MS in Spl. Edn., Bklyn. Coll., 1969; postgrad., Oxford (Eng.) U., 1974, N.Y.U., 1982. Cert. elem./spl. edn. tchr., N.Y. Tchr. Bd. Coop. Ednl. Svcs., Westbury, N.Y., 1966—; mem. adv. bd. Am. Biographical Inst. Inc., Raliegh, N.C., 1985—. Mem. ASCD, Am. Inst. of Parliamentarians, Royal Soc. Health, Phi Delta Kappa. Home: PO Box 346 Glen Jean WV 25846

BEVILL, TOM, retired congressman, lawyer; b. Townley, AL, Mar. 27, 1921; s. Herman and Fannie Lou (Fike) B.; m. Lou Betts, June 24, 1943; children: Susan B., Donald H., Patricia Lou. BS, U. Ala., 1943, LLB, 1948; LLD(hon.), U. Ala., Tuscaloosa, 1981, Livingston U., 1986; LLD (hon.), U. North Ala., 1991, Troy State U., 1992. Bar: Ala. 1949. Pvt. practice law Jasper, 1948-67; mem. Ala. Ho. of Reps., 1958-66; mem. 90th-104th Congresses from 4th Ala. dist., 1967-96, mem. appropriations com., ret., 1996. Mem. ABA, Ala. Bar Assn., Walker County Bar Assn. (past pres.), Am. Judicature Soc. Home: 411 Ridge Rd Jasper AL 35501

BEY, RICHARD DOUD, neurologist, electromyographer; b. Normal, Ill., Feb. 23, 1952; s. Douglas Rudolph and Dorothy (McCammon) B. BS, Beloit Coll., 1974; MD, Yale U., 1979. Diplomate Am. Bd. Psychiatry and Neurology, Am. Bd. Electrodiagnostic Med. Resident Mayo Clinic, Rochester, Minn., 1983; physician Smith & Bey PA, Winston-Salem, N.C. Home: 4011 D Whirla Way Ct Apt D Clemons NC 27012 Office: Smith & Bey PA 160 Charles Blvd Winston Salem NC 27103

BEYER, CRAIG FRANKLIN, ophthalmologist; b. St. Louis, May 2, 1958; s. Robert Franklin and Gaby B.; m. Larysa Roma Romanyshyn, mar. 23, 1985. BA in Biology, U. Mo., 1980; DO, U. Health Scis., Kansas City, Mo., 1984. Diplomate Am. Bd. Ophthalmology, Nat. Bd. Osteo. Physicians and Surgeons. Intern Univ. Med. Ctr., Plantation, Fla., 1984-85; resident in ophthalmology St. Louis U. Med. Ctr., 1985-88; fellow in cornea La. State U., New Orleans, 1988-90; dir. cornea svc. Deaconess Hosp., St. Louis, 1990. Contbr. articles to med. jours., chpts. to books. Grantee NIH, 1988-90. Fellow Am. Acad. Ophthalmology. Office: Deaconess Hosp 1237 Twin Peaks Cir Longmont CO 80503-2171

BEYER, DONALD STERNOFF, JR., state official; b. Trieste, Free Territory of Trieste, June 20, 1950; came to U.S., 1952; s. Donald Sternoff Sr. and Nancy Prew (McDonald) B.; m. Carolyn Anne McInerney, July 15, 1972 (div.); children: Donald III, Stephanie; m. Megan Carroll, Sept. 19, 1987; children: Clara, Grace. BA in Econs. magna cum laude, Williams Coll., 1972. Pres., v.p. and other positions Don Beyer Volvo, Falls Church, Va., 1974—; lt. gov. Commonwealth of Va., Richmond, 1990—; urban at large mem. Commonwealth Transp. Bd., Va., 1987-90; chmn. Va. Econ. Bridge Initiative, Va., 1990—. Chmn. Baliles for Gov., No. Va., 1985, Paul Simon for Pres., Va., 1988, Bill Clinton for Pres., Va., 1992; mem. 11th Dist. Dem. Com., Vienna, Va., 1992. Named Time Mag. Quality Dealer of Yr. for Va., 1991. Democrat. Episcopalian. Office: Office of Lt Gov 900 E Main St Richmond VA 23219-3513*

BEYLE, THAD LEWIS, political science educator, consultant; b. Syracuse, N.Y., May 11, 1934; s. Herman Carey and Madelon (McCulloch) B.; m. Patricia Fae Cain, Nov. 14, 1934; children: Carey, Jeffrey Lewis, Jonathan West, Aimee Maurine. AB, Syracuse U., 1956, AM, 1960; PhD, U. Ill., 1963. Asst. prof. polit. sci. Denison U., Granville, Ohio, 1963-64; faculty fellow Office of the Gov. of N.C., Raleigh, 1964-65; rsch. assoc. Study of Am. States, Duke U., Durham, N.C., 1965-67; asst. prof. polit. sci. U. N.C., Chapel Hill, 1967-69, assoc. prof., 1969-76, prof., 1976—; dir. Ctr. for Policy Rsch. Nat. Gov.'s Assn., 1974-76, sr. rsch. fellow, 1978-84; chmn. bd. dirs. N.C. Inst. Polit. Leadership. Editor: Governors and Hard Times, 1992; co-editor: Planning and Politics, 1969, The American Governor in Behavioral Perspective, 1972, Politics and Policy in North Carolina, 1975, Being Governor, 1983; editor State Government, annually 1985—, Gubernatorial Transitions, 1985, 89, Gubernatorial Re-elections, 1985-86, Governors and Hard Times, 1992. Mem. Am. Polit. Sci. Assn., Midwest Polit. Sci. Assn., So. Polit. Sci. Assn., Am. Soc. for Pub. Adminstrn. Democrat.

BHANDARI, ARVIND, oncologist; b. Sangrur, Punjab, India, Apr. 4, 1950; came to U.S., 1973; s. Girdhari Lal and Pushpa (Gandotra) B.; m. Anita Kanotra, Apr. 13, 1976; children: Sachin, Salil. Student, DAV Coll., Amritsar, India, 1966; MBBS, BChir, Indian Inst. Med. Scis., New Delhi, India, 1973. Diplomate Am. Bd. Internal Medicine, Am. Bd. Med. Oncology. Intern, then resident N.J. Med. Sch., Newark, 1973-76; fellow in oncology M.D. Anderson Hosp., Houston, 1976-78; physician Houston Cancer and Med. Ctr., 1978—. Mem. Am. Coll. Physicians, Am. Soc. Clin. Oncology, Tex. Med. Assn. Club: Sweetwater Country (Sugarland, Tex.). Home: 1722 Hodge Lake Ln Sugar Land TX 77478-4272 Office: Houston Cancer and Med Clinic 8200 Wednesbury Ln Ste 290 Houston TX 77074-2900

BHANDARI, BASANT, biochemist, molecular biologist, chemical engineer, food technologist, chemist; b. Rajasthan, India, Feb. 11, 1951; came to U.S., 1984, naturalized; s. B.R. and K. (Mehta) B.; m. Veena Bhandari, Feb. 17, 1981; children: Hanul, Naumit. BS, Udaipur (India) U., 1970; MS in Chemistry First Class, U. Udaipur, 1972, MTech. in Chem. Engring. Tech. 1st class, 1976; PhD in Biochemistry, U. Adelaide, Australia, 1981. Mgr., quality control engr. J.K. Industries Kankroli, India, 1977; product devel. scientist R&D unit Modern Bakeries India, Ltd., India, 1977-78; rsch. pool officer Coun. Sci. and Indsl. Rsch., U. Udaipur, New Delhi, 1981-82; Charles John Everard postdoctoral fellow Waite Rsch. Inst., Adelaide U., 1982-84; Am. Heart Assn. postdoctoral fellow Case Western Res. U. and VA Med. Ctr., Cleve., 1985, 86, rsch. assoc. depts. medicine and biochemistry, 1984-85, sr. rsch. assoc., 1987-88, instr. biochemistry in medicine, 1988-89; asst. prof. dept. biol. scis. U. Wis.-Parkside, Kenosha, 1989-90; asst. prof. dept. medicine U. Tex. Health Sci. Ctr., San Antonio, 1990—; jr. rsch. fellow dept. nuclear and radiochemistry Udaipur U., 1973-74, dept. chem. tech., U. Nagpur, India, 1974-76, biochem. engring. dept. Indian Inst. Tech. Delhi, New Delhi, 1977. Contbr. articles to nat. and internat. profl. jours., mags., newspapers and radio talk; achievements include herbal/plant rsch. in search for curing diseases of complex nature. Recipient William Cullross prize for best PhD thesis U. Adelaide, 1981; U. Adelaide postgrad. fellow, 1978-81, U. Oreg. Health Scis. Ctr. postgrad. fellow, 1981. Mem. Am. Soc. Biochemistry and Molecular Biology, Am. Soc. Nephrology. Home: 7322 Oak Manor Dr Unit 48 San Antonio TX 78229

BHATIA, D.M.S., geologist, educator. BSc, Jabalpur, 1959; M in Tech., Saugar, 1962; MSc, New Brunswick, 1970; PhD, U. Mo., Rolla, 1976. Registered profl. geologist. Asst. prof. U. Raipur, 1963-66; geologist New Brunswick Dept. Natural Resources, 1967, Brunswick Mining and Smelting, 1968-69; project mgr. New Ungava Iron Ore, 1970-72; geochemist Mo., 1973-76; prof. geology Austin Peay State U., Clarksville, Tenn., 1977—; pres., CEO Geotech. Cons. Internat., Inc., 1990—; cons. UN, 1976, Phillips Petroleum, 1977—, Internat. Oil and Gas, 1978—, Bendix Corp., 1978—, Union Carbide, 1979—, Internat. Chems., 1980—, Cumberland Exploration, 1983—, C. Howe & Assocs., 1983—, Sun Oil Co., 1988—, Mid-Valley Pipe Line, 1988—, Nashville Metro, 1989—, numerous local contracts, 1990—; liaison with Ky. Acad. Sci. for First Joint Meeting, 1994—; mem. Univ. Faculty Senate, 1981-84, 88-91, v.p., 1982, sec., 1988; mem. nat. environ. adv. com. Am. Geol. Inst., 1994—. Author 1 book on coal; mem. editl. bd. Geotimes, 1993—; contbr. articles to profl. jours. Mem. steering com. Montgomery County Dem. Party, 1993-95; mem. exec. com. Boy Scouts Am., Mid. Tenn., 1995; bd. dirs. Montgomery County Adult Lit. Program, 1988-94, S.E. U.S.A. Sikh Soc., 1986-88. Recipient fellowship Univ. Grants Commn. India, 1961-62, fellowship Geol. Survey Can. and Nat. Rsch. Coun., 1966-70, fellowship U.S. Geol. Survey, 1976, Big Apple award Tenn. Edn. Assn., 1982, fellowship Fulbright Found., 1989, grant NSF, 1990, 91; named Hon. Col. by Tenn. Gov. Fellow Am. Soc. Mining, Metallurgy and Exploration (geophysics com. 1993, geochemistry com. 1993—, program chmn. 1996, geology com. 1993—, rep. to Am. Geol. Inst. governing coun., program planning 1993—, edn. planning com. 1993—, Peele award 1993—); mem. AAUP, Nat. Assn. Geology Tchrs., Tenn. Acad. Sci. (chmn. Geology sect., chmn. membership com. 1995—, liaison with Ky. Acad. Sci. first joint meeting 1994—), Tenn. Groundwater Resources Assn., Tenn. Water Resources Assn. (chmn. internat. projects 1983-93, steering com. 1994), Rotary (dist. 6770 sec., Clarksville Sgt.-at-Arms 1989-90, treas. 1990-91, sec. 1991-92, Paul Harris fellow 1990). Democrat. Office: Geology Dept Austin Peay State Univ Clarksville TN 37044

BHATNAGAR, KUNWAR PRASAD, medical educator; b. Gwalior, India, Mar. 21, 1934; came to U.S., 1967; s. Narayan Swaroop and Bhagwati Devi B.; m. Indu, Apr. 28, 1961; children: Divya B. Rouben, Jyoti B. Burruss. BS, Agra U., 1956; MS, Vikram U., 1958; PhD, SUNY, Buffalo, 1972. Asst. prof., assoc. prof., prof. U. Louisville Sch. Medicine, Anatomical Scis. & Neurobiology, 1972—. Editor: Bat Rsch. News, 1982-86; guest editor: Microscopy Rsch. & Technique, 1992; contbr. articles to profl. jours. Fellow Max Planck Inst. Brain Rsch., 1978, 86. Hindu. Home: 2651 Kings Hwy Louisville KY 40205-2648 Office: U Louisville Sch Medicine Dept Anatomical Sci and Neurobiol Louisville KY 40292

BHATNAGAR, YOGENDRA MOHAN, biology educator; b. Gorakhpur, India, Feb. 5, 1945; came to U.S., 1968; s. Hirday Mohan and Ved Kumari Bhatnagar; m. Sheela Peter Shah, Aug. 30, 1974; 1 child, Pooja. BSc, U. Lucknow, India, 1962, MSc, 1964; postgrad., U. Copenhagen, Denmark, 1966-67; PhD, Boston Coll., 1974. Instr. Boston Coll., Chestnut Hill, Mass., 1973-74; rsch. fellow Harvard U. Med. Sch., Boston, 1974-76, rsch. assoc., 1976-77; sr. scientist EIC Corp., Newton, Mass., 1977-79; asst. prof. U. South Ala., Mobile, 1979-84, assoc. prof., 1984—; adj. lectr. Northeastern U., Boston, 1977-79, rsch. assoc., 1978-79; cons. Grambling (La.) State U., 1992—; presenter in field. Contbr. articles to profl. jours. Recipient Rsch. fellowship Govt. Denmark, Copenhagen, 1966, Rsch. fellowship The Population Coun., N.Y.C., 1974, Rsch. Career Devel. award NIH, Bethesda, Md., 1985; grantee NIH, 1980-87, 85-90. Mem. AAAS, Am. Soc. Biochemistry and Molecular Biology, Soc. for the Study Reproduction. Home: 1805 Ridge Ct Mobile AL 36609-3523 Office: U South Ala Coll Medicine 2042 MSB/SCB Mobile AL 36609

BHATTACHERJEE, PARIMAL, pharmacologist; b. Chittagong, Bangladesh, Feb. 14, 1937; s. Charu Ranjan and Kusum Bhattacherjee; m. Pratima Choudhuri, June 18, 1962; children: Charbak, Vasker. BS, Chittagong Govt. Coll., 1955; MS, Dhaka U., Bangladesh, 1959; PhD, London U., 1972. Prodn. mgr., with quality control pharm. industry Bangladesh, 1960-67; research asst. Inst. Ophthalmology, London, 1967-72; lectr. pharmacology Inst. Ophthalmology, 1972-78; vis. asst. prof. ophthalmology Coll. Physicians and Surgeons, Columbia U., N.Y.C., 1978-79; sr. lectr. pharmacology Inst. Ophthalmology, London, 1978-79; sr. scientist Wellcome Research Labs., Beckenham, England, 1979-84; sect. head biologicals dept. pharmacology Wellcome Research Labs., 1984-87, sr. research scientist dept. mediator pharmacology, 1987-90; vis. prof. Ky. Lions Eye Research Inst., U. Louisville Med. Ctr., Louisville, 1990; prof., 1974-79, 90—; tchr., bd. studies pharmacology U. London, 1974-79; organizer Symposium on Ocular Inflammation, 5th Internat. Congress for Eye Research, Eindoven, Netherlands, 1982, 6th Congress for Eye Research, Alicante, Spain, 1984; organizer 8th Internat. Congress for Eye Research, San Francisco, 1988; organizer Symposiums on the Inflammatory Process and Mediators, 9th Internat. Congress for Eye Research, Helsinki, 1990, 92. Co-author: The Leukotrienes, 1984, Ocular Effects of Eicosanoids and Related Substances, 1989, Interleukin 1 Inflammation and Disease, 1989, Lipid Mediators in Eye Inflammation, 1989; contbr. articles to profl. jours. UNESCO fellow, Belgium, 1963, Alexander Pigott Wernher Meml. Trust fellow Med. Research Coun., England, 1972; research grantee Med. Research Coun., England. Mem. British Pharmacological Soc., Assn. for Eye Research (Europe), Internat. Soc. Eye Research, Assn. for Research in Vision & Ophthalmology, Experimenta Eye Research (editorial bd.), Soc. for Drug Research, Inst. of Biology. Hindu. Office: U Louisville Ky Lions Eye Rsch Inst 301E E Muhammad Ali Blvd Louisville KY 40202-1511

BHAVSAR, SANATKUMAR NAVINCHANDRA, chemical engineer; b. Abmedabad, Gujrat, India, Nov. 7, 1954; arrived in the U.S., 1981; s. Navinchandra Gopaldas and Sushila (Bhogilal) B.; m. Nita Sanat, Feb. 24, 1981; children: Krishna, Sonya, Ami. BSChemE, U. Bombay, India, 1977; MSChemE, U. Ottawa, Can., 1980; MBA, Averett (Va.) Coll., 1995. Registered profl. engr., N.J., Del., Pa., Va. Asst. engr. Punit Tech. Svcs., Bombay, 1977-79; rsch. asst. U. Ottawa, Can., 1979-80; rsch. engr. U. Calgary, Can., 1980-81; quality assurance analyst Am. Cyanamid Co., Linden, N.J., 1982-84; supervising engr. N.J. Dept. Environ. Protection, Trenton, 1984-90; dir. environ., health and safety Yokohama Tire Corp., Salem, Va., 1990—. Mem. AIChE (environ. divsn.). Democrat. Hindu. Office: Yokohama Tire Corp 1500 Indiana St Salem VA 24153-7058

BIANCHI, LINDA LORRAINE, volunteer; b. Honolulu, Nov. 6, 1955; d. George Thomas and Barbara Lorraine Hooper; m. Michael David Bianchi, Nov. 18, 1978. BS, Tarleton State U., Stephenville, Tex., 1977. Contbr. articles to profl. jours., newspapers. Vol. Audie L. Murphy Meml. Vets. Hosp., San Antonio, ARC, Elf Louise Project, San Antonio; mem. Bisbee Coun. on Arts and Humanities. Recipient Vol. Svc. Pin, Dept. of Vets., San Antonio, Cert. of Appreciation, Bisbee coun. on the Arts and Humanities, Cert. of Achievement in Computer tech. for Physically Disabled, San Antonio Coll., 1992. Mem. Alamo PC Orgn. (v.p. membership, bd. dirs.), Epsilon Delta Pi, Rho Iota Delta.

BIANCHI, THOMAS DEVERELL, gastroenterologist; b. Rochester, N.Y., Jan. 3, 1952; s. Dominick Anthony and Jean Ann (Deverell) B.; m. Sharon E. Jones, June 1, 1975 (div. Oct. 1984); children: Andrew Dominick, Nicholas Anthony; m. Mary Elizabeth Carter, Nov. 7, 1987; children: Anthony Carter, Anna Elizabeth, Emily Nichole. BS, Jacksonville (Fla.) U., 1973; MD, U. Miami, 1977. Diplomate Am. Bd. Internal Medicine with subspecialty in gastroenterology. Intern in internal medicine U. Ala., Birmingham, 1971-78, resident in internal medicine, 1978-80; pvt. practice

Tallassee, Ala., 1980-87; fellow in gastroenterology U. Fla., Jacksonville, 1987-89; pvt. practice Cmty. Med. Arts Ctr., Tallassee, 1989—; med. staff Cmty. Hosp., Tallassee, 1980—. Mem. AMA, Elmore County Med. Soc. (treas. 1987—), Med. Soc. of Ala. Office: Community Medical Arts Ctr 875 Friendship Rd Tallassee AL 36078-1234

BIARD, CATHERINE, piano educator; b. Paris, Tex., Mar. 14, 1931; d. Hugh Lawson and Annelle (Varner) Palmer; m. James Herndon Biard, Mar. 28, 1948; children: Elizabeth, Richard, Robert Scott. AA, Paris Jr. Coll., 1977; BA in English, East Tex. State U., 1979. Women's editor Moore County News, Dumas, Tex., 1957-59; pub. svc. libr. Paris Pub. Libr., 1980-82; pvt. tchr. piano, Dumas, Paris, Valliant, Okla., 1955—. Ch. pianist Dumas Presbyn. Ch., 1954-70, Valliant Meth. Ch., 1990—; various dist. and local offices United Meth. Women, McAlester Dist., Okla., 1990—. Republican. Presbyterian. Homee: Box 202 Clyde's Tue Rd Valliant OK 74764

BIAS, DANA G., lawyer; b. Lexington, Ky., Mar. 12, 1959; d. Cyrus Dana and Betty Jo (Haddox) B. BA with highest honors, U. Louisville, 1981; JD magna cum laude, Boston U., 1984. Bar: Mass. 1985, N.Y. 1985, U.S. Dist. Ct. (so. and ea. dists.) N.Y. 1986, Ky. 1995. Counselor Mass. Half-Way Houses, Inc., Boston, 1982-83; sr. trial atty. Criminal Def. div. Legal Aid Soc., N.Y.C., 1984-89, mng. atty., 1989-94; sole practitioner Hauppauge, N.Y., 1995; sr. trial atty. Louisville-Jefferson County Pub. Defender Corp., 1995—; lectr. N.Y.C. Pub. Schs., 1989. Contbr. articles to profl. jours. Mem. ABA, ACLU, N.Y. State Bar Assn., Nat. Assn. Criminal Def. Lawyers, Mass. Bar Assn., Ky. Bar Assn., N.Y. Civil Liberties Union, Woodcock Soc., Mortar Bd., Phi Kappa Phi, Phi Eta Sigma. Democrat. Office: Louisville-Jefferson County Defender Corp 200 Civic Plz Louisville KY 40202

BIAS, JENNIFER MORRISON, editor; b. Lexington, Va., Apr. 22, 1970; d. Glenn Palmer Morrison and Wanda Jean (Irons) Dolan; m. Rodney Eugene Bias, Aug. 8, 1992; 1 child, Zachary Hunter. BA in journalism, Marshall U., 1992. Retail merchandiser Proctor and Gamble Distributing Co., Cinc., 1993; pub. rels., sales rep. Communications Connection, Inc., Ashland, Ky., 1993; asst. editor Lane Cons., Inc., Lexington, Ky., 1994; editor Lane Cons., Inc., 1994—. Editor: (mag.) The Lane Report, 1994—; freelance writer (qtrly. pub.) Site Selection Mag., 1996. PEO sisterhood mem. chpt. C PEO, Lexington, 1996. Democrat. Methodist. Office: Lane Consultants Inc 269 W Main St Ste 400 Lexington KY 40507-1759

BIAS, SHARON G., state commissioner. Commr. of banking State of W.Va. Office: Banking Div State Capital Rm 311 Charleston WV 25305*

BIBB, DANIEL ROLAND, antique painting restorer and conservator; b. Gadsden, Ala., June 10, 1951; s. Cassius Roland and Louise Selma B. Student, Jefferson State, 1969-70, DeKalb Coll., 1971-72. Sales cons. Macy's Antique Gallery, Atlanta, 1973; dir. Collector's Gallery, Atlanta, 1974-76, Connoisseur's Gallery, New Orleans, 1977-79; painting conservator Daniel R. Bibb Fine Painting Conservation & Restoration, Atlanta, 1980—; chief fund raiser Atlanta Rabbit Rescue; researcher for pvt. collectors and museums, Atlanta, 1977-89; listed conservator, New Orleans Museum List of Restorers, New Orleans, 1988. Discovered a lost major painting of Philip IV of Spain, from workshop of Valasquez; exhibited lost painting Atlanta High Mus. Art, 1980; publication of discovered paintin, High Mus. Monthly, 1980; conservator Anglo-Am. Art Mus., Baton Rouge, New Orleans Mus. Art.; owner Fabergè collection on loan to New Orleans Mus. Art, 1996. Fund raiser Am. Heart Assn., Atlanta, 1987, 88, March of Dimes, 1987, 88, Atlanta Rabbit Rescue, 1984-95; mem. High Mus. of Art, Atlanta; vol. ARC Disaster Relief Team, Atlanta, 1992, Art Care Art Auction for fight against AIDS, 1992, 93, chmn. Live Auction, 1993. Recipient Design award, Most Authentic Design, Patio Planters of the Vieux Carre, New Orleans, 1977. Mem. Nat. Trust for Historic Preservation. Republican. Baptist. Home and Office: Bibb Painting Restoration 807 Summit North Dr NE Atlanta GA 30324-5641

BIBLE, CARL RAYMOND, JR., electrical engineer; b. Cumberland, Md., Aug. 29, 1958; s. Carl Raymond Sr. and Patricia Ann (Nield) B.; m. Susan Mrvicin, Apr. 20, 1985; children: Rebecca Courtney, Brittany Faith. BSEE, U. Tenn., 1981. Registered profl. engr., Fla. Field engr. Fla. Power and Light, Miami, 1981-82; lead engr. Fla. Power and Light, Juno Beach, 1982-88; engring. supr. Fla. Power and Light, 1988-91, engring. mgr. Turkey Point site, 1991—. Fellow IEEE. Republican. Home: 164 Corrine Pl Key Largo FL 33037-4206 Office: Fla Power and Light PO Box 14000 North Palm Beach FL 33408-0420

BICE, JEANNETTE MUNROE, medical educator; b. Talladega, Ala., Sept. 17, 1950; d. William Jennings and Rachel (Joiner) Munroe; m. Paul Fredrick Savich, Aug. 18, 1979 (div. June 1981); m. James Watwood Bice, Dec. 2, 1983; children: Lindsey Suzanne, Rachel Lloyd. AA, Va. Intermont Coll., 1970; BS in Edn., Auburn (Ala.) U., 1972, postgrad., 1989-91; AA in Nursing, Hillsborough Cmty. Coll., 1978. RN, Fla. Sales hostess Walt Disney World, Orlando, Fla., 1973-75; educator Hillsborough Assn. for Retarded, Tampa, Fla., 1975-76; RN South Fla. Bapt. Hosp., Plant City, 1978-82; RN, head nurse Citizen's Bapt. Med. Ctr., Talladega, Ala., 1983-88, 88—; allied med. careers instr. Talladega City Vocat. Ctr., 1984—; advisor, regional host Health Occupations Students of Am., 1989—. Proof reader, cons. Diversified Health Occupations, 1995. Mem. Jr. Welfare League of Talladega, 1986-91; helper, spl. equestrians Ala. Inst. Deaf and Blind, Talladega, 1988-96. Mem. Talladega County Humane Soc. (bd. dirs. 1996—). Methodist. Home: 311 Creekside Circle Talladega AL 35160 Office: Talladega City Vocat Ctr 110 Piccadilly Cir Talladega AL 35160-3102

BICE, MICHAEL DAVID, retail and wholesale executive; b. Anderson, S.C., July 18, 1956; s. Johnnie Lee Richard and Virgie Ovaline (Martin) B.; m. Nancy Bice, 1993; children: Ansley Deann Bice, Adam Michael Bice, Kristin Kennedy, Rebekah Kennedy, John WilliamKennedy. Student, U.S. Merchant Marine Acad., 1974; degree, Tri-County Tech. Coll., 1981. Sales rep. Sav-A-Stop, Inc., Roanoke, Va., 1974-75, 76-77, 78-79; with mgmt. dept. Caper House Food Stores, Belton, S.C., 1975; material coord. Jeffrey Mfg., Belton, 1975-76; sales rep. Better Beer and Wine Co., Anderson, 1977-78; with mgmt. dept. Brown Shoe Stores, Anderson, 1979-81; ind. contractor Curtis Products Co., Anderson, 1981-85, sales rep., 1988-89; mgr. Curtis Products Co., Ashland, Va., 1989-91; project coord. Curtis Products Co., Alpharetta, Ga., 1992; CEO B & D Enterprises, Anderson, 1981-85; pres., COO Oriental Sources, Inc., Charlotte, N.C., 1985-87; CEO Jewelry Plus, Anderson, 1985-87; pres. Sales Plus, Anderson, SC, 1988—, Richmond, Va., 1989-91, Ashland, Va., 1989—; bd. dirs. Oriental Treasure Imports, Inc., Charlotte, 1985-91; pres. Maabe Possibilities, Inc., Anderson, 1992—; comml. mktg. dir., comml. accts. coord. Atlantic Coast Candy, Inc., Anderson, Roswell, Ga., Ashland, Va., 1992-94; v.p. sales, state mgr. Pubrs. Guild of S.C., Taylors, 1994-95; cons. Alliance for Affordable Health Care, S.C., N.C., Ga., 1995—; gen dir. Amcall, 1995—.

BICEHOUSE, HENRY JAMES, health physicist; b. New Castle, Pa., Feb. 8, 1943; s. Roy Hamilton and Carrie (Krepps) B.; m. Susan Evelyn Tannahill, Jan. 27, 1967; 1 child, Julia Anne. BS in Biochemistry, Pa. State U., 1965; BS in Biology, Incarnate Word Coll., 1969; MS in Radiol. Health, Temple U., 1970. Health and safety supr. ARCO Radiation Process Ctr., Quehanna, Pa., 1970-72; radiol. health physicist Pa. Dept. of Environ. Resources, Reading, Pa., 1972-78; radiol. engr. Westinghouse Hanford Co., Richland, Wash., 1978-82; health physicist U.S. Nuclear Regulatory Commn., King of Prussia, Pa., 1982-88; dir. regulatory compliance Quadrex Recycle Ctr., Oak Ridge, Tenn., 1988-92; corp. RSO Quadrex Corp., Oak Ridge, 1990—; cons. Automated Sci. Group, Inc., Oak Ridge, 1992—; chmn. task force on mamography Conf. Radiation Control Dirs., Reading, 1975-77. Vol. Knox County Sr. Citizen Ctr., Knoxville, 1990—; civil def. dir. Centre County, Pa., 1971-72. With USAF, 1965-68. Mem. AAAS (life), Am. Chem. Soc., Health Physics Soc. Home: 5805 Penshurst Ct Powell TN 37849-4969 Office: Automated Scis Group Inc 800 Oak Ridge Tpke Oak Ridge TN 37830-6927

BICK, DAVID GREER, healthcare marketing executive; b. Toledo, June 29, 1953; s. James D. and Carol Jean (Hermann) B.; m. Cynthia Brightfield; children from previous marriage: Jennifer Kelly, Jesse Quinn, Matthew Adam, Wylie Christine; stepchildren: Alec, Christopher. BE, U. Toledo, 1975; cert. health cons. Purdue U., 1981. Dist. mgr. Blue Cross N.W. Ohio, Tiffin, 1977-79, regional mgr., Sandusky, 1979-81, dir. sales, Toledo, 1981-82; v.p. mktg. Blue Cross/Blue Shield Cen. N.Y., Syracuse, 1983; exec. dir. Preview-Health Benefits Mgmt. of Ohio, Toledo, 1984-87, chief mktg. exec. HMO Health Ohio Blue Cross and Blue Shield of Ohio, 1984-87, v.p. sales and support svcs., mut. health svcs., 1988; v.p. sales and mktg. Family Health Plan HMO, 1989-95; v.p. gov. programs Blue Cross Blue Shield of Tex., 1995—. Author: (poetry) Paupers and Profiteers, Proud Words On a Dusty Shelf. Mem. People's Med. Soc., Toledo Zool. Soc., Toledo Mus. Art. Mem. Hastings Ctr.-Inst. and Soc. of Ethics and Life, Am. Mktg. Assn., N.W. Ohio Mktg. Assn. (pres.), Acad. for Health Svc. Mktg., U.S. Tennis Assn. (competition com., mktg. com., champs com.), U. Toledo Alumni Assn., Toledo C. of C., U. Toledo Rocket Club, Boilermaker Club (Purdue), U. Toledo Tower Club. Avocations: photography, golf, basketball, skiing, tennis. Roman Catholic. Home: 1339 Comanche Dr Allen TX 75013 Office: Blue Cross Blue Shield of Tex 901 S Central Expy Richardson TX 75080

BICKEL, STEPHEN DOUGLAS, insurance company executive; b. Lincoln, Nebr., Dec. 20, 1939; s. Myron Overton and Jane (Sawyer) B.; m. Linda Wall, Apr. 18, 1970; children: Stephanie, Loretta, Valerie. BA, Dartmouth Coll., 1962; LLB, U. Tex., 1965. V.p., actuary Am. Gen. Life Ins. Co., Houston, 1965-80; v.p., actuary Am. Gen. Corp., Houston, 1980-83, sr. v.p., actuary, 1983-87, exec. v.p., 1987-88; pres., chief exec. officer The Variable Annuity Life Ins. Co., Houston, 1988-94, chmn., CEO, 1994—. Fellow Soc. Actuaries; mem. Acad. Actuaries, Tex. Life Ins. Assn. (chmn. 1995—), Tex. Life, Accident, Health and Hosp. Svc. Ins. Guaranty Assn. (chmn. 1995—). Home: 55 Saddlebrook Ln Houston TX 77024-3404 Office: Variable Annuity Life Ins 2929 Allen Pky Houston TX 77019-2197

BICKEL, TED, JR., secondary school educator; b. Danville, Ky., Oct. 7, 1950; s. Theodore D. and Florence Alberta (Morgan) B.; m. Nancy Lou Ernst, Dec. 28, 1973; children: Ted W., Tim A. BS in Chemistry, U. Louisville, 1979, Cert. in Chemistry Tchg., 1983; MBA, Bellarmine Coll., 1981. Lab analyst (analytical) Harshaw Chem. Co., Louisville, 1973-74; lab analyst (R&D) Porter Paint Co., Louisville, 1974-77, Borden Chem. Co., Louisville, 1977-80; sales rep. Bio-RIA, Jeffersontown, Ky., 1981; instr. bus. U. Louisville, 1982-84; tchr. chemistry Oldham County H.S., Buckner, Ky., 1984-90; instr. Ky. Coll. Bus., Lousiville, 1990-91; gen. topics tchr. Ten Brusck Hosp., Lyndon, Ky., 1991-93; tchr. chemistry Trinity H.S., St. Matthews, Ky., 1993—. Activity dir. cub scouts Boy Scout Am., Fern Creek, Ky., 1996—; t-ball coach YMCA, Buechel, Ky., 1994; dir. coll. support camp Beulah Presbyn. Ch., Fern Creek, 1988—, choir mem., 1984—. Grantee Providean Ins. Co., Louisville, 1994, Eisenhower Math/Sci., 1993, 94. Mem. ASCD, Am. Chem. Soc., Nat. Sci. tchrs. Assn., Ky. Sci. Tchrs. Assn., Louisville Area Chem. Alliance, Kappa Delta Pi, Phi Delta Kappa. Presbyterian. Home: 6817 Holly Lake Dr Fern Creek KY 40291-3022 Office: Trinity High School 4011 Shelbyville Rd Saint Matthews KY 40207

BICKERSTAFF, MINA MARCH CLARK, university administrator; b. Crowley, Tex., Sept. 27, 1936; d. Winifred Perry and Clara Mae (Jarrett) Clark; m. Billy Frank Bickerstaff, June 12, 1954 (div. 1960); children: Billy Mark, Mina Gayle Bickerstaff Basaldu. AA, Tarrant County Jr. Coll., 1982; BBA, Dallas Bapt. U., 1991. Dir. pers. svcs. Southwestern Bapt. Theol. Sem., Ft. Worth, 1976—. Mem. Coll. and Univ. Pers. Assn., Seminary Woman's Club (past treas.), Alpha Chi. Baptist. Office: Southwestern Bapt Theol Sem PO Box 22000 Fort Worth TX 76122

BICKERTON, JANE ELIZABETH, university research coordinator; b. Shrewsbury, Shropshire, Eng., Apr. 16, 1949; came to U.S., 1978; d. Donald Samuel George and Lucy Mary (Hill) B.; m. Anthony Andrew Hudgins, Mar. 18, 1978 (div. Feb. 1995); children: Alexis Kathryn, Samantha Lucy. Grad. health visitor, North London U., 1977; BA, Oglethorpe U., 1980; MA, Ga. State U., 1991. RN, Ga.; grad. RN, U.K.; cert. family planning nurse, U.K. Nurse St. Bartholomews Hosp., London, 1967-72; housing advisor Shelter Housing Aid Ctr., London, 1973-76; owner, dir. Jane Bickerton Fine Arts, Atlanta, 1978-85; curator Ga. State U. Gallery, 1985; co-curator Arts Festival of Atlanta, 1995; coord. rsch. study Emory U., Atlanta, 1995—; co-presenter More Prodns., Ga. State U. Gallery; bd. dirs. Art Papers Inc., chmn., 1982-84, acting chmn., 1990—, art reviewer, 1993—; co-curator bathhouse, billboards, art-in transit Arts Festival Ga., 1995; co-prodr. grant Ga. Humanities Coun., 1989; adj. instr. Atlanta Coll. Art, 1993—; panelist NEA, 1993; part-time nurse Feminist Women's Health Ctr., 1980-90; pers. mgr., asst. mgr. Brit. Pavilion Shop, Expo '92, Spain; visual arts panelist Bur. Cultural Affairs, 1987; juror Arts Festival, Atlanta, 1989; coord. faculty exhbn. Atlanta Coll. Art, 1996. Author: (with John Fletcher) Guide to First-Time House Buyers, 1975; contbg. editor Art Papers, 1981-85; writer: "Suns", 1996. Vol. comty. worker, Guatemala, 1976; mem. adv. com. Arts Festival Atlanta, 1991-93; com. mem. Grady H.S. Parents, Tchrs. and Students Assn.; chmn. com. fine arts Inman Mid. Sch. PTA, 1990-92, Morningside Elem. Sch. PTA, 1986-88; bd. dirs. Pub. Domain, 1992—; ex-officio bd. dirs. The High Mus. Art, 1996. Mem. 20th Century Art Soc. at High Mus. (programming com. mem. 1993, bd. dirs. 1993—, v.p. 1994—, pres. 1996—). Home: 1036 High Point Dr Atlanta GA 30306

BICKFORD-WILCOX, BARBARA JEAN, elementary education educator, canvas fabricator; b. Manchester, N.H., Nov. 1, 1961; d. Robert Kent Bickford and Rosetta Irene Rash; children: Earl LaVerne Wilcox III, Nathan Robert Wilcox. AA, Brevard C.C., Cocoa, Fla.; BS, U. Ctrl. Fla. Cert. elem. tchr., primary tchr., Fla. Canvas fabricator Cape Marina, Cape Canaveral, Fla.; owner, operator B.J. Custons, Merritt Island, Fla.; tchr. Brevard County Sch. Bd., Melbourne, Fla. Den leader Cub Scouts, Boy Scouts Am., 1993—, treas., 1995—; Apple Corps vol., Merritt Island, 1993—. Mem. S.E. Early Childhood Assn. Home: 80 Rivercliff Ln Merritt Island FL 32952-4939

BIDLACK, JAMES ENDERBY, plant physiologist, plant anatomist; b. Mpls., Feb. 1, 1961; s. Verne Claude Jr. and Norma Ruth (Little) B. BS, Purdue U., 1984; MS, U. Ark., 1986; PhD, Iowa State U., 1990. Dir. ecology Resica Falls Scout Reservation, Marshall's Creek, Pa., 1978-81; lectr. demonstrator Purdue U., West Lafayette, Ind., 1982-84; lab. instr. U. Ark., Fayetteville, 1985-86, rsch. asst., 1984-86; rsch. asst. Iowa State U., Ames, 1986-90; asst. prof. U. Cen. Okla., Edmond, 1990—. Contbr. articles to profl. jours. Mem. AAUP (Disting. Scholar), Am. Soc. Agronomy, Sigma Xi, Gamma Sigma Delta. Republican. Presbyterian. Office: U Cen Okla Dept Biology Edmond OK 73034

BIEGEL, ALICE MARIE, secondary school educator; b. Blue Island, Ill., Sept. 12, 1947; d. Stanley and Lottie (Matras) Burczyk; m. Peter Leo Biegel, July 27, 1974; children: Kevin, Nicole, Robbie, Ryan. BS in Edn., Chgo. State U., 1968; MS in Edn., Gov.'s State U., 1980. Cert. math. tchr., Ill., Fla. Tchr. algebra Eisenhower High Sch., Blue Island, 1969-71; tchr. algebra and computer edn. Thornton Fractional North & South High Sch., Calumet City, Ill., 1971-76; tchr. geometry, algebra, dir. compensatory edn. Booker High Sch., Sarasota, 1988-90; tchr. algebra, chmn. math dept. Laurel Mid. Sch., Osprey, Fla., 1990-95; algebra tchr., chmn. dept. math. Larel Middle Sch., Osprey, Fla., 1992—; freshmen, jr. sponsor, prom sponsor, fgn. exchange sponsor; developer full yr. curriculum for measurements math course '75. Chmn. pub. rels. and grants com. Jr. League of Sarasota, 1988, 89-90. Recipient Tchr. Commendation award State of Ill., 1973. Mem. Nat. Coun. Tchrs. of Math., Sarasota Tchrs. of Math. Club. Roman Catholic. Home: 525 Freeling Dr Sarasota FL 34242-1019

BIEHLE, KAREN JEAN, pharmacist; b. Festus, Mo., July 18, 1959; d. Warren Day and Wilma Georgenia (Hedrick) Hargus; m. Scott Joseph Biehle, Aug. 22, 1981; children: Lauren Rachel, Heather Michelle. Student of pre-pharmacy, U. Mo., Columbia, Mo., 1977-79; BS in Pharmacy, U. Mo., Kans. City, Mo., 1982. Reg. Pharmicist. Pharmacy res. U. Iowa Hosp. & Clinics, Iowa City, Iowa, 1982-83; pharmacist Jewish Hosp. of St. Louis, St. Louis, 1983-86; pharmacy mgr. Foster Infusion Care, St. Louis, 1986-88; staff pharmacist Cardinal Glennon Children's Hosp., St. Louis, 1988-90; pres. Lauren's Specialty Foods, Inc., St. Louis, 1988-89; pharmacy mgr. Curaflex Health Svcs., St. Louis, 1989-91; asst. dir. Cobb Hosp. and Med. Ctr., Austell, Ga., 1991-94; asst. dir. pharmacy Publix Supermarkets, Marietta, Ga., 1994-96; acct. exec. Nats. Healthcare, Inc., Marietta, Ga., 1996—; preceptor St. Louis Coll. Pharmacy, 1984-91, U. Ga. Sch. Pharmacy, 1992. Vol. March of Dimes Walk-a-thon, 1985-90. Recipient Roche Pharmacy Communications Award, Roche Pharmaceuticals, Kans. City, 1982, I Dare You Award, 4-H Club, Nevada, Mo., 1976. Mem. Am. Soc. Hosp. Pharmacists, Kappa Epsilon, Alpha Delta Pi (St. Louis Alumnae pres. 1989-90). Republican. Baptist. Home: 2431 Westport Cir Marietta GA 30064-5707

BIELSS, OTTO WILLIAM, JR., secondary school educator; b. Weatherford, Tex., Nov. 12, 1933; s. Otto William and Ada Susan (Thomas) B.; m. Patsy Lee Woolsey, Dec. 23, 1958; children: Otto William III, Paul Lee. BA, Hardin-Simmons U., 1954; MS, N. Tex. State U., 1971; postgrad., So. Meth. U., 1957-58, U. Tex., Arlington, 1965-67, U. Tex., Dallas, 1984-87. Engr. Tex. Hwy. Dept., Weatherford, 1954, Gen. Dynamics Corp., Fort Worth, 1956-59; tchr. Tarleton State Coll., Stephenville, Tex., 1959-65; math. tchr. Highland Park High Sch., Dallas, 1965-72, Skyline High Sch., Dallas, 1972-90; travel cons. Travelco, Irving, Tex., 1990-96; asst. prof. math. Paul Quinn Coll., Dallas, 1994—; cluster coord. and dept. chairperson Skyline Math., 1983-90; instr. Dallas County C.C. Dist., various campuses, 1972—; grader coll. bd. advanced placement exams ETS. Author: Computer Mathematics, 1975; contbr. articles to profl. jours. Vol. various polit. campaigns, Stephenville, Tex., 1959-65, Irving, Tex., 1965—; bd. dirs. council airport noise, Irving, 1982—, Irving Community Concerts, 1991—. Served with U.S. Army, 1954-56, Korea. Grantee NSF, 1961, 67; recipient scholarship Hardin Simmon U., Abilene, Tex., 1951-54. Mem. AAUP, Math. Assn. Am., Greater Dallas Coun. Tchrs. (pres. 1974-76, bus. mgr. 1980-86, nat. rep. 1980-86), Tex. Coun. Tchrs. Math. (bus. mgr. 1980-86, pres. 1988-90), Nat. Coun. Tchrs. Math. (referee jour., rep.), Greater Dallas Tchrs. Math. (pres. 1988-90), Lions (bd. dirs. Irving 1985-87, treas. 1987-89, v.p. 1988-89, pres. 1989-91), Masons, Shriners (bd. dirs. 1988-89, 91, v.p. 1989-90, pres. 1990-91). Methodist. Home: 2609 Trinity St Irving TX 75062-5257

BIERNER, MARK WILLIAM, botanist, botanical garden director; b. Dallas, Aug. 22, 1946; s. Harold Irving and Zelda Mae (Cohen) B.; m. Judy Ann Finberg, June 16, 1968 (div. Aug., 1977); 1 child, Gann Alexander; m. Cassandra Ann James, May 11, 1986; 1 stepchild, Jameson Anthony Eynon James. BA, U. Tex., 1968, PhD, 1971. Asst. prof. U. Tenn., Knoxville, 1971-76, assoc. prof., 1976-79; dir. of prodn. Bierner & Son, Inc., Dallas, 1979-81; sci. editor St. Jude Children's Hosp., Memphis, 1982-84; exec. dir. Wild Basin Wilderness Preserve, Austin, Tex., 1985-88; lectr. S.W. Tex. State U., San Marcos, Tex., 1988-93; assoc. dir. rsch. Biosphere 2, Oracle, Ariz., 1993-94; exec. dir. Marie Selby Botanical Gardens, Sarasota, Fla., 1994—; cons. study of natural areas and special habitats The Uplands, 1987, vegitative survey s. congress at Slaughter Bus. Park, 1988, endangered species surveys six sites in Travis County, 1990; collector of plants for pharm. tests, U. Ariz., 1991, 92; study of impact on wetlands, suggestions on reduction of impact for Pleasant Valley Rd. improvements, City of Austin, 1992, mapping and mgmt. plan for the bracted twistflower, 1993. Contbr. over 30 articles and abstracts to profl. jours., chpts. to books and presented papers at sci. meetings and symposiums; edited 10 activities in Tex. Environ. Guide, 1990, 15 chpts. in Modern Biology, 1991, 3 Unit Features for Science Plus 1, 1992; edited figures and tables in Genetics, 1992. Recipient nmerous grants for sci. and conservation projects, from govt. agys., private founds., 1965— including Sarasota County Tourist Devel grant, 1995, Sarasota County Found. grant, 1995, Selby Found. grant 1995, State of Fla. grant, 1995; named Favorite Prof., S.W. Tex. State U., 1992. Mem. Am. Soc. Plant Taxonomists, Internat. Assn. for Plant Taxonomy, Botanical Soc. Am. (treas. phytochem. sect. 1975-79), Phytochem. Soc. N. Am., So. Appalachin Botanical Soc., Calif. Botanical Soc., Phi Beta Kappa, Sigma Xi (treas. U. Tenn. chpt. 1975-78), Phi Eta Sigma. Democrat. Jewish. Office: Marie Selby Bot Gardens 811 S Palm Ave Sarasota FL 34236-7726

BIERY, EVELYN HUDSON, lawyer; b. Lawton, Okla., Oct. 12, 1946; d. William Ray and Nellie Iris (Nunley) Hudson. BA in English and Latin summa cum laude, Abilene (Tex.) Christian U., 1968; JD, So. Meth. U., 1973. Bar: Tex. 1973, U.S. Dist. Ct. (we. dist.) Tex. 1975, U.S. Dist. Ct. (so. dist.) Tex. 1977, U.S. Dist. Ct. (no. dist.) Tex. 1979, U.S. Ct. Appeals (5th cir.) 1979, U.S. Ct. Appeals (11th cir.) 1981, U.S. Supreme Ct. 1981. Atty. Law Offices of Bruce Waitz, San Antonio, 1973-76; mem. LeLaurin & Adams, P.C., San Antonio, 1976-81; ptnr., head bankruptcy, reorganization and creditors' rights sect. Fulbright & Jaworski, San Antonio, 1981—, mem. policy com., 1996—; speaker on creditors' rights, bankruptcy and reorganization law at numerous seminars; lectr. Southwestern Grad. Sch. Banking, Dallas, 1980, La. State U. Sch. Banking, 1994; presiding officer, U. Tex. Sch. of Law Bankruptcy Conf., 1976, 94, State Bar Tex. Creditors' Rights Inst., 1985, State Bar Tex. Advanced Bus. Bankruptcy Law Inst., 1985, State Bar Tex. Inst. on Advising Officers, Dirs. and Ptnrs. in Troubled Bus., 1987, State Bar Tex. Advanced Creditors Rights Inst., 1988; pres. San Antonio Young Lawyers Assn., 1979-80; mem. bankruptcy adv. com. fifth cir. jud. coun., 1979-80; vice-chmn. bankruptcy com. Comml. Law League Am., 1981-83; mem. exec. bd. So. Meth. U. Sch. Law, 1983-91. Editor: Texas Collections Manual, 1978, Creditor's Rights in Texas, 2d edit., 1981; author: (with others) Collier Bankruptcy Practice Guide, 1993. Del. to U.S./Republic of China joint session on trade, investment and econ. law , Beijing, 1987; designated mem. Bankruptcy Judge Merit Screening Com. State of Tex. by Tex. State Bar Pres., 1979-82; patron McNay Mus., San Antonio; rsch. ptnr. Mind Sci. Found., San Antonio; diplomat World Affairs Coun., San Antonio. Recipient Outstanding Young Lawyer award San Antonio Young Lawyers Assn., 1979. Fellow Soc. of Internat. Bus. Fellow, Am. Coll. Bankruptcy Attys., Tex. Bar Found. (life), San Antonio Bar Found.; mem. Tex. Bar Assn. (chair bankruptcy com. 1982-83, chair corp., banking and bus. law sect. 1989-90), Tex. Assn. Bank Counsel (bd. dirs. 1988-90), San Antonio Young Lawyers Assn. (pres. 1979-80), Plaza Club San Antonio (bd. dirs. 1982—), Zonta (Chair Z club com. 1989-90), Order of Coif. Office: Fulbright & Jaworski 300 Convent St Ste 2200 San Antonio TX 78205-3723

BIESELE, JOHN JULIUS, biologist, educator; b. Waco, Tex., Mar. 24, 1918; s. Rudolph Leopold and Anna Emma (Jahn) B.; m. Marguerite Calfee McAfee, July 29, 1943 (dec. 1991); children: Marguerite Anne, Diana Terry, Elizabeth Jane; m. Esther Aline Eakin, Mar. 9, 1992. B.A. with highest honors, U. Tex., 1939, Ph.D., 1942. Fellow Internat. Cancer Research Found., U. Tex., 1942-43, Barnard Skin and Cancer Hosp., St. Louis, also; U. Pa., 1943-44, instr. zoology, 1943-44; temporary research assoc. dept. genetics Carnegie Instn. of Washington, Cold Spring Harbor, 1944-46; research assoc. biology dept. Mass. Inst. Tech., 1946-47; asst. Sloan-Kettering Inst. Cancer Research, 1946-47, research fellow, 1947, assoc., 1947-55, head cell growth sect., div. exptl. chemotherapy, 1947-58, mem., 1955-58, assoc. scientist div., 1959-78; asst. prof. anatomy Cornell U. Med. Sch., 1950-52; assoc. prof. biology Sloan-Kettering div. Cornell U. Grad. Sch. Med. Scis., 1952-55, prof. biology, 1955-58; prof. zoology, mem. grad. faculty U. Tex., Austin, 1958-78; also mem. faculty U. Tex. (Coll. Pharmacy), 1969-71, prof. edn., 1973-78; prof. emeritus zoology U. Tex., Austin, 1978—; cons. cell biology M.D. Anderson Hosp. and Tumor Inst., U. Tex. at Houston, 1958-72; dir. Genetics Found., 1959-78; mem. cell biology study sect. NIH, 1958-63; Sigma Xi lectr. NYU Grad. Sch. Arts and Scis., 1957; Mendel lectr. St. Peter's Coll., Jersey City, 1958; featured spkr. on first Earth Day, Old Westbury Campus of N.Y. Inst. Tech., 1970; Mendel Club lectr. Canisius Coll., Buffalo, 1971; mem. adv. com. rsch. etiology of cancer Am. Cancer Soc., 1961-64, pres. Travis County unit, 1966, mem. adv. com. on personnel for rsch., 1969-73; counsellor Cancer Internat. Rsch. Coop., Inc., 1962-90; mem. cancer rsch. tng. com. Nat. Cancer Inst., 1969-72; gen. chmn. Conf. Advancement Sci. and Math. Teaching, 1966. Author: Mitotic Poisons and the Cancer Problem, 1958; mem. editorial bd. Year Book Cancer, 1959-72; mem. editorial adv. bd. Cancer Rsch., 1960-64, assoc. editor, 1969-72; cons. editor: Am. Jour. Mental Deficiency, 1963-68; mem. editorial bd. The Jour. of Applied Nutrition, 1987-91; contbr. articles to profl. jours. Research Career award NIH, 1962, 67, 72, 77. Fellow N.Y., Tex. acads. scis., AAAS; mem. Am. Assn. Cancer Research (dir. 1960-63), Am. Soc. Cell Biology, Am. Inst. Biol. Scis., Phi Beta Kappa, Sigma Xi (pres. Tex. chpt. 1963-64), Phi Eta Sigma, Phi Kappa Phi. Home: 2500 Great Oaks Pky Austin TX 78756-2908

BIFERIE, DAN, art educator, digital artist; b. Miami, Dec. 17, 1950; s. Daniel Anthony and Ruth Teresa (Moderelli) B.; m. Kathryn Louise Horn, June 10, 1973; children: Danny, Billy, Robby. AS with high honors, Daytona Beach (Fla.) C.C., 1971; BFA summa cum laude, Ohio U., 1972, MFA, 1974. Prof. Daytona Beach (Fla.) C.C., 1975—, dir. Gallery of Fine Arts, 1978-91, chmn. visual arts dept., 1988-91. Photographer for book

Lakeland's Architectural Heritage, 1987. Founding mem. S.E. Mus. Photography, Daytona Beach, 1978-91; bd. dirs. Deland Mus. Art, Fla., 1980-84; ednl. advisor E. Leitz, Inc., Wetzlar, Germany, 1985; mem. Eastman Kodak Ednl. Adv. Coun., Rochester, N.Y., 1986-89; panelist visual arts fellowships Fla. Divsn. of Cultural Affairs, Tallahassee, 1989-91; pres. Arts Coun. Volusia County, Daytona Beach, 1991-94; com. mem. Volusia Vision, Inc., Daytona Beach, 1992-94. Sgt. USAFR. Individual Artists fellow Fla. Divsn. Cultural Affairs, 1995-96. Mem. Soc. for Photographic Edn. (pres. SE region 1977-84). Home: 333 S Dexter Ave Deland FL 32720 Office: Daytona Beach CC PO Box 2811 Daytona Beach FL 32120-2811

BIGDA, RUDOLPH A., business and financial consultant; b. Holyoke, Mass., Apr. 27, 1916; s. Alexander and Mary (Sakaske) B.; m. Josephine M. Baginski, June 22, 1946 (dec. July 1976); children: Donald R., Robert A.; m. Ann M. Willette, Dec. 9, 1981. BBA magna cum laude, Bryant Coll., 1935; postgrad., Dartmouth Coll., 1953. Vice pres. Parsons div. Am. Writing Paper Co., Holyoke, 1937-40; contr. F.W. Sickles div. Gen. Instrument Corp., Chicopee, Mass., 1946-54, Hano Bus. Forms Inc., Springfield, Mass., 1954-81; bus. and fin. cons. Palm Bay, Fla., 1981—; instr. Western New Eng. Coll., Springfield, 1974-75; bd. dirs. DRB Comms., Stamford, Conn.; counselor SCORE, Melbourne, Fla., 1983—. Bd. dirs. Pulaski Heights Old Age Housing, Holyoke. Col. AUS, 1941-46, mem. Res. ret. Recipient alumni award Bryant Coll., 1967. Mem. Inst. of Mgmt. Accts. (pres. Pioneer Valley chpt. 1972-74), Fin. Execs. Inst., Ret. Officers Assn. (pres. Pioneer Valley chpt. 1978-80), Am. Legion, Elks. Republican. Roman Catholic. Home and Office: 280 Berry Court NE Palm Bay FL 32907

BIGELOW, HONEY LYNN, postal employee; b. Lansing, Mich., Mar. 25, 1947; d. Harold Henry and Lillian Lula (Burgess) B. Student, Jefferson State U., Birmingham, Ala., 1974-76, U. Ala., 1976. Letter carrier U.S. Postal Svc., Birmingham, 1973—; participant Employee Involvement/Quality of Worklife Com., U.S. Post Office, Birmingham, 1976-95. Editor Br. 530 Bull., 1988-96. Active Covenant Met. Cmty. Ch. With U.S. Army, 1970-73, U.S. Army Res., 1983-88. Mem. Nat. Assn. Letter Carriers (fin. sec. 1989-95). Democrat. Office: US Postal Svc River Run PO Birmingham AL 35223

BIGGERS, NEAL BROOKS, JR., federal judge; b. Corinth, Miss., July 1, 1935; s. Neal Brooks and Sara (Cunningham) B.; 1 child, Sherron. BA, Millsaps Coll., 1956; JD, U. Miss., 1963. Sole practice Corinth, 1963-68; pros. atty. Alcorn County, 1964; dist. atty. 1st Jud. Dist. Miss., 1968-75, cir. judge, 1975-84; judge U.S. Dist. Ct. (no. dist.) Miss., Oxford, 1984—. Contbr. articles to profl. jours. Office: US Dist Ct PO Box 1238 Oxford MS 38655-1238

BIGGERS, PAULA BOWERS, medical/surgical nurse; b. Allendale, S.C., July 10, 1956; d. Paul Ford and Jessie (King) Bowers; m. William Alan Biggers Jr., Jan. 19, 1987. Student, U. S.C., 1974-75; A in Dental Assisting, Midlands Tech. Coll., 1975-76; BS in Nursing, U. S.C., 1979-82. RN, Tex., S.C., Miss.; cert. med.-surg. nurse, nephrology nurse. Asst. head nurse Richland Meml. Hosp., Columbia, S.C., 1982-84; asst. head nurse Dorn Vets. Hosp., Columbia, S.C., 1984-91; unit mgr. weekends Hermann Hosp., Houston, 1992-94, unit mgr., 1994-95; head nurse VA Hosp., Biloxi, Miss., 1995-96, performance mgmt. coord., 1996—; mem. procedure com. Dorn Vets. Hosp., Columbia, 1989-91, nurse quality control, 1990-91; preceptor hemodialysis unit Dorn Vets. Hosp., Columbia, 1989-91; instr. cardiopulmonary resuscitation ARC, Columbia, 1985-91; CPR instr., Houston, 1991—, unit guideline com., 1991—. Contbr. articles to profl. jours. Blood pressure screening ARC, Columbia, 1985-91. Mem. AACN (pub. rels. com. mid-state chpt. 1989-90, pres.-elect 1990-91, pres. 1991-92), Sigma Theta Tau. Republican. Baptist. Home: 251 Bayview Ave Biloxi MS 39530 Office: VA Hosp Pass Rd Biloxi MS 39531-2410

BIGGERS, WILLIAM JOSEPH, retired manufacturing company executive; b. Great Bend, Kans., Mar. 16, 1928; s. William Henry and Frances (Jack) B.; m. Eathil Bonner, Nov. 17, 1956 (div. July 1981); children: Frances, Patricia; m. Diane McLaughlin, Feb. 14, 1983; 1 child, Michael C. B.A., Duke U., 1949. C.P.A., Ga. Pub. acct., 1949-55; sec.-treas. Parker, Helms & Langston, Inc., Brunswick, Ga., 1955-59, Stuckey's, Inc., Eastman, Ga., 1959-60; sec.-treas., v.p. finance Curtis 1000 Inc., 1961-69; v.p. Am. Bus. Products, Inc., Atlanta, 1969-73, chief exec. officer, 1973-88, chmn. bd., 1983-94, chmn. exec. com., 1994—; bd dirs. Com. Publicly Owned Cos.; former trustee Ga. Coun. Econ. Edn., former mem. listed co. adv. com. N.Y. Stock Exch., Am. Stock Exch. Trustee Berry Coll.; bd. dirs. Atlanta Area coun. Boy Scouts Am. With USNR, 1946, with AUS, 1950-52. Mem. AICPA, NAM, Ga. Soc. CPAs, Fin. Execs. Inst., Am. Mgmt. Assn., Phoenix Soc. Atlanta, Capital City Club, Georgian Club, Marietta Country Club, Highlands Country Club, Rotary, Phi Kappa Psi. Office: Am Bus Products Inc Ste 1200 2100 Riveredge Pkwy NW Atlanta GA 30328-4656 Mailing Address: PO Box 105684 Atlanta GA 30348-5684

BIGGINS, PAUL ALEXANDRE, marketing professional; b. Cleve., Jan. 21, 1959; s. John and Annette (DeBeir-LeGrand) B.; children: Matthew Alexandre, Christopher Andrew. BSBA, Miami U., 1981. Account exec. Dean Witter Reynolds Inc., Dallas, 1983-85, Rauscher Pierce Refsnes Inc., Dallas, 1985; regional dir. Mut. Benefit Fin. Svcs., Dallas, 1985-87; regional v.p. Transam. Funds, Houston, 1987-91, MFS Fin. Svcs. Inc., Boston, 1991-93; regional dir. Invesco Svcs. Inc., Atlanta, 1993—. Mem. Internat. Assn. Fin. Planning (Dallas chpt.). Republican. Roman Catholic. Office: Invesco Svcs Inc 1355 Peachtree St NE Atlanta GA 30309-3269

BIGGS, ANTOINETTE BAILEY, real estate broker; b. Rhinebeck, N.Y., May 24, 1936; d. Donald Cheney and Felicita Mercedes (Rivera) Bailey; m. Robert Laney Bush, June 5, 1955 (div. Mar. 1971); children: Denise Lee Bailey McLeod, Lisa Anne Mooney, Amy Suzanne Curry, Patrick Laney Bush; m. Hubbard Kavanaugh Biggs, June 27, 1973. AA with honors, Polk C.C., Winter Haven, Fla., 1992; BA in Interpersonal Comm. cum laude, U. Ctrl. Fla., 1994; matriculated, Thomas M. Cooley Law Sch., 1995—. Cert. real estate brokerage mgr., real estate specialist. Legal sec. Fagan & Crouch, Attys., Gainesville, Fla., 1953-61; real estate salesperson Huskey Realty, Realtors, Maitland, Fla., 1968-70, Roberts & Gilman, Realtors, Maitland, 1970-73; real estate broker Hubbard K. Biggs, Realtor, Lake Wales, Fla., 1973-74; pres. Biggs Appraisal & Realty, Inc., Winter Haven, 1974-95, Biggs & Biggs, Inc., Winter Haven, fla., 1974—; pres. Lake Wales Bd. of Realtors, 1983, 84, also multiple chairmanships; edn. chmn. Winter Haven Bd. of Realtors, 1974, 81. mem. real estate adv. com. Polk C. C., 1980-93. Recipient Excellence in Ed. awards Winter Haven Bd. Realtors, 1974, 75, 76, 77, 81, 82, Realtor of Yr. award, 1984. Mem. DAR, Nat. Assn. Realtors, Lake Wales Bd. Realtors, Women's Coun. Realtors (v.p. 1980-81), Winter Haven Bd. Realtors, Phi Theta Kappa, Phi Kappa Phi, Golden Key Nat. Honor Soc. (pres. U. Ctrl. Fla. chpt. 1993-94). Republican. Roman Catholic. Home: 241 Volusia Dr Winter Haven FL 33884-1405 Office: Biggs & Biggs Inc Realtors 241 Volusia Dr Winter Haven FL 33884-1405

BIGGS-WILLIAMS, EVELYN ANN, librarian; b. Atmore, Ala., Sept. 27, 1950; d. John Henry and Mary Evelyn (Smith) Biggs; m. Michael Robin Williams, June 14, 1986. BS, U. South Ala., 1971; MLS, Fla. State U., 1972. Libr. Escambia Acad., Canoe, Ala., 1972-73; asst. libr. Jefferson Davis C.C., Brewton, Ala., 1973-91, libr., 1991-94, head libr., 1994—. Mem. ALA, Ala. Libr. Assn., Ala. Instnrl. Media Assn. (past pres.), Southeastern Libr. Assn. Methodist. Office: Jefferson Davis C C 220 Alco Dr Brewton AL 36424

BIGHAM, CYNTHIA DAWN, kindergarten educator; b. Lubbock, Tex., Apr. 29, 1966; d. Norman Dean and Evlyn Maxine (Taylor) B. BS in Elem. Edn., Tex. Tech. U., 1988. Cert. tchr., Tex. Early childhood tchr. Crosby (Tex.) Ind. Sch. Dist., 1989-90, kindergarten tchr., 1990-92, gifted/talented tchr., 1990-92, mentor tchr., 1991-92; kindergarten tchr. Goose Creek Consol. Ind. Sch. Dist., Baytown, Tex., 1992—. Mem. PTO, Alpha Delta Kappa. Office: Pumphrey Elem Sch 4901 Fairway Dr Baytown TX 77521-2911

BIGHAM, WANDA RUTH, college president; b. Barlow, Ky., June 19, 1935; d. Herbert Martin and Ada Florene (Baker) Durrett; m. William M. Bigham, Jr., June 7, 1958; children: William M. III, Janet Kaye, Julia Lynn. BME, Murray State U., 1956; MM, Morehead State U., 1971, MHE, 1973; EdD, U. Ky., 1978; cert., Inst. For Ednl. Mgmt. -Harvard U., 1982; LittD (hon.), Loras Coll., 1989. Dir. TRIO programs Morehead (Ky.) State U., 1972-85, assoc. dean acad. affairs, dir. instructional sys., 1982-85, acting dean grad. and spl. acad. programs, 1984-85; exec. asst. to pres. Emerson Coll., Boston, 1985, v.p. for devel., 1986; pres. Marycrest Coll., Davenport, Iowa, 1986-92, Huntingdon Coll., Montgomery, Ala., 1993—. Bd. dirs. Ala. World Affairs Coun., Montgomery, 1994—, Montgomery Symphony Orch., 1993—, Ala. Shakespeare Festival, 1996—, NASCUMC, 1996—; exec. com. Ctrl. Ala. chpt. ARC, Montgomery, 1995; mem. Leadership Ala., 1994—; co-chair Quad Cities Vision for the Future, Davenport, 1987-92. Recipient Pres.'s award Davenport C. of C., 1988, Women of Spirit and Note award Cmty. Com. of Davenport, 1991, Hope for Humanity award Jewish Fedn. of Q1, Rock Island, Ill., 1993; named to Alumni Hall of Fame, Morehead Stae U., 1988, Disting. Alumna, Murray State Coll., 1988. Mem. Am. Coun. on Edn. (mem. coun. of fellows, bd. dirs. 1994—, fellow in higher edn. adminstrn. 1983-84), Internat. Assn. Univ. Pres., Montgomery C. of C., Sigma Alpha Iota (Sword of Honor 1956), Phi Kappa Phi, Kappa Delta Pi. Home: 1393 Woodley Rd Montgomery AL 36106 Office: Huntingdon College 1500 E Fairview Ave Montgomery AL 36106-2114

BIGLER, ROSE JOHNSON, criminal justice educator; b. Marion, S.C., May 4, 1958; d. Kenneth Woodrow and Diana Louise (Arbogast) Johnson; m. David Warren Bigler, Aug. 16, 1992. BA in Sociology, Mercer U., 1981; MS in Criminal Justice, Northeastern U., 1982; PhD, Rutgers U., 1991; postgrad., U. Mich., 1991. Corr. Jacksonville (Fla.) Jour., 1976-77; tchg. asst., grad. asst. Coll. Criminal Justice Northeastern U., Boston, 1981-82; prodn. asst., writer Sta. WNEV-TV, Boston, 1982-83; prodn. asst. Sta. WJCT-TV, Jacksonville, 1984-85; tchg. asst. Grad. Sch. Criminal Justice, instr. Univ. Coll. Rutgers U., Newark, 1985-87, rsch. asst. Bur. Justice Assistance, 1987-88, tchg. asst. dept. sociology, 1988; asst. prof. social justice program U. Ill., Springfield, 1988-94; asst. prof. history, polit. sci., criminal justice Charleston (S.C.) So. U., 1994—; evaluation specialist for safe schs. Nat. Inst. Justice, Office of Juvenile Justice and Delinquency, and Dept. of Edn., Duval County Sch. Bd., Jacksonville, 1984; pub. spkr., cons. Citizens Against Crime, Jacksonville, 1984-85; ct. liaison counselor Juvenile Ct., Dept. Health and Rehab. Svcs., Jacksonville, 1985; intern UN, Visual Svcs., Film and TV Prodn., N.Y.C., 1986; adj. instr. dept. sociology, anthropology, urban studies and criminal justice Rutgers U., Newark, 1988; adj. instr. Montclair State Coll., Upper Montclair, N.J., 1988-89; presenter in field. Contbr. book revs., essays, and articles to profl. pubs. Vol., advance person Ted Kennedy Senate Reelection Campaign, Boston, 1982; vol. ARC, Macon, Ga., 1978-81. Named one of Outstanding Young Women of Am., Jacksonville Jour. Corr. of Yr., 1977; Mercer Univ. acad. scholar, 1977-81, Walter C. Russell scholar Rutgers U., 1988-89, postdoctorate vis. scholar U. Mich., 1991. Mem. Am. Soc. Criminology (sect. chair program com. 1995), Am. Sociology Assn., Nat. Orgn. for Victim Assistance, Am. Film Inst., Acad. Criminal Justice Scis., Ill. Criminal Justice Info. Authority, Alpha Phi Sigma, Phi Eta Sigma, Sigma Tau Gamma. Democrat. Office: Charleston So U 9200 University Blvd Charleston SC 29423

BIHUNIAK, JEANETTE LEE, medical records administrator; b. Bronx, Apr. 11, 1966; d. Garry and Regina (Wolozny) C. BSN, SUNY, Plattsburgh, 1988. RN, N.Y. Nurse med.-surg. Good Samaritan Hosp., Suffern, N.Y., 1988-90; nurse labor and delivery Good Samaritan Hosp., 1990-93; perinatal case mgr. Matria Healthcare Inc., Marietta, Ga., 1993-96, electronic patient record coord., 1996—.

BIKOWSKI, VERA ELLEN POLAKAS, speech pathologist; b. Cold Spring Harbor, N.J., Aug. 15, 1948; d. Anthony Joseph and Martha Rose (Rugala) Polakas; m. Michael John Bikowski, Dec. 20, 1969; children: David Michael, Paul Anthony. BA, CUNY, 1970, MEd, 1974. Speech pathologist N.Y.C. Bd. Edn., Bklyn., 1970-78, Franklin County Schs., Winchester, Tenn., 1983-84, Skills Devel. Services, Tullahoma, Tenn., 1986-88, Moore County Schs., Lynchburg, Tenn., 1987-88, Arab (Ala.) City Schs., 1988-89, Albertville (Ala.) City Schs., 1989-91, So. Euless (Tex.) Elem. Sch., 1991-94; speech pathologists Newport News (Va.) City Schs., 1994—. Home: 108 Birkdale Ct Yorktown VA 23693-5520

BILAS, RICHARD A., economist; b. Passaic, N.J., Feb. 3, 1935; s. Nestor Joseph and Helen Evelyn (Smith) B.; m. Janet Lianne Harris, June 23, 1956; children: Cathy, David, Ami. AB in Math., Duke U., 1956; PhD in Econs., U. Va., 1963. Asst., then assoc. prof. U. So. Calif., L.A., 1962-67; assoc. prof., then prof. Ga. State U., Atlanta, 1967-70; E.C. Reid prof. econs. Calif. State U., Bakersfield, 1970-87; commr. Calif. Energy Commn., Sacramento, 1987-95; Brock chair in energy econs. and policy Sarkeys Energy Ctr., Norman, Okla., 1995—; mem. Program on Workable Energy Regulation Bd., U. Calif., 1990—. Author: Microeconomics, 1967, 71, Problems in Microeconomics, 1972, Macroeconomics, 1974; mem. editl. bd. Western Econ. Assn.'s Contemporary Econ. Policy, 1990—. Active Rep. Ctrl. Com., Kern County, Calif., 1978-82. Nat. Def. fellow U. Va., 1959-62; recipient Honor cert. Freedoms Found., 1977, 79. Mem. Masons, Phi Beta Kappa. Republican. Episcopalian. Home: PO Box 722071 Norman OK 73070 Office: Sarkeys Energy Ctr 100 E Boyd Rm 510 Norman OK 73019-0628

BILBO, LINDA SUE HOLSTON, home health nurse; b. Poplarville, Miss., Mar. 20, 1955; d. Theo Gilmore Sr. and Dimple Bernice (Loveless) Holston; divorced; 1 child, Emily LeNore. Diploma, St. Dominic Sch. Nursing, 1976; postgrad., William Carey Coll., 1993—. RN, Miss., La. RN staff nurse med.-surg. Bogalusa (La.) Med. Ctr., 1976-78, Lakeside Hosp., Metairie, La., 1978-80; RN staff nurse ICU/CCU Jo Ellen Smith Hosp., New Orleans, 1980-81; RN staff nurse surgery West Jefferson Hosp., Marrero, La., 1981-82; RN staff nurse home health South Miss. Home Health, Hattiesburg, 1982—; instr. BLS Am. Heart, Miss. Children's Sun. Sch. tchr. 1st Bapt. Ch., 1990-95; active PTA, Poplarville, Miss. 1985-95, Poplarville Band Booster, 1991-95. Named Nat. Essay Contest winner Am. Jour. Nursing, 1993, 94. Mem. Miss. Nurses Assn. Home: PO Box 294 Poplarville MS 39470-0294 Office: South Miss Home Health PO Box 16929 Hattiesburg MS 39404-6929

BILES, DAVID WALLACE, lawyer; b. Dallas, Dec. 26, 1958; s. Adrain Ollie and Elisabeth Elaine (George) B.; m. Jane Jenkins, Mar. 3, 1990. BBA, U. North Tex., 1981; JD, U. Houston, 1984. Bar: Tex. 1984; cert. family law specialist. Assoc. atty. Bradshaw & Plummer, Houston, 1984-86; atty. Law Office of David W. Biles, Houston and Denton, Tex., 1986-91; mng. ptnr. Biles & Lock, P.C., Denton, Tex., 1991-94; ptnr. Biles & Bouschor, P.C., Denton, 1994—; trustee U. North Tex. Athletics. Contbr. articles to profl. jours. Lectr. Tex. Downtown Assn., Tex. Mainstreet Program; mem. Leadership Denton Alumni Assn.; treas., exec. com., trustee, corp. counsel Denton Festival Found., Inc.; exec. com., ex-officio dir., corp. counsel Denton Ctrl. Bus. Dist. Assn., Inc.; mem. Denton Community Theatre, Denton Hist. Soc., Denton County Commrs.' Property Com.; ex-officio exec. com., corp. counsel Denton Holiday Festival Assn., Inc.; chmn. Denton Streetscape Com. Mem. ABA (family law sect.), Tex. Acad. Family Law Specialists, Coll. State Bar Tex., State Bar Tex. (family law sect., litigation sect.), Denton County Bar Assn., Denton County Family Lawyers Assn. (bd. dirs.), U. North Tex. Alumni Assn. (Denton chpt. past pres.), Denton C. of C. (treas., exec. com., bd. dirs., past chmn. govt. affairs, Pres.'s Club 100). Office: Biles and Bouschor PC 512 W Hickory St Denton TX 76201-9095

BILES, MARILYN MARTA, painter; b. Wilmington, Del., Oct. 3, 1935; d. Albert Humbert and Anne Marie (DeRogatis) Marta; m. George Ronald Bower, June 30, 1956 (div. May 1970); children: Michele Bower Alvarado, Nancy Bower Guthrie, Randall William. Student Moore Coll. Art, 1953-54, St. Mary's Coll., 1959-61, Mus. Fine Arts, Houston, 1972-74. Art tchr. Contemporary Arts Mus., Houston, 1969-73, 80-81; head art dept. preprimary div. Duchesne Acad., Houston, 1970-72; project coord. Nan Fisher, Inc., Houston, 1983-84; one-woman shows include Brown & Scurlock Galleries, Beaumont, Tex., 1st Nat. City Bank, Houston, 1980, Christ Ch. Cathedral, 1981-82, Toni Jones Gallery, 1981, U. Houston, 1982, Station Gallery, Greenville, Del., 1984, Boyar Norton & Blair, 1986, Martha Turner Properties, 1986, Cancerfighters of Houston, 1991, R.S.V.P. Collection, Miami, Fla., 1993, Chateaux Piada, Bordeaux, France, 1993, Musée de la Commanderie d'Unet, Bordeaux, 1993, 1994, San Felipe Office Plz., Houston, 1996; group shows include: U. Houston, 1977, 79, Nat. Cape Coral Exhbn., Fla., 1979, Toni Jones Gallery, 1979, Assistance League of Houston, 1979, 80, Golden Crescent Gallery, Houston, 1984, Conrad Gallery, Galveston, Tex. 1991, Pima Coll. Tucson, La Sorbonne, Paris, 1992, Musée de la Commanderie d'Unet, Bordeaux, 1992, Spirit Echoes Gallery Invitational, Austin Tex., 1992, 2nd anniversary show, 1994, Hotel de Ville, Paris, 1993, Wirtz Gallery, Miami, Fla., 1993, New England Fine Arts Inst., Boston, 1993, Spirit Echoes Gallery, Austin, Tex., 1994; coord., designer art programs Spring Branch Schs., Houston, 1968-70; coord. art exhibits St. John the Divine Episcopal Ch., Houston. Bd. dirs. Spring Branch YWCA, Houston, 1973-74; docent Harris County Heritage Soc., Houston, 1970-72; mem. bd., v.p. Arcs Found., Inc., Houston, 1983; bd. dirs., gala chmn. Houston Grand Opera Guild, 1983-84, governing bd. assn., 1984-85, co-chmn. gala, 1985; founder, pres. Mus. Med. Sci. Assn., Houston, 1986-87; mem. com. Can-Do-It Charity Fundraiser, Peter W. Guenther Art History Scholarship Fund at U. Houston. Mem. Artists Equity (dir. Houston chpt. 1980), Art League Houston, Tex. Fine Arts Assn., Univ. Club Houston, Houston Racquet Club, World Trade Club (v.p. women's assn. 1974-75). Republican. Episcopalian. Home: 9337 Katy Fwy Ste 171 Houston TX 77024-1515

BILHARTZ, JAMES ROHN, JR., independent oil producer; b. Dallas, Nov. 19, 1955; m. Mary Patricia Callahan, May 21, 1976; children: Jennifer Lauren, James Rohn Daniel III. BS in Petroleum Engring., Tex. A&M U., 1978. Petroleum engr. Tenneco Oil Co., Denver, 1978-80; bus. devel. Tenneco Oil Co., Houston, 1980-81; v.p. JRB Oil & Gas Co., Duncanville, Tex., 1981-93, sr. v.p., 1994—. Bd. trustees Duncanville Ind. Sch. Dist., 1991, v.p., 1992, sec., 1993, v.p. sch. bd., 1994, pres. sch. bd., 1995, 96; pres. Duncanville Ind. Sch. Dist. Found., 1996. Mem. Soc. Petroleum Engrs., Mid Continent Oil and Gas Assn., Tex. Ind. Royalty Producers Orgn. Roman Catholic. Office: JRB Oil & Gas Co 627 Mercury Ave Duncanville TX 75137-2235

BILIRAKIS, MICHAEL, congressman, lawyer, business executive; b. Tarpon Springs, Fla., July 16, 1930; s. Emmanuel and Irene (Pikramenos) B.; m. Evelyn Miaoulis, Dec. 27, 1959; children: Emmanuel, Gus. BS in Engring., U. Pitts., 1959; student, George Washington U., 1959-60; JD, U. Fla., 1963; JD (hon.), Stetson U.; hon. degree, U. Tampa. Bar: Fla. 1964; cert. coll. tchr., Fla. Atty., small businessman Pinellas and Pasco Counties, Fla., 1968—; mem. 98th-104th Congresses from 9th Dist. Fla., 1983—; mem. energy and commerce com., veterans affairs com. Mem. Rep. Task Force on Social Security; co-chmn. Task Force on Infant Mortality; founder, charter pres. Tarpon Springs Vol. Ambulance Service; dir. Greek Studies program U. Fla.; dir. emeritus Juvenile Diabetes and Hospice; mem. Pres.' Coun. U. Fla. Sgt. USAF, 1951-55. Named Citizen of Yr. Greater Tarpon Springs, 1972-73, Man of Yr. United Way, 1989-90. Mem. Am. Legion (comdr. 1977-79), VFW, Amvets, USAF Sgts., NCOA, Air Force Assn., Greater Tarpon Springs C. of C. (past pres., dir.), Pinellas C. of C. (gov.), West Pasco Bar Assn., Am. Judicature Soc., Fla. Bar Assn., Gator Boosters, Fla. Blue Key (hon.), Mason (33 degree), Shriner, Jester, Moose, Elks, Rotary, Eastern Star, Phi Alpha Delta, Sigma Pi. Greek Orthodox. Lodges: Masons; Shriners; Moose; Tarpon Springs Rotary; Elks; Eastern Star; White Shrine of Jerusalem. Office: US Ho of Reps Rayburn House Ofc Bldg Washington DC 20515-0003

BILLETER, MARIANNE, pharmacy educator; b. Durham, N.C., Feb. 28, 1963; d. Ralph Leonard and Nancy Jane (Chambers) B. BS in Pharmacy, Purdue U., 1986, PharmD, 1987. Cert. pharmacotherapy specialist. Pharmacy extern Commd. Officer Student Tng. and Extern Program, USPHS-FDA, Rockville, Md., 1983; radiopharmacy extern Commd. Officer Student Tng. and Extern Program, USPHS-NIH, Bethesda, Md., 1984; pharmacy extern Indian Health Svc. Commd. Officer Student Tng. and Extern Program, USPHS, Tahlequah, Okla., 1985; pharmacist Beaumont Hosp., Royal Oak, Mich., 1986; pharmacy resident U. Ky., Lexington, 1987-89, fellow in infectious diseases, 1989-90; asst. prof. Xavier Univ. of L.A., New Orleans, 1990—; relief pharmacist Ochsner Med. Instns., New Orleans, 1991-96; cons. Abbott Labs., Abbott Park, Ill., 1991—. Contbr. chpts. to books and articles to profl. jours. Mem. Am. Assn. Colls. Pharmacy, Am. Coll. Clin. Pharmacy, Am. Soc. Health-Sys. Parmacists, La. Soc. Pharmacists, Soc. Health Sys. Infectious Diseases Pharmacists, Am. Soc. Microbiology. Office: Xavier Coll Pharmacy 7325 Palmetto St New Orleans LA 70125-1056

BILLICK, L. LARKIN, marketing executive; b. Des Moines, Sept. 15, 1948; s. Lyle Larkin and Florence Carlson B.; m. Kathryn Rose Gildner, Aug. 14, 1971; children: Kelly Lynne, Brett Larkin. BS, U. Kans., Lawrence, 1970; grad. Inst. Bank Mktg., U. So. Calif., La. State U., 1978. Group ins. trainee Bankers Life Co., Des Moines, 1970-71; nat. advt. rep. Stoner Broadcasting Co., Des Moines, 1971-74; advt. account supr. Mid-Am. Broadcasting, Des Moines, 1974-75; dir. pub. realtions and mktg. Iowa Bankers Assn., Des Moines, 1975-77; asst. v.p., advt. mgr. corp. staff Marine Banks, Milw., 1977-79, v.p. advt., 1979-81; pres. Billick Fin. Mktg. Group, 1981-82; 1979-81; sr. v.p. mktg. Univ. Savs. Assn., Houston, 1982-84; mgmt. supr. W.B. Doner Advt./S.W., Houston, 1984-86; pres. The Strategists, Inc., Houston, 1986-89, Rotan Mosle Div. Paine Webber, Inc., Houston, 1990-91, Oppenheimer & Co., Houston, 1991-94, LeMail Direct Marketing of Houston, 1994—. Bd. dirs. Grad. Inst. Bank Mktg., La. State U., 1978-79; chmn. comm. Milwaukee County Performing Arts Center, 1978-79; advt., promotion cons. to polit. candidates; chmn. comm. coun. United Performing Arts Fund Milw., 1978-79; dist. coord. State Del. for Jimmy Carter, 1972-80; chmn. comm. com. Milwaukee County coun. Boy Scouts Am., 1979-80; bd. dirs. Katy (Tex.) Nat. Little League, 1984-91, Katy Youth Football, 1984-86, Katy Taylor High Sch. Athletic Booster Club, 1989-94, pres., 1989-94, Pacesetters Drill Team Boosters Club, 1989-92, Nottingham Country Club Swim Team, 1984-92, Katy Bus. Assn., 1994—. Mem. Bank Mktg. Assn. (chmn. advt. council 1980-81, mem. nat. conv. com. 1980-82), Am. Bankers Assn. (mem. nat. mktg. conf. com. 1980), Am. Advt. Fedn. (public service com. 1980-81), Am. Mktg. Assn., U. Kans. Alumni Assn. (life), Milw. Advt. Club (v.p., bd. dirs. 1978-81). Republican. Roman Catholic. Home: 20531 Quail Chase Dr Katy TX 77450-5036 Office: 800 Tully Rd Ste 270 Houston TX 77079-5426

BILLINGS, HAROLD WAYNE, librarian, editor; b. Cain City, Tex., Nov. 12, 1931; s. Harold Ross and Katie Mae (Price) B.; m. Bernice Schneider, Sept. 10, 1954; children: Brenda, Geoffrey, Carol. B.A., Pan Am. Coll., 1953; M.L.S., U. Tex., 1957. Tchr. Pharr-San Juan-Alamo (Tex.) High Sch., 1953-54; catalog librarian U. Tex., Austin, 1954-57; asst. chief catalog librarian U. Tex., 1957-65, chief acquisitions librarian, 1965-67, asst. univ. librarian, 1967-72, asso. dir. gen. libraries, 1972-77, acting dir. gen. libraries, 1977-78, dir. gen. libraries, 1978—; sec. Tex. Bd. Libr. Examiners; mem. adv. com. Tex. Higher Edn. Coordinating Bd. Libr. Formula, 1987-92, acad. support formula adv. com., 1993-94; mem. steering com. Tex-Share Project, 1993-94; trustee Amigos Bibliographic Coun., 1980-83; chmn. Coun. Acad. Rsch. Librs., 1979-81; chmn. rsch. librs. adv. com. Online Computer Libr. Ctr. (OCLC), 1980-82, 87-88, mem. OCLC Users Coun.; bd. dirs. Ctr. Rsch. Librs., Chgo., 1989-96, Assn. Rsch. Librs., 1989-92; mem. Tex. Coun. State Univ. Librs., Assn. Rsch. Librs. Preservation Com., Collection Devel. Com., Coun. on Libr. Resources Preservation and Access Com., Coun. on Libr. Resources/Assn. Am. Pubs. Joint Working Group on Electronic Info., 1993-94; mem. adv. bd. Project Muse-Johns Hopkins U. Press, Balt., 1995—; project dir. numerous fed. grants. Author: Education of Librarians in Texas, 1956, Edward Dahlberg: American Ishmael of Letters, 1968, A Bibliography of Edward Dahlberg, 1972, The Shape of Shiel, 1865-1896, 1983, The Leafless American, 2d edit., 1986, Magic and Hypersystems, 1990, The Bionic Library, 1991, Supping with the Devil, 1993, The Information Ark, 1994, The Tomorrow Librarian, 1995; editor books in field; contbr. to jours.; mem. editorial bd. Libr. Chronicle, 1970—. Sec., trustee Littlefield Fund for So. History. Democrat. Office: U Tex Librs PO Box P Austin TX 78713-8916

BILLINGS, LETHA MARGUERITE, nurse; b. Navina, Okla., June 27, 1909; d. Edgar Hubert and Blanche Edith (Hubbard) Ladner; m. Carroll Humphrey, Aug. 15, 1928 (div. 1931); m. Ralph Melvin Billings, May 19, 1935 (dec. 1981); children: William Edgar, Betty Luella (dec.). Diploma, Okla. Meth. Hosp., Guthrie, Okla., 1929; student, Chgo. Lying-in Hosp., 1931-32, Cook County Hosp., Chgo., 1932. RN, Okla., Calif. Pvt. duty nurse Guthrie Hosp., Wesley Hosp., Oklahoma City, 1930-31; sch. nurse Logan County Schs. and Guthrie Schs., 1932-33; FERA adminstr. Logan County FERA, 1933-35; sch. nurse Guthrie Schs., 1936-38; night supr., mem. obstet. staff Mercy Hosp., Bakersfield, Calif., 1941-44; instr., trainer

Home Care, ARC, Woodward, Okla., 1949-55; co-owner Billings Advt. Assn., Woodward, 1950-75; cons. Woodard Nursing Ctr., 1989-91; supr. Woodward Meml. Hosp. and Health Ctr., 1952-84; local coord., long term care Am. Assn. Ret. Persons, Woodward, 1991—. Chmn. Christian Women's Fellowship, First Christian Ch., 1952. del., 1995; del. Rep. County Assn. Wooodward, 1991, White House Conf. on Aging, 1995; mem. Silver Haired Legislature form Dist. 11, Oklahoma City, 1988-92, mem. exec. com., 1990-92; mem. Okla. Health Planning Com., 1969-70; pres. adv. bd. Nutrition Coun.; health advocate, local coord. and long term care State Am. Assn. Retired Persons; mem. Okla. nursing com. ARC; mem. adv. coun. Area Agy. on Aging; vol. Sr. Ctr. Woodward. Named Outstanding Older Oklahoman State Conf. on Aging, 1993. Mem. ANA (econ. and gen. welfare com. 1958-61, study of functions com. 1962-64, chmn. nominating com. 1972, exec. com. pvt. duty sect. 1988-92), Okla. Nurses Assn. (pres. 1958, Nurse of Yr. 1959), Okla. Dist. 18 Nurses Assn., Okla. Fedn. Women's Clubs (past pres. 3rd dist., edn. chmn., health chmn. 1994), Okla. Congress Parents and Tchrs. (pres. 1964-67), PTA (nat., state life mem.), Order Ea. Star (treas., past matron), PEO (chpt. sec.), Ladies Elks. Home and Office: 1419 Hillcrest Dr Woodward OK 73801-4339

BILLINGS, ROGER LEWIS, oil company executive; b. Tulsa, Okla., Oct. 6, 1932; s. Arthur Lewis and Edra Mae (Duckworth) B.; m. Martha Carol Voight, Aug. 29, 1953; children: Victoria Martha Parks, Meg Yamamoto. B.S. in Geology, U. Okla., 1954, M.S. in Geology, 1956; M.B.A., Harvard U., 1968. Cert. petroleum geologist. Geologist Exxon, Rock Mountains and S.Am., 1955-66; mgr. planning Union Pacific, Los Angeles, 1968-72; v.p. gas and oil Mont. Power Co., Butte, 1972-78; v.p. exploration and prodn. KNEnergy, Lakewood, Colo., 1979-80; exec. v.p., chief operating officer Home Petroleum Corp., Houston, 1980-82; v.p. eastern region Aminoil Inc., Houston, 1982-85; exec. v.p., chief operating officer Plains Petroleum Co., Lakewood, 1985-88; pres., CEO L.B. Simmons Energy, Inc., Houston, 1989—; also bd. dirs. Mem. Am. Assn. Petroleum Geologists, Ind. Petroleum Assn. Am. Office: L B Simmons Energy Inc 5847 San Felipe St Ste 1890 Houston TX 77057-3009

BILLINGSLEY, JUDITH ANN SEAVEY, oncology nurse; b. Manchester, Conn., Aug. 4, 1947; d. John Frank and Carol Jean (Wood) Seavey; m. Michael Billingsley, June 7, 1969; children: Tamara Lynn, Tara Lynn. Diploma, Hartford Hosp. Sch. Nursing, 1968; student, Coll. of Albemarle, 1985-86, No. Va. C.C., 1990; grad. with honors, George Mason U., 1992. Cert. oncology nurse ANCC, 1995. Staff nurse ICU Manchester Meml. Hosp., 1968-69; staff nurse recovery rm. Burlingame (Calif.) Hosp. and Med. Ctr., 1972-73; staff nurse St. Joseph's Hosp., Atlanta, 1987-89; clin. nurse Alexandria (Va.) Hosp., 1989-91; admissions nurse Hospice of No. Va., 1991-92; neuro-oncology clin. rsch. nurse Winship Cancer Ctr. Emory U. Sch. Medicine, Atlanta, 1992—. Mem. Golden Key, Sigma Theta Tau, Alpha Chi. Home: 1273 Gray Squirrel Xing Marietta GA 30062-6275

BILLINGSLEY, NADINE YOUNG, genealogist; b. Geary, Okla., May 28, 1930; d. Hilyeard H. and Pearl (King) Young; m. Ray Verne Billingsley, Dec. 22, 1950; children: Leonard James, Dennis Lee, Sandra Renee. BS, Okla. State U., 1951. Home econ. tchr. Mulhall (Okla.) H.S., 1951-52, Roseville (N.C.) H.S., 1953-54; art tchr. (adults) Burma Am. Assn., Myanmar and Malawi, 1981-84. Author: My Kin, 1981, Brazos County Texas Births 1850-1910, 1993, Descendants of Joshua Jones and Solomon King 1771-1994, 1994; contbr. articles to profl. jours. Class leader Royal Bangkok Mus. Study Groups, Thailand, 1974-78; pres. St. Thomas Episcopal Women of the Ch., 1973-74. Recipient First of Show, Brazos Valley Art League, Bryan, Tex., 1973, Third of Show, 1974. Mem. AAUW (treas. Lubbock 1956-60), Am. Womens Club of Burma, 1960-62, UN Womens Club (Rome), Daus. of the Confederacy, Daus. of the Republic of Tex. (pres. Robert Henry chpt. 1993-97). Episcopal. Home: 706 Pershing College Station TX 77840

BILLINGSLEY, ROBERT THAINE, lawyer; b. Wichita, Kans., Jan. 9, 1954; s. Thaine Edward and Anita (Moore) B.; m. Anna Barron, Dec. 31, 1983; children: Carol Carothers, Leslie Hope. AB, Coll. of William and Mary, 1976; JD, U. Richmond, 1980. Bar: Va. 1980. Law clk. to presiding justice U.S. Dist. Ct., Roanoke, Va., 1980-81; assoc. McGuire, Woods & Battle, Richmond, Va., 1981-87, Hirschler, Fleischer, Weinberg, Cox & Allen, Richmond, Va., 1987—. Bd. editors The Virginia Lawyer, 1984-86; mem. adv. bd. U. Richmond Law Rev., 1986—; contbr. articles to profl. publs. Bd. dirs. Bethlehem Ctr., Richmond, 1985-89, United Meth. Found. of Va. Conf., Inc., 1993—, Hanover Indsl. Air Pk. Bus. Assn., 1994—; mem. adminstrv. bd. Trinity United Meth. Ch., Richmond, 1986-89, trustee, 1988—, chmn. bd. trustees, 1992-95, chmn. commitment campaign, 1995; team capt. United Way Greater Richmond, 1989, sect. chmn., 1991, divsn. chmn., 1993; mem. Leadership Metro Richmond Class, 1992-93; bd. dirs. Arts Coun. of Richmond, Inc., 1994—, exec. com., 1996—. Mem. ABA (litigation sect., state memnership chmn. young lawyers divsn. 1985-89, state membership chmn. 1989—), Va. Bar Assn. (com. on alternative dispute resolution), Va. State Bar Assn. (bd. govs. young lawyers conf. 1985-89, spl. com. on professionalism, legal edn., admission to bar), Richmond Bar Assn. (program com., vice chmn. 1990-91, chmn. 1991-92, adminstrn. of justice com. 1992—), William and Mary Alumni Assn. (bd. dirs. Richmond chpt. 1993-95), Richmond Jaycees (bd. dirs. 1984-86). Home: 305 Berwickshire Dr Richmond VA 23229-7301 Office: Hirschler Fleischer Weinberg Cox & Allen 701 E Byrd St Richmond VA 23219-4528

BILLINGTON, BARRY E., lawyer; b. Bruceton, Tenn., June 24, 1940; s. Charles Raymond and Edith Virginia (Bowles) B.; m. Bonnie Leslie Johnson, Oct. 16, 1971 (div. Mar. 23, 1990); children: Erin Alexis, Barry E. Jr. AB in Econs, Davidson Coll., 1964; JD, Emory U., 1968. Bar: Calif. 1969, Ga. 1971, U.S. Dist. Ct. (cen. dist.) Calif. 1969, U.S. Dist. Ct. (no. dist.) Ga. 1971. Assoc. Surr & Hellyer, San Bernardino, Calif., 1968-70; with Mfrs. Life Ins. Co., Atlanta, 1970-71; assoc. Carter, Ansley, Smith & McClendon, Atlanta, 1971-72; of counsel Raiford & Hills, Decatur, Ga., 1972-75; ptnr. Raiford, Hills, Billington & McKeithen, Atlanta, 1975-77; ptnr. Rich, Bass, Kidd, Witcher & Billington, Decatur, 1977-82; ptnr. Billington & Beasley, Decatur, 1982-83, ptnr. Billington & Turner, Atlanta, 1983-85, Barry E. Billington & Assocs., Atlanta, 1985—. Candidate for Ga. Ho. of Reps., 52d Dist., 1978, U.S. Congress, 4th Dist. Ga., 1980; Rep. publicity dir. San Bernardino County, 1969-70, San Bernardino County for Ronald Reagan Com., 1970; alt. del. Rep. Cen. Com. of Calif., 1969-70; chmn. 4th Dist. Conservative Caucus, 1977-79. With U.S. Army Mil. Police Corps, 1958-60. Editor Ga. Rep. Party Newsletter, 1968. Mem. Atlanta Bar Assn. (speaker's com., litigation, family law, criminal law sects. 1974-77), Decatur-DeKalb Bar Assn. (chmn. speaker's com. 1977-78), ABA (litigation sect. 1969—), Ga. Trial Lawyers Assn., Assn. Trial Lawyers Am. Home: 878 Sherwood Cir Forest Park GA 30050 Office: 3 Dunwoody Pk Ste 103 Atlanta GA 30338

BILLOUPS, EDD, medical administrator; b. Baton Rouge, Oct. 29, 1934; s. Leo and Louise (Myles) B.; m. divorced; children: Leo, Bunny, Sharon, Timothy, Shanya. BS in Biology, Grambling (La.) Coll., 1956; MA in Health Care Adminstrn., Ariz. State U., Scottsdale, 1976. Clin. specialist U.S. Army, 1956-73; instr. neurology nursing VA Med. Ctr., Phoenix, 1973-74, med. adminstrv. asst., 1974-80; med. adminstrv. specialist VA Med. Ctr., Wichita, Kans., 1980-81; operational chief, med. adminstrv. svc. VA Med. Ctr., Alexandria, La., 1981-82, asst. chief, med. adminstrv. svc., 1982-89; chief, med. adminstrv. svc. Dept. Vets. Affairs Med. Ctr., Alexandria, Va., 1989-90; asst. chief, med. adminstrv. svc. Dept. Vets. Affairs Med. Ctr., Alexandria, 1990-92; career counselor U.S. Army, Austin, Tex., 1964-66. Bd. dirs., ARC, United Way, Alcohol and Drug Abuse Coun., La. Organ Procurement Agy. Sgt. U.S. Army, 1956-73. Recipient Bronze Star cluster U.S. Army, DaNang, Vietnam, 1970. Mem. Toastmasters Internat. Republican. Baptist. Home: 6103 Saint Gabriel Ct Baton Rouge LA 70811-4118

BILLS, ROBERT E(DGAR), emeritus psychology educator; b. Nutley, N.J., Dec. 15, 1916; s. Willis Minard and Leah Catherine (Condit) B.; m. Annie Tarleton Carley, Dec. 22, 1944; children—Mary Ann Bills Niles, Leah Catherine Bills Hawkins. B.S., Western Ky. U., 1938; M.A., U. Ky., 1946; Ed.D., Columbia U, 1948. Tchr. sci. Breathitt County (Ky.) Bd. Edn., 1938-42; tchr. Anchorage Bd. Edn. (Ky.), 1943-44, prin., 1944-5; critic tchr. sci. U. Ky. Coll. Edn., 1945-46, faculty Coll. Arts and Scis., 1948-56, asst. prof. psychology, 1948-52, assoc. prof., 1952-56, chmn. div. biol. scis., 1950-51; prof. psychology, chmn. dept. Auburn U., 1956-61; prof. ednl. psychology U. Ala., 1961-69, rsch. prof. edn., 1969-79, rsch. prof. emeritus, 1979—, asst. dean rsch., 1961-63, interim dean Coll. Edn., 1963-65, dean, 1965-69, dean emeritus, 1979—; mem. council psychol. resources of South So. Regional Edn. Bd., 1953-56; chmn. Ky. Bd. Examiners Psychologists, 1954-56; vis. prof. U. Fla., 1953, 54, Mich. State U., 1956, U. Wash., 1963; lectr. in field. Bd. dirs. Southeastern Ednl. Corp., 1966-67; sec. Ala. Coalition for Better Edn., 1969-70, pres., 1971-72. Served with U.S. Army, 1943-44; with USCG Aux., 1982—. Recipient Outstanding Prof. award Coll. Edn. U. Ala., 1979; Ednl. Press Assn. award for disting. contbn. to ednl. journalism, 1982. Fellow Am. Psychol. Assn. (sec.-treas. div. 1963-66), Mid-South Edn. Research Assn. (v.p. 1978, pres. 1979), Assn. Supervision and Curriculum Devel. (dir. 1962-64), U.S. Coast Guard Aux (mem. nat. staff 1989—), Sigma Xi, Kappa Delta Pi, Psi Chi, Phi Delta Kappa. Author: Education for Intelligence or Failure?, 1982; contbr. chpts. to books, articles in field to profl. jours. Home: 3448 Tall Pines Cir Tuscaloosa AL 35405-5401

BIMSTEIN, BENJAMIN WILLIAM, caterer, chef; b. N.Y.C., Jan. 4, 1917; s. Reuben and Yetta (Plattner) B.; m. Mollie D. Goodman, June 29, 1941 (dec. Feb. 1961); children: Roberta Reinfeld, Laurence (dec. Oct. 1993); m. Mollie Shenkman, Aug. 6, 1961; stepchildren: Bennett Walstatter, David Walstatter. Cert. exec. chef. Owner Bim's Ice Sculptors of N.Y./Bim's Caterers, Richmond Hill, L.I., 1949-58; gen. mgr., dir. catering Leonards of Great Neck, N.Y., 1958-63; gen. mgr., culinary artist Golden Meadowbrook, Jericho, L.I., N.Y., 1967-76; dir. catering Chateaubriand, Westbury, L.I., N.Y., 1976-80; ice sculpter, food decor cons. Hotel Diplomat, Hallandale, Fla., 1980—; owner Ice Sculpture Display Co., Ft. Lauderdale, 1985—; corp. chef cons. Construction Caterers, Miami, Fla., 1985—; mfr., distbr. permanent ice sculpture molds worldwide, 1994—. Commd. ice sculptures for Lipton Tea Co., Fireman's Ins. Co., Ferrari Motor Co., Pres. Eisenhower, Brit. Queen's coronation ball, Caracas, Venezuela, Bacardi Rum Co., Wayne Heizinga, Fla. Panthers-Marlins, U.S. Navy Admiral's Ball, Burt O'Jacks Restaurant, others; contbr. articles to profl. jours.; featured in numerous full-page write-ups including rotogravure centerfold in N.Y. Daily News. Recipient Gold and Silver medals Nat. Hotel Expo, 1966, 72, 1st prize AVNET Foundry award Portrait Sculpture Nat. Sculpture Exposition, 1972, numerous others; duplicated Michael Angelo's David hand carved in ice, 1996, Rabbi Lehrman portrait Bust in ice, Miami, 1996. Mem. NRA (life mem., gallery pistol expert 1965), Am. Culinary Fedn. (cert., chmn., sec. 1951—, chef of yr. award Ft. Lauderdale 1994), Syosset Rotary Club (pres. 1976), Suburban Art League. Office: Ice Sculpture Display Co Ste 101 1719 White Hall Dr Fort Lauderdale FL 33324-6939

BINDER, BOB, lawyer; b. Paris, Tex., Nov. 17, 1944; s. Robert Thomas and Edna Louise (Risinger) B.; m. Andrea Marie Wangler, Dec., 1976 (div. 1979); m. Claudia Ann Scott, Nov. 20, 1982 (div. 1993); children: Margaux Diane, Paige Julienne. BBA, U. Tex., 1967, JD, 1972. Bd. cert. personal injury trial law, Tex. Bd. Legal Specialization. Ptnr. Binder Chapman & Hargadon, Austin, 1973-75; assoc. Harvey Lerer, L.A., 1975-76; sole practice Austin, 1976—; radio talk show host You and the Law with Bob Binder, Sta. KLBJ-AM, 1995—. Author: Earthly Pleasures of Wine, 1983. Tex. co-chair Tex. Vets. for Clinton/Gore, Austin, 1992; coun. mem. City Coun., Austin, 1973-75; student body pres. U. Tex., Austin, 1971-72; mem. airport adv. bd., Austin, 1995-97; pres. Cat Mountain Homeowners Assn., 1990-91. 1st lt. U.S. Army, 1967-69, Vietnam. Decorated Bronze Star. Mem. Capital Area Trial Lawyers Assn. (pres. 1991-92), Tex. Trial Lawyers Assn., U. Tex. Army ROTC Alumni Assn. (pres. 1991-92). Democrat. Home: 5821 Mount Bonnell Rd Austin TX 78731-3650 Office: Bob Binder & Assocs PC PO Box 1046 Austin TX 78767

BINFIELD, KEVIN SCOTT, English language educator; b. Wahoo, Nebr., Mar. 26, 1962; s. Glenn Richard and Marie Leona (Walcott) B.; m. Ramona Jean Smith, June 7, 1984. BA with high distinction in English, Nebr. Wesleyan U., 1984; MA in English, U. Nebr., 1987, PhD in English, 1993. Rsch. asst. U. Nebr., Lincoln, 1985-87, tchg. asst./instr., 1987-93; asst. prof. English Gardner-Webb U., Boiling Springs, N.C., 1993—. Contbr. articles to profl. jours. Recipient Tchg. Coun. Tchg. award U. Nebr., 1989, 91, 93; John McDonald Grad. fellow, 1992-93. Mem. MLA, Coll. English Assn., Keats-Shelley Assn., Am. Soc. for 18th Century Studies. Office: Gardner-Webb University Faculty Box 224 Boiling Springs NC 28017

BINFORD, JESSE STONE, JR., chemistry educator; b. Freeport, Tex., Nov. 1, 1928; s. Jesse Stone and Eglan Lee (Bracewell) B.; m. Lolita Ramona Fritz, June 8, 1955; children: Lincoln Bracewell, Jason Jolly. BA in Chemistry, Rice U., 1950, MA in Chemistry, 1952; PhD in Phys. Chemistry, U. Utah, 1955. Instr. chemistry U. Tex., Austin, 1955-58; asst. prof. U. of the Pacific, Stockton, Calif., 1958-60, assoc. prof., 1960-61; Fulbright prof., chmn. dept. chemistry Univ. Nacional Autonoma de Honduras, Tegucigalpa, 1968-69; vis. rsch. prof. Thermochemistry Lab., U. Lund, Sweden, 1971, researcher, 1982-83; rsch. fellow Chelsea Coll., U. London, 1983; assoc. prof. U. South Fla., Tampa, 1961-72, prof., 1972—; cons. Fla. consortium AID, Honduras, 1969, Exxon Prodn. Rsch. Co., Houston, 1974; chmn. State Univ. Faculty Senate Coun., Fla., 1972-76; dir. gen. chemistry program U. South Fla., 1978-82; vis. prof. dept. chem. engring. Rice U., 1993-94, rschr. Cox Lab. for Biomed. Engring., Inst. Bioscis. and Bioengring., 1993-94; mem. Inst. for Biomolecular Sci., U. South Fla. Author: (textbook) Foundations of Chemistry, 1977, 2nd edit., 1985; contbr. articles to profl. jours., 1956—. Active bicycle adv. com. Hillsborough County, Tampa, 1975-93, chairperson bicycle adv. com., 1990-93; faculty advisor U. South Fla. Bicycle Club, 1972—; coord. spl. tutoring program Danforth Found., Tampa, 1968. Grantee Petroleum Rsch. Fun, 1960-62, USPHS (NIH), 1966-68, Rsch. Corp., 1986. Mem. AAUP, AAAS, Am. Chem. Soc. (nat. and Fla. sect.), Calorimetry Conf., League Am. Wheelmen, Golden Key, Sigma Xi, Phi Beta Kappa, Phi Lambda Upsilon, Sigma Pi Sigma, Omicron Delta Kappa. Home: 1905 E 111th Ave Tampa FL 33612-6150 Office: U South Fla Dept Chemistry 4202 E Fowler Ave Tampa FL 33620-9900

BINGHAM, ELIZABETH ELLIOTT, librarian; b. Butler, Ala., June 29, 1948; d. James Howard and Emogene (Shamburger) Elliott; m. Clifton O. Bingham, Jr., Apr. 16, 1965 (div. Mar. 1977); 1 child, Clifton O. BS, La. State U.-Baton Rouge, 1970, MS, 1971. Reference libr. East Baton Rouge Parish Libr., 1970-74, head mid-city br., 1974-75, head adult svcs., 1975—; sec. task force White House Conf. on Librs. and Info. Svcs., 1994—, La. Endowment for Humanities, 1995-96, v.p. 1996-97. Contbr. articles to profl. jours. HEW fellow, 1975. Mem. Libr. Adminstrn. and Mgmt. Assn. (sec. 1994-96), Intellectual Freedom Round Table (treas. 1995-97), Am. Library Assn. (pres. Jr. Mem. Round Table 1979-80, mem. coun. 1994—), La. Library Assn. (treas. 1979-80, recipient Mid-Career award 1983, 1st v.p./pres.-elect 1989-90, pres. 1990-91), Southeastern Library Assn. Democrat. Presbyterian. Clubs: Altrusa Internat., Jr. League (Baton Rouge); Found. for Hist. La. Home: 14215 Harwood Ave Baton Rouge LA 70816-2714 Office: E Baton Rouge Parish Library 7711 Goodwood Blvd Baton Rouge LA 70806-7625

BINGHAM, GEORGE BARRY, JR., publishing and broadcasting executive; b. Louisville, Sept. 23, 1933; s. George Barry and Mary Clifford (Caperton) B.; m. Edith Wharton Stenhouse, Nov. 30, 1963; children: Emily Simms, Mary Caperton; adopted children: Philip John, Charles Wharton. A.B., Harvard U., 1956. Mgmt. trainee CBS, N.Y.C., 1958-59; researcher, field producer documentaries NBC, N.Y.C., Washington, 1959-62; formerly with Courier-Journal, Louisville Times; with Standard Gravure Corp., WHAS, Inc., Louisville, 1962-86; editor, pub. Courier-Jour. and Louisville Times, 1971-86; vice chmn. bd. WHAS, Inc.; pub. FineLine, 1989-91; owner, pub. Billy Goat Strut Pub., Louisville, 1989—. Active Actors Theatre Louisville, Greater Louisville Fund for Arts, Berea Coll., Isaac E. Bernheim Found., Ky. Opera Assn. Capt. USMC, 1956-58. Mem. Harvard Club, River Valley Club. Home: PO Box 64 Glenview KY 40025-9998 Office: Billy Goat Strut Pub 600 E Main St Louisville KY 40202-1011

BINKS, RONALD CARL, art educator, artist; b. Oak Lawn, Ill., Oct. 20, 1934; s. Harry Lewis and Charlien F. (Zuttermeister) B.; m. Lawsanna Henderson, Aug. 21, 1963; children: Justin L., Livia J. Pvt. study with Minor White, George Eastman House, 1954; summer study, Cummington Sch. of the Arts, 1955; BFA, R.I. Sch. Design, 1956; student, Hochschule fur Bildende Kunste, Berlin, 1956-58; MFA, Yale U., 1960. Prof. R.I. Sch. Design, Providence, 1962-76, head intermediate design, 1965-67, head film dept., 1967-72, dir. European program, 1972-74; dir. art div. U. Tex., San Antonio, 1976-83, prof. art, 1983—; exec. dir. R.I. Arts Festival, Providence, 1966; dir. art program Gov.'s Sch. of the Arts, Providence, 1968; chmn. bd. Nat. Coun. Art Adminstrs., 1982-84. Artist, exhibiting paintings and photography in nat. and internat. exhbns., 1956—; works in collections of Yale U.; R.I. Sch. Design Mus., Amon Carter Mus., San Antonio Mus. Art, Del Mar Coll., U. Tex. at San Antonio, West Tex. Mus. Art, and pvt. collections. Recipient prix de Rome, Am. Acad. in Rome, 1960-62; Hayes-Fulbright grantee, Berlin, 1956-58, Faculty Devel. grantee U. Tex. at San Antonio, 1984; Flaherty Found. fellow, Brattleboro, Vt., 1955. Office: U Tex at San Antonio 6900 N Loop FM 1604 San Antonio TX 78249

BINNS, WALTER GORDON, JR., investment management executive; b. Richmond, Va., June 8, 1929; s. Walter Gordon and Virginia Belle (Matheny) B.; m. Alberta Louise Fry, Apr. 1, 1972; 1 child, Amanda; 1 stepdau., Clarissa. AB, Coll. William and Mary, 1949; AM, Harvard U., 1951; MBA, NYU, 1959. Trainee Chase Nat. Bank, N.Y.C., 1953-54; with GM, N.Y.C., 1954-94, asst. treas., 1974-82, chief investment funds officer, 1982-94, v.p., 1986-94; pres., CEO GM Investment Mgmt. Corp., 1990-94; bd. dirs. Chgo. Mercantile Exch., Options Clearing Corp., Taubman Ctrs., Inc., Equity Fund Latin Am., Commonwealth Equity Fund; investment adv. com. N.Y. State Common Retirement Fund, 1987-94; mem. pension mgrs. adv. com. N.Y. Stock Exch., 1988-94; mem. Gov. Cuomo's Task Force on Pwnsion Fund Investment, 1988-89; mem. adv. com. Pwnsion Benefir Guaranty Corp., 1991-95; mem. adv. com. Chgo. Mercantile Exch., 1988-93, Chgo. Bd. Trade, 1992-93, Commodity Futures Trading Commn., 1992-94; chmn. investment adv. com. Va. Retirement Systems, 1994—; mem. fiduciary panel Prudential Ins. Co., 1994-95. Trustee ARC Retirement System, 1987-90, Citizens Budget Commn., N.Y.C., Endowment Assn., Coll. William and Mary, Med. Coll. Va. Found., Nat. Coun. Econ. Edn., 1982-94, Futures Ind. Assn., 1988-90; bd. dirs. Alcoholism Coun. Greater N.Y., 1982-92; bd. dirs. Cmty. Fund. of Bronxville, Eastchester Tuckahoe, Inc., 1986-92, Friends of Libr. Coll. William and Mary Coll., Fin. Execs. Rsch. Found., 1988-91, Christian Children's Fund, Nat. Coun. on Alcoholism and Drug Dependence, Vellore Christian Med. Coll. & Hosp. Bd. Mem. Fin. Execs. Inst. (chmn. com. on employee benefits 1977-80, com. on investment of employee benefits 1977-80, com. on investment of employee benefit assets 1985-88, treas. 1991-93), Bronxville Field Club, Harvard Club (N.Y.C.), Grolier Club, Commonwealth Club, Westwood Racquet Club, Phi Beta Kappa, Beta Gamma Sigma. Home: 115 Oxford Cir W Richmond VA 23221-3224 also: 120 Central Park S New York NY 10019 Office: PO Box 17308 Richmond VA 23226-7308

BIONDO, RAYMOND VITUS, dermatologist; b. N.Y.C., June 13, 1936; s. Joseph Pernice and Bena (Schwartz) B.; m. Mary McKinnon, Dec. 24, 1976. BA in Biology, U. No. Colo., 1960; MS in Biochemistry, U. Ark., 1963, BS in Medicine, 1967, MD, 1967. Diplomate Am. Bd. Dermatology. Asst. mgmt. analyst 38th USAF Hosp., Francis E. Warren AFB, Wyo., 1954-58; rsch. trainee NIH at U. Ark., Little Rock, 1961-63; rsch. biochemist VA Hosp., Little Rock, 1963-65; intern U. Cin. Med. Ctr., 1967-68; resident in dermatology U. Ark., Little Rock, 1968-71, asst. clin. prof. dermatology, 1971-90; pres. North Little Rock (Ark.) Dermatology Clinic, 1971-90. Contbr. rsch. articles to profl. publs. Mem. nat. adv. com. on scouting for the handicapped Boy Scouts Am., 1976-81, nat. chmn. med. exploring com., 1981-84, nat. coun., 1977—, nat. exploring com., 1977-92, nat. urban emphasis com. 1990—, nat. Jewish com. on scouting, 1981-84; mem. Ark. Kidney Disease Commn., 1979-83; bd. dirs. Cen. Ark. Health Systems Agy., 1984, Congregation B'nai Israel, Little Rock, 1982-84, Jewish Fedn. Ark., 1989-92; founder, pres. Am. Red Magen David for Israel, Ark., 1987-92. Staff officer USCG Aux. Flotilla, 1995. Recipient Outstanding Alumnus award U. No. Colo., 1977, Shofar award, 1992, William H. Spurgeon and Whitney M. Young awards Boy Scouts Am., 1981, Silver Antelope award, 1983, Silver Beaver award, 1977, Nat. Torch of Gold award, 1993, cert. of achievement in cmty. health promotion Ark. Dept. Health, 1983, vol. action award The White House, 1982, Gov.'s Vol. Excellence award, 1983, Ark. cert. appreciation for pub. svc., 1992, Father Joseph H. Biltz award Ark. Coun. Nat. Conf. of Christians & Jews, 1990, Nat. Disting. Svc. award Jewish War Vets. of the U.S., 1995; Golden Rule award finalist JC Penney Co./United Way of Pulaski County, 1996, Olympic Torch Relay nominee, 1996. Fellow Am. Acad. Dermatology (adv. bd. nat. dermatology program 1973-75); mem. AMA (physicians recognition award 1971-90, cert of appreciation 1984), Ark. Med. Soc. (ho. of dels. 1971—), Ark Dermatol. Soc. (pres. 1977), Pulaski County Med. Soc., Jewish War Vets U.S. (founder, comdr. Ark. post 436, nat. surgeon 1993-96, nat. asst. Boy Scout officer 1993-96, nat. White House liaison officer 1993-95, Judge Lawrence Gubow Meml. hon. mention 1989, Cert. of Appreciation Tex. dept. 1991, Cert. of Merit 1992, Chapel of Four Chaplains Legion of Honor 1994, Humanitarian award 1996) Sigma Xi, Alpha Omega Alpha. Jewish. Home: PO Box 6361 North Little Rock AR 72124-6361

BIRCH, ADOLPHO A., JR., judge; b. Washington, Sept. 22, 1932. BA, Howard U., 1956, JD, 1956. Bar: Tenn. 1957. Pvt. practice Nashville, 1958-66, asst. pub. defender, 1964-66, asst. dist. atty., 1966-69; judge Davidson County Gen. Sessions Ct., 1969-78, Tenn. Criminal Ct. (20th jud. dist.), 1978-87; former judge Tenn. Ct. Criminal Appeals; now chief justice Tenn. Supreme Ct., Nashville; assoc. prof. Nashville Sch. of Law. Served USNR, 1956-58. Mem. ABA, Nat. Bar Assn., Tenn. Bar Assn., Nashville Bar Assn., Napier Lobby Bar Assn. (past pres.). Office: 304 Supreme Ct Bldg 401 7th Ave N Nashville TN 37219-1406

BIRCHER, EDGAR ALLEN, lawyer; b. Springfield, Ohio, Apr. 28, 1934; s. John Clark and Ethel Ann (Speakman) B.; m. Lavinia Brock, Sept. 30, 1978; children: Douglas, Stephen, Todd, Karen. BA, Ohio Wesleyan U., 1956; JD, Ohio State U., 1961; postgrad., Columbia U., 1974, Stanford U., 1975. Bar: Ohio 1962, Tex. 1973. Assoc. Fuller, Seney, Henry & Hodge, Toledo, 1962-64; with Cooper Industries, Inc., Houston, 1964-88, v.p., 1977-88, gen. counsel, 1977-88; pres. Flex Law, Inc., Houston, 1988—; of counsel Evans & Kosut, Houston, Tex., 1995—. With USAF, 1956-59. Mem. Tex. Bar Assn., Yacht Club Galveston, Phi Delta Theta, Phi Delta Phi. Home: 1501 Harbor View Cir Galveston TX 77550-3119 Office: Four Greenspoint Ste 1600 16945 Northchase Dr Houston TX 77060

BIRD, LINDA W., realtor; b. Millington, Tenn., Mar. 19, 1952; d. Lawrence F. and Sara Teresa (Kori) Watermolen; m. Dennis Keith Bird, July 29, 1978; children: Kristin Ann, Lauren Elizabeth. BS, Fla. State U., 1974; MEd, Fla. Atlantic U., 1976. Broward County 4H coord. Fla. Cooperative Ext. Svc. U. Fla., Gainesville, 1974-76; sales rep. mgmt. tng. program Proctor and Gamble Distbg. Co., Cin., 1976; with mktg. mgmt. faculty Broward Community Coll., Ft. Lauderdale, Fla., 1978; pub. rels. coord. Port Everglades Authority, Ft. Lauderdale, 1978-80; flight attendant in charge Delta Air Lines, Miami, Fla., 1980-96; pres. Bird Realty, Inc., Ft. Lauderdale, 1984—. Pres. Kids in Distress Aux., 1986-87, Child Care Connection Aux., 1989-90; bd. dirs. Lakes Estates Homeowner Assn., 1982-93; chair Our House Jr. League Greater Ft. Lauderdale, Inc., 1994-95; mem. panel TV show 30 Below, 1972; troop coord. Girls Scouts USA, Pine Crest Sch. Fla. Jr. Coll. Presdl. scholar, Fla. Home Ext. scholar; named one of ten Women of Yr. Thousand Plus Club Am. Cancer Soc., 1986-87. Mem. Fort Lauderdale Panhellenic Assn. (tres. 1978), Delta Delta Delta (pres. 1988-90), Omicron Nu. Democrat. Methodist. Home: 2790 NE 57th Ct Fort Lauderdale FL 33308-2724 Office: Bird Realty Inc 2790 NE 57th Ct Fort Lauderdale FL 33308-2724

BIRD, WENDELL RALEIGH, lawyer; b. Atlanta, July 16, 1954; s. Raleigh Milton and R. Jean (Edwards) B. BA summa cum laude, Vanderbilt U., 1975; JD, Yale U., 1978. Bar: Ga. 1978, Ala. 1980, Calif. 1981, Fla. 1982, U.S. Ct. Appeals (2d, 3d, 4th, 5th, 6th, 7th, 8th, 9th, 10th and 11th cirs.) 1979-83, U.S. Supreme Ct. 1983. Law clk. to judge U.S. Ct. Appeals (4th cir.), Durham, N.C., 1978-79, U.S. Ct. Appeals (5th cir.), Birmingham, Ala., 1979-80; pvt. practice San Diego, 1980-82; atty. Parker, Johnson, Cook & Dunlevie, Atlanta, 1982-86; sr. ptnr. Bird & Assocs., P.C., Atlanta, 1986—; adj. prof. Emory U. Law Sch., Atlanta, 1985—; lectr. Washington Non-Profit Tax Conf., 1982, 84-86, 88—. Author: The Origin of Species Revisited, 2 vols., 1987; contbg. author: Federal Taxation of Exempt Organizations, 1994, CCH Federal Tax Service, 1988—; mem. bd. editors Yale U. Law Jour., 1977-78, others; contbr. articles to profl. jours. Bd. govs. Coun. for Nat. Policy, Washington, 1983—. Recipient Egger prize Yale U., 1978, Vanderbilt U. award, 1972. Mem. ABA (litigation sect., taxation sect., com. on exempt orgns., past chmn. subcom. on religious orgns., past chmn. subcom. on state and local taxes, chmn. subcom. on charitable contbns., sect. on econs. of law practice, sect. on real property probate and trust, com. charitable gifts), Am. Law Inst., Ga. Bar Assn., Fla. Bar Assn., Calif. Bar Assn., Ala. Bar Assn., Assn. Trial Lawyers Am., Phi Beta Kappa. Republican. Home: 92 Blackland Rd NW Atlanta GA 30342 Office: Bird & Assocs PC 1150 Monarch Plz 3414 Peachtree Rd NE Atlanta GA 30326-1113

BIRDSONG, ALTA MARIE, volunteer; b. Ft. Worth, July 18, 1934; d. Alton Roy and Artie Marguerite (Bentley) Flowers; m. Kenneth Layne Birdsong, Oct. 18, 1958; children: Suzanne Denise, Jeffrey Layne. BBA in Acctg. magna cum laude, U. North Tex., 1955. Cost engr. Tex. Instruments, Inc., Dallas, 1955-62; self-employed part-time acct. Atlanta, 1972—. Mem. DeKalb County Cmty. Rels. Com., 1981-93, chair, 1984-87; mem. Atlanta Regional Com. Adv. Group, 1981-88, Met. Atlanta United Way, 1985—; resource investment vol. sch. age children; chair Sch. Age Child Care Coun., 1987-90; mem. DeKalb County Task Force on Personal Care Homes, DeKalb County Task Force on Domestic Violence; mem. steering com. fo bond referendum DeKalb Bd. Edn.; mem. Vision 2020 Governance Stakeholders ARC, 1994-95. Recipient John H. Collier award for Camp Fire, 1991, Luther Halsey Gulick award for Camp Fire, 1993, Frederic E. Ruccius award for Camp Fire, 1993, Mortar Bd. Alumni Achievement award, 1991, Woman of Yr. award Atlanta Alumnae Panhellenic, 1983, Women Who Have Made a Difference award DeKalb YWCA, 1985. Mem. AAUW (divsn. pres. 1987-89, pres. elect 1987-89, mem. v.p. 1984-86, recording sec. 1982-84, assn. nominating com. 1993-97, chair 1995-97), Atlanta Coun. Camp Fire (pres. 1992-94, v.p. 1990-92, region fin. officer 1989-90, region nominating com. chair 1991-92), Atlanta Alumnae Panhellenic (pres. 1978-79, v.p. 1977-78), Freedoms Found. at Valley Forge (Atlanta chpt. pres. 1991-92, v.p. 1990-91, v.p. publicity 1988-89, treas. 1985-87, sec. 1983-85, ea.-so. region adv. 1994—), Nat. Women's Conf., Delta Gamma Alumnae (Atlanta chpt. 1st. v.p. 1985-87, treas. 1972-74, Oxford award 1992). Home: 5241 Manhasset Cv Atlanta GA 30338-3413

BIRDWELL, NANCY LEECH, developer; b. Abilene, Tex., Sept. 19, 1951; d. Glenn Houston and Lucy Grace (Gillean) Leech; m. John E. Birdwell III, Nov. 30, 1974; children: Lucy Laura, Megaen Lee. BA, Tex. Tech. U., 1974. Owner Duo Design, Lubbock, Tex., 1974-85; dir. corp. and found. rels. Tex. Tech. U., Lubbock, 1987, dir. health scis. ctr., 1989, asst. v.p. devel., 1989-91; dir. devel. Tex. Dept. Mental Health and Mental Retardation, Austin, 1993-94, Tex. Engring. Found., Austin, 1994-96; dir. devel. for corp. and found. rels. U. Tex., Austin, 1996—; cons. in field. Bd. dirs. Ranching Heritage Mus., Lubbock, 1978-90, Women of the West Mus., Boulder, Colo., 1994, Lubbock (Tex.) Cultural Affairs Coun. Named Outstanding Young Women of Am., 1978. Mem. Nat. Soc. Fund Raising Execs. (com. chair, conf. chair 1994), Coun. for Advancement and Support of Edn., Lubbock C. of C. (com. mem.), Pi Beta Phi (pres. alumnae club 1990, chmn. alumnae adv. com.). Presbyterian. Home: 2407 Hatley Dr Austin TX 78746-5750

BIRKHEAD, THOMAS LARRY, minister; b. Owensboro, Ky., Nov. 20, 1941; s. Thomas Butler and Ollie Mae (Brown) B.; m. Melva Jean Young, Oct. 18, 1968; 1 child, David. AB, Western Ky. U., 1963; MDiv, So. Bapt. Theol. Sem., 1968. Ordained to ministry So. Bapt. Conv., 1966. Pastor Mt. Vernon Bapt. Ch., Calhoun, Ky., 1966-69, Sorgho Bapt. Ch., Owensboro, 1969-73, Spottsville (Ky.) Bapt. Ch., 1973-82, Yelvington Bapt. Ch., Maceo, Ky., 1982-86, Ghent (Ky.) Bapt. Ch., 1986-93, Pond Run Bapt. Ch., Beaver Dam, Ky., 1993—; mem. exec. bd. Ky. Bapt. Conv., Middletown, 1988-91. Co-author: Ghent Baptist Church History 1800-1990, 1990. Asst. moderator exec. bd. Ohio County Bapt. Assn., 1995-96, moderator exec. bd., 1996—. Mem. Ohio County Ministerial Assn. (v.p. 1994—), Carroll County Mins. Assn. (treas. 1989-93). Democrat. Home and Office: 167 Burden Ln Beaver Dam KY 42320-9638

BIRMINGHAM, CAROLYN, recreation educator; b. Northhampton, Pa., Oct. 12, 1953; d. William Greason and Phoebe Ann (Thorne) B. BA, U. Rochester, 1975; MA, Ohio State U., 1984, PhD, 1989. Sr. instr. outdoor desegregation program Cleve. Bd. Edn., 1980; dir. sch. camp Cleve. Heights Bd. Edn., 1980; instr. Cleve. Heights Parks & Recreation, 1979-80; outdoor instr. Outward Bound, 1978-85; dir. outdoor adventure Bloomsburg (Pa.) State U., 1981; dir. wilderness program, lect. Earlham Coll., Richmond, Ind., 1981-82; asstantships Ohio State U., Columbus, 1983-87; asst. prof. recreation, coord. program Olivet (Mich.) Coll., 1987-89; asst. prof. recreation Christopher Newport Coll., Newport News, Va., 1989—; cons. in field. Editor: Winds from the Wilderness, 1981; author: Maps and Compass for Pirates and Others; contbr. articles to profl. jours. Vol. Newport News and Norfolk Cities Parks and Recreation, 1989-91, Jamestown Found., 1989-91. Recipient Fellowship Philanthropic Edn. Orgn., Ohio chpt., 1983-85, Grad. Student Alumni Rsch. award Ohio State U., 1989, Faculty Devel. grants Christopher Newport Coll., 1989, 90, 91. Mem. AAHPER and Dance, Va. Alliance for Health, Phys. Edn. and Recreation (chair recreation div.), Nat. Prks and Recreation Assn., Assn. for Experiential Edn. (editor conf. proceedings 1991), Va. Parks and Recreation Assn., Va. Coun. on Outdoor Adventure Edn. (bd. dirs., editor newsletter), Build Carilloneurs N.Am. (chair music exch. com.), Am. Sail Tng. Assn. Office: U Ill 1206 S 6th St Champaign IL 61820-6915

BIRNE, CINDY FRANK, business owner; b. Chgo., Nov. 13, 1956; d. Gordon D. and Paula (Feldman) Frank; m. Robert E. Birne, June 27, 1981. BA, Ohio State U., 1979. Creative coord. Point-Communications div. Tracy-Locke Advt., Dallas, 1983; asst. to Tex Schramm, pres. of Dallas Cowboys, 1984, sales and advt. rep., tour dir. Dallas Cowboys, 1985—; sports mktg., comml. endorsements agt. Talent Sports Internat., Dallas; founding mem., exec. dir. QB, Inc.-The Internat. Assn. Profl. Quarterbacks; rep. various high profile athletes; affiliated cons., pub. rels. mgmt. promotion mktg. Burson Marsteller Sports Ptnrs. Internat., Dallas; dir. pub. rels., mktg. Dupree/Miller Literary, Inc.; founder, owner custom design party invitations and greeting cards Cindy Birne Prodns., Dallas, 1993—. Active Ohio campaign Ronald Reagan for Pres., 1980-81; vol. Cystic Fibrosis Found.; event coord. Legends Sports Promotions, Tex. Shoot-Out Classic for Troy Aikman Found.-Juvenile Diabetes Children's Miracle Network, 1993-94; assoc. Thomas Cook Travel Million Dollar Shoot-Out-ARC, 1993; ann. fundraiser Ann. Nat. Coun. for Jewish Women; bd. dirs. Golden Acres Nursing Home for Jewish Aged, Dallas, 1993; assoc. Legends Sports Promotions.

BIRNEY, LEROY, minister; b. Dodge City, Kans., Jan. 13, 1942; s. Ralph David and Margaret (McColm) B.; m. Norma Campbell Kew, May 23, 1964 (div. Aug. 1993); children: Steven, Susana, Sara. BA, U. Kans., 1964; cert., Emmaus Bible Sch., Oak Park, Ill., 1965; MA in New Testament, Trinity Evang. Divinity Sch., 1968, MDiv, 1969; ThD, Internat. Sem., 1987. Ordained to ministry, 1969. Missionary Medellin, Colombia, 1970-74; missionary, founder Hermanos en Cristo Ch., Cartagena, Colombia, 1975-82, also bd. dirs.; missionary, founder Missionary Action, Inc., Cartagena, 1982-84; pres. Missionary Action, Inc., Bradenton, Fla., 1985—; missions pastor Covenant Life Assembly, Bradenton, 1986-88; pres., dir. Facultad Biblica Bet-el, Tegucigalpa, Honduras, 1987-91; founder Acción Misionera en Nicaragua, Diriamba, 1988—. Contbr. articles to religious jours. Faculty scholar Trinity Evang. Div. Sch., 1968, 69. Mem. Fellowship Christian Assemblies, Assn. Evang. Congregations, Assn. Internat. Missions Svcs., Phi Beta Kappa. Office: Missionary Action Inc PO Box 1027 Bradenton FL 34206-1027

BISBEE, GERALD ELFTMAN, JR., investment company executive; b. Waterloo, Iowa, July 12, 1942; s. Gerald Elftman Bisbee and Maxine Cole Prather; m. Linda Elaine Ude, Aug. 22, 1970; children: Gerald Elftman III, Katherine Elizabeth. BA, North Cen. Coll., Naperville, Ill., 1967; MBA, U. Pa., 1972; PhD, Yale U., 1975. Adminstr. Med. Ctr. Northwestern U., Chgo., 1968-70; asst. prof. Yale U., New Haven, 1974-78, assoc. dir. health svcs., 1975-78; pres. Hosp. Rsch. and Ednl. Trust, Chgo., 1978-84; v.p., shareholder Kidder, Peabody & Co., N.Y.C., 1984-88; chmn., chief exec. officer Hanger Orthopedic Group, New Canaan, Conn., 1988-89, Apache Med. Systems, Inc., Washington, 1989—; adj. prof. Northwestern U., Kellogg Sch. of Mgmt., Evanston, Ill., 1979-83; mem. visiting com. Harvard U. Health Svcs., Boston, 1986-92, exec. adv. com. Weatherhead Sch. of Mgmt. Health Systems Program, Case Western Res. U., Cleve., 1984-86; bd. dirs. Cerner Corp., Yamaichi Funds, Inc., Geriatrics and Med. Ctrs., Inc., Choate-Rosemary Hall. Author: (book) Multihospital Systems: Policy Issues for the Future, 1981, co-author: Managing the Finances of Health Institutions, 1980, Financing of Health Care, 1979, Musculo-skeletal Disorders: Their Frequency of Occurrence and Their Impact on the Population of the United States, 1978. Mem. adv. com. Waveney Care Ctr., New Canaan, 1987. Grantee USPHS, Washington, 1972-75. Mem. Yale Club (N.Y.). Home: 110 Wellesley Dr New Canaan CT 06840-3530 Office: Apache Med Systems 1650 Tysons Blvd Mc Lean VA 22102-3915

BISCHOFF, SUZANNE R., social services administrator; b. The Hague, The Netherlands, Jan. 31, 1950; d. Willem Fredrik Karel and Catarina (Telders) Bischoff van Heemkerck; m. Arie Marie Ryke, June 30, 1978. BA in Law, U. Utrecht, The Netherlands, D in Internat. Law. Officer, dep. head Ministry Fgn. Affairs, The Hague, The Netherlands, 1974-79; mem. Lower House Parliament, The Hague, 1979-81, mem. Senate, 1981-86; dir. internat. rels. Plan Internat., Greenwich, R.I., 1986-88; dir. UN Children's Fund, N.Y.C., 1988-91; exec. dir. Epilepsy Assn. Va., Charlottesville, Va., 1991—; mem. evaluation union UN Plan Internat., 1986—. Contbr. articles to profl. jours. Mem. Nat. Vol. Health Agys. (mem. pers. com. 1991, Honor award 1991), Epilepsy Found. Am., Charlottesville C. of C. Office: Epilepsy Assn Va Highlands Ctr Box BRH U Va Med Ctr Charlottesville VA 22908

BISHARA, AMIN TAWADROS, mechanical engineer, technical services executive; b. Cairo, Oct. 22, 1944; came to U.S., 1973; s. Tawadros and Fakha (Boules) B.; m. Suzi Guirguis, Aug. 27, 1977; children: James A., Robert A. BSME, Ain Shams U., Cairo, 1968; MSME, Poly. U. N.Y., 1976. Registered profl. engr., N.Y., Tex. Field engr. Gen. Engring. Co., Cairo, 1968-71; mech. engr. Enging. Co. for Indsl. Enterprises, Cairo, 1971-73; project engr. Cosentini Assocs., N.Y.C., 1973-76; sr. engr. Ebasco Svcs., Inc., N.Y.C., 1976-79, lead engr., 1979-84; chmn., chief exec. officer PTS Tech. Svcs., Inc., Hurst, Tex., 1985-96; mem. adv. bd. Entrepreuneurship Inst., Ft. Worth, 1990—. Mem. NSPE, Masons, Moslah Temple of Ft. Worth. Roman Catholic. Home: 2625 Brookridge Dr Hurst TX 76054

BISHER, JAMIE FURMAN, intelligence and security analyst, writer; b. Atlanta, Sept. 27, 1956; s. Furman and Montyne (Harrell) B.; m. Veronica Torres, Sept. 21, 1991; 1 child, Jamie F. III. BS, U.S. Air Force Acad., 1978; grad. cert. in Linguistics, Am. U., 1988; postgrad., Middle East Inst, USDA Grad. Sch. Staff engr. Sonic Scis., Arlington, Va., 1981-84; project mgr. Montyne Bisher & Assocs., Washington, 1984; freelance writer, 1983—; logistics analyst Advanced Comm. Systems, Inc., Arlington, 1984-91; sr. analyst Techmatics, inc., Arlington, 1991-94; cons. Washington, 1994-96; acquisition analyst TMA Corp., Arlington, 1996—. Contbr. articles to profl. jours. Vol. Washington Humane Soc., 1990—. Cadet USAF, 1974-78. Recipient Letter of Appreciation Naval Electronic Systems Engring. Activity, 1992. Mem. Nat. Intelligence Study Ctr., Assn. Nat. Security Alumni, Gorilla Found. Home: 4941 78th Ave Hyattsville MD 20784-1741

BISHNOI, UDAI RAM, agronomy and seed technology educator; b. Sukh Chain, Punjab, India, Aug. 15, 1942; came to U.S., naturalized, 1967; s. Ram Lal and Anchai Devi (Delu) B.; m. Sukh Devi Isarwal, May 11, 1966; children: Rita Rani, Raj Deep. BS, Rajasthan U., Jaipur, 1961; MS, Punjab Agrl. U., Ludhiana, 1963; PhD, Miss. State U., Starkville, 1971. Cert. profl. agronomist. Asst. prof. agronomy Rajasthan Agrl. U., Jobner, 1963-67; grad. rsch. asst. Seed Tech. Lab. Miss. State U., 1968-71; seed physiologist Hulsey Seed Labs., Inc., Decatur, Ga., 1971-72; assoc. prof. agronomy/seed tech. Ala. A&M U., Normal, 1972-80, prof., 1980—; seed technologist FAO/UN, Sudan and India, 1980, 88, 93; seed technologist, agronomist USAID/USDA-OICD, Keyna, Poland, 1980-83, 86; seed technologist, agronomist USAID, The Gambia, 1986, Denmark, 1995; mem., advisor promotion/tenure com. Ala. A&M U., Normal, 1991-93. Author: Handbook of Seed Technology, 1982; assoc. editor Agronomy Jour., 1994—, Egerton Coll. Rsch. Bull., 1981-83; contbr. over 70 rsch. papers to profl. jours.; author: (documentary video) Farming System Research-An Approach to Conserve Soil and Increase Income on Limited Resource Farms, 1988. Bd. chmn., trustees Huntsville (Ala.) India Assn., 1990-92; sec.-treas. Agrl. Scientists Indian Origin, 1988-91. Recipient Scholarships Govt. India, Miss. State and Egypt, 1961, 68, 71, Rsch. Grants USDA, USAID, USDoEd, CIMMYT, State Ala., 1972-95, Outstanding Farming Sys. Rsch. award Rural Devel. Ctr., Tuskegee (Ala.) U., 1987, Outstanding Rsch. Scientist award 1991. Fellow Am. Soc. Agronomy; mem. AAAS (bd. dirs. 1994-95), Crop Sci. Soc. Am., Assn. Ofcl. Seed Analysts. Hindu. Home: 6315 Havenwood Dr Huntsville AL 35802 Office: Ala A&M U Dept Plant & Soil Sci Meridian St Normal AL 35762

BISHOP, ALFRED CHILTON, JR., lawyer; b. Alexandria, Va., Oct. 3, 1942; s. Alfred Chilton and Margaret (Marshall) B.; divorced; 1 son, Alfred Chilton III; m. 2d Catherine Ann Keppel, May 17, 1980. B.A. with distinction, U. Va., 1965, LL.B., 1969; LL.M. in Taxation, Georgetown U., 1974. Bar: N.Y. 1970, U.S. Ct. Appeals (2d cir.) 1970, U.S. Tax Ct. 1971, U.S. Ct. Claims 1971, D.C. 1977. Assoc. Shearman and Sterling, N.Y.C., 1969-70; assoc. trial atty., Office of Chief Counsel IRS, Washington, 1970-74, sr. trial atty., 1974-80, sr. technician reviewer, 1980-81, br. chief, 1981—. Recipient Am. Jurisprudence award 1968, 1968. Mem. ABA (tax sec.), D.C. Bar Assn., Sr. Exec. Service Candidate Network (v.p. 1980-81, pres. 1981-82, dir. 1983), Sr. Exec. Assn., Phi Delta Phi. Episcopalian. Home: 7523 Thistledown Trl Fairfax Station VA 22039

BISHOP, AMELIA MORTON, freelance writer; b. Dallas, Dec. 31, 1920; d. Walter Pierce and Alice (Stanton) Morton; m. J. Ivyloy Bishop, Dec. 18, 1955; children: Dan, Judith. BA, U. Tex., El Paso, 1942; MRE, Southwestern Bapt. Theol. Sem., Ft. Worth, 1953. Reporter Hollywood (Calif.) Citizen-News, 1942-43; in advt. and pub. rels. New Orleans, 1943-48; Tex. state young people's sec. Woman's Missionary Union, Dallas, 1953-56; tchr. Plainview (Tex.) High Sch., 1963-80; instr. Wayland Bapt. U., Plainview, 1957-60, 81-83; freelance writer, 1960—; state v.p. Woman's Missionary Union of Tex., Dallas, 1980-84, state pres., 1984-88, nat. v.p., 1984-88. Author, photographer: The Gift and the Giver, 1984, The Flame and the Candle, 1987; contbr. numerous articles to publs. Recipient Tex. Bapt. Elder Statesman award Bapt. Gen. Conv. Tex., 1989. Democrat. Home: PO Box 163523 Austin TX 78716-3523

BISHOP, BARNEY TIPTON, III, political consultant, lobbyist; b. Panama City, Fla., Dec. 24, 1951; s. Barney and Margaret Lorraine (Rollo) B.; m. Shelby Lynn Stinson, Feb. 4, 1989. Student, Miami-Dade C.C., 1969-71; BS in Speech, Emerson Coll., 1973, postgrad. in Italy, 1973. Investigator Best & Sears, Attys. at Law, Orlando, Fla., 1975-76; chief investigator Alliance Investigative Agy., Winter Park, Fla., 1976-78; chmn., pres. TRAK Detective Agy., Inc., Orlando, 1978-83; regional ins. investigator Fla. Dept. Ins., Tallahassee, 1983, adminstrv. asst. to state ins. commr., 1983-84, state coord. consumer outreach program, 1984-87; regional coord. Acad. Fla. Trial Lawyers, Tallahassee, 1987-88, dir. legis. affairs, 1988, dir. fundraising, 1988-89, dir devel., 1990-91; dir devel. Fla. Lawyers Action Group, Tallahassee, 1991; exec. dir. Fla. Dem. Party, Tallahassee, 1991-93; mng. dir. Fla. Dem. Party Trustees, Tallahassee, 1993-94; pres., CEO Windsor Group, Tallahassee, 1993—; co-founder, chmn. Fla. Investigative and Security Trust Polit. Action Com., Orlando, 1981-83, also lobbyist; bd. dirs. Fla. Consumer Action Network, 1988—; spkr. on consumer advocacy. Chmn. Orlando Solicitations Rev. Bd., 1981-84; sec. Orlando Leadership Coun., 1981-83; v.p. Fla. Young Dems., Tallahassee, 1982-83, pres., 1983-84; mem. Seminole County Dem. Exec. Com., 1980-83, Leon County Dem. Exec. Com., 1983-86; bus. cons.-tchr. Jr. Achievement, 1982; chmn. patient advocacy task force Fla. divsn. Am. Cancer Soc., 1989; bd. dirs. Fla. Dem. Leadership Coun., 1993, exec. com., 1993, exec. v.p., 1993; apptd. state ins. commr. Fla. Hurricane Catastrophic Fund Adv. Coun., 1995. Recipient Lighthouse award Acad. Fla. Trial Lawyers, 1990, award of excellence, 1990; Young Dem. of Yr. award Fla. Young Dems., 1983; scholar Rotary Internat. Found., South Africa, 1983. Mem. Am. Assn. Polit. Cons., Fla. Assn. Pvt. Investigators (v.p. 1978-79, pres. 1979-80, newsletter editor 1981-83), Nat. Soc. Fund Raising Execs., Emerson Coll. Alumni Assn., Nat. Eagle Scout Assn., Tallahassee C. of C., Tallahassee Soc. of Assn. Execs., Capital City Jaycees (bd. dirs. 1983-86), Seminole Boosters, Capital Tiger Bay Club, Econ. Club of Fla., Gov.'s Club, Alpha Kappa, Alpha Phi Omega, Phi Rho Pi, Rho Delta Omega. Democrat. Methodist. Home: 10976 Luna Point Rd Tallahassee FL 32312-4906 Office: 501 E Tennessee St Tallahassee FL 32308-4906

BISHOP, BRUCE TAYLOR, lawyer; b. Hartford, Conn., Sept. 13, 1951; s. Robert Wright Sr. and Barbara (Taylor) B.; m. Sarah M. Bishop, Aug. 31, 1974; children: Elizabeth, Margaret. BA in Polit. Sci., Old Dominion U., 1973; JD, U. Va., Charlottesville, 1976. Bar: Va. 1977, U.S. Supreme Ct., Va. 1976, U.S. Dist. Ct. (ea. dist.) Va., U.S. Dist. Ct. (we. dist.) Va., U.S. Ct. Appeals (4th cir.). Law clk. to chief judge U.S. Dist. Ct. (ea. dist.) Va., 1976-77; assoc. Willcox & Savage, P.C., Norfolk, Va., 1977-82; ptnr. Willcox & Savage, P.C., Norfolk, 1983—; bd. dirs. Nautical Adventurs, Inc., Norfolk FistEvent, Ltd., 1981—, pres., 1982-85; mem. bd. visitors Old Dominion U., 1972-83, sec., 1979-81, chmn., mem. various coms.; speaker in field. Treas. Norfolk Reps., 1978-82, also mem. numerous coms.; bd. dirs., chmn. regional Key Club campaign United Way South Hampton Roads; chmn., co-chmn. United Negro Coll. Fund, 1981, Four Cities United Way Campaign; trustee Va. Stage Co., 1982; pres. Community Promotion Corp.; commr. Norfolk Redevel. and Housing Authority; active numerous other community orgns. Named Outstanding Young Man, Norfolk Jaycees; recipient Disting. Alumni award Old Dominion U., Dominion Vol. of Yr. award, 1993. Mem. ABA (mem. various sects.), Fed. Bar Assn. (pres. Tidewater chpt. 1980-81), Va. Assn. Def. Lawyers, Va. Bar Assn., Va. Trial Lawyers Assn., Norfolk-Portsmouth Bar Assn., Def. Rsch. Inst., Internat. Assn. Def. Counsel, Old Dominion U. Alumni Assn. (bd. dirs. 1978-83), Old Dominion U. Ednl. Found. (bd. dirs. 1987—), Norfolk C. of C. (chmn. downtown devel. com. 1980-81). Office: Wilcox & Savage PC One Commercial Place Norfolk VA 23510

BISHOP, BUDD HARRIS, museum administrator; b. Canton, Ga., Nov. 1, 1936; s. James M. and Mary E. (Ponder) B.; m. Julia Crowder, Nov. 30, 1968. A.B., Shorter Coll., Rome, Ga., 1958; M.F.A., U. Ga., 1960; student, Arts Adminstrn. Inst. Harvard, 1970. Instr. art Ensworth Sch., Nashville, 1961-63; dir. creative services Transit Advt. Assn., N.Y.C., 1964-66; dir. Hunter Mus. of Art, Chattanooga, 1966-76, Columbus (Ohio) Mus. Art, 1976-87, Samuel P. Harn Mus. Art, U. Fla., Gainesville, 1987—; vis. lectr. Vanderbilt U., 1962; past pres. bd. Intermuseum Conservation Lab., Oberlin, Ohio. Past trustee Fla. Arts Celebration, Gainesville; mem. Gainesville Art in Pub. Places Trust; mem. faculty Ctr. for Arts and Pub. Policy; bd. dirs. Fla. Assn. Mus. Found., Inc.; mem. nat. adv. bd. Philharm. Ctr. for Arts, Naples, Fla. Recipient gov.'s award Tenn. Art Commn., 1971, 73, Alumni Arts achievement award Shorter Coll., 1979, arts leadership award Columbus Day, 1986, Person of Yr. award in arts Gainesville Sun, 1995. Mem. Am. Assn. Museums, Assn. Art Mus. Dirs. (past trustee), Southeastern Museums Conf., Fla. Art Mus. Dirs. Assn. Office: U Fla Harn Mus Art PO Box 112700 Gainesville FL 32611-2700

BISHOP, CLAIRE DEARMENT, engineering librarian; b. Youngstown, Ohio, Oct. 12, 1937; d. Eugene Howard and Ruth (Bright) DeA.; m. Carl R. Meinstereifel, 1956 (div. 1964); children: Paul, Dawn; m. Olin Jerry Dewberry, Jr., 1974 (div. 1979); m. J. Bruce Bishop, May 6, 1992. B.S., Clarion State U., 1967; M.L.S., Ga. State U., 1977. Cert. libr. media specialist, Ga. Libr. Henry County, Stockbridge, Ga., 1967-69; head libr. Russell High Sch., East Point, Ga., 1969-84; engring. libr. Rockwell Internat., Duluth, Ga., 1984-88; rep. GIDEP, Corona, Calif., 1984-88; libr. Raytheon Co., 1990, MSD, Bristol, Tenn., 1988-90; owner rubber stamp store Claire's Collectables, St. Augustine. Author newsletter: Blueline. Mem. Mensa. Democrat. Avocations: computers, writing, information broker. Home: 238 Ravenswood Dr Saint Augustine FL 32095-3027

BISHOP, DAVID NOLAN, electrical engineer; b. Memphis, Jan. 14, 1940; s. Robert Allen Bishop and Sara Frances (Gammon) Bishop Marett; m. Lois Margaret Baudouin, Nov. 16, 1963; children: Julie Frances Bishop Malouse, Anne Marie Bishop Bryan. BSEE, Miss. State U., 1962, MSEE, 1965. Registered profl. engr., La., Miss., Tex., Fla. Constrn. engr. Chevron Oil Co., New Orleans, 1964-70, lead constrn. engr., 1970-72, sr. constrn. engr., 1972-78; staff elec. engr. Chevron U.S.A., Inc., New Orleans, 1978-82, sr. staff elec. engr., 1982-85, elec. engring. cons., 1985-92; facilities engring. elec. engring. cons. Chevron U.S.A. Prodn. Co., Houston, 1992-96, sr. elec. engring. cons., 1996—; offshore safety and anti-pollution equipment rep. Am. Petroleum Inst., 1982-86, mem. various coms.; mem. Nat. Elec. Code Panel 14, 1989—; instr. sch. elec. sys. oil and gas prodn. facilities Petroleum Ext. Svc., U. Tex., Austin, 1990—; mem. instrumentation craft com. New Orleans Regional Vocat. Tech. Inst., 1985-92; guest lectr. in field. Author: (book) Electrical Systems for Oil and Gas Production Facilities, 1988, 2d edit. 1992; contbr. articles to profl. jours. Asst. scoutmaster Boy Scouts Am., Metairie, La., 1964-69; adminstrv. bd. St. Matthew's United Meth. Ch., Metairie, 1974-76; adv. com. U. Tex., Austin, Petroleum Ext. Tex., 1980—; engring. adv. com. Miss. State U., 1982—, chmn. curriculum and rsch. subcom., 1986-89, sec., 1989-91, vice-chmn., 1992-93, chmn., 1993-94. With U.S. Army, Miss. N.G. Named Coll. Alumnus of Yr., Coll. Engring. Miss. State U., 1990, Disting. Engring. fellow, 1992, Chpt. Alumnus of Yr. Miss. State U. Alumni Assn., 1990. Fellow Instrument Soc. Am. (sect. pres. 1977-78, dist. v.p. 1983-85, chmn. coun. dist. v.p. 1984-85, v.p. stds. and practices 1988-90, host. com. chmn. ISA/90 1989-90, pres.-elect, sec. 1990-91, pres. 1991-92, chmn. honors and awards com. 1993-94, chmn. nominations com. 1994-95, New Orleans sect. Commendation award 1983-84, stds. and practices dept. Recognition Achievement award 1987-90, Stds. and Practices award 1995, Am. Nat. Standards Inst. meritorious svc. award 1995), Tau Beta Pi, Pi Eta Sigma, Eta Kappa Nu (student sect. pres. 1961-62), Omicron Delta Kappa. Republican. Home: 10 Mistflower Pl The Woodlands TX 77381-6117 Office: Chevron USA Prodn Co PO Box 1635 Houston TX 77251-1635

BISHOP, GENE HERBERT, corporate executive; b. Forest, Miss., May 3, 1930; s. Herbert Eugene and Lavonne (Little) B.; m. Kathy S. Bishop, May 27, 1983. BBA, U. Miss., Oxford, 1952. With First Nat. Bank, Dallas, 1954-69; sr. v.p., chmn. sr. loan com. First Nat. Bank, 1963-68, exec. v.p., 1968-69; pres., dir. SBIC subs. First Dallas Capital Corp.; pres. Lomas & Nettleton Fin. Corp., Dallas, 1969-75, Lomas & Nettleton Mortgage Investors, Dallas, 1969-75; chmn., CEO Merc. Nat. Bank, Dallas, 1975-81, MCorp., Dallas, 1975-90; vice-chmn., CFO Lomas Fin. Corp., 1990-91; pres., COO Lomas Mortgage USA, Dallas, 1990-91; chmn., CEO Life Ptnrs. Group, Inc., Dallas, 1991-94, also bd. dirs.; bd. dirs. Drew Industries, Inc., Liberté Investors, S.W. Airlines Co., Southwestern Pub. Svc. Co., First USA Inc., First USA Paymentech, Inc. Bd. dirs. State Fair Tex., Lighthouse for Blind, Dallas; trustee Children's Med. Ctr., Dallas Meth. Hosps. Found.; mem. Dallas Citizens Coun. 1st lt. USAF, 1952-54. Mem. Dallas Petroleum Club, Terpsichorean Club, Idlewild Club, Brook Hollow Golf Club, Eldorado Country Club. Methodist. Office: 1601 Elm St 47th Flr Dallas TX 75201

BISHOP, GEORGE ALBERT, psychiatrist; b. LaCrosse, Wis., Oct. 22, 1932; s. Albert Ferdinhan and Ida Lillian (Snolne) B.; m. Katherine Teresina Connor, Aug. 8, 1959; children: Frances, George Albert Jr., Mary, Margaret, Thomas, John. BS in Chem. Engring., Notre Dame U., 1954; MD, Marquette U., 1961. Bd. cert. psychiatry and neurology. Intern St. Thomas Hosp., Nashville, 1961-62; resident psychiatry Tulane Med. Sch., New Orleans, 1962-65; dir. chronic treatment area East La. State Hosp., 1965-68, dir. acute intermediate area, 1968-70, dir. acute intensive treatment area, 1970-72; asst. commr. mental health and substance abuse State La., 1976-82, psychiat. program adminstr. substance abuse, 1976-82; dir. adult and adolescent substance abuse treatment programs Greenwell Springs Hosp., 1976-82, acting chief exec. officer, clin. dir., 1976-80; psychiat. program adminstr. Mental Health Region II, 1985—; chief Bur. Substance Abuse, 1973-75; psychiat. program adminstr. Mental Health and Substance Abuse, Region II, 1982; psychiat. cons. Tulane Rsch. Ctr., East La. State Hosp., 1966-72, acting chief exec. officer, 1985, 86; asst. clin. prof. psychiatry Tulane U. Sch. Medicine, 1966—; cons. La. Tng. Inst., 1966-72; cons., dir. children's treatment svc. Baton Rouge Mental Health Treatment Ctr., 1965-72; psychiat. cons. St. Gabriel Women's Prison, 1972-79, East Baton Rouge Parish Prison, 1979—. With USAF, 1956-57. Fellow Am. Psychiat. Assn.; mem. La. Psychiat. Assn. (exec. advisor 1982—, v.p. 1982, 92), Baton Rouge Psychiat. Assn. (pres. 1975, 82, 92.). Home: 6142 Stratford Ave Baton Rouge LA 70808-3532 Office: 4615 Government St Baton Rouge LA 70806

BISHOP, MARY LOU, artist; b. Tulsa, Jan. 6, 1929; d. George W. and Frances Pearl (Hendrix) Nesmith; m. Thomas Ray Bishop, Sept. 1, 1951; children: Thomas R. Bishop II, Frances Joann Bishop Faber. Student, Columbia U., 1948; BA, U. Houston, 1949, MEd, 1951; student, U. Wash.,

1954; postgrad., U. Houston, 1983-84; pvt. studies with, James Jennings, Opal Walls, Ruth Pershing Uhler, Lowell Collins. Cert. tchr., Tex. Fine artist, painter specializing in portraits, 1951—, freelance artist, 1975—, pvt. tchr. pastels and oils; condr. portrait seminars Tidwell Art Ctr., Houston. Exhibited in one-woman shows in Washington, Ala., Tex.; group shows at Bellevue Arts Fair, Washington; represented in permanent collections at 1st Bapt. Ch., Houston, Unitarian Ch., Huntsville, Ala., also corp. and pvt. collections in U.S. and Europe; executed murals for Unitarian Ch., Huntsville. Recipient scholarship Houston Mus. Fine Art, 1939-50, numerous awards for art. Mem. AAUW, Houston Soc. Illustrators, Profl. Picture Framer's Assn., Phi Kappa Phi, Phi Theta Kappa, Kappa Delta Pi. Unitarian. Home: 4444 Victory Houston TX 77088

BISHOP, ROBERT WHITSITT, lawyer; b. Atlanta, Jan. 7, 1949; s. James Clarence and Dorothy Davis (Whitsitt) B.; m. Cynthia Graham, Aug. 23, 1970; children: Jessica Levesque, Joshua Davis, Amanda Joyce, Alexandra Kelt. Student, Duke U., 1966-68; BA with high distinction, U. Ky., Lexington, 1973; postgrad. George Washington U., 1973-74; JD, U. Ky., 1976. Bar: Ohio 1976, Ky. 1981. Mem. Squire, Sanders & Dempsey, Cleve., 1976-80, Barnett & Alagia, Louisville, 1980-84; ptnr. Greenebaum, Young, Treitz & Maggiolo, Louisville, 1984-87; founding mem. Friedman, Evans & Bishop, Louisville, 1987-88; ptnr. Amshoff, Amshoff, Evans, Bishop & Masters, Louisville, 1988; founding mem., ptnr. Evans, Bishop, Masters & Mullins, Louisville, 1989-93; founding mem., ptnr. Bishop & Wilson, Louisville, 1993—; founder, dir., officer Indoor Soccer of Louisville Inc., (The Louisville Thunder), 1984-85; bd. dirs., officer Louisville Thunder, Inc., 1985-87, Cen. Indoor Soccer League, 1984. Author: The Interdict. Bd. dirs., mem. pers. and fin. coms. Louisville Central Community Ctrs. Inc., 1985. Mem. ABA, Ky. Bar Assn., Ohio Bar Assn., Louisville Bar Assn. (chmn. fed. practice sect. 1987-88), Cleve. Bar Assn., Order of Coif, Phi Beta Kappa, Sigma Alpha Epsilon. Avocations: mountain and rock climbing, soccer, creative writing. Home: 3901 Glen Bluff Louisville KY 40222 Office: Bishop & Wilson 6520 Glenridge Park Pl Ste 6 Louisville KY 40222-3453

BISHOP, SANFORD DIXON, JR., congressman; b. Mobile, Ala., Feb. 4, 1947; s. Sanford Dixon Sr. and Minne (Slade) S. BA in Political Sci., Morehouse Coll., 1968; JD, Emory U., 1971. Ptnr. Bishop & Buckner, P.C., Columbus, Ga., 1972-92; mem. Ga. Ho. of Reps. from 94th Dist., 1976-90, Ga. State Senate, 1990-92, 103d Congress from 2d Ga. Dist., 1993—, 105th Congress from 2d Ga. Dist., 1996—; del. Dem. Nat. Conv. 1980, 84, 88; mem. Agrl. Com., Vets. Affairs Com.; chmn. Ga. legis. black caucus. Fellowship, 1971-72; named Man of the Yr., 1977, Black Georgian of the Yr., 1983, Most Influential Black Men in Ga., recipient Outstanding Legis. award Ga. NOW, 1983-84, Legis. Svc. award, Ga. Mcpl. Assn., 1984, 86. Mem. ABA, Nat. Bar Assn., Ga. Bar Assn., Ala. Bar Assn., Am. Judicature Soc., Shriners, Masons (32 degree), Phi Delta Phi, Pi Sigma Alpha, Kappa Alpha Psi. Democrat. Baptist. Office: US Ho of Reps 1632 Longworth House Office Bldg Washington DC 20515-1002 also: 4129 Roman Dr Columbus GA 31907-6229

BISHOP, SID GLENWOOD, union official; b. Gladehill, Va., Nov. 11, 1923; s. Clarence Glenwood and Lillian Helen (Onks) B.; grad. U.S. Naval Trade Sch., 1942; cert. in labor rels. Concord Coll., Athens, W.Va., 1961; m. Carol Faye Miller, Mar. 2, 1990. Telegraph operator Virginian R.R., 1946-47, C & O R.R., 1947-62; local chmn. Order R.R. Telegraphers, 1960-62, gen. chmn. C & O-Virginian R.R.'s, 1962-68; 2d v.p. Transp-Communication Employees Union, St. Louis, 1968-69; v.p. transp. communication div. Brotherhood Ry. and Airline Clks., Rockville, Md., 1969-73, asst. internat. v.p., 1973—; mem. subcom. Labor Rsch. Adv. Coun., Dept. Labor, 1975, mem. com. on productivity, tech., growth Bur. Labor Statistics, 1975-77. With USN, 1941-46. Mem. AFL-CIO, Can. Labor Congress, Hunting Hills Home Owners Assn., VFW, Chantilly Nat. Golf and Country Club, Elks, Masons, K.T., Shriners. Democrat. Home and Office: 108 Virginia Dare Ct Kill Devil Hills NC 27948-9017

BISHOP, (INA) SUE MARQUIS, psychiatric and mental health nurse educator, researcher, administrator; b. Charleston, W.Va., Sept. 30, 1939; d. Harold Edwin and Ina Mabel (Walkup) Marquis; m. Randal Young Bishop, Feb. 27, 1960: children: Jon Marquis, Heather Suzanne. RN, Norton Infirmary Sch. Nursing, 1960; BSN, Murray State U., 1963; MSN, Ind. U., 1967, PhD, 1983. RN, Ky., Ind., Fla., N.C. Ind. staff nurse psychiatry Norton Infirmary, Louisville, 1960-61; head nurse obstetrics, nursing supr. Murray (Ky.) Gen. Hosp., 1961-62; primary care nurse, crisis counselor infirmary Murray State U., 1962-63; staff nurse, clin. instr. Madison (Ind.) State Hosp., 1963-65; instr. through assoc. prof. Ind. U. Sch. Nursing, Indpls., 1967-89, developer child/adolescent psychiat., mental health nursing program, 1982-83, chairperson grad. dept., 1983-89; prof., asst. dean Coll. of Nursing U. South Fla., Tampa, 1989-91; dean Coll. Nursing U. N.C., Charlotte, 1992-95; dean U. N.C. Coll. of Nursing and Health Professions, Charlotte, 1995—; pvt. practice marital and family therapy, 1975-89; cons. in field. Founding editor-in-chief Jour. of Child and Adolescent Psychiatric and Mental Health Nursing, 1987-91; contbr. articles to profl. jours. NIHM trainee Ind. U., 1965-67, USPHS profl. nurse trainee Ind. U., 1977-78; recipient Youth Advocacy award Ind. Advs. for Child Psychiat. Nursing, 1987, Disting. Svc. award Ind. U. Sch. Nursing Alumni Assn., 1989, Nat. Youth Advocacy award Advs. for Child Psychiat. Nursing, 1990. Fellow Am. Acad. Nursing; mem. Am. Nurses Assn., Psychiat. Mental Health Nursing Coun., Soc. for Edn. and Rsch. in Psychiat. Mental Health Nursing (pres. 1988-90), Am. Assn. Marital and Family Therapy, So. Nursing Rsch. Soc., Sigma Theta Tau.

BISHOP, THOMAS RAY, retired mechanical engineer; b. Hutchinson, Kans., Oct. 26, 1925; s. Orren E. and Myrtle (Dale) Bish; m. Mary Lou Nesmith, Sept. 1, 1951; children: Thomas Ray II, Frances Joann. Student California (Pa.) State Tchrs. Coll., 1947-48; BS, U. Houston, 1953; postgrad. U. Wash., 1960-61; grad. Alexander Hamilton Bus. Inst., 1972. Rsch. engr. Boeing Co., Seattle, 1953-64, rsch. engr. Apollo program, 1964-69; asst. chief engr. Product div. Bowen Tools, Inc., Houston, 1969-75, chief engr., 1975-77, chief product engr., 1977-86; chief engr. rsch. and devel.; founder, pres. Tom Bishop Engrs., 1986—, oil field tool design and quality control programs, quality control engr. cons.; with U.S. Maritime Svc., 1943-44. Precinct committeeman King County (Wash.) Democratic Com., 1960. With USMCR, 1944-46. Decorated Purple Heart with Gold Star; named Engr. of Year, Boeing Aerospace Co., 1966, WHO Houston, State of Tex. Hall of Fame; recipient Excellence in Engrng. citation A.I.S.I., 1975. Registered profl. engr., Ala., La., Tex. Mem. Am. Soc. Quality Control, Tex. Soc. Profl. Engrs. Unitarian. Mason. Contbr. articles to profl. jours.; multi-patentee (16) oil field equipment field. Home and Office: 2202 Viking Dr Houston TX 77018-1728

BISHOP, WANDA CAROLINE, geriatrics nurse, medical/surgical nurse; b. Newark, July 18, 1937; d. Paul and Karolina (Werynska) Serafin; children: Carol Jean, Steven Michael; m. Eric J. Bishop, July 6, 1981. BSN, U. Cen. Okla., 1983, MEd in Gerontology, 1989. Cert. med. surg. nurse, gerontol. nurse. Med. office mgr. Henry J. Pearce, M.D., Edmond, Okla., 1969-81; staff nurse VA Med. Ctr., Oklahoma City, 1983-86; owner, adminstr. HomeCare Nursing Svcs., Inc., Edmond, 1985-89; dir. nursing Okla. Christian Home, Edmond, 1993-95. Mem. ANA (coun. gerontol. nursing), Okla. Nurses Assn. (govtl. activities com.), Ctrl. State U. Alumni Assn., Alphi Chi, Sigma Phi Omega. Home: 108 Woodbridge Cir Edmond OK 73003-4506

BISSADA, NABIL KADDIS, urologist, educator, researcher, author; b. Cairo, Egypt, Sept. 2, 1938; s. Kaddis B. and Negma Bissada; m. Samia Shafik Henain, July 23, 1967; children: Sally, Nancy, Mary, Amy, Andrew. M.D., Cairo U., 1963. Diplomate Am. Bd. Urology. Intern Cairo Univ. Hosp., 1964-65; resident in surgery Babelsharia Gen. Hosp., 1965-69; resident in urology U. N.C. Hosp., 1970-72, chief resident, 1972-73; asst. prof. urology U. Ark., 1973-77, assoc. prof., 1977-79; cons. urologist King Faisal Specialist Hosp. and Rsch. Ctr., Riyadh, Saudi Arabia, 1979-87; prof., chief urologic oncology Med. U. S.C., 1987—; chief urologic surgery Ralph H. Johnson Med. Ctr., 1987—; co-chmn. Div. U., U.S. Sect. Internat. Coll. Surgeons, 1989-91, chmn., 1991-93; frequent speaker to regional, nat. and internat. med. groups. Author: Lower Urinary Tract Function and Dysfunction: Diagnosis and Management, 1978; Pharmacology of the Urinary Tract and the Male Reproductive System, 1982; contbr. to hundreds of articles and books; pioneer, developer of several significant surgical and med. urologic treatment methods. Fellow ACS, Internat. Coll. Surgeons; mem. AMA, Am. Urol. Assn., Soc. Internat. D'Urologie, Soc. Urologic Oncology, Urodynamic Soc., Soc. Urology and Engrng., Carolina Urol. Soc. (pres.-elect 1996), Egypt Am. Urol. Assn. (pres. 1990-92), Arab Am. Urol. Assn. (pres. 1993—), Sigma Xi. Office: Med U of SC Med Ctr 171 Ashley Ave Charleston SC 29425-0001

BISSELL, LE CLAIR, medical researcher and writer; b. Ft. Monroe, Va., May 18, 1928. BA, U. Colo., 1950; MS in Libr. Sci., Columbia U., 1952, MD, 1963. Lic. physician, N.Y.; cert. pub. libr., N.Y. Intern, resident Roosevelt Hosp., N.Y.C., 1963-66, fellow in endocrinology and metabolism, 1966-68; libr. The N.Y. Pub. Libr., 1952-59; coord. to chief Smithers Alcoholism Treatment and Tng. Ctr./Roosevelt Hosp., N.Y.C., 1968-79; pres., chief exec. officer Edgehill-Newport, Inc., Newport, R.I., 1979-81, cons./researcher, 1981-82; self-employed writer, researcher, cons., lectr. Sanibel, Fla., 1982—; adv. coun. to Nat. Inst. on Alcohol Abuse and Alcoholism, 1970-81; mem. physician's com., Med. Soc. of the State N.Y., 1979-81; task force on alcoholism, Carter Mental Health Commn.; active N.Y. State Sen. Legislative Adv. Com. on Alcoholism, 1977-79; guest several radio and TV shows including Good Morning America, Not for Women Only, Hour Mag., Healthline, others: guest lectrs. numerous confs., summer schs., including AMA confs., Utah Sch. Alcohol and Drugs, Idaho Sch. Alcohol and Drugs, Rutgers Sch. Alcohol Studies, others. Author numerous audiotapes in field; co-author: (books) The Cat Who Drank Too Much, 1982, Alcoholism in the Professions, 1984, Ethics for Addiction Professionals, 1987, 2nd edit., 1994, To Care Enough: Intervention with Chemically Dependant Colleagues, 1989, Chemical Dependency in Nursing, The Deadly Diversion, 1988; contbr. articles to profl. jours. and profl. publs. Mem. ACLU, AMA (panel on alcoholism 1979-86, others), Gay and Lesbian Med. Assn., N.Y. Civil Liberties Union, Am. Med. Soc. on Alcoholism (past pres., bd. dirs., chair ethics com.), Am. Med. Women's Assn. (chair archives com.), Am. Med. Writers Assn., Amnesty Internat., R.I. Med. Soc. (impaired physician's com. 1979-82), Intercongl. Alcoholism Program (adv. bd.), Nat. Abortion Rights Action League, Planned Parenthood S.W. Fla. (bd. dirs.), others. Democrat.

BISSELL, MICHAEL GILBERT, pathologist; b. Ridgecrest, Calif., Mar. 5, 1947; s. Henry Robert and Margaret Alberta (Encell) Benefiel; m. Sherrie L. Lyons, Mar. 27, 1977 (div. June 1990); children: Cassandra, Grahame; m. Lita A. Hill, Nov. 29, 1991. BS in Chemistry, U. Ariz., 1969, BS in Math., 1969; MD, Stanford U., 1975, PhD in Neurobiol., 1977; MPH, U. Calif., Berkeley, 1978. Diplomate Am. Bd. Pathology. Resident Martinez VA Med. Ctr. U. Calif., Davis, 1978-81; rsch. fellow NIMH, Bethesda, Md., 1981-84; asst. prof. pathology U. Chgo. Med. Ctr., 1984-88; dir. clin. pathology City of Hope Nat. Med. Ctr., Duarte, Calif., 1988-91; v.p./med. dir. Nichols Inst. Reference Lab., San Juan Capistrano, Calif., 1991-93; dir. lab. medicine, assoc. prof. pathology U. Texas, 1993—; ptnr. Biomed.-Environ. Cons., Richland, Wash., 1989—; speaker in field. Contbr. articles to profl. jours. Activist/lectr. Calif. Physicians Alliance, San Francisco, 1988—. Fellow Am. Soc. Clin. Pathologists (course dir. annual meeting), Coll. Am. Pathologists, mem. Nat. Com. Clin. Lab. Standards, Am. Assn. Clin. Chemistry, Clin. Lab. Mgmt. Assn. (treas.), Physicians for Nat. Health Program (activist, lectr.), Sierra Club, Sigma Xi. Democrat. Office: U Tex Med Br 11th and Texas Ave Galveston TX 77555

BISSETTE, SAMUEL DELK, astronomer, artist, financial executive; b. Wilson, N.C., Aug. 10, 1921; s. Zachariah Coye and Annie Wright (Rice) B.; m. Ruby Graham Raynor, Sept. 8, 1943; children: Judy Sabra, David Coye. Student pub. schs., various coll. courses. With Peoples Fed. Savs. and Loan Assn., Wilmington, N.C., 1939-89, pres., chief exec. officer, 1959-77, chmn. bd., 1973-89, dir., 1954-89; visual artist, 1972—; one-man exhbns. FDIC Gallery, Washington, 1978, St. John's Mus. Art, Wilmington, N.C., 1974, 81, 84, Raleigh Civic Center, 1977, Fayetteville (N.C.) Mus. of Art, 1988, Discovery Pl., Charlotte, N.C., 1994; group show 82d Ann. U.S. Open Watercolor Exhbn., N.Y.C., 1982, N.C. Mus. Art, 1978; commd. by Wachovia Bank to execute 40 paintings Portrait of North Carolina, 1976; originated mosaic murals for Belk-Beery Co., Wilmington, 1979; originated exhbn. N.C. Circa 1900, 1983; traveling tour N.C. Mus., 1984-87; originated 35 piece exhbn. Images From the Microworld, 1991; created 60 painting exhbn. The Universe According to Earth, U.N.C., Wilmington, 1993; originator astro-microscopy, astro-photomicrography for astronomy, 1994; author: A Guide to Astromicroscopy, 1994, An Astromicroscopy Study of the Southern Hemisphere Sky, 1995. Trustee N.C. Mus. Art, Raleigh, 1980-85; chmn. N.C. Artists Exhbn., 1979. Served with USAAF, 1941-45. Mem. N.C. Watercolor Soc. (v.p. 1980), N.C. Art Soc. (dir. 1974-82), St. John's Mus. Art (pres. 1973-74). Republican. Baptist. Clubs: Cape Fear (pres. 1978), Cape Fear Country, Carolina Yacht (Wilmington). Address: 1939 S Live Oak Pky Wilmington NC 28403-5321

BISSIC, DAVID WAYNE, biologist, educator; b. Ruston, La., Oct. 9, 1958; s. Cato Walter Bissic and Murline Jeanette (Robinson) Rushing. BS, La. Tech. U., 1989, MS, 1992. Cert. tchr., La. Instr. sci. Green Oaks H.S., Shreveport, La., 1989; grad. asst. La. Tech. U., Ruston, 1990; instr. math., sci. Simsboro (La.) H.S., 1992-93; adj. prof. Grambling (La.) State U., 1993-94. Home: 8344 Hwy 80 Ruston LA 71270

BISSONETTE, WILLIAM THEADORE, SR., executive recruiter; b. Bombay, N.Y., Nov. 9, 1942; s. Floyd James and Marjorie (Cross) B.; m. Joyce Waite, Feb. 26, 1963 (div. June 1970); children: Elizabeth Ann, William Theadore Jr., Floyd James II, Rebecca Lynn; m. Susan Thomas, Jan. 11, 1972; children: Jackalyn Thomas, John Thomas Bissonette. BA in Liberal Arts, SUNY, Potsdam, 1967; postgrad., Ind. U., 1971, 72. Common laborer GE, Brockport, N.Y., 1960-61; bookkeeper, payroll Amerada Petroleum, N.Y.C., 1961-62; sales mgr. trainee Ency. Britannica, Potsdam, 1964-67; tchr., debate coach Pius X Cen High Sch., Saranac Lake, N.Y., 1964-67; tchr., debate coach North Country C.C., Saranac Lake, 1970-71; pres. gen. mgr. Scorpio Enterprises, Inc./Campus Chem. Co., Bloomington, Ind., 1972-83; cons., mgr. Bryant Bur., Knoxville, 1983-85; pres., gen. mgr. Bissonette & Assocs., Inc., Knoxville, 1986—. Fellowship Ind. U., 1967. Mem. Tenn. Assn. Pers. Recruiters and Cons. (bd. dirs. East Tenn. 1990, 91, Top Producer award 1988, 89, No. 1 Sales Recruiter award 1990, Million Dollar Circle award 1990, Nat. Golden Circle award 1990, 91). Republican. Roman Catholic. Home and Office: 1233 Courtfield Rd Knoxville TN 37922-6051

BISTER-BROOSEN, HELGA, German linguistics educator; b. Krefeld, Germany, July 22, 1947; came to U.S., 1975; d. Heinz and Helene Broosen; m. Klaus Bister, June 4, 1971 (div. Jan. 1985); m. Roland Willemyns, Sept. 30, 1991. MA, U. Münster, Germany, 1971; MAT, U. Cologne, Germany, 1973; PhD in Germanic Linguistics, U. Calif., Berkeley, 1986. Tchr. middle sch. and h.s., Cologne, 1971-76; tchg. asst. U. Calif., Berkeley, 1980-86; lectr. U. San Francisco County, San Francisco, 1985-86; lectr. Germanic linguistics U. N.C., Chapel Hill, 1986-88, asst. prof., 1988-94, assoc. prof., 1995—, asst. chair, supr. tchg. assts., dir. undergrad. lang. prog., 1986—; vis. prof. U. Duisburg, Germany, 1992, 97. Author monograph; co-author textbook Spektrum. Grammatik im Kontext, 1992, also workbook/lab. manual, instr.'s resource manual. Recipient rsch. and travel grants. Mem. MLA, AATG, AAUSC, ACTFEL, GAL, JVG, LSA. Office: U NC Chapel Hill Dept Germanic Langs 438 Dey Hall Chapel Hill NC 27599-3160

BITTEL, MURIEL HELENE, managing editor; b. N.Y.C., Mar. 22; d. Ernest Henry and Helen Minnie (Seibel) Albers; m. Robert Gifford Walcutt, June 15, 1946; children—Lynn Lowell Walcutt, Mark James Walcutt, Judith Anne Walcutt; m. Lester Robert Bittel, May 8, 1973. B.A., Douglass Coll. Feature writer Daily Home News, New Brunswick, N.J.; editor Fawcett Pubs., N.Y.C., 1940-46; pub. relations dir. Electrovox/Walco Inc., East Orange, N.J., 1946-62; mng. editor Acad. Hall Pubs., Bridgewater, Va., 1974—. Mng. editor: Ency. Profl. Mgmt., 1978; Handbook Profl. Mgrs., 1985, A Surprise in Every Corner, 1994, Island Adventures, 1995. Home: 106 Breezewood Ter Bridgewater VA 22812-1433

BITTING, GEORGE CAPEN, oil company executive; b. St. Louis, July 23, 1935; s. Kenneth Hills and Esther (Capen) B.; m. Carol Culver, Feb. 6, 1960; children: Carol, George, Christopher; m. Frances Baldwin, Jan. 22, 1994. AB, Brown U., Providence, 1957; JD, St. Louis U., 1963. Media buyer Gardner Advt. Co., St. Louis, 1958-59; salesman Universal Match Corp., St. Louis, 1960-63; lawyer Bryan Cave McPheeters & McRoberts, St. Louis, 1964-67; registered rep. Apache Corp., Mpls., 1968-71; v.p. spl. investments G.H. Walker & Co., N.Y.C., 1972-73; v.p. Wainoco Oil Co., Houston, 1974; pres. South Ranch Oil Co., Inc. & Oilfield Mgmt., Inc., St. Louis and Midland, Tex., 1974-88; pres., exploration mgr. Oilfield Mgmt., Inc., Midland, 1985—; prs. Nadir Corp., Midland, 1988—. With USAF Res., 1958-64. Mem. St. Louis Bar Assn., Mo. Bar Assn., St. Louis Country Club, Racquet Club (st. Louis), Sakonnet Golf Club (Little Compton, R.I., Petroleum Club (Midland, Tex.), Greentree Country Club (Midland). Address: 2011 Winfield Midland TX 79705 Office: Oilfield Mgmt Inc 414 W Texas Ste 206 Midland TX 79701-4416

BITTLE, POLLY ANN, nephrology nurse, researcher; b. Orlando, Fla., Jan. 15, 1963; d. James T. and Maybell (Wendel) B. ADN, Valencia Community Coll., Orlando, 1984, AA, 1986; BSN, U. South Fla., 1987. Cert. in CPR, emergency cardiac care. Clin. rsch. coord. nephrology, hypertension, cardiothoracic surgery U. South Fla. Coll. Medicine, Tampa, 1987—; interim dir. nursing U. South Fla. Dialysis Ctr., Tampa, 1994-95. Contbr. articles to profl. jours. Mem. Am. Heart Assn., Am. Nephrology Nurses Assn., Fla. Nurses Assn., Sigma Theta Tau, Phi Theta Kappa. Home: 4402 Bradley Ave Orlando FL 32839-1419

BIVENS, CONSTANCE ANN, elementary school educator; b. Madison, Ind., June 26, 1938; d. Nelson and Virginia (Cole) B. BS, George Peabody Coll. for Tchrs., now Vanderbilt U., 1960, MA, 1966; EdD, Nova U., Ft. Lauderdale, Fla., 1982. Cert. educator. Tchr. Broward County Schs., Ft. Lauderdale, Fla., 1960-61, 65—, Jefferson County Schs., Louisville, Ky., 1961-62, Ft. Knox (Ky.) Schs., 1962-64, Madison (Ind.) Consol. Schs., 1964-65; chmn. K-Adult Coun., Nova Schs., Ft. Lauderdale, 1976-78; cons. 1978-80. Author: Boots, Butterflies, and Dragons, 1982. Mem. Hollywood Hills United Meth. Ch., 1966—, mem. adminstrv. bd. Sing in Chancel Choir, pres. Sunday Sch. class, 1991-94, Walk to Emmaus, 1990, 91-92; active Children's Cancer Caring Ctr. Inc., Broward County chpt., 1986—, Hollywood Hist. Soc., Zool. Soc. Fla., Nat. Audubon Soc. Mem. AAUW, NEA, Fla. Reading Assn., Hist. Madison, Inc., Jefferson County Hist. Soc., Internat. Order King's Daus. and Sons, Irish Cultural Inst., Delta Kappa Gamma (internat. expansion com. 1986-88, chmn. internat. program of work com. 1988-90, internat. rep. World Confedn. Orgns. of Teaching profession 1989, chmn. S.E. regional conf. 1991, internat. nominations com. 1992—, chmn. 1994—, 1st v.p. Mu state 1993-95, Mu state pres. 1995-97, Sara Ferguson Achievement award 1990). Republican. Methodist. Home: 5516 Arthur St Hollywood FL 33021-4608 Office: Nova Blanche Forman Elem Sch 3521 Davie Rd Fort Lauderdale FL 33314-1604

BIXBY, ROBERT JAY, editor, writer; b. Mt. Pleasant, Mich., Nov. 9, 1952; m. Kathleen Mae Beal, July 30, 1971; children: Jennifer Marie, Steven Jay. BS, Ctrl. Mich. U., 1978; MSW, Western Mich. U., 1980; MFA, U. N.C., Greensboro, 1991. Social worker VA Med. Ctr., Battle Creek, Mich., 1980-87; editor GMI, Greensboro, 1987-96, KOZ inc., 1996—; pub. poetry books March St. Press; pub. semi-ann. lit. mag. Parting Gifts. With USN, 1972-76.

BIZOT, RICHARD BYRON, English language educator; b. Louisville, Dec. 6, 1939; s. Byron Jean and Rita (Moriarty) B.; m. Joyce Hellmann, Aug. 26, 1961; children: John Eric, Richard Byron Jr. BA in English, Bellarmine Coll., 1961; MA in English, U. Va., 1963, PhD in English, 1967. Instr. U. Notre Dame, Ind., 1965-67, asst. prof., 1967-72; assoc. prof. U. North Fla., Jacksonville, 1972-77, prof. English, 1977—, chmn. dept. lang. and lit., 1984-86, coord. MA in English program, 1992-96, coord. Irish Studies program, 1995—. Contbg. editor: Walter Pater: An Annotated Bibliography of Writings About Him, 1980; chmn. editorial bd. U. North Fla. Press, Jacksonville, 1973-91; mem. editorial bd. Univ. Press. Fla., Gainesville, 1991—, Working Papers in Irish Studies, Ft. Lauderdale, 1992—; contbr. articles and revs. to profl. jours. Mem. Jacksonville Community Coun., Inc., 1978—, chmn. Commissioned Study of Theatre Jacksonville, 1978-79. NDEA fellow U. Va., Charlottesville, 1961-64, NEH fellow, Washington, 1981-82; summer seminar grantee NEH, Washington, 1976, 79. Mem. MLA (regional del. 1992-94), South Atlantic MLA, Am. Conf. Irish Studies (exec. com. so. region 1992—), Internat. Assn. Study Anglo-Irish Lit. Democrat. Roman Catholic. Home: 5024 Brierwood Ct Jacksonville FL 32217-4501 Office: U North Fla Dept Lang & Lit Jacksonville FL 32224-2645

BIZZACK, JOHN W., protective services official; b. Harlan, Ky., Nov. 24, 1949. AA in Criminal Justice, Eastern Ky. U., 1971; BA in Bus. Adminstrn., LaSalle Adminstrn., 1988; PhD in Adminstrn. & Mgmt., Walden U. Div. law enforcement Fayette County Pub. Schs., Lexington, Ky., 1971-73; from uniform traffic officer to detective commdr. and chief's staff Lexington Fayette Urban County Govt., 1973—; adj. instr. U. Ky., Lexington C.C. Author: Police Management for the 1990s: A Practitioners Road Map, 1988, No Nonsense Leadership, 1991, Criminal Investigations: Managing for Results, 1992; editor: Issues in Policing: New Perspectives, 1992, Professionalism and Law Enforcement Accreditation, 1993, Authentic Leadership: Lifetime Tools that Make the Difference, 1995. Co-chair federal law enforcement coordination com., Ky. eastern dist.; co-chair law enforcement group for legis. change; mem. statewide task force on runaway and homeless youth; adv. coun. on student conduct Fayette County Schs.; trustee, vice-chair Millersburg Mil. Inst. Mem. Police Mgr.'s Assn., Internat. Assn. Chiefs of Police, Nat. Assn. Chiefs of Police, Lexington C. of C. (program coord.), Doctorate Assn., Southern Criminal Justice Assn., Acad. Criminal Justice Scis. Office: 150 E Main St Lexington KY 40507-1318

BIZZELL YARBROUGH, CINDY LEE, school counselor; b. Griffin, Ga., June 20, 1951; d. William Emerson and Senora Elizabeth (Henderson) B.; m. Gary Keith Phillips, Nov. 6, 1980 (div. Nov. 1990); m. Randy Yarbrough; 1 child, Delana Michelle. Student, North Ga. Coll., 1969-70; BA in Elem. Edn., West Ga. Coll., 1993, MS in Behavior Disorders, 1993; MS in Learning Disabilities, 1993, MS in Counseling and Ednl. Psychology, 1993. K-12 reading, math., sci. and elem. edn. tchr. Pike County Schs., Zebulon, Ga., 1972—; tchr., counselor of emotionally disturbed Pike County Elem. Sch., 1973—; tchr. of emotionally disturbed and behavior disorders Pike County H.S., 1993—; crisis counselor McIntosh Trail Mental Health Mental Retardation, 1994; cons. Alcoholics Anonymous, Griffin, 1982—, Pike County Coun. on Child Abuse, 1990—; lectr., presenter in field. Author: Hippotherapy for the Emotionally Disturbed, 1988; contbr. articles to profl. publs. Leader, instr. Girl Scouts U.S., Meansville, Ga., 1969-90; co-coord. Ga. Spl. Olympics, Pike County, 1980—; pres. Internat. Reading Assn., Griffin, 1978; asst. leader 4H, 1992-93; substitute Sunday sch. tchr. local Meth. Ch. Recipient Sci. award Ford Found., 1966; named Res. Champion Open Jumper, Dixieland Show Ctr., 1989. Mem. N.Am. Handicapped Riders Assn. (presenter), Profl. Assn. Ga. Educators. Democrat. Home: 734 Buck Creek Rd Griffin GA 30223-7915 Office: Pike County Schs Hwy 19 Zebulon GA 30295

BJONTEGARD, ARTHUR MARTIN, JR., foundation executive; b. Lynn, Mass., Mar. 23, 1938; s. Arthur M. and Irma W. (Cook) B.; m. Wilma Joy Golding, Oct. 15, 1966; children—Arthur M., Karla Kristin. B.A., Duke U., 1959; J.D., U. Va., 1962; postgrad., Stonier Grad. Sch. Banking, Rutgers U., 1966; grad. advanced mgmt. program, Harvard U. Sch. Bus., 1974. Bar: N.J. 1962, S.C. 1967. Bank examiner U.S. Treasury Dept., Richmond, Va., 1962-66; trust officer S.C. Nat. Bank, Columbia, 1966-74; sr. v.p. S.C. Nat. Bank, 1974-81; pres. S.C. Nat. Corp., Columbia, 1981-84; vice-chmn. S.C. Nat. Corp., 1984-92; pres. Ind. Colls. and Univs. of S.C. Inc., 1992—; commr. Columbia Housing Authority, 1995—. Pres. United Way of the Midlands, Columbia, 1984-85, S.C., 1986-87, Univ. Assocs., Columbia, 1984-85, Friday Luncheon Club, Columbia, 1984, Spring Valley Ednl. Found., 1986—, Ctrl. Carolina Community Found., 1990—; chmn. Columbia Community Resl. Coun., 1984, Fedn. of the Blind, 1992—. Named Vol. of Yr., Urban League, Columbia, 1984; recipient Order of Palmetto award, S.C. Gov., 1992. Mem. S.C. Bar Assn., Palmetto Soc., Thomas Jefferson Soc., S.C. C. of C., Forest Lake County Club, Palmetto Club, Spring Valley Country Club. Episcopalian. Office: Ind Colls and Univs of SC PO Box 12007 Columbia SC 29211-2007

BLACHMAN, MICHAEL JOEL, lawyer; b. Portsmouth, Va., Aug. 16, 1944; s. Zalmon I. and Rachel G. (Grossman) B.; m. Paula D. Levine, Nov. 23, 1969; children: Dara R., Erica Dale. BS, Am. U., 1966; JD, U. Tenn., 1969. Bar: Va. 1969, U.S. Dist. Ct. (ea. dist.) Va. 1971, U.S. Supreme Ct.

1974, U.S. Ct. Appeals (4th cir.) 1977. Asst. commonwealth's atty. Commonwealth of Va., Portsmouth, 1970-72; assoc. Bangel, Bangel & Bangel, Portsmouth, 1972-77, ptnr., 1977—; chmn. Portsmouth Juvenile Adv. Com., 1975-78. Mem. Va. Dem. Steering Com. 1980-85; vice chmn. Indsl. Devel. Authority and Port and Indsl. Commn., Portsmouth, 1987-89, chmn. 1989-93; bd. dirs. United Jewish Fedn. Tidewater, 1980—, v.p. 1989—. With USCGR, 1966-72. Recipient Young Leadership award United Jewish Fedn. Tidewater, 1983. Mem. ABA, Assn. Trial Lawyers Am., Va. Bar Assn., Va. Trial Lawyers Assn. (v.p. 1985-88, pres. 1989-90), So. Trial Lawyers Assn. (bd. dirs. 1993—), Portsmouth Bar Assn., Portsmouth C. of C., Kiwanis (bd. dirs. Portsmouth club 1973-75), B'nai B'rith. Jewish. Office: Bangel Bangel & Bangel PO Box 760 Portsmouth VA 23705-0760

BLACK, ALBERT GEORGE, English language educator; b. Northville, Mich., Aug. 22, 1928; s. William and Ruth Black; m. Mary Jared, June 9, 1950; children: Anne E., Alan R., Erich W. AB, U. Mich., 1952, MA, 1956, cert. tech. and profl. writing, 1977. Tchr., dept. head English high sch. Birmingham, Mich., 1952-58; fellow English U. Mich., Ann Arbor, 1958-60; campaign dir. Breakey for Supreme Ct. Mich., 1960; reporter Ypsilanti (Mich.) Press, 1960-61; assoc. editor Inst. Sci./Tech., U. Mich., Ann Arbor, 1961-62; instr. English Calif. State U., Long Beach, 1962-63, asst. prof., 1963-73, assoc. prof., 1973-88, prof. emeritus, 1988—; founder, dir. Calif. Assn. Faculty Tech./Profl. Writing, 1980-88; cel. Calif.Faculty Assn., L.A., 1975-82. Author: The Michigan Novel, 1963, Vigilant Balance, 1971; author, editor Asterisk, 1974-86; author, producer: (films) Process and Discovery: Group Composing, 1969, Boswell and Johnson: On Tour in the Hebrides, 1969, Samuel Johnson, Dramatic Theory, and Rasselas, 1977, Semiotics of American Signs, 1980, Enchanted Images: American Illustrations of Children's Books 1850-1925, 1987, A Child's Reading - Preparation for Technical Writing, 1987; co-editor Beginning, Middle and Ends of Technical Writing: Essays From Chicago, 1977. Commr. Boy Scouts Am., Ann Arbor, 1960-62; hon. Brit. friend Bodleian Libr., Oxford U., Eng., 1980—. Mem. AAUP (pres. Calif. Conf. 1982-83), Jane Austen Soc. (life, past pres. Southwestern U.S. 1986—), Soc. Tech. Comm. (sr.), Samuel Johnson Soc. (life). Home: PO Box 2873 Matthews NC 28106-2873

BLACK, B. R., educational administrator; b. Tampa, Fla., Apr. 6, 1942; s. R.C. and Gladys (Gaines) B.; m. Katy Black, Apr. 2, 1987; children: Amy Christine, Dale Rainer. AA, Marion (Ala.) Inst., 1962; BA, Fla. State U., 1964; MEd, Rollins Coll., 1974; EdD, Nova U., Ft. Lauderdale, Fla., 1988. Tchr. biology, chmn. sci. dept., asst. prin. high sch., 1970-85; supr. MIS, Sch. Bd. Polk County, Bartow, Fla., 1985-86, supr. instrnl. computing, 1986-93, dir. instrnl. tech., 1993—; presenter numerous workshops and confs. Author: Trouble Shooting Microcomputers; mem. nat. editl. adv. bd. Electronic Learning, 1989-92. Capt. U.S. Army, 1964-70. Mem. ASCD (ednl. futurists network 1989-95), Fla. Coun. Instnl. Tech. Leaders (sec. 1995—), Fla. Instnl. Computing Suprs. (bd. dirs. 1988-90, state chmn. 1989), Fla. Assn. for Computers in Edn., Fla. Assn. Ednl. Data Systems, Fla. ASCD, Internat. Soc. for Tech. in Edn., Phi Delta Kappa. Home: 3440 Whitman Cir Lakeland FL 33803-4240 Office: Sch Bd Polk County PO Box 391 Bartow FL 33830-0391

BLACK, BOBBY C., chaplain; b. Hartford, Ky., Apr. 27, 1933; s. Clifton Cornelius and Margaret Ruth (Smith) B.; m. Marybel Davis, Aug. 26, 1956; children: Lori Elizabeth, Brian Davis. BA, Ky. Wesleyan Coll., 1955; BD, Duke Div. Sch., 1959, MDiv, 1973; cert., Duke Med. Sch., 1959. Commd. 1st lt. USAF, 1959, advanced through grades to col., chaplain, 1959-83; space command chaplain USAF, Colorado Springs, Colo., 1983-87; ret. USAF, 1987; chaplain The Village Chapel, Pinehust, N.C., 1987—; dir. USAF Christian Encounter Conf., Va., Calif., N.C., 1970-79, Christian Leadership Conf., Spearfish, S.D., 1985; pres. Sr. USAF Chaplain Sch., Montgomery, Ala., 1973; preacher Outstanding Clergy Series, USAF Acad., 1984; dir. chaplaincy Moore Regional Hosp., 1987—. Decorated Def. Superior Svc. medal, Meritorious Svc. medal with three oak leaf clusters. Mem. N.C. Chaplain's Assn., Sandhill's Retired Officer's Assn. (chaplain 1989), N.C. Conf. U. Meth. Ch., Sandhill's Fellowship of Chs., Sandhills Men's Fellowship (bd. dirs. 1990—). Republican. Home: 15 Gray Fox Run Pinehurst NC 28374-9056 Office: The Village Chapel PO Box 1060 Pinehurst NC 28374-1060

BLACK, CLYDE EDWARD, radiologist; b. Birmingham, Ala., Nov. 29, 1938; s. Edward Wylie and Jorie Arlene (Aaron) B.; m. Evelyn Demetria Winslow; children: Edward, Eric, Allison. AB, Harvard U., 1960; MD, U. Ala., 1965. Resident diagnostic radiology U. Ala., Birmingham, 1968-70, chief resident radiology, 1971; radiologist Fulton Hosp., Atlanta, 1979, N.E. Regional Med. Ctr., Anniston, Ala., 1979—; chmn. Calhoun County Bd. Health, 1996. Bd. dirs. Westminster, Anniston, Ala., 1982-88; mem. Calhoun County Bd. of Health, Anniston, 1992—; elder First Presbyn. Ch., Anniston, 1985-88. Mem. AMA, Am. Coll. Radiology, Radiol. Soc. N. Am., So. Radiol. Assn., Calhoun County Med. Assn. (sec. 1986-87, v.p. 1988-89, pres. 1990-91). Republican. Office: Anniston Radiol Group PA 106 Med Arts Bldg Anniston AL 36201

BLACK, DANIEL HUGH, secondary school educator; b. Arab, Ala., July 4, 1947; s. Lehmon Ray and Lillian Geneve (Divine) B. BS, U. Ala., Tuscaloosa, 1970; MEd, Ala. A&M U., 1976; PhD, Vanderbilt U., 1981; MA, St. John's Coll., Annapolis, Md., 1988. Social studies tchr., advanced placement govt. tchr. Grissom High Sch., Huntsville, Ala., 1970—; adj. instr. history Calhoun C.C., 1982—, Ala. A&M U., 1989-94, Great Books in the Western World, U. Ala., Huntsville; essay reader advanced placement Am. govt. and politics exam. Ednl. Testing Svc., 1991-96. Mem. NEA, Ala. Edn. Assn., Huntsville Edn. Assn., Nat. Trust for Hist. Preservation (master class James Madison and Federalist Papers 1989), Phi Delta Kappa. Home: 1019 Old Monrovia Rd NW Apt 232 Huntsville AL 35806-3505 Office: Virgil I Grissom High Sch Bailey Cove Huntsville AL 35802

BLACK, DAVID CHARLES, astrophysicist; b. Waterloo, Iowa, May 14, 1943. BS, U. Minn., 1965, MS, 1967, PhD in Physics, 1970. Fellow NAS, 1970-72; rsch. scientist theoretical astrophysics Ames rsch. ctr. NASA, Houston, 1972—; chief scientist space sta. NASA, 1985—; dir. Lunar & Planetary Inst., Houston. Mem. AAAS, N.Y. Acad. Sci. Office: Lunar & Planetary Inst 3600 Bay Area Blvd Houston TX 77058

BLACK, D(EWITT) CARL(ISLE), JR., lawyer; b. Clarksdale, Miss., Aug. 17, 1930; s. DeWitt Carlisle Sr. and Alice Lucille (Hammond) B.; m. Ruth Buck Wallace, June 6, 1970; children: Elizabeth B. Smithson, D. Carl Black III. BA, Miss. Coll., 1951, LLB, 1963; MPA, Princeton U., 1953; LLM in Taxation, NYU, 1965. Bar: Miss. 1963, U.S. Dist. Ct. (so. dist.) Miss. 1963, U.S. Ct. Appeals (5th cir.) 1965. Rsch. asst. Pub. Affairs Rsch. Coun., Baton Rouge, 1956-57; asst. mgr., dir. rsch. Miss. Econ. Coun., Jackson, 1957-64; ptnr. Butler, Snow, O'Mara, Stevens & Cannada, Jackson, 1965—; chair Miss. Tax Inst., Jackson, 1987. Treas. New Stage Theatre, Jackson, 1965-69; pres. Miss. Symphony Orch. Assn., Jackson, 1985-86, Miss. Symphony Found., Jackson, 1989-92. Cpl. U.S. Army, 1953-55. Fellow Am. Coll. Tax Counsel; mem. So. Employee Benefits COnf., Miss. Bar Assn. (chair tax sect. 1989-90), Univ. Club, River Hills Club. Episcopalian. Home: 1704 Poplar Blvd Jackson MS 39202-2119 Office: 1700 Deposit Guaranty Plz Jackson MS 39201

BLACK, GEORGIA ANN, mathematics facilitator; b. DeSoto, Mo., Feb. 3, 1945; d. Walter Vernon and Mabel (Luebbers) Hardin; m. Gary R. Black Sr., Jan. 9, 1965; children: Gary Jr., Nancy, Walter, Kelly. AS, Mineral Area Coll., 1966; BS in Elem. Edn., U. Mo., 1969; M.Adminstrn. and Supervision, Southeast Mo. State U., 1979. Cert. tchr., Mo., Tex., supervision and mid-mgmt. Tchr. 4th grade Sacred Heart Sch., Festus, Mo., 1964-65; tchr. math. 7-8th grades Athena Sch., DeSoto, Mo., 1969-71, Spring Br. Ind. Sch. Dist., Houston, 1971-74; tchr. math. 7-9th grades Cen. R-111 Sch. Dist., Flat river, Mo., 1974-84; tchr. math. 7-8th grades El Paso (Tex.) Ind. Sch. Dist., 1984-91; asst. prin. Clardy Sch., 1991-93; instrnl. support math. facilitator El Paso (Tex.) Ind. Sch. Dist., 1993—. Sponsor Math. Club, 1990; campaign coord. U.S. Senate Race, St. Francois County, Mo., 1976. Named Tchr. of Yr. MacArthur Faculty, 1989-90. Mem. Greater El Paso Coun. Tchrs. Math. (treas. 1986-90).

BLACK, KAY FREEMAN, public affairs administrator; b. Biloxi, Miss., Feb. 3, 1936; d. Thomas Miller and Ellie Olivia (Collins) Freeman; m. Truman Nelson Pittman, Mar. 9, 1956 (div. 1961); 1 child, Susan Gail Pittman; m. David Dotson Black Jr., Dec. 30, 1965; 1 child, Maura Elaine Black. BS, U. So. Miss., 1956. Reporter Biloxi Gulfport Daily Herald, Biloxi, 1956-57; amusements editor State Times, Jackson, Miss., 1960-62; real estate editor, investigative reporter, polit. reporter Memphis Press Scimitar, 1962-83; exec. dir. Memphis City Coun., 1984-86; pub. affairs dir. Shelby County Sheriff, Memphis, 1986—. Mem. Shelby County Dem. Women, Memphis, 1963—, former pres.; former bd. dirs. Fedn. Dem. Women, Tenn.; co-chair fin. Shelby County Dem. Party, Memphis; mem., publicity chair Shelby Country Dem. Exec. Com., Memphis; county wide chair Am. Lung Assn. Christmas Seal Drive, 1992; bd. dirs. Family Svc. Recipient Malcolm Adams Journalism award for investigative reporting Memphis Lodge No. 27 of B&P Order of Elks, 1966, Upitan John W. Finney Meml. award for pub. svc. reporting, Upitan, 1972. Roman Catholic. Home: 11 S Reese St Memphis TN 38111-4605 Office: Shelby County Sheriff 201 Poplar Ave Rm 7-14 Memphis TN 38103-1947

BLACK, LAURA NEATH, language professional; b. Chgo., Dec. 3, 1949; d. James Gordon and Harriette Laverne (Lundgren) Neath; m. Michael Leon Vinson, Dec. 18, 1976 (div. Sept. 6, 1994); 1 child, John James Vinson; m. Ronnie Rex Black, Nov. 5, 1994. AB in English, Newberry (S.C.) Coll., 1971; MEd in Edn., U. S.C., 1972; PhD in Edn., 1980. Cert. Edn., English and Latin, Prin. H.S., S.C. Tchr. Dent Jr. H.S., Columbia, S.C., 1972-73, Summerville (S.C.) H.S., 1973-76, Lexington H.S., 1978-79; prof. Ctrl. Wesleyan Coll., S.C., 1980-87; tchr. Liberty (S.C.) H.S., 1987-91; prof., divsn. chair So. Wesleyan U., Central, S.C., 1991—; edtl. cons. Harper Collins Pub., N.Y.C., 1995—; adv. bd. ADEPT S.C. Dept. Edn., Columbia, 1993—. Contbr. author: First Printings of American Authors, 1980. Life mem. DAV Auxiliary, Bay Pines, Fla., 1965—. Named Faculty Mem. of Yr. So. Wesleyan U., Central, S.C., 1982, 86, Outstanding Young Alumna, Newberry (S.C.) Coll., 1984, Tchr. of Yr. Finalist Pickens County Schs., Easley, S.C., 1990. Mem. MLA, So. Atlantic MLA, Nat. Coun. Tchrs. English. Lutheran. Home: 480 Pin-du-Lac Dr Central SC 29630 Office: Southern Wesleyan U Wesleyan Dr Central SC 29630

BLACK, NORMAN WILLIAM, federal judge; b. Houston, Dec. 6, 1931; s. Dave and Minnie (Nathan) B.; m. Berne Rose Efron, Feb. 21, 1959; children: Elizabeth Ann, Diane Rebecca. B.B.A., U. Tex., Austin, 1953, J.D. (Frank Bobbitt scholar 1954), 1955. Bar: Tex. 1955. Law clk. to Houston judge, 1956; asst. U.S. atty. Houston, 1956-58, pvt. practice, 1958-76; U.S. magistrate, 1976-79; U.S. dist. judge So. Dist. Tex., Houston, 1979—; adj. prof. South Tex. Coll. Law. Served with AUS, 1955-56. Mem. Fed. Bar Assn., State Bar Tex., Houston Bar Assn., Houston Philos. Soc. Office: 11535 US Courthouse 515 Rusk St Houston TX 77002

BLACK, RHONDA STOUT, vocational special needs educator; b. Salt Lake City, Feb. 5, 1960; d. Doyle and Afton Glenna (Nebeker) Stout; m. Richard Terrell Black, Mar. 25, 1989. BS in Child-Family Devel. magna cum laude, U. Utah, 1982, BS in Psychology magna cum laude, 1982, MS in Spl. Edn., 1991, EdD in Occupl. Studies, 1996. Behavior specialist, instr. Columbus Community Ctr., Salt Lake City, 1984-85, program mgr. occupational skill tng., 1985-93; rsch. asst. U. Ga., Athens, 1993—; assoc. prof. U. Hawaii, Honolulu. Faculty scholar U. Utah, 1980-81. Mem. Am. Vocat. Assn., Am. Ednl. Rsch. Assn., Nat. Assn. Vocat. Spl. Needs Pers., Coun. for Exceptional Children (tchr. edn. and career devel. divsn. on mental retardation), Phi Beta Kappa, Phi Eta Sigma, Phi Kappa Phi, Phi Delta Kappa, Omicron Theta Tau. Democrat.

BLACK, ROBERT COLEMAN, judge, lawyer; b. Greenville, Ala., July 3, 1934; s. James Monroe and Mabel (Coleman) B.; m. Carolyn Musselwhite, Dec. 20, 1960; children: Elizabeth Anne, Robert C., Carolyn Jane. B.S. in Commerce and Bus. Adminstrn, U. Ala., 1960, LL.B., 1961. Bar: Ala. 1961. Law clk. to justice Ala. Supreme Ct., 1961-62; partner firm Hill, Hill, Carter, Flanco, Cole & Black, Montgomery, Ala., 1968—; spl. asst. atty. gen. Ala. Hill, Hill, Carter, Flanco, Cole & Black, 1969-79; judge Circuit Ct., 1979—; prof. law Jones Law Sch., Montgomery; instr. bus. law U. Ala. at Montgomery, Auburn U.; lectr. continuing legal edn. Ala. Bar Assn.; faculty Ala. Jud. Coll. City chmn. March of Dimes, 1966; Bd. dirs. March of Dimes Found., 1966-67, Montgomery YMCA, St. James Parrish Sch.; trustee Ala. Indsl. Sch. Served with USMCR, 1954-57. Mem. Ala. Bar Assn., Montgomery County Bar Assn. (chmn. exec. com. 1969-70, pres. 1971), Phi Delta Phi, Beta Gamma Sigma. Office: 425 S Perry St Montgomery AL 36104-4235

BLACK, ROBERT SAMUEL, engineering executive; b. Goodnight, Tex., Apr. 28, 1933; s. Alford Morris and Lillie Lynn (Radcliffe) B.; m. Linda Carol Pirtle, Mar. 14, 1959; children: Robert Andrew, Samuel Alan. BSEE, Tex. Tech. U., 1955. Registered profl. engr., Tex. Telecom. engr. Creole Petroleum Corp., Punto Fijo, Venezuela, 1955-57, Humble Pipe Line Co., Houston, 1957-65; engring. supr. Humble Oil & Refining Co., Houston, 1965-72; v.p. Exxon Comm. Co., Houston, 1972-90; pvt. practice Houston, 1990—; vice-chmn. Land Mobile Comm. Coun., Washington, 1970-72. Bd. dirs. Indsl. Telecom. Assn., Washington, 1985-90; Wycliffe Bible Translators, 1990—. Mem. Fellow- Radio Club Am., Am. Petroleum Inst. (chmn. telecomm. com. 1983-85), Energy Telecomms. and Elec. Assn. (pres. 1970-75). Baptist.

BLACK, SARAH JOANNA BRYAN, secondary school educator; b. Port Arthur, Tex., Sept. 30, 1948; d. Foster Paul and Evelyn June (Whetsel) Bryan; m. David Lee Black, Nov. 26, 1971; children: Bryan Joseph, Kelley Allison, David Neal. BA, U. Tex., 1971. Tchr. math. Robert E. Lee High Sch., Baytown, Tex., 1971-87;, 1987; tchr. math. Lee Coll., Baytown, 1987—, Ross S. Sterling High Sch., Baytown, 1987—. Pres. Svc. League, Baytown, 1980; pres. Peter McKenney Soc. C.A.R., Baytown, 1984; treas. PTA of Stephen F. Austin Elem., Baytown, 1984; mem. John Lewis chpt. DAR, Baytown, 1980—, Colonial Dames, Tex., 1980—; treas. East League Little League, Baytown, 1986; treas. Grace Meth. Ch. Women, Baytown, 1985; mem. Cedar Bayou Meth. Ch., 1988-90; pres. Cedar Bayou PTO, 1988; historian Sterling PTSO, 1989. Named Secondary Tchr. of Yr., GCC Ind. Sch. Dist., 1991; recipient Tex. Excellences award Outstanding H.S. Tchr., U. Tex. Ex-Student Assn., 1993, Seminole Pipeline Tchg. Achievement award, 1995. Mem. Baytown Classroom Tchrs. (treas.), Baytown Edn. Assn., San Jacinto Coun. Math. Tchrs., Nat. Coun. Tchrs. of Math., Tex. Execs. (bd. dirs.), Welfare League, Bay Area Panhellenic (rush chmn.), Alpha Xi Delta (area rush chmn.), Alpha Delta Kappa, Delta Kappa Gamma. Republican. Methodist. Home: 3702 Autumn Ln Baytown TX 77521-2707 Office: 300 W Baker Rd Baytown TX 77521-2301

BLACK, SHAUN DENNIS, biochemist, educator, software developer; b. Augusta, Ga., July 9, 1954; s. John Donald and Mary Leah (Keefe) B.; m. Carol Eileen Davison, Aug. 20, 1977; children: Sarah Kathleen, Theresa Christine, Matthew David, Angela Noel. BS in Biochemistry, U. Calif., Davis, 1976; MS in Biological Chemistry, U. Mich., 1978, PhD in Biological Chemistry, 1982. Postdoctoral fellow U. Mich., Ann Arbor, 1981-85, lectr., 1982-85; asst. prof. Ohio State U., Columbus, Ohio, 1985-92; assoc. prof. U. Tex. Health Ctr., Tyler, 1992—; researcher, full mem. Comprehensive Cancer Ctr. Ohio State U., Columbus, 1989-92; mem. faculty, mem. admissions com. Ohio State Biochemistry Program, Columbus, 1989-92; cons. U. Mich., Ann Arbor, 1986-91, U. Louisville, Ky, 1987, VA Mpls., 1988, W.Va. U., Wheeling, 1990. Editor Biotechniques, Peptide Research, Nat. Sci. Found., 1986—; contbr. many articles to profl. jours., chpts. to text books. Presenter chemistry demonstrations for preschs. and elem. schs., 1989—; leader Christian music ministries various chs., 1974—; guest spkr. Christian groups; mem. Tyler Cath. Sch. Bd., 1994-97. Recipient Calif. state scholarship, 1975-76, Merck pre-doctoral fellowship, Merck, Sharpe & Dohme, 1980-81; grantee State of Ohio, 1985, '86, '86-87, '88-89, '89-91; Am. Cancer Soc., 1986-87; NIH, 1988—. Mem. AAAS, The Protein Soc., Am. Soc. for Biochemistry and Molecular Biology, Am. Crystallographic Assn., Kappa Epsilon (advisor 1989-92). Roman Catholic. Office: U Tex Health Ctr at Tyler Dept Biochemistry PO Box 2003 Tyler TX 75710

BLACK, SHERYL ELAINE HALE, author; b. Covington, Ky., Sept. 18, 1947; d. Letcher Talmadge and Mary Nell (Quinn) Hale; children: Shawna Lee Futrelle Aiken, Lawrence Kelly Aiken; m. Caroll Don Black, Sept. 7, 1991. Student, St. Paul Hosp., Dallas, 1970, Amherst Careet Ct., Greenville, Tex., 1990. Respiratory therapist St. Paul Hosp, Dallas, 1969-71; exec. sec., receptionist D.P.A., Inc., Dallas, 1971-73; asst. mgr. Am. Condominium Corp., Dallas, 1973-75; head credit investigation dept. Triangle Pacific Cabinet, Dallas, 1975-77; head merchandiser Am. Greeting Card Corp., Dallas, 1979-80; owner, operator Midlakes Grocery, Royce City, Tex., 1980-81; exec. sec., receptionist Amherst Career Ctr., Greenville, 1990-91. Author: Is Christ Come?. . .In the Flesh?, 1993, Forgotten Lady, 1994, As She Lived...Who I Am!, 1994, Deceived by Default, 1994, Escape From Flesh, 1994, Proverbs for Success, 1995, (children's books) Buttons and Lacey, The Good Manners Bears, 1987, Pennelope Jones, 1993. Recipient Honor Soc. award Amherst Career Ctr., 1990. Democrat. Home: 104 S James Quinlan TX 75474

BLACK, SUZANNE WATKINS DUPUY, psychology educator; b. Farmville, Va., Aug. 25, 1939; d. Edward Laurecne and Mary Catherine (Little) DuPuy; m. George Donald Black, June 29, 1963; children: Matthew DuPuy, Edward Purnell. BA, U. Richmond, 1961; MS, Ind. U., 1963; postgrad., Va. Tech., 1985. Tchr. social studies Norfolk (Va.) City Schs., 1963-65; tchr. sacred studies St. Michael's Episcopal Sch., Richmond, Va., 1969-78; asst. registrar's office Va. Tech., Blacksburg, 1979-81; eligibility worker Montgomery County Social Svcs., Christiansburg, Va., 1981-85; rsch. assoc. "Va. View" Va. Tech., 1985-86; curriculum cons. Job Tng. and Placement Act Floyd Coll., Rome, Ga., 1987-88; coord., instr. Health Svc. Technician Program, Rome, Ga., 1988-93; instr. devel. psychology Floyd Coll., Rome, Ga., 1993-95, asst. prof., 1996—; workshop leader Shelter for Abused Children, Cartersville, Ga., 1994—; organizer local support group for Adults with Attention Deficit Disorder. Organizer, group leader Disciples of Christ in Cmty., St. Peter's Episcopal Ch., Rome, 1993-95; vol. Good Neighbors, Rome, 1990—; mem. Wednesday Book Club, Rome, 1987—. Mem. AAUP, APA, Psi Beta. Home: 305 E Fourth Ave Rome GA 30161 Office: Floyd Coll PO Box 1864 Rome GA 30162-1864

BLACK, TIMOTHY LEE, physician; b. Toccoa, Ga., Oct. 9, 1948; s. Robert N. and Kathryn A. (Harner) B.; m. Melinda Girdley, Sept. 28, 1985. BS, Wheaton Coll., 1971; MD, U. Tenn., 1979. Diplomate Am. Bd. Surgery. Intern, then resident in gen. surgery U. Tenn., 1979-84; fellow in pediatric surgery LeBonheur Children's Hosp., Memphis, Tenn., 1984-86; pediatric surgeon Pediatric Surg. Assn. of Ft. Worth, 1986—. Contbr. articles to profl. jours. Fellow ACS; mem. AMA, Am. Acad. Pediatrics, Am. Pediatric Surgery Assn., Ft. Worth Pediatric Soc. Office: Pediatric Surg Assn Ft Worth 800 8th Ave Ste 306 Fort Worth TX 76104-2602

BLACKBURN, CATHERINE ELAINE, lawyer, pharmacist; b. Columbus, Ohio, Nov. 5, 1953; d. Robert Jerome and Patricia Ann (Buchman) B. BS in Pharmacy with high distinction, U. Ky., 1978; JD with honors, Ohio State U., 1982. Bar: Ohio 1982, U.S. Dist. Ct. (so. dist.) Ohio 1983, Fla. 1992, U.S. Dist. Ct. (mid. dist.) Fla. 1992. Chief pharmacist Louisa (Ky.) Community Hosp., 1978; pharmacist Riverside Meth. Hosp., Columbus, 1978-82; law clk. Michael F. Colley Co., L.P.A., Columbus, 1980-82, assoc., 1982-87; asst. prof. law U. Louisville Sch. Law, 1987-91, assoc. prof. law, 1991-92; assoc. Wilkes & McHugh, Attys. at Law, Tampa, 1992—; workshop leader Ohio Drug Studies Inst., Columbus, 1982, 83, 14th Nat. Conf. on Women and the Law, Washington, D.C., 1983, 15th Nat. Conf., 1985; lectr./speaker Iowa Trial Lawyers Assn., Iowa City, 1984; speaker Nat. Assn. for Rights Protection and Advocacy Systems, Nat. Conf., Boston, 1986; lectr. legal writing Coll. Law Ohio State U., 1986; mem. aids edn. task force, subcom. on legal ethical issues U. Louisville, 1988—; speaker Nat. conf. Nat. Assn. Protection and Advocacy Systems, Washington, 1988, 16th Internat. Congress on Law and Mental Health, Toronto, 1990, Am. Pharm. Assn./Am. Soc. Pharmacy Law ann. meeting, New Orleans, 1991; cons. Ohio Legal Rights Svc., 1985—, Mich. Protection and Advocacy Svc., Lansing, 1988—, Advocacy Inc., Austin, Tex., 1989—. Staff writer, editor Ohio State U. Law Jour., 1980-82; contbr. articles to profl. jours. Trustee Women's Outreach for Women, Columbus, 1982-85, Amethyst, Inc., 1985-87; incorporator, treas. Columbus Career Women Inc., 1986-87. Fellow Am. Soc. Pharmacy Law (speaker ann. mtg. New Orleans 1991); mem. ABA, Assn. Trial Lawyers Am. (lectr., speaker 1982—), Acad. Fla. Trial Lawyers, Order of Coif, Phi Beta Kappa, Rho Chi Soc. Democrat.

BLACKBURN, JOHN GILMER, lawyer; b. Opelika, Ala., Oct. 21, 1927; s. John A. and Vera (Isley) B.; m. Phyllis Blackburn, May 12, 1951; children: Gay Blackburn Maloney, Allison Blackburn Akins, Lisa Blackburn Ayerst. BS in Acctg., Auburn U., 1950; JD, U. Ala., 1954; LLM in Taxation, NYU, 1956. Bar: Ala. 1954. Sole practice Decatur, Ala., 1955-79; ptnr. Blackburn, Maloney & Schuppert, P.C., Decatur, 1979—; lectr. various tax seminars. Mayor, City of Decatur, 1962-68; mem. exec. com. Ala. Dems.; chmn. Auburn U. Found.; chmn. Ala. Rev. Com. on Higher Edn. With U.S. Army, 1946-47, to 1st lt., 1951-52, ETO. Mem. ABA (com. on life ins., cos. sect. taxation), Ala. Bar Assn. (chmn. tax sect.). Methodist. Lodge: Kiwanis. Office: PO Box 1469 Decatur AL 35602-1469

BLACKBURN, ROGER LLOYD, lawyer; b. Mobile, Ala., Mar. 18, 1946; s. Rogers Hammock and Louise (Megahee) B.; m. Linda McNulty, Mar. 28, 1969. BA, U. Fla., 1968, JD, 1971. Bar: Fla. 1971, U.S. Dist. Ct. (so. dist.) Fla. 1972, U.S. Tax Ct. 1979. Ptnr. Blackwell, Walker & Gray, Miami, Fla., 1971-76, Leesfield & Blackburn, P.A., Miami, 1976-92; pvt. practice Miami, 1992—. Mem. ATLA, Fla. Bar Assn., Dade County Bar Assn. (bd. dirs. 1974-86), Acad. Fla. Trial Lawyers (bd. dirs. 1985-91, exec. com. 1989-91), Dade County Trial Lawyers Assn. (pres. 1985-86), Am. Bd. Trial Advocates (pres. Miami chpt. 1991-92, nat. bd. dirs., chmn. seminar com., diplomate), U. Fla. Law Ctr. Assn. (trustee 1986-95, trustee emeritus 1995—), U. Fla. Coll. Law Alumni Coun. (pres. 1984), Fla. Acad. Cert. Mediators, Fla. Blue Key. Democrat. Office: 6450 SW 100th St Miami FL 33156-3352

BLACKBURN, SADIE GWIN ALLEN, executive; b. San Angelo, Tex., Oct. 14, 1924; d. Harvey Hicks Allen and Helen (Harris) Weaver; m. Edward Albert Blackburn Jr., Feb. 25, 1946; children: Edward III, Catherine Ledyard, Robert Allen. BA, Rice U., 1945, MA, 1975. Bookkeeper, trust dept. State Nat. Bank, Houston; tchr. elem. sch. Galveston, Tex.; mng. ptnr. Storey Creek Partnership, Houston, 1989—; spl. projects dir. San Jacin; dir. master plan State Historial Park; lectr. in landscape design history. Co-author: Houston's Forgotten Heritage, 1822-1914, 1991; contbr. articles to gardening publs. Newsheet chmn. Jr. League, Galveston, 1950-53, art chmn., Houston Jr. League, 1957-58, mental health study com., 1959-61, 2d v.p., 1962-63, provisional chmn., 1962-63, interview chmn., 1963-64; adv. bd. Bayou Bend Gardens chmn. Mus. Fine Arts, 1973-74, Bayou Bend adv. com., 1987-89; v.p. Mental HEalth Assn., 1957-62; asst. treas. Child Guidance Assn., 1962-65; mem. Rice U. Hist. Commn., 1974-75. Recipient Sweet Briar Disting. Alumna award, 1991. Mem. Garden Club Am. (zone chmn. 1977-79, founders fund vice chmn. 1979-80, dir. 1980-82, rec. sec. 1982-84, v.p. 1984-86, archive co-chmn. 1986-87, 1st v.p. 1987-89, pres. 1989-91), Nat. Wildflower Rsch. Ctr., Nat. Parks and Conservation Assn., San Jacinto Mus. History (pres. bd. 1975-77). Republican. Epsicopalian.

BLACKBURN, TRACI MICHELLE, public relations assistant; b. Grand Island, Nebr., Nov. 21, 1969; d. James Robert and Norma Jean (Weinrich) B. Student, U. So. Miss., 1988-90; BA in Comm., U. Tulsa, 1992; M in Pub. Rels., U. So. Miss., 1995. Pub. affairs asst. Martin Marietta Manned Space Sys., New Orleans, 1991; pub. rels. asst. YMCA of Greater Tulsa, Okla., 1992; pub. affairs asst. Naval Oceanographic Office, Stennis Space Center, Miss., 1993—. Mem. Pub. Rels. Soc. Am. (assoc.), Pub. Rels. Student Soc. Am., Alpha Delta Pi (model pledge 1989). Lutheran. Home: 242 N Military Rd Slidell LA 70461

BLACKBURN, VICKIE CARLEE, vocational rehabilitation counselor; b. Hazard, Ky., Jan. 11, 1951; d. Moscoe James and Wynona Rose (Hawkins) B.; divorced; 1 child, Kelly Carlee Turner. BA, U. Ky., 1974, MA, 1976, Rank I in Learning Behavior Disorders, 1978. Tchr. spl. edn. Fayette County, Lexington, Ky., 1976-84; legal cons. Office of Exceptional Children, Frankfort, Ky., 1984-85, accreditation counselor, 1985-89; cons. Vocat. Rehab., Lexington, 1989—. Vol. Greater Lexington Conv. and Visitor's Bureau, 1989—, Lexington Host. Com., 1989—; mem. fund raising com. Am. Cancer Soc., 1989-91, Leukemia Soc., 1990-91, Lexington Children's Mus., 1991-92; bd. dirs. Lexington Child Abuse Coun., 1992—, chmn. fundraiser, 1992-93; bd. dirs. Ctrl. Ky. Women's Ctr., 1993-96, chmn. fundraiser, 1993-94; mem. pub. rels. bd. DISMAS Charities, Inc. 1992—; mem. publicity com. United Way Blue Grass Spl. Events, 1994; mem. domestic prevention com. Lexington Fayette Co. Gov., 1994; mem. Lexington Jr. League, 1994. Mem. Nat. Rehab. Assn., S.E. Region Nat. Rehab. Assn. (exhibitor com., publicity com., decoration com.), Ky. Rehab. Assn. (co-chair exhibitor com. 1993), Greater Lexington C. of C. (apple laison, ambassador program, athletic/bus. coun., mktg., promotion and advt. com., participant study on ctrl. adminstrn. Fayette County Bd. of Edn.). Office: Ky Workforce Devel Cabinet Vocat Rehab 627 W 4th St Lexington KY 40508-1207

BLACKLOCK, JERRY BOB, neurosurgeon; b. Wichita Falls, Tex., Oct. 30, 1951; s. Winston Lee and Flora Belle (Sims) B.; m. Helen Elizabeth Yerger, Jan. 3, 1974; children: Elaine, Caroline. BS, U. Ala., Tuscaloosa, 1974; MD, U. Miss., Jackson, 1979. Diplomate Am. Bd. Neurol. Surgery. Resident in neurosurgery U. Minn., Mpls., 1980-84; fellow NIH, Bethesda, Md., 1985; neurosurgeon M.D. Anderson Cancer Ctr., Houston, 1985-89; assoc. prof. Baylor Coll. of Medicine, Houston, 1989—. Author: (novel) After Thought, 1992; contbr. articles to profl. jours. Fellow ACS, Tex. Surg. Soc.; mem. Am. Assn. Neurol. Surgeons, Congress of Neurol. Surgeons, M.D. Anderson Assocs., Tex. Med. Assn. Office: Baylor Coll Medicine Dept Neurosurgery 6560 Fannin St Ste 944 Houston TX 77030-2706

BLACKMAN, JAMES TIMOTHY, automobile dealer; b. Lakeland, Fla., Dec. 10, 1951; s. James Ogden and Bernice (Green) B.; m. Martile Rebecca Sudduth, Feb. 5, 1983; children: Brittany Rebecca, Brooke Lansing, Molly Bernice, James Timothy Jr., Alexandra Elise. Student, U. Fla., 1969-71. Pres. Jim Blackman Ford, Sebring, Fla., 1972—, Sebring Leasing & Rent-A-Car, Inc., 1976—, Bros. Two Developers, Inc., Sebring, 1979—; pres. Capt. D's Seafood of Highlands and Okeechobee Counties., Shoney's of Highlands, Okeechobee & Hendry Counties. Crusade chmn. Am. Cancer Soc., Highland County, Fla., 1986—, pres. 1988—; chmn. Com. of 100, Sebring, 1977-78; co-chmn. Sebring C. of C., 1975-78; bd. dirs. Sebring Airport Authority, 1986—, chmn., 1988; bd. deacons 1st Presbyn. Ch., 1976—, past chmn. Mem. Fla. Automobile Dealers Assn. (bd. dirs. 1984-88). Democrat. Presbyterian. Lodge: Kiwanis (local pres. 1977-78). Home: 2808 Sunrise Dr Sebring FL 33872-2024 Office: Jim Blackman Ford Inc PO Box 433 3201 Us Highway 27 S Sebring FL 33870-5438

BLACKMON, MICHAEL EUGENE, minister; b. Camden, S.C., Sept. 26, 1951; s. Irvin Eugene and Betty Imogene (Ogburn) B.; m. Carol Ann Hamrick, June 28, 1980; 1 child, Daniel. AA, U. S.C., Lancaster, 1971; MEd, U. S.C., Columbia, 1994; BA, Furman U., 1973; MDiv, Southeastern Bapt. Sem., 1980. Cert. tchr., S.C. Youth min. Heath Springs (S.C.) Bapt. Ch., 1973; tchr. Lancaster Sch. Dist., 1973-76, coach, 1973-76; pastor Sandy Springs Bapt. Ch., Pelzer, S.C., 1980—. Mem. Lions (chaplain Piedmont club 1989-90, 3d v.p. 1996-97). Home: 371 Sandy Springs Rd Pelzer SC 29669 Office: Sandy Springs Bapt Ch 100 Snow Rd Pelzer SC 29669

BLACKMON, SUE ELLEN, journalism educator, publications adviser; b. Houston, July 18, 1955; d. Edward Carlton and Dorothy Ellen (Huffman) Hearon; m. Leslie Stephen Blackmon, Aug. 27, 1977; children: Shelbi Marie, Clinton Edward. BA in Tchg., Sam Houston State U., Huntsville, Tex., 1976. Cert. tchr., cert. journalism educator, Tex. Office asst. Sakowitz, Houston, 1976-77; tchr./adviser Cypress Fairbanks I.S.D., Houston, 1978-82, Channelview (Tex.) I.S.D., 1984-88, Klein I.S.D., Houston, 1988—; Workshop instr. Taylor Pub. Co., Houston, 1995—; yearbook/newspaper judge; conv. speaker. Author booklets. Mem. Journalism Edn. Assn., Assn. Tex. Photography Instrs., Tex. Assn. Journalism Educators, Nat. Scholastic Press Assn. (award of disting. merit 1994, 95), Interscholastic League Press Conf., Columbia Scholastic Press Advisers Assn., Tex. H.S. Press Assn. (State Champion Yearbook 1994). Baptist. Home: 14214 Cypress Green Cypress TX 77429 Office: Klein Forest HS 11400 Misty Valley Houston TX 77070

BLACKMON, WILLIE EDWARD BONEY, lawyer; b. Houston, Apr. 16, 1951; s. A.L. and Florence (Joseph) B. BBA in Mktg., Tex. A&M U., 1973; JD, Tex. Southern U., 1982. Bar: Nebr. 1984, Mich. 1985, U.S. Dist. Ct. (ea. dist.) Mich., 1984, U.S. Ct. Mil. Appeals 1984, U.S. Supreme Ct. 1987, Tex. 1989, U.S. Dist. Ct. (no. dist.) Tex. 1990, U.S. Dist. Ct. (so. dist.) Tex. 1993. Terr. sales mgr. Gillette Co., 1977-79; sales and mktg. coord. Drilco divsn. Smith Internat., 1973-77; legal intern Gulf Coast Legal Found., Houston, 1982; intern/ind. counsel City of Detroit, 1982-84; judge advocate USAF, Ellsworth AFB, Offutt AFB, S.D., 1984-89, USAFR, Reese AFB, Randolph AFB, Tex., 1989-94; dep. staff judge advocate Tex. Air N.G., Ellington Field, Tex., 1994—; sales agt. Destiny Telecom Internat. Inc., 1996—; asst. criminal dist. atty., Lubbock County, Tex., 1990-91; asst. criminal dist. atty., Harris County, Tex., 1991-92; pvt. practice, Houston, 1992—; assoc. mcpl. judge City of Houston, 1995—; admissions liaison officer USAF Acad., 1990—. Mem. Tex. Coalition Black Dems. Named to Tex. A&M U. Athletic Hall of Fame, 1994. Mem. ABA, State Bar Tex., Nebr. Bar Assn., State Bar Mich., Nat. Bar Assn., Tex. assn. African Am. Lawyers, Houston Lawyers Assn. (bd. dirs.), Mexican-Am. Bar Assn., Houston Bar Assn., Tex. Coalition Black Dems., Aggie Officers Assn., NAACP, Masons. Methodist. Office: 2715 Bissonnet St Ste 108 Houston TX 77005-1318

BLACKMORE, JAMES HERRALL, clergyman, educator, author; b. Warsaw, N.C., Feb. 15, 1916; s. Willie Richard and Martha Janie (Sansbury) B.; m. Ruth May Lillick, Jan. 26, 1945; children: Julia, John. BA cum laude, Wake Forest Coll., 1937; BD, Colgate Rochester Div. Sch., 1940; postgrad., Duke U., 1940-41, U. Iowa, 1949; PhD, U. Edinburgh, 1951. Ordained to ministry Bapt. Ch., 1940. Dir. religious edn. Parsells Ave. Bapt. ch., Rochester, N.Y., 1938-40; pastor King (N.C.) Bapt. Ch., 1941-43, Masonboro Bapt. ch., Wilmington, N.C., 1947-49, First Bapt. Ch., Spring Hope, N.C., 1951-61; dir. pub. rels. Southeastern Bapt. Theol. Sem., Wake Forest, N.C., 1963-69, dir. publs., spl. instr., 1969-83, prof. assoc. div. studies, 1983-84; editor Outlook, 1963-84; vis. prof. Southeastern Bapt. Theol. Sem., 1985-96. Author: The Cullom Lantern, A Biography of W.R. Cullom, 1963, A Preacher's Temptations, 1966, A reticule, A Collection of Short Stories and Essays, 1969, Sermons of Warsaw, 1975, Conversations About Jesus, 1977, The Wayfarer, 1977, Sermons at Masonboro, 1978, Biblical Orientation, 1981, Sermons at Spring Hope, 1983, The A.C. Reid Legacy, 1988, Reflections of the Temptations of Christ, 1992, others; contbr. articles to religious and learned jours., also to encys. Pres. Wilmington Ministerial Conf., 1948-49; moderator Tar River Bapt. Assn., 1960-61; sec. bd. dirs. Bibl. Recorder, 1959-62; chmn. hist. com. Bapt. State Conv., N.C., 1970-72. Served to maj. chaplain AUS, 1943-46. Mem. Bapt. Pub. Rels. Assn., Lions, Kappa Delta Alpha, Chi Eta Tau. Home: 209 S Wingate St Wake Forest NC 27587

BLACKSTOCK, LINDA MAHONEY, healthcare facility official, consultant; b. Port Arthur, Tex., May 31, 1947; d. Paul G. and Maurine A. (Farmer) Mahoney; m. Arlin L. Blackstock, Jan. 20, 1979. Student, San Antonio Coll., 1965-69, Incarnate Word Coll., 1974-75, Schreiner Coll.; BS, teaching cert., S.W. Tex. State U., 1971, MS in Health Professions in Health Adminstrn. and Rsch., 1992. Lic. dietitian, Tex. Hosp. dept. dir. Sid Peterson Hosp., Kerrville, Tex., 1978-85; cons. Kerrville Kidney Dialysis, 1982-83, Kimble Hosp., Junction, Tex., 1986-94, Comfort (Tex.) Garden Home, 1990-93, La Hacienda Drug Alcohol Treatment Ctr., Hunt, Tex., 1992—; performance improvement program specialist VA Med. Ctr., Kerrville, 1992—; leader seminar for healthcare profls. Kerrville Kidney Disease and Dialysis Ctr., spring 1983. Speaker seminar Kerrville chpt. Am. Cancer Soc., 1984. Recipient Acad. Excellence award Sch. Health Professions, S.W. Tex. State U., 1989, 90, 92. Mem. Am. Coll. Healthcare Execs., Am. Dietetic Assn. (registered), Tex. Dietetic Assn., Tex. Hosp. Assn., Tex. Soc. for Healthcare Quality, Phi Upsilon Omicron. Baptist.

BLACKWELL, BRUCE BEUFORD, lawyer; b. Gainesville, Fla., July 23, 1946; s. Benjamin Beuford and Doris Juanita (Heagy) B.; m. Julie McMillan, July 12, 1969; children: Blair Allison, Brooke McMillan. BA, Fla. State U., 1968, JD with honors, 1974. Bar: Fla. 1975, Ga. 1977, U.S. Supreme Ct. 1979, N.Y. 1980. Atty. So. Bell Tel. & Telegraph Co., Charlotte, N.C., 1975-76, Atlanta, 1976-78; antitrust atty. AT&T, Orlando and N.Y.C., 1978-80; atty. Sun Banks, Inc., Orlando, Fla., 1980; assoc. Peed & King, P.A., Orlando, 1980-84; shareholder King & Blackwell, P.A., Orlando, 1984—. Bd. dirs. Legal Aid Soc., Orlando, 1986-88; chmn. Winter Park (Fla.) Civil Svc. Bd., 1992-94; trustee Fla. State U. Found., 1985-86. Capt. USAF, 1968-72. Recipient award of excellence Legal Aid Soc., 1993, Judge J.C. Stone Pro Bono Disting. Svc. award, 1996. Mem. Fla. Bar (chmn. 9th cir. grievance com. 1985-87, chmn. mid-yr. meeting 1986, chmn. 9th cir. free arbitration com. 1992-94, bd. govs. 1994—, vice chair statewide disciplinary rev. com., access to cts. com. 1996-97, Pres.'s award for pro bono svc. 1996), Orange County Bar Assn. (exec. coun. 1983-86, pres. 1987-88), Fla. State U. Alumni Assn. (nat. pres. 1985-86), Orlando Touchdown Club (pres. 1996-97), Omicron Delta Kappa. Democrat. Presbyterian. Home: 1624 Roundelay Ln Winter Park FL 32789-4042 Office: PO Box 1631 Orlando FL 32802-1631

BLACKWELL, CECIL, science association executive; b. Enterprise, Miss., Oct. 29, 1924; s. George Dewey and Neely (Baggett) B.; m. Louise McLendon, May 27, 1944; children—Cecil Carl, Donna Lynn, Gregory Dale. B.S., Miss. State U., 1951; M.S., U. Md., 1955; postgrad., U. Ark., 1953-54. Asst. horticulturist Truck Crops Br. Expt. Sta., Crystal Springs, Miss., 1951; research asst. U. Md., College Park, 1951-52; instr., jr. horticulturist U. Ark., 1952-54; extension horticulturist U. Ga., 1954-56, head extension hort. dept., 1956-59; hort. editor Progressive Farmer, Birmingham, Ala., 1959-65; exec. dir. Am. Soc. Hort. Sci.; pub. Jour. Am. Soc. Hort. Sci., HortScience, St. Joseph, Mich., 1965-74, Mt. Vernon, Va., 1974-79, Alexandria, Va., 1979-88; exec. dir. emeritus Am. Soc. Hort. Sci., 1989—; cons., writer, 1989—. Author: (with L.A. Niven) Garden Book for the South, 1961. Served with USAAF, 1944-46. Decorated Air medal.; Gen. Edn. Bd. fellow Rockefeller Found., 1951-52. Fellow Am. Soc. Hort. Sci.; mem. AAAS, Internat. Soc. Hort Sci., Am. Inst. Biol. Scis., Royal Hort. Soc. (hon.), Alpha Zeta. Mem. Ch. of God. Address: 300 County Rd 475 Meridian MS 39301-8729

BLACKWELL, CHADWICK CARTER, elementary education educator; b. Fairfax, Va., Apr. 11, 1968; s. William Atwell and Patricia Anne (Keel) B. BS, James Madison U., 1991, MEd, 1993. Cert. tchr. grades 4-8. Sailing instr. Soundside Water Sports, Nags Head, N.C., 1990; health/athletic trainer Valley Wellness Ctr., Harrisonburg, Va., 1990-93; tchr. 5th grade Rocking County Sch., Harrisonburg, 1993—; mem. social studies curriculum leadership team Rockingham County Schs., Harrisonburg, 1993—; com. chairperson Sci./Tech. Team, Elkton, Va., 1993—; liaison Merck and Co./ Elkton Elem., 1993—. Inventor Earth Windows, 1994. Vol. trail crew Alaska State Pks., Juneau, 1994; advisor Student Theater Group, Elkton, 1994. Nationally ranked triathlete, 3d pl. Nat. Spring Triathlon, Florida Keys, 1992. Home: Rte 1 Box 804 Port Republic VA 24471

BLACKWELL, JOHN ADRIAN, JR., computer company executive; b. Tulsa, Aug. 1, 1940; s. John Adrian and Daisy Edith (Webb) B. MusB, Westminster Choir Coll., 1962, MusM, 1963. Minister of music 1st Presbyn. Ch., Warren, Ohio, 1963-68, Oklahoma City, 1968-79; artistic dir. Okla. Choral Assn., Oklahoma City, 1980-82; pres. Okla. Digital Technologies Inc., Oklahoma City, 1987-92; ptnr. JJ Enterprises (now Megabyn Assocs., Inc.); pres., co-owner JJ Enterprises (now Megabyn Assocs., Inc.), Oklahoma City, 1992—; program mgr. S. Systems Corp., Oklahoma City, 1995—; cons. Union Oil Co. Calif., Oklahoma City, 1989—; conductor Warren (Ohio) Symphony Orch., 1965-68; choral dir. NBC-TV Stars & Stripes Shows, Oklahoma City, 1975-76. Commd. ch. worker Presbyn. Ch. in the U.S.A., 1965. Recipient Paul Harris award Rotary Found., 1993. Mem. Rotary Internat. Home: 2413 NW 112th Ter Oklahoma City OK 73120-7202 Office: Megabyn Assocs 2413 NW 112th Ter Oklahoma City OK 73120

BLAEMIRE, ROBERT AARON, computer services executive; b. Hammond, Ind., Apr. 21, 1949; s. Robert Chester and Donna Mae (Chase) B.; m. Joanna Frances Caplan, Sept. 20, 1981; children: Nicholas Caplan Blaemire, Daniel Caplan Blaemire. BA, George Washington U., 1971, MA, 1975. Spl. asst. U.S. Senator Birch Bayh, Washington, 1967-81; pres. Commn. for Am. Principles, Washington, 1981; mktg. agt. Datatron, Washington, 1982; v.p. Below, Tobe & Assoc., Bethesda, Md., 1983-91; pres. Blaemire Comm., Reston, Va., 1991—. Contbr. articles to profl. jours. Democrat. Office: Blaemire Comm 1807 Michael Faraday Ct Reston VA 22090-5303

BLAIN, RICHARD EUGENE, JR., manufacturing engineer; b. Borger, Tex., Nov. 28, 1956; s. Richard Eugene Sr. and Sarah Ann (Pierce) B.; m. Brenda Diane Terrell Donaldson, Feb. 24, 1989 (div. Jan. 1993); 1 child, Richard Eugene III. Grad., Pampa (Tex.) High Sch., 1975. Cert. mfg. engr. Various duties Panhandle Indsl. Co., Pampa, 1972-74, various manual machines operator, 1974-79, CNC lathe operator, 1979-81, CNC machine ctr. operator/programmer, 1981-84, axix CNC machine ctr., operator/programmer/trainer, 1984-94; operator/programmer/trainer Crouse-Hinds Co. divsn. Cooper Industries, Amarillo, Tex., 1994—. Mem. Soc. Mfg. Engrs. (chmn. 1991-92), Pampa Masonic Lodge. Home: 3631 Brennan Blvd #13A Amarillo TX 79121-1647 Office: Crouse-Hinds Co Divsn Cooper Industries 1901 Farmer Ave Rt 5 Box 6 Amarillo TX 79118-6102

BLAIR, ELEANOR MARIE, artist, educator; b. Trenton, N.J., June 7, 1947; d. Hugh McGill and Eleanor Emma (Buckley) B.; m. Doran Michael Oster (div. 1983); children: Isaac, Daniel. BFA, Cooper Union, 1969. Artist, 1971—; art tchr. Alachua County Bd. of Edn., Gainesville, Fla., 1994—. Artist numerous posters 1982-91; represented in permanent collections in Mus. of Arts Sci., Daytona, Polk County Mus. of Art, Lakeland, Fla. Lectr. Harn Mus., Gainesville, 1993-94, Mus. Arts and Scis., Daytona, 1991. Recipient Vol. Artist of Yr. award City of Gainesville, 1991, Downtown Redevelopment award City of Gainesville, 92, Outstanding Creative Accomplishment award Nat. League of Am. Pen Women, 95. Episcopalian. Office: Eleanor Blair Studio 113 S Main St Gainesville FL 32601-6214

BLAIR, MARIE LENORE, retired elementary school educator; b. Maramec, Okla., Jan. 9, 1931; d. Virgil Clement and Ella Catherine (Leen) Strode; m. Freeman Joe Blair, Aug. 26, 1950; children: Elizabeth Ann Blair Crump, Roger Joe. BS, Okla. A&M Coll., 1956; MS, Okla. State U., 1961, postgrad., 1965-68. Reading specialist Pub. Schs. Stillwater (Okla.), 1966-88. Past bd. dirs. Okla. Reading Council. Mem. Internat., Okla., Cimarron (past pres.) reading assns., NEA, Okla. Edn. Assn., Stillwater Edn. Assn., Kappa Kappa Iota. Democrat. Mem. Disciples of Christ. Lodges: Demoley Mothers, Rainbow Mothers, Lahoma, White Shrine Jerusalem (past worthy high priestess). Order White Shrine Jerusalem (past supreme queen's attendant), Internat. Order of Rainbow for Girls (Okla. exec. com.), Order Eastern Star (past grand Martha, past grand rep. of Nebr. in Okla.). Home: RR 1 Maramec OK 74045-9801

BLAIR, RICHARD EUGENE, lawyer; b. Loudon, Tenn., Mar. 7, 1923; s. John Thomas and Minnie Laura (Jones) B.; m. Marjorie Ann Bechtel, Apr. 17, 1954; children: Catherine Elizabeth, Marilynne B. BA, U. Wash., 1948; JD, Georgetown U., 1956; LLM, So. Meth. U., 1962. Bar: Va. 1956, U.S. Supreme Ct. 1962, U.S. Dist. Ct. (ea. dist.) Va. 1972, U.S. Ct. Appeals (4th cir.) 1981. Commd. ensign, U.S. Navy, 1944, advanced through grades to capt., 1967, ret., 1972; sole practice, Fairfax, Va., 1972-79, Mc Lean, Va., 1979-82; of counsel Harrison, Golden & Hughes, P.C., Mc Lean, 1982-86; dir. Mc Lean Savs. & Loan Assn., 1977-88, gen. counsel, 1975-82; dir. McLean Fin. Corp., 1982-87; chmn. bd. dirs. Unifed Land Title Co., 1986-87; adj. prof. oil and gas law Georgetown U., 1962-75; vis. prof. Duke U. Law Sch., 1964-68. Contbr. articles to profl. jours. Recipient Navy Lawyer award Navy League U.S., 1961. Mem. Va. Bar Assn., Fairfax County Bar Assn., Va. Trial Lawyers Assn., Georgetown U. Law Sch. Alumni Assn. Republican. Presbyterian. Office: 1005 Galium Ct Mc Lean VA 22102-1106

BLAIR, RUTH REBA, government official; b. New Orleans, Aug. 21, 1934; d. Joseph Aloysius and Ruth (Labostrie) Porter; m. William Jennings Blair, Sept. 22, 1961; children: Joseph Vernon, Constance Eileen. AS in Bus. Adminstrn., Loyola U., New Orleans, 1980; BA in English, U. New Orleans, 1984; masters cert. in govt. contracting, George Washington U., 1992. Cert. assoc. contracts mgr.; cert. mem. fed. acquisition corps. Various positions Michoud Assembly Facility, New Orleans, 1964-84; contract specialist NASA, Marshall Space Flight Ctr, Ala., 1985-86; contracting officer USCG, New Orleans, 1986-87; contract adminstr. (supercomputers) Naval Rsch. Lab., Stennis Space Ctr., Miss., 1987—. author, adminstr. Primary Oceanographic Prediction System contract for Navy's Large Scale Computer Supercomputer System. Recipient Special Act award Naval Rsch. Lab., 1994. Mem. ABA (assoc., sects. pub. contracts law, bus. law, govt. and pub. sector lawyers div.), AAUW, Federally Employed Women. Home: 5815 Franklin Ave New Orleans LA 70122-6405 Office: Naval Rsch Lab S Contracts Office Code 3250/RPB Stennis Space Center MS 39529

BLAIR, SLOAN BLACKMON, lawyer; b. Groesbeck, Tex., Nov. 3, 1929; s. Sloan and Rosamond (Blackmon) B.; m. Eleanor Cuthrell, Nov. 17, 1953; children: Deborah, Mary Emily. BA, U. Tex., 1951, LLB, 1953. Bar: Tex., U.S. Dist. Ct. (no. and we. dists.) Tex., U.S. Ct. Appeals (5th cir.), U.S. Supreme Ct. Assoc. Cantey, Hanger, Johnson, Scarborough & Gooch, Ft. Worth, 1956-58; atty. Sinclair Refining Co., Chgo., 1958-60; assoc. Cantey, Hanger et al., Ft. Worth, 1960-62; ptnr. Cantey & Hanger, Ft. Worth, 1962—. Contbr. case notes to Tex. Law Rev. Bd. dirs. Goodwill Industries Ft. Worth, 1960's; mem. Ft. Worth Arts Coun., Tex. Heritage, Inc., Ft. Worth, State Bar Grievance Com., Ft. Worth, mid. 1960's, Tex. Bd. Law Examiners, Austin, 1977-83. Lt. (j.g.) USNR, 1953-56. Fellow Tex. Bar Found.; mem. ABA, Tex. Bar Assn., Tarrant County Bar Assn. (bd. dirs. 1970's), Tex. Assn. Bank Counsel, Phi Delta Phi. Republican. Methodist. Office: Cantey & Hanger 801 Cherry St Ste 2100 Fort Worth TX 76102-6821

BLAIR, TERRI JEAN, special education teacher; b. Robert Lee, Tex., Oct. 13, 1955; d. John Wesley and Nettie Geraldine (Davis) Kinsey; m. Joe Dee Blair, Jan. 26, 1974; children: Mandy Jo, Cody Joe, Garrett Wade. BS in Interdisciplinary Studies, Abilene Christian U., 1993. Dental asst. Office of Dr. Robert W. Hampton, Sweetwater, Tex., 1974-76; outpatient clk. Rolling Plains Meml. Hosp., Sweetwater, 1976-77; store mgr. Charlie's Angels Children's Wear, Sweetwater, 1977-80; elem. tchr. Blackwell County Ind. Sch. Dist., Blackwell, Tex., 1993-95, spl. edn. tchr., 1996—; coach elem. oral reading Univ. Iinterscholastic League, Blackwell, 1993—. Adult literacy educator College Heights Elem. Sch., Abilene (Tex.) Christian U., 1993; active PTO, Blackwell, 1996, FFA Booster Club, Blackwell, 1993—; parent supporter 4-H—Taylor County Horse Club, 1994—. Mem. Kappa Delta Pi. Democrat. Mem. Ch. of Christ. Home: 918 County Rd 198 Nolan TX 79537-1508

BLAISDELL, RUSSELL CARTER, minister, religious organization administrator; b. Chgo., Oct. 19, 1936; s. Russell Lloyd and Viola Evelyn (Hagen) B.; m. Anita Fay Cone, Jan. 4, 1964; children: David Scott, Valerie Ruth, Sarah Jane, John Milton. BA, U. Calif., Berkeley, 1959; MDiv, McCormick Theol. Sem., 1965. Ordained to ministry Presbyn. Ch. (U.S.A.), 1965. Pastor Community Presbyn Ch., Lawton, Iowa, 1965-73, 1st United Presbyn. Ch., Portage, Wis., 1973-79; assoc. dir. Presbyn. and Reformed Renewal Ministries Internat., Oklahoma City, 1979-91; assoc. gen. sec., assoc. dir. Presbyn. and Reformed Renewal Ministries Internat., Black Mountain, N.C., 1991—; chmn. Christian edn., N.W. Iowa Presbytery, Storm Lake, 1969-73; commr. 191st Gen. Assembly, United Presbyn. Ch. U.S.A., 1979; internat. dir. Spirit Alive and Alice in Christ for Congl. Renewal, 1990—; chmn. Congl. Devel. and Revitalization, Indian Nations Presbytery, Oklahoma City, 1985-87. Editor Renewal News, 1983-92; actor, singer Portage Players, 1974; organizer, singer, bd. dirs. Portage Ecumenical Chorus, 1974-79. 1st lt. USAF, 1959-62. Calif. Alumni scholar, 1954-55; Rotary scholar, 1954-57. Mem. Presbytery We. N.C., Kiwanis (bd. dirs. 1976-79). Republican. Office: Presbyn and Reformed Renewal Ministries Internat PO Box 429 Black Mountain NC 28711-0429

BLAISING, CRAIG ALAN, religious studies educator; b. San Antonio, Sept. 28, 1949; s. Claude Lawrence and Mildred Helen (Craig) B.; m. Diane Sue Garrison, May 31, 1975; children: Emily Grace, Jonathan Craig. BS, U. Tex., 1971; ThM, Dallas Theol. Sem., 1976, ThD, 1979; PhD, U. Aberdeen, Scotland, 1988. Lic. to ministry So. Bapt. Conv., 1972. Adj. prof. dept. religion U. Tex., Arlington, 1978; asst. prof. systematic theology Dallas Theol. Sem., 1980-85, assoc. prof., 1985-89, acting dept. chmn., 1988-89, prof., 1989-95; prof. So. Bapt. Theol. Sem., 1995—. Co-author: Progressive Dispensationalism, 1993; co-editor: Dispensationalism, Israel and the Church: The Search for Definition, 1992; contbr.: Bible Knowledge Commentary, 1985, Evangelical Dictionary of Theology, 1985, Handbook of Evangelical Theology, 1993; contbr. articles to religious jours. Rotary Found. fellow U. Aberdeen, 1978-79. Mem. AAAS, Am. Soc. Ch. History, Evang. Theol. Soc. (regional pres. 1986-87), Dispensational Study Group (pres. 1988-90), Am. Acad. Religion, Soc. Bibl. Lit., N.Am. Patristic Soc., Soc. for Study of Ea. Orthodoxy and Evangelicism, Tau Beta Pi. Office: So Bapt Theol Sem 2825 Lexington Rd Louisville KY 40280-0001

BLAKE, CHARLES HENRY, II, political science educator; b. St. Petersburg, Fla., Dec. 25, 1962; s. Charles Henry and Georgia Faye (Thomas) B.; m. Yolanda Elena Fernandez, June 27, 1992. AB magna cum laude, Davidson Coll., 1985; MA, Duke U., 1988, PhD, 1992. Instr. polit. sci. Duke U., Durham, N.C., 1987-92; asst. prof. James Madison U., Harrisonburg, Va., 1992—. Fulbright grantee, 1989-90, Tinker Found. grantee, 1988. Mem. Am. Polit. Sci. Assn., Latin Am. Studies Assn., Phi Beta Kappa. Office: James Madison U Dept Polit Sci Harrisonburg VA 22807

BLAKE, EDWARD LEONARD, JR., landscape architect; b. Bryn Mawr, Pa., Jan. 26, 1947; s. Edward Leonard Sr. and Charlotte (Claypoole) B.; m. Marilyn Moore (div. 1976); 1 child, Mathew; m. Marilyn Johnson; children: Matthew Moore, Benjamin. B Landscape Architecture, Miss. State U., 1970. Landscape architect Miller, Winry & Brooks, Louisville, 1970-73, Jack DeBoer Assocs., Wichita, Kans., 1974, Oblinger Smith Corp., Wichita, 1974-77, Sun House, Starkville, Miss., 1979-84; prof. landscape architecture Miss. State U., Starkville, 1977-84; dir. Crosby Arboretum, Picayune, Miss., 1984-94; vis. design critic grad. sch. design Harvard U., 1994. Author: Master Plan for Pinecote for Crosby Arboretum, 1994. Bd. dirs. Hattiesburg (Miss.) Civic Arts Coun., 1986-88; mem. Hattiesburg Tree Bd., 1993—. With USAR, 1970-75. Named Outstanding Alumnus of Landscape Archtl. dept. Miss. State U., 1990. Mem. Am. Soc. Landscape Architecture (Merit award 1977, 89, Honor award 1991). Home: 203 Williams St Hattiesburg MS 39401-2404

BLAKEMAN, CAROL ANN, medical/surgical nursing educator; b. Jacksonville, Fla., Aug. 17, 1954; d. John Raymond and Marion Alice (Lasher) B.; m. Key Miller Sargent, Mar. 22, 1984. AA, Fla. Jr. Coll., Jacksonville, 1974; BSN, U. South Fla., 1976; MSN, U. Fla., 1989. Cert. advanced RN practitioner, Fla. Staff and head nurse Bapt. Med. Ctr., Jacksonville, 1976-84; staff nurse Winter Haven (Fla.) Hosp., 1984-88; instr., assoc. prof., coord. Cen. Fla. C.C., Ocala, 1988—; on-call endoscopy nurse, Jacksonville, 1982-83; instr. Polk C.C., Winter Haven, Fla., 1987; cons. Student Nurses Assn., Ctrl. Fla. C.C., Ocala, 1989—, BCLS instr., 1988-91; judge competition Health Occupation Students Am., Orlando and Ocala, 1989-95; health examiner Nat. Youth Sports Program, Orlando, 1987. Mem. ANA, Fla. Nurses Assn., Dist. III Nurses Assn. (treas. 1993, pres. 1994—), Fla. Nursing Students Assn., Sigma Theta Tau, Phi Theta Kappa. Democrat. Roman Catholic. Home: 206 SE 44th Terrace Ocala FL 34471-8300

BLAKENEY, RAE, art historian, artist, writer, arts editor; b. Topeka, Kans., May 3, 1941; d. Charles W. and Stella M. Cox; m. William Spurlock, June 4, 1976. BA, Wright State U., 1976; PhD, Union Grad. Sch., Cin., 1987. Dir. pub. info. Dayton (Ohio) Art Inst., 1976-77; contbg. editor Midwest Art, 1976-78; dir. pub. info. Bank of Montecito, Santa Barbara, Calif., 1979-80; corr. Artweek, San Francisco, 1978-82; comms. editor and lectr. Grad. Sch. Urban and Pub. Affairs, U. Tex., Arlington, 1982-92; ind. writer and editor Ft. Worth, 1992—; curator of exhbn. or 20th century art Tex. Humanities Resource Ctr., Austin, 1985—; cons. to establish La Galerie des Cloitres, City of La Rochefoucauld, France, 1993—. Author: Language of the Self, 1987, Modern French Cooking, 1981; co-author, editor exhbn. cattalog; contbr. to artist's book. Recipient Juror's award Moudy Art Gallery, Ft. Worth, 1986, others. Home: 1201 Vincent St # 107 Fort Worth TX 76120 also: 3 rue Robiniere, La Rochefoucauld France 16110

BLALOCK, CARMEN, education educator; b. Birmingham, Ala., Dec. 16, 1947; d. Van Thomas Jr. and Helen Mavis (Swann) Fountain; m. Roger Blalock, Apr. 13, 1973; 1 child, Aytree. BS, U. Ala., 1972, MA, 1972, EdD, 1984. Instr. Calhoun C.C., Decatur, Ala., 1972—. Sec., treas. Bankhead Trail Riders Assn., Cullman, Ala., 1989—; pres. SHARE Club, Cullman, 1995; editor Tale of the Trail, Cullman, 1996. Home: 466 Co Rd 349 Logan AL 35098 Office: Calhoun Cmty Coll Hwy 31 N Decatur AL 35609

BLANCHARD, LAURA, emergency room nurse, rehabilitation nurse; b. Baton Rouge, Aug. 17, 1963; d. Alfred J. and Margaret Ann (Strickland) Blanchard; children: Allison, Megan, Lindsay. RN, Baton Rouge Gen. Sch. Nursing, 1987. Cert. emergency nurse, BLS, ACLS, pediatric ALS, pre-hosp. trauma life support, Am. Heart Assn. Staff nurse emergency rm. Our Lady of the Lake Regional Med. Ctr., Baton Rouge, 1988-92; charge nurse Med. Ctr. of Baton Rouge, 1992-93, nursing house supr., 1993-94; owner Diaz and Assocs. Med. Consulting Inc., Baton Rouge, 1994—; pres., adminstr. Comprehensive Outpatient Svcs. of Baton Rouge, a Medicare Comprehensive Outpatient Rehab. Facility, 1994—. Mem. Emergency Nurses Assn. (cert. emergency nurse), Home Health Nurses Assn. Address: 2326 Dogwood Glenn Cove Germantown TN 38139 Office: Comprehensive Outpatient Svcs 1850 S Sherwood Forest Blvd Baton Rouge LA 70816

BLANCHARD, LOUIS A., medical/surgical nurse, educator; b. Chgo., Dec. 28, 1924; s. Glenkern A. and Luella (Sheehan) B.; m. Hedy H. Blanchard, Aug. 3, 1963. Diploma in Nursing, U. Ill.-Cook County Sch., Chgo., 1953; BS in Psychology and Biology, Roosevelt U., Chgo., 1964; MEd, Xavier U., Cin., 1971; BSN with honors, Fla. Internat. U., 1979. RN, Fla. Charge nurse cystoscopic surg. Mercy Hosp., 1956; supr. o.r. St. Anne's Hosp., 1955-57; staff nurse Nat. Hosp. for Nervous Disease, Queen's Square, Holborn, London, Eng., 1958-60; DON Soverign Nursing Home, Chgo., 1967; instr. Fox River Pavillion Psychiat. Hosp., Chgo., 1969-73; instr. in anatomy and med.-surg. nursing Ravenswood Med. Ctr. Sch. of Nursing, Chgo., 1969-73; pvt. duty nurse Miami, Fla., 1979-92; bd. dirs. Nurse's Ofcl. Registry, Miami, 1974-79. Donor Hedy Blanchard nursing award Fla. Internat. U., 1990. Recipient cert. of appreciation Nurse's Ofcl. Registry, 1979, Fla. Internat. U. Alumni Assn., 1982. Mem. ANA, Fla. Nurses Assn. (treas. 5th dist. 1989-90), Xavier Alumni Assn., Sigma Theta Tau, Tau Delta Phi.

BLANCHARD, MARGARET ANN, journalism educator; b. Schenectady, N.Y., Sept. 4, 1943; d. Earl Chandler and Gladys Muriel (Hickok) B. AA, Palm Beach Jr. Coll., 1963; BS in Journalism, U. Fla., 1965, MA, 1970; PhD, U. N.C., 1981. Reporter Palm Beach Post Times, West Palm Beach, Fla., 1963-65, Miami Herald, Fort Lauderdale & Miami, Fla., 1966-69; grad. asst. Office Journalism and Comm. U. Fla., Gainesville, 1969-70; asst. prof. East Carolina U., Greenville, N.C., 1970-74; lectr., instr. Sch. of Journalism U. N.C., Chapel Hill, 1974-81, assoc. prof., 1982-88, prof., 1988—, William Rand Kenan, Jr., prof., 1993; panelist and presenter in field; coord. news writing course Sch. Journalism, U. N.C., Chapel Hill, 1983, mem. grad. admissions com., 1984-88, 91—, mem. adminstrv. bd., 1982-87, chair curriculum com., 1984-86, mem. entrance requirements com., 1986-87, dir. honors program, 1984-93, coord. doctoral program, 1993-94, dir. grad. studies, 1994—. Author: The Hutchins Commission, the Press and the Responsibility Concept, 1977, Exporting the First Amendment: The Press-Government Crusade of 1945-1952, 1986, Revolutionary Sparks: Freedom of Expression in Modern America, 1992; contbr. chpts. to books and numerous articles to profl. jours. Named Disting. Alumna, Coll. Journalism and Comm., U. Fla., 1993; recipient 1st prize 1st Amendment theory competition Law Divsn. Assn. for Edn. in Journalism, 1980, Baskette Mosse award for Faculty Devel., Assn. for Edn. in Journalism and Mass Comm., 1985, Frank Luther Mott-Kappa Tau Alpha Rsch. award, 1987, William C. Lassiter 1st Amendment award N.C. Press Assn., 1996; grantee U. N.C., 1983, 87, 92, Inst. for Rsch. in Social Scis., 1992. Mem. Assn. for Edn. in Journalism and Mass Comm., Soc. Profl. Journalists, Am. Journalism Historians Assn., Orgn. Am. Historians, Am. Soc. for Legal History, Phi Kappa Phi, Kappa Tau Alpha. Home: 102 Twisted Ct Hillsborough NC 27278-9332 Office: U NC Sch Journalism and Mass Comm CB 3365 Howell Hall Chapel Hill NC 27599

BLANCHARD, RICHARD EMILE, SR., management services executive, consultant; b. Thompson, Conn., July 13, 1928; s. Lionel A. and Bernadette L. (Jolicoeur) B.; m. Lorraine Patricia Lachapelle, July 3, 1954; children: Michele Welling, Richard E., Danielle Wornstaff, Marie Blanchard Oser, Robert Allen, Janine. BS in Biology, Providence Coll., 1952; postgrad. U. Conn. Sch. Law, West Hartford, 1952-53. Cert. Mgmt. Cons. Chemist Charles Pfizer Co., Inc., N.Y.C., 1953-56, med. salesman, 1956-60, coll. rels. mgr., 1960-63, pers. mgr., 1963-67; dir. manpower and orgn. devel. Sky Chef div. Am. Airlines, N.Y.C., 1967-70; dir. manpower ARA Svcs., Inc., Phila., 1970-72; v.p., 1972-76; v.p. pers. Jerrico, Inc., Lexington, Ky., 1976-78; chmn., CEO Career Mgmt., Inc., C.M. Temporary Svcs. and C.M. Mgmt. Svcs., Lexington, 1978—; cons. pers. svcs.; bd. dirs. U. Ky. Small Bus. Devel. Ctr.; chmn. adv. bd. U. Ky. C.C., 1987—; bd. dirs. Better Bus. Bur., 1985—, Ky. Higher Edn. Coun.; div. chmn. United Way, 1990, 92—; mem. adv. bd. C.C. div. U. Ky., Muscular Dystrophy Bluegrass coun.; v.p. Bluegrass Ednl. Work Coun., 1980—, Bluegrass Better Bus. Bur., 1990—, bd. dirs., past pres.; bd. dirs. Jr. Achievement, 1979—; bd. dirs. human rights commn., vice-chmn. 1991-94; bd. dirs. Ky. Econ. Devel. Coun.; co-chmn. bd. dirs. Bluegrass MS Soc., 1969. Served with USN, 1946-48. Mem. Inst. Mgmt. Cons., Am. Mgmt. Assn., Lexington C. of C. (bd. dirs.), Ky. State C. of C. (bd. dirs.), Ind. Temporary Svcs. Assn., Am. Soc. Pers. Assocs. (past pres. N.Y. chpt.), Ky. Assocs. Temporary Svcs. (past pres.), Nat. Assn. Temporary Svcs., Lexington Country Club, Exec. Fitness and Sports Ctr., Lexington Tennis Club, Rotary (bd. dirs. 1996—). Republican. Roman Catholic. Home: 628 Tally Rd Lexington KY 40502-2727 Office: Career Mgmt Inc CM Staffing Svcs 698 Perimeter Dr Ste 200 Lexington KY 40517-4141

BLANCHARD, TOWNSEND EUGENE, service companies executive; b. Du Quoin, Ill., Jan. 30, 1931; s. Townsend and Anna Belle (Jackson) B.; m. Norma Louise Barr, Dec. 18, 1960; children: John Barr, Susan Melody, Jayne Ann Blanchard Reishus, Stephen Eugene. BS, U. Ill., 1952; MBA, Harvard U., 1957. Cons. Ill. Sch. Bond Svc., Monticello, 1958-62; co-founder, treas., chief fin. officer Americana Nursing Ctrs., Monticello, 1962-75; v.p. fin., treas., CFO, chief of staff Cenco, Inc., Chgo., 1975-79; sr. v.p., CFO, bd. dirs. DynCorp., McLean, Va., 1979—; adv. dir. Landmark Sys., Inc., 1994—. Elder Presbyn. Ch.; bd. dirs. Combined Health Appeal, 1986—; bd. advisors Cameron Glen Care Facility, 1989-92. Lt. USNR, 1952-55. Decorated Spl. Commendation letter. Mem. Fin. Execs. Inst. (chpt. pres. 1988-89, nat. v.p. and bd. dirs. 1991-94), Internat. Platform Assn., U. Ill. Alumni Club, Harvard U. Bus. Sch. Club, Harvard Club Washington, Econ. Club Chgo., Am. Legion, Delta Sigma Phi (trustee nat. found. 1982-89, pres. nat. found. 1988-89, Harvey W. Herbert award 1975, Mr. Delta Sig award 1988). Home: PO Box 5389 McLean VA 22103-5389 Office: DynCorp 2000 Edmund Halley Dr Reston VA 20191-3468

BLANCHET-SADRI, FRANCINE, mathematician; b. Trois-Rivieres, Quebec, Can., July 25, 1953; came to U.S., 1990; d. Jean and Rolande (Delage) B.; m. Fereidoon Sadri, July 28, 1979; children: Ahmad, Hamid, Mariamme. BSc in Math., U. du Quebec a Trois-Rivieres, Quebec, Can., 1976; MS, Princeton U., 1979; PhD, McGill U., 1989. Rsch., teaching asst. U. du Quebec, Trois-Rivieres, Quebec, Can., 1974-76; lectr. U. du Quebec, 1976; rsch. asst. Princeton (N.J.) U., 1978; lectr. U. Tech. Isfahan, Iran, 1982-84, McGill U., Montreal, Quebec, 1988-89; asst. prof. U. N.C., Greensboro, 1990—. Contbr. articles to profl. jours. Recipient Rsch. Excellence award 1991; Natural Scis. and Engring. Coun. Can. postgrad. fellow, 1976-80, Fonds pour la Formation de Chercheurs et L'aide a la Recherche doctoral fellow, 1985-87, Natural Scis. and Engring. Rsch. Coun. Can. postdoctoral fellow, 1990; new faculty grantee U. N.C., Greensboro, 1990-91, NSF grantee, 1991-96. Mem. Am. Math. Soc., Assn. for Computing Machinery. Office: U NC Dept Math Greensboro NC 27412

BLANCO, JORGE DESIDERIO, physician, medical educator, researcher; b. La Habana, Cuba, Feb. 11, 1950; came to U.S., 1961; s. Victorino S. and Graciella G. (Garcia) B.; m. Teresa Ankewich, Aug. 23, 1980; children: Valerie Marie, Jay Matthew. BA in Natural Scis. with honors, Johns Hopkins U., 1971; MD, Vanderbilt U., 1975; cert. of mgmt. in health care, U. N.C., 1995. Diplomate Nat. Bd. Med. Examiners, Am. Bd. Ob-Gyn. (assoc. examiner gen. oral bds. 1991, examiner 1992—), sub-splty. Maternal-Fetal Medicine (examiner maternal-fetal medicine oral bds. 1995—); lic. physician, Tenn., Tex., Ga.; cert. Am. Bd. Med. Mgmt. Intern dept. ob-gyn. U. Tex. Health Sci. Ctr., San Antonio, 1975-76, resident dept. ob-gyn., 1976-79, adminstrv. chief resident, 1978-79, fellow in maternal-fetal medicine dept. ob-gyn., 1979-81, from asst. prof. to assoc. prof. dept. ob-gyn., 1979-85; prof. dept. ob-gyn. and reproductive scis. U. Tex. Health Sci. Ctr., Houston, 1989—, John T. Armstrong prof. dept. ob-gyn. and reproductive scis., 1990—; fellow in chlamydia lab. techniques U. Calif., San Francisco, 1981; assoc. clin. prof. Med. Coll. Ga., Augusta, 1986-87; prof. dept. ob-gyn. Tex. Tech. U. Health Scis. Ctr., Lubbock, 1987-89; dir. perinatology Meml. Med. Ctr., Savannah, Ga., 1985-87, assoc. dir. dept. ob-gyn. edn., 1985-87; dir. Perinatal Outreach and Edn. Project, Lubbock, 1988-89; dir. chlamydia rsch. lab. dept. ob-gyn. U. Tex. Health Sci. ctr., San Antonio, 1981-85, dir. sr. elective program dept. ob-gyn., 1983-85, coord. grand rounds conf. dept. ob-gyn., 1983-84; interim chmn. dept. ob-gyn. and reproductive scis. U. Tex. Med. Sch., Houston, 1993-94; mem. attending staff Med. Ctr. Hosp., San Antonio, 1979-85, Meml. Med. Ctr., Savannah, 1985-87, Lubbock (Tex.) Gen. Hosp., 1987-89, Hermann Hosp., Houston., 1989—, L.B.J. Gen. Hosp., Houston, 1990—; mem. consulting staff St. Joseph's Hosp., Houston, 1990—; cons. to U.S. Army Brooke Med. Ctr., Ft. Sam Houston, Tex., 1983-85; reviewer NIH study sect., 1995; expert cons. Ctrs. for Disease Control, Atlanta, 1989; expert cons. ob-gyn FDA, Washington, 1994—; participant NIH Conf. Pelvic Inflammatory Disease, Bethesda, Md., 1990; vis. prof. U. Kans. Sch. Medicine, Wichita, 1983, 89, U. Nebr. Sch. Medicine, Omaha, 1983, Creighton U. Sch. Medicine, Omaha, 1983, U. Mo. Sch. Medicine, Kansas City, 1983, La. State U., New Orleans, 1983, Shreveport, 1983, U. Tenn. Sch. Medicine, Chattanooga, 1984, Memphis, 1985, U. Okla. Sch. Medicine, Tulsa, 1984, U. Tex. Health Sci. Ctr., 1984, Rush-Presbyn.-St. Luke's Med. Ctr., Chgo., 1984, Loyola Med. Coll., Chgo., 1984, U. Chgo., 1984, Northwestern U. Sch. Medicine, Chgo., 1984, St. Louis U. Sch. Medicine, 1984, Washington U. Sch. Medicine, St. Louis, 1984, Baylor U. Sch. Medicine, Houston, 1984, 88, Vanderbilt U. Sch. Medicine, Nashville, 1984, Wright State U. Sch. Medicine, Dayton, Ohio, 1985, Wayne State U., Detroit, 1985, Johns Hopkins U., Balt., 1985, Med. Coll. Ohio, Toledo, 1987, 89, U. Mich. Sch. Medicine, Ann Arbor, 1989, Loma Linda U., San Bernardino, Calif., 1989, 91, Tex. Tech U. Health Scis. Ctr., Amarillo, Tex., 1990, 92, 93, U. Montreal Sch. Medicine, 1991, McGill U. Sch. Medicine, Montreal, 1991, U. Utah Sch. Medicine, 1992, U. Tex. Med. Br., Galveston, 1992, Baylor Med. Ctr., Dallas, 1992, U. Ottawa, Ont., Can., 1993, Hosp. for Sick Children, Toronto, 1993, McMaster U., Hamilton, Ont., Can., 1993; spkr. in field; study sect. reviewer Perinatal Emphasis Rsch. Cer. Nat. Insts. Child Health and Human Devel. NIH, 1995. Mem. editl. bd.: Infectious Diseases in Obstetrics and Gynecology, 1992—, Perinatal Advocate, 1988-89; reviewer: Am. Jour. Ob-Gyn., Ob-Gyn., Sexually Transmitted Diseases, Fertility and Sterility, Jour. of AMA.; contbr. numerous articles to med. jours., also abstracts and book chpts. Chmn. health professions adv. com. March of Dimes, Savannah, Ga., 1985-87, mem. health professions adv. com., Lubbock, Tex., 1988-89; med. advisor Young Parents Svcs. Orgn., Lubbock, 1988-89; mem. project adv. group Rev. Pub. Maternal and Child Health Svcs. in Harris County and Devel. Recommendations, U. Tex. Health Sci. Ctr. Houston-Sch. Pub. Health, March of Dimes Birth Defects Found., 1991. Fellow ACOG (faculty postgrad. courses on ob-gyn. infections 1982-83, 94-97); mem. Soc. for Gynecologic Investigation (sci. program com. 1990, 91, 92, 93, 95), Soc. Perinatal Obstetricians (sci. program com. 1992, 93, 94, 95, group leader spl. interest group on infectious diseases 1989, 90), Infectious Disease Soc. for Ob-Gyn. (nominating com. 1993-94, exec. coun. 1994—), Tex. Assn. Obstetricians and Gynecologists (exec. coun. 1994—), Am. Soc. Microbiology, Assn. of Profs. of Gynecology and Obstetrics, Am. Coll. Physician Execs., Tex. Perinatal Assn., Tex. Med. Assn., Phi Beta Kappa. Office: LBJ Hosp 5656 Kelley St Houston TX 77026-1967

BLANCO, JOSEFA JOAN-JUANA (JOSSIE BLANCO), social services administrator; b. Havana, Cuba, Jan. 31, 1954; came to U.S., 1962; d. Oscar Manuel and Josefa (Rodriguez) B.; m. John Franklin Hurt III, Nov. 18, 1979 (div. June 1985); children: John Franklin IV, Jeaninne Bernadette; m. Argelio M. Tejeda, Mar. 12, 1991; 1 child, Richard Manuel Tejeda. BA in Psychology and Religion, Fla. Internat. U., 1975, MA in Sch. Psychology, 1976, postgrad. in pub. adminstrn., from 1983; MS in Human Resource Adminstrn., Villanova U., 1979; PhD in Adminstrn., West Coast U. Lic. tchr., Fla.; tng. lic. clin. and child care svcs. Psychometrician Mailman Ctr. for Child Devel., U. Miami, 1975-76; supr. adoptions Health and Rehabilitative Svcs. Fla., Miami, 1972-75, 76-80; instr. psychology Draughons Jr. Coll., Memphis, 1980-81; spl. project dir. Children's Psychiat. Ctr., Miami, 1981-84; exec. dir. Community Habilitation Ctr., Miami, 1984-86; shelter dir. Miami Bridge, Inc., Miami, 1986-89; regional dir. Luth. Ministries Fla., Ft. Lauderdale, 1989-90; exec. dir. Residential Pla. at Blue Lagoon Inc., Miami, 1990; grant writer, researcher, speaker at confs., 1990—; instr. Dade County Pub. Sch. System, 1991—; health ctr. adminstr. Dade County Pub. Health Dept. State of Fla. Dept. Health and Rehab. Svcs., 1992-94; instr. Dade County Pub. System, 1994—; facilitator nat. confs. Nat. Justice Dept. Bd. dirs. S.E. Region Com. To Study AIDS and AIDS Prevention; mem. Adult Congregate Living Facility. Recipient award for svc. to runaways Fla. Network, 1989, plaque for work with troubled youth Friends Fla. Network, 1989; Miami Herald scholar, 1969. Mem. Residential Child Car Assn. (bd. dirs., chmn. advocacy com.), Fla. Network Youth and Family Svcs. (quality assurance com., tng. com.), NAFE. Republican. Roman Catholic. Address: 10521 SW 48th St Miami FL 33165-5649

BLANCO, KATHLEEN BABINEAUX, lieutenant governor; m. Raymond; 6 children. With La. State Legis. Dist. 45, 1984-88, mem. house edn. com., mem. house transp., hwys., and pub. works com.; mem. house edn. com., mem. house transp., hwys., and pub. works com. Pub. Svc. Commn., La., 1988-94, chair, 1993, 94; lt. gov. La. State Govt., 1995—. Address: PO Box 44243 Baton Rouge LA 70804*

BLAND, ANNIE RUTH (ANN BLAND), nursing educator; b. Bennett, N.C., Oct. 14, 1949; d. John Wesley and Mary Ida (Caviness) Brown; m. Chester Wayne Bland; 1 child, John Wayne; stepchildren: Jason Tyler, Adam Mathew. BS in Nursing, East Carolina U., Greenville, N.C., 1971; MS in Nursing, U. N.C. Chapel Hill, 1978; postgrad., U. S.C., 1996—. RN, N.C.; cert. clin. specialist in adult psychiat./mental health nursing; cert. BLS instr. Staff nurse VA Med. Ctr., Durham, N.C., 1974-75, 77-80; psychiat. clin. instr. Duke U. Med. Ctr., Durham, 1980-82, asst. head nurse, 1982-90, staff nurse, 1993—; psychiat. clin. nurse specialist John Umstead Hosp., Butner, N.C., 1990-93; psychiat. head nursing instr. Alamance C.C., Graham, N.C., 1994-96. Asst. Sunday sch. tchr. Mt. Hermon Bapt. Ch., Durham, 1994, 96—. With USN, 1971-74, capt. USNR, 1974—. Recipient award for nursing excellence Great 100 Orgn., Raleigh, N.C., 1991, Letter of Appreciation Am. Heart Assn., Chapel Hill, 1992. Mem. ANA, N.C. Nurses Assn. (sec. dist. 11, 1981), Naval Res. Assn., Assn. Mil. Surgeons U.S., U. N.C. Chapel Hill Alumni Assn. and Sch. Nursing, East Carolina U. Alumni Assn. and Sch. Nursing, Nat. Alliance for Mentally Ill, Epilepsy Found. Baptist. Home: 3226 Carriage Trl Hillsborough NC 27278-9554 Office: U South Carolina Coll of Nursing Columbia SC 29208

BLAND, CYNTHIA ZENOBIA, elementary school educator, writer; b. Harvey, Ill., Dec. 24, 1941; d. Prose Albert and Ann Marie (Thomas) M.; 1 child, Warren Maurice; m. Ernest Williams (div.); 1 child, Harlem Katsina; m. Ronald F. Shaw (div.); m. Roy Lewis (div.); m. Stephen J. Nolan (div.); children: Payge, Timi; m. Duane Lawrence Bland, Apr. 16, 1941. BS, U. Wis., 1971, postgrad., 1971. Tchr. Chgo. Bd. Edn., 1971-80, regular elem. tchr., tchr. regular English, tchr. h.s. ESOL, 1986-88; probation officer Cook County Adult Probation, Chgo., 1980-87; tchr. middle sch. DeKalb City Bd. Edn., Decatur, Ga., 1996—. Author: They Don't Clap for Me Anymore, 1995, Bitter Tears, 1995. Instr., group leader Afro-Am. Youth Found., Chgo., 1980; campaign for Jesse Jackson Dem. Party, Chgo., for Harold Washington, Anita Palmer. Home: 1434 Peachcrest Rd Decatur GA 30032

BLAND, GILBERT TYRONE, foodservice executive; b. Fredericksburg, Va., Mar. 10, 1955; s. Robert Edward and Ruth Elizabeth (Bumbry) B.; m. Rita Carol Henderson, Sept. 5, 1981; children: Robert David, Allison Michelle, Elizabeth Caroline. BS, James Madison U., 1977; MBA, Atlanta U., 1979. Banking officer Continential Ill. Bank, Chgo., 1979-83; v.p. Independence Bank, Chgo., 1983-85; pres. Tymark Enterprises Inc., Norfolk, Va., 1985—; pres. Burger King Minority Franchise Assn., Miami, Fla., 1988—; bd. dirs. Nat. Franchise Assn., Miami, 1988—, State of Va. Small Bus. Financing Authority, Richmond, 1990—. Chmn., exec. com., bd. advisors Old Dominion Univ. Sch. Bus., Norfolk, 1990, Va. Marine Sci. Mus. Found., Virginia Beach, 1991; trustee James Madison U. Found., 1992; bd. dirs. Hampton U. Bus. Adv. Ctr., Greater Norfolk Corp., Senatra Hosp. Norfolk, Chamber Group Plans, Inc., Norfolk State U. Athletic Found.; exec. bd. Tidewater Coun. Boy Scouts of Am. Recipient Community Svc. award Alpha Kappa Alpha, 1990, Norfolk Community Hosp., 1991. Mem. Beta Gamma Sigma. Baptist. Office: Tymark Enterprises Inc 223 E City Hall Ave Norfolk VA 23510-1728

BLAND, JAMES THEODORE, JR., lawyer; b. Memphis, June 16, 1950; s. James Theodore and Martha Frances (Downen) B.; m. Pattie L. Martin, Apr. 12, 1974. BBA magna cum laude, Memphis State U., 1972, JD, 1974. Bar: Tenn. 1975, U.S. Dist. Ct. (we. dist.) Tenn. 1976, U.S. Tax Ct. 1976, U.S. Supreme Ct. 1983, U.S. Ct. Claims 1987. Estate tax atty. IRS, Memphis, 1974-76; assoc. Armstrong, Allen, Braden, Goodman, McBride & Prewitt, Memphis, 1976-81, ptnr., 1981-91; pvt. practice Memphis, 1991—; instr. in taxation, bus. law State Tchr.'s Inst., Memphis, 1975-83; bd. dirs. Thomas W. Briggs Found., Memphis. Fellow Am. Coll. Trusts and Estate Counsel; mem. ABA (legis. initiatives com., taxation sect., specialization in estate planning real property, probate and trust sect., Achievement award 1983, 85), Fed. Bar Assn. (pres. 1987-88, 1st v.p. 1985-86, nat. coun. 1979—, bd. dirs. young lawyers div. 1979-84, pres. Memphis mid south chpt. 1979-80), Am. Assn. Atty.'s-CPAs, Tenn. Bar Assn. (chmn. tax sect. 1984-85, bd. govs. 1984-85, 89-90, 90-91), Tenn. Young Lawyers Conf. (bd. dirs. 1978—), Memphis Bar Assn. (bd. dirs. 1990-91), Tenn. Soc. CPA's. Republican. Methodist. Office: 4646 Poplar Ave Ste 320 Memphis TN 38117-4433

BLAND, LARRY IRVIN, historical documents editor; b. Indpls., Aug. 20, 1940; s. Harold Irvin and Emma Christian (Watt) B.; m. Joellen Ruth Kuerst, July 7, 1962; children: Neil David, Ryan Christopher. BS in Physics, Purdue U., 1962; MA in History, U. Wis., 1968, PhD, 1972. Engr., systems analyst P.R. Mallory Capacitor Co., Indpls., 1962-67; instr. history Gaston Coll., Dallas, N.C., 1971-76; NEH fellow in U.S. intellectual history U. Ill., Champaign, 1976-77; documentary editor George C. Marshall Found., Lexington, Va., 1977—. Editor: Papers of George Catlett Marshall, 1981—, Marshall Interviews and Reminiscences, 1991, Procs. Rockbridge Hist. Soc., 1980—; assoc. editor: Jour. Mil. History, 1988—. Mem. Alpha Sigma Phi. Office: George C Marshall Found VMI Parade PO Drawer 1600 Lexington VA 24450

BLANK, A(NDREW) RUSSELL, lawyer; b. Bklyn., June 13, 1945; s. Lawrence and Joan B.; children—Adam, Marisa. Student U. N.C., 1963-64; B.A., U. Fla., 1966, postgrad. Law Sch., 1966-68; J.D., U. Miami, 1970. Bar: Ga. 1971, Fla. 1970; cert. civil trial advocate Nat. Bd. Trial Advocacy. Law asst. Dist. Ct. Judge, Atlanta, 1970-72; ptnr. A Russell Blank & Assocs., P.C., 1985—. Contbr. articles to profl. jours. Mem. pub. adv. com. Atlanta Regional Commn., 1972-74. Recipient Merit award Ga. Bar Assn., 1981. Mem. Atlanta Bar Assn., Ga. Bar Assn., Ga. Trial Lawyers Assn. (officer), Lawyers Club Atlanta, ABA, Assn. Trial Lawyers Am., Fla. Bar Assn., Am. Bd. Trial Advocates (advocate, pres. Ga. chpt.). Office: 230 Peachtree St NW Ste 800 Atlanta GA 30303-1512

BLANKENBEKER, JOAN WINIFRED, communications/information management executive; b. Phila., Dec. 4, 1945; d. Henry Charles Ayton and Winifred M. Ayton Jacobs; m. Cleon Jerry Blankenbeker, Oct. 10, 1969; children: Robert Edgar, Jennifer Ellen. BA in History, Memphis State U., 1968; MS in Human Resource Mgmt., U. Utah, 1976. Hdqrs. squadron sect. comdr. Tactical Air Command Langley AFB, Hampton, Va., 1981-85; exec. asst. to dep. chief of staff Hdqs. Allied Forces, North (NATO), Oslo, 1985-88; chief pers. affairs Air Edn. and Tng. Command, Randolph AFB, Tex., 1988-91; dir., dep. dir., pers. programs, chief Dep. Chief of Staff for Pers. Hdqrs., San Antonio, 1988-91; comdr., dep. comdr. 3750 Support Group Sheppard AFB, Wichita Falls, Tex., 1991-92; dir. info. mgmt. Hdqs. Air Edn. and Tng. Command, San Antonio, 1992-95; dep. dir. comm. and info. Air Edn. and Tng. Command, San Antonio, 1996—; voting mem. Air Force Info. Mgmt. Policy Coun., San Antonio, 1992-96; bd. dirs. Air Force AFIT Info. Resource Mgmt., San Antonio; cons. Retiree Activities, 82 Tng. Wing, Sheppard AFB, Wichita Falls, 1991-92; chmn. hazardous waste sub-com. Sheppard AFB, Wichita Falls, 1991-92. Leader Girl Scouts U.S., New Braunfels, Tex., 1992-95; mem. Broad Investment Group of New Braunfels, 1996. Col. USAF. Named Air Tng. Command Mil. Sr. Pers. Mgr. of Yr., Comdr. ATC, Randolph AFB, 1989, Randolph AFB Most Outstanding Fed. Woman, Fed. Women's Program, 1989, Tactical Air Command's Outstanding Sr. Adminstrv. Officer, Comdr. TAC, Langley AFB, 1983. Mem. Armed Forces Comm. and Electronic Assn., New Braunfels C. of C., Beta Sigma Phi (pres., v.p., sect.-treas. 1969—). Republican. Episcopalian. Home: 2686 River Oaks New Braunfels TX 78132 Office: Hdqs AETC/SC 61 Main Cir Ste 2 Randolph AFB TX 78150-4545

BLANKENSHIP, DAVID LEE, aerospace executive; b. Las Vegas, N.Mex., Oct. 22, 1933; s. Lee R. and Ada Eva (Stites) B.; m. Joan Louise Lucas, June 5, 1953; children: Bruce Lee, Karen Louise Blankenship Roberts. B in Econs., U. Tulsa, 1955. With Rockwell Internat., 1962-95, dir. external affairs, 1983—; sr. v.p. Def. Techs. Inc., 1995—; bd. dirs. Community Bank and Trust Co.; chmn. Tulsa Joint Airport Zoning Bd. Bd. advisors Okla. Aviation and Space Hall of Fame and Mus.; governing bd. Spartan Sch. of Aeronautics. With USAF. Recipient Leadership award Nat. Mgmt. Assn., 1973; named to Daniel Webster H.S. Alumni Found. Disting. Alumni Hall of Fame. Mem. Air Force Assn. (nat. dir.), Nat. Air Force Assn. (pres., chmn. bd.), Okla. Air Force Assn., Okla. State C. of C. and Industry, Met. Tulsa C. of C., Oaks Country Club. Office: 7500 E Apache Tulsa OK 74115

BLANKENSHIP, DWIGHT DAVID, business owner; b. Ashland, Ky., Mar. 18, 1944; S. David Earl and Dorthy Irene (King) B.; m. Joyce Eddy, Mar. 1, 1969 (div. Oct. 1984); children: Dwight W., Cheryl L. Grad. high sch., Ashland, Ky. Owner, mgr. Royal Pool, Sarasota, Fla., 1970-72, Am. Indian Jewelry, Sarasota, Fla., 1972-78, Daves Enterprises, Big Pine Key, Fla., 1978-86, D & D Enterprises, Ocala, Fla., 1986—, Master Mktg. Prodn. Co., Bradenton, Fla., 1987—, Gold Designs, Bradenton, Fla., 1987—. Home: 6716 26th St W Bradenton FL 34207-5705 also: Gold Designs/ Master Mktg 1304 53rd Ave W Bradenton FL 34207-2861

BLANKENSHIP, RONNELLE EAVES, elementary education educator; b. Chattanooga, Aug. 2, 1949; d. Ronald Dennie and Bettye Jo (Walker) Eaves; m. Gary Steven Blankenship, Aug. 14, 1970; 1 child, Mark Garrett. BS in Elem. Edn., Middle Tenn. State U., 1970; postgrad., Stetson U., 1972, Chattanooga Community Coll., 1981; MEd in Adminstrn., U. Tenn., Chattanooga, 1975. Cert. tchr., Tenn., adminstr. Tchr. Titusville (Fla.) Pub. Schs., 1970-72, Hamilton County Schs., Chattanooga, 1972-94; asst. prin. McBrien Elem. Sch., Chattanooga, 1994-96; prin. Birchwood (Tenn.) Elem. Sch., 1996—; sch. coord. Reading is Fundamental program, 1986-89. Vol. usher Little Theatre of Chattanooga, 1988-95; bd. dirs. Youth Theatre Assn., Chattanooga, 1988-95, rec. sec., 1990-92; vol. Kids on the Block, Inc., Chattanooga, 1989—; mem. Think Tank com. Tenn. Edn. Commr., 1995. Named Tchr. of the Yr., Soddy-Daisy C. of C., 1988, Hamilton County Elem. Tchr. of Yr., 1992, East Tenn. Dist. Tchr. of Yr., 1992, Hixson C. of C. Tchr. of the Yr., 1992; recipient Life Membership award PTA, 1991, POGO Award for Gifted Edn., 1984, Milken Family Found. Nat. Educator award, 1993. Mem. NEA, Tenn. Edn. Assn., East Tenn. Edn. Assn., Internat. Reading Assn., Hamilton County Edn. Assn. (com., assoc. rep. 1989-91, Elem. Tchr. of the Yr. 1990), Alpha Delta Kappa (historian 1988-90, rec. sec. 1990-92). Home: 2322 Bending Oak Dr Chattanooga TN 37421-1519 Office: Birchwood Sch 5623 Highway 60 Birchwood TN 37308-5113

BLANKINSHIP, HENRY MASSIE, data processing executive; b. Providence, Sept. 27, 1949; s. Ernest Randolph and Henrietta (Massie) B.; m. Linda Ferber, Jan. 17, 1981; children: John Byron, Kevin Mark, Sara Jane. Student, Rollins Coll., 1962-63, U. Va., 1963-66. Mgmt. analyst First Va. Bankshares Corp., Falls Church, 1967-72; head systems planning br. Navy Recruiting Command, Arlington, Va., 1972-80; dir. def. techniques and tactics, head computer network devel. Bureau Naval Personel, 1980-83; head software engring. Navy Mil. Pers. Command, Arlington, Va., 1983-84; head Navy Pers. Data Systems, Arlington, 1984-88, Navy Pers. and Manpower Data Systems Mgmt., Arlington, 1988—. Nat. corr. Karate Illustrated Mag., 1976-79. Head Karate instr. YMCA, Fairfax County, Va.; police spl. teams cons., Fairfax County. Recipient Outstanding Navy Civilian Svc. award, 1976-82, 84, 86, 88-95, Gold Wreath USN, 1977, Navy Spl. Acts award, 1983; named Ea. Region Karate Champion. Mem. Am. Mgmt. Assn., Nat. Assn. Combative Arts, Am. Tae Kwon Do Assn., U.S. Karate Assn., Internat. Martial Arts Assn. (pres.), Taifung Martial Arts Assn. (chair bd. dirs.), U.S. Kickboxing Assn. Republican. Office: Navy

Pers & Manpower Data Systems Mgmt PO Box 1610 Arlington VA 22210-0910

BLANKS, NAOMI MAI, retired English language educator; b. Trezevant, Tenn., June 22, 1917; d. Hubbard Tazewell and Clara Clyde (Smith) Williamson; m. Jeff J. Blanks Jr., June 19, 1936 (dec.); children: Barbara, Jeff III, George (dec.). Student, Lambuth Coll., Jackson, Tenn., 1934-35; BA, Bethel Coll., McKenzie, Tenn., 1961; MA, George Peabody Coll., Nashville, 1966. Tchr. lang. arts Trezevant (Tenn.) Jr. High Sch., 1957-60; tchr. English McKenzie (Tenn.) High Sch., 1961-68; assoc. prof. English Bethel Coll., McKenzie, 1968-85; ret.; cons. lang. arts Harcourt Brace Jovanovich. Reviewer biography: T.S. Eliot: A Life, 1986, Waldo Emerson, 1982. Bd. dirs. Carroll County Devel. Ctr., Huntingdon, Tenn., 1976-88. NEH seminar grantee, 1980; NDEA fellow, 1965; recipient Alumni Svc. award, Bethel Coll., 1984, Tchr. of the Yr., 1975, 84. Mem. AAUP, So. Assn. Sec. Schs. and Colls. (evaluation com.), Delta Kappa Gamma (chpt. pres. 1970-72). Democrat. Methodist. Home: PO Box 186 Trezevant TN 38258-0186

BLANKSON, MARY LARTEY, pediatrician; b. Tutu, Ghana, Mar. 16, 1946; came to U.S., 1977; d. Richard Emmanuel and Christiana Karl (Odei) L.; m. Joe Harry Blankson, Jan. 20, 1973; children: Kwamena Abaka Blankson, Kwabena Lattey Blankson, Amma Amene Blankson. Pre-med. degree, U. Ghana, West Africa, 1967, MD, 1972; MPH in Maternal and Child Health, U. Minn., 1982. Diplomate Am. Bd. Pediatrics; cert. PALS; cert. instr. nursing child assessment. Rotating intern to instr. interns Korle Bu Teaching Hosp., Accra, Ghana, 1972-74, instr. for interns, primary care physician, sr. med. officer, 1976-77; intern to resident in pediatrics Harlem Hosp. Ctr., Columbia U., 1980; fellowship ambulatory pediatrics U Minn., 1982; primary care physician, preceptor med. students and nurses Bur. Maternal and Child Health, Mpls. Health Dept., 1980-83; pediatrician, mentor for nurse practitioners Child Care Clinic, U. Minn., 1982-83; pediatrician Community Univ. Health Care Ctr., U. Minn., Mpls., 1983-84; clin. instr. in pediatrics Dept. Pediatrics, U. Minn., 1984—; asst. prof. maternal and child health tng. program Sch. Pub. Health, U. Ala., Birmingham, 1985—; primary care pediatrician Jefferson County Health Dept., 1985—; courtesty staff privileges The Children's Hosp. of Ala., 1985—; physician (part-time) Cancer Detection Ctr., U. Minn., 1981-83; pediatrician (part-time) Group Health Inc., Mpls., 1982-83; faculty advisor to African students orgn. U. Ala., 1987-90, mem. ednl. policy com. sch. pub. health, 1988-92, mem. admission com., 1993—; mem. Pub. Health Area 8 Perinatal Adv. Com., 1988—. Adv. coun. Child Care Resources, 1993—; Head Start Health Adv. Com., 1993—; chairperson med. adv. com. Healthy Start Project, co-chairperson needs assessment com., 1991, adolescent pregnancy prevention com., 1992; pediatric cons. Health Care for the Homeless, 1989—; mem. Hold Out the Lifeline com., 1990—; mem. program planning com. Reuben-Lindh, Child Devel. Ctr., Mpls., 1982-84; adv. bd. UAB Daycare, 1989—; mem. com. on AIDS and Child Welfare Svcs., 1988; bd. dirs. Planned Parenthood of Ala., 1987-90. Recipient Nestle's Pediatric Prize, 1971, Arrington award for Svc. Birmingham's Mayor, 1991; Ghana Cocoa Mktg. Bd. scholarship, 1959-66. Fellow Am. Acad. Pediatrics; mem. APHA, Soc. for Pediatric Epidemiol. Rsch., Ambulatory Pediatric Assn., Nat. Coun. for Internat. Health, Assn. of Tchrs. of Maternal and Child Health, Ghana Med. Assn. Home: 544 Iroquois Dr Birmingham AL 35214-3729 Office: Jefferson County Dep Health No Health Ctr 2817 30th Ave N Birmingham AL 35207-4541

BLANTON, FRED, JR., lawyer; b. Muscle Shoals, Ala., July 2, 1919; s. Fred Sr. and Mary (Covington) B.; m. Mercer Potts McAvoy, Aug. 11, 1962. AB, Birmingham-So. Coll., 1939; JD, U. Va., 1942; postgrad., U. Ala., 1946, LLM in Taxation, 1979; postgrad., U. Mich., 1951. Sole practice, Birmingham, Ala., 1946-48, 54-83; prof. Dickinson Sch. Law, Carlisle, Pa., 1948-49; vis. prof. law U. Ala., Tuscaloosa, summer 1949; asst. prof. law U. Va., Charlottesville, 1949-51; assoc. Martin & Blakey, Attys., Birmingham, 1951-54; pvt. practice, Gardendale, Ala., 1983-93, Fultondale, Ala., 1994—. Contbr. articles to profl. jours. Served with USNR, 1942-46. Mem. Ala. Bar Assn. Republican. Episcopalian. Home: 1912 K C DeMent Ave Fultondale AL 35068-1249 Office: PO Box 15 Fultondale AL 35068-0015

BLANTON, HOOVER CLARENCE, lawyer; b. Green Sea, S.C., Oct. 13, 1925; s. Clarence Leo and Margaret (Hoover) B.; m. Cecilia Lopez, July 31, 1949; children: Lawson Hoover, Michael Lopez. J.D., U. S.C., 1953. Bar: S.C. 1953. Assoc. Whaley & McCutchen, Columbia, S.C., 1953-66; ptnr. McCutchen, Blanton, Rhodes and Johnson and predecessors, Columbia, 1967—; dir. Legal Aid Service Agy., Columbia, chmn. bd., 1972-73. Gen. counsel S.C. Rep. Conv., 1962; del. Rep. State Conv., 1962, 64, 66, 68, 70, 74; bd. dirs. Midlands Cmty. Action Agy., Columbia, vice chmn., 1972-73; bd. dirs. Wildewood Sch., 1976-78; mem. Gov.'s Legal Svcs. Adv. Coun., 1976-77, Commn. on Continuing Legal Edn. for Judiciary, 1977-84, Commn. on Continuing Lawyer Competence, 1988-92, Commn. on Continuing Legal Edn. and Specialization, 1992, sec. 1995, chmn., 1996; ordained deacon Baptist Ch. With USNR, 1942-46, 50-52. Mem. ABA. S.C. Bar (ho. of dels. 1975-76, chmn. fee disputes bd. 1977-81), Richland County Bar Assn. (pres. 1980), S.C. Def. Trial Attys. Assn., Def. Rsch. Inst., Assn. Def. Trial Attys. (state chmn. 1971-77, 80-95, exec. coun. 1977-80), Am. Bd. Trial Advs. (pres. S.C. chpts. 1989), Toastmasters Club (pres. 1959), Palmetto Club, Phi Delta Phi. Home: 3655 Deerfield Dr Columbia SC 29204-3730 Office: 1414 Lady St Columbia SC 29201-3304

BLANTON, PATRICIA LOUISE, periodontal surgeon; b. Clarksville, Tex., July 9, 1941; d. Ben E. and Mildred L. (Russell) B. MS, Baylor U., 1964, PhD, 1967, DDS, 1974, cert., 1975. Diplomate Am. Coll. Bd. Oral Medicine. Teaching asst. Baylor Coll. of Dentistry, Dallas, 1963-67, asst. prof., 1967-70, spl. instr., 1970-73, assoc. prof., 1974-76; resident periodontics VA Hosp., Dallas, 1975; prof. Baylor Coll. of Dentistry, Dallas, 1976-85, Baylor U. Grad. Sch., Dallas, 1976—; prof., chmn. Baylor Coll. of Dentistry, Dallas, 1983-85; cons. VA Hosp., Dallas, 1979-82; adj. prof. Baylor Coll. of Dentistry, Dallas, 1985—; cons. Commn. on Dental Accreditation and Coun. of Dental Edn., 1981—; v.p. State Anatomical Bd., Tex., 1983-85; mem. ADA-AADS Liaison Com., 1983—; chmn. Nat. Insts. Health, Oral Biology and Medicine Study Sect. II, 1985-86. Author: Periodontics for the G.P., 1977, Current Therapy in Dentistry, 1980, An Atlas of the Human Skull, 1980 (1st place honors 1981). Invited participant Am. Coun. on Edn., Austin, 1984; mem. liaison com. Dallas County Dental Soc.-Am. Cancer Soc., Dallas, 1976-78; bd. dirs. Dallas Dental Health Programs, 1992-93, S.W. Med. Found., 1992-93; bd. devel. Hardin-Simmons U., 1995—. Named one of Outstanding Young Women in Am., 1976. Fellow Am. Coll. Dentists, Internat. Coll. Dentists; mem. ADA (alt. del.), Tex. Dental Assn. (bd. dirs. 1995—), Am. Assn. Anatomists, Am. Acad. Periodontology, Am. Acad. Oral Medicine, Am. Acad. Osseointegration, S.W. Soc. Periodontology, Dallas County Dental Soc. (pres. 1992-93), Xi Psi Phi, Omicron Kappa Upsilon (pres. 1992-93). Office: 4514 Cole Ave Ste 902 Dallas TX 75205-4176

BLASCHKE, RENEE DHOSSCHE, alderman; b. San Antonio, Oct. 4, 1938; d. Raoul Albert Emil and Lillian Lenore (Parker) Dhossche; m. Kenneth Blaschke; children: Kenneth, Rex, Rochelle. Office mgr. Smithville (Tex.) Hosp., 1958-68; tax assessor, collector City of Smithville, 1968-76; mgr., buyer Ken's Rexall Pharmacy, Smithville, 1976-92, ret., 1992; alderman City of Smithville, 1977-82, 94—. Alderman City of Smithville, 1977-82, 94—; past pres. region X, bd. dirs. Tex. Mcpl. League; trustee, chmn. fin., chmn. adminstrv. bd. 1st United Meth. Ch., Smithville; active Boy Scouts Am., Girl Scouts U.S.; chmn. Smithville Bicentennial Commn., Smithville Sesquicentennial Commn., Smithville Centennial Com., bd. dirs. Keep Tex. Beautiful, Tex. Urban Forestry Coun., Smithville CFC, 1994—, Smithville Econ. Devel. Bd., 1994—; Smithville Tree Bd., Smithville Tree City USA, Keep Smithville Beautiful; sec.-treas. Trees for Tex. Gov.'s Task Force-Earth Day, 1990; devel. bd. Seton Hosp., 1979—. Named Garden Club Woman of Yr., State Fair Tex., 1993. Mem. Am. Pharm. Assn. Aux., Tex. Pharm. Assn. Aux., Tex. Garden Clubs (pres. 1991-93, life mem.), Nat. Coun. State Garden Clubs (master flower show judge, landscape design critic, presenter seminars, design cons.), U. Tex. Ex-Students (past pres.), Smithville Garden Club (pres.), Smithville C. of C. (city hostess, bd. dirs., chmn. econ. devel. bd. 1994—, pres. 1996—).

BLASI, ANTHONY JOSEPH, sociology educator, writer; b. Dayton, Ohio, Apr. 3, 1946; s. Emmanuel Anthony and Mary Ella (Marshall) B. BA, St. Edward's Univ., 1968; MA, Notre Dame Univ., 1971, PhD, 1974; MA, U St. Michael's Coll., 1985; ThD, Univ. of Toronto, 1986. Tchr. Notre Dame High Sch., Sherman Oaks, Calif., 1968-69, Holy Cross Sch., New Orleans, La., 1969-70; instr. St. Anselm Coll., Manchester, N.H., 1973-74; asst. prof. sociology DePauw Univ., Greencastle, Ind., 1974-75; vis. asst. prof. sociology U. Ala., Tuscaloosa, 1975-76; asst. prof. sociology U. Louisville, Ky., 1976-78; assoc. prof. sociology Daemen Coll., Amherst, N.H., 1978-80; asst. prof. sociology U. Hawaii, Hilo, 1986-90; assoc. prof. sociology Muskingum Coll., New Concord, Ohio, 1990-94; assoc. prof. Tenn. State U., 1994—. Author 11 books; contbr. articles to profl. jours. Precinet officer Dem. party, Hilo, Hawaii, 1988-90. Recipient William Rainey Harper Outstanding Scholar award Mustingim Coll., 1992. Mem. Credo Internat. (bd. dirs.), Inst. for Study Human Ideas on Utlimate Realtiy and Meaning (bd. dirs.), Am. Sociol. Assn., Assn. Sociology of Religion, So. Sociol. Soc., Soc. Sci. Study of Religion, Religious Rsch. Assn. Roman Catholic. Office: Tenn State U Dept Sociology 3500 John A Merritt Blvd Nashville TN 37209-1500

BLASINGAME, DONALD RAY (DON BLASINGAME), banker; b. Wills Point, Tex., Mar. 2, 1925; s. Scott Vernon and Clora Hayden (Vance) B.; m. Christine E. Razz, May 19, 1949 (div. Nov. 1980); children: Kathryn Lynn, Alan Ray; m. Mildred Claudia McBay, Nov. 25, 1981. Student, Trinity Valley Coll., 1949-51. Loan officer Tyler (Tex.) Prodn. Credit Assn., 1947-52; mgr. Fed. Land Bank Assn., Sulphur Springs, Tex., 1952-58; regional mgr., asst. v.p. Fed. Land Bank of Houston, 1958, v.p., 1974; pres. Fed. Land Bank Assn. of Tyler, 1974-84, dir., 1990—; dir. Citizens Nat. Bank, Wills Point, 1981-90, Farm Credit Bank of Tex., Austin, 1988-90; fin. and legis. cons., Tyler. Advisor Tex. Farm and Ranch Fin. Program, Austin, 1985; chmn. bd. commrs. South County Fire Prevention Dist. 1, 1996—. Named to Tex. Acad. of Honor in Agrl. Credit, 1994. Mem. East Tex. Fair Assn. (bd. dirs. 1980-90, pres. 1985-87), East Tex. Farm & Ranch Club (bd. dirs. 1977-81), Barb Wire Collector Soc., Masons (sec., jr. warden, sr. warden Wills Point lodge # 422 1984—). Methodist. Home and Office: 12214 Jaysid St Tyler TX 75706-8753

BLATE, MICHAEL, author, lecturer; b. Queens, N.Y., June 24, 1938; s. Martin Stanley and Sylvia (Lax) B.; m. Bonnie Gloria Baker, Oct. 18, 1958 (div. 1962); children: Laurie Sue, Keith Martin; m. Barbara Gail Watson, Oct. 13, 1975. Student, U. Miami, Oxford, Ohio, 1957, U. Miami, Coral Gables, Fla., 1959, U. Fla., 1962, Broward Community Coll., Davie, Fla., 1962. Registered principal, investment adviser. V.p. Western Water Co., Inc., Hollywood, Fla., 1959-65, Marina Products Mfg., Inc., Ft. Lauderdale, Fla., 1963-87; investment counsel pvt. practice, Davie, Fla., 1965-67; founder, reg. prin. officer M. Blate & Co., Davie, Fla., 1967-69; advisor Nova Convertible Inv. Fund, Ft. Lauderdale, Fla., 1969-88; founder, CEO Falkynor Communications, Davie, Fla., 1974-87; CEO Falkyn, Inc., Davie, Fla., 1987—; Author, radio-TV guest columnist The G-Jo Inst., Davie, Fla., 1975—; spokesperson, columnist, journalist, The G-Jo Inst., Hollywood, Fla., 1975—. Author: The Natural Healer's Acupressure Handbook Vol. I, II, 1978, How to Heal Yourself Using Hand Acupressure, How to Heal Yourself Using Foot Acupressure, Acugenics: Beat Stress in Five Minutes, The Tao of Health: The Way of Total Well-Being, 1982, When the Market Makes a Bottom, Vendanta for the 21st Century, 1995; columnist: Healthy & Natural Mag., Wolfe's Digest of Alternative Medicine, Townsend Letter for Doctors and Patients. Dir. United Fund of Broward County, Ft. Lauderdale, Fla., 1961; officer, dir. Jaycees, Hollywood, Fla., 1959-60; mem. Rotary Internat., W. Hollywood, Fla., 1968-70; founder, Vegetarian Gourmet Soc., Davie, Fla., 1982-88, Sathya Prema Charitable Found. Recipient Jaycee Key Man of Qtr. and Yr. awards, Hollywood, Fla., 1961, Kinsa Nat. Photographer's awards, Eastman Kodak, Fla., N.Y.C., N.Y., 1973-75. Office: The G Jo Institute PO Box 848060 Hollywood FL 33084-0060

BLATT, SOLOMON, JR., federal judge; b. Sumter, S.C., Aug. 20, 1921; s. Solomon and Ethel (Green) B.; m. Carolyn Gaden, Sept. 12, 1942; children—Gregory, Sheryl Blatt Hooper, Brian. AB, U. S.C., 1941, LLB, 1946, LLD (hon.), 1987; LLD (hon.), The Citadel, 1990, Coll. of Charleston, 1992. Bar: S.C., 1946. Ptnr. Blatt & Fales, Barnwell, S.C., 1946-71; judge U.S. Dist. Ct. S.C., Charleston, 1971-86, chief judge, 1986-90; sr. judge U.S. Dist. Ct. S.C., 1990—. Office: US Dist Ct SC PO Box 835 Charleston SC 29402-0835

BLAU, JUDITH RAE, sociology educator, researcher; b. Lansing, Mich., Apr. 27, 1942; d. Harold W. and Theda C. Fritz; m. Peter M. Blau, July 31, 1968; 1 child, Reva. BA, U. Chgo., 1964, MA, 1967; PhD, Northwestern U., 1972. From asst. to assoc. prof. SUNY, Albany, 1978-88; prof. U. N.C., Chapel Hill, 1988—; vis. assoc. prof. NYU, N.Y.C., 1986-87. Author: Architects and Firms, 1984, The Shape of Culture, 1989, Social Contracts and Economics Markets, 1993; co-editor: Art and Society, 1989. Rockefeller Found. Bellagio residency, 1988; rsch. grantee NSF, 1989-91, Am. Coun. Learned Socs., 1988; recipient Rsch. award NEA, 1986. Mem. Am. Sociol. Assn. (exec. coun. 1987-89, editor Rose monograph series 1993—). Home: 12 Cobb Ter Chapel Hill NC 27514-5741 Office: Univ of NC Dept Sociology Cb 3210 Hamilton Hall Chapel Hill NC 27599

BLAYDES, JAMES ELLIOTT, ophthalmologist; b. Bluefield, W.Va., Feb. 26, 1927; s. James Elliott Sr. and Mabel Lucetta (Hill) B.; children: James Elliott IV, William Mitchell, Stephen Hill, Elizabeth Boyd Blaydes Lewis; m. Anita G. Shrader, Sept. 25, 1976; 1 child, Jaime Brittany. AB, Princeton U., 1950; MD, U. Pa., 1954; postgrad., NYU, 1956. Intern Pa. Hosp., Phila., 1954-55; resident N.Y. Eye & Ear Infimary, N.Y.C., 1955-58, chief resident, 1957-58; asst. Blaydes Clinic, Bluefield, W.Va., 1950-58, ophthalmologist, 1958—, dir., owner, 1972—; bd. dirs. Blaydes Found., Bluefield, Columbia Ophthalmology Ctr. of Excellence, Bluefield; clin. prof. ophthalmology W.Va. U., Morgantown, 1987—; assoc. clin. prof. Marshall U., Huntington, W.Va., 1977—; cons. Norfolk So. Rlwy. Cons. editor Ophthalmology Mgmt., 1983—; mem. editorial adv. bd. Ocular Surgery News-Internat., 1982—; editor Phaco & Foldables; author: (with others) The Second Report on Cataract Surgery, 1971, Current Concepts in Cataract Surgery, 1974, rev. edits., 1976, 80, 82; contbr. articles to profl. jours. Named N.Y. Eye and Ear Infirmary Alumnus of Yr., 1990. Fellow Am. Coll. Eye Surgeons, Am. Acad. Ophthalmology (Hon. award 1979, Sr. Hon. award 1992); mem. Mercer County Med. Soc. (pres. 1967), W.Va. State Med. Assn., AMA, W.Va. Acad. Ophthalmology and Otolaryngology, Outpatient Ophthalmic Surg. Soc., Contact Lens Assn., Ophthalmologists, Am. Soc. Cataract and Refractive Surgery, China Vision Project Med. Adv. Bd., So. Med. Assn., PanAm. Med. Assn., Am. Assn. Ophthalmology, Am. Assn. Physicians and Surgeons, Soc. Eye Surgeons, N.Y. Eye and Ear Imfirmary Alumni Assn. Home: 908 Edgewood Rd Bluefield WV 24701-4209 Office: The Blaydes Clinic PO Box 1380 Bluefield WV 24701-1380

BLAYDES, WINIFRED JEAN, elementary school educator; b. Dallas, Sept. 2, 1947; d. James Wilfred and Betty Jacquelyn (Shirley) Stevenson; m. Mike Richardson, May 24, 1969 (div. 1985); children: Brynn Michelle, Darby Danielle; m. Barton Dudley Blaydes, June 14, 1987; children: Deborah Elizabeth, Preston Lawrence. BA, So. Meth. U., 1969; MS in Health and Phys. Edn., East Tex. State U., 1991. Elem. tchr. Spring Branch Ind. Sch. Dist., Houston, 1970-72, Southampton Elem. Sch., Houston, 1975-77; tchr. elem. phys. edn. Blueridge Elem. Sch., Fort Bend Sch. Dist., Houston, 1979-81, Plano (Tex.) Ind. Sch. Dist., 1982-83, Scofield Christian Sch., Dallas, 1985-88, Richardson (Tex.) Ind. Sch. Dist., 1988—; presenter workshops, insvcs., convs. in field; master tchr. phys. fitness program for underprivileged youth, 1985-87. coord. jump rope for heart Am. Heart Assn., Richardson, 1975—, bd. dirs., 1988—; ch. camp counselor Park Cities Bapt. Ch., Dallas, 1988; presenter, coach Jumpstarts, Tex. Scottish Rite Hosp., also other orgns., Dallas, 1987—. Named Tchr. of Yr., Ft. Bend Ind. Sch. Dist., 1980, 87, Richardson Tchr. of Yr. 1992; recipient award of Excellence in Tex. sch. health Tex. Dept. Health, 1991. Mem. AAHPERD (So. Dist. Elem. Phys. Educator of Yr. 1993), Tex. AHPERD (Tex. Elem. Phys. Educator of Yr. 1993, Phys. Edn. Pub. Info. award 1989), Kappa Delta Pi. Home: 2972 Warm Springs Ln Richardson TX 75082 Office: Classical Magnet Sch 701 Beltline Richardson TX 75080

BLAYLOCK, NEIL WINGFIELD, JR., applied statistics educator; b. Ft. Smith, Ark., Aug. 18, 1946; s. Neil Wingfield Sr. and Phyllis Catherine (Brown) B.; m. Naomi Josephine Smith, Aug. 25, 1968; children: Neil Wingfield III, Scott Allen, Adrian Philip, Paul Alexander. BA in Math., St. Mary's U., 1968; MS in Stats., U. Tex., San Antonio, 1987. Cert. tchr., Tex. High sch. math. tchr. San Antonio Ind. Sch. Dist., 1968-70; sr. engr. Martin Marietta Aerospace Corp., Orlando, Fla., 1972-79; prin. analyst S.W. Rsch. Inst., San Antonio, 1979—; evening faculty mem. U. Tex., San Antonio, 1987—. Contbr. articles to profl. jours. Com. chmn. Boy Scouts Am., San Antonio, 1982-93, asst. scoutmaster, 1993—. Fellow AIAA (assoc., chmn. S.W. Tex. sect. 1983, dep. dir. region IV 1991-95, nat. membership com. 1991—, bd. dirs. 1995—, Spl. Svc. award 1984, 95, 96, Disting. Achievement award 1989), Hypervelocity Impact Soc. (co-founder, nat. membership chmn. 1988-92), Am. Statis. Assn. Roman Catholic. Home: 7111 Moss Creek Dr San Antonio TX 78238-2725 Office: SW Rsch Inst 6220 Culebra Rd San Antonio TX 78238-5166

BLAZER, DAN GERMAN, psychiatrist, epidemiologist; b. Nashville, Feb. 23, 1944; s. Dan German and Mary Elizabeth (Owsley) B.; m. Sherrill Walls, Aug. 19, 1966; children: Dan German III, Natasha Leigh. BA, Vanderbilt U., 1965; MD, U. Tenn., 1969; MPH, U. N.C., 1979, PhD, 1980. Diplomate, Am. Bd. Psychiatry and Neurology. Fellow Montefiore Hosp. and Med. Ctr., N.Y.C., 1975-76; asst. prof., assoc. prof., then prof. psychiatry Duke U. Med. Ctr., Durham, N.C., 1976—, J.P. Gibbons prof. of psychiatry, 1990—; interim chair of psychiatry Duke U. Med. Ctr., 1990-93; dean of med. edn. Duke U., 1992—; prof. cmty. and family medicine Duke U. Med. Ctr., 1986—; chair, bd. dirs. Am. Geriatrics Soc., N.Y., 1983—; bd. dirs. ret. persons svcs. Am. Assn. Ret. Persons, Alexandria, Va., 1987-92, pres. Psychiat. Rsch. Soc., Salt Lake City, 1988; chmn. epidemiology and disease control study sect. NIH, Bethesda, Md., 1988—. Author: Depression in Late Life, 1993, Family Approach to Health Care in the Elderly, 1983, Life is Worth Living, 1987; editor: Handbook of Geriatric Psychiatry, 1980. Elder Brooks Ave. Ch. of Christ, Raleigh, N.C., 1982. Recipient Rsch. Career Devel. award, NIMH, 1977, Alex Haley award, East Tenn. Bapt. Hosp., Knoxville, 1986, Disting. Svc. award, U. N.C. Sch. Pub. Health, Chapel Hill, 1989. Fellow Am. Psychiat. Assn., Am. Coll. Psychiatrists, So. Psychiat. Assn., Gerontol. Soc. Am., Am. Psychopathol. Assn.; mem. Inst. of Medicine, Nat. Acad. Scis. Democrat. Office: Duke U Med Ctr PO Box 3005 Durham NC 27715-3005

BLAZIN, MICHAEL JOSEPH, banking executive; b. Lancashire, England, Nov. 22, 1955; came to U.S., 1957; s. Atlee Raymond and Felice Mary (Pado) B. BS, U.S. Naval Acad., 1977; MBA, Harvard U., 1985; MS, Johns Hopkins U., 1995. Cert. cash mgr., naval nuclear engr. Distbn. mgr. Procter & Gamble Mfg. Co., Balt., 1985-86; lockbox mgr. Equitable Bank, N.A., Balt., 1986-88, MNC Fin., Balt., 1988-93; project mgr. NationsBank, Balt., 1993-94, NationsBank Electronic Payments Svcs., Dallas, 1994—. Lt. USN, 1977-83. Mem. Treasury Mgmt. Assn., Naval Inst., Harvard Club (Dallas), Harvard Bus. Sch. Club (Dallas), VFW. Republican. Roman Catholic. Home: 2604 Hartman St Apt 5208 Dallas TX 75204-2673 Office: NationsBank MS TX1-609-21-04 1201 Main St 21st Fl Dallas TX 75202

BLECKE, ARTHUR EDWARD, principal; b. Oak Park, Ill., Sept. 21, 1926; s. Paul Gerard and Mathilda (Ziebell); m. June Audrey Eckholm, Jan. 22, 1949; children: William, Robert, Carol. B.S. in Phys. Edn., U. Ill., 1950; M.Edn., Loyola U., 1967. Tchr., coach Buckley High Sch., Ill., 1951-52, Paxton High Sch., Ill., 1952-53, Luther High Sch. North, Chgo., 1953-65, also dept. chmn.; asst. coach football and basketball Elmhurst Coll., Ill., 1965-66; dean, prin. Antioch Community High Sch., Ill., 1966-91; cons. in field; lectr. Contbr. articles to profl. jours. Mem. sanitary dist. Village of Lindenhurst, Ill., 1968-92; planning commn., 1967-77; chmn. long range planning com. and bldg. com. Bella Vista Luth. Ch. Served with U.S. Army, 1945. Recipient Hon. Mention Those Who Excel, Ill. State Bd. Edn., 1980; named Prin. of Yr. for Ill. Nat. Assn. of Secondary Sch. Prins., The Coun. of Chief State Sch. Officers, and the Burger King Corp., 1987. Mem. Lindenhurst Sanitary Dist. (pres. 1968-92), Ill. Prins. Assn. (dir. 1980-81, 83-84, herman graves award, 1991), Nat. Assn. Secondary Sch. Prins . Lutheran. Avocations: Golf; model building; model railroading.

BLEDSOE, MARY LOUISE, medical, surgical nurse; b. Sylacauga, Ala., May 21, 1935; d. Thomas Franklin and Beulah Mae (Vines) Borden; m. Ralph Johnson Bledsoe, June 28, 1958; children: Lynn, Steve, Johnny. LPN, N.F. Nunnelley Tech. Sch., Childersburg, Ala., 1971; AA, Alexander City (Ala.) Jr. Coll, 1989; BSN, Jacksonville (Ala.) State U., 1991. RN, Ala. Pediatric nurse Sylacauga Hosp., 1971-90; med./surg. staff nurse Coosa Valley Med. Ctr., Sylacauga, 1991-92, med./surg. chg. nurse, 1993-94; med./surg. staff nurse Coosa Valley Bapt. Med. Ctr., Sylacauga, 1994-96, charge nurse, 1996—. Musician/choir dir. Rising Star Bapt. Ch., Sylacauga, 1985-93, Mt. Olive Bapt. Ch., Childersburg, 1993-96. lMem. ANA, Ala. State Nurses Assn., Phi Theta Kappa. Baptist. Home: 980 Coaling Rd Sylacauga AL 35150-8743

BLEDSOE, ROBERT TERRELL, English language educator; b. Monticello, Ark., Nov. 14, 1944; s. John Truett and Helen (Millen) B. BA cum laude, Harvard U., 1966; MA, U. Kent, Canterbury, Eng., 1967; PhD, Princeton U., 1971. Asst. prof. English U. Tex., El Paso, 1971-76, assoc. prof., 1977-91, prof., 1991—, chair depts. English and philosophy, 1989-92, 96-99, dir. lit. program Dept. English, 1986-89; presenter papers in field; mem. peer rev. panels, grant reviewer NEH, Washington; pianist for various musical recitals, 1978—. Contbr. articles to profl. pubis. Bd. dirs. El Paso Symphony, 1992—, mem. artistic adv. com., 1992—, El Paso Pro Musica Chamber Choir and Orch., 1981-84; mem. Univ. Libr. cmty. adv. bd., 1988-91. NEH grantee, 1976, 83. Office: U Tex at El Paso English Dept El Paso TX 79968

BLEIDT, BARRY ANTHONY, pharmacy educator; b. South Charleston, W.Va., Mar. 29, 1951; s. Robert Anthony and Mary Frances (Gash) B.; 1 child, Brittany Alice. B in Gen. Studies, BS, U. Ky., 1974; PhD, U. Fla., 1982; PharmD, Xavier U., 1994. Registered pharmacist, Fla., La., Ga. Owner Health Resources Cons., Boston and Houston, 1979—; asst. prof. pharmacy Northeastern U., Boston, 1983-86; asst. prof. pharm. U. Houston, 1986-89; assoc. prof. pharmacy adminstrn. Xavier U., 1989-94; med. information scientist Astra/Merck Group, 1994-95; prin. investigator Upjohn Pharmacy Econs. Grant, Houston, 1988; faculty dir. Practicing Pharmacists Inst., Boston, 1983-86; project dir., host William S. Apple Mem. Program in Pharm., Houston, 1988. Contbr. articles to profl. jours.; guest editor Jour. Pharm. Mktg. and Mgmt., 1988; mem. editorial bd. Clin. Rsch. Reg. Affairs, 1983—. Mem. Assn. Colls. Pharmacy (parliamentarian 1983—), Am. Inst. History of Pharmacy, Ind. Pharm. Assn., Nat. Pharm. Assn. (life), Am. Pub. Health Assn., Fla. Blue Key, U. Fla. Hall of Fame, Nat. Eagle Scout Assn., Sigma Xi, Rho Chi, Omicron Delta Kappa, Phi Lambda Sigma. Home: 2038 Thornton Pl South Charleston WV 25303 Office: Health Resources Cons 2038 Thornton Pl South Charleston WV 25303

BLESSEN, KAREN ALYCE, free-lance illustrator, designer; b. Columbus, Nebr.. BFA, U. Nebr., 1973. Freelance illustrator, 1973-86; designer Dallas Morning News, 1986-89, freelance illustrator, designer, 1989—; owner, illustrator Karen Blessen Illustration, Dallas, 1989—. Rep. Tex. in Absolut Statehood series, Absolut; illustrator: Be An Angel, 1994. Recipient Pulitzer Prize for explanatory journalism, 1989; awards from N.Y. Art Dirs. Club, Soc. Newspaper Design, Dallas Press Club; commd. by Absolut to represent Tex. in Absolut Statehood series. Home and office: Karen Blessen Illustration 6327 Vickery Blvd Dallas TX 75214-3348

BLESSING, EDWARD WARFIELD, petroleum company executive; b. Glenridge, N.J., Oct. 6, 1936; s. Jess Edward Himes and Laura Louise (Warfield) Blessing; adopted s. Donald L. Blessing; m. Cynthia Harris, July 1, 1961 (div. 1969); m. Jeanne Kyle, Jan. 19, 1970 (div. 1980); 1 child, Megan Louise; m. Debra Jean Wayne, July 12, 1986. BA, San Diego State U., 1960; MBA, Harvard U., 1965. Rep. Shearson, Hammill & Co, La Jolla, Calif., 1961-63; cons. McKinsey & Co. Inc., San Francisco and L.A., 1965-68; assoc. mng. dir. Canadawide Investments, Vancouver, B.C. and Calgary, Alta., 1968-69; misc. investor energy and fin. related activities, 1969-75; mng. ptnr. Dexer Assocs., L.A. and Sharjah, United Arab Emirates, 1975-78; exec. v.p. Okla. Oil & Gas Co., Oklahoma City, 1978-80; pres. Blessing Petroleum Co., Blessing Oil Co., Oklahoma City, 1980-87; dir., pres., chief exec. officer Strategic Petroleum, Inc., Dallas, 1987-89; mng. ptnr. The Blessing Group, Dallas, 1989—; Vis. instr., adj. prof. U. Okla. Grad. Sch. Bus. Adminstrn.,

Oklahoma City, 1983-84. Res. dep. sheriff Okla. County Sheriff's Dept., Oklahoma City, 1986-87, Dallas County Sheriff's Dept., 1987-89; mem. Mayor's Adv. Com. on Crime, Dallas, 1988-91; Rep. candidate Calif. 79th Assembly Dist., 1960; hon. dir., chmn. bd. dirs. Calif. Pediatric Ctr., L.A., 1973—; mem. energy subcom. Okla. Dept. Commerce, Oklahoma City, 1987; mem. planning com. Okla. Gov.'s 1987 Energy Conf., Oklahoma City; chmn. stewardship com. Trinity Episcopal Ch. With USMC, 1960-61. Mem. Am. Assn. Petroleum Landmen, Ind. Petroleum Assn. Am. (exec. com., bd. trustees North Cen. Tex. region, fin. com., v.p., dir., Roustabout, mem. econs. policy com., crude oil policy com., econ. task force 1980—), Okla. Ind. Petroleum Assn., Tex. Ind. Producers and Royalty Owners Assn., Dallas C. of C. (energy subcom. 1987-90), Harvard Bus. Sch. Alumni Assn. (sponsor), Oklahoma City C. of C. (chmn. energy coun. 1982-87), Tex. Mid-Continent Oil and Gas Assn., North Tex. Oil and Gas Assn., Hard Hatters, Dallas Wildcat Com., Dallas Petroleum Club (bd. dirs.), Rotary Club Dallas. Episcopalian. Home: 6582 Briarmeade Dr Dallas TX 75240-7912 Office: The Blessing Group 1600 Three Lincoln Ctr 5430 Lyndon B Johnson Fwy Dallas TX 75240-2601

BLEVINS, ANDREA ELIZABETH, secondary education educator; b. Colorado Springs, Dec. 22, 1944; d. Sydney Stewart and Olive Elizabeth (Reed) McLean; m. Bobby Eldon Blevins, Nov. 15, 1969. BA in Polit. Sci. with Distinction, Wash. State U., 1966, MA, 1969; profl. cert., West Ga. Coll., 1982. Cert. polit. sci. tchr., middle grades tchr., Ga. Tchr. social studies, lang. arts, math. Clayton County Bd. Edn., Jonesboro, Ga., 1979—; swim team coach Pointe South Middle Sch., Jonesboro, 1982-94, mem. multicultural edn. com., 1990—, supr. sch. publs., 1982—. Recipient Hon. life membership for outstanding svc. to our children and youth Ga. PTA. Mem. AAUW, ASCD, Profl. Assn. Ga. Educators, Pi Sigma Alpha. Methodist. Home: 8282 Winston Way Jonesboro GA 30236-4057 Office: Pointe South Middle Sch 626 Flint River Rd Jonesboro GA 30236-3407

BLEVINS, CHARLES RUSSELL, publishing executive; b. Kittaning, Pa., Apr. 6, 1942; s. Clarence Ray and Elizabeth Sarah (Warren) B.; m. Gale Watkins Crittenden, Dec. 16, 1967; children: Charles Jr., Rush. BS, Ind. U., 1964. Asst. prodn. exec. Wall St. Jour., Cleve., D.C. and Princeton, 1964-71, Gannett Co. Inc., El Paso Agy., El Paso, Tex., 1971-76; prodn. exec. Rockford Newspapers, Rockland, Ill., 1976-77; corp. prodn. dir. Gannett Corp. Hdqrs., Rochester, N.Y., 1977-79; v.p., prodn. Gannett Corp. Hdqrs., Arlington, Va., 1979-89; chief exec. officer Blevins Harding Group, Vienna, Va., 1989—; speaker European Printing Conf., Newspaper Quality Meeting Conf.; chmn. Conf. Quality-Newspaper Assn., Conf. Research & Engring. Council, Chgo., Rsch. and Engring. Coun. Com. Graphic Arts Techs. Standards Unit Loading. Creator quality standards, operating procedures USA Today, 1981-86. Judge RIT/USA Today Quality Cup for Individuals and Teams, 1992—. Mem. Am. Newspaper Pub. Assn. (tech. com. 1985-89, officer internat. newspaper group 1989—), Rsch. and Engring. Coun. of Graphic Arts (v.p. 1985-94), Rochester Inst. Tech. Coun., W.Va. Inst. Tech. Adv. Coun., Inca Fiej Rsch. Assn. (press com.). Office: Blevins Harding Group 1617 Montmorency Dr Vienna VA 22182

BLEVINS, DONNA CATON, writer; b. Naha City, Okinawa, Japan, Jan. 13, 1965; came to U.S., 1967; d. Donald Herbert Jr. and Setsuko (Ukuda) Caton; m. Gary Lee Blevins, Feb. 29, 1992. BA in English, Ga. State U., 1991. Prin. dancer Ruth Mitchell Dance Co., Atlanta, 1976-83; paper distbr. U.S. A. Today newspaper, Roswell, Ga., 1983-84, Atlanta Jour./Constitution, 1986-88; optical technician Dr. John W. Hollier, O.D., Roswell, 1983-85; fitness instr. Am. Fitness Ctr., Roswell, Ga., 1984-86; waitress Kobe Steaks, Atlanta, 1988; air import specialist Nippon Express U.S.A., Inc., Atlanta, 1988-92; writer's asst., editor Laurie Lee Dovey, Alpharetta, Ga., 1992-93; freelance writer, photographer, 1993—; model for artist Lisa Iris, Atlanta, 1989; dancer TV comml. Ruth Mitchell Dance Co., 1980, Mr. Jr. Am. Contest, Atlanta, 1980; cons., Atlanta, 1993—, Plano, Tex., 1993-94, L.A., 1995—. Founder The Momo Newsletter, 1996; contbr. articles to mags. and newspapers. Pell grantee, 1984-85. Mem. Nat. Orgn. Outdoor Women, Dog Writers Assn. Am., Cat Writers Assn. (Excellence cert. for best cat photo 1994, Muse medallion 1994). Office: PO Box 135 Zachary LA 70791-0135

BLEVINS, GARY LYNN, architect, real estate broker, real estate appraiser; b. St. Charles, Ark., Feb. 17, 1941; s. Franklin Monroe and Frances Pauline (Breland) B. BS in Architecture, U. Tex., 1964, BArch, 1969; MBA, So. Meth. U., 1974; postgrad. U. Tex., Dallas, 1975-76. Registered architect, Tex., Fla.; lic. real estate broker, Tex.; cert. real estate appraiser, Tex.; lic. interior designer, Tex.; cert. Nat. Coun. Archtl. Registration Bds., Constrn. Specifications Inst. Draftsman, Omniplan Architects, Dallas, 1969-70; project mgr. STB Archs., Dallas, 1970-71; designer Architectonics, Inc., Dallas, 1971-72; arch. Envirodynamics, Inc., Dallas, 1972-75; arch./real estate broker Gary L. Blevins Co., Dallas, 1975-77, Trammell Crow Co., Dallas, 1977-83; arch., owner Gary L. Blevins, AIA; real estate broker, owner Gable Cos., 1983—; v.p., mgr. Farr Constrn. Co., Dallas, 1983-85, owner, 1994—; instr. architecture El Centro Coll., 1981-85; owner, head tennis profl. Dallas Tennis and Sports Club, 1987-90; mem. World Championship Tennis Adv. Bd. Tennis Profls., 1987-89; mem. profl. adv. panel KAEPA Sporting Equipment, 1987—; mem. retail adv. panel Tennis Buyers Guide mag., 1988—. Served with USN, 1964-67, Vietnam. Mem. AIA (coms. design, urban planning), Tex. Soc. Archs., Am. Planning Assn., Nat. Assn. Realtors, Tex. Assn. Realtors, Greater Dallas Assn. Realtors, Tex. Apt. Owners Assn. (NAR appraisal sect.), Bldg. Owners and Mgrs. Assn., Appraisal Inst., Constrn. Specifications Inst., The 500, Inc., Dallas Classic Guitar Soc. Dallas Mus. Art, Dallas Symphony Assn. So. Meth. U. M.B.A. Assn., U.S. Tennis Assn., Tex. Tennis Assn., Dallas Tennis Assn., Dallas Profl. Tennis Assn. Republican. Methodist. Office: 917 Tipperary Dallas TX 75218-2840

BLEVINS, LEON WILFORD, political science educator, minister; b. Brownfield, Tex., Oct. 2, 1937; s. Bernice Wilford and Virgie Opal (Bevers) B.; m. Shannah Pharr, Aug. 28, 1960; children: Tab, Keith, Shaleah. BA, Wayland Bapt. U., 1961; postgrad., Southwestern Bapt. Theol. Sem., Ft. Worth, 1961-63; MA, U. Tex., El Paso, 1967. Ordained to ministry So. Bapt. Conv., 1963. Pastor chs. Tex., N.Mex. and Calif., 1962-72; lectr., tchr. polit. sci. U. Tex., El Paso, 1965-67, Tex. Tech U., 1967-70, West Tex. State U., 1970-72; instr. polit. sci. El Paso Community Coll., 1972—. Author: A Topical Dictionary of American Government and Politics, 1973, Texas Government in National Perspective, 1986, also numerous text study guides and manuals; appeared as Jesus in ann. outdoor Easter Pageant, as Uncle Sam in parades and celebrations, numerous other characters. Mem. numerous hon. socs. in scholarship, pllit. sci., history, social sci., drama, and fgn. langs. Home: 10305 Ashwood Dr El Paso TX 79925-6313

BLEVINS, MELISSA FRANCES, library media specialist; b. Chattanooga, Oct. 17, 1967; d. Bobby C. Blevins and Judi L. (Maxwell) Bevil. BS in Edn., U. Ga., 1990; MEd, Middle Tenn. State U., 1992; postgrad., Tenn. State U., 1993—. Cert. sch. libr. media specialist K-12, social sci. edn., Tenn. Libr. media specialist Met. Nashville Pub. Schs., 1992—. Grantee Libr. Power Site DeWitt Wallace-Reader's Digest Fund, 1994. Mem. ALA, Tenn. Assn. of Sch. Librs., Kappa Delta Pi. Office: Tulip Grove Elem Sch 414 Tyler Dr Hermitage TN 37076-2144

BLICK, THOMAS EDWARD, JR., journalism educator, newspaper editor; b. Richmond, Va., July 2, 1945; S. Thomas Edward and Ida Lee (Craig) B.; m. Lynda Faye James, July 26, 1981. Student, Hampden-Sydney (Va.) Coll., 1963-64; BA in Math., U. Richmond, 1967; MA in Journalism, Pa. State U., 1980; PhD in Comms., U. Tenn., 1986. Tchr. math. Brunswick Acad., Lawrenceville, Va., 1967-69, 70-79; editor Brunswick Times-Gazette, Lawrenceville, Va., 1969-70; faculty journalism S.E. Mo. State U., Cape Girardeau, 1980-83; student publs. coord. Kennesaw State Coll., Marietta, Ga., 1986-90; assoc. prof. journalism La. Tech. U., Ruston, 1990—; yearbook judge Tenn. High Sch. Press Assn., Knoxville, 1991—; high sch. and coll. publs. judge Columbia Scholastic Press Assn., N.Y.C., 1979-83, 87-90; web site mgr. dept. journalism, campus newspaper La. Tech. U., Ruston, newsletter designer, editor coll. human ecology, 1990—. Newsletter designer/editor La. Tech. Alumni Found., Ruston, 1993—. Deacons and Sunday sch. tchr. Dolphin (Va.) Bapt. Ch., 1970-79, New Salem Bapt. Ch., Kennesaw, Ga., 1988-90; Sunday sch. dept. dir. Temple Bapt. Ch., Ruston, 1991-95. Mem. Soc. Profl. Journalists (chpt. advisor 1995—), Coll. Media Advisers (rsch. chmn. 1986—, Citation for Meritorious Svc. 1991, 92), Soc. for Newspaper Design (edn. com. 1990-92), Soc. for Collegiate Journalists (chpt. advisor 1980-83), Assn. for Edn. in Journalism and Mass Comm. (rsch. paper judge 1990—). Home: 1805 Wade Dr Ruston LA 71270-4855 Office: La Tech Univ Dept Journalism PO Box 10258 Ruston LA 71272

BLIGEN, CORINE ILLERY, elementary school educator; b. Manning, S.C.; m. Robert E. Bligen, Jr.; 2 daus. BA in Elem. Edn., Morris Coll., 1959; postgrad., S.C. State Coll., U. S.C., Francis Marion Coll., Presbyn. Sch. Christian Edn., New Harmony Presbytery; MA in Christian Edn., Internat. Bible Coll. and Seminary. Cert. spl. edn. tchr. for emotionally mentally handicapped. Tchr. Paxville (S.C.) Elem. Sch. Clarendon County Sch. Dist., 1959-64; tchr. Fleming Mid. Sch. Lee County Pub. Sch. Dist. # 1, Lynchburg, S.C., 1965-71; diagnostic prescriptive tchr. Lee County Pub. Sch., Bishopville, S.C., 1981-83; resource specialist Mt. Pleasant H.S. Lee County Pub. Sch. Dist., Elliott, S.C., 1981-87; substitute tchr. Lee County Pub. Schs., 1987-92; tchr. St. Jude Pvt. Sch. Diocese of Charleston, Sumter, S.C., 1993—; writing workshop leader Lee County Pub. Schs. Dist., presenter Young Writers Conf. Author poetry. Sunday sch. tchr. 2d Presbyn. Ch. (U.S.A.), Sumter, mem. Willing Workers Orgn., Christian edn. com., past dir., counselor summer camps, numerous other coms. Recipient Walker E. Solomon Human Rels. award, Outstanding Cmty. Svc. award Zeta Phi Beta, Martin Luther King, Jr. Devoted Svc. award, 1992, many other awards from various religious and civic orgns. Mem. Nat. Coun. Negro Women (Talent award 1982), Sumter Gallery Art, Sumter Poetry Club, Coun. Exceptional Children, Sumter Music Guild, Inc., Life Study Fellowship, Morris Coll. Alumni Assn., Internat. Soc. Poets, Inc., World of Poetry, Inc. Home: 231 Palmetto St Sumter SC 29150-6861

BLILEY, THOMAS JEROME, JR., congressman; b. Chesterfield County, Va., Jan. 28, 1932; s. Thomas J. and Carolyn F. Bliley; m. Mary Virginia Kelley, June 22, 1957; children: Mary Vaughan, Thomas Jerome III. B.A., Georgetown U., 1952. Pres. Joseph W. Bliley Funeral Home, 1972-80; mem. 97th-104th Congresses from 3rd (now 7th) Va. dist., Washington, D.C., 1981—; former ranking minority mem. D.C. com., now chmn. House Commerce Com.; vice-mayor Richmond City Council, 1968-70, mayor, 1970-77; past bd. dirs. Nat. League Cities; past pres. Va. Mcpl. League. Past bd. dirs. Crippled Children's Hosp.; past bd. dirs. St. Mary's Hosp.; bd. visitors Va. Commonwealth U. Served with USN. Republican. Roman Catholic.

BLISS, RONALD GLENN, lawyer; b. Buckeye, Ariz., Mar. 22, 1943; s. Glenn Francis Bliss and Jessie Marie (Waymire) Harrington; m. Charlene Wallace, Sept. 18, 1965; children: Erik, Jason. BS, USAF Acad., 1964; JD, Baylor U., 1976. Bar: Tex. 1976, U.S. Dist. Ct. (so. dist.) Tex. 1977, (no. dist.) Tex. 1981, (we. dist.) Tex. 1985, U.S. Ct. Appeals (5th cir.) 1979, (11th cir.) 1982, (D.C. cir.) 1982, U.S. Supreme Ct. 1980. Capt., fighter pilot USAF, U.S., Vietnam, 1964-74; prisoner of war Vietnam, 1966-73; assoc. Fulbright & Jaworski, Houston, 1976-84, ptnr., 1984—; mem. adv. com. So. Dist. Tex., 1992; acting chmn. Tex. Aerospace Commn., 1992-96. Contbr. to profl. jours. Pres. Norchester Club Inc., 1980; bd. dirs. Athletic Club Houston, 1984-85; bd. govs. Houston Center Club, 1987—. Mem. ABA, Tex. Bar Assn., Am. Intellectual Property Law Assn., Houston Intellectual Property Law Assn., Licensing Exec. Soc., 4th Allied POW Wing. Office: Fulbright & Jaworski LLP 1301 Mckinney St Houston TX 77010

BLITZ, PEGGY SANDERFUR, corporate travel management company official; b. Pitts., Apr. 12, 1940; d. Charles I. and Rebecca Polk (McBride) Wallace; m. Clark L. Blitz, Aug. 25, 1962 (div. Apr. 1974); children: Danette L., Jonathan D. BS, Ball State U., 1962; postgrad., No. Ill. U., 1976-77. Cert. speech therapist, spl. edn. tchr. Tchr. mentally retarded Anderson (Ind.) Pub. Schs., 1962-64; speech therapist Elgin (Ill.) Pub. Schs., 1964-66; pvt. practice speech therapy Elgin, 1966-68; tchr. mentally retarded Easter Seal Rehab. Ctr., Elgin, 1968-77; account exec. Whitehall Hotel, Chgo., 1977-79; regional mgr. IVI Travel Inc., Milw., 1979-85; sr. v.p. IVI Travel Inc., Dallas, 1985-88; pres. Travelmasters, Inc., Chgo., 1988-91; staff devel. Kemper Securities, Inc., Chgo., 1991-92; pres. Travel Mgmt. Cons., St. John, V.I., 1991—; property mgr. Short-Term Vacation Rentals, 1992—. Presbyterian. Home and Office: PO Box 8333 Cruz Bay VI 00831-8333

BLIWISE, DONALD LINN, neurology educator; b. Newark, June 14, 1952; s. Daniel and Ruth (Offenkrantz) B.; m. Nancy Gourash, Oct. 12, 1980; 1 child, Nathan Todd. BA cum laude, Clark U., 1974; MA, U. Chgo., 1978, PhD, 1982. Clin. rsch. assoc. Stanford (Calif.) Med. Sch., 1982-86, sr. clin. rsch. scientist, 1986-92; clin. asst. prof. psychiatry U. Calif., San Francisco, 1984-86; assoc. prof. neurology Emory U. Med. Sch., Atlanta, 1992—; cons. geriat. psychiatry task force Am. Psychiat. Assn., 1984, Oxford Med. Ltd., 1987, Discovery Health Cons., Sacramento, 1986, spl. study sect. NIH, 1988; adv. bd. Sch. Sleep Medicine, Palo Alto, Calif., 1991—; mem. MDA study sect. NIMH, 1992-96. Contbr. articles to profl. jours. Recipient Clin. Rsch. Trainee award NIMH, 1978-80; Rsch. grantee NIA, 1992-96. Fellow Am. Sleep Disorder Assn.; mem. AAAS, Am. Psychol. Assn., Gerontol. Soc. Am., INS, Sleep Rsch. Soc., Phi Beta Kappa. Office: Emory U Med Sch WMB 6000 Atlanta GA 30322

BLIZNAKOV, MILKA TCHERNEVA, architect; b. Varna, Bulgaria, Sept. 20, 1927; came to U.S., 1961, naturalized, 1966; d. Ivan Dimitrov and Maria Kesarova (Khorozova) Tchernev; m. Emile G. Bliznakov, Oct. 23, 1954 (div. Apr., 1974). Architect-engr. diploma, State Tech. U., Sofia, 1951; Ph.D., Engring.-Structural Inst., Sofia, 1959; Ph.D. in Architecture, Columbia U., 1971. Sr. researcher Ministry Heavy Industry, Sofia, 1950-53; pvt. practice architecture Sofia, 1954-59; assoc. architect Noel Combrisson, Paris, 1959-61; designer Perkins & Will Partnership, White Plains, N.Y., 1963-67; project architect Lathrop Douglass, N.Y.C., 1967-71; assoc. prof. architecture and planning Sch. Architecture, U. Tex., Austin, 1972-74; prof. Coll. Architecture, Va. Poly. Inst. and State U., Blacksburg, 1974—; prin. Blacksburg, 1975—; bd. dirs. founder Internat. Archives Women in Architecture, Va. Poly. Inst. and State U., The Parthena award, 1994. Prin. works include Speedwell Ave. Urban Renewal, Morristown, N.J., 1967-69, Wilmington (Del.) Urban Renewal, 1968-70, Springfield (Ill.) Ctrl. Area Devel., 1969-71, Arlington County (Va.) Redevel., 1975-77; author: (with others) Utopia e Modernitá, 1989, Reshaping Russian Architecture, 1990, Russian Housing in the Modern Age, 1993, Nietzsche and Soviet Culture, 1994, New Perspectives on Russian and Soviet Artistic Culture, 1994, Signs of Times, Culture and the Emblems of Apocalypse, 1996. William Kinne scholar, summer 1970, vis. scholar Inst. Advanced Russian Studies, The Wilson Ctr. of Smithsonian Instn., 1988; NEA grantee, 1973-74, Am. Beautiful Found. grantee, 1973, Internat. Rsch. and Exch. Bd. grantee, 1984-93; Fulbright Hays rsch. fellow, 1983-84, 91; recipient Parthend award, 1994. Mem. Internat. Archive Women in Architecture (founder, chair bd. dirs.), Am. Assn. Tchrs. Slavic and East European Langs., Soc. Archtl. Historians, Nat. Trust Hist. Preservation, Am. Assn. Advancement of Slavic Studies, Assn. Collegiate Schs. of Planning, Inst. Modern Russian Culture (chairperson architecture, co-founder, dir.), Assn. Collegiate Schs. of Architecture. Home: 2813 Tall Oaks Dr Blacksburg VA 24060-8109 Office: Coll Architecture Va Poly Inst And State Blacksburg VA 24061

BLOCK, ERNEST FRANCIS JONATHAN, surgeon; b. L.A., Jan. 17, 1961; s. Louis and Rosamunde Elisabeth (Herz) Finkelstein; m. Susan Carol Share, May 13, 1990; children: Geoffrey Jacob Hamilton, Andrew Isaac Leland. BA, Cornell U., 1982; MD, U. Miami, 1986. Diplomate Am. Bd. Surgery; cert. surg. critical care, ATLS state faculty. Intern Albert Einstein Med. Ctr., Phila., 1986-87, resident in surgery, 1987-91; fellow in critical care Jackson Meml. Hosp., Miami, 1991-92, fellow in trauma surgery, 1992-93; asst. prof. surgery La. State U. Med. Ctr., Shreveport, 1993—, dir. trauma critical care, 1993—; dir. Trauma Quality Assurance Program, Shreveport, 1993—; comms. com. SCCM Surg. sect. 1996—; presenter, lectr. in field. Contbr. articles to profl. jours.; prodr. med. motion pictures on operative techniques. Mem. MADD, Shreveport, 1994—. Rsch. grantee Pfizer Pharms., 1993-94, 94-95. Fellow ACS; mem. Soc. of Critical Care Medicine (Surgery sect. comms. com. 1996—), Shreveport Med. Soc. (emergency med. svcs. adv. com. 1993—), Ea. Assn. for the Surgery of Trauma (com. info. tech. com. 1996—), Am. Trauma Soc., Am. Inst. for Ultrasound in Medicine, Am. Assn. for the Advancement of Automotive Medicine, Southeastern Surg. Congress. Republican. Jewish. Home: 1231 Remington Circle Shreveport LA 71106 Office: LSUMC Surgery 1501 Kings Hwy Shreveport LA 71130

BLOCK, MICHAEL DAVID, minister; b. Albuquerque, Jan. 19, 1958; s. Isaac Edward and Lucy Mac (Waide) B.; m. Rebecca Lynn Hart, June 30, 1979; 1 child, Nathanael David. BA, Wayland Bapt. U., 1980; MDiv, Southwestern Bapt. Sem., 1983, PhD, 1990. Ordained to ministry Bapt. Ch., 1982. Min. music Finney Bapt. Ch., Plainview, Tex., 1978-79, Date St. Bapt. Ch., Plainview, Tex., 1979-80; pastor Levita Bapt. Ch., Gatesville, Tex., 1984-85, 1st Bapt. ch., Comanche, Okla., 1985-91, Crestwood Bapt. Ch., Oklahoma City, 1991-96, First Bapt. Ch., Monett, Mo., 1996—; lectr. Ministry Tng. Inst., Okla. Bapt. U., 1992-96. Basketball coach Youth Sports League, Duncan, 1989-90. Mem. Comanche C. of C. (coord. Christmas food baskets 1986-90), Mullins Bapt. Assn. (sec., dir. missions, search com. 1987-88, moderator 1987-89, chmn. budget com. 1990-91), Capital Bapt. Assh. (vice moderator 1992-94, chair com. on coms. 1994-95, pers. com. 1994-96, exec. com. 1992-94, continuing edn. com. 1992-94), Ministerial Alliance. Republican. Office: 412 4th Monett MO 65708

BLOCK, MITCHELL STERN, lawyer; b. Dallas, May 31, 1953; s. Richard E. Block and Phyllis (Katz) Harp; m. Sara Whitney Block, Apr. 7, 1984. BA, So. Meth. U., 1976, JD, 1980. Bar: Tex. 1980, U.S. Dist. Ct. (no. dist.) Tex., 1980. Law clk. A. J. Pope III, Esquire, Corpus Christi, Tex., 1971; law clk., then assoc. James A. Gandy, Esquire, Dallas, 1978-81; asst. county atty. Nolan County Atty.'s Office, Sweetwater, Tex., 1981; ptnr. Clark & Block, Snyder, Tex., 1981-82; pvt. practice Austin, Tex., 1982-83; assoc. Halperin & Marcus, N.Y.C., 1984, W. C. Roberts, Jr., Esquire, Dallas, 1985-86; asst. corp. Wyatt Cafeterias, Inc., Dallas, 1986-88, corp. atty., 1989-91, gen. counsel, v.p. real estate, sec., 1991-93; real estate atty. Morrison Restaurants Inc., Mobile, Ala., 1993-95; v.p., gen. counsel, sec. Morrison Fresh Cooking, Inc., Atlanta, 1996—. Mem. State Bar Tex. (corp. counsel sect., labor & employment law sect.), Dallas Bar Assn. (corp. counsel sect.), Internat. Coun. Shopping Ctrs. Office: Morrison Fresh Cooking Inc 4893 Riverdale Rd Ste 260 Atlanta GA 30337

BLOCK, OLIVER J., marine corps officer; b. Richmond, Va., Oct. 24, 1967; s. Dennis Buckley and Gwendolyn Mae (Bock) B. BS, U.S. Naval Acad., 1989; MBA, Loyola U., New Orleans, 1996. Commd. USMC, 1989—, advanced through grades to capt.; supply officer USMC, Yuma, Ariz., 1990-93; ops. officer, aide-de-camp 4th Force Svc. Support Group USMC, New Orleans, 1993—; water polo coach Tulane U.., New Orleans, 1996. Decorated Marine Corps Commendation Medal. Mem. U.S. Water Polo Assn., Alpha Sigma Nu. Home: 7731 Panola St New Orleans LA 70118

BLODER, LISA W., critical care nurse, mental health nurse; b. Birmingham, Ala., June 28, 1965; d. James A. and Audrey E. (Bryant) Weeks; m. Harald K. Bloder, Mar. 25, 1989; 1 child, Amanda. AS in Emergency Medicine, Trenholm St. Tech., 1984; ASN, Jefferson State Jr. Coll., 1987. RN, Ala., Fla.; cert. case mgr. Staf nurse Humana Hosp. East Mongtomery (Ala.); nurse mgr., dir. case mgr., dir. clin. assessment ctr. Laurel Oaks Hosp., Orlando, Fla., 1988-95; case mgr., dir. case mgmt. Ctrl. Fla. region Integrated Health Svcs. of Orlando, 1995—. Mem. Case Mgmt. Soc. of Am. Home: 16012 Four Lakes Ln Montverde FL 34756

BLOME, DOROTHY CARTER, pediatrics nurse; b. Dallas, Aug. 16, 1943; d. Paul Gilbert and Dorothy Mae (Lamb) Carter; div.; children: Craig A., Glenn C. BS, Tex. Woman's U., 1965; MN, Emory U., 1968; postgrad. pediatric nurse practitioner, U. Tex., Arlington, 1994. RN, CPNP, advanced nurse practitioner, Tex. Staff nurse pediatrics Parkland Meml. Hosp., Dallas, 1965, Bapt. Hosp., Pensacola, Fla., 1965; staff nurse Egleston Children's Hosp., Atlanta, 1966-67; staff nurse neonatal ICU Baylor Med. Ctr., Dallas, 1977; staff nurse, then head nurse pediatrics Richardson (Tex.) Med. Ctr., 1977-82; mem. faculty pediatric nursing Tex. Woman's U., Denton, 1982-88; clin. nurse specialist Children's Med. Ctr., Dallas, 1988-95; CPNP Devel. Pediatric Svcs., 1995—. Contbg. author: Nursing Care of Infants and Children, 1991. Mem. ANA, Tex. Nurses Assn. (Gt. 100 Nurse award 1992), Sigma Theta Tau. Office: Devel Pediatric Svcs Ste 604 8210 Walnut Hill Ln Dallas TX 75231

BLOMELEY, SHERRY LYNN, librarian; b. Miami, Fla., Aug. 23, 1948; d. William Stanley Jr. and Evelyn Virginia (Bennett) B. BA, Eckerd Coll., 1970; M of Libr., Emory U., 1971. Libr. Our Lady of Assumption Sch., Atlanta, 1971-72; rsch. libr. Andrew E. McColgan, Atlanta, 1972-73, Landauer Assocs., Atlanta, 1973-76; head law libr. Kutak, Rock & Huie, Atlanta, 1976-78, Jones, Bird & Howell, Atlanta, 1978-79; corp. libr. Mgmt. Sci. Am., Atlanta, 1979-83; real estate appraiser McColgan & Co., Atlanta, 1983-86; br. mgr. Cobb County Pub. Libr. System, Marietta, Ga., 1986—; trainer Cobb County Govt., 1991—, others; cons. in field. Mem. USCG Aux. Office: Kemp Meml Br Libr 4029 Due West Rd Marietta GA 30064-1021

BLOMGREN, DAVID KENNETH, dean, pastor; b. Rochelle, Ill., June 1, 1940; s. Darwin Wayne and Roslyn (Castle) B.; m. Susan Marie Blomgren, Nov. 3, 1961; children: Brenda Lynn, Bradley Wayne, Bryan Robert. BA, Tenn. Temple U., 1963; MA, U. Portland, 1969; MDiv, Western Cons. Bapt. Sem., 1967, ThM, 1968, DMin, 1976; ThD, Logos Grad. Sch., 1986; MACE, Luther Rice Sem., 1989. V.p. Portland (Oreg.) Bible Coll., 1967-71; pres. Logos Bible Coll. and Grad. Sch., Tampa, Fla., 1987-89; grad. dean Fla. Beacon Bible Coll., Largo, Fla., 1989—; sr. pastor Tampa Bay Christian Ctr., Brandon, Fla., 1983—; asst. mgr. Sta. KPAZ-TV Christian TV, Phoenix, 1971-73; advisor Victory Christian Univ., San Diego, 1990—. Author: The Song of the Lord, 1978, Prophetic Gatherings, 1979, Restoring God's Glory, 1985 (Bestseller 1987), Restoring Praise and Worship, 1989; exec. editor: The Trumpet Call Mag., 1989—. Chmn. Montavilla Community Assn., Portland, 1977-78. Mem. Mins. Fellowship Internat. (apostolic team Portland chpt. 1985—). Office: Tampa Bay Christian Ctr 3920 S Kings Ave Brandon FL 33511-7749

BLONDIN, JOAN, nephrologist educator; b. Beaumont, Tex., Nov. 28, 1936; d. Joseph Albert and Ona Mae (Williamson) B. BS, La. Tech U., 1959; MNS, Cornell U., 1961; MD, La. State U., 1969. Diplomate Am. Bd. Internal Medicine. Instr. U. Ala., Tuscaloosa, 1961-62; rsch. assoc. Cornell U., Ithaca, N.Y., 1962-63; asst. specialist La. State U., Baton Rouge, 1963-65; intern Barnes Hosp., St. Louis, 1969-70, resident, 1970-72; postdoctoral fellow Washington U., St. Louis, 1972-74, asst. prof., 1974-78; ptnr. Nephrology Cons., Monroe, La., 1978—; assoc. prof. La. State U., Shreveport, 1978-89; adj. prof. human ecology La. Tech. U., 1988; active staff St. Francis Med. Ctr., 1978—, North Monroe Community Hosp., 1984—, Glenwood Regional Med. Ctr., 1978, 92—; adj. prof. Coll. Pharmacy, Northeast La. U., 1996. Contbr. articles to profl. jours. Bd. dirs. Central Bank; bd. trustees Nat. Kidney Found. of La., 1988—; mem. La. Bd. Regents, 1989-94, chmn., 1992; med. dir. North La. Dialysis Ctr., 1992—, Ruston Kidney Ctr. Fellow La. Cancer Society, 1966, NIH, 1968. Mem. AAAS, ACP, End Stage Renal Disease (chmn. quality consensus com. 1994—), Internat. Soc. Nephrology, Am. Soc. Internal Medicine, Am. Soc. Nephrology, Am. Soc. Tropical Medicine and Hygiene, Am. Soc. Parenteral and Enteral Nutrition, Am. Heart Assn. (Coun. on Hypertension), Renal Physicians Assn. (bd. dirs., fin. com. 1991—), N.Y. Acad. Scis., La. State Med. Soc. (del. 1988—), Alpha Omega Alpha, Phi Kappa Phi, Sigma Xi, Omicron Nu. Republican. Episcopalian. Home: 301 Country Club Rd Monroe LA 71201-2562 Office: Nephrology Cons 711 Wood St Monroe LA 71201-7549

BLOODWORTH, VELDA JEAN, librarian, educator; b. Campobello, S.C., June 28, 1929; d. Lloyd Ernest and Nora Frances (McNeal) Burke; m. Clifford Burton Bloodworth, Aug. 14, 1949; children: Jill Henderson, Jackie Herschberger. BA, So. Coll., Collegedale, Tenn., 1967; MS, Fla. State U., 1968; MAT, Rollins Coll., 1979. Cert. tchr., Fla. Libr. Forest Lake Acad., Apopka, Fla., 1968-74, Rollins Coll., Winter Park, Fla., 1974—; cons. libr. Forest Lake Acad., Apopka, 1987-88. Editor, curator: (catalog for art mus. exhibit) Jessie B. Rittenhouse Poetry Collection, 1984. Mem. Fla. Libr. Assn., Beta Phi Mu. Home: 3162 Holiday Ave Apopka FL 32703 Office: Rollins Coll Olin Libr 1000 Holt Ave Winter Park FL 32789

BLOOM, CHARLES ROBERT, public relations professional; b. Emporia, Va., June 10, 1962; s. Richard Peyton and Lois Merle (Cohen) B.; m. Cynthia Renee Weaver, June 20, 1987; 1 child, Lindsay Taylor. BA in Journalism, U. S.C., 1985. Asst. sports info. dir. La. State U., Baton Rouge,

1985-87; assoc. sports info. dir. U. Miss., Oxford, 1987-88; sports info. dir. East Carolina U., Greenville, 1988-94, asst. dir. athletics, 1994-95; dir. media svcs. Southeastern Conf., Birmingham, Ala., 1995—; press asst. Games of the XXIII Olympiad, L.A., 1984;. Named to Outstanding Young Men of Am., Jaycees, 1987, 88. Mem. Coll. Sports Info. Dirs. Am. (editor brochures receiving nat. and regional honors), Football Writers Assn. Am., Nat. Assn. Collegiate Dirs. of Athletics (assoc.), Pub. Rels. Soc. Am., U.S. Basketball Writers Assn., Nat. Collegiate Baseball Writers Assn. (v.p.). Office: Southeastern Conf Birmingham AL 35200

BLOOM, STEPHEN EDWARD, marketing professional, consultant; b. Boston, Sept. 8, 1955; s. Alan Shale and Elinor Lois (Waldstein) B. BS in Mktg., Castleton (Vt.) State Coll., 1979. Asst. market analyst U.S. Lend Lease, Sarasota, Fla., 1980-81; mgr. product devel. Credit Mktg., Inc., Sarasota, 1981-82; pvt. practice cons. market research Sarasota, 1982-83; sr. brand mgr. Cook Bates Co., Inc. div. London Internat. U.S. Holdings, Inc., Sarasota, Fla., 1983-92; pres. B & P Internat., Inc., Sarasota, 1992—. Author: (catalog) Lite-R Line, 1985 (Addy award 1985). Mem. Am. Mgmt. Assn., Am. Mktg. Assn. Home: 8990 Huntington Pointe Dr Sarasota FL 34238 Office: B & P Internat Inc 2828 Proctor Rd Sarasota FL 34231-6423

BLOOMER, CAROLYN MITCHELL, cultural anthropologist; b. Wichita, Kans., Oct. 11, 1935; d. Donald Isaac and Kathrine (Reed) Mitchell; m. Richard Hutchison Bloomer, Aug. 19, 1955 (div. Apr. 18, 1973); children: Michael Bradford, Jennifer, Robert Reed, Carrie, Joshua David; m. Lynn Ernest Stauffer, Jr., Dec. 24, 1976. BA, Wichita State U., 1955; M. Art Edn., U. Hartford Art Sch., West Hartford, Conn., 1975; PhD, U. N.C., Chapel Hill, 1992. Tchr. art Parish Hill H.S., Chaplin, Conn., 1967-75; asst. prof. art and art edn. Monmouth U., West Long Branch, N.J., 1976-81; lectr. art edn. U. N.C., Chapel Hill, 1981-84; liberal arts faculty coord. cultural beliefs curriculum Ringling Coll. Art and Design, Sarasota, Fla., 1992—; coord., cultural exch. with China for artists and designers, Sarasota, 1991—; rsch. analyst, program trainer Performance Learning Sys., Westwood, N.J., 1975-79; lectr. in field. Author: Principles of Visual Perception, 1976, rev. edit., 1990; contbr. articles to profl. jours.; editl. writer Internat. Projects Assistance Svcs., Carrboro, N.C., 1990-92; exhibit designer Monmouth Mus., Lincroft, N.J., 1980-82, S.I. Children's Mus., 1978-80. Office of Internat. Programs/U. N.C. pre-dissertation travel awardee, 1988; U. N.C. Off-campus Dissertation fellow, 1989; Ringling Coll. Art and Design Profl. Devel. grantee, 1992—. Mem. Assn. Asian Studies, Am. Anthrop. Assn., Authors Guild, Southeastern Coll. Art Conf. Democrat. Daoist. Office: Ringling College of Art and Design 2700 N Tamiami Trl Sarasota FL 34234-5812

BLOSKAS, JOHN D., financial executive; b. Waco, Tex., July 13, 1928; s. George and Alvina (Schrader) B.; m. Anna Louise Nelson, Feb. 7, 1955; children: Suzzanne (dec.), John D., Kenneth Douglas. Exec. sec. Waco Jr. C. of C., 1953-55; assoc. editor Mexia (Tex.) Daily News, 1955-56; dir. publicity Valley C. of C., Weslaco, Tex., 1956-57; religion editor Houston Chronicle, 1957-58; v.p. pub. rels. annuity bd. So. Bapt. Conv., Dallas, 1984-92, v.p., endowment officer annuity bd., 1984-90; v.p. Lady Love Cosmetics, Dallas, 1984-90; retired, 1990, fin. mgmt. cons., 1990—. Author: Staying in the Black, Financially, Living Within Your Means; editor: THe Years Ahead. Served with USNR, 1945-49, 50-51. Mem. Southern Bapt. (past pres.), Tex. Bapt. Assn. (past pres.), Pub. Rels. Assn., Pub. Rels. Soc. Am. (accredited), Religious Pub. Rels. Coun., Sales and Mktg. Execs., Bapt. Devel. Officer's Assn., Assn. Bapt. Found. Execs., Dallas Estate Planning Coun., Fellowship Christians in Arts, Media and Entertainment. Home: 5602 Glenlivet Pl Greenville TX 75402-4205 Office: PO Box 11 Greenville TX 75403-0011

BLOUNT, CHARLES WILLIAM, III, lawyer; b. Independence, Mo., Nov. 14, 1946; s. Charles William and Mary Marguarette (Van Trump) B.; m. Susan Penny Smith Turner, Dec. 20, 1969 (div. Nov., 1987); children: Charles William IV, Chaille Elizabeth; m. Bonnie M. Harp., Jan. 1, 1991. BS in Journalism, U. Kans., 1968; JD cum laude, U. Toledo, 1981. Bar: Mo. 1981, U.S. Dist. Ct. (we. dist.) Mo. 1981, Tex. 1985, U.S. Dist. Ct. (no. dist.) Tex. 1988, U.S. Ct. Appeals (5th cir.) 1995. Litigation assoc. Shugart, Thomson & Kilroy, Kansas City, Mo., 1981-84, Hughes & Luce, Dallas, 1984-87; litigation assoc. Simpson & Dowd L.L.P., Dallas, 1987-91, ptnr., 1991-94; mem. Dowd & Blount, Dallas, 1994—. Bd. govs. Coll. Law U. Toledo, Ohio, 1980-81; trustee Episcopal Diocese We. Mo., Kansas City, 1983-84; mem., chmn. com. Boy Scouts of Am., Kansas City, 1983-84, Richardson, Tex., 1984-92. 1st lt. U.S. Army, 1968-72. Mem. Phi Kappa Phi, Phi Kappa Tau (pledge pres., social chmn., activities chmn., 1965—). Office: Dowd & Blount 2828 Woodside St Dallas TX 75204-2582

BLOUNT, THOMAS LEON, newspaper editor; b. Beaver Falls, Pa., June 13, 1935; s. Joseph Leon and Helen ELizabeth (Lawson) B.; m. Betty Lou Drogus, Sept. 9, 1957. BA in Journalism, U. Pitts., 1957. Reporter Wilmington (N.C.) Morning Star, 1957; asst. sports editor News Jour., Mansfield, Ohio, 1957-60; mng. editor Bedford (Pa.) Daily Gazette, 1960-61; sports editor The Idaho Statesman, Boise, 1961-64; copy desk chief Wichita (Kans.) Eagle, 1964-66; reporter, projects editor The News Tribune, Beaver Falls, Pa., 1966-69; mng. editor The News Tribune, Beaver Falls, 1969-78; editor Herald & Review, Decatur, Ill., 1978-89, High Point (N.C.) Enterprise, 1990—; publ. bd. Ea. Ill. U., Charleston, 1981-89; editor in residence Bradley U., Peoria, Ill., 1985; univ. and journalism orgn. seminar leader various topics, 1981—. Bd. vis. High Point U.; bd. dirs. Cities in Schs., High Point C. of C., 1992-94, Alcohol and Drug Action Coalition, 1994—; mem. Crimestoppers; mem. Forward High Point Strategic Plan, Triad Leadership Network; elder Three Presbyn. Ch. Mem. Pa. Assoc. Press mgmt. Editors (past pres.), Ill. Assoc. Press Editors (past pres.), N.C. Assoc. Press News Coun. (pres.), Am. Soc. Newspaper Editors, Internat. Home Furnishing Club, Rotary Club High Point. Republican. Presbyterian. Office: High Point Enterprise 210 Church Ave High Point NC 27262-4806

BLOUNT, WINTON MALCOLM, III, investment executive; b. Albany, Ga., Dec. 14, 1943; s. Winton Malcolm Jr. and Mary Katherine (Archibald) B.; m. Lucy Durr Dunn, June 6, 1970; children: Winton Malcolm IV, K. Stuart, William, Judkins. Student, U. Ala., 1962-63; B.A., U. South, 1966; M.B.A., U. Pa., 1968. With Blount Bros. Corp., Montgomery, Ala., 1968-73, project mgr., 1972-73; with Mercury Constrn. Corp., Montgomery, 1973-77; pres. Mercury Constrn. Corp., 1975-77; chief exec. officer, chmn. bd. Benjamin F. Shaw Co., Wilmington, Del., 1977-80; pres., chief operating officer Blount Internat., Ltd., Montgomery, 1980-83, pres., chief exec. officer, 1983-85; chmn., chief exec. officer Blount Internat., Ltd., 1985-87; sr. v.p. Blount Inc., 1985-87, vice chmn., 1987-89; chmn., chief exec. officer Winton Blount III & Assocs., 1989—; chmn., chief exec. officer Wright Plastics Co., 1989—, Cobb Pontiac-Cadillac & Royal Motor Co., 1990—, Blount-Strange Ford, Lincoln, Mercury, 1991—; bd. dirs. Dunn Constrn. Co., Birmingham, Ala. Mem. Fin. Com. Ala. Rep. com., 1980-82; bd. dirs. So. Rsch. Inst., 1995—, Montgomery YMCA, Episcopal High Sch., 1988-89, 95—, Ala. Pub. Affairs Rsch. Coun., 1979-83, Bus. Coun. Ala.; active Tukabatchee Area coun. Boy Scouts Am., 1980-83; bd. visitors U. Ala. Coll. Commerce and Bus. Adminstrn., 1983-88; mem. bd. control Com. of 100; mem. bd. Leadership Ala., 1989-93, 95—, Ala. Coun. on Econ. Edn. Mem. Chief Execs. Orgn., World Pres.'s Orgn., Young Pres.'s Orgn. (bd. dirs. 1978-94), Montgomery C. of C. (dir.), Del. C. of C. (dir. 1979-80), NAM (dir. 1982-85). Episcopalian. Office: PO Box 230039 Montgomery AL 36123-0039

BLOWERS, BOBBIE, entrepreneur; b. Cleve., Dec. 4, 1944; d. William Atmore and Sarah Esther (Woodruff) Hines; m. James William Ott, May 11, 1985 (div. 1990); m. Gordon Edward Blowers, Nov. 21, 1990; children: Kristina L., Jacklyn C. BS in Med. Tech., Ohio State U., 1966; MA in Psychology, U. Cin., 1989; postgrad., Miami U., Oxford, Ohio, 1989-93. Med. technologist in clin. chemistry/instr. Good Samaritan Hosp., Cin., 1966-67; rsch. biochemist VA Hosp., Cin., 1967-72, U. Cin., 1973, Children's Hosp., 1973-74; mktg. brand asst. Procter & Gamble, Cin., 1974-76; tech. brand mgr. Procter & Gamble, 1976-79, med. mktg. brand mgr., 1979-86, promotion mktg. mgr., 1986-87; v.p./cons., also dir. Orgn. Transformation Technologies, Milford, Ohio, 1988-90; yacht broker, finder, 1991-95; co-capt., organizer 5,000 mile cruise of U.S. waters, 1992-93; house/boat rehab. specialist, 1993—; adj. faculty Ea. Carolina U., 1996—; instr. Pamlico C.C., 1996—; mem. Nat. Ski Patrol, 1981-90. Contbr. articles to profl. jours. Organizer/researcher survey Group of Concerned Citizens for Milford Schs., 1989; counselor Battered Women's Shelter, Hamilton, Ohio, 1990-91. Mem. Neuse Sailing Assn. Home and Office: PO Box 852 Oriental NC 28571-0852

BLUE, CHARLOTTE ANN, intensive care nurse; b. Dallas, Oct. 17, 1947; d. Manza Derward and Charlotte LaVerne (Rains) Renfro; m. Samuel Hunter, Feb. 14, 1967 (div. 1970); 1 child, Samuel Allen Manza Hutner. Diploma, Terrell Sch. Vocat. Nursing, 1973; AA, Eastfield Coll., 1980; AAS in Nursing, El Centro Coll., 1985. ACLS, BLS. Staff vocat. nurse Alexander Hosp., Terrell, Tex., 1973-74, Gaston Episcopal Hosp., Dallas, 1974-76, Terrell State Hosp., 1977-78, Staff Builders Nursing Svc., Dallas, 1978-79; staff vocat. nurse Parkland Meml. Hosp., Dallas, 1980-81, staff nurse med. ICU, 1987-94; staff vocat. nurse ICU, telemetry unit Doctors Hosp., Dallas, 1976-77; charge nurse Ryburn Home for Aged, Dallas, 1981; vicat. nurse ICU Mesquite (Tex.) Physicians Hosp., 1982; staff nurse med. surg. unit Med. Ctr. of Mesquite, 1982-87; utilization mgmt. coord. Physicians Directed Quality Rev., Dallas, 1994—. Mem. AACCN. Episcopalian.

BLUE, KATHY JO, elementary school educator; b. Martinsburg, W.Va., Nov. 13, 1955; d. Daniel Walker and Agnes Rosalie (Hull) Tabler; m. John Kyner Blue, July 12, 1981; 1 child, Sarah Virginia. AS in Nursing, Shepherd Coll., Shepherdstown, W.Va., 1976; BA in Elem. Edn., Shepherd Coll., Sheperdstown, W.Va., 1979; MA, W.Va. U., 1988; reading authorization, 1988. Cert. profl. elem. tchr., tchr. gifted edn. 1-6, reading, W.Va. Nurse City Hosp., Inc., Martinsburg, 1976-78; substitute tchr. Jefferson and Berkeley counties, Charles Town, Martinsburg, 1979-80; elem. tchr. Morgan County Schs., Berkeley Springs, W.Va., 1980-81; substitute tchr. Jefferson County Schs., Charles Town, 1981-86, Chpt. I tchr. reading, 1986—; tutor, Shenandoah Junction, W.Va., 1989—. Recipient Regional Edn. Svc. Agy. Exemplary Teaching Technique in Lang. award, 1994; grantee W.Va. Edn. Fund, 1988, 89, 95. Mem. NEA, Internat. Reading Coun., W.Va. Reading Coun., Jefferson County Reading Assn., W.Va. Edn. Assn., Jefferson County Edn. Assn., Blue Ridge Elem. PTO, T.A. Lowery PTO, Order Ea. Star (worthy matron Shepherdstown 1983-84, 88-89), Alpha Delta Kappa. Republican. Methodist. Home: PO Box 112 Shenandoah Junction WV 25442-0112 Office: Blue Ridge Elem Sch RR 2 Box 362 Harpers Ferry WV 25425-9423

BLUESTEIN, EDWIN A., JR., lawyer; b. Hearne, Tex., Oct. 16, 1930; s. Edwin A. and Frances Grace (Ely) B.; m. Marsha Kay Meredith, Dec. 21, 1957; children: Boyd, Leslie. B.B.A., U. Tex., 1952, J.D., 1958. Bar: Tex. 1957, U.S. Ct. Appeals (5th cir.) 1960, U.S. Dist. Ct. (so. dist.)Tex. 1959, U.S. Dist. Ct. (ea. dist.)Tex. 1965, U.S. Supreme Ct. 1967, U.S. Ct. Appeals (11th cir.) 1982. Law clk. U.S. Dist. Ct., Houston, 1958-59; assoc. Fulbright & Jaworski, Houston, 1959-65, participating atty., 1965-71, ptnr., 1971—; head admiralty dept. Fulbright & Jaworski, 1984-93; sr. ptnr. Fulbright & Jaworski, Houston, 1990—; mem. permanent adv. bd. Tulane Admiralty Law Inst., New Orleans, 1983—; mem. planning com. Houston Marine Ins. Seminar, 1970-76; lectr. profl. seminars. Assoc. editor: American Maritime Cases; contbr. articles to profl. jours. Mem. Tex. Coastal Mgmt. Adv. Com., Austin, 1975-78; bd. dirs. Barbour's Cut Seafarers Ctr., 1992—, Houston Internat. Seafarers Ctr., 1993—. Served with U.S. Army, 1952-54. Recipient Yachtsman of Yr. award Houston Yacht Club, 1978; Eagle Scout, Boy Scouts Am., 1944. Mem. Tex. Bar Found., Maritime Law Assn. U.S. (mem. exec. com. 1980-83), Houston Mariners Club (pres. 1970), Southeastern Admiralty Law Inst. (dir. 1983-85, Houston C. of C. (chmn. ports and waterways com. 1978-79), Propeller Club U.S., Theta Xi (chpt. pres. 1952). Methodist. Club: Houston Yacht (commodore 1979-80). Home: 603 Bayridge Rd La Porte TX 77571-3512 Office: Fulbright & Jaworski 1301 Mckinney St Houston TX 77010

BLUITT, KAREN, technical manager, software engineer; b. N.Y.C., Oct. 25, 1957; d. James Bertrand and Beatrice (Kaufman) B.; m. Kenneth Mark Curry, Nov. 24, 1979 (div. Dec. 1991). BS, Fordham U., 1979; MBA, Calif. State Poly. U., 1982; postgrad., George Mason U. Software engr. Hughes Aircraft Co., Fullerton, Calif., 1979-81; microprocessor engr. Beckman Instruments Co., Fullerton, 1981-82, Singer Co., Glendale, Calif., 1982-83; sr. software engr. Sanders Assoc., Nashua, N.H., 1983-85; software project mgr. GTE Corp., Billerica, Mass., 1985-86; sr. software engr. Wang Labs, Lowell, Mass., 1986-87; project task leader Vanguard Rsch., Lexington, Mass., 1987-88; program mgr. Applied Rsch. & Engring., Bedford, Mass., 1989-91; program mgr. Sparta, McLean, Va., 1992-93; prin. software engr. Sci. Applications Internat., Arlington, Va., 1993-94; tech. mgr. CACI, Arlington, 1994-94, Booz-Allen & Hamilton, Vienna, Va., 1995, MRJ Tech. Solutions, Inc., Fairfax, Va., 1996—. 1st lt. USAR, 1979-88. Scholar Gov. N.Y. Scholarship Com., 1975-79; Beta Gamma Sigma scholar, 1978—. Mem. IEEE, AAUW, Am. Brokers Network, Assn. Computing Machinery, Data Processing Mgmt. Assn., Soc. Women Engrs. Office: MRJ Tech Solutions Inc 10560 Arrowhead Dr Fairfax VA 22030

BLUM, DONALD RALPH, editor, publisher; b. Cleve., Dec. 11, 1930; s. Frank Phillip and Frieda Marie (Kraker) B.; children: Robin, Van Eric, Mark, Ralph, Valery, Laura. BA, Kent State U., 1953, postgrad., 1955; postgrad., U. Akron, 1958. Editor Buyers Purchasing Digest, Cleve., 1960-66; v.p. Ashby & Assocs., Cleve., 1965-76; pres. Western Res. Advt., Asheville, N.C., 1970-80, W. N. Gates Co., Savannah, Ga., 1981-85; v.p. comms. Savannah C. of C., 1987-90; editor, pub. Savannah Bus. Jour., 1990—; cons. Tihama Advt., Jeddah, Saudi Arabia, 1983. Mem. Savannah Pubs. Assn. (pres. 1992—), Small Bus. Chamber of Savannah (sec. 1992—). Republican. Roman Catholic. Home: 909 E Victory Dr Savannah GA 31405-2423 Office: Savannah Bus Jour 6203 Abercorn St Ste 103E Savannah GA 31405-5526

BLUM, JACOB JOSEPH, physiologist, educator; b. Bklyn., Oct. 3, 1926; s. Paul and Anna (Brown) B.; m. Ruth Marsey, June 3, 1960; children: Mark, Douglas, lisa, Laura. BA, NYU, 1947; MS, U. Chgo., 1950, PhD, 1952. Mem. staff Naval Med. Rsch. Inst., Bethesda, Md., 1953-56; chief biophysics sect. gerontology br. NIH, Balt., 1958-62; prof. physiology Duke U., Durham, N.C., 1962—, James B. Duke prof., 1980—. With AUS, 1945-46. Merck postdoctoral fellow, 1952, Guggenheim fellow, 1969, Fogarty sr. internat. fellow, 1992. Mem. Am. Physiol. Soc., Soc. Protozoologists (pres. 1991). Home: 2525 Perkins Rd Durham NC 27706

BLUM, RICHARD ARTHUR, writer, media educator; b. Bklyn., July 28, 1943; w. Albert Elias and Eve (Griboff) B.; m. Barbara Fierstein, Sept. 16, 1967 (div. 1986); children: Jason Robert, Jennifer Rebecca; m. Ilene Shatoff, Sept. 2, 1995. BA, Fairleigh Dickinson U., 1965; MS, Boston U., 1968; PhD, U. So. Calif., 1977. Producer, dir., fellow Sta. WGBH-TV, Boston, 1965-67; program exec., writer, assoc. exec. producer Columbia Pictures-TV, L.A., 1968-74; instr. to asst. prof. U. Tex., Austin, 1974-78; sr. program officer NEH, Washington, 1978-82; sr. exec. producer Rainbow Programming Svc., N.Y.C., 1982; vis. faculty Harvard U., Cambridge, Mass., 1984-86; asst. prof. U. Md., College Park, 1984-88, assoc. prof., dir. RTUF Writing Program, dir. undergrad. studies, 1989-92; dir. TV and Film Writing Inst., U. Md., College Park, 1991-92; prof., dir. motion picture divsn. U. Ctrl. Fla., Orlando, 1993-95, prof., 1996—; mem. faculty Am. Film Inst. Workshops, 1982-86, The Writers Ctr., Bethesda, 1982-92. Author: Television Writing: From Concept to Contract, 1980, rev. edit., 1984, American Film Acting: The Stanislavski Heritage, 1984, Working Actors: The Craft of TV, Film and Stage Performance, 1989, (with Richard Lindheim) Primetime: Network TV Programming, 1987, (with Richard Lindheim) Inside Television Producing, 1991, Television and Screenwriting, 1994, 3d edit., 1995; co-author (screenplay with Frank Tavares) The Elton Project, 1992, Desert Fire, 1987; author (screenplay with A. Gerson) Sonja's Men, 1991. Judge Nicholl Screenwriting fellowships Acad. Motion Picture Arts and Scis., 1986-89, Corp. Pub. Broadcasting awards, 1988-90; bd. mem. Ctrl. Fla. Film Coun., 1992-95, Fla. Inst. for Film Edn., 1992-95, Ind. Prodrs. Project, Enzian Theatre-Fla. Film Festival Grants, 1995. Recipient Creative and Performing Arts award U. Md., 1986, Arts and Humanities award, 1987, Ford Found. award, 1988. Mem. Broadcast Edn. Assn., Univ. Film and Video Assn. Home: 3338 Hadleigh Crest Orlando FL 32817-2051 Office: U Ctrl Fla Divsn Motion Pictures PO Box 163120 Orlando FL 32816-3120

BLUM, UDO, botany educator; b. Ludenscheid, Westphalia, Germany, Nov. 29, 1939; s. Gerhard and Lydia B.; m. Mary Ann Schriefer, Aug. 25, 1968; children—Amy, Nicole. BA, Franklin Coll., 1962; MA, Ind. U.-Bloomington, 1965; PhD, U. Okla., 1968. Vis. asst. prof. U. Okla., Norman, 1968-69; asst. prof. N.C. State U., Raleigh, 1969-75, assoc. prof., 1975-80, prof. botany, 1980—, interim dept. head of botany, 1994-95. U.S. Dept. Agr. grantee, 1981-86. mem. editl. bd. Internat. Jour. Biometeorology, 1994—. Mem. Internat. Soc. Chem. Ecology, Internat. Soc. Biometeorology, Ecol. Soc. Am., Assn. Southeastern Biologists, N.C. Acad. Sci. Office: NC State U Dept Botany Box 7612 Raleigh NC 27695

BLUMBERG, EDWARD ROBERT, lawyer; b. Phila., Feb. 15, 1951. BA in Psychology, U. Ga., 1972; JD, Coll. William and Mary, 1975. Bar: Fla., 1975, U.S. Dist. Ct. Fla., 1975, U.S. Ct. Appeals, 1975, U.S. Supreme Ct., 1979. Assoc., Knight, Peters, Hoeveler & Pickle, Miami, Fla., 1977-76; ptnr. Deutsch & Blumberg, P.A., Miami, 1978—; adj. prof. U. Miami Sch. Paralegal Studies. Author: Proof of Negligence, Mathew Bender Florida Torts, 1988. Mem. ABA (ho. of dels. 1997—), ATLA, Dade County Bar Assn., Fla. State Bar (bd. govs., pres. elect 1996—), Acad. Fla. Trial Lawyers, Nat Bd. Trial Advocacy (cert. civil trial adv.). Office: Deutsch & Blumberg PA 100 Biscayne Blvd Fl 28 Miami FL 33132-2304

BLUMBERG, MICHAEL ZANGWILL, allergist; b. Phila., July 29, 1945; s. Jerome Blumberg and Vivian Rose (Liebman) Steiger; m. Barbara Sue Gurman, June 9, 1973; children: Jessica Lynn, Jason Mark. AB, Brandeis U., 1967; MD, Jefferson Med. Coll., 1971; postgrad., Med. Coll. Va., 1996—. Bd. cert. pediatrics, allergy and immunology. Intern, resident N.Y. Hosp., Cornell U. Med. Ctr., 1971-73; fellow in allergy and immunology Nat. Jewish Hosp.-U. Colo. Med. Ctr., 1973-75; chief allergy sect. major Scott Air Force Base, Ill., 1975-77; physician-ptnr. Va. Allergy, Asthma and Pulmonary Assn., Richmond, 1977—; intern, resident N.Y. Hosp.-Cornell U. Med. Ctr., 1971-73; asst. clin. prof. pediatrics Med. Coll. Va., Richmond, 1977—; chief of allergy Children's Hosp. of Richmond, 1987-96; med. advisor Rhone Poulenc Rorer, Allen Hansburys, Glaxo, Marion Merrell Dow Inc. Contbr. articles and abtracts to profl. jours.; contbg. editor: Review in Allergy, 1978; manuscript reviewer Asthma, 1995—. Bd. dirs. Jewish Cmty. Ctr., Richmond, 1984-87; exec. com. pres., bd. dirs., chmn. quality assurance bd. govs. Beth Shalom Home Va., Richmond, 1987—. Fellow Va. Allergy Soc. (program dir. 1989-90), Am. Coll. Allergy, Coll. Chest Physicians, Am. Acad. Pediatrics; mem. Am. Coll. Allergy Sports Medicine (practice stds. com. 1994-95), Am. Acad. Allergy, Am. Thoracic Soc., Friends of Brandeis Athletics, Masons. Jewish. Home: 1602 Swansbury Dr Richmond VA 23233-4628 Office: Va Allergy & Pulmonary Assocs 7605 Forest Ave Ste 102 Richmond VA 23229-4936

BLUMBERG, PHILIP FLAYDERMAN, real estate developer; b. Miami, Fla., Nov. 10, 1957; s. David and Lee (Dickens) B.; m. Lina Esther Waingortin, Apr. 13, 1986; children: David, Peter. BBA, U. N.C., 1979; MBA, Harvard U., 1983. Pres. Am. Ventures Corp., Miami, Fla., 1979—; mng. ptnr. Banyan Reach ltd., Cutler Ridge, Fla., 1979; pres. Realdata Info. Systems, Inc., Miami, 1984, Am. Ventures Realty Corp., Miami, 1985, Am. Ventures Realty Investors, Miami, 1990; chmn. exam. com. Profl. Savs. Bank, Coral Gables, Fla., 1985-87. Trustee Colony Performing Arts Theatre, Miami Beach, Fla., 1985; mem. U. Miami Venture Coun., Coral Gables, 1984; co-chmn. Japan-Miami Bus. Coun., 1987-94; trustee Beacon Coun., 1988—; bd. dirs. Downtown Devel. Authority, City of Miami, 1988-94, exec. com., 1992—, chmn. transp. com., 1988—; bd. dirs. Dade County Task Force on Empowerment & Enterprise Zones, 1993—, Brickell Area Assn., 1988—; mem. bd. trustees Temple Israel, 1989-93; chmn. Orange Bowl Spl. Events Com., 1993—; adv. coun. Orange Bowl Com., 1994—; chmn. Olympic Soccer Organizing Com., South Fla., 1993-96; bd. dirs. Dade County Transit 2020 Coalition, 1993—; mem. Tampa Bay Partnership, 1995—; bd. dirs. Greater Miami Fgn. Trade Zone, 1996—. Mem. Japan-Am. Soc. South Fla. (bd. dirs. 1988-89), Japan Soc. South Fla. (bd. dirs. 1990—), Greater Miami C. of C. (bd. govs. 1992—, exec. com. vice chmn. for bus. and industry/econ. devel. 1994—). Home: 10440 SW 53rd Ave Miami FL 33156 Office: Am Ventures Corp 255 Alhambra Cir Ste 1100 Coral Gables FL 33134

BLUME, JAMES DONALD, lawyer, consultant; b. St. Louis, Feb. 17, 1950; s. Donald David and Elizabeth Ann (Reitter) B.; m. Marilyn Rose Ender, Nov. 17, 1985. BA in Econs. cum laude, Cornell U., 1972; JD, U. Tex., 1975. Bar: Tex. 1975, U.S. Dist. Ct. (no., so., we. and ea. dists.) Tex. 1975, U.S. Ct. Appeals (5th and 11th cirs. 1975), U.S. Supreme Ct. 1989. Dir. rsch. charter revision com. City of Austin, Tex., 1975-76; staff atty. Tex. Dept. Comptroller, 1976-77, dir. claims, 1977-78, assoc. dep. comptroller, 1978-79; ptnr. Albach, Gutow, Rosenberg & Blume, Dallas, 1979-84, Gutow & Blume, P.C., Dallas, 1984-86, Mauro, Wendler, Sheets, Blume & Gutow, Dallas, 1986-90; pvt. practice, Dallas, 1990—; mem. State Unauthorized Practice Law Com., Dallas, 1986-90, regional chmn., 1987-90, state chmn., 1991—. Author: Hotel Occupancy Tax, 1984, Miscellaneous Occupation Tax, 1984, Federal Restrictions on Sales Tax, 1984. Pres. congregation St. Paul's Evang. and Ref. Ch., Dallas, 1984-85, 90-92; pres. NB, Tex. Assn. United Ch. of Christ, Dallas, 1987-89. Mem. ABA, Assn. Trial Lawyers Am., Tex. Trial Lawyers Assn., Texoma Sailing Club. Democrat.

BLUMENAU, IRIS WARECH, nursing consultant; b. Newark, Dec. 12, 1928; m. William Blumenau, Aug. 20, 1949 (dec.); 1 child, Bonnie Kaplan. Diploma, Newark Beth Israel Hosp., 1949; BA, Jersey City State Coll., 1975. Office mgr., bus. adminstr. Ctr. for Dermatology, P.A., West Orange, N.J., 1952-89; ret., 1989; pvt. cons. setting up and running med. office, 1989—.

BLUMENFELD, JOSHUA CHARLES, plant ecologist, editor, writer; b. Chgo., Aug. 18, 1967; s. Warren Stewart and Esther Edith (Richter) B. BA, U. Md., 1989; MS, U. Wis., 1992. Improvisational comedian Erasable, Inc., Washington, 1987-89; intern State Wis. Dept. Natural Resources, Madison, 1991; project coord. U. Wis., Madison, 1991-92; freelance writer Atlanta, 1992-94; editor, writer, plant ecologist Nat. Wildflower Rsch. Ctr., Austin, Tex., 1994—; legis. asst. Ho. of Reps., Washington, 1988; tchg. asst. U. Wis., Madison, 1990. Editor (newsletter) Wildflower, 1994—; contbr. articles to profl. jours. Mem. Ecol. Soc. Am. Office: Nat Wildflower Rsch Ctr 4801 La Crosse Ave Austin TX 78739

BLUMENTHAL, ARTHUR RICHARD, art museum director, art educator; b. Cleve., May 25, 1942; s. Sidney and Ann H. (Hirsch) B.; m. Kären Anderson Neustadt, May 22, 1993. BS in Art Edn., Kent State U., 1964; MA in Art History, NYU, 1966; Mus. Tng. Cert., NYU and Met. Mus., 1968; PhD in Fine Arts, NYU, 1984. Mus. intern Metro. Mus. Art, N.Y.C., 1966-67; curator Elvehjem Mus. Art U. Wis., Madison, 1968-74; curator art Hood Mus. Art Dartmouth Coll., Hanover, N.H., 1976-82; dir. The Art Gallery U. Md., College Park, 1982-84; dir. Cornell Fine Arts Mus. Rollins Coll., Winter Park, Fla., 1988—; reviewer gen. operating grant Inst. Mus. Svcs., 1992; judge Congl. Art Competition, Fla.'s 5th Dist., 1992, Crealde Sch. Art Student Exhibit, Winter Park, 1992, art dept. sr. show U. Ctrl. Fla., 1989; bd. dirs. Arts Svcs. Coun., Orlando, Fla. Author: Theater Art of the Medici, 1980, Giulio Parigi's Stage Designs, 1986, Theater Designs in the Collection of the Cooper-Hewitt Museum, 1986, (catalog) Italian Renaissance and Baroque Paintings in the Florida Museum, 1991; author, editor: (handbook) Treasures of the Cornell Fine Arts Museum, 1993; contbr. articles to profl. jours. Recipient Congress Meml. scholarship Ohio Edn. Assn., 1960-61, Ford Found. fellowship, NYU, 1965-67, Travel grant Am. Coun. Learned Societies, 1979, Spl. Project grant English-Speaking Union, 1991. Mem. Coll. Art Assn., Am. Assn. Mus. (accreditation com. 1993), S.E. Coll. Art Assn., Fla. Art Mus. Dirs. Assn. (exec. com. 1988—). Jewish.

BLUMENTHAL, MARK, organization administrator; b. Toledo, Sept. 4, 1946; s. Alfred and Frances (Schwartz) B.; m. Susan Ervin, 1971 (div. 1973); 1 child, Eva; m. Jacquelyn S. Small, 1978. BA in Govt. with honors, U. Tex., 1968. Editor/pub. HerbalGram, Austin, Tex., 1983—; exec. dir. Am. Bot. Coun., Austin, 1988—; sci. clin. advisor U. Tex. Ctr. for Alternative Medicine, Austin, 1996—. Editor: Commission E Monographs, 1996; editor HerbalGram, 1983; editl. adv. bd. Vegetarian Times, 1994—. Bd. dirs. Useful Wild Plants/Tex. Inc., Austin, 1992—, Amazon Ctr. for Environ. Edn. and Rsch. Found., Helena, Ala., 1995—. With USAR, 1970. Recipient Cliff Adler Heart and Bus. award, 1992, Industry Achievement award Tex. Herb Growers and Marketers Assn., 1994. Office: American Botanical Council PO Box 201660 Austin TX 78720-1660

BLUMSTEIN, JAMES FRANKLIN, legal educator, lawyer, consultant; b. Bklyn., Apr. 24, 1945; s. David and Rita (Sondheim) B.; m. Andree Kahn, June 25, 1971. BA in Econs., Yale U., 1966, MA in Econs., LLB, 1970. Bar: Tenn. 1970, U.S. Ct. Appeals (6th cir.) 1970, U.S. Dist. Ct. (mid. dist.) Tenn. 1971, U.S. Supreme Ct. 1974, N.Y. 1985. Instr. econs. New Haven Coll., 1967-68; pre-law adviser office of dean Yale U., New Haven, 1968-69; sr. pre-law adviser office of dean Yale U., 1969-70, asst. in instrn. law shc., 1969-70; asst. prof. law Vanderbilt U., Nashville, 1970-73; assoc. prof. Vanderbilt U., 1973-76, prof., 1976—, spl. advisor to chancellor for acad. affairs, 1984-85; assoc. dir. Vanderbilt Urban and Regional Devel. Ctr., 1970-72, dir. ctr., 1972-74; sr. rsch. assoc. Vanderbilt Inst. for Pub. Policy Studies, 1976-85, sr. fellow, 1985—, dir. health policy ctr., 1995—; Commonwealth Fund fellow, vis. assoc. prof. law and policy scis. law sch. Duke U. and Inst. of Policy Scis. and Pub. Affairs, 1974-75; vis. prof. health law med. sch. Dartmouth U., 1976, scholar-in-residence intermittently, 1976-78; John M. Olin vis. prof. sch. of law U. Pa., 1989; elected mem. Inst. Medicine NAS, 1990—; cons. law, health policy, civil and voting rights, land use, state taxation, torts; lectr. in field. Editor: (with Eddie J. Martin) The Urban Scene in the Seventies, 1974, (with Benjamin Walter) Growing Metropolis: Aspects of Development in Nashville, 1975, (with Lester Salamon) Growth Policy in the Eighties (Law and Contemporary Problems Symposium), 1979; (with Frank A. Sloan and James M. Perrin) Uncompensated Hospital Care: Rights and Responsibilities, 1986, (with Frank A. Sloan and James M. Perrin) Cost, Quality, and Access in Health Care: New Roles for Health Planning in a Competitive Environment, 1988; (with Frank A. Sloan) Organ Transplantation Policy: Issues and Prospects, 1989, (with Frank A. Sloan) Antitrust and Health Care Policy (Law and Contemporary Problems Symposium), 1989; mem. bd. editors Yale Law Jour., 1968-70; mem. editorial bd. Jour. Health Politics, Policy and Law, 1981—; mem. pub.'s adv. bd. Nashville Banner, 1982—; contbr. articles to profl. jours., op-ed articles to newspapers. Mem. Health Econs. Task Force, Middle Tenn. Health Sys. Agy., 1979; mem. adv. bd. LWV, 1979-80; mem. Nashville Mayor's Commn. on Crime, 1981; cons. Leadership Nashville, 1977—, Tenn. Motor Vehicle Commn., 1986-87, Leadership Music, 1989—; panelist Am. Arbitration Assn., 1977—; chmn. Tenn. adv. com. U.S. Commn. on Civil Rights, 1985-91, mem., 1991—; sec. Martin Luther King Jr. Holiday Com., State of Tenn., 1985-87; bd. dirs. Jewish Fedn. Nashville and Middle Tenn., 1981-90, mem. exec. com., 1988-90, chmn. cmty. rels. com., 1980-82, chmn. campus com., 1987-89; chmn. Yale Alumni Schs. Com. Middle Tenn., 1983—; mem Tenn. Gov.'s Task Force Medicaid, 1992-94; mem. adv. panel Office Tech. Assessment study of defensive medicine and use of med. tech., 1991-94; chmn. task force cost containment and med. malpractice Rand Corp., 1991-92; active Inst. Medicine Com. on Adequacy of Nursing Staffing, 1994-96. Bates Jr. fellow, 1968-69; grantee Ford Found./Rockefeller Found. Population Program, 1970-73, Health Policy grantee NCA Found., 1986-90; grantee State Justice Inst., 1991—, Robert Wood Johnson Found., 1994—; nominated Adminstr., Office Info. and Regulatory Affairs, Office Mgmt. and Budget, 1990; named One of Outstanding Young Men in Am. U.S. Jaycees, 1971; recipient award Univ. Rsch. Coun., 1971-72, 73-74, 79-80, 94-95, Earl Sutherland prize achievement in rsch. Vanderbilt U., 1992, Paul J. Hartman award Outstanding Prof., 1982. Mem. ABA (sec. sect. legal edn. and admissions to bar 1982-83 , chmn. subcom. on state and local taxation com. on corp. law and taxation sect. on corp., banking and bus. law 1983—, mem. accreditation com. sect. legal edn. and admissions to bar 1983-89, mem. com. on state and local taxation sect. on taxation 1983—), NAS (inst. of medicine), Assn. Am. Law Schs. (chmn. law, medicine and health care sect. 1987-88, mem. exec. com. 1988-92, 2d vice chmn. sect. local govt. law 1976-78, mem. sect. coun. 1980-86), Tenn. Bar Assn., N.Y. State Bar Assn., Nashville Bar Assn. (Liberty Bell award 1987), Hastings Ctr., Assn. for Pub. Policy Analysis and Mgmt., Assn. Yale Alumni (del.), Yale U. Law Sch. Alumni Assn. (exec. com. 1985-88), Univ. Club (Nashville). Home: 2113 Hampton Ave Nashville TN 37215-1401 Office: Vanderbilt U Law Sch 21st Ave S Nashville TN 37240

BLUNDE, MARY CATHERINE, admissions director; b. Rapid City, S.D., June 4, 1968; d. Wayne Harold and Carol Louise (Roberts) K.; m. Todd Alan Bunde, Sept. 7, 1996. BS in Elem. Edn., E. Tex. State U., 1991; MEd in Higher Edn. and Adminstrn., Coll. of Wm. and Mary, 1992. Cert. tchr., Tex. Admissions rep Lamar U., Beaumont, Tex., 1992-93; dir. admissions Paris (Tex.) Jr. Coll., 1993-95, Richmond (Va.) Meml. Hosp. Sch. of Nursing, 1995—; mem. Tex. Assn. Collegiate Registrars and Admissions Officers, 1992-95, mem. Va. Assoc. of Student Fin. Aid Adminstrn. Mem. C. of C. Leadership Lamar County, Paris, Tex., 1993-95. Mem. So. Assn. Collegiate Registrars and Admissions Officers, Va. Assn. of Collegiate Registrars and Admissions Officers. Republican. Episcopalian. Home: 864 Ventnor Dr Newport News VA 23608 Office: Richmond Meml Hosp Sch of Nursing 1300 Westwood Ave Richmond VA 23227

BLY, CHARLES ALBERT, nuclear engineer, research scientist; b. Winchester, Va., Jan. 11, 1952; s. Theodore and Nancy Irma (Fisher) B.; m. April Marie Monnen, July 24, 1976. BS in Nuclear Engring., U. Va., 1978, MS in Nuclear Engring., 1983; student, Nat. Acad. Nuclear Tng., 1992-93; postgrad. in nuclear engring., U. Va., 1994—. Nuclear reactor operator Nuclear Reactor Facility of the U. Va., Charlottesville, 1977-80, sr. reactor operator, 1980-83, rsch. engr., 1981-83; vis. engr. Brit. Nuclear Fuel Ltd. Springfields Works, Preston Lancashire, England, 1983; nuclear engr. Comml. Nuclear Fuel div. Westinghouse Electric, Pitts., 1983-92, Beaver Valley Power Sta. Duquesne Light Co., Shippingport, Pa., 1992-94; lead prof. Oak Ridge (Tenn.) Nat. Lab. Am. Tech. Inst., 1994-95; nuclear reactor staff Nuclear Reactor Facility of U. Va., Charlottesville, 1995—. Contbr. numerous articles to profl. jours. Candidate Shenandoah County (Va.) Bd. of Supervisor, 1975; mem. Ad Hoc Com. to Prevent Extension of I-66 Hwy. Through George Washington Nat. Forest, Strasburg, Va., 1979, Ad Hoc Com. to Preserve the Pitts. Aviary, 1991. Mem. ASME, IEEE, ASTM, AAAS, Am. Nuc. Soc., Am. Phys. Soc., ASM Internat., Assn. Energy Engrs., The Engring. Soc., Profl. Engr.'s Soc., Fedn. Am. Scientists, Engr.'s Soc. Western Pa., N.Y. Acad. Scis., Internat. Platform Assn. Democrat. Lutheran. Home: 777-D Mountainwood Rd Charlottesville VA 22902 Office: U Va Nuclear Reactor Facility Charlottesville VA 22903-2442

BLY, ROBERT MAURICE, lawyer; b. Connersville, Ind., Oct. 31, 1944; s. Karl H. and Faye Virginia (DeHoff) B.; m. Ann Patrice Gleason, Aug. 24, 1968; 1 child, Thomas Robert. BS, Ball State U., 1966; JD, U. Tenn., 1973. Bar: Ill. 1973, Ind. 1974, U.S. Dist. Ct. (so. dist.) Ind. 1974, U.S. Dist. Ct. (no. dist.) Ind. 1978, U.S. Supreme Ct. 1981, Tenn. 1991, U.S. Dist. Ct. (ea. dist.) Tenn. 1992. Pub. sch. tchr. Ind., 1966-71; regional counsel's staff Chgo. (Ill.) Title & Trust Co., 1973-75; dep. prosecutor Porter County Ind., Valparaiso, 1975-76; pvt. practice law Valparaiso and Kokomo, Ind., 1976-91, Knoxville, 1992—; adj. instr. Ind. U., Kokomo, 1987-91; del. Ho. of Dels., Ind. Bar Assn., Indpls., 1988; founder Southeast Estate Planning Inst.; guest lectr. in field. Columnist Fairfield Glade Sun, 1993-94. Pres. Vols. in Cmty. Svc., Kokomo, 1980-85; del. Ind. State Rep. Conv., Indpls., 1986; mem. Nat. Rep. Senatorial Com., Washington, 1993—. Mem. Nat. Network Estate Planning Attys., Tenn. Bar Assn. (tax, probate and trusts sect.), Assn. CLUs and ChFCs, Club LeConte (Knoxville). Episcopalian. Office: 9111 Cross Park Dr # D-200 Knoxville TN 37923-4506

BLYLER, WILLIAM EDWARD, lawyer; b. Youngstown, Ohio, Dec. 15, 1936; s. William Elmer and Rita Helen (Anderson) B.; m. Bess Ann Riggs, June 11, 1960 (div. Aug. 1972); children: Brett R., William B., Blake E.; m. Deborah Dobbins, Mar. 19, 1973 (div. Oct. 1979); 1 child, Jason L.; m. Diane Rohrsted, June 22, 1984. Student, U. Fla., 1954-56, JD, 1964; BA, Fla. State U., 1961. Bar: Fla. 1965. Law clk. to presiding justice Fla. Supreme Ct., Tallahassee, 1964-65; assoc. Patterson, Maloney & Frazier, Ft. Lauderdale, Fla., 1965-68, ptnr., 1968-74; ptnr. Patterson, Maloney, Blyler & Feige, Ft. Lauderdale, 1974-81; sole practice Coral Springs, Fla., 1981—. Served with U.S. Army, 1956-58. Mem. Fla. Bar Assn., Broward County Bar Assn., Phi Delta Phi. Democrat. Home: Apt 209 11306 NW 12th Ct Coral Springs FL 33071

BLYNN, GUY MARC, lawyer; b. Bklyn., May 26, 1945; s. S. Jerry and Viola T. Vogel Blynn; children: Daniel Scott, Harlan Sterling, Aaron Seth. BS in Econs. cum laude, U. Pa., Wharton Sch. of Fin. Commerce, 1967; JD cum laude, Harvard U., 1970. Bar: N.C., N.Y., U.S. Ct. of Appeals for Fed. Cir., U.S. Ct. of Appeals for the 2d Cir., U.S. Dist. Cts. for the Middle Dist. of N.C., Southern and Eastern Dist. N.Y. Assoc. Kaye, Scholer, Fierman, Hays & Handler, N.Y.C., 1970-78; assoc. counsel R.J. Reynolds Industries Inc., Winston Salem, N.C., 1978-79; sr. counsel RJR Nabisco Inc., Winston Salem, N.C., 1979-86; dep. gen. counsel R.J. Reynolds Tobacco Co., Winston Salem, N.C., 1986-1989, v.p., dep. gen. counsel, 1989—; lectr. Wake Forest U. Sch. of Law, 1980-93; cons. Dept. Commerce, 1987-90. Contbr. articles to profl. jours. Chmn. Brand Names Edn. Found., 1988-94; bd. dirs. N.C. Vol. Lawyers for the Arts, 1985-91, pres., 1987-91. Mem. ABA, Am. Arbitration Assn. (panel of arbitrators 1975-95), Carolina Patent Trademark & Copyright Law Assn. (v.p. 1979-80, pres. 1980-81), Am. Intellectul Property Law Assn. (chmn. taxation and fin. matters com. 1991-92), Am. Bar Assn. Forum Com. on Entertainment And Sports Industries, Assn. of Bar of City Of N.Y. (chmn. com. on trademarks and unfair competition 1975-78, subcommittee on patent and trademark office practice 1976-77), Anti-Defamation League of B'nai B'rith (N.C. regional adv. bd. 1987—, chmn. elect 1991-93, chmn. 1993—, vice chmn. 1990-91), U.S. Trademark Assn. (bd. dirs. 1982-90, v.p. 1984-85, exec. v.p. 1985-86, pres., chmn. 1986-87). Home: PO Box 20383 Winston Salem NC 27120-0383 Office: R J Reynolds Tobacco Co 401 N Main St Winston Salem NC 27101-3818

BLYSTONE, ROBERT VERNON, developmental cell biologist, educator, textbook consultant; b. El Paso, Tex., July 4, 1943; s. Edward Vernon and Cecilia (Mueller) B.; m. Donna Joan Moore, Mar. 26, 1964; 1 child, Daniel Vernon. BS in Biol. Sci., U. Tex., El Paso, 1965; MA in Zoology, U. Tex., Austin, 1968, PhD in Zoology, 1971. Instr. U. Tex., El Paso, 1965; teaching asst. U. Tex., Austin, 1965-68, NIH predoctoral fellow, 1968-70; asst. prof. biology Trinity U., San Antonio, 1971-76, assoc. prof., 1976-84, prof., 1984—, chmn. dept., 1984-86; dir. Biol. Visualization Lab., San Antonio, 1971—; cons. Ednl. Testing Svc., Princeton, N.J., also others; text and trade book cons., McGraw-Hill, 1987, Harper-Collins, 1991-93, Oxford U. Press, 1988, Addison-Wesley, 1987-91, also others. Contbr. numerous articles to profl. jours., chpts. to books. Asst. dir., dir., sec., v.p., historian Alamo Regional Sci. Fair, 1973-85; bd. dirs. Sci. Collaborative, San Antonio, 1987-95. Named Outstanding Prof. Trinity U. Student Body, 1982, Piper Prof. of Tex. Piper Found., 1986; Scott fellow for tchg., 1991; rsch. grantee USAF Office Sci. Rsch., 1990-91, NSF, 1991, 95. Fellow AAAS (film/book reviewer 1982—), Tex. Acad. Sci. (hon. life, exec. bd. 1976-79); mem. AAUP (treas. chpt. 1984-86), NSTA (coll. com. 1987-89), Am. Inst. Biol. Scis., Microscopy Soc. Am., Am. Soc. Cell Biology (edn. com. 1985-89, 91—), Nat. Assn. Biology Tchrs., Tex. Soc. Electron Microscopy (program chmn., assoc. jour. editor 1982-83), Assn. Computing Machinery (SIGGRAPH edn. com. 1994—), Sigma Xi (pres. chpt. 1990-91). Office: Trinity U Dept Biology 715 Stadium Dr San Antonio TX 78212-3104

BOARD, REBECCA RUTH BATCHELOR, software engineer; b. Goldsboro, N.C., Oct. 12, 1966; d. Robert Marshall and Ruth Victoria (Carlson) Batchelor; m. John Arnold Board Jr., Mar. 9, 1991. BSE, Duke U., 1988, MS, 1990. Teaching asst. Duke U., Durham, N.C., 1988-90; software engr. AAI Visual Sys., Durham, 1990—. Mem. IEEE, Assn. for Computing Machinery. Home: 10 Winslow Pl Chapel Hill NC 27514-9408 Office: AAI Visual Sys PO Box 13951 Research Triangle Park NC 27709

BOARDMAN, MARK SEYMOUR, lawyer; b. Birmingham, Ala., Mar. 16, 1958; s. Frank Seymour and Flora (Sarinopoulos) B.; m. Cathryn Dunkin, 1983; children:Wilson Paul, Joanna Christina. BA cum laude, U. Ala., 1979, JD, 1982. Bar: Ala. 1982, U.S. Dist. Ct. (no. dist.) Ala. 1982, U.S. Ct. Appeals (11th cir.) 1983, U.S. Supreme Ct. 1987. Assoc. Spain, Gillon, Riley, Tate & Etheredge, Birmingham, 1982-84; ptnr. Porterfield, Scholl, Bainbridge, Mims and Harper, P.A., Birmingham, 1984-93, Boardman & Tyra, P.C., Birmingham, 1993—. Sec. Holy Trinity Holy Cross Greek Orthodox Cathedral, 1987, treas., 1988-89, v.p., 1990, 96, pres. 1991-92, bd. auditors, 1994; mem. coun. Greek Orthodox Diocese of Atlanta, 1992-95; mem. Shelby County, Ala. Work Release Commn., sec., 1996—. Mem. ABA, Ala. State Bar, Shelby County Bar Assn. (treas. 1992-93, sec. 1994, v.p. 1995, pres. 1996), Birmingham Bar Assn., Am. Jud. Soc., Ala. Def. Lawyers Assn., Def. Rsch. Inst., Ala. Claims Assn., Order of Barristers, Phi Beta Kappa, Delta Sigma Rho-Tau Kappa Alpha, Pi Sigma Alpha. Greek Orthodox. Home: 1915 Wellington Rd Birmingham AL 35209-4026 Office: Boardman & Tyra PC PO Box 59465 Birmingham AL 35259-9465

BOARDMAN, MAUREEN BELL, community health nurse; b. Hartford, Conn., June 11, 1966; d. Jack Russell and Mary Elizabeth (Brumm) Bell; m. Byron Earl Boardman, June 4, 1988. BSN, U. Maine, Orono, 1988; MSN, U. Tenn., 1991. ACLS; cert. family nurse practitioner. Charge nurse med.-surg. divsn. Scott County Hosp., Oneida, Tenn., 1988-89, employee health nurse, 1989-92; RN team leader Oneida Home Health, 1989, Quality Home Health, Oneida, 1989-90; family nurse practitioner Straightfork Family Care Clinic, Pioneer, Tenn., 1992—; mem. child abuse rev. team Dept. Human Svcs., Huntsville, Tenn., 1993—. Med. advisor, liaison Scott County (Tenn.) Sch. Systems Sci. Fair Com., 1992—; bd. dirs., editor newsletter, 1993—, v.p., 1995-96 Appalachian Arts Coun., Oneida. Mem. Tenn. Nurses Assn. (del. to conv. 1994, 95, 96), Sigma Theta Tau (sec. Gamma Chi chpt. 1996-98). Roman Catholic. Home: RR 3 Box 213 Oneida TN 37841-9532 Office: Straightfork Family Care Clinic Rt 1 Box 320 Hwy 63 Pioneer TN 37847

BOARDMAN, ROBERT B., author; b. Key West, Fla., Sept. 18, 1943; s. Brewer Francis and Elizabeth Louise (Lewis) B. Student, U. Oreg., 1963, Portland State U., 1963-64, Idaho State U., 1964; BA in Econs., Whitman Coll., 1966. Mgmt. intern, computer systems analyst U.S. Bur. Labor Statis., Washington, 1966-68; systems supr. So. Pacific R.R., San Francisco, 1968-76; mgr. systems/programming Alaskan Data Systems, Anchorage, 1976-77; asst. acctg. mgr. So. Pacific R.R., San Francisco, 1977-80; systems analyst, distbn. mgr. Riviana Foods Inc., Houston, 1981-90. Author: Savior of Fire, 1992, The Trashers, 1993. Vol. coun. mem. Lighthouse of Houston, 1982-83; mng. dir. Nepénthe Project; treas. Com. to Elect Rob Thorn U.S. Ho. of Reps. Mem. Houston Space Inst. Libertarian. Home and Office: 2929 Hayes Rd Apt 1002 Houston TX 77082-2600

BOATMAN, DEBORAH ANN, hospice nurse; b. Muskogee, Okla., Sept. 8, 1955; d. John and Joanne Everitt; children: Will Boatman, Jeb Boatman. BA in Psychology, Northeastern State U., Tahlequah, Okla., 1981; BSN, U. Okla., 1985. Oncology staff nurse St. Francis Hosp., Tulsa, 1985; staff nurse St. John Hospice, Tulsa, 1986, St. Francis Hospice, Tulsa, 1986-94, Hospice of Okla. County, Oklahoma City, 1994—. Mem. Oncology Nursing Soc., Hospice Nurses Assn., Golden Key Honor Soc.

BOATRIGHT, JOANNA MORSON, computer programmer, analyst; b. Leland, Miss., Apr. 14, 1958; d. Andrew Alexander and Dorothy Rae (Brown) Morson; m. Greggory Deen Boatright, Nov. 11, 1989; 1 child from previous marriage, Joseph Andrew; 1 child, Deena Christina. B in tech., U. North Fla., 1985; BBA, U. Miss., 1980. Asst. acct. Baddau Inc., Memphis, 1979; customer service rep. Fine Jewelers Guild, Jacksonville, Fla., 1982-84, new accounts operator, 1984-85; coop. program analyst IRS, Jacksonville, 1985, programmer analyst, 1985-87, programmer/analyst in hardware/software Naval Regional Data Ctr., 1987; data designer Naval Computer and Telecommunications Sta., Jacksonville, 1987—. Recipient Letter of Commendation commanding officer NCTS, 1991, commander NCTC, 1991, under sec. Navy, 1991, Sec. Def., 1991. Mem. Phi Beta Phi, Delta Sigma. Republican. Mem. LDS Church. Home: 254 Oak Dr S Green Cove Springs FL 32043-8777

BOATWRIGHT, CHARLOTTE JEANNE, hospital marketing and public relations executive; b. Chattanooga, Dec. 12, 1937; d. Clifton Gentry and Veltina Novella (Braden) Blevins; m. Robert W. Boatwright; children: Lynn Kay, Janis Ann, Karen Jean, Mary Ruth, Melody Susan, April Celeste. Diploma, Erlanger Sch. Nursing, Chattanooga, 1963; BS, U. Tenn., Chattanooga, 1976, MEd, 1981; PhD, Columbia Pacific U., San Rafael, Calif., 1987. RN, Tenn. Surgeon's asst. William Robert Fowler, M.D., Chattanooga, 1963-64; instr. med.-surg. nursing Baroness Erlanger Hosp. Sch. Nursing, 1964-67, instr. fundamentals nursing, 1971-74, chmn. dept. mental health-psychiat. nursing, 1977-81; staff nurse Meml. Hosp., Chattanooga, 1967-68, nursing supr., 1968-70; dir. inservice edn. Hutcheson Med. Ctr., Ft. Oglethorpe, Ga., 1970-71; youth work cons. Sewanee Dist. Episcopal Chs., Chattanooga, 1975-76; dir. spl. projects North Park Hosp., Chattanooga, 1984-87, dir. mktg. and pub. rels., 1987—; pres. CBB Comms.; freelance writer. mem. dept. youth work Episcopal Diocese Tenn., 1975-77, mem. violence in soc. resource team; condr. adult ch. sch. groups St. Martin's Episcopal Ch., Chattanooga; vice chmn. Brynewood Park Cmty. Assn., 1985, 86; founder, chairperson Domestic Violence Coalition of Greater Chattanooga, 1994. Mem. Am. Coll. Healthcare Execs. (nominee), Tenn. Hosp. Assn., Tenn. Soc. for Hosp. Mktg. and Pub. Rels., Chattanooga C. of C., U. Tenn. Alumnae Assn., Columbia Pacific U. Alumnae Assn., Chi Sigma Iota. Republican.

BOAZMAN, FRANKLIN MEADOR, financial consultant; b. Dallas, Dec. 31, 1939; s. Howard Clark and Mary Elinor (Meador) B.; m. Tommie Sharon Cope, July 15, 1961 (div. Feb. 1974); children: Michael Louis, Terry Ann; m. Dianne Codone, Nov. 19, 1988. MBA, Tulane U., 1984. V.p. ops. Indsl. Uniform & Towel Co., Dallas, 1963-70; pres. Visual Presentations, Inc., Dallas, 1970-74; gen. mgr. Aratex Services, Inc., New Orleans, 1974-82, group mgr., 1982-86; pres. New Orleans Cons. Group, Ltd., 1985—. Mem. Met. Rep. Businessmen's Fedn. of New Orleans. Office: New Orleans Cons Group Ltd 401 Focis St Metairie LA 70005-3435

BOBO, GENELLE TANT (NELL BOBO), office administrator; b. Paulding County, Ga., Oct. 31, 1927; d. Richard Adolph and Mary Etta (Prance) Tant; m. William Ralph Bobo, May 1, 1948; children: William Richard, Thomas David (dec.). AS, Berry Coll., Mt. Berry, Ga., 1947. Exec. sec. Macon (Ga.) Kraft Co., 1951-54; med. sec. Drs. Loveman & Fleigleman, Louisville, 1954-55; tchr. Fulton County Schs., Palmetto, Ga., 1960-68; exec. sec. Rayloc, Atlanta, 1968-70; adminstrv. coord. U. Ga., Athens, 1970-77; assoc. to dir. Mission Svc. Corps, Home Mission Bd. So. Bapt. Conv., Atlanta, 1977-94; rschr., writer Sta. 11-TV, Atlanta, 1989. Author: Driven by a Dream, 1992. Philanthropy chmn. Exec. Women, Inc., Atlanta, 1968-69; mem. adv. coun. Baylor U., Waco, Tex., 1993—. Mem. NAFE. Baptist. Home: 87 Vickers Rd Fairburn GA 30213-1139 Office: 4200 N Point Pky Alpharetta GA 30202-4174

BOCK, JOHN LOUIS, architect; b. Richmond, Va., Aug. 17, 1945; s. Paul Hevener and Byrd (Johnson) B.; m. Carol Ann Chiocca, Feb. 5, 1983. Student Va. Poly. Inst., 1963-65; BS, Richmond Profl. Inst., 1968. Draftsman, G. Richard Brown, Architect, 1964-66; project capt. J. Henley Walker, Jr., Architect, 1966-69; tchr. mech. drawing Chesterfield County Schs., 1969-70; project architect J. Henley Walker, Jr., Architect, 1970-76, Harry S. Cruickshank, Architect, Richmond, 1976-77, Edward F. Sinnott & Son, Architect, Richmond, 1977-78; v.p., sec. Ernie Rose, Inc., Architects, Richmond, Va., 1978-91, also dir.; owners John L. Bock Architect, Mechanicsville, Va., 1991—. Mem. Constrn. Specifications Inst. (dir. Richmond chpt. 1981, 91, 93, 94, v.p. chpt.; award 1981, 83), Ducks Unltd. (chmn. Mechanicsville chpt. 1983-87, nat. sponsor 1983-91, Spl. award Va. com. 1986, Distng. Service award 1988). Episcopalian. Home: 8044 Shady Knoll Ln Mechanicsville VA 23111-2262

BOCKMAN, LINDA ANN, computer design analyst; b. Abilene, Tex., Oct. 18, 1947; d. Leon Lindberg and Vera Analee (Garrison) Bailey; m. Harold Dean Bockman, Sept. 20, 1966; children: Johnathan Lee, Carrie Michelle. BA in Journalism, Angelo State U., 1990. Owner Bockman's Cleaning Svc., San Angelo, Tex., 1978-85; ptnr. Skeeter's Garage, San Angelo, 1980-85; owner, designer, analyst, writer, editor Alpha Omega Pubs., San Angelo, Tex., 1991—; Reporter: Ram Page, 1988-90, Standard Times, 1989-90; writer, editor: Miles Messenger, 1990-91; newsletter editor: West Tex. Pipeline, Miles, 1991-94; contbr. polit. and info. stories to profl. publs.; adminstrv. asst. Angelo Air, San Angelo, Tex., 1994—; sec., founding mem. Support Svcs. Network, San Angelo, Tex., 1994—. Bd. dirs. Eastern Little League, San Angelo, 1976-79; sec., founding mem. Support Svcs. Network, San Angelo, 1994; newsletter editor West Tex. Pipeline, Miles, 1991-94; bd. dirs. Concho Valley Conf., San Angelo, 1988—. Wayland Yates Meml. scholar Angelo State U., 1990; named Outstanding Reporter, Ram Page, 1989. Mem. Nat. Desktop Pubs., Soc. Profl. Journalists (treas. 1988-90), Quick Printer's Assn. Baptist.

BOCKSTRUCK, LLOYD DEWITT, librarian; b. Vandalia, Ill., May 26, 1945; s. Harry Earl and Olive Elsie (Blankenship) B. AB cum laude, Greenville (Ill.) Coll., 1967; MA, So. Ill. U., 1969; MS, U. Ill., 1973; student, Samford U., 1973. Teaching asst. So. Ill. U., Carbondale, 1967-69; tchr. Mombasa (Kenya) Bapt. High Sch., 1969-71; teaching asst. U. Ill., Urbana, 1972-73; libr. Dallas Pub. Libr., 1973—; instr. Inst. Genealogy and Hist. Rsch., Samford U., Birmingham, Ala., 1973—; instr. Sch. Continuing Edn., So. Meth. U., Dallas, 1974-91; columnist Dallas Morning News, 1991—. Author: Virginia's Colonial Soldiers, 1988, Genealogical Research in Texas, 1992, Revolutionary War Bounty Land Grants Awarded by State Governments, 1996; contbr. articles to profl. jours. Recipient Scholarship Key award Phi Alpha Theta, 1967, History award DAR, 1989, Profl. award for hist. preservation Dallas County Hist. Commn., 1992; Nat. Geneal. Soc. fellow, 1992. Mem. ALA (life), SAR (libr. gen. 1981-83), SCW (gov. Tex. soc.), Soc. of the Cincinnati, Jamestowne Soc., Order of Ams. of Armorial Ancestry (registrar gen. 1993—), Order of Founders and Patriots of Am. (registrar gen. 1986—), Dallas Geneal. Soc. (dir. 1979—). Republican. Christian. Home: 3955 Buena Vista St Apt C Dallas TX 75204-1667 Office: Dallas Pub Libr 1515 Young St Dallas TX 75201-5411

BOCKWITZ, CYNTHIA LEE, psychologist, psychology/women's studies educator; b. Hallock, Minn., Apr. 11, 1954; d. Rodney Lee and Jeanette Yvonne (Vilen) B. AA in Arts and Scis., Richland Coll., 1983; BA in Psychology, U. Tex., Dallas, 1985; MA in Counseling Psychology, Tex. Woman's U., 1992. Lic. profl. counselor, Ga. Pers. adminstr. Automatic Data Processing, Miami, Fla., 1974-77; office mgr. G.A. Dexter Co., Atlanta, 1977-79; human resources mgr. No. Telecom, Atlanta and Dallas, 1979-84; mental health worker Timberlawn Psychiat. Hosp., Dallas, 1984-85; acct. NEC Am., Dallas, 1986-87; asst. program dir. Arbor Creek Hosp., Sherman, Tex., 1989; lic. profl. counselor Trinity Counseling Ctr., Carrollton, Tex., 1989-93, Atlanta, 1993—; adj. instr. psychology Tex. Woman's U., Denton, 1988-92; instr. psychology DeKalb Coll., Atlanta, 1993—; cons. The Resource Ctr., Atlanta, 1993-94, Laurel Heights Hosp., 1994—; mem. exec. com. Women Clinicians Network, Atlanta, 1994, 95. Mem. NOW (fin. contbr.), APA (assoc.), Am. Assn. for Marriage and Family Therapy (assoc.), Assn. for Women in Psychology, Ga. Marriage and Family Therapy Assn. (legis. com. 1993-94), Assn. for Play Therapy, Ga. Assn. for Play Therapy, Nat. Assn. of Masters in Psychology. Democrat. Home: 711 Tuxworth Cir Decatur GA 30033-5620 Office: Laurel Heights Hosp 934 Briarcliff Rd NE Atlanta GA 30306-2618

BOCKWOLDT, TODD SHANE, nuclear engineer; b. Spirit Lake, Iowa, July 31, 1967; s. Larry Ray and Gale Glee (Bobzien) B.; m. Margery Pitzer, June 9, 1990. BS in Nuclear Engring., Ga. Tech, 1989, MS in Nuclear Engring., 1990. Grad. rsch. asst. Ga. Inst. Technology, Atlanta, 1989-90; S5W (submarines) and A1G (carriers) fleet reactor engr. DOE/USN Naval Reactors Hdqrs., Arlington, Va., 1990-95; asst. naval reactors rep. Norfolk Naval Shipyard, Portsmouth, Va., 1995—; tech. program chmn. Am. Nuclear Soc. Student Conf., Atlanta, 1988; nuclear engring. rep. Mech. Engring. Student Adv. Com., Ga. Tech, 1988-89. Lt. USN, 1990—. Scholar NROTC, 1985-89, MCDAC, 1985-89, Am. Soc. Naval Engrs. scholar, 1987-89; recipient Gold medal Soc. Am. Mil. Engrs., 1988, Ga. Tech Honor award Soc. Am. Mil. Engrs., 1989, Outstanding Coll. Students of Am. award, 1989. Mem. Am. Nuclear Soc. (grad. scholar 1989-90), Tau Beta Pi, Mensa, Alpha Nu Sigma. Lutheran. Home: 3212 Buckthorn Ct Chesapeake VA 23323

BODDEKER, EDWARD WILLIAM, III, retired architect; b. Houston, Mar. 22, 1929; s. Edward William and Ruth Margaret (Cook) B.; m. Salee Noieam; 1 child, Mark Montagne. BArch, Tex. A&M U., 1951. Registered architect, Tex. Architect, MacKie & Kamrath, architects, Houston, 1960-63; architect Manned Spacecraft Center, NASA, Clear Lake, Tex., 1963-82 project design mgr., 1963-65, master planner, 1965-67, head master planning sect., 1967-68, head archtl. civil sect., engring. div., 1968-76, head facilities programs sect., 1976-77, chief facilities planning office, 1977-81, spl. asst. for facilities planning, 1981-82, ret., 1982. Bd. dirs., treas. Clear Creek Basin Authority, 1972-74. Served to 1st lt. Army Security Agy., AUS, 1952-54. Recipient Apollo and Skylab Achievement awards NASA, also NASA Gemini, Apollo, Skylab, Lunar Landing Team, Apollo Soyuz Test Project, Space Shuttle group achievement awards. Mem. AIA, Tex. Soc. Architects. Avocation: foreign travel. Home: 13915 Grosvenor St Houston TX 77034-5429

BODDIE, RICHARD LEE, agriculturalist, researcher; b. Minden, La., Sept. 26, 1946; s. Earnest Claude and Annie Gertrude (Norman) B.; m. Nancy Scharlene Thomas, Nov. 19, 1977; 1 child, Catherine Scharlene. BS in Wildlife Conservation and Mgmt., La. Tech. U., 1969. Enlisted U.S. Army, 1969; vet. and X-ray technician Ft. Sill (Okla.) Vet. Clinic; vet. technician 981st MP Co. U.S. Army, Rep. South Vietnam, 1970-71; vet. tech. Baumholder Vet. Clinic U.S. Army, Germany, 1975-76; rsch. assoc. Mastitis Rsch. Lab., Hill Farm Rsch. Sta. La. State U., Homer, 1976—; presenter in field. Contbr. over 90 articles and papers to sci. jours. Mem. Assn. Vet. Microbiologists, La. Dairy Fieldman's Assn., La. Farm Bur. Home: RR 1 Box 812 Dubberly LA 71024-9615 Office: La State U Agrl Ctr Hill Farm Rsch Sta RR 1 Box 10 Homer LA 71040-9604

BODENHEIMER, SALLY NELSON, reading educator; b. Bedford, Ind., Aug. 31, 1939; d. Paul Edwin Sr. and Sarah Kathryn (Scott) Nelson; m. Robert Edward Bodenheimer, June 24, 1961; children: Robert Edward, Marc Alan, Bryan Lee. BS, U. Tenn., Knoxville, 1961, postgrad.; postgrad., Northwestern U., Carson Newman Coll. Cert. tchr. K-3, 1-9, K-12, music. Interni Crow Island Elem., Winnetka, Ill., 1961-62; tchr. 1st grade Wilmot Elem Sch., Deerfield, Ill., 1962-63, Vestal Elem. Sch., Knoxville, 1981-82; 7th grade math. tchr. Knox County Schs., Doyle Middle Sch., Knoxville, 1982-83; kindergarten tchr. Mt. Olive Sch., Knoxville, 1983-93, chpt. I lang, reading, reading recovery tchr., 1993—, chpt. I Lang. Reading, Reading Recovery, 1993-95, tchr. kindergarten, 1995—. Recipient Knoxville Arts Coun. Art in Edn. award, Golden Apple award Knoxville News Sentinel, Outstanding Environ. Edn. award. 21st Century Classroom. Mem. NEA, ASCD, Tenn. Edn. Assn., Knox County Edn. Assn., Smoky Mountain Reading Assn., Internat. Reading Assn., Nat. Coun. Tchrs. Math., Smoky Mountain Math. Educators Assn., Nat. Sci. Tchrs. Assn., Music Educators Nat. Conf., East Tenn. Foxfire Tchrs. Network (steering com.), Greater Knoxville C. of C. (leadership edn., Best Tchr. award 1989, Best award 1996), Delta Kappa Gamma, Pi Labmda Theta, Sigma Alpha Iota. Home: 3335 Tipton Station Rd Knoxville TN 37920-9565

BODEY, GERALD PAUL, medical educator, physician; b. Hazelton, Pa., May 22, 1934; s. Allen Zartman and Marie Frances (Smith) B.; m. Nancy Louise Wiegner, Aug. 25, 1956; children: Robin Gayle Sparwasser, Gerald Paul Jr., Sharon Dawn Brantley. AB magna cum laude, Lafayette Coll., 1956; MD, Johns Hopkins U., 1960. Diplomate Nat. Bd. Med. Examiners; diplomate in internal medicine, med. oncology and infectious diseases Am. Bd. Internal Medicine. Intern Johns Hopkins U., Balt., 1960-61, resident, 1961-62; clin. assoc. Nat. Cancer Inst., Bethesda, Md., 1962-65; resident U. Wash., Seattle, 1965-66; internist, prof. U Tex. MDACC, Houston, 1975-95, chmn. dept. med. specialities, 1987-95; emeritus prof. medicine U. Tex. MDACC, Houston, 1995—; chief sect. infectious diseases U Tex. MDACC, Houston, 1981-95, chief chemotherapy, 1975-83, med. dir. Cancer Clin. Rsch. Ctr., 1977-81; mem. lunar quartine ops. team Apollo 11-14, Manned Spacecraft Ctr., NASA. Editl. acad. Internat. Jour. of Oncology; contbr. more than 1000 articles to profl. jours. Dir. Korean Collaborative Program, 1985-95; past trustee Benevolence Found. Nat. AIDS Prevention Inst.; past bd. dirs. Christian Coalition Reconciliation. Recipient Am. Chem. Soc. prize, 1956, Merck award, 1956, Robert B. Youngman Greek prize, 1956, Eugene Yourassowsky award U. Libre de Bruxelles, Belgium, 1995; Henry Strong Denison fellow Johns Hopkins Sch. Medicine, Balt., 1958-60. Fellow ACP, Am. Coll. Chest Physicians, Am. Coll. Clin. Pharmacology, Royal Coll. Medicine, Royal Soc. Promotion Health; mem. AMA, AAAS, Am. Assn. Cancer Rsch., Am. Soc. Clin. Oncology, Am. Soc. Clin. Pharmacology and Therapeutics,, Tex. Med. Assn., Houston Acad. Medicine, Houston Soc. Internal Medicine, Academia Peruana de Cirugia (hon.), Mediterranean Med. Soc. (hon.), Phi Beta Kappa, Sigma Chi. Presbyterian. Office: U Tex MDACC 1515 Holcome Houston TX 77030

BODGE, STEVEN ALTON, insurance special investigator; b. Parkersburg, W.Va., Sept. 2, 1956; s. Lloyd W. and Doris J. (Lynch) B.; m. Deidra Rae Bodge, Oct. 16, 1982; children: Megan Nicole, Eric Steven. AAS in Criminal Justice, Parkersburg Community Coll., W.Va., 1983; BA, Fairmont State Coll., 1984; postgrad., W.Va. U., 1989. Cert. fraud claim law assoc., cert. fraud examiner. Investigator The Parkersburg City Police, 1977-89; adj. faculty mem. W.Va. U., Parkersburg, 1985—; dir. safety and security The Pizza People Inc., Marietia, Ohio, 1989-92; investigator Westfield Ins. Co., 1992-96, Nemax Claims Svc., 1996—; cons. Wood County Sheltered Workshop, Parkersburg, 1990. Named Outstanding Young Officer Jaycees, 1984. Mem. FBI Nat. Acad. Assocs., Nat. Restaurant Assn., Ohio Crime Prevention Assn., Internat. Assn. Chiefs Police, Am. Soc. for Indsl. Security, Washington County Traffic Safety Program, Internat. Assn. Arson Investigators, Internat. Assn. Auto Theft Investigators, Soc. Profl. Ins. Investigators, Fraternal Order Police. Republican. Methodist. Office: Nemax Claims Svc 1409 Greenbrier St Charleston WV 25311-1055

BODIE, CAROL HOOVER, computer services professional; b. Orangeburg, S.C., Sept. 18, 1957; d. Richard and Lucy Virginia (Bolton) Hoover; m. Thomas Odom Bodie, Jr., May 20, 1978; children: Chadwick, Matthew. BS in Mgmt. Sci., U. S.C., 1980, MBA, 1984. Rsch. analyst S.C. Electric & Gas Co., Columbia, 1978-83, programmer analyst, 1983-89; systems analyst Dupont, Aiken, S.C., 1989; systems analyst Westinghouse Corp., Aiken, 1989-90, mgr., 1990—; basketball ofcl. O'Dell Weeks Parks & Recreation, 1991—. Softball coach Dixie Youth League, 1995—. Mem. Nat. Help Desk Inst., Nat. Fedn. Interscholastic Ofcls. Assn. (basketball ofcl. 1992—), Nat. Mgmt. Assn., Civitans (sec. 1981-82), S.C. H.S. League of Ofcls., Nat. Youth Sports Assn. Baptist. Home: 167 Cheltenham Dr Aiken SC 29803-6633 Office: Westinghouse Savannah River 1993 S Centennial Ave Aiken SC 19803

BODILY, SAMUEL EDWIN, business administration educator; children: Adam, Diana, Jill, Rachel. BS in Physics magna cum laude, Brigham Young U., 1971; SM, MIT, 1974, PhD, 1976. Instr. MIT, Cambridge, 1976; asst. prof. mgmt. sci. Boston U., 1976-77; from asst. prof. to assoc. prof. bus. adminstrn. U. Va., Charlottesville, 1981—, prof. bus. adminstrn., 1983—; course head, instr. IBM Corp., 1981—; vis. assoc. prof. U. Wash., Seattle, 1982-83; cons. in field. Author: (with R. Carraway, S.C. Frey Jr., P.E. Pfeifer) Quantitative Business Analysis Casebook, 1996, Modern Decision Making, 1985; (with Phillip E. Pfeifer) ModelWare, 1984; contbr. articles to profl. jours. 1st lt. U.S. Army, 1973. Home: 210 Chaucer Rd Charlottesville VA 22901-2215 Office: U Va Darden Grad Bus Sch PO Box 6550 Charlottesville VA 22906-6550

BODISCH, ROBERT JOHN, SR., state agency administrator; b. Boston, Mar. 24, 1951; s. Arpod Elmer and Lillian Marie (Comeau) B.; m. Sandra Lynn Cooke; children: James Rudolph, Joseph Ambrose; children from previous marriage: Robert John, Kenneth John. AS, U. Houston, 1976, BS, 1978. Cert. legal asst., Tex., master peace officer, Tex. Patrolman Harris County Sheriff's Office, Houston, 1973-75; lt. investigator Harris County Dist. Atty.'s Office, Houston, 1975-84; chief investigator Tex. State Prosecutor Coun., Austin, 1984; sr. criminal investigator Tex. Atty. Gen.'s Office, Austin, 1985-89; sr. polit. cons. Blythe-Nelson, Newton & Towery, Austin, 1989-90; pres. R.J. Bodisch & Assocs. Inc., Austin, 1991-96; dir. Tex. Narcotics Control Program, Office of Gov., 1996—. Contbr. chpt. to book, articles to profl. jours. Mem. Juvenile Justice Adv. Bd., Austin, 1990-91; mem. St. Mary's Sch. Bd., Taylor, Tex., 1995—. Sgt. USMC, 1969-78; col. Tex. State Guard, 1988—. Recipient Houston award Tex. State Guard, 1992, cert. of appreciation Crime Stoppers of Houston, 1983, Sam Houston Area coun. Boy Scouts Am., 1983. Mem. VFW (jr. vice comdr. 1995-96), State Guard Assn. U.S. (bd. dirs. 1992—, 1st v.p. 1994-95), Tex. State Guard Assn. (pres. 1992), Am. Legion (sr. vice comdr. 1994-96), Taylor Police Assn. (pres. 1994-95). Republican. Roman Catholic. Home: 117 E 6th St Taylor TX 76574

BODKIN, RUBY PATE, corporate executive, real estate broker, educator; b. Frostproof, Fla., Mar. 11, 1926; d. James Henry and Lucy Beatrice (Latham) P.; m. Lawrence Edward Bodkin Sr., Jan. 15, 1949; children: Karen Bodkin Snead, Cinda, Lawrence Jr. BA, Fla. State U., 1948; MA, U. Fla., 1972. Lic. real estate broker. Banker Barnett Bank, Avon Park, Fla., 1943-44, Lewis State Bank, Tallahassee, 1944-49; ins. underwriter Hunt Ins. Agy., Tallahassee, 1949-51; tchr. Duval County Sch. Bd., Jacksonville, Fla., 1952-77; pvt. practice realty Jacksonville, 1976—; tchr. Nassau County Sch. Bd., Jacksonville, 1978-83; sec., treas., v.p. Bodkin Corp., R&D/Inventions, Jacksonville, 1983—; assoc. Brooke Shields Innovative Designer Products, Inc., Kendall Park, N.J., 1988—. Author: Bodkin Bridge Course for Beginners, 1996. Mem. Jacksonville Symphony Guild, 1985—, Southside Jr. Woman's Club, Jacksonville, 1957—, Garden Club Jacksonville, 1976—; bd. dirs. (fin. dir.) Riverside Woman's Club of Jacksonville, 1991-92. Recipient 25 Yr. Service award Duval County Sch. Bd., 1976, Tchr. of Yr. award Bryceville Sch., 1981. Mem. N.E. Fla. Assn. Realtors, Fla. Assn. Realtors, Nat. Assn. Realtors, UDC, Am. Contract Bridge League, Fla. Edn. Assn. (pers. problems com. 1958), Duval County Classroom Tchrs. (v.p. membership 1957), Woman's Club Jacksonville Bridge Group, San Jose Country Club, Ponte Vedra Club, Friday Musicale. Baptist. Home: 1149 Molokai Rd Jacksonville FL 32216-3273 Office: Bodkin Jewelers & Appraisers PO Box 16482 Jacksonville FL 32245-6482

BODNAR-BALAHUTRAK, LYDIA, artist, educator; b. Cleve., May 6, 1951; d. Wolodymyr and Luba M. (Hurko) Bodnar; m. Michael B. Balahutrak, Jan. 8, 1977. BS, Kent State U., 1973; postgrad., Corcoran Sch. Art, Washington, 1976-77; MFA, George Washington U., 1977. Art specialist Parma (Ohio) City Pub. Schs., 1973-75; instr. San Jacinto Coll., Houston, 1977-79; art exhbns. coord. U. Houston, Clear Lake, Tex., 1981-82, lectr., 1979-82, 86-87, 92-94; vis. guest lectr. U. Pitts., 1983; guest artist/lectr. La. State U., 1989; guest lectr. Stephen F. Austin State U., Nacogdoches, Tex., 1991; guest lectr./artist residency Lviv State Inst. Fine and Applied Arts, Ukraine, 1991, 2d Internat. Painters' Symposium, Ukraine, 1993. One-woman shows include U. Houston at Clear Lake, 1985, Graham Gallery, Houston, 1988, Galveston (Tex.) Arts Ctr., 1993, Dallas Visual Arts Ctr., 1995, The Nave Mus. of Art, Victoria, Tex., 1995; exhibited in group shows at Bowling Green State U., 1995, Edith Baker Gallery, Dallas, 1991, 92, 93, Sherry French Gallery, N.Y.C., 1990, numerous others; represented in numerous pub. and pvt. collections; featured in newspapers and profl. publs. Grantee Scurlock Found., 1979, Harris and Eliza Kempner Fund, 1979, La Napoule (France) Art Found., 1985, La. State U. Guest Artist Series, 1989, Internat. Rsch. and Exchs. Bd., 1991; recipient Purchase award George Washington U., Washington, 1976, 1st Place award Nat. Small Painting and Drawing Competition, N.Y.C., 1983, Purchase award Hoyt Inst. Fine Arts, Pa., 1984, NEA Artist Hon. award Art League Houston, 1985, Creative Artist Program award Cultural Arts Coun. Houston, 1993.

BODNER, EMANUEL, industrial recycling company executive; b. Houston, July 25, 1947; s. Eugene and Eve (Pryzant) B.; m. Jennifer L. Holt, Sept. 13, 1981; children: Jessica Elyse, Jeremiah. BBA, U. Tex., Austin, 1969. V.p. Bodner Metal & Iron Corp., Houston, 1969-95, pres., 1995—. Contrb. articles to profl. jour. Bd. dirs. Tex. Rehab., 1985-91, Tex. Council on Disabilities, 1986-90; mem. Tex. Legis. Council, Citizens Adv. Commn. Study of Vocat. Rehab., 1970-72; mem. removal of archtl. barriers com. Tex. Rehab. Assn., 1971; mem. handicapped access program task force Tex. Dept. Human Resources, 1978-79; mem. bd. Tex. Rehab. Commn., 1985-91, bd. sec., 1990-91; mem. Tex. Gov.'s Com. on Employment of Handicapped, vice chmn. employment devel. sub-com. 1981-82; mem. new leadership exec. com. State of Israel Bonds, 1984; mem. Resource Group serving Tex. Task Force on Waste Mgmt. Policy, 1988; pres. Gulf Coast chpt. Inst. of Scrap Recycling Industries, 1989-91; chmn conv. 1987-89; bd. dirs. Tex. Rehab. Commn., 1985-91, sec., 1990-91; mem. solid waste fee team Tex. Water Commn., 1990-91; mem. Keep Tex. Beautiful; mem. steering com. Clean Houston Recycling Coun., 1991-92; apptd. chmn. long range planning com., Tex. State Bd. Physician Asst. Examiners, 1994—. Mem. Inst. Scrap Recycling Industries (bd. dirs. 1989-91, nat. pub. rels. com., nat. fgn. trade com., bd. dirs. Gulf Coast chpt. 1977-84, chmn. bd. dirs., 1991-93, Pres.'s plaque Gulf Coast chpt. 1991, chmn. chpt. pub. rels. com. 1978-83, editor Gulf Coast Reporter 1978-85, sec. Gulf Coast chpt. 1984-85, treas. 1985, 2d v.p. 1986-87, chmn. membership com. 1986-87, vice-chmn., 1992—, 1st v.p. and chair conv. com. 1987—, pres. 1989-91, chmn. conv. 1987-89, Outstanding award 1985, vice chmn. chpt. pres. com. 1990-91, vice chmn. membership com. 1990-91, chmn. bd. 1991-93), Ex-Students Assn. U. Tex., Shriners, Masons (32 deg.), Alpha Epsilon Pi (life). Jewish. Office: Bodner Metal & Iron Corp 3660 Schalker Dr Houston TX 77026-3525

BOE, MYRON TIMOTHY, lawyer; b. New Orleans, Oct. 30, 1948; s. Myron Roger and Elaine (Tracy) B. BA, U. Ark., 1970, JD, 1973; LLM in Labor, So. Methodist U., 1976. Bar: Ark. 1974, Tenn. 1977, U.S. Ct. Appeals (4th, 5th, 6th, 7th, 8th, 9th, 10th, 11th cirs.) 1978, U.S. Supreme Ct. 1978. City atty. City of Pine Bluff, Ark., 1974-75; sec.-treas. Ark. City Atty. Assn., 1975; labor atty. Weintraub-Dehart, Memphis, 1976-78; sr. ptnr. Rose Law Firm, Little Rock, 1980—. Author: Handling the Title VII Case Practical Tips for the Employer, 1980; contbr. book supplement: Employment Discrimination Law, 2d edit., 1983. Served to 2d lt. USAR, 1972-73. Recipient Florentino-Ramirez Internat. Law award, 1975. Fellow Ark. Bar Found., Ark. Bd. Legal Specialization (sec. 1982-85, chmn. 1985-89, labor, employment discrimination, civil rights).; mem. ABA (labor sect. 1974—, employment law com. 1974—), Ark. Bar Assn. (sec., chmn. labor sect. 1978-81, ho. of dels. 1979-82, Golden Gavel award 1983), Def. Rsch. Inst. (employment law com. 1982—), Am. Trial Lawyers Assn., Ark. Trial Lawyers Assn., Ark. Assn. Def. Counsel. Office: Rose Law Firm 120 E 4th St Little Rock AR 72201-2808

BOEGLIN, TIMOTHY RAY, minister; b. Dallas, Apr. 28, 1953; s. Charles Richard and Audrey Virginia (MacIntosh) B.; m. Suzanne Carol Sheppard, Dec. 12, 1986; 1 child, Andrew Skye. AB, Eastfield Coll., 1974; BA, Pontifical Coll. Josephinum, Columbus, Ohio, 1976; STB, Pontifical Coll. St. Thomas, Rome, 1979, MA, 1980. Ordained priest Roman Cath. Ch., 1980, minister United Meth. Ch., 1991. Pastor Roman Cath. Diocese, Ft. Worth, 1980-85; therapist Baylor U. Med. Ctr., Dallas, 1985-89; dir. Tarrant Coun., Arlington, Tex., 1988-89; interventionist CPC Millwood Hosp., Arlington, 1989-90; pastor United Meth. Ch., Ft. Worth, 1990—; co-founder Cath. Renewal Ctr., Ft. Worth, 1974; program host Chem. People TV show, 1989-91; mem. nominating com. West Dist., Ctrl. Tex. Conf. United Meth. Ch., 1995. Author: Epistles From Tim, 1980. Chmn. bd. Parents and Children Together, Ft. Worth, 1993—; chaplain AIDS Interfaith, Ft. Worth, 1993—; bd. dirs. Clergy-Interethnic Justice, Ft. Worth, 1994—. Home: 2005 Lipps Fort Worth TX 76134 Office: St Paul United Meth Ch 920 W Hammond Fort Worth TX 76115

BOEHM, JOHN CHARLES, music educator; b. Tampa, Fla., Oct. 13, 1948; s. T.S. Boehm and Mamie Boehm (Ausband) Mitchell; m. Nancy Perry, July 3, 1988; 1 child, Alison Boehm; stepchildren: Jason Cox, David Cox. AA, Gordon Mil. Coll., 1968; MusB, Carson-Newman Coll., 1971; MusM, Ga. State U., 1973. Choral dir. Richmond County Schs., Augusta, Ga., 1970-71, Fulton County Schs., Atlanta, 1971-72; instr. music Kennesaw (Ga.) Coll. (formerly Kennesaw Jr. Coll.), 1973-74; asst. prof., dir. music Atlanta Met. Coll. (formerly Atlanta Jr. Coll.), 1974—; contbg. writer, project staff mem. Atlanta jr. coll. humanities curriculum devel. pilot project and 3 yr. grant NEH, 1976, 78. Performing mem. Atlanta Symphony Orch. Chorus and Chamber Chorus, 1977-90. Mem. NARAS (voting mem., bd. govs. 1987-91, chmn. edn. com. 1987-89), Am. Choral Dirs. Assn. (life, state chair 2 yr. colls. 1983-85, state chair ethnic/minority concerns 1985-87, 89-91, so. divsn. chair 2 yr. colls. 1992—), Music Educators Nat. Conf., Ga. Music Educators Assn. (adjudicator 1982—, guest condr. 1982—), Phi Mu Alpha (life). Home: 1301 Dunwoody Ln NE Atlanta GA 30319-1515 Office: Atlanta Met Coll 1630 Stewart Ave SW Atlanta GA 30310-4448

BOEHM, RICHARD GLENNON, geography and planning educator, writer; b. St. Louis, Aug. 29, 1937; s. Frank A. and Ivy M. Boehm; m. R. Denise Blanchard; children: Brian, Lori, Mike, Laura, Mitch, Nick. BS in Edn., U. Mo., 1960, MA in Geography, 1962; PhD in Geography, U. Tex., 1975. From instr. to asst. prof. dept. geography and planning S.W. Tex. State U., San Marcos, 1963-71; from instr. to asst. prof. dept. geography U. Mo., Columbia, 1971-76, chmn. dept. geography, 1976-77; dir. Inst. for Corridor Studies S.W. Tex. State U., San Marcos, 1983—, prof., chmn. dept. geography, 1977-94; geography edn. cons. U.S. Dept. Edn., U.S. Dept. Def., AT&T Nat. Coun. on Crime and Delinquency, Ednl. Testing Svc., Nat. Geographic Soc., The Nat. Faculty, Nat. Coun. of Chief State Sch. Officers; assoc. fellow Nat. Ctr. for Juvenile Justice, Pitts., 1974-80; steering com. Geographic Edn. Nat. Implementation Project, 1984-87; mem. writing team joint nat. curriculum guidelines project Assn. Am. Geographers/Nat. Coun. Geographic Edn.; organized Summit I in Geographic Edn., 1993 and Summit II in Geographic Edn., 1995. Author: Exporting Cotton in Texas: Relationships of Ports and Inland Supply Points, 1975, Careers in Geography, 1990, Glencoe World Geography, 1995, (with others) Missouri's Transportation System: Condition, Capacity and Impediments to Efficiency, 1976, Principal Interaction Fields of Missouri Regional Centers, 1976, Transport Regulation in Missouri, 1978, Guidelines for Geographic Education: Elementary and Secondary Schools, 1984, World Geography: A Physical and Cultural Approach, 1989, 2d edit., 1992, Geography: The World and Its People, 1996; co-author: Geography for Life: National Standards in Geography, 1994. 2d lt. U.S. Army, 1960. Recipient Best Article award Jour. Geography, 1980, 87, Disting. Alumnus award U. Mo. Coll. Arts & Sci., 1996. Mem. Nat. Coun. Geographic Edn. (treas. 1977, local arrangements chmn. 1979, 2d v.p. 1980, 1st v.p. 1981, pres. 1983, editor Media Materials 1972-77, gen. editor slide libr. 1974-77, George J. Miller award 1991, Disting. Geographic Educator 1990, Disting. Tchg. Achievement award 1985), Nat. Geographic Soc. (co-coord. Tex. Alliance for Geographic Edn. 1986—), S.W. Tex. State U. (presdl. seminar award, 1995). Home: 733 Willow Ridge Dr San Marcos TX 78666 Office: S W Tex State U Dept Geography Planning San Marcos TX 78666

BOEKER, HERBERT RALPH, JR., urban planner; b. Cotulla, Tex., Dec. 4, 1951; s. Herbert Ralph and Doris (Franklin) B. BS in Sociology, Tex. A&M U., 1973, M in Urban and Regional Planning, 1975; MA in Energy and Mineral Resources, U. Tex., 1983. Project mgr. Tex. Dept. Water Resources, 1984-85, Tex. Water Commn., 1985-87; environ. coord. Gov.'s Office, Budget and Planning, Austin, Tex., 1987-89, asst. dep. dir. environ. planning, 1989; water resources planner Tex. Water Devel. Bd., Austin, 1990, unit head, policy, 1991-92, sect. chief, water rsch., 1992, sect. chief, water rsch. and policy, 1992-94, sect. chief, water policy, 1994—; mem. Nueces River Basin Clean Rivers steering com., Uvalde, Tex., 1992—; mem. Sulphur River Basin Authority steering com., Texarkana, 1992—; mem. Gov.'s Border Working Group, Austin, 1992; mentor Mickey Leland Environ. Internship Program, 1992. Contbr. chpt. to book. Recipient Disting. Svc. award State of Tex., 1989; recipient 1st Place student paper award, Mining and Metall. Soc. of N.Am., N.Y.C., 1982. Mem. Consortium for Rsch. on Mex., La Salle County Fair Assn., Assn. Former Students of Tex. A&M U., U. Tex. Friends of the U. Librs., Chihuahuan Desert Rsch. Inst. Baptist. Home: 2800 Bartons Bluff # 904 Austin TX 78746

BOENSCH, ARTHUR CRANWELL, lawyer; b. Charleston, S.C., Nov. 9, 1933; s. Frank Neville and Mary Alice (Cranwell) B.; m. Katherine Hume Lucas, June 16, 1956; children: Arthur Cranwell, Katherine Pierce, Alice Witt, Frances Murdaugh, Benjamin; m. 2d, Annelle Yvonne Beach, July 27, 1979. B.S. in Gen. Engring., U.S. Naval Acad., 1956; J.D., U. S.C., 1970. Bar: S.C. 1970, U.S. Dist. Ct. (so. dist.) Ga. 1970, U.S. Dist. Ct. S.C. 1971. Ptnr., Ackerman & Boensch, 1970-73, Bogoslow & Boensch, 1973-75; sole practice, Walterboro, S.C., 1975—; city recorder, mcpl. ct. judge, Walterboro, 1973-78. Chmn. Colleton County Alcohol and Drug Abuse Commn., 1991-96; dist. chmn. Boy Scouts Am., 1988-95; exec. bd. Coastal Carolina Council Boy Scouts Am., 1978—; vestry St. Jude's Episcopal Ch.; lay rector Cursillo Episcopal Diocese of S.C., 1989; del. Episcopal Conv. Diocese of S.C., 1995, 96. Served to lt. comdr. USN, 1956-67. Recipient Silver Beaver award and dist. award of merit Boy Scouts Am., 1982, James West fellow, 1996. Mem. S.C. Bar Assn. (chmn. lawyers caring about lawyers com. 1989-91), Phi Alpha Delta. Republican. Club: Rotary. Office: PO Box 258 Walterboro SC 29488-0258

BOERNER, JO M., real estate trainer; b. Wayne, Okla., Apr. 17, 1944; d. James Olman and Virgie M. (Jones) Whitaker; m. Buddy Dennis Boerner, July 3, 1964 (div. 1987); children: Christopher Alexander, James Dennis, Edward Floyd. Grad., Realtor Inst. Okla. State U., 1979. Cert. residential specialist. Assoc. Abide Realtors, Oklahoma City, 1976-83; br. mgr. Merrill Lynch Realtors, Oklahoma City, 1983-86; dir. career devel. Marolyn Pryor & Assocs., Oklahoma City, 1986-87; nat. tng. dir. Long & Foster, Realtors, Fairfax, Va., 1987—; regional v.p. Women's Coun. of Realtors, Chgo., 1987; bd. dir. Oklahoma City Bd. Realtors, 1984-85; instr. Realtors Inst. Okla. State U., 1987. Contbr. articles to profl. jours. Bd. govs. Wednesday's Child Found., Oklahoma City, 1987; mem. Allied Arts Coun., Oklahoma City, 1985-87, Realtors Polit. Action Com., Okla., 1984-87. Recipient State of Excellence award Okla. State Gov., 1987, Omega Tau Rho medal. Mem. Nat. Women's Coun. of Realtors (gov. bd. 1985-87), Nat. Assn. Realtors, Women's Coun. of Realtors (pres. 1985, gov. 1986), Va. Assn. Realtors, Siga Internat. (trustee 1982-83), Toastmasters. Republican. Office: Long & Foster Realtors 11351 Random Hills Rd Fairfax VA 22030-6081

BOERSCHMANN, JAMES F., hotel executive; b. Königsberg, Germany, June 10, 1928; s. Eduard and Ida Kaete (Stockman) B.; m. Gene Palacios; children: Frank, Karen Young-Boerschmann. Grad. in Bus. Adminstrn., U. Wilhemshaven/U. Berlin, Germany; cert. hotel adminstr., Holiday Inn U. Regional dir. ops. Allen & O'Hara Inc., Memphis; mgr. Hilton Hotel, Denver; gen. mgr. Sheraton Hotel, Columbus, Ohio; dir. ops. Leadership Lodging Corp., Rockville, Md.; gen. mgr. Mexico City, West Africa, Bali, Indonesia. Mem. Hotel Sales & Mktg. Assn. (treas. 1963). Republican. Roman Catholic. Home: 4280 Sand Fox Cove Memphis TN 38141-6877

BOERU, LAURENTIU MARIAN, health association executive; b. Braila, Romania, Nov. 23, 1955; came to U.S., 1990; s. Tanase Gheorghe Boeru and Olga Popescu; m. Marius Lucian Boeru, Apr. 28, 1978. MD, U. Iasi, Romania, 1981, MS in Biochemistry magna cum laude, 1981. Intern, physician Braila Dist. Hosp., 1981-84; resident in gen. surgery U. Bucharest, Romania, 1984-85; resident in gen. surgery Emergency Hosp., Braila, 1985-87, attending surgeon, 1987-90; dist. health min. Dept. Health & Human Svcs., Bucharest, 1989-90; asst. prof. Miami (Fla.) Christian Coll., 1990-91; prof. Arc Ventures, Inc., Miami, 1991-92; house physician Miami Children's Hosp., 1992-93; asst. to pres. Southeastern Health Mgmt. Assocs., Inc., Miami, 1993—; pres. Edge Healthcare Cons., Inc., 1994—. Baptist. Home: 11220 SW 180th St Miami FL 33157 Office: 600 W 20th St Hialeah FL 33012

BOETTCHER, ARMIN SCHLICK, lawyer, banker; b. East Bernard, Tex., Apr. 12, 1941; s. Clem C. and Frances Helene (Schlick) B.; m. Virginia Nan Barkley, Apr. 13, 1963; children: Lynn Frances, Laura Anne. BBA, U. Tex., Austin, 1963, JD, 1967. Various positions personal trust dept. Republic Bank Houston 1967-75, sr. v.p., trust officer, head trust dept., 1975-82; exec. v.p., dir. Union State Bank, East Bernard, Union Motor Co., Inc., East Bernard, 1982-93. Bd. dirs. Whispering Oaks Civic Club, 1980-85, pres., 1981. Mem. Houston Bus. and Estate Planning Council, Houston Bar Assns., U. Tex. Ex-Students Assn. (life), Meml. Forest Club (dir. 1981-83), Sigma Chi. Methodist. Office: 122 Warrenton Dr Houston TX 77024-6224

BOFILL, RANO SOLIDUM, physician; b. Panay, Capiz, The Philippines, Mar. 14, 1942; came to U.S., 1969; s. Saturnino Bernas and Consoladora (Solidum) B.; m. Judy Libo-On, May 27, 1972; children: Lora, Rano Libo-on II, Mariju. MD, U. Sto. Tomas, Manila, 1966. Pvt. practice Romney, W.Va., 1973-79; resident radiology Episcopal Hosp., Phila., 1980-82; chief resident radiology Germantown Hosp., Phila., 1982-83; assoc. radiologist Pleasant Valley Hosp., Point Pleasants, W.Va., 1984-89; chmn. credentials com., pres. exec. com., chmn. A.R. Hosp., Man, W.Va., 1984—, pres. med. staff, 1984—. Editor: newsletter, 1984—. Coord. health topic com. A.R. Hosp., Man, 1988. Lt. col. USAR, 1989. Fellow Am. Acad. Family Physicians, Am. Coll. Internat. Physicians (trustee 1985-87, treas. 1987—), Internat. Coll. of Surgeons; mem. Assn. Philippine Physicians Am. (del. 1989—), W.Va. Am. Coll. Internat. Physicians (founding pres. Point Pleasant 1984-85), Philippine Med. Assn. W.Va. (pres. Man 1989—). Roman Catholic. Home: 309 W Avis Ave Man WV 25635-1132

BOGGS, DANNY JULIAN, federal judge; b. Havana, Cuba, Oct. 23, 1944; s. Robert Lilburn and Yolanda (Pereda) B.; m. Judith Susan Solow, Dec. 23, 1967; children: Rebecca, David, Jonathan. A.B., Harvard Coll., Cambridge, Mass., 1965; J.D., U. Chgo., 1968; LLD (hon.), U. Detroit Mercy, 1994. Dep. commr. Ky. Dept. Econ. Security, 1969-70; legal counsel, adminstrv. asst. Gov. Ky., 1970-71; legis. counsel to Rep. legislators Ky. Gen. Assembly, 1972; asst. to solicitor gen. U.S. Dept. Justice, Washington, 1973-75; asst. to chmn. FPC, Washington, 1975-77; dep. minority counsel Senate Energy Com., Washington, 1977-79; of counsel Bushnell, Gage, et al., Washington, 1979-80; spl. asst. to Pres. White House, Washington, 1981-83; dep. sec. U.S. Dept. Energy, Washington, 1983-86; judge U.S. Ct. Appeals (6th cir.), Cin., 1986—; mem. adv. com. on appellate rules Jud. Conf. U.S., 1991-

94, com. on automation and tech., 1994—. Mem. vis. com. U. Chgo. Law Sch., 1984-87; del. Republican Nat. Conv., 1972; staff dir. energy subcom. Rep. Platform Com., 1980. Mem. ABA, Ky. Bar Assn., Mont Pelerin Soc., Phila. Soc., Order of Coif, Phi Delta Phi. Office: US Ct Appeals 220 US Courthouse 6th & Broadway Louisville KY 40202

BOGGS, DAVID GLENN, JR., early childhood educator; b. Greenville, S.C., June 5, 1969; s. David Glenn Sr. and Nettie Ann (Thompson) B. Student, Charleston So. U., 1987-91, Francis Marion U., Florence, S.C., 1992-93. Day camp dir. Grand Strand YMCA, Myrtle Beach, S.C., 1987-90, Lowell (Mass.) Cambodian Mission, 1991, River Valley Assn., Lake Havasu City, Ariz., 1992; presch. tchr. Florence Family YMCA, 1993—. Contbr. Around the World in 80 Ways, 1994. Mem. ASCD. Democrat. Presbyterian. Office: Florence Family YMCA 1700 S Rutherford Rd Florence SC 29505

BOGGS, JUDITH SUSAN, lawyer, health policy expert; b. Bklyn., Feb. 11, 1946; d. Robert Henry and Ethel (Shapiro) Solow; m. Danny Julian Boggs; children: Rebecca, David, Jonathan. BA cum laude, Bklyn. Coll., 1966; JD, U. Chgo., 1969. Bar: Ky. 1970. Human rights rep. Ky. Human Rights Commn., Frankfort, Ky., 1969; legal counsel Ky. Dept. Mental Health, Frankfort, 1970-73; sr. legal advisor Social and Rehabilitation Service, Washington, 1973-77; dir., health systems div. Health Care Fin. Adminstrn., Washington, 1978-82, special asst. to assoc. adminstr. for policy, 1982-86, spl. asst. to adminstr., 1986-87; sr. policy analyst The White House, Washington, 1987-89; of counsel Alagia, Day, Trautwein & Smith, Louisville, 1989-93; sr. v.p., gen. counsel Ky. Hosp. Assn., 1993-94; pvt. practice, 1994—. Mem. ABA, Ky. Bar Assn., Nat. Health Lawyers Assn., Am. Acad. Hosp. Attys.

BOGGS, WILLENE GRAYTHEN, art director, oil and gas broker, consultant; b. Vancouver, Wash., Mar. 10, 1939; d. William Louis and Zorah (Williams) Graythen; m. Ray Buck Glasgow, Feb. 8, 1964 (div. June 1969); m. Harry Maurice Boggs, May 23, 1993. BA in History, Centenary Coll., 1975; postgrad., La. State Law Sch., 1984, S.E. La. U., 1989. Tchr., educator St. Tam Parish Sch. Bd., Lacombe, La., 1964-65; abstractor St. Tam Parish Legal News, Covington, La., 1965-66, Kansas City Title Ins. Co., New Orleans, 1966-69, Lawyers Title Ins. Corp., New Orleans, 1975-77, Frawley, Wogan, Miller & Co., New Orleans, 1977-79; owner, mgr. Idea House and Sweet Home Antiques, Metairie, La., 1973-76; owner, mgr., abstractor, oil and gas broker Willene Glasgow & Assocs., Metairie, 1969-73; owner, mgr., abstractor Willene Glasgow & Assocs., Covington, La., 1979-93; pres. WCV Mgmt., Inc., Nashville, 1993-94; asst. to art dir. Bascom-Louise Gallery, Highlands, N.C., 1996. Author: Decoupage and Related Crafts, 1972; contbg. writer Times-Picayune, New Orleans, 1989. Bd. dirs. Air, Water and Earth Inst., Covington, 1989; bd. dirs., pres. Pontchartrain Area Recycling Coun., Inc., Covington, 1989, 90, 91, 92, 93; mem. Citizens Adv. Com. on Solid Waste, 1988, 89, 90, 91, 92; coord. Pontchartrain Area Recycling Conv., 1988; fund raiser March of Dimes, Am. Cancer Soc., Arthritis Found., others, 1986—. Named hon. sec. state State of La., 1987. Mem. AAUW (conf. chmn. 1988-89, 92-93, chmn. Ednl. Found. 1989-91, Mem. of Yr. award Covington-Mandeville br. 1989, v.p. membership 1991-93), Petroleum Landman's Assn., Covington C. of C. (legis. chmn. 1988—, Mem. of Yr. award 1988), Art League of Highlands (membership chmn. 1996, publicity chmn. 1997), Highlands-Cashiers Garden Club (v.p. membership 1997, 2d v.p. 1997). Home and Office: 145 Mount Lori Dr Highlands NC 28741

BOGGS, WILLIAM BRADY, quality engineering and applied statistics consultant; b. Atlanta, Nov. 15, 1943; s. William Brady and Callie Kathleen (Jordan) B.; m. Rebecca Lynn Taunton, Feb. 26, 1966; children: Jason Alan, Brian Daniel. BS in Physics, Ga. Inst. Tech., 1965; MS, Fla. State U., 1970, MBA, 1971; postgrad N.C. State U., 1979-80; diploma in Bible and Doctrine, Berean Sch. of Bible, 1985. Radar systems analyst Calspan Corp., Buffalo, 1972-74; sect. head research systems engring. BASF Corp. (formerly Am. Enka Co.), Enka, N.C., 1974-78, mgr. research systems engring., 1978-82, research staff statistician, 1982-83, engring. staff statistician, 1983-87, mgr. fibers div. statis. services, 1988-93; founder, pres. Alpha Quality Services, Inc., Candler, N.C., 1985—, Found. of Christian Leadership, 1993—, Adj. faculty, Mgmt. and Mathematics, Montreat Coll., 1996. Mem. editoral rev. bd., adminstrv. comm. Quality Progress mag.; book rev. Technometrics jour.; book reviewer: Quality Progress Mag.; contbr. papers to profl. conf. Sr. comr. Royal Rangers outpost 46 Christian ministry for boys, Asheville, 1984-85, sect. comdr. Gt. Smoky Mountain sect. N.C. dist., 1986-90; mem. elder West Asheville Assembly of God, 1982—, sch. bd. Rhema Christian Sch., Asheville, 1985-90. Capt. U.S. Army, 1965-68. Mulliken fellow, 1968-70, Fla. State U. fellow, 1970-71. Mem. Am. Soc. Quality Control (cert. quality engr., cert. quality auditor, chmn. sect. edn. com., sr. mem.), Am. Statis. Assn., Tau Beta Pi, Phi Kappa Phi, Sigma Pi Sigma, Pi Eta Sigma, Sigma Iota Epsilon, Beta Gamma Sigma. Mem. Assembly of God. Clubs: Full Gospel Businessmens Fellowship (treas. 1980, sec. 1981-82); Frontiersman Camping Fraternity N.C. Avocations: photography, computers, shooting sports. Home and Office: Alpha Quality Svcs Inc 767 Case Cove Rd Candler NC 28715-9283

BOGUCKI, RAYMOND SPENCER, lawyer; b. Hammond, Ind., Aug. 14, 1951; s. Raymond L. Bogucki & Bette J. Spencer; m. Vicki Kincheloe; children: Chant Graham, Anthony Dean. BA in Comms., U. Ky., 1976; JD, No. Ky. U., Highland Heights, 1980. Bar: Ky. 1980. Lawyer in pvt. practice Florence, Ky., 1980—, Augusta, Ky., 1981—, Maysville, Ky., 1994—; prof. No. Ky. U., Highland Heights, 1981-94. Served with USN, 1969-72. Mem. ABA, ATLA, Ky. Acad. Trial Attys. Roman Catholic. Office: PO Box 6206 Florence KY 41022-6206

BOHAM, KENNETH ARNOLD, academic administrator; b. Lake Forest, Ill., Mar. 27, 1955; s. Ora Conard Boham Jr. and Gertrude (Hughes) Outland; m. Betty Drew Crowder, June 9, 1984; children: Stephen Drew, Chelsea Hughes. BS, East Carolina U., Greenville, N.C., 1973-77; MEd, N.C. State U., 1982, EdD, 1988. Edn. specialist N.C. Dept. Correction, Raleigh, 1977-78; Northampton County continuing edn. coord. Halifax C.C., Weldon, N.C., 1978-82; dean extension and community svcs. Wake Tech. C.C., Raleigh, 1984-87, assoc. v.p. continuing edn., 1987-89, v.p. continuing edn., 1989-95; interim pres. Mayland C.C., 1994; pres. Caldwell C.C. and Tech. Inst., Hudson, N.C., 1995—. Mem. N.C. C.C. Adult Educators Assn. (treas. 1987-88, bd. dirs. 1988-91, pres. elect 1991-92, pres. 1992-93). Office: Caldwell CC and Tech Inst 2855 Hickory Blvd Hudson NC 28638

BOHANNAN, JULES KIRBY, printing company executive; b. Richmond, Va., June 21, 1917; s. Jules Kirby and Essie (Lambertson) B.; m. Lucyann Davis, June 28, 1941; children: Judy, Jay Kirby. Student, Syracuse U., 1946; BA, Kennedy-Western U., 1991. From order dept. staff to asst. mgr. Standard Salesbook Co., Inc., N.Y.C., 1936-49; mgr., dir. Standard Salesbook Co. Inc., 1949-51, v.p., 1950; exec. v.p. Newport Bus. Forms Co. Inc., Hampton, Va., 1951-59; pres. Newport Bus. Forms Co. Inc., 1960-62, dir., 1962-88; pres. Office Supply Inc., Hopewell, Va., 1950-62; ptnr. Paperconverters, Ltd., 1995—; bd. dirs. Printing Plates Inc. Chmn. safety com. Boy Scouts Am., 1958—; chmn. budget com. United Fund; chmn. bd. Tri-City Literacy Coun. With USNR, 1941-45. Mem. N.A.M. (mktg. com.), Nat. Ordnance Assn., Sales Execs. Club, Toastmasters, James River Country Club, Williamsburg Country Club. Episcopalian.

BOHANNON, CHARLES TAD, lawyer; b. Dallas, June 25, 1964; s. Charles Spencer and Donna Pauline (Smith) B.; m. Gayle Renee Alston, July 26, 1986. BA, Hendrix Coll., 1986; JD, U. Ark., Little Rock, 1992; LLM, Washington U., St. Louis, 1993. Bar: Ark. 1992, Tex. 1993, U.S. Dist. Ct. (ea. and we. dists.) Ark. 1992, U.S. Dist. Ct. (no. dist.) Tex. 1994, U.S. Ct. Appeals (5th and 8th cirs.) 1994, U.S. Tax Ct. 1994. Staff atty. U.S. Ct. Appeals (8th cir.), St. Louis, 1992-94; assoc. Gill Law Firm, Little Rock, 1994—. Contbr. articles to profl. jours. Mem. ABA, Ark. Bar Assn., Pulaski County Bar Assn., Ark. Trial Lawyers Assn., Nat. Transp. Safety Bd., Bar Assn. Fifth Cir., Bar Assn. State Bar of Tex., Am. Judicature Soc., Nat. Assn. Bond Lawyers, Ark. State Soccer Assn., Ctrl. Ark. Referees Assn., Aircraft Owners and Pilots Assn. Office: Gill Law Firm 3801 TCBY Twr 425 W Capitol Ave Little Rock AR 72201

BOHANNON, SARAH VIRGINIA, personnel operations technician; b. Roanoke, Va., Mar. 1, 1947; d. Laurence S. and Sarah Elizabeth (Smith) B. AA in Bus. Adminstrn. Mgmt., Nat. Bus. Coll., 1983. Pers. appointment clk. IRS, Richmond, Va., 1983-84; pers. ops. technician Commonwealth of Va., Richmond, 1985—. Mem. NAFE, Am. Biog. Inst. (life, dep. gov. 1991, hon. mem. rsch. bd. advisors 1991, mem. women's inner circle of achievement 1991), Va. Pub. Health Assn. Home: 2220 Clarke St Richmond VA 23228-6049 Office: Commonwealth of Va Dept of Tech Richmond VA 23219-2110

BOHANON, LUTHER L., federal judge; b. Ft. Smith, Ark., Aug. 9, 1901; s. William Joseph and Artelia (Campbell) B.; m. Marie Swatek, July 17, 1933; 1 son, Richard L. LLB, U. Okla., 1927; LLD (hon.), Oklahoma City U., 1991. Bar: Okla. 1927, U.S. Supreme Ct. 1937. Gen. practice law Seminole, Okla. and Oklahoma City, 1927-61; judge U.S. Dist. Ct. Okla. (no., ea., and we. dists.), 1961-74, sr. judge, 1974—. Mem. platform com. Democratic Nat. Conv., 1940. Served to maj. USAAF, 1942-45. Recipient citations and awards including citation from Okla. Senate and Ho. of Reps., 1979, Okla. County Bar Assn. and Jour. Record award, 1987, Humanitarian award NCCJ, 1991; Luther Bohanon Am. Inn of Ct. named in his honor Am. Inn of Ct. XXIII/U. Okla., 1991. Mem. U.S. Dist. Judges Assn. (10th cir.), Fed. Judges Assn., Okla. Bar Assn., Oklahoma County Bar Assn., Oklahoma City C. of C., Sigma Nu, Phi Alpha Delta. Methodist. Clubs: Mason (Shriner, 32 deg.), K.T, Jester, Kiwanis, Com.of 100, Men's Dinner Club. Home: 1617 Bedford Dr Oklahoma City OK 73116-5406 Office: US Dist Ct PO Box 1514 Oklahoma City OK 73101-1514

BOHJANEN, PAUL ROBERT, internist, scientist; b. Marquette, Mich., Aug. 29, 1963; s. Robert Raymond and Mabel Elsie (Junttila) B.; m. Kimberly Ann Lippman, June 25, 1988; 1 child, Robert Bruce. BS in Biochemistry, No. Mich. U., 1985; MD, U. Mich., 1993, PhD in Cell and Molecular Biology, 1993. Lab. asst. Marquette Gen. Hosp., 1981-85; lab. technician U. Mich. Hosps., Ann Arbor, 1985-86; rsch. scholar Howard Hughes Med. Inst., Bethesda, Md., 1987-89; internal medicine intern Duke U. Med. Ctr., Durham, N.C., 1993-94, internal medicine resident, 1994-96, infectious diseases fellow, 1996—. Contbr. articles to profl. jours. Counselor Bay Cliff Health Camp, Big Bay, Mich., 1984; asst. scoutmaster Boy Scouts Am. Troop 309, Marquette, 1981-85, chpt. chief Order of the Arrow, 1981-82. MD/PhD scholarship Life and Health Ins. Med. Rsch. Fund, 1989-93; postdoctoral fellowship for physicians Howard Hughes Med. Inst., 1995—; presdl. scholarship No. Mich. U., 1981-85; recipient Dean's award for Rsch. Excellence U. Mich., 1993. Mem. AMA, AAAS, Alpha Omega Alpha, Phi Kappa Phi. Office: Duke U Med Ctr Box 3686 Durham NC 27710

BOHLE, ROBERT HENRY, journalism educator; b. Oak Park, Ill., June 24, 1947; s. William Henry and Vivian Grace (Frasier) B.; m. Suzanne Egan, Mar. 12, 1994; children: Cameron Jay, Christopher Robert. BA in English cum laude, Calif. State U., Long Beach, 1970, MA in English lit., 1972; PhD in Comm., U. Tenn., 1984. Sports reporter and copy desk, copy clk., news copy clk. Long Beach Ind., 1968-72; tchr. English and journalism Monache High Sch., Porterville, Calif., 1972-74; instr., acting chmn. Orange Coast Coll., Costa Mesa, Calif., 1974-76; instr. Palomar Coll., San Marcos, Calif., 1976, Coll. of the Sequoias, Visalia, Calif., 1976-83; assoc. prof. Sch. of Mass Comm., Va. Commonwealth U., Richmond, 1983-95; dir. comms., chair dept. Comms. and Visual Arts U. North Fla., Jacksonville, 1995—; spkr. and presenter workshops and seminars; publ. and internet cons. Author: From News to Newsprint, 2d edit., 1992, Publication Design for Editors, 1990, (with others) Color in American Newspapers, 1986; contbr. numerous articles to profl. jours. Recipient Presdl. Citation Coll. Media Advisers, Inc., 1983, Outstanding Young Man in Am. award U.S. Jaycees, 1982, Gannett Found. Graduation scholarship, 1982; Freedom Forum Prof.'s Publ. grantee, 1992. Mem. Assn. for Edn. in Journalism and Mass Comm. (editl. adv. bd. Journalism and Mass Comm. Educator 1988—), Soc. Newspaper Design (mem. edn. com. 1985—, contbg. editor DESIGN jour. 1993-95), Soc. Profl. Journalists, Kappa Tau Alpha, Phi Kappa Phi.

BOHLKEN, DEBORAH KAY, banking executive, government consultant, lobbyist; b. Anchorage, Nov. 16, 1952; d. Darrell Richard and Gertrude Ann (Merkel) B. BA, U. Ark., 1975, MSW, 1977. Specialist community devel. State of Ark., Little Rock, 1976-77, supr. community area, 1977-78, mgr. evaluation and data processing, 1978-80; corp. analyst Systematics, Inc., Little Rock, 1980-83, mgr. corp. planning and rsch., 1983-85, group mgr. planning, rsch., Washington Congl. liasion, 1985-89, 91—, corp. mgr. legis. and regulatory, legal dept., 1990-91; mktg., planning and devel. mgr. Systematics, Inc., 1992-95; mgr. legis. and regulatory govt. svcs. Systematics Info. Svcs., Inc., Little Rock, 1992-95; v.p. ALLTEL Info. Svcs., Little Rock, 1994-95; pres. BCA, Inc., Little Rock, 1995—; pres. BCA, Inc., Little Rock, 1996. Contbr. articles and papers to profl. publs. Bd. dirs. Cen. Ark. Radiation Therapy Inst. Hotline, Little Rock, 1980-82, Cancer Soc., Little Rock, 1986-89; state chair Cansurmount, Little Rock, 1985-89. Nat. Juvenile Justice Law Enforcement Adminstrn. explimary data processing grantee, 1976-78. Mem. NAFE, Nat. Assn. Bank Svcs., Fin. Mgrs. Assn., Am. Mgmt. Assn. Methodist. Office: BCA Inc 1817 Foreman Dr Little Rock AR 72212

BOHN, BARBARA ANN, laboratory director; b. St. Louis, Nov. 24, 1943; d. Arthur John Joseph and Eleanor Caroline (Kinsman) B. BS in Med. Tech., Loyola U., New Orleans, 1965; MBA, Old Dominion U., 1984. Med. technologist Broward Gen. Med. Ctr., Ft. Lauderdale, Fla., 1965-66; microbiologist Duke U. Hosp., Durham, N.C., 1966-71; tech. lab. coord. Harvard Cmty. Health Plan, Cambridge, Mass., 1971-77; tech. lab. dir. Louise Obici Meml. Hosp., Suffolk, Va., 1977-89; lab. mgr. Orlando (Fla.) Health Care Group, 1989-91; technical lab dir. Metpath of Fla., 1992-93; technical cons. ASCP; planning analyst, chmn. Diagnosis Related Group task force, 1983-85; bd. dirs., sec. Edmarc, Inc., Suffolk, 1985-86, pres., bd. dirs., dir. 1986-87. Mem. adv. bd. Am. Hosp. Assn. Soc., Soc. for Hosp. Planning and Mktg.; dir. adv. bd. Western Tidewater Area Health Edn. Com., 1983—. Mem. Am. Soc. Clin. Pathologists (assoc.; program chmn. workshops Boston 1977), Clin. Lab. Mgmt. Assn. (fin. chmn. 1983), Hosp. Purchasing Svc. (pres. lab. com. 1983), Am. Hosp. Assn. Soc. for Hosp. Planning and Mktg., Beta Beta Beta. Avocations: piano, tennis, poetry. Address: 3635 Whitehall Dr Bldg 1-404 West Palm Beach FL 33401-1088

BOICE, MARGARET ROCKWELL (PEGGY BOICE), charitable organization executive; b. Boise, Idaho, June 27, 1947; d. Edward Henry and Mary Catherine (Bussey) B.; m. Gregory Morgan Jones, June 27, 1969 (div. 1974). BA, Baylor U., 1969; MSSW, U. Tex., Arlington, 1975, MA in Urban Studies, 1978. Lic. master social worker/advanced practitioner, Tex. Office asst. various doctors' offices, Houston, 1963-65; caseworker Meth. Children's Home, Waco, Tex., 1969-70, Florence Crittenton Home, Houston, 1970-71; pub. welfare worker Tex. Dept. Pub. Welfare, Denton, 1972-73; asst. HUD, Dallas, 1974-75; sr. planner Gov.'s Budget and Planning Office, State of Ga., Atlanta, 1975-77; coord. human resources Tex. Office State and Fed. Rels., Washington, 1977-79; sr. assoc., cons. Asst. Group for Human Resource Devel., Silver Spring, Md., 1979-80; dir. pub. policy United Way Tex., Austin, 1980—, convenor, organizer child care working group, 1986-93; mem. govt. rels. adv. com. United Way Am., Alexandria, Va., 1984-85; mem. fed. budget adv. com. Tex. Health and Human Svcs. Coordinating Coun., Austin, 1985-86, convenor, organizer state needs assessment com., 1988-90; mem. Tex. Legis. Subcom. on Child Care, 1989-91; mem. rate setting adv. com. Tex. Dept. Aging., 1990-91; mem. child care rate reimbursement methodologies steering com. Tex. Dept. Human Svcs., 1990-92; mem. project steering com. Gov.'s State Head Start Collaboration, 1990-92; mem. adv. com. Tex. Employment Commn. Child Care Clearinghouse, 1987-92. Author: Public Policy Handbook, 1990, 2d edit., 94; editor: (Booklets) Child Care in Texas, 1988. Organizer Baylor and Waco Vol. Orgn., 1968-69, Interagy. Human Svcs. Coun., Denton, 1972-73, CARE Coalition, child abuse prevention, Austin, 1983-87; organizer, mem. Tex. Mental Health Code Rewrite Com., 1983-85. Recipient cert. of Appreciation Coalition Mental and Devel. Disabilities, 1983, State of Tex., 1984-90, Tex. Maternal and Child Health Coalition, 1985, TEC Child Care Clearinghouse, 1991, Tex. Legis. Subcom. on Child Care, 1991, State Friend of Extension award Epsilon Sigma Phi, 1992, Cert. of Recognition for work on Tex. Head Start Collaboration Project, Tex. Gov. Ann Richards, 1993, Commendation, Tex. Child Care Working Group, 1993. Mem. Tex. Assn. for Edn. Young Children, Austin Assn. for Edn. Young Children (Jeannette Watson Pub. Policy award 1991). Office: United Way Tex 505 E Huntland Dr Ste 455 Austin TX 78752-3714

BOISAUBIN, EUGENE V., internist; b. St. Louis, Jan. 25, 1945; s. Eugene V. and Margaret T. (Titzler) B.; m. Jean Thorpe, Sept. 20, 1986; 1 child, Vincent. AB, Washington U., St. Louis, 1966; MD, U. Mo., 1971. Diplomate Am. Bd. Internal Medicine. Dir. gen. internal medicine Ben Taub Hosp., Houston, 1976-84, Meth. Hosp., Houston, 1984-93; clin. ethicist Robert Wood Johnson Found./U. Tex. Med. Br., Galveston, 1993—; intern and resident Baylor Coll. Medicine Hosps., Houston, 1971-75; mem. educating healthcare ethics nat. project U.S. Dept. Edn., 1992-95; cons. for ethics and med. care Tex. Bd. Med. Examiners, 1994-96. Contbr. over 80 articles to profl. jours., chpts. to books. Mem. AMA, Soc. Gen. Internal Medicine (regional chair 1982-86), Alpha Omega Alpha. Home: 2346 Gramercy Houston TX 77030 Office: University of Texas Medical Branch 301 University Galveston TX 77555-0572

BOKLAGE, CHARLES EDWARD, medical educator; b. Louisville, Aug. 25, 1944; s. George Charles and Mary Mildred (Buckman) B.; m. Sharon Ann Sias, 1964 (div. 1971); children—Leah, Anna; m. Diana Marie Hartwig, 1972 (div. 1977); children—Lara, Kelly; m. Cecilia Moore, 1978; children—Peyton, Georgia; m. Brenda Taylor Rhodes, 1992. A.B. summa cum laude, Bellarmine Coll., 1965; Ph.D., U. Calif.-San Diego, 1972. Research assoc. Kans. State U., 1972-75, instr., 1973-74, vis. asst. prof., 1974-75; fellow in med. genetics, biostats., neurobiology, and devel. psychology U. N.C., Chapel Hill, 1975-78; asst. prof. microbiology and genetics East Carolina U. Sch. Medicine, Greenville, 1978-85, assoc. prof., 1985—, dir. genetics program, 1982—, prof. genetics, 1989—, adj. prof. biology, 1990—, prof. pediatrics, 1991—. Bellarmine Coll. Pres.'s scholar, 1961-65; NSF fellow, 1964-65, 65-70; NIH trainee, 1970-72. Mem. Internat. Soc. for Twin Studies (founding mem.), Am. Soc. Human Genetics, Am. Statistical Assn., Internat. Neuropsychology Soc., N.C. Assn. Med. Genetics, Sigma Xi. Contbr. articles to profl. jours. Home: 200 Ravenwood Dr Greenville NC 27834-6737 Office: Brody Bldg East Carolina U Sch of Medicine Greenville NC 21858

BOLAND, BARBARA, counselor; b. Newberry, S.C., Sept. 19, 1955; d. James Andrew and Ivey Lee (Reynolds) Boland. BA, Winthrop U., 1976; MBA, The Citadel, 1980, MEd, 1991. Cert. tchr. middle and secondary social studies, guidance counselor elem. and secondary schs., Lion's Quest Internat. cert. educator; licensed profl. counselor. Tchr. Berkeley County schs., Moncks Corner, S.C., 1977-90, summer sch. tchr., 1980, 91; sch. guidance counselor Charleston (S.C.) County Sch. Sys., 1991-95; elementary sch. guidance counselor Charleston County Schs., Charleston Heights, S.C., 1991-95; tchr. adult edn. Berkeley County Schs., 1995; counselor S.C. Vocat. Rehab., Moncks Corner, 1995—; mem. student recognition com. PTA, Mary Ford Elem. Sch., 1991-95, mem. staff morale com., mem. cultural diversity com., mem. emphasis com. Mem. PTA, Sedgefield Mid. Sch., Goose Creek, S.C., 1977-90, "Just Say No" Club, Goose Creek, 1983-90. Grantee for drug edn. club, 1991, grantee for drug edn. magic show, 1993. Mem. AACD, Tri-County Assn. Counseling and Devel. Baptist. Home: 196 Bridgecreek Dr Goose Creek SC 29445-5214

BOLAND, LOIS WALKER, retired mathematician and computer systems analyst; b. Newton Center, Mass., Sept. 14, 1919; d. Charles Nelson and Nell Flora (Kruse) Walker; m. Ralph Montrose Boland, June 2, 1943; children: Charles Montrose, William Ralph (dec.), Ann Helen Boland Garner, Mark Alan Boland (dec.). BS, Stetson U., 1940; grad. fellow U. Ala., 1940-41; postgrad. U. Fla., 1948, 51-52, U. Mich., 1958, 65, U. Colo., 1966, 68, Air Force Computer Sch., Keesler AFB, Biloxi, Miss., 1974. Physics tchr., Lakeland Fla. High Sch., 1941-42; chemist, IM&CC, Mulberry, Fla., 1942-43; elec. engring. draftsman Tampa Ship Corp., Fla., 1943-46; math. tchr. Plant High Sch., Tampa, 1947-50; mathematician/computers, data reduction div. Patrick AFB, Fla., 1951-54; mathematician, computer supr. data reduction div. White Sands Missile Range, N.Mex., 1954-63; ops. research analyst Peterson AFB, Colo. Springs, Colo., 1963-78, ret., 1978. Author: AUPRE Computer Program Manual, 1963, 77; Askania Photheodolite Computer Manual, 1956; editor Q-Point mag., 1966. Elected mem. Democratic exec. com. Volusia County, Fla., 1984-89. Pioneer mathematician Pioneer Group White Sands Missile Range, 1985—; math. fellow U. Ala., 1940-41. Mem. Math. Assn. Am. (emeritus), AAUW (pres. DeLand chpt. 1984-86), ACBL Golden Master , 1995, Mensa, Am. Contract Bridge League. Clubs: Halifax, Lake Beresford Yacht. Avocations: writing; pianist; travel; duplicate bridge; swimming. Home: PO Box 215 Cassadaga FL 32706-0215

BOLAS, GERALD DOUGLAS, art museum administrator, art history educator; b. Los Angeles, Nov. 1, 1949; s. Norman Theodore and Elizabeth Louise (Douglas) B.; m. Deborah Jean Wohletz, Nov. 25, 1978; children: Ellen Claire, John David. BA, U. Calif.-Santa Barbara, 1972, MA, 1975; MPhil, CUNY, 1994. Tchg. asst. U. Calif.-Santa Barbara, 1973-74; NEH mus. intern Yale U. Art Gallery, New Haven, 1975-76, asst. to dir., 1976-77; dir. Washington U. Gallery of Art, St. Louis, 1977-88, Portland (Oreg.) Art Mus., 1988-92, Ackland Art Mus. at U. N.C., Chapel Hill, 1994—; adj. asst. prof. art history Washington U., 1982-88, U. N.C., Chapel Hill, 1994—; advisor Mo. Arts Coun., St. Louis, 1981-82; field reviewer Inst. Mus. Svcs., Washington, 1980-83; panelist NEA, 1989, NEH, 1990, 95, N.C. Arts Coun., 1995; bd. dirs. Asian Art Soc. of Washington U., 1983-88; mem. No. Calif. adv. com. Archives of Am. Art; active Lake Oswego Arts Commn., 1993-94. Author: Illustrated Checklist of Washington University Collection, 1981; contbr. to (books): Paris in Japan: The Japanese Encounter with European Painting, 1987; also contbr. articles to other publs.; numerous catalog forewords. Organizer numerous exhbns. Fellow Winterthur Mus. 1993, Smithsonian Instn., 1993. Mem. Coll. Art Assn., Assn. Art Mus. Dirs. Office: Ackland Art Mus Campus Box 3400 U NC Chapel Hill NC 27599-3400

BOLDOGH, ISTVAN, scientist, microbiology educator; b. Debrecen, Hungary, Nov. 23, 1946; s. Istvan and Jolan (Papp) B. M in Biochemistry, U. Natural Scis., Debrecen, 1970; D of Medicine and Biology, Med. U., Debrecen, 1974, PhD, 1974; Cand.D.Sc. in Medicine, Hungarian Acad. Scis., Budapest, 1986. Rsch. asst. prof. Med. U., Debrecen, 1974-78, rsch. assoc. prof., 1981-87; postdoctoral fellow U. N.C., Chapel Hill, 1978-80; Disting. McLaughlin fellow U. Tex. Med. Br., Galveston, 1988, vis. scientist, 1989-90, asst. prof., 1991, assoc. prof., 1991-96, prof., 1996—; sabbaticals Biol. Ctr. Hungarian Acad. Scis., Szeged, 1975, dept. exptl. virology Inst. Sera and Vaccines, Prague, 1978, dept. microbiology Wilhelm Pieck Med. U., Rostock, Germany, 1981; lectr. Sch. Allied Health Sci., Debrecen, 1981-87; lectr. in med. virology and bacteriology; presenter numerous nat. and internat. confs.; sci. rev. panelist Students Sci. Soc., Med. U. Debrecen, 1980-87, McLaughlin Fellowship Fund, U. Tex. Med. Br., Galveston, 1990—. Ad hoc referee Acta Microbiologica Hungarica, 1981—, Acta Virologica, 1981—, Hungarian Acad. Sci., 1986—, Archives of Virology, 1990—; contbr. chpts. to books, numerous articles to profl. jours. Recipient Excellence in Antibiotic Rsch. award Hungarian Pharm. Cos., Budapest, 1973, Excellence in Med. Microbiology Rsch. award Hungarian Acad. Sci., Budapest, 1978, Excellence in Med. Sci. award Hungarian Acad. Sci., 1985; grantee John Sealy Meml. Endowment Fund, 1991-94, U.S. EPA, 1992-95, NIH, 1994—, NIEHS, 1995—, U. Tex. Med. Br., 1993-94. Mem. AAAS, Am. Soc. Virology, Am. Assn. Cancer Rsch., European Assn. Cancer Rsch., Internat. Soc. Antiviral Rsch., N.Y. Acad. Scis., Hungarian Soc. Microbiology (Best Rsch. Presentation award 1975, Excellence in Med. Virology award 1981), Hungarian Oncol. Soc., Hungarian Soc. Antimicrobial Chemotherapy, Hungarian Astron. Soc., NRA, N.Am. Hunting Club, Sigma Xi. Roman Catholic. Office: Univ of Tex Med Br Dept Of Microbiology Galveston TX 77555

BOLDT, HEINZ, aerospace engineer; b. Schönfeld Krs. Friedeberg, Germany, July 12, 1923; s. August and Marie (Hamann) B.; m. Christa Friebel, Mar. 25, 1965; children: Pierre, Manon. Diploma in engring., Technische Universität, Berlin, 1951; student Wirtschaftsakademie, Berlin, 1953-57. Tech. dir. Borsig AG, Berlin, 1951-66; mem. exec. bd. for prodn., dir. Messerschmitt-Werke Flugzeug-Union Sud, München-Augsburg, Fed. Republic Germany, 1967-70; exec. bd. prodn., gen. proxi Messerschmitt-Werke Flugzeng Union Süd Klöckner-Humboldt-Deutz, Köln, Fed. Republic Germany, 1970-72; mem. exec. bd. for devel., constrn. and prodn. FAHR AG, Gottmadingen, Fed. Republic Germany, 1970-72; pres. VDI-Bodenseebezirksverein, Friedrichshafen, Germany, 1971-76 (Verein Deutscher Ingenieure); mem. exec. bd. Dornier GmbH, Munich, 1972-77; pres. Deutsche Industrieanlagen Gesellschaft mbH, Berlin, 1978-82; rep. Machinoexport. Holder over 100 patents in field. Served with German Army Air Force, 1942-45. Recipient Ring for Honour VDI-Ehrenring, 1962. Mem. Am. C. of C. Club: Club der Luftfahrt. Home: Golfclub The Oaks 280 Saratoga Ct Osprey FL 34229-9386 also: Waldenburger Strasse 9, 83024 Rosenheim Germany

BOLDUC, JEAN PLUMLEY, journalist, education activist; b. Hartford, Conn., Aug. 13, 1958; d. Peter Winslow and Elizabeth Josephine (Hamann) Plumley; m. Richard Allen Bolduc, Jan. 25, 1978; children: Brian Richard, Robert Allen. BA, U. N.C., 1994. Mktg. analyst Ctrl. Carolina Bank, Durham, N.C., 1984-87; computer trainer/cons. On Site Svcs., Chapel Hill, N.C., 1987-91; pres. Pub. Edn. Press, Inc., Hillsborough, N.C., 1994—; coord. safe schs. program Orange County Sheriff's Dept., Hillsborough, N.C., 1995-96; exec. dir. The Odyssey Project, Hillsborough, 1996—; mem. adv. bd. Project Graduation, Hillsborough, 1995-96; lit. jour. advisor Orange County Schs., Hillsborough, 1995-96. Chair Orange County Human Rels. Commn., 1989-91, Orange County Safe Schs. Task Force, 1993-95; chair subcom. Blue Ribbon Task Force on African-Am. Student Achievement, Chapel Hill Schs., 1991; pres. AIDS Svc. Agy., Inc., Chapel Hill, 1990-91, Sycamore Presch., Inc., Chapel Hill, 1993-94. Recipient Key to Chapel Hill for cmty. svc. Chapel Hill Town Coun., 1991. Home: 5519 Hideaway Dr Chapel Hill NC 27516 Office: Pub Edn Press Inc PO Box 1561 Hillsborough NC 27278

BOLEN, BETTYE SUE, academic administrator; b. Princeton, W.Va., Aug. 31, 1945; d. James Willard Conner and Trixie Gladys (Hill); m. Daniel Wayne Farley, Aug. 21, 1966 (div. 1983); children: Kathy Jo Quesenberry, Julia Anne Noland; m. Larry E. Bolen, Sr., Nov. 21, 1984. B in bus. edn., Concord Coll., 1966; M in counseling, guidance, W.Va. U., 1971; ednl. specialist degree, W.Va. Grad. Coll., 1996, M in adminstrn., 1996. Exec. sec. Kersey Mfg. Co.-Figie, Internat., Bluefield, Va., 1971-73, W.Va. Conf. United Meth. Ch., Princeton, 1973-78; couns. spl. edn. Mercer County Schs., Princeton, 1981—; coord., cons. Concord Coll., Athens, W.Va., 1994—; adj. faculty Bluefield State Coll., 1983-91; bd. dirs. So. W.Va. Reg. Primary Care Ctrs., Inc., So. W.Va. Reg. Health Coun., Inc., So. Health Mgmt., Inc., Appalachian OH-9, Inc.; co-coord. Mercer County Crisis Intervention Team; mem, prevention, edn. com. Mercer County Child Abuse; mem. Mercer County Sch. Health Coun., Mercer County Adolescent Health Task Force, Mercer County Spl. Edn. Adv. com.; coord. Mercer County Link, W.Va. Statewide Transition Sys. Change Project. Presenter in field. Bd. dirs. Civitan Internat., 1990-92; mem. Internat. Grants and Scholarship Com., 1994-97, chair, 1995-96; mem. admin. bd. First United Meth. Ch. Recipient Internat. Honor Key, 1994, Disting. Lt. Gov. award W.Va. Dist. 1982-83, Honor Key, Princeton Civitan Club 1982-83, Honor Key, W.Va. Dist. 1983-84, Gov.'s Honor Key, W.Va. Dist. 1987, Superior Recruitment award for Civitan Internat. 1991; named Civitan-of-Yr., W.Va. Dist., 1982-83; inductee Jr. Civitan Internat. Hall of Fame, 1993. Mem. Assn. for Supervision and Curriculum Devel., Nat. Vocational Assn., W.Va. Vocational Assn., Delta Kappa Gamma Internat. Edn. Soc. (exec. com. mem., 2nd v.p. 1996-98, chairperson, scholar. com. 1994-96). Methodist. Home: 304 Cardinal Ave Quail Valley Estates WV 24740 Office: Mercer County Schs 1403 Honaker Ave Princeton WV 24740

BOLEN, ERIC GEORGE, biology educator; b. Plainfield, N.J., Nov. 24, 1937; s. Wilbur Fraser and Doris (Wicks) B.; m. Rebecca Ann Woodhull, Aug. 20, 1967 (div. Jan. 1981); children: Brent F., Staci L.; m. Elizabeth Ann Danek, May 27, 1986. BS, U. Maine, Orono, 1959; MS, Utah State U., 1962, PhD, 1967. Instr. biology Tex. A&M U., Kingsville, 1965-66; asst. prof. dept. range & wildlife mgmt. Tex. Tech U., Lubbock, 1966-73, assoc. dean grad. sch., 1978-88; dean grad. sch. U. N.C., Wilmington, 1988-94, prof. biology, 1994—; Asst. dir. Welder Wildlife Found., 1973-78. Co-author: (coll. textbooks) Wildlife Ecology and Management, 1984, 3rd edit., 1995, Waterfowl Ecology and Management, 1994; contbr. over 170 articles to profl. jours., ency. Named Disting. Alumnus, U. Maine, 1991. Mem. Am. Ornithol. Union. Wilson Ornithol. Soc., Cooper Ornithol. Soc., Southwestern Assn. Naturalists, Wildlife Soc. Office: Univ NC Dept Biol Scis 601 S College Rd Wilmington NC 28403-3201

BOLENE, MARGARET ROSALIE STEELE, bacteriologist, civic worker; b. Kingfisher, Okla., July 11, 1923; d. Clarence R. and Harriet (White) Steele; student Oreg. State U., 1943-44; B.S., U. Okla., 1946; m. Robert V. Bolene, Feb. 6, 1948; children: Judith Kay, John Eric, Sally Sue, Janice Lynn, Daniel William. Technician bacteriology dept. Okla. Dept. Health, Oklahoma City, 1946-48; asst. bacteriologist Henry Ford Hosp., Detroit, 1948-49; bacteriol. cons., also asst. bus. mgr. Ponca Gynecology and Obstetrics, Inc., 1956-92, retired. Organizing dir. Bi-Racial Council, 1963; lay adviser Home Nursing Service, 1967-68; mem. exec. bd. PTA, 1956-71; active various community drives; sponsor Am. Field Service; patron Ponca Playhouse; bloodmobile vol. ARC; vol. Helpline. Republican precinct organizer, 1960. Mem. AAUW (treas. 1964-66), DAR (life, sec.-treas. 1961-67, 1st vice regent 1972-73, chpt. treas. 1974-84, chpt. chaplain 1991—, state schs. chmn. 1990-94), Kay-Noble County Med. Aux. (treas. 1957-58, 66-67), Ponca City Art Assn., Pioneer Hist. Soc., Okla. Heritage Assn., Okla. Hist. Soc., Daus. Founders and Patriots (life, state pres. 1980-84, registrar 1993—), Nat. Huguenot Soc., Hereditary Order First Families Mass. Daus. Am. Colonists (chpt. regent 1982-84, state flag chmn. 1990-92), Magna Charta Dames (treas. Okla. chpt. 1984), Order Colonial Physicians and Chirurgiens (life), Ancient and Honorable Arty. Co. Women Descs. Okla. Ct. (life, treas. 1983-84, registrar 1986—), Dames of Ct. of Honor, Colonial Dames of 17th Century, Daus. of Colonial Wars, Colonial Daus. 17th Century, U. Okla. Assn. (life), Lambda Tau, Phi Sigma, Alpha Lambda Delta. Presbyterian (elder 1983-86). Clubs: Ponca City Country, Ponca City Music, Red Rose Garden (pres. 1983-84, treas. 1993-95), Twentieth Century (rec. sec. 1992-94). Home: 2116 Juanito Ave Ponca City OK 74604-3813

BOLES, JOHN RAYMOND, secondary education educator; b. Montgomery, Ala., Dec. 9, 1940; s. Raymond Virgil and Mattie L. (Thomas) B.; m. Yvonne Y. Boles, Aug. 31, 1973; 1 child, David Y. BS summa cum laude, Troy State U., 1963; MS, Auburn U., 1971. Tchr. sci. Bullock Meml. Sch., Union Springs, Ala., 1971—. Dist. commr. Boy Scouts Am. Recipient Silver Beavee Boy Scouts Am., Eagle. Republican. Methodist. Home: 3515 Cottonwood Dr Montgomery AL 36109

BOLGE, GEORGE STEPHEN, museum director, exhibition design consultant; b. Trenton, N.J., Feb. 14, 1942; s. George R. and Grace M. (Rago) B.; m. Elizabeth Ann Stover, July 14, 1967 (div. 1983); 1 dau., Ann Elyse. B.A. and B.S., Rutgers U., 1964; M.A., NYU, 1967; Ph.D. (hon.), Nova U., 1986. Asst. curator ancient art Bklyn. Mus. Art, 1966-67; exec. dir. Mus. Art, Inc., Fort Lauderdale, Fla., 1970—; exhbn. cons. Fort Lauderdale Hist. Soc., 1978-79. Editor: (catalog) The Graphic Work of Renoir, 1975; author: (catalogs) Leon Kroll, 1980, Italian Art, 1981, Matta, 1983. Mem. Fort Lauderdale Community Appearance Bd., 1982, Fort Lauderdale Downtown Devel. Council, 1982—; bd. dirs. Broward County Arts Council, 1982, Art in Pub. Places, Broward County, 1982. Served to lt. USNR, 1967-69. Nat. Trust Hist. Preservation fellow, 1966. Mem. Fla. League Arts (dir. 1970-72), Fine Art Mus. Dirs. Assn. (state exec. com. 1982), Am. Assn. Mus., Coll. Art Assn. Democrat. Roman Catholic. Office: Mus of Art Inc 1 E Las Olas Blvd Fort Lauderdale FL 33301-1807

BOLI, FRED CLARK, academic administrator; b. Greenville, Ohio, Apr. 15, 1943; s. A. Eugene and I. Isabelle (Clark) B.; m. Diane Hawthorne, June 18, 1966; children: Nicole A., Scott M. BS in Engring. Mgmt., USAF Acad., 1965; MA in Internat. Rels. and Soviet Studies, U. Notre Dame, 1974; grad., Def. Lang. Inst., Monterey, Calif., 1975; PhD in Russian History and Def. Studies, U. Edinburgh, Scotland, 1995. Commd. 2d lt. USAF, 1965, advanced through grades to col., 1983; asst. air attaché Am. Embassy, Moscow, 1976-78; chief safety ops. and tng. 23d Tactical Fighting Wing (Flying Tigers), England AFB, La., 1980-82; chief Pacific-East Asia div. directorate of plans Hdqs. USAF, Washington, 1982-85; dep. dir., sr. fellow Strategic Concepts Devel. Ctr. Nat. Def. U., Washington, 1986-89; sr. mil. asst. to asst. sec. def. internat. security policy Office of Sec. of Def., Washington, 1989-92; ret., USAF, 1992; cons. Phoenix Inst. Russian and Eurasian Studies, BDM Internat., McLean, Va., 1992-94; sr. assoc. Nat. Inst. for Pub. Policy, Fairfax, Va., 1993-94; exec. dir. Democracy Inst., Fairfax, 1995—; lectr., presenter, condr. seminars in field, 1978—, including Royal Inst. for Def. Studies, Brussels, 1985, Royal Inst. for Internat. Studies, Edinburgh, 1986, PRC Nat. Def. U. Beijing, 1987, Va. Mil. Inst., Lexington, 1990, Mil. Acad. of Gen. Staff, Moscow, 1990, Kuznetsov Naval Acad., Leningrad, USSR, 1990, Nat. Intelligence Conf., 1990, Air War Coll., Maxwell AFB, Ala., 1990, Nat. Intelligence coun., 1996; chmn. nat. security strategy study group Nat. Def. U., also mem. strategy working group on President's NSC statement to Congress, 1986-89; mem. U.S.-Russian Ballistic Missle Counterproliferation Joint Study, 1994-95. Contbr. articles to profl. pubs. Asst. scoutmaster Boy Scouts Am., 1986-92. Decorated Silver Star, Def. Superior Svc. medal (2), Legion of Merit, DFC (2), Air medal (11), Vietnam Gallantry Cross with palm. Mem. Air Force Assn., USAF Acad. Assn. Grads., Order of Daedalians, Scottish Arts Club (hon.). Episcopalian.

BOLICH, GREGORY GORDON, humanities educator; b. Spokane, Wash., July 7, 1953; s. Glenn Gordon and Joanne G. (Stinger) B.; m. Barbara Jo Ranson, Apr. 8, 1976; children: April Louise, Alicia Layne, Amanda Larissa, Arielle Liron. BA in Philosophy and Religion, Seattle Pacific U., 1974, M of Christian Ministries in Ednl. Psychology, 1975; MA in Religion, Western Evang. Sem., 1977, MDiv in Christian Thought, 1978; PhD in Ednl. Leadership, Gonzaga U., 1983; PhD in Psychology, Union Inst., 1993. Mem. faculty Inland Empire Sch. of the Bible, Spokane, 1975-76; adminstr. First Evang. Free Ch., Spokane, 1978-79; pres. Christian Studies Inst., Cheney, 1979-89; grad. asst. research Gonzaga U., Spokane, 1981-83, staff mem. Ctr. for Research, 1981-83; psychology and religious studies faculty Cleve. Community Coll., 1993—; adj. faculty Grad. Schy. Union Inst., 1993—, Ea. Wash. U., 1985-93; doctoral rsch. asst. Gonzaga U., 1984-86; mentor Fuller Sem., Pasadena, Calif., 1984; elder shadle Park Presbyn. Ch., Spokane, 1982; rep. Presbyn. Ch., 1985-86; coord. Cheney Presbyn. Fellowship, 1986-89; exec. dir. Adult Survivors of Abuse, 1991-94. Author: Karth Barth and Evangelicalism, 1980, Authority and the Church, 1982, The Christian Scholar, 1986; co-author: Introduction to Religion, 1988, God in the Docket, 1992, Serving Human Experience: The Boundary Metaphor, 1993; also religious articles to profl. jours. and mags. Active Friends of Seven, Spokane, 1985-89, United Ministries in Higher Edn., Spokane, 1985-93; assoc. mem. YWCA, Spokane, 1984-85, Cheney United Ch. Christ, 1986—. Mem. APA, Bibl. Archaeology Soc., Internat. Thespian Soc., Soc. Bibl. Lit., N.W. Soc. Patristic and Koine Studies (v.p. 1986), Theology Forum (exec. officer 1981-84), Internat. Soc. for Traumatic Stress Studies, Alpha Kappa Sigma. Democrat. Jewish. Office: Social Studies Dept Cleve CC Shelby NC 28150

BOLIN, ROGER KENNETH, electronics executive; b. Zanesville, Ohio, Dec. 16, 1949; s. Kenneth L. and Agnes Catherine (Hill) B.; m. Linda Rose Kovach, Oct. 9, 1982; 1 child, Brian Kenneth. BS in Mktg., Ohio U., 1972. European sales mgr. Rothchilds/Pioneer, Frankfort, Germany, 1975-76; sales engr. Oler & Mdse. Inc., Dallas, 1976-83, Texet Semics, Allen, Tex., 1983-84; dir. sales, mktg. Airborn Electronics, Addison, Tex., 1984-87; v.p. sales Qualitron, Addison, Tex., 1987-90; exec. v.p. Magnetic Tech., Inc., Richardson, Tex., 1990—. Chmn. econ. devel. tech. bd. City of Plano (Tex.), 1988, mem. bd. landscape devel., 1990; bd. dirs. YMCA, Plano, 1989, Collin City Women's Shelter, Plano, 1988-89. Mem. Am. Elec. Assn. (chmn. mktg. com. 1987), Armed Forces Elec. Commn. Assn. (v.p. publicity 1990, v.p. corp. 1993-94). Republican. Roman Catholic. Home: 2616 Walnut Ln Plano TX 75075-3127 Office: Magnetic Tech Inc 1237 E Executive Dr Richardson TX 75081-2228

BOLING, EDWARD JOSEPH, university president emeritus, educator; b. Sevier County, Tenn., Feb. 19, 1922; s. Sam R. and Nerissa (Clark) B.; m. Carolyn Pierce, Aug. 8, 1950; children: Mark Edward, Brian Marshall, Steven Clark. BS in Accounting, U. Tenn., 1948, MS in Stats., 1950; EdD in Ednl. Adminstrn, Vanderbilt U., 1961; LLD (hon.), U. Richmond, 1984. With Wilby-Kinsy Theatre Corp., Knoxville, Tenn., 1940-41, Aluminum Co. Am., 1941-42; instr. statistics U. Tenn., 1948-50; research statistician Carbide & Carbon Chem. Corp., Oak Ridge, 1950; supr. source and fissionable materials accounting Carbide & Carbon Chem. Corp. (K-25 plant), 1951-54; budget dir. Tenn., 1955-59; commr. finance and adminstrn., 1959-61; v.p. U. Tenn., 1961-70, pres., 1970-88, pres. emeritus, 1988—, univ. prof., 1988-92; mem. So. Regional Edn. Bd., 1957061, 70-81, 83-90, 92—, mem. exec. com., 1974-75, 79-81, vice chmn., 1986-88; mem. Edn. Commn. of States, 1970-82; trustee, chmn. Am. Coll. Testing Program, 1983-85; dir. emeritus Allied Signal Corp., CSX, N.A. Philips, United Foods, Home Fed. Bank. Author: (with D. A. Gardiner) Forecasting University Enrollment, 1952, Methods of Objectifying The Allocation of Tax Funds to Tennessee State Colleges, 1961. Mem. Nat. Govs. Conf. Good Will Tour to Brazil and Argentina, 1960; Mem. com. on taxation Am. Council on Edn. Served with AUS, 1943-46, ETO. Mem. Am. Statis. Assn., Assn. Higher Edn., Nat. Assn. Land-Grant Colls. (com. on financing higher edn.), Am. Coll. Pub. Rels. Assn. (trustee chmn. com. taxation and philanthropy), Am. Coun. on Edn., Knoxville C. of C. (bd. dirs., chmn. bd. 1989-91), Tenn. Resource Valley (dir., chmn. bd. 1991-92, chmn. supr. com. 1992—, chmn. 21st century jobs initiative), Am. Legion, Phi Kappa Phi (Scholarship award 1947), Beta Gamma Sigma (charter pres. Alpha chpt. 1948), Phi Delta Kappa, Omicron Delta Kappa, Beta Alpha Psi. Democrat. Office: U Tenn System Andy Holt Towers Ste 731 Knoxville TN 37996

BOLING, JEWELL, retired government official; b. Randleman, N.C., Sept. 26, 1907; d. John Emmitt and Carrie (Ballard) B. Student, Women's Coll., U. N.C., 1926, Am. U., 1942, 51-52. Interviewer N.C. Employment Service, Winston-Salem, Asheboro, 1937-41; occupational analyst U.S. Dept. Labor, Washington, 1943-57, placement officer, 1957-58, employment service adviser, 1959-61, occupational analyst, 1962, employment service specialist counseling and testing, 1963-69, manpower devel. specialist, 1969-74, ret., 1974. Author: Counselor's Handbook, 1967; Counselor's Desk Aid, Eighteen Basic Vocational Directions, 1967; Handbook for New Careerists in Employment Security, 1971; contbr. articles to profl. publs. Recipient Meritorious Achievement award U.S. Dept. Labor, 1972. Mem. AAAS, ACA, ASCD, AAUW, Am. Rehab. Counseling Assn. (archivist 1964-68), Nat. Capital Astronomers (editor Star Dust 1949-58), Nat. Career Devel. Assn., Internat. Platform Assn., N.Y. Acad. Scis., Assn. Measurement in Counseling and Devel., Assn. Humanistic Psychology, Planetary Soc., Smithsonians, Sierra Club, Nature Conservancy, Audubon Naturalist Soc., Wilderness Soc. Address: 5071 US Highway 220 Bus N Randleman NC 27317-7655

BOLLICH, ELRIDGE NICHOLAS, investment executive; b. Eunice, La., Sept. 10, 1941; s. Nicholas Joseph and Caroline (Manuel) B.; m. Shirley Anne Yackel, July 14, 1973; children: Jennifer, Brian, Sandra. BBA in Fin., Tex. A&M U., 1963. Registered rep. N.Y. Stock Exchange. Asst. v.p. Rotan Mosle, Houston, 1969-74, v.p., 1975-86; 1st v.p. Rotan Mosle Paine Webber, Houston, 1986-88, Smith Barney, Houston, 1988—; dir. devel. bd. Nat. Commerce Bank, Houston, 1987-88. Cubmaster Boy Scouts Am., Houston, 1987-91; mem. troop com. troop 642 Boy Scouts Am., 1992—. 1st lt. U.S. Army, 1963-65, Vietnam, capt. USAR, 1967-69. Mem. Houston Security Dealers, Stock and Bond Club, Houston Racquet Club. Roman Catholic. Office: Smith Barney 5065 Westheimer Rd Ste 1200 Houston TX 77056-5605

BOLLMAN, JEANETTE VOGT, learning disabilities educator; b. Oklahoma City; d. Joseph Anthony and Marie Cecila (Schulte) Vogt; m. Jesse Verle Bollman; children: Jimmy Dale, Michael Keith, Stephen Joseph, Christopher Lee. BS in Elem. Edn., U. Okla., 1969; MEd in Learning Disabilities, U. Ctrl. Okla., 1973; MEd in Counseling Psychology, Cen. State U., 1982. Cert. sch. psychologist, psychometrist, reading specialist, learning disabilities, elem. edn., Gessell devel. examiner, Structure of the Intellect examiner, SW. Inst. Chem. Dependency, Nat. Assn. Sch. Psychologists. Tchr. classroom Oklahoma City Pub. Schs.; sch. psychologist Cen. State U., Edmond, Okla., Moore (Okla.) Pub. Schs., Edmond Pub. Schs.; tchr. classroom and learning disabilities Norman (Okla.) Pub. Schs.; presenter Internat. Learning Disabilities Conf., Atlanta and Miami, Nat. Assn. Sch. Psychologists, Nashville, State Coun. Exceptional Children; regional sch. psychologist Conf. Okla. Learning Disabilities Assn.; tchr. pilot project inclusionary teaching. Contbr. articles to profl. jours. Mem. Coun. for Exceptional Children (membership chmn.), Profl. Educators of Norman, Learning Disabilities Assn., Okla. Sch. Psychologists Assn., Nat. Assn. for Sch. Psychologists. Home: 1512 SW 82nd St Oklahoma City OK 73159-5918 Office: Bollman Cons PO Box 19075 Oklahoma City OK 73144-0075

BOLTON, BRIAN FRANKLYN, psychologist, educator; b. Evanston, Ill., Sept. 20, 1939. BA, U. Kansas City, 1961; PhD, U. Wis., 1968. Asst. prof. of rehab. Ill. Inst. Tech., Chgo., 1968-71; from asst. prof. to univ. prof. of rehab. U. Ark., Fayetteville, 1971—. Contbr. over 200 articles to profl. jours., chpts. to books. Recipient Burlington No. Disting. award U. Ark., 1986. Fellow APA (Roger Barker Disting. award 1988), Soc. for Personality Assessment. Office: Univ of Arkansas West Ave Annex Fayetteville AR 72701

BOLTON, ELAINE HAZLETON, gifted education educator, principal; b. Washington, Apr. 30, 1942; d. Lloyd Walter and Harriet Louise (Rosenzweig) H.; m. Herbert Alfred Bolton III, Aug. 21, 1965 (div. Mar. 1989); children: Brittany Charron, H.A. IV. BA, U. Puget Sound, 1964; MEd, U. Ga., 1968; EdS in Adminstrn./Supervision, Ga. State U., 1995. Cert. tchr. in early childhood edn., elem./mid. sch. edn., gifted/talented edn.; cert. adminstrn./supr NL-6. Intelligence rsch. technician Dept. Def., Ft. Meade, Md., 1964-65; tchr. Atlanta Pub. Schs., 1966-69; adminstrv. asst. to Sen. Virginia Shapard Ga. State Sen., Atlanta, 1976-78; tchr. Griffin-Spalding County Sch. System, Griffin, Ga., 1982—; participant Lower Saxony, Germany-Ga. Tchr. Exch. Program, 1993. Pres. Utility Club, Griffin, 1976, assoc. editor cookbook, 1981-82. Named Tchr. of Yr. Griffin-Spalding County Sch. System, 1994. Mem. ASCD, Future Stock, Ga. Assn. for Gifted (treas. 1994-97), Nat. Assn. Gifted Children, U. Puget Sound Nat. Alumni (bd. mem. 1994—), Phi Delta Kappa. Methodist. Home: 839 E Maddox Rd Griffin GA 30224-7424

BOLTON, JAN E., business executive. V.p. corp. sales and promotion Dillard Dept. Stores Inc., Little Rock. Office: Dillard Dept Stores Inc 1600 Central Rd Little Rock AR 72201

BOLTON, KEVIN MICHAEL, human resources executive; b. Boston, Oct. 10, 1951; s. Thomas James and Winifred Agnes (Burke) B.; m. Lynn Thompson, May 30, 1976; children: Neil, Philip, Madeleine. B. Gen. Studies, U. Mich., 1973. CLU; cert. assoc. in risk mgmt. Ins. Inst. Am. Sous-chef Club Switzerland, Fairbanks, Alaska, 1974-76; sales rep. Travelers Ins. Cos., Phoenix, 1977-78; assoc. Third Party Adminstrs., Phoenix, 1979-80; mgr employee benefits, pensions, ERISA reporting, 401K plans Dial Corp., Phoenix, 1981-86; sr. dir. compensation and benefits Greyhound Lines, Inc., Dallas, 1987-92; v.p. pers. liability mgmt. Pittston Coal Mgmt. Co., Lebanon, Va., 1992-94; pres. HR To Go, Dallas, 1994—; speaker Nat. Employee Benefit Inst., Soc. Ins. Rsch., IF of Employee Benefit Plans. Mem. Greater Phoenix Affordable Health Care Consortium, 1985-87. Mem. Internat. Found. Employee Benefit Plans (bd. dirs. 1988—, new product devel. com. 1988—), Am. Soc. CLU & ChFC, U. Mich. Alumni Soc., Tex. Longhorns Soccer Club (mgr.). Home and Office: 6622 Tulip Ln Dallas TX 75230-4153

BOLTON, ROBERT HARVEY, banker; b. Alexandria, La., June 19, 1908; s. James Wade and Mary (Calderwood) B.; m. Elsie Elizabeth McLundie (dec. Mar. 1987); children: Robert Harvey Jr., Elizabeth McLundie (Mrs. Robert Conery Hassinger), Mary Calderwood (Mrs. James Kelly Jennings Jr.); m. Abigail Crow Goodwin. BS, U. Pa., 1930. With credit dept. Guaranty Trust Co., N.Y.C., 1930-32; asst. cashier Rapides Bank & Trust Co., Alexandria, 1932-36, cashier, 1936-43, v.p., 1943-47, exec. v.p., 1947-56, pres., 1956-86, chmn., 1986-90, sr. chmn., 1990—, also bd. dirs.; bd. dirs. New Orleans br. Fed. Res. Bank Atlanta., 1979-81, First Commerce Corp., New Orleans; nat. bd. dirs. Robert Morris Assocs., 1943-45; La. rep. to Conf. State Bank Suprs., 1964-71. Mem. La. State U. Found., Pineville, devel. bd., Pres.'s club, bd. dirs. James C. Bolton Libr., Alexandria; fin. steering com. Attakapas coun. Boy Scouts Am., 1971-84; chmn. Rapides Parish chpt. ARC, 1943, Alexandria Little Theatre, 1942; hon. chmn. La. Coll. Quality Edge Dr. '95; bd. dirs. Rapides United Givers, Indsl. Devel. Bd. Ctrl. La.; mem. exec. com. Ctrl. Cities Devel. Com., Coun. for Better La., 1970—, Bus. and Indsl. Devel. Corp. La., 1971-73; mem. La. Bapt. Conv. Fedn. Bd., 1994-95; deacon Emmanuel Bapt. Ch., chmn. fin. com., chmn. Every Mem. Canvass, 1937-74; mem. citizen's adv. com. La. Spl. Edn. Ctr., La. Pub. Broadcasting; chmn., mem. St. Francis Cabrini Hosp. Found. Bd.; mem. Pub. Affairs Rsch. Coun. Recipient Disting. Svc. award Jr. C. of C., 1943, Humanitarian of Yr. award Arthritis Found., 1990, Disting. Svc. award La. Nat. Guard, Disting. Citizen award Boy Scouts Am., 1991, Outstanding Citizen award YWCA, 1992, Disting. Svc. award Trustees La. Coll., 1993, Rapides Arts & Humanities Cultural Advocate award, 1994. Mem. VFW, Am. Bankers Assn. (pres. state bank divsn. 1955), Mortgage Bankers Assn. (mem. Washington com. 1962-74), La. Bankers Assn. (pres. 1980, mem. legis. study com. 1950—, mem. fed. affairs com. 1971—), La. Mortgage Bankers Assn. (pres. 1952, mem. legis. com. 1970-74), U.S. C. of C. (mem. fin. com. 1964-71), Alexandria-Pineville C. of C. (pres. 1965, chmn. aviation com. 1972-84, military affairs com., econ. devel. com.), Am. Legion, Boston Club, Internat. House Club (New Orleans), Confrerie du Tastevin Club, Masons, Rotary (pres. Alexandria chpt. 1942, Govs. Choice award 1993-94). Home: 3200 Parkway Dr Alexandria LA 71301-4757 Office: Rapides Bank & Trust Co 400 Murray St PO Box 31 Alexandria LA 71309

BOLTON, WILLIAM J., food products executive; b. 1946. Pres. Jewel Food Stores, Melrose Park, Ill., 1991-95; corp. COO markets Am. Food Stores, 1995; chmn., CEO Bruno's Inc., Birmingham, Ala., 1995—. Office: Brunos Inc PO Box 2486 Birmingham AL 35201-2486

BOMAR, ROBERT LINTON, assistant principal; b. Americus, Ga., July 5, 1959; s. John Eugene and Blanche Alvenia (Shehee) B.; m. Laura Beth Elliott, June 27, 1987; i child, Sarah Beth. AA, Clayton Jr. Coll., Morrow, Ga., 1979; BA, U. Ga., 1981; MEd, Ga. State U., 1983, PhD, 1992. Tchr. social studies Henry County High Sch., McDonough, Ga., 1983-90; asst. prin. Locust Grove (Ga.) Elem. Sch., 1990-96, Wesley Lakes (Ga.) Elem. Sch., 1996—. Author: A Briefing Book for Hearings on Mexican Oil Imports and the Implications of Illegal Mexican Immigration, 1980 (William Jennings Bryan prize). Ptnr. Habitat for Humanity, Americus, 1986—; site coord. ann. campaign United Way, Locust Grove, 1990-96. Mem. ASCD, Prof. Assn. Ga. Educators, Foxfire Tchrs. Network, Kappa Delta Pi, Phi Kappa Phi, Phi Beta Kappa, Phi Delta Kappa. Presbyterian. Home: 578 Walter Moore Rd Jackson GA 30233-3610 Office: Wesley Lakes Elem Sch 2200 McDonough Pkwy Mc Donough GA 30253

BOMBA, ANNE KILLINGSWORTH, family relations and child development educator; b. Port Lavaca, Tex., Sept. 12, 1959; d. John Gilbert and Jane (Killingsworth) B. BS, Okla. State U., Stillwater, 1981, MS, 1987, PhD, 1989. Cert. in family and consumer scis.; cert. tchr., Okla. Kindergarten tchr. Tulsa Pub. Schs., 1981-85; asst. to editor Home Econs. Rsch. Jour., Stillwater, 1986; grad. asst., grad. assoc. in family rels. and child devel. Okla. State U., 1987-89; asst. prof. home econs. U. Miss., Oxford, 1989-95, assoc. prof. family and consumer scis., 1995—. Contbr. articles to profl. jours. Mem. AAUP, AAUW, Am. Assn. Family and Consumer Scis., Soc. for Rsch. in Child Devel., Nat. Assn. for Edn. Young Children, Nat. Coun. on Family Rels., So. Early Childhood Assn., Kappa Omicron Nu. Home: PO Box 1345 University MS 38677 Office: U Miss Dept Family and Consumer Scis 110 Meek Hall University MS 38677

BOMER, ELTON, state insurance commissioner; b. July 30, 1935; m. Ginny Bomer; 2 children. BBA in Bus. Mgmt., U. Houston, 1959. Computer sales and mktg. mgr. IBM Corp., 1965-74; mem. Tex. Ho. Reps., Austin, 1981-85; mem. bd. dirs. Sprint/United Telephone Midwest Corp., 1985-95; sr. v.p. East Tex. Nat. Bank, Palestine, Tex., 1990-95; mem. Tex. Ho. of Reps., Austin, 1991-95; commr. ins. Tex. Dept. Ins., Austin, 1995—. Named to Tex. Monthly 10 Best Legislators List, 1993. Office: Tex Dept Insur 333 Guadalupe St Austin TX 78714

BOMSTEIN, ALAN CHARLES, construction company executive; b. Balt., July 29, 1945; s. David Arthur and Dorothy Ruth (Seidel) B.; m. Nancy Sue Auerbach, Dec. 24, 1968; children: David, Joshua. Student, U. Md., 1962-66. V.p. Page Corp. div. U.S. Home Corp., Silver Spring, Md., 1967-72; nat. dir. mktg. U.S. Home Corp., Clearwater, Fla., 1973-74; pres. Creative Contractors, Inc., Clearwater, 1975—; Bd. dirs., vice-chmn. Citizens Bank Clearwater. Dir., chmn. long range planning com. Ruth Eckerd Hall Performing Arts Ctr. and Theatre, Clearwater, 1982-87; bd. govs. Morton Plant Hosp., Clearwater, 1988-94, mem. planning com., 1984, chmn., 1988-90, fin. com. 1990—, audit com., chmn., 1990-92, ad hoc Long Range Planning Com., 1990-94, chmn. bd. trustees, 1992-94; pres. Tampa Bay Forum, 1984-87; chmn. Clearwater Housing Devel. Corp., 1982—; chmn. Clearwater Downtown Devel. Bd., 1983-84; participant Leadership Fla.,

1983—; bd. dirs. Clearwater Marine Sci. Ctr., 1985-87, Clearwater Progress Inc., 1984-86, North Suncoast Bd. Fla. Orch., 1983-85, Fla. Aquarium, Tampa, 1987-90, Fla. Orch., 1988-89, Pinellas Sports Authority, appointed by County Commn., 1990—, sec., treas., 1992—; advisor Clearwater Phillies Baseball Club, 1985-87; gov.'s appointee Fla. Constrn. Lic. Bd., 1988-89; v.p. Pinellas County Jewish Fedn., 1987-88, bd. dirs. 1986-89; apptd. Pinellas County Bd. Adjustments, 1993—, Fla. 6th Cir. Jud. Nominations Com., 1994—, Clearwater High Speed Rail Commn., 1994—; bd. trustees U. South Fla., 1996—. Named Young Profl. of 1979 Building Design and Constrn. mag., 1979; recipient Liberty Bell award Clearwater Bar Assn., 1985, Community Service award, Award of Excellence in Archtl. Constrn. Fla. Chpt. AIA, 1984. Mem. Greater Clearwater C. of C. (bd. govs. 1980—, pres. 1985-86, Bilgore award 1991, Mr. Clearwater award 1991), Pinellas Suncoast C. of C. (exec. com. 1985-89, bd. govs. 1983-89, vice chmn. 1987-88), Jr. League of Clearwater-Dunedin (mem. adv. bd. 1987-90), Assoc. Gen. Contractors (bd. dirs. 1990-92), The Clearwater Club (bd. dirs. 1991-94), Rotary, Belleair Country Club, Tiger Bay Club. Republican. Jewish. Office: Creative Contractors Inc 620 Drew St Clearwater FL 34615-4108

BOND, BEVERLY KAY, fundraising executive; b. Charleston, W.Va.; d. Albert Flurnoy and Mary Jane (Harper) B.; m. William Lea, Jr., Nov. 24, 1984. B.Musicology, U. Mich., 1975; MBA, Vanderbilt U., 1993; postgrad., Vanderbilt U. Div. Sch., 1979-81. Account exec. Don Elliott & Assocs., Nashville, 1976-78; dir. corp. and found. rels. George Peabody Coll. for Tchrs., Nashville, 1978-79, dir. alumni and devel., 1979-81; dir. devel., alumni and pub. affairs Univ. Sch. of Nashville, 1980-81; dir. devel. George Peabody Coll. Vanderbilt U., Nashville, 1981-82, assoc. exec. dir. devel., 1982-88, exec. dir. univ. alumni and devel., 1988-96, assoc. vice chancellor, 1996—; asst. dir. music, sect. leader, soloist Ch. of the Advent, Nashville, 1988-91; dir. music and liturgy Ch. of Holy Rosary, Nashville, 1976-85; artist-in-the-schs. program project coord. NEH, 1974; tchr. humanities Huntsville (Ala.) city schs., 1975; writer Huntsville Times, 1968-70, 75; freelance media designer U. Ala., Huntsville, 1973. Bd. dirs., mem. policy com. Dismas, Inc., 1991—; chair Bishop's stewardship com. Cath. Diocese Nashville, 1990; mem. coun. W.O. Smith Music Sch., 1993—; v.p. Nashville Dismas House, 1989-90; devel. com. Tenn. Repertory Theater, 1993-94; pub. affairs com. YWCA, 1983-84; founder, dir. Cath. Cmty. Children's Choir, 1978-81; campaign capt. United Way of Mid. Tenn., 1982; mem. Nashville Symphony Chorus, 1976-79; vol. coord., media asst. Youth for Understanding, 1975. Recipient Columbia Press Assn. medal, 1971; Alliance Francias scholar, 1971. Mem. Coun. for Advancement and Support Edn. (ann. giving seminar coord. 1982), U. Mich. Alumni Assn. (chair Mich. ann. giving scholars program for middle Tenn. 1990). Home: 302 Windemere Woods Dr Nashville TN 37215-3231 Office: Vanderbilt Univ 105 Kirkland Hall Nashville TN 37240-0001

BOND, GORDON CREWS, college dean; b. Ft. Myers, Fla., Nov. 17, 1939; s. Henry C. and Hazel (Crews) B.; m. Stephanie Johns, Sept. 7, 1974; children: Michael, Annie. BS, Fla. State U., 1962, MA, 1963, PhD, 1966. Asst. prof. history U. So. Miss., Hattiesburg, 1966-67; asst. prof. history Auburn (Ala.) U., 1967-74, assoc. prof., 1974-80, prof., 1980—, head dept. history, 1985-91, assoc. dean liberal arts, 1991-92, dean Coll. Liberal Arts, 1992—. Author: The British Invasion of Holland in 1809, 1979. Mem. Rotary Internat. Office: Auburn U Coll Liberal Arts Auburn AL 36849

BOND, JAMES ANTHONY, toxicologist; b. Santa Monica, Calif., Sept. 11, 1952; s. John and Adriana (Tommasi) B.; m. Michele A. Medinsky, June 2, 1985. BA, Pomona Coll., Claremont, Calif., 1975; PhD, U. Wash., 1979. Diplomate Am. Bd. Toxicology. Postdoctoral fellow Chem. Industry Inst. Toxicology, Research Triangle Park, N.C., 1980-82, dept. head, 1989-95, program mgr., 1995—; toxicologist Inhalation Toxicology Rsch. Inst., Albuquerque, 1982-88, group supr., 1988-89; clin. asst. prof. U. N.Mex., Albuquerque, 1985-89; adj. prof. N.C. State U., Raleigh, 1992—; adj. assoc. prof. U. N.C., Chapel Hill, 1993—. Recipient Kenneth Morgareidge award Internat. Life Sci. Inst., 1990. Mem. Soc. of Toxicology (Young Investigator award 1992), Internat. Soc. Study of Xenobiotics, Am. Assn. Cancer Rsch., Am. Soc. Pharm. and Exptl. Therapeutics. Office: Chem Industry Inst Toxicology PO Box 12137 Research Triangle Park NC 27709

BOND, JOAN, elementary school educator; b. Americus, Ga., Dec. 24, 1945; d. Doyle Holden and Frances (Brown) B. BS in Elem. Edn., U. Ga., 1975, MEd, 1979, EdS, 1982. Clk. emergency room St. Mary's Hosp., Athens, Ga., 1963-64; receptionist, asst. Office Dr. Shu-Yun T. Tsao, Athens, 1964-66; tchr. remedial reading Danielsville (Ga.) Elem. Sch., 1975-76, primary tchr., 1975—. Tchr., dir. presch. Hull (Ga.) Bapt. Ch., 1970-84, asst. tchr. adult class, 1985—; mem. honor roll com. Danielsville Elem. Sch. PTO, 1990-92. Mem. Profl. Assn. Ga. Educators. Democrat. Home: 48 Glen Carrie Rd Hull GA 30646-9778 Office: Danielsville Elem Sch PO Box 67 Danielsville GA 30633-0067

BOND, JON ROY, political science educator; b. Chickasha, Okla., Dec. 30, 1946; s. Henry Lee and Othelle (Payne) B.; m. Patricia Anne Garner (div. Apr. 1989); 1 child, Lynn Elizabeth Bond; m. Wanda Karon Martin Frazier, July 11, 1992; children: Mika Karon Frazier, Monika Kara Frazier. BA, Okla. State U., 1969, MA, 1973; PhD, U. Ill., 1978. Prof. polit. sci. Tex. A&M U., 1976—. Co-author: Pres. in the Legislative Arena, 1990; co-editor: Jour. of Politics, 1993-97; contbr. articles to profl. jours. Precinct chair Brazos County Democratic Party, College Station, 1984-87. Mem. Am. Polit. Sci. Assn., Midwest Polit. Sci. Assn. (exec. coun. 1992-95), Southern Polit. Sci. Assn., Pi Sigma Alpha (exec. coun. 1994-98). Democrat. Methodist. Home: 1412 Frost Dr College Station TX 77845 Office: Tex A&M U Dept Polit Sci College Station TX 77843

BOND, JULIAN, civil rights leader; b. Nashville, Jan. 14, 1940; s. Horace Mann and Julia Agnes (Washington) B.; m. Pamela S. Horowitz, Mar. 17, 1990; children by previous marriage: Phyllis Jane, Horace Mann, Michael, Jeffrey, Julia. BA, Morehouse Coll., 1971; LLD (hon.), Dalhousie U., 1969, U. Bridgeport, 1969, Wesleyan U., Conn., 1969, U. Oreg., 1969, Syracuse U., 1970, Eastern Mich. U., 1971, Tuskegee Inst., 1971, Howard U., 1971, Morgan State U., 1971, Wilberforce U., 1971, Patterson State Coll., 1972, N.H. Coll., 1973, Detroit Inst. Tech., 1973; DCL (hon.), Lincoln (Pa.) U., 1970. A founder Com. Appeal for Human Rights, 1960, exec. sec., 1961; a founder Student Nonviolent Coordinating Com., 1960, communications dir., 1961-66; reporter, feature writer Atlanta Inquirer, 1960-61, mng. editor, 1963; mem. Ga. Ho. of Reps., from Fulton County, 1965-75, Ga. State Senate, 1975-87; vis. prof. history and politics Drexel U., 1988-89; Pappas fellow U. Pa., 1989; vis. prof. Harvard U., fall 1989, 91, U. Va., fall 1990, 1993—, Am. U., 1991—, Williams Coll., fall 1992; host Am.'s Black Forum. So. corr. Reporting Racial Equality Wars; narrator Parts 1 and 2, Eyes on the Prize. Bd. dirs. So. Conf. Edn. Fund, Robert F. Kennedy Meml. Fund, So. Regional Coun., Coun. for Liveable World, Ctr. for Community Change; pres. emeritus So. Poverty Law Ctr. Mem. NAACP (bd. dirs.). Office: 5435 41st Pl NW Washington DC 20015-2911

BOND, MYRON HUMPHREY, investment executive; b. Chickasha, Okla., Jan. 12, 1938; s. Reford and Jane Embick (Humphrey) B.; m. Janice Wootten, July 1, 1961; children: Richard Allen, Lori Elizabeth. BS in Petroleum Engring., U. Okla., 1961, MS in Petroleum Engring., 1965. Registered profl. engr., Okla. Staff engr. Exxon, Houston, 1960-68; sr. v.p. Paine Webber, Inc., Dallas, 1968—; pres., chmn. Four Bees Ranch Inc., 1989—; dir. Am. Pub. Communications, Inc., 1991-92. Bd. dirs. Dallas Epilepsy Assn., 1980-82, Dallas Campfire Girls, 1980-82. Lt. (s.g.) USN, 1961-64. Mem. Nat. Assn. Securities Dealers (prin., mem. Dist. 6 com. 1994-96), Dallas C. of C., Dallas Country Club, Brook Hollow Golf Club. Republican. Presbyterian. Home: 4515 Belfort Pl Dallas TX 75205-3619 Office: Paine Webber 5956 Sherry Ln Ste 1800 Dallas TX 75225-8029

BOND, RAE YOUNG, medical society administrator; b. Nampa, Idaho, Jan. 27, 1953; d. Edgar Otto and LeAnna Mae (Tague) Young; m. William C. Bond Jr., July 1, 1978; children: Daniel, John-Michael. BS, Towson State U., 1984. Reporter/editor/columnist Idaho Free Press, Nampa, 1971-76; reporter UPI, Boise, Idaho, 1976-77; press sec. U.S. Rep. Steve Symms, Washington, 1977-80; mng. editor Nat. Assn. Counties, Washington, 1980-82; pub. rels. cons. P.R. Concepts, Towson, Md., 1983-84; dir. pub. affairs Nat. Gov.'s Assn., Washington, 1984-94; exec. dir. Chattanooga/Hamilton County Med. Soc., Chattanooga, 1995—; sec.-treas. Physician Svcs., Inc., 1994—. Editor: Bringing Down the Barriers, 1987, Lessons From Europe, 1986; contbr. chpts. to books. Mem. Hamilton County Tenn-Care Com., Chattanooga, 1995-96; bd. dirs. America's Charities, No. Va., 1993-96; steering com. Internat. Youth Environ. Action Forum, Washington, 1990, Scenic City Women's Network, Chattanooga, 1996—; mem. leadership devel. program Chattanooga Resources Found., 1995; adv. bd. Hamilton County Cmty. Health Agy., 1995-96; mem. Chattanooga Mgr. of the Yr. Com., 1995-96; sec.-treas. Med. Found. Chattanooga, 1994—; pres. bd. Regional Sci. Fair, 1996-97; bd. dirs. Bapt. Home of Md., 1985-86; chair Idaho Helpline Assn., 1975; exec. com. D.C. Bapt. Conv., 1985-89; ch. organist, accompanist, children's choir dir., lay leader, 1985—; children's choir leader, Sunday sch. tchr., priorities and family life coms. Brainerd Bapt. Ch., Chattanooga, 1995—. Recipient writing/editl. awards Idaho Press Club, Idaho Press Women. Mem. Am. Assn. Med. Soc. Execs. (comm. com. 1995—), Am. Soc. Assn. Execs. (comm. com.), Med. Soc. Credential Verification Orgns. of Am. Baptist. Home: 205 Windmere Dr Chattanooga TN 37411 Office: Chattanooga/Hamilton County Med Soc 1917 E 3d St Chattanooga TN 37404

BOND, THOMAS JEFFERSON, JR., former federal agency administrator; b. Chattanooga, Aug. 27, 1936; s. Thomas Jefferson and Clara Emmalynne (Chisam) B.; m. Wilma W. McCrary, Mar. 14, 1959; children: Thomas Jefferson III, Julia Anne. BS in Edn., Tenn. Tech. U., 1958; MA in Biology, Vanderbilt U., 1959; postgrad., U. Louisville, Am. U., Antioch Sch. Law. Biology instr. U. Tenn., Chattanooga, 1959-60, 61-63, U. Louisville, 1963-64; various positions U.S. Dept. Interior, Washington, 1964-94; supervisory fish and wildlife biologist U.S. Dept. Interior, 1974-77, 78-81, staff asst. sec. land and water resources, 1977-78, trust svcs. officer ea. area bur. Indian affairs, 1981-92, dir. Office of Am. Indian Trust, 1993-94; ret., 1994; co-owner The Silver Ladle Ltd., Oakton, Va., Beaufort, S.C.; pres. Chisam Meml. Trust, Bond Meml. Trust. Congl. fellow, 1988-89, Exch. fellow, Can., 1989. Mem. NRA, SAR (various offices D.C. Soc. 1980—, nat. chmn. govt. rels. 1989-91, nat. chmn. congress planning 1991-93, v.p. gen. mid-Atlantic dist. 1993-94, registrar gen. 1994-96), Mensa, Westerners Club (publs. com. 1981—), Soc. War 1812, Continental Soc. Sons Indian Wars (gov. gen. 1993-95), Sons Am. Colonists (archivist gen. 1988-91, lt. gov. gen. 1991-93, vice gov. gen. 1993—), Nat. Soc. Children Am. Colonists (adult advisor hist., regional v.p.), Colonial Order Acorn, Soc. Colonial Wars, SCV, Sons Union Vets (assoc.), Mil. Order LoyaL Legion (companion), 1st Families Ga., Nat. Order of Blue and Gray, Heredity Order Loyalists and Patriots, Sovereign Mil. Order Temple Jerusalem (comdr.). Home: PO Box 1301 Vienna VA 22183-1301

BOND, WILMA MCCRARY, antique silver dealer, retired educator; b. Madison, Tenn., Sept. 17, 1938; d. Keller Brit and M. Lee (Reid) McCrary; m. Thomas Jefferson Bond Jr., Mar. 14, 1959; children: Thomas Jefferson III, Julia Anne. BS, Vanderbilt U., 1959; MA, Va. Tech. U., 1974. Cert. bus. edn. tchr., social studies, tchr., adminstrn., Va., Tenn., Ky., Fla., N.Mex. Sec. trust dept. 1st Tenn. Bank, Chattanooga, 1959-60; tchr. Hamilton County Pub. Schs., Chattanooga, 1960-61; exec. sec. to sr. ptnr. Witt, Gaither et al, Attys., Chattanooga, 1961-62; sec. Irvine Ins. Agy., Chattanooga, 1962; tchr. Hamilton County Pub. Schs., Chattanooga, 1962-63, Jefferson County Pub. Schs., Louisville, 1963-64, Fairfax County (Va.) Pub. Schs., 1967-69, Bernalillo County Pub. Schs., Albuquerque, 1969-72, Fairfax County Pub. Schs., 1972-95; ret., 1995; docent Smithsonian Instn. Mus. Am. History, Washington, 1977-82, 92—. Author (pamphlets) A Word to the Wives, 1967, Buenos Dias Amigos, 1970. Pres. Friends of Libr., Titusville, Fla., 1964-65. Mem. DAR, UDC, Nat. Order of Blue and Gray (founder, comdr. gen. 1990-96), Dame Commandeur Sovereign Mil. Order Temple of Jerusalem (counselor 1994-95), Daus. of Union Vets., Daus. of Loyal Legion of U.S., Ladies of Grand Army of Republic, Sons of Union Vets. Aux. Home: PO Box 1301 Vienna VA 22183-1301

BONDARENKO, HESPERIA AURA LOUIS, entrepreneur; b. Detroit, June 24, 1929; d. Arthur and Lola (Papadopoulou) Louis; m. William Bondarenko, Dec. 28, 1950; children: Marc, Fernande, Leif. Student, UCLA, 1962-64. Cert. comml. artist; cert. tchr., Ala. Designer Ernst Kern Co., Detroit, 1946-49, J.W. Knapp Co., Lansing, Mich., 1950-53; dir. interior visual merchandising Pizitz, Inc., Birmingham, Ala., 1968-75; photo stylist Bondarenko Photography, Birmingham, 1982-87; owner So. Postage Svcs., Birmingham, 1969—; designer Mich. Bell Tel., Detroit, 1952-53, Festival of Arts-Greece, Birmingham, 1969, Festival of Arts-Israel, Birmingham, 1972; designer display animation Horn's, Pitts., 1949. Dir. voter registration LWV, Birmingham, 1966-68; mem. Birmingham Mus. Art, 1988—, Nat. Mus. Women in Arts, 1989—. Mem. Internat. Assn. Postage Vendors, Ala. Retail Assn.

BONDINELL, STEPHANIE, counselor, former educational administrator; b. Passaic, N.J., Nov. 22, 1948; d. Peter Jr. and Gloria Lucille (Burden) Honcharuk; m. Paul Swanstrom Bondinell, July 31, 1971; 1 child, Paul Emil. BA, William Paterson Coll., 1970; MEd, Stetson U., 1983. Cert. elem. educator, Fla.; guidance counselor grades K-12, Fla. Tchr. Bloomingdale (N.J.) Bd. Edn., 1971-80; edn. dir. Fla. United Meth. Children's Home, Enterprise, 1982-89; guidance counselor Volusia County Sch. Bd., Deltona, Fla., 1989—. Sec. adv. com. Deltona Jr. High Sch., 1984-88; sec. Deltona Jr. PTA, 1982; vice-chmn. adv. com. Deltona Mid. Sch., 1988, chmn., 1989-91, chmn., 1991-92; mem. Deltona High Adv. Com., 1995-96; mem. secondary sch. task force Volusia County Sch. Bd., 1986—; mem. Volusia County Rep. Exec. Com., Rep. Presdl. Task Force; mem. state adv. bd. Fla. Future Educators Am., 1991-92. Acad. scholar Becton, Dickinson & Co., N.J., 1966; N.J. State scholar, 1966-70; named girls state rep. Am. Legion, N.J., 1966, Tchr. of Yr. Deltona Lakes, 1991, 95; recipient Vol. Svc. award Volusia County Sch. Bd., Deland, 1985. Mem. ASCD, AAUW, Coun. Exceptional Children, Divsn. for Learning Disabilities, Fla. Assn. Counseling and Devel., N.J. Edn. Assn., Volusia Tchrs. Orgn., Internat. Platform Assn., Deltona Civic Assn., Deltona Rep. Club (v.p. 1991), 4 Townes Federated Rep. Women's Club (sec., v.p.), Stetson Univ. Alumni Assn. Home: 1810 W Cooper Dr Deltona FL 32725-3623 Office: Volusia County Sch Bd 2022 Adelia Blvd Deltona FL 32725-3976

BONDS, SOPHIA JANE RIDDLE, geriatrics, medical/surgical nurse; b. Prentiss County, Miss., July 28, 1937; d. Cleatis Ross and Nona Exie (Palmer) Riddle; m. Joseph Luther Bonds, Sr., Jan. 21, 1956; children: Theresa Regina Bonds Peters, Joseph Luther, Jr., Michael Timothy, Sheila Elaine Bonds Ryan, Terry Jane Bonds Lee. LPN, Northeast Miss. Jr. Coll., 1968, ADN, 1980. RN, Miss. Asst. head nurse Magnolia Hosp., Corinth, Miss.; head nurse Aletha Lodge, Booneville, Miss.; supr. Alcorn County Care Inn, Corinth; staff nurse swingbed Bapt. Meml. Hosp., Booneville; mem. Miss. State Dept. Health. Mem. ANA.

BONDY, KATHLEEN NOWAK, nursing educator; b. South Bend, Ind., Apr. 1, 1942; d. Edward Frank and Helen Isabel (Kaminski) Nowak; m. Warren H. Bondy, Aug. 17, 1973 (dec. Dec. 1977). Diploma in Nursing, Holy Cross Ctrl. Sch. Nursing, South Bend, 1963; BSN, St. Louis U., 1966; MS, Boston U., 1970; PhD, NYU, 1976. Cert. rehab. nurse. Instr. Peter Bent Brigham Sch. Nursing, Boston, 1967-68; rehab. clin. specialist Newton Wellesley Hosp., Newton Lower Falls, Mass., 1970-72; asst. prof. Adelphi U., Garden City, N.Y., 1975-78; assoc. prof. U. Wis., Madison, 1978-93; postdoctoral rsch. fellow U. Pitts., 1991-93; prof. nursing U. Ctrl. Ark., Conway, 1993—. Editl. bd. Rehab. Nursing Jour., 1981-86; author/prodr. videotapes: Evaluation of Clinical Performance, 1981; contbr. articles to profl. jours. Spencer Found. grantee, 1979-80. Mem. Assn. Rehab. Nurses (bd. dirs. 1981-85, Outstanding Svc. award 1981, 85, Recognition for Editl. Bd. work 1992). Roman Catholic. Office: Univ of Central Arkansas 201 Donaghey Ave Conway AR 72035-5001

BONESIO, WOODROW MICHAEL, lawyer; b. Hereford, Tex., Dec. 27, 1943; s. Harold Andre and Elizabeth (Ireland) B.; m. Michaele Ann Dougherty; children: Elizabeth Eaton, Jo Kristin, William Michael. B.A., Austin Coll., 1966; J.D., U. Houston, 1971. Bar: Tex. 1971, U.S. Dist. Ct. (we., no., so., and ea. dists.) Tex. 1973, U.S. Ct. Appeals (5th cir.) 1973, U.S. Ct. Appeals (11th cir.) 1981. Law clk. to U.S. dist. Judge Western Dist. Tex., San Antonio, 1971-73; ptnr. Akin, Gump, Strauss, Hauer & Feld, Dallas, 1973-92, Kuntz & Bonesio LLP, Dallas, 1992—; speaker profl. confs. Democratic precinct chmn. Dallas County; mem. Dallas County Dem. Exec. Com., 1982—; elder Northminster Presbyterian Ch., 1981-85; bd. dirs. Grace Presbytery Devel. Bd., 1986-88. Fellow Tex. Bar Found.; mem. ABA, Fed. Bar Assn., Am. Judicature Soc., Dallas Bar Assn., Dallas Assn. Def. Counsel, Order of Barons, Austin Coll. Alumni Assn. (bd. dirs. 1983-88), U. Houston Law Alumni Assn. (chpt. pres. 1982), Vocal Majority (bd. dirs. 1990—), Soc. for Preservation and Encouragement Barber Shop Quartet Singing in Am. (internat. chorus champions 1975, 79, 82, 85, 88, 91, 94), Lake Highlands Exch. Club, Phi Alpha Delta. Office: Kuntz & Bonesio LLP 1717 Main St Ste 4050 Dallas TX 75201-4639

BONEY, LESLIE NORWOOD, III, state agency administrator; b. Wilmington, N.C., Oct. 13, 1959; s. Leslie Norwood and Lillian Maxwell (Bellamy) B.; m. Margaret Murchison Autry, Aug. 6, 1994. BA, Amherst Coll., 1981. Instr. Waynflete Sch., Portland, Maine, 1981-82; tchr. Va. Episcopal Sch., Lynchburg, 1982-84; anchor, reporter Clay Comms., Wilmington, 1984-87; producer, reporter Capitol Broadcasting, Raleigh, N.C., 1987-93; from dep. press sec. to dir. cmty. involvement Office of Gov. State of N.C., Raleigh, 1993—; Stephen min., 1992—; Klingenstein tchg. fellow Columbia U., N.Y.C., 1983. Bd. dirs. Crabtree Valley Youth Leadership, Raleigh, 1995—, N.C. Symphony, Wilmington, 1984-85, Lower Cape Fear Arts Coun., Wilmington, 1983-85. Recipient outstanding newswriting awards Radio TV News Dirs. Assn., 1987, 89, 92; grad. Leadership Raleigh, 1991. Mem. Leadership Raleigh Alumni Assn. (pres.-elect). Democrat. Methodist. Home: 610 Dixie Tr Raleigh NC 27607 Office: 121 W Jones St Raleigh NC 27603

BONFIELD, BARBARA GOLDSTEIN, municipal agency administrator; b. Lincoln, Ala., Jan. 12, 1937; d. Samuel Jacob and Margaret (Embry) Goldstein; m. Robert Lawrence Bonfield, Feb. 26, 1959; children: Barney, Susan. BA, Ala. Coll., 1958; MSW, U. Ala., 1976. Lic. cert. social worker. Social worker Jefferson County Dept. Pub. Welfare, Birmingham, Ala., 1958-59; child welfare worker Children's Aid Soc., Birmingham, 1960-71; human resources officer Jefferson County Commn., Birmingham, 1976-77, dir. agea agy. on aging, 1977—. Recipient Community Svc. award B'nai B'rith Women, Birmingham, 1983, Social Worker of Yr. award Ala. Conf. Social Work, 1993, State of Ala. Sr. Citizen Hall of Fame award 1993. Fellow Gerontol. Soc. Am.; mem. NASW (Social Worker of Yr. Birmingham chpt. 1978), Ala. Gerontol. Soc. (Profl. of Yr. 1986), Nat. Assn. Area Agys. on Aging, Southeastern Assn. Area Agys. on Aging (sec., bd. dirs. 1981), Acad. Cert. Social Workers. Democrat. Jewish. Home: 233 Beech Cir Birmingham AL 35213-2021 Office: 2601 Highland Ave S Birmingham AL 35205-1707

BONHAM-YEAMAN, DORIA, law educator; b. Los Angeles, June 10, 1932; d. Carl Herschel and Edna Mae (Jones) Bonham; widowed; children: Carl Q., Doria Valerie-Constance. BA, U. Tenn., 1953, JD, 1957, MA, 1958; EdS in Computer Edn., Barry U., 1984. Instr. bus. law Palm Beach Jr. Coll., Lake Worth, Fla., 1960-69; instr. legal environment Fla. Atlantic U., Boca Raton, 1969-73; lectr. bus. law Fla. Internat. U., North Miami, 1973-83, assoc. prof. bus. law, 1983—. Editor: Anglo-Am. Law Conf., 1980; Developing Global Corporate Strategies, 1981; editorial bd. Attys. Computer Report, 1984-85, Jour. Legal Studies Edn., 1985—. Contbr. articles to profl. jours. Bd. dirs. Palm Beach County Assn. for Deaf Children, 1960-63; mem. Fla. Commn. on Status of Women, Tallahassee, 1969-70; mem. Broward County Democratic Exec. Com., 1982—; pres. Dem. Women's Club Broward County, 1981; mem. Marine Coun. of Greater Miami, 1978—, Svc. award, 1979. Recipient Faculty Devel. award Fla. Internat. U., Miami, 1980; grantee Notre Dame Law Sch., London, summer 1980. Mem. AAUW (pres. Palm Beach county chpt. 1965-66), U.S. Coun. for Internat. Bus., No. Dade C. of C., Acad. Legal Studies in Bus., Alpha Chi Omega (alumnae club pres. 1968-71), Tau Kappa Alpha. Episcopalian. Office: Fla Internat U Law Dept North Miami FL 33181

BONIFAZI, STEPHEN, chemist; b. Hartford, Conn., Oct. 31, 1924; s. Camillo and Carrie (Mortensen) B.; BS, Trinity Coll., Hartford, 1947; postgrad. Okla. U., 1943-44, Rensselaer Poly. Inst., 1955-58; m. Joan Rose Dunlop, Dec. 19, 1959; 1 dau., Karen Stephanie. Sr. chemist Pratt & Whitney Aircraft Co., East Hartford, Conn., 1950-56, supr. chemistry, 1956-58, project chemist, West Palm Beach, Fla., 1958-63, gen. supr. chemistry, 1963-78, fuels and lubricants specialist, 1978-86, cons. 1986—. Served with inf. AUS, 1943-45; ETO. Decorated Bronze Star medal. Mem. ASME, ASTM, Am. Chem. Soc., Am. Soc. Lubrication Engrs., Am. Soc. Mech. Engrs., Internat. Assn. for Hydrogen Energy, Coordinating Research Council, Sigma Pi Sigma. Contbr. articles to sci. jours. Home and Office: 516 Kingfish Rd North Palm Beach FL 33408-4316

BONILLA, JAMES JOSEPH, international marketing director; b. Managua, Nicaragua, Nov. 26, 1949; s. Dora Gutierrez Salcido; m. Sonia Ramirez, Oct. 18, 1972; children: James Joseph, Alexander, Stefanie. BA in Polit. Sci., U. Calif., Berkeley, 1974; MA in Internat. Rels., George Washington U., 1976. Regional dir. Logetronics, Inc., Springfield, Va., 1976-88; v.p.; Autografica Corp., Miami, Fla., 1988-90; internat. mktg. dir. The Assoc. Press, Miami, 1990—; congl. intern U.S. Ho. of Reps. Inter-Am. Rels. Subcom., Washington, 1975. Ford Found. scholar U. Calif., Berkeley; Wolcott Found. fellow George Washington U. Roman Catholic. Home: 19631 SW 136th Ave Miami FL 33177 Office: AP 9100 NW 36th St # 104 Miami FL 33178-2432

BONIOL, EDDIE EUGENE, investments executive; b. Port Arthur, Tex., Sept. 14, 1931; s. Willie Bernice and Leila Evelina (Chase) B.; diploma in acctg. Tyler Comml. Coll., 1949; student Baylor U., 1955-56, La. Coll., 1956, SUNY, 1981—; m. Margaret Faye Aguillard, Feb. 5, 1966; children: Joe Ed, Mark Eugene, Liesl Michelle. Various positions Comml. Credit Co., Bus. Services Group, Balt., 1959-73, area dir., 1970-73; freelance mgmt. cons. Dallas, 1973; v.p. Tex. Western Fin. Corp., Dallas, 1974-76; asst. v.p. Citicorp Bus. Credit Inc., Dallas, 1976-78; v.p. fin. and adminstrn., also chief fin. officer Superior Iron Works & Supply Co. Inc., Shreveport, La., 1978-80; sr. v.p., chief fin. officer Latham Resources Corp., Shreveport, 1980-81; pres. Decca Leasing Corp., Shreveport, 1981—; chmn., chief exec. officer Red River & Gulf Resources, Inc., Shreveport, 1982—; pres. Med. Bus. Services, Inc., Shreveport, 1982-86; cons. in field. Trustee La. Coll., 1984-90, vice-chmn., 1987-90. Served with USN, 1950-53. Cert. credit analyst, credit and fin. analyst. Mem. Lions (gov. dist. 8L 1989-90, founder, 1st pres. LeCompte, La. club, 1959, pres. North Shreveport club 1986-87, founder, 1st pres. South Shreveport club 1988-89). Republican. Baptist. Home: 8606 Rampart Pl Shreveport LA 71106-6228 Office: PO Box 6079 Shreveport LA 71136-6079

BONNARENS, JOSEPH KEITH, trade association administrator, pharmacist; b. Lakeview, Oreg., Nov. 18, 1966; s. Theodore Joseph B. and Frances Yvonne Stewart; m. Daria Delfino, Mar. 24, 1995. Student in pharmacy, science, Oreg. State U., 1990. Staff pharmacist Profl. Pharmacy, St. Helens, Oreg., 1990-91, Emanuel Hosp., Portland, 1991; exec. resident Am. Soc. Hosp. Pharmacists, Bethesda, Md., 1991-92, coord. exec. mgmt. seminar, 1992; assoc. dir. student affairs Nat. Assn. Retail Druggists, Alexandria, Va., 1992-94, dir. student affairs, 1994-96, assoc. dir. mgmt. svcs., 1994-96; Invited Young Pharmacist Leadership Conf. U. Tex. Coll. Pharmacy, Austin, 1993-96. Editor, contbr.: (quarterly jour.) The New Independent, 1994-95. Chmn. planning com. Am. Soc. Hosp. Pharmacists Found. Walter Jones Golf Classic, Bethesda, Md., 1996, Inter Organizational Coun. Student Affairs, Washington, 1995. Home: 18131 Chalet Dr #201 Germantown MD 20874

BONNER, ANNIE STUCKEY, secondary educator; b. Danville, Ga., Aug. 12, 1945; d. R.C. and Lucille (Watkins) Stuckey; m. Clark Bonner, Apr. 24, 1970; children: Chastity Ayanna, Timethia Jamille. BA, Paine Coll., 1966; MS, Fort Valley State Coll., 1973; edn. specialist, Ga. So. U., 1986. Tchr. Calhoun H.S., Irwinton, Ga., 1966-84, Laurens County Bd. of Edn., Dublin, Ga., 1984—; chairperson, bd. dirs. RVI Enrichment Camp, Atlanta, 1991. Grad. Dublin-Laurens Leadership, 1994; adv. bd. Laurens County Spl. Olympics, Dublin, 1986—; v.p. Dublin Laurens Black Festival; campaign helper Dublin City coun. Race, 1991—, Laurens County Bd. of Edn., 1992—; bd. dirs. Dublin-Laurens Libr. Bd., 1996. Named Black Woman of the Yr. Dublin Laurens Black Festival, 1992. Mem. Dublin Laurens Black Festival (v.p. 1994—), Ga. Vocat. Assn. (treas. spl. needs personnel 1995, Order of the Ea. Star, Order of the Golden Circle, Delta Sigma Theta. Home: 1057 Highway 199 South Dublin GA 31027

BONNER, DONNA PACE, real estate investments, consultant, volunteer; b. Yorktown, Tex., Aug. 22, 1932; d. Lloyd Benjamin and Delia Anna (Bourssa) Pace; m. E.V. Neal Bonner, Oct. 11, 1952 (dec. Nov. 1990); children: E.V. Jr., Terese Bonner Youngblood, Andrew, L. Pace. BS, U. Tex., 1954, postgrad., 1955-56. Speech tchr. Harlingen (Tex.) Ind. Sch. Dist., 1958-60; ptnr. Toytown, Harlingen, Tex., 1962-67, Roby & Lyn Children, Harlingen, Tex., 1967-74; owner Wally's Shoes, Harlingen, Tex., 1974-85; cons. Bonner & Bonner, Harlingen, Tex., 1990-94; motivational speaker, Harlingen, Rio Grande, 1975-94. Pres. Harlingen Jr. League, 1971; dir. Shepard's Ctr., 1988-93, Harlingen Libr. Bd., 1972-87, Tex. MHMR Vol. Coun., 1987-89; pres. Harlingen PTA, 1977; dir. Tex. State Tech. Coll. Devel. Bd., 1987-94, St. Anthony Endowment, 1985-94; elected city councilwoman City of Harlingen, 1986-94. Named Spirit of Am. Woman, J.C. Penney, 1989, Woman of Yr., Zonta Club, 1993, Leadership Tex., 1988; named among 100 Disting. Vols., Assn. Jr. Leagues Internat., 1995. Mem. Rotary Internat., Harlingen Country Club. Roman Catholic. Office: Bonner & Bonner PO Box 288 Harlingen TX 78551-0288

BONNER, MARY ELAINE, psychologist; b. Augusta, Ark., Nov. 11, 1940; d. Robert Carl and Dorothy Elaine (McAlexander) Walker; m. J. Darell Bonner, Dec. 22, 1961 (div. Aug. 1982); children: David, Stephen, Holly Bonner Ford; m. Michael E. Hale, Feb. 3, 1990. BS in edn., U. Ctrl. Ark., 1968, MSc in edn., 1972; PhD, U. Miss., 1986. Cert. psychologist Ark. Bd. Examiners in Psychology. Libr. supr. North Little Rock (Ark.) Pub. Schs., 1968-70; reading tchr. Conway (Ark.) Pub. Schs., 1970-72; reading supr. Pulaski Acad., Little Rock, 1972-75; private practive, psychol. examiner Little Rock, 1980-84; psychologist Bridgeway Hosp., North Little Rock, 1987-89, Counseling Clinic, Inc., Benton, Ark., 1989—. Contbr. articles to profl. jours. First vice regent Nat. Soc. Daughters of Am. Revolution, Little Rock, 1994-96; mem. Overlook Neighborhood Assn., Little Rock, 1995-96. Mem. Ark. Psychol. Assn., Am. Acad. Forensic Examiners, Ballet Ark., Phi Mu. Republican. Episcopalian. Home: 24 Hearthside Dr Little Rock AR 72207 Office: Counseling Clinic Inc 307 E Sevier St Benton AR 72015

BONNER, PHILLIP RAY, foundation executive; b. Ashland, Ala.; s. George Samuel and Dorothy Hilma (Ray) B.; m. Sheila Farish, Jan. 8, 1972; children: Sheila Farish Bonner, Meredith R., Carrie Spencer. BA, Auburn U. Exec. dir. State of Ala. Gas Commn., 1959-64; pub. rels. cons., 1965-70; regional dir. Muscular Dystrophy, Memphis and Atlanta, 1971-82; nat. telethon coord. Arthritis Found., Atlanta, 1982; pres., CEO Ga. chpt. Arthritis Found., 1983—; continuing med. edn. provider Ga. Rheumatology Soc., Med. Assn. Ga., Atlanta. Bd. dirs. Phoenix Soc., Atlanta. Mem. Nat. Soc. Fund Raising Execs., Ga. Soc. Fund Raising Execs., Ga. Soc. Assn. Execs., Lambda Chi Alpha. Republican. Roman Catholic. Office: Arthritis Found Ga Chpt 550 Pharr Rd NE Ste 550 Atlanta GA 30305-3428

BONTOS, GEORGE EMMANUEL, physician; b. Alton, Ill., Dec. 7, 1924; s. Emmanuel Anthony and Lillian (Saris) Bontzolakis; B.A., U. Chgo., 1949; M.D., U. Athens (Greece), 1968; m. Athena M. Teregis, Sept. 21, 1952; children—E. Christopher, Elizabeth Ann. Research asso. Chgo. State Hosp., 1969; intern Wheeling (W.Va.) Hosp., 1970-71, resident, 1971-73; practice medicine specializing in family medicine, Wheeling, 1973—; pres. med.-dental staff Wheeling Hosp., 1987-88; sr. attending Wheeling Hosp., Ohio Valley Med. Center; sr. attending staff, instr. dept. family practice, chief dept. family practice Wheeling Hosp.; plant physician Wheeling-Pitts. Steel Corp. Bd. dirs. Wheeling chpt. ARC, 1975, Health Plan Upper Ohio Valley, Vis. Nurses Assn. Ohio County, 1976; v.p. bd. dirs. HMO-IPA Health Plan of Upper Ohio Valley; past pres. bd. trustees, ch. coun. St. John The Divine Ch. With U.S. Army, 1945-46; Korea. Diplomate Am. Bd. Family Practice. Fellow Am. Acad. Family Physicians, Am. Geriatrics Soc.; mem. AMA (Recognition award 1975, 78, 80, 82, 85, 88), So. Med. Assn., W.Va. Med. Assn., Ohio County Med. Soc. (pres. 1985), Ohio County Found. Med. Care, Pan-Cretan Assn. Am. (gov. dist. III). Republican. Greek Orthodox. Lodges: Masons (32 degree), Jesters, Scottish Rite, Shriners. Home: 3 Stratford Dr Apt 302 Wheeling WV 26003-6148 Office: 2427 Warwood Ave Wheeling WV 26003-7250

BONURA, LARRY SAMUEL, writer; b. Galveston, Tex., Jan. 4, 1950; s. Leo Bonura and Beatrice Sadie (Maiorka) Immel; m. Marilyn Esther Ward, Feb. 17, 1990; 1 child, Sean Joseph Sullins. BS in Journalism, U. Kans., 1977; MA in Am. History, Emporia (Kans.) State U., 1982. Asst. libr. U. Kans. Librs., Lawrence, 1975-77; instr. Butler County Community Coll., El Dorado, Kans., 1982-83; dir. Bike Libr., Emporia, 1977-84; mng. editor Agora Assocs., Balt., 1983-84; dir. Word Workers, Richardson, Tex., 1984—; mgr. editorial svcs. Convex Computer Corp., Richardson, 1987-94; sr. instr. No. Telecom Meridian Info. Products, Richardson, 1994-95; instr. Richland C.C., Dallas, 1988-91; leader seminar Solutions Inc., Boston, 1991-93; lectr. 2d World Congress on Sports Documentation, Vienna, Austria, 1982. Author: Fruit of a Fleeting Joy, 1975, Desktop Publisher's Dictionary, 1989, Desktop Publisher's Thesaurus, 1990, Indexing Technical Documents, 1991, The Art of Indexing, 1994. Mem. Arapaho Elem. PTA, 1993-96, mem. Arapaho Elem. PTA, 1996—; coach Richardson Sports Inc., 1990-95. Mem. Am. Soc. Indexers (pres. D.C. chpt. 1985), Soc. for Tech. Comm., Dallas Sci. Mus., Dallas Hist. Soc., The Authors Guild, Nat. Trust for Hist. Preservation, Pi Gamma Mu. Home: 806 Clearwater Dr Richardson TX 75080-5032 Office: PO Box 831038 Richardson TX 75083-1038

BONZAGNI, VINCENT FRANCIS, program administrator, analyst, researcher; b. Boston, Dec. 10, 1952; s. Augustine Joseph and Augusta M. (Giarla) B.; m. Marie T. Rainville, Aug. 27, 1972 (div. Sept. 1982); 1 child, Gina Theresa; m. Donna J. Bachtell, May 14, 1988; stepchildren: Allison, Neil. BS in Math., Lowell (Mass.) Tech. Inst., 1974. Retail store mgr. Consumer Value Stores, 1974-76; claims adminstr. Social Security Adminstrn., 1976-79; quality assurance specialist Social Security Adminstrn., Boston, 1979-83; disability analyst Social Security Adminstrn., Arlington, Va., 1983-88; program adminstr. Corp. for Open Systems, McLean, Va., 1988-91; sr. hearings and appeals analyst Social Security Adminstrn., Falls Church, Va., 1991—; self-employed researcher and crossword puzzle cons., 1982—. Author: The Mensa Book of Lists, 1992, The Mensa Book of Lists II, 1996; co-author: A History of Mensa, 1990. Treas. Maplewood Village Condo. Assn., 1989-93. Mem. Mensa (local treas. 1986-90, local pres. 1990-91, nat. historian 1989—, nat. SIGs officer 1989-91, internat. archivist 1992—), Intertel, Nat. Puzzlers League. Democrat. Home: 4737 Parkman Ct Annandale VA 22003-5046 Office: OHA 5107 Leesburg Pike Falls Church VA 22041-3234

BOOK, JOHN KENNETH (KENNY BOOK), retail store owner; b. Hillsboro, Ill., June 26, 1950; s. Vern Ray Book and Pearl Iva (Foster) Book Alford; m. Betty L. Christy, Dec. 23, 1981; children: Elizabeth Marie Dunn Rose, Leslie Michelle Dunn. Assoc. in Acctg., Ky. Bus. Coll., 1974. Laborer, Lexington (Ky.) Army Depot, 1968-70; machine operator A.O. Smith, Mt. Sterling, Ky., 1971-72; laborer Irvin Industries, Lexington, 1973-75; owner Kenny's Signs & Bus. Svcs., Winchester, Ky., 1977-90, Kenny's Bookkeeping & Tax Svc., Winchester, 1990—; rsch. bd. advisors ABI. Active Winchester Sch. Bd., 1976, 78; candidate for commr. City of Winchester, 1977, 79, 81, 83, 87, elected commr., 1989, reelected, 1993, 96, candidate for mayor, 1985. Named to Hon. Order Ky. Cols., 1973. Mem. Ky. Sheriff's Assn. (hon.). Democrat. Office: Kenny's Bookkeeping & Tax Svc PO Box 840 Winchester KY 40392-0840

BOOKER, LARRY FRANK, accountant; b. Mobile, Ala., May 22, 1950; s. Frank and Helen Louise Booker; m. Prudence E. Porter, Sept. 1, 1972; children: Jennifer Erin, Meggan Leah. BA, U. South Ala., 1972; student, U. N.C., 1976-77. Lic. pub. acct., Ala. Rsch. economist Rsch. Triangle Inst., Durham, N.C., 1974-76; with Providence Hosp., Mobile, 1978-80; pvt. practice acctg. Mobile, 1981—; enrolled IRS. Vol. Jr. Achievement. Mem. Nat. Assn. Accts., Nat. Assn. Tax Practitioners, Nat. Soc. Pub. Accts., Ala. Assn. Pub. Accts. (past dist. pres., bd. dirs.), Accreditation Coun. in Acctg. and Taxation (accredited in taxation and accountancy). Lodge: Kiwanis. Home: 6436 Brindlewood Ct Mobile AL 36608-3837 Office: 750 Downtowner Loop W Ste B Mobile AL 36609-5500

BOOKER, LEWIS THOMAS, lawyer; b. Richmond, Va., Sept. 22, 1929; s. Russell Eubank and Leslie Quarles (Sessoms) B.; m. Nancy Electa Brogden, Sept. 29, 1956; children: Lewis Thomas Jr., Virginia Frances, Claiborne Brogden, John Quarles. B.A., U. Richmond, 1950, LL.D., 1977; J.D., Harvard U., 1953. Bar: Va. 1953, U.S. Ct. Mil. Appeals 1954, U.S. Supreme Ct. 1958, D.C. 1980, N.Y. 1985. Assoc. Hunton & Williams, Richmond, Va., 1956-63; ptnr. Hunton & Williams, 1963-95, sr. coun., 1995—; substitute Judge 13th Dist., Va., 1996—; lectr. in law Seinan Gakuin U., Fukuoka, Japan, 1985; vis. lectr. in law St. Thomas U., Miami, Fla., 1993. Mem. Va. Coun. on Human Rights, 19878; commr. chmn. Richmond Redevel. and Housing Authority, 1961-70; trustee U. Richmond, 1972—, rector, 1973-77, 81-85, 91-94, vice rector, 1985-87, chmn. exec. commn., 1977-81; trustee Va. Inst. Sci. Rsch., 1981-94, Richmond Symphony, 1987-92, Rouse-Bottom Found., 1989—; mem. Coun. Richmond Symphony, 1995, Westminster-Canterbury Found. Richmond, 1995—, Robins Found., 1996—. Fellow Am. Coll. Trial Lawyers, Am. Bar Found.; mem. ABA, Va. Bar Assn., Richmond Bar Assn., Westwood Racquet Club. Democrat. Baptist. Office: Hunton & Williams East Tower Riverfront Pla 951 E Byrd St Richmond VA 23219-4040

BOOKER, MONROE JAMES, small business owner; b. Howenwald, Tenn., Nov. 21, 1921; s. William Garfield and Hattie (Witherspoon) B.; m. Mary Pope, May 27, 1950; children: Claudia, Charlotte, Janet, Gwen, Cyrus, Linda, Brenda, Robert, Joe, Sherry, Karen, Barry. Ptnr. Booker Bros., Franklin, Tenn., 196—; ptnr. JMP&B Real Estate, Franklin, 1960-95; owner Booker Mobile Home Park, Franklin, 1969—. Author: Thoughts From the Coffee Table, 1995. With U.S. Army, 1942-45, South Pacific. Recipient Spl. Recognition for Child Rearing Pres. George Bush, 1989.

BOOKER, SHIRLEY RUTH, entertainment specialist; b. Center, Tex., Oct. 15, 1947; d. Preston and Elminer Brittian; m. Charles Seach, Jan. 3, 1967 (div.); 1 child, Charles Seach Jr.; m. Patrick Henry Booker, Dec. 31, 1975; 1 child, Roshon Booker. BS in Social Work, U. Ctrl. Tex., 1992. Recreation specialist Community Recreation Divsn., Ft. Hood, Tex., 1974-88; comml. entertainment specialist Community Recreation Divsn., Ft. Hood, 1988—; cons. in field; rest and recuperation coord. S.W. Asia Theatre during Operation Desert Storm. Author: (jour.) Desert Storm/A Time to Love, 1992. Recipient Desert shield, Desert Storm medal Dept. of Def., 1992, Dept. of Army Comdr.'s award, 1985, Cert. of achievement, 1991, Superior Civilian Svc. award, 1991. Democrat. Mem. Assembly of God Ch. Home: 1310 Hammond Dr Killeen TX 76543-5220 Office: Hdqs and III Corps Bldg 1001 Rm 217 W/DPCA Fort Hood TX 76544

BOONE, ALICIA KAY LANIER, marketing communications consultant, writer; b. Ft. Worth, Sept. 3, 1941; d. John David and Reba Louise (Smith) Lanier; m. William T. Boone, July 22, 1967 (div. June 1988); children: Katherine, Suzanne, Lisa, Norma, Matthew. Student, Abilene (Tex.) Christian U., 1959-60, North Tex. State U., 1960-64; BA in Sociology cum laude, U. Tex., Dallas, 1993. Reporter Daily Oklahoman/Oklahoma City Times, 1964-66; feature writer Houston Post, 1967; info. rep. Okla. Dept. Inst., Social and Rehab. Services, Oklahoma City, 1967-73; dir. pub. info. United Way Mecklenburg-Union, Charlotte, N.C., 1974-76; account mgr., sr. writer Epley Assocs./Pub. Relations, Charlotte, 1977-78; account mgr. Yarbrough Co./Advt., Pub. Relations, Dallas, 1979-82; owner Boone & Assoc./Pub. Relations and Advt., Richardson, Tex., 1982-88; v.p. Yarbrough Co./Advt., Dallas, 1988-90; owner The Creative Solution, Dallas, 1990—; bd. dirs Hope Cottage, 1993-95; pub. Adoption Triad Forum, 1993—. Author, editor History of Child Welfare In Oklahoma, 1976. Mem. SBA (region VI adv. coun. 1990-94), Pub. Rels. Soc. Am., Assn. Women Entrepreneurs of Dallas (pres. 1987-88), Richardson C. of C. (editor newsletter 1986-87), Dallas Women in Bus. (Advt. of Yr. 1988), Small Bus. Congress in Dallas (co-chair 1988).

BOONE, CELIA TRIMBLE, lawyer; b. Clovis, N.Mex., Mar. 3, 1953; d. George Harold and Barbara Ruth (Foster) T.; m. Billy W. Boone, Apr. 21, 1990. BS, Ea. N.Mex. U., 1976, MA, 1977; JD, St. Mary's U., San Antonio, 1982. Bar: Tex. 1982, U.S. Dist. Ct. (no. dist.) Tex. 1983, U.S. Ct. Appeals (5th cir.) 1985, U.S. Supreme Ct. 1986. Instr. English, Eastern N.Mex. U., Portales, 1977-78; editor Curry County Times, Clovis, 1978-79; assoc. Schulz & Robertson, Abilene, Tex., 1982-85, Scarborough, Black, Tarpley & Scarborough, 1985-87; ptnr. Scarborough, Black, Tarpley & Trimble, Abilene, Tex., 1988-90, Scarborough, Black, Tarpley & Boone, 1990-94, of counsel Scarborough, Tarpley, Boone & Fouts, 1994-96; prin. Law Office of Celia Trimble Boone, , Abilene, 1996—; instr. legal rsch. and writing St. Mary's Sch. Law, 1981-82. Legal adv. to bd. dirs. Abilene Kennel Club, 1983-85; mem. landmarks commn. City of Abilene, 1989-90. Recipient Outstanding Young Lawyer of Abilene, 1988. Mem. ABA, State Bar Tex. (mem. disciplinary rev. com. 1989-93), Am. Trial Lawyers Assn., Tex. Trial Lawyers Assn., Tex. Criminal Def. Lawyers Assn., Tex. Acad. Family Law Specialists, Tex. Bd. Legal Specialization (cert. 1987), Abilene Bar Assn. (bd. dirs. 1985-86, 87-88, sec./treas. 1985-86), Abilene Young Lawyers Assn. (bd. dirs. 1985-86, 87-89, treas. 1985-86, pres.-elect 1987-88, pres. 1988-89), NOW, ACLU, Phi Alpha Delta. Democrat. Avocations: needlework, gardening. Office: 104 Pine St Ste 705 Abilene TX 79601

BOONE, GEORGE STREET, retired lawyer; b. Elkton, Ky., Aug. 27, 1918; s. Benjamin Edwards Jr. and Susan Marion (Street) B.; m. Joy Bale; children: Shelby Bale, Barbara Bale, Daryl Vann, Richard, Bradley, Phillip. BA, Vanderbilt U., 1940, LLB, 1941; LLM, Columbia U., 1946. Pvt. practice, ret. Chmn. Ky. Bicentennial Ency. Com.; vice chmn. Ky. Bicentennial Com., Ky. Legislature Study of Ky. Constitution. Named Outstanding Freshman Rep., Ky. Gen. Assembly, 1972. Mem. Ky. Bar Assn. (mem. com. on U.S. Bicentennial celebration), Ky. Hist. Soc. (pres. 1990-91), Athenaeum, Rotary, Filson Club. Home: 402 W Main Elkton KY 42220

BOONE, JOHN LEWIS, religious organization administrator; b. Elkton, Ky., Oct. 5, 1927; s. Benjamin Edwards and Manie (Street) B.; m. Sally Hardcastle, Dec. 30, 1952; children: Sally Boone Wieland, John L. Jr., Martha Boone Bland. BA, Vanderbilt U., 1949. CLU. Chmn. bd. Presbyns. for Democracy and Religious Freedom, 1985—; mem. South Ctrl. Fin. Assocs. Author Presbyn. Mainstream newspaper, 1986—. Recipient Faith and Freedom award Presbyns. for Democracy and Religious Freedom, Washington, 1990; named Man of the Yr., Tenn. Assn. of Life Underwriters, 1989. Mem. Nashville Chpt. CLUs (pres. 1957), Nashville Assn. of Life Underwriters (pres. 1955). Republican. Office: South Ctrl Fin Assocs 30 Burton Hills Blvd Ste 300 Nashville TN 37215-6140

BOONE, O. RILEY, retired surgeon; b. Franklin County, Va., July 19, 1936; s. Irvin Cline and Maggie Elizabeth (Bowman) B.; m. Judith Ann Ault, Oct. 14, 1988; 3 children. BS, William and Mary Coll., 1961; MD, Med. Coll. Va., 1961. Diplomate Am. Bd. Surgery. Dep. chief dept. surgery USPHS Hosp., Balt., 1966-67; asst. chief dept. surgery USPHS Hosp., San Francisco, 1967-68; dep. chief surgery USPHS Hosp., Norfolk, Va., 1968-69; pvt. practice Bethesda, Md., 1969-71, Leesburg, Va., 1971-95; chief of staff Loudoun Hosp. Ctr., 1978-79. Comdr. USPHS, 1961-69. Fellow ACS (mem. Va. chpt., coun. mem. 1982-84); mem. AMA, Med. Soc. Va., No. Va. Found. Med. Care (pres. 1978-79), Loudoun County Med. Soc. (pres. 1973-74), Kiwanis Club Leesburg.

BOONE, RICHARD WINSTON, SR., lawyer; b. Washington, July 19, 1941; s. Henry Shaffer and Anne Catherine (Huehne) B.; m. Jean Knox Logan, Dec. 17, 1966; children: Elizabeth Anne, Richard Winston, Jr., Katheryn Jeanne. B.A. with honors, U. Ala., 1963; J.D., Georgetown U., 1970. Bar: Va. 1970, D.C., 1970, U.S. Ct. Claims 1975, U.S. Ct. Appeals (D.C. cir.) 1970, U.S. Ct. Appeals (2d cir.) 1973, U.S. Ct. Appeals (4th cir.) 1972, U.S. Supreme Ct. 1974, Md. 1984. Ptnr. Carr, Jordan, Coyne & Savits, Washington, 1977-81; shareholder, dir. Wilkes, Artis, Hedrick & Lane, Washington, 1981-84; pres. Richard W. Boone, P.C., McLean, Va., 1984-95, pres. The Law Offices of Richard W. Boone, 1995—. Capt. USAR, 1964-67. Mem. ABA, Am. Soc. Hosp. Risk Mgrs., Am. Acad. Hosp. Attys., Def. Research Inst., D.C. Def. Lawyers Assn., Va. Trial Lawyers Assn., Assn. Trial Lawyers Am., Barristers Assn. Avocations: model railroading, personal computer.

BOOP, FREDERICK ALAN, neurosurgeon; b. Memphis, Mar. 28, 1956; s. Warren Clark and Nancy Ruth (Ogden) B.; m. Lee Ann Dunlap, June 14, 1986; children: Sarah Elizabeth, Scott Harris. BA, U. Ark., 1979; MD, U. Ark., Little Rock, 1983. Diplomate Am. Bd. Neurol. Surgery. Intern gen. surgery U. Tex. Health Sci. Ctr., San Antonio, 1983-84, resident neurosurgery, 1984-89; resident neurology rotation, hon. asst. house officer Inst. Neurology, Nat. Hosp., London, 1986; pediatric neurosurgery rotation resident Hosp. Sick Children, Toronto, Ont., Can., 1987; fellow epilepsy and functional neurosurgery U. Minn., Mpls., 1989; fellow pediatric neurosurgery Ark. Children's Hosp., U. Ark. Med. Scis., Little Rock, 1990; vice chief pediatric neurosurgery Ark. Children's Hosp., Little Rock, 1990-91, chief, 1992—; asst. prof. neurosurgery, asst. prof. anatomy U. Ark. Med. Scis., Little Rock, 1990-95, assoc. prof. neurosurgery and anatomy, 1995—; mem. steering com. Ark. Comprehensive Epilepsy Program, 1991. Contbr. articles to profl. jours. Fellow ACS; mem. Am. Assn. Neurol. Surgeons, Am. Epilepsy Soc., Congress Neurol. Surgeons, Nat. Assn. Epilepsy Ctrs. (bd. dirs. 1992, chmn. nominating com. 1993), N.Am. Skull Base Soc., Soc. Neurol. Surgeons, N.Y. Acad. Scis., Pulaski County Med. Soc., Ark. State Med. Soc., Robert Watson Soc. (sec. 1991), Soc. Neurosci. (pres. Ark. chpt. 1993), Am. Soc. Pediatric Neurosurgons, Neurosurg. Soc. Am. Office: Ark Childrens Hosp 800 Marshall St Little Rock AR 72202-3510

BOOSER, DANIEL JAMES, physician, oncologist; b. Middletown, Pa., Dec. 12, 1941; s. James Henry and Edith Maude (Metzger) B.; m. Kathryn Joyce Tremblay (div. 1981); m. Helene Alicia Yakimetz, Nov. 10, 1985; children: James Eric, Timothy John, Kenneth Charles. BA, Swarthmore (Pa.) Coll., 1963; MD, Yale U., 1967. Diplomate Am. Bd. Internal Medicine, Am. Bd. Med. Oncology. Med. oncologist King Faisal Specialist Hosp., Riyadh, Saudi Arabia, 1976-78; asst. internist, asst. prof. M.D. Anderson Cancer Ctr., Houston, 1979-81; med. oncologist King Faisal Specialist Hosp, Riyadh, Saudi Arabia, 1982-89; assoc. internist, asst. prof. M.D. Anderson Cancer Ctr., Houston, 1990—. Lt. USNR, 1969-70, Vietnam. Fellow Royal Coll. Physicians Can.; mem. ACP, Can. Oncology Soc., European Soc. med. Oncology, Am. Soc. Clin. Oncology. Office: M D Anderson Cancer Ctr Box 56 Houston TX 77030

BOOTH, GORDON DEAN, JR., lawyer; b. Columbus, Ga., June 25, 1939; s. Gordon Dean and Lois Mildred (Bray) B.; m. Katherine Morris Campbell, June 17, 1961; children: Mary Katherine Williams, Abigail Kilgore Curvino, Sarah Elizabeth, Margaret Campbell. BA, Emory U., 1961, JD, 1964, LLM, 1973. Bar: Ga. 1964, D.C. 1977, U.S. Supreme Ct. 1973. Pvt. practice Atlanta, 1964-96; ptnr. Schreeder, Wheeler & Flint, Atlanta, 1995—; bd. dirs., v.p. Stallion Music Inc., Nashville, BAA USA, Inc.; chmn. CPS Systems, Inc., Dallas; trustee, sec. Inst. for Polit. Econ., Washington. Contbr. articles to profl. jours. Trustee Met. Atlanta Crime Commn., 1977-80, chmn., 1979-80; mem. assembly for arts and scis. Emory Coll., 1971-86, chmn., 1983. Mem. Internat. Bar Assn. (coun. sect. bus. law 1974-88, chmn. aero. law com. 1971-86), State Bar Ga., Capital City Club, Piedmont Driving Club, Univ. Club, Advocates Club, Sigma Chi. Home and Office: Schreeder Wheeler & Flint 1600 Chandler Bldg 127 Peachtree St Atlanta GA 30303

BOOTH, HILDA EARL FERGUSON, clinical psychologist, Spanish educator; b. Pinehurst, N.C., Aug. 14, 1943; d. Arthur C. and Edna Estelle (Henry) Ferguson; m. Thomas Gilbert Booth, Oct. 25, 1966 (dec. Apr. 1990). AA, Montreat-Anderson Coll., 1963; BA, Pembroke State U., 1965; MS, Valdosta State U., 1985; postgrad. U. S.C., 1991. Lic. profl. counselor, S.C., cert. counselor, hypnotherapist; Spanish instr. C.C., Lake City, Fla., 1983-86; clin. counselor Columbia Counseling, Lake City, Fla., 1985-87; children's psychologist I Coastal Empire Mental Health Ctr., Allendale, S.C., 1987; psychologist II, 1988; office mgr., 1987-91; pvt. practice, Allendale, 1989-91; mem. assessment team, mutual health cons. Richland Meml. Hosp., Richland Springs; spl. svcs. coord., area coord. Allendale office, 1989; dir. women FORSPRO (Spain), Coral Gables, Fla., 1984-88; aquatics instr. Harbison Recreation Ctr., 1993; aquatics leader Nat. Arthritis Found., 1994; mem. mobile assessment team Richland Meml. Hosp., Richland Springs. 1994; emergency services staff Mental Health, Lake City, 1985-87; mem. Children at Risk team, Children' s Advocacy team, 1987-91. Mem. extension community planning com. City of Allendale, 1989-91, Shandon Presbyn. Ch.; pres. Protestant Women of Chapel, Nfld., Can., 1969, Church Women United, Lake City, 1976; deacon First Presby. Ch., Lake City, 1976-86, chmn. bd. deacons, 1982, elder 1985; elder Allendale Presby. Ch. 1988—, clk. of session, 1989—, tchr. Sunday sch., 1994; mem. LWV. Served to lt. (j.g.) USN, 1965-67. Fellow Internat. Biog. Assn.; Mem. NAFFE, AAUW, SEICUS, Inter-Am. Soc. of Psychology, Am. Legion (life), Nat. Beta Club, Soc. Noetic Scis., Robert Burns Soc. Republican. Avocations: painting, swimming, travel, reading, Spanish. Home and Office: 3134 Prentice Ave Columbia SC 29205-3940

BOOTH, JANE SCHUELE, real estate broker, executive; b. Cleve.; d. Norman Andrew and Frances Ruth (Hankey) Schuele; m. George Warren Booth, Dec. 6, 1968. AA, Stephens Coll., 1946; student, U. Mo., 1946-47. Lic. real estate broker, Fla. Assoc. J.M. Mathes Inc., N.Y.C., 1947-48; dept. supr. Lord and Taylor, Scarsdale, N.Y., 1948-50; art coord. J. Walter Thompson, Inc., N.Y.C., 1953-58; art buyer SSC&B Inc. Advt., N.Y.C., 1959-80; pres. Jane Schuele Booth Realty, Ocala, Fla., 1982—. Mem. Fla. Thoroughbred Fillies, Ocala, 1980—; charter mem., trustee Royal Dames for Cancer Rsch., Inc., Ocala, 1986—; treas. Ladies Aux. Fla. H.C.H. Inc., Ocala, 1986-90; bd. visitors Fla. Horsemen's Children's Home, Inc., 1983-90. Mem. Ocala/Marion County Assn. Realtors, Ocala/Marion County C. of C. (agribus./equine com.), Nat. Assn. Realtors, Fla. Assn. Realtors, Estates Club. Home: 1771 SW 55th Street Rd Ocala FL 34474-5933 Office: PO Box 5538 Ocala FL 34478-5538

BOOTH, LINDA LEIGH, vocational educator; b. Dallas, May 12, 1953; d. Federico Rose and Gladys Ruth (Petty) Buenrostro; m. Joe Henry Booth Jr., May 24, 1985; children: Kathryn Leigh, Elizabeth Rose. BS in Home Econs., Abilene Christian U., 1985. Instr. Abilene (Tex.) Ind. Sch. Dist., 1988—; mem. edn. vocat. adv. bd. Abilene Ind. Sch. Dist., Abilene, 1991—, mem. textbook selection com., 1990-91. Judge Future Homemakers of Am., Abilene, 1987-88; mem. children's ministries com. Univ. Ch. of Christ, 1993. Mem. Am. Vocat. Assn., Tex. Vocat. Spl. Needs Assn., Vocat. Home Econs. Tchrs. Assn. of Tex. (alt. dir. 1996—), Tex. Restaurant Assn., Abilene Restaurant Assn., Tex. Classroom Tchrs. Assn., Assn. Tex. Profl. Educators, Hospitality Educators Assn. Tex., Future Homemakers Am. Home: 709 Deborah Dr Abilene TX 79601-5535 Office: Abilene HS 2800 N 6th St Abilene TX 79603-7125

BOOTH, ROBERT HARRISON, association executive; b. Wichita, Kans., Oct. 30, 1932; s. Arch N. and Wilma G. (Harrison) B.; m. Barbara DeLapp, July 17, 1954; children: Susan, Robert Jr. BA, Duke U., 1954. Pres., CEO Durham (N.C.) C. of C.; sales adminstr. ALCOA, Atlanta and Charlotte, N.C., 1957-60; civic affairs mgr. Charlotte C. of C., 1960-65; exec. v.p. Durham (N.C.) C. of C., 1965-89, pres., CEO, 1990—. Mem. U.S. C. of C. Execs., So. C. of C. Execs., N.C. C. of C. (pres.), Rotary (pres. 1994). Republican. Presbyterian. Office: Greater Durham C of C PO Box 3829 Durham NC 27702-3829

BOOTH, RONNIE LEE, college official, educator; b. Aiken, S.C., June 27, 1955; s. Dewey Harvie and Hazel Sylvia (Strickland) B.; m. Sara Lorraine Merriett, Aug. 9, 1980; children: Erin Marie, Ashley Riane. BS, U. S.C., 1976; MA in Christian Edn., Gordon-Conwell Theol. Sem., South Hamilton, Mass., 1983; MEd, U. S.C., 1984, PhD, 1990. Dir. fin. aid Columbia (S.C.) Internat. U., 1984-86; fin. aid counselor Clemson (S.C.) U., 1986; asst. dir. fin. aid U. S.C., Columbia, 1986-87; from dir. fin. aid to dean students Aiken Tech. Coll., 1988-92; dir. admissions & enrollment mgmt. Gordon-Conwell Theol. Sem., 1992-94; v.p. student affairs and continuing edn., asst. prof. Piedmont Coll., Demorest, Ga., 1994—. Elder Presbyn. Ch. Am., 1988—; mem. S.C. Rep. Party, Aiken, 1991-92. Mem. Am. Assn. Collegiate Registrars and Admissions Officers, Nat. Assn. Student Pers. Adminstrs., Rotary, Phi Delta Kappa. Office: Piedmont Coll 165 Central Ave Demorest GA 30535

BOOTH, ROSEMARY, management educator; b. New Rochelle, N.Y., Mar. 23, 1941; d. Robert Roche and Margaret Mary (Hogan) B. BA, Marquette U., 1962; MBA, Iona Coll., 1971; PhD, U. Ky., 1991. Sec. IBM, White Plains, N.Y., 1965-69; word processing mgr. IBM, N.Y.C., 1969-71; communications profl. IBM, Franklin Lakes, N.J., 1971-79; info. mgr. IBM, Lexington, Ky., 1979-89; IBM faculty loan Midway Coll., Lexington, Ky., 1988-89; asst. prof. U. N.C., Charlotte, 1991—; instr. United Way Leadership Devel. Program, Lexington, 1985-87. Bd. dirs. YWCA, Lexington, 1981-87, Vol. Ctr. Blue Grass, Lexington, 1986-90; adv. bd. Charlotte Vol.

Ctr., 1994-95. Mem. Acad. Mgmt., Speech Comm. Assn., Assn. Bus. Comm. Home: 9503 Marsena Ct Charlotte NC 28213-3760 Office: U NC Dept Mgmt Charlotte NC 28223

BOOTH, WENDY CHRISTINA, nursing educator; b. Montreal, Que., Can., Aug. 28, 1944; d. Lester John and Josephine Louise (Tock) B. Diploma, Montreal Gen. Hosp., 1966; BSN, U. Ala., Birmingham, 1985, MSN, 1988. RN, Ala. Staff nurse orthopedic, trauma unit Montreal Gen. Hosp., 1966-67; staff nurse pediatric unit Foothills Provincial Hosp., Calgary, Alta., Can., 1967-68; staff nurse pediatrics The Queen's Med. Ctr., Honolulu, 1969-71, staff nurse surg. ICU, open heart surgery unit, 1971-75, asst. head nurse, 1975-78, head nurse, 1978-83; staff, relief charge nurse surg. ICU U. Ala. Hosp., Birmingham, 1983-88, supplemental staff nurse, 1987-89, nursing case mgr. aftercare, 1988; nursing dir. for 5 counties Ala. Dept. Pub. Health Area III, Pelham, 1989-95; clin. instr. cmty. health nursing U. Ala., Birmingham, 1995—. Contbr. articles to profl. jours. Lt. comdr. USNR. Mem. ALPHA, AACN, ANA, Naval Res. Assn., U. Ala. Birmingham Alumnae Assn., Sigma Theta Tau (Nu chpt.). Home: 4109 Brookmont Dr Birmingham AL 35210-4102

BOOTHBY, MARK R., immunologist; b. Evanston, Ill., Aug. 16, 1955; s. William and Ruth Boothby; m. Jin Chen; 1 child, Ian Chen. BS, U. Wis., 1976; MD, Washington U., 1983, PhD in Molecular Biology, 1983. Intern in medicine U. Colo., Denver, 1983-84, resident in medicine, 1984-86; rsch. fellow med. sch. Harvard U., Boston, 1986-88, postdoctoral fellow sch. pub. health, 1986-89, instr. medicine, 1988-89, asst. prof. immunology sch. pub. health, asst. prof. medicine med. sch., 1990-92, rsch. assoc. dept. cancer biology, 1989; clin. fellow rheumatology Brigham and Women's Hosp., Boston, 1986-89, assoc. rheumatologist, 1989-92; asst. prof. immunology, asst. prof. medicine Vanderbilt U., Nashville, 1992—; mem. part time med. staff Vanderbilt U. Hosp., Nashville, 1992. Peer reviewer Immunity Jour. Immunology, Jour. Biol. Chemistry, Molecular and Cellular Biology, Oncogene; contbr. articles to profl. jours. Recipient Hilda Duggan arthritis investigator award Arthritis Found., 1989, 1st ind. rsch. support in transition award NIH, 1989; spl. fellow Leukemia Soc. A., 1991; Baxter scholar in immunology Baxter Found., 1992, scholar Leukemia Soc. Am., 1995, NIH RO1. Mem. AAAS, Am. Assn. Immunologists, Phi Beta Kappa, Alpha Omega Alpha. Office: Vanderbilt U Dept Microbiology and Immunology 1161 21st Ave S Nashville TN 37203

BOOTHE, LEON ESTEL, university president emeritus; b. Carthage, Mo., Feb. 1, 1938; s. Harold Estel and Merle Jane (Hood) B.; m. Nancy Janes, Aug. 20, 1960; children: Cynthia, Diana and Cheri (twins). B.S. (Curators' scholar), U. Mo., 1960, M.A., 1962; Ph.D. in History, U. Ill., 1966; LL.D. (hon.), Kyung Hee U., Korea, St. Thomas Inst. Advanced Study, 1985. Tchr. history Valparaiso (Ind.) High Sch., 1960-61; asst. prof. history U. Miss., Oxford, 1965-68; assoc. prof. U. Miss., 1968-70; assoc. prof. history George Mason Coll., U. Va. (now George Mason U.), Fairfax, 1970-73, prof. history, 1973-80, assoc. dean, 1970-71, dean, 1971-72, dean coll. arts and scis., 1972-80; provost, v.p. acad. affairs Ill. State U., Normal, 1980-83; pres. No. Ky. U., Highland Heights, 1983-96, pres. emeritus, 1996—; bd. dirs. Am. Assn. of State Colls. and Univs., 1990-93, chmn., 1993, Coun. Internat. Edn. Exchange, 1993, Jessie Stewart Found., 1990, Greater Cin. Consortium Colls. and Univs., 1988-91, Commn. on Internat. Edn. of Am. Coun. Edn., 1988—. Former mem. adv. bd. Cin. Coun. World Affairs; bd. trustees Cin.-Kharkiv Project, hon. mem., 1995-96; bd. dirs. Met. YMCA, Met. Cin. chpt. ARC, McLean County Heart Assn., McLean County United Way, INROADS/Cin., Inc., Nat. Conf. Christians and Jews, 1983—, Cin.'s Enjoy the Arts, 1988-90; vice chmn. No. Ky. United Way, chair, 1988; Greater Cin. YMCA; mem. steering com. Cin. Bicentennial; chmn. Multiple Sclerosis Soc. Gifts Campaign; mem. steering and exec. coms. Cin. Youth Collaborative; co-chair blue ribbon econ. devel. study No. Ky. Area Devel. Dist.; mem. Leukemia Soc.; bd. dirs. Greater Cin. Conv. and Visitor's Bur., 1989—; bd. dirs., mem. exec. com., vice-chair cmty. edn. svcs., 1989-90, Cin. chpt. ARC, Wood Hudson Cancer Rsch. Lab. Inc., 1987-92; chmn. Ky. Bicentnnial Com., 1990, chmn. steering com., 1992; chmn. Leadership Ky. Class; trustee Greater Cin. United Way and Cmty. Chest, 1991; steering com. greater Cin. summit on racism, 1994. NEH postdoctoral fellow, 1967-68; scholar Diplomat Seminars Dept. State; recipient Coll. Liberal Arts & Scis. award U. Ill., 1988, Alumni Coun. Pres.'s Spl. Recognition award No. Ky. U., 1989, Alumni award U. Mo., 1989, Walter R. Dunlevey Frontiersman award, 1994, Disting. Citizens Citation award NCCJ, Disting. Pub. Svc. award No. Ky. U. Found., 1995. Mem. Soc. Historians for Am. Fgn. Rels., McLean County Assn. for Commerce and Industry, Am. Assn. State Colls. and Univs. (internat. programs com. 1986—), No. Ky. C. of C. (Walter R. Dunlevey-Frontierman award 1994), Greater Cin. C. of C. (asst. sec.-treas. 1989), Rotary, Masons, Sigma Rho Sigma, Omicron Delta Kappa, Phi Alpha Theta, Phi Delta Kappa. Home: 1 University Blvd Highland Heights KY 41076-9010 Office: No Ky U Office of Pres 800 Ken Lucas Ctr Highland Heights KY 41099-8002

BOOTLE, WILLIAM AUGUSTUS, retired federal judge; b. Colleton County, S.C., Aug. 19, 1902; s. Philip Lorraine and Laura Lilla (Benton) B.; m. Virginia Childs, Nov. 24, 1928; children: William Augustus, Ann, James C. A.B., Mercer U., 1924, LL.B., 1925, LL.D., 1982. Bar: Ga. 1925. Since practiced in Macon; U.S. dist. atty. Middle Ga. Dist., 1929-33; mem. firm Carlisle & Bootle, 1933-54; acting dean Law Sch., Mercer U., 1933-37, part-time prof. law, 1928-43; judge U.S. Dist. Ct. for Middle Dist. Ga., Macon, 1954-81; sr. judge U.S. Dist. Ct. for Middle Dist. Ga., 1972-81. Trustee Mercer U., 1933-79, chmn. exec. com., 1941-46, 48-53, life trustee, 1994—; trustee Walter F. George Sch. Law Found., 1961—, v.p., 1963-64, 83-86, pres., 1964-66, 86-88. Recipient Disting. Alumnus award Mercer U., 1971, Disting. Alumnus award Walter F. George Sch. Law, 1986. Mem. Phi Alpha Delta, Phi Delta Theta. Republican. Baptist. Clubs: Masons, Shriners, Civitan (pres. 1936).

BOPP, CHARLES DANIEL, retired chemical engineer; b. Decatur, Ill., Feb. 4, 1923; s. Charles Daniel and Edna (Rybolt) B.; m. Mary Elizabeth McLeod, Mar. 24, 1971 (dec. Jan. 1992). BSChemE, Purdue U., 1944. Chemist Oak Ridge, Tenn., 1944-48; devel. engr. Oak Ridge Nat. Lab., Oak Ridge, 1948-92. Mem. AIChE, AAAS, Am. Chem. Soc., Am. Ceramic Soc., Am. Nuclear Soc. (reviewer nuclear tech.). Home: 72 Outer Dr Oak Ridge TN 37830 Office: ORNL PO Box X Oak Ridge TN 37830

BOPP, EMERY, art and design educator, artist, sculptor; b. Corry, Pa., May 13, 1924; s. Emery Jacob B. and Katherine Ann Woodward; m. Marian Edith Meyer, May 29, 1948; children: Sue Ann marie, Laurie Kay, Jay Morgan. Cert. Illustration, Pratt Inst., 1949; BFA, Yale U., 1951; student, Inst. Fine Arts, 1951-52; MFA, Rochester Inst. Tech., 1967. Prof. art Bob Jones U., Greenville, S.C., 1951-55, 94—, chmn. divsn. art, 1955-94, chmn. emeritas, 1994—; Co-founder, pres. bd. Hamptos III Gallery Ltd., Taylors, S.C., 1970—. With USNR, 1943-46. Recipient Best In Show Hunter Gallery Regional, Chatto, Tenn., 1966, Mus. Purchase award Greenville County Mus. Art, S.C., 1967, Select award Southeastern Regional H.S., Atlanta, 1970. Home: 10 Sennet Dr Greenville SC 29609 Office: Bob Jones U 1700 Wade Hampton Blvd Greenville SC 29614

BORCHARDT, DUKE, federal labor relations professional; b. Pinneberg, Germany, Mar. 29, 1941; came to the U.S., 1954; s. Karl Heinrich and Martha (Kreuzfeld) B.; m. Nancy Ann Saskas, Dec. 26, 1964; children: Lisa Marie Borchardt Baker, Marc. JD, La Salle U., 1968. Adminstrv. specialist N.Y. NG, Rocky Point, 1964-74, Fla. NG, Orlando, 1974-78; recruiting and retention specialist Fla. NG, St. Augustine, 1978-83, pers. mgmt. specialist, 1983, labor rels. mgr., 1983—; discipline and adverse action appeal hearing examiner Nat. Guard Bur., 1989—, chmn. labor rels. adv. coun., 1995—. Arbitrator 1st time juvenile offenders 7th Jud. Cir. State's Atty., St. Augustine, 1984—, guardian ad litem, 1989—, vice chair, 1992—; bd. dirs. St. Johns County Blood Bank, St. Augustine, 1994—; vice chair St. Johns County Juvenile Justice Com., St. Augustine, 1994—; mem. mental health/substance abuse adv. com. St. Johns County, 1988—, mem. health & human svcs. adv. coun., 1995—. Republican. Roman Catholic. Home: 7 Grandview Rd Saint Augustine FL 32084-5339 Office: Fla NG Saint Francis Barracks PO Box 1008 Saint Augustine FL 32085-1008

BORCHARDT, PAUL DOUGLAS, recreational executive; b. Osage, Iowa, Nov. 2, 1942; s. Raymond E. and Olive M. (Johnson) B.; m. Paula Ruth Roads, June 8, 1965; children: Rebecca, Kristen, Keira, Paige. BBA, U. Okla., 1965; MBA, West Tex. State U., 1973. Gen. mgr., pres. Wonderland Amusements Inc., Amarillo, Tex., 1969—; pres. Borchardt's Coin Machines Inc., Amarillo, 1969—; owner Buffalo Nickel Family Fun Inc., 1996—. Bd. dirs. Panhandle Hotel/Motel Assn., Amarillo, 1982-86, Tex. War on Drugs, 1993-96; mem. fin. adv. bd. Golden Spread coun. Boy Scouts Am., 1993-94; founding bd. dirs. Amarillo Drug Task Force, 1993. Mem. Internat. Assn. Amusement Parks and Attractions (bd. dirs. 1983-87, 88-91, chmn. pub. rels. com. 1986, fin. com. 1994-95, sustaining fin. com. 1994), Amusement Music Operators Am., Amusement Music Operators Tex. (v.p. 1987-88, pres. 1988-90), Am. Mktg. Assn. (bd. dirs. Amarillo chpt. 1987-88), Amarillo C. of C. (chmn. conv. and tourism coun. 1988-90, exec. bd. 1989, Community Asset award 1989, Vol. of the Yr. award 1990, bus. com. of C. of C., 1994-96), Amarillo Exec. Assn. (pres. 1979-80, treas. 1977-78), Rotary (chmn. art show 1990, bd. dirs. 1992-95), Rotary Club Amarillo (pres. 1994-95). Democrat. Lutheran. Home: 3915 Kileen Dr Amarillo TX 79109-3921 Office: Wonderland Amusements Inc PO Box 2325 Amarillo TX 79105-2325

BORCHERS, KAREN LILY, child welfare administrator; b. Detroit, Apr. 4, 1940; d. Albert Oscar and Lily Louise (Denzler) B. BA in Psychology and Sociology, Mich. State U., 1961; AM in Social Svc. Adminstrn., U. Chgo., 1964; MS in Spl. Edn. Adminstrn., No. Ill. U., 1976; EdD in Early Childhood Edn./Adminstrn., Nova U., 1982. Cert. social worker. Child welfare worker Ill. Dept. Children & Family Svcs., Rockford, 1962-65; sch. social worker Komarek Schs., N. Riverside, Ill., 1965-67; exec. dir. Seguin Sch., Berwyn, Ill., 1967-72, Seguin Tng. Ctr., Cicero, Ill., 1967-72; adminstr. Orchard Hill, Madison, Wis., 1972-76; exec. dir. Children's Home Soc. Fla., West Palm Beach, 1976—; pres. Pathways to Growth, Inc., West Palm Beach, 1986—. Pres., founder Masterworks Chorus of the Palm Beaches, West Palm Beach, 1978—, Teen Musical Theatre, Inc., West Palm Beach, 1984—, Internat. Children's Chorus of the Palm Beaches, West Palm Beach, 1988-90; pres. Palm Beach Regional Achievement Ctr., West Palm Beach, 1979-84. Recipient Excellence in Health and Social Svcs. award Palm Beach County Commn., 1979. Mem. NASW, Civitan, Mensa. Home: 11984 Suellen Cir West Palm Beach FL 33414-6274 Office: Childrens Home Soc Fla 3600 Broadway West Palm Beach FL 33407-4844

BORDEAUX, PIERRE WILLIAM HARRISTON (PETER BORDEAUX), beverage alcohol company executive; b. Neptune, N.J., Aug. 1, 1948; s. Robert Joseph and Nell Mae (Harriston) B.; m. Mary Marta King, Dec. 13, 1980; children: Pierre W.H. Jr., Charles Parker C. BS, Cornell U., 1970; JD, Tulane U., 1974. Bar: La., 1974, U.S. Dist. Ct. (ea. dist.) 1975. Fin. analyst First Commerce Corp., New Orleans, 1974-75; project mgr. mayor's office policy planning and analysis City of New Orleans, 1975; v.p. mktg. Gulf Consol. Internat., Inc., Houston, 1975-76; pvt. practice cons. mktg. and fin. Houston, 1976, New Orleans, 1979-80; spl. asst. to pres. Tulane U., New Orleans, 1976-80; exec. v.p., gen. mgr., pres., chief exec. officer Sazerac Co., Inc., New Orleans, 1980—; owner, chmn. bd. dirs. Bailey Lumber Co., Bluefield, W.Va., 1986-89; pres. PWB Corp., New Orleans, 1986-89, Peter Bordeaux and Co., New Orleans, 1986—; mem. dean's coun. Tulane Law Sch.; adj. prof. Tulane Bus. Sch.; chmn. Hibernia Nat. Bank Internat. Adv. Bd., Am. Craft Brewing Internat., 1996—. Bd. dirs. Japan Garden Soc., New Orleans, Japan-L.A. Friendship Found.; chmn. Ambrew Internat., Bermuda. Mem. ABA, La. Bar Assn., Keepers of Quaich (Scotland), Kingussie Golf Club (Scotland), Hurlingham Club (London), New Orleans Country Club, World Trade Assn. (bd. dirs.), Nat. Assn. Beverage Importers (bd. dirs.). Republican. Episcopalian. Office: Sazerac Co Inc PO Box 52821 New Orleans LA 70152-2821

BORDELON, ALVIN JOSEPH, JR., lawyer; b. New Orleans, Nov. 1, 1945; s. Alvin Joseph and Mildred (Quarella) B.; m. Brigid Catherine Hannon Burns (div.); m. Selma Elizabeth Schmidt, Nov. 8, 1975; children: Peter Jude, Emily Aprill. BA in English, U. New Orleans, 1968; JD, Loyola U., New Orleans, 1973. Bar: La. 1973, U.S. Ct. Appeals (5th cir.) 1975, U.S. Supreme Ct. 1983. Landman Chevron Oil Co., New Orleans, 1973-74; pvt. practice New Orleans, 1974-75; ptnr. Douglas, Favre & Bordelon, New Orleans, 1975-76, Monroe & Lemann, New Orleans, 1976-81; sr. ptnr. Bordelon, Hamlin & Theriot, New Orleans, 1981—; labor negotiator St. Tammany Parish Sch. Bd., Covington, La., 1991—, St. Bernard Parish Sch. Bd., Chalmette, La., 1986—; instr. criminal justice Loyola City Coll., 1975-76, Loyola U. Sch. Law, 1976-77. Mng. editor Loyola Law Rev., 1972-73. Chmn. Alcoholic Beverage Control Bd., New Orleans, 1983-84; mem. Mayor's Commn. on Crime, New Orleans, 1979; pres. Faubourg St. John Neighborhood Assn., New Orleans, 1977-80. With U.S. Army, 1968-70. Recipient Outstanding Civic Leadership award La. State Senate, Baton Rouge, 1982; named Short Story Competition 1st Place winner Writer's Digest, 1993. Mem. Profl. Assn. of Dive Instrs., La. Bar Assn. Republican. Roman Catholic. Office: Bordelon Hamlin & Theriot 701 S Peters St New Orleans LA 70130

BORDEN, EUGENE OWEN, software engineer; b. Muncie, Ind., Mar. 8, 1959; s. Mitchell Petrick Jr. and Freda Eileen (Smith) B.; m. Mary Elizabeth McCarter, Aug. 7, 1993; children: Christopher Lee, Samuel Eugene, Hannah Elyse. BA in Computer Sci., U. Tenn., 1987, MBA in Mgmt., 1993. Engring. programmer CTI Pet Systems, Knoxville, Tenn., 1987-88; software engr. CTI Pet Systems, Knoxville, 1988-92, quality assurance software engr., 1992-94; validation and verification specialist Perceptics Westinghouse Corp., Knoxville, 1994-95; project mgr. Perceptics Northrop Grumman, Knoxville, 1995-96, product mgr., 1996—; chmn. employee recognition com. CTI Pet Sys., Knoxville, 1991-93. Bd. dirs. Spl. Olympics, Knoxville, 1991-93; panel mem. allocations com. United Way, Knoxville, 1992—, mem. nominating com., 1994—. Mem. Assn. for Computing Machinery, Assn. for Software Design. Republican. Mormon. Home: 1133 Sanders Rd Knoxville TN 37923-2036 Office: Perceptics Northrop Grumman 725 Pellissippi Pky Knoxville TN 37932-3322

BORDEN, WILLIAM HENRY, lawyer; b. Wilmington, Del., Mar. 14, 1954; s. James Benjamin and Rita Hattie (Doerrmann) B.; m. Ann Caroline Adams, Dec. 30, 1978; children: Caroline, James. BA in Biology and Psychology, U. N.C., 1976, JD, 1980. Bar: N.C. 1980, Calif. 1987. Assoc. atty. gen. N.C. Atty. Gen.'s Office, Goldsboro, 1980-83; asst. atty. gen. N.C. Atty. Gen.'s Office, Morganton, 1987-91, Raleigh, 1991—. Maj. USMC, 1983-87; mem. USMCR, 1987—. Office: NC Dept Justice PO Box 629 Raleigh NC 27609

BOREHAM, ROLAND STANFORD, JR., electric motor company executive; b. L.A., Sept. 2, 1924; s. Roland S. and Anita K. (Brown) B.; m. Judith P. Boreham; children: Debra Rhea, Anita Katherine. B.A. in Physics, UCLA, 1947, postgrad., 1951-54; PhD (hon.), U. Ozarks, 1986, U. Oklahoma City, 1991. Ptnr. R.S. Boreham & Co. (mfr.'s rep. for Baldor Electric Co.), L.A., 1948-61; v.p. sales Baldor Electric Co., Ft. Smith, Ark., 1961-70, exec. v.p., 1970-75, pres., 1975-81, chief exec. officer, chmn. bd., 1975—. Trustee U. Ozarks, Clarksville, Ark., 1981—, Sparks Regional Med. Ctr., Ft. Smith, 1981—; dir. United Way, Ft. Smith, 1984-87, Gov.'s Commn. on Literacy, Little Rock, 1989—. 1st lt. USAAF, 1943-46, PTO. Mem. Am. Bus. Conf. (bd. dirs.). Republican. Presbyterian. Office: Baldor Electric Co 5711 S 7th St Fort Smith AR 72901

BOREN, DAVID LYLE, academic administrator; b. Washington, DC, Apr. 21, 1941; s. Lyle H. and Christine (McKown) B.; m. Molly Shi, Dec. 1977; children: David Daniel, Carrie Christine. B.A. summa cum laude, Yale, 1963; M.A. (Rhodes scholar), Oxford (Eng.) U., 1965; J.D. (Bledsoe Meml. prize as outstanding law grad.), U. Okla., 1968. Bar: Okla. 1968. Asst. to dir. liaison Office Civil and Def. Moblzn., Washington, 1960-62; propaganda analyst Soviet affairs USIA, Washington, 1962-63; mem. Speakers Bur. Am. Embassy, London, Eng., 1963-65; mem. residential counseling staff U. Okla., 1965-66; practiced in Seminole, 1968-74; prof. polit. sci., chair divsn. social scis. Okla. Bapt. U., Shawnee, 1969-74; mem. Okla. Ho. of Reps., 1967-75; gov. Okla., 1975-79; mem. U.S. Senate from Okla., 1979-94; pres. U. Okla., Norman, 1994—; mem. Senate Fin. Com., Senate Agrl. Com.; chmn. Senate Select Com. on Intelligence, govt. dept. Okla. Bapt. U., 1969-74. Del. Dem. Nat. Conv., 1968, 76, 84, 88; trustee Yale U., 1989. Named One of 10 Outstanding Young Men in U.S., U.S. Jaycees, 1967. Mem. Assn. U.S. Rhodes Scholars, Phi Beta Kappa. Methodist. Office: U Okla 660 Parrington Oval Norman OK 73019-3070

BOREN, EDWARD DANIEL, priest; b. Indpls., Sept. 2, 1936; s. Edward Daniel and Mary Ann (Foreman) B. BA in Philosophy and Psychology, Quincy Coll., 1960; STB in Theology, Antonianum (Rome), Teutopolis, Ill., 1964; MA in Math. Edn., U. Tex., San Antonio, 1978. Ordained priest Roman Cath. Ch., 1964. Tchr., math. dept. head, registrar Hales Franciscan High Sch., Chgo., 1965-74; tchr., dept. head St. Francis Acad., San Antonio, 1974-85; pastor Sacred Heart Ch., Von Ormy, Tex., 1976-86; tchr. Holy Cross/St. Gerard, San Antonio, 1986-88; asst. pastor, tchr. St. Joseph's, San Antonio, 1988-89; pastor Sacred Heart Ch., Falfurrias, Tex., 1989-90, Our Lady of Guadalupe, Bay City, Tex., 1990—; advisor St. Joseph's Sch., 1988-89. Moderator Medina River Watershed Coalition, Von Ormy, 1982-85. Mem. Nat. Coun. Tchrs. of Math, Assn. for Supervision and Curriculum Devel., Math. Assn. Am. Roman Catholic. Home: 1412 12th St Bay City TX 77414-3834 Office: Our Lady of Guadalupe 1412 12th St Bay City TX 77414-3834

BOREN, LYNDA SUE, gifted education educator; b. Leesville, La., Apr. 1, 1941; d. Leonard and Doris (Ford) Schoenberger; m. James Lewis Boren, Sept. 1, 1961; 1 child, Lynda Carolyn. BA, U. New Orleans, 1971, MA, 1973; PhD, Tulane U., 1979. Prof. Northwestern State U., Natchitoches, La., 1987-89; propr. Colony Country House, New Llano, La., 1992-94; tchr. of gifted Leesville (La.) H.S., 1992—; vis. prof. Newcomb Coll., Tulane U., New Orleans, 1979-83, U. Erlangen-Nuremburg, Germany, 1981-82, Middlebury (Vt.) Coll., 1983-84, Ga. Inst. Tech., Atlanta, 1985-87, Srinakharinwirot U., Bangkok, 1989-90; mem. planning com. 1st Kate Chopin Internat. Conf., Natchitoches, La., 1987-89; Fulbright lectr. USIA and Bd. Fgn. Scholars, 1981-82, 89-90. Author: Eurydice Reclaimed: Language, Gender and Voice in Henry James, 1989; co-editor, author: Kate Chopin Reconsidered, 1992; contbr. numerous articles to profl. jours. Founding mem. John F. Kennedy libr. Recipient awards for watercolors; Mellon fellow Tulane U., 1977-78; NEH seminar fellow Princeton U., 1986. Mem. MLA, AAUW, DAR, IPA, Fulbright Alumni Assn., Women in the Arts, Art Guild, Audubon Soc. Democrat. Home: 1492 Ford's Dairy Rd New Llano LA 71461

BOREN, WILLIAM MEREDITH, manufacturing executive; b. San Antonio, Oct. 23, 1924; s. Thomas Loyd and Verda (Locke) B.; m. Molly Brasfield Sarver, Dec. 3, 1976; children: Susan, Patricia, Janet, Jenny, Burton, Cliff. Student, Tex. A&M U., 1942-43, Rice U., 1943-44; B.S. in Mech. Engring., Tex. U., 1949. Vice pres., gen. mgr. Rolo Mfg. Co., Houston, 1949-54; mgr. sales engring. Black, Sivalls & Bryson, Houston, Oklahoma City, 1955-64; vice chmn., dir., mem. exec. com. Big Three Industries, Inc., Houston, 1965—; chmn. Bowen Tool Co., Houston.; bd. dirs. Engring. Adv. Coun., Tex. U.; dir. Air Liquide Am. Corp.; dir. Electric Reliability Coun. Tex. Inventor Classic Bridge game. Trustee S.W. Rsch. Inst., San Antonio; bd. dirs. Coun. Econ. Edn.; mem. chancellor's coun. U. Tex. Lt. (j.g.) USN, 1943-46. Named Disting. Grad. Engring. Dept., U. Tex., 1992. Mem. Internat. Oxygen Mfrs. Assn. (chmn.), French-Am. C. of C. (bd. dirs.), Tau Beta Pi, Pi Tau Sigma. Republican. Home: 2906 Midlane St Houston TX 77027-4912 Office: Air Liquide Am Corp 3535 W 12th St PO Box 3047 Houston TX 77253-3047

BORG, JOSEPH PHILIP, lawyer; b. N.Y.C., Nov. 20, 1952; s. Philip Joseph and Dorothy Ann (Chircop) B.; widowed; 1 child, Chelly. BS in Polit. Sci., CCNY, 1974; JD, Hofstra U., 1977. Bar: N.Y. 1978, Ala. 1978, Fla. 1979, U.S. Dist. Ct. (no. dist.) Ala., U.S. Dist. Ct. (mid. dist.) Ala., U.S. Dist. Ct. (no. dist.) Fla., U.S. Dist. Ct. (mid. dist.) Fla., U.S. Ct. Appeals (5th cir.), U.S. Ct. Appeals (11th cir.), U.S. Supreme Ct. Asst. corp. counsel Hagan Industries, Inc., Montgomery, Ala., 1977-79; corp. counsel, legal officer First Ala. Bank of Montgomery, 1979-85; pntr. Capouano, Wampold, Prestwood & Sansone, P.A., Montgomery, 1985-94; dir. Ala. Securities Commn., Montgomery, AL, 1994—; prof. law uniform comml. code Faulkner U.; lectr. Jones Bar Review Course, Ala. Continuing Ed. Program. Bd. dirs. Consumer Credit Counseling Svc. of Ala., Inc., 1981-85, pres. , 1982-84; bd. dirs. Ala. Youth Found., 1982-85, programs chmn., 1983-84. Mem. ABA, N.Y. State Bar Assn., Ala. State Bar Assn., Fla. State Bar Assn., Am. Trial Lawyers Assn., N.Y. Trial Lawyers Assn., Montgomery County Bar Assn., Montgomery County Trial Lawyers Assn., Montgomery County Young Lawyers Assn. (sec. 1984, v.p. 1985), N.Y. Acad. Sci. Home: 2656 Woodley Rd Montgomery AL 36111-2835 Office: Ala Securities Commn 770 Washington St Ste 570 Montgomery AL 36104-3816

BORGER, JAMES ANDREW, pediatric surgeon; b. Nashville, Nov. 10, 1942; s. Bruno and Marianne B.; m. Lisa Sharp, Dec. 2, 1972; children: Christopher Longstreth, Ashley Field, Joshua Cady. BA, Vanderbilt U., 1964; Md, U. Tenn., 1968. Diplomate Am. Bd. Surgery with spl. competence in pediatric surgery. Pediatric surgeon pvt. practice, Boston, 1977-83; chmn. surgery All Children's Hosp., St. Petersburg, Fla., 1983-89; assoc. surgeon in chief Nemonrs Children's Clinic, Jacksonville, Fla., 1989-95; chief divsn. pediatric surgery Nemours Children's Clinic, Jacksonville, Fla., 1995—. Contbr. numerous articles to profl. jours. Bd. dirs. Bapt. Health System Found., Jacksonville, 1990—; mem. community bd. Am. Cancer Soc., Jacksonville, 1990—. Mem. ACS, Am. Pediatric Surg. Assn., Am. Acad. Pediatrics, Rotary Club South Jacksonville, Timmuquana Country Club. Republican. Home: 1880 Shadowlawn St Jacksonville FL 32205-9430 Office: Nemonrs Childrens Clinic 807 Nira St Jacksonville FL 32207-8426

BORGKVIST, JOSEPH, JR., minister; b. Portsmouth, N.H., Jan. 13, 1944; s. Joseph Sr. Borgkvist and Virginia Mae (Moulton) Roy; m. Jo-Ann Marie Fenn, Aug. 19, 1967; children: Joseph Christian, Rebecca Ann. A of Div. Pastoral Ministry, New Orleans Bapt. Theol. Sem., 1978. Ordained to ministry So. Bapt. Conv., 1971. Min. of youth and edn. Northside Bapt. Ch., Valdosta, Ga., 1978-80; assoc. pastor, min. edn. White Oak Bapt. Ch., Greenville, S.C., 1980-83; pastor Hillside Bapt. Ch., Fountain Inn, S.C., 1983-85; min. edn. First Bapt. Ch., West Columbia, S.C., 1985-87; assoc. pastor, min. edn. West Side Bapt. Ch., West Columbia, 1987-92; ch. devel. dir. Lexington (S.C.) Bapt. Assn., 1992—; minister edn./adminstrn. Lake Murray Bapt. Ch., Lexington, 1992-94; pastor Northwood Bapt. Ch., Lexington, 1994—; conf. leader S.C. Bapt. Conv., Columbia, 1983—, Sun. Sch. growth specialist, 1983—, youth retreat speaker, 1977—, ASSISTeam dir. Lexington (S.C.) Bapt. Assn., 1988—. Contbr. (book) 100 Great Growth Ideas, 1990; contbr. articles to profl. jours. Com. mem. Adv. com. to S.C. Dept. of Youth Svcs. Trustees, Columbia, 1987—; founder, chmn. bd. dirs. REACH Inc., West Columbia, S.C. With U.S. Army, 1964-67, Vietnam. Named Outstanding Direct Svc. Vol. of Yr. S.C. Dept. Youth Svcs., 1987. Mem. Religious Edn. and Music Assn. (pres. 1989-90), S.C. Bapt. religious Edn. Assn. (v.p. 1987-88, pres. 1988-89). Home: 1715 B Ave West Columbia SC 29169-5603 Office: Northwood Baptist Church 5236 Sunset Blvd Lexington SC 29072

BORKAN, WILLIAM NOAH, biomedical electronics company executive; b. Miami Beach, Fla., Apr. 29, 1956; s. Martin Solomon and Annabelle (Hoffman) B.; m. Vivienne Eliane; children: Martin and Kenneth. Student, Carnegie Mellon U., 1977; PhD, Sussex Coll. Tech., 1979; married. Tech., Dominicks' Radio & TV Co., Miami Beach, 1971-74; computer programmer Mt. Sinai Hosp., Miami Beach, 1973-74; chief studio engr. WGMA, Hollywood, Fla., 1973-74; disc. jockey WBUS-FM, Miami Beach, 1974; chief rec. engr. Dukoff Recording Studios', Miami, 1974-75; rec. studio design and constrn. TSI, Hollywood, Fla., 1975-77; chief design engr. Lumonics Co., Miami, 1974; svc. mgr. 21st Century Electronics Co., Miami, 1975; lab. tech. Carnegie-Mellon U.; mgr. Tech. Electronics Co., Pitts., 1976; pres. Borktronics Co. Miami, 1974-84; cons. specialist in neurobiometrics St. Barnabas Hosp., N.Y.C., 1978-83; rec. studio designer FXL Studios, Sunrise, Fla., 1978; pres., CEO Electronic Diagnostics, Inc., 1978-83, pres., CEO NeuroMed, Inc., 1980-95, Nice Tech., Inc., 1989-96, Electrovest, 1996—; pres. Master Angler, Inc., 1990—; mem. coll. curricular coms. E.E. Dept. Grantee Carnegie Corp. and Carnegie Mellon U. Named Fla. Inc. Mag. Entrepreneur of Yr., 1992. Mem. Am. Soc. Heating, Refrigeration and Air Conditioning Engrs., Assn. Energy Engrs., Soc. Automotive Engrs., Assn. for Advancement Med. Instrumentation, AAAS, N.Y. Acad. Scis., Audio Engring. Soc. Author publs. in field; various U.S. and fgn. patents in energy and healthcare fields. Home: 3364 NE 167th St Miami FL 33160-3850 Office: Electrovest 12000 Biscayne Blvd Ste 502 Miami FL 33181

BORKOSKY, BRUCE GLENN, psychologist; b. Anchorage, Nov. 5, 1954; s. Glenn Edson and Gwendolyn (Copening) B. BA, Ohio Wesleyan U.,

1978; MS, U. Dayton, 1984, Miami (Fla.) Inst. Psychology, 1990; D in Psychology, Miami (Fla.) Inst. Psychology, 1992. Cert. hypnotherapist. Mgr. Domino's Pizza, Raleigh, N.C., 1978-81; computer programmer GMAC, Dayton, 1981-84; planner IBM Corp., Boca Raton, Fla., 1984-91; counseling intern Ctr. For Group Counseling, Delray Beach, Fla., 1991—; pvt. practice, 1994-95; bd. dirs. Word Mastering, Inc., Delray Beach, Fla.; pres. Pers. Devel., Boynton Beach, Fla.; instr. Indian River C.C., 1993—. Landmark edn. therapist on-call, 1993—; psychologist Eckerd Youth Devel. Ctr., 1993—, Okeechobee Counseling Ctr., 1994—. Mem. APA, IEEE, Assn. Computing Machinery, Am. Assn. Individual Investors, Fla. Psychol. Assn., Mensa, Psi Chi. Home: 6209 Country Fair Cir Boynton Beach FL 33437-2808 Office: PO Box 2828 Okeechobee FL 34973-2828

BORLAUG, NORMAN ERNEST, agricultural scientist; b. Cresco, IA, Mar. 25, 1914; s. Henry O. and Clara (Vaala) B.; m. Margaret G. Gibson, Sept. 24, 1937; children: Norma Jean (Mrs. Richard H. Rhoda), William Gibson. BS in Forestry, U. Minnesota, Minneapolis, 1937, MS in Plant Pathology, 1940, PhD in Plant Pathology, 1941; ScD (honoris causa), Punjab (India) Agrl. U., 1969, Kanpur U., India, Royal Norwegian Agrl. Coll., Luther Coll., 1970, Michigan State U., U. de la Plata, Argentina, Uttar Pradesh Agrl. U., India, 1971; Sc.D. (honoris causa), U. Arizona, Phoenix, 1972, U. Florida, 1973, U. Católica de Chile, 1974, U. Hohenheim, Germany, 1976, U. Agr., Lyallpur, Faisalabad, Pakistan, 1978, Columbia U., N.Y.C., 1980, Ohio State U., Columbus, 1981, U. Minnesota, Minneapolis, 1982, U. Notre Dame, 1987, Oreg. State U., 1988, U. Tulsa, 1991; L.H.D., Gustavus Adolphus Coll., 1971, Iowa State U., 1992; LL.D. (hon.), New Mexico State U., 1973; D. of Agriculture (hon.), Tufts U., 1982; D. of Agricultural Sciences (hon.), U. Agricultural Sciences, Hungary, 1980, Tokyo U. Agriculture, 1981; D. Agricultural Sciences (hon.), U. Nacional Pedro Henriques Turena, Dominican Republic, U. Cen. del Estes, Dominican Republic, 1983; D. Honoris Causa, U. Mayor de San Simón, Bolivia, U. de Buenos Aires, 1983, U. de Cordoba, Spain, U. Politécnica de Catalunya, Barcelon, Spain, 1986, Colegio Postgraduadas, Mexico, 1990; Rector U. Dubuque, 1992-93; honoris causa, U. Studi de Bologna, Italy, 1991, Warsaw Agrl. U., Poland, 1993. With U.S. Forest Service, 1935-38; instr. U. Minn., 1941; microbiologist E.I. DuPont de Nemours, 1942-44; research scientist in charge wheat improvement Coop. Mexican Agrl. Program, Mexican Ministry Agr. Rockefeller Found., Mexico, 1944-60; assoc. dir. assigned to Inter-Am. Food Crop Program Rockefeller Found., 1960-63; dir. wheat research and prodn. program Internat. Maize and Wheat Improvement Ctr., Mexico City, 1964-79; cons. Internat. Maize and Wheat Improvement Ctr., 1980—; disting. prof. agricultural sciences TexasA & M Univ, College Station, Tex.; cons., collaborator Inst. Nacional de Investigationes Agricolas, Mexican Ministry Agr., 1960-64; cons. FAO, North Africa and Asia, 1960; ex-officio cons. wheat research and prodn. problems to govts. in Latin Am., Africa, Asia, 1960—; mem. Citizen's Commn. on Sci., Law and Food Supply, 1973, Commn. Critical Choices for Am., 1973, Council Agr. Sci. and Tech., 1973—, Presdl. Commn. on World Hunger U.S.A., 1978-79, Presdl. Coun. Advisers Sci and Tech., 1990-93; dir. Population Crisis Com., 1971-92; asesor especial Fundacion para Estudios de la Poblacion A.C., Mexico, 1971-80; mem. adv. council Renewable Natural Resources Found., 1973; A.D. White Disting. prof.-at-large Cornell U., 1983-85; Disting. prof. Internat. Agr., Dept. Soil & Crop Scis., Tex. A&M U., Jan.-May, 1984—; adj. prof. dept. biology Emory U., Atlanta, 1991-92; advisor The Population Inst., U.S.A., 1978; bd. trustees Winrock Internat. U.S.A.; life fellow Rockefeller Found., 1983—. Recipient Disting. Service awards Wheat Producers Assns., and state govts. Mexican States of Guanajuato, Queretaro, Sonora, Tlaxcala and Zacatecas, 1954-60; Recognition award Agrl. Inst. Can., 1966; Recognition award Instituto Nacional de Tecnologia Agropecuaria de Marcos Juarez, Argentina, 1968; Sci. Service award El Colegio de Ingenieros Agronomos de Mexico, 1970; Outstanding Achievement award U. Minn., 1959; E.C. Stakman award, 1961; named Uncle of Paul Bunyan, 1969; recipient Disting. Citizen award Cresco Centennial Com., 1966; Nat. Disting. Service award Am. Agrl. Editors Assn., 1967; Genetics and Plant Breeding award Nat. Council Comml. Plant Breeders, 1968; Star of Distinction Govt. of Pakistan, 1968; citation and street named in honor Citizens of Sonora and Rotary Club, 1968; Internat. Agronomy award Am. Soc. Agronomy, 1968; Distinguished Service award Wheat Farmers of Punjab, Haryana and Himachal Pradesh, 1969; Nobel Peace prize, 1970; Diploma de Merito El Instituto Tecnologico y de Estudios Superiores de Monterrey, Mexico, 1971; medalla y Diploma de Merito Antonio Narro Escuela Superior de Agricultura de la U. de Coahuila, Mexico, 1971; Diploma de Merito Escuela Superior de Agricultura Hermanos Escobar, Mexico, 1973; award for service to agr. Am. Farm Bur. Fedn., 1971; Outstanding Agrl. Achievement award World Farm Found., 1971; Medal of Merit Italian Wheat Scientists, 1971; Service award for outstanding contbn. to alleviation of world hunger 8th Latin Am. Food Prodn. Conf., 1972; Nat. award for Agrl. Excellence in Sci. Nat. Agri-Mktg. Assn., 1982, Disting. Achievement award Council for Agrl. Scis. and Tech., 1982; inaugural lectr., medal recipient Dr. S.B. Hendrick's Meml. Lectureship., 1981, other honored lecturships; named to Halls of Fame Oreg. State U. Agrl., 1981, Agrl. Nat. Ctr., Bonner Springs, Kans., 1984, Scandinavian-Am., U.S.A., 1986, Nat. Wrestling, 1992; dedicated in his name Norman E. Borlaug Centro de Capitación y Formación de Agrs., Santa Cruz, Bolivia, 1983, Borlaug Hall U. Minn., 1985, Borlaug Bldg. Internat. Maize and Wheat Improvement Ctr., 1986; numerous other honors and awards from govts., ednl. instns., citizens groups. Hon. fellow Indian Soc. Genetics and Plant Breeding; mem. Nat. Acad. Sci., Am. Soc. Agronomy (1st Internat. Service award 1960, 1st hon. life mem.), Am. Assn. Cereal Chemists (hon. life mem., Meritorious Service award 1969), Crop Sci. Soc. Am. (hon. life mem.), Soil Sci. Soc. Am. (hon. life mem.), Sociedad de Agronomia do Rio Grande do Sul Brazil (hon.), India Nat. Sci. Acad. (fgn.), Royal Agrl. Soc. Eng. (hon.), Royal Soc. Edinburgh (hon.), Hungarian Acad. Sci. (hon.), Royal Swedish Acad. Agr. and Forestry (fgn.), Academia Nacional de Agronomia y Veterinaria (Argentina), Sasakaws African Assn. (pres. 1986—); hon. academician N.I. Vavilov Acad. Agrl. Scis. Lenin Order (USSR.), Am. Council on Sci. and Health (trustee 1978—), Internat. Food Policy Research Inst. (trustee 1976-82), Royal Soc. Eng., Chinese Acad. Agrl. Sci., 1994. Home: 15611 Ranchita Dr Dallas TX 75248-4982 Office: Tex A&M U Dept Soil & Crop Science College Station TX 77843*

BORLEIS, HERBERT WILLIAM, pharmaceutical company executive; b. Balt., Sept. 5, 1937; s. Herbert Henry and Elmyra Elizabeth (Feuchter) B.; m. Patricia Ann Allen, Mar. 28, 1964; children: Robyn, David, H. William. AB, Transylvania U., 1960. Asst. v.p. personnel and pub. relations Chevron Oil, Perth Amboy, N.J., 1960-66; sales analyst Squibb Corp., N.Y.C., 1966-68; market research analyst Winthrop Labs, N.Y.C., 1968-69; sr. market analyst Beecham, Bristol, Tenn., 1969-73; mgr. mktg. research Bristol-Myers, Syracuse, N.Y., 1973-81; v.p., gen. mgr., dir. strategic planning Rorer Group div. Kremers-Urban Co., Inc., Port Washington, Wis., 1981-86; pres. Kremers-Urban Co., Milw., 1986—, also bd. dirs.; founder, pres. Procon Corp., Milw., 1988—; pres. Freedom Village, Milw., 1989—; bd. dirs. Friendship Living Cens., Inc., Brookfield; v.p. adminstrn. Friendship Village, Milw., 1987—. Patentee spl. drug delivery applicator, 1985. Active United Way, Syracuse, 1978, Milw., 1983-85, Nat. Ileitis and Colitus Found., Milw., 1984-85; elder Elmbrook Ch., Brookfield, Wis. Served with U.S. Army, 1961-63. Recipient Progress award Milw. United Way, 1983, Commendation award Nat. Ileitis and Colitis Found., 1984, 85, Wis. Gov.'s New Product award, 1987. Mem. Pharm. Mktg. Research Assn., Pharm. Mfg. Assn., Pharm. Research Group, Nat. Wholesale Druggist Assn., World Trade Info. Bur., Wis. Mfrs. and Commerce Assn. (mem. com. for gov. cost control), Milw. C. of C. Office: Kremers-Urban Co Inc 7300 W Dean Rd Milwaukee WI 53223-2637

BORN, ALLEN, mining executive; b. Durango, Colo., July 4, 1933; s. C. S. and Bertha G. (Tausch) B.; m. Patricia Beaubien, Mar. 23, 1953; children: Michael, Scott (dec.), Brett. B.S. in Metallurgy and Geology, U. Tex.-El Paso, 1958; D Engring. (hon.), Colo. Sch. Mines, 1992. Exploration geologist El Paso Natural Gas, Tex., 1958-60; metallurgist Vanadium Corp. Am., 1960-62; gen. foreman Pima Mining, 1962-64; asst. supt. MolyCorp, 1964-67; chief metallurgist and supt., mgr. AMAX Inc., N.Y.C., 1967-76; pres., chief exec. officer Can. Tungsten Mining Corp. Ltd., 1976-81; pres. AMAX of Can. Ltd., 1977-81; pres., chmn., chief exec. officer Placer Devel. Ltd., Vancouver, B.C., Can., 1981-85; pres., chief operating officer AMAX Inc., N.Y.C., 1985—, chief exec. officer, 1986—, chmn., 1988—; also bd. dirs.; chmn. bd., CEO Alumax Inc., 19936; bd. dirs. Amax Gold Inc., Internat. Primary Aluminum Inst., AK Steel Holding Corp.; chmn. Aluminum Assn.; co-chmn. bd. Cyprus Amax Minerals Co. Contbr. numerous articles to mining jours. Bd. trustees Robert W. Woodruff Arts Ctr. Served with U.S. Army, 1952-55. Named CEO of Yr. in mining industry, 1986, 91, 92, silver award all industry Fin. World Mag., 1986. Mem. AIME, Nat. Mining Assn., Sky Club, Vancouver Club, Atlanta Athletic Club. Republican. Office: ALUMAX 5655 Peachtree Pky Norcross GA 30092-2812*

BORN, ETHEL WOLFE, church worker; b. Kasson, W.Va., Jan. 6, 1924; d. Otto Guy and Nancy Grace (Nestor) Wolfe; m. Harry Edward Born, Apr. 4, 1944 (dec. Aug. 1992); children: Rosemary Ellen (dec.), Barbara Anne Born Craig. Student, Ecumenical Inst., Geneva, 1983; BA, Mary Baldwin Coll., 1991. Author: A Tangled Web--A Search for Answers to the Question of Palestine, 1989, By My Spirit, Methodist Protestant Women in Mission, 1879-1939, 1990; contbr. articles to religious publs. Va. pres. United Meth. Women, 1972-76; bd. dirs. United Meth. Gen. Bd. Global Ministries, N.Y.C., 1976-84, v.p. women's divsn., 1980-84, v.p. com. on relief, 1980-84, Mid. East cons. women's divsn., 1984-88; chmn. N.Am. Coordinating Com. for Non-govtl. Orgns. UN Symposium, N.Y.C., 1986, 87; pres. N.Am. area, asst. world treas. World Fedn. Meth. Women, 1986-91, archivist, 1992—; mem. United Meth. Gen. Comm. Christian Unity and Inter-Religious Concerns, N.Y.C., 1988-96; mem. interfaith commn. Nat. Coun. Chs. of Christ, 1996-2001. Mem. Nat. LEague Am. Pen Women, Nat. Assn. Parliamentarians. Home: 3789 Knollridge Rd Salem VA 24153-1938

BORNFELD, STEVE IRA, journalist; b. Bronx, N.Y., May 4, 1957; s. Jerry and Rita (Engler) B. AA in Liberal Arts, Westchester C.C., Valhalla, N.Y., 1977; BS in Journalism, Mercy Coll., 1984. Reporter, columnist, mag. writer Gannett Suburban Newspapers, White Plains, N.Y., 1983-88; feature writer York (Pa.) Dispatch, 1989; tv writer, columnist Albany (N.Y.) Times Union, 1990-93; tv writer N.Y. Post, N.Y.C., 1994; free lance tv writer Boston Herald, 1995, Electronic Newsstand-World Wide Web, 1995; entertainment writer, tv. and radio columnist Chattanooga Times, 1995—; mem. TV Critics Assn., 1990-95. Active B'nai Zion Synagogue, Chattanooga, 1996. Recipient Alumni award Mercy Coll., Dobbs Ferry, N.Y., 1986. Mem. Soc. Profl. Journalists. Home: Apt P-173 936 Mountain Creek Rd Chattanooga TN 37405 Office: Chattanooga Times 100 E 10th St Chattanooga TN 37402-4230

BORSOS, ERIKA, cardiac care, medical/surgical nurse; b. Bakonycsernye, Hungary, May 8, 1952; d. John and Elizabeth (Nyevrikel) B. ADN, Thornton Community Coll., 1974, AS, 1979; BSN cum laude, U. S. Fla., 1984; candidate MSN, Andrews U., Berrien Springs, Mich., 1996—. RN Fla., Ind., Ill.;cert. BLS, ACLS Am. Heart Assn. Staff nurse, relief charge nurse, float nurse Ingalls Meml. Hosp., Harvey, Ill., 1974-79; staff nurse, team leader, float nurse Sarasota (Fla.) Meml. Hosp., 1979-84; staff nurse, clin. nurse I, cardiac catheter recovery nurse, preceptor Bon Secours Venice (Fla.) Hosp., 1985—. Editor, writer Cardiac Courier. Vol. pub. edn. Am. Cancer Soc., Sarasota Fla., 1983-90. Ill. State scholar, 1970. Mem. AACN, NLN (advocacy), Inst. Noetic Sci., Venice Hosp. Found., Folk Dance Coun., Sigma Theta Tau, Phi Theta Kappa (scholar). Home: 7416 Bounty Dr Sarasota FL 34231-7920

BORSTEIN, JEANNE ERWIN, secondary school educator; b. Charleston, W.Va., Dec. 4, 1946; d. Eugene D. and Olive V. (Starkey) Erwin; 1 child, Tiffany. BS, W.Va. U., 1968; MEd summa cum laude, U. North Fla., 1989, EdD summa cum laude, 1995. Cert. lang. arts 7-12, Fla. Tchr. lang. arts and creative writing Wolfson High Sch., Jacksonville, Fla., 1982-92; tchr. lang. arts/theory of knowledge/rsch./creative writing Stanton Coll. Prep. Sch., Jacksonville, 1992-95; co-dir. Jaxwrite, Nat. Writing Inst. for Tchrs., 1992-95, dir. Jaxwrite Insvc. Program, 1992-96; coord. Instnl. Design for Duval Co. Schs., 1996—. Author: Teacher Guidebook for Creative Writing II, 1990; contbr. articles and poetry to jours.; writer advanced creative writing curriculum. Recipient outstanding curriculum project award U. North Fla., 1990, Wolfson Tchr. of Yr. award, 1991, Wolfson Most Valuable Tchr. award, 1991, Dilsey award, 1991. Mem. ASCD, Nat. Coun. Tchrs. English, Fla. Coun. Tchrs. English, Duval County Tchrs. English, Phi Kappa Phi, Phi Delta Kappa. Office: Duval County Sch Bd Bdlg 1701 Prudential Dr Jacksonville FL 32207-8152

BORUM, OLIN HENRY, realtor, former government official; b. Spencer, N.C., Nov. 3, 1917; s. Oscar Henry and Marjorie Mae (Leigh) B.; m. Beatrice Star Comulada, Nov. 14, 1944; children: Pamela Leigh, Robin Olin, Denis Richard. BS, U. N.C., 1938, MA, 1947, PhD, 1949; postgrad., U. Md., 1940-41. Rsch. chemist E.I. duPont de Nemours & Co., Phila. Lab., 1949-50; interim rsch. asst. prof. Cancer Rsch. Lab., U. Fla., 1950; instr., asst. prof. chemistry U.S. Mil. Acad., 1952-55; rsch. adminstr. U.S. Army Chem. Corps R&D Command, Washington, 1956-60; rsch. adminstr. U.S. Army Material Command, Washington, 1964-76; realtor assoc. Unique Properties, Alexandria, Va., 1974-79; realtor, assoc. broker The J. Edwards Co., Inc., Alexandria, 1979-82; prin. broker Olin H. Borum Realty, 1982—; tchr. chemistry U. Va., Arlington, Va., 1966-68; tchg. fellow U. Md., 1940-41; grad. asst., tchg. fellow U. N.C., 1946-49. Adult scouter Nat. Capital Area council Boy Scouts Am., 1964-75, unit commr., 1968-75; sec. Mt. Vernon (Va.) Civic Assn., 1965-66; mem. Com. of 33 (nat. adv. group Nat. Sojourners, Inc.), 1962-71, chmn., 1969-71. Nat. trustee Nat. Sojourners, Inc., 1971-73. 2d lt. to maj. AUS, 1941-46; as maj. USAF, 1951-56, lt. col., 1960-64. Recipient cert. of Achievement Dept. Army, 1971. Fellow Am. Inst. Chemists; mem. Am. Chem. Soc., Masons, K.T. Shriners, Phi Beta Kappa, Sigma Xi. Presbyn. Contbr. articles to profl. jours. Home: 9002 Volunteer Dr Alexandria VA 22309-2921 Office: 6641 Backlick Rd Springfield VA 22150-2710

BORUM, RODNEY LEE, financial business executive; b. High Point, N.C., Sept. 30, 1929; s. Carl Macy and Etta (Sullivan) B.; m. Helen Marie Rigby, June 27, 1953; children: Richard Harlan, Sarah Elizabeth. Student, U. N.C., 1947-49; BS, U.S. Naval Acad., 1953. Design-devel. engr. GE, Syracuse, N.Y., 1956-58; design-devel. engr. GE, Cape Kennedy, Fla., 1956-58, missile test condr., 1958-60, mgr. ground equipment engr., 1960-61, mgr. ea. test range engring., 1961-65; adminstr. Bus. and Def. Svcs. Adminstrn.-Dept. Commerce, 1966-69; pres. Printing Industries Am., Arlington, Va., 1969-85, staff cons., 1985-86, mem. exec. com., 1969-85, dir.; pres. W.H. Rigby Cons., 1985-86; exec. v.p. Amasek Inc., Cocoa, Fla., 1986-87; assoc. Fin. Svcs. Orgn., Cocoa, Fla., 1987—; sec. Graphic Arts Show Corp.; dir. Inter-Comprint Ltd., Strangers Cay, Ltd.; mem. governing bd. Comprints Internat.; Rep. candidate 11th dist. U.S. congress, Fla., 1988-90; ops. mgr. COVIX Corp.; mgmt. cons. 1990—; exec. v.p. Pearl of Va., Inc. Mem. exec. coun. Cub Scouts Am., 1965; bd. dirs., v.p. Brevard County (Fla.) United Fund, 1964-65; bd. dirs. Brevard Beaches Concert Assn., 1965; mem. edn. coun. bd. dirs. Graphic Arts Tech. Found., Pitts., 1970-86; trustee, founder Graphic Arts Edn. and Rsch. Trust Fund, Arlington, Va., 1978-85; candidate for U.S. Ho. of Reps. from 11th dist. Fla., 1988. 1st lt. USAF, 1953-56. Named Boss of Yr., C. of C., 1965; recipient Bausch and Lomb Sci. award, 1947, Am. Legion award, 1952. Mem. U.S. Naval Inst., U.S. Naval Acad. Alumni Assn., Graphic Arts Coun. N.Am. (bd. dirs. 1977—), Phi Eta Sigma. Methodist.

BOSAH, FRANCIS N., molecular biochemist, educator; b. Onitsha, Anambra, Nigeria, Sept. 13, 1959; s. Michael and Comfort (Odiari) B. BS, Shaw U., 1985; MS, N.C. Ctrl. U., 1988; PhD, Clark Atlanta U., 1995. Rsch. asst. N.C. Ctrl. U., Durham, 1985-88, instr., 1988-90; rsch. assoc. Rsch. Triangle Inst., Research Triangle Park, N.C., 1989-90; rsch. assoc. dept. biochemistry Morehouse Sch. Medicine, Atlanta, 1990-95, NASA postdoctoral rsch. fellow dept. medicine, 1995—; coord. health career Atlanta Met. Coll., 1993-94, instr., 1993—; presenter in field. Author abstracts and pubis. in field. Recipient Minority Biochem. Rsch. Support award, 1990-93. Mem. AAAS, Am. Soc. for Cell Biology, Am. Physiol. Soc. (predoctoral fellow 1993-95), Am. Chem. Soc., N.Y. Acad. Scis., Minority Biomed. Rsch. Soc., Beta Kappa Chi. Roman Catholic. Office: Morehouse Sch Medicine Dept Medicine 720 Westview Dr SW Atlanta GA 30310-1427

BOSHART, EDGAR DAVID, editor, journalist, photographer; b. Carthage, N.Y., July 19, 1949; s. Eli Boshart and Edwina (Noftsier) Manchester. AAS, Rochester Inst Tech, 1969; BS, Rochester Inst. Tech., 1972; cert. in religious edn., Unification Theol. Sem., Kingston, N.Y., 1976. Tech. analyst Am. Cyanamid Corp., Bound Brook, N.J., 1970-71; chemist Xerox Corp., Rochester, N.Y., 1971-72; reporter News World, N.Y.C. & Washington, 1978-80; reporter, editor Oliphant Washington News Svc., 1981-83; reporter, writer, editor Foster Natural Gas Report, Washington, 1983—; owner, photographer PhotoSpeak Prodns., Arlington, Va., 1986—. Mem. Nat. Press Club, Natural Gas Roundtable, No. Va. Photographic Soc. (bd. dirs., field trip coord.), Internat. Platform Assn., Wedding and Portrait Photographers Internat., Phi Kappa Phi Honor Soc. Home: 4501 Arlington Blvd Apt 209 Arlington VA 22203-2739 Office: Foster Assocs 1015 15th St NW Ste 1100 Washington DC 20005-2605

BOSSE, GEORGE MICHAEL, emergency medicine physician; b. Dayton, Ohio, Aug. 3, 1956; s. George and Eva Christa (Hutmacher) B.; m. Bari Elaine Ennis, May 24, 1986; children: Victoria Ann, Alexander George. BA magna cum laude, Duke U., 1978; MD magna cum laude, U. Louisville, 1983. Diplomate Am. Bd. Internal Medicine, Am. Bd. Emergency Medicine, Am. Bd. Med. Toxicology. Intern, resident in internal medicine U. Fla., Gainesville, 1983-86; resident in emergency medicine UCLA Med. Ctr., 1986-89; preceptor in med. toxicology L.A. Poison Ctr., 1987-89; preceptor in med. toxicology Ky. Regional Poison Ctr., Louisville, 1989-90, asst. med. dir., 1990—; from asst. prof. to assoc. prof. emergency medicine U. Louisville Sch. Medicine, 1995—. Fellow Am. Coll. Emergency Physicians; mem. Am. Acad. Clin. Toxicology, Soc. Acad. Emergency Medicine, Am. Acad. Emergency Medicine, Alpha Omega Alpha. Office: U Louisville Sch Medicine Dept Emergency Medicine Louisville KY 40292

BOSSIER, ALBERT LOUIS, JR., shipbuilding company executive; b. Gramercy, La., Nov. 29, 1932; s. Albert Louis and Alba Marie (Dufresne) B.; m. Jo Ann Decedue, Jan. 11, 1958; children—Albert Louis III, Brian, Donna, Steven. BS, La. State U., 1954, BSEE, 1956; J.D., Loyola U., New Orleans, 1971. Registered profl. engr., La. With Avondale Shipyards, Inc., New Orleans, 1957—, elec. supt., 1961-67, gen. plant supt., 1967-69, v.p. prodn. ops., 1969-72, exec. v.p., 1972-78; with Avondale Shipyards, Inc., Westwego, La., 1985—; pres. Avondale Shipyards, Inc., New Orleans, 1987—, chmn., CEO, dir., 1987—, also bd. dirs., 1987—. Bd. dirs. Better Bus. Bur. of New Orleans, C. of C. of New Orleans and River Regions. Served as 1st lt. Signal Corps AUS, 1956. Mem. ABA, La. Bar Assn., Am. Welding Soc., Navy League of U.S. (pres. Greater New Orleans council 1981—). Club: Propeller (New Orleans).

BOSSMAN, DAVID A., trade association administrator. Pres.-treas. Am. Feed Industry Assn., Arlington, Va., 1992—. Mem. Internat. Feed Industry Fedn. (v.p.), Latin Am. Balanced Feed Assn. (bd. dirs.), Animal Industry Found. (sec. treas.), Nat. Risk Retention Assn. (past chmn.). Office: Am. Feed Industry Assn 1501 Wilson Blvd Ste 1100 Arlington VA 22209

BOST, JOHN ROWAN, retired manufacturing executive, engineer; b. Spartanburg, S.C., May 9, 1922; s. John Rowan and May Netta (Swink) Bost-McDaniel; m. Martha Angela Simmons, June 8, 1963; children: John Rowan III, Warren Vincent. Aircraft fabrication grad., Anderson Airplane Sch., 1941-42; student spl. courses, USN, 1942-60. Assembler, leadman Goodyear Aircraft, Akron, Ohio, 1942; aviation chief metalsmith USN, 1942-46; v.p., sec., supt. Greenwood (S.C.) Meml. Gardens, 1950-56; owner, pres., engr. B & H Industries, Laurens, S.C., 1959-62; engr. The Torrington Co., Clinton, S.C., 1961-75; engr. and developer Byars Machine Co., Laurens, S.C., 1979-86; pres., engr. Downey Bost Corp., Fountain Inn, S.C., 1986-94; ret., 1994; owner, organizer NIFTI Industries Corp., Laurens, 1994-96; instr. Greenville (S.C.) Tech. Coll., 1962-82; instr. numerous cos., 1962—. Inventor and patentee in field. Baptist. Home: 102 Clemson St PO Box 902 Laurens SC 29360 Office: NIFTI Industries Corp 40 Lucas Ave PO Box 902 Laurens SC 29360

BOST, SUZANNE MICHELLE, humanities educator; b. Chgo., June 15, 1970; d. Jonathan Robert and Mary Anne (Cassidy) B. BA in English with honors, U. Tex., Austin, 1992; MA, Vanderbilt U., 1993, postgrad., 1995. Accounts mgr., receptionist House of Tutors, Austin, 1991-92; English tutor U. Tex. Learning Skills Ctr., Austin, 1991-92; instr. dept. English Vanderbilt U., Nashville, 1992—; adj. faculty Nashville Tech. Coll., 1996; creative writing instr. Aquinas Coll., Nashville, 1996; participant, poet Writer's Circle, Austin, 1990-92, Women's Words, Austin, 1991-92. Contbr. poetry to lit. jours.; poetry editor: Analecta, 1991. English dept. rep. to grad. student coun. Vanderbilt U., 1994-96, to liberal arts coun. U. Tex., 1991-92. Mellon fellow Vanderbilt U., 1996—, grad. fellow, 1992-96, Phi Kappa Phi fellow, 1992; scholar Sigma Tau Delta, 1991. Mem. MLA, Am. Studies Assn., Coll. English Assn., Phi Beta Kappa, Sigma Tau Delta (pres. U. Tex. chpt. 1990-92), Phi Kappa Phi. Democrat. Roman Catholic. Office: Vanderbilt U Dept English Box 1654 Sta B Nashville TN 37235

BOSTED, DOROTHY STACK, public relations executive; b. Newark, Apr. 6, 1953; d. Richard Joseph and Dorothy Marie (Irvin) Stack; m. Kenneth James Bosted, Aug. 22, 1976; 1 child, Danielle Whitney. Student, Lyndon State Coll., 1971-73; BA, NYU, 1975. Reporter The Daily Advance, Succasunna, N.J., 1974-75; producer, tech. intern Manhattan Cable TV, N.Y.C., 1975; editorial asst. Calif. Sch. Employees Assn., San Jose, 1975-76; news dir., anchor UA-Columbia Cablevision, Oakland, N.J., 1977-79; dir. pub. relations Overlook Hosp., Summit, N.J., 1981-84; pres. Dorothy Bosted Pub. Relations, Harding Twp., N.J., 1984-86; dir. pub. relations, communications Middlesex County Coll., Edison, N.J., 1986-88; mgr. corp. communications Hoechst Celanese Corp., Bridgewater, N.J., 1988-89; ptnr. Bosted-Burton Assocs., Coral Springs, Fla., 1986—; cons. Coral Springs, 1986—. Co-author: Writing with Impact, 1986; contbr. articles to N.Y. Times, various mags. Seminar leader Kinnelon (N.J.) Enrichment Program, 1978; trustee Middlesex County Coll. Found., Edison, 1986-88; bd. dirs. Middlesex County Coll. Alumni Assn., 1986-88. Recipient News Program ACE award Nat. Cable TV Assn., 1979, Spectrum of Talent merit award Internat. Assn. Bus. Communicators, 1982, Percy award N.J. Hosp. Mktg. and Pub. Relations Assn., 1982, 84, Tribute to Women and Industry award YWCA, Ridgewood, N.J., 1979; Mennen Co. scholar, 1971, Neighborhood House scholar, 1971, KP scholar, 1971. Mem. Tribute to Women and Industry Mgmt. Forum (v.p. pub. rels. Ridgewood chpt. 1986-87, bd. dirs. cen. N.J. chpt. 1989-91), Pub. Rels. Soc. Am. (editor N.J. chpt. newsletter 1987-89, bd. dirs. N.J. chpt. 1989-91). Home: 8738 NW 19th Dr Coral Springs FL 33071-6155

BOSTIC, JACQUELINE WHITING, management consultant, retired postmaster, association executive; b. Houston, Jan. 3, 1938; d. Samuel and Martha (Countee) Whiting; m. Joseph W. Bostic, July 15, 1960 (dec. 1991); children: Shelby Lance, Ursula Jimmison, Kirksten Sinclair, Jacqueline F. Student, Fisk U., Hofstra Coll.; BA in Psychology, Tex. So. U., Houston. Libr. asst. N.Y. Pub. Libr., 1958-59; edn. specialist U.S. Postal Svc., 1967-74, investigator so. region, 1974-86; officer-in-charge U.S. Postal Svc., Highlands, Tex., 1980; postmaster U.S. Postal Svc., Porter, Tex., 1986-92; officer-in-charge U.S. Postal Svc., Pearland, Tex., 1988; comms. mgr. U.S. Postal Svc., 1990; pres. Mgmt.-Orgn. Cons., 1992—; substitute tchr. Houston Ind. Sch. Dist., 1968-70; chmn. bd. dirs. Houston Postal Credit Union, 1990-92; lectr. mgmt. seminars, 1968—; chmn. bd. dirs. Antioch Project Reach, 1996—. Editor Intercom, Jack & Jill Am. Found. Nat. v.p. Jack & Jill Am., Inc., 1982-86; bd. dirs. Jack & Jill Am. Found.; nat. bd. dirs. YWCA of U.S.A., 1987-94, vol. mgmt. trainer, 1981—; pres. and chmn. bd. dirs. Houston Met. YWCA, 1982-86; active A-PLUS, UNCF, Telethon Gala; trustee Antioch Missionary Bapt. Ch., YWCA Retirement Fund; commnr. Clean Houston Commn.; legis. rep. Tex. Postal Workers. Recipient Black Houstonians Making History award, 1986, Dist. Achievement award Nat. Coun. Negro Women, Civic award Houston chpt. YWCA, Outstanding Svc. award United Negro Coll. Fund; named Vol. of Yr., Houston chpt. YWCA, Outstanding Vol., United Way/YWCA, Outstanding Jiller, Jack & Jill Am., Inc.; named to Pres.'s Cir., Houston C. of C. Mem. AFL-CIO (pres. Clerk Craft, Am. Postal Workers Union 1980-82, mem. ctrl. labor coun., bd. dirs. Tex. chpt.), NAACP, HMAC (bd. dirs.), NAFE, Nat. League Postmasters, Nat. Assn. Postmasters, Am. Bus. and Profl. Women, Network, United Negro Coll. Fund (Outstanding Svc. award), Rotary, Booker T. Washington Alumni Assn., Fisk Univ. Alumni Club, East Montgomery County C. of C., Delta Sigma Theta (bd. dirs., pres. Houston met. chpt. 1982-86, v.p. Delta Edn. and Charitable Found. 1992—). Home: 4410 Roseneath Dr Houston TX 77021-1617

BOSTICK, BRIAN, publishing executive, book; b. Feb. 25, 1972. B in Aviation Mgmt., Auburn U., 1994. Author, pub. Bostick Publs., Memphis, 1993-96; co-pub. FedEx Aviation Svcs., 1996—. Author: (series) Fleet Facts,

1993-96; co-pub. Comml. Jet Fleets, 1996—. Office: 2005 Corporate Ave 1st Fl Memphis TN 38132

BOSTICK, CHARLES DENT, lawyer, educator; b. Gainesville, Ga., Dec. 28, 1931; s. Jared Sullivan and Charlotte Catherine (Dent) B.; m. Susan Oliver, Sept. 8, 1956; children: Susan, Alan. Student, Emory-at-Oxford U., 1948-49; B.A., Mercer U., 1952, J.D., 1958. Bar: Ga. 1957, Tenn. 1974, U.S. Dist. Ct. (no. dist.) Ga. 1958, U.S. Ct. Appeals (5th cir.) 1959. Individual practice law Gainesville, Ga., 1958-66; asst. prof. law U. Fla., Gainesville, 1966-68, assoc. prof., 1968; assoc. prof. Vanderbilt U., Nashville, 1968-71, prof., 1971—, assoc. dean, dir. admissions, 1975-79, acting dean, 1979-80, dean, 1980-85; retired, 1992; vis. prof. law U. Leeds, Eng., 1985-86, prof. law emeritus, dean emeritus Sch. Law, 1992. Served to lt. USNR, 1952-55. Mem. Tenn. Bar. Assn. Episcopalian. Office: Vanderbilt U Sch Law 21st Ave S Nashville TN 37240

BOSTON, BILLIE, costume designer, costume history educator; b. Oklahoma City, Sept. 22, 1939; d. William Barrett and Margaret Emeline (Townsend) Long; m. William Clayton Boston, Jr., Jan. 20, 1962; children: Kathryn Gray, William Clayton III. BFA, U. Okla., 1961, MFA, 1962. Asst. to designer Karinski of N.Y., N.Y.C., 1966-67; prof. costume history Oklahoma City U., 1987—; rep. Arts Coun., Oklahoma City, 1987-90, Arts Festival, Oklahoma City, 1972-80; dir. ETC Theater, Oklahoma City SW Coll., 1979-83; actress Lyric Theatre, Oklahoma City, 1979-81. Exhibited in group shows at Taos, N.Mex., Santa Fe; represented in permanent collections in Dallas, Taos, Santa Fe, Tulsa, N.Y.C., La Jolla; costume designer Ballet Okla., Oklahoma City, 1979-84, Agnes DeMillie's Rodeo Ballet Okla., 1982, Royal Ballet Flanders, 1983, Pitts. Ballet, 1983, BBC's Childrens Prodn., 1984, 86, Lyric Theatre, Oklahoma City, 1987-95, Red Oak Music Theatre, Lakewood, N.J., 1988, Winter Olympics, 1988, Miss Am. Pageant, 1988, for JoAnne Worley in Hello Dolly, San Francisco Opera Circus, 1991, Jupiter (Fla.) Theatre, 1991—, Mame prodn. Conn. Broadway Theatre, 1991-92, Mobile (Ala.) Light Opera, 1992, The Boy Friend, Temple U., Japan, 1995, The Sound of Music, Lyric Stage, Dallas, 1995, Annie Get Your Gun, Guys and Dolls with Vic Damone, 1995, Westbury Flash Valley Forge Music Fair. Rep. Speakers Bur. Oklahoma City for Ballet, 1979-85; judge State Hist. Speech Tournament, Oklahoma City, 1985-87; chmn. State of Okla. Conf. on Tchr./Student Relationships, Oklahoma City, 1981. Recipient Gov.'s Achievement award, 1988, Lady in the News award, 1987. Mem. Alpha Chi Omega (house corp. bd. 1986-90). Methodist. Home: 1701 Camden Way Oklahoma City OK 73116-5121

BOSTON, BRUCE ORMAND, writer, editor, publications consultant; b. New Castle, Pa., Aug. 11, 1940; s. John Ormand and Williamina (Loudon) B.; m. Sandra Waymer, June 8, 1963 (div. 1973); children: Aaron Clark, Nathan Waymer, Kyle Richard; m. Jean Nelson, Dec. 23, 1989. BA, Muskingum Coll., 1962; BDiv, Princeton Theol. Sem., 1968, PhD, 1973. Instr. theology St. Joseph's Coll., Phila., 1972-73; assoc. Colloquy of Reston, Va., 1973-78; pres. Wordsmith, Inc., Reston, 1976—; publs. developer Coun. for Exceptional Children, Reston, 1973-75; asst. chief clk. com. on vets. affairs U.S. Senate, Washington, 1976; communications coun. Reston Assn., 1986-89. Author: The Sorcerer's Apprentice, 1976, (with Fortna) Testing the Gifted Child, 1976, (with Orloff) Preparing to Teach the Gifted and Talented, 2 vols., 1980, (with Cox and Daniel) Educating Able Learners, 1985, Language on a Leash, 1988, The Cutting Edge of Common Sense, 1993, Arts Education for the 21st Century American Economy, 1994, The Arts and Education: Partners in Achieving Our Natural Education Goals, 1995, Connections: Integrating the High School Curriculum through the Arts, 1996; editor: A Resource Manual on Educating the Gifted and Talented, 1975, Gifted and Talented: Developing Elementary and Secondary School Programs, 1975, STET! Tricks of the Trade for Writers and Editors, 1986, Perspectives on Implementation: Arts Education Standards for America's Students, 1994, also numerous articles and scripts. Pres. Fairfax Farms Cmty. Assn., 1980-81; mem. Reston Task Force on Town Governance, 1988—; lay preacher Episc. Diocese Va., 1984—; sr. warden St. Anne's Episc. Ch., Reston, 1990-92; bd. dirs. Episc. Awareness Ctr. on Handicaps, Washington, 1986-89, Cmty. Svc. Learning Ctr., Springfield, Mass., 1992-96. Recipient Achievement award Edn. Press Assn., 1986, 91, 1st place award Editor's Forum, 1986, 2d place award, 1991, Golden Eagle awards Coun. for Internat. Non-Theatrical Events, 1977, 84; Danforth Found. fellow, 1962-64, United Presbyn. Grad. fellow, 1968, Kent fellow in religion. Mem. Assn. Editorial Bus., Washington Ind. Writers (bd. dirs. 1982-84), Rotary (bd. dirs. Reston chpt. 1988-90). Democrat.

BOSTON, HOLLIS BUFORD, JR., retired military officer; b. Athens, Ala., Sept. 29, 1930; s. Hollis Buford Sr. and Opie (Hargrove) B.; m. Nancy Thomas Delbridge, Dec. 27, 1955; children: Elizabeth Lynn Boston Chesnutt, James Warren, John David. BBA, Baylor U., 1958; M Polit. Sci., Auburn U., 1972. Commd. 2d lt. USAF, 1953, advanced through grades to col., 1972, ret., 1975; sr. assoc. Program Control Corp., Van Nuys, Calif., 1977-89. Author: Estate Papers of Jones Boston, 1995. Chmn. planning com. City of Montgomery, Ala., 1983; pres. Capital City Kiwanis Club, Montgomery, 1987. Mem. Natchez Trace Geneal. Soc., Smith County Tenn. Hist. Assn., Sons of the Republic of Tex., Sigma Alpha Epsilon. Republican. Episcopalian. Home: 2341 Wentworth Dr Montgomery AL 36106

BOSTON, JOHN ARMISTEAD, psychiatrist, educator; b. Washington, July 3, 1924; s. John Armistead and Margaret Edith (Hill) B.; m. M. Louise Morgon, Nov. 11, 1950 (div. Sept. 1972); m. Deloris L. Miller Smith, Apr. 17, 1992; children: Paula, Diane, David, Gail Boston, Steven M. Smith, Bryan A. Smith. Student, Va. Mil. Acad., 1942-43, Duke U., 1943, U. Ga., 1943-45; MD, Temple U., 1948. Dir. Austin (Tex.) Child Guidance Clinic, 1956-63; asst. prof. State U. Iowa Sch. Medicine, Iowa City, 1963; pvt. practice Austin, 1963-91; acting med. dir. Travis County Mental Health/Mental Retardation Ctr., Austin, 1992-94; locum tenums Vista Corp., 1993-95; with Tex. Dept. Correction/Skyview Unit, Rusk, 1995—; clin. asst. prof. U. Tex. Med. Br., Galveston, 1985—; lectr. Sch. Social Work, U. Tex., Austin, 1964-70; sec.-treas. bd. dirs. Travis County Mental Health/Mental Retardation Ctr., Austin, 1973. Lt. USNR, 1950-52. Fellow Am. Psychiat. Assn. (life), Acad. Child and Adolescent Psychiatry; mem. Tex. Soc. Child Psychiatry (pres. 1970), Austin Psychiat. Soc. (pres. 1968). Republican. Episcopalian. Home: 3209 Piney Point Dr Jacksonville TX 75766

BOSTON, WILLIAM CLAYTON, lawyer; b. Hobart, Okla., Nov. 29, 1934; s. William Clayton and Dollie Jane (Gibbs) B.; m. Billie Gail Long, Jan. 20, 1962; children: Kathryn Gray, William Clayton III. BS, Okla. State U., 1958; LLB, U. Okla., 1961; LLM, NYU, 1967. Bar: Okla. 1961. Assoc. Mosteller, Fellers, Andrews, Snider & Baggett, Oklahoma City, 1962-64; ptnr. Fellers, Snider, Baggett, Blankenship & Boston, Oklahoma City, 1968-69, Andrews, Davis, Legg, Bixler, Milsten & Murrah, Oklahoma City, 1972-86; pvt. practice, Oklahoma City, 1986—. Contbr. articles to profl. jours.; mem. adv. bd. The Jour. of Air Law and Commerce, 1995—. Past pres. and trustee Ballet Okla.; past v.p., bd. dirs. Oklahoma City Arts Coun.; past trustee Nichols Hills (Okla.) Methodist Ch.; past trustee, chmn. Okla. Found. for the Humanities; past trustee, vice-chmn., sec. Humanites in Okla., Inc., 1992-95. With U.S. Army, 1954-56. Mem. ABA (chmn. subcom. on aircraft fin., chmn. aircraft fin. and contract divsn. forum on air and space law), Fed. Bar Assn., Internat. Bar Assn., Inter-Pacific Bar Assn., Okla. State Bar Assn., Oklahoma County Bar Assn. Home: 1701 Camden Way Oklahoma City OK 73116-5121 Office: 4005 NW Expressway St Oklahoma City OK 73116-1679

BOSWELL, GEORGE MARION, JR., orthopedist, health care facility administrator; b. Dallas, May 12, 1920; s. George Marion and Viola (Scarbrough) B.; m. Veta M. Fuller, Oct. 30, 1958; children: Brianna Boswell Brown, Kama Boswell Koudelka, Maia Boswell. BS, Tex. Tech U., 1940; MD, U. Tex., Southwestern Dallas, 1950. Diplomate Am. Acad. Orthopaedic Surgery. Intern Parkland Hosp., Dallas, 1950-51; resident gen. surgeryand orthopedic surgery Parkland, Baylor and Scottish Rite Hosps., Dallas, 1951-55; practice medicine specializing in orthopedics Dallas, 1955—; v.p. med. affairs Baylor Health Care System, Dallas, 1982-86; dir. orthopaedic clin. studies Baylor U. Med. Ctr., 1995—; pres., owner Bee Aviation Inc., Dallas, 1968—, Boswell Realty Inc., Dallas, 1971—; lectr., cons. on health care delivery. Contbr. articles to profl. jours. Fellow ACS; mem. AMA, Am. Acad. Orthopaedic Surgery (Key Man U.S. Congress 1980—), Am. Hosp. Assn., Tex. Hosp. Assn. (Key Man Tex. Legislature 1980—, council on hosp. staffs), Flying Physicians (pres. Tex. 1960-64). Republican. Methodist. Club: Cresent (Dallas). Home: 7249 Wabash Ave Dallas TX 75214-3535 Office: Baylor U Med Ctr Dept Orthopaedic Surgery 3500 Gaston Ave Dallas TX 75246

BOSWELL, JOHN HOWARD, lawyer; b. Houston, Mar. 22, 1932; s. Henry Oliver and Opal Everest (Wineburg) B.; m. Sharon Lee Ueckert, Dec. 19, 1959; children—John Brooke, Mark Richard. B.B.A., U. Houston, 1955; J.D., U. Houston, 1963. Bar: Tex. 1962, U.S. Supreme Ct. 1970, U.S. Ct. Appeals (5th cir.) 1970; cert. civil trial advocate Nat. Bd. Trial Advocacy, Tex. Bd. Legal Specialization. Sr. shareholder Boswell and Hallmark, P.C., Houston; lectr. State Bar Tex. Continuing Legal Edn. Program, 1978-84, Pepperdine U. Coll. Law; faculty Tex. Coll. of Trial Advocacy, 1980-90. Served to lt. USNR, 1955-58. Mem. Am. Bd. Trial Advocates, Internat. Assn. Ins. Counsel, Tex. Assn. Def. Counsel, Def. Research Inst. Home: 405 Chapelwood Ct Houston TX 77024-6737 Office: 1100 Louisiana St # 2100 Houston TX 77002

BOSWELL, TOMMIE C., middle school educator; b. Gainesboro, Tenn., Nov. 8, 1942; d. Tommy and Ethel (Draper) Cassetty; m. Neal Stanley Boswell, Aug. 28, 1965; children: Brian Andrew, James Travis. AA, Cumberland U., Lebanon, Tenn., 1962; BS, Tenn. Technol. U., 1965; MAT, Rollins Coll., Winter Park, Fla., 1980, EdS, 1984. Cert. tchr. English, social studies; cert. adminstrv. supr. Tchr. English and social studies Beaumont Middle Sch., Kissimmee, Fla., 1965-72, tchr. social studies, 1978-89; tchr. social studies Neptune Middle sch., Kissimmee, 1989—; team leader 8th Grade Acad. Team "Challengers", Kissimmee, 1994—. Founding pres. Canterbury Lane Neighborhood Assn., Kissimmee, 1988; mem. N.M.S. Program Improvement Coun., Kissimmee, 1994—. Named Social Studies Tchr. of the Yr., Fla. Coun. for Social Studies, 1984, 86, 89, Outstanding Tchr. of Am. History, Joshua Stevens chpt. DAR, Kissimmee, 1982; Delta Kappa Gamma scholar, 1980. Mem. Upper Cumberland Geneal. Soc. Republican. Methodist. Office: Neptune Middle Sch 2727 Neptune Rd Kissimmee FL 34744-6237

BOSWORTH, WILLIAM POSEY, physician, physical education educator; b. Valdosta, Ga., Mar. 23, 1935; s. Paul Brooks and Myra Mae (Posey) B.; m. Wanda Marie Grimm; 1 child, Lynne Marie. BS, U. Tampa, 1957; MEd, Springfield (Mass.) Coll., 1961; postgrad., Orlando (Fla.) Jr. Coll., 1968; DO, U. Health Scis., Kansas City, Mo., 1972. Phys. edn. tchr., jr. high sch. tchr. Duval County Sch. Bd., Jacksonville, Fla., 1959-62; gen. practice, Jacksonville, 1974—; physician athletic team, 1975—. Mem. Duval County Sch. Bd., Jacksonville, 1986-90, Jacksonville Sports Com., 1981-86, Duval County Hosp. Authority, 1982-86, Fla. Gov.'s Coun. on Phys. Fitness and Sports, 1985-93, Fla. Sunshine State Games Found., 1990—. Capt. M.C. USNR, 1969—. Named Gen. Practitioner of Yr. Fla. Soc. Am. Coll. Family Physicians, 1982, Health Educator of Yr., Duval County Coalition Against Tobacco, 1991; recipient physician's recognition award AMA, 1988, 91, 94, vol. svc. 35-yr. gold pin award AAU/USA, 1988, Navy Commendation Medal, 1991. Mem. Fla. Med. Assn., Fla. Soc. Sons of Am. Revolution (pres. 1980, meritorious svc. medal Jacksonville chpt. 1986), Duval County Med. Soc., Duval County Acad. Family Physicians (treas., v.p., pres.), Assn. Mil. Surgeons U.S., Freedoms Found. at Valley Forge (pres. Jacksonville chpt. 1995—). Office: 9765 San Jose Blvd Jacksonville FL 32257-5443

BOTT, KENNETH FRANCIS, JR., microbiology educator; b. Albany, N.Y., Dec. 19, 1936; s. Kenneth F. and Eva (Button) B.; m. Lacala Hall, July 8, 1990; m. Patricia Weiler, June 18, 1960; children: Allison Eva, Kenneth Alan. BS in Biology, St. Lawrence U., Canton, N.Y., 1958; MS in Microbiology, Syracuse (N.Y.) U., 1960, PhD in Microbiology, 1963; postgrad. virology, U. Chgo., 1963-64. Instr. dept. microbiology and The Coll. U. Chgo., 1964-67, asst. prof. dept. microbiology and The Coll., 1967-71; assoc. prof. dept. bacteriology and immunology U. N.C., Chapel Hill, 1971-80, prof. dept. microbiology and immunology, 1980—, mem. curriculum in genetics, 1972—, chmn. curriculum in genetics, 1985-91, mem. adminstrv. bd. Grad. Sch., 1985-92; Am. Soc. Engring. Edn.-NASA summer faculty fellow Stanford U., 1969; vis. prof., Fulbright grantee U. Paris XI, Orsay, France, 1971; CNRS sponsored Chercheur Associe Institut Pasteur, Paris, 1977; vis. researcher, Fulbright grantee Centre Genetique Moleculaire, CNRS Gif sur Yvette, France, 1982. Contbr. articles to profl. jours. Merck & Co. Found. grantee U. Chgo., 1969. Mem. AAAS, AAUP, Am. Soc. Microbiology (chmn. found. lectr. com. 1986-89, pres. N.C. br. 1978-79), Sigma Xi (sec. U. Chgo. chpt. 1967-68). Office: U NC Med Sch Dept Microbiology Chapel Hill NC 27599-7290

BOTTORFF, DENNIS C., banker; b. Clarksville, Ind., Sept. 19, 1944; s. Irvin H. and Lucille H. B.; m. Jean Brewington, Aug. 21, 1964; children: Todd, Chad. BE, Vanderbilt U., 1966; MBA, Northwestern U., Evanston, Ill., 1968. Pres. Commerce Union Bank, Nashville; also exec. v.p. Commerce Union Corp., Nashville; chmn., chief exec. officer Commerce Union Bank and Commerce Union Corp., Nashville, 1984-87; vice chmn., chief oper. officer Sovran Fin. Corp., Norfolk, Va., 1988-89, pres., chief oper. officer, 1989-90; pres., chief oper. officer C&S/Sovran Corp., Norfolk, Va., 1990—, C&S/Sovran Corp. (merger Citizens & So. Corp. and Sovran Fin. Corp. 1990), 1990—; chmn., pres., CEO, dir. 1st Am. Corp., Nashville, 1991—; bd. advisors The Jack C. Massey Grad. Sch. Bus., Belmont, Coll., Nashville; bd. dirs. Shoney's Inc., Ingram Industries. Bd. dirs. Inroads, Tenn. Tomorrow; trustee, mem. investment com. Vanderbilt U., Nashville. Mem. Am. Bankers Assn. (bd. dirs.), Am. Bankers Coun. (bd. dirs.), Tenn. Bankers Assn. (bd. dirs.), Bankers Roundtable (bd. dirs.), Nashville Area C. of C. (bd. dirs.), The Hundred Club (Nashville), Belle Meade Country Club, Cumberland Club. Presbyterian. Home: 1314 Chickering Rd Nashville TN 37215-4522 Office: First Am Corp First Am Ctr 4th and Union St Nashville TN 37237-0615

BOTWAY, LLOYD FREDERICK, computer scientist, consultant; b. Flushing, N.Y., June 18, 1947; s. Albert Harold and Alice Rebecca (Halperin) B. BS, Tufts U., 1968; MS, U. Colo., 1970. Programmer Anaconda Co., Butte, Mont., 1970-72; systems analyst U. Mo., Columbia, 1972-77; tech. dir. Dataphase Systems, Inc., Kansas City, Mo., 1977-80; pres. Liberty Logic Corp., Pasadena, Md., 1980-84; computer scientist Computer Scis. Corp., Balt., 1984-86; dir. MIS Internat. Clin. Labs., Nashville, 1986-88; dir. info. systems Nat. Health Labs., Nashville, 1988-94; v.p. Corning Nichols Inst., San Juan Capistrano, Calif., 1994—; Cons. Internat. Clin. Labs., Nashville, 1981-85; grad. asst. Dale Carnegie. Contbr. articles to profl. jours., co-author: (reference pamphlet) Latex Command Summary, 1985. Libertarian candidate for U.S. Ho. of Reps. from 5th Tenn. Dist., 1994. Mem. IEEE, Toastmasters. Office: Corning Nichols Inst 33608 Ortega Hwy San Juan Capistrano CA 92675-2042

BOTWINICK, RITA STEINHARDT, history educator; b. Winzig, Germany, July 22, 1923; came to U.S., 1939; d. Heymann and Rosa (Moses) Steinhardt; m. Leonard Botwinick, Dec. 19, 1946; children: Ronnie Botwinick Londner, David. BA in Journalism, U. S.C., 1945; MA in History, Bklyn. Coll., 1953; PhD in History, St. John's U., 1973. Tchr. Herriks Sr. High Sch., Roslyn, N.Y., 1956-79; prof. history Sacred Heart U., Fairfield, Conn., 1980-86, Fla. Atlantic U., Boca Raton, 1987—; lectr. in field. Author: Winzig Germany 1933-1946: The History of a Town under the Third Reich, 1992, A History of the Holocaust; From Ideology to Annihilation, 1995. Active Bridgeport (Conn.) Jewish Ctr., 1982-86.

BOUCHER, GEORGE, aquarium administrator. Pres. Miami (Fla.) Seaquarium. Office: Miami Seaquarium 4400 Rickenbacker Cswy Miami FL 33149-1032

BOUCHER, LARRY GENE, sports association commissioner; b. Bowling Green, Ky., Jan. 23, 1947; s. Larry Gene and Virginia Elizabeth (Miller) B.; m. Paula Ann Feeback, Oct. 4, 1949 (div. Feb. 1996); children: Brooke Renee, Brenna Ann. BS in Bus. Edn., Ea. Ky. U., 1970. Unemployment ins. examiner Human Resource Cabinet Ky., Frankfort, 1972-73; budget/policy analyst Ky. Transp. Cabinet, Frankfort, 1973-87, br. mgr. mgmt. svcs., 1987-91; asst. commr. Ky. H.S. Athletic Assn., Lexington, 1991—; mem. Am. Govtl. Accts., Frankfort, 1984-87. Mem. allocation com. Frankfort/Franklin County United Way, 1987-91. Mem. Church of Christ. Home: Apt 2911 4030 Tates Creek Rd Lexington KY 40517 Office: Ky H S Athletic Assn 2280 Executive Dr Lexington KY 40505-4808

BOUCHER, MILDRED EILEEN, state agency administrator; b. Chelsea, Mass., Dec. 8, 1928; d. William Brennan and Lillian Beatrice (Baggs) Hudson; m. Lawrence Clifford Boucher, Oct. 4, 1947 (dec. 1980); children: Katherine, Lawrence, Deborah, Jayne, Lyle, Constance. AA with honors, Indian River Community Coll., Fort Pierce, Fla., 1982, AS, 1983; BS in Applied Tech. magna cum laude, Fla. Inst. Tech., 1984. Tchr., head sci. dept. Peace Corps, Republic of Kiribati, 1984-85; environ. health specialist State of Fla., Port St. Lucie, 1989—; chmn. St. Lucie County Environ. Control. Hearing Bd., Fort Pierce, 1985-89. Editor: The Electrolyte, 1982. Active diabetic screening, Fort Pierce, Port St. Lucie, 1982, 83; mem. village coun. Rongorongo Maneaba, Beru Island, Republic of Kiribati, 1985. Mem. Am. Soc. Clin. Pathologists (registrant), Fla. Pub. Health Assn., Alpha Epsilon Soc. Republican. Methodist. Home: 1879 SE Vesthaven Ct Port Saint Lucie FL 34952-8814 Office: HRS-Saint Lucie County Health Unit 714 Avenue C Fort Pierce FL 34950-4189

BOUCHILLON, JOHN RAY, education coordinator, real estate executive; b. Covington, Ga., Sept. 3, 1943; s. John Ray and Mary Reid (Death) B.; m. Martha Jo Logue, Dec. 18, 1965; children: Trey, Monica, Beth. BA, LaGrange Coll., 1965; MEd, Ga. Coll., 1969. Tchr. chemistry Baldwin County, Milledgeville, Ga., 1965-71, career coordinator, 1971-72; dir. career edn. Liberty County, Hinesville, Ga., 1972-75; career edn. cons. Ga. Dept. Edn., Atlanta, 1975-86, quality basic education field administr., 1986-87, coordinator local strategic planning, 1987-92, sch. support team leader, 1992—; dir. sch. support svcs., asst. dir. quality and sch. support divsn.; chmn. career edn. adv. com. Ga. So. Coll., Statesboro, 1972-73; dir.-at-large guidance div. Ga. Vocat. Assn., Atlanta, 1976; sec.-treas. Ga. Vocat. Guidance Assn., 1976, pres., 1979. Co-editor: (newsletter) Ga. Pupil Personnel, 1975; editor: (newsletter) Ga. Personnel and Guidance, 1977-78; mem. editorial bd. Jour. Career Edn., 1978-80, Future Mag., 1978, Chronicle Guidance Corp., 1987-89. Mem. Ga. Sch. Counselors Assn. (Gov's. award for Govt. Svc.), Internat. Soc. Ednl. Planners (bd. dirs. 1987-91). Democrat. Methodist. Avocations: photography, woodworking. Home: 4276 Village Green Cir Conyers GA 30208 Office: Ga Dept Edn 1754 Twin Towers E Atlanta GA 30334

BOUDINOT, FRANK DOUGLAS, pharmaceutics educator; b. New Brunswick, N.J., Mar. 31, 1956; s. Frank Lins and Dorothy Jean (Libourel) B.; m. Sarah Garrett, Sept. 1992; 1 child, Frank Garrett. BS in Biology, Springfield Coll., 1978; PhD in Pharmaceutics, SUNY, Buffalo, 1986. Vet. technician Afton Animal Hosp., Williamsville, N.Y., 1978-79; rsch. technician SUNY-Millard Fillmore Hosp., Buffalo, 1979-80; grad. asst. SUNY, 1980-85; asst. prof. pharmaceutics U. Ga., Athens, 1986-90, assoc. prof., 1990—, head dept. pharm., 1992—; cons. Assn. Minority Profl. Health Schs., Drug Devel. Group for AIDS, Tex. So. U. Coll. Pharmacy and Health Scis., Oneida Rsch. Svcs., Inc. Mem. editl. bd. Jour. Pharmacy Tchg., 1989—, Biopharm. and Drug Disposition, Eng., 1994—; referee Jour. Pharm. Scis., 1988—, Jour. Pharm. Rsch., 1989—, Antimicrobial Agts. and Cehmotherapy, 1993—; contbr. over 80 articles to sci. jours. Bd. dirs. Oconee Animal Shelter, Watkinsville, Ga., 1986-88; vice chair govt. svcs. subcom. Oconee 2000, Waktinsville, 1986-87; del. Ga. State Rep. Conv., Atlanta, 1989, 91, 92; event svcs. staff vol. 1996 Summer Olympic Games, Athens, Ga. NIH grantee, 1987, 90, U.S. FDA grantee, 1989; named one of Outstanding Young Men of Am., 1987. Mem. Am. Assn. Pharm. Scientists, Am. Assn. Colls. Pharmacy (del. 1989-90, mem. profl. affairs com. 1990-91), Am. Soc. Microbiology, Rho Chi. Episcopalian. Office: U Ga Coll Pharmacy Brooks Dr Athens GA 30602

BOUDREAU, DIANE ELAINE, business educator; b. Miami, Fla., Nov. 19, 1954; d. Harold and Margaret (Snitman) B. BS in Nursing, Brenan Coll., Gainesville, Ga., 1981, MBA, 1985. RN, Fla. Supr. Miami Children's Hosp., 1990; DON Internat. Air Ambulance, Miami, 1992; clin. specialist Bapt. Hosp., Miami, 1994; prof. bus. Trinity Internat. U., Miami, 1994—; newsletter editor AWPC, Miami, 1989-96; mem. Dade County Coalition for Immunization, Miami, 1993-94. Author: (video) Use of the Apnea Monitor, 1993. Mem. bd. Miami Youth Mus., 1994. Capt. USAF, 1985-89. Named Alumni of Yr. Brenan Coll., 1988. Mem. DAV. Presbyterian.

BOUDREAUX, MARK MICHAEL, graphic designer; b. New Orleans, Apr. 25, 1961; s. Lloyd Charles and Ruby Marie (Burmastrer) B. BA, U. New Orleans, 1992. Designer, owner, dir. Mouepro Design Studio, New Orleans, 1995—. Creator comic strip White House Mouse, 1994-95; illustrator (children's book) Squirkle McGurkle, 1996. Mem. Alpha Theta Epsilon. Home and Studio: 4524 Charlene Dr New Orleans LA 70127

BOUILLET, SARA ELIZABETH, hospital administrator, marketing professional; b. Ft. Knox, Ky., July 8, 1967; d. John Emile Bouillet and Sara Frances (Deese) Snider; children: Sara GeorgeAnna, George Andrew IV. BS in Merchandising, East Carolina U., 1989. Mgmt. trainee, buyer Belk, The Washington Plaza, Washington, N.C., 1990; writer, fund raiser Pirate Club East Carolina U., Greenville, N.C., 1991-92; dir. of cmty. rels. Beaufort County Hosp., Washington, 1992—; exec. asst. to chancellor ECU News Bur. and Pub. Rels. Office, Washington. Mem. Am. Healthcare Philanthropy, Carolinas Healthcare Pub. Rels. and Mktg. Soc., N.C. Hosp. Assn., C of C. Office: Beaufort County Hosp 628 E 12th St Washington NC 27889

BOUILLIANT-LINET, FRANCIS JACQUES, global management consultant; b. Garches, France, Aug. 20, 1932; came to U.S., 1977; s. Jacques Achille and Virginia Sutton (McKee) B.-L.; m. Carolyn Jeanine Taylor, Nov. 17, 1978. Diploma in sci., Admiral Farragut Acad., 1948; post., Hautes Etudes Commerciales, Paris, 1949, Duke U., 1949-50. Mgmt. trainee Harry Ferguson Cos., Europe, 1951-53; sales promotion mgr. Massey-Harris-Ferguson, Paris, 1957-59; gen. programs mgr. Massey Ferguson Ltd., Coventry, Eng., 1959-63; coord. office of pres. Massey Ferguson Ltd., Toronto, Ont., Can., 1963-65; group product mgr. Massey Ferguson Ltd., Toronto, 1966-68; dir. internat. logistics Allis Chalmers Corp., Milw., 1968-71; joint mng. dir. LePiol, s.a.r.l., Cannes, France, 1971-77; chmn. bd., chief exec. officer FBL, Inc., Hurtsboro, Ala., 1977—, also bd. dirs.; exec. dir. H.J. Crawley, Ltd., Leamington, Eng., 1961-66; bd. dirs. F.J.B., Inc., Thermal, Calif. Author: (manual) The New Product Process, 1963; trademark registrant for "Rent-a-Boss." Assoc. mem. Nat. Trust for Hist. Preservation, Washington, 1982; charter founder Ronald Reagan Rep. Ctr., Washington, 1987. With French Armed Forces, 1953-54, 56-57. Mem. Am. Soc. Agrl. Engrs. (affiliate), Brit. Inst. Mgmt., Calif. Farm Bur. Fedn., Ala. Farm Bur. Fedn., Ala. Sheriff's Assn. (hon.), Capital City Club, Midland (Ga.) Fox Hounds. Office: FBL Inc PO Box 298 Hurtsboro AL 36860-0298

BOULDEN, DORATHY ANN, genealogist; b. El Dorado, Ark., May 18, 1959; d. Thomas James and Pearlie Ruth (Bradley) Pierce; m. Albert Craig Boulden, June 21, 1981. Grad., U. Ark., 1980, El Dorado Coll., 1983. Cert. in surg. tech. Clk., typist U.S. Corps. Engrs., Little Rock, 1977-79; scrub nurse St. Vincent's Infirmary, Little Rock, 1980-82; clk., staff genealogist Barton Libr., El Dorado, Ark., 1984—; bd. dirs. Southwest Ark. Regional Archives, Washington. Editor: Tracks and Traces, 1992. Asst. pianist Zion Watch Bapt. Ch., El Dorado, 1984—, fin. sec., 1990—. Mem. Ark. Geneal. Soc. (bd. dirs. 1994—), Union County Geneal. Soc. (sec., publicity chair 1991-93). Office: Barton Libr 200 E 5th El Dorado AR 71730

BOULEY, EUGENE EDWARD, JR., criminal justice and sociology educator; b. Woonsocket, R.I., May 24, 1941; s. Eugene Edward and Rita Cora Jane (Tavernier) B.; m. Theresa Isabelle Gaudreau, Jan. 11, 1964; children: Edward Paul, Danielle Marie. BA in Edn.-Math., Providence Coll., 1962; MA in Criminology and Corrections, Sam Houston State U., Huntsville, Tex., 1971, PhD in Criminal Justice, 1995. Commd. U.S. Army, 1962-92, advanced through grades to col., ret. 1992; div. chief Directorate of Combat Devel. U.S. Army Mil. Police Sch., Ft. McClellan, Ala., 1978-79; comdr. 11th Mil. Police Bn. Ft. McClellan, Ala., 1979-81; advisor 43d Mil. Police Brigade, R.I. Army N.G., Providence, 1981-84; Army attache Am. Embassy, Buenos Aires, 1985-88; def. and Army attache Am. Embassy, Bogota, Colombia, 1988-90; chief L.Am. div. Directorate for Attaches, Def. Intelligence Agy., Washington, 1990-92; asst. instr. Coll. Criminal Justice, Sam Houston State U., Huntsville, 1993-95; asst. prof. criminal justice dept. govt. and sociology Ga. Coll. and State U., Milledgeville, 1995—; instr. Canal Zone br. Fla. State U., Ft. Davis, 1976-77. Decorated Bronze Star medal, Legion of Merit, Army Commendation medal with oak leaf cluster, Def. Superior Svc. medal with oak leaf cluster, Army Meritorious Svc. medal with

3 oak leaf clusters; Orden de Mayo al Merito Militar in the grade of Comemdador, Pres. of Republic of Argentina, 1988, Orden del Merito Militar General Jose Maria Cordoba, Chief of Staff of Army of Republic of Colombia, 1990. Mem. Am. Soc. Criminology, Acad. Criminal Justice Scis., Am. Soc. Indsl. Security, Elks. Home: 3089 Heritage Rd Milledgeville GA 31061 Office: Ga Coll and State U Dept Govt/Sociology Campus Box 18 Milledgeville GA 31061

BOULTINGHOUSE, (DANNIE) CAROL, business development specialist; b. Dallas, Sept. 11, 1954; d. Daniel Calvin and Mary Bennette (Temple) Wilkinson; m. Steven Ed Boultinghouse, Feb. 21, 1981 (div. June 1986); 1 child, Brian Steven. AD in Liberal Arts, Eastfield C.C., Mesquite, Tex., 1975; student, Abilene Christian Coll., Garland, Tex., 1976-77. Various secretarial positions Dallas, 1974-80; sec. CIGNA Internat., Dallas, 1980-83, underwriting asst., 1983-85, assoc. underwriter, 1985-87, account rep., 1987-92, bus. devel. specialist, 1992—. Mem. Marine Corps League Aux. Roman Catholic. Home: 3039 Sharpview Ln Dallas TX 75228-6084 Office: CIGNA Internat 600 Las Colinas Blvd E Ste 950 Irving TX 75039-5633

BOUMA, ARNOLD HEIKO, geology educator, consultant; b. Groningen, The Netherlands, Sept. 5, 1932; came to U.S., 1966; s. Pier and Trientje (Eissens) B.; m. Mechelina H. Kampers, Jan. 15, 1960; children: Mark A., N. Robert, Lars O. BS in Geology, U. Groningen, 1956; MS in Geology, U. Utrecht, The Netherlands, 1959, PhD in Sedimentology, 1961. Cert. petroleum geologist. Lectr. U. Utrecht, 1963-66; assoc. and full prof. Tex. A&M U., College Station, 1966-75; sr. rsch. geologist U.S. Geol. Survey, Menlo Park, Calif., 1976-79; geologist in charge U.S. Geol. Survey, Corpus Christi, 1979-81; sr. rsch. scientist, mgr. Gulf Oil Co., Pitts. and Houston, Tex., 1981-85; sr. rsch. scientist Chevron Oil Co., Houston, La Habra, Calif., 1985-88; prof. sedimentary geology La. State U., Baton Rouge, 1988—; cons. Geo-Marine Cons., Inc., Baton Rouge, 1989—. Author: Sedimentology of Flysch Deposits, 1962, Methods for the Study of Sedimentary Structures, 1969; editor numerous books and jours. Lt. Dutch Army, 1952-54. Recipient Outstanding Educator award Gulf Coast Assn. Geol. Socs., 1992; U. Utrecht fellow, 1961-62, Fulbright fellow Scripps Inst. Oceanography, La Jolla, Calif., 1962-63. Fellow AAAS; mem. Am. Assn. Petroleum Geologists, Soc. Econ. Paleontologists and Mineralogists (F.P. Shepard award for Excellence in Marine Geology 1982), Internat. Assn. Sedimentologists (treas. 1961-66), Baton Rouge Geol. Soc., Houston Geol. Soc. Home: 2841 Twelve Oaks Ave Baton Rouge LA 70820-5718 Office: La State U Dept Geology and Geophysics Baton Rouge LA 70803

BOUNDS, SARAH ETHELINE, historian; b. Huntsville, Ala., Nov. 5, 1942; d. Leo Deltis and Alice Etheline (Boone) Bounds; AB, Birmingham-So. Coll., 1963; MA, U. Ala., Tuscaloosa, 1965, Ed.S. in History, 1971, PhD, 1977. Tchr. social studies Huntsville City Schs., 1963, 65-66, 71-74; residence hall adv., dir. univ. housing U. Ala., Tuscaloosa, 1963-65, 68-71; instr. history N.E. State Jr. Coll., Rainsville, Ala., 1966-68; instr. history U. Ala., Huntsville, 1975, 78-80, 85—, dir. Weeden House Mus., 1981-83; asst. prof. edn., supr. student tchrs. U. North Ala., Florence, 1978. Mem. AAUW, Assn. Tchrs. Educators, Nat. Council Tchrs. Social Studies, NEA, Ala. Hist. Assn., Ala. Assn. Historians, Ala. Assn. Tchrs. Educators, Huntsville Hist. Soc., Historic Huntsville Found., Alpha Delta Kappa (state pres. Ala. 1990-92, regional sec. 1991-93, internat. mem. com. 1993—), Kappa Delta Pi, Phi Alpha Theta. Methodist. Club: Huntsville Pilot (pres. 1990-91, club builder 1991-93, Ala. dist. lt. gov. 1995-96, Ala. dist. gov.-elect 1996—). Home: 1100 Bob Wallace Ave SE Huntsville AL 35801-2807

BOURGEOIS, PATRICIA ANN, middle school educator; b. N.Y.C., Aug. 25, 1952; d. John Patrick and Ellen Patricia (Park) Roche; m. Bruce David Bourgeois, Aug. 26, 1972; children: Larisa, Sean, Nicole. BS, Fairleigh Dickinson U., 1974; M., U. Houston, 1990. Cert. spl. edn. tchr., Tex. Life skills tchr. Humble (Tex.) Ind. Sch. Dist., 1989-92; tchr. students with autism Aldine (Tex.) Ind. Sch. Dist., 1992—. Mem. Tex. Assn. for Persons with Severe Handicaps (bd. dirs. 1991-94), Assn. for Persons with Severe Handicaps, Coun. for Exceptional Children. Roman Catholic. Home: 8706 Donys Dr Houston TX 77040-1547

BOURGEOIS, PATRICIA MCLIN, women's health and pediatrics nurse, educator; b. Hammond, La., Mar. 12, 1941; d. Lannie McLin and Mary (Lossett) Nicolay; m. Charles Bourgeois, June 10, 1962; children: Deborah, Cynthia, Terry Kay, Lori, Betsy. BSN, McNeese State U., 1962; MSN, Northwestern State U., Natchitoches, La., 1980. Cert. clin. nurse specialist, nursing child assessment, La. Office nurse pediatrics Green Clinic, Ruston, La., 1962-63; staff nurse ob-gyn. Lincoln Gen. Hosp., Ruston, 1963-64; staff nurse nursery St. Francis Cabrini Hosp., Alexandria, La., 1966-67; prof. maternal/child nursing La. Tech. U., Ruston, 1975—; part-time office nurse Green Clinic, 1975-93; part-time resident nurse Methodist Children's Home, Ruston, 1990—. Vice chairperson La. Coalition for Maternal/Infant Health, Baton Rouge, 1989-91; pres. Ruston Civic Guild, 1990. Grantee, March of Dimes, Monroe, La., 1984. Mem. ANA (del. 1991-93), La. State Nurses Assn. (sec. 1991-93, pres. 1994-95). Democrat. Roman Catholic. Home: 2703 Belcara Dr Ruston LA 71270-2401 Office: La Tech Univ PO Box 3152 TS Ruston LA 71272

BOURGEOIS, PATRICK LYALL, philosophy educator; b. Baton Rouge, Mar. 17, 1940; s. Eugene Oliver Bourgeois and Una Sarah Chauvin; m. Mary Margaret Hallaron, Aug. 21, 1968; children: Daniel Patrick, Margaret Mary. BA in Philosophy, Notre Dame Sem., 1962, MA in Religion, 1964; MA in Liturgical Theology, Notre Dame U., 1965; PhD in Philosophy, Duquesne U., 1970. Instr. theology Duquesne U., Pitts., 1965-67; from instr. philosophy to asst. prof. to assoc. prof. Loyola U., New Orleans, 1968-78, prof., 1978—. Author: Can Catholics be Charismatic?, 1976, The Religious Within Experience and Existence: A Phenomenologist Investigation, 1990, Toward a Common Vision: Mead and Merleau-Ponty, 1991; co-author: Pragmatism and Phenomenology, 1980, Thematic Studies in Phenomenology and Pragmatism, 1983, others; contbr. numerous articles to profl. jours. NEH rsch. grantee, 1988-89. Mem. Am. Cath. Philos. Assn., Soc. for Phenomenology and Existential Philosophy, So. Soc. for Philosophy and Psychology, Gabriel Marcel Soc. Roman Catholic. Office: Loyola U Box 196 New Orleans LA 70124

BOURGEOIS, PRISCILLA ELZEY, educational administrator; b. Natchez, Miss., Oct. 4, 1952; d. John Patrick and Patsy Ruth (Broussard) Elzey; 1 child, Stephanie Priscilla. BA, U. Southwestern La., 1974; MEd, U. New Orleans, 1979, postgrad., 1982. Cert. elem. tchr., mentally retarded, learning disabled, supr. student tchrs., socially maladjusted and emotionally disturbed edn., prin., parish or city sch. supr. instrn., reading specialist, spl. sch. prin., mild, moderate elem. and secondary edn., severe-profound parish or city sch. supr., La. Prin. John Martyn Sch., Jefferson Parish Sch. System, Metairie, La., ednl. strategist; prin. Waggaman (La.) Sch. Jefferson Parish Sch. System. Active community orgns. Recipient appreciation award Coun. for Exceptional Children, 1984, 89. Mem. NAESP, La. Assn. Sch. Execs., Phi Delta Kappa.

BOURGEOIS, ROGER ROBERT, fire protection systems company executive; b. Thibodaux, La., July 22, 1943; s. Abel Leonard and Leonie (Babin) B.; m. Diane Lee Miller, July 12, 1969 (div. 1972); m. Carolyn Marie Cunningham, June 21, 1979; children: Steven, Lea Ann, Terry, Jerri Lynn. BS in Indsl. Tech., La. State U., 1966. Constrn. engr. Exxon Pipeline Co., Raceland, La., 1969-75; mgr. Delta Fire Systems, Houma, La., 1975-84; pres. Bourgeois & Assocs., Inc., Houma, 1984—. Contbr. articles on fire protection to trade jours. Mem. Rep. Presdl. Task Force, Houma, 1966. With USAF, 1967-69. Mem. Nat. Fire Protection Assn. (committeeman), Fire Suppression Systems Assn. (pres. 1990-91, bd. mem. 1984-91, svc. award 1989), Am. Soc. Safety Engrs. (sec.-treas. 1984—), Instrument Soc. Am., Soc. Fire Protection Engrs. (past pres. La. chpt.), Houma-Terrebonne C. of C. (bd. dirs.), La. Automatic Fire Alarm Assn. (founder, pres. 1993-94). Republican. Roman Catholic. Office: Bourgeois & Assocs Inc Sta 1 Box 10157 Houma LA 70363

BOURGEOIS, SUSAN K., critical care nurse; b. Aberdeen, Miss., Apr. 22, 1955; d. Robert and Doris (Willis) King; m. Kenneth Bourgeois, Jan. 7, 1978. AD, Memphis State U., 1977; postgrad., Union U. Cert. critical care nurse; cert. nursing adminstr. Staff nurse Bapt. Meml. Hosp., Memphis, supr. telemetry, supr. cardiovascular-thoracic intensive care unit. Mem. AACN.

BOURGOYNE, ADAM THEODORE, JR., petroleum engineering educator; b. Baton Rouge, July 1, 1944; s. Adam Theodore and Marceline (Navarre) B.; m. Kathryn Daspit, Jan. 22, 1966; children: Darryl, Dwayne, Tammy, Ben, Brad, Tracey. B.S., La. State U., 1966, M.S., 1967, Ph.D., 1969. Registered profl. engr., La. Sr. systems engr. Continental Oil Co., Houston, 1969-70; asst. prof. petroleum engring. La. State U., Baton Rouge, 1970-74, assoc. prof., 1974-79, prof., 1979—, chmn. dept., 1979-83; dir. IADC Blowout Control Sch., Baton Rouge, 1980-83; pres. B & A, Inc., 1982-83; v.p. Coastal Petroleum Assocs., Inc., Baton Rouge, 1980-82. Author: Applied Drilling Engineering, 1983; inventor well control process. Mem. AIME-Soc. Petroleum Engrs. (disting. achievement for petroleum engring. faculty award 1981), Am. Petroleum Inst., Nat. Soc. Petroleum Engrs. (dir.), Tau Beta Pi, Pi Epsilon Tau. Democrat. Roman Catholic. Home: 6006 Boone Ave Baton Rouge LA 70808-5005 Office: Dept Petroleum Engring La State Univ Baton Rouge LA 70803

BOURJAILY, VANCE, novelist; b. Cleve., Sept. 17, 1922; s. Monte Ferris and Barbara (Webb) B.; m. Bettina Yensen, 1946; children: Anna (sec.), Philip, Robin; m. Yasmin Mogul, 1985; 1 child, Omar. A.B., Bowdoin Coll., 1947. Newspaperman, TV dramatist, playwright, lectr.; prof. U. Ariz., U. Iowa Writers Workshop, 1958-80; co-founder, editor Discovery, 1951-53; cultural mission to S.Am. auspices State Dept., 1959, 73; Boyd prof. La. State U., Baton Rouge, 1985—; Disting. vis. prof. Oreg. State U., summer 1968; vis. prof. U. Ariz., 1977-78. Author: The End of My Life, 1947, The Hound of Earth, 1953, The Violated, 1958, Confessions of a Spent Youth, 1960, (non-fiction) The Unnatural Enemy, 1963, The Man Who Knew Kennedy, 1967, Brill Among the Ruins, 1970 (nominated Nat. Book Award for fiction 1971),(non-fiction) Country Matters, 1973, Now Playing at Canterbury, 1976, A Game Men Play, 1980, The Great Fake Book, 1987, Old Soldier, 1990, Fishing By Mail: The Outdoor Life of a Father and Son, 1993. Mem. campaign staff Hughes for Senate, 1968. Served with Am. Field Service, 1942-44; Served with AUS, 1944-46. Recipient Academy Award in lit., American Academy of Arts and Letters, 1993. Office: William Morris Agy care Owen Laster 1350 Avenue Of The Americas New York NY 10019-4702

BOURKE, WILLIAM OLIVER, retired metal company executive; b. Chgo., Apr. 12, 1927; s. Robert Emmett and Mable Elizabeth (D'Arcy) B.; m. Elizabeth Philbey, Sept. 4, 1970; children: Judith A., Andrew E., Edward A. Student, U. Ill., 1944-45; B.S. in Commerce, DePaul U., 1951. With Ford Motor Co., Dearborn, Mich., 1956-60, nat. distbn. mgr., 1960-64; gen. sales mgr. Ford Can., Toronto, Ontario, 1964-67; asst. mng. dir. Ford Australia, Melbourne, 1967-70, mgr. dir., 1970-71; pres. Ford Asia-Pacific and South Africa, Inc., Melbourne, 1971-72, Ford Asia-Pacific, Inc., Melbourne, 1972-73; pres. Europe, Inc., 1973-75, chmn. bd., 1975-80; exec. v.p. Ford N.Am. Automotive Ops., Dearborn, 1980-81, also bd. dirs.; exec. v.p. Reynolds Metals Co., Richmond, Va., 1981-83, pres., COO, 1983-86, pres., CEO, 1986-88, chmn. bd., CEO, 1988-92; bd. dirs. Premark Internat., Inc., Merrill Lynch, Sonat, Inc., Tupperware Corp. 1st lt. M.I., U.S. Army, 1944-48. Office: Reynolds Metals Co 6601 W Broad St Richmond VA 23230-1701

BOURLAND, D(ELPHUS) DAVID, JR., linguist; b. Wichita Falls, Tex., June 6, 1928; s. Delphus David and Margaret (Hawley) B.; m. Elizabeth Jagush, Oct. 16, 1981; children by previous marriages: David III, Meda, Ruskin, Ileana. AB, Harvard U., 1951, MBA, 1953; lic. in English linguistics, U. Costa Rica, 1973. Ops. analyst Ops. Evaluation Group MIT, Washington, 1955-61; with various corps., 1961-65; pres. IR Assocs., Inc., San Diego, 1965-69, Semantics Rsch. Corp., Washington, 1969-71; from instr. to assoc. prof. U. Costa Rica, San Jose, 1971-80; pres. Semantics Rsch. Corp., Wichita Falls, Tex., 1994—; trustee Inst. Gen. Semantics, 1964-89. Author: Introduccion a la Tagmemica, 1974; co-author: An Advanced Course in Squirrelly Semantics: A Coloring Book for Some Adults, 1993, Not So Great Moments in the Lives of Great Men and Women, 1994; editor Gen. Semantics Bull., 1964-70; co-editor: To Be or Not: An E-Prime Anthology, 1991, More E-Prime: To Be or Not II, 1994, E-Prime III!, 1997; contbr. articles to profl. publs. Lt. USNR, 1953-65. Korzybski fellow Inst. Gen. Semantics, 1949-50. Mem. Inst. Gen. Semantics, Internat. Soc. Gen. Semantics (contbg. editor Et Cetera, bd. dirs. 1993—, v.p. devel. 1995—), Am. Legion (comdr. dept. Panama Canal 1979-81, post comdr. Costa Rica 1980-84), Sons Am. Legions (nat. adjutant 1985, 86), Forty and Eight (nat. exec. com. 1983-86), Harvard Faculty Club, Harvard Club Boston, Univ. Club of Wichita Falls, Wichita Falls Country Club, Sons. Confederate Vets., Wichita Falls Yacht Club. Republican. Home: 1517 Celia Dr Wichita Falls TX 76302-3515

BOUTROS, LINDA NELENE WILEY, medical/surgical nurse; b. New Orleans, Aug. 31, 1951; d. Robert Vernon and Marye Dell (Adcock) Wiley; m. Eddy Boutros, Dec. 23, 1972; children: Scott, Mark, Natalie. BS in Nursing, U. S.W. La., 1973. RN, coord./supr. of nursing Kelsey Seybold Clinic, Missouri City, Tex., 1982-86; RN, head nurse S.W. Pediatric Ctr., Sugarland, Tex., 1986-87; RN, nursing supr. Westshore Hosp., Tampa, Fla., 1988-89; med.-surg. nurse Centurion Hosp., Carrollwood, Tampa, 1989-90, asst. head nurse med., 1990-91; relief supr. Centurion Hosp., Carrollwood, Tampa, 1991, dir. surg. nursing svcs., 1992-93; nurse mgr. surg. floor, relief supr. Univ. Cmty. Hosp. Carrollwood, Tampa, Fla., 1993—. Mem. ANA, Fla. Nurses Assn. Home: 502 Brooktree Ct Lutz FL 33549-4427 Office: Univ Cmty Hosp Carrollwood 7171 N Dale Mabry Hwy Tampa FL 33614-2670

BOUTTE, DAVID GRAY, oil industry executive, lawyer; b. Kingman, Ariz., Sept. 6, 1944; s. Riley Joseph and Audray Echo (Bowden) B.; m. Caroline Ruth Regitko, June 27, 1981; children: Ryan Gray, Gray Douglas, Banks David Gray. BA in History, Calif. State U., Long Beach, 1966; JD, U. So. Calif., 1972. Bar: Calif. 1973, U.S. Ct. Appeals (9th cir.) 1973, D.C. 1976, U.S. Supreme Ct. 1976, U.S. Ct. Appeals (D.C. cir.) 1976. Asst. to chief engr. Norris Industries, Inc., L.A., 1964-66; law clk. to Hon. Judge Walter Ely U.S. Ct. Appeals (9th cir.), L.A., 1972-73; law clk. to Hon. Warren Burger U.S. Supreme Ct., Washington, 1973-74; assoc. O'Melveny & Myers, L.A., 1974-78; dir. staff task force U.S. Dept. Def., Washington, 1978-80; gen. counsel alt. energy div. Mobil Oil Corp., N.Y.C., 1980-83; mgr. planning coordination Mobil Chem. Co., Stamford, Conn., 1983-86; gen. counsel internat. div. Mobil Oil Corp., 1986-90; assoc. gen. counsel mktg. and refining div. Mobil Oil Corp., Fairfax, Va., 1989-90, div. exec. internat. div., 1990-93, gen. mgr. environ., health & safety, govt. rels., 1993—. Editor-in-chief So. Calif. Law Rev., 1971-72. Commr. L.A. Pub. Commn. on County Govt., 1974-75; trustee The Washington Opera, Hudson Inst., Japan-Am. Soc.; bd. dirs. Marine Preservation Assn., Coun. of the Ams.; bd. govs. Nat. Ctr. for APEC; steering com. U.S. Coun. for Internat. Bus., environ. com.; mem. adv. coun. The Asia Soc., CARE, Nat. Mus. Women in Arts. Decorated Purple Heart. Mem. Order of Coif, Sleepy Hollow Country Club (Scarborough, N.Y.). Republican. Episcopalian. Office: 27640 Villa Rd Easton MD 21601

BOVARNICK, BENNETT, lawyer, management consultant; b. Lawrence, Mass., June 22, 1924; s. Jacob and Rose C. (Fineman) B.; m. Evelyn Singer, Dec. 28, 1948; children: Deborah, Ellen, Daniel. BS in Engring., Calif. Inst. Tech., 1946; AM and PhD in Physics, Boston U., 1949, 58, LLM in Taxation, 1979; JD, New Eng. Sch. Law, 1978. Bar: Mass 1978, FLa. 1979. Jr. engr. Boston U., 1948-49, instr., 1949-50; physicist U.S. Navy Underwater Sound Lab., New London, Conn., 1950-51; materials engr. U.S. Army Watertown (Mass.) Arsenal, 1951-59; materials scientist Raytheon Co., Waltham, Mass., 1959-61; sr. materials engr. Arthur D. Little, Inc., Cambridge, Mass., 1961-74; ind. mgmt. cons. Arthur D. Little, Inc., Newton, Mass, 1974-79; pvt. practice Miami, Fla., 1979-85, Boca Raton, Fla., 1985—; gen. counsel New Horizons Cmty. Mental Health Ctr., Inc., Miami, 1981—, New Horizons Found., Inc., Boca Raton, 1983—. Sec. of Army research fellow, 1957. Mem. Fla. Bar Assn., Mass. Bar Assn. Jewish. Home: 3945 NW 27th Ave Boca Raton FL 33434-4436 Office: 2200 Corporate Blvd NW Ste 303 Boca Raton FL 33431-7307

BOVENDER, JACK OLIVER, JR., health care executive; b. Winston Salem, N.C., Aug. 16, 1945; s. Jack Oliver Sr. and Eva Louise (Westmoreland) B.; m. Barbara Ann Tuttle; 1 child, Richard Spencer. AB, Duke U., 1967, MHA, 1969. Asst. adminstr. Community Gen. Hosp., Thomasville, N.C., 1972-75; assoc. adminstr. West Fla. Regional Med. Ctr., Pensacola, 1975-77; adminstr. Largo Med. Ctr., Largo, Fla., 1977-80, West Fla. Regional Med. Ctr., Pensacola, 1980-85; div. v.p. Hosp. Corp. Am., Atlanta, 1985-87; pres., group ops. Hosp. Corp. Am., Nashville, 1987-91; sr. v.p., operations Hospital Corp. of America, Nashville, TN, now exec. v.p., COO. Mem. editorial bd. Jour. of Health Adminstrn. Edn., Washington, 1987—, Health Adminstrn. Press, Ann Arbor, Mich., 1988—. Bd. dirs. United Way, Pensacola, 1984; sr. warden and vestryman Christ Ch., Pensacola, 1982-85. Lt. USN, 1969-72. Fellow Am. Coll. Healthcare Execs.; mem. Pensacola C. of C. (bd. dirs. 1984), Leadership Nashville, Duke U. Hosp. and Health Adminstrn. Alumni Coun. (pres. 1986-87), Duke U. Gen. Alumni Bd., Rotary (Largo, Pensacola). Republican. Episcopalian. Home: 6517 Radcliff Dr Nashville TN 37221-3716 Office: HCA Health SVCS of Virginia 1602 Skipwith Rd Richmond VA 23229

BOWDEN, ANN, bibliographer, educator; b. East Orange, N.J., Feb. 7, 1924; d. William and Anna Elisabeth (Herrstrom) Haddon; m. Edwin Turner Bowden, June 12, 1948; children: Elisabeth Bowden Ward, Susan Turner, Edwin Eric; m. William Burton Todd, Nov. 23, 1969. BA, Radcliffe Coll., 1948; MS in Library Services, Columbia U., 1951; PhD, U. Tex., 1975. Cataloger, reference asst. Yale U., 1948-53; manuscript cataloger, rare book librarian, librarian Humanities Research Ctr., librarian Acad. Ctr., U. Tex., Austin, 1958-63, lectr., sr. lectr. Grad. Sch. Library and Info. Sci., 1964-85, 88-89; coordinator adult services Austin Pub. Library, 1963-67, asst. dir., 1967-71, dep. dir., 1971-77, assoc. dir., 1977-86; bd. dirs. Tex. Info. Exchange, Houston, 1977-78; bd. dirs. AMIGOS Bibliog. Council, Dallas, 1978-82, chmn. bd., 1980-81, trustee emeritus, 1986—; chmn. AMIGOS '85 Plan, 1984-86; scholar in residence Rockefeller Found. Villa Serbelloni, Bellagio, Italy, 1986, Ransom Ctr. scholar U. Tex., Austin, 1990—; Zachariah Polson fellow Libr. Co. of Phila., 1990. Author (with W.B. Todd) Tauchnitz International Editions in English, 1988; editor: T.E. Lawrence Fifty Letters: 1921-1935, 1962; Maps and Atlases, 1978; assoc. editor Papers of the Bibliographical Soc. Am., 1967-82; contbr. articles to profl. jours. Served as cpl. USMC Women's Res., 1944-46. Mem. ALA (council 1975-79), Assn. Coll. and Research Libraries (chmn. rare book and manuscript sect. 1975-76), Tex. Library Assn. (chmn. publs. com. 1965-71), Bibliog. Soc. Am., Phi Kappa Phi, Kappa Tau Alpha. Club: Grolier (N.Y.C.).

BOWDEN, ELBERT VICTOR, banking, finance and economics educator, author; b. Wrightsville, N.C., Nov. 25, 1924; s. James Owen and Dovie Ellen (Phelps) B.; m. Doris Adele Fales (div.); children: Elbert V. Jr., Richard Ashley, Doris Ellen, Jack Bryson, William Austin, Joyce Leigh; m. Judith Louise Holbert; children: Kristen R., Amy L. BA in Econs. and Polit. Sci. with high distinction, U. Conn., 1950; MA in Econs., Duke U., 1952, PhD in Econs., 1957. Grad. asst. dept. econs. Duke U., Durham, N.C., 1950-53, instr. dept. econs., 1953-54, 55-56; rsch. assoc. Bur. Bus. Rsch. U. Ky., Lexington, 1954-55; assoc. prof. Norfolk (Va.) Coll. of William and Mary (name now Old Donimion U.), 1956-59, prof., chmn. dept. econs., 1959-63; prof. econs. Elmira (N.Y.) Coll., 1963-64, SUNY, Fredonia, 1970-75; exec. dir. Upper Peninsula Com. for Area Progress, Escanaba, Mich., 1964-65; chief economist, chief of mission Robert R. Nathan Assocs. Trust Terr. Econ. Devel. Team, Saipan, Mariana Islands, 1965-67; assoc. prof., rsch. economist Tex. A&M U., 1967-70; chief econ. adviser, project mgr. Fiji Regional Planning Project UN, Suva, 1975-77; prof. econs. and fin., chair banking Appalachian State U., Boone, N.C., 1977—, Alfred T. Adams disting. prof., 1992—; dir. Houston-Galveston (Tex.) Area Project Fed. Water Pollution Control Adminstrn. and Tex. Water Quality Bd., 1967-69; testifier Interstate Commerce Commn., U.S. Senate Pub. Works Com., U.S. Senate Com. on Interior and Insular Affairs, 1964-66; asst. Blue Ridge Electric Membership Corp.; speaker Olean (N.Y.) Bus. Inst., 1979; cons., presenter seminars, workshops in field. Author: Economics, 1960, rev. edit., 1969, Economics in Perspective, 1974, 3rd rev. edit., 1990, Economics: The Science of Common Sense, 1974, 8th edit., 1995, Money, Banking and the Financial System, 1989, numerous others; co-author: (with Judith Holbert) Revolution in Banking: Regulatory Changes, The New Competitive Environment and the New World for the Financial Services Industry in the 1980s, 1980, rev. 1984; contbr. articles, papers, book revs. to profl. publs. and orgns. Mem. fin. com. City of Seven Devils, N.C., 1982-85; asst. N.C. Dept. Marine Fisheries; adv. bd. Statewide Taxpayers Ednl. Coalition. With U.S. Mcht. Marine, 1943-46, ATO and PTO. Ford Found. fellow, 1960. Mem. AAAS, AAUP, Nat. Assn. Bus. Econs. (U.S. and Carolinas chpts.), Am. Bus. Communication Assn., Am. Econ. Assn., Am. Fin. Assn. (com. 1960-61), Atlantic Econ. Soc., Community Colls. Social Scis. Assn., Ea. Fin. Assn., Fin. Mgmt. Assn., N.Am. Econs. and Fin. Assn., Regional Sci. Assn., So. Econ. Assn., So. Fin. Assn., So. Regional Sci. Assn., Southwestern Social Sci. Assn. (chmn. interdisciplinary symposium on urban and regional problem solving 1970), Western Econ. Assn., Western Regional Sci. Assn. (program planning com.). Home: PO Box 1461 Boone NC 28607-1461 Office: Appalachian State U Coll Bus Banking Chair Boone NC 28608

BOWDEN, JAMES ALVIN, construction company financial executive; b. Vernal, Utah, Mar. 19, 1948; s. Alvin George and Erva (Kirk) B.; m. Jane Ruth Taylor, May 31, 1973; children: Scott James, Julie, Jeffrey Taylor, Camille, Timothy Kirk. BS in Civil Engring., Brigham Young U., 1972, MBA, 1974. Planning analyst Morrison Knudsen Corp., Boise, 1974, asst. mgr. corp. planning, 1974-75, mgr. fin. analysis, 1975-78, asst. treas., 1978-83, v.p. fin. real estate subs., 1983-84, treas., 1984-86, v.p. and treas., 1986-89; sr. v.p., chief fin. officer J.A. Jones, Inc., 1990—, also bd. dirs.; bd. dirs. Palmer & Cay of the Carolinas, Hebel S.W.; spl. instr. Boise State U., 1977-78. Bd. dirs. Boise chpt. ARC, 1982-89, treas., 1984-86, vice chmn. 1986-87, chmn. 1987-88, nat. nominating com. 1989-91; bd. dirs. Greater Carolinas chpt. ARC, 1991—, treas. 1992-93, chmn. elect., 1993, chmn., 1994-96; Charlotte World Affairs Coun., 1990—; pres. Idaho Edn. Project, 1990; mem. United Way, Boise, 1980-85; bd. dirs. Fundsy, 1989-91; mem. alumni bd. Brigham Young U. Sch. Mgmt, 1987-90. Mem. Beta Gamma Sigma. Republican. Mormon. Home: 2720 Flintgrove Rd Charlotte NC 28226-5621 Office: J A Jones Inc One South Executive Pk J A Jones Dr Charlotte NC 28287

BOWDEN, NANCY BUTLER, school administrator; d. Rogers Davis and Lilla Ann (Yarbrough) B.; m. Robert C. Bowden, 1970 (div. 1981); 1 child, Linda Camille. BA in English, Spanish, Southwest Tex. U., 1964; MEd in Counseling, U. Houston, 1972, EdD in Curriculum Instrn., 1978, postgrad., 1979. Cert. profl. mid-mgmt. adminstrv., Tex., profl. supr., Tex., profl. reading specialist, Tex., profl. coun., Tex., elem. gen. English Spanish, Tex., high sch. English Spanish, Tex. Tchr., Spanish, English, reading Bowie Jr. High Sch., Odessa, Tex., 1964-65; tchr., reading Nimitz Jr. High Sch., San Antonio, 1965-66; tchr., Spanish Chofu High Sch., Tokyo, 1966-68; tchr., English, speech Carverdale High Sch., Houston, 1968-69; tchr., English Clear Creek High Sch., League City, Tex., 1969-71; instr., curriculum instrn. dept. U. Houston, University Park, 1974-75, 76-77; asst. prof. U. Houston at Clear Lake, Clear Lake, 1978-86; asst. prin. Travis Elem. Sch., Baytown, Tex., 1986-92; reading specialist Metcalf Elem. Sch., Houston, 1992-93; asst. prin. Holmsley Elem. Sch., Houston, 1993—; adj. faculty mem. U. Houston, 1989, 90, lectr., 1975-76, 77-78; presenter in field. Contbr. articles to profl. jours. Mem. Nat. Assn. Elem. Sch. Prins., Nat. Coun. Tchrs. English, Internat. Reading Assn., Tex. Elem. Sch. Prins. Suprs. Assn., Tex. State Reading Assn., Greater Houston Area Reading Coun., Bay Area Reading Coun. (past. pres.), Assn. Supervision Curriculum Devel., Kappa Delta Pi. Home: 14111 Queensbury Ln Houston TX 77079-3228 Office: Holmsley Elem Sch 7315 Hudson Oaks Dr Houston TX 77095-1149

BOWDRE, PAUL REID, protective services official, consultant; b. N.Y.C., Aug. 27, 1958; s. Philip Ross and Inge Elenore (Eckert) B. BS, Western Carolina U., 1981; cert. in Social Gerontology, U. N.C.-Asheville, 1981; MPS in Gerontology, Coll. Boca Raton, Fla., 1988; PhD, Nova Southeastern U., 1994. Cert. fraud examiner. Rsch. asst. Mo. Gerontology Inst., Columbia, 1981-83; asst. swim coach U. Mo., Columbia, 1981-83, teaching asst. Dept. Sociology, 1982-83; pub. safety officer North Palm Beach Dept. Pub. Safety, Fla., 1983-85; nat. and olympic swim coach Federcion Nacional de Natacion, Guatemala, May-Aug. 1984; police officer ops. div. Town of Palm Beach, 1985, field tng. officer, 1985-86, detective organized crime, vice and narcotics unit, 1986-91, sgt. patrol div., 1991, organized crime, vice and narcotics unit, 1991-93, profl. standards unit, 1993, capt. law enforcement divsn., 1994-95; sr. inspector Inspector Gen.'s Office Fla. Dept. Corrections, 1995—; cons. in field. Author: (with others) Death & Dying: In-Home Care-

A Teaching Curriculum, 1983, Safety: In-Home Care-A Teaching Curriculum, 1983; contbr. articles to profl. publs. Asst. scoutmaster Troop 132 Gulf Stream coun. Boy Scouts Am., 1981-84; trustee North Palm Beach Police and Fire Pension Bd., 1984-85. Research grantee Sigma Xi, 1981. Mem. Acad. Criminal Justice Scis., Am. Soc. Law Enforcement Trainers, So. Criminal Justice Assn., Nat. Eagle Scout Assn., Nat. Assn. Bunco Investigators, Am. Soc. Criminology, Midwest Sociol. Soc. (student dir. 1981-82), Am. Sociol. Assn. (regional newsletter reporter 1982-83), Gerontol. Soc. Am. (Biol. scis. sect. com. member 1983), Gerontol. Soc. Fla., The Catamount Club, Alpha Kappa Delta, Sigma Phi Omega. Democrat. Baptist. Home: 1145 Duncan Cir # 104 West Palm Beach FL 33418-8035 Office: Fla Dept Corrections Inspect Gen's Office 189 SE 3rd Ave Ste 1 Delray Beach FL 33483-4541

BOWEN, BILL MONROE, educational administrator; b. Kingsport, Tenn., June 7, 1940; s. Freda Arbutus Short, Nov. 13, 1977; children: Timmy, Terry, Tina, Billy Jr. AA, Lees McRae Coll., Banner Elk, N.C., 1961; BS, East Tenn. State U., 1964; MA, Nova Southeastern U., Ft. Lauderdale, Fla., 1995. Cert. tchr. early childhood devel. Tchr./coach Boone's Creek H.S., Gray, Tenn., 1964-67, Johnson City (Tenn.) South Jr. H.S., 1967-68, Church Hill (Tenn.) H.S., 1968-69, Lynn View H.S., Kingsport, Tenn., 1969-72, Science Hill H.S., Johnson City, 1972-73; recreation supr. City of Johnson City, 1973-74; profl. fundraiser NASCO, Inc., Springfield, Tenn., 1974-75; dir. ACC, Inc., Appalachia, Va., 1975-76; exec. dir. A.R.C.H.S. Inc. (Appalachian Regional Cmty. Head Start), Norton, Va., 1976—; co-founder Star of David, Inc., Keokee, Va., 1983—, David's Tabernacle, Appalachia, 1991—; founder Quad County Head Start, Norton, 1989—. Author: No Place to Go, 1979, Lonesome Pine Preacher, 1982, Blue Candy Heart, 1984, Jews of Babylon, 1990. Recipient Citizenship award Women's Athletic Assn., Banner Elk, 1961, 100% award East Tenn. State U., 1964, Leadership and Guidance award Wise County Norton Head Start, Norton, Va., 1982, Devoted Effort award, 1992, Child's Best Friend award, 1992, Progress award, Coeburn, Va., 1982. Mem. Va. Coun. Head Start Dirs., Assn. for Childhood Edn., Nat. Assn. Edn. Young Children, Am. Assn. for Edn. Young Children, Kiwanis. Office: ARCHS Inc 736 Park Ave Norton VA 24273

BOWEN, DUDLEY HOLLINGSWORTH, JR., federal judge; b. Augusta, Ga., June 25, 1941. A.B. in Fgn. Lang., U. Ga., 1964, LL.B., 1965; profesor invitado (hon.), Universidad Externada de Bogotá, 1987. Bar: Ga. 1965. Pvt. practice law Augusta, 1968-72; bankruptcy judge U.S. Dist. Ct. (so. dist.), 1972-75, judge, 1979—; ptnr. firm Dye, Miller, Bowen & Tucker, Augusta, 1975-79; bd. dirs. Southeastern Bankruptcy Law Inst., 1976-87; mem. Ct. Security Com. Jud. Conf. U.S., 1987-92. Mem. bd. visitors U. Ga. Sch. Law, 1987-90. Served to 1st lt. inf., U.S. Army, 1966-68. Decorated Commendation medal. Mem. State Bar Ga. (chmn. bankruptcy law sect. 1977), Fed. Judges Assn. (bd. dirs. 1985-90), 11th Cir. Dist. Judges Assn. (sec.-treas. 1988-89, pres. elect 1989-90, pres. 1991-92). Presbyterian. Office: US Dist Ct PO Box 2106 Augusta GA 30903-2106

BOWEN, EVA JOYCE (EVA JOYCE JONES), evaluation program educator, consultant; b. Gordon, Ga., Oct. 21, 1934; d. Emmett Jackson and Bessie Mabel (Brooks) Jones; m. J.W. Bowen; children: Agnes Irene B. Williams, John Paul, James Madison. AB in Religious Edn., Tift Coll., 1955; cert. elem. edn., Mercer U., 1963, M in Elem. Edn. and Reading, 1972; cert. in gifted edn., Ga. Southwestern Coll., 1982; EdS in Adminstrn. and Supervision, U. Ga., 1984. Tchr. Norman Park (Ga.) High Sch., 1955-56, Bibb County Sch. System, Macon, Ga., 1957-68; lead tchr. Dodge County Sch. System, Eastman, Ga., 1968-74; reading cons. Heart of Ga., Eastman, 1974-89; prof. Ga. Southwestern Coll., Americus, 1979-81, Mercer U., Eastman, 1986; tchr. evaluation program, trainer Ga. Dept. Edn., Eastman, 1988-92; coord. media staff devel. Heart of Ga., Eastman, 1974-89; developer, coord. Dist. Authors Day Celebration, 1985-89; trainer Learning Styles, Eastman, 1981-89; developer, trainer summer reading program, 1982-85; adj. prof. Mercer U., 1989-92; freelance ednl. cons., 1988-94. Editor: The Fourth B, 1968, Best of the Best, 1988; contbr. articles to profl. jours. Dist. leader Ga. 4-H Club, Eastman, 1970-74; pres. Heart of Ga. Reading Coun., Dublin, 1983; pres. Ga. Coun. Reading Cons., 1983-85, Ga. Reading Coun., Atlanta, 1988-89. Recipient Tchr. of Yr. award Dodge County Sch. System, 1973, Ga. Reading Leadership award, 1985, Annette P. Hopson Svc. award, 1992; named to Ga. Reading Hall of Fame, 1992. Mem. Internat. Reading Assn., Ga. Coun. of Internat. Reading Assn., Heart of Ga. Reading Coun., Delta Kappa Gamma Soc. 9chair com.), Kappa Delta Epsilon (pres., advisor Macon chpt. 1968-74). Democrat. Baptist. Home: PO Box 11324 Macon GA 31212-1324

BOWEN, JOHN W., business executive; b. 1954. With Bank of Dawson, Ga., 1975-80, Morris State Bank, Dublin, Ga., 1980-83; pres. Universal Blanchers Inc., Blakely, Ga., 1983—. Office: Universal Blanchers Inc Hwy 62 Industrial Park Blakely GA 31723

BOWEN, KIRA L., plant pathologist; b. Scranton, Pa., Oct. 10, 1958; d. Lee Roland and Celia (Wisniewski) B. BS in Plant Sci., Pa. State U., 1980; MS in Plant Pathology, U. Minn., 1983; PhD in Plant Pathology, U. Ill., 1987. Lab. asst. dept. plant pathology Pa. State U., University Park, 1977-79; grad. rsch. asst. dept. plant pathology U. Minn., St. Paul, 1980-83; cons. Asian Vegetable Rsch. and Devel. Ctr., Shanhua, Taiwan, China, 1983; rsch. asst. dept. plant pathology U. Ill., Urbana, 1983-87; rsch. affiliate USDA-ARS, dept. plant pathology N.C. State U., Raleigh, 1987-88; asst. prof., assoc. grad. faculty dept. plant pathology Auburn (Ala.) U., 1988-93, assoc. prof., grad. faculty dept. plant pathology, 1993—, mem. senate, 1990-93; vis. scientist Internat. Rsch. Ctr. for Maize and Wheat Improvement Hdqrs., El Batan, Mex., 1982. Author: (with P.S. Teng) The Cereal Rusts, Vol. II, 1985, Crop Loss Assessment and Pest Management, 1987; assoc. editor: Phytopathology jour., 1991-93; edit. com. Highlights of Agricultural Rsch. quarterly rsch. report; contbr. articles to profl. jours. Mem. Auburn Women's Caucus, 1989—, sec., 1992-94, co-chmn., 1994—. Grantee Ala. Feed Grains Assn., 1990, USDA, 1991, 93, Southeastern Poultry and Egg Assn., 1991, So. Regional IPM, 1991, 92, Sustainable Agrl. Rsch. and Edn., 1993-96, Nat. Rsch. Initiative Competitive Grants Program: Agrl. Systems, 1996. Mem. Am. Peanut Rsch. and Edn. Soc., Am. Phytopathological Soc. Office: Auburn U Dept Plant Pathology 209 Life Scis Auburn AL 36849

BOWEN, MARCIA KAY, customs house broker; b. Bradford, Pa., July 20, 1957; d. George W. Allen Jr. and Katherine (Jema) Allen; m. Glenn Edward Rollins, June 26, 1975 (div. 1979); m. Michael James Bowen, Dec. 27, 1983; children: James Derek, Kodie Ann. Student Houston Community Coll., 1978-81, Am. Mgmt. Assn., 1984-85. Lic. customs house broker. Asst. mgr. W.R. Zanes & Co. of La., Inc., Houston, 1975-76; sec. Westchester Corp., Houston, 1973-75; import br. mgr. Schenkers Internat., Inc., Houston, 1976-85; br. mgr. F.W. Myers & Co., Inc., El Paso, 1985-88, regional mgr., 1989-91; v.p. Southwest region The Myers Group (US) Inc., 1992—. Mem. NAFE, Houston Customs House Brokers Assn. (sec. 1977-79, mem. U.S. customs com. 1979-83), El Paso Customs House Brokers Assn. (v.p. 1994), Houston Freight Forwarders Assn., El Paso Fgn. Trade Zone Assn., Soc. Global Trade Execs., El Paso/Juarez Transp. and Distbn. Assn., Inc., El Paso Custon Brokers Assn. (v.p. 1994). Roman Catholic. Office: The Myers Group (US) Inc 34 Spur Dr El Paso TX 79906-5308

BOWEN, RAY MORRIS, academic administrator, engineering educator; b. Ft. Worth, Mar. 30, 1936; s. Winfred Herbert and Elizabeth (Williams) B; m. Sara Elizabeth Gibbens, July 5, 1958; children: Raymond Morris, Marguerite Elizabeth. BS in Mech. Engring., Texas A&M U., 1958, PhD in Engring., 1961; MS in Mech. Engring, Calif. Inst. Tech., 1959. Registered profl. engr., Tex., Ky. Assoc. prof. Mech. Engring. La. State U., Baton Rouge, 1965-67; prof. Mech. Engring. Rice U., Houston, 1967-83, chmn. dept., 1972-77; dir. divsn. NSF, Washington, 1982-83, from acting asst. dir., engr. to dep. asst. dir., engr., 1990-91; prof. Engring., dean U. Ky., Lexington, 1983-89; v.p. acad. affairs Okla. State U., Stillwater, Okla., 1991-93; interim pres. Okla. State U., Stillwater, 1992-93; pres. Tex. A&M U., College Station, 1993—; mem. staff Sandia Corp., Albuquerque, summers 1966, 67, 72, cons., 1970-78; cons. U.S. Army Ballistic Rsch. Lab, Aberdeen Proving Ground, Md., 1970, Sun Oil Co., Albuquerque, 1974-75. Author: Introduction to Continuum Mechanics for Engineers, 1989; co-author: Introduction to Vectors and Tensors, Vols. I and II, 1976; contbg. author: Rational Thermodynamics, 1984; contbr. articles to profl. jours. Capt. USAF, 1961-64. Fellow Johns Hopkins U., 1964-65;. Fellow ASME (ad hoc vis. list Accreditation Bd. Engring. and Tech. 1977-83, bd. profl. devel. 1984-90, coun. edn. 1986—, nominating com. 1988-90, assoc. editor Jour. Applied Mechanics 1990-93); mem. NSF (adv. bd. divsn. mechanics and structural systems), Am. Soc. Engring. Edn., Soc. Natural Philosophy, Soc. Engring. Sci., U. Ky. Inst. Mines and Minerals Rsch. (bd. dirs. 1983-89), U.Ky. Transp. Ctr. (bd. dirs. 1984-89), Stillwater C. of C., Soc. Scholars Johns Hopkins U., Tau Beta Pi, Phi Kappa Phi, Sigma Xi. Office: Tex A&M Univ Rudder Tower Room 805 Office of Pres College Station TX 77843-1246

BOWER, DOUGLAS WILLIAM, pastoral counselor, psychotherapist, clergyman; b. Niagara Falls, N.Y., Jan. 6, 1948; s. Charles Henry Bower and Phyllis June (Rank) Ayres; m. Cheryl Stewart, May 25, 1980; children: Katherine Elizabeth, Erin Colleen. AA, Manatee Jr. Coll., Bradenton, Fla., 1969; BS, Oglethorpe U., 1972; PhD, U. Ga., 1989. RN, Ga.; ordained to ministry United Meth. Ch., 1980; cert. counselor, Ga. Nurse Northside Hosp., Atlanta, 1970-80; assoc. pastor lst United Meth. Ch., Griffin, Ga., 1980-82; pastor, pastoral counselor Oconee Street United Meth. Ch., Athens, Ga., 1982-86; dir. Counseling Ministeries, Athens, 1986—. Contbr. articles to profl. jours. Mem. ACA, Assn. for Religious and Value Issues in Counseling, Person-Centered Assn., N.E. Ga. Mental Health Assn. Republican. Office: Counseling Ministries PO Box 209 Crawford GA 30630-0209

BOWER, PHILIP JEFFREY, cardiologist, administrator; b. Kenmore, N.Y., Nov. 23, 1935; s. Philip Graydon and Evelyn (McLoney) B.; m. Ann Bruce Weaver, Aug. 9, 1958; children: Elizabeth Ann, Susan Lynn. BA, U. Va., 1957; MD, Johns Hopkins U., 1961. Diplomate Am. Bd. Internal Medicine, subsplty. cardiology. Intern in medicine U. N.C., Chapel Hill, 1961-62; resident in medicine Johns Hopkins Hosp., Balt., 1962-63; resident in medicine Mayo Clinic, Rochester, Minn., 1965-66, resident in cardiology, 1966-68; staff physician cardiology Ochsner Clinic, New Orleans, La., 1968-78; dir. cardiology, dir. cardiac catheterization lab. East Jefferson Hosp., Metairie, La., 1978—; instr. medicine U. Ga. Sch. Medicine, 1963-65, Tulane U., New Orleans, 1970-74; clin. asst. prof. medicine La. State U., New Orleans, 1974—; clin. prof. medicine Tulane U., New Orleans, 1983—; bd. dirs. East Jefferson Gen. Hosp. Found.; faculty mem. Advanced Cardiac Life Support Affiliate; cons. Scimed., 1988—; adv. bd. Advanced Catheter Sys., 1988—; presenter in field. Contbr. articles to profl. jours. Capt. U.S. Army, 1963-65. Fellow ACP, Am. Coll. Chest Physicians, Am. Coll. Cardiology, Soc. Cardiac Angiography and Interventions; mem. AMA, Am. Heart Assn. (bd. dirs. 1979-83, fellow Coun. Clin. Cardiology), Am. Soc. Echocardiography, So. Med. Assn., La. Med. Soc., La. Heart Assn. (chmn. physician edn. com. pres.-elect 1976, pres. 1977), Jefferson Parish Med. Soc., Phi Kappa Psi, Phi Chi. Home: 199 Sauve Rd River Ridge LA 70123-1933 Office: East Jefferson Hosp Dept Cardiology 4200 Houma Blvd Metairie LA 70006-2970

BOWERS, CAROLYN POWERS, business and office education educator; b. Clarksville, Tenn., Dec. 11, 1945; d. Carl Liberty and Margaret Eudora (Poyner) Powers; m. William Michael Bowers, June 27, 1963; chlidren: Laurie Lynn Bowers Swift, Margaret Alice Bowers Hooper. BS, Austin Peay State U., 1967, MA in Edn., 1975; postgrad., U. Tenn. Cert. tchr., Tenn. Tchr. bus. and office edn. Clarksville (Tenn.) High Sch., 1969-74, 94—, tchr. stenography lab, compuerized acctg. software tools, 1974-84; tchr. data processing Clarksville Vo-Tech Ctr., 1984-94, liason staff, 1990-93; mem. state steering com. Tenn. Tchrs. Study Coun., 1980-82; pres., v.p., sec. Curriculum Coordinating Com., 1983-89; advisor Bus. Profls. Am., Clarksville High Sch. and Vocat. Tech. Ctr. chpt., 1984-94. Tchr. CCD Immaculate Conception Ch., Clarksville, 1971-72, mem., 1964—; sponsor Future Tchrs. Am., 1994-95. Mem. NEA, Nat. Bus. Edn. Assn., Am. Vocat. Assn., Tenn. Bus. Edn. Assn., Tenn. Edn. Assn., Tenn. Vocat. Assn. (bd. dirs. bus. edn. 1992-94), Tenn. Office Edn. Tchrs. Assn. (pres. 1995-96), Clarksville Montgomery County Edn. Assn. (v.p., sec., treas., editor newsletter, Adopt-A-Sch. Coun. 1990—). Home: 2210 Springlot Rd Clarksville TN 37043-2205 Office: Clarksville High Sch 151 Richview Rd Clarksville TN 37043-4723

BOWERS, ELLIOTT TOULMIN, university president; b. Oklahoma City, Aug. 22, 1919; s. Lloyd and Enah (McDonald) B.; m. Frances Marie Handley, May 29, 1940; children—Linda Lu Rushing, Cynthia Ann Bowers Kimmel. B.S., Sam Houston State U., 1941, M.A., 1942; Ed.D., U. Houston, 1959. Dir. music Huntsville High Sch., 1937-42; mem. faculty Sam Houston State U., 1946-89, v.p. univ. affairs and dean of students, 1964-70, acting pres., 1963-64, pres., 1970-89, pres. emeritus, 1990—; dir. First Nat. Bank, Huntsville, Tex. Mem. Tex. Criminal Justice Council; bd. dirs. Sam Houston Area council Boy Scouts Am., Salvation Army, Am. Cancer Soc.; pres. bd. Wesley Found., 1962-63. Served with USAAF, 1943-46. Mem. Assn. Higher Edn., Huntsville C. of C. (past pres.), Masons, K.T., SAR, Alpha Phi Omega, Kappa Delta Pi, Phi Mu Alpha. Home: 1802 16th St Huntsville TX 77340-4205

BOWERS, MICHAEL JOSEPH, state attorney general; b. Jackson County, Ga., Oct. 7, 1941; s. Carl Ernest and Janie Ruth (Bolton) B.; m. Bette Rose Corley, June 8, 1963; children: Carl Wayne, Bruce Edward, Michelle Lisa. B.S., U.S. Mil. Acad., 1963; M.S., Stanford U., 1965; M.B.A., U. Utah-Wiesbaden, Germany, 1970; J.D., U. Ga., 1974. Bar: Ga. 1974. Sr. asst. atty. gen. State of Ga., Atlanta, 1975-81, atty. gen., 1981—. Served to capt. USAF, 1963-70. Mem. Lawyers Club, Kiwanis. Republican. Methodist. Home: 817 Allgood Rd Stone Mountain GA 30083-4803 Office: State Ga Dept Law 40 Capitol Sq SW Atlanta GA 30334-1300

BOWERS, PATRICIA NEWSOME, communications executive; b. Baton Rouge, June 21, 1944; d. Carl Allen and Sue Mayre (Powell) Newsome; m. Robert Lloyd Bowers Jr., Aug. 19, 1967 (div. Nov. 1979); children: Paige Ivy, Katherine Elizabeth. BJ, La. State U., 1967. Sr. writer, editor Litton Industries, Pascagoula, Miss., 1978-80; sr. presentations supr. Martin Marietta Aerospace, Orlando, Fla., 1980-81; mgr. presentations Martin Marietta Aerospace, Balt., 1981-85, mgr. pub. rels., 1985-90; dir. pub. rels. and corp. comm. Contraves USA, Pitts., 1990-92; sr. mgr. sector comms. Harris Electronic sys. sector Harris Corp., Melbourne, Fla., 1992-95; dir. mktg. and pub. rels. Intracoastal Health Systems, Inc., West Palm Beach, Fla., 1995—. Coach Parkville Recreation Council, Balt., 1985-87; bd. dirs. Salvation Army, Human Resources Devel. Agy. Balt. County, Brevard Symphony Youth Orch.; adv. bd. Nat. Aquarium in Balt.; active Brevard Leadership. Mem. Pub. Rels. Soc. Am. (bd. dirs. Chesapeake conf. 1987, Silver Anvil Judge, 1991, 92), Nat. Press Club, Navy League (bd. dirs. Balt. council 1986-87), Balt. County C. of C. (leadership program 1986-87), Pitts. Press Club, Forum Club of Palm Beach. Republican. Episcopalian. Office: Intracoastal Health Systems Inc 1309 N Flagler Dr West Palm Beach FL 33401-3406

BOWERS, THOMAS DANIEL, JR., policeman; b. Mexia, Tex., Jan. 14, 1949; s. Thomas D. and Elva Mae Bowers; m. Johnnie Mae Gatewood, June 5, 1971 (div. July 1975); children: Danielle, Nicole, Thomas, Stephen. A, U. Md., European divsn., 1974; BS, SUNY, Albany, 1975; MS, Abilene (Tex.) Christian U., 1977. Cert. law officer, Tex. Sgt. police Dallas Police Dept., 1974—; instr. tap South Dallas Cultural Ctr., 1991-92; tap dancer Bowers Dance, Dallas, 1991—; instr. tap and ballroom Dallas Black Dance Theater, 1992-93. Author: Issues in Afro-American Tap Dance, 1992; author revs. and songs. Singer choir Shileds of Faith, Dallas, 1990; vol. singer, dancer Dallas Ind. Sch. Dist. Staff sgt. USAF, 1967-74, Vietnam. Recipient User Freindley award City of Dallas, 1989. Mem. Am. Numismatic Assn., Tex. Peace Officer Assn., Dallas Police Assn., Masons. Democrat. Baptist. Office: Bowers Dance PO Box 224144 Dallas TX 75222-4144

BOWERSOX, CHRISTINA A., public relations executive; b. Pensacola, Fla., Mar. 7, 1955; d. William Crowell and Aline Mercedes (Day) B.;. BA in Comms., Springhill Coll., 1973-77. Announcer WLPR-FM, Mobile, Ala., 1978-81; talk show host, prodn. mgr. WKRG-AM, Mobile, Ala., 1981-85; freelance reporter Voice of Am., Washington, 1985; pub. rels. dir. Mobile Pub. Libr., 1986—; pub. affairs host WPMI-TV, Mobile, Ala., 1987-89. Contbr. article to Mobile Bay Monthly. Mem. adv. com. blood svcs. ARC, Mobile, Ala., 1981-92; mem. com. edn. Challenge 2000, Mobile, 1991-94; pres. exec. bd. Joe Jefferson Players, 1993-95, bd. dirs., 1995—. Mem. Pub. Rels. Coun. Ala. (student affairs, spl. projects Mobile chpt.), Nat. Soc. Fundraising Execs. Home: 261 Morgan Ave Mobile AL 36606 Office: Mobile Pub Libr 700 Government St Mobile AL 36602-1403

BOWLBY, ROGER LOUIS, economist, educator, researcher; b. Shiawassee County, Mich., Oct. 22, 1929; s. Jay Faxon and Ada Rose (Mühlbach) B.; m. Sylva Macrides, Oct. 31, 1953; children: Gavin Jay, Larry Brier. BA, Mich. State U., 1950, MA, 1951; PhD, U. Tex., 1958. Grad. asst. econs. Mich. State U., East Lansing, 1950-51; teaching fellow in econs. U. Tex., Austin, 1951-53, econs. instr., 1956-57; econs. instr. Iowa State U., Ames, 1957-58; asst. prof. econs. Mich. State U., East Lansing, 1958-63; labor economist Dept. Labor, Washington, 1963-65; from assoc. prof. to prof. econs. U. Tenn., Knoxville, 1965-96, prof. emeritus, 1996—; part-time instr. U. Md. Overseas, Molesworth AFB, Eng., 1956; labor expert Internat. Labour Office, Geneva, 1971, 74, 77, 86, 88. Contbr. articles to profl. jours. With U.S. Army, 1953-55. Mem. Am. Econ. Assn., Indsl. Rels. Rsch. Assn. Home: 2520 Tall Pine Ln Knoxville TN 37920-2849 Office: U Tenn Dept Econs Knoxville TN 37996

BOWLES, BETTY JONES, business education educator; b. Richmond, Va., June 10, 1947; d. Robert Lee and Blanche (Williamson) Jones; m. Norman Lee Bowles Sr., Feb. 14, 1970; children: Ruth Anne, Lee, Danny. BS, Va. Commonwealth U., 1969; M Humanities, U. Richmond, 1989. Cert. postgrad. profl., Va. Tchr. Lee Davis H.S., Mechanicsville, Va., 1969-72, 73-74, 84-87; sec. Battlefield Park Elem. Sch., Mechanicsville, 1972-73; sec. Stonewall Jackson Jr. H.S., Mechanicsville, 1982-84, tchr., 1987-91; tchr., dept. chair Atlee H.S., Mechanicsville, 1991—; mem. adv. bd. Commonwealth Coll., Richmond, Va., 1993—; presenter staff devel. workshop, activities on block scheduling pub. schs. in Va., 1993-94;, Walled Lake, Mich., 1994; Fayetteville, N.C., 1995; mem. Va.-Russia Tchr. Exchange in Moscow, 1995. Lit. sec. Cool Spring Bapt. Ch., Mechanicsville, 1988—. Named Vocat. Tchr. of Yr. Mechanicsville Rotary Club, 1994. Mem. Nat. Bus. Edn. Assn., So. Bus. Edn. Assn., Va. Bus. Edn. Assn., Va. Vocat. Assn. Baptist. Office: Atlee HS 9414 Atlee Station Rd Mechanicsville VA 23111-2600

BOWLES, STEFFANIE NOREEN, elementary school educator; b. Louisville, Mar. 2, 1967; d. James Stanley and Bonnie Lou (Messmore) B.; m. Scott Talbott Richards, Dec. 17, 1994; children: Nicolas Irie, Alexander Carl. BA in Art and Psychology, Transylvania U., 1988; MFA, Savannah Coll. of Art/Design, 1992; MEd, Ga. So. U., 1995. Cert. tchr. emotional/behavior disorders, specific learning disorders K-12, Ga. Tchr. Savannah-Chatham County Bd. Edn., 1992—. mem. Title One Schoolwide Reform Com., Garrison Elem. Sch., Savannah, 1995-96. Recipient HOPE scholarship, State of Ga., 1995-96. Democrat. Methodist. Home: 27 Nancy Pl Savannah GA 31406 Office: Garrison Elem Sch 768 W Jones St Savannah GA 31401-3116

BOWLING, JAMES CHANDLER, retired executive, farmer, philanthropist; b. Covington, Ky., Mar. 29, 1928; s. Van Dorn and Belinda (Johnson) B.; m. Ann Jones, Oct. 20, 1951; children: Belinda, Nancy, James Jr., Stephanie. B.S., U. Louisville, 1951; LL.D. (hon.), Murray U., 1976, U. Ky., 1981. With Philip Morris, Inc., N.Y.C., 1948-86, various positions from campus rep. to v.p. sales and corp. relations; then exec. v.p., group v.p.., dir. mktg., sr. v.p., bd. dir. Miller Brewing Co., Seven Up Co., until 1986; bd. dirs., mem. exec. com. Tobacco Inst., Washington., until 1984; sr. adv. bd. Burson-Marsteller, 1986-95; advisor USIA, 1980-92; bd. dirs. Cherokee Farms, Union Trust, Darien, Conn., Centurion, Inc., Centurion Stables, Inc.; chmn. bd. dirs. Pub. Rels. News., 1986-88; chmn. Bowling Investments, Inc. Author: How To Improve Your Personal Relations, 1959. Mem. nat. coun. Boy Scouts Am., 1961—; trustee Boy Scout Mus.; justice of peace, Rowayton, Conn., 1960-68; chmn. Pub. Affairs Coun., Washington; bd. overseers U. Louisville; bd. dirs., past pres. and chmn. Keep Am. Beautiful, 1966-80; bd. dirs. Nat. Automatic Merchandising Assn., Ky. Ind. Coll. Found., Nat. Tennis Found. Hall of Fame, Sanders Brown Found., Ky. Ctr. Aging, Country Music Hall Fame, 1956, U. Ky. Devel. Coun.; trustee, vice chmn. Berea Coll., Midway Coll. Recipient Kolodny award as outstanding young exec. in tobacco industry, 1963; named U.S. Young Businessman of Year St. John's U., 1967, Outstanding Alumnus U. Louisville, 1970, 86, 90, Kentuckian of Year, 1977; elected to Tobacco Industry Hall of Fame, 1976. Mem. Nat. Assn. Tobacco Distbg. (bd. dirs. exec. mgmt. div.), Pub. Rels. Soc. Am. Sales Execs. Club N.Y., The Kentuckians (past pres.), Laymen's Nat. Bible Assn. (v.p., bd. dirs.), World Press Inst., Lambda Chi Alpha (found. v.p., pres.), Wee Burn Country Club, Union League Club, John's Island Club, Windsor Club. Episcopalian. Home: 400 Ocean Rd Apt 170 Vero Beach FL 32963-3231 Home (summer): 18 Tokeneke Trl Darien CT 06820-6127

BOWLING, JOHN ROBERT, osteopathic physician, educator; b. Columbus, Ohio, Feb. 18, 1943; s. Ardyce Saul and Wilma Garcia (Snider) B.; m. Janet Lou Bowman, July 10, 1965; children: Jack Robert, James Richard, Jason Russell. BS, Ohio U., 1965; DO, Kirksville (Mo.) Coll. Osteopathic Medicine, 1969. Diplomate Am. Osteo. Bd. Family Practice. Rotating intern Drs. Hosp., Columbus, 1969-70; gen. practice osteo. medicine Lancaster, Ohio, 1970-88; clin. assoc. prof. Ohio U. Coll. Osteo. Medicine, Athens, 1977-88; med. dir. Lancaster Health Care Ctr., 1980-88; assoc. prof. dept. family medicine U. N. Tex. Health Sci. Ctr. Coll. Osteopathic Medicine, Ft. Worth, 1988—, interim chmn. dept. family medicine, 1991, vice chmn. dept., 1991-95, course dir. core clin. clerkship in family practice, 1991—, mem. steering com. Catchum project, mem. exec. coun. of faculty, 1992, 96, mem. curriculum com., 1993-95; mem. admissions com. U. North Tex. Health Sci. Ctr. Coll. Osteo. Medicine, Ft. Worth, 1989—; mem. sr. attending staff Doctors Hosp., 1970-88, co-dir. family practice residency program, 1979, acting dir., 1980; chmn. dept. medicine Lancaster Fairfield Cmty. Hosp., 1975, sec. med. staff, 1982-83, pres., 1985; active staff Osteo. Med. Ctr. Tex., 1988—; team physician Bloom Carroll (Ohio) Sch., 1973-88;. Pres., bd. dirs. Montessori Presch., Lancaster, 1975; chmn. youth basketball com. YMCA, Lancaster; former youth coord., tchr., mem. adminstrv. bd. United Meth. Ch., Lancaster. Named Outstanding Advisor, Tex. Coll. Osteo. Medicine, 1992, Osteo. Family Physician of Yr., State of Tex., 1996. Mem. Am. Coll. Osteo. Family Physicians (com. on evaluation and edn. 1991—, program chmn. nat. conv. 1995); mem. Am. Osteo. Assn., Ohio Osteo. Assn., Am. Acad. Osteopathy, Tex. Osteo. Med. Assn. (program chmn. state conv. 1994, 95), Tex. Med. Assn. (preventive medicine task force 1993-94). Methodist. Home: 6001 Lansford Ln Colleyville TX 76034-5230 Office: U North Tex Health Sci Ctr College Osteo Medicine 3500 Camp Bowie Blvd Fort Worth TX 76107-2644

BOWMAN, CATHERINE MCKENZIE, lawyer; b. Tampa, Fla., Nov. 10, 1962; d. Herbert Alonzo and Joan Bates (Baggs) McKenzie; m. Donald Campbell Bowman, Jr., May 21, 1988; children: Hunter Hall, Sarah McKenzie. BA in Psychology and Sociology, Vanderbilt U., 1984; JD, U. Ga., 1987. Bar: Ga. 1987, U.S. Dist. Ct. (so. dist.) Ga. 1987. Assoc. Ranitz, Mahoney, Forbes & Coolidge, P.C., Savannah, Ga., 1987-91; ptnr. Forbes and Bowman, 1991—. Bd. dirs. Greenbriar Children's Ctr., exec. com. 1995, pres. 1996; active Jr. League Savannah; mem. Leadership Savannah, 1994-96. Mem. Ga. Def. Lawyers Assn., Savannah Claims Assn., Savannah Young Lawyers Assn. (pres. 1996—), 2000 Club (membership chair 1990-91, pres. 1992), South Atlantic Found. (bd. dirs. 1992). Home: 21 Jameswood Ave Savannah GA 31406-5219 Office: Forbes and Bowman PO Box 13929 7505 Waters Ave Ste D-14 Savannah GA 31406

BOWMAN, DANIEL OLIVER, psychologist; b. Holly Hill, S.C., Feb. 1, 1931; s. John Daniel and Pansy (Mizzell) B. BA in Music, Furman U., 1951; MEd, U. S.C., 1952; PhD, U. Ga., 1963. Lic. psychologist, S.C. Tchr., English, French Summerville (S.C.) High Sch., 1952-53; chmn. English dept., sr. guidance counselor Boys High Sch., Anderson, S.C., 1955-61; instr. psychology U. Ga., Athens, 1961-63; asst. prof. psychology The Citadel, Charleston, S.C., 1963-66; assoc. prof. psychology, counselor to corps cadets The Citadel, 1966-69, prof. psychology, dir. grad. studies, 1969-77, prof., head dept. psychology, 1977-91, Arland D. Williams prof. psychology, 1991-96; cons. Charleston County Sheriff's Dept., 1985-94, Berkeley County Sch. System, Moncks Corner, S.C., 1977-89. Chmn. Charleston County Mental Retardation Bd., 1988-90. Mem. Am. Psychol. Assn. Am. Psychol. Soc. (charter mem.), AAUP, Nat. Assn. Sch. Psychologists, Southeastern Psychol. Assn., S.C. Psychol. Assn. (pres. 1990-91, Outstanding Contbrs. Psychology

1988), Phi Kappa Phi (pres. 1979-80), Phi Delta Kappa. Home: 6 Fort Royal Ave Charleston SC 29407-6012

BOWMAN, JAMES ROBERT, communications and public relations executive; b. Commerce, Tex., Apr. 14, 1945; s. William Lafayette and Dana Jean (Longshore) B.; m. Joan Mary Baca, Aug. 16, 1971; children: Christopher Michael (dec.), Allison Leigh. BA in Journalism, North Tex. State U., 1967; MA in Journalism, East Tex. State U., 1971. Instr. English U. Ark., Monticello, 1967-69; news bur. mgr. East Tex. State U., Commerce, 1969-72; comm. dir. Tex. A&I Univ. Sys., Kingsville, 1972-74; adminstrv. officer Republic Bank, Dallas, 1974-77, asst. v.p., 1977-79, v.p., 1979-80; freelance pub. rels. Dallas, 1980-82; sr. acct. exec. Bozell & Jacobs Pub. Rels., Dallas, 1982; comm. dir. Coldwell Banker Relocation Mgmt. Svcs., Inc., Dallas, 1982-83; sr. acct. exec. Engleman CO., Dallas, 1983-85; v.p. mktg. svcs. Vantage Cos., Dallas, 1985-87; sr. acct. exec., chief editor C. Pharr & Co., Dallas, 1987-89; mgr. fin. comm. LTV Corp., Dallas, 1989-92; v.p. corp. comm. Southwest Securities, Inc., Dallas, 1992—; founder All Star Baseball Fantasy League, co-champ 1991, 92. Mem. Soc. Profl. Journalists, Press Club Dallas (Found. scholar 1966-67, Katie award 1992), Advt. and Pub. Rels. Roundtable Securities Industry Assn. Office: Southwest Securities Inc Ste 3500 1201 Elm St Dallas TX 75270-2134

BOWMAN, JAMES VAUGHN, journalist; b. Kane, Pa., July 24, 1948; s. Vaughn Vowinkle and Ruth Ide (Benscoter) B.; m. Dianne Elizabeth Snow, Mar. 26, 1970 (div. Oct. 1990); children: Vaughn Charles Snow Bowman, Helen Margaret Bowman, Stephen James Bowman, John David Bowman; m. Karlyn Texie Herbolsheimer, Dec. 23, 1992. BA, Lebanon Valley Coll., 1971, Cambridge (Eng.) U., 1975; MA, Cambridge (Eng.) U., 1979. Asst. dept. pub. rels. Lebanon Valley Coll., Annville, Pa., 1971, dir. publs., 1971-73; schoolmaster Westminster Sch., London, 1980; schoolmaster Portsmouth (Eng.) Grammar Sch., 1980-89, head gen. studies, 1986-89; Am. corr. The Spectator, London, 1989-91; Am. editor Times Lit. Supplement, London, 1991—; film critic The American Spectator, Arlington, Va., 1990—; media critic The New Criterion, N.Y.C., 1993—. Contbr. articles to newspapers including The Wall Street Journal, The Washington Post, National Review, The National Interest, Reason, The Washington Times, The Daily Telegraph, The Sunday Telegraph, The Evening Standard, The American Enterprise. Republican. Roman Catholic. Home and Office: PO Box 19604 Alexandria VA 22320-0604

BOWMAN, JULIETTE JOSEPH, interior decorator, gourmet food consultant; b. Albany, Ga., Aug. 9, 1923; d. Solomon and Asma (Metrie) Joseph; m. David Stroud Bowman, Jan. 18, 1948; children: David, Steven, Denise. Student, Miss. State Coll. for Women, 1960. Buyer, bookkeeper Manhattan Fruit Co. and Deli, Albany, 1945-48; purchasing agent various German and English antique dealers, 1954-58, 61-64; buyer Atlanta Mdse. Mart. and Apparel Mart, 1974—, Atlanta Decorative Arts Ctr., 1974—, Atlanta Gift Mart, 1974—; interior decorator, personal shopper, Atlanta, 1974—; society edutor Comml. Dispatch, Columbus, Mass., 1960; decorator The Party Ctr., Atlanta, 1984-86; gourmet food cons. Atlanta, 1983, 84, Sta. WPBA-TV, Atlanta, 1986; owner Juliette's Gourmet Pantry, Buckhead Design Ctr., Atlanta, 1995—. Bd. dirs. Freedom Found. Valley Forge, Alliance Theater Guild, High Mus. Art Affiliates, Atlanta Coun., Better Films Guild, Pro-Mozart Soc., Repertory Opera Co.; mem. Rabun Gap-Nacoochee Guild Atlanta, Atlanta Ballet Guild, Atlanta Symphony Guild, Salvation Army Guild, Ga. Trust for Hist. Preservation, Atlanta Hist. Soc., 100 Club Atlanta, Atlanta Music Club. Named hon. Lt. Col. for contbns. to arts in Atlanta, State of Ga. Mem. Frog Club (pres., founder). Home: 30 Karland Dr NW Atlanta GA 30305-1124

BOWMAN, LAURA CATHERINE, pediatric oncologist; b. Amarillo, Tex., July 25, 1956; d. Edward John and Joyce Esther B.; children: David, Catherine. BA in Biology and Chemistry, Ind. U., 1977, MD, 1981. Diplomate Am. Bd. Pediatrics, sub.-bd. pediatric hematology-oncology. Resident in pediatrics Med. U. of S.C., Charleston, 1981-84; fellow, pediatric hematology/oncology St. Jude Children's Hosp., Memphis, Tenn., 1984-87, asst. mem., 1987-93, assoc. mem., 1993—; asst. prof. pediatrics U. Tenn., Memphis, 1987-93, assoc. prof. pediatrics, 1993—. Mem. Pediatric Oncology Group (Chgo.). Democrat. Soc. of Friends.

BOWMAN, LYNNE BARNETT, medical librarian; b. Shelbyville, Ky., Apr. 12, 1954; d. James Robert and Alice Louise (Harrison) Barnett; m. Howard Wayne Bowman, Mar. 5, 1987. AB, U. Louisville, 1976; MSLS, U. Ky., Lexington, 1978. Med. libr. U. Ky., Lexington, 1978—. Mem. Health Scis. OCLC Users Group (recording sec. 1991-92), Med. Libr. Assn., Ky. Libr. Assn. Spl. Librs. Sect. (sec. 1981-82, 90-91, treas. 1985-86), Midwest Chpt. Med. Libr. Assn., Beta Phi Mu, Phi Kappa Phi. Office: U Ky Med Ctr Libr 800 Rose St Lexington KY 40536-0084

BOWMAN, RICHARD ANDREW, business owner; b. Newcomb, Tenn., Mar. 9, 1936; s. Carl Clinton and Precious Joy (Lay) Bowman; m. Revonna Mae Hoover, June 24, 1955 (dec. 1971); children: Richard Andrew II, Laura Marie, David Anthony; m. Joyce Lynn Rouse, Sept. 22, 1973. Student, Howard Coll., 1954-55, Tenn. Tech. U., 1955, U. Tenn., 1955-68. Sr. rsch. technician Union Carbide Nuclear Corp., Oak Ridge, Tenn., 1956-69; sales engr. Chem-Form Corp., Pampano Beach, Fla., 1969-72; sales mgr. ECM div. Howmet Corp., Rockwall, Tex., 1972-73; EDM product mgr. POCO Graphite, Decatur, Tex., 1973-74; v.p. gen. mgr. Gordon Equipment & Supply, Dallas, 1974-83; pres./owner Bodic Industries, Garland, Tex., 1983—. Patentee freeze dried nuclear fuel; devel. prodn. mfg. method for cardiovascular stents. Mem. Soc. Mfg. Engrs. (sr.), So. Indsl. Dist. Assn., Electro-Chem. Machining, Electro Discharge Machining, Indsl. Distbn. Assn. Office: Bodic Industries Inc 2410 Executive Dr Garland TX 75041-6123

BOWMAN, SHEARER DAVIS, historian, educator; b. Richmond, Va., July 9, 1949; s. Shearer Calvin and Carolyn Allen (Davis) B.; m. Norma Lee Willey, Aug. 12, 1972; children: Kate, Will. BA, U. Va., 1971; MA, U. Calif., 1976, PhD, 1986. Vis. asst. prof. Hampden-Sydney (Va.) Coll., 1981-84, asst. prof., 1984-86; asst. prof. U. Tex., Austin, 1986-93, assoc. prof., 1993—, assoc. chair dept. hist., 1995—; mem. panel of experts U.S. Info. Agy., Washington, 1991-92. Author: Masters and Lords, 1993; editl. bd. Va. Magazine Hist. Biography, 1995—; contbr. articles to profl. jours. Pres. sch. bd. All Sts. Episcopal Day Sch., Austin, 1989-90, bd. trustees Samaritan Counseling Ctr., Austin, 1992; active elder on session First Pres. Ch., Austin, 1989-91, 93-95. Mem. So. Hist. Assn. (life), Phi Beta Kappa, Phi Alpha Theta. Presbyterian. Office: Dept Hist Univ Tex Austin TX 78712-1163

BOWMAN, STEPHEN WAYNE, quality assurance engineer, consultant; b. Charlotte, N.C., Oct. 3, 1949; s. John Wayne and Dagmar Katharine (Hege) B.; m. Patricia Faye Waldron, June 17, 1972 (div. 1988); 1 child, Jennifer Leigh. BS in Physics, Ga. Inst. Tech., 1972, MS in Nuclear Engring., 1974. Registered profl. engr., Tex.; cert. quality sys. lead auditor (RAB). Quality assurance engr. GE, Schenectady, N.Y., 1978-81; mgr. IEEE qualification program Stewart and Stevenson Svcs., Houston, 1981-86, mgr. nuclear projects, 1984-86; sr. engr. Pacific Engring. Corp., Portland, Oreg., 1988-89; pres. Bowman and Assocs., Kingwood, Tex., 1986—; project quality assurance mgr. M.W. Kellogg Co., Houston, 1990-96; sr. ptnr. Internat. Mgmt. Systems Co., 1992—; chmn. curriculum adv. bd. dept. mfg. technology Houston C.C., 1984-87. Contbr. articles to profl. publs. 1st lt. U.S. Army, 1975-78. Mem. Am. Nuclear Soc., Am. Soc. Quality Control, Houston Engring. and Sci. Soc. Home: 1915 Crystal Springs Dr Kingwood TX 77339-3339

BOWMAN, SUSAN, writer. BA with honors, Auburn U., 1984; MFA, U. Ala., 1990. Asst. editor Resurrection Cath. Ctr., Montgomery, Ala., 1983-84; pvt. tutor, editor, 1988-90; consulting editor Ctr. Rsch. Ednl. Accountability and Tchr. Evaluation, 1991; writer, editor Coll. Edn. U. Ala., 1989-92; advt. cons., freelance writer, editor, 1992—; adj. instr., temporary asst. prof., grad. teaching asst., tutor Dept. English U. Ala., 1984-90; vis. artist Eufaula (Ala.) Sch. Sytem, 1988; presenter in field. Contbr. articles to profl. jours.; author of poems. Home and Office: 3007 Green Grove Dr NE Tuscaloosa AL 35404-2115

BOWNE, SHIRLEE PEARSON, credit union executive, real estate executive; b. High Shoals Twp., N.C., Mar. 11, 1936; d. Lloyd E. Pearson and Parnell (James) Garland; divorced; 1 child, Gregory Charles. Grad. high sch., Gaffney, S.C. Various secretarial positions, 1955-64; sales repr., pres. Real Estate Marketers, Inc., Tallahassee, FL, 1964-80; chief exec. officer Shirlee Bowne Mktg. & Devel. Inc., Tallahassee, 1980-91; vice chmn. Nat. Credit Union Adminstrn., Washington, 1991—; Consult. in field. Treas. Rep. Party Fla., 1988-91. Episcopalian.

BOWTON, DAVID LOWELL, physician; b. Long Beach, Calif., Mar. 7, 1950; s. F. Lowell and Harriet (Richter) B.; m. Pamela Carol Hassel, Oct. 5, 1974; children: Erica, Lindsay. BS, Univ. Ill., 1971, MD, 1975. Diplomate Am. Bd. Internal Medicine, Diplomate Am. Bd. Critical Care Medicine, Diplomate Am. Bd. Pulmonary Disease. Assoc. prof. medicine and anesthesia Bowman Gray Sch. Medicine, Winston-Salem, N.C., 1989—; medical dir. respiratory care N.C. Bapt. Hosp., Winston-Salem, N.C., 1987—, medical dir. intensive care unit, 1994—; dir. asthma clinic Wake Forest Univ. Physicians, Winston-Salem, N.C., 1992—. Fellow Am. Coll. Chest Physicians, Am. Coll. Critical Care Medicine; mem. Am. Thoracic Soc. Office: Pulmonary and Critical Care Medical Ctr Blvd Winston Salem NC 27157-1054

BOWYER, CHARLES LESTER, chaplain; b. Richwood, W.Va., June 3, 1939; s. Charles Cicero and Delores Irene (Seward) B. BA, Berea (Ky.) Coll., 1961; MDiv, Episcopal Theol. Seminary, Lexington, Ky., 1964; D of Ministry, Grad. Theol. Found. at, Notre Dame, 1991; PhD in Pastoral Psychology, La Salle U., Mandeville, La., 1995. Ordained to ministry Episcopal Ch. as deacon, 1964, as priest, 1965; lic. alcohol and drug addiction counselor. Curate St. Mary's Episcopal Ch., Big Spring, Tex., 1964-66; vicar St. John's Episcopal Ch., Snyder, Tex., 1966-75; assoc. rector St. Paul's Episcopal Ch., Lubbock, Tex., 1975-84; chaplain and addiction counselor St. Mary of the Plains Hosp., Lubbock, 1986—; sec. Episcopal Diocese of Northwest Tex., Lubbock, exec. com., mem. living and end. commn.; synod del. The Seventh Episcopal Providence. Editor/author: Alcoholism: A Spiritual Disease, 1991. Grad. Theol. Found. fellow. Mem. Tex. Assn. Alcohol and Drug Addiction Counselors, Nat. Assn. Alcohol and Drug Addiction Counselors, Soc. of St. Paul, Delta Phi Alpha. Home: PO Box 98178 Lubbock TX 79499-8178 Office: St Mary of Plains Hosp Dept Pastoral Care 4000 24th St Lubbock TX 79410-1894

BOWYER, SHIRLEY CAROLINE SMITH, accountant; b. Greenville, Ala., Nov. 3, 1949; d. Newton B. Smith and Alma Caroline (Kummel) Smith; m. Patrick E. Bowyer, May 1, 1981 (div. July 1983). Student, Faulkner Jr. Coll., Bay Minette, Ala., 1968-70; BA in Acctg., Fin. and Mgmt., U. West Fla., 1972. Payroll adminstr. Cook Constrn. Co., Inc., Jackson, Miss., 1972-73; acctg. supr. Starco Corp., Jackson, 1973-74; acct., credit mgr. Equipment, Inc., Jackson, 1974-76; field office mgr., asst. to project engr. Algernon Blair, Inc., Montgomery, Ala., 1976-78; instr. bus. subjects Phillips Coll., Jackson, Miss., 1977; acct., office mgr. Chandler Ford Sales, Inc., DeQueen, Ark., 1978-80; field office mgr. Zellner Constrn. Co., Inc., Memphis, 1980-81; mgr. Das A. Borden & Co., Muscle Shoals, Ala., 1981-82; asst. adminstr., credit mgr. S.F. Parker & Co., P.C., CPA's, Foley, Ala., 1982-86; acct. City of Gulf Shores, Ala., 1986-92, acctg. mgr., 1992—. Mem. South Baldwin Hosp. Aux., Foley, 1990. Recipient Cert. of Commendation, City of Gulf Shores, 1989. Mem. Govt. Fin. Officers Assn. Ala., Ala. Assn. Pub. Accts., Am. Soc. Women Accts., Mcpl. Treas. Assn. of U.S. and Can. Methodist. Home: Mimosa Pl 106 S Beech St Foley AL 36535

BOX, DWAIN D., former judge; b. Stuart, Okla., Sept. 15, 1916; s. William Autry and Vera (Johnson) B.; m. Doris Louise Nordstrom, July 27, 1946; children: Kenneth Dwain, Dennis Rae. Student, Oklahoma City Law Sch., 1939; LL.B., Cumberland U., 1940. Bar: Okla. 1940. Pvt. practice law, 1940-46, 52-56; judge Ct. Common Pleas, Oklahoma County, 1956-68; asso. dist. ct. judge, 1968-71; judge Ct. Appeals of State of Okla., Oklahoma City, 1971-83, ret. subject to assignment, 1983; Rep. Okla. Legislature, 1947-50. Sec. Oklahoma County Election Bd., 1954-56. Served with AUS, 1940-45, 50-52. Decorated Bronze Star medal with oak leaf cluster. Mem. Okla. Bar Assn., Oklahoma County Bar Assn., Okla. Jud. Conf. Baptist.

BOX, JAY KEITH, college administrator; b. Crane, Tex., Mar. 14, 1954; s. Melvin Odell and Ruth Marie (Moore) B.; m. Beverley Gayle Zimmerman, Nov. 25, 1978; 1 child, Jason. AA, Howard Coll., 1974; BS, S.W. Tex. State U., 1976; MEd, Tex. Tech. U., 1985; DEd, Baylor U., 1994. Tennis coach, health and phys. edn. tchr. Ft. Stockton (Tex.) H.S., 1976-80; tennis coach, history tchr. Coronado H.S., Lubbock, Tex., 1980-84; men's and women's tennis coach Odessa (Tex.) Coll., 1984-91, chair, phys. edn., 1987-94, dir. instnl. rsch. and effectiveness, 1994-96; v.p. instrn. McLennan C.C., Waco, Tex., 1996—. Bd. dirs. Am. Hart Assn., 1995; pres., bd. dirs. St. John's Episcopal Sch., Odessa, 1991-95; pres., rep. Odesso Coll. Faculty Senate, Odessa, 1991-94. Mem. Soc. of Coll. and Univ. Planners (regional comm. dir. 1995), So. Assn. of Instnl. Rschrs., Tex. Assn. of Instnl. Rschrs., Tex. Jr. Coll. Tchrs. Assn., Intercollegiate Tennis Assn. (nat. ranking chmn. 1984-91, Coach of Yr. 1989), Tex. Tennis Coaching Assn. (v.p. 1981-84, Coach of the Yr. 1984, 89). Episcopalian. Office: Odessa Coll 201 W University Odessa TX 79764

BOX, JOHN HAROLD, architect, educator, academic dean; b. Commerce, Tex., Aug. 18, 1929; s. E.O. and Mary Emma (Haynes) B.; m. Dorothy Jean Baldwin, Jan. 19, 1952 (div. Jan. 1971); children: Richard B., Kenneth W., Gregory V.; m. Eden Van Zandt, Apr. 9, 1977; stepchildren: William D., Kate V.Z. BArch, U. Tex., 1950. Apprentice O'Neil Ford (architects), San Antonio, 1948; designer Broad & Nelson (architects), Dallas, 1954-56; assoc. Harrell & Hamilton (architects), Dallas, 1956-57; ptnr. Pratt, Box, Henderson & Ptnrs. (architects), Dallas, 1957-83, Box Architects, Austin, 1983—; prof., 1st dean Sch. Architecture and Environ. Design, U. Tex., Arlington, 1971-76; prof., dean Sch. Architecture, U. Tex., Austin, 1976-92, Moody prof., 1983—; Chmn. design of city task force Goals for Dallas, 1968-70; chmn. Goals Achievement Com., 1970—; chmn. design com. Greater Dallas Planning Council, 1969; v.p. Save Open Space, 1970. Prin. works include: St. Stephen's Meth. Ch., Dallas, 1962, Great Hall of Apparel Mart, Dallas, 1965, Quadrangle Shopping Ctr., Dallas, 1965, Garden Ctr., Dallas, 1970; master plan Griffin Sq., Dallas, 1971; Marsh House, Austin, 1982; Co-author: Prairies Yield, 1962, Goals for Dallas Proposals for Design of City, 1970. Bd. dirs. Dallas Chamber Music Soc., 1960-76, Austin Symphony, 1982-90, Laguna Gloria Art Mus., 1984-90, Austin History Ctr., 1984-88; regional dir. Assn. Collegiate Schs. Architecture, 1975-78. Served to lt. C.E. Corps, USNR, 1955. Co-recipient Enrico Fermi Meml. Archtl. Competition prize, 1957; Grand prize Homes for Better Living Competition, 1959; Tex. Architecture Found. grantee, 1957. Fellow AIA (pres. Dallas 1967, nat. dir. 1975-78); mem. Tex. Soc. Architects (v.p., commr. edn. and research 1971, design awards 1964-66, 68, 70, 71, 82), Phi Kappa Phi, Alpha Rho Chi, Sigma Nu. Episcopalian. Studio: 7 Nob Hill Cir Austin TX 78746-3603

BOXER, ROBERT JACOB, chemist, educator, science writer; b. N.Y.C., Apr. 9, 1935; s. Nathan and Frieda (Walkin) B.; m. Riette Hirsch, Nov. 28, 1963; children: Mark Alan, Deborah Allison. BS in Chemistry, Bklyn. Coll., 1956; PhD in Organic Chemistry, Rutgers U., 1961. Asst. prof. chemistry Oglethorpe Coll., Atlanta, 1961-62, assoc. prof., 1962-64; assoc. prof. chemistry Ga. So. U., Statesboro, 1964-72, prof., 1972—. Author: Graduate Record Examination-Chemistry, 1984; editor: Organic Chemistry Exam File, 1988. Home: 211 Henderson St Statesboro GA 30458-5432 Office: Ga So U Rte 301 S Statesboro GA 30460

BOYCE, EMILY STEWART, retired library and information science educator; b. Raleigh, N.C., Aug. 18, 1933; d. Harry and May (Fallon) B. BS, East Carolina U., 1955, MA, 1961; MS in Library Sci., U. N.C., 1968; postgrad., Cath. U. Am., 1977. Librarian Tileston Jr. High Sch., Wilmington, N.C., 1955-57; children's librarian Wilmington Pub. Library, 1957-58; asst. librarian Joyner Library East Carolina U., Greenville, N.C., 1959-61, librarian III, 1962-63; ednl. supr. II ednl. media div. N.C. State Dept. Pub. Instrn., Raleigh, 1961-62; assoc. prof. dept. library and info. scis. East Carolina U., Raleigh, 1964-76, prof., 1976-92, chmn. dept., 1982-89; retired, 1992; cons. So. Assn. Colls. and Schs., Raleigh, 1975—. Mem. Pitt County Hist. Preservation Soc., Greenville, Pitt County Mental Health Assn. Mem. ALA, AAUW, N.C. Library Assn., Southeastern Library Assn., Assn. Library and Info. Sci. Educators, Spl. Libraries Assn., LWV, NOW. Democrat. Home: 99 Moody Cove Rd Weaverville NC 28787-9746

BOYCE, HENRY WORTH, III, portfolio manager, financial consultant; b. Conway, S.C., Sept. 21, 1953; s. H(enry) Worth Jr. and Jean (Murphy) B.; m. Melinda Jane Ayton, Jan. 26, 1980; children: Erin Frazer, Henry Worth IV. BS, Wake Forest U., 1975; MBA in Fin., Stetson U., 1977. Cert. fin. analyst. Supr. treasury issues Fed. Res. Bank, Miami, Fla., 1977-79; fin. cons. Prudential, Miami Beach, Fla., 1979-91; portfolio mgr. Smith Barney, Miami, 1991—. Co-author monthly newsletter The Earnings Statement, 1993, 94. Mem. Miami Soc. Fin. Analysts (pres. 1994), Wake Forest Alumni Assn. Home: 1421 Harrison St Hollywood FL 33020 Office: Smith Barney 1000 E Hallandale Beach Blvd Hallandale FL 33009-4430

BOYCE, WILLIAM HENRY, former urologist, educator; b. Ansonville, N.C., Sept. 22, 1918; s. William Henry and Louise Lockhart (Gaddy) B.; m. Anna Doris Shore, June 6, 1948; children: W. Lockhart, Catharine L. Boyce Baldwin, Anna Barbara Boyce Howard, Frederick Shore. BS in Biology and Chemistry, Davidson Coll., 1940; MD, Vanderbilt U., 1944; DSc (hon.), Davidson Coll., 1982. Intern dept. surgery Bowman Gray Sch. Medicine N.C. Bapt. Hosp., Winston Salem, 1944-45, asst. resident dept. surgery Bowman Gray Sch. Medicine, 1947; asst. resident dept. urology James Buchanan Brady Found. N.Y. Hosp., Cornell Med. Ctr., N.Y.C., 1948-49; asst. resident dept. urology U. Va. Hosp., Charlottesville, 1950-51, chief resident urology, 1951-52; chief urologic svcs. N.C. Bapt. Hosp., 1960-83; instr. surgery/urology Bowman Gray Sch. Medicine Wake Forest U., Winston Salem, 1952-56, asst. prof., 1956-58, assoc. prof., 1958-60, prof. and chmn. sect. urology dept. surgery, 1960-83, prof. surgery/urology, 1983-89, prof. emeritus, 1989—; with dept. clinics N.C. Bapt. Hosp., 1952-89; staff surgeon urology City Meml. Hosp., Winston Salem, 1952-71, Kate Bitting Reynolds Meml. Hosp., Winston Salem, 1952-71; attending urologist Forsyth Meml. Hosp., Winston Salem, 1971-83, mem. courtesy staff, 1983—; mem. courtesy staff R. J. Reynolds-Patrick County Meml. Hosp., Stuart, Va., 1989-91; cons., rschr. John A. Hartford Found., Inc., N.Y., Robert Woods Johnson Found., Bowman Gray Found., Vitel Found., Vichy, France, Henry Wilson Found., NIH; lectr. in field. Author: (with others) Prostatic Ultrasonography, 1990, Common Problems in Infections and Stones, 1991, Mastery of Surgery, 2d edit., 1992; consulting editor, Urologic Surgery, 4th edit., 1991; contbr. articles to profl. jours. Capt. USMC, 1945-47, MTO. Recipient Svc. to Mankind award Sertoma Internat., 1966, Cline Golden Eagle award Coun. Internat. Non-Theatrical Events, 1980, Disting. Alumnus award Vanderbilt U. Sch. Medicine, 1989, Keyes medal Am. Assn. Genito-Urinary Surgeons, 1992, Dornier Innovative Rsch. award Am. Found. Urol. Disease, Inc., 1992; William H. Boyce Professorship of Urology, Wake Forest U., 1989. Fellow Am. Coll. Surgeons (hon., bd. govs. 1975-78, adv. coun. urology, residency rev. com. urology 1980-83), Am. Inst. Ultrasound in Medicine (hon.); mem. AMA (residency rev. com. urology 1980-83), AAAS, Am. Urol. Assn. (hon., chmn. edn. com. 1963-65, residency rev. com. urology 1980-83, rsch. com. 1956-62, Hugh Hampton Young award 1974, Mary Hugh and Russell Scott award 1986), Am. Surg. Assn. (hon.), Am. Assn. Genitourinary Surgeons (hon., pres. 1984, Barringer medal 1981), Am. Bd. Urology (diplomat, examiner 1960-65, trustee 1980-86, pres. 1985-86, rep. to Am. Bd. Med. Specialties 1980-86, residency rev. com. urology 1980-83), Med. Soc. Va., N.Y. Acad. Scis., N.C. Med. Soc. (hon.), So. Soc. Clin. Rsch., European Intrarenal Surg. Soc. (founding mem. 1976), Pan-Pacific Surg. Assn., Societe D'Urologie Internationale, Clin. Soc. Genitourinary Surgeons (pres. 1982), Soc. Exptl. Biology and Medicine, Soc. Univ. Surgeons, Soc. Univ. Urologists (founding mem., pres. 1965, rep. to Am. Assn. Med. Colls. 1965-75, residency rev. com. urology 1980-83), Soc. Sigma Xi, Alpha Omega Alpha. Independent. Presbyterian. Home: RR 2 Box 150 Stuart VA 24171-9506 Office: Bowman Gray Sch Medicine Medical Center Blvd Winston Salem NC 27157

BOYD, BARBARA JEAN, librarian; b. Monroe, La., July 14, 1954; d. Rube and Ora Lee (Renfro) Robinson; m. William Chester Boyd, June 25; children: Chaundra, Cameron, Chelsea. Student, U. Wis., Eau Claire, 1972-73; BS in Libr. Sci., U. Wis., Oshkosh, 1979; M in Libr. and Info. Sci., U. Wis., Milw., 1989. Libr. tech. asst. Legis. Reference Bureau City of Milw., 1980-89, libr. I, 1989-91; br. mgr., libr. II W.L.D. Johnson Br. Houston Pub. Libr., 1991—. Recipient Positive Action Program for Minority Groups Stipend award Spl. Librs. Assn., 1987-88; Libr. Career Tng. fellow U. Wis., 1987-88. Mem. ALA, BCALA (3d nat. conf. African Am. Librs. planning com., 3d evaluation com.). Office: Houston Pub Libr 3511 Reed Rd Houston TX 77051-2333

BOYD, B(EVERLEY) RANDOLPH, lawyer; b. Richmond, Va., Mar. 8, 1947; s. Henry Armistead and Mary Archer (Randolph) B.; m. Julia Murray Williams, May 14, 1977; children: Peter Armistead Randolph, Alexander Page Monroe. BA, Williams Coll., 1969; JD, U. Va., 1972. Bar: Va. 1973, U.S. Dist. Ct. (ea. and we. dists.) Va. 1974, U.S. Ct. Appeals (4th cir.) 1986. Ptnr. Boyd & Boyd, Richmond, 1973-79, Randolph, Boyd, Cherry & Vaughan, Richmond, 1979—; Commonwealth's atty. Charles City County Va., 1976—; v.p., sec. James River Assn., Richmond, 1984—. Capt. USAR, 1972-82. Mem. Va. Bar Assn., Va. Trial Lawyers Assn. Democrat. Episcopalian. Home: 4545 Kimages Wharf Rd Charles City VA 23030-3331 Office: Randolph Boyd Cherry & Vaughan 14 E Main St Richmond VA 23219-2110

BOYD, BILL GERALD, business executive; b. Penrose, Wyo., Nov. 5, 1939; s. Ward Carson and Mary (Shumway) B.; m. Susan Margaret Spencer, May 29, 1969; children: Kyle, Kelly, Jacquelyn, Scott. BA, Brigham Young U., 1966; MA, Ball State U., 1973; EdS, Troy State U., 1979; program mgr. diploma, Def. System Mgmt. Coll., 1981. Computer systems analyst Seattle, 1966-74; asst. prof. U. Iowa, Iowa City, 1974-79; mgr. software/hardward computer systems Colorado Springs, Colo., 1979-83; mgr. Oklahoma City, Okla., 1983-92; pres. Boyd Enterprises, Edmond, Okla., 1992—. Lt. col. USAF, 1966—. Mem. Phi Delta Kappa. Republican. Mem. LDS Ch. Home: 5400 Sudbury Ln Oklahoma City OK 73135 Office: Boyd Enterprises 3327 S Boulevard Edmond OK 73013

BOYD, CARL, history educator; b. Phila., Mar. 27, 1936. AB, Ind. U., 1962, AM, 1963; PhD, U. Calif., Davis, 1971. Instr., asst. prof. Ohio State U., Columbus, 1969-75; asst. prof., assoc. prof. history Old Dominion U., Norfolk, Va., 1975-85, prof., 1985-95, Univ. eminent scholar, 1994—, dir. grad. program in history, 1991-94, Louis I. Jaffé prof. history, 1995—; vis. scholar U.S. Army Ctr. Mil. History, Washington, 1987-89; vis. Inst. for Advances Study, Princeton, N.J., summer 1993; vis. scholar-in-residence Nat. Security Agy., 1996—; reviewer scholarly articles and numerous books, 1966—; presenter at profl. confs., 1974—; commentator or session chmn. over 40 nat. acad. confs., 1977—. Author: The Extraordinary Envoy: General Hiroshi Oshima and Diplomacy in the Third Reich, 1934-39, 1980, 2d edit., 1982, Hitler's Japanese Confidant: General Oshima Hiroshi and MAGIC Intelligence from Berlin, 1941-45, 1993 (selection History Book Club 1993), Am. Command of the Sea Through Garriers, Codes and the Silent Service: World War II and Beyond, 1995; co-author: The Japanese Submarine Force and World War II, 1995; contbr. articles to profl. jours., chpts. to books. With Submarine Svc., USN, 1954-58. Recipient rsch. awards Old Dominion U., 1977-84, 93, rsch. fellow, summer 1979, Am. Philos. Soc., 1990. Mem. Internat. Naval Rsch. Orgn., Soc. for Mil. History, So. Hist. Assn., U.S. Commn. on Mil. History, U.S. Naval Inst., WWII Studies Assn., Phi Kappa Phi. Home: 1229 Rockbridge Ave Norfolk VA 23508-1337 Office: Old Dominion U Dept History Norfolk VA 23529

BOYD, CLAUDE COLLINS, educational specialist, consultant; b. Kent, Tex., May 25, 1924; s. Edward Clarke and Nora (Morris) B.; m. Frances Arline Haley, Jan. 22, 1955; children: David Chand, Anese Nasim Boyd Forsyth, Mark Kevin, Kimberly Ann Boyd Surgeon. BA, Tex. A&M U., 1948; MEd, U. Tex., 1957, EdD, 1961. Cert. elem. tchr., prin., supt., Tex. Elem. sch. tchr. Culberson County Ind. Sch. Dist., Van Horn, Tex.; elem. sch. prin. The Austin (Tex.) Ind. Sch. Dist.; elem sch. bilingual tchr. Ector County Ind Sch. Dist., Odessa, Tex.; assoc. prof. Ind. U., Bloomington; curriculum specialist USAID, Guatemala City, Guatemala; project specialist in edn. The Ford Found., N.Y.C.; assoc. prof. edn. Pa. State U., Erie; edn. specialist Devel. Assocs., Inc., Washington; internat. edn. advisor/cons. U.S. Agy. for Internat. Devel., San Salvador; edn. adminstr., curriculum advisor U.S. Agy. for Internat. Devel., La Paz, Bolivia; Dominican Republic; edn.

adminstr., curriculum advisor U.S. Agy. for Internat. Devel., Dominican Republic; free-lance edn. advisor, cons., worldwide svc. Odessa, Tex.; tchr. edn. specialist InterAm. Devel. Bank, Santo Domingo, Dominican Republic; ednl. supervision specialist InterAmerican Devel. Bank, Santo Domingo, Dominican Republic; substitute tchr. K-12, Ector County ISD, Odessa, Tex. Recipient Grand Order of Edn., Pres. of Rep. of Bolivia. Mem. ASCD, Phi Delta Kappa (past pres. Mu chpt.). Home: 2426 E 21st St Odessa TX 79761-1703

BOYD, DAN STEWART, lawyer; b. Waco, Tex., Sept. 30, 1949; s. Will Carr and Elizabeth Lockey (Stanton) B.; m. Terry Mae Riddlesperger, Mar. 20, 1976; children: Daniel James, Caroline Elizabeth, Catherine Terry. BA with honors, U. Tex., 1972, JD with honors, 1975. Bar: Tex. 1975, U.S. Dist. Ct. (so. dist.) Tex. 1976, U.S. Dist. Ct. (ea. dist.) Tex. 1978, U.S. Dist. Ct. (no. dist.) Tex. 1982, U.S. Ct. Appeals (5th cir.) 1978, U.S. Ct. Appeals (11th cir.) 1978, U.S. Supreme Ct. 1979. Assoc. Vinson & Elkins, Houston, 1975-81, Johnson & Swanson, Dallas, 1982; ptnr. Johnson & Gibbs, P.C. (formerly Johnson & Swanson), Dallas, 1982-93, Baker & McKenzie, Dallas, 1993—. Contbr. articles to legal jours. Bd. dirs. F.D. Roosevelt Four Freedoms Found., N.Y.C., 1986-87, Franklin and Eleanor Roosevelt Inst., Hyde Park, N.Y., 1987—. Fellow Tex. Bar Found.; mem. Tex. Young Lawyers Assn. (bd. dirs. 1980-82), Houston Young Lawyers Assn. (bd. dirs. 1979-80, Outstanding Dir. award 1980), Dallas Bar Assn. (chmn. bus. litigation sect. 1990), Friars Soc., Lancers Club (Dallas), Exch. Athletic Club (Dallas), Royal Oaks Country Club (Dallas). Methodist. Home: 3829 Southwestern Blvd Dallas TX 75225-7121 Office: Baker & McKenzie 2001 Ross Ave Ste 4500 Dallas TX 75201-2974

BOYD, DANNY DOUGLASS, financial counselor; b. Olustee, Okla., Oct. 18, 1933; s. Robert and Juanita Henrietta (Crawford) B.; B.A. magna cum laude, Abilene Christian U., 1954; M.A. in Linguistics, U. Tex., Arlington, 1976; CLU, chartered fin. cons.; cert. fin. planner; m. Mary Ann Thomas, Jan. 25, 1953; children: Robert Lee, Rebecca Dyann Boyd McCully, Scott Thomas, Douglas Dean. Min. Chs. of Christ, Ardmore, Okla., 1954-56, Velma, Okla., 1956-57, Cisco, Tex., 1958-60, Utrecht, Netherlands, 1960-65, Wilmington, Del., 1965-69, Dallas, 1969-71; v.p. Nat. Comp Assocs., Dallas, 1972-77; marriage and family counselor Adaptive Counseling Assocs., Dallas, 1977-94; fin. counselor CIGNA Ind. Fin. Svcs. Co., 1979-92, Dan Boyd & Assocs., 1992—; mng. dir. Fin. Edn. Assocs., Tex., 1994—; exec. v.p. WampumWare, Inc., 1996—; exec. v.p. WampumWare, Inc., 1996—; founder Chair of Bible, Cisco Jr. Coll., 1959. Bd. dirs. Skyline High Sch. PTA, 1971; intervenor for integrated neighborhoods fed. dist. ct. desegregation suit, Dallas, 1977. Mem. Am. Assn. CLUs and Chartered Fin. Cons. (Dallas chpt.). Republican.

BOYD, ELEANOR DREHER, director of community services; b. Columbia, S.C., Apr. 15, 1964; d. Julius Clarence I and Donna (Greer) Dreher; m. Lawrence Martin Boyd, Jul. 23, 1988. BA in political sci., Clemson Univ., 1986; MPA, Memphis State Univ., 1993. Cert. paralegal. Paralegal corp. & regulatory Willoughey Hoefer, Columbia, S.C., 1987-89; devel. coord. Hemophilia Found., Memphis, Tenn., 1990-92; internship City of Germantown, Germantown, Tenn., 1992; internship program dir. Met. Inter-Faith Assn., Memphis, 1993; dir. program svcs. March of Dimes of W. Tenn., Memphis, 1993—. Pres. Clemson Alumni Club, Memphis, 1993-94; active Jr. League Memphis, 1994. Mem. Am. Soc. Pub. Adminstrn., Pi Alpha Alpha (pres. 1993-94). Republican. Home: 5105 Lynbar Ave Memphis TN 38117

BOYD, EMILIE LOU, elementary school educator, consultant; b. Millvale, Pa., July 14, 1935; d. Ralph William and Melba Margaret (Cochran) Popp; m. Thomas Boyd, Aug. 25, 1957 (div. Feb. 1969); children: Michael Thomas, Elizabeth Michelle Boyd Spalding. BS, Pa. State U., 1957; MEd, U. Tex., 1959; postgrad., Am. U., 1973. Cert. elem., spl. reading tchr., prin., supr. spl. edn., Tex., Va. Tchr., reading specialist El Paso (Tex.) Pub. Schs., 1958-69; asst. prin., prin. Fairfax (Va.) Pub. Schs., 1970-71, 75-76, specialist learning disabilities, 1973-75; dir. Summer Learning Disabilities Inst., Fairfax, 1971-76; bd. dirs. Staff Devel. Inst., Fairfax, 1975-76; developer Intensive readiness Staff Devel. Inst., 1981-84; counselor elem. sch., 1984-89; learning disabilities specialist Marshall Rd. Sch., 1989—; speaker on remedial reading and tech. Va. Tech. Conv., 1994. Author: (film) Learning Disabilities Childhood Resources. Mem. Nat. Assn. Mini Enthusiasts (editor newsletter 1986—), Fairfax Miniature Enthusiasts (editor newsletter 1986—), Pi Lambda Theta, Delta Gamma Delta, Pi Delta Gamma, Phi Delta Kappa. Roman Catholic.

BOYD, GORDON PAYNE, television news reporter, anchor; b. Lexington, Ky., May 6, 1962; s. Charles Payne and Mary (Thurman) B. BS in Journalism, Northwestern U., 1984. Regional reporter WTVO-TV, Rockford, Ill., 1984-86, WAVE-TV, Louisville, 1986-89; producer WLEX-TV, Lexington, 1990; weekend anchor WKXT-TV, Knoxville, Tenn., 1990-91; sr. reporter KSLA-TV, Shreveport, La., 1991-93; capitol bur. chief WKYT-TV, Lexington, 1993—; reporter, anchor WTVQ-TV, Lexington, 1995; primary anchor WGEM-TV, Quincy, Ill., 1996. Recipient 1st Pl. Newscast award AP, 1990, 3d Pl. News Series award AP, 1991, 2d Pl. Spot News award AP, 1993, 1st Pl. Features award AP, 1994. Mem. Soc. Profl. Journalists, Radio-TV News Dirs. Assn. Office: Sta WKYT-TV Channel 27 Winchester Rd Lexington KY 40555

BOYD, GREGORY, theater director; b. San Francisco, Apr. 14, 1951; s. Donald Crawford and Anita Cecilia (Carroll) B.; m. Laurie Brown, June 30, 1973 (div. Jan. 1981). AB, U. Calif., Berkeley, 1973; MFA, Carnegie-Mellon U., 1975. Dir. Other Stage Williamstown (Mass.) Theatre Festival, 1975-86; artistic dir. Playmakers Repertory Co., Chapel Hill, N.C., 1981-84, Stagewest, Springfield, Mass., 1984-89, Alley Theatre, Houston, 1989—. Actor Berkeley Repertory Theatre, 1972-76; dir., author (mus. play) Svengali, 1991; dir. (mus. play) Jekyll & Hyde, 1990, over 30 prodns. classic plays, 1975-89. Panelist NEA, Washington, 1991, Tex. Commn. on Arts, Austin, 1990-91. Mem. Actors' Equity Assn., Soc. Stage Dirs. and Choreographers. Office: Alley Theatre 615 Texas St Houston TX 77002-2710

BOYD, HERBERT REED, JR., dentist; b. Petersburg, Va., Sept. 15, 1925; s. Herbert Reed and Eula Jesse (Arnold) B.; m. Beverly Jane Lackey, Aug. 5, 1950; children: Herbert Reed III, Stuart Arnold, Amy Lewis. BA, U. Richmond, 1972; DDS, Med. Coll. Va., 1948. Dental intern in oral surgery Med. Coll. Va. Hosps., Richmond, 1948-49; instr. crown and bridge prosthodontics Med. Coll. Va., Richmond, 1951-53; asst. prof. Med. Coll. Va., 1953-56, assoc. prof., 1956-61, asst. clin. prof. periodontics, 1964-70; pvt. practice Petersburg, Va., 1961—. Capt. U.S. Army, 1949-51, lt. col. 1962. Fellow Va. Dental Assn.; mem. ADA, Southside Va. Dental Assn. (pres. 1977), Am. Coll. Dentists, Internat. Coll. Dentists, Am. Acad. Medicine, Pierre Fauchard Acad., Med. Coll. Va. Alumni Assn. (pres. 1977), U. Richmond Alumni Assn., Boatwright Soc. U. Richmond, U.S. Lighthouse Soc. (adv. bd. Chesapeake chpt. 1992—), Petersburg C. of C., McKee Dental Study Club Richmond, Rotary (pres. 1976-77), Omicron Kappa Upsilon, Psi Omega, Phi Kappa Sigma. Home: 1200 Northampton Rd Petersburg VA 23805-1932 Office: 23 Goodrich Ave Petersburg VA 23805-2119

BOYD, JAMES ROBERT, oil company executive; b. Nashville, July 29, 1946; s. James Clinton and Mary Avon (Motlow) B.; m. Elise White, June 27, 1970; children: Elizabeth, Mary Franklin. BSEE, U. Ky., 1969; MBA, NYU, 1972. Sales engr. Westinghouse Electric Co., N.Y.C. and St. Louis, 1970-75; mgr. generation sales Westinghouse Electric Co., St. Louis, 1975-77; cons. planning Westinghouse Electric Co., Pitts., 1977-79, mgr. div. planning, 1979-81; mgr. strategic planning Ashland (Ky.) Oil Co., 1982-84, dir. corp. planning, 1984-86, sr. v.p. , group oper. officer, 1989—; sr. v.p. adminstrn. Ashland Exploration, Houston, 1986-87, pres., 1987-89. Office: Ashland Oil Inc PO Box 391 Ashland KY 41105-0391

BOYD, JANE GAIL, program director; b. Bentonville, Ark., Oct. 26, 1960; d. James Carson and Frances Grace (Gammon) B. BS in Edn., U. Ark., 1984; postgrad., East Tex. State U., 1985. Tchr. drama, speech Ark. H.S., Texarkana, 1984-88; dir. debate and forensics Grapevine (Tex.) H.S., 1988—; coach championship team Univ. Interscholastic League Cross-Exam. Debate, 1993-94. Chair Task Force Comm., Grapevine, 1993-94; mem. polit. action com. NEA, Texarkana, 1987-88. Named Ark. Young Speech Tchr. of Yr., 1985. Mem. Nat. Debate Coaches Assn. (Barton scholar 1992), Tex. Forensic Assn., Nat. Forensic League (Diamond coach, dist. chmn. 1992-94, dist. com. 1990-92), U. Ark. Alumni Assn. Democrat. Presbyterian. Office: Grapevine High Sch 3223 Mustang Dr Grapevine TX 76051-5962

BOYD, JULIA MARGARET (MRS. SHELTON B. BOYD), lay church worker; b. Newton Grove, N.C., Mar. 7, 1921; d. Isaiah and Mary Lela (Blackman) Tart; m. Shelton Bickett Boyd, Feb. 21, 1944; children: Mary (Mrs. Edward Southerland III), Deborah (Mrs. John Wayne Pearson). BS, East Carolina U., 1942. V.p. WSCS, Lillington (N.C.) U. Meth. Ch., 1948-49; pres. Woman's Soc. Christian Svc., Mt. Olive, N.C., 1951-55, 59-61; sec. various coms. WSCS, 1st United Meth. Ch., Mt. Olive, N.C., from 1950, mem., sec. adminstrv. bd. and coun. ministries, from 1955, mem. local work area on edn., 1960-82, chmn., 1971-75, chmn. spiritual growth, 1971-75, mem. fin. com., 1985-87, 90-96; counselor United Meth. Youth Fellowship, 1960-67; adult del. Nat. Convocation Meth. Youth, 1964; pres. Goldsboro dist. United Meth. Women, 1955-59; mem. N.C. Conf. Bd. Edn., 1964-72; mem. N.C. Coun. on Youth Ministries, 1964-82, chmn., 1972-76; mem. adult staff youth, sr. high mins., 1972-92; mem. N.C. Conf. Coun. on Ministries, 1972-82; mem. Goldsboro dist. Coun. on Ministries, 1970—, sec., 1971—; also coord. youth ministries Goldsboro dist., 1964-82; del. SEJ Youth Conf., Arlington, Va., 1976, SEJ Leadership Devel. Workshop, Lake Junaluska, 1977; lay rep. Goldsboro dist. Conf. Coun. on Ministries, 1982-92, ann. conf. United Meth. Ch., 1985, 87, 90, 96, dist. trustee, 1993—; rep. N.C. Christian Advocate, 1985—; bd. dirs. Meth. Home for Children, 1993-96; mem., sec. dist. adv. com. Fremont Youth Home, 1988-96. Editor Meth. Messenger, 1965-68. Pres. PTA, Mt. Olive, 1955-56, Mt. Olive High Sch. and So. Wayne High Sch. Band Patron's Club, 1964-66; leader Girl Scouts U.S.A., 1956-57; active Community Chest. Named Lay Person of Yr. N.C. Conf. United Meth. Ch., 1979, (with husband) Outstanding Sr. Citizens of Mt. Olive, 1990; recipient cert. appreciation United Meth. Youth Fellowship, 1980, 83. Mem. Women's Aux. of N.C. Pharm. Assn. (corr. sec. 1976-77, rec. sec. 1977-78, 2d v.p. 1978-79, 1st v.p. 1979-80, pres. 1980-81, mem. nominating com. 1988-95, mins. com. 1988-89, hospitality com. 1989), United Meth. Women (mem. hist. com. Goldsboro dist. 1984, chairperson 1989, 94, v.p. local chpt. 1988-89), So. Wayne Country Club. Home: 400 W Main St Mount Olive NC 28365-2018

BOYD, KENNETH WADE, publishing company executive, consultant; b. Jacksonville, Fla., Oct. 2, 1938; s. Wade Julius and Hariett Lucile (Rogers) B.; m. Linda Jean Adams, Dec. 29, 1962; 1 child, Lara Christine. BA in History, The Citadel, 1960; MS in LS, Drexel Inst. Tech., 1962. Extension librarian Flint River Regional Library, Griffin, Ga., 1962-64; acquisitions librarian Atlanta Pub. Library, 1964-65; v.p. sales Am. Library Line, Atlanta, 1965-68; mgr. Josten's Libr. Supplies, Atlanta, 1968-72; southeastern sales rep. Congl. Info. Svc., Washington, 1972-75; pub., pres. Cherokee Pub. Co.-Larlin Corp., Marietta, Ga., 1975—; mem. adv. bd. Coun. Authors and Journalists, Atlanta, 1987—. Author, compiler: Vermont Historic Markers, 1989, Georgia Historical Markers, 3 Vols., 1990. Trustee Walker Sch., Marietta, 1982—; bd. dirs. Reach of Song, Gainesville, Ga., 1988—. 2d lt. U.S. Army. Named Pub. of Yr., Ga. chpt. Nat. League Am. Pen Women, 1987. Mem. Ga. Book Pubs. Assn. (pres.), ALA, Southeastern Libr. Assn., Ga. Libr. Assn., Metro Atlanta Libr. Assn. (v.p., pres. 1967-68). Republican. Office: Cherokee Pub Co-Larlin Corp 2151 Dixie Ave Smyrna GA 30080-1266

BOYD, LOWE ADLAI, academic administrator; b. Dunedin, Fla., Aug. 25, 1935; s. Robert Ulric and Elizabeth Pearl (Lowe) B.; m. Laura Louise Teague, May 22, 1957 (div. June 3, 1971); children: Adlai II, Rebekah Louise; m. Sandra Jean Bolt, June 13, 1971 (div. Aug. 3, 1995); 1 child, John Jennings. BA, Maryville Coll.; MDiv, Union Theol. Sem., Richmond, Va., 1960; MEdn, Presbyn. Sch. Christian Edn., Richmond, Va., 1961; PhD, Temple U., 1978. Asst pastor 1st Presbyn. Ch., Raleigh, N.C., 1961-64; asst. pastor, min. edn. 1st Presbyn. Ch., Norfolk, Va., 1964-65, Miami Shores (Fla.) Presbyn. Ch., 1965-67; dean of students Lenoir Rhyne Coll., Hickory, N.C., 1967-68; dean of students, asst. prof. philosophy King Coll., Bristol, Tenn., 1968-71; dir. edn. and tng. Western Carolina Ctr., Morganton, N.C., 1971-74; from assoc. dir. edn. and tng. to dir. tng. Temple/Woodhaven Ctr., Phila., 1974-77; assoc. prof., dir. Fla. Mental Health Inst., Tampa, 1978-81; chair dept. child and family studies U. South Fla., Tampa, 1981-90, faculty dept. spl. edn., 1985—, acad. adminstr., 1991—; adj. prof. Temple U., Phila., 1974-77, Appalachian State U., Boone, N.C., 1972-74. Author: A Study of Foster Care in Florida, 1989, Integrating Systems of Care for Children, 1994; contbr. articles to profl. jours. Adv. com. Tampa Springs H.S., 1993-96, chair, 1995-96, Networks for Severely Emotionally Disturbed, Pinellas, 1981—; exec. com. Hillsboro Constituency for Children, Tampa, 1982—, pres., 1994-96. Grantee Fla. State Legislature, 1987-88, Fla. Dept. Edn., 1988-91, NIMH, 1991-95. Mem. NRC Child Welfare Am. Democrat. Home: PO Box 6749 Ozona FL 34660 Office: U South Fla MHC 4-218 Fla Mental Health Inst 13301 Bruce B Downs Blvd Tampa FL 33612

BOYD, MOLLY DENISE, librarian, English educator; b. Perryville, Ark., Apr. 5, 1965; d. Jimmie Richard and Zelma Ione (Minyard) Johnson; m. Jim H. Boyd, Jr., Aug. 23, 1986; 1 child, Georgia Mae. BS in Interior Design, U. Ark., 1987, MA in English Arts, 1992; PhD in English Arts, U. S.C., 1995. Librarian Washington County Law Libr., Fayetteville, Ark., 1986—; tchg. asst. U. Ark., Fayetteville, 1989-91, U. S.C., Columbia, 1991-95; data mgmt. asst. Editype Bus. Svcs., Fayetteville, 1991—; instr. N.W. Ark. C.C., Fayetteville, 1996—. Contbr. articles to profl. jours. Mem. MLA, William Gilmore Simms Soc., Soc. for Study of So. Lit. Home: 215 E Davidson Fayetteville AR 72701

BOYD, MORTON, banker; b. Louisville, June 7, 1936; s. Morton and Pauline Boyd; m. Anne Theobald; children—Anne Chambers, Robert Morton. B.A., U. Va., grad. Stonier Grad. Sch. Banking, 1964. With First Nat. Bank of Louisville, 1959—, pres., chief adminstrv. officer, 1981—, also bd. dirs.; exec. v.p. First Ky. Nat. Corp., pres., 1987—, chief exec. officer, 1988—; chief exec. officer Nat. City Corp. (merged with First Nat. Bank of Louisville), Cleve., 1988—; also bd. dirs. holding co. First Ky. Nat. Corp.; chmn., chief exec. officer First Ky. Nat. Corp. (now Nat. City Bank Ky.); bd. dirs. Nat. City Bank, Ky., chmn., CEO; chmn. bd. dirs. Greater Louisville Con. devel. Parnership, The Housing Partnership; exec. v.p. Nat. City Corp. Mem. Louisville fund for the Arts, 1984—; bd. overseers U. Louisville; trustee Bellarmine Coll. Served to 2d lt. U.S. Army, 1958-59. Mem. Assn. Res. City Bankers, The Bankers Roundtable. Episcopalian. Office: Nat City Bank Ky 101 S 5th St Louisville KY 40202-3103

BOYD, ROBERT FRIEND, lawyer; b. Richmond, Va., May 11, 1927; s. Oscar Linwood and Ruby (Friend) B.; m. Sara Grace Miller, Sept. 20, 1952; children: Robert Friend Jr., David M., Mary Boyd Horton, James M. AB, Coll. of William and Mary, 1950, JD, 1952. Bar: Va. 1952. Pvt. practice Norfolk, Va., 1955—; chmn. Boyd & Boyd, P.C., Norfolk, 1957—; commr. Chancery for Cir. Ct., Norfolk, 1967—, Cir. Ct. Chesapeake, Va., 1967—; bd. dirs. Holnam, Inc. Chmn. adv. com. Norfolk City Coun., 1966-71; trustee, vice chmn., mem. exec. com. Va. Wesleyan Coll.; trustee, v.p. Randolph-Macon Acad.; trustee William and Mary Endowment Assn., United Meth. Found. Va.; pres. bd. trustees Coll. of William and Mary Law Sch.; bd. dirs. Greater Norfolk Corp., Norfolk Mcpl. Hosp.; chmn. bd. Va. Cultural Found.; vice chmn., trustee Walk Thru The Bible Ministries, Atlanta; pres. Kiwanis, Norfolk, Am. Heart Assn. Mem. ABA (com. on corp. counsel, bus. law sect.), Nat. Assn. Coll. and Univ. Attys., Va. Bar Assn. (chmn. judiciary com.), Va. Trial Lawyers Assn. (v.p.), Masons, Shriners, Tau Kappa Alpha. Home: 3199 Adam Keeling Rd Virginia Beach VA 23454-1000 Office: 1 Commercial Pl Norfolk VA 23510-2103

BOYD, WILLIAM DOUGLAS, JR., library science educator, clergyman; b. Pulaski, Tenn., Dec. 15, 1929; s. William Douglas and Lula May (Scott) B.; m. Margaret Woolfolk, July 16, 1966; 1 child, Julia Woolfolk. BA, Rhodes Coll., 1952; BD, Union Theol. Sem., N.Y.C., 1955; ThM, Princeton Theol. Sem., 1958; MLS, Ind. U., 1972, PhD, 1975. Ordained to ministry, 1956. Pastor First Presbyn. Ch., Mt. Pleasant, Tenn., 1956-63; asst. pastor Ind. Presbyn. Ch., Birmingham, Ala., 1963-67; asst. law librarian Ind. U., Bloomington, 1972-73; asst. prof. library sci. U. So. Miss., Hattiesburg, 1973-77, assoc. prof., 1977-95; with The Presbyn. Ch., Vernal, Miss., 1992—; reviewer pub. library program NEH, 1978. Translator: (L. Buzás) German Library History 800 1945, 1986, Schottenloher, Books and the Western World, 1989; contbr. articles to profl. jours. Mem. Presbytery of Miss., Citizens for Justice Com. Mem. ALA, SAR (sec. Miss. 1985-88, 2d v.p. 1988-90, pres. Isaac Carter chpt. 1994), Tenn. Libr. Assn. (vice chmn. trustees and friends sect. 1962-63), Mil. Order Stars and Bars, Sons of Confederate Vets., Krewe of Zeus, Hattiesburg Country Club, Omicron Delta Kappa, Beta Phi Mu. Democrat. Home: 114 Sangria Dr Hattiesburg MS 39402-3044

BOYDEN, CHRISTOPHER WAYNE, lawyer, divorce mediator; b. Orange, Calif., Jan. 4, 1952; s. H. Paul and Louise Rosemonde (Falvey) B.; m. Karen Marie Sigler, Aug. 9, 1981 (div. Dec. 1989); children: Kacie Marie, Matthew Paul; m. Bonnie Lee Boren, May 4, 1990. BA magna cum laude, Fairleigh Dickinson U., 1975; JD cum laude, Seton Hall Law Sch., 1978. Bar: N.J. 1978, Fla. 1979. Tchr. polit. sci. Vail Dean Sch., Elizabeth, N.J., 1973-75; law clk. to judge N.J. Superior Ct., Morristown, 1978-79; ptnr. Boyden & Laufer, Attys., North Palm Beach, Fla., 1979—; prof. bus. law Palm Beach Bus. Coll., Lake Worth, Fla., 1979-83. Author: Your Changing 4th Amendment Rights, 1982; author numerous poems and songs. Mem. ABA, N.J. State Bar Assn., Fla. Bar, Palm Beach County Bar Assn. Democrat. Office: 321 Northlake Blvd Ste 107 North Palm Beach FL 33408

BOYER, VINCENT LEE, aerospace executive; b. Dallas, Oct. 16, 1956; s. Donald Boyer and Patricia Carolyn (Bills) Bloodsworth; m. Sandra Kay Mayo, Feb. 26, 1974 (div. 1992); children: John Vincent, Donald Lee, Vincent Lee Jr., Whitney Alexandra; m. Vanessa Bradbury, Nov. 7, 1992. AS, Eastfield Coll., Mesquite, Tex., 1980; BS, Abilene Christian U., 1983; MS summa cum laude, Amber U., 1988, MBA, 1988, PhD, 1989. Cert. quality analyst, quality auditor; registered ISO assessor; lic. pvt. investigator, Tex. Engring. mgr. STL Electronics, Dallas, 1977-79, TEC Electronics, Dallas, 1979-80; quality engr. Boeing Electronics, Irving, Tex., 1980-82; systems engr. Searle Optical Lab., Dallas, 1982-83; sr. engr. E-Systems, Inc., Garland, Tex., 1983-88; dir. quality assurance UTL Corp., Dallas, 1988-92; engring. documentation mgr. Electrocom Automation, Arlington, 1992—, documenation dir., 1996—; cons. The Carmen Group, Inc., Plano, Tex., 1990—. Author: Software Quality Manual, 1994. Precinct rep. Collin County Reps., Plano, 1990; com. mem. Cub Scout Pack 285, Plano, 1991; v.p. St. Paul's Sports Assn., Richardson, Tex., 1988. With U.S. Army, 1973-76. Mem. IEEE (book rev. author, standards com. mem. 1984-86), Am. Soc. Quality Control (sr., chmn. policy com. 1990—, assoc. newsletter editor 1991-96). Republican. Roman Catholic. Home: PO Box 6514 Arlington TX 76005 Office: Electrocom Automation LP 2910 Avenue F Arlington TX 76011-5214

BOYER, WILLIAM EDWARD, manufacturing professional; b. Silverton, Oreg., Aug. 4, 1931; s. William E. and Dorothy Marie (Gandy) B.; m. Evelyn Delores Holbert, June 6, 1951 (div. June 1969); m. Lorene Holt, Dec. 30, 1970; children: Richard, John, James, Diane, Claudette, Brenda. BSIE, Oreg. State, 1956. Registered mfg. engr. Sr. indsl. engr. Willamette Iron & Steel, Portland, Oreg., 1955-66; v.p., chief engr. S. Patkay & Assocs., El Monte, Calif., 1966-81; mfg. mgr. Barry Controls, Burbank, Calif., 1981-93; with Selective Consulting, Murphy, N.C., 1993—; mgmt. cons. various orgns., 1966-81. Home: RR 1 Box 232C Murphy NC 28906-9133 Office: Creek Side Dr Murphy NC 28906

BOYES, PATRICE FLINCHBAUGH, lawyer, environmental executive; b. York, Pa., Aug. 1, 1957; d. Glenn Dale Flinchbaugh and Patricia Ann (Frey) Shultz; m. Stephen Richard Boyes, June 23, 1984. BA, Dickinson Coll., 1978; MA, U. Mich., 1980; JD, U. Fla., 1991. Bar: Fla. 1991, Fed. 1994. Law clk. Rakusin & Ivey, Gainesville, Fla., 1989; summer assoc. Hopping, Boyd, Green & Sams, Tallahassee, Fla., 1990; gen. counsel GeoSolutions, Inc., Gainesville/Tallahassee, Fla., 1986—; pres. Boyes & Assocs., P.A., Gainesville, Fla., 1991—, Wildcat Tech. Svc., Inc., 1995—; vice-chmn. City's Hist. Preservation Adv. Bd.; vol. Kanapaha Bot. Gardens; counsel Duckpond Neighboorhood Assn.; pres. Wildcat Tech. Svcs., Inc., Gainesville, 1995—. Pres. Hist. Gainesville, Inc.; vice chair City's Hist. Preservation Adv. Bd.; vol. Kanapha Bot. Gardens; counsel Duckpond Neighborhood Assn., Inc. Recipient Keystone Press award Pa. Soc. Newspaper Editors and Pubs., 1981, City Beautification award, 1994, Hist. Preservation award, 1994, Fla. Trust for Hist. Preservation award, 1996; grad. fellow Modern Media Inst., St. Petersburg, Fla. Mem. ABA, Fla. Bar Assn. (pub. interest com. for environ. and land use sect.), Fla. Trial Lawyers Assn., 8th Jud. Cir. Bar Assn., Fla. Assn. Women Lawyers, Pi Delta Epsilon. Office: GeoSolutions Inc 602 S Main St Gainesville FL 32601-6718

BOYES, STEPHEN RICHARD, hydrogeologic consultant; b. Evanston, Ill., May 17, 1950; s. Will W. and Beth (Henry) B.; m. Patrice Lynne Flinchbaugh, June 23, 1984. AA, U. South Fla., 1972, BA, 1974. Lic. profl. geologist, Fla. Geophys. engr. seismic process ctr. Geophys. Svcs., Inc., Midland, Tex., 1974; geophys. engr. field ops. Geophys. Svcs., Inc., Chickasha, Okla., 1975; geophys. engr. Geophys. Svcs., Inc., Saudi, Arabia, 1975-77; geologist Fla. Dept. Environ. Regulations, Tallahassee, 1978-82; hydrogeologist Fla. Dept. Environ. Regulations, Tampa, 1982-84; sr. hydrogeologist Groundwater Technology, Tampa, 1984-86, Handex Corp., Odenton, Md., 1986; pres. GeoSolutions, Inc., Gainesville, Fla., 1986—. Contbr. to profl. publs. Mem. Nat. Groundwater Assn., Heritage Club.

BOYETT-THOMPSON, C. CHRISTINE, secondary education educator; b. Aurora, Colo., May 3, 1964; d. Bobby Earl and Sandra Kay (Boteler) Boyett; m. Stephen Edward Thompson, June 8, 1985; children: Victoria Caroline Thompson, Madeleine Alexandra Thompson. BA, S.W. Tex. State U., San Marcos, 1986; MA, Sam Houston State U., Huntsville, Tex., 1990. Prof. English Tomball (Tex.) Coll., 1991-95; tchr. English St. Thomas' Episcopal Sch., Houston, 1994—. Troop leader Girl Scouts U.S., 1995—. Named Outstanding Sr. Women, S.W. Tex. State U., 1986. Mem. Gamma Phi Beta. Republican. Episcopalian. Home: 15510 W Barbara Cir Houston TX 77071 Office: St Thomas' Episcopal Sch 4900 Jackwood Houston TX 77096

BOYKIN, BETTY RUTH CARROLL, mortgage loan officer, bank executive; b. Mobile, Ala., Dec. 14, 1943; d. John Calvin Sr. and Zimmie Mae (Burdette) Carroll; m. William Henry Boykin Jr., Sept. 9, 1961; children: Helen Carroll Boykin Ferris, John William. Student, Auburn U., 1961-62, U. Fla., 1969-72, Santa Fe C.C., 1972-90; BSBA, U. Mo., St. Louis, 1992. Asst. v.p., loan officer Guaranty Fed. Savs. and Loan, Gainesville, Fla., 1973-80; mortgage loan officer Fortune Mortgage Corp., Gainesville, 1980-86; mgr. Svc. Title Corp., Gainesville, 1986-87; account exec. Fla. Fed. Savs. Bank, Gainesville, 1987-88; banking officer 1st Union Nat. Bank (merger Fla. Nat. Bank), Gainesville, 1988-90; br. mgr., mortgage loan officer 1st Fed. Bank Mortgage Lending, Huntsville, Ala., 1993—; dir. Sys. Dynamics, Inc., 1980-89, AMJ, Inc., 1980-83; instr. mortgage lending Inst. Fin. Edn., Gainesville, 1986. Amb. PBS, Gainesville, 1989-90; chmn. loan com. Neighborhood Housing Svcs., Inc., Gainesville, 1985-90; dir. Gainesville Homebuilder's Homeowners Warranty Coun., 1984-86. Recipient Outstanding Svc. award Neighborhood Housing Svcs., Inc., 1985-90. Mem. Am. Mgmt. Assn., Am. Mktg. Assn., Mortgage Bankers Assn. North Ctrl. Fla. (v.p., pres.-elect 1989-90), Mortgage Officers Soc. (pres. Dist. IV 1980-81), Mortgage Bankers Assn. Huntsville (co-chair program com. 1994—), Women's Coun. Realtors, Huntsville/Madison County Builders Assn. (assocs. coun. mem., mem. women's coun.), Huntsville Bd. Realtors (affiliate), Huntsville C. of C., Gainesville C. of C., Delta Sigma Pi. Home: 35 Revere Way Huntsville AL 35801-2847 Office: First Fed Mortgage 2310 Market Pl SW Ste B Huntsville AL 35801-5250

BOYKIN, JOSEPH FLOYD, JR., librarian; b. Pensacola, Fla., Nov. 7, 1940; s. Joseph Floyd and Delree (Bailey) B.; m. Evelyn Louise Larson, Aug. 3, 1963; children: Suzanne Michelle, Pamela Denise. Student, Pensacola Jr. Coll., 1958-60; B.S., Fla. State U., 1962, M.S., 1965. Lic. pvt. pilot. Asst. to librarian U. N.C., Charlotte, 1965-68; acting head librarian U. N.C., 1968-70; dir. library, 1970-81; dean libraries Clemson (S.C.) U., 1981—; bd. dirs. Southeastern Libr. Network, Inc., 1975-78, 96—, chmn., 1977-78. Trustee OCLC Online Computer Library Ctr., Inc., 1980-86; trustee OCLC Users Council, 1978-82, 89-92, pres., 1978-80. Democrat. Baptist. Democrat. Baptist. Lodge: Sertoma (Clemson) (v.p., pres.). Home: 307 Bent Oak Ln Central SC 29630-9460 Office: Clemson Univ Robert Muldrow Cooper Clemson SC 29634

BOYLAN, KEVIN BERNARD, neurologist; b. Arlington, Mass., Aug. 20, 1956; s. Charles Vincent and Edith Murial (Aho) B. BA in Social Sci., U. Calif., Irvine, 1979, BS in Biology cum laude, 1979; MD, U. Calif., San Francisco, 1983. Diplomate Nat. Bd. Med. Examiners, Am. Bd. Med. Genetics, Am. Bd. Psychiatry and Neurology, also Sub.-Bd. Clin. Electrophysiology, Am. Bd. Electrodiagnostic Medicine. Intern Johns Hopkins Hosp., Balt., 1983-84; fellow neurology U. Calif., San Francisco, 1984-87, fellow med. genetics, 1985-87, resident, 1987-90, fellow neuromuscular diseas Johns Hopkins Hosp, 1990-91; instr. neurology Johns Hopkins U., 1991; asst. prof. Mayo Grad. Sch. Medicine, Jacksonville, Fla., 1992—; assoc. cons. Mayo Clinic, Jacksonville, Fla., 1992-94, cons., 1994—, 1994—; dir. EMG lab. Mayo Clinic, 1994—; dir. Muscular Dystrophy Assn. Clinic N.E. Fla., 1994—. Contbr. numerous articles to profl. jours. Multiple Sclerosis fellow Nat. Multiple Sclerosis Soc., 1984-87, Charles A. Dana fellow Charles A. Dana Found., 1990-91. Mem. AMA, AAAS, Am. Soc. Human Genetics, Am. Acad. Neurology, Fla. Med. Assn., Duval County Med. Assn. Office: Mayo Clinic Dept Neur 4500 San Pablo Rd S Jacksonville FL 32224-1865

BOYLAN, MICHELLE MARIE OBIE, medical surgical nurse; b. St. Louis, Jan. 22, 1962; d. James Martin and Yvonne Marie (DeLoof) Obie; m. Steven Arthur Boylan, June 5, 1962; children: Paige Brittany, Courtney Marie, Brandon James. BSN, Marquette U., 1984; MA, Webster U., 1996. RN. Commd. 2d lt. U.S. Army, 1984, advanced through grades to maj., 1994; pediatrics charge nurse William Beaumont Army Med. Ctr., El Paso, 1984-86, neonatal ICU charge nurse, 1986-87; asst. head nurse pediatrics 98th Gen. Hosp., Neurenberg, Germany, 1987-88; head nurse 98th Gen.Hosp., Neurenberg, Germany, 1987-90, U.S. Army Ft. Huachuca, Sierra Vista, Ariz., 1990-92; head nurse Winn Army Cmty. Hosp., Ft. Stewart, Ga., 1992—, infection control/quality improvement nurse, 1994—, chief patient support divsn., chief quality mgmt. divsn.; lectr. in field. Decorated Army Commendation medal with 3 oak leaf clusters, Meritorious Svc. medal with 1 oak leaf cluster. Mem. Am. Profls. in Infection Control. Roman Catholic. Home: 870 Piros Dr Colorado Springs CO 80922 Office: Evans Army Cmty Hosp Fort Carson CO 80913

BOYLE, SUSAN JEAN HIGLE, elementary school educator; b. Tarrytown, N.Y., June 15, 1956; d. George Edward and Barbara Jean (Deverill) Higle. BA in Psychology, Elem. Edn., Ladycliff Coll., 1978; MS in Learning Disabilities, Fordham U., 1980; EdS in Ednl. Leadership, Stetson U., 1988. Cert. tchr., Fla. Tchr. St. Ursula Sch., Mt. Vernon, N.Y., 1978-81, Blue Lake Elem. Sch., DeLand, Fla., 1982-86, Deltona (Fla.) Lakes Elem., 1986-88, Discovery Elem. Sch., Deltona, 1988-89, Tomoka Elem. Sch., Ormond Beach, Fla., 1989-90, Ormond Beach Mid. Sch., 1990—; mem. discipline task force, Volusia County Schs., 1989, health task force, 1989. Eucharistic minister St. Brendan Ch. TOPS grantee, 1985, 86. Mem. Phi Delta Kappa, Daytona Beach Hummel Collectors Club. Office: Ormond Beach Mid Sch 151 Domicilio Ave Ormond Beach FL 32174-3918

BOYLES, HARLAN EDWARD, state official; b. Lincoln County, N.C., May 6, 1929; s. Curtis E. and Kate S. B.; m. Frankie Wilder, May 17, 1952; children—Phyllis Godwin, Lynn Boyles Butler, Harlan Edward Jr. Student, U. Ga., 1947-48; B.B.A. in Acctg, U. N.C., 1951. C.P.A., N.C. Corp. tax auditor N.C. Dept. Revenue, 1951-56; exec. sec., local govt. com. N.C. Tax Rev. Bd., 1956-76, dep. treas., 1960-76; treas. State of N.C., 1977—; mem. Council of State; mem. mcpl. securities rulemaking bd. SEC, 1975-77. Mem. adv. bd. Raleigh Salvation Army; chmn. Local Govt. Commn.; chmn. State Banking Commn., Tax Rev. Bd.; mem. State Bd. Edn., State Bd. Community Colls., N.C. Capital Planning Commn., others. Mem. N.C. Assn. CPAs, Nat. Assn. State Auditors, Comptrs. and Treas. (past pres., exec. dir.), Raleigh C. of C. (past bd. dirs.), N.C. State Employees Assn., N.C. Young Dems. Club, Execs. of Raleigh Club (past pres.), Rotary (past pres.). Democrat. Presbyterian (deacon, elder, treas., clk.). Home: 1924 Fairfield Dr Raleigh NC 27608-2720 Office: Treasurer's Dept 325 N Salisbury St Raleigh NC 27603-1388

BOYLES, WILLIAM ARCHER, lawyer; b. Lakeland, Fla., Aug. 16, 1951; s. Jesse V. and Louise (Archer) B.; m. Laura M. Rose, June 12, 1977; children: William Archer Jr., John H. BSBA, U. Fla., 1973, JD, 1976, LLM in Taxation, 1978. Bar: Fla. 1977, U.S. Tax Ct. 1978, U.S. Dist. Ct. (mid. dist.) Fla. 1979; CPA, Fla. Assoc. Gray, Harris & Robinson, P.A., Orlando, Fla., 1978-82, ptnr., 1982—; mem. Cen. Fla. Estate Planning Coun. Bd. dirs. Christian Family Svcs., Inc., Gainesville, Fla., 1977-86, Ctrl. Fla. YMCA, Orlando, 1979-81; treas. Univ. Blvd. Ch. of Christ, Orlando, 1979-88; bd. dirs., treas. Orlando Shakespeare Festival, Inc., 1989—, bd. dirs., 1992, 2d v.p., 1992-95; bd. dirs. Better Bus. Bur. Ctrl. Fla., 1994-96, chair-elect, exec. com. 1994, 95; mem. Planned Giving Coun. Ctrl. Fla. Mem. ABA, Fla. Bar (exec. coun. tax sect.), Orange County Bar Assn., AICPA, Fla. Inst. CPA's, Am. Assn. Atty.-CPA's, Small Bus. Coun. Am. (polit. action com.), Econs. Club, Citrus Club. Republican. Office: Gray Harris & Robinson 201 E Pine St Ste 1200 Orlando FL 32801-2725

BOYLL, JAMIE FRANCES, ecologist; b. Jackson, Miss., Sept. 22, 1949; d. James Ellis and Frances (Trull) Fowler; m. Guy Lee Boyll, June 12, 1971; children: Guy Lee III, Jill Fowler. BA in Edn., U. Miss., 1971; MA in Counseling, Jackson State U., 1977. Mem. nuclear waste policy adv. coun. State of Miss., Jackson, 1979-83; ecologist Miss. Environ. Mgmt. Orgn., Jackson, 1983—, chmn., 1987—, lobbyist, civic speaker, 1988-90. Grantee Youth Project, 1983. Episcopalian. Home: 72 Bear Creek Rd Asheville NC 28806-1604 Office: Environ Coalition of Miss PO Box 10006 Jackson MS 39286-0006

BOYNTON, FREDERICK GEORGE, lawyer; b. Yokohama, Japan, May 9, 1948; s. Fred Wenderoth and Buelah Eleanor (Nygaard) B.; m. Nancy Jeanne McLendon, Aug. 3, 1985; children: Emily Margaret, Charlotte Clayton, Susan Jeanne. BA, The Citadel, 1970; JD, Tulane U., 1973. Bar: SC 1973, Ga. 1976, U.S. Dist. Ct. Ga. 1976, U.S. Ct. Appeals (5th and 11th cirs.). Assoc. Smith, Gambrell & Russell, and predecessors, Atlanta, 1976-82, ptnr., 1982-88; sole practice, Atlanta, 1988—. Author: Criminal Defense Techniques, 1976; editor articles Tulane Sch. Law Rev. Mem. exec. com. Southside Progress Assn., Atlanta, 1983-84, Leadership Sandy Springs, 1989-90; bd. dirs. Atlanta Union Mission, 1990—, mem. exec. com., 1991, sec., 1992. Served to capt. JAGC, U.S. Army, 1973-76. Fellow Ga. Bar Found.; mem. ABA, Fed. Bar Assn. (pres. Atlanta chpt. 1981-82, mem. exec. com. 1982—, dep. chmn. adminstrv. law sect. 1986-87, bd. dirs. younger lawyers div. 1981-84, v.p. 11th Cir. 1985-87), State Bar Ga. (chmn. adminstrv. law sect. 1987-88), Lawyers Club of Atlanta, Order of Coif. Republican. Baptist. Home: 4860 Northway Dr NE Atlanta GA 30342-2424 Office: Bldg 16 Ste 100 750 Hammond Dr Atlanta GA 30328-5501

BOYNTON, REX POWELL, trade association executive; b. Hartford, Conn., June 14, 1951; s. Homer Austin and Alice Evelynne (Powell) B.; m. Lynn Davis, Oct. 1, 1983; children: Blake Homer, Brittany Evelyn, Brenna Powell. Student polit. sci., U. R.I., 1974. Asst. press sec. Congressman Bob Price, Washington, 1974; campaign mgr. Congressman Bob Price, Pampa, Tex., 1976; asst. dept. head and environ. lobbyist Greater Washington Bd. Trade, 1977-80; div. dir. Soc. Am. Florists, Alexandria, Va., 1980-84; asst. exec. v.p. Mach. Dealers Nat. Assn., Silver Spring, Md., 1984-86; exec. dir. U.S. Marshals Found., McLean, Va., 1987-89, Profl. Picture Framers Assn., Richmond, Va., 1989—; seminar leader Strategic Planning, 1989-91. Contbr. articles to profl. jours. Pres. Branch Drive Home Owners Assn., Hendron, Va., 1981-83; bd. dirs. Towlston Meadows Homeowners Assn., Vienna, Va., 1984-85. Mem. Am. Soc. Assn. Execs., Va. Soc. Assn. Execs. Republican. Presbyterian. Office: 4305 Sarellen Rd Richmond VA 23231-4311

BOYSEN, THOMAS CYRIL, school system administrator; b. Sioux Falls, S.D., Nov. 16, 1940; s. Cyril Joseph and Dolores Margaret (Parry) B.; m. PoChan Mar, Aug. 25, 1964 (div. 1980); children: Thomas C., Anne-Marie Lee; m. Laurie Louise Shaffer, June 25, 1983. BA in History, Stanford U., 1962; Diploma in Grad. Edn., Makerere U., Kampala, Uganda, Africa, 1964; EdD in Edn. Adminstrn., Harvard U., 1969. Geography master Kabaa High Sch., Thika, Kenya, Africa, 1964-66; dir. adminstrn. Bellevue Pub. Schs., Wash., 1968-70; supt. schs. Pasco Sch. Dist. Wash., 1970-73, Pelham Pub. Schs., N.Y., 1973-77, Redlands United Sch. Dist., Calif., 1977-80, Conejo Valley Unified Sch. Dist., Thousand Oaks, Calif., 1980-87, San Diego County Schs., 1987-90, Ky. Commn. Edn., 1991-95, sr. v.p. edn., 1995—.

BOYT, PATRICK ELMER, farmer, real estate executive; b. Liberty, Tex., Sept. 22, 1940; s. Elmer Vernon and Kathleen (Nelson) B.; B.S. in C.E., U. Tex., 1963; m. Elizabeth Ruth Jefferson, June 16, 1962; children: Jefferson Elmer, Mark Cecil. Owner, mng. ptnr. Boyt Properties, mng. ptnr. Kathleen N. Boyt Family Ltd. Partnership; dir. First State Bank, Liberty, 1978-89, Beaumont State Bank, 1969-78, Farm Credit Banks of Tex., 1986-88; mem. Coun. on Small Bus. and Agr. of Fed. Reserve Bank of Dallas, 1989-94; mng. ptnr. Kathleen N. Boyt Family Ltd. Partnership, 1996—. Bd. dirs. Beaumont Art Mus., 1973—, Devers Ind. Sch. Dist., 1974-90; mem. Tex. Commn. for Arts, 1978-81; bd. dirs. Kersting Meml. Hosp., 1976-83; supr. Lower Trinity Soil and Water Conservation Dist., 1972-90. Democrat. Presbyterian. Home: 5672 Longwood St Beaumont TX 77707-1891 Office: PO Box 575 Devers TX 77538-0575

BOZACK, MICHAEL JAMES, physicist; b. Lansing, Mich., June 19, 1952; s. Joseph J. Bozack and Helen Pauline (Shutes) Roblee. BS and MS in Physics, Mich. State U., 1977; MA in Theology, Western Conservative Bapt. Sem, Portland, Oreg., 1979; PhD in Physics, Oreg. Grad. Inst. Sci. Tech., Portland, 1985. Physicist Tektronix, Inc., Portland, 1978; postdoctoral rsch. assoc. dept. chemistry U. Pitts., 1985-87; dir. surface sci. lab. Intel Corp., Hillsboro, Oreg., 1987-88; asst. prof. physics Auburn (Ala.) U., 1988-93; assoc. prof. Physics Auburn U., 1994—; Adj. prof. physics Oreg. Grad. Inst., 1988-93. Contbr. 70 articles to profl. jours., 60 papers at various seminars. Mem. Am. Vacuum Soc., Am. Phys. Soc., Materials Rsch. Soc. Baptist. Office: Auburn U Dept Physics Auburn AL 36849

BOZALIS, JOHN RUSSELL, physician; b. St. Louis, Sept. 19, 1939; s. George Sauter and Ruth (Russell) B.; m. Sharon Louise Sabo, June 21, 1963; children: John Jr., David L., Diana. BA, U. Okla., 1961, MD, 1965; MS, U. Mich., 1971. Diplomate Am. Bd. Internal Medicine, Am. Bd. Allergy and Immunology. Intern Henry Ford Hosp., Detroit, 1965-66, resident, 1966-68, chief resident, 1968-69; fellow in allergy-immunology U. Mich., Ann Arbor, 1969-71, instr., 1969-71; clin. asst. prof. U. Tex., San Antonio, 1972-73; pvt. practice Okla. Allergy Clinic, Oklahoma City, 1973—; clin. instr. Coll. Medicine, U. Okla., 1973, clin. asst. prof., 1977-83, clin. assoc. prof., 1983-89, clin. prof., 1989—; mem. courtesy staff Mercy Hosp., Bapt. Hosp., Deaconess Hosp., St. Anthony Hosp., Presbyn. Hosp., Children's Hosp., Okla. Tchg. Hosp., S.W. Med. Ctr. Trustee Casady Sch., 1977-85, United Way Okla. City, chmn. profl. divsn. 1983, Okla. Health Scis. Found.; bd. dirs. Infant Ctr., 1983-86, Allied Arts Okla. City, 1984-86, 92, Hosp. Hospitality House, 1983-86; vice chmn. health scis. ctr. U. Okla. Centennial Commn.; bd. trustees McGee Eye Inst., mem. search com. for chmn. dept. ophthalmology and dir., 1991; active Com. of 100, 1991; bd. trustees Okla. City Pub. Schs. Found., 1989—, Okla. Orthopedic and Arthritis Found., Inc., Bone and Joint Hosp., 1993. Maj. USAF, 1971-73. Recipient Regents' Alumni award U. Okla., 1992; named Physician of Yr.-Pvt. Practice, U. Okla. Coll. of Medicine Alumni Assn., 1993. Fellow ACP, Am. Coll. Chest Physicians, Am. Acad. Allergy; mem. AMA, Am. Thoracic Soc., Okla. State Med. Assn. (del. 1992), Okla. Lung Assn., Okla. Thoracic Soc. (pres. 1979), John M. Sheldon Soc., Okla. County Med. Soc. (editor Bull. 1978-83, chmn. orientation com. 1989—, pres. 1996, bd. trustees 1996—), Osler Soc. (pres. 1984), Okla. City Acad. Medicine, Robert M. Bird Soc., U. Okla. Coll. Medicine Alumni Assn. (chmn. rsch. com., pres. 1983-85), Okla. City C. of C. (bd. dirs. 1988-90). Republican. Episcopal. Office: Okla Allergy Clin Inc PO Box 26827 Oklahoma City OK 73126-0827

BOZE, BETSY VOGEL, marketing educator, dean; b. Shreveport, La., Sept. 18, 1953; d. Leroy Vogel and Betty Gray (Garrett) Vogel McDonald; children: Christopher Lee, Broox Garrett Vogel Boze, Lee Gray Boze. BS in Psychology, So. Meth. U., 1974; postgrad., Am. Grad. Sch. Internat. Mgmt., 1975; MBA, So. Meth. U., 1975; PhD, U. Ark., 1984. Lectr. U. Md., 1975, 78-80; asst. prof. St. Bonaventure U., Olean, N.Y., 1977-78; instr. U. Ark., Fayetteville, 1979-83; asst. prof. Centenary Coll. of La., Shreveport, 1983-89; assoc. prof., chair dept. bus. adminstrn. U. Alaska, Anchorage, 1989-94; dean, prof. mktg. U. Tex., Brownsville, 1994—; pres. Boze & Assocs., Shreveport and Anchorage, 1983-94; dir. Women in Mgmt. Conf., Shreveport, 1983-89; mem. adv. coun. Hispanic Ednl. Telecomms. Sys., San Juan, P.R., 1995—; co-dir. Tex. Transp. Inst. Ctr. for Ports and Waterways, 1994—; vis. faculty Portland State U. on Khaborosk, Russia, 1994. Mem. editl. bd. Jour. for Not-for-Profit Mktg., 1990—; contbr. articles to profl. jours., chpts. to textbooks. V.p. Atlantic Mktg. Assn., Orlando, Fla., 1988-90; pres. Susitna coun. Girl Scouts U.S., Anchorage, 1992-94, Wish Upon a Star, Shreveport, 1988-90; mem. program com. Commonwealth North, Anchorage, 1989-94. U.S. Dept. Edn. Internat. fellow U. Hawaii, 1990. Mem. Leadership Tex., AAUP, AAUW, Petroleum Club of Anchorage, Delta Delta Delta (pres. alumnae chpt. 1989-92). Methodist. Home: 1409 Avenida Santa Ana Rancho Viejo TX 78575 Office: U Tex Brownsville 80 Fort Brown Brownsville TX 78520

BOZEMAN, ROSS ELLIOT, engineering executive; b. New Orleans, Feb. 16, 1967; s. Robert Ray and Rita (Findley) B. BS cum laude, La. Tech. Inst., 1990. Assoc. vessel engr. Litwin Engrs. and Constructors, Houston, 1990-94, vessel engr., 1994-96; engring. mgr. Bergaila Engring. Svcs., Inc., Houston, 1996—. Mem. ASME (assoc.), Tau Beta Pi. Home: 8623 Rose Garden Dr Houston TX 77083

BOZIC, WILLIAM JOSEPH, JR., secondary school educator; b. Pitts., July 27, 1964; s. William Joseph B. Storey and Barbara Ann Greene; m. Julissa Diana Gonzalez, Dec. 21, 1993. BA in History, U. Fla., 1986, MEd, 1987. Tchr. Brevard County Schs., Melbourne, Fla., 1987-93, Houston Ind. Sch. Dist., 1993-94; tchr. Tomball (Tex.) Ind. Sch. Dist., 1994—. Mem. SAR, SCV. Republican. Roman Catholic. Home: 16226 Cypress Valley Dr Cypress TX 77429-1620 Office: Tomball High Sch 30330 Quinn Rd Tomball TX 77375-4314

BRAASCH, STEVEN MARK, advertising executive; b. Omaha, Nebr., June 8, 1954; s. Jack Oliver and Jane (McCleneghan) B.; m. Jennifer Locke, Aug. 7, 1976; children: Mark, Heather. BS in Advt., U. Tex., 1976. Acct. mgr., writer Ray Hall Advt., Austin, 1974-76; acct. mgr. Tracy-Locke, Dallas, 1976-77; acct. supr. Bozell, Dallas, 1977-80; pres. Braasch & Assocs., Dallas, 1981-85; sr. v.p. Anderson Thompson, Dallas, 1985-86; sr. v.p., dir. GSD & M, Austin, 1986—; pres. SJB Resoures, Austin, SJB Interests, McBe, JM Duke, Brazos Valley Breeder's, Inc., Dallas and Austin. Contbr. articles to profl. jours. Bd. dirs. Austin Am. Heart Assn. Carbomedics Fundraiser, 1994; v.p. North Dallas Am. Heart Assn. Fundraiser, Dallas, 1986-87; vol., supporter Austin Ronald McDonald KLRU, Austin, 1987—; mem. Am. Cancer Soc., U. Tex. Longhorn Found. Named Outstanding Advt. Intern Dallas Advt. League, 1975, Top Promotions Exec. Am. Soc. Mktg. and Promotions Execs., 1986. Mem. Am. Soc. Advertisers, U. Tex. Alumni Assn., Barton Creek Country Club, Seton Forum, Phi Gamma Delta. Office: GSD & M PO Box 164181 Austin TX 78716-4181

BRACE, JEANETTE WARNING, nurse educator; b. Buffalo, Nov. 21, 1938; d. Henry and Pearl Warning; m. Richard C. Brace, Apr. 21, 1958; children: Richard, Kimberly, Randall, Kristen. RN, Buffalo Gen. Hosp., 1958; BSN, Incarnate Word Coll., 1976; MSN, U. Tex. Health Sci., 1977. RN, N.Y., Ohio, Pa., W.Va.; cert. geriatrics nurse. Staff nurse Buffalo Gen. Hosp., 1958-59, NorthWest Cmty. Hosp., Arlington Hgts., Ill., 1962-64, St. Lukes Hosp., Bethlehem, Pa., 1971-73; program mgr., nurse cons. Tex. Dept. Human Svcs., San Antonio, 1977-86; site dir., assessor Area Agy. Aging, Cambridge, Ohio, 1987-92; asst. prof. nursing West Liberty (W.Va.) State Coll., 1992—; cons. program excellence Ohio Bd. Regents, Columbus, 1988. Bd. dirs. St. Johns Med. Ctr., Steubenville, Ohio, 1988-90; history nurse ARC, Steubenville, 1991-93. Mem. ANA, Am. Soc. on Aging, Ohio Nurses Assn. (nurse evaluator 1992-94), W.Va. Aging Alliance, Pilot Club of Steubenville (pres. 1996—). Office: West Liberty State Coll Main Hall Nursing Dept West Liberty WV 26074

BRACHMAN, LEON HAROLD, chemical company executive; m. Fay Rosenthal; children: Debbye Rice, Wendy B. Fisher, Ellen Brachman, Marshall Brachman. BS in Astronomy, Harvard Coll., 1942. Pres. Petrochemicals Co., Inc., 1968-79, Computerized Bus. Systems, Inc., Huileries Caraibes, S.A., Marco Chem. Co.; chmn. steering com. U. North Tex. Coll. of Pub. Health and Pub. Health Policy; adv. coun. Health Sci. Ctr. at Fort Worth. Pres. Fort Worth Chamber Music Soc., Fort Worth Hebrew Day Sch., Casa Manana Musicals of Fort Worth, 1973-76, Fort Worth Symphony Orch. Assn., 1979-82, exec. com.; pres., campaign chmn. Fort Worth Jewish Fedn.; pres., bd. dirs. Ahavath Sholom Synagogue; exec. com. Arts Coun. of Fort Worth and Tarrant County; nat. vice chmn. United Jewish Appeal; past chmn. bd. All Saints Episcopal Hosps.; chmn. Tarrant County Appraisal Dist., 1985-91. Mem. Am. Chem. Soc., Am. Oil Chemists Soc., Assn. of the Pulp and Paper Industry, Soaring Soc. of Am. Home: 3720 Autumn Dr Fort Worth TX 76109-2613 Office: 2108 West Fwy Fort Worth TX 76102-4329

BRACHMAN, MALCOLM K., oil company executive; b. Ft. Worth, Dec. 9, 1926; s. Solomon and Etta (Katzenstein) B.; m. Minda Fay Delugach, Sept. 4, 1951; children: Lynn, Malcolm K. Jr., Lisa. BA, Yale U., 1945; MA, Harvard U., 1947, PhD, 1949. CLU. Asst. prof. So. Meth. U., Dallas, 1949-50; assoc. physicist Argonne Nat. Lab., Chgo., 1950-53; rsch. staff Tex. Instruments, Inc., Dallas, 1953-54; v.p. Pioneer Am. Ins. Co., Ft. Worth, 1954-61, pres., 1961-73, chmn. bd., chief exec. officer, 1973-79; pres. N.W. Oil Co., Dallas, 1956—; chmn. adv. coun. Econ. Growth Ctr. Yale U. Capt. USAAF, 1950-57. Fellow Am. Phys. Soc., Soc. Petroleum Engrs., Am. Math. Soc.; sr. mem. IEEE, Soc. Exploration Geophysics; mem. Petroleum Club. Jewish. Home: 3510 Turtle Creek Blvd Apt 16F Dallas TX 75219-5545 Office: NW Oil Co 3232 Mckinney Ave Ste 770 Dallas TX 75204-2429

BRACK, JACQUES, language educator, linguistics researcher, author; b. Warsaw, Poland, Jan. 11, 1921; came to U.S., 1943; s. Baron Eliezer von Brachfeld and Baila Gitla Bursztyn; m. Marianne Dahmen, Feb. 17, 1943 (div. Mar. 1973); 1 child, Fanchon Faye B. Godynick; m. Simone Lallemand. MA, Sorbonne, Paris, 1990. Cert. tchr. French, Spanish and English, N.C. Travel supr. Am. Express, 1949-58; v.p., ptnr. Translloyd Travel, N.Y.C. and Amsterdam, 1959-61; founder, 1st pres. Marianne du Breaux Cosmetics, N.Y.C. and Paris, 1966-67; gen. mgr. three hotels, various locations, 1967-70; travel dir. Escorts, various locations, 1970; co-founder, v.p., asst. cruise dir. Costa Line, Holland Am. Line, 1970-73; founder, 1st pres. Eurocontact Lang. Inst., Paris, 1974-81; prof. Johnson C. Smith U., Charlotte, N.C., 1982-90, Craven C.C., New Bern, N.C., 1982-90, East Carolina U. Extension, Morehead, N.C., 1991-94; freelance travel tours dir. Co-author: Frigidity or All About Love, 1995, The Crudified From Paris, 1996, others. Missionary, United Meth. Ch., Vanceboro, N.C. Mem. Am. Legion, Cercle Militaire des Officiers, Benevolent Assn. of French Security Agts., Am. Soc. Travel Agts., Internat. Air Travel Assn., Alliance Francaise of Carteret Craven. Home: 812-A Old Cherry Point Rd New Bern NC 28560 also: 7 rue du Disque, Paris France 75013

BRACKEN, LOUIS EVERETT, retired sales executive, health services executive; b. Altoona, Pa., July 1, 1947; s. Everett William and Antonnette Virginia (DeFalco) B.; children: William Joseph, Jennifer Lynn. BS, U. Md., 1970. Sales trainee DeVilbiss Co., Somerset, Pa., 1970; dist. sales rep. DeVilbiss Co., 1970-71, dist. sales mgr., 1971-75, regional sales mgr., 1976-82; pres. Health Care Equipment Mktg. Assocs., Inc., Scituate, Mass., 1982-94; v.p. Associated Home Health Care Svcs., Inc., Everett, Mass., 1988-94; retired, 1994; co-founder Home Strategic Planning, Inc., Boston, 1981-83, Mass. Rehab. Svcs., Inc., Randolph, Mass., 1981, Health Care Distbn. Svcs., Inc., Hanover, Mass., 1984, Associated Home Health Svcs., Inc., Everett, 1985, Health Care Billing Systems, Inc., Hanover, 1985, Continuing Med. Corp. Inc., Providence, 1987, Nat. Homecare Purchasing Network, Boca Raton, Fla., 1990, Health Care Equipment Leasing Ltd., Boca Raton, 1991. Dir. U.S. Jr. Chamber of Congress in Scituate, Scituate, Mass., 1978-81; head coach Pop Warner in Scituate, 1978. Grantee U. Md., 1965-70. Mem. Boys Club (Altoona, Pa., pres.). Republican. Roman Catholic. Office: PO Box 579 Boca Raton FL 33429-0579

BRACKEN, MARILYN CASEY, environmental company executive; b. Pitts., Nov. 5, 1935; d. Dennis Arthur and Dorothy (Connolly) Casey; m. Harry Jerome Bracken Jr., July 13, 1957; children: Michael Farrell, Steven Gray, Ann Bracken Kelsey, Margaret Bracken Barrett. BS in Chemistry, Carnegie Inst. Tech., Pitts., 1957; MA in Pub. Adminstrn. Tech. Mgmt., Am. U., 1967, PhD in Pub. Adminstrn. Tech. Mgmt., 1971. Chemist Melpar Inc., Falls Church, Va., 1957-58, Nat. Bur. Standards, Washington, 1962-64; student trainee biol. scis. com. project George Washington Univ., Washington, 1966-70; cons. Nat. Libr. Medicine, Bethesda, 1970-71; info. sys. analyst Nat. Agrl. Libr., Beltsville, Md., 1971-72; info. sys. analyst office info. sys. USDA, Washington, 1972-73; dir. divsn. scientific coordination bur. biomedical sci. U.S. Consumer Product Safety Commn., Bethesda, 1973-76; assoc. dept. head environ. chemistry and biology The MITRE Corp., McLean, Va., 1976-77, dept. head Energy and Environ. Info. Systems, 1977-78; dep. asst. adminstr. program integration and info. Office Pesticides and Toxic Substances, U.S. EPA, Washington, 1978-80, assoc. asst. adminstr. toxics integration, 1980-83; v.p. product testing and liability Environ. Testing & Certification Co., Edison, N.J., 1983-88; sr. v.p. spl. projects Metcalf & Eddy, Wakefield, Mass., 1988-89; pres. Metcalf & Eddy de Puerto Rico, San Juan, 1989-91; pres. South region Air & Water Techs. Inc., Sunrise, Fla., 1991-92; sr. v.p. fed. programs Air & Water Techs. Inc., Chevy Chase, Md., 1992-93; v.p. mktg. and bus. devel. Applied Biosci. Internat., Inc., Arlington, Va., 1993-94; pres. PARAGON Global Svcs., Arlington, 1993—, Bracker Assocs. L.L.C., Md., 1995—; nat. corr. Internat. Registry for Potentially Toxic Chems., UN Environ. Program, 1978-83; chmn. Toxic Substances Data Com.-U.S. Govt., 1978-83; chmn. mgmt. com. Spl. Program on Control of Chemicals OECD, 1978-80; U.S. chmn. Project on Identity and Control of Toxic Substances, U.S.-Japan Environ. Agreement, 1978-83; mem. program adv. com. Internat. Program on Chem. Safety, WHO, 1982-83; mem. toxicology info. program com. NAS, 1984-92, com. on biotech. nomenclature, 1986-87, com. to evaluate mass balance info. and facilities handling toxic substances, 1987-91; others. Contbr. chpt. to book and articles to profl. jours. Recipient chmn.'s spl. citation U.S. Consumer Product Safety Commn., 1976, Disting. Alumna award Am. U., 1978, Presdl. Rank award U.S. Govt., 1980; tng. grantee Nat. Libr. Medicine, NIH, 1966-70. Fellow AAAS (chmn. sect. info., computing and comm. 1981-82); mem. Soc. Am. Mil. Engrs. (v.p. Washington post 1993-94, dir., 1995—), Am. Soc. Info. Sci. (councilor), Am. Chem. Soc. Office: PO Box 151048 Chevy Chase MD 20815-4206

BRACKETT, COLQUITT PRATER, JR., judge; b. Norfolk, Va., Feb. 24, 1946; s. Colquitt Prater Sr. and Antoinette Gladys (Cacace) B.; m. Pamela Susan Colwell, Oct. 11, 1969 (dec. Aug. 1978); 1 child, Susan Elizabeth; m. Frances Sybil Langford, Jan. 1, 1982. BS, U. Ga., 1966, MA, 1968, JD, 1973, LLM, 1976. Bar: Ga. 1973, U.S. Dist. Ct. (so. dist.) Ga. 1974, U.S. Dist. Ct. (mid. dist.) Ga. 1977, U.S. Supreme Ct. 1980, Tenn. 1987. Assoc. Surrett & CoCroft, Augusta, Ga., 1972-74; ptnr. Surrett & Brackett, Augusta, 1974-76; mem. faculty Sch. Law, U. Ga., Athens, 1977-82; mng. ptnr. Brackett, Prince & Neufeld, Athens, 1982-90; adminstrv. law judge Ga. Dept. Med. Assistance, Athens, 1990—; hearing officer Ga. State Bd. Edn., 1979-91; v.p. Mus. Dolls & Gifts, Inc., Pigeon Forge, Tenn., 1983—. Author: Court Administration, 1972. Pres. Athens Clarke Mental Health Assn., 1985; chmn. bd. dirs. N.E. Ga. Mental Health Assn., 1989-90; bd. dirs. Coalition For The Blue Ridge Pkwy., 1994—. Mem. Ga. State Bar Assn., Ga. Assn. Adminstrv. Law Judges (bd. dirs. 1990-91), Ga. Trial Lawyers Assn., Western Cir. Bar Assn. Episcopalian. Office: 505 Woodlawn Ave Athens GA 30606-4359

BRACKETT, JAMES VINCENT, electrical engineer; b. Billings, Mont., June 4, 1959; s. Perry Chester and Lillian Helen Kaczmarski (Clinton) B.; m. Elizabeth Andrea Hein, June 16, 1991. BSEE, Mont. State U., 1981. Cert. telecommunications engr. Mem. tech. staff Hughes Aircraft Corp., El Segundo, Calif., 1980; electronics engr. Harry Diamond Labs., Adelphi, Md., 1985-91; elec. engr., phys. scientist Def. Spl. Weapons Agy., Alexandria, Va., 1991-94; safety engr. Def. Nuclear Agy., Alexandria, Va., 1994, chief assessment sect., 1994—. Contbr. articles to profl. jours.; co-author mil. standards and handbooks. Capt. U.S. Army, 1981-85. Mem. IEEE, U. Md. Sq. UMs (del. 1991-92), Nat. Assn. Radio and Telecom. Engrs., Masons. Home: 8542 Electric Ave Vienna VA 22182 Office: Defense Spl Weapons Agy 6801 Telegraph Rd Alexandria VA 22310

BRACKIN, HENRY BRYAN, JR., psychiatrist; b. Raleigh, N.C., Nov. 3, 1924; s. Henry Bryan and Rachel Pauline (Luker) B.; m. Eva Drucilla Cato, Oct. 15, 1948; children: Henry Bryan III, John Curtis, Robert Lewis. BA, Vanderbilt U., 1944, MD, 1947. Diplomate Am. Bd. Psychiatry and Neurology. Intern St. Thomas Hosp., Nashvile, 1947-48; resident surgery Nashville Gen. Hosp.,

1948-50; resident psychiatry Perry Point (Md.) VA Hosp., 1950, U.S. Naval Hosp., Oakland, Calif., 1951-52, Hosp. U. Pa., Phila., 1952-54; pvt. practice psychiatry Nashville, 1954—; staff Madison Hosp., 1954-73, pres., 1960's, chief psychiat.; staff park View Hosp. (now Centennial Med. Ctr.), Columbia, 1973—, chief of psychiatry staff, 1977-81, 85-91, bd. trustees, 1973-87, 95-96; cons. Vanderbilt U. Hosp., 1954—, Bapt. Hosp., 1954-96, Nashville Gen. Hosp., 1954-75, St. Thomas Hosp., 1954-95; asst. prof. clin. psychiatry Vanderbilt Med. Sch., 1954—. Fellow Am. Psychiat. Assn. (life, dep. rep. from area V to assembly exec. com. 1969-73, rep. 1973-77, parliamentarian 1977-78, trustee 1978-81); mem. AMA, Nashville Acad. Medicine (former mem. mental health, legis. coms.), Tenn. Med. Assn., So. Med. Assn. (life), Tenn. Psychiat. Assn. (offices include pres. 1969-70, dep. rep. to Am. Psychiat. Assn. Assembly 1963-66, rep. 1966-69, pres. mid-Tenn. chpt. 1980, Pres. award 1991), So. Psychiat. Assn. (chmn. program com. 1966, site com. 1974, 77, parliamentarian 1980-84, chmn. bd. regents 1983-84, pres. 1985). Republican. Methodist. Home: 137 Prospect Hill Nashville TN 37205-4721 Office: 310 25th Ave N Nashville TN 37203-1515

BRACKIN, PHYLLIS JEAN, recruiting professional; b. Aliquippa, Pa., Oct. 5, 1946; d. Matthew Edward and Trula Estelle (Venable) Plonka; children: Keith, Kevin. Student, Georgetown U., 1966, U. S. Fla., 1981. Librarian Def. Intelligence Agy., Washington, 1966-70, Aerospace Corp., Los Angeles, 1975-78; personnel mgr. Badger Engrs. Inc., Tampa, Fla., 1979-85; dir. career devel. PTC Inst., Tampa, 1985-86; dir. mktg. & pub. rels. DSI Staff RX, Inc., Clearwater, Fla., 1986—. Author: Personal Skills Development, How to Hire Eagles, 1988, Recruitment Services: A Viable Option, 1988, How to Get a Job and Keep It, 1990, Are We Having Fun Yet?, Celebrate Your Profession, 1992, Are You Hiring Ziggers or Zaggers?, Celebrate You!, 1994. Mem. NAFE, ASTD, Fla. Soc. Pers. Cons., Am. Healthcare Radiology Adminstrs. Republican. Roman Catholic. Home: 8207 Olivewood Pl Tampa FL 33615-5718

BRACKMEYER, MELLODY S., oncology and emergency medicine nurse; b. Watsonville, Calif., June 8, 1950; d. Frank T. and Ruby (Velazquez) Cabral; children: Dale, Daniel, Jill. Diploma, United Nurses Sch., San Bernardino, Calif., 1971; student, Clinton (Iowa) Community Coll.; ADN, N.E. Iowa Tech. Inst., Peosta, 1982; student, U. Dubuque, Ark. State U. Cert. oncology nurse, emergency nurse, pediat. nurse. Weekend charge nurse in pediatrics St. Joseph Mercy Hosp., Clinton; clin. nurse for edn. John L. McClellan VA Hosp., Little Rock, nurse mgr. in oncology; oncology nurse out-patient clinic Ark. Children's Hosp., Little Rock; staff nurse bone marrow transplant unit Ark. Children's Hosp.; part-time home health nurse Olsten Kimberly Quality Care. Vol. ARC, 1995. Capt. Army Nurse Corps, 1984—. Recipient Fitness award 807th med. Brigade, 1988, 89. Mem. Oncology Nurses Soc., Assn. Mil. Surgeons U.S. Home: 3800 Lochridge Rd North Little Rock AR 72116-8331

BRADDOCK, DONALD LAYTON, SR., lawyer, accountant; b. Jacksonville, Fla., Dec. 14, 1941; s. John Reddon and Harriet (Burgess) B.; children: Stella Helene Knowlton, Leslie Ann, Donald Layton Jr. BS in Bus. Adminstrn., U. Fla., 1963, JD, 1967. Bar: Fla. 1968, U.S. Dist. Ct. (mid. and no. dists.) Fla. 1968, U.S. Tax Ct. 1970, U.S. Ct. Appeals (5th cir.) 1968, U.S. Ct. Appeals (4th and 11th cirs.) 1983, U.S. Supreme Ct., 1976; registered real estate broker. Staff acct. Coopers and Lybrand, CPAs, 1964-65, Keith C. Austin, CPA, 1965-67; assoc. Kent, Durden & Kent, attys. at law, 1967-71; sole practice, 1971-73; ptnr. Howell, Kirby, Montgomery, D'Aiuto & Dean, attys. at law, 1974-76; pres. Howell, Liles, Braddock & Milton, attys. at law, Jacksonville, Fla., 1976-88; ret., 1988; bd. dirs., mem. exec. com. Fla. Lawyers Mutual Ins. Co.; bd. dirs., pres. Doctors Lake Marina, Inc., SafeStop, Inc., Mandarin Realty; pres., dir. Donald J. Braddock Chartered, 1970—. Bd. dirs. Jacksonville Vocat. Edn. Authority, 1971-75; mem. Jacksonville Bicentennial Commn., 1976; bd. govs. Fla. Bar Found., 1984-86, sec.-treas., 1986-88; sec., dir. Laurel Grove Plantation, Inc., 1988—, Safe Stop, Inc., 1991—; pres., dir. Doctors Lake Marina, Inc., 1993—. Served with Air N.G., 1963-69. Mem. Fla. Bar (bd. govs. young lawyers sect. 1972-77), Fla. Inst. CPAs, Jacksonville C. of C. (com. of 100), Jacksonville Bar Assn. (pres. 1983-84, bd. govs. 1978-84), U. Fla. Alumni Assn. (pres. 1975, bd. dirs. 1968-75), Fla. Blue Key, Friars Club, Phi Delta Phi, Alpha Tau Omega. Republican. Baptist. Office: PO Box 57385 Jacksonville FL 32241-7385

BRADEN, JOHN A., accountant; b. Houston, Feb. 9, 1945; s. John Earl and Marjorie (Wilson) B.; m. Leilani D. Fowler, Dec. 9, 1972; children: Meredith, Alana. BBA, U. Houston, 1967. CPA, Tex. Sr. acct. Haskins & Sells, Houston, 1967-71; pres. John A. Braden, Houston, 1971-86, Braden & Kikis, Houston, 1986-96, John A. Braden & Co., Houston, 1996—. Contbr. articles to profl. jours. Bd. dirs., treas. Northampton Mcpl. Utility Dist., Spring, Tex., 1986—; pres., commr. Harris County Rural Fire Protection Dist. # 1, 1989-92; officer parent orgn. Klein Oak H.S., 1986-94; chmn. audit com., mem. adminstrv. bd., fin. com., found. trustee, choir pres. Klein United Meth. Ch., Spring. Mem. AICPA's, Tex. Soc. CPA's (bd. dirs., com. chmn. 1969—), Houston Chpt. CPA's (bd. dirs., com. chmn. 1969—, v.p. 1990-91), Houston Estate adn Fin. Forum, Soc. Exploration Geophysicists, Planned Giving Coun. Houston. Republican. Home: 6107 Knollview Dr Spring TX 77389-3748 Office: John A Braden & Co Ste 840 12941 Interstate 45N Houston TX 77060

BRADEN, THOMAS WARDELL, news commentator; b. Greene, Iowa, Feb. 22, 1918; s. Thomas Wardell and Louise (Garl) B.; m. Joan E. Ridley, Dec. 18, 1948; children: David, Mary, Joan, Susan, Nancy, Elizabeth, Thomas Wardell III, Nicholas R. AB, Dartmouth Coll., 1940, AM, 1964; LittD, Franklin Coll. Ind., 1979. Newspaperman; instr. English Dartmouth, 1946, asst. to pres. and asst. prof., 1947-48; exec. sec. Mus. Modern Art, N.Y.C., 1949; dir. Am. Com. on United Europe, 1950; editor, pub. Blade Tribune, Oceanside, Calif., 1954-68; columnist Los Angeles Times Syndicate, 1968-86; commentator CNN, CBS, NBC, 1978-89. Author: (with Stewart Alsop) Sub-Rosa, 1946, Eight is Enough, 1975. Mem. Calif. Bd. Edn., 1959-67; past. pres. Trustee Calif. State Coll., 1961-64, Dartmouth, 1964-74, Carnegie Endowment, 1970-82. Served with King's Royal Rifle Corps Brit. Army, Africa and Italy, 1941-44; trans. to inf. AUS, 1944. *

BRADFORD, DENNIS DOYLE, textiles executive, real estate broker; b. Tulsa, Sept. 5, 1945; s. Doyle Earl and Elta (Price) B.; m. Richie Deloris Dawson. BSBA in Econs., U. Tulsa, 1969. Sales and mktg. rep. Xerox Corp., Oklahoma City, 1969-72; comml. loan officer Mager Mortgage Co., Oklahoma City, 1973-74; pvt. practice real estate Oklahoma City, 1973—; pres., owner Bradford Oil Co., Oklahoma City, 1977-80; pres. Blazer Oil Co., Oklahoma City, 1980-84; v.p. Petro So., Inc., Tampa Fla., 1983-84; ptnr. Coachman Inns, Oklahoma City, 1981-86; chmn., chief exec. officer Coachman Inc., Oklahoma City, 1985—; pres., CEO Olympia Mills Corp., Guaynabo, P.R., 1995—; mem. nat. adv. coun. to U.S. SBA, Washington, 1986. Bd. dirs. Okla. Med. Ctr. Found., 1989—; bd. dirs., sec. Okla. Air and Space Mus., 1989—, v.p. 1991-92, pres. 1992-93; mem. Local Selective Svc. Bd., Oklahoma City. Mem. Nat. Cowboy Hall of Fame, Okla. Heritage Assn., Okla. County Hist. Soc., Air Force Assn., Navy League, Young Pres.'s Orgn. (chmn. 1993-94, N.Am. spl. projects officer 1993-94), Oklahoma City C. of C., Balloon Fedn. Am., Oklahoma City Golf and Country Club, Clearwater Club. Republican. Methodist. Office: Coachman Inc 301 NW 63rd St Ste 500 Oklahoma City OK 73116-7906

BRADFORD, JAMES WARREN, JR., manufacturing executive; b. Newport News, Va., May 3, 1947; s. James Warren and Blanche B.; m. Susan Garrision; children: Geoffrey, Emily, Alexander, Laura. BA, U. Fla., 1969; JD, Vanderbilt U., 1973. Pvt. practice, 1973; ptnr. Hunter, Smith & Davis, Kingsport, Tenn., 1973-84; v.p., gen. counsel AGF Industries, Inc., Kingsport, 1984-92, pres., 1992—. Co-author: An Introduction of Academic Unionism for College Administrators. Chmn. 1st Broad St. United Meth. Child Care, Kingsport, Dream Team, 1992; mem. exec. bd. Holston Valley Hosp. and Med. Ctr., Kingsport. Mem. ABA, Tenn. Bar Assn., Kingsport Bar Assn., Kingsport C. of C. Home: 1422 Watauga St Kingsport TN 37664-2563 Office: AFG Industries Inc 1400 Lincoln St Kingsport TN 37660-5174*

BRADFORD, LOUISE MATHILDE, social services administrator; b. Alexandria, La., Aug. 3, 1925; d. Henry Aaron and Ruby (Pearson) B. BS, La. Poly. Inst., 1945; cert. in social work, La. State U., 1949; MS, Columbia U., 1953; postgrad., Tulane U., 1962, 64, La. State U., 1967; cert., U. Pa., 1966. Diplomate Am. Bd. Clin. Social Work; cert. social worker Acad. Cert. Social Workers. With La. Dept. Pub. Welfare, Alexandria, 1945-78; welfare caseworker La. Dept. Pub. Welfare, Alexandria, La., 1950-53; children's caseworker La. Dept. Pub. Welfare, Alexandria, 1957-59, child welfare cons., 1959-73, social svcs. cons., 1973-78, state cons. day care, 1963-66; dir. social svcs. St. Mary's Tng. Sch., Alexandria, 1978—; del. Nat. Day Care Conf., Washington, 1964; mem. early childhood edn. com. So. States Work Conf., Daytona Beach, Fla., 1968; mem. La. adv. com. 1970 White House Conf. on Children, also del.; mem. So. region planning com. Child Welfare League Am., 1970-73; mem. profl. adv. com. Cenla chpt. Parents Without Partners, 1970-95; adj. asst. prof. sociology La. Coll. Pineville, 1969-85; lectr. Kindergarten Workshop, 1970-72; mem. La. 4-C Steering Com.; social svcs. cons. La. Spl. Edn. Ctr., Alexandria, 1980-86; del. Internat. Conf. on Social Welfare, Nairobi, 1974, Jerusalem, 1978, Hong Kong, 1980, Brighton, 1982, Montreal, 1984. Bd. dirs. Cenla Cmty. Action Com., Alexandria, 1966-68; mem. kindergarten bd. Meth. Ch., 1967-87, ofcl. bd., 1974-75, 77-81, 83-85, 96—. Recipient Social Worker of Yr. award Alexandria br. NASW La. Conf. Social Welfare, 1984, Hilda C. Simon award, 1987, George Freeman award, 1987. Mem. NASW, DAR, Acad. Cert. Social Workers, La. Bd. Cert. Social Workers, So. La. Assn. Children Under Six, La. Conf. Social Welfare (George Freeman award 1987, Hilda C. Simon award 1987), Internat. Coun. on Social Welfare, Am. Pub. Welfare Assn. (S.W. region planning com. 1965), Am. Assn. on Mental Retardation (La. social work chair 1989-94), DAR, Ctrl. La. Pre-Sch. Assn. (dir. 1967-70), Rapides Golf and Country Club. Home: 5807 Joyce St Alexandria LA 71302-2510 Office: PO Box 7768 Alexandria LA 71306-0768

BRADFORD, MICHAEL LEE, religious organization administrator, clergyman; b. Johnson City, Tenn., May 4, 1942; s. Harry B. Bradford and Geneva Elizabeth (Lethco) Williams; m. Julia Ann Garrett, June 6, 1966; children: Stephen Allen, Rachel Leigh. BA, Milligan Coll., 1965; postgrad., Emmanuel Sch. of Religion, 1965-71, U. Louisville, 1985—. Ordained to ministry Christian Ch., 1965; accredited resident mgr. Inst. Real Estate Mgmt.; lic. nursing home adminstr., Ky., Tenn. Minister West Walnut St. Christian Ch., Johnson City, 1963-65, Poplar Ridge Christian Ch., Piney Flats, Tenn., 1966-71, East End Christian Ch., Bristol, Va., 1971-73; supt. East Tenn. Christian Home, Elizabethton, 1973-77; sr. minister Camden Ave. Christian Ch., Louisville, 1977-84; devel. officer, dir. communications Christian Ch. Homes of Ky. Inc., Louisville, 1984-86, mgr. Friendship House, 1986-90; dir. property mgmt., 1990—; asst. adminstr. Appalachian Christian Villages, Johnson City, 1991—; chmn. emergency assistance South Louisville Community Ministry, 1979-82; bd. advisors Milligan Coll., Tenn., 1985—; mem. adv. coun. Lifespan. Bd. dirs. Neighborhood Devel. Corp. for Old Louisville. Named Hon. Col. Gov.'s Staff, State of Ky., 1981. Mem. Louisville Area Mins. Assn. (sec. 1979-80), N.Am. Christian Conv. (nat. com. 1981-84, 87-90, 91—, chmn. local arrangements 1981, 89), Ky. Assn. Homes for Aging, Tenn. Assn. Homes for Aging (state ednl. com.), Nat. Soc. Fund Raising Execs. (bd. dirs. Mountain Empire chpt., chmn. found. dr. 1995), So. Assn. HUD Mgmt. Agts., East Tenn. Christian Mins. Assn. (v.p. 1992), Johnson City C. of C. (amb. task force 1993—, chmn. amb. task force 1994), Ruritan (sec. 1968-69), Lions (v.p. 1977). Republican. Home: 115 Beechnut St Apt I-11 Johnson City TN 37601-1542 Office: Appalachian Christian Village 2012 Sherwood Dr Johnson City TN 37601-3238

BRADFORD, REAGAN HOWARD, JR., ophthalmology educator; b. Lawton, Okla., July 31, 1954; s. Reagan Howard Sr. and Conita Ann (Hargraves) B.; m. Cynthia Ann McGough, Apr. 22, 1988. BS, U. Okla., 1976; MD, U. Okla., Oklahoma City, 1980. Diplomate Am. Bd. Ophthalmology. Intern Bapt. Med. Ctr., Oklahoma City, 1980-81; resident Dean A. McGee Eye Inst. U. Okla., 1981-84; fellow in vitreo retina Bascom Palmer Eye Inst. U. Miami, Fla., 1984-85; assoc. clinical prof. Dean A. McGee Eye Inst., U. Okla., Oklahoma City, 1985—. Author: (with others) Basics of Neurophthalmology; contbr. articles to profl. jours. Fellow Am. Acad. Ophthalmology; mem. Okla. County Med. Soc., Okla. State Med. Assn., AMA, Okla. State Acad. Ophthalmology. Republican. Baptist. Office: Dean A McGee Eye Inst 608 Stanton L Young Blvd Oklahoma City OK 73104-5014

BRADFORD, WILLIAM EDWARD, oil field equipment manufacturing company executive; b. Dallas, Jan. 8, 1935; m. JoDeane Browning, Aug. 18, 1955; children: William B., A. Kathleen, Jon E. B.S. in Geology, Centenary Coll., 1958; grad. exec. devel. course, Tex. A&M U., 1975. Salesman Hycalog, Inc., 1958-61; v.p., gen. partner Analytical Logging, Inc., 1961-70; with Dresser Industries, Inc., 1970—, dir., pres., 1979-80, group pres., 1980-83, v.p. ops., 1983-84, sr. v.p., 1984—; pres., chief exec. officer Dresser Rand, Corning, N.Y. Mem. Soc. Petroleum Engrs., Am. Assn. Petroleum Geologists, Petroleum Equipment Suppliers Assn., AAAS, Assn. Oilwell Drilling Contractors, Internat. Petroleum Assn., Nat. Ocean Industries Assn., Tex. Mid-Continentant Oil and Gas Assn. Republican. Presbyterian. Clubs: Petroleum, Raveneaux Country, Houston, University (Houston); Champions Golf, Heritage. Office: Dresser Industries Inc PO Box 718 Dallas TX 75221-0718*

BRADIE, BRIAN DAVID, mathematics educator; b. Hempstead, N.Y., Dec. 30, 1964. BS in Math. and Computer Sci., Clarkson U., 1986, MS in Applied Math., 1988, PhD in Applied Math., 1990. Grad. rsch. asst., grad. teaching asst. Clarkson U., Dept. Math. and Computer Sci., Potsdam, N.Y., 1987-90; rsch. asst. prof. Clarkson U., Dept. Math. and Computer Sci., Potsdam, 1990-91; J. Willard Gibbs instr. Yale U. Dept. Math., New Haven, 1991-93; asst. prof. Christopher Newport U., Newport News, Va., 1993—. Contbr. articles to profl. jours. Recipient Outstanding Grad. Teaching Asst. award Clarkson U. Mem. Am. Math. Soc., Math. Assn. Am., Soc. for Indsl. and Applied Mathematicians, Pi Mu Epsilon, Eta Kappa Nu (outstanding undergrad. teaching asst. award). Home: 26 Franklin Rd Newport News VA 23601-4509 Office: Christopher Newport U Dept Math 50 Shoe Ln Newport News VA 23606-2998

BRADIE, PETER RICHARD, lawyer, engineer; b. Bklyn., Feb. 19, 1937; s. Alexander Robert and Blanche Isabelle (Silverman) B.; m. Anna Barbara Corcoran, Jan. 22, 1960; children: Suzanne J., Barbara L., Michell S. BSME, Fairleigh Dickinson U., 1960; JD, South Tex. Coll. Law, 1978. Bar: Tex. 1978, U.S. Dist. Ct. (so. dist.) Tex. 1981; registered profl. engr., Ala. Performance engr. Pratt & Whitney Aircraft, West Palm Beach, Fla., 1961-63; sr. engr. Hayes Internat. Corp., Huntsville, Ala., 1963-64, Lockheed Missiles and Space, Huntsville, 1964-68; fluidics engr. Double A Products Co., Manchester, Mich., 1968-69; cons. Spectrum Controls, Montvale, N.J., 1969-72; sr. project mgr. Materials Research Corp., Orangebury, N.Y., 1972-74; sr. contracts adminstr. Brown & Root Inc., Houston, 1974-85; sole practice Houston, 1985-91; ptnr. Bradie, Bradie & Bradie, Houston, 1991—; counsel Inverness Forest C.A, Houston, 1978-80; sr. counsel Raymond-Brown & Raymond-Molem, J.V., Houston, 1982-84. Contbr. articles on fluidic controls to mags.; patentee. Dem. committeeman Bergen County, Haworth, N.J., 1959; del. Harris County Reps., Houston, 1984; officer, bd. dirs. Inverness Forest Civic Assn., Houston, 1975-78. Served to 2d lt. USMCR, 1958-61. Mem. Tex. Bar Assn., Houston Bar Assn., Houston N.W. Bar Assn. (treas. 1986, bd. dirs. 1988, sec. 1988, pres.-elect 1988-89, pres. 1990-91), Assn. Trial Lawyers Am., Houston Trial Lawyers Assn., Comml. Law League Am., Rotary Club (Montvale bd. dirs. 1973-74), Am. Inn of Ct. Republican. Jewish. Home: 22007 Kenchester Dr Houston TX 77073-1315 Office: 3845 Fm 1960 Rd W Ste 330 Houston TX 77068-3519

BRADISH, WARREN ALLEN, internal auditor, operations analyst, management consultant; b. Adrian, Mich., June 9, 1937; s. Calvin Gamber and Florence Helen (Schulze) B.; m. Setsuko Arimatsu, May 18, 1959 (div.); children—Donna, John, Bradly, Jacqueline; m. 2d, Roberta Mary Kalil, Sept. 26, 1969. BA in Bus. Adminstrn. summa cum laude, St. Leo Coll., 1977; MA in Bus. Mgmt., Central Mich. U., 1980. Enlisted in U.S. Army, 1956, comd. officer, advanced through ranks to maj., 1976, intelligence officer, ret., 1976; edn. and tng. officer, State of Ga., 1977; mgmt. cons. Gov's. office, Ga., 1977-80, dir. investigations Sec. State, 1980-82, dir. surveillance, specialized investigative services, 1982-83; internal auditor/ops. analyst Ga. Dept. Revenue, 1983-84, govt. security specialist, Ft. McPherson, Ga., 1984-88; intelligence ops. specialist MacDill, AFB, Fla. 1988—; adj. prof. St. Leo Coll. Decorated Bronze Star. Mem. Assn. Former Intelligence Officers, Spl. Forces Decade Assn., Disabled Vets. Am., Sigma Iota. Home: 4841 Foxshire Cir Tampa FL 33624-4309

BRADLEY, CHARLES ERNEST, educational leadership consultant, music educator; b. Aurora, Colo., Oct. 20, 1962; s. Ernest Rayford and Mickey Marie (Cook) B. BS cum laude, Asbury Coll., 1985. Cert. facilitative leader. Music specialist Hillsborough County Schs., Tampa, Fla., 1985-94; profl. tng. specialist Fla. Dept. Edn., 1992—; leadership cons., ednl. cons./trainer, program coord. West Cen. Ednl. Leadership Network, Tampa, 1994-95; coord. instrnl. pers. Manatee County Schs., 1995—; chmn. Assemblies Com., Tampa, 1985—, ARea IX Music Coun., Tampa, 1986-87, Mid. Sch. Task Force, 1989-90; co-chmn. Site-Based Decision Making Com., graduation com. Very Spl. Arts Hillsborough County, 1989-90, chmn., 1991-92, coord., 1991—; cons. Music in Exceptional Edn., 1993—; Team Facilitation cons., 1993—. Composer: Sonata in G Minor, 1980, Sonata in B Minor, 1984, Five American Scenes, 1984, Two Anglican Office Anthems, 1989, Five Liurgical Alleluias, 1989-90, Who Am I, cantata, 1990, Three Early American Hymns for Choirs, 1991, Medieval Cortege (organ), 1994. Choirmaster, organist St. Anne of Grace Episcopal Ch., Seminole, Fla., 1986-91; organist/music dir. St. Andrews Presbyn. Ch., Dunedin, Fla., 1991-94, organist, 1994—. Recipient Mayor's Cert. merit, Mayor's Alliance for the Handicapped, 1988, Very Spl. Arts/Hillsborough County Schs. Achievement award, 1992; Tech. Retrofit grantee State of Fla., 1993, Competitive Tech. grantee, 1994. Mem. ASCD, Am. Guild Organists (governing body, 1989—, sub-dean, 1991—), Music Educators Nat. Conf., Fla. Music Educators Assn., Fla. Elem. Music Educators Assn., Stratford Shakespeare Soc., Gen. Music Nat. Assn., Royal Sch. Ch. Music, Internat. Interactive Comm. Soc. Republican. Home: 6565 Exeter Ct Seminole FL 34642-6509 Office: West Ctrl Ednl Leadership Network 12493 Telecom Dr Tampa FL 33637-0913

BRADLEY, CHARLES HENRY, linguistic anthropologist; b. Balt., Dec. 26, 1930; s. George Downer and Lydia Hallam (Read) B.; m. Barbara Leah Brown, Aug. 29, 1952; children: Charles, David, Mark, Eric, Scott. BA, Wheaton Coll., 1953, MA, 1956; PhD, Cornell U., 1965. From field researcher to cons. Summer Inst. Linguistics, Mex., 1956-80; prof. anthropology Judson Coll., Elgin, Ill., 1980-86; from. internat. anthropology coord. to field researcher cons Summer Inst. Linguistics, Dallas, 1980—; vis. prof. linguistics Gordon Coll., Wenham, Mass., 1973-74; adj. prof. linguistics U. Okla., Norman, 1978-83, 87. Author: A Linguistic Sketch of Jicaltepec Mixtec, 1970; co-editor: Studies in the Mixtecan Languages, 1988, 90, 91, 92. Trustee Internat. Mus. Cultures, Inc., Dallas, 1986—. Nat. fgn. lang. fellow U.S. Dept. Edn., 1962. Fellow An. Anthropol. Assn., Soc. Applied Anthropology; mem. Linguistic Soc. Am., Am. Ethnol. Soc., Soc. Cultural Anthropology, Soc. Linguistic Anthropology. Home: 3811 Kentucky Ct Grand Prairie TX 75052 Office: Summer Inst Linguistics 7500 W Camp Wisdom Rd Dallas TX 75236

BRADLEY, DARNITA SUE, community health nurse; b. Marshalltown, Iowa, Aug. 2, 1957; d. Max Loran and Myra Dell (Sturtz) Mulcahy; m. Therrell James Bradley, Dec. 3, 1982; children: James Loran, Kevin Paul. ADN with honors, George Wallace Community Coll., Dothan, Ala., 1985. RN, asst. head nurse Southeast Ala. Med. Ctr., Dothan; RN, ICU Dale County Hosp., Ozark, Ala.; nurse III, pub. health Dale County Health Dept., Ozark, Ala. Sgt. U.S. Army, 1975-82. Mem. Phi Theta Kappa.

BRADLEY, DON BELL, III, marketing educator; b. Taylorville, Ill., Jan. 20, 1945; s. Don Bell Jr. and Anna V. (Anderson) B.; m. Janice M. McClain, June 4, 1966; children: Christina, Angie, Don IV. BS, Bowling Green State U., 1968; MS, Ind. State U., 1971; PhD, U. Mo., 1978. Mktg. edn. coord. Wawasee High Sch., Syracuse, Ind., 1968-69; asst. prof. mktg. Vincennes (Ind.) U., 1969-73; mid-mgmt. coord., dir. banking and svc. programs Longview C.C., Lee's Summit, Mo., 1973-76; asst. prof. mgmt. and mktg., head dept. Western Ky. U., Bowling Green, 1977-82; prof. mktg., dir. externship U. Cen. Ark., Conway, Ark., 1982—; exec. dir. Small Bus. Advancement Nat. Ctr., U. Ctrl. Ark., Conway, 1990—; mem. SBA, Washington, Youth Entrepreneurship Task Force. Author: Dynamic Retailing, 1990; editor: SBIDA News, 1990-92; mem. editorial bd. Jour. Small Bus. Mgmt., 1987—, Jour. Bus. & Entrepreneurship, Jour. Small Bus. Strategy. V.p., sec. The Gideons Internat., Conway, 1982—, family life coordinator United Meth. Ch., Conway, 1984—. Fellow Southwestern Small Bus. Inst. (sec.-treas. 1986-87, v.p. 1987-89, pres. 1989-90), Small Bus. Inst. Dirs. Assn. (nat. pres. 1990-91); mem. Ark. Mfg. Ext. Network (bd. dirs., coord. coun.), Nat. Assn. Purchasing Mgrs. (Ark. chpt. treas. 1987-88, sec. 1988-89, v.p. 1989-91, pres. 1991-92), So. Mktg. Assn., Southwestern Mktg. Assn., Midwest Mktg. Assn., Ark. Soc. for Quality Control (mktg. and publicity dir.), Am. Mktg. Assn., Internat. Coun. for Small Bus. (v.p. pubs.), Kiwanis (bd. dirs. 1985—). Democrat. Home: 12 Kensington Dr Conway AR 72032-7224 Office: U Ctrl Ark Mktg and Mgmt Dept Conway AR 72035

BRADLEY, DOUGLAS OLIVER, school principal; b. Richmond, Va., Dec. 29; s. Douglas O. Sr. and Dorothy (Harris) B.; m. Mary Garnett, Aug. 12, 1972. BS, Va. State U., Petersburg, 1972, MEd, 1974, CAGS, 1991; EdD, Va. Tech. U., 1996. Cert. tchr., adminstr., Va. Tchr. Petersburg Pub. Schs., 1972-90, Henrico County Schs., Richmond, 1990-91; asst. prin. Nottoway (Va.) H.S., 1991-92; prin. Nottoway Mid. Sch., 1992—; treas. Southside Prins. Mid.-Sch. Conf., Va., 1993-94. Served as sgt. USAF, 1965-68. Recipient service and performance awards. Mem. NEA, Va. Edn. Assn., Nottoway Edn. Assn., Nat. Assn. Secondary Sch. Prins., Kappa Alpha Psi. Baptist. Office: Nottoway Middle Sch PO Box 93 Nottoway VA 23955-0093

BRADLEY, JUDY FAYE, elementary school educator; b. New Orleans, Aug. 26, 1950; d. Hunter L. and Virginia C. (Glaser) B. BA, McNeese Coll., 1978, MEd, 1981; diploma, Inst. Children's Lit., 1992. Cert. elem. sch. counselor, La. Tchr., counselor St. Margaret Elem. Cath. Sch., Lake Charles, La., 1978-84; dir. edn. Sylvan Learning Ctr., Lake Charles, 1984-88; tchr. Rosa Fondel Elem. Sch. (formerly Eastwood Elem. Sch.), Lake Charles, 1988—; coord. Rainbows for All Children program Eastwood Elem. Sch., 1990-92; Cayenne Crawfish mascot Sta. KPLC-TV, 1990—; Discoveries facilitator Sta., 1993-94. Named Outstanding Young Educator, Lake Charles Jaycees, 1983-84; Tchr. of Yr. nominee, 1992-93. Office: Rosa Fondel Elem Sch 2903 Opelousas St Lake Charles LA 70615-2761

BRADLEY, NOLEN EUGENE, JR., personnel executive, educator; b. Memphis, Nov. 29, 1925; s. Nolen Eugene and Anice Pearl (Luther) B.; m. Eloise Mullins, Jan. 7, 1947; children: Sharon (Mrs. Edward W. Vanderpool), Diana (Mrs. Wiley M. Rutledge), Nolen Eugene III, David Lee. BS, Memphis State U., 1951, MA, 1952; EdD, U. Tenn., 1966. Instr. polit. sci. Memphis State U., 1951-52; tchr. English Messick High Sch., Memphis, 1952-56; asst. dean admissions Memphis State U., 1956-64; dir. State Agy. for Title I, Higher Edn. Act, 1965, Div. Continuing Edn., U. Tenn., 1966-70; dean instrn. Vol. State Community Coll., Gallatin, Tenn., 1970-78; tutor, ednl. cons., 1978-79; pers. asst. Hoeganaes Corp., Gallatin, 1979-80; pers. mgr. Hoeganaes Corp., 1980-82; dir. pers. Music Village U.S.A., Hendersonville, Tenn., 1984—. Contbr. articles to profl. jours. Deacon Bapt. ch., 1966—. With AUS, 1944-46, ETO. Mem. Am. Assn. Sch. Adminstrs., Tenn. Adult Edn. Assn., Tenn. Edn. Assn., Omicron Delta Kappa, Pi Delta Epsilon, Phi Delta Kappa, Phi Kappa Phi. Democrat. Lion. Home: 907 Harris Dr Gallatin TN 37066-3462

BRADLEY, ROBERT EDWARD LEE, JR., energy economist, public policy professional; b. Houston, June 17, 1955; s. Robert Lee and Margaret (Lockett) B.; m. Nancy Capps, July 16, 1983; children: Catherine, Robert III. BA in Econs. with honors, Rollins Coll., 1977; MA in Econs., U. Houston, 1980; PhD in Polit. Economy with distinction, Internat. Coll., L.A., 1985. Credit analyst Capital Bank, Houston, 1979-81; adj. scholar energy rsch. Cato Inst., Washington, 1981-85; strategic planning analyst HNG-Interstate Pipeline Co., Houston, 1985-86; mktg. analyst Transwestern Pipeline Co., Houston, 1986-87, sr. mktg. analyst, 1987-89, mgr. market planning, 1989-93, market devel. specialist, 1993-95, dir. pub. policy analysis, 1995—; pres. Inst. Energy Rsch., Houston, 1989—; lectr. various confs., 1979—. Author: The Mirage of Oil Protection, 1989, Oil, Gas and Government: The U.S. Experience, 1996; editor: Done In Oil (J. Howard Marshall II autobiography), 1994; contbr. articles to profl. jours., chpts. to books. Fellow Inst. Humane Studies-Tex., George Mason U., Fairfax, Va., 1985—, program dir. Inst. Humane Studies-Tex., 1985-89; founding trustee Future of Freedom Found., Fairfax, 1987-95; active Resource Bank, Heritage

Found., Washington, 1991—, Acad. Resources Network, Tex. Pub. Policy Found., San Antonio, 1991—; advisor Am. Legis. Exch. Coun., 1995—; acad. advisor Free Enterprise Inst., Houston, 1994—. Adj. scholar Cato Inst., 1986—. Mem. Internat. Assn. Energy Econs., River Oaks Country Club (Houston), Allegro. Libertarian-Republican. Presbyterian. Home: 6219 Olympia Dr Houston TX 77057-3527

BRADLEY, SANDRA LYNN, nursing administrator; b. Lubbock, Tex., Oct. 16, 1959; m. Clayton Allen Bradley, Feb. 11, 1994; children: Chelsea, Stephanie, Chance, Rachael. Cert. vocat. nursing, Frank Phillips Coll., 1980; BSN, Tex. Tech U., 1995. RN, Tex.; lic. vocat. nurse, Tex. Nurse aide Dumas (Tex.) Meml. Home, 1978-79, lic. vocat. nurse, 1980-81; lic. vocat. nurse K.W. Pieratt, M.D., Dumas, 1981-82; LPN Pawnee (Okla.) Mcpl. Hosp., 1982-84; LPN, child birth educator Dr. James P. Riemer, Pawnee, 1984-88; lic. vocat. nurse (med.-surg.) Meth. Hosp., Lubbock, 1988-91, lic. vocat. nurse (cardiac telemetry), 1991-94; RN supr. home health divsn. South Plains Cmty. Action Assn., 1995; program dir./coord. Alternative Home Health Svcs., Lubbock, Tex., 1995—. Mem. AACN (West Tex. chpt.), Nat. League Nursing, Nurse Ambs.

BRADSHAW, JAMES EDWARD, automotive company executive, consultant; b. Waco, Tex., Aug. 18, 1940; s. Leo Herman Sr. and Eleanor Rose (Cogdell) B.; m. Ouida P. Massey; children: Robin Louise, Dorenda and Dorette (twins), James E. Jr., Cogdell O'Neal. BBA in Mktg. and Fin., Baylor U., 1963. Ptnr. Cogdell's Westview, Waco, 1960-64, Kennedy-David & Assocs., Waco, 1966-68; sales rep. Fed.-Mogul Corp., Detroit, 1964-66; pres. Cogdell Auto Supply Co., Inc., Ft. Worth, 1968-77; chmn. bd. dirs. Auto Supply Co., Inc., Ft. Worth, 1979—; mayor pro tem City of Ft. Worth, 1977-79. Bd. dirs. Big Bros./Big Sisters Tarrant County, United Way, Jr. Achievement, Tarrant County Coun. Alcohol and Drug Abuse, Tex. Mcpl. League, Austin, 1976-78; mem. adv. bd. dirs. Betty Ford Ctr.; mem. cmty. devel. steering com. Nat. League Cities, 1978-79; chmn. Tarrant County March of Dimes, Ft. Worth, 1979, Future Pres. Orgn., Kansas City, Mo., 1974; councilman City of Ft. Worth, 1975-77, mem. zoning commn., 1974-75; Republican. candidate 12th Congl. Dist., 1980. Named to Ten to Watch, D mag., 1977. Mem. Colonial Country Club, Petroleum Club, Masons, Shriners. Methodist. Home: 4613 Briarhaven Rd Fort Worth TX 76109-4609 Office: PO Box 100338 Fort Worth TX 76185-0338

BRADSHAW, JEFFREY, company executive; b. Concord, N.C., Mar. 3, 1947; s. Clarence Ernest and Marie (Groomes) B.; m. Jennifer L. Bradshaw, Oct. 22, 1966 (div. 1978); children: Kelly Todd, Jeffrey Shannon, Bryan Scott; m. Sharon Ann Bradshaw, Feb. 4, 1983. BA, U. N.C., 1970, MBA, 1972. Strategic planner GE Co., Conn., 1972-78; nat. dir. mktg. Santavicca Corp., Boca Raton, Fla., 1978-82; CEO Bradshaw Group, Richmond, Va., 1983—; pres., CEO Satellites Direct Inc., Concord, N.C., 1986-94, Fin. Funding Group, 1994—; bd. dirs., officer Health Care Mgmt. Co., Richmond, Va., 1983—; cons., officer Lighthouse Corp. of Am., Charlotte, N.C., 1988—; cons. Med. Cos. Inc. of N.C., JSB Internat. Contbr. articles to profl. jours. Mem. Am. Cons. Assn. (Cons. of Yr. 1980), Va. Staffing Assn. (pres. 1988-90, Man of Yr. 1989), Nat. C. of C., Am. Assn. Health Care Profls. Republican. Assemblies of God. Home: 141 Wilson St NE Concord NC 28025-3444

BRADSHAW, OTABEL, secondary school educator; b. Magnolia, Ark., Oct. 27, 1922; d. Grover Cleveland and Mae (Staggs) Peterson; AA, Magnolia A&M Coll., 1950; BS in Edn., So. State Coll., 1953; MS in Edn., Henderson State U., 1975; postgrad. U. Ark.; PhD, Kensington U., 1983; m. Charles Howard Bradshaw, Aug. 14, 1948; children: Susan Charla, Michael Howard. Tchr., English and drama Walkers Creek Schs., Taylor Ark., 1945-46, primary grades Locust Baypere Schs., Camden, Ark., 1946-52, 2d grade Fairview Sch., Camden, 1962-73; tchr. 1st grade Harmony Grove Sch., Camden, 1973-83, coordinator Title IX, gifted children and handicapped; tchr. East Camden Accelerated Sch., 1983—; cons. econ. edn. workshop U. Ark., Fayetteville. Life mem., sec., historian chmn. bicentennial com. PTA; active vol. fund-raising drives Am. Cancer Soc., Birth Defects Soc.; leader Missionary Soc., Camden 1st United Methodist Ch.; mem. Camden and Ouachita County Library bd., 1974-77; active Boys Club Aux. Recipient Disting. Alumni Award So. Ark. U., 1981, Valley Forge Tchr. medal and George Washington Honor medal Freedom Found., 1973; Achievement citation Kazanian Found., 1969, citation for ednl. leadership Pres. of U.S., 1976, 77; profl. achievement citation Internat. Paper Co. Found., 1981. Mem. Assn. Supervision and Curriculum Devel. (speaker San Francisco conf.), NEA, Ark. Edn. Assn. (speaker 1969), Harmony Grove Edn. Assn. (pres. 1978-79), Nat. Council for Social Studies (mem. sexism com.), Am. Assn. Adminstrs., Alpha Delta Kappa (outstanding mem.). Club: Tate Park Garden (sec.). Home: 3188 Roseman Rd Camden AR 71701

BRADSHAW, ROD ERIC, personnel consultant; b. Washington, May 29, 1951; s. Howard Vernon and Ona A. (Joyce) B.; m. Rebecca Lynn Bell, Mar. 20, 1974 (div. 1981). AA, Charles County Community Coll., 1971; BA, U. Md., 1973; M Human Resource Mgmt. with honors, Pepperdine U., 1981. Personnel cons. Career Devel. Corp., Atlanta, 1977-79, regional office mgr., 1979-82, prin., mgr., 1982-93; pres. Bradshaw & Assocs., 1993—. Asst. to pres. Christopher's Corner Cmty. Assn., Marietta, Ga., 1978-79, chmn. planning com., 1979; rep. Gov.'s Environ. Symposium, Smithsonian Inst., 1971; fund raiser, charter mem. High Mus. Art, Atlanta, 1979—; mem. Envoy to 1996 Atlanta Olympic Games. Recipient J.P. Rice Scholarship, 1971; named one of Outstanding Young Men Am., Atlanta C. of C., 1985. Mem. Nat. Assn. Pers. Cons. (cert.), Am. Mgmt. Assn., Internat. Platform Assn., Am. Legion, Atlanta Ski Club, Omicron Delta Kappa, Delta Tau Delta. Republican. Home: 4903 Township Overlook Marietta GA 30066-5001 Office: Bradshaw & Assocs 1850 Parkway Pl Ste 420 Marietta GA 30067-8222

BRADSHAW, WILLIAM C., museum director. BA in Secondary Edn. Social Studies, U. Fla.; M in Liberal Studies Museum Emphasis, U. Okla. Program advisor La. State U. Union, Baton Rouge, 1965-68; curator jr. ctr. Valentine Mus., Richmond, Va., 1968-71; exec. dir. Peninsula Nature and Sci. Ctr., Newport News, Va., 1971-78, Cumberland Sci. Mus., Nashville, Tenn., 1978-93; v.p. for programs and exhibits The Franklin Mus., Phila., 1994; exec. dir. Ark. Mus. Sci. and History, Little Rock, 1994—; co-founder regional Mus. Coun. of Va. Peninsula; co-founder, past pres. Va. History and Mus. Fedn.; past treas. Southeastern Mus. Coun.; co-founder and sec. Sci. Mus. Assn. Ea. Va.; past pres. Intermus. Coun. of Nashville. Mem. Am. Assn. for State and Local History, Nat. Sci. Tchrs. Assn., Am. Assn. of Mus., Assn. Sci. and Tech. Ctrs., Rotary Club of Little Rock. Office: Ark Mus Sci and Hist. McArthur Park Little Rock AR 72202

BRADUNAS, JOHN JOSEPH, marine corps officer; b. Hartford, Conn., Dec. 28, 1955; s. Edward Anthony and Florence Eleanor Mae (Martel) B. BS in EE, Cornell U., 1977; MS in Systems Mgmt., U. So. Calif., 1985; MA in Nat. Security Affairs, Georgetown U., 1988; MS in EE, Naval Postgrad. Sch., Monterey, Calif., 1990. Cert. mil. acquisition specialist. Commd. 2nd lt. USMC, 1977, advanced through grades to maj., 1989; with Def. Intelligency Agy., Arlington, Va., 1986-88; assigned to Naval Postgrad. Sch., Monterey, Calif., 1988-90; with Marine Corps Systems Command, Quantico, Va., 1990-93, 22d Marine Expeditionary Unit, Camp Lejeune, N.C., 1993-95; participant UN Humanitarian Ops., Bosnia-Hercegovina, Somalia; combat devel. command USMC, Quantico, Va., 1995—. Inventor laser diode power driver. Vol. genealogist Nat. Archives, Washington, 1990-93; reader for the blind Washington Ear, Rockville, Md., 1990. Decorated Navy Commendation medals, Joint Svc. Achievement medal, Def. Meritorious Svc. medal. Mem. IEEE, Armed Forces Comms. and Electronics Assn., Soc. Young Intel Profls., Eta Kappa Nu. Home: 7054 Solomon Seal Ct Springfield VA 22152-3150 Office: MC Combat Devel Command 3300 Russell Rd Quantico VA 22134-5021

BRADY, JAMES JOSEPH, economics educator; b. Jersey City, Mar. 2, 1936; s. James and Anna (Shine) B.; m. Sheila Hartney, July 24, 1965; children: Matthew, Michael, James. BA, U. Notre Dame, 1959, MA in Econs., 1963, PhD in Econs., 1969. Profl. baseball player Detroit Tigers, 1955-60; asst. prof. econs. Ind. U., South Bend, 1965-69; asst. prof., assoc. prof., prof. econs. Old Dominion U., Norfolk, Va., 1969-79; dean Coll. Arts and Scis. Jacksonville (Fla.) U., 1979-83, dean Coll. Bus., 1983-84, v.p. acad. affairs, 1984-88, pres.-elect, 1988-89, pres., 1989-95, prof. econs., 1995—; spl. master Fla. Pub. Employees Rels. Commn., Tallahassee, 1985—; pvt. labor cons., Jacksonville, 1978-88. Author: Arbitration Principles: Layoffs, 1989; co-author: Transportation Noise Pollution, 1970. Bd. dirs. Jacksonville Symphony, 1991—, ARC, Jacksonville, 1992—, Instn. for World Capitalism. With U.S. Army, 1959-61. NASA grantee, Norfolk, Va., 1970. Mem. Am. Arbitration Assn. (labor arbitrator 1965—, comml. arbitrator 1987-89), Soc. Profls. in Dispute Resolution, Jacksonville C. of C. (bd. dirs. 1989—), Rotary (bd. dirs. 1994—). Home: 4454 Maywood Dr Jacksonville FL 32277-1036 Office: Jacksonville U Coll of Bus 2800 University Blvd N Jacksonville FL 32211-3321

BRADY, JENNIE M., wholesale and retail sales professional; b. Tampa, Fla., May 4, 1948; raised by William Jackson and Mattie Estelle (Garrett) Amason; children: Velma Mychelle (Shelly) Amann, Theresa Victoria, 4 stepchildren. Student, Mo. Western State Coll.; cert. bus. adminstrn., Coastal Tng. Svc. Nurse's aide Manhattan Convalescent Ctr., Tampa, Fla., 1983-84; office mgr. Sun Saver Solar Glass Tinting, Tampa, 1986; technician Westshore Grooming Inc., Tampa, 1987-88, Holiday Pet Inn, Tampa, 1987-88; DAV rep., svc. officer VA Hosp., Birmingham, Ala., 1990; owner, operator Bradamas Farms and Myjoy Kennels, Heflin, Ala., 1988—; legal sec. Forrester and Assocs., Piedmont, Ala., 1995. Bd. dirs. Pony Express Hist. Assn., 1972-78; legis. chmn. counselor Girls' State, parliamentarian Am. Legion Aux., 1972-81; jr. activities chmn., legis. chmn. DAV Aux., 1981-90; jr. vice comdr., sr. vice comdr. VFW Aux., 1981-90; bd. dirs., pres., sec., treas., archivist Buchanan County Hist. Soc., 1974-78. Recipient numerous awards for vol. efforts; recipient various recruitment awards and citations from Disabled Am. Vets. Mem. NAFE, Wildlife Rescue, Nat. Cockatiel Soc., Am. Fedn. Aviculture, Southeastern Aviculturists Assn., Am. Cockatiel Soc., Internat. Lorinae Soc. (studbook keeper for red lory), Soc. Parrot Breeders and Exhibitors, Internat. Platform Assn. Home: Bradamas Farms 1081 County Rd 404 Heflin AL 36264

BRADY, KIMBERLY ANN, editorial director; b. Omaha, Sept. 22, 1956; d. John Henry and Margaret Florence (Swatek) Robinson; 1 child, Jonathan Charles Brady. Student, Corcoran Sch. Art, Washington, 1974-75, George Mason U., 1974-76, Christopher Newport Coll., Newport News, Va., 1976-79. Editor-in-chief student newspaper Christopher Newport Coll., 1977-79; photojournalist Gloucester-Matthews Gazette-Jour., Gloucester, Va., 1979-80; mng. editor Journal of Analytical Toxicology Preston Publs., Niles, Ill., 1980-81; mng. editor Darkroom Techniques and Creative Camera Preston Publs., 1981-84; art dir., prodn. mgr. Profl. Photographers of Am., Des Plaines, Ill., 1984-86; sr. editor Professional Photographer Profl. Photographers of Am., 1990-91; editor-in-chief PHOTO Electronic Imaging Profl. Photographers of Am., Des Plaines, Atlanta, 1991-94; editorial dir. Atlanta, 1994—; editorial cons., photographer, graphic artist Chgo., 1986-90; instr. Winona Internat. Sch. Profl. Photography, Mt. Prospect, Ill., 1987; judge photography competitions, Chgo., 1981-84, electronic imaging competition, L.A., 1993-95. Exec. dir. Lake Shore Sr. Svc. Ctr., Chgo., 1988-93; vol. Adult Literacy Program, Chgo., 1988; coord. Mayor Harold Washington campaign, Chgo., 1983. Recipient Va. Press Assn. Journalism award, 1979, Christopher Newport Coll. Journalism award, 1977-78. Mem. Profl. Photographers of Am. Office: Profl Photographers of Am 57 Forsyth St NW Ste 1600 Atlanta GA 30303-2206

BRADY, MICHAEL JAY, environmental engineer, geologist; b. Kenton, Ohio, July 16, 1946; s. Ernest Kenneth and Faith Catherine (Heward) B.; m. Karen Ann Smith, Sept. 23, 1973; children: Kathleen, Lorraine, Michael II. BS in Geological Engring., Mich. Tech. U., 1969. Registered profl. engr., Miss., Ohio, Colo., Ariz., Ala.; profl. geologist, Tenn. Project engr. Inspiration Copper Co., Christmas, Ariz., 1969-72; sr. project engr. Inspiration Copper Co., Miami, Ariz., 1973-76; sr. mining engr. Phelps-Dodge Corp., Tyrone, N.Mex., 1972-73; mine, mill maintenance engr. Texasgulf Inc., Aurora, N.C., 1976-79; chief engr. Anschutz Mining Corp., Denver, 1979-82; sr. tech. specialist SOHIO, Cleve., 1983-85; mgr. geosci. Browning-Ferris Industries, Houston, 1985-94; cons. Environ. and Petroleum Cons., Jackson, Miss., 1994—; rep. Inst. Chemical Waste Mgmt., Washington, 1987-88, Nat. Solid Waste Mgmt. Assn., Washington, 1988-89; pub. rels. mem. BFI-Katy Wildlife Refuge, Tex., 1993-94. Co-author: AICHE-Resource Recovery of Municipal Solid Waste, 1988. Asst. scoutmaster Troop 300 Boy Scouts Am., 1994-95. Mem. Soc. Mining Engrs., Houston Geol. Soc., Copper Country Lodge, Tucson Lodge of Perfection (class pres.). Republican. Methodist. Home: 917 Audubon Point Dr Brandon MS 39042 Office: Environ and Petroleum Cons 291 Hwy 51 Ste D6 Ridgeland MS

BRADY, RUPERT JOSEPH, lawyer; b. Washington, Jan. 24, 1932; s. John Bernard and Mary Catherine (Rupert) B.; m. Maureen Mary MacIntosh, Apr. 20, 1954; children: Rupert Joseph Jr., Laureen Zegowitz, Kevin, Warren, Jeanine Hartnett, Jacqueline Rada, Brian, Barton. BEE, Cath. U. Am., 1953; JD, Georgetown U., 1959. Bar: Md. 1961, U.S. Ct. Appeals (D.C. cir.) 1964, U.S. Patent Trademark Office 1961, D.C. 1962, U.S. Supreme Ct. 1969, U.S. Ct. Appeals (fed. cir.) 1961. Elec. engr. Sperry Gyroscope Co., L.I., 1953-56; patent specifications writer John B. Brady, patent atty., 1956-59; patent agt. B.P. Fishburne, Jr., Washington, 1959-61; pvt. practice patent agt., Washington, Md., 1961; practice, Washington, 1961—; sr. ptnr. Brady, O'Boyle & Gates, Washington and Chevy Chase, Md., 1963-95; of counsel Birch, Stewart, Kolasch & Birch, LLP, Va., 1996—; v.p. Minist-O-Media, Inc. Mem. ABA, Am. Intellectual Property Law Assn., Md. Patent Law Assn. Republican. Roman Catholic. Club: Senator's Alumni. Patentee crane, booms, moldboard support assembly. Home: 7201 Pyle Rd Bethesda MD 20817-5623 Office: Birch Stewart Kolasch & Birch LLP 8110 Gatehouse Rd Ste 500E Falls Church VA 22040

BRADY, VIRGINIA WINEGAR, retired school librarian; b. Warren, Ark., Feb. 1, 1920; d. Marcus Gordon and Ruth Elmira (Tucker) W.; m. Carl Boyd Brady, Feb. 14, 1947; 1 child, Melissa Anne Brady Davis. BS in Edn., U. Houston, 1957; MS in Edn. and Libr. Sci., Sam Houston U., 1965. Cert. libr., Tex. World history tchr. North Forest Ind. Sch. Dist., Houston, 1957-60, high sch. libr., 1961-67, jr. high libr., 1970-78; edn. libr. U. Houston, 1968-69; ret., 1978. Author: Pilgrimage to the Past, 1992, Guidelines to Library Instruction Grades 1-12, 1969; contbr. hist. essays to profl. publs. Mem. Montgomery County Rep. Women, Conroe, Tex., 1990—; chmn. libr. com. First United Meth. Ch., Conroe, 1991—. Mem. Tex. Libr. Assn., Soc. Mayflower Descendants, Nat. Soc. Colonial Dames XVIIC (chpt. pres. 1993-95), U.S. Daus 1812 (chpt. registrar 1994-95, treas. 1991-93), Mary Ball Washington Mus. and Libr., Williamsburg Found. Republican. Methodist.

BRADY-BLACK, WANDALENE, secondary school educator; b. Oklahoma City, Aug. 16, 1938; d. Walter Jacque Brady and Mable Griffin; m. Luke J. Black, Dec. 23, 1957 (dec. 1987); children: Luke J., Eric S., Ieshia L. BS in Oral Comm., U. Ctrl. Okla., 1979. Cert. spl. edn. and oral comm. tchr. Tchr. Oklahoma City Pub. Sch. System, 1980—; sponsor sr. and jr. classes Douglass High Sch., Oklahoma City, 1984-87, jr. class Capitol Hill High Sch., Oklahoma City, 1993; dir. Capitol Hill Intensity Performance Group, 1990—. Principal artwork includes (paintings) The Lifestyle Series, 1988; author: (short story) The Reunion, 1993. Pres. pack troop 281 Boy Scouts Am., Oklahoma City, 1972-75; deaconess Evang. Bapt. Ch., 1978—, WMU pres. 1979-82, min. edn., 1983-85, dir. activities, 1986-93; fund raiser Disabled Vets., Oklahoma City, 1989—, HIV-AIDS Found., 1991—, Am. Cancer Soc., 1992—; voter registrar Oklahoma County Bd. Elections, 1993. Mem. Alpha Kappa Alpha. Democrat. Office: Capitol Hill High Sch 500 SW 36th St Oklahoma City OK 73109-6699

BRAGAN, JOHN FREDERICK, emergency physician; b. Salem, Mass., July 17, 1950; s. James Aloyisius and Christine (Quealy) B.; m. Sylvia Magaña, May 17, 1975; children: Janine, Jennifer, John Jr., Jessica, Janna, Jamie. BA, Boston Coll., 1973; MD, Autonoma U., Mexico, 1978. Diplomate Am. Bd. Emergency Medicine; cert., instr. advanced cardiac life support; cert. advanced trauma life support, pediatric advanced life support. Intern Cooper Med. Ctr., Camden, N.J., 1978-79; resident Meml. Med. Ctr., Corpus Christi, Tex., 1979-80; chief dept. emergency medicine Southwest Gen. Hosp., San Antonio, 1984-92, chief of staff, 1993; pres., med. dir. Texem Emergency Physicians, San Antonio, 1986—; pres., owner Stat Transcription Svc., San Antonio, 1986—; med. dir. Columbia Health Svc., Inc., Tex., 1993—; mem. medical staff Valley Bapt. Regional, Harlingen, Tex., 1980, Brownwood (Tex.) Med. Ctr., 1980, Met. Hosp., San Antonio, 1982, Bapt. Hosp. Sys., San Antonio, 1983, San Antonio Regional Hosp., 1991, Santa Rosa N.W. Hosp., San Antonio, 1992, Santa Rosa Hosp., San Antonio, 1992; clin. coord. First Aid Safety Tng. Ednl. Program, San Antonio, 1984—; bd. dirs. Columbia Health Svcs., Inc., Texem Med. Mgmt., Inc., Med. Diversified Svcs., Inc.; chmn. Exec. Quality Assurance, Emergency Dept., Nominating Com., San Antonio, 1984—; consulting physician Martial Arts Assn., Houston, 1985—. Med. vol. Ananda Marga Med. Relief Orgn., 1988—; instr. blackbelt Kuk Sool Won Martial Arts Ctr., San Antonio, 1990—; chmn. bd. trustees S.W. Gen. Hosp. Fellow Am. Coll. Emergency Physicians, Am. Acad. Emergency Medicine; mem. AMA, Tex. Med. Assn., Bexar County Med. Soc. Office: Texem Emergency Physicians 15600 San Pedro Ave Ste 107 San Antonio TX 78232-3738

BRAGG, ELLIS MEREDITH, JR., lawyer; b. Washington, Jan. 30, 1947; s. Ellis Meredith Sr. and Lucille (Tingstrum) B.; m. Judith Owens, Aug. 18, 1968; children: Michael Andrew, Jennifer Meredith. BA, King Coll., 1969; JD, Wake Forest U., 1973. Bar: N.C. 1973, U.S. Dist. Ct. (we. and mid. dists.) N.C. 1974, U.S. Ct. Appeals (4th cir.) 1980. Assoc. Bailey, Brackett & Brackett, P.A., Charlotte, N.C., 1973-76; ptnr. Howard & Bragg, Charlotte, 1976-77, McConnell, Howard, Johnson, Pruitt, Jenkins & Bragg, Charlotte, 1977-79; sole practice Charlotte, 1979—. Dist. chmn. Mecklenburg County Dems., Charlotte, 1978; coach youth soccer program YMCA, Charlotte, 1982-83; mem. Headstart Policy Council, Charlotte, 1985—. Mem. ABA, N.C. Bar Assn., N.C. Acad. Trial Lawyers. Presbyterian. Home: 6407 Honegger Dr Charlotte NC 28211-4718 Office: 500 E Morehead St Ste 210 Charlotte NC 28202-2606

BRAILSFORD, JUNE EVELYN, musician, educator; b. Wiergate, Tex., Apr. 11, 1939; d. Lonnie and Jessie (Coleman) Samuel; m. Marvin Delano Brailsford, Dec. 23, 1960; children: Marvin Delano, Keith, Cynthia. BA in Music, Prairie View A & M U., Tex., 1960; MA in Music, Trenton (N.J.) State Coll., 1981; postgrad., Jacksonville State U., summer 1971, Lamar U., Beaumont, Tex., summer 1963, Juilliard Sch., summer 1994. Jr. high music tchr. Lincoln Jr. High Sch., Beaumont, Tex., 1960-61; organist/choir dir. various chs., various locations, 1962-82; dir. adult edn. Morris County Human Resources, Dover, N.J., 1980-82; band and choral dir. Zweibruecken Am. High Sch., Ger., 1982-84; vocal soloist and pianist Am. Women's Activities, Ger., 1986-87; dir. female choir U.S. Army War Coll., 1978-79, U.S. Air Force Skylarks, Sembach, Ger., 1976-77. Hostess/fundraiser Quad City Symphony Guild 75th Ur., Rock Island, 1989, Links, Inc. Beautillion Scholarship, 1989, Installation Vol. Coord. Cons., Ft. Belvoir, Va., 1990-91; minister music First Bapt. Ch., Vienna, Va., 1995; active numerous charitable orgns. Recipient Molly Pitcher award U.S. Army F.A. Officers, 1986, Outstanding Civilian Svc. award Dept. Army, 1990, Disting. Civilian Svc. award Dept. Army, 1992. Mem. AAUW, NAACP (life mem. No. Va. Fairfax County chpt.), Music/Etude Club, Rock Island Arsenal Hist. Soc. (hon. mem.), Quad City Symphony Guild (USO com.). Baptist. Home: 15865 W Bayaud Dr Golden CO 80401

BRAMBLE, RONALD LEE, lawyer, business and legal consultant; b. Pauls Valley, Okla., Sept. 9, 1937; s. Homer Lee and Ethyle Juanita (Stephens) B.; m. Kathryn Louise Seiler, July 2, 1960; children: Julia Dawn, Kristin Lee. AA, San Antonio Coll., 1957; BS, Trinity U., 1959, MS, 1964; JD, St. Mary's U., 1975; DBA, Ind. No. U., 1973. Mgr., buyer Fed-Mart, Inc., San Antonio, 1959-61; tchr. bus. San Antonio Ind. Sch. Dist., 1961-65, edn. coordinator, bus. tng. specialist, 1965-67; assoc. prof., chmn. dept. mgmt. San Antonio Coll., 1967-73; prin. Ron Bramble Assocs., San Antonio, 1967-77; pres. Adminstrv. Research Assocs., Inc., 1977-82; v.p. PIA, Inc., 1982-83; v.p. fin. Solar 21 Corp., 1983-84, sr. staff Ausburn, Astoria & Seale (formerly Ausburn, O'Neill & Assocs.), San Antonio, 1984-89; pvt. practice, 1990—; cons., comptr. TEL-STAR Systems, Inc., 1993-95; v.p. MegaTronics Internat. Corp., 1995—; lectr. bus., edn. and ch. groups, 1965—. Cons. editor: Prentice-Hall, Inc., Englewood Cliffs, N.J., 1969-71; contbr. articles to profl. jours. Cert. lay speaker Meth. Ch. Served with AUS, 1959. Recipient Wall Street Jour. award Trinity U., 1959, U.S. Law Week award St. Mary's Sch. of Law, 1975. Mem. ABA, San Antonio C. of C., Adminstrv. Mgmt. Soc. (pres. 1966-68, Merit award 1968), Bus. Edn. Tchrs. Assn. (pres. 1964), Sales and Mktg. Execs. San Antonio (bd. dirs. 1967-68, Disting. Salesman award 1967), Internat. Platform Assn., Internat. Assn. Cons. to Bus., Nat. Assn. Bus. Economists, Acad. Mgmt., Christian Legal Soc., Comml. Law League Am., Toastmasters, Phi Delta Phi, Lions. Republican. Home: 127 Palo Duro St San Antonio TX 78232-3026

BRAME, TRACEY ANNE, elementary education educator; b. Hopkinsville, Ky., Feb. 13, 1971; d. John Thomas Jr. and Timmie Bronaugh (Leavell) B. BS in Edn., Austin Peay State U., 1993. Cert. elem. tchr. Tchr. 4th grade Pembroke (Ky.) Elem. Sch., 1994—; sponsor Just Say No club, chmn. math. com., mem. curriculum com. Pembroke Elem., 1994—. Youth leader, Sunday sch. tchr. Pembroke Bapt. Ch., 1993—. Mem. NEA, Ky. Edn. Assn., Christian County Edn. Assn., Chi Omega. Democrat. Office: Pembroke Elem Sch PO Box 100 Pembroke KY 42266

BRAMLETT, JOYCE FIELDER, mathematics educator; b. Cochran, Ga., Mar. 24, 1933; d. Harley Leslie and Christine (Scott) Fielder; B.S., Ga. State U., 1963, postgrad., 1980—; M.A.T., Emory U., 1970; Ed.S., U. Ga., 1977; m. Kenneth Earl Bramlett, Dec. 19, 1986; children by previous marriage: Phillip, Timothy, Elizabeth, Susan. Bench electronics mechanic Lockheed Aircraft, Marietta, Ga., 1951-56; buyer and supr. non-prescription drugs E. Marietta Drug Co., 1956-63; tchr. math. Marietta H.S., 1963-66; tchr. math. East Cobb Middle Sch., 1966-70; math. supr. k-12 Cobb County Bd. Edn., 1970-81, Title I project writer, coord., 1974-75; pvt. practice ednl. cons., 1982—; owner, op. White's Florist and Greenhouses, 1967-70; part-time math. instr. So. Tech. Coll., 1980-82, instr., 1982-85; tchr. math. Campbell H.S., 1985-87, Oakwood High Sch., 1987-93, Mt. Paran Christian Sch., 1993—, chair math. dept.; real estate agent Am.'s Realty, 1991—. Mem. St. Joseph Sch. Bd. Edn., 1977-79. NSF grantee, 1967-70. Mem. ASCD, Nat. Coun. Tchrs. Math, Ga. Coun. Tchrs. Math, Metro Math Club, Cobb County Adminstrv. Assn., Ga. Coun. Suprs. Math., U. Ga. Alumni Assn., Ga. State Alumni Assn., Emory U. Alumni Assn., Delta Kappa Gamma, Mu Rho Sigma. Club: Eastern Star. Home and Office: 107 Mt Calvary Rd Marietta GA 30064-1919

BRAMLETT, PAUL KENT, lawyer; b. Tupelo, Miss., May 31, 1944; s. Virgil Preston and McDuff (Goggans) B.; m. Shirley Marie Wilhelm, June 14, 1966; children: Paul Kent II (dec.), Robert Preston. AA with honors, Itawamba Jr. Coll., Fulton, Miss., 1962-64; BA, David Lipscomb Coll., 1966; postgrad., George Peabody Coll., 1966; JD, U. Miss., 1969. Bar: Miss. 1969, Tenn. 1980, U.S. Dist. Ct. (no. dist.) Miss. 1969, U.S. Dist. Ct. (we. dist.) Tenn. 1976, U.S. Dist. Ct. (mid. dist.) Tenn. 1980, U.S. Dist. Ct. (so. dist.) Miss. 1983, U.S. Dist. Ct. (we. dist.) Ky. 1988, U.S. Ct. Appeals (5th cir.) 1974, U.S. Ct. Appeals (6th cir.) 1980, U.S. Ct. Appeals (11th cir.) 1981, U.S. Supreme Ct. 1974. Pvt. practice Tupelo, Miss., 1969-80, Nashville, 1980—. Mem. ABA, Assn. Trial Lawyers Am., Miss. Trial Lawyers Assn. (bd. govs. 1976-79), Tenn. Bar Assn., Miss. Bar Assn. (pub. info. com. 1979-81), Nashville Bar Assn. (fed. ct. com. 1980-81), Am. Arbitration Assn. (comml. panel), Civitan Club (past gov. and legal counsel no. dist. Miss.). Mem. Ch. of Christ. Office: PO Box 150734 2828 Stouffer Tower Nashville TN 37215-0734

BRAMLETT, SHIRLEY MARIE WILHELM, interior decorator, artist; b. Scottsboro, Ala., June 14, 1945; d. Robert David and Alta (Reeves) Wilhelm; m. Paul Kent Bramlett, June 5, 1966; children: Paul Kent II (dec.), Robert Preston. BS, David Lipscomb U., 1966; postgrad., U. Miss., 1966-68; pvt. study art, 1976—. Decorator The Anchorage House, Oxford, Miss., 1966-67, Interiors by Shirley, Tupelo, Miss., 1971-80; tchr. Oxford City Schs., 1967-69; decorator, buyer Donald Furniture, Tupelo, 1969-71; owner, importer Bramblewood Interiors & Antiques, Belden, Miss., 1976-80; owner, decorator, artist The Cottage on Caldwell, Inc., Nashville, 1980—. Represented in art galleries Gallery Fine Art, Destin, Fla., Lyzon Gallery, Nashville, Magic Memories, Franklin, Tenn., elegant Creations Gallery, Brentwood, Tenn.; introduced and presented House of Parliament, Luxembourg; commd. for watercolor print fortnightly Musicale of Miss., 1991-92; European representation by Internet Internat. Bd. dirs. Found. for Christian Edn., 1988—, Ea. European Missions, Vienna, Austria, 1986— (commd. for watercolor print used in internat. fundraising); del. Miss. Dem. caucus, 1970; fundraiser Agape Artist, 1991. Named Woman of Decade, David Lipscomb Coll., 1986, one of Outstanding Young Women of Am.,

1979; selected Centennial Artist, David Lipscomb U., Nashville, 1991, one of ten Master Tenn. Artists, Lyzon Gallery, Nashville, 1991. Mem. Nat. Mus. Women in Arts, Tenn. Watercolor Soc., Nat. Soc. Tole and Decorative Painters, Green Hills Garden Club (cover artist for nat. conv. garden clubs 1985), Assoc. Ladies Lipscomb (bd. dirs. 1991-92). Mem. Ch. of Christ. Home: 930 Caldwell Ln Nashville TN 37204-4016

BRAMMER, BARBARA ALLISON, secondary school educator, consultant; b. Pitts., Sept. 3, 1942; d. Harry Harlan Allison and Valedina J. (Kouloumbrides) Vorkapic; m. Wetsel Jerry Brammer, Jan. 14, 1968; 1 child, Jeffrey Scott. AA, Valencia Community Coll., 1975; BS in Limnology, Fla. Tech. U., 1977; Ms in Adminstrn. and Supervision, Nova U., 1982, postgrad., 1990—. Tchr. Maynard Evans High Sch., Orlando, Fla., 1977-87; facilitator Valencia Community Coll., Orlando, 1987; tchr. Miami Killian Sr. High Sch., 1987-88, Dade County Sci. Zoo Magnet, Miami, Fla., 1988-89; facilitator Miami Dade Community coll., 1989; tchr. Homestead (Fla.) Sr. High Sch., 1989—; cons. documentary Pub. TV, Orlando, 1982. Author: Marine Science, 1980. Bd. dirs. Butler Chain Conservation Assn., Windermere, Fla., 1983-84. Cpl. USMC, 1960-62. Mem. NSTA, Nat. Marine Educators Assn., United Tchrs. Dade, Fla. Assn. Sci. Tchrs., Fla. Marine Educators Assn. (treas. membership chmn. 1986-88, bd. dirs. 1988-91, Outstanding Marine Sci. Educator award 1995-96), NOAA Tchr. in the Sea Soc., Beta Sigma Phi. Republican. Home: 15022 SW 74th Pl Miami FL 33158-2139 Office: Homestead Sr High Sch 2351 SE 12th Ave Homestead FL 33034-3511

BRANAN, CAROLYN BENNER, accountant, lawyer; b. Wiesbaden, Fed. Republic Germany, Mar. 7, 1953; d. Huebert Harrison and Kathryn Wilfreda (Diggs) Benner; m. Ralph Edward Lovejoy II; children: Lynn, Katherine Ann. BA in Philosophy, U. S.C., 1973, JD, 1976. Bar: S.C. 1977, U.S. Dist. Ct. S.C. 1977, U.S. Ct. Appeals (4th cir.) 1977; CPA, N.C. Sole practice law, Columbia, S.C., 1977-79, assoc. Deloitte Haskins & Sells, Charlotte, N.C.; exec. fin. counseling regional dir., 1987-89; sr. mgr. in charge Carolina's Personal Fin. Planning, 1989-91, ptnr. in charge, 1991—; ptnr. in charge personal tax and fin. planning practice S.E. Area KPMG Peat Marwick, 1993—; cons. Gov.'s Bus. Council Task Force on Infrastructure Financing, 1983. Contbr. articles to profl. jours. Former mem. exec. com., former treas., v.p., chmn. budget com., bd. dirs. Opera Carolina, 1981-89; exec. com. mayor's study com. Performing Arts Ctr., Charlotte, 1983-85; former mem. bd. dirs., chmn. performing arts Springfest, Charlotte, 1982-86; fin. chmn. Opening of New Charlotte Transit Mall, 1984-85; bus. adv. coun. Queens Coll., Charlotte, 1984-90; bd. trustees St. Peter's Ch., 1988—; chmn. endowment com., bd. dir. grants com. Arts and Sci. Coun., Charlotte and Necklenburg, N.C., 1992-96; chmn. structure com., bd. dir. Daniel Jonathan Stowe Conservancy, Daniel Stowe Bot. Garden, 1990—. Mem. ABA (former chmn. important devels., former chmn. gen. acctg. matters, regulated pub. utilities, 1984-90, tax sect. 1984-91), AICPA, N.C. Bar Assn., S.C. Bar Assn., Charlotte Estate Planning Council, Nat. Assn. Accts. (bd. dirs., dir. profl. devel., dir. community affairs 1979-84), S.C. Assn. CPAs, N.C. Assn. CPAs, Founders Soc. of Charlotte Opera Assn. (life), Golden Circle (bd. dirs. 1988-90), Charlotte City Club, Rotary (treas., Charlotte North 1989-91). Presbyterian. Home: 19209 Hidden Cove Ln Cornelius NC 28031 Office: KPMG Peat Marwick 2800 Two First Union Ctr Charlotte NC 28282

BRANA-SHUTE, GARY, anthropology educator, educational director; b. Ossining, N.Y., June 19, 1945; s. Monroe B. and Vivian W. (Madden) Shute; m. Rosemary A. Brana, Dec. 12, 1972. BS, SUNY, Oswego, 1967; MA, U. Mich., 1969; PhD, U. Fla., 1974. Prof. anthropology Fla. Internat. U., Miami, 1980-81, Coll. Charleston, S.C., 1981-85, U. Utrecht, The Netherlands, 1987-90, U. S.C., Beaufort, 1990-91; prof. Fgn. Svc. Inst.; prof. anthropology George Washington U.; election observer/Suriname Orgn. Am. States, Washington, 1991, 96; election observer/Guyana Pres. Jimmy Carter Ctr., Atlanta, 1992. Author: Crime and Punishment in the Caribbean, 1980, One the Corner: Male Social Life in Paramaribo, 1989, Resistance and Rebellion in Suriname, 1990. Named Fulbright-Hays scholar, Suriname, 1979. Fellow Am. Anthropol. Assn., Caribbean Studies Assn. Democrat. Home: 23 Windsor Charleston SC 29407-5351 Office: Fgn Svc Inst 4000 Arlington Blvd Arlington VA 22204-1586

BRANCH, JOHN CURTIS, biology educator, lawyer; b. Buffalo, Okla., Oct. 1, 1934; s. Ernest Samuel and Ethel Imogene (Parsons) B.; m. Jacqueline Joyce Davis, July 20, 1960; children: Kim Renee, Karla Jean, Kay Lynn. BS, Northwestern Okla. State U., 1959; MS, U. Okla., 1963, PhD, 1965; JD, Okla. City U., 1980. Bar: Okla. 1980. Asst. prof. biology dept. Okla. City U., 1964-67, assoc. prof. biology dept., 1967-75, prof. biology dept., 1975—. With U.S. Army, 1955-57. Mem. Okla. County Bar Assn., Okla. Acad. Sci., Okla. Bar Assn., Beta Beta Beta. Methodist. Home: 2705 Abbey Rd Oklahoma City OK 73120-2702 Office: John C Branch PC 6803 S Western Ave # 300 Oklahoma City OK 73139-1814 Office: Okla City U Dept Biology 2501 N Blackwelder Ave Oklahoma City OK 73106-1402

BRANCH, THOMAS BROUGHTON, III, lawyer; b. Atlanta, June 5, 1936; s. Thomas Broughton Jr. and Alfred Iverson (Dews) B.; m. Trudi Schroetter, Dec. 27, 1963; children: Maria Barbara, Thomas B. IV. BA cum laude, Washington and Lee U., 1958, JD, 1960. Bar: Ga. 1960, U.S. Dist. Ct. (no. dist.) Ga. 1960, U.S. Ct. Appeals (5th cir.) 1960, U.S. Dist. Ct. (mid. dist.) Ga. 1980, U.S. Ct. Appeals (11th cir.) 1980, U.S. Dist. Ct. (so. dist.) N.Y. 1984, U.S. Ct. Appeals (2d cir.) 1984, U.S. Supreme Ct. 1991. Assoc. Kilpatrick & Cody, Atlanta, 1960-63; ptnr. Greene, Buckley et al, Atlanta, 1963-79, Wildman, Harrold, Allen, Dixon & Branch, Atlanta, 1979-89, Branch, Pike & Ganz, Atlanta, 1990-95, Holland & Knight, Atlanta, 1995—; asst. prof. Woodrow Wilson Law Sch., Atlanta, 1964-68; trustee Washington and Lee U., Lexington, Va., 1979-90, trustee emeritus, 1991—; trustee, chmn. Atlanta Lawyers Found., Atlanta, 1980-81, Atlantis Aurora, Inc., 1970-74. Mem. Citizens Adv. Council on Urban Devel., Atlanta, 1977; trustee The Children's Sch., Inc., Atlanta, 1980-85; elder, clk. First Presbyn. Ch., Atlanta, 1967-79, 81-85. Served to capt. U.S. Army, 1958-66. Mem. ABA, Ga. Bar Assn., Atlanta Bar Assn. (mem. jud. selection and tenure com. 1988—), Am. Jud. Soc., Atlanta Lawyers Club (pres. 1976-77), Bleckley Inn of Ct. (master), Def. Rsch. Inst., Ansley Golf Club (pres., bd. dirs. 1976-87). Home: 160 The Prado NE Atlanta GA 30309-3388 Office: Holland & Knight 2 Midtown Plz 15th Fl 1360 Peachtree St NE Atlanta GA 30309-3214

BRANCH, WILLIAM TERRELL, urologist, educator; b. Paragould, Ark., Dec. 7, 1937; s. William Owen and Mary Rose (Dempsey) B.; m. Mary Fletcher Cox, Dec. 11, 1965; children: Ashley Tucker, William T., Steven K. BS, Ark. State U., 1964; BS, U. Ark., 1966, MD, 1971. Diplomate Am. Bd. Urology. Adminstrv. asst. mental retardation planning project State of Ark., Little Rock, 1964-66; intern U. South Fla. Sch. Medicine Affiliated Hosps., Tampa, 1971-72, resident in surgery, 1972-73, resident in urology, 1973-75, chief resident in urology, 1975-76, clin. prof. urology, 1976—, mem. adv. bd. Suncoast Ednl. Telecommunications Systems, 1982; practice medicine specializing in urology, Tampa, 1976—; mem. staff, sec. urology Tampa Gen. Hosp., 1976-78, vice chief urology, 1978-80, chief urology, 1980-82; mem. staff, co-chief surgery Meml. Hosp. Tampa, 1978-80, vice chief med. staff, 1980-82, chief med. staff, 1982-84, trustee, 1983-88, also bd. dirs., vice chmn. bd. dirs. 1987-88; cons. in urology James A. Haley VA Hosp., Tampa, 1978—; mem. staff St. Joseph's Hosp., Tampa, 1976—, Tampa Gen. Hosp.; cons. staff Women's Hosp. Tampa; adv. bd. Glendale Fed. Savs., 1983-85, Beneficial Harbour Island Savs. Bank, 1985-87, South Trust Bank, 1988—, also bd. dirs., exec. com., chair audit com. Author: (with others) Mental Retardation in Arkansas 1964-66: A Demographic Study, 1966; cons. editor Jour. Fla. Med. Assn., 1978-93. Bd. dirs. Tampa Ballet, 1980, Tampa Charity Horse Show Bd. Dirs. Assn., 1985-87; United Way, Tampa, 1983-90, mem. exec. com., 1984-88; mem. med. adv. bd. Nat. Kidney Found. of Fla., Inc., 1983-90; mem. Tampa Bay Super Bowl Task Force; mem. adv. bd. dirs. Salvation Army; founding chmn. Kettle com., vice chmn. adv. bd. dirs. Recipient Disting. Alumnus award Ark. State U., 1986. Fellow ACS (credit com. Region IV, Fla. chpt. 1982—, exec. com. Fla. chpt. 1985—, sec./treas. 1987-88, pres.-elect 1989-90, pres. 1990-92); mem. ACS (gov. 1990-96, bd. gov. chpt. activities com. 1991-96, alt. 1993, chmn. nomination com. 1995, chmn. applications com. region IV), Am. Urol. Assn., Royal Soc. Medicine (affiliate), Fla. Med. Assn. (del. 1983, 88-96), Fla. Urol. Soc. (Milton Copeland award 1976, exec. com. 1978-82), Hillsborough County Med. Assn. (exec. com. 1978-81, treas. 1981-82, sec. 1983-84), Fla. Quality Med. Assurance, Inc. (bd. dirs., treas., chmn. exec. com. 1995, chmn. bd. govs.), Southeastern Surg. Congress, Greater Tampa C. of C. (dir. 1982-86, 87-90, chmn. med. meetings task force 1983-84, Super Star award 1983), Tampa Hist. Soc., Hillsborough County Med. Soc. (pres. polit. action com. 1986-87, 88-89). Clubs: Tampa Yacht and Country (gov. 1984-87), Centre of Tampa (founding mem. 1988-93, bd. dirs., chmn. membership com.), Univ., Ye Mystic Krewe of Gasparilla (bd. dirs. 1991—, 1st lt. 1988-89, lord chamberlain 1994-95, chmn. exec. com. 1995-96, capt. 1996—). Home: 909 S Golfview Ave Tampa FL 33629-5221 Office: 2919 W Swann Ave Ste 303 Tampa FL 33609-4051

BRAND, FRANK AMERY, retired electronics company executive; b. Bklyn., June 26, 1924; s. Charles A. and Louise S.; m. Elaine M. Donohue, June 29, 1946; children: Kathleen Ann, Nancy Jeanne, Frank A. Jr., Robert Edward, Jeannette Marie, Thomas Patrick. BS, Poly. Inst. Bklyn., 1950, MS, 1958; PhD, UCLA, 1970. Dir. R&D programs in microwave semiconductor and quantum electronic devices U.S. Army Electronics Command, 1950-67, chief Integrated Electronics div., 1967-71; exec. v.p., COO M/A-Com, Inc., Burlington, Mass., 1982-86, acting CEO, 1986-87, sr. v.p., chief tech. officer, 1987-91; cons., 1991-95, ret., 1995; adj. prof. Monmouth Coll., 1958-70. Fellow IEEE (life), Bd. Fellows of Poly. U.; mem. Deans Coun. UCLA. Home: 249 Alexander Palm Rd Boca Raton FL 33432-7906

BRANDÃO, FRANK RAPOSO, counselor; b. Vila da Povoacão, Azores, Portugal, Oct. 22, 1946; came to U.S., 1967; s. Carlos Soares and Isaltina Pacheco (Raposo) Brandão; m. Colleen Louise Campbell, Mar. 25, 1972; children: Tina, Benjamin, Marcia, Teresa. BS, Husson Coll., 1975; MS, Mankato State U., 1977, EdS, 1985; EdD, U. North Fla., 1995. Cert. ednl. adminstr., guidance counselor, Fla. Counselor North Shore C.C., Danvers, Mass., 1977-80, Melrose (Minn.) H.S., 1980-82, Corwith (Iowa)-Luvern Schs., 1983-84; prin. Clinton (Minn.) H.S., 1984-85, Wellcome H.S., Garden City, Minn., 1985-86; counselor Flagler County Schs., Bunnell, Fla., 1986-96, St. Johns County Schs., St. Augustine, Fla., 1996—. With USMC, 1969-71. Named Counselor of Yr. Volusia-Flagler Counseling Assn., 1993, Sports Hall of Fame Husson Coll., 1994. Mem. ASCD, Nat. Assn. Multicultural Edn., Fla. Assn. Counseling and Devel., Phi Delta Kappa, Phi Kappa Phi. Roman Catholic. Home: 14 Patchogue Ln Palm Coast FL 32164

BRANDEL, RALPH EDWARD, management consultant; b. Cleve., Sept. 15, 1922; s. Wallace Lester Andrew and Marion (Coulton) B.; m. Dorothy Lucille Alspach, Jul. 14, 1945. BS, U. Md., 1954; MS, Rensselaer Polytech. Inst., 1960; postgrad., American U., Washington, 1970-72. With USMC, 1942-69, commd. 2d lt., 1944, advanced through grades to col., 1968, inf. officer, 1944, arty. officer, 1945, photointerpretation intelligence officer, 1945, engr. officer, 1949-67; S-4 logistics, S-3 ops., 1st Engr. Bn., 1st Marine Divsn. Fleet Marine Force Pacific, 1954-56; asst. prof. naval sci. Rensselaer Poly. Inst., Troy, N.Y., 1957-60; cmdg. officer 2d MarDiv engrs. Cuban Crisis, 1962-63, tng. plans officer for 4 Korean Armed Forces, 1963-64; Def. Depot Ogden dir. installation svcs. USMC, 1964-67; head officer plans HQMC USMC, Washington, 1968-69; ret. USMC Hdqrs., Washington, 1969; v.p., sec., treas. Va. Pharms. Co., Inc., Fairfax, 1974-84; cons., 1984—. Decorated Joint Svcs. Commendation medal, Navy Commendation medal, Army Commendation medal. Mem. VFW (life), Am. Legion (life), Nat. Assn. Atomic Vets. (life), Retired Officers Assn. (life), Toastmasters. Episcopalian. Home and Office: Oakdale Park 8606 Janet Ln Vienna VA 22180-6864

BRANDIS, ROYALL, economist, educator; b. Richmond, Va., Mar. 8, 1920; s. Roland Buford and Ruby Inez (Parsley) B.; m. Mary Lorraine Arnold, Oct. 18, 1941; children: Mary Elizabeth, Margaret Royall. AB, U. Richmond, 1940; MA, Duke U., 1947, PhD, 1952. War regulations analyst E.I. du Pont de Nemours and Co., Wilmington, Del., 1941-43; fgn. trade economist Nat. Cotton Coun., Washington, 1947-49; instr. econs. Duke U., 1949-52; asst. prof. U. Ill., 1952-56, assoc. prof., 1956-61, prof., 1961-84, prof. emeritus, 1984—. Author: Economics: Principles and Policy, 1959, 63, Economia: Principios y Politica, 1962, Principles of Economics, 1968, 72, Principios de Economia, 1972, Current Economic Problems, 1972. With USN, 1943-46. Mem. History of Econs. Soc. (pres. 1979-80), Midwest Econs. Assn. (pres. 1975-76), So. Econ. Assn. Presbyterian. Home: Apt 327 12191 Clipper Dr Lake Ridge VA 22192 Office: Dept Econs U Ill Commerce West 1206 S 6th St Champaign IL 61820

BRANDL, ERNEST DAVID, civil engineer; b. Hartford, Conn., Feb. 29, 1952; s. Ernest and Jean Margaret (McCutcheon) B.; m. Kathryn Farmer, Aug. 16, 1986; children: Rebecca, Adam. BSCE cum laude, U. Conn., 1970-74; MBA, Auburn (Ala.) U., 1979. Registered profl. engr. Miss., Tex., N.Mex., Colo., La., Ark., Iowa, Mont, Utah, Kans., Wis., Minn., Ohio, Wyo., Ind., Mo., Okla., Mich. Field engr. Bechtel Power Corp., Grand Gulf, Miss., 1974-77, Procon Inc., Tuskegee, Ala., 1977-78; sales/design mgr. Schnabel Found. Co., Chgo., 1979-82, Houston, 1982-85; br. mgr. Shnabel Found. Co., Houston, 1985-88, S.W. regional mgr., 1988-89, v.p., 1989—. Co-patentee in field. Mem. ASCE, NSPE. Office: Schnabel Found Co 11231 Richmond Ave Ste D109 Houston TX 77082-2673

BRANDON, DIANE LAINE, personal empowerment consultant, writer; b. New Orleans, Apr. 3, 1948; d. Daniel Morris and Shirley Adele (Carr) B. AB in French, Duke U., 1970; postgrad., U. N.C., 1972-73. Tutor in French studies Geneva, 1969; accounts payable profl. Gulf States Theatres, New Orleans, 1970-71; bilingual exec. sec. So. Shipbldg. Corp., Slidell, La., 1971-72; narrator U. N.C. Sch. Medicine, Chapel Hill, 1974-75; rsch. asst. Rsch. Triangle Inst., Research Triangle Park, N.C., 1976-77; sec. and sales coord. Edward Weck & Co., Inc., Durham, N.C., 1977-78; mgr., sales adminstrn. Edward Week & Co., Inc., Durham, N.C., 1978-83; owner Theatrics, Chapel Hill, 1983-87; voice tchr., performer Chapel Hill, 1987—, spiritual and empowerment cons., writer, 1992—; guest appearances various radio stas., Boston, Balt., Greensboro, Wilmington, N.C., Winston-Salem, N.C., 1994-95; workshop tchr. Charlotte, Greensboro and Chapel Hill, 1993—; v.p. employee activities com. Edward Weck & Co., Durham, 1979-80, mem. planning com. morale campaign, 1979. Contbr. articles to jours.; co-author-producer (Children's Show) Where Are the Animals?; writer-producer: (cassette audio tape) Yes, You Can Sing, 1995. Mem. adv. bd. Brightleaf Music Workshop, Durham, 1992—; bd. dirs., recording sec. Durham Theatre Guild, N.C., 1974-76; mem. merchant com. Am. Dance Festival, Durham, 1984; mem. Silver Reels Com. Internat. TV Assn., 1992; judge for student talent contest No. H.S./Githesn Jr. High, Durham, 1986-87. Named Vol. of Yr. Brightleaf Music Workshop, 1994. Mem. Inst. Noetic Scis., Intelligentsia Metaphysica, Spirit in Bus., Internat. Assn. Near-Death Studies. Democrat. Office: PO Box 16034 Chapel Hill NC 27516

BRANDON, ELVIS DENBY, III, financial planner; b. Memphis, Aug. 11, 1954; s. Elvis Denby Jr. and Helen (Deupree) B.; m. Sarah Buntin, Mar. 15, 1980; children: Elizabeth Holt, William Denby, Mary Buntin. BBA, So. Meth. U., 1976; MBA, Memphis State U., 1979. Cert. fin. planner; CLU; chartered fin. cons. Mgmt. candidate First Tenn. Bank, NA, Memphis, 1979-80; sr. credit analyst Banc Texas/Dallas NA, 1980-82; asst. v.p., comml. loan officer Banc Texas/Sherman NA, 1982; pres. Denby Brandon Orgn., Inc., Memphis, 1982—; v.p. Branco Planning Co., Inc., Memphis, 1982—; adj. faculty Coll. for Fin. Planning, Denver, 1984-85. Deacon Idlewild Presb. Ch. Mem. NASD (registered prin.), Am. Soc. CLUs and Chartered Fin. Cons., Inst. Cert. Fin. Planners. Presbyterian. Home: 5953 Brierdale Ave Memphis TN 38120-2345 Office: Branco Planning Co Inc 3100 Walnut Grove Rd Ste 404 Memphis TN 38111-3530

BRANDON, RICHARD LEONARD, health care consultant; b. Winston Salem, N.C., Oct. 1, 1951; s. Richard Jack and Ruth Leola (Leonard) B.; m. Debra Marie Huffman, Aug. 11, 1973; children: Richard, Michael. B in Indsl. Engring., N.C. State U., 1974, M in Indsl. Engring., 1988. Registered profl. engr., N.C. Methods engr. Scovill Mfg., Wake Forest, N.C., 1973-74; plant engr. Sorensen-Christian Industries, Angier, N.C., 1974-77; mfg. engr. Stanadyne Corp., Sanford, N.C., 1977-82; mgmt. engr. II U. N.C. Hosps., Chapel Hill, 1982-89; dir. mgmt. engring. Mary Imogene Bassett Hosp., Cooperstown, N.Y., 1990-93; mgr., consulting svcs. Premier Healthcare Alliance, 1993—; MIT task force Vol. Hosps. Am., Syracuse, N.Y., 1990-93; cons. in field, 1986-89, 93—. Sr. warden St. Bartholomew's Episcopal Ch., Pittsboro, N.C., 1988; H.S. varsity basketball ofcl., 1991—. Mem. Inst. Indsl. Engrs. (sr.), Soc. Health Systems, Accreditation Bd. Engring. Tech., Health Info. Mgmt. Systems Soc. (sr.). Republican. Home: 2826 Winton Dr Hillsborough NC 27278-9632 Office: 122 S Churton St Hillsborough NC 27278

BRANDS, JAMES EDWIN, medical products executive; b. Lebanon, Ind., July 5, 1937; s. Edwin Herman and Pearl Irene (Brown) B.; m. Gail Marian Knight, Sept. 12, 1959; children: Jeffrey, Scot, Alan, Susan. AB, Wesleyan U., Middletown, Conn., 1959; MBA, U. Chgo., 1961; JD, Kennedy-Western U., Boise, Idaho, 1992. CPA, Mo. Staff acct., mgr. Arthur Andersen & Co., Chgo., 1961-71; ptnr. Arthur Andersen & Co., St. Louis, 1971-82; sr. v.p. Scherer-Storz, Inc., St. Louis, 1982-86; vice chmn., CFO Scherer Healthcare Inc., Atlanta, 1982-95; exec. v.p. Scherer Sci. Ltd., Atlanta, 1986-95; bd. dirs., v.p. Ramco Fluid Svcs., Inc., Atlanta, BodyCare Inc., Atlanta, Maximum Benefits, LLC, Atlanta; bd. dirs., pres. Throwleigh Technologies LLC, Atlanta; bd. dirs. Ga. Am. Land Co., Atlanta, Creative Beverages, Inc., Evansville, Ind.; bd. dirs., CEO Marquest Med. Products, Inc., Denver, 1993-95; owner, mgr. Brands & Co., 1981—. Mem. AICPA, Mo. Soc. CPAs, Bellerive Country Club (St. Louis), Atlanta Nat. Golf Club. Republican. Presbyterian. Home: 4330 Bancroft Valley Alpharetta GA 30202-5175 Office: PO Box 767655 Roswell GA 30076-7655

BRANDT, EDWARD WILLIAM, III, nonprofit organization executive, consultant; b. Lewistown, Pa., Sept. 20, 1945; s. Edward William and Betty (Harmon) B.; m. Janice Cosbey, Nov. 30, 1968; children: Derek Edward, Danielle Jacqueline. BA, Trinity Coll., Dunedin, Fla., 1968; grad. studies, Harvard U., 1972-73, 78. Sr. minister First Bapt. Ch., New Carrollton, Md., 1975-85; sr. v.p. Fazio Internat. Ltd., Washington, 1985-88; exec. dir. The Pet Care Trust, Washington, 1988-95; exec. v.p. Missing Kids Internat., McLean, Va., 1996—. V.p. Montgomery Village (Md.) Found., 1991-95. Mem. Am. Soc. Assn. Execs., Am. Assn. Counselors, McLean Va. C. of C. Republican. Presbyterian. Home: 19746 Greenside Terr Montgomery Village MD 20879 Office: Missing Kids Internat Inc 6707 Old Dominion Dr # 200 Mc Lean VA 22101

BRANDT, I. MARVIN, chemist, engineer; b. Shreveport, La., Nov. 26, 1942; s. David and Esta (Epstein) B. BS in Chemistry, Centenary Coll., 1965; postgrad., U. Tex., 1968-70. Gen. mgr. Am. Pipe and Supply, Shreveport, 1970-73; researcher Shell Oil, Houston, 1973-75; rsch. tech. svc. trainer NL Baroid, Houston, 1975-79; rschr., tech. svc. engr., tng. coord. Arco Oil & Gas Co., worldwide, 1979-86; specialist, project mgr. Petrolite Corp., St. Louis, 1986-90; sr. engr., tng. mgr., environ. coord. Marathon Oil Co., Houston, 1990—; cons. for drilling and environ. projects Dallas, S.Am., Cen. Am., Tex., Calif., Russia, N. Sea, Mid. East, Africa, Alaska, Australia, New Zealand, China. Contbr. articles to profl. jours.; patentee in field. Active Am. Cancer Soc., Houston, Denver, St. Louis, Morris Animal Found., Denver, Am. Heart Assn. Recipient Grad. Tching. fellowship, U. Tex., Austin, 1968-70, Robert Welch Rsch. grant, U. Tex., Austin, 1969. Mem. Soc. Petroleum Engrs. (program chmn.), Internat. Assn. Drilling Contractors, Am. Chem. Soc., Am. Petroleum Inst. (numerous subcoms. for drilling and environment), Am. Assn. Drilling Engrs. (chmn. drilling com.), Planning Com. for Petro-Safe, N.Y. Acad. Scis., Internat. Platform Assn. Home: PO Box 571844 Houston TX 77257 Office: 5555 San Felipe St Houston TX 77056-2725

BRANDT, JAMES CARL, research organization executive; b. Fargo, N.D., Aug. 16, 1947; s. Roland Henning and Juliet (Kretzschmar) B.; m. Janie Rhorer. Student, U. East Anglia, Norwich, Eng., 1967-68; BA with distinction, U. Colo., 1969; MSW, Tulane U., 1971. Rsch. assoc. City Coun. Rsch. Staff, New Orleans, 1970-71; planning dir. Mayor's Criminal Justice Coordinating Coun., New Orleans, 1971-74; asst. dir., sr. assoc. Inst. for Govtl. Studies, Loyola U., New Orleans, 1974-78; dep. dir. Downtown Devel. Dist., New Orleans, 1978-81; v.p. planning and adminstrn. La. World Exposition Inc., New Orleans, 1981-84; pres. Brandt & Assocs., Mgmt. Svcs. for Assns. and Orgns., New Orleans, 1984-87; exec. dir. Bur. Govtl. Rsch., New Orleans, 1987—; adj. faculty Tulane U., New Orleans, 1977-81, U. New Orleans Coll. Urban and Pub. Affairs, 1992-93. Contbr. articles to profl. jours. Mem. bd. advisors Govtl. Leadership Inst. at U. New Orleans; pres. bd. dirs. Nat. Govtl. Rsch. Assn., 1995-96; mem. Met. Area Com.; bd. dirs., cons. Jr. Achievement of New Orleans; bd. dirs., mem. exec. com. La. Ctr. for the Pub. Interest; vice chmn. govtl. affairs com. New Orleans Area Coun.; bd. dirs. Citizens for Quality Nursing Home Care. Named to Outstanding Young Men of Am., 1980; Shoe-Smith scholar Colo. U.; Regent's scholar U. East Anglia; HEW trainee, 1971. Mem. Am. Planning Assn., Am. Soc. Assn. Execs., New Orleans Coun. Bus. Economists, The Chamber--New Orleans and the River Region, La. Soc. Assn. Execs., World Trade Ctr., Orleans Intercommunity Coun., Pub. Affairs Rsch. Coun. La., Am. Soc. for Pub. Adminstrn., Young Leadership Coun., La. Coun. for Fiscal Reform, Phi Beta Kappa. Office: Bur Govtl Rsch 225 Baronne Ste 600 New Orleans LA 70112

BRANDT, MITZI MARIANNE, educational specialist; b. St. Louis, Dec. 21, 1932; d. Vernon Osborn and Kathleen Louisa (Everett) Young; m. William Eugene Brandt Jr., Dec. 16, 1951; children: William Eugene III, Shelley, Susan, Shauna. BS, Wright State U., 1975, M in Reading, 1976; alphabetic phonics therapy cert., Neuhaus Edn. Ctr., Houston, 1993. Tchr. 2d grade Fairborn (Ohio) City Schs., 1975-82; tchr. 3d grade Clear Creek Ind. Sch. Dist., Clear Lake, Tex., 1982-89, ednl. specialist, 1989—; mem. advanced dyslexia therapist tng. Neuhaus Edn. Ctr., Houston, 1991. Rep. Leukemia Soc. of Am., Houston, 1985-90. Mem. Tex. Tchrs. Assn. (chairperson Houston chpt. 1984-87), Clear Creek Educators Assn. (rep. 1983-86), Orton Dyslexic Soc. Office: Ferguson Elem 1910 S Compass Rose Blvd League City TX 77573-6642

BRANDT, WILLIAM ARTHUR, JR., consulting executive; b. Chgo., Sept. 5, 1949; s. William Arthur and Joan Virginia (Ashworth) B.; m. Patrice Bugelas, Jan. 19, 1980; children: Katherine Ashworth, William George, Joan Patrice, John Peter. BA with honors, St. Louis U., 1971; MA, U. Chgo., 1972, postgrad., 1972-74. Asst. to pres. Pyro Mining Co., Chgo., 1972-74; commentator Sta. WBBM-AM, Chgo., 1977; with Melaniphy & Assocs., Inc., Chgo., 1975-76; pres., cons. Devel. Specialists, Inc., Chgo., 1976—; mem. adv. bd. Sociol. Abstracts, Inc., San Diego, 1979-83. Contbr. articles to profl. jours. Trustee Fenwick H.S., 1991-94, Comml. Law League of Am., Internat. Coun. Shopping Ctrs., Nat. Assn. Bankruptcy Trustees, Ill. Sociol. Assn., Midwest Sociol. Soc., Urban Land Inst. LaVerne Noyes scholar, 1971-74. Mem. Am. Bankruptcy Inst. (bd. dirs.), Am. Sociol. Assn., Monroe Club, Amelia Island Plantation Club, Union League Club Chgo., City Club of Miami, sust. fellow of Art Inst. of Chicago, gov. mem. Chicago Symphony, Clinton/Gore '96 Natl. Finance Bd., mnging. trustee Democratic Natl. Comm., maj. trust mem. Democratic Senatorial Campaign Comm., life mem. Zoological Soc. of the Miami Metro Zoo. Democrat. Roman Catholic. Home: 1000 Venetian Way Unit 702 Miami FL 33139 also: Amelia Island Plantation 6518 Beachwood Rd Amelia Island FL 32034-9103 also: 1134 Sheridan Rd Winnetka IL 60093-1538 also: 182 Temple Ave Apt 24 Old Orchard Beach ME 04064-1265 Office: 3 First Nat Plz Ste 2300 Chicago IL 60602 also: 200 S Biscayne Blvd Ste 900 Miami FL 33131-2321 also: Devonshire House, 146 Bishopsgate, London EC2M 4JX, England also: Wells Fargo Ctr 333 S Grand Ave Ste 2010 Los Angeles CA 90071-1524 also: Two Oliver St 5th Fl Boston MA 02109-4901

BRANDT, WILLIAM PAUL, pilot; b. Dallas, Nov. 15, 1954; s. John Henry and Theresa Jean (Pool) B.; m. Susan Elaine Turley, Oct. 1, 1977; children: Carolyn Elaine, Annesly Elizabeth, Clayton Robert. BS in History, USAF Acad., 1977; postgrad., U. Phoenix, 1995—. Cert. airline transport pilot, FAA. Commd. 2d lt. USAF, 1977, advanced through grades to maj., 1991, ret., 1986; systems engr., program mgr. Tex. Instruments, Dallas, 1986-90; pilot Fed. Express, Memphis, Tenn., 1990—. Contbr. columns to newspapers: What Bill Thinks, 1994-96. Del. 10th Senatorial Dist. Conv., Fort Worth, 1988; chief of staff Anderson for Congress, Fort Worth, 1996; del. State Rep. Conv., San Antonio, 1996; media cons. Stacy for Mayor, Southlake, Tex., 1996; mem. spkrs. bur. Tarrant County Dole for Pres., 1996. With USAFR. Mem. Air Force Assn., CAL-20 Assn., Heritage Found., Order of Dadaeliens, Southlake C. of C. Lutheran. Home: 808 Victoria Ln Southlake TX 76092

BRANHAM, GRADY EUGENE, principal; b. Birmingham, Ala., June 19, 1947; s. Grady B. and Pauline (Kelley) B.; m. Joy Canavan, Mar. 26, 1983;

children: Joy Elizabeth, Gralynn. BS, Birmingham (Ala.) So. Coll., 1969; MEd, Montevallo (Ala.) U., 1976; PhD, U.N.A., St. Louis, 1988. Prin. Dallas Christian Sch., Selma, Ala., 1970-84, Briarwood Christian High Sch., Birmingham, Ala., 1984—. V.p. Community Concert Assn., Selma, 1980-84. Named Patriot of Yr., Patriotic Am. Youth, Jackson, Miss., 1982. Mem. Am. Soc. Interior Design. Office: Briarwood Christian High 6255 Cahaba Valley Rd Birmingham AL 35242-4915

BRANHAM, PAMELA HELEN, special education educator; b. Knoxville, Tenn., July 24, 1960; d. John Author and Nancy Carolyn (Garth) Thomas. BS in Spl. Edn., U. Tenn., 1983, MS in Spl. Edn., 1986. Cert. tchr., Tenn., Fla., Ky., Ind. Interpreter, hearing specialist Knoxville County Schs., 1987-88; tchr. hearing impaired Pasco County Sch., Spring Hill, Fla., 1988-93; tchr. emotionally handicapped and hearing impaired Charlestown (Ind.) High Sch., 1993-95; tchr. of emotionally and mentally handicapped Pine View Mid. Sch., Land O' Lakes, Fla., 1995—. Mem. Nat. Assn. of the Deaf, Fla. Registry of Interpreters for the Deaf, Alexander Graham Bell Assn. for Deaf. Presbyterian. Office: Pine View Mid Sch 5334 Parkway Blvd Land O'Lakes FL 34639

BRANN, RICHARD ROLAND, lawyer; b. Olney, Ill., June 9, 1943; s. Roland John and Margaret (McVay) B.; m. Penny Sue Farrington, June 5, 1965; children: Wesley R., Patrick T. BA, Miss. State U., 1965; JD, U. Tex., 1968. Bar: Tex. 1968, U.S. Dist. Ct. (so., no., ea. and we. dists.) Tex. 1970, U.S. Ct. Appeals (5th and 11th cirs.) 1973, U.S. Supreme Ct. 1973; bd. cert. in labor and employment law Tex. Bd. Legal Specialization. Assoc. Baker & Botts, Houston, 1968-76, ptnr., 1976—; chmn. fed. judiciary rels. com. State Bar Tex., 1996-97; chmn. Houston Mgmt. Lawyers Forum, Houston, 1981. Editor: Tex. Assn. of Bus. and C. of C. Labor Law Quarterly Rev., Tex. Labor Letter, 1994. With USMC, 1961-66. Mem. ABA, Tex. Bar Assn., Tex. Bar Coll., Houston Bar Assn. (chmn.-elect labor and employment law sect. 1996-97), Def. Rsch. Inst., Houston Club, Plaza Club, Phi Kappa Phi. Republican. Methodist. Office: Baker & Botts 3000 One Shell Plaza 910 Louisiana St Houston TX 77002-4995

BRANNON, TREVA LEE (WOOD), insurance company executive; b. Burleson, Tex., Oct. 6, 1932; d. William Albert and Virginia May (Garner) Wood; m. Lone J. Brannon, Aug. 3, 1951 (dec. Apr. 1989); 1 child, Ralph Eugene. Grad. high sch., Godley, Tex. Acctg. clk. Internat. Svcs. Life Ins. Co., Ft. Worth, 1950-63; sec. John Hancock Life Ins. Co., Ft. Worth, 1963-64; asst. v.p. Olympic Life Ins. Co., Ft. Worth, 1964-70; v.p. Transport Life Ins. Co., Ft. Worth, 1970—. Mem. Soc. Ins. Licensing Adminstrs. Home: 349 Heirloom Dr Fort Worth TX 76134-3950 Office: Transport Life Ins Co 714 Main St Fort Worth TX 76102-5217

BRANNON, WILLIAM LESTER, JR., neurologist, educator; b. Olar, S.C., Jan. 11, 1936; s. William Lester and Lena Mae (Brigman) B.; m. Darrell Meeks, June 13, 1959; children: Debra Brannon DeMarco, William Bert, Victoria Brannon-Diaz. AB, U. S.C., 1957; MD, Med. U. S.C., 1961. Commd. ensign U.S. Navy, 1966, advanced through grades to capt., 1980; chmn. dept. neurology Nat. Naval Med. Ctr., Bethesda, Md., 1969-79; assoc. prof. neurology Georgetown U. Sch. medicine, Washington, 1969-79; prof. neurology Uniformed Svc. U. Health Scis., Bethesda, 1974-79, chmn. dept. neurology, 1978-79; dir. clin. svcs. Naval Regional Med. Ctr., Charleston, S.C., 1979-80; ret. U.S. Navy, 1980; clin. prof. neurology Med. U. S.C., Charleston, 1979-80; vice chair, dir. neurology U. S.C. Sch. Medicine, Columbia, 1980—; neurology cons. to attending physician U.S. Capitol and White House, 1970-79, to Surgeon Gen. U.S. Navy, 1970-79. Contbr. articles to sci. and med. reports. Fellow ACP, Am. Acad. Neurology, Am. Electroencephalography Soc. Democrat. Methodist. Office: U SC Sch Medicine 3555 Harden St Columbia SC 29203

BRANSON, ROBERT EARL, marketing economist; b. Dallas, Dec. 3, 1918; s. R. Earl and Gertrude (Smith) B.; children: Donald, Richard. BS, So. Meth. U., 1941; MPA, Harvard U., 1948, MA, 1949, PhD, 1954. Economist War Food Adminstrn., USDA, Dallas, 1941-43; economist, statistician USDA, Washington, 1943-55; assoc. prof., prof. Tex. A&M U., College Sta., Tex., 1955-80; dir., Tex. Agr. Mkt. Research Ctr. Tex. A&M U., College Sta., 1969-88; pres. Branson Research Assoc., Inc., Bryan, Tex., 1985—, Agribusiness Analysts, Bryan, 1985—; prof. emeritus Tex. A&M U., College Sta., 1987—; mktg. economist research cons. U. P.R., 1949-51, Argentina Eco Planning Staff, Foreign Agr. Service, USDA, Bryon/College Station Tex. 2020 Vision Area Planning Com. Author: Intro Agriculture and Marketing, 1983; contbr. articles to profl. jours. With U.S. Army, 1944-45. Mem. Am. Mktg. Assn., So. Agr. Econ. Assn. (Life Mem. award 1989), Kiwanis (College Station pres. 1982). Methodist. Home: 2511 Broadmoor Dr Bryan TX 77802-2804 Office: Branson Rsch Assoc Inc 1806 Wilde Oak Circle Bryan TX 77802-4402

BRANTLEY, JEFFREY GARLAND, health science facility administrator; b. Rocky Mount, N.C., Nov. 4, 1949; s. Roy Garland and Irene (Cockrell) B.; m. Mary Mathews, Nov. 21, 1981. BA in History, Davidson Coll., 1971; MD, U. N.C., 1977. Diplomate Am. Bd. Psychiatry. Resident in psychiatry U. Calif., Irvine, 1981; pvt. practice psychiatry Laguna Niguel, Calif., 1981-82, Durham, N.C., 1985-87; med. dir. Hospice Orange County, Laguna Niguel, 1982; clin. dir. Durham County Mental Health Ctr., Durham, N.C., 1982-89; freelance cons., educator Durham, 1990—; clin. assoc. dept. psychiatry U. Calif., Irvine, 1981-82; consulting assoc. Dept. Psychiatry Duke U., 1983—. Mem. Am. Psychiat. Assn., N.C. Psychiat. Assn., Am. Soc. Clin. Hypnosis, Physicians for Social Responsibility. Democrat. Buddhist. Home: 1109 Huntsman Dr Durham NC 27713-2370 Office: 201 Providence Rd Chapel Hill NC 27514

BRANTLEY, JERRY LEE, JR., systems programmer; b. Farmington, N.Mex., June 25, 1962; s. Jerry Lee and Katherine Noreen (Braun) B.; m. Beryl Jeannette Adams, Jan. 27, 1984; children: Krystina Jeannette, Kevin Thomas Adams, Katherine Nicole, Kayla LeeAnne. Student, Troy State U., Montgomery, Ala., 1981-83. Programmer, analyst Sperry Corp., Montgomery, 1984-86; systems analyst Unisys Corp., Montgomery, 1986-89; sr. systems programmer Soc. Internat. Telecommunications Aeronautiques, College Park, Ga., 1989-91; sr. software engr. Computer Maintenance Corp., College Park, 1991—; pres. Encore Solutions, Inc., 1994—. Active children's ch. tchr. With USAF, 1980-84. Recipient hon. mention USE Program Libr. Interchange, 1991. Republican. Mem. Assembly of God. Office: CMC 5136 Southridge Pky Ste 100 College Park GA 30349-5969

BRANTLEY, JOHN KENNETH, government official, pilot; b. Austell, Ga., Feb. 8, 1942; s. Hudson Lee and Evelyn Pearl (Jackson) B.; m. Linda Hendrick, May 6, 1960; children: Jeanette, John Kenneth Jr., Candyon, Brandyon, Summer, Holly. Student, Kennesaw Coll., 1966-67. Charter and instr. pilot, Atlanta, 1966-71; air traffic controller Air Traffic Control, FAA, Hampton, Ga., 1968-71; aviation safety insp. flight stds. FAA, Jacksonville, Fla., from 1971, Atlanta; examiner Bd. Civil Svc. Examiners, Atlanta, 1977-82. Author: The Matilda Archer Story, 1986, The Records of the Church at Williams Creek, 1995. Recipient 1st prize in writing Genealogist Digest, 1988. Mem. Brantley Assn. Am. (founder, pres. 1987—).

BRANTLEY, STEPHEN GRANT, pathologist; b. Raleigh, N.C., Nov. 27, 1957; s. Herbert and Juanita (Grant) B. BS with honors, U. N.C., 1980; MD, Med. U. S.C., 1984. Diplomate Am. Bd. Pathology. Residency in pathology U. Pitts. Med. Sch., 1984-88; pathologist Tampa (Fla.) Gen. Hosp., 1988—; med. dir. labs. Vencor Hosp., Tampa, 1990—; clin. asst. prof. U. South Fla. Coll. Medicine, Tampa, 1988—. Bd. dirs. Tampa Bay Chamber Orch., Tampa, 1993—; exec. com. mem. Rep. Party of Hillsborough County, Tampa, 1989—. Mem. Coll. Am. Pathologists, Am. Soc. Clin. Pathologists, Am. Soc. Transplant Physicians, Internat. Soc. for Heart Transplantation. Republican. Episcopalian. Office: Ruffolo Hooper and Assocs 112 N East St Ste D Tampa FL 33602-4108

BRANTLEY, WILLIAM OLIVER, JR., English language educator; b. Atlanta, Aug. 15, 1955; s. William Sr. and Grace (Josey) B. BA in English, Ga. State U., 1977, MA in English, 1981; PhD in English, U. Wis., 1991. Teaching asst. Dept. of English U. Wis., Madison, 1984-88; Brittain fellow in writing Sch. of Lit., Comm., Culture Ga. Inst. Tech., 1988-91; vis. lectr. Interdisciplinary Writing Program U. Calif., Santa Barbara, 1991-92; asst. prof. English Middle Tenn. State U., Murfreesboro, 1992—. Author: (book) Feminine Sense in Southern Memoir: Smith, Glasgow, Welty, Hellman, Porter and Hurston, 1993, Conversations With Pauline Kael, 1996. Recipient Ga. Press Assn. award First Place Best Feature Article, 1979, Brittain Fellowship in Writing Ga. Inst. Tech., 1988-91, Eudora Welty prize, 1992. Mem. MLA, Am. Lit. Assn., Soc. for Study of So. Lit., Ellen Glasgow Soc., Eudora Welty Soc., Katherine Anne Porter Soc. Home: 4225 Harding Pike # 305 Nashville TN 37205 Office: Middle Tenn State U Dept of English Murfreesboro TN 37132

BRANTON, DAVID CARL, secondary school educator, consultant; b. Alexandria, La., June 16, 1948; s. Carl Roan and Florine (Dickerson) B.; m. Cynthia Ann Clayton, June 25, 1976; children: Rebecca, Andrew. BM in Edn., La. State U., 1971, MA, 1992; MRE, New Orleans Bapt. Sem., 1978. Cert. instrumental music, computer sci. and literacy tchr., gifted edn. tchr., La. Tchr. Buras (La.) High Sch., 1971-75, Denham Springs (La.) High Sch., 1975-76, Alexandria Sr. High Sch., 1986-87; youth pastor Forest Highlands Bapt. Ch., Little Rock, 1978-80; youth pastor 1st Bapt. Ch., Russellville, Ark., 1980-83, Winnfield, La., 1984-85; technician Terminix, Baton Rouge, 1984-85; tchr. McKinley High Sch., Baton Rouge, 1987—. Named hon. mayor Baton Rouge City Coun., 1992. Republican. Home: 9121 Cedar Springs Ave Denham Springs LA 70726-6123 Office: McKinley High Sch 800 E Mckinley St Baton Rouge LA 70802-6852

BRASHEARS, KENT BAKER, interior designer; b. Tulsa, Mar. 24, 1953; s. Vol Jr. and Helen Virginia (Baker) B. Student, Wake Forest Coll., 1969, U. Ga., 1970; BS, U. Mo., 1975. Asst. designer Cyril Gerac Interiors, Houston, 1975-76; staff designer Foley's Interior Design Studio, Houston, 1976-78, Rova Interiors, Houston, 1978-81; project designer Allison/Walker Interests, Houston, 1981-85; chief exec. officer Galveston (Tex.) Gallery, 1985—. Author, illustrator: The Frog Manual, 1982. Bd. dirs. Galveston Hist. Found., homes tour chmn.; bd. dirs., mem. Artwalk com., pres. Galveston Arts Ctr.; commr. City of Galveston Commn. for the Arts. Mem. Am. Soc. Interior Designers (program chmn., bd. dirs. Tex. gulf coast chpt.), Tex. Assn. for Interior Design, Am. Orchid Soc., Knights of Regina (color guard), Diana Found. (hon.), Delta Upsilon. Methodist. Home: RR 1 Box 1962T Galveston TX 77554-9801 Office: Galveston Gallery 1825 Rosenberg St Galveston TX 77550

BRASHEARS, WILFORD SESSION, JR., retired metals company executive, priest; b. Coral Gables, Fla., Sept. 30, 1925; s. Wilford Session Brashears and Minnie Marie (Turner) Brashears Maloney; m. Bee Jacqueline Boulogne, Jan. 25, 1953 (dec.). BS, U. Tex., 1946, BA, 1948; postgrad., St. Mary's U.; MA, Loyola U., 1989. Ordained to priest Roman Cath. Ch., 1982. Environ. engr. ASARCO, Inc., Amarillo, Tex., 1948-89, ret., 1991; pres., chief exec. officer King of Kings Mines, Inc., Amarillo, 1989—; assoc. pastor St. Mary's Ch., Amarillo, 1984—. Holder of seven French noble titles. Republican. Lodge: Rotary. Home: 1505 S Rusk St Amarillo TX 79102-2321 Office: King of Kings Mines Inc 1200 S Washington St Amarillo TX 79102-1645

BRASHER, GEORGE WALTER, physician; b. Jackson, Tenn., Dec. 7, 1936; s. George W. and Verla S. Brasher; m. Martha S. Brasher, Dec. 23, 1960; children: Suzanne Cheshier, George Brasher, John Brasher, David Brasher. BA, Lambuth U., 1959; MD, U. Tenn., 1961. Diplomate Am. Bd. Allergy and Immunology, Am. Bd. Pediatrics. Cons. Scott & White Clinic & Hosp., Temple, Tex., 1966—; dir. Allergy and Immunology Scott & White Clinic and Hosp., Temple. Tex., 1975—; prof. Medicine and Pediatrics Tex. A&M U. Coll. of Medicine, Temple, Tex., 1977—. Contbr. articles to profl. jours. Fellow Am. Acad. Allergy and Immunology, Am. Acad. Pediatrics, Am. Coll. Allergy and Immunology; mem. AMA, Tex. Med. Assn., Bell County Med. Soc., Tex. Allergy Soc. Office: Scott & White Clinic & Hosp 2401 S 31st St Temple TX 76508-0001

BRASHIER, EDWARD MARTIN, environmental consultant; b. New Iberia, La., Sept. 30, 1954; s. Martin Lee and Ann Elizabeth Brashier; m. Deborah W. Brashier, July 15, 1977 (div. 1987); children: Shannon E., Edward Martin II, Joseph L. II; m. Debra A. Dillard, Nov. 1994; 1 child, Sunny Ann. AS, Jones Jr. Coll., Ellsville, Miss., 1974; BS, MS, U. Miss., 1976; student, Kensington U., 1990; JD, LaSalle U., 1995. Chemist Fla. Machine & Fdry., Jacksonville, 1976, Union Carbide, Woodbine, Ga., 1976-77; sr. chemist Nilok Chem., Memphis, 1977-78; tech. mgr. Chem. Waste Mgmt., Emelle, Ala., 1978-83; dir. Am. Nukem, Rock Hill, S.C., 1983-86; regional environ. mgr. Layne Western, Rock Hill, 1986-87; project mgr. Westinghouse Environ., Pitts., 1987-88; sr. environ. scientist Dames & Moore, Boca Raton, Fla., 1988-91; nat. sales mgr. Mo. Fuel Recycler Inc./Continental Cement Co. divsn. Scancem, Hanible, 1991-93; sr. project mgr. Jones Edmunds & Assocs., Gainesville, Fla., 1994-96; ind. environ. cons. Waynesboro, Miss., 1996—. Editor and tech. advisor, editor various manuals on toxic and hazardous substances. Bd. dirs. Rock Hill (S.C.) Sch. Bd., 1985-86. Fellow Am. Inst. Chemists; mem. Am. Chem. Soc., Am. Water Wks. Assn., Am. Indsl. Hygiene Assn., WHO, Nat. Assn. Environ. Profls., Am. Soc. Safety Engrs. Democrat. Methodist. Home: 808 Spring St Waynesboro MS 39367

BRASSEAUX, CARL ANTHONY, historian; b. Opelousas, La., Aug. 19, 1951; s. Ferdinand and Odile Valajean (Johnson) B.; m. Glenda M. Melancon, July 21, 1973; children: Ryan Andre, David Marc, Aimee Elizabeth. BA in Polit. Sci., U. S.W. La., 1974, MA in History, 1975; PhD, U. Paris, 1982. Asst. dir. ctr. La. studies U. S.W. La., Lafayette, 1975—; curator Colonial Records Collection, U. S.W. La., Lafayette, 1980—, assoc. prof. history, 1994—; cons. La. Park Svc., Baton Rouge, 1984, Nat. Park Svc., Washington, 1987-88, U.S. Corps. Engrs., New Orleans, 1995; mng. editor La. History, 1993—. Freelance editor Scribner's Ref. Divsn., N.Y.C., 1991-92; author: Denis-Nicolas Foucault and the New Orleans Rebellion of 1786, 1987, In Search of Evangelin: Origins and Evolution of the Evangelin Myth, 1989, Lafayette, Where Yesterday meets Tomorrow: An Illustrated History, 1990, The Foreign French: French Immigration into the Mississippi Valley, 1820-1900, Vol. I, 1990, Vol. II, 1992, Vol. III, 1993; Scattered to the Wind: Dispersal and Wanderings of the Acadians, 1755-1809, 1991, Acadian to Cajun: Transformation of a People, 1803-1877, 1994, A Refuge for All Ages: Immigration in Louisiana History, 1996; co-author: The Courthouses of Louisiana, 1977, A Bibliography of Acadian History, Literature and Genealogy, 1955-85, 1986, A Bibliography of Scholarly Literature on Colonial Louisiana and New France, 1992, Crevass: The 1927 Flood in Acadiana, 1994, Creoles of Color in the Bayou Country, 1995; co-editor: A Franco-American Overview: Louisiana, Vol. V, 1981, Vol. VI 1981, Vol. VII: The Postbellum Period, 1982, Vol. VIII: French louisiana in the Twentieth Century, 1982; translator, editor, annotator, compiler many other works; contbr. over 85 articles to profl. jours., chpts. to books. Office: Ctr La Studies 302 E St Mary Blvd Lafayette LA 70506

BRASWELL, JACKIE TERRY, medical, surgical nurse; b. Raleigh, N.C., Oct. 15, 1961; d. Charles Thurman and Laura (Russell) Terry; 1 child, Matthew Russell Braswell. BSN, U. N.C., 1983. Cert. BCLS, med. surgical nursing ANA. Staff nurse orthopedics/neurology unit Wake County Med. Ctr., Raleigh, staff nurse cardiac telemetry step-down unit; asst. head nurse orthopedics unit Raleigh Community Hosp., staff nurse telemetry unit; charge nurse vent unit IHS, Raleigh, 1993-95. Mem. ANA, NCNA.

BRASWELL, KERN F., protective services official; b. Linden, Tex., May 13, 1956; s. August Kern Braswell and Wanda Lee (Fant) Baldwin. BS, U. Tulsa, 1979. Cert. arson investigator, fire svc. instr., Okla. Firefighter Tulsa Fire Dept., 1980-84, fire equipment operator, 1984-88, tng. officer, 1988-89, adminstrv. staff officer, 1989-91; fire capt., 1991—; mem. fire tech. adv. bd. Tulsa Jr. Coll., 1985—; bd. dirs. Tulsa Firefighters Pension Bd., 1988-91. Author: (weekly newspaper column) Healthy, Wealthy and Wise, 1987-88; editor newsletter The Tulsa Fire Fighter, 1988; producer, dir. Sta. TFD-TV, 1989-91; contbr. articles to profl. jours. Bd. dirs. Litchfield Homeowners Assn., 1994. Recipient Certs. Achievement Nat. Fire Acad., 1988, 89, 91, 93, 94, 95, Cert. Achievement Emergency Mgmt. Inst., 1990, 91. Mem. Internat. Assn. Firefighters (v.p. Local 176 1987-88), Profl. Firefighters Okla. (conv. del. 1988), Nat. Fire Protection Assn., Okla. State Fire Fighters Assn., Women in the Fire Svc., Fire Marshal's Assn. Okla., Fire Svc. Instrs. of Okla. Democrat. Office: Tulsa Fire Dept 411 S Frankfort Ave Tulsa OK 74120-3011

BRASWELL, RANDY LEE, educational administrator; b. Tifton, Ga., June 28, 1958; s. William James and Betty (Hutchinson) B.; m. Claire L. Waldhour, July 14, 1984; children: Sarah, Luke, Anna, Mary Esther. AS, Andrew Coll., 1978; BS, Ga. Southwestern Coll., 1980; Master's degree, U. Ga., 1982; PhD, Ga. State U., 1996. Rsch. technician U. Ga./USDA, Tifton, 1982-88; dir. instnl. rsch. Gordon Coll., Barnesville, Ga., 1988—. Sunday sch. tchr. Fellowship Bapt. Ch., Thomaston, Ga., 1991—, pianist, 1992—. Mem. Am. Assn. Higher Edn., Assn. for Instnl. Rsch., Ga. Instnl. Rsch. and Planning Coun. Southern Baptist. Home: 47 Hill Crest Dr Thomaston GA 30286 Office: Gordon Coll 419 College Dr Barnesville GA 30204

BRASWELL, WALTER E., U.S. attorney. Sr. litigation officer U.S. Dist. Ct. (no. dist.) Ala., Birmingham, 1995S. Office: US Attorney for No Dist Alabama Federal Bldg 1800 5th Ave N Birmingham AL 35203-2111*

BRATTON, IDA FRANK, secondary school educator; b. Glasgow, Ky., Aug. 31, 1933; d. Edmund Bates and Robbie Davis (Hume) Button; m. Robert Franklin Bratton, June 20, 1954; 1 son, Timothy Andrew. B.A., Western Ky. U., 1959, M.A., 1962. Cert. secondary tchr., Ky. Tchr. math. and sci. Gottschalk Jr. High Sch., Louisville, 1959-65; tchr. math. Iroquois High Sch., Louisville, 1965-79; tchr. Waggener High Sch., Louisville, 1979—, chair math. dept. co-chair sch. based decision making coun. Waggener High Sch. Mem. NEA, Ky. Edn. Assn., Jefferson County Tchrs. Assn., AAUW. Democrat. Methodist. Avocations: travel, needle crafts. Home: 304 Paddington Ct Louisville KY 40222-5541 Office: Waggener High Sch 330 S Hubbards Ln Louisville KY 40207-4011

BRATTON, WILLIAM EDWARD, electronics executive, management consultant; b. Dallas, Oct. 25, 1919; s. William E. and Edna (Walker) B.; m. Betty Thume, May 30, 1942; children: Dale, Janet, Donna. AB in Econs., Stanford U., 1940; MBA, Harvard U., 1945. From v.p. to pres. Librascope, Glendale, Calif., 1947-63; v.p., gen. mgr. Ampex, Culver City, Calif., 1963-66; pres. Guidance Tech., Santa Monica, Calif., 1967-68; v.p. electronics div. Gen. Dynamics, San Diego, 1969-72; pres. Theta Cable T.V., Santa Monica, 1974-82; pres., chief exec. officer Stagecoach Properties, Salado, Tex., 1959—. Served to lt. (j.g.) USNR, 1944-46. Republican. Episcopalian. Club: El Niguel Country (Laguna, Calif.) (pres. 1978-79).

BRAUDAWAY, GARY WAYNE, secondary school educator; b. Ft. Worth, Nov. 28, 1955; s. Clarence Albert and Martha Jean (Lutz) B. BA, Hardin-Simmons U., 1982; postgrad., North Tex. State U., 1983, 95; cert. ESL tchr., Tex. Wesleyan U., 1986; postgrad., Middlebury Coll., 1992, U. North Tex. Cert. secondary tchr., Tex., applied learning tchr. FWISD. Secondary English lang. arts tchr. Ft. Worth Ind. Sch. Dist., 1983—; presenter Keystone Writing and Reasoning Project, Ft. Worth, 1991-96; cons. Spencer Found., Chgo., 1994, Write to Change, Clemson (S.C.) U., 1995-96. Recipient Writing for the Cmty. award Bingham Trust/Clemson U., 1992, Tex. Excellence for Outstanding H.S. Tchr., U. Tex., 1993. Mem. ASCD, NEA, Ft. Worth Edn. Assn., Nat. Coun. Tchrs. English, Tex. State Tchr. Assn., United Educators Assn. Baptist. Home: 7704 Trimble Dr Fort Worth TX 76134-4647 Office: Applied Learning Acad 3201 South Hills Fort Worth TX 76109

BRAUER, GWENDOLYN GAIL, real estate broker; b. Middletown, Ohio; d. Robert J. and Mary M. (Kurry) Flynn; 1 child, John. CFP. Sales assoc. Better Homes Realty, Fairfax County, Va., 1976-81, Town & Country Properties, Fairfax County, 1981-84, ReMax Xecutex Real Estate, Fairfax County, 1984—. Mem. Nat. Assn. Realtors (cert. residential specialist, Million Dollar Sales Club 1980—), Employee Relocation Coun. (cert. relocation profl.), Internat. Bd. CFPs, No. Va. Assn. Realtors (Top Producers Club 1985—), Va. Assn. Realtors, Remax 100 Club (Hall of Fame 1994—). Home: 2627 Five Oaks Rd Vienna VA 22181 Office: ReMax Xecutex Real Estate 2911 Hunter Mill Rd Ste 101 Oakton VA 22124-1719

BRAUN, JANET K., biologist; b. Kittery, Maine, June 8, 1956; d. William Karl George and Ruth Elizabeth (Hundley) B. BS, Memphis State U., 1978, MS, 1982; PhD, U. Okla., 1992. Curatorial specialist Okla. Mus. Natural History, Norman, 1983-96, staff curator, 1996—. Contbg. author: Latin American Mammalogy, 1991, Biology of the Heteromyidae, 1993; editor: GIS Applications in Mammalogy, 1993. Gen. Conservation Survey grantee Inst. Mus. Svcs., 1989, 94, Rsch. grantee U.S. Constrn. Engring. Rsch. Lab., 1989, 90; Fulbright scholar, 1995-96. Mem. Am. Soc. Mammalogists, Southwestern Assn. Naturalists, Soc. Systematic Biology, Sigma Xi. Democrat. Office: Okla Mus Natural History 1335 Asp Ave Norman OK 73019-0606

BRAUN, MARY LUCILE DEKLE (LUCY BRAUN), therapist, consultant, counselor; b. Tampa, Fla.; d. Guthrie J. and Lucile (Culpepper) Dekle; children: John Ryan, Matthew Joseph, Jeffrey William, Douglas Edwin. AB, Brenau Coll.; MA, U. Cen. Fla.; EdD, U. Fla. Cert. ins. rehab. specialist; lic. mental health counselor; lic. marriage and family therapist; nationally cert. counselor. Coord. Orange County Child Abuse Prevention, Orlando, Fla., 1983-88; cons. Displaced Homemaker Program, Orlando, 1989—, DCS, Oviedo, Fla., 1990-92; adj. prof. U. Ctrl. Fla., Orlando, 1989—; clin. dir. Response Sexual Abuse Treatment Program, 1993-95; mem. adv. bd. Fla. Hosp. Women's Ctr., Orlando, 1989—; bd. dirs. Parent Resource Ctr., Orlando, Children With Attention Deficit Disorders, Orlando, 1989—. Author: Someone Heard, 1987, Humor Us Soup, 1989; contbg. author: Death from Child Abuse, 1986, Personality Types of Abusive Parents, 1993. Sustaining mem. Jr. League of Orlando and Winter Park, Fla., 1989—. Program recipient Community Svc. award Walt Disney World, 1987. Mem. ACA, Fla. Counseling Assn., Nat. Bd. Cir. Counselors, Phi Kappa Phi, Kappa Delta Pi, Chi Sigma Iota.

BRAUN, ROBERT FREDERICK, publishing executive; b. Saginaw, Mich., Jan. 7, 1927; s. Martin M. and Edna M. (Ahlgrim) B.; m. Doris M. Veitengruber, July 10, 1948; children: Marsha, Lynn, Judy, Martin. BA, Mich. State U, 1948. Gen. mgr. Braun Builders, Saginaw, 1948-62, Crosland Co., Winston Salem, N.C., 1963-69; investment strategist Integon Corp., Winston Salem, 1969-82; pub. Braun's Sys., Lewisville, N.C., 1969—. Worker, United We Stand, N.C., 1996. With U.S. Army, 1944-46. Lutheran. Home & Office: 127 Linder Dr Homosassa FL 34446

BRAWER, MARC HARRIS, lawyer; b. N.Y.C., June 11, 1946; s. Leonard and Diana R. Brawer; m. Susan L. Brunswick, Nov. 23, 1975; 3 children. BA, Queens Coll., 1967; JD, Bklyn. Law Sch., 1969. Bar: N.Y. 1970, Fla. 1978, U.S. Dist. Ct. (ea. and so. dists.) N.Y. 1974, U.S. Ct. Appeals (2nd cir.) 1974, U.S. Supreme Ct. 1975, U.S. Dist. Ct. (so. dist.) Fla. 1981, U.S. Ct. Appeals (5th cir.) 1980; cert. marital and family lawyer. Staff atty. Legal Aid Soc., N.Y.C., 1972-78; ptnr. Meyerson Resnicoff & Brawer, N.Y.C., 1978-83, Meyerson & Brawer, Tamarac, Fla., 1983-84; head firm Marc H. Brawer, Sunrise, Fla., 1984—; of counsel Resnicoff, Samanowitz & Brawer, Great Neck, N.Y., 1985-91; adj. prof. family law St. Thomas Law Sch., 1992; spkr. various orgns. and colls., 1980-96. Contbr. articles to profl. jours., 1970-84. Fellow Am. Acad. Matrimonial Lawyers; mem. Broward County Bar Assn., Queens County Bar Assn. (cert. of svc. 1982-83), Fla. Bar (sec. Family Law Commentator). Office: 7771 W Oakland Park Blvd Fort Lauderdale FL 33351-6749

BRAY, CAROLYN SCOTT, educational administrator; b. Childress, Tex., May 19, 1938; d. Alonzo Lee and Frankie Lucile (Wood) Scott; m. John Graham Bray, Jr., Aug. 24, 1957 (div. May 1980); children: Caron Lynn, Kimberly Anne, David William. BS, Baylor U., 1960; MEd, Hardin-Simmons U., 1981; PhD, U. North Tex., 1985. Registered med. technologist. Adj. prof. bus. comm. Hardin-Simmons U., 1981-84; dir. career placement, 1979-82, assoc. dean students, 1982-85; assoc. dir. career planning and placement U. North Tex., Denton, 1985-95, adj. prof. higher edn. adminstrn., mem. Mentor program; dir. career svcs. U. Tex. at Dallas, Richardson, 1995—. mem. U. North Tex. League for Profl. Women, 1985-95; mem. pers. com. First Bapt. Ch., 1992-95; bd. dirs. Irving Christian Counseling, Inc., 1993-95. Mem. Am. Assn. for Employment in Edn., (bd. dirs. 1989-94, treas. 1994-95), S.W. Assn. Colls. & Employers, Co-chmn. Tech. Com., (vice chair ops. 1992, 93, chair ann. conf. registration, 1991, 92), Tex. MBA Consortium (treas. 1993-95, co-chmn. 1995-96, Tex. Am. Assn.

for Employer of Edn., Staffing (v.p. 1986-87, pres. 1987-88), Nat. Assn. Colls. & Employers, North Cen. Tex. Assn. Sch. Pers. Adminstrs. and Univ. Placement Pers. (pres. 1987-88, sec. 1988-95), Denton C. of C. (pub. rels. com. 1988-95), Dallas Human Resources Mgmt. Assn., Leadership Denton (co-dir. curriculum 1988-89, chair membership selection com. 1990, 93, 94, steering com. 1990, 93, 94, Denton Cultural Arts Assn., Kappa Kappa Gamma (chpt. advisor, chmn. adv. bd. Zeta Sigma chpt. 1987-93). Republican. Avocations: skiing, tennis, golf, reading. Office: U Tex at Dallas Box 830688, LF 11 Richardson TX 75083-0688

BRAY, CHADWICK MCFALL, journalist; b. Mauldin, S.C., Mar. 10, 1972; s. Dillard Watson and Juanita Ann (Jones) B. BA in Journalism, U. S.C., 1994. Cotton assoc. W.E. Dunvant & Co.-Ea., Greenville, S.C., 1991-93; intern Congress Daily, Washington, S.C., 1993, Augusta (Ga.) Chronicle, 1993, AP, Columbia, S.C., 1996; assoc. UPS, Columbia, 1993; tchg. asst. U. S.C., Columbia, 1993-94; obituary clk. The State newspaper, Columbia, 1993-94; staff writer The Augusta Chronicle, 1994—. Assoc. advisor Exporer Post # 2029, 1996. Mem. Soc. Profl. Journalists. Methodist. Home: 1536-B Hamilton Dr Aiken SC 29803 Office: Augusta Chronicle 123 Pendleton St NW Aiken SC 29801

BRAYBROOKE, DAVID, philosopher, educator; b. Hackettstown, N.J., Oct. 18, 1924; s. Walter Leonard and Netta Rose (Foyle) B.; m. Alice Boyd Noble, Dec. 31, 1948 (div. 1982); children: Nicholas, Geoffrey, Elizabeth Page; m. Margaret Eva Odell, July 1, 1984 (div. 1994); m. Michiko Gomyo, Dec. 22, 1994. Student, Hobart Coll., 1941-43, New Sch. Social Research, 1942, Downing Coll., Cambridge, 1945, Columbia U., 1946; BA, Harvard U., 1948; MA, Cornell U., 1951, PhD, 1953; postgrad. (Am. Council Learned Socs. fellow), New Coll., Oxford, 1952-53; postgrad. (Rockefeller Found. grantee), Balliol Coll., Oxford, 1959-60. Instr. history and lit. Hobart and William Smith Colls., Geneva, N.Y., 1948-50; teaching fellow econs. Cornell U., Ithaca, N.Y., 1950-52; instr. philosophy U. Mich., Ann Arbor, 1953-54, Bowdoin Coll., Brunswick, Maine, 1954-56; asst. prof. philosophy Yale U., New Haven, 1956-63; asso. prof. philosophy and politics Dalhousie U., Halifax, N.S., Can., 1963-65; prof. Dalhousie U., 1965-88, McCulloch prof. philosophy and politics, 1988-90, prof. emeritus, 1990—; dean liberal arts Bridgeport (Conn.) Engring. Inst., 1961-63; Centennial Commn. chair liberal arts U. Tex., Austin, 1990—; vis. prof. philosophy U. Pitts., 1965, 66, U. Toronto, Can., 1966-67, Bowling Green State U. (Ohio), 1982, U. Waterloo, 1985; vis. prof. polit. sci. Hill Found., U. Minn., Mpls., 1971, U. Calif., Irvine, 1980, U. Chgo., 1984, Murphy Inst. Pol. Economy Tulane U., 1988; mem. Council Philos. Studies, 1974-79. Author: (with C.E. Lindblom) A Strategy of Decision: Policy Evaluation as a Social Process, 1963, Three Tests for Democracy: Personal Rights, Human Welfare, Collective Preference, 1968, Traffic Congestion Goes Through the Issue-Machine, 1974, Ethics in the World of Business, 1983, Philosophy of Social Science, 1987, Meeting Needs, 1987, (with B. Brown and P.K. Schotch) Logic on the Track of Social Change, 1995; contbr. articles to profl. jours.; editor: Philosophical Problems of the Social Sciences, 1965; monograph series Philosophy in Canada, 1973-78; Social Rules, 1996; cons. editor Philos. Studies, 1972-76; mem. editl. bd. Am. Polit. Sci. Rev., 1970-72; Ethics, 1979-89; Dialogue, 1974-78, 81-90. Mem. nat. acad. adv. panel Can. Council, Ottawa, 1968-71; chmn. Town Democratic Com., Guilford, Conn., 1961-62. Served with AUS, 1943-46. Guggenheim fellow, 1962-63; Social Scis. and Humanities Research Council Can. fellow, 1978-79, 85-86; vis. fellow Wolfson Coll., Cambridge, 1985-86, Cecil and Ida Green prof. U. B.C., 1986; John Milton Scott prof. Queen's U., 1988. Fellow Royal Soc. Can.; mem. Can. Philos. Assn. (pres. 1971-72), Can. Assn. Univ. Tchrs. (pres. 1975-76), Can. Polit. Sci. Assn., Am. Polit. Sci. Assn. (v.p. 1981-82), Am. Philos. Assn. (exec. com. Eastern div. 1976-79), Am. Soc. Polit. and Legal Philosophy, Friends of the Lake Dist. (life), Amnesty Internat., Phi Beta Kappa. Address: 1500 Scenic Dr Apt 300 Austin TX 78703-2050 also: 1 Prince St #510, Dartmouth, NS Canada B2Y 4L3

BRAZDA, FREDERICK WICKS, pathologist; b. New Orleans, Dec. 17, 1945; s. Fred George and Helen Josephine (Wicks) B.; student U. Chgo., 1962-64; B.S. cum laude, Tulane U., 1966; M.D., La. State U., 1970; m. Margaret Mary Hubbell, Sept. 8, 1973; children—Geoffrey Frederick, Gretchen Marie, Gregory Paul. Intern, then resident in pathology La. State U. div. Charity Hosp., New Orleans, 1970-75; pathologist Hotel Dieu Hosp., New Orleans, 1975-92, dir. Sch. Med. Tech., 1976-83; assoc. med. dir. Am. Bio-sci. Labs., New Orleans, 1983-84, Smith Kline Bio-sci. Labs., New Orleans, 1985-89; tech. dir. Smith Kline Beecham Clin. Labs., New Orleans, 1990-94; pathologist, tech. dir. Univ. Hosp. Lab., New Orleans, 1993-95, Med. Ctr. La. at New Orleans U. Campus Lab., 1995—; cons. St. Tammany Parish Hosp., Covington, La., Riverside Hosp., Franklinton, La, 1976-84; asst. prof. clin. pathology and med. tech. La. State U. Med. Center, New Orleans, 1976-93, prof. clin. pathology La. State U. Med. Ctr., New Orleans, 1994—. Diplomate Am. Bd. Pathology. Fellow Nat. Acad. Clin. Biochemistry; mem. AMA, Am. Soc. Clin. Pathologists, Coll. Am. Pathologists, Am. Assn. Clin. Chemistry, Nat. Acad. Clin. Biochemistry, So. Med. Assn., La. Med. Soc., La. Pathology Soc., Orleans Parish Med. Soc., Greater New Orleans Pathology Soc., Clin. Lab. Mgmt. Assn., La. Civil Service League, Friends of City Park, Friends of Zoo, Friends of Aquarium, Friends of Charity Hosp., New Orleans Mus. Art, Les Amis du Vin, Phi Beta Kappa, Alpha Omega Alpha, Phi Beta Pi. Democrat. Roman Catholic. Home: 422 Hector Ave Metairie LA 70005-4412 Office: 2025 Gravier St Ste 200 New Orleans LA 70112-2256

BRAZIEL, SUSAN LANSDOWN, mental health/rehabilitation nurse, administrator; b. Ringgold, La., Sept. 18, 1950; d. W.N. and Norma Jean (Halter) Lansdown; children: Samuel Eliot III, Jordan Alexis. Diploma with honors, St. Dominic's-Jackson Meml. Sch. Nursing, Jackson, Miss., 1971. Evening supr. Phil Smalley Children's Ctr. Cen. State-Griffin Meml. Hosp., Norman, Okla., 1972-74; coord. crisis intervention inpatient svcs. Heart of Tex. Region Mental Helath/Mental Retardation Ctr., Waco, 1975-79; dir. nursing Waco Ctr. for Youth, 1979-88; dir. child psychiat. unit Presbyn. Hosp. Dallas, 1988-90, coord. child/adolescent psychiatric svcs., 1990-91, coord. chronic pain rehab. program, 1991-93; dir. clin. svcs. Spring Creek Rehab. Hosp., Dallas, 1993-94; coord. comprehensive pain rehab., supr. outpatient rehab. Med. City Dallas Hosp., 1994—. Mem. Tex. Nurses Assn., ANA.

BRAZIER, MARY MARGARET, psychology educator, researcher; b. New Orleans, Feb. 4, 1956; d. Robert Whiting and Margaret Long (Mc Waters) B. BA, Loyola U., New Orleans, 1977; MS, Tulane U., 1985, PhD, 1986. Assoc. prof. Loyola U., 1986—. NSF grantee, 1987. Mem. APA, Am. Psychol. Soc., Southeastern Psychol. Assn., Southwestern Psychol. Assn. (coun. 1988—), So. Soc. Philosophy and Psychology (exec. coun. 1989-92). Roman Catholic. Office: Loyola U Dept Psychology 6363 Saint Charles Ave New Orleans LA 70118-6143

BRDLIK, CAROLA EMILIE, accountant; b. Wuerzburg, Germany, Mar. 11, 1930; came to U.S., 1952; d. Ludwig Leonard and Hildegard Maria (Leipold) Baumeister; m. Joseph A. Brdlik; children: Margaret Louise, Charles Joseph. BA, Oberrealschule Bamberg, Fed. Republic Germany, 1948; MA, Bavarian Interpreter Coll., Fed. Republic Germany, 1949; Cert., Internat. Accts. Soc., Chgo., 1955. Interpreter, exec. sec. NCWC Amberg, Schweinfurt, Ludwigsburg and Munich, Fed. Republic Germany, 1949-52; exec. sec. Red Ball Van Lines, Jamaica, N.Y., 1952; interpreter Griffin Rutgers Inc., N.Y.C., 1952-53; office mgr., exec. sec. Rehab. Ctr. Summit Co., Inc., Akron, 1953-56; pvt. practice acctg. Cuyahoga Falls, Ohio, 1956-61, Uniontown, Ohio, 1961-81; sec., treas. Omaca, Inc., Uniontown and Deerfield Beach (Fla.), 1981-86; pres. Omaca, Inc., Uniontown and Jupiter, 1986—; sec.-treas. Shipe Landscaping, Inc., Greensburg, Ohio, 1968-92, Sattler Machine Products, Copley, Ohio, 1981-88; asst. treas. Mar-Lynn Lake Park, Inc., Streetsboro, Ohio, 1969—. Bd. dirs., trustee Czechoslovak Refugees, Cleve. and Cin., 1968. Mem. Nat. Soc. Tax Profls. (cert. accredited taxation and accountancy), Nat. Soc. Pub. Accts., Nat. Assn. Tax Preparer's, Nat. Assn. Enrolled Agts., Fla. Soc. Enrolled Agts., Fla. Soc. Acctg. and Tax Profls. Roman Catholic.

BREAUNE, JOSEPH GEORGE, retired lawyer, judge; b. El Paso, Aug. 13, 1915; s. Horace Malcolm abd Carrie Anna (Andrews) B.; m. Ruth Virginia Williams, June 23, 1939; children: Glenda Gayle King, Roberta Lea Crum. AB in Econs. and Govt., Okla. U., 1940, LLB, 1942. Bar: Okla. 1944. Pvt. practice Miami, Okla., 1946-50, 52-61, 1967-87; dist. judge State of Okla., Miami, 1961-67, assoc. dist. judge, 1987-92; mem. exec. com. teen ct., Ottawa County, Okla., 1993—. Elder, deacon, Sunday sch. tchr. Presbyn. Ch., Miami, 1947-50, 53-68; chmn. Ottawa County ARC, Miami, 1960-65; chmn. advancement com. Boy Scouts Am., Bartlesville, Okla., 1958-68; organizer, chmn. Ottawa County Rural Water Dist. #2, Miami, 1965-85; leader 4-H Club, Miami, 1960—; organizer, chmn. Friendship House and Sheltered Workshop, Miami, 1955-65. Major U.S. Army, 1943-44, 50-52. Mem. Okla. Bar Assn., Ottawa County Bar Assn. (pres. 1948-49), Masons (worshipful master), Shriners, Lions, York Rite, Am. Legion, VFW. Democrat. Home: RR 3 Box 150 Miami OK 74354-9541

BREAUX, DAVID LEE, retired military officer; b. Breaux Bridge, La., Dec. 10, 1954; s. Louis N. and Willa Mae (Leblanc) B.; m. Kathy Frith, May 27, 1972; 1 child, Amber Nichol. Grad., Officer Candidate Sch., 1975, Army Inst. of Profl. Devel., Ft. Eusts, Va., 1985, U.S. Army Command & Staff Coll., Ft. Leavenworth, Kans., 1988, Liberty U., Lynchburg, Va., 1989. Officer 256th Inf. Brigade (MECH), Lafayette, La., 1975-96; office mgr. S.E. Water Dist. of Vermilion Parish, 1996—. Treas. Abbeville Bumper Zone Vol. Fire Dept., 1987—. Mem. N.G. Assn. of U.S., N.G. of La., Assn. of the U.S. Army, Nat. Mem. Smithsonian Assocs. Democrat. Roman Catholic. Home: 13815 Lynnedale Rd Abbeville LA 70510-8516

BREAUX, JOHN B., senator, former congressman; b. Crowley, La., Mar. 1, 1944; s. Ezra H., Jr. and Katherine (Berlinger) B.; m. Lois Gail Daigle, Aug. 1, 1964; children: John B., William Lloyd, Elizabeth Andre, Julia Agnes. B.A. in Polit. Sci, U. Southwestern La., 1964; J.D., La. State U., 1967. Bar: La. 1967. Ptnr. Brown, McKernan, Ingram & Breaux, 1967-68; legis. asst. to Congressman Edwin W. Edwards, 1968-69, dist. asst., 1969-72; mem. 92d-99th Congresses from 7th Dist. La., 1972-86; U.S. Senator from La. Washington, 1987—; mem. Fin. com., 1990—; mem. Commerce com., Spl. Com. on Aging; chmn. Nat. Water Alliance, 1987-88, Nat. Dem. Senatorial Campaign Com., 1989-90, Dem. Leadership Coun., 1991-93. Recipient Am. Legion award; Moot Ct. finalist La. State U., 1966; Neptune award Am. Oceanic Orgn., 1980. Mem. La. Bar Assn., Crowley Jr. C. of C., La. Jr. C. of C., Pi Lambda Beta, Phi Alpha Delta, Lambda Chi Alpha. Office: US Senate 516 Hart Senate Bldg Washington DC 20510-1803

BREAUX, PAUL JOSEPH, lawyer, pharmacist; b. Franklin, La., Mar. 11, 1942; s. Sidney J. and Irene (Bodin) B.; m. Marilyn Anne Jones, Aug. 21, 1965; children: Jason E., James P. BS in Pharmacy, Northeast La. U., 1965; JD, La, State U., 1972. Bar: La. 1972, U.S. Supreme Ct. 1975. Pharmacist Belanger's Pharmacy, Morgan City, La., 1965-66, Clinic Pharmacy, Morgan City, La., 1966-69; pvt. practice of law Lafayette, La., 1972-73, 93—; assoc. Allen, Gooch, Bourgeois, Breaux, Robison, Theunissen Attys., Lafayette, 1973-75; ptnr. Allen, Gooch, Bourgeois, Breaux, Robison & Theunissen, Lafayette, 1975-93; sec., bd. dirs. Bank of Lafayette. Bd. dirs. Lafayette Community Health Care Clinic, 1992—; mem. Gov.'s Universal Health Care Law Reform Commn., 1992—; active Boy Scouts Am., 1984-92. Mem. ABA, La. Bar Assn., Lafayette Parish Bar Assn., La. Bankers Assn. (mem. bank counsel com. 1983-85, 88-90, La. banking code legislation revision com. 1983), Am. Land Title Assn., Am. Pharm. Assn., La. Pharmacists Assn. (bd. dirs. 1991—, Pharmacist of Yr. award 1992), Nat. Assn. Retail Druggists, Am. Soc. Law and Medicine, Am. Soc. Pharmacy Law, Nat. Health Lawyers Assn., Acad. Hosp. Attys. of Am. Hosp. Assn., Soc. Hosp. Attys. of La. Hosp. Assn., Lafayette C. of C., Kappa Psi, Phi Eta Sigma. Republican. Roman Catholic. Office: 600 Jefferson St Ste 503 Lafayette LA 70501-6964

BRECHT, BLAINE RICHARD, manufacturing company executive; b. Plainfield, N.J., Feb. 6, 1958; s. Joseph Thomas and Gloria Maria (Calabrese) B. BSBA, The Citadel, 1980; cert., The Quality Coll., Orlando, Fla., 1987. Cert. lead assessor Registrar Accreditation Bd. Mgmt. trainee Milliken & Co., Bostic, N.C., 1980-81; texturing shift mgr. Milliken & Co., Saluda, S.C., 1981-83, knit, dye and packing shift mgr., 1983-84, quality control supr., 1984-85; asst. quality control mgr. Collins & Aikman, Graham, N.C., 1985-87, div. mgr. quality services, 1987; div. mgr. planning and customer service Burlington Industries, Madison, N.C., 1987-88, engr. process improvement, tech. service, 1988-89; dir. quality assurance Dixie Yarns, Inc., Threads USA div., Gastonia, N.C., 1989-94; quality assurance mgr. U.S. Label, Greensboro, N.C., 1994—; team mem. Small Bus. Adminstrn., 1979-80. Sunday sch. tchr. Glen Hope Bapt. Ch., Burlington, N.C., 1985-87, dir. brotherhood, 1987—, mem. bd. deacons, 1996—. Named one of Outstanding Young Men in Am., 1984. Mem. Am. Soc. Quality Control (sr.; cert. quality auditor). Republican. Home: 2604 Regents Park Ln Greensboro NC 27455-2237

BRECKE, BARRY JOHN, weed scientist, researcher, educator; b. Milw., Jan. 16, 1947; s. Melvin Albert and Marie Catherine (Goerg) B.; m. Gayle Linda Naggatz, June 14, 1969; children: Darren John, Suzanne Marie. PhD, Cornell U., 1976. Asst. prof. U. Fla., Gainesville, 1976-81, assoc. prof., 1981—. Author: (chpt) Model Crop Systems: Sorghum, Napiergrass, 1988, Weed Management in Peanuts, 1990, Management of Weeds, 1995; assoc. editor Weed Tech., 1993-96; contbr. articles, referee to Weed Tech., Peanut Sci., Weed Sci., 1980—. With U.S. Army, 1970-72. Grantee USDA, 1987-89, Cotton Inc., 1992-96, Ctr. for Integrated Pest Mgmt., 1995-96. Mem. Am. Soc. Agronomy, So. Weed Sci. Soc., Am. Peanut Rsch. and Edn. Soc., Weed Sci. Soc. Am., Internat. Weed Sci. Soc., Fla. Weed Sci. Soc. (pres. 1979). Roman Catholic. Office: West Fla Rsch and Edn Ctr 4253 Experiment Dr Hwy 182 Jay FL 32565-9524

BRECKINRIDGE, SCOTT DUDLEY, JR., retired law educator; b. Washington, Apr. 17, 1917; s. Scott Dudley and Gertrude Ashby (Bayne) B.; m. Helen Virden Babbitt, Aug. 29, 1942. BA, U. Ky., 1940, LLB, 1941. Atty. Breckinridge & Breckinridge, Lexington, Ky., 1947-53; employee Ctrl. Intelligence Agy., Washington, 1953-79, deputy inspector gen., 1972-79; lectr. U. Ky., Lexington, 1980-86. Co-author: Sword Play, 1941; author: CIA and U.S. Intelligence System, 1986, CIA and The Cold War, 1993. Asst. sec. gen. Soc. Cin., Washington, 1971-76; exec. com. U. Ky. Libr. Assoc., Lexington, 1985—, Ky. Hist. Soc., Frankfort, Ky., 1988-92; bd. dirs. The Filson Club, Louisville, Ky., 1991-93. Recipient Disting. Intellegence medal Ctrl. Intellegence Agy., Washington, 1977, 79; Disting. Svc. award Ky. Hist. Soc., 1990. Mem. Ky. Bar Assn., Del. State Soc. of Cin., U.S. Fencing Assn. (v.p. 1949-52). Home: 395 Redding Rd Apt 13 Lexington KY 40517-2369

BREDEHOFT, ELAINE CHARLSON, lawyer; b. Fergus Falls, Minn., Nov. 22, 1958; d. Curtis Lyle and Marilyn Anne (Nesbitt) Charlson; m. John Michael Bredehoft, Aug. 6, 1983; children: Alexandra Charlson, Michelle Charlson. BA, U. Ariz., 1981; JD, Cath. U. Am., 1984. Bar: Va. 1984, U.S. Ct. Appeals (4th cir.) 1984, U.S. Bankruptcy Ct. (ea. dist.) Va. 1987, D.C. 1994, U.S. Ct. Appeals (D.C. cir.) 1994. Assoc. Walton and Adams, McLean, Va., 1984-88, ptnr., 1988-91; ptnr. Charlson & Bredehoft, P.C., Reston, Va., 1991—; spkr. Fairfax Bar Assn. CLE, 1992—, VB Assn. CLE, 1993—, 12th Ann. Multistate Labor and Employment Law Seminar, 1994, Va. CLE Ann. Employment Law Update, 1993-96, Va. Women's Trial Lawyers Assn. Ann. Conf., 1994, Va. Bar Assn. Labor and Employment Conf., 1994-96, Va. Trial Lawyers Assn., 1995, Va. Law Found., 1995. Bd. dirs. Va. Commn. on Women and Minorities in the Legal System, 1987-90, sec., 1988-90. Mem. Va. Bar Assn. (exec. com. young lawyers sect., litigation com., nominating com., chmn. model jud. com.), Va. Trial Lawyers Assn. (vice chmn. 1997 ann. conv., com. on long range planning 1996—), Fairfax Bar Assn., Minn. State Soc., George Mason Inns of Ct. (master 1996—). Republican. Office: Charlson & Bredehoft PC 11260 Roger Bacon Dr Ste 201 Reston VA 20190-5203

BREDEHOFT, JOHN MICHAEL, lawyer; b. N.Y.C., Feb. 22, 1958; s. John William and Viola (Struhar) B.; m. Elaine Charlson, Aug. 6, 1983; children: Alexandra Charlson, Michelle Charlson. AB magna cum laude, Harvard Coll., 1980, JD cum laude, 1983. Bar: D.C. 1983, U.S. Dist. Ct. D.C. 1985, U.S. Ct. Appeals (D.C. cir.) 1985, U.S. Ct. Appeals (1st cir.) 1986, U.S. Supreme Ct. 1987, U.S. Ct. Appeals (9th cir.) 1988, U.S. Ct. Appeals (3d and 5th cir.) 1989, U.S. Tax Ct. 1989, U.S. Ct. Appeals (4th Cir.) 1990, U.S. Dist. Ct. Mont. 1991, Va. 1992, U.S. Dist. Ct. (ea. dist.) Va. 1992. Assoc. Cleary, Gottlieb, Steen & Hamilton, Washington, 1983-91; prin. Charlson & Bredehoft, Fairfax, Va., 1991—. Bd. dirs. Falls Brook Assn., Herndon, Va., 1988-91; nat. class 1983 reunion gift chmn. Harvard Law Sch. Fund, Cambridge, 1988, class agt., 1994—; mem. Harvard Debate Centennial Com., 1992. Mem. ABA, Va. Bar Assn., Fairfax Bar Assn., Va. Trial Lawyers Assn., Met. Washington Employment Lawyers' Assn. (Lawyer of Yr. 1996). Office: 11260 Roger Bacon Dr Ste 201 Reston VA 20190-5203

BREDESEN, PHILIP NORMAN, mayor; b. Oceanport, N.J., Nov. 21, 1943; s. Philip Norman and Norma (Walborn) B.; m. Andrea Conte, Nov. 22, 1974; 1 child, Benjamin. AB in Physics, Harvard U., 1967. Computer programmer Itek Corp., Lexington, Mass., 1967-70; dir. systems devel. Searle Medidata, Lexington, 1970-73; div. mgr. Searle Medidata, London, 1973-75; dir. spl. project Hosp. Affiliates Internat., Nashville, 1975-78; v.p. internat. div. INA Health Care Group, Nashville, 1978-80; chmn. and chief exec. officer HealthAmerica Corp., Nashville, 1980-86; chmn., co-founder Coventry Corp., Nashville, 1986-90; chmn. Clin. Pharms., Nashville, 1986-93; mayor Met. Nashville and Davidson County, 1991—. Bd. dirs. Nashville Symphony, 1985-91, Univ. Sch. Nashville, 1986-95, United Cerebral Palsy, 1988-92, United Way of Middle Tenn., 1984—, Tenn. State U. Found.; founder Nashville's Table, 1989, bd. dirs., 1989-91; candidate for mayor Nashville, 1987, 91, Dem. nominee for gov., 1994. Democrat. Presbyterian. Home: 1724 Chickering Rd Nashville TN 37215-4908 Office: Office of the Mayor Public Sq 107 Metro Courthouse Nashville TN 37201

BREDFELDT, JOHN CREIGHTON, economist, financial analyst, retired air force officer; b. Great Bend, Kans., Oct. 31, 1947; s. Willis John and Geraldine Elizabeth (Creighton) B.; m. Barbara Elaine Gutow, June 6, 1984; children: Jason Caulter, Bryan Thomas. BBA, Wichita State U., 1969, MA in Econs., 1971; PhD in Pub. Adminstrn. La Salle U., 1995; grad., Air Command and Staff Coll., 1984, Nat. Def. U., 1987. Dir. Brennan Halls, Wichita State U., 1969-71; commd. 2d lt. U.S. Air Force, 1971, advanced through grades to lt. col. 1987, ret., 1993; budget/cost ananlyst Aero. System div., Dayton, Ohio, 1971-76; insp. Air Force IG, Andrews AFB, Md., 1976-79; chief economist Dir. Programs AF/PRP, Pentagon, Va., 1979-83; chief cost analyst div. U.S. Air Force Europe, 1985-87; dep. dir. program control, engine program office, Dayton, 1987-89; dir. program control spl. ops. forces, 1989-93; prin. econs./fin. analyst Modern Techs. Corp. Warner Robins, Ga., 1993—; instr. econs. Wichita State U., 1969-71; bus. prof. Bowie State Coll., 1980-83; econs. instr. European divsn. U. Md., Germany, 1985-87, Sinclair C.C., Dayton, 1988-93, Macon (Ga.) Coll., 1994—; adj. prof. Mercer U., 1996—. Contbr. articles to profl. jours. Rep., Sunday sch. tchr. Ramstein Protestant Parish Council Germany, 1984-86; asst. scout master Ramstein council Boy Scouts Am., 1984-87; v.p. St. Timothy Lutheran Ch., Dayton, 1989-91. Mem. Assn. Govt. Accts., Soc. Cost Estimating and Analysis, Am. Soc. Mil. Comptrollers. Lutheran. Avocations: micro-economics, golfing, tennis, racquetball, reading.

BREE, GERMAINE, French literature educator; b. France, Oct. 2, 1907; came to U.S., 1926, naturalized, 1952; d. Walter and Lois Marguerite (Andrault) B. Licence, U. Paris, 1930, Diplôme d'Etudes Supérieures, 1931, Agregation, 1932; postgrad., Bryn Mawr Coll., 1931-32; D.Litt., Smith Coll., 1960, Mt. Holyoke Coll., 1963, Allegheny Coll., 1963, Duke U., 1964, Colby Coll., 1964, Oberlin Coll., 1966, Dickinson U., 1968, Rutgers U., 1969, Wake Forest U., 1970, Brown U., 1971, U. Mass., 1976, Kalamazoo Coll., 1977, Washington U., 1978, U. of the South, 1979, Boston Coll., 1979, U. Wis.-Madison, 1981; L.H.D., Wilson Coll., 1960; LL.D., Middlebury Coll., 1965, U. Mich., 1971, Davis-Elkins Coll., 1972, U. Wis. at Milw., 1973, N.Y. U., 1975; LL.D. (all hon.). Tchr. Algeria, 1932-36; from lectr. to prof. Bryn Mawr Coll., 1936-53; faculty French summer sch. Middlebury Coll., 1937, 40, 41, 46; chmn. dept. French Washington Sq. Coll., 1953-60; head Romance lang. dept., grad. sch. arts and sci. N.Y. U., 1954-60, head dept. Romance langs. and Russian, 1958-60; Vilas prof. U. Wis. Inst. for Research in Humanities, Madison, 1960-73; Kenan prof. of Humanities Wake Forest U., Winston-Salem, N.C., 1973-84, Kenan prof. of Humanities emerita, 1984—; Disting. vis. prof. Ohio State U., 1981; Whitney Oates vis. prof. Princeton U., 1983; Bernhardt vis. prof. Williams Coll., fall 1983; mem. panel translation Nat. Endowment Humanities, 1978-79; cons. lang. depts. Conn. Coll., 1979; Mem. adv. bd. Am. Council Learned Socs. Author: Marcel Proust, 1952, André Gide, 1953, Camus, 1959, rev. edit., 1961, Twentieth Century French Literature: An Anthology of Prose and Poetry, 1961, (with Margaret Guiton) An Age of Fiction, (with Micheline Dufau) Voix d'aujourd'hui, 1964, The World of Marcel Proust, 1966, (with Alex Kroff) Twentieth Century French Drama, 1969, (with G. Bernauer) Defeat and Beyond, An Anthology of French Wartime Writing (1940-1945), 1970, Camus and Sartre: Crisis and Commitment, 1972, Women Writers in France, 1973, Littérature Française, Vol. 16, XX Siecle c.2, 1920-1970, 1978, others; editor series of French poets in transl. Wake Forest U. Press, 1989, L'univers fabuleux de Jean-Marie Le Clézio, 1990; contbr. (with G. Bernauer) articles to profl. publs.; book revs. to New Republic. Served with French Army, 1943-45. Decorated Bronze Star; chevalier Legion of Honor (France); commandeur dans l'Ordre des Palmes Académiques. Mem. MLA (pres. 1975), AAUP, PEN, Am. Assn. Tchrs. French, Société des Professeurs Français, Am. Philos. Soc., Alliance Française, Nat. Council Humanities, Am. Acad. Arts and Sci.

BREEDEN, BETTY LONETA, secondary school educator; b. Subiaco, Ark., May 29, 1944; d. William Homer and Lillie Mae (Keech) Scrudder; m. Leonard Jerry Breeden, July 11, 1973; 1 child, Sherri Dawn. BS, Ark. Tech. U., 1967; postgrad., Henderson State U., Arkadelphia, Ark., 1969, U. Ark., 1978, 94, U. Ctrl. Ark. Cert. tchr. secondary math., biology, physics, gen. sci., secondary edn., Ark. Tchr. sci. and math. Fourche Valley H.S., Briggsville, Ark., 1966-70, County Line H.S., Branch, Ark., 1970-76, Van Buren (Ark.) Sch. Sys., 1976—; participant MSM Summer Inst., 1996. Choir mem., tchr., vacation Bible sch. dir. Calvary Missionary Bapt. Ch., Van Buren, 1979—. NSF grantee, 1969; Ark. Sch. for Math. and Sci. AC2E Summer Inst. participant, 1994. Mem. Nat. Coun. Tchrs. Math., Ark. Sch. for Math and Sci. Office: Coleman Jr High Sch 821 E Pointer Trl Van Buren AR 72956-2309

BREEDEN, DAVID MARION, English language educator, writer; b. Granite City, Ill., Mar. 23, 1958; s. Marion W. and Mary Elizabeth (Woolard) B.; m. Joan M. Bishop, Aug. 15, 1983; children: Audrey, Jesse, Patrick. AA, Southeastern Ill. Coll., 1978; BA, So. Ill. U., 1982; MFA, U. Iowa, 1985; PhD, U. So. Miss., 1988. Teaching asst. So. Ill. U., 1981-83; substitute tchr. Iowa City Pub. Schs., 1983-85; teaching asst. U. So. Miss., 1985-88; prof. Ark. State U., Jonesboro, 1988-91, Schreiner Coll., Kerrville, Tex., 1991—. Author: Picnics, 1983, Hey, Schleimann, 1989, Doubled-Headed End Wrench, 1991, Building A Boat, 1995, The Guiltless Traveler, 1996; editor: Context South, 1988—; contbr. articles and revs. to profl. jours. and newspapers; author weekly newspaper column. Pres. Unitarian Universalist Fellowship, 1990-91; humanities advisor N.E. Ark. Poetry Found.; bd. dirs. Jonesboro Humanities Coun.; humanities advisor Salons of Kerrville. Mem. Coord. Coun. Lit. Presses, Tex. Assn. Creative Writing Tchrs., MLA, PEN Ctr. West, Kiwanis. Democrat. Home: PO Box 4504 Kerrville TX 78028

BREEDING, J. ERNEST, JR., physicist, travel consultant, photographer; b. Peoria, Ill., Mar. 17, 1938; s. J. Ernest Breeding, Sr. and Ruth Irene (Saddoris) Hoffman; m. Barbara Ellen Walker, June 6, 1970 (div. 1989); 1 child, Della Grace; m. Rebecca Darden, May 19, 1990; stepchildren: David Benefield, Michael Benefield. Student, Simpson Coll., 1956-59; BA, Drake U., 1960; postgrad., U. Tenn., 1960-61; PhD, Colombia U., 1972. Grad. tchg. asst. U. Tenn., Knoxville, 1960-61; physicist Naval Coastal Systems Ctr., Panama City, Fla., 1962-78; grad. rsch. asst. Lamont-Doherty Earth Observatory of Colombia U., Palisades, N.Y., 1965-70; assoc. prof. oceanography and ocean engring. Fla. Inst. Tech., Melbourne, 1979-87; oceanographer, mathematician Naval Oceanographic Office, Stennis Space Ctr., Miss., 1988; rsch. physicist Naval Rsch. Lab., Stennis Space Ctr., 1988—; owner World Class Travel & Tours, 1994—; vis. assoc. prof. Fla. State U., Tallahassee, 1977-79; mem. adv. bd. Summit Travel Group, Inc., Winston-Salem, N.C., 1996—. Contbr. articles to profl. jours. Bd. trustees, pres. Am. Homesteading Found., Melbourne Village, Fla., 1986-88. Mem. Am. Geophys. Union, Soc. Exploration Geophysicists, Acoustical Soc. Am., Am. Meterol. Soc., Am. Assn. Physics Tchrs., AAAS, Sigma Xi, Sigma Pi Sigma. Republican. Home and Office: 115 Blackbeard Dr Slidell LA 70461-2721 Office: Naval Rsch Lab Stennis Space Center MS 39529-5004 Office: World Class Travel and Tours 115 Blackbeard Dr Slidell LA 70461

BREEDLOVE, MICHAEL ALAN, archivist; b. Selma, Ala., Jan. 7, 1952; s. John Will and Mary Watson (Griffith) B.; m. E. Brooks Taylor, Aug. 29, 1992. BA in History, U. Ala., 1979, MA in History, 1981; PhD in U.S. History, Am. Univ., Washington, 1990. Archivist, mus. curator Ala. Power Co., 1984-85; archivist Ala. Dept. Archives and History, Montgomery, 1985-88, archivist, head spl. collections, 1988-91; archivist, head govt. records Ala. Dept. Archives and History, 1991—; supr. Records Ctr. State Ala. Microform Storage Preservation Vault, 1996—; adj. prof. history U. Ala., Birmingham, 1984-85, Auburn U., Montgomery, 1991, Troy State U., Montgomery, 1992, Ala. State U., 1992—; mem. adv. coun. Biog. Guide to Ala. Lit., 1991-95; presenter in field. Editor Jour. of Hist. Studies, 1982-83; contbr. articles to profl. jours. Statewide judge Citizen Bee Competition, Montgomery, 1993. Recipient Grad. assistantship U. Ala., Birmingham, 1979-80, DAR scholarship, 1980, Grad. teaching assistantship Am. Univ., 1981-82, 82-83, Hurst fellowship Am. Univ., 1981-82, 82-83. Mem. Soc. Am. Archivists (participated as mem. steering com. govt. records sect., 1994—, vice chair, 1995-96, chair 1996-97), Ala. Hist. Assn. (treas. 1992-, local hist. soc. award com. 1990-91), So. Hist. Assn. (membership com. 1989-90), Soc. Ala. Archivists (chmn. local arrangements 1987, treas. 1987-92), Ala. Assn. Historians, West Elmore County Hist. Soc., Montgomery County Hist. Soc. Episcopalian. Office: Ala Dept Archives & History 624 Washington Ave Montgomery AL 36130-0024

BREEN, DAVID HART, lawyer; b. Ottawa, Ont., Can., Mar. 27, 1960; came to U.S., Aug. 19, 1978; naturalized, 1993; s. Harold John and Margaret Rae (Hart) B.; m. Pamela Annette Mitchell, Sept. 17, 1988; 1 child, Matthew Mitchell. BA cum laude, U. S.C., 1982, JD, 1986. Bar: S.C., U.S. Dist. Ct. S.C., U.S. Ct. Appeals (4th cir.), U.S. Bankruptcy Ct. S.C. 1987. Law clk. to Hon. Don S. Rushing U.S. Cir. Ct. (6th cir.), S.C., 1986-87; sr. ptnr. David H. Breen, P.A., Myrtle Beach, 1988—; C.J.A. panel atty. U.S. Dist. Ct. S.C., 1991—. Campaign asst. Joe Clark for Prime Minister, Ottawa, 1975-76. Mem. ABA, S.C. Trial Lawyers Assn., Assn. Trial Lawyers Am., S.C. Bar Assn., Horry County Bar Assn., Oshawa Gun Club, Phi Delta Phi. Methodist. Home: Prestwick Country Club 2187 N Berwick Dr Myrtle Beach SC 29575-5815 Office: 4603 Oleander Dr Ste 5 Myrtle Beach SC 29577-5738

BRENDER, JEAN DIANE, epidemiologist, nurse; b. Bellingham, Wash., Nov. 23, 1951; d. Otto and Jennie Wilma Tolsma; m. Dennis Ray Brender, Aug. 30, 1975; 1 child, Valerie. BSN summa cum laude, Whitworth Coll., 1974; M of Nursing, U. Wash., 1979, PhD of Epidemiology, 1983. RN, Tex. Staff nurse, infection control Sacred Heart Med. Ctr., Spokane, Wash., 1974-80; instr. nursing Intercollegiate Ctr. for Nursing Edn., Spokane, 1979-80, asst. prof. nursing, 1982-84; teaching asst. epidemiology U. Wash., Seattle, 1981-82; rsch. health scientist Audie L. Murphy Vets. Hosp., San Antonio, 1984-85; staff epidemiologist bur. epidemiology Tex. Dept. Health, Austin, 1986-87, acting program dir. environ. epidemiology program, 1987, dir. environ. epidemiology program, 1987-93, dir. noncommunicable disease epidemiology and toxicology, 1993—, also state environ. epidemiologist; bd. dirs. Agriculture Resources Protection Authority; state environ. epidemiologist; adj. instr. allied health scis. and health adminstrn. S.W. Tex. State U., 1986-90; adj. asst. prof. epidemiology U. Tex. Health Sci. Ctr.-Houston Sch. Pub. Health, 1985-93, adj. assoc. prof., 1993—. Contbr. articles to profl. jours. Tchr., mem. adult choir St. Martin's Luth. Ch., Austin, 1991—. Recipient H.E.A.L.T.H. award, 1994; grantee in field. Mem. Soc. Epidemiologic Rsch., Coun. State and Territorial Epidemiologists, Exec. Women in Tex. Govt. Home: 6902 Alder Cv Austin TX 78750-8161 Office: Tex Dept Health 1100 W 49th St Austin TX 78756-3101

BRENDSEL, LELAND C., federal mortgage company executive; b. Sioux Falls, S.D.; married. D in Fin., Northwestern U. Prof. U. Utah; economist Farm Credit Banks, Fed. Home Loan Bank, Des Moines; exec. v.p., CFO Fed. Home Loan Mortgage Corp., McLean, Va., 1982, pres., 1990, chmn., CEO, 1990—. Office: Fed Home Loan Mortgage Corp 8200 Jones Branch Dr Mc Lean VA 22102-3107*

BRENNAN, EILEEN HUGHES, nurse; b. Atlanta, Sept. 26, 1951; m. David Lee Altizer, May 11, 1974 (div. Dec. 1978); m. Scott Curtis Brennan, Feb. 6, 1982; 1 child, Bonnie Joy. Student, North Ga. Coll., 1969-70; diploma, Ga. Bapt. Sch. Nursing, 1973; student, Tift Coll., 1970-73, Ga. State U., 1980-85, SUNY, Albany, 1986-91, Brenau Univ., 1994—. RN, Ga.; CNOR. Orthopedic charge nurse Grady Meml. Hosp., Atlanta, 1974; operating room nurse DePaul Hosp., Norfolk, Va., 1974-76; nurse orthopedics Cabell Huntington (W.Va.) Hosp., 1976; surg. charge nurse VA Hosp., Huntington, 1976-77; nurse VA Hosp., Decatur, Ga., 1978-82, team leader oper room, 1979—, mem. operating room open heart team, 1986-88, 89-91; orthopedic nurse specialist Peachtree Orthopedic Clinic, Atlanta, 1982; operating room charge nurse Drs. Meml. Hosp., Atlanta, 1982-85, chmn. operating room policy and procedures, 1982-84, 94—; vascular rsch. coord. # 141 Co-operative Study-a-Multi-Ctr. VA Study, Decatur, Ga., 1988-89, # 362, 1991-93; acting temporary chair Nursing Svc. Narcotic Inventory Com., 1994-95, team leader genitourological svc., 1995—. Developed multi-media slide presentation for the Perioperative Patient as well as a pamphlet for preop teaching purposes, 1979, rev., 1985; editor: urology pamphlet, 1986, Open Heart Instrumentation, 1987; wrote and presented slide teaching program for coop. study (a multi-ctr. Dept. VA study), 1993. Vol. ARC, Atlanta, 1970-, Am. Heart Assn., Atlanta, 1987-88, Atlanta Lung As., 1985-88, Am. Lung Assn., Atlanta, 1988-91, Outreach Com., 1995—, North Fulton County Cmty. Charities, including Thanksgiving lunch, Brown Bag Cmty. Food Bank, Clothes Closet, Homestretch, Battered Women's Shelter, Adopt a Christmas Family, 1991—, co-chmn. of Flea Mkt. horse show for charities, 1995—. Recipient Cert., United Fund Campaign, Atlanta, 1981, Spl. Incentive award VA Med. Ctr., Decatur, Ga., 1981, Performance award Nurse Profl. Standards Bd., Decatur, 1987, Achievement award, 1987. Mem. Assn. Operating Room Nurses (co-chmn. Project Alpha 1986-87, spl. com. ethics, HIV task force). Episcopalian. Home: 9250 Brumbelow Crossing Way Alpharetta GA 30202-6193

BRENNAN, LEONARD ALFRED, research scientist, administrator; b. Westerly, R.I., Aug. 2, 1957; s. Leonard Alfred Brennan Jr. and Louise (Gagne) Ladd; m. Teresa Leigh Pruden, Jan. 1, 1980; adopted children: Jessica, Michele. BS, Evergreen State Coll., 1981; MS, Humboldt State U., 1984; PhD, U. Calif., Berkeley, 1989. Technician USDA Forest Svc., Arcata, Calif., 1984-85; biologist Calif. Dept. Food & Agr., Ukiah, 1985; rsch. asst. U. Calif., Berkeley, 1986-89; lectr. Humboldt State U., Arcata, 1989-90; rsch. scientist dept. wildlife and fisheries Miss. State U., Mississippi State, 1990-93; dir. rsch. Tall Timbers Rsch. Station, Tallahassee, Fla., 1993—; Habitat ecology cons. The Chukar Found., Boise, 1989—. Author: (chpt.) The Use of Multivariate Statistics for Developing Habitat Suitability Index Models, 1986, The Use of Guilds and Guild-Indicator Species for Assessing Habitat Suitability, 1986, Arthropod Sampling Methods in Ornithology: Goals and Pitfalls, 1989, Influence of Sample Size on Interpretation of Foraging Patterns by Chestnut-backed Chickadee, The Habitat Concept in Ornithology: Theory and Applications; contbr. articles to profl. jours. U. Calif. fellow, 1987; grantee Calif. Dept. Forestry, Internat. Quail Found., USDA Forest Svc.; San Francisco Bay Area chpt. Wildlife Soc. scholar, 1984; judge Mendocino County Pub. Schs. Sci. Fair, Laytonville, Calif., 1988, Miss. Sci. and Engring. Fair, Miss., 1990-91. Mem. AAAS, Am. Ornithologists' Union, Assn. Field Ornithologists, Cooper Ornithological Soc., Ecol. Soc. Am., Wildlife Soc. (faculty advisor Miss. chpt.), Miss. Wildlife Fedn., Pacific N.W. Bird and Mammal Soc., Wilson Ornithological Soc., Ottawa Field Naturalists' Club. Office: Tall Timbers Rsch Sta RR 1 Box 678 Tallahassee FL 32312-9712

BRENNAN, TERESA PRUDEN, freelance editor, indexer, educator; b. Norfolk, Va., Mar. 27, 1958; d. Muriel Albert Pruden and Nora A. (Forehand) Rhodes; m. Leonard A. Brennan III, Jan. 1, 1980; adopted children: Jessica L., Michelle L. BA in Environ. Studies, Evergreen State Coll., 1982. Cert. tchr., Calif. Wilderness info. specialist Nez Perce Nat. Forest, White Bird, Idaho, summer 1977; youth conservation corps crew leader, environ. ednl. instr. Mt. Spokane (Wash.) State Park, summer 1978, Green Mountain Nat. Forest, Danby, Vt., summer 1980; presch. tchr. Driftwood Day Care Ctr., Olympia, Wash., fall 1979, 80; arts and crafts specialist, counselor Easter Seal Soc. Camp, Boulder Creek, Calif., summer 1982; elem. sch. tchr. Laytonville (Calif.) Unified Sch. Dist., 1983-90, music dir. sch. plays, 1989; tech. asst. Univ. Libr. Miss. State U., 1990-92, dept. supr. Univ. Libr., 1992-93; sci. indexer Tall Timbers Rsch., Inc., Tallahassee, 1993-95; Calif. State mentor tchr. in lang. arts, 1985-86. Co-author: ECONEWS: newsletter of the Northcoast Environ. Ctr., 1982, Sterling Coll. Newsletter, 1990; author, editor: District-Wide Continuum Grades K-8, 1986; co-editor Proc. of the 1994 and 1995 Tall Timbers Game Bird Seminar. Vol. instr. elem. student writing Killearn Lakes Elem., Tallahassee, 1995—; alumni admissions rep. Sterling Coll., Craftsbury Common, Vt., 1992, vol. alumni admissions rep., 1992-94; environ. edn. co-chair Youth Ednl. Svcs., Vols., Arcata, Calif., spring 1982; vol. women's clinic Evergreen State Coll., Olympia, Wash., 1977-78; presch. vol. Humboldt State U., Arcata, 1982; music dir. for sch. plays. Recipient scholarships Sterling Sch., 1975, Va. Polytechnic Inst. and State U., 1976. Mem. ALA (assoc.), Soc. of Children's Book Writers and Illustrators, Nat. Wildlife Fedn. Home: RR 1 Box 679 Tallahassee FL 32312-9713 Office: Tall Timbers Rsch Inc RR 1 Box 678 Tallahassee FL 32312-9712

BRENNER, EDGAR H., legal administrator; b. N.Y.C., Jan. 4, 1930; s. Louis and Bertha B. (Guttman) B.; m. Janet Maybin, Aug. 4, 1979; children from previous marriage—Charles S., David M., Paul R. B.A., Carleton Coll., 1951; J.D., Yale U., 1954. Bar: D.C. 1954, U.S. Ct. Claims 1957, U.S. Supreme Ct. 1957. Mem. 2d Hoover Commn. Legal Task Force, Washington, 1954; trial atty. U.S. Dept. Justice, Washington, 1954-57; assoc. Arnold & Porter, Washington, 1957-62, ptnr., 1962-89; nat. dir. The Behavioral Law Ctr., Washington, 1989—; vis. rsch. prof. law Nat. Law Ctr., George Washington U., 1993—; chmn. conf. com. Alternative Dispute Resolution, 1990-91. Contbr. articles to profl. jours. Commr. Fairfax County Econ. Devel. Corp., Va., 1963-78; pres., bd. dirs. Stella and Charles Guttman Found., N.Y.C., Ams. for Med. Progress, Arlington, Va. Fellow Coll. Problems of Drug Dependency. Fellow Coll. Problems Drug Dependency; mem. ABA (chmn. arbitration com. litigation sect. 1984-87), D.C. Bar Assn., Yale Club, Explorers Club (N.Y.C.). Democrat. Home: 340 Persimmon Ln Washington VA 22747-9707 Office: 4620 Lee Hwy Ste 216 Arlington VA 22207-3400

BRENNER, ERIC RICHARD, epidemiologist; b. Boston, Oct. 18, 1944; m. Karlann Puerschner, June 8, 1969; children: Joel, Alexander. BA in French Lit., U. Calif., Berkeley, 1966; MD, Dartmouth U., 1973. Diplomate Am. Bd. Internal Medicine, Am. Bd. Infectious Disease. Resident in internal medicine Mt. Zion Hosp., San Francisco, 1973-75; dir. outpatient med. svcs. Tuberculosis Control Divsn. S.C. State Health Dept., Columbia, 1976-78; fellow in infectious disease U. S.C., 1978-80; med. officer Tuberculosis Control Divsn. Ctrs. for Disease Control, Atlanta, 1980-82; asst. chief Bur. Disease Control S.C. State Health Dept., Columbia, 1982-85; med. officer Expanded Program on Immunization WHO, Geneva, 1985-86; asst. prof. dept. community health & tropical medicine U. Geneva, 1986-89, charge de cours Dept. Community Health and Tropical Medicine, 1991—; cons. med. epidemiologist EPI Resources, Columbia, 1989—; med. epidemiologist S.C. Dept. Health and Environ. Control, Columbia, 1992—; presented papers Ctr. for Disease Control Nat. Tuberculosis Conf., Atlanta, 1977, 84, 2d Internat. Conf. on Nosocomial Infections, Atlanta, 1980, Intersci. Conf. on Antimicrobial Agts. and Chemotherapy, New Orleans, 1980, Chgo., 1981; adj. assoc. prof. internal medicine U. S.C., 1985, assoc. clin. prof., 1989—; conducted spl. projects WHO Global Program on AIDS, Geneva, 1987, 89, Washington, 1990; with internat. health missions Geneva, 1986-88, Thailand, 1985, Sri Lanka, 1986, among others. Contbr. articles to profl. jours. Mem. Internat. Union Against Tuberculosis and Lung Disease, Am. Soc. for Microbiology, S.C. Pub. Health Assn. Home: 724 Holly St Columbia SC 29205-1852 Office: SC Dept Health Environ Box 101106 1751 Calhoun St Columbia SC 29211

BRENNER, ESTHER HANNAH, elementary school educator; b. N.Y.C., Apr. 12, 1940; d. Israel Eli and Elsie (Lipschitz) B. BEd, U. Miami, 1963. Cert. tchr., Fla. Elem. tchr. Dade County Bd. Pub. Instrn., Miami, Fla., 1963-96; ret. Dade County Bd. Pub. Instrn., Miami, 1996; youth coord. Red Cross, 1996—. Unit chmn. Jackson Meml. Hosp., Miami, 1963-73; instr. trainer first aid and CPR, Greater Miami chpt. ARC, 1987—, chmn. safety svcs. Homestead br., 1989-92, chmn. nursing and health programs S.W. br., youth chmn., 1988-90, vol. youth coord., 1996—, disaster shelter mgr.; adult trainer South Fla. coun. Girl Scouts USA, 1987—, master trainer, 1995. Recipient Appreciation plaque Adv. for Victims, 1985, Clara Barton Honor award, 1985, Ayme Carroll Meml. award, 1988, Plaque of Appreciation, PTA, 1989, Health and Safety award ARC, 1989, Woman of Yr. award Am. Cancer Soc., 1990—, Sarah Cullipher award, 1992, Appreciation Pin, Girl Scouts of Am., 1992, Honor Pin, Girl Scouts of Am., 1995. Mem. NSTA, Fla. Assn. Sci. Tchrs., Dade County Sci. Tchrs. Assn. (Sci. Tchr. of Yr. award 1994), Advs. for Victims (plaque of appreciation 1987), Gamma Sigma Sigma (past historian, sec., v.p., pres. Greater Miami chpt., bd. dirs. so. region 1975-79, nat. pub. rels. dir. 1979-83, Woman of Yr. award 1973, Outstanding Alumnae award 1977, Disting. Svc. award 1987). Democrat. Jewish. Home: 12310 SW 111th S Canal Street Miami FL 33186-4826

BRENNER, RENA CLAUDY, communications executive; b. Camden, N.J.; d. John Lawler and Louretta (Du Fresene) Morgan; m. Edgar W. Claudy (div. 1968); 1 child, Renee; m. Millard Brenner, Nov. 6, 1971 (dec. 1975); children: Sally, Malcolm, Hugh. Student, U. Pa., 1978, U. Mich., 1983. Reporter Tribune-Telegram, Salt Lake City, 1943-45, Times Chronicle, Jenkintown, Pa., 1950-55; free-lance writer Enfield, Pa., 1955-60; pub. relations dir., advt. mgr. Gen. Atronics/Magnavox, Phila., 1960-70; mgr. corp. pub. relations ITE-Imperial, Phila., 1970-73, dir. corp. comm., 1973-76; dir. corp. comm. Parker-Hannifin Corp., Cleve., 1976-83, v.p. corp. comm., 1983-85; pres. Brenner Assocs., Clearwater, Fla., 1986—. Recipient Creative Direction award Phila. Club Advt. Women, 1970, Clarion award Women in Communications, 1982, Gold Key award Pub. Relations News, 1984. Mem. Bus. Profl. Advt. Assn. (life), Pub. Relations Soc. Am. (life), Nat. Investors Relations Inst.. Office: Brenner Assocs 1501 Gulf Blvd Apt 607 Clearwater FL 34630-2903

BRENT, ALLAN RUDOLPH, advertising agency executive; b. L.A., Feb. 3, 1918; s. Joseph Maximilian Bernstein and Belle (Rudolph) Brent; m. Joleene Adalie Margules, Dec. 17, 1941 (dec.); 1 child, Joanna. BA, Brown U., 1938; tchg. credential, UCLA, 1940. Cert. elem. tchr., Calif. Vice prin. Haydock Sch., Oxnard, Calif., 1940-41; v.p. Herbert Benjamin Assocs., Baton Rouge, 1946-50, exec. v.p., 1952-83; adj. prof. So. U., Baton Rouge, 1980-84, La. State U., Baton Rouge, 1981-85. Lt. col. USAF, 1942-46, 51-52. Recipient Printers Ink medal Advt. Fedn. Am., 1965. Mem. Sales and Mktg. Club, Advt. Club Baton Rouge (pres. 1961-62), Svc. Corps Retired Execs. (pres. 1985-86), Kiwanis Club Capital City (pres. 1960-61), City Club Baton Rouge (bd. mem. 1970-72). Jewish. Home: 3930 Floyd Dr Baton Rouge LA 70808

BRENT, FRANK NEVIL, state agency administrator; b. Roanoke, Va., Apr. 29, 1934; s. Frank Nevil and Elizabeth Lois (Pinkard) B.; m. Janeen Patricia Elizabeth Bayley, July 6, 1957; children: Michael Ashby Victor, Andrew John. AA in Acctg., Va. So. Coll., 1955; BS in Psychology, U. Md. in Europe, 1975; MBA in Mgmt., Ga. State U., 1985. Commd. 2d lt. USAF, 1957, advanced through grades to lt. col., 1975; flight examiner, instr. USAF, various locations, 1957-69; spl. projects and reconnaissance briefing officer USAF, Vietnam, 1970-71; chief tactics and elec. warfare USAF, Huntingdonshire, U.K., 1971-75; chief target prediction and interpretation 5th Bomb Wing, Minot, N.D., 1975-76; ret., 1976; dir. adminstrv. svcs. Ga. Emergency Mgmt. Agy., Atlanta, 1977—; guest lectr., Royal Coll. Air Warfare, Eng., 1971-75; mem. adj. faculty Nat. Emergency Tng. Ctr., Emergency Mgmt. Inst. Author tng. manuals, operations plans. Sr. warden, St. Stephens Episcopal Ch., Jacksonville, Ark., 1965-67; warden, St. Catherines Episcopal Ch., Marietta, Ga., 1983-86. Decorated, Bronze Star medal, Air medal, DFC. Mem. Emergency Mgmt. Assn. Ga., Nat. Emergency Mgmt. Assn., Am. Mgmt. Assn. Republican. Office: Ga Emergency Mgmt Agy PO Box 18055 Atlanta GA 30316-0055

BRENT, HAL PRESTON, sales executive; b. Jackson, Miss., Dec. 30, 1955; s. Mildred (Newman) Brent. BBA, U. Miss., 1978; postgrad., Marine Corps Jet Pilot, 1981. Sales rep. Control Data, Avon, Conn., 1984-87, sales mgr., 1987-89, v.p. sales, 1989-92; v.p. sales & mktg. PC-Excel, 1992-93; dir. ARETE Group, Ltd. Investment Banking, 1994-96; CEO Media Exch. Group, Coconut Creek, Fla., 1996—; v.p. sales and mktg. Smith, Gardner & Assocs., 1996—; bd. dirs. PC-Excel, 1992-94. Capt. USMC, 1978-84, Korea and CBI. Home: 5440 Lyons Rd Unit 110 Coconut Creek FL 33073

BRENTLINGER, WILLIAM BROCK, college dean; b. Flora, Ill., Aug. 21, 1926; s. Arthur Kenneth and Frances (Maxwell) B.; m. Barbara Jean Weir, Dec. 29, 1946; children: Gregory, Gary, Rebecca Anne, Garth, Barbara Sue. Student, Washington U., 1946-47; A.B., Greenville Coll., 1950; M.A., Ind. State U., 1951; Ph.D., U. Ill., 1959. Instr. speech Greenville Coll., 1951-59, chmn. dept., 1959-62, dean of coll., 1962-69, dean coll. fine arts and comm., 1969-92; interim pres. Lamar U., Beaumont, Tex., 1992-93; asst. to pres. Lamar U., Beaumont, 1993—; cons. higher edn. Served with USNR, 1944-46. Recipient tchr. study award Danforth Found., 1957. Mem. Internat. Council Fine Arts Deans, Speech Communication Assn. Am., Tex. Speech Assn., Tex. Assn. Coll. Tchrs., Tex. Council Arts in Edn. (pres.), Phi Kappa Phi. Baptist. Club: Rotary (Beaumont). Home: 6530 Salem Cir Beaumont TX 77706-5552 Office: Lamar U PO Box 10001 Beaumont TX 77710-0001

BRENTON, HAROLD L., physician; b. Des Moines, Dec. 13, 1924; s. Harry LaVerne and Vera Mae (Hawbaker) B.; m. Martha Berch Willard, June 14, 1948; children: Douglas, Bradley, Marla K. Veenstra, Randall. MD, Bowman Gray Sch. Medicine, 1948. Diplomate Am. Bd. Internal Medicine. Straight med. intern N.C. Bapt. Hosp., Winston Salem, 1949-50; intern U. Iowa Hosps., Iowa City, 1949-50, resident internal medicine, 1952-54; physician Linvill Clinic, Columbia City, Ind., 1954-59; internist dept. medicine Park Clinic, Mason City, Iowa, 1959-88; ret., 1988; physician Vets. Hosp., Big Springs, Tex., 1991-92; dir. VA Mobile Clinic, Fayetteville (N.C.) VA Med. Ctr., 1992-95, ret., 1995; sec. Whitley County Med. Soc., Columbia City, 1958-59; chief of staff North Iowa Med. Ctr., Mason City, 1975-80; chmn. Park Clinic, Mason City, 1976-78, 81-82; dir. med. Mobile Health Clinic, Fayetteville (N.C.) VA Med. Ctr., 1992-95. Author: Park Clinic Iowa's Oldest Multispecialty Group, 1992. Pres. North Iowa Racquet Club, Mason City, 1976-80, North Iowa Fair Assn., Mason City, 1977-84. Capt. U.S. Army, 1950-52. Decorated Paratrooper wings, 82nd Airborne Divsn., Ft. Bragg, 1950, Bronze star Eighth Army Med. Corps, Korea, 1952. Mem. AMA, Iowa State Med. Soc., Cerro Gordo Med. Soc. (various positions including pres. 1974), Korean War Vets. Assn., Wake Forest Alumni Assn., Iowa Alumni Assn., Alpha Omega Alpha. Republican. Methodist. Home and Office: PO Box 4687 Emerald Isle NC 28594-4687

BRESLAUER, CHARLES S., chemical company executive; b. N.Y.C., Mar. 13, 1925; s. Lewis R. and Anna (Helen) B.; m. Carol Sweet; children: Ann Louise, Robert Ardon, Kenneth Charles. BA, U. Mich., 1948. V.p. Seaboard Vermiculite Corp., West Palm Beach, Fla., 1952-56; product mgr. Zonolite Co., Chgo., 1956-60; regional mgr. Zonolite Co., Boca Raton, Fla., 1960-67; gen. mgr. Concrete Products Div. W.R. Grace & Co., Brunswick, Ga., 1967-71; regional mgr. Concrete Products Group, W.R. Grace & Co., Pompano Beach, Fla., 1971-92; v.p. Darex Puerto Rico, Inc. subs. W.R. Grace & Co., San Juan, P.R., 1980-92; pres. Bermuda Roof Co., Inc., Fort Lauderdale, Fla. 1983—. Patentee Portland cement wood flake structural panels, ultra lightweight mortar for roof and floor tiles. Liaison officer USAF Acad., South Fla., 1960-70. Lt. col. USAF ret. Mem. Jaycees (pres. Delray Beach, Fla. 1956), Air Force Assn. (charter mem.), Reserve Officers Assn. (life mem.). Home: 10709 SE Flotilla Ct Hobe Sound FL 33455-3220 Office: Bermuda Roof Co Inc 1499 W Palmetto Park Rd Boca Raton FL 33486-3328

BRESLAW, ELAINE GELLIS, history educator; b. N.Y.C., June 27, 1932; d. Max and Mary (Belenke) Gellis; m. Jerome Breslaw, Mar. 19, 1956 (div. May 1978); children: Joseph (dec.), Karl; m. John Muldowny, May 15, 1993. BA, Hunter Coll., 1954; MA, Smith Coll., 1956; MLS, Pratt Inst., Bklyn., 1964; PhD, U. Md., 1973. Libr. asst. Bklyn. Pub. Libr., 1959-60; reference libr. Catonsville (Md.) Cmty. Coll., 1964-65; reference libr. Morgan State U., Balt., 1965-66, prof. history, 1966-94; vis. prof. history U. Tenn., Knoxville, 1994—; faculty assoc. John Hopkins U., Balt., 1980—; vis. prof. history, Fulbright scholar U. West Indies, Barbados, 1989-90; project evaluator Md. Humanities Coun., Balt., 1986-87; cons. Ednl. Testing Svc., Princeton, N.J., 1981—. Author: Tituba, Reluctant Witch of Salem, 1996; editor: Records of the Tuesday Club, 1988; contbr. articles to profl. jours. Mem. Am. Hist. Assn., Southeastern Am. Soc. 18th Century Studies, Assn. Caribbean Historians, Md. Hist. Soc. Home: 10900 Harbour Park Ln Knoxville TN 37922 Office: U Tenn History Dept Knoxville TN 37996

BRESLIN, DAVID DUNBAR, elementary educator; b. Fairfax, Va., Oct. 17, 1969; s. Judson and Wendy (Worsky) B. BA in Elem. Edn., Ohio Wesleyan U., 1993. 5th, 6th and 8th grade history tchr. Chesapeake Acad., Irvington, Va., 1993-94, 5th grade history, reading, math, English, health tchr., 1994—. Mem. youth com., bd. dirs. Grace Episcopal Ch., Kilmarnock, Va., 1994—, jr. high youth group leader, 1994-95. Home: PO Box 104 Weems VA 22576 Office: Chesapeake Acad PO Box 8 Irvington VA 22480

BRESLIN, ELVIRA MADDEN, lawyer, educator; b. Phila., Oct. 28, 1943; d. Daniel Joseph and Elvira Rose (Leichner) Madden; m. John Anthony Breslin, June 19, 1971; children: Kristen, John A.V. AB in English, Secondary Edn., Chestnut Hill Coll., Phila., 1961-65; MA in High Sch. Adminstrn., Villanova (Pa.) U., 1968; JD, Cath. U. Am., Washington, 1990; LLM in Taxation, Villanova U., 1996. Bar: Pa. 1991, U.S. Dist. Ct. Pa. 1994, U.S. Ct. Appeals (3d cir.) 1994, D.C. 1992, U.S. Dist. Ct. D.C. 1992, U.S. Tax Ct. 1996. Tchr. Baldwin-Whitehall Pub. Schs./Cheltenham Pub. Schs., Pa., 1965-75; educator, prin. certification, tchr. Fairfax County (Va.) Pub. Schs., 1979-94; tchr. Thomas Jefferson H.S. for Sci. and Tech., 1979-94, Gov's. Sch. for Gifted, 1979-94; computer/paralegal specialist Personnel Pool, Washington, 1987; rsch. assoc. Meade & Assocs., Fairfax, 1988, Akin, Gump, Strauss, Hauer & Feld, Washington, 1988; law clk. Fedn. of Tax Adminstrs., Washington, 1989, Beins, Axelrod, Osborne & Mooney, Washington, 1989-90; pvt. practice Washington and Pa., 1991—; rsch. assoc. Villanova U., 1994; legal/computer specialist Nat. Acad. Scis., Smithsonian Instn., Steptoe & Johnson, Akin, Gump, Strauss, Hauer & Feld, Office of Ind. Counsel; legal resource/rsch. specialist Dir. Testing and Evaluation, Walnut Hill Ctr. Mem. Oakton Glen (Va.) Homeowners Neighborhood Watch, 1987—, Oakton Glen Homeowners Assn., 1979—; mem., religious instr. Our Lady of Good Counsel Roman Cath. Ch., Vienna; judge moot ct. competitions Cath. U. Columbus Sch. Law, Washington, 1993—; exec. treas. Thomas Jefferson H.S. for Sci. and Tech., also investment advisor. Mem. ABA (tax sect. and legal edn. sect.), Fed. Bar Assn. (tax sect.), D.C. Bar Assn. (tax sects.), Pa. Bar Assn. (tax sects., legal edn., edn. coms. and taxation coms.). Home and Office: 2655 Oakton Glen Dr Vienna VA 22181

BRESSLER, MARCUS N., consulting engineer; b. Havana, Cuba, July 31, 1929; came to U.S., 1942; s. Isaac and Augustine (Draiman) B.; m. Sondra Kipnes, Nov. 7, 1954; children: Eric L., Lisa A., Karen J. Lee. B of Mech. Engring., Cornell U., 1952; MSME, Case Inst. Tech., 1960. Registered profl. engr., Ohio, Tenn. Stress analysis engr. The Babcock & Wilcox Co., Barberton, Ohio, 1955-66; design engr. Lenape Forge, West Chester, Pa., 1966-70; mgr., product design and devel. engr. Taylor Forge, Cicero, Ill., 1970-71; supr. codes, standards and materials TVA, Knoxville, 1971-79; sr. engring. specialist TVA, 1979-88; pres. M.N. Bressler, PE, Inc., Knoxville, 1988—. Served to 1st lt. U.S. Army, 1952-54, capt. USAR, 1957. Recipient Bernard F. Langer Nuclear Codes and Standards award Am. Soc. Mech. Engrs., 1992, J. Hall Taylor medal for Pressure Technology Codes and Stds. Outstanding Contbns., 1996. Fellow ASME (boiler and pressure vessel main com., bd. accreditation and cert., Century medallion 1980). Home and Office: M N Bressler PE Inc 829 Chateaugay Rd Knoxville TN 37923-2017

BRETHAUER, WILLIAM RUSSELL, JR., claim investigator; b. Pitts., Apr. 5, 1953; s. William Russell Brethauer Sr. and Cecelia Helen Geldrich-Brethauer; m. Barbara L. Summers, Mar. 8, 1980; children: Laura Diane, Stacy Lynn. BA magna cum laude, Thiel Coll., 1975; grad., Inst. Paralegal Tng., Phila., 1976. Cert. paralegal, casualty-property claim law assoc. Claim rep. St. Paul Cos. Inc., Ft. Washington, Pa., 1977-80; claim supr. St. Paul Cos. Inc., San Jose, 1980-84, St. Paul, 1980-84; spl. claim investigator St. Paul Cos. Inc., Orlando, Fla., 1984—; intern WQED-TV, Pitts., 1974; mem. Fla. adv. com. arson prevention, Maitland, 1984—. Author: (novel) Boardwalk, 1991, (book) If I Were A Horse, They'd Shoot Me, 1993, My

Enemies, Small Devils, 1993, Insurance Fraud: Deceit & Ingenuity, 1992; asst. prodr.: (multi-media program) When to Say When, 1974. Libertarian. Zen Buddhist. Home and Office: PO Box 621329 Oviedo FL 32762-1329

BRETT, MAUVICE WINSLOW, retired educational administrator, consultant; b. Xenia, Ohio, May 24, 1924; d. Perle Alonzo and Lurena Belle (Hamilton) W.; m. John Woodrow Brett, Sept. 20, 1943; children: Diane, John, Anthony, Loretta. BS in Psychology, Howard U., 1944, MS in Psychology, 1946; PhD in English, Union Grad. Sch., Cin., 1978. Tchr. English, Hertford County Schs., Winton, N.C., 1959-76, ednl. supr., 1977-80, dir. personnel, 1981-87, asst. supt., 1988-89; ret., 1989; cons. N.C. Coun. English Tchrs., Charlotte, 1979; com. mem. quality assurance program N.C. State Dept. Pub. Instn., Raleigh, 1980-81; bd. visitors Chowan Coll., 1991—; mem. found. bd. Roanoke-Chowan C.C., 1991—; adj. prof. psychology Roanoke-Chowan C.C., 1992—, Chowan Coll., 1993—, East Carolina U., 1994—. Sec. Hertford County Arts Coun., 1977; mem. Hertford County 400th Anniversary Com., 1982-83; trustee Elizabeth City State U., 1983-91. Mem. N.C. Assn. Sch. Adminstrs. (dist. rep.), Am. Assn. Sch. Adminstrs., N.C. ASCD, Bus. and Profl. Women's Club, Rotary, Delta Sigma Theta. Home: RR 2 Box 260A Ahoskie NC 27910-9563 Office: Chowan Coll PO Box 1848 Murfreesboro NC 27855

BRETT, THOMAS RUTHERFORD, federal judge; b. Oklahoma City, Oct. 2, 1931; s. John A. and Norma (Dougherty) B.; m. Mary Jean James, Aug. 26, 1952; children: Laura Elizabeth Brett Tribble, James Ford, Susan Marie Brett Crump, Maricarolyn Swab. B.B.A., U. Okla., 1953, LL.B., 1957, J.D., 1971. Bar: Okla. 1957. Asst. county atty. Tulsa, 1957; mem. firm Hudson, Hudson, Wheaton, Kyle & Brett, Tulsa, 1958-69, Jones, Givens, Brett, Gotcher, Doyle & Bogan, 1969-79; judge U.S. Dist. Ct. (no. dist.) Okla., Tulsa, 1979—. Bd. regents U. Okla., 1971-78; mem. adv. bd. Salvation Army; trustee Okla. Bar Found. Col. JAG, USAR, 1953-83. Fellow Am. Coll. Trial Lawyers, Am. Bar Found.; mem. Okla. Bar Assn. (pres. 1970), Tulsa County Bar Assn. (pres. 1965), Am. Judicature Soc., U. Okla. Coll. Law Alumni Assn. (bd. dirs.), Order of Coif (hon.), Phi Alpha Delta. Democrat. Office: US Dist Ct US Courthouse 333 W 4th St Rm 4508 Tulsa OK 74103-3819

BRETTELL, CAROLINE B., anthropology educator; b. Montreal, Que., Can., June 11, 1950; came to U.S., 1967; d. Jacques Louis and Zoe (Browne-Clayton) Bieler; m. Richard Robson Brettell, June 9, 1973. BA, Yale U., 1971; MA, Brown U., 1972, PhD, 1978. Instr. U. Tex., Austin, 1976-78, postdoctoral rsch. assoc. Population Rsch. Ctr., 1978-80; lectr. Loyola U., Chgo., 1983-88; project dir. and rsch. assoc. Newberry Libr., Chgo., 1984-88; dir. women's studies So. Meth. U., Dallas, 1989-94; vis. assoc. prof. So. Meth. U., 1988-91, assoc. prof., 1991-93, prof., 1993—, chair dept. anthropology, 1994—. Author: Men Who Migrate, Women Who Wait, 1986, We Have Already Cried Many Tears, 1982, revised edit., 1995; co-author: Painters and Peasants, 1983, Gender in Cross-Cultural Perspective, 1992, Gender and Health: An International Perspective, 1995; editor: When They Read What We Write: The Politics of Ethnography, 1993; co-editor: International Migration: The Female Experience, and others. Recipient numerous grants including NIH, 1978, Wenner Gren Found., 1979, NEH, 1984, Social Sci. Rsch. Coun., 1988, 96, Am. Phil. Soc., 1990 and others. Mem. Soc. Sci. History Assn. (exec. com. 1988-92), Am. Anthropol. Assn., Soc. for Anthropology of Europe (pres.-elect 1994-96, pres. 1996-98), Coun. for European Studies (steering com. 1988-92, exec. com. 1994—), Literacy Instrs. for Tex. (pres. bd. dirs. 1994-95). Home: 5522 Montrose Dr Dallas TX 75209-5610 Office: Dept Anthropology So Meth U Dallas TX 75275

BRETT-MAJOR, LIN, lawyer, mediator, arbitrator, lecturer; b. N.Y.C., Sept. 21, 1943; d. B.L. and Edith H. Brett; children from previous marriage: Dania S., David M. BA, U. Mich., 1965; JD cum laude, Nova Law Ctr., 1978; postgrad., Harvard U., 1993. Bar: Fla. 1978, U.S. Ct. Appeals (5th and 11th cirs.) 1981, U.S. Tax Ct. 1981, U.S. Dist. Ct. (so., mid. and no. dist.) Fla. 1982, U.S. Supreme Ct. 1984, U.S. Dist. Ct. (mid., so. and no. dists.) Fla. 1984, U.S. Ct. Mil. Appeals 1990. Internat. communications asst. Mitsui and Co., Ltd., N.Y.C., 1962; with dept. pub. relations and devel. St. Rita's Hosp., Lima, Ohio, 1965-66; reporter The Lima News, 1969-70; honors intern U.S. Atty.'s Office, Miami, 1977; pvt. practice, Ft. Lauderdale, Fla., 1979-93; alternative dispute resolution mediator Conflict Solutions, Boca Raton, Fla., 1993—; participant Gov.'s Conf. on World Trade, Miami and Jacksonville, Fla., 1984, Unidroit Workshop Devel. Pvt. Internat. Comml. Law, 1992; spkr. trial and negotiation trade Bus. Owner's Conf., Hollywood, Fla., 1986, Nova U. Law Ctr., 1988, ABA Nat. Conv., Toronto, 1988, Fla. Atlantic U., 1989, CPA Club, 1992, ABA Sect. Meeting, Bal Harbor, Fla., 1996. Contbr. articles to profl. jours. on internat. anti-trust law. Bd. dirs. Neurol. Rehab. Ctr., Broward Navy Days; mem. Ft. Lauderdale Opera Soc., 1986, Ft. Lauderdale Mus. Art, 1985, Opera Guild, 1990—; Dept. Def. ESGR Com., 1996—. Recipient Silver Key award ABA, 1977. Mem. ABA, FBA, ATLA, Fla. Bar Assn. (mil. law com. 1989—, chmn. legis. issues subcom. 1990-92, media-law com. 1991-93), Broward County Bar Assn., Internat. Platform Assn., U.S. Fencing Assn., U. Mich. Alumni Assn. (Gold Coast pres. 1988-90, S.E. U.S. dist. v.p., sec.-treas. 1992-95, pres. 1995—), Ft. Lauderdale C. of C., Palm Beach C. of C., U.S. Propeller Club (nat. del. Port Everglades, Fla. 1981). Republican. Office: Conflict Solutions 1515 N Federal Hwy Ste 418 Boca Raton FL 33432-1954

BREVOORT, RICHARD WILLIAM, public relations executive; b. Bklyn., Nov. 7, 1937; s. Patricia Gallivan. Student, Hunter Coll.; CUNY. Supervising adjustor The Home Ins. Co., 1960-66; dir. weight and measures City of N.Y., 1966, deputy commr. markets, 1966-68, 1st deputy commr. commerce, 1968-69, asst. adminstr. econ. devel., 1969-70, commr. tax collection, 1970-75; dir. program-minority N.Y. State Senate, Albany, 1975-77, sec. to minority, 1977-83; v.p. The Whitney Leadership Group, Inc., 1991—; pres. The Hudson Agy., Inc., Cape Coral, Fla., 1984—; bd. dirs. N.Y.C. Convention Ctr. Corp., 1982-84; mem. N.Y. State Task Force on Cigarette Bootlegging, 1976, N.Y. State Econ. Stblzn. Bd., 1970; mem. adv. coun. to N.Y.C. supt. schs., 1968-69. With U.S. Army, 1957-60. Mem. Am. Mgmt. Assn., Am. Soc. Pub. Adminstrn., Soc. Advancement Mgmt., Adminstrv. Mgmt. Soc. Office: Hudson Agy 4818 Coronado Pky Cape Coral FL 33904-9526

BREWER, ERNEST ANDREW, JR., elementary education educator; b. West Palm Beach, Fla., Oct. 21, 1968; s. Ernest Andrew and Louise Fredonia (Hobbs) B. BA in Edn., U. Fla., 1992, MEd, 1993. Tchr. Gardendale Elem. Magnet Sch., Merritt Island, Fla., 1994—; Mem. sch. improvement com. Gardendale Elem. Magnet Sch., Merritt Island, 1994—, tchr. rep. Democrat. Methodist. Home: 3024 Winchester Dr Cocoa FL 32926

BREWER, GAY, poet, English language and literature educator; b. Louisville, Apr. 3, 1965. BA in English, U. Louisville, 1985; MA in English, Ohio State U., 1988, PhD in English, 1992. Teaching assoc. Ohio State U., 1986-92, instr. creative activities program, 1991; instr. arts and scis. divsn. Indian Hills Coll., 1992-93; asst. prof. English Mid. Tenn. State U., Murfreesboro, 1993—; presenter in field. Music critic Louisville Courier-Jour., 1991, 93; weekly columnist, arts editor Louisville Cardinal, 1984; found. editor, literary Journ., Poems & Plays, 1993; author books, literary criticism: A Detective in Distress: Philip Marlowe's Domestic Dream, 1989, David Mamet and Film: Illusion/Disillusion in a Wounded Land, 1993, Laughing Like Hell: The Harrowing Satires of Jim Thompson, 1996; author poetry chapbooks: Zócalo, 1991, Book Lover, 1991, The Woman and the White Dog, 1994, Presently A Beast, 1996, Predator in the House, 1996; author plays JFK Rudolph, and A Life with Fear in It, 1992, Undertakings, 1993, Meisner, 1993; author 300 pub. poems; reviewer books; contbr. articles to profl. jours. Fundacion Valparaiso residency grantee, Almeria, Spain, 1995; Hawthornden Castle residency fellow, Midlothian, Scotland, 1996. Office: Mid Tenn State U Dept English PO Box 70 Murfreesboro TN 37132

BREWER, JAMES WILLIAM, mathematics educator; b. West Palm Beach, Fla., May 29, 1942; s. William Ferrell and Martha Elizabeth (Grimes) B.; m. Deborah Ann Phelps, Dec. 27, 1973 (div. Mar. 1987); m. Virginia Gayle Ganther, Aug. 5, 1989; children: Deborah Lynn, Jill Diane, Amy Webb, James C.B., David R., Thomas. AB, Fla. State U., 1964, MS, 1966, PhD, 1968. Asst. prof. math. Va. Polytech. Inst., Blacksburg, 1968-70; prof. math. U. Kans., Lawrence, 1970-85, Fla. Atlantic U., Boca Raton, 1985—. Author: Power Series Over Commutative Rings, 1981; co-author: Linear Systems over Commutative Rings, 1986; co-editor: Proceedings of the Kansas Commutative Algebra Conference, 1973, Emmy Noether: A Tribute to Her Life and Work, 1981; contbr. articles to profl. jours. Mem. Am. Math. Soc. Home: 11 NW 24th Ct Delray Beach FL 33444 Office: Fla Atlantic U 777 Glades Rd Boca Raton FL 33431-6424

BREWER, JOYCE MARIE, nurse midwife; b. New Orleans, Jan. 23, 1949; d. Harrison J. Holloway and Melvey Raye Coyle Langston; m. John Money Brewer, July 22, 1972. ADN, Hinds Jr. Coll., Raymond, Miss., 1978; CNM, MS, U. Miss., 1982; BSN, SUNY; MSN, U. Miss., 1996. RN, Miss.; cert. nurse midwife perinatal, family nurse practitioner. Nurse midwife Kuhn Meml. Hosp., Vicksburg, Miss., 1983; dir. nurse midwifery svcs. Meth. Hosp. of Mid-Miss., Lexington, 1983-85; clin. supr. Miss. Bapt. Med. Ctr., Jackson, 1985-87; nurse, midwife newborn nursery U. Miss. Med. Ctr., Jackson, Miss., 1990-93, pediatric HIV/AIDS case mgr., 1993-96; nurse midwife Madison County Med. Ctr., Canton, Miss., 1996—; instr. in CPR and first aid. Mem. ANA, ACNM, ARC, Childbirth Edn. Assn. Metro Jackson, Internat. Childbirth Edn. Assn., Assn. Nurses in AIDS Care, Miss. Nurses Assn. Office: Women's Health Svcs/Primary Care Clinic Carthage Madison County Med Ctr PO Box 530 Carthage MS 39051

BREWER, LEWIS GORDON, judge, lawyer, educator; b. New Martinsville, W.Va., Sept. 6, 1946; s. Harvey Lee and Ruth Carolyn (Zimmerman) B; m. Kathryn Anne Yunker, May 25, 1985. B.A., W.Va. U., 1968, J.D., 1971; LL.M., George Washington U., 1979. Bar: W.Va. 1971, Calif. 1978. Commd. 2d lt. USAF, 1968, advanced through grades to Col., 1988; dep. staff judge adv., Travis AFB, Calif., 1976-78, chief civil law San Antonio Air Logistics Center, Kelly AFB, Tex., 1979-83, staff judge adv., MacDill AFB, Fla., 1983-86; chief Air Force Cen. Labor Law Office, Randolph AFB, Tex., 1987-88, dep. staff judge adv. Air Tng. Command, 1988-89; staff judge adv. 7th Air Force, Osan AFB, Korea, 1989-91, 45 Space Wing Patrick AFB, Fla., 1991-93; adminstrv. law judge W.Va. Edn. & State Employee Grievance Bd., Charleston, 1993—; instr. bus. law No. Mich. U., Marquette, 1972, Solano Coll., Suisun City, Calif., 1978; instr. labor law Webster U., Ft. Sam Houston, 1983. Decorated Air Force Commendation medal, Meritorious Service medal, Legion of Merit. Mem. ABA, W.Va. Bar Assn., State Bar Calif., W.Va. U. Alumni Assn., George Washington U. Alumni Assn. Methodist. Home: 528 Sheridan Cir Charleston WV 25314-1063 Office: 808 Greenbrier St Charleston WV 25311

BREWER, PAMELA SUE DIDLAKE, English and Latin languages educator; b. Shreveport, La., Oct. 2, 1948; d. Ralph Hunter and Lorraine S. (McLaurin) Didlake; m. Robert Nelson Sellers, Jan. 5, 1969 (div. March 1982); 1 child, John Robert; m. Gary Russel Brewer, Dec. 15, 1984. BA, Mississippi Coll., 1981, MS in Edn., 1987; postgrad., Jesus Coll., Cambridge U., England, 1982, U. So. Mississippi, 1987—. Cert. tchr. Miss. Sec., vocat. edn. dept. Miss. State Dept. Edn., 1969; tchr. Grandview Kindergarten, Pearl, Miss., 1973-76; sec. to group agency supr. Mutual of N.Y., Jackson, Miss., 1977; secondary English, Latin tchr. Northwest Rankin Attendance Ctr., Brandon, Miss., 1981-84; Latin, social studies tchr. Jackson Preparatory Sch., Miss., 1984-85; world history, Latin, secondary English Raleigh Attendance Ctr., Miss., 1985-88; instr. Latin, advanced placement English Brookhaven High Sch., Miss., 1989—. Troop leader, organizer, bus. adminstr. for day camp, cookie chmn., tgn. com., leader trainer, Girl Scouts of Am., 1970-80; bd. dirs. Multiple Sclerosis Soc. Miss., 1979-80. Recipient Star Tchr. award Miss. Econ. Coun., 1993; grantee NEH. Mem. MLA, NEA, Miss. Assn. Educators, Nat. Coun. Tchrs. of English, Am. Classical League, Miss. Philol. Assn., Ark. Philol. Assn., La. Philol. Assn., Jane Austin Soc. N.Am., William Blake Soc., Early Modern Cultural Studies, Phi Theta Kappa, Delta Kappa Pi, Sigma Tau Delta, Alpha Mu Gamma, Phi Delta Kappa. Episcopalian. Home: 21168 Highway 51 Crystal Springs MS 39059-9165

BREWER, RICKY LEE, investment broker, estate planner; b. Amarillo, Tex., June 20, 1948; s. Murry Lee and Carmelia (Grantham) B.; m. Kathy Jean Hall, Apr. 5, 1974; children: Ricky Lee II, Robert Neil. Student, Hardin-Simmons U., 1967-68, Tex. Tex. U., 1968-70. Account rep. CIT Fin., Lubbock, Tex., 1970-71; collection officer Cleburne (Tex.) Nat. Bank, 1971-73; salesman Baldwin Piano and Organ, Lubbock, 1973-75; owner Averitt Music Co., Lubbock, 1975-80, Piano Warehouse, Lubbock, 1980-84; agy. mgr. La. Farm Bur., Gonzales, 1984-88, Tex. Farm Bur., Bonham, 1988-92; investment broker A.G. Edwards & Sons, Inc., McKinney, Tex., 1992—. Mem. Bonham C. of C. (bd. dirs. 1991—), Bonham Rotary Club (pres. elect 1990, pres. 1991). Republican. Baptist. Home: 401 High Meadow Dr Mc Kinney TX 75070-3633 Office: A G Edwards & Sons Inc 1836 W Virginia St Ste 102 Mc Kinney TX 75069-7868

BREWER, SHERYL ANNE, social worker, dental hygienist; b. Orlando, Fla., Jan. 9, 1946; d. Allen Frank Jr. and Nell Marian (Thompson) B. BS in Dental Hygiene, Tex. Woman's U., 1973; MSSW, U. Tex., Arlington, 1982; postgrad., Tex. Woman's U., 1991. Cert. social worker, Acad. Cert. Social Workers; lic. master social worker; lic. marriage and family therapists; lic. and cert. chem. dependency specialist; registered dental hygienist; cert. in clin. hypnosis. Dental hygienist Dr. J.A. Hardgrave, Crowley, Tex., 1976-89, Dr. Jack Martin, 1992—; exec. asst. Dr. R.J. Shaeffer, Ft. Worth, 1980-92; instr. social work various univs., 1980-96; instr. Tarrant County Jr. Coll., Ft. Worth, 1985-96; pvt. practice Ft. Worth, Arlington, 1987—; cons. Women's Ctr. Tarrant County, 1981-89, Rubicon, Ft. Worth, 1985-90; lectr. Nat. Orgn. for Victim Assistance, Washington, 1985—. Mem. Tarrant Coun. Alcoholism and Drug Abuse, Women of All Saints, Ctr. for the Prevention of Sexual and Domestic Violence; counselor Women's Ctr. of Tarrant County, 1981-87. Mem. NASW, APHA, Am. Assn. World Health, Am. Soc. Clin. Hypnosis, Am. Dental Hygienist Assn., Nat. Orgn. Victim Assistance, Fla. Dental Hygienist Assn., Tex. Dental Hygienist Assn., Tarrant County Psychol. Assn., Nat. Assn. Coun. for Children, Eta Sigma Gamma. Episcopalian. Address: PO Box 690371 Orlando FL 32869-0371

BREWER, WILLIAM ROBERT, JR., army acquistion administrator, federal specialist; b. Clinton, Ill., Sept. 2, 1940; s. William Robert and Mable (Florence Bartelmay) B. Grad. high sch., Minooka, Ill. Contract specialist U.S. Army, Rock Island, Ill., 1973-77; chief contract adminstrn. U.S. Army, Independence, Mo., 1977-81; chief contracts div. C.E. U.S. Army, Kansas City, 1981-84; dir. contracting GSA, Kansas City, Mo., 1984-86; insp. gen. Chief Acquisitions Inspection div. C.E. U.S. Army, Washington, 1986-91; dir. contracting C.E. U.S. Army, Winchester, Va., 1991—. Editor: Should Cost Analysis of Holston Army Ammunition Plant, 1976, Should Cost Analysis of Lake City Army Ammunition Plant, 1980, various insp. gen. reports. With U.S. Army, 1964-66. Recipient Presdl. award Pres. U.S., 1979, hon. recognition SBA, 1980, U.S. Armyh Comdrs. medal, 1991, 92, 94. Mem. Nat. Contract Mgmt. Assn. (treas. 1983-84 Kansas City chpt. speaker 1986—), Fed. Mgrs. Assn., Soc. Profl. Compts. Office: US Army CE Transatlantic Div Attn: CE+AD-CT PO Box 2250 Winchester VA 22601-1450

BREWER, WILLIAM WALLACE, dentist; b. Anadarko, Okla., July 17, 1937; s. Wallace and Daisey Edna (Dean) B.; m. Harriet Ann Hackett, Dec. 21, 1958; children: Brian, Shelley. ASc, Eastern Okla. A&M U., 1958; BA, Central State Coll., 1960; DDS, U. Tenn., 1968; MPH, U. Okla., 1992. Pvt. practice dentistry, Oklahoma City, 1968—. Fellow Acad. Gen. Dentistry (pres. Okla. chpt. 1973), Internat. Coll. Dentists; Col. USAR, (Ret). mem. ADA (del. 1990), Okla. Dental Assn. (pres. 1990), Am. Assn. Dental Examiners, Assn. Mil. Surgeons U.S., Res. Officers Assn., Army Reserve Sr. Commanders Assn., U. Tenn. Coll. Dentistry Alumni Assn. (trustee 1983—), Registered Dentists of Okla. (bd. govs. 1979-85, pres. 1984—), Lions Club (pres. N.W. Oklahoma City chpt. 1983-84, zone chmn. Okla. chpt. 1984-85, cabinet sec., treas. 1989-90). Democrat. Methodist. Avocations: running, quail hunting, flying. Home: 8232 NW 114th St Oklahoma City OK 73162-2005 Office: 4801 Richmond Sq Oklahoma City OK 73118

BREWSTER, CLARK OTTO, lawyer; b. Marlette, Mich., Nov. 5, 1956; s. Charles W. and June V. (Hoff) B.; m. Deborah K. Trowhill, Aug. 3, 1974; m. Cassie Mae, Corbin Clark. BA cum laude, Cen. Mich. U., 1977; JD with honor, Tulsa U., 1980. Bar: Okla. 1981, U.S. Dist. Ct. (no. and ea. dists.) Okla. 1982, Tex. 1993. Assoc. Riddle and Assocs., Tulsa, 1981, Braly and McEachin, Tulsa, 1981-82; ptnr. Brewster & Shallcross, Tulsa, 1982—; bd. dirs. Redy Corp., Tulsa, Cottontail Oil Corp., Tulsa; trustee Travis Kerr Magana Trust, Tulsa, 1985—. Mem. ABA, ATLA, Okla. Bar Assn., Okla. Trial Lawyers Assn. (v.p. 1996), Tulsa County Bar Assn., Order of Curule chair, Order of Barristers. Home: 2109 E 30th St Tulsa OK 74114 Office: Brewster Shallcross & DeAngelis 2021 S Lewis Ave Ste 675 Tulsa OK 74104

BREWSTER, OLIVE NESBITT, retired librarian; b. San Antonio, July 19, 1924; d. Charles Henry and Olive Agatha (Nesbitt) B.; B.A., Our Lady of Lake Coll., 1945, B.S. in L.S., 1946. Asst. librarian aeromed. library U.S. Air Force Sch. Aviation Medicine, Randolph AFB, Tex., 1946-60, chief cataloger aeromed. library Sch. Aerospace Medicine, Brooks AFB, Tex., 1960-83, chief tech. processing, 1983-88; ret., 1988. Mem. ALA, Am. Soc. Indexers, Mensa. Anglican. Home: 1906 Schley Ave San Antonio TX 78210-4332

BREWTON, DUDLEY CORNELIUS, JR., school administrator; b. Pensacola, Fla., Sept. 30, 1936; s. Dudley Cornelius and Dorothy (Harris) B.; m. Irene Catherine Kalfas, May 4, 1957; children: Cheryl Ann, Dudley III, Christopher (dec.), Joseph. BS in Bus., Fla. State U., 1964, MS in Edn. Adminstrn., 1971. Acct. Williams, Sheffield, Waterson, CPAs, Tallahassee, 1965-66; fin. specialist Fla. Dept. Edn., Tallahassee, 1966-81, adminstr. fin. mgmt. sect., 1981-90; asst. supt. bus. and fin. Duval County Sch. Bd., Jacksonville, Fla., 1990-94; retired, 1994. Mem. Assn. of Sch. Bus. Ofcls., Fla. Assn. of Sch. Bus. Ofcls. (dir. 1986-90), Fla. Sch. Fin. Officers Assn. Democrat. Roman Catholic.

BRIAN, A(LEXIS) MORGAN, JR., lawyer; b. New Orleans, Oct. 4, 1928; s. Alexis Morgan and Evelyn (Thibaut) B.; m. Elizabeth Louise Graham, 1951; children—Robert Morgan, Ellen Graham. B.A., La. State U., 1949, J.D., 1956; M.S., Trinity U., 1954. Bar: La. 1956, U.S. Supreme Ct. 1971. Assoc. Deutsch, Kerrigan & Stiles, New Orleans, 1956-60, ptnr., 1961-79; sr. ptnr. Brian, Simon, Peragine, Smith & Redfearn, New Orleans, 1979-82; sr. ptnr. Fawer, Brian, Hardy & Zatzkis, New Orleans, 1982-86; pvt. practice, New Orleans, 1986—; spl. asst. to La. Atty. Gen., 1982-87; speaker profl. seminars; lectr. Inst. Continuing Legal Edn., La. State U. Law Ctr., 1972—. Local merit badge counselor Boy Scouts Am., 1963—; bd. dirs. Goodwill Industries New Orleans, 1969-84, v.p. and mem. exec. com., 1975-77, mem. adv. bd., 1978, 86—; life deacon, trustee, lay preacher, Bible tchr., mem. coms. First Baptist Ch. New Orleans; speaker at convs., confs. So. Bapt. Conv., 1956—, La. Bapt. Conv., 1956—, Am. Platform Assn.; past pres., bd. trustees New Orleans Bapt. Theol. Sem., 1961-74; bd. dirs. New Orleans Bapt. Theol. Sem. Found., 1972-81, Inter-Varsity Christian Fellowship, 1974—, La. State U. Found., 1976-81; mem. nat. legal adv. council Ams. United for Separation of Ch. and State, 1977—. Served with USAF, 1951-55. Recipient Boss of Yr. award New Orleans Legal Secs. Assn., 1966. Mem. ABA (TIPS fidelity and surety com., forum com. contstrn. industry), La. State Bar Assn. (asst. examiner com. on bar admissions 1968-89, fidelity, surety and constrn. sect. 1991—), New Orleans Bar Assn., Internat. Assn. Def. Counsel (vice chmn. fidelity and surety com. 1978-79, architects, engrs. and constrn. litigation com., advocacy com.), La. Assn. Def. Counsel, Def. Research Inst., Am. Arbitration Assn. (arbitrator 1970—), La. Civil Svc. League, Internat. House, La. State U. Alumni Fedn. (life), Trinity U. Alumni Assn., La. State U. Law Ctr. Alumni Assn. (life), Upper Carrollton Neighborhood Assn. (v.p. 1976), Christian Legal Soc., Theta Xi, Phi Delta Phi. Democrat. Contbr. articles to legal jours. Home: 5216 Pitt St New Orleans LA 70115-4107 Office: 700 Camp St New Orleans LA 70130-3702

BRICKER, HARVEY MILLER, anthropology educator; b. Johnstown, Pa., June 29, 1940; s. George Harry and Florence Helen (Miller) B.; m. Victoria Evelyne Reifler, Dec. 27, 1964. BA, Hamilton Coll., 1962; MA, Harvard U., 1963, PhD, 1973. Successively instr., asst. prof., assoc. prof. to prof. anthropology Tulane U., New Orleans, 1969—. Co-author: The Analysis of Certain Major Classes of Upper Palaeolithic Tools, 1969, Excavation of the Abri Pataud: The Perigordian VI Assemblage, 1984; co-editor: Hunting and Animal Exploitation in the Later Palaeolithic and Mesolithic of Eurasia, 1993; editor: La Paléolithique Supérieur de l'abri Pataud (Dordogne), 1995; contbr. articles on French prehistory and Maya archaeoastronomy to profl. jours. Decorated Order Palmes Académiques (France). Fellow AAAS; mem. Am. Anthrop. Assn., Soc. Am. Archaeology, Soc. French Prehistory. Office: Tulane U Dept Anthropology New Orleans LA 70118

BRICKHILL, WILLIAM LEE, international finance consultant; b. Rahway, N.J., Oct. 13, 1937; s. William Welch and Wilma Eloise (Gay) Mumford; m. Margaret A. Stempel, June 16, 1961 (div. 1971); children: William L., Barbara A., Cynthia A., Robert L.; m. Joan Marie Ward, May 19, 1988. Student, U. Ga., 1957, Sophia U., Tokyo, 1958-60; BBA, George Washington U., 1970. Lic. comml. and instrument rated pilot. Internat. specialist Am. Security & Trust Co., Washington, 1960-62; loan officer Export-Import Bank of U.S., Washington, 1962-90, dep. mgr. contract adminstrn., 1990-91, dep. v.p. contract adminstrn., 1991-94, ret., 1994; cons. internat. fin., 1994—. Contbr. articles to profl. jours. With U.S. Army, 1956-58, Germany. Mem. Nat. Capital Bromeliad Soc. (1st v.p. 1991—), Nat. Capital Orchid Soc., Gem, Mineral and Lapidary Soc. (bd. dirs., v.p. 1965-75). Roman Catholic. Home and Office: 6338 Phyllis Ln Alexandria VA 22312-6402

BRIDGES, DAVID MANNING, lawyer; b. Berkeley, Calif., May 22, 1936; s. Robert Lysle and Alice Marion (Rodenberger) B.; m. Carmen Galante de Bridges, Aug. 16, 1973; children: David, Stuart. AB, U. Calif., Berkeley, 1957, JD, 1962. Assoc. Thelen, Marrin, Johnson & Bridges, San Francisco, 1962-70, ptnr., 1970-94; mng. ptnr. Thelen, Marrin, Johnson & Bridges, Houston, 1981-91. Served as lt. (j.g.) USN, 1957-59. Mem. ABA, State Bar of Tex., Tex. Bar Assn., Houston Bar Assn., Internat. Bar Assn., Houston Club, Coronado Club, Pacific-Union Club. Office: 1111 Bagby St Fl 24 Houston TX 77002-2551

BRIDGES, EDWIN CLIFFORD, state official; b. Greenville, S.C., Oct. 18, 1945; s. Henry A. and Elizabeth (Bruce) B.; m. Martha Callison; 3 children. B.A., Furman U., Greenville, S.C., 1967; M.A., U. Chgo., 1969, Ph.D., 1981. Tchr. Social Studies Greenville, S.C., 1968-70; hist. resources cons. Ga. Dept. Natural Resources, Atlanta, 1973-75; instr. Ga. Inst. Tech., Atlanta, part-time, 1973-75; asst. to dir. Ga. Dept. Archives and History, Atlanta, 1976-78, asst. dir., 1978-82; dir. Ala. Dept. Archives and History, Montgomery, 1982—, chmn. State Records Commn., Local Govt. Records Commn.; coordinator Ala. Hist. Records Adv. Bd.; sec. Gov.'s Mansion Adv. Bd., 1991-92; Mem. bd. Ala. Preservation Alliance; active Ala. Hist. Commn., Ala. Hist. Assn., Nat. Hist. Pubs. and Records Commn., 1988, rsch. libr. com. Coun. on Libr. Resources, Rsch. Librs. Group, 1993—, rsch. adv. coun. Auburn U., Govt. Coun. Info. Tech. Author: (with others) Georgia Signers of the Declaration of Independence, 1981, Documenting America, 1984. Fellow Soc. Am. Archivists (mem. Standards Bd. 1991-2); mem. So. Hist. Assn., Nat. Assn. Govt. Archives and Records Adminstrs. (treas. 1980-85, v.p. 1990-92). Home: 3336 Wiley Rd Montgomery AL 36106-3224 Office: Ala Dept Archives & History 624 Washington Ave Montgomery AL 36130-0024*

BRIDGES, LEROY W., retired state agency administrator, consultant; b. Idabel, Okla., Oct. 12, 1927; s. Clem Millard and Edna Mae (Matkin) B.; m. Ellen Harper, Aug. 15, 1975; children from a previous marriage: Carol Ann, Shirley Walker, Robert L. BS in Pub. Adminstrn., Oklahoma City U., 1981. Asst. dir. mktg. divsn. Okla. Dept. Agr., Oklahoma City, 1954-58; dir. orgn. Okla. Farm Bur. Fedn., Oklahoma City, 1958-70; chief adminstrv. officer Ariz. Farm Bur. Fedn., Phoenix, 1970-78; adminstrv. officer pub. affairs Okla. Dept. of Mental Health, Oklahoma City, 1980-90; cons. Yukon, Okla., 1990—; bd. dirs Change to Change, Red Earth, Inc., founding incorporator, exec. com. Co-chmn. Okla. cultural diversities and econ. devel. task force Okla. Futures; mem. ad hoc com. Native Am. Cultural and Ednl. Ctr.; chmn. subcom. Gov.'s Coun. Health Care Delivery; mem. guardianship task force state of Okla.; mem. Let's Get the Job Done com., fine arts bldg. com. Okla. City U.; vol. cons. numerous fund raising projects including Employment and Edn. Ministry, Am. Indian Lang. and Culture Preservation, Country Heritage Theme Park, El Reno, Pol. Comm. Ctr.; trustee Okla. City U., former mem. adv. bd.; mem. adv. bd. bur. govt. and pub. svcs. Ctrl. State U.; chmn. adv. bd. New Destiny; regent Redlands C.C.; chmn., mem. adv. coun. Polit. Comms. Ctr., U. Okla. Recipient award for Outstanding Vol. Activity Boy Scouts Am.; named twice Disting. Alumni Okla. City U.; Leroy Bridges scholarship named in his honor, Competency Based Degree Program. Mem. Okla. City U. Alumni Assn. (past pres.), UN Assn. (bd. dirs., v.p.

Oklahoma City chpt.), Pol. Sci. Club, Sundowners, Redlands C.C. Alumni and Friends Assn. (pres.), Rotary (pres., Rotarian of Yr. 1993-94, Outstanding Rotarian 1994-95), Red, Red Rose Frat., Phi Alpha Theta. Home: 11613 SW 3rd Ter Yukon OK 73099-6717

BRIDGES, ROBERT GOLTRA, obstetrics-gynecologist; b. Muskogee, Okla., Dec. 20, 1932; s. William Goltra Bridges and Geneva Harriet (Bohannan) Juday; children: Cheryl Anne Bridges, Diana Lynn Bridges. BS in Microbiology, U. Okla., 1954, MD, 1958. Intern U. Tex. Med. Br., Galveston, 1958-59; ob-gyn. resident U. Tex. Med. Br., 1959-62; pvt. practice San Angelo (Tex.) Med. and Surg., 1964-76, Angelo Clin. Assn., San Angelo, 1976-78, Women's Clinic of San Angelo, 1978-85; pvt. practice gynecology Coll. Hills Women's Clinic, San Angelo, 1985-92, West Tex. Med. Assocs., San Angelo, 1992—; physician advisor, cons. Family Planning of San Angelo, 1985—; clinic physician Angelo State U., 1988—. Past dist. dir. Am. Cancer Soc., San Angelo, 1966; past pres. San Angelo Photography Club, 1983, 84. Capt. USAF, 1962-64. Fellow Am. Coll. Ob-Gyn.; mem. Willard R. Cooke Ob-Gyn. Soc., Am. Assn. Gynecol. Laparoscopy, Am. assn. for Colposcopy and Colpomicroscopy, Tex. Assn. of Ob.-Gyn. (past v.p.), Tex. Med. Assn. Republican. Office: West Tex Med Assocs 3555 Knickerbocker Rd San Angelo TX 76904

BRIDGEWATER, HERBERT JEREMIAH, JR., radio host; b. Atlanta, July 3, 1942; s. Herbert Bridgewater and Mary Sallie (Clark) Bridgewater-Hughes. B.A., Clark Coll., Atlanta, 1968; postgrad., Atlanta U.; L.H.D., Faith Coll., 1978; LL.D., Heed U., 1978. Tchr. bus. edn. and English Atlanta Pub. Sch. System, 1964-67; relocation and family svcs. cons. Atlanta Housing Authority, 1967-70; columnist, writer Atlanta Daily World, 1968—, Lovely Atlanta; consumer protection specialist FTC, Atlanta, 1970-83; pres. Bridgewater's Personnel Service, 1971—; assoc. prof. bus. edn. and mass communication Clark Coll., instr., 1983-86; instr. Atlanta Jr. Coll., 1986—, The Univ. System of Ga., 1986—; with reservations sales Delta Airline Inc., Atlanta, 1984—; host radio program Enlightenment (WGKA-AM), 1975-79; host pub. affairs program Confrontation WZGC FM and WIGO AM, 1975-79, WYZE AM, 1979—; TV talk show host Bridging the Gap. Mem. Epilepsy Found. Am., Nat. Urban League, Big Bros. Council of Atlanta, Met. Boys Clubs of Atlanta, YMCA, NAACP; active So. Christian Leadership Conf., Ga. and nationwide civil rights movements; bd. dirs. Atlanta Dance Theater, Ralph C. Robinson Atlanta Boys Club, Proposition Theater Co., Am. Cancer Soc., Just-Us Theatre Task Force. Recipient Pres.'s award Clark Coll. United Negro Coll. Fund, 1960, 61, Best Citizens award Delta Sigma Theta, 1962, Humanitarian award Future Soc. Orgn., 1975, award Atlanta Dance Theatre, 1978-79, also; Met. Atlanta Boys Club; FTC Superior service medal, 1978; Bronner Bros. Nat. Beauticians Conv. Excellence in Communication award, 1978; named One of Most Outstanding Young Men in Am., Nat. Jr. C. of C., 1969, One of Most Eligible Bachelors in Am., 1970, One of 1,000 Successful Black Americans, 1973; both Ebony Mag.; One of 10 Outstanding Young People of Atlanta, 1977-78; One of 20 Most Progressive Young People in Atlanta, 1977; Herbert Bridgewater Day proclaimed in his honor Atlanta. Mem. Atlanta Jr. C. of C., Young Men on the Go, Clark Coll. Alumni Assn., Clark Coll. Assn., Heritage Valley Community Civic Orgn., Hungry Club Forum, Internat. Assn. for African Heritage and Black Identity (founding). Baptist (founder, chmn. bd. jr. deacons). Home: 3569 Rolling Green Rdg SW Atlanta GA 30331-2323 Office: Delta Airlines Inc Bldg A-2 Reservations Sales PO Box 45007 Hartsfield Internat Airport Atlanta GA 30320

BRIEF, ARTHUR PAUL, business educator; b. Newark, Aug. 4, 1946; s. Nathan and Lillian (Cantor) B.; m. Rose Woolner, June 14, 1970; 1 child, Laura Rebecca. BS in Indsl. Mgmt., U. Tenn., 1968; MS in Mgmt. & Orgn., U. Wis., 1971, PhD in Mgmt. & Orgn., 1974. Asst. prof. U. Ky. Coll. Bus., 1974-75; Asst. prof. U. Iowa Coll. Bus. Adminstrn., 1975-78, assoc. prof., 1978-80; assoc. prof. NYU Stern Sch. Bus., 1980-83, prof., 1983-89; Cecil and Ida Green honors prof. Tex. Christian U., 1988; prof. Tulane U. Freeman Sch. Bus., 1989—; dir. William B. and Evelyn Burkenroad Inst., 1990—, Norman Mayer prof. bus., 1991-94; Lawrence Martin chair bus., 1994—; lectr. U. Wis., Madison, 1971-72, 73-74; Fulbright/FLAD chair orgnl. behavior, Lisbon, fall 1995; rsch. assoc. U. Iowa Health Svc. Rsch. Ctr., 1979-80, NYU Inst. Retail Mgmt., 1982-84; adj. prof. Tulane U., Dept. Psychology; vis. prof. Ctr. HEC-ISA, France, 1990, Helsinki Sch. Econs., Finland, 1992; mgmt. trainee State Med. Soc. Wis., 1968-69; staff assoc. Gov.'s Health Policy and Planning Task Force, State of Wis., 1972-73; presenter in field. Contbr. chpts. to books and articles to profl. jours. Recipient Erich Sternberg award, 1991; rsch. grantee Peat, Marwick, Mitchell & Co., 1979; vis. scholar Ctr. Surveys, Methods and Analysis, Mannheim, Germany, 1993; Giblin fellow, 1989. Fellow Am. Psychol. Assn.; mem. Am. Psychol. Soc., Am. Sociological Assn., Soc. Organizational Behavior, MESO, Acad. Mgmt., Soc. Psychol. Study Social Issues. Office: Tulane U Freeman Sch Bus New Orleans LA 70118

BRIGANCE, MARCELENA, critical care nurse; b. Mobile, Ala., Sept. 16, 1941; d. Maurice Jr. and Dorothy (Bell) B.; children: Monica Renee Burch, Alana Jeanne Burch. Student, Samford U., 1959-60, 61-62; BSN, U. Wash., 1975. RN, Ala.; CEN; cert. ACLS instr.; cert. TNCC; cert. PALS. Staff nurse surg. ICU, med. ICU, CCU Harborview Med. Ctr., Seattle, 1975-77; staff nurse, supr. oral surg. U. Wash., Seattle, 1979-81; staff nurse emergency room, mobile intensive care nurse Sequoia Hosp., Redwood City, Calif., 1983-87; staff nurse emergency dept. Springhill Meml. Hosp., Mobile, Ala., 1987-91; staff nurse emergency rm. Thomas Hosp., Mobile, 1992-93; PRN emergency nurse Providence and Knollwood Emergency Rm., Mobile, 1992—; emergency rm. nurse Springhill Hosp., 1992-95, Knollwood Park Hosp., 1995—.

BRIGGMAN, JESSIE B., special education educator; b. Branchville, S.C., May 7, 1945; d. Jesse and Louise (McCormick) Bowman; m. Lemuel D. Briggman, Aug. 21, 1970; children: Wydreda JaVonne, Lemetrius Deon. BA, Claflin Coll., Orangeburg, S.C., 1970; MEd, S.C. State Coll., Orangeburg, 1985, postgrad., 1987. Cert. in social studies, learning disabilities, educable mentally retarded, trainable mentally retarded. Tchr. social studies Orangeburg Dist. 7, Elloree, S.C.; spl. edn. tchr. Orangeburg Dist. 5; spl. edn. tchr. transitiona social adjustment students Orangeburg-Wilkinson H.S. Acitve Orangeburg-Wilkinson H.S. PTSA. Tchr. grantee State of S.C., 1987-88. Mem. NEA, S.C. Edn. Assn., Orangeburg Edn. Assn., Coun. Exceptional Children, Assn. for Children With Learning Disabilities, Zeta Phi Beta. Home: 1275 Cherokee St SW Orangeburg SC 29115-7634

BRIGGS, ARLEEN FRANCES, mental health nurse, educator; b. Bklyn., Sept. 4, 1939; d. Thomas Frances and Margaret Elizabeth (McCann) Whelan; (div.); children: Lisa J., Jon M., Kara J., Lora M. Diploma in Nursing, Helene Fuld Sch. Nursing, 1960; BSN, Coll. Santa Fe, 1987; MSN in Nursing Adminstrn., U. N.Mex., 1993. RN; ANA cert. adult psychiat. and mental health nurse. Staff Helene Fuld Hosp., Trenton, N.J., 1960-61; supr. psychiatry Trenton (N.J.) State Hosp., 1960-61; 1st lt. USAF, 1961-63; supr. med. surg. Coeur de Alene (Idaho) Hosp., 1966-67, Centinella Hosp., Hawthorne, Calif., 1967-68, Laguna Meml. Hosp., Laguna Beach, Calif., 1968-70; staff operating rm. Mission Cmty. Hosp., Mission Viejo, Calif., 1970-77; supr., educator Las Vegas Med. Ctr., 1977-94; asst. prof. McNeese State U., Lake Charles, La., 1994—; mem. Recovering Nurse Program Adv. Com., Bon, La., 1995—. Director, author: (program) Research Cooperative Care of PT with Two Psychiatric Diagnoses, 1993. Chairperson Regional Bd. Nursing-Diversion Program, Las Vegas, 1989-94; intervention nurse alcoholism Alcoholics Anonymous-McNeese, Lake Charels, 1990—, Las Vegas, N. Mex.; counsellor Reach to Recovery, Lake Charles, 1994—; psychiatric counselor HIV patient, 1989—. Recipient award Bd. of Nursing, 1994. Mem. Nat. Soc. Addictions Nursing, Nat. Soc. Medicine, Law and Ethics, Sigma Theta Tau. Office: McNeese State U PO Box 90415 Lake Charles LA 70609

BRIGGS, STEVEN ROSS, university director; b. Hamilton, Ohio, Nov. 15, 1969; s. Steven Paul and Nanceen Paula (Hertel) B.; m. Laura Iline Sockrider, Aug. 22, 1992. BA, Ball State U., 1992; MA in Edn., Western Ky. U., 1995. Meat cutter Waterson's Grocery, Syracuse, Ind., 1987-90; resident asst. Ball State U., Muncie, Ind., 1990-92; residence hall dir. Western Ky. U., Bowling Green, 1992—. Mem. So. Assn. of Coll. Student Adminstrs. (presenter 1993), Student Affairs Grad. Assn. (mem. steering com. 1992—). Democrat. Home: Western Ky Univ 1 Big Red Way PO Box 8371 Bowling Green KY 42101 Office: Western Ky Univ Dept of Residence Life 431 Potter Hall Bowling Green KY 42101

BRIGHT, JEPTHA BARNARD (BARNEY), sculptor; b. Shelbyville, Ky., July 8, 1927; s. Jeptha Barnard and Deanie Ray (Wakefield) B.; m. Gayle Sandefur Royce, Nov. 5, 1971; children: Leslie, Becky, Jep, Michael. Student, Davidson Coll., 1945, U. Louisville, 1946, Art Ctr. Sch., Louisville, 1947-48. Pres. Bright Studio, Inc., Louisville, 1990—. Prin. works include 13' bronze sculpture of Julius Erving, 1989, design and sculpture of 40' Louisville Clock, 1976; numerous bronze busts, 1955—. With USNR, 1945-46. Named Artist of Yr., Sta. WAVE-TV, Louisville, 1967-81; recipient Life Time Achievement award Gov. of Ky., 1989, many 1st pl. awards in regional exhbns., 1946-53. Mem. Ky. Arts Coun. Studio: Bright Studio Inc 2031 Frankfort Ave Louisville KY 40206

BRIGHT, JERLENE ANN, information systems programs administrator; b. Norman, Okla., July 4, 1942; d. Hoyt David and Pearl J. Little; Asso. in Bus., Okla. Sch. Banking and Bus., 1964; student U. Okla., 1974-76; m. James Bright, July 25, 1959; children—Bridget, Michelle, Erika. Project coordinator U. Okla. Computing Center, 1965-68, dir. info. systems programs U. Okla., Norman, 1968-84; data processing dir. Dwight's Energydata, Inc., 1984—; dir. Dwight's DPDS Svcs.participant UN energy meetings and workshops to third world meetings. Contbr. numerous papers and articles to profl. jours. Mem. Soc. Petroleum Engrs., Am. Assn. Petroleum Geologists, Oklahoma City Geology Soc. Home: 4317 Lyrewood Ln Norman OK 73072-4412

BRIGHT, JOSEPH CONVERSE, lawyer; b. Richmond, Va., July 28, 1940; s. Joseph Elliott and Marion (Converse) B.; m. Jill Giddens, May 5, 1989; children: Thomas Converse, Elizabeth Chase. BA, U. Va., 1962; LLB, U. Ga., 1965. Bar: Ga. 1964, U.S. Dist. Ct. (so. dist.) Ga. 1965, U.S. Dist. Ct. (mid. dist.) Ga. 1967, U.S. Dist. Ct. (no. dist.) Ga. 1983, U.S. Ct. Appeals (5th cir.) 1965, Fla. 1976, U.S. Dist. Ct. (mid. dist.) Fla. 1982, U.S. Supreme Ct. 1976, U.S. Ct. Appeals (11th cir.) 1981. Assoc. Joseph B. Bergen, Savannah, Ga., 1965-67; sole practice Valdosta, Ga., 1967-69; ptnr. Blackburn & Bright, Valdosta, 1969-91; pvt. practice Valdosta, 1991—; instr. part time Valdosta State Coll., 1967-81. Fellow Am. Bd. Criminal Lawyers, Am. Coll. Trial Lawyers; mem. ATLA, Am. Bd. Trial Advocacy (advocate), Nat. Assn. Criminal Def. Lawyers, Ga. Trial Lawyers Assn. (v.p.). Office: PO Box 5889 Valdosta GA 31603-5889

BRIGHTMIRE, PAUL WILLIAM, retired judge; b. Washington, Mo., June 12, 1924; s. Quinton Claude and Alvena Matilda (Wehr) B.; m. Lorene E. Edwards, Nov. 7, 1952; children: Deborah Sue, William Paul, Jon Edward, Christina Ann, Thomas Christopher. B.A., U. Tulsa, 1949, J.D., 1951. Bar: Okla. 1951, U.S. Supreme Ct. 1973. Mem. firm Rogers & Brightmire, 1954-57, Brightmire & Asso., Tulsa, 1957-70; judge Okla. Ct. Appeals, Div. 2, Tulsa, 1971-94, presiding judge, 1971-75; spl. justice Supreme Ct. Okla.; vice chief judge Okla. Ct. Appeals, 1989, chief judge, 1990-94; vis. prof. med. jurisprudence Okla. Coll. Osteo. Medicine and Surgery, 1975-82. Founding editor: Tulsa Lawyer, 1962-64; editor in chief: Advocate, 1967-70. Served to 2d lt. USNR, USAR, 1943-46, 51. Recipient Outstanding Svc. award Okla. Ct. Appeals, 1990. Fellow Internat. Acad. Law and Sci.; mem. Am. Trial Lawyers Assn., Okla. Trial Lawyers Assn. (pres. 1967, Outstanding Service award 1968, Appellate Judge of Yr. award 1991), Okla. Bar Assn. (Outstanding Service award 1969), Tulsa County Bar Assn. (Outstanding Service award 1965, exec. com. 1962-64), Am. Inns of Ct. (master emeritus), Tulsa Press Club, Kappa Sigma, Phi Beta Gamma, Pi Kappa Delta. Lodge: Masons (32 deg., Shriner). Home: 4041 S Birmingham Ave Tulsa OK 74105-8230 Address: PO Box 2763 Tulsa OK 74101-2763

BRIGHTWELL, REBECCA LYNN, marketing professional; b. Athens, Ga., Feb. 15, 1964; d. Thomas Jackson and Juanita (George) B. MBA, Brenau Coll., 1991; postgrad., U. Ctrl. Fla. Coord. mktg. Sea Pines Resort, Hilton Head Island, S.C., 1988-90, Walt Disney World, Lake Buena Vista, Fla., 1990—; cons. State Bot. Garden Ga., Athens, 1987, ARC, Athens, 1989. Author newsletter Bus. Briefs, 1988, Inside Sea Pines, 1991; editor newsletter The PR Paper, 1988-89. Engring. scholar Profl. Women's Found., 1991; recipient Leadership award Hugh O'Brian Found., 1982, Leadership award Jaycees, 1982. Mem. NAFE, Orlando Mktg. Assn., Alpha Gamma Delta. Republican. Office: Walt Disney World Co/Mktg Sunbank Bldg Ste 310 1675 Buena Vista Lake Buena Vista FL 32830

BRILL, EARL HUBERT, clergyman, educator; b. Abington, Pa., Nov. 17, 1925; s. Joseph and Stella Ellsworth (Scheer) B.; m. Ruth Madelyn Ball, Feb. 26, 1952 (div. Apr. 1983); children: Lesley Elizabeth, Grace Elaine, Kenneth Edward; m. Margaret Simpson Pickett, Jan. 14, 1984. AB, U. Pa., 1951; BTh, Phila. Divinity Sch., 1956; MTh, Princeton Theol. Sem., 1958; PhD, Am. U., 1969. Ordained deacon Episc. Ch., 1956, priest, 1956. Vicar Ch. Epiphany, Royersford, Pa., 1956-59; Episc. chaplain U. Pa., Phila., 1959-61; Episc. chaplain Am. U., Washington, 1961-71, dir. Am. studies program, asst. prof. history, 1971-74; canon Washington Cathedral, 1974-83; dir. deacon formation Episc. Diocese N.C., Raleigh, N.C., 1984—; trustee Phila. Divinity Sch., 1964-68, 72-74, Washington Theol. Consortium, 1975-78, Episc. Divinity Sch., Cambridge, Mass., 1974-79, Ch. Pension Fund, N.Y.C., 1988—; dir. studies Coll. Preachers, Washington, 1974-83; Episc. chaplain Duke Univ., Durham, N.C., 1984-91. Author: Creative Edge of American Protestantism, 1966, Sex is Dead-And Other Postmortems, 1967, The Future of the American Past, 1975, The Christian Moral Vision, 1979. Mem. Dem. Ctrl. Com., Washington, 1968-72; bd. dirs. Ams. Dem. Action, Washington, 1965-74, Sister Cities of Durham, 1989-95. With U.S. Army, 1943-46. Danforth Found. fellow, 1964-65, 68-69. Mem. N.C. Episc. Clergy Assn. (bd. dir. 1985), Hist. Soc. Episc. Ch. (editl. bd. 1980—). Home and Office: 1108 Anderson St Durham NC 27705

BRINDLEY, JOAN HARRIET, elementary educator; b. Temple, Tex., Apr. 28, 1950; d. George Valter and Cleo Harriet (Love) B. BS in Elem. Edn., S.W. U., Georgetown, Tex., 1971; MS in Edn., Baylor U., 1979. Cert. edn. adminstr., Kindergarten tchr., Tex. First grade tchr. Austin (Tex.) Ind. Sch. Dist., 1971-72; kindergarten tchr. Temple (Tex.) Ind. Sch. Dist., 1973-75, first grade tchr., 1975-88, kindergarten and first grade tchr., 1988-89; 2nd grade tchr. Killeen (Tex.) Ind. Sch. Dist., 1990-91, gifted and talented tchr. 1st grade, 1991—. Mem. Tex. Assn. of Supervision and Curriculum Devel. (v.p. 1988-89), Tex. Classroom Tchrs. Assn. (pres. 1989-90), Temple Classroom Tchrs. Assn. (pres. 1979-80), Temple Jr. League, Temple Civic Theatre, Delta Kappa Gamma (pres. Lambda chpt. 1988-90), Phi Delta Kappa (v.p. cen. Tex. chpt. 1987-88). Democrat. Baptist. Home: 720 W Nugent Ave Temple TX 76501-1926 Office: Killeen Ind Sch Dist 500 Mountain Lion Rd Killeen TX 76543-2061

BRINE, DOLORES RANDOLPH, chemist; b. Marion, N.C., Nov. 26, 1945; d. Carl Lee and Addie (Ritter) Randolph; m. George Atkins Brine, Aug. 31, 1968. BS, Duke U., 1968. Rsch. chemist Research Triangle Inst., Research Triangle Park, N.C., 1968—. Contbr. articles to profl. jours., chpts. to books. Mem. Am. Chem. Soc. Episcopalian. Home: 6505 Hunters Ln Durham NC 27713-9738

BRINKLEY, DONALD R., oil industry executive; b. 1937. BA, Culver Stockton Coll., 1959; BS, U. Mo., 1960. V.p. transp. Standard Oil Co., Cleve., 1960-87; pres., CEO Colonial Pipeline Co., Atlanta, 1987—. Office: Colonial Pipeline Co 945 E Paces Ferry Rd NE Atlanta GA 30326-1125

BRINKLEY, GLENDA WILLIS, medical/surgical nurse, women's health nurse; b. Gore Springs, Miss., Dec. 23, 1961; d. Stark Willis and Loree Conley; m. Timothy L. Brinkley, Sept. 15, 1984; children: Victoria Celeste, Tia Danielle. BSN, Miss. U. for Women, 1987; BS in Biology, Miss. Valley U., 1984. RN, Miss.; cert. perinatal nurse. Edn. coord. Clay County Med. Ctr. Named to Outstanding Young Women of Am., 1987. Mem. Assn. Women's Health, Obstetrics, and Neonatal Nursing, Assn. Profls. in Infection Control, Sigma Theta Tau Internat.

BRINKLEY, JACK THOMAS, lawyer, former congressman; b. Faceville, Ga., Dec. 22, 1930; s. Lonnie Elester and Pauline (Spearman) B.; m. Alma Lois Kite, May 29, 1955; children: Jack Thomas, Fred Alen II. Student, Young Harris Coll., 1947-49, Okla. A. and M. Coll., 1952; LL.B. cum laude, U. Ga., 1959. Bar: Ga. 1958, D.C. 1973. Sch. tchr. Ga., 1949-51; assoc. firm Young, Hollis & Moseley, Columbus, Ga., 1959-61; partner firm Coffin & Brinkley, Columbus, 1961-66; mem. Ga. Ho. Reps., 1965-66; sr. ptnr. Brinkley and Brinkley, 1983-95, of counsel, 1996—; mem. 90th-97th Congresses from 3d Ga. dist.; chmn. mil. facilities and installations subcom. 97th Congress; mem. Ga. Ho. Rep., 1965-66. Trustee Young Harris Coll. Mem. Ga. Bar Assn., Columbus Bar Assn., Young Lawyers Club of Columbus (pres. 1963-64), Blue Key, Civitan Club, Masons. Democrat. Baptist. Office: Corporate Ctr Ste 901 Columbus GA 31902

BRINKMANN, ROBERT JOSEPH, association administrator, lawyer; b. Cin., Dec. 25, 1950; s. Robert Harry and Helen R. (Streuwing) B.; m. Claire Jeanne LeFreche, July 28, 1976; children: Christopher, Julia. BA, U. Notre Dame, 1972; postgrad., Alliance Française, 1974-75; AM, Brown U., 1977; JD, Loyola U., Los Angeles, 1980. Bar: Calif. 1980, D.C. 1981, U.S. Ct. Appeals (D.C. and 9th cirs.) 1981, U.S. Supreme Ct. 1984, U.S. Ct. Appeals (6th cir.) 1987. Tchr. secondary schs., Los Angeles and Paris, 1974-77; assoc. Hedrick & Lane, Washington, 1980-82; gen. counsel Nat. Newspaper Assn., Washington, 1982-92; exec. dir. Red Tag News Publs. Assn., 1990-92; v.p., postal and regulatory affairs Newspaper Assn. Am., Reston, Va., 1992—; mem. faculty Am. Press. Inst., Reston, Va., 1982—; lectr. U. Md. Mem. ABA, Fed. Communications Bar Assn. (former vice chmn. postal affairs com.). Roman Catholic. Home: 8207 Thoreau Dr Bethesda MD 20817-3161 Office: Newspaper Assn Am National Press Bldg 529 14th St NW Washington DC 20045-1402

BRINSON, GAY CRESWELL, JR., lawyer; b. Kingsville, Tex., June 13, 1925; s. Gay Creswell and Lelia (Wendelkin) B.; m. Bette Lee Butter, June 17, 1979; children from former marriage: Thomas Wade, Mary Kaye. Student, U. Ill.-Chgo., 1947-48; B.S., U. Houston, 1953, J.D., 1957. Bar: Tex. 1957, U.S. Dist. Ct. (so. dist.) Tex. 1959, U.S. Dist. Ct. (ea. dist.) Tex. 1965, U.S. Dist. Ct. (no. dist.) Tex. 1990, U.S. Ct. Appeals (5th cir.) 1962, U.S. Supreme Ct. 1974; diplomate Am. Bd. Trial Advocates, Am. Bd. Profl. Liability Attys. Spl. agt. FBI, Washington and Salt Lake City, 1957-59; trial atty. Liberty Mut. Ins. Co., Houston, 1959-62; assoc. Horace Brown, Houston, 1962-64; assoc. Vinson & Elkins, Houston, 1964-67, ptnr., 1967-91; of counsel McFall, Sherwood & Sheehy, Houston, 1992—; lectr. U. Houston Coll. Law, 1964-65; mem. staff Tex. Coll. Trial Advocacy, Houston, 1978-86; prosecutor Harris County Grievance Com.-State Bar Tex., Houston, 1965-70. Served with AUS, 1943-46, ETO. Fellow Tex. Bar Found. (life); mem. Tex. Acad. Family Law Specialists (cert.), Tex. Assn. Def. Counsel, Tex. Bd. Legal Specialization (cert.), Fedn. Ins. Counsel, Nat. Bd. Trial Advocacy (cert.), Houston Ctr. Club, Phi Delta Phi. Home: 3740 Del Monte Dr Houston TX 77019-3018 Office: McFall, Sherwood & Sheehy 2500 2 Houston Ctr 909 Fannin St Houston TX 77010

BRINSON, RALPH ALAN, physician, pediatrician, neonatologist; b. Jackson, Miss., Dec. 31, 1954; s. Ralph C. and Catherine May (Shumaker) B.; m. Pamela Gail Barnett, Nov. 9, 1985; children: Rebecca Gail, Matthew Alan, Jessica Michelle. MD, U. Miss., Jackson, 1980. Diplomate Am. Bd. Pediatrics, sub-bd. Neonatal-Perinatal Medicine. Resident in pediatrics U. Ky., Lexington, 1980-83, fellow in neonatal-perinatal medicine, 1983-85; staff neonatologist Ochsner Clinic, New Orleans, 1985-87, Bapt. Hosp., Montgomery, Ala., 1987-89; pvt. practice neonatal-perinatal medicine, ptnr. North Miss. Neonatology, Tupelo, Miss., 1989-95; pvt. practice Methodist Hosp., Hattiesburg, Miss., 1995—; instr. Coll. Allied Health, U. Ky., 1982-84; instr. neonatal nurse practitioner program Ochsner Clinic, New Orleans, 1986-87; clin. instr. respiratory therapy Itawamba C.C., Tupelo, 1991, 92. Contbr. articles to profl. jours. Treas. First Evang. Ch., Tupelo, 1990-91. Fellow Am. Acad. Pediatrics; mem. AMA, Christian Med. and Dental Soc., So. Perinatal Assn. Office: 5003 Hardy St Ste 302 Hattiesburg MS 39402-1308

BRISCOE, CONSTANCE YVONNE, writer; b. Washington, Dec. 31, 1952; d. Leroy Fabian and Alyce Levenia (Redmond) B. BS, Hampton U., 1974; MPA, Am. U., 1978. Rsch. analyst Analytic Svcs., Inc., Arlington, Va., 1977-81; assoc. editor Jt. Ctr. Polit. and Econ. Studies, Washington, 1981-90; mng. editor Gallaudet U., Washington, 1990-94. Author: Sisters and Lovers, 1994, Big Girls Don't Cry, 1996.

BRISTER, BILL H., lawyer, former bankruptcy judge; b. Sieper, La., Mar. 5, 1930; s. Clayton Houston and Era (Price) B.; m. Carolyn Lee McDowell, June 11, 1955; children—Jeff, Julie. B.S. in Chemistry, Northwestern State U. Natchitoches, La., 1948; J.D., U. Tex., 1958. Bar: Tex. 1957, U.S. Dist. Ct. (no. dist.) Tex. 1959, U.S. Ct. Appeals (5th cir.) 1971, U.S. Supreme Ct. 1971. Pvt. practice, Lubbock, Tex., 1958-79; bankruptcy judge U.S. Dist. Ct. (no. dist.) Tex., 1979-85; of counsel Winstead, Sechrest & Minick and predecessor firm, 1986—. Served to col. USMCR, 1951-52. Office: Winstead Sechrest & Minick 5400 Renaissance Tower 1201 Elm St Dallas TX 75270

BRISTER, COMMODORE WEBSTER, JR., religion educator; b. Pineville, La., Jan. 15, 1926; m. Gloria Nugent, Mar. 28, 1946; 1 child, Mark Allen. BA, La. Coll., 1947; postgrad., La. State U., 1948-49; BD, New Orleans Bapt. Sem., 1952, MDiv, 1973; ThD, Southwestern Bapt. Sem., 1957, PhD, 1974; postdoctoral studies, N.C. Bapt. Sch. Pastoral Care, 1960, Tex. Christian U., 1961-62, Princeton Theol. Sem., 1962-63, 67, Union Theol. Sem., N.Y.C., 1962-63, 67, S.W. Med. Sch., 1969-70, Oxford (Eng.) U., 1978. Ordained to ministry Bapt. Ch.; lic. profl. counselor, Tex. Alumni sec. La. Coll., 1947-48; pastor Folsom (La.) Bapt. Ch., 1950-52, Ethel (La.) Bapt. Ch., 1952-53, Haltom Rd. Bapt. Ch., Ft. Worth, 1954-57; Disting. prof. pastoral ministry Southwestern Bapt. Theol. Sem., Ft. Worth, 1957—; guest lectr. Internat. Bapt. Theol. Sem., Cali, Colombia, 1990, New Zealand Bapt. Theol. Coll., Auckland, 1990, Whitley Coll. of U. Melbourne, Australia, 1990, Kenya Bapt. Theol. Coll., 1991. Author: Pastoral Care in the Church, rev. edit., 1992, People Who Care, Dealing With Doubt, It's Tough Growing Up, Life Under Pressure: Dealing With Stress in Marriage, The Promise of Counseling, Take Care, Becoming You, Beginning Your Ministry, Caring for the Caregivers, Change Happens: Finding Your Way Through Life's Transitions; (with others) Southwestern Sermons, Everyday, Five Minutes With God When Trouble Comes, Toward Creative Urban Strategy, Contemporary Trends in Christian Thought, Broadman Devotional Annual, An Approach to Christian Ethics; contbr. to: Holman Study Bible; contbr. articles to Pastoral Psychology, Home Life, other religious jours. With armed forces, ETO, 1944-45. Fellow La. State U., 1948-49, Southwestern Med. Sch., 1969-70. Mem. Soc. Pastoral Theology, Assn. Couples for Marriage Enrichment, Assn. for Clin. Pastoral Edn., Bapt. World Alliance (commn. on ch. leadership). Office: Southwestern Bapt Theol Sem PO Box 22000 Fort Worth TX 76122

BRISTOW, WALTER JAMES, JR., retired judge; b. Columbia, S.C., Oct. 14, 1924; s. Walter James and Caroline Belser (Melton) B.; m. Katherine Stewart Mullins, Sept. 12, 1952; children: Walter James III, Katherine Mullins (dec.). Student Va. Mil. Inst., 1941-43; AB, U. N.C., 1947; LLB cum laude, U. S.C., 1947-49; LLM, Harvard U., 1950. Mem. Marchant, Bristow & Bates, 1953-76; mem. S.C. Ho. of Reps., 1956-58; mem. S.C. Senate, 1958-76; resident judge 5th Jud. Cir. Ct. S.C., 1976-88; ret. 1988; nat. pres. Conf. Ins. Legislators, 1974-75. Trustee Elvira Wright Fund for Crippled Children. Served with AUS, 1943-45; ETO; brig. gen. S.C. Army N.G. Decorated Meritorious Service medal. Mem. ABA, Wig and Robe, Capital City Club, Cotillion Club, Forest Lake Club, Palmetto Club, Columbia Ball Club, Sertoma, Alpha Tau Omega. Democrat. Office: PO Box 1147 Columbia SC 29202-1147

BRISTOW, WILLIAM ARTHUR, artist, educator; b. San Antonio, Feb. 1, 1937; s. Edgar Allen and Sue Agnes (Wood) B.; m. Wilanna O. Blanton, Aug. 2, 1958; 1 child, Elizabeth Ann Bristow Krouse. BFA, U. Tex., 1958; MFA, U. Fla., 1960. Instr. art U. Fla., Gainesville, 1959-60; instr. San Antonio Art Inst., 1960-61; prof. art Trinity U., San Antonio, 1960—; artist, tchr. Ghost Ranch, Abiqui, N.Mex., summers 1967, 68. Works represented in permanent collections at Dallas and Houston Mus. of Fine Arts; designer mural for Frost Nat. Bank, 1974; designer, fabricator U.S. Pavilion Fountain, 1968; included in Tex. Project, Archives of Am. Art, 1983; contbr. articles to art pubs. Piper prof. Piper Found., 1983; Scott fellow Trinity U., 1989. Mem. Coppini Acad. (hon. lifetime), San Antonio Watercolor Group (hon. lifetime). Episcopalian. Home: 344 Wildrose Ave San Antonio TX 78209-

3817 Office: Trinity U Dept Art 715 Stadium Dr San Antonio TX 78212-3104

BRITT, W. EARL, federal judge; b. McDonald, N.C., Dec. 7, 1932; s. Dudley H. and Martha Mae (Hall) B.; m. Judith Moore, Apr. 17, 1976. Student, Campbell Jr. Coll., 1952; BS, Wake Forest U., 1956, JD, 1958. Bar: N.C. 1958. Pvt. practice law Fairmont, N.C., 1959-72, Lumberton, N.C., 1972-80; judge U.S. Dist. Ct. (ea. dist.) N.C., from 1980, chief judge, 1983-90; mem. Jud. Conf. Com. on Automation and Tech., 1990-95; 4th cir. dist. judge rep. to Jud. Conf. U.S., 1991—. Trustee Southeastern Community Coll., 1965-70, Southeastern Gen. Hosp., Lumberton, 1965-69, Pembroke State U., 1967-72; bd. govs. U. N.C. Served with U.S. Army, 1953-55. Mem. N.C. Bar Assn., Fed. Judges Assn. (bd. dirs., v.p. , pres. 1995-97). Baptist. Office: US Dist Ct PO Box 27504 Raleigh NC 27611-7504

BRITTAIN, CLAY D., golf club executive; b. 1929. With Chesterfield Inn, Myrtle Beach, S.C., 1951—; ptnr. Ocean Front Investors, Myrtle Beach, 1988; prin. Coastal Corp., Myrtle Beach; chmn. bd. Myrtle Beach Nat. Golf Club; owner, operator motel. Office: Myrtle Beach Nat Golf Club 1203 48th Ave N Ste 200 Myrtle Beach SC 29577

BRITTAIN, JACK OLIVER, lawyer; b. Greenwood, La., Sept. 24, 1928; s. Clarence Lafitte and Irene Geneva (Humphries) B.; m. Ann Marie Williams, Nov. 25, 1955; children: Jack Jr., Marguerite, Rebecca, Lala, Eliza, John, Mary Jane. BA, La. Tech. U., 1949; JD, La. State U., 1957. Bar: La. 1957, U.S. Dist. Ct. La. 1960, U.S. Ct. Appeals (5th cir. 1961). Assoc. Watson & Williams, Natchitoches, La., 1957-61; ptnr. Watson, Williams & Brittain, Natchitoches, 1961-70; sr. ptnr. Brittain, Williams, McGlathery, Passman & Sylvester, Natchitoches, 1970-91, Brittain and Sylvester, Natchitocches, 1992—. Maj., U.S. Army, 1951-53. Mem. La. Assn. of Def. Counsel (bd. dirs.), Fedn. of Ins. and Corp. Cons., Def. Rsch. Inst. (co-chmn.), Rotary, Natchitoches Parish C. of C. (named Man of Yr. 1965), Jr. C. of C. (named Man of Yr. 1963). Democrat. Methodist. Home: 919 Parkway Dr Natchitoches LA 71457-2059 Office: Brittain & Sylvester 113 E 5th St PO Box 2059 Natchitoches LA 71457

BRITTAIN, JERRY LEE, naval officer, neuropsychologist; b. Bossier City, La., Aug. 4, 1947; s. Melvin Houston and Reba Cleo (Eaves) B.; m. Judith Lynn Justice, Mar. 18, 1988. BA in Psychology, Villanova U., 1972; BS in Biology, Centenary Meth. Coll., 1974; MA in Counseling Psychology, La. Tech U., 1975; PhD in Clin. Psychology, Calif. Sch. Profl. Psychology, Frenso, 1978. Lic. clin. psychologist, Calif., Va. Commd. officer USN, 1979, advanced through grades to comdr., neuropsychologist, 1979—; neuropsychologist Naval Hosp., Portsmouth, Va., 1989—. Pres. Colonial Place/Riverview Civic League, Norfolk, Va., 1992-94. Mem. Nat. Acad. Neuropsychology, Internat. Neuropsychology Assn., Va. Head Injury Found. Republican. Home: 520 Pennsylvania Ave Norfolk VA 23508-2835 Office: Navy Med Clin Annapolis MD 21402-5050

BRITTON, LAURENCE GEORGE, research scientist; b. Hampton Court, Eng., Sept. 26, 1951; came to U.S., 1981; s. George and Barbara Mavis (Card) B.; m. Helen Lynn Grass, Apr. 16, 1983 (div. 1987); 1 child, Robert; m. Carol-Ann Kirby, Jan. 6, 1995. BS with 1st class honors, U. Leeds, Eng., 1974; PhD in Fuel and Combustion Sci., U. Leeds, 1977. Chartered engr., Eng. Rsch. fellow dept. elec. engring. U. Southhampton, Eng., 1978-81; sr. combustion scientist Union Carbide Corp. Tech. Ctr., South Charleston, W.Va., 1981-84; project scientist process fire and explosion hazards Union Carbide Corp. Tech. Ctr., South Charleston, 1984-89, rsch. scientist, 1990—; guest lectr. Coll. Grad. Studies, Sch. Engring. and Sci., U. W.Va., 1991-94; mem. fueling systems com. U. K. Ministry Def., 1978-81; speaker at profl. metings and symposia; mem. U.S. Coast Guard/U.S. Dept. Transp. Static Electricity Adv. Group, 1993—. Contbr. articles to sci. jours. Fellow Inst. Energy; mem. AICHE (mem. editl. rev. bd. Process Safety Progress 1993—, William H. Doyle award 1986, 89), Combustion Inst., Ctr. for Chem. Process Safety (engring. design practices com. 1988-93, reactive materials storage and handling com. 1990—, design basis for process safety sys. com. 1993—), Nat. Fire Protection Assn. (explosion protection sys. com., hazardous chems. com. static electricity com., properties of flammable liquids com.), Chem. Mfrs. Assn. (flame resistant clothing issues group 1995), Chem. Mfrs. Assn./Am. Petroleum Inst. (reactive hazards tech. task force 1995). Office: Union Carbide Corp Tech Ctr PO Box 8361 South Charleston WV 25303

BRITTON, PATRICIA ANN, nursing educator, nursing administrator; b. Waterbury, Conn., Mar. 23, 1955; d. Albert L. and Ida A. (Ciriello) Valente; m. Ronald J. Britton, June 20, 1981; children: Matthew Ronald, Laura Patricia. BSN, U. Conn., 1977; MS, Western Conn. State U., 1983, MSN, 1991. Cert. nursing administr. Staffing coord. St. Mary's Hosp., Waterbury, Conn., 1983-85; asst. supr. psychiatry Waterbury (Conn.) Hosp., 1986-88; program coord., dir. RSP program Danbury (Conn.) Hosp., 1988-90; dir. nursing I Greater Bridgeport (Conn.) Community Mental Health Ctr., 1991-92; clin. nursing educator Mattatuck Community Coll., Waterbury, Conn., 1991-92; med. mgmt. coord. ITT Hartford Ins. Co., 1992-93; asst. prof. nursing Barry U., Miami Shores, Fla., 1993-95; dir. nursing The Renfrew Ctr., Coconut Creek, Fla., 1995-96; nursing edn. cons. Fla. Bd. Nursing, Jacksonville, 1996—. Book reviewer Jour. of Nursing and Healthcare, 1992—. Mem. ANA, Conn. Nurses Assn., Sigma Theta Tau (manuscript reviewer Image 1993—).

BRITTON, WESLEY ALAN, English language educator; b. Munich, Sept. 29, 1953; came to the U.S., 1955; s. Royce J. and Betty Ruth (Somers) B. BA in English, Calif. U. Pa., 1977; MA in English, U. North Tex., 1986, PhD, 1990. News dir. Calif. U. Pa., 1975-77; prin. Wes Britton Advt. Agy., Dallas, 1977-79; pub. rels. dir. VISTA, Dallas, 1982-83; teaching fellow U. North Tex., Denton, 1983-90, prof. English, 1990-92; instr. Paul Quinn Coll., Dallas, 1991-93; prof. Bacone C.C., Muskoqee, Okla., Southeast Okla. Coll., Durant Cooke C.C., 1993-94, Grayson C.C., Sherman, Tex., 1994—; cons. Wentwork Films, Washington, 1991; instr. Cedar Valley Community Coll., Dallas, 1992; bd. dirs. KNON, Dallas, 1992. Contbr. poetry, plays, articles to profl. jours., ency. entries and indices. Trustee Assn. Individuals with Disabilities, Dallas, 1981-83; adv. bd. North Tex. Radio for Blind, Dallas, 1983; writer, producer Sta. KERA-Fm Radio, Dallas, 1978-79. Mem. MLA, North Tex. Interdisciplinary Forum (pres. 1990-91), Grad. Students in English (v.p. 1988-89), Rsch. Soc. Am. Periodicals, Texoma Area Poetry Soc. (program dirs. 1995—), Mark Twain Circle Am., Friends Mark Twain Ctr., We. Lit. Assn., Sigma Tau Delta. Democrat. Home: 9536 Meadowknoll Dr Dallas TX 75243-6114

BRIUER, ELKE MOERSCH, editor; b. Darmstadt, Germany, Feb. 20, 1943; came to U.S., 1962; d. Karl Wilhelm and Ilse (Hohorst) Moersch; divorced; children: Patricia Mae Monroe, Kenneth Frank Gaston; m. Frederick L. Briuer, Oct. 9, 1986. BA in German cum laude, U. Md., 1977, postgrad., 1984; postgrad., U.T., 1980; MS in Comm., Miss. Coll., 1992. Accredited pub. rels. profl. Pub. affairs officer Med. Ctr. 97th Gen. Hosp., Frankfurt, Germany, 1982-84; supr. pub. affairs officer USMCA, Aschaffenburg, Germany, 1984-86; pub. affairs specialist 5th rctg. brigade U.S. Army, San Antonio, 1986-88; writer, editor (Technology Transfer Specialist) U.S. Army Engr. Waterways Expt. Sta., Vicksburg, 1988—. Author: (recruitment pamphlet) The Quick Answer Book of U.S. Army Recruiting Support Command Exhibits, 1989, (booklet) The Young Scientist's Introduction to Wetlands, 1993; dir. (video) The Black Swamp, 1995; editor: Caduceus, Ad Libs, Wetlands Rsch. Program Bull., 1991—; writer, editor: (multi-media CD-ROM) Wetlands Rsch. Program Summary, 1991-94; contbr. numerous articles to newspapers and mags. Sec. Vicksburg Art Assn., 1990-91, newsletter editor, 1990-93; mem. Soc. Wetland Sci., 1991—, Miss. Heritage Trust, 1991—, Heritage Herald editor, 1994—; 2d v.p. Vicksburg Cmty. Concert Assn., 1994-96. Mem. So. Pub. Rels. Fedn., Pub. Rels. Assn. Miss. Office: US Army Engr Waterways Expt Sta CEWES-IM-MV-E 3909 Halls Ferry Rd Vicksburg MS 39180-6133

BRIZENDINE, ANTHONY LEWIS, civil engineering educator; b. Bluefield, W.Va., Apr. 27, 1962; s. Donald Lewis B. and Erma Louise (Stowers) Havens; m. Laora Eugenia Dauberman, July 13, 1991; children: Lauren Renia, Elizabeth Kaitlyn, Courtney Elaine. AAS, Wytheville C.C., 1987; BS, Bluefield State Coll., 1989; MSCE, Va. Poly. Inst. and State U., 1990; postgrad. in engring., W.Va. U. Draftsman, detailer Peters Equipment Co., Inc., Bluefield, 1981-85, design engr., 1985-87, project civil engr., 1987-89; instr. Wytheville (Va.) C.C., 1991; instr. Fairmont (W.Va.) State Coll., 1991-93, asst. prof., 1993-95, dir. honors program, 1994—, assoc. prof., 1996—; cons. U.S. Army Corps Engrs., Vicksburg, Miss., 1992-94; advisor ASCE Student Orgn. Fairmont State Coll., 1991—. Grantee NSF/WV EPSCOR, 1993, 94, 95; recipient W.Va. Young Civil Engr. of Yr. award, 1995. Mem. ASTM, ASCE (nat. tech. curricula and accreditation com. 1996-2000, v.p. W.Va. sect. 1994, pres. W.V.A. Northern Br., 1996, pres. W.Va. sect. 1996-97, sec./treas. 1993, del. mgmt. conf. 1995, chairperson W.Va. sect. continuing edn., pres. No. W.Va. br. 1996, pres.-elect 1995), Am. Soc. Engring. Educators, Am. Soc. Hwy. Engrs., Internat. Soc. Soil Mechanics and Found. Engrs. Home: PO Box 1043 Fairmont WV 26555 Office: Fairmont State Coll 1201 Locust Ave Fairmont WV 26554

BROAD, DAVID BENJAMIN, sociologist; b. Bklyn., Oct. 30, 1946; s. Monroe M. and Frances (Buxbaum) Wegner; m. Judy Diann Dawdy, Aug. 11, 1989. BS, U. Houston, 1971, MA, 1973; MS, Canisius Coll., 1987; PhD, SUNY, 1985. Lectr. in sociology Niagara C.C., Sanborn, N.Y., 1974-77; instr. sociology Buffalo State Coll., 1977-84; asst. prof. sociology Canisius Coll., Buffalo, 1984-87; assoc. prof. sociology Adams State Coll., Alamosa, Colo., 1987-89; prof. sociology William Penn Coll., Oskaloosa, Iowa, 1989-91; prof., head dept. Tenn. State U., 1991—. Author: (with others) Jock: Male Identity and Sport, 1980; editor: Student, Self and Society, 1996; contbr. articles to profl. jours. Named Coach of Yr. Nat. Assn. of Intercollegiate Athletics, 1987, 88; recipient Gold medal Empire State Games, 1987. Mem. AAUP, Popular Culture Assn., So. Sociol. Soc. Office: Tenn State Univ Dept Sociology Nashville TN 37209

BROADHEAD, JAMES LOWELL, electrical power industry executive; b. New Rochelle, N.Y., Nov. 28, 1935; s. Clarence James and Mabel Roseader (Bowser) B.; m. Sharon Ann Rulon, May 6, 1967; children: Jeffrey Thorton, Kristen Ann, Carolyn Mary, Catherine Lee. B.M.E., Cornell U., 1958; LL.B., Columbia U., 1963. Bar: N.Y. 1963. Mech. engr. sales dept. Ingersoll-Rand Co., 1958-59; asso. Debevoise, Plimpton, Lyons & Gates, N.Y.C., 1963-68; asst. sec. St. Joe Minerals Corp., N.Y.C., 1968-70, sec., 1970-77, gen. counsel, 1973-74, v.p. devel., 1976-77, exec. v.p., 1980-81, pres., 1981-82, also dir.; sr. vp. GTE Corp., Stamford, Conn., 1984-88; also pres. GTE Corp. telephone ops., Stamford, Conn., 1984-88; pres., CEO, chmn. bd. Fla. Power & Light Co./FPL Group, Inc., West Palm Beach, Fla., 1989—; chmn., CEO Energy Rsch. Corp., Danbury, Conn., 1973-74; v.p. St. Joe Petroleum Co., N.Y.C., 1974-76; pres. St. Joe Zinc Co., Pitts., 1977-80; exec. v.p., dir. U.S. Industries, 1983; dir. Pittston Co., Barnett Banks, Inc., Delta Air Lines, Inc. Editor: Columbia Law Rev., 1963. Served with U.S. Army, 1960-61. Club: Union League, Middlesex. Office: FPL Group Inc 700 Universe Blvd Juno Beach FL 33408-2657

BROADHEAD, JOSEPH JAMES, airline company executive; b. Chgo., Sept. 2, 1944; s. Joseph James and Ruth Irene (Snell) B.; m. Patricia Ann Tousignant, Aug. 12, 1967; children: Robert James, Scott Patrick. BS in Geology, U. Kans., 1967. 1st officer Fed. Express Corp., Memphis, 1974-79, capt., 1980, project mgr. DA-20, 1980-82, project mgr. B-727, 1982-84, check airman B-727, 1984-86, asst. chief pilot, 1986—. asst. coach Bartlett (Tenn.) Jr. Pros Soccer, 1986. Served to lt. USN, 1967-73. Republican. Methodist. Club: Investors Unltd. (Memphis) (pres. 1983). Office: Fed Express Corp PO Box 727 Memphis TN 38194-0001

BROADRICK, STEVEN MARK, manufacturing executive; b. Odessa, Tex., Oct. 13, 1957; s. Archie Ewin and Mary Helen (Arthur) B.; m. Cherie Janice Charping, Oct. 13, 1989. Pre-med., Tex. Tech. U., 1976-79; B in Bus. Adminstrn. and Mgmt., U. Houston, 1996. Sales rep. Bovaird Supply Co., Houston, Galveston, 1981-86; regional rep. Durabla Mfg. Co., Houston, 1988-89; account exec. Hahn & Clay, Houston, 1990—. Home: 9630 FM 1488 Magnolia TX 77355-1410

BROCK, EUNICE LEE MILLER, realtor; b. Memphis, Mar. 17, 1930; d. Glendon Lee and Kellner (Carter) Miller; children: Clifton Michael, Douglas Martin, Melinda Kellner. BS, Miss. Univ. for Women, 1951; MS, U. N.C., 1964. Cert. residential specialist. Writer I. P. Callison, San Diego, 1952-54; real estate broker Mel Rashkis & Assocs. Inc., Chapel Hill, N.C., 1963-81; real estate prin. Little, Bryan, Worth, Lucas & Brock Inc., Chapel Hill, 1981-86, Eunice Brock & Assocs., Chapel Hill, 1989-95; gen. ptnr. The Fountains, 1989-95; chmn. bd. dirs. Brock & Hall Real Estate, Chapel Hill, 1995—; cons. Cameron Glen, Chapel Hill, 1985-90, West Franklin Perservation Ptnr., Chapel Hill, 1986—, West Rosemary Ptnrs., 1989-92. Real estate columnist Chapel Hill Newspaper, 1980—; contbr. articles to profl. jours. Chmn. Recreation Commn., Chapel Hill, 1974, Chapel Hill Appearance Commn., 1978. Pub. Pvt. Ptnr., 1986—, Downtown Commn., 1987—; v.p., chairperson Town of Chapel Hill Bicentennial, 1993-94; bd. visitors U. N.C. Libr. Sch., 1993—; writer Web Site for Brock & Hall Real Estate, 1995. Mem. Nat. Assn. Realtors, Realtors Nat. Mktg. Inst., Chapel Hill Bd. Realtors (v.p. 1980). Democrat. Presbyterian. Office: Brock & Hall Real Estate 311 W Rosemary St Chapel Hill NC 27516-2514

BROCK, HELEN RACHEL MCCOY, retired mental health and community health nurse; b. Cromwell, Okla., Dec. 10, 1924; d. Samuel Robert Lee and Ire Etta (Pounds) McCoy; m. Clois Lee Brock, Sept. 29, 1963; children: Dwayne, Joyce, Peggy, Ricki, Stacey. AS, Southwestern Union Coll., Keene, Tex., 1968; BS in Nursing, Union Coll., Lincoln, Nebr., 1970; postgrad., Vernon Regional Jr. Coll., Tex., 1972, 76; MPH, Loma Linda (Calif.) U., 1983. Cert. ARC nurse. Dir. nursing Chillicothe (Tex.) Clinic-Hosp., 1970-77, Pike County Hosp., Waverly, Ohio, 1977-79, Marion County Hosp., Jefferson, Tex., 1979-81; nurse III, nursing unit supr, patient health educator Vernon State Hosp., Maximum Security for Criminally Insane, 1981-96; retired, 1996; nurse, admissions and assessments Texhoma Community Health Svcs., 1987-94. Mem. Am. Nurses Assn., Tex. Nurses Assn. Home: PO Box 238 Chillicothe TX 79225-0238

BROCK, KERRY LYNN, broadcast executive; b. Ft. Lewis, Wash., Feb. 4, 1957; d. Frank Harvey and Carol Jean (Carpenter) B.; m. John Michael Seigenthaler, Jan. 4, 1992. BA in Speech, Communications, Washington State U., Pullman, 1979. Anchor, reporter KNDU TV, Kennewick, Wash., 1979-80, KIVI TV, Boise, Ind., 1980-81, WOWT TV, Omaha, 1981-83, KOMO TV, Seattle, 1983-93; broadcasting, programming dir. First Amendment Ctr. Vanderbilt U., Nashville, 1993—. Moderator (TV program) Freedom Speaks. Bd. dirs. Wash. State Leukemia Soc., Seattle, 1986-93, Sinking Creek Film Festival, Nashville, 1993—; trustee Wash. State U., Pullman, 1990—; adv. bd. dirs. Seattle Jr. League, 1992-93. Mem. NATAS (bd. dirs.), Soc. Profl. Journalists, Radio and TV News Dirs. Assn., Internat. Women's Media Found., Nat. Press Club. Office: The Freedom Forum First Amendment Ctr 1207 18th Ave S Nashville TN 37212-2807

BROCK, LAURA KRUEGER, accountant; b. Waukegan, Ill., Feb. 22, 1955; d. George Edward and Joan Eileen (Fellows) Krueger; m. James C. Brock, Jr., Sept. 27, 1980; children: Brittney Lynn, Tyson James. AA, St. Petersburg (Fla.) Jr. Coll., 1975; BS in Acctg., Fla. State U., 1978. CPA; cert. fraud examiner. Staff acct. Harper, Van Scoik Co. CPA, Clearwater, Fla., 1978-84, mgr., 1984-88, ptnr., 1989-95; mem. audit dept. Gregory, Sharer & Stuart, St. Petersburg, 1995—; mem. task force contributed capital Govt. Acctg. Stds. Bd., N.Y.C., 1991-96; chmn. audit com. Clearwater Jr. Woman's Club, 1988-92, pres., 1985, treas., 1984, bd. dirs., 1984-87. Trustee Archdiocese Miami/ Diocese St. Petersburg/ Diocese Venice pension plan, 1993—; mem. fin. coun. St. Petersburg Cath. Diocese, 1994-96; campaign treas. St. Petersburg Jr. Coll. Yes com., 1995; pres. Blessed Sacrament Sch. Bd., Seminole, 1994, bd. dirs., 1992-96. Recipient Judy Lutz Leadership award Clearwater Jr. Woman's Club, 1985, Clearwater Panhellenic Achievement award, 1994. Mem. AICPA, Am. Women's Soc. CPAs (charter, pres. 1990-91, v.p. 1989-90, treas. 1983-84, 88-89, scholarship chair 1991-92, bd. dirs. 1984-85, 89-91), Fla. Inst. CPAs (bd. govs. 1993-96, not-for-profit com. 1995—, pres. West Coast chpt. 1993-94, sec. 1991-92, treas. 1990-91, bd. dirs. 1987-95), Fla. Govt. Fin. Officers Assn. (Gulf Coast chpt.), Assn. Cert. Fraud Examiners (dir. 1995-96, v.p. 1996—), Clearwater Alumnae Panhellenic (corr. sec. 1991-92, recording sec. 1992-93, treas. 1993, v.p. 1994, pres. 1995-96), Rotary, Delta Delta Delta (del. 1990-94, treas. 1987-91, pres. 1986). Republican. Roman Catholic. Home: 12276 106th Ave N Largo FL 33778 Office: Gregory Sharer & Stuart 100 2d Ave South #606 Saint Petersburg FL 33701

BROCK, PAUL WARRINGTON, lawyer; b. Mobile, Ala., Feb. 23, 1928; s. Glen Porter and Esther (Goodwin) B.; m. Grace Leigh Blasingame, Sept. 4, 1948 (dec. June 1960); children—Paul W., Bette Leigh, Valerie Grace; m. Louise Morris Shearer, July 6, 1962; children—Louise Shearer, Richard Goodwin. Student, Ala. Poly. Inst., 1944; B.S., U. Ala., 1948, J.D., 1950. Bar: Ala. 1950. Practiced in Mobile, 1953—; mem. Hand, Arendall & Bedsole, 1953-56, Hand, Arendall, Bedsole, Greaves & Johnston, 1956-95, hand, Arendall, L.L.C., 1996—. Served to 2d lt. USAF, 1952-53. Recipient Nat. Balfour award Sigma Chi, 1946-47. Mem. ABA, Internat. Assn. Ins. and Def. Counsel, Assn. Def. Trial Attys., Ala. Bar Assn., Mobile Bar Assn., Am. Coll. Trial Lawyers, Am. Bar Found., Ala. Def. Lawyers Assn. (past pres.), Def. Rsch. Inst. (past pres.), Nat. Assn. R.R. Trial Counsel, Mobile Am. Inn of Ct. (past pres.), Omicron Delta Kappa, Beta Gamma Sigma. Republican. Episcopalian. Home: 4768 Bexley Ln Mobile AL 36608-2482 Office: PO Box 123 Mobile AL 36601-0123

BROCKMAN, LESLIE RICHARD, social worker; b. St. Paul, Aug. 10, 1940; s. Leslie Blair Brockman and Mary Emma (Miller) Hemenway; m. Rosemarie Lemus, Aug. 18, 1962; 1 child, Christopher Scott. BA, Loyola U. of L.A., 1963; MS, Troy (Ala.) State U., 1977; MS in Social Work, U. Tex., Arlington, 1984. Lic. profl. counselor; lic. chem. dependency counselor, marriage and family therapist, master social worker; advanced clin. practitioner ACSW; diplomate clin. social work; cert. cognitive-behavioral therapist; cert. compulsive gambling counselor, criminal justice specialist; diplomate Am. Acad. Forensic Counseling. Exec. dir. Family Assessment Consultation Therapy Svc., Ft. Worth, 1984—; commd. 2d lt. USAF, 1963, advanced through grades to maj., retired, 1983. Fellow NASW (diplomate), Am. Bd. Med. Psychotherapists (diplomate); mem. ACA, Am. Assn. Marriage and Family Therapists, Am. Mental Health Counselors Assn., Am. Assn. Behavioral Therapists, Internat. Assn. Marriage and Family Therapists, Nat. Assn. Forensic Counseling. Home: 6400 Trail Lake Dr Fort Worth TX 76133-4810 Office: FACTS Inc 2821 Lackland Rd # 300A Fort Worth TX 76116

BRODALE, LOUISE LADO, medical, post surgery and geriatrics nurse; b. Cleve., Dec. 2, 1924; d. Louis G. and Velma Susan (Palady) Lado; m. Roger M. Brodale, Sept. 18, 1953; 4 children. Diploma, Maumee Valley Hosp., Toledo, 1947; AA, Tarrant County Jr. Coll., Ft. Worth, 1974, AAS, 1976; BSN, Tex. Christian U., 1980, MA in Liberal Arts, 1984; diploma fashion merchandising, Internat. Corr. Schs., 1991, diploma dressmaking and design, 1993. RN, Tex., Ohio; cert. tchr., Tex. Head nurse med. ward San Antonio Tuberculoses Hosp., 1962-69; supr. Campbell-White Co., Forest Hill, Tex., 1986, Forest Hill Nursing Home, Ft. Worth, 1986; with Home Care Svc. Am., 1986-89, geriatrics nurse, 1990-93. With Nurse Corps U.S. Army, 1947-51; capt. USAF, 1951-54. Home: 3805 Kimberly Ln Fort Worth TX 76133-2020

BRODEUR, THOMAS J., information systems specialist; b. Washington, June 30, 1955; s. Harold Hills and Marie Norma (Chabot) B.; m. Mary Patricia Rader, June 12, 1982; 1 child, Michelle Marie. BA in Comm., Va. Polytechnic Inst. & State U., 1978; attended, George Mason U., 1979, Corcoran Sch. Fine Art, 1979. Prodr., dir. David Taylor Naval Ship Rsch. and Devel. Ctr.; dir, publs. dept. BDM Corp., Riyadh, Saudi Arabia, 1985-89; project mgr. Skyho Am., Inc., 1989-91; mgr. Women's Med. Group, P.A., 1991-93; dir. adminstrn. Premier Family Care, P.A., 1993-94; mgr. computer ops. Barnett Brass & Copper, 1994—; pub. speaker numerous presentations. Home: 2949 Sanctuary Blvd Jaxville Bch FL 32250-2567 Office: Barnett Brass & Copper 3333 Lenox Ave Jacksonville FL 32254-4225

BRODIE, HARLOW KEITH HAMMOND, psychiatrist, educator; b. Stamford, Conn., Aug. 24, 1939; s. Lawrence Sheldon and Elizabeth White (Hammond) B.; m. Brenda Ann Barrowclough, Jan. 26, 1967; children: Melissa Verduin, Cameron Keith, Tyler Hammond, Bryson Barrowclough. AB, Princeton U., 1961; MD, Columbia U., 1965; LLD hon., U. Richmond, 1987; LHD (hon.), High Point U., 1992. Diplomate Am. Bd. Psychiatry and Neurology. Intern Ochsner Found. Hosp., New Orleans, 1965-66; resident in psychiatry Columbia-Presbyn. Med. Center, N.Y.C., 1966-68; clin. assoc. intramural research program NIMH, 1968-70; asst. prof. psychiatry, dir. gen. clin. research center Stanford U. Med. Sch., 1970-74; prof. psychiatry, chmn. dept. Duke U. Med. Sch., 1974-82, James B. Duke prof. psychiatry and behavioral scis., 1981—, prof. dept. psychology, prof. law, 1980—; psychiatrist-in-chief Duke U. Med. Center, 1974-82; chancellor Duke U., 1982-85, pres., 1985-93, pres. emeritus, 1993—; mem. Pres. Biomed. Rsch. Panel, 1975; mem. Carnegie Coun. on Adolescent Devel., 1986—; trustee Com. for Econ. Devel., 1986—, mem. subcom. on edn. and child devel., 1990; trustee Nat. Humanities Ctr., 1988-93; mem. nat. rev. and adv. panel for improving campus race rels. Ford Found., 1990—; mem. subcom. on Edn. on Child Devel. Com., 1990; bd. dirs. Inst. of Medicine, Mental Health and Behavioral Medicine, 1981-83, chmn., 1981-82; mem. Com. on Leadership Devel., Am. Coun. on Edn., 1990-93; chmn. Com. on Substance Abuse and Mental Health Issues in AIDS Rsch., 1992—. Co-author: The Importance of Mental Health Services to General Health Care, 1979, Modern Clinical Psychiatry, 1982; co-editor: American Handbook of Psychiatry, vols. 6, 7 and 8, 1975, 81, 86, Controversy in Psychiatry, 1978, Psychiatry at the Crossroads, 1980, Critical Problems in Psychiatry, 1982, Signs and Symptoms in Psychiatry, 1983, Consultation-Liaison Psychiatry and Behavioral Medicine, 1986, AIDS and Behavior: An Integrated Approach, 1994; assoc. editor: Am. Jour. Psychiatry. Recipient Disting. Med. Alumni award Columbia U., 1985, Disting. Alumnus award Ochsner Found. Hosp., 1984, Strecker award Inst. of Pa. Hosp., 1980, N.C. award for sci., 1990, William C. Menninger Meml. award ACP, 1994. Fellow Royal Soc. of Medicine; mem. Am. Psychiat. Assn. (sec. 1977-81, pres. 1982-83), Inst. Medicine, Royal Coll. Psychiatrists, Soc. Biol. Psychiatry (A.E. Bennet rsch. award 1970). Home: 63 Beverly Dr Durham NC 27707-2223 Office: Duke U Office of Pres Emeritus 205 E Duke Bldg Durham NC 27708

BRODSKY, LEWIS, psychiatrist, educator; b. Mont., Que., Can., Nov. 24, 1942; came to U.S., 1967; s. Abraham and Zora (Schaizik) B.; m. Frances Mary Daly, Sept. 24, 1965 (div. 1978); children: Boris Michael, Deborah Anne, Aaron Phillip. BSc in Biochemistry with honors, McGill U., Mont., 1963; MD, U. Ottawa, Can., 1967. Lic. psychiatrist, Calif. Fla., Ga. Hawaii, Mich., Ont., Can. Extern in psychiatry Ottawa Gen. Hosp., 1966; gen. rotating intern Sinai Hosp. Detroit, 1967-68, resident dept. psychiatry, 1968-70, chief resident, 1970-71, teaching fellow, rsch. assoc., 1971-72, asst. chief in patient svc., 1972-73, chief day hosp. svc. dept. psychiatry, 1973-74, chief intake and emergency svc. dept. psychiatry, 1974-76, 81-83, dir. edn. dept. psychiatry, 1976-77, acting chief liason psychiatry dept. psychiatry, 1977-78, now mem. courtesy staff; chief emergency response program dept. psychiatry Mt. Carmel Mercy Hosp., Detroit, 1974-76, chief emergency response program, 1981-83; pvt. practice psychiatry Tallahassee, Fla., 1983—; chmn. dept. psychiatry Tallahassee Meml. Regional Med. Ctr., 1990-91, med. dir. psychiat. emergency response program, 1990—, mem. active staff, chmn. dept. psychiatry, 1993-94; mem. courtesy staff Tallahassee Community Hosp.; editor U. Ottowa Psychiat. Jour., 1965-66; sec. house staff coun. Sinai Hosp Detroit, 1968, intern and resident recruitment com., 1968, 71-73, cardiac care com., 1972-73, ad hoc com. for ambulatory care, 1974-75, edn. com. dept. psychiatry, 1975-77, 81-83, cancer com., 1977-78; mem. substance abuse com. Mt. Carmel Mercy Hosp., 1981-83; mem. spinal cord injury com. Tallahassee Meml Regional Med. Ctr., 1985—, emergency svcs. com., 1986—, sleep disorder adv. com., 1986—, ultilization rev. com., 1985-86, 87-88, pharmacy and therapeutics com., 1986-87; asst. clin. prof. sch. human medicine dept. psychiatry Mich. State U., 1972-76; instr. sch. medicine dept. psychiatry Wayne State U., 1973-77, asst. prof., 1978-84; asst. prof. dept. human svcs. and studies Fla. State U., Tallahassee, 1984-85, assoc. prof. sch. nursing, 1988—; assoc. in medicine coll. medicine U. Fla., 1985—; mem. Am. Coll. Psychiatrists Psychiatry Resident-in-Tng. examination, youth and families case rev. com. on dept. health and rehab. svcs. State of Fla., 1983-85; presenter papers in field; lectr. in field. Contbr. over 30 articles to profl. and sci. jours. U. Ottawa scholar, 1964-65, Med. Rsch. Coun Can. scholar, 1965; recipient Physicians Recognition award AMA, 1970-86, 88-91. Mem. Am. Assn. for Emergency Psychiatry, Am. Psychiat. Assn. (steering com. for 5th edit. psychiat. knowledge and skills self-assessment program 1982-85), Am. Physicians Fellowship, Am. Group Psychotherapy Assn., Am. Assn. for

Geriatric Psychiatry, Internat. Psychosomatics Inst., Assn. Acad. Psychiatry, Capital Psychiat. Soc. (pres.-elect 1992-94), Can. Psychiat. Assn., Coll. Physicians and Surgeons Ont., Fla. Psychiat. Soc., Royal Soc. Health. Republican. Jewish. Office: 1407 M D Ln Ste B Tallahassee FL 32308-5375

BRODSKY, LEWIS CARL, federal agency administrator; b. Bklyn., Nov. 20, 1946; s. Jack and Beatrice (Solorsy) B.; m. Cathy-Jane Cooperman, June 16, 19868; children: James, Jordanna M. BA, Hofstra U., 1968; MS, CUNY, Bklyn., 1970. Prodn. asst. news ABC-TV, N.Y.C., 1966-67; tchr. N.Y.C. Bd. Edn., 1971-72; chief pub. affairs Headquarters USAR, Washington, 1975-80, 82-86; dir. info. divsn. USDA Agrl. Mktg., Washington, 1980-82; asst. dir. pub. affairs Selective Svc. Sys., Arlington, Va., 1986-93; dir. pub. and congl. affairs Selective Svc. Sys., Arlington, 1993—. Prodr. All for One, 1979; editor-in-chief Army Res. Mag., 1982; project dir. pub. rels. campaign First Musters Since Civil War, 1986, Silver Anvil award Pub. Rels. Soc. Am., 1986. Bd. dirs., publicity chmn. Springvale (Va.) Civic Assn., 1980-96; mem. exec. com. Va. ESGR com., Richmond, 1981-96. Lt. col. USAR, 1968-96. Mem. Nat. Assn. Govt. Communicators (v.p. adminstrn. 1989, pres. 1990, Disting. Svc. award 1993), Res. Officers Assn. (life). Office: Selective Svc Sys 1515 Wilson Blvd Arlington VA 22209

BROHAMMER, RICHARD FREDERIC, psychiatrist; b. Rockford, Ill., Nov. 9, 1934; s. Joseph C. and Marthe Marie (Ringuette) B.; m. Shirley Ruth Noble, June 22, 1956; children: Richard Frederic II, Renee Marie, Rory Christopher. PhB, U. Detroit, 1960; MD, U. Fla., 1964; postgrad. basic tng. diving medicine, Internat. Underwater Explorers Soc., 1973, advanced tng. diving medicine, 1974. Diplomate Am. Bd. Psychiatry and Neurology. Rsch. fellow tropical medicine La. State U., Costa Rica, 1963, Ctrl. Am., 1968; intern Duval Med. Ctr., Jacksonville, Fla., 1964-65; resident psychiatry U. Fla., 1965-68; practice medicine specializing in psychiatry, Ft. Lauderdale, Fla., 1968-93; mem. staff Broward Gen. Med. Ctr., 1968—, Imperial Point Med. Ctr., 1974—, Holy Cross Hosp., 1968—; chmn. dept. psychiatry Imperial Point Hosp., 1975-80, Holy Cross Hosp., 1981-83. Served with USAF, 1954-58, Korea. Mem. AMA (pres. student chpt. 1961-64), Broward County (Fla.) Med. Assn., Broward County Psychiat. Soc., Undersea Adventurers, Internat. Soc. Diving Medicine. Republican. Roman Catholic.

BROMBERG, ALAN ROBERT, law educator; b. Dallas, Nov. 24, 1928; s. Alfred L. and Juanita (Kramer) B.; m. Anne Ruggles, July 26, 1959. A.B., Harvard U., 1949; J.D., Yale U., 1952. Bar: Tex. 1952. Assoc. firm Carrington, Gowan, Johnson, Bromberg and Leeds, Dallas, 1952-56; atty. and cons., 1956-76; of counsel firm Jenkens & Gilchrist, P.C., 1976—; asst. prof. law So. Meth. U., 1956-58, assoc. prof., 1958-62, prof., 1962-83, Univ. Disting. prof., 1983—, mem. presdl. search group, 1971-72; faculty adviser Southwestern Law Jour., 1958-65; sr. fellow Yale U. Law Faculty, 1966-67; vis. prof. Stanford U., 1972-73; mem. adv. bd. U. Calif. Securities Regulation Inst., 1973-78, 79-87; counsel Internat. Data Systems, Inc., 1961-65, sec., dir., 1963-65; mem. Tex. Legis. Council Bus. and Commerce Code Adv. Com., 1966-67. Author: Supplementary Materials on Texas Corporations, 3d edit, 1971, Partnership Primer-Problems and Planning, 1961, Materials on Corporate Securities and Finance—A Growing Company's Search for Funds, 2d edit, 1965, Securities Fraud and Commodities Fraud, Vols. 1-7, 1967-93, 2nd edit., 1994, Crane and Bromberg on Partnership, 1968, Bromberg and Ribstein on Partnership, Vols. 1-2, 1988, Vols. 3-4, 1994, Bromberg and Ribstein on Limited Liability Partnerships and the Revised Uniform Partnership Act, 1995; mem. ednl. publs. adv. bd., Matthew Bender & Co., 1977-95, chmn., 1981-94; contbr. articles and revs. to law and bar jours.; adv. editor: Rev. Securities and Commodities Regulation, 1969—, Securities Regulation Law Jour, 1973—, Jour. Corp. Law, 1976—, Derivatives: Tax, Regulation, Finance, 1995—. Sec., bd. dirs. Community Arts Fund, 1963-73; gen. atty. Dallas Mus. Contemporary Arts, 1956-63; bd. dirs. Dallas Theater Center, 1955-73, sec., 1957-66, fin. com., 1957-65, mem. exec. com., 1957-70, 79-85, life, 1973—, v.p., trustee endowment fund, 1974-85; trustee Found. for the Arts, 1996—. Served as cpl. U.S. Army, 1952-54. Mem. ABA (coms. commodities, partnerships, fed. regulation securities), Dallas Bar Assn. (chmn. com. uniform partnership act 1959-61, libr. com. 1981-83), Tex. Bar Assn. (chmn. sect. corp. banking and bus. law 1967-68, vice chmn. 1965-67, com. corps. 1957—, mem. com. securities 1965—, chmn. 1965-69, mem. com. partnerships 1957—, chmn. 1979-81), Am. Law Inst. (life), Southwestern Legal Found. (co-chmn. securities com. 1982-85), Tex. Bus. Law Found. (bd. dirs. 1988—, co-chmn. legis. com. 1994—). Office: So Meth U Sch Law Dallas TX 75275-0116 also: 1445 Ross Ave Ste 3200 Dallas TX 75202-2799

BRONFIN, FRED, lawyer; b. New Orleans, Nov. 30, 1918; s. Philip and Edith M. B.; m. Carolyn Pick; children by previous marriage: Daniel R., Kenneth A. BA, Tulane U., 1938, JD, 1941. Bar: La. 1941, U.S. Dist. Ct. (ea. dist.) La. 1941, U.S. Ct. Appeals (5th cir.) 1951, U.S. Supreme Ct. 1973. Assoc. Rittenberg & Rittenberg, New Orleans, 1946-48; ptnr. Rittenberg, Weinstein & Bronfin, New Orleans, 1948-56; ptnr. Weinstein & Bronfin, New Orleans, 1956-62; ptnr. Bronfin, Heller, Steinberg & Berins and predecessor Bronfin, Heller, Feldman & Steinberg, New Orleans (now Bronfin & Heller), 1962-91, of counsel, 1991; dist. counsel B'nai B'rith. Served with USN, 1942-46. Mem. Orleans Bar Assn., La. Bar Assn., ABA, Estate Planning Council, Order of Coif, Phi Beta Kappa. Mem. editorial bd. Tulane Law Rev., 1939-41. Office: Bronfin & Heller LLC 650 Poydras St Ste 2500 New Orleans LA 70130-3379

BRONIS, STEPHEN J., lawyer; b. Miami, Fla., Feb. 23, 1947; s. Larry and Thelma (Berger) B.; children: Jason Michael, Tyler Adam, Kenneth Lawrence. BSBA, U. Fla., 1969; JD, Duke U., 1972. Bar: Fla. 1972, D.C. 1973, U.S. Dist. Ct. (so. dist.) Fla. 1973, U.S. Ct. Appeals (5th cir.) 1977, U.S. Supreme Ct. 1978, U.S. Ct. Appeals (11th cir.) 1981, U.S. Dist. Ct. (mid. dist.) Fla. 1989, Colo. 1994, U.S. Dist. Ct. Colo. 1996, U.S. Ct. Appeals (10th cir.) 1996. Asst. pub. defender 11th Jud. Cir. Fla., Miami, 1972-75; ptnr. Rosen & Bronis, P.A., Miami, 1975-77, Rosen, Portela, Bronis, et al., Miami, 1977-82, Bronis & Potela, P.A., Miami, 1982-90; pvt. practice, 1990-93; ptnr. Davis, Scott, Weber & Edwards, 1993-95, Zuckerman, Spaeder, Taylor & Evans, 1996—. mem. faculty Nat. Inst. of Trial Adv., U. N.C., Yeshiva U, Nova Sch. Law. Contbr. articles to profl. jours. Recipient Am. Jurisprudence award Bancroft-Whitney Co., 1972, cert. of Appreciation Fla. Shorthand Reporters Assn., 1984, Outstanding Service award Fla. Criminal Def. Attys. Assn., 1981. Mem. Fla. Criminal Def. Attys. Assn. (pres. 1980-81), Am. Bd. Criminal Lawyers (v.p. 1981-82), Assn. Trial Lawyers Am., Nat. Criminal Def. Attys. Assn., Calif. Attys. Criminal Justice, Acad. Fla. Trial Lawyers (criminal law sect. dir.). Democrat. Home: 2 Grove Isle Dr Apt 307 Miami FL 33133-4102 Office: 201 S Biscayne Blvd Ste 900 Miami FL 33131-4326

BRONKEMA, FREDERICK HOLLANDER, retired minister and church official; b. Albany, N.Y., Feb. 1, 1934; s. Frederick and Sadie (Hollander) B.; m. Marguerite Cobble, June 5, 1959; children: Frederick David, Timothy Dunning, John Hollander, Robert Kelton. BA magna cum laude, Whitworth Coll., 1956; MDiv, Princeton Theol. Sem., 1959, ThM, 1965; postgrad., New Coll., U. Edinburgh, Scotland, 1959-60, Union Theol. Sem., 1971-72, Ctr. for Intercultural Documentation, Cuernavaca, Mex., 1972. Ordained to ministry United Presbyn. Ch. in U.S.A., 1960. Asst. min. Craigsbank Ch. of Scotland, Edinburgh, 1959-60; min. Atlantic Highlands (N.J.) Presbyn. Ch., 1960-63; assoc. min. Red Clay Creek Presbyn. Ch., Wilmington, Del., 1963-65; fraternal worker United Presbyn. Ch., Lisbon and Figueira de Foz, Portugal, 1966-71; dir. Reconciliation Ecumenical Ctr., Figueira de Foz, 1966-71; prof. Evang. Theol. Sem., Carcavelos, Portugal, 1967-70; missionary Christian Ch. (Disciples of Christ) and Commn.; assoc., fraternal worker United Presbyn. Ch., Rome, 1972-76; dir., mng. editor The Future of Missionary Enterprise, documentation/publs. project Internat. Documentation and Communication Ctr., Rome, 1972-76, assoc. gen. sec., 1974-76; U.S.A. rep. Ecumenical Devel. Coop. Soc., N.Y.C., 1977-86; fraternal worker, missionary Presbyn. Ch. (U.S.A.) and Christian Ch. (Disciples of Christ); coord. Program and Ctr. Reconciliation, Honduran Christian Commn. for Devel., Tegucigalpa, 1986-88; dir. Human Rights Office, Nat. Coun. Chs. of Christ in U.S.A., N.Y.C., 1989-93; ret., 1994; pres. Ecumenical Group of Portugal, 1967-69; cons. Commn. on World Mission and Evangelism, World Coun. Chs., 1973-75, advisor cen. com. meeting, Geneva, 1984; advisor 7th Assembly of Luth. World Fedn., Budapest, Hungary, 1984. Contbr. articles to ch. jours. Mem. Ecumenical Assn. of Acads. and Laity Ctrs. in Europe. Democrat. Home: PO Box 483 Penney Farms FL 32079

BRONNER, SHEBA, director private school, modeling instructor; b. Kansas City, Mo., Aug. 28, 1948; d. Louis James Copeland and Juanita (Washington) Harris; m. Vernon C. Hughes, Jr., June 25, 1966 (div. Jan., 1975); children: Stacy, Terrance, Vernon; m. Rev. Lorenzo Bronner, Dec. 23, 1988. BBA, Denver C.C., 1966-67; profl. model cert., John Powers Modeling Sch., N.Y.C. Keypunch operator Internal Rev. Svc., Kansas City, Mo., 1966-67; sr. Keypunch operator First Nat. Bank, Kansas City, 1967-70, Denver, 1970-75; modeling instr. Barbizon Modeling Sch., Denver, 1971-77, Atlanta, 1978-80; word processing supr. Manning, Selvage & Lee, Atlanta, 1978-83; dir., founder Profl. Elegance, Inc., Atlanta, 1983—. Author: (autobiography) Lifting As We Climb: A Century of Spiritual LIving by Madam R.V. Melville. 1900—, 1995. Edn. chair E. Atlanta Cmty. Assn., Atlanta, 1988-91, the Atlanta Project, 1991-94; del. Neighborhood Planning Unit, Atlanta, 1990-91. Named Super Citizen of Month, TBS Channel 17, Atlanta, 1995. Mem. Nat. Coun. Negro Women (Cmty. Leader of Yr. 1996), Atlanta Bus. League. Democrat. Spiritualist. Office: Profl Elegance Inc 461 Flat Shoals Ave SE Atlanta GA 30316

BRONSON, FRANKLIN H., zoology educator; b. Pawnee City, Nebr., Apr. 6, 1932; s. Harry and Vida (Shanklin) B.; m. Virginia Rowe, Nov. 14, 1951 (div. 1975); children—Barbara Ann, Steven Michael; m. Rebecca Barnett, Nov. 16, 1978. B.S., Kans. State U., 1956, M.S., 1957; Ph.D., Pa. State U., 1961. Assoc. staff scientist Jackson Lab., Bar Harbor, Maine, 1961-65, staff scientist, 1965-68; assoc. prof. U. Tex., Austin, 1968-72, prof., 1972—, dir. Inst. Reproductive Biology, 1978—; cons. NIH, NSF. Author: Mammalian Reproductive Biology, 1989; contbr. articles to profl. jours. Home: 2725 Trail Of The Madrones Austin TX 78746-2344

BRONWELL, NANCY BROOKER, writer; b. Columbia, S.C., Oct. 11, 1921; d. Norton Wardlaw and Lucile Duty (Michaux) Brooker; m. Alvin Wayne Bronwell, June 21, 1943 (div. Mar. 1975); children: Betsy Randolph Bronwell Jones, Cynthia Alison. BS, Mary Washington Coll., 1942; postgrad., U. Ky., 1942-43, Tex. Tech. U., 1965, 87. Tchr. English, phys. edn. Louisville Pub. Schs., 1943-46; sec. edn. dept. Jos. S. Seagram & Sons Inc., Louisville, 1945-46; sec. to sales mgr. Marshall Field Corp., Chgo., 1946; sec. to dir. purchases Jos. E. Seagram & Sons., Inc., 1946-48; freelance writer Lubbock, Tex., 1978—. Author: Lubbock: A Pictorial History, 1980. Cofounder, bd. dirs. Young Women's Christian Assn., Lubbock, 1953; vol. Lubbock Jr. League, Lubbock Symphony Orch., Palsy Ctr., ARC, Tech. Mus., St. Paul's Ch. Mem. South Plains Writers Guild, Lubbock Heritage Assn. (Excellence award 1981), DAR, Friends of Libr. (life). Republican. Episcopalian. Home and Office: 4108 18th St # A Lubbock TX 79416-6009

BROOKE, GEORGE MERCER, JR., historian, educator; b. Tokyo, Oct. 21, 1914; (parents Am. citizens); s. George Mercer and Isabel Elsie (Tilton) B.; m. Frances Fleming Bailey, June 13, 1942; children: George Mercer III, Marion Bailey Brooke Philpott. BA in Liberal Arts, Va. Mil. Inst., 1936; MA in History, Washington and Lee U., 1942; PhD in History, U. N.C., 1955. Spl. agent Md. Casualty Co., Balt., 1936-41; history instr. Va. Mil. Inst., Lexington, 1942-43, from asst. prof. to prof., 1948-80, prof. emeritus, 1980—; history instr. Washington & Lee U., Lexington, 1946-47. Author: John M. Brooke, Naval Scientist, 1980, General Lee's Church, 1984, John M. Brooke's Pacific Cruise, 1986; contbr. numerous articles to profl. publs. Chmn. Citizen-Soldier Meml. Va. Mil. Inst., 1983-84, Sesquicentennial celebration, 1986-89; unit pres. Am. Cancer Soc., 1980-82; pres. Stonewall Jackson area coun. Boy Scouts Am., 1964-67. 1st lt. U.S. Army, 1943-46, PTO. Fulbright rsch. scholar Keio U., 1962-63; Fulbright teaching grantee Nat. Taiwan U., 1963; recipient Silver Beaver award Boy Scouts Am., 1967, Citizen-Scouter of Yr. award, 1989. Mem. SAR, So. Hist. Assn., Assn. for Preservation Va. Antiquities (br. pres. 1975-77), Soc. of the Cin. (standing com. 1984-87), Rockbridge Hist. Soc. (pres. 1960-62, author procs. 1989), English Speaking Union (br. pres. 1980-82), Internat. House of Japan, Am. Legion, Phi Beta Kappa, Kappa Alpha Order. Republican. Episcopalian. Home: 405 Jackson Ave Lexington VA 24450-1905

BROOKER, LENA EPPS, human relations program administrator; b. Lumberton, N.C., Oct. 13, 1941; d. Frank Howard and Grace Evelyn (Smith) Epps; m. James Dennis Brooker, July 30, 1966; children: Lora, Lindsey. AB, Meredith Coll., Raleigh, N.C., 1962. Cert. elem. sch. tchr., N.C. Elem. sch. tchr., Charlotte, Robeson County, N.C., Winchester, Va., Chevy Chase, Md., Raleigh, 1962-75; coord. human svcs. program N.C. Commn. Indian Affairs, Raleigh, 1975-78; planner, adminstr. human svcs. program N.C. Dept. Natural Resources and Community Devel., Raleigh, 1978-86; dir. diversity mgmt. The Women's Ctr., Raleigh, 1990-96; dir. diversity program 1st Citizens Bank, Raleigh, 1996—; developer model program U.S. Dept. Labor, Raleigh, 1976; presenter Pres.'s Commn. on Status of Women, Raleigh, 1979; facilitator Internat. Yr. of Woman, Winston-Salem, N.C., 1977; speaker on status of Am. Indians to univs., schs., chs. and orgns., 1975—. Contbg. writer The Carolina Call. Chaplain, entertainment chmn. Dem. Women Wake County, Raleigh, 1989-91; mem. Task Force on Native Am. Ministry N.C. Conf. United Meth. Ch., chmn. ethnic minority local ch. concerns com., 1988-91, mem. bd. evangelism, 1986-91, audit com. coun. fin. and adminstrn., 1990-91, coun. ministries, 1992-94, mem. bishops task force on staff and structure, 1993-95; mem. Wake County Mammography Task Force, 1990-93; mem. cultural diversity com. Wake County Arts Coun., 1990; bd. dirs. Internat. Festival Raleigh, 1990-91, Triangle OIC, 1991-93, N.C. Civil Liberties Union, 1992-94, United Arts Coun. Wake County, 1996, sec. 1996; mem. steering com. for Yr. of native Am., N.C. Mus. Natural History, 1986; mem. city of Raleigh Human Resources & Human Rels. Commn., 1990-93; pres. bd. dirs. Women's Fund of N.C., 1993—; bd. advisors Heritage Arts Found., 1993, N.Am. Health Edn. Fund, 1994—, Women's Leadership Inst., Bennett Coll., 1995—. Grantee N.C. Arts Coun., Duke-Semans Fine Arts Found., 1986; recipient Personal Advocacy for Women in N.C. Carpathian award N.C. Equity, 1993. Mem. N.C. Natural Scis. Soc. (bd. dirs. 1987-90), Triangle Native Am. Soc. (past coord. spl. projects), Meredith Coll. Alumne Assn. (bd. dirs. 1994-95). Home: 2110 Fairview Rd Raleigh NC 27608-2235 Office: 1st Citizens Bank PO Box 27131 Raleigh NC 27611-7131

BROOKER, SUSAN GAY, employment consulting firm executive; b. Washington, Sept. 4, 1949; d. Robert Morris and Mildred Ruby (Parler) B. BA, St. Mary's Coll., St. Mary's City, Md., 1971. News editor WPGC Radio, Lanham, Md., 1971; mgr. trainee Household Fin. Corp., Silver Spring, Md., 1972; career counselor Place-All, Bethesda, Md., 1972-73; exec. v.p. New Places, Inc./ Get-A-Job, Washington, 1973-89; employment cons., owner, pres. SGB Consultants, Reston, Va., 1989—; mem. Emploibank, Washington, 1978-79. Outreach vestry chair Grace Episcopal Ch., 1992-94; conservation chairperson Silver Spring Woman's Club, 1993-94. Recipient Cert. Appreciation U.S. Fish and Wildlife Assn., 1985, Cert. of Recognition Chaplaincy Assocs., Howard Gen. Hosp, Letter of Appreciation Pres. Bill Clinton, 1996. Mem. Pell-Capital Pers. Svc. Asssn. (cert.), St. Mary's Coll. (Md.) Alumni Assn. (bd. dirs. 1987-91). Democrat. Home and Office: 2209 Coppersmith Sq Reston VA 20191-2305

BROOKES, CAROLYN JESSEN, early childhood education educator; b. Orlando, Fla., June 16, 1946; d. Thomas M. and Hilda Marie (Hanson) Jessen: m. Edward N. Brookes, Aug. 8, 1970 (dec. Oct. 1990); 1 child, Donna Marie. BA, U. So. Fla., 1969; MS, Nova U., 1990. Asst. dir., dir. lower schs. Gables Acad., Winter Park, Fla., 1973-83; tchr. Orange County Pub. Schs., Orlando, 1983—, early childhood resource tchr., high-scope trainer, 1983-92, coord. edn. homeless children and youth program, 1992-95; coord. mentor tchr. program U. Ctrl. Fla. and Orange County Pub. Schs.; parent educator, adj. instr. U. Ctrl. Fla.; ednl. cons.; distance educator Ednl. Mgmt. Group, Phoenix, 1994-96. Contbr. article to profl. publ. Mem. ASCD, Assn. for Childhood Edn. Internat., Nat. Assn. for Edn. Young Children, So. Early Childhood Assn. (trainer), Orange County Assn. for Edn. Young Children, Phi Delta Kappa. Home: 265 Lazy Acres Ln Longwood FL 32750 Office: Orange County Pub Schs 445 W Amelia St Orlando FL 32801-1127

BROOKES, DAVID ALEXANDER, pilot, educator, computer consultant, entrepreneur; b. N.Y.C., Nov. 8, 1968; s. Malcolm John and Barbara Jane (Schonwald) B. BA, Columbia U., 1990; MS, London Sch. Econs., 1992. Cert. flight instr., FAA. Landman Oklatex, Pompano Beach, Fla., 1989-94; flight instr. Pompano Air Ctr., Pompano Beach, Fla., 1994-95; computer cons. Pompano Beach, Fla., 1995—, flight instr., 1995—; pilot, photographer Boots Aerial Photography, Pompano Beach, Fla., 1996—; tchr., tutor, Pompano Beach, 1994—. Author: Pain, 1993, Earth is My Home, 1994. 1st Dan black belt Tae Kwon Do Club, N.Y.C., 1986-90. Mem. Mensa. Home and Office: 2742 NE Third St Pompano Beach FL 33062

BROOKES, KIMBERLY ANN, perinatal/neonatal clinical nurse specialist; b. Montgomery County, Md., Nov. 26, 1967; d. Walter Wilson and Margaret Joan (Ewell) B. BA in Biology, Sweet Briar Coll., 1989; BSN, Johns Hopkins U., 1990; MSN, Old Dominion U., 1996. RN, RNA, Va. Nurse neonatal ICU Children's Hosp of Kings Daus., Norfolk, Va., 1990-91; staff nurse level II and III neonatal ICU U. Tenn. Med. Ctr., Knoxville, 1991-93; staff nurse LDRP, newborn nursery, level II nursery St. Peters Hosp., Helena, Mont., 1993-95. Mem. AWHONN, TANN (pres.-elect), Nat. Assn. Neonatal Nursing. Home: 1704 Lanckfield Mews Virginia Beach VA 23455

BROOKINS, JAMES ROBERT, customer service professional; b. Huntington, W.Va., Aug. 29, 1942; s. Robert Frank and Maxine Patricia (Searls) B.; m. Marie Elizabeth Smith, Sept. 1, 1965 (div. Jan. 1973); children: Leah Lynette, Joseph Christopher, James Christopher; m. Deborah Sue Sabin, Apr. 29, 1978. Student, Black Hills State Tchrs. Coll., 1961-63. Bookkeeper Bonham Sales and Electric, Mansfield, Ohio, 1965-67; customer svc. rep. Weyerhaeuser Corp., Mt. Vernon, Ohio, 1967-71, Boise Cascade Corp., Marion, Ohio, 1971-72; asst. customer svc. mgr. KEM Mfg. Co., Tucker, Ga., 1972-76, sales rep., 1976-77; customer svc. rep., mgr. Stone Container Corp., Lithonia, Ga., 1977-81; customer svc. rep., terr. mgr. Internat. Paper Co., Statesville, N.C., 1982-84; sr. customer svc. rep. Internat. Paper Co., Stockbridge, Ga., 1984-86, mgr. customer svc., 1987-92, product estimator, 1984-86, coord. order tracking sys., 1985-87, adminstrv. asst. to sales mgr., 1987; mgr. customer svc. Four M Mfg. Group, Stockbridge, 1992-96; customer svc. rep. Ga. Box divsn. Pratt Industries, Jackson, 1996—. With USAF, 1961-65. Lodge: Moose. Home: 1589 Canberra Dr Stone Mountain GA 30088-3629 Office: Ga Box divsn Pratt Industries 192 Bunch Rd Jackson GA 30233

BROOKS, ANN, medical librarian; b. Clarksville, Ark., July 16, 1941; d. John Davis and Edith Louise (Thompson) Nettleship; m. Roger Carl Pfaffenberger, Jr., June 13, 1963 (div. 1984); 1 child, Janelle Bretten; m. Lloyd William Brooks, Jr., Apr. 3, 1987. BS, Calif. State Poly. U., 1964; MLS, U. Pitts., 1975; MBA, Tex. Christian U., 1989. Cataloger George Washington U. Libr., Washington, 1975; sr. cataloger divsn. blind and physically handicapped Libr. of Congress, Washington, 1976; head of reference engring. and phys. sci. libr. U. Md., College Park, 1976-78; reference libr. Tex. Christian U., Fort Worth, 1978; extramural svcs. U. No. Tex. Health Sci. Ctr., Fort Worth, 1979-91; assoc. dir. Gibson D. Lewis Health Sci. Libr. U. No. Tex., Fort Worth, 1991—. Contbr. articles to profl. jours. Mem. Med. Libr. Assn. (rsch. com. south ctrl. sect. 1980—), Tex. Libr. Assn. (grantee 1979), Beta Phi Mu. Republican. Office: Gibson D Lewis Health Sci Libr U North Tex Health Sci Ctr 3500 Camp Bowie Blvd Fort Worth TX 76107

BROOKS, ANNE LEE, assistant principal, educator; b. Richmond, Ind., July 16, 1948; d. Walter Issac and Nina Rose (Maple) B. BS, Ind. U., 1970, MS, 1973. Cert. tchr., prin. Tchr. English, phys. edn. Shelby Eastern Schs., Shelbyville, Ind., 1970-72; tchr. English, phys. edn. Loudoun County Schs., Leesburg, Va., 1973-76, dean, tchr., 1976-89, asst. prin., 1989—; resident asst. dept. resident life Ind. U., Bloomington, 1972-73. Camp dir. Lake Erie Girl Scout coun., Cleve., 1973, 74; com. chair London Towne Homeowners Assn., Centreville, Va., 1981-84; organizer Neighborhood Watch, Centreville, 1980-85; bd. sec. No. Va. Audubon Soc., Fairfax, Va., 1983-84; coordinator Christmas Bird Count Nat. Audubon, Fairfax, 1984-86. Named Outstanding Young Educator, Shelby Ea. Schs., Shelbyville, Ind., 1983; finalist Agnes Meyer Outstanding Tchr. award Washington Post, 1988; recipient Presdl. Silver award Nat. Coaches Mag. and Franklin Life Ins., 1988. Mem. NEA, Cardinal Basketball Ofcls. Assn., Va. Assn. Tchrs. English (pres. NATE, State Svc. award 1991), Va. High Sch. Coaching Assn., Alpha Delta Kappa (state v.p. 1988-90, state pres.-elect 1990-92, state pres. 1992—, regional scholarship chair 1990-92, regional membership tng. cons. 1992-94), Ind. U. Alumni Club, Arena State Angels, Coun. of Pres.'s (pres.). Mem. Soc. of Friends. Home: 5503 Village Center Dr Centreville VA 20120-1661 Office: Broad Run HS 21670 Ashburn Rd Ashburn VA 20147

BROOKS, CARLA JO, financial services manager; b. Cedar Rapids, Iowa, July 9, 1956; d. Carleton Paul and Gladys Jane (Benning) Groszkruger; m. Thomas Robert Brooks, Sept. 28, 1979; children: Chera MoRae, Erica Love, Heather Joyzelle, Victoria JoLee. BA, Coe Coll., 1978; MS, U. Tex., Dallas, 1983. Fin. analyst Fed. Res. Bank of Dallas, 1978-83, mgr., 1983-85; sr. mgr. KPMG Peat Marwick LLP, Dallas, 1985—; instr. FRS Bd. Govs., Washington, 1985-87, 96; instr. Southwestern Grad. Sch. Banking, Dallas. Republican. Methodist. Club: P.E.O. (Richardson, Tex.). Office: KPMG Peat Marwick LLP 200 Crescent Ct Ste 300 Dallas TX 75201-7830

BROOKS, CARSON EUGENE, electrical engineer; b. Evansville, Ind., Jan. 17, 1956; s. Gary Wayne and Dorothy Rose (Schmitzer) B.; m. LouEllen Marie Fisher, July 1, 1989 (div. Aug. 1993). BSEE, Auburn U., 1979. Tech. staff mem. Tex. Instruments, Dallas, 1979-82, Alcatel Network Systems, Richardson, Tex., 1982—. Home: 2807 Capella Cir Garland TX 75044-6229

BROOKS, CLAYBOURNE LENOR, JR., adult education educator, youth pastor; b. Miami, Fla., Oct. 18, 1959; s. C.L. and Eleanor (Davis) B. AA, Miami Dade C.C., 1978; 0BS, Pacific Western U., 1989; postgrad., Trinity Internat. U., Miami, 19995—. Ordained to ministry Bapt. Ch., 1995. Tchr. adult edn. Lindsey Hopkins Tech. Edn. Ctr., Miami, 1979-82; tchr. phys. edn. Miami Gardens Elem. Sch., Carol City, Fla., 1986-87, Lake Stevens Elem. Sch., Opa Locka, Fla., 1987-88; substitute tchr. Dade County Pub. Schs., Miami, 1983-85, tchr. adult edn., 1995—; CEO, C.L. Brooks, Jr. Ministries Inc. Global Evangelistic Outreach. Contbr. to anthology. Chmn. bd. Family Support Svcs. Network, Inc., Miami, 1996—. C.L. Brooks, Jr. Day proclaimed in his honor City of Miami, Met. Dade County and State of Fla., 1990. Mem. Fla. Assn. Health, Phys. Edn. and Recreation, Dade County Assn. Health, Phys. Edn. and Recreation, Nat. Assn. Religious Profls. Republican. Home: 3931 NW 177th St Miami FL 33055 Office: 3931 Northwest 177th St Opa Locka FL 33056-3853

BROOKS, DANIEL F., historic site director. Dir. Arlington House Historic Gardens. Office: Arlington House 331 Cotton Ave SW Birmingham AL 35211-1465*

BROOKS, E. R. (DICK BROOKS), utility company executive; b. Slaton, Tex., 1937; m. Martha Garrett; 2 children. BSEE, Tex. Tech U., 1961; postgrad., Harvard U., 1985, U. Mich. Engr. West Tex. Utilities Co., Abilene, 1961-82; v.p. customer svcs. West Tex. Utilities Co., 1980-82; v.p. engring. Ctrl. Power & Light Co., 1982-83; chief engring. officer, sr. v.p. Cen. Power & Light Co., 1983-86, pres., CEO, 1986-87; exec. v.p. elec. ops. Cen. & S.W. Corp., Dallas, 1987, exec. v.p., 1988-89, chmn., pres., CEO, 1990—; also past pres., CEO Cen. & S.W. Svcs., Inc.; also pres., CEO Transok, Inc.; various positions West Tex. U. Engring. Dept. Trustee Dallas Theater Ctr.; mem. exec. bd. Cir. Ten Coun. Boy Scouts Am.; exec. bd. United Way of Met. Dallas; deacon Park Cities Bapt. Ch., Dallas; trustee Dallas Symphony; past chair Tex. Coun. Econ. Edn.; chmn. N.Am. Elec. Reliability Coun. Named Disting. Engr. award Tex. Tech U., 1988. Mem. Assn. Elec. Cos. Tex. (mem. exec. bd.), Tex. Rsch. League, Tex. C. of C. Office: Cen and SW Corp PO Box 660164 1616 Woodall Rodgers Fwy Dallas TX 75266

BROOKS, FRED, executive recreational facility; b. 1942. Staff Walt Disney Prodns., 1967-72, Ringling Bros., Haines City, Fla., 1972-73; real estate agt. Caldwell Bankers, Newport Beach, Calif., 1973-77, N. Hollywood, Calif., 1977-81; owner, mgr. Western Consolidated Equities, Orange, Calif., 1981-89; exec. Battaglia & Assocs., Irvine, Calif., 1989-90; staff Main Street Sta., Las Vegas, Nev., 1989-90; pres. Wet n' Wild Florida, Inc., Orlando, Fla., 1992—. Office: Wet n Wild Fla Inc 6200 Internat Dr Orlando FL 32810

BROOKS, HENRY FRANKLIN, real estate company executive; b. Kinston, N.C., Nov. 26, 1934; s. Frederick P. and Octavia (Broome) B.; m. Sandra Broadhurst, June 25, 1960; children: James Phillips, Richard

Franklin. BS in Bus. Econs., U. N.C., 1957. Sec.-treas. Brooks Svc. Co. Inc., Kinston, 1961—; pres. Rental Tool Co. Inc., Kinston, 1963-87, Brooks & Brooks Ltd., Kinston, 1972—; ptnr. Brooks Distbg. Co., Kinston, 1965—. Asst. scoutmaster Boy Scouts Am., 1974-86; pres. dental parents U. N.C., Chapel Hill, 1993-94; chmn. ofcl. bd. Queen St. United Meth. Ch., Kinston, 1977; chmn. trustees bldg. com. Meth. Retirement Homes of N.C., Durham, 1987-91; pres. Kinston Fedn. of Chs., 1990-91; mem. local bd. N.C. Symphony, 1990-95; mem. Met. Opera Guild, 1994—. Mem. Am. Forestry Assn., Tobacco Growers Assn. of N.C., Lenoir County Livestock Devel. Assn., Nat. Frame Builders Assn., Lenoir County Hist. Assn. (pres. elect 1997-98), Alpha Kappa Psi (treas. 1956-57). Home and Office: 2210 Riley Rd Kinston NC 28504

BROOKS, JACK BASCOM, congressman; b. Crowley, La., Dec. 18, 1922; s. Edward Chachere and Grace Marie (Pipes) B.; m. Charlotte Collins, Dec. 15, 1960; children: Jack Edward, Katherine Inez, Kimberly Grace. AA, Lamar Jr. Coll., Beaumont, Tex., 1939-41; BJ, U. Tex., 1943, JD, 1949. Bar: Tex. 1949. Mem. Tex. Legislature, 1946-50, 83d-89th Congresses from 2d Tex. dist., 90th-103rd Congresses from 9th Tex. dist., Washington, D.C., 1967-94. Author, Lamar Coll. bill, 1949. Served from pvt. to 1st lt. USMCR, 1942-46; col. Res. ret. Mem. ABA, State Bar Tex., Am. Legion, VFW, Sigma Delta Chi. Home: 1029 East Dr Beaumont TX 77706-4738 Office: US Ho of Reps 3535 Calder Third Flr Beaumont TX 77705

BROOKS, JAMES JOE, III, accountant; b. Augusta, Ga., July 15, 1948; s. James J. Jr. and Pattie (D.) B. AA, Mid. Ga. Coll., Cochran, 1968; BBA in Acctg., Ga. So. Coll., Statesboro, 1970. CPA, Ga. Internal auditor Ga. Dept. Transp., Atlanta, 1972-77; staff acct. Webb, Dreher & Clark, Atlanta, 1977-78, Gaddis & Eidson, Atlanta, 1978-80; contr. Food Svcs., Inc., Atlanta, 1980-81; pvt. practice Atlanta, 1981—; cons. in field. Coach First Bapt. Ch. of Atlanta softball team, 1985-86, 90—. Mem. Personal Computers Users Group, Ga. Soc. CPA's, Ga. Real Estate Investor Assn., Northcrest Swim & Tennis Club (bd. dirs. 1989—). Republican. Home: 3532 Bowling Green Way Atlanta GA 30340-4187

BROOKS, JEFFREY MARTIN, marketing and sales executive; b. Charlotte, N.C., Oct. 14, 1958; s. Jack M. and Margaret Anne (Reap) B.; m. Kim Marie Whitaker, Sept. 26, 1981; 2 children: Justin Jeffrey Whitaker, Evan Martin Whitaker. BSBA in Acctg., East Carolina U.; MS in Econs., N.C. State U. Staff acct. Ernst & Whinney, Raleigh, N.C., 1980-82; account rep. Data Gen. Corp., Charlotte, 1982-85; mgr. systems mktg. AT&T Charlotte, 1985-86; pres. Fastfly Corp., 1985-89; dir. sales and distbn. Vanguard Cellular Systems, Inc., Greensboro, N.C., 1989-94; v.p. mktg. and sales So. Comm. (subs. The So. Co.), Atlanta, 1994—; cons. Charlotte Hornets, GTE. Vol. Jr. Achievement; mem. Johns Creek United Meth. Ch. Mem. Nat. Assn. Accts., AICPA, Aircraft Owners and Pilots Assn., Nat. Air Transp. Assn., Nat. Bus. Aircraft Assn. Home: 10635 Oxford Mill Cir Alpharetta GA 30202-6369 Office: The So Co 64 Perimeter Ctr E Atlanta GA 30346-2205

BROOKS, JERRY CLAUDE, safety engineer, educator; b. College Park, Ga., Apr. 23, 1936; s. John Bennett and Mattie Mae (Timms) B.; BS, Ga. Inst. Tech., 1958; m. Peggy Sue Thornton, Feb. 26, 1961; children: Apryll Denise, Jerry Claude, Susan Vereen. Safety engr. Cotton Producers Assn., Atlanta, 1959-64, dir. safety and loss control, 1964-70; dir. corporate protection Gold Kist, Inc., Atlanta, 1970-81; dir. corporate safety J.P. Stevens, 1981-84, dir. Safety and Security, 1984-86, dir. health and safety, 1986-88, dir. loss control Am. Yarn Spinners Assn., 1988-89; dir. safety Springs Industries, Inc., 1989—; instr., Ga. Safety Inst., Athens, Ga., 1971—. Bd. dirs. Greater Lithonia (Ga.) Homeowners Assn., Ga. Soc. Prevention of Blindness, Ga. Safety Coun. Served with AUS, 1958-59. Mem. Am. Soc. Safety Engrs. (chpt. pres. 1968-69, regional v.p. 1974-76), Nat. Safety Coun. (gen. chmn. fertilizer sect. 1969-70, gen. chmn. textile sec. 1985-87, Disting. Svc. to Safety award 1989, Palmetto chpt. pres. 1994), So. Safety Conf. (v.p. bus. and industry 1968-74, pres. 1974), Am. Textile Mfrs. Inst. (chmn. safety and health com 1991-93), Am. Soc. Indsl. Security, S.C. Occupational Safety Coun. (bd. mem. 1994—), Ga. Bus. and Industry Assn. (dir., named outstanding mem. 1981), Internat. Assn. Hazard Control Mgrs. (chpt. pres. 1979-80). Clubs: Masons, Rosicrucians; Exchange (pres. 1969-70; Book of Golden Deeds award 1981) (Lithonia). Home: 105 Saint Gaudens Ct Kings Mountain NC 28086-7754 Office: Springs Industries Inc PO Box 70 Fort Mill SC 29716-0070

BROOKS, LESLIE GENE, association executive; b. Fletcher, Okla., June 15, 1936; s. Frank and Ethel Earlene (Spears) B.; m. Nancy Carmen, Aug. 15, 1970; 1 child, Steven. MusB in Piano, Okla. Bapt. U.; MusM, PhD in Music Adminstrn., U. Okla. Dept. chmn. Cameron State U., Lawton, Okla., 1962-69, Midwestern State U., Wichita Falls, Tex., 1969-75, U. Ark., Little Rock, 1975-77; nat. exec. dir. Am. Choral Dirs. Assn., Lawton, 1977—, nat. conv. chmn., 1973. Recipient Profile in Excellence award Okla. Bapt. U., 1986, Disting. Alumni award 1996. Mem. Internat. Fedn. Choral Music (sec.-gen. 1982—), Music Tchrs. Nat. Assn. (nat. choral chmn. 1971-73, chmn. music in higher edn. 1974-75). Democrat. Baptist. Avocations: skiing, travel. Office: Am Choral Dirs Assn 502 SW 38th St PO Box 6310 Lawton OK 73506

BROOKS, LLOYD WILLIAM, JR., osteopath, interventional cardiologist, educator; b. Amarillo, Tex., Nov. 4, 1949; s. Lloyd William and Tina Margaret (Roe) B.; m. Ann Nettleship, Apr. 3, 1987. BS, U. Tex., 1972; DO cum laude, Tex. Coll. Osteo. Medicine, 1985. Diplomate Am. Osteo. Bd. Internal Medicine; bd. cert. in internal medicine & cardiology. Intern Dallas-Ft. Worth Med. Ctr., 1985; resident in internal medicine Ft. Worth Osteo. Med. Ctr., 1986-88; fellow in cardiology Detroit Heart Inst.; fellow in angioplasty and interventional cardiology Riverside Meth. Hosp., Columbus, Ohio; pvt. practice Ft. Worth, 1990—; pvt. practice, pres. Ft. Worth Heart and Vascular Inst.; chief of medicine Osteo. Med. Ctr. of Tex.; clin. asst. prof. U. North Tex. Health Sci. Ctr., Ft. Worth, 1991—. Contbr. articles to med. jours. Fellow Am. Coll. Cardiology; mem. AMA, Am. Osteo. Assn., Am. Coll. Osteo. Internists (diplomate). Office: Ft Worth Heart & Vascular 1002 Montgomery St Ste 200 Fort Worth TX 76107-2693

BROOKS, MARK D., company executive. Chmn. Brooks-Baine Golf, Inc. Address: # 707 1320 S University Dr Fort Worth TX 76107

BROOKS, MARY MCLEOD, retired early childhood education educator; b. St. Johnsbury, Vt., Aug. 13, 1911; d. Jonas Hastings and Annie Maude Elizabeth (McLeod) B. BA, Smith Coll., 1933; postgrad., Merill-Palmer Sch., 1934-35; MA, Columbia U., 1942. Nursery sch. tchr. Vassar Inst. Euthenics, Poughkeepsie, N.Y., 1933; dir., tchr. pvt. nursery sch. St. Johnsbury, Vt., 1933-34; counselor Merrill-Palmer Camp, Detroit, 1935; dir., asst. prof. Hillsdale (Mich.) Coll. Nursery Sch., 1935-38; dir., assoc. prof. Berea (Ky.) Coll. Nursery Sch., 1938-41; dir., asst. prof. Wheaton Coll. Nursery Sch., Norton, Mass., 1942-48; teaching fellow dept. early childhood edn. Tchrs. Coll. of Columbia U., N.Y.C., 1948-49; instr. Eliot-Pearson Sch., Tufts U., Medford, Mass., 1949-50; supr. student tchrs. dept. early chilhood edn. Tchrs. Coll., Columbia U., N.Y.C., 1949-51; prof., dir. Goddard Coll. Nursery Sch., Plainfield, Vt., 1950-52; asst. to curator Mus. Nat. Hist., St. Johnsbury, 1952-54; dir. admissions Eliot-Pearson Sch. Tufts U., Medford, Mass., 1954-55; dir. children's activities Children's Hosp. Phila., 1955-61, coord. children's activities, 1965-72; supr. program autistic nursery sch., 1956-58; dir. Child Study Ctr. Nursery Sch., Phila., 1961-65. Editor: Jour. New England Assn. Nursery Edn., 1950-54; contbr. articles to profl. jours. Overseer, 1st day com. Religious Soc. of Friends, Phila., 1969-73; trustee Clearwater (Fla.) Soc. of Friends, 1978—; active Common Cause, 1970—, ARC, 1973—, Sr. Citizens of Clearwater, 1974—, Amnesty Internat., 1985-96, Tampa Bay Orch., 1992—; historian, vol. Hospice of Fla. Suncoast, 1978-95; historian Spouse Abuse Shelter, Clearwater, 1981—. In honor of her long svc. to Hospice, Mary McLeod Brooks award presented annually to oustanding vol. of Hospice of Fla. Suncoast. Mem. Assn. for Care of Children's Health (founder, charter mem., hon. mem., chmn. Internat. conf. 1967, v.p. 1970-73, historian 1973-80), Child Life Coun. Inc. (charter), Fla. Assn. Child Life Profls., Fla. Assn. Child Life (hon. mem., founder, Coalition Child Life and Therapeutic Rels. (hon. mem.). Quaker. Home: 901 Seminole Blvd Apt 431 Largo FL 33770-7448

BROOKS, NEAL, agricultural services executive; b. 1939. With J.R. Brooks and Son, Inc., Homestead, Fla., 1961—, now pres. Office: J R Brooks & Son Inc 18400 SW 256th St Homestead FL 33031-1892

BROOKS, NEILS WILLARD, vocational/adult education educator; b. Marion, N.C., Apr. 24, 1956; s. Jay Willard and Risberth Joan (Arrowood) B.; m. Jenny Mae Fulcher, Oct. 17, 1978; children: Neils Willard II, Jennifer Beth. BSBA, Gardner-Webb U., 1978; MEd in Adminstrn./Supervision, East Tenn. State U., 1986; EdD in Ednl. Leadership, Nova Southeastern U., 1993. Project engr. Stanley Furniture Corp., Stanleytown, Va., 1978-79; retail sales Legget Dept. Stores, Martinsville, Va., 1979-80; tchr. Henry County Pub. Schs., Collisville, Va., 1980-84; stockbroker J.C. Bradford & Co., Martinsville, 1984-85; sales mgr. Patrick Henry Chryler Plymouth Dealer, Martinsville, 1985; tchr. Bristol (Va.) Pub. Schs., 1985-87; prin., asst. vocat. dir. Accomack (Va.) County Schs., 1987-89; dir. vocat. and adult edn. York County Pub. Schs., Yorktown, Va., 1989-92; state dir., vocat., adult and employment tng. svcs. Commonwealth Va. Dept. Edn., Richmond, 1992—; ex-officio mem. Va. Bd. of Correctional Edn., Richmond, 1993—; bd. dirs. So. Regional Edn. Bd. High Schs. That Work Consortium, Atlanta, 1992—; parliamentarian, exec. com. Vocat. Tech. Edn. Consortium of States, Atlanta, 1992—; mem. Va. Tech. Prep. Exec. Com., Richmond, 1992—. Named Alumnus of Yr. Gardner-Webb U., 1994; Nat. Sr. Exec. fellowship Dewitt Wallace and Nat. Vocat. Tech. Edn. Founds., John Hopkins U., 1993; recipient Disting. Svc. awards Va. Congress of Parents and Tchrs., 1992, VA FHA/HERO, 1992. Mem. Nat. Assn. of State Dirs. of Vocat. Tech. Edn. (sec.-treas., bd. dirs. 1992—, Disting. Svc., 1996), Nat. Vocat. Tech. Edn. Found. (sec.-treas.), Am. Vocat. Assn., Va. Assn. of Vocat. Adminstrn., Va. Vocat. Assn., Masons. Baptist. Home: 3800 Danewood Dr Richmond VA 23233 Office: Va Dept of Edn PO Box 2120 Richmond VA 23218

BROOKS, PAL, business executive. Pres. Brooks Tropicals, Inc., Homestead, Fla. Office: Brooks Tropicals Inc PO Box 900160 Homestead FL 33090

BROOKS, PHYLLIS M. BRITTO, gerontological nurse, nursing educator; b. New Orleans, Nov. 1, 1939; d. Joseph Phillip and Evelyn (Richard) Britto; m. Frank K. Brooks, Dec. 27, 1958; 1 child, Frank K. Jr. Diploma in Nursing, St. Joseph Sch. Nursing, Tacoma, 1972; AA, Tacoma Community Coll., 1972; BSN, Nazareth Coll., Kalamazoo, Mich., 1980; MSN, Mich. State U., 1983. RN, Tex., Mich. Head nurse ICU and progressive care unit Battle Creek (Mich.) Community Hosp.; staff nurse ICU Ingham Med. Ctr., Lansing, Mich.; clin. nurse specialist Mich. State U. Family Practice Dept., East Lansing, Mich.; instr. nursing edn. Audie L. Murphy Meml. Vets. Hosp., San Antonio; researcher in field. Mem. ANA (cert. clin. specialist gerontology, nursing continuing edn. and staff devel.), Sigma Theta Tau (Delta Alpha chpt.). Home: 15254 Moonlit Grove San Antonio TX 78247-2942

BROOKS, ROBERT FRANKLIN, SR., lawyer; b. Richmond, Va., July 13, 1939; s. Robert Noel Brooks and Annie Mae (Edwards) Miles; m. Patricia Wilson, May 6, 1972; children: Robert Franklin Jr., Thomas Noel, Courtenay M. Brooks Rainey. BA, U. Richmond, 1961, M of Humanities, 1993; JD, 1964. Bar: Va. 1964, N.Y. 1985, U.S. Dist. Ct. (ea. and we. dists.) Va. 1964, U.S. Ct. Appeals (4th cir.) 1965, U.S. Ct. Appeals (5th cir.) 1972, (2d cir.) 1979, (11th cir.) 1981, D.C. 1977, U.S. Supreme Ct. 1979. Assoc. Hunton & Williams, Richmond, 1964-71, ptnr., 1971—; chmn. sect. II 3d Dist. Com., 1983; mem. rules evidence com. Supreme Ct. Va., 1984-85; mem. Fourth Cir. Judicial Conf. Trustee U. Richmond. Fellow ABA, Am. Coll. Trial Lawyers (com. atty.-client relationships 1983-91, chmn. Va. state com. 1993-94), Am. Bar Found., Va. Law Found.; mem. N.Y. Bar Assn., D.C. Bar Assn., Va. State Bar (coun. 1986—, bd. govs. litigation sect. 1984-90, sec. 1985-86, chmn. 1986-87, com. lawyer fin. responsibility 1986-89, nominating com. 1990, spl. com. election methods 1989, chmn. bench-bar rels. com. 1987-88, faculty professionalism course 1988-90, governance com. 1990-91), Richmond Bar Assn. (chmn. judiciary com. 1985-87, chmm. com. on unprofl. conduct 1979-80, com. on improvement of adminstrn. of justice 1981-84), Va. Bar Assn. (profl. responsibility com. 1981-84, 87—), Va. Trial Lawyers Assn. Home: 500 Kilmarnock Dr Richmond VA 23229-8102 Office: Hunton & Williams Riverfront Plz East Tower 951 E Byrd St Richmond VA 23219-4040

BROOKS, SHELLY ANN, minister, osteopath; b. Ft. Worth, May 24, 1962; d. Donald Lee and Florine Estelle (Dougan) B. BS, Tex. Wesleyan U., 1984; DO, U. North Tex., 1988; MDiv, So. Meth. U., 1994. Diplomate Tex. Bd. Med. Examiners; ordained deacon Meth Ch. Family practice intern Family Practice Ctr., Waco, Tex., 1988-89; family practice physician MediCenter, Waco, Tex., 1989-92; assoc. pastor Ctrl. United Meth. Ch., Waco, Tex., 1992-94; pastor 1st United Meth. Ch., Ranger, Tex., 1994—. Bd. dirs. Ctrl. Tex. Sr. Adult Ministries, Waco, 1994. Recipient McFadden scholarship, 1980-84, Am. Osteo. Assn. scholarship, 1984-85, Nicholson scholarship, 1989-94. Mem. Ctrl. Tex. Conf. United Meth. Ch. (probationary mem.), Tex. Osteo. Med. Assn., Tex. Med. Found. Home: 1220 Meadowbrook St Ranger TX 76470-2904 Office: 1st United Meth Ch PO Box 155 Ranger TX 76470-0155

BROOKS, STEVE, business executive; b. 1956. Pres. Razorback Farms, Inc., Springdale, Ariz. Office: Razorbacks Farms inc W Shady Grove Rd Springdale AR 72764

BROOKS, THOMAS JOSEPH, JR., preventive medicine educator; b. Starkville, Miss., May 23, 1916; s. Thomas Joseph and Lelia Adeline (Perkins) B.; m. Mary Alice Pollard; children: Thomas Joseph III, Michael Pollard, Mary Browning, Melinda Anne. BS, U. Fla., 1937; MS, U. Tenn., 1939; PhD, U. N.C., 1942; MD, Wake Forest U., 1945. Diplomate Am. Bd. Med. Microbiology. Instr. bacteriology and parasitology Sch. Medicine Wake Forest U., Winston-Salem, N.C., 1942-45; intern Wake Forest U. and N.C. Bapt. Hosp., 1945-46; assoc. prof. pharmacology Sch. Medicine U. Miss., Oxford, 1947-48; med. officer assigned to VA Hosp. USNR, Lake City, Fla., 1946-47; officer-in-charge streptococcal diseases research unit U.S. Naval Tng. Ctr., Bainbridge, Md., 1953-55; prof., chmn. dept. preventive medicine U. Miss. Sch. Medicine, Jackson, 1952-81, prof. emeritus, 1981—; cons. Miss. State Dept. Health, 1981—; vis. prof. preventive medicine sch. medicine U. Costa Rica, San Jose, 1962-63, faculty medicine Keio U., Tokyo, 1968, faculty medicine Trinity Coll., U. Dublin, Ireland, 1979; vis. prof. pub. health faculty medicine Kyoto U., Japan, 1968-69; invited lectr. sch. medicine U. N.D., Grand Forks, 1971; physician-in-chief Univ. Hosp., Fla. State U., 1948-52; asst. dean in charge student affairs sch. medicine U. Miss., 1956-73; UN cons. in med. edn., India, 1966. Author: Essentials of Medical Parasitology, 1963; co-editor: Control of Communicable Diseases in Man, 11th edit., 1970, 12th edit., 1975; contbr. articles to profl. jours. Past pres. Jackson (Miss.) Photographic Soc., Jackson Amateur Radio Club; cons. to rector Universidad Industrial de Santander, Bucaramanga, Colombia, 1968; chmn. admissions com. Sch. Medicine, U. Miss., 1955-65. Gilchist Meml. scholar 1936-37, band scholar 1934-37 U. Fla.; teaching fellow parasitology dept. zoology U. Tenn., 1937-39, teaching fellow parasitology sch. medicine U. N.C., 1939-42, fellow in tropical medicine La. State U. 1956-60, Alan Gregg fellow in med. edn. China Med. Bd. N.Y., 1968-69; Assn. Am. Med. Colls. grantee sch. tropical medicine Tulane U., 1943, Assn. Am. Med. Colls. grantee for study tropical diseases Latin Am., 1944, Rockefeller Found. Travel grantee, 1952. Fellow Royal Soc. Health Eng.; mem. Am. Pub. Health Assn. (com. on communicable diseases 1968-75, nominating com. epidemiology sect. 1975, coun. internat. health div. 1978-81, chmn. nominating com. coun. internat. health div. 1981), Miss. Pub. Health Assn., U. Tenn. Hon. Biol. Soc. (pres. 1938-39), Omicron Delta Kappa, Sigma Xi. Presbyterian. Home: 750 Lenox Dr Jackson MS 39211-4105

BROOKSHIRE, JERRY HARDMAN, historian, educator; b. Athens, Ga., Oct. 17, 1943; s. James Knox and Leclare (Hardman) B.; m. Judy Allen Heiman, Sept. 7, 1968; children: Michael David, Ryan James. BA, U. Ga., 1965; MA, Vanderbilt U., 1967, PhD, 1970. Mil. historian U.S. Mil. Acad., West Point, N.Y., 1970-72; prof. history Mid. Tenn. State U., Murfreesboro, 1972—, acting chair, dept. history, 1991-92. Author: Clement Attlee, 1995; contbr. articles to profl. jours. Coord. Tenn. 4th Dist. Common Cause, Murfreesboro, 1976-77; Tenn. dir. Nat. History Day, 1980-81. Capt. U.S. Army, 1970-72. Mem. AAUP, Am. Hist. Assn., N.Am. Conf. Brit. Studies, Phi Kappa Phi, Phi Beta Kappa. Methodist. Home: 3074 E Compton Rd Murfreesboro TN 37130-6849 Office: Mid Tenn State U Dept History Murfreesboro TN 37132

BROOME, JACK HARRISON, insurance executive; b. Fort Worth, Apr. 1, 1933; s. Riley J. and Frankie (Dell) B.; m. Millie Dean Lloyd, Apr. 8, 1953; children: Bonnie, Susan, Jack Jr. Diploma in adjusting, Ins. Inst. Am., 1968. Field claim supr. Crum & Forster Ins. Co., Dallas, 1960-74; br. mgr. Hammerman & Gainer, Dallas, 1974-78; v.p. claims Union Standard Ins. Co., Dallas, 1978-82; pres. Jack Broome & Assocs., Inc., San Antonio, 1982—. Home: 6330 Mary Jamison St San Antonio TX 78238-2336 Office: 4100 E Piedras Dr Ste 116 San Antonio TX 78228-1425

BROOME, MICHAEL CORTES, college administrator; b. Ringgold, Ga., Apr. 28, 1948; s. Cortes Carna and Frances Margaret (Lockhart) B.; m. Charlotte Lou Stackhouse, Aug. 6, 1989; children from previous marriage: Stephen, Paul. BA, U. Tenn., 1970; MA, Fla. State U., 1972; PhD, U. S.C., 1988. Law clk., proofreader Swafford and Taylor, Chattanooga, Tenn., 1967-70; instr., asst. prof. English dept. Columbia (S.C.) Coll., 1973-82, assoc. prof., 1986-92, assoc. dean, 1992—; dir. tng. devel. Nat. Guard Prof. Edn. Ctr., North Little Rock, Ark., 1982-85; editor The Stelter Co., Des Moines, 1989-90; cons. interdis. writing Williamsburg Tech. Coll., Kingstree, 1990; cons. strategic planning Am. Ins. Agy., Fort Mill, S.C., 1992; cons. State Pers. Tng. Dept., 1978-81. Author: (with others) The Vanity Fair Gallery, 1979, A Literary Map of South Carolina, 1993. Big Bro., interviewer Richland County Family Ct., Columbia, 1974-75; vol. trainer United Way of S.C., Columbia, 1990. With S.C. Nat. Guard, 1974-95, ret. lt. col. Named Outstanding Tchg. Asst. English Dept. Fla. State, 1973; named Outstanding Young Men of Am. U.S. C. of C., 1976, Ky. Col. Gov. of Ky., 1985. Mem. S.C. Assn. of Developmental Educators (pres. 1982), Nat. Coun. of Tchr. of English, Nat. Guard Assn. of S.C., Nat. Guard Assn. of U.S., S.C. Higher Edn. Assessment Network (chair fiscal adv. com. 1995). Democrat. United Methodist. Home: 6118 Hampton Leas Ln Columbia SC 29209 Office: Columbia Coll Columbia College Dr Columbia SC 29203

BROOME, RANDALL, evangelist; b. Hattiesburg, Miss., June 9, 1954; s. Eugene Wallace and Doris Vonceil (Lucas) B.; m. Barbara Ann Kelly, Dec. 18, 1976; children: Christopher Randall, Kelli Kristi Anna. BMin, Fla. Bapt. Theol. Coll., Graceville, Fla., 1981; MDiv, New Orleans Bapt. Sem., 1984, DMin, 1996. Lic. to ministry So. Bapt. Conv., 1976, ordained to ministry So. Bapt. Conv., 1979. Pastor Unity Bapt. Ch., Chipley, Fla., 1979-81, Good Hope Bapt. Ch., Franklinton, La., 1983-84, Oconee Bapt. Ch., Commerce, Ga., 1984-87, 1st Bapt. Ch. of Arabi, La., 1987-90; evangelist, pres. World Evangelism, Inc., Chalmette, La., 1990—. Contbr. articles to religion mags. With U.S. Air Force, 1973-75. Mem. Living Dividends Investment Club (founder, presiding officer 1989-90). Republican. Home and Office: 2208 Legend Dr Meraux LA 70075-2829

BROOTEN, KENNETH EDWARD, JR., lawyer; b. Kirkland, Wash., Oct. 17, 1942; s. Kenneth Edward Sr. and Sadie Josephine (Assad) B.; m. Patricia Anne Folsom, Aug. 29, 1965 (div. Apr. 1986); children: Michelle Catherine, Justin Kenneth. Diploma, Lewis Sch. Hotel, Restaurant and Club Mgmt., Washington, 1963; student, U. Md., 1964-66; AA, Sante Fe Community Coll., Gainesville, Fla., 1969; BS in Journalism with highest honors, U. Fla., 1971, MA in Journalism and Communications with highest honors, 1972, JD with honors, 1975; law student, U. Idaho, 1972-73; diploma, Inst. Legal Scis., Polish Acad. Scis., Warsaw, 1974; student, Trinity Coll., U. Cambridge, England, 1974. Bar: Fla., D.C., U.S. Dist. Ct. (no., mid. and so. dists.) Fla., U.S. Dist. Ct. D.C., U.S. Tax Ct., U.S. Ct. Appeals (5th, 9th, 11th and D.C. circs.), U.S. Supreme Ct., Trial Counsel Her Majesty's Govt. of United Kingdom. Asst. to several Congressmen U.S. Ho. of Reps., Washington, 1962-67; adminstrv. asst. VA Cen. Office, Washington, 1967; adminstrv. officer VA Hosp., Gainesville, Fla., 1967-72; ptnr. Carter & Brooten, P.A., Gainesville, Fla., 1975-78, Brooten & Fleisher, Chartered, Washington and Gainesville, Fla., 1978-80; sole practice Washington and Gainesville, 1980-86, Washington, 1987-88, Washington and Orlando, Fla., 1988-91, Washington and Winter Park, Fla., 1991—; permanent spl. counsel, acting chief counsel, dir. Select Com. Assassinations U.S. Ho. of Reps., 1976-77; counsel Her Majesty's Govt. of U.K. (in U.S.). Author: Malpractice Guide to Avoidance and Treatment, 1987; episode writher TV series Simon and Simon; nat. columnist Pvt. Practice, 1988-90, Physicians Mgmt., 1991-93; commentator Med. News Network, 1993-94; contbr. more than 200 articles to profl. jours. Served with USCGR, 1960-68. Named one of Outstanding Young Men Am., U.S. Jaycees, 1977. Mem. Fla. Bar Assn., D.C. Bar Assn., Am. Coll. Legal Medicine, Sigma Delta Chi. Roman Catholic. Office: 631 W Fairbanks Ave Winter Park FL 32789-4710 also: 1350 Connecticut Ave NW Ste 905 Washington DC 20036-1701

BROPHY, GILBERT THOMAS, lawyer; b. Southampton, N.Y., July 15, 1926; s. Joseph Lester and Helen Veronica (Scholtz) B.; m. Canora Woodham Brophy, Sept. 3, 1957; m. Isabel Blair Porter; children: Laure Porter Thompson, Erin Woodham Brophy. BS with high honors, U. Fla., 1949; LLB, George Washington U., 1960; postgrad. Grad. Law Sch., U. Miami, 1970-73. Bar: Fla. 1960, D.C. 1974; U.S. Dist. Ct. D.C., 1970. Title examiner Jesse Phillips Klinge & Kendrick, Arlington, Va., 1959-60; ptnr. Beall, Beall & Brophy, Palm Beach, Fla., 1962-65; asst. city atty. West Palm Beach (Fla.), 1965-67; ptnr. Brophy & Skrandel, Palm Beach, 1968-70, Brophy & Aksomitas, Tequesta, Fla., 1974-75, Brophy, Genovese & Sayler, Jupiter, Fla., 1977-78, Brophy & Genovese, 1978-83; town atty. Lantana (Fla.), 1967-70; judge ad litem Village of Tequesta, 1970-72; town atty. Jupiter, 1974-75. Bd. dirs., disaster chmn. ARC, Palm Beach; past corr. sec. Palm Beach County Hist. Soc.; del. Fla. Caucus for Presidency, 1979, 87; mem. Rep. Com. Martin County, 1984-87. Served with AUS, 1944-46 Europe, 1951-54 Japan and Korea. Recipent Dedicated Service plaque Town of Jupiter, 1975. Mem.NRA (life), Attys. Title Ins. Fund, Palm Beach County Bar Assn., Nat. Mil. Intelligence Assn., Nat. CIC Assn., Assn. Former Intelligence Officers (life), Challenge Inc., Kappa Sigma Alumni Assn. Clubs: Rotary (pres. 1977-78, dist. 6930 ethics chair-4 way test), University (Washington); Elks, Everglades Rifle and Pistol (hon. life). Home: Villas on Green #504 717 S Us Hwy 1 Jupiter FL 33477-5975 Office: Parkway Plz 810 Saturn St Ste 16 Jupiter FL 33477-4456

BROST, GERARD ROBERT, mental health counselor, addictions professional, educator; b. Evanston, Ill., Sept. 30, 1949; s. Andrew Joseph and Zoe Wilhelmena (Dreis) B. BS, Western Mich. U., 1975, MA, 1976. Cert. behavior analyst, Fla.; cert. math. tchr., Fla.; lic. mental health counselor, cert. addictions profl. Tchg. asst. U. Fla., Gainesville, 1979-85; clin. supr. Alcothon House, Gainesville, 1983-85; psychologist Sunland Ctr., Gainesville, 1985-88; rehab. therapist N.E. Fla. State Hosp., MacClenny, 1988; therapist Marion Citrus Mental Health, Ocala, Fla., 1988-89; lectr. Ctrl. Fla. C.C., Ocala, 1987-90; psychol. specialist Marion Correctional Inst., Lowell, Fla., 1989-90; psychologist N.E. Fla. State Hosp., Macclenny, 1989-90; behavior analyst Behaviortek, Gainesville, 1989-90; fin. cons. Corp. Securities Group Inc., Maitland, Fla., 1990-91; registered rep. Waddell & Reed Fin. Svcs., Winter Park, Fla., 1990-91; ind. mktg. rep. Excel Telecom., Orlando, Fla., 1991; sr. therapist Lakeside Alternatives, Orlando, Fla., 1991-94; mental health counselor, addictions profl. Tampa Bay Consortium, Tampa, 1994-95; clin. assessment counselor Heart of Fla. Behavioral Ctr., Lakeland, 1993-95; mental health counselor Daylight of West Fla. Inc., Lakeland, 1995—; mental health counselor, addictions profl. Continuum Behavioral Healthcare, Tampa, Fla., 1996—; guest Sta. WCJB-TV, 1983; mental health counselor Continuum Behavioral Healthcare, Tampa, 1996. Mem. Food Bank, Gainesville, 1989-90; youth vol. Interface Youth Program, Gainesville, 1982-85; substance abuse vol. Corner Drugstore, Inc., Gainesville, 1983-84; crisis intervention vol. Alachua County Crisis Ctr., Gainesville, 1983. Recipient Outstanding Svc. award Transitions Substance Abuse Program, 1983, Interface Youth Program, 1985. Mem. Fla. Alcohol and Drug Abuse Assn., Dozenal Soc. Am., Dozenal Soc. Great Britain, Am. Literacy Coun., Affiliated Inventors Found., Math. Soc. Am., Am. Assn. Christian Counselors, Christian Assn. Psychol. Studies, World Future Soc., Nat. Assn. Masters in Psychology, Fla. Assn. Masters in Psychology. Home: 9631 Voyles Loop Polk City FL 33868-9732 Office: Daylight of W Fla Inc 1530 Kennedy Blvd Lakeland FL 33809

BROTH, RAY, retail executive; b. N.Y.C., Jan. 27, 1930; s. Abraham Lewis and Dorothy (Rand) B.; m. Beverly Rosenblatt, June 30, 1951; children:

Penny Cheryl, Caryn, Donna Elyse, Fran Susan. Grad. high sch., Pensacola, Fla. Receiving & inventory clk. Peerless Camera Stores, N.Y.C., 1952, repair svcs. clk., 1953, salesman, 1954-55, buyer, 1956, sales mgr., 1958; pres. Scopus, Inc., N.Y.C., 1957; store mgr. Peerless Camera Stores, Pitts., 1959-60; exec. v.p. Willoughby/Peerless Camera Stores, N.Y.C., 1961-76; pres., chief exec. officer Sarasota (Fla.) Camera Exch. & Video Ctr., 1976—; trustee Photo Mktg. Assocs.; charter mem. Eastman Kodak Medalist Bd., 1989. Bd. dirs. Sarasota Manatee Community Orch., 1990—. Staff sgt. USMC, 1948-52. Named Dealer of Yr. by Photo Trade News-Dealer Publ., 1988, Bus. Person of Yr. by Sarasota County C. of C., 1989; named to Hon. Order of Ky. Cols., 1989. Office: Sarasota Camera Exch & Video Ctr 1055 S Tamiami Trl Sarasota FL 34236-9100

BROTHERS, JOHN ALFRED, oil company executive; b. Huntington, W.Va., Nov. 10, 1940; s. John Luther and Genevieve (Monti) B.; m. Paula Sprague Benson, June 21, 1975. B.S., Va. Poly. Inst., 1962, M.S., 1965, Ph.D., 1966; postgrad advanced mgmt. program, Harvard U., 1981. With Internat. Nickel Co., 1962-64; with Ashland Oil, Inc., Ky., 1966—; sr. v.p. Ashland Oil, Inc., 1983-87; sr. v.p., group operating officer Ashland Oil Inc., 1987—; with Ashland Chem. Co., Columbus, Ohio, 1974-88; pres. Ashland Chem. Co., Columbus, 1983-88; bd. dirs. Key Bank, Cleve., Geon Co., Cleve, Drew Chem. Co., Ashland Coal, Inc.; adj. prof. engring. Ohio State U., 1978—; pres. bus. adv. coun., 1981—. Bd. dirs. Columbus Mus. Art, Columbus Children's Hosp., Ohio Dominican Coll., 1984—. NSF fellow, 1965-66; named Outstanding Young Man U.S. C. of C., 1972. Mem. Am. Petroleum Inst., Chem. Mfrs. Assn., Columbus C. of C. (bd. dirs.), Tau Beta Pi, Phi Kappa Phi. Republican. Clubs: Scioto Country, Rolling Rock, Muirfield Country, Mill Reef, Columbus. Office: Ashland Oil Inc PO Box 391 Ashland KY 41105-0391

BROTHERTON, ANN CASKEY, financial advisor; b. Louisville, Oct. 29, 1929; d. Marion William and Edith (Maxwell) C.; m. William Thurlow Weed Brotherton, Jr., June 17, 1950; children: Elizabeth Brotherton Gorrell, William Brotherton III, Laura. BA, Randolph-Macon Woman's Coll., 1948; MA, Duke U., 1950. Registered gen. securities rep.; lic. life ins. agt. Fin. advisor Prudential Securities, Charleston, W.Va., 1985—. Assoc. producer TV program Is Kanawha County for Me, 1980; chmn. events conflict mgmt. Kanawha County Dialogue, 1976-80. Bd. dirs., chair W.Va. Ednl. Broadcasting Authority, Garnet Sch. Cmty. Adv. Bd., 1979-92; sustaining mem. Assn. Jr. Leagues of Am., 1955—; bd. dirs. W.Va. Exec. Enterprise Conf., 1988—, Leadership W.Va., 1988—, W.Va. Pub. Broadcasting Found.; bd. dirs. Arthur B. Hodges Found., 1993—; trustee U. Charleston, 1994—; chair W.Va. Techcorps and Net Day, 1996—. Recipient Vol. Activist award Nat. Ctr. for Voluntary Action, 1977, Svc. award Charleston Area C. of C., 1983. Mem. W.Va. C. of C. (bd. dirs. 1990—, exec. com. 1992—, chmn. edn. com. 1993—), W.Va. Ednl. Broadcasting Authority (chmn.), Nat. Assn. Pub. TV Stas./Assn. for Pub. Broadcasting. Democrat. Episcopalian. Home: 1205 Colonial Way Charleston WV 25314-1921 Office: 1200 Laidley Tower Charleston WV 25301-2149

BROTZEN, FRANZ RICHARD, materials science educator; b. Berlin, July 4, 1915; came to U.S., 1941; s. Georg and Lena (Pacully) B.; m. Frances Burke Ridgway, Jan. 31, 1950; children: Franz Ridgway, Julie Ridgway. B.S. in Metall. Engring., Case Inst. Tech., 1950, M.S., 1953, Ph.D., 1954. Salesman a Quimica Bayer Ltda., Rio de Janeiro, Brazil, 1934-41; mfrs. rep. R.G. Le Tourneau, Inc., Longview, Tex., 1947-48; sr. research assoc. Case Inst. Tech., Cleve., 1951-54; mem. faculty Rice U., Houston, 1954—, prof. materials sci., 1959-88, prof. emeritus, 1988—, dean engring., 1962-66, master Brown Coll., 1977-82; vis. prof. Max Planck Inst., Stuttgart, W.Ger., 1960-61, 73-74, Fed. Poly. Inst., Zurich, Switzerland, 1966-67, U. Lausanne, (Switzerland), 1981. Author papers in field. Chmn. Houston Contemporary Arts Assn., 1964-65. Served to 1st lt. AUS, 1942-46. Recipient Sr. Scientist award W. German Govt., 1973-74; Guggenheim fellow, 1960-61. Fellow Am. Soc. Metals (chmn. Houston chpt. 1980-81); mem. AIME, Am. Phys. Soc., Soc. Engring. Sci., Sigma Xi, Tau Beta Pi. Home: 2701 Bellefontaine St # H Houston TX 77025 Office: Rice U Dept Materials Sci PO Box 1892 Houston TX 77251-1892

BROUCEK, WILLIAM SAMUEL, printing plant executive; b. Statesboro, Ga., July 27, 1950; s. Jack Wolf and Emily Louise (Kupferschmid) B.; m. Sara Carolyn Bennett, May 10, 1975; children: Samuel Josiah, William Bennett. BBA, Ga. So. U., 1972. Adminstr. Willingway Hosp., Statesboro, Ga., 1972-73; dept. mgr. Deluxe Check Printers, Inc., Jacksonville, Fla., 1975-78, asst. prodn. mgr., 1978-82, asst. plant mgr., 1982-83, mgr. Atlanta plant, 1984—. Bd. dirs. Ga. So. U. Alumni Assn., Statesboro, 1980-81; vol. Am. Cancer Soc., Jacksonville, 1981-83, Leadership Dekalb, 1992-93, bd. dirs. 1994—, Dekalb Initiative, 1993—; elder, trustee Eastminster Presbyn. Ch.; bd. dirs. Am. Heart Assn. Mem. Stone Mountain Indsl. Park Assn., DeKalb County C. of C., Aircraft Owners and Pilots Assn., Nantucket Swim and Racquet Club (Lilburn, Ga.). Republican. Avocations: aviation, old cars. Home: PO Box 1337 Tucker GA 30085-1337

BROUGH, JAMES A., airport terminal executive; b. 1938. BBA, Tex. A & M Coll., 1960. Commd. officer U.S. Navy, 1961-68; with Lockheed-GA, Marietta, Ga., 1968-69, RCA, West Palm Beach, Fla., 1969-71, Holland Oil, Fort Worth, 1971-72, Indpls. Airport Authority, Indpls., 1972-73, La Crosse (Wis.) Airport, 1973-75; exec. dir. Lexington-Fayette Union County Airport Bd., Lexington, Ky., 1975-87; with Birmingham (Ala.) Airport Authority, 1987—, now exec. dir. Office: Birmingham Internat Airport 5900 Messer Airport Hwy Birmingham AL 35212-1046

BROUGH, RICHARD BURRELL, retired graphic design educator, artist; b. Salmon, Idaho, May 31, 1920; s. Albert Burrell and Ruby (Wyant) B.; m. Hazel Waterman, July 31, 1946; children: Carol Ann Brough Henley, Richard B. Jr., Gregory Robert. Cert., Chouinard Art Inst., L.A., 1948; LHD (hon.), U. Ala., Tuscaloosa, 1993. Freelancee graphic designer, L.A., 1947; 0prof. graphic design art dept. U. Ala., 1948-87; freelance artist, Tuscaloosa, 1987—. Works exhibited at Met. Mus. Art, N.Y., 1950, Littlehouse Art Ctr., Homewood, Ala., 1985; represented in corp. collections. Sgt. USAAF, 1941-46, ETO. Recipient award for outstanding commitment to tchg. Nat. Alumni Assn. U. Ala., 1985, Disting. Career award Soc. for Fine Arts, U. Ala., 1992. Mem. Water Color Soc. Ala. (hon. life), Tuscaloosa Advt. Fedn. (hon. life), Tex. Watercolor Soc. Home and Studio: 17 Elmire Dr Tuscaloosa AL 35405

BROUGHTON, HELEN REED, science educator; b. Marion, Ark., June 27, 1945; d. Frank Reed and Annie (Watson) Anderson; m. Charles Lee Broughton, Dec. 26, 1965; children: Charles II, Clifford, Camille. BS, U. Ark. Pine Bluff, 1966; MS, Memphis State U., 1973, EdD, 1984. Tchr. Harvey (Ill.) Sch. Dist., 1967-68, West Memphis (Ark.) Sch. Dist., 1968-71, Memphis City Schs., 1971—. Author: Take Back Your Neighborhood, 1994. Fellow Dept. Energy, 1989, NASA, 1991-92; recipient Image award NAACP, 1989; named Tchr. of Yr. NABSE, 1994. Mem. NEA, Tenn. Edn. Assn., Tenn. Sci. Tchrs. Assn. (rep. dist. 9 1992-94, Outstanding Chpt. award 1994), Memphis Edn. Assn., Memphis Orgn. Sci. Tchrs. (co-founder 1992, pres. 1992-94, Presdl. award 1994). Home: 195 Southhill Ave Memphis TN 38109

BROUILLETTE, ALBERT C., watermedia painter, educator; b. Holyoke, Mass., Jan. 9, 1924; s. Eugene and Delia Leona (Spinks) B.; m. Mary Kathleen Ross, June 3, 1946; children: Maureen, Michael, Andrew, Ann. Student, Am. Sch. Comml. Art, Dallas, 1948-50. Watermedia painter. Author: The Evolving Picture, 1987; works exhibited in various exhbns. including Am. Watercolor Exhbn., N.Y.C., 1991, Am. Watercolor Internat. Waters Exbhn., 1991, Nat. Acad. Design, N.Y.C., 1993, Taipei, Taiwan Exhbn., 1994, San Diego Watercolor Soc., 1995. With U.S. Army, 1943-45, ETO. Mem. Nat. Acad. (William Payton award 1975, 92), Am. Watercolor Soc. (Dolphin fellow 1979, Gold medal of honor 1986, Bronze medal of honor 1993), Nat. Watercolor Soc., Southwestern Watercolor Soc., Tex. Watercolor Soc., Rocky Mountain Nat. Watercolor Soc. Home: 1300 Sunset Ct Arlington TX 76013

BROUSE, MICHAEL, petroleum engineer, management consultant; b. Houston, Aug. 16, 1937; s. William Gaston and Mattye (Palmo) B.; m. Maribeth Colleen Collins (div. Mar. 1978); children: Michele Christine, Marea Celeste (dec.), Michael Eric; m. Lesley Ann Barrett, Apr. 27, 1981. AA, Wharton County Jr. Coll., Tex., 1957; BSc in Petroleum and Natural Gas Engr., Tex. A&I U., 1961. From petroleum engr. trainee to drilling engr. trainee Phillips Petroleum Co., Tex., La., 1961-64; from petroleum engr. sr. grade to European drilling mgr. Amoco Internat. Oil Co., various nat. & internat., 1965-76; v.p., gen. mgr. Oilfield Cons. Internat., London, 1976-82; drilling mgr. Neddrill B.V., Rotterdam, The Netherlands, 1982; ops. mgr. Neddrill B.V., Rotterdam, 1983-84, mgmt. advisor/spl. projects, 1984-86; sr. v.p. ops. Golden Engring., Inc., Houston, 1986-89; pres., co-owner United Oil Cons. Internat. S.A., Houston, 1989-90; v.p., gen. mgr. Triton Engring. Svcs. Co., Houston, 1990-92; cons. Mike Brouse Enterprises, Houston, 1993—; exec. v.p., gen. mgr. Tesco Drilling Tech. (U.S.) Inc., 1994—; sr. v.p. Tesco Corp. of Can., 1994—; advisor, former edit. com. mem. World Oil and Ocean Industry Mag., Houston, 1987-92. Inventor in field; contbr. articles to profl. jours. Mem. Am. Assn. Drilling Engrs., Soc. Petroleum Engrs., Tau Beta Pi (sec.), Alpha Chi. Home: 201 Vanderpool Ln Apt 66 Houston TX 77024-6125

BROUSSARD, RAY F., history educator; b. Lafayette, La., Apr. 22, 1926; s. Andrew F. and Lucille (Moss) B.; m. Ernestine E. Gonzales, Nov. 25, 1951; children: Charles Timothy, Edward Michael, David Christopher. BA, Southwestern La. Inst., 1949; MA, U. Tex., 1952, PhD, 1959. Head fgn. lang. dept. S.W. Tex. Jr. coll., Uvalde, 1952-55; instr. Howard County Jr. Coll., Big Spring, Tex., 1955-57; tchg. asst. U. Tex., Austin, 1957-59; dir. Centro Colombo Americano, Cartagena, Colombia, 1959-61; asst. prof. Miss. State U., Starkville, 1961-66; assoc. prof. history U. Ga., Athens, 1966—. Author: (monograph) San Antonio During Texas Rep, 1966; editor Friends and Neighbors newsletter, 1996. Bd. dirs. Camp Halliuah, Athens, 1970-80, Clarke Fed. Credit Union, Athens, 1971-82, Cath. Social Svcs., Athens, 1995—; mem. parish coun. St. Joseph Ch., Athens, 1980—. With USN, 1943-51. Mem. Nat. Social Sci. Assn. (bd. dirs. 1990-96), S.E. Conf. of L.Am. Studies, Conf. of L.Am. History. Roman Catholic. Home: 155 Hancock Ln Athens GA 30605 Office: University of Georgia Dept of History Athens GA 30602

BROUSSARD, WILLIAM JOSEPH, physician, cattleman, environmentalist; b. Abbeville, La., Feb. 14, 1934; s. Alphe Alcide and Odile Perpetue (Cade) B.; m. Margaret Lucile Reynolds, Apr. 3, 1933; children: Dianne, M. Lynn, Allen, Laura. BS, La. State U., Baton Rouge, 1955; MD, U. Minn., 1959. Diplomate Am. Bd. Ophthalomology. Pvt. practice medicine Melbourne (Fla.) Eye Assocs., 1967—; pres. med. staff Melbourne Eye Assocs., 1967; bd. dirs. Space Coast PPO. Bd. dirs. Civic Music Assn., Melbourne, 1970-83, Scrubland Trust, 1992—; mem. pvt. landowners com. Ecosystem Mgmt., State of Fla., 1994. Fellow ACS, Am. Acad. Ophthalmology (ethics com. 1986-88); mem. AMA, Nat. Cattlemen's Assn., Fla. Soc. Ophthalmology (pres. 1983), Fla. Cattleman's Assn., Fla. Med. Assn., Found. Beefmaster Assn. (pres. 1988), Allen Broussard Conservancy, Inc. Home: 3660 N Riverside Dr Melbourne FL 32903-4424 Office: Melbourne Eye Assocs 502 E New Haven Ave Melbourne FL 32901-5427

BROWDER, JOHN GLEN, congressman, educator; b. Sumter, SC, Jan. 15, 1943; s. Archie Calvin and Ila (Frierson); m. Sara Rebecca Moore; 1 child, Jenny Rebecca. BA in History, Presbyn. Coll., 1965; MA in Polit. Sci., Emory U., 1971, PhD in Polit. Sci., 1971. Asst. in pub. relations Presbyn. Coll., Clinton, S.C., 1965; sportswriter The Atlanta Jour., 1966; investigator U.S. Civil Service Commn., Atlanta, 1966-68; prof. polit. sci. Jacksonville (Ala.) State U., 1971-87; mem. Ala. Ho. of Reps., Montgomery, 1982-86; sec. of state State of Ala., Montgomery, 1987-89; mem. 101st-104th Congresses from 3d Ala. dist., Washington, 1989—. Mem. Am. Polit. Sci. Assn., So. Polit. Sci. Assn. Democrat. Methodist. Home: 517 Pelham Rd N Jacksonville AL 36265-1825 Office: US Ho of Reps 2344 Rayburn HOB Washington DC 20515

BROWER, DAVID JOHN, lawyer, urban planner, educator; b. Holland, Mich., Sept. 11, 1930; s. John J. and Helen (Olson) B.; m. Lou Ann Brown, Nov. 26, 1960; children: Timothy Seth, David John, II, Ann Lacey. B.A., U. Mich., 1956, J.D., 1960. Bar: Ill. 1960, Mich. 1961, Ind. 1961, U.S. Supreme Ct. 1971. Asst. dir. div. community planning Ind. U., Bloomington, 1960-70; rsch. prof. dept. city and regional planning U. N.C., Chapel Hill, 1970—, assoc. dir. Ctr. for Urban and Regional Studies, 1970-94; pres. Coastal Resources Collaborative, Ltd., Chapel Hill and Manteo, N.C., 1980—; counsel Robinson & Cole, Hartford, Conn., 1986—. Author: (with others) Constitutional Issues of Growth Management, 1978; Growth Management, 1984, Managing Development in Small Towns, 1984, Special Area Management, 1985, Catastrophic Coastal Storms, 1989, Understanding Growth Management, 1989, Coastal Zone Management: An Evaluation, 1991, An Introduction to Coastal Zone Management, 1994. Mem. Am. Planning Assn. (bd. dirs. 1982-85, chmn.-founder planning and law div. 1978, co-chmn. substainable devel. group 1995—), Am. Inst. Cert. Planners. Democrat. Episcopalian. Home: 612 Shadylawn Rd Chapel Hill NC 27514-2009 Office: U NC CB # 3140 Chapel Hill NC 27599-3140

BROWER, JANICE KATHLEEN, library technician; b. Chgo., July 29, 1952; d. Gerald B. and Emily (Kavicky) B. AA, Lincoln Coll., 1973; BS, Ill. State U., 1975; postgrad., U. Okla., 1984-86. Libr. assoc. Chgo. Pub. Libr., 1975-80, 81-83; libr. technician U. Okla. Biol. Sta., Norman, 1987, Okla. Dept. of Corrections Ouachita Correctional Ctr., Hodgen, 1987—. Lutheran. Office: Ouachita Correctional Ctr HC 63 Box 5390 Hodgen OK 74939

BROWN, A.C., JR., electrical engineer; b. Fort Smith, Ark., June 12, 1959; s. A.C. and Welela Eve (Graham) B.; m. Kimberly Karol Elliott, May 7, 1983; children: Alexis Colbea, A.C. III, Elliott Graham. BSEE, U. Ark., 1982. Cert. profl. engr., Tex.; cert. energy mgr. Asst. to div. supt. Tex. Power and Light, Sherman, 1983-84; T&D engr. TU Electric, Sherman, 1984-85; oper. engr. TU Electric, Tyler, Tex., 1985-87; engr. TU Electric, Lancaster, Tex., 1987-89; staff engr. TU Electric, Dallas, 1989-92, account exec., 1992—. Co. coord. United Way, Dallas, 1991, spkr. of yr., 1994. Mem. NSPE, Assn. Energy Engrs., Toastmasters Internat. (area gov. 1994-95, divsn. gov. 1995—), Rotary (sec. 1995—). Baptist. Home: 301 Creekwood Dr Lancaster TX 75146-3405 Office: TU Electric 1506 Commerce St Ste 13E Dallas TX 75201-4929

BROWN, ALETHA FERN, author, poet; b. Atwater, Calif., May 27, 1931; d. Charles Clinton and Hazel Pearl (Fugate) Kruse; m. Duncan Ray Brown, July 18, 1959 (dec. Aug. 1993); children: Joyce Evon Hoffman Brown, Gary Leslie Hoffman Brown, Michelle Renee Brown. Student, Northwest Bible Coll., Seattle, 1949. Libr. Bellevue (Wash.) H.S., 1946-49; cons. Children's Ct. Yakima, Wash., 1980-90; owner, operator DAG Ice Cream, Salem, Oreg., 1976-78, Wapato, Wash., 1978-95. Author: (poetry) Sea of Treasures, 1995 (Merit award Nat. Libr. of Poetry), Best Poems of 1996, 1995 (Editor's Choice award Nat. Libr. of Poetry), Dear God-Help Us to Know You, 1996, Hangin' Out with the STARS, in My Galaxy, 1996. Publicity chmn. PTA (Oreg. & Wash.), 1957-58, 1976-78; foster parent Oreg. & Wash., 1962-91; active Assemblies for the Baha'i Faith. Mem. Internat. Soc. of Poets (Merit award 1996). Home: 1407 Jackson Downs Blvd Nashville TN 37214

BROWN, AMY BENSON, English language and literature educator; b. York, S.C., May 21, 1966; d. James Francis and Linda Gayle (Skipper) B.; m. Brian Mendelsohn; 1 child, Caida Mendelsohn. BA in English magna cum laude, U. S.C., 1988; MA in English and Am. Lit., Rutgers U., 1990; PhD in English and Am. Lit., Emory U., 1995. Vis. asst. prof. State U. West Ga. Contbr. articles, revs. to profl. publs. Mem. MLA, So. Atlantic MLA, Toni Morrison Soc., Phi Beta Kappa. Home: 2058 Howard Cir NE Atlanta GA 30307 Office: English Dept State U of West Ga Carrollton GA 30118

BROWN, ANDREW M., otolaryngologist, allergist; b. Columbus, Ga., July 7, 1932; s. Leonard Franklin and Arizona Ruth (Embrey) B.; m. Peggy Jean Inzer; children: Sarah Embrey Brown Hughes, Franklin Inzer; m. Renalda Joan Holcomb, June 23, 1985. BA cum laude, Baylor U., 1954; BS, U. Ala., 1958; MD, Med. Coll. Ala., 1962. Intern Lloyd Noland Found. Hosp., Fairfield, Ala., 1962-63; resident Barnes & Allied Hosp., Washington Hosp., St. Louis, 1983-67; pvt. practice Ear Nose & Throat Assocs. of Gadsden, P.A., Ala., 1970—; with Odess & Brown, Otolaryngologists, Birmingham, Ala., 1967-70. Office: 515 S 3d St Gadsden AL 35901-5301

BROWN, ANN LENORA, community development consultant; b. Austin, Tex., Aug. 29, 1955; d. William Alley and Ann Dyke (Shafer) B.; m. Robert William Lukeman, May 21, 1988; 1 child, Dancy Ann Lukeman. BArch, U. Tex., 1983. Main st. project dir. City of Brenham, Tex., 1983-86; owner, cons. TEXANA Devel. & Design Co., Galveston, Tex., 1980—; dir. residential programs and arch. svcs. Galveston Hist. Found., 1988-91; realtor Barney Rapp, Inc. Realtors, Galveston, 1995—; urban planner City of Galveston, 1996—; mus. exhibit U.S. Corps of Engrs., 1992; cmty. devel. cons. Galveston and Houston neighborhoods, 1991—; faculty mem. Coll. Arch., U. Houston hist. preservation program, 1991-93. Archtl. illustrator calendar med. br. U. Tex., Galveston, 1991. Chair Broadway Redevel. Com., Galveston, 1990-93; founder, exec. dir. Galveston Affordable Housing, 1991-96; bd. dirs., pres. Galveston Housing Fin. Corp., 1992—. Recipient Preservation award Tex. Hist. Commn., 1986. Mem. AIA (assoc., tri-chair urban design 1991, chair hist. resources 1990-93), Tex. Cmty. Devel. Assn. Tex. (steering com. Tex. Devel. Inst. 1991-92). Episcopalian.

BROWN, ASHMUN N., priest; b. Yakima, Wash., June 9, 1930; s. Nathaniel Usher and Marie Adair (Flynn) B.; m. Suzanne Hengesch, Oct. 28, 1953 (div. 1973); children: Mara Kate Routh, Lisa Ann, Mark, Fred J.; m. Rita L. Rodda, May 23, 1981. JD cum laude, Boston U., 1958; LLM, U. Mich., 1959; D Ministry, Grad. Theol. Found., 1989. Bar: Mass. 1959, Fla. 1967, U.S. Supreme Ct., 1972; ordained priest Episc. Ch., 1991. Chancellor Canterbury Retreat and Conf. Ctr., Oviedo, Fla., 1981—; vice chancellor, mem. ct. array Diocese of Cen. Fla., Orlando, 1988-91; deacon Cathedral Ch. of St. Luke, Orlando, 1984-91, assoc. priest, 1991-94; pres., dean Inst. for Christian Studies, Orlando, 1985-92; gen. counsel Univ. Cen. Fla., Orlando, 1980-94, chaplain, 1990-93; vicar St. Francis Ch., Bushnell, Fla., 1994—; diocesan bd. Diocese of Cen. Fla., Orlando, 1987-89, sexuality commn., 1990-91; bd. dirs. Inst. for Youth Ministry, Orlando. Contbr. articles to newspapers. Mem. Disabled Am. Vets., Orlando, 1989—. Lt. U.S. Signal Corps, 1951-53. Rome scholar Boston Univ. Law Sch., 1957-58, Cook fellow Univ. Mich., Ann Arbor, 1959. Mem. Fla. Bar Assn., Mass. Bar Assn. Democrat. Episcopalian. Home: PO Box 1089 Bushnell FL 33513-1089 Office: St Francis Episcopal Ch PO Box 566 Bushnell FL 33513

BROWN, BAILEY, federal judge; b. Memphis, June 16, 1917; s. Joshua Goodlett and Lillian (Pearcy) B.; m. Doris Frances Lawhorn., Dec. 24, 1964; 1 son, Bailey, Jr. A.B., U. Mich., 1939; LL.B., Harvard U., 1942. Bar: Tenn. 1941. Ptnr. Burch, Porter, Johnson & Brown, Memphis, 1946-61; judge U.S. Dist. Ct. (we. dist.) Tenn., Memphis, 1961-79, chief judge, 1966-79; sr. judge (6th cir.) U.S. Ct. Appeals, 1979—; mem. Jud. Conf. Com. on Ct. Adminstrn., 1969-75, 78-84; past chmn. Subcom. on Judicial Improvements; past mem. ad hoc com. studying Cameras in the Courtroom; guest lectr. Rhodes Coll., Memphis. Pres. Memphis Symphony, 1958-60, Memphis Pub. Affairs Forum, 1955. Lt. USNR, 1942-46. Recipient Charles A. Rond Outstanding Judge of Yr. award Young Lawyers Memphis and Shelby County Bar Assns., 1977. Mem. Memphis and Shelby County Bar Assn. (Liberty Bell award 1971, Ann. Dedication and Achievement award Criminal Law Sect. 1979). Episcopalian (vestryman). Office: US Ct Appeals 1116 Federal Bldg 167 N Main St Memphis TN 38103-1816

BROWN, BARBARA JEAN, special and secondary education educator; b. Midland, Tex., Nov. 3, 1945; d. John Joseph and Sarah Beryl (Seely) Sury; m. Samuel Bradford Brown III, June 30, 1984. BA in English, U. Tex., Arlington, 1967, MAT, 1979. Cert. gifted and English tchr., Tex., Fla. With Euless (Tex.) Jr. High Sch./Hurst-Euless-Bedford Ind. Sch. Dist., 1967-84, Edgewater High Sch./Orange County Sch. Bd., Orlando, Fla., 1984-86; educator Lakeview Mid. Sch./Seminole County Sch. Bd., Sanford, Fla., 1986—; curriculum writer Hurst-Euless-Bedford Ind. Sch. Dist., Hurst, mem. curriculum and dist. policy devel. com.; curriculum writer Seminole County Sch. Bd.; presenter Tex. Gifted Conf., Houston. Seminole County Sch. Bd. grantee, 1987-88, Svc. award, 1991, finalist, 1989-93; recipient Tchr. Merit award Walt Disney World Co., 1990-92; named Prominent Educator of Tex., 1983, Tchr. of the Yr., Coun. for Exceptional Children, 1991. Mem. NEA, Nat. Assn. Gifted Children, PTA, Fla. Scholastic Press Assn., Orlando Area City Panhellenic, Phi Mu (pres. Winter Park-Orlando chpt. 1988-91, nat. state day chmn. 1993-94), Sigma Tau Delta, Sigma Delta Phi. Roman Catholic. Home: 107 Hatfield Ct Longwood FL 32779-4606 Office: Lakeview Mid Sch 21 Lakeview Ave Sanford FL 32773-5331

BROWN, BARBARA S., environmental scientist; b. Newark, Aug. 5, 1951; d. Louis and Louise (Mumper) Stein; children: Kristin Leigh, Andrew Hayden. Student Am. U., 1969-71; BS in Biology, U. Miami, 1976, postgrad. Staff scientist Environ. Sci. and Engring., Inc., Miami, 1978-86; dir. environ. crimes unit Dade County Environ. Resource Mgmt., 1986—. Mem. Nat. Assn. Environ. Profls.

BROWN, BARRY STEPHEN, research psychologist; b. Bklyn., Sept. 26, 1937; s. Isidore Brook and Barbara (Drazin) B.; m. Ann J. Foley, Feb. 25, 1961; children: Rebecca, David, Mariam. AB, Bklyn. Coll., 1958; MS, Western Res. U., Cleve., 1959, PhD, 1963. Chief divsn. rsch. and stats. D.C. Dept. Human Resources, 1974-75; chief svcs. rsch. br. Nat. Inst. on Drug Abuse, Rockville, Md., 1975-82, dir. divsn. clin. rsch., 1982-85, dir. divsn. prevention and comms., 1985-86; chief treatment and early intervention rsch. br. Nat. Inst. on Drug Abuse, Balt., 1986-88; chief cmty. rsch. br. Nat. Inst. on Drug Abuse, Rockville, 1989-92; vis. scientist Tex. Christian U., Ft. Worth, 1993—; adj. prof. U. N.C., Wilmington, 1993—; chair steering com. Nat. Inst. on Drug Abuse and Nat. Devel. and Rsch. Insts., 1995—; Nat. Inst. on Drug Abuse; adv. bd. Nat. Tech. Ctr. for Substance Abuse Needs Assessment, Boston, 1993—, Ctr. for Therapeutic Cmty. Rsch., N.Y.C., 1993—; cons. Nat. Devel. & Rsch. Insts., N.Y.C., 1993—. Editor: Handbook on Risk of AIDS, 1993. Recipient award Nat. Assn. of State Alcohol and Drug Abuse Dirs., 1986, USPHS, 1979; Nat. Inst. on Drug Abuse grantee, 1994. 96. Mem. Soc. Psychologists in Addictive Behaviors. Home: PO Box 1695 Carolina Beach NC 28428-1695

BROWN, BENJAMIN THOMAS, urologist, educator; b. Beckley, W.Va., Sept. 30, 1948; s. Benjamin Porter Jr. and Nancy Jo (Ballengee) B.; m. Kimberlee Timbrook; children: Elizabeth Timbrook, James Schuyler. Student, Johns Hopkins U., 1966-69; MD, W.Va. U., 1973. Diplomate Am. Bd. Urology. Surg. intern W.Va. U., Morgantown, 1973-74, resident in medicine, 1974-75; resident in urology U. Miami (Fla.), 1975-78; pvt. practice Daytona Beach, Fla., 1978—; chief surgery Meml. Hosp, Ormond Beach, Fla., 1980-82, chief staff, 1986-87; chief urology Halifax Med. Ctr., Daytona Beach, 1982-84; clin. asst. prof. urology U. South Fla., Tampa, 1979—. Contbr. numerous articles to med. jours. Pres. I-Care, child abuse, Daytona Beach, 1988; vice chmn. adminstrv. bd. United Meth. Ch., 1990-91, pastor, mem. pastor-parish rels. com., 1990-94; bd. dirs. Am. Cancer Soc., 1993—, 2d v.p., 1994-97; bd. dirs. Ptnrs. for Cmty. Health, 1993—, v.p., 1996-97; bd. dirs. Volusia County Coop. Health Group, 1991—, vice chmn., 1993-94, chmn., 1994-97. Fellow ACS; mem. AMA, Am. Urol. Assn. (bd. dirs. Southeastern sect. 1994—, bd. rep. to exec. com. 1996—), Fla. Urol. Soc. (exec. com. 1990—, chmn. bylaws com. 1992-94, membership 1994-96), Underwater Med. Soc., Fla. Med. Assn. (Volusia County del. 1990—), Volusia County Med. Soc. (sec. 1990-91, pres.-elect 1991-92, pres. 1992-93, chmn. bd. govs. 1994-95), Daytona Beach Quarterback Club (team physician 1987), Univ. Club Volusia County (bd. dirs. 1986-89), Tiger Bay Club (2d v.p. 1995-97), Volusia County (bd. dirs.), Rotary, Masons. Republican. Home: 602 Riverside Dr Ormond Beach FL 32176-7714 Office: Atlantic Urol Assocs 545 Health Blvd Daytona Beach FL 32114-1493

BROWN, BERTHA FAYE, early childhood and elementary school educator; b. Burnsville, W.Va., July 2, 1966; d. John L. and Patricia Ann (Godfrey) Dennison; m. Jeffery Wayne Brown, July 2, 1988. B.Elem. and Early Childhood Edn., Glenville (W.Va.) State Coll., 1984-88; postgrad., W. Va. U., 1992-96. Substitute tchr. Braxton County Bd. Edn., Sutton, W.Va., 1988-89; kindergarten tchr. Webster County Bd. Edn., Webster Springs, W.Va., 1989-91, Even-Start tchr., 1991-93, tchr. 6th grade, 1993-96; prekindergarten tchr. Braxton County Bd. of Edn., 1996—; facilitator Gov.'s Inst., Charleston, W.Va., summer 1996, Parkersburg, W.Va., summer 1995. Mem. adminstrv. coun. Burnsville (W.Va.) United Meth. Ch., 1983-93, leader youth group, 1990-91. Mem. W.Va. Edn. Assn., W.Va. Fedn. Tchrs. Democrat.

BROWN, BETH MARIE, dietitian, hospital administrator; b. Pigeon, Mich., Oct. 2, 1952; d. Walton Durwood and Marion Anita (Schweitzer) B. BS, Cen. Mich. U., 1974; MS, S.W. Tex. State U., 1990. Registered dietitian; diplomate ACHE. Clin. dietitian Leonard Hosp., N.Y., 1975-76; edn. and staff devel. dietitian VA Med. Ctr., Iron Mtn., Mich., 1976-79, chief food prodn. & svc., 1979-81; chief adminstrv. dietetic svc. VA Med. Ctr., Phila., 1981-83; chief dietetic svc. VA Med. Ctr., Butler, Pa., 1983-86, Temple, Tex., 1986-94; adminstrv. officer managed care South Tex. Vets. Health Care System, San Antonio, 1995—; adj. lectr. Tex. A&M U., Temple, 1986-94. Mem. Big. T Toastmasters, Temple, 1989-93, assoc. dir. trainee, San Antonio,1994; bd. dirs. Altrusa Internat. of Temple, 1989-92, Butler Meals-on-Wheels, 1983-86. Recipient Pride & Pub. Svc. award Dept. Vets. Affairs, 1991, Leadership VA award, 1990; named Competent Toastmaster, 1990, Outstanding Young Woman of Am., 1988, Excellence in Improving Svc. to the Pub., 1979. Mem. Am. Coll. Healthcare Execs., Am. Dietetic Assn., Cen. Tex. Dietetic Assn. (officer 1987-89), Tex. Hosp. Assn., Tex. Dietetic Assn. Lutheran. Home: 3147 Morning Tr San Antonio TX 78247 Office: South Tex Vets Health Care System 7400 Merton Minter St San Antonio TX 78284-5700

BROWN, BETSY ETHERIDGE, dean; b. Statesville, N.C., Aug. 2, 1950; d. Guy Wetmore and Elizabeth (Hackney) Etheridge; m. Homer L. Brown, Aug. 13, 1972 (dec. Mar. 1987); 1 child, Elizabeth Leigh; m. Lawrence C. Timbs, Jr., July 30, 1995. BS in English, Appalachian State U., 1972; MA in English, Ohio State U., 1974, PhD in English, 1978. Cert. tchr., N.C. Asst. prof. English Pa. State U., University Park, 1978-85; asst. to v.p. Queens Coll., Charlotte, N.C., 1987-89, Winthrop U., Rock Hill, S.C., 1990-92; assoc. v.p. Winthrop U., Rock Hill, 1992-94, dean Coll. Arts and Scis., 1994—; bd. mem. Cmty. Bd. for Women's Svcs., Rock Hill, 1994—. Recipient Mgmt. Devel. Program award Harvard Grad. Sch. Edn., 1992, Forum award Am. Coun. on Edn.-Nat. Idenfification Program, 1995; Fulbright grantee, Bonn, Germany, 1994. Mem. AAUW, S.C. Women in Higher Edn. Adminstrn. (bd. sec. 1994—). Office: Winthrop Univ 107 Kinard Rock Hill SC 29733

BROWN, BILLY CHARLIE, secondary school educator; b. Cookeville, Tenn., Feb. 20, 1947; s. Joe Homer and Sallie Mable (Hendrickson) B. BS in Forestry, BS in Edn., U. Tenn., 1969, EdD in Curriculum and Instruction, 1979; MA in Secondary Sci. Edn., Tenn. Tech. U., 1973, EdS in Secondary Sci. Edn., 1976. Cert. secondary sci. tchr., Ga., Tenn., Ky. Tchr., dept. chair Westwood Jr. High Sch., Manchester, Tenn., 1970-77; tchr., coach Feldwood High Sch., College Park, Ga., 1979-84; tchr., sci. Shiloh High Sch., Lithonia, Ga., 1984-87; coord. environ. energy sci. edn. ctr. U. Tenn., Knoxville, 1987-88; assoc. prof. Ky. Wesleyan Coll., Owensboro, 1990-93; with Cobb County Schs., Marietta, Ga., 1993—; vis. asst. prof. U. Tenn., Knoxville, 1988-90; co-dir. Ctr. for Environ./Energy/Sci. Edn., U. Tenn., Knoxville, 1988-90; sci. cons. area sch. dists. Ky. Wesleyan Coll., Owensboro, 1990-93; dir. Elem. Sci. Leadership Inst., Oak Ridge Nat. Lab., 1993—. Contbr. articles to profl. jours. Named Outstanding Classroom Tchr., Tenn. Edn. Assn., 1975. Mem. Nat. Sci. Tchr. Assn. (Outstanding Sci. Educator nominee 1991), Nat. Coun. Tchrs. Math., Mid-East Regional Assn. Educators Tchrs. Sci. Home: 3410 Windcliff Dr Marietta GA 30067

BROWN, BONNIE MARYETTA, lawyer; b. North Plainfield, N.J., Oct. 31, 1953; d. Robert Jeffrey and Diana (Parket) B. AB, Washington U., St. Louis, 1975; JD, U. Louisville, 1978. Bar: Ky. 1978, U.S. Dist. Ct. (we. dist.) Ky. 1979, U.S. Dist. Ct. (ea. dist.) Ky. 1993. Pvt. practice Louisville, 1978—; lectr., seminar leader various profl., ednl., govtl. and civic groups; cons. marital rape; registered lobbyist 1994 Ky. Gen. Assembly for Ky. Assn. Marriage and Family Therapy. Editor Ky. Appellate Handbook, 1985; contbr. articles to profl. jours. Vol. legal panel Ky. Civil Liberties Union, Louisville, 1984—; author, chief lobbyist Marital Rape Bill, Ky. Coalition Against Rape and Sexual Assault, 1982—, Sexual Harassment bill, 1996; vol. advisor Louisville RAPE Relief Ctr., 1975—; treas. Family Support Group/Family Readiness Program. of USAR, 1994—. Recipient Cert. Spl. Recognition RAPE Relief Ctr., 1980, Cert. Outstanding Contbn., Louisville YMCA, 1983, Cert. of Appreciation, James Graham Brown Cancer Ctr., 1984, Decade of Svc. award YMCA/Rape Relief Ctr., Outstanding Victim Adv. award Fayette County Govt., 1990, cert. of Recognition Jefferson County Family Ct., 1995. Mem. ABA (family law sect., apptd. to appellate handbook com., jud. adminstrn. divsn. lawyers conf.), Ky. Bar Assn. (family law sect. vice-chair 1994-95, chair-elect 1995-96, chair 1996—, seminar spkr., task force solo practitioners and small law firms 1992, chair subcom. on law office automation and networking, Continuing Legal Edn. award 1981, 93), Louisville Bar Assn. (liaison to mental health sect., organizer marital rape seminar, chmn. family law sect., mediation com. property divsn., seminar spkr., organizer joint custody child abuse seminars, solo practitioner and small law firm sect., chair 1995, pro bono consortium), Ky. Acad. Trial Attys. (spkr. seminar, editor The Advocate family law sect.), Bus. and Profl. Women (pres. River City chpt.), Ky. Fedn. (legis. chair 1986-87, 90-92, legal counsel 1992, 96, lobby corps chair 1993-95), Louisville Internat. Cultural Ctr., Women Lawyers Assn. Jefferson County. Republican. Office: Nat City Tower 101 S 5th St Ste 3850 Louisville KY 40202-3121

BROWN, BRAD, museum administrator. Dir. Mus. Coastal History, St. Simons, Ga. Office: Mus Coastal History 101 12th St Saint Simons GA 31522-4821

BROWN, BRENT BURRIS, data processing executive; b. Lake Charles, La., Oct. 7, 1963; s. Cecil Ray and Stella (Burris) B.; m. Sharon Rose Clay, May 27, 1989. BS in Math. cum laude, La. Tech. U., 1986. Systems engr. Electronic Data Systems, Flint, Mich., 1986-87; data processing trainee Systematics Info. Svc., Little Rock, 1987-88, sr. client svcs. specialist, 1988-91, conversions mgr., 1991-93; product mgr. Systematics Info. Svcs. Inc., Little Rock, 1993-94; client svcs. mgr. Systematics Info. Svcs., Little Rock, 1994-95; product mgr. Alltel Info. Svcs., Little Rock, 1995, asst. acct. mgr., 1996—. Contbr. articles to profl. jours. Bd. dirs. Big Bros./Big Sisters of Pulaski County, Little Rock, 1993—, vol, 1989—; active Jr. Achievement of Ark., 1991—. Mem. Soc. for Tech. Communication, La. Tech. Alumni Assn., Pi Mu Epsilon, Gamma Beta Phi. Republican. Methodist. Home: 191 Pebble Beach Dr Little Rock AR 72212-2647 Office: Alltel Info Svcs Inc One Allied Dr B4F3 Little Rock AR 72202

BROWN, CALLIE CORRINNE WRATHER, medical, surgical nurse, derma-technologist; b. Rutherford County, Tenn., July 1, 1934; d. Horace Palmer and Gola Kate (Jones) Wrather; m. Trenton Larry Brown, Sept. 7, 1957; children: Bradley Trenton, Brenda Calantha, Gerald Truman. RN, East Tenn. Bapt. Hosp. Sch. Nursing, 1956; student, U. Tenn., 1953, 54, 62. RN, Tenn., N.C., S.C., Pa., Ohio, Ind. Supr. Maury County Hosp., Columbia, Tenn., 1957; office nurse Acuff Clinic, Knoxville, 1957-60; staff nurse oper. rm. East Tenn. Bapt. Hosp., Knoxville, 1961; plant nurse, stenographer wear-ever divsn. Aluminum Co. Am., Chillicothe, Ohio, 1964; pub. health nurse Blount County Health Dept., Maryville, Tenn., 1961-68; supr. Richmond (Ind.) State Hosp., 1970-71; staff nurse Med. Pers. Pool, Pitts., 1971-76, Aide Health Svc., Pitts., 1980-83; store mgr. Furniture Factory Outlet World of Waxhaw, N.C., Columbia, S.C. and Hickory, N.C., 1983-89; staff, charge nurse, designated facilitator St. Joseph's Hosp., Asheville, N.C., 1991—; pres., derma-technologist Derma-Graphics of Asheville, Inc., 1992—. Instr. mother and baby care, home nursing, swimming ARC, Columbia, Knoxville and Maryville, Tenn., 1957-60's; treas. Independence PTA, Aliquippa, Pa., 1978-80; pres. Hopewell Jr. High Parent, Tchr. and Student Assn., Aliquippa, 1980-83; mem. choir various chs., 1960-78. Mem. ANA, Nat. League Nursing (advocacy), Am. Coun. Dermagraphic Rsch. (diplomat), Soc. Permanent Cosmetic Profls., MCN Micropigmentation Assn. Baptist. Home: 73 Old Concord Rd Fletcher NC 28732-9421 Office: Derma-Graphics of Asheville Inc 73 Old Concord Rd Fletcher NC 28732 also: St Joseph's Hosp Biltmore Ave Asheville NC 28801

BROWN, CAROL RENTIERS, health facility administrator; b. Miami, Fla., Dec. 22, 1931; d. William W. and Margaret (Driggers) Rentiers; m. R. Robert Brown, Jan. 8, 1955; children: Kati Schardl, R. Robert Jr., Joan Kaplan. Diploma, St. Francis Xavier Sch. Nsg., Charleston, S.C., 1952. RN, S.C., Fla. Asst. supr. surg. floor Victoria Hosp., Miami, Fla., 1952-55; staff nurse surg./obstetrical floor Bay Meml. Hosp., Panama City, 1955; pub. health nurse Bay County (Fla.) Health Dept., 1960-62; social worker HRS Social and Econ. Svcs., 1964-78; staff nurse, mem. utilization rev. com. Health and Rehab. Svcs., 1978-79, human svc. analyst, 1979-87; staff nurse psychiat./geriatric unit Fla. State Hosp., 1988, sr. human svc. program analyst, 1988-90; health care risk mgr. Fla. State Hosp., Chattahoochee, Fla., 1990—. Recipient Davis Productivity award, 1991.

BROWN, CAROLYN BREWER, family nurse practitioner; b. DeKalb County, Ala., May 20, 1950; d. Thomas Cecil and Nancy Fay (Reed) Brewer; children: Daphne Luann, Charles Nathan. ADN, N.E. State Jr. Coll., 1982; BSN cum laude, U. Ala., Huntsville, 1990, MSN, 1994. RN, Ala.; cert. FNP. Nurse practitioner Jackson County Rural Health, Scottsboro, Ala., 96—; FNP Jackson County Rural Health Project, Scottsboro, Ala.; clin. nursing instr. N.E. St. C.C., Rainsville, Ala. Mem. ANA, ASNSA, Ala. Nurse Practitioners Coun., Sigma Theta Tau.

BROWN, CHRIS, telecommunications company executive; b. Knoxville, Tenn., Dec. 17, 1949; s. John Harding and Marie (Long) B.; m. June Darlene Scott, June 12, 1976; children: Wendy Tegreeny Hugg, Kathleen. BSEE, U. Tenn., 1972. Project engr. RCA Corp., Camden, N.J., 1972-77; sales mgr. Harris Corp., Quincy, Ill., 1977-84; internat. sales mgr. Andrew Corp., Orland Park, Ill., 1984-94; sr. v.p. internat. sales Calif. Microwave, Houston, 1994—. Mem. IEEE, Soc. of Motion Picture and TV Engrs., Appalachian Trail Conf., Lionel Collectors Club of Am. Republican. Methodist. Home: PO Box 885 Stafford TX 77497 Office: Calif Microwave 4000 Greenbriar Stafford TX 77477

BROWN, CLAUDE LAMAR, JR., psychiatrist, educator; b. Mobile, Ala., Mar. 12, 1923; s. Claude Lamar and Pauline Johanna (Phifer) B.; m. Catherine McRaney, May 2, 1979; children by previous marriage—Claude Lamar, Paul William, Christianna Lori. B.S., Tulane U., 1943, M.D., 1945. Diplomate Am. Bd. Psychiatry and Neurology. Intern, City Hosp. Mobile, 1945-46; resident in psychiatry Menninger Found. Sch. Psychiatry, Topeka, 1948-51; practice medicine specializing in psychiatry, Mobile, 1951—; mem. staff Mobile Infirmary, Providence Hosp., Doctors Hosp., U. Med. Center Hosp., Southland Hosp., Mobile; clin. prof. psychiatry U. South Ala. Sch. Medicine, 1973—; mem. Ala. Mental Health Bd., 1959-71, chmn., 1967-69. Served to lt. USNR, 1946-48. Fellow Am. Psychiat. Assn.; mem. AMA, Ala. State Med. Assn., Ala. Dist. Br. Am. Psychiat. Assn. (pres. 1981), Mobile County Med. Soc. (pres. 1962). Methodist. Club: Mobile Yacht. Contbr. articles to profl. and popular publs. Office: 176 Louiselle St Mobile AL 36607-3510

BROWN, CLIFTON, business executive; b. 1946. Farmer Trenton, N.C., 1967—; pres. Jones County Cotton Gin, Inc., Trenton, N.C. Office: Jones County Cotton Gin Inc. 888 Nobles Ln Trenton NC 28585

BROWN, CONNIE YATES, small business owner; b. Carthage, Mo., Apr. 29, 1947; d. Charles Lee and Eunice Jane (Farmer) Yates; m. Larry Edward Brown, June 19, 1982 (div. 1993); stepchild, Tammy Lynn Brown. BS, Pittsburg State U., 1969. Cert. home economist. With White Shield Oil and Gas/Petro-Lewis, Tulsa, 1969-74, dept. supt., 1971-74; with Southwestern Bell Telephone Co., 1975-79; owner, mgr. Abbyco, Inc., rental, sales carpet cleaning equipment, Tulsa, 1977—, Conpro, Inc., 1991-94; sec. R.D.R. Assn. Inc.; mem. Rug Doctor adv. com., 1991—; lectr. in field. Active Okla. Rep. Party. Named Rookie of Yr., Tulsa div. Southwestern Bell Yellow Pages, 1976; sales award winner Rug Doctor Licensee of Yr., 1981, 85. Mem. Home Economists in Bus., Am. Home Econs. Assn., Met. Tulsa C. of C., Associated Specialists in Cleaning and Restoration, Tulsa Alumnae Panhellenic (bd. dirs., treas.), Pitts. State U. Alumni Assn. (past pres. Tulsa chpt.), NAWBO, Tulsa Exec. Exch., Order of Rainbow for Girls, Phi Upsilon Omicron, Alpha Gamma Delta (nat. dir. alumnae devel. 1984-86, coord. alumnae philanthropy 1990, 91, rush cons. 1991-96, chmn. internat. membership com. 1996). Home: 7806 S Evanston Ave Tulsa OK 74136-8703 Office: Abbyco Inc 8600 S Lewis Ave Tulsa OK 74137-3200

BROWN, CORRINE, congresswoman; b. Jacksonville, Fla., Nov. 11, 1946; 1 child, Shantrel. BS, Fla. A & M U., 1969; EdS, U. Fla., 1974. Former mem. Fla. Ho. of Reps; del. Nat. Dem. Conv., 1988; mem. 103rd-104th Congress from 3rd Fla. dist., 1993—, mem. transp. and infrastructure com. aviation, surface transp., mem. VA com. hosp. and health care. Mem. Sigma Gamma Rho. Baptist. Home: 314 Palmetto St Jacksonville FL 32202-2619 Office: US Ho of Reps 1610 Longworth House Office Bldg Washington DC 20515-0903

BROWN, CRAIG JAY, ophthalmologist; b. Fayetteville, Ark., Feb. 11, 1951; s. Connell Jean and Erma Dexter (Taylor) B.; m. Patricia Ruth Davis, Aug. 31, 1974. BS in Zoology, U. Ark., 1973, MD, 1977. Diplomate Am. Bd. Ophthalmology. Intern Bapt. Med. Ctr., Nalerigu, Ghana, 1977-78; resident in ophthalmology U. Mo., Columbia, 1978-81; practice medicine specializing in ophthalmology, Fayetteville, 1981—; attending physician Washington Regional Hosp., Fayetteville, 1981—. Contbr. articles to profl. jours. Justice of Peace for Washington County, Ark., 1972. Fellow Am. Coll. of Surgeons, Am. Acad. Ophthalmology; mem. AMA, Ark. Med. Soc. Methodist. Avocations: invertebrate paleontology, medieval studies. Home: 10 Ranch Dr Fayetteville AR 72703-3036 Office: 594 E Milsap Fayetteville AR 72701

BROWN, DEE ALEXANDER, author; b. La., 1908; s. Daniel Alexander and Lulu (Cranford) B.; m. Sara B. Stroud, Aug. 1, 1934; children—James Mitchell, Linda. B.S., George Washington U., 1937; M.S., U. Ill., 1951. Librarian Dept. Agr., Washington, 1934-42, Aberdeen Proving Ground, Md., 1945-48; agrl. librarian U. Ill. at Urbana, 1948-72, prof., 1962-75. Author: Wave High the Banner, 1942, Grierson's Raid, 1954, Yellowhorse, 1956, Cavalry Scout, 1957, The Gentle Tamers: Women of the Old Wild West, 1958, The Bold Cavaliers, 1959, They Went Thataway, 1960, (with M.F. Schmitt) Fighting Indians of the West, 1948, Trail Driving Days, 1952, The Settler's West, 1955, Fort Phil Kearny, 1962, The Galvanized Yankees, 1963, Showdown at Little Big Horn, 1964, The Girl from Fort Wicked, 1964, The Year of the Century, 1966, Action at Beecher Island, 1967, Bury My Heart at Wounded Knee, 1971, Andrew Jackson and the Battle of New Orleans, 1972, The Westerners, 1974, Tepee Tales, 1979, Creek Mary's Blood, 1980, The American Spa, 1982, Killdeer Mountain, 1983, Conspiracy of Knaves, 1987, Wondrous Times on the Frontier, 1991, When the Century Was Young, 1993, The American West, 1994, (with Mort Künstler) Images of the Old West, 1996; on-camera narrator: The Wild West, 1993, The Real West, 1993-95, other documentaries of the Am. West; contbr.: Growing Up Western, 1990; editor: Agricultural History, 1956-58, Pawnee, Blackfoot and Cheyenne, 1961. Served with AUS, 1942-45. Recipient A.L.A. Clarence Day award, 1971, Christopher award, 1971, Illinoisian of Yr., Ill. News Broadcasters Assn., 1972, W.W.A. Golden Saddleman award, 1984. Mem. Authors Guild, Soc. Am. Historians, Western Writers Am., Beta Phi Mu. Home: 7 Overlook Dr Little Rock AR 72207-1619

BROWN, DICK ERIE, genealogist, archivist; b. Richlands, Va., May 29, 1953; s. Erie Montgomery and Beulah (Wise) B. BA, Emory & Henry Coll., 1979. Genealogist Wolf Hills Rsch., Abingdon, Va., 1982—; archival researcher Holston Conf. Archives, Emory, Va., 1993-95; archivist Circuit Ct. Chancery Papers, Washington County, Va., 1996—. Compiler: Marriages of Washington County, Virgina, 1781-1853, 1994, Unfiled Court Papers, 1994; co-editor: Roads of Washington County, Va. 1836, 1983. Regional dir. Over-mountain Victory Trail Assn., Va., 1995. Methodist. Home: PO Box 723 410 Stone Mill Rd SW Abingdon VA 24210-3057 Office: Clks Office Cir Ct Washington County 189 E Main St PO Box 289 Abingdon VA 24212

BROWN, DONALD JAMES, JR., insurance company executive; b. Inglewood, Calif., Sept. 30, 1955; s. Donald James and Kathleen Elizabeth (McKillips) B.; m. Joan Colleen Brewer, June 25, 1977 (div. May 1985); 1 child, Randy. BA, Calif. State U., Long Beach, 1979. Estimator, supt. Home Improvement Builders, Santa Ana, Calif., 1979; asst. supt. Village Home of Calif., Santa Ana, 1980; claim rep. Aetna Life & Casualty, Orange, Calif., 1980-82, sr. claim rep., 1982-85; property specialist Aetna Life & Casualty, Woodland Hills, Calif., 1985-86; regional supr. United Pacific Ins. Co., Glendale, Calif., 1986-88; regional gen. adjuster Reliance Ins. Co., Glendale, 1988-90; regional property examiner Reliance Ins. Co., Durham, N.C., 1990-92; property claim mgr. Home Ins. Co., Maitland, Fla., 1992-95; gen. adjuster Zurich Ins. Group, Longwood, Fla., 1995—; mem. membership com. Orange County Adjuster's Assn., Anaheim, Calif., 1983-84. Republican. Office: Zurich-Am Ins Group PO Box 915245 Longwood FL 32791-5245

BROWN, ELIZABETH TAYLOR, psychology educator; b. Cleve., Jan. 2, 1930; d. Talmadge Andrew and Alberta Lois (Carter) Guy; m. Eugene Donaldson Taylor, Sept. 9, 1954 (div. Sept. 1963); 1 child, Eugene Guy; m. Dallas Coverdale Brown, Jr., Sept. 5, 1985. BA, Ohio State U., 1952; PhD, Washington U., St. Louis, 1968. Lic. clin. psychologist, Ohio, W.Va. Staff psychologist Standard Oil Ohio, 1963-65; lectr. Case Western Res. U., Cleve., 1964-66, asst. prof., 1968-71; instr. Cleve. State U., 1964-68, assoc. prof., 1971-85; prof. psychology W.Va. State Coll., Institute, 1985—, chairperson dept. psychology, 1985-93; cons. psychologist Juvenile Ct. Cuyanoga County, Cleve., 1966-67; mem. personnel Rsch. Inc., Cleve., 1966-81. Contbr. articles to profl. jours. Bd. dirs. LWV, St. Louis, 1960-63, Arts & Edn. Coun., St. Louis, 1960-63. Mem. Links Inc., Alpha Kappa Alpha. Home: 400 Bibby St # E Charleston WV 25301-1151 Office: WVa State Coll Campus Box 170 Institute WV 25112

BROWN, ERNEST LEE, education educator; b. Pensacola, Fla., June 24, 1932; s. Annie B. (Brown) Pate. BS, Fla. A&M U., 1954, MEd, 1966; postgrad., U. Okla., 1970; PhD, Fla. State U., 1975. Cert. tchr. math. and sci., cert. vis. tchr., cert. in ednl. leadership, Fla. Tchr. math. and sci. Escambia County (Fla.) Sch. Bd., Pensacola, 1957-68, vis. tchr., 1968-70; prin. N.B. Cook Elem. Sch., Pensacola, 1970-74; grad. asst. Fla. State U., Tallahassee, 1973-74, interim prin. Developmental Rsch. Sch., 1974-75, prin., 1975-86; dir. Developmental Rsch. Sch. Fla. A&M U., Tallahassee, 1986-89, dir. student tchg., 1989-91, assoc. prof. of ednl. leadership, 1991—; mem. adminstrv. coun., mem. adv. bd. Developmental Rsch. Sch. Fla. State U., 1974-86; mem. task force on lab. schs. Fla. State Dept. Edn., Tallahassee, 1980; mem. state adv. com. Fla. Statewide Com. on Program Assessment, Tallahassee, 1979-80; mem. rev. com. Fla. Ednl. Leadership Exam program U. South Fla., Tampa, 1993. Contbr. articles to edn. publs. Mem. customer svc. panel Barnett Bank, Tallahassee, 1995. NSF fellow Bklyn. Coll., 1959, Kellogg Found. fellow, 1965-66. Mem. Phi Delta Kappa, Kappa Alpha Psi (life, alumni). Democrat. Baptist. Home: 106 Dixie Dr Tallahassee FL 32304

BROWN, FRANCES ANNE, nurse, therapist; b. Newport News, Va., Feb. 13, 1946; d. Quincy and Frances (Williams) B. AA in Nursing, Chowan Coll., 1968; BS in Profl. Arts, St. Joseph's Coll., North Windham, Ma., 1980; student, Graceland Coll., Lamoni, Iowa, 1995—. RN, N.C., Va. Staff nurse in psychiatry Duke U. Med. Cen., Durham, N.C., 1968-71; head nurse in psychiatry Duke U. Med. Cen., Durham, 1971-76; pvt. practice counseling Chapel Hill, N.C., 1976-90; trainer assertiveness Durham (N.C.) Tech. Inst., Duke U. Med. Ctr., Piedmont Tech. U., 1980-83; nurse Isle Wight County Sch., Smithfield (Va.) Elem. Sch., 1991; clin. nursing supr. Riverside Convalescent Ctr., Smithfield, Va., 1991-94; nursing supr. evenings James River Conv. Ctr. Va. Health Svcs., Newport News, Va., 1994-95; evening charge nurse youth svcs. Columbia Peninsula Ctr. for Behavioral Health, Hampton, Va., 1995—; cons. Ctr. Wellbeing, Carrboro, 1987; photographer Alderman's Galleries, Durham, House of Frames, Durham; distbr. Success Motivation Inst. Co-chair Orange County Domicilliary Home Adv. Com., 1985-87; bd. dirs. Orange County Rape Crisis Cen., chair 1986-87; ordained priest Order Melchizedek, 1990. Mem. APA, NOW (publicity/photography com. 1981-92), Nat. Assn. Women Bus. Owners (cons. 1987, sec. 1987-89), Chapel Hill/Carrboro C. of C. (mem. speakers bur., cons. 1981-87), N.C. Soc. Clin. Hypnosis, Internat. Platform Assn., Women Moose. Home: 104 Lumar Rd Smithfield VA 23430-1434 Office: Columbia Peninsula Ctr Behavioral Health 2244 Executive Dr Hampton VA 23666

BROWN, FRANK REGINALD, III, pediatrician, educator; b. Kansas City, Mo., Oct. 15, 1943; s. Frank R. Jr. and Charlotte Elaine (Snider) B.; m. Martha Ann Wilson, Jan. 23, 1988; children: Frank R. IV, Riggs Wilson. BS in Chemistry, Stanford U., 1965, MS in Chemistry, 1967; PhD in Biol. Chemistry, Harvard U., 1971; MD, Washington U., 1975. Diplomate Am. Bd. Pediatrics. Rsch. assoc. Washington U. Sch. of Medicine, St. Louis, 1972-73; instr. pediatrics Johns Hopkins Med. Instns., Balt., 1980-81, asst. prof. pediatrics, 1981-84; assoc. prof. pediatrics Med. U. S.C., Charleston, 1984-88, prof. pediatrics, 1988-93; prof. pediatrics Baylor Coll. Medicine, 1993—; dir. Meyer Ctr for Devel. Pediatrics, Tex. Children's Hosp., Houston, 1993—; dir. div. devel. disabilities Med. U. S.C., also Vince Mosely Ctr. for Handicapped Children, Charleston. Author: Diagnosis and Management of Learning Disabilities, 1992, 96; editor Jour. of Learning Disabilities, Mental Retardation and Devel. Disabilities Rsch. Revs. Bd. dirs. S.C. Spl. Olympics, Columbia, 1987-90; advisor Joseph P. Kennedy Jr. Found. for Mental Retardation, Washington. Named Joseph P. Kennedy Jr. scholar for mental retardation, Joseph P. Kennedy Jr. Found., Washington, 1982, sr. fellow Nat. Multiple Sclerosis, N.Y., 1986, Jeffrey Edwin Gilliam Prof., Med. U. S.C., 1988-93. Fellow Am. Acad. Pediatrics; mem. Am. chem. Soc., Soc. for Devel. Pediatrics, Phi Beta Kappa, Sigma Xi, Alpha Omega Alpha. Home: 545 Begonia St Bellaire TX 77401-5005 Office: Texas Childrens Hosp Meyer Ctr 6621 Fannin St Houston TX 77030-2303

BROWN, FREDERICK WILLIAM, III, psychiatrist; b. Lansing, Mich., July 4, 1943; s. Frederick William and Dorothy Harriet (Lewis) B.; m. Sandra J. Avenell. BA, U. Mich., 1965; MD, Wayne State U., 1969. Diplomate Nat. Bd. Med. Examiners, Am. Bd. Psychiatry and Neurology, Am. Bd. Adolescent Psychiatry. Intern Detroit Gen. Hosp., 1969-70; resident in psychiatry U. Wis., Madison, 1970-73; staff psychiatrist Dept. Mental Health Wilford Hall USAF Med. Ctr., Lackland AFB, Tex., 1973-74, chief Psychiatry Consultation Svc. Dept. Mental Health, 1974-77; staff psychiatrist Audie L. Murphy VA Hosp., San Antonio, 1977-80; clinic psychiatrist Dimmit County Mental Health Ctr., Carrizo Springs, Tex., 1979-94; pvt. practice psychiatry San Antonio, 1979-94; med. dir. Alamo Mental Health, 1994—. Contbr. articles to profl. jours. Maj. USAF, 1977-80. Mem. AMA, Am. Psychiat. Assn. (Bexar County chpt. Tex. Dist. br.), Am. Soc. Adolescent Psychiatry, Am. Soc. Clin. Psychopharmacology, Nat. Assn. Neuro-Liguistic Programming, Tex. Med. Assn. Office: Alamo Mental Health Group 14500 San Pedro Ave Ste 203 San Antonio TX 78232-4354

BROWN, GARY ALLEN, defense analysis company executive; b. Lincoln, Nebr., Aug. 31, 1938; s. Kenneth Wesley and Erma Bethine (Barker) B.; m. Anita Katharine Jacobsen, May 8, 1959; children: Allen Ernst, Brian Kenneth. BS in Systems Sci., U. West Fla., 1971. Enlisted man USAF, 1956, advanced through grades to master sgt., 1974; ret., 1977; math tchr. Meigs Middle Sch., Shalimar, Fla., 1977-78; sr. programmer ASI Systems Internat., Ft. Walton Beach, Fla., 1977-88; v.p., dir. ASI Systems Internat., Ft. Walton Beach, 1988—. Councilman Niceville (Fla.) City Coun., 1981—; dir. Okaloosa County Gas Dist., Valparaiso, Fla., 1983—. Mem. Niceville-Valparaiso C. of C. Home: 504 Wexford Dr Niceville FL 32578-1765 Office: ASI Systems Internat 838 Eglin Pky NE Ste 421 Fort Walton Beach FL 32547-3908

BROWN, GLENN EDWARD, minister, tennis educator; b. Louisville, Ky., Apr. 23, 1961; s. Joseph William and Doris Jean (Bindner) B.; Patsy Annette Kahafer, Aug. 3, 1991; 1 child, Hannah Elizabeth. BA in Polit. Sci., U. Louisville, 1983. Ordained to ministry, Assemblies of God, 1996; cert. tennis profl. U.S. Profl. Tennis Assn., U.S. Profl. Tennis Registry. Electrician helper, electrician Reliance Electric Co., Louisville, Ky., 1974-83; tennis profl. Louisville (Ky.) Indoor Racquet Club, 1983-88; head pro Owl Creek, Louisville, 1986-88; minister, children's pastor Evangel. Christian Life Ctr., Louisville, 1987-92, youth pastor, 1988-89, jr. high pastor, 1992-94, asst. bus. adminstr., 1994—, recreation dir., 1988—, royal ranger boys dir., 1993—, Taekwondo leader, 1996—. Author: America's #1 Prayer Guide for all Ages, 1993. Lifeguard, attendant Jefferson County Bd. Health, 1977—. Mem. U.S. Profl. Tennis Assn., U.S. Profl. Tennis Registry, U.S. Chung Do Kwan Assn., Ky. Real Estate (realtor). Republican. Office: Evangel Christian Life Ctr 5400 Minors Ln Louisville KY 40219-3019

BROWN, HARDIN, occupational health nurse; b. Memphis, July 6, 1955. ADN, Memphis State U., 1976; BSN, U. Neb. Med. Ctr., 1978; MPA, Portland (Oreg.) State U., 1984; MSN, Oreg. Health Scis. U., 1985. RN, Oreg., Tenn. DON svcs. Beverly Enterprises, Portland, 1981-82; instr. Meth. Sch. Nursing, Memphis, 1992-94, occupational health nurse, 1994—;

rsch. assessment of staff turnover nursing assts. Oreg. Geriatric Nursing Homes. Mem. ARC. Lt. USN, 1985-90, USNR, 1990-92. Mem. Nat. Assn. Orthopaedic Nurses, Assn. Mil. Surgeons of U.S., Navy Nurse Corps Assn., Am. Assn. Occupational Health Nurses, Sigma Theta Tau.

BROWN, HARLEY MITCHELL, retired computer company executive, writer; b. Mt. Belvieu, Tex., Oct. 15, 1929; s. Hardy Mack and Eva Leandor (Warden) B.; m. Marjorie Rae Fite, Aug. 21, 1925; children: Deborah Diane Morel, Marjorie Joann Guin, Sallie Annette, Raylena Jean Ehlert. 9th grade, W. Columbia High Sch., Tex., 1946. Computer programmer U.S. Navy, 1947-58; chief systems and programming U.S. Bur. Customs, Washington, 1958-68; nat. systems mgr. Stromberg-Carlson, Houston, 1968-73; v.p. mktg. Compass Micromation, Houston, 1973-87; pres. Comtex Data Svcs., Inc., Houston, 1987-91; columnist The Kountze (Tex.) News, 1992—; dir. Comtex Data Svcs., Inc., Houston, 1991—; guest lectr. Univ. Houston. Author: Hard Times in Hardin County, 1992, Pulpit Humor, 1995. With USN, 1946-58. Republican. Home: Apt 513 3201 Kari Ln Greenville TX 75402-7203

BROWN, HENRY, chemist; b. Jersey City, Apr. 5, 1907; s. Mayer and Kate (Hearsh) B.; m. Harriet Stone; children: Paula, Dennis. AB, U. Kans., 1928; MS, PhD, U. Mich., 1933. Chemist Udylite Corp., Detroit, 1934-50, dir. rsch., 1950-72; rsch. chemist Manhattan Project Columbia U., N.Y.C., 1943-45. Author: (with others) Modern Electroplating 3rd edit., 1974; contbr. numerous articles to profl. jours., 1932-71. Bd. dirs. Sinai Hosp., Detroit, 1965. Recipient Carl Heussner award Am. Electroplaters Soc., Detroit, 1953, George Hogaboom award, 1963, AES Sci. Achievement award, 1968, Westinghouse prize Inst. of Metal Finishing of Great Britain, 1970; named to Outstanding Inventors List, State of Mich. 1968. Fellow Am. Inst. Chemists; mem. N.Y. Acad. Scis, Am. Chem. Soc. (Midgely Gold Medal 1971), Sigma Xi. Jewish. Home: Apt 502 5270 Gulf Of Mexico Dr Longboat Key FL 34228-2018

BROWN, JACQUELINE LEY WHITE, lawyer; b. Blue Island, Ill., Apr. 14, 1948; d. William Raymond and June Irene (Cowing) L.; m. Arthur Lee White, May 2, 1970 (div. Mar. 1982); m. William John Brown, May 7, 1988. BA, U. Fla., 1969; MA, Rider Coll., 1977; JD, Stetson U., 1992. Bar: Fla. 1992. From supr. to dir. social services Steuben County (N.Y.) Dept. Social Services, Bath, N.Y., 1970-75; from sr. to prin. N.J. Dept. Pub. Welfare, Trenton, N.J., 1975-78; mgmt. cons., nat. seminar leader sales and mktg. Nathaniel Hills & Assocs., Raleigh, N.C., 1978-79; from dir. mktg. to v.p. Concord Mgmt. Systems, Tampa, Fla., 1979-88; labor and employment def. atty. Zinober & McCrea, P.A., Tampa, 1992—; cons. Action Planning Assocs., Trenton, 1976-78; bd. dirs. Tex. Instruments Users Group, 1983-84; bd. dirs., pres. Data Bus., St. Peterburg, 1985-88; sspeaker in field. Contbr. articles to profl. jours. Mem. NAFE, ABA (labor and employment law sect.), Fla. Bar Assn., Indsl. Labor Rels. Rsch. Assn. Democrat. Methodist. Home: 1 Beach Dr SE Apt 2101-02 Saint Petersburg FL 33701-3963

BROWN, JAMES BARROW, bishop; b. El Dorado, Ark., Sept. 26, 1932; s. John Alexander and Ella May (Langham) B.; m. Mary Joanna Strausser, Oct. 3, 1970; 2 daus., Clare Elizabeth, Mary Laura. B.S., La. State U., 1954; B.D., Austin Presbyn. Sem., Austin, Tex., 1957; D.D., U. of South, Sewanee, Tenn., 1976. Ordained priest Episcopal Ch., 1965; teaching fellow Princeton Theol. Sem., 1962-64; curate chs. in La., 1965-70, archdeacon of, 1971-76, bishop of, 1976—. Served as chaplain AUS, 1957-59. Alumni fellow Austin Presbyn. Sem., 1957; recipient Sam Bailey Hicks prize, 1957. Mem. La. Clergy Assn., Phi Delta Theta. Club: Rotary. Address: 1623 7th St New Orleans LA 70115-4411

BROWN, JAMES H., JR., state insurance commissioner, lawyer; b. May 6, 1940. BA, U. N.C.; JD, Tulane U. Bar: La. 1966. Pvt. practice, 1966—; mem. La. State Senate, 1972-80; sec. of state State of La., 1980-87; mem. Brook, Morial, Cassibry, Fraiche, Pizza, Baton Rouge/New Orleans, 1987-91; commr. ins. State of La., 1991—. Del. La. Constl. Conv., 1973. Democrat. Presbyterian. Office: Brooke Morial Ste 500 9100 Bluebonnet Centre Blvd Baton Rouge LA 70809-2985

BROWN, JAMES ROY, retail executive; b. Broken Arrow, Okla., Nov. 24, 1950; s. Roy Thelbert and Betty Anne (Ice) B.; m. Eva Jane Boggs, June 25, 1970; children: Courtney James, Ava Lauren. AA in Fine Arts, Tulsa Jr. Coll., 1971. Stocker Doc's Food Stores, Inc., Bixby, Okla., 1962-69, produce mgr., 1969-72, meat mgr., 1972, store mgr., 1972-85, v.p., 1979, pres. and owner, 1983—; pres. and owner Bixby True Value, 1986-92. Mem. adv. com. for vocat. edn. Bixby High Sch., 1986-87; mem. bd. Family YMCA, 1988, chmn. bldg. fund; v.p. Bixby Endowment Fund, 1991—; bd. dirs. Okla. Grocers Edn. Found., 1991. Named Outstanding Employer Okla. chpt. Distributive Edn. Clubs Am., 1986. Mem. Okla. Grocers Assn. (bd. dirs. 1989), Bixby C. of C. (v.p. 1971-72, 87-88, prs. 1973, 88-89), Bixby Jaycees (Jaycee of Month award 1971, Jaycee of Quarter award 1982), Optimists (v.p. 1982, Optimist of Yr. award 1976). Democrat. Baptist. Home: 45 W 5th St Bixby OK 74008-4536 Office: Doc's Food Stores Inc 211 N Cabaniss Ave Bixby OK 74008-4390

BROWN, JANET LOUISE, continuing education specialist; b. Mobile, Ala., June 25, 1944; d. Benjamin James Simms and Ethel (Gardener) Coleman; m. Felton Page; children: James Earl Brown III, Daraka Ghamal Brown. BA in Sociology and Psychology, Ala. State U., 1966; MSW, U. Hawaii, 1971; PhD in Adult and Continuing Edn., Kans. State U., 1993. Adjunct prof. Kans. State U., Manhattan, 1974-78; chief, tng. and devel. U.S. Mil. Acad., Ft. Riley, Kans., 1979-84; personnel mgmt. specialist U.S. Army Materiel Command, Alexandria, Va., 1985-87; chief, career mgmt. office U.S. Total Army Personnel Command, Alexandria, Va., 1987-90, chief, civilian acquisition mgmt. branch, 1990—; chair Mil. Edn. Com., Washington; Marshall U. Parent Com., Huntington, W.Va. Mem. editorial bd. Adult Learning Mag., 1993—. Recipient Outstanding Performance awards, Ft. Riley, Kans., 1974, comdr.'s award, Ft. Riley, 1978, Significant Accomplishment award U.S. Mil. Acad., 1982, Exceptional Performance, 1983, Spl. Act award Army Materiel Command, 1987, Exceptional Performance awards U.S. Total Army Pers. Command, 1988-95, Outstanding Svc. medallion Am. Assn. Adult and Continuing Edn., 1995. Mem. NAACP, Army Women's Profl. Assn., Am. Assn. for Adult and Continuing Edn., Rappahannock-Frederickburg Rotary Club (bd. dirs. 1995—, chair internat. svc. com.), Delta Sigma Theta. Home: 160 Winding Creek Rd Stafford VA 22554-3915

BROWN, JANET MCNALLEY, retirement plan consultant; b. Denver, May 16, 1960; d. Michael Collins and Sharon Bess (Cook) McNalley. Student, Mt. Holyoke Coll., 1978-79; BA in Econs. with honors, Mills Coll., Oakland, Calif., 1982; MA in Social Scis., U. Calif., Irvine, 1987, elem. teaching credential, 1988. Teaching asst. U. Calif., Irvine, 1986-88; employee benefits adminstr. Western Co. N.Am., Ft. Worth, 1988-89; trust officer Ameritrust Tex. N.A., Ft. Worth, 1989-90; thrift and profit sharing analyst Burlington No. R.R., Ft. Worth, 1990-93; assoc. human resources group Coopers & Lybrand, Dallas, 1993-94; pension coord. Bell Helicopter Textron, Inc., Ft. Worth, 1994-95; adminstr., cons. Rogers & Assocs., Ft. Worth, 1995—. Dem. del., Ft. Worth, 1990; mem. Liberty Coalition, Bluebonnet Pl. Neighborhood Assn. (newsletter editor); neighborhood crime prevention coord. Citizens on Patrol. Mem. AAUW (membership v.p. 1990-92, charter Eleanor Roosevelt Found. 1990-92), Am. Soc. pension Actuaries (qualified pension adminstr., cert. pension cons.). Home: 3408 Cockrell Ave Fort Worth TX 76109-3003 Office: Rogers & Assocs 424 S Summit Ave Fort Worth TX 76104

BROWN, JERRY MILFORD, medical company executive; b. Anderson, S.C., Apr. 30, 1938; s. James Milford and Jane Elizabeth (McCord) B.; m. Alice Alberta Thompson, July 30, 1960; children—John Milford, Allen Thompson. B.S., Furman U., 1960; M.A. in Biology, Wake Forest U., 1963, Temple U., 1967; Ph.D. in Physiology, Dental Sch., U. Md., 1972. Commd. lt. U.S. Army, 1960, advanced through grades to lt. col., 1980; research instr. Hahnemann Med. Coll., Phila., 1967-68; sect. leader, exptl. medicine div. Biomed. Lab., Edgewood Arsenal, Md., 1967-68; instr. anatomy Med. Sch., U. Md., Balt., 1970-77; sect. leader, exptl. medicine div. U.S. Army Research Inst. Environ. Medicine, Natick, Mass., 1973-76; dep. dir. U.S. Army Med. Intelligence and Info. Agy., Ft. Detrick, Md., 1976-80; dir. internat. health affairs Dept. Def., Washington, 1980-84; editor Mgmt. and Info. Study, Office of Surgeon Gen., 1984; chief plans ops. security, 2nd Gen. Hosp., Federal Republic of Germany, 1984-87; med. co-ordinator, Fed. Emergeny Mgmt. Agy, Washington, 1987-90, nat. disaster med. system staff, bd. govs. Nat. Council Internat. Health, 1980-90; cons. and spl. asst. to the pres. Bio Technology Gen. Corp., Iselin, N.J., 1991—; pres., COO NeuroSurg. Internat., 1995—; v.p., chief oper. officer M/D Frontiers, Springfield, Va., 1990—; pres. Automated Med. Products, Inc., 1990—; v.p. Automated Systems, 1991—; assoc. dir. rsch. nat. study ctr. for trauma and emergency medicine U. Md.; U.S. mem. Internat. Com. of Mil. Medicine and Pharmacy, 1981-87; U.S. mil. mem. Joint Civil/Mil. Med. Working Group U.S., NATO, 1981—; mem. program planning com. Internat. Assembly on Emergency Med. Services, Balt., 1984; congress lobbyist; cons. in field. Contbr. articles to med. jours; pub. books in field of philately. Commr., Explorer Scouts, Natick, Mass., 1975-76; trustee Cardinal Spellman Philatlic Mus., Weston, Mass., 1980—. Decorated Meritorious Service medal with 3 oak leaf clusters, Legion of Merit; recipient gold medal Res. Officers Assn., 1960. Mem. Electron Microscopy Soc. Am., Am. Stamp Dealers Assn., Central Atlantic Stamp Dealers Assn. (pres. 1977-81), Research and Engring. Soc. Am., Balt. Philatelic Soc., Sigma Alpha Epsilon, Sigma Xi. Republican. Baptist.

BROWN, JOAN HALL, elementary school educator; b. Montgomery, Ala., Sept. 12; d. Leo Nathaniel and Bertha (Glaze) Hall; m. Tyrone Brown, Aug. 25, 1984. BS in Elem. Edn. cum laude, Ala. State U.; MEd cum laude, Auburn U., Montgomery, 1989. Cert. tchr., Ala. Tchr. Resurrection Sch., Montgomery, 1985-89, St. John the Bapt. Cath. Sch., Montgomery, 1989-91; tchr., former asst. prin. St. John Resurrection Cath. Sch., Montgomery, 1991-94; tchr. Highland Gardens Elem. Sch., Montgomery, 1994—; mem. sch. bd. Resurrection Sch., 1987-88, advisor, editor sch. newspaper; textbook com. Mobile Diocese, Montgomery, 1985-87, mem. English proficiency com., 1991-92; coord. State Spelling Bees, 1989, St. John the Bapt. Cath. Sch., 1990-91, St. John Resurrection Cath. Sch., 1991-94, textbook com. 1993-94; fin. com. Highland Gardens Sch., v.p. programs. Mem. Resurrection Cath. Ch.; mem. Montgomery County PTA. Grantee Arts Coun. Montgomery, 1991, 93, 94. Mem. NEA, Ala. Edn. Assn., Capitol Area Reading Educator, Nat. Honor Soc., Deka Philos. Svc. Orgn. (v.p. 1985—), Internat. Reading Assn., Kappa Delta Pi. Democrat. Roman Catholic. Home: 705 N Pass Rd Montgomery AL 36110-2906

BROWN, JOHN GRACEN, writer; b. Martinsburg, W.Va., Oct. 8, 1936; s. Yeakley Arthur and Virgil Marion (Waters) B. BS in Edn., So. Ill. U., 1961, MS in Edn., 1962. Cert. guidance counselor, Wis. Tchr. Phillips (Wis.) High Sch., 1962-63; guidance dir. Milton-Milton Junction (Wis.) H.S., 1963-64; freelance writer, 1964—. Author: Variation in Verse, 1975, A Sojourn of the Spirit, 1981, Passages in the Wind, 1985, Eight Dramas, 1991, The Search, 1994; poems used as lyrics by more than 150 composers worldwide. Mem. ASCAP. Home: 430 Virginia Ave Martinsburg WV 25401-2630

BROWN, JOHN HALL, architect; b. Houston, June 6, 1910; s. John Clyde and Ida Rand (Wilson) B.; m. Hilda Lee Hardy (dec. Dec. 1976); children: John, Margaret Brown Londolt; m. Dorris Asel. BS in Architecture, Tex. A&M, 1933, postgrad., 1934. Registered architect, Tex. Prin. John Hall Brown, Architect, Sherman, Tex., 1946; ptnr. Brown & Chapman Architects, Richardson, Tex., 1948-67; ptnr. Brown, Brown & Assocs., Richardson, 1967-93, chmn. bd. dirs., 1993—. Bd. dirs. Itasca Children's Home, Tex.; commr. Arts Commn., Richardson, 1990-95. Lt. col. USAF, 1939-46. Recipient Dist. Svc. award Arts Commn. Richardson, 1984-94. Mem. Artists and Craftsmen Assn., S.W. Watercolor Soc. Presbyterian. Home: 17007 Graystone Dallas TX 75248

BROWN, JOHN WAYNE, lawyer; b. East Orange, N.J., Nov. 17, 1949; s. John Edison and Margaret Patricia B.; m. Donna Potts, Nov. 18, 1978; children: Savannah Jane, Justin Taylor, Molly Ross. BA cum laude, Meth. Coll., 1971; JD, Wake Forest U., 1974; M in Law and Taxation, William and Mary Coll., 1980. Bar: Va. 1974, U.S. Dist. Ct. (ea. dist.) Va. 1975, U.S. Supreme Ct 1980, U.S. Tax Ct. 1980, U.S. Ct. Appeals (4th cir.) 1981. Pvt. practice Chesapeake, Va., 1974-75; asst. dep. commonwealth atty. Commonwealth Atty's Office, Chesapeake, 1975-80; ptnr. Gordon & Brown, Chesapeake, 1980-86; pvt. practice Chesapeake, 1986—; bd. dirs. Br. Bank and Trust, Crime Line, Inc., Chesapeake. Co. chmn. Sch. Bond Referendum, Chesapeake. Mem. Va. State Bar Assn., Va. Trial Lawyers Assn., Chesapeake Bar Assn., South Norfolk Ruritan Club, Rotary. Democrat. Methodist. Office: The 411 Bldg 440 Woodards Ford Rd Chesapeake VA 23322-4307

BROWN, JOHN Y., state official. BA in History magna cum laude, Bellarmine Coll., Louisville, Ky., 1988; JD with distinction, U. Ky. Coll. Law, Lexington, 1992. Summer assoc. Stoll, Keenon & Park Law Firm, Lexington, Ky., 1990, Brown, Todd & Heyburn Law Firm, Louisville, Ky., 1991; dir. franchising Roasters Franchise Corp., Fort Lauderdale, Fla., 1992-94; sec. of state Commonwealth of Ky., Frankfort, 1996—; grad. asst. Dale Carnegie Tng., 1987-92. Mem. ABA, Ky. Bar Assn. Home: 221 Sequoya Rd Louisville KY 40207 Office: 700 Capitol Ave Frankfort KY 40601-3410

BROWN, KAREN LYNN, elementary education educator; b. Dallas, May 18, 1949; d. Samuel Henry and Janice A. (Hornbaker) Hampton; m. DeWayne L. Brown, June 13, 1969; children: Marcie L., Lonnie D. BA, Ariz. State U., 1971. Cert. Ariz., Iowa, Tex. Tchr. Pendergast Sch., Tolleson, Ariz., 1971-74, BGM Elem. Sch., Brooklyn, Iowa, 82-84, Union Hill Ind. Sch. Dist., Gilmer, Tex., 1986—. Bd. dirs. Am. Cancer Soc., Gilmer, Camp Deer Run, Winnsboro, Tex. Mem. Ch. of Christ. Home: Rt 11 Box 11198 Gilmer TX 75644

BROWN, KATHY ALICE, broadcast journalist; b. Maryville, Mo., July 20, 1958; d. Herbert Dale and Roberta Jean (Keever) B. BS in Broadcast and Bus., N.W. Mo. State U., 1979. Journalist Newsweek Video, N.Y.C., 1980; anchor, reporter WSAZ-TV, Huntington, W.Va., 1980-94; mng. editor WSAZ-TV, Charleston, W.Va., 1994—. Chmn. bd. dirs. Huntington AIDS Task Force, 1987-88; bd. dirs. W.Va. Mobile Med. Unit, 1988—, Charleston Pub. Safety Coun., 1995—, Ky. Health Found., Frankfort, 1990—, Huntington Hospitality House, 1994-95. Recipient Best Spot News award AP, 1988, Best Documentary award AP, 1988, Best Coverage of Issue award AP, 1988, Best Spot News award AP, 1990, Best Continuing Coverage award AP, 1991, Journalist of Yr. award W.Va. Trial Lawyers Assn., 1992, Lee Enterprises, 1994, Disting. Citizen award Cabell County Commn., 1993, Best Pub. Affairs award AP, 1993, Best Investigation award AP, 1994. Mem. Soc. Profl. Journalists, Investigative Reporters and Editors, W.Va. Associated Press Broadcasters (bd. dirs.), Radio and TV News Dirs. Assn. (Bruce Palmer scholar 1979, BGest Continuing Coverage award 1991). Home: 1518 Huron Terr Charleston WV 25311 Office: WSAZ-TV 111 Columbia Ave Charleston WV 25302

BROWN, KEVIN JAMES, real estate broker; b. Sheboygan, Wis., July 12, 1952; s. Keith Hammond and Jean Lois (Van Ouwerkerk) B.; m. Ana Ligia Arevalo, Mar. 14, 1986. BA in English, Denison U., 1974; doctoral candidate, U. Tenn., 1995; MBA in Mgmt., Pepperdine U., 1980. Mgr. Flying Tiger Line, San Francisco, 1978-81; founder, pres. Angel Enterprises, Foster City, Calif., 1981-83; mgr. aerospace mktg. CF Airfreight, Inglewood, Calif., 1983-85; regional mgr. TNT Express divsn. Kwikasair, Inglewood, Calif., 1985; gen. mgr. Three Way Corp., Hawthorne, Calif., 1985-86; v.p. ops. Boardroom Bus. Products, Costa Mesa, Calif., 1986-88; dist. mgr. Nat. Inst. Bus. Mgmt., L.A., 1988; ind. contractor, realtor, broker Culver City, Calif., 1988-91; mng. broker. br. mgr. Vol. Realty Co., Knoxville, Tenn., 1991-93; franchise devel. sr. market analyst Coldwell Banker Residential Affiliates, Mission Viejo, Calif., 1993-96. Featured guest Sta. WIVK, 1992. Named Hon. Ky. Col., 1993. Mem. ACLU, ASPCA, Acad. Mktg. Sci., Am. Mktg. Assn., Amnesty Internat., Nat. Assn. Realtors, Pub. Citizen, Tenn. Assn. Realtors, World Future Soc., Wolf Edn. and Rsch. Ctr., Common Cause, Denison U. Alumni Assn., Pepperdine U. Alumni Assn., Silver Saddle Homeowners Assn., So. Poverty Law Ctr., U. Tenn. Grad. Student Assn. Democrat. Home: PO Box 52587 Knoxville TN 37950

BROWN, L(ARRY) EDDIE, tax practitioner, real estate broker, financial planner; b. Hanging Limb, Tenn., Aug. 31, 1941; s. Earl and Lois Ovoca (Norrod) B.; m. Lillian Virginia Edwards, Feb. 9, 1965; children: Clifford Bruce, Michael Dwayne, Jennifer Noelle. BBA, Ga. State U., 1974, MBA, 1976. Cert. tax profl.; accredited tax advisor, enrolled agent. Mgmt. trainee Citizens Bank, Cookeville, Tenn., 1963-65; office mgr. Redisco, Tampa, Fla., 1965-67; methods analyst Delta Air Lines, Atlanta, 1967-83; owner Brown Enterprises, College Park, Ga., 1971—; pres. So. Heritage Properties, Inc., 1984—; instr. Ga. State U., 1976-80. Bd. dirs. Ga. Spl. Olympics, Atlanta, 1983-90; Ga. del. White House Conf. on Small Bus., 1995. With USAF, 1959-63. Mem. Nat. Soc. Tax Profls. (Ga. state com. 1994—), Nat. Assn. Tax Practitioners (Ga. bd. dirs. 1994—), Nat. Soc. Pub. Accts., Ga. Assn. Pub. Accts. (pres. So. Cres. chpt. 1993-95, bd. govs. 1994—, 1st v.p. 1996—), Internat. Assn. Fin. Planners, Nat. Assn. Securities Dealers, Atlanta Bd. Realtors. Mormon. Clubs: Civitan (pres. Airport-Southside, Atlanta 1982-83, treas. Airport Area, Atlanta 1979-81, Civitan of Yr. chpt. 1982, bd. dirs. Ga. dist. north 1984-86, trustee Ga. dist. North Found. 1985-88), Masons. Office: Brown Enterprises 392 N Glynn Fayetteville GA 30214

BROWN, LEE R., minister; b. Memphis, June 4, 1949; s. Mitchell Anderson and Emma (Ross) B.; m. Charles Etta Jackson, Feb. 24, 1979; children: Felicha, Le'Carl. MDiv, Memphis Theol. Sem., 1992; DD (hon.), Tenn. Sch. Religion, 1993. Ordained to ministry Nat. Bapt. Conv. U.S.A., 1971. Asst. pastor Oak Grove Bapt. Ch., Memphis, 1975-79; sr. pastor Springdale Bapt. Ch., Memphis, 1979—; fellow D Ministry program United Theol. Sem., Dayton, Ohio, 1994. Trustee Skyland Land Devel., Memphis, 1988-89; alt. mem., vice-chmn. Tenn. Selective Svc. Local Bd., Nashville, 1989—; bd. dirs. Habitat for Humanity/Mid South, Memphis, Memphis Ch. Health Ctr., TVA Cmty. Rels. Com., NAACP PAC, Nat. Civil Rights Mus., Memphis Trust Fund, Mid-South chpt. ARC, Nat. Congress Black Chs.; mem. Downtown Memphis Ministry, Inc.; mem. steering com. on ednl. stds. Memphis City Schs.; mem. minority adv. com. U. Memphis; chmn. ann. fund campaign LeMoyne-Owen Coll., 1992-93; past mem. curriculum com./v.p. student and rsch. com., others; mem. transitional team Intergovernmental Com. Mayor Herenton, mem. Black on Black Chrome Task Force; chmn. Memphis Black United Fund of the Nat. Black United Fund, Inc.; dean Greater Memphis Sunday Sch. and Nurture for Bapt. Chs. Congress. Recipient Community Svc. award Shankman Hill Civic Club, Memphis, 1987, Outstanding Citizen award Memphis Housing Authority, 1989; named Hon. City Councilman, Memphis City Coun., 1986, one of 10 Best Dressed Men of Memphis, Tri-State Def., 1986. Mem. Memphis Dist. Assn. (pres. 1990—), Memphis Bapt. Ministerial Assn. (v.p. 1989-91, pres. 1991-93), Memphis African-Am. Ecumenical Assn. (bd. dirs. 1988—), Tenn. BM&E Conv. Congress (faculty), Nat. Bapt. Congress Christian Edn. Home: 2740 Lakecrest Cir Memphis TN 38127-8438 Office: Springdale Bapt Ch 1193 Springdale St Memphis TN 38108-2235

BROWN, LINDA LOCKETT, nutrition management executive, nutrition consultant; b. Jacksonville, Fla., Jan. 8, 1954; d. Willie James and Katie Lee (Taylor) Lockett; m. Thomas Lee Brown, Dec. 18, 1982; children: Ashanti, William, Timothy. BS in Agr., U. Fla., 1975, M of Agr., 1981. Lic. profl. nutritionist; cert. food svc. dir. III; registered dietitian. Chemist/microbiologist Green Giant Co., Alachua, Fla., 1975-77; lab. technologist II U. Fla., Gainesville, 1977-81, extension agt. I, Ft. Myers, 1981-85, extension agt. II, 1985-87, West Palm Beach, 1987-88; pres. CINET, Inc., 1985—, nutritionist head start, Jacksonville Fla.; area supr. Palm Beach County Sch. Food Svc., 1988-90; adj. prof. Palm Beach Community coll., 1990, Fla. C.C., Jacksonville, 1993—; dir. sch. food svc. St. Johns County, 1990—; nutrition cons. Congregate Meals, Ft. Myers, 1984-87, Serenity House, Ft. Myers, 1985-87; cons. Performax, 1989—; vis. prof. U. Fla. Coop. Ext. Svc., Clay County, 1996—; treas. St. Augustine chpt. Internat. Food Svc. Execs. Assn., 1993—; apptd. by gov. Fla. Health and Human Svcs. Bd., elected vice chair, 1993-94, chair, 1994-96. Columnist Palm Beach Post, 1989—; contbr. articles to profl. jours.; host nutrition digest radio show Sta. WZNZ-AM, Jacksonville, Fla., 1996—. Mem. exec. bd. Community Coordinating Coun., Ft. Myers, 1985; Am. Heart Assn., Palm Beach, 1989-90; co-founder Friends of Hearing Impaired Youth, Gainesville, 1976; tutor-coord. Sampson, Gainesville, 1973; mem. Jr. League, Ft. Myers, 1987; mem. Jr. League, Palm Beach, Fla., 1987-90, mem. edn. tng. com., community rsch. com. 1989-90; mem. nutrition com. Am. Heart Assn., Palm Beach, 1989—. State U. System Bd. Regents grantee, 1980. Mem. NAFE, Soc. Nutrition Edn. (legis. network chmn.), Am. Diabetes Assn. (mem. profl. adv. com. Jacksonville affiliate 1996), Am. Dietetic Assn. (network of blacks in nutrition, chair legis. com. 1988-89, chair nominating 1989, sec. 1989-90, state profl. recruitment coord.), Fla. Dietetic Assn. (chair minority issues com., chair membership 1987-88, chair edn. and registration 1988-90, state profl. recruitment coord. rep. Fla. chpt., chair nominating com. 1994—), Palm Beach Dietetic Assn. (community nutrition chair 1988-89, chair legis. com. 1989-90), Caloosa Dietetic Assn. (sec.), Nat. Speakers Assn., Sch. Food Svcs. Assn. (1988—), Nat. Assn. Extension Home Econs. Agts., Internat. Platform Assn., Jacksonville Dietetic Assn., Nutrition Today Soc., Alpha Zeta, Epsilon Sigma Phi. Club: Greater Palm Beaches Bus. and Profl. Women (minority student mentor, role model mentor), Nat. Speakers Assn., N. Fla. Profl. Speakers Assn. Avocations: singing, violin. Office: 2234 George Wythe Rd Orange Park FL 32073-8507

BROWN, LOIS HEFFINGTON, health facility administrator; b. Little Rock, Mar. 28, 1940; d. Carl Otis and Opal (Shock) Heffington; M. Ivy Roy Brown, June 21, 1984; children: Carletta Jo Rice, Roby Lynn Rice, Pherby Allison Graham, Phelan Missy Graham. Student, Guilford Tech. Community Coll., Jamestown, N.C., 1974-75, 77, 80. Cert. hearing aid specialist. Sec. Berger Enterprises, West Memphis, Ark., 1962-65; office mgr. Beltone Hearing Aid Ctr., Greensboro, N.C., 1975-81; owner Hearing Care Ctr., Cullman, Ala., 1982-85, Miracle-Ear Ctr., Cullman, Decatur, Fultondale, Jasper and Birmingham, Ala., 1985-87; pres. L&I Corp., Cullman, Decatur, Fultondale, Jasper and Birmingham, 1987-90, L & I Corp. Miracle Ear Ctr., Cullman, Decatur, Jasper, Ala., 1991-93; owner Conway (Ark.) Hearing Aid Ctr., 1994—, Beltone Hearing Aid Ctr., Conway, 1995-96; distbr. Showcase Distbg. Co., Conway, North Little Rock, Ark. Gov.-appointed Ala. Bd. Hearing, chmn. of the bd., 1989-91. Mem. Nat. Hearing Aid Soc., Ark. Hearing Soc. (sec. 1996—), Ala. Hearing Aid Dealers Assn. (sec. 1984-86, v.p. 1986-88, bd. dirs. 1988-91), Ark. Hearing Aid Dealers Assn., Women´of the Moose. Republican. Baptist. Home: 199 Highway 107 Enola AR 72047-8101

BROWN, LYNDA NELL, nursing educator; b. Humphreys County, Miss., Oct. 6, 1943; d. A. C. and Elizabeth (Holloway) Merchant; m. Walter U. Brown, Oct. 11, 1963; children: Rebecca E., Darren K., Sarah E. BSN, U. Miss., 1965; MS in Nursing, Boston U., 1974, EdD, 1977. Asst. prof. Boston Coll., Chestnut Hill, Mass., Vanderbilt U., Nashville; assoc. prof. U. Akron, Ohio, U. Ky., Lexington. Contbr. articles to profl. publs. Mem. ANA, Nat. League Nursing, ARN , Sigma Theta Tau (Excellence in Nursing award Delta Omega chpt., dist. lectr.).

BROWN, MARGARET MARY, special education educator; b. Wilmington, Del., Jan. 8, 1951; d. Daniel Joseph and Colleen Mary (Kirkley) B. BS in Elem. Edn., U. Del., 1973; MEd in Spl. Edn., Loyola Coll., Balt., 1980; MEd in Ednl. Leadership, U. South Fla., 1989. Dorm supr. Benedictine Sch. for Exceptional children, Ridgely, Md., 1974-75, tchr., dorm supr., 1975-76, 77-81; tchr. St. Catherine Siena Elem. Sch., Wilmington, Del., 1976-77; tchr. educable mentally handicapped Sch. Bd. Hilsborough County, Tampa, Fla., 1982-93, accelerated literacy tchr., 1993—. Bd. dirs. adult edn. St. Francis of Assisi, Seffner, Fla., 1989-92. Mem. Internat. Reading Assn., Fla. Reading Assn. Roman Catholic. Home: 2220 Glen Mist Dr Valrico FL 33594-5523 Office: Dover Elem Sch 3035 Nelson Ave Dover FL 33527-5151

BROWN, MARILYN BRANCH, retired educational administrator; b. Richmond, Va., Apr. 11, 1944; d. Elbert LeRoy and Edna Harriett (Eley) Branch; m. Winfred Wayland Brown, Jr., June 19, 1982; 1 dau., Lesli Antoinette; 1 dau. by previous marriage, Kara Rachelle Lancaster-Gay. B.S., Va. State U., 1966; M.S., U. Nebr., 1968; postgrad., U. Ala., Va. Commonwealth U. Nat. Tchr. Corps intern U. Nebr. at Omaha and Omaha Pub. Schs., 1966-68; tchr. McKlenburg County Pub. Schs., Boydton, Va., 1968-71; community organizer model cities health planning Capital Area Comprehensive Health Planning Coun., Richmond, Va., 1971-72; asst. dir. com. mental health mental retardation svcs. bd. Va. Dept. Mental Health & Mental Retardation, Richmond, 1972-75, spl. edn. dir., 1975-76; civil rights coord. Va. Dept. Social Svcs., Richmond, 1976-88, chmn. EEO adv. com., 1984-88; supr. spl edn. compliance Va. Dept. Edn., 1988-92; chmn. adv. com. on Black adoption Va. Dept. Social Svcs. Program coord. Swansboro Bapt. Ch., Richmond, 1979—; mem. Swansboro Ensemble, 1974—. Recipient Youth Motivation Commendation, Nat. Alliance of Bus., 1983. Fellow Am.

Orthopsychiat. Assn.; mem. Am. Assn. Affirmative Action, Black Adminstrs. in Child Welfare, Alliance for Black Social Welfare, Psi Chi, Alpha Kappa Alpha. Baptist. Home: 5500 Larrymore Dr Richmond VA 23225-6020

BROWN, MARTIN ADIN, job search consultant; b. Plymouth, N.H., June 18, 1940; s. Martin A. Jr. and Ann Marie (Louesque) B.; m. Susan Jackson Brown, Dec. 14, 1963 (div. Nov. 1991); m. Kristine E. Wisely, Nov. 9, 1991; children: Martin II, Michael, Amanda. BA in History, Middlebury (Vt.) Coll., 1962; MA in Bus., Ctrl. Mich. U., 1981. Commd. 2d lt. U.S. Army, advanced through grades to lt. col., 1979, ret., 1987; CEO, v.p. Consult Wise, Newport News, Va., 1991—; job cons. USAF, Langley AFB, Va., 1992-95; sr. counselor Resource Cons. Inc., Hampton, Va., 1995—; adj. prof. Thoman Nelson C.C., Hampton, Va., 1988—, Christopher Newport Univ., Newport News, 1988—, Hampton (Va.) U., 1987—, Saint Leo Coll., Langley AFB, 1982—; cons., trainer C&W Assocs. Inc., Newport News, 1987—, People to People, Newport News, 1992—, chairperson, 1992—; soccer referee Nat. Intercollegient Assn. of Soccer Referees, Newport News, 1982—. Decorated Bronze star, Air medal. Mem. Toastmasters Internat. Democrat. Roman Catholic. Home: 16 Blacksmythe Ln Newport News VA 23602-7465 Office: RCI at NASA Langley Rsch Ctr GA Langley Blvd Hampton VA 23681

BROWN, MICHAEL STUART, geneticist, educator, administrator; b. N.Y.C., N.Y., Apr. 13, 1941; s. Harvey and Evelyn (Katz) B.; m. Alice Lapin, June 21, 1964; children: Elizabeth Jane, Sara Ellen. BA, U. Pa., 1962, MD, 1966; DSc (hon.), Rensselaer Poly. Inst., 1982, U. Chgo., 1982, U. Pa., 1986, U. Buenos Aires, 1988, U. Paris, 1988, So. Meth. U., 1993. Intern, then resident in medicine Mass. Gen. Hosp., Boston, 1966-68; served with USPHS, 1968-70; clin. assoc. NIH, 1968-71; asst. prof. U. Tex. Southwestern Med. Sch., Dallas, 1971-74; Paul J. Thomas prof. genetics, dir. Ctr. for Molecular Diseases, 1977—; mem. med. adv. bd. Howard Hughes Med. Inst., Scripps Inst., Salk Inst., Meml. Sloan-Kettering Hosp. Co-editor: The Metabolic Basis of Inherited Disease, 1983. Trustee U. Pa., Lamplighter Sch. Recipient Pfizer award Am. Chem. Soc., 1976, Passano award Passano Found., 1978, Lounsbery award U.S. Nat. Acad. Scis., 1979; Lita Annenberg Hazen award, 1982, Albert Lasker Med. Rsch. award, 1985, Horwitz prize, 1985, Nobel Prize in Medicine or Physiology, 1985, Nat. Medal of Sci. U.S., 1988. Mem. Nat. Acad. Scis., Am. Soc. Clin. Investigation, Assn. Am. Physicians, Harvey Soc., Royal Acad. Scis. (fgn. mem.). Office: U Tex Health Sci Ctr Dept Molecular Genetics 5323 Harry Hines Blvd Dallas TX 75235-9046*

BROWN, MICHELLE RENEE, interior designer; b. Lincoln, Nebr., Apr. 30, 1964; d. John Allen and Audrey Claudine (Baker) Rider; m. Edward Daniel Brown, Nov. 19, 1988; 1 child, William Andrew. Student, East Tenn. State U., 1982-84, 1985-87; BA in Home Econs., Tenn. Tech. U., 1986; MA in Interior Design, U. Ky., 1988; postgrad., W.Va. U., 1990-91 summers. Cert. Nat. Coun. for Interior Design Qualification, Home Economist, 1990. Teaching asst. U. Ky., Lexington, Ky., 1986-88; interior designer Interiors, Morgantown, W.Va., 1990—; asst. prof., interior design W.Va. U., Morgantown, 1988-95. Design Projects include: W.Va. U. Academic Affairs Office Design, U. Health Svcs. Records and Nurses Area, U. Svcs Ctr. Ctrl Adminstrn., Office Layout, Divsn. Family Resources Breakroom, Stalnaker Hall, Arnold Hall, Math Dept, Wise Library, Duncan Library; Hawkins County Courthouse Extension, Tenn.; Fairmont State Coll. Learning Resource Ctr.; Calvary Baptist Ch.; C&P Telephone Co., Morgantown, W.Va. Recipient Faculty Scholarship award Tenn. Tech. U., 1985-86, Outstanding Tchr. award W.Va. U., 1993. Mem. Am. Soc. Interior Designers, Am. Home Econs. Assn., W.Va. Home Econs. Assn., Phi Kappa Phi, Phi Upsilon Omicron. Home: 79 Gans St Westover WV 26505-4512 Office: Interiors 19 Ashebrooke Sq Morgantown WV 26505

BROWN, MITCHELL W., protective services official. Chief of police Raleigh, N.C. Office: Police Dept 110 S McDowell St Raleigh NC 27602

BROWN, MONIKA CHRISTIANE BARGMANN, English language educator; b. Friedberg, Germany, Aug. 17, 1950; came to U.S., 1955; d. Rolf E. and Ilse M. (Heckenbach) B.; m. Robert Warren Brown, July 20, 1974; 1 child, Sarah Elisabeth. BA in English and French, U. Ga., Athens, 1970; MA in English, Duke U., 1972, PhD in English, 1981. Cert. secondary tchr. Tchr. English Dekalb County Schs., Atlanta, 1970-71; lectr. in English U. Münster (Germany), 1975-77; instr. in English Winthrop Coll., Rock Hill, S.C., 1980-82; lectr. in English Pembroke (N.C.) State U., 1982-85, asst. prof. English, 1985-92, assoc. prof. English, 1992—. Contbr. chpts. to books, articles to profl. jours. and mags. Music/choir dir. St. David's Episcopal Ch., Laurinburg, N.C., 1988—. NEH summer grantee. Mem. MLA, Philol. Assn. of the Carolinas (sec.-treas. 1992-95), Nat. Coun. of Tchrs. of English, Coll. Conf. for Composition and Comm., N.C. English Tchrs. Assn. Democrat. Office: Pembroke State U One University Dr Pembroke NC 28372

BROWN, NAN MARIE, clergywoman; b. Winton, N.C., Jan. 2, 1931; d. Richard and Aberdeen Elizebeth (Clanton) Watford; m. Joseph Linwood Blunt, June 9, 1947 (dec. Sept. 1970); children: Linette, Joseph Linwood Jr., Alvin; m. Frank Coolige Brown, Oct. 2, 1972; stepchildren: Ameedah Ali, Sami Nuridden. BS, D.C. Tchrs. Coll., 1972; MDiv magna cum laude, Va. Union U., 1982, D Ministry in Ch. Adminstrn., 1993. Ordained to ministry Bapt. Ch., 1980. Clk., sec., adminstr. Dept. Commerce and AEC, Suitland, Germantown, Md., 1960-65; program analyst Job Corps, U.S. Office Econs., Washington, 1965-67; licensing asst. U.S. Nuclear Regulatory Commn., Bethesda, Md., 1967-72, pers. mgmt. analyst, 1972-74; mgr. nat. fed. women's program U.S. Dept. Energy, Germantown, 1974-76; nat. dir. fed. women's program U.S. Dept. Interior, Washington, 1979; asst. pastor Pleasant Grove Bapt. Ch., Columbia, Va., 1975-83; pastor Mt. Level Bapt. Ch., Dinwiddie, Va., 1983-87, New Hope Bapt Ch., Esmont, Va., 1987-89; founder, pastor The Way of Cross Bapt. Ch., Palmyra, Va., 1989—; cons. Nan M. Brown Assocs., bus. cons.; vol. cons., reviewer AIDS proposals for funding Va. Health Dept., Richmond, 1979-89; founder, dir. Children's Saturday Enrichment Program, Palmyra, 1990—; mem. gen. bd. Bapt. Gen. Conv. Va., mem. social concerns com., 1990; vice moderator Slate River Bapt. Assn., 1995—. Author: (devotionals) The Word in Season, 1986, The Patience To Wait, Vol. I, 1988, Vol. II, 1992; contbg. author: Wise Women Bearing Gifts, 1988, Those Preachin' Women, 1988, Sister to Sister, 1995. Founder, pres. Black Women in Sisterhood for Action, Washington, 1979-82; vol. chaplain Martha Jefferson Hosp., Charlottesville, Va., 1993—; bd. dirs. AIDS Support Group, Charlottesville, 1990; mem. Fluvanna County Minority Health Coalition, 1993—. Named Disting. Black Woman, Black Women in Sisterhood for Action, 1982; recipient recognition for cmty. svc. Interfrat. Coun., Charlottesville, 1993, award for excellence Sister Care Internat., 1995, spl. achievement and cmty. svc. award Charlottesville Tribune, 1996. Mem. NAACP (pres. Fluvanna County chpt. 1979-81, cert. of appreciation 1994), Va. Women in Ministry (founder, pres. 1983-88, chaplain, Founder's award 1986, 90, 95). Home: PO Box 39 Rt 2 Box 1785 Kents Store VA 23084 Office: Way of Cross Bapt Ch State Rt 640 Palmyra VA 23084

BROWN, NAOMI YANAGI, publisher, author; b. Horomushiro Island, Hokkaido, Japan, June 10, 1920; came to U.S., 1951; d. Saisaku and Sawa (Horikoshi) Yanagi; m. Clayton Benjamin Earl Brown. Student, Showa Women's Coll., Tokyo, 1937-39. Prin., pub. Yucca Books, El Paso, Tex. Author book of haiku: Seasons' Enigma, 1989. Mem. Western Writers of Am. (assoc.), Nat. League Am. Pen Women, El Paso Writers' League, Mt. Franklin Corral Westerners Internat., El Paso County Hist. Soc., American Mus., El Paso Mus. Art. Home: 7772 Cedar Breaks Ln El Paso TX 79904-3522

BROWN, NORMAN JAMES, financial manager; b. Concord, N.H., May 12, 1942; s. Gilman D. and Katherine (Tucker) B.; m. Catherine Murphy, Sept. 17, 1983. BBS cum laude, N.H. Coll., 1968. CPA, Tenn. Acct. Peat Marwick Mitchell & Co., Portland, Me., 1968-69; audit mgr. Internal Audit Service div. VA, Washington, 1969-77; fin. mgr. regional office VA, Nashville, 1980—; supr. auditor Office Inspector Gen., Austin, Tex., 1977-80. With USAF, 1960-64. Mem. Assn. Govtl. Accts., Mid. Tenn. Fed. Exec. Assn., Moose. Republican. Mem. LDS Ch. Home: PO Box 22604 Nashville TN 37202-2604 Office: VA Regional Office 110 9th Ave S Nashville TN 37203-3817

BROWN, OLIVE PATRICIA, nursing consultant; b. Tucson, July 21, 1932; d. Cyril George and Olive M. (Peterson) Hanley; m. Charles Eugene Brown, Jan. 15, 1955; children: Charlotte D., Charlene B., Charmaine G. Diploma nursing, Good Samaritan Hosp., Phoenix, 1953; BS, U. Houston, 1973; MA, Ariz. State U., 1976; PhD, U. N.Mex., 1990. Staff nurse emergency rm Meml. Hosp., Houston, 1963-73; operating rm. nurse U. N.Mex. Hosp., Albuquerque, 1973; staff nurse rsch. unit Phoenix Indian Hosp., 1974-76; charge nurse, staff nurse gen. med. unit Alburqerque Indian Hosp., 1976-78; nursing cons., asst. dir. nursing Indian Health Svc., USPHS, Santa Fe, N.Mex., 1978-86; nursing cons., chmn. patient edn. and incident com. Santa Fe Indian Hosp., 1987-88; survey and cert. program review specialist Health Care Fin. Adminstrs., Dallas, 1989—; mem. adv. com. on continuing edn. to Bd. Nursing, 1979. Cadre mem. ARC. Capt. USPHS, 1975—. Teenage health and health edn. grantee. Mem. ANA, Commd. Corps Profl. Orgn., N.Mex. Nurses Assn. (past nurse practice com., coninuing edn. com., self-directed study chmn.), Sigma Theta Tau. Home: 450 Live Oak Ln NE Albuquerque NM 87122-1423

BROWN, OPAL DIANN, medical technologist, nurse; b. Gassaway, W.Va., Aug. 9, 1958; d. Albert Lee and Elizabeth Lee (Kidd) Persinger; m. Thomas David Brown, July 31,1993. BS in Med. Tech., W.Va. U., 1981; BSN, U. S.C., 1993. Med. technologist Biomed. Reference Labs., Fairmont, W.Va., 1981-82, Fairmont (W.Va.) Gen. Hosp., 1982, B.G. Thimmappa, M.D., Inc., Bridgeport, W.Va., 1982-83, Pocahontas Meml. Hosp., Marlinton, W.Va., 1984-87, Alexandria (Va.) Hosp., 1987-88, Richland Meml. Hosp., Columbia, S.C., 1988—; part-time RN Midlands Regional Ctr., S.C. Dept. of Disabilities and Spl. Needs, Columbia, 1994—. Mem. Am. Soc. Clin. Pathologists, Sigma Theta Tau. Democrat. Presbyterian. Home: 232 Laurel Meadows Dr West Columbia SC 29169-2361

BROWN, ORVAL ERIC, otolaryngologist; b. Milw., Apr. 16, 1951. BS summa cum laude, Tex. A&M U., 1973; MD, U. Tex. Southwestern Med. Sch., 1977. Intern in gen. surgery U. Tex. Southwestern Med. Ctr., Dallas, 1977-78, resident in otolaryngology, 1978-82; assoc. prof. clin. otorhinolaryngology U. Tex. Southwestern Med. Sch., Dallas, 1982—, chmn. divsn. pediatric otorhinolaryngology, 1990—; attending staff Parkland Meml. Hosp., Dallas, 1982—, Children's Med. Ctr., Dallas, 1982—, VA Hosp., Dallas, 1982—, John Peter Smith Hosp., Fort Worth, 1982—; mem. vis. teaching staff St. Paul Med. Ctr., Dallas, 1983—; mem. cons. staff Presbyn. Hosp., Dallas, 1985—, Tex. Scottish Rite Hosp. for Crippled Children, 1985—; lectr. in field. Contbr. articles to profl. jours. Bd. dirs. United Cerebral Palsy Assn. Dallas, 1985-88, 2d v.p., 1987—; mem. profl. adv. bd. Dallas Assn. for Parent Edn., 1985—; chmn. med. coverage task force otolaryngology Tex. Dept. Health State Crippled Children's Svcs., 1987-88. Grantee NIH, 1982-85, 84-87, 87-89, Smith, Kline and French Labs., 1987-88, Eli Lilly and Co., 1988, 89. Fellow ACS, Am. Acad. Otolaryngology, Soc. for Ear, Nose and Throat Advances in Children (pres. 1992), Am. Acad. Pediatrics; mem. AMA, Dallas County Med. Soc., Dallas Acad. Otolaryngology, Am. Soc. Pediatric Otolaryngology (charter), Deafness Rsch. Found. (Centurion). Home: 5320 Pebblebrook Dr Dallas TX 75229 Office: U Tex Southwestern Med Sch Dept ENT 5323 Harry Hines Blvd Dallas TX 75235-9035

BROWN, PATRICIA ANN, child health nurse; b. Kokomo, Ind., Apr. 4, 1938; d. John Conrad and Marie L. (Landseadel) B. BSN, Ind. U., 1959, MSN, 1969; Pediatric Nurse Assoc., U. Tenn., 1976. Staff nurse, asst. head nurse Ind. U. Children's Hosp., Indpls., 1960-66; chief nurse Child Devel. Ctr., Memphis, 1966-67; instr., asst. prof. child health nursing Ctr. for Health Scis., U. Tenn., Memphis, 1969-73; asst. prof. child health nursing U. Tenn., Knoxville, 1973-75, U. Tenn. Ctr. for Health Scis., Memphis, 1975-84; child health nursing faculty Holmes Jr. Coll., Grenada, Miss., 1985-89; dir. nursing East Ark. C.C., Forrest City, Ark., 1989—; chairperson Nursing Faculty Coun., Memphis. Hospice vol. Hospice of Memphis, 1981-84. Mem. Nat. League for Nursing, Tenn. Nurses Assn. (chairperson Maternal Child Health), Ark. State Bd. Nursing, Coun. Nursing Adminstrs. of Nursing Edn. Programs in Ark. (chairperson assoc. degree nursing coun. 1992-94), Ind. U. Alumni, Sigma Theta Tau, Pi Lambda Theta. Methodist. Home: 6984 Loddon Cove Memphis TN 38119-8517 Office: East Ark CC 1700 New Castle Rd Forrest City AR 72335-2204

BROWN, PATRICIA L., art educator, artist; b. Frankfurt am Main, Germany, Apr. 1, 1952; came to U.S., 1956; d. Johann Mueller and Margot Gertrude (Hennig) Lorance; m. James Ohl Brown, Aug. 8, 1973; children: Shannon Leigh, Christopher Ohl. BS in Art, Delta State U., 1974; MFA with honors, U. Ga., 1982. Cert. tchr., Miss. Asst. prof. art Delta State U., Cleveland, Miss., 1989—, gallery dir., 1994—; bd. dirs. Am. Craft Coun. S.E., 1996—; instr. workshop Paperworks '93, Arrowmont Sch., 1993; researcher in textiles, South Am., 1990, 93; lectr. 1st Tuesday Lectr. Series, Cleveland, Miss., 1990. V.p., Bolivar County Humane Soc., Cleveland, Miss., 1993-95. Faculty Devel. grant Delta State U., 1992; artist fellow Miss. Arts Commn., 1992; recipient Purchase award Cottonlandia Mus., Greenwood, Miss., 1995, Ark. Arts Ctr. Coll., Little Rock, 1996. Methodist. Home: 1515 Bella Vista Rd Cleveland MS 38732 Office: Delta State U Art Dept Sunflower Dr Cleveland MS 38733

BROWN, PAUL FERRELL, writer; b. Fairfax, VA, Oct. 10, 1972; s. Philip Thomas and Janice Eileen (Ferrell) B. BA in English, Coll. Wm. and Mary, 1994, MA in English, 1995. Record rev. writer The LaFayette Ledger, Williamsburg, Va., 1987-90; feature writer, editor editorial page The LaFayette Ledger, Williamsburg, 1989-90; co-editor poetry Imprints Coll. William and Mary lit. mag., Williamsburg, 1989-90; asst. coll. William and Mary, Williamsburg, 1994-95; freelance writer Williamsburg, Va., 1996—. Vol. The Pines Convalescent Ctr., Williamsburg, Va., 1989. Mem. Phi Beta Kappa, Alph Kappa Delta, Phi Eta Sigma, Alpha Lambda Delta. Democrat.

BROWN, PAUL NEELEY, federal judge; b. Denison, Tex., Oct. 4, 1926; s. Arthur Chester and Nora Frances (Hunter) B.; m. Frances Morehead, May 8, 1955; children: Paul Gregory, David H. II. JD, U. Tex., 1950. Assoc. Keith & Brown, Sherman, Tex., 1951-53; ptnr. Brown & Brown, Sherman, 1953; asst. U.S. atty. for Ea. Dist. Tex. Texarkana and Tyler, Tex., 1953-59; U.S. atty. Ea. Dist. Tex., Tyler, 1959-61; ptnr. Brown & Brown and Brown Brothers & Perkins, Sherman, 1961-65, Brown and Perkins, Sherman, 1965; sole practice, Sherman, 1965-67; ptnr. Brown & Hill, Sherman, 1967, Brown Kennedy Hill & Minshew, Sherman, 1967-71, Brown & Hill, Sherman, 1971-76, Brown Hill Ellis & Brown, Sherman, 1976-85; U.S. dist. judge U.S. Dist. Ct. (ea. dist.) Tex., Sherman, 1985—. Served with USN, 1944-46, 50-51. Fellow Tex. Bar Found.; mem. Rotary. Presbyterian. Office: US Dist Ct Fed Bldg 101 E Pecan St # 9 Sherman TX 75090-5989

BROWN, PAULA KINNEY, heating and air conditioning contractor; b. Portsmith, Va., June 19, 1953; d. Curtis Wade and Joan (Glascoe) Kinney; m. Wayne Howard Brown, Feb. 12, 1983; children: Rebecca Jo, Raina Jaye. AS, Lake Sumter Community Coll., 1973, 77; student Lake County Area Vocat. Ctr., 1979, 80. Cert. air conditioning and heating contrator. Pres. Kinney's Air Conditioning and Heating, Leesburg, Fla., 1981—, head computer system operator, 1986—, office mgr; sec.-treas. Wayne's Paint & Body, Inc., Leesburg, 1995—. Mem. adv. com. for Area Lake Air Conditioning and Heating Vo-Tech. Sch., Eustis, Fla., 1981-82, 1993—. Mem. Ch. of Christ. Home: 5 Lonesome Pine Trl Yalaha FL 34797-3058 Office: Kinney's Air Conditioning & Heating Inc 409 N 13th St Leesburg FL 34748-4968 also: Wayne's Paint & Body Inc 3831 W Main St Leesburg FL 34748

BROWN, PERRY EDMOND, academic administrator; b. West Palm Beach, Fla., Dec. 28, 1964; s. Kenneth Eugene and Laurel Ann (Snyder) B.; m. Debra Denise Collins, Sept. 6, 1986; children: Jordan Spencer, Ethan Edmond. AA, Lake Sumter C.C., 1987; BS, Palm Beach Atlantic Coll., 1990; MBA, Baylor U., 1992. Agy. mgmt., sales Ken Brown Ins. Agy., Inc., Wildwood, Fla., 1982-87; grad. admission dir. Palm Beach Atlantic Coll., West Palm Beach, Fla., 1988-91; dir. exec. MBA program Baylor U., Waco, Tex., 1991-95; dir. corp. rels. and career svcs. U. Fla., Gainesville, 1995—. Bd. dirs. ARC, Waco, 1993-95; faculty advisor Baylor U. Coll.Reps., Waco, 1993-94; mem. bd. advisors Salvation Army, Gainesville, 1996—; state committeeman Alachua County Rep. Ctrl. Com. Fla., 1996—. Lt. (j.g.) USNR, 1993—. Mem. Fin. Mgmt. Assn., Baylor U. Alumni Assn., Omicron Delta Epsilon, Sigma Iota Epsilon. Republican. Baptist. Office: U Fla MBA Programs PO Box 117152 Gainesville FL 32611-7152

BROWN, RAYMOND JESSIE, financial and insurance company executive; b. La., Nov. 29, 1944; s. Clarence and Katherine (Foster) B.; m. Syndee D. Williams, July 26, 1992; children: Shawn, Carmen. BA in Govt. and Speech, Southeastern U., Hammond, La., 1967; postgrad., La. State U. Asst. mgr. CIT, Baton Rouge, 1967-71, Thrift Funds, Baton Rouge, 1971-72; mgr. Blazer Fin., Baton Rouge, 1972-73; v.p. Fidelity Fin. Svc., Baton Rouge, 1973-82; chief exec. officer CFC-City Fin. Corp., Baton Rouge, 1982—; pres., chief exec. officer City Life and Casualty, Baton Rouge; treas. Baton Rouge Lenders Exchange, 1982, pres., 1983. Mem. La. Ind. Fin. Assn. (bd. govs. 1984-88, exec. com. 1988—). Republican. Roman Catholic. Office: City Fin Corp 5235 Florida Blvd # E Baton Rouge LA 70806-4149

BROWN, RENÉ LILLIAN, medical librarian; b. Balt., July 16, 1952; d. Robert Leo and Dorothy Lillian (Pincott) Tabb; m. William Ambrose Brown III, May 22, 1976; 1 child, Hazel Louise. BA in Philosophy, Washington Coll., Chestertown, Md., 1974; MLS, George Peabody Coll., 1975. Student libr. asst. George Peabody Coll., Nashville, 1974-75; asst. cataloger Portsmouth (Va.) Pub. Libr., 1975-78, head cataloging dept., 1978-80; med. libr. Maryview Hosp., Portsmouth, 1986-96. Sec. Mayor's Sister City Commn., Portsmouth, 1993-96; adult trainer Girl Scouts, Colonial Coast, 1991—, leader, 1988—; mem. Friends Portsmouth Pub. Libr., 1980-96; newsletter editor Maryview Aux., Portsmouth, 1993-95. Mem. Va. Libr. Assn., Med. Libr. Assn., Tidewater Health Sci. Librs. (chair 1992-93). Home: 26337 Hanging Tree Rd Courtland VA 23837

BROWN, RICK DEAN, engineer, consultant; b. Defiance, Ohio, Apr. 10, 1949; s. Welhelm David and Joyce Elaine (Dyer) B.; m. Scarlett F. Chadic, Sept. 17, 1985; children: Judy, Clinton, Eva, Erich. BS, Defiance Coll., 1971; MS, D Chiropratic, Palmer Coll., Davenport, Iowa, 1975. Cert. tchr., Ohio; cert. valuation appraiser. Lab. chemist Johns-Manville Inc., Defiance, 1917-71; tchr. secondary sch. Holgate (Ohio) Local Sch. Sys., 1971-72; dir. prodn. facility S-K Tool Co. Inc., Johnson City, Tenn., 1972-75; pvt. practice, Bryan, Ohio, 1976-78; engring. cons. Brown Cons., Essex Junction, Vt., 1978-94; mgr. quality assurance Network Solutions Inc., Oklahoma City, 1994-95, facility dir., 1995; bus. strategy advisor DynaCom Info. Sys. Inc., Moore, Okla., 1995—; engring. cons. advisor Brown Cons. Inc., Bethany, Okla., 1995—; sr. quality engr. Raytheon Aircraft Co., Wichita, Kans., 1996—; curriculum advisor NEA, Washington, 1971-73; quality assurance sys. cons. GTE, Sacramento, 1994-95; contract analysts cons. Dept. Def., Washington, 1994-95; mem. exec. steering com. Network Solutions Security Commn., Herndon, Va., 1994-95. Author: Teaching Manual for Statistical Process Control, 1993; inventor HOH fuel source carburation, ceramic coating of engine and transmission components. V.p. Joy Pub. Sch. Sys. Bd. Edn., 1981-83. Fellow Am. Soc. Engring.; mem. Am. Soc. for Quality Control, Am. Soc. for Nondestructive Testing (chpt. advisor 1992-93), Nat. Jaycees, Toastmasters (sr. v.p. instrn. Oklahoma City 1995-96), Lions, Odd Fellows. Republican. Roman Catholic. Home and Office: 504 E School St Rose Hill KS 67133

BROWN, ROBERT FREDERICK, industrial systems engineer, technology applications, industrial systems and management systems consultant; b. N.Y.C., Nov. 8, 1944; s. Robert Joseph and Ruth Mildred (Mueller) B.; m. Susan Maria Juneman, Nov. 27, 1993; children from previous marriage: Dana Marguerite, Cristina Ruth. BS, Kans. State U., 1970, MS, 1971; MBA, U. Richmond, 1976. Cert. in systems integration; cert. project mgmt. profl.; cert. master hazardous materials mgr. Indsl. engr. Philip Morris USA, Richmond, Va., 1972-77; mgr. indsl. engring. Consolidated Aluminum, St. Louis, 1977-78; mgr. system engr. System Devel. Corp., Oak Ridge, Tenn., 1978-84; project dir. Roy F. Weston Inc., West Chester, Pa., 1984-86; project mgr. Systematic Mgmt. Svcs., Inc., Oak Ridge, Tenn., 1986-88; v.p. Systematic Mgmt. Svcs., Inc., Oak Ridge, 1988-91; mgr. Tenera, L.P., 1991-92; regional dir. Pragmatics Inc., Oak Ridge, 1992-95; ind. cons. tech. devel. and applications, 1996—. Pres. Crestwood Farms Resident Assn., Richmond, 1976. With U.S. Army, 1966-69, Vietnam. Mem. NSPE, Am. Soc. Engring. Mgmt., Inst. Indsl. Engrs. (chpt. pres. 1969—), Am. Soc. Cost Engrs., U.S. Power Squadron (comdr. 1984-85), Nat. Contract Mgmt. Assn., Project Mgmt. Inst., Nat. Corvette Restorers Soc., Am. Soc. Quality Control, Soc. Am. Value Engrs., Am. Nuclear Soc., Nat. Coun. Sys. Engring., Order of Engr., Am. Mensa, Rotary. Office: 118 Ridgeway Ctr Oak Ridge TN 37830-6926

BROWN, ROBERT HOWARD, customer support specialist; b. Greenville, Tex., Dec. 29, 1967; s. Lanny Howard Brown and Judy (Nelson) Manning. Student, East Tex. State U., 1986-90. Sales clk. Braum's Ice Cream, Greenville, Tex., 1985-88; researcher, teller State Nat. Bank, Caddo Mills, Tex., 1986-87; credit mgr. DSC King Saver, Greenville, 1988-90; customer svc. rep. OmniSys/Bluff Creek Systems, Greenville, 1990-91; customer support technician Health Care Computer Corp., Ft. Worth, 1991-92, Summers Press, Inc., Bedford, Tex., 1992—; cons. Griffin Communications, Little Creek Acres/Casa Linda Garage, Quinlan, Tex., 1991. Democrat. Baptist.

BROWN, ROBERT LAIDLAW, state supreme court justice; b. Houston, June 30, 1941; s. Robert Raymond and Warwick (Rust) B.; m. Charlotte Banks, June 18, 1966; 1 child, Stuart Laidlaw. BA, U. of the South, 1963; MA in English and Comparative Lit., Columbia U., 1965; JD, U. Va., 1968. Bar: Ark. 1968, U.S. Dist. Ct. (ea. and we. divs.) Ark. 1968. Assoc. Chowning, Mitchell, Hamilton & Burrow, Little Rock, 1968-71; dep. prosecuting atty. 6th Jud. Dist., Prosecuting Atty. Office, Little Rock, 1971-72; legal aide Office Gov. Dale Bumpers, Little Rock, 1972-75; legis. asst. U.S. Senator Dale Bumpers, Washington, 1975-77; adminstrv. asst. Congressman Jim Guy Tucker, Washington, 1977-78; ptnr. Harrison & Brown, P.A., Little Rock, 1978-85; pvt. practice law, 1985-91; assoc. justice Ark. Supreme Ct., Little Rock, 1991—. Contbr. articles to profl. jours. Trustee U. of the South, Sewanee, Tenn., 1983-89, mem. bd. regents, 1989-95. Mem. ABA, Ark. Bar Assn., Ark. Bar Found. (cert. of recognition 1981). Episcopalian.

BROWN, ROBERT LAWRENCE, research plant pathologist; b. Chgo., Jan. 4, 1947; s. Robert and Susie (Carmichael) B.; m. Marcia Carrie Wilson, Oct. 6, 1973 (div. May 1992); 1 child, Karma; m. Shirley Marie Jackson, July 10, 1993; 1 child, R. Jovan Bell. BS, Iowa Wesleyan Coll., 1970; MS, U. Wyo., 1976; PhD, Rutgers U., 1984. Staff coord. Rutgers Coop. Ext., Newark, 1978-79, asst. prof., 1979-83; instr. Franklyn K. Lane High Sch., Queens, N.Y., 1984-85, Rutgers-Cook Coll., New Brunswick, N.J., 1984-87; spl. programs counselor Rutgers-Cook Coll., New Brunswick, 1988-89; rsch. geneticist USDA-Agrl. Rsch. Svc.-So. Regional Rsch. Ctr., New Orleans, 1989-93; rsch. plant pathologist USDA-ARS-SRRC, New Orleans, 1993—; grad. faculty affiliate in plant pathology and crop physiology La. State U., Baton Rouge, 1994—; instr. Seton Hall U., South Orange, N.J., 1986-87, Immaculate Conception High Sch., Montclair, N.J., 1986-88. Contbr. articles to profl. jours. Vol. reading tutor Operation Mainstream Adult Literacy Program, New Orleans, 1990-92; vol. Youth Motivation Task Force Program, Xavier U., La., 1994. Mem. Am. Phytopathological Soc., So. Region Info. Exch. Group (chair 1995), So. Corn Improvement Conf., N.Y. Acad. Scis., Sigma Xi. Office: USDA Agrl Rsch Svc So Regional Rsch Ctr 1100 Robert E Lee Blvd New Orleans LA 70124-4305

BROWN, ROBERT WILLIAM, small business owner, musician; b. Matador, Tex., Oct. 23, 1945; s. Silas Carlisle and Austella (Miller) B. Student, West Tex. State U., 1964-68. Mem. The Three Notes Band, Matador, Tex., 1960-61; session guitarist Norman Petty Studio, Clovis, N.M., 1964; bandleader The Gemini Five Band, Amarillo, Tex., 1964-66; backup guitarist The Crossroads Club, Amarillo, Tex., 1970; songwriter Al Galico Music, Nashville, 1975; owner Ash St. Violin Shop, Plainview, Tex., 1981-85; founder, owner Brown-Robin Music, Plainview, Tex., 1995—; regional rep. Vose Artists Archives, Brookline, Mass., 1989-90. Author: Brown's Index of Southwestern Painters, 1995; composer: Brown's Collection of Songs, 1994, Brown's New Collection, 1996. Recipient Purchase award Ranching Heritage Ctr., Lubbock, 1986, Frick Art Reference Libr., N.Y.C., 1989, Art Acceptance award N.Y. Hist. Soc., 1984, Art Rsch. citation

Worthington Pump Co., N.J., 1979. Mem. The West Winds (Canyon, Tex.). Baptist. Office: Robert Brown Enterprises 614 Ash St Plainview TX 79072

BROWN, ROBIN COTTEN, otolaryngologist; b. Birmingham, Ala., Mar. 14, 1934; s. Percy Rivers and Katherine Austin (Kelley) B.; m. Jan Stuart Mercer, Aug. 30, 1956; children: deirdre, Robin Cotten Jr., Stuart, Stephen. BS in Zoology, Tulane U., 1955, MD, 1959. Diplomate Am. Bd. Otolaryngology. Rsch. asst. in pharmacology Tulane U., New Orleans, 1957-59; intern Touro Infirmary, New Orleans, 1959-60; resident in otolaryngology U. Ill., Chgo., 1960-64; surg. fellow Oschsner Found. Hosp., New Orleans, 1960-61; otolaryngology resident Ill. Rsch. Hosp., Chgo., 1961-64; pvt. practice Ear, Nose & Throat Assocs., Ft. Myers, Fla., 1964—; pres. med. staff Lee Meml. Hosp., Ft. Myers, 1970-71. Author: Florida's Fossils, 1988, Florida's First People, 1994. Bd. dirs. Ft. Myers Hist. Mus., 1992—, Mus. of Fla. History, Tallahassee, 1995-96. Mem. Lee County Med. Soc. (sec. 1965-67), Rotary (bd. trustees 1989-95), Phi Beta Kappa. Office: Ear Nose & Throat Associates 3487 Broadway Fort Myers FL 33901-7213

BROWN, RODGER ALAN, meteorologist, researcher; b. Ellicottville, N.Y., Mar. 24, 1937; s. Ellsworth LeRoy and Gladys Lucille Brown; m. Diane Priscilla McLeod, June 27, 1959; children: Christopher, Elizabeth, Katherine. BS, Antioch Coll., 1960; MS, U. Chgo., 1962; PhD, U. Okla., 1989. Resident observer Mt. Washington (N.H.) Obs., 1955-56, Blue Hill Meteorol. Obs., Milton, Mass., 1956; student aide U.S. Weather Bur., Washington, 1957; rawinsonde observer U.S. Weather Bur., Little America V, Antarctica, 1957-59; lab. asst. Antioch Coll., Yellow Springs, Ohio, 1959-60; rsch. asst. U. Chgo., 1960-65; rsch. meteorologist Cornell Aero. Lab., Buffalo, 1965-70, Wave Propagation Lab., Boulder, Colo., 1970, Nat. Severe Storms Lab., Norman, Okla., 1970—. Contbr. articles to profl. jours. and ency. Active Boy Scouts Am., Norman, 1972—; bd. dirs. My Friend's House, Norman, 1989-90, 94-96. Fellow Royal Meteorol. Soc.; mem. Nat. Weather Assn. (sec. 1994, v.p. 1996), Am. Meteorol. Soc. (chair severe storms com. 1980-82), Am. Geophys. Union, Sigma Xi. Home: 2232 Crestmont Ave Norman OK 73069-6418 Office: Nat Severe Storms Lab 1313 Halley Cir Norman OK 73069-8480

BROWN, RONALD CHRIS, telecommunications executive; b. Knoxville, Tenn., Dec. 17, 1949; s. John Harding and Marie (Long) B.; m. June Darlene Scott, June 12, 1976; children: Wendy Caprice Hug, Kathleen Alicia. BSEE, U. Tenn., 1972. Chief engr. Ctr. for Ednl. Devel., Tallahassee, 1972-74; sr. engr. RCA corp., Camden, N.J., 1974-77; sales mgr. Harris Corp., Quincy, Ill., 1977-84; internat. sales mgr. Andrew Corp., Orland Park, Ill., 1984-94; sr. v.p. internat. sales Calif. Microwave MNS Div., Houston, 1994—. Mem. IEEE, Soc. Motion Picture and TV Engrs. Home: PO Box 885 Stafford TX 77497-0885 Office: Calif Microwave MNS Div 4000 Greenbriar Stafford TX 77477

BROWN, RONALD CONKLIN, history educator; b. Brownwood, Tex., Apr. 25, 1945; s. Glenn Lamar and June Day (Conklin) B.; m. Judith Dianne Hardin, Aug. 2, 1969; 1 child, Brian Russell. AB, Wabash Coll., 1967; AM, U. Ill., 1968, PhD, 1975. From instr. history to assoc. prof. history S.W. Tex. State U., San Marcos, 1975-85, prof. history, 1985—, dir. honors program, 1980-95, acting dean Coll. Gen. Studies, 1995—. Author: Hard Rock Miners: The Intermountain West, 1979; Beacon on the Hill: Southwest Texas State U., 1979. Scoutmaster Boy Scouts Am., San Marcos, 1987—; active First Presbyn. Ch., San Marcos. Mem. Am. Hist. Assn., Nat. Collegiate Honors Coun, Western History Assn., Mining History Assn. (coun. 1990-92, treas. 1992—), Great Plains Regional Honors Coun. (pres. 1985-86), Rotary of Greater San Marcos (sec./treas. 1989-90, v.p. 1990-91, pres. 1992-93). Democrat. Home: 823 Willow Creek Cir San Marcos TX 78666-5061 Office: Coll Gen Studies SW Tex State U 601 University Dr San Marcos TX 78666-4684

BROWN, RONALD ELLSWORTH, SR., software engineer, consultant; b. Williamston, N.C., Sept. 10, 1954; s. Joseph Ellsworth Lewis and Nellie Faye (Brown) Slade; children: Ronald Ellsworth Jr., Shierina Anjel. BA in Computer Sci., N.C. A&T State U., 1988. Cert. netware engr. Maintenance Technicon Sci. Ctr., Tarrytown, N.Y., 1972-73; air cargo specialist USAF, Tokyo, 1973-82; salesman Combined Ins. Co., Raleigh, N.C., 1988-89; from telecom. network analyst to software engr. Am. Airlines, Inc., Ft. Worth, Cary, N.C., 1989-92; programmer analyst Inmar Enterprises, Inc., Winston-Salem, N.C., 1993-94; sr. field sys. engr. Info. Handling Svcs., Arlington, Va., 1994—; sys. developer, CEO REB Enterprises, Winston-Salem, 1988—; fitness cons. Lifestyles, 1988; freelance computer cons. to small bus., 1982-84. Vol. Rainbow Coalition, Greensboro, N.C., 1984, YMCA, Greensboro, 1986. Recipient meritorious svc. medal USAF, 1977, longevity awards 1976-82. Mem. IEEE, Nat. Soc. Black Engrs. (assoc. publ. editor 1986-88). Democrat. Office: 2341 Jefferson Davis Hwy Ste 113178 Arlington VA 22202

BROWN, RONALD KAYE, civil engineer, minister; b. San Antonio, Jan. 21, 1949; s. William K. and Mavis Margie (Shields) B.; m. Carolyn Nadene Dibrell, Apr. 12, 1969 (div. Jan. 1994); children: Leonard Kieth, Zachary Aaron; m. Panzia Belice Adams Pullam, June 15, 1995; children: J'Anzia Masad Pullam, Josiah Joel Pullam. BSCE, Tex. A&I U., 1974; DD, Guadalupe Bapt. Theol. Sem., 1989. Registered profl. engr., Tex. Engr. Entex, Inc., Houston, 1974-76; jr. engr. drainage divsn. San Antonio Dept. Pub. Works, 1976-77; pvt. practice engring. cons., 1977-78, 81-82; asst. resident engr. Tex. State Dept. Hwys. and Pub. Transp., San Antonio, 1978-81; engr. dept. pub. works City of San Antonio, 1982-84, engr. dept. environ. mgmt., 1984-88; sr. engr. engring. dept. San Antonio Water Sys., 1988—; pastor St. Phillip Bapt. Ch., San Antonio, 1982—; v.p. Guadalupe Bapt. Theol. Sem., 1993—. Author: User's Manual for Hydrology and Hydraulic Software for San Antonio, 1984; author, editor: Enoch, 1995. Office: St Phillip Bapt Ch 205 Bargas St San Antonio TX 78210

BROWN, RONALD STEPHEN, dental educator, clinician; b. Washington, Feb. 15, 1946; s. Norman and Selma Regina (Hidnert) B.; m. Sylvia L. Lesse, Dec. 26, 1978; children: Elaine Michelle, Benjamin Jeffrey. Student, U. Md., 1964-67; DDS, Georgetown U., 1971, MS in Pharmacology, 1988. Diplomate Am. Bd. Oral Medicine. Pvt. practice dentistry Brown and Berger, Fairfax, Va., 1975-85; clin. instr. dentistry Georgetown U., Washington, 1976-85, adj. asst. prof., 1988-89, clin. assoc. prof., 1995—; assoc. prof. U. Tex., Houston, 1989-94; asst. prof. Howard U., Washington, 1995—. Mem. editorial bd. Oral Surgery Oral Medicine Oral Pathology, 1995—; author more than 8 monographs and book chpts., some 40 articles in profl. jours. Capt. U.S. Army, 1971-73. NIH grantee, 1986, 93. Mem. AAAS, ADA, Am. Acad. Oral Medicine (sec. 1993—, Disting. Svc. award 1988, 90), N.Y. Acad. Sci., Orgn. Tchrs. Oral Diagnosis, D.C. Dental Soc. Home: 631 S 29th St Arlington VA 22202

BROWN, RUBYE ELLEN, retired nursing administrator; b. Milam County, Tex., Feb. 21, 1925; d. Henry Clarence and Carrie (Kyle) Spence; m. Elbert Howard Brown, Sept. 21, 1946; 1 child, Bert. Diploma in nursing, Brackenridge Hosp., Austin, Tex., 1946. RN, Tex. County health nurse State of Tex., Cameron; county sch. nurse Milam County, Cameron; head nurse Richards Meml. Hosp., Rockdale, Tex.; ret.; nurse church camp in summers. Mem. ANA. Home: PO Box 1292 Rockdale TX 76567-1292

BROWN, RUBYE GOLSBY, secondary education educator, artist; b. Youngstown, Ohio; d. Clifford and Augusta Bell (Blalock) Golsby; m. Robert L. Brown; children: Harlean J. Preston, Charles, Louis, Carson, Gloria, Robin, Debbie. BA in Edn., Youngstown (Ohio) State Coll., 1956, BS, 1979, MS in Sociology, Edn. and Adminstrn., 1981; Cert. in History and Govtl. Econs., Youngstown State U., 1989. Credit mgr. Klivan's, Youngstown, 1953-56; sec. City Hall, Treasurer's Office, Youngstown, 1956; substitute tchr. Chaney High Sch., Youngstown, 1981-92; tchr. Round Rock High Sch., 1992—; instr. Austin (Tex.) Community Coll., 1993—; owner Custom Craft, Austin, 1993—; instr. in art, pub. speaker on crime and drug abuse. Mem. Ohio State Bd. Health, 1980—; pres. Mahoning County Courtwatch, 1987—; ednl. specialist Police Dept. Task Force, Youngstown, 1989—; vol. Olin E. Teaque Detention Ctr. Recipient Health Care award, Columbus State Bd. Health, 1988. Mem. Am. Soc. Curriculum and Devel., Am. Univ. and Coll. Women. Democrat. Baptist.

BROWN, SAMUEL, retired corporate executive; b. Mobile, Ala., Mar. 2, 1908; s. Milton Leopold and Edna (Solomon) B.; m. Carolyn Elkan Greenfield, Nov. 2, 1930 (dec. Oct. 1989); children: Milton Leopold, Maxine Phyllis Brown Feibelman, Carol Lynn Brown Robinson. BS, U. Ala., 1929. Mng. ptnr. Brown & Brown, Mobile, 1935-42, owner, 1942-45; pres. Brown & Brown, Inc., Mobile, 1954-84; pres. Brownfield Investment Corp., Mobile, 1954, also bd. dirs.; pres. Brown and Brown of Del., Inc., Wilmington, 1984—, also bd. dirs.; pres. Greenfield Lands, Inc., Atlanta, 1981—, also bd. dirs. Author: The Rotary Club of Mobile, Alabama, 1914-1986; also articles. Pres. Rotary, Mobile, 1955-56, bd. trustees Mobile Pub. Libr., 1964. Recipient Disting. Svc. award Ala. Soc. for Crippled Children, 1973. Mem. Indsl. Fabrics Assn. (hon. life), Mobile Country Club. Republican. Jewish.

BROWN, SARA LOU, accounting firm executive; b. Houston, Oct. 11, 1942; d. William Hale and Ruth Elizabeth (Hearon) Rutherford; m. Joseph Kurth Brown, Dec. 21, 1965 (div. Mar. 1979); 1 child, Derek Kurth. B.A., Rice U., 1964; M.B.A., U. Tex., 1966. CPA, Tex. Mem. staff KPMG Peat Marwick, Houston, 1966-69, mgr., 1969-73, ptnr., 1973—. Treas. Zool. Soc. Houston, 1989-96, Houston Grand Opera, 1973-74, Parks and Recreation Bd., City of West University Place, Tex., 1983, 84. Mem. Am. Inst. C.P.A.s, Tex. Soc. C.P.A.s. Home: 2701 Mid Lane St Houston TX 77027-4907 Office: KPMG Peat Marwick LLP PO Box 4545 Houston TX 77210-4545

BROWN, SARAH RUTH, accountant, educator; b. Chattanooga, July 3, 1956; d. Elmon Huey Sr. and Janie Margaret (Stevens) B. BS, Athens State Coll., 1977; MBA, U. North Ala., 1981; D of Bus. Adminstrn., Miss. State U., 1990. CPA, Ala. Staff acct. Garrard, Humphries, and Snow CPAs, Muscle Shoals, Ala., 1978-80; div. acct. State of Ala. Hwy. Dept., Tuscumbia, 1980-84; grad. asst. Miss. State U., Starkville, 1984-85; instr. U. North Ala., Florence, 1985-90, asst. prof., 1990-92, assoc. prof., 1992—, eminent scholar chair sch. bus., 1994-95. Recipient research grant U. North Ala., 1987. Mem. AICPA, AAUP, Nat. Assn. Accts. (dir. ednl. projects 1986-87, comty. responsibilities 1987-89, v.p. profl. edn. 1990-91), Am. Acctg. Assn., Midsouth Inst. Accts., Ala. Assn. Acctg. Educators, Pi Tau Chi, Beta Gamma Sigma. Methodist. Home: Rt 13 Box 296 Florence AL 35630 Office: U North Ala Box 5206 Florence AL 35632

BROWN, SHARON ELIZABETH, software engineer; b. Lynn, Mass., Nov. 23, 1960; d. Leland James Brown and Vail (Wilkinson) Bartelson. B-SChemE, U. Mass., 1983. Software engr. K&L Automation div. Daniel Industry, Tucson, 1983-86, sr. software engr., 1986-87, asst. mgr. software systems, 1987; software mgr. Daniel Automation, Houston, 1987-91; sr. software engr. Praxis Instruments, Inc., Houston, 1991-93, Dresser Measurement, Houston, 1993—. Mem. NSPE, ISA. Republican. Home: 5735 Henniker Dr Houston TX 77041-6589 Office: Dresser Industries Inc PO Box 42176 Houston TX 77242-2176

BROWN, STEPHEN NEAL, computer engineer; b. Austin, Tex., July 30, 1952; s. Edward James and Alice Marie (Stewart) B. BS in Mech. Engring., U. Tex., 1975, MS in Mech. Engring., 1978, MS in Elec. Engring., 1984, PhD in Computer Engring., 1989. Registered profl. engr., Tex. Jr. engr. IBM, Austin, 1975-76, assoc. engr., scientist, 1976-79, sr. assoc. engr., scientist, 1979-89, devel. staff engr., 1989-92; pres. Knowledge Innovations, Inc., Austin, 1992—; grad. rsch. asst. II, U. Tex.-Austin, 1984-85. Team leader CD, San Antonio, 1969; aquatic dir. summer camp Boy Scouts Am., Kerrville, Tex., 1973. Recipient Eagle Scout award Boy Scouts Am., 1969. Mem. IEEE Computer Soc., Assn. Computing Machinery, ASME (1st Place award for paper 1975), Tau Beta Pi, Eta Kappa Nu. Avocation: travel. Home: 14307 Richard Walker Blvd Austin TX 78728-6863 Office: Knowledge Innovations Inc 14307 Richard Walker Blvd Austin TX 78728-6863

BROWN, STEVEN THOMAS, state regulatory policy director; b. Monticello, Fla., Mar. 31, 1961; s. Homer Thomas and Brenda (Leviner) B.; m. Alisa Walleen Senterfit, Feb. 28, 1987; children: David Gregory, Emily Kaytlin. AA in Bus. Adminstrn., Tallahassee Community Coll., Tallahassee, Fla., 1981; BA in Econs., Fla. State U., 1983, BA in Internat. Affairs, 1983; MBA, Nova U., 1992. Fiscal clk. II Dept. Adminstrn. State of Fla., Tallahassee, 1983-84; mgr. trainee Winn Dixe Inc., Tallahassee, 1982-86; pers. aide Dept. Adminstrn. State of Fla., Tallahassee, 1984-85, benefit cal. specialist, 1986-88; regulatory analyst I Fla. Pub. Svc. Commn., Tallahassee, 1988-89, regulatory analyst II, 1989-91, regulatory analyst III, 1991-92, regulatory analyst supr., 1992-96; dir. state regulatory policy Intermedia Comms., Tampa, Fla., 1996—. Named Mr. Woodman, Woodman of the World, 1984. Home: 2108 Golf Manor Blvd Valrico FL 33594 Office: Intermedia Comm Corp Hdqs 3625 Queen Palm Dr Tampa FL 33619-1309

BROWN, TED LEON, JR., investment company executive; b. Lawrence, Kans., Jan. 14, 1956; s. Ted Leon and Simona (Garcia) B.; m. Cynthia Marie Fulmer, Jan. 26, 1974 (div. 1983); children: Chauntel M., Donald E.; m. Cynthia Jean Ford (div. 1993); children: Mark W. Kurta, Jennifer L. Kurta; m. Anne E. Scott, Aug. 19, 1995; 1 child, Amber Scott. Grad. high sch. Produce mgr. Pantry Pride, Lauderhill, Fla., 1971-77; asst. grocery mgr. Albertsons South Co., Plantation, Fla., 1977-79; pres. Brown & Brown Investments Inc., Ft. Lauderdale, Fla., 1980-91, Advent Investments Inc., Tamarac, 1990-92, Safeguard Investments Inc., Coral Springs, Fla., 1995—. Chmn. adv. bd. Pinewood Elem. Sch., North Lauderdale, 1987-89; exec. dir. Fla. Lions Eye Bank, Miami, 1989-91; chmn. Boy Scouts Am., North Lauderdale, 1987. Recipient Landscape Excellence award,, City of Boca Raton, 1989, Landscape Maint. award, Tishman Speyer Properties, 1990, Gov.'s Achievement award, Lions, 1989. Mem. Lions (pres. Tamarac 1990-91). Home and Office: 12109 Royal Palm Blvd Coral Springs FL 33065

BROWN, (WILLIAM) THEODORE, JR., lawyer, writer; b. Memphis, June 7, 1949; s. William Theodore and Florence Aileen (Collins) B. BS summa cum laude, U. Tenn., 1971; JD, Vanderbilt U., 1978. Staff asst. U.S. Senator Albert Gore, Sr., Washington, 1969, 70; rsch. asst. Andrew Jackson Papers Project, Washington, Hermitage, Tenn., 1974-77; assoc. editor Legal Papers of Andrew Jackson, Hermitage, 1977-79; law clk. to Hon. Russell H. Hippe, Jr. U.S. Bankruptcy Ct., Nashville, 1979-81; atty. Kilpatrick & Cody, Atlanta, 1981-93, Reece & Assocs., Atlanta, 1993—; Estes Kefauver Scholars lectr. Hiwassee Coll., 1995. Co-editor Legal Papers of Andrew Jackson, 1979-87; contbr. articles to profl. jours. Bd. trustees Ga. Legal History Found., Atlanta, 1988-92, chmn. ann. Woodrow Wilsn dinner, 1988-89; bd. dirs. Atlanta Vanderbilt Club, 1994-96, co-chmn. lecture series com., 1995; mem. Ga. steering com. Albert Gore Jr. for Pres., 1988. Mem. Orgn. Am. Historians, So. Hist. Assn., State Bar Ga., State Bar Tenn., Phi Beta Kappa, Phi Kappa Phi, Phi Eta Sigma. Democrat. Home: 2058 River Heights Walk Marietta GA 30067 Office: Reece & Assocs 245 Peachtree Center Ave Ste 2150 Atlanta GA 30303

BROWN, TIMOTHY WAYNE, urban planner; b. New Albany, Ind., Jan. 27, 1960; s. Leonard and Patricia Ann (Whitman) Brown. BS in Aviation Adminstrn., Ind. State U., 1981; MPA, U. Ctrl. Fla., 1990. Intern in planning dept. City of Winter Park (Fla.), 1988; planning intern in gen. planning divsn. East Ctrl. Fla. Regional Planning Coun., 1989; grad. asst. in student affairs office U. Ctrl. Fla., 1989-90; planning intern Solin and Assocs., Inc., 1990; planner City of Tarpon Springs (Fla.), 1990-93, City of Largo (Fla.), 1993-96; sr. planner City of Port Orange, Fla., 1996—. Contbr. articles to profl. jours. Participant internat. planning exch. Am. Planning Assn./Royal Town Planning Inst., Eng. Staff sgt. U.S. Army, 1984-87, USAR, 1987—. Named one of Outstanding Coll. Students of Am.; Hoosier scholar. Mem. ASPA, Am. Planning Assn. (treas. 3 terms Suncoast sect., sec. 1 term), Am. Inst. Cert. Planners, Fla. Planning and Zoning Assn., Pub. Adminstrn. Student Assn. (pres.), Student Vets. Assn. (v.p.), 1000 Friends of Fla., Alpha Phi Omega (life), Alpha Eta Rho, Omicron Delta Kappa. Methodist. Home: 2050 S Ridgewood Ave #L8 South Daytona FL 32119 Office: City of Port Orange Cmty Devel 1000 City Center Cir Port Orange FL 32119-4144

BROWN, VIRGIL JACKSON, minister; b. Argyle, Tex., May 28, 1944; s. Virgil Jackson and Essie Marie (Taylor) B.; m. Nancy Marie Hilton, Aug. 15, 1969; children: David, Stephanie, Philip. BS in Secondary Edn., U. N. Tex., 1971; MDiv, Southwestern Bapt. Sem., 1975, MA in Religious Edn., 1986. Ordained to ministry So. Bapt. Conv., 1972. Pastor Spring Creek Bapt. Ch., Weatherford, Tex., 1972-74, Center Point Bapt. Ch., Denton, Tex., 1974-76, 1st So. Bapt. Ch., Arkansas City, Kans., 1976-80, Martin Springs Bapt. Ch., Sulphur Springs, Tex., 1980-85, Garden Acres Bapt. Ch., Ft. Worth, 1985-88, 1st Bapt. Ch. Jacinto City, Houston, 1988—; chmn., Vietnamese Resettlement Com., Denton Bapt. Assn., 1975-76; mem. exec. bd. Kans./Nebr. Bapt. Conv., 1978-78; vice moderator Rehoboth Bapt. Assn., 1982-84. Chmn. bd. Helping Hands Jacinto City, 1990-91; mem. ch. ext. com. Union Assn., 1991-94; chaplain Tex. State Guard, 1992—; mem. Lay Renewal Ministry, Holland, Fed. Republic of Germany, 1994; vol. Mission to Belgium, 1995. Recipient Outstanding Contbn. award Progressive Farmer Mag., 1982. Office: 1st Bapt Ch Jacinto City 10701 Wiggins St Houston TX 77029-2515

BROWN, WADE EDWARD, lawyer; b. Blowing Rock, N.C., Nov. 5, 1907; s. Jefferson Davis and Etta Cornelia (Suddreth) B.; m. Euzelia Smart (dec.); children: Margaret Rose Johnson, Wade Edward, Sarah Baity. Student Mars Hill Coll., 1928; JD, Wake Forest U., 1931. Bar: N.C. 1930. Pvt. practice, Boone, N.C., 1931—; chmn. N.C. Bd. Paroles, Raleigh, 1967-72; cons. Atty. Gen., N.C. Dept. Justice, 1973; mem. N.C. Senate, 1947-49; mem. N.C. Ho. Reps., 1951-53; mayor Town of Boone, 1961-67; with student legal svcs., Appalachian State U. Chmn., Watauga County Hosp.; active Boone Merchants Assn.; mem. gen. bd. Bapt. State Conv. N.C.; trustee Wake Forest U., Appalachian State U., Bapt. Found. N.C. Bapt. State Conv.; founder Watanga County Pub. Libr., 1996—. Office: 221 W King St PO Box 1776 Boone NC 28607

BROWN, WALLACE LAMAR, design engineer; b. Banks, Ala., Sept. 21, 1926; s. William Lewis and Nancy Bama (HendersoN) B.; m. Bobby Jean Green, Mar. 24, 1950; children: Alan Lamar, Joy Lynn Brown Sanders. M in Engring. cum laude, U. Okla., 1963, U. Okla., 1964. Linesman United Telephone & Telegraph, Brundidge, Ala., 1947-50; commd. 2d lt. USAF, 1950, advanced through grades to maj., 1965, pilot, 1950-68, ret., 1968; chief engr. Metric Systems Corp., Ft. Walton Beach, Fla., 1969-80; pvt. practice Guntersville, Ala., 1980—. Author: The Endless Hours, 1961; contbr. articles to profl. jours.; patentee rapid assembly of munitions systems. With inf. Med. Corps, U.S. Army, 1944-46. Decorated Air medal, Air Force Commendation medal, Prisoner of War medal. Mem. Air Commando Assn., Ret. Officers Assn., Res. Officers Assn., Air Resupply and Communications Assn. Home: 5024 Neely Ave Guntersville AL 35976-8102

BROWN, WILLIAM A., lawyer; b. Memphis, Nov. 6, 1957; s. Winn D. Sr. and Annie Ruth (Hurt) B.; m. Mary Lee Walker, Dec. 27, 1980. BBA, U. Miss., 1978, JD, 1981. Bar: Miss. 1981, U.S. Dist. Ct. (no. and so. dists.) Miss. 1981, U.S. Dist. Ct. (we. dist.) Tenn. 1987. Ptnr., pres. Walker, Brown & Brown, P.A., Hernando, Miss., 1981—. Pres. DeSoto Literacy Coun., Hernando, 1988, Am. Cancer Soc., Hernando, 1988, DeSoto County Econ. Devel. Coun., 1995—; mem. Leadership 2000, 1990-91. James O. Eastland scholar, 1978-81. Mem. Miss. Bar Assn. (bd. dirs. young lawyers sect. 1988-89), DeSoto County Bar Assn. (v.p. 1988-89, pres. 1996-97), Rotary (pres. Hernando chpt. 1989-90), Boy Scouts Am., N.W. Miss. (membership chmn. 1990, activities chmn. 1991), Am. Arbitration Assn. Methodist. Home: PO Box 276 Hernando MS 38632-0276 Office: Walker Brown & Brown PA PO Box 276 Hernando MS 38632-0276

BROWN, WILLIAM ARTHUR, editor-in-chief; b. N.Y.C., Dec. 12, 1961; s. Malcom Nelson and Lucille Marian (Forbes) B. BA, Harvard U., 1992. Script writer The Paladin Group, L.A., 1981-83; advising editor Cool Beans Mag., San Francisco, 1983-87; founder, editor Dream Whip Publs., Lubbock, Tex., 1987—. Author: 10 Ways In (To) No Where, 1986, The Beanbag & Other Chairs, 1989, My Ride Up Your Canals, 1993. Vol. Lubbock Book Militia. Mem. Order of Elks and Cats (dean 1985-86, Most Favorable Dean 1985), UFO Adventure Tours. Office: Dream Whip Publs Internat PO Box 53832 Lubbock TX 79453

BROWN, WILLIAM LARRY, manufacturing engineer; b. Anderson, S.C., Mar. 1, 1941; s. John Fred and Ossie Irene (Thrasher) B.; m. Dianne Craig Marcom, June 26, 1941; children: Leah Denise, David Larry. AS, Jackson (Tenn.) State C.C., 1975; BS, Lambuth Coll., 1977; MS, West Tex. A&M U., 1986. Cable splicer Gen. Telephone of Fla., Tampa, 1962-63; aircraft mechanic Fairchild Hiller, St. Petersburg, Fla., 1963-67; ins. salesman Life Ins. of Ga., Tampa, 1967; munitions inspector Milan (Tenn.) Army Ammunition Plant, 1968; process engr. Owens-Corning, Jackson, 1969-78; product/mfg. engr. Owens-Corning, Amarillo, Tex., 1979—. With USAF, 1959-63. Home: 5905 Pelman Pl Amarillo TX 79109 Office: Owens-Corning 1701 Hollywood Rd Amarillo TX 79114

BROWN, WILLIS ELLSWORTH, JR., neurosurgeon, educator; b. Ann Arbor, Mich., Dec. 12, 1938; s. Willis Ellsworth and Dorothy Ethel (Anderson) B.; m. Elizabeth Ann Bliedung, Dec. 28, 1960; children: Willis Ellsworth III, Lisa Ann. BA cum laude, Vanderbilt U., 1960, MD, 1963. Diplomate Am. Bd. Neurol. Surgery. Surgical intern and resident Vanderbilt U., Nashville, 1963-65; clin. assoc. Nat. Cancer Inst., Bethesda, Md., 1965-68; neurosurg. resident U. Minn., Mnpls., 1968-73, instr. neurosurgery, 1973-74; asst. prof. U. Tex. Health Sci. Ctr., San Antonio, Tex., 1974-80, assoc. prof., 1980-89, prof., 1989—; cons. Wilford Hall USAF Med. Ctr., San Antonio, 1989—. Co-editor: Clinical Neurosurgery, 1982; author in field; contbr. articles to profl. jours. Pres. Alamo Hts. Rotary, San Antonio, 1985, St. Luke's Episc. Sch. Bd., San Antonio, 1980-81; v.p. bd. trustees Tex. Military Inst., San Antonio, 1981-83; sr. warden St. Luke's Epis. Ch., San Antonio, 1979. Lt. Commdr. USPHS, 1965-68. Fellow ACS; mem. Am. Assn. Neurol. Surgeons (membership chmn. 1987), Am. Acad. Neurol. Surgery, Neurol. Soc. Am. (membership chmn. 1992-93, sec. 1995-98), So. Neurosurg. Soc. (pres. 1989-90), Soc. U. Neurosurgeons (pres. 1987-88), Soc. Neurol. Surgeons. Episcopalian. Office: Neurosurgery U Tex Ctr 7703 Floyd Curl Dr San Antonio TX 78284-7843

BROWNE, HARRY, writer, investment advisor; b. N.Y.C., June 17, 1933; s. Edson Bradford and Cecil Margaret (Davis) B.; m. Gloria Frances Maxwell, June 9, 1953 (div. 1964); 1 child, Autumn Lee; m. Pamela Lanier Wolfe, Nov. 2, 1985. Grad. high sch., Van Nuys, Calif. Various sales and advt. positions L.A., 1956-67; investment advisor U.S., Can. and Switzerland, 1967—; cons. Permanent Portfolio Fund, Austin, Tex., 1982—. Author: How You Can Profit from the Coming Devaluation, 1970, How I Found Freedom in an Unfree World, 1973, You Can Profit From a Monetary Crisis, 1974, Harry Browne's Complete Guide to Swiss Banks, 1976, New Profits from the Monetary Crisis, 1978, Investment Rule #1, 1985, Why the Best-Laid Investment Plans Usually Go Wrong, 1987, The Economic Time Bomb, 1989, (with Terry Coxon) Inflation-Proofing Your Investments, 1981, Why Government Doesn't Work, 1995. Libertarian Part cand. for U.S. Pres., 1996. With U.S. Army, 1953-56. Office: PO Box 50829 Nashville TN 37205

BROWNELL, BLAINE ALLISON, university administrator, history educator; b. Birmingham, Ala., Nov. 12, 1942; s. Blaine Jr. and Annette (Holmes) B.; m. Mardi Ann Taylor, Aug. 21, 1964; children—Blaine, Allison. B.A., Washington & Lee U., 1965; M.A., U. N. C., 1967, Ph.D., 1969. Asst. prof. Purdue U., West Lafayette, Ind., 1969-74; assoc. prof., chmn. dept. U. Ala., Birmingham, 1974-78, prof., 1980-90, dean grad. sch., 1978-84, dean social and behavioral scis., 1984-90; provost, v.p. for acad. affairs U. North Tex., Denton, 1990—; sr. fellow Johns Hopkins U., Balt., 1971-72; Fulbright lectr. Hiroshima U., Japan, 1977-78; dir. U. Ala. Ctr. Internat. Programs, 1980-90. Author: The Urban Ethos...., 1975, City in Southern History, 1977, Urban America, 1979, 2d edit., 1990, The Urban Nation 1920-80, 1981; editor Jour. Urban History, 1976-90, assoc. editor, 1990-95. Mem. Birmingham City Planning Commn., 1975-77, Jefferson County Planning Commn., 1975-77, Dallas Com. Fgn. Rels., 1990—; chmn. Birmingham Coun. on Fgn. Rels., 1988-90. Mem. Am. Hist. Assn., Orgn. Am. Historians, So. Hist. Assn., Philos. Soc. Tex. Democrat. Presbyterian. Home: 2900 Santa Monica Dr Denton TX 76205-8518 Office: U North Tex Office of Provost and VP Acad Affairs PO Box 13707 Denton TX 76203-3707

BROWNING, MARY ANN PIZZA, reading specialist; b. Amityville, N.Y., Jan. 2, 1947; d. Leonard Joseph and Mary Lucille Pizza; m. Philip Y. Browning, Jr., July 26, 1969; children: Carol Ann, Jennifer, Michael, Lee Ann, Philip Y. III. BS in Social Sci./Edn., Molloy Coll., Rockville centre, N.Y., 1968; MEd in Reading Edn., U. Md., 1974; postgrad., Nova

Southweastern U., Ft. Lauderdale, Fla. Cert. elem. tchr., reading specialist, N.Y., Calif., Ga. Tchr. West Point (N.Y.) Elem. Sch., 1968-71, Coll. of Charleston Ext., Ft. Stewart, Ga., 1974-75; reading specialist/tchr. Ft. Stewart Dependent Sch., 1975-76; reading specialist Del Rey Woods Sch., Monterey, Calif., 1977-80; kindergarten tchr. Seoul (Korea) Am. Elem. Sch., 1982-83, reading specialist, 1989-91; adult edn. tchr. Monterey Peninsula Unified Dist., 1984-89; reading specialist Flat Rock Mid. Sch., Fayette County, Ga., 1991-92; reading specialist, remedial tchr. Huddleston Elem. Sch., Fayette County, 1992—; lectr. in field. Editor Army Cmty. Svc. newsletter, 1977-80. Mem. Child Devel. Bd., Ft. Ord, Calif., 1983-89; pub. rels. chmn. ARC, Ft. Ord, 1985-89, Girl Scouts U.S., Ft. Ord, 1984-89; bldg. rep. United Way Campaign, Fayette County, Ga., 1995-96; mem. PTO, Sandy Creek H.S. Mem. ASCD, Internat. Reading Assn. (mem. Ga. coun. 1991—), Profl. Assn. Ga. Educators, USMA West Point Parents' Club. Roman Catholic. Office: Huddleston Elementary School 200 McIntosh Trail Peachtree City GA 30269

BROWNING, PETER CRANE, packaging company executive; b. Boston, Sept. 2, 1941; s. Ralph Leslie and Nancy (Crane) B.; m. Carole Ann Shegog, Dec. 14, 1963 (div. 1974); children: Christina, Jennifer; m. Kathryn Ann Klucharich, July 27, 1974; children: Kimberly, Peter. AB in History, Colgate U., 1963; MBA, U. Chgo., 1976. Salesman, mktg. mgr. White Cap div. Continental Can, Northbrook, Ill., 1964-75; mgr. mktg. Conally Venture div. Continental Can, 1975-79; gen. mktg. and sales mgr. Bondware div. Continental Can, 1979-81, v.p., gen. mgr., 1981-84; v.p. gen. mgr. White Cap. div. Continental Can, 1984-86, exec. v.p., oper. officer, 1987-89; pres., CEO Gold Bond Bldg. Products div. Nat. Gypsum Co., Charlotte, N.C., 1989-90, Nat. Gypsum Co., Dallas, 1990—, Aancor Holdings Inc., Dallas, 1990—; chmn. bd. dirs., CEO Nat. Gypsum Co. parent co. Aancor Holdings, Inc., 1991-93; exec. v.p. Sonoco Products Co., Hartsville, S.C., 1993-96, pres., COO, 1996—, also bd. dirs.; bd. dirs. Phoenix Home Life Mut. Ins. Co., Loctite Corp., First Union Nat. Bank S.C., Pelican Cos. Mem. bd. visitors McColl Sch. Bus./Queens Coll., Davidson Coll.; mem. coun. on Grad. Sch./U. Chgo.; mem. exec. bd. Pee Dee Area coun. Boy Scouts Am.; trustee Presbyn. Hosp. Found. Mem. NAM (exec. com., bd. dirs.), Conf. Bd., Quail Hollow Country Club. Republican. Episcopalian. Home: 1400 W Carolina Ave Hartsville SC 29550-4902 Office: Sonoco Products Co 1 N 2nd St Hartsville SC 29550-3300

BROWNLEY, MARTINE WATSON, English language educator; b. Spartanburg, S.C., July 27, 1947; d. Floyd Irving Brownley and Martine Newlin Watson. BA, Agnes Scott Coll., 1969; MA, Harvard U., 1971, PhD, 1975. From asst. prof. to assoc. prof. Emory U., Atlanta, 1975-86, prof., 1986—; dir. Brit. studies program, Emory U., Atlanta, 1988, 90, dir. grad. studies, 1988, 91, assoc. chair English dept., 1989-91, dir. women's studies, 1992-96. Author: Clarendon and the Rhetoric of Historical Form, 1985; editor: Mothering the Mind, 1984, Two Dialogues...by Clarendon, 1984. Grad. fellow Harvard U., 1970-75, Am. Soc. for Eighteenth Century Studies fellow William Andrews Clark Libr., 1985, fellow Am. Philos. Soc., 1987, univ. tchr. fellow NEH, 1988-89. Office: Emory U Dept English Atlanta GA 30322

BROWN-WYNN, KATHY ALLISON, process control engineer, database administrator; b. Springfield, Mass., June 16, 1961; d. Gordon Seymour and Yvonne (Boylton) B.; m. James Earl Wynn, Jr., Dec. 20, 1987; children: Kharim Asha, James Earl III. AS, Springfield Tech. C.C., 1981, BS in Mgmt. Info. Systems, 1984; postgrad., Am. Internat. Coll., 1994—. Systems mgr. Springfield (Mass.) Sch. Dept., 1985-87; programmer II Dow Jones and Co., Inc., Chicopee, Mass., 1987-89; database adminstr., process control engr. City of Fort Lauderdale (Fla.) Utilities, 1989—. Mem. NAFE. Home: 18144 SW 28th St Miramar FL 33029-5153 Office: Fort Lauderdale Utilities 949 NW 38th St Fort Lauderdale FL 33309-5920

BROYLES, BONITA EILEEN, nursing educator; b. Ross County, Ohio, Sept. 29, 1948; d. Arthur Runnels and Mary Elizabeth (Page) Brookie; m. Roger F. Broyles, Dec. 29, 1984; children: Michael Richard Brown, Jeffrey Allen Brown. BSN, Ohio State U., 1970; MA with honors, N.C. Cen. U., Durham, 1988; EdD summa cum laude, LaSalle U., 1996. ADN instr., CPR instr. Piedmont C.C., Roxboro, N.C.; instr. nursing Watts Sch. Nursing, Durham; res. float staff nurse Durham County Gen. Hosp., Durham; dir. practical nursing edn., instr. Piedmont C.C., Roxboro, N.C.; maternity patient tchr. Mt. Carmel Med. Ctr., Columbus, Ohio; vice chmn. assoc. degree nursing faculty Piedmont Community Coll., 1990—. Contbr. articles to profl. jours. Named ADN Educator of Yr. N.C. Assoc. Degree Nursing Coun., 1993. Office: Piedmont CC Sch Nursing College St Roxboro NC 27573

BROYLES, J(OHN) ALLEN, clergyman; b. Johnson City, Tenn., Jan. 13, 1934; s. Joseph Warren and Edith Verna (Allen) B.; m. Dolores Anne Pettit, June 2, 1956; 1 child, Marianne Aweagon. BA, U. of Redlands, 1956; STB, Boston U., 1959, PhD, 1964. Ordained elder Meth. Ch., 1964. Pastor 1st Meth. Ch., Boothbay Harbor, Maine, 1962-65, Orono (Maine) Meth. Ch., 1965-68, Crawford Meml. United Meth. Ch., Winchester, Mass., 1968-70; chmn. dept. religion Oklahoma City U., 1970-72; pastor Lexington (Mass.) United Meth. Ch., 1972-77; exec. dir. United Meth. Neighborhood Ctrs., Memphis, 1977-79; pastor Fountain Ave. United Meth. Ch., Paducah, Ky., 1979-81; chaplain U. Tenn. Med. Units, Memphis, 1981-84; pastor Union Ave. United Meth. Ch., Memphis, 1984-88, Wesleyan Hills United Meth. Ch., Memphis, 1988—; mem. instl. rev. com., ethical adv. com. Meth. Hosp., Memphis, 1988—; dist. dir. Ch. and Soc., 1988—. Author: The John Birch Society, 1964, paperback edit., 1966; contbr. articles to social issues publs. Chair Gov.'s Task Force on Intergovtl. Welfare, 1966-68; pres. Lexington Ministers Assn., 1975-76, Paducah Ministers Assn., 1980-81, Memphis Ministers Assn., 1994-95; elder Meth. Ch., 1964—. Mem. Soc. Christian Ethics, Leadership Memphis. Home: 515 Melody Ln Memphis TN 38120-2457 Office: Wesleyan Hills United Meth Ch 390 S Yates Rd Memphis TN 38120-2432

BROYLES, ROBERT HERMAN, biochemistry and molecular biology educator; b. Kingsport, Tenn., Feb. 16, 1943; s. Herman Harrison and Nancy (Larkin) Broyles; m. J. Dianne Fields, Sept. 3, 1966; children: David C., James R. BS in Chemistry, Wake Forest Coll., 1965; postgrad., Marine Biolog. Lab., Mass., 1969; PhD in Biochemistry, Wake Forest U., 1970; postdoctoral studies, Fla. State U., 1970-72. Rsch. asst. dept. biology Bowman Gray Sch. Medicine, Winston-Salem, N.C., 1966; rsch. assoc. dept. chemistry Fla. State U., Tallahassee, 1970-72; asst. prof. dept. zoology U. Wis.-Milw., 1972-77; assoc. prof. dental biochemistry U. Okla. Health Scis. Ctr., 1977—, prof. biochemistry and molecular biology, 1985—; mem. Ctr. for Gt. Lakes Studies, U. Wis.-Milw., 1975-77; assoc. prof. dept. biochemistry and molecular biology U. Okla. Health Scis. Ctr., 1977-85; adj. prof. dept. pediatrics U. Okla. Coll. Medicine, 1988—, asst. dir. MD/PhD program, 1991—; sr. scientist divsn. kidney, urol. and hematol. diseases and lab. of chem. biology NIH, 1989, 90; invited participant workshop NSF, 1973, confs., NIH, 1978, 80, 82, 84, 86, 88, 90, 92, 94; lectr. Marine Biol. Lab., 1983; vis. sr. scientist NIH, 1989-91; mentor numerous rsch. students; mem. numerous univ. and profl. coms.; presenter in field. Contbr. numerous articles to profl. jours. Hon. scholar Wake Forest Coll., 1961-63; Title IV Predoctoral fellow NDEA, 1965-68; Wilder fellow Bowman Gray Sch. Medicine, 1968-70, postdoctoral fellow NIH, 1970-72; recipient numerous research grants. Mem. AAAS, Am. Soc. Cell Biology, Am. Soc. Biolog. Chemists, Am. Soc. Hematology, Am. Soc. Zoologists, N.Y. Acad. Scis., Soc. Devel. Biologists, Sigma Xi (chpt. pres.-elect 1988-89, 91-92, pres. 1992-93). Unitarian. Office: U Okla Health Scis Ctr Dept Biochemistry/Molecular Biology 940 Stanton L Young Blvd Rm 853 Oklahoma City OK 73104-5042

BROYLES, RUTH RUTLEDGE, principal; b. Sullivan County, Tenn., July 15, 1912; d. Floyd Lylburn and Ethel Sally (Gross) Rutledge; m. David Lafayette Broyles, Aug. 15, 1937 (dec. Oct. 1980); children: Nancy Ann Broyles McCracken, Edwin Joseph, Dava Lee Broyles Russell. BS, East Tenn. State U., 1934, MA, 1968. Cert. English and biology tchr., Tenn., elem. edn. supr., supt. cert. Tchr. English Jonesborough (Tenn.) High Sch., 1934-38; tchr. 3d and 4th grades Telford (Tenn.) Elem. Sch., 1956-57; tchr. 3d grade Midway Elem. Sch., Jonesborough, 1957-62; tchr. 5th grade Jonesborough Elem. Sch., 1962-67; supr. tchr. corp. program East Tenn. State U., Johnson City, 1967-69; prin. Cherokee Elem. Sch., Johnson City, 1969-78, ret., 1978. County commr. Washington County Ct., 1980-90; chairperson Jonesborough Civic Trust, 1982-85, Watauga Regional Libr. Bd., Washington County, 1982-87, Washington County/Jonesborough Mus., Jonesborough, 1984—, Tenn. Homecoming 1986, 1985-86; mem. Washington County Libr. Bd., 1991—; mem. fin. com. Washington County Bd. Edn., 1991—; historian Washington County, 1991—; elder, Sunday sch. tchr., chair Christian edn. com. Jonesborough (Tenn.) Presbyn. Ch., 1989-91; moderator Presbyn. Women, chair adminstrv. com. Holston Presbytery, Kingsport, Tenn.; historian Synod of Living Waters Presbyn. Women, Brentwood, Tenn.; mem. Synod of Living Waters Ministry Divsn., Brentwood; mem. ch. coun. Tusculum Coll., Greenville, Tenn.; mem. Bicentennial com. for Washington County State of Tenn., 1993—. Named Woman of the Yr., Bus. and Profl. Women , Jonesborough, Tenn. 1975, Hon. Col., State of Tenn., 1989; Ruth Rutledge Broyles Scholarship Fund for tng. tchrs. named in her honor, 1994. Mem. Tenn. Ret. Tchrs. (state pres. 1985-86, Nashville 1978—, legis. asst. East Tenn. 1991—, Plaque 1985-86), N.E. Tenn. Tourism Coun. (chair, Silver Tray 1989, Outstanding Svc. award 1993), Tenn. Congress Parents and Tchrs. (v.p. Nashville 1948-69), Tenn. Libr. Assn. (trustee Nashville 1984-85), Washington County Ret. Tchrs. (life, chmn. scholarship com. 1991—), Tenn. Ret. Tchrs. Assn., Washington County Hist. Soc. (pres. 1994—). Presbyterian. Home: 241 Brethern Church Dr Jonesborough TN 37659

BROYLES, WAYMON CARROLL, health facility administrator, educator; b. Sparta, Tenn., Nov. 21, 1943; s. Waymon Eurrell and Virgie Mae (Howard) B.; m. Patricia Ann Hutchings, Mar. 20, 1966; 1 child, Angela Renée. BS, Tenn. Tech. U., 1966, MBA, 1978. Cert. in mental health Assn. Mental Health Adminstrs. Acct. Thomas Industries, Sparta, 1968-69; dir. adminstrv. svcs. Plateau Mental Health Ctr., Cookeville, Tenn., 1969—; mem. adj. staff Tenn. Tech. U. Sch. Bus., Cookeville, 1989-91. Vol. United Way, 1990, 91. 1st lt. U.S. Army, 1966-68. Mem. Tenn. Assn. Mental Health Adminstrs. (pres. 1975-76), Assn. Mental Health Adminstrs. (pres. 1990, past-pres. 1991, bd. govs. 1984-89). Baptist. Office: Plateau Mental Health Ctr Burgess Falls Rd And W Cookeville TN 38502

BROZOVSKY, JOHN A., accounting educator; b. Spokane, Wash., Apr. 30, 1951; s. Victor Jerald and Orise (Watson) B.; m. Sue Ellen King, Apr. 14, 1984; 1 child, Joseph Victor. AAS, Spokane C.C., 1971; BBA, U. Tex., 1975, M in Profl. Acctg., 1978; PhD in Bus. Adminstrn., U. Colo., 1990. CPA, Tex.; cert. data processor; cert. computer programmer. Computer programmer U. Tex., Austin, 1974-77; computer programmer II Tex. State Health Dept., Austin, 1978-80; EDP auditor City of Austin, 1980-81; sr. internal auditor Enserch Corp., Dallas, 1981-83; lectr. Calif. State U., Fresno, 1983-86; rsch. and teaching asst U. Colo., Boulder, 1986-89; asst. prof. Va. Tech., Blacksburg, 1989-96, assoc. prof., 1996—; presenter in field. Contbr. articles to profl. jours. Am. Accctg. Assn. fellow, 1986, Gerald Hart fellow, 1987; grantee Calif. CPA Found., 1986-89, AICPA, 1988, Pamplin, 1992. Mem. Am. Acctg. Assn., Am. Econ. Assn., Am. Tax Assn., Nat. Tax Assn., Inst. Mgmt. Accts. (coach nat. championship team student case competition 1995, nat. finalists 1996). Home: 9000 Newport Rd Catawba VA 24070 Office: Va Tech Pamplin # 3007 Blacksburg VA 24061

BRUBAKER, BERYL MAE HARTZLER, administrator, educator; b. Belleville, Pa., May 13, 1942; d. C. Clayton and Mamie Kathryn (Kauffman) Hartzler; m. J. Mark Brubaker, May 20, 1967; children: Heather Carmel, Patricia Ann. BS, Case Western Res. U., 1967; MS, U. Pa., 1969; DSc in Nursing, U. Ala., Birmingham, 1984. Staff nurse Lewistown Hosp., Lewistown, Pa., 1964-65, 67; instr. U. Pa., Phila., 1969-70; prof. Ea. Mennonite U., Harrisonburg, Va., 1970-94, v.p. enrollment mgmt., 1994—; accreditation visitor Nat. League for Nursing, N.Y.C., 1986-89. Co-author: A Life of Wholeness, 1993; editor: Bioethics and the Beginning of Life, 1990; contbr. articles to profl. jours. Bd. dirs. Mennonite Mut. Aid, Goshen, Ind., 1985—; Harrisonburg-Rockingham County Free Health Clinic, 1990—. Recipient Isabel McIsaac award Nurses' Ednl. Funds, N.Y., 1980. Mem. ANA, Va Nurses Assn., Mennonite Nurses Assn., Sigma Theta Tau, Pi Lambda Theta, Phi Delta Kappa. Home: 965 Broadview Dr Harrisonburg VA 22801-4956 Office: Ea Mennonite U 1200 Park Rd Harrisonburg VA 22801-2404

BRUCE, RICKIE JOSEPH, secondary school educator, gifted and talented educator; b. Houma, La., Aug. 30, 1951. BA, Nicholls State U., Thibodaux, La., 1974; MA, U. Southwestern La., 1980; postgrad., La. State U., Baton Rouge. Cert. in English, math., academically gifted. Tchr. English and math. South Lafourche High Sch., Lafourche Parish Sch. Bd., Thibodaux, 1977-80; writer-in-residence Ouachita Parish Sch. Bd., Monroe, La., 1983; writer-in-schs. St. Charles Parish Pub. Schs., Luling, La., 1980-83; tchr. English and fine arts Destrehan High Sch., St. Charles Parish Pub. Schs., Luling, 1983—; tchr. on spl. assignment St. Charles Parish Pub. Schs., Luling, 1994—; co-dir. nat. writing project La. State U. Summer Inst., St. Charles Parish, 1990-94; tchr. cons. writing project Outcome Based edn.; instr.-in-residence Southeastern La. U., 1995-96; mem. writing com. La. English/Lang. Arts Stds. and Benchmarks, 1995-96. Contbr. poetry and short stories to lit. mags. Recipient Outstanding Tchr. award Am. Petroleum Inst., 1990, Disting. Teaching award La. Scholars' Coll., 1992, Excellence in Edn. award New Orleans and River Region Chamber and Cox Comms., 1994-95. Mem. Am. Fedn. Tchrs., Nat. Coun. Tchrs. English (La. state judge program to recognize excellence in student lit. mags.), La. Reading Assn., La. Fedn. Tchrs. Home: 205 River Oaks Dr Apt A Destrehan LA 70047-3510

BRUCE, SAMUEL BYRD, management consultant; b. Rome, Ga., Sept. 30, 1949; s. Milburn Homer Jr. and Dess Mae (Baldwin) B.; m. Virginia Christine Roberts, Sept. 26, 1970; children: Scott Samuel Woodruff, Tanya Christine. BS with honors, U. So. Miss., 1976; M in Mass. Comm., U. S.C., 1980. Registered broker securities, ins. and mortgages. Commd. 2d lt. U.S. Army, 1970, advanced through grades to maj., 1981, ret., 1989; pub. affairs cons. Sec. of Army; media spokesman Dept. Army, Washington, 1981-84; chief of staff, co-chmn. bus. and edn. task force State Dept. Edn., 1990-91; sr. cons., sr. dir., pres. Sam Bruce Internat., Lexington, S.C.; mem. Sr. Communicators Workshop, Washington; cons. Dept. of Def.; lectr. Fed. Emergency Mgmt. Agy. Inst., U. London; liaison mem. Columbia Organizing Com., 1993—; spokesman Air Fla. Crash/Recovery operation Dept. of Def., Washington, 1983; speaker, workshop leader dist. II conf. Internat. Assn. Bus. Communicators; contracting officers tech. rep. Army Standard Info. Mgmt. System. Mem. S.C. Rep. Party, 1988—, S.C. Policy Coun., 1993—; vice chrmn. Lexington Co. GOP 1995—; pres. Hollow Creek Precinct, Lexington County, 1991-93; pres 1994-95, v.p., sec. we. conf. Luth. Men, 1993—, treas., 1991-92; coun. mem. Lake Murray-Shore Rd. Community Assn., 1990-92, St. Pauls Luth. Ch., 1990-93; mem. econ. devel. task force Lexington County Planning for Future, 1992—; mem. World Cup Ski Patrol, Lauterbrunnen, Switzerland, 1984, 85; dir. Great Gribble Getaway, 1985—; divsn. advisor Nat. Ski Patrol, 1972—; mem. com. 100 Luth. Men in Mission, 1989—, Ctrl. Midlands Econ. Alliance, 1990—; participant Campbell Cup, S.C., 1992, 93; candidate S.C. State Senate, 1992. Recipient Silver Merit Star award Nat. Ski Patrol System, 1984, U.S. Meritorious Svc. medal (3), U.S. Humanitarian Svc. medal. Mem. Lexington Bus. Assn., U. S.C. Alumni Assn., Am. Legion, Nat. Eagle Scout Assn. (life), Greater Columbia C. of C. (innovation task force 1989—), Lexington C. of C., First Tuesday Club, Univ. Club (Columbia), Order of DeMolay (life), Alpha Phi Omega (life). Republican. Lutheran. Office: PO Box 502 Lexington SC 29071-0502

BRUCE-JUHLKE, DEBBIE, nursing consultant, social worker; b. Hughes Springs, Tex., Oct. 24, 1954; d. Norman L. and Arthur L. Bruce; m. Timothy Juhlke; children: Shay'La, Arthur II, Jonathan. AS, Tyler (Tex.) Jr. Coll., 1975; nursing diploma, Tex. Ea. Sch. Nursing, 1976; BS, Am. Tech. U., 1987. Emergency rm. nurse Mother Frances Hosp., Tyler, 1976-81; pub. health nurse Tyler (Tex.) Smith County Health Dept., 1981-84; nurse Girling Home Health, Temple, Tex., 1986-89; adult protective svcs. specialist Tex. Dept. Protective & Regulatory Svcs., Belton, 1988-94; dir. Am. Nat. Home Health, Killeen, Tex., 1994—; nursing dir. Advantage Adult Day Care and Health Svcs., Inc., Harker Heights, Tex., 1995—. Home: 1402 Wild Vine Cove Round Rock TX 78664

BRUCKER, JANET MARY, nurse; b. London, May 26, 1946; came to U.S., 1953; d. George Edward and Elsie Maud (Sharp) Blain; m. Dennis Jack Brucker, July 8, 1967 (div. 1978); children: Stephen Jack (dec.), Denise Michelle. Diploma in nursing, M.B. Johnson Sch. Nursing, 1967; student, San Jacinto Coll., 1979-82; BSN, U. Tex., Houston, 1984; MS in Nursing Adminstrn., Tex. Woman's U., 1988. RN, Tex.; cert. neuroscience nurse. Staff nurse pediatrics Mount Sinai Hosp., Cleve., 1967-71; staff nurse Rainbow Babies and Children's Hosp., Cleve., 1971-73; night charge nurse pediatrics Clear Lake (Tex.) Hosp., 1973; head nurse Bay Area Pediatric Assocs., Clear Lake City, 1973-78; staff nurse, night charge nurse pediatric intensive care Tex. Children's Hosp., Houston, 1978, unit tchr., pediatric intensive care, 1978-79, charge nurse Jr. League Clinic, 1979-80, asst. nurse mgr. pediatric neurosurgery/neurology, 1980-86, staff devel. coord., 1986-90, asst. dir. nursing, 1990—; clin. instr. pediatrics Houston Bapt. U., 1988—, U. Tex. Health Sci. Ctr. Sch. Nursing, Houston, 1988—; speaker in field. Contbr. numerous articles to profl. jours. Mem. NAFE, Am. Assn. Neurosci. Nurses (chmn. social activities S.E. Tex. chpt. 1985, membership chmn. 1984), Continuing Edn. League, Health Meeting Planners Houston, Soc. Pediatric Nurses (nat. bd. mem. 1993-95, v.p. 1995-97), Am. Assn. Neurol. Surgeons (assoc.), Epilepsy Assn. (sec., profl. adv. bd., 1995-97), Sigma Theta Tau (pres. Eta Phi chpt. 1992-94). Episcopalian. Home: 2326 Swift Blvd Houston TX 77030 Office: Tex Children's Hosp 6621 Fannin St Houston TX 77030-2303

BRUESS, CLINT E., academic administrator; b. Duluth, Minn., Sept. 7, 1941; s. Ray W. and Gladys (Lawrence) B.; m. Susan Jo Laing, Aug. 16, 1981. BS, Macalester Coll., 1963; MA, U. Md., 1965; EdD, Temple U., 1968. Cert. health edn. specialist. Assoc. prof. health edn. West Chester (Pa.) State U., 1968-70; chair dept. health sci. Towson (Md.) State U., 1970-78; dir. sch. health edn. project Nat. Ctr. for Health Edn., San Francisco, 1978-81; chair dept. health edn. and phys. edn. U. Ala., Birmingham, 1981-87, dean Sch. Edn., 1987—. Co-author: Sexuality Education: Theory and Practice, 1981, 3d edit., 1994, Healthy Decisions, 1994, Decisions for Health, 1985, 4th edit. 1995, Sexuality: Insights and Issues, 1986, 3d edit., 1993. V.p. personnel Exch. Club Ctr. for Prevention of Child Abuse, Birmingham, 1995—; bd. dirs. Birmingham Exch. Club, 1994—, Leadership Birmingham, 1995-96. Fellow Am. Sch. Health Assn. (disting. svc. award 1987); mem. Assn. for Advancement of Health Edn. (profl. svc. award 1988), Soc. Pub. Health Educators, Am. Assn. Higher Edn., Health Educator's Assn. Ala. (named health educator of yr. 1987), Eta Sigma Gamma. Office: Sch Edn UAB Station Birmingham AL 35294

BRUFF, BEVERLY OLIVE, public relations consultant; b. San Antonio, Dec. 15, 1926; d. Albert Griffith and Hazel Olive (Smith) B. BA, Tulane U., 1948; postgrad. Our Lady of Lake Coll., 1956, Okla. Center for Continuing Edn., 1960-70. Asst. dir. New Orleans Theatre Guild, 1948-50; dist. dir. San Antonio Area coun. Girl Scouts Am., 1958-70, public rels. dir., 1970-83; free-lance pub. rels., 1983—; mem. Coun. of Pres., v.p., 1981-82, 84—; mem. Coun. of Internat. Rels. Zoning commr. Hill Country Village, Tex., 1973-76, 83-85, 88—; councilwoman Hill Country Village, 1985-88; bd. dirs. Animal Def. League, Camp Fire, Inc. Mem. Pub. Rels. Soc. Am., Tex. Pub. Rels. Assn. (Silver Spur award), Women in Communications (historian 1969-70, v.p. 1970-71, treas. 1971-73), Tex. Press Women (recipient state writing contest awards 1971, 72, 73, 74, mem. exec. bd. dirs. 1970-71, 73-74, dist. treas. 1972-73, dist. v.p. 1973), Nat. Fedn. Press Women, Internat. Assn. Bus. Communicators, Speech Arts of San Antonio (pres. 1964-66, 70-72, 84—, dir. 1964-72, 88—, chmn. bd. dirs. 1966-69), Am. Women in Radio and TV (dir. chpt. 1974, sec. 1975, pres. 1979-80), San Antonio Soc. Fund Raising Execs., Assn. Girl Scout Exec. Staff. (exec. bd. 1963-72, nat. bd. 1972-74). Home: 508 Tomahawk Trl San Antonio TX 78232-3620

BRUMBACK, ROGER ALAN, neuropathologist, researcher; b. Washington, Feb. 15, 1948; s. Oscar Benjamin and Frances Elaine (Neufeld) B.; m. Mary Helen Skinner, Apr. 26, 1969; children: Darryl Wyatt, Audrey Christine, Owen Eliot. BS, Pa. State U., 1967; MD, Pa. State U., Hershey, 1971. Diplomate Nat. Bd. Med. Examiners, Am. Bd. Pediatrics, Am. Bd. Psychiatry and Neurology, Am. Bd. Pathology; cert. clin. electroencephalography. Pediatric intern Johns Hopkins Hosp., Balt., 1971-72, pediatric asst. resident, 1972-73; fellow in pediatrics Johns Hopkins U. Sch. Medicine, Balt., 1971-73; asst. resident neurology Barnes Hosp., St. Louis, 1973-74; fellow in pediatric neurology Washington U., St. Louis Children's Hosp., 1973-75; clin. assoc. neurology and exptl. neuropathology med. neurology br. Nat. Inst. Neurol. and Communicative Disorders and Stroke, Nat. Insts. of Health, Bethesda, Md., 1975-77; clin. instr. neurology and pediatrics U. Pitts., 1977-78; asst. prof. neurology U. N.D., Fargo, 1978-79, asst. prof. pediatrics, 1978-82, assoc. prof. neurology, 1980-82; resident/fellow anatomic pathology and neuropathology svcs. Strong Meml. Hosp., U. Rochester (N.Y.), 1982-86; assoc. prof. pathology U. Okla., Oklahoma City, 1986-89, prof. pathology, 1989—, chief neuropathology sect. Health Scis. Ctr., 1987—; chief neurology svc. V.A. Med. Ctr., Fargo, 1978-82; dir. Muscular Dystrophy Assn. Clinic, Fargo, 1978-82, co-dir., Oklahoma City, 1988-91; adj. assoc. prof. pediatrics U. Okla., 1986-90, adj. assoc. prof. psychiatry and behavioral scis., 1986-91, adj. prof. pediatrics, 1990—, adj. prof. psychiatry and behavioral sci., 1991—, adj. prof. neurology 1991—; clin. care cons. dermatology br. Nat. Cancer Inst., 1987—. Author: (with W.H. Olson, G. Gascon, L.A. Christoferson) Practical Neurology for the Primary Care Physician, 1981, (with J.W. Gerst) The Neuromuscular Junction, 1984, (with R.W. Leech) Color Atlas of Muscle Histochemistry, 1984, (with R.M. Herndon) The Cerebrospinal Fluid, 1989, (with M.H. Brumback) The Dietary Fiber Weight Control Handbook, 1989, (with R.W. Leech) Hydrocephalus: Current Clinical Concepts, 1991, Neurology and Clinical Neuroscience, 1993, (with W.H. Olson, G. Gascon, V. Iyer) Handbook of Symptom-Oriented Neurology, 2nd edit., 1994, (with R.W. Leech) Neuropathology and Basic Neuroscience, 1995; chief editor Jour. Child Neurology, 1986—; mem. editorial bd. Jour. Geriatric Psychiatry and Neurology, 1990—, Biomed. Rsch. India, 1990—, Neuropsychiatry, Neuropsychology and Behavioral Neurology, 1994—. With USPHS, 1975-77. Mem. Am. Acad. Neurology, Am. Assn. Electrodiagnostic Medicine, Am. Assn. Neuropathologists, Am. Neurol. Assn., Child Neurology Soc., Coun. Biology Editors, Internat. Child Neurology Assn., Soc. for Exptl. Neuropathology (sec.-treas. 1988-93, pres. 1995—), Behavioral Neurology Soc. (councillor 1990-91, sec.-treas. 1991-93, pres. 1993-95). Republican. Lutheran. Home: 4014 Hidden Hill Rd Norman OK 73072-3013 Office: Okla U Health Sci Ctr Dept Pathology BMSB Rm 451 940 S L Young Blvd PO Box 26901 Oklahoma City OK 73190

BRUMBACK PATTERSON, CATHY JEAN, psychologist; b. Birmingham, Ala., Oct. 15, 1953; d. Roy Clifton and Violet Lorraine (Wesley) Brumback; m. Louis Loomis Patterson, June 10, 1987; children: Catherine Elizabeth Patterson, Allyson Brumback Patterson. BA, U. Ala., Tuscaloosa, 1975; MA, U. Ala., Birmingham, 1977; EdS, Ga. State U., 1985, PhD, 1986. Diplomate Am. Bd. Profl. Psychology, Am. Bd. Forensic Examiners; lic. psychologist; cert. sch. psychologist. Tchr. Jefferson County Bd. Edn., Birmingham, 1975-76, Birmingham (Ala.) Bd. Edn., 1976-77, Baldwin County Bd. Edn., Bay Minette, Ala., 1977-79; psychometrist Regional Edn. Svc. Ctr., Bartlesville, Okla., 1979-81, Union Pub. Schs., Tulsa, 1981-82, Forsyth County Schs., 1982-84; sch. psychologist Atlanta (Ga.) Pub. Schs., 1984-87; pvt. practice psychologist Northport, Ala., 1987-94, Fairhope, Ala., 1994—; grad. rsch. asst. Ga. State U., Atlanta, 1982, 85, instr., 1986; instr. U. Ala., Tuscaloosa, 1988-90. Named Mrs. Ala., Mrs. Am. Assn., 1979, Outstanding Young Women of Am., 1982, 87, 89; recipient Outstanding Doctoral Student award Ga. Assn. Sch. Psychologists, 1987. Fellow Am. Acad. Sch. Psychology; mem. AAUW, APA, Ala. Psychol. Assn., Nat. Regiter Health Svc. Providers, Montrose Garden Club, Bayside Acad. Parents Orgn. , Rock Creek Country Club, Rotary, Phi Delta Kappa, Kappa Delta Pi. Home: PO Box 687 Montrose AL 36559-0687 Office: 22787 Highway 98 Bldg A Fairhope AL 36532-3339

BRUMELLE, KENNETH COY, retail store owner; b. Odessa, Tex., Mar. 18, 1945; s. Clarence Lee and Leota (Jones) B.; m. Sharon Jean Suther, Dec. 21, 1967; 1 child Jenni Rebecca. AS, Odessa Coll., 1966; BBA, Tex. Tech U., 1968. Buyer trainee Sanger Harris, Dallas, 1969-71, buyer, 1971-73; buyer White House Dept. Stores, Beaumont, Tex., 1973-74; mdse. mgr. White House Dept. Stores, Beaumont, 1974-77; owner Outlaw Jean Store, Odessa, Tex., 1977—. Bd. dirs. Better Bus. Bur., 1991—. With U.S. Army, 1968-69, Tex. N.G., 1969-74. Mem. Nat. Fedn. Ind. Bus., Tex. Retail Mchts. Assn. (bd. dirs. 1987—), Tex. Retail Assn. (state chmn. membership com. 1991—), Odessa C. of C., Optimist (v.p. Odessa club), Masons. Republican. Methodist. Home: 1809 E 52nd St Odessa TX 79762-4547 Office: Outlaw Jean Store 4101 E 42d Bldg E-31 Odessa TX 79762

BRUMFIELD, WILLIAM CRAFT, Slavic studies educator; b. Charlotte, N.C., June 28, 1944; s. Lewis F. and Pauline Elizabeth (Craft) B. BA, Tulane U., 1966; PhD in Slavic langs., U. Calif., Berkeley, 1973. Vis. lectr. U. Wis., Madison, 1973-74; asst. prof. Harvard U., Cambridge, Mass., 1974-80; assoc. prof. Tulane U., New Orleans, 1984-91, prof. Slavic langs., 1992—; resident dir. Am. Coun. Tchrs. of Russian Pushkin Inst. Program, Moscow, 1979-80; co-dir. Summer Inst. for Coll. Faculty, NEH, 1994; lectr. on architecture, photography and lit. at museums and univs throughout U.S. and Europe. Author: Gold in Azure: One Thousand Years of Russian Architecture, 1983, The Origins of Modernism in Russian Architecture, 1991, A History of Russian Architecture, 1993, An Architectural Survey of St. Petersburg: 1840-1916, 1994, Lost Russia: Photographing the Ruins of Russian Architecture, 1995; editor, contbr.: Reshaping Russian Architecture: Western Technology, Utopian Dreams, 1990, Christianity and the Arts in Russia, 1991, Russian Housing in the Modern Age: Design and Social History, 1993; contbr. articles to profl. jours.; represented in permanent collections at Photographic Archives, Nat. Gallery Art, Washington. Woodrow Wilson fellow, 1966, NEH fellow Nat. Humanities Ctr., 1992-93; sr. exch. scholar Internat. Rsch. Exchs. Bd./Am. Coun. Learned Socs. U.S.-USSR Exch., Moscow, 1983-84, rsch. scholar Kennan Inst., Washington, 1989. Mem. Am. Assn. Advancement Slavic Studies, Soc. Archtl. Historians, Inst. Modern Russian Culture (head photography sect.), Am. Coun. Tchrs. of Russian, Soc. of Historians of East European and Russian Art and Architecture. Office: Tulane U Slavic Dept New Orleans LA 70118

BRUMGARDT, JOHN RAYMOND, museum administrator; b. Riverside, Calif., Feb. 3, 1946; s. Reuben R. and Grace (Taylor) B.; m. Doris Ann Tarasko, Dec. 20, 1969; children—Jennifer, Thomas. B.A. in History, U. Calif.-Riverside, 1967, M.A. in History, 1968, Ph.D. in History, 1974; Mgmt. Devel. Cert., U. Colo., Boulder, 1981; LettD (hon.), Coll. of Charleston, 1991. County historian Riverside Mus., Calif., 1974-76; head history div. Riverside County Parks Dept., 1976-78; dir. Mus. of Western Colo., Grand Junction, Colo., 1978-84, The Charleston Mus., S.C., 1984—; adj. prof. Chapman Coll. REC, Orange, Calif., 1973-78; instr. history Riverside City Coll., Calif., 1973, U. Calif.-Riverside, 1977; teaching asst. history U. Calif., Riverside, 1969, 72-74; assoc. in history Coll. of Charleston, 1989—. Author: People of the Magic Waters, 1981; editor: Civil War Nurse, 1980; contbr. articles to profl. jours. Chmn. Riverside County Bicentennial Commn., Calif., 1975-76, Airport Art Com., Grand Junction, Colo., 1983-84; active Airport Art Com., Charleston, S.C., 1984-87; chmn. S.C. Abandoned Cultural Property Bd., 1987-89; pres. Mountain-Plains Mus. Assn., 1983-84.. 1st lt. U.S. Army, 1970-72. Haynes Found. fellow, 1968; grantee in field. Mem. Am. Assn. Mus. (accreditation team), S.E. Mus. Conf. (coun. mem. 1987-92, treas. 1990-92), S.C. Fedn. Mus. (v.p. 1985-87, pres. 1987-89), Rotary, Phi Beta Kappa. Lutheran. Lodge: Rotary. Office: Charleston Mus 360 Meeting St Charleston SC 29403-6235

BRUMM, MARCIA COWLES, pharmacist; b. Cleve., Nov. 22, 1921; d. Forest Eugene and Vivian Curtis (Bonnallie) Cowles; m. Joseph Norris Brumm, Apr. 27, 1962 (dec.). BS, Case Western Res. U., 1944. Lic. pharmacist, Ohio, Calif., Ariz., Colo. Pharmacist Am. Pharm. Assn., Washington, 1944-70. Active United Meth. Women, Port St. Lucie; vol. U. Fla. Ext. Svc. Recipient Cert. 1000 Hours Vol. Work, U. Fla., Port St. Lucie, 1989. Mem. AAUW, Am. Assn. Hosp. Pharmacists in Ohio (treas. 1952-56), Gen. Fedn. Woman's Club (pres. St. Lucie chpt.). Democrat. Home: 42 Dawn Flower Cir Lehigh Acres FL 33936

BRUNDAGE, STEPHANIE CAROL, physician; b. Washington, Aug. 27, 1946; d. Robert Sayles and Marjorie Abbie (Snowden) B.; m. Alan Kaplan, Dec. 4, 1964 (div. 1980); children: Elena, Jonathan; m. James Kenneth Harkins Jr., July 13, 1985. AA, Miami-Dade C.C., 1976; BS, Barry U., 1979; MD, U. Miami, 1982; MPH, U. S.C., 1992. Resident in family practice U. Miami (Fla.) Jackson Meml. Hosp., 1982-85; physician S.E. Miss. Rural Health, New Augusta, 1985-89; physician, med. dir. Brittons Neck Health Care Assn., Conway, S.C., 1989-92; physician Nat. Emergency Svcs., Shaw AFB, S.C., 1992-94; assoc. dir., mem. faculty Ctr. for Family Medicine Greenville (S.C.) Hosp. System, 1994—; asst. prof. family and preventive medicine U. S.C., Columbia, 1995; asst. prof. family medicine Med. U. S.C., Charleston, 1995. Fellow Am. Acad. Family Physicians; mem. AMA, APHA, S.C. Acad. Family Physicians, S.C. Med. Assn., Greenville County Med. Soc. Presbyterian. Office: Greenville Meml Hosp Ctr for Family Medicine 701 Grove Rd Greenville SC 29640

BRUNK, SAMUEL FREDERICK, oncologist; b. Harrisonburg, Va., Dec. 21, 1932; s. Harry Anthony and Lena Gertrude (Burkholder) B.; m. Mary Priscilla Bauman, June 24, 1976; children: Samuel, Jill, Geoffrey, Heather, Kirsten, Peter, Christopher, Andrew, Paul, Barbara. BS, Ea. Mennonite Coll., 1955; MD, U. Va., 1959; MS in Pharmacology, U. Iowa, 1967. Diplomate Am. Bd. Internal Medicine, Am. Bd. Internal Medicine in Med. Oncology. Straight med. intern U. Va., Charlottesville, 1959-60; resident in chest diseases Blue Ridge Sanatorium, Charlottesville, 1960-61; resident in internal medicine U. Iowa, Iowa City, 1962-64, fellow in clin. pharmacology (oncology), 1964-65, 66-67, asst. prof. internal medicine, 1967-72; assoc. prof. internal medicine, 1972-76; fellow in medicine (oncology) Johns Hopkins U., Balt., 1965-66; clin. assoc. prof. med. Okla. State U. Coll. Osteo; vis. physician bone marrow transplantation unit Fred Hutchinson Cancer Treatment Ctr., U. Wash., Seattle, 1975; practice medicine specializing in med. oncology Des Moines, 1976-94; attending physician Iowa Luth. Hosp., 1976-94, Iowa Meth. Med. Ctr., 1976-94, Charter Hosp., 1976-94, Mercy Hosp. Med. Ctr., 1976-94; dir. med. oncology Hahne Regional Cancer Ctr., DuBois, Pa., 1994; attending physician DuBois Regional Med. Ctr., 1994; dir. Pa. Cmty. Cancer Care, 1995; attending physician St. Mary's Regional Med. Ctr., 1994; med. oncologist Cancer Treatment Ctr., Tulsa, Okla., 1995—; attending physician Meml. Med. Ctr., Tulsa, Okla., 1995—; chief of staff Iowa Luth. Hosp., 1990, chmn. dept. internal medicine, 1988; cons. physician Des Moines Gen. Osteo. Hosp., 1976-94; prin. investigator Iowa Oncology Rsch. Assn. in assn. with N. Cen. Cancer Treatment Group and Ea. Coop. Oncology Group, 1978-83; prin. investigator Iowa Oncology Rsch. Assn. Comty. Clin. Oncology Program, 1983-84; mem. cancer care com. St. Mary's, Pa., 1995. Contbr. articles to profl. jours. Bd. dirs. Iowa div. Am. Cancer Soc., 1971-89, Johnson County chpt., 1968-72. Mosby scholar, U. Va., 1959. Fellow ACP, Am. Coll. Clin. Pharmacology; mem. AMA, Okla. Medical Soc., Tulsa County Medical Soc., Iowa Thoracic Soc., Am. Thoracic Soc., Iowa Clin. Med. Soc., Am. Fedn. Clin. Rsch., Iowa Heart Assn., Am. Assn. Cancer Edn., Am. Soc. Hematology, Am. Soc. Clin. Pharmacology and Therapeutics, Cen. Soc. Clin. Rsch., Raven Soc., Alpha Omega Alpha. Roman Catholic. Home: 2929 E 69th St Tulsa OK 74136-4541

BRUNNER, KENNETH AUGUST, educational consultant, author; b. Milw., Feb. 10, 1921; s. Leo Gustav and Emma Dorothea (Jens) B.; m. Eva Sue Womack, May 1, 1943; children: Robert Alan, Carol Jean Rankin, Richard Jens (dec.), Conrad Stephen. AB, U. Ga., 1947; MA, U. Wis., 1956; EdD, U. Fla., 1956. Instr. polit. sci. Ga. State U., Atlanta, 1948-50; vocat. counselor, placement dir. St. Petersburg (Fla.) Jr. Coll., 1955-58; jr. coll. specialist U.S. Office Edn., Washington, 1958-65; prof. higher edn. So. Ill. U., Carbondale, 1965-68; prof. and chmn. dept. higher edn. U. Mo., Columbia, 1968-71; regional commr. U.S. Office Edn., Atlanta, 1971-78; edn. cons., writer Atlanta, 1978—; pres. coun. univs. and colls. Am. Assn. Cmty. and Jr. Colls., 1970-71. Author guides; contbr. articles to profl. jours. Treas., trustee Ga. Fed./Mil. Retiree Coalition, Atlanta, 1992—. 1st lt. U.S. Army, 1940-46; capt. USAF, 1950-53, lt. col. ret. U. Fla. Grad. Coun. fellow, 1954-55. Mem. Res. Officers Assn. (life), Ga. Dept. of Res. Officers Assn. (chmn. retirement affairs com. 1990-96), Nat. Assn. Ret. Fed. Employees (dist. officer region 4 Ga. Fedn. 1989-92, pres. Dunwoody chpt. 1987-89), Sigma Chi (life), Phi Beta Kappa, Phi Kappa Phi, Phi Eta Sigma, Delta Phi Alpha, Kappa Delta Pi, Phi Delta Kappa. Office: PO Box 450141 Atlanta GA 31145-0141

BRUNNER, RONALD GENE, trade association administrator; b. Carthage, Mo., Oct. 10, 1947; s. Otis John and Alice Maxine (Richardson) B.; m. Diana Louise Davis, Aug. 11, 1967; children: Di Rhronda, Amber. BS in Mech. Engring., U. Mo., 1970. Reg. profl. engr., Okla. Project engr. Cities Svc. Oil & Gas, Tulsa, Okla., 1970-76; project mgr. Cities Svc. Oil & Gas, Tulsa, 1976-82; measurement mgr. Occidental Oil & Gas, Tulsa, 1982-89; sr. project mgr. Edeco Engrs., Tulsa, 1989-94; dir. tech. svcs., corp. sec. Gas Processors Assn., Tulsa, 1994—. Contbr. articles to profl. jours. With U.S. Army, 1970. Mem. Am. Petroleum Inst. (Citation for Svc. 1989, 90). Office: Gas Processors Assn 6526 E 60th St Tulsa OK 74145

BRUNO, RONALD G., food service executive; b. 1951; married. BS, U. Ala., 1974. With Bruno's Inc., Birmingham, Ala., chmn. bd., CEO, 1990—; pres. Bruno Capital Management Corp. Office: Bruno Capital Management Corp Two Perimeter Pk S Ste 300E Birmingham AL 25243

BRUNS, DAVID EUGENE, medical educator, researcher; b. St. Louis, Dec. 12, 1941; s. Eugene H. and Ellen E. (Johnson) B.; m. M. Elizabeth Hirst; children: Elizabeth, David. BSChemE, Washington U., 1963, AB, 1965; MD, St. Louis U., 1973. Diplomate Nat. Bd. Med. Examiners. Instr. pathology Sch. Medicine Washington U., St. Louis, 1973-77, vis. prof. pathology, 1985-86; asst. prof. U. Va., Charlottesville, 1977-81, assoc. dir. of clin. chem. and toxicology, 1977—, assoc. prof. dept. pathology, 1981-90, prof. pathology Sch. Medicine, 1990—; exec. coun. Acad. of Clin. Lab. Physicians and Scientists, Salt Lake City, 1990-93. Editor Clin. Chemistry, Washington, 1990—; contbr. articles to profl. jours., 1975—; inventor Immunochemical Assays for Human Amylase Isoenzymes and Related Monoclonal Antibodies, 1993. Recipient Israel Diamond Lecture award Brown U. Sch. of Med., 1990, Sunderman award Clin. Scientist of the Year, Assn. of Clin. Scientists, 1987, Outstanding Contbns. to Rsch. award Am. Assn. for Clin. Chemistry, 1987. Office: Am Assn for Clin Chem Univ Station PO Box 3757 Charlottesville VA 22903-0757

BRUNS, MICHAEL, transportation company executive; b. 1951. Student, U. Ill., Chgo., 1972-74. With Crow Flight Motor Express, Chgo., 1974-78, Spector-Red Ball Motor Freight, Memphis, 1979-81, Intermodal Transp., Memphis, 1981-83; with Comtrak Inc., Memphis, 1983—, pres. Office: Comtrak Inc 5660 Universal Dr Memphis TN 38118-7923

BRUNSON, JAMES MCDUFFIE, SR., management consultant; b. Charleston, S.C., Jan. 2, 1950; s. James S. and Juliet (Norred) B.; m. Winifred Elaine Ford, Dec. 21, 1974; children: Mack, Jack, Katie, Lissie. BS in Commerce, U. Va., 1971; MBA in Fin., Ga. State U., 1973; exec. cert., Rutgers U., 1985. Mktg. officer 1st Nat. Bank Atlanta, 1971-75; auditor Seidman & Seidman, Atlanta, 1975; v.p. Branch Banking & Trust, Wilson, N.C., 1975-79, Payment Systems Inc., Atlanta, 1979-80, 1st Ky. Nat. Corp., Louisville, 1980-86; pres., founder Fin. Info. Products, Bethesda, Md., 1986-90; ptnr. Deloitte & Touche Consulting Group, Washington, 1990—; mem. faculty Grad. Sch. Bank Mktg., Boulder, Colo., 1987-88, Grad. Sch. Banking, Boulder, 1989—. Editor: Telephone Bill Paying, 1986; programmer Fin. Mgmt. Software, 1984; contbr. articles to banking jours. Vice chmn. Southeaster Econ. Project, Atlanta, 1972-74; mayor City of Broeck Pointe, Ky., 1982-85. Office: Deloitte & Touche Consulting Group 1900 M St NW Washington DC 20036

BRUNSON, JOHN SOLES, lawyer; b. Houston, Jan. 8, 1934; s. Nathan Bryant and Jonnie E. (McMillian) B.; BBA, Baylor U., 1956, LLB, 1958, JD, 1965; m. Joan Erwin, Dec. 26, 1953: children: W. Mark, Dana Ruth. Bar: Tex., 1958, U.S. Supreme Ct., 1961; assoc. Dillingham, Schleider & Lewis, Houston, 1958-64; ptnr. Brunson & Brill, Houston, 1964-70, Baker, Heard & Brunson, Houston, 1970-72, Brunson & Erwin, Houston, 1972-84; pres. New Asia Products, Inc.; chmn. Clavis Investment Corp.; bd. dirs. Supply Resources Internat. Pty. Ltd. Mem. Harris County (Tex.) Dem. Exec. Com., 1959-65, Tex. Dem. Exec. Com., 1968-74; mem. exec. bd. Bapt. Gen. Conv. Tex., 1988-94; trustee First Bapt. Acad. Mem. ABA, State Bar Tex., Houston Bar Assn. Office: 7555 Katy Fwy Apt 69 Houston TX 77024-2119

BRUSCO, LYNNE PATRICIA, secondary education educator, administrator; b. Pitts., Mar. 12, 1971; d. Arthur M. and Margaret (Murphy) B. BA in English and Secondary Edn., Purdue U., 1993; postgrad., Middlebury Coll., 1995—. Tchr. lang. arts Cmty. Sch. Naples, Fla., 1994-95, tchr. secondary English, dean student, 1995—; presenter in field Collier County Young Authors' Conf., Naples, 1995, Nat. Assn. Ind. Schs. Conf., Washington, 1996; panelist Fla. Arts in Edn., Tallahassee, 1996. Mem. Collier County Arts Coun., 1995—. DeWitt E. and Vera M. Hooker fellow Fla. Coun. Ind. Schs. Mem. MLA, Am. Philol. Assn., Nat. Coun. Tchrs. English, Nat. Assn. Women in Edn., Purdue U. Alumni Assn. Episcopalian. Office: Cmty Sch Naples 3251 Pine Ridge Rd Naples FL 33942

BRUWELHEIDE, DALE A., business executive; b. 1949. Grad., U. South Fla., 1975. With Arthur Young CPAs, Tampa, Fla., 1977-78, CF Industries, Bartow, Fla., 1978-84, Ewell Industries, Lakeland, Fla., 1984-91; v.p., treas., CFO Orange-Co., Inc., Bartow, Fla., 1991—. Office: Orange-Co Inc 2020 US Highway 17 S Bartow FL 33830-7525

BRYAN, GLORIA ELAINE, beauty and fashion consultant; b. St. Catherine, Jamaica, Nov. 18, 1946; d. Roy Donovan and Lucille (Claffee) Sutherland; m. John Harold Bryan, Apr. 16, 1966 (div. Dec. 1985); children: John Harold Jr., Donna Maria, Paul Ivanhoe. Cert., Leons Sch. Beauty, Kingston, Jamaica, 1972, Jim Williams Clinic, Manhattan, N.Y., 1978; student, Jim Williams Clinic, 1985. Salon owner Ultimo Beauty Salons, Inc., Hempstead, N.Y., 1980-85; cosmetics cons. M&M Co., Uniondale, N.Y., 1980—; beauty cons. various salons, 1991-96; techr. cosmotology Libs Sch., 1989, 91; beauty cons. various community beauty salons. Pentecostal. Club: Jack Lalanne Rockville Ctr. Home and Office: 15422 Evergreen Grove Dr Houston TX 77083-5468

BRYAN, JAMES EDWIN, JR., forester, consultant; b. Calhoun, La., Dec. 14, 1917; s. James Edwin and Annie Lee (Scales) B.; m. Leta Colvin, Jan. 11, 1941; children: Marsha Lee, James Ansley. BS in Forestry, La. State U., Baton Rouge, 1938. Registered forester, Miss. Instr. forestry Ala. Poly. Inst., Auburn, 1939-40, 1941-42; chief forester L.N. Dantzler Lumber Co., Perkinston, Miss., 1945-66; dist. supr., wood supr. Internat. Paper Co., Wiggins, Miss., 1967-74; cons. forester Bryan Enterprises, Inc., Wiggins, 1975-86; chmn. bd. dirs. Bank of Wiggins, 1990—; adv. dir. Bank of Wiggins, 1972-90; bd. dirs. Harrison Life Ins. Co., Gulfport. Trustee Miss. Gulf Coast C.C., Perkinston, 1976—; mem. Miss. State Forestry Commn., Jackson, 1981-86; bd. dirs. Pearl River Basin Devel. Dist., Jackson, 1981-86; mem. Pine Break Recreation Assn., Wiggins, 1969—. Maj. inf. U.S. Army, 1941-45, 50-52. Decorated Bronze Star medal (2). Fellow Soc. Am. Foresters (chmn. Gulf States sect. 1951, named Outstanding Forester 1975, Golden Membership award 1986); mem. Miss. Forestry Assn. (chair 1962). Methodist. Home: 306N Critz Wiggins MS 39577

BRYAN, JESSE DWAIN, minister, missionary; b. Downsville, La., Oct. 11, 1936; s. Elijah B. and Mary A. Bryan; m. Beverly Ann Bailey, June 7, 1958; 1 child, Allaric Dwain; 1 adopted child, Debra Michelle. BA, La. Tech. U., 1961, MA, 1975; BD, New Orleans Theol. Sem., 1964, DMin, 1980. Ordained to ministry, Bapt. Ch., 1957; commd. fgn. missionary, 1965. Pastor Hico Bapt. Ch., Dubach, La., 1958-60, 1st Bapt. Ch., Choudrant, La., 1960-65; fgn. missionary Fgn. Mission Bd., So. Bapt. Conv., El Paso, Tex., and Spain, 1965—; field missionary, pastor 1st Bapt. Ch., Bilbao, Spain, 1965-71; mgr. Bapt. Bookstore, Bapt. Spanish Pub. House Dist., Barcelona, Spain, 1971-76; dir. sales Bapt. Spanish Pub. House, El Paso, 1977-78, dir. distbn., 1979-85, dir. mktg., 1986-90, dir. communications, 1990-91, dir. mgmt. svcs. and fin. div., 1991—; interim pastor Sunrise Bapt. Ch., El Paso, 1989-93, 1st Bapt. Ch., Anthony, N.Mex., 1988-89, Bethel Bapt. Ch., Alamogordo, N.Mex., 1987-88; chaplain Sun Valley Hosp. (now Columbia Behavioral Ctr.), El Paso, 1989—. Editor, contbr. El Obrero Cristiano, 1977-78. Fellow Bapt. Pub. Rels. Assn., Christian Bookseller's Assn., Spanish Evang. Pub. Assn. Democrat. Home: 4545 Rl Shoemaker Dr El Paso TX 79924-6820 Office: Bapt Spanish Pub House 7000 Alabama PO Box 4255 El Paso TX 79914-4255

BRYAN, JOHN STEWART, III, newspaper publisher; b. Richmond, Va., May 4, 1938; s. David Tennant and Mary Davidson Bryan; m. Alice Pyle Zimmer, 1963 (div. 1985); children: Elizabeth Talbott, Anna Saulsbury; m. Lisa-Margaret Stevenson, 1993. BA, U. Va., 1960. Former advt. salesman Burlington (Vt.) Free Press; former reporter The Tampa (Fla.) Times; pub. The Tampa Tribune and Times, Fla., 1976-77, Richmond Times-Dispatch, Richmond News Leader, Va., 1978—; bd. dirs. Media Gen., Inc., Richmond, 1974—, vice-chmn., exec. v.p., 1985—, chmn., pres., CEO, 1990—; bd. dirs. Mut. Ins. Co., Bermuda. Past pres. Tampa Bay Art Ctr., Tampa Citizens Safety Coun., Tampa United Way, Gulf Coast Symphony, Jr. Achievement Richmond, Goodwill Industries Richmond; chmn. United Way Greater Richmond, 1984; trustee Va. Found. Ind. Coll., chmn., 1993-95; trustee Inst. Bill of Rights Law, Coll. William and Mary, Va. Commonwealth U. Found., J. Sargeant Reynolds C.C. Found., Maymont Found., Found. Am. Communications. With USMC, 1960-62. Mem. SAR, S.R., Soc. of Cin., Fla. Soc. Newspapers Editors (life), So. Newspapers Pub. Assn. (found. chmn. 1978-79, pres. 1981-82), Fla. Press Assn. (life, pres. 1971-72, Disting. Svc. award 1975), Va. Press Assn. (bd. dirs. 1980-86), Newspaper Advt. Bur. (chmn. 1991-92), Newspaper Assn. of Am., Soc. Profl. Journalists, World Bus. Coun., Va. Bus. Coun., Fla. Coun. of 100, Bohemian Club, Country Club Va., Commonwealth Club, Tampa Yacht and Country Club. Home: 4608 Sulgrave Rd Richmond VA 23221-3119 Office: Media Gen Inc 333 E Grace St Richmond VA 23293-1000

BRYAN, MARY ANN, interior designer; b. Dallas, Nov. 16, 1929; d. William C. and Harriet E. (Carter) Green; m. Frank Wingfield Bryan, Aug. 31, 1957; children: Frank Wingfield, Elizabeth F. BS in Interior Design U. Tex., 1950. Head of stock Foleys Dept. Store, Houston, 1952-53, asst. buyer, 1953-54, buyer, 1955-60, exec. tng. dir., 1960-61; owner, pres. The Bryan Design Assocs., Inc., Houston, 1961-96; mem. interior design Tex. Bd. Archtl. Examiners, 1993—. Trustee Houston Art Inst.; mem. interior design adv. bd. Stephen F. Austin Coll., Houston C.C.; U.S. del. Friendship Among Women; dir. profl. devel NCIDQ. Mem. Am. Soc. Interior Designers (nat. bd. dirs. 1984-86, 91-92, pres. Gulf Coast chpt. 1975), Chi Omega. Republican. Home: 5120 Woodway St 8009 Houston TX 77056

BRYAN, ROBERT FESSLER, former investment analyst; b. New Castle, Pa., Jan. 19, 1913; s. Harry A. and Nell (Fessler) B.; m. Elaine A. Norwood, Sept. 7, 1940; children: Diane Elaine Bryan Lyon, Barbara Norwood Bryan Bardo; m. Dorothy Darr MacKenzie, Aug. 11, 1961; m. Gertrude B. Bruneau, Feb. 10, 1978. AB summa cum laude, Oberlin Coll., 1934; PhD, Yale, 1939. Instr. econs. Yale U., 1935-36, 37-39, Princeton U., 1936-37; economist Lionel D. Edie & Co., Inc., N.Y.C., 1939-40; asst. v.p. Lionel D. Edie & Co., Inc., 1943-45, v.p., 1946-48; price exec., rubber br. OPA, 1941-42; economist Goodyear Aircraft Corp., Akron, Ohio, 1943; with J.H. Whitney & Co., N.Y.C., 1948-50; partner J.H. Whitney & Co., 1951-59; financial v.p., treas., dir. Whitney Communications Corp., 1959-69; ptnr. Whitcom Investment Co., 1967-69. Mem. exec. com. Yale Grad. Sch. Council, 1969-73; trustee Oberlin Coll., 1960-70. Mem. Am. Mgmt. Assn. (fin. coun. 1952-55), Gulfstream Golf Club, Gulfstream Bath and Tennis Club, Ocean Club, Ekwanok Country Club, Phi Beta Kappa. Home: 200 N Ocean Blvd Delray Beach FL 33483-7126

BRYANS, JOHN ARMOND, artist, art educator; b. Marion, Ohio, July 21, 1925; s. Ralph Armond and Frances Annetta (Kilbury) B.; m. Christina S., Jan. 23, 1960; children: Marshall, Estella Bryans-Munson. Student, Ringling Sch. Art, 1947-49, Jerry Farnsworth Studio, 1950. Reporter Marion Star, 1944-46; clk. Armour & Co., 1951, Southern Distributors, Washington, 1951-52, Bur. Medicine and Surgery, US Navy, Washington, 1952-58; instr. Hill's Art Sch., Arlington, Va., 1952-77; instr., dir. art dept. McLean (Va.) Arts Ctr., 1963-73, 77—; guest instr. Md. Coll. Art & Design, Silver Spring, 1981-82, Midfearn Sch., Ardgay, Scotland, 1990; co-founder, dir. Painting in the Mountains, Burnsville, N.C., 1965-83; artist in residence Foundry United Meth. Ch., Washington, 1960-80. One-man shows include New Georgetown Gallery, Washington, 1954, Asheville (N.C.) Mus., 1956, Silver Spring (Md.) Gallery, 1958, Kerst Gallery, Arlington, Va., 1960, Decoy Book Shop, Kennett Sq., Pa., 1963, Hodges Gallery, Alexandria, Va., 1967, Spectrum Gallery, washington, 1968, 70, 72, 74, 76, 78, 80, 82, 84, 86, 88, 91, 94, Granary Gallery, Martha's Vineyard, Mass., 1981, Best of Everything, Potomac, Md., 1986, Clin. Ctr. Gallery NIH, Bethesda, Md., 1989, Brian Logan Gallery, Washington, 1991, Lowndes/Valdosta Arts Ctr., Ga., 1992, Hayden Gallery, Burnsville, 1993, others; group shows include Am. Art League, 1953, 58, 59, 60, 65, Corcoran Gallery Area Show, 1955, 56, 58, Soc. Washington Artists, 1955, 57, Balt. Mus. Area Show, 1957, Washington Watercolor Assn., 1957, 61, 62, 63, Va. Mus., 1965, Balt. Watercolor Soc., 1979, 85, 86, 87, 89, 92, 94, Springfield (Mo.) Mus., 1989, 95, 96, Md. Fedn. Arts, 1992, 93, Perry House Gallery, Alexandria, 1993, 95, numerous others; monthly exhibit Art League Gallery, Alexandria, 1993—; spl. shows, murals; represented in permanent collections: Beebe Meml. Hosp., Lewes, Del., Atlantic Food Svcs., Manassas, Va., Monsanto Chem. Co., Washington, U.S. Nuclear Regulatory Commn., Rockville, Md., Sallie Mae, Washington, Abilene (Tex.) Mus., Columbus (Ga.) Mus., Internat. Brotherhood Electrical Workers, Washington, Wall St. Jour. Washington Office, C. of C., Burnsville, Triton Enterprises, Greensboro, N.C., others. Cpl. USAF, 1946-48. Mem. Southern Watercolor Soc., Va. Watercolor Soc., Ky. Watercolor Soc., Ga. Watercolor Soc. Home: 2264 N Vernon St Arlington VA 22207-4049 Office: McLean Arts Ctr 1437 Emerson Ave Mc Lean VA 22101-5706

BRYANT, BARRETT RICHARD, computer and information sciences educator; b. Chgo., Feb. 25, 1961; s. Cullan Charles and Mary Lou (Richardson) B. BS, U. Ark., Little Rock, 1979; MS, Northwestern U., 1980, PhD, 1983. Asst. prof. U. Ala., Birmingham, 1983-88, assoc. prof., 1988—; vis. researcher Ibaraki U., Hitachi, Japan, 1987; vis. scientist IBM, San Jose, Calif., 1991-92; rsch. assoc. Rome Lab., N.Y., 1993. Contbr. articles to profl. jours. Recipient Instrumentation and Lab. Improvement grant Nat. Sci. Found., 1993-95. Mem. Ala. Acad. Sci. (chmn. engring., computer sci. sect. 1989-92), Assn. Computational Linguistics, Assn. Computing Machinery (lectr. 1993-96, Disting. Lectr. award 1995, mem. spl. interest group applied computing, programming langs., program chmn. symposium in applied computing, editor-in-chief SIGAPP Applied Computing Rev. 1996—), IEEE Computer Soc. Office: U Ala-Birmingham Dept Computer Info Scis 1300 University Blvd Birmingham AL 35233

BRYANT, CECIL FARRIS, lawyer, retired insurance company executive; b. Ocala, Fla., July 26, 1914; s. Charles Cecil and Lela Margaret (Farris) B.; m. Julia Burnett, Sept. 18, 1940; children: Julie Lovett, Cecilia Ann, Allison Adair. Student, Emory U., 1931-32; B.S., U. Fla., 1935; J.D., Harvard U., 1938; LL.D. (hon.), Rollins Coll., Fla. State U., U. Fla., Fla. Atlantic U., Fla. So. Coll. Bar: Fla., U.S. Supreme Ct. Auditor Fla. Comptroller's Office, 1939-40; of counsel Bryant, Miller & Olive, Tallahassee; pres., chmn. bd. Voyager Life Ins. Co., Jacksonville, 1965-85; mem. Fla. Ho. of Reps., 1942, 46-55, speaker of ho., 1953; del. Dem. Nat. Conv., 1952, 60, 68, alt. del., 1964, chmn. Fla. delegation, 1964; gov. State of Fla., 1961-65. Dir. Office of Emergency Planning, 1966-67; mem. Nat. Security Council, 1966-67; chmn. adv. Commn. on Intergovtl. Relations, 1966-69; U.S. rep. NATO, 1967. Served with USN, 1942-46. Named Most Valuable Mem. Fla. Ho. of Reps., 1949, 51, 53, Most Valuable Mem. Fla. Ho. of Reps. St. Petersburg Times Poll, 1949, 51, 55; recipient Top Mgmt. award Sales and Mktg. Execs. Assn., 1976, Clayton Nonce Powell award Fla. Pub. Defenders, 1988, Silver Beaver award Boy Scouts Am. Mem. Fla. Bar Assn., Am. Legion, VFW, Fla. Council of 100, Phi Delta Phi, Alpha Kappa Psi, Kappa Delta Pi, Alpha Phi Omega, Alpha Tau Omega. Methodist. Clubs: Rotary, Elks, Masons, Shriners.

BRYANT, DENNIS MICHAEL, insurance executive; b. Austin, Tex., June 30, 1947; s. L.D. and Mildred (Perkins) B.; m. Nancy Louthan, Apr. 17, 1976; children: Michael, Sarah. BS, Trinity U., 1970. Sales mgr. Southland Equipment Co., Houston, 1973-74; mgr., equipment specialist Briggs Weaver Co., San Antonio, 1974-81; life ins. specialist N.Y. Life Ins. Co., San Antonio, 1981-85; territorial ins. specialist Merrill Lynch Life Agy., San Antonio, 1985-86; life and group ins. mgr. Cen. Fin. Ins. Svcs., San Antonio, 1986—; owner Bryant Agy./Trinity Fin. Concepts, San Antonio, 1988—; chmn. Focus on Growth, 1993—; chmn. Focus on Growth, Inc. Active Project Any Baby Can, San Antonio, 1983—, pres. 1984-85. 1st lt. U.S. Army, 1971-73. Republican. Home: 5305 E 101st Pl Tulsa OK 74137

BRYANT, GAY DAVIS, office systems educator; b. Carrollton, Ga., Feb. 11, 1948; d. Duke Jr. and Dorothy (Emert) Davis; m. David Perry Bryant, Apr. 20, 1973; children: Lee Davis, Ann Rae. BS, West Ga. Coll., 1970; MS, U. Tenn., 1971. Cert. office automation profl. Assoc. prof. Roane State C.C., Harriman, Tenn., 1971-85, Pellissippi State Tech. C.C., Knoxville, Tenn., 1985—; cons. Knoxville (Tenn.) Utility Bd., 1990-94; mem. adv. bd. Knox County Schs., Knoxville, 1986—, Knoxville Area Urban League, 1990-

94; mem. admissions bd., curriculum specialist U. Tenn. Tech. and Adult Edn., Knoxville, 1990-94. Author: Introduction to Word Perfect, 1995. Recipient Excellence in Teaching award Nat. Inst. for Staff and Orgnl. Devel., 1994, Master Presenter award, 1994. Mem. Nat. Coun. Instrnl. Adminstrs., Tenn. Bus. Edn. Assn. (pres., treas. 1985—, editl. rev. bd. 1993—), Office Automation Soc. Internat., Profl. Secs. Internat., So. Bus. Edn. Assn., Nat. Bus. Edn. Assn., Delta Pi Epsilon (sponsor 1992—). Baptist. Office: Pellissippi State Tech CC 10915 Hardin Valley Rd Knoxville TN 37932-1412

BRYANT, GEORGE MACON, chemist; b. Anniston, Ala., Aug. 3, 1926; s. Fred Boyd and Jessie Elizabeth (Macon) B.; m. Mary Lee Miles, Sept. 9, 1950; children—Fred Boyd II, George Macon. B.S. in Physics, Auburn U., 1948; M.S., Inst. Textile Tech., 1950; Ph.D., Princeton U., 1954. Research chemist research and devel. ctr. Union Carbide Corp., South Charleston, W.Va., 1954-58, group leader, 1958-66, assoc. dir., 1966-75, corp. research fellow, 1975-86, cons. 1986—. Served with USN, 1944-46. Mem. Am. Chem. Soc. (award for sci. achievement 1979), Am. Assn. Textile Chemists (Milson award 1982), Fiber Soc. (award for disting. early achievement 1964), Sigma Xi, Phi Kappa Phi. Democrat. Presbyterian. Contbr. articles to profl. jours.; patentee in field. Home: 1204 Williamsburg Way Charleston WV 25314-1938

BRYANT, GEORGE OTHELLO, III, journalist; b. Omaha, Aug. 29, 1955; s. George Sr. and Hazel Marie (Rountree) B.; m. Yvonne Mckenzie Brown, Nov. 12, 1983 (div. Sept. 1990). BS in Telecomms. Arts, Iowa State U., 1978. News reporter Sta. WOI-TV, Ames, Iowa, 1976-79; news reporter, anchor Sta. WCIA-TV, Champaign, Ill., 1979-82; news reporter Stae. WMC-TV, Memphis, 1982-84; news reporter, anchor Stat. WAGA-tV, Atlanta, 1984-88; sports anchor, reporter WGNX-TV, Atlanta, 1988-92; pres. Devine Comms., Atlanta, 1992-94; producer, writer Cable News Network, Atlanta, 1994—. Vol. Martin Luther King Jr. Fed. Holiday, Atlanta, 1984; bd. dirs. 100 Black Men of Atlanta, Inc., 1987—, YMCA, Atlanta, 1992—. Mem. Nat. Acad. Arts and Scis. (contest judge 1991-92, Sports Reporting Emmy 1989, Feature Reporting Emmy 1990, Gen. Reporting Emmy 1990), Ga. Assn. Press (contest judge 1991-92), Atlanta Assn. Black Journalists, Soc. Profl. Journalists (contest judge 1991-92), Omega Psi Phi. Home: PO Box 8312 Atlanta GA 30306-0312

BRYANT, HERBERT MCCOY, JR. (HERBIE DELANEY), statistician; b. Sebring, Fla., Aug. 8, 1943; s. Herbert McCoy Bryant and Evelyn Lanel Smith Bryant DeLaney; stepson of Edgar A. DeLaney Jr. BA, U. South Fla., 1972. Computer operator data processing ctr. City of Tampa, Fla., 1972-73; sr. sci. programmer, statistical analyst S.W. Fla. Water Mgmt. Dist., Brooksville, Fla., 1973—. V.p. Unitarian Universalist Ch. of Tampa, 1977; judge state sci. fair Fla. Found. for Future Scientists, Gainesville, 1993-95; mem. citizens adv. coun. Tampa Bay Regional Transp. Authority, 1978. With USAF, 1961-65. Mem. APHA, Am. Statis. Assn., Soc. Epidemiology Rsch., Sys. Dynamics Soc., Amnesty Internat., Internat. Environmetrics Soc., World Future Soc., Tiger Bay Club Tampa. Democrat. Home: 14410 Hellenic Dr # F-16 Tampa FL 33613-2846 Office: SW Fla Water Mgmt Dist 7601 Highway 301 N Bldg 2 Tampa FL 33637-6758

BRYANT, IRA HOUSTON, III, lawyer; b. San Antonio, Aug. 30, 1942; s. Ira Houston and Florence (Kimberlin) B.; m. Judith Ann Bryant, Mar. 13, 1971; children—Ira Houston IV, Andrew Nelson, Jennifer Ann. B.A., Oklahoma City U., 1965, J.D., 1973. Bar: Okla., 1973. Physicist, White Sands Missile Range, N.Mex., 1965-70; ins. adjuster U.S. Fidelity & Guaranty Co., Oklahoma City, 1971-72; assoc. Robert Leyton Wheeler, Inc., Oklahoma City, 1973-77, Kerr, Davis, Irvine, Krasnow, Rhodes & Semtner, Oklahoma City, 1977-79; ptnr. Bryant & Scribner, Oklahoma City, 1979-83, Claunch, Bryant & Scribner, 1983-91; pvt. practice, 1991—. Mem. Oklahoma City Mineral Lawyers Soc., Oklahoma City Title Attys. Assn., Phi Delta Phi. Republican. Methodist. Club: Sportsman's Country (Oklahoma City). Office: 7800 Lyrewood Ln #151 Oklahoma City OK 73132

BRYANT, JACQUELINE EOLA, educational consultant specialist; b. Norfolk, Va., Oct. 26, 1949; d. James Thomas Sr. and Wincie (Jackson) B. BS, Old Dominion U.; MA, George Washington U.; postgrad., Va. Polytech. Inst., U. Va. Cons., coord. supr. Fibachu Corp., Norfolk, Va., 1978-79; tchr. English, chmn. dept. Virginia Beach (Va.) City Schs., 1981-83, lang. arts coord. Mid. Sch., 1983-90; cons., ednl. specialist Target Communications Inc., Norfolk, 1989-90; dir. reading/lang. arts Dallas Ind. Sch. Dist., 1990-94; tchr. Larkspur Mid. Sch., Virginia Beach, 1994-95; nat. key accounts coord. McDougal Littell/Houghton Mifflin Co., Evanston, Ill., 1995—. Contbr. articles to profl. jours. Mem. ASCD, Internat. Reading Assn., Va. Assn. Tchrs. English (pres. 1985), Nat. Coun. Tchrs. of English (bd. dirs. 1984, chair com. to evaluate curriculum guide); Conf. on English Edn. (chair com. minority educators, mem. tchr. preparation and cert. com.), Phi Delta Kappa. Home: 4821 Gatwick Dr Virginia Beach VA 23462-6437

BRYANT, JAMES CECIL, JR., academic administrator; b. Lake Wales, Fla., Oct. 21, 1931; s. James Cecil and Mary Lou (McCranie) B.; m. Marion Lois Carnett, June 19, 1955; children: David Mixon, Albert Carnett. BA, Stetson U., 1954; BD/MDiv, So. Bapt. Theol. Sem., 1958; MA, U. Miami, 1961; PhD, U. Ky., 1967. Asst. prof. English Fla. State U., Tallahassee, 1967-73; prof. English Mercer U., Atlanta, 1973-92; historian, spl. asst. to pres. Mercer U., Macon, Ga., 1992—. Author 13 books; contbr. articles to profl. jours., mags. and newspapers. Chaplain, editor Yaarab Shrine Temple, 1975—. Mem. Soc. Profl. Journalists, Scottish Rite, Masons, York Rite, Kiwanis (com. mem. 1986—), Atlanta Press Club. Home and Office: 1470 Leafmore Pl Decatur GA 30033-2023

BRYANT, JOHN HULON, education educator; b. Oklahoma City, Apr. 30, 1941; s. Glenn Henry and Bernice (Cochran) B.; m. Linda Sue Carhart, Oct. 17, 1943; 1 child, Mary Ellen. BArch, Okla. State U., 1964; MArch, U. Ill., 1968. Registered architect, Okla. Architect The Benham Group, Oklahoma City and L.A., 1964-70; alumni prof.dept. architecture Auburn (Ala.) U., 1970-76; head architecture dept. Okla. State U., Stillwater, 1977-86, prof. architecture dept., 1986—; vis. scholar U. Hawaii, Honolulu, 1981; cons., lectr. People's Republic China, 1984. Co-author: (with Harold N. Cones) The Zenith Trans-Oceanic: The Royalty of Radios, 1994; editor Scholarly Jour. F.T. Proceedings, 1988—; producer, dir. ednl. TV, 1986; contbr. articles to profl. jours. Sr. Fulbright Rsch. scholar Fulbright Commn., 1976-77. Mem. AIA (cons., del. People's Rep. China 1979). Methodist. Home: RR 5 Box 14 Stillwater OK 74074-9301 Office: Okla State U 101 Architecture Bldg Stillwater OK 74078-0185

BRYANT, KERI LYNN, German language educator; b. Stockton, Calif., June 14, 1964; d. Larry Jean and Jessie Anne (Leimbach) B. BA, Kenyon Coll., 1987; MA, Columbia U., 1987, U. Pa., 1991; PhD, U. Pa., 1994. German instr. High Mowing Sch., Wilton, N.H., 1987-89; lectr. U. Pa., Phila., 1994-95; asst. prof. German Murray (Ky.) State U., 1995—. Co-author: Alles Klar?, 1996. Mem. MLA, AAUW (v.p. 1996—), Am. Assn. of Tchrs. of German. Home: 1420 S Michelle Dr Murray KY 42071 Office: Murray State Univ Dept Fgn Lang Box 9 Murray KY 42071

BRYANT, LAURA MILITZER, artist; b. Detroit, Mar. 3, 1955; d. Paul Herman and Kanella (George) Militzer; m. Matthew T. Bryant, May 25, 1980. BFA summa cum laude, U. Mich., 1978. Pres., owner, founder Prism, Buffalo, 1983-92; pres., owner Prism, St. Petersburg, Fla., 1992—. Active Emily's List, 1990—, Mus. Fine Arts, St. Petersburg, 1992—, Fla. Gulf Coast Art Ctr., 1994—. Individual artist grantee State of Fla., 1994; individual artist fellow Nat. Endowment for Arts, 1992; recipient Best of Show award Hilton Head Art League, 1995, award of distinction Handweavers Guild Am., 1995. Mem. Am. Craft Coun., Knitting Guild Am. (tchr. 1995-96), Nat. Needlework Assn., Fla. Craftsmen (mem. various coms. 1993—). Office: Prism 2595 30th Ave N Saint Petersburg FL 33713-2925

BRYANT, MARY ROSELYN GLASGOW, visual arts educator; b. Ackerman, Miss., Jan. 2, 1939; d. Thomas Rawls and Charlene Tate (Senter) Glasgow; m. Henry G. Bryant Jr., June 28, 1961; children: Salita S. Hank, Harlin G. BFA, Miss. U. for Women, 1961; MEd, U. S.C., 1992; specialist in supervisin, Regional Ednl. Svc. Agy., 1996. Visual arts instr. Sego Mid. Sch., Augusta, Ga., 1962-66, Evans (Ga.) Mid. Sch., 1980—; arts instr. Augusta (Ga.) Coll., Kids Coll., summer 1993; sponsor yearbook Evans Mid. Sch., 1985—, mem. awards ceremony com., 1994—, chmn. Christmas craft fair, 1992, 93. Penny arts chmn. Augusta Jr. Women's Club, 1974-78, 2d v.p., com. chmn., 1967-78; past pres., bd. dirs. West Augusta Women's Club, Augusta, 1982—; past pres. Willow Wood Garden Club, Evans, 1970-80, Ga. Podiatry Aux., Atlanta, 1963—; chair, soloist 1st Bapt. Ch. Evans, 1970—; deacon, 1990-93. Named Homemaker of Yr., Columbia County, 1971. Mem. Nat. Art Edn. Assn., Ga. Art Edn. Assn., Profl. Assn. Ga. Educators. Republican. Home: Rt 1 Box 303 Peckerwood Farm Dr Evans GA 30809 Office: Evans Mid Sch 2418 Washington Rd Evans GA 30809

BRYANT, PATTY ANN, foundation executive, public relations executive; b. Manhattan, Kans., Jan. 28, 1950; d. William Paul and Lois Florence (Diehl) Trenkle; m. Terrence W. Ryan; m. Robert William Bryant, Oct. 4, 1980; 1 child, Cheryl Ann. BS in Journalism, Kans. State U., 1972. Salesclerk parttime Keller's TOO, Manhattan, Kans., 1969-73; travel agt. Harvey Travel, Houston, 1973-74; food editor Skagit Valley Herald Newspaper, Mount Vernon, Wash., 1974-75; asst. mktg. dir. First Fed. Savs. & Loan Assn., Mount Vernon, Wash., 1975-76; freelance writer LaConner, Wash., 1976-78; travel agt. Montrose (Colo.) World Travel, 1978-79; copyeditor, salesperson KUBC AM-FM Radio and KWDE-FM Radio, Montrose, 1978-80, 80-81; pub. rels. advt. cons. Patty A. Bryant Comm., Amarillo, Tex., 1981-90; exec. v.p., gen. mgr. Musical Drama "TEXAS" and Tex. Panhandle Heritage Found., Canyon, 1992-94, pres., gen. mgr., 1994—. Conf. and visitors coun. bd. Amarillo C. of C., 1988—, Conv. & Tourism chmn., 1989—, convs. com. chmn., 1989-90, tourism com. chmn., 1988-89, quality of life coun., 1989-94, chmn. com. vice chmn., 1987-88; Tex. leadership conv. steering com. Leadership Amarillo Alumnae, 1987-89, bd. dirs., 1988-91; 1st v.p. Panhandle-Plains Hist. Mus. Aux., 1986-88, pres., 1988-90; bd. dirs. Panhandle-Plains Hist. Soc., 1989-93; bd. dirs. Lone Star Ballet, 1990—, comm. chmn., 1990, nominating com. chmn. 1992-93, 95-96; apptd. by Gov. George Bush to Tex. Dept. Commerce policy bd. Recipient Leadership award Tex. Rural Electric Women's Assn., 1988, Disting. Svc. award 1996, Outstanding Contbns. to Tourism award Amarillo C. of C., 1989, Spotlight on Excellence award Nat. Coun. Rural Electric Communicators, 1991, Addie award of Merit, Amarillo Advt. Fedn., 1992, Gold Addie award Amarillo Advt. Fedn., 1993, Career Achievement award Amarillo Women's Network, 1992, 93, Merit Addie award 1994; named Globe News Good Neighbor, 1989; named for Outstanding Achievement in the Arts, Amarillo C. of C. Arts Com., 1992. Mem. AAUP, Nat. Rural Electric Women's Assn. (sec.-treas. 1983-85, v.p. 1985-87, pres. 1987-89), Farm Women's Leadership Network, Leadership Tex., Leadership Tex. Alumnae Assn. (bd. dirs. 1991-94, sec. 1991-92), Am. Mktg. Assn., Am. Assn. Am. Travel Editors, BBB Amarillo (bd. dirs. 1991-93), Rotary Club of Canyon (bd. dirs. 1991—, pres. 1996-97). Methodist. Home: PO Box 9897 Amarillo TX 79105-5897 Office: Tex Panhandle Heritage Found PO Box 268 Canyon TX 79015-0268

BRYANT, PERRIN CRANFORD, pilot; b. Birmingham, Ala., Jan. 1, 1941; s. Phillip Nelson and Alice Mildred (Cranford) B.; m. Patricia Ann Thompson, Oct. 20, 1963; children: Perrin Cranford II, Ann Renee, Susan Lee, Samantha Jo. BS, Auburn (Ala.) U., 1963; student, Air Command and Staff Coll., 1980, Air War Coll., 1987. With Thompson & Assocs., Birmingham, Ala., 1968-76; motel mgr. Thompson Motels Inc., Birmingham, Ala., 1972-76; pilot SouthTrust Corp., Birmingham, Ala., 1976-88, chief pilot, 1988—. Capt. USAF, 1963-68; lt. col. Ala. Air N.G., 1973—. Named Mgr. of the Yr., Rodeway Inn, Inc., 1974. Mem. Quiet Birdmen. Office: SouthTrust Corp 4427 E Lake Blvd Birmingham AL 35217-4033

BRYANT, WINSTON, state attorney general; b. Donaldson, Ark., Oct. 3, 1938. B.A. in Bus. Adminstrn, Ouachita Bapt. U., 1960; LL.B., U. Ark., 1963; LL.M. in Adminstrv. Law, George Washington U., 1970. Bar: Ark. 1963. Individual practice law Malvern, Ark., 1964-66, 71-75; atty. Ark. Ins. Commn., 1966; asst. U.S. atty. for Eastern Dist. Ark., 1967; legis. asst. to Senator from Ark., 1968-71; dep. pros. atty. Hot Spring County, Ark., 1971-75; mem. Ark. Ho. of Reps., 1973-76; sec. of state State of Ark., Little Rock, 1976-80; lt. gov. State of Ark., 1981-91, atty. gen., 1991—; instr. polit. sci. Ouachita Bapt. U., 1971-73, Henderson (Ark.) State U., 1973—. Mem. Ark. Youth Svcs. Planning Adv. Coun., 1974, Ark. Gov.'s Ad Hoc Com. on Workmen's Compensation, 1975. Served to capt., inf. U.S. Army, 1963-64. Mem. ABA, Ark. Bar Assn. (ho. of dels.), Malvern C. of C. (pres. 1972), Am. Legion, Ark. Farm Bur. Baptist. Office: Office of Atty Gen 323 Center St Little Rock AR 72201-2605

BRYSON, MARION RITCHIE, army scientist; b. Centralia, Mo., Aug. 26, 1927; d. Thomas Raymond and Helen Price (Pool) B.; m. Lenora Jane Kalips, July 22, 1947 (div. Aug. 1992); children: Rosalyn Irby, Nina Harmon, Kevin, Richard; m. Winona Villanueva, Oct. 16, 1993; children: Christopher Luna, Noelani Luna. BS in Edn., U. Mo., 1949, MA, 1950; PhD, Iowa State U., 1958. Tchr. Elgin (Ill.) High Sch., 1950-52; instr. U. Idaho, Moscow, 1952-53, Drake U., Des Moines, 1953-55; rsch. assoc. Iowa State U., Ames, 1955-58; researcher, asst. prof., assoc. prof. Duke U., Durham, N.C., 1958-68; tech. dir. Inst. Systems, Ft. Belvoir, Va., 1968-72; scientific advisor Combat Devels. Experimentation Command, Ft. Ord, Calif., 1972-83; dir. Combat Experiment Camp, Ft. Ord, Calif., 1983-91; tech. dir. Test & Experimental Command, Ft. Hood, Tex., 1991-94. Contbr. tech. papers to tech. jours. With U.S. Army, 1946-47. Fellow Mil. Oper. Rsch. Soc. (pres. 1976-77).

BRYSON, PAULA KAY, secondary school educator; b. New Albany, Ind., Oct. 4, 1945; d. Paul Lomax and Sarah (Shope) B.; m. Walter Randall Scruggs, Oct. 2, 1965 (div. 1983); children: Randall Scott Scruggs, Vance Andrew Bryson. BSBA in Mktg., Western Carolina U., 1971, cert. in Teaching, 1988, MA in Edn., 1989. Cert. secondary sch. tchr., N.C. Area sec. N.C. State Hwy. Commn., Waynesville, 1966-67; dep. sec. Western Carolina U., Cullowhee, 1967-71; office mgr. Akzo Am., Asheville, N.C., 1971-88; sec. tchr. Asheville High Sch., Asheville, 1989—; instr. A-B C.C., Asheville, 1990—. Sponsor Maggie BMW Nat. Motorcycle Rally. Mem. N.C. Bus. & Profl. Women (pres. Asheville chpt. 1990-91, state bd. dirs. 1991-93, dist. dir. 1992-93, Woman of Yr. 1991), Nat. Bus. Edn. Assn., Am. Vocat. Assn., N.C. Assn. Edn., N.C. Bus. Edn. Assn., N.C. Vocat. Assn., Western Carolina Women's Coalition (v.p. 1992-94), N.C. State Dept. Pub. Instruction (program leadership coun. bus. edn.), Kappa Delta Pi, Beta Sigma Phi. Methodist. Home: 16 W Baird Mountain Rd Asheville NC 28804-1126 Office: Asheville High Sch 419 Mcdowell St Asheville NC 28803-2610

BUCCIERO, JOSEPH MARIO, JR., executive engineering firm; b. Phila., Mar. 27, 1948; s. Joseph Mario Sr. and Carmela (Biscari) B.; m. Nancy Louise Arnquist, Aug. 19, 1972; children: Paul Joseph, Mark Benjamin. BS, Villanova U., 1969. Software programmer, project software engr. Leeds and Northrup Co., North Wales, Pa., 1969-72; applications engr. Leeds and Northrup Co., North Wales, 1972-74; systems cons. Macro Corp., Horsham, Pa., 1974-76; consulting engr. Macro Corp., Horsham, 1976-82, sr. consulting engr., 1982-89; strategic bus. unit mgr. Cegelec ESCA, Bellevue, Wash., 1989-90; prin. cons. KEMA-ECC, Fairfax, Va., 1990—; bus. area mgr. KEMA-ECC, Fairfax, 1991—; v.p. KEMA-ECC, Inc., Fairfax, 1992—. Contbr. articles to profl. jours. Ch. coun. pres. Little Zion Luth. Ch., Telford, Pa., 1980-85. Mem. IEEE (sr. mem.). Home: 6619 Mccambell Cluster Centreville VA 20120-3731

BUCCINO, MARGUERITE, management consultant, free lance writer; b. Stamford, Conn., Feb. 12, 1953; d. Francesco and Celeste (Totaro) B.; m. Alfredo Tamez, Jan 3, 1992; 1 child, Bianca Lucia Tamez-Buccino. BS in Fin., La. State U., 1983; MBA, U. Tex., Arlington, 1986. Asst. to treas. Snyder Oil Ptnrs., Fort Worth, 1984; fin. cons. Merrill Lynch, Dallas, 1984-89; bus. mgr. CBI Labs., Dallas, 1990-92; pvt. practice mgmt. cons. specializing in personal care products Dallas, 1992—. Mem. Friendly Visitor Program, VNA, Dallas, 1991—. Mem. Italian Club of Dallas (treas. 1989-90), U. Tex. Arlington MBA Alumni Assn. (program coord. 1989-90). Home and Office: 9957 Dresden Dr Dallas TX 75220-6303

BUCHANAN, EDWARD A., education educator; b. Newark, Aug. 28, 1937; s. Osborne B. and Edna Dorothy (Weber) B.; m. Gladys J. Buchanan, Aug. 28, 1965; children Roger, Becky. AB, Rutgers U., 1959; MRE, N.Y. Theol. Sem., 1962; EdD, So. Bapt. Theol. Sem., 1970. Tchr. Cen. Sch., Middlesex, N.J.; assoc. prof. psychology and edn. Grand Rapids (Mich.) Bapt. Coll.; dean of acad. affairs, prof. Lancaster (Pa.) Bible Coll.; prof. edn., dir. continuing edn. Bethel Theol. Sem., St. Paul; prof. edn. Southeastern Bapt. Theol. Sem., Wake Forest, N.C. Contbr. articles to profl. jours. Mem. APA, ASCD, Am. Ednl. Rsch. Assn., Nat. Soc. Study of Edn. Home: 1113 Silent Brook Rd Wake Forest NC 27587-7145

BUCHANAN, HARRIETTE CUTTINO, humanities educator; b. St. Augustine, Fla., June 5, 1942; d. John Tindal and Nell Parrot (Seabrook) Cuttino; m. Baird Lee Buchanan, Jan. 13, 1973; 1 child, Ian Baird. BA, Boston U., 1964; MA, East Carolina U., 1965; PhD in Am. Lit., U. N.C., 1974. Instr. in English East Carolina U., Greenville, N.C., 1965-67; asst. prof. interdisciplinary studies Appalachian State U., 1983-90, assoc. prof., 1990-96, prof., 1996—; lectr. N.C. Libr. Assn., Duke U. Office Continuing Edn., 1984—; coord. videotutoring program learning assistance program Appalachian State U., 1987-93. Asst. editor: Jour. Health Care Mktg., 1980-83; editorial advisor: Appalachian Bus. Rev., 1980-83; guest editor: Jour. Developmental and Remedial Edn., 1981-82; contbr. articles and revs. to profl. jours. Named for inclusion in Women of Letters, A Group Portrait of North Carolina Writers, 1992; recipient award for outstanding svc. to students Nat. Assn. for Developmental Edn., 1989. Mem. MLA, Nat. Assn. for Devel. Edn. (archivist 1992—), Am. Studies Assn., Coll. English Assn., Conf. on Coll. Composition and Comm., Nat. Coun. Tchrs. English, N.C.-Va. Coll. English Assn. (pres.-elect 1993-94, pres. 1994-95), N.C. Assn. for Devel. Studies (pres. 1990-91, membership co-chmn. 1992-94), South Atlantic MLA, N.C. Assn. for Women in Edn., N.C. Coun. Ednl. Opportunity Programs, N.C. Lit. and Hist. Assn., N.C. Writers Network, Philol. Assn. Carolinas, also others. Home: 194 Eastview St Boone NC 28607-3612

BUCHANAN, JAMES MCGILL, economist, educator; b. Murfreesboro, TN, Oct. 2, 1919; s. James McGill and Lila (Scott) B.; m. Anne Bakke, Oct. 5, 1945. BS, Middle Tenn. State Coll., 1940; MA, U. Tenn., 1941; PhD, U. Chgo., 1948; D honoris causa, U. Giessen, 1982, U. Zurich, 1984, George Mason U., U. Valencia, New U. Lisbon, 1987, Ball State U., 1988, City U., London, 1988, Lycoming Coll., 1992, Free U., Rome, 1993, U. Bucharest, 1994, Acad. Econ. Studies, Romania, 1994, U. Catania, 1994, U. Porto, 1995, U. Valladolid (Spain), 1996. Assoc. prof. U. Tenn., 1948-50, prof. econs., 1950-51; prof. Fla. State U., 1951-56; prof. U. Va., 1956-62, Paul G. McIntyre prof. econs., 1962-68, chmn. dept., 1956-62; prof. UCLA, 1968-69; univ. disting. prof. Va. Poly. Inst., 1969-83, George Mason U., 1983—; adv. dir. Ctr. for Pub. Choice, 1969—; Fulbright rsch. scholar, Italy, 1955-56; Ford Faculty rsch. fellow, 1959-60; Fulbright vis. prof. Cambridge U., 1961-62. Author: (with C.L. Allen and M.R. Colberg) Prices, Income and Public Policy, 954, Public Principles of Public Debt, 1958, The Public Finances, 1960, Fiscal Theory and Political Economy, 1960, (with G. Tullock) The Calculus of Consent, 1962, Public Finance in Democratic Process, 1966, The Demand and Supply of Public Goods, 1968, Cost and Choice, 1969, (with N. Devletoglou) Academia in Anarchy, 1970; Editor: (with R. Tollison) Theory of Public Choice, 1972, (with G.F. Thirlby) LSE Essays on Cost, 1973, The Limits of Liberty, 1975, (with R. Wagner) Democracy in Deficit, 1977, Freedom in Constitutional Contract, 1978, What Should Economists Do?, 1979, (with G. Brennan) The Power to Tax, 1980; (with G. Brennan) The Reason of Rules, 1985; Liberty Market and State, 1985, Economics: Between Predictive Science and Moral Philosophy, 1987, Explorations in Constitutional Economics, 1989, Economics and Ethics of Constitutional Order, 1991, Better than Plowing, 1992, Ethics and Economic Progress, 1994; editor: (with Yong Yoon) Return to Increasing Returns, 1994; contbr. articles to profl. jours. Lt. USNR, 1941-46. Decorated Bronze Star; recipient Seidman award, 1984, Nobel Prize in Econs., 1986. Fellow Am. Acad. Arts and Scis.; mem. Am. Econ. Assn. (exec. com. 1966-69, v.p. 1971, dist. fellow 1983—), So. Econ. Assn. (pres. 1963), Western Econ. Assn. (pres. 1983), Mt. Pelerin Soc. (pres. 1984-86). Home: PO Box G Blacksburg VA 24063-1021 Office: George Mason U Buchanan House Mail Stop 1 E6 Fairfax VA 22030-4443

BUCHANAN, JO ANN, social worker, educator; b. Dallas, Aug. 28, 1960. BA, So. Meth. U., 1982; MS, Emporia State U., 1984; MS in social work, U. Tex., 1987. Lic. social worker, Ky. Counselor Denton (Tex.) County Friends of the Family, 1984-85, clin. dir., 1988-89; counselor Arlington (Tex.) Women's Shelter, 1986-87, Rape Crisis Program/Women's Ctr. of Tarrant County, Fort Worth, Tex., 1987; treatment dir. Oak Grove Treatment Ctr., Burleson, Tex., 1987-88; pvt. prac. psychotherapist Dallas, 1989-93; instr. psychology Prestonsburg (Ky.) Cmty. Coll., 1993-95; asst. prof. social work Cumberland Coll., Williamsburg, Ky., 1995—. Mem. Nat. Assn. of Social Workers (Acad. of Certified Social Workers (ACSW). Office: Cumberland Coll 6000 College Station Dr Williamsburg KY 40769

BUCHANAN, ORENA GREGG, community health nurse; b. Greenville, S.C., Feb. 15, 1935; d. Roy Q. and Evie Mae (Pressley) Gregg; m. Verl Lea Buchanan, Sept. 14, 1954; 1 child, Christine Orena Buchanan Woody. Diploma, Spartanburg (S.C.) Gen. Hosp., 1956. Pub. health nurse Spartanburg Health Dept., 1979; pub. health nurse Richland County Health Dept., Columbia, S.C., 1979-80; home health pub. health nurse Charleston County Health Dept., Charleston, S.C., 1981-84; home health pub. health nurse, team leader Charleston County Health Dept., North Charleston, S.C., 1984-95; supr. Berkeley County Health Dept., Moncks Corner, S.C., 1993-95; supervisor Charleston County Health Dept., S.C., 195—. Mem. S.C. State Employees Assn. Office: Charleston County Health 1946 Savage Rd Ste 300E Charleston SC 29407

BUCHANAN, RANDAL THOMAS, supplier relations director; b. Oakland, Calif., June 17, 1948; s.Thomas H. and Ramona B. B.; m. Ruby Dunbar, June 10, 1989. BS in Fin., San Jose State U., 1970, MBA, 1973. Materials mgr., supr. and planner Semiconductor Div. Nat. Semiconductor Corp., Santa Clara, Calif., 1973-78, mgr. subcontract assembly ops., 1978-81, mgr. of materials Dyna-Craft Div., 1981-83, dir. of materials Dyna-Craft Div., 1983-85, dir. of mktg., 1985-86; mgr. of adminstrv. svcs. Mil. Aerospace Div. Nat. Semiconductor Corp., Tucson, Ariz., 1986-89; mgr. partnering programs Sematech (affiliated with Nat. Semiconductor Corp.), Austin, Tex., 1990-91, dir. procurement & contracting, 1991—. Office: Sematech 2706 Montopolis Dr Austin TX 78741-6408

BUCHANAN, RAY ALLEN, clergyman; b. Houston, Jan. 8, 1947; s. Wilbur Allen and Louise (Zwahr) B.; m. Marian Kelly, Aug. 5, 1967; children: Peter Andrew, Amy Krysteen. BA, U. N.C., Wilmington, 1972; MDiv, Southeastern Bapt. Theol. Seminary, 1976; DD, Shenandoah Coll., 1990. Ordained to ministry United Meth. Ch., 1977. Pastor North Mecklenburg United Meth. Ch., Union Level, Va., 1973-77, Oak Hall (Va.) United Meth. Ch., 1977-79, Bedford (Va.) Cir. United Meth. Ch., 1979-81; co-founder, co-dir. Soc. St. Andrew, Big Island, Va., 1979—; mem. Va. ann. conf. United Meth. Ch. Co-editor Gleanings, 1986; co-author: Prepare the Way of the Coed, 1986; author: Pass the Potatoes, 1987; contbr. articles, poems to various publs. Vice pres. bd. trustees Sedalia Fin Arts Ctr.; mem. Lynchburg Dist. Coun. on Ministries; chaplain Clan Buchanan Soc. in U.S.; commr. Mid-Atlantic Region Clan Buchanan Soc. Internat.; pres. Clar Innis Found.; mem. nat. com. for World Food Day; co-organizer Va. Congress on Hunger. Recipient Disting. Alumnus award U. N.C.-Wilmington, 1985, Real Am. Hero award Maxwell House, 1992. Home: RR 1 Box 867 Big Island VA 24526-9746

BUCHER, FRANÇOIS, art history educator; b. Lausanne, Switzerland, June 11, 1927; came to U.S., 1952; s. Alois J. and Gabrielle (Zundel) B.; divorced; 2 children. PhD, Bern (Switzerland) U., Bern, Switzerland, 1955. With U. Minn., 1952-53, Yale U., 1954-60, Brown U., 1960-62, Princeton U., 1963-69, SUNY, Binghamton, 1970-77; prof. medieval art and architecture Fla. State U., Tallahassee; dir. Soc. Arch. Historians, 1964-67; mem. Exec. Coun. of Arts, State of N.J., 1965-70; pres. Internat. Ctr. Medieval Art, 1966-70; vis. prof. Ctr. d'Etudes Supérieures Mediévales, Poitiers, 1968; co-dir. Ctr. Medieval and Early Renaissance Studies, SUNY, Binghamton, 1973-77, sr. fellow, 1975—; mem. exec. coun. Southeastern Medieval Assn., 1983-86; pres. Nautilus Found., Lloyd, Fla., 1989—, mem. exec. coun.; mem. Archtl. Rsch. Ctr., 1993—; active numerous coms. Fla. State U., Tallahassee. Author: Notre-Dame de Bonmont und die ersten Zisterzienserabteien der Schweiz, 1957, Josef Albers, Trotz der Geraden, 1961, Josef Albers, Despite Straight Lines, 1969, 2d edit., 1977, paperback edit., 1978, Japanese edit., 1987, The Pamplona Bibles, 1970, Architector, The Lodge and Sketch-Books of Medieval Architects, 1979, The Traveler's Key to Medieval France, 1986,

A Blazing End, 1984, paperback edit., 1986; founder, editor Gesta jour., 1961-70; contbr. articles to profl. jours. Chmn. Planning Bd., Millstone, N.J., 1964-70; trustee Interfuture, 1968—. With Swiss Armed Forces, 1948-51. Guggenheim fellow, 1956, 66, Inst. for Advanced Study fellow, 1962-63, Southeastern Inst. for Medieval and Renaissance Studies fellow, 1967; life fellow Internat. Ctr. Medieval Art, 1975—; Disting. scholar S.C. Coll., 1968-69, Faculty Exch. scholar SUNY, 1976-77. Democrat. Home: PO Box 368 Lloyd FL 32337-0368 Office: Fla State U History Of Art Dept Tallahassee FL 32306

BUCHHOLZ, ANGELA MARIE, rehabilitation nurse; b. Tonawanda, N.Y., Mar. 29, 1971; d. Victor Walter and Helen Irene (Shalaty) B. BSN, U. Memphis, 1994. RN, Tenn. Unit sec. Jackson (Tenn.)-Madison County Gen. Hosp., 1990, nursing asst., 1992; nurse technician St. Francis Hosp., Memphis, 1993-94; registered nurse Jackson (Tenn.)-Madison County Gen. Hosp., 1994—. Youth advisor St. Mary's Cath. Youth Program, Jackson, 1994. Mem. ANA, Nat. League Nursing. Republican. Roman Catholic. Home: 151 Linda Vista Dr Jackson TN 38301-4263

BUCHHOLZ, DONALD ALDEN, stock brokerage company executive; b. LaPorte, Tex., Mar. 10, 1929; s. Fred T. and Chrystine (McCombs) B.; m. Ruth Vernon, May 17, 1958; children: Robert, Chrystine Louise. BBA, North Tex. U., 1952. C.P.A., Tex. Acct., staff auditor Peat, Marwick & Mitchell, Dallas, 1952-54; asst. sec.-treas., chief acct. ICT Discount Corp., 1954-56; comptroller Eppler-Guerin & Turner, Inc., 1956-59; ptnr. Cheshier-Buchholz (pub. accountants), 1959-60; comptroller, sec. Parker Ford, Inc. (stock brokers), Dallas, 1960-63, also dir., 1962-63; v.p., chief adminstrv. officer, sec. Weber, Hall, Cobb & Caudle, Inc., Dallas, 1963-72, also bd. dirs.; ptnr., chmn. bd. Southwest Securities Group, 1972—; chmn. bd. Buckley Oil Co., Dallas, 1994—, First Savs. Bank, Arlington, Tex., 1994—; bd. govs. N.Y. Stock Exch., 1969-71; assoc. mem. Am. Stock Exch.; mem. Chgo. Bd. Trade, Midwest Stock Exch. Trustee Garland Ind. Sch. Bd., 1971-74, pres., 1973-74; trustee Dallas County C.C. Dist., 1982—, pres., 1990-91; bd. dirs. Garland Meml. Hosp., 1981-85, Garland Meml. Hosp. Found., 1981—, Alliance of Higher Edn., 1994—, Coun. for Higher Edn. Accreditation, 1996—, Dallas Citizens Coun.; mem. adv. bd. Baylor U., 1991-94. Mem. Nat. Security Dealers Assn. (chmn. bus. conduct com. dist. 6 1985-87, bd. govs. 1988-91), Securities Industry Assn. (exec. com. south cen. dist. 1986—, exec. bd. 1990-93), Dallas Security Dealers Assn. (sec. 1961), Tex. Stock and Bond Dealers Assn. (treas. 1982, v.p. 1986-87, pres. 1987-88), Lakewood Country Club, Ea. Hills Country Club, City Club Dallas, Kiwanis (pres. 1957-58), Nat. Coun. of Policy Advisors. Baptist. Home: 3627 Glenbrook Ct Garland TX 75041-5101 Office: SW Securities Inc 1201 Elm St Ste 4300 Dallas TX 75270-2134

BUCHKO, MICHAEL SCOTT, construction executive; b. Washington, June 10, 1946; s. Joe and Martha Virginia (Gicker) B.; m. Linda Leigh Bateman, Aug. 20, 1968 (div. Nov. 1975); m. Janice DeLaquil, May 21, 1976; 1 child, Allison Michelle. BS, Frederick Coll., 1968; postgrad. in contract law, No. Va. Comm. Coll., 1976. V.p. The Shade Shop, Inc., Sterling, Va., 1968-78; v.p., owner Fairfax Home Window Products, Inc., Manassas, Va., 1978—, also bd. dirs.; v.p., owner Fairfax (Va.) Home Decorating Ctr., Inc., 1980—, also bd. dirs.; owner Fairfax Home Joint Venture, Manassas, 1985—, also bd. dirs.; v.p., owner Uncle Sam's Express, Inc., Washington, 1987—. Mem. Nat. Bldrs. Assn., Va. Bldrs. Assn. Episcopalian. Home: 127 Chesterfield Pl SW Leesburg VA 20175-2700 also: 14870 Patuxent Ave Solomons MD 20688 Office: Fairfax Home Window Products 9411 West St Manassas VA 22110-5507

BUCHMAN, KENNETH WILLIAM, lawyer; b. Plant City, Fla., Nov. 20, 1956; s. Paul Sidney and Beryle (Solomon) B.; m. MarDee H. Buchman, May 9, 1985; 1 child, Katherine Elizabeth. AA, U. Fla., 1976, BBA, 1978, JD, 1981. Bar: Fla. 1981; U.S. Dist. Ct. (mid. dist.) Fla. 1981; U.S. Ct. Appeals (11th cir.) 1986; U.S. Supreme Ct. 1988; bd. certified in City, County and Local Govt. Law. Ptnr. Buchman and Buchman, Plant City, 1981-85, Buchman and Buchman, P.A., Plant City, 1985-91; sole practitioner Plant City, 1991—; city atty. City of San Antonio, Fla., 1995—; asst. city atty. City of Plant City, 1982-91, city atty., 1991—. Mem. Fla. Mcpl. Attys. Assn. (steering com. 1984-85), Attys. Title Ins. Fund, Kiwanis (pres. Plant City club 1986-87), Olin S. Wright Masons (Plant City), Plant City Bar Assn. Democrat. Jewish. Office: 212 N Collins St Plant City FL 33566-3314

BUCHMEYER, JERRY, federal judge; b. Overton, Tex., Sept. 5, 1933. Student, Kilgore Jr. Coll., 1953; B.A., U. Tex., 1955, LL.B., 1957. Bar: Tex. 1957. Assoc. Thompson, Knight, Simmons & Bullion, Dallas, 1958-63, ptnr., 1963-66, sr. ptnr., 1968-79; judge U.S. Dist. Ct. (no. dist.) Tex., Dallas, 1979-94, chief judge, 1995—. Mem. ABA, Dallas Bar Assn. (pres. 1979), State Bar Tex. (chmn. com. 1978-79, dir. 1982-84, 94-95). Office: US Dist Courthouse 1100 Commerce St Rm 15 E6 Dallas TX 75242-1027*

BUCKAWAY, WILLIAM ALLEN, JR., lawyer; b. Bowling Green, Ky., Dec. 3, 1934; s. William Allen and Kathryn Anne (Scoggin) B.; m. Bette Joan Cross, July 27, 1963; 1 child, William Allen III. AB, Centre Coll. of Ky., 1956; JD, U. Louisville, 1961. Bar: Ky. 1961, U.S. Dist Ct. (we. dist.) Ky. 1981, U.S. Dist. Ct. (ea. dist.) Ky. 1986, U.S. Supreme Ct. 1975. Assoc. Tilford, Dobbins, Caye & Alexander, Louisville, 1961-78; ptnr. Tilford, Dobbins, Alexander, Buckaway & Black, Louisville, 1978—; atty. Masonic Homes of Ky., Louisville, 1985—; gen. counsel Kosair Charitites. Elder 2d Presbyn. Ch., Louisville, 1975; emeritus mem. bd. govs. Lexington (Ky.) unit Shriners Hosp. for Cripled Children, 1986, sec., 1989-94; adj. John Hunt Morgan Camp, 1993-96. With USNR, 1956-58. Named Disting. Alumnus U. Louisville Sch. Law, 1986, Centre Coll., 1986. Mem. SAR, Soc. of the Cin. in State the of Va., Sons Confederate Vets., Masons (33 deg., past master Crescent Hill lodge 1967, chmn. jurisprudence and law com. imperial coun. Shrine of N.Am. 1989-91), Kosair Shrine Temple (potentate 1986), Rotary, Soc. Colonial Wars, Soc. War of 1812, Sigma Chi, Phi Alpha Delta. Home: 1761 Sulgrave Rd Louisville KY 40205-1643 Office: Tilford Dobbins et al 1400 One Riverfront Plz Louisville KY 40205

BUCKELEW, ROBIN BROWNE, aerospace engineer; b. York, Pa., Mar. 14, 1947; d. Grant Hugh and Frances (Coleman) Browne; m. William Paul Buckelew, June 5, 1971; children: Leon, Christina. BS in Aerospace Engring., U. Ala., 1970; MS in Engring., U. Ala., Huntsville, 1977, PhD in Engring., 1994. Registered profl. engr., Ala. Aerospace engr. U.S. Army Missile Command, Redstone Arsenal, Ala., 1970-74; systems engr. U.S. Army Missile Intelligence Agy., Huntsville, Ala., 1974-81; group leader air vehicle Sentry U.S. Army Ballistics Missile Def. System Command, Huntsville, 1981-83, interceptor engr. High Endoatmospheric Def. Interceptor, 1983-85; chief air vehicle div. HEDI project U.S. Army Strategic Def. Command, Huntsville, 1985-88, chief Ground Based Interceptor Experiment Office, 1988-91, chief engr. HEDI project, 1991-92; dir. Sys. Directorate, U.S. Army Space and Strategic Def. Command, Huntsville, 1993-94, dir. Engring. and Sys. Directorate, 1994-95; dir. Missile Def. Battle Integration Ctr., 1995—. Contbr. articles to AIAA conf. proceedings. Bd. dirs. Trinity Personal Growth Ctr., Huntsville, 1990-92. Named Strategic Def. Engr. of Yr., NSPE, 1990, Disting. Engring. fellow U. Ala., 1993, State of Ala. Engring. Hall of Fame, 1995; recipient Superior Civilian Svc. award U.S. Army, 1991, Outstanding Alumna award U. Ala., Huntsville, 1996. Fellow AIAA (assoc.); mem. Capstone Engring. Soc. (bd. dirs. dist. 4), Sigma Xi. Methodist. Home: 117 Bel Air Rd SE Huntsville AL 35802-3107 Office: US Army Space Strategic Def Command Huntsville AL 35807

BUCKLA, ROBERT JOSEPH, college administrator, consultant; b. Endicott, N.Y., Aug. 16, 1962; s. John and Irene Ann (Straka) B. BA, St. Bonaventure U., 1984; MEd, Vanderbilt U., 1994. Dir. devel. Doane Stuart Sch., Albany, N.Y., 1985-87; dir. alumni and devel. Ctrl. Cath. High Sch., Lawrence, Mass., 1987-89; dir. devel. Theol. Coll./Cath. U., Washington, 1989-93; v.p. instnl. advancement Averett Coll., Danville, Va., 1995—; cons. Africa U., Old Mutare, Zimbabwe, 1994, Kersey & Assocs., Bethesda, Md., 1992-93. Vol., spkr. Coun. for Advancement and Support of Edn., Washington, 1985—; pres.'s adv. coun. on journalism St. Bonaventure U., 1991—, endowment com., 1992-94; vol. campaign to elect Sharon Pratt Kelly, Washington, 1992; cons. Men Stopping Violence, Atlanta, 1994—. Mem. St. Bonaventure U. Alumni Assn., Capital Rowing Club (bd. dirs. 1991-93), Vanderbilt U. Rowing Club. Home: 112 W Orange St Hillsborough NC 27278

BUCKLEW, NEIL S., educator, past university president; b. Morgantown, W.Va., Oct. 23, 1940; s. Douglas Earl and Lanah L. (Martin) B.; m. Iona Bucklew; children—Elizabeth, Jennifer, Jeffrey, Gayle, Cara. A.B., U. Mo.; M.S., U. N.C.; Ph.D. (grad. fellow), U. Wis. Dir. personnel Duke U., 1964-66; dir. employee relations U. Wis., 1966-70; prof., v.p. Central Mich. U., Mt. Pleasant, 1970-76; prof., provost Ohio U., Athens, 1976-80; pres. U. Mont., Missoula, 1981-86, W.Va. U., 1986-95; prof. W.Va. U., Morgantown, 1995—; vis. rsch. fellow Pa. State U.; arbitrator in field. Author: Public Sector Collective Bargaining, Planning in Higher Education. Mem. Nat. Assn. State Univs. and Land Grant Colls. Office: West Va U Coll Bus PO Box 6025 Morgantown WV 26506-7920

BUCKLEW, SUSAN CAWTHON, federal judge; b. 1942. BA, Fla. State U., 1964; MA, U. So. Fla., 1968; JD, Stetson U., 1977; LLD (hon.), Stetson Coll. Law, 1994. Tchr. Plant High Sch., 1964-65, 70-72, Seminole High Sch., 1965-67, Chamberlain High Sch., 1969; instr. Hillsborough C.C., 1974-75; corp. legal counsel Jim Walter Corp., 1978-82; county ct. judge Hillsborough County, 1982-86; circuit ct. judge 13th Jud. Circuit, 1986-93; judge U.S. Dist. Ct. (mid. dist.) Fla., 1993—; mem. Gender Bias Study Commn., 1988-90, Fla. Bar Bench Bar Commn., 1990-92; bd. overseers Stetson Coll. Law, 1994—. Recipient award Disting Svc., Fla. Coun. Crime and Delinquincy, 1990, Disting. Alumnus award Stetson Lawyers Assn., 1994. Mem. ABA, Fla. Gar Assn., Fla. Assn. Women Lawyers, Hillsborough Assn. Women Lawyers (award Outstanding Pub. Svc. ADvancing Status Women 1991), Hillsborough County Bar Assn. (Robert W. Patton Outstanding Jursit award young lawyer's sect. 1990), Fla. State U. Alumni Assn., Am. Inns Ct. (LII, William Glenn Terrell chpt.), Athena Soc., Tampa Club, Delta Delta Delta Alumnae. Office: US Dist Ct 611 N Florida Ave Rm 109 Tampa FL 33602-4500

BUCKLEY, BETTY BOB, journalist, consultant; b. Tonkawa, Okla., Nov. 1, 1925; d. Clinton Sawyer and Mary Powell (Barnes) Diltz; m. Ernest Lynn Buckley, Aug. 17, 1946 (dec. Aug. 1989); children: Betty Lynn, Patrick Joe and Michael Jay (twins), Norman Lee. Student, Tex. Tech U., 1943-46, S.D. State U., 1946, Tex. Christian U., 1966; BA in Communication, U. Tex., Arlington, 1983. Reporter Big Spring (Tex.) Herald, 1942-43; society reporter Lubbock (Tex.) Avalanche Jour., 1944; reporter Mercury-Chronicle, Manhattan, Kans., 1948, Ft. Worth Press, 1951; columnist Moroccan Courier, Casablanca, Morocco, 1953; asst. editor Gen. Dynamics News, Ft. Worth, 1968-71; dir. pub. rels. Casa Manana Theatre, Ft. Worth, 1975-82; tchr. pub. rels. S.D. State U., Brookings, 1986; freelance pub. rels. cons. Brookings, 1988-89. Recipient Casa Manana award for Humanitarian Support, 1996. Mem. AAUW, PEO, Women in Communication (pres. Ft. Worth chpt. 1957-59, 92-93, Outstanding mem. Ft. Worth chpt. 1977). Methodist. Home: 6808 Riverridge Rd Fort Worth TX 76116-9355

BUCKLEY, CHARLES ROBINSON, III, lawyer; b. Richmond, Va., Oct. 9, 1942; s. Charles Robinson and Eleanor (Small) B.; m. Virginia Lee, Apr. 17, 1971; children: Richard, Rebecca. BS, U. N.C., 1965, JD, 1969. Bars: N.C. 1969, U.S. Supreme Ct., 1979. Asst. city atty. City of Charlotte (N.C.), 1969-78; ptnr. Constangy, Goines, Buckley & Boyd, 1978-81, Taylor & Buckley, Charlotte, 1981-85; ptnr. Buckley Mcmullen & Buie, P.A., 1994—; town atty. Town of Matthew (N.C.), 1978—; faculty Ctrl. Piedmont C.C., 1970. Bd. dirs. Charlotte City Employees Credit Union, 1974-78; pres. PTA, 1980-82. Recipient Certificate of Merit, City of Charlotte, 1982. Mem. N.C. Bar Assn., N.C. Assn. Mun. Attys. (dir. 1979-81, 2d v.p. 1995—), Phi Alpha Delta. Democrat. Lutheran. Club: Optimist (pres. 1982-83). Home: 6813 Linda Lake Dr Charlotte NC 28215-4019

BUCKLEY, LINDA TIBBETTS, public relations executive; b. Hartford, Conn., Dec. 2, 1954; d. Wesley Frederick and Noreen Philomena (Lowe) T.; m. Robert Bruce Buckley, Sr., Nov. 9, 1985; children: Brendan Patrick, Robert Bruce Jr. Student, U. South Fla., 1973-74. Office mgr. Inside Sports Mag. (divsn. Newsweek), L.A., 1979-80; sr. researcher, reporter Newsweek mag., L.A., 1980-92; dep. editor Newsweek on Campus, L.A., 1987-89; mgr. publicity and pub. rels. Universal Studios Fla., Orlando, 1992-94, dir. publicity and pub. rels., 1994—. Mem. L.A. Mayor's Christopher Columbus Bicentennial Com., 1990; bd. dirs. Reseda (Calif.) Homeowners Assn., 1987-91; asst. campaign mgr. L.A. City Coun. Candidate Peter Ireland, 1988; mem. adv. bd. Camp Good Days and Spl. Times. Recipient Spl. award Matsushita Pub. Rels. Competition, 1992, 2 Awards of Merit, Internat. Assn. Bus. Communicators, 1994. Mem. Pub. Rels. Soc. Am., Fla. Pub. Rels. Assn. Democrat. Roman Catholic. Home: 239 Lake Ellen Dr Casselberry FL 32707-2913 Office: Universal Studios Fla 1000 Universal Studios Plz Orlando FL 32819-7601

BUCKLEY, PAMELA KAY, academic organization administrator. BA in English, U. Evansville, 1964; MAT, U. Louisville, 1970; EdD in Curriculum and Instrn., U. Houston, 1977. Sr. instr. manpower devel. div. The Gulf Bank, Kuwait, 1984-85; faculty developer staff instructional devel. dept. Houston Community Coll. System, 1985-88; co-dir. Commonwealth Ctr. for Edn. Tchrs. James Madison U., Harrisonburg, 1988-92, assoc. prof. Coll. of Edn. and Psychology, 1988-92; program staff devel. coord. U. Houston Tchr. Corps Project, 1978-80; various ednl. positions, 1964-78; assoc. rsch. scientist Far West Lab. for Ednl. R&D, San Francisco, 1980; assoc. project dir. U. Houston Tchr. Corps Project, 1981; tng. mgr. tng. div. City of Houston Civil Svc. Dept., 1981-83; sr. tng. specialist tng. div. Kuwait Inst. for Sci. Rsch.; dir. Eisenhower Math/Sci. Consortium, 1992—. Contbr. articles and revs. to profl. jours. Mem. ASTD, ASCD, Am. Ednl. Rsch. Assn., Assn. Tchr. Educators, Phi Delta Kappa. Home: 5402 Morning Dove Ln Cross Lanes WV 25313-1111

BUCKLEY, STEPHANIE DENISE, health care executive; b. Tulsa, Sept. 19, 1961; d. Richard Harvey and Judith Carol (Holtzinger) Welcher; m. Jeffery Lee Taylor, June 16, 1990 (div. July 1992); m. Dennis Ray Buckley, Oct. 30, 1995. BS, Okla. State U., 1983; MA, U. Okla., 1994. Reporter The Daily O'collegian, Stillwater, Okla., 1980-83; news anchor KOSU-FM, Stillwater, 1981, KRXO-FM, Stillwater, 1982; asst. producer KTVY-TV, Oklahoma City, 1983-84; anchor/reporter KTEN, Ada, Okla., 1985-86; producer America's Shopping Channel, Oklahoma City, 1987; pub. rels. coordinator S.W. Med. Ctr. Okla., Oklahoma City, 1988-89, pub. rels. assoc., 1990-91, mgr. pub. rels. and devel., 1991-93; exec. dir., CEO Neighborhood Alliance, Oklahoma City, 1994-95; cmty. devel. assoc. Integris Health, Oklahoma City, 1995—; cons. on brochure, Women to Woman, 1990. Mem. comms. com. United Way, Oklahoma City, 1989-90; bd. dirs. Nat. Clown and Laughter Hall of Fame, 1989—; bd. dirs. HUGS, 1992-94, Firesafe Found., 1994—, Internat. Ctr. for Humor and Health, 1995—, contact, 1996; bd. dirs. Youth Build Oklahoma City, 1996; mem. Jr. Hospitality. Recipient Good Guy award, KTVY-TV, 1988, 89. Mem. Women in Comms. (v.p. 1981-82), Am. Hosp. Assn., Okla. Hosp. Assn., Am. Soc. Health Care Mktg. and Pub. Rels., Pub. Rels. Soc. Am., Oklahoma City C. of C., South Oklahoma City C. of C., Lions Internat., Am. Bus. Clubs (bd. dirs.), Rotary Internat. (group study exch. to Queensland, Australia 1995), West Oklahoma City Rotary Club, Oklahoma City Rose Garden Club. Methodist. Office: Integris Health C-30 3366 Northwest Expressway Oklahoma City OK 73112

BUCKLIN, LEONARD HERBERT, lawyer; b. Mpls., Apr. 17, 1933; s. Leonard A. and Lilah B. (Nordland) B.; m. Charla Lee Bucklin; children: Karen, Anne, David, Douglas, Lea, Gregory. BS in Law, U. Minn., 1955, JD, 1957. Bar: Minn. 1957, U.S. Dist. Ct. Minn. 1957, N.D. 1960, U.S. Dist. Ct. N.D. 1960, U.S. Ct. Appeals (8th cir.) 1971, U.S. Supreme Ct. 1973, Colo. 1989, U.S. Dist. Ct. Colo. 1989, Tex. 1992, U.S. Dist. Ct. Tex. 1993. Ptnr. Larson, Loevinger, Lindquist, Freeman & Fraser, Mpls., 1957-60, Zuger & Bucklin, Bismarck, N.D., 1960-87; pres., Bucklin Trial Lawyers, P.C., 1988-95; of counsel Bucklin and Klemine, Bismarck, N.D., 1992—, Allison and Huerta, Corpus Christi, 1992—; lectr. on product liability to various groups; mem. Joint Trial Procedures Com. N.D. Supreme Ct., 1977-92. Fellow Internat. Acad. Trial Lawyers (bd. dirs.); mem. ABA (litigation sect.), UNOS (patient affairs and ethics coms.), ATLA, Am. Acad. Forensic Scientists, State Bar Tex. (litigation sect.), Tex. Trial Lawyers Assn., Corpus Christi Bar Assn., Rotary Club Corpus Christi (Paul Harris Fellow), Order of Coif, Phi Delta Phi, Delta Sigma Rho, Town Club Corpus Christi. Author: Civil Practice of North Dakota, 1975, ann. supplements, 1976-92. Methodist. Home: 4350 Ocean Dr Apt 703 Corpus Christi TX 78412-2570 Office: 920 Leopard St Corpus Christi TX 78401-2423

BUCKMAN, MARY WARNER, promotions and public relations executive; b. Ft. Madison, Iowa, Mar. 6, 1946; d. George Franklin and Virginia Ruth (Brown) W.; m. James Patrick Buckman, Dec, 18, 1966 (div. 1975); David Jeffery, Bradley Christopher, Duane Anthony, Joseph Claude, Jody. Student, Northeast State U., 1964-66, Mary Crest Coll., 1968-69. Dist. mgr. Beaumont (Tex.) Enterprise Jour., 1978-79, jour. city mgr., 1979-80, mgr. circulation and promotion, 1980-82; mgr. sales and circulation Gannett Newspaper Prodn. Co., Shreveport, La., 1982-84, dir. promotion and pub. relations, 1985—. Contbr. articles to profl. jours. Mem. Shreveport Speakers Bur.; bd. mem. Teen Challenge, 1985—, Coalition for Parent Edn., 1985—, Shreveport Mayor's comn. U.S. Constitution Bicentennial, 1987. Recipient Community Service award Internat. Promotion Assn., 1983, Editorial and Circulation award Internat. Promotion Assn., 1983. Mem. Adtv. Federation, Internat. Newspaper Mktg. Assn., Nat. Research Council. Mem. Assembly of God Ch. Office: Dir Promo & Pub Relations Gannett Newspaper Prodn Co Shreveport LA 71102

BUCKNER, JOHN KENDRICK, aerospace engineer; b. Indpls., June 13, 1936; s. Roland Kendrick and Lucille (Cave) B.; m. Nancy Ann Smith, June 13, 1974; children: James Kendrick, Bari Kay, Kendrick Ann. BA in Math., DePauw U., 1958; MS in Aero-Engring., Stanford U., 1960. Aerodynamics sr. engr. Gen. Dynamics, Ft. Worth, 1960-69, supr. aerodyns., 1969-75, aircraft project engr., 1975-77, mgr. flight controls, 1977-80, dir. advanced programs, 1980-89, v.p. spl. programs, 1989-95; com. mem. Nat. Rsch. Coun./Naval Studies Bd., Washington, 1990, Aeronautics and Space Engring. Bd., 1992-96; mem. aerospace rsch. and tech. subcom. aeronautics adv. com. NASA, Washington, 1988-93. Bd. dirs. Am. Heart Assn., Ft. Worth, 1990—, chmn., 1995-96. Fellow AIAA (assoc., chmn. aircraft design tech. com. 1990-92, pub. policy com. 1988—). Home: 5401 Benbridge Dr Fort Worth TX 76107-3209

BUCKNER-REITMAN, JOYCE, psychologist, educator; b. Benton, Ark., Sept. 25, 1937; d. Waymond Floyd Pannell and Willie Evelyn (Wright) Whitley; m. John W. Buckner, Aug. 29, 1958 (div. 1970); children: Cheryl, John, Chris; m. Sanford Reitman, Aug. 13, 1994. BA, Ouachita Bapt. Coll., 1959; MS in Edn., Henderson State U., 1964; PhD, North Tex. State U., 1970. Lic. psychologist, Tex., marriage and family therapist; cert. Nat. Registry Health Svc. Providers in Psychology; master trainer in imago relationship therapy. Assoc. prof. U. Tex., Arlington, 1970-80, chmn. dept. edn., 1976-78; pvt. practice psychology, Arlington, 1974—; dir., chief profl. officer Southwest Inst. Relationship Devel., Weatherford, Tex.; author, profl. speaker; appeared on internat. TV shows, including Oprah Winfrey Show. Mem. APA, Nat. Assn. for Imago Relationship Therapy (pres.), Nat. Speakers Assn., Am. Assn. Marital and Family Therapy. Home: 2208 Farmer Rd Weatherford TX 76087

BUCKRHAM, GAIL WILLIAMS, children's librarian; b. Clinton, N.C., Nov. 29, 1945; d. Lisker and Pauline (Lockamy) Williams; m. J.P. Buckrham, Nov. 11, 1976 (dec. Jan. 1991). BS, N.C. Ctrl. U., 1967. Libr. Sampson H.S., Clinton, N.C., 1967-68, Eaton-Johnson Elem., Henderson, N.C., 1968-70; house mother Ctrl. Orphanage, Oxford, N.C., 1970 summer; sec., bookkeeper Payton Funeral Home, Dunn, N.C., 1970-74; dir. Ezzell Day Care Ctr., Clinton, N.C., 1974-78; children's libr. Sampson-Clinton (N.C.) Libr., 1978—; sec. Sampson County Employee Com., Clinton, 1988-92, Headstart Adv. Coun., Clinton, 1980-89. Mem. Sampson County Voter's League, Clinton, 1980—; sec. Sampson County Handicapped, Clinton, 1993—. Recipient Svc. award Nat. Assn. of Counties Awards, 1980, Outstanding Svc. award Regional Tchrs. Family Svc., 1985; named Sampson County Employee of Yr., 1990. Mem. Nat. Western Assembly of Chs. (min. of music 1980—). Home: 1877 H B Lewis Rd Clinton NC 28328

BUCKWALTER, ALAN ROLAND, III, banker; b. N.Y.C., Feb. 21, 1947; s. Alan Roland Jr. and Mary (Ackerman) B.; m. Linda Marie Castellano, June 15, 1969 (div. 1979); 1 child, Lisa Jeanine; m. Helen Aline Kraft, Aug. 29, 1981; children: Robert Alan, Katherine Anne, William Roland. Diploma, Valley Forge Mil. Acad., 1966; BA, Fairleigh Dickinson Coll., 1970; postgrad., Stanford U., 1985. Mng. dir. Chem. Bank, N.Y.C., 1970-90; pres. Tex. Commerce Bank, Houston, 1990—; vice chair Tex. Commerce Bankshares, Inc. Trustee Valley Forge Mil. Acad.; bd. dirs. We. Nat. Corp., Am. Energy Ptnrs. Ltd., Houston Symphony, Salvation Army, Houston. Mem. ARC, Houston Club, Sweetwater Country Club, Briar Club, Coronada Club, River Oaks Country Club. Home: 3325 Del Monte Dr Houston TX 77019-3103 Office: Tex Commerce Bank NA 712 Main St Houston TX 77002-3223

BUCY, J. FRED, JR., retired electronics company executive; b. Tahoka, Tex., July 29, 1928; s. J. Fred and Ethel (Montgomery) B.; m. Odetta Greer, Jan. 25, 1947; children: J. Fred, Roxanne, Diane. B.Physics, Tex. Tech. U., 1951; M.Physics, U. Tex., 1953; DSc (hon.), Tex. Tech U., 1994. With Tex. Instruments, Inc., Dallas, 1953-85, corp. v.p., 1963-67, corp. group v.p. components, 1967-72, exec. v.p., 1972-75, exec. v.p., chief operating officer, 1975-76, pres., chief operating officer, 1976-84, pres., chief exec. officer, dir., 1984-85; cons. Tex. Instruments, Inc., 1985—; dir. Thomas Group, Inc., Optical Data Systems, Inc., Hypres, Inc., Southwest Rsch. Inst.; cons., chmn. Tex. Nat. Rsch. Lab. Com. Patentee in field. Mem. Tech. Assessment of U.S. Congress; mem. Comptroller Gen.'sPanel, Pres.'s Commn. for Nat. Agenda for 80's, comm. chmn. Nat. Rsch. Coun., Washington; mem. bd. regents Tex. Tech U., Health Sci. Ctr. Tex. Tech U., 1973-91; chmn. bd. regents Tex. Tech U. and Health Sci. Ctr., 1980-82, 89-90; mem. adv. com. rsch. Tex.Higher Edn. Coordinating Bd.; external adv com. Arnold O. and Mabel M. Beckman Inst. Advanced Sci. Tech., U. Ill.; adv. coun. Woodrow Wilson Internat. Ctr. for Scholars, Washington; chmn. Tex. Sci. Adv. Coun.; nat. chmn. Enterprise Campaign Tex. Tech U.; mem. vis. com. Russian Rsch. Ctr., Harvard U.; mem. physics vis. com. MIT. Recipient Disting. Engr. award Tex. Tech U., 1972, Disting. Alumnus award, 1991. Fellow IEEE; mem. NAE, Am. Inst. Physics, Soc. Exploration Geophysicists, Conf. Bd., Sigma Pi Sigma, Tau Beta Pi, Cosmos Club (Washington), Dallas Petroleum Club. Address: PO Box 780929 Dallas TX 75378-0929

BUDD, DAVID GLENN, lawyer; b. Dayton, Ohio, May 19, 1934; s. Glenn E. and Anna Elizabeth (Purdy) B.; m. Barbarann Dumbaugh, Apr. 4, 1964; children: Anne Elizabeth, David Glenn II. AB with honors, Ohio U., 1959; JD with honors, U. Cin., 1962. Bar: Ohio 1962, U.S. Dist. Ct. (so. dist.) Ohio 1963, U.S. Dist. Ct. (no. dist.) Ohio 1967, U.S. Supreme Ct. 1967, Fla. 1980, U.S. Dist. Ct. (mid. dist.) Fla. 1981, U.S. Tax Ct. 1989. Assoc. Young, Pryor, Lynn, Strickland & Falke, Dayton, 1962-65; trial atty. U.S. Dept. Justice, Cleve., 1965-67; chief antitrust sect. Atty. Gen. Ohio, Columbus, Ohio, 1967-69; ptnr., sr. corp. atty. Cox & Brandabur Attys., Xenia, Ohio, 1969-74; asst. v.p., asst. sec. law Jim Walter Corp., Tampa, Fla., 1974-76; sec., gen. counsel, asst. treas. Gardinier Big River, Inc., Gardinier, Inc., Tampa, 1976-80; assoc. Young, Van Assenderp, Varnadoe & Benton, P.A., Naples, Fla., 1981-84; ptnr. Van Koughnet & Budd, Naples, 1984-85; sr. ptnr. Budd, Hines & Thompson, Naples, 1985-88, Budd & Thompson, Naples, 1989-92, Budd, Thompson & Zuccaro, Naples, 1993-95, Budd & Zuccaro, Naples, 1996—; legal counsel to bd. dirs. of numerous corps. Vol. Legal Aid Soc., Xenia, 1972; active Newcomen Soc. N.Am. With USN, 1952-54. Mem. ABA (bus. law sect.), Fla. Bar Assn., Collier County Bar Assn., Blue Key Club, Omicron Delta Kappa, Pi Gamma Mu, Phi Kappa Tau. Republican. Home: 3757 Fountainhead Ln Naples FL 34103 Office: Budd & Zuccaro 3033 Riviera Dr Ste 201 Naples FL 34103-2750

BUDD, ISABELLE AMELIA, research economist; b. Granite City, Ill., Feb. 8, 1923; d. Floyd Harry and Amelia Frederica (Bradvogel) Marx; BS, U. Mo., 1944; postgrad. U. Wis., 1946; m. Louis John Budd, Mar. 3, 1945; children: Catherine Lou, David Harry. Research economist Ralston Purina Co., St. Louis, 1945-46; govtl. legislator, Durham, N.C., 1975-79; fin. and govtl. cons., Durham, 1972-88. Troop leader Girl Scouts U.S.A., 1955-61; mem. environ. concerns com. Duke U., Durham, 1972-77, co-chmn., 1974-75; mem. Durham City Council, 1975-79; Durham del. Council Govts., 1976-78; mem. exec. com. regional govt. criminal justice com., 1976-78; chmn. personnel policy com. regional govt., 1977-78; bd. dirs. Durham County Sr.

Citizens Coordinating Council, 1982-85, Raleigh-Durham Internat. Airport Authority, 1983-85; chmn. bd. trustees Raleigh-Durham Firemen's Relief Fund, 1983-89. Mem. AAUW (life), N.C. Center for Public Policy Research, Greater Durham C. of C., S.W. Durham Assn. (charter mem., treas. 1973-76), Mark Twain Circle of Am. (founding mem. 1986, govt. advisor), Nat. Trust for Historic Preservation, Historic Preservation Soc. Durham (charter mem.), N.C. Mus. Life and Sci., Friends of Duke U. Library (life), Ind. Scholars Assn. (life). Author articles on estates. Home: 2753 Mcdowell Rd Durham NC 27705-5715

BUDDINGTON, PATRICIA ARRINGTON, engineer; b. Takoma Park, Md., Dec. 25, 1950; d. Warren and Elsie (Miller) B. BS, Northrop Inst. Tech., 1973; MS, Fla. Inst. Tech., 1986. With Air Force Systems Command, Edwards AFB, Calif., 1973-78; various positions Boeing Def. & Space Group, Huntsville, Ala., 1978-81, test engr. reaction control system inertial upper stage, 1981-86, lead engr. microgravity material processing facility, 1986-88, task leader advanced civil space systems, 1988—. Mem. AIAA (assoc. fellow). Office: Boeing Spl Projects PO Box 240002 (JN-04) 499 Boeing Blvd Huntsville AL 35824-6402

BUDGE, MARCIA CHARLENE, family nurse practitioner; b. Goodland, Kans., Feb. 10, 1952; d. Edwin J. and Bonnie L. (Walker) Carleton; m. Marc R. Budge, May 7, 1977; 1 child, Steven R. ADN, Barton County Community Coll., 1983; cert. primary care nurse practitioner, U. Kans., 1986. RN, Kans., Tex.; cert. advanced RN practitioner, Kans.; cert. advanced nurse practitioner, Tex.; cert. pediatric & gerontol. nurse practitioner ANCC. Supr. and staff nurse St. John (Kans.) Dist. Hosp., 1983-85; staff nurse spl. care unit and obstetrics Pratt (Kans.) Regional Med. Ctr., 1986; advanced nurse practitioner, family nurse practitioner Med. Ctr. PA, Hutchinson, Kans., 1986-90; advanced nurse and family nurse practitioner Sterling (Kans.) Med. Ctr., 1990-92; advanced nurse practitioner Bapt. Hosp. Rural Health Clinic, Liberty, Tex., 1992-94; clinic dir. U. Tex. Med. Br. Regional Maternal and Child Health Program Walker County Maternal and Child Health Ctr., Huntsville, 1994—, Walker County Maternal and Child Health Ctr., 1994—; mem. tech. adv. group Study of EACH/RPCH Concept in Kans., 1990-92. Chairperson bd. dirs. St. John Hosp. Dist. No. 1, 1991-92. Mem. Coun. Nurses in Advanced Practice, Am. Acad. Nurse Practitioners (cert. family nurse practitioner), Kans. Nurses Assn. (sec. advanced practice conf. group), Tex. Nurses Assn., Coastal Area Health Edn. Coop. (bd. dirs. 1993—). Home: 307 Brenda Ln Conroe TX 77385-9004 Office: Walker County Maternal & Child Health Ctr 1217 Ave M Huntsville TX 77340

BUDILOVSKY, SUSAN ANDREA, journalist; b. Dallas, Dec. 12, 1972; d. Ivan and Jitka Eva (Nadvornik) B. BS in Journalism, U. North Tex., 1996. Customer svc. rep. Comdata Corp., Carrollton, Tex., 1991-96; edn. reporter, journalist Denton (Tex.) Record-Chronicle, 1996—. Mem. Soc. Profl. Journalists (coms. 1992—). Office: Denton Record-Chronicle 314 E Hickory St Denton TX 76201

BUDKA, JAMES D., lawyer, educator; b. N.C., Jan. 13, 1942; s. Gerald D. Jr. and Theresa Diane (Winnie) B.; m. Judith M. Zuraski, Apr. 4, 1970; children: Shawn, Rob, Sue, Roxanne. BS cum laude, N.C. State U., 1963; JD, U. Tex., 1966. Bar: Tex. 1967, U.S. Tax Ct. 1980. Assoc. White & Reynolds, Austin, 1967-71; ptnr. White, Reynolds & Budka, Austin, 1971-82; pvt. practice Austin, 1983—; adj. law prof. U. Tex., 1986—. Contbr. articles to profl. jours.; editor Tax Law Today Jour., 1977-83. Active PTA, Am. Cancer Soc. Mem. ABA, State Bar of Tex. Democrat. Roman Catholic. Office: Werik Tower 781 W 57th St Ste 201 Austin TX 78751

BUDLONG, THOMAS FRANCIS, JR., library administrator; b. Anchorage, Aug. 6, 1948; s. Thomas F. and Isabel M. (Mulchahey) B.; m. Debra A. Skopczynski, May 25, 1979. BA, Loyola U. of the South, 1970; M Librarianship, Emory U., 1973. Cert. libr., Ga. Reference libr. Atlanta-Fulton Pub. Libr., 1973-74, asst. head film dept., 1974-78, head video dept., 1978-80, mgr. Hobgood-Palmer br., 1980-88, asst. ctrl. libr. adminstr., 1988-90, acting ctrl. libr. adminstr., 1990-91, mgr. video svcs. dept., 1991-92, ops. mgr. regional svcs. team, 1992-93, mgr. Buckhead br., 1993—; panelist various intellectual freedom programs, 1980—. Cons.: Censorship in the South: A Report of Four States, 1980-85; video reviewer: Libr. Jour., 1993—. Mem. ALA (chair intellectual freedom roundtable 1992-93), Libr. Adminstrn. and Mgmt. Assn. (cultural diversity com. 1993—), Pub. Libr. Assn., Libr. Info. and Tech. Assn., Southeastern Libr. Assn., Ga. Libr. Assn. (exec. bd. dirs. 1987-89, treas. 1995-98), Ga. Video Libr. Assn. (co-founder 1978), Ga. First Amendment Found. (bd. dirs. 1994—). Democrat. Home: 949 Rupley Dr NE Atlanta GA 30306-3818 Office: Atlanta-Fulton Pub Libr 269 Buckhead Ave NE Atlanta GA 30305-2224

BUDNIK, PATRICIA MC NULTY, elementary education educator; b. Riverside, N.J., July 2, 1936; d. Norbert E. and Mabel E. (Seifert) McNulty; divorced; children: Barry J., Scott D. BEd, U. Miami, Coral Gables, Fla., 1967, MEd, 1972; EdD, Nova U., 1991. Elem. tchr. Dade County Pub. Schs., Miami, Fla., 1967—; English tchr. Hunan Edn. Coll., Changsha, China, 1994, 95, 96; adj. faculty Nova Southeastern U., Ft. Lauderdale, Fla. Contbr. articles to profl. jours. Mem. choir, Evangelism Explosion Team St. Andrews Presbyn. Ch., Sunday sch. supt. Grantee Found. Excellence Pub. Edn., 1986, 87, Broward Community Found., 1990. Mem. Nat. Assn. Edn. Young Children, Assn. Childhood Edn. Internat., Internat. Reading Assn., Fla. Reading Assn., United Tchrs. Dade (bldg. steward). Home: 1820 N 45th Ave Hollywood FL 33021-4104 Office: Skyway Elem Sch 4555 NW 206th Ter Opa Locka FL 33055-1248

BUERSCHINGER, CHARLES ALBERT, state commissioner; b. San Juan, P.R., Nov. 2, 1945; s. Harold Francis Buerschinger and Olga Antonia (Willoughby) McKeever; m. Merrylyn Anne Straube, Jan. 12, 1974 (div. Nov. 1992); m. Mary Anne Rickhoff, Oct. 12, 1993. BBA, U. Tex., 1969; MBA, Southwest Tex. State U., 1974; postgrad., U.S. Army Command Coll., Ft. Leavenworth, Kans., 1984. Acct. Fgn. Motors, Austin, Tex., 1973-75; from supervising svc. officer to dep. adminstr. Tex. Vets. Commn., Austin, 1975-89, dep. dir., 1989—. Capt. U.S. Army, 1969-73. Mem. VFW (svc. officer), DAV, Am. Legion (svc. officer), Tex. Caissons Assn., Tex. State Agy. Bus. Adminstrs. Assn., U.S. Army Res. Assn. (lt. col.), Meeting Planners Internat. (bd. dir.), Jaguar Club Austin (founder, v.p.). Democrat. Office: Tex Vets Commn PO Box 12277 Austin TX 78711-2277

BUFORD, EVELYN CLAUDENE SHILLING, jewelry specialist, merchandising professional; b. Fort Worth, Sept. 21, 1940; d. Claude and Winnie Evelyn (Mote) Hodges; student Hill Jr. Coll., 1975-76, Tarrant County (Tex.) Jr. Coll., 1992-93; m. William J. Buford, Mar. 1982; children by previous marriage: Vincent Shilling, Kathryn Lynn Shilling La Chappelle. With Imperial Printing Co., Inc., Ft. Worth, 1964-70, 77-79, gen. sales mgr. comml. div., 1982-90, corp. sec., 1977-79; with Tarrant County Hosp. Dist., Fort Worth, 1973-77, asst. to asst. adminstr., 1981-84; merchandising asst. J.C. Penney Co., 1989—. Mem. Exec. Women Internat. (dir., publs. chmn., v.p. 1984, pres. 1985, chmn. adv. com. 1986, 87, scholarship dir. 1988-93, corp. publ. com. 1988-89, dir. S. ctrl. region 1993-94). Republican. Methodist. Home: 1025 Kenneth Ln Burleson TX 76028-8375 Office: JC Penney Co Hurst TX 76053

BUFORD, ROBERT PEGRAM, lawyer; b. Roanoke Rapids, N.C., Sept. 7, 1925; s. Robert Pegram and Edith (Rawlings) B.; m. Anne Bliss Whitehead, June 26, 1948; children: Robert, Bliss, Peyton. LLB, U. Va., 1950. Bar: Va. 1949. sr. counsel Hunton & Williams, Richmond, Va. Bd. visitors U. Va., Charlottesville, 1972-80; chmn. Met. Richmond C. of C., 1973; vice chmn., bd. trustees St. Paul's Coll., Lawrenceville, Va., 1977-85. Lt. (j.g.) USNR, 1943-46. Recipient Disting. Service award Jr. C. of C., 1961, Va. Profl. Assn., 1965, Good Govt. award Richmond First Club, 1967. Fellow Am. Bar Found., Va. Law Found.; mem. ABA, Va. Bar (assoc.), Country Club of Va., Commonwealth Club. Home: 506 Kilmarnock Dr Richmond VA 23229-8102 Office: Hunton & Williams Riverfront Pla E Tower 951 E Byrd St Richmond VA 23219-4040

BUGG, KEITH EDWARD, computer software developer, software company executive; b. Ashland, Ky., Feb. 18, 1952; s. Walter Edward and Sally (Worthington) B. BS in Math., Morehead State U., 1974. Mathematician Goodyear Atomic Corp., Piketon, Ohio, 1981-83; sr. systems analyst Sci. Applications Internat. Corp., Oak Ridge, Tenn., 1983-88, Am. Computer Profls., Columbia, S.C., 1988-90, Analysas Corp., Oak Ridge, 1990-94; pres. Tristar Systems, Inc., Oak Ridge, 1993—. Author: The Visual C++ Construction Kit, 1994; contbr. articles to trade mags. Sgt. U.S. Army, 1977-80. Mem. Assn. Computing Machinery. Libertarian. Baptist. Home and Office: Tristar Systems Inc 122 Morningside Dr Oak Ridge TN 37830-8320

BUGG, WILLIAM ADOLPHUS, JR., real estate executive; b. Atlanta, Aug. 1, 1937; s. William Adolphus and Anne Louise (Page) Bugg; m. Nina Gordon Wilkerson, Apr. 20, 1963; children: William III, Robert. BA, Vanderbilt U., 1959; MBA, Ga. State U., 1967. Broker Adair Realty Co., Atlanta, 1973-77; ptnr. Bugg, Coppedge, Ghertner & McWilliams, Atlanta, 1977; exec. mng. dir., south/ctrl. region Cushman & Wakefield, Inc., Atlanta, 1977-92, exec. mng. dir. internat., exec. com., nat. mgmt. com., 1993-94; pres. Bugg Properties, Inc., 1993—; mgr. Bugg Lambeat Properties, LLC, 1995—. Bd. dirs. Atlanta Symphony Orch. League, Atlanta Opera Co.; mem. exec. coun. Boy Scouts Am. Capt. USNR, ret. Mem. Urban Land Inst., Atlanta C. of C. (past bd. dirs.), Ctrl. Atlanta Progress (past bd. dirs.), Midtown Alliance (past bd. dirs.), Atlanta Bd. Realtors (Alvin B. Cates award 1975, 76), Atlanta Sales and Mktg. Execs. (Disting. Salesman award), Capital City Club, Vanderbilt U. Atlanta Alumni, Ga. State U. Alumni. Republican. Episcopalian. Office: Bugg Properties Inc 471 W Wesley Rd Atlanta GA 30305

BUGGIE, FREDERICK DENMAN, management consultant; b. Toledo, Mar. 27, 1929; s. Horace and Loraine (Denman) B.; BA, Yale U., 1956; MBA, George Washington U., 1961; m. Betty Jo Chilcote, Sept. 7, 1951; children: Martha Louise Buggie Kenney, John Chilcote. Sales engr. Alcoa, Balt. and Phila., 1956-66; pres. Gt. Lakes Rsch. Inst., Erie, Pa., 1967-69; mktg. mgr. Technicon Instruments, Tarrytown, N.Y., 1969-71; program mgr. Innotech, Norwalk, Conn., 1971-74; pres. Inomation Divsn. Van Dyck Corp., 1974-76; pres. Strategic Innovations Internat., Lake Wylie, S.C., 1976—, SII Strategic Innovations A.G., Lausanne, Switzerland; founder, chmn. Strategic Innovations Internat. Ltd., Keele, Staffordshire, England, Strategic Innovations B.V., The Hague, The Netherlands; conf. leader, lectr.; adj. prof. various univs. Served with USAF, 1950-54. Mem. Assn. Corp. Growth, Strategic Leadership Forum, Comml. Devel. Assn., Product Devel. Mgmt. Assn., Inst. of Dirs. Clubs: Tower, Yale (London, Charlotte, N.Y.C.). Author: New Product Development Strategies, 1981; contbr. over 50 articles to profl. jours. Home: 8 Sunrise Pt Lake Wylie SC 29710 Office: Strategic Innovations Internat 12 Executive Ct Lake Wylie SC 29710-9338

BUHAIN, WILFREDO JAVIER, medical educator; b. Bacoor, Cavite, Philippines, Oct. 12, 1940; m. Carlota Torres; children: Ronald, Edgar. AA, BS, U. Philippines, 1959, MD, 1964. Diplomate Am. Bd. Internal Medicine, Am. Bd. Pulmonary Diseases. Rsch. fellow in cardiology U. Philippines, Philippine Gen. Hosp., 1964-65; rotating intern Queens Hosp. Ctr., N.Y.C., 1965-66, resident in internal medicine, 1965-68; clin. fellow in pulmonary diseases Hosp. of U. Pa., 1968-69, chief pulmonary function lab. dept. medicine, 1971-72; rsch. fellow in pulmonary diseases Hosp. of U. Pa., VA Hosp., Phila., 1969-71; assoc. in medicine, cardiovascular-pulmonary div. med. dept. U. Pa. Sch. Medicine, 1971-72; assoc. in medicine, dept. medicine Mt. Sinai Sch. Medicine, CUNY, 1972-74; clin. instr. medicine Georgetown U., 1976-95; chief pulmonary function lab. dept. medicine Mt. Sinai Hosp. Svcs./City Hosp. Ctr. at Elmhurst, 1973-74; med. dir. respiratory therapy dept. Mt. Vernon Hosp., 1978—, chmn. dept. medicine, 1987-88, pres. med. staff, 1996—; mem. exec. com. Alexandria Hosp., 1983. Contbr. articles to profl. jours. Queensborough Soc. grantee; Pa. Thoracic Soc. grantee. Fellow ACP, Am. Coll. Chest Physicians; mem. AMA, Am. Soc. Internal Medicine, Am. Thoracic Soc., Am. Fedn. Clin. Rsch., Alexandria Med. Soc., Va. Med. Soc., Philippine Med. Assn. (exec. dir., past pres. Metro-Washington), Assn. Philippine Physicians in Am. Office: 6300 Stevenson Ave Apt B Alexandria VA 22304-3576

BUI, LONG VAN, church custodian, translator; b. Cao Xa, Vietnam, May 1, 1940; came to U.S., 1985; s. So Van and Ninh Thi (Nguyen) B.; m. Dung Thi Le, May 14, 1970; children: Van Thanh Bui, Long Ba Bui. Student, U. Dalat, Vietnam, 1960; AA, Houston C.C., 1991. High sch. tchr. Vietnam, 1964, mil. svc., 1965-75, detainee, 1975-81; grocery store cashier Houston, 1986; custodian Spring Branch Community Ch., Houston, 1986—. Editor: Holy Family newsletter of Youth Better Found., Houston, 1993—; translator Medjugoje The Message into Vietnamese, 1993, Fatima the Great Sign into Vietnamese, 1994. Capt. Vietnamese Army, 1965-75. Mem. Youth Better Found. Roman Catholic. Home: # 2303 8801 Hammerly Blvd Apt 2303 Houston TX 77080-6507 Office: Youth Better Found 12923 Harwin Dr Houston TX 77072-1017

BUI, QUINN VAN, community health promotion specialist; b. Vanh Thiet, Vietnam, Aug. 3, 1968; came to U.S., 1975; s. Sia Van and Thom T. (Nguyen) B. BS, St. Vincent Coll., Latrobe, Pa., 1990; MS, Slippery Rock U., 1993; MPH, U. Pitts., 1994. Mgr. health edn. Slippery Rock U., 1990-93; mem. program staff, statis. cons. Spina Bifida Assn. Western Pa., Pitts., 1993-95; rschr. U. Pitts., 1994, cons. to learning team Med. Ctr., 1994; cmty. health program specialist W.Va. Bur. for Pub. Health, Charleston, 1994—; gymnastics instr., Parkersburg, W.Va, 1994—; adj. prof. medicine W.Va. U. Cmty. Med. Sch., 1996—; bd. dirs. W.Va. Health Edn. Coun., Charleston, 1995—. Mem. W.Va. Pub. Health Assn. (at-large). Republican. Roman Catholic. Home: 1101 14th St Apt 3 Vienna WV 26105 Office: WV Bur for Pub Health 914 Market St Ste 303 Parkersburg WV 26101

BUICE, BONNIE CARL, lawyer, priest; b. East Point, Ga., May 20, 1932; s. Bonnie Carl and Mahalia Elizabeth (Ramsey) B.; m. Patterson Nall, Dec. 14, 1957 (div. Apr. 1982); children: Merrianne, Shannon, Samuel, William, Christopher; m. Hulane E. George, Feb. 18, 1984. AB, Mercer U., 1954, JD, 1957; MA in Theology, U. Notre Dame, 1975. Bar: Ga. 1954, U.S. Dist. Ct. (no. dist.) Ga. 1957, U.S. Dist. Ct. (mid. dist.) Ga. 1983, U.S. Ct. Appeals (11th cir.) 1991; ordained priest Episcopal Ch., 1975. Assoc. Nall, Miller, Cadenhead & Dennis, Atlanta, 1957-61; ptnr. Robinson, Buice, Harben & Strickland, Gainesville, Ga., 1961-74; curate Holy Trinity Parish, Decatur, Ga., 1975-79; rector St. Francis Ch., Macon, Ga., 1979-84; ptnr. George & Buice, Milledgeville, Ga., 1984-86, Waddell, Emerson, George & Buice, Milledgeville, 1986-94, Waddell, Emerson & Buice, Milledgeville, 1994—; assoc. priest St. Stephens Episcopal Ch., Milledgeville, 1986-91; rector St. James Episcopal Ch, Macon, 1992—. Mem. Ocmulgee Bar Assn. (pres. 1991-92), Baldwin County Bar Assn. (treas. 1991-92). Home: 115 Maplewood Ave SW Milledgeville GA 31061-3646 Office: Waddell Emerson & Buice PO Box 630 Milledgeville GA 31061-0630

BUIS, PATRICIA FRANCES, geology educator, researcher; b. Jersey City, Dec. 29, 1953; d. George Herman Buis and Marie Agnes Fitzsimmons. BA in Geology, Rutgers U., 1976; MA in Geology, Queens Coll., 1983; PhD in Geology, U. Pitts., 1988; MS in Mining Engring., Mich. Tech. U., 1994, PhD in Mining Engring., 1995. Coal quality geochemist Pa. Geologic Survey, Harrisburg, 1989-91; asst. prof. U. Miss., Oxford, 1994-96, Japanese Sci. and Tech. Mgmt. Program scholar, 1996—; cons., reviewer of sci. textbooks prior to pub. Winston-Rinehart, Austin, Tex., 1994—. Dept. Edn. doctoral fellow in mining Mich. Tech. U., 1991-95, Provost Predoctoral fellow U. Pitts., 1988; Dept. Edn. grantee Mich. Tech. U., 1993; nat. merit scholar Schering-Plough, Rutgers U., 1971-75. Mem. Soc. Exploration Geochemistry, Nat. Water Wells Assn., Am. Mineralogist, Sigma Xi.

BUJONES, FERNANDO CALLEIRO, ballet dancer; b. Miami, Fla., Mar. 9, 1955; s. Fernando and Marie (Calleiro) B.; m. Marcia Kibitschek, June 8, 1980; 1 dau., Alejandra Patricia Kubitschek. Grad., Profl. Children's Sch., 1972. Mem. Sch. Am. Ballet, 1967-72; mem. corps de ballet Am. Ballet Theatre, 1972-73, soloist, 1973-74, prin. dancer, 1974-85, guest prin., 1976; assoc. artistic dir. Rio de Janeiro Opera House, from 1986; prin. guest artist Boston Ballet, from 1987; artistic dir. Ballet Miss., Jackson, to 1994, Bay Ballet Theatre, Tampa, Fla., 1994—; guest tchr. schs.; restaged Jacob's Pillow Festival, 1973; prin. Bujones, Ltd.; guest artist Joffrey Ballet, Royal Swedish Ballet, Stuttgart Ballet, Nat. Ballet Can., Royal Ballet (London), Rome Opera Ballet, Deutsche Oper Ballet, others; choreographer Grand Pas Romantique, 1985; created role, Alexander the Great (Maurice Bejart), 1987; guest artist Paris Opera, Royal Danish Ballet. Danced farewell performance Met. Opera House, 1995. Recipient Varna Gold medal and tech. achievement award, 1974; Key to City Ft. Worth, 1975; Dance Mag. award, 1982, Fla. prize, 1986, N.Y. Times award, 1986, Elliott Norton award Boston Theatre, 1992; Fernando Calleiro Bujones Day proclaimed in his honor City of Boston, 1991. Mem. Movimento Democratico Brazil. Roman Catholic.

BUKANTZ, SAMUEL CHARLES, physician, educator; b. N.Y.C., Sept. 12, 1911; s. Barnett and Bertha (Stelson) B.; m. A. Jewell Williams, Apr. 5, 1941; children: Jessica, Dorothy. BS, Washington Sq. Coll., N.Y. U., 1930; MD, NYU, 1934. Intern in pathology Mt. Sinai Hosp., N.Y.C., 1934-35; intern in medicine Mt. Sinai Hosp., 1935-36, house physician, resident, 1936-38; assoc. prof. medicine Washington U., St. Louis, 1946-58; fellow in allergy Washington U., 1946-47; assoc. prof. medicine U. Colo., 1958-63; dir. medicine and research Children's Asthma Research Inst. and Hosp., 1958-63; assoc. prof. clin. medicine N.Y. U., 1963-72; prof. medicine U. South Fla., 1972—, head div. allergy and immunology, 1972-82, emeritus dir., prof. med. microbiology and immunology, 1982—, 96—; pvt. practice medicine specializing in allergy and immunology N.Y.C., 1938-40, 66-72, St. Louis, 1954-58, Tampa, Fla., 1972-82; chief sect. allergy and clin. immunology VA Hosp., Tampa, 1972-82. Editor: Hosp. Practice, 1968—; Contbr. numerous articles on allergy and immunology to profl. jours. Served with AUS, 1941-46. Lucius Littauer and Parmelee fellow in pneumonia research, 1938-41; NIH grantee, 1947-63. Fellow ACP, AAAS; mem. Am. Coll. Chest Physicians, Am. Soc. Clin. Investigation, Cen. Soc. Clin. Rsch., Am. Acad. Allergy, Am. Coll. Allergy, Alpha Omega Alpha. Democrat. Jewish. Home: 4940 W San Rafael St Tampa FL 33629-5404 Office: U South Fla Coll of Medicine 12901 Bruce B Downs Blvd Tampa FL 33612-4745

BUKOVSKY, ANTONIN VACLAV, physician, obstetrician, gynecologist, educator; b. Prague, Czechoslovakia, Oct. 3, 1944; came to U.S., 1990; s. Antonin and Irena (Kleinhamplova) B.; m. Kornelie Hurychova, Aug. 15, 1964 (div. Apr. 1965) 1 child, Kornelie; m. Eva Mukensnablova, Mar. 26, 1971; children: Alena, Antonin, Anna. MD, Charles U., Prague, 1969, PhD, 1980, DSc, 1989. Physician, obstetrician/gynecologist NIH, Jindrichuv, Czechoslovakia, 1970-74; researcher Inst. Care Mother and Child, Prague, 1975-90, Meth. Hosp., Indpls., 1990-91, U. Tenn. Med. Ctr., Knoxville, 1991—; asst. prof. U. Tenn. Med. Ctr., 1994—. Contbr. more than 130 articles to profl. jours. Lt. Czechoslovakian Mil., 1969-70. Mem. AAAS, Soc. for the Sutdy of Reproduction, N.Y. Acad. Scis. Home: 11720 N Williamsburg Dr Knoxville TN 37922 Office: U Tenn Med Ctr Dept Ob-Gyn 1924 Alcoa Hwy Knoxville TN 37920-1511

BUKSA, IRENA, language and literature educator; b. Wolka-Zapalovska, Poland, Mar. 20, 1961; d. Piotr and Katarzyna (Czetyrbok) Bazylewicz; m. Peter Buksa, Feb. 5, 1985; 1 child, Orest. MA, Warsaw U., 1985; D of Arts, Syracuse U., 1991. Instr. UAH, Huntsville, 1990-91; asst. prof., 1991-96, assoc. prof., 1996—; internat. aerospace edn.: Russian space sci. program asst. translator, UAH, Huntsville, Ala., 1991—; coord. Russian Study Program Abroad, UAH, 1994—. Reviewer in field; contbr. chpts. to books, articles to profl. jours. Faculty adv. UAH Slovo-Slavic Club, 1992—. Named Rsch. Stipend Kiev State U., 1991; fellowship, scholarship Syracuse U., 990-97. Mem. MLA, Am. Assn. of Tchrs. of and Slavic East European Langs., Am. Assn. for Advancement of Slavic Studies. Office: Univ Ala in Huntsville 4705 University Dr Huntsville AL 35899

BULACH, CLETUS RALPH, education educator; b. St. Leon, Ind., Aug. 23, 1938; s. Clarence and Bertha (Kraus) B.; m. Lillian Margaret Harper, June 10, 1962 (div. Nov. 1976); children: Christine, Katherine, Lisa, Gregory; m. Joan Beverly Roberts, Nov. 14, 1979; 1 child, William Roberts. EdB, U. Cin., 1964; postgrad., U. Minn., 1965; MEd, Xavier U., 1967; EdD, U. Cin., 1974; postgrad., U. Idaho, 1972. Cert. supt., Ohio, Ky., cert. tchr., Ohio, Ky. Visual aids dir., tchr. German Western Hills High Sch., Cin., 1967-70; bldg. adminstr. Schwab Jr. High Sch., Cin., 1970-71; asst. supt. for curriculum and instrn. Wilmington City Schs., 1973-76; supt. Little Miami Local Schs., Warren County, Ohio, 1976-79, New Lexington City Schs., 1979-86, Norton City Schs., 1986-90; assoc. prof. Murray State U., 1990-93, State U. of West Ga., Carrollton, 1993—; adminstr. Diagnostic Ctr. for Ga., 1994—; program assoc. for staff devel. U. Cin., 1972-73; curriculum specialist Hamilton County Bd. Edn., 1972-73; adj. asst. prof. psychology Wilmington Coll., 1976-79; adj. asst. prof. edn. adminstrn., Ohio U., 1985; adj. assoc. prof. U. Akron, 1987-89; condr. workshops in instrl. improvement, mgmt., human rels. conflict mgmt.; rsch. sch. climate, group openness, group trust; exec. sec. Western Ky. Coalition for Sch. Based Decision-Making, 1992—; mem. Western Ky. Ednl. Cooperative, 1990—; chmn. Tri-County Ednl. Media Resource Ctr., 1980-81, Southeast Ohio Special Edn. Com., 1982-83. Contbr. articles to profl. publs. Speaker Chrysler Motors 27th Ann. Youth Award dinner, 1989; pres. Norton City Schs. Scholarship Endowment Fund, 1988-90; mem. citizen's task force Summit Energy Storage Project, 1988-90; bd. dirs. econ. devel. and ednl. tng. Akron Regional Devel. Bd., 1987-88. With USAF. Mem. ASCD, Am. Assn. Sch. Adminstrs., Am. Coun. Hypnotist Examiners, Nat. Staff Devel. Coun., Nat. Coun. Profs. of Edn. Adminstrn., Univ. Assn. Edn. Profs., Ga. Assn. of Sch. Supts., Ga. Assn. of Ednl. Leaders, Carrollton Rotary Club, Perry County C. of C. (v.p. 1983, 84, pres. 1985), Junction City Am. Legion, Norton Kiwanis (pres.-elect 1990), Phi Delta Kappa. Office: State U of West Ga Dept Ednl Leadership Carrollton GA 30118-5030

BULCKEN, CAROLYN ANNE BROOKS, retired special education educator; b. Balt., Jan. 10, 1933; d. Roland Bowers and Evelyn Mabel (Peters) Brooks; m. George W. Bulcken, Nov. 23, 1952 (div. Apr. 1989); children: Cheryl Bulcken Sawyer, Cynthia Bulcken Coker, George W. III, Richard B. BS, Towson State U., 1955; MS, U. Houston, Clear Lake, 1977. Cert. ednl. diagnostician, spl. edn. and elem. tchr., Tex., Md. Tchr. Balt. County Schs., 1955-59; T Friendswood (Tex.) Ind. Sch. Dist., 1965-67; tchr., dept. chair Dickinson (Tex.) Ind. Sch. Dist., 1969-77; ednl. diagnostician Galveston (Tex.) Ind. Sch. Dist., 1977-87, diagnostic learning specialist, 1987-94. Fulbright chmn. Inst. for Internat. Edn., Houston. Recipient cert. of appreciation U.S. Info. Agy. Mem. NEA, Tex. State Tchrs. Assn., Mensa (proctor coord. Gulf Coast chpt.), Tex. Ednl. Diagnosticians Assn., Houston Met. Ednl. Diagnosticians Assn., Order Eastern Star, Phi Kappa Phi, Phi Delta Kappa, Kappa Delta Pi, Beta Sigma Phi.

BULISON, JERRY WAYNE, superintendent; b. Centerville, Tenn., June 11, 1949; m. Eva Ernestine Coleman, Sept. 8, 1971; children: Janeen, Greg. AA, Martin Coll.; BS, MTSU, MEd. Tchr., coach Hickman Middle Sch., Centerville, 1972-79, Unionville (Tenn.) H.S., 1979-85; prin. East Hickman Elem. Sch., Lyles, Tenn., 1985-90; vocat. dir. Hickman County H.S., Centerville, Tenn., 1990-96; trustee Martin Coll. Bd., 1995—. Named Citizen of Yr. Hickman County, 1991, Outstanding Young Man of Yr. 1974, Educator of Yr. Bedford County, 1984. Mem. Hickman Edn. Assn. (pres. 1993-95), Masons, Tenn. Def. Force (maj. 1989—), Lions Club (past pres. Centerville, Tenn., 1993-94, past pres. Unionville, Tenn., 1984-85), Civitan Club (past pres. 1978-79), Martin Coll. Alumni (pres. 1995—). Methodist. Home: 2602 Shadylawn Dr Centerville TN 37033

BULL, FRANK JAMES, architect; b. Chattanooga, June 25, 1922; s. Louis H. and Augusta (Clausius) B.; m. Betty Frances Graham, May 7, 1949; 1 child, Birney O'Brian. BS in Architecture, Ga. Inst. Tech., 1948, BArch, 1949. Registered architect, Ga., Fla., Ala., Miss.; cert. Nat. Coun. Archtl. Registration Bds. Pilot Pan Am. World Airways, N.Y., Fla., 1942-46; architect Aeck Assocs. Architects, Atlanta, 1948-57; ptnr. Bull & Kenney Architects, Atlanta, 1957-88, Bull, Brown & Kilgo, Architects, Atlanta, 1988—; cons. Fed. Republic of Germany Embassy, Washington, 1986-93; archtl. cons. for golf clubhouse Quinta do Peru, Sesimbra, Portugal and Palheiro Golfe, Funchal, Madeira Island, Portugal, 1991; lectr. in field. Co-author: Asbestos Abatement: Vol. 5 The Sourcebook on Asbestos Diseases, 1991; contbr. articles to profl. jours.; prin. works include Sanctuary for Holy Innocents Episc. Ch., Atlanta, Atlanta Speech Sch. and Clin., Hummel Hall Episc. H.S., Alexandria, Va., Jekyll Island Golf Clubhouse, McLarty Hall, Tull Hall, Turner Gymnasium, Westminster Schs., Atlanta, Dunwoody Country Club, Atlanta, East Lake Golf Clubhouse Restoration, Atlanta, others. Charter trustee Holy Innocents Episcopal Sch., Atlanta, 1962-68, chmn., 1966; founder Galloway Schs., Atlanta, 1969-75. Recipient Rambusch prize Ecole de Beaux Arts, 1940. Mem. AIA (treas. Atlanta chpt. 1976-78, bd. dirs. Ga. assn. 1971-74), Am. Arbitration Assn. (mem. nat. panel constrn. industry arbitrators 1977—), Nat. Asbestos Coun. (founder, charter v.p., bd. dirs. 1983-86, 89-90, treas. 1987, exec. com. 1983-87), Cherokee Town and Country Club (charter, bd. govs. 1976-79, chmn. capital appropriations com., chmn. green com.), Omicron Delta Kappa, Tau Beta Pi, Phi Kappa Phi, Phi Eta Sigma, ANAK, Beta Theta Pi. Republican. Episcopalian. Home: 34 Willow Gln NE Atlanta GA 30342-2000 Office: Bull Brown & Kilgo Architects AIA 2815 Clearview Pl Ste 100 Atlanta GA 30340-2131

BULL, MARY MALEY, radio executive; b. Munich, Mar. 26, 1956; came to U.S., 1956; d. John David and Mary (Kline) M.; m. Steven Tremaine, May 23, 1981; children: Ellen, Emily, Stephanie. BA in History & Music, Trinity U., San Antonio, Tex., 1978. Exec. trainee Joskes' of Tex., San Antonio, 1978-79; office mgr. Advance Mktg., Dallas, 1979-80; acct. exec., asst. advt. mgr., advt. dir. Fisher Publs., San Antonio, 1980-88; sr. account mgr. KSMG-FM, San Antonio, 1988—. Actress Harlequin Theatres, San Antonio, 1979—, San Antonio Little Theatre, 1985—, St. Andrew's Players, 1982—; model various Tex. TV commls., mags., newspapers. Mem. adminstrv. bd., family ministries chmn., St. Andrews Meth. Ch., San Antonio, mem. applause support group, choir pres., 1989, mem. bell choir, dir. children's choir, 1993—; active Girl Scouts USA, 1992—, leader, 1994—. Recipient Nat. Presby. scholarship Nat. Presby. Ch., 1974-78, Dow Jones Writing award Dow Jones, 1974, Addy award, 1989; named Top Salesman Recorder-Times, 1982-84, one of Outstanding Young Women Am., 1983, 85, 87. Mem. San Antonio Advt. Fedn. (bd. dirs. 1988-94, 2d v.p. 1989-90, 1st v.p. 1990-91, pres. 1991-92, 10th dist. dir. 1992-93), Women in Comm., San Antonio Radio and Broadcast Execs., Suburban Newspaper Am. Club. Republican. Methodist. Office: KSMG-FM Radio 8930 Fourwinds Dr Ste 500 San Antonio TX 78239-1973

BULL, WALTER STEPHEN, police officer; b. Collingswood, N.J., May 17, 1933; s. Walter Stephen and Mabelle (Miller) B.; m. Dolores Ruth Kinkade, June 19, 1954; children: Douglas, Donald, Diana, Daniel, David, Dwayne. AAS, Amarillo Coll., 1977, AS, 1978; BS, Wayland Bapt. U., 1978; MA, West Tex. State U., 1982. Advanced cert. Tex. Commn. Law Enforcement Tng. and Edn. Lt. Amarillo (Tex.) Police Dept., 1957-91; ret. Staff sgt. USAF, 1952-56. Mem. Internat. Assn. Chiefs Police (life), Tex. Police Assn., Air Force Assn., Law Enforcement Lions Club, Am Legion (life, post, dis. and div. comdr.). Home: 1915 Manhattan St Amarillo TX 79103-4222

BULLA, BEN F., retired manufacturing company executive; b. Asheboro, N.C., Sept. 4, 1920; s. Franklin Michaux and Margaret Ola (Shoffner) B.; m. June Moore, Aug. 2, 1946; children: Gregory Franklin, Beth Marie. Student, High Point (N.C.) Coll., 1938-40, U. N.C., Chapel Hill. Treas., asst. sec. Sellers Mfg. Co., Saxapahaw, N.C., Jordan Spinning Co., Saxapahaw. Author: Textiles and Politics: Life of B. Everett Jordan, 1992. Lay del. N.C. Ann. Conf., Meth. Ch., Sun. sch. supt., lay leader; mem. Conf. Bd. of Laity, conf. com. on social concerns, long range planning; pres. So. Alamance High Sch. PTA; chmn. Alamance County Com. for Better Schs.; dir. Alamance County Mental Health Assn.; trustee Alamance County Hist. Mus.; leader Saxapahaw Meml. Assn. (recipient So. Alamance County Community svc. award); pres. Cherokee Coun., Boy Scouts Am., 1983-84. Recipient Silver Beaver, Order of the Arrow, God and Svc. award Boy Scouts Am., 1984, Vigil honor Boy Scouts Am., Svc. to Mankind award Sertoma.

BULLARD, EDGAR JOHN, III, museum director; b. L.A., Sept. 15, 1942; s. Edgar John and Katherine Elizabeth (Dreisbach) B. BA, UCLA, 1965, MA, 1968; LHD (hon.), Loyola U., New Orleans, 1987. Asst. to dir., curator spl. projects Nat. Gallery Art, Washington, 1968-73; dir. New Orleans Mus. Art, 1973—; alternate mem. Citizens Stamp Adv. Com., 1969-71; mem. mus. adv. panel Nat. Endowment for Arts, 1974-77. Author: Edgar Degas, 1971, John Sloan 1871-1951, 1971, Mary Cassatt: Oils and Pastels, 1972, A Panorama of American Painting, 1975. Nerdrum: The Drawings, 1994. Bd. dirs. La. Cultural Alliance, 1988-91, New Orleans Jazz and Heritage Found., 1974-78; trustee Ga. Mus. Art, U. Ga., Athens, 1975-80, Kneisel Hall String and Ensemble Music Sch., Blue Hill, Maine, 1986—, La. Soc. for Prevention Cruelty to Animals, 1986-93; mem. New Orleans Commns. for Bicentennial U.S. Constn., 1987. Decorated Order of Republic of Egypt, 1979, Officer Am. Soc. Venerable Order St. John Jerusalem, 1990, chevalier Order of Arts and Lettres of France, 1994; Samuel H. Kress Found. fellow, 1967-68; recipient Mayor's Art award, 1993. Mem. Assn. Art Mus. Dirs., Am. Assn. Mus. (bd. dirs. 1996—), Coll. Art Assn. Democrat. Episcopalian. Home: 1805 Milan St New Orleans LA 70115-5443 also: Greenlea Reach Rd Deer Isle ME 04627 Office: New Orleans Mus Art PO Box 19123 New Orleans LA 70179-0123

BULLARD, JAMES JERDAN, broadcast executive; b. Red Bay, Ala., May 21, 1937; s. James Carl and Daisy Pearl (Jerdan) B.; m. Linda Jean Hosey Nesmith, Aug. 16, 1974; children: Tena Renee Nesmith Simmons, Jeana Rae Nesmith Russell. BA in Comm., U. Ala., 1958. V.p., gen. mgr. County Broadcasting Co., Inc., Sta WARF, Jasper, Ala., 1958-65; gen. mgr. Sta. WPTX, Lexington Park, Md., 1966; v.p. gen. mgr. Cullman (Ala.) Broadcasting Co., Inc., Sta. WKUL, 1967-78, Etowah Broadcasting, Inc., Sta. WAAX, Gadsden, Ala., 1978-80, Park City Comm. of Ala., Sta. WZZK FM, Birmingham, 1980-82, Katz Broadcasting of Ala., Sta. WZZK FM, Birmingham, 1982-86; v.p., gen. mgr. NewCity Comm. of Ala., Sta. WZZK FM, Birmingham, 1986-93; sr. v.p., gen. mgr. NewCity Comm. of Ala. Inc., Stas. WZZK AM/FM, WODL FM, Birmingham, 1993—. Past bd. dirs. Benefit Ala. Sheriff's Boys and Girls Ranches; Razzberry Awards fund raiser Birmingham Press Club. Named Alumnus of Yr., U. Ala. Coll. Comm., 1988, Broadcaster of Yr., Ala. Broadcaster's Assn., 1990. Mem. Country Music Assn. (Medium Market Gen. Mgr. of Yr. 1989, 90), Acad. Country Music, U. Ala. Alumni Assn., Coll. Comm. Alumni Assn., Birmingham Ad Club. Home: 1195 Country Club Cir Birmingham AL 35244-1473 Office: New City Comm of Ala Inc 530 Beacon Pky W Ste 300 Birmingham AL 35209-3196

BULLARD, JOHN MOORE, religion educator, church musician; b. Winston-Salem, N.C., May 6, 1932; s. Hoke Vogler and May Evangeline (Moore) B. AB, U. N.C., 1953, AM, 1955; MDiv, Yale U., 1957, PhD, 1962. Ordained to ministry United Meth. Ch., 1955. Asst. in instrn. Yale U., New Haven, 1957-61; asst. prof. religion Wofford Coll., Spartanburg, S.C., 1961-65, assoc. prof., 1965-70, Albert C. Outler prof. religion, 1970—, chmn. dept., 1962—, faculty sec., 1988—; minister music (organist-choirmaster) Cen. United Meth. Ch., Spartanburg, 1961-72, Bethel United Meth. Ch., 1972-88, Second Presbyn. Ch., Spartanburg, 1994, Palmetto Moravian Fellowship, 1994—; lectr. Eureka Coll., 1967, Furman U., 1982, Barton Coll., 1992; vis. prof. Biblical Lit. U. N.C., Chapel Hill, 1966, 67, U. N.C. at Charlotte, summer 1974; vis. prof. comparative religion Converse Coll., Spartanburg, S.C., 1984. Contbr. articles to Interpreter's Dictionary of Bibl. Interpretation and profl. jours. With Naval ROTC, 1950-52. Grantee NEH summer seminar Harvard U., 1982, U. Pa., 1986, Yale U., 1987; Fulbright-Hays grantee, Pakistan 1973, Fund for the Study of Gt. Religions in Asia, 1970-71; James fellow Yale U.; NEH/Wofford rsch. grantee U. London, 1975; named to Ky. Cols.; Dana Fellow Emory Univ's. Grad. Inst. Liberal Arts, 1989-90. Mem. Soc. Bibl. Lit. (pres. so. sect. 1968-69), Am. Acad. Religion, Am. Guild Organists (dean chpt. 1965-67), Organ Hist. Soc., S.C. Acad. Religion (pres. 1974-75), Southeastern Hist. Keyboard Soc., New Bach Soc. (Leipzig), Moravian Music Found., Phi Mu Alpha Sinfonia. Avocation: early keyboard music. Home: 104 Hickman Ct Hillbrook Forest Spartanburg SC 29307 Office: Wofford Coll Dept Religion 429 N Church St Spartanburg SC 29303-3612

BULLARD, MARY ELLEN, retired religious study center administrator; b. Elkin, N.C., Jan. 12, 1926; d. Roy Brannoch and Mattie Reid (Doughton) H.; m. John Carson Bullard Sr., Apr. 27, 1957; children: John Carson Jr., Roy Harrell. BS, U. N.C., Greensboro, 1947; postgrad., Union Theol. Sem., N.Y.C., 1956; MA, Troy State U., Montgomery, Ala., 1979. Dir. women's and girls' work Gilvin Roth YMCA, Elkin, 1947-49; dir. Christian edn. 1st United Meth. Ch., Salisbury, N.C., 1949-51, Charlotte, N.C., 1951-55; dir. youth ministry United Meth. Ch., Western N.C. Conf., 1956-57; dir. ednl. ministries, div. continuing edn. Huntingdon Coll., 1979-88; dir. U.S. office Bibl. Resources Study Ctr., Inc., Jerusalem, 1988-92; bd. dirs. Ch. Women United Ala., 1970-71; del. World Meth. Coun., 13th World Meth. Conf., Dublin, 1976; mem. 15th World Meth. Conf., Nairobi, Kenya, 1986, 16th World Meth. Conf., Singapore, 1991, exec. com., 1991—, 17th World Meth. Conf., Rio de Janeiro, World Evangelism Inst., 1991—; del. Gen. Conf. United Meth. Ch., St. Louis, 1988, Louisville, 1992; del. Southeastern Jurisdictional Conf., United Meth. Ch., Lake Junaluska, N.C., 1988, 92, 96; mem. gen. coun. fin. and adminstrn. United Meth. Ch., 1992—. Bd. dirs. LWV, Montgomery, 1966-70, Am. Cancer Soc., Montgomery, 1975-81, Ala. Dept. Youth Svcs., Mt. Meigs Campus Chapel, 1984-86; mem. Montgomery Symphony League, 1984-96; mem. adv. bd. Resurrection Cath. Mission, 1993—; mem. Nat. Vision 2000 Long-Range Dream Team, United Meth. Ch., 1995—; del. Southeastern Jurisdictional Conf., The United Meth. Ch., 1988, 92, 96; bd. trustees Ala. West Fla. Con. The United Meth. Ch., 1995—. Recipient award of recognition Bd. Edn. We. N.C. Conf. The United Methodist Ch., 1956, Christian Higher Edn., Ala.-West Fla. Conf. United Meth. Ch., 1975, Conf. Coun. on Ministries, Ala. West Fla. Conf., 1987, Candler Sch. of Theology, Emory U., 1990, Alice Lee award Ala. West Fla. Conf. United Meth. Ch., 1994. Mem. Christian Educators Fellowship, Kappa Delta Pi. Home: 3359 Warrenton Rd Montgomery AL 36111-1736

BULLER, JEFFREY LYNN, associate dean; b. Milw., Sept. 9, 1954; s. Richard Martin and Marian (Stelzner) B.; m. Ruth Francis Osier, July 24, 1976 (div. Apr. 1990); m. Sandra Clemmons McClain, Aug. 24, 1996. BA, U. Notre Dame, 1976; MA, U. Wis., 1977, PhD, 1981. Asst. prof. classics Loras Coll., Dubuque, Iowa, 1981-88, assoc. prof., 1988-90; asst. dean Ga. So. U., Statesboro, 1990-93, assoc. dean, 1993—; chairperson Ga. Art and Sci. Deans, 1994-96. Contbr. articles to profl. jours. Fulbright fellow USIA, Washington, 1985. Mem. Classical Assn. Mid. West and South (mem. regional exec. bd. 1989-94, Ovatio award 1996), Phi Beta Kappa, Phi Kappa Phi. Office: Ga So Univ PO Box 8142 Statesboro GA 30460-8142

BULLIVANT, KEITH, modern German literature educator; b. Derby, England, Feb. 11, 1941; s. Norman Henry and Mabel Amanda (Foster) B.; m. Jean Cicely Henderson, Sept. 4, 1965; children: John-Paul, Matthew. BA, U. Birmingham, 1963, PhD, 1968. Asst. prof. U. Birmingham, U.K., 1965-70; assoc. prof. U. Warwick, U.K., 1970-88; prof. U. Fla., Gainesville, 1989—, chair, 1993—; disting. vis. prof. N.Mex. State U., Las Cruces, 1989; joint dir. German Summer Sch. in the S.E. Author: Realism Today, 1987, The Future of German Literature, 1994; contbr. chpts. to books, articles to profl. pubs.; editl. bd. de Gruyter, N.Y.C., Berlin, 1994—. Mem. MLA, Am. Assn. of Tchrs. of German, German Studies Assn., South Atlantic MLA. Office: Dept German U Fla Gainesville FL 32611

BULLOCK, FRANK WILLIAM, JR., federal judge; b. Oxford, N.C., Nov. 3, 1938; s. Frank William and Wilma Jackson (Long) B.; m. Frances Dockery Haywood, May 5, 1984; 1 child, Frank William III. B.S. in Bus. Adminstrn., U. N.C., 1961, LL.B., 1963. Bar: N.C. 1963. Assoc. Maupin, Taylor & Ellis, Raleigh, N.C., 1964-68; asst. dir. Adminstrv. Office of Cts. of N.C., Raleigh, 1968-73; ptnr. Douglas, Ravenel, Hardy, Crihfield & Bullock, Greensboro, N.C., 1973-82; judge U.S. Dist. Ct. N.C., Greensboro, 1982—, chief judge, 1992—. Mem. bd. editors N.C. Law Rev., 1962-63; contbr. articles to profl. jours. Mem. N.C. Bar Assn., Greensboro Bar Assn., N.C. Soc. of Cin. Republican. Presbyterian. Clubs: Greensboro Country. Office: US Dist Ct PO Box 3223 Greensboro NC 27402-3223*

BULLOCK, JERRY D., company executive; b. 1930. BS in Petroleum Engring., La. State U., 1951, BS in Geology, 1952. With Exxon Corp.; sr. v.p. Coastal Corp., 1981—. Office: Coastal Oil & Gas Corp 9 E Greenway Plz Houston TX 77046

BULLOCK, JERRY MCKEE, retired military officer, consultant, educator; b. Ralls, Tex., June 2, 1932; s. Arthur Vaughn and Lillian McKee B.; m. Velma Lucille Young, Aug. 30, 1954; children: Ronnie Jay, Randy Ross, Roddy McKee, Kathy L. Bullock Chiro, Kevin L., Kelly L. Bullock Wheeler, Kristie E. Bullock Tumlinson. BA, East Tex. State U., 1954; grad., Indsl. Coll. Armed Forces, 1978, Air War Coll., 1977; MA, Webster U., 1981. Lic. profl. counselor, Tex. Commd. 2d lt. USAF, 1954, advanced through grades to col., 1974, dep. chief security police, ret., 1981; exec. dir. Family and Marriage Counseling, San Marcos, Tex., 1981-83; dir. human resources Tracor Aerospace, Austin, Tex., 1983-90; cons., owner Creative Edn. Inst., San Marcos, 1990-95. Author: Short History of the Air Force Security Police; staff writer San Marcos Bus. Jour., Corridor Bus. Jour., San Marcos Daily Record; contbr. articles toprofl. jours. Active Industry, Edn. Task Force, Austin, 1989-91, State Human Resources Com., 1989-91, Bicycle Advocacy Coalition, 1991; pastor, CEO Hill Country Faith Ministries, 1992—. Decorated Legion of Merit with 3 oak leaf clusters, Bronze Star. Mem. Air Force Security Police Assn. (chmn. bd. dirs. 1986-92, exec. dir. 1992—), Tex. Assn. Bus. (bd. dirs. 1990-92, state exec. com. 1991). Republican. Baptist. Home: 818 Willow Creek Cir San Marcos TX 78666-5060 Office: Hill Country Church 2001 River Rd San Marcos TX 78666

BULLOCK, ROBERT B., air transportation executive. Exec. dir. Greater Orlando (Fla.) Aviation Authority. Office: Greater Orlando Aviation Authority One Airport Blvd Orlando FL 32827-4399

BULLOCK, ROBERT D. (BOB BULLOCK), lawyer, lieutenant governor, state legislator; b. Hillsboro, Tex., July 10, 1929; s. Thomas A. and Ruth (Mitchell) B.; m. Jan. Felts Teague; children: Lindy Bullock Ward, Robert Douglas Jr., Kimberly Teague. AA, Hill Coll., 1949; BA, Tex. Tech U., 1958; JD Baylor U., 1958, D of Humanities in Medicine (hon.), 1992. Bar: Tex. 1958, U.S. Dist. Ct. (so. and ea. dists.) Tex. 1960, U.S. Dist. Ct. (we. dist.) Tex. 1961, U.S. Ct. Appeals (5th cir.) 1972. Sole practice, Hillsboro, Tex., 1957-59, Tyler, Tex., 1960-61, Austin, Tex., 1961-67; asst. atty. gen. State of Tex., Austin, 1967-68, legal counsel, office of gov., 1969-71, sec. of state, 1971-73, comptr. pub. accounts, 1975-91; lt. gov. State of Tex., 1991—; pres. Tex. State Senate. Mem. Tex. Ho. of Reps., 1956-59; mem. Legis. Budget Bd., Legis. Coun., Interstate Oil Compact Commn., Impact 2000; chair Tex. State Dem. Leadership Coun.; mem. Sesquicentennial Coun. of 150 Baylor U. Served with USAF, 1951-54, Korea. Recipient Louisville Gold Medal award Mcpl. Fin. Officers Assn., 1978, Leon Rothenberg Pub. Svc. award Fed. Tax Adminstrs., 1989, Legis. award Clean Water Action and Clean Water Fund, 1991, Pub. Svc. award Common Cause, 1991, Outstanding Legislator of Yr. award Houston Police Patrolman's Union, 1991, Legislator of Yr. award Sportsmen Conservations of Tex., 1991, Champion of Children award Tex. Collation for Juvenile Justice, 1991, Elected Ofcl. award Tex. Human Rights Found., 1991, Leadership award Assn. Retarded Citizens, 1992, Friend Edn. award Tex. Classroom Tchrs. Assn., Elves Smith Meml. award Alcoholic Rehab. Ctr. Bexar County, Pub. Ofcl. award Tex. Pub. Power Assn., 1992, Bill Hobby award Tex. Abortion Rights Action League, 1992, Mirabeau B. Lamar medal Assn. Tex. Colls. and Univs., 1993; named Mr. South Tex., Washington Birthday Celebration Assn., 1993, Better than the Best in 73d Legislature, Tex. Monthly Mag., 1993, Outstanding Legislator of Yr., Tex. Jr. Coll. Tchrs. Assn., 1994, Frank C. Erwin award U. Tex., 1994, Baylor Lawyer of Yr., 1994, Outstanding Svcs. to Librs. award Tex. Libr. Assn., 1994, Legislator of Yr. 1994, Achievement in Support of Tort Reform Tex. Civil Justice League, 1995, Hats Off award Tex. Ind. Prodrs. and Royalty Owners Assn., 1995, Gov. Allan Shivers Pub. Svc. award Austin Headliners' Found., 1995, award of excellence Tex. Assn. Symphony Orchs., 1996, Santa Rita award, U. Tex. Bd. of Regents, 1996, Disting. Public Servants award, Tex. U. Ctr. for Public Svc., 1996, Merit award for 1996, award of Excellence, Nat. Junior Coll. Athletic Assn., and numerous others; honored by People First!, 1993, Exec. Dirs. Tex. Coun. Family Violence, Tex. Family Planning Assn., 1993, honored Bob Bullock Endowed Scholarship Blinn Coll., 1994; named to Nat. Jaycee Hall of Leadership, 1993, others. Mem. NRA (life), State Bar Tex., Tex. Trial Lawyers Assn., Travis County Bar Assn., Am. Legion, Tex. State Hist. Assn., Baylor Law Alumni Assn. (life), Masons (33d degree). Democrat. Office: Office of Lt Gov Box 12068 Capitol Station Austin TX 78711-2068

BULMAHN, LYNN, journalist, freelance writer; b. Waco, Tex., Feb. 18, 1955; d. Franklin Harrold and Louise (Stolte) B. BA, SW Tex. State U., 1977. Med., health, feature writer and gen. assignment reporter Waco Tribune Herald, 1977—; vis. journalist fellowship Duke U., 1991. Bd. trustees Unity Ch. of Living Christ, Hewitt, Tex. Recipient Anson Jones Merit citation, Tex. Med. Assn., 1978, 91, Outstanding Contbn. award Nat. Found. March of Dimes, 1980, Pub. Health award for media excellence Tex. Pub. Health Assn., 1980, 85, 88, 89, 90, 91, 92, 93, 94, 95, First Place award Readers Digest Mag. Workshop Tex. Competition, 1981, Feature Writing award North and East Tex. Press Assn., 1983, Media Appreciation award McLennan County Med. Assn., 1985, Journalism Excellence award Am. Cancer Soc., 1989, 91, Silver Star of Tex. award Tex. Hosp. Assn., 1989, 92, Newspaper award, Mental Health Assn., 1989, 90, 91, 94, 95, Anson Jones award Tex. Med. Assn., 1992; co-recipient Tex. Katie award Press Club Dallas, 1993. Office: Waco Tribune-Herald 900 Franklin Ave Waco TX 76701-1906

BULOW, JACK FAYE, library director; b. Elmira, N.Y., June 7, 1942; m. June Burwell, May 22, 1971. Associates degree, Corning (N.Y.) C.C., 1968; BA, U. Ala., Birmingham, 1971; MLS, U. Ala., Tuscaloosa, 1973. Community svcs. libr. Birmingham Pub. Libr., 1973-77, assoc. dir., 1977-93, dir., 1993—. Developer Books-by-Mail program, Birmingham and Jefferson County, 1976; participant exec. in residence program Birmingham-Southern Coll., 1987, Leadership Birmingham, 1992; elected as del. White House Conf. on Libr. and Info. Svc., Washington, 1991; elected as regional rep. White House Conf. on Libr. and Info. Svcs. Task Force, Washington, 1992; bd. dirs. Birmingham Internat. Ednl. Film Festival, 1992—, Literacy Coun. Ctrl. Ala., Birmingham, 1993—; mem. Nat. League Cities, Washington, 1993—; mem. long range planning com. Birmingham Mus. Art, 1993—; mem. cultural fafairs com. Operation New Birmingham, 1988—; patron Cahaba River Soc. Birmingham, 1992—. With USCG, 1960-64. Recipient Forestry Recognition award Ala. Forestry Commn., 1977. Mem. ALA (mem.-at-large fund raising fin. devel. sect. 1994), Am. Hist. Print Collectors Soc., Am. Mgmt. Assn., Nat. Soc. Fund Raising Execs., Southeastern Libr. Assn., Ala. Libr. Assn. (pres. 1995). Office: Birmingham Pub Libr 2100 Park Pl Birmingham AL 35203-2744

BUMAGAT, FERDINAND MENDOZA, military physician; b. Davao, Philippines, Nov. 22, 1941; came to U.S., 1966; s. Guillermo and Rosa (Mendoza) B.; m. Mary Catherine Fletcher, Nov. 20, 1973; children: William, Annabel, Melody, Marybeth. MD, U. Philippines, Manila, 1966. Diplomate Am. Bd. Internal Medicine. Intern St. Peter's Hosp., Albany, N.Y., 1966-67; resident in internal medicine Grace Hosp., Detroit, 1967-70; fellow endocrinology Wayne State U., Detroit, 1970-71; attending physician Met. Hosp., Detroit, 1971-76; commd. lt. USN, 1966, advanced through grades to comdr., 1978; staff internist Naval Regional Med. Ctr., Long Beach, Calif., 1976-80; dir. clin. svc. Naval Regional Med. Ctr., Subic Bay, Philippines, 1980-82; staff internist Naval Hosp., Orlando, Fla., 1982-85; head internal medicine dept. Naval Hosp., Oak Harbor, Wash., 1985-88; dir. med. svcs. Naval Hosp., Naples, Italy, 1988-91; head internal medicine dept. Naval Hosp., Pensacola, Fla., 1991-94. Mem. Assn. Philippine Physicians of the Fla. Panhandle, KC. Republican. Roman Catholic. Office: Navy Hosp Pensacola FL 32512

BUMGARDNER, CLOYD JEFFREY, school principal; b. Lorain, Ohio, Feb. 4, 1964; s. Cloyd Otis and Lois Christina (Todd) B. BS, Eastern Ky. U., 1987, MS, 1990. Cert. sch. adminstr., Ky. Sci. tchr. Pulaski County Schs., Somerset, Ky., 1990-93; asst. prin. Calloway County Schs., Murray, Ky., 1993-94; prin. Calloway County Mid. Sch., Murray, 1994—; adj. faculty U. Ky., 1990-93, Somerset C.C., 1990-93, Ea. Ky. U., Richmond, 1992-93; environ. cons. Am.-Russian Eco-bridge Team, Murray, 1994—; content adv. bd. mem. Ky. Dept. Edn., Frankfort, 1994-96. Contbr. articles to profl. jours. Fundraiser Am. Heart Assn., Murray, 1995, Internat. Assn. Lions Clubs, Murray, 1994—; mem. Ky. Col. Commn., Gov. State of Ky., 1995. Named Hon. Capt. of Ky. Lake, Judge Exec. of Calloway County, 1995. Mem. NEA, Nat. Alliance for Restructuring Edn., Nat. Assn. Secondary Sch. Prins., Ky. Assn. Environ. Edn., Internat. Assn. Lions Clubs, Ky. Acad. Scis., Phi Delta Kappa. Republican. Office: Calloway County Middle School 2108A College Farm Rd Murray KY 42071-8805

BUMGARDNER, JAMES ARLISS, artist, educator; b. Winston-Salem, N.C., Mar. 25, 1935; s. Edgar E. and Alma Faye (Preston) B.; m. Judith Joy, May 28, 1960; 1 child, Rhea Maya. BFA, Va. Commonwealth U., 1957. Prof. Va. Commonwealth U., Richmond, 1958—. Recipient Spl. award in painting N.C. Mus., 1958, 59, 60, 62, Cert. of Distinction, Va. Mus. Fine Art, 1959, 61, 63, 77, Purchase prize Southeastern Ctr. Contemporary Art, 1977, Purchase prize N.C. Mus., 1957. Home: 406 N Allen Ave Richmond VA 23220-2902

BUMGARNER, EDWARD SCOTT, quality assurance professional; b. Wyneewood, Okla., Dec. 1, 1944; s. Thomas Scott and Geneva Florence (Wells) B.; m. Carolyn Bonnell Denton, Jan. 17, 1969 (div. 1980); 1 child, Alicia Bonnell; m. Nettie Elizabeth Edwards, Nov. 1, 1986; 1 stepchild, Vanna Kay Foster. AB, Richland Coll., 1977. Group leader Tex. Instruments, Inc., Dallas, 1966-78; production planner Tex. Instruments, Inc., Sherman, Tex., 1980-82; production operator Tex. Instruments, Inc., Sherman, 1982-88, quality control, 1988-95; quality control MEMC Southwest, Inc., Sherman, 1995—; owner, operator Tuition Sources, Sherman, 1991—, Southwest Mktg., Sherman, 1993—. Mem. Oxford Club, Highlander Club. Protestant. Office: Southwest Mktg 209 Iowa Sherman TX 75090

BUMP, LARRY J., international engineering and construction company executive; b. Salem, Ill., Dec. 13, 1939; s. Joseph Ernest and Mary Emma (Withers) B.; m. Linda L. Johnson, 1965; chidlren: Tina, Terry, Tricia. BS in Acctg., Okla. State U., 1964. Project mgr. Neill-Price Internat., Inc., Benghazi, Libya, 1964-67; exec. v.p. Neill-Price Internat., Inc., London, 1967-71; pres., chief exec. officer Banister Price Internat., Inc., Tehran, Iran, 1971-77; chmn., chief exec. officer Heerema Holding Co. Inc., Geneva, 1985-88, Willbros Group, Inc., Tulsa, 1977—; pres. Internat. Pipe Line Contractors Assocs., Paris, 1984-86; bd. dirs. Divsn. Fintube Corp., Tulsa. Gov. Okla. State U. Found., Stillwater, Okla., 1989—; trustee Tulsa Boys Home Found., 1988—; mem. Okla. State U. Centennial Commn., Stillwater, 1989—. Recipient Disting. Alumnus award Okla. State U. Alumni Assn., 1989; inductee Hall of Fame Okla. State U. Coll. Bus. Adminstrn., 1992. Office: Willbros USA Inc 2431 E 61st St Ste 700 Tulsa OK 74136-1235

BUMPERS, DALE L., senator, former governor; b. Charleston, AR, Aug. 12, 1925; s. William Rufus and Lattie (Jones) B.; m. Betty Lou Flanagan, Sept. 4, 1949; children: Dale Brent, William Mark, Margaret Brooke. Student, U. Ark., 1943, 46-48; J.D., Northwestern U., 1951. Bar: Ark. 1952. Pres. Charleston Hardware and Furniture Co., 1951-56; pvt. practice Charleston, 1952-70; operator Angus cattle farm, 1966-70; gov. of Ark., 1970-74; U.S. senator from Ark., 1975—. Pres. Charleston Sch. Bd., 1969-70. Sgt. USMC, 1943-46. Mem. Charleston C. of C. (pres.). Methodist. Office: US Senate 229 Dirksen Senate Bldg Washington DC 20510

BUMPOUS, EARLE THOMAS, III, concrete products company executive; b. Selma, Ala., Nov. 26, 1943; s. Earle Thomas and Lillian Patricia (Curtis) B.; m. Joyce Marie Rudolph, May 8, 1961 (div. Apr. 1968); 1 child, Earle Thomas IV; m. Beverly Ann Stephenson, June 8, 1968 (div. Jan. 1995); 1 child, Tylah Ann; m. Marcella Jean Quinn, July 15, 1995. Student, U. Tenn., 1961-62, Belmont Coll., Nashville, 1962-63; grad., Nashville Area Tech., 1971. Cert. welder. Underground welder Mid-Continent Resources, Carbondale, Colo., 1972-76; welding supr. Peterbilt Motors Co., Madison, Tenn., 1976-78; welder Carbondale (Colo.) Mine Svcs., 1978-80; steel fabricator Raber Industries, Ft. Myers, Fla., 1980-82; v.p. Cement Industries, Inc., Ft. Myers, 1983—; Inventor angle-cut concrete saw. Emergency radio operator Am. Radio Relay League, Ft. Myers, 1989. Capt. U.S. Army, 1963-70, Korea. Mem. Am. Soc. Safety Engrs., Gulf Coast Concrete and Products Assn., Fla. Employers Safety Assn. (committeeman 1987-88), S.W. Fla. Safety Coun. (bd. dirs. 1988-91, v.p. 1990-91), Ft. Myers Amateur Radio Club, Am. Legion, NRA. Home: 6741 Circle Dr Fort Myers FL 33905 Office: Cement Industries Inc 2709 Jeffcott St Fort Myers FL 33901-5337

BUMPUS, FLOYD DAVID, JR., microcomputer analyst; b. Little Rock, Aug. 18, 1952; s. Floyd David and Wilma Ruth (Bishop) B.; m. Bonnie Suzanne Buckner, June 22, 1991; 1 child, Jamie Suzanne Jay. BS in Computer Sci., Math., U. Mary Hardin Baylor, 1993. Enlisted U.S. Army, 1970, advanced through grades to staff sgt., 1980, resigned, 1984; mechanic's helper Otis Elevator, Little Rock, 1984-87; microcomputer analyst Bell County, Belton, Tex., 1987—. Mem. Temple Amateur Radio Club (vol. examiner coord.), Am. Radio Relay League (vol. FCC examiner, ofcl. observer North Tex. sect.). Republican. Mem. Ch. of Christ. Home: 214

Berry Dr Salado TX 76571-9575 Office: Bell County Info Systems 411 E Central Ave # 669 Belton TX 76513-3241

BUMPUS, JAMIE EDWARD, newspaper copy editor; b. Union City, Tenn., Nov. 27, 1969; s. James Earl and Bettye Jean (Norman) B. BA, U. Tenn., Martin, 1993. Exec. editor The Pacer, Martin, Tenn., 1992-93; sports editor The Fulton (Ky.) Leader, 1993-95; color commentator WOBT-TV, Union City, Tenn., 1996; county reporter The Jackson (Tenn.) Sun, 1996; news dir. WCMT-AM-FM and WCDZ-FM, Martin, 1996; copy editor State Gazette, Dyersburg, Tenn., 1996—. Pres. Soc. Profl. Journalists, Martin, 1991-93. Recipient 1st pl. Class I Best Sports Story, Ky. Press Assn., 1994, 2d pl. Class I Best Sports Feature, 1994, 2d pl. Region 12 Best Sports Story, Soc. Profl. Journalists, 1993; named Outstanding Mem. Soc. Profl. Journalists, 1993. Republican. Mem. Ch. of Christ. Home: 737 Campground Rd Troy TN 38260 Office: State Gazette 294 Hwy 51 Bypass N Dyersburg TN 38025

BUNCH, FRANKLIN SWOPE, architect; b. Madison, Ind., Jan. 4, 1913; s. Walker Franklin and Susan Beatrice (Swope) B.; m. Virginia Aurelia Boggs, June 8, 1937; children: Franklin Swope, Dean Boggs. B.S. in Arch, U. Fla., 1934. Draftsman, designer, architect and constrn. supr. various Fla. architects, 1934-41; archtl. engr. U.S. Engrs. Dist. Office, Jacksonville, Fla., 1942-43, Jacksonville Naval Air Sta., 1944-45; partner Kemp, Bunch & Jackson Architects, Inc., Jacksonville, 1946-69; sr. v.p. Kemp, Bunch & Jackson Architects, Inc., 1970-82; Pres. Fla. Bd. Architecture, 1959-61; mem. com. on exams. Nat. Council Archtl. Registration Bds., 1961-62; pres. bldg. code adv. bd., Jacksonville, 1949-68, mem. examining com., from 1949; chmn. bldg. codes adjustment bd. Jacksonville Consol. Govt.; mem. housing com. Jacksonville Council on Aging, 1962. Projects include S. Central Home Office Prudential Ins. Co. Am., gen. offices Seaboard Coast Line R.R., Fla. State Prison, Starke, Hdqrs. Bldg. State Rd. Dept., Tallahassee. Pres. Little Theatre of Jacksonville, 1952-53. Fellow AIA (emeritus); mem. Fla. Assn. Architects (pres. 1947-48, now emeritus), Jacksonville Jr. C. of C. (chmn. luncheon club 1938), Jacksonville Area C. of C. (chmn. city, county, state affairs com. 1963, chmn. fed. assistance 1949-68), Phi Kappa Tau. Baptist.

BUNDY, CHARLES ALAN, foundation executive; b. Cheraw, S.C., Jan. 5, 1930; s. Jackson Corbett and Ruby Jones (Hughes) B.; m. Margaret Ellen Jackson, Feb. 27, 1954; children: Charles Alan, Robert Jackson, Dan Hughes. AB, Wofford Coll., 1951; DH (hon.), Charleston So. Coll. Mgr. prodn. planning J.P. Stevens & Co., Inc., Rockingham, N.C., 1951-54; mgr. Jesup (Ga.) C. of C., 1954-56, Lancaster (S.C.) C. of C., 1956-61; dist. mgr. U.S. C. of C., Birmingham, Ala., 1961-65; exec. v.p. Macon (Ga.) C. of C., 1965-71, Greg Enterprises, Lancaster, 1971-72; pres. Springs Found., Inc. and Close Found., Inc., Lancaster, 1972—. Chmn. S.C. Parks, Recreation and Tourism Commn., 1983-89; mem. S.C. Coordinating Coun. for Econ. Devel., 1986-89, Coun. on Founds.; past chmn. S.E. Coun. Founds.; trustee Columbia Coll., 1976-88, S.C. Found. Ind. Colls., 1982-93; chmn. bd. 1st Meth. Ch., 1978, 79; chmn. Gov.'s Freshwater Wetlands Forum, 1989; mem. State Govt. Reorgn. Commn., 1991; chmn. Lancaster County Strategic Plan, 1990; bd. dirs. Springs Meml. Hosp., S.C. Hosp. Assn.; trustee, treas. J. Marion Sims Found., Inc. Mem. Lancaster County C. of C. (past pres.), Rotary (past pres.). Home: 518 Briarwood Rd Lancaster SC 29720-1802 Office: Springs Found Inc 104 E Springs St PO Box 460 Lancaster SC 29721

BUNE, KAREN LOUISE, criminal justice official; b. Washington, Mar. 6, 1954; d. Harry and Eleanor Mary (White) B. BA in Am. Studies cum laude, Am. U., 1976, MS in Adminstrn. of Justice with distinction, 1978. Notary pub., Va. Case mgr. Arlington (Va.) Alcohol Safety Action Program, 1979-94; victim specialist Office of Commonwealth Atty., Arlington, Va., 1994—; case mgr. regional rep. of case mgmt. com. of Dirs. Assn. Commn. on Va. Alcohol Safety Action Program, Richmond, 1980-81, 84-85, 88-89, mem. subcom. studying treatment issues, 1988-94; chair career guidance subcom. alumni adv. com. Sch. Pub. Affairs Am. U., Washington, 1991-94. Sch. of Justice rep. alumni adv. com. Coll. Pub. Affairs, Am. U. Washington, 1982-86, chmn. student rels., 1982-86, mem. alumni steering com., 1991—. Recipient spl. achievement award Dept. Navy, 1973, merit award Arlington County, 1986, Woman of the Yr. Am. Biog. Inst., 1990, inducted into Hall of Fame for outstanding achievement in case management. Mem. ASPA (No. Va. chpt. coun.), NAFE, APHA, AAUW, Nat. Assn. Chiefs Police (award of merit 1986), Nat. Criminal Justice Assn., Nat. Orgn. Victim Assistance, Am. Police Hall of Fame (cert. of appreciation 1985), Acad. Criminal Justice Scis., So. Criminal Justice Assn., Am. Soc. Criminology, Va. Sheriffs Inst., No. Va. Crime Prevention Assn., No. Va. Fraternal Order Police, Va. Assn. Female Execs., Internat. Platform Assn., Am. U. Alumni Assn. (immediate past pres. sch. pub. affairs chpt. 1994-96), Women of Washington, Phi Kappa Phi, Phi Alpha Alpha, Phi Delta Gamma (1st v.p. 1981-82). Home: 926 16th St S Arlington VA 22202-2606 Office: Office of Commonwealth Atty 1425 N Court House Rd Arlington VA 22201-2605

BUNGE, RICHARD PAUL, cell biologist, educator; b. Madison, S.D., Apr. 15, 1932; married, 1956; 2 children. BA, U. Wis., 1954, MS, 1956, MD, 1960. Asst. anatomist U. Wis., 1954-57, instr., 1957-58; from asst. prof. to assoc. prof. anatomy, coll. physicians and surgeons Columbia U., 1962-70; prof. anatomy sch. medicine Washington U., St. Louis, 1970-89; sci. dir. Miami project/paralysis divsn., prof. neurosurg. cell biology anatomy Miami (Fla.) U., 1989—; vis. prof. Harvard Med. Sch., 1968-69; Nat. Multiple Sclerosis Soc. fellow surgeon Coll. Physicians and Surgeonas, Columbua U., 1960-62. Co-author: Peripheral Neuropathy, 2 vols., 2d edit., 1984; co-editor: Spinal Cord Reconstruction, 1983, Current Issues in Neural Regeneration Research, 1988. Recipient Lederle Med. Faculty award, 1964-67. Mem. Am. Assn. Anatomy, Am. Soc. Cell Biology, Am. Assn. Neuropathology, Tissue Culture Assn., Soc. Neuroscience. Office: U Miami Miami Project to Cure Paralysis 1600 NW 10th Ave # R48 Miami FL 33136-1015

BUNKER-SOLER, ANTONIO LUIS, physician; b. Cagua, P.R., Oct. 2, 1948. BS, U. P.R., Mayaguez, 1970; MD, U. P.R., San Juan, 1974. Diplomate Am. Bd. Allergy and Immunology, Am. Bd. Pediatrics. Commd. 2d lt. U.S. Army, 1973, advanced through grades to lt. col.; resident in pediatrics Brooke AMC, San Antonio, 1977; with pediatric svc. SHAPE, Belgium, 1977-79; various positions U.S. Army, Ft. Campbell, Ky., 1981-83, Ft. Hood, Tex., 1988-89; chief allergy-immunology svc. U.S. Army, Frankfurt, Germany, 1989-92; asst. chief allergy-immunology svc. U.S. Army, El Paso, Tex., 1992-94; various positions EAMC, Ga., 1983-88; pediatric pulmonary fellow Tex. Children's Hosp., Houston, 1994-95; pvt. practice Tampa, 1996—; asst. clin. prof. MCG, Augusta, Ga., 1983-88; allergy cons. southeastern region CONUS, 1984-88, 7th MEDCOM, Europe, 1989-92, allergy cons.; presenter in field. Contbr. articles to profl. jours. Active Asthma and Allergy Support Group, Augusta, 1985-87. Decorated Army Commendation medal with oak leaf cluster, Order of Mil. Med. Merit; Allergy fellow Fitzsimons AMC, 1981. Fellow Am. Coll. Asthma, Allergy and Immunology, Tex. Med. Assn., Mil. Allergists (Dura Pharm. award 1987); mem. AMA, Am. Acad. Pediatrics, Am. Acad. Allergy and Immunology, Am. Thoracic Soc. Office: 14310 N Dale Mabry Hwy Ste 260 Tampa FL 33618-2059

BUNNELL, GEORGE ELI, lawyer; b. Miami, Fla., Apr. 28, 1938; s. George A. and Lillian E. (Hurley) B.; m. Dianne Railton, Dec. 1, 1990; children: Kelley, Courtney. BA, U. Fla., 1960, LLB, 1962. Bar: Fla. 1963, U.S. Dist. Ct. (so. dist.) Fla. 1963, U.S. Ct. Appeals (11th cir.) 1982, U.S. Supreme Ct. 1970. Assoc., Nicholson, Howard & Brawner, Miami, 1963-64; assoc. Dean, Adams, George & Wood, Miami, 1964-67, ptnr., 1968-71; officer, dir. Huebner, Shaw & Bunnell, P.A., Fort Lauderdale, Fla., 1972-77; pres., dir. Bunnell, Woulfe, Kirschbaum, Keller & McIntyre, P.A., Fort Lauderdale, 1977—. Mem. advance office staff White House, 1974-76; mem. City of Fort Lauderdale Marine Adv. Bd., 1974-76, City of Fort Lauderdale Civil Svc. Bd., 1977-79; bd. dirs., sec. Ft. Lauderdale Mus. Art, 1990—. Mem. Internat. Assn. Ins. Counsel, Am. Coll. Trial Lawyers, Am. Bd. Trial Advs. (pres. Ft. Lauderdale chpt. 1992), Def. Rsch. Inst., Fla. Def. Lawyers Assn., Broward County Bar Assn. Republican. Clubs: Lago Mar Beach, Lauderdale Yacht (Fort Lauderdale). Office: Bunnell Woulfe Kirschbaum Keller & McIntyre PA 888 E Las Olas Blvd # 4 Fort Lauderdale FL 33301-2272

BUNNER, PATRICIA ANDREA, lawyer; b. Fairmont, W.Va., Sept. 16, 1953; d. Scott Randolph and Virginia Lenore (Keck) B. AB in History & English magna cum laude, W.Va. U., 1975, JD, 1978; postgrad., Internat. Bible Sem., Trinity Theol. Sem., 1995—; DD, Am. Inst. Theology, 1996; postgrad. in Psychology, LaSalle U., 1995; postgrad., Pacific Universal Life Ch., 1995, Andover Newton Theol. Sem., 1995—, W.Va. U., 1996—. Bar: W.Va. 1978, U.S. Dist. Ct. (so. dist.) W.Va. 1978, U.S. Dist. Ct. (no. dist.) W.Va. 1985, U.S. Ct. Claims 1990, U.S. Supreme Ct. 1989; ordained to ministry Universal Life Ch., 1996, World Christian Ch., 1996; cert. Christian counselor, 1986—. Mem. staff Dem. Nat. Com., Washington, 1978-79; assoc. Gailor, Elias & Matz, Washington, 1979-81, N.Y. State Bankers Assn., N.Y.C., 1981-83; ptnr. Bunner & Bunner, Fairview, W.Va., 1984—; exec. dir. N.Y. State Consumer Mortgage Rev. Bd.; chmn. dist. VIII Consumer Mortgage Rev. Com., N.Y.C., 1982-83; cons. atty. Energy Cons. Assocs., Spring Harbor, N.Y., 1981; of counsel Monongahela (W.Va.) Soil Conservation Dist., 1985. Author: How Charley Methency Broke the Four Minute Mile, 1971, Across the Bennefield Prong, 1973, German Anti-Semitism, Bismarck Through Weimar, 1973, N.Y. State Bankers Assn. Legis. Directory, 1983, Through a Glass Darkly, A Compendium of Film Noir, 1996, The Influence of the Seventeenth Century Scientific Revolution on Anglo-American Law, 1996, Rene Descartes, Phenomenologist, 1996. Pres. Monongalia County Dem. Women, 1987-89; sec. Monongalia County Devel. Authority, 1984-91; pres. United Taxpayers Assn., Inc., W.Va., 1985-88; bd. dirs. W.Va. U. Morgantown, 1974-75; active W.Va. State Dem. Exec. Com., 1990, 94. Rilla Moran Woods fellow Nat. Fedn. Dem. Women, Washington, 1978. Mem. ABA (vice chmn. legal econs. and new lawyers coms. 1986-87, litigation sect., 1st amendment rights and media law com., gen. practice com., corps. and banking com.), W.Va. Bar Assn. (com. econs. of law practice 1987—), Assn. Trial Lawyers Am., W.Va. Trial Lawyers Assn., N.Y. State Bar Assn., Monongalia County Bar Assn., Marion County Bar Assn., W.Va. Criminal Def. Lawyers Assn., Women's Info. Ctr. (founding), LWV, NAFE, W.Va. Alliance for Women's Studies (founding), Bus. and Profl. Women (bd. dirs.), Climates, Inc., Monongalia County Hist. Soc., Clay-Battelle Alumni Assn., W.Va. Coll. Law Alumni Assn., Nat. Rifle Assn. (life), Nature Conservancy, Nat. Arbor Day Found., World Wildlife Fund, Am. Farmland Trust, AAUW, Sierra Club, Audobon Soc., Young Dems. Club W.Va. (sec. 1976), Phi Alpha Theta (chpt. pres. 1974-75), Phi Beta Kappa, Zeta Phi Eta, Alpha Rho (chpt. pres. 1974). Mem. Ch. of Christ. Club: Woman's (bd. dirs. Morgantown chpt. 1986—). Home: RR 2 Box 341 Fairview WV 26570-9449

BUNNER, WILLIAM KECK, lawyer; b. Fairmont, W.Va., Sept. 2, 1949; s. Scott Randolph and Virginia Lenore (Keck) B. BS in Secondary Edn. magna cum laude, W.Va. U., 1970, MA in History, 1973, JD, 1978. Bar: W.Va. 1978, U.S. Dist. Ct. (so. dist.) W.Va. 1978, U.S. Dist. Ct. (no. dist.) W.Va. 1985. Tchr. Monongalia County Bd. Edn., Morgantown, W.Va., 1970-78; contract lawyer dept. fin. and adminstrn. State of W.Va., Charleston, 1978-79; pvt. practice law Fairview, W.Va., 1979-84; pres. Farm Home Svc., Inc., 1983—; ptnr. Bunner & Bunner, Morgantown and Fairview, 1984-92; pres. Climates, 1988—. Pres. Monongalia County Young Dems., 1974; parliamentarian Monongalia County Dem. Exec. Com., 1982-94; counsel, parliamentarian Young Dem. Clubs W.Va., 1974-77; bd. dirs., supr. Monongahela Soil Conservation Dist., 1982—; advisor West Run Watershed Improvement Dist., 1983—; mem. W.Va. Commn. on Rural Abandoned Mines, Rural Alliance, Monongalia County Solid Waste Auth., 1989—, also chmn., 1990-92. Mem. ABA, Monongalia County Bar Assn., Assn. Rural Conservation, Soil Conservation Soc. Am., United Taxpayers' Assn. (counsel), Monongalia County Hist. Soc., Marion County Hist. Soc., Marion County Bar Assn., W.Va. Trial Lawyers Assn, Phi Alpha Delta, Phi Alpha Theta. Democrat. Home and Office: RR 2 Box 341 Fairview WV 26570-9449

BUNT, RANDOLPH CEDRIC, mechanical engineer; b. Pascagoula, Miss., Dec. 3, 1958; s. Cedric and Linda Lou (McGuire) B.; m. Raechel Amy Ellis, May 15, 1982; children: Ashley Michele, Ryan Christian, Raechel Victoria. BME, Auburn U., 1979, MS, 1982. Registered profl. engr., Ala., Ga. Asst. engr. So. Co. Svcs., Birmingham, Ala., 1982-84, engr. II, 1984-86, engr. I, 1986-87, sr. engr., 1987-88; sr. engr. Ga. Power Co., Birmingham, 1988-89; project engr. So. Nuclear Oper. Co., Birmingham, 1989—; project mgr. Ga. Power Co., Atlanta and Birmingham, 1987-89; chmn. GE Nuclear Turbine Conf., 1993-95. Trustee Friends of Moody Schs.; chmn., co-founder GE Nuclear Turbine Users Group; vice chmn. Fairbanks Morse Owners Group, 1994-96, chmn. 1996—; stewardship chmn. Moody United Meth. Ch., 1995—; capt. Birmingham Amateur Hockey Assn., 1985. Mem. ASME, NSPE, Am. Nuclear Soc., Ala. Soc. Profl. Engrs. (chmn. student engring. yr. com. 1987-92, chmn. Math Counts program 1990-95, sec. 1992-93, v.p. 1993-95, pres. 1995—, co-chmn. 1993 conf., Young Engr. of Yr. 1991), Birmingham Eng ring. Coun. (chmn. Discover E 1993-95, treas. 1995-96, sec. 1996—), So. Nuclear Nat. Mgmt. Assn. (treas. 1991-92, bd. dirs. 1994-95), Terry Turbine Users Group (vice chmn. 1993—). Republican. Methodist. Home: 1005 Muscadine Cir Leeds AL 35094-1027 Office: So Nuclear Oper Co 42 Inverness Center Pky Birmingham AL 35242-4809

BUNTEN, BRENDA ARLENE, geriatrics nurse; b. Paris, Ill., May 7, 1947; d. Arthur Ray Sr. and Maxine L. (Bacon) B. A in Arts and Scis., Lakeland Coll., Mattoon, Ill., 1968; ADN, Kapiolani C.C., Honolulu, 1992. Charge nurse Meml. Med. Ctr., Springfield, Ill., 1968-76, Mattoon Health Care Ctr., 1977-79; agy. nurse Kahu Malama, Inc., Honolulu, 1983; charge nurse, staff devel. coord., infection control officer Hale Nani Health Ctr., Honolulu, 1979-93, also nursing staff scheduler, supr., 1979-93; unit mgr. Randal Mill Manor, Arlington, Tex., 1994—; supr. Heritage Oaks, Arlington, Tex., 1994—; fundraiser Challenger Run Hawaii, Honolulu, 1986—; co-owner, cons. retail sales Sunset Enterprises, Honolulu, 1982—. Mem. USS Lancelot, Citizens Police Acad. Alumni Assn., Citizens Fire Dept. Alumni Assn., Alpha Kappa Psi, Beta Sigma Phi (pres. 1985-86). Home: 2009 Newbury Dr Arlington TX 76014-3616

BUNTING, GARY GLENN, operations research analyst, educator; b. Toledo, Ohio, Mar. 19, 1947; s. Glenn Rose and Maxine (Hunt) B.; m. Glenda Marlene Mechum, Aug. 23, 1974; children: Wendy Daniele, Bradley Glenn, Max Alan, Morgan Cecile. BS, Auburn U., 1969; MS, Troy State U., 1977. Research analyst City of Jacksonville, Fla., 1972-76; ops. research analyst U.S. Army Aviation Ctr., Ft. Rucker, Ala., 1976-78, U.S. Army Tng. Support Ctr., Ft. Eustis, Va., 1978-80, USAF Tactical Air Warfare Ctr., Eglin AFB, Fla., 1980-85, Office Sec. Def. Tng. and Performance Data Ctr., Orlando, Fla., 1985-92; chief ops. analysis Spl/ Missions Operational Test and Evaluation Ctr.; adj. assoc. prof. U. West Fla., Ft. Walton Beach, 1982, Troy State U., Ft. Walton Beach, 1983—. Contbr. articles to profl. jours. Served with U.S. Army, 1969-71. Recipient Civilian Excellence award, USAF Tactical Air Warfare Ctr. and Air Force Assn., 1983. Mem. Air Force Assn. Republican. Lodge: Elks. Avocations: reading, photography. Home: 306 Northampton Cir Fort Walton Beach FL 32547-1468 Office: 606 Cruz Ave Hurlburt Field FL 32544-5708

BUNTON, LUCIUS DESHA, III, federal judge; b. Del Rio, Tex., Dec. 1, 1924; s. Lucius Desha and Avis Maurine (Fisher) B.; m. Mary Jane Carsey, June 18, 1947; children: Cathryne Avis Bunton Warner, Lucius Desha. Student, U. Chgo., 1943-44; BA, U. Tex., Austin, 1947, JD, 1950. Bar: Tex. 1949. Individual practice law Uvalde, Tex., 1950; assoc. firm H.O. Metcalfe, Marfa, Tex., 1951-54; dist. atty. 83d Jud. Dist. Tex., 1954-59; mem. firm Shafer, Gilliland, Davis, Bunton & McCollum, Odessa, Tex., 1959-79; judge U.S. Dist. Ct. (we. dist.) Tex., Midland, 1979-87, chief judge, 1987-92, sr. judge, 1989—; mem. jud. resources com., 1989-94. Trustee Ector County (Tex.) Ind. Sch. Dist., 1967-76 . With inf. U.S. Army, 1943-46. Mem. Tex. Bar Found. (charter), Am. Bar Assn., Am. Bar Found., Am. Coll. Probate Counsel, Am. Acad. Matrimonial Lawyers, State Bar Tex. (chmn. 1971-72, v.p. 1973-74, pres.-elect 1979), Masons. Baptist.

BUNZL, RUDOLPH HANS, retired diversified manufacturing company executive; b. Vienna, Austria, July 20, 1922; came to U.S., 1940, naturalized, 1944; s. Robert Max and Nellie Margaret (Burian) B.; m. Rema R. Templeton, Apr. 6, 1947; children: Ann Mary Bunzl Kamoe, Carol Elizabeth Bunzl Showker; m. Esther R. Mendelsohn, Nov. 14, 1970. BSChemE, Ga. Inst. Tech., 1943; MA in History, U. Richmond, 1994. With Shell Chem. Co., Calif., 1943-54; v.p. Am. Filtrona Corp., Richmond, Va., 1954-59, pres., 1959-83, CEO, 1983-87, chmn. bd., 1987-95. Trustee Richmond Symphony Found., Greater Richmond Cmty. Found., Sheltering Arms Rehab. Hosp., Sci. Mus. Va. Found. With U.S. Army, 1944-46. Mem. AICE. Office: 5540 Falmouth St Ste 305 Richmond VA 23230-1800

BUOCH, WILLIAM THOMAS, corporate executive; b. Atlanta, Mar. 2, 1923; m. Jean Cleste Wright; children: Steven T., David W., William Mark. Student, Ga. State U., 1946-54. Pres. Buoch Enterprises Inc., Atlanta, 1954—. Office: Buoch Enterprises Inc 2871 Main St PO Box 90862 Atlanta GA 30364

BUOY, WILLIAM EDWARD, JR., electronics designer, consultant; b. Houston, Dec. 15, 1946; s. William Edward Sr. and Mary Elizbeth (Meyer) B.; m. Linda Gayle Mueller, 1968 (div. 1978); children: Bernhardt Louis, Tammy Renee; m. Darlene Kay Turner, July 19, 1980; children: Quinn, Shannon. Student, Lee Jr. Coll., Baytown, Tex., 1966-67, San Jacinto Jr. Coll., Pasadena, Tex., 1967-68, U. Houston, 1968-69, Nat. Radio Inst., Washington, 1979. Technician, installer Lamkin Assocs., Houston, 1972-77; design engr., project technician Vetco Pipeline Svcs., Houston, 1977-93; design engr., technician Pulse Radar, Inc., Houston, 1993—. With U.S. Army, 1969-72, Europe. Mem. Am. Legion, Am. Radio Relay League, Nat. Assn. Radio and Telecomms. Engrs., Houston Area League of PC Users.

BURAND, STEPHEN HAROLD, civil engineer; b. Toledo, Nov. 27, 1955; s. Harold and Janet Mae (Grunst) B.; m. Janis Porter, July 17, 1976 (div.); 1 child, Adam; m. Janet Leigh Wood, June 4, 1983; children: Courtney, Crista. BSCE, U. Toledo, 1977. Registered profl. engr. Ga., Fla., Ala., Md., Tenn., S.C. Design engr. Atlantic Steel Corp., Atlanta, 1977-79; lead civil, structural engr. Dravo Engring. Co., Atlanta, 1979-83, sr. civil, structural engr., 1985-87; sr. civil, structural engr. McBurney Corp., Atlanta, 1983-85; mgr. civil and structural dept. Dean Oliver Assoc., Duluth, Ga., 1987-89; mgr., v.p., prin. Promation Inc., Norcross, Ga., 1989-95; regional mgr. Larson Engring. Ga., Atlanta, 1995—. Mem. ASCE, Am. Concrete Inst., Nat. Soc. Profl. Engrs., Ga. Soc. Profl. Engrs., Pulp and Paper Inst., Lions Club, Tau Beta Pi (hon.), Chi Epsilon (hon.). Republican. Lutheran. Home: 1955 Quail Hollow Dr Cumming GA 30131 Office: Precision Engring Co 1955 Quail Hollow Dr Cumming GA 30131

BURBANK, KERSHAW, writer; b. Flushing, N.Y., Jan. 1, 1914; s. Robert Abraham and Lillian Cassels (DuBose) B.; m. Elizabeth E. Hapworth, Mar. 1942 (div.); children: Kershaw Jr., Thorne Burbank Taylor; m. Sally Page Williams Crawford, May 30, 1951 (div.); m. Barbara Bennett, Dec. 16, 1961 (dec. Jan. 1985); 1 child, Bennett. BA, Yale U., 1937. Accredited pub. rels. profl. Unitman MGM Studios, Culver City, Calif., 1937-39; asst. to v.p. 20th Century-Fox Film Corp., N.Y., Calif., 1941-44; dir. nat. promotion Richard Condon Inc., N.Y.C., 1945; sr. ptnr. Burbank Assocs., N.Y.C., 1945-48; dir. pub. info. Colonial Williamsburg (Va.), Inc., 1948-51; advisor pub. affairs Office of the Rockefeller Family, N.Y.C., 1951-61; v.p., sec. Channel 13 Ednl. Broadcasting Corp., N.Y.C., 1961-65; exec. v.p., dir. Infoplan Internat., N.Y.C., 1965-69; mng. dir. Weightman Assocs., Phila., 1969-74; v.p. The Franklin Inst., Phila., 1974-79; cons. Sleepy Hollow Restorations, Tarrytown, N.Y., 1961-64, 69-74, Palisades Interstate Pkwy., N.Y., N.J., 1961-64. Author: A Pleasant Land to See, 1973; contbr. articles to nat. mags. Trustee Elsie Lee Garthwaite Meml. Found., Rosemont, Pa., 1970—, CRC Found., Delray Beach, Fla., 1990-94; bd. dirs. Crossroads Club (non-profit orgn.), Delray Beach, 1988-90, Bethesda Hosp. Assn., Delray Beach, 1983-85; chmn. Coalition of Pa. Museums, 1979-80. Episcopalian. Home: 125 MacFarlane Dr Delray Beach FL 33483-6803

BURBRIDGE, ANN ARNOLD, elementary school educator; b. Galesburg, Ill., Sept. 13, 1947; d. Adis Michael and Janet Louise (Frymire) Arnold; m. Robert Arthur Burbridge, June 27, 1970; children: Britt, Michael, Mark. BMEd, Augustana Coll., 1969; MMEd, Tex. Tech. U., 1987, postgrad.; Kodaly cert. levels 1, 2 and 3, Silver Lake Coll., 1990; advanced Kodaly cert., U. North Tex., 1993; postgrad., Tex. Tech U.; choral music experience level I cert., London; choral music experience level II cert., No. Ill. U., 1995, choral music experience level III cert., 1996. Cert. music tchr. Tchr. Washington Jr. High Sch., Chicago Heights, Ill.; music tchr. Mountain Home AFB (Idaho) Presch. and Kindergarten, Christ the King Cathedral Sch., Lubbock, Tex.; tchr. music Nat Williams Elem. Sch. Lubbock Ind. Sch. Dist.; mem. campus performance objectives com., author curriculum materials for elem. music; dist. mentor; scorer Tex. Master Tchr. Exam.; author, cons. essential knowledge and skills Tex. Edn. Agy. Tchr. Working Group: Web. Resources & Texas Carriculum, Tex. Edn. Network; clinician/presenter in field. Author: Fundamentals of Music, 1987; author, cons. Silver Burdett Ginn Publ. Co. Bd. mem. Llano Estacado Friends of Piano Found. Recipient Disting. Svc. award Lubbock Jaycees, Innovative Teaching Strategy award, LISD. Mem. Am. Choral Dirs. Assn., Am. Orff-Schulwerk Assn., Orgn. Am. Kodaly Educators, Music Educators Nat. Conf. (nat. registered and cert.), Kodaly Educators Tex., Tex. Music Educators Assn. (state chair elem. music 1995—, past region XVI chair), Tex. Classroom Tchrs. Assn. (rep.), Lubbock Elem. Music Tchrs. Assn. (treas.), Choristers Guild, Phi Delta Kappa (past v.p. programs and del. Llano Estacado chpt.).

BURCH, JACK EDWARD, JR., organization executive; b. Jersey City, N.J., July 4, 1945; s. Jack Edward and Patricia Alice (O'Dell) B.; m. Margaret Kerr Holt, Aug. 26, 1967; 1 child, Jack Edward III. BA in Econs., Rhodes Coll., 1967. Cert. community action profl. Country dir. Peace Corps, Washington, 1967-75; pres. Appalachian Leadership and Community Outreach, Hazard, Ky., 1975-79; exec. dir. Community Action Coun., Lexington, Ky., 1979—; bd. dirs. Community Ventures Corp., Lexington; pres. WinterCare Energy Fund, Lexington, 1983—; CEO, Community Action Coun. Housing Corp., Lexington, 1990—; cons. in field. Author: Controlling Unemployment Costs: A Handbook for Head Start Grantees, 1988, Fuel Funds: A Community Response to Low-Income Energy Problems, 1990, Comparative Analysis of the Community Reinvestment Activities of Lexington's Financial Institutions, 1991. Bd. dirs. Mountain Assn. for Cmty. Econ. Devel., Berea, Ky., 1977-88, Hope Ctr., 1990—, ARC of Blue Grass, Lexington, 1989-95; bd. dirs. Nat. Fuel Funds Network, Pitts., 1986-91, sec., 1990-91; bd. dirs. Federated Transp. Svcs. Bluegrass, Lexington, 1981-95, sec., 1991-95; mem. Cmty. Reinvestment Alliance Lexington, 1988-94; mem. Commn. on Race Rels., Lexington, 1991—, co-chmn., 1993-96; mem. planning coun. Mayor's Career Resource and Tng. Ctr., 1985—, also others, Equity coun. Fayette County Pub. Schs., 1994—. Named Hon. Order of Ky. Cols., Gov., 1983; recipient outstanding Contrbn. award SE Assn. Community Action Agys., 1989, Performance award U.S. Dept. Housing and Urban Devel., 1992. Mem. Ky. Head Start Assn. (chairperson grantees unemployment ins. reimbursement trust 1984—), Ky. Assn. Cmty. Action (bd. dirs. 1979—, pres. 1982-83). Democrat.

BURCH, JOHN CHRISTOPHER, JR., investment banker; b. Nashville, Jan. 18, 1940; s. John Christopher and Frances Vivian (Harris) B.; m. Susan Marie Klein, Sept. 13, 1969; children: Frances Marie, Christina Polk, John Christopher III. BA, Vanderbilt U., 1966. Credit analyst Bank N.Y., N.Y.C., 1966-70; v.p. instl. sales Loeb Rhoades & Co., N.Y.C., 1970-75, J.C. Bradford & Co., Nashville, 1976-82; mng. dir. Equitable Securities Corp., Nashville, 1982—. Active Com. Fgn. Relations, Nashville, 1976, N.C. Soc. Cin., Raleigh, 1979. With U.S. Army, 1962-65. Mem. Nashville Security Dealers Assn., Assn. Investment Mgmt. and Rsch., Belle Meade Country Club, Cumberland Club (Nashville). Episcopalian. Home: 705 Hillwood Blvd Nashville TN 37205-1315 Office: Equitable Securities Corp Nashville City Ctr 511 Union St Ste 800 Nashville TN 37219-1729

BURCH, JOHN RUSSELL, technical services librarian; b. Peoria, Ill., Mar. 22, 1968; s. John Russell and Idalia Amparo (Murgas) B.; m. Samantha Jo Bailey, July 1, 1989; children: Morgan Lourrae, Alexandra Christine, Christopher Simpson. BA in History, Berea (Ky.) Coll., 1990; MS in Libr. Sci., U. Ky., 1992. Grad. asst. U. Ky. Agrl. Libr., Lexington, 1991-92; govt. documents libr. So. Ark. U., Magnolia, 1992-93; reference libr. Cumberland Coll., Williamsburg, Ky., 1993-95, pub. svcs. libr., 1995, tech. svcs. libr., 1995—. Mem. ALA, Assn. Coll. and Rsch. Librs., Ky. Libr. Assn., ASCUE, Phi Alpha Theta. Republican. Home: 173 Hutton Dr Williamsburg KY 40769 Office: Cumberland Coll Hagan Libr 821 Walnut St Williamsburg KY 40769-1338

BURCH, LUCIUS EDWARD, JR., lawyer; b. Nashville, Jan. 25, 1912; s. Lucius Edward and Sarah (Cooper) B.; m. Elsie Caldwell, Dec. 27, 1935;

children: Sarah Polk (Mrs. John F. Gratz, Jr.), Elsie Caldwell Burch Donald, Edith Montague (Mrs. Burch Caywood), Lucia Newell Doggrell (dec.). B.A., Vanderbilt U., 1934, LL.B., 1936; DHL (hon.), Rhodes Coll., 1986. Bar: Tenn. 1936. Since practiced in Memphis; sr. ptnr. Burch, Porter & Johnson, 1947—; dir. Nat. Commerce Bancorp., Nat. Bank of Commerce. Author articles. Bd. dirs. Nat. Park Found., 1980-86, Memphis Civic Research Com., 1947-67; mem. Plough Park Devel. Bd.; chmn. Leadership Memphis; founder, charter mem. Memphis Com. Community Relations, 1958-59, pres., 1959; chmn. Tenn. Game and Fish Commn., 1949-55; pres. Tenn. Conservation League, 1955-56; mem. Nat. Council Atlantic Union, 1949—; adv. com. Internat. Movement Atlantic Union, 1961—; mem. devel. council Vanderbilt U. Law Sch., 1968—; Del. Democratic Nat. Conv., 1952; mem. Tenn. Dem. Exec. Com., 1962, 74-81, Tenn. Racing Commn., 1988-91; trustee Edward J. Meeman Found.; bd. govs. Assn. Advancement Aging Research, 1968—. Recipient Cartter-Patten award Tenn. Conservation League, 1956; cert. of merit Memphis Urban League, 1952; Humanitarian award NCCJ, 1985; Disting. Alumni award Vanderbilt Law Sch., 1988. Fellow Am. Coll. Trial Lawyers, Am. Bar Found.; mem. ABA, Tenn. Bar Assn. (gov. 1958), Memphis and Shelby County Bar Assn. (dir. 1962-63, Lawyer's Lawyer award 1993), Tenn. Acad. Sci. (hon. life), Tenn. Hist. Soc., West Tenn. Hist. Soc. Clubs: Memphis Country, Wolf River Soc. (Memphis) (founder, 1st pres.). Home: Whiteacre Farm 1000 W Poplar Ave Collierville TN 38017-2505 Office: 130 Court Ave Memphis TN 38103-2217

BURCH, SHARRON LEE STEWART, woman's health nurse; b. Washington, Dec. 19, 1944; d. David A. Jr. and Ruthanna (Craig) Stewart; m. Donald Victor Burch, Aug. 27, 1966; children: Elizabeth Katherine, Craig Donald. BSN, Vanderbilt U., 1966; M in Nursing, U. Miss. Med. Ctr., Jackson, 1975. RN, Miss. Staff nurse Druid City Hosp., Tuscaloosa, Ala., 1966-69; instr. insvc. edn. U. Hosp., Jackson, Miss., 1969-71; specialized nurse cons. Miss. Bd. Health, Jackson, 1972-74; instr. ADN Miss. Gulf Coast Jr. Coll., Biloxi, Miss., 1975-81, Hinds Community Coll., Jackson, 1982-91; staff nurse Rankin Med. Ctr., 1987—. Contbr. articles to profl. jours. Mem. ANA, Orgn. for Advvancement ADN (chmn. ad hoc competency validation com. 1983-91, 1st vice chmn. tech. com. on state of art curricula for vocat. and tech. programs for health and personal svcs. 1991—), Miss. Nurses Assn., Sigma Theta Tau. Home: 784 Benwick Dr Brandon MS 39042-8112

BURCHAM, RANDALL PARKS, lawyer, farmer; b. Union City, Tenn., July 20, 1917; s. John Simps and Myrtle Caldwell (Howard) B.; m. Hellon Owens, Sept. 30, 1945; children—Randall Parks Jr., Susan. Student Murray State Coll. (Ky.), 1934-38, U. Miss., 1938-39; LL.B., Cumberland U., Lebanon, Tenn., 1940; J.D., Samford U., Birmingham, 1969. Bar: Tenn. 1941. Sole practice, Union City, 1941; atty. U.S. Govt., Nashville, 1945-49; owner Interstate Oil Co., Fulton, Ky., 1949-53; ptnr. Burcham & Fox, Union City, 1953—. Del., Tenn. Constitutional Conv., Nashville, 1971. Served to comdr. U.S. Navy, 1941-45. Fellow Am. Coll. Probate Counsel; mem. ABA, Tenn. Bar Assn. (bd. govs. 1969-72). Democrat. Methodist.

BURCHFIELD, DONALD FRANCIS, safety engineer, recreation administrator, consultant; b. Rockwood, Tenn., Dec. 7, 1932; s. George Farris and Nannie Bell (Rasnick) B.; m. Mary Katherine Adams, Dec. 19, 1964; children: Timothy Freeman, Margaret. BS, Tenn. Technol. U., 1956; MA, Murray (Ky.) State U., 1969; Dir. Recreation, Ind. U., 1972; PhD, Columbia Pacific U., 1988. Cert. camp dir., recreation adminstr., profl. safety engr., secondary sch. tchr., Ind., Ala., Tenn. Tchr., coach Knox County Schs., Knoxville, Tenn., 1959-64; various positions TVA, Golden Pond, Ky., 1964-80; safety engr. TVA, Muscle Shoals, Ala., 1980-87; water recreation safety coord. TVA, Knoxville, 1987-90; adj. prof. in recreation U. N. Ala., Florence, 1990-94; safety engr. Northwest Envirocon-Reynolds Metal Co., Muscle Shoals, Ala., 1994—; bd. dirs. Nat. Ctr. for Aquatic Safety Edn., Athens, Tenn.; chmn. ednl. activities Nat. Water Safety Congress, Washington, 1966—, bd. dirs.; cons. Leisure Craft Counseling and Camping, Urbana, Ill., 1970—; mem. task force Tenn. Safety Coun., 1986—. Producer, dir. multimedia program Essentials of Nature Trails, 1970; editor: Handbook for Water Recreation Safety Instruction, 1981; author: (with others) profl. manuals. Flotilla comdr USCG Aux., Florence, Ala., 1972—. Master sgt. U.S. Army, 1956-58. Recipient Butler Community Service award 100th div. U.S. Army, 1972, regional water safety achievement award Nat. Water Safety Congress, 1982. Mem. Am. Soc. Safety Engrs., Am. Camping Assn. (coord. environ. edn., 1978-82), Am. Assn. Health Phys. Edn. and Recreation (chmn. water safety, 1968-76), Nat. Recreation and Parks Assn. (chmn. ch. sec. 1976-80, outdoor safety, 1982-84), Nat. Wildlife Fedn. (Conservation Educator of Yr.), Nature Conservancy, Kiwanis (v.p. Murray chpt. 1964-68), Order of Arrow (advisor 1972-76), Shriners. Republican. Episcopalian. Home: 103 Meadow Hill Rd Sheffield AL 35660-6816 Office: Northwest Environcon Inc 503 W State St Ste 4 Muscle Shoals AL 35661-2839

BURD, JOHN STEPHEN, academic administrator, music educator; b. Lock Haven, Pa., Apr. 6, 1939; s. John Wilson and Lily (Fye) B.; m. Patricia Ayers, June 3, 1961; children: Catherine Elizabeth, Emily Susanne. B in Music Edn., Greenville Coll., 1961; MS in Music, Butler U./Christian Theo. Sem., 1964; PhD, Ind. State U., 1971. Adj. music instr. Rose Hulman Inst. Tech., Terre Haute, Ind., 1969-71; assoc. prof. Greenville (Ill.) Coll., 1971-76; prof. edn. Lindenwood Coll., St. Charles, Mo., 1976-80; v.p. acad. affairs Maryville U., St. Louis, Mo., 1980-85; pres. Brenau U., Gainesville, Ga., 1985—; team evaluator Nat. Coun. Accreditation Tchr. Edn., 1979-84; mem. exec. coun. Women's Coll. Coalition, 1989-92, NAICU Commn. on State Rels. Bd., 1991-93, 94—; adv. bd. Wachovia Bank, Gainesville. Editor: New Voices in Education, 1969-71; contbr. articles to profl. jours. Choir dir. Ctr. Presbyn. Ch., St. Louis, 1984-85, Maryville U., St. Louis, 1983-85; v.p. Christian Arts, Inc., N.J., 1965—; mem. adv. bd. N.E. Ga. Med. Ctr.; bd. dirs. Gainesville Symphony, Crawford W. Long Mus. Recipient Outstanding Young Alumnus award Greenville Coll., 1982, Disting. Alumnus award, 1991. Mem. Am. Assn. Tchr. Edn., Am. Assn. Higher Edn., So. Assn. Women's Colls. (pres. 1988-89), Ga. Found. Ind. Colls. (exec. bd. 1986—, vice chmn. 1993), Ga. Assn. Colls. (pres. 1989-90), Gainesville C. of C. (bd. dirs. 1985—). Methodist. Office: Brenau U 1 Centennial Cir Gainesville GA 30501-3668

BURD, SHIRLEY FARLEY, clinical specialist, mental health nurse; b. Pluckemin, N.J.; d. Raymond and Katherine Kiser (Horton) Farley; m. Robert L. Burd, Nov. 30, 1957. Diploma, Somerset Hosp. Sch. Nursing, Somerville, N.J.; BS, Rutgers U. Coll. Nursing, 1956, MS, 1958; EdD, Rutgers U. Grad. Sch. Edn., 1966. Asst. prof. Rutgers U. Coll. Nursing, Newark, 1957-63; prof., chair dept., dir. dept. grad. program Vanderbilt U., Nashville, 1967-72; prof., dept. chair U. Tenn. Coll. Nursing, Memphis, 1972-90; pvt. practice, psychiat. mental health nurse cons. self-employed, Germantown, Tenn.; prof. emeritus; mem. Tenn. Bd. Examiners, Nursing Home Adminstrs., 1990-96; cons. Health Care Financing Adminstrn., 1991-95. Vol., vice chair appropriations com. United Way Greater Memphis, 1980—; commr. Sr. Citizen Adv. Commn. City Germantown, Tenn. Named Disting. lectr. Sigma Theta Tau; first recipient Pres.'s award Am. Nurses' Credentialing Ctr. Fellow Am. Acad. Nursing.

BURDETTE, CAROL JANICE, gerontology nursing administrator; b. Glens Falls, N.Y., Sept. 22, 1936; d. Edward J. Johnson and Daisy M. (Minor) Griffin; m. Edward L. Burdette, Mar. 6, 1981; children: Keith Noseworthy, Scott Noseworthy, Debra Colombo. Student, Bklyn. Meth. Hosp., 1954-57; BS, Coll. of St. Francis, 1990, MS, 1995. Cert. in gerontology; cert. CDON/LTC dir. nursing/long term care. Utilization review coord. Norwich (Conn.) Hosp., 1973-81, med. review nurse I, 1980-81; allergy nurse Drs. Clinic, Vero Beach, Fla., 1981-83; dir. nursing Fla. Bapt. Retirement Ctr., Vero Beach, 1984—. Contbr. articles to profl. jours. Mem. Nat. Assn. Dirs. of Nursing Adminstrn. (cert.), Fla. Assn. Dirs. of Nursing Adminstrn. (pres.), Nat. Gerontol. Nurses Assn., Am. Soc. Long Term Care Dirs. Nursing, Nat. Assn. Gerontological Nursing. Home: 7000 20th St Lot 911 Vero Beach FL 32966-8878 Office: Fla Bapt Retirement Ctr P O Box 460 1006 33rd St Vero Beach FL 32960-6910

BURDETTE, JANE ELIZABETH, nonprofit association executive, consultant; b. Huntington, W.Va., Aug. 17, 1955; d. C. Richard and Jewel Kathryn (Wagner) B. AAS, Parkersburg Community Coll., W.Va., 1976; BA, Glenville State Coll., W.Va., 1978; MA, W.Va. U., 1984. Fund raiser, recruiter Muscular Dystrophy Assn., Charleston, W.Va., 1973, 74, 75; sec., bookkeeper Nationwide Ins. Co., Parkersburg, 1975; v.p. Burdette Funeral Home, Parkersburg, 1976-85; intake and referral specialist Wood County Sheltered Workshop, Parkersburg, 1984-85; exec. dir. YWCA, Parkersburg, 1985-91; cons. in field, 1991—. Bd. dirs. Sheltered Workshop, Parkersburg, 1982-86, Western Dist. Guidance Ctr., Parkersburg, 1984-94; vol. St. Joseph's Hosp., 1991—; mem. W.Va. Coun. Ind. Living, 1992-94; mem. W.Va Muscular Distrophy Assn. task force on disability issues, 1992—; bd. advisors, vice chmn. Parkersburg Community Coll., 1980-89, Domestic Violence Interdisciplinary adv. com., 1987, Just Say No, 1987-91; chmn. Wood County Commn. on Crime, Delinquency and Corrections, Parkersburg, 1985—; chmn. Mid Ohio Valley United Fund Agy., 1986 Heads; v.p. Jr. League of Parkersburg, 1989—; mem. Sanctuary Soc., 1991—, All Saints Guild, 1991-95, St. Margaret Mary Parish Coun., 1992—; bd. dirs., v.p. Cmty. Svc. Coun., 1985-96; bd. dirs. Parkersburg Transit Authority, 1994—; liaison Gov. Commn. on Disabled Persons, Charleston, W.Va., 1981-85; mem. Career Adv. Network, 1987-91; treas. W.Va. Women's Conf., 1987; exec. com. W.Va. chpt. Muscular Dystrophy Assn., 1987—; mem. We've Been There Parent Support Group, 1987-90; v.p. A Spl. Wish Found., 1988—; mem. Parkersburg Consumer Adv. Group; mem. founding com. Banquet of Wealth, 1988-91; bd. dirs. Horizon's Ind. Living Ctr., v.p., 1990—; past transition plan team leader Wood County Bd. Edn.; past liason Internat. Yr. Disabled Persons; past treas. and program chmn. Gov.'s Conf.; former pres. Y Teen Club, YWCA; former adv. com. Mountwood Pk. White Oak Village, Organ Donor Com., 1989. Named Miss Wheelchair W.Va., 1981, Outstanding Young Woman of Yr. for W.Va., 1981, Outstanding Young Woman of the Yr, 1986; recipient Kenneth Hieges award Muscular Dystrophy Assn., 1982, Outstanding Citizen award Frat. Order of Police, 1984, Community Service award Moose Lodge, 1995, Cert. Appreciation State W.Va., Gov. Jay Rockefeller, Cert. Appreciation Am. Legion Aux., Trail of New Beginning award, Banquet of Wealth Trial Blazer award YWCA/Altrusa, 1989, Personal Achievement award for W.Va., MDA, 1993, 94, Mary Harriman Community Leadership award Jr. League Internat., 1994, Jennings Randolph award W.Va. Rehab. Assn., 1996; named W.Va.'s Disabled Profl. Woman of Yr. Pilot Internats., 1989, Hometown Hero Sta. WSAZ-TV, 1993, One Who Makes a Difference, Sta. WTAP, 1994, Profl. and Bus. Woman's Internat. Hall of Fame, 1995;. Mem. NAFE, Toastmasters (Comm. and Leadership award 1989). Democrat. Roman Catholic. Avocation: designing. Home: 2500 Brooklyn Dr Parkersburg WV 26101-2913

BURDETTE, WILLIAM JAMES, bank executive, lawyer; b. Salt Lake City, Feb. 8, 1962; s. Walter James and Kathryn Mary (Lynch) B. BBA, U. Tex., 1984; MBA, Tex. A&M U., 1987; JD, South Tex. Coll. Law, 1995. Bar: Tex. 1995. Campus news editor Daily Texan, Austin, 1982; credit analyst First City, Tex.-Houston, N.A., 1987-88, banking rep., 1988-89, banking officer, 1989-90, asst. v.p., 1990-92; with Btler & Binion, LLP, Houston, 1996. Note and comment editor South Tex. Law Rev., 1994-95; asst. editor Corp. Counsel Rev., 1994; contbr. articles to profl. jours. U. Tex. scholar. Mem. Order of Lytae, Phi Delta Phi.

BURDINE, JOHN A., hospital administrator, nuclear medicine educator; b. Austin, Tex., Feb. 7, 1936; married; 3 children. BA, U. Tex., 1959; MD, U. Tex., Galveston, 1961. Diplomate Am. Be. Nuclear Medicine (orgnl. exam. com. 1971, bd. dirs. 1978—, chmn. certifyng exam. com. 1980-81, 81-82, editorial bd. Jour. Nuclear Medicine, 1973-81). Intern Med. Ctr. Ind. U., 1961-62; resident nuclear medicine, internal medicine U. Tex., Galveston, 1962-65; active med. staff St. Luke's Episcopal Hosp.-Tex. Children's Hosp., Houston, 1969-90; chief nuclear medicine svc. St. Luke's Episcopal Hosp.-Tex. Children's Hosp., Tex. Heart Inst., Houston, 1969-85; chief exec. officer, head adminstr. St. Luke's Episcopal Hosp., Houston, 1984-87, pres., chief exec. officer, 1986-91, vice chmn., chief exec. officer, 1991-95; also bd. dirs. St. Luke's Episcopal Hosp., 1991-94; cons. St. Luke's Hosp., 1991—; courtesy staff Tex. Children's Hosp., 1992—; asst. prof. dept. radiology Baylor Coll. Medicine, 1965-68, acting chmn. dept. radiology, 1968-71, chief nuclear medicine dept., 1965-95, assoc. prof. dept. radiology, 1968-74, prof. dept. radiology, 1974—, acting dir. sect. nuclear medicine dept. medicine, 1979-80, prof. dept. medicine, 1979—, mem. exec. faculty com., 1968-71, mem. com. human experimentation, 1969-71, chmn. radiosotope com., 1970-74, mem., 1966-82, other coms.; sec. Tex. Radiation Adv. Bd., 1981-86, exec. com., 1982-86, med. com., 1982-86, radioactive waste com., 1982-86, fee rules com., 1982-83; chmn. radioisotope com. Meth. Hosp., 1979-80, active med. staff, 1979-84, courtesy med. staff, 1984—, acting med. dir. radioisotope lab., 1979-80; chief nuclear medicine sect. Harris County Hosp. Dist., 1965-83; mem. forward planning com. Tex. Med. Ctr., 1986—; trustee Tex. Heart Inst., 1985—. Editorial bd. Cardiovascular Disease, 1974; contbr. book chpts., abstracts, papers. Bd. dirs. Houston Symphony Orch., 1987-88. Fellow Am. Coll. Nuclear Physicians (orgn. com. 1973-74, chmn. radioassay & radiopharmacy com. 1975-76, DOE speaker's bur. 1981-85), mem. AMA (rep. coun. nuclear medicine 1976-77), AAUP, Harris County Med. Assn., Tex. Med. Assn. (vice chmn. com. nuclear medicine 1968-71, chmn. 1971-78, others), Tex. Assn. Physicians in Nuclear Medicine, Soc. Nuclear Medicine (pres. 1982-83, southwestern chpt. trustee 1972-80, mem. numerous coms.), Phi Beta Kappa, Phi Eta Sigma, Alpha Epsilon Delta. Home: 347 Hunters Trail Houston TX 77024 Office: St Luke's Episcopal Hosp PO Box 20269 Houston TX 77225-0269

BURFORD, ALEXANDER MITCHELL, JR., physician; b. Memphis, Mar. 21, 1929; s. Alexander Mitchell and Mary Young (Tittle) B.; BS, Florence (Ala.) State Coll. (now U. North Ala.), 1951; MD, U. Tenn., Memphis, 1957. Intern, U. Tenn., Knoxville, 1957-58, resident in pathology, Memphis, 1958-62; assoc. pathologist Eliza Coffee Meml. Hosp., Florence, Ala., 1962-73, dir. lab., chief pathology, 1973-95, mem. med. staff, 1962—; practice medicine specializing in pathology, 1958—, Florence Pathology Svcs., 1983—. Active Florence Tree Commn., 1987-92, Am. Chestnut Found., 1985—, Mars Hill Bible Sch. Endowment Assn., 1985—, Nat. Arbor Day Found.; mem. pres. cabinet U. North Ala., 1992—; mem. alumni coun. Coll. Medicine U. Tenn. Mem. AMA, Ala. Urban Forestry Assn., Ala. Forest Owner's Assn., Tree City USA, Med. Assn. Ala., Ala. Assn. Pathologists (pres. 1974-75), Coll. Am. Pathologists (del. 1972-90), Am. Soc. Clin. Pathologists, Am. Assn. Blood Banks, Am. Forestry Assn., Am. Rifleman Assn., Nat. Wildlife Fedn., Lauderdale County Med. Assn., Shoals Symphony Assn. (bd. dirs. 1993—), Florence C. of C., Friends of Florence-Lauderdale Pub. Libr. (pres. 1993-95), Audubon Soc., Lions Club (past pres. local chpt. 1962-70, dep. dist. gov.), Alpha Kappa Kappa, Kappa Mu Epsilon, Alpha Psi Omega. Home: 652 Howell St Florence AL 35630-3537 Office: Eliza Coffee Meml Hosp PO Box 818 Florence AL 35631-0818

BURGER, ANDRÉ ERIC, computing system project manager; b. Cheltenham, Eng., Sept. 18, 1937; s. Eric Felix and Marie Louise (Ramseyer) B.; m. Ruth Homer, Apr. 21, 1965; children: Clive André, Jason Paul, Christopher Robert. BS with Gen. Honors, U. Leeds, Yorkshire, Eng., 1961. Chartered engr. Staff programmer, field systems engr. IBM U.K., London, 1961-68, devel. mgr., 1969-73; adv. programmer IBM U.K., Endicott, N.Y., 1973-79; devel. mgr. IBM, Charlotte, N.C., 1979-82, sr. devel. mgr., 1983-92, sr. programmer, 1993; v.p. model banking program NationsBank, Charlotte, 1994-95; gen. bank systems support Nationsbank, Charlotte, 1996—. Sec., dir. Ramblewood Soccer, Inc., Charlotte, 1993—. Recipient IBM Divisional award, 1981, 84, NB Go the Extra Mile award, 1995. Mem. Brit. Computer Soc., The Engring. Coun. Office: NationsBank NC1-004-04-06 Charlotte NC 28255

BURGER, CHARLES DWAYNE, physician; b. Paducah, Ky., June 6, 1959; s. Guy and Marie (Spencer) B. Student, Carson-Newman Coll., 1977-78; BA in Chemistry, U. Tenn., 1981, postgrad., 1981-82; MD, Bowman Gray Sch. Medicine, 1985. Diplomate internal medicine, pulmonary disease, critical care, sleep medicine; lic. physician, Fla. Resident internal medicine Vanderbilt U. Hosps., Nashville, 1985-88; fellow pulonary and critical care Mayo Grad. Sch., Rochester, Minn., 1988-91; med. dir. Flagler Career Inst. Respiratory Therapy, Jacksonville, Fla., 1991—; cons. thoracic disease, critical care and sleep Mayo Clinic, Jacksonville, Fla., 1991—, chmn. dept. crit. care, 1995—; med. dirs. respiratory therapy St. Lukes' Hosp., chief pulmonary medicine; asst. prof. Mayo Med. Sch., 1990—. Contbr. articles to profl. jours., chpts. to books. Pulmonary fellow; recipient Young Investigator award Am. Sleep Disorders Assn., 1990. Mem. AMA, Am. Coll. Chest Physicians, Am. Thoracic Soc., Sigma Xi, Alpha Omega Alpha. Republican. Baptist. Home: 116 Meadowcrest Ln Ponte Vedra Beach FL 32082 Office: Mayo Clinic Jacksonville Divsn Thoracic Disease 4500 San Pablo Rd S Jacksonville FL 32224-1865

BURGESS, C(HARLES) CONEY, bank executive; b. Brookhaven, Miss., Oct. 2, 1937; s. Coney and Johnnie Margaret (Campbell) B.; m. Cornelia Jane Slemp, Apr. 26, 1964; children: Charles Coney, Cornelius Campbell, Carson Herring, Charlotte Amelia. BS in Geology, Miss. State U., 1960; postgrad., U. Miss., 1964. Geologist Texaco, 1964; ranching, real estate, 1982; pres., bd. dirs., mem. exec. com. Monrch Trust Co., 1982; chmn. bd. Herring Bancorp, Vernon, Tex.; officer, bd. dirs. Zircon, Inc., Amarillo; pres., bd. dirs. Burgess-Herring Ranch Co.; pres. Chain-C & Cattle, Flagg Land & Cattle Co., Castro County, Tex., Rebel Ranches, Brookhaven, Miss.; bd. dirs. Ultra Plating Corp., Green Bay, Wis. Bd. adv. Tex. Tech. U., Lubbock, Tex.; chmn. bd., com. Cal Farley's Boys Ranch and Girlstown, 1986, bd. trustees, Marine Military Acad., Tex., 1992; pres., bd. trustees, Symphony Bd. Amarillo, 1993-94; bd. trustees, Panhandle Plains Historical Soc., bd. trustees, investment com. Panhandle Plains Mus., Canyon, Tex. Mem. Tex. & Southwestern Cattle Raisers (dir., v.p.), Am. Quarter Horse Assn. (chmn. mktg. & pub. info. com., 1992-94), Panhandle Livestock Assn. (past pres., exec. com. dirú, Ranching Heritage Assn. (bd. overseers), Ranching Heritage Assn. (bd. endowment, trustee), Nat. Cattlemens Assn. (dir., com. mem.), Rotary Club (pres., dir. 1992-93), Amarillo C. of C. (com. mem.), Southwestern Pub. Svc.(dir.), Amarillo, Tex. Presbyterian. Home: 3001 S Lipscomb St Amarillo TX 79109-3533 Office: 1608 S Polk St Amarillo TX 79102-3149

BURGESS, DIANE GLENN, real estate broker, paralegal; b. Mar. 5, 1935; d. Howard Glenn and Emma Kathie (Higham) King; m. Raymond H. Symanski, Apr. 23, 1955 (div. 1968); children: Raymond H. Jr., Jeffrey H.; m. L. Michael Burgess, July 19, 1985. Student, Strayer's Coll., Washington. Subrogation supr., paralegal Carr, Jordan, Coyne & Savits, Washington, 1972-82; property mgr. Lewis & Silverman, Fairfax, Va., 1982-87; owner, v.p. Burgess Custom Builders, Inc., Vienna, Va., 1985—; owner, real estate broker, pres. ERA-House of Burgesses, Inc., Vienna, 1988—; tng. and recruiting dir. ERA-House of Burgesses. Chmn. ERA-MDA Ann. Golf Tournament, 1989-90; campaign mgr. Warren Barry for County Court Clerk, Fairfax; vol. Linwood Holton for U.S. Senate, Fairfax, John Warner for U.S. Senate, Fairfax, ARC, 1968-89. Recipient Recognition award Over 500 ARC, 1968-69, 5 gold medals Masters East Coast Championship, 1979. Mem. GMW Broker Coun. (ERA Broker Coun. 1989—), North Va. Assn. Realtors (pub. rels. com.), Colonial Rep. Women's Club (pres. 1994-95).

BURGESS, HARVEY WAITES, journalist; b. Charlotte, N.C., June 11, 1948; s. Fay Robert and Pauline (Stewart) B.; m. Anne Marie Hege, Sept. 20, 1969 (div. 1977); children: Tracey, Robert, Chris; m. Julie Ann Britt, Oct. 1, 1983. Student, N.C. State U., 1966-70. Sports editor News-Messenger, Hamlet, N.C., 1970-73; editor Lumberton (N.C.) Post, 1973-76; news dir. Sta. WTSB, Lumberton, 1976-79; writer Robesonian Newspaper, Lumberton, 1979-82; editor Bladen Jour., Elizabethtown, N.C., 1982-83; writer Ind.-Mail, Anderson, S.C., 1983-85; columnist Charlotte Leader, 1985-89; pres. Charlotte Bur., 1990—. Co-author: Video Movie Guide, 1989; (novel) Perfect Poison, 1992. Pres. Carmel Civitan Club, Charlotte, 1987; dir. Read Up Charlotte, 1990—. Recipient Editorial Excellence award N.C. Press Assn., 1976, McKissick award S.C. Press Assn., 1985, Column Writing award Nat. Assn. Non-Daily Papers, 1987. Mem. Fraternal Order Police. Republican. Methodist. Home: 7306 Colby Ct Charlotte NC 28226-4426 Office: Charlotte Bur 600 E 4th St Ste 241 Charlotte NC 28202-2870

BURGESS, LESTER PHILLIPS, quality assurance manager; b. Oklahoma City, Oct. 10, 1946; s. Lester Phillips Jr. and Neva Algean (Rogers) B.; m. Linda J. Lindsay, Dec. 28, 1968; children: Phillips Royce, Kristina Danielle, Theresa Michelle. Student, U. R.I., 1966-67, Metals Engring. Inst., 1968, U. Akron, U. So. Calif., 1988-89; AA, North Harris County Coll., 1988; BS in Econs., U. Houston, 1991, MBA, 1994. Metallurgical technician Leesona Corp., Warwick, R.I., 1969-71, mfg. metallurgist, 1971-74; mgr. quality control McEvoy Oilfield Equipment Co., Houston, 1974-77; chief inspector bolt divsn. Standco Industries Inc., Houston, 1977-80, corp. quality assurance mgr., 1980-90, corp. quality assurance mgr., safety dir., 1990—; quality assurance/quality control mgr. U.S. Bolt Mfrs., Inc., Houston, 1994—. Mem. ASTM (Cert. of Appreciation), ASME (mem. gasket com., Cert. Acclamation), ASM Internat., Am. Soc. for Quality Control, Energy Rubber Group divsn. Am. Chem. Soc., Nat. Assn. Corrosion Engrs., Tex. Assn. Bus. Environ. Com.

BURGESS, MARGARET LOUISE, elementary education educator; b. Monterey, Tenn., Dec. 9, 1952; d. Luther Benjamin and Margaret Wilma (Taylor) Atkinson; m. James Richard Burgess, June 4, 1973; children: William Benjamin, Cortis Blaine. BS in elementary edn., Tenn. Tech., 1970-73. Tchr. first grade Fentress County Bd. Edn., Jamestown, Tenn., 1973-74; tchr. kindergarten Cumberland County Bd. Edn., Crossville, Tenn., 1974-80; tchr. Dept. Defense, Germany, 1980-84; tchr. fourth, fifth, sixth grade Cath. Dioceses, El Paso, Tex., 1985-87; tchr. first grade Am. Cmty. Sch., Abu Dabi, UAE, 1987-90; tchr. Sylvan Learning Ctr., Huntsville, Ala., 1991; tchr. second grade Huntsville City, 1991—. Leader Cub Scout Boy Scouts Am., Abu Dhabi, 1987-89; chmn. Cub Scout Boy Scouts Am., Abu Dhabi, 1989-90; PTA tchr. rep. PTA Bd., Huntsville, 1994—. Recipient Tchr. of Yr. award Tchrs. and Staff Univ. Place, Huntsville, 1995-96. Mem. Nat. Edn. Assn., Ala. Edn. Assn. Home: 261 Dan West Rd Union Grove AL 35175

BURGESS, MARVIN FRANKLIN, human resources specialist, consultant; b. Heathsville, Va., Mar. 18, 1932; s. Marvin Judson and Emma Elizabeth (Bradberry) B.; m. Beatrice Ione Hildahl, Feb. 7, 1932; children: Michael Marvin, Linda Ione. BA in Math. and Physics, U. Richmond, 1953; postgrad., Va. Tech., 1953-54; MA in Sociology and Psychology, Duke U., 1962. Commd. USCGR, 1956, advanced through grades to capt., dist. insp., port security, adminstr., ret., 1992; NASA engr. Langley Rsch. Ctr., Hampton, Va., 1954-84; cons. outplacement Career Dynamics II, Virginia Beach, Va., 1984—; adj. prof. sociology Christopher Newport Coll., Newport News, 1970-72; mgmt. and planning cons. U.S. Dept. Transp., Washington, 1972-80; funding, mgmt., productivity cons. NASA, 1965-84; spkr. in field. Author: Rebuilding Downtrodden Job Market and Madhouse Society, 1996. Post comdr. Am. Legion, Yorktown, Va., 1977-81; chmn., pres. PTA Yorkshire Acad., York County, Va., 1968-69; mgr. Little League and Am. Legion Baseball, York County, 1970-80; player Chesapeake League semi-pro baseball, Northern Neck, Va., 1951-56; mem. govt. com. Kiwanis, Yorktown, 1968-70. Methodist. Home: 130 Mill Ln Yorktown VA 23692 Office: Career Dynamics II 1 Columbus Ctr Ste 673 Virginia Beach VA 23462

BURGESS, ROBERT LESTER, JR., telephone company executive; b. Lafayette, La., July 28, 1949; s. Robert L. and Dorothy (Hollier) B.; m. Juliet Ann Trimble, Mar. 9, 1974; children: Andrea, Briana, Elysia, Maisie. BS in Math., U. Southwestern La., 1970; MBA, Nova U., 1983. Various positions South Cen. Bell, Lafayette, La., 1972-78, New Orleans, 1978-81; industry mgr. AT&T, New Orleans, 1981-83, region mgr., 1983-85; region mgr. AT&T, Atlanta, 1985-86, Century Cellunet, Inc., Shreveport, La., 1986-89; v.p. ops. Century Cellunet, Inc., Monroe, La., 1989-92; v.p. network svcs. Century Cellunet, Inc., Monroe, 1992-93, v.p. corp. svcs., 1993—; mem. coun. leaders AT&T, Morristown, N.J., 1979, 85, 86. Bd. dirs. Little Theatre of Monroe, La.; mem. Gov.'s Task for on Telecom. Lt. USNR, 1971-76. Mem. Execs. Assn., Rotary. Home: PO Box 4065 Monroe LA 71211-4065

BURGESS, ROBERT RONALD, human resources executive; b. Memphis, Dec. 2, 1943; s. Doyle Eugene Burgess and Mildred Burgess (Sparks) Hamill; m. Suzie Strong, June 28, 1985; 1 child, Mary Weldon. BS in Psychology, Memphis State U., 1967, MEd, 1975, EdD (ABD), 1979. Dir. Teen Challenge, Vienna, Austria, 1971-73; religious affairs coord. Memphis State U., 1973-80; dir. human resources The Peabody, Memphis, 1980-81, GE/RCA, Memphis, N.Y.C., 1981-86; exec. dir. The Promus Companies, Memphis, 1986—; chmn. coord. coun. Profl. Religious Assn. in Higher Edn., N.Y.C., 1978-79. Editor: Dialogue on Campus, 1978. Fund raiser WKNO Edn. T.V., Memphis, 1989, United Way, Memphis, 1988. With U.S. Army, 1969-71. Recipient Disting. Svc. award U.S. Army, Berlin, 1971. Mem. Human Resources Assn., Human Resources Planning Soc. (corp. sponsor 1989—),

Economics Club, Rotary. Home: 3780 Walnut Grove Rd Memphis TN 38111-6822 Office: Promus 1023 Cherry Rd Memphis TN 38117-5423

BURGHARDT, WALTER FRANCIS, JR., veterinarian; b. Columbus, Ohio, Sept. 18, 1952; s. Walter Francis and Helen Wanda (Watrobinski) B.; m. Charleen S. Horkott, July 24, 1993; stepchildren: Joel Webster, Christopher Webster. BA, Fla. Atlantic U., 1974, MA, 1975; DVM, U. Fla., 1980; PhD in Biopsychology, U. Md., 1988. Prin. investigator, dept. exec. officer Armed Forces Radiobiology Research Inst., Bethesda, Md., 1980-84; animal behavior cons. Behavior Clin. for Animals, Washington, 1985-95; assoc. veterinarian Colonial Animal Hosp., Boynton Beach, Fla., 1985; chief mil. pub. health 482d Med. Squadron, Homestead AFB, Fla., 1984-95; hosp. dir. Abacus Animal Hosp., Coral Springs, Fla., 1985-95; chief pub. health 433 Med. Squadron, Kelly AFB, Tex., 1995—; chief behavioral medicine and mil. working dog studies Mil. Working Dog Vet. Svc., Lackland AFB, Tex., 1995—; cons. Whittle Communications (Purina), Am. Vet. Med. Assn., Reader's Digest. Contbg. writer Pet Supplies Mktg.; contbr. articles and papers in field. Capt. USAF, 1980-84, maj. Res. Research fellow U. Fla. Coll. Vet. Medicine, 1977. Mem. AVMA, APA, Am. Vet. Soc. Animal Behavior (sec.-treas. 1984-88, pres. 1989-92), Animal Behavior Soc., Assn. Mil. Surgeons U.S., Broward County Vet. Med. Assn. (pres.-elect), Res. Officers Assn., Mensa, Blue Key. Republican. Presbyterian. Office: 341 TRS/SGV 1219 Knight St Lackland AFB TX 78236-5631

BURGHDUFF, JOHN BRIAN, mathematics educator; b. Augusta, Ga., July 16, 1958; s. Richard Dean and Betty Kay (Hebeler) B. BS in Applied Maths., Tex. A&M U., 1980; MS in Maths., Ohio State U., 1982; PhD in Math., U. Houston, 1994. Teaching asst. Tex. A&M U., College Station, 1978-80, Ohio State U., Columbus, 1980-82; instr. San Jacinto Coll., Houston, 1982-88, U. Houston, 1988-92; prof. Kingwood Coll., 1992—. Vol. youth dir. League City (Tex.) Ch. of Christ, 1982-86; faculty sponsor San Jacinto Coll. Bapt. Student Union, Houston, 1982-86; vol. Magnificat House Homeless Shelter, Houston, 1989—. Mem. Math. Assn. Am., Am. Math. Soc., Inst. for Combinatorics and its Applications. Democrat. Baptist. Home: 2600 Westridge St Apt 364 Houston TX 77054-1545 Office: Kingwood Coll Dept Math Kingwood TX 77339

BURGIN, MAX EDWARD, minister, military officer; b. Forest City, N.C., Feb. 26, 1934; s. Robert Cheek and Nannie Bell (Harris) B.; m. Mickie Jean Kelly, June 30, 1962; children: Kelli Lynn, Edward Lee. BA, Wake Forest U., 1959; BD, Southwestern Bapt. Theol. Sem., 1962; MA, L.I. U., 1974; D Ministry, N.Y. Theol. Sem., 1976. Ordained to ministry Bapt. Ch., 1962. Pastor Union Bapt. Ch., Shelby, N.C., 1963-65; commd. 1st lt. U.S. Army, 1963, advanced through grades to col., 1985; dir. dept. ministry and pastoral care Walter Reed Army Med. Ctr., Washington, 1986-91; ret., 1991; dir. clin. pastoral edn. program VA Med. Ctr., Asheville, N.C., 1992—. Contbr. articles to profl. jours. Chmn. personnel com. Sch. Bd., Fort Benning, Ga., 1978-81. Decorated Bronze Star, Nat. Def. Ribbon, 2 Legion of Merit, 5 Meritorious Svc. medals, 5 Army Commendations. Fellow Coll. of Chaplains. Home: 167 Stroud Rd Ellenboro NC 28040-5798

BURGOS, HECTOR HUGO, trading company executive; b. Mexico City, D.F., Dec. 1, 1954; came to U.S., 1989; s. Jose H. and Luz Maria (Esparza) B.; m. Myrna O. Marten, Oct. 25, 1979; children: Myrna, Hugo, Hector, Mariel. BBA, U. Iberoamericana, Mexico City, 1976; MBA, U. Tex., 1979; postgrad., Harvard U., 1987. Strategic planning mgr. IEM Westinghouse, Mexico City, 1974-77; mng. dir., capital markets dir. Operadora De Bolsa, Mexico City, 1980-88; CEO, mng. dir. Aigle Internat., Laredo, Tex., 1989-90; ptnr., CEO Agronegocios SA de CV, San Antonio, 1990-92; chmn. Buosa SA de CV, Santa Fe, Mex., 1992—; ptnr., bd. dirs. Bursamex S.A. de CV, Operadora de Franquicini SA, Banca Quadrum SA de C.V., Bursamex S.A. do C.V., Promotora Hidalguense S.A., Buosa S.A. do C.V., Video Prima S.A. do C.V., TV Azteca, Ferrioni SA. Mem. Young Pres.'s Orgn., Harvard Club. Home: 7 Morning Downs San Antonio TX 78257-1228 Office: 1284 Monte Caucaso, Mexico City 11000, Mexico

BURGOS-SASSCER, RUTH, college president; b. N.Y.C., Sept. 5, 1931; m. Donald Sasscer, June 14, 1958; children: Timothy, James, Julie, David. BA, Maryville (Tenn.) Coll., 1953; MA, Columbia U., 1956; PhD, Fla. State U., 1987. Mem. faculty Inter-Am. U., P.R., 1968-71; dept. chair U. P.R., Aguadilla, 1972-76; dir. non-traditional programs Cen. Adminstrn. Regional Coll. U. P.R., 1976-81; dir., dean, chief exec. officer U. P.R., Aguadilla, 1981-85; v.p. faculty and instrn. Harry S. Truman Coll., Chgo., 1988-93; pres. San Antonio Coll., 1993—; bd. dirs. Assn. Ho. of Chgo., Nat. Hispanic Coun. Community Colls. Pres. Commn. for Women's Affairs, Office of the Gov. of P.R., San Juan, 1979-81. Mem. Am. Assn. C.C., Assn. Women in C.C., Internat. Consortium for Ednl. and Econ. Devel. Presbyterian. Home: 2646 Chestnut Bnd San Antonio TX 78232-4659 Office: San Antonio Coll 1300 San Pedro Ave San Antonio TX 78212-4201

BURIAN, PETER HART, literature and classics educator, translator; b. Hanover, N.H., July 18, 1943; s. Hermann Martin and Gladys (Hart) B.; m. Maura Elizabeth High; children: Alexander, Martin. BA with high honors, U. Mich., 1964; MA, Princeton U., 1968, PhD, 1971. Instr. classical studies Duke U., Durham, N.C., 1968-71, asst. prof., 1971-77, assoc. prof., 1977-96; prof. Duke U., Durham, 1996—; chmn. program in comparative lit. Duke U., Durham, N.C., 1985-88; asst. prof. Intercollegiate Ctr., Rome, 1975-76; vis. prof. Dartmouth Coll., Hanover, 1989. Editor: Aristophanes' Birds, 1991; translator: Suppliant Maidens (Aeschylus), 1991, (with B. Swann) Phoenician Women (Euripides), 1981; contbr. numerous articles and revs. to scholarly jours. Coord. Amnesty Internation Group 63, Durham, 1985-88; bd. dirs. Carolina Justice Policy Ctr., Durham, 1993—, pres., 1995—. Woodrow Wilson fellow, 1964-65, Fulbright fellow U. Innsbruck, Austria, 1966-67, fellow NEH, Florence, Italy, 1972-73, Ctr. for Hellenic Studies, Washington, 1980-81. Fellow U. N.C. Inst. for Arts and Humanities; mem. Am. Philol. Assn., Classical Assn. Mid. West and South, Vergilian Soc. Am. (dir. summer sch. in Italy 1980), Soc. for Lit. and Sci. Office: Duke U Dept Classical Studies 236 Allen CB 90103 Durham NC 27708

BURK, JAMES STEVEN, sociologist, trust company officer; b. Balt., Oct. 9, 1948; s. John Franklin and Peggy Gladys Burk; m. Patricia Andrea Garcia, Oct. 21, 1967; children: Jacqualine Lee, Theodore Michael. BS, Towson State U., 1975; MA, U. Chgo., 1978, PhD, 1982. Asst. trust officer Equitable Trust Co., Balt., 1969-76; lectr. U. Chgo., 1980-81; vis. asst. prof. McGill U., Montreal, Can., 1981-83; vis. asst. prof. Tex. A&M U., College Station, 1983-84, asst. prof., 1984-90, assoc. prof., 1990—; mem. adv. coun. Mil. Studies Inst., Tex. A&M Univ., College Station. Author: Values in the Marketplace, 1988; editor: On Social Organization and Social Control, 1991, The Military in New Times, 1994; editor Armed Forces and Society, 1995—, book rev. editor, 1992-94; mem. editorial bd. Am. Jour. Sociology, 1990-92. Recipient Disting. Teaching award Assn. Former Students of Tex. A&M Univ., 1990. Fellow Inter-Univ. Seminar on Armed Forces and Soc. (exec. coun. 1992—); mem. Am. Sociol. Assn., Southwestern Social Sci. Assn. Democrat. Presbyterian. Office: Tex A&M Univ Dept Sociology College Station TX 77843-4351

BURK, JOHN EDWARD, architect; b. Lexington, Ky., Nov. 25, 1949; s. John C. and Marie Burk; m. Patty Copper, (div. 1987); children: Tracy, Wesley; m. Pam D. Smith, Aug. 19, 1989 (div. 1994). Student, Ea. Ky. U., 1968-70; BS in Architecture, U. Ky., 1975. Registered architect, Fla., Ga., N.C., Pa., S.C., Ala., Ohio, Tenn., Ky.; lic. gen. contractor, Fla., N.C., S.C., Va., Tenn. Carpenter Smith-Haggard Lumber Co., Lexington, 1966-71, foreman, 1973-74; archtl. draftsperson Paul J. Kissel, ARchitect, Lexington, 1972-73, Chrisman-Miller-Wallace, Architects, Lexington, Ky., 1974-75; intern architect Leon E. Browning, Architect, Lexington, Ky., 1975-78, Ken Hiler Builder, Inc., Lexington, Ky., 1978-79; architect Clofgelter & Assocs., Architects, Lexington, Ky., 1979-83; staff architect Sherman/Carter/Barnhart, Architects, Lexington, Ky., 1984-88; sr. architect/mktg. mgr. Takenaka Internat., Ltd., N.Y.C., 1988-92; pres. Just Accommodations, Atlanta, 1993—; prin. John Burk, Arch., Lexington, 1980-84; instr. Lexington Tech. Inst., 1982; adv. bd. Interdisciplinary Human Devel. Inst., U. Ky., 1990-91; cons. S.E. Disability and Bus. Tech. Ctr.; cons. multiple chem. hypersensitivity MCS Referral and Resources; mem. Self-Advocacy Network, Concrete Change, Fulton County ADA Coord. Com., DeKalb County Adv. Com. on Disabilities. Mem. AIA, Japan/Am. Soc. (Atlanta chpt.), Constrn. Specifications Inst. (Cert. of Appreciation award 1980-91), ADA Exch. (trustee Ga. chpt.), Human Ecology Action League, Chem. Injury Info. Network, Greater Atlanta Home Builders Assn. Home and Office: 3693 Raven Way Duluth GA 30136

BURK, SYLVIA JOAN, petroleum landman, freelance writer; b. Dallas, Oct. 16, 1928; d. Guy Thomas and Sylvia (Herrin) Ricketts; m. R. B. Murray, Jr., Sept. 7, 1951 (div. Jan. 1961); children: Jeffery Randolph, Brian BeVaughn; m. Bryan Burk, Apr. 26, 1973. BA, So. Meth. U., Dallas, 1950, MLA, 1974; postgrad. U. So. Calif., 1973-74. Cert. profl. landman. Landman, E. B. Germany & Sons, Dallas, 1970-73; asst. mgr. real estate Atlantic Richfield Co., L.A., 1973-74; landman GoldKing Prodn. Co., Houston, 1974-76; oil and gas cons./landman, co-owner Burk Properties, Burk Ednl. Properties, Houston, 1976—. Author: Petroleum Lands and Leasing, 1983; contbr. articles and photographs to profl. jours.; photographer; Author's Guild, 1984-93. Active Planning and Zoning Commn., Sugar Land, Tex., 1990-92; vol. media staff Economic Summit Industrialized Nations, Houston, 1990. Mem. Foremost Women 20th Century, Am. Assn. Petroleum Landmen (dir. 1980-82, 2d v.p. 1982-83, 71-94), Houston Assn. Petroleum Landmen (dir. 1976), Sweetwater Country Club, Huisache Club (pres. elect), The Houston Forum, HAPL Aux. (treas.). Republican. Presbyterian.

BURKE, CHARLES MICHAEL, military officer; b. Denver, June 28, 1944; s. Charles Martin and Gwendolyn Rae (Smith) B.; m. Mary Kathleen Flanagan, Feb. 17, 1968; children: Michael Kevin, Marueen Catherine, Shannon Colleen. BS in Bus., U. Tampa, 1974. Commd. 2d lt. U.S. Army, 1967, advanced through grades to brig. gen., 1990; comdr. 228th attack helicopter bn. U.S. Army, Ft. Hood, Tex., 1983-85, dep. comdr. 6th cavalry brigade, 1985-87; chief concepts and doctrine divsn. hdqs. Dept. of Army-Pentagon, Washington, 1988-90; comdr. combat aviation brigade 3d armored divsn. U.S. Army, Hanau, Fed. Republic Germany, 1990-92; dep. asst. comdt. U.S. Army Aviation Sch., Ft. Rucker, Ala., 1992-93; asst. chief of staff G-3 and chief of staff III U.S. Army Corps., Fort Hood, Tex., 1993-95; dep. chief of staff for support HQ Landsouth, Verona, Italy, 1996—. Contbr. articles to profl. jours. Decorated Silver Star, Legion of Merit, Bronze Star, Air Medal, Meritorious Svc. medal U.S. Army. Mem. Army Aviation Assn. Am. (chpt. pres. 1968-94). Republican. Roman Catholic. Home: 6604 Todd St Fort Hood TX 76544-1331 Office: US Army III Corps Hdqs Fort Hood TX 76544

BURKE, JOHN JEFFREY, librarian; b. Niagara Falls, N.Y., July 29, 1969; s. John Edward and Candace Lily (Hildebrandt) B.; m. Lynne Katherine Siemsen, July 6, 1991. BA in History, Mich. State U., 1991; MS in Libr. Sci., U. Tenn., 1993. Reference libr. Fairmont (W.Va.) State Coll., 1993—. Author: Learning the Internet, 1996. Grantee Fairmont State Coll., 1996. Mem. ALA. Democrat. Baptist. Home: 1103 Village Way Fairmont WV 26554 Office: Fairmont State Coll Libr Locust Ave Fairmont WV 26554

BURKE, KIERAN E., business executive; b. 1957. V.p. Drexel Burnham Lambert Group, Inc., N.Y.C., 1978-87, vice chmn., mng. dir., 1987-89; chmn. bd., CEO Premier Parks, Inc., Oklahoma City, 1989—. Office: Premier Parks Inc 11501 NE Expressway St Oklahoma City OK 73131

BURKE, MARGUERITE JODI LARCOMBE, writer, computer consultant; b. Pasadena, Calif.; d. Richard Albert and Marguerite (Colella) L.; m. M. Theodore Jockers, Dec. 5, 1954 (div. Nov. 1969); children: Richard Larcombe, Sir Blair; m. Roger Eugene Burke, Dec. 5, 1969. BA, Columbia U., 1949. Model Ford Agy., N.Y.C., 1949-54; freelance writer Savannah, Ga., 1969-80; pres. Jodi Larcombe Assocs., Murfreesboro, N.C., 1970—; freelance computer programmer Murfreesboro, 1981—; exec. asst. Resinall Corp., Severn, N.C., 1981—, computer programmer, 1981-89. Author: Sailing Cookbook, 1979; contbr. numerous articles to mags.; dir. Shotgun Theater Prodns., 1995. Dir. Shotgun Theater Prodns., N.Y., 1996—. Mem. Met. Opera Oncore Soc., Am. Film Soc., Met Opera Patron Assn. (2d century cir.), Met. Opera Nat. Coun., N.Y.C. Opera. Home: 306 Holly Hill Rd Murfreesboro NC 27855-2110 Office: Jodi Larcombe Assocs 306 Holly Hill Rd Murfreesboro NC 27855-2110

BURKE, MARIANNE MARSH, editor; b. Baton Rouge, Mar. 28, 1958; d. Bobby Lee and Gladys Mary (Rieder) Marsh; 1 child, Connor Levi. BS, La. State U., 1981. Lab. analyst La. Dept. Agr., Baton Rouge, 1982-84, mktg. specialist, 1984-88; seafood advt. and promotions dir. La. Seafood Promotions and Mktg. Bd., Baton Rouge, 1988-90; assoc. editor La. Conservationist Mag., La. Dept. Wildlife & Fisheries, Baton Rouge, 1990—. Mem. Outdoor Writers Assn. Am., La. Outdoor Writers Assn. Home: 1432 Wellington Dr Baton Rouge LA 70815-5339 Office: La Conservationist Mag PO Box 98000 Baton Rouge LA 70898-9000

BURKE, THOMAS WILLIAM, executive benefits consulting company official; b. Harmon, Ill., Aug. 1, 1947; s. John William and Mary Eileen (Long) B.; m. Mary Ellen Bosau, Nov. 27, 1970; children: Kelly, Colleen, Shannon, Tommy, Michael. BS, St. Joseph's Coll., Collegeville, Ind., 1969. CLU; ChFC; CFP; lic. ins. counselor. Asst. mgr. Conn. Gen., Chgo., 1970-77; v.p. Fin. Industries, Austin, Tex., 1977; pres. T.W. Burke Assocs., Austin, 1978-87; dir. advanced underwriting SunLife, Dallas, 1988-92; pres. Hefner Assocs., Richardson, Tex., 1992—; tchr. continuing edn. ABA, Tex. Soc. for CPA's and Atty. CPA's, U. Tex., 1986—. Coach Little League, 1991—; bd. advisor St. Joseph's Coll. Mem. Nat. Assn. Life Underwriters, Nat. Assn. Securities Dealers, Assn. Advanced Life Underwriters, Soc. CLU's, Dallas C. of C. (govt. affairs com. 1993-94), Million Dollar Round Table. Roman Catholic. Office: Hefner & Assocs 600 W Campbell Ste 7 Richardson TX 75080-3357

BURKE, TOM CLIFTON, marketing executive; b. Weatherford, Tex., Aug. 30, 1954; s. John Gary and Betty Jean (Thomas) B.; m. Mary Eileen Freese, May 26, 1979. BA, Tex. Christian U., 1976. Staff writer, columnist Orange (Tex.) Leader Daily Newspaper, 1976-77; asst. editor Open Road Mag., Ft. Worth, 1977-78; dir. pub. rels., mktg. Cen. Freight Lines Inc., Waco, Tex., 1978-96; sr. assoc. Ctr. for Occupl. Rsch. and Devel., Waco, Tex., 1996—. Mayor City of Hewitt, Tex., 1985-86, mem. City Coun., 1984-89, Planning and Zoning Commn., 1982-84; mem. Greater Hewitt Econ. Devel. Team, 1986—, chmn., 1987, 88, 89, Cen. Tex. Bus and Truck Transp. Legis. Edn. Group, Waco, Tex., 1980-96, chmn., 1981, 84. Recipient Top 100 Mgmt. Achievement award Fleet Owner Mag., 1981, Silver Spur award Tex. Pub. Relations Assn., 1984, 2 Awards of Excellence, Am. Advt. Fedn., 1986. Mem. Internat. Assn. Bus. Communicators (award of merit 1981, 83, 87), Pub. Rels. Soc. Am. (pres. Waco chpt. 95, chair-elect S.W. dist., Tex. star award, accredited 1989), Waco Advt. Club (awards of excellence 1986, 2 Addy awards 1986, Telly award 1993), Am. Trucking Assns., Inc. (past chmn. pub. rels. coun., mem. communications adv. com., pub. rels. award of yr. 1980, 81, 83, employee publ. award 1981, 82, 83, 84), Tex. Motor Transp. Assn. (edn. com., chmn. pub. rels. com.), Hewitt C. of C. (bd. dirs. 1985-87, 91-94). Republican. Roman Catholic. Lodges: Lions (pres. 1983-84), Masons, Scottish Rite, Shriners. Home: 1100 Dendron Dr Hewitt TX 76643-3913 Office: Ctr Occupl Rsch & Devel PO Box 21689 Waco TX 76702-1689

BURKE, WILLIAM TEMPLE, JR., lawyer; b. San Antonio, Oct. 30, 1935; s. William Temple and Adelaide H. (Raba) B.; m. Mary Sue Johnson, June 8, 1957; children: William Patrick, Michael Edmond, Karen Elizabeth. B.B.A., St. Mary's U., San Antonio, J.D., 1961. Bar: Tex. 1961. Practice law Dallas; founder, pres. Burke Wright & Keiffer, P.C., 1985—. Pres., founder Dallas Assn. KC, 1968-69; v.p., co-founder, dir. Tex. Cath. Credit Union, 1966-69, vice chmn. bd. dirs., 1990-91 (Man of Yr., 1969-70); grand knight, trustee Dallas Coun. 799 KC, 1964-69; v.p., dir. Dallas Optimists Club, 1965-66 (Mem. of Yr., 1966, Pres.'s award, 1968); dist. exemplar 4th degree KC, 1968-89; pres., dir. Dallas County Small Bus. Devel. Center, 1965-66; v.p. Dallas County Hist. Survey Com., 1966; pres. Dallas Mil. Govt. Assn., 1962-63; pres. men's club St. Patrick's Parish Roman Cath. Ch., 1963, prin. jr. high sch. Christian devel. program, 1970, chmn. scout troop com., 1976-78, chmn. fin. com., 1984-87, mem. bldg. com., 1978-87, chmn. bd. consultors, 1978-81; bd. dirs. Dallas County War on Poverty, 1965-66; trustee Montserrat Jesuit Retreat House, 1995—, treas., 1996—; vice chair Cath. Commn. Appeal Diocese of Dallas, 1993—. Served to 1st lt. AUS, 1958-60; capt. Res. ret. Mem. ABA, Tex. Bar Assn., Dallas Bar Assn. (chmn. bankruptcy and comml. law sect. 1976-77, 86-87, courthouse liaison com. 1985—, lectr. 1985—), Am. Bankruptcy Inst., Dallas C. of C., Serra Club (v.p. Met. Dallas 1995—, Outstanding Mem. of Yr. 1996), Internat. Order Alhambra (exemplar 1978-95), Dallas City Club, Phi Delta Phi, Tau Delta Sigma. Home: 9751 Larchcrest Dr Dallas TX 75238-2112 Office: 2900 Renaissance Tower Dallas TX 75287-5943

BURKETT, BEN VERN, SR., aircraft support company executive; b. Jay, Okla., Aug. 12, 1944; s. Grelie Burkett and Grace Delean Townsend; divorced; children: Sonya Reneé, Ben V II. AIT, Belvoir, Va., 1965. V.p. mfg. Porta Kamp Mfg. Co., Houston, 1969-83; CEO The Burkett Co., Houston, 1983—; bd. dirs. The Battery Co., Jerusalem. Inventor water activated battery. Bd. dirs. Houston County Fair, Harris County, Tex., 1984; mem. quality bd. Omega House, Houston, 1993. With U.S. Army, 1965-67. Recipient Svc. award UN Command, 1967. Republican. Baptist.

BURKHART, DORTHEA DAVENPORT, language educator; b. Salisbury, N.C., July 3, 1944; d. John Allen and Dorothy Dean (Hester) Davenport; m. Thad L. Burkhart, July 25, 1964; 1 child, Thad Allen. BA, U. N.C., Greensboro, 1967; MA, U. N.C., Chapel Hill, 1969. Eng. tchr. East Davidson, Thomasville, N.C., 1968-69; Eng. instr. Davidson County C.C., Lexington, N.C., 1969—. Pres. Davidson County Arts Coun., Lexington, 1980. Recipient First Union Bank award, 1986. Mem. N.C. Conf. Cmty. Coll. Eng. Instr. Democrat. Home: 1975 E Holly Grove Lexington NC 27292 Office: Davidson Co CC Lexington NC 27292

BURMAN, MARSHA LINKWALD, lighting manufacturing executive, marketing development professional; b. Balt., Jan. 9, 1949; d. William and Lena (Ronin) Linkwald; m. Robert Schlosser, July 2, 1972 (div. 1980); children: Melanie, David. BS in Edn. cum laude, Kent State U., 1970, MA in Sociology summa cum laude, 1971. Cert. in secondary edn., Ohio. Spl. project dir. tng. and rsch. ctr. Planned Parenthood, Chgo., 1978; with mgmt. edn. ctr. Gould, Inc., Chgo., 1979, program adminstr., 1979-80; sys. trainer Lithonia Lighting, 1981; mgr. tng. and edn. Lithonia Lighting, Chgo., 1981-86; dir. mktg., tng. and devel., corp. tng., mgr. Lithonia Lighting Ctr., Atlanta, 1986—. Author: (booklet) Putting Your Best Foot Forward (award Am. Soc. Tng. and Devel.), 1982; author, editor: Dictionary of Lighting Industry Terminology, 1989, 3d edit., 1990. U.S. Office Edn. grantee, 1971. Mem. ASTD (bd. dirs. 1982, spl. projects dir. Atlanta chpt. 1982, Vol. of Yr., Cmty. Leader Am. 1987, 89, 92), Tng. Dirs. Roundtable (founding mem.), Lithonia Lighting Mgmt. Club (v.p. 1982-83), Toastmasters. Office: Lithonia Lighting Div Nat Svc Industries 1400 Lester Rd NW Conyers GA 30207-3908

BURMESTER, JOSEPH KIRK, iformation technology executive, consultant; b. DeKalb, Ill., May 30, 1946; s. Willard H. and Mary-Lou (Hiatt) B.; m. Rebecca J. Readinger, Sept. 7, 1968; children: Leslie A., Matthew A. BS in Math., Bowling Green State U., 1968, MBA, 1969. CPA, Ohio, Mo. Instr. Bowling Green (Ohio) State U., 1969-72; sr. mgr. Arthur Andersen & Co., Cleve., 1972-81; sr. v.p. Capitol Am. Life Ins. Co., Cleve., 1982; ptnr. KPMG-Peat Marwick, St. Louis, 1982-90; v.p. Wright Systems Inc., Plymouth, Mich., 1990; v.p., cons. Integral Sys., Inc., Walnut Creek, Calif., 1990-92; gen. mgr. Integral Midrange, Raleigh, N.C., 1992-93; pres. Neumenon, Inc., Raleigh, N.C., 1994; v.p. Realogic, Cleve., 1995—. Gen. mgr. Cleve. Bus. Show, 1980; treas. Westhaven, Cleve., 1980-82; elder Presbyterian Ch. Mem. AICPA, Assn. for Sys. Mgmt. (chpt. pres. 1978-79, 85-86), Mo. Soc. CPAs, N.C. Roadrunners Club. Democrat. Presbyterian. Home: 625 Downpatrick Ln Raleigh NC 27615-1518 Office: Realogic Inc 600 Superior Ave E Ste 2300 Cleveland OH 44114-2611

BURNETT, CASSIE WAGNON, middle school educator; b. Atlanta, Aug. 31, 1950; d. Lovic Pierce and Virginia (Slaughter) Wagnon; m. Irvin D. Burnett, Sept. 26, 1970; children: Bryan, Brittany. BA, Oglethorpe U., 1971; MEd, Ga. State U., 1975. Tchr. elem. sch. Dekalb County Bd. Edn., Decatur, Ga., 1971-81; tchr. jr. high sch. Greater Atlanta Christian Sch., Norcross, Ga., 1982—; sponsor History Club, 1992—; co-sponsor Joy Club, 1990-92. Home: 5071 Hodgkins Pl SW Lilburn GA 30247-7313 Office: Greater Atlantic Christian Sch PO Box 4277 Indian Trail Rd Norcross GA 30091-4277

BURNETT, PAUL DAVID, small business owner; b. Arlington, Tex., Sept. 19, 1963; s. Paul W. and Joyce (Childers) B.; m. Jeri Dee Walker, June 23, 1989; children: Kayli Danielle, Brayden Paul, Makenzie Dee. BBA, Tex. Christian U., 1985, MBA, 1989. V.p. Burnett's Staffing, Arlington, Tex., 1985—; owner Burnett Ventures, Arlington, 1990—. Dir. Vol. Adv. Com., Arlington, 1991—. Mem. Tex. Assn. Pers. Cons. (bd. dirs. 1991), Metroplex Assn. Pers. Cons. (bd. dirs. 1991—), Nat. Assn. Pers. Cons., Nat. Assn. Temporary Cons., Execs. Unltd., Southwest Task Force. Home: 4321 Greenwood Ln Grapevine TX 76051-6719 Office: Burnetts Staffing 2710 Avenue E Arlington TX 76011-5206

BURNETT, ROSA SCOTT, librarian; b. Utica, Miss., Oct. 28, 1945; d. Winfield and Ida Mae (Page) Scott; children: Michelle, Michael. A, Utica Jr. Coll., 1964; BS, Miss. Valley State U., 1966; MLS, U. Miss., Oxford, 1974. Libr. Patton Ln. High Sch., Batesville, Miss., 1966-67, Booker T. Washington Elem. Sch., Clarksdale, Miss., 1967-69; asst. libr. Coahoma Jr. Coll., Clarksdale, Miss., 1969-74; dir. Learning Resource Ctr. Miss. Indsl. Coll., Holly Springs, 1974-76; dean libr. svcs. State Tech. Inst. Memphis, 1976—. Editor: (newsletter) Academic Support, 1989. Chair person speaker's bur. Memphis in May Internat. Festival, 1987, bd. dirs., 1989, exec. com., 1990; pres. Ladies on Fire for Christ, Memphis, 1989-90; bd. dir. nominating com. Tenn.-Ark.-Miss. Girl Scout Coun., 1992, chair, 1994—; v.p. Memphis Area Black Librs. Caucus, 1996. Mem. ALA, Tenn. Libr. Assn., Tenn. Bd. Regents Libr. Dirs. (pres. 1987-88), Am. Vocat. Assn., Memphis Libr. Coun. (sec. 1988-89, v.p., pres. elect 1991-92, pres. 1992-93), Utica Nat. Alumni Assn. (sec. 1991-93, pres. elect 1993-95, pres. 1995-97), Memphis Area Black Librs. Caucus (pres.-elect 1995-96). Baptist. Office: State Tech Inst Memphis 5983 Macon Cv Memphis TN 38134-7642

BURNETT, SUSAN WALK, personnel service company owner; b. Galveston, Tex., Aug. 21, 1946; d. Joe Decker and Ruth Corinne (Lowe) Walk; m. Rusty Burnett, Dec. 27, 1973; stepchildren—Barbara, Sara. B.A. in Journalism, U. Ark.-Fayetteville, 1968. Asst. pub. relations mgr. sta. KATV, Little Rock, 1968-69; speech writer Assoc. Milk Producers, Inc., Little Rock, 1969-70; mgr. Allied Personnel, Houston, 1970-74; owner Burnett Cos. Consol., Inc., Houston, 1974—. exec. bd. dirs. Arthritis Found. Recipient Appreciation awards Lyndon Johnson Space Ctr., NASA, 1983, State of Tex., 1984, Top Houston Woman Bus. Owner award Nat. Assn. Women Bus. Owners, 1996; named one of 10 Women on the Move in Houston, Houston Chronicle, 1996. Mem. Tex. Assn. Personnel Cons. (v.p. 1985), Houston Assn. Personnel Cons. (pres. 1986, v.p. 1985, Outstanding Contbn. to Placement Industry award 1995), Nat. Assn. Personnel Cons., Chi Omega Alumnae. Republican. Methodist. Avocations: Reading; golf; flying; sailing. Office: Burnett Cos Consol Inc 9800 Richmond Ave Ste 800 Houston TX 77042-4544

BURNETTE, JAMES THOMAS, lawyer; b. Stuart, Va., Apr. 7, 1959; s. Edwin Lee and Marye Joanne (Minter) B.; m. Sarah Katherine Kelly, Dec. 2, 1989; children: Sarah Elizabeth, Thomas Pullen. BS, Campbell U., 1981; JD, Wake Forest U., 1984. Bar: N.C. 1985. Atty. Womble Carlyle Sandridge & Rice, Winston-Salem, N.C., 1985-86; ptnr. Edmundson & Burnette, Oxford, N.C., 1986—; atty. City of Oxford, 1995—. Mem. ATLA, N.C. Acad. Trial Lawyers, N.C. State Bar, N.C. Bar Assn., South Granville Country Club (bd. dirs.), Thorndale Country Club, Capital City Club. Episcopalian. Home: 4129 Salem Farm Rd Oxford NC 27565-9199 Office: Edmundson & Burnette 146 Main St Bldg Oxford NC 27565-3353

BURNETTT, E. C., III, state supreme court justice. Justice S.C. Supreme Ct., Columbia. Office: SC Supreme Ct PO Box 11330 Columbia SC 29211

BURNEY, CURTIS MICHAEL, oceanographer, educator; b. Beatrice, Nebr., Sept. 26, 1947; s. Curtis Norris and Mary Jane Burney; m. Joyce Ann Johnson, May 19, 1972; children: Martha, James, Ruth. BS in Biology, Nebr. Wesleyan U., 1969; MS in Oceanography, U. R.I., 1976, PhD in Oceanography, 1980. Tchr., lab. asst. in gen. bacteriology biology dept. Nebr. Wesleyan U., 1969; rsch. asst. Grad. Sch. Oceanography U. R.I.,

Kingston, 1974-80, rsch. assoc., 1980-81; asst. prof. oceanography Oceanographic Ctr. Nova Southeastern U., Dania, Fla., 1981-88; assoc. prof. oceanography Nova U., Dania, Fla., 1988—, co-adminstr. Inst. Marine and Coastal Studies, 1983—. Contbr. articles to profl. publs. With USN, 1970-74. Grantee NSF, Broward County, Fla., 1989-96, Forman Found. and Tindall Hammock Drainage and Irrigation Dist. Republican. Office: Nova Southeastern U Oceanographic Ctr 8000 N Ocean Dr Dania FL 33004-3033

BURNHAM, J. V., sales executive; b. Pascagoula, Miss., May 23, 1923; s. George Luther and Eli Vashti (Hough) B.; m. Patti Lauri Latham, May 18, 1946; children: James Steven, Jon Douglas, Richard Scott, Bruce Edward, Vernon Alan. AA, Jones County (Miss.) Jr. Coll., 1946; AS, Rochester Inst. Tech., 1948; BS, U. Houston, 1951, MEd, 1953. Mgr. The Progress-Item, Ellisville, Miss., 1948-50; asst. prof., asst. mgr. U. Houston Journalism and Printing Plant, 1950-57; estimator, product supt. purchasing Chas. P. Young Co., Houston, 1957-67, asst. sec.-treas., 1967-69, v.p. sales, 1969-91, sr. v.p., 1991—. Assoc. editor Am. Oceanography, 1968-71; southwest corr. Inland Printer and Nat. Lithographer, 1952-60. Pres. Printing Industries of Gulf Coast, Houston, 1971-73; chmn. emeritus, bd. dirs. Tex. Printing Edn. Found., Houston; vice chmn., bd. dirs. Mus. of Printing History, Houston; mem. Rep. Presdl. Task Force, Nat. Rep. Senatorial Com. Order of Merit, Nat. Rep. Congl. Com., Rep. Nat. Com. (chmn.'s adv. bd.), Rep. Party of Tex., Rep. Nat. Candidate Trust, The Heritage Found., Gramm Senate Club, The Concord Coalition. Lt. USNR, 1943-46. Recipient Scouters award Boy Scouts Am., 1960, Scouters Key award, 1965, Wood Badge award, 1964; named Man of Yr., Houston Graphics Soc., 1968, Printing Industry of Gulf Coast, 1970. Mem. NRA (life), AARP, Am. Fedn. Police, Gun Owners Am., Second Amendment Found., USS Constitution Mus. Found., Houston Advt. Club, Pres's. Club of Chas. P. Young Co. (charter, Outstanding Sales Achievement award), Houston Lithographic Club, U.S. Hist. Soc. (life), Nat. Eagle Scout Assn. (life), Tex. State Rifle Assn. (life), Tex. Police Officers Assn., Naval Airship. Assn., Rep.-Presdl. Legion of Merit, Am. Legion, Living Bank, U. Houston Alumni (life), Jones County Jr. Coll. Alumni (life), Rochester Inst. Tech. Alumni Assn., U.S. Golf Assn., Houston Golf Assn., 100 Club Houston, Braeburn Country Club, Hummel Collecters Club (Houston), The Landing at Seven Coves (Conroe, Tex.), NRA Whittington Ctr. Founders Club, Santa Fe Trail Gun Club (life), Houston Craftsmens Club (hon. life., past pres., Ben Franklin award 1971), Crime Stoppers of Houston (gold cir. mem.), Pinto Horse Assn. Am., Ducks Unltd., U.S. Navy Meml. FOund., Naval Aviation Mus. Found., U.S. Navy Pub. Affairs Alumni Assn. (life). Republican. Methodist.

BURNHAM, JUDITH F., medical librarian; b. Louisville, Sept. 18, 1948; d. Thomas W. and Norma (Boldt) Fell; m. Gilbert E. Burnham, Jr., June 24, 1967; children: Brian Gilbert, Shawn David. AA, Western Okla. C.C., 1968; BS magna cum laude, U. South Ala., 1988; MLS, U. So. Miss., 1989. Info. svcs. libr. biomed. libr. U. South Ala., Mobile, 1989-91, UMC site coord. biomedical libr., 1991-95, asst. dir. for regional svcs., 1995—. Contbr. articles to profl. jours. Nat. Libr. Medicine grantee, 1993. Mem. Ala. Libr. Assn. (mem. rsch. com. 1995-97, chair coll. univ. and spl. libr. divsn. program planning com. 1993-94, mem. CUS program planning com., 1992-93, nom. com. CUS, 1985, sec. health scis. roundtable, 1984-86, EBSCO scholar 1988), Bay Area Libr. Assn. (pres. 1992), Ala. Health Librs. Assn. (pres.-elect 1994, pres. 1995, mem.-at-large 1991-93, sec. 1991, chair directory com. 1990, panelist ann. mtg. 1990, awards com. 1995-96), Med. Libr. Assn. (so. chpt. chair, govtl. rels. com. 1995-96, chair mem. com. nursing and allied health resource sect. 1993-95, mem. com. 1992-93, rsch. com. 1995—, Continuing Edn. award 1992), Acad. Health Info. Profls. (assoc.), Beta Phi Mu, Gamma Beta Phi, Phi Kappa Phi (pres. chpt. 194 1993-95). Home: 3726 Bay Front Rd Mobile AL 36605-3701 Office: U So Ala Med Ctr 2451 Fillingim St Mobile AL 36617-2238

BURNHAM, TOM, state school system administrator; b. Jackson, Miss., May 5, 1946; 1 child, Cassandra Burnham Vanderford. BSBA, Miss. Coll., Clinton, 1969, MEd; EdS, Delta State U., Cleveland, Miss., 1983, EdD, 1985. Cert. in social studies adminstrn., Miss. Tchr., dept. chair Pearl (Miss.) High Sch., 1969-72; asst. prin. McLuarin Jr. High, Pearl, 1973-86; prin. Solomon Jr. High, Greenville, Miss., 1986-87; supt. Biloxi (Miss.) Pub. Schs., 1987-92; state supt. edn. Miss. Dept. Edn., Jackson, 1992—. Mem. Am. Assn. Sch. Adminstrs., Miss. Profl. Educators, Harrison County United Way, Phi Delta Kappa. Baptist. Office: Miss Dept Edn 550 High St Jackson MS 39201-1113

BURNS, BARBARA BELTON, investment company executive; b. Fredericktown, Mo., Dec. 10, 1944; d. Clyde Monroe and Mary Celestial (Anderson) Belton; m. Larry J. Bohannon; Mar. 27, 1963 (div.); 1 child, Timothy Joseph; m. Donald Edward Burns, Nov. 1, 1980; stepchildren: Brian Edward, David Keone (dec.). Student, Ohio State U., 1970-75. Dir. nat. sales Am. Way, Chgo., 1976-77; recruiter Bell & Howell Schs., Columbus, Ohio, 1978-80; pres., founder Bardon Investment Corp., Naples, Fla., 1980-90; founder Cambridge Mgmt. Co., Columbus, 1983-86; pres., CEO Charter's Total Wardrobe Care, Columbus, 1984-89; founder, exec. Phoenix Bus. Group, Inc., 1990—. Treas. Vicace-Columbus Symphony, 1981-82; fundraiser Grant Hosp., Columbus, 1986; chmn. Impresarios/Opera Columbus, 1986-87; founding mem. Columbus Women's Bd., 1986-87; mem. devel. com. Babe Zaharias/Am. Cancer Soc.; auction chmn. Opera Ball-Opera/Columbus, 1989; tennis tournament chmn. NABOR Scholarship Fund, 1990, 91; mem. Philharmonic Chorale, Naples, Fla., 1992; spokesperson Diabetes Found. Collier Co., Fla., 1992—, pres., 1994; elder Vanderbilt Presbyn. Ch., 1994; prs. Diabetes Found., Inc., 1994—. Named Entrepreneur of Yr. Arthur Young/Venture mag., 1988, Outstanding Vol. Opera Columbus, 1986, Vol. of Yr. Diabetes Found., 1994; recipient Design award Reynoldsburg C. of C., 1988. Mem. Naples C. of C. (new bus. com. 1990—). Republican.

BURNS, BEBE LYN, journalist; b. Baytown, Tex., Nov. 2, 1952; d. L.L. and Edith Elizabeth (Smith) B.; m. George Frederick Rhodes Jr., Nov. 30, 1980; 1 child, Elizabeth Kathleen. BA, U. Houston, 1974; MS in Journalism, Northwestern U., 1975. Reporter, anchor Sta. WSPA-TV, Spartanburg, S.C., 1975-76, Sta. KHOU-TV, Houston, 1976-79; reporter Sta. KTVI-TV, St. Louis, 1979-82; bus. reporter Sta. KPRC-TV, Houston, 1982-95; prin. Burns Kopatic, Houston, 1996—. Bd. dirs. Presbyn. Sch., 1996—, Houston Area Parkinson's Soc., 1991-95, CanCare of Houston, Inc., 1995—; founding mem. Greater Houston Women's Found.; active Friends of Fleming Park, Boulevard Oaks Civic Assn. Recipient awards Headliners Club Tex. 1988, Tex. AP Broadcasters, 1988, Am. Women in Radio & TV, 1988, Press Club Houston, 1987, 88, Press Club Dallas, 1981, 93, Employee award for help to jobless Tex. Employment Commn., 1993, Bus. Advocacy award North Harris-Montgomery C.C. Dist. & Bus. & Industry Coun., 1993; named one of Women on the Move Houston Post and Tex. Exec. Women, 1988, Small Bus. Media Advocate of Yr. SBA, 1992. Mem. Soc. Profl. Journalists. Methodist. Office: Burns Kopatic 5599 San Felipe Ste 1210 Houston TX 77056

BURNS, CASSANDRA STROUD, prosecutor; b. Lynchburg, Va., May 22, 1960; d. James Wesley and Jeanette Lou (Garner) Stroud; m. Stephen Burns; children: Leila Jeanette, India Veronica. BA, U. Va., 1982; JD, N.C. Cen. U., 1985. Bar: Va. 1986, N.J. 1986, U.S. Dist. Ct. (ea. dist.) Va. 1987, U.S. Ct. Appeals (4th cir.) 1987, U.S. Bankruptcy Ct. (ea. dist.) Va. 1987. Law clk. Office Atty. Gen. State of Va., Richmond, summer 1984; law intern Office Dist. Atty. State of N.C., Durham, 1985; staff atty. Tidewater Legal Aid Soc., Chesapeake, Va., 1987-89; asst. atty. Commonwealth of Va., Petersburg, 1989-90; assoc. atty. Bland and Stroud, Petersburg, 1990; asst. pub. defender City of Petersburg, 1990-91; Commonwealth's atty. City of Petersburg, Va., 1991—; founder BED Task Force on Babies Exposed to Drugs, 1991. Sec. Chesapeake Task Force Coun. on Youth Svcs., 1987-89; ch. directress and organist; mem. NAACP. Mem. Va. Bar Assn. (mem. coun. 1993—), Old Dominion Bar Assn., Va. Assn. Commonwealth Attys. (bd. dirs., mem. coun. 1993—), Legal Svcs. Corp. Va. (bd. dirs.), Soutside Va. Legal Aid Soc. (bd. dirs.), Petersburg Bar Assn., Petersburg Jaycees, Order Eastern Star, Peterburg C. of C., Phi Alpha Delta, Alpha Kappa Alpha. Democrat. Baptist. Club: Buddies (Lynchburg). Home: 326 N Park Dr Petersburg VA 23805-2442 Office: Commonwealth's Atty 39 Bollingbrook St Petersburg VA 23803-4548

BURNS, CHESTER RAY, medical history educator; b. Nashville, Dec. 5, 1937; s. Leslie Andrew and Margaret (Drake) B.; m. Ann Christine Griffey, Aug. 31, 1962; children: Christine, Derek. BA, Vanderbilt U., 1959, MD, 1963; PhD, Johns Hopkins U., 1969. Asst. prof. history medicine U. Tex. Med. Br., Galveston, 1969-71, James Wade Rockwell asst. prof. history medicine, 1971-75, James Wade Rockwell assoc. prof., 1975-79, James Wade Rockwell prof., 1979—; cons. Nat. Ctr. for Health Svcs. Rsch., Washington, 1976-78; mem. nat. bd. cons. NEH, Washington, 1978-83. Editor: Humanism in Medicine, 1973, Legacies in Ethics and Medicine, 1977, Legacies in Law and Medicine, 1977; author numerous essays. Bd. dirs. The Grand 1894 Opera House, Galveston, 1986-88. Mem. Am. Assn. for History of Medicine (exec. coun. 1972-75), Soc. for Health and Human Values (pres. 1975-76), Am. Osler Soc. (bd. govs. 1984-87), Internat. Soc. for History of Medicine (treas. 1991—), Tex. State Hist. Assn. (exec. coun. 1993—), Rotary (pres. Galveston club 1980-81, gov. Dist. 5910, 1993-94). Democrat. Methodist. Office: U Tex Med Br Rm 2 208 Ashbel Smith Bldg Galveston TX 77555-1311

BURNS, DIANE, gifted education educator; b. N.Y.C., Feb. 20, 1946; d. John A. and Virginia Mae (Ridenour) De Gaetano; 1 child, Michele Young; m. Frank Anthony Burns, Apr. 6, 1980; 1 child, Michael John. BA, SUNY, New Paltz, 1968; MEd, U. Ctrl. Fla., 1984. Cert. tchr. elem., early childhood and gifted edn., Fla. Tchr. grade 3 Three Village Sch. Dist., Setauket, N.Y., 1968-69; reading tchr. Am. Heritage Sch., Hollywood, Fla., 1971-74; tchr. various grades Oak Park Elem., Leesburg, Fla., 1975-87; tchr. gifted 3d and 4th grades Dabney Elem., Leesburg, 1987-95; tchr. 3d grade Treadway Elem. Sch., Leesburg, Fla., 1995—; pvt. tutor, Leesburg. Author, editor: The Time Shifters, 1990 (Fla. Assn. of Gifted grant). Soloist, choir mem. Chancel Choir-Morrison United Meth. Ch., Leesburg, 1986—. Named Fla. Merit Master tchr. State of Fla., Tallahassee, 1983. Mem. Fla. Assn. Gifted, Lake County Edn. Assn., Lake County Reading Coun., Alpha Delta Kappa (chaplain 1986-88). Republican. Home: 819 Palm Ave Leesburg FL 34748-6857 Office: Treadway Elem Sch 10619 Treadway School Rd Leesburg FL 34788-4675

BURNS, GARY ALLEN, forester, consultant, appraiser; b. Haverhill, Mass., Apr. 15, 1945; s. J. D. and Margaret Carma (Besso) B. BS in Forestry, U. N.H., 1967; MS in Forestry, Stephen F. Austin State U., 1993. Owner Burns Forestry, Crockett, Tex., 1970—, Burns and Assocs., Crockett, 1985—. Contbr. articles to profl. jours. Chmn. Houston County (Tex.) Forestry Com., 1977-87; mem. Planning and Zoning Com., Crockett, Tex., 1980-81; pres. Trinity Valley Audubon Soc., Crockett, 1981-82; pres. Crockett (Tex.) Rotary Club, 1986-87. Recipient Forest award Houston County Program Bldg. Com., 1981. Mem. Am. Soc. Appraisers (sr. mem., internat. bd. examiners 1986-93), Soc. Am. Foresters (chmn. Tex. chpt. 1984), Assn. Consulting Foresters (chmn. Tex.-La. chpt. 1983-84), Tex. Forestry Assn. (dir. 1982-84, 87-89). Home: PO Box 1227 Crockett TX 75835 Office: Burns Forestry 316 N 5th St Crockett TX 75835-1504

BURNS, GROVER PRESTON, retired physicist; b. nr. Hurricane, W.Va., Apr. 25, 1918; s. Joshua Alexander and Virgie (Meadows) B.; m. Julia Belle Foster, Nov. 4, 1941; children: Julia Corinne Burns Jefferson, Grover Preston. AB, Marshall U., 1937; postgrad., Duke U., 1939-40; MS, W.Va. U., 1941; postgrad., U. Md., 1946; DSc (hon.), Colo. State Christian Coll., 1973. Tchr. high sch., W.Va., 1937-40; fellow W.Va. U., 1940-41; instr. physics U. Conn., 1941-42; asst. prof. Miss. State Coll., 1942-44, acting head physics dept., 1944-45; asst. prof. physics Tex. Tech. Coll., 1946; assoc. prof. math. Marshall U., 1946-47; research physicist Naval Research Lab., Washington, 1947-48; asst. prof., chmn. physics dept. Mary Washington Coll., 1948-68; assoc. prof., chmn., 1968-69; supr. statis. analysis sect. Am. Viscose div. FMC Corp., 1950-67; pres. Burns Enterprises Inc., Fredericksburg, Va., 1958—; mathematician Naval Surface Weapons Ctr., 1967-81; staff mathematician Unisys Corp., 1982-87; cons. FMC Corp., 1984-86. Author: A Story of My Life, 1988reviewer Am. Jour. Pysics; contbr. articles to profl. jours.; patentee in thermometers, conductivity testers and star finders. Served with AUS, 1945-46. Mem. Phys. Soc., AAUP, Am. Assn. Physics Tchrs. Home: 600 Virginia Ave Fredericksburg VA 22401-3447

BURNS, JOSEPH CHARLES, plant physiologist and educator; b. Iowa City, Iowa, Feb. 16, 1937; s. Lawrence E. and Dora G. (Schroder) B.; m. Marijane L. Connell, Nov. 17, 1956; children: Joan T., Dann M., Patricia L., Leah M., Ann K., Shawn P. BS in Agronomy, Iowa State U., 1960, MS in Crop Prodn., 1963; PhD in Plant Physiology/Animal Nutrition, Purdue U., 1966. Dist. sales mgr. Bow-Key Feed Co., Des Moines, 1961; rsch. asst. Iowa State U., Ames, 1961-63, Purdue U., West Lafayette, Ind., 1963-64; rsch. assoc. Purdue U., West Lafayette, 1964-66; asst. prof. forage physiology Tex. A&M U., College Station, 1966; plant physiologist USDA-Agrl. Rsch. Svc., Raleigh, N.C., 1967—; asst. prof. crop sci. and animal sci. N.C. State U., Raleigh, 1967-71, assoc. prof., 1971-76, prof., 1976—. Contbr. articles to profl. jours. With U.S. Army, 1954-56. Fellow Am. Soc. Agronomy, Crop Sci. Soc. Am.; mem. Am. Forage and Grass Land Coun. (Merit Cert. 1984), Sigma Xi, Gamma Sigma Delta. Office: USDA-ARS Box 7620 1119 Williams Hall Raleigh NC 27695

BURNS, LAURA ELIZABETH, editor; b. Houston, Feb. 21, 1942; d. Bruce and Evelyn Virginia (Sims) McNeil; m. Frederick Grant Burns, Aug. 31, 1963 (div.); children: Bruce Frederick Burns, Edward McNeil Burns; m. John Seveir Koloen, May 31, 1990. B of Journalism, U. Tex., 1963. Editor of pubs. Tex. Sch. for the Deaf, Austin, 1964-66; proofreader U. Tex. Press, Austin, 1966-67; asst. editor Applied Mechanics Revs., San Antonio, 1967-68; freelance writer, 1975-80; copy editor Midland (Tex.) Reporter-Telegram, 1979; info. specialist Tex. Commn. on Alcoholism, Austin, 1979-85; editor MICROpendium Mag., Round Rock, Tex., 1984—, Austin Health Fitness Mag., 1988-93; bd. dirs. Burns-Koloen Communications, Round Rock, v.p., 1985—; treas. DDJ&L Pub., Austin, sec., 1990-91. Contbr. articles to profl. jours. Sec. Career Women's Assn. of Round Rock, 1989; Round Rock Parent Tchr. Student Assn. Mem. Round Rock Talented and Gifted Assn. (bd. dirs. 1989-93), Chisholm Trail Midday Sertoma Club (bd. dirs.), Round Rock Toastmasters (cert.; v.p. comms.). Methodist. Office: Burns Koloen Communications PO Box 1343 Round Rock TX 78680-1343

BURNS, LESLIE KAYE, documentary video producer and director; b. Columbus, Miss., Sept. 21, 1953; d. Fayette Charles Jr. and Mary Theo (Wright) B. BFA in Printmaking/Advt. Art cum laude, Miss. U. for Women, 1975; MFA in Photography/Printmaking, U. Ala., 1978. Multi-image producer, photographer Pitluk Group Advt. Agy., San Antonio, 1981-87; dir. media prodn. Inst. Texan Cultures U. Tex., San Antonio, 1987—. Producer, dir., writer/co-writer numerous documentaries and ednl. videos including From the Ground Up: Theirs to Tell, Ours to Share, 1989, Panna Maria; The Heart of Polish Texans, 1990 (San Antonio Conservation Soc. citation), Circle of Life: The Alabama-Coushattas, 1991 (San Antonio Conservation Assn. citation, 41st Ann. Columbus Internat. Film and Video Festival honoree), Tex. Folklife Festival 1991-95 :30 Pub. Svc. Announcement (1st Pl. Internat. Festivals Assn. Media Competition 1991, Mktg. award Tex. Festivals Assn. 1991, 92), Train Your Brain: A Science, Engineering, and Mathematics Video, 1991, "I Remember...": The Impact of World War II on Children in Texas, 1991, The Day of the Dead, 1991 (San Antonio Conservation Soc. citation 1992, 41st Ann. Columbus Internat. Film and Video Festival honoree, Am. Assn. Mus. Muse award 3rd place cultural studies divsn. 1993), Big City Trail: The Urban Indians of Texas, 1992 (42d Annual Columbus Internat. Film and Video Festival honoree), Texas Children's Festival Promotional Video, 1992, People of the Sun: The Tiguas of Ysleta, 1992 (Soc. Visual Anthropology Film and Video Festival honoree 1993, 42d Annual Columbus Internat. Film and Video Festival honoree), Tejanos: Quiènes somos?, 1993, Noki Pematiedeni (To Have a New Life), 1993, Scientists Are Everywhere!, 1994, Tex. Folklife Festival Promotional Video, 1995, Tex. Folklife Festival 1995 Pub. Svc. Announcement (1st place Pinnacle award Internat. Festivals and Events Assn. 1995), Workin' From Can't to Can't: African-American Cowboys in Texas, 1995 (Am. Assn. Mus. Muse award 2d place cultural studies divsn. 1996, Women in Comms., Inc. San Antonio profl. chpt. award of excellence TV documentary program, 1996, 44th Ann. Columbus Internat. Film and Video Festival Bronze plaque), American Indians in Texas Today, an Interactive Multimedia Exhibit, 1996 (Multimedia Prodr. mag. Top 100 of 1996). Mem. Am. Assn. Museums. Office: U Tex Inst Texan Cultures 801 S Bowie St San Antonio TX 78205-3209

BURNS, MARION G., management consultant, retired council executive; b. Tonawanda, N.Y., July 22, 1924; d. Herbert E. and Gertrude V. (Bristow) B. BA, Bethany Coll., W. Va., 1945; MS, Sch. Applied Social Sci. Western Res. U., 1948. Case worker family welfare dept. Salvation Army, Buffalo, 1945-46; dist. dir., functional dir. tng. and camping Akron (Ohio) Area Girl Scout Coun., 1948-53; exec. dir. Girl Scouts DuPage County Coun., Glen Ellyn, Ill., 1953-67, Seal of Ohio Girl Scout Coun., Columbus, 1967-71; mgmt. cons. Region V Girl Scouts U.S., Shawnee Mission, Kans., 1972-79; assoc. dir. ednl. svcs. Girl Scouts U.S., N.Y.C., 1979-82; interim exec. dir. Girl Scouts U.S., Tex. Wash., Ill., N.Y., 1983-87; exec. dir. Lake Erie Girl Scout Coun., Cleve., 1987-90; vol. mgmt. cons. Oklahoma City, 1991—. Mem. exec. com. coun. agy. execs. United Way Svcs., Cleve., 1989-90; mem. World Found. for Girl Guides and Girl Scouts, N.Y.C.; mem. Friends of Sangam Com., 1992—; life mem. Girl Scouts U.S.A; pres.'s assoc. Bethany Coll., 1995-96. Mem. NASW (cert. appreciation TEX 1984), Acad. Cert. Social Workers, Assn. Girl Scout Profl. Workers (pres. 1961-63, 64-66, v.p. 1957-60, Hall of Fame 1987), Zeta Tau Alpha (Theta chpt. Bethany Coll. Disting. Alumni Achievement award for youth svcs. Mem. Christian Ch. Home: 3021 Willow Brook Rd Oklahoma City OK 73120-5724

BURNS, MARTHA A., association management company executive; b. Dover, N.J., May 3, 1942; d. William Edwin and Phyllis M. (Coates) B. BS, U. Bridgeport, 1964; MEd, Penn State U., 1967, EdD, 1971. Sr. resident Penn State U., University Pk., Pa., 1964-65; asst. coord. Penn State U., University Pk., 1965-66, asst. dean, coord., 1966-68; rsch. asst. Ctr. for Study of Higher Edn., University Pk., 1968-71; dir. One World Project, Washington, 1971-72; dir. edn. found. programs AAUW, Washington, 1972-76; prof. George Washington U., Washington, 1976-91; pres. Integrated Options, Inc., Alexandria, Va., 1984—; adv. com. U.S. Dept. Edn., Protection Sexual Harassment in Higher Edn., 1977-79; jury chairperson Coun. for Advancement & Support of Edn., Washington, 1980-82. Co-author: (monograph) Student Activism in American Higher Education, 1970, Handbook for Human Service Programs, 1972; author: (monograph) New Careers in Human Service, 1971; contbr. articles to profl. jours. Recipient Excellence in Edn. award Penn State U., 1990, Rsch. grant George Washington U.,1977. Mem. Am. Assn. for Higher Edn., Am. Coll. Personnel Assn., Nat. Assn. Student Personnel Adminstr. Methodist. Office: Integrated Options Inc PO Box 10280 Alexandria VA 22310-0280

BURNS, MITCHEL ANTHONY, transportation services company executive; b. Las Vegas, Nev., Nov. 1, 1942; s. Mitchel and Zella (Pulsipher) B.; m. Joyce Jordan, Nov. 14, 1962; children: Jill, Mitchel, Shauna. BS in Bus. Mgmt, Brigham Young U., 1964; MBA in Fin., U. Calif., Berkeley, 1965; hon. doctorate, Fla. Internat. U., 1989. With Mobil Oil Corp., N.Y.C., 1965-74, controller, 1970-72, cost-of-living coordinator, 1973, fin. analysis mgr., 1973-74; with Ryder System, Inc., Miami, Fla., 1974—, exec. v.p., chief fin. officer, 1978-79, pres., chief ops. officer, 1979-83, pres., chief exec. officer, 1983-85, chmn., pres., chief exec. officer, 1985—, also bd. dirs.; exec. v.p., CFO, pres. Ryder Truck Rental, Inc., 1980-81; bd. dirs. J.C. Penney Co., Inc., Pfizer Inc., The Chase Manhattan Corp., The Chase Manhattan Bank, N.A.; mem. nat. adv. coun. sch. mgmt. Brigham Young U., 1981—. mem. bd. visitors Grad. Sch. Bus. Adminstrn., U. N.C., Chapel Hill, 1988-93; mem. bd. overseers Wharton Sch., 1989-94; assoc. trustee U. Pa., 1989-94; bd. dirs., trustee United Way Dade County, Fla., 1981—, chmn., 1991-93, Dade County campaign, 1988, bd. govs., 1989-92, chmn. S.E. region United Way of Am., 1989-92; trustee Nat. Urban League, 1984-94, chmn., 1987-89, vice chmn., 1989-94, hon. trustee, 1994—. Named Marketer of Yr. Acad. Mktg. Sci., 1983, Americanism award Anti-Defamation League, 1984, Bus. Leader of Yr. The Miami News, 1985, Ricks Coll. Bus. Leader of the Century, 1989, Fin. World CEO of Decade in Transp., Freight & Leasing, 1989, CEO of Yr., 1984, 85, 87, Bus. Leadership Hall of Fame, 1987; recipient Boneh Yisroel award Greater Miami Jewish Fedn., 1989, Silver medallion award Nat. Conf. Christians & Jews, 1988, Community Svc. award Advt. Fedn. Gt. Miami, 1987, Joseph Wharton Bus. Statesman award Wharton Sch. Club, 1987, Jesse Knight Indsl. Citizenship award Brigham Young U., 1988, Robert W. Laidlaw Humanitarian award Epilepsy Found. South Fla., 1989, Good Scout award Boy Scouts Am., 1990., Sand in my Shoes award Greater Miami C. of C., 1991, Equal Opportunity award Nat. Urban League, 1992, Humanitarian of Yr. award ARC, 1993. Mem. Bus. Coun., Bus. Roundtable (policy com.), Bus.-Higher Edn. Forum. Office: Ryder System Inc 3600 NW 82nd Ave Miami FL 33166-6623

BURNS, PAT ACKERMAN GONIA, information systems specialist, software engineer; b. Birmingham, Ala., July 16, 1938; d. Richard Lee and Hattie Eugenia (Bragg) Ackerman; m. Robert Edward Gonia, June 4, 1957 (div. Jan. 1973); children: Deborah Hayes, Junita Grantham, Ronald Gonia; m. James Clayton Burns, June 23, 1984 (dec. Dec. 1989). BS in Math., U. Ala., 1970, postgrad., 1971-77. Cert. secondary tchr., Ala. Missionary United Meth. Bd. of Missions, Sumatra, Indonesia, 1961-64; homebound tchr. Huntsville (Ala.) City Schs., 1970-75; mem. tech. staff Gen. Rsch. Corp., Huntsville, 1975-79; rsch. scientist Nichols Rsch. Corp., Huntsville, 1979-84, mgr. personnel div., 1984-87, mgmt. info. systems dept. head, 1987-90, dir. info. systems div., 1990-95; program mgr. MIS and tech. MIS U.S. Army Space and Strategic Defense Systems, 1990-93; mem. adv. com. Drake Tech. Sch., Huntsville, 1988-94; program mgr. USASDC MIS//TMIS, 1990-94. Mem. PTA, Huntsville, 1994, Ch. Women United, Huntsville, Cmty. Chorus, Huntsville. Mem. IEEE, NAFE, Data Processing Mgmt. Assn., Assn. Pers. Adminstrs., Am. Computer Soc., Huntsville C. of C. (spkr. 1986-95). Democrat. Methodist. Office: Nichols Rsch Corp 4040 Memorial Pky SW Huntsville AL 35802-1396

BURNS, PAUL YODER, forester, educator; b. Tulsa, Okla., July 4, 1920; s. Paul Patchin and Mary Emily (Knowles) B.; m. Kathleen Iola Chase, Dec. 4, 1942; children: Virginia B. Belland, Margaret B. Feierabend, Nancy B. McNeill. BS, U. Tulsa, 1941; M in Forestry, Yale U., 1946, PhD, 1949. Asst., assoc. prof. U. Mo., Columbia, 1948-55; prof. forestry La. State U., Baton Rouge, 1955-86, prof. emeritus of forestry, 1986-96; dir. sch. forestry La. State U., Baton Rouge, 1955-76; commr. La. Forestry Commn., Baton Rouge, 1955-76. Editor: Forest Management in Plan & Practice, 1956, Southern Forest Soils, 1959; co-editor: Southern Forestry in Practice, 1977, Christmas Tree Production & Marketing, 1983. Pres. bd. dirs. La. State U. YMCA-YWCA, Baton Rouge, 1957-59; mem. La. Conf. Ch. Bd., Baton Rouge, 1967-73; pres. La. Coun. Human Rels., Baton Rouge, 1987-89; chair bd. dirs. The FISH Good Samaritans, Baton Rouge, 1996. Recipient Disting. Alumnus award U. Tulsa, 1974, Humanitarian award Baton Rouge Coun. Human Rels., 1984, Peacemaking award, Bienville House Ctr. for Peace, Baton Rouge, 1991, Brotherhood award Baton Rouge chpt. NCCJ, 1995. Fellow Soc. Am. Foresters, La. Soc. Am. Foresters (chmn. 1990, Disting Svc. to Forestry 1989), Phi Kappa Phi, Sigma Xi, Xi Sigma, Pi. Presbyterian. Home: 2137 Cedardale Baton Rouge LA 70808 Office: Sch Forestry Wildlife and Fisheries La State Univ Baton Rouge LA 70803

BURNS, ROBERT, JR., architect, freelance writer, artist; b. Jackson, Miss., Jan. 29, 1936; s. Robert Sr. and Grace Hortense (Inmon) B. BS in Architecture, Ga. Inst. Tech., 1959, BArch, 1960. Registered architect, Miss. Architect Overstreet, Ware & Lewis, Jackson, 1961-70, Ware, Lewis & Eaton, Jackson, 1970-71, Jones & Haas, Jackson, 1971-74, Leon Burton & Assocs., Jackson, 1974-75, Glenn Albritton Designer, Jackson, 1975-83, Breland & Farmer, Jackson, 1983-84, The Plan House, Jackson, 1984-86; part-time tchr. art dept. Miss. Coll., 1987; architect Johnny Wynne & Assocs., Ltd., Jackson, 1995-96. Tenor soloist 1st Bapt. Ch., Jackson, 1967-68, 1st Christian Ch., Jackson, 1968-71, Covenant Presbyn. Ch., Jackson, 1971-74, Galloway Meml. United Meth. Ch., 1989-91, Northminster Bapt. Ch., Jackson, 1995—, St. Luke's United Meth. Ch., Jackson, 1991-94, song leader, 1991-94; mem. Friends of the Gallery, Mcpl. Art Gallery, Jackson, 1981-93; mem. rev. panel Arts Alliance of Miss., 1989. Sgt. USAR, 1961-67. Mem. Am. Hemerocallis Soc., Inc. Republican. Baptist. Home: 609 Broadway Ave Jackson MS 39216-3206

BURNS, SALLY ANN, medical association administrator; b. Findlay, Ohio, Dec. 13, 1959; d. Van Larson and Marian (Delia) B. Student, Findlay Coll., 1980-82, Bowling Green State U., 1982-83; AAS, Houston C.C., 1985. Lic. physical therapist asst., Tex. Intern in clin. studies various Hosps., Houston, 1984-85; patient care Spring Br. Meml. Hosp., Houston, 1985-86; pres. Burns Phys. Therapy Clinic, Inc., Houston, 1986—; pres., bd. dirs. Phys. Therapy Plus, Inc., Houston, 1988—; pres. FYI Med. Suppliers, Inc.,

1991—, Pain Stop Inc., 1994—; pres. FYI Med. Suppliers, Inc., 1991—, FYI Med., Inc., 1991, Pain Stop, Inc., 1994—; mem. adv. com. Houston C.C. Sys. Physical Therapist Asst. Program. Author: Physical Therapy for Multiple Sclerosis. Mem. adv. com. Houston C.C. Sys. Phys. Therapist Asst. Program. Mem. Inst. for Profl. Health Svc. Administrs. (charter mem.), Am. Judicature Soc., Am. Phys. Therapy Assn., Tex. Phys. Therapy Assn., Community Health Administrn. Home: 1914 Potomac Dr Houston TX 77057-2922 Office: Phys Therapy Plus Inc 3303 Audley St Houston TX 77098-1921

BURNS, SANDRA, lawyer, educator; b. Bryan, Tex., Aug. 9, 1949; d. Clyde W. and Bert (Rychlik) B.; 1 son, Scott. BS, U. Houston, 1970; MA, U. Tex.-Austin, 1972, PhD, 1975; JD, St. Mary's U., 1978. Bar: Tex. 1978; cert. tchr., adminstr., supr. instrn., Tex. Tchr. Austin (Tex.) Ind. Sch. Dist., 1970-71; prof. child devel./family life and home econs. edn. Coll. Nutrition, Textiles and Human Devel. Tex. Woman's U., Denton, 1974-75; instrnl. devel. asst. Office of Ednl. Resources div. instrnl. devel. U. Tex. Health Sci. San Antonio, 1976-77; legis. aide William T. Moore, Tex. Senate, Austin, fall, 1978, com. clk.-counsel, spring, 1979; legal cons. Colombotti & Assocs., Aberdeen, Scotland, 1980; corp. counsel 1st Internat. Oil and Gas, Inc., 1983; contracted atty. Humble Exploration Co., Inc., Dallas, 1984; assoc. Smith, Underwood, Dallas, 1986-88; pvt. practice, Dallas, 1988—; atty. contracted to Republic Energy Inc., Bryan, Tex., 1981-82, ARCO, Dallas, 1985; vis. lectr. Tex. A&M U., fall 1981, summer, 1981; lectr. home econ. Our Lady of the Lake Coll., San Antonio, fall, 1975. Mem. ABA, State Bar of Tex., Phi Delta Kappa. Contbr. articles on law and edn. to profl. jours. Office: 8300 Douglas Ave Ste 800 Dallas TX 75225-5826

BURNS, STEPHEN REDDING, golf course architect; b. Troy, Ohio, Nov. 6, 1958; s. John Vernon and Nancy (Caroline Natalie) (Grimm) B.; m. Laraine (Dorothy Laraine) Brazell, July 25, 1987. BS in Landscape Architecture, Ohio State U., 1981. Registered landscape architect, Fla., S.C. Golf course architect Charles F. Ankrom, Inc., Stuart, Fla., 1981, Fazio Golf Course Designers, Inc., Jupiter, Fla., 1981-88; owner, golf course architect Burns Golf Design, Fernandina Beach, Fla., 1988—; golf course designer Club de Golf, Malinalco, 1992, Hawks Nest Golf Club, 1993, Fox Meadow Golf and Country Club, 1994, Laura S. Walker State Park Golf Course, 1995. Mem. Am. Soc. Landscape Architects, Nat. Golf Found., Donald Ross Soc. Presbyterian. Home and Office: Burns Golf Design 5449 Marshview Ln Fernandina Beach FL 32034-5445

BURNS, THERESA LOUISE, children's books author and illustrator; b. Chgo., Jan. 14, 1961; m. Edward Maler, Sept. 16, 1995. BFA, Calif. Coll. Arts and Crafts, 1983. Designer The Idea Source, South Hampton, N.Y., The Metro Opera Guild N.Y.C., Buddy L Toys, N.Y.C., Anva Internat., San Francisco, The Albatross Restaurant, N.Y.C., East End Clothing Co., N.Y.C., The Game Room, N.Y.C., The Person Planet Gallery, N.J., The Ocean Beach Grill and Hotel, N.Y.C., The Crystal Shop, Soho, N.Y.C.; illustrated editls. Standard Oil, Boy Scouts Am., Solaris Hills Newspaper, The Shrine Circus, Hughs Catering, Soc. Children's Book Writers, Key West Mag.; owner, designer TS Tees. Author, illustrator: You're Not My Cat, 1989; illustrator: Frog Frolics, 1991, Little New Kangaroo, 1993, Travis and The Better Mousetrap, 1995, Carla's Diary, 1996; spot illustrator ednl. publs. Silver, Burdett & Ginn, 1994; exhbns. include one woman shows at Solaris Hill Design Studio, Key West, Kenny Goodmans Gallery, Fire Island, N.Y., The Crytal Shop, Stone House Gallery, Mtn. Home, Ark., The Sun Bank Internat. Ctr., Miami. Mem. Graphic Artist Guild, Soc. Children's Book Writers and Illustrators, South Fla. Book Group.

BURNS, THOMAS DAVID, small business owner; b. Winston-Salem, N.C., Apr. 22, 1926; s. Charles Harvey and Ruth (Graves) B.; m. Jean Whisnant, Aug. 9, 1947. Co-founder, pres. Sci. Hobbies, Inc., Charlotte, N.C., 1961-83, Sci. and Nature Distbrs., Inc., Matthews, N.C., 1983-89, Sci. Ednl. Products, Inc., Matthews, 1989—. Inventor in field; author, prod., photographer slide documentaries; photographer, designer poster; author, illustrator coloring and activity books. With USN, 1944-46, Pacific. Home and Office: PO Box 128 Matthews NC 28106

BURNSIDE, MADELEINE HILDING, museum director, educator; b. London, Oct. 18, 1948; came to U.S., 1970; d. George William Augustin Burnside and Signe Winifreda (Nyman) Smyth; m. William Joseph Lukan, May 18, 1973. BA, U. Warwick, Eng., 1970; PhD, U. Calif., Santa Cruz, 1976. Editorial assoc. Art News mag., N.Y.C., 1976-79, Arts mag., N.Y.C., 1979-80; performance critic Soho Weekly mag., N.Y.C., 1977-78; freelance curator Bronx Mus. Fine Arts, 1977-80; dir. Islip (N.Y.) Art Mus., 1980-91; assoc. prof. Dowling Coll., Oakdale, N.Y., 1985-91; exec. dir. Mel Fisher Maritime Heritage Soc., Key West, Fla., 1991—; assoc. prof. Union Inst., 1995—. Bd. dirs. People Take Action Against AIDS, Bellport, N.Y., 1988-90, Stopping AIDS Together, 1990—, Key West Bus. Guild, 1994—, Fla. Assn. Museums, 1995—. Harkness Found. fellow, 1970, Ford Found. fellow, 1973; NEA grantee, 1980. Mem. Media Alliance. Home: 536 White St Key West FL 33040 Office: Mel Fisher Maritime Heritage Soc 200 Greene St Key West FL 33040-6516

BURR, RICHARD M., congressman; b. Charlottesville, Va., Nov. 30, 1955; m. Brooke Burr; children: Tyler, William. BA in Comm., Wake Forest U., 1978. Nat. sales mgr. Carswell Distributing, 1978-94; state co-chmn. N.C. Taxpayers United, 1993-94; mem. 104th Congress from 5th N.C. dist., 1995—. Republican. Office: US House Reps 1431 Longworth HOB Washington DC 20515-3305

BURR, TIMOTHY FULLER, lawyer; b. New Bedford, Mass., Oct. 18, 1952; s. John Thayer and Joan (Ames) B.; AB, Harvard U., 1975; JD, U. Miami, 1979; m. Marguerite Conti, Feb. 28, 1981; children: Emily Ames, Lisa Conti, David Thayer. Bar: La. 1979, Tex. 1993, Fla. 1996, U.S. Supreme Ct., U.S. Cir. Ct., U.S. Dist. Ct.; mng. dir. firm Galloway, Johnson, Tompkins & Burr, New Orleans, 1987—, admiralty and litigation atty., 1979—. Past chmn. St. Tammary Parish Zoning Bd. Mem. La. Bar Assn., Tex. Bar Assn., Fla. Bar Assn., Maritime Law Assn. U.S., Tammany Yacht Club, Pensacola Yacht Club. Republican. Home: 208 Pine Tree Dr Gulf Breeze FL 32561 Office: Galloway Johnson Tompkins and Burr 4040 1 Shell Sq Ste 4040 New Orleans LA 70139 also: 55 Baybridge Gulf Breeze FL 32561

BURRELL, NANCY BRADBURY, retail executive; b. Evanston, Ill., June 12, 1948; d. David Hamlin III and Nancy Bradbury (Blunt) B.; m. Jeffrey John Kommuck, Nov. 27, 1987. BS magna cum laude, Boston U., 1970; MSLS, Case Western Res. U., Cleve., 1974; MPH, U. South Fla., 1987. Ordained minister Found. Ch. of the New Birth. Reference libr. Case Western Res. U., Cleve., 1974-78; libr. adult svcs. Manatee & Sarasota Counties, Fla., 1978-82; dir. libr. svcs. U. Sarasota, Fla., 1982-84, 92-93; reference libr. U. South Fla., 1986-88; mgr. Gen. Nutrition Ctr., 1993, owner, 1993—; pres. Ibid Inc., Sarasota, 1981—. Home: 6045 Marella Ct Sarasota FL 34243-2650

BURRELL, VICTOR GREGORY, JR., marine scientist; b. Wilmington, N.C., Sept. 12, 1925; s. Victor Gregory and Agnes Mildred (Townsend) B.; m. Katherine Stackley; Jan. 7, 1956; children: Cheri, Cathey, Charlene, Sarah. BS, Coll. Charleston, 1949; MA, Coll. William and Mary, 1968, PhD, 1972. Rsch. assoc. Va. Inst. Marine Sci., Gloucester Point, 1966-68, asst. marine scientist, 1968-70, assoc. marine scientist, 1970-72; assoc. marine scientist S.C. Marine Resources Rsch. Inst., Charleston, 1972-73, assoc. marine scientist, asst. dir., 1973-74, sr. marine scientist, dir., 1974-91, dir. emeritus, 1991—. Contbr. numerous articles to profl. jours. With USN, 1943-46, PTO. Mem. Nat. Shell Fisheries Assn. (pres. 1982-83, hon. life mem. 1992), Estuarine Rsch. Fedn. (sec. 1975-77), Gulf and Caribbean Fisheries Inst., Southeastern Estuarine Rsch. Soc. (pres. 1986-88, hon. mem. 1990). Episcopalian. Office: SC Marine Resources Rsch Inst PO Box 12559 Charleston SC 29422-2559

BURRIS, BETTY PRICE, banker; b. High Point, N.C., Oct. 22, 1942; d. Samuel and Eloise (Little) Walls; m. Ray T. Price, Jan. 3, 1963 (div. 1977); children: Melinda Ann Price Pinson, Teresa Gail Price; m. James C. Burris, Jr., Dec. 20, 1980. BSBA and Econs., High Point Coll., 1987; MS in Adult Edn., N.C. Agr. and Tech. State U., 1989; postgrad., U. N.C., Greensboro, Va. Tech. Sr. collections coord. Wachovia Bank of N.C. & Trust Co., N.A., Greensboro, N.C., 1973-92. Treas. Friends of High Point Theatre, 1979-96; High Point chair United Negro Coll. Fund campaign Bennett Coll., 1987-93; mem. Dem. Women of Guilford County; mem. adv. com. Project Blueprint United Way of Greater High Point; mem. capital bonds steering com. City of High Point; bd. dirs. Adams Meml. YWCA; advocate N.C. Equity Women's Agenda; mem. High Point Human Rels. Commn.; mem. adv. com. High Point Police Dept.; commr. High Point Housing Authority; founder Race Rels. Network Group.; mem. Selective Svc. Bd. Mem. AAUW (treas. High Point br. 1987-93, pres. High Point br. 1994, chair legal advocacy fund, legal advocacy fund devel. com.), N.C. Adult Edn. Assn. Democrat. Methodist. Home: 1454 Finsbury Ln High Point NC 27260-4233

BURRIS, CRAVEN ALLEN, education educator; b. Wingate, N.C., Sept. 11, 1929; s. Craven Cullom and Virginia Neulin (Currie) B.; m. Jane Russell Burris, June 19, 1955; children: Christa Cullom, David Allen. AA, Wingate Coll., 1949; BS, Wake Forest U., 1951; BDiv, Southeastern Bapt. Sem., Wake Forest, N.C., 1958; MA, Duke U., 1959, PhD, 1964. Prof. history and govt. Gardner-Webb Coll., Boiling Springs, N.C., 1958-66; prof. history, govt. and interdisciplinary studies St. Andrews Presbyn. Coll., Laurinburg, N.C., 1966-69; v.p., dean of coll.; prof. history and politics Meredith Coll., Raleigh, N.C., 1969—, acting pres., 1971. Contbr. articles to profl. jours. Precinct ofcr. State Conv. del., N.C. Dem. Party, 1969, 71; pres., dir. Tammy Lynn Found./Retarded Children, Raleigh, 1980—. Lt. USNR, 1951-55, Italy. Recipient Disting. Alumni award Wingate Coll., 1983, Fulbright Study Trip, U.S. Govt., Pakistan, 1973. Mem. Civitan Internat. (v.p. bd. dirs. 1970—), Lions Club (editor 1965), Masons. Baptist. Home: 1322 Duplin Rd Raleigh NC 27607 Office: Meredith Coll 3800 Hillsborough St Raleigh NC 27607

BURRIS, FRANCES WHITE, personnel director; b. Cuero, Tex., Oct. 18, 1933; d. Marian Cecil and Dorothy Christine (Pruetz) White; m. Berlie Burris Jr, Mar. 8, 1958 (div. 1982); children: William Alan, Joel Maurice. BA, Mary Hardin Baylor Coll., Belton, Tex., 1955; M in Eng., Trinity U., San Antonio, 1959. Cert. tchr., Tex. Elem. tchr. East and Mt. Houston Independent Sch. Dist., 1956, Edgewood Ind. Sch. Dist., San Antonio, 1956-57, 58-59; tchr. Edna (Tex.) Ind. Sch. Dist., 1957-58; elem. tchr. Northside Ind. Sch. Dist., San Antonio, 1960-62, Southside Schs., San Antonio, 1962-63; mgr. Michael's Dept. Store, Houston, 1980-81; eligibility worker Tex. Dept. Human Resources, Houston, 1981—. Mem. Meridith Manor Civic Club, Houston, 1966-78, Settlers Valley Civic Club, Katy, Tex., 1979-81. Mem. Tex. State Employees Union (exec. bd. 1984—, del. gen. assembly 1984-96, lobbyist 1985—). Democrat. Baptist. Club: Bridge (Houston).

BURRIS, JOHNNY CLARK, law educator; b. Paris, Ky., May 21, 1953; s. John Curtis and Ada (Sargent) B.; m. Jane Wright, July 1975 (div. Sept. 1980); m. Cathy Jackson, Mar. 1981 (div. Feb. 1984); m. Nancy Nevius, Aug. 6, 1985; 1 child, Sarah Nevius. BA, U. Ky., 1975; JD, No. Ky. U., 1978; LLM, Columbia U., 1984. Bar: Ky. 1978, U.S. Ct. Appeals (6th cir.) 1978, Ohio 1979, U.S. Dist. Ct. (ea. dist.) Ky. 1979, U.S. Ct. Appeals (11th cir.) 1987. Law clk. to presiding justice Ky. Supreme Ct., Frankfort, 1978-79; asst. atty. Commonwealth Atty. Kenton County, Covington, Ky., 1979; asst. dean Nova Southeastern U. Shepard Broad Law Ctr., Ft. Lauderdale, Fla., 1979-84; asst. prof. law Nova U. Ctr. Study of Law, Ft. Lauderdale, Fla., 1981-87, assoc. prof. law, 1987-89, prof. law, 1989—. Mem. No. Ky. Law Rev., 1976-78. Mem. ABA, Ky. Bar Assn., Fed. Bar Assn., Fla. Bar Assn. (affiliate), Omicron Delta Kappa. Office: Nova Southeastern U Shepard Broad Law Ctr 3305 Coll Ave Fort Lauderdale FL 33314-7721

BURRIS, KENNETH WAYNE, biologist, educator; b. Salisbury, N.C., Nov. 22, 1941; s. Ira J.B. and Dorothy Virginia (Rodgers) B.; m. Peggy Rogister Whitt, June 7, 1964; children: Kenneth Wayne Jr., Susan M. BS, High Point U., 1964; MA, East Carolina U., 1968; postgrad., N.C. State U., 1973-75. Specialist environ. health Moore County Health Dept., Carthage, N.C., 1964-65; instr. biology Mitchell Coll., Statesville, N.C., 1967-68; assoc. prof. biology Louisburg (N.C.) Coll., 1968-75; prof. biology Sandhills C.C., Pinehurst, N.C., 1975—. Author: Laboratory Exercises for Microbiology, 1985; co-author: Diseases of Fish, 1974; contbr. articles to profl. jours. Grantee NSF, 1969, 71. Mem. AAUP, Human Anatomy and Physiology Soc., Phi Theta Kappa (Horizon award 1995, advisor 1991—). Democrat. Home: 530 North Seven Lakes NC 27376 Office: Sandhills Cmty Coll 2200 Airport Rd Pinehurst NC 28374

BURROUGHS, JACK EUGENE, dentist, management consultant; b. Harlingen, Tex., Nov. 24, 1946; s. Jack Eugene and Virginia (Ayoub) B.; children by previous marriage—Brian A., Brad A.; m. Laura; children: Kyle, Tiffany. BS, U. Tex. Arlington, 1969, DDS, U. Tex. Dental Br. Houston, 1973. Practice dentistry, Houston, 1973—; seminar leader, cons. Quest, Dallas, 1983—. Contbr. articles to profl. jours. Recipient Speaker awards Aspen Med.-Dental Conf., 1982, 83, 84, N.Am. Med.-Dental Assn., 1984, Am. Internat. Seminars, 1984. Fellow Acad. Gen. Dentistry; mem. ADA, Tex. Dental Assn., Houston Dist. Dental Soc., Houston Northwest C. of C. (bd. dirs.). Republican. Mem. Christian Ch. Clubs: Exchange (bd. dirs.), Toastmasters (officer). Office: 17200 Red Oak Dr Houston TX 77090-2642

BURROWS, EMILY ANN, neonatal nurse; b. Spokane, Wash., June 30, 1960; d. James Aaron and Agnes Cecilia (Wilke) McKenzie; m. Carl Douglas Burrows, Feb. 7, 1981; children: Cassandra Lynn, Timothy Carl. ADN, Amarillo Coll., 1982. RN, Tex.; cert. neonatal cardiac life support. Staff nurse Upjohn Co., Amarillo, Tex., 1986-87, High Plains Bapt. Hosp., Amarillo, 1987-88; nurse infant care specialist Tex. Tech U Health Sci. Ctr., Amarillo, 1988-90; staff nurse N.W. Tex. Hosp., Amarillo, 1982—. Spkr. babies and you March of Dimes, 1994. Mem. Nat. Assn. Neonatal Nurses, Tex. Nurse Assn. Roman Catholic. Home: 2009 S Roberts St Amarillo TX 79103-2106

BURROWS, VIRGINIA MOORE, paralegal; b. Morehead City, N.C., Dec. 5, 1956; d. John Mercer Sr. and Virginia Duncan (Chadwick) Moore; m. Perry King Burrows, Mar. 5, 1988. BS in Bus. Edn., East Carolina U., 1978, MEd, 1980; AAS in Paralegal Tech., Pitt Community Coll., 1992. Cert. legal asst. 1993, specialist in real estate 1995. Legal sec. Richard L. Stanley, Beaufort, N.C., 1981; legal sec. Dennis M. Marquardt, Morehead City, 1981-83, paralegal, 1983-85; paralegal Bennett, McConkey, Thompson, Marquardt & Wallace, P.A., Morehead City, 1985-88; legal asst. Ward & Smith, P.A., Greenville, N.C., 1988-93; paralegal Hutson Hughes & Powell, P.A., Durham, 1993—. Mem. Nat. Assn. Legal Assts., N.C. Paralegal Assn. (treas. 1996), Profl. Legal Assts. Inc., Durham-Orange Paralegal Assn. (1st v.p. 1994, treas. 1995). Democrat. Methodist. Office: Hutson Hughes & Powell PA PO Drawer 2252-A Durham NC 27702

BURRUSS, TERRY GENE, architect; b. Little Rock, Dec. 30, 1950; s. Alvin Eugene and Fern (Pelton) B.; m. Merilyn Kloss, Dec. 20, 1981; children: Mamie Christine, Gracie Aline. BArch, BA, U. Ark., 1973. Registered architect, Ark. Intern architect firm Robinson and Wassell, Inc., Little Rock, 1973-75; practice architecture Evo-Tech Prodn., Little Rock, and I.D.E.A., Eureka Springs, Ark., 1976-78; architect Store Planning Assos., San Francisco, 1978; asso. Design 3, Architects, Little Rock, Ark., 1979; v.p., div. mgr. Mehlburger, Tanner, Renshaw and Assocs., Little Rock, 1980-84; v.p. Mehlburger, Tanner, Robinson & Assocs., 1984-87; pres. Terry Burruss, Architects, 1987—; instr. Hatha Yoga Community Edn. Program, 1976-77, St. Francis House, Little Rock, 1978, Parapsychology Ctr., 1978-79. Mem. Ark. Environ. Barriers Coun.; chmn. ministerial rels. Unity Ch. of Little Rock, 1986-87, pres. bd. dirs., 1987; pres. Montessori Children's Ctr. Parent Tchrs. Orgn., 1986-87; pres. Unity Ch., 1987, Cen. High Neighborhood Assn., 1989-90; mem. adv. com. Gov's. Mansion Area, 1989—. Mem. AIA (state chmn. 1981), Nat. Trust Historic Preservation, Ark. Solar Coalition, U. Ark. Alumni Assn., Little Rock Jaycees (dir. 1981-83, sec. 1982-83), chmn. TV auction 1982). Alpha Phi Omega, Pi Kappa Alpha. Author: Flow Gently Sweet Alpha, 1972, Inflatables, An Alternative to the Deflated Classroom, 1973, Accessibility Guidelines for Meeting and Lodging Facilities, 1981, "Housing for the Developmental Disabled", 1986. Home: 12 Tallyho Ln Little Rock AR 72227-2416 Office: 1202 Main St Ste 230 Little Rock AR 72202-5057

BURSON, BETSY LEE, librarian; b. Olney, Tex., Dec. 16, 1942; d. James Hollis and Lora Elizabeth (Talbott) B.; m. Winston Rabb Henderson, June 26, 1976. BS in Edn., Kans. State Tchrs. Coll., 1964; MLS, Tex. Woman's U., 1967, PhD in Libr. Info. Studies, 1987. With Phoenix Pub. Libr., 1967-74; libr. dir. Glendale (Ariz.) Pub. Libr., 1974-75; project archivist Phoenix History Project, 1975-77; adj. faculty U. Ariz., Tucson, 1979, Tex. Woman's U., Denton, 1980; libr. cons. La. State Libr., Baton Rouge, 1982-85; libr. dir. El Paso (Tex.) Pub. Libr., 1987-90, Arlington (Tex.) Pub. Libr., 1990—. Named Librarian of the Yr. Tex. Library Assn., 1995. Office: Arlington Pub Libr 101 E Abram St Arlington TX 76010-1102

BURSON, BYRON LYNN, geneticist; b. Hobart, Okla., Feb. 24, 1940; s. Isaac D. and Annice P. (Hill) B.; m. Linda Sharon Conrad, July 2, 1961; children: Laura Ann Burson Koehler, Byron Lynn II. BS in Agronomy, Okla. State U., 1962; MS in Cytogenetics and Plant Breeding, Tex. A&M U., 1965, PhD in Cytogenetics and Plant Breeding, 1967. Grad. asst. dept. soil and crop scis. Tex. A&M U., College Sta., 1965-67; asst. prof. dept. agronomy Miss. State U., Miss. State, 1967-71, assoc. prof. dept. agronomy, 1971-75; rsch. geneticist grassland, soil and water rsch. lab. USDA-Agrl. Rsch. Svc., Temple, Tex., 1975-93; rsch. geneticist southern crops rsch. lab. USDA-Agrl. Rsch. Svc., College Sta., 1993—; mem. Nat. Forage and Turf Grass Crop Adv. Com., 1986—, chmn. subcom. warm-season grasses, 1986-91, chmn. com., 1991-95; advisor Miss. Agrl. and Forestry Experiment Sta. PIPD-Beef Com., 1974; chmn. Southern Pasture and Forage Breeders Group, 1974, program chmn., 1976; sec. Grass Breeders' Work Planning Conf., 1982-84, pres.-elect 1984-86, pres., 1986-88; mem. grad. faculty Tex. A&M U., 1981, 92; mem. grad. coms. Miss. State U., Tex. A&M U.; cons. in field. Contbr. articles to profl. jours. Nat. Def. Edn. Act fellow Tex. A&M U., 1962-65; Travel grantee Fulbright Commn., 1982. Fellow Am. Soc. Agronomy (state membership com. 1967-75), Crop Sci. Soc. Am. (preservation plant germplasm com. 1983-85, chmn. 1985, ad hoc com. crop common and sci. names 1986-87, assoc. editor crop sci. editorial bd. 1987-90); mem. Am. Genetic Assn., Genetics Soc. Can., Alpha Zeta, Gamma Sigma Delta, Phi Kappa Phi, Sigma Xi (com. constn. and by-laws 1970-71, exec. com. 1971-75, sec. 1973-74, Rsch. award 1974). Office: USDA Agrl Rsch Svc Dept Soil & Crop Scis Tex A&M U College Station TX 77843-2474

BURT, ALLEN DANIEL, artist; b. Owensboro, Ky., Aug. 17, 1930; s. Harold Allan and Catherine Eleanor (Coulter) B.; m. Anne Warren, May 31, 1935; 1 child, Barbara. Student, Kansas. State Coll., 1949, 50, Trinity U., 1955, 56, S.W. Tex. State U., 1965. Artist, 1949—; tchr. watercolor numerous workshops; painting instr. Hill Country Arts Found., Artists and Craftsmen Associated-Dallas, Brownsville Art League, Watercolor Art Soc. Ft. Worth, Midland Art Assn., Tex., So. Ariz. Watercolor Guild, Tucson, Ardmore Art Guild, Okla., Amarillo Art Assn., Tex., No. Ariz. Watercolor Soc., Sedona, Watercolor Soc. Ind., Indpls. Exhibited in group shows at Nat. Acad. Galleries, N.Y., Knickerbocker Artists, N.Y. (Argmari/Arches/Rives Paper award 1991, Gold Medal Honor award 1992), Hudson Valley Art Assn., White Plains, N.Y., Salmagundi Club, N.Y., Nat. Arts Club, N.Y., Audubon Artists, N.Y. (Alice Melrose award 1990, Winsor & Newton award 1993, Silver Medal Honor award 1994)), Rocky Mountain Nat. Watermedia, Golden, Colo.(The Colorist award 1995), La. Watercolor Soc., New Orleans, Watercolor West, Glendale, Calif. (Founders award 1991, Juror's award 1994), Midwest Watercolor Soc., Green Bay, Wis. (Mcpl. Art League Chgo. award 1991), Nat. Watercolor Soc., Brea, Calif. (Jurors award, St. Cuthbert's Paper Mill award 1995), Am. Watercolor Soc., N.Y. (Clara Stroud Meml. award 1993), S.W. Watercolor Soc., Coppini Acad. Fine Arts, Tex. Watercolor Soc., La. Watercolor Soc., Nat. Acad. Design, others. Sgt. U.S. Army, 1951-54. Recipient Excellence award We. Fedn. Watercolor Socs., 1988, 90, 92, El Cajon Art Assn. award 12th Ann. San Diego Watercolor Soc. Award Exhbn., 1991, Jack Richeson award 18th Ann. Exhbn., 1995. Mem. Am. Watercolor Soc., Nat. Watercolor Soc., Allied Artists Am. (Gold Medal Honor award 78th Ann. Exhbn. 1991, Jane Peterson Meml. award 80th Ann. Exhbn. 1994, David Wu and Elsie Vect-Key award 82d Ann. Exhbn. 1996), Audubon Artists, Knickerbocker Artists, SW Watercolor Soc. (tchr.). Home and Office: 2110 West Ln # B Kerrville TX 78028-3838

BURT, ROBERT HAMPTON, composer, music publisher; b. Biloxi, Miss., Nov. 15, 1940; s. William Thomas Burt, Jr. and Mary Alice (White) Burt-Bedell. BMus, Sam Houston U., 1963. Music tchr. Houston Ind. Sch. Dist., 1964-66; performer Houston Harpsichord Soc., pres. 1988-89; owner Burt's of Houston, 1993. Author: Stepping Stones Book One, 1996, Stepping Stones Book Two, 1996; composer sheet solos. Ssgt. USAF Res., 1964-73. Charles Wakefield Cadman Grad. fellow U. Redlands, Calif., 1963-64; recipient Am. Spirit Honor medal USAF. Home and Office: 2604 Ridgewood Houston TX 77006

BURT, WALLACE JOSEPH, JR., insurance company executive; b. Burlington, Iowa, Apr. 1, 1924; s. Wallace Joseph and Lela (Catlow) B.; m. Alice Olmsted, June 22, 1946; children: Lockwood, David, Virginia. student Iowa State Coll., 1942, U. Wis., 1945. V.p., dir. 1st Ins. Fin. Co., Des Moines, 1946-50, Northeastern Ins. Co., Hartford, Conn., 1950-59; pres., owner Hail Reinsurance Mgmt., Inc., Ormond Beach, Fla., 1960-89; chmn. Burt & Scheld, Inc., Ormond Beach, 1961-89; chmn. U.S. br. Hamburg Internat. Reins. Co., 1976-81; chmn. First N.Y. Syndicate Corp., 1979-89, W.J. Burt Mgmt., Inc., N.Y.C., 1979-89; pres. Ormond Reins. Co., 1976-92, Oceanside RE Group, Inc., 1989; dir., v.p. Barnett Bank, Ormond Beach; underwriting mem. Lloyd's of London; dir. N.Y. Ins. Exchange, 1983-84. Trustee, pres. Ormond Beach Meml. Hosp. Served to 1st lt. USAAF, World War II. Decorated D.F.C., Purple Heart, Air medal with 5 oak leaf clusters. Home: 222 Riverside Dr Ormond Beach FL 32176-6504 Office: 140 S Atlantic Ave Ormond Beach FL 32176-6689

BURTI, CHRISTOPHER LOUIS, lawyer; b. Muroc, Calif., Oct. 15, 1950; s. Louis Burti and Johanna Renate (Schmidt) Landa; m. Linda Carol Pipkin, Sept. 15, 1973; children: Christopher Louis Jr., Erika Pipkin. BSBA, East Carolina U., 1975; JD, U. N.C., 1979. Bar: N.C. 1979, U.S. Dist. Ct. (ea. dist.) N.C. 1983. Assoc. Lewis, Lewis & Lewis, Farmville, N.C., 1979-82; ptnr. Lewis & Burti, Farmville, 1982-94; regional v.p., legal counsel Statewide Title, Inc., Greenville, N.C., 1994—; atty. Town of Farmville, N.C., 1982-94, Town of Falkland, 1989—. Bd. dirs. Farmville Child Devel. Ctr., 1983-84, Farmville Cmty. Arts Coun., 1983-84, Farmville Charitable Svcs., 1987-89; cubmaster Farmville Troop 25 Boy Scouts Am. With U.S. Army, 1970-72. Mem. N.C. Bar Assn., N.C. Mcpl. Attys. Assn. (bd. dirs. 1988-89, chmn. cable communications com. 1991), Pitt County Bar Assn., Nat. Inst. Mcpl. Law Officers (mcpl. utilities com.), Phi Kappa Phi, Beta Gamma Sigma, Phi Sigma Pi, Farmville C. of C. (bd. dirs. 1982-83). Democrat. Episcopalian. Club: Farmville Country. Lodge: Masons. Office: Statewide Title Inc 150 E Arlington Blvd Greenville NC 27858-5019

BURTOFT, JOHN NELSON, JR., cardiovascular physician assistant; b. Pitts., Jan. 29, 1944; s. John Nelson Sr. and Elizabeth Louise (Lyons) B.; m. Jo Ann Stewart, Aug. 16, 1963 (div. Apr. 1966); 1 child, John Nelson III; m. Artie Ann Spilman, Sept. 19, 1966 (div. Dec. 1969); 1 child, Bonnie Beth; m. Sandra Ellen Bishop, Jan. 28, 1971; 1 child, Tracy Lynne. Grad., Sch. Health Care Sci., Sheppard AFB, 1975; grad. clin. preceptorship, Naval Hosp., 1976; BS, U. Nebr., Omaha, 1977. Physician asst. USN, 1961-80; retired chief warrant officer, 1980; surg. intern, resident Montefiore Hosp., Bronx, N.Y., 1980-82; cardiovascular physician asst. Cen. Ill. Cardiac Surgery Assocs., Peoria, Ill., 1982-83, Sanger Clinic, Charlotte, N.C., 1983-89, Dr. R. Carlton, Hickory, N.C., 1989-92, Mid-Atlantic Cardiothoracic Surgeons, Ltd., Norfolk, Va., 1992-93, C.V.T. Surgery, Baton Rouge, La., 1993—. Fellow Am. Acad. Physician Assts., Assn. Physician Assts. in Cardiovascular Surgery, L.A. Acad. Physician Assts. Office: 7777 Hennessy Blvd Ste 108 Baton Rouge LA 70808-4363

BURTON, BARBARA ABLE, psychotherapist; b. Columbia, S.C.; d. Eugene Walter Able and Mary Louise (Chadwick) Cantelou; 1 child, Stacia Louise. BA in Psychology, Ga. State U.; MSW, U. Ala., 1970. Diplomate Am. Bd. Examiners in Clin. Social Work, Internat. Acad. Behavioral Medicine, Counseling and Psychotherapy; cert. Am. Acad. Cert. Social Workers, NASW, diplomate clin. social work. Assoc. exec. dir. Positive Maturity, Inc., Birmingham, Ala., 1970-72; comm. org. planner Community Svc. Council, INc., Birmingham, Ala., 1972-75; adj. faculty U. Ala., Tuscaloosa, Ala., 1975-77; dir. Ensley Outpatient Drug Abuse Clinic, Birmingham, Ala., 1975-77, Sch. of Social Work, Miles Coll., Birmingham, Ala., 1977-78; prog. mgr. and clin. cons. Goodwill Industries of Ala.,

Birmingham, Ala., 1977-81; pvt. practice New Orleans, 1983--; cons. Omega Internat. Inst., New Orleans, 1988--. Author: Love Me, Love Me Not, and Other Matters That Matter, 1990. Past chmn. Policy and Program Com. Birmingham Urban League; Ala. Adv. Com. on Social Svcs.; Ala. Com. for the Dev. of Higher Ed.; Ala. Conf. of Social Work. NIMH fellow Inst. on Human Sexuality, U. Hawaii, 1976. Mem. Am. Assn. Sex Educators, Counselors and Therapists, Nat. Assn. Social Workers, Pvt. Practitioners Unit of New Orleans, Acad. Cert. Social Workers, Internat. Platform Com., Psi Chi. Office: 1631 Constantinople St New Orleans LA 70115-4707

BURTON, CAROL NYSTROM, newborn nursery nurse; b. Columbus, Ohio, Apr. 11, 1942; d. Roland Maynard and Sara Frances (Pace) Nystrom; m. John A. Burton, Nov. 13, 1976 (dec. Feb. 1996); 1 child, Daniel Roland. ADN, Amarillo Coll., 1971; BSN, West Tex. State U., 1976. RN, Tex.; cert. instr. adult and infant CPR; cert. childbirth educator. Orthoneurol. nursing High Plains Bapt. Hosp., Amarillo, Tex., 1970-76, relief supr., 1985—, nurse II newborn nursery, 1976—; instr. in field. Mem. Orthopedic Nurses Assn. (nat. pres. 1975-76, nat. pres.-elect 1974-75, pres. local chpt. 1973-74).

BURTON, CHARLES, elementary school principal; b. Tulsa, Oct. 30, 1942; s. Charles and Flossie (Rogers) B.; m. Barbara Ann Burton; 1 child, Charles III. BS in Edn., Langston (Okla.) U., 1965; MEd, U. Ctrl. Okla., 1969. Cert. tchr., elem. prin., Okla. Tchr. Harmony Elem. Sch., Oklahoma City, West Nichols Hills Elem. Sch., Oklahoma City; asst. prin. Polk Elem. Sch., Oklahoma City; prin. Martin Luther King Elem. Sch., Oklahoma City, Oakridge Elem. Sch., Oklahoma City; asst. prin. Classen 5th Elem. Sch., Oklahoma City, Eugene Field Elem. Sch., Oklahoma City; prin. Gatewood Elem. Sch., Oklahoma City. Commr. Game and Fish, Oklahoma City; mem. Leadership Oklahoma City; mem. Profl. Responsibility Tribunal, State of Okla. Bar Assn. Recipient Cert. of Appreciation, Thrive Ctr., 1990, Mayor of Oklahoma City, 1994. Mem. Am. Fedn. Sch. Adminstrs., Nat. Elem. Prins. Assn., Am. Fedn. Musicians, Kappa Alpha Psi. Democrat. Roman Catholic. Home: 1144 NE 59th St Oklahoma City OK 73111

BURTON, JOE ELLA, elementary educator, dance educator; b. Georgetown, S.C., Apr. 8, 1934; d. Joseph Alfred and Mary Ellen (Gordon) Brown; m. Riley James Burton, Nov. 23, 1960; children: Angelique Cornelia, Francell Olevia. BS, Grambling Coll., 1954; MA, U. Mich., 1960; postgrad., N.E. La. U., 1972. Cert. elem. tchr., spl. edn. tchr., Ga., La. Tchr., dance instr. J.S. Clark Elem. Sch., Monroe, La., 1954-82, Henry Grady H.S., Atlanta, 1982-91; tchr. Minnie Ruffin Elem. Sch., Monroe, 1991-92; tchr., dance instr. Little Flower Acad., Monroe, 1992—; supr. student tchrs. Grambling (La.) Coll., 1959-80, instr., summer 1987; Headstart instr. Little Flower Ctr., Monroe, summer 1965, Martin Temple Ctr., Monroe, summer 1966, Antioch Bapt. Ctr., Monroe, summer 1967; rep. LSWB, Inc., Kenner, Ala., 1996—; coord. demonstrations for area convs. La. Edn. Assn., 1958. Composer song for Headstart; co-author: Colntributors of Ouachita Parish (A History of Blacks to Commemorate the Bicentennial of the U.S.A.), 1976, (ednl. game) JEB Method of Teaching Number Concepts to the Blind, 1995. Youth orgn. sponsor Martin Temple C.M.E. Ch., Monroe, 1960; coord. debutante tea activities Les Martinique Social Club, Monroe, 1967; bd. dirs., asst. leader Girl Scouts U.S., Monroe, 1956; instr. dance workshops N.E. La. U., 1979-82; coord. beauty pageant Monroe Newsleader, 1969. Recipient numerous certs., trophies, plaques for choreography and speaking, 1954—. Mem. Delta Sigma Theta (pres. local chpt. 1956-57). Home: 1709 Dilling St Monroe LA 71202

BURTON, JOHN JACOB, retired real estate company executive appraiser; b. N.Y.C., Dec. 31, 1912; s. Fannie (Rosenfeld) Burton; m. Sylvia R. Carlin, Oct. 12, 1940 (dec. 1981); children: Frances Lee, Barbara, Spencer, Gerald K. BS in Physics with honors, L.I. U., 1935, DSc (hon.), 1987; MAI, Columbia U., 1937. Lic. real estate broker, Fla. With Manpower Commn. Sci. & Specialized Personnel, N.Y., N.J., 1942-46; owner, mgr. John J. Burton Real Estate, Mortgages & Appraisals, Boston, 1946-50, John J. Burton Gen. Real Estate & Appraisals, Hollywood, Fla., 1950-92; ptrn. Am. Title Corp.; ret., 1995; personal aide col. to gov. State of Mass., 1966-68; trustee Broward County Investment Trust, Dania, Fla.; co-founder Technion, Israel. A founder Jewish Chapel at U.S. Mil. Acad. West Point, N.Y.; mem. exec. com. Broward County Rep. Com., 1958-74. Recipient Presdl. Medals of Merit, 1985, 90, 93; John J. Burton Molecular Biology Lab., L.I. U. named in his honor (founder), 1987; Rep. Presdl. Legion of Merit, 1985, 94. Mem. AAAS, Internat. Orgn. Real Estate Appraisers (sr.), Nat. Assn. Real Estate Appraisers (cert.), Fla. Assn. Cert. Real Estate Appraisers, U.S. Navy League Commodore, Security and Intelligence Fund. (founder), Naval Intelligence Profls., Mil. Order of the World Wars (life mem.), Masons (32 degree), Shriners, B'nai B'rith. Jewish. Home: 3800 S Ocean Dr Hollywood FL 33019-2927

BURTON, JOHN LEE, SR., banker; b. Blaine, Ky., Mar. 30, 1927; s. H.G. and Gladys Marie (Gambill) B.; student Morehead State U., 1943-44; m. Guinola Hill Oct. 3, 1945; children: John Lee, Joseph Edward. Mcht., farmer, 1944-46; banker, 1946—. With Peoples Security Bank, Louisa, Ky., 1946—, pres., 1964—; pres., dir. Grayson Rural Electric Coop. (Ky.), 1950—; pres., dir. Foothills Rural Telephone Coop., Staffordsville, Ky., 1966—; vice chmn., dir. East Ky. Power Corp., Winchester. Advisor, Ky. Gov.'s Econ. Devel. Commn., 1976; past agrl. chmn. Lawrence County; past mem. jury com. and election com. of Lawrence Co. Named hon. clk. Ct. Appeals Ky., 1976; hon. treas. State of Ky., 1978, hon. sec. state, 1980. Mem. Ky. Bankers Assn. (past sec., v.p., pres. group 9), Ind. Community Bankers Ky., Ky. Hist. Soc. Mem. Ch. of Christ. Office: PO Box 60 Louisa KY 41230-0060

BURTON, MELVIN KEITH, librarian; b. St. Louis, July 21, 1952; s. Marvin Everett and Ethel Pernelia (Norrington) B.; m. Roberta Lea Stewart, Aug. 24, 1975; children: Andrew, Melanie. BA, Ctrl. Meth. Coll., 1973; MLS, U. Mo., 1974. Children's libr. Natrona County Libr., Casper, Wyo., 1976-79, Phoenix Pub. Libr., 1979-81; children's libr. St. Louis Pub. Libr., 1981-88, br. libr. mgr., 1988-90; supr. childrens svcs. Gaston-Lincoln Regional Libr., Gastonia, N.C., 1990—; mem. commn. on svcs. to children with spl. needs ALA, Chgo., 1977; mem. Caldecott Award Com., Chgo., 1981-82; pres. Met. Libr. Assn., Charlotte, N.C., 1994. Storyteller (cassettes) Storytelling Kaleidoscope, 1978. Bd. mem., adv. bd. mem. Yeatman Cmty. Sch., St. Louis, 1986-87; mem. Historic Hyde Park, St. Louis, 1987-90; bd. mem. Hyde Park Housing Orgn., St. Louis, 1989-90. 3M-JMRT Profl. Devel. grantee JMRT of ALA, Chgo., 1978. Mem. N.C. Libr. Assn. (bd. mem. children's svcs. sect. 1990-96), Metrolina Libr. Assn., Gaston Chordweavers (v.p. membership 1995-96). Methodist. Home: 540 Jones St Stanley NC 28164 Office: Gaston-Lincoln Regional Libr 1555 E Garrison Blvd Gastonia NC 28054

BURTON, RICHARD MAX, management and healthcare educator; b. Rushville, Ill., Aug. 12, 1939; s. Arlie H. and Mabel E. (Hoyt) B.; m. Nadine Ferdman; 1 child, Aziel. BS, U. Ill., 1961, MBA, 1963, D in Bus. Adminstrn., 1967. Asst. prof. Naval Postgrad. Sch., Monterey, Calif., 1967-70; prof. Duke U., Durham, N.C., 1970—, program dir. health svcs. mgmt., 1991—; chmn. bd. trustees Durham County Hosp. Corp., 1987-89. Co-author: Designing Efficient Organizations, 1984, Innovation and Entrepreneurship in Organizations, 1986, Organizational Responses to the New Business Conditions, 1989, Strategic Organizational Diagnosis and Design: Developing the Ory for Application, 1995; editor: Mgmt. Sci., 1986—; contbr. articles to profl. jours. Exec. dir. LEAD Adv. Coun., Durham, 1985-93; chmn. acad. coun. Duke U., 1992-94. Office: Duke U Fuqua Sch Bus Durham NC 27706

BURTON, RON D., educational foundation executive; b. Duncan, Okla., Sept. 22, 1946; s. Alton Head, Jr. and Nola Marie (Duvall) B.; B.B.A. in Acctg., U. Okla., 1969, J.D., 1974; m. Jetta Ellen Stewart, Sept. 1, 1967; children—Ronna Ellen, Josh Andrew. Bar: Okla. 1974. Acct. III, then dir. deferred giving U. Okla., Norman, 1969-78, trust officer, 1978-87; treas., then assoc. exec. dir. U. Okla. Found., 1970-78, exec. dir., sec., 1978—. Ward 1 rep. Norman City Charter Revision Com., 1979-80; chmn. Sooner dist. Last Frontier coun. Boy Scouts Am., 1984-87; bd. dirs., Norman Pub. Sch. Found., 1984—, treas. 1984-88, pres. 1988-90; bd. dirs. U. Okla. Fed. Credit Union, 1975-90, pres., 1978-86. Recipient Silver Beaver award Boy Scouts Am., 1988. With USAR, 1971-72. Mem. Am. Bar Assn., Okla. Bar Assn., Cleveland County Bar Assn., Rotary (bd. dirs. Norman club 1982-91, pres. 1983-84, dist. gov. 1987-88), Rotary Found. (cons. devel. com. 1989—, citation for meritorious svc. 1989, Rotary Internat., (coun. on legis. 1992, election review comm. 1992—). Democrat. Christian Scientist. Office: 100 W Timberdell Rd Norman OK 73019-5070

BURTON, SCOT, marketing educator; b. Houston, Feb. 24, 1953; s. William James and Mary (Tilley) B.; m. Jana Louise Keller, Apr. 3, 1982. BBA, U. Tex., 1974, MBA, 1976; PhD, U. Houston, 1985. V.p. consumer research Tex. Commerce Bank, Houston, 1977-81; fellow, research asst. U. Houston, 1982-85; assoc. prof. mktg. La. State U., Baton Rouge, 1986-92; assoc. prof., Wal-Mart chair in mktg. U. Ark., Fayetteville, 1993—; cons. in field. Contbr. articles to profl. jours. Mem. Am. Mktg. Assn., Assn. Consumer Rsch., Acad. Mktg. Sci. Office: U Ark Dept Mktg Badm # 302 Fayetteville AR 72701

BURTON, SHEAROR FAY, school system administrator, educator, computer consultant; b. Eastpoint, Fla., Dec. 10, 1938; d. George Wilburn and Mary Virginia (Segree) Creamer; m. Thomas Eliot Gordon, Oct. 6, 1956 (div. Apr. 1969); children: Brenda Gale, Pamela Faith; m. Orlis Luell Burton, Dec. 25, 1969. AA, Gulf Coast Community Coll., Panama City, Fla., 1969; BA, Fla. State U., 1972; MA, U. West Fla., 1979. Cert. tchr., Fla. Tchr. aide Chapman Elem. Sch., Apalachicola, Fla., 1966-67, sec., 1967-71; libr. Brown Elem. Sch., Eastpoint, Fla., 1972-73; media specialist Apalachicola High Sch., 1972-90; dist. adminstr. Franklin County Sch. Dist., Apalachicola, 1990—; adj. instr. Gulf Coast Community Coll., Panama City, 1987-89, Apalachicola coord., 1990-91; dir. Drug Free Schs. Adv. Coun., Apalachicola, 1989—; mem. Franklin County Literacy Bd., Apalachicola, 1989—; trainer Disadvantaged Youth Program, Apalachicola, 1990-91. Author: (computer program) Winner's Edge, 1989; editor: (book) Classic Creamer Cookery, 1996, (newsletter) Good New's Report, 1991. Recipient Literacy Program Goal Achievement award Fla. Dept. Edn., Tallahassee, 1991. Mem. Fla. Assn. Sch. Adminstrs., Fla. Assn. Media in Edn., Fla. Literacy Coalition, Franklin County Literacy Bd., Philaco Woman's Club (parliamentarian 1988), Kappa Delta Pi, Delta Kappa Gamma (Alpha Lambda chpt. coor. sec. 1988). Baptist. Office: Franklin County Schs 155 Avenue E Apalachicola FL 32320-2069

BURZYNSKI, STANISLAW RAJMUND, internist; b. Lublin, Poland, Jan. 23, 1943; s. Grzegorz and Zofia Miroslawa (Radzikowski) B.; came to U.S., 1970; M.D. with distinction, Med. Acad., Lublin, 1967, Ph.D., 1968. Teaching asst. Med. Acad. Lublin, 1962-67; intern, resident in internal medicine, Med. Acad., 1967-70; research assoc. Baylor U., 1970-72, asst. prof., 1972-77; pvt. practice specializing in internal medicine, Houston, 1977—; dir. Burzynski Research Lab., 1977-83; pres. Burzynski Research Inst., Inc., 1983—. Nat. Cancer Inst. grantee, 1974 West Found. grantee, 1975. Mem. AAAS, Am. Assn. Cancer Research, AMA, Harris County Med. Soc., Polish Nat. Alliance (pres. Houston chpt. 1974-75), Soc. Neurosci., Tex. Med. Assn., Sigma Xi. Roman Catholic. Contbr. articles profl. jours. Discoverer of antineoplastons components of biochem. def. system against cancer; described structure of Ameletin, 1st substance known to be responsible for remembering sound in animal's brain; invented new treatment for cancer, AIDS, viral infections, autoimmune diseases, neurofibromatosis, and Parkinson's disease. Home: 20 W Rivercrest Dr Houston TX 77042-2127 Office: 12000 Richmond Ave Houston TX 77082-2431

BURZYNSKI, TADEUSZ, engineering executive; b. Lublin, Poland, Oct. 18, 1932; came to U.S., 1981; s. Gregory and Zofia (Radzikoski) B.; m. Zofia Leszczuk, Feb. 2, 1954; 1 child, Anna. BEE, Acad. Min. and Metall., 1958; MSEE, Fed. U., Brazil, 1981. Constrn. mgr. Tech. and Elec. State Co., Krakow, Poland, 1958-66; gen. mgr. Elektromontaz State Co., Krakow, 1966-73; gen. pres. The Housing Plant, Krakow, 1973-75; dir. elec. dept. Intecnial, Erechim, Brasil, 1975-81; constrn. mgr. Intecnial, Houston, 1981-82; chief engr., sr. v.p. Burzynski Rsch. Inst. Inc., Houston, 1982—. Contbr. articles to profl. jours. Recipient First prize Polish Nat. Com. Sci. and Techique, 1967, Golden medal City Krakow, 1967, personal thanks Pres. Brasil, 1978. Mem. Nat. Soc. Profl. Engrs., Nat. Fire Protection Assn., N.Y. Acad. Scis. Roman Catholic. Home: 6000 Reims Rd Apt 3505 Houston TX 77036-3054 Office: Burzynski Rsch Inst 12707 Trinity St Stafford TX 77477-4212

BUSBICE, BILL A., JR., transportation company executive; b. 1955. With Acme Truck Lines, Broussard, La., 1976-82, Ace Transp. Inc., Broussard, from 1982; pres. Dynasty Transp. Inc., Broussard. Office: Ace Transportation Inc 3721 Highway 90 E Broussard LA 70518-3206

BUSBY, MARK BAYLESS, university administrator, educator, writer; b. Ennis, Tex., Nov. 30, 1945; s. James Henry and Monte Allene (Scott) B.; m. Linda Barbara Whitehouse, Sept. 6, 1967; 1 child, Joshua William. BA, Tex. A&M U., 1967, MA, 1969; PhD, U. Colo., 1977. Asst. prof. English Tex. A&M U., College Station, 1977-83, assoc. prof. English, 1983-91; prof. English Southwest Tex. State U., San Marcos, 1993—, dir. Ctr. for Study of Southwest, 1991—. Author: Ralph Ellison, 1991, Larry McMurtry and The West: An Ambivalent Relationship, 1995; editor: The Frontier Experience and the American Dream, 1989, New Growth/2: Contemporary Short Stories by Texas Writers, 1995. 1st lt. U.S. Army, 1969-71. Recipient fellowship NEH, 1996. Mem. Western Am. Lit. Assn. (exec. coun. 1987-90). Home: 115 Cedar Springs Wimberley TX 78676 Office: Southwest Tex State Univ Ctr for Study of Southwest San Marcos TX 78666

BUSBY, SHANNON NIXON, special education educator; b. Gainesville, Tex., Nov. 30, 1955; d. James H. and Helen M. (Ross) Nixon; m. Larry W. Busby, Apr. 3, 1982; 1 child, James Ross. BS in Home Econs. Edn., Tex. Tech U., 1977; MEd, Sul Ross State U., Alpine, Tex., 1982. Cert. profl. ednl. diagnostian, tchr. of lang. and/or learning disabilities, tchr. of vocat. homemaking. Home econ. tchr. Pecos (Tex.)-Barstow-Toyah Ind. Sch. Dist., 1978-83, ednl. diagnostian spl. edn. dept., 1983—; exec. dir. West of the Pecos Guild, Inc., 1995—; interior design cons. L.W. Busby and Co., Pecos, 1989—; bd. dirs. Dept. Mental Health and Mental Retardation, Pecos, 1980-83. Chairperson Tex. War on Drugs, Pecos, 1980-83. Mem. AAUW (local pres. 1982-86, local v.p. 1978-81, Tex. state bd. dirs. 1982-83), Tex. Ednl. Diagnosticians Assn. (sec. region 18), Tex. Soc. for Autistic Citizens. Home: 1519 S Mary St Pecos TX 79772-5615

BUSCH, NOEL HENRY, banker; b. Jordan, Minn., Dec. 9, 1940; s. Albert Meinrad and Hildegarde Sophie (Bauer) B.; m. Bertina Nancy Lee Helgeson, July 9, 1966; children: Maria Renee, Lavinia Christine, Owen Martin, Mark Allen, Amineh Adrienne. BA, U. Minn., 1965. Legis. and bus. devel. counsel various trade assns., 1966-71; CEO Ind. Bankers Minn., Mpls., 1972-75; prin. organizer, founding dir., CEO Ind. State Bank Minn., Mpls., 1975-81; chmn. bd. Ind. Bankers Credit Corp., Mpls., 1980-82; pres. Ind. Bancservices Exch., Mpls., 1981-82; founding dir., pres., CEO, chmn. exec. com. Ind. Bankers Bank Fla., Orlando, 1982-94; chmn., treas. Busch & Co. Resource Strategies, Inc., 1994—; chmn. Bankers Bank Coun.; founding dir., pres. Bankers' Bancorp of Fla., 1989-94; prin. organizer, founding exec. officer bankers bank movement; publ. Pine Hills Press, 1995—; Fla. rep. Apt. Home Equity Program, Inc., 1994—. Named Banker Advocate of Yr. Orlando C. of C., 1985, Fin. Services Advocate of Yr. U.S. Small Bus. Adminstrn., Jacksonville, Fla., 1985. Republican.

BUSCHER, HENRY N., secondary school educator; b. Chanute, Kans., May 25, 1937; m. Barbara Adine Gready, June 12, 1963; children: Briana, Wendy, Thomas. AA, Chanute Jr. Coll., 1957; BS, Kans. State Coll., 1961; MS, U. Okla., 1963, PhD, 1965. Tchg. cert. secondary sci. Rsch. assoc. Sch. Tropical Medicine, San Juan, P.R., 1965-66, Inst. Internat. Medicine, Lahore, West Pakistan, 1966-68; prof. biology Austin Coll., Sherman, Tex., 1968-78; asst. acad. dean Bee County Coll., Beeville, Tex., 1980-83; instr. Houston Ind. Sch. Dist., 1987-89; asst. prof. U. Alaska, Bethel, 1989-90; instr. Brenham (Tex.) Ind. Sch. Dist., 1990-91; chair dept. sci. Monsignor Kelly H.S., Beaumont, Tex., 1991—. Served in U.S. Army, 1957-59, Germany. NIH fellow, 1963-65, NSF fellow, 1960, 63; NSF grantee, 1961-62, U.S. Dept. Edn. grantee, 1990. Office: Monsignor Kelly HS 5950 Kelly Dr Beaumont TX 77707

BUSFIELD, ROGER MELVIL, JR., retired trade association executive, educator; b. Ft. Worth, Feb. 4, 1926; s. Roger Melvil and Julia Mabel (Clark) B.; m. Jean Wilson, Mar. 26, 1948 (div. Oct. 1960); children: Terry Jean, Roger Melvil III, Timothy Clark; m. Virginia Bailey, Dec. 1, 1962 (dec. July 1991); 1 child, Julia Lucille; m. Addie Howard Davis, June 17, 1995. Student, U. Tex., 1943, 46; BA, Southwestern U., 1947, MA, 1948; PhD, Fla. State U., 1954. Asst. prof. Southwestern U., 1947-49; instr. U. Ala., 1949-50, Fla. State U., 1950-54; asst. prof. speech Mich. State U., 1954-60; editl. svcs. specialist Oldsmobile divsn. Gen. Motors Corp., Lansing, Mich., 1960; gen. publs. supr. Consumers Power Co., Jackson, Mich., 1960-61; assoc. dir. Mich. Hosp. Assn., Lansing, 1961-73; exec. dir. Ark. Hosp. Assn., Little Rock, 1973-81, pres., 1981-94, pres. emeritus, 1994—; adj. prof. health svcs. mgmt. Webster U., 1979—. Trustee, Ctrl. Mich. U., 1967-73, chmn., 1970; mem. Mich. Gov.'s Commn. on Higher Edn., 1972-74; mem. Ark. Gov.'s Emergency Med. Svcs. Adv. Coun., 1975-94, chmn., 1978-84; mem. Ark. Gov.'s Task Force on Rural Hosps., 1988-89, Ark. Dept. of Health Long Range Planning Com., 1988-89; chmn. AIDS adv. com. Ark. Dept. Health, 1990—; mem. Ark. Gov.'s Task Force Health Care Reform, 1993-96; chmn. Health Data Task Force, Ark. Resources Comm., 1994—; mem. adv. bd. Ark. Pediat. Facility, 1995-96. Served with USMC, 1943-46. Named Tex. Outstanding Author, Theta Sigma Phi, 1958; recipient Disting. Alumnus award Southwestern U., 1971; Senate-House Concurrent Resolution of Tribute, Mich. Legis., 1973; Bd. Trustees award Am. Hosp. Assn., 1994; Merit award Ark. Hosp. Assn., 1994. Mem. Am. Soc. Assn. Execs., Ark. Soc. Assn. Execs. (pres. 1981-82), Pub. Rels. Assn. Mich. (pres. 1966), Speech Comm. Assn., Am. Coll. Health Care Execs., State Hosp. Assn. Exec. Forum (sec., treas. 1989, pres. 1991), Am. Hosp. Assn. (coun. legis. 1975-77, coun. allied and govtl. rels. 1983-86), Rotary (Little Rock). Methodist. Author: The Playwright's Art, 1958, Arabic transl., 1964; (with others) The Children's Theatre, 1960; editor Theatre Arts Bibliography, 1964; contbr. articles to profl. jours.; author profl. motion picture scenarios. Home: PO Box 25212 Little Rock AR 72221-5212

BUSH, ARTHUR JOE, mining engineer, educator; b. Washington, Mar. 27, 1922; s. Arthur Edward and Cassie (Rice) B.; m. Margaret Elizabeth Strausser, Dec. 25, 1956; children: Beryl Candice, Diane Denise. BS, Mining Engring., Mo. Sch. Mines, 1947; MS, 1963; MS Urban Planning, Transp., Purdue U., 1970. Registered profl. engr., Mo., Ind., Ky. Asst. mining engr. Fredericktown Lead Co., Mo., 1947-49; mining engr. Solvay Process Div., Allied Chem. & Dye Corp., Prairie du Rocher, Ill., 1949-53; acting asst. quarry supt., 1950-53; mining engr. Internat. Salt Co., Retsof, N.Y., 1953-55; engr. Frazier-Davis Constrn. Co., Morgantown, Pa., Marion, Ill., 1955-56; chief engr. Baroid Div., Nat. Lead Co., Malvern, Ark., 1956-60, instr., engring. graphics, U. Mo., Rolla., 1962-65; asst. prof. civil engring. Tri-State U., Angola, Ind., 1965-72; city coordinator, city engr. Kendallville, Ind., 1972-73; asso. prof. engring. tech. Western Ky. U., Bowling Green, 1974-87; cons. on mining engring. Co-author: Black Powder to Black Gold. Served to 1st lt., U.S. Army, 1943-46. Decorated Silver Star with oak leaf cluster. Mem. AIME, ASCE, Soc. Engring. Edn., Am. Rd. Builders Assn., Ky. Soc. Profl. Engrs., Nat. Soc. Profl. Engrs., Mammoth Cave chpt. Profl. Engrs., Am. Fencers Assn., Hobson House Assn., Am. Soc. Explosives Engrs., Steuben County Hist. Soc. Sertoma (Lewis B. Hershey chpt.), Sigma Xi, Pi Kappa Alpha, Sigma Gamma Epsilon, Tau Beta Pi. Clubs: Rolla Arts Group, Arts Alliance Bowling Green., So. Ky. Past-Finders. Research in fields of explosives and dynamic creep. Home: 1927 Price Ave Bowling Green KY 42104

BUSH, BARBARA PIERCE, volunteer, wife of former President of the United States; b. Rye, N.Y., June 8, 1925; d. Marvin and Pauline (Robinson) Pierce; m. George Herbert Walker Bush, Jan. 6, 1945; children: George Walker, John Ellis, Neil Mallon, Marvin Pierce, Dorothy Walker. Student, Smith Coll., 1943-44; hon. degrees, Stritch Coll., Milw., 1981, Mt. Vernon Coll., Washington, 1981, Hood Coll., Frederick, Md., 1983, Howard U., Washington, 1987, Judson Coll., Marion, Ala., 1988, Bennett Coll., Greensboro, N.C., 1989, Smith Coll., 1989, Morehouse Sch. Medicine, 1989. Author: C. Fred Story; Millie's Book; Barbara Bush: A Memoir, 1994. Hon. chair adv. bd. Reading is Fundamental; hon. mem. Bus. Coun. for Effective Literacy; mem. adv. coun. Soc. of Meml. Sloan-Kettering Cancer Ctr.; hon. mem. bd. dirs. Children's Oncology Svcs. of Met. Washington, The Washington Home, The Kingsbury Ctr.; hon. chmn. nat. adv. coun. Literacy Vols. of Am., Nat. Sch. Vols. Program; sponsor Laubach Literacy Internat.; nat. hon. chmn. Leukemia Soc. of Am.; hon. mem. bd. trustees Morehouse Sch. of Medicine; hon. nat. chmn. Nat. Organ Donor Awareness Week, 1982-86; pres. Ladies of the Senate, 1981-88; mem. women's com. Smithsonian Assocs., Tex. Fedn. of Rep. Women, life mem., hon. mem.; hon. chairperson for the Nat. Com. on Literacy and Edn. United Way, Barbara Bush Found. for Family Literacy, Washington Parent Group Fund, Girls Clubs of Am., 10th anniversay Harvest Nat. Food Bank Network; hon. chmn. Nat. Com. for the Prevention of Child Abuse and Childhelp U.S.A.; hon. pres. Girl Scouts U.S; hon. chair Nat. Com. for Adoption; mem. bd. trustees Mayo Clinic Found.; hon. chair Read Am., Boarder Baby Project; mem. bd. visitors M. D. Anderson Cancer Ctr.; hon. chair Leukemia Soc. Am., Children's Literacy Initiative; hon. mem. Reading is Fundamental; ambassador at large Americares; honorary mem. Barbara Bush Found. for Family Literacy. Recipient Nat. Outstanding Mother of Yr. award, 1984, Woman of Yr. award USO, 1986, Disting. Leadership award United Negro Coll. Fund 1986, Disting. Am. Woman award Coll. Mt. St. Joseph, 1987, Free Spirit award Freedom Forum, 1995. Mem. Tex. Fedn. Rep. Women (life), Internat. II Club (Washington), Magic Circle Rep. Women's Club (Houston), YWCA. Episcopalian. Office: 10000 Memorial Dr Houston TX 77024-3422*

BUSH, GEORGE HERBERT WALKER, former President of the United States; b. Milton, Mass., June 12, 1924; s. Prescott Sheldon and Dorothy (Walker) B.; m. Barbara Pierce, Jan. 6, 1945; children: George W., John E., Neil M., Marvin P., Dorothy W. Koch. BA in Econs., Yale U., 1948; numerous other hon. degrees. Co-founder Bush-Overbey Oil Devel. Co., 1951; Co-founder, dir. Zapata Petroleum Corp., Midland, 1953-59; pres. Zapata Off Shore Co., Houston, 1956-64; chmn. bd. Zapata Off Shore Co., 1964-66; mem. 90th-91st Congresses from 7th Dist. Tex., 1967-71, Ways and Means com.; U.S. amb. to UN, 1971-73; chmn. Rep. Nat. Com., 1973-74; chief U.S. Liaison Office Peking, People's Republic China, 1974-75; dir. CIA, 1976-77; adj. prof. adminstrv. sci. Rice U., Houston, 1978; V.P. of U.S., 1981-89, Pres. of U.S., 1989-93. Del. Rep. Nat. Conv., 1964, 69; Rep. candidate U.S. senator from Tex., 1964, 70. Lt. (j.g.), pilot USN, WWII. Decorated D.F.C., Air medals (3). Office: 10000 Memorial Dr Houston TX 77024-3422

BUSH, GEORGE W., governor; s. George Herbert and Barbara (Pierce) B.; m. Laura; children: Barbara and Jenna (twins). BA in History, Yale U., 1968; MBA, Harvard U., 1975. Founder, mgr. Spectrum 7 Energy Corp. (merger with Harken Energy Corp. 1986), Midland, Tex.; dir. Harken Energy Corp.; gov. State of Tex., 1994—. With Tex. Air N.G. Recipient Big D award Dallas All Sports Assn., 1989. Office: Office Gov State Capitol PO Box 12428 Austin TX 78711*

BUSH, JILL LOBDILL, artist; b. Grand Island, Nebr., May 11, 1942; d. Oran Russell and Sylvia Salome (Dobbs) Lobdill; m. William Richard Bush, Aug. 28, 1963; children: Jennifer Wynn, Beau Richard. B in Advt. Art and Design, Tex. Tech. U., 1964. art juror Trinity Arts Guild, Ft. Worth, 1973, Gen. Dynamics Recreation Area, Ft. Worth, 1973, Eastside Creative Arts Club, Ft. Worth, 1977, Gregg Art Guild's Silver Anniv. Show, 1982, L&L Gallery, 1982, Mayfest, Ft. Worth, 1992, 93, 94, Tex. Coll. Osteopathic Medicine, Ft. Worth chpt. Composers, Authors and Artists Am., 1992; demonstrator, lectr., tchr. in field. One-woman shows include Latch String Gallery, Ft. Worth, 1975, Moulton Galleries, Ft. Smith, Ark., 1980, L&L Gallery, Longview, Tex., 1982, Southwestern Regional Ballet Festival, Evelyn Siegel Gallery, Ft. Worth, 1986; exhibited in group shows at Odyssey Gallery, Ft. Worth, 1972, L&L Gallery, 1974, 87, 89, 91, Latch String Gallery, Ft. Worth, 1976, Evelyn Siegel Gallery, 1984-85, 92, 1st Ann. Main St. Tex. Invitational Art Show, Ft. Worth, 1986, 3d Salon des Pastellists, Lille, France, 1987, Ashland (Ky.) Area Gallery, 1989; featured artist Moulton Galleries spring show, 1986, L&L Gallery 25th anniv. show, 1993; represented in permanent collection Duncanville (Tex.) H.S., St. Joseph's Hosp., Ft. Worth, So. La. State U., Holt Crock Clinic, Ft. Smith, Ft. Worth Women's Club, 1st Fed. Savs. Loan, Ft. Smith, Darby's Ranger's Mus., Ft. Smith, Cooper Clinic, Ft. Smith, Drawing Bd., Dallas, Carlton Card divsn. Am. Greeting Cards, Dallas, Tex. Christian U., Ft. Worth, Harris Meth. Hosp., Hurst-Euless-Bedford, Tex., St. Joseph's Hosp., Ft. Worth; contbr.

paintings to books Pastel Interpretations, 1992, Still Life Techniques, 1993, The Art of Pastel Portraiture, 1996. Recipient 1st place Heritage Hall Competition, Ft. Worth, 1969, Circuit award Jurors' Choice award, citation award Tex. Fine Arts Assn., 1972, Schwann Weber award PSA 8th Ann. Competition N.Y., 1980, PSA award, San Marcus, 1980, Pastel Soc. Southwest 1st place & honorable mention, 1985, PSA Ann. N.Y. Pruchase award, 1994. Mem. Pastel Soc. Am. (signature, award, hon. mention 1979, Schwann Weber award, 1980), Nat. League Am. Pen Women, Pastel Soc. S.W. (1st place award, hon. mention 1985). Home: 6440 Curzon Ave Fort Worth TX 76116-4402

BUSH, JOHN WILLIAM, federal transportation official; b. Columbus, Ohio, Sept. 17, 1909; s. William Hayden and Esther (Brushart) B.; m. Mary Elizabeth Van Doren, June 4, 1932 (dec. 1958); children: Jan Hayden (Mrs. Richard L. Jennings), Emily Van Doren Bush; m. Dorothy Vredenburgh, Jan. 13, 1962 (dec. 1991). BSBA, Va. Poly. Inst., 1931. With Standard Oil Co. La., 1932-37, T.K. Brushart Oil Co., Portsmouth, Ohio, 1937-49; pres. Ohio System Inc., 1946—, dir. purchasing Ohio,, 1949-57; dir. commerce, 1959-61; commr. ICC, 1961-71, chmn., 1966; spl. transp. adviser Senate Commerce Com., 1971—; mem. gov.'s adv. coun. Fla., 1957-59; v.p. Coastal Petroleum Co., 1972-89; bd. dirs. Can. So. Petroleum Ltd., 1972-89, R.C. Williams & Co., Inc., N.Y.C.; chmn. bd. Old Judge Foods Corp., St. Louis, 1988-91. Mem. Ohio Small Bus. Commn., 1954-56, Ohio Water Pollution Control Bd., 1954-56; mem. Fla. Gov.'s adv. coun., 1989-90; councilman, Portsmouth, 1941-44; Dem. nominee for Congress, 1974; dir. Ohio Vietnam Vets. Bonus Commn., 1973-74. Mem. Nat. Assn. State Purchasing Ofcls. (pres. 1954). Address: Box C104 106 Moorings Park Dr Naples FL 33942-2157

BUSH, MITCHELL LESTER, JR., retired federal agency administrator; b. Syracuse, N.Y., Feb. 1, 1936; s. Mitchell Lester Bush and Sarah Margaret (Skenandore) Gonyea. Grad. h.s., Lawrence, Kans. Tribal enrollment specialist Bur. Indian Affairs, Washington, 1962, 66; area tribal enrollment officer Bur. Indian Affairs, Anadarko, Okla., 1964-65; acting chief Bur. Tribal Enrollment Svcs., Washington, 1982, chief, 1983, ret., 1991. Co-editor: American Indian Society Cookbook, 1974, 2nd edit., 1984. Vice chairperson Va. Coun. on Indians, Richmond, 1989-95. With U.S. Army, 1958-61. Recipient Points of Light cert., award for Outstanding Pub. Svc. to U.S.A., U.S. Sec. of Interior, Washington, 1990, Maharishi award Maharishi U., Washington, 1985. Mem. Am. Indian Soc. (founder, pres. 1966-91, editor newsletter 1991—, Disting. Svc. award 1971, 90, Outstanding Elder/Advisor award 1996). Methodist. Home: 22258 Cool Water Dr Ruther Glen VA 22546 Office: AIS Newsletter 22226 Cool Water Dr Ruther Glen VA 22546

BUSH, ROBERT G., III, lawyer, state legislator; b. Kansas City, Mo., Jan. 15, 1936; s. Robert G. and Margaret Irene (Woolard) B.; m. Wanda Lou Baker, Jan. 20, 1962; 1 child, Sherry O'Shea Cornell. B.A., Kans. U., 1957; J.D., So. Meth. U., 1963. Bar: Tex. 1963, U.S. Dist. Ct. (ea. dist.) Tex. 1964, U.S. Ct. Appeals (5th cir.) 1974, U.S. Supreme Ct. 1974; sole practice, Sherman, 1967—; Bancroft-Whitney Practice Cons., Right to Die Directives, 1988-94; mem. Tex. Ho. of Reps., 1977-87, majority leader House Democratic Caucus, 1981-85, chmn. judiciary com., 1981-87; instr. Grayson County Jr. Coll., 1968-72. Served with U.S. Army, 1958-59. Fellow Tex. Bar Found.; mem. Tex. Trial Lawyers Assn. (past assoc. dir.). Episcopalian.

BUSH, ROBERT THOMAS, shipping company executive; b. Newbury, Berkshire, Eng., May 18, 1928; came to U.S., 1968; s. Randolph George and Catherine Ellen (Benger) B.; m. Haydee Ojeda, Jan. 23, 1966; children: Allan David, Linda Martha, Grace Katherine. Master Mariner, Southampton (Eng.) U., 1953. Shipmaster Burmah Oil Co., Rangoon, Burma, 1955-60; marine surveyor Sydney, Australia, 1960-68; terminal supt. Exportadora De Sal, Cedros Island, Mex., 1968-70; marine mgr. Balfour Williamson, London, 1970-73; sr. marine advisor Aramco, Saudi Arabia, 1974-76; ops. mgr. Mercantile & Marine (Tex.) Inc., Houston, 1976-80; sr. marine advisor Phillips Petroleum Co., Bartlesville, Okla., 1980-86; gen. mgr. Universe Tankships (Del.) Inc., N.Y.C., 1986-94; pres. Neptune Marine Consultants (Ams.) Inc., Dickinson, Tex., 1994—. Contbr. numerous articles to profl. jours. Charter mem. Better World Soc., Washington, 1988; tutor Literacy Vols. Am., Edison, N.J., 1988—; founder Friends of the Sea, N.Y., 1991. Mem. N.Y. Acad. Sci., Nautical Inst. of London. Home: 427-1 Sunset Dr Dickinson TX 77539

BUSH, THOMAS NORMAN, lawyer; b. Lancaster County, Va., Nov. 13, 1947; s. T. Edwin and Willie Ann (Landman) B.; m. Carolyn Sue Brown; children: Jason, Jennifer. BS in Acctg., Va. Tech, 1970; JD, U. Richmond, 1977. Bar: Va. Staff acct. Peat Marwick, Richmond, Va., 1970-71; sr. auditor U.S. Army, Frankfurt, Germany, 1972-74; pvt. practice acctg. Richmond, 1974-77; tax mgr. Coopers & Lybrand, Richmond, 1977-81; v.p., tax counsel James River Corp., Richmond, 1981—; Mem. adv. bd. dept. acctg. Va. Tech., 1991—. V.p. James River Found., 1993—; chmn. corp. matching gift U. Richmond Annual Fund steering com., 1996—; mem. dept. acctg. adv. bd. Va. Tech., 1991—; mem. steering com. Ctr. for Leadership, Govt. and Global Econs., 1996—. Mem. ABA, AICPA, Va. State Bar, Internat. Fiscal Assn., Am. Forest and Paper Assn. (tax com. 1986-94), Tax Execs. Inst. (pres. Va. chpt. 1989-90, regional v.p. 1995-96, bd. dirs. 1993-96, nominating com. 1996—, IRS adminstrv. affairs com. 1996—, nominating com. 1996-97, IRS adminstrv. affairs com. 1996—), Tax Found. (program com. 1996—), Va. Soc. CPAs, Va. Mfrs. Assn. (tax com. 1988—), Civitan (pres. West End Richmond 1982). Methodist. Home: 10007 Ashbridge Pl Richmond VA 23233-5402 Office: James River Corp PO Box 2218 120 Tredegar St Richmond VA 23218-2218

BUSS, GLENN RICHARD, agricultural researcher; b. Easton, Pa., Apr. 12, 1940; s. Paul R. and Evelyn A. (Roth) B.; m. Nelda Weidman, Apr. 2, 1961; children: Paula L., Gary R. BS in Agronomy, Pa. State U., 1962, MS in Genetics, 1964, PhD in Genetics, 1967. Prof. Va. Tech., Blacksburg, 1967—. Mem. Am. Soc. Agronomy, Crop Sci. Soc. of Am., Am. Genetic Assn. Lutheran. Office: CSES Dept Blacksburg VA 24061

BUSSLER, ROBERT BRUCE, management consultant; b. Ramey, Pa., Apr. 7, 1925; s. Arthur and Mary Eleanor (McCrossin) B.; m. Evelyn Louise Murrell, June 28, 1952; children: Mary Louise, Janice Lynn. BEE, George Washington U., 1950. Electronics engr. Melpar, Inc., Falls Church, Va., 1953-55; elec. engr. Bur. of Ships, Washington, 1955-59; value engr. Bur. Naval Weapons, Washington, 1959-66; br. head Naval Air Systems Command, Washington, 1966-80; dir. engring., v.p. Nat. Systems Mgmt. Corp., Arlington, Va., 1980-89; pres., chmn. bd. dirs. REMAR, Inc., Alexandria, Va., 1990—. Lt. comdr. USNR, 1943-52, PTO. Mem. Free and Accepted Masons (Worshipful Master 1975), Royal Arch Masons Internat. (com. chmn., Bronze medal 1975, Grand High Priest 1980). Republican. Methodist. Home and Office: 2515 Page Ter Alexandria VA 22302-2714

BUSTAMANTE, NESTOR, lawyer; b. Havana, Cuba, Apr. 20, 1960; came to the U.S., 1961; s. Nestor and Clara Rosa (Sanchez) B.; m. Marilyn Gonzalez, Sept. 20, 1986; children: Tiffany Alexandra, Nestor C. AA, U. Fla., 1980, BS in Journalism, 1982, JD, 1985. Bar: Fla. 1986, U.S. Dist. Ct. (so. dist.) Fla. 1989, U.S. Supreme Ct. 1991. Asst. state atty. State Atty.'s Office 11th Cir., Miami, 1986-88; juvenile serious offender prosecutor State Atty.'s Office, Miami, 1987-88, spl. prosecutor, gang prosecutor, 1987-88; asst. divsn. chief State Atty.'s Office-11th Jud. Cir., Miami, 1987-88; of counsel Fernandez-Caubi, Fernandez & Aguilar et al., Miami, 1988-89; atty. Leiby, Ferencik, Libanoff & Brandt, Ft. Lauderdale, Fla., 1989—; mem. code and rules of evidence com. The Fla. Bar, 1989-90. Contbr. articles to newsletters. Named Hon. mem. Quien es Quien Publs., Inc., N.Y.C., 1990. Mem. ATLA (scoring judge nat. finals student trial advocacy competition 1994, 95), Fed. Bar Assn., Dade County Bar Assn. (mem. juvenile divsn. com. 1988-92, mem. media and pub. rels. com. 1989-91, mem. constrn. law com. 1990-91), Phi Delta Phi, U. Fla. Alumni Assn. Office: Leiby Ferencik Libanoff & Brandt 150 S Pine Island Rd Ste 400 Fort Lauderdale FL 33324-2667

BUSTER, ALAN ADAIR, control engineer; b. Houston, May 30, 1918; s. Edwin Crozier and Eva Lea (Shelby) B.; m. Virginia Anne Clarkson, Oct. 1, 1945; children: Anne Shelby Windsor, Alan A. Jr. BSChE, Rice U., 1949; postgrad., U. Houston, 1958-59; dipl., Army Command/Gen. Staff Coll., Ft. Leavenworth, Kans., 1960. Registered profl. engr., Calif., Tex. Artilleryman, flying cadet, air photo officer U.S. Army, 1936-47, res. instr.; lt. col. Army Corps Engrs., Houston, Paris, Germany, 1947-78; rsch. lab. technician, refining technologist Shell Oil Co., Deer Park, Tex., 1947-52; chem. engr. Crown Ctrl. Petroleum Corp., Pasadena, Tex., 1952-60; process analyst Thompson-Ramo-Wooldridge, L.A., 1960-63; chef de projet Feyzin, Cie des Machines Bull, Paris, 1963-65; engr. computer control GE, Houston, 1965-74; engr. consulting control Honeywell, Houston, 1974-86; ret., 1986. Contbr. articles to profl. jours. Leader Boy Scouts Am., 1938-58; hon. life mem. Oxford U. Rover Crew, 1945. Mem. AIChE, Am. Chem. Soc., Instrument Soc. Am., 7th Photo Group Assn. Home: 3502 Elk Cliff Pass San Antonio TX 78247-4463

BUSTER, JOHN EDMOND, gynecologist, medical researcher; b. Oxnard, Calif., July 18, 1941; s. Edmound B. and Beatrice (Keller) B.; m. Frances Bunn (dec.). Student, Stanford U., 1959-62; MD, UCLA, 1966. Diplomate Am. Bd. Gynecology. Intern., Harbor UCLA Med. Ctr., Torrance, 1966-67, resident, 1967-71, research fellow, 1971-73, faculty, 1975—; prof. obstetrics and gynecology UCLA Sch. Medicine, 1983, dir. divsn. reproductive endocrinology; prof. obstetrics and gynecology U. Tenn., Memphis, 1987—; prof. ob-gyn. Baylor Coll. Medicine, Houston, 1994—; dir. research group human embryo transplants UCLA; examiner Am. Bd. Obstetrics and Gynecology. Contbr. articles to profl. jours. Served to lt. col., U.S. Army, 1973-75. Mem. Am. Gynecologic & Obstetrics Soc., Soc. for Gynecologic Investigation. Presbyterian. Office: Baylor Coll Medicine 6550 Fannin St Ste 801 Houston TX 77030-2719

BUTCHER, BRUCE CAMERON, lawyer; b. N.Y.C., Feb. 17, 1947; s. John Richard and Dorothy Helen (Wehner) B.; m. Kathryn Ann Fiddler, Oct. 12, 1979; 1 child, Kristen Ann. BS, Belknap Coll., 1969; JD, St. John's U., N.Y.C., 1972. Bar: N.Y. 1973, U.S. Dist. Ct. (so. dist.) N.Y. 1974, La. 1980, U.S. Dist. Ct. (ea. dist.) La. 1980, U.S. Ct. Appeals (5th and 11th cirs.) 1981, Tex. 1993. Assoc. Laporte and Meyers, N.Y.C., 1972-73; asst. chief contract div. Corp. Counsel's Office City of N.Y., 1973-79; ptnr. Chaffe, McCall, Phillips, Toler & Sarpy, New Orleans, 1980-84; prin. Bruce C. Butcher, P.C., Metairie, La., 1985-93; of counsel Smith Martin & Schneider, New Orleans, 1993-94; gen. coun. The Vulvan Group, Burmingham, Ala., 1994-95, Favalora Constructors, Inc., 1995—; pres. and gen. counsel Tailgators Restaurant, LLC, New Orleans, LA. Mem. ABA (regional chmn. pub. report 1975, state chmn. pub. contracts sect. 1984-95, cert. of performance 1975), La. Bar Assn., Am. Arbitration Assn., New Orleans Country Club, New Orleans Squash Club, Crescent Club. Home: 344 Homestead Ave Metairie LA 70005-3707 Office: 933 Metairie Rd Metairie LA 70005

BUTCHER, CARMEN JULIE-ANN ORTIZ, medicine and nephrology educator; b. Johnson City, Fla.; d. Juan M. Ortiz de Valderrama and Carmen Maria Garcia Vera; m. Albert Interian, July 27, 1979 (div. Mar. 1991); children: Albert Michael, Allan Thomas; m. Jeffrey William Butcher, June 15, 1992; 1 child, William Morgan Webb. BS magna cum laude, U. Miami, 1978, MD, 1982. Diplomate Am. Bd. Internal Medicine, Am. Bd. Nephrology. Resident in internal medicine U. Miami-(Fla.) Jackson Meml. Hosp., 1982-85, fellow in nephrology, 1986-89, asst. prof. clin. medicine and nephrology, 1989-93, assoc. prof., 1993—; med. bd. Nat. Kidney Found., Fla., 1993—, chair med. adv. bd. Contbr. articles to med. jours. Mem. health adv. coun. Miami Visitors Bur., 1991-94. Fellow ACP; mem. Am. Soc. Nephrology, Internat. Soc. Nephrology, Am. Fed. Clinic Res., Alpha Omega Alpha.

BUTCHER, HARRY WILLIAM, security and investigation company executive; b. Frederick, Okla., May 15, 1948; s. Harry William Hobbs and Alice Marie (Brownrigg) Butcher Able; m. Jeanne McPherren, June 24, 1972; children: Jonathan Hobbs, Megan Rachel. BS, Okla. State U., 1970; postgrad., 1971. Agt. Pinkerton, Inc., Oklahoma City, 1971-73; mgr. investigation Pinkerton, Inc., Dallas, 1973-75; mgr. Pinkerton, Inc., Baton Rouge, 1975-77, Memphis, 1977-78; mgr., dist. Pinkerton, Inc., Houston, 1978-79; v.p. Mark Lipman Div., Memphis, 1979-84; regional dir. Pinkerton, Inc., Dallas, 1984-88; dir., group investigation Pinkerton, Inc., Ft. Worth, 1988-89, dir. nat. accounts, 1990-91; v.p. domestic and internat. sales, 1991-96; sr. v.p. domestic and internat. sales Pinkerton, Inc., Ft. Worth, 1996—. Co-editor: (nat. sales tng. program) Pinkerton Selling Skills. Mem. Am. Soc. Indsl. Security (chmn., dir. programs), Am. Mgmt. Assn. (pres.'s assn.), Pres.'s Club (N.Y.C.). Republican. Southern Baptist. Office: Pinkerton Inc Ste 100 4150 International Plz Fort Worth TX 76109-4805

BUTCHER-TOWZEY, DAVID, public relations executive; b. Phila., Feb. 1, 1948; s. Herman J. Jr. and Dorothy (O'Malley) B.; m. Phyllis J. Towzey, Apr. 12, 1986; children: Thomas Phillip, Megan Dar. BA in English, LaSalle U., 1970. Sports reporter The Daily Intelligencer, Doylestown, Pa., 1971-72; pub. rels. assoc. Am. Cancer Soc., Phila., 1972-73; dir. pub. rels. ARC, Phila., 1973-83; co-owner Butcher and Towzey Pub. Rels., Moorestown, N.J., 1983-86; pub. rels. officer Core States Fin. Corp., Phila., 1986-87; v.p., gen. mgr. Healy & Co. Pub. Rels., Tampa, Fla., 1987-89; v.p. corp. communications Invest Fin. Corp., Tampa, 1989-90; prin. Langley & Butcher Pub. Rels., Tampa, 1990—; pres. Shareholder Commn. of Fla., Inc., St. Petersburg; mem. Super Box XXV Media Task Force, Tampa, 1991. Contbr. articles to profl. jours. Founding mem. Coun. of Communicators, Phila., 1979; vice chmn. environ. commn. West Deptford Twp. Mcpl. Govt., N.J., 1986; bd. dirs. Kingsway Sch., Haddonfield, N.J., 1987; bd. dirs., chair pub. rels. ARC, Tampa, 1988-92. Recipient 1st Pl. award Internat. Assn. Bus. Communicators, 1975. Mem. Pub. Rels. Soc. Am. (accredited mem., counselors acad., exec. com., social svc. sec. 1980, bd. dirs. Tampa chpt. 1988—, del. nat. assembly 1993—), Fla. Pub. Rels. Assn. Democrat. Roman Catholic. Home: 1336 54th Ave NE Saint Petersburg FL 33703-3225 Office: 270 1st Ave S Ste 300 Saint Petersburg FL 33701-4306

BUTHOD, MARY CLARE, school administrator; b. Tulsa, Aug. 20, 1945; d. Arthur Paul and Mary Rudelle (Dougherty) B. MA in Teaching, Tulsa U., 1969; M Christian Spirituality, Creighton U., 1981. Joined Order of St. Benedict. Asst. tchr. HeadStart, Tulsa, 1966; tchr. Madalene Parish Sch., Tulsa, 1968-69, Monte Cassino Pvt. Sch., Tulsa, 1969-79; prin. Monte Cassino Elem. Sch., Tulsa, 1979-86; dir. Monte Cassino Sch., Tulsa, 1986—; mem. convent coun. Benedictine Sisters, Tulsa, 1975-88, dir. formation programa, 1983—. Mem. State Congl. Ednl. Com., Tulsa, 1989-90; co-chair for edn. and human devel. Tulsa Coalition Against Illegal Use of Drugs, 1990-91; mem. adv. com. Schs. Attuned, U. N.C. Recognized for Excellence in Edn. U.S. Dept. Edn., 1993-94. Mem. Tulsa Reading Coun. (sec. 1975-77), Nat. Cath. Edn. Assn., Delta Kappa Gamma. Home: 220 S Lewis Ave Tulsa OK 74104-1918 Office: Monte Cassino Sch 2206 S Lewis Ave Tulsa OK 74114-3117

BUTKIN, ROBERT, state treasurer. Treas. State of Okla., Oklahoma City. Office: State of Okla Treas Office 217 State Capitol 2300 N Lincoln Oklahoma City OK 73105

BUTLER, ABBEY J., pharmaceutical distribution company executive; b. 1938. Co-chmn., co-CEO Nat. Intergroup, Inc., Carrollton, Tex. Office: Foxmeyer Health 1220 Senlac Dr Carrollton TX 75006-7019

BUTLER, ALLEN TODD, poet; b. Portsmouth, Va., May 6, 1961; s. William and Doreathe Butler. BS in Mass Comm., Norfolk (Va.) State Coll., 1986. Distributor Norfolk Jour. & Guide; office worker Seven Seas, Norfolk; driver, packer L & U Moving Co., Virginia Beach, Va.; writer Christian Introduction, Virginia Beach. Author: Reflections, 1995, Know Your Enemy, 1995. Mem. The 12 Tribes of Israel, Oakwood Chapel Ch., Norfolk, 1991. Recipient Golden Poet award World of Poetry, Sacramento, 1989-91, Disting. Achievement award DJ Music Svcs., Chgo., 1983-84. Mem. The Writers Club (v.p. 1981-82), Top Records Songwriters Assn., Songwriter Club of Am. Home: 3200 Locust Ave Norfolk VA 23413

BUTLER, CAROL KING, advertising executive; b. Charlotte, N.C., May 29, 1952; d. Charles Snowden Watts and Marion (Thomas) King; m. James Rodney Butler, Aug. 12, 1972 (div. 1975). Student U. N.C., Greensboro, 1970-72. Sales rep. Sta.-WKIX, Raleigh, N.C., 1978-82, N.C. Box, Inc., Raleigh, 1982-84; radio sales account exec. WRAL-FM, Raleigh, 1984-88, team sales mgr., 1989; prin. Butler-Smith Assocs., Raleigh, 1988-89; ind. programming and video producer, Raleigh, 1989-90; prin., freelance presentation/video script writer, producer and sales person, Carol Butler Sales Writer/Photographer, 1991—; sales mgr. BW Territory of Lifetouch, 1996. Mem. NAFE. Democrat. Mem. Unity Ch. Avocations: water skiing, golf, tennis, boating, bicycling. Home: 6616 English Ivy Ln Raleigh NC 27615-6303

BUTLER, CHARLES RANDOLPH, JR., federal judge; b. 1940. BA, Washington and Lee U., 1962; LLB, U. Ala., 1966. Assoc. Hamilton Butler Riddick and LaTour, Mobile, Alal., 1966-69; asst. pub. defender Mobile County, 1969-70, dist. atty., 1971-75; ptnr Butler and Sullivan, Mobile, 1975-84; ptnr. Hamilton Butler Riddick Tarlton and Sullivan P.C., Mobile, 1984-88; dist. judge U.S. Dist. Ct. (so. dist.) Ala., Mobile, 1988-94, chief dist. judge, 1994—; adj. prof. criminal justice program U. So. Ala., 1972-76; mem. Judicial Conf. Criminal Law Com. Active Ala. Wildlife Fedn. (named Gov.'s Water Conservationist of Yr. 1975), Mobile County Wildlife and Conservation Assn., Gulf Coast Conservation Assn., UMS Prep. Sch. Alumni Assn. 1st lt. USAR, 1962-64. Named One of Outstanding Young Men of Am., Mobile County Jaycees, 1971. Mem. Ala. Bar Assn., Mobile County Bar Assn., Judicial Coun. 11th Cir. (judicial conf. com. on criminal law). Office: US Dist Ct 113 Saint Joseph St Mobile AL 36602-3606

BUTLER, CHARLES THOMAS, museum director, curator; b. Pearisburg, Va., Apr. 20, 1951; s. John Thomas Butler and Luenette (Evans) Hughes; m. Marilyn Laufer, Oct. 28, 1979. BA cum laude, U. Del., 1976; postgrad., U. N.Mex., Albuquerque, 1976-78. Asst. dir. Sioux City (Iowa) Art Ctr., 1979-85; exec. dir. Mitchell Mus., Mt. Vernon, Ill., 1985-88, Huntington (W.Va.) Mus. Art, 1988-94, Columbus (Ga.) Mus., 1994—. Author: New Talent/New York, 1984, Gary Bowling Paintings, 1987, Recent Graphics from American Print Shops, 1986, Out of the Mainstream: Photographs by Dick Arentz, 1991. Bd. dirs. Historic Columbus Found. Uptown Columbus, 1995, Southeastern Mus. Conf., 1990—. Mem. SEMC, Am. Assn. Mus., Rotary. Office: Columbus Mus 1251 Wynnton Rd Columbus GA 31906-2810

BUTLER, DAVID RAY, geography educator; b. Lincoln, Nebr., Apr. 14, 1952; s. Ray W. and Marian L. (Harbor) B.; m. Janet A. Baseman, Dec. 30, 1976; 1 child, William Butler. BA summa cum laude, U. Nebr., 1974, MS, 1976; PhD, U. Kans., 1982. Asst. prof. Okla. State U., Stillwater, 1982-86; from asst. prof. to Gen. Sandy Beaver assoc. prof. U. Ga., Athens, 1986-92; assoc. prof. U. N.C., Chapel Hill, 1992—; editl. bd. Resource Publs. in Geography, 1991-94, 95—, The Southeastern Geographer, 1991-95, 96—. Author: Zoogeomorphology, 1995; contbr. articles to profl. jours. Mem. Assn. Am. Geographers, Internat. Mtn. Soc., Am. Quaternary Assn. Lutheran. Office: U NC Dept Geography Chapel Hill NC 27599-3220

BUTLER, DONALD B., surgery educator, mediator; b. Houston, Feb. 5, 1919; s. Leo G. and Mary D. (Cohen) B.; m. Madeleine; children:Lind Martin, Kent, Bruce, Lauri. BA in Biology with honors, Rice U., 1940; BM, MD, MS in Physiology, Northwestern U., 1943; JD, South Tex. Coll. Law, 1989. Diplomate Am. Bd. Surgery; bar: Tex., 1991, U.S. Dist. Ct. (so. dist.) Tex. 1991. Abbott rsch. fellow Northwestern U., 1942-43, asst. in physiology, 1942-44; intern Cin. Gen. Hosp., 1944-45; surgery fellow Mayo Found., Rochester, Minn., 1947-51; pvt. practice surgeon, 1951-91; clin. assoc. prof. surgery coll. medicine Baylor U., Houston, 1951—; assoc. chief surgery St. Luke's Episc. Hosp., Houston, 1957-91; chmn. bd., organizing founder Ctr. Pavilion Hosp., Houston, 1965-69, co-founder, chmn. malpractice def. com., 1971-73; exec. med. dir. patient care rev. Harris County Hosp. Dist., Houston, 1988-91; clin. assoc. prof. surgery sch. medicine U. Tex., Houston, 1989—; acting. med. dir. surg. suites, cons. Tampa (Fla.) Gen. Hosp., 1991-92; med.-legal cons., 1988—; mem. exec. com. adv. coun. Ctr. for Conflict Analysis and Mgmt., sch. bus. and pub. adminstrn. U. Houston, Clear Lake. Capt. U.S. Army Med. Corps, 1945-46. Named Hon. Indian Chief, Cherokee Tenn. Water Tribe, 1991. Mem. AMA, ACS, ABA, Am. Arbitration Assn. (panel neutrals), Am. Coll. Physician Execs., Am. Med. Peer Rev. Assn., Am. Coll. MEd. Quality, Am. Soc. Law and Medicine, Nat. Assn. Quality Assurance Profls., Internat. Coll. Surgeons, Nat. Urol. Assn. Mex. (hon.), Soc. Profls. in Dispute Resolution (assoc.), Soc. Med. Assn., State Bar Tex., Tex. Soc. Gastroenterologists and Proctologists, Tex. Surg. Soc., Tex. Soc. for Quality Assurance, Tex. Med. Found., Houston Surg. Soc., Priestley Soc. (pres. 1971-72), Dr.'s Mayo Soc., Mayo Found. Alumni Assn., Coll. State Bar Tex., Phi Beta Kappa, Alpha Omega Alpha, Sigma Xi, Phi Delta Epsilon. Home: 415 Bayridge Rd Morgans Point TX 77571-3508 Office: PO Box 1165 La Porte TX 77572-1165

BUTLER, DOUGLAS JAMES, academic librarian; b. Buffalo, Aug. 13, 1952; s. David Milton and Ruth Harriet (Gretzinger) B.; m. Janet G. Johnson, May 13, 1974; children: Rebecca, Rachel, Mark, Matthew. BA, Sterling (Kans.) Coll., 1974; MLS, SUNY, Geneseo, 1975; postgrad., Ind. U., 1983. Cataloger Phila. Coll. of Bible, 1975-76; libr. dir. Washington Bible Coll., Lanham, Md., 1976; catalog libr. Asbury Coll., Wilmore, Ky., 1977—. Editor: Christian Periodical Index, 1986—. Mem. Ky. Libr. Assn., Assn. Christian Librs. (bd. dirs. 1985-92), Wilmore Lions Club (pres. 1995-96, dir. 1996—). Republican. Methodist. Home: 202 S Walnut St Wilmore KY 40390 Office: Asbury Coll 1 Macklem Dr Wilmore KY 40390

BUTLER, HOWARD EDWARD, quality assurance professional; b. Middletown, Ohio, Apr. 15, 1923; s. Howard Herman and Ida Esther (Moore) B.; m. Barbara Jean Burroughs, May 15, 1948; children: Sue, John, James, Richard. B in Indsl. Engring., GMI Engring. & Mgmt. Inst., 1948. From quality engr. to supt. reliability and quality GM, Dayton, Ohio, 1948-80; owner Quality Control Svcs., Co., Hilton Head Island, S.C., 1981—; com. mem. statis. quality control GM, Detroit, 1950-54, quality and reliability stds., 1970-80, brake sys. reliability com. mem., 1976-80; presenter in field. Co-author: Statistical Process Control Simplified: Practical Steps to Quality, 1986, Statistical Process Control Simplified Workbook, 1990, Statistical Process Control Simplified for Services: Practical Tools for Continuous Quality Improvement, 1991. Chmn. Kettering (Ohio) Sch. Adv. Coun., 1968. With USN, 1945-46. Mem. Am. Soc. for Quality Control (sr. mem., cert. quality engr.). Home and Office: 6 Edgewood Dr Hilton Head Island SC 29926-6701

BUTLER, JAMES HANSEL, periodontist; b. Canton, Ohio, Dec. 7, 1936; s. Hansel Harmon and Mary Frances (Kelley) B.; m. Carol Teegardin, July 28, 1961; children: Catherine J., Matthew T., Sarah A. BA, Denison U., 1958; DDS, Ohio State U., 1962; MS, U. Rochester, 1967. From asst. prof. to assoc. prof. U. Minn., Mpls., 1967-74; from assoc. prof. to prof. Va. Commonwealth U. Sch. Dentistry, Richmond, 1974—; vis. prof. King Saud U., Riyadh, Saudi Arabia, 1985-86, 82; leader skill devel. group Va. Commonwealth U. 1992-96, dir. primary care clinic, 1988-92, interim dir. clinics, 1983-85, chmn. dept. gen. dentistry, 1981-88. Sunday sch. supt. Trinity Lutheran Ch., Richmond, 1975-77, pres. congregation, 1979-81, 88-90. Dental officer USAF, 1962-64. Fellow Internat. Coll. Dentists, Am. Coll. Dentists; mem. Internat. Assn. Dental Rsch., Am. Assn. Dental Schs., Am. Dental Assn., Va. Dental Assn., Am. Acad. Periodontology, Psi Omega, Omicron Kappa Upsilon, Sigma Xi. Republican. Office: Va Commonwealth U Dentistry 521 N 11th St Box 980566 Richmond VA 23298

BUTLER, JODY TALLEY, gifted education educator; b. Columbus, Ga., Mar. 14, 1958; d. Bill Ray and Jacqueline (Hay) T.; m. Danny Butler. BS in Edn., West Ga. Coll., 1979, MEd, 1982; EdD, Auburn U., 1988. Cert. tchr., Ga. Tchr. Cen. Primary Sch., Carrollton, 1979-88; tchr. gifted student program QUEST Cen. Middle Sch., Carrollton, 1988—; co-owner Hay's Mill Antiques, Ga., 1994—. Mem. Internat. Reading Assn., Ga. Ptnrs. in Edn. Coun., Profl. Asshn. Ga. Educators, Carroll County Cmty. Chorus, Phi Delta Kappa (Dissertation of Yr. award 1989), Phi Kappa Phi, Alpha Gamma Delta. Presbyterian. Office: Ctrl Middle Sch 155 Whooping Creek Rd Carrollton GA 30116-8999

BUTLER, JOHN PAUL, sales professional; b. Lexington, S.C., Sept. 6, 1935; s. Albert G. and Alma J. (Braswell) B.; m. Clare Vestal, Nov. 8, 1958 (div. 1978); children: Cathy, Tom, Frank. BSME (NROTC scholar), U. S.C., 1957; MBA, U. Conn., 1965. Sr. engr. Pratt & Whitney Aircraft, East Hartford, Conn., 1960-65; engring. supr. Westinghouse Electric Corp., Pitts., 1966-70, mktg. supr., 1971-76; dir. sales and mktg. Morgan div. Amca, Alliance, Ohio, 1977-78; sales dir. Mid-East, Westinghouse Electric Corp., Orlando, Fla., 1979-84; pres. Butler Assocs., Orlando, 1984-86; mgr. Tandy

Corp., Tampa, Fla., 1987—. Committeeman Rep. Com. Lt. USN, 1957-60. Mem. ASME. Methodist. Contbr. articles to profl. jours.; patentee in field. Home: 4712 Olive Branch Rd Apt 415 Orlando FL 32811-7247 Office: Tandy Corp 5130 Eisenhower Blvd Ste 170 Tampa FL 33634-6312

BUTLER, MARY ANNE, school principal; b. Savannah, Ga., Dec. 13, 1946; d. John George and Mary Catherine (Winters) B. BS, Armstrong State Coll., 1967; MEd, Ga. State U., 1972; EdS, Ga. So. Coll., 1984. Cert. tchr., Ga. Tchr. Chatham-Savannah Bd. Edn., 1969-70, spl. edn. tchr., 1970-73, coord. behavior disorders, 1973-81; prin. Blessed Sacrament Sch., Savannah, 1981—; cons. pre-sch. and extended-day sch. programs. Grantee Ga. Dept. Edn., 1970, U.S. Dept. Edn., 1971. Mem. NEA, Mental Health Assn. Coastal Empire (sec. 1975, pres. 1978), Coun. Exceptional Children, Nat. Cath. Edn. Assn., Delta Kappa Gamma, Phi Kappa Phi. Democrat. Roman Catholic. Home: 517 E 53rd St Savannah GA 31405-3511 Office: Blessed Sacrament Sch 1003 E Victory Dr Savannah GA 31405-2425

BUTLER, MERLIN GENE, physician, medical geneticist, educator; b. Atkinson, Nebr., Aug. 2, 1952; s. Garold Melvin and Berdena June (Sandall) B.; m. Ranae Ilene Kisker, Oct. 2, 1976; children: Michelle Ranae, Brian Gene. BA with very high distinction, Chadron State Coll., 1974, BS with very high distinction, 1975; MD, U. Nebr., Omaha, 1978; MS, U. Nebr., Lincoln, 1980; PhD, Ind. U., Indpls., 1984. Supervising physician Med. Info. Svcs., Omaha, 1978-80; rsch. assoc. dept. biology U. Notre Dame, South Bend, Ind., 1983-84; med. dir. North Ctrl. Ind. Regional Genetics Ctr., South Bend, 1983-84; dir. cytogenetics Meml. Hosp., South Bend, 1983-84; NIH postdoctoral fellow dept. med. genetics Sch. Medicine Ind. U., Indpls., 1980-83, adj. asst. prof. dept. med. genetics Sch. Medicine, 1984; asst. prof. dept. pediatrics Sch. Medicine Vanderbilt U., Nashville, 1984-90, dir. regional genetics program Sch. Medicine, 1984—, dir. Cytogenetics Lab. dept. pediatrics Sch. Medicine, 1989—, assoc. prof. dept. pediatrics, 1990—, assoc. prof. dept. pathology, 1991—, investigator John F. Kennedy Ctr. Rsch. on Edn. and Human Devel., Peabody Coll., 1987—; assoc. dir. Inst. Behavior and Genetics; assoc. prof. dept. orthopedics U. Indpls., 1994—; adj. assoc. prof. dept. pediatrics Meharry Med. Coll., Nashville, 1988—; genetics cons. Baptist Hosp., Nashville, 1985—, Westside Hosp., Nashville, 1985—, Nashville Gen. Hosp., 1985—; mem. epidemiology genetic diseases subcom. Ind. State Bd. Health, 1983-84; faculty interviewer Vanderbilt U., 1987; peer reviewer Am. Jour. Human Genetics, Am. Jour. Med. Genetics, Clin. Genetics, Am. Jour. Diseases of Children, Dysmorphology and Clin. Genetics, Am. Jour. Mental Retardation, Jour. Pediatrics, So. Med. Jour., Human Mutations, Cancer Genetics and Cytogenetics, Pediatrics, Genomics, Prader-Willi Perspectives; mem. ad-hoc grant review com. NIH, 1990—, craniofacial assessment team Vanderbilt U., 1992—; lectr., presenter in field. Author: Fragile X Syndrome: A Major Cause of X-Linked Mental Retardation, 1988, 1989; author: (with others) Genetics for the Medically Oriented, 1983, Novak's Textbook of Gynecology, 11th edit., 1988, Birth Defects Encyclopedia, 1990, Prader-Willi Syndrome and Other Chromosome 15q Deletion Disorders, 1992, Human Genetics: New Perspectives, 1994, 1992 International Fragile X Conference Proceedings, 1992, Prader-Willi and Angelman Syndromes Examples of Genetic Imprinting in Man, 1994; mem. editorial bd. Prader-Willi Perspectives, 1992—; contbr. numerous articles to profl. jours. including Nature and New England Jour. Medicine. Grant reviewer March of Dimes Birth Defects Found., 1985—. Recipient Disting. Svc. award Chadron State Coll., 1986, Teaching award Osler Inst., 1989; grantee Univ. Rsch. Coun., 1985, 92-93, Tenn. Dept. Mental Health and Mental Retardation, 1986-91, Clin. Nutrition Rsch. Unit, 1986-88, Joseph P. Kennedy, Jr. Found., 1988, 89—, Clin. Rsch. Ctr. Meharry Med. Coll., 1989—, Dept. Pathology, 1992-93, Orthopedic Rsch. Edn. Found., 1993—, NIH, 1995—; Cancer Rsch. grantee Ind. U. Med. Ctr., 1980, Biomed. Rsch. Support grantee, 1985, 88, 89—, Clin. Rsch. grantee March of Dimes Birth Defects Found., 1987, 88, 90-92, Lyle V. Andrews Meml. scholar, 1974. Fellow Am. Coll. Med. Genetics (founder, diplomate, lab. practice subcom. 1993); mem. AMA (Physician Recognition award 1984, 87), AAAS, Am. Bd. Med. Genetics (cert. clin. genetics and clin. cytogenetics), Am. Genetics Assn., Am. Soc. Human Genetics (cytogenetics resource com. 1992—), Am. Fedn. Clin. Rsch., Coll. Am. Pathologists (cytogenetics resource com. 1992—, molecular pathology resource com. 1993—), So. Med. Assn., Davidson County Pediatric Soc., Prader-Willi Syndrome Assn. (med. rsch. task force 1985—, diagnostic task force 1991—), Sigma Xi, Phi Chi. Home: 8218 Twin Springs Ct Brentwood TN 37027-6723 Office: Vanderbilt U Sch Med Divsn Genetics DD-2205 Medical Center N Nashville TN 37232-2578

BUTLER, MICHAEL WARD, economics educator; b. Great Bend, Kans., June 11, 1939; s. George Ward and Mary Jane (Lambert) B.; m. Regina Ann Hammond, Sept. 8, 1995; 1 child, Alexander Ward. BSBA, Fort Hays State U., 1963, MS in Econs., 1964; PhD in Econs., U. Ark., 1974. Diplomate, bd. cert. forensic examiner. Data processing sales rep. IBM, Wichita, Kans., 1964-66; instr. econs. Butler County C.C., El Dorado, Kans., 1964-70; asst. prof. econs. U. North Ala., Florence, 1973-75, assoc. prof. econs., 1975-78, prof. econs., 1978—; referee Jour. Forensic Econs., Kansas City, Mo., 1988—; editl. adv. Ark. Bus. Econs. Rev., Fayetteville, Ark., 1976—; editl. bd. Am. Bd. of Forensic Examiners, Springfield, Mo., 1995—. Editor: Jour. Legal Econs., 1991-96. Recipient Outstanding Achievement award Am. Higher Ed., 1985; Distinguished Serv. award Ala. C. of C., Montgomery, 1976. Mem. Nat. Assn. Forensic Economists, Am. Bd. Forensic Examiners, Am. Rehab. Econs. Assoc. (adv. bd. 1992-94), MidSouth Acad. Econs. and Fin. (pres. 85-86), Am. Acad. Econ. Fin. Experts (pres. 94—, Svc. award 1995), Am. Econs. Assn., Am. Statis. Assn., C. of C. of the Shoals. Home: 462 Ridgecliff Dr Florence AL 35630 Office: U North Ala Box 5077 Florence AL 35632

BUTLER, QUINCY GASQUE, musician; b. Winchester, Va., May 31, 1935; d. Quincy Damon and Ruth Lavinia (Beaty) Gasque; m. Raymond Kenneth Butler, June 23, 1956; children: Ruth Wendell Butler Forstall, Raymond Kenneth III, Damon Gasque, Courtney Canair. BA cum laude, Randolph-Macon Women's Coll., 1956; AA summa cum laude, No. Va. C.C., 1982; MM, Cath. U. Am., 1985; student, Westminster Choir Coll. Social studies tchr., 1956-57; music dir., founder handbell program bell camp and concerts St. Alban's Episcopal Ch., Annandale, Va., 1976-91, mem. vestry, 1996—; chorus tchr. No. Va. C.C., 1986; dir. Musica Viva Oratorio Soc. Washington, 1989-90; founder, music dir. Alban Chorale, 1989—; piano tchr. Falls Church, Va., 1961—; judge Nat. Piano Guild Auditions; clinician local and nat. level teaching various classes in handbell techniques. Vol. Jr. League No. Va., chmn. thrift shop, pres., 1976-77, projects chmn., 1995-96; mem. Dominion Guild, Inc. Mem. Am. Coll. Musicians (cert. piano tchr.), Nat. Assn. Music Tchrs., No. Va. Music Tchrs. Assn., Va. Music Tchrs. Assn., Springfield Music Club, Va. Fedn. Music Clubs, Nat. Fedn. Music Clubs, Am. Guild English Handbell Ringers, Inc. (chmn. area III festival conf. 1989-91, chmn. area III 1991-93, nat. bd. dirs. 1990-93, chmn. adult festival conf. area III 1994-95), Choral Arts Soc. (singer 1965-76), Oratorio Soc. Washington (singer 1985—). Episcopalian. Home and Office: 3613 Bent Branch Ct Falls Church VA 22041-1005

BUTLER, ROBERT OLEN, writer, educator; b. Granite City, Ill., Jan. 20, 1945; s. Robert Olen Sr. and Lucille Frances (Hall) B.; m. Carol Supplee, Aug. 10, 1968 (div. Jan. 1972); m. Marylin Geller, July 1, 1972 (div. July 1987); 1 child, Joshua Robert; m. Maureen Donlan, July 21, 1987 (div. Mar. 1995); m. Elizabeth Dewberry, Apr. 23, 1995. BS summa cum laude in Oral Interpretation, Northwestern U., 1967; MA in Playwriting, U. Iowa, 1969; postgrad., New Sch. Social Rsch., 1979-81; LHD, McNeese State U., 1994. Editor-in-chief Energy User News, N.Y.C., 1975-85; assoc. prof., then prof. fiction writing McNeese State U., Lake Charles, La., 1985—; prof. McNeese State U., 1993—; summer faculty Iowa Summer Writing Festival U. Iowa, Port Townsend (Wash.) Writers Conf., New Orleans Writers' Conf., Southampton Writers' Conf., Long Island U., N.Y., Hofstra U. Summer Writing Conf., Hempstead, N.Y., others, 1988—. Author: The Alleys of Eden, 1981 (also wrote screenplay 1991-92), Sun Dogs, 1982, Countrymen of Bones, 1983, On Distant Ground, 1985, Wabash, 1987, The Deuce, 1989, (short story collection) A Good Scent from a Strange Mountain, 1992 (Pulitzer Prize for fiction 1993, Richard and Hilda Rosenthal Found. award Am. Acad. Arts & Letters 1993, nominee PEN/Faulkner award 1993, Notable Book 1993 Notable Books Coun. Am. Libr. Assn.), They Whisper, 1994, Tabloid Dreams, 1996; author numerous short stories; works translated to 12 langs.; contbr. articles, book reviews to jours., newspapers. Sgt. U.S. Army, 1969-72, Vietnam. Recipient Emily Clark Balch award best work fiction, 1990 Va. Quar. Rev., 1991, TuDo Chinh Kien award outstanding contbns. Am. culture by Vietnam vet. Vietnam Vets. Am., 1987, Medal of Merit, Lotos Club, 1996; grantee NEA, 1994; fellow John Simon Guggenheim Found., 1993. Mem. PEN. Office: Dept of Lang Arts McNeese State U PO Box 92655 Lake Charles LA 70609

BUTLER, SHEILA MORRIS, occupational health nurse; b. Paducah, Ky., Sept. 12, 1944; d. Edwin Morris and Beatrice Aileen (Hobbs) Word; m. Benjamin Edward Butler, Dec. 4, 1976; 1 child, Michelle Renee. ADN, Paducah Jr. Coll., 1966. Cert. occupational health nurse, Am. Bd. Occupational Health, occupational hearing conservationist. Staff nurse Marshall County Hosp., Benton, Ky., 1966-67; shift nursing supr. Parkview Hosp., Dyersburg, Tenn., 1967-69, obstet. nursing supr., 1969-72; clin. nursing instr. State of Tenn. Dept. of Edn., Nashville, 1968-69; charge nurse Dravo-Groves-NEwberg, Hamlettsburg, Ill., 1972-74; surg. nurse Western Bapt. Hosp., Paducah, Ky., 1974-76; ophthalmic asst. Dr. Harry Abell, Jr., Paducah, Ky., 1976-83; occupational health cons. self-employed, Paducah, Ky., 1983-86; plant nurse Air Products & Chemicals, Inc., Calvert City, Ky., 1986—; bd. dirs. Nat. Nurses Soc. on Addiction, 1983-84; Am. Bd. Occupational Health Nurses, 1994—; sec. Jackson Purchase Oper. Nurses, Paducah, 1975-76; cmty. asst. panel Agy. for Toxic Substance and Disease Registry of CDC, Atlanta, 1991—; pres. Jackson Purchase Occupational Health Nurse, 1993—. Mem. Nat. Arbor Day Found. Named Student Nurse of Yr., Circle K-Paducah Jr. Coll., 1966, Ky. Col., Gov. Louie B. Nunn, 1971—; recipient Chem. Group Recognition award Air Products & Chems., 1990, 91. Mem. NAFE, Am. Assn. Occupational Health Nurses (pres. Jackson Purchase sect. 1993—, assoc. bd. dirs. 1994—), Civil Def. of McCracken County, Order of Ea. Star, Esther # 5 Ruth, Daus. of the Nile Neith Temple, Chinese Shar-Pei Club of Am. Democrat. Baptist. Home: 248 Hayes St Benton KY 42025-6649 Office: Air Products & Chemicals PO Box 97 Calvert City KY 42029-0097

BUTLER, SHIRLEY ANN, social worker; b. New Orleans, Apr. 18, 1951; d. John and Will A. (Powell) Cain; children: Chander Lynn, Twann Gerald-Lynn. BSW, So. U. New Orleans, 1980, MSW, 1991. Lic. practical nurse; cert. phlebologist; qualified mental retardation profl. Social worker intern Comty. Svc. Ctr., New Orleans, 1979, VA Hosp. New Orleans, 1979-80; social worker Hope Haven/Madonna Manor, Marrero, La., 1980-81; tchr. Orleans Parish Sch. Bd., New Orleans, 1981-87; psychiat. technician River Oaks Mental Hosp., West Harahan, La., 1981-82; counselor Vols. of Am. of New Orleans, 1987-89; mental retardation profl. Met. Developmental Ctr., Belle Chase, La., 1989-92; case mgr. No AIDS Task Force, New Orleans, 1992-93; nurse St. Anna Nursing Home, New Orleans, 1993-94, Meds Force, 1994—, St. Charles Manor, 1994—; social worker intern Carrollton Hollgrove Comty. Ctr., New Orleans, 1977. Contbr. rsch. articles to profl. jours. Active People's Inst. for Survival and Beyond, New Orleans, 1990—. Mem. NASW, Acad. Cert. Baccalaureate Social Workers. Democrat. Baptist. Home: 9412 Fig St New Orleans LA 70118-1723

BUTLER, STEVEN RAY, history educator, historian, genealogist; b. Dallas, June 5, 1949; s. Raymond Joe Butler and Ida Louise (Jenkins) Pirman; m. Anita Rose Wilson, Sept. 3, 1970; children: Benjamin Tate, Nathan James. AA, R.I. Jr. Coll., Warwick, 1974; BA, R.I. Coll., 1976. Cert. tchr., Tex. Clk. Delta Steel Bldg. Co., Dallas, 1976-77; travel agt. Am. Express Travel svc., London, 1978-82, Internat. travel Advisors, Richardson, Tex., 1983-84, World Bus. Travel, Dallas, 1984-85; dir. edn. Regional Travel Tng. Ctr., Dallas, 1985-89; dir. Acad. for Careers in Travel, Plano, Tex., 1989-91; tchr. U.S. history Austin Acad., Garland, Tex., 1991-93; writer/rschr. Descendants of Mex. War Vets., Richardson, Tex., 1993-94; instr. Richland Coll., Dallas, 1994—. Editor Mex. War Jour., 1991—, The Am. Eagle, 1989—; author: How to Find Your Mexican War Ancestor, 1990, Historic Sites of the Mexican War in Texas, 1995; editor/compiler: Historical and Genealogical Handbook of Freestone County, Texas, 1992, A Complete Roster of Mexican War Officers, 1994, A Documentary History of the Mexican War, 1995; author/compiler: Alabama Volunteers in the Mexican War, 1996; world wide web site adminstr. Descendants of Mexican War Veterans. Adv. bd. Palo Alto Nat. Park Com., Brownsville, Tex., 1991—. With USN, 1968-71. Mem. Descendants of Mex. War Vets. (pres. 1989—), Sons of Confed. Vets. Democrat. Office: Descendants of Mexican War Veterans PO Box 830482 Richardson TX 75083-0482

BUTLER, SUZANNE B., secondary education educator; b. Waco, Tex., June 8, 1955; d. Leo Weldon and Ruth Virginia (Dyer) Sumblin; m. Lawrence A. Baca, Dec. 28, 1974 (div. Dec. 1987); m. Samuel J. Butler, June 6, 1988; children: Bryan V. Baca, Amanda E., Elijah J. BA, U. Okla., 1976, MS, 1979. Cert. elem. edn. with mid. sch. endorsements; cert. photo-finishing technician. Grad. asst. dept. psychology U. Okla., Norman, 1977-80; photographer F2 Photography, Del City, Okla., 1980-87; mgr. Shirron Enterprises, Nassau, The Bahamas, 1988-91; tchr. Oklahoma City Pub. Schs., 1994—. Contbr. articles to profl. jours., photographs to books and mags. Vol. Head Start, Norman, 1993-94. Mem. Kappa Delta Pi. Office: Moon Mid Sch 1901 NE 13th St Oklahoma City OK 73117

BUTLER, THOMAS PARKE, internist, oncologist; b. Chgo., Apr. 12, 1945; s. Robert Elliott and Barbara Jane (Parke) B.; m. Ann Johnson Benedict; 1 child, Whitney Elizabeth. BA magna cum laude, Oberlin Coll., 1967; MD, Case Western Reserv U., 1971. Diplomate Am. Bd. Internal Medicine, Am. Bd. Oncology. Intern internal medicine R.I. Hosp., Providence, 1971-72; sr. asst. surgeon, rsch. assoc. USPHS, Nat. Cancer Inst., Bethesda, Md., 1972-74; resident Georgetown U. Hosp., Washington, 1974-76, fellow in med. cncology, 1976-78; pvt. practice specializing in oncology and hematology Arlington-Fairfax Oncology-Hematology P.C., Arlington, Va., 1978—; clin. assoc. prof. medicine Georgetown U. Sch. of Medicine, Washington, 1982—; med. dir. oncology unit, Arlington Hosp., 1983—, exec. com. 1988—. Contbr. articles and abstracts to profl. jours. Mem. county bd. Am. Cancer Soc., Arlington, 1980—. Sr. asst. surgeon USPHS, 1972-74. Recipient Golden Apple Teaching award, Georgetown U. Med. Sch., 1981. Fellow Am. Coll. Physicians; mem. AMA, Va. Med. Soc., Am. Soc. Internal Medicine, Va. Soc. Internal Medicine, Am. Assn. for Cancer Rsch., Am. Soc. Clin. Oncolo gy, Washington Golf and Country Club, Sigma Xi. Office: Arlington-Fairfax Hematology Oncology 1715 N George Mason Dr Arlington VA 22205-3609

BUTLER, VICKIE BURKHART, college official; b. Knoxville, Tenn., May 22, 1955; d. James Claude and Ruth Adelia (Pratt) B.; m. Benjamin Larry Butler, Jan. 7, 1984; 1 stepson, Benjamin Brent. BS, Carson-Newman Coll., 1976; MS, U. Tenn., 1979. Cert. tchr. Tchr. Knox County Sch. System, Knoxville, 1976-82; state vol. coord. Tenn. Dept. Human Svcs., Nashville, 1982-89; dir. alumni rels. Carson-Newman Coll., Jefferson City, Tenn., 1989—; mem. Tenn. Advancement Resources Coun., 1989—; cons.; workshop leader; program builder; grad. Tenn. Leadership, 1990. Author: (manual) DHS Volunteer Services, 1982. Pianist, dir. bell choir 1st United Meth. Ch., Newport, 1985—, sec. nominations and personnel com. mem. Fellow Lab. for Learning; mem. Gamma Sigma Sigma, Phi Lambda Theta, Kappa Delta Pi. Office: Carson Newman Coll Russell Ave Jefferson City TN 37760

BUTTERFIELD, CHARLES EDWARD, JR., educational consultant; b. Urbana, Ill., Mar. 31, 1928; s. Charles E. and Bessie J. (Winters) B.; BS, U. Ill., 1951, MS, 1953; postgrad. (NSF/AAAS fellow) Mich State U., 1959, 64-65, 72, Duke U., 1958, No. Ill. U., 1958-59, Knox Coll., 1962, Fla. State U., 1969, U. Colo., 1970; m. Gayle Coberley, Jan. 27, 1952; children: Jeffrey M., Carey J. Field exec. Nottawa Trails council Boy Scouts Am., Battle Creek, Mich., 1953-54; instr. sci. Gardner-South Wilmington Twp. H.S., Gardner, Ill., 1954-59, Lake Park H.S., Medinah, Ill., 1959-65; sr. sci. project editor Singer/Random House Pub. Co., 1965-68; sci. supr. Ramsey (N.J.) Pub. Schs., 1968-82; cons. Rand McNally Pubs., 1972-80; sci. edn. cons., 1981—; mem. sci. adv. bd. Raintree Pubs., Milw., 1981-86; assoc. Thomas A. Edison Found., 1981-88; condr. various workshops for sci. teaching, 1965—. Pres., Bd. Edn., Gardner, Ill., 1956-57; pres. Foxwood Village FMO, 1988-90; treas., bd. dirs. Highland Fairways POA, 1993-96; co-project dir., fin. officer suprs. programs NSF/NSSA/PEEC, 1979-83; judge Seiko Youth Challenge, 1994, 95. With USN and USMC, 1946-48. Recipient Allendale (N.J.) Cmty. Lifesaving award, 1976; fellow 1st Southeastern NASA Aerospace Conf., 1961. Contbg. author: NSSA Sourcebook for Science Supervisors, 2nd edit., 1976, 3d edit., 1988. Fellow AAAS; mem. NEA, Nat. Sci. Suprs. Assn. (pres. 1977-78, mem. exec. com. 1974-80, mem. editl. adv. bd. 1986-91, sr. staff mem. various other confs.-U. Calif. 1979, U. Iowa 1979-80, Outstanding Svc. award 1990), Nat. Sci. Tchrs. Assn. (exec. bd. 1977-78, Disting. Svc. Sci. Edn. citation 1981), N.J. Sci. Tchrs. Assn., N.J. Sci. Suprs. Assn. (Disting. Svc. award 1982), Cmty. Assn. Inst., Ramsey Suprs. Assn. (founding pres. 1980-81), Bergen County Sci. Suprs. Assn. (pres. 1971-73, Outstanding Svc. award 1974, 78), Sch. Sci. and Math. Assn., Am. Inst. Biol. Scis., Nat. Assn. Biol. Tchrs., Coun. Elem. Sci. Internat., Assn. Edn. Tchrs. Sci., N.J. Prins. and Suprs. Assn., Am. Assn. Notaries, Nat. Notary Assn., Cmty. Assns. Inst., 1st Marine Divsn. Assn., Am. Legion, USN Meml. Found., Mensa, Masons, DeMolay (chevalier), Order of Ea. Star, Psi Chi. Office: 53 Cardinal Dr Oakland NJ 07436-3911

BUTTERWORTH, ROBERT A., state attorney general; b. Passaic, N.J., Aug. 20, 1942; m. Marta Prado. BA, BS, U. Fla.; JD, U. Miami. Prosecutor Fla., 1970-74; circuit and county judge, 1974-78; sheriff Broward County Sheriff's Office, 1978-82; head Fla. Dept. Hwy. Safety and Motor Vehicles, Tallahassee, 1982-84; mayor City of Sunrise, 1984-87; atty. gen. State of Fla., Tallahassee, 1987—. Office: Capitol Dept Legal Affairs Tallahassee FL 32399-1050

BUTTON, JAMES DAVID, II, physics educator; b. Hopewell, Va., Oct. 26, 1944; s. James David and Elizabeth (Cleere) B.; m. Beverly Luz, June 16, 1973; children: James David III, Elizabeth Lee. BS, Randolph-Macon, 1967; MEd, U. Va., 1971. Cert. secondary education, Va. Physics and chemistry tchr. Prince William County, Manassas, Va., 1968-79, G/T resource staff, 1979-82, physics tchr., 1982-87, 88—; asst. prin. Manassas City, 1987-88. Edn. deacon Ch. of Christ, Manassas, 1995—. Mem. Am. Assn. Physics Tchrs., Phi Delta Kappa (v.p. mem.). Home: 9378 Fernwood Ct Manassas VA 20110

BUTTS, TERRY LUCAS, state supreme court justice; b. Patsburg, Ala., Feb. 15, 1944; s. Ezra Lucas and Nata V. (Watson) B.; m. Suzanne Croley, Mar. 7, 1987; children: Kells Carroll, Casey L. Carroll. BS, Troy State U., 1979; JD, U. Ala., 1968. Bar: Ala. 1968. Pvt. practice Elba, Ala., 1968-76; judge City of Elba, 1969-74, Coffee County, Elba, 1974-76; circuit judge Coffee and Pike Counties, 1976-94; justice Ala. Supreme Ct., Montgomery, 1995—. Office: Ala Supreme Ct 300 Dexter Ave Montgomery AL 36104-3741

BUTZNER, JOHN DECKER, JR., federal judge; b. Scranton, Pa., Oct. 2, 1917. B.A., U. Scranton, 1939; LL.B., U. Va., 1941. Bar: Va. bar 1941. Pvt. practice law Fredericksburg, 1941-58; judge 15th and 39th Jud. Cir. of Va., 1958-62; U.S. judge Ea. Dist. Va., 1962-67; cir. judge U.S. Ct. Appeals (4th cir.), Richmond, Va., 1967—; judge for appointment of ind. counsel U.S. Ct. Appeals for D.C. Cir., 1988—. Served with USAAF, 1942-45.

BUZZARD, SIR ANTHONY FARQUHAR, religion educator; b. Godalming, Surrey, Eng., June 28, 1935; came to U.S., 1981; s. Anthony W. and Margaret E. (Knapp) B.; m. Barbara Jean Arnold, July 21, 1970; children: Sarah J., Claire J., Heather E. MA in Modern Langs., Oxford U., 1960; ThM, Bethany Theol. Coll., 1990. Tchr. fgn. langs. Am. Sch., London, 1974-81; lectr. in Bible Oregon (Ill.) Bible Coll. (now Atlanta Bible Coll.), Morrow, Ga., 1982—; coord. Restoration Fellowship, Oregon, 1981—. Author: The Coming Kingdom of the Messiah: A Solution to the Riddle of the New Testament, 1988, The Doctrine of the Trinity: Christianity's Self-Inflicted Wound, 1994, Our Fathers Who Aren't in Heaven: The Forgotten Christianity of Jesus the Jew, 1995. Home: 185 Summerville Dr Brooks GA 30205-9709

BYARS, MERLENE HUTTO, accountant, visual artist, writer, publisher; b. West Columbia, S.C., Nov. 8, 1931; d. Gideon Thomas and Nettie (Fail) Hutto; m. Alvin Willard Byars, June 10, 1950 (dec.); children: Alvin Gregg, Robin Mark, Jay C., Blaine Derrick. Student, Palmer Coll., Midlands Tech., U. S.C., 1988—; diploma in Journalism, Internat. Corr. Sch., 1995, Longridge Writers Group, 1995. Acct. State of S.C., 1964-93; ret., 1993; pres. Merlene Hutto Byars Enterprises, Cayce, 1993—; designer Collegiate Licensing Co., U.S. Trademark, 1989—. Pub. Lintheads, 1986, Olympia-Pacific: The Way It was 1895-1970, 1981; Did Jesus Drive a Pickup Truck, 1993, The Plantation Era in South Carolina; pub., produr. (play) Lintheads and Hard Times, 1986; creator quilt which hung in S.C. State Capital for bicentennial celebration, 1988; designer Saxe Gotha Twp. Flag, 1993; author: The State of South Carolina Scrap Book, Orangeburg District, 1990, A Scrap Book of South Carolina, Dutch Fork, Saxe Gotha, Lexington County, 1994. Life mem. Women's Missionary Soc., United Luth. Ch., 1954—; mem. edn. found. U. S.C., 1969-93; treas. Airport H.S. Booster Club, 1969-76; sec. Saxe Gotha Hist. Soc., Lexington County, 1994-96. Recipient numerous awards for quilting S.C. State Fair, 1976—, Cert. for rose rsch. test panel Jackson and Perkins, 1982, Formost Women in Comm. award, 1969-70, Cayce Amb. award, City of Cayce, 1994. Fellow Internat. Biog. Assn.; mem. Cayce Mus. History (contbr. books, award for contribution 1987), S.C. State Mus. Home: 1842 Evelyn St Cayce SC 29033-2008

BYAS, TERESA ANN URANGA, healthcare professional; b. Plainview, Tex., Mar. 20, 1955; d. Adam T. and Lucy (Sandoval) Uranga; m. Wesley W. Byas, Sept. 11, 1972 (div. 1992); children: Chad W., Christina Ann. Student, Tarrant County Jr. Coll., 1982-83, 87-88, 95—, Tex. Wesleyan U., 1983-88. Teller Allied Nat. Bank (now named 1st Interstate), Ft. Worth, 1985-87, Nowlin Savs. and Loans (now named Comerica), Ft. Worth, 1987-88; missionary United Meth. Ch. Global Bd. World Missions, Brazil, 1988-91; asst. mgr. Bag 'n Baggage, Ft. Worth, 1991-92, store mgr., 1992-93; med. record clerical coord. Total Home Health Svcs., Inc., Ft. Worth, 1993-94; nurses aide Total Home Svcs. In Med. Home Health, 1994-95, Nurture Care, Ft. Worth, Tex., 1995—; with svc. desk The Home Depot Store, Ft. Worth, 1996—. Mem. Women's Polit. Caucus, Ft. Worth, United Meth. Women's Group; hon. mem. Westcliff United Meth. Women's Group (chpt. named in her honor 1991). Mem. Am. Bus. Women's Assn. Democrat. Home: 3117 Sondra Dr # 207D Fort Worth TX 76107 Office: The Home Depot 4850 SW Loop 820 Fort Worth TX 76109

BYBEE, JAY SCOTT, lawyer, educator; b. Oakland, Calif., Oct. 27, 1953; s. Rowan Scott and Joan (Hickman) B.; m. Dianna Jean Greer, Feb. 15, 1986; children: Scott, David, Alyssa, Ryan. BA, Brigham Young U., 1977, JD, 1980. Bar: D.C. 1981, U.S. Ct. Appeals (4th cir.) 1983, U.S. Supreme Ct. 1985, U.S. Ct. Appeals (5th cir.) 1986, U.S. Ct. Appeals (2d, 9th, 10th and D.C. cirs.) 1987. Law clk. to judge U.S. Ct. Appeals (4th cir.), 1980-81; assoc. Sidley & Austin, Washington, 1981-84; atty., advisor U.S. Dept. Justice, Washington, 1984-89; assoc. counsel to Pres. of U.S. The White House, 1989-91; assoc. prof. law La. State U., Baton Rouge, 1991—. Contbr. articles to profl. jours. Missionary Mormon Ch., Santiago, Chile, 1973-75. Edwin S. Hinckley scholar, Brigham Young U., 1976-77. Mem. Phi Kappa Phi. Home: 6516 Millstone Ave Baton Rouge LA 70808-5112

BYERS, WILLIAM SEWELL, electrical engineer, educator; b. Ironton, Ohio, Oct. 3, 1925; s. William T. and Anna M. (Sewell) B.; m. Marjorie E. Reidel, Dec. 28, 1946; children: Thomas William, Robert M., Catherine G. BEE, Ohio State U., 1951; MBA, Rollins Coll., 1966; MEng, Pa. State U., 1969, MEd, 1972; EdD, Nova Southeastern U., 1976; DEng. Open U., 1978; LLD (hon.), Frank Ross Stewart U., 1981. Registered profl. engr., Fla. Broadcast engr. Crosley Broadcasting Corp., Columbus, Ohio, 1949-51; dist. engr. GE. Co., Syracuse, N.Y., 1951-55; staff engr., engring. mgr. Martin Marietta Aerospace Corp., Orlando, Fla., 1955-75; assoc. prof. elec. engring. tech. U. Ala., Tuscaloosa, 1975-81, prof. and coord. elec. engring. tech., 1981-83; prof., chmn. engring. tech. Murray State U. (Ky.), 1983-84, U. Central Fla., Brevard Campus, Cocoa, 1984—, prof., coord. electronics engring. program, 1988—; acad. advisor tech. Institut National d'Electricite et d'Electronique at Boumerdes, Algeria, 1977-78; former adj. faculty Seminole Jr. Coll., Fla. So. Coll., Valencia Community Coll. Amateur radio operator. Nat. Sci. Found. grantee, 1968-69; pres. United Faculty Fla. U. Cen. Fla., 1994—. Mem. IEEE (sr. life, past chmn. canaveral sect.), Soc. Wireless Pioneers (life), Am. Soc. for Engring. Edn. (past vice chmn. engring. tech. div., past chmn. internat. div.), Capstone Engring. Soc., Pa. State Amateur Radio Club (hon. life), Tau Alpha Pi, Eta Kappa Nu. Home: 3928 Carnaby Dr Oviedo FL 32765-5114 Office: U Cen Fla 1519 Clearlake Rd Cocoa FL 32922-6503

BYFORD, JAMES LLOYD, dean; b. Trenton, Tenn., Sept. 2, 1943; s. Lloyd G. and Virgie (Sammons) B.; m. Daryl J. Holley, Oct. 5, 1963; children: Julie, Brad. BS in Agriculture, U. Tenn., 1966; PhD in Wildlife, Forestry, Fisheries, Auburn U., 1970. Rsch. asst. Coop. Wildlife Rsch. Unit Auburn (Ala.) U., 1966-69; tchg. asst. dept. zoology Auburn U., 1968-69; extension wildlife specialist U. Ga., Athens, 1969-72; assoc. prof. forestry, wildlife, and fisheries U. Tenn., Knoxville, 1972-77, prof., 1977-87, acting dept. head, 1985-86; dean Sch. Agrl. and Human Environ. U. Tenn., Martin, 1987—; cons. and presenter in field. Author 4 videos including Conservation Music Video, 1994. Pres. Lions Club, 1976, 82, v.p., 1981; bd. dirs. Tenn. Purebred Sheep Producers Assn., 1981-82, Seymour Community Citizens Assn. (founding), 1982; pres. High BLuff PTA, 1976-77. Recipient Nat. Disting. Agrl. Svc. award Alpha Gamma Rho, 1992, Friendmaker award Girl Scouts Am., 1990, Tenn. Wildlife Profl. award Tenn. chpt. Wildlife Soc., 1985, Ext. award Tenn. chpt. Gamma Sigma Delta, 1983, Pub. Svc. award Tenn. Higher Edn. Commn., 1995; named Cons. of Yr., Tenn. Conservation League, 1981. Mem. Internat. Sci. & Edn. Coun. (tech. assistance com. 1990-91), Internat. Assn. Fish & Wildlife Agys. (extension edn. com. 1982-83), Nat. Assn. State & Univ. Land Grant Colls. (fish & wildlife com. 1991—), The Wildlife Soc. (cert. wildlife biologist, profl. devel. com. 1989-92, animal damage control com. 1985-89, nat. ext. com. policy 4-H nat. resources subcom. 1980-81, program com. nat. ext. wildlife and fisheries conf. 1977, 84, other coms., mem. numerous coms. SE Sect. including profl. affairs 1985—, pres. 1979-81, chmn. confs., workshops, Spl. Recognition award 1995), Tenn. Hunters for Hungry (exec. bd. 1991—), Tenn. Assn. 4-H Workers (state v.p. 1985, dist. v.p. 1979), Tenn. Assn. Agrl. Agts. & Specialists (chmn. 4-H youth com. 1982-85, pub. info. awards com. 1981-82), Tenn. Assn. Colls. & Tchrs. Agriculture (scholarship com. 1989—), Ga. Fisheries Workers Assn. (sec./treas. 1971). Office: U Tenn Sch Agrl and Human Environ Martin TN 38238-0001

BYLER, JENNIFER CURTIS, marketing consultant, publisher, editor; b. Athens, Ga., Aug. 11, 1958; d. John L. and Patricia Ann (Baker) Curtis; m. Gary C. Byler; children: Sarah Alexandra, Georgia Cate, Emma Grace. BS in Mktg., U. Ariz., 1981. Cons. Congl. Candidates, Wis., N.J., Ariz., Wis., N.J., Washington, 1980-88; fin. dir. Pima County Rep. Com., Tucson, 1981; editor Spl. Indsl. Radio Service Assn., Rosslyn, Va., 1981-82; account exec. The Viguerie Co., Falls Church, Va., 1983, 85; assoc. Herman Pirchner Assocs., Great Falls, Va., 1985-86; pres. The Mktg. Dept., Inc., Alexandria, Va., 1986—; pub., editor Redskin Rev., 1990-95; bd. dirs. Conservative Leadership Pac, Springfield, Va., 1985—. Author: VFW Political Action Handbook, 1987. Mem. Arlington Young Reps., treas., 1982-83, polit. vice chmn., 1985, vol. coord. leadership conf. 1984; exec. dir. Com. for Responsible Youth Politics, 1984; mem. Virginia Beach Rep. City Com., 1989—; mem. state ctrl. com. Rep. Party of Va., 1992—; mem. Princess Anne GOP Women, 1996; mem. Jr. League Norfolk/Virginia Beach, 1988-90; vice chairwomen eastern dist. Rep. Party of Va., 1996—; bd. advisors Va. VOter Integrity Project, 1996; vol. coord. YRNF Leadership Conf., 1994. Mem. Nat. Fedn. Ind. Businesses, Tusk & Trunk Club (pres. 1994—). Episcopalian. Home: 4529 Old Princess Anne Rd Virginia Beach VA 23462-7902

BYLES, ROBERT VALMORE, manufacturing company executive; b. Robeline, La., Dec. 7, 1937; s. Robert S. and Ann (Murray) B.; m. Mary E. Hornsby, Sept. 14, 1954; children: Robert V. Jr., Rebecca Kay, Raymond Gale, Aaron Blake. Student, Northwestern State U., Natchitochos, La., 1955-57, La. Tech. U., 1957-58. Ptnr. Byles Bros. Welding and Tractor Co., Many, La., 1960-72; owner, pres. R.V. Byles Industries, Many, 1972-80, R.V. Byles Enterprises, Inc., Many, 1980—; ptnr. Byles Internat., Shreveport, La., 1984—; pres. West La. Hot Mix Asphalt, Inc., Many, 1986—. Chmn. Sabine Parish Dem. Exec. Com., 1968-79; mem. Repub. State Cen. Com., 1979-94; chief Many Fire Dept., 1965-69. Served with USN, 1959-60. Named one of Outstanding Young Men Am., 1970. Mem. La. Assn. Bus. and Industry, Am. Soc. Concrete Constrn., Nat. Fedn. Bus. and Industry, Sabine Parish C. of C. (bd. dirs. 1966—, pres. 1969-70), Many Jaycees (pres. 1970-71, Outstanding Young Men of Am. 1970). Republican. Methodist. Lodge: Shriners (pres. 1988). Office: RV Byles Enterprises Inc 1750 Robby St Many LA 71449-2923

BYNES, FRANK HOWARD, JR., physician; b. Savannah, Ga., Dec. 3, 1950; s. Frank Howard and Frenchye (Mason) B.; m. Janice Ratta, July 24, 1987; children: Patricia, Frenchye. BS, Savannah State Coll., 1972; MD, Meharry Med. Coll. Resident gen. surgery Staten Island (N.Y.) Hosp., 1978-82; resident internal medicine N.Y. infirmary Beekam Downtown Hosp., N.Y.C., 1983-86; dir. medicine USAF Sheppard Regional Hosp., Sheppard AFB, Tex., 1986-87; pvt. practice internal medicine N.Y.C., 1987-90; attending physician Bronx (N.Y.) Lebanon Hosp., 1990-93; pvt. practice intenral medicine Savannah, Ga., 1994—. Maj. USAF, 1986-87. Mem. AMA, AAAS, ACP, N.Y. Acad. Scis., Assn. Mil. Surgeons of U.S., Alpha Phi Alpha.

BYNUM, RICHARD CARY, publishing consultant, author; b. Atlanta, Mar. 15, 1937; s. Paul Cary and Ethel Avious (Rutherford) B.; m. Brenda Sue Storey, Apr. 12, 1964; children: Brennon Franklin, Quinlan Ashby. BFA, U. Ga., 1962; MA, CUNY, 1973. Prodn. editor Holt, Rinehart and Winston, N.Y.C., 1965-67; publ. mgr. Assn. Am. U. Presses, N.Y.C., 1967-69; mng. editor R.R. Bowker Co., N.Y.C., 1969-73; founding dir. Ga. State U. Bus. Press, Atlanta, 1973-95. Author: Cabbagetown: 3 Women, 1984, Six Short Plays, 1993; editor: Scholarly Books in America, 1968-69. With USAR. Recipient John Golden award CUNY, 1972, Sparks award Ga. State U., 1985, medal AAUP, 1995. Mem. Dramatists Guild, Soc. for Scholarly Publ., S.E. Playwrights Project. Office: Ga State U University Plz Atlanta GA 30303

BYRD, ANDREW WAYNE, investment company executive; b. Nashville, Apr. 16, 1954; s. Benjamin F. and Allison (Caldwell) B.; m. Marianne Menefee; children: Marianne, Valere, Andrew Jr. BA, Vanderbilt U., 1976, JD, 1979; LLM, Georgetown U., 1981. Bar: Tenn., 1979, U.S. Dist. Ct. (mid. dist.) Tenn. 1979. Atty. Stokes & Bartholomew, Nashville, 1981-84; exec. v.p. Gen. Cap Am. Inc., 1987-94; exec. v.p. Gen. Capital Corp., Nashville, 1984-89, pres., 1989-94; pres. Andrew W. Byrd & Co., LLC, 1994—. Mem. Leadership Nashville, 1984-85; deacon 1st Presbyn. Ch., 1982-92; bd. dirs. Tenn. divsn. Am. Cancer Soc., 1982-88, 92—, Cheekwood, 1987-93; bd. dirs. Boy Scouts of Am., Mid. Tenn. Coun., 1995—; chmn. bd. dirs. Vanderbilt Children's Hosp., 1987-93. Mem. ABA, Tenn. Bar Assn., Nashville Bar Assn., Nashville C. of C., Cumberland Club Nashville, Exch. Club (pres. 1993-94). Democrat. Home: 4419 Harding Pl Nashville TN 37205-4530 Office: Andrew W Byrd & Co 201 4th Ave N Ste 1250 Nashville TN 37219-2014

BYRD, GARY ELLIS, lawyer; b. Dothan, Ala., Mar. 8, 1957; m. Emily Marie Reid; children: Elizabeth, Virginia and Victoria (twins). BS in Pre-Law and Am. History summa cum laude, Troy State U., 1979; JD, U. Ala., 1982. Bar: Ga. (no. and middle dists.) 1983, U.S. Dist. Ct. (no. and so. dists), Ga., U.S. Ct. Appeals. Pntr. Bishoff & Byrd, Talbotton, Ga., 1982—; assoc. Bunn & Kirby, Hamilton, Ga., 1993—; ptnr. Bunn & Byrd, Hamilton, Ga., 1996—; chmn. bd. dirs. Talbot County Law Libr., Talbotton, 1992-95. Contbr. numerous articles to newspapers and profl. jours., chpt. to book; author City of Woodland city code, 1986. Bd. dirs. Chattahoochie-Flint RESA, Americus, Ga., 1986-87, Pine Mountain Regional Arts Coun., Manchester, Ga., 1986-88; pres., chmn. exec. com. Talbot County 2000 Group, Talbotton, 1987-88; coach debate team dept. social studies Manchester (Ga.) H.S., 1982; chmn. appropriations com. Harris County YMCA, Hamilton, 1994, 95, 96, bd. dirs. 1994, 95, 96; mem. budget com. City of Talbotton, 1989-92, councilman, 1985-92, mem. policy adv. com., 1986-92, vol. fireman, 1982-93; ct. apptd. adminstr. City of Geneva, Ga., 1992; mem. adv. com. Am. Security Coun., Washington, 1976-82. Recipient Outstanding Svc. award Talbot County Jaycees, 1983,. Mem. Ga. Bar Assn., Ga. Mcpl. Assn. (atty.'s sect.), Talbot County C. of C. (chmn. membership com. 1992-93, bd. dirs. 1993), Troy State U. Alumni Assn. (membership com. East Ala./West Ctrl. Ga. chpt. 1993-96, Phi Kappa Phi, Phi Alpha Theta (State Hist. Rsch. award 1979). Home: PO Box 119 Hamilton GA 31811 Office: 103 N College St PO Box 489 Hamilton GA 31811

BYRD, GENE GILBERT, astronomer, educator; b. Kosse, Tex., Oct. 19, 1945; s. Charlie C. and Adice (Mathis) B.; m. Kathryn Cline, May 15, 1971; children: Jeannette, Dana. BS in Physics, Tex. A&M U., 1968; PhD in Astronomy, U. Tex., 1974. Prof. astronomy U. Ala., Tuscaloosa, 1974—. Contbr. articles to profl. jours. Mem. Divsn. on Dynamical Astronomy (nat. chair 1991). Office: U Ala Dept Physics/Astronomy Tuscaloosa AL 35487-0324

BYRD, GWENDOLYN PAULINE, school system superintendent; b. Mobile, Ala., July 21, 1943; d. Marley and Frances (Ramsay) B. BS in History, Marillac Coll., St. Louis, 1966; MA in Sch. Adminstrn., DePaul U., 1975. Tchr. St. Matthias Sch., St. Louis, 1966-70; prin., tchr. Cathedral Elem. Sch., Natchez, Miss., 1970-74; prin. St. Francis De Sales Sch., Lake Zurich, Ill., 1974-77; curriculum coord. for sch. system Archdiocese of Mobile, 1977-83, sch. supt., 1983—. Chairperson Little Flower Liturgy Com., Mobile, 1980—; pvt. sch. rep. to adv. com. on tchr. edn. State of Ala., 1983—; adv. bd. Cath. Svc. Ctr., Mobile, 1989—; v.p. bd. dirs. Mobile Mental Health Assn., 1990—; bd. dirs. L'Arche Cmty., 1992—. Named Outstanding Career Woman, Gayfer's Career Club, 1985, Outstanding Supt., Ala. Assn. Learning Disabilities, 1988, Disting. Diocesan Leader Today's Cath. Tchr. Mag., 1992. Mem. Nat. Cath. Edn. Assn., Chief Adminstrs. Cath. Edn. (regional rep. 1995), CACE (exec. com. 1996), Phi Delta Kappa. Office: Office Cath Schs PO Box 129 Mobile AL 36601-0129

BYRD, IDA FAY, college official; b. Harmony, N.C., May 28, 1938; d. Nelson Hall and Tracy Jane (Groce) Caudle; m. Kenneth Edwin Byrd, Aug. 27, 1959; children: Teressa Rene Byrd McGuire, Edwin Scott. BA, Appalachian State U., Boone, N.C., 1959, MA, 1961, EdS, 1972; EdD, Nova U., 1976. Cert. libr., tchr., adminstr., N.C. Tchr., libr. Jonesville (N.C.) High Sch., 1959-61; libr. Jonesville Sch. Dist., 1961-64; instr. learning resources Marshall U., Huntington, W.Va., 1964-66; dir. learning resources Wilkes C.C., Wilkesboro, N.C., 1966—. Mem. Wilkes County Bd. Edn., 1978-92, chmn., 1990-92; del. White House Conf. on Literacy, Productivity and Democracy, Washington, 1991; bd. dirs. Adult Devel. Activity Program, North Wilkesboro, N.C., 1981-93. Recipient Disting. Svc. award Piedmont Fed. Savs. & Loan, 1989, cert. of excellence Wilkes Bd. Edn., 1991; grantee Kellogg Found., 1973, James Larkin Pearson Libr., 1983, Appalachian Region Commn., Smith Reynolds Found., 1983. Baptist. Home: PO Box 148 Roaring River NC 28669-0148

BYRD, ISAAC K., JR., lawyer. BA Polit. Sci./Sociology magna cum laude, Tougaloo Coll., 1973; JD, Northwestern U., 1976. Staff atty. Swift & Co. Legal Dept., Chgo., 1976-78; assoc. Banks & Nichols, Jackson, Miss., 1978-80; ptnr. Banks & Nichols, Jackson, 1980-81, Owens & Byrd, Jackson, 1982-86; pvt. practice Byrd & Assocs., Jackson, 1986—; part-time instr. polit. sci. Tougaloo Coll., 1980, bd. trustees, 1987—; bd. dirs. Miss. Dept. Corrections, 1984-88, vice-chmn., 1986-88; apptd. Chancery Ct. judge Hinds County, Miss., 1989. First black Chancery judge in Miss. Bd. dirs. Arts Alliance, New Stage Theater, Ballet Miss.; campaign coord. former gov. William Winter, 1979; active Miss. Mus. Art-Rembrandt Soc., Hinds County Dem. Exec. Com., 1980-85; campaign mgr. Shirley Watson for Jackson City Commr., 1984; gen. counsel Miss. State Conf. of the NAACP. Recipient Miss. Outstanding 4-H Leadership award, 1969, Father Walter Legal scholarship, Indianola, Miss., 1973, 74, NAACP State Vernon Dahmer award, 1985, Thelma Sanders Milestone award Jackson Minority Bus., 1992, Faces of Courage award Medgar Evers Statue Fund, 1992; named Hinds County Trial Lawyers Assn. Outstanding Trial Lawyer, 1984, Tougaloo Coll. Alumnus of Yr., 1984. Mem. ABA, Nat. Bar Assn., Miss. Bar Assn. (vice-chmn., state bar disciplinary adv. com.), Assn. Trial Lawyers Am. (bd. govs. 1992, publs. com., standing com., birth trauma litigation group, minority caucus del., sexual abuse litigation group, M Club), Miss. Trial Lawyers Assn. (bd. mem., Pres.'s Club, exec. com. ATLA del.), Magnolia Bar Assn. (legis. com., platinum circle mem., continuing legal edn. chmn. 1992-93), NAACP (life), ACLU Miss. (bd. mem.), Alpha Phi Alpha. Home: 449 W Northside Dr Jackson MS 39206-4637

BYRD, JULIE ANDERSON, nurse; b. San Diego, Feb. 18, 1949; d. Asa Lee and Connie (Alderete) Anderson; m. Richard Allan Byrd, June 8, 1970. Diploma, Mercy Coll. Nursing, San Diego, 1970. RN; registered diagnostic cardiac sonographer; registered vascular technologist. Staff nurse Howard Meml. Hosp., Biloxi, Miss., 1971, Santa Rosa Med. Ctr., San Antonio, 1972; office nurse Dr. Mario Cardenas, Princeton, W.Va., 1973-74; acting head nurse Radford (Va.) Community Hosp., 1975; staff nurse Nurses Ctrl. Registry, Phoenix, 1976, Greenbrier Valley Med. Ctr., Ronceverte, W.Va., 1981-82; chief noninvasive cardiovascular lab. The Greenbrier Clinic, While Sulphur Springs, W.Va., 1976-91; nurse for adolescent child care agy. Davis-Stuart Inc., Lewisburg, W.Va., 1992—. Recipient Am. Legion Sch. award, 1964. Mem. Soc. Vascular Tech., Greenbrier Health Club, Calif. Scholarship Fedn. (life). Democrat. Roman Catholic. Home: PO Box 647 Lewisburg WV 24901-0647 Office: Davis-Stuart Rte 2 Box 188-A Lewisburg WV 24901

BYRD, LARRY DONALD, behavioral pharmacologist; b. Salisbury, N.C., July 14, 1936; s. Donald Thomas and Mildred (Gardner) B.; m. Corrinne Williams, Dec. 23, 1961; children: Kay, Lynn, Renee, Andrew. AB, E. Carolina U., Greenville, N.C., 1962; MA, E. Carolina U., 1964; PhD, U. N.C., 1968; postgrad., Harvard U., 1967-70. Faculty E. Carolina U., 1962-64; tchg. and rsch. asst. exptl. psychology U. N.C., Chapel Hill, 1964-67; rsch. fellow pharmacology, instr. psychobiology Harvard Med. Sch., 1967-70; assoc. scientist Lab. Psychobiology New Eng. Reg. Primate Rsch. Ctr., 1969-74; psychobiologist, chmn. divsn. primate behavior Yerkes Primate Rsch. Ctr., Emory U., Atlanta, 1974-79, assoc. rsch. prof., chmn. divsn. primate behavior, 1979-80, lectr. dept. psychology, 1974-81, assoc. rsch. prof., chief divsn. behavioral biology, 1980-82; prof., chief divsn. behavioral biology Emory U., Atlanta, 1982—; prof., chief divsn. behavioral biology Yerkes Primate Rsch. Ctr., Emory U., Atlanta, 1981-95, prof. dept. pharmacology, 1995—; adj. prof. dept. psychology Emory U., 1981—; cons. Dept. Pharmacological and Physiol. Scis. U. Chgo., 1973, MIT Press, Cambridge, 1975, Nat. Ctr. for Toxicological Rsch. FDA, Jefferson, Ark., 1976-77, S.W. Found. for Rsch. and Edn., San Antonio, 1977, Naval Aerospace Med. Rsch. Lab. U.S. Naval Air Sta., Pensacola, Fla., 1977, G.D. Searle and Co., Skokie, Ill., 1986, Battelle Meml. Inst., Columbus, Ohio, 1989-94; mem. spl. rev. com. Contract Rev. Unit Nat. Inst. on Drug Abuse, Lexington, Ky., 1979-81, mem. spl. rev. com. biomed. rsch. rev. com., 1981-82, spl. rev. cons. clin., behavioral and psychosocial rsch. rev. com., 1981-82, mem., 1982-85, chmn., 1984-85, others; spl. rev. cons. dept. medicine and surgery VA, Washington, 1983, NSF, Washington, 1984, div. of rsch. resources NIH, Washington, 1983, mem. spl. study sect. div. rsch. grants, 1984, panel mem. Workshop on Implemenation of Pub. Health Svc. Policy on Humane Care and Use of Lab. Animals, 1989, others; panel mem. USPHS Animal Welfare Forum Alcohol, Drug Abuse and Mental Health Adminstrn., 1985; active numerous other career related orgns. Editorial bd. Jour. Exptl. Analysis of Behavior, 1969-79, 87-91; assoc. editor Jour. Exptl. Analysis of Behavior, 1970-76; cons. editor Am. Jour. Primatology, 1980-83; editor Psychopharmacology Newsletter, 1976-82; editorial advisor Jour. Pharmacology and Exptl. Therapeutics, Jour. Exptl. Analysis of Behavior, others; contbr. numerous articles to profl. jours. Mem. sci. adv. com. Nat. Families in Action, 1991—. Recipient Outstanding Alumnus award, E. Carolina U., 1977, Disting. Alumnus award, U. N.C., 1987. Fellow AAAS, Am. Psychol. Assn. (exec. com. psychopharmacology divsn. 1976-95, neurobehavioral toxicity test standards com. 1980—, coord. Young Psychopharmacologist award 1985-95, bd. sci. affairs com. on animals in rsch. and ethics 1990-93); mem. Am. Assn. Accreditation Lab. Animal Care (trustee 1990—, exec. com. 1991—, sec. 1993, vice chmn. 1994-96, chmn. 1996—), Am. Soc. Pharmacology and Exptl. Therapeutics, Nat. Families in Action (sci. adv. com. 1991—), Am. Soc. Primatologist, Behavioral Pharmacology Soc. (pres. 1984-86), Soc. Exptl. Analysis of Behavior (v.p. 1975-76, bd. dirs. 1970-78), European Behavioral Pharmacology Soc., Southeastern Pharmacology Soc., Am Pub. Health Assn., Behavioral Toxicology Soc., Southeastern Assn. for Behavior Analysis, Internat. Study Group Investigating Drugs as Reinforcers, Emory Neurosci. Group, Phi Sigma Pi. Home: 1026 Viking Dr Stone Mountain GA 30083-1707 Office: Yerkes Primate Rsch Ctr Emory U Atlanta GA 30322

BYRD, LAVERNE, elementary school educator; b. Spartanburg, S.C., Oct. 2, 1957; d. James and Mary (Johnson) Scurry; m. Bennie Lee Byrd, May 4, 1957; 1 child, Krysti Lee Byrd. AA, Spartanburg Meth. Coll., 1977; BS, Winthrop Coll., 1979; MEd, Converse Coll., 1983, EdS, 1986, cert. Edn. Specialist, 1986. Counselor's asst. Alcohol and Drug Abuse Com., Spartanburg, 1973-75; counselor Piedmont Community Actions, Spartanburg, 1975-80; tchr. Goucher Elem. Sch., Gaffney, S.C., 1980-81, Pauline (S.C.) Glenn Springs Sch., 1981-85, Jesse S. Bobo Elem. Sch., Spartanburg, 1985—; mem. Edn. Improvement Act Implementation Council, Spartanburg, 1984-86; cons. SMC Career Panel, Spartanburg, 1987. Tchr. Sunday sch., Spartanburg, S.C., 1986—. Mem. Delta Sigma Theta. Democrat. Baptist. Home: 1600 Fowler Rd Woodruff SC 29388-8654

BYRD, LINDA LOU FITZGERALD, elementary education educator; b. Ft. Benning, Ga., Apr. 10, 1956; d. Donald Carl and Bobbie Jane (Oliver) Fitzgerald; m. James Anthony Holt, Aug. 16, 1975 (div. June 1991); 1 child, Laura Leigh; m. Richard Wayne Byrd, July 1, 1993. AA, Hopkinsville Community Coll., Ky., 1976; BS, Western Ky. U., 1979; MA, Murray (Ky.) State U., 1984. Cert. elem. tchr., Ky. Math/sci. demonstration tchr. K-12 Hopkins County Schs., Madisonville, Ky., 1979—; math. cons. K-12, workshop presenter Hopkins County Sch. System, Madisonville, 1982-95, Badgett Ctr. Ednl. Enhancement; tchr. trainer Ky. K-8 Math. Specialist Program and 4-5 Sci. Specialist Program, 1990-93. Grantee NSF, 1990, 93. Mem. Nat. Coun. Tchrs. Math. (presenter regional conf. Paducah 1993), Nat. Sci. Tchr. Assn., Internat. Reading Assn., Ky. Coun. Tchrs. Math. (conf. presider 1990), Ken-Lake Coun. Tchrs. Math., Western Ky. Math.-Sci. Alliance (bd. dirs., elem. rep.). Democrat. Baptist. Home: 2201 S Main St Madisonville KY 42431-3307 Office: Hopkins County Bd Edn 320 S Seminary St Madisonville KY 42431-2424

BYRD, LINWARD TONNETT, lawyer, rancher; b. Hamburg, Ark., June 25, 1921; s. Charley E. and Arrie (Montgomery) B.; m. Reba Ann Rowe, Dec. 22, 1965; 1 child, Jana Lynn. LLB, U. Tex., 1950. Bar: Tex. 1950, U.S. Dist. Ct. (we. dist.) Tex. 1956, U.S. Ct. Appeals (5th cir.) 1965, U.S. Ct. Appeals (11th cir.) 1981. Sr. ptnr. Byrd, Davis & Eisenberg, Austin, Tex., 1959—. With USN, 1942-43. Fellow Am. Trial Lawyers Found., Tex. Bar Found., Am. Coll. Trial Lawyers; mem. Assn. Trial Lawyers Am., Am. Bd. Trial Advs. (adv.), Tex. Trial Lawyers Assn., State Bar Tex., Travis County Bar Assn. (lifetime disting. achievement award), Travis County Young Lawyers Assn. (lifetime disting. achievement award). Baptist. Home: 3110 Maywood Ave Austin TX 78703-1133 Office: Byrd Davis & Eisenberg 707 W 34th St Austin TX 78705-1204

BYRD, MARY JANE, education educator; b. Topeka, Apr. 21, 1946; d. Vernon Thomas and Mary Elizabeth (Caldwell) Wharton; m. Gerald David Byrd, June 24, 1965; children: Kari, Juli, Cori. BS, U. So. Ala., 1980, MBA, 1984; D of Bus. Adminstrn., Nova Southeastern U., 1991. Dental asst. Gerald E. Berger, DMD, Mobile, Ala., 1963-65; dental hygenist Robert P. Hall, DMD, Mobile, Ala., 1965-66; teller Am. Nat. Bank, Mobile, Ala., 1972-75; office mgr. Byrd Surveying, Inc., Mobile, Ala., 1975-80; div. acct. cafeteria Morrison, Inc., Mobile, Ala., 1980-82; mgmt. cons. pvt. practice Mobile, Ala., 1982-84; lectr. acctg. U. South Ala., Mobile, Ala., 1984; asst. prof. acctg. & mgmt. Univ. Mobile, Mobile, Ala., 1984-89; assoc. prof. acctg. and mgmt. Mobile Coll., 1989-95; prof. mgmt., 1995—; reviewer Internat. Jour. Pub. Adminstrn., 1991—; dir. Nat. Assn. Accts., Mobile, 1986-89. Author: Supervisory Management Study Guide/Southwestern, 1993, 2d edit., 1997, Small Business Management: An Entrepreneur's Guide to Success/Irwin, 1994, 2d edit. 1997, Human Resource Management, Dame, 1995; contbr. articles to profl. jours. Named Assoc. of the Month, Home Builders Assn., 1986, Charles S. Dismukes Outstanding Mem., Nat. Assn. Accts. Mem. AAUW, Acad. Mgmt., Am. Bus. Women Assn., Assn. for Bus. Grad. Dirs., Mortgage Lenders Assn., So. Acad. Mgmt. Office: Univ Mobile PO Box 13220 Mobile AL 36663-0220

BYRD, SANDRA JUDITH, information scientist; b. Detroit, July 14, 1960; d. Brian Kenneth and Ruth (Jocaitas) Paukstys; m. Michael Keith Byrd, Nov. 23, 1985; children: Kristin Michelle, Adam Keith. BA, So. Ill. U., 1994. Asst. mgr. Colony West Swim Club, 1979, mgr., summers, 1980-82; aquatic supr. So. Ill. U., Carbondale, 1982; asst. mgr. Body Shop, Vero Beach, Fla., 1984; office mgr. Insta-Med Clinics, Inc., Vero Beach, 1984; receptionist Redgate Communications Corp., Vero Beach, 1985, circulation asst., 1985-87, circulation mgr., 1987-88; circulation dir. TT Pubs., Inc., Longwood, Fla., 1988-89; supr. of nursing payroll Orlando (Fla.) Regional Med. Ctr., 1989—, computer specialist nursing adminstrn. computer support, 1990-91; info. specialist dept. ops. improvement Orlando Regional Healthcare System, 1993-96; bus. mgr. Treasure Coast Diagnostics, Inc., 1987-88. Ill. State scholar, 1979-82. Mem. NAFE. Home and Office: 180 SE Duxbury Ave Port Saint Lucie FL 34983

BYRD, WALTER RAYMOND, court counselor; b. Greensboro, N.C., Nov. 20, 1944; s. Walter Warren and Janie May (Moses) B.; m. Delphine Matthews, Apr. 1965 (div. July 1969); children: Walter Jr., Patrick; m. Tresca Mitchell, Aug. 14, 1970; 1 child, Janet. BA, N.C. Coll., Durham, 1967. Social worker Rockingham Dept. Social Svcs., Reidsville, N.C., 1967-69, Guilford County Dept. Social Svcs., Greensboro, 1969-71; ct. counselor Jevenile Svcs. Divsn., Greensboro, 1971-91, ct. counselor supr., 1991-95; chief ct. counselor Jevenile Svcs. Divsn., Winston-Salem, 1995—. Chmn. Guilford County Conf. for Children, Greensboro, 1991-92; mem. social wk. adv. bd. N.C. State U., U. N.C.-Greensboro, 1985-93; pres. Nat. Black Child Devel. Inst., Greensboro, 1984-88. Recipient Meritorious Svc. award Lincoln Mid. Sch. of Sci., Math. and Tech., Greensboro, 1988-89, Leadership award Nat. Black Child Devel. Inst., 1984. Mem. N.C. Assn. Ct. Counselors (sec. 1990-91), Alpha delta Mu. Lutheran. Home: 1408 Paxton Ct Greensboro NC 27120-0443

BYRD, WILLIAM C., architect. Office: Willard C Byrd & Assoc 3400 Peachtree Rd NE Ste 1637 Atlanta GA 30326-1107

BYRNE, GRANVILLE BLAND, III, lawyer; b. San Antonio, Jan. 26, 1952; s. Granville Bland and Mary (Dowling) B.; divorced; children: Peyton Smith, Fulton Buckner. AB, U. N.C., Chapel Hill, 1974; JD, Harvard U., 1978. Bar: Ga. 1978, U.S. Dist. Ct. (no. dist.) Ga. 1978, U.S. Ct. Appeals (5th cir.) 1978, U.S. Ct. Appeals (11th cir.) 1981. Assoc. Swift, Currie, McGhee & Hiers, Atlanta, 1978-84, ptnr., 1984-94; prin. Byrne, Eldridge, Moore & Davis, P.C., Atlanta, 1994—; bd. dirs. Compeer Atlanta, Inc., chmn., 1996—; bd. dirs. Cagle's, Inc. Elder, mem. session 1st Presbyn. Ch. Atlanta, 1993-96. Mem. ABA, Ga. Bar Assn., Atlanta Bar Assn. Democrat. Presbyterian. Home: 2664 Birchwood Dr NE Atlanta GA 30305-3822 Office: Byrne Eldridge Moore & Davis PC 3340 Peachtree Rd NE Atlanta GA 30326-1000

BYRNES, THOMAS RAYMOND, JR., osteopath; b. Ft. Meade, Md., Aug. 18, 1956; s. Thomas Raymond and Jeanne Marie (Lavis) B.; m. Kathleen Ann Jory, Jan. 7, 1984; children: Erin Marie, Christopher Mason. Student, Tanana Valley C.C., Fairbanks, Alaska, 1977-85, U. Alaska, 1978-85; BSc in Sports Medicine, Pepperdine U., 1983; DO, Kirksville Coll. Osteo. Medicine, 1992. Cert. athletic trainer; Diplomate Am. Bd. Family Practice. Human performance lab. technician, athletic trainer Pepperdine U., Malibu, Calif., 1980-82; asst. athletic trainer U. Alaska, Fairbanks, 1983-85; spl. edn. tchrs. aide North Star Borough Sch. Dist., Fairbanks, 1985-87; teaching fellow Kirksville (Mo.) Coll. Osteo. Medicine, 1989-92; resident Warren Hosp., Phillipsburg, N.J., 1992-95; family practice physician, med. supr. Soldier Family Health Clinic, Fort Stewart, Ga., 1995—. Commd. 2d lt. U.S. Army 1988, advanced through grades to capt., 1992—. Mem. Am. Acad. Osteopathy, Am. Osteo. Assn., Am. Acad. Family Practitioners, Assn. Mil. Osteo. Physicians and Surgeons, Cranial Acad. Home: PO Box 1122 Richmond Hill GA 31324-1122 Office: Soldier Family Health Clinic MEDDAC Fort Stewart GA 31314

BYRON, H. THOMAS, JR., veterinarian, educator; b. Troy, N.Y., Feb. 13, 1944; s. Henry Thomas and Mary Katherine (Hayes) B.; m. E. Lee Kimball, May 18, 1966; children: H. Thomas III, Chase Kimball, Lee Hayes. BS, Stonehill Coll., 1965; MS, U. Fla., 1973; DVM, Auburn U., 1977. Intern Animal Med. Clinic, Lakeland, Fla., 1977; resident in radiology, instr. Auburn (Ala.) U., 1977-79; chief staff Ctrl. Animal Hosp., Tampa, Fla., 1979-80; founder Fruitville Vet. Clinic, Sarasota, Fla., 1980-94; chief vet., dir. animal programs Circus World, Haines City, Fla., 1981-83; pvt. practice Bus. Resource Group, Sarasota, Fla., 1994—; liasion S.W. Fla. Vet. Med. Assn., Humane Soc., 1984-92; cons. Ringling Bros., Barnum and Bailey Circus, Venice, Fla., 1986—, Busch Gardens, TAmpa, 1984—, Roberts Bros. Circus, Hanneford Circus, Coronas Circus, Hoxie Bros. Circus, Sarasota, 1979—,

Circus Vargas Internat., L.A., 1984—, Parc Safari, Hemingford, Que., Can., 1993; lectr. U. Fla. Vet. Sch., 1989—, mem. adv. coun. Coll. Vet. Medicine, 1991—. Contbr. articles to profl. jours. Troop leader Boy Scouts Am., Auburn, Sarasota, 1977-81, scoutmaster, packmaster; vet. chmn. Sarasota United Way, 1980—; lectr., vol. Sarasota County Schs., 1980—; mem. Sarasota County rabies control com. Pub. Health Dept., 1980-92; founding mem. Sarasota County Animal Welfare Adv. Com., 1992; bd. dirs. Sarasota Girls' Choir, 1987-89, Pine View Sch. Parents' Assn. Bd., 1990—; bd. dirs., pres. Sunset Royale Condominium Assn., Siesta Key, Fla., 1988-89, 91-93. Lt. USNR. Recipient Aux. award AVMA, 1977, recognition award Sarasota County Commrs., 1993; Alexander Hamilton scholar Stonehill Coll., 1964-65; fellow NAS, 1972-73, Geraldine Page wildlife fellow, 1987. Mem. Fla. Pub. Health Assn., Fla. Vet. Medicine Assn. (fin. com. 1982-86, bd. dirs. 1986-92, chmn. legis. com. 1982-90, Gold Star award 1988), S.W. Fla. Vet. Med. Assn. (bd. dirs., sec.-treas., v.p., pres. 1980-85), Aquatic Animal Vet. Assn., Zoo Animal Vet. Assn., Sarasota C. of C. (legis. com. 1986-91), Phi Zeta. Republican. Roman Catholic. Home and Office: 653 Sinclair Dr Sarasota FL 34240-9367

BYRON, JOSEPH WINSTON, pharmacologist; b. N.Y.C., Apr. 23, 1930; s. Joseph Adolphos and Florence Augusta (Coull) B.; 1 child, Annette. BS, Fordham U., 1952; MS, Phila. Coll. Pharmacy and Sci., 1955; PhD, U. Buffalo, 1960. Sr. rsch. scientist Paterson Cancer Rsch. Inst., Manchester, U.K., 1962-65; prin. rsch. scientist Paterson Cancer Rsch. Inst., Manchester, 1965-73; assoc. prof. U. Md. Med. Sch., Balt., 1973-76, prof. pharmacology, 1976-82; prof., chmn. pharmacology Meharry Med. Coll., Nashville, 1982—; mem. bd. sci. counselors NIOSH, CDC, Atlanta, 1991—, Divsn. Cancer Treatment, Nat. Cancer Inst., 1980-82; mem. com. Nat. Bd. Med. Examiners, Phila., 1989-90; nat. rsch. coun. fellowship panelist, Washington, 1986-90; mem. evaluation panel Ford Found. Predoctoral Fellowships for Minorities in Biol. Scis., 1996—. Editorial bd. mem.: Exptl. Hematology, 1975-78, Internat. Jour. of Cell Cloning, 1983-88; contbr. over 60 articles to profl. jours. and books. Recipient Postdoctoral fellowship NSF, 1959-60, Am. Cancer Soc., 1961-62. Mem. Internat. Soc. for Exptl. Hematology (mem. coun. 1978-81), Am. Soc. for Pharmacology and Exptl. Therapeutics. Office: Meharry Med Coll 1005 D B Todd Jr Blvd Nashville TN 37208

CABALLERO, CESAR, librarian; b. Puebla, Mex., May 26, 1949; arrived in U.S., 1958; s. Arnulfo and Rafaela (Alonso) C.; m. Carol Brey Caballero, Sept. 2, 1995. BBA in Acctg., U. Tex. El Paso, 1972; MLS, U. Tex., Austin, 1974. Assoc. univ. librarian U. Tex. El Paso, 1974-75; head Circulation Dept., 1976-78, head Spl. Collections Dept., 1979-80; pub. svcs. coord. El Paso C.C., 1990-92; assoc. univ. libr. U. Tex. El Paso, 1993—; mem. Adv. com. Ctr. for Inter-Am. and Border Studies, El Paso, Tex., 1984-86; v.p. Visions, El Paso, 1994—. Author: Chicano Organizations Directory, 1985, The Border Finder, 1987, (chpt.) Hispanic Archives, 1994. Chmn. Bd. dirs., El Paso Pub. Libr., 1982-83; pres. El Concilio de El Paso, 1981-85, Toastmasters Internat., 1986; mem. Police Adv. Com., El Paso, 1987-88. Mem. ALA, Reforma, Phi Kappa Phi. Home: 12065 Jose Cisneros El Paso TX 79936

CABANAS, ELIZABETH ANN, nutritionist; b. Port Arthur, Tex., Oct. 27, 1948; d. William Rosser and Frances Merle (Block) Thornton. BS, U. Tex., 1971; MPH, U. Hawaii, 1973; postgrad., Tex. Woman's U., 1991—. Registered dietitian. Clin. nutritionist Family Planning Inst. Kapiolani Hosp., Honolulu, 1972-74; dietitian Kauikeolani Children's Hosp.-Pacific Inst. Rehab. Medicine, Honolulu, 1974-75; dietitian San Antonio Ind. Schs., 1975-84, asst. food service adminstr., 1984-89; coord. equipment and facilities Dallas Ind. Sch., 1990-91; dietitian SureQuest Solutions in Software, Richardson, Tex., 1990-91; nutritionist div. endocrinology, metabolism and hypertension, clin. studies unit rsch. nutritionist, asst. prof. dept. health promotion & gerontology U. Tex. Med. Br., Galveston, 1991—; lectr. nutrition U. Hawaii, Honolulu, 1974-75, St. Mary's U., San Antonio Coll., 1984-90; adj. faculty Tex. Woman's U., 1994—; cons. nutritionist, 1980—; presenter in field. Contbr. papers to profl. jours. Recipient diabetes educator recognition Eli Lilly & Co., 1994. Mem. Am. Dietetic Assn., Am. Assn. Diabetes Educators, Assn. Sch. Bus. Ofcls. Internat., Nutrition and Food Svc. Mgmt. Com., Am. Diabetes Assn. (adv. com. U. Tex. Med. Br. children's diabetes mgmt. program 1993—, mem. Galveston County diabetes support group 1991—, Disting. Svc. award 1995, mem. Galveston County Outreach adv. com., UTMB rep. 1996—), Coun. Nutritional Scis. and Metabolism (profl. sect., non-peer rev. com. 1993-94), Tex. Sch. Food Svc. Assn. (dist. bd. dirs. 1977-78), Tex. Nutrition Coun. (nominating com. 1996-99, sports and cardiovasc. nutritionists practice group, Tex. gerontol. nutritionists practice group), Houston Area Dietetic Assn. (legis. network com. 1995—), San Antonio Sch. Food Svc. Assn. (com. chmn. 1975-89), Tex. Assn. Sch. Bus. Ofcls., Tex. Restaurant Assn., San Antonio Area Food Svc. Adminstrs. Assn. (pres. 1989-90), Assn. Profls. in Positions of Leadership in Edn., Dallas Dietetic Assn. (cons. nutritionists practice group, chmn. 1990-91), San Antonio Mus. Assn., Randolph C. of C., Grand Opera House, Galveston (patron), Galveston Hist. Found., Space City Ski Club, Sierra Club, Hawaii Club (chmn. entertainment com. 1983). Republican. Methodist. Home: 711 Holiday Dr Apt 75 Galveston TX 77550-5579 Office: Univ Tex Med Br Rte 1060 301 University Blvd Galveston TX 77555-1060

CABEY, ALFRED ARTHUR, JR., business owner, publisher; b. N.Y.C., Nov. 23, 1935; s. Alfred Arthur Sr. and Consuelo Louise (Wynns) C.; m. Loretta Arline Summers, June 1, 1957 (div. Feb. 1974); children: Dawn, Jihad, Khadijah, Lateefah; m. Sally Willie Street, May 1, 1974 (div. 1993); m. Clara H. Page, Sept. 25, 1993. Student, Kennesaw Jr. Coll., 1973, DeKalb Community Coll., 1974. Owner Holiday Limousine Svc., Atlanta, 1978—, Alfred's Photographers, Atlanta, 1978—, Holiday Pubs., Atlanta, 1988—; motivatioal speaker DeKalb County Schs., 1987—, John F. Kennedy Mid. Sch., Atlanta, 1988—, Grad. Sch. learning disabilities program Ga. State U.; conv. speaker Ga. Coun. of the Blind, 1989; cons. on adult literacy State of Ga.; mem. Study of Adult Literacy panel Ga. State U., adv. bd. Howard Schs., Inc. and Project Read, 1991; panelist Ga. Family Literacy Symposium, 1991. Author: Spirit of the Heart, 1987. Active DeKalb (Ga.) Coun. for the Arts, 1988—; mem. focus com., rep. computer tech. and instructional resource material Ga. Dept. Tech. and Adult Edn., 1990-91; advisor to trainers IBM's Principles of the Alphabet Literacy System. Portraiture, N.Y. Inst. Photography, 1965. Mem. Internat. Platform Speakers Assn., Internat. Soc. Poets, Golden Poets Soc. of the World of Poetry (award 1991). Democrat. Islam. Home: 1747 Fayetteville Ct SE Atlanta GA 30316-2908

CABRERA-MENDEZ, FABIO, psychiatrist; b. Garzon, Huila, Colombia, May 10, 1943; came to U.S., 1971; s. Victor Felix Cabrera-Muñoz and Trinidad Mendez-Buendia; m. Clara Alicia Garcia, Aug. 5, 1967 (div. Jan. 1982); children: Diana Patricia Cabrera-Garcia; m. Merle Ester Reyes-Ortiz, Nov. 7, 1986; 1 child, Victor Ernesto Fabio. MD, Nat. U. Colombia, Bogota, 1968; MBA, Troy State U., 1986. Med. dir. Caprecom, Bogota, 1968-70; instr. preventive medicine U. Javeriana, Bogota, 1970-71; health ctr. dir. Bogota Health Dept., 1970-71; resident in pathology CWL Hosp., Emory U., Atlanta, 1971-73; resident in psychiatry Emory U., Atlanta, 1973-75; chief resident in psychiatry Grady Meml. Hosp., Atlanta, 1975-76; med. dir. West Fulton M.H.C., Atlanta, 1976-80; dir. A&D program Lowndes Co., Valdosta, Ga., 1980-90; chief psychiatrist D.C. of Fla. (MCI), Lowel, 1992-94, Cen. Fla. Regulation Ctr., Orlando, 1994-95. Col. USAFR, 1978. Mem. Am. Psychiat. Assn., Assn. of Mil. Surgeons of U.S. (life), Aerospace Med. Assn. Republican. Roman Catholic. Home and Office: 9126 NW 49th Avenue Rd Ocala FL 34482-1280

CACCAMISE, ALFRED EDWARD, real estate executive; b. LeRoy, N.Y., June 9, 1919; s. Joseph Peter and Rose Marie (Petrella) C.; m. Louise Ball, July 7, 1974. Student, Officers' Candidate Sch., Camp Davis, N.C., 1943, Cen. Calif. Comml. Coll., 1946-47. Lumber co. and hardware store owner Chili, N.Y., 1956-65; motel owner DeLand, Fla., 1965-71; real estate salesman DeLand, 1974-75, real estate investments co. owner, 1972—; real estate broker Alliance Realty, DeLand, 1976—. Served with U.S. Army, 1940-46. Recipient John McCready award Community Outreach Services, DeLand, 1979, 81. Mem. Nat. Assn. Realtors, Fla. Assn. Realtors, DeLand and West Volusia Bd. Realtors (bd. dirs. 1978-79, grievance com. chmn. 1983, bldg. com. chmn. 1985-87), Alhambra Villas Home Owners' Assn. (pres. 1979-80), DeLand C. of C., DeLand Com. of 100. Democrat. Roman Catholic. Lodge: Kiwanis (Sav-a-Life chmn. 1977, membership chmn. 1979), Lions (charter). Home: PO Box 241 Deland FL 32721-0241 Office: Alliance Realty 1122 N Woodland Blvd Deland FL 32720

CACCAMISE, GENEVRA LOUISE BALL (MRS. ALFRED E. CACCAMISE), retired librarian; b. Mayville, N.Y., July 22, 1934; d. Herbert Oscar and Genevra (Green) Ball; m. Alfred E. Caccamise, July 7, 1974. BA, Stetson U., DeLand, Fla., 1956; MLS, Syracuse U., 1967. Tchr. grammar sch., Sanford, Fla., 1956-57, elem. sch., Longwood, Fla., 1957-58; tchr., libr. Enterprise (Fla.) Sch., 1958-63; libr., media specialist Boston Ave. Sch., DeLand, 1963-82; head media specialist Blue Lake Sch., DeLand, 1982-87, ret., 1987. Author Volusia County manual Instructing the Library Assistant, 1965, Echoes of Yesterday: A History of the DeLand Area Public Library, 1912-1995, 1995. Charter mem. West Volusia Meml. Hosp. aux., DeLand, 1962-81; leader Girl Scout U.S., 1955-56; area dir. Fla. Edn. Assn., Volusia county, 1963-65; bd. dirs. Alhambra Villas Home Owners Assn., 1972-75; bd. trustees DeLand Pub. Library, 1977-86, sec., 1978-80, v.p., 1980-82, pres. 1982-84; v.p. Friends of DeLand Pub. Library, 1987, pres., 1989, 90, 95, 96, bd. dirs., 1991—, newsletter editor 1992-95; charter mem. Guild of the DeLand Mus. Art, v.p., 1990, pres. 1991-92, mem. Guild of bd. dirs. 1991—, mus. bd. dirs., 1991-95; co-orgn. chmn. Friends DeLand Mus. Art, 1993. Mem. AAUW (2d v.p. chpt. 1965-67, rec. sec. 1961-65, 78-80, pres. 1980-82, parliamentarian 1982-84), Assn. Childhood Edn. (1st v.p. 1965-66, corr. sec. 1963-65), DAR (chpt. registrar 1969-80, asst. chief page Continental Congress, Washington 1962-65), Fla. Libr. Assn., Bus. & Profl. Women's Club (corr. sec. DeLand 1968-71, 2d v.p. 1969-70), Stetson U. Alumni Assn. (class chmn. for ann. fund drive 1968), Volusia County Assn. Media in Edn. (treas. 1977), Volusia County Retired Educators Assn. (pres. Unit II 1988-90, scholarship chmn. 1992-95), Soc. of Mayflower Descendants (lt. gov. Francis Cook Colony 1988-90), Pilgrim John Howland Soc., Colonial Dames XVII Century, Magna Charta Dames, Nat. Soc. New Eng. Women (v.p. Daytona Beach Colony 1990-91), Hibiscus Garden Circle (treas. 1988-89, v.p. 1990-93, 96—), Delta Kappa Gamma (pres. Beta Psi chpt. 1982-84), Nat. Soc. of U.S. Daus. of 1812. (rec. sec. Peacock chpt. 1989-90), DeLand Garden Club (corresponding sec. 1993-95, editor newsletter 1993-95), W. Volusia Hist. Soc. (sec. 1996, libr. 1995-96, bd. dirs.), Fla. Hist. Soc. Democrat. Episcopalian. Address: PO Box 241 Deland FL 32721

CADWALDER, HUGH MAURICE, psychology educator; b. Mt. Ayer, Iowa, July 1, 1924; s. Hugh M. and Mary (Crouch) C.; m. Melba Atwood, May 22, 1944 (div. 1975); children: Mark M., Mindy M.; m. Dianna Renfro-Reeves, May 15, 1980. MA, Baylor U., Waco, Tex., 1955, PhD, 1962; DD, Houston Bible Coll., 1963; ArtsD (hon.), Inst. Applied Rsch., London, 1970. Lic. master social worker, Tex., chem. dependency counselor, Tex.; cert. compulsive gambling specialist, Tex., clin. assoc. Am. Bd. Med. Psychotherapists, cert. criminal justice specialist; master addictions counselor; ordained to ministry Bapt. Ch., 1944. Instr. psychology Baylor U., Waco, Tex., 1955-62; acad. dean Southwestern Agrl. Coll., Waxahachie, Tex., 1962-64; sr. minister Christian Life Community Ch., Dallas, 1964-69, 1st Assembly of God Ch., Corpus Christi, Tex., 1969-74; mem. faculty dept. psychology San Jacinto Coll., Pasadena, Tex., 1974—; seminar dir. Cadwalder Behavioral Ctr., Houston, 1982-90; staff psychologist Charter Hosp., Sugar Land, Tex., 1990-95; full staff mem. Bellaire (Tex.) Gen. Hosp., 1993—, Forest Springs Hosp., Houston, 1988-95; seminar dir. Sharpstown Christian Singles, Houston, 1975-92; v.p. 1st Colony Mcpl. Utility Dist. 6, Sugar Land, 1988-96; host radio talk show Sta. KTEK. Author: Some Psychological Determinants Involved in Religious Attitudes, 1965, The Spiritual Dimension of Recovery from Addiction, 1988, Emotional Adhesions and Their Cure, 1989, Some Current Trends in the Mental Health Field, Or What To Do until the Psychiatrist Arrives with the Paramedics, 1995. Pres. bd. Community Ednl. TV Network, 1989-92; bd. dirs. Cadwalder Behavioral Ctr.; mem. Rep. Presdl. Task Force. Mem. NASW, Am. Assn. Coll. Profs., Am. Pub. Health Assn., Community Coll. Humanities Assn., Am. Assn. Retired Persons, Tex. Jr. Coll. Tchrs. Assn., Am. Assn. Christian Counselors, Am. Bd. Med. Psychotherapy, Am. Coun. on Alcoholism, Am. Assn. Coll. Profs., Community Coll. Humanities Assn., Harris County Sheriff's Deputies Assn. (cert. hon. membership 1985), Nat. Mental Health Assn., N.Y. Acad. Sci., Tex. Assn. Social Workers, Nat. Asns. Ind. Bus., Forum Club Houston, Phi Delta Kappa. Office: Cadwalder Counseling 7324 Southwest Fwy Ste 850 Houston TX 77074-2037

CADWALLADER, CHESTER SAMUEL, JR., missions educator; b. Waco, Tex., Dec. 21, 1920; s. Chester Samuel and Carrie Francis (Kendall) C.; m. Dorothy Bell, Sept. 3, 1943; children: Chester Seth, Paul David, Ralph Aldes, Martha Faye, Gloria Ruth. BA, Baylor U., 1942; ThM, Southwestern Bapt. Theol. Sem., Ft. Worth, 1945, New Orleans Bapt. Theol. Sem., 1951; grad., Spanish Lang. Sch., San Jose, Costa Rica, 1953; PhD, Mid-Am. Bapt. Theol. Sem., Memphis, 1996. Pastor College Pl. Bapt. Ch., Monroe, La., 1944-52; teaching fellow New Orleans Bapt. Theol. Sem., 1950-51; missionary Fgn. Mission Bd., So. Bapt. Conv., Guatemala, El Salvador, 1952-80; prof. missions Mid-Am. Bapt. Theol. Sem., 1983-90; adj. prof. Criswell Coll., Dallas, 1990-95, Southwestern Bapt. Theol. Sem., 1990—; ethnic cons. Tarrant Bapt. Assn., Ft. Worth, 1990-96; cons. Spanish-speaking chs., North Cen. Tex., 1990-94; dir. discipleship Kenya mission, summer 1991. Author: Earthquakes and Missions, 1991. Named Alumnus of Yr., Mid-Am. Bapt. Theol. Sem., 1991. Mem. Near East Archaeol. Soc. (officer Memphis chpt. 1988—). Republican. Home: 6319 Brookgate Dr Arlington TX 76016-3708 Office: Tate Springs Bapt Ch 4201 Little Rd Arlington TX 76016-5602

CADWALLADER, DONALD ELTON, pharmacy educator; b. Buffalo, June 14, 1931; s. Donald E. and Catherine E. (Russell) C.; m. Cecelia Vidis, Feb. 13, 1961; children—Susan, Keith, Lynn. B.S. in Pharmacy, U. Buffalo, 1953; M.S. in Medicinal Chemistry, U. Ga., 1955; Ph.D. in Pharmaceutics, U. Fla., 1957. Research assoc. pharmacy dept. Sterling Winthrop Research Inst., Rensselaer, N.Y., 1958-60; sect. head pharmacy dept. White Labs., Kenilworth, N.J., 1960-61; asst. prof. Sch. Pharmacy U. Ga., 1961-64, assoc. prof., 1964-68, prof., 1968-77, prof., head dept. pharmacy, 1977-80, prof., 1980-90, head dept. pharmaceutics, 1991, part-time prof., prof. emeritus pharmaceutics. Author: Biopharmaceutics and Drug Interactions, 3d edit., 1983. Fellow AAAS, Am. Assn. Pharm. Scis., Acad. Pharm. Scis.; mem. Am. Pharm. Assn., Am. Assn. Colls. of Pharmacy, Sigma Xi. Home: 470 Brookwood Dr Athens GA 30605-3851 Office: U Ga Coll Pharmacy Athens GA 30602

CAFFEE, MARCUS PAT, publishing company executive; b. Tulsa, Feb. 23, 1948; s. Malcolm Wesley and Martha Marjorie (Deming) C.; m. Virginia Maureen Gladden, May 31, 1975; 1 child, Katheryn Elizabeth. Student, Tulsa U., 1965-66, Okla. State U., 1966-67, 77-78. Pres. Computer Sales & Svc., Tulsa, 1972-75; owner Data Mgmt. Systems, Tulsa and Houston, 1975-77; staff analyst Okla. State U., Stillwater, 1977-78; project leader Ranger Ins. Cos., Houston, 1979-80; group mgr. corp. and fin. svcs. Am. Gen. Life Ins., Houston, 1980-82; mgr. systems devel. U. Tex. Health Sci. Ctr., Houston, 1982-84; owner Marcus Caffee, Cons., Conroe, Tex., 1984-89; pres., chief exec. officer Emcee Systems, Inc., 1989-90; dir. ops. I.C. Svcs., St. Petersburg, Fla., 1989-91; pvt. practice computer consulting Largo, Fla., 1991-95; pres., chmn. bd. Web Pub. Assocs., Inc., Ft. Worth, 1995—; dir. ops. AIM Am., Fort Worth, 1996—; spkr. in field. Author: Time Scaled Real Time Simulators, U.S. Navy, 1970, Satelite Data Communication Criteria Between Mainframe Computer Sites, Am. General 1981, Evaluation, Justification and Purchasing Guidelines for MicroComputers and Word Processors, U. Texas Health Science Ctr. at Houston 1982; copyright computer operaing system IBOL, 1972, integrated bus. software Office Master!, 1988, 89; author, editor bus. newsletter Read Me, 1986, 89, 91. Mem. Montgomery County Econ. Devel. Team, 1987; mem. adminstrv. bd. First United Meth. Ch., Conroe, 1987, instr. computer literacy, 1985-87. With USN, 1967-71. Mem. Airman's Aero Club, Rotary (Conroe chpt., guest speaker 1988). Republican. Office: Aim Am 4301 Empire Fort Worth TX 76155

CAFFEE, VIRGINIA MAUREEN, secretary; b. Kansas City, Mo., Feb. 25, 1948; d. Frederick Arthur Gladden and Ethel Elizabeth (Keithly) Courier; m. Jack B. Todd Jr., May 13, 1967 (div. Dec. 1973); m. Marcus Pat Caffee, May 31, 1975; 1 child, Katheryn Elizabeth. Student, Ctrl. Mo. State U., 1966-73, Okla. State U., 1977-78; BBA in Bus. Edn., Sam Houston State U., 1985. Cert. profl. sec., 1975. Land abstractor Johnson County Title Co., Warrensburg, Mo., 1967-68; dept. sec., bus. placement office Ctrl. Mo. State U., Warrensburg, 1968-69; exec. sec. European Exchange System, Giessen, Germany, 1969-70; confidential sec. Consolidated Freightways, Kansas City, 1972-73; exec. sec. Behring Internat., Houston, 1974-75; sr. sec. Tenneco Oil Co.-E&P, Houston, 1979-84; exec. sec. St. Petersburg (Fla.) Hilton & Towers, 1989-90; adminstrv. mgr. Tampa Bay Engring., Clearwater, Fla., 1990-92; office mgr., WP trainer Marcus Caffee, Consulting, Largo, Fla., 1992-95; sr. adminstrv. asst. BMH Inc., Dallas, 1995—; ad hoc instr. St. Petersburg (Fla.) Jr. Coll., 1993, Profl. Secs. Internat. chpt. liaison for CPS rev. course, 1993-94; presenter in field. Editor (performance programs) Suncoast Singers, 1991-94 (Cmty. Svc. award Arts Coun. Co-op 1993), Clearwater Cmty. Chorus, 1993-95, Ft. Worth Civic Chorus, Fall 1995, (newsletters) Clearwater Sparkler, 1992-93 (1st pl. award 1993), Fla. Divsn. The Secretariat, 1993-94; editor: Livin, Lovin, Laughin, 1995. Sec. Montgomery County Choral Soc., Conroe, Tex., 1986-88, publicity co-chmn., 1987-89; pres. Anona Meth. Ch. Choir, Largo, 1990-91. Named Sec. of Yr. Profl. Secs. Internat. Inc. Clearwater chpt., 1994; recipient Mo. State Tchrs. scholarship Mo. Congress Parents and Tchrs., 1966. Mem. NAFE, Profl. Secs. Internat. (chmn. secs. week, sec. Clearwater chpt. 1992-93, pres. 1994, chmn. seminar and v.p. Clearwater chpt. 1992-93, workshop spkr. Fla. divsn. 1993, program spkr. St. Petersburg chpt. 1993, alt. del. to internat. conv. 1993, alt. del. to divsn. meeting 1993, 94, del. dist. conv. 1994, Sec. of Yr. 1994-95, del. Fla. divsn. meeting 1995, program spkr. Trinity chpt. 1996, alt. Tex.-La. meeting 1996, del. to 1996 internat. conv., chmn. audit com. Denton chpt. 1996, divsn. treas. Tex.-La. divsn. 1996), CPS Soc. Tex. (roster chmn. 1983-85). Republican. Methodist. Office: BMH Inc 4004 Beltline Rd #125 Dallas TX 75244

CAFFEY, JAMES ENOCH, civil engineer; b. Rockdale, Tex., May 5, 1934; s. Enoch Arden and Leevicy Viola (Stephens) C.; m. Patricia Louise Latham, June 4, 1960; children: Jeffrey E., Jeanne Erin, Jerald E. BSCE, Tex. A&M U., 1955, MSCE, 1956; PhD, Colo. State U., 1965. Registered profl. engr., Tex.; registered profl. sanitarian, Tex. Prof. U. Tex., Arlington, 1959-74; dept. head Turner, Collier & Braden, Inc., Houston, 1974-76; assoc. Rady and Assocs., Inc., Ft. Worth, 1976-85; pres. Caffey Engring., Inc., Arlington, 1985—; asst. city engr. City of Arlington, 1991—; adv. bd. Cancer Rsch. Found. North Tex., Arlington, 1990-91. Capt. USAF, 1956-59; mem. USAFR, 1959-68. Fellow ASCE, Am. Water Resources Assn. (charter, bd. dirs. 1973-75); mem. NSPE, Am. Geophys. Union, Am. Inst. Hydrology (profl.), Kiwanis, Phi Eta Sigma, Tau Beta Pi, Phi Kappa Phi, Chi Epsilon. Baptist.

CAGGINS, RUTH PORTER, nurse, educator; b. Natchez, Miss., July 11, 1945; d. Henry Chapelle and Corinne Sadie (Baines) Porter; m. Don Randolph Caggins, July 1, 1978; children: Elva Rene, Don Randolph, Myles Thomas Chapelle. BS, Dillard U., New Orleans, 1967; MA, NYU, 1973; PhD Tex. Woman's U., 1992. Staff nurse Montefiore Hosp., Bronx, 1968-70, head nurse, 1970-72; nurse clinician Met. Hosp., N.Y.C., 1973-74, clin. supr., 1974-76; asst. prof. U. So. La., Lafayette, 1976-78; assoc. prof. Prairie View A&M U. Coll. Nursing, Houston, 1978—, apptd. project dir. LIFT Ctr. Active The Links Inc., Houston, 1982—, Cultural Arts Coun., Houston, Nat. Black Leadership Initiative on Cancer, Houston. Recipient Tchg. Excellence award Nat. Inst. Staff and Orgnl. Devel., 1992-93. Mem. ANA (clin. ethnic/racial minority fellow 1989-92, post doctoral proposal devel. program 1995), Nat. Black Nurses Assn., A.K. Rice Inst. (assoc. Ctrl. States Ctr., Tex. Ctr.), Assn. Black Nursing Faculty in Higher Edn. (Dissertation award 1990), Sigma Theta Tau, Delta Sigma Theta, Chi Eta Phi. Democrat. Baptist. Avocations: singing, sewing, traveling, aerobics, writing. Home: 5602 Goettee Cir Houston TX 77091-4523 Office: Prairie View A&M U Coll Nursing 6436 Fannin St Houston TX 77030-1519

CAGLE, JOHN B., marketing educator; b. London, Tenn., June 16, 1963; s. Johnny R. and Berna Dean (Embry) C.; m. Cynthia Gail Woods, Dec. 1, 1985; children: Laura Caitlin, Jacob Ronald. AA, Hiwassee Coll., 1983; BS in Bus. and Mktg. Edn., U. Tenn., 1993. Dir. admissions Hiwassee Coll., Madisonville, Tenn., 1986-88; mktg. tchr./coord. Jefferson County H.S., Dandridge, Tenn., 1993—. Mem. NEA, Jefferson County Edn. Assn. (award of excellence 1996), Tenn. Edn. Assn., Mktg. Edn. Assn., Tenn. Vocat. Assn., Am. Vocat. Assn. Office: Jefferson County High Sch 115 W Dumplin Valley Rd Dandridge TN 37725-4501

CAGLE, PAULETTE BERNICE, mental health administrator and psychologist; b. Ft. Worth, July 14, 1944; d. James Frank and Cordelia Pauline (Bourke) C. BS, North Tex. State U., 1972; MA, So. Meth. U., 1976. Lic. chem. dependency counselor; cert. diagnostic and evaluation psychologist; qualified mental health profl. Part-time psychometrist Jack Waxler, Psychologist, Richardson, Tex., 1973-77; social worker Vernon (Tex.) State Hosp., 1977-78, psychologist, 1978-88; adminstr. tech. programs Wichita Falls (Tex.) State Hosp., 1988-91, assoc. dir. mgmt. and support, 1991-96; assoc. dir. mgmt. and support Rolling Plains Socs., Tex., 1996—; cons. mem. quality improvement coun. Vernon State Hosp., 1992-96. Co-founder and mem. Cmty. Svcs. Quality Assurance Dirs. of Tex., 1993—; designated contact Mental Health Disaster Assistance, Austin, 1994—; mem. Wichita County Mental Health Assn., 1992—. Named Sister of the Yr. Sisterhood of Freedom, 1991. Mem. Am. Counseling Assn., Am. Mental Health Counselors Assn., Tex. Assn. Alcoholism and Drug Abuse Counselors, Internat. Assn. of Marriage and Family Counselors. Office: Texas Dept Mental Health Wichita Falls State Hosp PO Box 300 Wichita Falls TX 76307-0300

CAGLE, TERRY DEE, clergyman; b. Charlotte, N.C., June 7, 1955; s. James Clarence and Jean (Belk) C.; m. Julia Ann Conner, June 30, 1979; children: Julia Lynn, Christopher Terry, Benjamin Conner. BA, Gardner-Webb U., 1979; MDiv, Southeastern Bapt. Theol. Sem., 1982. Ordained to ministry So. Bapt. Conv., 1982. Pastor Mountain Creek Bapt. Ch., Oxford, N.C., 1982-85, Southside Bapt. Ch., Gaffney, S.C., 1985-88, Pleasant Ridge Bapt. Ch., Boiling Springs, N.C., 1988—; adj. prof. O.T. Gardner-Webb U., Boiling Springs, 1989—; mem. Christian Life com. King Mountain Bapt. Assn., Shelby, N.C.; v.p. Greater Gaffney Ministerial Fellowship, 1987-88. Mem. Boiling Springs Area Rotary Club (v.p. elect, club svc. chmn. 1989-94), Shelby Amateur Radio Club (repeater com. 1994—). Home: 203 Gordon Ave # 1084 Boiling Springs NC 28017 Office: Pleasant Ridge Bapt Ch 198 Pleasant Ridge Church Rd Shelby NC 28152-9022

CAHELA, ROXANNE BOWDEN, home health nurse; b. Anniston, Ala., Nov. 24, 1963; d. Johnny Jeff and Naomi Wynelle (Craft) Bowden; m. Roy Wade Cahela, Dec. 8, 1984; children: Jessica Renee, Brandon Wade. BSN, U. Ala., Birmingham, 1986. Cardiovascular intensive care, open heart recovery nurse Med. Ctr. East, Birmingham, 1986-87; spl. care unit staff nurse Boaz-Albertville Med. Ctr., Boaz, Ala., 1987-89; home health nurse coord. Etowah County Health Dept., Gadsden, Ala., 1989-95; Area 5 home health mgr., Dept. Pub. Health State of Ala., Gadsden, 1995—. Bd. dirs. Caregivers in the Middle Inc. Support Group, Gadsden, 1993-94; coun. agy. execs. United Way, 1994-95. Mem. Home Health Care Nurses Assn. Republican. Baptist. Home: 1116 Broadwell Rd Boaz AL 35956 Office: Ala Dept Pub Health Area 5 PO Box 8425 Gadsden AL 35952

CAHOON, SUSAN ALICE, lawyer; b. Jacksonville, Fla., Oct. 14, 1948; d. Robert Harold and Alice (Dubberly) C. BA, Emory U., 1968; JD, Harvard U., 1971. Bar: Ga. 1971, U.S. Dist. Ct. (no. dist.) Ga. 1971, U.S. Dist. Ct. (no. & ea. dists.) Tex. 1977, U.S. Dist. Ct. (mid. dist.) Ga. 1978, U.S. Dist. Ct. (we. dist.) Wis. 1979, U.S. Supreme Ct. 1979, U.S. Ct. Appeals (4th cir.) 1980, U.S. Dist. Ct. (so. dist.) Ga. 1981, U.S. Ct. Appeals (5th, 11th & D.C. cirs.) 1981, U.S. Ct. Appeals (6th cir.) 1983. Assoc. Kilpatrick & Cody, Atlanta, 1971-76, ptnr., 1977—. Contbr. articles to law revs., chpts. to books. Chmn. Stone Mountain Park Authority, Atlanta, 1984-93; v.p. Fulton County Divsn. Am. Heart Assn., Atlanta, 1992-93, pres., 1993-95; v.p. USO Coun. Ga., Inc., Atlanta, 1992—; bd. dirs. Atlanta Conv. & Visitors Bur., 1992—, vice chmn. 1996, Metro Atlanta Crime Commn., 1990-92, Fed. Defender PRogram, 1987-92; pres. Atlanta Area Alumni Club, 1975; mem. Leadership Atlanta, 1982, LeadershipGa., 1989. Fellow Am. Coll. Trial Lawyers, Am. Bar Found., Ga. Bar Found.; mem. ABA (litigation sect. com. chair 1986-88, com. chair 1995—), Ga. Bar Assn. (com. chair 1980-81), Atlanta Bar Assn. (bd. dirs. 1981-87, Leadership award 1991), D.C. Bar Assn., Am. Law Inst., Phi Beta Kappa, Omicron Delta Kappa, Lumpkin Inns of Ct. (master bencher). Baptist. Home: 2040 Old Dominion Rd Atlanta GA 30350-4619 Office: Kilpatrick & Cody 1100 Peachtree St NE Ste 2800 Atlanta GA 30309-4528

CAIN, CHARLES E., manager administrator; b. Augusta, Ga., Aug. 5, 1953; s. John H. Sr. and Lou Arrie Washington. BA, Ky. State U., 1975; MSW in adminstrn., U. Mich., 1979; MPH, U. Calif., 1981, DPH, 1987. Cert. instr. Calif. Community Coll. Credential Masters Level in Labor, Indsl. Rels. Children, youth project Med. Coll.Ga., Augusta; coord. adolescent health, pediatrics dept. Med. Coll.Ga.; foster care specialist Children's Home Soc., San Francisco; instr. San Francisco Community Coll.; program dir. Alternative Family Svcs., San Francisco; Adminstrv. dir., univ. affiliated program dept. pediatrics U. Tex. Southwestern Med. Ctr., Dallas, Tex.; regional maternal #2, chief health cons., dept. health and human svcs. U.S. Pub. Health Svc. Region V Div. ion, Chicago, IL.; bur. chief health and human svcs. Houston (tex.) Dept. Health and Human Svcs.; exec. dir. Nat. Resource Ctr. on Cultural Competency. Contbr. articles to profl. jours. Vol. Am. Red Cross. Recipient U. Calif. Grossman Rsch. award. Mem. Nat. Black Child Devel. Inst., Am. Pub. Health Assn., Omega Psi Phi.

CAIN, DARREN LEE, internist; b. Gamaliel, Ky., June 12, 1967; s. Tim Lee Cain and Mildred Edith (Fletcher) Sizemore. BS, Western Ky. U., 1989; MD, U. Louisville, 1993. Intern U. Louisville, 1993-94, resident in internal medicine, 1994-96, attending physician dept. medicine, 1996—. Mem. AMA, ACP, Ky. Med. Assn., Jefferson County Med. Soc.

CAIN, DONALD EZELL, judge; b. San Marcos, Tex., Oct. 8, 1921; s. Erie Montclair and Betty Belle (Howell) C.; m. Betty Anne Culberson, June 14, 1952; children: David, Dale Cain Husen, Donald Ezell, Randolph. A.S., North Tex. Agrl. Coll., 1941; B.B.A., U. Tex., 1943, LL.B., 1948; postgrad., Nat. Jud. Coll., Reno, 1974, 78, 82. Bar: Tex. 1948. With contracts dept. Convair, Ft. Worth, 1948-50; pvt. practice law Pampa, Tex., 1951-76; county atty. Gray County, Tex., 1955-68, county judge, 1971-77; dist. judge 223rd Dist. Ct. Tex., 1977-91; sr. dist. judge State of Tex., 1991—. Pres. Adobe Walls coun. Boy Scouts Am., 1957-59; bd. dirs. Pampa United Fund, 1956-60. Served from ensign to lt. USNR, 1943-46; as lt., 1950-51. Recipient Silver Beaver award Boy Scouts Am., 1958. Fellow Tex. Bar Found.; mem. ABA, Tex. Bar Assn., Gray County Bar Assn. (pres. 1968), Am. Judicature Soc., Tex. Judges and Commrs. Assn., Panhandle County Judges and Commrs. Assn. (pres. 1975), Pampa C. of C. (dir. 1959-60), Phi Alpha Delta. Democrat. Baptist. Clubs: Masons, Rotary (pres. 1958-59), Pampa Country. Home: 1826 Williston St Pampa TX 79065-3602

CAIN, FRANK, electrical engineer; b. Bklyn., June 3, 1944; s. Louis and Jean C.; m. Marcia Ellen Sachs, Oct. 3, 1965; children: Lou Michael, Lori Beth. AAS, N.Y. Tech. Coll., 1965; BSEE, N.Y. Inst. Tech., 1970; MS, U. So. Fla., 1974. Engring. tech. Hazeltine Electronics Corp., Greenlawn, N.Y., 1965-70; from instrumental design engr. to total quality staff engr. Honeywell, Clearwater, Fla., 1970—; adv. bd. St. Petersburg Jr. Coll., 1980—; former chair bd. Sci. Ctr. Pinellas County. Mem. Am. Soc. Quality Control (cert. reliability engr.). Jewish. Home: 3075 Roberta St Largo FL 33771 Office: Honeywell 13350 US19 N Clearwater FL 34624

CAIN, LAURENCE SUTHERLAND, physics educator, consultant; b. Washington, Feb. 4, 1946; s. Leighton Aubrey and Beatrice (Sutherland) C.; m. Mary Jane Dimmock, Aug. 21, 1971; children—Rebecca Anne, Peter Laurence. B.S., Wake Forest U., 1968; M.S. in Physics, U. Va., 1970, Ph.D. in Physics, 1973. Research assoc. U. N.C., Chapel Hill, 1973-76, lectr., 1976-78; asst. prof. physics Davidson Coll. (N.C.), 1978-85, assoc. prof., 1985-88, assoc. prof., chmn. Dept. Physics, 1988-91; prof., chmn. dept. physics, 1991—; vis. prof. Wake Forest U., Winston-Salem, N.C., summer 1979; faculty research participant Dept. Energy, 1986-87; cons. in field. Bd. dirs. North Mecklenburg Child Devel. Assn., 1979-85, treas., 1982-85. NSF Research Equipment grantee, 1981; grantee Research Corp., 1981, 83, 85, 86. Mem. Am. Phys. Soc. (treas. southeastern sect. 1991—), Am. Assn. Physics Tchrs., AAAS, Sigma Xi, Phi Beta Kappa, Kappa Mu Epsilon. Democrat. Presbyterian. Contbr. articles to profl. jours. Office: Davidson Coll Dept Physics Davidson NC 28036

CAIN, MICHAEL DEAN, research forester; b. Pascagoula, Miss., Nov. 9, 1946; s. Thomas R. and Bennie (Gleghorn) C. AS, Perkinston (Miss.) Jr. Coll., 1966; BS, Miss. State U., 1969; MS, La. State U., 1973. Registered forester, Miss. Rsch. forester So. Rsch. Sta., Pineville, La., 1975-78, Crossett, Ark., 1978-87, Monticello, Ark., 1987—. Contbr. articles to Forest Sci., So. Jour. Applied Forestry, Forest Ecology and Mgmt., Internat. Jour. Wildland Fire, New Forests, Nat. Areas Jour., Can. Jour. Forest Rsch., Am. Midland Naturalist, The Cons., Soc. Am. Foresters Conf. Procs., Procs. of the So. Weed Sci. Soc., univ. rsch. publs., USDA Forest Svc. rsch. publs. With U.S. Army, 1969-71. Mem. Soc. Am. Foresters, Weed Sci. Soc. Am., So. Weed Sci. Soc., Ecol. Soc. Am., Internat. Assn. Wildland Fire, Soc. for Conservation Biology. Office: So Rsch Sta PO Box 3516 Monticello AR 71656-3516

CAIN, ROSEMARY PRINCE, Montessori educator; b. Tuscaloosa, Ala., Dec. 18, 1954; d. Benny Andrew and Mary C. (McCollum) Prince; divorced; children: Michael, Christopher, Latheria, Kelvin, Jamey, Mary. BS, U. Ala., 1996. Tchr. Univ. Place Montessori Sch. Leader Tombigbee coun. Girl Scouts U.S., Tuscaloosa. Mem. Coun. for Learning Disabilities, Phi Kappa Phi. Baptist. Home: 11077 Longbow Dr Tuscaloosa AL 35405

CAINE, CURTIS WEBB, anesthesiologist; b. New Orleans, Oct. 13, 1921; s. Ansel Marion Sr. and Pearl (Jacobs) C.; m. Evelyn Lucile Johnson, Sept. 24, 1940; children: Curtis Jr., Edsel, Gary, Carol. BS, Tulane U., 1942, MD, 1944. Diplomate Am. Bd. Anesthesiology. Intern So. Bapt. Hosp., New Orleans, 1944-45; resident in anesthesiology Charity Hosp., New Orleans, 1945-46; pvt. practice Jackson, Miss., 1948—; staff physician Miss. Bapt. Med. Ctr., chief of staff, 1957; staff physician St. Dominics Med. Ctr., Meth. Med. Ctr., Womans Hosp., U. Med. Ctr., River Oaks Health Sys., Surgicare of Jackson, Miss. Surg. Ctr.; clin. asst. prof. anesthesiology, U. Miss. Med. Sch. Patentee in field; contbr. articles to profl. jours. Sr. deacon First Bapt. Ch., Jackson, 1954—. With USNR, 1942-47; lt. col. Miss. CAP. Named Man of Yr. Miss. Women for Constl. Govt., 1971, 89, Nat. Women for Constl. Govt.; recipient Freedom award Congress of Freedom, Liberty Amendment award, 1964. Fellow Am. Coll. Anesthesiologists, Internat. Coll. Anesthesiologists; mem. AMA, NRA, Flying Physicians Assn. (life pres. 1969-70, Airman of Yr. award 1979), So. Soc. Anesthesiologists (founder), La. Med. Soc., la. Soc. Anesthesiologists, Anesthesia History Assn., Miss. Soc. Anesthesiologists (founder, pres. 1950-51, Outstanding Svc. award 1975), Assn. Am. Physicians and Surgeons (life, pres. 1980-81), Internat. Anesthesia Rsch. Soc., Jackson Anesthesiology Forum (founder), Exptl. Aviation Assn., Aircraft Owners and Pilots Assn., Jackson C. of C., Miss. Econ. Coun., Jackson Opera Assn., So. Econ. Coun., U. Club., Country Club Jackson, Kappa Sigma. Home: 712 Forest Point Dr Brandon MS 39042 Office: 1543 Brobridge Dr Jackson MS 39211-2114

CAINE, ROBERT, electrical engineer; b. Pitts., Dec. 29, 1946; s. Robert B. and Irene K. (Fullerton) C.; m. Katie A. Brier, 1971 (div. 1975); m. Leilana V. Gomez, May 31, 1982. BSEE, Villanova U., 1969; postgrad. in telecomms., George Washington U., 1988. Elec. engr. PEPCO, 1969-70, Bernard Johnson, 1970-72, Bechtel, 1972-73; sr. elec. engr. DeLeuw Cather Co., 1973-74, E.C. Ernst, 1974-79, Heery Internat., 1979-82; sr. contract adminstr. Dynalectric, 1982-84; prin. Leo A. Daly, 1985-93, Tilden, Lobnitz and Cooper, Orlando, Fla., 1993—; engring. contracts include The World Bank, Washington, Army Corps of Engrs., Beltsville Info. Ctr., Duke U. Hosp., Peat, Marwick & Main, Washington, Chevy Chase Ctr., Washington, Lincoln Theatre, Washington, NASA, Beltsville, Md., Standard Federal, Laurel, Md., others; lectr. in field. Contbr. articles to profl. jours. Mem. NSPE, IEEE, TMACA (pres. 1988), IES. Office: Tilden Lobnitz Cooper 1717 S Orange Ave Orlando FL 32806-2944

CALAMITA, KATHRYN ELIZABETH, nursing administrator; b. Portland, Maine, Oct. 12, 1943; d. Maurice Daniel and Eleanor Elizabeth (Sullivan) Casey; m. John Joseph Calamita, Jan. 9, 1965; children: Angela Marie, Carla Anne, Daniel John. RN, Mercy Hosp. Sch. Nursing, Springfield, Mass., 1964; student, Midwestern State U., Wichita Falls, Tex., 1979-86, Vernon Regional Coll., 1987; BS in Bus., St. Joseph's Coll., Windham, Maine, 1992. Staff nurse Mercy Hosp., Springfield, 1964; med/surg. nurse Wichita Gen. Hosp., Wichita Falls, Tex., 1976-77, nurse ICU, 1977-79, supr. dept. nursing, 1979-86, assoc. adminstr. nursing dept., 1986-92; health facility adminstr. Wichita Falls Rehab. Hosp., 1992; rehab. nurse Bay Convalescent and Rehab. Ctr., Panama City, Fla., 1993-94; asst. DON L.A. Wagner Nursing and Rehab. Ctr., Panama City, Fla., 1994—. Mem. ANA (cert. in mgmt., 1995), FNA. Democrat. Roman Catholic.

CALAWAY, DENNIS LOUIS, insurance company executive, real estate broker, financial executice; b. Helena, Ark., Dec. 10, 1960; s. Carl Jr. and Mary Jean (Taylor) C.; m. Elizabeth Anne Suiter, July 16, 1988; children: Sean Joseph, Katherine Elizabeth, Bridget Marie. BS in Bus. Adminstrn., Ark. State U., 1983, MBA, 1988. Registered health underwriter; life underwriter tng. coun. fellow; lic. real estate broker, Ark.; registered employee benefit cons. Ops. mgr. Churchill Truck Lines, Jonesboro and Litte Rock, Ark., 1983-85; rep. Mut. of Omaha Cos., Jonesboro, 1985-88; pres. Profl. Ins. Svcs., Inc., 1988—; gen. agt. State Life Ins. Co. of Ind., Time Ins. Co. and United Am. Ins. Co., 1988—, Security Gen. Life Ins. Co., 1989—, GPM Life Ins. Co., 1991—; prin. broker Calaway Realty Co., 1992—; pres. Profl. Fin. Svcs., Inc., 1993—; CFO, Davis Electric Motors, Inc., 1993-94; co-founder TDI Bearing & Supply, Inc., 1994; account exec., indsl. benefit cons. Health Choice of Jonesboro, Inc./Meth. Hosp. of Jonesboro, 1995—; CFO, Davis Electric Motors, Inc., 1993-94; benefit cons. Health Choice of Jonesboro, 1995. Chief counsellor Columbian Squire Cir., 1988—; mem. pastoral coun. Blessed Sacrament Cath. Ch., 1990-92, founder, pres. Soc. St. Therese, 1975—; mem. fin. com. Blessed Sacrament Cath. Sch., 1994-95. Fellow Life Underwriters Tng. Coun. (instr. 1990-91, moderator 1991, chmn. 1991-92, Amb. Club, Silver Club); mem. Nat. Assn. Health Underwriters, Nat. Soc. Human Resource Mgmt., N.E. Ark. Soc. Human Resource Mgmt., Gen. Agts. and Mgrs. Conf., Nat. Assn. Life Underwriters, Jonesboro Assn. Life Underwriters (sec.-treas. 1o86-88, pres.-elect 1988-89, pres. 1989—, health chmn. 1992—), Assn. Health Ins. Agts., KC (treas. 1982-83, 84-87, faithful scribe 1983-84, faithful navigator 1986-88, grand knight 1981-83, faithful adm. 1989-90, faithful trustee 1991—, Ark. youth dir. 1989-92, chmn. Ark. squires 1989-92, Knight of Yr. award 1982, 88), Lions, Beta Gamma Sigma, Omicron Delta Epsilon, Gamma Iota Sigma. Home: PO Box 1 State University AR 72467-0001 Office: Profl Ins Svcs Inc PO Box 419 Jonesboro AR 72403-0419 also: Profl Fin Svcs Inc PO Box 419 Jonesboro AR 72403-0419 also: CSA Mktg Inc PO Box 2700 State University AR 72467-2700

CALDWELL, BILLY RAY, geologist; b. Newellton, La., Apr. 20, 1932; s. Leslie Richardson and Helen Merle (Clark) C.; m. Carolyn Marie Heath; children: Caryn, Jeana, Craig. BA, Tex. Christian U., 1954, MA, 1970. Cert. petroleum geologist, cert. profl. geologist. Geologist, Geol. Engring. Svc. Co., Ft. Worth, Tex., 1954-60; sci. tchr. Ft. Worth and Lake Worth Sch. Dists., 1960-63; mgr. Outdoor Living, 1963-71; instr. geology Tarrant County Jr. Coll., Ft. Worth, 1971—; petroleum and environ. geologist cons., Ft. Worth, 1971—. Bd. dirs. Ft. Worth and Tarrant County Homebuilders Assn., 1973; co-chmn. Fort Worth Environ. Coun. Named Dir. of Yr., Ft. Worth Jaycees, 1966-67. Mem. Am. Inst. Profl. Geologists, Am. Assn. Petroleum Geologists, Geol. Soc. Am., Ft. Worth Geol. Soc., Soc. Profl. Well Log Analysts, Ft. Worth C. of C. (environ. com). Republican. Baptist. Avocations: traveling, ch. work. Home: 305 Bodart Ln Fort Worth TX 76108-3804 Office: PO Box 150989 Fort Worth TX 76108-0989

CALDWELL, CLAUD REID, lawyer; b. Augusta, Ga., Sept. 18, 1909; s. John Mars and Ethel (Bennett) C.; student Acad. Richmond County, 1922-26; m. Josephine F. Clarke, June 30, 1940; children: Claud R., Kathryn C., James W. Bar: Ga. 1932, U.S. Supreme Ct. Ga. 1949, Ga. Ct. Appeals 1949, U.S. Dist. Ct. 1934, U.S. Ct. Appeals (5th cir.) 1953, U.S. Ct. Appeals (11th cir.) 1981, U.S. Supreme Ct. 1968. Pvt. practice, Augusta, 1934-95; ret. 1995; judge Mcpl. Ct., City of Augusta, 1948-49. Pres., Richmond County Ind. Party, 1950-51; bd. dirs. Augusta chpt. ARC, YMCA; chmn. Augusta council Boy Scouts Am., 1949-50. With AUS, 1941-45; ETO; col. USAR (ret.). Recipient Distinguished Pistol Marksman award U.S. Army, 1965. Mem. ABA, Ga. State Bar. Assn., Augusta Bar Assns., Ga. Sport Shooting Assn. (dir., past pres.), Augusta-Richmond County Hist. Mus., Mil. Order World Wars, Nat. Sojourners, Heroes of '96 (Gen. Oglethorpe chpt.), Res. Officers Assn. (Augusta chpt.), Am. Legion, Sons of Confederacy, Assn. U.S. Army, Masons, Augusta Country Club. Presbyn. (deacon).

CALDWELL, DONALD WILSON, communications executive; b. Franklin, Tenn., Nov. 10, 1945; s. Wilson Troxler and Carolyn (Jamison) C.; m. Elizabeth Sue Caldwell, Sept. 2, 1967; children: Lori Elissa, Karyn Luisa. BS, Tenn. Tech. U., 1967; MS, West Va. U., 1969; postgrad., U. Tenn., 1976-78. Sales promotion mgr. Cummins Engine Co., Columbus, Ind., 1979-83; dir. comms. Calspan Corp., Buffalo, 1983-84; mktg. mgr. Cummings Inc., Nashville, 1984-85; instr. mktg. Belmont U., Nashville, 1985-87; exec. v.p. Royal Tapestry Inc., Nashville, 1987; tng. specialist No. Telecom, Inc., Nashville, 1988-89, pub. affairs mgr., 1989—; bd. dirs. Boston Coll. Ctr. for Corp. Cmty. Rels., The So. Cos. Chmn. corp. ptnrs. Fisk U., Nashville, 1992-94; program chmn., contbns. coun. The Conf. Bd., N.Y.C., 1994; chmn. bd. dirs. Sr. Citizens, Inc., Nashville, 1993-94; chmn. Cable TV Commn., City of Columbus, 1982-83; bd. dirs. Pencil Found., Nashville, 1994—; chmn. comms. com. United Way, Nashville, 1991-92. Lt. col. USAR, 1967—. Named Outstanding Young Man of Am., Oym Found., 1974, 88. Mem. Pub. Rels. Soc. Am., Am. Mgmt. Assn., Sigma Delta Chi, Omicron Delta Kappa. Baptist. Office: No Telecom Inc 200 Athens Way Nashville TN 37228-1308

CALDWELL, DONNA FRANCES, elementary education educator; b. Somerset, Ky., Sept. 7, 1955; d. henry S. and LaVerne (Eubank) Keith; m. Raymond D. Caldwell; 1 child, Molly E. A in Libr. Sci., U. Ky., 1975; BS in Elem. Edn., Ea. Ky. U., 1988, M in Elem. Edn., 1993. Chiropractic asst. McNevin Chiropractic Clinic, Somerset, Ky., 1976-78; sec. State Farm Ins., Somerset, 1978-80; ins. agt. Lafavers Ins., Somerset, 1981-86; tchr. Pulaski County Bd. Edn., Somerset, 1988—; team leader No. Middle Sch. Named Tchr. of Yr., Somerset C. of C., 1995. Republican. Member Church of Christ. Office: No Middle Sch 650 Oak Leaf Ln Somerset KY 42503-4652

CALDWELL, HAPPY, religious organization executive. Address: Ste 502 10801 Executive Center Dr Little Rock AR 72211

CALDWELL, JOHN ALVIS, JR., experimental psychologist; b. New Orleans, June 16, 1955; s. John Alvis and Patsy Ruth (Richardson) C.; m. Jo Lynn Woodard, July 18, 1981. BA cum laude, Troy State U., 1976; MS in Psychology, U. South Ala., 1979; PhD in Psychology, U. So. Miss., 1984. Psychologist II Eufaula (Ala.) Adolescent Adjustment Ctr., 1979-80, coord. drug-free clinic, 1980-81; asst. dir. behavioral med. lab. Children's Hosp. Nat. Med. Ctr., Washington, 1984-86; rsch. psychologist U.S. Army Aeromed. Rsch. Lab., Ft. Rucker, Ala., 1986—; sec., chief edn. working group 19 NATO Adv. Group R&D, 1991-94; math. and sci. adv. com. mem. Troy State U., 1992—; adj. faculty U.S. Army Sch. Aerospace Medicine, 1996—. Spl. guest editor Biol. Psychology, Amsterdam, 1994; jour. referee Aviation Space and Environ. Med., 1992—; contbr. articles to profl. jours. Dir. ch. choir St. John Cath. Ch., Enterprise, Ala., 1991—; vol. counselor Wiregrass Emergency Pregnancy Svc., Daleville, Ala., 1992; choir mem. Enterprise com. choir ARL Christmas choir, Enterprise, 1991, Ft. Rucker, 1992-93. Named Outstanding Young Man in Am., 1981; recipient Writing award U.S. Army Aviation Med. Assn., 1996. Mem. AAAS, Am. Psychol. Soc., Soc. for Psychophysiol. Rsch., Psi Chi (v.p. 1976, Achievement award 1976), Sigma Xi. Republican. Roman Catholic. Home: RR 1 Box 110 Jack AL 36346-9731 Office: US Army Aeromed Rsch Lab PO Box 620577 Fort Rucker AL 36362-0577

CALDWELL, JUDY CAROL, advertising executive, public relations executive; b. Nashville, Dec. 28, 1946; d. Thomas and Sarah Elizabeth Carter; 1 child, Jessica. BS, Wayne State U., 1969. Tchr. Bailey Mid. Sch., West Haven, Conn., 1969-72; editorial asst. Vanderbilt U., Nashville, 1973-74; editor, graphics designer, field researcher Urban Observatory of Met. Nashville, 1974-77; account exec. Holden and Co., Nashville, 1977-79; bus. tchr. Federated States of Micronesia, 1979-80; dir. advt. Am. Assn. for State and Local History, Nashville, 1980-81; dir. prodn. Mktg. Communications Co., Nashville, 1981-83; ptnr. Victory Images of Tenn., Inc., Nashville, 1990-92; owner, pres. Ridge Hill Corp., Nashville, 1983—.

CALDWELL, LEE ANN, history educator; b. Augusta, Ga., Sept. 21, 1949; d. Joseph Lawton and Peggy (Sheram) C.; m. Richard Edgar Swann; 1 child, Richard Caldwell Swann. AA, Gulf Park Coll., 1968; AB, U. Tenn., 1970; MA, U. Ga., 1976, PhD, 1986. Grad. asst. U. Ga., Athens, 1975-78; dir. Augusta (Ga.) Heritage Trust, 1978-81; assoc. prof. history Paine Coll., Augusta, 1980-91, Augusta State U., 1991—. Contbr. articles to profl. jours. Mem. exec. bd. Leadership Augusta, 1980-92, 93-95; bd. dirs. Richmond County Hist. Soc., Augusta, v.p., 1996, pres., 1997; mem. adv. bd. Main St. Program, Augusta, 1990—; bd. trustees Historic Augusta, 1970-92, 94—; bd. dirs. Augusta Arts Coun., 1996—. Recipient J.W. Brown award Paine Coll., 1993. Mem. So. Assn. Women Historians, So. Hist. Assn., Ga. Hist. Soc., Ga. Assn. Historians. Democrat. Methodist. Office: Augusta Coll 2500 Walton Way Augusta GA 30904-4562

CALDWELL, PAULA DAY, telecommunications executive; b. Colorado Springs, Colo., Nov. 11, 1954; d. Taylor Arnold Day and Constance Theo (Jenkins) Day; m. Michael Anthony Caldwell, Feb. 21, 1981. BS, Lindenwood Coll., 1981; MBA, Dallas Bapt. U., 1986. Exec. sec. Minority Econ. Devel. Agy., St. Louis, 1974-76; adminstrv. asst. New Age Fed. Savs. and Loan, St. Louis, 1976-78; bookkeeper Family Planning Council, 1978-81; sr. account mgr. AT&T Corp., Dallas, 1981-92; staff mgr. to sales v.p. AT&T Corp., Dallas, 1993; nat. sales mgr. AT&T Corp., 1994. Home: PO Box 763845 Dallas TX 75376-3845 Office: AT&T Corp 5th Fl 5501 Lyndon B Johnson Fwy Dallas TX 75240-6202

CALDWELL, ROSSIE JUANITA BROWER, library service educator; b. Columbia, S.C., Nov. 4, 1917; d. Rossie Lee and Henrietta Olivia (Irby) Brower; m. Harlowe Evans Caldwell, Aug. 6, 1943 (dec. 1983); 1 adopted dau., Rossie Laverne Caldwell Jenkins. BA magna cum laude, Claflin Coll., 1937; MS, S.C. State Coll., 1952; MSLS, U. Ill., 1959. Tchr., libr. Reed St. High Sch., Anderson, S.C., 1937-39, Emmett Scott High Sch., Rock Hill, S.C., 1939-42, Wilkinson High Sch., Orangeburg, S.C., 1942-43, librarian, 1945-57; civilian pers. War Dept., Tuskegee Army Air Field, 1943-45; asst. prof. then assoc. prof. library service dept. S.C. State Coll., Orangeburg, 1957-83. Contbr. to book in field; author articles. Life mem. NAACP; trustee, Christian advocate The United Meth. Ch. in S.C., 1978-86; assoc. mem. Orangeburg Regional Hosp. Aux; comm. chairperson Trinity United Meth. Ch. Named to Scroll of Honor, Lambda Sigma, 1988; recipient Presdl. citation Claflin Coll., 1989, also numerous ann. vol. work citations. Mem. ALA (continuing life mem.), ALA Black Caucus (emeritus), AAUP (emeritus), VFW Aux. (aux.), S.C. Library Assn. (hon.), AAUW (editor Orangeburg chpt. bull.), Friends of the Library, Palmetto Med. Dental Pharmaceutical Assn. Aux. (historian, state pres., Woman of Yr. 1972), Sigma Pi Phi (archousa), Phi Delta Kappa, Beta Phi Mu (hon.), Alpha Kappa Alpha (life). Clubs: Links (archivist, historian), As You Like It Bridge, Daus. of Isis, Forerunners Club (coord., founder), Golden Scholarship Club. Home: 1320 Ward Ln NE Orangeburg SC 29115-1342

CALDWELL, THOMAS HOWELL, JR., accountant, financial management consultant; b. Wichita Falls, Tex., Feb. 5, 1934; s. Thomas Howell and LaVerne Louise C.; m. Bernell Irons, Apr. 12, 1968 (div. Jan. 1979); 1 child, Thomas Howell III (dec.). BA in Religion, Baylor U., 1956; postgrad., Tex. Christian U., 1958-63, North Tex. State U., 1973-75; LLD (hon.), London Inst. Applied Rsch., 1994. Cert. internal auditor. Tech. writer Gen. Dynamics, Ft. Worth, 1956-60; asst. dir. pers. Harris Hosp., Ft. Worth, 1960-62; with fiduciary tax sect. 1st Nat. Bank, Ft. Worth, 1962-64; jr. acct. various CPA's, Dallas, 1964-65; auditor Def. Contract Audit Agy., Dallas, 1965-74; tax appraiser, mcpl. acct. City of McKinney, Tex., 1974-75; systems acct. USDA, Dallas, 1975-83; auditor U.S. Army C.E., Dallas, 1983-86; acct. rep. IRS, Dallas, 1986-87; systems acct. Def. Fin. & Acctg. Svc., Dallas, 1987-93; fin. mgmt. cons. Caldwell Fin. Mgmt. Cons., Dallas, 1993—. Mem. jr. bd. 1st Bapt. Ch., Dallas. With USAFR, 1957-63. Mem., bd. dirs., treas. Desc. Vets. Mexican War, (bd. dirs., treas.), Baylor U. Ex-Students Assn., Masons, Shriners. Republican. Home and Office: 10822 Pagewood Dr Dallas TX 75230-4468

CALDWELL, WILLIAM MCNEILLY, insurance agent; b. Kingston, Pa., Dec. 31, 1953; s. William Parks and Lois Elizabeth (McNeilly) C.; m. Paula Teresa Harvey; 1 child, William Harvey. BS in Econs., U. Pa., 1976. CLU, ChFC. Rep. Equitable Life, Austin, Tex., 1976-78, agt., registered rep., 1983-90; agt. Southland Life, Austin, 1978; dir. mktg. div. ins. trust Automotive Svc. Assn., Bedford, Tex., 1978-83; mng. rep. Covenant Life, Austin, 1990-94; Sibley & Assocs. Fin. Group; ptnr. Sibley Fin. Group, Austin, 1994—; moderator Life Underwriter Tng. Coun., Austin, 1987-96. Deacon 1st Presbyn. Ch. Austin, 1989-92. Fellow Life Underwriter Tng. Coun.; mem. Am. Soc. CLU and ChFC (bd. dirs. Austin chpt. 1988), Exch. Club Austin (past pres. 1989-90). Office: 505 E Huntland Dr Ste 510 Austin TX 78752

CALEVAS, HARRY POWELL, management consultant; b. Williamsburg, Va., Nov. 18, 1918; s. Gus and Elizabeth (Powell) C.; m. Betty Nicoolette Chronaker, July 4, 1939 (wid. Nov. 1989); children: Phillip H., Stanley P.; m. Lillian Ida Satrum. Mech. Engring. Diploma, Case Sch. Applied Scis., Cleve., 1939; MBA, Pacific Western U., 1980, D Bus. Adminstrn., 1985. Lic. real estate broker, real estate property mgr., Fla. Real Estate Commn. V.p., gen. mgr. Radisson Hotel, Mpls., 1949-53; v.p. Banker Life & Casualty, Chgo., 1953-63; pres. Fla. Bd. Trade, Ft. Lauderdale, 1963-95. Author: Condominium Management Handbook, 1985, The Wandering Moon, 1994, Positive Way to Profit, 1965; author twelve cookbooks/internat. food recipes, 1960. Capt. Merchant Marines, ATO. Mem. Am. Legion, SAR, Decendants George Washington, Optimist Club (bd. dirs. 1990-96). Republican. Baptist. Home: 5680 North A1A Vero Beach FL 32963

CALHOUN, DEBORAH LYNN, emergency room nurse, consultant; b. Tulsa, Aug. 6, 1958; d. Charles Cooper Calhoun and Delores Susan (Deardorf) Metzger. BSN, Clemson U., 1982. RN, S.C.; cert. instr. ACLS, Am. Heart Assn., TNCC instr.; CEN; clin. coord. EMS and cmty. svcs., hyperbaric medicine. Staff nurse, clin. nurse III Roper Hosp., Charleston, S.C., 1982—; owner Charleston Med.-Lega. Consulting, 1994—; clin. coord. EMS/Cmty. Svcs. and Hyperbaric Medicine, Roper Hosp.; clin. coord. emergency svcs. Roper Hosp. North. Instr. ENCARE, 1993. Mem. ENA, TNCC, S.C. Emergency Nurses Assn. (pres. 1994, ann. symposium chair 1996), Low Country Emergency Nurses Assn. (pres. 1991. 92). Republican. Episcopalian. Home: 1212 Gilmore Rd Charleston SC 29407-5333 Office: Roper Hosp 316 Calhoun St Charleston SC 29401-1113

CALHOUN, HAROLD, architect; b. Mineral Springs, Ark., Oct. 11, 1906; s. Albert Sidney and Willie (Reeder) C.; m. Annie Louise Robertson, Dec. 3, 1932; 1 dau., Nancy Ann (dec.). B.A., Rice U., 1932. Freelance delineator and archtl. draftsman, 1925-29; organized firm Wirtz & Calhoun (architects), 1932; with Robert & Co. (architects and engrs. on design of Corpus Christi Naval Air Center), Corpus Christi, Tex., 1940-43; vis. critic, grad. students archtl. dept. Rice U., 1946; with Wirtz, Calhoun, Tungate & Jackson, Houston, 1947-66, Calhoun, Tungate & Jackson, Houston, 1966-75, Calhoun, Tungate, Jackson & Dill, Houston, 1975—. Served to lt. (s.g.) USNR, 1943-46. Recipient first hon. mention House Beautiful competition, 1946; 3d prize Georgia Builds competition, 1947; certificate of award Houston chpt. A.I.A., 1947; hon. mention, 1953; award of merit Tex. Soc. Architects, 1954; architecture of merit award, 1960. Fellow AIA; mem. Tex. Soc. Architects (past pres.), Houston Engring. and Sci. Soc., La Sociedad de Arquitectos Mexicanos (hon.), Masons, Lions. Baptist (deacon). Home: 1 Concord Cir Houston TX 77024-6309 Office: CTJ&D Architects 6200 Savoy Dr Ste 630 Houston TX 77036-3315

CALHOUN, LINDA PALMON (LINDA C. PALMON), cardiologist; b. Phila., June 4, 1959; d. Florentina Perez and Socorro (Abela) Palmon; m. Timothy John Calhoun, Oct. 13, 1990. BS in Biology magna cum laude, Georgetown U., 1981, MD cum laude, 1985. Diplomate Am. Bd. Internal Medicine, Am. Bd. Cardiovascular Disease. Intern, then resident in internal medicine N.C. Meml. Hosp., U. N.C., Chapel Hill, 1985-88; fellow in cardiology Hosp. U. Pa., Phila., 1988-92; cardiologist Wilmington (N.C.) Health Assocs., P.A., 1992—; cardiologist New Hanover Regional Med. Ctr., 1992—; cardiologist, med. dir. spl. testing Cape Fear Meml. Hosp., 1993—; clin. instr. U. N.C., Wilmington, 1992—. Contbr. articles to profl. jours. Fellow Am. Coll. Cardiology; mem. Am. Heart Assn. (clin. cardiology coun., Rsch. Fellow award 1990, 91), Am. Soc. Echocardiography, Am. Assn. Nuclear Cardiology, N.C. Med. Soc., Alpha Omega Alpha, Phi Beta Kappa. Roman Catholic. Office: Wilmington Health Assocs PA 1202 Medical Center Dr Wilmington NC 28401-7307

CALHOUN, PATRICIA HANSON, secondary education educator; b. Detroit, Apr. 29, 1940; d. James William and Gordie Eugenia (Wiggins) H.; m. Hubert Calhoun, Jr., July 27, 1956; children: Phillip Wayne, Debra Jean, Donna Marie. BS in Comprehensive Bus. Edn., West Georgia Coll., 1981, MEd in Comprehensive Bus. Edn., 1982, EdS in Comprehensive Bus. Edn., 1984. Cert. tchr., performance based tchr., comprehensive bus. educator, Ga. Tchr. bus. edn. Bowdon (Ga.) H.S., 1982, Carroll County (Ga.) Vocat.-Tech. Sch., 1982-85, Chattahoochee Tech. Inst., Marietta, Ga., 1986-91, Paulding County H.S., Dallas, Ga., 1982-91; tchr. bus. edn. East Paulding H.S., Dallas, 1991—, also coord. coop. bus. edn., head dept. vocat. edn., 1991—; advisor Future Bus. Leaders Am., Dallas, 1984—. Mem. NEA, Ga. Assn. Educators, Ga. Bus. Edn. Assn., Nat. Bus. Edn. Assn., Nat. Vocat. Assn., Ga. Vocat. Assn., Phi Kappa Phi, Kappa Delta Pi. Republican. Home: 724 Burns Rd Carrollton GA 30117-2518 Office: East Paulding High Sch 6800 Dragstrip Rd Dallas GA 30132-4552

CALHOUN, PEGGY JOAN, fundraising executive; b. La Salle, Ill., Sept. 14, 1957; d. Floyd Anthony and Sophia (Regula) Sarwinski; m. James R. Calhoun, Apr. 19, 1989. Student, Ill. Valley C.C., Oglesby, 1975, So. Ill. U., 1976, 77; MA, St. Mary's Coll., Minn., 1994. Assoc. dir. United Way, Sarasota, Fla., 1979-85; devel. dir. Boy Scouts Am., Sarasota, 1985-86; assoc. campaign dir. United Way, Ft. Lauderdale, Fla., 1986-87; dir. devel. YMCA, Sarasota, 1987-88, Salvation Army, Ft. Lauderdale, 1988-91, Diabetes Rsch. Inst. Found., U. Miami Sch. Medicine, 1992-93; pres. Calhoun & Co., Inc., Ft. Lauderdale, 1993—; instr. Nova U., Ft. Lauderdale, 1991-93, Barry U., 1996—. Com. mem. United Way, 1988-91. Mem. Nat. Soc. Fund Raising Execs. (cert., pres., bd. dirs. 1990, Outstanding Profl. Fund Raiser 1991, bd. dirs. 1990—, pres. 1996), Women's Exec. Com. (mentor), Broward Planned Giving Coun. (bd. dirs. 1991), Pub. Rels. Soc. Am. (pres. 1993, bd. dirs. 1991—). Republican. Home and Office: 2741 NE 57th Ct Fort Lauderdale FL 33308-2723

CALHOUN, SCOTT DOUGLAS, lawyer; b. Aurora, Ill., May 1, 1959; s. Ellsworth L. Calhoun and Mary Louise (Mummert) Wire; m. Gloria Jean Fulvi, Aug. 1, 1987; 1 child, John Daniel. BA cum laude, Knox Coll., 1981; JD, Coll. of William and Mary, 1984. Bar: Ga. 1984, U.S. Dist. Ct. (no. dist.) Ga. 1984, U.S. Ct. Appeals (11th cir.) 1984. Assoc. Swift, Currie, McGhee & Hiers, Atlanta, 1984-90, ptnr., 1990-92; pvt. practice, Atlanta, 1992-94; prin. Byrne, Eldridge, Moore & Davis, P.C., Atlanta, 1994-95; ptnr. Mozley, Finlayson & Loggins, 1996—; seminar spkr. in field, 1995—. Bd. dirs. Atlanta Symphony Assocs., 1991, Wildwood Civic Assn., Atlanta, 1991; elder, mem. session Trinity Presbyn. Ch., Atlanta, 1994. Mem. Mortar Bd. Office: Mozley Finlayson & Loggins Ste 900 5605 Glenridge Dr NE Atlanta GA 30342

CALIENES, ARMANDO LUIS, SR., information technology executive; b. Remedios, Cuba, Oct. 22, 1940; s. Leonides F. and Mercedes Maria (Mulkay) C.; m. Martha R. Nunez de Villavicencio; children: Armando R., Richard J., Christine M. BSEE, U. Del., 1969; MS in Engring., U. South Fla., 1973; MBA, Barry U., 1979. Equipment supr., engr. GTE of Fla., Tampa, 1969-71, engr., data processing mgr., 1971-73; sr. applications analyst Control Data Corp., Coral Gables, Fla., 1973-76; sr. tech. rep. GE Info. Svcs., Coral Gables, 1976-78, sr. account mgr., 1978-80; sr. account mgr. GE Info. Svcs., Miami, 1985-88; sr. account exec. United Info. Svcs., Miami, 1980-82; dir. Master Mgmt. Info. Sys. program St. Thomas U., Miami, 1984-86; pres., CEO SPEC Info. Svcs., Miami, 1982-85, MTE Info Svcs.-IBMAGENT, Miami, 1989—; IBM authorized agt., 1989—. Mem. Computer Soc. of IEEE, Planning Inst., Assn. MBA Execs., Toastmasters. Republican. Roman Catholic. Home: 1435 SW 104th Ave Miami FL 33174-2753

CALIRI, DAVID JOSEPH, retired lawyer, insurance agent; b. Lawrence, Mass., Dec. 12, 1929; s. Joseph and June Hazel (Rothera) C.; m. Saralou Debnam, Aug. 29, 1958; children: Linda, Donna, Paul, James, John. BA, Harvard Coll., 1951; LLB, Harvard U., 1954. Bar: N.J. Assoc. Gardner & Williams, Passaic, N.J., 1957-59; ptnr. Gardner & Williams, 1959-64, Williams, Gardner, Caliri, Miller & Otley, Wayne, N.J., 1964-71, Williams, Caliri, Miller & Otley, Wayne, 1971-86; N.C. life and ins. health ind. agt. Author: The Pine and the Thistle, 1989. Pres. bd. edn., Wayne, 1964-70; chmn., mem. Scholarship and Honors Bd., Wayne, 1972-86; dir. Lennilenape coun. Girl Scouts Am., 1970-82; coord. Presbyn. of the Palisades, Teaneck, N.J., 1974-76; chmn. Moore County Dem. Party, 1992—; elder Bethesda Presbyn. Ch., 1988-91, 93-95. With U.S. Army, 1955-56. Home: 700 E Indiana Ave Southern Pines NC 28387-6643

CALKINS, JOANN RUBY, nursing administrator; b. Mich., June 28, 1934; d. William Russell and Imajean (Dunkle) Armentrout; m. James W. Calkins, 1952; children: Russell, Jill, Cindy; m. W. Arthur Brindle, May 7, 1983. AS, Delta Coll., 1964, BS, Cen. Mich. U., 1972, MA, 1977. Staff nurse, L.P.N. clin. instr., asst. dir. Sch. Nursing, Midland (Mich.) Hosp., 1964-71; dir. nursing, dir. substance abuse unit Gladwin (Mich.) Hosp., 1972-76; prin. Calkins Profl. Counseling & Cons., Harrison, Mich., 1976-78, part-time, 1978-83; dir. nursing svc. Ctrl. Mich. Cmty. Hosp., Mt. Pleasant, 1978-83; dir. nursing Oaklawn Hosp., Marshall, Mich., 1983-87; asst. adminstr. profl. svcs. DON Betsy Johnson Meml. Hosp., Dunn, N.C., 1987-93, v.p. profl. svcs., 1993-95, pub. rels., 1995—; coord. Harnett County Alliance for Sch. Health Ctrs., 1995—; part-time prin. W. Arthur and Assocs. Cons.; conducted workshops Mich. Dept. Pub. Health, Mich. Hosp. Assn.; exec. dir. Holistic Health Agy., 1977-82. Trustee Mid-Mich. C.C.; vol. counselor student nurses Cen. Carolina Coll., 1988-93; friends of the libr., 1995; mem. health task force for Harnett County HelpNet; adv. bd. to schs. of nursing Johnston C.C., Sampson C.C., Cen. Carolina C.C.; mem. adv. bd. St. Joseph of the Pines Home Health Agy., 1988-93; cert. layity spkr. Meth. Ch., 1994; mem. adv. bd. Harnett County Coop. Ext., 1996—; bd. dirs. Harnett divsn. Am. Heart Assn., 1996—. Recipient Murial A. Grimmason Nursing Scholarship award, 1962; Cert. nursing adminstr. Mem. Mich. Soc. Hosp. Nursing Adminstrs. (mem. steering com. 1979-80, dir., 14 county rep. 1980-83, pres. 1983-84, chmn. devel. com.), Mich. Nurses Assn., Am. Orgn. Nurse Execs., N.C. Orgn. Nurse Execs. (exec. bd. dirs. 1990-93), Carolinas Healthcare Pub. Rels. and Mktg. Soc., Lioness Internat. (3d v.p. 1985).

CALLAGHAN, KAREN ANN, sociology educator; b. Phila., July 3, 1957; d. Thomas Edward and Lois Louise (King) Callaghan; m. John William Murphy, Nov. 10, 1981. BA, La Salle Coll., Phila., 1979; MA, Ohio State U., 1981, PhD, 1986. Dir. program evaluation Consol. Youth Svcs., Jonesboro, Ark., 1984-86; dir. therapeutic foster care program George W. Jackson Cmty. Mental Health Ctr., Jonesboro, 1986-89; asst. prof. sociology Barry U., Miami Shores, Fla., 1989-95, assoc. prof., 1995—, chair dept. sociology, 1993—; adj. asst. prof. U. Miami, Coral Gables, Fla., 1989. Co-author: The Politics of Culture, 1995; editor: Ideals of Feminine Beauty, 1994; contbr. chpt. to book, articles to profl. jours. Judge, Golden Drum Scholarship, Miami, 1991—. Mem. Am. Sociol. Assn. Office: Barry U Dept Sociology 11300 NE 2nd Ave Miami FL 33161-6628

CALLAHAM, BETTY ELGIN, librarian; b. Honea Path, S.C., Oct. 8, 1929; d. John Winfred and Alice (Dodson) C. B.A., Duke U., 1950; M.A., Emory U., 1954, Master Librarianship, 1961. Tchr. pub. schs. N.C., Ga. and S.C., 1951-60; field svcs. libr. S.C. State Libr., 1961-64, adult cons., 1964-65, dir. field svcs., 1965-74, dep. libr., 1974-79, dir., 1979-90, ret., 1990; Conf. coord. Gov.'s Conf. on Pub. Librs., 1965, S.C. White House Conf. Libr. and Info. Svcs., 1978-79; del. White House Conf. Libr. and Info. Svcs., 1979; mem. OCLC Users Coun., 1982-84, 86-87; chair del. SOLINET, 1983-84; bd. dirs. Southeastern Libr. Network, 1984-88, vice chmn., 1985-86, chmn. bd. 1986-87. Active S.C. Hist. Soc. Mem. ALA (coun. 1977-80), S.C. Libr. Assn. (fed. rels. coord. 1976-80, chmn. pub. libr. sect. 1985, mem. legis. com. 1984-90, v.p., pres.-elect 1987-88, pres. 1988-89, Intellectual Freedom award 1986, Educator of Yr. award 1987), Nat. Trust Hist. Preservation, Riverbanks Zool. Soc., Hist. Columbia Soc., Friends S.C. State Mus., Friends McKissick Mus., Friends Richland County Pub. Libr. Home: 733 Poinsettia St Columbia SC 29205-2067

CALLAHAN, BARBARA, television journalist, consultant. Honors program, Manhattanville Coll., Purchase, N.Y.; BA, Wellesley (Mass.) Coll. Assoc. prodr., writer, assignment editor CBS Inc, St. Louis, 1973-76; reporter, anchor, asst. news dir. Pulitzer Broadcasting, St. Louis, 1976-80; program host, anchor Hubbard Broadcasting, St. Petersburg, Fla., 1980-86; anchor, reporter Media Gen., Tampa, Fla., 1986-93, Sta. WTOG-TV, St. Petersburg, 1993—. Co-founder, spokesperson Gtr. Tampa Bay Breast Screening Project, Am. Cancer. Soc., 1987-93; spokesperson Buddy Check Program, 1993—. Recipient DuPont-Columbia citation for excellence, local Emmy awards; named Communicator of Yr., Fla. divsn. Am. Cancer Soc. Mem. Soc. Profl. Journalists (chpt. pres. 1990-91), Am. Women in Radio and Television, Radio-Television News Dirs. Assn. (assoc.). Office: WTOG-TV 365 105th Ter NE Saint Petersburg FL 33716-3330

CALLAHAN, COLLEEN RUTH, museum curator, educator, consultant; b. Northampton, Mass., Jan. 24, 1948; d. Frederick David and Ruth Eleanor (Mitchell) C.; m. Powell William Peck, Jr., Sept. 6, 1987 (div. Jan. 1993). BA, Smith Coll., 1969; MA, NYU, 1985. Costume asst. St. Louis Repertory Theatre, 1969-70; costume shop mgr. Hartford (Conn.) Stage Co., 1970-72, St. Louis Repertory Theatre, 1972-74; costume shop mgr., instr. Temple U., Phila., 1974-82; design faculty N.C. Sch. of Arts, Winston-Salem, N.C., 1982-85; curator costumes, textiles The Valentine Mus., Richmond, Va., 1985—; cons. Colonial Williamsburg (Va.) Found., 1991, Hampton (Va.) Rds. History Ctr., 1992, Oakland (Calif.) Mus., 1994; guest curator William King Regional Arts Ctr., Abingdon, Va., 1992. Contbr. articles to profl. jours. Co-pres. Smith Coll. Club, Richmond, 1991-95. Recipient Summer Inst. fellowship Mus. Early So. Decorative Arts, 1984, Grad. assistanship Metro. Mus. Art, 1983, Achievement award in costume rsch. Am. Theatre Assn., 1981. Mem. Costume Soc. Am. (nat. bd. dirs. 1988—, regional pres. 1990-94, nat. pres. 1996—). Office: The Valentine Museum 1015 E Clay St Richmond VA 23219-1527

CALLAHAN, GARY LUTHER, music educator, researcher; b. Fostoria, Ohio, June 27, 1950; s. Walter F. Sr. and Mary L. (Davis) C.; m. Linda Florence, Apr. 2, 1983; children: Jesse Alan, Jolita Ashlee. B in Music Edn., Wittenberg U., 1972; M in Music Edn., U. Mich., 1978; PhD, Ohio State U., 1986. With Springfield (Ohio) Pub. Schs., 1974-77, Johnson C. Smith U., Charlotte, N.C., 1979-83, Alabama A&M U., Normal, 1986-88, Eastmoor High Sch., Columbus, Ohio, 1988-90; dir. bands, prof. Elizabeth City (N.C.) State U., 1990—; juror all state band auditions N.C. Sr. High, Durham, 1981, 35th talent hunt Omega Psi Phi, Charlotte, N.C., 1981, solo and ensemble contest Ala. Band Dir. Assn., Huntsville, 1987, 88. With U.S. Army, 1972-74. Recipient Commendation, Dept. of Army, 1974, Commendation, Ohio House Reps., 1985. Mem. Ctrl Intercollegiate Athletic Assn. Band Dirs. Assn., Coll. Band Dirs. Nat. Assn., Music Educators Nat. Conf., Intercollegiate Music Assn. (treas. 1991-96, guest condr. IMA conf., Winston-Salem, N.C. 1996), Nat. Black Music Caucus, N.C. Music Educators Assn. (pres. dist. XV 1991-95), Coun. Rsch. Music Edn., Phi Kappa Lambda, Phi Kappa Phi. Office: Elizabeth City State U Campus Box 810 Elizabeth City NC 27909

CALLAHAN, JAMES K., fire chief. BA in Social Sci., U. South Fla.; M in Pub. Adminstrn., Troy State U.; grad., Nat. Fire Acad. With Fire Dept., St. Petersburg, Fla., 1970-81, lt., 1981-83, capt., 1983-85, fire marshall, 1985-87, asst. chief, 1987-90, chief, 1996—; chief Hillsborough County (Fla.) Fire Dept., 1990-96; mem. steering com. State of Fla. Fire Rescue Disaster Response Com. With USMC, Vietnam. Mem. Internat. Fire Chiefs Assn., Fla. Fire Chiefs Assn., Fla. Fire Marshal's Assn., Pinellas County Fire Chiefs Assn. Office: 400 ML King St S Saint Petersburg FL 33701

CALLAHAN, LESLIE GRIFFIN, JR., engineer educator; b. Pocomoke City, Md., July 27, 1923; s. Leslie Griffin Sr. and Ruth (Parks) C.; m. Annette Hodges, Dec. 20, 1994 (dec. June 1988); children: Susan Ruth, Leslie Griffin III; m. Dorothy Warren, Oct. 21, 1989. Student, Washington Coll., 1940-41; BS, U.S. Mil. Acad., 1944; MSEE, U. Pa., 1951, PhD, 1961. Advanced through grades to col. U.S. Army, 1944-69, ret., 1969; prof. engring. Ga. Inst. Tech., Atlanta, 1969—. Mem. Ops. Rsch. Soc. Am., Armed Forces Comm. Assn. Republican. Episcopalian. Home: 7110 Duncourtney Dr NE Atlanta GA 30328-1211 Office: Ga Inst Tech Sch Engring North Ave Atlanta GA 30332

CALLAHAN, RICHARD DEAN, career officer; b. Norwood, Mass., Oct. 1, 1965; s. George Warren and Nancy Lou (Hallet) C.; m. Rebecca Lynne Wood, June 22, 1989; children: Nicholas Robert, Alida Johanna. Student, Massassat C.C., Brockton, Mass., 1990; BA, Bridgewater State Coll., 1994. Cert. secondary tchr., Mass. Prodn. mgr. Deseret Pallet, Foxboro, Mass., 1988-90; commd. USMC, 1988; E-1, E-5 USMC, Camp Edwards, Mass., 1988-95; O-1 USMC, Quantico, Va., 1995—; student tchr. Chelsea (Mass.) H.S., 1994. Leader Boy Scouts Am., N. Dartmouth, Mass., 1992-95, Stafford, Va., 1995-96; missionary LDS Ch., 1986-88. Dr. Henry Rosen Meml. Scholarship, 1994, All Am. Collegiate scholar, 1992. Mem. LDS Ch. Home: PO Box 12544 Yuma AZ 85365-0544

CALLAHAN, RICKEY DON, business owner; b. Dallas, Mar. 17, 1956; s. Dayton Easton and Alice Jane (Holloway) C. AA, Eastfield Coll., 1976; BA in Polit. Sci., U. Tex.-Dallas, 1978; MBA in Gen. Mgmt., Amber U., 1986. Cert. secondary tchr., Tex. Real estate assoc. ERA Sage Realty, Inc., Dallas, 1979-80, First Mark Real Estate, Dallas, 1980-81; adminstrv. asst. Dallas Precious Metal Plating, Inc., Garland, Tex., 1981-84; legis. asst. to state rep. Alvin R. Granoff, Dallas, 1984-87; owner, broker Callahan Properties, Dallas, 1987—. Pres. Dallas County East Dem. Orgn., 1986-88, Clean Dallas-S.E., Inc., 1987-88, Tex. Jr. C. of C. Found.; bd. dirs. Dallas Conv. and Visitors Bur., 1995—; mem. Dallas Bond Campaign Com., 1995; bd. dirs. S.E. Emergency Food Ctr., 1996. Mem. Nat. Assn.Realtors, Tex. Assn. Realtors, S.E. Dallas C. of C. (bd. dirs. 1987—, vice chmn. econ. devel. 1991-92, chmn. 1994-95), U. Tex. Dallas Alumni Assn., Amber U. Alumni Assn., Tex. Jaycees (dist. dir. 1981-82, Prestigious J.C.I. Senator award #38931, pres. Mesquite chpt. 1980-81, 82-83, bd. dirs. Dallas 1990-91), N. Tex. Comml. Assn. Realtors, Phi Theta Kappa. Democrat. Baptist. Office: Callahan Properties 8344 E R L Thornton Fwy Ste 308 Dallas TX 75228-7134

CALLAHAN, SONNY (H.L. CALLAHAN), congressman; b. Mobile, Ala., Sept. 11, 1932; m. Karen Reed; children: Scott, Patrick, Shawn Mattei, Chris, Cameron (dec.), Kelly. Grad., McGill Inst. Pres., chmn. bd., chief exec. officer Finch Cos., Mobile and Montgomery, Ala., 1964-84; mem. Ala. Ho. of Reps., 1970-78, chmn. Mobile County delegation; mem. Ala. Senate, 1978-82, 99th-104th Congresses from 1st Ala. dist.; mem. appropriations com., chmn. subcom. on fgn. ops. Served with USN, 1952-54. Mem. Mobile Area C. of C., Ala. Movers Assn., Ala. Trucking Assn., Kiwanis, Optimists. Office: 2970 Cottage Hill Rd Ste 126 Mobile AL 36606-4749 Office: US Ho of Reps 2418 Rayburn Bldg Washington DC 20515-0005*

CALLAIS, ELAINE DENISE ROGERS, accountant; b. Cleveland, Tenn., Dec. 30, 1962; d. Eddie L. and Dennie Jo (Richards) R.; m. Edwin T. Callais Jr.; 1 child, Rachel Savannah. BS cum laude, Tenn. Wesleyan Coll., 1985. CPA, Ga. Asst. contr. Luesing Group, Inc., Atlanta, 1985-90; dir. acctg./fin.-interior design divsn. Life Care Ctrs. Am., Cleveland, Tenn., 1990—. Co-author: (manual) Policies and Procedures of the Luesing Group, Inc., 1988, Life Care Centers of America Accounts Receivable Financial Manual, 1993. Vol. United Way, Cleveland, 1991, ARC, Cleveland, 1978-82. Mem. AICPA, Tenn. Wesleyan Coll. Bd. Alumni, Beta Sigma Phi, Sigma Kappa (pres. 1984-85). Republican. Presbyterian. Home: 1111 Cookdale Tr Cleveland TN 37312 Office: Life Care Ctrs Am 3570 Keith St NW Cleveland TN 37312-4309

CALLAN, JOSEPH PATRICK, social service administrator; b. Washington, July 29, 1944; s. G. Christopher and Mary Jane (Gorsuch) C.; m. Judith Marie Bell, June 14, 1980; children: Kimberly Jane, Kathleen Marie. AA, St. Petersburg (Fla.) Jr. Coll., 1964; BA, U. So. Fla., 1972, MSW, 1985; MS, Nova U., 1985. Group work supr. Eckerd Found., Clearwater, Fla., 1968-72, dir. tng., 1977-83; coord. Collier County Mental Health, Naples, Fla., 1972-76; pvt. practice psychotherapy Tampa, Fla., 1985-87; dir., owner Univ. Psychotherapy Group, P.A., Tampa, 1987—; psychotherapist Employee Assistance Programs and Sex Therapy, Tampa, 1987—; vis. faculty U. So. Fla., Tampa, 1987—; pres. Tng. and Edn. Ctr., Naples, 1972-77, Immokalee (Fla.) Adult Refuge, 1972-77; cons. social svcs. agys. Tampa area, 1987—. Sgt. U.S. Army, 1966-72. Mem. NASW, Am. Acad. Clin. Sexologists, Collier County Assn. Retarded Citizens (charter), Fla. Soc. Clin. Social Work, U. So. Fla. Social Work Alumni Assn. (pres. 1986-88), Phi Kappa Phi, Pi Gamma Mu. Home: 3450 Lake Padgett Dr Land O'Lakes FL 34639-6514 Office: Univ Psychotherapy Group PA 5208 E Fowler Ave Ste E Tampa FL 33617-2152

CALLENDER, JOHN FRANCIS, lawyer; b. Jacksonville, Fla., May 3, 1944; s. Francis Louis and Ethel (McLean) C.; m. Susan Carithers, June 13, 1969; children: John Francis Jr., Susanna McLean. AB cum laude, Davidson Coll., 1966; MA, U. N.C., 1969; JD with distinction, Duke U., 1976. Bar: Fla. 1976, U.S. Supreme Ct. 1982; Fla. bd. cert. civil trial lawyer, cert. cir. ct. mediator. Asst. states atty. State of Fla., Jacksonville, 1980-81; ptnr. Turner, Ford & Callender, P.A., Jacksonville, 1981-84; pvt. practice Jacksonville, 1984—. Pres. Mental Health Clinic Jacksonville, Inc., 1985; bd. dirs. Vol. Jacksonville, Inc., 1981-84. Served with U.S. Army, 1970-73. Fellow Am. Soc. Papyrologists, 1969. Fellow Acad. Fla. Trial Lawyers; mem. ABA, FBA, ATLA, jacksonville Bar Assn., Fla. yacht Club, River Club, Rotary (pres.-elect), Phi Beta Kappa Alumni Assn. of N.E. Fla. (treas.). Democrat. Episcopalian. Home: 1745 Woodmere Dr Jacksonville FL 32210-2233 Office: 1301 Riverplace Blvd Ste 2105 Jacksonville FL 32207-9026

CALLENDER, NORMA ANNE, psychology educator, counselor; b. Huntsville, Tex., May 10, 1933; d. C. W. Carswell and Nell Ruth (Collard) Hughes Bost; m. B.G. Callender, 1951 (div. 1964); remarried 1967 (div. 1973); children: Teresa Elizabeth, Leslie Gemey, Shannah Hughes, Kelly Mari; m. E. Purfurst, June 1965 (div. Aug. 1965). BS, U. Houston, 1969; MA, U. Houston at Clear Lake, 1977; postgrad. U. Houston, 1970, Lamar U., 1972-73, Tex. So. U., 1971, St. Thomas U., 1985, 86, U. Houston-Clear Lake, 1979, 87, 89-93, San Jacinto Coll., 1988, 89, 94. Aerospace Inst., NASA, Johnson Space Ctr., 1986. Cert. profl. reading specialist, Tex.; lic. profl. counselor. Tchr., Houston Ind. Schs., 1969-70; co-counselor and instr. Ellington AFB, Houston, 1971; tchr. Clear Creek Schs., League City, Tex., 1970-86; cons., LPC intern Guidance Ctr., Pasadena (Tex.) Ind. Sch. Dist., 1993-95; part-time instr. San Jacinto Coll., Pasadena, Tex., 1980-81, 91-93; univ. adj., U. Houston, Clear Lake, 1986-91; owner, dir. Bay Area Tutoring and Reading Clinic, Clear Lake City, Tex., 1970—, Bay Area Tng. Assocs, 1982—, Bay Area Family Counseling, 1995—; cons. in field, 1994—. Contbr. poetry to profl. jours. State advisor U.S. Congl. Adv. Bd., 1985-87; vol., bd. dirs. Family Outreach Ctr., 1989-92; vol. Bay Area Coun. on Drugs and Alcohol, Nassau Bay, Tex., 1993-94; bd. dirs. Ballet San Jacinto, 1985-87; adv. bd. Cmty. Ednl. TV, 1990-92. Recipient Franklin award U. Houston, 1965-67; Delta Kappa Gamma/Beta Omicron scholar, 1967-68; PTA scholar, 1973; Berwin scholar, 1976; Mary Gibbs Jones scholar, 1976-77; Found. Econ. Edn. scholar, 1976; Insts. Achievement Human Potential scholar, Phila., 1987. Mem. APA (assoc.), ACA, Clear Creek Educators Assn. (past, honorarium 1976, 77, 85), Assn. Bus. and Profl. Women (mem. cmty. and ednl. affairs com.), Internat. Reading Assn., U. Houston Alumni Assn. (life), Leadership Clear Lake Alumni Assn. (charter, program and projects com mem. 1986-87, edn. com. 1985), Houston Mental Health Assn., Houston Psychol. Assn., Houston World Affairs Coun., Kappa Delta Pi, Phi Delta Kappa, Phi Kappa Phi (life), Psi Chi (life). Mem. Life Tabernacle Ch. Office: 1234 Bay Area Blvd Ste R Houston TX 77058-2538

CALLNER, BRUCE WARREN, lawyer; b. Camden, N.J., Sept. 20, 1948; s. Phillip David and Miriam June (Caplan) C.; m. Janet Adams, Apr. 25, 1970 (div. Dec. 1982); children: David, Michelle; m. Kathy Lynne Portnoy, Mar. 9, 1983; 1 child, Samantha. BS in Psychology, Western Mich. U., 1970; JD, U. Notre Dame, 1974. Bar: Ga. 1974, U.S. Dist. Ct. (no. dist.) Ga. 1975, U.S. Ct. Appeals (5th cir.) 1975, U.S. Ct. Appeals (11th cir.) 1981. Ptnr. Nall & Miller, Atlanta, 1974-81, Alembik, Fine & Callner, P.A., Atlanta, 1981—; lectr. law Emory U., Atlanta. Author: Georgia Domestic Relations Casefinder, 1990. Vol. numerous legal orgns. Mem. ABA (family law and litigation sects.), Ga. Bar Assn. (family law and litigation sects.), Atlanta Bar Assn. (family law, litigation and sects., speaker's bur.); fellow Am. Acad. Matrimonial Lawyers, Nat. Council Family Relations, Southeastern Council Family Relations, NOW, Assn. Family Conciliation Cts. Democrat. Jewish. Home: 956 Heritage Hls Decatur GA 30033-4146 Office: Alembik Fine & Callner PA 4th Fl Marquis One Tower 245 Peachtree Center Ave NE Atlanta GA 30303-1222

CALOGERO, PASCAL FRANK, JR., state supreme court chief justice; b. New Orleans, Nov. 9, 1931; s. Pascal Frank and Louise (Moore) C.; children—Deborah Ann Calogero Applebaum, David, Pascal III, Elizabeth, Thomas, Michael, Stephen, Gerald, Katherine, Christine. Student, Loyola U., New Orleans, 1949-51, J.D., 1954; ML in the Jud. Process, U. Va., 1992; DLL (hon.), Loyola U., New Orleans. Bar: La. Ptnr. Landrieu, Calogero & Kronlage, 1958-69, Calogero & Kronlage, 1969-73; gen. counsel La. Stadium and Expn. Dist., 1970-73; assoc. justice Supreme Ct. La., New Orleans, 1973-90, chief justice, 1990—. Mem. La. Democratic State Central Com., 1963-71; mem. subcom. on del. selection La. Dem. Party, 1971; del. Dem. Nat. Conv., 1968. Served to capt. JAGC U.S. Army, 1954-57. Recipient Disting. Jurist award La. Bar Founds., 1991; Judge Bob Jones Meml. award, Am. Judges Assn., 1995. Mem. ABA, La. Bar Assn., New Orleans Bar Assn., Greater New Orleans Trial Lawyers Assn. (v.p. 1967-69), Order of the Coif. Office: Supreme Ct La 301 Loyola Ave New Orleans LA 70112-1800

CALVER, RICHARD ALLEN, college dean; b. Chillicothe, Ohio, Feb. 16, 1939; s. Catherine Mae (Roush) Bryan; m. Susan Jane Yost, Oct. 9, 1988. Student U. Hawaii, 1959-61; BSBA, W.Va. U., 1963; MS in Bus., Va. Commonwealth U., 1970; C.A.G.S.E., Va. Tech. U., 1983, EdD in Comm. Coll. Edn., Va. Tech. Coll., 1984. Mgmt. trainee Sears Roebuck & Co., 1963, Reuben H. Donnelley Corp., 1963-64, state publs. and customer relations mgr., 1964-68; state job analyst Va. Div. Personnel, Richmond, 1968-70; dean adminstrv. services S.W. Va. Community Coll., Richlands, 1970-88; dean adminstrv. svcs. Thomas Nelson Community Coll., Hampton, Va., 1988—, interim pres., 1994-95; mem. accreditation teams So. Assn. Colls. and Schs. and Mid. States Assn. Mem. Lebanon (Va.) Town Council, 1978-82; mem. special edn. adv. com. Russell County Sch. Bd., 1984-88, Va. Peninsula Inst. Leadership Program, 1989. With USAF, 1957-61. Mem. Nat. Assn. Coll. and Univ. Bus. Officers, Nat. Council Community Coll. Bus. Officers (Regional Outstanding Bus. Officer 1990, nat. bd. mem.), So. Assn. Coll. and Univ. Bus. Officers, Ea. Assn. Coll. and U. Bus. Officers, Coll. and Univ. Pers. Assn., Va. Peninsula Mil. Affairs Coun., Delta Tau Delta, Phi Kappa Phi, Phi Theta Kappa (hon.). Methodist. Lodges: Lions (pres. Lebanon club 1976-77), Shriners (pres. club 1974-75), Scottish Rite (32 deg.), Masons. Home: 443 Warner Hall Pl Newport News VA 23608-9304 Office: PO Box 9407 Hampton VA 23670-0407

CALVERT, JENNIFER HAMILTON, freelance writer, photographer; b. Knoxville, Tenn., Dec. 17, 1939; d. Samuel Barton, Jr. and Marie (Ogle) Hamilton; m. Lawrence Lamar Calvert, May 29, 1962; children: Lawrence Lamar Jr., Laura Lee Calvert Hubbard. BS in Journalism, U. Tenn., 1961. Contbr. articles to numerous newspapers, mags. and literary jours.; guest panelist on TV and radio programs; exhbns. include Nat. Geographic Soc., Washington, EPCOT Ctr., Lake Buena Vista, Fla., 1993-94; guest editor: Mademoiselle mag., 1961. Recipient Spl. Merit award Kodak Internat. Newspaper Snapshot award, 1993, prize The Knoxville News-Sentinel, 1993, 1st pl. award The Oak Ridger (Tenn.) Photo Contest, 1993, 2d place, 1992, Silver Pen award The Knoxville Jour., 1985, 86, The Jean Lieberman Poetry prize Children's Mus. of Oak Ridge, Tenn., 1980, prize for fiction, Seventeen mag., 1959. Home: 111 Amanda Dr Oak Ridge TN 37830-7813

CALVERT, LINDA DARNELL, women's health nurse, educator; b. Huntsville, Tex., Nov. 5, 1960; d. Gary Mac and Jimmie Jo (Park) C. BSN, Harding U., Searcy, Ark., 1983; MS in Nursing, West Tex. State U., 1988. RN, Tex.; cert. in perinatal nursing, clin. nurse specialist in family nursing. Charge nurse, labor and delivery Huntsville (Tex.) Meml. Hosp., 1983-84; staff nurse, relief charge nurse in labor and delivery Scott and White Meml. Hosp., Temple, Tex., 1984-86; staff nurse, relief charge nurse Meth. Hosp. of Lubbock, Tex., 1986-88; jr. med.-surg. instr. Meth. Hosp. Sch. Nursing, Lubbock, 1988-91; instr. Abilene (Tex.) Intercollegiate Sch. Nursing, 1991-93, asst. prof., 1993—. Mem. health profl. adv. com. March of Dimes, Abilene; USPHS trainee, 1987-88. Named Outstanding Alumnae Harding U. Sch. Nursing, 1995, One of Outstanding Young Women of Am., 1987. Mem. Assn. Women's Health Obstetrical Neonatal Nursing, Nat. League for Nursing, Tex. Perinatal Assn., Health Educators Resource Network Abilene, Sigma Theta Tau, Alpha Chi. Home: 3218 Winter Hawk Abilene TX 79606

CAMACHO, ALFREDO, accountant; b. Havana, Cuba, Sept. 18, 1951; came to U.S., 1961; s. Alberto and Silvia Maria (San Pedro) C.; m. Maria Rodriguez, June 24, 1972; 1 child, Jorge Alfredo. BBA, Fla. Internat. U., 1975, MS in Taxation, 1984. CPA, Fla. Acct., auditor Oppenheim, Appel, Dixon & Co., Miami, Fla., 1973-79; sr. auditor Aristar, Inc., Coral Gables, Fla., 1979-80; controller Wynne Bldg. Corp., Miami, 1980—; tchr. Mercy Coll., Miami, 1979. Mem. Am. Inst. CPA's, Fla. Inst. CPA's. Democrat. Roman Catholic. Office: Wynne Bldg Corp 12804 SW 122nd Ave Miami FL 33186-6203

CAMAYD-FREIXAS, YOEL, management, strategy & planning consultant; b. Holguin, Oriente, Cuba, Nov. 27, 1948; came to U.S., 1962; s. Alberto and Olga (Freixas) Camayd; m. Ana Maria Perez, Jan. 2, 1982; 1 child, Cristina de la Prat Camayd. BA summa cum laude, U. Mundial, San Juan, P.R., 1970; MEd, Northeastern U., 1972; MA, Boston Coll., 1978, PhD, 1982. Planner Multi-Svc. Ctr., New Bedford, Mass., 1971-74; psychologist Jamaica Plain Outreach Program, Boston, 1975-78, program dir., 1978-80, exec. dir., 1980-81; asst. prof. grad. sch. urban studies and planning MIT, Cambridge, 1982-86; sr. officer Office R & D Boston Pub. Schs., 1985-87; pres. Boston R & D, 1987-90; bd. chmn. Pavers & Tiles of Fla., Inc., Miami, 1987-91; exec. v.p. Health & Hosps. Corp., N.Y.C., 1990-91; bd. chmn., mng. dir. Nurse Referrals, Inc., N.Y.C., 1990-91; mng. ptnr. Camayd Cons., Miami, Fla., 1992—. Author: The Costs of Opportunity, 1983 (award Psi Chi 1983), Hispanics in Massachusetts, 1987, Effective Dropout Prevention, 1987, Crisis in Miami, 1988, Latino Health in New York City, 1992, Affordability Controls in Affordable Housing and Disaster Relief, 1995. Mem., co-chmn. Mass. Legislature Commn. on Hispanic Affairs, Boston, 1984-88; co-chmn. add-ons com. Mass. Dem. Com., Boston, 1985-90; bd. dirs. United Way Massachusetts Bay, Boston, 1986-90; pres. Mass. Coalition for Electoral Reform, Boston, 1987-90. Recipient nat. community svc. award Coalition Hispanic Human Svc. Orgns., 1980, gubernatorial citation State of Mass., 1988, 90, commendation Boston City Coun., 1990, legis. citation Mass. Ho. of Reps., 1990.

CAMBRICE, ROBERT LOUIS, lawyer; b. Houston, Nov. 23, 1947; s. Eugene and Edna Bertha (Jackson) C.; m. Christine Jackson, Jan. 7, 1972; children: Bryan, Graham. BA cum laude, Tex. So. U., 1969; JD, U. Tex.-Austin, 1972. Bar: Tex. 1973, U.S. Dist. Ct. (so. dist.) Tex. 1975, U.S. Ct. Apls. (5th cir.) 1975, U.S. Ct. Apls. (11th cir.) 1981, U.S. Sup. Ct. 1981. Asst. atty. City of Houston, 1974-76; sole practice, Houston, 1976-81; asst. atty. Harris County, Tex., 1981-85, City of Houston, 1986—; sr. trial atty. City of Houston Legal Dept., 1990-92, chief def. litigation dept., 1992— . Earl Warren fellow, 1969-72. Mem. ABA, NAACP, Nat. Bar Assn., Alpha Kappa Mu. Roman Catholic.

CAMERON, CARROLL DUNHAM, writer; b. Miami, Oct. 31, 1940; d. John Paul and Eva Ruth (Dunlap) D.; m. Billy Leo Cameron, Feb. 27, 1971. AA, Miami Dade C.C., 1968; BA in English, Fla. Atlantic U., 1970; MA in English, U. Miami, 1972. Dental hygienist various dentists, 1960-75; clin. instr. Miami Dade C.C., 1970-74; founder, dir., officer Health Studies Inst., Inc., 1983-92; founder, pres. Home Study Educators, Inc., 1992—; writer continuing edn. courses, 1982—. Vol. rschr. Fla. Hist. Survey; career day spkr. various Miami Area Schs.; spkr. Nat. Children's Dental Health Week. Mem. Am. Dental Hygiene Soc., East Coast Dental Hygiene Soc. (past pres., Brass Roses award 1996), Fla. Dental Hygiene Soc. (trustee). Office: Home Study Educators PO Box 652838 Miami FL 33265-2838

CAMERON, DANIEL FORREST, communications executive; b. Santa Monica, Calif., Mar. 8, 1944; s. Dan W. and Bonnie (Forrest) C.; m. Sharon Tompos, June 1, 1968; children: Daniel Christian, Stephen Forrest. BSBA, U. Tulsa, 1974; MBA, Morehead (Ky.) State U., 1978, MA, 1981; PhD, U. Ky., 1989. Editor Appalachian News-Express, Pikeville, Ky., 1976-77; coord. mining tech. program Pikeville (Ky.) Coll., 1977-78, Morehead State U., 1978-85; dir. devel. and pub. rels. Monte Cassino Sch., Tulsa, 1986-89; exec. dir. coll. advancement Coll. Osteo. Medicine Okla. State U., Tulsa, 1989-92; pres. D. Forrest Cameron and Assocs., Tulsa, 1992—; cons. Home of Hope, Inc., Vinita, Okla., 1987—. Editor: Kentucky Underground Coal Mine Guidebook, 1985; editor, pub. Greater Tulsa Reporter Newspapers (Union Boundary, Jenks Gazette and Tulsa Free Press), 1993—. Pres. Comet Jr. Athletic Assn., Tulsa, 1989; co-founder Collegiate Assn. for Mining Edn., Lexington, Ky., 1983; bd. dirs. U. Tulsa Golden Hurricane Club, 1993-95. Mem. U. Tulsa Alumni Assn., Tulsa Green Country Rotary Club (pres. 1994-95).

CAMERON, GLENN NILSSON, real estate broker; b. Orange, N.J., Apr. 20, 1956; s. John Richardson and Alma (Nilsson) C. BA in History, Wheaton (Ill.) Coll., 1978; ThM in Biblical Studies, Dallas Theol. Sem., 1983. Lic. real estate broker, Tex. Real estate developer shopping ctrs. and apts. Hunsicker & Assocs., Dallas, 1983-85; dir. comml. investment brokerage Donald Kinney & Assocs., Dallas, 1985-86; dir. sales So. Classical Homes/Northtown Sq., Dallas, 1986-87, Glenn Cameron & Co., Residential Real Estate Brokerage, Dallas, 1987-90; broker assoc. Realty Execs., Residential Real Estate Brokerage, Plano & Dallas, Tex., 1990-95; dir. sales Martin Raymond Homes Inc., 1995—. Mem. So. Meth. U. Internat. Friendship Program, 1985-87, Lone Star Masters Swim Team, 1983-89, North Dallas Aquatics, 1989—; vol. Lifewalk, Black Tie Dinner; mem. Tex. Human Rights Found., Human Rights Campaign Fund; vol. AIDS Svcs. Denton County, HIV counselor. Named to Outstanding Young Men of Am., 1983-87. Mem. Nat. Assn. Realtors, Tex. Assn. Realtors, Greater Dallas Assn. Realtors, Nat. Human Rights Found., Arete, Collin County Assn. Realtors, Dallas Songwriters Assn., Dallas Dance Assn., Realty Execs. Internat., Exec. Club. Home: 5335 Bent Tree Forest Unit 209 Dallas TX 75248 Office: Martin Raymond Houses PO Box 797512 Dallas TX 75379

CAMERON, KRISTEN ELLEN SCHMIDT, nurse, construction company executive, educator; b. Waterbury, Conn., Mar. 11, 1953; d. William Thomas and Shirley Ellen (Peck) Schmidt; m. Roderick P. Cameron, Feb. 12, 1972; children: Sara Ellen, James Ryan. Diploma in practical nursing, Eli Whitney Tech., 1973; ASN, Pasco Hernando C.C., Brooksville, Fla., 1987; BSN, Fla. So. Coll., Lakeland, 1992; MS, U. So. Fla., 1994. RN, Fla. Office nurse J.B. Forman, MD, New Haven, 1973-74; staff nurse Hewitt Meml. Hosp., Shelton, Conn., 1979-80; medication nurse Zephyr Haven Nursing Home, Zephyrhills, Fla., 1982-85; utilization rev. coordinator East Pasco Med. Ctr., Zephyrhills, 1985-86; staff nurse East Pasco Med. Ctr., Zephyrhills, Fla., 1987—; sec., treas. Sunscape Builders Inc., Ridge Manor, Fla., 1986—; clin. coord. med.-surg. East Pasco Med. Ctr., Zephyrhills, 1988-90, adminstrv. asst., 1990; field RN Gulf Coast Home Health Svc., 1990-91; lab. facilitator RN program Pasco Hernando C.C., Brooksville, Fla., 1991, instr. RN program, faculty advisor student nurse's orgn., 1992—; mem. nursing celebration com. East Pasco Med. Ctr., 1987-90, chmn., 1989, sec. nursing guild, 1990; participant APHA Nat. Conv., Washington, 1994. Mem. Ridge Manor Fla. Blood Bank, 1986—, Ridge Manor Property Assn., 1985—, East Pasco Adventist Ednl. Ctr. Home and Sch. Assn., Dade City, Fla. 1987-88; editor Dade City Seventh Day Adventist Ch. newsletter; bd. dirs. East Pasco Adventist Ednl. Ctr., Dade City, 1983—, newsletter editor 1986, 87. Mem. APHA, Fla. Nurses Assn., Greater Hernando County C. of C., Hernando County Builders Assn., Alumni Assn. Fla. So. Coll., Alumni Assn. U. So. Fla., Sigma Theta Tau, Phi Kappa Phi. Republican. Home: 33408 Pennsylvania Ave Ridge Manor FL 33525-9044

CAMERON, NAN, nurse; b. Washington, Pa., Sept. 15, 1953; d. Wilfred Robert and Nan (James) C.; 1 child, Dewayne Cameron. BSN, U. Ky., 1977; MSN, Gwynedd Mercy Coll., 1987. RN, W.Va. Dir. staff devel. Guiffre' Med. Ctr., Phila., 1980-83; clin., editor Springhouse (Pa.) Corp., 1983-84; patient care coord. Albert Einstein Med. Ctr., Phila., 1984-86; div. dir. St. Mary Hosp., Phila., 1986-88; adminstrv. asst. inpatient nursing St. Patrick Hosp., Lake Charles, La., 1988-90; nurse adminstr. Drs. Hosp., Healthtrust, Inc., Moblie, Ala., 1990; asst. adminstr. nursing USA Drs. Hosp., Moblie, Ala., 1990-93; v.p. nursing Greenbrier Valley Med. Ctr., Ronceverte, W.Va., 1993-96; COO Columbia Hosp., Maysville, Ky., 1996—; mem. faculty Thomas Jefferson U., Phila., 1988. Clin. editor: Emergencies, 1985, Neoplastic Disorders, 1985. Mem. ANA (cert. nursing adminstr., advanced), Am. Orgn. Nurse Execs., Oncology Nursing Soc., Am. Coll. Healthcare Execs. Home: 1233 Lewis St Maysville KY 41056 Office: Columbia Hosp Maysville 989 Medical Park Dr Maysville KY 41056

CAMERON, WILLIAM DUNCAN, plastics company executive; b. Harrell, N.C., June 14, 1925; s. Paul Archiebald and Atwood (Herring) C.; m. Betty Gibson, Oct. 3, 1953; children: Phillip MacDonald, Colleen Kay. Student Duke U., 1945-49. Chmn. emeritus Reef Industries Inc., Houston. Pres. bd. trustees Trinity Episcopal Sch., Galveston, Tex., 1981-82; trustee William Temple Found., 1987-90. Served with U.S. Army, 1943-45. Mem. Houston C. of C. (chmn. mfg. com. 1967), Rotary, Galveston Artillery, Bob Smith Yacht. Home: PO Box 310 Smith Ranch Rd Cuero TX 77954-0310 Office: Reef Industries Inc 9209 Almeda Genoa Rd Houston TX 77075-2339

CAMESE, WANDA GREEN, nurse; b. New Orleans, Sept. 30, 1954; d. Elton Warren and Ida Mae (Smith) Lorio; m. Alton M. Green, June 4, 1977 (dec.); children: Nicole Uchenna, Ashley; m. Earl August Camese, Oct. 12, 1991. AS, La. State U., 1979, MSN, 1992; BS in Nursing, Dillard U., 1989. RN, La. Staff nurse Charity Hosp., New Orleans, 1979-80; nursing supr. St. Claude Gen. Hosp., New Orleans, 1980-82; unit supr. DePaul Hosp., New Orleans, 1981-82; dir. nursing Quality Care, New Orleans, 1981; head nurse Charity Hosp., New Orleans, 1982-83; unit patient mgr. New Orleans Gen. Hosp., 1984-86; charge nurse St. Charles Gen. Hosp., New Orleans, 1986-89; quality assurance coord. Charity Hosp., New Orleans, 1989-91; instr. Charity Sch. Nursing, New Orleans, 1991-95; adminstr. Family of Families Home Health Svcs. Inc., 1995—; cons. and instr. in field. Pres. Ladies Unltd. Civic, New Orleans, 1981-86; nurse vol. Health Fair, New Orleans, 1983-85; parent vol. PTA; bd. dirs. New Orleans East YMCA. Mem. NAACP, ANA, New Orleans Dist. Nursing Assn., Nat. Black Nurses Assn., Nat. League for Nurses, Nat. C. of C. for Women, Santa Filomena Nursing Assn., New Orleans Assn. Quality Assurance Professions, La. Pub. Health Assn., Gamma Phi Delta (first Anti-Basileum 1989, v.p. 1989, chpt. Basileus 1994). Democrat. Baptist. Home: 4401 Werner Dr New Orleans LA 70126-4545 Office: Delgado Community Coll Charity Sch Nursing 450 S Claiborne Ave New Orleans LA 70112-1310

CAMNER, HOWARD, author, poet; b. Miami, Fla., Jan. 14, 1957; s. Edward I. and Ida (Puldy) C. BA in English, Fla. Internat. U., 1982; LittD (hon.), London Sch. Applied Rsch., 1995. Cert. English tchr., Fla. Editor Southwind Mag., Miami, Fla., 1976-78; performance poet Writers' Exch., N.Y.C., 1979-81; freelance writer various publications, Miami, 1982-84; screenwriter Harris Prodns., L.A., 1985-89; TV prodr., host Century Cable, L.A., 1986-88; writing instr. Dade County Schs., Miami, 1990—. Author: (poems) Notes from the Eye of a Hurricane, 1979, Transitions, 1980, Scattered Shadows, 1980, Road Note Elegy, 1980, A Work in Progress, 1981, Poetry from Hell to Breakfast, 1981, Midnight at the Laundromat, 1983, Hard Times on Easy Street, 1987, Madman in the Alley, 1989, Stray Dog Wail, 1991, Banned in Babylon, 1993, Jammed Zipper, 1994, Bed of Nails, 1995, Brutal Delicacies, 1996; contbr. to anthology: Florida in Poetry, 1995, also over 100 lit. collections. Mem. Nat. Writers Assn., Acad. of Am. Poets, Poets and Writers, Inc., Poetry Soc. of Am., So. Fla. Poetry Inst. Home: 10440 SW 76th St Miami FL 33173

CAMP, ALETHEA TAYLOR, correctional program specialist; b. Wingo, Ky., Nov. 12, 1938; d. Wayne Thomas and Ethel Virginia (Austin) Taylor; children: Donna Paul, Sean Richard. BA, Murray State U., 1961; MA, So. Ill. U., 1975. Tchr. McLean and Hopkins (Ky.) County Schs., 1961-64; instr. homebound Harrisburg (Ill.) Community Sch. Dist., 1971-73; counselor evaluation Coleman Rehab. Ctr., Shawneetown, Ill., 1974-75; counselor corrections and parole Dept. Corrections, State Ill., Springfield, 1975-77, supr. casework, 1977, supr. parole, 1977-80; asst. warden programs Dept. Corrections, State Ill., Hillsboro, 1980-84, warden, 1984-91; correctional program specialist Nat. Inst. Corrections, Washington, 1991-95. Mem. NAFE, Assn. Exec. Women in Corrections, Am. Correctional Assn., N. Am. Wardens Assn.

CAMP, EHNEY ADDISON, III, investment banking executive; b. Birmingham, Ala., June 28, 1942; s. Ehney Addison and Mildred Fletcher (Tillman) C.; m. Patricia Jane Hough, Sept. 17, 1966; children: Ehney Addison IV, Margaret Strader. BA, Dartmouth Coll., 1964. Sr. v.p. Cobbs, Allen & Hall Mortgage Co., Inc., Birmingham, 1965-72; v.p., gen. mgr. The Rime Cos., Birmingham, 1972-75; pres. Camp & Co., Birmingham, 1975-96; prin. Addison Investments, LLC, Birmingham, 1996—; bd. dirs. AmSouth Corp., Birmingham, Vesta Ins. Group, Inc. Past bd. dirs. Community Chest/United Way, Jefferson, Walker and Shelby Counties, Better Bus. Bur., Greater Birmingham; pres., past trustee Civic Club Found., Inc.; bd. dirs. Birmingham Football Found.; mem. pres.'s coun. U. Ala., bd. visitors Sch. of Commerce. Mem. Am. Mortgage Bankers Assn. (income property com.), Ala. Mortgage Bankers Assn. (reas. 1985, sec. 1986, v.p. 1987, Pres. 1988), Mountain Brook Club (bd. govs. 1976-77, 89-95, pres. 1994), Birmingham County Club, The Club (bd. dirs., fin. chmn. 1987-90), Wade Hampton Golf Club (bd. dirs. 1996—), Shoal Creek Club (bd. govs. 1983-93), Kiwanis (bd. dirs. 1977-78, 82-83, sec. 1983-84, v.p. 1985-86, pres. 1986-87). Methodist. Home: 3510 Victoria Rd Birmingham AL 35223-1404 Office: Addison Investments 6 Office Park Cir Ste 100 Birmingham AL 35223-2540

CAMP, JACK TARPLEY, JR., federal judge; b. Newnan, Ga., Oct. 30, 1943; s. Jack Tarpley and Sophia (Stephens) C.; m. Elizabeth Thomas, Apr. 24, 1976; children: Thomas Henry, Sophia Rose. BA, The Citadel, Charleston, S.C., 1965; MA, U. Va., 1967, JD, 1973. Bar: Ala. 1973, Ga. 1975. Atty. Cabaniss, Johnston, Dumas & O'Neal, Birmingham, Ala., 1973-75, Glover & Davis, P.A., Newnan, 1975-88; U.S. dist. judge Atlanta, 1988—; mgr. family timber land holdings. Mem. Newnan Hist. Soc., 1975—, Ga. Trust for Hist. Preservation, Atlanta, 1975—. Capt. U.S. Army, 1967-70, Vietnam. Decorated Bronze Star; Ford Found. fellow, 1965-66. Mem. Ga. State Bar (bd. govs. 1987-89), Newnan-Coweta Bar Assn. (pres. 1978), Fed. Judges Assn., Kiwanis. Presbyterian. Office: US Dist Ct 2142 US Courthouse 75 Spring St SW Atlanta GA 30303-3309

CAMP, JOSEPH SHELTON, JR., film producer, director, writer; b. St. Louis, Apr. 20, 1939; s. Joseph Shelton and Ruth Wilhelmena (McLaulin) C.; m. Andrea Carolyn Hopkins, Aug. 7, 1960; children: Joseph Shelton III, Brandon Andrew. BBA, U. Miss., 1961. Jr. account exec. McCann-Erickson Advt., Houston, 1961-62; owner Joe Camp Real Estate, Houston, 1962-64; account exec. Norsworthy-Mercer, Dallas, 1964-69; dir. TV comls. Jamieson Film Co., Dallas, 1969-71; founder, pres., writer, producer, dir. feature films Mulberry Square Prodns., Inc., Dallas, 1971-90, Gulfport, Miss., 1991-94, Chapel Hill, N.C., 1994—. Producer, dir., writer films including Benji, 1974, Hawmps, 1976, For the Love of Benji, 1977, The Double McGuffin, 1979, Oh Heavenly Dog, 1980, Benji The Hunted, 1987; TV spls. The Phenomenon of Benji, 1978, Benji's Very Own Christmas Story, 1978, Benji at Work, 1980, Benji (Takes a Dive) at Marineland, 1981; TV series Benji, Zax and the Alien Prince, 1983; author: Underdog, 1993. Bd. trustees Piney Woods Country Life Sch., Warren Wilson Coll.; adv. bd. N.C. Sch. of Arts, Sch. of Film Making. Mem. Dir.'s Guild Am., Writer's Guild Am. Home: 39512 Glenn Glade Chapel Hill NC 27514

CAMP, RICHARD GLENN, special education educator, coach; b. Ft. Payne, Ala., Apr. 5, 1968; s. Terry Glenn and Jane Marie (Groat) C.; m. Jennifer Suzanne Allen, Mar. 25, 1995. BS in Spl. Edn., Jacksonville (Ala.) State U., 1994. Tchr. spl. edn. Calhoun County Bd. Edn., Anniston, Ala., 1994-95; tchr. second chance program, football and wrestling coach Ft. Payne City Schs., 1995—. Mem. NEA, Ala. Edn. Assn. Democrat. Methodist.

CAMP, THOMAS EDWARD, retired librarian; b. Haynesville, La., July 12, 1929; s. Charles Walter and Annie Laura (Brazzel) C.; m. Elizabeth Anne Sowar, Sept. 4, 1952; children: Anne Winifred, Thomas David. BA, Centenary Coll. Shreveport, 1950; M.L.S., La. State U., 1953. Binding asst. La. State U. Library, Baton Rouge, 1951-53; circulation librarian Perkins Sch. Theology Bridwell Library, So. Meth. U., Dallas, 1955-57; librarian Sch. Theology, U. of South, Sewanee, Tenn., 1957-93, assoc. univ. librarian, 1976-93, acting univ. librarian, 1981-82. Co-author: Using Theological Libraries and Books, 1963; contbr. articles to profl. jours. Pres. Franklin County Assn. for Retarded, 1971-72. Served with AUS, 1953-55. Mem. ALA, Am. Theol. Library Assn. (exec. sec. 1965-67), Tenn. Library Assn. Democrat. Episcopalian. Home: 209 Carruthers Rd PO Box 820 Sewanee TN 37375-0820

CAMP, THOMAS HARLEY, economist; b. Charlotte, N.C., Aug. 13, 1929; s. Thomas Franklin and Agnes Mae (Davis) C.; m. Frances Ann Rogers, Mar. 20, 1953; children: Thomas Harley Jr., Landon G. BSc, U. N.C., 1956; postgrad, Am. U., 1965-67. Industry econ. USDA, Washington, 1959-70; location leader USDA, Austin, Tex., 1970-74; rsch. leader USDA, College Station, Tex., 1974-86; program leader USDA, Weslaco, Tex., 1986-88; agrl. mktg. specialist USDA, Lane, Okla., 1988-90; cons. Georgetown, Tex., 1990—. Author, co-author 44 sci. publs.; contbr. articles to profl. jours. Cubmaster Boy Scouts Am., Springfield, Va., 1965-69, asst. scoutmaster, 1966-70, scoutmaster, Round Rock, Tex., 1970-72, asst. scoutmaster, Austin, 1972-74. With USN, 1946-51, Korea. Mem. Am. Soc. Agrl. Engrs., Animal Air Transp. Assn., Food Distbn. Rsch. Soc., Transp. Rsch. Forum, Masons. Methodist. Home and Office: 230 Mesa Dr Georgetown TX 78628-1529

CAMP, VIRGINIA ANN, medical/surgical nurse; b. Chgo., Dec. 25, 1946; d. Victor S. and Annabelle (Todd) Rakow; m. Carey D. Camp, Dec. 28, 1974; children: Kimberly Ann, Alison Marie. RN, St. Paul Sch. Nursing, Dallas, 1967; BS, Incarnate Word Coll., San Antonio, 1975. Commd. 2d lt. U.S. Army, 1969—, advanced through grades to lt. col., 1980; staff nurse Walter Reed, Washington, 1986, Newborn Nursery, 1969-70; staff nurse med./surg. Martin Army Hosp., Ft. Benning, Ga., 1970-71; head nurse operating rm. U.S. Army, Ireland Army Hosp., Ft. Knox, Ky., 1979-84; staff nurse oper. rm. U.S. Army Hosp., Ft. Campbell, Ky., 1971-73, Brook Army Med. Ctr., Ft. Sam Houston, Tex., 1975-76; head nurse oper. rm. 2d Gen. Hosp., Landstuhl, Fed. Republic Germany, 1977-79; chief operating rm./CMS nursing sect. Bayne-Jones Army Hosp., Ft. Polk, La., 1984-86, 97th Gen. Hosp., Frankfurt, Fed. Republic Germany, 1986-89, Ireland Army Hosp.; ret., 1990; nurse mgr. operating room Humana Hosp. Med. Cities Dallas, 1990-91; staff nurse oper. rm. Dallas, 1992-95; asst. nurse mgr. OR/CSS Medical City, Dallas, 1995—. Mem. TSHSPP, Assn. Operating Rm. Nurses (cert.), Assn. Mil. Surgeons, Ret. Officers Assn., Nat. Assn. Uniformed Svcs.

CAMPBELL, B(OBBY) JACK, university official; b. Fort Worth, Oct. 12, 1929; s. Jack Bryan and Ruby Opal (Lamberth) C.; m. Frances Carol Alexander, Aug. 24, 1957; children: Carol Stuart Davis, John William Campbell. BA, Tex. Christian U., 1951, MA, 1953; PhD, U. N.C., 1960. Asst. dir. U. N.C. Inst. of Govt., Chapel Hill, 1957-59; chief accident rsch. br. Cornell U. Aero. Lab., Buffalo, 1959-66; dir. U. N.C. Hwy. Safety Rsch. Ctr., Chapel Hill, 1966-91, sr. investigator, dir. emeritus, 1992—; chmn. com. accident stats. Nat. Safety Coun., 1964-68; chmn. nat. motor vehicle safety adv. coun. U.S. Dept. Transp., 1975-76, mem., 1987-89, chmn. nat. driver register adv. com., 1983-86; chmn. panel on automotive assessment into 21st century U.S. Congress Office Tech. Assessment, 1976-77; chmn. com. to study CB radios on buses NRC, 1983-84, mem. com. to identify measures to improve safety of sch. bus transp., 1987-88; chmn. Global Traffic Safety Trust, Melbourne, Australia, 1988-92; lectr. or cons. in Australia, Azerbaijan, Brazil, Can., China, Denmark, Dominica, France, India, Hong Kong, Japan, Republic of Korea, Malawi, Malaysia, New Zealand, Russia, Saudi Arabia, Spain, Switzerland, Uruguay. Author: Driver Improvement: The Point System, 1958, Reducing Traffic Injury: A Global Challenge, 1988; (with others) Collier's Encyclopedia, 1962, Human Factors in Technology, 1963, Trauma and the Automobile, 1966, Traffic Safety: A National Problem, 1967, Key Issues in Highway Loss Reducation, 1970, Restraint Technologies: Rear Seat Occupant Protection, 1987; contbr. numerous articles to profl. jours. Sgt. U.S. Army, 1948-49. Recipient Gerin Medal for Rsch. Internat. Assn. for Accident and Traffic Medicine, 1992, Gustafson Leadership award Hwy. Users Fedn., 1989, Volvo Internat. Traffic Safety award, 1988, Volvo Pub. Safety award 1984, Disting. Svc. award Am. Assn. for Automotive Medicine, 1978, N.C. Pub. Health Assn., 1972, Alvah Lauer award Human Factors Soc., 1976, Met. Rsch. award Commendation Nat. Safety Coun., 1971, 60. Home: 502 Belmont St Chapel Hill NC 27514-3000

CAMPBELL, BRIAN SCOTT, army officer; b. Union City, Pa., Mar. 14, 1959; s. Paul Ralph and Beverly Jean (Allen) C.; m. Susan Carol Palone, Nov. 26, 1988. BS, Edinboro U. Pa., 1980; postgrad., U. Scranton, 1980-81; DO, Phila. Coll. Osteo. Medicine, 1985; MPH, U. Tenn., 1992, U.S. Army Command & Gen. Staff Coll., 1996. Diplomate Am. Bd. Preventative Medicine, Am. Osteo. Bd. Preventive Medicine, Nat. Bd. Examiners for Osteo. Physicians and Surgeons, Pa. State Bd. Examiners. Enlisted USMC, 1976; commd. 2d lt. U.S. Army, 1981, advanced through grades to lt. col., 1996; specialist in occupational, environ. and aerospace medicine U.S. Ctrl. Command, McDill AFB, Fla., 1996—. Author: University of Tennessee Wellness Handbook; contbr. articles to profl. jours. Instr. Baize Sch. Karate, Clarksville, Tenn., 1988—. Health Professions scholar, 1981; decorated Bronze Star. Mem. NRA (life), Aerospace Med. Assn., Am. Osteo. Coll. Preventive Medicine, Wilderness Med. Soc., Soc. U.S. Army Flight Surgeons (life), Am. Osteo. Assn., Assn. Mil. Osteo. Physicians and Surgeons, U.S. Judo Assn. (Black Belt, patron life), United Bujutsu Fedn. (black belt), Okinawan Karate-Do Union (black belt), Beta Beta Beta. Republican.

CAMPBELL, CARL DAVID, oil industry executive, landman; b. Oklahoma City, July 4, 1959; s. David Gwynne and Janet Gay (Newland) C. B in Bus. Admninstrn., U. Okla., 1982. Cert. profl. landman, scuba diver, licensed pilot. Land cons. Leede Exploration, Okla. City, 1978, 79; lease broker W.M. Bryan, Inc., Okla. City, 1980, 81; corp. sec., land mgr. Earth Hawk Exploration, Inc., Okla. City, 1980-96, v.p., 1996—; landman PetroCorp, Okla. City, 1983-87; mid-continent divsn. landman Petrocorp, Okla. City, 1987-91; Gulf Coast divsn. landman Petrocorp, Houston, 1991-92; Gulf, Rockies, Can. divsn. landman PetroCorp, Houston, 1993—. Mem. Cherokee Nation Okla., Tahlequah, 1979—. Mem. Am. Assn. Petroleum Landmen, Houston Assn. Petroleum Landmen, Canadian Assn. Petroleum Landmen, Okla. Ind. Petroleum Assn., Okla. City Assn. Petroleum Landmen, Houston Soc., U. Okla. Found. Assocs., First Families Tenn. (charter), Cherokee Hist. Soc. (charter mem. heritage coun. 1982—), Houston Mus. Fine Arts, Aircraft Owners and Pilots Assn., Phi Gamma Delta. Republican. Presbyterian. Home: 1701 Hermann Dr Ste 2204 Houston TX 77004 Office: PetroCorp Ste 300 N Atrium 160800 Greenspoint Park Dr Houston TX 77060-2391

CAMPBELL, CAROL ANN, newspaper library manager; b. Woodville, Okla., Mar. 4, 1940; d. William Ferges and Alma May (Harrison) Jones; m. Floyd H. Stevenson, Oct. 15, 1957 (div. 1962); children: Timothy L., Eric N.; m. Max N. Campbell, Oct. 15, 1965. Grad. high sch., Midwest City, Okla. With Okla. Pub. Co., Oklahoma City, 1968—, asst. libr., 1984-88, staff writer, 1988-90, instr. new equipment, 1990-91, mem. electronic page layout staff, 1991-92, libr. mgr., 1992—. Active Freedom of Info. Okla., Oklahoma City, 1992—. Mem. Spl. Librs. Assn. (nat. and Okla. chpts., Okla. pres.-elect 1994-95, mem. news div. tech. com.). Office: Okla Pub Co 9000 Broadway Ext Oklahoma City OK 73114-3708 also: Okla Pub Co PO Box 25125 Oklahoma City OK 73125-0125

CAMPBELL, CATHERINE LYNN, elementary school educator; b. Lynchburg, Va., Mar. 16, 1961; d. Tomie Eawell Campbell and Barbara (Arthur) McCraw. BA, Sweet Briar Coll., 1983; postgrad., U. Va. Cert. elem. tchr., Va. Tchr. Amherst (Va.) County Pub. Schs., 1984—. Mem. Nat. Honor Soc. Home: 107 Cedar Crest Townhouses Madison Heights VA 24572-2471 Office: Amherst County Pub Schs Amherst VA 24521

CAMPBELL, CHARLES ALTON, manufacturing corporate executive; b. Brunswick, Ga., Mar. 10, 1944; s. Rayford Monroe and Cecelia Elizabeth (Camilla) C.; B Indsl. Engring., Ga. Inst. Tech., 1966; MBA, Harvard U., 1973; m. Mary Alla Traber, Aug. 15, 1970; children—Christine Beensen, Elizabeth Traber, Charles Traber. Mgr. ops. projects Camak Lumber Ops., ITT Rayonier, Thomson, Ga., 1974-75, mgr. ops. projects Wood Products Group, N.Y.C., 1975-77, dir. chems. devel. parent co., 1977-79, dir. operational planning and control, Seattle, 1979-80; pres. Fox Mfg. Co., Rome, Ga., 1980-81, Camtec, Inc., Rome, 1981-88; chmn. bd. Universal Ceramics, Inc., Adairsville, Ga., 1984-87; exec. v.p. Saunders, Inc., Birmingham, Ala., 1987-88, pres., chief oper. officer, 1988-90; pres. N.Am. Tech. Corp., Birmingham, 1990—. Lt. C.E., USNR, 1967-69. Episcopalian. Club: Mountain Brook (Ala.) Swim and Tennis. Lodge: Rotary (Birmingham). Home: 3725 Briar Oak Cir Birmingham AL 35223-2826 Office: NAm Tech Corp PO Box 43462 Birmingham AL 35243-0462

CAMPBELL, CLAIR GILLILAND, lawyer; b. Aberdeen, Md., Nov. 27, 1961; d. Bobby Eugene and Sara Frances (Matkins) G. BA, U. Ala., 1982; JD, Cumberland U., 1985. Bar: N.C. 1985, U.S. Dist. Ct. (we. and mid.

dists.) N.C. 1985, S.C. 1986. Ptnr. Karney, Campbell & Karney, Charlotte, N.C., 1985-91; ptnr. Campbell & Taylor, 1991—, Charlotte, N.C., 1996—; instr. Paralegal Inst., Queens, Coll., 1990; participant Wild Dolphin Project. Author: Twas the Night Before the Orange Bowl, 1988. Mem. ABA, ATLA, Mecklenburg County Bar Assn. (program coord. edn. com. 1986-88, panel televised lawyers discussion 1991, mem. speakers forum com. 1992, silent ptnr.), N.C. Acad. Trial Lawyers, Ducks Unltd., Cumberland Alumni Assn. (reunion com. 1989-90), DAR (vice regent 1993-94), Nat. Soc. Colonial Dames (sec. 1995—), Nat. Soc. Magna Charta Dames, Alpha Omicron Pi (sec. 1994—). Home: 3915 Pomfret Ln Charlotte NC 28211-3729 Office: Campbell & Taylor 717 East Blvd Charlotte NC 28203

CAMPBELL, CLAIRE PATRICIA, nurse practitioner, educator; b. Jan. 10, 1933; d. Hugh Paul and Clara Louise (Bell) Campbell. Student So. Meth. U., 1956-57; BS in Nursing, U. Tex. Sch. Nursing-Galveston, 1959, Family Nurse Practitioner, 1979, cert., 1984, 89; MS in Nursing, Tex. Woman's U. Sch. Nursing, 1971. Staff nurse Parkland Meml. Hosp., Dallas County Hosp. Dist., 1955-70, head nurse gen. surgery, chest surgery, neurosurgery, orthopedics, and internal medicine, until 1970; instr. nursing Tex. Woman's U. Sch. Nursing, Dallas, 1971-72; rschr. nursing diagnosis, Dallas, 1972-77; FNP Otis Engring. Health Svc., Dallas, 1979-86, nurse practitioner pain mgmt. program Dallas Rehab. Inst., 1986-95, HealthSouth SubAcute Unit, 1995—; adj. asst. prof. U. Tex. Sch. Nursing, Arlington, 1976—; cons. nursing diagnosis. Author: Nursing Diagnosis and Intervention in Nursing Practice, 1st edit., 1978, 2d edit., 1984. Mem. ANA, Tex. Nurses Assn. - Dist. 4, North Am. Nursing Diagnosis Assn., Sigma Theta Tau. Roman Catholic.

CAMPBELL, CURTIS MILTON, associate engineer, technician; b. Birmingham, Ala., July 13, 1961; s. Norman Joseph and Eva Nell (Carlton) C.; m. Gay Lee Bradley, May 15, 1985 (div. May, 1990). Assoc. ASEET, Cleve. Inst. Electronics, 1993. Cert. electronic technician ISCET; lic. gen. radiotelephone operator, 1995. Technician SCI Systems, Huntsville, Ala., 1981-83; engring. aid So. Techs., Huntsville, 1983-84, Universal Data Systems, Huntsville, 1984-86; instr. electronics So. Jr. Coll., Huntsville, 1986-87; component engr. Comptronix Corp., Guntersville, Ala., 1987; technician III B, PLC systems programmer Keyes Fibre, Van Leer, Albvertville, Ala., 1988-89; technician sr. r.f. Lash-Ade, Inc., Guntersville, 1989-95; head-end supr. dBtronics, Spartanburg, S.C., 1995—. Co-author: (manual) SR84 Storage Reliability of Missile Materiel, 1984. Petty officer US Navy, 1980-81.

CAMPBELL, DIANNE, social worker; b. Little Rock, Apr. 19, 1961; d. George Emerson and Anna Claire (Janes) C. BA in Psychology, U. Colo., 1979-83; MSW, U. Ark., 1984-86. Lic. Clin. Social Worker, Ark. Pub. health investigator Ark. Dept. Health, Little Rock, 1988-90; med. social worker U. Ark Med. Scis., Little Rock, 1990-93; psychiat. social worker Little Rock Cmty. Mental Health Ctr., 1993-94; renal social worker Little Rock Dialysis, 1994—; rschr., lobbyist Little Rock Dialysis, 1995; appointee med. rev. bd. End Stage Renal Disease Network 13, 1996—. Mem. Acad. Cert. Soc. Workers. Democrat. Presbyterian. Office: Little Rock Dialysis Ste 100 10310 W Markham Little Rock AR 72205

CAMPBELL, DONNA MARIE, telecommunications executive; b. Somerville, N.J., Oct. 7, 1949; d. Howard E. and Joyce E. Bilbee; m. Charles Edward Campbell, Mar. 28, 1969; children: Carla Marie, Bradley James. Attended, Eckerd Coll. Bus. Mgmt., St. Petersburg, 1988. Personnel adminstr. The Bradenton Herald, 1979-82; dir. telecommunications HCA Blake Hosp., Bradenton, Fla., 1982-88; corp. mgr. telecomm. Snelling & Snelling Internat., Sarasota, Fla., 1988-90; mgr. telecomm. and ops. mgr. Health Resource Network Sarasota (Fla.) Meml. Hosp., 1990-94; dir. The Health Resource Network, 1994—; mem. SunHealth Alliance Task Force, 1991. Mem. Am. Bus. Women's Assn. (sec. 1983, pres. 1984, woman of yr. 1985), West Fla. Hosp. Comm. Assn. (sec. 1984-85, pres. 1986-87), Am. Hosp. Assn. (guest speaker nat. conf. 1991), IBX Users' Group (attendant console foucs com. 1993-94, nat. conf. hostess 1995, mem. exec. bd. 1995), Fla. Pub. Interest Rsch. Group, Am. Coalition for the Homeless. Republican. Baptist. Office: Sarasota Meml Hosp 1700 S Tamiami Trl Sarasota FL 34239-3509

CAMPBELL, G. DOUGLAS, medical educator; b. Jackson, Miss., May 20, 1951; s. Guy D. and Margaret F. Campbell; m. Laura Casteel, July 29, 1987. Student, U. Miss., 1969-72, MD, 1976. Resident U. Miss. Sch. Medicine, Jackson, 1976-79, instr. dept. internal medicine, 1979-80, asst. dir. student health, 1979-81, asst. prof. dept. internal medicine, 1980-81; fellow U. Tex. Health Sci. Ctr., San Antonio, 1981-83; asst. prof. dept. internal medicine U. Ark. for Med. Scis., Little Rock, 1985-90, asst. prof. dept. microbiology and immunology, 1987-90; assoc. prof. dept. medicine La. State U. Med. Ctr., Shreveport, 1990—, program dir. pulmonary diseases dept. medicine, 1990—, acting chief divsn. pulmonary and critical care medicine, 1992-94, chief divsn. pulmonary and critical care medicine, 1994—; staff physician med. svc. VA Med. Ctr., Jackson, 1979-81, dir. diabetes sect., 1980-81, med. student coord. med. svc., 1980-81, asst. environ. health officer, 1980-81; staff physician med. svc. John L. McClellan VA Hosp., Little Rock, 1985-90; staff physician med. svc. Overton Brooks VA Hosp., Shreveport, 1990—. Named Outstanding Young Men in Am., 1981; recipient Disting. Svc. award Disabled Am. Vets., 1990; postdoctoral fellowship in microbiology and infectious diseases U. Calgary Health Sci. Ctr., 1983-85. Fellow ACP, Am. Coll. Chest Physicians; mem. Am. Soc. Microbiology, Am. Thoracic Soc., Med. Mycological Soc. Ams., Sigma Xi. Office: La State Univ Pulmonary Medicine Shreveport LA 71130

CAMPBELL, GEORGE EMERSON, lawyer; b. Piggott, Ark., Sept. 23, 1932; s. Sid and Mae (Harris) C.; m. Anna Claire Janes, June 22, 1960 (dec. Mar. 1971); children: Dianne, Carole; m. Joan Stafford Rule, Apr. 7, 1973. J.D., U. Ark., Fayetteville, 1955. Bar: Ark. 1955, U.S. Supreme Ct. 1971. Law clk. to judge Ark. Supreme Ct., 1959-60; assoc. Kirsch, Cathey & Brown, Paragould, Ark., 1955; mem. Rose Law Firm, P.A., Little Rock, 1960—; Del. 7th Ark. Constl. Conv., 1969-70; regional v.p. Nat. Mcpl. League, 1974-86; mem. Ark. Ednl. TV Commn., 1976-92, chmn., 1980-82, 88-91; bd. dirs. Ark. Ednl. TV Found., 1984-92, chmn., 1988-91. Chmn. bd. Pulaski County Law Libr., 1980—; bd. dirs. Ark. Arts Ctr., 1991-95, sec. 1992-93), Ark. Symphony Orch. Soc., 1982-87, Ark. Capital Corp., Ark. Cert. Devel. Corp., Downtown Partnership; bd. dirs. Youth Home Inc., 1986-92, pres., 1991-92. With USNR, 1955-77, ret.. Mem. ABA, Ark. Bar Assn., Pulaski County Bar Assn., Am. Law Inst., Am. Judicature Soc., Nat. Assn. Bond Lawyers. Office: Rose Law Firm PA 120 E 4th St Little Rock AR 72201-2808

CAMPBELL, GEORGE LEROY, utilities executive; b. Ray, Ariz., Sept. 11, 1940; s. George Howard and Ynez Lois (Hersey) C.; m. Jane Leiby (div.); 1 child, George Leroy Jr.; m. Pamela Ann Meacomes, Aug. 1, 1987. BSBA, U. Ariz., 1963; MBA in Fin., Calif. State U., Long Beach, 1966; cert. in info. mgmt., UCLA. Credit analyst Security Pacific Bank, Los Angeles, 1965-66; fin. analyst So. Calif. Edison, Los Angeles, 1966-69; fin. acct. Fla. Power Corp., St. Petersburg, 1969-73, mgr. investor relations, 1973-82, dir. pub. affairs, 1982-86, v.p., 1987—; adj. instr. U. South Fla., 1974. pres. St. Petersburg Jaycees, 1974; v.p. Pinellas County United Way, 1981, also bd. dirs.; troop chmn. Boy Scouts Am., Pinellas County coun., St. Petersburg, 1979; bd. dirs. Fla. Taxwatch, 1983—. Served with USAFR, 1963-69;. Mem. Pub. Affairs Coun. (bd. dirs. 1987—), U.S. C. of C., Nat. Assn. Mfrs., Fla. C. of C., Associated Industries Fla., St. Petersburg Hist. Soc. (bd. dirs. 1988—), Capitol Hill Club. Club: Capitol Hill (Washington). Office: Fla Power Corp 3201 34th St S Saint Petersburg FL 33711-3828

CAMPBELL, GLENDA GAIL, medical and surgical nurse; b. Graham, Tex., July 28, 1953; d. Austin Bell and Margaret Louise (Ward) C. AA, Cisco (Tex.) Jr. Coll., 1974; BSN cum laude, Midwestern State U., 1992. Cert. NRP, PALS, TNCCP, ACLS. Asst. in lab. Graham Gen. Hosp., 1969-71; magnetic tape machine operator Graham Magnetics, 1972-73; sec./draftsman Dresser Atlas, 1974-84; sec. Campbell Rathole Drlg., Inc., 1984-91; clin. asst. Graham (Tex.) Gen. Hosp., 1991; grad. nurse, staff nurse RN Graham Gen. Hosp., 1992—. Recipient Nat. Collegiate Nursing award Midwestern State U., 1992. Mem. Nat. Student Nurses Assn., Midwestern State U. Nursing Honors Soc., Christian Broadcasting Network, Nat. Humane Edn. Soc., Nat. Bus. Assn., Sigma Theta Tau, Tex. Gamma Chpt. of Alpha Chi. Republican. Home: PO Box 52 Graham TX 76450-0052

CAMPBELL, GROVER STOLLENWERCK, university official; b. Dallas, May 6, 1954; s. Frank Whitney and Elizabeth Ann (Stollenwerck) C.; m. Nancy L. Bauerle, Dec. 5, 1981; children: Logan Bauerle, Lee Hillman. BJ, U. Tex., 1977, MBA, 1986. Asst. sgt. at arms Tex. House Reps., Austin, 1973-74; adminstrv. asst. State Rep. Herman Adams, Austin, 1974-78; spl. asst. govtl. rels. U. Tex. System, Austin, 1978-84; vice chancellor U. Houston System, 1984—. Exec. prodr. The Capitol Report, Sta. KUHT. Mem. Austin Heritage Soc., 1982-86, Sta. KLRU Action Com., Austin, 1982-84, Les Patrons of the Paramount, Austin, 1982-85, Symphony Sq. Com., Austin. Named Outstanding Young Man in Am. U.S. Jaycess, 1980. Mem. Am. Assn. Univ. Adminstrs., Nat. Assn. State Univs. and Land-Grant Colls., Coun. for Advancement and Support of Edn., Pub. Affairs Assocs., Houston C. of C., Beta Gamma Sigma. Home: 1510 Westover Rd Austin TX 78703-1912 Office: U Houston System 1005 Congress Ave Ste 820 Austin TX 78701-2415

CAMPBELL, HILTON EARL, reliability engineer; b. Driggs, Idaho, Mar. 6, 1960; s. Phil J. and Betty Ruth (Hall) C.; m. Paulette Piquet, June 13, 1980; children: Hilton Eugene, Heather, William Ian, Felicia Marie. BS in Indsl. Tech., So. Ill. U., 1988. Asst. materials mgr. Logan (Utah) Regional Hosp., 1980-82; integrated avionics specialist USAF, RAF Upper Heyford, U.K., 1982-88; tech. reliability test devel. Compaq Computer Corp., Houston, 1988-89; engr. Compaq Computer Corp., 1989-91; mgr. engring. evaluation sys. Compaq Computer Corp., Houston, 1991-93; reliability project mgr. Compaq Computer Corp., 1993-95; field engring. mgr., 1995—; cons., designer Campbell Software Prodns., Houston, 1992—; analyst Tex. Air Nat. Guard, Houston, 1988-94. Scoutmaster Boy Scouts Am., Houston, 1991-94; soccer, basketball coach YMCA, Houston, 1989-93. Mem. IEEE, Nat. Guard Assn. Tex., Houston Computer Artists and Animators. Home: 9303 Zurich Ct Houston TX 77070-2029 Office: Compaq Computer Corp 20555 SH 249 M/S 040106 Houston TX 77070

CAMPBELL, JAMES ALBERT BARTON, marketing executive; b. Chattanooga, Tenn., Nov. 2, 1940; s. James Harry and Elizabeth Tipton (Johnson) C.; m. Julia Madge Clark, Sept. 12, 1964; children: Richard Barton, Julia Clark. BS, Princeton U., 1962; grad., U.S. Army Command Gen. Staff Coll., 1975, U.S. Army War Coll., 1985. Devel. engr. DuPont Co., Wilmington, Del., 1964-66; mktg. specialist Formex Co., Greeneville, Tenn., 1966-67; field sales engr. Reynolds Metals Co., Richmond, Va., 1967-70; regional sales rep. Reynolds Metals Co., Charlotte, N.C., 1970-74; mktg. mgr. Reynolds Metals Co., Richmond, 1975-81, mgr. market planning, 1982-84, market group mgr., 1984-86, mktg. svcs. mgr., 1986-93, mgr. sales and mktg. svcs., 1994-96, mem. pres.'s task force on corp. definition, 1996—, chmn. access definition team, 1996; founder, owner Priceless Pages Christian Bookstore, Richmond, 1983-90; light postal vehicle task force Aluminum Assn., N.Y.C., 1978-79; advisor Marine Pleasure Boat Assn., Chgo., 1984. Pres. Res. Officers Assn., Richmond, 1987, area 3 dir., 1988, state v.p. Army, 1992-93; exec. com. Assn. U.S. Army, Richmond, 1988-90; mil. advisor State of Va. Com. Employer Support Guard and Res.; mem. exec. com. Young Life, 1988-92; bd. dirs. Encounter Ministries; elder local Presbyn. Ch. Col. USAR ret. Decorated Legion of Merit, Meritorious Svc. medal with two oak leaf clusters, Army Commendation medal, Army Achievement medal with oak leaf cluster. Mem. SCV (Ga. comdr. 1969-70, Va. lt. comdr. 1992-96, chmn. nat. strategy planning com. 1994-96, chmn. centennial nat. conv. 1996), Gideons Internat. (local pres., v.p., sec. 1969-90), Jeb Stuart Camp (comdr. 1991-92), Res. Officers Assn. (dir. membership and ROTC affairs 1997—). Home: 2211 Heathland Dr Midlothian VA 23113-4183 Office: Reynolds Metals Co 6601 W Broad St Richmond VA 23230-1701

CAMPBELL, JEFFERSON HOLLAND, English language educator; b. Beaumont, Tex., Jan. 19, 1931; s. William Holland and Eula Mildred (Owens) C.; m. Shelia Ann Trapp, Sept. 4, 1952; children: Cary Elizabeth, Susan Holland, William Charles. AA, Lamar Coll., 1950; BA, So. Meth. U., 1952; BD, Perkins Sch. Theol., 1955; PhD, Duke U., 1963. Prof., chmn. English dept. Southwestern U., Georgetown, Tex., 1962-74, Midwestern State U., Wichita Falls, Tex., 1974—; chmn. faculty devel. com. Humanities CLEP Exam., Princeton, N.J., 1972-77; chmn. writing exam Tex. Acad. Skills Coun., Austin, 1986-88. Author: John Howard Griffin, 1970, Updike's Novels: Thorns Spell Word, 1987. Mem. MLA (south ctrl. sect. chmn. 1972, 75, 91), Am. Studies Assn. Tex. (pres. 1971, v.p., councillor), Conf. Coll. Tchrs. English (pres. 1974, councillor). Democrat. Methodist. Office: Midwestern State Univ 3410 Taft Wichita Falls TX 76308

CAMPBELL, JOAN VIRGINIA LOWEKE, secondary school educator, language educator; b. Detroit, Nov. 8, 1942; d. George Paul and Lolamae (Weians) L.; m. James Bachelder Campbell, July 26, 1975; 1 child, James Bachelder Loweke. BA in German, French, Hope Coll., 1965; student, U. Cologne (Germany), 1964, U. Salzburg (Austria), 1968, U. Stuttgart (Germany), 1970-71, Sampere Inst., Madrid, 1982, Millersville (Pa.) State U., 1983, 84, 90, Va. Poly. Inst. and State U., 1976-77, 80-84. Cert. secondary tchr., Mich., Kans., Va. Tchr. French and German I, II Grand Haven (Mich.) Jr. H.S., 1965-69; asst. instr. elementary and intermediate German U. Kans., Lawrence, 1969-70, 71-72; tchr. German I, II Ctrl. Jr. H.S., Lawrence, Kans., 1972-74; tchr. French I, II, sr. English Oskaloosa (Kans.) H.S., 1974-75; tchr. German I-IV Highland Park H.S., Topeka, 1975-76; tchr. French I-V, Spanish I Blacksburg (Va.) H.S., 1977—; tchr. French, Spanish YMCS evening courses, Blacksburg, Va., 1976-80; mem. audio visual com. Montgomery County Fgn. Lang. Collaborative Group, Blacksburg, 1984-87; chaperone Am. Inst. Fgn. Study, Germany, France, Spain, 1968-82, area adminstr. summer and winter programs abroad, We. Mich., 1968-69; chaperone Ednl. Adventures, Montreal, 1984, 90-91, 93-94, Montgomery County Schs.; presenter in field. Author: The Gothic Cathedral, 1995. Mem. Internat. Host Family Orgn. Va. Poly. Inst. and State U., Blacksburg, 1977—;. Fulbright exch. fellow U. Kans., 1970-71, Fulbright fellow Goethe Insts., 1976, Rockefeller fellow Rockefeller Assn. and Nat. Endowment Humanities, 1986, NDEA fellow, 1966; recognized as Va. Gov.'s Sch. Outstanding Educator, 1990. Mem. Am. Assn. Tchrs. French (state and region IV U.S. Recognition effort, dedication and high scores on nat. French exams, 1988, 96, founder La Soc. Hon. de Français for Outstanding Students in French Blacksburg chpt. 1977, state com.),Am. Assn. Tchrs. Spanish and Portuguese, Am. Assn. Tchrs. German (Va. exec. com. sec. 1977-83, co-chmn. nat. German exams Va. chpt. 1984-87, state nominating com. 1984-87, chmn. 1984-85), Nat. Assn. Edn. (Blacksburg H.S. rep. 1980-82), Va. Assn. Edn., Montgomery County Assn. Edn., Assn. Supervision and Curriculum Devel., Fgn. Lang. Assn. Va. (life). Republican. Presbyterian. Home: 3003 McLean Ct Blacksburg VA 24060 Office: Blacksburg HS Patrick Henry Dr Blacksburg VA 24060

CAMPBELL, JOHN ROY, animal scientist educator, academic administrator; b. Goodman, Mo., June 14, 1933; s. Carl J. and Helen (Nicoletti) C.; m. Eunice Vieten, Aug. 7, 1954; children: Karen L., Kathy L., Keith L. BS, U. Mo., 1955; MS, U. Mo., Columbia, 1956, PhD, 1960. Instr. dairy sci. U. Mo., Columbia, 1960-61, asst. prof., 1961-65, assoc. prof., 1965-68, prof., from 1968; assoc. dean, dir. resident instrn. Coll. Agr., U. Ill., Urbana-Champaign, 1977-83; dean Coll. Agr. U. Ill., Urbana, 1983-88; pres. Okla. State U., Stillwater, 1988—. Author: (with J.F. Lasley) The Science of Animals That Serve Humanity, 1969, 3d edit., 1985, In Touch with Students, 1972, (with R.T. Marshall) The Science of Providing Milk for Man, 1975; Reclaiming A Lost Heritage...Land-Grant and Other Higher Education Initiatives for the Twenty-First Century, 1995. Recipient Gamma Sigma Delta Superior Teaching award, 1967, Gamma Sigma Delta Internat. award for disting. svc. to agr., 1985, Coll. Osteo. Medicine Okla. State U. Disting. Svc. award, 1992. Mem. Am. Dairy Sci. Assn. (dir. 1975-78, 80-86, pres. 1980-81, Ralston Purina Disting. Teaching award 1973, Award of Honor 1987), Nat. Assn. Coll. Tchrs. Agr. (Ensminger Interstate Disting. Tchr. award 1973, Teaching fellow 1973, Disting. Educator award 1990, Nat. Assn. State and Univ. and Land-Grant Colls. (commns. on home econs. and vet. medicine, com. on water resources, coun. of presidents), Okla. Futures, Gamma Sigma Delta. Office: Okla State U 105 CITD Stillwater OK 74075-9618

CAMPBELL, KERMIT ERNEST, assistant professor; b. Freeport, Tex., Nov. 29, 1960; s. Major Ernest and Laverne (Griggs) C.; m. Betsy Ching-Hsuan Lin, Sept. 3, 1993. BA with honors, U. Tex., 1984; MA in English, U. of Houston, 1988; PhD in English, Ohio State U., 1993. Fgn. tchr. South China Inst. Tech., Guangzhou, 1985-86; tchg. asst. U. Houston, 1987-88; tchg. assoc. Ohio State U., Columbus, 1988-93; asst. prof. U. Tex., Austin, 1993—; lectr. in field including South Africa, Italy and Canada, 1987—. Area coord./host, Nat. Coun. of Tchrs. of English Black Caucus African Am. Read-in Chain, Ohio State U., 1990-92; minority outreach coord., U. Tex., 1994—. Recipient Regent's Acad. Challenge grant, Ohio State U., 1990-91, Honorable Mention in Ford Found.; Fellow NRC, 1991, Dissertation fellow, Presdl. fellow Ohio State U., 1992-93. Mem. MLA, Can. Soc. for Study of Rhetoric, Coll. Composition and Comm., Internat. Soc. for the History of Rhetoric, Nat. Coun. Tchrs. of English Black Caucus, Nat. Coun. Tchrs. English, Rhetoric Soc. of Am., Assn. for Rhetoric and Comm. in Southern Africa. Office: U Tex Dvsn Rhetoric & Composition Parlin 3 Austin TX 78712-1122

CAMPBELL, MARGARET GEORGESON, retired librarian; b. Dayton, Ohio, Apr. 22, 1913; d. Andrew Gilbertson and Jessie (Taylor) C. BA, Ohio Wesleyan U., 1935; MLS, Western Res. U., 1952. Med. technologist Mt. Sinai Hosp., Cleve., 1936-39; med. technologist S.C. State Bd. Health, Columbia, 1939-45; club dir. ARC, Munich, Germany, 1945-46, Kunsan, Taegu, Korea, 1947-50; libr. U.S. Army Spl. Svcs., Germany, France, 1952-54; libr. dir. Shaker Heights (Ohio) Pub. Librs., ret., 1975; auditing student U. South Fla., Tampa, 1986—. Libr. vol. Sarasota (Fla.) Pub. Libr., 1976-78; interviewer Met. Ministries, Reading for the Blind, WUSF Radio, 1990—; vol. sr. care Univ. Cmty. Hosp., 1984—. Mem. Delta Zeta. Methodist. Home: 4000 E Fletcher Ave Apt G309 Tampa FL 33613-4818

CAMPBELL, NANCY COLENE, magazine editor; b. Te Puke, New Zealand, May 27, 1941; came to U.S., 1991; d. Ivan Verdun and Joyce Kathleen (Grant) Bowen; m. Charles Colin Campbell, Mar. 4, 1963; children: Wesley, Stephen, Evangeline, Rocklyn, Pearl, Serene. Founder, editor Above Rubies mag., Palmerston, New Zealand, 1977-82, Gold Coast Queensland, Australia, 1982-91, Franklin, Tenn., 1991—. Home: 4150 Clovercroft Rd Franklin TN 37067 Office: Above Rubies PO Box 351 Franklin TN 37011-0351

CAMPBELL, POLLYANN S., lawyer; b. Zanesville, Ohio, Oct. 26, 1949; d. Walter Frederick and and Ann Marie (Heiss) Stuenkel; m. John William Campbell II, Apr. 3, 1970 (div. Oct. 1990); children: Georgia Ann, John William III. BA cum laude, Shorter Coll., 1970; JD magna cum laude, Woodrow Wilson Coll. of Law, 1981. Bar: Ga. 1981, U.S. Dist. Ct. (no. dist.) Ga. 1981. Assoc. Lipshutz, Frankel, Greenblatt, King and Cohen, Atlanta, 1982-85; dist. underwriter, counsel Stewart Title Guaranty Co., Atlanta, 1985-87; state counsel Transamerica Title Ins. Co., Atlanta, 1987-90; appointed div. counsel Commonwealth Land Title Ins. Co. and Transamerica Title Ins. Co., Atlanta, 1990—; appointed Ga. State Counsel, 1996—; presenter Ga. Real Estate Closing Attys. Assn. seminar, 1991, Commonwealth Land Title Ins. Co. seminar, 1992, other seminars. Editor-in-chief Woodrow Wilson Jour. Law, 1979-81. Mem. coun. Luth. Ch. of Nativity, Austell, Ga., 1982, 89-91, pres., 1990-91; mem. Rudisill Meml. Handbell Choir. Mem. ABA, Ga. Bar Assn., Atlanta Bar Assn., Am. Land Title Assn. (former state ct. mem. of judiciary com.). Office: Commonwealth Land Title Ins Co Transam Title Ins Co 990 Hammond Dr NE Ste 770 Atlanta GA 30328-5510

CAMPBELL, RANDOLPH BLUFORD, historian, educator; b. Charlottesville, Va., Nov. 16, 1940; s. John Landon and Virginia Lewis (Lyon) C.; m. Diana Snow Campbell, June 9, 1962; children: James Landon, Jonathan Clay. BS, U. Va., 1961, MA in History, 1963, PhD in History, 1966. Instr. Va. Poly. Inst., Blacksburg, 1963-64, Madison Coll., Harrisonburg, Va., 1966; from asst. prof. to prof. U. North Tex., Denton, 1969-77, prof., 1977-88, regents prof., 1988—. Mem. editl. adv. bd. U. North Tex. Press, Denton; author: A Southern Community in Crisis: harrison County, Texas, 1850-1880, 1983, An Empire for Slavery: The Peculiar Institution in Texas, 1821-1865, 1989, Sam Houston and the American Southwest, 1993. Recipient Summerfield Roberts award Sons of Rep. Tex., 1990, Friends of Dallas Pub. Libr. award Tex. Inst. Letters, 1990. Mem. Tex. State Hist. Assn. (mem. editl. bd. 1987-96, pres. 1993-94, Tullis award 1990), So. Hist. Assn. (mem. editl. bd. 1980-84, Ramsdell award 1974), Orgn. Am. Historians. Democrat. Home: 924 Imperial Dr Denton TX 76201 Office: Dept History Univ North Tex PO Box 13735 Denton TX 76203

CAMPBELL, ROBERT LYNDSAY, II, psychology educator; b. Dubuque, Iowa, July 31, 1953; s. Robert Lyndsay and Susan Valeria (Altman) C.; m. Jolie Marie LaChance, Feb. 1983 (div. Mar. 1985); m. Heidi Martha Friedberg, June 22, 1991; 1 child, Kyla Alexandra. BA in Social Rels., Harvard U., 1974; PhD in Devel. Psychology, U. Tex., 1986. Teaching asst. dept. psychology U. Tex., Austin, 1978-80, 83, rsch. asst. Children's Rsch. Ctr., 1984; rsch. assoc. S.W. Ednl. Devel. Lab., Austin, 1980-82; mem. rsch. staff User Interface Inst., IBM T.J. Watson Rsch. Ctr., Yorktown Heights, N.Y., 1985-91; asst. prof. psychology Clemson (S.C.) U., 1991-93, assoc. prof., 1993—; conf. presenter, spkr. in field, 1983—; mem. conf. panels; article reviewer CHI Conf. Procs., Cognitive Devel., Devel. Rev., Human Devel., Jour. Exptl. and Theoretical Artificial Intelligence, New Ideas in Psychology. Author: (with M.H. Bickhard) Knowing Levels and Developmental Stages, 1986; author: The Earthly Recordings of Sun Ra, 1994; regular jazz and blues reviewer Cadence mag., 1992-96; contbr. chpts. to books, articles to profl. jours. Rsch. grantee Clemson U., 1993. Mem. Cognitive Sci. Soc., Internat. Soc. for Study of Behavioral Devel., Philosophy of Sci. Assn., Soc. for Philosophy and Psychology, Soc. for Rsch. in Child Devel., Inst. of Objectivist Studies, Sigma Xi. Office: Clemson U Dept Psychology Clemson SC 29634

CAMPBELL, SELAURA JOY, lawyer; b. Oklahoma City, Mar. 25, 1944; d. John Moore III and Gyda (Hallum) C. AA, Stephens Coll., 1963; BA, U. Okla., 1965; MEd, Chapel Hill U., 1974; JD, N.C. Cen. U., 1978; postgrad. atty. mediation courses, South Tex. Sch. of Law, Houston, 1991, Atty. Mediators Inst./Dallas, Dallas, 1992. Bar: Ariz 1983; lic. real estate broker, N.C.; cert. tchr. N.C. With flight svc. dept. Pan Am. World Airways, N.Y.C., 1966-91; lawyer Am. Women's Legal Clinic, Phoenix, 1987; charter mem. Sony Corp. Indsl. Mgmt. Seminar, 1981; guest del. Rep. Nat. Conv., Houston, 1992; judge all-law sch. mediation competition for Tex., South Tex. Sch. Law, Houston, 1994. Mem. N.C. Cen. U. Law Rev., 1977-78. People-to-People del. People's Republic of China, 1987; guest del. Rep. Nat. Conv., Houston, 1992. Mem. Ariz. Bar Assn., Humane Soc. U.S., Nat. Wildlife Fedn., People for the Ethical Treatment of Animals, Amnesty Internat., Phi Alpha Delta. Republican. Episcopalian. Home: 206 Taft Ave Cleveland TX 77327-4539

CAMPBELL, THOMAS DOUGLAS, lawyer, consultant; b. N.Y.C., Jan. 5, 1951; s. Edward Thomas and Dorothy Alice (Moore) C.; m. Mary Anne Campbell, Dec. 22, 1978; 1 child, Kristen Anne. BA, U. Del., 1972; JD, U. Pa., 1976. Bar: Del. 1977. Law clk. Law Offices Bayard Brill & Handleman, Wilmington, Del., 1974-77; Washington rep. Std. Oil Co. (Ind.), 1978-85; pres. Thomas D. Campbell and Assocs., Inc., 1985—; govt. affairs rep. Northeastern U.S., Std. Oil Co. Ind., 1977-78. Served with U.S. Army, 1968-69, Del. Air N.G., 1969-77. Mem. ABA, Del. Bar Assn., Congl. Awards Found. (chmn. bd. dirs.), Nat. Trust for Historic Preservation, Phi Beta Kappa, Phi Kappa Phi, Omicron Delta Epsilon, Omicron Delta Kappa. Republican. Episcopalian. Home: 517 Queen St Alexandria VA 22314-2512 Office: 113 S Alfred St Alexandria VA 22314-3001

CAMPBELL, TIMOTHY LEE, airport executive; b. Pittsburg, Kans., Jan. 16, 1947; m. Marilyn Johnson; children: Kristen, megan. BA in Urban and Regional Planning, U. Colo., M in Urban and Regional Planning. Accredited airport exec. Asst. to dir. aviation Mass. Port Authority, Boston, 1974-77; exec. dir. Patrick Henry Internat. Airport, Newport News, Va., 1977-80, Metro Knoxville Airport Authority, Knoxville, Tenn., 1980-84; dir. aviation Ft. Lauderdale/Hollywood Internat. Airport, Ft. Lauderdale, Fla., 1984-87; exec. v.p. Metro Nashville Airport Authority, 1987—. Mem. Am. Assn. airport Execs. (2d vice chmn. 1992-93, 1st vice chmn. 1993-94, chmn. 1994-95, past pres. S.E. chpt.), Tenn. Assn. Carrier Airports (pres. 9191-93), Airport Operators Coun. (past bd. dirs.). Office: Metro Nashville Airport 1 Terminal Dr Ste 501 Nashville TN 37214-4110

CAMPBELL, VALERIE LYNN, veterinarian; b. Buffalo, May 19, 1958; d. Joseph Richard and Thanya Thea (Loehner) C.; m. Donald Kenneth Nichols, June 2, 1984; 1 child, Geoffrey Campbell Nichols. BS in Biology, Mary Washington Coll., 1980; DVM, Va.-Md. Regional Coll. Vet. Medicine, 1984. Assoc. veterinarian Bowie (Md.) Animal Hosp., 1984-85, Prince Frederick (Md.) Animal Hosp., 1985-89; owner, veterinarian Blue Ridge Vet. Assocs., Purcellville, Va., 1989—. Mem. Am. Vet. Med. Assn. Home: RR 1 Box 122A Purcellville VA 22132-9507 Office: Blue Ridge Vet Assn 101 A Maple Ave PO Box 939 Purcellville VA 22132

CAMPBELL, WILLIAM BUFORD, JR., materials engineer, chemist, forensic consultant; b. Clarksdale, Miss., Nov. 23, 1935; s. William Buford and Bertha Lucille (Atkins) C.; m. Joan E. Stakem, June 29, 1963 (div. 1983); children: Lisa Anne, William Buford II, Heather Katherine, Matthew Rush (dec.). B in Ceramic Engring., Ga. Inst. Tech., 1958, MS in Engring., 1960; AM in Mineralogy, Inorganic Chemistry, Harvard U., 1962; PhD in Materials Engring., Ohio State U., 1967; postgrad., MIT, 1963-65, Ohio State U., 1969-72, NYU, 1980. Registered profl. engr., Ga., Ala. Asst. prof. dept. ceramic engring. Ohio State U., Columbus, 1967-69, assoc. prof., 1969-74; chief biomed. engring. dept. Doctor's Hosp., Morristown, Tenn., 1974-76; assoc. prof. engring. sci. and mechanics U. Tenn., Knoxville, 1974-77; sr. ptnr. Campbell, Churchill, Zimmerman & Assocs., Cons., Knoxville, 1977-84; cons., pvt. practice Biomed. Engring. and Forensic Sci., Knoxville, 1984—; ptnr. Brae Arden Farms Ltd., Phila., Tenn., 1979-83, tech. dir., chief exec. officer Southeastern Mobility Co., Inc., Phila., Tenn., 1977-84; founder Biomed. Systems Inc., Knoxville, 1986; project engr. TVA, 1987-89; dir. EPRI Ctr. for Materials Fabrication, Battelle Meml. Inst., Columbus, Ohio, 1989-90, dir., program mgr. Innovation and Tech. Transfer, Battelle Meml. Inst., Columbus, 1990; mng. ptnr. Performance Cons., 1991—. Patentee: Holds 3 U.S. Patents; contbr. articles to profl. jours. Mem. Adminstrv. Bd. Bearden United Meth. Ch., 1982-85; chmn. exec. com. The Ch. of the Redeemer, Concord, Tenn., 1985-87; mem. fin. com. Americans for Responsible Govt, 1984-85, fin. com. 50th Am. Presidential Inaugural, 1984-85, Nat. Adv. Bd. on Tech. and the Disabled; trustee Lakeshore Mental Health Insts., Dept. Mental Health, State of Tenn., 1986—; bd. dirs. Vols. of Am., Knoxville, 1987-90; adv. bd. Knoxville Mus. Art, 1987-88; mem. Tenn. Sci. and Tech. Adv. Coun., State Tenn., 1993—. Capt. Tenn. Def. Force. Recipient Cert. Recognition, NASA, 1973, Freeman award Am. Coun. for the Blind, 1976. Fellow Am. Inst. Chemists (cert. chemist), Am. Acad. Forensic Sci., Am. Ceramic Soc. (abstracter and reviewer 1962—, nat. programs and meetings com. 1968-72, div. chmn. 1969-70, other offices, life mem.); mem. ASTM (liaison mem. for ceramics and med., surg. materials and devices 1975—), Nat. Soc. Profl. Engrs., Am. Soc. for Engring. Edn., Am. Soc. for Nondestructive Testing, Nat. Inst. Ceramic Engrs. (life), Phi Lambda Upsilon, Tau Beta Pi (Eminent Engr. 1974), Sigma Xi (rsch. awards 1958, 60, 71), KERAMOS, others. Republican. Office: Performance Cons PO Box 51825 Knoxville TN 37950-1825

CAMPELLO, VALERIA VANDELLI, fashion designer and importer, publisher; b. Carpi, Italy, Sept. 19, 1950; d. Vilmos and Franca (Orlandi) Vandelli; m. Ugo Riccardo Campello, Sept. 11, 1976; children: Silvia, Guido Enrico, Stefano Vilmos. Dottore in Legge, U. Modena, Italy, 1977. Tchr. Istituto Tecnico Commerciale, Prodenone, Italy, 1978-79; fashion designer, importer Cosabella, Miami, Fla., 1983—; pub. Casa & Estilo Internacional, Miami, 1994—. Promoter opera concerts to Italy, New World Sch. of the Arts, 1995. Vol., sponsor Miami City Ballet, 1994-95; bd. dirs. Miami Ballet, 1995; mem. adv. bd. Cinema Italiano Oggi, Miami, 1993-95. Office: Cosabella 12186 SW 128th St Miami FL 33186-5230

CAMPOLETTANO, THOMAS ALFRED, financial analyst; b. Long Island City, N.Y., Feb. 13, 1946; s. Barney and Mary (Felner) C.; m. Kathy Lee Clemons, Mar. 19, 1989; 1 stepchild, Christopher; children by previous marriage: Lisa, Jennifer, Tricia. AAS, Nassau Coll., 1971; BA, U. South Fla., 1977; postgrad., Am. Grad. U., 1980-85, Touro Coll., 1980-85. Cert. profl. contract mgr. Cost/price analyst Grumman Aero. Corp., Bethpage, N.Y., 1963-70; sr. cost/price analyst Potter Instrument Co., Plainview, N.Y., 1970-73; prin. fin. analyst, govt. liaison Space Systems div. Honeywell, Inc., Clearwater, Fla., 1973—; prof. Honeywell Fed. Contracting Tng. program (recipient 1992 Honeywell Fin. Achievement award). Author: Profit Proposal Initiatives, 1990; co-author: Weighted Guidelines Profit, 1984. With USN, 1963-66, Vietnam. Recipient Apollo Space Program commendation, NASA, 1969. Mem. Nat. Contract Mgmt. Assn., Fin. Exec. Inst. (mem. com. on govt. bus. 1985), U.S. Track & Field, Road Runners Club Am. Republican. Roman Catholic. Home: 8412 Parkwood Blvd Seminole FL 33777-2710 Office: Honeywell Inc 13350 Us Highway 19 N Clearwater FL 34624-7226

CANADY, CHARLES T., congressman, lawyer; b. Lakeland, Fla., June 22, 1954. BA, Haverford Coll., 1976; JD, Yale U., 1979. Mem. 44th dis. Fla. Ho. of Reps., 1984-90; majority whip Fla. Ho. of Reps, 1986-88, mem. Marketable Record Title Act Study Commn., 1985-86; mem. 103d-104th Congress 12th Fla. dist., 1992; mem. counsel Ctrl. Fla. Regional Coun., 1983-84. V.p. United Cerebral Palsy, Polk County, 1982-83; bd. dirs. Big Brothers & Big Sisters, 1984-85. Recipient Allen Morris award Fla. Ho. of Reps., 1986, Legislator of the Yr. Fla. Assn. Realtors, 1986, Spec Leadership award Save Our Home and Lands, 1986; named Most Valuable Legislator in Growth Mgmt. Fla. Regional Coun. Assn. Mem. ABA, Lakeland Bar Assn., Lakeland C. of C., Winter Haven C. of C. Republican. Presbyterian. Office: US Ho Reps 1222 Longworth Washington DC 20515

CANALES, LUIS I., gastroenterologist; b. Detroit, Nov. 2, 1958. BA, U. Tex., 1980; MD, U. Tex., Galveston, 1984. Diplomate Am. Bd. Internal Medicine, subspecialty gastroenterology. Intern internal medicine William Beaumont Army Med. Ctr., El Paso, Tex., 1984-85; resident internal medicine William Beaumont Army Med. Ctr., El Paso, 1985-87; fellow gastroenterology Brooke Army Med.Ctr., San Antonio, 1989-91; staff internal medicine Darnall Army Med. Ctr., 1987-89, blood and tissue com., 1988-89; staff gastroenterologist Landsthul Army Med. Ctr., 1991-93; staff gastroenterologist, internist Med. Ctr. Baton Rouge, La., 1993-94; staff gastroenterologist Ocshner Clinic Baton Rouge, 1993-94, Diagnostic Clinic Houston, 1994—. Contbr. articles to profl. jours. Home: 4900 Braeburn Dr Bellaire TX 77401-5316

CANARY, NANCY HALLIDAY, lawyer; b. Cleve., Apr. 21, 1941; d. Robert Fraser and Nanna (Hall) Halliday; m. Sumner Canary, Dec. 1975 (dec. Jan. 1979). BA, Case Western Res. U., 1963; JD, Cleve. State U., 1968. Bar: Ohio 1968, Fla. 1972, U.S. Dist. Ct. (no. dist.) Ohio 1975, U.S. Supreme Ct. 1974. Law clk. to presiding judge Ohio Ct. Appeals, Cleve., 1968-69; ptnr. McDonald, Hopkins & Hardy, Cleve., 1969-83, Thompson, Hine and Flory, Cleve., 1984—. Trustee Beck Ctr. for Cultural Arts, Lakewood, Ohio, 1980-90, Ohio Motorists Assn., 1989—, Ohio Chamber Orch.; trustee, mem. devel. adv. com. Fairview Gen. Hosp., Cleve., 1980—; chairperson Sumner Canary Lectureship com. Case Western Res. U. Law Sch.; bd. dirs. Comerica Bank & Trust Co., F.S.B., 1993—. Mem. Ohio State Bar Assn., Cleve. Bar Assn., Palm Beach County Bar Assn., Estate Planning Coun. Cleve., Estate Planning Coun. Palm Beach County, Gulf Stream (Fla.) Golf Club, Westwood Country Club (Cleve.). Republican. Home: 12500 Edgewater Dr Cleveland OH 44107-1677 also: 200 N Ocean Blvd Delray Beach FL 33483-7126 Office: Thompson Hine and Flory 1100 Nat City Bank Bldg 629 Euclid Ave Cleveland OH 44114-3003

CANCALOSI, MARK FRANCIS, pharmacist; b. Scranton, Pa., Dec. 13, 1954; s. Joseph James and Dorothy Theresa (Calleo) C. BS in Pharmacy, Arnold and Marie Schwartz Coll. Pharmacy, Bklyn., 1978, MS in Biomed. Communications, 1986. Registered pharmacist, N.J., Fla. Pharmacist Hosp. Pharmacy, Paterson, N.J., 1980, Singac Pharmacy & Surg., Little Falls, N.J., 1980-81, Bergen Pharmacy, Englewood, N.J., 1984-86, Gateway Discount Drugs, Boynton Beach, Fla., 1986; staff pharmacist Englewood (Fla.) Hosp., 1980, 86, Holy Name Hosp., Teaneck, N.J., 1981-86; dir. pharmacy HCA Univ. Pavilion Hosp., Tamarac, Fla., 1988-93; sr. staff pharmacist West Boca Med. Ctr., Boca Raton, Fla., 1987-88, pharmacy supr., 1993-95, pharmacy dir., 1995—. Mem. Am. Pharm. Assn., Am. Soc. Hosp. Pharmacists, Fla. Soc. Hosp. Pharmacists, Palm Beach Soc. Hosp. Pharmacists (pres. 1989-90), N.J. Soc. Hosp. Pharmacists (sec. North chpt. 1983-86), Boca Raton Hist. Soc., Met. Mus. Art, KC, Rho Chi. Republican. Roman Catholic. Home: 10262 Islander Dr Boca Raton FL 33498-6306 Office: West Boca Med Ctr 21644 State Road 7 Boca Raton FL 33428-1842

CANCER, CATHY LYNN, elementary education educator; b. Vidalia, Ga., July 10, 1963; d. Jessie and Hattie Lee Hunt; m. Anthony Gerald Cancer, June 8, 1990; 1 child, Hunter Tyrez. BBA, Savannah State Coll., 1987; Tchg. Cert., Ga. So. U., 1989, MEd in Sch. Nursing, 1996. Elem. tchr. Toombs County Bd. Edn., Lyons, Ga., 1989—; bus. cons. H&K Package Store, Lyons, 1989—. Fellow ASCD, GSCA. Home: 117 Cascade Dr Lyons GA 30436-1634

CANCINO, ENRIQUE ALBERTO, management consulting company executive; b. Santiago, Chile, Jan. 18, 1947; came to U.S., 1966; s. Domingo Enrique and Graciela Elena (Chüden) C.; m. Mary Lamar Gutierrez, May 29, 1971; children: Aracely, Richard, Gabriel, Sebastian. BS in Indsl. Engring., St. Mary's U., San Antonio, 1971. Mgr. indsl. tng. Compañia de Acero del Pacifico, Concepcion, Chile, 1972-76; mgr. mfg. tng. Coca-Cola Foods, Houston, 1976-80; sr. tng. cons. Fluor Engrs., Houston, 1980-82; quality program coord., cons. Atlantic-Richfield Corp., L.A., 1982-85; mfg. tng. mgr. Frito-Lay, Inc., Plano, Tex., 1985-87; tng. supt. Cape Horn Methanol, Ltd., Punta Arenas, Chile, 1987-89; pres., COO Directions Internat., Plano, 1989—; pres., CEO Graphic Direction, Inc., Plano, 1991—. Mem. Orgn. Devel. Network. Roman Catholic. Office: Directions Internat Inc 2329 Coit Rd Ste B Plano TX 75075-3796

CANFIELD, CONSTANCE DALE, accountant, nurse; b. Fairmont, W.Va., May 2, 1940; d. Robert Alman and Dorothy Jane (Motter) C. RN, Fairmont Gen. Hosp., 1961; Flight Nurse Diploma, Sch. Aerospace Med., 1967; BS in Acctg., Rollins Coll., Winter Park, Fla., 1979; student, Stetson U., 1975-76, Fla. Inst. Tech., 1976-77; grad., Army Comd. Gen. Staff Coll., Ft. Levenworth Kans., 1991. RN, Fla. Prin. C. D. Canfield, Acct., Melbourne, Fla., 1979-90; acct. C.D. Canfield, Acct., Melbourne, Fla., 1991—. Gov.'s appointee Women in Mil. for Am. Meml. Found., Washington, 1991; gov.'s escort Fla. Freedom Festival, Inc., Tallahassee, 1991; state coord. VietNam Women's Meml. Project, Inc., Washington, 1986—; bd. dirs. Space Coast Philharmonic Orch., Cocoa, Fla., 1989—; adminstrv. bd. United Meth. Ch., Melbourne, 1987—; musician Melbourne Mcpl. Band, 1980-90, Space Coast Philharmonic Orch., 1986-87; vol. attendant Harbor City Ambulance Squad., 1991. With USAF, 1963-70, U.S. Army, 1970-75, maj. USAR, N.G., 1989—. Decorated Air Force Commendation medal, VietNam Campaign Medal with four bronze stars, Vietnam Service Medal, Vietnam Medal of Honor 1st class, Cross Gallantry. Mem. AACN, Nat. Soc. Tax Profls., Nat. Soc. Pub. Accts., Fla. Assn. Ind. Accts. (sec. space coast chpt. 1992-93), Internat. Biog. Assn. (life), VFW (life), Vietnam Vets. of Brevard, Inc. (life), Emergency Rm. Nurses Assn., N.G. Officers Assn., Fla. Hist. Soc., U.S. C. of C., Fla. Home Builders Assn., Internat. Lions Club, Soc. Brevard Profl. Womens Network. Republican. Methodist. Office: CD Canfield Acct 834 Sarno Rd Melbourne FL 32935-5028

CANFIELD, GLENN, JR., metallurgical engineer; b. Springfield, Ill., Sept. 20, 1935; s. Glenn Sr. and Ruth (Kestel) C.; m. Beverly Joyce Brown, June 18, 1955 (div. 1981); children: Cheryl Lee, Charisse Marie, Glenn III (dec.), Derek Ethan; m. Virginia Nell Davis, June 28, 1982. Assoc. in Sci., Springfield Jr. Coll., 1957; BS in Metall. Engring., U. Ill., 1959; MBA, U. Tex., Tyler, 1987. Registered profl. engr., Tex. Sr. mfg. engr. Westinghouse Electric Co., Cheswick, Pa., 1961-63; supr. quality control Latrobe (Pa.) Steel Co., 1963-69; mgr. spl. products Crucible Specialty Metals, Syracuse, N.Y., 1969-73; mgr. product constrn. Lone Star (Tex.) Steel, 1974-76, supt. melting, 1976-86; pres. Thermo-Tech Co., Longview, Tex., 1986—; mng. dir. The Plum Group, Longview, 1986—; pres. Canfield & Assocs., Longview, 1986—; chmn. Canfield Engring. Inc., Longview, 1987—; bd. dirs. Dickson, Inc., Longview. Editor: The Americanist Newsletter, 1962-66, The Plum Index of Steel, 1986—; pub.: (newspaper) The Plum Crier, 1961-64, the Melt Shop Messenger; author tech. papers on deoxidation. Chmn. Plum Twp. (Pa.) Rep. Com., 1962-65; chmn. Gregg County Rep. Com., 1991—, chmn. ballot security, 1988; sec. Am. Party, N.Y., 1968-72; chmn. Tax Reform Immediately Com., Longview, 1980-84. With USN, 1952-56, Korea. Recipient Thomas Jefferson award Constl. Party Pa., 1966, Senatorial Medal of Freedom, 1994. Mem. NSPE, Am. Soc. for Engring. Mgmt., Am. Computer Mgrs. Assn., Am. Soc. for Metals, Am. Inst. Metall. Engrs. (Silver award 1980). Baptist. Home: 303 Ramblewood Pl Longview TX 75605-3352 Office: Canfield Cos PO Box 9955 Longview TX 75608-9955

CANIPE, STEPHEN LEE, educational administrator; b. Lincolnton, N.C., Jan. 9, 1946; s. Clayton Lee and Edna Jeanette (Farmer) C.; BS in Biology cum laude, Appalachian State U., 1968; MS in Biology (NSF fellow), Mich. State U., 1973; EdD in Ednl. Adminstrn., Duke U., 1982; m. Sharon Wilbourne, Apr. 1, 1972; children: Martha Murray, David Jacob. Lab. asst. USPHS, Savannah, Ga., 1968-69; tchr. high sch. biology Charlotte, N.C., 1969-76, asst. prin., 1976-77; N.C. sci. cons., Raleigh, 1977-78; supr. ednl. svcs. Duke Power Co., Charlotte, N.C., 1978-79, dir. employee communications, 1979-81, dir. adminstrn. and devel., 1981-83; prin. West Lincoln Sr. High Sch., Lincolnton, N.C., 1983-86, prin. Lincoln County Sch. of Tech., 1987-93; dir. media and tech. Mooresville (N.C.) Sch. Dist., 1993-94; prin. J.M. Alexander Mid. Sch., Charlotte-Mecklenburg Sch. Dist., 1994—; instr. Cen. Piedmont Community Coll., 1976-78; adj. prof. Gaston Coll., 1984—; cons. Project ALIVE, 1979-81; instr., prin. exec. program U. N.C., Chapel Hill, 1991—; apptd. gov.'s Adv. Coun. for Tech. and Vocat. Edn., 1991—, Gov.'s permanent com. on Work Force Preparedness, 1992—; state chmn. Telecommunications Users Networked for Edn., 1991; pres. Lakeshore Cons. Charter mem. Metrolina Environ. Concern Assn., 1970-77; mem. mayor's energy adv. com., 1979. Mem. NEA, ASCD, N.C. Alliance Sci. and Math. (tchr. edn. adv. com. 1992), Nat. Vocat. Assn., Rotary, Civitan, Phi Delta Kappa, Kappa Delta Pi, Beta Beta Beta. Episcopalian. Author: Valuing the Environment, 1975, High School Animal Behavior, 1977, School Retrofit Analysis System, 1983. Home: 3916 Fox Run Denver NC 28037-9168 Office: 12201 Hambright Rd Huntersville NC 28078-7670

CANN, SHARON LEE, health science librarian; b. Ft. Riley, Kans., Aug. 14, 1935; d. Roman S. and Cora Elon (George) Foote; m. Donald Clair Cann, May 16, 1964. Student Sophia U., Tokyo, 1955-57; BA, Calif. State U., Sacramento, 1959; MSLS, Atlanta U., 1977; EdD, U. Ga., 1995. Cert. health scis. libr. Recreation worker ARC, Korea, Morocco, France, 1960-64; shelflister Libr. Congress Washington, 1967-69; tchr. Lang. Ctr., Taipei, Taiwan, 1971-73; libr. tech. asst. Emory U., Atlanta, 1974-76; health sci. libr. Northside Hosp., Atlanta, 1977-85; libr. cons., 1985-86; libr. area health edn. ctr., learning resource ctr. Morehouse Sch. Medicine, 1985-86; edn. libr. Ga. State U., 1986-93; head libr. Ga. Bapt. Coll. Nursing, 1993—. Editor Update, publ. Ga. Health Scis. Libr. Assn., 1981; contbr. articles to publs. Chmn. Calif. Christian Youth in Govt Seminar, 1958. Named Alumni Top Twenty Calif. State U.Sacramento, 1959. Mem. ALA, AAUW, Med. Libr. Assn., Spl. Libr. Assn. (dir. South Atlantic chpt. 1985-87), Ga. Libr. Assn. (spl. libr. divsn. chmn. 1983-85), Ga. Health Scis. Libr. Assn. (chmn. 1981-82), Atlanta Health Sci. Libr. (chmn. 1979, 95), Am. Numis. Assn., ARC Overseas Assn. Home: 5520 Morning Creek Cir Atlanta GA 30349-3538

CANNELLA, DEBORAH FABBRI, elementary school educator; b. Statesville, N.C., Sept. 7, 1949; d. Raymond Joseph and Sylvia (Sides) Fabbri; m. S.J. Garciga, Apr. 16, 1970 (div. 1990); children: Jennifer, Melissa, Bryan; m. Frank Cannella, July 1, 1994. Student, U. So. Fla., 1970, 91—; Presch. Edn. degree, Montessori Inst. Am., 1984; BS in acctg., U. So. Fla., 1995. Cert. Montessori Presch. Edn., Kansas City, Mo. Tchr. presch. Montessori Acad. of Temple Terr., Fla., 1982-87; tchr. 1st grade St. John's Parish Day Sch., Tampa, Fla., 1987—. Facilitator Bay Area Assn. Ind. Schs. Profl. Day, 1990, mem. program com., 1990-92; bd. dirs. Tampa Prep. Parent's, grad. reception, 1987-88. Mem. Assn. for Childhood Edn., Tampa Mus. of Art, Tampa Bay Performing Arts Ctr., Mus. Sci. and Tech. Episcopalian. Office: St John's Parish Day Sch 906 S Orleans Ave Tampa FL 33606-2941

CANNELLA, KATHLEEN ANN SILVA, nursing educator, researcher; b. Durham, N.C., Apr. 1, 1949; d. Joseph Andrew Silva and Lurene (Chapman) Brinser; m. Sam Chris Cannella, May 1, 1971; 1 child, Elizabeth Karen. Diploma, Md. Gen. Hosp. Sch. Nursing, 1970; BS cum laude, Ga. State U., 1974; MN, Emory U., 1975; MS in Community Counseling, PhD, Ga. State U., 1987. Instr. Piedmont Hosp. Sch. Nursing, Atlanta, 1976-83, Ga. Bapt. Hosp. Sch. Nursing, Atlanta, 1983-85; clin. examiner, cons. So. Performance Assessment Ctr., Univ. State N.Y., 1989—; rsch. health scientist, rehab. rsch. and devel. unit VA Med. Ctr., Decatur, Ga., 1990-91; assoc. prof. North Ga. Coll., Dahlonega, Ga., 1988-91; assoc. prof. Nell Hodgson Sch. Nursing Emory U., 1992-94, postdoct. fellow pulmonary and critical care medicine Sch. Medicine, 1996—; nurse rschr. Vets. Affairs Med. Ctr., Decatur, Ga., 1992-94, clin. specialist pulmonary and critical care medicine, 1994-96, nurse rschr., 1996—; postdoctoral fellow pulmonary and critical care medicine Emory U. Sch. Medicine, Atlanta, 1996—. Contbr. articles to profl. jours. Grantee in field. Mem. ANA, So. Nursing Rsch. Soc., Am. Ednl. Rsch. Assn., Ga. Ednl. Rsch. Assn., Soc. Urologic Nurses & Assocs., Am. Heart Assn., Ga. Heart Assn., Sigma Theta Tau (Alpha Epsilon and Epsilon Alpha chpts.). Home: 2016 Fisher Trl NE Atlanta GA 30345-3429

CANNON, DANNIE PARKER, special education educator; b. Knoxville, Tenn., Sept. 19, 1951; d. Tommie Isaac and Mary (Halliburton) Parker; m. Robert Kyle Cannon Sr., Aug. 2, 1975; children: Thomas Parker, Jonathan Ray, Robert Kyle Jr., Dan Cameron. BS in Edn., U. Tenn., 1973, MS, 1975. Cert. tchr. emotionally disburbed, neurologically impaired, learning and behavior disorders. Tchr. 2d and 3d grade Farragut Primary, Knoxville, 1973-75; elem. resource tchr. Brown Sch., Louisville, 1975; spl. edn. resource tchr. Waggener High Sch., Louisville, 1975-95; tchr. 2nd and 3d grades St. Matthews Elem. Sch., Louisville, 1995—; tchr. exptl. program U. Tenn., Knoxville, 1972-73; project tchr. CAEVEP-CSDC Project, Louisville, 1977-78. Sunday sch. tchr. Hurstbourne Bapt. Ch., Louisville, 1984-86, Pleasant Grove Bapt. Ch., Louisville, 1987-90. Fellow NEA, Parents Tchrs. Students Assn., Ky. Edn. Assn., Jefferson County Tchrs. Assn. Republican. Baptist. Home: 10611 Kinross Ct Louisville KY 40243-1760 Office: St Matthews Elem Sch 601 Browns Ln Louisville KY 40207-4043

CANNON, DOUGLAS ROBERT, investment executive, federal government appointee; b. Apr. 17, 1954; s. Robert A. and Lola M. Cannon; m. Ursula Swiatkowski, May 4, 1991. BS, U. Pa., 1975; MBA, Harvard U., 1982. CFA. Investment analyst Rauscher Pierce Refsnes, Inc., Dallas, 1976-80; policy analyst OMB, Exec. Office of the Pres., Washington, 1983-85; staff mem. The White House Working Group on Privatization, Washington, 1984-85; leveraged buyout advisor T.F. Industries, Inc., Washington, 1985-86; sr. staff mem. White House Office Policy Devel., Washington, 1987-88; staff mem. Office of the Pres.-Elect, Washington, 1988-89; dep. exec. dir. Pension Benefit Guaranty Corp., Washington, 1989-91, Cannon Investment Svcs., 1991-94; sr. cons. SEI Corp., 1994-95; mng. dir. Benefit Capital Inc., 1995-96; sr. investment analyst Venswold, King and Assocs., Houston, 1996—. Mem. fin. com. Tower for Senate, Tex., 1978, Dallas County steering com. Reagan/Bush Campaign, 1980, Gramm 96 Com., Tex., 1991—. Mem. Reagan Alumni Assn., Harvard Bus. Sch. Club (v.p. Washington chpt. 1985-87, 91-92). Methodist. Office: 1980 Post Oak Blvd Ste 2400 Houston TX 77056-3898

CANNON, HUGH, lawyer; b. Albemarle, N.C., Oct. 11, 1931; s. Hubert Napoleon and Nettie (Harris) C.; A.B., Davidson Coll., 1953; B.A. (Rhodes scholar) Oxford U., 1955, M.A., 1960; LL.B., Harvard U., 1958; children: John Stuart, Marshall, Martha Janet. Bar: N.C., 1958, D.C., 1978, S.C., 1979; mem. staff U. N.C. Inst. Govt., Chapel Hill, 1959; mem. firm Sanford, Phillips, McCoy & Weaver, Fayetteville, 1960; asst. to Gov. of N.C., Raleigh, 1961; dir. adminstrn. State of N.C., 1962-65, state budget officer, 1963; mem. and mng. ptnr. law firm Sanford, Cannon, Adams & McCullough, Raleigh, 1965-79; individual practice law, Charleston, S.C., 1979—; mem. Everett, Gaskins, Hancock and Stevens attys., Raleigh, 1990—; v.p. fin. Palmetto Ford, Inc., Charleston, 1979—. Parliamentarian NEA, 1965—; pres. Friends of Coll., Raleigh, 1963; alt. del. Democratic Nat. Conv., 1964; chief parliamentarian, 1976, 80, 84, 88, 92, 96; bd. govs. U. N.C., 1972-81; trustee Davidson Coll., 1966-74, N.C. Sch. Arts, 1963-72. Author: Cannon's Concise Guide to Rules of Order, 1992. Mem. Phi Beta Kappa, Omicron Delta Kappa, Phi Gamma Delta. Democrat. Episcopalian. Home: PO Box 31820 Charleston SC 29417-1820 Office: 1625 Savannah Hwy Charleston SC 29407-2236

CANNON, ISABELLA WALTON, mayor; b. Dunfermline, Scotland, May 12, 1904; came to U.S., 1916; d. James and Helen Bett (Seaman) Walton; m. Claude M. Cannon. BA, Elon Coll., 1924, LLD (hon.), 1978. Tchr. pub. schs.; head dept. stats. French Purchase Commn., Washington; fin. officer UN, Washington; with N.C. State U. Library; mayor of Raleigh, N.C., 1977-79. V.p. Women in Bus. Adv. Council, N.C. Conservation Council, Women's Polit. Caucus; charter mem. Wake County Dem. Women; organizer, pres. Univ. Park Assn., Raleigh; civic sponsor, mem. bldg. com. Raleigh Little Theatre; mem. Univ. Neighborhood Planning Council, N.C. Child Advocacy, N.C. Commn. Bicentennial of U.S.; bd. dirs. Mordecai Sq. Hist. Soc.; chmn. Wade CAC; mem. devel. bd. YWCA Acad. of Women; chairperson Keep Am. Clean Sweep; bd. dirs. Raleigh Symphony Orch.; mem. Women's Forum of N.C.; mem. Coll. Presdl. Electors, Centennial Com.; bd. dirs., historian St. Luke's Home, Raleigh liaison RSVP bd., Raleigh Bicentennial Task Force 1988-92, Martin Luther King Jr. Celebration Com., 1989-92; precinct chair numerous polit. orgns. Recipient. Disting. Alumnus award Elon Coll., 1983, Medallion award, 1991, Isabella Cannon Rm. named in her honor Elon Coll., 1987, Isabella Cannon Leadership Fellows Program established in 1991, Lifetime Achievement award Theatre in the Park, Govt. award YWCA Acad. Women, 1988, Role Model Leader award N.C. State U., 1991, Mentor of Distinction award Women Bus. Adv. Coun., 1994; Isabella Cannon Arboretum Intership established in her honor N.C. State U., 1991. Mem. N.C. Sr. Citizens Assn. (pres.), Elon Coll. Alumni Assn., Delta Kappa Gamma. Mem. United Ch. of Christ.

CANNON, MAJOR TOM, special education educator; b. Anniston, Ala., Nov. 11, 1932; s. Thomas Albert and Sallie Mae (James) C. BA in Religion, Samford U., 1961; postgrad., So. Bapt. Theol. Sem., 1961-62, Tulane U., 1962-63, Auburn U., 1963-64; MEd in Counseling, U. Ga., 1968; postgrad., S.C. State Coll., 1979-80, 80-81. Cert. prin., guidance counselor, spl. edn. tchr., S.C. English tchr. North Whitfield H.S., Dalton, Ga., 1964-65, Savannah (Ga.) H.S., 1965-66; guidance counselor Savannah Pub. Schs., 1966-79; dir. spl. svcs. Marlboro County Sch. Dist., Bennettsville, S.C., 1979-80, coord. programs for handicapped, 1980-81; tchr. trainable mentally retarded Edisto Mid. Sch., Orangeburg, S.C., 1981-86; tchr. learning disabled Norman C. Toole Mid. Sch., Charleston, S.C., 1986-88; tchr. learning disabled Berkeley Mid. Sch., Moncks Corner, S.C., 1988—, chmn. dept. spl. edn., 1991-94; specialist learning disabilities Berkeley County Sch. Dist., Moncks Corner, 1995—; labor resources technician City of Savannah, 1979; presenter in field; mem. Strategic Planning Com. for Berkeley County Sch. Dist. Sch. Improvement Coun., 1993-96. Contbr. poetry to Great Poems of the Western World, 1990, Our World's Favorite Gold and Silver Poems, 1991, Perceptions, 1994, Am. Poetry Annual, 1994; author resource manuals and videotaped lessons. Charter Rep. Nat. Com., 1992—, Rep. Presdl. Task Force, 1989—, Rep. Nat. Commn. on Am. Agenda, 1996, Nat. Rep. Senatorial Com., 1996; at-large del. Rep. Party Platform Planning Com.; mem. Ga. Com. on Children and Youth, 1968. With USN, 1953-57. Recipient Nat. Def. Edn. award U.S. Office of Edn., 1966-67, GE Found. award, 1971, Rep. Presdl. Legion of Merit, 1992-96, Rep. Presdl. award, 1994, Rep. Presdl. Order of Merit, 1996. Mem. Nat. Authors Registry, Coun. for Exceptional Children, Am. Personnel and Guidance Assn., Am. Sch. Counselors Assn. (Ga. coord.), Nat. Edn. Assn., Nat. Assn. Sch. Counselors., Am. Legion, Ga. Assn. Educators, Ga. Personnel and Guidance Assn., Sierra Club, Nature Conservancy, Nat. Resources Def. Coun., World Wildlife Soc., Phi Delta Kappa, Kappa Delta Pi. Republican. Baptist. Home: 324 Tulane Dr Ladson SC 29456-6235

CANNON, ROBERT EUGENE, librarian, public administrator, fund raiser; b. Elkhorn, Wis., Dec. 20, 1945; s. Wendell Eugene and Louise Marie (Bredehoeft) C.; m. Miriam Ruth Hillson, May 25, 1974; 1 child, Allison. BA in Music, Calif. State U., L.A., 1967; postgrad. Ariz. State U., 1967-68; MLS, U. So. Calif., 1970; M in Pub. Adminstrn., San Diego State U., 1978. Adult svcs. libr. Tucson Pub. Libr., 1969-70, Altadena Libr. Dist., 1970-71; head tech. processing, regional coord. San Diego County Libr., 1971-76; asst. dir. Tulare County Libr., Visalia, Calif., 1976-78; dir. Kern County Libr., Bakersfield, Calif., 1978-86; exec. dir. Pub. Libr. of Charlotte and MacKlenburg County, N.C., 1986—; mem. bd. dirs. Mecklenburg County Law and Govt. Libr., Inc.; sec.-treas. Pub. Lib. Charlotte and Mecklenburg County, 1986—; sec. Mus. New South, 1991-93, bd. dirs., 1991—; former mem. Leadership Charlotte; founder Novello Festival of Reading, 1991—,

ProSearch Info. Svc., 1991-96; founder Internat. Bus. Libr., 1994—, Virtual Libr., 1995—; co-founder Charlotte's Web, 1995—; bd. visitors Sch. Info. and Libr. Sci. U. N.C., Chapel Hill; steering com. Charlotte Alliance Info. Referral Svcs. Named N.C. Libr. Dir. of Yr. N.C. Pub. Libr. Dirs. Assn., 1995. Mem. Am. Libr. Assn., N.C. Libr. Assn., Charlotte/Mecklenburg Coalition for Literacy, 1988-89, Kern County Hist. Records Commn. (vice chmn. 1978-86), Nat. Soc. Fund Raising Execs., Southeastern Libr. Assn. (treas., chmn. conf. com. 1993-95), Mecklenburg Hist. Assn. Office: Pub Libr Charlotte & Mecklenburg County 310 N Tryon St Charlotte NC 28202-2139

CANO, MARIO STEPHEN, lawyer; b. Miami, Fla., Sept. 2, 1953; s. Mario Arturo Cano and Irene H. Moreno; m. Johanna Marie Van Rossum, Oct. 13, 1979. AA, Miami Dade Jr. Coll., 1973; BA, Fla. Internat. U., 1975; JD, U. Santa Clara, 1978. Bar: Fla. 1979, U.S. Dist. Ct. (so. dist.) Fla. 1979, U.S. Ct. Claims 1979, U.S. Tax Ct. 1979, U.S. Ct. Mil. Appeals 1979, U.S. Ct. Appeals (9th cir.) 1979, U.S. Dist. Ct. (no. and mid. dists.) Fla. 1980, U.S. Dist. Ct (no. dist.) Calif. 1980, U.S. Ct. Appeals (3d cir.) 1980, U.S. Ct. Internat. Trade 1981, U.S. Ct. Appeals (11th cir.) 1981, U.S. Ct. Appeals (6th and 10th cirs.) 1983, U.S. Supreme Ct. 1983, Nebr. 1984, U.S. Dist. Ct. Nebr. 1984, U.S. Dist. Ct. (no. dist.) Okla. 1984, U.S. Dist. Ct. Hawaii 1984, U.S. Ct. Appeals (2d, 4th, 5th, 7th 8th and D.C. cirs.) 1984, N.Y. 1985, U.S. Dist. Ct (no., we., ea. and so. dists.) N.Y. 1985, U.S. Ct. Appeals (1st cir.) 1987, U.S. Dist. Ct. (no. and so. dist.) Tex. 1988, U.S. Dist. Ct. (ea. dist.) Wis. 1988, U.S. Dist. Ct. (we. dist.) Pa. 1988, U.S. Dist. Ct. (no. dist.) Ill. 1991. Assoc. Orta and Assocs., Miami, 1979-80, Law Office of J. Ramirez, Coral Gables, Fla., 1980, Law Office of I.G. Lichter, Miami, 1980-82, Gelb & Spatz, Miami, 1982; pvt. practice, Coral Gables, 1982—. Mem. ABA, Coral Gables Bar Assn., Cuban Am. Bar Assn., InterAm. Bar Assn., Nat. Assn. Criminal Def. Lawyers, Alliance Francaise de Miami, Friends of the Netherlands Assn., Holland-Fla. C. of C., Brit. Fla. C. of C. Democrat. Office: 2121 Ponce De Leon Blvd Miami FL 33134-5224

CANO, MARTA MENDENDEZ, securities company executive, financial consultant; b. Havana, Cuba, July 29, 1941; came to U.S., 1961; d. Jose F. and Maria C. (Llanio) Menendez; m. Peter J. Cano, Nov. 30, 1960 (div. Jan. 1982); children: Marta, Eileen, Marianne, Peter, Andres. BA in English cum laude, U. Havana, 1961; MEd, U. P.R., 1970. Lic. securities profl., mgmt., life and health ins., notary pub. Dir. ESOL program Colegio Rosa-Bel, Bayamon, P.R., 1966-75; v.p. import/export Distribuidora Delmar, Inc., Bayamon, 1975-79; advanced sales specialist Sun Life of Can., Morristown, N.J., 1980-87; sr. fin. cons. Smith Barney, West Palm Beach, Fla., 1987-94; v.p. investments Prudential Securities, Inc., North Palm Beach, Fla., 1995—; speaker in field. Founder Hispanic Coalition, Palm Beach County; nominated bd. dirs. Pal, Beach County, 1994; participant Directions 94, 1994; bd. commrs. Palm Beach County Health Care Spl. Taxing Dist., 1993—, Housing Authorities, City of West Palm Beach, 1994—; bd. dirs. Citizens Adv. for Health and Human Svcs., Palm Beach County, 1993—, Palm Beach County Budget Task Force, 1991—; mem. St. Ignatius Cathedral Parish coun., 1989-91; mem. Healthy Start Coalition, 1991—, others. Mem. Internat. Businessmean's Assn. (v.p. 1989-93), Internat. Assn. Fin. Planners. Roman Catholic. Office: Prudential Securities Inc 200 PGA Blvd Ste 2104 West Palm Beach FL 33408

CANSLER, DENISE ANN, real estate executive; b. St. Louis, Apr. 19, 1959; d. Jerold Fredrick and Sandra Louise (Hartling) Wesling; m. Lowell Todd Cansler, June 28, 1996. Student, Mo. So. State Coll., 1977-78, Comml. Coll., 1980-86, Northlake Coll., 1986-87, Comml. Investment Real Estate Inst., Chgo., 1991-94. Lic. real estate broker, Okla., Tex., Ark.; lic. auctioneer, Tex.; cert. comml. investment member. Comml. real estate agt. GLA & Assocs., Dallas, 1980-82; dir. mktg. Beltway Devel. Co., Dallas, 1982-86; v.p. Montfort Mgmt., Inc., Dallas, 1986-87; pres. Comml. Property Svcs., Dallas, 1987-90; dir. sales comml. real estate Tipton Group, Dallas, 1990-91; sr. v.p. sales mgmt., comml. real estate mktg. and investment banking Kennedy-Wilson, Internat., Dallas, 1991-94; v.p. client svcs. Prentiss Properties, Ltd., Inc., 1995—; regional dir. Wells Fargo, 1996—; speaker Inst. Real Estate Mgmt., 1992, Nat. Assn. Indsl. Office Parks, Internat. Assn. Corp. Real Estate Execs., Comml. Investment Brokers Group; comml. real estate advisor, property and asset mgr. Vol. campaign Addison (Tex.) City Coun., 1982-86, Cumberland Children's Home, Denton, Tex., 1990-92; vol. road com. Argyle City Coun., 1990. Mem. Nat. Assn. Indsl. Office Parks, Real Estate Transfers-Dallas, Internat. Assn. Corp. Real Estate Execs., Asset Mgrs. Breakfast Group (sponsor Dallas chpt. 1991—, San Antonio chpt. 1991—), Cert. Comml. Investment (mem. North Tex. chpt. 1991—), Addison Bus. Assn. Home: 2771 Harbinger Ln Dallas TX 75287-5904

CANTILO, PATRICK HERRERA, lawyer; b. Santiago, Chile, Mar. 19, 1954; came to U.S., 1965; s. Luis M. and Yvonne (Cantilo) Herrera-Cantilo; m. Kathryn Gail Goltra, June 18, 1977; children: Michael, Daniel, Nicholas. BA, U. Tex., 1977, JD, 1980. Bar: Tex. 1980, U.S. Dist. Ct. (we. dist.) Tex. 1983, U.S. Dist. Ct. (no. dist.) Tex. 1988, U.S. Dist. Ct. (ea. and so. dists.) Tex. 1989, U.S. Ct. Appeals (5th cir.) 1989, U.S. Ct. Appeals (4th cir.) 1994, U.S. Supreme Ct. 1994. Counsel to receiver Tex. Bd. Ins., Austin, 1980-83; assoc. Davis & Davis P.C., Austin, 1983-85; ptnr. Davis, Cantilo, Welch & Ewbank, Austin, 1985-86; of counsel Freytag, Perry, LaForce, Rubinstein & Teofan, Austin, 1986-87; ptnr. Rubinstein & Perry, Austin, 1987-93, Cantilo, Maisel & Hubbard L.L.P., Austin, 1993—; chmn. fin. subcom. HMO adv. com. Tex. Bd. Ins., 1986. Contbr. articles to profl. jours. Mem. ABA, Tex. Bar Assn., Travis County Bar Assn., Austin Young Lawyers Assn., Nat. Assn. Ins. Commrs. (liquidators task force adv. com. 1985, chmn. fin. subcom., adv. com. HMO 1986, mem. receiver's handbook com. 1991), Soc. Ins. Receiver's Charter Prin., Nat. Assn. HMO Regulators-Nat. Assn. Ins. Commrs. (joint com., adv. com. 1986, continuation of benefits working group, contracts and svcs. 1989). Democrat. Roman Catholic. Home: 4508 Anikawi Dr Austin TX 78746-1628

CANTLIFFE, DANIEL JAMES, horticulture educator; b. N.Y.C., Oct. 31, 1943; s. Sarah Lucretia Keesler C.; m. Elizabeth F. Lapetina, June 5, 1965; children: Christine, Deanna, Danielle, Cheri. MS, Purdue U., 1967, PhD, 1971. Asst. prof. horticulture U. Fla., Gainesville, 1974-76, assoc. prof., 1976-81, prof., 1981—, asst. chair dept., 1983-84, acting chair dept., 1984-85, chmn. dept., 1985-92, acting chair dept. fruit crops, 1991-92, chair dept. hort. scis., 1992—; vis. prof. U. Hawaii, Honolulu, 1979-80; sci. cons. Sun Seeds Genetics, Hollister, Calif., 1987, Pillsbury Co., 1987—, Teltech Inc., Bloomington, Minn., 1988—. Author: (with others) Tissue Culture Propagation Development, 1985, Development of Artificial Seeds, 1987, Somatic Embryos as a Tool for Synthetics, 1990, Automated Evaluation of Somatic, 1991, Micropropagation of Sweet Potato, 1991. Recipient Rsch. award Fla. Fruit and Vegetable Assn., Orlando, 1986, Alumni Achievement award Delaware Valley Coll., Doylestown, 1990. Fellow Am. Soc. Host. Sci. (v.p. rsch. 1991—, pres.-elect 1993-94, pres. 1994-95, chmn. 1995-96, Outstanding Grad. Educator award 1991); mem. Fla. State Hort. Soc. (v.p. vegetable sect. 1984-85, pres. 1991-92, chairperson exec. com. 1992-93), Fla. Seed Assn. (hon.), Internat. Soc. Horticulture, Am. Soc. Plant Physiologists, Sigma Xi, Delta Tau Alpha, Phi Kappa Phi, Gamma Sigma Delta, Phi Beta Delta. Office: U of Fla Hort Sciences Dept 1251 Fifield Hall Gainesville FL 32611-2092

CANTRELL, DOUGLAS EUGENE, history educator, author; b. Whitewood, Va., May 24, 1959; s. Charles Anderson Cantrell and Norma Lovus Davis; m. Lisa Ann Sanders, July 29, 1988. BA, Berea Coll., 1982; MA, U. Ky., 1985. Student tchr. Harlan (Ky.) High Sch., 1983; grad. asst. U. Ky., Lexington, 1983-87, instr. history, 1988; instr. history Elizabethtown (Ky.) C.C., U. Ky., 1987-91, asst. prof. history, 1991—; presenter papers in field. Co-editor: Ky. History Jour., 1987; contbr. articles and book revs. to prof. jours. Mem. Ky. Hist. Soc., Ky. Assn. Tchrs. History (mem. exec. bd. 1991—, pres. 1994—), Orgn. Am. Historians, So. Hist. Assn., Appalachian Studies Assn., Filson Club. Home: 627 Jacquelin Ct Elizabethtown KY 42701-2699 Office: Elizabethtown CC 600 College Street Rd Elizabethtown KY 42701-3053

CANTRELL, FRANKIE L., retired medical and surgical nurse, educator; b. Huntsville, Ala., Apr. 4, 1929; d. Frank and Laura Jane (Moore) Mitchell; m. Theodore Cantrell, Aug. 6, 1950; children: Frank, Linda. BSN, Loma Linda (Calif.) U., 1953; BA, Oakwood Coll., 1950; MS, Ga. State U., Atlanta, 1974; postgrad., U. Ala. Coll. Nursing. Oper. rm. nurse White Meml. Hosp., L.A., 1953-55; missionary nurse practitioner, health instr. Liberia and Nigeria, 1955-68; DON Victory Lake Nursing Home, Hyde Park, N.Y., 1970-71; coord. of Med. Surg. Nursing Piedmont Hosp. Sch. of Nursing, Atlanta, 1974-76; insvc. and continuing edn. coord. Smyrna (Ga.) Hosp., Ga., 1976-80; coord. nursing svcs., RN-in-charge Seventh-day Adventist Health Svcs., Nairobi, Kenya, East Africa, 1980-86; nursing coord. II, dept. nursing Oakwood Coll., Huntsville, Ala., 1988-91; primary nurse North Ala. Rehab. Hosp., Huntsville, 1991-94; ret., 1994; vol. rschr. Oakwood Coll. Archives. Mem. Nat. League Nursing, Assn. Seventh-day Adventist Nurses. Home: 3101 Jordan Ln NW Huntsville AL 35816-1026

CANTRELL, LUTHER E., JR., lawyer; b. Nashville, Aug. 6, 1933; s. Luther E. and Hattie Mai (Cassetty) C.; m. Barbara Ann Richardson, Oct. 4, 1960; children: Luther III, Timothy Richard, Christopher Thomas. BS in fin. and econs., U. Tenn., 1960; LLD, Nashville Sch. Law, 1965. Bar: Tenn., U.S. Dist. Ct. (mid. dist.) Tenn., U.S. Ct. Appeals (6th cir.), U.S. Supreme Ct. Assoc. Smith, Ortale & Smith, Nashville, 1965-70, Taylor, Schlater & Smith, Nashville, 1970-72; ptnr. Smith, Smith & Cantrell, Nashville, 1972-73, Smith, Davies, Smith & Cantrell, Nashville, 1973-84, Davies, Cantrell, Humphreys & McCoy, Nashville, 1984—. Cpl. U.S. Army, 1954-55. Named Disting. Alumni Nashville Sch. Law, 1996. Mem. Tenn. Def. Lawyers Assn., Def. Rsch. Inst., Atlanta Claims Assn., Nashville Bar Assn., Tenn. Bar Assn., U.S. Supreme Ct Historical Soc., U. Tenn. Alumni Assn., Nashville Sch. Law Alumni Assn. (pres. 1971), Shriners, Am. Legion, Masons, Scottish Rite Masons, Optimist Club (pres. 1969, lt. gov. 1970-71, Honor Club 1969), Crime Stoppers Inc. (bd. dirs.). Home: 2813 Glenoaks Dr Nashville TN 37214-1605 Office: Davies Cantrell Humphreys & McCoy 150 2nd Ave N Nashville TN 37201-1934

CANTRELL, SHARRON CAULK, secondary school educator; b. Columbia, Tenn., Oct. 2, 1947; d. Tom English and Beulah (Goodin) Caulk; m. William Terry Cantrell, Mar. 18, 1989; 1 child, Jordan; children from previous marriage: Christopher, George English, Steffenee Copley. BA George Peabody Coll. Tchrs., 1970; MS Vanderbilt U., 1980; EdS Mid. Tenn. State U., 1986. Tchr., Ft. Campbell Jr. High Sch., Ky., 1970-71, Whitthorne Jr. High Sch., Columbia, Tenn., 1977-86, Spring Hill (Tenn.) High Sch., 1986—; chmn. edn. Homecoming '86 Maury County Schs., Columbia, 1984-86. Mem. NEA, AAUW (pres. Tenn. div. 1983-85), Maury County Edn. Assn. (pres. 1983-84), Tenn. Edn. Assn., Assn. for Preservation Tenn. Antiquities, Maury County C. of C., Friends of Children's Hosp., Phi Delta Kappa. Mem. Ch. of Christ. Home: 5299 Main St Spring Hill TN 37174-2449 Office: Spring Hill High Sch 1 Raider Ln Columbia TN 38401-7346

CANTRELL, WESLEY EUGENE, SR., office equipment company executive; b. 1935. AS So. Coll. Tech., 1955. With Lanier Business Products, Inc., 1955-87, v.p., 1966-72, exec. v.p., 1972-77, pres., dir. 1977-87; pres., chief exec. officer Lanier Worldwide, Inc. (formerly Harris 3M), Atlanta, 1987—. Office: Lanier Worldwide Inc 2300 Parklake Dr NE Atlanta GA 30345-2808

CANTWELL, DON, artistic director; b. Charleston, S.C., July 10, 1935; s. James Richard Jr. and Helen (Thompson) C.; m. Patricia Downs; children: Kimberly S., Dewey C. Jr., Joshua Paul. Grad. high sch., Charleston. Dir. Charleston Ballet Sch., 1969—; artistic dir. Charleston Ballet Theatre, 1969—. Mem. Southeastern Ballet Assn. (v.p. 1981-82, 85-86, pres. 1983-84, 86-87, chmn. bd. 1984-85, 87-88).

CANTWELL, THOMAS, geophysicist, electrical engineer; b. Buffalo, June 25, 1927; s. Thomas and Helen (Robinson) C.; children: Elizabeth Raye, Thomas III, Douglas. BSChemE, MIT, 1948, MSChemE, 1949; MBA, Harvard, Boston, 1951; PhD in Earth Sci., MIT, 1960. Registered profl. engr., Tex.; lic. geologist, Calif. Project engr. nuclear engring. dept. MIT, Cambridge, 1951-58, mem. faculty, 1958-65; pres. Mandrel Industries, Houston, 1966-70, Petroleum Holdings, Inc., Houston, 1970-78, Ind. Exploration, Inc., Houston, 1978-84, Tech. Computer Graphics, Inc., Houston, 1984—. With U.S. Army, 1946-47. Fellow Royal Geographic Soc.; mem. IEEE, Soc. Exploration Geophysicists, Am. Assn. Petroleum Geologists. Home: 3949 Ann Arbor Dr Houston TX 77063-6301 Office: Tech Computer Graphics Inc 3949 Ann Arbor Dr Houston TX 77063-6301

CANUP, SHERRIE MARGARET, foreign languages educator; b. Thomaston, Ga., Dec. 18, 1946; d. J.B. and Lucille Evelyn (Parham) C. BA, Ga. Coll., 1969, MEd, 1976; EdS, West Ga. Coll., 1990. Tchr. Griffin (Ga.)-Spalding County Sch. System, 1969-91; head. dept. fgn. lang. Griffin H.S., 1992—. Mem. NEA, Ga. Assn. Educators, Fgn. Lang. Assn. Ga., Profl. Assn. Ga. Educators, Griffin Spalding Assn. Educators. Republican. Home: 1110 W Poplar St Apt K4 Griffin GA 30224-2666 Office: Griffin HS 1617 W Poplar St Griffin GA 30224-2038

CAPALDI, NICHOLAS, philosophy educator; b. Phila., May 5, 1939; s. Edward and Mildred (Izzi) C. BA, U. Pa., 1960; PhD, Columbia U., 1965. Prof. philosophy Queens Coll., CUNY, 1967-91; McFarlin prof. philosophy U. Tulsa, 1991—. Author: David Hume: Newtonian Philosopher, 1975, Hume's Place in Moral Philosophy, 1989; editor Pub. Affairs Quar., 1991-94. Grantee NEH, 1978-79. Mem. Am. Polit. Sci. Assn. Republican. Roman Catholic. Office: U Tulsa Dept Philosophy 600 S College Ave Tulsa OK 74104-3126

CAPDEVIELLE, XAVIER O., entrepreneur, aviation consultant; b. Paris, Aug. 26, 1956; came to U.S., 1991; s. Marcel and Monique (Poulet) C.; m. Martine Valluy, June 7, 1983; 1 child, Victoria. MBA, Inst. Européen des Affairs, 1981. Lic. comml. pilot. Mgr. fin. Satam Brazil, Rio de Janeiro, 1981-82, gen. mgr., 1982-83; gen. mgr. Satam Argentina, Buenos Aires, 1984-88; pres., CEO Cader S.A., Buenos Aires, 1988-93, So. Cross Group, Miami, Fla., 1991—. 1st. lt. French Air Force, 1977-79. Mem. Aeroclub France (rep. Paris 1991), Grove Isle Yacht and Tennis (Miami), Buenos Aires Lawn Tennis. Home: 3 Grove Isle Dr Apt 307 Miami FL 33133-4109 Office: So Cross Group 3191 Coral Way Ste 605 Miami FL 33145-3222

CAPERTON, RICHARD WALTON, automobile repair company executive; b. Waynesburg, Pa., Jan. 11, 1948; s. Walton Greene Caperton and Sareta (Campbell) Garetson ; m. Elizabeth Anne Till, Apr. 14, 1987; children: Richard Walton Jr., Christa Elizabeth. Grad. high sch., Naples, Fla. Asst. mgr. W.T. Grant Co., Naples, 1967-75; pres., chief exec. officer, gen. mgr. R&R Automotive Inc., Naples, 1975-95, CEO, 1996; pres., chief exec. officer AAMGO Auto Parts Inc., Naples, 1987-91; pres. Caperton Properties, 1977—, Nu U Mktg., 1991-95; instr. J.L. Walker Votech, 1996—. Bd. dirs. East Naples Civic Assn., 1979-80; v.p. Fla. Sports Park, Naples, 1987; mem. adv. bd. J. L. Walker VoTech, 1991-95; apptd. to Fla. New Motor Vehicle Arbitration Bd., 1994-97. Fellow Automobile Svc. Assn., Rotary (bd. dirs. Naples East 1987-96, v.p. Naples East 1990-91, pres. 1996—). Republican. Mem. Unity Ch. Home: 1703 Daisy Ln Naples FL 34105

CAPERTON, W. GASTON, governor; b. W.Va., 1940; m. Rachael Worby; children: Gat, John. Grad., Univ. N.C., 1963. Pres. McDonough Caperton Ins. Group, 1976—; gov. W.Va., 1989—. Founder, past pres. W.Va. Edn. Fund. Office: Office of Gov State Capital Bldg Charleston WV 25305*

CAPES, DAVID BRYAN, theology educator; b. Atlanta, Dec. 16, 1955; s. Tasker Lee and Shirley (Melson) C.; m. Cathy Ann Hall, May 7, 1977; children: David Bryan, Daniel Ryan, Jordan Michael. BA, Mercer U., 1978; MDiv, Southwestern Sem., Fort Worth, Tex., 1982, PhD, 1990. Ordained, 1983. Minister Dunwoody (Ga.) Bapt. Ch., 1976-79; instr. Union U., Memphis, 1989-91; pastor Hibbit Bapt. Ch., Whitesboro, Tex., 1983-86, Eastwood Bapt. Ch., Memphis, 1986-90; asst. prof. Houston Bapt. U., 1990—; cons. Shelby County Bapt. Assn., Memphis, 1988-90. Author: Old Testament Yahweh Texts in Paul's Christology, 1992. Fellow Inst. for Bibl. Rsch.; mem. Soc. Bibl. Lit. Office: Houston Bapt U 7502 Fondren Rd Houston TX 77074-3204

CAPES, RICHARD EDWARD, artist, publisher; b. Atlanta, Nov. 6, 1942; s. James Edward and Helen Capes. Student, Oglethorpe U.; BS in Art Edn., U. Ga., 1966, MEd in Art Edn., 1969. Asst. prof. art U. So. Miss., Hattiesburg, 1970-72, Morehead (Ky.) State U., 1972-74; dir. Capes Studio Fla., Sarasota, 1975—; cons. Lazer Works Corp., Bradenton, Fla., 1978-79. One man shows include Hist. Wiggins Bldg., Bradenton, 1990, Siesta Kay Exhibition, 1993; exhibited in group shows at Addison Gallery Am. Art, Andover, Mass., 1972, Stagecoach Gallery, Albuquerque, 1973, Okla. Mus. Art, 1975, Springville (Utah) Mus. Art, 1975, Sarasota Art Assn., 1980, Jacksonville (Fla.) Art Mus., 1981, U. Tampa, 1986, Longboat Key Art Ctr., 1992, Creative Edge Gallery, Bradenton, 1992, Collectors Gallery, Venice, Fla., 1992; author, artist: Richard Capes Drawings Capture Siesta Key: An Artistic Tour of the Island, 1993; works featured in The American Freedom Train Series, 1974, 200 Years, 1976, Major Graphic Commission for the City of Venice, Florida, 1992, numerous others. Artist Easter Seals Soc., Sarasota, 1991-92; design artist Lighthouse for Blind, Sarasota, 1993. With USAF. Travel scholar Nat. Found. for Humanities/U. Ga., 1967; Art Edn. Rsch. fellow U.S. Govt., 1969-70; recipient 1st and 2nd pl. in drawing awards Ford Motor Co., 1957, 1st and 3rd pl. in drawing awards, 1959, Bancour award Argus Gallery, 1965, 2d pl. in drawing award Edgewater Art Exhbn., 1972. Mem. Fla Artists Group (Hamel Meml. award 1981), Sarasota Art Assn. (v.p. 1978, First Place award 1983, awards 1980, 82, 84), Longboat Key Art Assn., Arts & Crafts Guild Sarasota, Sarasota Alliance for Historic Preservation, Sarasota County Arts Coun., Anna Maria Island Art League, Manataa Art League, Phi Beta Kappa. Home and Office: 2116 Florinda St Sarasota FL 34231-4413

CAPLAN, MERRY WASSOM, non-profit educational corporation executive; b. Atlanta, Sept. 28, 1944; d. Bruner Edward and Claire Roberta (Mullally) Wassom; m. W. Ryckman Caplan, Feb. 18, 1982; children: Thomas Matthews, Merry Ashley, Craig Freyhan, Michael Ryckman. Student, La. State U., Baton Rouge, 1963-65; BFA, U. Houston, 1976; M of Religious Edn., Loyola U., New Orleans, 1990; PhD in Environ. Theology, Union Inst., Cin., 1993. Lic. real estate sales agt., broker; cert. in interior design. Archtl. interior design coord. for mcpl. projects Cimini, Merick, Bruns and Counce Architects and Engrs., 1976-78; tchr. 1st grade St. Louis King of France Cath. Sch., New Orleans, 1978-79; v.p. comml. div., sales assoc. Latter & Blum, Inc., 1979-86; v.p., sales assoc., assoc. broker John Kushner and Assocs., Inc., 1986-92; ind. cons. for wildlife rehab. and wilderness sanctuaries, 1992-93; pres., founder Community Earth, Inc., Metairie, La., 1993-94. Past bd. dirs. Advocacy Ctr. for Elderly and Disabled; bd. dirs., chmn. environ. com., organizer recycling program Lakewood Property Owners Assn. Recipient numerous awards Real Estate Bd. New Orleans, including Emerald award, Realtor Assoc. of Yr. award, Gold Supersalesperson award, Poche-Waguespack award. Mem. Humane Soc. U.S., Gulf States Humane Educators, Assn. Profs. and Rschrs. in Religious Edn., Nat. Assn. for Advancement of Humane and Environ. Edn., Nat. Wildlife Rehabilitators Assn., New Eng. Anti-Vivisection Soc. (bd. dirs.), People for Ethical Treatment of Animals, La. Soc. for Prevention of Cruelty to Animals, St. Tammany Human Soc (bd. dirs., chmn. humane edn. com.), Real Estate Bd. New Orleans, Women's Coun. of Realtors, Women's Profl. Coun., La. Realtors Assn. (past bd. dirs.). Office: Cmty Earth Ins Ste 310 4740 S I 10 Service Rd W Metairie LA 70001-1273

CAPLINGER, JAMES CLAIR, theatrical producer; b. Elkins, W.Va.; s. James Clair and Mazie Ellen (Lewis) C. BFA, Fla. Atlantic U., Boca Raton, 1981, MAT, 1992; postgrad., Ohio U.; degree, Northwood U., Dallas, Yestermorrow Sch. of Architecture, Vt. Vocalist Greater Miami Opera Assn., Coral Gables, Fla., 1978-83, Palm Beach (Fla.) Opera, 1983-85; vocalist, instr., condr., dir. workshops, 1985—; instr. chamber vocal ensemble and opera workshop Fla. Atlantic U. Conducting experience includes Fla. Atlantic U. Chamber Vocal Ensemble, Our Lady of Mercy Cath. Ch. Choir, Nova High Sch. Chorualus and Wind Ensemble; directing experience includes workshops and revs.; profl. performances include Paper Mill Playhouse, N.Y.C., St. John's Episcopal Ch., N.Y.C., Greater Miami Opera Assn., Civic Opera of the Palm Beaches, Versaille Hotel, Miami, Mallory Sq. Theatre Key West, Northwood Inst. Theater, Ft. Lauderdale Opera Guild, Parker Playhouse, Ft. Lauderdale, Miami Oratorio Soc. Civic responsibility includes the restoration of turn of the century structures and the preservation of the character of neighborhoods containing those structures: Sailboat Bend Hist. Dist. Master Plan and Infrastructure Coms. Recipient numerous music and voice awards and scholarships. Mem. Wagner Soc. N.Y., Lambda Legal Def. and Edn. Fund., Phi Kappa Phi. Unitarian/Universalist. Home: 202 Adams St Nelsonville OH 45764

CAPONE, ANTONIO, psychiatrist; b. Afragola, Naples, Italy, Feb. 18, 1926; came to U.S., 1954; s. Giulio and Giovanna (Fico) C.; m. Maria Morello, Mar. 21, 1957; children: Antonio Jr., John, Walter. MD, U. Naples, 1953. Diplomate Am. Bd. Med. Psychotherapists, Am. Bd. Psychiatry and Neurology, Internat. Acad. Behavioral Medicine, Am. Bd. Forensic Examiners. Intern Ospedale Incurabili, Naples, 1953-54, St. Francis Hosp., Jersey City, 1954-55; resident physician St. Clare's Hosp., Denville, N.J., 1955-56; hon. staff Butler Hosp., Providence, 1995—; chief psychiatry John E. Fogarty Meml. Hosp., North Smithfield, R.I., 1969-79, Pawtucket (R.I.) Meml. Hosp., 1971-80, St. Joseph Hosp., Providence, 1971-94; clin. asst. prof. psychiatry and human behavior Brown U. Med. Sch., Providence, 1980-95; med. dir. St. Joseph Ctr. for Psychiat. Svcs., Providence, 1987-94; hon. staff St. Joseph Hosp., Providence, 1995—, Pawtucket Meml. Hosp., 1995—; cons. John E. Fogarty Meml. Hosp., North Smithfield, 1995—; chief psychiat. cons. R.I. Divsn. Vocat. Rehab., Providence, 1967-72; med. advisor Dept. HEW, 1967-95; clin. elective course leader Brown Med. Sch., Providence, 1980-95. Contbr. articles to profl. jours. Various presentations on mental health and alcoholism, Lions Club, Kiwanis, TV, and radio. Fellow Am. Psychiat. Assn. (pres. R.I. dist. br. 1968-70, mem. peer rev. com. 1982-95, mem. fellowship com. 1984-95, mem. ad hoc on referral svc. 1987-88); mem. AMA, R.I. Med. Soc., Providence Med. Assn., Psychiatry and Neurology, Pan Am. Med. Assn., Am. Soc. Vienna. Roman Catholic. Office: PO Box 8988 Atlanta GA 30306-8988

CAPPELLE, ANN ALEACE, recreation therapist; b. Roanoke, Va., Apr. 13, 1961; d. John Junior Bryant and Alice Margaret (Davis) Rice. BS, Longwood Coll., 1983; M of Pub. Adminstrn., Auburn U., 1988. Cert. therapeutic recreation specialist. Recreation therapist VA Med. Ctr., Tuskegee, Ala., 1983-89; therapeutic recreation cons. VA Med. Ctr., Montgomery, Ala., 1984-89, recreation therapist, VA Med Ctr., Houston, 1989-90, lead therapist, 1990-95, supervisory recreation therapist, 1995—, EEO persons with disabilities program mgr., 1991-95; therapeutic recreation instr. Houston C.C., 1995—; adj. prof. Ala. State U., Montgomery, 1988-89. Recipient Superior Performance award, 1983, 90, 91, 92, Outstanding Performance award, 1984, 86, 87, 88, 93, 94, Spl. Recognition cert. U.S. Congress, 1985, Quality Increase award, 1995. Mem. AAUW, Lone Star Therapeutic Recreation Assn. (pres.), Houston Employee Assn. (treas.), Am. Therapeutic Recreation Assn., Alpha Sigma Phi, Delta Psi Kappa, Phi Kappa Phi. Avocations: reading, cooking, crossword puzzles, walking. Office: VA Med Ctr Rec Therapy Vol Svc RTVS 2002 Holcombe Blvd Houston TX 77030-4211

CAPPS, JAMES LEIGH, II, lawyer, military career officer; b. Brunswick, Ga., Dec. 17, 1956; s. Thomas Edwin Sr. and Betty Marie (Greenhill) C.; m. Nancy Ann Fisher, June 25, 1978; children: Bonnie Lynn, James Leigh III. AA, Seminole C.C., Sanford, Fla., 1976; BA in History, U. Cen. Fla., 1981; JD, U. Fla., 1987. Bar: Fla. 1987, U.S. Ct. Mil. Appeals 1988, Colo. 1990. Enlisted USAF, 1977, advanced through grades to capt., 1985; med. svc. specialist USAF, MacDill AFB, Fla., 1977-79; air weapons dir. USAF, Germany, 1982-84; claims officer USAF, Homestead AFB, Fla., 1987-88, area def. counsel, 1988-90; dep. staff judge adv. USAF, Onizuka AFB, Calif., 1990-93; atty. office of state atty. 18th Jud. Ct., Sanford, Fla., 1994; assoc. Dominick Salfi Law Offices, Maitland, Fla., 1993-94, of counsel, 1994-96; pvt. practice, 1996—; assigned to 16th Air Force Hdqs., Aviano AFB, Italy, Operation Joint Endeavor, 1996. Maj. USAFR, 1993—. Democrat.

CAPPS, PATRICIA, communications and psychology educator, counselor; b. Greenville, Miss., Dec. 21, 1951; d. John A. and Mary Frances (Baker) C. BA, U. West Fla., 1972; MS, Ind. U., 1975. Exec. asst. Gov's. Office/Bus. Assistance, Tallahassee, Fla., 1980-81; legis. officer St. Petersburg Jr. Coll., Clearwater, Fla., 1981-82, instr., program coord. Bus. Adminstrn., 1982-85; exec. dir. Bay Area Consortium for Bus. and Higher Edn., Clearwater, 1985-86; asst. prof., dir. entrepreneurship program St. Petersburg Jr. Coll., 1986-89, assoc. prof., counselor, 1989—. Appointee Gov.'s Commn. on Status of Women, Tallahassee, 1978-80; bd. dirs. Mental Health Assn. Pinellas County, St. Petersburg, 1985-86; active Nat. Conf./Citizen Involvement, L.A., 1985; cons. trainer Woman to Woman alcohol awareness program Assn. Jr. Leagues Internat., 1987-90; community v.p. Jr. League Clearwater-Dunedin, 1991-92. Mem. Internat. Assn. of Bus. Communicators. Democrat. Office: St Petersburg Jr Coll 2465 Drew St Clearwater FL 34625-2816

CAPPS, RUSSELL CRAIG, controller; b. Alexandria, Va., May 18, 1965; s. Robert Lewis and Mary Louise (Smith) C. BBA in Acctg., Radford U., 1989; postgrad., Marymount U., 1996—. Staff acct. Bruner, Kane & McCarthy, Alexandria, Va., 1987-91; acct. mgr Whitman-Walker Clinic, Washington, 1991-93; asst. contr. Soc. for Human Resource Mgmt., Alexandria, 1993—. Mem. Am. Soc. Assn. Execs. (mem. edn. com. 1995-96), Crystal City Jaycees (bd. dirs. 1995—, bd. dirs. 1995-96). Democrat. Baptist. Office: Soc for Human Resource Mgmt 606 N Washington St Alexandria VA 22314

CAPPS, THOMAS EDWARD, utilities company executive, lawyer; b. Wilmington, N.C., Oct. 31, 1935; s. Edward S. Jr. and Agnes (Rhodes) C.; m. Jane Paden, Sept. 13, 1963; children: Ashley R., Leigh C. AB, U. N.C., 1958, JD, 1965. Bar: Fla. 1975, N.C. 1966. Sr. counsel Carolina Power & Light Co., Raleigh, N.C., 1970-74; v.p., gen. counsel Boston Edison Co., 1974-75; sr. ptnr. Steel Hector & Davis, Miami, Fla., 1975-84; exec. v.p. Va. Power, Richmond, 1984-86; pres. Dominion Resources, Inc., Richmond, 1986—, chief exec. officer, 1990—, chmn. bd. dirs., 1992—; bd. dirs. Bassett (Va.) Furniture Industries, Inc., NationsBank Corp., Petersburg Long Distance, Inc. Bd. dirs. Va. Blood Svcs., 1986. Lt. USCG, 1959-62. Mem. ABA, Bd. of Bar Overseers, N.C. Bar Assn., Fla. Bar Assn., Mass. Bar Assn. Episcopalian. Office: Dominion Resources Inc PO Box 26532 Richmond VA 23261-6532

CAPRARO, FRANZ, accountant; b. Uder-Eichsfeld, Thuringia, Germany, Nov. 19, 1941; came to U.S., 1959; s. Ernst Capraro and Lia (Loeschmann) Baeuscher; m. Daniela DiPauli, Dec. 26, 1964; 1 child, Monica L. BBA cum laude, U. Miami, 1964. CPA, Fla. Ptnr. Deloitte Haskins & Sells (name now Deloitte & Touche), Miami, 1966-84; exec. v.p. The Wolfson Initiative Corp., Miami, 1984-95; v.p. The Novecento Corp., Miami, 1984-95, Washington Storage Co., Miami, 1984-95, The Foundlings, Inc., Miami Beach, 1984-95, The Hampton Roads, Inc., Miami Beach, 1984-95; pvt. practice acctg. Davie, Fla., 1995—; treas. The Jour. of Decorative and Propaganda Arts, Miami, 1986—; attended Nat. Security Forum, U.S. Air War Coll., Montgomery, Ala., 1993. Mem. exec. com. U. Miami Citizens Bd., Coral Gables, 1987—; treas. Mitchell Wolfson Family Found., Miami, 1985—; bd. dirs. Louis Wolfson II Media History Ctr., Miami, 1987-95; trustee Greater Miami Opera Fin. Com., 1991-96. 1st lt. U.S. Army Fin. Corps, France, 1965-66. Recipient Certificate of Appreciation City of Miami Beach, 1987; named Honorary Conch City of Key West, 1987. Mem. AICPA, Fla. Inst. CPAs, Schlaraffia Costa Aurea (treas. 1986-87), U.S. Air War Coll. Alumni Assn. (life). Roman Catholic. Home: 2821 SW 116th Ave Fort Lauderdale FL 33330-1418 Office: Franz Capraro CPA 2821 SW 116th Ave Davie FL 33330-1418

CAPUTI, MARIE ANTOINETTE, university official; b. Newport, R.I., Aug. 14, 1935; d. Saverio and Madeline (Esposito) C. AB, Barnard Coll., 1957; MS in Social Work, Columbia U., 1959; PhD, St. Louis U., 1978. Lic. social worker, Fla. Field instr. Columbia U., N.Y.C., 1962-64; social worker ob.-gyn. dept. Bronx (N.Y.) Mcpl. Hosp., 1964-65; generic supr. Maimonides Med. Ctr., Bklyn., 1965-75; asst. prof. Grad. Sch. of Social Work U. Wis., Madison, 1978-83; instr. dept. continuing edn. Edgewood Coll., Madison, Wis., 1982-85; asst. prof., dir. faculty svcs. region II Cardinal Stritch Coll., Milw., 1984-89; ptnr. Midwest Ctr. for Human Svcs., Madison, 1982-89; assoc. prof., dir. grad. and continuing edn. St. Thomas U., Miami, Fla., 1989-92, coord. Earth Literacy Programs, 1993-94; asst. to v.p. for acad. affairs Lynn U., Boca Raton, Fla., 1993, dir. Instnl. Rsch., Instnl. Effectiveness, 1994—; faculty mentor Walden U., 1993—; researcher, specialist U. Wis. Survery Rsch. Lab., Madison, 1982-84; rsch. cons. North Chicago VA Med. Ctr., 1984-89; cons. U. Wis. Hosp. & Clinics, Madison, 1987; adj. asst. prof. NYU Grad. Sch. Social Work, N.Y.C., 1967-69. Contbr. articles to profl. jours. Lavanburg Cornerhouse scholar, 1957-59; VA fellow, 1975-78. Mem. NASW, AAUW, Assn. of Institutional Rsch. Democrat. Home: 7120 SW 41st Pl Davie FL 33314-3182 Office: Lynn U 3601 N Military Trl Boca Raton FL 33431-5507

CAPWELL, RICHARD LEONARD, English language educator; b. East Greenwich, R.I., May 6, 1920; s. Walter Henry and Grace (Knowles) C.; m. Margaret Ruth Johnston, Dec. 19, 1959; children—Richard Johnston, Alton Robert. A.B., Brown U., 1942; M.A., Yale, 1946; Ph.D., Duke, 1964. Instr. Adm. Billard Acad., New London, Conn., 1942-44; instr. Milton (Mass.) Acad., 1944-45, U. Mo., Columbia, 1946-49, Ohio Wesleyan U., Delaware, 1952-54; asst. prof. 17th Century English lit. East Carolina U., Greenville, N.C., 1957-64; assoc. prof. East Carolina U., 1964-66, prof., 1966-85, prof. emeritus, 1985—, dean Coll. Arts and Scis., 1969-80. Contbg. editor Abstracts of English Studies, 1961-85. Mem. MLA, South Atlantic MLA, Conf., Phi Beta Kappa, Phi Kappa Phi. Methodist. Club: Greenville Golf and Country. Home: 2701 Pickett Rd Apt 2039 Durham NC 27705

CARABELLO, BLASE ANTHONY, cardiology educator; b. Reading, Pa., Aug. 5, 1947; s. Charles Anthony and Fern June (Houck) C.; m. Susan Jane Beidman, Aug. 15, 1970 (div. June 1977); 1 child, Charles; m. Catherine Wheatley, Apr. 9, 1989; children: Nicholas, Blaise. BA, Gettsburg Coll., 1969; MD, Temple U., 1973. Diplomate Am. Bd. Internal Medicine, Am. Bd. Cardiology. Intern in Medicine Mass. Gen. Hosp., Boston, 1973-74, resident in Medicine Harvard Med. Sch., 1974-75, sr. resident in Medicine Harvard Med. Sch., 1975-76; fellow in Cardiology Peter Bent Brigham Hosp., Boston, 1976-78, cardiologist, 1978-79; asst. prof. Medicine U. Va. Hosp., Charlottesville, 1979-81; dir. Diagnostic Cardiology Temple U., Phila., 1981-85; prof. Medicine Med. U. S.C., Charleston, 1985-95, dir. clin. rsch., 1990—; Charles Ezra Daniel prof. medicine U. S.C., Charleston, 1995—. Author: Cardiology Pearls, 1993; contbr. articles to profl. jours. Beta-Blockade grantee Pub. Health Svc., 1988-89, Dept. Va. Pub. Health grantee, 1989-94. Fellow Am. Coll. Cardiology, Am. Heart Assn. (coun. on circulation, chmn. com. on cardiac catheterization); mem. Am. Soc. Clin. Investigation, Alpha Omega Alpha. Home: 528 Island Walk W Mount Pleasant SC 29464 Office: Dept Cardiology Med U SC 171 Ashley Ave Charleston SC 29425-0001

CARACCIOLO, FRANCIS SAMUEL, management consultant; b. Phila., Jan. 18, 1929; s. Francis Charles and Constance (Achuff) C.; m. Clara Slater Caracciolo, Sept. 3, 1965; children: Addison L., Gloria Ann. AA, George Washington U., 1950, AB in Psychology, 1952, MA in Pyschology, 1954. Jr. exec. Gen. Motors Acceptance Corp., Washington, 1953-55; ednl. specialist Army Dept., Washington, 1955-57; dir. profl. devel., mgmt. skills Navy Dept., Washington, 1957-59, dir. adminstrn. and managerial programs, 1959-60; assoc. dir. mgmt. intern programs CSC, Washington, 1960-62, dir. mgmt. sci. programs, 1962-63; dir. Exec. Seminar Ctr. CSC, Kings Pt., N.Y., 1963-64; spl. asst. to dir. Office Career Devel., Washington, 1964-65; dir. ednl. programs Office Tech. Assistance Equal Employment Opportunity Commn., Washington, 1965-67; program specialist pub. adminstrn. Ford Found., New Delhi, 1967-70; dir. office tng. support Peace Corps, Washington, 1970; asst. adminstr Office Manpower Devel. and Tng., Social and Rehab. Svcs., HEW, Washington, 1970-73; dir. internat. exchange programs R & D, Social and Rehab. Svcs, HEW, Washington, 1973-79; team leader pub. svc. improvement UN Devel. Programs, Jamaica, W.I., 1979-80; asst. to dir. Nat. Inst. Handicapped Rsch., U.S. Dept. Edn., Washington, 1980-81; dir. spl. rehab. programs Rehab. Svcs. Adminstrn., U.S. Dept. Edn., Washington, 1981-89; prin. Ft. Myers Beach, FL, 1989—; founder Indian Soc. for Tng. and Devel., New Delhi, 1970; pres. Three Continents Ltd., Vienna, Va., 1973-76. Mem. Nat. Italian Am. Found. (coun. of 1000), Am. Soc. for Pub. Adminstrn. Republican. Roman Catholic. Home and Office: 6145 Court St Fort Myers Beach FL 33931-4301

CARAVATI, CHARLES MARTIN, dermatologist; b. Richmond, Va., May 9, 1937; s. Charles Martin and Mary Virginia (Dore) C.; m. Betty Noland, Aug. 31, 1963; children: Charles M. III, Elizabeth Caravati Butler, Nancy Caravati Jordan. BA, U. Va., 1959, MD, 1963. Diplomate Am. Bd. Dermatology. Resident in dermatology U. Va., Charlottesville, 1966-68, chief resident dermatology, 1968-69; founder, pres. Dermatology Assocs. Va., Richmond, 1969—; pres., chmn. bd. dirs. Richmond Acad. Medicine, 1980-82; bd. visitors U. Va., 1994—. Bd. dirs. Sheltering Arms Rehab. Hosp., 1990-95, St. Joseph's Villa, 1982-85. Fellow Am. Acad. Dermatology; mem. AMA (chair Va. delegation 1991—), Med. Soc. Va. (pres. 1985-86), Va. Dermatol. Soc., Richmond Dermatol. Soc. Republican. Roman Catholic. Home: 931 Broad St Rd Manakin-Sabot VA 23103 Office: Dermatology Assocs Va 5600 Grove Ave Richmond VA 23226

CARAWAY, GEORGE MICHAEL, transportation executive; b. Meridian, Miss., Nov. 9, 1953; s. George Mason and Bobbye Jo (Smith) C.; m. Gayle Jeanann Rodgers, Sept. 24, 1988; children: Taylor Michael, George Wesley, Hailey Joann. AS, East Ctrl. Jr. Coll., 1973; BS, Miss. State U., 1977. From salesperson to ops. mgr. Motion Industries, Inc., Birmingham, 1978-86; from purchasing agt. to procurement dir. Miss. Dept. Transp., Jackson, 1986—. Mem. Miss. Assn. Govtl. Purchasing Agts. (1st v.p. 1993). Baptist. Office: Miss Dept Transp 401 N West St # 1068 Jackson MS 39201-1010

CARBALLO, PEDRO PABLO, cardiologist; b. Artemisa, Cuba, Apr. 21, 1953; came to U.S., 1963; s. Pedro V. and Ofelia B. (Hernandez) C.; m. Maria T. Pol, Aug. 13, 1982; children: Suzanne E., Sarah A., Paul A. AA, Miami Dade Community Coll., 1974; BA, Northwestern U., 1976, MS, 1977; MD, U. Ill., Chgo., 1981. Diplomate Am. Bd. Internal Medicine, Am. Bd. Cardiovascular Medicine. Resident Ill. Masonic Med. Ctr., Chgo., 1981-84, fellow, 1984-86, dir., Intensive Care Units, 1986-92; pvt. practice Chgo., 1986-92; cardiologist Family First Med. Ctrs., Dade & Broward Counties, Fla., 1992—. Fellow Am. Coll. Cardiology, Am. Coll. Chest Physicians; mem. Alpha Omega Alpha, Beta Beta Beta. Roman Catholic. Office: 9732 SW 24th St Miami FL 33165-7513

CARBONE, ROBERT JAMES, family practice physician; b. Hartford, Conn., Aug. 17, 1930; s. Rocco James and Agnes Eve (Miscavich) C.; m. Dorothy Mildred Saffomilla, Apr. 11, 1953; children: Kama, Kerry, Kim. BA, U. Conn., 1952, MA, 1953, PhD, 1956; MD, U. Juarez, Mex., 1978. Diplomate Am. Bd. Family Practice. Physicist MIT/Lincoln Lab., Lexington, Mass., 1956-72, Philips, Eindhoven, The Netherlands, 1968-69; group leader Los Alamos (N.M.) Nat. Lab., 1972-80; asst. prof. family practice residency East Tenn. State U., Johnson City, 1982-84; assoc. dir. family practice residency Hamot Med. Ctr., Erie, Pa., 1984-89; dir. family practice residency La. State U., Mandeville, 1989-90; med. dir. residency Polyclin. Med. Ctr., Harrisburg, Pa., 1990-91; pvt. practice Johnson City, Tenn., 1991—. Fellow Am. Acad. Family Practice; mem. AMA, Sigma Xi. Home and Office: 1 Red Fern Cir Johnson City TN 37604

CARD, HUGH CLEVELAND, III, city official; b. Ft. Worth, Tex., Oct. 20, 1960; s. Hugh C. and Betty (Barns) C.; m. Jane M. Goodrich, Aug. 6, 1983; children: Madison Rose, Marjorie V. BBA, Berea (Ky.) Coll., 1984; M.Urban Affairs, U. Tex., Arlington, 1986, ABD, 1988. Lic. Grade B ground water, Tex. Natural Resources Conservation Commn. Adminstrv. intern Ky. Legis. Rsch. Commn., Frankfort, Tex., 1983-84, City Mgr. Office, Lancaster, Tex., 1984; instr. VTI Paralegal Sch., Arlington, Tex., 1986-88; grad. rsch. asst. Inst. Urban Studies U. Tex., Arlington, 1984-88; adminstrv. intern pub. works dept., water utilities divsn. City of Irving, Tex., 1988, adminstrv. analyst pub. works dept., water utilities divsn., 1988-90, water quality & prodn. supr. pub. works dept., divsn. water utilities, 1990—. Contbr. articles to profl. jours. Asst. scoutmaster Boy Scouts Am., 1990-96; rep. V.M. Ehulers Scholarship Bd., 1994—. Recipient Meritorious Svc. award VTI Paralegal Sch., 1988; named to Outstanding Young Men of Am., 1985; named Hon. Sec. of State, State of Ky., 1982. Mem. Am. soc. Pub. Adminstrs., Am. Water Works Assn., Tex. Water Utility Assn. (chmn. membership com. 1994—), White Rock Water Utility Assn. (pres. 1992). Home: 2618 Fifth Ave Fort Worth TX 76110-3001 Office: City of Irving PO Box 152288 Irving TX 75015-2288

CARDENAS, NORMA ALICIA, secondary school orchestra director, violist, violinist; b. Edinburg, Tex., May 1, 1952; d. Jesus Maria and Rose Mary (Hon) C. BA, Pan American U., 1974. Orch. dir. North Jr. High Sch., Edinburg, 1974-80, Edinburg Jr. High Sch., 1980-85, South Jr. High Sch., Edinburg, 1985—; violist, violinist Valley Symphony Orch., Edinburg, 1965—, South Tex. Chamber Orch., Edinburg, 1980—, Valley Sinfonette, Edinburg, 1990—; mem., mgr. The Silken Strings, Edinburg, 1974—; SBDM coun. sec. South Jr. High Sch., 1996—. Mem. South Tex. Symphony Assn., Edinburg, 1976—. Mem. Tex. Music Educators Assn. (treas. 1982-86, 94—), Tex. Orch. Dirs. Assn., Am. Strings Tchrs. Assn., Tex. Classroom Tchrs. Assn., Mu Phi Epsilon (sec. 1978-82). Democrat. Roman Catholic. Home: 303 W Fay St Edinburg TX 78539-4328 Office: South Jr H S 601 W Freddy Gonzalez Dr Edinburg TX 78539-6133

CARDER, LARRY WILLIAM, display and exhibit executive; b. Cumberland, Md., July 2, 1958; s. Kenneth Milton and Patricia Ann (Terry) C.; m. Terrill Ann Brockway, Aug. 13, 1983; children: Mandy Lynn, Casey James. Student, The Citadel, 1977-81. Jr. engr. Gen. Dynamics, Charleston, S.C., 1981; designer Ralph M. Parsons, Pasadena, Calif., 1981-82; gen. mgr. KMC/Alco, Culver City, Calif., 1982-88; pres. Exhibit Systems Calif., Culver City, 1988-90; v.p. Subia, Hawthorne, Calif., 1990-91; nat. sales mgr. N/S Corp., Inglewood, Calif., 1991; div. mgr. Exhibit Group, L.A., 1992-93; pres. Carolina Exhibits, Irmo, S.C., 1994—; cons. R&K Industries, Inc., Inglewood, Calif., 1988. Bid. dirs., coach Culver City Babe Ruth, 1985-88; baseball scout Kansas City Royals Baseball Club, 1995—. With USMC, 1979-80. Recipient Design award Nimlok, 1989. Mem. Mil. Order of The Stars and Bars, SCV, Sons of Union Civil War Vets. Republican. Home and office: 15 Castle Vale Ct Irmo SC 29063-2615

CARDER, THOMAS ALLEN, nuclear energy industry emergency planner, educator; b. Marion, Ind., June 6, 1949; s. Otto Leroy and Mary Madeline (Dobson) C.; m. Barbara Gail Rice, June 24, 1978; children: Damian Bruce, Eric Thomas, Kimberly Rose. Student, Ind. U., 1970-72, 76, Ky. Coll. Tech., 1967-68, So. Ill. U., 1986—. Registered emergency med. technician, Ind., Pa., Va., Ill. Cyclotron project technician Ind. U., Bloomington, 1971-73; radiation safety officer, instr., technician Ind. Emergency Mgmt. Agy., Indpls., 1973-81; coord. emergency planning North Anna Power Sta., Mineral, Va., 1981-82; nuclear specialist Energy Cons., Inc., Harrisburg, Pa., 1982-84; emergency planner Ill. Power Co., Clinton, 1984-88; sr. emergency planner Tex. Utilities, Comanche Peak Sta., 1988-95; pres., CEO Childcare Action Project Christian Analysis of Am. Culture, 1995—; radiation safety adv., mem. Mahomet (Ill.) Emergency Svcs. and Disaster Agy., 1985-88. Author: Handling of Radiation Accident Patients by Paramedical and Hospital Personnel, 1981, 2d edit., 1991, Strengths/Needs Analysis Project, 1994. Mem. Health Physics Soc. Baptist. Home: PO Box 177 Granbury TX 76048-0177

CARDIN, CHARLES EDWARD, lawyer; b. Barnesville, Ga., Aug. 22, 1929; s. Roscoe Levi and Mary (Robinson) C.; m. Jean McCorvey, Dec. 23, 1951; 1 child, Leslie Jean Cardin Pruchnicki. Student, Auburn U., 1950-52; BBA, U. Ga., 1955; postgrad. law, Emory U., 1962-68; JD, John Marshall Law Sch., 1985. Bar: Ga. 1985, U.S. Dist. Ct. (no. dist.) Ga. 1985, U.S. Ct. Appeals (11th cir.) 1985, U.S. Supreme Ct. 1989. Middle and sr. mgr. Pitney Bowes Co., Stamford, Conn., 1967-85; assoc. Wall & Noonan, Roswell, Ga., 1985-87, Atlanta, 1985-87; pvt. practice Norcross, Ga., 1987—; v.p., gen. counsel Primary Care Physicians Group, P.C., Atlanta, 1985—. With USAF, 1947-50. Mem. ABA, State Bar Ga., Atlanta Bar Assn., Assn. Trial Lawyers Am., Sigma Delta Kappa, Delta Chi. Democrat. Methodist. Home: 4800 Coppedge Trl Duluth GA 30136-2970

CARDIN, JACKSON EUGENE, commodities trader; b. Barnesville, Ga., June 3, 1933; s. R.L. and Mary Robinson Cardin; m. Patricia Pittard, 1959 (div. 1981); children: Richard, Jody, Michael; m. Cynthia Buck, Jan. 1, 1983; 1 child, John Pattison. BBA, U. Ga., 1958, MBA, 1959. Cert. commodity trading advisor. Mgmt. trainee Am. Oil Co., Atlanta, 1960-62; N.Am. rep. Mettler Instrument Corp., 1963-73; pres. South By S.E., Inc., Basel, Switzerland, 1973-77; br. mgr. Conticommodity Svcs., New Orleans, 1977-84; pres. Active Cycles, Inc., Atlanta, 1984—; instr. Emery U., Atlanta, 1978, Ogletharp U., Atlanta, 1979, U. New Orleans, 1983. Author: Basic Training for Commodity Traders, 1988, A Personal Financial Catalog, 1989. Chair Econ. Task Force Atlanta, 1975. With U.S. Army, 1953-55. Recipient Am. Spirit of Honor medal C. of C., 1953; Rayonair scholar, 1959. Mem. Nat. Futures Assn., New Orleans Bd. of Trade, Leadership Atlanta Alumni, New Orleans Exec. Club. Office: Active Cycles Inc Ste 2150 6855 Jimmy Carter Blvd Norcross GA 30071

CARDINA, CLAIRE ARMSTRONG, archivist, records manager; b. Montclair, N.J., June 13, 1931; d. Cole Alexander and Florence Maida (Brown) Armstrong; m. William John Johnson, June 9, 1951 (div. 1980); children: James Benjamin, Glenn Alexander; m. Daniel John Cardina, Oct. 5, 1985. BA, Gettysburg Coll., 1951; MLS, Rutgers U., 1970. Cert. archivist, records mgr. Svc. rep. C&P Telephone Co., Hyattsville, Md., 1951-54, N.J. Bell Telephone Co., East Orange, 1954-56; coorespondent AT&T, N.Y.C., 1956-60; librarian Madison Jr. Sch., Madison, N.J., 1970-72; media specialist Miles Elem. Sch., Tampa, Fla., 1972-82; records Mgr. City of Tampa, 1982-87, archivist, records mgr., 1987—; adj. prof. Hillsborough C.C., Tampa, 1994-96, mem. office sys. tech. adv. com., 1986-91; adj. prof. U. South Fla. Sch. Libr. and Info. Sci., Tampa, 1992-93; mem. Fla. Hist. Records Adv. Bd., Tallahasssee, 1983-86, adv. com., 1995—. Author records management manuals, leaflets for govtl. and profl. orgns. Bd. dirs., pres. Friends of Tampa/Hillsborough County Pub. Libr., Tampa, 1978—; mem. Pres.'s Round Table Orgns. Greater Tampa, 1983-84; mem. adv. com. City of Tampa Archives, 1989—; mem. adv. coun. Tampa Bay History Ctr., 1993—; del. Tampa Sister Cities Com., 1993. Mem. Assn. Records Mgrs. and Adminstrs. (nominating com. 1995—, internat. conf. program com. 1987-94, asst. chair 1993, chair 1994, co-chair mcpl. and county govt. industry action com. 1990-94, internat. chair micrographics subcom. 1986-88, chmn. bd. dirs. Tampa Bay chpt. 1986-87, pres. 1985-86, Mem. of the Yr. 1986, 92), Inst. Cert. Records Mgrs., Soc. Am. Archivists, Soc. Fla. Archivists (founding bd. dirs. 1988-90, 92-93, v.p. 1990-91, pres. 1991-92), Nat. Assn. Govt. Archivists and Records Adminstrs. (local govt. records com. 1986-91, mem. com. 1994—), Fla. Records Mgmt. Assn. (bd. dirs. 1993-94, 95-96, pres. 1994-95), Tampa (Fla.) Hist. Soc. (bd. dirs. 1996—), Assn. for Info. and Image Mgmt., Network Exec. Women (historian 1991—, bd. dirs. Compass Project 1991—), Tampa Bay History Ctr. Advisory Com., 1994—, Archives Awareness Week Council (Pres. 1993), Acad. Cert. Archivists, Toastmasters Internat. (Able Toastmaster), Tampa Bay Rutgers Club (sec. 1990-94). Republican. Presbyterian. Office: City of Tampa 1104 E Twiggs St Tampa FL 33602-3136

CARDOSO, ANTHONY ANTONIO, artist, educator; b. Tampa, Fla., Sept. 13, 1930; s. Frank T. and Nancy (Messina) C.; m. Martha Rodriguez, 1954; children: Michele Denise, Toni Lynn. BS in Art Edn., U. Tampa, 1954; BFA, Minn. Art Inst., 1965; MA, U. South Fla., 1975; PhD. in Art, Elysion Coll. Calif., 1981. Art instr., head fine arts dept. Jefferson High Sch., Tampa, 1952-67, Leto H.S., Tampa, 1967—, instr. adult art edn., 1965—; bd. dirs., supr. art Hillsboro County Schs.; rep. Tampa Art Council; artist, 1952-87. One-man shows include Warren's Gallery, Tampa, 1974, 75, 76, Tampa Realist Gallery, Tampa, 1975; group shows include Rotunda Gallery, London, Eng., 1973, Raymon Duncan Galleries, Paris, France, 1973, Brussels (Belgium) Internat., 1973; represented in permanent collections Minn. Mus., St. Paul, Tampa Sports Authority Art Collection, Tampa Arts' Coun.; executed murals Tampa Sports Authority Stadium, 1972, Suncoast Credit Union Bldg., Tampa, 1975. Recipient Prix de Paris Art award Raymon Duncan Galleries, 1970, Salon of 50 States award Ligoa Duncan Gallery, N.Y.C., 1970, Latham Found. Internat. Art award, 1964, XXII Bienniel Traveling award Smithsonian Instn., 1968-69, Purchase award Minn. Mus., 1971, 1st award Fla. State Fair, 1967, Gold medal Accademia Italia, 1981-82, Medallion Merit, Internat. Parliament, Italy, 1984, Statue of Vittoria award for centro studi and ricerche, Italy, 1988, Accademia D'Europa, Premio Palma D'Oro D' Europa, Italy, 1989—, El Prado Gallery, 1990—, Merit award Festival of Arts Hillsborough County Tampa, 1994-96. Democrat. Roman Catholic. Home and Studio: 3208 W Nassau St Tampa FL 33607-5145 Office: El Prado Art Gallery 4307 W El Prado Blvd Tampa FL 33629-8404

CARDWELL, HAROLD DOUGLAS, SR., rehabilitation specialist; b. Varnell, Ga., July 17, 1926; s. Arlie Amber and Hettie Ellen (Eledge) C.; m. Priscilla Dean Rumley, July 3, 1954; children: Harold Douglas, Jr., Ruth Ellen Cardwell-Landau. AA, Daytona Beach C.C., 1972; student, U. Fla., 1970; BA, Fla. Tech. U., 1974; postgrad., Clemson U., 1975. Registered landscape architect, Fla. Chem. operator Fercleve Chem. Corp., Oak Ridge, Tenn., 1945-46; draftsman C.M. Price Constrn. Co., Daytona Beach, Fla., 1947-48; bookkeeper, expediter W.A. Cardwell Constrn. Co., Gatlinburg, Tenn., 1948-49; office mgr., sales rep. J.H. Gordon Lumber Co., St. Augustine, Fla., 1949-51; asst. mgr. King Bros. Lumber Co., St. Augustine, 1951-56; pvt. practice landscape architect Port Orange, Fla., 1956-67; sr. rehab. specialist State of Fla. Divsn. of Blind Svcs., Daytona Beach, 1967—. Vice chmn. Daytona Beach Preservation Bd., 1987—; adv. mem. task force Daytona Beach City Govt., 1987; vice chmn. Volusia County Hist. Commn., Deland, Fla., 1989-92; mem. adv. bd. Volusia County Hist. Preservation Bd., Deland, 1992-94; adv. mem. Flagler Centennial Com., Tallahassee, Fla., 1986; pres. Fla. Anthropol. Soc., Gainesville, 1988-89. Recipient Historian of Yr. award Volusia County Hist. Commn., 1988, Lazarus award for Preservation, Fla. Anthropol. Soc., 1988. Mem. Am. Hort. Therapy Assn. (registered hort. therapist, nat. treas. 1978-80), Fla. Nurserymen and Growers Assn. (bd. dirs. 1963-64, 68-69), Halifax Hist. Soc. (bd. dirs. 1974—), Fla. Hist. Soc., Lions (Pres.' award in leadership Port Orange/South Halifax club 1988). Democrat. Methodist. Home: 1343 Woodbine St Daytona Beach FL 32114 Office: State of Fla Divsn Blind Svcs 1111 Willis Ave Daytona Beach FL 32114-2808

CARDWELL, SUE POOLE, reclamation services company executive; b. Clearfield, Pa., Oct. 31, 1952; d. Robert Thomas Poole and Alice Katz Jost, Mary B. (Edwards) (stepmother) and Patricia Alice (Coleman) (stepmother) P.; m. Charles Howard Cardwell, Nov. 24, 1979; children: Jonathon Aaron, Jacqueline Leigh. Clk.-typist Ky. Dept. Mines and Minerals, 1974; sr. reclamation insp. div. reclamation Ky. Dept. Natural Resources, Madisonville, 1974-77; pres. Reclamation Svcs. Unltd., Inc., Madisonville, 1977—; chmn. West Ky. adv. group Office Surface Mining, Dept. Interior, 1979—; adv. bd. U. Ky. Symposium on Surface Mining Reclamation and Hydrology, also mem. exec. adv. com.; mem. Ky. Adv. Com. on Strip Mine Regulation, 1979—; mem. exec. bd. Ky. Task Force on Exploited and Missing Children; bd. dirs., sec. Ky. Alliance for Missing and Exploited Children; mem. Rep. Senatorial Inner Circle, 1984—; mem. fin. com. St. Joseph's Ch., Central City, Ky., also chmn. social concerns com., mem. parish coun., 1995—; pres. PTA, Madison, Ky, 1989—. Served with WAC, 1972-73. Named hon. Ky. col.; named to W.Va. Ship of State. Mem. West Ky. Coal Operators Assn. (dir.), West Ky. Assn. Gen. Contractors, Hazardous Materials Control Rsch. Inst., Mining and Reclamation Council Am. (chmn. reclamation subcom.), Profl. Reclamation Assn. Am. (bd. dirs., charter), World Safety Assn., W.Va. Surface Mine Assn., Nat. Reclamation Assn. West Ky., West Ky. Constrn. Assn. of Associated Gen. Contractors, West Ky. Constrn. Assn. (bd. dirs.); contbg. editor Ky. Coal Jour. Office: 701 Temple St Central City KY 42330-2130

CARDWELL, THOMAS AUGUSTA, III, scientist, retired career officer, executive; b. Oklahoma City, July 25, 1943; s. Thomas Augusta Jr. and Hilda Ogreta (Box) C.; m. T.J. Hopkins, 1992; children: Jill Suzanne, Mark Christopher, Robert M. Hopkins, Kevin D. Hopkins. BBA, Tex. A&M U., 1965; MS, U. So. Calif., 1976; PhD, Pacific Western U., L.A., 1988; DLitt (hon.), London Inst. for Applied Rsch., 1993. Commd. 2d lt. USAF, 1965, advanced through grades to col., 1982; ret., 1993; F-4 fighter pilot 390th Tactical Fighter Squadron USAF, Da Nang Air Base, Republic of Vietnam, 1967; F-106 pilot 11th Fighter Interceptor Squadron USAF, Duluth, Minn., 1968-72; ASTRA dep. chief staff for sys. and logistics USAF, Washington, 1973-74; dir. acad. tng. and pubs. Interceptor Weapons Sch. USAF, Tyndall AFB, Fla., 1974-77; program and planning officer USAF, Washington, 1977-81; dep. comdr. ops. 323d Flying Tng. Wing USAF, Mather AFB, Calif., 1982-84; chief strategy div. Orgn. of Joint Chiefs of Staff, Washington, 1984-85; comdr. 601st Tactical Control Wing USAF, Semach Air Base, Germany, 1985-87; asst. dep. chief staff for plans and prog. U.S. Air Forces in Europe, Ramstein Air Base, Germany, 1987-88; dep. asst. chief staff and vice comdr. Air Force Ctr. for Studies and Analyses, Washington, 1988-90; comdr. Air Force Studies and Analyses Agy., Washington, 1990-93; sr. program mgr. joint and comml. programs Sci. Applications Internat. Corp., McLean, Va., 1993-95, divsn. mgr. command and control ops.; v.p., ops. mgr. C2 Ops., McLean, Va., 1995-96; v.p. internat. and comml. bus. devel. ADSI Ops., 1996—; lectr. in field. Author: Command Structure for Theater Warfare, 1984, 2d edit., 1991, Air Land Combat -- An Organization for Joint Warfare,

1992, Global Reach -- Global Power, 1995; contbr. articles to profl. jours. Donor Washington Performing Arts Soc.; mem. Washington Opera Guild, Wolf Trap Assocs., Kennedy Ctr. Stars, Libr. Congress Assocs., Corcoran Gallery of Art, Air Mus. Britain. Decorated Legion of Merit, DFC, Air Medal. Mem. Nat. Air and Space Soc. (founder), Studies and Analyses Assn., Air Force Assn., Red River Valley Fighter Pilot Assn., Air Force Mus., Mil. Ops. Rsch. Soc., Assn. Former Students Tex. A&M U., Air War Coll. Alumni Assn., Armed Forces Communication and Electronics Assn., Tex. State Soc. Washington, Tex. Breakfast Club of Washington, Assn. Old Crows, Am. Legion, VFW, Order of Daedalians (flight adj. 1978-80, vice flight capt. 1987-88), Mil. Order of World Wars. Republican. Episcopalian. Home: 2385 N Danville St Arlington VA 22207-4923 Office: Sci Applications Internat Corp 1710 Goodridge Dr Mc Lean VA 22102-3701

CAREY, ROBERT MUNSON, university dean, physician; b. Lexington, Ky., Aug. 13, 1940; s. Henry Ames and Eleanor Day (Munson) C.; m. Theodora Vann Hereford, Aug. 24, 1963; children: Adonice Ames, Alicia Vann, Robert Josiah Hereford. BS, U. Ky., 1962; MD, Vanderbilt U., 1965. Diplomate Am. Bd. Internal Medicine, Am. Bd. Endocrinology and Metabolism, Nat. Bd. Med. Examiners. Intern in medicine U. Va. Hosp., Charlottesville, 1966; jr. asst. resident in medicine N.Y. Hosp.-Cornell Med. Ctr., N.Y.C., 1968-69, sr. asst. resident, 1969-70; instr. endocrinology, dept. medicine Vanderbilt U. Sch. Medicine, Nashville, 1970-72; postdoctoral fellow in medicine St. Mary's Hosp. Med. Sch., London, 1972-73; asst. prof. internal medicine, endocrinology and metabolism U. Va. Sch. Medicine, Charlottesville, 1973-76, assoc. prof., 1976-80, prof., 1980—, James Carroll Flippin prof. medical sci. and dean, 1986—, assoc. dir. Clin. Rsch. Ctr., 1975-86, head. div. endocrinology and metabolism, dept. internal medicine, 1978-86, chmn. gen. faculty, chmn. med. adv. com., chmn. exec. com., 1986—; attending staff U. Va. Hosp., Charlottesville, 1973—, pres. clin. staff, 1977-79, vice chmn. med. policy com., 1986—, adv. bd. 1986—; mem. study sect. on exptl. cardiovascular scis. NIH, 1982-85; mem. cardiovascular and renal adv. com. USDA, 1988—; vis. prof. div. nephrology, U. Miami Med. Sch., Fla., 1979, 83, 84, Hosp. das Clinicas da Univ., Fed. do Ceara, Forteleza, Brazil, 1981, hypertension div. Mt. Sinai Sch. Medicine, N.Y.C., 1981, div. pediatric endocrinology N.Y. Hosp.-Cornell Med. Ctr., 1981, dept. endocrinology St. Vincent's Hosp., Univ. Coll., Dublin, Ireland, 1982, depts. physiology and endocrinology Mayo Grad. Sch. Medicine, Rochester, Minn., 1984, div. rsch. Cleve. Clinic Found., 1984, Genentech, Inc., San Francisco, 1984, divs. endocrinology and metabolism U. Mass., U. Pa. Sch. Medicine, Boston U. Med. Sch., 1984, U. N.C. Sch. Medicine, 1985, Harvard Med. Sch., Boston, 1987, Jefferson Med. Coll., 1988; Bley Stein vis. prof. endocrinology U. So. Calif., 1987; Pfizer vis. prof. in pharmacology U. Chgo., 1988; co-organizer 3d Internat. Meeting on Peripheral Actions of Dopamine, Charlottesville, 1989; v.p. Va. Ambulatory Surgery, Inc., 1986—; speaker, presenter numerous nat. and internat. profl. meetings and congresses. Author: (with E.D. Vaughn) Adrenal Disorders, 1988; co-editor: Hypertension: An Endocrine Disease, 1985; mem. editorial bd. Jour. Clin. Endocronlogy and Metabolism, 1981-84, Hypertension jour., 1983-84, Am. Jour. Physiology: Heart and Circulatory Physiology, 1987-89, Am. Jour. Hypertension, 1987—; author over 150 articles, revs., papers for profl. jours., contbr. 19 chpts. to books. Mem. exec. com. and fin. com. U. Va. Health Services Found., 1986—; bd. dirs. Va. Kidney Stone Found., Inc., 1986—, The Harrison Found., Inc. U. Va., 1986—, Dyslexia Ctr., Charlottesville, 1986—. Surgeon (lt. comdr.) USPHS, 1966-68, res., 1968—. Recipient Attending Physician of Yr. awrd dept. internal medicine U. Va. Med. Ctr., 1983-84, Disting. Alumnus award and Founder's medal Vanderbilt U.; USPHS fellow Vanderbilt U., 1970-72; recipient numerous NIH grants as co-prin. and prin. investigator, 1972—. Fellow Am. Coll. Physicians (program com. regional meeting 1987), Coun. for High Blood Pressure Rsch. AMA (program com. 1984-86, exec. and long rang planning coms. 1992—); mem. Inst. Medicine of NAS, Am. Heart Assn. (established investigator 1975-80), Va. affiliate Am. Heart Assn. (bd. dirs. 1977-83, pres. 1979-80, Disting. Service award), The Endocrine Soc. (fin. com. 1988—, chair devel. com. 1991-92), Am. Fedn. Clin. Rsch. (so. sect. councilor 1978-81, nominating com. 1982), So. Soc. Clin. Investigation (nominating com. 1982, sec.-treas. 1985-86), Inter-Am. Soc. for Hypertension, Am. Soc. Clin. Investigation, Am. Clin. and Climatol. Assn., Am. Soc. Hypertension (intersocietal affairs com. 1986—), Internat. Soc. Hypertension, Assn. Am. Physicians, AMA, Albemarle County Med. Soc., Med. Soc. Va., Assn. Am. Med. Coll.s Coun. of Deans, Inst. of Medicine, Nat. Acad. of Scis., The Raven Soc., Alpha Omega Alpha (Disting. Med. Alumnus award Vanderbilt U. 1994). Home: Pavilion Vi East Lawn Charlottesville VA 22903 Office: U of Va Sch Medicine Med Ctr Box 395 Makim Charlottesville VA 22908

CARGO, RUSSELL ALLEN, art executive; b. Youngstown, Ohio, Dec. 7, 1948; s. Benjamin Rosser and Martha Virginia (Harnar) C.; m. Elizabeth Ann Bryant, Dec. 28, 1971; children: Elizabeth Rosser, Sarah Bryant. BA, Tex. Christian U., 1971; MA, So. Meth. U., 1977; MSBA, Boston U., 1982; PhD, U. Colo., 1990. Mus. preparator Indpls. Mus. of Art, 1971-72; registrar Carpenter Hochman Gallery, Dallas, Tex., 1976-77; curator The Art Ctr., Waco, Tex., 1977-79; various civilian mgr. positions USAF, 1979-86; adminstr. Colo. Speaks Out on Health Ctr. Health Ethics and Policy, Denver, 1986-88; devel. cons. Colo. Springs Fine Arts Ctr., 1988-89; dean acad. affairs and pres. San Antonio Art. Inst., 1989-92; sr. fellow Hemisphere Inst. for Pub. Svc., San Antonio, 1982-83; founder, pres., CEO Tech. Design and Devel. Corp., Inc., San Antonio, 1992—, also bd. dirs.; lectr. art history overseas program U. Md., Heidelberg, Germany, 1979-83; adj. lectr. art history San Antonio Art Inst., 1984-86; adj. asst. prof. engring. and social and policy scis. U. Tex., San Antonio, 1992-93; coord. nonprofit mgmt. program George Mason U., Fairfax, Va., 1994—; rsch. assoc. Ctr. for Mus. Studies, Smithsonian Instn., 1994—; fund raiser for numerous cultural and recreational programs. Contbr. articles to jours. in field, chpt. to book. Pres. bd. govs. Citizens for Arts H.S. San Antonio, 1992-93; strategic planning task force, 1992; participant San Antonio Civic Leaders Tour, Wright-Patterson AFB, Ohio, 1992; bd. dirs. San Antonio 2000, 1992—; adv. bd. Fairfax Conservatory Music and Art, 1993-95; planning com. San Antonio New Schs. Devel. Found., 1992-93. 1st lt. U.S. Army, 1972-74. Recipient scholarship Meadows Sch. of Arts. So. Meth. U., 1975-77, Doctoral fellowship Colo. Commn. on Higher Edn., 1986-88; cert. lesiure profl. Nat. Recreation and Park Assn., 1986. Mem. Am. Assn. Mus. (com. on mus. profl. tng.), Am. Soc. Pub. Adminstrn. (v.p. So. Tex. chpt.), DESIGN San Antonio (founding mem.), Pi Alpha Alpha. Home: 10836 Burr Oak Way Burke VA 22015-2419 Office: George Mason U Dept Pub & Internat Affairs 4400 University Dr Fairfax VA 22030-4443

CARINE, EDWIN THOMAS, actor, playwright; b. Queens, N.Y., Jan. 10, 1918; s. Edwin Thomas and Marion Ann (Deebach) C.; m. Lucille Lorretta Welch, Aug. 22, 1941 (dec. June 1982); children: Edwin, Eugene, Kathleen. BS, St. John's Coll., Bklyn., 1938, JSD, 1940; MS in Edn., St. John's Coll., Queens, 1949. Bar: N.Y. 1940. Pvt. practice, Queens, 1940-41; dir. student pers. Coll. Aeros., La Guardia Airport, N.Y., 1941-45; dir. admissions Hofstra U., Hempstead, N.Y., 1946-57; assoc. regional dir. Coll. Bd., N.Y.C., 1966-68, regional dir., 1969-81; freelance actor and playwright, Davenport, Fla., 1982—. Author: (plays) Taketori and the Shining Princess, 1991, Maggie and Madge, 1992, Borderline, 1993, Aunt Amelia's Deed, 1994, Cypress Trace, 1995, Fanfare, The Spa, 1996; appeared on stage in Heaven Can Wait, Corpse, I'm Not Rappaport, Social Security, Painting Churches, Funny Girl, Theatre Winter Haven, Fla., Look Homeward Angel, Icehouse Theatre, Fla.; in commls. for Cookin' Good Chicken, Opry Land, Astoria Fed. Savs. & Loan, Fla. Health Care, U.S. League Savs. Inst.; TV/video appearances Clarissa Explains It All, Beach Blast Sing-A-Long, Sea Quest. Staff sgt. USAAF, 1941-45. Recipient Best Featured Actor awards Ice House Theatre and Theatre Winter Haven.

CARL, ROBERT E., marketing company executive; b. Independence, Mo., Sept. 1, 1927; s. Elmer T. Carl and Marion R. (Pack) C.; BS, U. Kans., 1950; cert. in real estate So. Meth. U., 1965, cert. in mktg., 1990; cert. in investment analysis N.Y. Inst. Fin., 1967; m. Linda Arlene Sutton, Aug. 30, 1967; children—Melanie Ruth, Robert Brady, Camber Carleen. V.p.. sales promotion Riverside Press, Inc., Dallas, 1951-54; pres., chief operating officer Jones-Carl, Inc., Dallas, 1954-62; v.p. mktg. communications Modern Am. Corp., Dallas, 1962-70; v.p. sales Dunn Properties of Tex., Inc., Dallas, 1970-71; sr. v.p. mktg. svcs. Vantage Cos., Dallas, 1971-84; pres. Mktg. Mgmt. Systems, Dallas, 1984-90; v.p. The Premium Group, Inc., 1990-92; mem. Dallas Cable TV Bd., 1981-83. Founder, exec. dir. Preston Ctr. Assn., 1991-93. Recipient legion of honor degree Internat. Supreme Council of Order of De Molay, 1957; Silver Anvil award Pub. Relations Soc. Am., 1958. Mem. Sales and Mktg. Execs. Dallas (pres. 1976-77, Disting. Salesman's award 1954), S.W. Found. Free Enterprise (pres. 1975-76), Tex. Indsl. Devel. Coun., Nat. Assn. Corp. Real Estate Execs., Sales and Mktg. Execs. Internat. (sr. v.p.), Nat. Assn. Indsl. and Office Parks. Republican. Baptist. Clubs: Big D. Toastmaster (pres. 1966), Press, Dallas, Pk. City (bd. govs. 1989-92), Masons (32nd degree), Shriners. Contbr. articles to profl. jours. Home: 4209 Gloster Rd Dallas TX 75220-3819

CARLAY, RONALD LEON, mechanical engineer; b. Greenwood, S.C., May 28, 1939; s. Ralph Leon and Emmie (Buzhardt) C.; m. Patricia Biggerstaff, July 20, 1962 (div. 1980); children: Marion Patricia, Ronald L., Shannon Wells; m. Melissa Kate Ficklin, June 22, 1991. BSME, Clemson U., 1961; MBA, Furman U., 1975. Registered profl. engr., S.C.; cert. mfg. engr. Design engr. Duff-Norton Co., Charlotte, N.C., 1961-64; project engr. The Torrington Co., Clinton, S.C., 1965-69; plant engr. The Torrington Co., Honea Path, S.C., 1969-71; engring. mgr. The Torrington Co., Clinton, S.C., 1971-75, supt., 1975-84, mfg. mgr., 1984-87; project mgr. The Torrington Co., Torrington, Conn., 1987-89; staff engr., project mgr. CRS Sirrine Engring. Cons., Greenville, S.C., 1989-94; engr., project mgr Jacobs Sirrine, Greenville, 1994—. Contbr. articles to profl. jours. Charter mem. Rep. Presdl. Task Force, Washington, 1990—. Mem. ASME, NSPE, ASM, Water Pollution Control Fedn., Am. Water Works Assn., Soc. Mfg. Engrs., Assn. Energy Engrs., S.C. C. of C. (bd. dirs. 1982-83). Methodist. Home: RR 1 Box 123 Waterloo SC 29384-9718 Office: Jacobs Sirrine PO Box 5456 1041 E Butler Rd Greenville SC 29607-5725

CARLE, ERICA See PETER, JANET

CARLIN, STEWART HENRY, accounting executive; b. Colo. Springs, Colo., Dec. 27, 1952; s. William Henry and Jean (Stewart) C.; m. Martha Self, June 10, 1978; children: Melissa, Kristyn. BS in Indsl. Mgmt., Ga. Tech, 1974; BS in Acctg., Stetson U., 1975. CPA, Fla. Mgr. G,P,H, & D, CPAs, Daytona Beach, Fla., 1975-78; treas. Carlin's TV & Appliance, Daytona Beach, Fla., 1978-83; controller Atlanta News Agy., Atlanta, 1983-85; controller, treas. Camelot Distbg. Co., Atlanta, 1985-89; controller CISU, Atlanta, 1989-90; pres. Acctg. Consultants of Cobb, Marietta, Ga., 1990—; chmn. Olympic CPA Vols., Atlanta, 1990—; co-chmn. Course Ops., Marietta, 1991-96, Charity Ball/Silent Auction, Atlanta, 1991-96. Mem. Scottish Rite Festival, Atlanta, 1990-96, CPAs in Industry, Govt. & Edn., Atlanta, 1985-96, chmn. 1992-94; v.p. Hospice, 1992-94, pres. Marietta Rotary Club, 1995-96, mem. fin. com. Mt. Zion Meth. Ch., 1990-96, recreation com., 1990-94, adminstrn. coun., 1992-96. Mem. AICPA, Ga. Soc. CPAs, Marietta Metro Rotary Club. Republican. Office: Acctg Consultants of Cobb 191 Lawrence St Ste 503 Marietta GA 30060-1659

CARLISLE, ERVIN FREDERICK, university provost, educator; b. Delaware, Ohio, Mar. 20, 1935; s. Ervin Frederick C. and Winnifred (Lucas) Pope; children: Lindy, Rebecca, Ginna, Jana; m. Barbara, Sept. 28, 1973. B.A., Ohio Wesleyan U., 1956; M.A., Ohio State U., 1957; Ph.D., Ind. U., 1963. Mem. faculty Ohio U., Athens, 1962-63, DePauw U., Greencastle, Ind., 1963-66; asst. prof. dept. English Mich. State U., East Lansing, 1966-68, assoc. prof., assoc. chmn. dept. English, 1968-72, prof., 1972-79, chmn. dept. English, 1979-81, asst. to pres., 1981-85; provost, exec. v.p. for acad. affairs Miami U., Oxford, Ohio, 1985-89; sr. v.p., provost Va. Poly. Inst. and State U., Blacksburg, 1989-94; William E. Lavery prof. Va. Poly. Inst. and State U., 1995—. Editor: American Poetry and Prose, 1970; author: The Uncertain Self, 1973, Loren Eiseley, 1983. Served to 1st lt. USAF, 1957-60. NEH fellow, 1972-73; NEH grantee, 1978, 80. Mem. MLA (chmn. lit. and sci. div. 1983). Home: Three Meadow Mountain Rt 1 Box 74 Newport VA 24128 Office: Dept English Va Poly Inst and State U Blacksburg VA 24061

CARLISLE, PATRICIA KINLEY, mortgage company executive, paralegal; b. Royston, Ga., Sept. 21, 1949; d. Luther Clark Kinley and Ann Busby Carey; children: Angela Renee, William Clark, Matthew Vincent. Grad., Suburban Inst. Real Estate, Tucker, Ga., 1978; grad. with honors, Lanier Tech. Sch., Oakwood, Ga., 1983; postgrad., Gainesville Coll., 1986, Maryville Coll., 1986. Lic. real estate salesperson, Ga. Fin. analyst, then pers. mgr. Citicorp Acceptance Co., Inc., St. Louis, 1983-89; exec. v.p., v.p. purchasing, regional sales mgr. George-Ingraham Corp., Stone Mountain, Ga., 1989-90; sr. loan officer Terrace Mortgage Co., Atlanta, 1990-92; dir. client svcs. Feagin & Assocs., P.C., 1992-96, Atlanta, 1996—; dir. client svcs. Feagin & Assocs., PL, 1996—; rsch. bd. advisors Am. Biog. Inst., Inc. Mem. NAFE, Forsyth County Bd. Realtors, Aircraft Owners and Pilots Assn., Female Execs. North Atlanta, AAPMW, Ga. Mortgage Brokers Assn., MBAG. Home: PO Box 467364 Atlanta GA 31146-7364

CARLS, STEPHEN DOUGLAS, history educator; b. Mpls., Feb. 15, 1944; s. Ernest Paul and Eleanor Louise (Schwerdfeger) C.; m. Alice-Catherine Maire, June 25, 1977; children: Philip Stephen, Elizabeth Eleanor, Paul Victor-James. BA, Wheaton Coll., 1966; MA, U. Minn., 1968, PhD, 1982. Tchg. asst. U. Minn., Mpls., 1970-71; asst. prof. history Sterling (Kans.) Coll., 1971-81, assoc. prof., 1981-83; assoc. prof. Union U., Jackson, Tenn., 1983-90, prof., chairperson dept. history and polit. sci., 1990—. Author: Louis Loucheur and the Shaping of Modern France, 1993; contbr. book revs. to Historian, 1985—. So. Regional Edn. Bd. grantee, 1985; recipient Faculty Mem. of Yr. award Union U. chpt. Lambda Chi Alpha, 1987. Mem. Am. Hist. Assn., Coun. for European Studies, Soc. for French Hist. Studies, Econ. and Bus. Hist. Soc., Western Soc. for French History, West Tenn. Hist. Soc., Phi Alpha Theta (faculty sponsor Delta Psi chpt. 1983—), Pi Gamma Mu (faculty sponsor Kans. Zeta chpt. 1975-76, 78-83). Home: 59 Lesa Dr Jackson TN 38305 Office: Union Univ Dept History Jackson TN 38305-3697

CARLSMITH, ROGER SNEDDEN, chemistry and energy conservation researcher; b. N.Y.C., Oct. 2, 1925; s. Leonard Eldon and Hope (Snedden) C.; m. Thelma Kathleen Sutton, July 31, 1954; children: David, Nancy Lynn. AB in Chemistry cum laude, Harvard, 1948; MSCE, MIT, 1950. Rsch. engr. Oak Ridge (Tenn.) Nat. Lab., 1950-62, group leader, 1962-70, sect. mgr., 1970-78, prog. dir. conservation and renewable energy, 1978-94; ret., 1994; mem. Gov.'s Energy Task Force, Tenn., 1972-74, adv. com. Fed. Power Commn., Washington, 1973; bd. dirs. Am. Coun. Energy Efficient Economy., Washington. Author: (book with others) World Energy Conference Survey of Energy Resourses, 1974. Sgt. USAF, 1943-46. Recipient Sadi Carnot medal for achievements in energy conservation rsch. Dept. Energy, 1996. Mem. AAAS, Sierra Club, The Wilderness Soc. Home: 1052 W Outer Dr Oak Ridge TN 37830-8641

CARLSON, BRUCE HERBERT, interim personnel company executive; b. Chgo., Sept. 14, 1946; s. Kenneth Herbert and Fern Gwendolyn (Krause) C.; m. Candace Jo Stefani, Sept. 18, 1971; children: Scott Kenneth, Chad Christopher. BA, No. Ill. U., 1968, M of Bus., 1971. Program coord. No. Ill. U., DeKalb, 1968-72; program dir. Ga. Inst. Tech., Atlanta, 1972-73; budget analyst DeKalb County, Decatur, Ga., 1973-74, adminstr. budget, 1974-78; v.p. mgmt. Intex Products, Inc., Greenville, S.C., 1978-81; v.p. fin. Package Supply Co., Greenville, S.C., 1981-83, exec. v.p., 1983-88; v.p./pres. Interim Personnel, Greenville, S.C., 1988—. Bd. dirs. U. S.C., Spartanburg, 1987—, Higher Edn. Consortium, Greenville, 1989-90; bd. regents Leadership Greenville, 1990-91; chmn. bd. deacons 4th Presbyn. Ch., Greenville, 1993—. Mem. Anderson Sertoma Club, Greenville Country Club, Rotary (Paul Harris fellow), Delta Upsilon. Republican. Home: 170 Ingleoak Ln Greenville SC 29615-3151 Office: Interim Personnel Healthcare 300 University Rdg Greenville SC 29601-3645

CARLSON, J(OHN) PHILIP, lawyer; b. Shickley, Nebr., Apr. 16, 1915; s. Christopher Theodore and Klara Louise (Blomquist) C.; m. Maryjo Suverkrup, Oct. 14, 1950. Student Luther Coll., 1931-33; AB, Wayne State Coll., 1935; MA, Columbia U., 1967; JD, Georgetown U., 1951. Bar: D.C. 1952, U.S. Dist. Ct. D.C. 1952, U.S. Ct. Appeals D.C. cir. 1952, U.S. Supreme Ct. 1957, U.S. Ct. Mil. Appeals 1970, D.C. Ct. Appeals 1972. Tchr., athletic coach high schs. of Bristow, Nebr., 1935-37, Carroll, Nebr., 1937-38, Ashland, Nebr., 1938-42; vets. rels. advisor OPA, Washington, 1946-47; tng. specialist Dept. Navy, 1947-56; minority counsel House Com. on Govt. Ops., 1956-80; pvt. practice, Washington, 1980-93. Bd. dirs. Fellowship Sq. Found., Reston, Va., 1961-86, Peter Muehlenberg Meml. Assn., 1972-86. Capt. USAAF, 1942-45; ETO. Congl. Staff fellow Am. Polit. Sci. Assn., 1964-65, 66-67; Decorated D.F.C., Air medal with oak leaf cluster; recipient Meritorious Svc. award Am. Nat. Standards Inst., 1984, Meritorious Svc. award Fellowship Square Found., 1986. Mem. ABA, Fed. Bar Assn., D.C. Bar Assn., Am. Judicature Soc., Am. Econ. Assn., Air Force Assn., Res. Officers Assn., Metropolitan Club, Capitol Hill Club, George Town Club, Nat. Econs. Club, Belle Haven Country Club. Republican. Lutheran. Home: 2206 Belle Haven Rd Alexandria VA 22307-1115

CARLSON, ROBERT ARTHUR, engineer; b. Chgo., Nov. 24, 1937; s. Arthur Axel Falke and Francis Elizabeth C.; m. Mary Rose Johnson; 1 child, Robert Arthur II. AAS, CCAF, 1983; BA in Bus. Adminstrn., Wayland Baptist U., 1980, BS in Civil Engring. Tech., 1980; MA in Mgmt., Webster U., 1986. Topographic surveyor U.S. Army, 1955-58; engring. asst. USAF, 1958-84; constrn. rep. Naval ROICC, Corpus Christi, Tex., 1984-86; chief master planning pub. works Naval Air Station, Corpus Christi, 1986-87; dir. maintenance pub. works. Naval Air Station, 1987-88; chief master planning Engring. & Housing, Mianz, Germany, 1988-90; chief roads & grounds 21 TAACOM, Kaiserlautern, Germany, 1990-91; chief bldg. & grounds 21 TAACOM, 1991-92; chief planning pub. works Naval Air Sta., 1992-96; dep. to dir. Pub. Works Directorate, Pusan, Korea, 1996—. Treas. First Bapt. Ch., Corpus Christi, 1992-96. Recipient meritorious svcs. medals (3) USAF, joint svc. medal NATO, 1980, Vietnam svc. and campaign medal USAF, 1972, commendation medal, 1978. Mem. Soc. Am. Mil. Engrs. (v.p. 1992-93), Air Force Sgts. Assn., Air Force Assn. Democrat. Home: 730 Mariana Dr Corpus Christi TX 78418-4777 Office: Pusan DPW 20 Supgp Unit 15181 Box 271 APO AP 96259-0220 also: Directorate of Pub Works Unit #15181 APO AP 96259-0270

CARLTON, BRADLEY JOSEPH, medical educator; b. Mayfield, Ky., Feb. 3, 1967; s. Billy Joe and Pauline Isabelle (Green) C. AS, Jackson (Tenn.) State C.C., 1989; BS, Coll. of St. Francis, Joliet, Ill., 1996. Asst. clin. instr. Jackson-Madison County Gen. Hosp., Jackson, 1988-93, staff radiologic technologist, 1993-94, radiology clin. instr., 1994—; clin. instr. radiology Pitt C.C., Greenville, N.C., 1993. Mem. radiology adv. com. Jackson State C.C., 1990—, allied health adv. com., 1990—; pres. Radiology Endowment Fund of Jackson-Madison County Gen. Hosp., 1993—. Recipient Mallinckrodt award Meth. Hosp. of Dyersburg, Tenn., 1988. Mem. Am. Soc. Radiologic Technologists, Tenn. Soc. radiology Technologists (Dist. V pres. 1989-91). Office: Jackson-Madison County Gen Hosp 708 W Forest Ave Jackson TN 38301-3901

CARLTON, JENNIFER LENORE, elementary education educator; b. Austell, Ga., July 2, 1968; d. Harrison A. and Pamela L. (Heard) C. BS, Kennesaw State Coll., 1993. Cert. pre-kindergarten-5th grade. Tchr. kindergarten spl. instrnl. assistance Douglas County Schs., Douglasville, Ga., 1993—. Sunday sch. tchr. Macland Presbyn., Powder Springs, Ga., 1993—. Mem. Nat. Assn. Educators. Home: 2273 Warren Dr Austell GA 30001

CARLTON, PATRICK WILLIAM, educational administration educator; b. Gadsden, Ala., July 10, 1937; s. Peter A. and Lois (Williams) C.; m. Janet Reeve Carlton, June 1977; children: Alice Anne, Jennifer Joy. AA, Louisburg (N.C.) Coll., 1957; BA, U. N.C., 1959, EdM, 1961, PhD, 1966; postgrad., U. Oreg., 1967; MA in History, Shippensburg (Pa.) U., 1992. Sci. tchr. Arlington (Va.) County and San Diego Pub. Schs., 1960-63; asst. prin. Chapel Hill Schs., Chapel Hill, N.C., 1964-66; fed. grants officer U.S. Office Edn., Washington, 1967-69; dir. sponsored programs Coll. Edn. NYU, 1969-71; dir. edn. research services U. Pacific, Stockton, Calif., 1971-74; assoc. prof. ednl. adminstrn. Va. Poly. Inst. and State U., Blacksburg, 1974—; interim dir. edn and outreach U. Office of Internat. Programs Va. Tech., 1996—. Author: The Collective Dilemma, 1969; contbr. articles to profl. jours. Col. USAR, 1955-92. Mem. Am. Assn. Sch. Adminstrs., Am. Arbitration Assn., Oral History Assn., Rotary, Phi Delta Kappa. Home: PO Box 11177 Blacksburg VA 24062 Office: Va Poly Inst and State U Coll Edn Blacksburg VA 24061

CARMACK, COMER ASTON, JR., steel company executive; b. Phenix City, Ala., June 26, 1932; s. Comer Aston and Mary Kate (Mills) C.; AS, Marion Mil. Inst., 1951; BS, Ala. Poly. Inst., 1954; m. Blanche Yarbrough, Nov. 30, 1957; children: Comer Aston, Mary Kate. Project mgr. Muscogee Iron Works, Columbus, Ga., 1956-58, v.p. engring., 1958-73, pres., 1973-91, chmn. bd. dirs. 1991—; pres. Universal Drives & Svcs., 1985-89; pres. M.K. Realty, Columbus, 1985-91, chmn. bd. dirs. 1991—. Past bd. dirs. Better Bus. Bur. With USAFR, 1954-56. Registered profl. engr., Calif. Mem. ASTM, Nat. Soc. Profl. Engrs., Ga. Soc. Profl. Engrs., Ga. Archtl. and Engring. Soc. (past pres., bd. dir. Columbus chpt.), Order of Engr., Chattahooche Valley Safety Soc., Columbus Country Club. Methodist. Office: Muscogee Iron Works 1324 11th Ave Columbus GA 31901-2202

CARMAN, PATRICIA DOBBS, language educator; b. Detroit, Sept. 24, 1950; d. John M. and Mary Sue (Guice) Dobbs; m. Don Claud Carman, July 16, 1972; 1 child, Zachary Andrew. BA, Ga. Southwestern U., 1972; MEd, Ga. State U., 1975. Tchr. English Jonesboro (Ga.) H.S., 1972-79; instr. English Clayton State Coll., Morrow, Ga., 1981-87, West Ga. Coll., Carrollton, 1987-93, McIntosh H.S., Peachtree City, Ga., 1993—.

CARMANY, SANDRA GARRETT, city council member; b. Greensboro, N.C., Jan. 20, 1949; d. Joseph Lee and Edna Mae (Underwood) G.; m. Robert Millard Carmany, Mar. 23, 1968; children: Robert Scott, Mark Edward, Michael Sean. Student, N.C. State U., Raleigh, 1967-68. Clerical Potomac Temporaries, Arlington, Va., 1968; media asst. Greensboro (N.C.) Pub. Schs., 1981-88; statis. analyst Dr. Carl Shartner, Winston Salem, N.C., 1989-90; grant adminstrn. N.C. PTA, Raleigh, 1987-92; city council member City of Greensboro, N.C., 1991—. Mem. N.C. Women's Polit. Caucus, Women in Mcpl. Govt., City of Greensboro; pres. N.C. PTA, 1994—, bd. dirs., 1994—. Named N.C. PTA life mem. D.L. Jones PTA, Greensboro, 1984, Nat. PTA, 1996. Mem. Enrichment Fund for Guilford County Schs. Republican. Methodist. Office: Greensboro City Council PO Box 3136 Greensboro NC 27402-3136

CARMEAN, E. A., JR., art museum director, art historian; b. Springfield, Ill., Jan. 25, 1945; s. E.A. Sr. and Helen E. (Marker) C.; m. Janet Anderson Yantis, June 7, 1970 (dec. 1977); 1 child, Elizabeth Anne; m. Mary Kathryn Shelton, Apr. 27, 1991. BA in Art History and Philosophy, MacMurray Coll., 1967; DFA (hon.), Macmurray Coll., 1983; MA in Art History, U. Ill., 1970. Lectr. in art history U. Ill., Urbana, 1969-70; art instr. Ft. Berthold Indian Reservation, Berthold, N.D., 1970-71; curator 20th Century art Mus. Fine Arts, Houston, 1971-74, Nat. Gallery of Art, Washington, 1974-84; dir. Modern Art Mus., Ft. Worth, 1984-91, Brooks Mus. of Art, Memphis, 1992—; vis. prof. art history Rice U., Houston, 1971-74, George Washington U., Washington, 1974-78; former chmn. adv. com. North Tex. Inst. Visual Arts Edn.; former mem. Ft. Worth Cultural Dist. Com., Archtl. Adv. Com. Ft. Worth Zoo. Films: (participant, partial narrator) Helen Frankenthaler, 1977, (spl. advisor, narrator) Picasso: The Saltimbanques, 1981, (co-dir., narrator) David Smith, 1983 (Emmy award for best direction of documentary 1984), (spl. advisor, narrator) Je Suis le Cahier: The Sketchbooks of Picasso, 1987; patentee in field; author catalogues; contbr. articles to profl. jours. Art advisor Calvary Episcopal Ch., Memphis; mem. downtown redevel. com. City of Memphis. NEA fellow, 1973, John Simon Guggenheim fellow, 1978; rsch. grantee NEA, 1971, 73. Mem. Am. Mus. Assn., Assn. Art Mus. Dirs., Internat. Coun. Mus., Coll. Art Assn., Friends of Catalogue Raisonne. Home: Mud Island 954 Harbor View Dr Memphis TN 38103 Office: Memphis Brooks Mus Art 1934 Poplar Ave Memphis TN 38104-2756

CARMICHAEL, DONALD RAY, artist, educator; b. Elnora, Ind., Dec. 26, 1922; s. Ora and Mary Mildred (Edmondson) C.; m. Beulah Frances Bunker, Dec. 20, 1947; children: Susan Lynn, Daniel Ray, Catherine Joan, Rodger Ora, Patricia Ann. BFA, Ind. U.-Purdue U., Indpls., 1951; MFA, U. Tenn., 1975. Lab. technician Lindeman Corp., Indpls., 1951-56; color stylist Lindeman Corp., Galax, Va., 1956-61; sales rep. Lindeman Corp., Jackson, Tenn., 1961-69; instr. art Union U., Jackson, 1969-74; advisor visual arts Tenn. Arts Commn., Nashville, 1969-74, chmn. visual arts, 1974-76; field rep. Tenn. Arts Commn., 1976-78; dir. Tarble Arts Ctr., Ea. Ill. U., Charleston, Ill., 1978-85; lectr. in field. Featured paintings at Artists USA, 1972-73; one-man shows include Union U., Tenn., 1969, Internat. Festival, Fulton, Ky., 1970, Tusculum Coll., Tenn., 1970, U. Ark., Little Rock, 1971,

McClung Mus. U. Tenn., Knoxville, 1975, Carnegie Ctr. for Arts and History, Jackson, Tenn., 1986, Kress Internat. Plz., Sarasota, Fla., 1987, Venice Art Ctr., Fla., 1987; exhibited in group shows at Cheekwood Fine Arts Ctr., Nashville, 1967, Kottler Gallery, N.Y.C., 1971, 23rd Grand Prix Internat., Deauville, France, 1972, Bertrand Russell Centenary Rotunda Gallery, London, 1972, 9th Grand Prix, Cannes, France, 1973, Springfield Art Ctr., Mo., 1974, 6th Ann. Tenn. Watercolor Soc. Hunter Mus., Chattanooga, 1976, Foothills Art Ctr., Golden, Colo., 1976, Longboat Key Art Ctr., Fla., 1986, Internat. Soc. Marine Painters Marine Mus. at Fall River, Mass., 1991, Crooked Tree Arts Coun. Petoskey, Mich., 1992, others; represented in permanent collections Tenn. State Mus., McClung Mus., U. Tenn., Bristol Art Ctr., Tenn., Tarble Arts Ctr. EIU, Charleston, Ill., Venice Arts Ctr., Fla., Jackson Pub. Libr., Casey Jones Railroad Mus., Tenn. Bd. dirs. Ctrl. Ill. Arts Consortium, Springfield, 1979-85, program chmn., 1982-83; pres. Venice (Fla.) Art Ctr., 1993-94, bd. dirs., exhbn. chmn., 1987-93; divsn. chmn. Goals for City of Jackson, 1972; mem. planning com. New Civic Ctr., Jackson, 1972. Sgt. U.S. Army, 1942-45. Mem. Suncoast Watercolor Soc., Fla. Watercolor Soc., Kiwanis (bd. dirs., editor newsletter 1986-96, pres. 1993-94), Elks. Republican. Methodist. Home: 860 Stewart St Englewood FL 34223-2844

CARMICHAEL, JOHN CRAIG, JR., career counselor; b. Ft. Knox, Ky., Apr. 13, 1953; s. John Craig and Sara Alice (Booher) C.; m. Barbara Louise Werth, Aug. 18, 1984; 1 child, Jonathan Christian. BA, Western Ky. U., 1980, MEd, 1981. Employment counselor Ky. Dept. Human Resources, Bowling Green, 1980-81; residence hall dir. East Tex. State U., Commerce, 1981-84; career specialist, human devel. instr. Richland Coll., Dallas, 1987—; lectr. Richland Coll. Spkrs. Bur., 1993—; cons. Pvt. Industry Coun., Dallas, 1994—. Recipient Nat. Inst. for Staff and Orgnl. Devel. award for Tchg. Excellence, C.C. Leadership Program, U. Tex., Austin, 1994. Mem. ASCD, Tex. C.C. Tchrs. Assn. Democrat. Episcopalian. Home: 3306 Heathercrest Dr Garland TX 75044 Office: Richland College 12800 Abrams Rd Dallas TX 75243

CARMICHAEL, MIRIAM WILLENA, neurologist, educator, consultant; b. Birmingham, Ala., Oct. 21, 1925; m. Shirley Powell Lingo, Apr. 22, 1960; 1 child, Stuart Patrick Lingo. BA in Music/Sociology, Converse Coll., 1946; postgrad., U. Richmond, 1946-47; MD, Med. Coll. Va., 1951. Diplomate Am. Bd. Psychiatry and Neurology in Neurology, with Spl. Competence in Child Neurology. Rotating intern U. Wis. Hosp., Madison, 1951-52; jr. asst., asst. resident in medicine Med. Coll. Va., Richmond, 1952-54; jr. asst. resident in neurology Neurol. Inst. N.Y.-Columbia Presbyn. Med. Ctr., 1954-55; asst. resident in neurology Mass. Gen. Hosp., Boston, 1955-56, neuropathology fellow, 1956-57; rsch. fellow in neuropharmacology Coll. Physicians & Surgeons-Presbyn. Hosp. Med. Ctr., 1959-60; neurologist Richmond Meml. Hosp., 1960—; pvt. practice adult and child neurology Richmond, 1960—; neurologist Med. Coll. Va. Hosp., 1957-58; Exptl. Drug Program, 1959-60, U. Va. Hosp., 1960-76; cons. Sheltering Arms Hosp., 1964-80, Stuart Cir. Hosp., 1960—, St. Mary's Hosp., 1970—, C&E Clinic-Anderson Clinic, 1960—, Child Devel. Clinic State Health Dept., 1957—, Richmond Met. Hosp., 198-93, Children's Hosp., 1960—; teaching fellow Harvard Med. Sch., 1956-57; asst. prof. neurology Med. Coll. Va., 1957-58, asst. in neurology Exptl. Drug Clinic Epilepsy Coll. Physicians & Surgeons-Columbia U. Presbyn. Med. Ctr., 1959-60; asst. clin. prof. neurology U. Va., Charlottesville, 1960-70, lectr. pediatric neurology, assoc. prof. neurology, 1970-76; med. dir. Bur. Crippled Children's Neurology Clinic Richmond Area Master Clinic Va. State Dept. Health, 1957—; asst. examiner Am. Bd. Psychiatry and Neurology, 1965-70, examiner, 1981; mem. steering com. Va. Coun. Health and the Handicapped Child, 1961—; mem. adv. coun. for learning disabilities project Chesterfield County Schs., 1968; mem. prof. adv. bd. Epilepsy Soc. Va., 1978-; dir. Neurologically Impaired Individual Symposium Series. Co-author: Neurologic Manifestations of Chronic Pulmonary Insufficiency, 1957; contbr. articles to profl. jours. Bd. dirs. Buford Acad., 1967-74, Ginter Park Ch.'s Child Care Ctrs., Inc. NIH Trainee award, 1959-60. Mem. AMA, Am. Acad. Neurology, Va. Med. Soc., Richmond Acad. Medicine, Va. Neurol. Soc., Assn. Rsch. in Nervous and Mental Disease, Am. Epilepsy Soc., Richmond Pediatric Soc., Assn. Childhood Edn. Internat. (med. advisor Richmond br. 1964-66, pres. 1966-68, bd. dirs. 1969-74), Royal Soc. Medicine (London), Gamma Sigma, Alpha Sigma Sigma. Office: 1400 Westwood Ave Richmond VA 23227-4627

CARMICLE, LINDA HARPER, psychotherapist; b. Westmore, Tenn., Oct. 20, 1937; d. Noel Franklin and Mary Frank (Caldwell) Harper; m. Jerrel B. Carmicle, June 2, 1956; children: Roxanna Linn Carmicle Lynch, Jerry Noel. AA, St. Petersburg Jr. Coll., 1968; BSW with honors, Tex. Women's U., 1975, MA, 1977; PhD in Psychology, Fielding Inst., Santa Barbara, Calif., 1992. Lic. profl. counselor, marriage and family therapist; cert. eating disorder specialist, chem. dependency specialist; cert. group psychotherapist; supr. for LPCs. Dir. Galaxy Ctr., Garland, Tex., 1975-78; counselor Saudi Arabia Internat. Sch., Daharan, 1978, Dallas County Family Ct. Counselors, Dallas, 1979-83; pvt. practice psychotherapy Dallas and Plano, Tex., 1983—; mem. faculty S.W. Group Psychotherapy Inst., 1995; mem. adj. faculty Tex. Women's U., Denton, 1976-78, rep. Coun. on Social Work Edn., 1977. Contbr. articles to profl. jours. Active Custer Rd. United Meth. Ch. Mem. Am. Group Psychotherapy Assn., Am. Assn. Marriage and Family Therapy, Tex. Assn. Counseling Devel., Tex. Assn. Marriage and Family Therapy, Dallas Group Psychotherapy Soc. (chair program com.), Internat. Assn. Transactional Analysis, Internat. Assn. Eating Disorder Profls. Democrat. Methodist. Home: 3005 Saddlehead Dr Plano TX 75075-1529 Office: 2301 Ohio Dr Ste 215 Plano TX 75093-3902

CARMODE, RALPH E., communications educator. BA in Radio-TV Motion Pictures, U. N.C., 1960; MA in Comms., Brigham Young U., 1966; PhD in Speech Comms., Pa. State U., 1986. Cert. secondary tchr. journalism, speech, and drama, Utah. TV dir., prodn. asst. WTVD, Durham, N.C., 1959-61; TV producer/dir. Weber County Sch. Dist., Ogden, Utah, 1965-66, KLRN/U. Tex., Austin and San Antonio, 1966-68, WQED/WQEX-TV, Pitts., 1968; TV dir. WIIC-TV (now WPXI), Pitts., 1968-73; asst. prof., instr. Pa. State U., Wilkes-Barre/Univ. Park, 1974-80; TV prodn. mgr. WVIA-TV, Wilkes Barre and Scranton, Pa., 1979-80; assoc. prof. Divsn. Head Miss. U. for Women, Columbus, 1980-84; assoc. prof., journalism R-TV Murray (Ky.) State U., 1984-87; prof. comms. Jacksonville (Ala.) State U., 1987—. Conductor TV workshops for Boys and Girls Clubs, Calhoun County, Ala., 1995-96, Anniston Mid. Sch., Ala., 1996; oratory judge Am. Legion, Bay Minnette, Ala., 1993. Mem. Assn. for Edn. in Journalism and Mass Comm., Broadcast Edn. Assn. LDS. Office: Jacksonville State U 700 Pelham Rd N Jacksonville AL 36265-1602

CARMODY, EDMOND, bishop; b. Moyvane, Kerry, Ireland, Jan. 12, 1934. Student, St. Brendan's Coll., Killarney, St. Patrick Seminary, Carlow, Ireland. Ordained priest San Antonio, 1957; missionary Peru, 1984-89; consecrated titular bishop Mortlach, 1988; consecrated aux. bishop San Antonio, 1988; consecrated bishop Tyler, Tex., 1992. Office: Diocese of Tyler Chancery 1015 ESE Loop 323 Tyler TX 75701-9663

CARMODY, THOMAS ROSWELL, business products company executive; b. Cleve., May 18, 1933; s. Thomas R. and Mary (Farrell) C.; m. Grace Marie Wagner, Aug. 25, 1956; children—Thomas, John, Michael. B.B.A., John Carroll U., 1956. Adminstrv. mgr. Curtis 1000 Inc., Houston, 1962-68; div. mgr. Curtis 1000 Inc., Lawrence, Kans., 1969-75, regional exec. v.p., 1976-81; exec. v.p. Am. Bus. Products, Inc., Atlanta, 1982-84; chief exec. officer, 1988; pres. Am. Bus. Products, Inc., Atlanta, 1985-94, chmn., 1994—, also bd. dirs. Served to 1st lt. U.S. Army, 1957-59. Mem. Atlanta Rotary Club, Capital City Country Club. Republican. Roman Catholic.

CARMODY, VICTOR WALLACE, JR., lawyer; b. Jackson, Miss., Aug. 29, 1945; s. Victor Wallace and Mary Elizabeth (Alexander) C.; m. Suzanne Hackney, Mar. 24, 1975 (div. 1981); m. Dona Louise Leach, Aug. 31, 1983; children: T.J., Tripp. Student, Miss. State U., 1963-67; JD, Miss. Coll., 1979. Bar: Miss. 1980. Lt. Jackson (Miss.) Police Dept., 1973-80; ptnr. Stanfield, Carmody & Clark, Jackson, 1978—; founder, bd. regents Nat. Coll. for DUI Def. Capt. U.S. Army, 1967-80. Mem. Am. Corrections Assn. (legal issues in jail sect. 1987—), Miss. Bar Assn., Hinds County Bar Assn., Miss. Atty.'s for Constitutional Justice. Baptist. Home: 1426 Windrose Pointe Brandon MS 39042 Office: Stanfield Carmody & Clark The Court St Bldg 514 E Court St Jackson MS 39201-5001

CARMONY, JANET CAROLYN (JANET CAROLYN KOPF), sales and marketing executive; b. San Francisco, Oct. 30, 1946; d. Richard Kenneth Carmoney and Nancy Ruth (Doud) Carmoney Brown. Student Sonoma State Coll., 1964-65. Owner Small World Travel, Mill Valley, Calif., 1970-75; co-owner Entrerprises Unltd., Riverside/Orange County, Calif., 1977-80; pres. Sequoia Internat., Houston, 1989—. Recipient multiple travel industry awards, 1970-75, award 10th Am. Song Festival, 1983. Mem. NAFE, Internat. Platform Assn., Rotary (bd. dirs. Houston), Internat. Knife and Fork Club (bd. dirs.). Republican. Presbyterian. Club: Orange County Sabre (founding bd. dirs., past v.p.).

CARNAHAN, ROBERT NARVELL, lawyer; b. Littlefield, Tex., Nov. 22, 1928; s. C.D. and Wilma L. (Hartness) C.; children from previous marriage: Cynthia, Michael, Christopher; m. Natalie Kay Kowalik, May 8, 1993. BBA, Tex. Tech. Coll., 1950; JD with honors, U. Tex.-Austin, 1957. Bar. Tex. 1956. Asst. county atty. Potter County, Tex., Amarillo; ptnr. Stokes, Carnahan & Fields, Amarillo; sole practice, Corpus Christi, Tex. Contbr. articles to profl. jours. 1st lt. USAF, 1954. Mem. State Bar Tex., Nueces County Bar Assn., Tex. Trial Lawyers Assn., Tex. Assn. Criminal Def. Lawyers, Am. Judicature Assn. Office: Law Offices of Carnahan 730 Wilson Plz Corpus Christi TX 78476

CARNELL, CLAUDE MITCHELL, JR., academic administrator; b. Woodroff, S.C., Apr. 27, 1934; s. Claude M. Sr. and Edith I. (Gossett) C.; m. Elizabeth Jean Frei, July 6, 1957 (dec.); children: Elizabeth Suzanne Carnell Smith, Claude Michael. AA, Mars Hill Coll., 1954; BA, Furman U., 1956; MA, U. Ala., 1958; PhD, La. State U., 1972; HHD, Lander Coll., 1988. Instr. Furman U., Greenville, S.C., 1958-59; speech/lang. pathologist Soc. for Crippled Children, Wheeling, W.Va., 1959-60; chief speech pathologist Cerebral Palsy Assn. Baton Rouge, 1960-64; exec. dir. Charleston (S.C.) Speech and Hearing Ctr., 1964—; adj. prof. La. State U., Baton Rouge, 1962-64, Webster U., Charleston, 1980—, Charleston So. U., 1993-94, 96; chmn. John A. Hamrick Lectureship in Bapt. History, 1996; pub. adv. com. Med. U. of the S.C. Coll. of Health Professions, 1995—. Author: Development, Management, and Evaluation of Community Speech and Hearing Centers, 1976, Speaking in Church Made Simple, 1985; contbr. articles to profl. jours. Sunday sch. tchr. First Bapt. Ch., Charleston, 1973—; bd. dirs. Clown's Bazaar, Charleston, 1987—. Fellow Am. Speech-Lang.-Hearing Assn. (congrl. action state chmn. 1970-95); mem. Nat. Spkrs. Assn., S.C. Speech-Lang.-Hearing Assn. (past pres.), Assn. for the Blind (adv. bd. 1992-95), Network Speech and Hearing Adminstrs. (chmn. 1993-96), Optimist Club (past pres., past v.p.). Home: 2444 Birkenhead Rd Charleston SC 29414-5440 Office: Charleston Speech & Hearing Ctr 3815 W Montague Ave North Charleston SC 29418

CARNER, WILLIAM JOHN, banker; b. Springfield, Mo., Aug. 9, 1948; s. John Wilson and Willie Marie (Moore) C.; m. Dorothy Jean Edwards, June 12, 1976; children: Kimberly Jean, John Edwards Carner. AB, Drury Coll., 1970; MBA, U. Mo., 1972, PhD, 1989. Mktg. rep. 1st Nat. Bank Memphis, 1972-73; asst. br. mgr. Bank of Am., L.A., 1973-74; dir. mktg. Commerce Bank, Springfield, Mo., 1974-76; affiliate mktg. mgr. 1st Union Bancorp., St. Louis, 1976-78; pres. Carner & Assocs., Springfield, Mo., 1977—; exec. v.p. Exch. Resources, Ltd., Atlanta, 1992-94; pres. Carner Info. Resources, Inc., 1995—; instr. Drury Coll., 1975, 84-86, U. Mo., Columbia, 1986-88; asst. prof. SW Mo. State U., 1988-90; assoc. prof. St. Edwards U., 1991-96; adj. asst. prof. U. Tex., 1992—; bd. dirs. Ozark Pub. Telecommunications, Inc. 1982-88, sec., 1984-85, treas., 1985-86, vice chmn. 1986-87, chmn., 1987-88. Bd. dirs. Am. Cancer Soc., Greene County, Mo., 1974-82, crusade chmn., 1982-83, publicity chmn., 1974-78; bd. dirs. Springfield (Mo.) Muscular Dystrophy Assn., 1975-76, Greater Ozarks council Camp Fire Girls, 1980-81, Chameleon Puppet Theatre, 1988-89, Downtown Springfield Assn., 1989-90. Mem. Bank Mktg. Assn. (service mem. council 1985-88), Mo. Banker's Assn. (instr. Gen. Banking sch.), Fin. Instns. Mktg. Assn. (chmn. service mem. com.), Drury Coll. Alumni Assn. (v.p. 1985-86, pres. 1986-87). Democrat. Mem. Christian Ch. (Disciples of Christ). Club: Hickory Hills Country. Lodges: Masons, Shriners. Home: 2910 Montebello Ct Austin TX 78746-6816 Office: PO Box 160757 Austin TX 78716-0757

CARNES, JULIE E., federal judge; b. Atlanta, Oct. 31, 1950; m. Stephen S. Cowen. AB, U. Ga., 1972, JD, 1975. Bar: Ga. 1975. Law clk. to Hon. Lewis R. Morgan U.S. Ct. Appeals (5th cir.), 1975-77; asst. U.S. Atty. U.S. Dist. Ct. (no. dist.), Ga., 1978-90; spl. counsel U.S. Sentencing Commn., 1989, commr., 1990—; judge U.S. Dist. Ct. (no. dist.), 1992—. Office: US Courthouse 75 Spring St Ste 2167 Atlanta GA 30303

CARNEY, STEPHEN CHRISTOPHER, newspaper reporter; b. St. Petersburg, Fla., June 2, 1964; s. Thomas Michael and Dolores (Russell) Mitchell C. AS, Santa Fe C.C., Gainesville, Fla., 1988; BS, U. Fla., 1993. Reporter The Ind. Fla. Alligator, Gainesville, 1987-89, mng. editor, 1989; reporter The Daily Comml., Leesburg, Fla., 1990, asst. city editor, 1991; reporter The Ledger, Lakeland, Fla., 1993—. Mem. ACLU, Sierra Club, The Nature Conservancy, Amnesty Internat. Democrat. Roman Catholic. Home: 175 Lake Morton Dr Lakeland FL 33801-5323 Office: The Ledger 401 South Missouri Ave Lakeland FL 33801

CARO, CHARLES CRAWFORD, microcomputer company executive, international consultant; b. Champaign, Ill., Feb. 15, 1946; s. William Crawford and Marian Dell (Heischmidt) C.; m. Sallye Simons, Dec. 18, 1977 (div. 1987); 1 child, Mark Christopher. BA, U. South Fla., 1973, MA, 1976. Program support specialist Bendix/Siyanco, Riyadh, Saudi Arabia, 1973-74; chmn., chief exec. officer Caro Internat. Trade and Rels. Corp., Tampa, Fla. and Jeddah, Saudi Arabia, 1976-79, dir., 1976-79; mng. dir. Architect Lee Scarfone Assocs., Al-Khobar, Saudi Arabia, 1979-80; exec. dir. Caro Rsch. Assocs., Tampa, 1980—; dir., v.p. Chancelogic, Inc., Tampa and London, 1989-93; v.p., pres., dir. Pro-C Incorporated (formerly Chancelogic, Inc.), Tampa and London, 1993—; v.p. sales/mktg. Pro-C Inc., Tampa and London, 1996—; pres., CEO C3DS, Inc., Tampa, 1987-88, Microfine Inc., Tampa, 1983-84, also bd. dirs.; bd. dirs. Action Cons. Svcs., Inc., Brandon, Fla.; pres. Select Singles System, Inc., Tampa, 1989-91. Editor Internat. Round Table, 1987—, mng. editor, 1995—; contbr. articles to pubis. in field. Mem. Hillsborough Dem. Exec. Com., Tampa, 1982—, Hillsborough County Minority Bus. Enterprise Citizen Part. Com., Tampa, 1988-95, Royal Patronage in Principality of Hutt River Province, 1995—; pres. Drug Abuse Awareness Group, 1987; pres., dir., exec. dir. Communities Against Substance Abuse, Inc., 1988-90; treas. Coun. Downtown Chs., Tampa, 1991—; newly apptd. to bd. dirs. Communities Helping Children Found., Inc., 1993; scoutmaster Boy Scouts Am., 1994—. Mem. World Inst. Achievement (life), Assn. Computing Machinery (computers and soc. spl. interest group), Internat. Platform Assn., Stephen Minister, Am. Legion, Tiger Bay of Tampa Bay Club, Phi Kappa Phi, Pi Sigma Alpha. Episcopalian. Office: Pro-C Inc Ste 350 100 W Kennedy Blvd Tampa FL 33602-5832

CARON, SIMONE MARIE, history educator; b. Central Falls, R.I., Oct. 18, 1961; d. Leo Oscar and Eva Marie (Glaude) C.; m. Christopher Morse O'Neill, Aug. 18, 1991; 1 child, Quaid Camire Caron-O'Neill. BA in History, Bridgewater State Coll., 1983; MA in History, Northeastern U., 1985; PhD in History, Clark U., 1989. Teaching asst. Northeastern U., 1983-85, vis. instr., 1988; teaching asst. Clark U., 1985-87, vis. instr., 1988-89; vis. instr. Worcester Polytechnic Inst., 1987-90; vis. asst. prof. U. Mass., 1990, Coll. of William and Mary, 1990-91; asst. prof. history Wake Forest U., Winston-Salem, N.C., 1991—, pre-law advisor, mem. Truman scholarship com., 1993—, lower div. advisor, 1992—; papers presented at Clark U., 1988, Am. Antiquarian Soc., 1991, Southwestern Social Sci. Assn., Austin, 1992, New Orleans, 1993, Wake Forest U., 1993, New Eng. Hist. Assn., Hartford, Conn., 1994, Northeast Popular Culture Assn., 1995; book reviewer Jour. Asian and African Studies, 1994, Jour. of the History of Sexuality, 1995. Contbr. articles to profl. jours. Participant fundraising cookout Battered Women's Shelter, Winston-Salem, 1993; cons. March of Dimes for Birth Defects and Birth Control Policy Display, 1992. Mem. Orgn. Am. Historians, Omicron Delta Kappa (award 1994, Reid-Doyle prize for excellence in tchg. 1995). Democrat. Office: Wake Forest U PO Box 7806 Winston Salem NC 27109-7806

CARPENTER, BETTE JOAN, business educator; b. Amarillo, Tex., Sept. 4, 1942; d. Curtis LeVerne and Hazel (Colgrove) Edwards; m. Cecil Clark Carpenter, July 24, 1975; children: Lisa Renee Neese, Leslie Joan. BBA, West Tex. State U., 1963, MBE, 1984. Cert. tchr., Tex., profl. sec. Tchr. Tex. Panhandle Ind. Sch. Dist., 1964-66; sec. City of Amarillo, 1974-75; instr. Amarillo Coll., 1974-76, West Tex. State U., Canyon, 1982-86, 90-92, Wayland Bapt. U., Plainview, Tex., 1984-87; tchr. Canyon Ind. Sch. Dist., 1986-90; instr. West Tex. A&M U., Canyon, 1990—; writer curriculum and textbook materials Tex. Edn. Agy., Austin, 1987-95, presenter, Houston, 1988, 90, 91, Irving, 1989, Dallas, 1992, 93, 94, 95. Author: (with others) Business Computer Applications, 1989, Business Computer Programming, 1989, Microcomputer Applications, 1990, Business Computer Applications with Integration of Learning Styles, 1994. Fellow Cert. Pub. Sec. Acad.; mem. NEA, Tex. Bus. Edn. Assn. (exec. sec. 1987—), Tex. Faculty Assn., Tex. State Tchrs. Assn., Tex. Compter Edn. Assn., Phi Gamma Nu, Pi Omega Pi. Baptist. Home: 3500 Kileen Dr Amarillo TX 79109-3918 Office: West Tex A&M U Dept Mgmt Mktg and Gen Bus Canyon TX 79016

CARPENTER, BRUCE NEIL, engineering executive; b. Wayne, Nebr., Nov. 4, 1933; s. Wayne Blair and Helen Alta Carpenter; m. Eva Ann Carpeenter, Feb. 1957 (dec. Feb. 1981); children: Julie, Kevin, Cynthia, Lori; m. Barbara Elizabeth Goetz, July 19, 1982. BS in Petroleum Geology, Mo. Sch. Mines & Metallurgy, 1956. Logging engr. Schlumberger Well Survey Corp., Houma, La., 1956-57; sr. logging engr. Schlumberger Well Survey Corp., Houma, 1958-59; field engr. gen. Schlumberger Well Survey Corp., Evansville, Ind., 1959-60; sr. rsch. engr. Schlumberger Doll Rsch. Ctr., Ridgefield, Conn., 1960-78; patent agt. Schlumberger Doll Rsch. Ctr., Ridgefield, 1978-79; dist. log analyst Am. Natural Resources, Oklahoma City, 1979-82; exploration mgr. Am. Trading and Prodn., Oklahoma City, 1982-86; consulting log analyst Target Reservoir Analysis, Oklahoma City, 1986-93; owner Log Experts, Edmond, Okla., 1993—. Contbr. articles to profl. jours. 1st lt. USAR, 1957-62. Mem. Am. Assn. Petroleum Geologists, Soc. Profl. Well Log Analusts (various offices local chpt.), Soc. Petroleum Engrs., Soc. Ind. Profl. Earth Scientists, Blue Key, Kappa Alpha, Sigma Phi Epsilon. Republican. Methodist. Home: 1204 Brookhaven Dr Edmond OK 73034-4845 Office: Log Experts 300 N Broadway St Edmond OK 73034-3682

CARPENTER, CHARLES ELFORD, JR., lawyer; b. Greenville, S.C., Nov. 3, 1944; s. Charles Elford and Mary Charlotte (Campbell) C.; m. Nancy Townsend, June 8, 1968; children: Charlotte Elizabeth, John Morrison. BA, Furman U., 1966; JD, U. Va., 1969; MPA, U. S.C., 1976. Bar: Va. 1969, S.C. 1972, U.S. Dist. Ct. S.C. 1974, U.S. Ct. Appeals (4th cir.) 1978, U.S. Ct. Appeals (11th cir.) 1984, U.S. Supreme Ct. 1983. Assoc. Leatherwood, Walker, Todd & Mann, Greenville, 1969, Richardson, Plowden, Grier & Howser, Columbia, S.C., 1974-78; ptnr. Richardson, Plowden, Carpenter & Robinson, P.A., Columbia, S.C., 1978—; mem. com. on grievances and discipline S.C. Supreme Ct., 1986-89; spkr. Law Seminars, Inc., Columbia, 1987, Outline for Post-Trial Practice, 1988, 89, 90; mem. S.C. Supreme Ct. Bd. Law Examiners. Editor Appeal and Error, S.C. Jurisprudence; contbr. articles to legal jours. Mem. bd. visitors Presbyn. Coll., Clinton, S.C., 1983-87; trustee James H. Hammond Sch., Columbia, 1986-89, Trinity Presbytery; pres. A.C. Flora PTO; elder Eastminster Presbyn. Ch. Capt. U.S. Army, 1969-72. Fellow Am. Acad. Appellate Lawyers; mem. ABA (speaker appellate process program 1990, editor Appellate Practice Jour. 1989—, co-chair oral arguement subcom. litigation sect.), S.C. Bar Assn. (mem. Richland County fee dispute com. 1984-88, speaker 1987, appellate practice, panel mem. proposed rules of appellate practicefor S.C. Bar ann. meeting 1989, mem. practice and procedure com., health and hosp. law subcom., appellate rules subcom., chmn. merit selection of judges subcom., alternative dispute resolution com. 1993—), Richland County Bar Assn., S.C. Def. Trial Attys. (chmn. amicus curiae com. 1981-85), Forest Lake Club, St. Andrews Soc., Tarantella Club, Columbia Ball Club, Torch Club (pres.). Office: Richardson Plowden Carpenter & Robinson PA 1600 Marion St, PO Dwr 7788 Columbia SC 29202

CARPENTER, CHARLES FRANCIS, lawyer; b. Raleigh, N.C., Apr. 3, 1957; s. William Lester and Mattie Frances (Wallace) C.; m. Heidi Ann Athanas, June 14, 1980. BA with honors, U. N.C., 1979, JD, 1982. Bar: N.C. 1982, U.S. Dist. Ct. (mid. dist.) N.C. 1982, U.S. Dist. Ct. (ea. dist.) N.C. 1986, U.S. Ct. Appeals (4th cir.) 1986, U.S. Dist. Ct. (we. dist.) N.C. 1988. Assoc. Newsom, Graham, Hedrick, Murray, Bryson & Kennon, Durham, N.C., 1982-87; ptnr. Newsom, Graham, Hedrick, Bryson & Kennon, Durham, 1988-93; prin. Charles F. Carpenter, P.A., Durham, 1993—. Trustee Resurrection United Meth. Ch., 1986—; trustee N.C. Ann. Conf. United Meth., 1993—; mem. exec. bd. Occoneechee coun. Boy Scouts Am., 1988—; pres. 3d Regt. Foot Guards, Ltd., 1984—. Mem. ABA, N.C. State Bar, N.C. Bar Assn., Durham County Bar Assn. (medico-legal com. 1994—), Order of the Old Well, Durham C. of C., Phi Beta Kappa. Democrat. Home: 1325 Arnette Ave Durham NC 27707-1601 Office: 905 W Main St Ste 24-E Durham NC 27701-2054

CARPENTER, DAVID ALLAN, lawyer; b. Cambridge, Mass., May 16, 1951; s. David Lawrence and Jane (Boucher) C.; m. Nancy Joan Surdyka, Apr. 29, 1973. BS in Bus. Adminstrn., Bucknell U., Lewisburg, Pa., 1972; MBA in Fin., Temple U., Phila., 1975; JD, Rutgers U., 1981. Banking officer Girard Bank, Phila., 1972-77, mng. ptnr., 1983-85, mng. ptnr. Mid Atlantic region, 1985-89, mng. ptnr. Atlantic region, 1989-92; ptnr. dir. litigation and claims svcs. Coopers & Lybrand, Phila., 1987-92; nat. dir. fin. adv. svcs. Coopers & Lybrand, Boston, 1992-94; founding ptnr. Ptnrs. for Mkt. Leadership, Inc., Atlanta, 1995—. Co-editor: Proving and Pricing Construction Claims, 1990, Environmental Dispute Handbook, 1991; contbr. articles to profl. jours., chpts. to books. Mem. Inst. Mgmt. Consultants, Turnaround Mgmt. Assn., Beta Gamma Sigma. Office: Ptnrs for Mkt Leadership Inc 100 Galleria Pky NW Ste 400 Atlanta GA 30339-3122

CARPENTER, DELBERT STANLEY, educational administration educator; b. Wichita Falls, Tex., May 18, 1950; s. Delbert Stanley Sr. and Ruby Elizabeth (Green) S.; m. Noralyn Gray, July 13, 1973 (div. Mar. 1986); m. Janet Ann Stewart, July 15, 1989 (div. June 1993); m. Linda Jan Meerdink Evans, June 15, 1994; 1 child, Susanne Gray Carpenter; stepchildren: Robert Scott Evans, Peter Clark Evans. BS, Tarleton State U., 1972; MS, East Tex. State U., 1975; PhD, U. Ga., 1979. Actuarial technician A.S. Hansen, Inc., Dallas, 1972-74; grad. asst. cen. housing office East Tex. State U., Commerce, 1974-75; men's resident dir. Oglethorpe U., Atlanta, 1975-77; grad. asst. counseling and human devel. dept. U. Ga., Athens, 1977-79; dean students U. Ark., Monticello, 1979-81; asst. dir. devel. Tex. A&M U., College Station, 1982-84, asst. prof. edn1. adminstrn., 1985-89, assoc. prof., 1989-95, prof., 1995—. Mem. editl. bds. various profl. jours.; contbr. articles to profl. jours. Named Outstanding Doctoral Alumnus, Students Affairs Adminstrn. U. Ga., 1995, Disting. Tchg. award Assn. Former Students Coll. of Edn., 1996. Mem. Assn. for the Study Higher Edn. (exec. dir. 1987—, Disting. Svc. award 1996), Am. Coll. Pers. Assocs. (Annuit Coeptis award 1995), Nat. Assn. Student Pers. Adminstrn., South Assn. for Coll. Student Affairs, Alpha Phi Omega (pres., bd. dirs. 1986-90, Nat. Disting. Svc. award 1990), Alpha Chi. Home: 1111 12th Man Cir College Station TX 77845 Office: Tex A&M U 222 Harrington College Station TX 77843

CARPENTER, GORDON RUSSELL, lawyer, banker; b. Denton, Tex., Feb. 6, 1920; s. Solomon Lafayette and Grace L. (Fowler) C.; m. Muriel E. James, Sept. 18, 1943 (dec.); m. 2d, Mary Alice Borah, Aug. 4, 1962. B.S., North Tex. State U., 1940; postgrad. Georgetown U. Law Sch., 1941-42; LL.B., So. Meth. U., 1948. Bar: Tex. 1947, U.S. Supreme Ct. 1960. Announcer radio sta. KDNT, Denton, 1940-41; spl. agt. FBI, 1941-46; exec. sec. Southwestern Legal Found., Dallas, 1947-56, exec. dir., 1956-58; adminstrv. asst. to dean So. Meth. U. Law Sch., 1951-58, asst. prof. law, 1956-58; trust officer 1st Nat. Bank, Dallas, 1958-60, v.p., 1960-79; v.p., sr. fin. planning officer InterFirst Bank Dallas, 1979-84. Bd. regents Tex. Sch. Trust Banking, 1981-82; bd. trustees Hatton W. Sumners Found., 1959-85, exec. dir. 1985—; chmn. North Tex. State U. Ednl. Found.; chmn. Luth. Med. System of Tex. Found., 1980-83; vice chmn. Farmers Br. Hosp. Authority, 1976-77. Recipient Pres.'s award State Bar Tex., 1963, Bd. Dirs. award, 1971. Fellow Tex. Bar Found.; mem. ABA (chmn. publs. com. mineral and natural resources law sect. 1958-64, chmn. membership com. 1963-64), State Bar Tex. (chmn. continuing legal edn. com. 1952-54, 58-66, chmn. real estate, probate and trust law sect. 1964-65), Dallas Bar Assn. (dir. 1960-61, 65-66, chmn. centennial com. 1972-73), Dallas Bar Found. (trustee, sec.-treas.), Tex. Bankers Assn. (chmn. trust div. 1980-81), Soc. Former Spl. Agts. FBI (pres. 1963), Delta Theta Phi. Republican. Presbyterian. Clubs: Brookhaven

Country, Masons. Office: Ste 2800 325 N Saint Paul St Dallas TX 75201-3817

CARPENTER, JAMES GASTON, trade association administrator; b. Charlotte, N.C., Dec. 13, 1945; s. James Gaston and Sara Ellen (Miller) C.; children: Alison Dawn, Mary Elizabeth. AA, U. N.C., 1967, BA, 1971; MA, U. S.C., 1973. Cmty. planner Southeast Ga. Area Planning Co., Waycross, 1973-74; dep. dir. Beaufort Co. Planning Co., Beaufort, S.C., 1974-77; cmty. devel. dir. City of York (S.C.), 1977-80, city mgr., 1980-82; v.p. pub. affairs Charlotte (N.C.) C. of C., 1982-85; exec. v.p. S.C. Bus. and Industry Polit. Edn. Com., Columbia, 1985-91; pres. Printing Industry of Carolinas, Charlotte, N.C., 1991-93, Union County C. of C., Monroe, N.C., 1993—. Bd. dirs. N.C. C. of C. Self Insurers Fund, 1994—, Union County Cmty. Arts Coun., 1996—. Served with USNG, 1967-74. Mem. Monroe Rotary Club (chair program com. 1993—), Columbia Rotary Club (chair newsletter com. 1986-91). Republican. Presbyterian. Home: 225 Water Oak Ln Matthews NC 28105 Office: Union County C of C PO Box 1789 Monroe NC 28111

CARPENTER, JOHN TOPHAM, JR., medical educator; b. Shreveport, La., Sept. 25, 1942; s. John Topham and Anna Belle (Thomas) C.; m. Sandra Ann Moore, June 2, 1984; 1 child, Claire Elizabeth. BA, Johns Hopkins U., 1964; MD, Tulane U., 1968. Diplomate Am. Bd. Internal Medicine, Med. Oncology, Hematology; diplomate hematology Am. Bd. Pathology. From asst. prof. medicine to assoc. prof. medicine U. Ala., Birmingham, 1973-86, prof. medicine, 1986—. Bd. dirs. Ala. divsn. Am. Cancer Soc., prof. clin. oncology, 1987-91. Fellow ACP; mem. Am. Soc. Clin. Oncology, Am. Soc. Hematology. Episcopalian. Office: Divsn Hematology/Oncology U Ala Birmingham Station Birmingham AL 35294-3280

CARPENTER, JUDITH K., health careers educator; b. Detroit, Nov. 2, 1940; d. Willis Emerson and Naomi Jean (Bergquist) Borders; m. Kenneth Robert Carpenter, May 13, 1961; children: Lisa Ann, Brent Sean. Diploma, Butterworth Sch. Nursing, Grand Rapids, Mich., 1961; BS in Edn., U. Tenn., 1985, MS in Edn., 1989. RN, Mich., Tenn.; lic. tchr., Tenn. Staff nurse Butterworth Hosp., Grand Rapids, 1961-62, Tampa (Fla.) Gen. Hosp., 1962-63, Henry County Hosp., New Castle, Ind., 1963-64, East Tenn. Bapt. Hosp., Knoxville, 1964-65, Laughlin Hosp., Greenville, Tenn., 1969-72; dir. edn., supr. Laughlin Hosp., 1972-88; health careers educator Ctr. for Tech., Greenville, 1988—. Mem. Am. Vocat. Assn., East Tenn. Health Sci. Coun. Lutheran. Home: 182 Britton Ave Greeneville TN 37743 Office: Ctr for Tech 1121 Hall Henard Rd Greeneville TN 37743

CARPENTER, NAN COOKE, English language educator; b. Louisa County, Va., July 29, 1912; s. Charles Richard and Nan (Cooke) C. B in music, Hollins Coll., 1937; MA in musicology, U. N.C., 1941; MA in Eng., Yale U., 1945, PhD in music history, 1948. Music tchr. Blair Jr. High Sch., Norfolk, Va., 1935-40; Eng. prof. U. Mont., Missoula, 1948-63, Southern Ill. U., Carbondale, 1963-64; music prof. Syracuse (N.Y.) U., 1964-65; Eng. prof. Ga. Southwestern Coll., Americus, 1965-66; Eng. prof. U. Ga., Athens, 1966-70, comp. lit. prof., 1970-80, chmn. comp. lit. dept., 1975-80. Author: Rabelais and Music, 1954, Music in the Medieval and Renaissance Universities, 1958, John Skelton, 1969, A Quiver of Quizzez for Quidnuncs, 1985. Officer Athens Humane Soc., 1968—; reader, pianist Recording for Blind, Athens, 1968—. Fellow ASLS, 1954-55. Home: PO Box 410 Yorktown VA 23690

CARPENTER, ROBERT JAMES, JR., medical educator; b. Dallas, Nov. 7, 1945; s. Robert James Sr. and Lottie Pearl (Newton) C.; m. Addie Flowers, Aug. 27, 1970; 1 child, Craig B. Student, Oak Ridge Assoc. Univs., 1967; BA in Biology/Chemistry magna cum laude, Hardin-Simmons U., 1968; postgrad., U. Tex., Houston, 1968; MD with honors, Baylor Coll. Medicine, 1973. Diplomate Am. Bd. Obstetrics and Gynecology, subspecialty Maternal Fetal Medicine. Rotating intern Baylor Coll. Medicine, Houston, 1973-74, resident in ob/gyn, 1974-76, chief resident in ob/gyn, 1976-77, fellow in maternal fetal medicine, 1977-79; ultrasound and fetoscopy obstetrician Yale U., New Haven, 1977; asst. attending obstetrician/gynecologist Harris County Hosp. Dist., Ben Taub Gen. Hosp., Houston, 1977—, St. Luke's Episc. Hosp., Houston, 1977—; attending ob-gyn. Meth. Hosp., Houston, 1978—; attending physician surgery svc. VA Hosp., Houston, 1980-94; mem. courtesy staff Hermann Hosp., Houston, 1980-85, Woman's Hosp. Tex., Houston, 1979—; lectr. in field; asst. prof. dept. ob/gyn Baylor Coll. Medicine, 1979, assoc. prof., 1987, program dir. maternal fetal medicine, 1991, asst. prof. Inst. Molecular Genetics, 1985. Author numerous book chpts., articles, abstracts, revs. in field. Comdr. USN, 1962-93. Fellow Am. Coll. Obstetricians and Gynecologists; mem. Soc. Perinatal Obstetricians, Ctrl. Assn. Ob/Gyn, Am. Soc. Human Genetics, Fetoscopy Study Group, Internat. Fetal Medicine and Surgery Soc., Am. Inst. Ultrasound in Medicine, Am. Diabetes Assn., Harris County Med. Soc. (med. student com.), Tex. Med. Assn., Tex. Perinatal Assn. Baptist. Office: 6624 Fannin St Ste 2720 Houston TX 77030-2312

CARPENTER, STANLEY HAMMACK, retired military aviation organization executive; b. Hattiesburg, Miss., Jan. 21, 1926; s. Henry Herbert and Esther Mae (Cooper) C.; m. Catherine Jane Sadler, Nov. 29, 1946; children: Stanley Hammack, Louise N., Catherine D., Mary C. BS, Tulane U., 1946; U.S. Naval Postgrad. Sch., 1956; Aero. Engr., Calif. Inst. Tech., 1957; MS, U. So. Calif., 1982; cert. safety profl.; Enlisted U.S. Navy, 1944. Commd. 2d lt. U.S. Marine Corps, 1946, advanced through grades to col., 1968; comdg. officer Marine Detachment USS Breckinridge (AP-176), 1948-49; Korean combat tours in amphibian tractors, 1950-51, Skyraider and Bird Dog pilot, 1953-54; aircraft maintenance officer, Edenton, N.C., 1957-58; liaison officer Naval Weapons Center, China Lake, Calif., 1959-62; comdg. officer air base squadron Far East, 1962, A4E Squadron, 1963-65; aide to asst. sec. navy for research devel., 1965-68; Viet Nam combat tour officer in charge Chu-Lai Air Base, comdg. officer Marine Wing Support Group, 1968-69; staff officer, dir. def. research engring., 1969-71; asst. chief of staff and div. chief Marine Corps Devel. Center, Quantico, Va., 1971-74; ret., 1974; aero. engr., sr. program mgr. Unified Industries, Inc., Springfield, Va., 1975-86; exec. dir. Marine Corps Aviation Assn., 1988-93. Decorated Legion of Merit, Air medal. Mem. Marine Corps Aviation Assn., First Marine Div. Assn., Marine Corps Assn., Assn. Naval Aviation, Tailhook Assn., Marine Corps Res. Officers Assn., Ret. Officers Assn., Marine Corps League, Navy League, Marine Corps Hist. Found., Naval Aviation Mus. Found., U.S. Naval Inst., Chosin Few, Aircraft Owners and Pilots Assn., Tulane U. Alumni Assn., Calif. Inst. Tech. Alumni Assn., U. So. Calif. Alumni Assn., Order of Daedalians, Phi Beta Kappa, Omicron Delta Kappa, Kappa Sigma, Kappa Delta Phi. Roman Catholic. Home: 8404 Bound Brook Ln Alexandria VA 22309-2136

CARPENTER, SUSAN, modeling and talent agency owner; b. Clarksville, Tenn.; d. Dallas W. Chester and Ellen Ruth McGregor. Student, St. Mary's Coll., San Jose State Coll., John Robert Powers. Former model Calif.; dir. John Powers Schs., Calif.; founder, dir. Jo-Susan Modeling/Finishing Sch. and Agy., Nashville; Recipient W.S.M. Civic award Cerebral Palsy Chmn., Nashville. Chmn. Belle Meade Mansion Christmas Party, Nashville; civic leader various charity functions, Nashville, Nashville Showcase Decorators, Vanderbilt Children's Hosp., Nashville. Home: 6666 Brookmont Ter Nashville TN 37205 Office: Jo Susan Sch & Agy Park Place 2817 W End Ave Nashville TN 37203-1440

CARPENTER, SYLVIA JO, surgical nurse; b. Mt. Airy, N.C., Mar. 13, 1957; d. Billy Grey and Peggy L. (Beck) Smith; m. Christopher Lee Carpenter, Aug. 6, 1988; children: Adrianne Brooke, Stephen Charles. AAS, Miss. Gulf Coast Jr. Coll., 1978. RN, N.C. Staff nurse oper. rm. No. Surry Hosp., Mt. Airy, 1979-91; staff nurse cardiothoracic surgery N.C. Bapt. Hosp., Winston-Salem, 1992-93; pub. health nurse Surry County Health Dept., 1993—. Assn. dir. Girls in Action, Surry County, N.C., 1987-90; dir. Women's Missionary Union, Mt. Airy, 1990-92. Recipient N.C. Nurse Gt. 100 award, 1994. Mem. Assn. Oper. Rm. Nurses (cert., bd. dirs. Cen. N.C. chpt. 1988-89, sec., 1989-91, pres., 1992-93), N.C. Bapt. Nurse Fellowship. Democrat. Baptist. Home: 2187 W Pine St Mount Airy NC 27030-8793

CARPENTER-MASON, BEVERLY NADINE, health care/quality assurance nurse consultant; b. Pitts., May 23, 1933; d. Frank Carpenter and Thelma Deresa (Williams) Carpenter Smith; m. Sherman Robert Robinson Jr., Dec. 26, 1953 (div. Jan. 1959); 1 child, Keith Michael; m. David Solomon Mason Jr., Sept. 10, 1960; 1 child, Tamara Nadina. Grad. in nursing, Shadyside Hosp. Sch. Nursing, Pitts.; BS, St. Joseph's Coll., North Windham, Maine, 1979; MS, So. Ill. U., 1981; PhD, Columbia Pacific U., 1995. RN, Pa., D.C., Fla. Staff nurse med. surgery, ob-gyn neonatology and pediatrics Pa., N.Y., Wyo., Colo. and Washington, 1954-68; mgr. clinician dermatol. svcs. Malcolm Grow Med. Ctr., Camp Spring, Md., 1968-71; pediatric nurse practitioner Dept. Human Resources, Washington, 1971-73; asst. dir. nursing Glenn Dale Hosp., Md., 1973-81; nursing coord. medicaid div. Forest Haven Ctr., Laurel, Md., 1981-83, spl. asst. to supr. for med. svcs., 1983-84; spl. asst. to supt. for quality assurance Burr. Habilitation Svcs., Laurel, 1984-89; exec. asst. quality assurance coord. Mental Retardation Devel. Disabilities Adminstrn., Washington, 1989-91; also bd. dirs., 1989—; asst. treas. Am. Bd. Quality Assurance Utilization Rev. Physicians, 1988-94, chair exam. com., 1990-93; ret. Mental Retardation Devel. Disabilities Adminstrn., Washington, 1991; bd. dirs. Quality Mgmt. Audits, Inc., 1991-94; coord. quality assurance health svcs. div. UPARC, Clearwater, Fla., 1993-94; owner, prin. BCM Assocs., 1992—; cons., lectr. in field; case study editor, mem. jour. editorial bd. Am. Coll. Med. Quality, 1985—, chmn. publs. com., 1987—, asst. treas., 1988-93; mem. Am. Bd. Quality Assurance and Utilization Rev. Physicians, 1984—; chief proctor ABQAURP exam. com., 1995—; mem. exec. com. Am. Found. for Edn. in Healthcare Quality, 1995—. Contbr. articles to profl. jours. Mem., star donor ARC Blood Drive, Washington, Md., 1975-91; chair nominations com. Prince Georges Nat. Coun. Negro Women, Md., 1984-85. Recipient awards Dept. Air Force and D.C. Govt., 1966-92, Della Robbia Gold medallion Am. Acad. Pediatrics, 1972, John P. Lamb Jr. Meml. Lectureship award East Tenn. State Y., 1988, Woman of Yr., 1990, 91, 92, 93, 94, 95, 96. Mem. NAFE, Am. Assn. Mental Retardation (conf. lectr. 1988), Am. Coll. Utilization Rev. Physicians, Assn. Retarded Citizens, Healthcare Quality Inst., Top Ladies of Distinction (1st v.p. 1986-91), Internat. Platform Assn., Order Ea. Star (Achievement award Deborah chpt. 1991), Am. Bd. Quality Assurance Utilization Rev. Physicians (Chmn. of Yr. award 1992, presdl. citation, Calvin R. Openshaw Svc. award 1993). Democrat.

CARPER, WILLIAM BARCLAY, management educator; b. Winchester, Va., Apr. 3, 1946; s. Roy Silas and Evadnyr Joyce (Arthur) C.; m. Brenda Carol Campbell, Aug. 20, 1966 (div. Sept. 1994); children: Melissa Paige, Jonathan Barclay. BA, U. Va., 1968; MBA, Coll. William & Mary, 1976; PhD, Va. Poly. Inst. and State U., 1979. Instr. Va. Poly. Inst. and State U., Blacksburg, 1976-79; asst. prof. Auburn (Ala.) U., 1979-81, George Mason U., Fairfax, Va., 1981-87; assoc. prof. mgmt. Ga. So. U., Statesboro, 1987-92, prof., 1992-95, dept. head., 1987-90, assoc. dean., 1989-95; dir. ctr. for mgmt. devel., 1993-94; dean Coll. Bus. U. West Fla., Pensacola, 1995—, prof. mgmt., 1995—; dir. small bus. programs George Mason Inst., 1983-85; pres. Strategic Mgmt. Systems, Inc., Satesboro, 1987—; cons. Nat. Health Advisors, Ltd., McLean, Va., 1983-95, Can. Mfrs. Inst., Washington, 1986-95. Jour. reviewer Acad. Mgmt. Rev., Jour. Mgmt., Rev. Bus. and Econ. Rsch., Mgmt. Sci.; mem. editorial rev. bd. Jour. Global Info. Mgmt., Jour. of Mktg. and Theory Practice; contbr. articles to profl. jours. USAFR advisor Montgomery County Composite Squadron CAP, Blacksburg, 1977-79; coach Youth League Soccer and Football, Auburn, Ala. and Vienna, Va., 1980-86; mem. exec. com. cub scouts Boy Scouts Am., Vienna, 1982-83; pres. Statesboro High Sch. Quarterback Club, 1991-92. Decorated DFC, Air medal with 3 oak leaf clusters; recipient Disting. Faculty Mem. award George Mason U., 1984; SBA grantee, 1983-84, Commonwealth of Va. grantee, 1984-86, State of Ga. grantee, 1994-95. Mem. Acad. Mgmt. (dissertation award com.), Ea. Acad. Mgmt., So. Mgmt. Assn. (program com. 1981-82, bd. dirs. 1989-92, mem. teaching excellence com. 1992-94), Decision Scis. Inst. (program com. 1991-92), S.E. Region Decision Scis. Inst. (program com. 1985-86, v.p. industry liaison 1986-87, v.p. planning and devel. 1987-88, sec. 1990-91, coun. mem. 1992—, coun. chair 1994—, nominations com. 1996), Inst. Mgmt. Sci. (editor Southeastern chpt. Proceedings Jour. 1987, coun. 1986—, program chmn. 1986-87, sec.-treas. 1987-88, v.p. 1988-89, pres. 1989-90, Disting. Svc. award 1992), Soc. Advancement Mgmt. (Disting. Svc. award 1985), Aircraft Owners and Pilots Assn., Mid-Day Optimist Club (membership dir. 1989-91, bd. dirs. 1989-91), 5 Flags Rotary, Delta Sigma Phi, and others. Methodist. Office: Dean's Office Coll of Bus U West Fla Pensacola FL 32514-5752

CARR, BEN W., JR., academic administrator. Chancellor U. Kentucky C. C. Sys., Lexington, Ky. Office: Community Coll System Office of the Chancellor 17 Breckinridge Hall Lexington KY 40506

CARR, BESSIE, retired middle school educator; b. Nathalie, Va., Oct. 10, 1920; d. Henry C. and Sirlena (Ewell) C. BS, Elizabeth City Coll., N.C., 1942; MA, Columbia U. Tchrs. Coll., 1948, PhD, 1950, EdD, 1952. Cert. adminstr., supr., tchr. Prin. pub. sch., Halifax, Va., 1942-47, Nathalie-Halifax County, Va., 1947-51; prof. edn. So. U., Baton Rouge, 1952-53; supr. schs. Lackland Schs., Cin., 1953-54; prof. edn. Wilberforce U., Ohio, 1954-55; tchr. Leland Sch., Pittsfield, Mass., 1956-60; chair math. dept., tchr. Lakeland Mid. Sch., N.Y., 1961-83. Founder, organizer, sponsor 1st Math Bowl and Math Forum in area, 1970-76; founder Dr. Bessie Carr award Halifax County Sr. High Sch., 1962. Mem. Nat. Women's Hall of Fame. Mem. AAUW (auditor 1970-85), Delta Kappa Gamma (auditor internat. 1970-76), Assn. Suprs. of Math. (chair coordinating council 1976-80), Ret. Tchrs. Assn., Black Women Bus. and Profl. Assn. (charter mem. Senegal, Africa chpt.). Democrat. Avocations: travel, photography, souvenirs.

CARR, EDWARD A., lawyer; b. Borger, Tex., July 31, 1962. AB with distinction, Stanford U., 1984; JD, UCLA, 1987. Bar: Tex. 1988, D.C. 1989, U.S. Dist. Ct. (so. dist.) Tex. 1989, U.S. Ct. Appeals (5th cir.) 1989, U.S. Ct. Appeals (fed. cir.) 1989. Assoc. Vinson & Elkins, Houston, 1988—. Contbr. articles to profl. jours. Fellow Tex. Bar Found. (life); Mem. ABA (sects. antitrust law, litigation), Am. Judicature Soc. (life), Coll. State Bar Tex., D.C. Bar, Fed. Bar Assn. (sect. fed. litigation), State Bar Tex., Houston Bar Assn. Address: Vinson & Elkins LLP 2300 First City Tower 1001 Fannin Houston TX 77002-6760

CARR, ELIZABETH DAVIS-JACKSON, town clerk; b. Plymouth, N.C., May 13, 1932; d. Raleigh Sherman and Lillian Blanche (Davis) Jackson; m. Joseph Hargrove Bryan, Dec. 24, 1953; children: Joanna Davis, Peter-Michael. BA, East Carolina U., 1953. Dir. Clinton (N.C.) C. of C., 1972-82; investments, venture capital Carr & Assocs., Inc., Atlantic Beach, N.C., 1985—; town clk. Pine Knoll Shores, N.C., 1995—; bd. dirs. First Citizens Bank & Trust, Clinton, 1982-84; bd. realtors Carteret County, 1989-91. Democrat. Presbyn.

CARR, GERALD PAUL, former astronaut, business executive, former marine officer; b. Denver, Aug. 22, 1932; s. Thomas Ernest and Freda (Wright) C.; divorced; children: Jennifer, Jamee, Jeffrey, John, Jessica, Joshua; m. Patricia Musick, Sept. 14, 1979. BS in Mech. Engring., U. So. Calif., 1954; BS in Aero. Engring., U.S. Naval Postgrad. Sch., 1961; MS in Aero. Engring., Princeton U., 1962; DSc (hon.), St. Louis U., 1976. Registered profl. engr., Tex. Commd. 2d lt. USMC, 1954, advanced through grades to col., 1974, ret., 1975; jet fighter pilot U.S., Mediterranean, Far East, 1956-65; astronaut NASA, Houston, 1966-77; comdr. 3d Skylab Manned Mission, 1973-74; sr. v.p. CAMUS, Inc., Huntsville, Ark.; adv. bd. Nat. Space Soc., Space Dermatology Found., Eldorado Bank. Bd. trustees U. of the Ozarks. Recipient Group Achievement award NASA, 1971, Distinguished Service medal, 1974; Gold medal City of Chgo., 1974; Gold medal City of N.Y., 1974; Alumni Merit award U. So. Calif., 1974; Distinguished Eagle Scout award Boy Scouts Am., 1974; Robert J. Collier Trophy, 1974; Robert H. Goddard Meml. trophy, 1975; FAI Gold Space medal; others. Fellow Am. Astronautical Soc. (Flight Achievement award 1975); mem. NSPE, Marine Corps Assn., Marine Corps Aviation Assn., Soc. Exptl. Test Pilots, U. So. Calif. Alumni Assn., Tau Kappa Epsilon. Presbyterian. Home and Office: PO Box 919 Huntsville AR 72740-0919

CARR, HOWARD ERNEST, retired insurance agency executive; b. Johnson City, Tenn., Oct. 4, 1908; s. William Alexander and Gertrude (Feathers) C.; BS, E. Tenn. State U., 1929; MEd, Duke, 1935; postgrad. U. N.C., 1938-39; m. Thelma Northcutt, June 11, 1937 (dec. Oct. 1972); 1 son, Howard Ernest. Supt., Washington Coll. (Tenn.), 1929-35; ednl. advisor U.S. Office Edn., Ft. Oglethorpe, Ga., 1935-37; prin. Greensboro (N.C.) city schs., 1937-42; dir. activities First Presbyn. Ch., Greensboro, 1946-47; with Jefferson Standard Life Ins. Co., Greensboro, 1947—, spl. rep., 1947-54, supr. agy. Greensboro, 1964, mgr., 1964-67; pres. Everett's Lake Corp. Chmn. Guilford County Bd. Edn., 1950-77; vice chmn. N.C. Gov's Com. Edn., 1956-60; N.C. rep. White House Conf. Edn., 1955. Mem. adv. com. Greensboro div. Guilford Coll., 1958—; head Guilford County Cancer Drive, 1956, bd. dirs. Cancer Soc., 1956—; v.p. N.C. State Sch. Bds. Assn., 1959-61; bd. dirs. Greensboro Jr. Mus., 1956-62, Tannenbaum Sternberger Found. Lt. USNR, 1942-46, asst. head motion picture dept., Washington; to capt., 1951-54, as head motion picture dept; ret. as capt., 1968. Recipient Nat. Quality award Nat. Assn. Life Underwriters, 1948, Nat. Honor award East Tenn. State U., 1993; named Boss of the Year, Lou-Celin chpt. Am. Bus. Woman's Assn., 1967; W.H. Andrews, Jr. award, 1985; named Man of Yr., 1988. Mem. Nat., N.C. (pres. 1964-65; Man of Year award 1969), Greensboro (pres. 1956-57) assns. life underwriters, N.C. Leaders Club, Greensboro C. of C. (chmn. edn. com. 1960-62). Presbyn. (elder). Mason (32 deg.), Kiwanian (pres. Greensboro 1951). Author: History of Higher Education in East Tennessee, 1935. Home: 4100 Well Spring Dr Apt 2111 Greensboro NC 27410-8800

CARR, JESSE METTEAU, III, lawyer, engineering executive; b. Roanoke, Va., Sept. 3, 1952; s. Jesse Metteau Jr. and Martha Ann (Niday) C.; m. Amelia Kathryn Tynes, May 6, 1983 (div. Oct. 1985). BSEE, La. State U., 1974, JD, 1977. Bar: La. 1978, Tex. 1979; registered profl. engr., Tex., Wash., Oreg., Pa., Ind., La., Miss. Elec. engr. Southeastern Chem., Reserve, La., 1974-77; control systems engr. J.E. Sirrine Co., Houston, 1977-83; pvt. practice cons. Houston, 1983-84; control systems engr. Jacobs Engring., Houston, 1985-86; mng. gen. ptnr. Carr/Sperry Design, Houston, 1985-87, Tech. Ventures Group, Houston, 1987-90; v.p. Intellex Corp., Houston, 1986-92, pres., 1992—, also bd. dirs.; mng. gen. ptnr. Tech. Ventures Group, Houston, 1987-90; v.p. East Tex. Co., Inc., 1994—; bd. dirs. Mimics Inc., Houston, East Tex. Co., Washington, Ga. Cub Scout leader Boy Scouts Am., Houston, 1987-90. Mem. IEEE, ABA, La. Bar Assn., Tex. Bar Assn., Am. Inst. Chem. Engrs., Internat. Soc. Pharm. Engrs., Am. Soc. Agrl. Engrs., S.W. Assn. Biotech. Cos., Instrument Soc. Am., Assn. Energy Engrs., Tau Beta Pi, Omicron Delta Kappa, Eta Kappa Nu. Republican. Methodist.

CARR, MIKE, English language educator; b. Columbus, Ga., Feb. 2, 1953; s. Howard Sylvester and Mamie Talitha (Spivey) C.; m. Carol Goodale, June 6, 1977 (div. Dec. 1981). BA, Columbus Coll., 1992; MA, W.Va. U., 1994. Dir. tng. and instrn. Search, Tracking and Rescue Dogs, Augusta, Ga., 1975-93; program coord. intensive English program W.Va. U., Morgantown, 1993—. Author: Tales From the Basement, 1990. Recipient U.S. Jaycees Speak Up award, 1979, Regional Drama Festival award 1st place, 1972. Mem. TESOL, Assn. Curriculum Devel., Grad. Student Assn. Office: W Va U Dept Fgn Lang PO Box 6298 Morgantown WV 26506-6298

CARR, OSCAR CLARK, III, lawyer; b. Memphis, Apr. 9, 1951; s. Oscar Clark Carr Jr. and Billie (Fisher) Carr Houghton; m. Mary Leatherman, Aug. 4, 1973; children: Camilla Fisher, Oscar Clark V. BA in English with distinction, U. Va., 1973; JD with distinction, Emory U., 1976. Bar: Tenn. 1976, U.S. Dist. Ct. (we. dist.) Tenn. 1977, U.S. Dist. Ct. (no. dist.) Miss. 1977, U.S. Ct. Appeals (6th cir.) 1985, U.S. Ct. Appeals (5th cir.) 1995. Assoc. firm Glankler Brown, PLLC (formerly Glankler, Brown, Gilliland, Chase, Robinson & Raines), Memphis, 1976-82, ptnr., 1982—. Bd. dirs. Memphis Ballet Soc., 1980, Memphis-Shelby County Unit Am. Cancer Soc., 1985—, Memphis Oral Sch. for Deaf, 1988-91; treas., vestryman St. John's Episcopal Ch., Memphis, 1988-91, sr. warden, 1991; mem. Commn. on Ministry Diocese of West Tenn., 1987-90, King of Carnival Memphis, 1994. Mem. ABA, Tenn. Bar Assn.(western dist. coun. environ. law 1992—), Memphis and Shelby County Bar Assn. (bd. dirs. 1985-87), U. Va. Alumni Assn., Memphis Country Club. Office: Glankler Brown PLLC 1700 One Commerce Sq Memphis TN 38103

CARR, PATRICIA ANN, community health nurse; b. Teaneck, N.J., Dec. 6, 1949; d. John O. and Elizabeth (Nestor) Olsen. Diploma, Mt. Sinai Hosp. Sch. Nursing, N.Y.C., 1970. RN, Ga., Fla. Asst. DON Taylor Meml. Hosp., Hawkinsville, Ga., 1979-81; staff nurse ICU Shands Teaching Hosp., Gainesville, Fla., 1981-82; staff nurse Venice Hosp., 1982-84; field nurse Fla. Home Health Svcs. Sarasota Inc., 1986-93; regulatory compliance coord. Fla. Home Health Svcs., Sarasota, 1993-96; program clin. coord. Cmty. AIDS Network, Inc., Sarasota, 1996—. Contbr. articles to publs. Mem. Assn. Nurses in AIDS Care, Home Health Nurses Assn., AACN, APHA, Intravenous Nurses Soc., Assn. Practitioners in Infection Control. Office: Cmty AIDS Network Inc 150 East Ave South Sarasota FL 34237

CARR, PATRICIA WARREN, adult education educator; b. Mobile, Ala., Mar. 24, 1947; d. Bedford Forrest and Mary Catherine (Warren) Slaughter; m. John Lyle Carr, Sept. 26, 1970; children: Caroline Elise, Joshua Bedford. BS in Edn., Auburn U., 1968, MEd, 1971. Tchr. DeKalb County Schs., Atlanta, 1969-70; counselor Dept. Defense Schs., Okinawa, Japan, 1972-75; tchr. Jefferson County Schs., Jefferson, Ga., 1975-76; counselor Clarke County Schs., Athens, Ga., 1976-78; tchr. Fairfax County Schs., Adult and Community Edn., Fairfax, Va., 1980—; instrnl. supr. Vol. Learning Program; coord. Enrichment for Srs. Program Fairfax Area Agy. on Aging and Adult and Cmty. Edn., 1985-89; cons. State Va. Dept. Edn., 1984—, Va. Assn. Adult and Cmty. Edn., 1987, Commn. on Adult Basic Edn., 1988; instr. George Mason U., Fairfax, 1985. Tchr. Met. Meml. United Meth. Ch., Washington, 1981—; co-leader McClean, Va. troop Girl Scouts U.S., 1985-88. Mem. Am. Assn. Adult and Community Edn., Smithsonian Nat. Assocs., No. Va. Assn. Vol. Adminstrs., Va. Assn. Adult and Community Edn., Greater Washington Reading Coun. Methodist. Office: Fairfax County Adult & Community Edn Woodson Adult Ctr 9525 Main St Fairfax VA 22031

CARR, ROBERT KIMBREL, technology consultant; b. Greenville, Miss., Mar. 22, 1943; s. Robert Broadwell and Roberta (Kimbrel) C.; m. Melissa Roberta Moore, June 26, 1965 (dec. May 1977); children: Catherine Kelly, Jennifer, Robert D. BA, U. Calif., Berkeley, 1966. With U.S. Fgn. Svc. U.S. Dept. State, Washington, 1966-82, dep. asst. sec. state, 1989-90; counselor adminstrn. U.S. Embassy, Jeddah, Saudi Arabia, 1982-84; counselor sci. and tech. U.S. Embassy, Cairo, 1984-86, U.S. Mission to OECD, Paris, 1986-89; staff mem. Los Alamos (N.Mex.) Nat. Lab., 1990-92; tech. cons. Burke, Va., 1992—. Author: Measurement and Evaluation of Federal Technology Transfer, 1995; contbr. articles to profl. jours., chpt. to book. Pres. Smoke Rise Homes Assn., Fairfax Station, Va., 1996. Home and Office: 5765-F Burke Ctr Pky # 149 Burke VA 22015

CARR, THOMAS ELDRIDGE, lawyer; b. Austin, Tex., Aug. 16, 1953; s. Peter Gordon and Margaret (Johnson) C.; children: Christopher Allen, Austin Thomas. BA, Tex. Tech U., 1975, JD, 1977. Bar: Tex. 1978, U.S. Dist. Ct. (no. and we. dist.) Tex. 1978, U.S. Ct. Appeals (5th cir.) 1981, U.S. Supreme Ct. 1982. Assoc. Morgan, Gambill & Owen, Ft. Worth, 1978-81; ptnr. Morgan, Owen, & Carr, Ft. Worth, 1981-85; ptnr. Quillin, Owen & Thompson, Ft. Worth, 1985-87; ptnr. Owen, Wilson & Carr, Ft. Worth, 1987-91; ptnr. Owen & Carr, Ft. Worth, 1991-94; ptnr. Lane, Ray, Wilson, Carr & Steves, Ft. Worth, 1994—. Co-author: Of Counsel to Classrooms: A Resource Guide to Assist Attorneys and Teachers in Law Focused Education. Active Benbrook City Council, Tex., 1984-86, Benbrook Park and Recreation Bd., 1981-84; mem. exec. bd. Longhorn coun. Boy Scouts Am., 1983-86; mem. Home Rule Charter Commn., Benbrook, 1983. Selected Outstanding Young Lawyer of Tarrant County, 1990. Mem. ABA (chmn. com), Ft. Worth Tarrant County Young Lawyers Assn. (pres. 1983), State Bar Tex. (chmn. sch. law sect. 1991, treas., sec. 1988), Tex. Young Lawyers Assn. (bd. dirs. 1984-86), Ridglea Country Club. Office: 6115 Camp Bowie Blvd # 200 Fort Worth TX 76116-5522

CARR-ALLEN, ELIZABETH, real estate and mortgage broker, metaphysician; b. Ithaca, N.Y., May 24, 1939; d. John Franklin II and Helen Louise (Ziegler) C.; m. Robert Kern Mansur, Sept. 7, 1970 (div. 1982). Student U. Rochester, 1957-60; BA, U. Edinburgh, Scotland, 1962, MA in English Lit., 1962; postgrad. NYU, 1966, 77; grad. Realtors Inst. Lic. real estate broker, Fla.; cert. residential specialist. With various advt. and pub. rels. firms, N.Y.C., 1962-72; dir. comm. Unishield, Inc., N.Y.C., 1972-74; dir. pub. rels. Thermasol Ltd., N.Y.C., 1974-76; v.p., CFO Sports Mktg., Inc., N.Y.C., 1976-80; sales dir. Found. Investments, Highland Beach, Fla., 1980-85; dir. mktg. Concordia Properties, Highland Beach, 1985-86; pres.

Sunstone Realty, Inc., Boca Raton, 1987-94; pres. World Investors Realty, 1995—. Mem. NRA, NAFE, AULV Nat. Assn. Realtors, Fla. Assn. Realtors, Women's Coun. Realtors, South Palm Beach Assn. Realtors, Mensa, Intertel. Avocations: motorcycling, scuba diving, pistol/rifle shooting, crystals, healing. Home: 8705 Eagle Run Dr Boca Raton FL 33434-5433

CARRELL, DANIEL ALLAN, lawyer; b. Louisville, Jan. 2, 1941; s. Elmer N. and Mary F. (Pfingst) C.; m. Janis M. Wilhelm, July 3, 1976; children: Mary Monroe, Courtney Adele. AB, Davidson Coll., 1963; BA, Oxford U., 1965, MA, 1969; JD, Stanford U., 1968. Bar: Va. 1972, U.S. Dist. Ct. (ea. dist.) Va. 1972, U.S. Ct. Appeals (4th cir.) 1975, U.S. Dist. Ct. (we. dist.) Va. 1985. Asst. prof. U.S. Mil. Acad., West Point, N.Y., 1968-71; assoc. Hunton & Williams, Richmond, Va., 1971-79, ptnr., 1979-95; exec. v.p., gen. counsel The Ark Envelope Co., L.L.C., Richmond, Va., 1994—; prin. Carrell & Rice, Richmond, Va., 1996—. Active Richmond Rep. Com., 1974—; co-counsel Dalton for Gov. campaign, Richmond, 1977; counsel Obenshain for Senate campaign, Richmond, 1978; treas. Va. Victory '92; state fin. chmn., mem. fin. com., state ctrl. com. and budget com. Rep. Party Va., 1993-96; bd. dirs. Southampton Citizens Assn., 1985—, v.p., 1985-94; pres. Davidson Coll. Alumni Assn., 1987-88; trustee Davidson Coll., 1987-88; bd. dirs. Needles Eye Ministries, 1986-90, mem. adv. bd., 1990—. Rhodes scholar, 1962; recipient Award of Merit Sports Illustrated Mag., 1963. Mem. ABA (chmn. exemption and Noerr Doctrine com. 1986-87, antitrust sect.), Va. Bar Assn. (chmn. young lawyers joint law-related edn. com. 1978-79, young lawyers fellow award 1980), Va. State Bar (chmn. com. on legal edn. and admission to bar 1984-91, bd. govs. sect. edn. lawyers 1992—), Richmond Bar Assn., Christian Legal Soc., Westwood Club. Presbyterian. Home: 3724 Custis Rd Richmond VA 23225-1102 Office: Carrell & Rice 7275 Glen Forest Dr Richmond VA 23226

CARRERA, VICTOR MANUEL, lawyer; b. Rio Grande City, Tex., Nov. 20, 1954; s. Eladio and Ines Olivia (Guerra) C. BS, U. Tex., 1975, BA with honors, 1976, JD, 1979. Bar: Tex. 1979, U.S. Dist. Ct. (so. dist.) Tex. 1980, U.S. Ct. Appeals (5th cir.) 1986; cert. civil trial law, personal injury trial law, civil appellate law, Tex. Assoc. Cardenas & Whitis, McAllen, Tex., 1979-80; briefing atty. U.S. Dist. Ct. (so. dist.) Tex., Brownsville, 1980-81; assoc. Keys, Russell & Seaman, Corpus Christi, Tex., 1981-84; assoc. Wood, Boykin, Wolter & Keys, Corpus Christi, 1984-86, ptnr., 1986-88; participating mem. Law Offices of Ramon Garcia, P.C., Edinburg, Tex., 1988-90; ptnr. Munoz, Hockema & Reed, McAllen, Tex., 1990—; lectr. South Tex. Coll. Law, Houston, 1987, U. Houston, 1989-90, 96, State Bar Tex., 1992. Mng. editor Tex. Internat. Law Jour., 1978-79. Recipient Outstanding Individual Contbn. award Vol. Lawyers of Coastal Bend, 1985. Mem. Tex. Bar Assn., Tex. Trial Lawyers Assn. (dir., lectr. 1993-94), Hidalgo County Bar Assn., McAllen Tower Club. Democrat. Home: 1208 Xanthisma Ave Mcallen TX 78504-3520 Office: Munoz Hockema & Reed 1109 Nolana PO Box 9600 Mcallen TX 78502-9600

CARRERE, CHARLES SCOTT, judge; b. Dublin, Ga., Sept. 26, 1937; 1 son, Daniel Austin. B.A., U. Ga., 1959; LL.B., Stetson U., 1961. Bar: Fla. 1961, Ga. 1960. Law clk. U.S. Dist. Judge, Orlando, Fla., 1962-63; asst. U.S. atty. Middle Dist. Fla., 1963-66, 68-69, chief trial atty., 1965-66, 68-69; ptnr. Harrison, Greene, Mann, Rowe & Stanton, 1970-80; judge Pinellas County, Fla., 1980—. Mem. State Bar Ga., Fla. Bar, Phi Beta Kappa. Presbyterian. Address: PO Box 22034 Gateway Mall Sta Saint Petersburg FL 33742 Office: 150 5th St N 335 County Bldg Saint Petersburg FL 33701

CARRICO, HARRY LEE, state supreme court chief justice; b. Washington, Sept. 4, 1916; s. William Temple and Nellie Nadalia (Willett) C.; m. Betty Lou Peck, May 18, 1940 (dec. 1987); 1 child, Lucretia Ann; m. Lynn Brackenridge, July 1, 1994. Jr. cert., George Washington U., 1938, JD, 1942, LLD, 1987; LLD, U. Richmond, 1973, Coll. William & Mary, 1993. Bar: Va. 1941. With Rust & Rust, Fairfax, Va., 1941-43; trial justice Fairfax, Va., 1943-51, pvt. practice law, 1951-56; judge 16th Jud. Cir., Va., 1956-61; justice Va. Supreme Ct., Richmond, 1961-81, chief justice, 1981—; chmn. bd dirs. Nat. Ctr. for State Cts., 1989-90. With USNR, 1945-46. Recipient Alumni Profl. Achievement award George Washington U., 1981. Mem. McNeill Law Soc., Conf. Chief Justices (bd. dirs. 1985—, 1st v.p. 1987, pres.-elect. 1988, pres. 1989-90, co-chair nat. jud. coun. 1991—), Order of Coif, Phi Delta Phi, Omicron Delta Kappa. Episcopalian. Office: Va Supreme Ct PO Box 1315 Richmond VA 23210-1315

CARRIER, RONALD EDWIN, university administrator; b. Bluff City, Tenn., Aug. 18, 1932; s. James Murphy and Melissa (Miller) C.; m. Edith Marie Johnson, Sept. 7, 1955; children: Michael Lavon, Linda Lois Carrier Frazee, Jennine Marie Thomas. BS, Ea. Tenn. State U., 1955; MS in Econs., U. Ill., 1957, PhD in Econs., 1960. Assoc. prof. econs. U. Miss., Oxford, 1960-63; dir., prof. Bur. Bus. and Econ. Research, Memphis State U., 1963-66, provost, v.p. acad. affairs, 1966-71; pres. James Madison U., Harrisonburg, Va., 1971—, Ctr. for Innovative Tech., Herndon, Va., 1986-87; vice chmn. bd. dirs. Leader Fed. Savs. Bank, Memphis; bd. dirs. Universal Systems Inc., Universal Corp.; chmn. Coun. Pres.'s Va. Colls., 1975, Ctr. for Innovative Tech., Universal Systems, Inc. Author: Plant Locations: A Theory and Explanations, 1968; contbr. articles and monographs to profl. publs. Mem. White House Conf. Balance Econ. Growth; mem. Va. Indsl. Facilities Study Commn., 1972-75; chmn. Va. Land Use Adv. Com., 1974-77, Va. Gov.'s Electricity Costs Commn., 1975—; mem. Va. Gov.'s Energy Resource Adv. Commn., 1975-76, Gov.'s Regulatory Reform Adv. Bd., 1983, Joint Subcom. to Study Coal Slurry Pipeline Feasibility, 1983; bd. dirs. WVPT Pub. TV. Earheart fellow 1958-60; recipient Ben Franklin award Memphis Printing Industry, 1966, faculty award East Tenn. State U., 1955, Disting. Svc. award Jr. C. of C., 1965, Virginian of Yr. award Va. Assn. Broadcasters, 1982; named Outstanding Virginian, FHA, 1990; cultural laureate Va.; named Outstanding Virginian FFA, 1991. Mem. Assn. Higher Edn. Execs., Omicron Delta Kappa, Omicron Delta Gamma, Sigma Phi Epsilon. Methodist. Home: 916 Oak Hill Dr Harrisonburg VA 22801-3320 Office: James Madison U Office of President Harrisonburg VA 22807

CARRIGAN, JOHN DONLEY, retired secondary educator; b. Warren, Ohio, Oct. 14, 1927; m. Marian Joy Silman, Aug. 5, 1950; children: Timothy, David, Shawn, Kelly, Laurie. BS in Edn., U. Md., 1955. High sch. tchr. Balt., 1955-57; owner, pres. Carrigan Office Trailers, Towson, Md., 1957-85; real estate sales agt., Captiva Island, Fla., 1985-90; substitute tchr. Lee County Bd. Edn., Fort Myers, Fla., 1995—. Sec. adv. bd. Balt. Bullets, 1967-74; commr. U.S. Flag Football League, Balt., 1976-93. Named to Hall of Fame Am. Football Assn., 1990, U.S. Flag Football League, 1994. Mem. Lions (founder all-star football game Sanibel, Fla. 1989-94), Rotary (founder all-star football game Fort Myers 1994-96), First Marine Divsn. Assn., 2d Marine Divsn. Assn. (v.p. 1985-90), China Marine Assn., NFL Alumni Assn., VFW (life). Roman Catholic. Home: 9861 Mainsail Ct Fort Myers FL 33919

CARRILLO, GERALDINE MARY DEEHAN, trauma, medical/surgical and women's health nurse; b. Lima, Ohio, Oct. 9, 1958; d. Joseph Gerard and Mairead (Gunn) D. ADN with honors, Lima Tech. Coll., 1985; BSN magna cum laude, Armstrong State Coll., Savannah, Ga. Cert. med.-surg. nurse. Office mgr. physician's office, Lima, 1978-85; asst. head nurse Candler Gen. Hosp., Savannah, 1985-91; dir. quality assurance and infection control Northland Terr., Columbus, Ohio, 1992-93; trauma surg. nurse Wilford Hall Med. Ctr., San Antonio, 1993—. Mem. Internat. Mgmt. Coun., Sigma Theta Tau.

CARRINGTON, BESSIE MEEK, librarian; b. Houston, Oct. 17, 1931; d. James H. and Bessie B. Meek; m. Paul D. Carrington, Aug. 2, 1952; children: Clark, Mary, William J., Emily. BA, U. Tex., 1956; MLS, U. Mich., 1972. Libr. HUD, N.Y.C., 1972-73; reference libr. Detroit Pub. Libr., 1973-76; asst. br. libr. Ann Arbor (Mich.) Pub. Libr., 1976-78; reference libr. Duke U., Durham, N.C., 1979-94; adj. prof. U. Mich., Ann Arbor, 1976, U. N.C., Chapel Hill, 1989, 91, 92. Author: Guide to Reference Books, 11th edit., 1996; contbr. articles to profl. jours.; reviewer. Mem. ALA, Am. Econs. Assn., Am. Soc. for Info. Sci., N.C. Libr. Assn., Alpha Lambda Delta, Phi beta Kappa. Home: 1616 Pinecrest Rd Durham NC 27705-5832

CARRINGTON, PAUL DEWITT, lawyer, educator; b. Dallas, June 12, 1931; s. Paul and Frances Ellen (DeWitt) C.; m. Bessie Meek, Aug., 1952; children: Clark DeWitt, Mary Carrington Coults, William James, Emily Carrington Bell. BA, U. Tex., 1952; LLB, Harvard U., 1955. Bar: Tex. 1955, Ohio 1962, Mich. 1967. Practice Dallas, 1955; teaching fellow Harvard U., 1957-58; asst. prof. law U. Wyo., 1958-60, Ind. U., 1960-62; assoc. prof. Ohio State U., 1962-65; prof. U. Mich., 1965-78; dean Duke U. Sch. Law, Durham, N.C., 1978-88, prof., 1978—; reporter civil rules adv. com. Jud. Conf. of U.S., 1985-92. Author: (with Meador and Rosenberg) Justice on Appeal, 1977, Appellate Courts, 1994, Civil Procedure, 1977, 3d edit., 1983. Mem. Ann Arbor (Mich.) Bd. Edn., 1970-73; pres. Pvt. Adjudication Ctr., Inc., 1988-94, chmn., 1995—. With U.S. Army, 1955-57. Guggenheim fellow, 1988-89. Fellow Am. Bar Found.; mem. ABA, Am. Law Inst. Episcopalian. Office: Duke U Sch Law Durham NC 27708-0362

CARROLL, ANGELA CHRISTINE, vocational and home economics educator; b. Hazard, Ky., May 3, 1970; d. Ronald and Janice Crystal Lee (Collier) Fields; m. Steven Carroll, Sept. 24, 1994. BS in Home Econs. Edn., Ea. Ky. U., 1993. Tchr. home econs. Jackson County Bd. Edn., McKee, Ky., 1993-94, chair home econs. dept., 1994—, tech. prep. coord., 1994—; Future Homemakers of Am. advisor Jackson County H.S., McKee, 1993-95. Chair, mem. Jackson County Fair Bd., McKee, 1994-95; mem. 4-H Adv. Coun., McKee, 1994-95, PTA, 1994-95. Mem. NEA, Ky. Tchr. Assn., Ky. Vocat. Home Econs. Tchrs. Assn. (nominating com. 1994-95). Baptist. Home: Box 850 Hwy 421 N Mc Kee KY 40447 Office: Jackson County H S PO Box 427 Mc Kee KY 40447

CARROLL, ANN ELIZABETH, newspaper editor, retired; b. Pocahontas, Ark., Aug. 29, 1922; d. Warren Lee and Thelma (Martin) Blankenship; widow; children: Carol Ann, William N., Patrick W. Student, U. Ark., 1939-40. Editor to mgr., owner Pocahontas Star Herald, 1963-88, editor emeritus, part-time staff, 1988—. Lay minister United Meth. Ch., N. Ark. Conf.; alderperson Pocahontas City Coun., 1989—; vice-chmn. Randolph County Dem. Com., Pocahontas, 1965-95; commr. Ark. Commemorative Com., Little Rock, 1977-82, Ark. Rural Devel., 1990-94, Ark. Martin Luther King Com., Little Rock., 1995—; mem. Commn. Race and Religion, North Ark. Conf., United Meth. Ch., 1991—. Recipient various newspaper and writing awards Ark. Press Assn., 1963-88; finalist Golden Dozen Internat., Internat. Conf. Newspaper Editors, 1969. Home: 207 N Van Bibber Pocahontas AR 72455

CARROLL, BARBARA ANNE, radiologist, educator; b. Beaumont, Tex., Oct. 20, 1945; d. Theron Demp and Annette Ione (Anderson) C.; m. Olaf T. von Ramm. BA, U. Tex., 1967; MD, Stanford U., 1972. Intern, Stanford Hosp., Palo Alto, Calif., 1972, resident, 1973-76; research asst. Genetics Found., U. Tex., Austin, 1963-67; teaching asst. NSF Summer Biology Workshop, Austin, 1967; clinician Planned Parenthood, Santa Clara, Calif., 1973-76; instr. extension div. U. Calif.-Santa Cruz, 1972-76; asst. prof. radiology Stanford U. Med. Sch., Palo Alto, 1977-84, assoc. prof. radiology, 1984-85; chief diagnostic ultrasound, 1977-85; assoc. prof. radiology Duke U., Durham, N.C., 1985-92, prof. radiology, 1992—; cons. Searle, Santa Clara, 1977-78, Diasonics, Inc., Santa Clara, 1979-83, NIH, 1981-84, Acuson, 1984—. Contbr. articles to various publs.; reviewer numerous med. jours., 1982—; assoc. editor Radiology Jour., 1986—, Investigative Radiology, 1989-95, AJR, 1994—, Academic Radiology, 1995—, Jour. of Ultrasound in Medicine, 1990—. Bd. dirs. Planned Parenthood Santa Clara County, 1975-76. Agnes Axtell Moule Faculty scholar, 1979-84; recipient Cancer and Med. Rsch. Found. award, 1980. Fellow Am. Inst. Ultrasound in Medicine (bd. govs. 1987-90, Presdl. Recognition award 1988); mem. Soc. Radiologists in Ultrasound, Am. Coll. Radiology (commn. on ultrasound, 1989—, commn. on stds., 1994—), Radiologic Soc. N.Am. (sci. exhibits com.), sci. advisor rsch. and edn. fund), Am. Roentgen Ray Soc., Assn. Women Radiologists, Assn. Univ. Radiologists, Venezuelan Ultrasound Soc. (hon.), N.C. Ultrasound Soc. (faculty adv. 1986—), Phi Beta Kappa. Presbyterian. Office: Duke U Med Sch Dept Radiology PO Box 3808 Durham NC 27710-0001

CARROLL, CAROLE MAKEIG, sociology educator, researcher; b. Amarillo, Tex., Dec. 30, 1941; d. Clay Lee and Anne Louise (Makeig) Cochran; m. D. Frederic Carroll, Aug. 15, 1968 (dec. July 1978); children: Ellen Makeig, Katheryn Carroll Ward. Student, Baylor U., 1960-61; BA, So. Meth. U., 1964; MA, North Tex. State U., 1966; postgrad., U. Ariz., 1966-69. RN, Tenn. Sociology prof. Mid. Tenn. State U., Murfreesboro, 1969—; chair, bd. dirs. Hospice Murfreesboro, 1983—; cons. Domestic Violence Program, 1986-88, Episcopal Diocese Tenn., Nashville, 1987—. Coauthor: Methods of Sociological Research, 1971; editor: Community Services, 1988; co-editor: My Sociology Book, 1974; contbr. articles to profl. jours. Coun. mem. Diocese Tenn. Episcopal Aging Coun., Nashville, 1982-87; bd. dirs. Murfreesboro Health Care Ctr. Adv. Bd., 1982-83, Foster Care Rev. Bd., Rutherford County, Tenn., 1984-90, Affirmative Aging Program, Nashville, 1986-89; vestry mem. St. Paul's Episcopal Ch., 1991-94. Grantee Mid. Tenn. State U. Pub. Svc. Com., 1985-86, 88, Instructional Devel. Com., 1985, 89. Mem. Population Reference Bur., Popular Culture Assn., Popular Culture Assn. of South, So. Sociol. Soc., Mid-South Sociol. Assn. Democrat. Home: 5350 Browns Mill Rd Lascassas TN 37085-4623 Office: Mid Tenn State U PO Box 10 Murfreesboro TN 37132-0010

CARROLL, EDWARD PERRY, instrumental music educator, conductor; b. Sarasota, Fla., Dec. 17, 1934; s. Oliver Henry Perry and Sarah Theodosia (Amsden) C.; m. Rosa Marion Harvey, Dec. 30, 1965; 1 child, Kathryn Susan. MusB, Baylor U., 1957; M of Ch. Music, So. Bapt. Sem., 1970; EdD in Ch. Music, New Orleans Bapt. Sem., 1979. Bandsman USAF, U.S. and Spain, 1957-66; coll. instrumental tchr. Brewton Parker Coll., Mt. Vernon, Ga., 1970-73; prof. music Anderson (S.C.) Coll., 1975—; condr. Anderson Symphony Orch., 1975—; mus. dir. Anderson Cmty. Theatre, 1976-94. Mem. wing staff CAP, Anderson & Columbia, S.C., 1986—. With USAF, 1957-66. Mem. Music Educators Nat. Conf., Nat. Assn. Coll. Wind and Percussive Instrs., Hymn Soc. U.S. and Can., Internat. Trombone Assn., So. Bapt. Music Conf., Coop. Bapt. Fellowship Ch. Music Conf., Kappa Kappa Psi (life mem., pres. 1956-57), Phi Mu Alpha (life mem., pledgemaster 1955-56). Home: 126 Foxcroft Way Anderson SC 29621-2547

CARROLL, EDWIN WINFORD, architect; b. Elizabeth, La., Mar. 6, 1912; s. Rupert A. and Maude Marie (Ping) C.; m. Alyce Moter Outlaw, Mar. 27, 1937. B.Arch., U. Tex., 1936. Designer, draftsman Trost & Trost (architects), El Paso, Tex., 1936-41; architect, supt. bldgs. El Paso Pub. Schs., 1941-45; partner Carroll, Daeuble Du Sang & Rand, El Paso, 1945—; chmn. Tex. Bd. Archtl. Exam., 1953; vice chmn. internat. border devel. commn. A.I.A. and; Sociedad de Arquitectos Mexicanos, 1960-63; mem. El Paso Bldg. Code Bd., 1951—, chmn., 1953; pres. Am. del. XI Congress of Fedn. Pan-Am. Architects, 1965. Prin. works include engring.-biol. sci. complex, liberal arts bldg., Sun Bowl stadium, Geology Bldg., all at U. Tex. at El Paso, El Paso Civic Center, Hotel Dieu Sch. Nursing, Tex. hdqrs. bldg. Mountain Bell Co; Providence Meml. Hosp. Ambulatory Care Ctr., El Paso, Tex. Tech U. Health and Sci. Ctr., El Paso, Queen of Peace Cath. Ch., El Paso; also others in, N.Mex., Ariz., Tex., Mexico. Pres. Tex. Archtl. Found., 1958-59, 78-79; mem. Tex. Western Coll. Mission 1973. Fellow AIA (chmn. nat. border planning com. 1964-66); mem. Tex. Soc. Architects (pres. 1954, Pitts award 1983), Sociedad de Arquitectos Mexicanos (hon.), U. Tex. Ex-Students Assn. (chancellor's council). Mem. Christian Ch. (elder, past pres. congregation). Clubs: El Paso Country (pres. bd. govs. 1957), Coronado Country (pres. 1967, 68). Office: 122 Castellano Dr El Paso TX 79912

CARROLL, IRWIN DIXON, engineer; b. Many, La., Nov. 6, 1934; s. Andrew Dixon and Elizabeth Margaret (Irwin) C.; m. Claudia Laverne Bratcher, June 27, 1958; children: Richard Irwin, Claudia Elizabeth. BS in Mech. Engring., So. Methodist U., 1957, MS in Elec. Engring., 1967. Registered profl. engr., Tex. Design engr. Tex. Instruments, Dallas, 1957-66, engring. supr., 1966-71, engring. mgr., 1971-75, ops. mgr., 1975-77, European div. mgr., 1977-79, mfg. ops. mgr., 1979-80, dept. mgr., 1980-85; dept. mgr. George A. Greene Co., Campbell, Calif., 1985-86; cons. engr. Irwin Carroll Assocs., Dallas, 1986-88; dir. joint devel. programs, site mgr. Applied Materials, Inc., Austin, Tex., 1988—; tech. program dir. Semiconductor Equip. and Materials Inst., Dallas, 1983-85, speaker Zurich, Switzerland, 1986; mem. semiconductor adv. com. U.S. Dept. Commerce, 1990—. Chmn. Zion Luth. Sch. Bd., Dallas, 1985-89; bd. dirs. Jr. Achievement of Ctrl. Tex., 1991-93, Japan-Am. Soc. of Austin, 1990—, Austin Symphony Orch., 1994—; pres. Austin Children's Mus., 1991—; active Austin Choral Union, 1994—. Mem. ASME, Greater Austin C. of C. (bd. dirs. 1991—), Rotary. Lutheran. Home: 3222 Tarryhollow Dr Austin TX 78703-1639 Office: Applied Materials Inc PO Box 149146 9700 Hwy 290 E Austin TX 78714-9146

CARROLL, JOAN LOUISE, home health and hospice nurse; b. Warsaw, N.Y., Jan. 27, 1932; d. Clifford Preston and Donna Mariette (Shaw) Hayden; m. John S. Rooney, June 30, 1952 (div. 1968); children: John, James, Matthew, Donna, Lorilee; m. Frank Hamlin Carroll, May 5, 1978. Nursing diploma, Highland Hosp., Rochester, N.Y., 1953. RN, Fla. Staff nurse Desoto Meml. Hosp., Arcadia, Fla., 1970-71, asst. head nurse ICU, 1971-73, emergency rm. supr., 1973-78; mem. staff Upjohn Healthcare, Port Charlotte, Fla., 1978-79, adminstr., 1979-85; clin. supr. Upjohn Healthcare, Port Charlotte, 1985-89; mem. staff Hospice S.W. Fla., Port Charlotte, 1991, patient/family care coord., 1992-93; hospice admitting nurse, 1994-95, ret., 1995; pres. Charsoto, Port Charlotte, 1983-85. Active ARC, Am. Cancer Soc., Am. Lung Assn., various community orgns., Port Charlotte, 1975—. Home: PO Box 9118 Port Charlotte FL 33949-9118

CARROLL, JOHN MILLAR, computer science and psychology educator; b. Bethlehem, Pa., Oct. 10, 1950; s. John Millar and Jane (Morris) C.; m. mary Beth Rosson, Feb. 12, 1983; 1 child, Erin Marissa. BA in Math. and Info. Sci., Lehigh U., 1972; MA in Psychology, Columbia U., 1974, PhD in Psychology, 1976. Scientist IBM Rsch., Yorktown Heights, N.Y., 1976-83, mgr., 1983-94; prof., dept. head Va. Poly. Inst. and State U., Blacksburg, 1994—, dir. Ctr. for Human-Computer Interaction, 1995—. Author 10 books; mem. numerous editl. and adv. bds.; contbr. over 150 articles to profl. jours. Recipient Rigo award Assn. for Computing Machinery, 1994.

CARROLL, MICHAEL M., academic dean, mechanical engineering educator; b. Thurles, County Tipperary, Ireland, Dec. 8, 1936; came to U.S. 1960; s. Timothy and Catherine (Gleeson) C.; m. Carolyn F. Gahagan, Oct. 31, 1964; children—Patricia, Timothy J. B.A., Univ. Coll., Galway, Ireland, 1958, M.A., 1959; Ph.D., Brown U., 1964; DSc, Nat. U. Ireland, 1979, LLD (hon), 1992. Asst. prof. mech. engring. U. Calif., Berkeley, 1965-69, assoc. prof., 1969-73, prof., 1973-83; Shell disting. chair Shell Cos. Found., 1983-88; dean George R. Brown Sch. Engring., Burton J. and Ann McMurtry prof. engring. Rice U., Houston, 1988—; cons. TerraTek Labs., Salt Lake City, 1976-84, Thoratec Lab., Berkeley, Calif., 1976-84, Sci. Applications Internat., La Jolla, Calif., 1984—, JAG Industries, Trinidad, Calif., 1984—, Sandia Labs., Albuquerque, 1991—, Brit. Petroleum, Houston, 1991—. Contbr. articles to profl. jours.; mem. editorial bds. of tech. jours. Fellow ASME, Am. Acad. Mechanics (pres. 1994-95), Am. Acad. Arts and Scis.; mem. NAE, Am. Soc. Engring. Edn. (gov. bd., deans coun. 1992—), Soc. Engring. Sci. (bd. dirs., v.p., pres.), Sigma Xi. Roman Catholic. Home: 3227 Robinson Rd Missouri City TX 77459-3246 Office: Rice U George R Brown Sch Engring 6100 Main St MS 364 Houston TX 77005-1892

CARROLL, ROGER CLINTON, medical biology educator; b. Mt. Clemens, Mich., Sept. 28, 1947; s. Lee Stanley and Evelyn Marie (Badgett) C.; m. Andrea Kristine Skrec, Sept. 13, 1969; children: Brian Roger, Alicia Helene. BS, Cornell U., 1969, PhD, 1977. Rsch. assoc. U. Calif. San Diego, LaJolla, 1976-78; rsch. assoc. U. Okla. Health Sci. Ctr., Oklahoma City, 1978-79, asst. prof. dept. pathology, 1979-80, adj. asst. prof. dept. biochemistry, dept. physiology, 1980-84; assoc. prof. dept. med. biology U. Tenn. Med. Ctr., Knoxville, 1984-90, prof. dept. med. biology, 1990—, prof. dept. surgery, 1993—; asst. mem. Okla. Med. Rsch. Found. (Merrick award 1984), Oklahoma City, 1982-84; cons. Nat. Heart Lung and Blood Inst., 1985— (grantee 1980-90). Contbr. articles to profl. jours., chpts. to books. Mem. Am. Heart Assn. (thrombosis coun., rsch. com. chmn., peer rev. com. chmn., Tenn. affiliate, grantee 1981-84, 1987—), Internat. Soc. on Thrombosis and Haemostasis, Sigma Xi. Democrat. Roman Catholic. Home: 706 Ala Dr Knoxville TN 37920-6364 Office: U Tenn Med Ctr Grad Sch Medicine 1924 Alcoa Hwy Knoxville TN 37920-1511

CARROLL, ROY, academic administrator; b. England, Arkansas, Dec. 8, 1929; m. Eleanor Kate Moorefield, 1953; children: Jane, Linda. BA cum laude, Ouachita Baptist Univ., 1951; MA, Vanderbilt Univ., 1959, PhD, 1964. Math. tchr. Baker High Sch., Columbus, Ga., 1955; asst. prof. History and Political Sci. Mercer Univ., Macon, Ga., 1959-65; prof. History, chmn. Dept. Hist. and Political Sci. Armstrong State Coll., Savannah, Ga., 1965-69; prof. History, chmn. Dept. History Appalachian State Univ., Boone, N.C., 1969-79; v.p. planning gen. adminstrn. U. N.C. System, 1991-96; sr. v.p., v.p. acad. affairs, 1996—; interim chancellor U. N.C., Asheville, 1990-91; mem. N.C. Justice Edn. and Tng. Standards Commn., 1979-90, chmn. Planning Com. of the Commn., 1981-88; mem. adv. bd. Inst. Transp. Rsch. and Edn., Rsch. Triangle Park, 1980—; mem. bd. dirs. Western N.C. Devel. Assn., 1990-91, N.C. State Employees Credit Union, 1990-91. Contbr. articles to profl. jours. infantry officer U.S. Army, 1951-53, Japan, Korea. Fulbright scholar, Eng., 1958-59. Home: 15 Clover Dr Chapel Hill NC 27514-2509 Office: U North Carolina Gen Adminstrn POB 2688 Chapel Hill NC 27515-2688

CARROLL, STEPHEN DOUGLAS, chemist, research specialist; b. Clarendon, Ark., Nov. 2, 1943; s. Albert Genson and Wilma Mae (Hill) C.; m. Nonnie Lee Dyer, June 8, 1991; children: Geoffrey Genson, Raymond Loyd. BA, Hendrix Coll., 1965; MS, U. Ark., 1970. Del. chemist Chicopee Mfg. Co., North Little Rock, Ark., 1969-73, Mgr. Quality Assurance, 1973-80; cons. self employed, Clarendon, Ark., 1980-82; rsch. asst. U. Ark., Marianna, 1982-87, rsch. specialist, 1987—. Mem. Am. Chem. Soc. Democrat. Methodist. Office: U Ark Highway 1 Byp Marianna AR 72360

CARROLL, WILLIAM ALEXANDER, political scientist, educator; b. Providence, July 25, 1923; s. Charles Vincent and Winifred Louise (Martin) C.; m. Alice Middleton, Dec. 27, 1958 (dec. June 1992). BA, Brown U., 1948; MA, Georgetown U., 1950, PhD, 1963. Barrister at Law of the Middle Temple. Social studies tchr. B.M.C. Durfee High Sch., Fall River, Mass., 1950-53; fellow Georgetown U., Washington, 1953-55, rsch. analyst, 1955-58; instr. polit. sci. Oglethorpe U., Atlanta, 1958-59, asst. prof., 1959-62; prof. Frostburg (Md.) State Coll., 1963-68; prof. Guilford Coll., Greensboro, N.C., 1968-93, prof. emeritus, 1993—. Co-author, editor: American Constitutional Rights: Cases, Documents and Commentary, 1991. With U.S. Army, 1943-45. Mem. Am. Polit. Sci. Assn., AAUP, English Speaking Union U.S. (pres. Greensboro br. 1983-85, chmn. region IV 1986-89, bd. dirs. 1990—). Roman Catholic. Office: Guilford Coll 5800 W Friendly Ave Greensboro NC 27410-4108

CARROLL-DOVENMUEHLE, BETTYE TURPIN, counselor; b. Baton Rouge, La., Sept. 17, 1943; d. Baynard T. Jr. and Mary Elizabeth (Barnett) Turpin; m. Robert H. Dovenmuehle, July 31, 1988. BA, La. State U., 1964; MEd, U. N.C., Greensboro, 1989. Instr. Rockingham C.C., Wentworth, N.C., 1969-73; exec. dir. Eden (N.C.) Child Devel. Ctr., 1973-76; cons. Office for Children, Greensboro, 1976-77; trainer N.C. State Tng. Office for Head Start, Greensboro, 1977-80; counselor Fellowship Hall, Greensboro, 1980-86; rehab. counselor, behavior modification therapist The Hatcher Ctr., Danville, Va., 1989—; vol. therapist Mental Health Assocs., 1990—. Mem. ACA, Nat. Bd. Cert. Counselors, Va. Psychol. Assn., Assn. Nondirective Counselors, Nat. Assn. Drug Abuse Counselors, Va. Counselors Assn. Home: 147 Acorn Ln Danville VA 24541-6201

CARRON, MAUDEE LILYAN, painter, sculptor, writer; b. Melville, La., Oct. 1, 1912; d. Albert Hilliard and Zora Trisha (King) Carron; widowed; 1 son. Studies with Ola McNeill Davidson, Creative Arts Sch., 1934-35. guest curator Art Mus. S.E. Tex., Beaumont, 1990; billboards designer Art Mus. S.E. Tex. Opening, Beaumont, 1990; guest lectr. Deep South Writers' and Artists' Conf., U. S.W. La., Lafayette, 1969. One-woman shows include Gresham Gallery, New Orleans, 1938, Little Gallery, New Orleans, 1940, Wilson Meml. Art Ctr., Beaumont, Tex., 1971, Gates Gallery, Port Arthur, Tex., 1973, Scurlock Gallery, Beaumont, 1974, Angelina Coll., Lufkin, Tex., 1978, Beaumont Art League, 1984, Galerie Kunstraum, West Berlin, Germany, 1985, Little Gallery, New Orleans, 1985, Art Mus. S.E. Tex., Beaumont, 1988, Hooks Epstein Galleries, Houston, 1992; exhibited in group shows at Mus. Fine Arts Houston, 1938, Little Gallery, 1945, Mcpl. Arts Gallery, Jackson, Miss., 1947, 51, Witte Meml. Mus., San Antonio, 1953, Beaumont Art Mus., 1956, 64, Dallas Mus. Fine Arts, 1959, The Roswell (N.Mex.) Mus. and Art Ctr., 1962, Laguna Gloria Art Mus., 1966, Mobile

(Ala.) Art Gallery, 1968, Collector's Guild, Orange, Tex., 1970, Tex. Union Fine Arts Gallery, U. Tex. Austin, 1971, The Art Zoo, Gates Gallery, Port Arthur, Tex., 1973, Blaffer Gallery, U. Houston, 1977, Art League Houston, 1980, Beaumont Art League, 1982 (hon. mention), Gates Libr., Port Arthur, 1984, 25th Ann. Tri-State Art Exhbn., Beaumont, 1986, Hooks-Epstein Galleries, 1989, The Designs Industry Found. AIDS, Houston, 1991, Dishman Art Gallery, Retrospective Lamar U., Beaumont, 1992, Lamar U., 1993, numerous others; represented in permanent collections Art Mus. SE Tex., Beaumont, Beaumont Art League, Centennial Mus., Corpus Christi, Dishman Art Gallery, Gulf Oil, James Johnson Sweeney Estate, Mobil Oil, Southwestern U.; pvt. collection Western Savings Bank. Recipient Hon. Mention award Tex. Fine Art Assn., 1943, award 1st Ann. Art Assn. Lake Charles (La.) Area Show, 1962, Juror's Choice award Tex. Fine Arts Assn., 1966, award 13th Beaumont Art Mus. Ann. Exhibit, 1969, award Tex. Fine Arts Assn., Austin, 1969, Juror's 5th Citation, Hon. Mention award Tex. Fine Arts Assn., 1969, award Houston Pub. Libr., 1977, Gulf Oil Purchase award, Houston, 1980, Hon. Mention, Purchase award Gallery Port Arthur Pub. Libr., 1981, Mobil Oil Found. Purchase awards, 1986, 90, Juror's award 25th Ann. Baytown, Tex., 1991. Home: RR 6 Box 300 Beaumont TX 77705-9644

CARSIA, GENE VINCENT, physician; b. Hazelton, Pa., Nov. 10, 1961; s. Gene Vincent and Dolores Louise (Knelly) C. BS, U. Pitts., 1984; DO, U. Health Scis., Kansas City, Mo., 1988. Diplomate Am. Bd. Osteopathy; cert. Am. Osteopathic Bd. Family Practice. Resident family practice Dallas Family Hosp., 1988-91; pvt. practice Arlington, Tex., 1993—. Mem. Am. Osteopathic Assn., Am. Coll. Gen. Practitioners, Tex. Med. Assn., Tarrant County Med. Soc. Republican. Roman Catholic. Office: 3295 S Cooper St Arlington TX 76015-2328

CARSON, ALBERT GUS, IV, video producer; b. Baton Rouge, Feb. 25, 1960; s. Albert G. III and Joy Monteal (Baragona) C. BS in Fin., La. Tech. U., 1983. With cinematography and publicity depts. La. Tech. U., Ruston, 1980-83; mgr. Group W Cable, Baker, La., 1983-86; pres., producer TREB Prodns., Baker, 1986—; v.p. Enviro News, 1991-94. Dir., producer numerous TV shows including 5-Star Wrestling, 1990, Open House, 1987, Let's Talk It Over and My Home Town, 1983-86, Live Election Returns, 1984, 88, Zachary on the Grow, 1983-84, Speak Out Louisiana, 1992, We Walk by Faith, 1993, Ark of Safety, 1992-93, Inside Gospel Outreach, 1992, Inspirational Joy, 1992-93, Louisiana Gospel Music, 1992-93, Living for Jesus, 1992-93, I Think Myself Happy, 1993-95, The Voice of Faith, 1993—, Provost Adventures, 1993—, Inspiration Up Life Gospel Show, 1994, Dreams Do Come True, 1995—. Bd. dirs. Baker Little Theatre, pres., 1987-89; bd. dirs. La. the Beautiful, 1991-94. Recipient Vision award for Best Polit. comml. & Best Svc. comml. Mem. Rotary (pres. Baker chpt. 1989-90, Paul Harris award 1990, Rotarian of Yr. 1989), Baker Civic Club, Baker C. of C. (bd. dirs. 1983-84), DARE. Republican. Mem. Christian Ch. Office: TREB Prodns 3121 Van Buren Ste C Baker LA 70714

CARSON, BARBARA GILBERT, college educator, consultant; b. Lancaster, Pa., July 7, 1941; d. Joe Capp and Anna Elizabeth Gilbert; m. Cary Carson, June 19, 1965; 1 child, Anna Purcell. AB, Brown U., 1963; MA, U. Del., 1965. Assoc. prof., lectr. Am. Studies The George Washington U., 1975-94; assoc. prof. lecturer Coll. William & Mary, Williamsburg, Va., 1982-94. Author: The Governor's Palace, 1982, Ambitious Appetites, 1991.

CARSON, CULLEY CLYDE, III, urologist; b. Westerly, R.I., Feb. 25, 1945; s. Culley Clyde, Jr., and Dorothy (Scarborough) C.; B.S., Trinity Coll., 1967; M.D., George Washington U., 1971; m. Mary Jo McDonald, Aug. 10, 1970; children—Culley Clyde IV, Hilary. Intern, Dartmouth Med. Center, 1971-72, resident in surgery, 1971-73; fellow in urology Mayo Clinic, 1975-78; instr. urology U. Minn. Mayo Med. Sch., 1978; asst. prof. urology Duke U. Med. Center, Durham, N.C., 1978-84, assoc. prof., 1984-88, prof. 1988-93; prof. and chmn. urology U. N.C., 1993—; chief urology Durham VA Hosp. Served to maj. M.C., USAF, 1973-75. Am. Heart Assn. research fellow, 1969; O'Dea travel fellow, 1978; recipient Calvin Klopp research award, 1971, Friedman research prize, 1971, Cristol Mayo Alumni award, 1992; named Command Flight Surgeon of Yr., USAF, 1974. Diplomate Am. Bd. Urology. Fellow ACS; mem. AMA, Am. Urol. Assn., Internat. Sociétéd'Urologie, Am. Fertility Soc., Univ. Urol. Forum, AAAS, N.Y. Acad. Scis., Mayo Alumni Assn., Sigma Xi, Psi Chi, Alpha Omega Alpha. Clubs: Gov's., Carolina, Trinity (Hartford). Author: Endourology, 1985, Atlas of Urologic Endoscopy, 1986, Impotence, 1992, Complications of Invasive Procedures, 1995; contbr. chpts. in urol. texts. Home: 2719 Spencer St Durham NC 27705-5720 Office: Duke University Medical Center Durham NC 27710

CARSON, DAVID COSTLEY, psychologist, health care administrator; b. Dallas, Oct. 18, 1921; s. William Henry and Eula Lee (Costley) C.; BA, So. Meth. U., 1943; postgrad. U. Chgo., 1943-46; MA, U. Tex., 1950, postgrad., 1950-52; m. Barbara Dame, Aug. 22, 1946; children: Jonathan David, Laurel, Bruce Alan. Psychologist, Tex. State Youth Devel. Council, Austin, 1952-53; counselor, planner Tex. Edn. Agy., Austin, 1953-67; project dir. Planning Commn. for Vocat. Rehab., Olympia, Wash., 1967-70; exec. dir. Group Health Coop. S. Central Wis., Madison, 1972-76; pres. Austin Health Maintenance Orgn., Inc., 1978-84; cons. health care adminstrn., 1969—; pres. WindWatts, Inc., 1974—. Sec. Dane County Arts Commn., 1975-78; pres., bd. dirs. Austin Ballet Soc., 1955-67; pres. bd. trustees McDade Ind. Sch. Dist., 1986-89, pres. 1986-87. With M.C., U.S. Army, 1946-48. VA fellow, 1948-49. Mem. AAAS, Nat. Audubon Soc. (bd. dirs. 1991-94), Audubon Council Tex. (pres. 1986-88), Bastrop County Audubon Soc. (pres. 1986-87), Phi Delta Kappa, Psi Chi. Author: Satellite HMO, 1972; Rehabilitation Advance, 1969; co-author: Rehabilitation in Washington State, 1968. Home and Office: PO Box 4856 Mc Dade TX 78650-4856

CARSON, MARGARET MARIE, gas industry executive, marketing professional; b. Windber, Pa., Dec. 30, 1944; d. Peter and Margaret (Olenik) Buben; m. Claude Carson, Dec. 30, 1967 (div. 1974); m. Brian Charles Scruby, June 6, 1975; stepchildren: Debbie, Victor, Chris, Kenneth. BA, U. Pitts., 1971; MS in Mgmt., Houston Bapt. U., 1985. Petroleum analyst Gulf Oil Co., Pitts., 1973-75, crude oil analyst, 1971-74, environ. coordinator, 1974-79, mgr. oil acquistition, Houston, 1980-84, mktg. dir., 1985; sales dir. Cabot Cons. Group, Houston, 1985-86; dir. competitor analysis and corporate strategy dept., Enron Corp., Houston, 1987—; adj. prof. bus tech. Houston Community Coll., 1985-91. Columnist: The Collegian, 1984-85. Bd. dirs. Indiana U., Pa., 1980-81. Mem. Am. Competitiveness Soc. (bd. dirs.), Internat. Energy Economists, Gas Processors Assn. (speaker tech. sessions 1985-94), Gas Rsch. Inst., Univ. Club.

CARSON, VIRGINIA HILL, oil and gas executive; b. L.A., Dec. 4, 1928; d. Percy Albert McCord and Flora May (Newking) Schultz; m. John Carson, Dec. 30, 1950 (dec.). BA in Internat. Relations, U. Calif., Berkeley, 1949; postgrad. Stanford U., 1948, UCLA, 1951. Gen. office worker UN, San Francisco, 1949; ind. oil and gas profl., U.S., Can., Cuba, 1953-73; supr., specialist Sun Exploration & Prodn. Co. (name changed to Oryx Energy Co.), Dallas, 1978-83, profl. analyst, 1983-92; lit. rschr. and freelance editor, 1992—. Mem. Dallas Coun. World Affairs, 1984—, Dallas Mus. Fine Arts, 1984—; vol. North Tex. Taping and Radio for the Blind, 1992—, Thanks Giving Sq., 1996—. Nominated to pres.'s coun. Am. Inst. Mgmt., N.Y.C., 1974. Address: PO Box 12530 Dallas TX 75225-0530

CARSTENS, PER HENRIK BECHER, pathology educator; b. Copenhagen, Denmark, Jan. 22, 1939; s. Niels Jacob Becher and Erna Kathrine (Jensen) C.; m. Nellie Holm, Mar. 20, 1965. MD, U. Copenhagen, 1965. Diplomate in anat. pathology Am. Bd. Pathology. Asst. prof. U. Louisville, 1972-76, assoc. prof., 1976-83, full prof., 1983—. Mem. editorial bd. Ultrastructural Pathology, 1985—; contbr. articles to profl. jours. Recipient fellowship U. Copenhagen, 1962-65. Fellow Arthur Purdy Stout Soc. for Surg. Pathologists; mem. AMA, Internat. Acad. Pathology, Soc. for Diagnostic Ultrastructural Pathology, Renal Pathology Soc. Home: 4904 Clovernook Rd Louisville KY 40207-1116 Office: Univ Louisville Dept Pathology Mdr Bldg 208 Louisville KY 40243

CARTAYA, MARIO, architect; b. Havana, Cuba, Sept. 9, 1951; s. Juan Ignacio and Leida Isaura (Mateo) C.; m. Pamela Lynn Phares, Aug. 1, 1981; children: Lesli Lynn, Mario Marcos. BArch magna cum laude, U. Fla., 1974, M of Constrn., 1975. Owner, prin., pres. Cartaya and Assocs. Architects, Ft. Lauderdale, Fla., 1978—; chmn. dept. architecture Broward Community Coll., Ft. Lauderdale, 1978-83, instr. architecture, 1984-91. Prin. works include various projects for Sch. Bds. of Broward, Dade and Palm Beach Counties, Lake Carol Townhouses (300 units, phases 1 thru 5), Miami Lakes, Fla., Potamkin Dodge, Hialeah, Fla., Radiology Assocs., P.A., Ft. Lauderdale, Jefferson Ward Hdqrs., Auto Svc. Bldg. and 7 Dept. Stores, Miami, Fla., Marlin Shopping Ctr., Suniland, Fla., Cen. Disposal Ctr., Waste Mgmt., Inc., Pompano Beach, Fla. Mem. Svc. Acad. (Naval) Selection Team, 1986—; past pres. Hispanic Am. Dems., Broward County, 1989-91; active United Way, 1990-92, Imperial Point Hosp. Cmty. Rels. Bd.; co-chair bd. trustees Broward C.C., 1991—; treas. Holy Cross Hosp. Instl. Rev. Com. Recipient L. Clayton Nance Meml. award Broward County Commrs., 1981. Mem. AIA (sec. 1982-85), U.S. C. of C., Latin C. of C. Roman Catholic. Office: Cartaya and Assocs Architec 3077 E Commercial Blvd Fort Lauderdale FL 33308-4311

CARTE, SUZANNE LEWIS, elementary school educator; b. S. Charleston, W.Va., Nov. 16, 1943; d. Carson Richard and Thelma Lee (Dew) Lewis; m. John Herman Carte, Sept. 1, 1962; children: John Kevin, Jennifer Kristin, Samuel Jefferson. BS, W.Va. State Coll., 1973; student W.Va. Coll. Grad. Studies, 1976-86. Tchr., Kanawha County Schs., Charleston, W.Va., 1978, tchr. history, 1979-81, tchr. intensive svc. unit, 1981, tchr. 6th grade, 1982-86, tchr. social studies, 1986—, cheer coach, 1987—; cheer coach, dir. state high sch. cheer competition W.Va. Secondary Schs. Activity Commn.; cheer coach U. Charleston. Home: Coal River Rd Saint Albans WV 25177 Office: Hayes Jr High Sch 830 Strawberry Rd Saint Albans WV 25177-3331

CARTEE, MARVIN LEWIS, corporate senior security officer; b. Spartanburg County, S.C., Feb. 1, 1940; s. James Curtis and Lillie Mae (McCright) C.; m. Erika Franziska Schmidt, June 2, 1990; children: Lisa Diane, Rebecca JoAnn, Rhonda Maxine, Marvin Lewis Jr. Br. mgr. Columbus (Ga.) Ledger-Enquirer, 1980-82; security officer Security Engrs., Birmingham, Ala., 1982-88; sr. security officer AFLAC, Inc., Columbus, 1988—. With U.S. Army, 1957-80. Recipient Golden Poet award World of Poetry, 1988-92. Home: 7087 Stoneybrook Dr Columbus GA 31909-6006

CARTEE, THOMAS EDWARD, JR., financial consultant; b. Largo, Fla., Jan. 30, 1960; s. Thomas Edward and JoAnne (Todd) C.; m. Kathryn Armecia Stokes, Aug. 6, 1983; children: Thomas Edward III, John Caleb. AB in Econs., Davidson Coll., 1982; MBA, U. N.C., 1984. Assoc. account rep. First Nat. Bank Chgo., 1984-85; credit analyst, account rep. Swiss Bank Corp., Chgo., 1985, asst. treas., head credit dept., 1986-87, asst. v.p., account officer, 1988-89, v.p. corp. banking, 1989-91; analyst Banc One Capital Corp., Columbus, Ohio, 1992-93; fin. cons. Jennings & Assocs., Winston-Salem, N.C., 1994—; assoc. Robert Morris Assocs., Chgo., 1986-87; registered rep. Ogilvie Security Advisors Corp., 1995—. Treas. Clifton Pl. Condominium Assn., Chgo., 1985-86; mem. Lake Bluff Adv. Com., 1988-90. Mem. Chgo. Coun. on Fgn. Rels. (com. on fgn. affairs 1990-91), U. N.C. Alumni Assn. Republican. Office: 3000 Bethesda Pl Ste 803 Winston Salem NC 27103

CARTER, ALAN BRUCE, psychiatrist; b. Mpls., July 27, 1936. AB, Duke U., 1958, MD, 1962; grad. psychoanalytic tng. program, U. N.C./Duke U., 1985. Diplomate Am. Bd. Pediatrics, Am. Bd. Psychiatry and Neurology; lic. physician, N.C. Intern in pediatrics Duke U. Med. Ctr., Durham, N.C., 1962-63, resident in pediatrics, 1966-67, resident in psychiatry, 1967-70, fellow in child psychiatry, 1969-71; resident in pediatrics U. Colo. Med. Ctr., Denver, 1963-64; pvt. practice child, adolescent and adult psychiatry Raleigh, 1971—; psychiat. cons. Lee-Harnet Community Mental Health Ctr., Sanford and Buies Creek, N.C., 1971-72, Wilson-Greene Community Mental Health Ctr., Wilson, N.C., 1971-75, Wake County Mental Health Ctr., Raleigh, 1975-77, Life Enrichment Ctr., Raleigh, 1979—, Child and Adolescent Mental Health Clinic, Fayetteville, N.C., 1991-95; supr. psychotherapy to Fellows in Child Psychiatry, Child Psychiatry Divsn. Dorothea Dix Hosp., Raleigh, 1971-75; pvt. practice Wake Meml. and Holly Hill Hosps., Raleigh, 1976-84. With M.C. U.S. Army, 1964-66. Mem. Am. Assn. Psychiat. Svcs. for Children (Cert. of Recognition 1971). Office: 1004 Dresser Ct Ste 107 Raleigh NC 27609-7325

CARTER, CARL DOUGLAS, public relations executive; b. Birmingham, Ala., Nov. 19, 1953; s. Loren Kemp and Thelma Brown (Harwell) C.; m. Katherine Smith, June 19, 1976; children: Todd, Lindsay. BA in Comm., U. Ala., 1976. Gen. assignment reporter The Birmingham (Ala.) News, 1976-78, religion editor, 1978-82, night city editor, bus. editor, 1983; staff mgr. media rels. BellSouth, Birmingham, 1984-86; mgr. media rels. BellSouth Enterprises, Atlanta, 1986; mgr. employee comm. Bell South Enterprises, Atlanta, 1987-88; mgr. employee publs. South Ctrl. Bell, Birmingham, 1988-90, BellSouth Telecom., Birmingham and Atlanta, 1990-95; pres. Carter-Harwell Pub. Rels., 1995—. Chmn. Irondale (Ala.) Libr. Bd., 1984; publicity/advt. dir. Hoover (Ala.) Quality Schs. Referendum, 1989; mem. curriculum adv. com., Hoover, 1991—, Hoover (Ala.) 2000 Com., 1993. Recipient numerous state, local and regional awards for newswriting and public relations. Mem. Pub. Rels. Soc. Am. Home: 1758 Strollaway Ln Birmingham AL 35226-2600 Office: Carter-Harwell Pub Rels 1758 Strollaway Ln Birmingham AL 35226-2600

CARTER, CRAIG NASH, veterinary epidemiologist, educator, researcher, software developer; b. Gary, Ind., Mar. 20, 1949; s. Frank Lynn and Harriet May (Nash) C. AA Computer Sci., Riverside (Calif.) City Coll., 1972; BS in Vet. Sci. magna cum, Tex. A&M U., 1980, DVM cum laude, 1981, MS in Epidemiology, 1985, PhD in Pub. Health, 1993. Diplomate Am. Coll. Vet. Preventive Medicine. Computer systems engr. U.S. Navy, Civilian, Mechanicsburg, Pa., 1976-77; computer specialist USAF, Civilian, Universal City, Tex., 1977-78; vet. clinical assoc. Tex. Vet. Med. Diagonstic Labs, College Station, Tex., 1981-83; vet. epidemiologists, adj. prof. Tex. A&M U., College Station, 1983-88, adj. prof., 1988—; head dept. epidemiology and informatics, chief info. officer Tex. Vet. Med. Diagnostic Labs, College Station, 1988—; pres. Am. Vet. Acad. Disaster Medicine, 1988—; pres. Carter-Melloy Corp., 1989—; presenter more than 50 nat. and internat. sci. presentations. Contbr. 40 articles to profl. jours.; inventor in field. Capt. USAFR, Vietnam, Desert Storm. Mem. Am. Coll. Vet. Informatics (pres. 1990-92), Am. Vet. Computer Soc. (pres. 1987-90), Am. Vet. Med. Assn., Tex. Vet. Med. Assn., Am. Assn. Vet. Labs. Diagnostic Med., Internat. Vet. Acad. Disaster Med., U.S. Animal Health Assn. Democrat. Congregationalist. Home: 3107 Manorwood Dr Bryan TX 77801-4204 Office: 4801 Indian School Rd NE Albuquerque NM 87110-3928

CARTER, DALE WILLIAM, psychologist; b. Woodbury, N.J., Jan. 27, 1949; s. Charles Elmer and Dorothy Adele (Seibold) C. BS, Wake Forest U., 1971; MS, Radford U., 1976; PhD, U. Ga., 1982. Tchr. Gaston Day Sch., Gastonia, N.C., 1971-73, Charlotte (N.C.) Country Day Sch., 1973-74; psychologist Roanoke County Schs., Salem, Va., 1976-83; psychologist Gwinnett County Schs., Lawrenceville, Ga., 1983-94, coord. psychol. svcs., 1994—; pvt. practice Lilburn, Ga., 1985-93, Norcross, Ga., 1994—; adj. prof. Mercer U., Atlanta, 1984-85; cons. N.E. Consulting Ctr., Lawrenceville, 1985-92; intern supervision Gwinnett County Schs., Lawrenceville, 1985—. Mem. APA (div. sch. psychology), Ga. Assn. Sch. Psychologists, Nat. Assn. Sch. Psychologists, Beta Beta Beta, Kappa Delta Pi, Phi Kappa Phi. Home: 280 Sageglen Rd Lawrenceville GA 30244-5249 Office: Gwinnett County Schs 52 Gwinnett Dr SW Lawrenceville GA 30245-5624

CARTER, DANIEL ROLAND, lawyer; b. Shreveport, La., Aug. 6, 1956; s. Jerry Glen and Sandra Jane (Roland) Griffith; m. Lauri Ann Witek, Nov. 13, 1993. BA Polit. Sci., La. Tech. U., 1979, BSChemE, 1983; JD, South Tex. Coll. Law, Houston, 1991. Bar: Tex. 1991, U.S. Dist. Ct. (so., no., ea. and we. dists.) Tex. Prodn. engr. Transco Exploration & Prodn. Co., Houston, 1982-83; transmission engr. Transcontinental Gas Pipe Line Corp., Houston, 1984-87, environ. engr., 1987-88, sr. environ. engr., 1988-91, atty., 1991-95; sr. assoc. Phillips & Akers, Houston, 1995—; bd. dirs. La. Tech. Centennial Devel. Com., Ruston, La. Tech. Alumni Assn., Ruston, Music for Healing and Transition Program, Houston. Mem. Tex. Assn. Def. Counsel, Tex. Bar Assn., Houston Bar Assn., Tex. Soc. Profl. Engrs., Phi Delta Phi, Tau Beta Pi, Phi Alpha Theta, Order of the Lytae. Republican. Baptist. Home: 1706 Lofty Maple Trail Kingwood TX 77345 Office: Phillips & Akers 3200 Southwest Fwy Houston TX 77027

CARTER, DAVID EDWARD, communications executive; b. Ashland, Ky., Nov. 24, 1942; s. Victor Byron and Lillie Elzena (Clarke) C.; m. Linda Louise Gibson, May 31, 1969; children: Christa Ann, Lauren Louise. AB, U. Ky., 1965; MS, Ohio U., 1967; MBA, Syracuse U., 1995; SMM, Harvard Bus. Sch., 1995. Dir. advt. Wheeler & Williams Co., Ashland, 1965-66; instr. U. Ky., 1967-70; dir. communications Ky. Electric Steel Co., Ashland, 1970-77; pres. David E. Carter Inc., Ashland, 1977—; pres. Hollywood Ky. Corp. div. David E. Carter, Inc., Ashland, Bangkok, Jakarta, Caracas, Hong Kong, 1986—; bd. dirs. Home Fed. Savs. & Loan Assn., Ashland, Decathlon Corp., Hanover Pub. Co.; exec. adv. bd. Ohio U. Sch. Bus.; alumni bd. dirs. U. Ky. Sch. Journalism; adj. prof. Thammasat U., Bangkok, 1992—. Scoutmaster, Tri-State Area Council Boy Scouts Am., 1970-77, dist. commr., 1977-78, recipient dist. award of merit, 1975, Recipient Clio award, N.Y.C., 1980, Disting. Alumnus award Ashland Community Coll., 1990. Mem. Nat. Acad. TV Arts and Scis. (3 Emmys for writing TV programs 1987), N.Y. Art Dirs. Club (2 Emmys for producing pub. TV program 1990, Am. Inst. Graphic Arts. Republican. Methodist. Author: It's Not the Money—It's The Principle, 1975, Book of American Trade Marks, 11 vols., 1972-89, Designing Corporate Symbols, 1975, Corporate Identity Manuals, 1976, Letterheads 7 vols., 1977-89, Ideas for Editors, 1977, Letterheads 5 vols. 1979-89, American Corporate Identity 5 vols. 1985-89, Designing Corporate Identity for Small Companies, 1985, How to Improve Your Corporate Identity, 1986, Logos of Major American Companies, 1989, International Corporate Design Symbols, 1990, Logos of Major World Corporations, 1990, World Corporate Identity, 1990; writer, producer: (TV series) Sassafrass, 1987-88; producer more than 12 sketches for The Johnny Carson Show, 1989-91 (2 Emmys, 1991). Avocations: sports collectibles, golf, photography. Home: 4727 Southern Hills Dr Ashland KY 41102-8213 also: 3225 W Gulf Dr # B-301 Sanibel FL 33957-5652 Office: PO Box 2500 Ashland KY 41105-2500

CARTER, DAVID LUCION, medical services administrator; b. Lumberton, N.C., Nov. 24, 1950; s. Robert Elise and Lucille (Hunt) C.; m. Opal Sue Cook, Dec. 2, 1972; children: Tanya Naomi, Tonya Lucille, Dana Carol, Davita Sue. AA in Music, Sandhills C.C., 1972. Custom kitchen designer Sears, Balt., 1971-72; emergency med. tech. City of Lumberton (N.C.) Fire Dept., 1974-84; emergency svcs. dir., enhanced 900 coord. Robeson County Fire Dept., Lumberton, 1985—; instr. N.C. Divsn. Emergency Mgmt., Raleigh, 1986—, pres. 1993—; cons. in field, 1990—. V.p. Boys and Girls Clubs, Lumberton, 1995; chmn. bd. dirs. Outdoor Drama, Pembroke, N.C., 1989—; cmdr. County Search and Rescue Team, Robeson County, 1986—; mem. Vis. Bur., Lumberton, 1991-95. Recipient gov.'s award of excellence State N.C., 1989. Democrat. Pentecostal. Office: Robeson County Emergency 108 W 8th St Lumberton SC 28358

CARTER, DONALD LEE, computer services executive; b. Charlotte, N.C., Nov. 6, 1937; s. Edward Martin and Pearl Mae (Foster) C.; m. Judith Ann Barfield, Dec. 15, 1960; children: Beverly Ann Carter Mills, Daniel Scott, Donna Elizabeth Carter Jones. AA in Elec. Engring., Charlotte Coll., 1961; BA in Nat. Sci. and Math., Thomas A. Edison State Coll., 1987. Programmer, analyst Piedmont Natural Gas Co., Charlotte, 1961-66; with American & Efird, Inc., Mt. Holly, N.C., 1966-72; mgr. systems and programming Am. & Efird, Inc., Mt. Holly, N.C., 1972-87, v.p. computer svcs. div., 1987—. Mem. Masons. Republican. Home: 7817 Ritter Dr Charlotte NC 28270-2772 Office: American & Efird Inc 22 American St # 507 Mount Holly NC 28120-2150

CARTER, ED, construction company executive; b. 1943. Comml. pilot, 1964-80; with McKnight Constrn., Augusta, Ga., 1981-85; v.p. ACC Constrn. Co. Inc., Augusta, 1986—. Office: ACC Constrn Co Inc Ste B 635 NW Frontage Rd Augusta GA 30907

CARTER, EDITH HOUSTON, statistician, educator; b. Charlotte, N.C., Oct. 12, 1936; d. Z. and Ellie (Hartsell) Houston; BS, Appalachian State U., 1959, MA, 1960; PhD, Va. Poly. Inst. and State U., 1976; m. Fletcher F. Carter, Apr. 2, 1961. Transcript analyst Fla. Dept. Edn., Tallahassee, 1961-65; instr. Radford U., 1969-70, 91-94, asst. prof., 1994—; prof. New River C.C., Dublin, Va., 1970-83, dir. instl. research, 1974-78, asst. dean Coll. Arts and Scis., 1978-79, statistician, 1979-83. Violist New River Valley Symphony, Va. Poly. Inst. and State U. Orch., Radford U. Orch., S.W. Va. Opera Soc. Orch.; sec./treas. Radford New River Valley chpt. Am. Sewing Guild, 1991-94, pres., 1994-96. Mem. Am. Ednl. Rsch. Assn., State and Regional Ednl. Rsch. Assn. (sec./treas. 1989-93, pres. 1993-95), Assn. Instl. Research (exec. bd. 1976-78), Southeastern Assn. C.C. Rsch. (exec. bd. 1976-78, Outstanding Service award, Disting. Service award 1981), Nat. Coun. Rsch. and Planning (Outstanding Svc. award 1992), Coll. Music Soc., Am. String Tchrs. Assn., Va. Ednl. Rsch. Assn. (pres.-elect 1996—), Va. Fedn. Women's Clubs (dir. 1968-70), Va. Tech. U. Alumni (pres. New River Valley chpt. 1982-83), Radford Jr. Woman's Club (pres. 1967-68). Methodist. Clubs: Radford Garden. Editor Community Coll. Jour. Research and Planning, 1981-93, Am. Assn. Community Colls. Jour. (rsch. review editor 1991—), Newsletter Southeastern Assn. C.C. Research, 1972—; mem. editorial bd. C.C. Rev., 1990-93. Home: 6924 Radford Univ Radford VA 24142 Office: Radford U Russell Hall Radford VA 24142

CARTER, ERIC VINCENT, marketing educator; b. Detroit, Aug. 12, 1960; s. Fred M. and Catherine Evelyn (Walker) C., Herbert Lewis (stepfather); m. Janice May Stephenson, Oct. 16, 1993. BS in Mktg., GMI Engring. and Mgmt. Inst., Flint, 1983; MBA in Internat. Bus., Columbia U., 1987; PhD in Mktg. and Cybernetics, George Washington U., 1995. Sales mgr. GM Parts Divsn. GM, Detroit, 1983-86; corp. mktg. cons. GE, Bridgeport, Conn., 1987-88; office automation cons. Mobil Oil Co., N.Y.C., 1988; mktg. prof. Howard U. Sch. Bus., Washington, 1988-93, Morehouse Coll., Atlanta, 1993—; mktg. cons. Quality Edn. Devel., N.Y.C., 1988, Project Africa, Alexandria, Va., 1991-92, African Greeting Card Collective, Washington, 1992—. Contbr. articles to profl. jours., poetry to Am. Poetry Anthology, 1990. Named to Outstanding Young Men of Am., 1986, 87. Fellow Nat. Consortium for Ednl. Access; mem. NAACP, Am. Mktg. Assn., Soc. History of Tech., Inst. Noetic Scis., Am. Soc. for Cybernetics, Internat. Interactive Comms. Soc., World Future Soc., Alpha Phi Alpha. Home: 1367 Middlesex Ave Atlanta GA 30306 Office: Dept Econs and Bus Adminstn Morehouse Coll Atlanta GA 30314

CARTER, FRANCES B., secondary school educator; b. Lynchburg, Va.; m. Clarence H. Carter, June 15, 1968. BA, Va. Union U., 1966; MEd, Lynchburg Coll., 1974. Cert. tchr., Va. Tchr. English, Lynchburg City Schs.; presenter Nat. Conf. on Multicultural Edn., New Orleans, 1992, Va. Med. Sch. Assn. Ann. Conf., Richmond, 1994; chairperson, coord. for brotherhood and cultural diversity month activities Linkhorne Middle Sch., 1994-95, 95-96, 96—, chairperson recognition com., 1994-95. Team leader Unit 1 Linkhorne Mid. Sch., Grade 7, 1991-92; mem. Supt.'s Pers. Adv. Com. for Lynchburg City Schs., 1996—. Named Mid. Sch. Tchr. of Yr., Lynchburg Pub. Schs., 1990. Mem. NEA (Cert. of Appreciation 1995), Va. Edn. Assn. (Cert. of Appreciation), Lynchburg Edn. Assn. (Cert. of Appreciation), Nat. Coun. Tchrs. English (Cert. of Achievement 1995), Phi Delta Kappa.

CARTER, FRANK GUERRANT, JR., graphic design educator; b. Winston-Salem, N.C., July 31, 1950; s. Frank Guerrant and Dura (Shelton) C.; divorced; children: Christie Lynn, Carrie Anne. BA, U. N.C., Chapel Hill, 1971; MEd, U. N.C., Greensboro, 1977. Pub. info. officer Greensboro Pub. Schs., 1972-73; program dir. Danville (Va.) Cablevision Co., 1973-75, spl. projects dir., 1982-84; H.S. tchr. Caswell County Schs., Yanceyville, N.C., 1980-82, Rockingham County Schs., Wentworth, N.C., 1980-82; coll. instr. Alamance C.C., Graham, N.C., 1985—; advt. cons. Frank Carter Assocs., Ruffin, N.C., 1973-77; pres., pub. CHN Comms. Corp., Yanceyville, N.C., 1981-85. Editor, pub. the County Mag., 1981-84, The Caswell Citizen newspaper, 1983-84. Bd. dirs. Caswell County Arts Coun., Yanceyville, 1979; mem. Rockingham County Theatre Guild, Reidsville, N.C., 1992-95. Mem. Assn. Graphic Design Educators, Phi Kappa Sigma (sec. bd. trustees). Democrat. Methodist. Home: PO Box 115 Ruffin NC 27326 Office: Alamance CC PO Box 8000 Graham NC 27253

CARTER, GAIL MARIE, special education educator; b. Como, Miss., June 18, 1962; d. Clarence and Lula Mae (Campbell) Taylor; m. Reginald Latrell Carter, Jr., Apr. 4, 1984 (div. Sept. 17. 1994). BA in Spl. Edn., U. Miss., 1984, MEd in Ednl. Leadership, 1996. Substitute tchr. N. Panola Sch. Dist., Sardis, Miss., 1985; spl. edn. tchr. S. Panola Sch. Dist., Batesville, Miss., 1985—. Mem. Coun. Exceptional Children (divsn. learning disabilities), Coun. Adminstrn. Spl. Edn., Assn. Supervision Curriculum Devel. Baptist. Home: Star Rte Box 176A Sardis MS 38666 Office: S Panola Sch Dist College St Batesville MS 38606

CARTER, HARRIET VANESSA, public relations specialist, congressional aide; b. N.Y.C.; d. Gerard Frederick and Eugenia Carter. BA in Spanish magna cum laude, Tulane U., 1969; MEd in Spanish, U. Ill., 1974; postgrad., U. D'Aix en Provence, France, 1972, U. Nice, France, 1974, U. Montreal, 1979, U. Vienna, 1980. Spanish tchr. King Philip Jr. H.S., West Hartford, Conn., 1971-76, Irvington (N.Y.) H.S., 1976-77, Closter (N.J.) Village Sch., 1977-78; Spanish tchr., coordinator academic awards program Benjamin Sch., North Palm Beach, Fla., 1978-81; asst. to clin. dean, pub. relations coordinator, med. residency coordinator Am. U. of Caribbean Sch. of Medicine, Miami, Fla., 1981-84; asst. dir. admissions Ross U. Sch. of Medicine, N.Y.C., 1984; coord. ednl. tng., asst. to pres. United Schs. of Am., Miami, 1985-86; pvt. practice Miami, 1986—; coord. divsn. Latino studies Fla. Internat. U., Miami, 1987-88, promotions cons. in broadcasting, 1989-90, TV prodr., exec. asst. to program dir., 1990-91; TV prodr., co-host series Volunteer Miami Sta. WLRN-TV, 1991-92; congl. aide, 1993—; Pub. rels. mgr. Voyager mag., Lake Park, Fla., 1981-82; instr. med. Spanish U. Conn. Med. Sch., Farmington, 1974, Mt. Sinai Hosp., Hartford, 1973; teaching asst. in Spanish U. Ill., Urbana, 1970-71, fellow, 1970. Founder, editor (newsletter) Focus on Multi-Cultural Happenings, 1975-76; editor (newsletter) American University of the Caribbean School of Medicine, 1981-84; contbr. articles to profl. jours. Participant Hispanic leadership tng. program Cuban-Am. Nat. Coun., Miami, 1988; mem. pub. rels. and comms. com. Leadership Miami, 1989—; vol. Miracle Telethon, Miami Children's Hosp., 1986, Jerry Lewis Labor Day Telethon, 1989, 93, 94, 95, auction Sta. WLRN-TV, Miami, 1990-94, vol.-a-thon for United Way Dade County, Sta. WPLG-TV, 1991; guide So. Gov.'s Conf., Miami, 1985; active Greater Miami Ambs. Corps, 1985-92, Coun. Internat. Visitors Greater Miami. Semi-finalist Miss Teenage Am. Contest; recipient recognition award U.S. Ho. of Reps., 1991, cert. of merit for commitment to cmty. svc. Pres. of U.S., 1991; fellow U. Ill., 1969-70; scholar Govt. of Austria, 1980. Mem. NATAS, AAUW (co-chmn. com. on women 1980-81), Phi Beta Kappa, Phi Delta Kappa. Office: 9357 Fontainebleau Blvd Ste 202 Miami FL 33172-4275

CARTER, JAMES A., finance executive; b. Lakeland, Fla., July 25, 1926; s. William and LaTrelle (Morgan) C.; m. Mary Lois Barnes, Aug. 26, 1950; children: James A. Jr., Jeffrey M. BA in English Lit., The Citadel, 1950. Trainee to pres. various CIGNA corp. cos., Phila., 1954-80; pres. Lumbermens Mut. Ins. Co., Mansfield, Ohio, 1980-82; sr. Am. officer, exec. v.p. Tokio Marine and Fire Ins. Co., N.Y.C., 1982-84; pres. First Southern Ins. Co., Tampa, Fla., 1984-86; owner J.A. Carters Co., Inc., Tampa, 1986-90; pres. Mgmt. Advisors Inc., 1991. Contbg. author: Business Insurance Handbook, 1980. Lt. col. U.S. Army infantry, 1945-46, WWII, 51-53, Korea. Decorated Combat Infantry badge and others. Democrat. Methodist. Home and Office: 1215 S Roxmere Rd Tampa FL 33629-4225

CARTER, JAMES CLARENCE, university administrator; b. N.Y.C., Aug. 1, 1927; s. James Clarence and Elizabeth (Dillon) C. BS in Physics, Spring Hill Coll., 1952; MS in Physics, Fordham U., 1953; STL in Theology, Woodstock Coll., 1959; PhD in Physics, Cath. U. Am., 1956. Ordained priest Roman Cath. Ch., 1958. Instr., asst. prof. Physics Loyola U., New Orleans, 1960-67; assoc. prof. of Physics Loyola U., 1967—, v.p., 1970-74, pres., 1974-95, chancellor, 1995—; bd. dirs. Met. Area Com.; mem. higher edn. facilities com. State La., 1971-73, Am. Council's Commn. on Leadership in Higher Edn., 1975-78; bd. trustees Loyola U. Chgo., 1981-90; chmn. Mayor's Com. Ednl. Uses CATV, 1972. Contbr. articles to profl. jours. Mem. adv. com. New Orleans Pub. Library for the NEH Grant, 1975; bd. dirs. Greater New Orleans Area United Way, 1976-82, La. Ednl. TV Authority, 1977-83. Recipient Torch of Liberty award Anti-Defamation League of B'nai B'rith, 1983. Mem. Palmes Academiques, So. Assn. of Colls. and Schs. (exec. council of the commn. on colls.), Am. Phys. Soc., Am. Assn. Physics Tchrs., Assn. Jesuit Colls. and Univs. (chmn. acad. v.p. conf. 1971-74), Nat. Assn. Ind. Colls. and Univs. (bd. dirs. 1977-82), Am. Council Edn., Sigma Xi. Office: Loyola U Office of Chancellor 6363 Saint Charles Ave New Orleans LA 70118-6143

CARTER, JAMES HARRISON, chemist, research director; b. Biloxi, Miss., July 4, 1945; s. James Harrison and Virginia Kay (Crouch) C.; m. Nina Kay Spurrier, Aug. 7, 1965; children: Christine Elizabeth, James Daniel. BS in Chemistry, Ga. Inst. Tech., 1966, PhD in Organic Chemistry, 1970. Assoc. dir. Med. Lab. Assocs., Birmingham, Ala., 1970-71; gen. mgr. Biomed. Products Corp., Ft. Lauderdale, Fla., 1971-75; profl. lab. cons. self-employed Ft. Lauderdale, Fla., 1975-78; rsch. scientist Coulter Electronics, Inc., Miami, 1978-84, dir. diagnostics rsch., 1984—; staff cons. Cambridge Diagnostic Products, Ft. Lauderdale, 1975—. Fellow Nat. Acad. Clin. Biochemistry; mem. Am. Soc. for Cell Biology, Am. Assn. Clin. Chemistry, Am. Peptide Soc., The Protein Soc., Soc. for Gen. Physiology, Internat. Soc. Lab. Hematology. Republican. Baptist. Office: Coulter Corp M/C 22-ao1 PO Box 169015 Miami FL 33116-9015

CARTER, JAMES SUMTER, oil company executive, tree farmer; b. Rock Hill, S.C., June 3, 1948; s. James Roy Jr. and Sumter Inez (McWatters) C.; m. Melinda Ruth Roberts, Mar. 25, 1972; children: James Sumter Jr., Stephanie Jane, Lauren Elizabeth. BSME, Clemson U., 1970; MBA, Tulane U., 1974. Various mktg. positions Exxon Co. USA, Houston, 1974-79; dist. mgr. Exxon Co. USA, Linden, N.J., 1980-81; adv. Exxon Corp., N.Y.C., 1982-83; analysis mgr. Exxon Internat., Florham Pk, N.J., 1984-85; coord. mgr. Exxon Co. USA, Houston, 1986, exec. asst. to pres., 1987, distbn. mgr., 1988, downstream planning mgr., 1989, fuel products mgr., 1990-96, v.p. mktg., 1996—. Bd. dirs. Clemson U. Found., 1996—, BBB, 1996—. Lt. U.S. Army, 1971-72. John Jay assoc. Columbia U. Mem. Am. Petroleum Inst., Petroleum Marketers Edn. Found. (bd. dirs. 1990-92), Forest Farmers Assn., Ben Tilman Soc., Petroleum Club Houston, Tau Beta Pi, Beta Gamma Sigma. Republican. Methodist. Office: Exxon USA 800 Bell St Houston TX 77002-7426

CARTER, JAMES THOMAS, contractor; b. N.Y.C., Dec. 27, 1952; s. Wendell Green and Carolyn Elizabeth (Smith) C.; m. Mary Jane Zellers, Oct. 8, 1985. Cert. airline transport pilot, flight instr., FAA. Charter pilot, flight instr. Pompano Air Ctr., Pompano Beach, Fla., 1976-78; profl. pilot Profl. Pilot Svcs., Ft. Lauderdale, Fla., 1978-79; aviation operative CIA, 1978-79; pres., pilot Carter Charter Co., Inc., Ft. Lauderdale, 1979-92; novelist Ft. Lauderdale, 1992-94; account exec. Power Line Components, Inc., Lighthouse Point, Fla., 1994-96; exec. dir. Advanced Tech., Inc., Ft. Lauderdale, 1996—; mem. missile program Lockheed Missile and Space, Huntsville, Ala., 1995—, HRC program Smithsonian Astrophys. Obs., Cambridge, Mass., 1995-96, MIL-STAR program Electromagnetic Scis., Norcross, Ga., 1995—, J-STARS program, 1996—. Author: Operation: Deepcover, 1994, A Twist of Fate, 1995, Stiletto, 1996, (poetry) Twilight, 1995, Christmas in the Snow, 1996. Recipient Editor's Choice award Nat. Libr. Poetry, 1996. Mem. Aircraft Owners and Pilots Assn., Internat. Soc. Poets (disting.). Democrat. Presbyterian. Home: PO Box 030265 Fort Lauderdale FL 33303 Office: Advanced Tech Components Inc Ste 102 2717 E Oakland Park Blvd Fort Lauderdale FL 33306

CARTER, JIMMY (JAMES EARL CARTER, JR.), former President of United States; b. Plains, Ga., Oct. 1, 1924; s. James Earl and Lillian (Gordy) C.; m. Rosalynn Smith, July 7, 1946; children: John William, James Earl III, Donnel Jeffrey, Amy Lynn. Student, Ga. Southwestern Coll., 1941-42, Ga. Inst. Tech., 1942-43; BS, U.S. Naval Acad., 1946 (class of 1947); postgrad., Union Coll., 1952-53; LLD (hon.), Morris Brown Coll., 1972, Morehouse Coll., 1972, U. Notre Dame, 1977, Emory U., 1979, Kwansei Gakuin U., Japan, 1981, Ga. Southwestern Coll., 1981, N.Y. Law Sch., 1985, Bates Coll., 1985, Centre Coll., 1987, Creighton U., 1987; DEng (hon.), Ga. Inst. Tech., 1979; PhD (hon.), Weizmann Inst. Sci., 1980, Tel Aviv U., 1983, Haifa U., 1987; DHL (hon.), Cen. Conn. State U., 1985. Farmer, warehouseman Plains, Ga., 1953-77; mem. Ga. Senate, 1963-67; gov. State of Ga., Atlanta, 1971-75; President of United States, 1977-81; disting. prof. Emory U., Atlanta, 1982—; leader internat. observer teams Panama, 1989, Nicaragua, 1990, Dominican Republic, 1990, Haiti, 1990; host peace negotiations Ethiopia, 1989. Author: Why Not the Best?, 1975, A Government as Good as Its People, 1977, Keeping Faith/Memoirs of a President, 1982, Negotiation: The Alternative to Hostility, 1984, The Blood of Abraham, 1985, (with Rosalynn Carter) Everything to Gain: Making the Most of the Rest of Your Life, 1987, An Outdoor Journal, 1988, Turning Point: A Candidate, A State, and a Nation Come of Age, 1992, Talking Peace: A Vision for the Next Generation, 1993, Always a Reckoning, 1995. Mem. Sumter County (Ga.) Sch. Bd., 1955-62, chmn., 1960-62; mem. Americus and Sumter County Hosp. Authority, 1956-70; mem. Sumter County (Ga.) Library Bd., 1961; chmn. congl. campaign com. Dem. Nat. Com., 1974; founder Carter Ctr. Emory U., 1982; bd. dirs. Habitat for Humanity, 1984-87; chmn. bd. trustees Carter Ctr., Inc., 1986—, Carter-Menil Human Rights Found., 1986—, Global 2000 Inc., 1986—; chmn. Coun. of Freely-Elected Heads of Govt., 1986—; chmn. Coun. Internat. Negotiation Network, 1991—. Served to lt. USN, 1946-53. Recipient Gold medal Internat. Inst. Human Rights, 1979, Internat. Mediation medal Am. Arbitration Assn., 1979, Martin Luther King Jr. Nonviolent Peace prize, 1979, Internat. Human Rights award Synagogue Coun. Am., 1979, Conservationist of Yr. award, 1979, Harry S. Truman Pub. Svc. award, 1981, Ansel Adams Conservation award Wilderness Soc., 1982, Disting. Svc. award So. Bapt. Conv., 1982, Human Rights award Internat. League for Human Rights, 1983, World Meth. Peace award, 1985, Albert Schweitzer prize for Humanitarianism, 1987, Edwin C. Whitehead award Nat. Ctr. for Health Edn., 1989, Jefferson award Am. Inst. Pub. Svc., 1990, Phila. Liberty medal, 1990, Spirit of Am. award Nat. Coun. for Social Studies, 1990, Physicians for Social Responsibility award, 1991, Aristotle prize Alexander S. Onassis Found., 1991, Félix Houphouët-Boigny Peace prize UNESCO, 1995. Office: Carter Ctr 1 Copenhill Ave NE Atlanta GA 30307-1400*

CARTER, JOSEPH CARLYLE, JR., lawyer; b. Mayfield, Ky., June 3, 1927; s. Joseph Carlyle and Cynthia Elizabeth (Stokes) C.; m. Dianne C. Dinwiddie, July 15, 1949; children: Joseph Carlyle, Hugh D., William H., Henry S., Dianne C. BA, U. Va., 1948, LLB, 1951. Bar: Va. 1951. Since practiced in Richmond; assoc. firm Hunton & Williams, Richmond, 1951-58, ptnr., 1958-93; mng. ptnr. Hunton & Williams, 1972-82; sr. counsel Hunton & Williams, Richmond, 1993—; dir. Albemarle Corp., 1994-96, Ethyl Corp., 1974-94. Active elder 2d Presbyn. Ch., Richmond, 1962—; chmn. Richmond Pub. Libr. Bd., 1967-77, active, 1980-85; vice-chmn. Richard City Sch. Bd., 1990-94; trustee Colonial Williamsburg Found., 1977-93, Med. Coll. Va. Found., 1976—, pres., 1984-87; trustee, pres. U. Va. Law Sch. Found., 1985—. Recipient Algernon Sidney Sullivan award, 1948. Mem. ABA, Va. Bar Assn., Richmond Bar Assn., Am. Law Inst., Am. Judicature Soc., Newcomen Soc. Presbyterian. Clubs: Commonwealth (Richmond), Country of Va. (Richmond). Home: 5102 Harlan Cir Richmond VA 23226-1637 Office: Hunton & Williams 951 E Byrd St Richmond VA 23219-4074

CARTER, JOSEPH HENRY, SR., writer, museum manager; b. Enid, Okla., July 18, 1932; s. Dwight Henry and Margaret Alice (Wilson) C.; m. Beverly Roxanna Blood (dec.); children: Joseph Henry, Russell N., Valerie A.; m. Michelle K. Lefebvre, Sept. 11, 1992. B in Econs., U. Tulsa, 1957, B in Journalism, 1959. Reporter Sapulpa (Okla.) Herald, Honolulu Advertiser; assoc. editor Okla. Jour.; corr. UPI; mem. Presidential Staff, Washington, 1960's, 70's; congrl. aide; chief of staff Gov. David Hall, Oklahoma City; v.p. Cameron U., Lawton, Okla., 1985-89; pres. Will Rogers Heritage Trust, Claremore, Okla., 1989—; dir. Will Rogers Meml., Claremore, 1989—. Author: Never Met a Man I Didn't Like: The Life and Writings of Will Rogers, 1991. Past mem. bd. dirs. Okla C. of C., Okla. Heritage Assn.; mem. Nat. Dem. Club. With U.S. Army, 1952-54. Mem. Tulsa Press Club, Tulsa Gridiron, Masons, Elks. Methodist. Office: Will Rogers Meml PO Box 157 Claremore OK 74018-0157

CARTER, L. PHILIP, neurosurgeon, consultant; b. St. Louis, Feb. 26, 1939; s. Russell G. and Dorothy Ruth (Zerwick) C.; m. Marcia L. Carlson, Aug. 26, 1960 (div. Apr., 1989); children: Kristin, Melinda, Chad Philip; m. Colleen L. Harrington, Oct. 20, 1990. MD, Washington U., St. Louis, 1964. Active staff Barrow Neurol. Inst., Phoenix, 1976-88, dir. microsurg. lab., 1978-88, chief cerebral vascular surgery, 1983-88; prof. neurosurgery, chief neurosurg. svcs. Coll. Medicine U. Ariz., Tucson, 1988-93; prof., chmn. dept. neurosurgery U. Okla. Health Sci. Ctr., Oklahoma City, 1993-96; clin. prof. neurosurgery Coll. Medicine, U. Ariz., Tucson, 1997—; med. cons. Flowtronics, Inc., Phoenix, 1980—; vis. prof. Japan Neurosurg. Soc., Kyoto, 1983. Editor: Neurovascular Surgery, 1994; co-editor: Cerebral Revascularization for Stroke, 1985; contbr. articles to profl. jours. Cons. Ariz. Head Injury Found., 1988-93, Ariz. Epilepsy Found., 1973-75. Capt. USAF, 1965-67. Recipient Internat. Coll. Surgeons fellowship, 1973, Ariz. Disease Control for the Study of Treatment of Stroke grant, 1986. Fellow ACS, Am. Heart Assn.; mem. Am. Assn. Neurol. Surgeons, Soc. Neurol. Surgeons, Rocky Mountain Neurosurg. Soc., Ariz. Neurol. Soc. (sec.-treas. 1985-91), We. Neurosurg. Soc. (program chmn. 1990, 95). Republican. Home: 3778 N Camina Lea Maria Tucson AZ 85716 Office: Northwest Hosp Med Plz 1980 W Hospital Dr Ste 300 Tucson AZ 85704

CARTER, LOUVENIA MCGEE, nursing educator; b. Bradley, Oct. 12, 1934; d. Henry Battle and Emma (Cox) McGee; m. Harvey L. Carter Jr., Jan. 15, 1956; children: Harvey III, Christopher, Richard, Robert. Diploma, Northwestern State Coll., Natchitoches, La., 1955; BSN, Northwestern State Coll., 1961, MSN, 1979; PhD, Tex. Women's U., 1990. Svc. dir. Upjohn Health Care Svcs., Shreveport, La., 1979-81; staff nurse VA Med. Ctr., Shreveport, 1955-56, 60, 82; prof. Northwestern State U., Shreveport, 1982—. Mem. ANA (cert. in nursing adminstrn.), Nat. Conf. Gerontol. Nurse Practitioners, Sigma Theta Tau. Home: 830 Erie St Shreveport LA 71106-1506

CARTER, MARILYN RAY, nurse; b. Galveston, Tex., May 25, 1931; d. Raymond J. and Elizabeth E. (Weyer) Hansen; m. Wade V. Carter, Jr., Feb. 21, 1957; children: Renee, Wade, Kim, Vanette. R.N., St. Mary's Sch. Nursing, 1951. Head nurse VA Hosp., Houston, 1953-56; psychiat. nurse Panama Canal Co., Balboa, C.Z., 1956-79; charge nurse Starlight Hosp., Center Point, Tex., 1982—; reporter Canal Record, 1981-82. Founder, chmn. Hill Country Zonian's Assn., Kerrville, 1979-82; chmn. Hill Country Youth Ranch Charity Ball, 1977; poll clk. local, fed. elections, 1981-83. Contbr. to cookbooks. Vol. Salvation Army, 1979-82, Cowboy Artists Am. Mus. Named Nurse of Yr., VA Hosp., Houston, 1954; recipient Outstanding Job Performance award U.S. Civil Service, 1968. Mem. Native Plant Soc. Tex., Tex. Nurses Assn., Panama Canal Soc. Fla., Am. Assn. Ret. Persons. Lutheran. Club: Hill Country Zonians.

CARTER, MARY KATHLEEN, pharmacologist, educator, researcher; b. Franklinton, La., July 11, 1922; d. Elijah Augustus and Ora Victoria (Kemp) C. BA in Chemistry, Tulane U., 1949, MS in Pharmacology, 1953; PhD in Pharmacology, Vanderbilt U., 1955. Tchg. asst. Tulane U., New Orleans, 1949-52; rsch. asst. Vanderbilt U. Med. Sch., Nashville, 1952-55; rsch. assoc. Med. Ctr. U. Kans., Kansas City, 1955-57; instr. Tulane U., 1957-59, asst. prof., 1959-62, assoc. prof., 1962-73, prof., 1973-84, prof. emeritus, 1984—; bd. dirs. (adult literacy program) Upgrade Tangipahoa, Inc. Contbr. over 50 articles to profl. jours. Recipient Postdoctoral fellowship USPHS, 1955-57, Sr. Rsch. fellowship USPHS, 1957-62. Mem. Am. Soc. Pharmacology and Exptl. Therapeutics, Sigma Xi. Democrat. Baptist. Home: 77139 N River Rd Kentwood LA 70444

CARTER, PAULA STANLEY, special education educator; b. Wilmington, N.C., Nov. 29, 1950; d. Lawrence Paul and Theresa Olivia (Bullard) S.; m. Stanley Wayne Carter, Sept. 13, 1975; 1 child, Marina Kostyleva. Student, U. N.C., 1969-71; BA in Theology, Berkshire Christian Coll., 1974; MEd, U. North Fla., 1979. Cert. K-12 spl. learning disabilities. Tchr., vol. assoc. Ogden Christian Acad., Wilmington, N.C., 1972-73; thcr. pre-sch. neurol. impaired Southburry (Conn.) Tng. Sch., 1973-74; GED tchr. Fla. Jr. Coll., Jacksonville, 1975-76; presch. tchr. United Cerebral Palsy, Jacksonville, 1976-78; career counselor City of Jacksonville, 1978-81; exceptional edn. tchr. Duval County Schs., Jacksonville, 1981—; cons., advisor Nursing Home Adv. Bd., Jacksonville, 1986-88; rep. Duval Tchrs. Assn., Jacksonville, 1992-93. Author: Parent-Student Handbook John Love Elementary, 1991, Elementary Government - Magnet Program Course, 1991, Tips for Teachers of E.S.E. Students, 1993, Classroom Motivator Henry F. Kite Elementary School, 1994. Pres. Advent Christian Youth Assn., Wilmington, 1967-69; pres. Coun. on Aging/Advocates, Jacksonville, 1986-88; v.p. Opportunity Devel., Inc., Jacksonville, 1985-90; rep. Telethon Easter Seals Assn., Jacksonville, 1981-90; rep., vol. Duval Assn. Retarded Citizens Spl. Olympics, Jacksonville, 1974-79; vol. civic, polit., tchr. assns., 1974—; host parent Edn. Exch. Program, 1981—; tchr. single adult denomination Sunday Sch.; active Under BluePrint 2000 Goal V, Fla., 1995-96; chair Victory Over Violence program Duval County Sch. # 37, 1995-96, safety patrol dir., chair Zeroing Prevention Drug Abuse. Fellowship grantee Advent Christian Delegation, Wilmington, 1969; recipient Supt.'s Bronze Key Club award United Way Assn., Jacksonville, 1991-92, Cert. of Achievement Am. Fedn. Tchrs., AFL-CIO, 1993-94. Mem. ASCD, Coun. Exceptional Children, Dinsmore Improvement Assn., Delta Kappa Gamma (v.p. coord. coun. 1994—, pres. 1992—, pres. coord. coun. 1996—, Pres.'s award 1994). Democrat. Baptist. Home: PO Box 83 Jacksonville FL 32219-0083 Office: Henry F Kite Elem 9430 Lem Turner Rd Jacksonville FL 32208-1569

CARTER, REBECCA GAIL, medical, surgical nurse; b. Fayetteville, N.C., May 28, 1961; d. Edward Delano and Katharina Maria (Scheder) Comer; m. Ted Lee Carter, Jr., Apr. 19, 1980; children: Christopher Allen, Rachael Lauren. AA, Fayetteville Tech. Inst., 1984; student, Barton Coll. Cert. CPR instr. Nursing asst. Highland House Nursing Home, Fayetteville, N.C., 1972-80; staff nurse Good Hope Hosp., Erwin, N.C., 1984-85; from staff nurse to head nurse Highsmith-Rainey Meml. Hosp., Fayetteville, 1987-93, clin. dir., 1993-95, nurse mgr. 4th fl. surg., 1995—; documentation chmn. Highsmith Hosp., 1989—, mem. bioethics com., 1990, mgr. nurse adminstrn. computer system, 1992. Office: Highsmith Rainey Meml Hosp 150 Robeson St Fayetteville NC 28301-5570

CARTER, RICHARD DENNIS, lawyer, educator; b. Newburgh, N.Y., Feb. 17, 1949; s. Edward Francis and Catherine Florence (Harding) C. BA, Pace U., 1977; JD, George Washington U., 1980. Bar: D.C. 1980, Va. 1991, Md. 1991, U.S. Dist. Ct. D.C. 1981, U.S. Dist. Ct. Md. 1990, U.S. Dist. Ct. (ea. dist.) Wis. 1994, U.S. Dist. Ct. Ariz. 1994, U.S. Ct. Appeals (4th cir.) 1991, U.S. Supreme Ct. 1987. Supervising atty., adj. prof. law D.C. Law Students in Ct., Washington, 1980-90, dep. dir., 1981-85, exec. dir., 1985-90; adj. prof. trial advocacy Georgetown U., Washington, 1982—; ptnr. Cunningham and Hudgins, Alexandria, Va., 1990, Hudgins, Carter & Coleman, Alexandria, 1990—. Contbr. articles to profl. jours. Mem. ABA, D.C. Bar Assn., Washington Bar Assn., Alexandria Bar Assn., Am. Inns of Ct. Episcopalian. Home: 6 Muirs Ct Alexandria VA 22314-2415 Office: Hudgins Carter & Coleman 515 King St Ste 440 Alexandria VA 22314-3103

CARTER, RODNEY, corporate finance executive; b. Roswell, N.Mex., Oct. 17, 1957; s. Powhatan Jr. and Beverly Jean (Tucker) C.; m. Dawn Denise Howes, Aug. 1, 1981; children: Meghan Alyssa, Brandon Matthew. BA, Tex. Tech U., 1980; MBA, So. Meth. U., 1983; M. in Internat. Mgmt., Am. Grad. Sch. Internat. Mgmt., Glendale, Ariz., 1983. Comml. banking officer Rep. Bank Dallas, N.A., 1983-86; asst. v.p. AmeriTrust Co., Dallas, 1986-87; financing project mgr. J.C. Penney Co., Inc., Dallas, 1988-90, corp. financing dir., 1990-92; mgr. fin. planning J.C. Penney Co., Inc., Plano, Tex., 1992-94; sr. v.p. fin. and planning, treas. J.C. Penney Life Ins. Co., Plano, 1994—; fin. cons. North Am. Sound, Dallas, 1982, Jordan & Johnson, Inc., Dallas, 1986; bd. dirs. Fin. Exec. Inst. Advisor Jr. Achievement, Dallas, 1983-84; account vol. United Way, Dallas, 1983-86. Mem. Dallas C. of C. (internat. com. 1984-88). Republican. Mem. Ch. of Christ. Home: 5977 Willowross Way Plano TX 75093 Office: JC Penney Life Ins Co 2700 W Plano Pky Plano TX 75075-8205

CARTER, ROSALYNN SMITH, wife of former President of United States; b. Plains, Ga., Aug. 18, 1927; d. Edgar and Allie (Murray) Smith; m. James Earl Carter, Jr., July 7, 1946; children: John William, James Earl III, Donnel Jeffrey, Amy Lynn. Grad., Ga. Southwestern Coll.; DHL (hon.), Morehouse Coll., 1980; LLD (hon.), U. Notre Dame, 1987. Disting. fellow Inst. Women's Studies Emory U., Atlanta, 1990—; vice chair, bd. dirs. The Carter Ctr., chair Mental Health Task Force Carter Ctr.; pres., bd. dirs. Rosalynn Carter Inst. of Ga. Southwestern State U.; co-founder Every Child by Two Campaign for Early Immunization. Author: First Lady from Plains, 1984, (with Jimmy Carter) Everything to Gain: Making the Most of the Rest of Your Life, 1987, Helping Yourself Help Others: A Book for Caregivers, 1994. Bd. dirs. Friendship Force; bd. advisors Habitat for Humanity; trustee Menninger Found.; hon. trustee Scottish Rite Children's Med. Ctr.; m. Ga. Gov.'s Commn. to Improve Svcs. for Mentally and Emotionally Handicapped, 1971; hon. chmn. Pres.'s Commn. on Mental Health, 1977-78. Recipient Vol. of Decade award Nat. Mental Health Assn., 1980, Predsl. Citation APA, 1982, Nathan S. Kline medal of merit Internat. Com. Against Mental Illness, 1984, Disting. Alumnus award Am. Assn. State Colls. and Univs., 1987, Dorothea Dix award Mental Illness Found., 1988, Dean's award Columbia U. Coll. Physicians and Surgeons, 1991, Notre Dame award for internat. humanitarian svc., 1992, Eleanor Roosevelt Living World award Peace Links, 1992, Nat. Caring award, The Caring Inst., 1995, Kiwanis World Svc. medal, Kiwanis Internat. Found., 1995, Jefferson award Am. Inst. for Pub. Svc., 1996. Hon. fellow Am. Psychiat. Assn.

CARTER, RUSSELL PAUL, JR., chemist; b. Trenton, N.J., June 5, 1927; s. Russell Paul and Helena Fredrika (Gellin) C.; m. June Marie Watlington, June 16, 1951; children: Richard, Paul. BS in Chemistry, Lehigh U., Bethlehem, Pa., 1952; MS in Polymer Chemistry, Akron (Ohio) U., 1960. Mfg. employee Heyden Chem. Corp., Princeton, N.J., 1951-52; rsch. chemist Goodyear Tire & Rubber Co., Akron, Ohio, 1952-57, compounder, 1959-69; group leader tech. svc. Goodyear Aerospace Corp., Akron, 1969-75; rsch. chemist Mobay Chem. Corp., New Martinsville, W.Va., 1975-80, sr. rsch. chemist, 1980-86; rsch. specialist Mobay Corp., New Martinsville, 1986-94; ret., 1995; cons. Pliotron Corp. Am., Niagara Falls, N.Y., Toronto, Ont., Can., 1963-79. Patentee in field. Active Humane Soc., New Martinsville, Halt Out of State Garbage Environ. Group, Wetzel County. With AUS, 1957-59. Mem. Soc. Plastics Engrs., Masons (coach 1960-67). Home: 12 Orchard Dr New Martinsville WV 26155-2818

CARTER, SARALEE LESSMAN, immunologist, microbiologist; b. Chgo., Feb. 19, 1951; d. Julius A. and Ida (Oiring) Lessman; B.A., National Coll., 1971; m. John B. Carter, Oct. 7, 1979; children: Robert Oiring, Mollie. Supr. lab. immunology Weiss Meml. Hosp., Chgo., 1973-80; lab. immunology supr. Henrotin Hosp., Chgo., 1980-84; tech. dir. Lexington Med. Labs., West Columbia, S.C., 1984—; mem. nat. workshop faculty Am. Soc. Clin. Pathologists; clin. instr. faculty Med. U. S.C. Mem. Am. Soc. Clin. Pathologists (subspecialty cert. in microbiology and immunology, cert. med. technologist). Researcher Legionnaires Disease and mycoplasma pneumonia World Soc. Pathologists, Jerusalem, Israel, 1980. Contbr. articles to profl. jours.; Mem. Rep. Senoritorial Inner Circle, co-chmn. S.C. Young Profls. for George Bush. Office: 110 Medical Ln E Ste 100 West Columbia SC 29169-4817

CARTER, STEPHEN EDWARD, lawyer; b. Louisa, Ky., Feb. 11, 1954; s. Edward Carter and Ima Jean (Workman) Heraldson; m. Roxanne Swank, May 4, 1973; 1 child, McKenzie. BA, Ohio State U., 1975; JD, Capital U., 1980. Bar: Ohio 1980, U.S. Dist. Ct. (so. dist.) Ohio 1982, U.S. Ct. Appeals (6th cir.) 1985, U.S. Supreme Ct. 1985, S.C. 1989, U.S. Dist. Ct. S.C. 1990. Assoc. Federico, Myers & Enz, Columbus, Ohio, 1980; pvt. practice law Circleville, Ohio, 1981-84; ptnr. Dumm & Carter, Circleville, 1984-87, Farthing, Carter & Dumm, Circleville, 1987-89, McNair Law Firm, Hilton Head Island, S.C., 1990-92, Bethea, Jordan & Griffin, P.A., Hilton Head Island, 1992—. Mem. ABA (litigation sect.), Ohio Bar Assn., Assn. Trial Lawyers Am., Ohio Acad. Trial Lawyers, Leadership Hilton Head. Office: Bethea Jordan & Griffin PA 23 Shelter Cove Ln Ste 400 Hilton Head Island SC 29928-3542

CARTER, THOMAS ALLEN, engineering executive, consultant; b. Cin., July 12, 1935; s. Fernando Albert and Mary Gladys (Gover) C.; m. Janet Tucker, Oct. 14, 1956; children: Barry Everett, Duane Allen, Sarita Anne. AB, Jones Coll., 1980, BBA, 1982. Cert. constrn. insp. Enlisted USN, 1954, advanced through grades to master chief, ret., 1976; contract adminstr. Red Lobster Restaurants, Orlando, Fla., 1976-78; pvt. practice Orlando, 1978-80; sec. Blacando Devel. Corp., Orlando, 1980-84; chief engr. D.A.M.S., Inc., Orlando, 1984-91, SA Williams Inc, Orlando, 1991—. Mem.

Fleet Res. Assn., Rafman Club Orlando, Am. Legion. Democrat. Methodist. Office: SA Williams Inc 7041 Grand National Dr Ste 128G Orlando FL 32819-8379

CARTER, THOMAS SMITH, JR., retired railroad executive; b. Dallas, June 6, 1921; s. Thomas S. and Mattie (Dowel) C.; m. Janet R. Hostetter, July 3, 1946 (dec. 1981); children: Diane Carter Petersen, Susan Canter Estes, Charles T., Carol Carter Koehler. BS in Civil Engring., So. Meth. U., 1944; MS in Engring. Mgmt., Kans. U., 1991. Registered profl. engr., Mo., Kans., Okla., Tex., La., Ark. Various positions Mo. Kans. Tex. R.R., 1941-44, 46-54, chief engr., 1954-61, v.p. ops., 1961-66; v.p. Kansas City So. Ry. Co., La. and Ark. Ry. Co., 1966-74; pres. Kansas City So. Ry. Co., 1973-86, also bd. dirs., chmn. bd., 1981-91; pres. La. and Ark. Ry. Co., 1974-86, also bd. dirs., chmn. bd., 1981-91, CEO, 1981-91; bd. dirs. Kansas City So. Industries, 1974-96, Georgetown Rail Equipment Co., Assn. Am. R.R.'s, 1980-90, Snead Rsch. Inst., Tex.-Mex. Ry. Co.; adj. prof. Rockhurst Coll., 1992-93; instr. Johnson County C.C., 1992-93. With C.E., AUS, 1944-46. Fellow ASCE; mem. Am. Ry. Engring. Assn. (life), NSPE, Hide-A-Way Lake Club. Home: 131 Clubview Dr Lindale TX 75771-5054

CARTER, THOMASINE E., principal, academic program administrator; b. Norfolk, Va., Sept. 2, 1949; d. Thomas and Carrie (Mann) Easter; m. John B. Carter, Oct. 27, 1973. BS in Elem. Edn., Va. State U., 1972; MS in Supervision and Adminstrn., Longwood Coll., 1980; postgrad., Va. Tech. U. Tchr. Halifax County Pub. Schs., Danville (Va.) Pub. Schs.; asst. prin. E.A. Gibson Mid. Sch. Danville (Va.) City Schs., prin. Forest Hills Elem. Sch.; coord. chpt. 1 program Danville Pub. Schs. Mem. ASCD, Nat. Assn. Elem. Sch. Prins., Danville Prin's. Assn., Delta Sigma Theta, Phi Delta Kappa. Home: 543 Rosemary Ln Danville VA 24541-4529

CARTER, WILLIAM KEMP, accounting educator; b. L.A., Oct. 31, 1951; s. Elijah Albert and Warrene Stansel (Hyner) C.; m. Imelda Frances Smith, May 25, 1974; children: Richard William, Craig Warren. BSBA, U. So. Miss., 1973, MS in Acctg., 1974; PhD, Okla. State U., 1977. CPA, Miss. Asst. prof. acctg. McIntire Sch. of Commerce, U. Va., Charlottesville, 1978-81, assoc. prof., 1981—, acctg. area coord., dir. grad. studies, 1983-86; mem. univ. retirement com. U. Va., 1995-96, chair com. on faculty benefits, 1989-96, chair subcom. on long-term disability, 1987-88, assessment com., McIntire Sch. of Commerce, 1993-95, grad. admissions and programs com., 1993-94, chair grad. program com., 1983-86, mem. 1982-86, mem. task force to write a statement of mission and objectives, 1983-84, faculty v.p. Beta Alpha Psi, Delta Mu chpt., 1988-89, 96—, asst. faculty v.p., 1987-88, mem. maj. field examining coms. for DBA candidates, 1981-82, sec. 1981-82; ad hoc reviewer Jour. of Acctg. Case Rsch., 1995, Acctg. Horizons, 1995, The Jour. of Cost Analysis, 1986-88, The Accounting Review, 1983-84; cons. Inst. of Chartered Fin. Analysts, 1981; mem. rev. com. M.B. Washington Rsch. grant U. West Fla., 1989, 1990. Author: (with others) Cost Accounting, 1994, Solutions Manual, 1994, Instructor Manual, 1994; cons. editor Cost Accounting: Planning and Control, 1991, Solutions Manual; contbr. articles to profl. jours.; editl. bd. Jour. of Acctg. Edn., 1987-94, The Acctg. Rev., 1984-85; regular reviewer Jour. of Acctg. Edn., 1987; referee Jour. of Cost Analysis, 1988-89. Recipient Fellowship award to Instrs. in Acctg. The Haskins and Sells Found., 1975; fellowship Am. Acctg. Assn. Doctoral Consortium, 1975. Mem. AICPA, Am. Acctg. Assn. (mgmt. acctg. sect., membership com. 1979-80, chair edn. resources com. mgmt. acctg. sect. 1992-93), Inst. of Mgmt. Accts., Omicron Delta Kappa, Beta Alpha Psi, Beta Gamma Sigma. Office: U Va McIntire Sch Commerce Monroe Hall UVA Charlottesville VA 22903

CARTER COVINGTON, CLAUDIA MCGINNIS, literary manager, educational director; b. Greenwich, Conn., Dec. 1, 1951; d. Homer Monroe and Mary Louise (Durant) Carter; m. George Carruthers Covington, July 23, 1977; children: Tyler Carruthers, Alexander Carter, Abigail Stedman. BFA in Theatre Arts, Stephens Coll., 1972; grad., Neighborhood Playhouse Sch., 1975. Creative activities instr. Prichard (Ala.) Elem. Sch., 1975; dance and theatre instr. Town Sch., N.Y.C., 1976; 7th and 8th grade speech and drama tchr. Westminster Schs., Atlanta, 1976-77; counselor Abortion and Pregnancy Testing, Albuquerque, 1978-79; head of drama, drama instr. 5th to 12th grades Albuquerque Acad., 1979-80; counselor, dir. Women's Pavilion, Greensboro, N.C., 1980-81; dir. Pennyfeather Players, Durham and Orange County, N.C., 1981-84; literary mgr., dir. of ednl. outreach Charlotte (N.C.) Repertory Theatre, 1985—; creative dramatics instr. Tom Ray Ctr., Charlotte, 1994; outreach edn. instr. Spirit Square Ctr. for Performing Arts, Charlotte, 1994—; artistic dir. Cities at Peace, 1994—. Appeared in various stage prodns. at Charlotte Repertory Theatre, N.C. Shakespeare Festival, Tiffany's Attic, Utah, Vortex Theatre, N.Mex., Trinity Players, Atlanta, Neighborhood Playhouse, N.Y.C., Agassiz Theatre, Cambridge, Mass., also in comml. and indsl. film; dir. stage prodns. at Charlotte Festival New Plays in Am., Charlotte Repertory Theatre, Children's Theatre of Charlotte; contbr. poems to various publs. Named Best Actress in Comedy, Creative Loafing Mag., 1991, Best Dir. of Comedy, Creative Loafing Mag., 1992, Best Supporting Actress in Comedy, Creative Loafing Mag., 1995. Mem. Literary Mgrs. and Dramaturgs Assn. Democrat. Presbyterian. Home: 801 Edgehill Rd Charlotte NC 28207

CARTIER, BRIAN EVANS, association executive; b. Providence, Apr. 12, 1950; s. Clarence Joseph and Mary Anna (Evans) C. BA, R.I. Coll., 1972; MEd, Springfield (Mass.) Coll., 1973. Exec. dir. Arthritis Found. Conn., Hartford, 1976-78, dep. exec. dir. N.Y. chpt., N.Y.C., 1979; exec. dir. Found. for Chiropractic Edn. and Research, Arlington, Va., 1979-90; exec. dir. Nat. Ct. Reporters Assn., 1990—. Mem. Am. Mgmt. Assn.(cert. assn. exec.), Am. Soc. Assn. Execs, Greater Washington Soc. Assn. Execs., U.S. C. of C. Republican. Roman Catholic. Home: 10108 Waterside Dr Burke VA 22015-3931 Office: NCRA 8224 Old Courthouse Rd Vienna VA 22182-3808

CARTLIDGE, SHRILEY ANN BELL, school administrator; b. Indianola, Miss., July 26, 1940; d. Albert and Betty (Newsome) Bell; 1 child, Carol W. Rowe; m. Arthur J. Cartlidge, Mar. 16, 1991. BS, Miss. Valley State U., Itta Bena, 1964; MEd, Delta State U., Cleveland, Miss., 1975. Tchr. English Greenville (Miss.) Pub. Schs., 1964-93, chmn. dept. English, 1971-87, dist. chmn. dept. English, 1987-93; instr. supr. Yazoo City (Miss.) Schs., 1993-94, chpt. 1 coord., 1994-96; dir. fed. programs, 1996—; tchr./cons. Writing Across the Curriculum, MAS (state testing sys.). Bd. dirs. Miss. PTA, 1987—, v.p. edn., 1993-95, editor bull., 1993-95, state treas., 1995—. Mem. NEA, Nat. Coun. Tchrs. English, Internat. Reading Assn., Miss. Assn. Sch. Adminstrs., Eta Phi Beta (past pres., sec.). Baptist. Office: Yazoo City Mcpl School 1133 Calhoun Ave Yazoo City MS 39194-2939

CART-ROGERS, KATHERINE COOPER, emergency nurse; b. Jacksonville, Tex., Aug. 7, 1948; d. Raymond Jesse and June (Walker) Cooper; m. Frank E. Rogers, Sept. 25, 1981; 1 child, Natalie Christine Cart. Med. Technologist, St. Mary's, Galveston, Tex., 1967; BS in Nursing, Stephen F. Austin U., Nacogdoches, Tex., 1989; MA in Mgmt., Regent U., Virginia Beach, Va., 1995. Cert. CPR, Emergency Nurse, ACLS, instr. trauma nurse core course. Pharmacology-toxicology researcher U. Tex. Med. Br., Galveston, 1967-68, Ohio State U., Columbus, 1968-72; physicians asst., lab. supr. Newborn Meml. Hosp., Jacksonville, 1975-78; lab. mgr. East Tex. Med. Ctr., Rusk, 1978-87; lab. supr. Nacogdoches Meml. Hosp., 1987-89, emergency rm. nurse, 1989-91; emergency rm. chrge nurse Kingwood (Tex.) Pla. Hosp., 1991-92; nursing cons. Thorstenson Eye Clinic, Nacogdoches, 1991-92; dir. surg. svcs. Thorstenson Ambulatory Surgery Ctr., Nacogdoches, 1992-93, dir. emergency svcs., trauma coord., 1992—, employee health dir., 1994, dir. admissions, 1995, dir. rural health clinic, 1996—; dir. rural health clinic Nan Travis Meml. Hosp., 1992—. Mem. AACCN, Emergency Nurses Assn., Tex. Trauma Coords., Tex. Regional Adv. Coun. for Trauma Area G. Home: 310 N Mound St Nacogdoches TX 75961-5032

CARTWRIGHT, BONNIE REED, secondary school educator; b. Norfolk, Va., Mar. 5, 1969; d. John Grant and Juanita (Rushing) Reed; m. James Alton Cartwright, Apr. 3, 1993; 1 child, Zachary James. BS in Elem. and Mid. Sch. Edn. magna cum laude, Old Dominion U., 1991. Cert. tchr., Va. Instr. sci. Norfolk Pub. Schs., 1991—; head dept. grade-level sci. instrn., Norfolk, 1995—, mem. staff devel. com., 1994—. Dir., prodr.: (instructional video) Under the Sea, 1992 (1st pl. Nat. Media Festival 1993). Mem. PTA Lafayette Winona Mid. Sch., Norfolk, 1991—. Mem. NEA, Va. Edn. Assn., Edn. Assn. Norfolk, Phi Kappa Phi. Baptist. Office: Lafayette Winona Mid Sch 1701 Alsace Ave Norfolk VA 23509

CARTWRIGHT, CHARLES NELSON, lawyer; b. Ft. Worth, July 22, 1933; s. Charles L. and Mildred (Epperson) C.; student U. Houston, 1952; m. Suzanne Oberwetter, Sept. 5, 1956; 1 son, Charles Rea. BA, U. Tex., 1956, JD, 1960. Bar: Tex. 1960. Asst. city atty. Corpus Christi, Tex., 1960-63; assoc. Utter & Chase, Corpus Christi, 1964-67, ptnr., 1967-73; mem. firm Howard, McDowell & Cartwright, Corpus Christi, 1973-76, Prichard, Peeler & Cartwright, Corpus Christi, 1976—; instr. real estate law Del Mar Coll., Corpus Christi, 1965-68, guest lectr., 1968-70. Mem. City Zoning and Planning Commn. Corpus Christi, 1970-76, chmn., 1973-76; chmn. adv. bd. Mcpl. Legal Studies Ctr., 1982-84; rsch. fellow Southwestern Legal Found., Dallas, 1978—, mem., 1973—. V.P. Dispute Resolution Svcs. Nueces County. Co-author: Texas Civil Trial Handbook, 1984. Bd. dirs. Nueces County Dispute Resolution Svcs., 1993—. Served to 2d lt. AUS, 1957. Fellow Tex. Bar Found. (life); mem. Nueces County Bar Assn. (pres. 1975-76), State Bar Tex. (past chmn. continuing legal edn., dir. State Bar Coll. 1984-87), Nueces County Trial Lawyers Assn. (dir. 1970-71), Tex. Assn. Mediators, Tex. Assn. Bank Counsel, Ind. Banker Assn. Tex., Corpus Christi C. of C., Leadership Corpus Christi, NRA, Rotary, Masons. Home: 334 Cape Hatteras Dr Corpus Christi TX 78412-2628 Office: Prichard Peeler & Cartwright Am Bank Plz 1130 711 N Carancahua St Corpus Christi TX 78475-1102

CARTWRIGHT, TALULA ELIZABETH, writing and career development educator, communication and leadership consultant; b. Asheville, N.C., Oct. 25, 1947; d. Ralph and Sarah Helen (Medford) C.; m. Edwin Byram Crabtree, May 23, 1976 (div. Sept. 1984); children: Charity, Baxter; m. Richard Thomas England, Apr. 27, 1986; 1 child, Isaac. BA, U. N.C., 1971, MEd, 1974, EdD, 1988. Instr. McDowell Tech. Inst., Marion, N.C., 1972-73, Guilford Tech. C.C., Jamestown, N.C., 1973-89, Guilford Coll., Greensboro, N.C., 1982-87, U. N.C.-Greensboro, 1982-87, N.C. A&T State U., Greensboro, 1984-85; cons. Communication Assocs., Lenoir, Shelby, Asheboro, 1981—; dean continuing edn. Caldwell C.C., Lenoir, N.C., 1989-92; v.p. acad. programs Cleve. C.C., 1992-95; program assoc. Ctr. for Creative Leadership, Greensboro, N.C., 1996—; mem. bd. dirs. N.C. Quality Coun., Carolinas Quality Consortium, Parents-As-Tchrs.; mem. funding bd. United Way; chmn. bd. dirs. Cleve. Abuse Prevetion Coun. Precinct chmn. Dem. Party, Greensboro, 1973-74. Winfield scholar U. N.C. at Greensboro, 1970; recipient Escheats award U. N.C.-Greensboro, 1971; Tchr. of Yr. award Greensboro Tech. C.C. Edn. Assn., 1982, Edn. Honor Roll award, 1989; Civitan Citizenship award, 1966; winner Human Rights Writing Contest, 1988, 89. Mem. NAFE, ASCD, NCAE (pres. local unit 1988-89, chair higher edn. commn. 1989-90, 92-95), Am. Coun. Edn., N.C. Assn. C.C. Adult Edn. Assn., Am. Assn. Women in C.C., Women's Adminstrs. in N.C. (exec. bd. 1995), Higher Edn., N.C. Assn. Colls. & Univs., Am. Mgmt.

CARTY, BRIAN CLIFFORD, family practice physician; b. Glen Ridge, N.J., Nov. 24, 1962; s. Joseph Charles and Muriel Calista (Bolden) C. BS, MIT, 1985, BS in Chem. Engring. and Biology, 1985; MD, Bowman Gray Sch. Medicine, 1990. Diplomate Am. Bd. Family Practice. Resident Franklin Sq. Hosp. Ctr., Balt., 1990-93; physician Mount Vernon Med. Group, Alexandria, Va., 1993—. Mem. AMA, Am. Acad. Family Physicians, Va. Acad. Family Physicians. Democrat. Roman Catholic. Home: 6215 Winham Hill Rd Alexandria VA 22315 Office: Mount Vernon Med Group 6287 Franconia Rd Alexandria VA 22310

CARUTHERS, J. C., religious association executive. Exec. dir. Fellowship of Conservative So. Baptists. Address: 6850 Hammock Rd Naples FL 33962

CARVER, CHARLES RAY, retired information systems company executive; b. Foreman, Ark., Oct. 10, 1929; s. Andrew Jackson and Ada Cowlin (Nolen) C.; m. Grace Isabelle Jean, Nov. 16, 1930 (dec. Nov. 10, 1994); children: Edward Arnold, Linda Diane, Wanda Susan. Student, U. Md., Europe, 1951-54, 60-63, George Washington U., 1972-74, U. Ark., 1976. Commd. USAF, advanced through grades, dir. systems and programming, 1946-69; sr. systems rep. RCA Corp., Washington, 1969-70; program mgr. U.S. Postal Service, Washington, 1970-74, Norman, Okla., 1974-89; pres., CEO, ret. owner Mgmt. Info. Systems Devel., Inc., Norman, 1980—; cons. Office Automation, 1970—. Author: ADP Standards, 1970, ADP Information Systems, 1973, ADP Management, 1980. Mem. Assn. Govt. Accts., Assn. Computer Programmers and Analysts, Retired Enlisted and Officer Assns. Democrat. Baptist. Home and Office: 2209 Morgan Dr Norman OK 73069-6528

CARVER, HAZEL OATES, music educator, editor; b. LaFollette, Tenn., Apr. 30, 1918; d. Benjamin Franklin and Velma Lee (Ross) Oates; m. Marvin Gill Carver, June 21, 1939 (dec. May 1970); children: Keith Ross, Jean, Cathryn. AB, Western Ky. U., Bowling Green, 1938, MA, 1962. Music tchr. Hughes-Kirk Consol. Sch., Beechmont, Ky., 1938-42; band and choral dir. Russellville (Ky.) H.S., 1943-77; editor Ky. Music Educators Assn. Mag., Russellville, 1977-96; organist First Bapt. Ch., Russellville, 1986-96; piano, violin instr. Hazel Carver Music Studio, Russellville, 1977—; bd. dirs., adjudicator Ky. Music Educators Assn., 1977—; adjudicator Hall of Fame Nat. Piano Guild Auditions, various states, 1977—, Natl. Fedn. of Music Clubs, 1977—, Tenn. Assn. of Music Tchrs., Ky. Music Tchrs. Assn. Editor Bluegrass Music News (Ky. Music Educators Assn. jour., Outstanding Jour. award Music Educators Nat. Conf. 1988), 1977—. Pres. Logan County Arts Assn., Russellville, 1977-81; founder, bd. dirs. The deGraffenried Chorale, 1977-81. Recipient Cert. of Achievement, Ky. Ho. of Reps., 1996. Mem. Ky. Music Educators Assn. (Dist. Svc. award 1980, Ky. colonel award 1982, Gold Note award 1982, Spl. Svc. award 1996), Logan County C. of C. Democrat. Baptist. Home: 1007 Granville Lane Russellville KY 42276-1034

CARVER, JOAN SACKNITZ, university dean; b. Spokane, Wash., Jan. 22, 1931; d. Weldon and Mabel (Swanson) S.; m. Jay Randall Carver, June 25, 1955; 1 child, James Randall (dec.). BA, Barnard Coll., 1953; MA, U. N.C., 1957; PhD, U. Fla., 1965. Exec. sec. Iranian del. to UN, N.Y.C., 1953-55; tchr. Lake Shore Jr. High Sch., Jacksonville, Fla., 1956-57; office mgr. Bartram Sch., Jacksonville, 1957-58; from asst. to assoc. prof. Jacksonville U., 1958-60, 63-75, prof., 1975—, chmn. div. social scis., 1982-83, dean Coll. Arts and Scis., 1983—, dir. Taft Seminars in Practical Politics, 1968-78; instr. employee seminars City of Jacksonville, 1969-82; evaluator ABT Assocs., Boston, 1975; mem. reaffirmation coms. So. Assn. Colls., Atlanta, 1983-94. Contbr. articles to profl. jours. Sec., bd. dirs. Jacksonville Cmty. Coun., Inc., 1976-80; commr. 1st Appellate dist. Jud. Nominating Commn., Tallahassee, 1983-87; commr. Jacksonville Mayor's Com. on Status of Women, 1984-88; bd. trustees St. John's Country Day Sch., Orange Park, Fla., 1984—, pres., 1993-95; chair career opportunities subcom. Def. Adv. Com. on Women in Svc., Washington, 1991-93. Recipient Prof. of Yr. award Jacksonville, U., 1972, EVE award for achievement in edn. Fla. Times Union, Jacksonville, 1982; Seven Coll. Conf. nat. scholar Barnard Coll., 1949-53; grad. fellow U. Fla., 1960-63. Mem. Fla. Polit. Sci. Assn. (pres. 1975-76), Am. Soc. for Pub. Adminstrn. (pres. N.E. Fla. chpt. 1987-88), Women's Caucus for Polit. Sci.-South (pres. 1981-82), So. Polit. Sci. Assn. (membership chmn. 1983-91, rec. sec. 1993-94), Jacksonville Women's Network (pres. 1987-90), Phi Beta Kappa. Democrat. Episcopalian. Home: 46 15th St Jacksonville FL 32233-5722 Office: Jacksonville U 2800 University Blvd N Jacksonville FL 32211-3321

CARWISE, EDWARD ROLAND, information systems specialist, retired military officer; b. Live Oak, Fla., Sept. 22, 1940; s. Dolphus and Georgain (Williams) C.; m. Thelma Theresa Colbert, Aug. 17, 1962; children—Wendie, Curtis, Edward. B.S., Bethune-Cookman Coll., 1962; M.S. in Mgmt., Air Force Inst. Tech., Dayton, 1967. Commd. 2d lt., U.S. Air Force, 1963, advanced through grades to col., 1990—; staff officer Def. Comm. Agy., Washington, 1969-72, exec. officer U.S. CINCEUR, Stuttgart, Ger., 1972-75; comdr. Communications Squadron, San Antonio, 1975-77; dep. comdr. Communications Group, Adana, Turkey, 1977-79; comdr. Communications Squadron, Glendale, Ariz., 1979-80; dir. Hdqrs. U.S. Air Force, Washington, 1981-84; vice comdr. Continental Communications Div., Rome, NY, 1984-85, comdr., 1985-87; chief of staff, inspector gen. Def. Info. Systems Agy., Arlington, Va., 1987-89; asst. dept. dir., Def. Intelligence Agy, Washington, 1989-90; mktg. mgr. Universal Automation Labs, Silver Spring, Md., 1990-91; dir. Morris Brown Rsch. Inst., Morris Brown Coll., Atlanta, 1991-93; mem. exec. staff Computer Scis. Corp., 1993—. Bd. dirs. Bolling Fed. Credit Union, 1983-84; mem. Smithsonian Assocs., Washington, 1979—. Mem. Air Force Assn., Armed Forces Communications-Electronics Assn., Omega Psi Phi. Baptist. Home: 7205 Thomas Dr Upper Marlboro MD 20772-4336 Office: Computer Scis Corp 6565 Arlington Blvd Falls Church VA 22042-3000

CASALS, RAFAEL GABRIEL, assistant city manager; b. Havana, Cuba, Oct. 7, 1968; came to U.S., 1968; s. Rafael Maricio and Dora (Giaveran) C.; m. Gwen Bullock, July 1, 1995. AA, Miami-Dade C.C., 1988; student, Fla. Atlantic U., Boca Raton, 1995—. Computer analyst City of Florida City, Fla., 1985-86, bookkeeper, 1986-87, fin. officer, 1986-87, fin. officer utilities dept., 1987-88, adminstrv. asst. to city mgr., 1989-92, asst. city mgr., 1992—. Named Hurricane Hero, State of Fla., South Dade area, 1992. Mem. Internat. City Mgrs. Assn. Office: City of Florida City 404 W Palm Dr Florida City FL 33034-3346

CASANOVA-LUCENA, MARIA ANTONIA, computer engineer; b. Cienfuegos, Las Villas, Cuba, Jan. 1, 1954; came to U.S., 1979; d. Manuel José and Loida Eugenia (Ojeda) Casanova; m. Angel de Jesus Lucena, Aug. 12, 1978; 1 child, Ingrid. BSEE cum laude, U. Miami, 1985. Software engr. Martin Marietta Corp., Orlando, Fla., 1986-89; computer engr., mgr. software acquisition, Tng. Sys. divsn. Naval Air Warfare Ctr., Orlando, 1989—. Mem. IEEE, Golden Key, Sigma Xi, Tau Beta Pi, Eta Kappa Nu, Phi Kappa Phi. Home: 3212 Lake George Cove Dr Orlando FL 32812-6844 Office: Naval Air Warfare Ctr Tng Sys Divsn Code 242 12350 Research Pky Orlando FL 32826-3261

CASASANTA, MARY FRANCES, medical/surgical nurse; b. Ft. Jay, N.Y., June 17, 1962; d. John Joseph and Marlene Ann (Maiwald) C. BSN, West Tex. State U., 1984. RN, Tex. Nurse St. Anthony's Hosp., Amarillo, Tex.; nurse orthopedics unit Spohn Hosp., Corpus Christi, Tex.; autotransfusionist/perfusion asst. Harbor Perfusion, Inc., Corpus Christi, Tex.; orthopedics nurse Bay Area Med. Ctr.; coustal infusion therapist Bayside Home Health. Mem. Nat. Assn. Orthopaedic Nurses.

CASE, CHARLES DIXON, lawyer; b. Manning, S.C., Mar. 23, 1952; s. James E. and Jennie (Stout) C.; m. Margie Toy, Aug. 28, 1982; children: J. Everett II, Elliot T. BS in Physics, N.C. State U., 1973; JD, Harvard U., 1977. Bar: N.C. 1977, U.S. Dist. Ct. (mid. and we. dists.) N.C., U.S. Supreme Ct. Environ. atty., ptnr. Moore & Van Allen, 1977-92; ptnr. Hunton & Williams, Raleigh, N.C., 1992—; adj. prof. law Campbell U., Buies Creek, N.C., 1981-84; hearing officer N.C. Safety and Health Rev. Bd., Raleigh, 1981-84; chmn. Wake County Bd. Adjustment, Raleigh, 1979-83; mem. N.C. Hazardous Waste Study Commn., 1982. Co-author: Toxic Tort and Hazardous Substance Litigation, 1995; contbr. articles to profl. jours. Pres. Coll. Phys. and Math. Scis. Found., N.C. State U. 1994-95, bd. dirs., 1991—; bd. dirs. Jr. Achievement Ea. N.C., 1994—; mem. bd. visitors N.C. State U., 1995—. Home: 1540 Carr St Raleigh NC 27608-2302 Office: Hunton & Williams PO Box 109 Raleigh NC 27602-0109

CASE, THOMAS LOUIS, lawyer; b. Dallas, June 14, 1947; s. Donald L. and Ellen (Hanson) C.; m. Bonnie Nally, July 8, 1972. BA, Vanderbilt U., 1969, JD, 1972; cert. civil trial law, Tex. Bd. Legal Specialization. Bar: Tex. 1972, U.S. Dist. Ct. (no. dist.) Tex. 1973, U.S. Dist. Ct. (we. and ea. dists.) Tex. 1978, U.S. Dist. Ct. (so. dist.) Tex. 1979, U.S. Dist. Ct. (ea. dist.) Ark. 1981, U.S. Ct. Appeals (5th cir.) 1977, U.S. Supreme Ct. 1978, U.S. Ct. Appeals (8th cir.) 1984, U.S. Ct. Appeals (11th cir.) 1981. Assoc. Johnson, Bromberg, Leeds & Riggs, Dallas, 1972-77; ptnr. Bickel & Case, Dallas, 1977-84, St. Claire & Case, Dallas, 1984-93, Thomas L. Case & Assocs., P.C., Dallas, 1993—. Mem. ABA, Tex. Bar Assn., Tex. Assn. Def. Coun., Dallas Assn. of Def. Counsel, Dallas Bar Assn. Office: Thomas L. Case & Assocs PC Ste 1450 5910 N Central Expy Dallas TX 75206-5125

CASELLAS, JOACHIM, art gallery executive; b. Gerona, Spain, Aug. 1, 1927; came to U.S., 1954; s. Juan and Dolores Farre (Carrera) C.; m. Elizabeth Reed Brannon, Mar. 17, 1952 (dec. Dec. 1984); m. Janice Mary Bezverkov, May 29, 1990. BA, Gerona Coll., 1948; MA, Sacred Heart Coll., 1953. Curator Mus. Provincial, Gerona, Spain, 1952; art appraiser Feist Co., N.Y.C., 1952-68, Mahan Co., New Orleans, 1968-72; pres. Casell Gallery, New Orleans, 1972—. One-man shows include Ft. Walton (Fla.) Beach Mus. Art, 1987. Mem. Ocean Springs Yacht Club. Republican. Episcopalian. Home: 107 Shearwater Dr Ocean Springs MS 39564-4828 Office: Casell Gallery 818 Royal St New Orleans LA 70116-3115

CASEY, BEVERLY ANN, postmaster; b. Decaturville, Tenn., Aug. 6, 1949; d. Willie Hugh and Lillian Blanche (Ivy) Tillman; m. John Robert Casey, Jan. 19, 1969 (div. 1982); children—John Gary, Kimberly Jean. Student Jackson State Community Coll., 1982-84. Sec. State of Tenn., Western Institute, 1969-76; post office clk. U.S. Postal Service, Western Institute, 1977-82, postmaster, 1982-84; postmaster U.S. Postal Service, Pickwick Dam, Tenn., 1984—; officer-in-charge U.S. Postal Service, Michie, Tenn., 1984. Bd. dirs. Pickwick Med. Clinic, 1986; vol. Hardeman chpt. Saint Jude, Bolivar, Tenn., 1983, Hospice, 1996; mem. parents advancement com. Wesleyan Coll., 1991-94; town chmn. Reelfoot council Girl Scouts U.S., 1980-84, activities chmn., 1980-84, recipient Appreciation award, 1983. Named Outstanding 3d Class Postmaster 380 area U.S. Postal Service, 1984; recipient Vol. Service award Cystic Fibrosis Found., Tenn. Chpt., 1982, Vol. Appreciation Cert. Western Mental Health, 1984. Mem. Nat. League of Postmasters (v.p. Tenn. br. 1984-86), 380 Postmasters Assn. (pres. 1983-84), U.S. Postal Service (dir.-at-large women's adv. coun. 1983-88). Baptist. Avocations: walking; tennis. Home: PO Box 363 Pickwick Dam TN 38365-0363 Office: US Postal Service Pickwick Dam TN 38365

CASEY, DAVID ROBERT, lawyer; b. Wichita Falls, Tex., Dec. 1, 1945; s. Robert Joseph and Betty Lou (Baily) C.; m. Sue C. Hartness; children: Kristen Boenicke, Ryan B. BBA, North Tex. State U., 1968; JD, Tex. Tech., Lubbock, 1971. Bar: Tex. 1971, U.S. Dist. Ct. (no. dist.) Tex. 1972. Assoc. King & Massey, Ft. Worth, 1972-78; ptnr. Naler & Casey, Hurst, Tex., 1978-80; prin. Law Office David R. Casey, Hurst, Tex., 1980—. Mcpl. judge City of North Richland Hills, Tex., 1980-85, judge teen ct., 1992—. Mem. ABA, Tex. Assn. Bank Counsel, Tex. Bar Assn., Tarrant County Bar Assn. Office: 1840 Norwood Plaza Ct Ste 102 Hurst TX 76054-3749

CASEY, JAMES FRANCIS, management consultant; b. Boston, May 22, 1935; s. James Francis and Elizabeth Mary (MacNeil) C.; m. Margaret Ann Flaherty, Jan. 22, 1977. BA in Philosophy cum laude, Weston Coll., 1957, BS/MS in Physics cum laude, 1962. Sales mgr. Xerox Corp., Stamford, Conn., 1963-79; dir. mktg. Computervision Corp., Bedford, Mass., 1979-82; v.p. CTX Corp., Sunnyvale, Calif., 1982-83; mktg. mgr. Hewlett-Packard Corp., Palo Alto, Calif., 1983-86; group mgr. Digital Equipment Corp., Maynard, Mass., 1986-92; mng. ptnr. Synergy Cons., Austin, Tex., 1992—; prin. The Technology Group, Austin, 1996—; cons. numerous clients, including Hewlett-Packard Co., Ceridian, Lexis-Nexis, Raster Graphics, Inc., others. Patron San Francisco Opera Co., 1982-92, San Francisco Orch., 1982-91; friend Boston Symphony Orch., 1976-81. Mem. Greater Austin C. of C., Xerox-X, Am. Mgmt. Assn. (bd. dirs. 1962-65), Am. Electronic Assn. (mktg. com. chmn. 1989-91), Del. Valley Reprographic Soc. (v.p.1965-69), Jr. C. of C. (pres. Phila. chpt. 1965-69). Home: 10123 Treasure Island Dr Austin TX 78730 Office: 111 Congress Ave Ste 1200 Austin TX 78701

CASEY, JOHN DUDLEY, writer, English language educator; b. Worcester, Mass., Jan. 18, 1939; s. Joseph Edward and Constance (Dudley) C.; m. Jane Barnes, June 10, 1967 (div. 1980); children: Maud, Nell; m. Rosamond Pinchot Pittman, June 27, 1982; children: Clare, Julia. BA, Harvard U., 1962, LLB, 1965; MFA, U. Iowa, 1968. Prof. English U. Va., Charlottesville, 1972-92; lit. executor Estate of Breece D'J Pancake, 1979—; resident scholar Am. Acad. in Rome, 1990-91. Author: An American Romance, 1977 (runner up Ernest Hemingway award 1977), Testimony and Demeanor, 1979 (Friends Am. Lit. award 1980), Spartina, 1989 (Nat. Book awrad 1989), Supper at the Black Pearl, 1995; contbr. stories (O. Henry awrd 1989), essays maj. nat. mags. including New Yorker, Esquire. With USAF, 1959-60. Guggenheim fellow, 1979-80, Nat. Endowment for Arts fellow, 1983, resident Am. Acad. in Rome, 1990-91; grantee Strauss living AAAL,

1993—. Mem. PEN, Nat. Writers Union. Office: U Va Dept English Wilson Hall Charlottesville VA 22903-3289 Office: William Morris Agy care Michael Carlisle 1350 6th Ave C New York NY 10019

CASEY, JOSEPH PATRICK, county official; b. Washington, Apr. 28, 1964; s. Joseph P. and Anne Marie (Longo) C.; m. Suzanne Wheatall, July 28, 1990; children: Harrison, Patrick. BS, U. Richmond, 1986; M in Pub. Adminstrn., Va. Commonwealth U., 1995. CPA. Acct. KPMG Peat Marwick, Richmond, 1986-90; fin. dir. Hanover County, Va., 1990—. Human svcs. planning bd. United Way, Richmond, 1990—; Big Brother, Richmond, 1988-95; mem. West of the Blvd. Assn., 1990-95. Mem. Am. Inst. CPAs, Govt. Fin. Officers Assn., Va. Govt. Fin. Officers Assn. Office: County of Hanover PO Box 470 Hanover VA 23069

CASEY, LINDA HALEY, cardiopulmonary nurse; b. Scottsburg, Ind., Sept. 14, 1946; d. Howard L. and Mamie Rebecca (Martin) Haley; m. Marvin I. Casey, Sept. 1, 1967; children: Christopher, Andrew, Marlynn. BSN, Ind. U., New Albany, 1989. RN, Ind. Asst. supr. Jewish Hosp., Louisville, 1989—. Mem. Sigma Theta Tau, Alpha Chi (mem. exec. bd. 1988). Home: 3013 Beech Grove Ct Apt 1 Jeffersonville IN 47130-5863 Office: Jewish Hosp Col H Sanders Unit 217 E Chestnut St # 5W Louisville KY 40202-1821

CASEY, MARTIN, newspaper editor; b. Plainview, Tex., May 24, 1939; s. Orman W. and Mary Ruth (Patterson) C.; m. Sharon M. Stoos, Feb. 5, 1971; children: Jennifer, Erin, Patrick. BS in Tech. Journalism, Colo. State U., 1962; MS in Journalism, Northwestern U., 1963. Reporter Waterloo (Iowa) Daily Courier, 1963-65; reporter, local polit. writer, Washington corr. The Dallas Morning News, 1965-69; Congl. staff press sec. U.S. Congress, Washington, 1969-75; with Am. Newspaper Pubs. Assn., Reston, Va., 1976-92, mgr. govt. and internat. affairs, 1985-89, dir. circulation and readership, 1989-90, v.p. circulation and readership, 1990-92; dir. Washington Journalism Ctr., 1992-93; editor Media Express, 1994-95; editor Loudoun Times-Mirror, Leesburg, Va., 1996—; instr. history of mass comm. Univ. Coll., U. Md., College Park, 1985-87, instr. in writing for mass media & editing for mass media U. Md. Coll. Journalism, 1994; vis. lectr. in pub. comms. U.S. Naval Acad., 1977-78. Served with U.S. Army Res., 1957-64. Mem. Soc. Profl. Journalists, Leadership Loudoun. Home: 12007 Vale Rd Oakton VA 22124-2221

CASEY, RONALD BRUCE, journalist; b. Birmingham, AL, Aug. 21, 1951; s. J. B. and Ruby Lois (Sizemore) C.; m. Margaret Griffin Brooke, Feb. 3, 1979; children: Jefferson Brooke, Anna Heviges. BA, U. Ala., Tuscaloosa, 1973. Reporter Birmingham News, 1973-77, asst. city editor, 1977-79, edtorial writer, 1979-90, editor editorial page, 1990—. Bd. dirs. Family and Child Svcs., Birmingham, 1991—; mem. Leadership Birmingham. Recipient Nat. Headliners award Atlantic City Soc. Profl. Journalists, 1991, Pulitzer prize for editl. writing, 1991, Journalist of Yr. award Troy (Ala.) State U., 1993, award for editl. writing Nat. Edn. Writers Assn., 1995. Mem. Nat. Conf. Editorial Writers. Office: Birmingham News PO Box 2553 Birmingham AL 35202-2553

CASH, CAROL VIVIAN, sociologist; b. Port Arthur, Tex., Jan. 22, 1929; d. Mano Nathan and Floris Duval (Akin) C.; m. Robert Morrow Welch, Dec. 21, 1951 (div. 1966); children: Catherine Carol, Robert M. III, Candice Claire. AA, Lamar Jr. Coll., 1951; BS in Sociology, U. Houston, 1971. Sec. Port Arthur SS Co., 1948-50; with Gov's Office State of Tex., Austin, 1951-52; legal sec. Wesley W. West, Houston, 1953-55. Author numerous children's books. Active Houston area Boy Scouts Am., Girl Scouts U.S., 1960-76, Port Arthur Hist. Soc.; mem. Tex. Sesquicentennial Com., 1986; active in restoration of Tex. historic homes. Mem. AAUW (chmn. Port Arthur fund raiser 1982), Tex. Artist Mus. Soc., Planetary Soc., Fed. Women's Clubs, Writer's Club (v.p. 1983-84, pres. 1984-85, treas. 1985-90), U. Houston Alumni Assn.

CASH, RALPH EUGENE, psychologist; b. Knoxville, June 1, 1947; s. Ralph Leon and Alice Kathryn (Barnawell) C.; m. Dana V. Wallace, June 10, 1972; 1 child, Christopher David. BS, U. Tenn., 1968; MA, NYU, 1974, PhD, 1979. Lic. psychologist, Fla. Psychologist in tng. Bellevue Psychiat. Hosp., N.Y.C., 1972-73; psychology intern Flatlands Community Mental Health Ctr., Bklyn., 1973-74, psychotherapist, 1974-75; cons., sch. psychologist Broward County (Fla.) Pub. Schs., 1976-79, program coord., 1979-80; pvt. practice psychologist Hollywood, Fla., 1980—; adj. prof. Nova U., Ft. Lauderdale, Fla., 1980; bd. dirs. Assn. Drug Abuse Prevention and Treatment, Tamarac, Fla., 1980—. With U.S. Army, 1969-71. Mem. Am. Psychol. Assn., Fla. Assn. Sch. Psychologists (exec. bd. 1980-95, pres.-elect 1995-96, pres. 1996-97), Broward Assn. Sch. Psychologists (founding mem., past pres., v.p.), Nat. Assn. Sch. Psychologists, Hollywood C. of C., Phi Beta Kappa, Phi Delta Kappa, Phi Eta Sigma, Phi Mu Alpha. Office: 2699 Stirling Rd Ste 305B Fort Lauderdale FL 33312-6546

CASH, SANDRA KAY, critical care nurse; b. Shiloh, Ohio, Sept. 9, 1938; d. Stanley M. and Inez L. (Winely) Moser; children: Michael Allen, Kevin Lee. Diploma, Christ Hosp. Sch. Nursing, Cin., 1959; BSN, Tenn. State U., 1985. Cert. cardiovascular nurse; ACLS. Surg. intensive care nurse Donelson Hosp., Nashville; nursing supr. Clermont County Hosp., Cin. instr. home nursing ARC.

CASHION, JOE MASON, home health care administrator; b. Lynchburg, Tenn., Jan. 24, 1938; s. C. Rufus Cashion and Mary (Mason) Templeton; m. Mary Soroka, July 31, 1973; children: Michael David, Steven Andrew. BS, U. Tenn., 1961; MBA, George Washington U., 1963; postgrad., Syracuse U., 1963, Cornell U., 1969. Adminstr. resident East Tenn. Baptist Hosp., Knoxville, 1962-63, asst. adminstr., 1965-66; Peace Corps hosp. adminstr. Dyer Maternity Ctr., Monrovia, Liberia, 1963-65; hosp. adminstr. Arabian Am. Oil Co., Dhahran, Saudi Arabia, 1966-73, Franklin County Hosp. & Nursing Home, Winchester, Tenn., 1973-75; pres. Mid. Tenn. Home Health Svc., Winchester, 1975—; health care cons. Trans World Airlines, Dubai, Hosp. Corp. Am., Saudi Arabia, Saudi Arabian Ministry of Health, Nat. Pub. Health Service, Liberia; mem. home health care profl. exchange to Republic of China with People-to-People program Spokane, Wash., 1987. Fellow Royal Soc. Health (London); mem. Nat. Assn. Home Care, Am. Coll. Healthcare Execs. (cert. healthcare exec.). Mem. Ch. of Christ. Lodge: Rotary (pres. Winchester 1979-80). Home: PO Box 399 Winchester TN 37398-0399 Office: Mid Tenn Home Health Svc PO Box 399 Winchester TN 37398-0399

CASHMAN, JOHN A., business executive; b. 1941. Bloodstock agt. L.I., N.Y., 1964-80; pres. Castleton, Inc., Lexington, Ky., 1980—. Office: Castleton Inc 2469 Iron Works Rd Lexington KY 40511-8432

CASHMAN, PAUL WALKER, writer, editor; b. Port Chester, N.Y., Jan. 30, 1964; s. Robert Walter Cashman and Loralee Jean Brundage Goetze. BS in Computer Sci., West Ga. Coll., Carrollton, 1986. Sr. applications programmer CBTCorp./Ashford Inst., Dunwoody, Ga., 1986-87; pres. Internat. Michael Moorcock Appreciation Soc., Atlanta, 1988-94, pres. emeritus, 1994—; editor-in-chief DCI, Inc./Dragon*Con, Atlanta, 1990—; dir. publs. Dragon*Con, Atlanta, 1990-96; membership dir. Inception-Storm Constantine Info. Svc., London, 1996—. Contbr. short story to Elric--Tales for the White Wolf, 1994; contbr. to periodical The Megaflow Manifesto, 1988-94. Mem. The Planetary Soc., World Sci. Fiction Soc., Wraeththu Online (coord.). Libertarian. Office: Inception Storm Constantine Info Svc PO Box 451433 Atlanta GA 31145-9433

CASKEY, CHARLES THOMAS, biology and genetics educator; b. Lancaster, S.C., Sept. 22, 1938; m. Peggy Ann Pearce, 1960; children: Clifton, Caroline. Student, U. S.C., 1956-58; MD, Duke U., 1963; DSc (hon.), U. S.C., 1993. Diplomate Am. Bd. Internal Medicine. Intern, resident dept. medicine Duke Med. Sch., 1963-65; rsch. assoc. Nat. Heart & Lung Inst., Bethesda, Md., 1965-67, head sect. med. genetics, 1970-71; sr. investigator Lab. Biomed. Genetics NIH, Bethesda, 1967-70; chief sect. med. genetics, prof. medicine, prof. biochemistry Baylor Coll. Medicine, Houston, 1971—, investigator Howard Hughes Med. Inst., 1976—, dir. Robert J. Kleberg, Jr. Ctr. for Human Genetics, 1980-94, dir. med. scientist tng. program, 1982-93, prof. cell biology, 1982-94, dir. and prof. molecular genetics Inst. Molecular Genetics, 1985-92, prof. molecular genetics Inst. Molecular Genetics, 1985-94, Henry and Emma Meyer chmn. molecular genetics, 1987-94, dir. Human Genome Ctr., 1991-94, chmn. dept. molecular and human genetics, 1994—; sr. v.p. rsch. Merck Rsch. Labs., 1995—; Josiah Macy, Jr. faculty scholar Med. Rsch. Coun. Cambridge (Eng.) U., 1979-80; dir. NATO ASI on Somatic Cell Genetics, 1980-81, NATO/EMBO/FEBS Spetsai European Molecular Biology Course, 1983, 87; Bernard Sachs lectr. Child Neurology Soc., 1993; Roy E. Moon disting. lectr. sci. Angelo State U., 1994; Samuel Rudin disting. vis. prof. Columbia U., N.Y.C., 1994; mem. biochem. test com. Nat. Bd. Med. Examiners, 1977-81, chmn. biochem. test com., 1981-84, mem. coord. com. for FLEX, 1984-86, mem.-at-large, 1984-88; chmn. sci. adv. bd. Xytronyx Inc., 1984-90; acad. assoc. Nichols Inst., 1987-92; liason mem. program adv. com. on human genome NIH, 1989-92; chair adv. panel forensic uses DNA tests U.S. Congress Office Tech. Assessment, 1989-90; mem. mapping the human genome adv. com. U.S. Dept. Energy, 1986-89; mem. adv. panel mapping the human genome U.S. Congress Office Tech. Assessment, 1987-88; mem. human genome coord. com. Dept. Energy, 1989-94. Author: Somatic Cell Genetics, 1982; author: (with others) Prebiotic and Biochemical Evolution, 1971, Frontiers of Biology: The Mechanism of Protein Synthesis and Its Regulation, 1972, The Enzymes, 1974, The Kidney in Systemic Disease, 1976, Protein Synthesis, 1976, Molecular Mechanisms of Protein Biosynthesis, 1977, Tay-Sachs Disease Screening and Prevention, 1977, Nonsense Mutations and tRNA Suppressors, 1979, Strauss and Welt Diseases of the Kidney, 3d edit., 1979, Gene Amplification, 1982, Internal Medicine, 1983, Advances in Gene Technology: Human Genetic Disorders, 1984, After Barney Clark: Reflections on the Utah Artificial Heart Program, 1984, Pediatric Neurology, 1986, Clinical Endocrinology, 1986, Gene Transfer, 1986, Molecular Biology of Homo Sapiens, 1986, Medical and Experimental Mammalian Genetics: A Perspective, 1987, Human Genetics, 1987, Molecular Neurobiology in Neurology and Psychiatry, 1987, Current Neurology, vol. 9, 1988, Textbook of Internal Medicine, 1988, Nucleic Acid Probes in Diagnosis of Human Genetic Diseases, 1988, Molecular Genetics of Brain, Nerve, and Muscle, 1989, Molecular Genetics of Diseases of Brain, Nerve, and Muscle, 1989, The Metabolic Basis of Inherited Disease, 6th edit., 1989, PCR Technology: Principles and Applications of DNA Amplification, 1989, The Polymerase Chain Reaction, 1989, PCR Protocols: A Guide to Methods and Applications, 1989, Genetic Engineering, Principles and Methods, vol. 11, 1989, The Science and Practice of Pediatric Cardiology, vol. 1, 1990, Ribosomes and Protein Synthesis: A Practical Approach, 1990, Etiology of Human Disease at the DNA Level, 1991, PCR: A Practical Approach, 1991, Neurodegenerative Disorders: Mechanisms and Prospects for Therapy, 1991, Reproductive Risks and Prenatal Diagnosis, 1991, Antisense RNA and DNA, 1991, Biomonitoring and Carcinogen Risk Assessment, 1991, Legal and Ethical Issues Raised by the Human Genome Project, 1991, Advances in Forensic Haemogenetics, 1992, Gene Mapping - Using Law and Ethics as Guides, 1992, The Code of Codes, 1992, Antisense Strategies, 1992, Molecular Basis of Neurology, 1993, Genetic Engineering, Principles and Methods, 1993, Genetics and Society, 1993, numerous other chpts. to books; mem. editorial bd. Archives Biochemistry and Biophysics, 1975-78, Jour. Biol. Chemistry, 1978-83, Annals Intenal Medicine, 1980-83, Molecular Biology and Medicine, 1982-90, Somatic Cell and Molecular Genetics, 1983-94, Trends in Genetics, 1985-90, Genomics, 1987-90, Molecular and Cell Biology, 1988-90, Human Gene Therapy, 1990—, Jour. AMA, 1991-94, Genetic Epidemiology, 1992-94, Human Mutation, 1992—, Circulation, 1993—; mem. bd. reviewing editors Sci., 1991—. Mem. Human Genome Orgn., 1988—, pres., 1993—; mem. task force on genetics Muscular Dystrophy Assn., 1989-94. With USPHS, 1965-67. Recipient Borden Rsch. award, Disting. Alumnus award Duke U. Med. Sch., 1991, Wadsworth award N.Y. State Dept. Health, 1992, Svc. Merchandise Leadership award Muscular Dystrophy Assn., 1992, Basic Biomed. Rsch. prize Giovanni Lorenzini Med. Found., 1993, Lucy Wortham James Basic Rsch. award Soc. Surg. Oncology, 1994, Norberto Montalbetti Milan award, 1994, The Coriell medal Coriell Inst., 1995, 5th Milano award in memory of Norberto Montalbetti, 1995. Fellow AMA (founding), AAAS (sci. innovation program com. 1991-93), Am. Coll. Physicians, Am. Acad. Microbiology, Royal Soc. Medicine Found.; mem. Nat. Acad. Scis., Am. Fedn. Clin. Rsch., Am. Soc. Biochemistry and Molecular Biology, Am. Soc. Clin. Investigation, Am. Soc. Human Genetics, Am. Soc. Cell Biology, Am. Coll. Med. Genetics, Assn. Am. Physicians, Fedn. Am. Socs. for Exptl. Biology, N.Y. Acad. Scis., So. Soc. Clin. Investigation, Soc. Inherited Metabolic Disorders, Inst. Medicine Nat. Acad. Scis., Royal Soc. Medicine, Baylor Med. Alumni Assn. (disting. faculty mem. 1993), Alpha Omega Alpha. Home: 6402 Belmont St Houston TX 77005-3802 Office: Merck Rsch Labs Sumneytown Pike West Point PA 19486

CASLER, FREDERICK CLAIR, academic administrator, law enforcement educator; b. Corry, Pa., Mar. 7, 1946; s. Clair O. and Helen M. (Church) C.; m. Janice L. Newrick, Nov. 26, 1983; 1 child, Frederick Clair Jr. AA, Miami-Dade Jr. Coll., 1970; BGS, Rollins Coll., 1975, MS in Criminal Justice, 1979; cert., Kissimmee Police Acad., 1974, 88; postgrad.in Philosophy, Fla. Tech. U., 1995—. Cert. tchr., Fla. Tchr. criminal justice Orange County Schs., Orlando, Fla.; tchr., work experience coord. Osceola County Schs., Kissimmee, Fla.; police-sch. liaison officer Kissimmee Police Dept./Osceola County Schs.; vocat. adult and community education tchr. Kissimmee Police Acad./Osceola Dist. Schs.; coord. Kissimmee Criminal Justice Acad. Adviser various youth orgns. including SADD, Just Say No Club; mem. Osceola County Rep. Exec. Com.; cubmaster Boy Scouts Am. Mem. NEA, Am. Fedn. of Police, Internat. Conf. of Police Officers, Am. Soc. Law Enforcement Trainers, Nat. Assn. Chiefs Police, Fla. Assn. Sch. Resource Officers, Fla. Tchrs. Assn., Osceola County Tchrs. Assn., Fla. Criminal Justice Tng. Officers Assn., Fla. Peace Officers Assn., Internat. Conf. Police Chaplains, Am. Legion (post comdr. 1973), Kiwanis Club (dir.), Masons, Shriners, Scottish Rite, Police Acad. Alumni Assn., Am. Police Hall of Fame, Am. Criminal Justice Assn., NRA (life), Am. Assn. Christian Counselors, Lambda Alpha Epsilon , Alpha Omega Epsilon (chpt. pres. 1996), Phi Delta Kappa.

CASO, PHILIP MICHAEL, financial services company executive, educator; b. N.Y.C., June 19, 1958; m. Suzanne Marie Marcil, Nov. 30, 1987. BS, NYU, 1981; postgrad., N.Y. Inst. Fin., N.Y.C., 1982, 83. Cert. arbitrator, Nat. Assn. Securities Dealers (series 7, 63, 4, 24, 8); lic. Dept. Ins., Life, Health and Annuity, Fla. Gen. mgr. Hallmark & Holland, Inc., N.Y.C., 1980-81; officer ops. mgr. Citicorp Capital Markets Group, N.Y.C., 1981-83; v.p. investments, registered rep. various fin. firms, 1983-86; v.p., br. mgr. Rosenkrantz, Lyon & Ross, Inc. and predecessor cos., Chgo., 1986-89; resident mgr., fin. cons. Merrill Lynch, Pierce, Fenner & Smith, Inc., Pompano Beach, Miami Beach, Fla., 1989—; instr. Broward Community Coll., CUNY, others, 1981-89; fin. expert, lectr. Celebrity Cruises, Miami, Fla., 1990—. Bd. curriculum advisors Broward Community Coll., Coconut Creek, Fla., 1990-91; founding mem. Fla. Grand Opera Leadership Coun., 1993—. Mem. Sales and Mktg. Execs. Internat. (past pres., So. Fla. chpt.), Am. Arbitration Assn., Fla. Bar Com., Latin Bldrs. Assn., Miami Beach C. of C.

CASON, DICK KENDALL, physician; b. Beaumont, Tex., June 27, 1922; s. Dick Kendall and Maurine (Mills) C.; m. Maxine Skocdopole, Apr. 4, 1946; children: Dick Mills, Alma Christine. BA Rice U., 1945; MD U. Tex., 1945. Intern Kings County Hosp., Bklyn., 1945-46; med. resident Meth. Hosp. Dallas, 1948-49; gen. practice medicine, Hillsboro, Tex., 1949-94; charter mem. Am. Bd. Family Practice. Pres. Hillsboro Indsl. Devel. Found., 1955-60, 79—; past mem. regional adv. com. Dallas Civic Opera Co.; parish vis. 1st Presbyn. Ch., Hillsboro, Tex., 1994—. Served from 1st lt. to capt., AUS, 1946-48. Fellow Royal Soc. Health (Eng.); mem. Hill County Med. Soc. (pres. 1951), Tex. Med. Assn. (alt. del. to AMA 1980-84, del. 1984-94), Am. Acad. Gen. Practice, N.Y. Acad. Sci., Internat. Horn Soc., C. of C., Hill County Soc. Crippled Children. Presbyterian (elder). Clubs: Hillsboro Country, Rotary (pres. Hillsboro 1955). Contbr. articles to profl. jours. Home: 1303 Park Dr Hillsboro TX 76645-2633

CASS, BARBARA FAY, elementary school educator; b. Vernon, Tex., Jan. 24, 1949; d. Jester Earl and Sylvia Louise (Bowden) Hunt; m. Millard Don Cass, Jan. 21, 1966; 1 child, Paula Sue Cass Threatt. BS, Tex. Tech U., 1985. Sec. Dr. Johnson, Plainview, Tex., 1973; receptionist Dr. T.M. Trimble, Wylie, Tex., 1973-75, Dr. Thomas Neal, Lubbock, Tex., 1987-88; bookkeeper Aledo (Tex.) Counter Top, 1976-77; receptionist med. records and ins. clk. care unit Trinity Oaks Hosp., Ft. Worth, 1977-78; substitute tchr. Lubbock Ind. Sch. Dist., 1986-87, DeSoto (Tex.) Ind. Sch. Dist., 1988-89; kindergarten tchr. home econs. Tyler St. Christian Acad., Dallas, 1989-94; tchr. 1st grade Robinwood Christian Acad., Seagoville, Tex., 1994—. Baptist. Home: 603 FM 740N Forney TX 75126

CASSCELLS, SAMUEL WARD, III, cardiologist, educator; b. Wilmington, Del., Mar. 18, 1952; s. Samuel Ward and Oleda (Dyson) C.; m. Roxanne Bell, Feb. 10, 1990; children: Sam, Henry. BS cum laude, Yale U., 1974; MD magna cum laude, Harvard U., 1979. Intern then resident Beth Israel Hosp., Boston, 1979-82; cardiology fellow Mass. Gen. Hosp., Boston, 1982-85; Kaiser fellow clin. epidemiology Brigham and Women's Hosp. and Harvard Sch. Pub. Health, 1984-85; rsch. fellow Nat. Heart, Lung, and Blood Inst., Bethesda, Md., 1985-91; vis. scientist Scripps Inst. Medicine and Sci., LaJolla, Calif., 1991-92; chief cardiology, T.R. and M. O'Driscoll Levy prof. medicine U. Tex. Med. Sch., Houston, 1994—; chief cardiology Hermann Hosp., Houston, 1994—; assoc. dir. cardiol. rsch. Tex. Heart Inst. and St. Luke's Episc. Hosp., Houston, 1992—; med. dir. U. Tex. Telemedicine; founder Prizm Pharms., La Jolla, 1992—; cons. FDA, Advanced Rsch. Project Agy., NASA, NIH, VA. Mem. editl. bd. Circulation, 1992—, Am. Jour. Cardiology, 1992—, Tex. Heart Inst. Jour., 1992—, Vascular Medicine, 1995—, U.T. Lifetime Newsletter, 1996—; contbr. numerous articles to profl. jours. Mem. Am. Heart Assn. (Houston bd. dirs. 1992-96), Am. Fedn. Clin. Rsch., Am. Soc. Cell Biology, Soc. Vascular Biol. Medicine (bd. dirs.), Houston Cardiology Soc. (pres. 1995-96), Am. Coll. Cardiology, Assn. Univ. Cardiologists, Assn. Profs. of Cardiology, Chevy Chase (Md.) Club, Union Boat Club (Boston), Vicmead Hunt Club, Farmington Country Club (Charlottesville, Va.), City Tavern Club (Washington). Office: U Tex Med Sch 6431 Fannin St Houston TX 77030-1501

CASSEL, JOHN ELDEN, accountant; b. Verden, Okla., Apr. 24, 1934; s. Elbert Emry and Erma Ruth (McDowell) C.; m. Mary Lou Malcom, June 3, 1953; children—John Elden, James Edward, Jerald Eugene. Plant mgr., also asst. gen. mgr. Baker and Taylor Co., Oklahoma City, 1966-71; paymaster, office mgr. Robberson Steel Co., Oklahoma City, 1971-76; pvt. investor, 1976—. Democrat. Methodist. Home: 2332 NW 118th St Oklahoma City OK 73120-7404

CASSELL, ROBERT BERNARD, council executive; b. Chattanooga, Tenn., Feb. 16, 1918; s. Samuel and Kathryn Gwendolyn (Lesser) C.; m. Vylva Holland, May 27, 1943 (dec. Jan. 1984); 1 child, Robert H.; m. Angela Vandoren, June 20, 1987. BA, U. Chattanooga, 1937; MA, Vanderbilt U., 1938. Cert. econ. developer. Sr. indsl. developer, dir. rsch. Tenn. Indsl. & Agrl. Devel. Commn., Nashville, 1946-60; prin. rsch. scientist Ga. Inst. Tech., Atlanta, 1960-81; exec. dir. So. Econ. Devel. Coun., Atlanta, 1967-93; v.p. Am. Travel Network, Atlanta, 1988-95. Author: Evaluating Economic Development Programs, 1982, Community Economic Development, 1981, Economic Analysis of Appalachian Georgia, 1980; editor Georgia Development News, 1962-75; contbr. articles to profl. jours. Cpl. U.S. Army, 1942-46. Recipient Award for Professionalism, Ga. Indsl. Developers, 1984, Outstanding Svc. award Ga. Tech. Rsch. Inst., 1992. Mem. Am. Econ. Devel. Coun. (pres. 1971, Ednl. Merit award 1986, Spl. Recognition Ednl. Indsl. Devel. award 1975), Ga. Indsl. Developers Assn., So. Econ. Devel. Coun. (pres. 1968). Home: 3599 Greystone Cir Atlanta GA 30341-5856

CASSENS, SUSAN FORGET, artist; b. Ft. Pierce, Fla., May 11, 1956; d. Louis Conrad and Joan Hancock Forget; m. Steven Dale Cassens, Mar. 4, 1979; children: Christopher, Michael, Scott. AA, U. Fla., 1976; BA in Edn. with honors, Fla. Atlantic U., 1978. Tchr. Garden City Elem., Ft. Pierce, 1978-79; owner Brush Strokes Art Gallery, Ft. Pierce, 1993-95; co-owner Indian River Crafters Guild, Ft. Pierce, 1995—; bd. mem. St. Lucie County Cultural Affairs Coun., Ft. Pierce, 1993, chair, 1996—. Cover artist: Cracker Cuisine, 1993; exhbns. include A.E. Backus Gallery, Ft. Pierce, Treasure Coast Art Gallery, Ft. Pierce. Chpt. sec. Philanthropic Ednl. Orgn., Ft. Pierce, 1987, chpt. pres., 1989; mem. Vero Beach Ctr. for the Arts, A.E. Backus Art Gallery, Mainstreet (Ft. Pierce) Inc., St. Lucie Hist. Soc.; chair St. Lucie Mural Soc., Ft. Pierce, 1994. Mem. Nat. Mus. of Women in the Arts (charter mem.), Vero Beach Art Club, Heathcote Botanical Gardens (charter mem.). Presbyterian. Home: PO Box 593 Fort Pierce FL 34954-0593 Office: Indian River Crafters Guild 201 N 2nd St Fort Pierce FL 34950-4407

CASSIBRY, FRED JAMES, lawyer, retired federal court judge; b. D'Lo, Miss., Sept. 26, 1918; s. Reginald E. and Lelia (Garner) C.; m. Lorraine E. Patterson, Dec. 21, 1940; 1 dau., Elizabeth; m. Muriel D. Belsome, Feb. 13, 1974; 1 dau., Cathryn. BA, Tulane U., 1941, LLB, 1943. Bar: La. 1944. Pvt. practice New Orleans, 1947-61, 87-94; mem. firms Cassibry & Zengel, 1946-47, Dymond & Cassibry, 1950-55, Cassibry, Jackson & Hess, 1955-61; judge Civil Dist. Ct., Parish of Orleans, 1961-66, U.S. Dist. Ct., Eastern Dist. La., 1966-87; ptnr. Brook Morial Cassibry Pizza and vanLoon, New Orleans, 1987-94; bd. dirs. La. Econ. Devel. and Gaming Corp., New Orleans; mem. com. on jud. ethics La. Supreme Ct., 1965-66; instr. fed. procedure Tulane U., 1975. Mem. city council, New Orleans, 1954-60; mem. bd. commrs. New Orleans City Park, 1962-68; Del. Democratic Nat. Conv., 1956. Served from ensign to lt. (j.g.) USNR, 1944-46. Recipient Disting. Am. award Nat. Football Found. and Hall of Fame, 1988; named to Tulane U. Athletic Hall of Fame, 1988. Mem. ABA, Fed. Bar Assn., La. Bar Assn., New Orleans Bar Assn., La. Dist. Judges Assn. (pres. 1963), U.S. 5th Cir. Dist. Judges Assn. (pres. 1974-75), Tulane U. Alumni Assn. (mem. exec. com. 1962-65, Outstanding Law Alumnus award 1976), Blue Key, Order of Coif (hon.), Sigma Chi. Home: 734 Crystal St New Orleans LA 70124-3608

CASSIDY, DOROTHY ANN, special education educator; b. Burke County, N.C., July 1, 1947; d. Roscoe and Mary Etta Junie (Spakes) Pruitt; m. Kenneth Howard Cassidy, Dec. 21, 1970 (div. Dec. 1981); 1 child, Kenneth Wayne. BA in Polit. Sci., U.N.C., 1970; MEd in Spl. Edn., U. Va., 1982; postgrad., U.S.C., 1986—. Homebound tchr. Pittsylvania County Schs., Chatham, Va., 1975-79, learning disabilities, resource tchr., 1979-82; county resource thcr. Brunswick County Schs., Southport, N.C., 1982-85; tchr. learning disabilities and visually impaired Horry County Schs., Conway, S.C., 1985—, self-contained experimental tchr., 1994—. Recipient awards tchr. incentive program S.C. Bd. Edn., 1988-90; scholar Rotary Club, Myrtle Beach, S.C., 1991. Mem. NEA, Coun. Exceptional Children(divsn. learning disabilities, divsn. vidually handicapped, divsn. internat. spl. edn. and svcs.), Assn. Children with Learning Disabilities, Orton Dyslexia Soc., S.C. Edn. Assn., Horry county Edn. Assn., Meher Spiritual Ctr. Democrat. Methodist. Home: 2406 Bert Dr North Myrtle Beach SC 29582-4322

CASSIDY, TERRENCE PATRICK, JR., engineering consultant; b. Honolulu, May 21, 1964; s. Terrence Patrick Sr. and Lorraine C. BS Marine Engring., U.S. Merchant Marine Acad., 1987. Third asst. engr. Crowley Maritime, Ft. Lauderdale, Fla., 1987-89; second asst. engr. D2-Meba-Amo, Dania, Fla., 1989-91, first asst. engr., 1991-92; project engr. Spectec Gen., Irvine, Calif., 1991; sr. project engr., corp. sec. Impact Engring., Inc., Ft. Lauderdale, 1992—; v.p. Impact Engring. Inc., 1995—, also bd. dirs.; corp. sec. Impact Engring. Equipment, Inc., Ft. Lauderdale, 1993—, v.p., 1995—; also bd. dirs. Impact Engring. Equipment, Inc.; chief fin. officer Qualtair, Inc., Seattle, 1994-95; bd. dirs. Qualtair, Inc. Lt. USNR. Mem. Soc. Naval Architects and Marine Engrs., Nat. Assn. Self-Employed, Nat. Fedn. Ind. Bus. Republican. Roman Catholic. Office: Impact Engring Inc 1511 E Commercial Blvd Ste 2 Fort Lauderdale FL 33334-5717

CASTAGNA, WILLIAM JOHN, federal judge. Student, U. Pa., 1941-43; LLB, JD, U. Fla., 1949. Bar: Fla. 1949. Sole practice Morehead, Pallot & Forrest, Miami, 1949-50; pvt. practice Clearwater, 1951-53, 54-65, 69; assoc. Castagna & Satterfield, Clearwater, 1951-53, Castagna, Satterfield & Stamathis, Clearwater, 1953, Castagna & Korones, 1965-68; ptnr. MacKenzie, Castagna, Bennison & Gardner, 1970-79; judge U.S. Dist. Judge (mid. dist.) Fla., 1979—, now sr. judge. Democrat.

CASTALDI, FRANK JAMES, environmental engineer, consultant; b. Elizabeth, N.J., May 24, 1947; s. Frank James and Anita (Arditi) C.; m. Keerocha Srithavatch, July 2, 1981; 1 child, Ann Elizabeth. BS in Civil Engring., N.J. Inst. Tech., 1969; ME in Environ. Engring., Manhattan Coll., Bronx, N.Y., 1971; PhD in Civil (Environ.) Engring., U. Tex., 1976. Registered profl. engr., Tex. Engr. Alexander Potter Assocs., N.Y.C., 1969; rsch. assoc. Manhattan Coll., 1969-71; design engr. Buck, Seifert and Jost Engrs., Englewood Cliffs, N.J., 1971-72; rsch. asst. U. Tex., Austin, 1972-76; project mgr., engr. Engring. Sci., Inc., Austin, 1976-84; sr. engr. Radian Corp., Austin, 1984-86, sr. staff engr., group leader, 1986-90, prin. engr., 1990—; chmn. Synfuels Wastewater Biotreatment Workshop Morgantown (W.Va.) Energy Tech. Ctr., 1983. Co-author: Applied Biotechnology for Site Remediation, 1994, Microbial Processes for Bioremediation, 1995; patentee in field. Mem. ASCE, Water Environ. Fedn., Internat. Assn. Water Quality, Air and Waste Mgmt. Assn. Roman Catholic. Office: Radian Internat LLC 8501 N Mopac Blvd Austin TX 78759

CASTALNO, PAUL C., theatre educator, author; b. Hartford, Conn., May 19, 1950; s. Rowe A. and Marion (Macdonald) C.; m. Molly McKeown, Dec. 16, 1989; children: Andrew, Peter. BFA, U. Conn., 1972; MFA, Stanford U., 1973; PhD in Theatre, Ohio State U., 1989. Dir. new playwrights program U. Ala., Tuscaloosa, 1989—, head MFA Playwrighting Dramatizing program, 1989—; editor theatre symposium U. Ala. Press, 1993-96; chair new play project SETC, 1990-93. Author: The Early Commedia dell Arte, 1994, Playwriting 2000, 1996; editor: Voice of the Dramaturg, 1995, Theatrical Spare and Dramatic Place, 1996; author jour. articles. Lilly fellow, 1990-91; NEH fellow, 1994. Mem. MLA, Am. Soc. Theatre Rsch., Assn. Theatre in Higher Edn., So. Writers Project. Office: U Ala Dept Theatre 115 RJ Tuscaloosa AL 35487

CASTEEL, DIANN BROWN, elementary school educator; b. Greeneville, Tenn., Dec. 16, 1953; d. Harold James Brown and Clara Ruth (Phillips) Johnston; m. Everette Kenneth Casteel, Oct. 7, 1972; children: Trisha DiAnn, Mary Camille, Cheyenne James. BS, East Tenn. State U., 1973, MA, 1976, EdD, 1994. Cert. tchr., Tenn. Tchr. Greene County Bd. Edn., Greeneville, 1973-90; dir. Project Choice, Greeneville-Greene County Ctr. for Tech., 1990-91; tchr. Doak Sch., Tusculum Sta., Tenn., 1992—; founder Iowa-Tenn. Student Exch. Program, Dayton and Greeneville, 1986-87; secondary educator, evening instr. Tusculum Coll., Greenville, Tenn., Guidance and Assessment for Single Parent/Displaced Homemaker Program, 1989-90. Founder, conor Hay Relief Program, Tenn., 1986-87; leader 4-H Club, Baileyton Elem. Sch., 1985-88; mem. Ottway United Meth. Ch., Greenville, 1985-92; v.p. Ottway United Meth. Women, Greeneville, pres., 1976; mem. women's group study exch. to India, Rotary Internat., 1989; mem. 1st Christian Ch., Greenville, Tenn., 1992—. Recipient Horse of Yr. award Appalachian Horse Show Assn., 1967, Outstanding Citizen award Ruritan Nat., 1986, 4-H Emerald Club Leader award, 1987, DIANA award Epsilon Sigma Alpha, 1990, Book of Golden Deeds award Greeneville (Tenn.) Exchange Club, 1992. Mem. NEA, Greene County Edn. Assn., East Tenn. Edn. Assn., Tenn. Edn. Assn., Internat. Platform Assn., U.S.S. Greenville, Inc., Kappa Delta Pi, Phi Delta Kappa. Democrat. Home: 2545 Flatwoods Rd Greeneville TN 37745-8582 Office: Chuckey Elem Sch 1605 Chuckey Hwy Chuckey TN 37641

CASTEEN, JOHN THOMAS, III, university president; b. Portsmouth, Va., Dec. 11, 1943; s. John Thomas and Naomi Irene (Anderson) C.; children: John Thomas IV, Elizabeth, Lars. BA with high honors, U. Va., 1965, MA, 1966, PhD, 1970; LLD, Shenandoah Coll. and Conservatory Music, 1984; DHL, Bentley Coll., 1992; hon. degree, Piedmont (Va.) C.C., 1992; DPA, Bridgewater Coll., 1993; D honoris causa, U. Athens, Greece, 1996. Asst. prof. English U. Calif., Berkeley, 1970-75; assoc. prof., dean admissions U. Va., Charlottesville, 1975-82; adj. prof. Va. Commonwealth U., Richmond, 1982-85; prof. English, pres. U. Conn., Storrs, 1985-90; pres. U. Va., 1990—, George M. Kaufman presdl. prof., prof. of English, 1990—; bd. dirs. Am. Coun. on Edn., Jefferson Bankshares, Inc., Nellie Mae, Connie Lee, Inc., Allied Concrete Co. Author: 16 Stories, 1981; contbr. articles to various publs. Sec. edn. Commonwealth of Va., Richmond, 1982-85; trustee Mariner's Mus., 1990—, Coll. Entrance Exam Bd., N.Y.C., 1980-90, chmn. 1986-88; mem. So. Regional Edn. Bd., 1982-85. New Eng. Bd. of Higher Edn., 1986-90; mem. nat. adv. com. Nat. Domestic Violence Media Campaign, 1992—. Mem. So. Assn. Colls. and Schs. (chair commn. on colls. 1995, 96), Assn. Governing Bds. Colls. and Schs. (coun. of pres. 1992—), Raven Soc. (Raven award, Outstanding Virginian 1993), Keswick Club, Farmington County Club, Commonwealth Club (Richmond), Phi Beta Kappa. Episcopalian. Office: U Va Office of Pres Madison Hall PO Box 9011 Charlottesville VA 22906-9011

CASTERLOW, GILBERT, JR., mathematics educator; b. Rich Square, N.C., Oct. 28, 1948; s. Gilbert and Juanita (Joyner) C.; m. Patricia Ann Vaughan, June 2, 1979; children: Bonita K., Laveda M., Marguita V. BS in Math. Edn., N.C. A&T State U., Greensboro, 1970, MS in Math. Edn., 1971; PhD in Curriculum and Instrn., Pa. State U., State College, 1980. Grad. asst. N.C. A&T State U., Greensboro, 1970-71, instr. math., 1971-77, math/computer edn. coord., 1980—, math. cons., 1984—, assoc. prof., 1986-91, prof., 1991—; adj. instr. Bennett Coll., Greensboro, 1973-74, Winston Salem (N.C.) State U., 1981-83; grad. asst. Pa. State U., State College, 1977-80; math. edn. coord. Saturday Acad. Program, Greensboro, 1981-94; bd. dirs., 1994—; math. edn. coord. Greensboro Area Math. and Sci. Edn. Ctr., 1984—; math. edn. cons. Bennington Corp., SDPI, Greensboro Coll., 1980—; presenter various local, state & nat. confs.; bd. govs. U. N.C. System. Co-author: The AM-BC Saturday Academy, 1988; contbr. articles to profl. jours.; condr. rsch. in the use of calculators, computers and other technologies to enhance math. instruction. Vol. Greensboro-Guilford County Area Schs., 1970—, Income Tax Assistance Program, Greensboro, 1980—; pres., v.p., chmn. Gen. Greene and Lincoln Mid. Schs. and Dudley H.S., Greensboro, 1985—; mem., tutor, Sunday sch. tchr., trustee East White Oak Bapt. Ch., Greensboro, 1992—. Recipient Excellence in Teaching award U. N.C. Bd. Gov's., 1996; several funded grants, numerous appreciation and svc. awards from schs. and orgns. Mem. NAACP, ASCD, Math. Assn. Am. (regional rep. 1986—), Nat. Coun. Tchrs. Math. (testbook reviewer 1988—), N.C. Coun. Tchrs. Math. (v.p. colls. 1985-87, pres. Ctrl. Region 1993-95, W.W. Rankin Meml. award for excellence in math. edn. 1994), Am. Bowling Congress, Greater Greensboro Bowling Assn., Triad Scratch Bowling League (pres.), Kappa Delta Pi (Presdl. Excellence award 1977), Pi Mu Epsilon, Phi Delta Kappa, Alpha Kappa Mu. Democrat. Baptist. Home: 4229 Queen Beth Dr Greensboro NC 27405-6360 Office: NC AT&T U Dept Math Marteena Hall Greensboro NC 27411

CASTILLO, ANGEL, JR., lawyer; b. Havana, Cuba, Nov. 29, 1946; came to U.S., 1960; s. Angel and Graciela (Blanco) C. m. Stormie G. Stafford, Dec. 16, 1977; children: Arielle Caridad, Angel Marti. BA, Stetson U., 1968; JD with high honors, U. Fla., 1978; LLM, Yale U., 1980. Bar: Fla. 1979, U.S. Supreme Ct. 1982. Various positions in pub. and journalism, 1968-80; legal affairs reporter The N.Y. Times, N.Y.C., 1980-81; assoc. Shutts & Bowen, Miami, Fla., 1981-83; sr. assoc. Morgan, Lewis & Bockius, Miami, 1983-86; ptnr. Soto & Castillo, Miami, 1987-89, Castillo, Stafford & Wald, Miami, 1989—; exec. asst. to chmn. Ways and Means Com., Fla. Senate, Tallahassee, 1978-79; mem. jud. nominating com. Fla.Dist. Ct. Appeal (3d dist.), 1992-95. Exec. editor U. Fla. Law Rev., 1978. Del. Creative Crime Control Conf., Fla., 1982. Mem. ABA, Dade County Bar Assn. (chmn. internat. law com.), Cuban-Am. Bar Assn., Hispanic Nat. Bar Assn., Inter-Am. Bar Assn., Order of Coif, Phi Kappa Phi. Office: Castillo Stafford & Wald 1320 S Dixie Hwy Ste 450 Miami FL 33146-2925

CASTILLO, TOMAS FRANKLIN, secondary school educator; b. Havana, Cuba, Sept. 5, 1959; came to U.S., 1959; s. Franklin Tomas and Bertalina (Reyes) C.; m. Yolanda Lucille Castro, Sept. 22, 1990; children: Nicole Jennifer, Jessica Casey. BS, Springhill Coll., Mobile, Ala., 1981; MS in Edn., U. Miami, Coral Gables, Fla., 1992. Cert. tchr. biology, chemistry, gifted, Fla. Rsch. scientist asst. U. Miami/Coulter Diagnostics, 1982-83, Dept. Pharm., U. South Ala., Mobile, 1983-85; sales rep. Mario's Castings/Met. Life, Miami, 1985-86; 1st aid/CPR instr. ARC, Miami, 1987-92; tchr. math, English, computers PSI Inst. of Miami, 1988-90; tchr. sci. Homestead (Fla.) Mid. Sch., 1990-91, S.W. Miami Sr. H.S., Miami, 1991—; tutor sci. and math. Tutoring Assocs., Miami, 1992—; union steward United Tchrs. of dade, Miami, 1992-95; tchr. edn. rep. Tchr. Ednl. Ctr., Miami, 1991—. Committeeman Rep. Party of Dade County, Miami, 1995-96; baptism instr. St. Augustine's Cath. Ch., Coral Gables, Fla., 1993-95. Lance cpl. USMC, 1986-92. NIH grantee, 1992, NSF grantee, 1993; Woodrow Wilson fellow, 1994; recipient NEWMAST award NASA/Nat. Sci. tchrs. Assn., 1996, Leadership Miami, Greater Miami C. of C., 1990. Mem. Southwest Faculty Assn. (pres. 1994-95), Marine Corps League (adj. paymaster 1988-91, jr. vice comdt./sr. vice comdt. 1992-94, unit comdt. 1996-97), Young Marines of Dade (trainer, exec. officer 1987-94), KC (rec. sec. 1984-86, dir. family activities). Home: 14600 SW 122d Pl Miami FL 33186

CASTLE, VERNON CHARLES, recording company executive; b. Whitewater, Wis., May 17, 1931; s. Erwin Ellesworth and Anne Bertha (Nelson) C.; B.Ed., U. Wis., Whitewater, 1951; m. Mary Lou Hill, Mar. 19, 1983. Profl. entertainer, musician, 1956-65; pres. Castle Prodns., Inc., Lake Geneva, Wis., 1966-79, Castle Rec., 1972-78, Recreational Recs., Ltd., 1972-77, 81-82; leader Last Dance Band, 1980-92; broadcast advt. cons., 1979-92; contr. Mary Castle Co. Ltd., 1986-89. Served with Adj. Gen. Corps, U.S. Army, 1952-55. Mem. Am. Small Bus. Assn. (exec. dir. 1992-96).

CASTLEBERRY ROBERTS, SHARON ELAINE, business consultant; b. Knoxville, Tenn., Mar. 6, 1954; d. Claude Benson and Margaret Leah (Clabough) Castleberry; children: Shaun Kory Roberts, Kimberly Castle Roberts. Student, U. Tenn., Knoxville, Roane State C.C.; ABS in Acctg., Knoxville Bus. Coll., 1976; BS in Applied Orgnl. Mgmt., Tusculum Coll., 1994. Acct. Koppers Co., Inc., Oak Ridge, Tenn., 1982-83, Helen Ross McNabb Ctr., Knoxville, 1983-85; cons., pvt. contractor Cherokee Mental Health Ctr., Morristown, Tenn., 1986; v.p., co-owner Roberts Enterprises, Inc., Oak Ridge, 1985-88; bus. mgr. Planned Parenthood of East Tenn., Inc., Oak Ridge, 1988-90; v.p. of bus. devel. Right Assocs., Knoxville, 1990—. Mem. Venture Exchange Forum (mem. exec. com.), NOW, Rotary. Home: 467 Bramblewood Ln Knoxville TN 37922 Office: Right Assocs 1111 Northshore Dr NW Knoxville TN 37919-4005

CASTLE-HASAN, ELIZABETH E., religious organization administrator; b. Balt., Nov. 1, 1950; d. John Thomas and Elizabeth Eliza (Wilson) Castle; m. Osborne Samuel James, Jr., Dec. 20, 1980 (div. Nov. 1993); children: Claudia C. Boulware, Richsharia D. Boulware, Kurtson E. Boulware, Curtis R. Boulware II; m. Edward N. Hasan, Dec. 12, 1994. AA in Criminal Justice, Valencia C.C., 1982; D of Systematic Theology (hon.), Interdenominational Theol. Sem. and Coll. of Theism, 1990; student, Love of God Theol. Sem., 1996—. Account exec. Sta. WEBB, Balt., 1975-77; liaison coord. Balt. City Jail, 1977-79; case mgr. Health and Rehabilitative Svcs., Cocoa, Fla., 1980-88; CEO Yissakar Ministries, Gainesville, Fla., 1989-94, Jabbok Ministries, Gainesville, 1991-94, Resurrected Life Ministries, Inc., Sarasota, Fla., 1994—; pres. The House of Bavaka (formerly, The House of La E'Shika), Sarasota, 1992—; CEO Resurrected Life Ministries Inc., 1994—, HEAT Ministries, 1996; bd. dirs. Jay Ministries, West Palm Beach, Fla., 1993. Author: The Prophet's Fast, 1996; co-author: Reflections in Lace, 1992; author: (poetry) Power, 1990 (honorary mention 1990); columnist, religious editor Mahogany Revue, Ocala, Fla., 1992-93; author short story, 1987 (honorary mention 1987); contbr. articles to newspaper. Chairperson com. for Aged and Disabled Persons, Gainesville, 1993, Sarasota Employment and Econ. Devel., 1996; chmn. grant com. Student Adv. Com. of Howard Bishop Mid. Sch., Gainesville, 1993; candidate City Commr. Dist. I, Gainesville, 1993, 95; mem. leadership bd. Sarasota County Coalition for the Homeless, 1994—, mem. exec. bd., 1995; mem. exec. com. Democratic Club, Sarasota, 1994; pres., bd. dirs. Family Self-Sufficiency Project, Sarasota, 1994—; cmty. liasion for Newtown Task Force; bd. dirs. Common Ground Cmty. Assn.; mem. Nat. Coalition Neighborhood Women. Recipient 1st Willie Bruton award U. Ctrl. Fla., 1982, Dr. Martin L. King scholarship, 1982. Mem. NAFE, Nat. Coalition of Neighborhood Women, God's Women of Power (pres. 1993), Gainesville Women's Network, Royal Venice Assn., Phi Beta Kappa, Chi Epsilon. Democrat. Office: Venice Housing Authority PO Box 49796 Sarasota FL 34230-6796

CASTLEMAN, TONYA KAY, journalist; b. Flint, Mich., June 15, 1964; d. Thomas Earl and Kay Janis (Corey) Snowball; m. Byron Thomas Castleman, July 29, 1985 (div. 1995); 1 child, Naomi Michelle. BA in Mass Communications, U. South Fla., 1987. Art specialist U.S. DOD Schs., Fort Davis, Panama, 1986-87; corr. St. Petersburg (Fla.) Times, 1987, copy editor II, 1995-96; tchr. English as a second lang. Colegio Internat., Del Caribe, Panama, 1987-88; sect. editor Fort Campbell (Ky.) Courier, 1989-90; copy editor Ky. New Era, Hopkinsville, 1991-93, Insight Mag., Washington, 1993-94; news editor Washington Times Weekly, 1994-95; freelance journalist Palmetto, Fla., 1996—. Illustrator: Puzzles for Kids By Kids, 1978; contbr.: Word Puzzles for Kids, 1978, Puzzles for Kids By Kids, 1978. Active dist. communications Cogioba dist. Boy Scouts Am., Clarksville, Tenn., 1990, explorer's leader journalism, 1990. Gov. honors scholar Eckerd Coll., 1981; recipient 1st place award Picnic With the Pops Pennyroyal Arts Coun., 1993; newswriting and editing fellow Poynter Inst. for Media Studies, 1983. Mem. AAUW, Soc. Profl. Journalists, Kappa Delta (parliamentarian Delta Eta chpt. 1985). Republican. Jewish. Home: 1503 Lantana Ct Palmetto FL 34221

CASTNER, NANCY MILLER, ambulatory services nurse; b. Dayton, Ohio, Oct. 1, 1947; d. Ernest Richard and Constance Lee (Allison) Miller; m. Lee Castner, Dec. 28, 1985 (dec. 1989); children: John, Mark. Diploma in nursing, Jackson Meml. Hosp. Sch., 1968; BSN, Tenn. State U., 1984; MSN, Vanderbilt U., 1989. RN, Tenn.; cert. ACLS Am. Heart Assn., cert. trauma nurse core curriculum Emergency Nurses Assn., CEN Emergency Nurses Assn. Staff nurse CCU St. Mary's Hosp., Knoxville, Tenn., 1968-72; staff nurse CCU, ambulatory svcs. Vanderbilt Hosp., Nashville, 1974-81; patient edn. nurse West Side Hosp., Nashville, 1981-86; nurse, cons. Am. Healthcorp, Nashville, 1986-87; staff nurse ambulatory svcs. VA Hosp., Nashville, 1987—; trainer, leader self-help course Arthritis Found., Nashville, 1981—; guest lectr. rheumatology nursing Vanderbilt U., 1984-91, nurse practitioner preceptor, 1990—; rheumatology nurse cons. Vanderbilt Health Care Rsch., Nashville, 1984-91. Contbr. articles to profl. publs. Recipient Vol. of Yr. award Mid-East Tenn. div. Arthritis Found., 1983, Nat. Vol. award, 1983, award for excellence in nursing VA So. Region, 1991. Mem. Arthritis Found. (regional chair pub. edn. 1980-83, bd. dirs. 1980-85, 86-88), Arthritis Health Professions Assn. (region rep. 1981-82, pres. 1982), Emergency Nurses' Assn., Sigma Theta Tau. Republican. Roman Catholic. Home: 1101 Davidson Rd Nashville TN 37205-1025 Office: Nashville VA Med Ctr 1310 24th Ave S Nashville TN 37212-2637

CASTOR, BETTY, academic administrator. Pres. Univ. South Fla., Tampa. *

CASTOR, CAROL JEAN, artist, teacher; b. Bend, Oreg., Feb. 3, 1944; d. Keith and Lena (Morara) Morrison; 1 child, William Franklin. BFA, U. Okla., 1967; postgrad., U. Tulsa, summer 1976, Art Student's League of N.Y., N.Y.C., summer 1984. Dir. art dept. Jefferson Jr. High Sch., Oklahoma City, 1967-68; art instr. Vinita (Okla.) High Sch., 1976-80; profl. artist specializing in commd. portraiture Carol Castor Art Studio, Vinita, 1980—, profl. artist commd. for portraits of Native Ams. & Cowboys, 1980—; maintains Window Gallery on Mainstreet Vinita; Mem. bd. dirs. Craig Gen. Hosp., 1995—. Represented in permanent collections at Vinita Pub. Libr., Craig Gen. Hosp., Vinita, 1st Nat. Bank & Trust, Vinita, Cowgirl Hall of Fame and Western Heritage Ctr., Ft. Worth, Okla. Hall of Fame, Oklahoma City, Okla. U. Med. Sch., Oklahoma City, Oklahoma U. Law Sch., Norman, Okla. U. Pharmacy Sch., Oklahoma City; featured in 2nd edit. of American Artists: An Illustrated Survey of Leading Contemporaries; portraits represented by Grand Ctrl. Galleries, N.Y. Mem. Mayor's Adv. Com., Vinita, 1972-74; mem. bldg. com. Vinita Pub. Libr., 1974-75; charter mem. Vinita chpt. Okla. Alliance for Mentally Ill, 1986—; organizer, mem. com. Young Life, Vinita, 1987—; mem. com. for chronically and mentally ill Vinita Day Ctr. Inc., 1987—; organizer Ea. Trails Art Assn., 1972—; bd. dirs. Craig Gen. Hosp., 1995—. Recipient Cmty. Svc. award Vinita C. of C., 1984, named to Hall of Fame, 1993. Mem. AAUW (pres. Vinita chpt. 1972-74, Best banner award nat. conv. 1979, Women of Achievement award 1985), P.E.O., Am. Soc. Portrait Artists. Democrat. Episcopalian. Home and Studio: 121 Jennie Ln Vinita OK 74301

CASWELL, JEFFRY CLAXTON, financial executive; b. Columbia, S.C., June 8, 1959; s. Lewis Milton and Sylvia Naomi (Davis) C. BS in Acctg., U. S.C., 1982. Acctg. supr. Richland Meml. Hosp., Columbia, 1983-85, sr. acct., 1985-87; contr. Pacific Nuclear Systems Inc., Columbia, 1987-88; contr., chief fin. officer W.O. Blackstone & Co., Inc., Columbia, 1988-96; v.p. fin., adminstrn. W.O. Blackstone & Co., Inc., 5, 1996—. Campaign rep. United Way, Columbia, 1988-93. Mem. Inst. Mgmt. Accts., Contruction Fin. Mgrs. Assn. Republican. Home: 3618 Hanson Ave Columbia SC 29204 Office: WO Blackstone & Co Inc 425 Huger St Columbia SC 29201-5223

CATALAND, LOUIS S., lawyer; b. Columbus, Ohio, Jan. 22, 1966; s. Samuel and Penny (Parthemos) C. BS in Econs., U. Mich., 1988; JD, Ohio State U., 1991. Bar: Ohio 1991, Ga. 1994. Atty. Vorys Sater Seymour & Pease, Columbus, 1991-94, Kilpatrick & Cody, Atlanta, 1994-95, Fleming Drummond & Ray, Atlanta, 1995—. Mentor Midtown Bus. Alliance, Atlanta, 1994—. Mem. Columbus Bar Assn. Greek Orthodox. Home: 216 Berkeley Run Atlanta GA 30342 Office: Fleming Drummond & Ray 1360 Peachtree St Ste 930 Atlanta GA 30309

CATANESE, ANTHONY JAMES, academic administrator; b. New Brunswick, N.J., Oct. 18, 1942; s. Anthony James and Josephine Marlene (Barone) C.; m. Sara Jean Phillips, Oct. 23, 1968; children: Mark Anthony, Michael Scott, Mark Alexander. BA, Rutgers U., 1963; M in Urban Planning, NYU, 1965; PhD, U. Wis., 1968. Asst. prof. city planning Ga. Inst. Tech., Atlanta, 1967-78, assoc. prof., 1968-73, chmn. doctoral studies com., 1970-73; James A. Ryder prof. transp. and planning, dir. Ryder program in transp. U. Miami, Coral Gables, Fla., 1973-75; dean Sch. Architecture and Urban Planning U. Wis., Milw., 1975-82; prof. architecture and urban planning, provost Pratt Inst., N.Y.C., 1982-84; dean Coll. Architecture, U. Fla., Gainesville, 1984-89; pres. Fla. Atlantic U., Boca Raton, 1989—, pres., prof., 1990—; sr. Fulbright prof., Colombia, 1971-72; sr. cons. State of Wis., 1965-67, sr. planner State of N.J., 1963-67; pres. A. J. Catanese & Assocs., Inc., 1967—; mem. pres. commn. NCAA, 1991-93. Author: Scientific Methods of Urban Analysis, 1972, New Perspectives on Urban Transportatio Research, 1972, Systematic Planning-Theory and Applications, 1970, Planners and Local Politics: Impossible Dreams, 1973, Urban Transportation in South Florida, 1974, Personality, Politics and Planning, 1978, Introduction to Urban Planning, 1979, Introduction to Architecture, 1979, The Politics of Planning and Development, 1984, Uban Planning, 1988; contbr. articles to profl. jours. Chmn. Mid. DeKalb County Dem. Party, 1969-71, mem. 5th Congl. Dist. Dem. caucus, 1971; aide-de-camp Gov.'s Office, State of Ga., 1971-72; mem. Ga. Dunes Studies Commn., 1972-73; bd. dirs. Archtl. Rsch. Ctrs. Consortium, 1976—; mem. Urban Policy Task Force, Carter presdl. campaign, 1976, 80; pres. Park West Redevel. Corp., 1976-78; chmn. Milw. City Plan Commn., 1978-82; bd. dirs. Goals for Milw. 2000, 1978-82, Environ. Edn. Found. Fla.; chmn. Gainesville (Fla.) Planning Bd., 1986-89. With USAR, 1961-63. Recipient fellowships State of N.J. Act of 1927, 1962-63, Werner Hegemann Found., 1963-65, Wis. Alumni Rsch. Found., 1965-68, Richard King Mellon Trust, 1966-67, Ford Found., 1967, Nat. Endowment Arts, 1980. Mem. Am. Inst. Planners (bd. govs., v.p. 1971-74), Am. Inst. Cert. Planners (mem. exec. com. 1971-74), Am. Planning Assn., Transp. Rsch. Bd., Regional Sci. Assn., Am. Acad. Polit. and Social Scis., Assn. Coll. Schs. Planning, Heritage Club, Wycliff Club, Tower Club. Office: Fla Atlantic U 777 Glades Rd PO Box 3091 Boca Raton FL 33431-0991

CATANZARO, TONY, dancer; b. Bklyn.; s. Archie Achilles and Elvira (Alessandra) C.; 1 child, Maya Vanesa. Student, Performing Arts, N.Y.C., 1961-64. Artistic dir. Bay Ballet Theatre, Tampa, Fla., 1994-95; mem. dance panel Mass. Coun. for Arts and Humanities, 1978-80; mem. Com. for Pub. Action for Arts; mem. blue ribbon com. for Mass. arts lottery bill Spl. Commn. on Performing Arts; mem. hon. com. Dance/New Eng.; Am. team coach Varna Internat. Ballet Competition, 1994; staged first Nutcracker in Medellin, Colombia, 1995 (first nutcracker ever in S.A.). Appeared with modern dance cos. Paul Sanansardo Co., 1963-64, Pearl Lang Co., 1966-70, Norman Walker, 1963-70, Harkness Ballet Co. II, 1967, N.J. Ballet Co., 1968-69, Ala. Ballet Co., 1969, Boston Ballet Co., 1969-70, 73-76, Joffrey Ballet, 1970-73, Dennis Waynes Dancers, Boston, 1977-78, artistic dir., choreographer, Boston Ballet Ensemble, 1980-81; prin. dancer, Boston Ballet Co., 1980-82; artistic dir. Ballet Acad. of Miami, 1984—, Ballet Theatre of Miami, 1985—, Ballet Theatre of Miami Ensemble, 1989—; leading dance roles in (Broadway) Annie Get Your Gun, 1966, Golden Boy; London Palaedium, 1968. Team coach for Am. team Internat. Ballet Competition, Varna, Bulgaria, 1994. With USNG, 1967-70. Office: 1809 Ponce De Leon Blvd Miami FL 33134-4418

CATARSI, CHARLOTTE MARIE, pharmacist; b. Richmond, Va., Apr. 2, 1965; d. Louis Peter Catarsi Jr. and Patricia Ann (Crockett) Jenkins. Grad., Va. Commonwealth U., 1995. Ins. underwriter Progressive Ins., Richmond, 1985-88; pharmacy technician Bellevue Pharmacy, Richmond, 1988-95; pharmacist Bellevue Pharmacy, 1995—. Mem. Am. Pharm. Assn., Am. Soc. Health System Pharmacists, Phi Delta Chi. Republican. Baptist. Office: 4038 Macarthur Ave Richmond VA 23227-4051

CATASUS, JOSE MAGIN PEREZ, school psychologist; b. Santiago, Oriente, Cuba, Jan. 18, 1942; came to U.S., 1960; s. Magin Perez and Teresa (Losada) C.; m. Carol Lee Getty, Sept. 15, 1962 (div. Nov. 30, 1967); 1 child, Magin Scott; m. Lina Teresa Jubran, Nov. 13, 1982; children: Cristina Teresa, Adam Benjamin. AA, Miami-Dade Jr. Coll., 1971; BS, Fla. Internat. U., 1974, MS, 1976; PhD, Fla. State U., 1981. Cert. sch. psychologist, Fla. Med. technologist Quillian & Assocs., Coral Gables, Fla., 1965-74; screening specialist Dade County Schs., Miami, 1974-76; psychometrist Med. Psychiatric Ctr., Miami, 1974-77; specialist sch. psychology Palm Beach County Schs., W. Palm Beach, Fla., 1977-78; clin. instr. Fla. Internat. U., Miami, 1980-81, visiting instr., 1981-82; vis. instr. U. Fla., Gainesville, 1982-83; lead sch. psychologist Alachua County Schs., Gainesville, 1983—; cons. in field; adv. com. mem. Vocat. Edn. Fla. Internat. U., Miami, 1981-82. Founder Psychol. Svcs. Grad. Student Assn., Miami, 1975; coord. guest speakers XVI InterAm. Congress of Psychology, Miami, 1976; bd. dirs. Hispanic Human Resource Coun., West Palm Beach, 1977-78. Recipient Doctoral Fellowship Fla. State U., 1978. Mem. Nat. Assn. Sch. Psychologists, Fla. Assn. Sch. Psychologists, Fla. Soc. for Med. Technology. Democrat. Roman Catholic. Home: 6800 NW 26th Pl Gainesville FL 32606-6339 Office: Alachua County Schs Psychoednl Svcs 620 E University Ave Gainesville FL 32601-5448

CATE, CATHERINE ELEANOR, college administrator, educator; b. Knoxville, Tenn., Nov. 27, 1968; d. Robert William and Carolyn Alice (Milligan) Pounders; m. Mark Edwin Cate, Aug. 7, 1993. BA in Am. Studies, U. Tenn., 1990, MS in Higher Edn., 1992. Coord. student activities, residence hall dir. Maryville (Tenn.) Coll., 1990-93, dir. campus programs, 1993-96; asst. dean of students, 1996—; exptl. edn. facilitator Mountain Challenge, Maryville, 1992—. Tutor Adult Basic Edn., Blount County, Tenn., 1994—; bd. dirs. Haven House Shelter, Maryville, 1995—. Named one of Outstanding Coll. Students of Am., 1990, Outstanding Women of Am., 1991. Mem. Nat. Orientation Dirs. Assn., Assn. Student Judicial Affairs, So. Assn. Coll. Student Affairs. Democrat. Methodist. Office: Maryville Coll 502 E Lamar Alexander Pkwy Maryville TN 37804-5907

CATER, ALICE RUTH WALLACE, real estate educator, broker; b. Kilgore, Tex., June 16, 1935; d. Clarence C. and Mary Alice (Johnson) Wallace; m. Otis Earl Cater, Jr., Aug. 26, 1961 (dec. Sept. 1988); 1 child, Clarence Wallace. BBA, So. Meth. U., 1957; MBA, U. Tex., 1959. Lic. real estate broker, Tex. Instr. McNeese State U., Lake Charles, La., 1959-63; prof. No. Mich. U., Marquette, 1964-65, U. Guam, Agana, 1967-69; broker Cater Real Estate, Beaumont, Tex., 1971—; coord. real estate Lamar U., Beaumont, 1974—, instr. II, 1974-79; instr. III Lamar U., 1979-84, instr. IV, 1984—. Recipient Regents Merit award Lamar U., 1979, Pres.'s Leadership award, 1983, Teaching Excellence award, 1985, 87; rsch. grantee Tex. Real Estate Ctr., Tex. A&M U., 1974-79; named to Outstanding Young Women of Am., 1965. Mem. Am. Fin. Assn., Tex. Real Estate Tchrs. Assn. (charter, state pres. 1978-79, merit award 1982), Real Estate Educators Assn., Tex. Coll. Mgmt. Educators Assn., Tex. Assn. Coll. Tchrs., Sales and Mktg. Execs. Club, Lamar U. Women's Club. Methodist. Home: 5858 Meadow Way Beaumont TX 77707-1832 Office: Lamar U 4400 Martin Luther King Pkwy PO Box 10043 Beaumont TX 77710

CATES, DENNIS LYNN, education educator; b. Dallas, Nov. 25, 1946; s. Robert N. and Wanda June (Boyd) C.; m. Sue Anne Sadler, Aug. 9, 1975. BA, Tex. Tech U., 1968, MEd, 1976, EdD, 1986; MA, Sul Ross State U., 1981. Cert. secondary edn. tchr., deficient vision, learning disabilities, mental retardation, supervision, mid-mgmt., orientation and mobility instr. Tchr. Eagle Pass (Tex.) Ind. Sch. Dist., Beeville (Tex.) Ind. Sch. Dist., Levelland (Tex.) Ind. Sch. Dist.; teaching asst. Tex. Tech. U., Lubbock; asst.

prof. West Tex. State U., Canyon, 1986-89; asst. prof. U. S.C., Columbia, 1989-95, dir. Ctr. for Excellence in Spl. Edn. Tech., 1992-93; assoc. prof. Cameron U., Lawton, Okla., 1995—; presenter numerous profl. confs. Contbr. articles to profl. jours. Sgt. USAF, 1969-73. Consultation Tchrs. grantee, 1981-82. Mem. ASCD, AAUP, Nat. Coun. for Social Studies, Nat. Coun. Geographic Edn., Am. Assn. Mental Retardation, Internat. Assn. Spl. Edn., Am. Ednl. Rsch. Assn., Coun. for Exceptional Children (bd. dirs., constn. and elections com. of tchr. edn. divsn.), Assn. Edn. and Rehab. for Blind and Visually Impaired (bylaws com. Divsn. 17, newsletter editor Divsn. 3), Phi Delta Kappa. Office: Cameron U Dept Edn Lawton OK 73505

CATES, HAROLD THOMAS, aircraft and electronics company executive; b. Key West, Fla., Aug. 24, 1941; s. Joseph Livingston and Dorothy Louise (Whitehead) C.; m. Sue Cotton, Aug. 24, 1971; children: Harold Joseph, Kimberly Lisa, Andrew Franklin, Joseph Franklin, Robyn Marie, Erik Cotton. BSEE, Valparaiso U., 1963; MSEE, U. N.Mex., 1965, PhDEE, 1967. Registered profl. engr., Fla. Rsch. assoc. and asst. Bur. Engring. Rsch., U. N.Mex., Albuquerque, 1963-67, instr., asst. prof. elec. engring., 1967-68; rsch. asst. Kirtland AFB and Sandia Labs., Albuquerque, 1963-67; program dir., chief engr. Martin-Marietta Co., Orlando, Fla., 1968-87; v.p., asst. gen. mgr. E-Systems, Inc., Greenville, Tex., 1987-91; v.p. tech. ops. Martin Marietta, Orlando, Fla., 1991-92, v.p. fire control systems, lantirn program, 1992-93, v.p. fire control systems, 1993—; pres. Spectrum Engring., Testing & Cons., Key West, Fla., 1973—; vis. prof. Rollins Coll., Winter Park, Fla., Fla. Inst. Tech., Melbourne. Patentee process for preparing nuclear hardened semicondrs. and microelectronic devices. Mem. IEEE (sr.), Air Force Assn., Theta Chi, Sigma Chi. Home: 4085 Conway Place Cir Orlando FL 32812-7988 Office: Lockheed Martin Electronics & Missiles MP-540 5600 Sand Lake Rd Orlando FL 32819-8907

CATES, MARIAN WARD, Christian Science practitioner; b. Richmond, Va., Sept. 2, 1947; d. Mitchell Dresner and Marian Granville (Sharwood) C.; m. Carl Ray Schilt, Dec. 13, 1970 (div. 1980). BA, Hollins Coll., 1969, MA, 1979. Cert., Christian Sci. Bd. Edn. Tchr. St. Agnes Sch., Alexandria, Va., 1979-72; freelance writer Richmond, Va., 1983—; artistic dir. Green Alley Theater Co., Richmond, 1986-88; English instr. Va. Union U., Richmond, 1989-90; Christian Science practitioner Springfield, Va., 1988—. Contbr. articles to Christian Science jours. 1990--. Home: 7800-E Harrowgate Cir Springfield VA 22152-3805

CATLETT, JAMES STEPHEN, archivist, librarian; b. Laurinburg, N.C., Sept. 12, 1951; s. James Levi and Emilie Lucille (Bunch) C.; m. Leslie Wright Foushee, Aug. 21, 1971; children: Evan Bradshaw, Emilie Jean-Marie. BA in History, U. N.C., Greensboro, 1973, MA in History, 1975; MSLS, U. N.C., Chapel Hill, 1977. Asst. manuscripts libr. Am. Philos. Soc. Libr., Phila., 1977-78, manuscripts libr., 1980-86, assoc. libr., 1986; archivist Greensboro Hist. Mus., 1986—; lectr. dept. history U. N.C., Greensboro, 1989—; reviewer NEH, Washington, 1980. Author, editor: A New Guide to the Collections in the American Philosophical Society Library, 1987; author: Army Town: Greensboro, 1943-1946, 1994; contbr. numerous articles to profl. jours. Mem. Soc. Am. Archivists, Soc. N.C. Archivists (mem. exec. bd. 1989-90). Home: 2400 Walker Ave Greensboro NC 27403 Office: Greensboro Hist Mus 130 Summit Ave Greensboro NC 27401

CATO, JAMES ANTHONY, newspaper editor; b. Aug. 18, 1945; s. Gordon and Hazel Louise (Gheen) C.; m. Susan Delores Fairfax, Mar. 14, 1970; children: Jason Anthony, Justin Fairfax, Courtney Elizabeth. BA in Journalism, U. S.C., Columbia, 1972. Sports editor, photographer The Chester (S.C.) Reporter, 1969-71; asst. mng. editor The Lancaster (S.C.) News, 1973-74; editor The Field & Herald, Conway, S.C., 1974-77; exec. news editor The Index Jour., Greenwood, S.C., 1977-78; news editor The Sun News, Myrtle Beach, S.C., 1978-79, mng. editor, 1979-80; mng. editor The Beaufort (S.C.) Gazette, 1980, editor, 1980—. Alumnus Leadership S.C., Columbia, 1982; advisor student newspaper U. S.C., Beaufort, 1985—. Staff Sgt. U.S. Army, 1965-69, Vietnam. Mem. Am. Soc. Newspaper Editors, Nat. Conf. Editorial Writers, Nat. Newspaper Assn. (contest com. mem. 1977, 1st place award 1974), S.C. Press Assn. (chmn. weekly div. 1977, exec. com. 1984-86, bd. dirs., numerous 1st and 2nd place awards), S.C. Associated Press News Coun. (pres. 1987, 1st place award 1976, 3rd place award 1979), Rotary Club Port Royal (pres. 1993, Paul Harris fellow 1994). Episcopalian. Home: 2603 Ivy Ln Beaufort SC 29902-6424 Office: The Beaufort Gazette PO Box 399 Beaufort SC 29901-0399

CATO, SANDRA WARD, critical care nurse; b. Monroe, La., Apr. 27, 1962; d. Ralph Darrell and Gail Francis (Fleming) Ward; m. Bobby Wayne Cato, Apr. 29, 1983; children: Jake Edward, Jason Wayne. ADN, La. Tech. U., 1987. RN, La.; CCRN. Staff nurse med. ICU, St. Francis Med. Ctr., Monroe, 1987-88, staff nurse surg. ICU, 1989-90, charge nurse cardiovasc. recovery unit, 1991-93, unit coord., case mgr., 1993-95; cardiac nurse adminstr., 1995—. Named Outstanding Critical Care Nurse surg. ICU, St. Francis Med. Ctr., 1989. Mem. AACN. Home: 617 Northwood Dr West Monroe LA 71291-1684

CATRON, JAMES OTIS, college counseling administrator, social science educator; b. Ancon, Panama, July 21, 1942; s. James Otis and Eletheer (Besley) C.; m. Sylvia Leigh Thomas, Aug. 13, 1966; children: Kristen Elise, Steven James. BA, Emory & Henry Coll., 1964; MA, Appalachian State Tchrs. Coll., 1966. Tchr. Wilkes Central High Sch., North Wilkesboro, N.C., 1965-66; instr. history North Fla. Jr. Coll., Madison, 1966-90, prof. history, polit. sci., philosophy, 1990-93, dir. counseling, 1993—; com. mem. Commn. on Colls., So. Assn. Schs., 1990-93. Contbr. articles to profl. jours. Pres. Madison C. of C., 1985; mayor City of Madison, 1991-92; commr., com. man Dem. Com., Madison, 1978-93. Named Outstanding Young Man, Madison, 1975. Mem. Fla. Polit. Sci. Assn., Rotary Club (pres. 1982), Elks. Democrat. Methodist. Home: 903 Park Cir Madison FL 32340-3101

CATSIS, JOHN R., communications educator; b. Evanston, Ill., July 9, 1933; s. Harry Lucas and Barbara Vera (Halkioupoulo) C.; m. Connie Louise Thibeau, Sept. 6, 1969; 1 child, Alexander Thibeau. BS in Journalism, Northwestern U., 1957, MS, 1959. News dir./anchor KPRC-AM TV, Houston, 1961-65, 67-70; news dir. KTRH-AM, Houston, 1973-74; transp. reporter KHOU-TV, Houston, 1974-76; pres., gen. mgr., stockholder KIVA-TV, Farmington, N.Mex., 1977-81; pres., stockholder KYKN-FM, Grants, N.Mex., 1978-81; owner, pres. KIVA FM, Santa Fe, Albuquerque, 1981-86; co-owner The Sabio Group, Santa Fe, 1986—; exec. prodr. WMTW-TV, Portland, Maine, 1988-90; assoc. prof. Okla. State U., Stillwater, 1990—. Author: Guide to Vancouver, 1973, Hunter's Handbook, 1986, Sports Broadcasting, 1996. Chmn. Town Forum 2000, Farmington, 1980. With U.S. Army, 1953-55. Recipient Sid Lasher award Houston Jr. C. of C., 1976; Okla. State U. Dean's Incentive grantee, 1991, 92, 93. Mem. Outdoor Writers Assn. Am., Rocky Mountain Outdoor Writers and Photographers Assn. (bd. dirs. 1985-88, 95—, Selected Works award 1993). Office: Oklahoma State University Sch Journalism/Broadcasting Stillwater OK 74078-4053

CAUDELL, LOUIE C., JR., police chief; b. Munich, Germany, Sept. 7, 1947; s. Louie C. Sr and Myrtis Madeline (Burcham) C.; m. Tommie D. Attlesey, May 31, 1969; children: Stephen, David, Jennifer. BA in English, Va. Mil. Inst., 1969; MS in Human Rels. & Bus., Abilene Christian U., 1980. From police officer to acting chief of police Dallas Police Dept., 1972-88; chief-of-police Little Rock Police Dept., 1988—. Capt. U.S. Army, 1970-72. Mem. Internat. Assn. Chiefs of Police, FBI Nat. Acad. Assocs., N. Tex. Police Chief's Assn., Little Rock Air Force Base Community Coun., Vietnam Vets. Am., Rotary, Shriners, Masons. Republican. Methodist. Office: Little Rock Police Dept 700 W Markham St Little Rock AR 72201-1304

CAUDILL, SAMUEL PATTON, statistician; b. Oklahoma City, Mar. 4, 1949; s. Woodrow Wilson and Margie Elese (Conner) C.; m. Marcia Elaine Wilson, Apr. 17, 1982; children: Rebecca Elese, Hannah Diann. BS in Math. with highest honors, U. Tex., Arlington, 1971; MS in Stats., Okla. State U., 1975, PhD in Stats., 1977. Missionary journeyman Fgn. Mission Bd. of So. Bapt. Conv., 1971-73; grad. teaching asst. Okla. State U., 1973-74; grad. rsch. asst. HEW, Okla. State Dept. Vocat. and Tech. Edn., 1974-75, Evaluation Team for Ctr. Local Govt. Tech. Project, NSF, 1976, USAF, 1976; grad. teaching asst. Okla. State U., 1976-77; statistician lab. program office Ctrs. Disease Control, Atlanta, 1977-85, math. statistician divsn. environ. health lab. scis.; mem. statis. awards com. Ctrs. Disease Control, 1992, 93; mem. seminar com. Environ. Health Lab. Scis., 1992, 93; asst. statistician Shepard Sci. award com. for Best Ctrs. Disease Control Publ., 1988, 89, sr. statistician, 1990. Contbr. articles to profl. jours. Recipient Best Statis. Pub. award Ctrs. Disease Control and Agy. for Toxic Substances and Disease Registry, 1993. Mem. Am. Statis. Assn. (instl. rep. 1976). Baptist.

CAUDILL, WILLIAM HOWARD, lawyer; b. Memphis, Mar. 18, 1951; s. John W. Caudill and Elizabeth (Rivers) Stayton; m. Chris Looney, Sept. 2, 1978; children: Lucy L., W. Christopher. BSBA, U. Ark., 1973; M in Pub. Acctg., U. Tex., 1977, JD, 1978. Bar: Tex. 1978, U.S. Dist. Ct. (so. dist.) Tex. 1978, U.S. Tax Ct. 1978, U.S. Claims Ct. 1978, U.S. Ct. Appeals (5th cir.) 1978; CPA. Assoc. Fulbright & Jaworski, Houston, 1982-86, ptnr., 1986—. Vestry, treas., sec. St. John the Divine Episc. Ch., Houston, 1982-86, 89-93. Mem. ABA (chair spl. projects subcom., partnership com., tax sect. 1994-95), State Bar Tex. (sec. 1989, bd. dirs. taxation sect. 1987-92, chair-elect 1990, chair 1991-92, dir. advanced tax law course 1986-87). Episcopalian. Office: Fulbright & Jaworski 1301 Mckinney St Ste 5100 Houston TX 77010

CAUDILL HOUSEL, JUDY L., emergency nurse, administrator; b. Williamsport, Pa., Feb. 5, 1949; d. Dale S. and Betty (Crosby) Betz; m. William E. Housel Jr.; 1 child, Ray Allen. AS, Fla. Jr. Coll. Jacksonville, 1971; AA, Brevard Community Coll., 1989. Cert. emergency nurse; trainer instr. BLS; ACLS instr. Charge nurse emergency dept. Univ. Hosp., Jacksonville; office nurse, scrub nurse to pvt. practice physician Ft. Myers, Fla.; supr. emergency dept. Parrish Med. Ctr., Titusville, Fla.; staff nurse Presbyterian Hosp., Charlotte, N.C.; mgr. emergency dept. Lake Norman Hosp., Mooresville, N.C., 1992-94; staff nurse Upstate Carolina Med. Ctr., Gaffney, S.C., 1994-95, Fla. Hosp. East, Orlando, 1996—; active. Brevard County EMS Coun., Brevard County CPR/ECC Coun., BCC/EMT Paramedic Adv. Coun. Active Brevard County Commn. Against Sexual Assault. Mem. Emergency Nurse Assn.

CAULFIELD, HENRY JOHN, physics educator. BA in Physics, Rice U., 1958; PhD in Physics, Iowa State U., 1962. Staff scientist Cen. Rsch. Labs. Tex. Instrument Inc., Dallas, 1962-67; tech. dirs. night vision dept. Raytheon Co., Melville, N.Y., 1968; prin. scientist Sperry Rand Rsch. Ctr., 1968-72; mgr. laser tech. dept. Block Engring. Inc., 1972-77; pres. Innovative Optics, Caulfield Cons., 1981-85; dir Ctr. for Applied Optics U. Ala., Huntsville, 1985-91; University Eminent Scholar, prof. physics Ala. Agrl. and Mech. U., Normal, 1991—; adj. prof. U. Louis Pasteur, France, Degli Studi di Cagliari, Italy, U. Ala., Huntsville; bd. dirs. Helen Keller Eye Rsch. Inst., Innovision Phys. Optics Corp., Ala. Cryogenic Engring., Nodal Systems Corp., Inn Edge Tech., Tech. Resources Inc., The Holos Corp., Am. Propylaea Corp., N.E. Photosciences, AIA Optical Info. Processing team; mem. patent bd. Applied Optics, evaluation bd. NAS, NBS, adv. com. Mus. Holography, N.Y.C., hon. exec. bd. Nat. Inst. for Engring. Tech., Frederick, Md.; chmn. bd. Loki; curator Holography Works, N.Y. Mus. Holography, 1984; tchr. course Optical Info. Processing, Munich, Paris, London, Tel Aviv, 1986; tchr. course Strategic Infrared Systems, U. Ala., Huntsville, 1986. Author: (with Sun Lu) The Applications of Holography, 1972, (with Gregory Gheen) Optical Computing, 1990; editor: (with Jean Robillard) Industrial Applications of Holography, (with Christopher Tocci) Optical Interconnection Foundations and Applications, 1994, (with Mustafa A.G. Abushagur) Fourier Optics, 1995; editor: editor: Optical Memory and Neural Networks; former editor: Optical Engring.; former mem. editl. bd. Fiber and Integrated Optics, Applied Optics (info. processing editl. adv. bd., Laser Focus, Holography News, Microwave and Optical Tech. Letters, Jour. Neural Network, Computing Internat., Jour. Optical Computing, Optical Computing and Processing Jour., Math. Imaging; series editor: PWS Kent Pub. Co., 1988; publ. bd. Acad. Press; contbr. articles to profl. jours., chpts. to books, presentations to confs. and seminars; patentee in field. Fellow Optical Soc. Am. (Eastman lectr. 1982, 92), Soc. Photooptical-Instrumentational Engrs. (Svc. award, Gov.'s award, pres.'s award, Gabor award); mem. IEEE (sr.). Address: Ala A&M U PO Box 285 Normal AL 35762-0285

CAUSEY, ENID RUTHERFORTH, library director, educator; b. Sherburn-in-Elmet, Eng., Dec. 24, 1937; came to U.S., 1958; d. John George and Maud (Stakes) Rutherforth; m. William Carl Causey Jr., Dec. 7, 1957; children: Christina Marjorie, William Carl III, Angela Noelle. BA summa cum laude, Charleston So. U., 1973; M Libr., U. S.C., 1975, PhD, 1992. Asst. reference libr. Charleston (S.C.) So. U., 1975-83, head tech. svcs., 1983-85, dir. libr., 1985—, asst. prof. libr. sci., 1975-92, assoc. prof., 1992—, project dir. for self-study, 1992-95, acad. advisor, 1975—; asst. prof. libr. sci. Charleston Southern U., 1975-92, assoc. prof., 1992—, project dir. for self-study, 1992—, academic advisor, 1975—. Vol. organist, choir dir. Messiah Evang. Luth. Ch., Hanahan, S.C., 1963—, pres. congl. coun., 1996—; mem. dir.'s com. Charleston Acad. Libr. Consortium; chmn. libr. sect. acad. area assessment network S.C. Higher Edn. Assessment Network, 1991. Recipient Tribute to Women and Industry award YWCA of Greater Charleston, 1994, Outstanding Faculty award Charleston So. U., 1994. Mem. ALA, Am. Guild Organists, S.C. Libr. Assn. (chair coll. & univ. sect. 1990), Beta Phi Mu. Home: 230 Candleberry Circle Goose Creek SC 29445 Office: Charleston Southern U PO Box 118087 Charleston SC 29423-8087

CAUTHEN, CARMEN WIMBERLEY, legislative staff member, jewelry designer; b. Raleigh, N.C., Aug. 4, 1959; d. William Peele and Cliffornia (Grady) Wimberley; m. Ricky Leon Cauthen, May 26, 1990; 1 child, Kena Elizabeth. Student, Ga. Inst. Tech., 1977-78; BA in Polit. Sci., N.C. State U., Raleigh, 1986. Asst. sgt.-at-arms N.C. Ho. of Reps., Raleigh, 1981, 82, computer calendar clk., various yrs.; owner, jewelry designer Accessories and Things, Raleigh, 1984—; sec. Coll. Humanities/Social Sci. N.C. State U., Raleigh, 1989-91; owner bookkeeping/typing svc. CTYPE, Raleigh, 1990—; jour. clk. N.C. Ho. of Reps., Raleigh, 1992-94, adminstrv. clk., 1992—. Mem. Am. Soc. Legis. Clks. and Secs. Democrat. Christian. Home: 703 Latta St Raleigh NC 27607-7203 Office: NC Gen Assembly House Prin Clks Office Legis Bldg Jones St Raleigh NC 27603-5924

CAUTHEN, CHARLES EDWARD, JR., retail executive, business consultant; b. Columbia, S.C., Oct. 26, 1931; s. Charles Edward and Rachel (Macaulay) C.; m. Hazel Electa Peery, June 13, 1959; children: Portia Cauthen White, Rachel Cauthen Rohrer, Sara Cauthen Landfear, Sidney Cauthen Bullard. BA, Wofford Coll., 1952; cert. Charlotte Meml. Hosp. Sch. Hosp. Adminstrn., 1956; MS in Bus. Adminstrn. and Labor Mgmt., Kennedy-Western U., 1986, PhD in Bus. Adminstrn., 1986; LLD, Montreat-Anderson Coll., 1991. Asst. adminstr. Union Meml. Hosp., Monroe, N.C., 1956-58; adminstr. Lowrance Hosp., Inc., Mooresville, N.C., 1958-61; v.p., mgr. Va. Acme Market, Bluefield, W.Va., 1961-68; v.p. Acme Markets and A-Mart Stores, (name now Acme Markets of Tazewell, Va., Inc.), North Tazewell, Va., 1965-87, exec. v.p., 1968-71, pres., 1971-87; provost King Coll., Bristol, Tenn., 1987-89, pres., 1989-92; cons. for bus. and instns., 1992—; pres. Doran Devel. Corp., 1971-87, Big A Market, Inc., 1981-87. Author: Evaluation of the Small Company For Strategic Planning, Merger or Acquisition, 1987. Deacon, elder, trustee Westminster Presbyn. Ch., Bluefield, W.Va.; mem. Internat. Adv. Coun. Han Nam U., Korea, 1991; mem. exec. bd. Sequoyah Coun. Boy Scouts Am.; bd. dirs. Internat. Inst. Christian Studies, 1993—, Family Inst., 1994—. Served to 1st lt. AUS, 1952-54. Decorated Army Commendation medal, Combat Med. badge. Mem. W.Va. Assn. Retail Grocers (v.p., dir. 1968-82), Va. Food Dealers Assn. (dir. 1978), Bluefield Sales Exec. Club (dir. 1965-67), Rotary (bd. dirs. 1966). Republican. Home and Office: 1626 King College Rd Bristol TN 37620-2735

CAUTHEN, H(ARVEY) E(LLINGTON), JR., governmental relations consultant, agriculturist; b. Montgomery, Ala., Sept. 25, 1949; s. Harvey E. Cauthen and Elizabeth (Smith) Launder; m. Florence Minor Mangum, Aug. 29, 1981; children: Belle Churchwell Cauthen, Eugene Preston Mangum Cauthen. BS, U. Ala., Tuscaloosa, 1978. Various positions Ala. Govt., Montgomery, 1970-81; govtl. rels. cons. Montgomery and Washington, 1984—; bd. dirs. South Ala. State Fair, Montgomery, 1982—, Am. Brahman Cattle Breeders Assn., Houston, 1980-86. Mem. Ala. Dem. Exec. Com., 1986—. Mem. Kiwanis. Presbyterian. Home: RR 1 Box 360 Montgomery AL 36105-9733 Office: PO Box 250266 Montgomery AL 36125-0266

CAUTHEN, REA KIMBRELL, JR., engineer; b. Rock Hill, S.C., Dec. 9, 1953; s. Rea Kimbrell Sr. and Frances (Sullivan) C.; m. Kaye Holley, June 21, 1980; 1 child, Rea Kimbrell III. BSE, U. S.C., 1977, MSE, 1986. Registered profl. engr., S.C. Engr. S.C. Dept. Health and Environ. Control, Columbia, 1978-84; asst. dir. S.C. Dept. Health and Environ. Control, Aiken, 1984-87, dir., 1987-91; sr. engr. Westinghouse Savannah River Co., Aiken, S.C., 1991-93, mgr. environ. compliance, 1993—. Named Employee of Yr., S.C. Dept. Health and Environ. Control, 1986. Mem. S.C. Soc. Profl. Engrs. (v.p. Aiken chpt. 1989-90, pres. Aiken chpt. 1990-91, bd. dirs. 1991-93). Presbyterian. Office: Westinghouse Savannah Co Rm 704-S PO Box 616 Aiken SC 29802-0616

CAUTHORNE-BURNETTE, TAMERA DIANNE, family nurse practitioner, healthcare consultant; b. Richmond, Va., Apr. 13, 1961; d. Robert Francis Cauthorne and Lois Avery (Lloyd) Cumashot; m. William Nichols Burnette, Dec. 3, 1983. BSN, U. Va., 1983; postgrad., Med. U. S.C., 1988; MSN, Old Dominion U., 1993, grad. cert. in women's studies, 1994; postgrad., Med. Coll. Va., 1994—. RN, Va.; family nurse practitioner. Staff nurse, charge nurse gynecology-oncology unit U. Va. Med. Ctr., Charlottesville, 1983, staff nurse, charge nurse high-risk labor and delivery, ICU, 1984-85; staff nurse, charge nurse, preceptor med. ICU Med. U. S.C., 1985-87, staff nurse ICU, 1988; staff nurse, charge nurse med.-surg. ICU, progressive care Stuart Cir. Hosp., Richmond, Va., 1988-90; staff nurse pediatric and neonatal ICU Childrens' Hosp. of the King's Dau., Norfolk, Va., 1990, staff nurse, team leader neonatal ICU, 1990-91; pvt. health care cons., 1993—; with Delmar Pub., 1994—; pres. The Foxmont Co., LLC, 1995—; with Sussex Ctrl. Health Ctr., 1995; men's responsibility clinic coord. Planned Parenthood, 1996; cons. Old Dominion U. Coll. Health Sci., Sch. Nursing, 1993—, undergrad. clin. facility, 1994—; condr. analysis of Russian and Ukrainian health care system; breast self-exam instr. Am. Cancer Soc., 1982—; presenter at profl. confs.; mng. mem. The Foxmont Co., L.L.C.; mem. adj. faculty Sch. Nursing U. Va., 1996. Contbg. author for med. texts Delmar Pub.; contbr. articles to profl. jours. Vol. Ronald McDonald House, 1980-83; docent Spoleto Festival USA, 1984-92, MacArthur Meml. Mus., 1991; vol. receptionist info. ctr. Gibbes Art Gallery, 1987-89; vol. ARC Blood Donation Ctr., 1986-92; mem. U. Va. Coll. of Health Scis. Coun. Fellow Internat. Pedagogical Acad./Moswoc. Order of Omega Nat. Honor Soc.; mem. AACN, DAR, AAUW, Va. Coalition for Nurse Practitioners, U. Va. Sch. Nursing Alumnae Assn. (pres., CEO 1994—), Jr. League Va. (chair state pub. affairs com.), Virginians Patient Choice Coalition, Jr. League Norfolk and Virginia Beach (state pub. affairs vice chmn./lobbyist 1995), Daus. of Confederacy, Carolina Art Assn., S.C. Hist. Soc., Confederate Meml. Lit. Soc., U. Va. Coll. Health Scis. Coun., Alpha Delta Pi (chmn. nat. panhellenic rels. com., nat. by-laws and resolutions com.), Sigma Theta Tau.

CAVALLARO, JOSEPH JOHN, microbiologist; b. Lawrence, Mass., Mar. 18, 1932; s. John and Salvatrice (Zappala) C.; m. Kathleen Frances Kraus, Dec. 2, 1972; children: Theresa Margaret, Sandra Marie, Elizabeth Camille, Danielle Kay, Gina Kathleen. BS, Tufts U., 1952; MS, U. Mass., 1954; PhD, U. Mich., 1966. Pub. health sanitarian Hartford (Conn.) Health Dept., 1954-55, 57-61; teaching assoc. dept. microbiology U. Mass., Amherst, 1961-62; rsch. virologist Med. Rsch. Labs., Charles Pfizer & Co., Groton, Conn., 1966-67; rsch. assoc. dept. epidemiology Sch. Pub. Health, U. Mich., Ann Arbor, 1967-70; microbiologist, diagnostic immunology tng. br. Ctrs. for Disease Control, Atlanta, 1971-86, research microbiologist anaerobic bacteria br., Ctrs. for Disease Control, 1986—; lectr. resident pathologists Grady Meml. Hosp., Atlanta, 1975; asst. prof. pathology Morehouse Sch. Medicine, 1982-85, clin. assoc. prof., 1986—; adj. asst. prof. pathology and lab. medicine Emory U. Sch. of Medicine, 1985—; cons. Pan Am. Health Orgn., Colombia and Brazil, 1976, 77. Served with M.C., AUS, 1955-57. Registered specialist microbiologist Nat. Registry Microbiologist, Am. Acad. Microbiology. Fellow Am. Acad. Microbiology; mem. Am. Soc. Microbiology, Am. Assn. Immunologists, N.Y. Acad. Sci., KC, Sigma Xi. Democrat. Roman Catholic. Prin. author/co-author over 11 lab. manuals; contbr. articles to profl. jours., chpts. to books. Home: 1325 Balsam Dr Decatur GA 30033-2905 Office: 1600 Clifton Rd Atlanta GA 30333

CAVANAGH, JOHN JOSEPH, JR. (JACK CAVANAGH), investment broker, consultant; b. Bayside, N.Y., Feb. 5, 1942; s. John Joseph Sr. and Wanda W. (Weidemeyer) C.; m. Martha Marlowe, June 25, 1961; children: Dawn, Kelly, Jacqueline, Heidi, Trey. BA in Bus. Adminstrn. in Econs., German, Elon Coll., 1964; MBA in Econs., Mktg., Appalachian State U., 1965. Registered rep., SEC. Chmn., CEO N.C. First Flight, Inc., Winston-Salem, N.C., 1991-93; investment rep. Edward D. Jones & Co., Winston-Salem, N.C., 1992—; bd. dirs. N.C. Small Bus. and Tech. Devel. Ctrs.; mem. N.C. Employment Security Commn.; trustee Winston-Salem State U., Glade Valley Sch., Inc.; mem. bd. advisors Lees McRae Coll., Cannon Meml. Hosp. TV investment show host Minding Your Own Bus. Alderman Winston-Salem City Coun., 1977-80; senator N.C. State, 1980-82; bd. dirs. Ctrl. YMCA, Small Bus. Revolving Loan Com., City of Winston-Salem, Winston-Salem Swim Club, Inc., Winston-Salem Tennis Club, Inc., Reynolds Toastmasters Club, Inc.; chmn. Forsyth County Rep. Party; pres. Mac Wood Sch., Kidney Found. Forsyth County, Youth for Christ, Inc.; mem. Operation Mobilization, Europe; elder Presbyn. Ch. Mem. Winston-Salem Assn. Life Underwriters (pres.), N.C. Assn. Life Underwriters (v.p.). Office: Edward D Jones and Co 101 S Stratford Rd Ste 103 Winston Salem NC 27104-4224

CAVE, JOHN DAVID, religious studies educator, researcher; b. Atlanta, Nov. 27, 1957; s. John David and Laura Jean (Carden) C.; m. Peggy Tucker, Mar. 4, 1955; 1 child, Jonathan David. BA, N.C. State U., 1979; MDiv, So. Sem., Louisville, 1985, PhD, 1989. Instr. Spalding U., Louisville, 1989-90, U. Wis., Oshkosh, 1990-91, No. Ky. U., Highland Heights, 1992—, Xavier U., Ohio, 1995, Hebrew Union Coll., Jewish Inst. Religion, Interfaith Acad., 1994—; devel. fellow, Cin. Ctr. for Developmental Disorders Children's Hosp. Med. Ctr.; mktg. cons. Internat. Visitors Ctr., Cin., 1983; minister Spain, 1980-82, Germa ny, 1983, P.R., 1985. Author: Mircea Eliade's Vision for a New Humanism, 1993. Mem. Am. Acad. Religion. Home and Office: 83 Pleasant Ridge Ave Fort Mitchell KY 41017-2861

CAVE, KIRK CLARK, engineer, computer specialist; b. Atchison, Kans., Nov. 16, 1957; s. Ralph Donald and Betty Leona (Steele) C.; m. Doris J. Ramsey, Apr. 13, 1985. AS, Mo. Western State Coll., 1983, BS in Tech., 1984; BS in Computer Sci., U. Tex., Dallas, 1994. Registered profl. engr., Mo. Elec. engr. Midwest Grain Products, Atchison and Pekin, Kans. and Ill., 1984-86; computer aided design specialist Seismic Engring. Co., Dallas, 1986—; sys. analyst MCI Telecomms., Richardson, Tex., 1994—; advisor product adv. com. EC & M Mag., N.Y.C., 1985-86. Republican. Methodist. Home: 2109 Argonne Dr Carrollton TX 75007-5518 Office: Seismic Engring Co 2659 Nova Dr Dallas TX 75229-2220

CAVE, SKIP, company executive. Dir. R&D Intervoice, Inc. Address: 17811 Waterview Pkwy Dallas TX 75252

CAVES, PEGGY, medical/surgical nurse; b. Lodi, Calif., July 19, 1945; d. Burnerd Clette and Thelma Jean (Humphrey) Hamilton; m. Virgil Wayne Caves, Feb. 14, 1978 (div. June 28, 1995); children: Rhonda Pilcher Miller, Kelly Pilcher Rainwater, Shelly Pilcher Dennis; stepchildren: Shelly Deanne White, Leo Wayne, Karrie Ausbrooks, Billy. LPN, Kiamichi Vo-Tech, Hugo, Okla., 1982; Assoc. degree Sch. Nursing, Ea. Okla. State Coll., 1996. RN, Okla. Staff nurse Pushmataha Hosp., Antlers, Okla., Texoma Med. Ctr., Denison; dr. nursing Antlers (Okla.) Nursing Home; staff nurse Presby. Hosp., Oklahoma City; dir. nursing Choctaw Nursing Home, Antlers, Okla., 1992-93; staff nurse Med. Ctr. of Southeastern Okla., Durant, Okla., 1992; staff nurse outpatient dept., emergency room Choctaw Nation Hosp., Talihina, Okla., 1993-94; pvt. duty field nurse Superior Home Health, Talihina, 1994-95; dir. nurses Choctaw Nation Nursing Home, 1994—; dir. nursing Choctaw Nation Nursing Home; field nurse Happy Hearts Home Health, Antlers, Okla., 1995—, staff nurse Pushmataha Hosp. Home: PO Box 872 Antlers OK 74523-0872

CAWLEY, CHARLES NASH, enviromental scientist; b. Shreveport, La., Aug. 21, 1937; s. Charles Preston and Carnall (Nash) C. BA, U. Okla., 1960, MA, 1970; MS, U. Tex.-Dallas, Richardson, 1976, PhD, 1978. Registered environ. mgr.; cert. environ. profl. Project leader Tex. Woman's U. Research Inst., Denton, 1964-73; gen. ptnr. Southwest Textile Lab., Denton,

1973-77; research assoc. U. Tex.-Dallas, 1978; asst. prof. Cornell U., Ithaca, N.Y., 1979-83; prin. scientist Hanford Ops. div. Rockwell Internat., Richland, Wash., 1983-87, Westinghouse Corp., Richland, 1987-88; licensing supr. Bechtel Nat. Inc., Oak Ridge, 1988-95; pres. Environ. Sci. and Systems, 1995—; cons. Saint St. Cons., Oak Ridge, Tenn., 1984—. Contbr. articles in field to profl. jours. Served with U.S. Army, 1962-64. Mem. AAAS, Soc. Risk Analysis, N.Y. Acad. Sci., Am. Nuclear Soc., Health Physics Soc., Nat. Assn. Environ. Profls. (cert. environ. profl.), Nat. Registry Environ. Profls. (registered environ. mgr.), Am. Statis. Assn., Sigma Xi, Delta Upsilon. Home: 130 Brandeis Ln Oak Ridge TN 37830-7601 Office: Bechtel Environmental Inc Oak Ridge TN 37831-0350

CAWOOD, GARY KENNETH, photography educator; b. Chattanooga, Jan. 17, 1947; s. Kenneth Garnett and Minnie Christine (Malos) C.; m. Teresa Louise Taft, Feb. 1,1 986 (div. Apr. 1988). BArch, Auburn (Ala.) U., 1970; MFA, East Tenn. State U., Johnson City, 1976. Designer Hayes B. Fleming, Architect, Johnson City, 1970-75; asst. prof. photography La. Tech. U., Ruston, 1976-80, assoc. prof. photography, 1980-85; assoc. prof. photography U. Ark., Little Rock, 1985—. Author: Scenes Unseen, 1990. Recipient Eugene Feldman award Print Club, 1986, Publ. award Soc. for Contemporary Photography, 1988; Nat. Endowment for Arts fellow, 1982, Ark. Arts Coun. fellow, 1991—, Mid-Am. Arts Alliance fellow, 1995; U. Ark. Rsch. grantee, 1986. Mem. Soc. for Photographic Edn. (regional chair 1983-84), Phi Kappa Phi. Democrat. Home: 1703 Fair Park Blvd Little Rock AR 72204-2719 Office: U Little Rock Dept of Art 2801 S University Ave Little Rock AR 72204-1000

CAWOOD, MERTON CAMPBELL, investment management executive; b. Johnson City, Tenn., Nov. 1, 1947; s. Clarence Allen and Julia (McCorkle) C. BS, U. Va., 1970; MBA, Temple U., 1990. CFA. Asst. v.p. Girard Bank, Phila., 1971-76, Wachovia Bank & Trust Co., Winston-Salem, N.C., 1976-78; pres. Salem Investment Counselors, Winston-Salem, 1978-84; gen. ptnr. Venture First Assocs., Winston-Salem, 1984-89; investment rep. Alex Brown and Sons, Inc., Winston-Salem, 1989-96; ind. broker, investment advisor LPL Fin. Svcs., Clemmons, N.C., 1996—; adj. prof. U. N.C. Grad. Sch. Bus., Chapel Hill, 1989; bd. dirs. N.C. Biotech. Ctr., also numerous pvt. cos.; grader CFA Inst., Charlottesville, Va. With U.S. Army, 1970-71. Mem. N.C. Soc. Fin. Analysts (pres. 1984-85), Coun. Entrepreneurial Devel., Piedmont Entrepreneurs Network (founder). Home: 794 Gateshaven Ln Winston Salem NC 27103-9783 Office: LPL Fin Svcs PO Box 947 Clemmons NC 27012

CAWTHON, FRANK H., retired construction company executive; b. Kissimmee, Fla., Apr. 3, 1930; s. Benjamin Hill and Eva Elizabeth (Mullins) C.; m. Mary Elizabeth Dickert, July 10, 1959; 1 child, Frank H. Grad. high sch. Asst. sec.-treas. Orange Belt Truck & Tractor, Orlando, Fla., 1948-52, Murdock Constrn. Co., Inc., Orlando, 1954-59; sec.-treas. Amick Constrn. Co., Inc., Orlando, 1959-90; ret., 1990; bd. dirs. Amick Constrn. Co., Inc. Bd. dirs. Conway Little League, Orlando, 1977. With U.S. Army, 1952-54. Mem. Cen. Fla. Rd. Bldrs. Assn. Democrat. Lutheran. Home: 391 Brushwood Ln Casselberry FL 32708-4955 Office: Amick Constrn Co 401 Ferguson Dr Orlando FL 32805-1009

CAYLOR, DEE JERLYN, accountant; b. Calhoun, Ga., Dec. 22, 1942; d. George Herbert and Annie Mae (Shirley) Darnell; widowed; children: Mark Gerald, George Alexander, Gregory Wayne. Student, Am. Inst. Banking, 1961, Dalton Jr. Coll., 1979, Continual Learning Inst., Nashville, 1985. Accredited resident mgr. Owner, operator Age Olde Traditions, Antiques, Calhoun, 1980-83; resident mgr. Allied Mgmt. Co., Nashville, 1984-85; acct. Vawter, Gammon, Norris & Collins, Nashville, 1986, Robert Half & Accountemps, Nashville, 1987-88; resident mgr. Carter Co., Nashville, 1989—; office mgr. Bridal Path Wedding Chapel, Nashville, 1991—; acct. Gaddy, Gaydou & Assoc., 1993; pvt. practice acct. Nashville, 1994—; resident mgr. Natchez Village Apts., 1995—. Exec. dir. spl. TV musical Tribute to Women in Country Music, 1990. Mem. Women of Music and Entertainment Network (founder, pres. 1988-94), Nashville Apt. Assn. (community svc. com. 1990). Republican.

CAYTON, MARY EVELYN, clergyman; b. Morgantown, W. Va., July 7, 1926; d. Adam Johnson and Dorothy Ena (Bigler) C. Student, Internat. Bible Coll., San Antonio, Tex., 1955. Ordained minister Full Gospel Denomination, 1958. Founder, pastor Morgantown (W.Va.) Revival Ctr., 1956-92; staff, controller's office W.Va. U., Morgantown, 1951-55, '58-84; chmn. Morgantown Revival Ctr. Assn., 1956—. Home and Office: Morgantown Revival Ctr RR 3 Box 542A Morgantown WV 26505-9538

CAYWOOD, BUD, association administrator. Exec. dir. Am. Soc. Furniture Designers, High Point, N.C. Office: Am Soc Furniture Designers PO Box 2688 High Point NC 27261

CAZALAS, MARY REBECCA WILLIAMS, lawyer, nurse; b. Atlanta, Nov. 11, 1927; d. George Edgar and Mary Annie (Slappey) Williams; m. Albert Joseph Cazalas (dec.). R.N., St. Joseph's Infirmary Sch. Nursing, Atlanta, 1948; BS in Pre-medicine, Oglethorpe U., 1954; MS in Anatomy, Emory U., 1960; JD, Loyola U., 1967. Gen. duty nurse, 1948-68; instr. maternity nursing St. Joseph's Infirmary Sch. Nursing, 1954-59; med. researcher in urology Tulane U. Sch. Medicine, 1961-65; legal researcher for presiding judge La. Ct. Appeals (4th cir.), 1965-71; sole practice, 1967-71; asst. U.S. atty., New Orleans, 1971-79; sr. trial atty. EEOC, New Orleans, 1979-84; owner Cazalas Apts., New Orleans, 1962—; lectr. in field. Contbr. articles to med. and legal publs. Bd. advisors Loyola U. Sch. Law, New Orleans, 1974, v.p. adv. bd., 1975; mem. New Orleans Drug Abuse Adv. Com., 1976-80, task force Area Agy. on Aging, 1976-80, pres.'s coun. Loyola U., 1978—, adv. bd. Odyssey House, Inc., New Orleans, 1973; chmn. women's com. Fed. Exec. Bd., 1974; bd. dirs. Bethlehem House of Bread, 1975-79. Named Hon. La. State Senator, 1974; recipient Superior Performance award U.S. Dept. Justice, 1974, Cert. Appreciation Fed. Exec. Bd., 1975, 76, 77, 78, Rev. E.A. Doyle award, 1976, commendation for teaching Guam Legislature, 1977, Career Achievement award Mount de Sales Acad., 1995. Mem. Am. Judicature Soc., La. State Bar Assn., Fed. Bus. Assn. (v.p. 1976—, pres. 1976-78, bd. dirs. 1972-75), Fed. Bar Assn. (1st v.p. 1973, pres. New Orleans chpt. 1974-75, nat. coun. 1974-79), Assn. Women Lawyers, Nat. Health Lawyers Assn., DAR, Bus. and Profl. Women's Club, Am. Heart Assn., Emory Alumni Assn., Oglethorpe U. Alumni Assn., Loyola U. Alumni Assn. (bd. dirs. 1974-75, 1977, v.p. 1976), Jefferson Parish Hist. Soc., Phi Delta Delta (merged with Phi Alpha Delta, pres. 1970-72, bd. dirs., vice justice 1974-75), Sierra Club, Zonta, Alpha Epsilon Delta, Phi Sigma, Leconte Hon. Sci. Soc. Democrat.

CAZAYOUX, CHARLES, airport executive. Airport mgr. New Orleans Internat. Airport. Office: New Orleans Internat Airport PO Box 20007 New Orleans LA 70141-0007

CAZEL, HUGH ALLEN, industrial engineer, educator; b. Asheville, N.C., Aug. 6, 1923; s. Fred Augustus and Agnes (Petrie) C.; BS in Indsl. Engring., N.C. State U., 1948, M Indsl. Engring., 1972; m. Edna Faye Hawkins, Sept. 2, 1944; children: Audre Elizabeth, Hugh Petrie, Susan Margaret, Steven Sidney. Service mgr. Cazel Auto Svc. Co., Asheville, 1948-51; sales rep. Snap-On Tools Corp., Kenosha, Wis., 1951; estimator, cost acct. Std. Designers, Inc., Asheville, N.C., 1951-52; designer Robotyper Corp., Hendersonville, N.C., 1952-53; engr. Western Electric Co., Burlington, N.C., 1953-74; alt. rep. configuration mgmt. subcom. Electronic Industries Assn., 1970-72; mgr. engring. So. Bell Telephone Co., Atlanta, 1974-79, ret., 1979; ptnr. Engring. Unltd., 1963—; instr. math. Elon Coll., 1956-59; instr. engring. graphics and design Ga. Inst. Tech., 1977-87, ret., 1987; instr. constrn. blue print reading DeKalb C.C., 1981-87; project engr. Dept. Def. Election poll worker, 1960-93; mem. Dekalb County (Ga.) Adv. Com., 1979-82; dir. Glendale Townhouses Assn., chmn., 1979-80; mem. adminstrv. bd. 1st United Meth. Ch., Decatur, 1976-86; interviewer Decatur Emergency Assistance Ministry, 1990-92; lay mem. Ea. N.C. Annual Conf. United Meth. Ch., 1965-73; vol. Dept. Vets. Affairs Med. Ctr., Durham, N.C., 1993—; mem. adminstrv. bd. Asbury United Methodist Ch., 1993—. Served with AUS, 1943-46, ETO. Registered profl. engr., N.C., Ga. Mem. AAAS, Am. Inst. Indsl. Engrs. (pres. Raleigh, N.C. chpt. 1963-64), Nat. Soc. Profl. Engrs., Profl. Engrs. N.C. (pres. North Piedmont chpt. 1972-73, state bd. dirs. 1970-73), Ga. Profl. Engrs. in Industry (chmn. 1976), Ga. Soc. Profl. Engrs. (Ga. Engr. of Yr. in Industry 1976; energy com. 1979-86), Telephone Pioneers Am. (life mem. club, pres. Dixie chpt. 1991-92), Rep. Club, Odd Fellows, Rotary, Lions (local sec. 1991-96). Patentee ultra low frequency sound generator for deep sea, 1972. Home: 2720 Twin Lakes Dr Greensboro NC 27407-4717

CECI, LOUIS J., former state supreme court justice; b. N.Y.C., Sept. 10, 1927; s. Louis and Filomena C.; m. Shirley; children—Joseph, Geraldine, David; children by previous marriage: Kristin, Remy, Louis. Ph.B., Marquette U., 1951, J.D., 1954. Bar: Wis. 1954, U.S. Dist. Ct. (ea. dist.) Wis. 1954, U.S. Dist. Ct. (we. dist.) Wis. 1987. Sole practice Milw., 1954-58, 63-68; asst. city atty. City of Milw., 1958-63; mem. Wis. Assembly, Madison, 1965-66; judge Milw. County Ct., 1968-73, Milw. Circuit Ct., 1973-82; justice Wis. Supreme Ct., Madison, 1982-93, retired, 1993; res. judge State of Wis., 1993—; lectr. Wis. Jud. Confs., 1970-79. Lectr. Badger Boys State, Ripon, Wis., 1961, 1982-84; asst. dist. commr. Boy Scouts Am., 1962. Recipient Wis. Civic Recognition PLAV, Milw., 1970; recipient Community Improvement Pompeii Men's Club, Milw., 1971, Good Govt. Milw Jaycees, 1973, Community-Judiciary Pompeii Men's Club, 1982. Mem. ABA, Wis. Bar Assn., Dane County Bar Assn., Milw. County Bar Assn., Waukesha County Bar Assn., Am. Legion (comdr. 1962-63).

CECIL, ALLAN, corporate communications executive. Sr. v.p. corp. comm. and investor rels. Sonoco Products, Hartsville, S.C. Office: Sonoco Products One N 2d St Hartsville SC 29551

CECIL, BONNIE SUSAN, elementary education educator; b. Louisville, Sept. 29, 1951; d. Robert Lawrence and Mary Hedwig (Kluesner) C. BA in Edn., U. Ky., 1973; MS in Edn., Ind. U., 1978; postgrad., U. Louisville, 1988—. Tchr. grades 1-4 Roosevelt Community Sch., Jefferson County, Ky., 1972-80; tchr. ages 6 and 7 Wandle Primary Sch., London, 1980-81; tchr. 1st grade Foster Elem. Sch., Jefferson County, 1981-82; tchr. ages 5-8 Brown Sch. Primary, Jefferson County, 1982—; co-dir., instr. writing process for tchrs. Ky. Writing Insts. I and II, Boone County, 1986-88; instr. writing process insvc. Jefferson County Pub. Schs., 1988-89, workshop presenter on environ. edn., 1990, 92, supr. student tchrs., 1989-90, 92, 94; instr. lang. arts U. Louisville, 1990-91; participant Fulbright Tchr. Exch. Program, London, 1980-81, Brown Sch. Dream Team, 1992; presenter ann. conf. Ky. Assn. Edn. Young Children-Louisville Assn. for Children Under Seven, 1990; presenter Cmty. Learning Resource Conf., 1992; participant Louisville Writing Project, 1984-85, premier class Leadership Edn., 1986-87. Tchr. rep. J. Graham Brown Sch. PTSA, 1983-90, 92—; bd. dirs. Roosevelt Cmty. Sch., Inc., 1973-76; creater, dir. summer reading and writing program Portland Mus., Louisville, 1985; treas. Louisville Homefront Performances, Inc., 1986-87, sec., 1988-90, bd. dirs. 1984—. Recipient Golden Apple Achievement award Ashland Oil Co., 1989, Individual Tchr. Achievement award, 1992, Nat. Educator award Milken Family Found., 1994, Excel award WHAS-TV and PNC Bank, 1995; named Jefferson County Elem. Tchr. of Yr., 1992, Ky. Elem. Tchr. of Yr., 1993, Ky. Tchr. of Yr., 1993; grantee Ky. Arts Coun., 1986-87, Jefferson County Pub. Schs.-U. Louisville, 1989-91, U. Louisville, 1991. Mem. ASCD, NEA, Assn. Childhood Edn. Internat., Nat. Coun. Tchrs. English (conf. presenter 1988, chmn., presenter nat. conf. 1992), Ky. Edn. Assn., Jefferson County Tchrs. Assn., Leadership Edn. Alumni Assn. Office: J Graham Brown Sch 546 S 1st St Louisville KY 40202-1816

CECIL, JOHN DAVID, lawyer; b. Charleston, W.Va., Nov. 16, 1941; s. John Dexter and Agnes (Graham) C.; m. Jacquelyn Elaine Roush, Dec. 20, 1969; children: John Kenneth, Jennifer Nicole, Jana Michelle. BA in History and Polit. Sci., W.Va. U., 1963, JD, 1970. Bar: W.Va. 1970, U.S. Dist. Ct. (no. and so. dists.) W.Va., U.S. Ct. Appeals (4th cir.) 1975, U.S. Surpeme Ct. 1980. Trial counsel Legal Aid of Charleston, W.Va., 1970-72; law clk. W.Va. Supreme Ct. Appeals, Charleston, 1972-74; state dir. W.Va. Legal Svcs. Plan, Charleston, 1974-77; counsel Sprouse & Cecil, Charleston, 1977-79; ptnr. Cecil, Pearson & Barth, Charleston, 1980-84; sr. ptnr. Cecil, Barth & Thompson, Charleston, 1984-93; ptnr. Armada & Cecil, Hurricane, W.Va., 1993—. State dir. W.Va. Legal Svcs. Plan, Charleston, 1974-77; chmn. Hayes Parent Assn., St. Albans, W.Va., 1990-92; counsel W.Va. Pub. Energy Authority, Charleston, 1990—. With U.S. Army, 1963-66. Mem. ABA, Am. Trial Lawyers Am. Home: 526 Everest Ave Saint Albans WV 25177-2672 Office: Armada & Cecil 3972 Teays Valley Rd Hurricane WV 25526-9796

CECIL, MAXINE, critical care nurse; b. Healdton, Okla., Sept. 25, 1921; d. James Albert and Clara (Phelps) Metz; children: Harold E. Seals, James Michael Seals, David Ray Smith. LPN, Seventh Day Adventist Hosp., Ardmore, Okla., 1954; ADN cum laude, No. Okla. Coll., Tonkawa, Okla., 1979. RN, Okla. LPN Seventh Day Adventist Hosp., Ardmore, 1953-66; LPN, charge nurse at nursing homes Ardmore, 1966-74; LPN and RN Johnston Meml. Hosp., Tishomingo, Okla., 1974-80; RN Meml. Hosp. So. Okla., Ardmore, Okla., 1980-84; charge nurse Love County Med. Ctr., Marietta, Okla., 1988-90; charge nurse, RN Lakeland Manor, Inc., Ardmore, 1982—; nurse Meml. Convalescent Home, Ardmore, 1990—; pres. LPN Assn for Carter, Love, Johnston and Marshall Counties, 1963-70; mem. state bd. LPNs, 1968. Instr. first aid ARC, Ardmore, 1960-62; pathfinder dir. Seventh Day Adventist Ch., Ardmore.

CECIL, WILLIAM A. V., SR., landmark director; married; 2 children. Degree, Harvard U. Rep. Chase Manhattan Bank, N.Y.C., officer internat. dept.; former founding chmn. Asheville (N.C.)/Buncombe County Tourism Devel. Authority; former pres. Asheville (N.C.) C. of C.; former chmn. bd. dirs., founder Hist. House Assn. Am. (now merged with Nat. Trust for Hist. Preservation); now pres. Biltmore Co., Asheville, N.C.; pres. Biltmore Estate Wine Co., Asheville; bd. dirs. Pub. Svc. Natural Gas Co. Past pres. N.C. Travel Coun.; bd. dirs. N.C. Citizens for Bus. and Industry. Recipient Charles J. Parker Travel award N.C. Travel Coun., 1974. Mem. Carolina Motor Club (bd. dirs.). Office: Biltmore Estate One North Pack Square Asheville NC 28801

CEDEL, MELINDA IRENE, violinist, educator; b. Ft. Worth, July 31, 1957; d. Albert and Emilia Florence (Sylvester) C. Student, N.C. Sch. Arts, 1974-77; MusB Edn., U. S.C., 1979. Cert. tchr., S.C. Tchr. music Charleston (S.C.) County Pub. Schs., 1979-92; pvt. tchr. music, 1983—; concertmaster Brunswick (Ga.) Civic Orch., 1993—, pers. mgr., 1995-96. Performed with Florence Symphony, Columbia Philharm., S.C. Chamber Orch., Augusta Symphony, Savannah (Ga.) Symphony, Hilton Head (S.C.) Symphony, Jacksonville Summer Symphonetta, Valdosta (Ga.) Symphony Orch.; musician Charleston Symphony, 1979—, Charleston Symphony Chamber Orch., Long Bay (S.C.) Symphony; musician, mgr. Charlestowne String Quartet, 1983-92; condr. Charleston County Prep. Orch., 1983-84; performer Piccolo Spoleto, 1980-91; co-dir. Charleston County Strolling Strings; pers. mgr. Brunswick (Ga.) Civic Orch., 1995-96. Mem. Am. Fedn. Musicians, Am. String Tchrs. Assn., Suzuki Assn. of the Ams., Inc., Mensa, Kappa Phi Kappa. Home: 220 Five Pounds Rd Saint Simons GA 31522

CEFALU, MARY ANN, banker; b. Amite, La., May 16, 1923; d. Charles Vincent Genco and Pauline Misita; children: Vincent, Ursula, Charles, Paulette, Nick Jr., William, Joseph, Ann Kay, Francis. BA, Southeastern La. U., 1973, MEd, 1975. cert. tchr., La. Bookkeeper Misita and Son, Amite, 1940-43; sec. N. Cefalu Co., Inc. Feed Mfrs.-Real Estate, Amite, 1944-72; pres. N. Cefalu Co., Inc., Amite, 1972—; comptr., also bd. dirs. Cen. Progressive Bank, Amite, 1972-81; bd. dirs. 1st Guaranty Bank, Hammond, La., chmn., 1982—. Active choir, organist, mem. altar and rosary guild St. Helena Ch., Amite, 1945—; mem. ladies aux. St. Mater Dolorosa Ch.; bd. dirs. Lallie Kemp Hosp., Independence, La., 1990, Indsl. Search Com., Amite, 1990; pres. Amite C. of C., 1985. Named Woman of Yr., BPW, Hammond, 1984. Democrat. Roman Catholic. Office: N Cefalu Co Inc 100 S 2nd St Amite LA 70422-2706

CEIPS, KATHLEEN MCCARTHY, nurse consultant, healthcare manager; b. New Orleans, Aug. 15, 1947; d. Edward Joseph and Helen Ruth (Mohrmann) McCarthy; m. Melvin Juris Ceips, Dec. 24, 1979; 1 child, Maija Anna. RN, Charity Hosp. Sch. Nursing, New Orleans, 1979; student, U. New Orleans, 1975-78. RN, La. Charge nurse Charity Hosp., New Orleans, 1980-81; night charge nurse Allied Health Svcs., Metairie, La., 1981-82; staff nurse Am. Nursing Svcs., Metairie, La., 1982-84; dir. nursing HSA-Greenbrier Hosp., Covington, La., 1984-86; ind. cons., 1986—; ind. cons., pres. Alternative Healthcare and Alternative Nursing Mgmt., Mandeville, La., 1986—; co-founder, pres. Alternative Healthcare Assn., Mandeville, 1993—; founder, pres. Alternative Nursing Mgmt. Svcs., Inc., Mandeville, 1994—; pvt. cons. in field; sec., adv. bd. Deaf Action Ctr., New Orleans, 1991-92; adv. bd. mem. Dept. of Health, Baton Rouge, 1993—. Co-author: (tng. course) State of Louisiana Certified Medication Attendant and manual of Teaching Techniques, 1993. Mem. ANA, NAFE, Devel. Disabilities Nurses Assn., Nat. Nurses in Bus. Republican. Roman Catholic. Office: Alternative Nursing Mgmt PO Box 432 Mandeville LA 70470-0432

CEKAUSKAS, CYNTHIA DANUTE, social worker; b. Detroit, Mar. 24, 1954; d. Vladas Algimantas and Isabel Gana (Stasiulis) C. BA in Sociology, Madonna Coll., Livonia, Mich., 1976; MSW, U. Mich., 1979. Bd. cert. social worker, La.; lic. clin. social worker, Fla. Psychiat. social worker Charity Hosp. New Orleans, 1982-84; social worker child and adolescent svc. DePaul Hosp., New Orleans, 1986-87; social worker, family advocacy programmgr. Army Cmty. Svcs., Friedberg, Fed. Republic Germany, 1988-89; social worker, mgr. family adv. program, chmn. family adv. case mgmt. team Cmty. Counseling Ctr., Camp Zama, Japan, 1989-90; social worker, exceptional family mem. program mgr. Army Cmty. Svcs., Bamberg, Germany, 1990-91; alt. family adv., on-call crisis counselor Desert Storm Army Cmty. Svcs., Bamberg, Fed. Republic Germany, 1990-91; social worker, family advocacy rep., head dept. family adv. Naval Med. Clinic, New Orleans, 1991-96; presenter child abuse prevention Bad Nauheim Elem. Sch., 1988-89. Contbr. articles to newspapers. Hosp. corpsman USN, 1979-82. Recipient Customer Svc. award Giessen Mil. Cmty., 1988-89, Friend Bad Nauheim Elem. Sch. award, 1989, commendation for exceptional svc. Cam Zama, 1990, Scroll of Appreciation for Desert Storm/Desert Shield, Bamberg, Germany, 1990-91, Outstanding Performance award, 1993, 94, Presdl. Sports Award for racewalking, 1996, for aerobic dance, 1996. Mem. NAFE, NASW, NOW, Acad. Cert. Social Workers, Federally Employed Women, New Orleans Track Club, Greater New Orleans Runners' Assn., Am. Racewalk Assn., Nat. Audubon Soc. Democrat. Roman Catholic. Home: 102 Amy Ln Chipley FL 32428

CELELLA, JAN GERDING, legislative staff member; b. Cin., Dec. 10, 1935; d. Carlyn Henry and Kathryn Josephine (Simon) Wodraska; m. Philip Gary Celella, Apr. 8, 1989; children: Thomas Allen, Timothy James, Peggy Ann, Pamela Rose. Student, Thomas More Coll., 1972-75. Field rep. Congressman John B. Breckinridge, 6th Dist., Ky., 1973-79; dist. rep. Senator Wendell H. Ford of Ky., Covington, 1979—; Co-founder The Resource Bank. Contbr. articles to profl. jours. Bd. mem. No. Ky. U. ReEntry Ctr.; dir. Covington-Cin. Suspension Bridge Com.; bd. overseers Redwood Sch.; bd. mem. Louise Southgate Women's Ctr.; mem. Elder Concerns Forum, Summit on Ky. Women, Women's Health Seminar Com.; mem. Elder Abuse Prevention Task Force, United Way; bd. dirs. March of Dimes Birth Defect Found. Named Outstanding Woman Ky. Post/No. Ky. U., 1988; recipient Walter L. Pieschel award C. of C., 1989, No. Ky. Area Devel. Dist. Cmty. Leadership award, 1992. Mem. Am. Bus. Women's Assn., No. Ky. C. of C. (transp. com.). Democrat. Roman Catholic. Home: PO Box 1327 Covington KY 41012 Office: US Senator Wendell Ford 19 Federal Bldg Covington KY 41011

CELLA, EUGENE JOSEPH, state official. BA in History, U. N.C., 1970; JD, Stetson U., 1974. Bar: Fla. 1972, U.S. Supreme Ct. 1979, N.C. 1981, U.S. Ct. Appeals (4th cir.) 1985. Law clk. to Hon. Orie L. Phillips U.S. Ct. Appeals (10th cir.), Denver, 1974-75; atty. Law Offices of Robert W. Pope, St. Petersburg, Fla., 1975-76; atty. securities fraud unit Office of the Fla. Comptr., Dept. Banking and Fin., Tallahassee, 1976-77, gen. counsel, 1977-80; pvt. practice Orlando, Fla., 1980-81, Chapel Hill, N.C., 1981-84; chief enforcement atty. enforcement sect. N.C. Dept. of Sec. of State Securities Divsn., Raleigh, 1984-91, dep. securities adminstr., 1991—. Mem. ABA, N.C. Bar Assn. Address: 6425 Dixon Dr Raleigh NC 27609-3651 Office: Dept Securities Admin 300 N Salisbury St Raleigh NC 27603-5925

CELMER, VIRGINIA, psychologist; b. Detroit, June 26, 1945; d. Charles and Stella (Kopicko) C. BA in English, Marygrove Coll., 1968; MA in Theological Studies, St. Louis U., 1977; PhD in Counseling Psychology, Tex. Tech. U., 1986. Lic. psychologist; lic. chem. dependency counselor; cert. diplomate in managed care; cert. alcoholism and drug abuse counselor; internat. cert. alcoholism and drug abuse counselor; cert. group psychotherapist. Chaplain Mercy Ctr. for Health Care Svcs., Aurora, Ill., 1977-81; grad. asst. counselor U. Counseling Ctr., Tex. Tech. U., Lubbock, 1982-86, pre-doctoral intern in counseling psychology, 1985-86; post-doctoral intern Consultation Ctr., San Antonio, 1986-89, staff psychologist, 1989-90; pvt. practice psychologist San Antonio, 1989—; instr. dept. psychology Tex. Tech. U., Lubbock, 1981-85, Oblate Sch. Theology, San Antonio, 1989-90. Contbr. articles to profl. jours. Mem. APA, Tex. Psychol. Assn., Bexar County Psychol. Assn., Am. Group Psychotherapy Assn., San Antonio Group Psychotherapy Assn., Nat. Assn. Alcoholism and Drug Abuse Counselors, Tex. Assn. Alcoholism and Drug Abuse Counselors, Leadership Conf. Women Religious (region XII), Intercongregational Leadership Group San Antonio. Office: 1603 Babcock Rd Ste 270 San Antonio TX 78229-4750

CENSITS, RICHARD JOHN, business consultant; b. Allentown, Pa., May 20, 1937; s. Stephen A. and Theresa M. Censits; m. Linda A. Malin, June 21, 1958; children: Debra, Mark, David. BS in Econs., U. Pa., 1958; MBA, Lehigh U., 1964. Sr. auditor Arthur Andersen & Co., 1958-62; mgr. acctg. Air Products & Chems., 1962-64; contr. Hamilton Watch Co., Lancaster, Pa., 1964-69; v.p., contr. IU Internat., Phila., 1969-75; v.p., CFO Campbell Soup Co., Camden, N.J., 1975-86; CEO, chmn. MedQuist Inc., Marlton, N.J., 1986-95; bd. dirs. Checkpoint Sys., Inc., Energy North Inc., MedQuist Inc. Mem. undergrad. adv. bd. Wharton Sch., U. Pa.; health sys. trustee U. Pa.; trustee U. Pa. Mem. The Club of Pelican Bay. Home and Office: 688 Annemore Ln Naples FL 34108

CENTERBAR, ALBERTA ELAINE, education educator; b. Ilion, N.Y., Dec. 8, 1949; d. Raymond A. and Gladys J. (Orcutt) Pettengill; m. Richard E. Centerbar, Nov. 2, 1985. BFA, Fla. Atlantic U., 1971, MEd, 1975, EdS, 1993, EdD, 1995. Tchr. 3d grade St. Anastasia Sch., Ft. Pierce, Fla., 1971-74; spl. edn. tchr. St. Lucie County Schs., Ft. Pierce, 1975-80, music specialist, 1980—; adminstr./dir. First United Meth. Ch., Ft. Pierce, 1971-81; adj. prof. (undergrad.) Fla. Atlantic U., Boca Raton, 1990—, adj. prof. (grad.), rsch. specialist, 1993—; tchr. evaluator Fla. performance mgmt. cert. St. Lucie County Schs., 1990—; evaluator, rsch. specialist S.E. Assn. Colls. and Schs., Fla., 1993; revised state cert. tchr. exam. Guest organist chs. from Fla. to Ga., 1981—; accompanist local theater and state band groups, 1975—; adminstrv. bd. First United Meth. Ch., Ft. Pierce, 1971— ; chair and vice chair edn. leadership adv. coun. Fla. Atlantic U., 1991-94, co-chair Prof. of Yr. selection com., 1993. Phi Kappa Phi Nat. Grad. scholar, 1992—. Mem. AAUW, ASCD, Fla. Music Educators Assn. Home: 1923 S Ocean Dr Fort Pierce FL 34949-3362 Office: Village Green Elem School 1700 SE Lennard Rd Port Saint Lucie FL 34952-6535 Also: Fla Atlantic Univ 500 NW University Blvd Port Saint Lucie FL 34986

CENTERS, BONNIE JEAN, nursing administrator; b. Mt. Sterling, Ky., June 23, 1947; d. Harrison Williams and Viola (Alfrey) Conway; m. Arlie Edward Centers, Feb. 5, 1962; 1 child, Arlie Edward Jr. AAS, Morehead State U., 1980. RN, Ky.; cert. rehab. nurse; cert. case mgr.; cert. ACLS instr., BCLS instr. Staff nurse CCU/ICU Mary Chiles Hosp., Mt. Sterling, 1980-83, staff nurse surgery/preceptor, 1983-90; asst. dir. nursing svc. Winchester (Ky.) Health Care Ctr., 1990-92, case mgr. subacute, 1992-95; nurse, ref. liaison Cardinal Hill Rehab. Hosp., Lexington, Ky., 1995—; method of instrn. instr. nurses aides Montgomery Area Vocat. Sch., Mt. Sterling, 1989-91, cert. medication aide instr., 1991-92; speaker in field; mem. faculty conf. on rehab. continuum U. Ky., Lexington, 1994; cons. Christopher East Health Care Facility, 1994; field reviewer Joint Accreditation on Hosps., Cert. and Accreditation for Rehab. Facilities. Co-author tng. manual: Nurse Management, 1991; author orientation programs Guardian Angel, 1991, Nurse Aide Orientation, 1991. Vol. Big Bros./Big Sisters, Winchester, 1991-94, Winchester Health Care, 1991-94. Mem. Assn. Rehab. Nursing, Internat. Case Mgmt. Assn. Home: 865 Bedford Rd PO Box 101 Jeffersonville KY 40337

CENTNER-CONLON, CAROLINE ELIZABETH, social worker, educator; b. Rochester, N.Y., Feb. 12, 1955; d. William and Dorothy (Gardner)

Centner. BS, Syracuse U., 1977; MS in Social Adminstrn., Case Western U., 1979. Cert. sch. social worker, social worker, N.Y. Med. social worker Millard Fillmore Hosp., Buffalo, 1979-80; social worker Hillside Children's Ctr., Rochester, 1980-85; sch. social worker Bd. Coop. Ednl. Svcs. 1, Rochester, 1986-91, Pinellas Sch. Dist., 1991—; adj. prof. dept. social work SUNY, Brockport, 1990-91. Bd. dirs. Rochester-Monroe Effective Parenting Info. for Children, Inc., 1985, Jr. League, Rochester, 1990-91. Mem. Acad. Cert. Social Workers. Home: 1931 Beckett Lake Dr Clearwater FL 34623-4407 Office: Pinellas City Schs Area #1 Student Svcs 525 Pennsylvania Palm Harbor FL 34624

CEPEDA, JOSEPH CHERUBINI, geology educator; b. Del Rio, Tex., Apr. 19, 1948; s. Jose and Elvira (Cherubini) C. BS, U. Tex., 1970; MS, N.Mex. Inst. Mining & Tech., 1972; PhD, U. Tex., 1977. Instr. Appalachian State U., Boone, N.C., 1976-77; from asst. prof. to prof. West Tex. A&M U., Canyon, 1977—; Field camp dir. West Tex., A&M U., 1984-87. Author: Physical Geology Laboratory Exercises, 1984, Introduction to Minerals and Rocks, 1994. Mem. Am. Water Resources Assn., Soc. Wetland Scientists, Geol. Soc. Am., N.Mex. Geol. Soc. Home: PO Box 162 WT Sta Canyon TX 79016

CERBIN, CAROLYN MCATEE, transportation executive, writer; b. Wichita, Kans., June 7, 1957; d. Harold Douglas and Geraldine (Switzer) McAtee; m. David Edward Cerbin, Sept. 26, 1976; children: Greg David, Andrea Michelle. BA, U. Utah, 1978; MBA, U. Fla., 1990. Reporter, editor The Deseret News, Salt Lake City, 1978-79; copy editor, make-up editor Phoenix Gazette, 1979-83; Sunday editor The Dallas Morning News, 1983-88; editor Orlando (Fla.) Bus. Jour., 1990-91; pres. My Chauffeur After-Sch. Shuttle, Inc., Orlando, 1991—. Vol. Clinton-Gore Campaign, Orange County, Fla., 1992; del. Fla. State Dem. Com. Conf., Orlando, 1993; mem. Orange County Dem. Exec. Com.; mem. Concord Coalition; mem. adult bd. WEEKENDS Winter Park. Recipient 1st Pl. award AP Mng. Editors, 1984; co-recipient Pulitzer prize, 1986. Mem. Orange County Dem. Women's Club Fla. Inc. (exec. bd.). Office: My Chauffeur After Sch Shuttle Inc PO Box 5163 Winter Park FL 32793-5163

CERRI, ROBERT NOEL, photographer; b. Boston, Dec. 25, 1947; s. Lawrence Alfred and Angelina (Arena) C. BA, Georgetown Coll., 1972. Dir., head counselor The Open Door, Boca Raton, Fla., 1972-77; actor, model Miami, 1977-79; photojournalist Newsweek/Nat. Geographic, Miami, 1979-85; comml. advt. photographer Miami, 1985—; pres. Robert Cerri Photography, Miami, NY, LA, Orlando, The Caribbean. Mem. Acad. Model Aeronautics, Tasters Guild, U.S. Golf Assn. Republican. Office: Robert Cerri Photography PO Box 801536 Aventura FL 33280

CESARIO, SANDRA KAY, women's health nurse, educator; b. Racine, Wis., May 3, 1955; d. Harold J. and Bernice (Ittner) Block; m. Robert J. Cesario, May 29, 1976; children: Tony, Anna. RN, St. Luke's Hosp., Racine, Wis., 1976; BSN, Ft. Hayes State U., Hays, Kans., 1985; MS, U. Okla., 1989; postgrad., Tex. Womans U., 1995—. Nursery charge nurse Kirksville (Mo.) Osteopathic Hosp., 1976-77; staff nurse NICU St. Joseph's Hosp., Milw., 1977-78; ob staff nurse N. Colo. Med. Ctr., Greeley, 1981-82; ob nursing instr. Luna Vo-Tech., Las Vegas, N.Mex., 1980-81; ob insvc. coord. Guymon (Okla.) Meml. Hosp., 1983; coord. ob nurse residency prog. Indian Health Svc., Oklahoma City, 1989-92; asst. prof. U. Okla., 1992—; mem. adj. clin. faculty Langston U., 1994—. Mem. Assn. Womens Health Obstetrics and Neonatal Nursing, Okla. Nurses Assn., Am. Nurses Assn., Sigma Theta Tau. Home: 3106 Cedar Ave Claremore OK 74017-5919

CESSAC, JOYCE EVE LABORDE, elementary school educator; b. Bordelonville, La., Feb. 7, 1934; d. Adras Paul and Blanche C. (Bordelon) LaBorde; m. Albert J. Cessac; children: Cheri McBurnett, Stephen, Kenneth, Denise Long, Kevin, Nannette Baucom, Chris. BS in Edn., Loyola U., 1954; MS in Curriculum and Early Childhood, Corpus Christi State U., 1979. Cert. elem. tchr., La., Tex. Tchr. Ursuline Acad., New Orleans; owner, tchr. Kiddie Kollege Kindergarten, Sour Lake, Tex.; tchr. St. Luke's Day Sch., Corpus Christi, Tex., Taft (Tex.) Sch. Dist., Gregory-Portland (Tex.) Ind. Sch. Dist. Mem. Dela Kappa Gamma. Home: 106 Blanco Dr Portland TX 78374-1302 Office: East Cliff Sch 200 Fulton Pl Portland TX 78374-1326

CETRON, MARVIN JEROME, management executive; b. Bklyn., July 5, 1930; s. Jack Student and Gertrude Leah C.; m. Gloria Rita Wasserman, June 29, 1955; children: Edward Jack, Adam Bruce. B.S. in Indsl. Engring and Indsl. Psychology, Pa. State U., 1952; MBA, Columbia U., 1959; PhD in Rsch. and Devel. Mgmt, Am. U., 1970. Civilian with U.S. Navy, 1951-71, chief rsch. and devel. planning Naval Material command, 1963-71; founder, pres. Forecasting Internat. Ltd., Arlington, Va., 1971—; adj. prof. Am. U., M.I.T., Ga. Inst. Tech.; Mem. research and devel. adv. com. USCG, 1974—. Author: Technological Forecasting: A Practical Approach, 1969, Technical Resource Management: Quantitative Methods, 1970, The Science of Managing Organized Technology, 4 vols, 1971, Industrial Applications of Technological Forecasting: Its Use in Research and Development Management, 1971, The Navy Technological Forcast, 3d edit, 1970, Technology Assessment in a Dynamic Environment, 1972, The Methodology of Technology Assessment, 1972, Quantitative Decision-aiding Techniques for Research and Development Management, 1972, Proc. NATO Advanced Study Institute on Technology Transfer, 1974, Industrial Technology Transfer, 1977, Encounters with the Future, A Forecast of Life into the 21st Century, 1982, Jobs with a Future, 1984, Schools of the Future, 1985, The Future of American Business, 1985; Great Job Shakeout: How to Find a New Career after the Crash, 1988, America at the Turn of the Century, 1989, American Renaissance: Our Lives at the Turn of the 21st Century, 1989, Educational Renaissance: How to Improve Our School by Turn of the 21st Century, 1990, Crystal Globe: The Have and the Have-Not of the New World Order, 1991; editor in chief Tech. Assessment Jour., 1971-78. Served with USCG, 1954-56. Mem. Ops. Rsch. Soc. Am., IEEE, Tech. and Indsl. Mgmt. Soc., World Future Soc. Office: 1001 N Highland St Arlington VA 22201-2142

CEVASCO, FRANCIS MICHAEL, international business consultant; b. N.Y.C., Mar. 24, 1941; s. Frank Michael and Helen Josephine (Goodock) C.; m. Linda Margaret Hamilton, Aug. 3, 1963; children: Michael, Kevin. BSCE, Polytechnic U., 1963; MSE, George Washington U., 1970. Staff engr. Aurnhammer Assocs., Summit, N.J., 1963; project leader Belvoir Rsch. and Devel. Ctr., Ft. Belvoir, Va., 1967-77; staff engr. Office of the Program Mgt. Container Distbn. Systems, Alexandria, Va., 1977-78; sr. policy advisor HQ Army Material Command, Alexandria, Va., 1979; asst. dep. under sec. def. for internat. devel. and prodn. Dept. Def., Washington, 1980-90; mng. dir. Internat. Ptnrships. Group, Arlington, Va., 1990—. Contbr. articles to profl. jours.; co-inventor air transportable ship mooring system. Treas., bd. dirs. Shouse Village Community Assn., Vienna, Va., 1982-83. Capt. U.S. Army Corps Engrs., 1964-67. Decorated Bronze Star, Comdrs.'s Cross Order of Merit Pres. Fed. Republic of Germany, 1988, Comdr. Order of House of Orange Queen of Netherlands, 1988; recipient Rank of Meritorious Exec. Pres. of U.S., 1989, Disting. Alumni Polytechnic U., 1990. Mem. AAAS, Am. Friends of Turkey, Am. Legion. Republican. Roman Catholic. Home: 7308 Hooking Rd Mc Lean VA 22101-2718 Office: INTERPAR Ste 1109 1215 Jefferson Davis Hwy Arlington VA 22202-4302

CHABACK, JOSEPH JOHN, oil industry researcher; b. Elizabeth, N.J., July 18, 1946; s. Joseph John and Helen Gertrude (Ayers) C.; m. Lucia Katherine Plese, Dec. 22, 1973. BSChemE, Lehigh U., 1968; MS, Washington U., 1971, DSc, 1973. Engr. Exxon Rsch. and Engring. Co., Bayton, Tex., 1973-76; rsch. assoc. Thermodynamics Rsch. Ctr. Tex. A&M U., 1976-78; rsch. engr. Columbia Gas System Svc. Corp., Columbus, Ohio, 1978-81; sr. rsch. engr. Amoco Prodn. Co., Tulsa, 1981-84, staff rsch. engr., 1984-87, rsch. assoc., 1987—. Contbr. articles to profl. jours.; patentee in field. Mem. AIChE, Am. Chem. Soc., Soc. Petroleum Engrs., Toastmasters Internat. (club pres.). Office: Amoco Prodn Co PO Box 3385 Tulsa OK 74102-3385

CHABROW, PENN BENJAMIN, lawyer; b. Phila., Feb. 16, 1939; s. Benjamin Penn and Annette (Shapiro) C.; m. Sheila Sue Steinberg, June 18, 1961; children: Michael Penn, Carolyn Debra, Frederick Penn. BS, Muhlenberg Coll., Allentown, Pa., 1959; JD, George Washington U., 1962, LLM in Taxation, 1968; postgrad. in econs. Harvard U. Bar: Va. 1963, D.C. 1964, U.S. Ct. Appeals (D.C. cir.) 1964, U.S. Tax Ct. 1964, U.S. Supreme Ct. 1966, Fla. 1972, U.S. Ct. Claims 1974, U.S. Ct. Appeals (5th and 11th cirs.) 1981; bd. cert. tax atty., Fla. Tax law specialist IRS, Washington, 1961-67; tax counsel C. of C. U.S., Washington, 1967-74; pvt. practice, Miami, Fla., 1974—; shareholder Wampler, Buchanan & Breen, P.A., Miami, 1993—; pres. Forum Realty Co., Phila., Pure Poultry Enterprises, Inc., Miami, Heartland Farms of Fla., Inc.; lectr. fed. taxation Barry U. Grad. Sch. of Bus., 1977-81. Fellow Am. Coll. Tax Counsel; mem. ABA, Fla. Bar Assn., Fed. Bar Assn., Va. Bar Assn., D.C. Bar Assn., Greater Miami Estate Planning Coun., Muhlenberg Coll. Internat. Vis. Com., Phi Alpha Delta, Phi Sigma Tau. Contbr. articles profl. jours. Office: 777 Brickell Ave Ste 900 Miami FL 33131-2807

CHABROW, SHEILA SUE, English language educator; b. Chgo., Mar. 24, 1940; d. Fred and Florence (Arenson) Steinberg; m. Penn Benjamin Chabrow, June 18, 1961; children: Michael Penn, Carolyn Debra, Frederick Penn; BA, U. Miami (Fla.), 1961; student Harvard U., 1960-61, George Washington U., 1961-62, Va. Poly. Inst., 1972-74; MS, Barry U., 1976. Writer, No. Va. Newspapers, Fairfax, 1969-73; dir. Olam Tikvah Sch., Fairfax, 1973-74; tchr. Palmetto Sr. H.S., Miami, 1979-80; instr. psychology Barry U., Miami, 1980-81; instr. intensive English, U. Miami, Coral Gables, Fla., 1981—; instr. English Fla. Internat. U., 1986-89; v.p. Cutler Bay Estates, Miami, 1975-76, Parent Co-Op. Preschools Internat., 1972-73; pres. No. Va. Co-Op. Schs., 1969-70. Mem. Women in Communications, AAUW (sec. Annandale, Va. 1972), Theta Sigma Phi. Office: U Miami Dept Intensive English Coral Gables FL 33146

CHACE, WILLIAM MURDOUGH, university administrator; b. Newport News, Va., Sept. 3, 1938; s. William Emerson and Grace Elizabeth (Murdough) C.; m. JoAn Elizabeth Johnstone, Sept. 5, 1964; children: William Johnstone, Katherine Elizabeth. BA in English, Haverford Coll., 1961; MA in English, U. Calif., Berkeley, 1963; PhD in English, U. Calif., 1968; LLD (hon.), Amherst Coll., 1990, William Coll., 1992. Instr. Stillman Coll., Tuscaloosa, Ala., 1963-64; teaching asst. U. Calif., Berkeley, 1964-66, acting instr., 1967-68; asst. prof. English Stanford (Calif.) U., 1968-74, assoc. prof., 1974-80, prof., 1980, assoc. dean Sch. Humanities and Scis., 1981-85, vice provost for acad. planning and devel., 1985-88; pres. Wesleyan U., Middletown, Conn., 1988-94, Emory U., Atlanta, 1994—; cons. to Hewlett-Packard, Hallmark Cards Inc., Hawaiian Ednl. Fund, Midwestern Mgmt. Assn.; vis. prof. The Coll. Aboard the Delta Queen, 1979, 80, 82, The Coll. in We. Europe and Brit. Isles, 1985; lectr. to Libr. Assocs. of Stanford U., 1976, 6th Internat. James Joyce Symposium, Dublin, 1977, MLA Ann. Conv., 1977, 78, Tufts U. Symposium, 1978, English Conf. of U. Calif., Berkeley, 1979, Eighth Internat. James Joyce Symposium, Dublin, 1982, IBM Internat. Bus. and Acad. Conf., Monte Carlo, 1984, Ezra Pound Centennial Colloquium, San Jose State U., 1985, Ann. Meeting of the Assn. of Grad. Liberal Studies Programs, St. Louis, 1986, Chico State U., La. State U., 1987, U. Utah Sch. of Medicine Pub. Lecture series, 1987, Northern Calif. Sci. Meeting of Am. Coll. Physicians, Monterey, Calif., 1987, 13th Internat. James Joyce Symposium, 1992; presenter Joyce and History conf. Yale U., 1990. Author: James Joyce: A Collection of Critical Essays, 1973, The Political Identities of Ezra Pound and T.S. Eliot, 1973, Lionel Trilling: Criticism and Politics, 1980, (with others) Graham Greene: A Revaluation, 1990; editor: (with Peter Collier) Justice Denied: The Black Man in White America, 1970, An Introduction to Literature, 1985, (with JoAn E. Chace) Making It New, 1972; contbr. numerous scholarly articles, revs. to profl. jours. Office: Emory U Office of Pres Atlanta GA 30322

CHADWELL, JAMES RUSSELL, JR., comptroller; b. Shelbyville, Ky., Dec. 29, 1948; s. James Russell and Martha (Cinnamond) C.; m. Cecilia Pearce, Dec. 4, 1993; children: Cameron, Ellen, Jackson, Aaron. BS in Math., Ea. Ky. U., 1970; BBA in Acctg., U. Cen. Fla., 1975; MBA, U. Louisville, 1981. CPA, Ky. Auditor Ky. State Auditor's Office, Frankfort, 1975-80, audit mgr., 1981-84; comptr. Ky. Tchr.'s Retirement System, Frankfort, 1984—. Bd. dirs. Commonwealth Credit Union, 1988—, sec.-treas., 1992—. With U.S. Army, 1970-72. Mem. AICPA, Ky. Soc. CPAs, Assn. Govt. Accts. (pres. 1981-82, treas. 1983-84), Govt. Fin. Officers Assn. (spl. rev. com. 1991), Frankfort Earthday Alliance (treas.), U. Louisville Capital Region Alumni Club (pres. 1993-94, treas. 1994—, Bicentennial com.), Sigma Chi. Democrat. Episcopalian. Office: Ky Tchrs Retirement System 479 Versailles Rd Frankfort KY 40601-3868

CHADWICK, CHARLES WILLIAM, veterinarian; b. Jackson, Miss., Mar. 8, 1912; s. Hudson and Anne Louise (Eley) C.; m. Evelyn Elizabeth Clark, June 14, 1938; children: Charles Eley, Martha Ann, Evelyn Elizabeth, William Lyon, Hudson Barnett, Clara Gene. Student, Hinds Jr. Coll., 1933; DVM, Tex. A&M U., 1938. Veterinarian U.S. Bur. Animal Industry, Jacksonville, Fla., 1938-42; pvt. practice vet. medicine Jackson, 1946-90; cons. veterinarian Union Stock Yards, Jackson, 1946-76. Cartoonist, contbr. articles to vet. jours. Bd. dirs. Jackson YMCA; v.p. Southwest Jackson Improvement Assn.; trustee Forest Hill Sch., Jackson, 1955-56; parental councilman Wilkins Sch., Jackson, 1963-69; adminstrv. bd. Forest Hill United Meth. Ch., Jackson. Served with Vet. Corps AUS, 1942-45. Mem. AVMA (honor roll), Miss. Vet. Medicine Assn. (life), Miss. Cattlemens' Assn., SCV, Tex. A&M Former Students Assn. Lodges: Masons, Shriners. Home and Office: 1426 Raymond Rd Jackson MS 39204-4358

CHADWICK, NANENIA ELAINE B., mental health nurse; b. Jesup, Ga., Aug. 28, 1949; d. L. H. and Ruby D. (Jones) Brannen; m. Thomas F. Chadwick, Aug. 31, 1968; children: Tara Y., Lyle T. ASN, Brunswick (Ga.) Coll., 1969; BS, Ga. State U., 1983, MS, 1989; postgrad., Med. Coll. Ga. Cert. adult psychiatric/mental health specialist. Nursing supr. ABC Home Health Agy., Brunswick; head nurse intervention unit Windy Hill Hosp., Marietta, Ga.; night supr. Ridgeview Inst., Smyrna, Ga.; head nurse adult psychiat. unit Brawner Psychiat. Inst., Smyrna; clin. nurse specialist, researcher Grady Meml. Hosp., Atlanta; mem. faculty MCG, Athens, Ga. Piedmont Hosp. scholar. Mem. ANA, Ga. Nurse's Assn., Metro Atlanta Advance Psychiatric Nurse Group, Nurses in Bus., Sigma Theta Tau.

CHADWICK, ROBERT, lawyer, judge; b. Jackson, Miss., Apr. 5, 1924; s. Hudson and Annie (Eley) C.; m. Helen Faye Josey, Apr. 5, 1953; children: Robert Hudson, Celia, Dan, Lea Ann, Robin. BA, Auburn U., 1950; JD, Miss. Coll., 1957; postgrad., U. So. Calif., 1973, 75-76. Bar: Miss. 1963, U.S. Supreme Ct. 1970, U.S. Ct. Mil. Appeals 1975, Ky. 1980, U.S. Dist Ct. (ea. dist.) Ky. 1987. Chief regulation staff div. pesticide regulation USDA, Washington, 1965-70; atty., ecologist div. enforcement EPA, Washington, 1970-75, chmn. com. pesticide misuse rev., 1975-79; asst. gen. counsel Presdl. Clemency Bd. White House Dept. Justice, Washington, 1975; pvt. practice law Frankfort, Ky., 1980-82, 83—; law judge parole bd. Corrections Cabinet, Frankfort, 1982-83; asst. dir. div. hazardous materials Ky. Dept. Natural Resources and Environ. Protection, Frankfort, 1983—; chmn. bd. Exis, Inc.; staff atty., gen. counsel Ky. Cabinet for Human Resources, 1989-90. Pres. PTA Oxon Hill (Md.) Jr. High Sch., 1974, Frankfort Audubon Soc., 1981-83. Cpl. U.S. Army, 1943-45. Mem. ABA, Nat. Assn. Adminstrv. Law Judges, Miss. State Bar Assn., Ky. State Bar Assn., Franklin County Bar Assn., VFW, Masons. Home and Office: 16 Ryswick Ln Frankfort KY 40601-3848

CHAE, DON B., judge, educator; b. Kwangju, Korea, Aug. 27, 1937; came to U.S., 1960; s. He Byong and Woo Ae (Park) C.; m. Yoon Jung Lee, Aug. 14, 1950; children: Donald, Sue, Sarah, Michael. BA, Chonnam Nat. U., 1959; MA, U. Pa., 1962; PhD, U. Tex., 1972; JD, So. Meth. U. Law Sch., 1980. Bar: Tex. 1980, U.S. Dist. Cts., U.S. Tax Ct., Immigration Ct. From asst. to assoc. prof. Chonnam Nat. U., Kwangju, 1962-69; instr. Tarrant County Jr. Coll., Ft. Worth, 1975-80; pvt. practice law Dallas, 1980-94; judge Dallas Mcpl. Ct., 1995—; bd. dirs. Dallas Dispute Mediation Svc., 1994—; immigration and nationality com. State Bar Tex., Austin, 1993—; adminstr. Am. Studies Inst., Kwangju, 1966-72. Chmn. human rights commn. Fedn. of Korean-Am. Assocs. in U.S.A., 1993—, Korean-Am. Scholarship, Inc., Dallas, 1993—, Korean-Am. Fedn. Southwest, 1991—; mem. Overseas Korean Leaderhip Conf., 1996—. Mem. ABA, Am. Immigration Lawyers, Asian-Am. Bar Assn. Dallas (bd. dirs. 1992—), Asian-Am. C. of C. Dallas. Office: Chae & Assocs PC 2828 Forest Ln #1100 Dallas TX 75234

CHAFEE, INGRID ROBERTA HOOVER COLEMAN, French language educator; b. Evanston, Ill., Dec. 12, 1934; d. Richard Thomas and Ingrid (Krogvig) Hoover; m. Samuel Henry Coleman III, Sept. 10, 1958 (wid. Oct. 1974); children: Robert D., Charles E.; m. Nathaniel Chafee, July 8, 1989. AB, Western Coll. of Miami, Oxford, 1956; MA, U. Va., 1959; PhD, Emory U., 1980. Part-time instr. Ga. State U., Atlanta, 1976-81; asst. prof. Morehouse Coll., Atlanta, 1981-83, 1990-95, assoc. prof., 1995—; tech. writer, trainer Am. Software, Inc., Atlanta, 1984-90; coord. European Program, Morehouse Ctr. for Internat. Studies, Atlanta, 1994-96; jour. referee Jour. of Assn. for W. Ga. Coll., 1996. Contbr. articles to profl. jours. Coord. prisoner of conscience coms., Amnesty Internat., Atlanta, 1983-87. Mem. MLA, South Atlantic Modern Lang. Assn., Am. Assn. Tchrs. of French, Phi Beta Kappa. Democrat. Home: 476 Princeton Way NE Atlanta GA 30307 Office: Morehouse Coll Dept Modern Fgn Langs 830 Westview Dr SW Atlanta GA 30314

CHAFFIN, LYLE DWAIN, semiconductor integrated circuits executive; b. Woodward, Okla., May 26, 1940; s. Elmer David and Lula Marie (Lucas) C.; m. Loretta ExaLynn Sigle, Aug. 30, 1963; children: Alan Dane, Ashly Scott. BS in Physics, Okla. State U., 1962, MSEE, 1965. Semiconductor process engr. Tex. Instruments Inc., Dallas, 1965-67, semiconductor design engr., 1967-68; product engring. mgr. Tex. Instruments Inc., Sherman, 1968-74, engring. program mgr., 1974-77, dept. mgr., 1977-82, div. mgr., 1982-86, v.p. semiconductor U.S. product mgr., 1986-87, v.p. semiconductor worldwide product mgr., 1987—; mem. engring. adv. coun. Okla. Christian U. Sci. and Arts, Edmond, 1989—, vice chmn. bd. devel., 1992. Elder Western Heights Ch. of Christ, Sherman, 1976—. Mem. Sherman C. of C. Republican. Home: 2511 Nantucket Dr Sherman TX 75092-2240

CHAIN, BOBBY LEE, electrical contractor, former mayor; b. Hattiesburg, Miss., Sept. 19, 1929; s. Zollie Lee and Grace (Sellers) C.; ; m. Betty Sue Green, June 30, 1967; children: Robin Ann, Laura Grace, Bobby Lee, John Webster. BS, U. So. Miss., Hattiesburg, 1974; DBA (hon.), William Carey Coll., Hattiesburg. Chief electrician Miss. Power & Light Co., Natchez, 1950-53; asst. to gen. supt. atomic energy plant Allegany Electric Co., Oak Ridge, 1954-55; owner, chmn. bd. Chain Electric Co., Hattiesburg, 1955, Chain Lighting & Appliance Co., Hattiesburg, 1960; owner, pres. Chainco, Inc., oil properties, Hattiesburg, 1974—; bd. dirs. Deposit Guaranty Nat. Bank, Jackson, Deposit Guaranty Corp., Jackson; adv. dir. Deposit Guaranty Nat. Bank, Hattiesburg; mem. Interstate Oil Compact Commn., 1972—; mem. nat. adv. coun. SBA, 1966-67; bd. dirs. Miss. Econ. Coun., 1991—; mayor city of Hattiesburg, 1980-85. Bd. dirs. Pub. Sch. Forum Miss.; past mem., past pres. Miss. Trustees Instns. Higher Learning; past mem. So. Regional Edn. Bd., MIssissippians for Quality Edn.; chmn. Commn. on Efficiency in Govt., Miss. Econ. Coun.; mem. Miss. State Workforce Devel. Coun.; chmn. Pearl River County Dist. Workforce Coun. Recipient Disting. Svc. award U. So. Miss., 1976, Hub award, 1979, Continuous Outstanding Svc. award, 1980, Liberty Bell award Forrest County Bar Assn., 1980, Svc. to Edn. award Phi Delta Kappa, 1980, Disting. Citizen award Pine Burr Area Coun. Boy Scouts Am., 1995; named to Hall U. So. Miss., Miss. Bus. Hall of Fame, 1994; Bobby L. Chain Tech. Ctr. named in his honor; Bobby L. Chain Hattiesburg Mcpl. Airport named in his honor; Paul Harris fellow Rotary Internat., 1990. Mem. Newcomen Soc. N.Am., U. So. Miss. Alumni Assn. (Outstanding Svc. award 1972, Sales and Mktg. Man of Yr. award 1981), Hattiesburg C. of C. (past dir.), Miss. Bus. Roundtable, Kiwanis, Hattiesburg Country Club (past pres.), U. So. Miss. Century Club, Shriners, Univ. Club, Plimsoll Club (New Orleans), Omicron Delta Kappa, Beta Gamma Sigma. Baptist. Home: 312 6th Ave Hattiesburg MS 39401-4240 Office: PO Box 2058 Hattiesburg MS 39403-2058

CHAIT, ANDREA MELINDA, special education educator; b. Buffalo, May 7, 1970; d. Marvin and Rochelle (Benatovich) C. BS in Health Edn., Ithaca (N.Y.) Coll., 1992; MEd in Spl. Edn., U. Fla., 1995. Cert. tchr. health edn., N.Y.; cert. N.Y. State Mandatory Child Abuse and Neglect Tng. Program K-12; cert. tchr. spl. edn., Ga. Substitute tchr. Cortland (N.Y.) H.S., 1992; tchrs. aid/substitute Stanley G. Falk, Cheektowaga, N.Y., 1993; pvt. spl. edn. tutor Buffalo and Gainesville, 1992—; behavioral disorders tchr. Paul D. West Middle Sch., East Point, Ga., 1995-96; chairperson discipline com. spl. edn. dept. Paul P. West Middle Sch., East Point, Ga., 1995—. Vol. Task Force for Battered Women, Ithaca, 1991, nursing homes, Ithaca, 1991-92, Human Rights Orgn., Gainesville, 1993-94. Mem. ASCD, Coun. for Exceptional Children, Coun. for Children with Behavioral Disorders, Pi Lambda Theta, Kappa Delta Pi, Phi Kappa Phi. Jewish. Home: 823 SW 56th Ter Gainesville FL 32607

CHAKKO, SIMON C., cardiologist, educator; b. Kerala, India, Sept. 30, 1950; came to U.S., 1975; MB, BS, St. John's Med. Coll., Bangalore, India, 1974. Diplomate Am. Bd. Internal Medicine; sub-splty. cardiovasc. diseases. Intern St. Martha's Hosp. St. John's Med. Coll., 1973-74, resident, 1974-75; intern Jersey City (N.J.) Med. Ctr., 1976-77, resident, 1977-78, fellow in cardiology, 1978-79; fellow in cardiology Temple U. Hosp., Phila., 1979-81, clin. instr., 1979-81; from asst. prof. to assoc. prof. U. Va., Charlottesville, 1981-88; assoc. prof. clin. medicine U. Miami, Fla., 1988-92, assoc. prof. medicine, 1992—; assoc. chief cardiology VA Med. Ctr., Salem, Va., 1981-87, chief, 1987-88, chief coronary care unit, Miami, 1988-89, chief non-invasive cardiac labs., 1989—; attending staff physician divsn. cardiology Jackson Meml. Hosp., Miami, 1988—, U. Miami Hosps. and Clinics, 1988—. Contbr. chpts. to books and articles to profl. jours.; referee reviewer: Am. Heart Jour., Chest, Jour. Am. Coll. Cardiology Clin. Cardiology. Mem. community leadership club U. Miami United Way Campaign, 1989, 90, 91. Recipient Physicians Recognition award AMA, 1982—. Fellow Am. Coll. Cardiology, ACP; mem. Am. Fedn. for Clin. Rsch., AM. Soc. Echocardiography, Am. Heart Assn. Scientific Coun. on Clin. Cardiology. Home: 10027 SW 126th St Miami FL 33176-4848 Office: VA Med Ctr 111-A Cardiology Miami FL 33176

CHAKRABARTY, SUBHAS, medical educator; b. Kwantung, China, Sept. 21, 1946; came to U.S., 1968; m. Lila Adhikari, Dec. 29, 1970; 1 child, Justin Alexander. BS in Biology/Psychology, U. N.D., 1973, MS in Microbiology/Biochemistry, 1974; PhD in Immunology, U. Manitoba, Can., 1980. Postgrad. cancer biology and pharmacology Baylor Coll. Medicine, Houston, 1980-84, asst. prof. pharmacology, 1984-90; asst. biologist, asst. prof. lab. medicine U. Tex. M.D. Anderson Cancer Ctr., Houston, 1990-93, asst. prof. tumor biology, 1991-93; assoc. prof. lab. medicine and tumor biology, 1993—; cons. Bristol-Myers Co., 1983-89; adj. asst. prof. pharmacology Baylor Coll. Medicine, Houston, 1990-93; faculty mem. U. Tex. Allied Health Sci. Ctr., Grad. Sch. Biomed. Scis., Houston, 1991—; presenter in field. Contbr. chpts. to books and articles to profl. jours. Recipient Undergrad. tuition scholarship U. N.D., Grand Forks, 1972-73, Bd. Higher Edn. scholarships U. N.D., Grand Forks, 1974-75, other numerous grants. Mem. AAAS, Am. Assn. for Cancer Rsch., Am. Soc. for Cell Biology, Metastasis Rsch. Soc. Home: 1915 Oakhurst Pky Sugar Land TX 77479-3268 Office: Univ Tex MD Anderson Cancer Ctr 1515 Holcombe Blvd Houston TX 77030-4009

CHAKRAVARTHY, UPEN SHARMA, computer science educator; b. Bangalore, Karnataka, India, Jan. 13, 1952; came to U.S., 1979; s. Ananthachar and Jayamma Chakravarthy; m. Shubha Iyengar, Jan. 19, 1983; 1 child, Tejas. B in Engring., Indian Inst. Sci., Bangalore, 1973; M in Tech., Indian Inst. Tech., Bombay, 1975; MS, U. Md., 1981, PhD, 1985. Sci. officer Tata Inst. Fundamental Rsch., Bombay, 1975-78; tchg. asst., rsch. asst., instr. U. Md., College Park, 1979-85; computer scientist Computer Corp. Am., Cambridge, Mass., 1985-88; mem. tech. staff Xerox Advanced Info. Tech., Cambridge, 1988-89; assoc. prof. U. Fla., Gainesville, 1989—. Recipient nat. scholarship and commonwealth scholarship Ministry of Edn., India, 1979. Mem. IEEE, Am. Assn. Artificial Intelligence, Assn. for Computing Machinery. Office: Univ Fla Database Ctr 470 CSE Gainesville FL 32611

CHALAM, ANN, healthcare administrator. Patient care svcs. adminstr. Cancer Ctr. U. Va. Health Sci. Ctr., Charlottesville. Office: U Va Health Sci Ctr Box 334 Charlottesville VA 22908

CHALFANT, WILLIAM ARTHUR, petroleum landman; b. Bismark, N.D., July 24, 1954; s. Wesley and Doris Fern (Meyer) C.; m. Karen Wood Bryant, Feb. 18, 1978 (div. 1988); m. Katherine Sappington, Aug. 28, 1992; children:

Paul, Matthew. Degree in Fin., Tex. A&M, 1976. Cert. profl. landman, cert. mediator, Tex. Owner Chalfant Properties Inc., Midland, Tex., 1976—. Deacon 1st Presbyn. Ch., 1993—; bd. dirs. Midland Presbyn. Mission, 1995—, v.p., 1996. Mem. Am. Assn. Petroleum Landmen (CPL test subcom. 1991), Permian Basin Landman Assn. (bd. dirs. 1992-93, sec. 1993-94, 1st v.p. 1994-95, pres. 1995-96). Office: Chalfant Properties Inc 1502 N Big Spring Midland TX 79701-4417

CHALK, JOHN ALLEN, SR., lawyer; b. Lexington, Tenn., Jan. 16, 1937. A.A., Freed-Hardeman Coll., 1956; B.S., Tenn. Tech. U., 1962, M.A., 1967; J.D., U. Tex., 1973. Bar: Tex. 1973, D.C. 1977; ordained to ministry Ch. of Christ, 1956; cert. advanced mediator Dispute Resolution Svcs. of Tarrant County, Tex.; Tex. Ct.-Approved Mediator. Pastor chs. Dayton, Ohio, 1956-60, Cookeville, Tenn., 1960-66, Abilene, Tex., 1966-71; assoc. Rhodes and Seamster, Abilene, 1973-74, Rhodes and Doscher, Abilene, 1974; ptnr. Rhodes, Doscher, Chalk and Heatherly,, Abilene, 1975-78; gen. counsel La Jet, Inc., Abilene, 1978-84, also v.p., sec; exec. v.p. Dabney Corp., 1984-86; pres. Dabney Capital, 1984-86; assoc. Gandy, Michener, Swindle, Whitaker & Pratt, Ft. Worth, 1986, ptnr., 1987-93; ptnr. Michener Larimore Swindle Whitaker Flowers Sawyer Reynolds & Chalk, Ft. Worth, 1993—; pres. Equity, Inc., 1982-90; bd. dirs. Osteo. Health Sys. Tex., Inc.; mem. strategic alliances com. for edn. Nat. Ct. Reporters Assn., 1994-95; advanced mediator Dispute Resolution Svcs. Tarrant County, Tex. Author: The Praying Christ, 1964, Three American Revolutions, 1970, Jesus' Church, 1970, The Christian Family, 1973, Great Biblical Doctrines, 1973, The Devil, You Say!, 1974; author numerous articles on U.S. Dept. Edn. postsecondary regulations, also articles on religion. Trustee Abilene Regional Mental Health Retardation Ctr., 1978-80, Christian Scholarship Found., Inc., Atlanta, 1980—, chmn. bd., 1992-93; chmn. Ailene Bicentennial Com., 1975-76; mem. nat. adv. coun. Am. United for Separation of Ch. and State, 1979-82, pres. bd. trustees, 1981-82; mem. nat. devel. coun. Abilene Christian U.; featured spkr. radio and TV programs Herald of Truth, 1966-69; trustee Osteo. Health Care Found., Inc., Ft. Worth, 1987—, sec.-treas., 1990-91, sr. v.p., pres.-elect, 1991-92, pres., 1992-93; mem. Strategy for 2000, City of Ft. Worth, 1995—. Fellow Coll. of State Bar Tex., Tex. Bar Found.; mem. ABA (acting assoc. editor, mem. editl. bd. Family Adv. 1977-78), FBA, Am. Arbitration Assn. (panel arbitrators and mediators), Internat. Ctrs. for Arbitration (panel arbitrators and mediators), Tarrant County Assn. Mediators, Tex. Ct.-Approved Mediators, Tex. Bar Assn., State Bar Tex., Ft. Worth Bar Assn. Home: 3601 Verde Vista Ct W Aledo TX 76008-3679 Office: Michener Larimore Swindle Whitaker 3500 City Ctr II Fort Worth TX 76102-4140

CHALMERS, KIMBERLY, artist, educator. BFA, U. Southwestern La., 1971; MFA, Fla. State U., 1973. Tchg. asst. Fla. State U., Tallahassee, 1971-73; prof. art Coker Coll., Hartsville, S.C., 1973—, chair dept. art, 1985—; designer; adj. prof. U. Southwestern La., Lafayette, 1980; studio resident Mus. Internat. de Electrografia, Cuenca, Spain, 1992; participant conf. Irish Mus. Modern Art, Dublin, 1993; vis. lectr. Kawaijuku Art Inst., Tokyo, 1995, Daito Bunka U., Tokyo and Higashimatsuyama, Japan, 1995; exhbns. coord. Kalmia Arts, Hartsville Arts Coun., 1974-82; dir. Darlington County Summer Program for Gifted and Talented in Art, 1988; founder, dir. Art Dept. Gallery, 1973-80, New Gallery, 1980-83, Bell Art Gallery, 1983-94; lectr., presenter orgns. including Coker Artists, Spkrs. Bur., 1974—; juror art competitions, 1974—. One-person shows include Francis Marion Coll., Florence, S.C., 1974, 78, 85, U. North Fla., Jacksonville, 1974, Coker Coll., 1975, Concord Coll., Athens, W.Va., 1976, Mckissick Mus., Columbia, S.C., 1977, Studio C Gallery, New Orleans, 1983, Cecilia Coker Bell Gallery, Hartsville, 1984, Florence Mus., 1986, Augusta (Ga.) Coll., 1987, Cheraw (S.C.) Arts Commn. Gallery, 1987, U. Tenn., Chattanooga, 1987, U. Western Carolina, Cullowhee, N.C., 1988, Auburn (Ala.) U., 1989, 7th St. Gallery, Charlotte, N.C., 1991, Mus. Internat. de Electrografia, 1992, YMCA, Hartsville, 1992, County Mayo Libr., Castlebar, Ireland, 1993, Space Map Gallery, Kawaijuku Art Inst., Tokyo, 1995, Daito Bunka U., 1995; exhibited in group and juried exhbns., most recently at Stanback Mus. Art, Orangeburg, S.C., 1988, Grand Palais, Paris, 1988, Inst. Contemporary Art, London, 1988, S.C. State Mus., 1989, 94, Florence Mus. Art, 1989, Francis Marion U., 1994, S.E. Ctr. for Contemporary Art, N.C., 1994. S.E. Arts Fedn. regional fellow Nat. Endowment for Arts, 1994, Fulbright fellow, Japan, 1980. Home: 1500 Ballentine Ave Hartsville SC 29550 Office: Coker Coll Dept Art 300 E College Ave Hartsville SC 29550

CHAMBERLAIN, CHARLES FRANK, artist, educator; b. Brockton, Mass., Aug. 7, 1942; s. William Smith and Bertha Louise (Hansler) C.; m. Linda Chloe Cheney, Jan. 3, 1968; children: Gabrielle Elizabeth, Pamela Chloe. BFA, Mass. Coll. Art, Boston, 1964; MFA, SUNY, Alfred, 1967. Instr. U. N.H., Durham, 1966-67; prof. art East Carolina U., Greenville, N.C., 1967—; chair arts commn. Episcopal Diocese of East Carolina, Kinston, N.C., 1988—. Exhibitor pottery at Crafts Multiples, Washington, 1978; exhibitor ceramic art at Rocky Mt. Art Ctr., 1996, Henri Gallery, Washington, 1965; artist Stations of the Cross, St. Paul's Ch., Greenville, N.C., 1965. Mem. Nat. Coun. Edn. Ceramic Art. Democrat. Office: East Carolina U Sch Art Greenville NC 27858-4353

CHAMBERLAIN, ENRIQUE KING, library director; b. Laredo, Tex., May 3, 1943; s. Richard King and Francisca (Perez) C. AA, Laredo Jr. Coll., 1963; BA, U. North Tex., 1965; MA, EdD, East Tex. State U., 1982. Libr. Dallas Ind. Sch. Dist., 1965-66, North Lake Coll., Irving, Tex., 1966—; chmn. 25th anniversary com., chmn. archives com. for 25th anniversary com. Dallas County C.C. Dist., 1991. Named Minnie Piper Prof., Tex., 1988. Mem. North Lake Coll. Faculty Assn. (pres. 1983-85), Dallas County C.C. Faculty Assn. (v.p. 1983-85), Phi Theta Kappa. Democrat. Roman Catholic. Office: North Lake Coll 5001 N Macarthur Blvd Irving TX 75038-3804

CHAMBERLAIN, JOHN MEREDITH, health facility executive, consultant; b. Little Rock, Apr. 27, 1950; s. Charles Thomton and Frances (Goodlett) C.; m. Debra Lee McAden, May 21, 1981; children: Jason Meredith, Frances Elizabeth. BA, Westminster Coll., Fulton, Mo., 1972; M of Health Adm., Washington U., St. Louis, 1985. Group leader Mallinckrodt, Inc., St. Louis, 1972-76, ops. mgr., 1978-82; plant mgr. Mallinckrodt, Inc., Beaufort, N.C., 1976-78; mgr. customer compliance Sigma Chem. Co., St. Louis, 1982-83; cons. Warner Health Svcs., St. Louis, 1983-85; dir. mktg. St. Louis Children's Hosp., St. Louis, 1985-87; asst. adminstr. Lakeview Hosp., Bountiful, Utah, 1987, Drs. Hosp. of Sarasota, Sarasota, Fla., 1987-90; med. staff liaison, chief devel. officer Glenwood Regional Med. Ctr., West Monroe, La., 1990-93, sr. v.p., chief operating officer, 1993-95; assoc. adminstr. ops. Med. Ctr. Hosp., Odessa, Tex., 1995—; ptnr. Med. Devel. Svcs., Sarasota, 1989—. Active Leadership La., Leadership Ouachita, Leadership Odessa. Fellow Am. Coll. Healthcare Execs., Rotary; mem. Am. Hosp. Assn. Republican. Unitarian.

CHAMBERLAIN, WILLIAM RHODE, county official; b. Clarendon, Tex., Feb. 1, 1944; s. William Park and Norma Evelyn (Rhode) C.; m. Brenda Kay Lane, Nov. 28, 1963; children: Shalane Chamberlain Wesley, Sheri Chamberlain Cooper. Student, Tex. A&M U., 1988-94, Amarillo (Tex.) Jr. Coll., 1993, Midwestern State U., 1993. County commr. Donley County, Clarendon, 1979—; dir. Shamrock Savs. and Loans, Amarillo, 1985-88; v.p. Panhandle Grant Com., Amarillo, 1987; pres. Panhandle Judges and Commrs., Amarillo, 1990; conf. com. mem. West Tex. Judges and Commrs., 1990-92, chmn. nominations com., 1994. Mem. Free Mason (past master 1978, 32 Lubbock dist. dep. 1982). Democrat. Methodist. Home: HC 5 Box 40 Clarendon TX 79226-9322

CHAMBERLIN, SHELIA DIANE, office administrator; b. Richmond, Ky., Nov. 11, 1964; d. Jerry and Rachel (Northern) Rose; m. Frank Chamberlin; children: Brandy, Chad, Megan, Renae, Rachel. Grad., Madison Ctrl. H.S., Richmond, 1982. Cashier Days Inn, Richmond, 1982-83; sec. Ea. Ky. U., Richmond, 1983-85; with data entry dept. 1st Image, Berea, Ky., 1986-90, 93-94; sec. 1st Am. Mobile Homes, Richmond, 1990-91. Author: (poetry) Inspirations, 1995, Mists of Enchantment, 1995, Treasured Poems of America, 1995, Impressions, 1995. Home: 144 Rose Ln Richmond KY 40475

CHAMBERS, CAROL TOBEY, elementary school educator; b. L.A., July 17, 1947; d. Joseph Richard and Jean Doris (Neal) Tobey; m. Joseph Price Chambers, June 8, 1973; 1 child, Ryan Leigh. Student, Ohio State U., 1965-67; BS in Edn., George Peabody Coll. Tchrs., 1969; postgrad., U. Tenn., 1971, Belmont U., 1971, 88, 96, Tenn. State U., 1980-83, Vanderbilt U., 1986, 92, Trevecca Coll., 1978, 89, 90, Tenn. Arts Acad., 1989, 94-96. Cert. tchr. elem. edn., elem. art, Tenn. Tchr. 4th grade Metro-Nashville Pub. Sch., Nashville, 1969-70, tchr. art, music, 1970-71; tchr. 5th grade Harding Acad., Nashville, 1971-75, tchr. art, 1977—; presenter workshops Mid-So. Assn. Ind. Schs., Nashville, 1986; vis. com. Oak Hill Sch., So. Assn. Colls. and Schs., Nashville, 1990, St. Berbard Acad., 1991; chair planning com. Harding Acad., Nashville, 1992-94, mem. 25th anniversary com.; fine arts chair St. Cecilia Acad. Parents Club, Nashville, 1991-93, mem. Parents Club; cofounder Art Tchrs. Guild, Nashville; organizer Youth Art Month Exhibit, Nashville, 1992—. V.p. in charge of art Children's Internat. Edn. Ctr., Nashville, 1985-90; cons. Cheekwood Fine Arts Ctr. and Bot. Gardens Edn. Dept., Nashville, 1987—; prodr. parent's seminar 1st Bapt. Ch., 1986. Outstanding Tchr. of Humanities grantee Tenn. Humanities Couns., 1988. Mem. Nat. Art Edn. Assn., Tenn. Art Edn. Assn., Nat. Mus. Women in the Arts (charter). Baptist. Home: 722 Starlit Rd Nashville TN 37205-1210 Office: 170 Windsor Dr Nashville TN 37205-3719

CHAMBERS, DALE, mechanical engineer; b. Welch, W.Va., Jan. 7, 1953; s. Chester and Jannigee (Dutton) C.; m. Norma Jeanne Ogden, Nov. 5, 1971; children: Brian, Marshall. BSME, Va. Poly. Inst., 1976; MBA, U. Richmond, 1989. Registered profl. engr., Va., Calif., N.C., Miss., Maine, Pa. Design engr. Babcock & Wilcox, Lynchburg, Va., 1976-77; engr. Wiley & Wilson, Lynchburg, 1977-82; sr. engr. Velzy Assocs., Richmond, Va., 1982-84; staff engr. Va. Power, Richmond, 1984-86; v.p. REFCOM Corp., Richmond, 1986-88; project mgr. Black & Veatch, Richmond, 1988-89, regional office mgr., 1989-91; pres. Chambers Engring., Inc., Richmond, 1991-92; dist. mktg. mgr. Smith Environ. Techs. Corp., Richmond, 1992-95, dist. mgr., 1995—. Coach Tuckahoe Little League Baseball. Mem. ASME (solid waste processing div., membership chmn. Richmond chpt. 1992-93), ASHRAE, Am. Rwy. Engring. Assn., Va. Econ. Developers Assn., Richmond Engrs. Club, Assn. Am. Railroads (environ. ops. subcom.), Soc. Am. Mil. Engrs. Republican. Home: 12609 Wilde Lake Ct Richmond VA 23233-3381 Office: Smith Technology Corp PO Box 17497 Washington DC 20041-0497

CHAMBERS, IMOGENE KLUTTS, school system administrator, financial consultant; b. Paden, Okla., Aug. 6, 1928; d. Odes and Lillie (Southard) Klutts; BA, East Central State U., 1948; MS, Okla. State U., 1974, EdD, 1980; m. Richard Lee Chambers, May 27, 1949. High sch. math. tchr. Marlow (Okla.) Sch. Dist., 1948-49; with Bartlesville (Okla.) Sch. Dist., 1950-94, asst. supt. bus. affairs, treas. Ind. Sch. Dist. 30, 1977-87, treas., 1985-94; fin. acctg. cons. Okla. State Dept. Edn., 1987-92; dir. Plaza Nat. Bank, 1984-94; adv. dir. Bank Okla., 1994-96. Bd. dirs. Mutual Girls Club, 1981—; treas. Okla. Schs. Ins. Assn., 1982—, adminstr., 1993—. Mem. Okla. Assn. Sch. Bus. Ofcls., Assn. Sch. Bus. Ofcls. Internat., Okla. Assn. Retired Sch. Adminstrs., Okla. State U. Alumni Assn., E. Ctrl. Univ. Alumni Assn. (bd. dirs. 1994-96), Rotary. Democrat. Methodist. Home and Office: 911 SE Greystone Pl Bartlesville OK 74006-5141

CHAMBERS, JOHNNIE LOIS, elementary school educator, rancher; b. Crocket County, Tex., Sept. 28, 1929; d. Robert Leo and Lois K. (Slaughter) Tucker; m. R. Boyd Chambers; children: Theresa A., Glyn Robert, Boyd James, John Trox. BEd, Sul Ross State U., Alpine, Tex., 1971. Tchr. 1st and 2d grades Candelaria (Tex.) Elem. Sch., 1971-73; head tchr. K-8 Ruidosa (Tex.) Elem. Sch., 1973-77; head tchr. K-8 Presidio Ind. Sch. Dist. at Candelaria Elem. Sch., 1977-91, tchr. 2d and 3d grades, 1991-93, tchr. pre-kindergarten, kindergarten and 1st grade, 1993—; acting prin. Candelaria Elem. & Jr. High, 1995—; mem. sight-base decision making, Presidio, 1991-94; mem. Chihuahuan Desert Rsch. Inst., Alpine, 1982-94. Leader Boy Scouts Am., Ruidosa and Candelaria, 1973-91, Cub Scout leader, 1973-91;chpt. mem. Sheriffs Assn. Tex., Austin, 1980. Recipient awards Boy Scouts Am., 1969, 83, winner Litter Gitter award, 1994-95. Mem. Tex. State Tchrs. Assn., Phi Alpha Theta. Home and Office: Number 1 Education Ave Candelaria TX 79843

CHAMBERS, JUDITH TARNPOLL, speech pathologist; b. Newark, Mar. 17, 1940; d. Morris and grace Annette (Lambeck) Tarnpoll; m. John Darby Chambers, May 29, 1977; 1 child, Joshua. BA, Rutgers U., 1964; MA, Columbia U., 1966. Cert. audiologist, N.Y., Conn. Speech and lang. therapist League Sch., Bklyn.; lang. therapist BOCES, Elmsford, N.Y.; chief audiologist Royal Victoria Hosp., Montreal, Que., Can.; ind. dispensing audiologist Bridgeport, Conn. Mem. Am. Speech-Lang.-Hearing Assn., Acad. Dispensing Audiologists, Am. Acad. Audiology (charter mem.).

CHAMBERS, JULIUS LEVONNE, academic administrator, lawyer; b. Montgomery County, N.C., Oct. 6, 1936. BA, N.C. Central U., 1958; MA, U. Mich., 1959; LLB, U. N.C., 1962; LLM, Columbia U., 1963. Bar: N.C. 1962, N.Y. 1986. Ptnr. Chambers, Ferguson, Watt, Wallas, Adkins, & Fuller, Charlotte, N.C., 1964-84; dir., counsel NAACP Legal Def. and Ednl. Fund, N.Y.C, 1984-92; chancellor N.C. Ctrl. U., Durham, N.C., 1993—; bd. dirs. RJR Nabisco Holdings. Trustee N.J. State Bd. of Higher Edn.; bd. visitors Harvard U., Columbia Law Sch.; trustee U. Pa., mem. bd. overseers Law Sch.; bd. dirs. Children's Def. Fund, Legal Aid Soc. N.Y. Mem. ABA (bd. editors ABA jour.), N.C. Bar Assn., Mecklenburg County Bar Assn., N.Y. State Bar Assn., Assn. of Bar of City of N.Y., Nat. Bar Assn., Assn. Black Lawyers N.C., Order of Coif, Order of Golden Fleece, Phi Alpha Theta. Office: NC Ctrl U 1801 Fayetteville St Durham NC 27707-3129

CHAMBERS, LINDA DIANNE THOMPSON, social worker; b. Mexia, Tex., Apr. 21, 1953; d. Lee and Essie Mae (Hopes) Thompson; m. George Edward Chambers, Nov. 30, 1978; 1 child, Brandon. AS cum laude, Navarro Coll., Tex., 1974; B in Social Work magna cum laude, Tex. Woman's U., 1976; cert. gerontology and Human Svcs. Mgmt., Sam Houston U., 1982; M in Social Work, U. Tex.-Arlington, 1990. Lic. marriage and family therapist, social worker-advanced practitioner; cert. family life ducator; registered sex offender treatment provider. Mem. social work staff Dept. Human Resources, Ft. Worth, Tex., 1975, Children's Med. Ctr., Dallas, 1976, Mexia State Sch., Tex., 1976-93, Methodist Home, Waco, Tex., 1993-96, Tex. Dept. Health, Waco, 1996—, Parkview Regional Hosp., 1996—, Pres., Raven Exquisites, Mexia, 1983-84, sec.-treas., 1984-85; bd. dirs. Limestone County Child Welfare Bd., Hospice, Inc.; pres. bd. dirs. Limestone County unit Am. Cancer Soc.; bd. dirs. Gibbs Meml. Libr., Teen Pregnancy Prevention Coun., Childcare Mgmt. Svcs.; mem. Tex. Dem. Women; vol. McLennan County Pub. Health Dist. AIDS Clinic; coord., founder Limestone County Teen Parent Program; co-founder Limestone County Parenting Coalition; mem. Limestone County Youth Adv. Com.; PTO sec. Ctrl. Tex. Literacy Coalition, 1992—; vol. Ctr. for Action Against Sexual Assault, Family Abuse Ctr.; mem. Tex. Hist. Found., Nat. Mus. Women in Arts, 1985—; Recipient numerous awards for scholarship and profl. excellence. Fellow Internat. Biog. Assn. (dep. bd. gov., life); mem. Am. Sociol. Soc. (sec. 1975-76), Univ. Woman's Assn., Am. Childhood Edn. Internat., Nat. Assn. Social Workers, NAFE, Am. Assn. Mental Retardation, Nat. Assn. Future Women, Am. Soc. Profl. and Exec. Women, Nat. Assn. Negro Bus. and Profl. Women's Clubs, AAUW, Tex. Woman's U. Nat. Alumnae Assn., Mortar Bd. Honor Soc. (sec.-treas. 1975-76), Tex. Soc. Clin. Social Workers, Internat. Platform Assn., Internat. Assn. Bus. and Profl. Women, Am. Biog. Assn. (dep. bd. govs.), Nat. Mus. Women Arts, Los Amigos, Limestone County Parenting Coalition (co-founder), Phi Theta Kappa, Alpha Kappa Delta, Alpha Delta Mu, Young Dems. Club. Avocations: reading, gardening, gourmet cooking. Home: 102 Harding Mexia TX 76667

CHAMBERS, RAY WAYNE, security and loss control consultant; b. Cascade, W.Va., June 22, 1931; s. Robert and Mildred Ethel (Starrett) C.; m. Joan Roberta Tilley, Apr. 7, 1952; children: Rebecca H. Frase, Bonita I. Knight, Diana L. Sobalvarro. Cert. protection profl., mgmt. cons. Enlisted U.S. Army, 1949, advanced through grades to lt. col., 1971; sgt.-maj. tank battalion U.S. Army, Republic of Korea, 1952-53; U.S. Army, Europe, 1956-60, 62-65, 67-70; intelligence battalion ops. officer U.S. Army, Socialist Republic of Vietnam, 1966-67; dep. chief staff ops., intelligence command U.S. Army, ret., 1973; v.p. loss prevention Little Gen. Store div. Gen. Host Corp., Tampa, Fla., 1973-84; pres. Assets Protection Systems Assocs., Inc., Largo, Fla., 1985—; loss control cons. JRB Investigations Inc., Largo, 1986-87. Contbr. articles to profl. jours.. Bd. dirs. Del Prado Imperial Assn., Largo, chmn. neighborhood watch com., 1983-88. Decorated Bronze Star, Legion of Merit. Mem. Am. Soc. Indsl. Security (chmn. 1975-76, cert. 1976), Internat. Assn. Profl. Security Cons. (exec. dir. 1990-93), Retail Grocers Assn. Fla. (chmn. crime prevention 1983-85), Pinellas Assn. Pvt. Investigators (pres. 1986), Fla. Crime Prevention Officers Assn., Nat. Assn. Convenience Stores, Internat. Found. for Protection Officers, Assn. Counter Intelligence Corps Vets, Inst. Mgmt. Cons. Republican. Home and Office: Assets Protection Sys Assoc Inc 11113 Bella Loma Dr Largo FL 34644-4622

CHAMBERS, ROBERT WILLIAM, financial company executive; b. Atlanta, Apr. 4, 1943; s. Robert William Chambers and Mary Emily (Martin) Nalley; m. Wendy Ann Treneer, Dec. 28, 1967 (div. 1979); 1 child, Robert William III. AB, Princeton U., 1965; MA, Indiana U., 1970, PhD, 1974. Assoc. instr. Ind. U., Bloomington, 1970-73; instr. Kans. State U., Manhattan, 1973-74; gen. mgr. Standard Cellulose Products Inc., Atlanta, 1974-75; mgr. sales, ops. Disposable Plastic Systems Inc., Marietta, Ga., 1975-77; asst. v.p., account exec. instl. sales Robinson-Humphrey Co. Inc., Atlanta, 1977-80; columnist, fin. reporter Atlanta Journal, 1980-81; account exec. Hill and Knowlton (J. Walter Thompson Group), Atlanta, 1981-83; sr. v.p., sales mgr. eastern div. Colonial Investment Svcs. Inc., Atlanta, 1983-90; sr. fin. cons. The Gwent Group, Atlanta, 1990-92; v.p., treas. Rabun Gap Film Corp., Atlanta, 1993—; dir. Bus. Svcs. Div. Porraro and Assocs., Atlanta, 1993-95; mgr. accts. divsn. Atlanta Rsch. and Trading, 1994-95; regional mktg. dir. Stephens, Inc., Atlanta, 1996—; S.E. U.S. correspondent The Economist, London, 1978-83. Episcopal. Clubs: Piedmont Driving, Nine O'Clocks (Atlanta). Home: 335 Franklin Rd NE Atlanta GA 30342 Office: RWC Ltd PO Box 20211 Atlanta GA 30325-0211

CHAMBERS, THOMAS EDWARD, college president, psychologist; b. Cleve., Aug. 1, 1934; s. James Clyde and Mary Celestine (Malone) C. BA, U. Notre Dame, 1956, MA, 1962, PhD, 1976; MA, Holy Cross Coll., 1961. Lic. counselor, Ohio, La. Dir. student residences U. Notre Dame, Ind., 1969-73, dir. student activities, 1973-74, asst. v.p. student affairs, 1974-76; v.p. acad. affiars Ursuline Coll., Cleve., 1976-87; pres. Our Lady of Holy Cross Coll., New Orleans, 1987—; founder Internat. Student Leadership Inst., 1968; mem. exec. com. Sta. WLAE-TV, New Orleans, 1987—. Editor: For Leaders Only, 1975. Mem. exec. com. Met. Area Com., New Orleans, 1987—; bd. dirs. King's Coll., Wilkes-Barre, Pa., 1989—, St. Joseph Sem. Coll.; trustee Gilmour Acad., Cleve., 1978—, United Way. Recipient Nat. League Nursing award of Ohio Nat. League Nursing, 1986, Trustee award Cathedral High Sch., 1987. Mem. Am. Psychol. Assn., Am. Cath. Colls. and Univs., Plimsoll Club, Internat. House Club. Roman Catholic. Office: Our Lady of Holy Cross Coll 4123 Woodland Dr New Orleans LA 70131-7337

CHAMBLISS, LAVONDA JO EASTUP, writer, poet, songwriter; b. Valdasta, Tex., Aug. 29, 1931; d. Ira Albert and Maxine Lottie (Box) Greer; m. Admah C. Eastup, Jr., Dec. 12, 1948 (div. Oct. 1985); children: Lana Kay, Reggie Dale, Allen Ray, Debra Darlene; m. James Connely Chambliss, Jan. 16, 1993. Grad. h.s. Author: Two Wheels to Glory--The Gentle Giant, 1982, Silver Teardrops and Golden Manna, Great Poems of the Western World, 1990, (with others) The World of Poetry Anthology, 1991, Who's Who in Poetry, Vol. III, 1991, Gold and Silver Poems, 1992, Poems that Will Live Forever, 1993, Great Poems of Our Time, 1993, Our World's Favorite Poems, Who's Who in Poetry, 1993, Outstanding Poets of 1994; contbr. poetry to books, including: On the Threshold of a Dream, Vol. 3, 1992, Selected Works of Our World's Best Poets, 4 poems made into songs and released by Rainbow Records, 1991, 92. Recipient numerous awards and plaques for poetry. Mem. Little Black Book Poetry Soc. of Hunt County, Tex., Internat. Soc. Poets (hon.). Republican. Baptist.

CHAMINGS, PATRICIA ANN, nurse, educator; b. Lakeland, Fla., June 21, 1940; d. Roy John and Esther Delilah (O'Steen) C. Diploma, Orange Meml. Hosp., 1961; BSN, U. Fla., 1964, M of Nursing, 1965; PhD, George Peabody Coll., 1978. Cert. nurse adminstr. advanced. Dir., assoc. prof. grad. program Vanderbilt U., Nashville, 1976-84; asst. dean Emory U., Atlanta, 1984-85; prof. U. N.C., Greensboro, 1985—, dean, 1985-90, dir. anesthesia edn. project, 1989-92; bd. trustees Wesley Long Cmty. Hosp., 1989-96; bd. dirs. N.C. Ctr. for Nursing, Health Svc. Ministry, N.C. Commn. on Mental health, Devel. Disabilities and Substance Abuse Svcs., 1993-96. Named N.C. Nurse Educator of Yr., 1988; advanced nurse tng. grantee USPHS, 1989-91. Fellow Am. acad. Nursing; mem. Sigma Theta Tau Internat.

CHAMOT, DENNIS, research organization executive; b. Bklyn., June 5, 1943; s. Joe and Sarah C.; m. Judith Ornstein, May 19, 1974; children: Jonathan, Joshua. BS in Chemistry, Poly. Inst. Bklyn., 1964, MS in Chemistry, 1964; PhD in Chemistry, U. Ill., 1969; MBA, U. Pa., 1974. Rsch. chemist E.I. duPont de Nemours and Co., Wilmington, Del., 1969-73; asst. to exec. sec. coun. unions for profl. employees AFL-CIO, Washington, 1974-77, asst. dir. dept. for profl. employees, 1977-84, assoc. dir. dept., 1984-90, exec. asst. to pres. dept., 1990-94; assoc. exec. dir. Commn. on Engring. and Tech. Sys., NRC, Washington, 1994—; mem. com. on computer aided mfg., assembly of engring. NRC, 1980-81, mem. com. on edn. and utilization of engr., 1982-85, mem. panel on tech. and women's employment, 1984-86, mem. commn. on engring. and tech. sys., 1985-92, mem. com. on rev. of info. sys. modernization of IRS, 1990-94, mem. coordinating coun. for edn., 1991-92, mem. com. to study impact of info. tech. on performance of svc. activities, 1991-93, mem. nat. com. on sci. edn. stds. and assessment, 1992-94, mem. com. on internat. stds., conformity assessment and U.S. trade policy, 1993-95, acting dir. bd. on infrastructure and constructed environ., 1994-95, acting dir. bd. on engring. edn., 1995; mem. pub. understanding of sci. adv. com. NSF, 1977-79, chmn. informal sci. edn. oversight com., 1985-86, mem. adv. coun., 1984-89; mem. adj. faculty George Mason U., Fairfax, Va., 1983, 84; adj. asst. prof. Univ. Coll. U. Md., College Park, 1993—; mem. external rev. com. Nat. Inst. Occupl. Safety and Health; mem. adv. panel on info. tech., automation and the workplace Office Tech. Assessment, U.S. Congress, 1982-84; mem. nat. adv. com. for tng. in new tech. Work in Am. Inst., 1985-87; mem. rev. panel Ctr. on Edn. Quality of Workforce, U.S. Dept. Edn., 1990; provider testimony various congl. hearings, 1982, 83, 87; participant, presenter numerous profl. confs. and symposia, most recently tech. summit Berkeley Round Table on Internat. Economy, San Francisco, 1993, presdl. colloquium on chem. rsch. environ. in next century, Washington, 1994. Contbr. many articles to profl. publs. Recipient Charles Gordon award Chem. Soc. Washington, 1986; travel grantee Swedish Inst., 1984; Mary E. Switzer meml. scholar Nat. Rehab. Assn., 1989. Fellow AAAS; mem. Am. Chem. Soc. (councilor 1975—, soc. com. on profl. rels. 1988-89, chmn. subcom. on career support and mem. assistance 1990-91, chmn. subcom. on career support 1989, cons. 1992-93, chmn. com. on Project Seed 1992—, chmn. divsn. profl. rels. 1982, chmn. mem. adv. bd. 1973, mem. com. on econ. status 1978-86, mem. task force on occupl. health and safety 1987-94, Henry Hill award 1992, chmn. subcom. on fed. policy agenda 1996—), Soc. for Occupl. and Environ. Health (sec.-treas. 1978-82, plaque 1982), Sigma Xi, Phi Kappa Phi, Phi Lambda Upsilon. Office: NRC 2101 Constitution Ave NW Washington DC 20418

CHAMPION, CHARLES HOWELL, JR., army officer; b. Canton, Ga., Feb. 17, 1944; s. Charles Howell and Ethel Marie (Cooper) C.; m. Patricia Ann Little, Nov. 24, 1965; children: Charles Howell III, Danielle, Christopher, Jonathan, Alicia. BS in Biology, North Ga. Coll., 1967; MA in Health Facilities Mgmt., Webster U., 1977. Commd. 2d lt. U.S. Army, 1966, advanced through grades to col., 1989; asst. chief schedules acad. ops. Med. Field Svc. Sch., Ft. Sam Houston, Tex., 1967-68; commanding officer 3/45 Med. Air Ambulance, Long Binh, Vietnam, 1969-70, 15th Med. Air Ambulance, Grafenwoehr, Germany, 1971-74; force devel. test officer Acad. Health Scis., Ft. Sam Houston, Tex., 1975-80; med. tng. liason officer Tng. and Doctrine Command, Ft. Monroe, Va., 1980-84; chief force modernization Office Surgeon Gen., Washington, 1984-88, chief doctrine, policy and orgn., 1988-90; dep. command surgeon U.S. Army Forces Command, Ft. McPherson, Ga., 1990—; sr. faculty mem. Col. John R. Sperandeo Plans, Ops. Profl. Postgrad. Short Course, Denver, 1991, 93, 95; bd. dirs. Med. Svc. Corps U.S.A., Washington, 1992-94. Inducted into Order of Mil. Med. Merit, 1988. Mem. Assn. Mil. Surgeons, Assn. U.S. Army, Army Aviation Assn. Am., Dustoff Assn., Retired Officers Assn., Army War Coll. Alumni Assn. Roman Catholic. Home: 2800 Chelsea Pl Marietta GA 30064-1288 Office: US Army Forces Command Fort McPherson GA 30330

CHAMPION, LAURIE, English literature educator; b. Dallas, Oct. 23, 1959; d. Jerry and Patricia Beatrice (Andrews) Champion; m. Thomas W. Brumley, Jan. 13, 1978; children: Brooke Renee Brumley, Billy Bob Brumley. BA in Psychology, U. Tex., Dallas, 1987, MA in Humanities, 1991; MA in English, U. North Tex., Denton, 1992, PhD in English, 1994. Prof. English, dir. honors Sul Ross State U., Alpine, Tex., 1994—. Editor: The Critical Response to Mark Twain's Huckleberry Finn, 1991, The Critical Response to Eudora Welty's Fiction, 1994; contbr. essays to jours. and anthologies; author short stories, reviews and essays reviews. Office: Sul Ross State U Box C-89 Alpine TX 79832

CHAMPLIN, WILLIAM GLEN, clinical microbiologist-immunologist; b. Rogers, Ark., Sept. 10, 1923; s. Glen and Anna Champlin; m. Helen Elizabeth Garner, Feb. 2, 1951; 1 child, Steven. BS, N.E. Okla. State U., 1948; MS, U. Ark., 1965, PhD, 1971. Lab. dir. VA Med. Ctr., Fayetteville, Ark., 1955-65, clin. microbiologist, lab. dir., 1965-80; cons. ANL Med. Lab. Wash. Regional Med. Ctr. VA Med. Ctr., 1965-90; edn. coord. Antaeus Inst. Sch. Med. Tech., 1980-90; vis. prof. microbiology U. Ark., 1978-85. With U.S. Army, 1943-45. Mem. Am. Acad. Microbiology (specialist), Am. Soc. Clin. Pathologists (specialist), Sigma Xi.

CHAN, DONALD PIN-KWAN, orthopaedic surgeon, educator; b. Rangoon, Burma, Jan. 21, 1937; s. Charles Y.C. and Josephine (Golamco) C.; m. Dorothy Chan, July 31, 1966; children: Joanne, Elaine. BS, U. Rangoon, Burma, 1955, MD, 1960. Intern medicine U. Hong Kong, 1960-61, resident surgery and orthopaedics, 1961-68; resident orthopaedic surgery U. Vt., 1968-71; assoc. orthopaedist Strong Meml. Hosp., Rochester, N.Y., 1972-80, sr. assoc. orthopaedist, 1980-86, attending orthopaedist, 1986—; asst. prof. U. Rochester, 1972-80, assoc. prof., 1980-87, prof., 1987-93; prof., head of divsn. spine surgery U. Va., Charlottesville, 1994—; dir. Goldstein Fellowship, Rochester, Orthopaedic Clin. Svcs., Rochester; chief sect. spine surgery dept. orthopaedics, Rochester, 1993. Contbr. articles on clin. rsch. related to the spine. Bd. dirs. Rochester Chinese Assn., 1991. Traveling fellow Scoliosis Rsch. Soc. Fellow ACS, Am. Acad. Orthopaedic Surgeons, Am. Orthopaedic Assn., Scoliosis Rsch. Soc. (1st v.p. 1995); mem. AMA, N.Am. Spine Soc., Am. Spinal Injury Assn., Ea. Orthopaedic Assn. Office: Univ Va Health Scis Ctr PO Box 159 Charlottesville VA 22902-0159

CHAN, KA WAH, physician; b. Hong Kong, Nov. 27, 1949; came to U.S., 1992; s. Kan Pun and Chuen Ping (Chow) C.; m. Eva Y. Ling, Jan. 25, 1980; children: Wynette, Aaron. MB, BS, U. Hong Kong, 1968-73. Cert. in Pediatrics, Can., Hematlogy; diplomate Am. Bd. Pediatrics. Asst. prof. pediatrics U. British Columbia, Vancouver, 1981-86, assoc. prof. pediatrics, 1986-92; prof. pediatrics U. Tex. Anderson Cancer Ctr., Houston, 1992—, section chief bone marrow transplantation in pediatrics, 1992—; dir. Canadian Bone Marrow Transplant Coop. Group, Ottawa, Ont., Can., 1986-92; cons. Canadian Red Cross Rsch. Review, Ottawa, Ont., Can., 1987-92; vis. prof. Quong Zhou (China) Children's Hosp., 1987. Fellow Royal Coll. Physicians and Surgeons of Can., Am. Acad. Pediatrics. Office: MD Anderson Cancer Ctr 1515 Holcombe Blvd Houston TX 77030-4009

CHAN, KWAI SHING, materials engineer, researcher; b. Hong Kong, Feb. 2, 1955; came to U.S., 1973; s. Mau F. and Sau L. (Siu) C.; m. Ing M. Oei, June 5, 1982; children: Candace Kay, Kara Lynn, Stacey Karmen, Aaron Eugene. BS in Metall. Engring., Mich. Technol. U., 1976, MS in Metall. Engring., 1978, PhD in Metall. Engring., 1980. Jr. rsch. engr. Olin Material Rsch. Lab., New Haven, 1976; postdoctoral affiliate Stanford (Calif.) U., 1980-82; rsch. engr. S.W. Rsch. Inst., San Antonio, 1982-85, sr. engr., 1985-88, prin. engr., 1988-92, staff engr., 1992-96; inst. scientist, 1996—; vis. scholar Harvard U., Cambridge, Mass., 1991; bd. rev. Metall. Transactions A, Pitts., 1992—. Co-editor: Forming Limit Diagrams: Concepts, Methods and Applications, 1989, Micromechanics of Advanced Materials; contbr. articles to profl. jours. Mem. ASCE (Alfred Noble prize 1991), ASME (assoc. editor Jour. Engring. Materials and Tech. 1993—), ASM Internat. (Marcus A. Grossmann award 1986, 94), Am. Inst. Mining and Petroleum Engrs. (Rossiter M. Raymond Meml. award 1990), Minerals, Metals & Materials Soc., Am. Ceramic Soc., Sigma Xi, Alpha Sigma Mu. Office: SW Rsch Inst PO Drawer 28510 6220 Culebra Rd San Antonio TX 78238-5166

CHAN, PHILIP, dermatologist, army officer; b. Oceanside, N.Y., Oct. 14, 1946; s. Walter O. and Ann (Yee) C. BA, Harvard U., 1968; MD, Columbia U., 1972. Diplomate Am. Bd. Dermatology. Commd. capt. U.S. Army, 1973, advanced through grades to col., 1987; dermatologist Martin Army Cmty. Hosp., Ft. Benning, Ga., 1995—; adj. asst. prof. Uniformed Svcs. U. of Health Scis., 1995—; mem. cancer com. Martin Army Hosp., 1995-96. Editor (govt. pub.) Procs. of Vesicant Workshops, 1987; contbr. articles to profl. jours. Fellow Am. Acad. Dermatology; mem. AMA, Mensa, Assn. of Mil. Dermatologists. Home: 1285 Whisperwood Dr Columbus GA 31907 Office: Martin Army Cmty Hosp PO Box 56100 Derm Svc Fort Benning GA 31905

CHAN, TAT WING, computer science educator; b. Hong Kong, Mar. 3, 1965; s. Che Tim and Lau Ching (Fong) C. BSc, U. S.W. La., 1987, MS, 1989, PhD, 1994. Teaching asst. U. S.W. La., Lafayette, 1988-90, computer lab. mgr., 1991, lectr., 1992—; faculty mem. Fayetteville (N.C.) State U. Contbr. papers to profl. jours. and conf. procs. Mem. IEEE, Assn. Computing Machinery. Home: 956 Andrews Rd # A Fayetteville NC 28311-1118 Office: Fayetteville State U Dept Math and Computer Sci Fayetteville NC 28311

CHAN, WAN-KANG WILL, mechanical engineer; b. Canton, China, Nov. 3, 1946; came to U.S., 1964; s. Kin and Pui Lee (Tam) C.; m. Tai-May Yuen, Aug. 30, 1979; children: Allen, Margaret. BSME, N.J. Inst. Tech., 1972; MSME, N.Y. Poly. Inst., 1976, MS in Mgmt., 1980. Cons. mech. engr. Gibbs & Cox Naval Architects, N.Y.C., 1971—; design engr. Rosenblatt Naval Architect, N.Y.C., 1975-76, Ebasco Svc. Engring., N.Y.C., 1977-78, Stone & Webster Engring., N.Y.C., 1978-80; project engr. Pa. Power and Light Co., Allentown, 1980-82; design engr. Bechtel Engring., Limerick Power Plant, Pa., 1982-84; project engr. U.S. Dept. Navy, Arlington, Va., 1985—. Author: Tai-Chi-Chuan (Total Exercise), 1993; asst. dir., actor (Chinese stage play in U.S.) Emperor's Daughter, 1967. Founder, bd. dirs., chmn. Hong Kong Student Assn., N.Y.C., 1968-80; vice prin. Transfiguration Chinese Lang. Sch., N.Y.C., 1968-72; founder, instr., dir. Will Chan's Inst. Kung Fu and Tai-Chi-Chuan, Burke, Va., 1974—; advisor U.S. Confedn. Kung Fu and Chinese Martial Art, Md., 1993—; bd. dirs. Wei-Hua Chinese Sch., Annandale, Va., 1991-95. Republican. Roman Catholic. Home: 9804 John Robert Way Fairfax VA 22032 Office: US Dept Navy PMS 380 (NAVSEA) 2531 Jefferson Davis Hwy Arlington VA 22202

CHANCE, JANE, English literature educator; b. Neosho, Mo., Oct. 26, 1945; d. Donald William and Julia (Mile) C.; m. Dennis Carl Nitzsche, June, 1966 (div. Mar. 1969); 1 child, Therese; m. Paolo Passaro, Apr. 30, 1981; children: Antony Damian, Joseph Sebastian. BA in English with honors and highest distinction, Purdue U., 1967; AM in English, U. Ill., 1968, PhD in English, 1971. Lectr. U. Saskatchewan, Can., 1971-72, asst. prof., 1972-73; asst. prof. Rice U., Houston, 1973-77, assoc. prof., 1977-80, prof., 1980—; hon. rsch. fellow U. Coll. U. London, 1977-78; sec., Scientia, 1982-83, acting dir., 1983-84; dir. NEH Summer Seminar for Coll. Tchrs., 1985, NEH Inst. for Coll. Tchrs. on Medieval Women, 1997; pres. TEAMS, 1986-89; dir. med. studies program Rice U., 1986-92; resident Rockefeller Found., Bellagio, Italy, 1988; mem. Sch. Hist. Studies Inst. for Advanced Study, Princeton U., 1988-89; vis. rsch. fellow Inst. for Advanced Studies in Humanities, U. Edinburgh, summer, 1994; Eccles fellow Humanities Ctr. U. Utah, 1994-95; plenary spkr. Rocky Mountain Med. and Renaissance Assn., 1995. Author: The Genius Figure in Antiquity and the Middle Ages, 1975, Tolkien's Art: A Mythology for England, 1979, Woman as Hero in Old English Literature, 1986, The Lord of the Rings: The Mythology of Power, 1992, Medieval Mythography: From Roman North Africa to the School of Chartres, Vol. 1, 1994 (South Ctrl. MLA book prize 1994), The Mythographic Chaucer: The Fabulation of Sexual Politics, 1995; translator: Christine de Pizan's Letter of Othea to Hector, 1990; editor: The Mythographic Art: Classical Fable and the Rise of the Vernacular in Early France and England, 1990, Medievalism in the Twentieth Century, Studies in Medievalism, vol. 2:2, 1983, The Inklings and Others, vol. 3:3, 1990; editor: Gender and Text in the Later Middle Ages, 1996; co-editor: Mapping the Cosmos, 1985, Approaches to Teaching Sir Gawain, 1986; series editor Focus Libr. Medieval Women, 1988—. NEH fellow, 1977-78, Guggenheim fellow, 1980-81, ACLS Travel grantee, 1982, Rice U. Mellon leave, 1988, Rice U. Disting. Faculty Tchg. fellow, 1995. Mem. AAUP (chpt. sec., treas. 1975-76), Scientia (acting dir. 1983-84, sec. 1982-83), Tex. Faculty Assn. (exec. com. 1995—). Home: 2306 Wroxton Rd Houston TX 77005-1538 Office: Rice U Dept English MS 30 6100 S Main St Houston TX 77005-1892

CHANCELLOR, JOANN, lawyer, legal association administrator. Adminstr., sec.-treas. So. Poverty Law Ctr., Montgomery, Ala. Office: So Poverty Law Ctr 400 Washington St Montgomery AL 36104-4344

CHANDLER, BEN, attorney general. Atty. gen. Office Atty. Gen., Frankfort, Ky. Office: Office Atty Gen State Capitol Bldg Rm 116 Frankfort KY 40601

CHANDLER, CLAYTON WINTHROP, III, city manager; b. Augusta, Ga., Apr. 7, 1948; s. Clayton Winthrop and Helen (Battle) C.; m. Shirley Martin, Jan. 17, 1972; children: Robert, David, Christopher. AB in Journalism, U. Ga., 1970, M in Pub. Adminstrn., 1977. Asst. fin. dir. City of Greenville, S.C., 1975-77; mgmt. cons. fin. Appalachian Council Govts., Greenville, S.C., 1977-78; asst. city mgr. City of North Myrtle Beach, S.C., 1978-79; city mgr. City of Waterville, Ohio, 1979-84, City of Mansfield, Tex., 1984—; cons. fin. S.C. Appalachian Council Govts., City of Greenville, 1977-78; cons. trainer North Cen. Regional Tng. Ctr., Arlington, Tex., 1985—; lectr. Bowling Green (Ohio) State U., 1979-84; mem. internship com. Bowling Green State U., 1981-84. Author, cons.: Model Revenue Policy Business License Regulations, 1977, Model Classification Compensation Plan, 1977, Operational Efficiency Study Spartinburg County, 1978. Mem. Mansfield Econ. Devel. Commn.; treas., trustee Lucas County Improvement Corp., Toledo, 1979-84. Named Entrepreneur of the Yr. of Metroplex Region, Inc. Mag., 1992. Mem. Mansfield C. of C. (bd. dirs.), Internat. City Mgrs. Assn., Govt. Fin. Officers Assn. (Disting. Budget Presentation award 1985), Internat. Personnel Mgmt. Assn., Nat. Pub. Employee Labor Relations Assn. Methodist. Home: 1515 Berkeley Dr Mansfield TX 76063-2946 Office: City of Mansfield 1305 E Broad St Mansfield TX 76063-1804

CHANDLER, GORDON HAROLD, minister; b. Calhoun County, Ala., Dec. 24, 1932; s. Gordon Russell and Kathleen Maudie (Green) C.; m. Hazel Blackwell, Dec. 25, 1951; children: Cathy Miranda, Gordon Harold, Jr. BS, Auburn U., 1952; BD, So. Bapt. Theol. Sem., 1956, MDiv, 1973; DD (hon.), Judson Coll., 1980. Pastor Pine Bower Bapt. Ch., Cedartown, Ga., 1955-57, Paden Bapt. Ch., Gadsden, Ala., 1957-81; dir. of missions Calhoun Bapt. Assn., Anniston, Ala., 1981-89; exec. dir. Madison Bapt. Assn., Huntsville, Ala., 1989—. Editor INFO, 1989— (Exceptional Merit award); contbr. articles to profl. jours. Dir., tchr. Samford U. Ext. Divsn., Gadsden and Anniston, Ala., 1966-86; mem., vice chmn. bd. dirs. Bapt. Med. Ctr., Gadsden, 1973-81, Human Relations Coun., 1978-81. Mem. Gadsden C. of C., Ala. Bapt. Conf. of Dirs. of Missions (pres. 1989-90), Greater Huntsville Mins. Assn. (sec. 1993, treas. 1994). Home: 7803 Ferncliffe Dr SE Huntsville AL 35802 Office: Madison Bapt Assn 2318 Whitesburg Dr S Huntsville AL 35801-3818

CHANDLER, IRA ANSEL, computer technician; b. Miami Beach, Fla., Oct. 13, 1953; s. William Anson and Gertrude Chandler; m. Katherine Belinda Griffin; children: Sunny Lee, Laura Reneé. BA in Mass Communications, AA in Electronic Music, U. South Fla., 1975. IBM bus. ptnr. for AS/400 midrange computer products ROI Corp., Atlanta, 1988—; computer cons. Ga. Bur. Investigation, GE neutron div., No. Telecom, Avery Graphics, State of Ga. DOAS, U.S. FDA, Ctr. for Disease Control, Sandia Labs, Lillie Rubin Affiliates, Litton/Kimball Systems, A.L. Williams, Owens/Corning Fiberglas, Atlanta, MCI Mail, Atlanta, NDC, Atlanta. Assoc. editor: PC Publ. Mag., 1986-87, Computing Today, 1986-87; tech. editor Que publs.; contbr. programs and revs. to on-line database, articles to Systems 3X World, MicroTimes, BIX; documentor Ashton-Tate Multi-User dBASE, Toshiba printer manuals, PC Mart product catalog. Mem. Profl. Software Programmers Assn., Internat. Assn. Builders and Contractors (cons. 1985—). Jewish. Home: 2884 Anderson Cir Smyrna GA 30080-3621

CHANDLER, J. HAROLD, insurance company executive; b. 1949. MBA, U. S.C. With Citizens & So. Nat. Bank S.C., Columbia, 1972-88, Citizens & So. Nat. Bank, Atlanta, 1988-91, NationsBank Corp., Atlanta, 1992-93; pres., CEO Provident Life & Accident Ins. Co., Chattanooga, Tenn., 1993—, also bd. dirs.; bd. dirs. AmSouth Bancorporation, Herman Miller, Inc., Healthsource, Inc. Office: Provident Life & Accident Ins Co 1 Fountain Sq Chattanooga TN 37402-1307

CHANDLER, JOAN MARY, humanities educator; b. Balham, England; came to U.S., 1968; d. John Gibbs and Gwen Claudia (Skilton) C. BA with honors, U. Cambridge, 1958; MA, Bryn Mawr Coll., 1959, U. Cambridge, 1962; PhD, U. Tex., 1972. Tchr. secondary schs., 1950-55, 59-60; lectr. Homerton Coll., Cambridge, 1960-64; dept. chair West Midlands Coll. Edn., Walsall, 1965-66; assoc. dean women U. Keele, 1966-68; asst. prof. U. Mass., Amherst, 1972-75; assoc. prof., prof. U. Tex., Dallas, 1975—, program head Am. studies, 1977-89, dir. undergrad. studies Sch. Arts and Humanities, 1977-80. Author: America Since Independence, 1965, Settlement of the American West, 1972, Television and National Sport, 1988; contbr. articles to profl. publs. Sophia Adelaide Turle scholar, 1955-58; English Speaking Union fellow, 1958-59. Fellow Am. Anthrop. Assn., Am. Studies Assn., Popular Culture Soc., N.Am. Soc. Sport History (bd. dirs., pub. bd. dirs.), N.Am. Soc. Sociology of Sport, Tex. State Hist. Assn. Home: 4138 Beaver Brook Ln Dallas TX 75229-5350 Office: U Tex PO Box 830688 Richardson TX 75083-0688

CHANDLER, LAWRENCE BRADFORD, JR., lawyer; b. New Bedford, Mass., June 20, 1942; s. Lawrence Bradford and Anne (Crane) C.; m. Madeleine Bibeau, Sept. 7, 1963 (div. June 1984); children: Dawn, Colleen, Brad; m. Cynthia Korn Howe, May 11, 1985. BS in Bus. Adminstrn., Boston Coll., 1963; LLB, U. Va., 1966, JD, 1970. Bar: Mass. 1966, U.S. Supreme Ct. 1967, Va. 1970, W.Va. 1993; diplomate Nat. Bd. Trial Advocacy; advocate Am. Bd. Trial Advocates. Ptnr. Chandler, Franklin & O'Bryan, Charlottesville, Va., 1971—. Pres. Western Va. Chpt., 1992-93. Capt. U.S. Army, 1967-71. Mem. ABA, ATLA (chair state dels. 1993-94, exec. com. 1993-94, bd. govs. 1995—), Va. Trial Lawyers Assn. (pres. 1985-86), Am. Bd. Trial Advs. (pres. Va. chpt.), Charlottesville Bar Assn., Assn. U.S. Army (pres. 1971-73), Am. Coll. Legal Medicine, Am. Soc. on Law, Medicine and Ethics, Am. Assn. Profl. Liability Attys. Roman Catholic. Home: 1445 Old Ballard Rd Charlottesville VA 22901-9469 Office: Chandler Franklin & O'Bryan PO Box 6747 Charlottesville VA 22906-6747

CHANDLER, MARCIA SHAW BARNARD, farmer; b. Arlington, Mass., Aug. 22, 1934; d. John Alden and Grace Winifred (Copeland) Barnard; m. Samuel Butler Chandler, Aug. 31, 1952 (dec. 1986); children: Shawn Chandler Seddinger, Mark Thurmond, Matthew Butler. BA, Francis Marion Coll., Florence, S.C., 1976; MEd, U. S.C., 1985. Resource person United Cerebral Palsy of S.C., Dillon, 1976-79; instr. English Horry-Georgetown Tech. Coll., Conway, S.C., 1980-81; farm owner, mgr. Dillon. Author: (with others) Best of Old Farmer's Almanac, First 200 Years, 1991; cover artist So. Bell Telephone Directory, 1988, 90. Bd. dirs., publicist, artist Dillon County Theatre, Inc., 1985—; publicist, bd. dirs., artist MacArthur Ave. Players, Dillon, 1990—; bd. dirs. Friends of Francis Marion U., 1985—; pres. Dillon Area Arts Coun., 1980-85, Jr. Charity League of Dillon, 1960-75; nat. poetry judge DAR, 1982. Recipient Honorable Commendation for civic involvement S.C. Ho. Reps., Mar. 22, 1990. Mem. Cousteau Soc., Ctr. Environ. Edn., Internat. Fund Animal Welfare, World Wildlife Fund, Nature Conservancy, Sea Shepherd Conservation Soc. Home: 309 E Reaves Ave Dillon SC 29536-1919

CHANDLER, MARLENE MERRITT, construction executive; b. Greenville, S.C., Dec. 13, 1949; d. Harvey Allen and Gladys Iona (Stewart) Merritt; m. Charles Mack Owens, June 8, 1968 (div. Oct. 1984); 1 child, Heather Michelle; m. Ray Lewis Chandler, Apr. 25, 1985. Grad. high sch., Piedmont, S.C. Asst. billing and computer operator Dillard Paper Co., Greenville, 1968-70; exec. asst. Daniel Constrn. Co., Greenville, 1970-74; co. sec., pres. asst. M.L. Garrett Constrn. Co., Greenville, 1974-78; asst. to purchasing mgr. P.Y.A. Monarch Co., Inc., Greenville, 1978-83; mgr., owner, pres. RAM Builders, Easley, S.C., 1985—; owner, pres. RAM Builders of Greenville, Inc., Greenville, 1986—. Author poem: Poetry Contest, 1989. Tutor Greenville Lit. Assocs., Inc., 1988-90; dir. S.C.'s Living Doll Pageant, S.C.'s Most Beautiful Girl Pageant, S.C.'s Baby of the Yr., S.C.'s Baby Bumpkin Contest. Named Mrs. I Love You Greenville, Greenville Bus. Assn., 1981, Mrs. S.C., S.C. Little Miss/Beauty Pageant, Greenville, 1982. Republican. Baptist. Home and Office: RAM Builders Greenville Inc 10129 Anderson Rd Easley SC 29642-8237

CHANDLER, MARY M. SZEGEDY, principal; b. Gyor, Hungary, Sept. 12, 1948; d. Laszlo and Elizabeth (Rado) Szegedy; m. Drake E. Chandler, Aug. 22, 1970; 1 child, Jenny. BS in Edn., Ind. U., Ft. Wayne, 1970; MAT, Emory U., 1975; EdS, U. Ga., 1980; PhD, Ga. State U., 1986. Cert. adminstrn. and supr. Tchr. 6th grade Whiteland (Ind.) Sch. Dist.; asst. prin., tchr. Cobb Bd. Edn., Marietta, Ga.; tchr. 7th grade DeKalb County, DeKalb, Ga.; prin. middle sch. Fulton County Bd. Edn., Atlanta, prin. H.S., 1986-91, 91-94; cons. Ga. State U., Atlanta, 1994—. Mem. ASCD, Prins. Ctr. Ga. State U. (bd. dirs. 1986-92), Phi Delta Kappa. Office: Ga State U Ctr Sch Improvement 1 Park Pl S Ste 215 Atlanta GA 30303-2911

CHANDLER, SADIE ARNETTE, state educational administrator, consultant; b. Port St. Joe, Fla., July 5, 1933; d. David Crockett and Roxie Mae (Whitehead) Arnette; m. James William Herschel Chandler, Jr., Sept. 16, 1956; children—Richard Allan, Kathi Lynn Morris. B.A., Stetson U., 1956; M.Ed., Middle Tenn. State U., 1969, Ed. S.,1982. Tchr., choral dir. Franklin County High Sch., Winchester, Tenn., 1965-69, guidance counselor, 1969-77; instr. Motlow State Community Coll., Tullahoma, Tenn., 1971-74; tch. acad. for profl. devel. Tenn. Dept. Edn., Nashville, 1978-80; dir. Tenn. Tchr. Acads., 1980—; cons. Univ. Counselor, Murfreesboro, Tenn., 1970, 74, 75; mem. nat. task force career edn. communication, Washington, 1979; bd. dirs. Nat. Council States Inservice Edn., Tenn., 1984-88; dir. div. of State Edn. Agy., 1990; task force dir. State Plan Career Edn., 1978, Tenn. Instructional Model, 1984. Recipient Outstanding Service award Franklin County Jaycees, 1976. Mem. Tenn. Assn. Suprs. and Curriculum, South Tenn. Pers. and Guidance Assn. (pres., counselor 1976), Middle Tenn. Edn. Assn. (chmn., Counselor of Yr. award 1966-67), Bus. and Profl. Women, Ky. and Tenn. Cols. Assn. (hon.), Phi Delta Kappa, Delta Kappa Gamma (pres. 1980-82). Methodist. Avocations: music, writing, ednl. consulting, organist. Home: RR 1 Decherd TN 37324-9801 Office: Tenn Dept Edn Gateway Plz 7th Fl James Robertson Pky Nashville TN 37203

CHANEY, COURTLAND MERLYN, management educator, psychologist, consultant; b. Baton Rouge, Sept. 29, 1952; s. Merlyn Thompson and Virginia May (Slocum) C.; m. Colette Juliette Duysens, Dec. 2, 1982; 1 child, Christopher Laurence. BS, La. State U., 1974, MA, 1978, PhD, 1980. Lic. psychologist, La.; cert. sr. profl. in human resources; registered orgn. devel. profl. Grocery mgr. Krogers, Inc., Baton Rouge, 1971; resident counselor Calcusearch, Inc., Baton Rouge, 1976; teaching asst. La. State U., Baton Rouge, 1977-79, rsch. asst., 1978, instr. dept. psychology, 1977-79, instr., adviser dept. mgmt., instr. exec. edn. program, 1983—; lectr. European div. U. Md., Heidelberg, Germany, 1980-82; acad. adviser Cen. Mich. U., New Orleans, 1984-88, adj. faculty, 1984-88; pres. Human Resource Mgmt. Assocs., Inc., Baton Rouge, 1984—; presenter in field. Contbr. articles to profl. jours. Recipient Outstanding Tchr. of Mgmt. award bus. students La. State U, 1989, Outstanding In-Class Teaching award Student Govt. Assn., 1989, Outstanding Human Resource Profl. award, 1995, Greater Baton Rouge Soc. for Human Resource Mgmt. Mem. APA, Acad. Mgmt., Soc. for Human Resource Mgmt., Soc. for Indsl. and Orgnl. Psychology, Am. Psychol. Soc., Internat. Registry Orgnl. Devel. Profls., La. Soc. Human Resource Mgmt. (state coun. 1992—, dir.-at-large 1992—), Greater Baton Rouge Soc. for Human Resource Mgmt. (chmn. edn. com. 1990—), Greater Baton Rouge C. of C. (corp., ad hoc com. Internat. Resource Ctr. 1987-90). Office: La State U Dept Mgmt Cedar Ave # 3158 Baton Rouge LA 70805-7877

CHANG, AARON CHAUNCEY, trade association administrator; b. Livington, N.J., July 22, 1971; s. Tinchiu and Lily (Liew) C. BA in Polit. Sci., George Washington U., 1993, MA in Polit. Mgmt., 1993. Page Ho. of Reps., Washington, 1987-88; asst. to chief of staff Congressman Jack Buechner, Washington, 1989-91; asst. to assoc. adminstr. Gen. Svcs. Adminstr., Washington, 1991-93; spl. asst. to pres., CEO Nat. Assn. of Chain Drug Stores, Alexandria, Va., 1993—. Various polit. campaigns; event coord. Richard Nixon Libr. and Ctr., Yorba Linda, Calif., Washington, 1990—. Mem. Orgn. Chinese Ams., George Washington U. Alumni Assn. Republican. Baptist. Office: Nat Assn of Chain Drug Stores 413 N Lee St Alexandria VA 22314

CHANG, KUNYA, food products executive. Dir. R&D Savannah (Ga.) Foods & Industries, Inc. Office: Savannah Foods & Industries Inc 2 E Bryan St Savannah GA 31401

CHANH, TRAN CONG, immunologist; b. Go-Cong, South Vietnam, May 12, 1949; came to U.S., 1967; s. Tran C. Dang and Vo Thi Minh; m. Celita de Lacerda Coutinho, Mar. 29, 1974; children: Eric, Tanya. BS in Biology, Am. U., 1971; MS in Microbiology, U. Hawaii, 1976, PhD in Immunology, 1980. Postdoctoral fellow U. Ala., Birmingham, 1980-83; asst. prof. Georgetown U. Med. Sch., Washington, 1983-86; assoc. scientist dept. virology and immunology S.W. Found. for Biomed. Rsch., San Antonio, 1986-90, scientist, 1990—. Grantee U.S. Army Med. R. and D. Command, 1983—, Nat. Heart, Blood and Lung Inst., NIH, 1989—. Office: SW Found for Biomed Rsch PO Box 28147 West Loop 401 at Military San Antonio TX 78228-0147

CHAO, CHING YUAN, economics educator; b. Shaoshing, Chekiang, China, Dec. 5, 1921; came to the U.S., 1969; s. Jin Ho and Wang Shih Chao; m. Nelly Chin Chuku, Sept. 28, 1947; children: Amy Hsiao Ming Chao Chang, Hsiao Lin Chao Tharp. Student, Nat. Chekiang (China) U., 1941-43; BS, Nat. Ying-Shih U., Chekiang, 1945; MS, Iowa State U., 1961, PhD, 1963. Teaching asst. Fukien Provincial Agr. Coll., Fuchow, Fukien, China, 1945-46; prof. Nat. Taiwan U., Taipei, 1946-63; vis. assoc. prof. Dalhousie U., Halifax, N.S., 1964-68; assoc. prof. St. Mary U., Halifax, 1968-69, Mich. Tech. U., Houghton, Mich., 1969-72; prof. Jackson (Miss.) State U., 1972—; vis. scholar Nanking and Chekiang Univs., China, 1980; Am. del. in agrl. econs. to USSR, Citizen Amb. Program, Moscow, 1989. Author: Farm Management, 1960; editor: (procs.) Papers of First Annual Economic Research Symposium, 1992, Papers of Second Annual Economic Research Symposium, 1993, Papers of Third Annual Economic Research Symposium, 1994, Papers of Fourth Annual Economic Research Symposium, 1995; contbr. articles to profl. jours. Recipient fellowship Agrl. Econ. State Dept., U.S., 1953-54, scholarship Rockfeller Found., Iowa State U., 1959-62. Mem. Am. Econ. Assn., Am. Agrl. Econs. Assn., Acad. Econs. and Fin. (exec. bd., program area coord., session chair, discussant, bd. mem. editors 1986—), Southwestern Soc. Economists (session chair, discussant), Southwestern Econs. Assn. (session chair, discussant), Nat. Chekiang U. Alumni Assn. North Am. (southeast dist. coord. USA), Phi Tau Phi. Office: Jackson State Univ Dept Econ Fin & Gen Bus PO Box 17760 Lynch St Jackson MS 39217

CHAO, JAMES LEE, chemist; b. Lafayette, Ind., Sept. 4, 1954; s. Tai Siang and Hsiang Lin (Lee) C.; m. Juliana Meimei Ma, Apr. 4, 1992. BS in Chemistry, U. Ill., 1975, MS in Chemistry, 1976; PhD in Chemistry, U. Calif., Berkeley, 1980. Applications scientist IBM Instruments, Inc., Danbury, Conn., 1980-87; vis. assoc. prof. dept. chemistry Duke U., Durham, N.C., 1986-87, adj. asst. prof. dept. chemistry, 1987-91, adj. assoc. prof., 1992—; advisory scientist IBM Corp., Research Triangle Park, N.C., 1987—; cons. Lab. for Laser Energetics, U. Rochester, N.Y., 1979-80; postdoctoral fellow Lab. for Chem. Biodynamics, Lawrence Berkeley Lab., 1980; referee Applied Spectroscopy, 1982—, Applied Physics Letters, Jour. Applied Physics, 1989—; grant referee N.C. Biotech. Ctr., 1991—. Contbr. articles to profl. jours. Recipient Marcus E. Hobbs. Svc. award, 1995; Edmund James scholar, 1972-75, Dow Chem. scholar, 1977. Fellow N.Y. Acad. Scis., Am. Inst. Chemists; mem. Am. Chem. Soc. (chmn. N.C. sect. 1991, councillor 1993—), Soc. for Applied Spectroscopy, Coblentz Soc., Triangle Coun. Engring. and Sci. Socs. (treas. 1992-94), Sigma Xi. Home: 7424 Ridgefield Dr Durham NC 27713-9503 Office: IBM Corp Dept CMZA 061 PO Box 12195 Research Triangle Park NC 27709

CHAPA, JORGE, university dean. BA in Biology with honors, U. Chgo., 1975; MA in Sociology, U. Calif., Berkeley, 1979, MA in Demography, 1983, PhD in Sociology, 1988. Asst. prof. U. Tex., Austin, 1988-92, assoc. prof. Lyndon B. Johnson Sch. Pub. Affairs, 1993—, assoc. dean and dir. grad. opportunity program, 1993—; rsch. scholar Tomas Rivera Ctr., San Antonio, 1988-93; Martin Luther King-Cesar Chavez-Rosa Parks vis. scholar Julian Samora Rsch. Inst., Mich. State U., East Lansing, summer 1992, seminar dir. Inter-Univ. Consortium for Polit. and Social Rsch., summer 1990-92; lectr. in field. Co-author: The Economy of the Urban Ethnic Enclave, 1991, Assessing Molecular and Atomic Scale Technologies, 1989, The Burden of Support, 1988; article reviewer Jour. AMA, Social Sci. Quar., Internat. Migration Rev., Jour. Policy Analysis and Mgmt., Jour. Hispanic Behavioral Success; contbr. numerous articles to profl. jours., chpts. to books. Mem. adv. com. Social Sci. Rsch. Coun. Multi-City Study on Urban Inequality, Russell Sage Found., 1990. Grantee Tex. Dept. Health, Tomas Rivera Ctr., Project Quest-MacTiger, Social Sci. Rsch. Coun., Tex. Rsch. League; Nat. Rsch. Coun. postdoctoral fellow, 1991-92. Office: Univ of Texas LBJ Sch Pub Affairs Austin TX 78713

CHAPEL, THERON THEODORE, quality assurance engineer; b. Jackson County, Mich., Jan. 31, 1918; s. Theron Eugene and Monica Iris (Paton) C.; m. Lucy Eldredge, 1946 (dec.); m. Sue Smith, 1990 (div. Aug. 1995); children: Robert, James. BA, Albion Coll., Mich., 1938; BSE, U. Mich., 1940. Analytical chemist Minn. Mining & Mfg. Co., Detroit, 1940-41; rubber compounder, 1941-43; research/devel. chemist The Simoniz Co., Chgo., 1946-51; quality control supr. The Simoniz Co., Chgo. and Kankakee, Ill., 1951-53; process devel. engr. Armour Pharm. Labs., Bradley, Ill., 1954-56; product control supr. Acheson Colloids Co., Port Huron, Mich., 1956-61; material treatment and processes quality control rep. Inspector of Naval Material, Chgo., 1962-63; shipbuilding quality control rep., supr. shipbuilding USN, Bay City, Mich., 1963-70; quality assurance specialist supr. Shipbuilding, Conversion & Repair USN, Pascagoula, Miss., 1970-72, quality assurance engr. supr. Shipbuilding, Conversion & Repair, 1972-93; ret. Shipbuilding, Conversion & Repair, USN, Pascagoula, Miss., 1993. With U.S. Army, 1943-46. Mem. LDS Ch. Home: 5300 Beardslee St Moss Point MS 39563-2108

CHAPIN, DIANE LOUISE, cardiac care nurse; b. Berwick, Pa., Oct. 8, 1952; d. A. Richard and Esther Elizabeth (Remphrey) C.; m. James Yeatts, June 11, 1977 (div. Mar. 1983). Diploma, Williamsport (Pa.) Sch. Nursing, 1973; BS in Edn., Bloomsburg State Coll., 1975. CCRN; cert. provider/instr. BCLS and ACLS. Charge nurse orthopedics Geisinger Med. Ctr., Danville, Pa., 1974-77, charge nurse urology, 1980-81; charge nurse psychiatry DePaul Hosp., Norfolk, Va., 1977-78; home health nurse John D. Archibald Meml. Hosp., Thomasville, Ga., 1982-83; med. staff/charge nurse Tallahassee Community Hosp., 1981-82, supr., 1984-86, nurse educator ICU, 1986-87, asst. nurse mgr. ICU, 1987-90; nurse mgr. critical care unit HCA Palmyra Med. Ctr., Albany, Ga., 1990-93; dir. critical care Palmyra Med. Ctr., Albany, 1993—; grad. cons. area 4 Student Nurse Assn. Pa., 1973-74; developer restorative nurse program in home health, 1981; co-developer critical care internship program, 1991. Mem. AACN. Methodist. Home: 171 Archie Dr Albany GA 31707-1711

CHAPIN, FRED, airport executive. Dir. ops. Charleston (S.C.) Internat. Airport. Office: Charleston Internat Airport Charleston Cty Aviation Authorty Box 101 5500 International Blvd Charleston SC 29418-6911

CHAPIN, SUZANNE PHILLIPS, retired psychologist; b. Syracuse, N.Y., Aug. 9, 1930; d. Harold Bridge and Charlotte Virginia (Warner) Phillips; m. Richard Hilton Chapin, June 13, 1953 (div. 1964); children: Bruce Phillips Chapin, Linda Chapin Fry. BA, Syracuse U., 1952; MA, Columbia U., 1965. Statis. asst. Syracuse Bd. of Edn., 1952-53; psychol. examiner Stamford (Conn.) Pub. Schs., 1965-68, psychologist Head Start program, 1967-68; psychologist Southbury (Conn.) Tng. Sch., 1968-74, Onondaga Assn. for the Retarded, Syracuse, 1974, Harlem Valley Psychiatric Ctr., Wingdale, N.Y., 1974-93, Mid-Hudson Psychiat. Ctr., New Hampton, 1993; ret., 1993. Mem. LWV, Audubon Soc., Sierra Club. Democrat. Home: 10 S Bearwood Dr Palmyra VA 22963

CHAPMAN, CHARLES W., music educator; b. Ardmore, Okla., Oct. 7, 1936; s. Alton Blain and Jalie Eleanor (Goodwin) C.; m. Sarabelle Janette Bray; children: Sara Eleanor, Jennifer Ruth. B of Music Edn., U. Okla., 1958, M of Music Edn., 1962; PhD in Music, U. Tex., 1971. Vocal music dir. Vinita Pub. Schs., Okla., 1958-62; music teaching asst. U. Tex., Austin, 1968-70; prof. music Southwestern Okla. State U., Weatherford, Okla., 1962—, coord. vocal choral divsn. dept. music, 1975-87, chair dept. music, 1987—; workshops Tri State Festival Chorus, Okla., 1993, Jr. High Western Okla. Honor Choir, 1994. Contbr. to profl. jours. Sr. warden St. Mark's Episcopal Ch., Weatherford, 1979-81, 84-85, 89-90, jr. warden, 1981-83, organist, 1979—, ch. treas., 1991-92; chair comm. on music Episcopal Diocese of Okla., 1980-85, mem., 1980—, mem. comm. on missions, 1978-80, vice chair task force, 1994. Recipient Tchr. of the Year award Okla. Edn. Assn, 1974, Outstanding Okla. Music Educator award Okla. Secondary Schs. Activies Assn., 1992. Mem. Am. Choral Dirs. Assn. (pres. 1980-82, editor state newsletter 1982-83, ch. music rep. 1994—, Okla. Dir. of Distinction award 1981), Alliance for Arts Edn. (chair 1982-85), Nat. Assn. Tchrs. of Singing (dist. gov. for Okla. 1991—, gov. Texoma region 1995—), Am. Guild Organists, Okla. Music Educators Assn. (editor Okla. Music News 1992—, Hall of Fame 1995), Phi Mu Alpha Sinfonia, Pi Kappa Lambda, Kappa Kappa Psi. Democrat. Episcopalian. Home: 621 N Broadway St Weatherford OK 73096-3847 Office: Southwestern Okla State U Music Dept 100 Campus Dr Weatherford OK 73096-3001

CHAPMAN, DAN G., minister; b. Brownwood, Tex., Jan. 29, 1939; s. Bert A. and Mary Louise (Pelton) C.; m. Delores Sue Thomas,June 20, 1964; 1 child, Jason Carter. BTh, Internat. Sem., 1985, MTh, 1988, DM, 1989; DTh, Sch. Bible Theology, 1989. Ordained to ministry Pentecostal Ch. God. Dist. youth dir. S.W. Tex. Dist. Pentecostal Ch. God, San Marcos, 1971-79, sectional presbyter S.W. Tex. Dist., 1986—, dir. Christian Edn. S.W. Tex. Dist., 1988-90; internat. evangelist Pentecostal Ch. God, Joplin, Mo., 1979-83; adminstr. Trinity Day Care, Early, Tex., 1983—; prin. Trinity Christian Acad., Early, 1983—; sr. pastor Trinity Chapel Ch., Early, 1983—; area advisor Heart of tex. Area Aglow, Killeen, 1987—; chaplain Police and Fire Depts., Brownwood, 1987—. Author: Youth Leadership and Development, 1978. Mem. Tex. Youth Coun. Adv. Bd., Brownwood, 1991—, Noah Project Bd., Brownwood, 1991—; pres. Ctrl. Tex. Christian Conf.; Tex. rep. Internat. Conf. Police Chaplains. With U.S. Army, 1961-63. Mem. Internat. Conf. Police Chaplains, Internat. Assn. Trauma Counselors, Early C. of C. (pres.), Lions Club (pres. 1969-70). Home: 207 Crescent Dr Brownwood TX 76802-8916 Office: Trinity Chapel Ch 1040 Early Blvd PO Box 3246 Brownwood TX 76803

CHAPMAN, HUGH MCMASTER, banker; b. Spartanburg, S.C., Sept. 11, 1932; s. James Alfred and Martha (Marshall) C.; m. Anne Allston Morrison, Dec. 27, 1958 (dec. Mar. 1993); children: Anne Allston, Rachel Buchanan, Mary Morrison. BSBA, U. N.C., 1955. With Citizens & So. Nat. Bank S.C., 1958—, pres., 1971-74, chmn. bd., 1974-91; pres. Citizens & So. Corp., Atlanta, 1986-91; vice chmn. C&S/Sovran Corp., 1990-91; chmn. Nations Bank S., 1992—; bd. dirs. SCANA Corp., Inman Mills. Trustee Thomas Jefferson Meml. Found., Duke Endowment. 1st lt. USAF, 1955-57. Office: Nations Bank South 55 Nationsbank Plz Atlanta GA 30308*

CHAPMAN, J. MILTON, lawyer; b. Fairfield, Ill., Mar. 9, 1962; s. Howard Max and Tressa Imogene (Sniderwin) C.; m. Tami Lynette Upton, Aug. 9, 1986; 1 child, Lauren Elisabeth. BA, Baylor U., 1984, JD, 1986. Bar: Tex. 1986; lic. realtor. Assoc. McKay, Smith, Robins, Russell & Rigsby, P.C., Victoria, Tex., 1986-90, Anderson, Smith, Null, Stofer & Murphree, Victoria, 1990—. Pres. Boys and Girls Club of Victoria, 1995—, Victoria Livestock Show Scholarship Found., 1991-96; bd. dirs., treas. Victoria C. of C., 1991-93; dir. Minority and Bus. Alliance for Higher Edn., Victoria, 1993—; dir., treas. Making the Grade Pub. Edn. Found., Victoria, 1994—; deacon First Bapt. Ch., Victoria, 1994—. Mem. Rotary (Paul Harris fellow 1994, pres. Victoria chpt. 1995-96, Rotarian of Yr. award Area 1, dist. 5930 1995-96, sec. 1996-97, benefactor 1996). Home: 116 Buckingham Victoria TX 77904 Office: Anderson Smith Null Stofer & Murphree LLP 1 OConnor Plz 7th Fl Victoria TX 77902

CHAPMAN, JAMES PAUL, university official; b. Cleve., Nov. 11, 1943; s. Paul Edward and Alice (McDevitt) C.; m. Patricia Ann Daniel, Dec. 30, 1967; children: J. Daniel, Andrew A. BA, St. Meinrad Coll., 1965; MS in Edn., Ind. U., 1967, MA, 1967, PhD, 1972. Asst. dir. acad. affairs Madisonville Community Coll., 1972-74; asst. univ. budget dir. U. Ky., Lexington, 1974-76, spl. asst. to v.p. acad. affairs, 1975-80, asst. v.p. acad. affairs, 1981-82, asst. vice chancellor adminstrn., 1982-89, asst. chancellor, 1990-96, adj. prof. honors, 1994—, adj. prof. classics, 1995—, vice chancellor pub. svc. and outreach, 1996—; acad. cons. Indonesia, 1988, Croatia, 1994; coord. Coll. Bus. Mgmt. Inst., Lexington, 1987-91. Forum moderator Sta. WKYT-TV, Lexington, 1980-94. Co-chair Task Force Equality Pub. Schs., Fayette County, Ky., 1988-89; bd. dirs. Bluegrass chpt. NCCJ, Lexington, 1988-90; mem. Lexington Commn. Race Rels., 1988—; trustee, overseer St. Meinrad Coll., 1991—. Capt. U.S. Army, 1968-71, Vietnam. Decorated Bronze Star. Mem. So. Assn. Coll. and Univ. Bus. Officers, Assn. Gen. and Liberal Studies (exec. bd. 1984-86). Home: 1840 Traveller Rd Lexington KY 40504-2006 Office: U Ky 101 Glass Ave Lexington KY 40505-4109

CHAPMAN, JEFFERSON, museum director; b. Kinston, N.C., Mar. 13, 1943; married; 2 children. BA in Anthropology, Yale U., 1965; MAT in History and Edn., Brown U., 1968; MA in Anthropology, U. N.C., 1973, PhD in Anthropology, 1975. Tchr. Webb Sch., Knoxville, Tenn., 1965-67, tchr., chmn. social studies dept., 1968-71, tchr. summer enrichment program, 1969, dir. Field Sch. in Archaeology, 1970-71; rsch. asst. prof. dept. anthropology U. Tenn., Knoxville, 1975—, rsch. assoc. prof., 1984—, curator archaeology Frank H. McClung Mus., 1981-90, dir., 1990—; part time tchr. Webb Sch. Knoxville, 1981—; peer reviewer Delores Archaeol. Project, Southwestern Colo., U.S. Dept. Interior, Water and Power Resources Sv. Project; periodic peer reviewer proposals submitted to Nat. Geog. Sof., NSF, NEH; chmn. Tenn. Archaeol. Adv. Coun., 1988—. Contbr. articles to profl. jours. Bd. advocates Planned Parenthood Assn. Knox County, 1985—; trustee Webb Sch. Knoxville, 1975-81, chmn., 1986—; bd. dirs. Knoxville Symphony Soc., 1977—; bd. dirs. Lamar House-Bijou, 1982-90, exec. officer, 1983-90; bd. dirs. Tenn. Children's Dance Ensemble, 1984-88, Thompson Ctr., 1984—; mem. Knoxville Bicentennial Hist. Com., 1990-91; mem. dir. search com. Knoxville Mus. Art, 1989, 91; mem. Arts Coun. Adv. Panel, 1984-86. Recipient Outstanding Young Educator award Farragut Jaycees, 1971, Disting. Alumnus award Webb Sch. Knoxville, 1991; named hon. fellow Lower Miss. Survey, Peabody Mus., Harvard U., 1987. Fellow Am. Anthropol. Assn.; mem. Am. Assn. Museums, Am. Soc. Conservation Archaeology (exec. bd. 1981-83), Archaeol. Soc. Am. (pres. East Tenn. chpt. 1982-83), Archaeol. Soc. N.C., Assn. Field Archaeology, Coun. Mus. Anthropology, Ala. Archaeol. Soc., Museums of Knoxville (treas. 1990—), Soc. Am. Archaeology (nominating com. 1983-90), Soc. Historic Archaeology, Soc. Profl. Archeologists (dir. at large 1981-83), Southeastern Archaeol. Conf., Southeastern Mus. Conf., Tenn. Anthropol. Assn. Home: 2229 Duncan Rd Knoxville TN 37919-9112 Office: Frank H McClung Mus U Tenn Circle Park Dr Knoxville TN 37996-3200

CHAPMAN, JENNIFER BOERSEMA, elementary school educator; b. Savannah, Ga., Sept. 26, 1964; d. John Martin and Sandra Rose (Stewart) Boersema; m. Edward Clay Chapman, May 12, 1984. BA, Winston-Salem State U., 1993. Cert. English tchr., N.C. Telephone inquiry operator Nat. Heritage Ins. Co., Austin, Tex., 1984-85; sec. Unifi, Inc., Yadkinville, N.C., 1986-88, ins. rep., 1988-89; customer asst. Sara Lee/Hanes Mill Outlet, Winston-Salem, N.C., 1989-93; pre-algebra tutor Winston-Salem State U., 1991-92; 8th grade comm. skills tchr. Winston-Salem/Forsyth County Schs., 1993—; newspaper reporters' advisor Mineral Springs Mid. Sch., Winston-Salem, 1993-95, yearbook advisor, 1994-95, mem. social/benevolence com., 1993-95. Home: 2599 US Hwy 64 E Mocksville NC 27028

CHAPMAN, LUREE, health care administrator; b. Hall County, Ga., Feb. 10, 1964; d. David Dwight and Patricia (Underwood) Oliver; m. David Tyrone Chapman Jr., May 28, 1988. AS in Nursing, North Ga. Coll., 1984; BSN, Brenau Coll., 1991; MS, family nurse practitioner, Ga. State U., 1994. RN, Ga.; cert. critical care nurse, emergency nurse. Charge nurse med. floor Lanier Park Hosp., Gainesville, Ga.; charge nurse ICU-CCU Lanier Park Hosp., Gainesville, staff nurse cardiac catheter lab, physicians nurse; family nurse practitioner Gainesville Cardiology.

CHAPMAN, RANDALL ALLEN, research engineer; b. Detroit, Feb. 4, 1954; s. William Neal and Barbara Joan (Cox) C.; m. Deborah Jean Bridgman, Aug. 1, 1992; 1 child, William Graham. BS in Chemistry cum laude, Ctrl. Mich. U., 1976; MS in Chem. Engring., Mich. State U., 1984, PhD in Chem. Engring., 1986. Rsch. lab. technician Ctrl. Mich. U., Mt. Pleasant, 1974; rsch. chemist Cook Paint and Varnish, Detroit, 1977-78; rsch. asst. Mich. State U., East Lansing, 1979-85; aerospace engr. NASA-Lewis Rsch. Ctr., Cleve., 1981; vis. prof. U. Ill., Urbana, 1986-89; faculty fellow NASA-LeRC, Cleve., 1988-89; prin. investigator Ctr. for Space Transp. and Applied Rsch., Tullahoma, Tenn., 1991-93; rsch. engr. Sverdrup Tech., Tullahoma, Tenn., 1990—; cons. Air Force Studies Bd., Washington, 1986-87; peer review com. NASA-Langley Rsch. Ctr., Hampton, Va., 1994; mem. study group Civilian Space Fusion Program, Washington, 1988. Contbr. articles to profl. jours. Precinct del., Clawson, Mich., 1972-76. Mem. AIAA (student conf. judge Southeastern region 1994), Nat. Space Soc., Sigma Xi. Office: Sverdrup Tech 1088 Ave C Arnold AFB TN 37389-6700

CHAPMAN, ROBERT FOSTER, federal judge; b. Inman, S.C., Apr. 24, 1926; s. James Alfred and Martha (Marshall) C.; m. Mary Winston Gwathmey, Dec. 21, 1951; children: Edward, Foster, Winston. BS, U. S.C., 1945, LLB, 1949, LLD (hon.), 1986. Bar: S.C. 1949. Asso. firm Butler & Moore, Spartanburg, 1949-51; partner firm Butler, Chapman & Morgan, Spartanburg, 1953-71; U.S. dist. judge for S.C., 1971-81, U.S. cir. judge, 1981—. Chmn. S.C. Republican Party, 1961-63. Served to lt. USNR, 1943-46, 51-53. Recipient Nat. Patriot's award Congl. Medal of Honor Soc., 1985. Fellow Am. Coll. Trial Lawyers. Presbyn. (ruling elder). Home: 1822 Fair St Camden SC 29020-2721 Office: US Ct Appeals 4th Ct PO Box 7097 Columbia SC 29202-7097

CHAPMAN, WAYNE KENNETH, English language educator; b. Portland, Oreg., Mar. 5, 1950; s. Kenneth Frederick and Rachel Eunice (Waehlte) C.; m. Janet Marilyn Manson, Sept. 24, 1974; children: Charis Elaine Manson, William Gaelan Manson. BS, Portland State U., 1972, MA, 1977; PhD in English, Wash. State U., 1988. Instr., editl. asst. Wash. State U., 1986-88, instr., 1991 spring; instr. Kans. State U., 1989, 90 fall; assoc. prof. Clemson U., 1991—; vis. Fulbright scholar dept. english, U. London, Royal Holloway and Bedford New Coll., 1990, U. London, U. Sussex, spring 1989; faculty sec. English dept. Clemson U., 1992—, libr. liaison, 1993—, chair vis. splrs. com., 1993—, mem., 1991—, faculty hiring com. Wash. State U., 1985-86, English chaor search com., 1986-87, assoc. dir. writing lab., spring 1984; coord. 6th ann. Va. Woolf Conf., 1996. Author: Yeats and English Renaissance Literature, 1991; contbr. numerous articles to profl. jours. Mem. MLA, Am. Conf. for Irish Studies, Virginia Woolf Soc. Home: 225 Heather Dr Central SC 29630-8736 Office: Dept English Clemson U PO Box 341503 Clemson SC 29634-1503

CHAPPELL, BARBARA KELLY, child welfare consultant; b. Columbia, S.C., Oct. 17, 1940; d. Arthur Lee and Katherine (Martin) Kelly; 1 child, Kelly Katherine. BA in English and Edn., U. S.C., 1962, MSW, 1974. Tchr. English, Dept. Edn., Honolulu, 1962-65, Alamo Heights High Sch., San Antonio, 1965-67; caseworker Dept. Social Services, Columbia, S.C., 1969-70; supr. Juvenile Placement and Aftercare, Columbia, 1970-72; child welfare cons. Edna McConnell Clark Found., N.Y.C., 1974-75; dir. Children's Foster Care Rev. Bd. System, Columbia, 1975-85; child welfare cons., 1985-89; adminstr. Dept. Human Resources and Juvenile Svcs., Balt., 1989-92; exec. dir. New Pathways, Inc., Balt., 1992—; lectr. in field. Contbr. articles to profl. jours. Coordinator Child's Rights to Parents, Columbia, 1970-75. Epsicopalian. Home and Office: 3215 Girardeau Ave Columbia SC 29204-3314

CHAPPELL, CLOVIS GILLHAM, JR., lawyer; b. Waverly, Tenn., Sept. 13, 1911; s. Clovis Gillham and Cecil (Hart) C.; m. Pauline Mikell LaRoche, Oct. 28, 1938; children: Carolyn (Mrs. D.W. Light III), Polly (Mrs. F. Ferrell Davis), Marian (Mrs. David Scott Miles). Student, Rhodes Coll., 1929-30; B.A., So. Methodist U., 1934, LL.B., 1936. Bar: Tex. 1936. Landman Humble Oil & Refining Co., 1938-44; atty. Baker & Botts, Houston, 1944-50; ptnr. Stubbeman, McRae, Sealy & Laughlin, Midland, 1950-59; ptnr. Lynch, Chappell & Alsup, Midland, 1959-90, of counsel, 1991—; Past sec., dir. Tex. Am. Oil Corp., Midland. Contbr. articles to profl. jours. Past mem. bd. visitors So. Meth. U. Law Sch.; former trustee 1st United Meth. Ch., Midland, Tex. Fellow Am. Coll. Probate Counsel; mem. Am., Tex., Midland County bar assns., Pi Kappa Alpha. Methodist. Home: 1605 Bedford Dr Midland TX 79701-5704 Office: Lynch Chappell & Alsup 300 N Marienfeld St Midland TX 79701-4345

CHAPPELL, DANNY MICHAEL, lawyer; b. Chilhowie, Va., July 4, 1956; s. Glen Jack and Dorothy Susan (Wolfe) C. BBA with honors, U. Tex., 1981; JD, U. Houston, 1984. Bar: Tex. 1985, D.C. 1988, U.S. Ct. Mil. Appeals 1986, U.S. Ct. Appeals (5th cir.) 1988, U.S. Dist. Ct. (so. dist.) Tex. 1988, U.S. Supreme Ct. 1988, U.S. Dist. Ct. (ea. dist.) Tex. 1992. Assoc. Baker Brown Sharman & Parker, Houston, 1988-92; atty. Southwestern Bell Telephone Co., Bellaire, Tex., 1992—; chief prosecutor, Ft. Eustis, Va., 1986-88; spl. prosecutor U.S. Army Judge Advocate Gen.'s Corp, Ft. Dix, N.J., 1987. Capt. U.S. Army, 1985-88. Recipient Meritorious Svc. medal, 1988. Mem. ABA, Houston Bar Assn., Coll. of State Bar of Tex., Advocates, Phi Delta Phi, Beta Gamma Sigma. Office: Southwestern Bell Telephone Legal Dept 6500 West Loop S # 55 Bellaire TX 77401-3503

CHAPPELL, KIMBERLY ANN, elementary education educator; b. Savannah, Ga., May 25, 1966; d. Frank, Jr. and Annie Claudia (Coleman) C. AB in polit. sci., U. Ga., 1988; M in pub. adminstrn., Savannah State Coll., 1990. Cert. tchr., Ga. Tchr. fourth grade Savannah Bd. Edn., 1989-92, reading recovery tchr. leader, 1992—. Contbr. articles to profl. jours. Mem. Alpha Kappa Alpha, Phi Delta Kappa. Democrat. Roman Catholic. Home: 3104 College St Savannah GA 31404 Office: Savannah Bd Edn 208 Bull St Rm 303 Savannah GA 31401-3901

CHAPPELL, MILTON LEROY, lawyer; b. Accra, Ghana, Mar. 25, 1951; (parents Am. citizens); s. Derwood Lee and Helen Jean (Freeman) C.; m. Margot Cecelia Shields, Dec. 18, 1972; children: Marton Gerald, Monet Louise. BA summa cum laude, Columbia Union Coll., 1973; JD, Cath. U., 1976; diploma, Nat. Inst. Trial Advocacy, Boulder, Colo., 1978; cert., U. Miami, 1982. Bar: Md. 1976, D.C. 1977, U.S. Ct. Appeals (4th, 5th, 9th and D.C. cirs.) 1977, U.S. Dist. Ct. D.C. 1978, U.S. Ct. Appeals (6th cir.) 1979, U.S. Supreme Ct. 1980, U.S. Ct. Appeals (11th cir.) 1981, U.S. Dist. Ct. Md. 1982, U.S. Ct. Appeals (7th cir.) 1988, U.S. Dist. Ct. (no. dist.) Calif., 1990. Sole practice Silver Spring, Md., 1976—; staff atty. Nat. Right to Work Legal Def. Found., Springfield, Va., 1976—; lectr. Columbia Union Coll., Takoma Park, Md., 1976-77; legal cons. JNA Elem. Sch., Takoma Park, 1980-83; gen. counsel Playgrounds Unltd., Inc., 1988—, Internat. Play Equipment Mfrs. Assn., Inc., 1995—; participant play settings subcom. recreation access adv. com. U.S. Archtl. and Transp. Barriers Compliance Bd., 1993-94. Contbr. to Ohio No. U. Law Rev., Govt. Union Rev. Mem. Hillandale Civic Assn., Silver Spring, 1980—; legal cons., bd. dirs. Silver Spring Seventh-day Adventist Ch., 1976-84, Takoma Park.; participant U.S. Arch. and Trans. Barriers Compliance Bd., Recreation Access Adv. Com., Play Settings subcom., 1993-94. Mem. ABA, Md. Bar Assn. D.C. Bar assn. (assoc.). Home: 10321 Royal Rd Silver Spring MD 20903-1616 Office: Nat Right to Work Legal Def Found 8001 Braddock Rd # 600 Springfield VA 22151-2110

CHAPPLE, ABBY, consumer comunications consultant; b. N.Y.C., Aug. 17, 1939; d. Adolph Emil and Thelma (Pierce) Klueppelberg; m. Ross Victor Chapple (div.); m. Robert Alan Mewhinney (div.); m. David Marshall Walker. BA, Am. U., 1961, postgrad., 1961-65. Reporter Washington Star, 1966-81; pres. Chapple/Mewhinney Assocs., Annapolis, Md., 1981-82; spl. asst. to chmn. Consumer Product Safety Commn., Washington, 1982-85; pres. Consumer Comm., Annapolis, W.Va., 1985—. Recipient Media award Dallas Mkt. Ctr., 1978, Home Furnishngs Hall Fame, 1979, Am. Soc. Interior Designers, 1985, Chmn.'s award Consumer Product Safety Commn., 1984. Mem. Soc. Consumer Affairs Profls., Internat. Furnishings and Design Assn. (Presdl. commendation 1991), Nat. Assn. Bus. Women, Women in Comm. (pres. Md. chpt. 1994). Republican. Jewish. Home: PO Box 370 Great Cacapon WV 25422-0370 Office: Consumer Comms PO Box 370 Great Cacapon WV 25422

CHAPURA, JOHN ROBERT, computer scientist; b. Endicott, N.Y., Nov. 30, 1958; s. John Cyril and Frances Geraldine (Levanda) C.; m. Elizabeth Ann Griffin, Aug. 8, 1992; 2 children: John Griffin, David Michael. BS, Le Moyne Coll., 1980; MS, Binghamton U., 1995. Engr. IBM Corp., Endicott, N.Y., 1982-93; tchg. asst. Binghamton (N.Y.) U., 1993-94; sr. systems analyst Excelis, Inc., Dallas, 1995—. Inventor: Fluid Application Device, 1995. Mem. IEEE Computer Soc., Assn. Computing Machinery, Epsilon Pi. Home: 2334 Vega St Grand Prairie TX 75050

CHARBONNEAU, ARMAND BERNARD, real estate developer; b. Plattsburgh, N.Y., Jan. 26, 1957; s. Armand Bernard and Beatrice Marie C.; m. Lauren Elizabeth Danisch, May 29, 1982; children: Luke Alexander, Claire Reneé. BS in Mech. Engring., U. Hartford, 1979; MBA, U. North Tex., 1984. Lic. real estate broker, Tex.; lic. comml. pilot. Design engr. Tex. Instruments, Dallas, 1979-82; real estate broker Greenhill Fin. Corp., Dallas, 1984-85; securities wholesaler Wagner Properties, Dallas, 1985-86; v.p., dir. acquisitions Lincoln Property Co./Lowe Enterprises, Dallas, 1988-93; apt. developer Fairfield Devel., Grand Praire, Tex., 1993—. Mem. BYU Mgmt. Soc. (bd. dirs. 1991-93). Home: 6551 Lange Cir Dallas TX 75214-2419 Office: Fairfield Residential ABC 2045 N Highway 360 Ste 250 Grand Prairie TX 75050-1403

CHARKATZ, HARRY MARVIN, psychiatrist; b. Balt., June 18, 1940; s. Allan A. and Harriette D. (Livingston) C.; m. Susan Joy Busch, June 14, 1964; children: Perry, Lawrence, Holly. AA, George Washington U., 1957-60; BS in Medicine, Northwestern U., 1961, MD, 1964. Attending psychiatrist Luth. Gen. Hosp., Park Ridge, Ill., 1972-92, Holy Family Hosp., Des Plaines, Ill., 1972-92; clin. asst. prof., attending psychiatrist U. Ill., Chgo., 1974-90; attending psychiatrist Houston Med. Ctr., Warner Robins, Ga., 1992—. Cpt. U.S. Army, 1965-67. Mem. Am. Psychiatric Assn. Office: Psychiatric Health Svcs 1047 N Houston Rd Warner Robins GA 31093-1505

CHARLES, ANNE M., English language educator; b. Houston, May 14, 1951; d. Kenneth John and Anne Marie (Reilly) C. BA, Barnard Coll., 1973; MA, Purdue U., 1978; PhD, U. Wis., 1997. Proofreader, paralegal Reid & Priest, N.Y.C., 1973-75; bursar Boston Conservatory of Music, 1979-80; from verification specialist to preparedness coord. Somerville Cambridge (Mass.) Econ. Opportunity Com., 1980-84; instr. English U. New Orleans, 1989—; dir. Women's Ctr. U. New Orleans, 1993-94, steering com., 1994-95, steering com. women's studies program, 1993-94. Co-editor: (mag.) The Second Wave: A Magazine of Ongoing Feminism, 1980-82. Mem. Nat. Women's Studies Assn., MLA (v.p. gay and lesbian caucus 1994-95, pres. 1995—, women's caucus), Ctr. for Lesbian & Gay Studies. Democrat. Office: U New Orleans English Dept Lakefront New Orleans LA 70148

CHARLES, HOWARD CLIFTON, JR., public warehousing executive; b. Winston-Salem, N.C., Mar. 31, 1918; s. Howard Clifton Sr. and Jessie Mae (Idol) C.; m. Rachel Louise Charles, June 14, 1941; children: Rachel Diana Phillips, Janie Leah McKnight. AA, Mars Hill (N.C.) Coll., 1939. Mgr. Firestone Home & Auto Store, Reidsville, N.C., 1946-48; mgr. Ctrl. Carolina Warehouses, Inc., Greensboro, N.C., 1949-55, CEO, pres., 1955-80, chmn. bd., 1980—. Trustee Mars Hill Coll., 1987—; bd. dirs. Chapels for the Retarded Ctrs. in N.C., 1976-88; deacon First Bapt. Ch., Greensboro, 1980-84, Sunday Sch. tchr., 1956—. Served to maj. USAAC, 1941-45, to lt. col. Res. ret. Named Alumnus of Yr., Mars Hill Coll., 1996. Mem. Ret. Officers Assn. (pres. 1990), N.C. Warehousemen's Assn. (pres. 1975), Toastmasters (pres. 1957), Kiwanis. Republican. Office: Ctrl Carolina Warehouses Inc PO Box 20107 Greensboro NC 27420

CHARLES, JOEL, forensic audio and video tape analyst, voice identification consultant; b. Phila., Jan. 12, 1914; s. Samuel William and Minnie (Fink) Blumenstein; m. Lillian DuBowe, May 31, 1938 (div. 1964); children: Mark Blumenstein, Richard Blumenstein; m. Nancy Sher, Oct. 24, 1988. BSChemE, Drexel U., 1938. Pres. The Charles Agy., Phila., 1938-42,

45-64; physicist Naval Air Exptl. Station, Phila., 1942-45; pres. The Dento-Med. Tapes, Upper Darby, Pa., 1957-73, Associated TV Prodns., Inc., Phila., 1948-52, Computerized Electronic Edn., Upper Darby, Pa., 1969-73; dir. continuing edn., media instructional methodology Pa. Coll. of Podiatric Medicine, Phila., 1973-77; pvt. practice, audio and video tape analysis and voice identification cons. Plantation, Fla., 1977-96; Coral Springs, Fla., 1996—; expert witness on tape recordings in over 250 trials; seminar lectr. Tex. Criminal Def. Lawyers Inst., La. Pub. Def. Criminal Lit. Seminar, Broward Criminal Def. Lawyers Assn., Dade Criminal Def. Lawyers Assn., Phoenix Pub. Defenders, Dade Fed. Pub. Defenders. Contbr. articles to profl. jours. Mem. NACDL (assoc.), Nat. Forensic Ctr., Internat. Assn. for Forensic Phonetics, Am. Fedn. Musicians, Am. Dialect Soc., Audio Engring. Soc. (chmn. forensic tape com.). Home and Office: St Johns Woods 1109 NW 97th Dr Coral Springs FL 33071

CHARLES, JOHN FRANKLYN, marriage and family therapist, clergyman; b. St. Paul's, Antigua, W.I., Sept. 10, 1937; came to U.S., 1978; s. Christopher Cornelius and Celestine Rebecca (James) C.; m. Delpha Louista Buntin, Dec. 19, 1982. B.Div., U. London, 1976; M.S.Ed., U. Miami, Fla., 1979, Ed.S., 1981; Ph.D., Calif. Coast Coll., 1985; EdD U. Miami, Fla., 1989. Ordained to ministry United Methodist Ch., 1974. Tchr. Grammar Sch., St. John's, Antiqua, 1959-67; chaplain, tutor Wesley Coll., Belize City, Belize, 1971-72; minister religion Meth. Ch., W.I., Road Town, 1972-78; vocat. counselor CETA, U. Miami, Coral Gables, Fla., 1980-82; psychometrist, psychologist Consortium, Miami, 1981-85; marriage therapist Charles' Cons. Bur., Miami, 1983—; assessor Magistrate Ct., Brit. V.I., 1976-78; cons. Corrections Ctr., Miami, 1980-81. Mem. U.S. Presdl. Task Force, 1984; pres. Gideons Internat., Antigua, 1962-67. Meth. Conf. scholar, 1968; U. Miami grantee, 1980. Mem. Am. Assn. Counseling and Devel., Fla. Assn. Counseling and Devel., Am. Assn. Specialists in Group Work. Avocations: travel; swimming; yoga; table tennis; international affairs. Office: PO Box 248631 Miami FL 33124-8631

CHARLESWORTH, ERNEST NEAL, allergist, dermatologist, immunologist, educator; b. Denver, June 11, 1945; s. Albert Ernest and Wilma Nadine (Wright) C.; m. Margaret Louise Gay, July 12, 1969; children: Richard Neil, Mark Edward. BS, U. Houston, 1967; MD, U. Tex., 1971. Diplomate Am. Bd. Allergy and Immunology, Am. Bd. Dermatology, Am. Bd. Internal Medicine, Diagnostic Lab. Immunology Bd. Commd. capt. USAF, 1971, advanced through grades to col., 1987;, ret. 1996; intern in medicine Wilford Hall USAF Med. Ctr., Lackland AFB, Tex., 1971-72, resident in dermatology, 1973-76, resident in internal medicine, 1984-86; staff dermatologist USAF Med. Ctr., Keesler AFB, Miss., 1976-78; pvt. practice in dermatology Jackson, Miss., 1978-81; clin. faculty dept. medicine U. Miss. Med. Sch., Jackson, 1979-81; chief dermatology svc. USAF Regional Med. Ctr., Clark Air Base, The Philippines, 1981-84; fellow in allergy and immunology Johns Hopkins U. Sch. Medicine, Balt., 1986-89, clin. faculty divsn. allergy and clin. immunology, 1988-89; asst. chief allergy-immunology svc. Wilford Hall USAF Med. Ctr., Lackland AFB, 1989-95; assoc. prof. medicine Uniformed Svcs. Univ. of The Health Scis., Bethesda, Md., 1990-92; clin. assoc. prof. U. Tex. Health Sci. Ctr., San Antonio, 1990-92; allergist/dermatologist Brenham (Tex.) Clinic Assn., 1995—; cons. to surgeon gen. for dermatology PACAF Med. Command, Hickam AFB, Hawaii, 1981-84; presenter Harold S. Nelson Allergy-Immunology Symposium, Fitsimons Army Med. Ctr., Aurora, Colo., Johns Hopkins Asthma and Allergy Ctr., Balt., 16th Hawaii Dermatology Seminar, Maui. Contbr. articles to Arch. Dermatology, Jour. Mil. Assn. Dermatology, Jour. Clin. Investigation, Internat. Arch. Allergy Immunology, Insights in Allergy, Jour. Pediatrics, Jour. Investigative Dermatology. Recipient Clemens Von Pirquet Rsch. award Am. Coll. Allergy and Immunology, 1987. Fellow ACP (presenter), Am. Acad. Dermatology, Am. Coll. Allergy (presenter); mem. Am. Acad. Allergy and Immunology (dermatologic disease interest sect., presenter, Young Investigator award 1989), Assn. Air Force Allergists, Soc. Air Force Physicians, Soc. Investigative Dermatology, San Antonio Allergy Soc. (sec.). Episcopalian. Home: 806 E Mansfield Brenham TX 77833 Office: Brenham Clinic Assn 600 N Park Brenham TX 77833

CHARLEY, NANCY JEAN, communications professional; b. LaCrosse, Wis., Jan. 6, 1956. A in Bus. Adminstrn., Midway Coll., 1992, A in Computer Info. Systems, 1993, BBA, 1994, postgrad. Office mgr. for neurologist, Lexington, Ky., 1985-88; health unit coord. acute care hosp., Lexington, 1979-91, health unit coord. trainer, 1992-93, coord. order comms., order mgmt. trainer mgmt. info. system, 1988-95; system support analyst Mgmt. Info. Systems, 1994-96, sys. support analyst, patient auditor trainer, 1996—; freelance cons. Mem. Nat. Assn. Health Unit Coords. (support cons. 1990, edn. bd. 1990-95, chmn. continuing edn. com. 1991-93, mem. several ad hoc coms.), Midway Coll. Alumnae Assn. Office: Baptist Healthcare Systems 4007 Kresge Way Louisville KY 40207-4604

CHARLIP, RALPH BLAIR, career officer; b. Detroit, July 16, 1952; s. Jack Edward and Dorothea (Steinman) C.; m. Cynthia Lanell Sallas, May 23, 1987. BA, U. Ariz., 1976, MPA, 1977. Commd. 2nd lt. USAF, 1978, advanced through grades to lt. col., 1994; squadron comdr. USAF Regional Hosp., Langley AFB, Va., 1978-79, dir. patient adminstrn., 1979-80, plant mgr., 1980-81; dir. med. resource mgmt. USAF Clinic Andersen, Andersen AFB, Guam, 1981-82; dir. patient adminstrn. Malcolm Grow USAF Med. Ctr., Andrews AFB, Md., 1983-84; intern Data Systems Design Ctr., Gunter AFB, Ala., 1984-85; health policy devel. officer USAF Hdqs., Bolling AFB, Washington, 1985-89; dir. patient adminstrn. USAF Med. Ctr., Wright-Patterson AFB, Ohio, 1989-92; assoc. dir. med. svcs. Air Nat. Guard Hqrs., Andrews AFB, 1992-94; dir. plans integration and mktg. Dept. Def. Health Svcs. Region VII, Ft. Bliss, Tex., 1994-96; comdr. 423 Clinic, Upwood, U.K., 1996—. Author (book) Your Health Benefits, 1989. Fellow Am. Coll. Healthcare Execs.; mem. Assn. Quality and Participation, Am. Acad. of Med. Adminstrs. Office: 423 Clinic/SC Box 223 Unit 5610 APO AE 09470

CHARLTON, GORDON TALIAFERRO, JR., retired bishop; b. San Antonio, Sept. 29, 1923; s. Gordon Taliaferro and Enid Lynn (Jones) C.; m. Landon Cutler Crump, Dec. 23, 1948; children—Virginia, David, Duncan. B.A., U. Tex-Austin, 1944; M.Div., Va. Sem., 1949, D.D. (hon.), 1974. Ordained priest Episcopal Ch. Asst. rector St. James Ch., Houston, 1949-51; rector St. Mathews Ch., Fairbanks, Alaska, 1951-54; personnel sec. Overseas dept. Nat. Council Episcopal Ch., N.Y.C., 1954-58; rector Christ Ch., Mexico City, 1958-63, St. Andrews Ch., Wilmington, Del., 1963-67; asst. dean Va. Sem., Alexandria, 1967-73; dean Sem. of Southwest, Austin, Tex., 1973-82; Suffragan bishop Episcopal Diocese of Tex., Houston, 1982-89, ret., 1989. Served to lt. (j.g.) USNR, 1943-46; PTO. Episcopalian.

CHASE, EMERY JOHN, JR., nuclear engineer, researcher; b. St. Albans, Vt., Dec. 27, 1943; s. Emery J. and Rita M. (Tatro) C.; m. Eleanora M. Fitzwilliam, June 3, 1995; children: Emery J. III, Kenneth D., Heather M. BS, U.S. Mil. Acad., West Point, N.Y., 1965; MS in Nuclear Engring., MIT, 1967; MS in Bus. Adminstrn., U. No. Colo., 1978. Registered profl. engr., Colo., Va. Commd. 2d lt. U.S. Army, 1965-92, advanced through grades to col.; asst. prof. physics USAF Acad., Colorado Springs, Colo., 1972-75; analyst, engr. Engr. Sch., Ft. Belvoir, Va., 1977-78; spl. asst. nuclear Office of Sec. of Def., Washington, 1978-81; comdr. Engr. Battalian, Darmstadt, Germany, 1981-84; asst. corps engr. Vth U.S. Corps, Frankfurt, Germany, 1983-84; rsch. asst. testing Def. Nuclear Agy., Washington, 1984-86, dir. nuclear assessments and applications, 1986-89; exec. asst. OSD Office of Sec. of Def., Washington, 1989-92; dir. Ctr. for Verification Rsch./SAIC, Newington, Va., 1992—; lectr. Inter-Am. Def. Coll., Ft. McNair, 1988-92. AEC fellow, 1965, Sr. Ofcls. in Nat. Security award Harvard U., Boston, 1988. Mem. NSPE, Soc. Mil. Engrs., Arms Control Assn., Alumni Assn. U.S. Mil. Acad., MIT Alumni Assn., Harvard U. Alumni Assn. Home: 3701 Del Mar Dr Woodbridge VA 22193 Office: Ctr for Verification Rsch SAIC 8500 Cinderbed Rd Newington VA 22122

CHASE, HELEN LOUISE, banker; b. Waukegan, Ill., Sept. 29, 1943; d. David William and Ruth Virginia (Sawyer) C. BA, U. Ill., 1965. Sec., exec. sec. Foote, Cone and Belding, Chgo., 1965-66; various positions Continental Bank, Chgo., 1966-73, internat. banking officer, 1973-76, 2nd v.p., 1976-77; Brazil rep. Continental Bank, Sao Paulo, 1977-80; 2nd v.p., sect. head Far East group Continental Bank Internat., N.Y.C., 1980-81; 2nd v.p. internat. div. Continental Bank, Chgo., 1981-83; v.p. N.Am. Union Trust Bank (now Signet Bank), Balt., 1983-84; v.p., mgr. internat. ops. Signet Bank, Balt., 1984-89; v.p. internat. dept. Meridian Bank, Lancaster, Pa., 1989-92, v.p., mgr. internat. ops., 1992-94; pvt. practice internat. fin. cons., 1994-95; v.p., mgr. internat. divsn. Compass Bank, Birmingham, Ala., 1995—. Mem. bus. adv. bd. Millersville U.

CHASE, JEAN COX, retired English language educator; b. Charlottesville, Va., July 2, 1925; d. Joseph Lee and Wirt (Davidson) Cox; m. John Bryant Chase Jr., June 16, 1951 (dec. June 1978); children: Nancy Davidson Chase, Jean Cox Chase. BA magna cum laude, U. N.C. Woman's Coll., 1946; MA in Eng. Lang. and Lit., U. Mich., 1947; postgrad., U. Va., 1950, 53, various univs. Cert. tchr., Va., N.C. Instr. English Carroll Coll., Waukesha, Wis., 1947-49, housemother, 1948-49; teaching asst. English U. Wis., Madison, 1949; editorial proof reader Michie Legal Publs., Charlottesville, Va., 1951; tchr. of English and Latin Lane High Sch., Charlottesville, Va., 1950-53; critic tchr. for sch. edn. in English U. Va., Charlottesville, Va., 1951; tutor Chapel Hill, N.C., 1958-66; teaching English, gifted, remedial Jordan High Sch., Durham, N.C., 1966; tchr. English Orange County High Sch., Hillsborough, N.C., 1966-67; instr. Cen. Piedmont Community Coll., Charlotte, N.C., 1970-87; co-chmn. fall faculty conf., Cen. Piedmont Community Coll., 1974, vice-chmn. faculty senate, 1976-77, chmn., 1977-78, chmn. writing across the curriculum, 1980-84 and others; judge Charlotte Writers Club Contest, 1984. Co-editor, author: The Communication Course, 1974; contbg. author, The Jane Doe Papers, 1977, Women of Mecklenburg: Making a Difference, 1980. Active N.C. state legis. coun., N.C. Coun. Women's Orgns., World Affairs Conf. Planning Com., Univ. League, Jr. Svc. League, Creative Retirement Hilton Head, Dem. Party of Hilton Head, others; vol. English, Latin tutor. Recipient scholarship U. Mich., Ann Arbor, 1946-47, fellowship Nat. Endowment for Humanities, Carnegie Mellon Univ., Pitts., 1981. Mem. MLA, AAUW (various offices, coms. Hilton Head br.), Nat. Coun. Tchrs. English, Great Books Study Group, Opera Guild Study Group, Daus. of the King (life), Phi Beta Kappa, Kappa Delta Pi, Chi Omega (advisor local chpt. 1959-69), others. Episcopalian. Home: 300 Wood Haven Dr Apt 3405 Hilton Head Island SC 29928-7516

CHASE, JEANNE NORMAN, artist, educator; b. Spokane, Wash., Feb. 15, 1929; d. John Henry and Violet Inez (Crosby) Norman; m. David Carl Chase, July 4, 1964. BFA in Painting, Calif. State U., Northridge, 1959. Instr. painting and drawing Ringling Sch. Art and Design, Sarasota, Fla., 1978-94, chmn. fine arts dept., 1983-85; condr. workshops Ringling Workshop Series, Wildacres Retreat, N.C., 1984, 85; lectr. in field. Group and one-woman shows include Rauchbach Gallery, Bal Harbour, Fla., 1981, 83, Boca Grande (Fla.) Gallery, 1982, Tatem Gallery, Ft. Lauderdale, 1986, 87, St. Boniface Conservatory of Arts, Sarasota, 1988, Helios Gallery, Naples, Fla., 1989, Manatee C.C. Fine Arts Gallery, 1988, Phillips Gallery, Sanibel, Fla., 1991, Mickelson Gallery, Washington, 1989-94, others; nat. and internat. juried competitions Ridge Crest Art Assn., Winter Haven, Fla., 1980, Mason Keane Gallery, N.Y.C., 1981 (Best of Show), Tampa (Fla.) Mus. of Arts, 1982, El Paso Mus. Art, 1982, Columbia-Greene C.C., Hudson, N.Y., 1982, Edison C.C., Ft. Myers, Fla., 1982, 85, The Soc. of the Four Arts, Palm Beach, Fla., 1982, 87, The Capitol Gallery, Tallahassee, Fla., 1986, Tampa Mus., 1988, Binnewater Arts Ctr., N.Y.C., 1988, others.; represented in permanent collections former Pres. Jimmy and Roslyn Carter, Grace Lemon (collector), Indonesia, Bendix Avionies, Dr. and Mrs. Victor Maitland, Fla., Ringling Sch. Art and Design, Mr. and Mrs. E. Howland Swift III, Va., Chatahoochie Mus. Art, Ga., Dr. Artine Artinian, Fla., George Whitman, Shakespeare and Co., Paris, Veroingue Rabin Le Gall E'cole des Beaux-Arts, Paris, Donahoe Swift Assn., N.Y.C.; works published in book American Artists, an Illustrated Survey of Leading Contemporary Americans, 1986; subject in books: Female Artists in the United States: a Research and Resource File, 1986, 88, Artists and Their Cats, 1990, Drawings, Hylton-Leech Gallery, Sarasota, Fla., 1996; subject numerous newspaper articles; TV and video interviews: Focus on the Arts, Channel 4, 1980, A Fabric of Our Own Making, Ga. State U., 1981, Introduction to Jeanne Norman Chase, local sta., St. Augustine, Fla., 1991. Mem. Fla. Artists Group. Recipient Merit award Foster Harmon Gallery, Sarasota, 1991. Mem. Fla. Artists Group. Studio: 1602 Bay Rd Sarasota FL 34239-6808

CHASE, VICTORIA BYLER, mechanical engineer; b. Dallas, Dec. 19, 1954; d. Edwin Carl Byler Sr. and Annie Orlena Hurlburt; m. Warren Chase, Apr. 9, 1988; 1 child, Joseph Scott. BSME, So. Meth. U., 1979; MS in Human Devel., U. Tex., Dallas, 1992. Registered profl. engr., Tex. Design drafter Tex. Instruments, Inc., Dallas, 1973-78, mech. design engr., 1979, lead mech. engr., 1983-85; project engr. Exxon Co., U.S.A., Houston, 1980-81; sr. project engr. Exxon Co., U.S.A., Tyler, Tex., 1981-83; engring. mgr. Tng. Gallery, Inc., Dallas, 1986; lead packaging engr. Boeing Electronics, Inc., Irving, Tex., 1987-88; sr. mech. engr. Sci. Communications, Garland, Tex., 1988-89. Mem. Tex. Soc. Profl. Engrs., Pi Tau Sigma. Presbyterian. Home: 500 Harvest Glen Richardson TX 75081

CHASE, WILLIAM M., academic administrator; b. Newport News, Va., 1938; m. JoAn Johnstone; children: Will, Kati. Bachelor's degree with honors, Haverford Coll., 1961; MLitt, U. Calif., Berkeley, 1963; DLitt, U. Calif., 1968; hon. degree, Amherst Coll., Williams Coll. Instr. U. Calif., Berkeley; prof. of English Stanford U., assoc. dean Sch. Humanities and Scis., 1981, vice provost for acad. planning and devel., 1985-88; pres. Wesleyan U., 1988-94; Emory U., 1994—. Author: The Political Identities of Ezra Pound and T.S. Eliot, Lionel Trilling: Criticism and Policies; editor: Justice Denied: The Black Man in White America, James Joyce: A Collection of Critical Essays, An Introduction to Literature, (poetry anthology) Making It New. Recipient Richard W. Lyman award Stanford Alumni Assn., 1986; Woodrow Wilson nat. fellow. Office: Emory U Atlanta GA 30322

CHASSAY, ROGER PAUL, JR., engineering executive, project manager; b. Chgo., Aug. 30, 1938; s. Roger Paul Sr. and Ruth Ruby (Taylor) C.; m. Katheryne Faye Roper, Jan. 1961 (div. Mar. 1988); children: Cynthia, Terri, Donald, Dean, Paul, Brett; m. Judith Marie Armstrong, Mar. 1990; stepchildren: Angela, Dana. BS, La. State U., 1961; postgrad., Ohio State U., 1962. F8U-3 fighter wing designer Dallas, 1958; aerospace engr. Saturn & Skylab Program Offices NASA/Marshall Space Flight Ctr., Huntsville, Ala., 1964-74; SPAR project mgr. NASA/Marshall Space Flight Ctr., Huntsville, 1974-77, mgr. integration/ test office Microgravity Projects Office, 1977-82; mgr. experiment carriers office Microgravity Projects Office, NASA/Marshall Space Flight Ctr., Huntsville, 1982-86, dep. mgr. Microgravity Projects Office, 1986-88; mgr. space sta. and advanced projects office Microgravity Projects Office NASA/Marshall Space Flight Ctr., Huntsville, 1988-94; chmn. orbiter motion subcom. NASA, 1984-86, ctr. rep. flight assignments working group, Huntsville and Washington, 1985-86, chmn. space sta. microgravity requirements integration group, Huntsville, 1990-94. Author: Application of Mathematics to the XB70 Bomber, 1963, Low-g Measurements by NASA, 1986, Processing Materials in Space: History and Future, 1987, (chpt.) Low Gravity Materials Experiments in Space Sta., 1989, Cooperation Between NASA and ESA for the First Microgravity Materials Science Glovebox, 1992; author, editor: (NASA movie) Space Processing Applications Rocket Project, 1979. Sr. arbitrator Better Bus. Bur., Huntsville, 1987—; pres. Holy Spirit Ch. Coun., Huntsville, 1982, N.E. Ala. Ch. Coun., Huntsville, 1984-85; scoutmaster Boy Scouts Am., Dayton, Ohio, 1963; clarinetist Huntsville Concert Band, 1987-91, 93—. Capt. USAF, 1961-64. Assoc. fellow AIAA. Office: NASA Marshall Space Flight Ctr/#FA31 Huntsville AL 35812

CHASTAIN, DENISE JEAN, process improvement engineer; b. Casper, Wyo., Dec. 12, 1961; d. Jerry and Nancy Gayle (Stewart) C. BAChemE, Ga. Inst. Tech., 1986. Registered profl. engr., Ga. Product devel. engr. Ga. Pacific, Atlanta, 1986-89; process engr. Lockwood Greene Engrs., Atlanta, 1989-94; process improvement engr. Ga. Pacific, Atlanta, 1994—. Named Young Engr. of Yr., Ga., 1994, to Coun. of Outstanding Young Alumni, Ga. Inst. Tech., 1995. Mem. AIChE (sec. 1989-90, vice chmn. 1990-91, chmn. 1991-93), Engrs. for Edn. (nat. profl. devel. com. and subcom. for profl. standards).

CHASTAIN, SHIRLEY PERKINS, nursing administrator, medical/surgical nurse; b. Cin., Apr. 28, 1930; d. Warren Langdon Jr. and Ruth Virginia (Washburn) Perkins; m. David Franklin Chastain Jr., Apr. 28, 1956; children: David III, John, Mark, Ann. Diploma, Jewish Hosp. Sch. Nursing, Cin., 1950; BSN, Med. Coll. of Ga., 1977; MS, Ga. State U., 1981. Dir. nurses Inst. for Chronic Illness, Cin., Home for Jewish Aged, Cin., The Jewish Home, Atlanta; nursing supr. Kennestone Hosp., Marietta, Ga., staff nurse oncology unit; ret., 1992; researcher incidence of urinary tract infrctions in a nursing home setting. Mem. ANA, Ga. State Nurses' Assn., Am. Soc. on Aging, Sigma Theta Tau. Home: 662 Monticello Way Marietta GA 30067-5520

CHATTERJEE, SANKAR, geology educator; b. Calcutta, India, May 28, 1943; arrived in U.S., 1976; s. Prafulla and Biva (Banerjee) C.; m. Sibani Mitra, Feb. 4, 1971; children: Soumya, Shuvu. BS, Jadaupur U., Calcutta, 1962, MS, 1964; PhD, Calcutta U., 1970; postdoctoral, Smithsonian Inst., 1978. Lectr., asst. prof. Indian Statis. Inst., Calcutta, 1968-75; asst. prof. George Washington U., Washington, 1976-78; asst. prof., curator Tex. Tech. U., Lubbock, 1976-78, assoc. prof., curator, 1984-87, prof., curator, 1987-94, Paul Whitfield Horn prof., 1994—; vis. prof. U. Calif., Berkeley, 1976, U. Tubingen, Germany, 1991-92; curator of paleontology Mus. Tex. Tech. U., Lubbock, 1979—; rsch. assoc. Smithsonian Inst., 1979—. Author: Antarctica, 1985, New Concepts in Global Tectonics, 1992; contbr. numerous articles to profl. jours. Recipient Antarctic Svc. medal Dept. State, 1982, Sci. Achievement award Tex. Senate, 1991, Headliner award Women in Comm., 1992; grantee NSF, Nat. Geog. Soc., Am. Mus. Natural History, Field Mus. Natural History. Fellow Geol. Soc. Am.; mem. Antarctical Soc., Sigma Xi. Office: Mus of Tex Tech Univ 4th and Indiana Lubbock TX 79409

CHATTERJEE, SUNIL K., cancer research scientist; b. Calcutta, Aug. 7, 1940; came to U.S., 1966; s. Bhupendra Nath and Parimal Bala (Banerjee) C.; m. Malaya Bhattacharya, Oct. 25, 1972; children: Indranil, Sumana. BS, Presidency Coll., Calcutta, 1959; MS, U. Calcutta, 1961, PhD, 1966. Postdoctoral fellow dept. microbiology U. Pa., Phila., 1966-68; rsch. assoc. Inst. Cancer Rsch., Fox Chase/Phila., 1968-69; rsch. officer U. Calcutta, 1969-71; rsch. fellow Max-Planck Inst., Goettingen, W. Germany, 1971-72; asst. cancer rsch. scientist dept. pathology Roswell Park Cancer Inst., 1972-73, cancer rsch. scientist I, 1973-76, cancer rsch. scientist III, 1976-86, 87-93; assoc. prof. dept. ob/gyn U. Ky., Lexington, 1993—; guest scientist Divsn. Oncology, Stanford (Calif.) U., 1993. Contbr. articles to profl. jours. Grantee Elsa U. Pardee Found., 1991-93, Am. Cancer Soc., 1992, Audrey Lippman Cancer Rsch. Fund, 1990-92, NIH, 1991-94, Ephrain McDowell Cancer Found., 1993-94. Democrat. Hindu. Home: 2400 The Woods Ln Lexington KY 40502-6596 Office: Univ Ky 800 Rose St Lexington KY 40536-0001

CHATTIN, GILBERT MARSHALL, financial analyst; b. Decherd, Tenn., Jan. 13, 1914; s. Murrell Emmett and Lena Katherine (Jones) C.; m. Hester Stroud, June 18, 1938; 1 child, Marsha Jane. BA, U South Sewanee, 1937; JD, Blackstone Sch. Law, 1965. Chief credit analyst, mgr. city dept. Dun and Bradstreet, Inc., Knoxville, Tenn., 1938-43; ptnr. A&A Service and Supply Co., Atlanta, 1946-70; chief auditor Ga. Dept. Health, 1963-72; chief auditor, audit mgr. Ga. Dept. Human Resources, 1972-84; corp. auditor Ga. Dept. Revenue, 1955-63; pvt. practice fin. analyst, investor, cons., 1955—. Served with AUS, 1943-46, ETO. Mem. NRA, Am. Assn. Individual Investors, Nat. Assn. Investors, Am. Numismatic Assn., Phi Gamma Delta. Mem. Ch. of Christ.

CHAU, HIN-FAI, electrical engineer; b. Hong Kong, Jan. 6, 1964; s. Tat Hung and Kwei Sin (Ho) C. BSc in Engring., U. Hong Kong, 1985; MS in Engring., U. Mich., 1986, PhD in Elec. Engring., 1992. Trainee technician Lambda Tele-equipment Ltd., Hong Kong, 1984; rsch. asst. U. Mich., Ann Arbor, 1986-92; mem. tech. staff Tex. Instruments, Inc., Dallas, 1992—. Chmn. Chinese Group in the 15th and 16th Multi-Ethnic Festival of Ann Arbor, 1987, 88. Mem. IEEE, Tau Beta Pi. Home: 801 Legacy Dr Apt 2412 Plano TX 75023 Office: Tex Instruments Inc Corp R&D PO Box 655936 MS 134 Dallas TX 75265

CHAUDHRY, ABDUL GHAFOOR, surgeon; b. Lahore, Pakistan, Dec. 12, 1947; came to U.S., 1974; m. Fauzia Jabeen, Jan. 15, 1983; children: Sulemon, Imrom, Saba. MD, King Edward Med. Coll., Lahore, Pakistan, 1970. House surgeon May Hosps., Labon, Pakistan, 1971; mem. Mobile Surg. Team, Pakistan, 1971-74; rotating intern Perth Amboy (N.J.) Gen. Hosp., 1974-75; resident gen. surgery The Meth. Hosp., Bklyn., 1975-79; cardiothoracic surgeon Boston U. Med. Ctr., 1979-81; cardiothoracic surgeon pediats. The Children's Hosp. Med. Ctr., Boston, 1981; cardiovascular, thoracic surgeon Raleigh (N.C.) Cardiovascular and Thoracic, Inc. Mem. AMA, N.C. Med. Soc., Wake County Med. Soc. Office: Raleigh Cardiovascular & Th 2800 Blue Ridge Rd #306 Raleigh NC 27607

CHAVARRIA, DOLORES ESPARZA, financial service executive; b. Levelland, Tex., Nov. 13, 1952; d. Thomas Medina and Hermenejilda (Estrada) Esparza; m. Margarito R. Grimaldo (div. Feb. 1975); children: Maurice Patrick, Margarito; m. Frank Sedillo Chavarria; 1 child, Mecca Esparza. AS, South Plains C.C., 1977; student, Tex. Tech U., 1977-78. Notary public, Tex. Supr. cen. supply South Park Med. Ctr., Lubbock, Tex., 1980-84, dir. materials mgmt. dept., 1984-90; buyer City of Lubbock, 1990-94, recruiter, 1994—; prin. D.E.E. Enterprises, Lubbock, 1992—. Chmn. S.W. Voter's Registration, Lubbock, 1988. Mem. Nat. Assn. Purchasing Mgmt. (2d v.p. South Plains chpt.), Am. Bus. Women's Assn., Tex. Purchasing Mgmt. Assn., Hispanic Assn. of Women. Democrat. Roman Catholic. Office: 1625 13th St Lubbock TX 79401-3830

CHAVEZ, J. ANTHONY, lawyer; b. Auburn, Calif., Oct. 5, 1955; s. Marco Antonio and Barbara Ann (Lawrence) Chavez-Rivas. BA, U. Calif., Santa Barbara, 1977; JD, Stanford U., 1981. Bar: Calif. 1981, Tex. 1982, U.S. Dist. Ct. (so. and no. dists.) Calif. 1982, (cen. dist.) Calif. 1983, U.S. Dist. Ct. (so. dist.) Tex. 1982, (we. dist.) Tex. 1983, (no. dist.) Tex. 1991, N.Y. 1986, U.S. Dist. Ct. (ea. and so. dists.) N.Y. 1986, U.S. Supreme Ct. 1986. With legal dept. Exxon Co. U.S.A., Houston, 1981-85, N.Y.C., 1985-86; assoc. gen. counsel Sybron Corp., Saddlebrook, N.J., 1986-88, Crown Equipment Corp., New Bremen, Ohio, 1989-90; trial atty. Exxon Co. U.S.A., Houston, 1990-92; counsel Exxon Chem. Co., Houston, 1992-95, Exxon Exploration Co., Houston, 1995—. Contbr. articles to profl. jours. Chancellor's scholar U. Calif., 1976, Univ. Svc. award U. Calif., Santa Barbara, 1977. Mem. ABA (antitrust, criminal justice and litigation sects., white collar crime com., criminal litigation com.), Houston Bar Assn. (vice chair antitrust and trade regulation sect.), Coll. State Bar Tex. Republican. Home: 9 Woodsborough Cir Houston TX 77055 Office: Exxon Exploration Co PO Box 4778 233 Benmar Houston TX 77210-4778

CHAVEZ, JANIE IGNACIA, education educator; b. Monterrey, Mex., July 31, 1946; came to U.S., 1955, naturalized, 1985; d. Guadalupe C. and Josefa (Cuevas) C. Student, Gulf Coast Bus Coll., 1968; BS in Elem. Edn., Tex. So. U., 1984. Cert. tchr., Tex. Typist Concentrated Employment Co., Houston, 1969-71; bookkeeper Phillips 66, Houston, 1971-73; sec. Highlands Ins., Houston, 1974-78; tchr. aide Houston Ind. Sch. Dist., 1978-83, bilingual tchr., 1984-86; substitute tchr. McAllen (Tex.) Ind. Sch. Dist., 1987—; computer cons, CIA Lab., Houston, 1981. Leader, Valley Interfaith, Weslaco-McAllen, 1987; v.p. Roosevelt Elem. PTA, McAllen, 1988-89. Mem. Nat. Tchrs. Assn., Am. Assn. Ret. Persons, Smithsonian Instn., NAFE, Fatima Crusader, Sacred Heart Auto League. Home: 3008 Lucille Ave Mcallen TX 78503-8632

CHAVEZ, VICTOR MANUEL, process engineer; b. Trujillo, Peru, Mar. 10, 1946; came to U.S., 1976; s. Alfonso Manuel Chavez and Paulina Leon Flores; m. Carmen Rosa Herrera, July 19, 1974; children: Leslie, Natalie, Valerie. BSChemE, UNMSM, Lima, Peru, 1970; engring. degree in petrochimie, U. Libre, Brussels, 1976. Registered profl. engr., Tex. Process engr. Nueces Petrochem., Corpus Christi, Tex., 1977-80; sr. process engr. HDR, Houston, 1980-82, Litwin Engrs. & Constrn., Houston, 1982-84; lead process engr. M.W. Kellogg, Houston, 1984-91; process engr. specialist Va. Indonesia Co., Houston and Bontang, Indonesia, 1991-96; prin. process engr. Fluor Daniel, Houston, 1996—. Mem. AIChE, NSPE. Home: 14714 Charlmont Dr Houston TX 77083

CHAVIS, LARRY EUGENE, mayor; b. Richmond, Va., Sept. 10, 1950; s. Horace and Patricia C.; m. Edna Keys, July 31, 1994; 1 child, Mickia

Kemyon Williams. BSBA, Va. Commonwealth U., 1975. Coun. mem. City of Richmond, Va., 1992—, vice mayor, 1992-94, mayor, 1996—; chair orgnl. devel. com. City of Richmond, 1996—, legis. com., 1996—; appointing authority City of Richmond Sister Cities Commn.; mem. Leadership Metro Richmond, Joint Housing Task Force, Gov.'s Task Force-Revitalization of Urban Areas; co-chmn. Metro Regional Crime Task Force; pres. Richmond Renaissance; mem. Blackwell Safe Haven; bd. dirs. Va. Biotech. Rsch. Park, Richmond, Weed and Seed, Inc., Richmond; pres., CEO Chavis Transfer, Inc., PATCO Trucking, Inc. Mem. U.S. Conf. Mayors, Nat. League of Cities (econ. and cmty. devel. steering com.). Home: 5231 Bemiss Rd Richmond VA 23224 Office: Office of Mayor 900 E Broad St Ste 201 Richmond VA 23219

CHEATHAM, DAVID ALAN, internist; b. Amarillo, Tex., Jan. 10, 1949; s. Roy Francis and Nell (Spann) C.; m. Barbara Elise Beckmann, July 31, 1970; children: Jeff, Chris, Brian. BS, Tex. Tech. U., 1971; MD, U. Tex., 1975. Pvt. practice internal medicine Dallas, 1978—. Mem. AMA, Am. Soc. Internal Medicine, Tex. Med. Assn. Home: 3609 Whiffletree Dr Plano TX 75023-6038 Office: 8335 Walnut Hill Ln Ste 105 Dallas TX 75231-4213

CHEATHAM, PATRICK SEALE, engineering executive; b. Dothan, Ala., Aug. 12, 1949; s. Jesse Richard and Mary Ila (Poyner) C.; m. Judith Gill Knopp, Oct. 11, 1974; children: Alexander Knopp, Margaret Leigh. BS in Physics, Auburn (Ala.) U., 1971; MS in Optical Sci., U. Ariz., 1974, PhD in Optical Sci., 1976. Optical designer Vivitar, Santa Monica, Calif., 1975-77; mem. tech. staff The Aerospace Corp., L.A., 1977-80, sys. dir., 1984-91; sys. dir. The Aerospace Corp., Herndon, Va., 1991—; sr. analyst Pacific-Sierra Rsch. Corp., Santa Monica, Calif., 1984-91. Contbr. articles to profl. jours. Mem. McLean Symphony Orch. Mem. SPIE, Soc. for Info. Display, Optical Soc. Am. Episcopalian. Office: The Aerospace Corp 13873 Park Center Dr #187 Herndon VA 22071

CHEATHAM, ROBERT CARL, SR., city manager; b. Frostproof, Fla., Feb. 14, 1935; s. Milton Rufus Cheatham and Mabel Alice (Morris) Hester; m. Barbara Ann Lamb, Aug. 23, 1953 (div. 1993); 1 child, Robert Carl, Jr.; m. Kathryn Grace Hart, Dec. 18, 1994. AS, Polk Cmty. Coll., Winter Haven, 1969; BS, U. Ala., 1984; MPA, U. South Fla., 1995. Utilities dept. City of Lake Wales (Fla.), 1958-67, dir. pub. works, 1967-69, city mgr., 1969-75; city mgr. City of Anniston (Ala.), 1975-87, City of Winter Haven (Fla.), 1987—; adv. bd. pub. adminstrn. U. South Fla., Lakeland, 1991—. Contbr. articles to various works. Pres. Ridge League of Municipialities, Lake Wales, 1980. Recipient Outstanding Alumnus award Polk Cmty. Coll., Winter Haven, 1989, Outstanding Administrator of Yr. Montgomery chpt. ASPA, 1981. Mem. Internat. City Mgrs. Assn., Am. Soc. Pub. Adminstrn., Ala. City Mgrs. Assn. (state pres. 1980, 86), Kiwanis Club (pres. 1974), Fla. City Mgrs. Assn. Presbyterian. Home: 824 Howard Terr NW Winter Haven FL 33881 Office: City of Winter Haven PO Box 2277 Winter Haven FL 33883

CHEATHAM, VALERIE MEADOR, clinical dietitian; b. Huntington, W.Va., June 17, 1957; d. Phillip Jarrell and Anna Lee (Law) Meador; m. Edward Lee McCallum, May 13, 1978 (div. 1990); children: Shaun Jeffrey, Briana Marie; m. Miles W. Cheatham III, Oct. 26, 1990. BS in Biology, James Madison U., 1979; MS in Nutrition, Clemson U., 1986. Registered dietitian, 1987. Cytotechnologist Roanoke (Va.) Meml. Hosp., 1979-80; greenhouse mgr. Greenwood Nurseries, Princeton, W.Va., 1980-81; vet. technician Lewisburg (W.Va.) Animal Hosp., 1981-82; rsch. asst. Clemson (S.C.) U., 1984-86; clin. dietician Anderson (S.C.) Meml. Hosp., 1986-87, asst. food svc. dir., 1987-91, nutritionist III dept. health and environ. control, 1994—; nutritionist Dept. Health and Environ. Control Anderson County (S.C.) Health Dept., 1994—; dir. maternal and child health programs Anderson County Appalachia I Health Dist., 1996—. Mem. Am. Dietetic Assn., Am. Soc. Hosp. Food Svc. Adminstrs. (pres. Palmetto chpt. 1991—), Piedmont Dist. Dietetics Assn. (sec.), S.C. Dietetics Assn., S.C. Pub. Health Assn. Home: 111 Yorkshire Dr Anderson SC 29625-2521 Office: Dept Health Environ Control 200 McGee Rd Anderson SC 29625-2104

CHECHUCK, BETTY JEAN, critical care nurse; b. Harriman, Tenn., Feb. 28, 1955; d. Charles E. and Elizabeth Jane (Crump) Raymond. Student, State Vo-Tech, Harriman, 1982, Roane State Community Coll., Harriman. Staff nurse ICU, CCU, cardiac rehab. Chamberlain Meml. Hosp., Rockwood, Tenn.; charge nurse Spring City (Tenn.) Health Care; staff nurse intensive care-coronary care unit Loudon (Tenn.) County Meml. Hosp.; charge nurse Marshall Voss Health Care, Harriman, Tenn.; staff nurse Roane County Ambulance Svc., staff nurse with pediat. nursing specialists, Nashville, 1992, Elk Valley Health Svcs., Fayetteville, Tenn., 1994. Home: 125 Stevens Cir Rockwood TN 37854

CHECKI, JOHN JOSEPH, JR., financial services company executive; b. Passaic, N.J., Jan. 16, 1948; s. John J. and Clara Ann (Gentile) C.; m. Kathleen Mandell, Aug. 1, 1969 (div. 1980); children: Stephanie, John J. III; m. Janice Miller, Mar. 30, 1980; children: Chris, Carrie Sanders. BBA in Acctg., U. Tex., Arlington, 1975; BA in Econs., Tex. Christian U., Fort Worth, 1970. CPA, Tex., CFP. Gen. acct. Enserch Corp., Dallas, 1973-76; instr. Northwood Inst., Cedar Hill, Tex., 1976-77, Dallas C.C. Dist., 1976-79; pvt. practice acctg., 1981-86; tax mgr. Edgewood Investments, Carrollton, Tex., 1986-89; mng. prin., sr. fin. advisor Am. Express Fin. Advisors, Richardson, Tex., 1989-95; registered prin., br. mgr. Securities Am., Inc., Plano, Tex., 1995—. Author, critic Dallas Times Herald, 1977-79; author novels. Pres. PTA, Dallas, 1982; scoutmaster Boy Scouts Am., Dallas, 1983. With U.S. Army, 1971. Mem. Internat. Assn. Fin. Planners (edn. com. 1995), Tex. Soc. CPAs, Dallas Estate Planning Coun., Toastmasters (pres. Big D club). Home: 1705 Baylor Richardson TX 75081 Office: John J Checki Jr & Assocs 101 E Park Ste 715 Plano TX 75074

CHEE, SHIRLEY, real estate broker; b. Ridley Park, Pa., Dec. 29, 1941; d. Richard E. and Lillian G. (Laudeman) Foehl; married, Nov. 26, 1967 (div. Nov. 1986). BS, Susquehanna U., 1963; grad., Real Estate Inst., 1975, postgrad., 1976-77. Music tchr. Nether Providence (Pa.) Sch. System, 1963-65, Anne Arundel Sch. System, Annapolis, Md., 1965-67; 1st cellist Annapolis Symphony Orch., 1967; bank teller Guaranty Bank & Trust Co., Morgan City, La., 1967-68; real estate agt. Joe J. Relle, Inc., Gretna, La., 1969-71; real estate broker Clyde Casey Real Estate, Inc., Gretna, 1972-75; pres. Chee, Inc. Realtors, 1976—, Harvey, La., 1976—; pres. West Bank Profl. Real Estate Sch., Inc., Gretna, 1976-87; mem. merger task force New Orleans and Jefferson Bds. Realtors, 1992. Chmn. small bus. Am. Cancer Soc., New Orleans, 1978, 79; pres. West Bank Rep. Women's Club, Gretna, 1976; mem. Harvey Canal Indsl. Assn., 1988. Mem. Jefferson Bd. Realtors (chmn. edn. 1979, dir. 1989-90, chmn. profl. standards 1989, 91), La. Realtors Assn., Nat. Assn. Realtors, ERA-S.E. La. Brokers Coun. (pres. 1990, sec. 1989-90, treas. 1990, Multi-Million Dollar award 1989), New Orleans Met. Assn. Realtors (bd. dirs. 1993-94). Home: 728 Hickory St Terrytown LA 70056-5113 Office: Chee Inc Realtors 1600 4th St Harvey LA 70058-4410

CHEEK, ARTHUR LEE, marketing professional; b. Raleigh, N.C., Aug. 6, 1940; s. Arthur Lee Sr. and Margaret Louise (Bradburn) C.; m. Sandra Lee Tigges, July 21, 1958 (wid. Sept. 1971); children: Michael Sidney, Robert Bruce; m. Sheila Ann Waters, June 27, 1987. Comml. pilot. Capt. Air America, Inc., Far East, 1965-66; corp. pilot Am. Enka Corp., Asheville, N.C., 1966-68; capt. TWA/Saudi Arabian Airlines, Jidda, Saudia Arabia, 1968-71; owner Custom Homes, Inc., Asheville, 1971-80; corporate pilot SEU Constrn., Inc., Cape Coral, Fla., 1980-85, contract adminstr., 1985-89, v.p. contract adminstrn and constrn. litigation support svcs., 1989—; v.p., gen. mgr. Coral Rock, Inc., Punta Gorda, Fla., 1994—, West Coast Industries, Ft. Myers, Fla., 1990—, Advantage Transp., Punta Gorda, Fla., 1994—; constrn. litig. faciliator, 1994—; constrn. and contract litig. facilitator, cons., 1996—; ind. rep. Rexall Showcase Internat., 1996—, Telecom Network Internat., Nu-Concepts in Travel, 1996; COO A&S Enterprises. With U.S. Army, 1957-65, ETO. Mem. Masons. Republican. Office: A&S Enterprises 1535 SW 58th Ln Cape Coral FL 33914

CHEEK, GORRELL PAUL, computer engineer; b. Fayetteville, N.C., June 11, 1965; s. Joseph Gorrell Cheek and Brigitta Balada Redlin. BS in Computer Sci., S.W. Tex. State U., 1987; MS in Computer Sci., U. Va., 1990. Commd. 2nd lt. Signal Corps, U.S. Army, 1987, advanced through grades to capt., 1992; platoon leader U.S. Army, Korea, 1987-90; automation test officer U.S. Army, Ft. Hood, Tex., 1990; comm./computer analyst U.S. Army, Saudi Arabia, 1990; exec. officer, bn. signal officer, brigade signal officer U.S. Army, Ft. Hood, 1991-93; comm./computer integration and evaluation officer, comdr. U.S. Army, Ft. Gordon, Ga., 1993-96, resigned, 1996; computer engr. Corning, Inc., Wilmington, N.C., 1996—. Mem. ACM, IEEE, Armed Forces Comms. and Electronics Assn., Signal Corps Regimental Assn. Episcopalian. Home: 4103 Hearthside Dr Wilmington NC 28412 Office: Corning Inc 310 N College Rd Wilmington NC 28405

CHEEK, RONALD EDWARD, artist; b. Greenville, S.C., Dec. 6, 1942; s. William Claude and Ruby Elizabeth (Holliday) C. Student, Art Students League, N.Y.C., 1961-64, New Sch. Social Rsch., N.Y.C., 1961-62; Diploma Fine Arts, BFA, Ringling Sch. Art and Design, 1971; postgrad., Tex. A&M U. Kingsville, 1972-73. Tchr. art Sarasota (Fla.) County Tech. Inst., 1978-90, Manatee County Art League Sch., Bradenton, Fla., 1978-90, Manatee Area Vocat. Tech. Ctr., Bradenton, 1978-86, Sarasota Visual Art Ctr., 1991-94, Manatee C.C., Bradenton, 1996—, Pickens County Mus. Art and History, Pickens, S.C., 1996—; chmn. exhibitions Ringling Sch. Art Alumni Bd., 1980-83. One-man shows include Tex. A&M U. Kingsville, Tex., 1973, Banks Haley Art Mus., Albany, Ga., 1978, Columbia (S.C.) Mus. Art, 1978, Van Wezel Performing Arts Hall, Sarasota, Fla., 1978, Florence (S.C.) Mus. Art, 1978, Manatee County (Fla.) Ctrl. Libr., Bradenton, 1980, The Citadel Mus., Charleston, S.C., 1981, Manatee C.C., Bradenton, 1983, Pickens County (S.C.) Mus. Art, 1984, Selby Pub. Libr. Gallery, Sarasota, 1986, Greenville County (S.C.) Mus. Art, 1989, Greenville Art Ctr., 1990, Anderson County (S.C.) Art Ctr., 1991, numerous others; two man show Rhoades Art Gallery, Sarasota, 1971; three-man show St. Petersburg (Fla.) Pub. Libr. Art Gallery, 1977; spl. exhbns. Longboat Key (Fla.) Art Ctr., 1979, 85, 86, Sarasota Visual Art Ctr., 1990, (travelling) Blair-Murrah Exhbns., Kansas City, 1992, Longwood Gardens, Kennett Sq., Pa., 1992, Cartwright Ctr., U. Wis., Lacrosse, 1993, Nat. Historic Oreg. Trail Interpretive Ctr., 1994, numerous others; represented in permanent collections Polk Mus., Lakeland, Fla., Columbia (S.C.) Mus. Art, Jasper Rand Art Mus., Westfield, Mass., Sioux Indian Mus., Rapid City, S.D., S.C. State Mus., Columbia, others. Sgt. USARPAC, 1964-66. Recipient Best in Show award and 1st Place in Landscape, City of Sarasota, 1969, 1st Place in Portrait, Venice (Fla.) Area Art League, 1971, Merit award 1979, 1st Place award 1981, 2d Best in Show award 1st Place in Painting and 2d Place in Mixed Media, Anderson (S.C.) Art Assn., 1973, 3d Place award Art League Manatee County, 1975, Merit award 1977, Merit award Sarasota Art Assn., 1976, 83, First Place award Old Hyde Park Art Ctr., 1982, 1st Place award Venice Art Ctr., 1982, 3d Place award, 1989, Merit award 1990, 92, numerous others. Studio: 617 E Main St Easley SC 29640-3151

CHEEK, SIDNEY MICHAEL, retired military officer; b. Greensboro, N.C., Apr. 22, 1956; s. Gilmer L. and Dorothy M. (McPherson) C.; m. Martha Virginia Wohlford, Feb. 23, 1968; 1 child, Sidney Michael Jr. B of History and Polit. Sci., SUNY, 1982; MPA, Valdosta (Ga.) State U., 1994; postgrad., Va. Polytech. Inst., Blacksburg, 1995—. Commd. ensign USN, 1974, advanced through grades to lt. cmdr., 1982, ret., 1995. Mem. Blacksburg Stiders, Am. Soc. of Pub. Adminstrn. (SW Va. chpt.), Acad. of Polit. Sci. Home: 187 Huntington Ln Blacksburg VA 24060 Office: Va Polytech Inst Coll of Arch & Urban Study Blacksburg VA 24061-0520

CHEEK, WILL T(OMPKINS), investor; b. Nashville, Oct. 4, 1943; s. Will T. Sr. and Bessie (Courtwright) C.; m. Brenda Dunlap (div. 1970); children: William, Catherine; m. Joan Beddingfield, 1976. BA, Middle Tenn. State U., 1965; MA, U. Ala., 1966. Dir. rsch. div. indsl. devel. State of Tenn., Nashville, 1966-70; pub. The Tenn. Report, Nashville, 1970-72; pres. Will T. Cheek Cons., Nashville, 1972-77; entrepreneur diversified investments, Nashville, 1977—; farmer Am. Gen. Acres, Williamsport, Tenn., 1983—. Sec. Tenn. Dem. com., 1973-94, vice chmn., 1994-95, chmn. 1995—, mem. subcom. on constrn., rules and by-laws, 1974; bd. dirs. Tenn. Indsl. and Agrl. Devel. Commn., Nashville, 1979-83; trustee Mid. Tenn. State U. Found., Murfreesboro, 1985-91; bd. dirs. Nashville Family Shelter, 1988-94, Tenn. Environ. Action Fund, pres., 1993-94. Mem. Tenn. Fruit and Vegetable Growers Soc., Tenn. Cattleman's Assn., Pi Gamma Mu. Home: 712 Enquirer Ave Nashville TN 37205-3724 Office: Am Gen Acres 3930 Robinson Rd Williamsport TN 38487

CHEEK, WILLIAM SHIELDS, JR., protective services official; b. Nashville, Oct. 25, 1942; s. William Shields and Josephine Elizabeth (Womack) C.; m. Kathleen Glynneth Brisby, June 22, 1969; children: Heather Elizabeth, Rebecca Caroline. AA, Daytona Beach (Fla.) Jr. Coll., 1965; BS, Fla. State U., 1968; MS, U. Louisville, 1980. Dist. supr. Daytona Beach News-Jour., 1963-65; res. patrolman Daytona Beach Police Dept., 1964-65; patrolman police dept. Fla. State U., Tallahassee, 1965-67; patrolman Tallahassee Police Dept., 1967-68; spl. agent Naval Investigative Svc., Alexandria, Va., 1968-71, Health Edn. & Welfare, Washington, 1971; spl. agt. FBI, Phila., 1971-72, Ashland, Ky., 1972-74, Louisville, 1974-95, Jacksonville, Fla., 1996—; adj. prof. Ea. Ky. U., Richmond, 1984-95; adj faculty mem. med. sch. U. Louisville, 1987-95. Bd. dirs. Area-Wide Alcohol/Drug Rehab. Edn. & Enforcement Coun., 1990-95. Lt. (j.g.) USN, 1968-70. Recipient Law Enforcement Commendation medal SAR, 1991; named Alumnus of Month Daytona Beach Jr. Coll., 1972, 75, Ky. Col., Commonwealth of Ky., 1974, Hon. Chief of Police, Shively, Ky. Police Dept., 1986, Col. Aide De Camp, Ky. State Police, 1992; Rsch. grantee U. Louisville, 1986-90. Mem. Ky. Chiefs Police (officers sect., mem. publs. com. 1986-88), Ky. Peace Officers Assn. (bd. dirs. 1984-95), Ky. Crime Prevention Assn. (bd. dirs. 1984-95, pres. 1990-95), Internat. Assn. Chiefs Police (vice chmn., chmn. pub. info. 1987—), Jaycees (Daytona Beach), Elks, Pi Kappa Alpha (silver chpt. 1986). Republican. Presbyterian. Office: US Dept Justice FBI 7820 Arlington Expy Ste 200 Jacksonville FL 32211-7400

CHELEOTIS, TASSOS GEORGE, lawyer; b. Miami, May 18, 1956; s. George T. and Marie (Hoffman) C.; m. Deborah Hollie Presner, Apr. 26, 1987; children: Courtney A., Alyssa R. AA in Computer Systems, Miami Dade C.C., 1977; BA in Econs., Fla. Internat. U., 1980; JD, Nova Law Ctr., 1983. Bar: Fla. 1983, U.S. Tax Ct. 1984, U.S. Dist. Ct. (so. dist.) Fla. 1984, U.S. Ct. Appeals (11th cir.) 1984, U.S. Dist. Ct. (mid. dist.) Fla. 1994. Assoc. Lyons & Farrar P.A., Miami, 1983-84; sr. atty. 3rd Dist. Ct. of Appeals, Miami, 1984-90; clk. of ct. U.S. Dist. Ct. (so. dist.), Fla., 1990-94, spl. asst. ct. adminstr., 1994—; mem. jud. evaluation com. Fla. Bar, 1989-90; mem. civil justice reform act com. U.S. Dist. Ct. (so. dist.) Fla., 1991-96, mem. criminal justice act com., 1993—, mem. mediation com. 1993—, mem. local rules com., 1994—; guest lectr. Fla. Bar on Fed. Practice Rev., 1992-96, U. Miami Alternative Legal Careers, 1993, U.S. State Dept. Bahamian Islands Modernization Project, 1994, 95, 96. Mem. Fed. Bar Assn. (mem. exec. bd. S. Fla. chpt. 1993-96, 2d v.p. 1996—), Am. Soc. for Quality Control (Fla. State Gov's. Sterling Coun. Examiner, 1995—). Office: US Dist Ct So Dist Fla 301 N Miami Ave Ste 150 Miami FL 33128-7700

CHELLGREN, PAUL WILBUR, petroleum company executive; b. Tullahoma, Tenn., Jan. 18, 1943; s. Wilbur E. and Kathryn L. (Berquist) C.; m. Sheila Mary McManus, Nov. 21, 1970; children: Sarah, Matthew, Jane. BS, U. Ky., 1964; MBA, Harvard U., 1966; diploma in devel. econ., Univ. Coll., Oxford, Eng., 1967. Assoc. McKinsey & Co., Washington and London, 1967-68; ops. analyst Office Sec. Def., Washington, 1968-70; adminstrv. asst. Boise Cascade Corp., Idaho, 1970-71; div. gen. mgr. Boise Cascade Corp., L.A., 1971-72; pres. Universal Capital Corp., Kansas City, Mo., 1972-74; exec. asst. to chmn. Ashland (Ky.) Inc., 1974-77; adminstrv. v.p. Ashland Chem. Co., Columbus, Ohio, 1977-78, group v.p., 1978-80; sr. v.p., group operating officer Ashland Inc., 1980-88; sr. v.p., CFO Ashland Oil Inc., 1988-92, pres., COO, 1992-96, pres., CEO, 1996-97, chmn., CEO, 1997—; bd. dirs. Ashland Inc., Ashland Coal, Inc., PNC Bank Corp., U. Ky., Centre Coll. Past pres., trustee Huntington (W.Va.) Mus. Art; chmn. Leadership Tri-State; bd. dirs., sec.-treas. Am. Friends of Univ. Coll. Oxford, Inc.; bd. dirs., vice chmn. Nat. Found. Advancement in the Arts; bd. dirs. Found. for Tri-State Community. 1st lt. U.S. Army, 1968-70. Mem. Am. Petroleum Inst. (bd. dirs.), Nat. Petroleum Refiners Assn., Soc. Chem. Industry, Chem. Mfrs. Assn. (former dir.), Am. Indsl. Health Coun. (former dir.), Melamine Chems., Inc., (former bd. dirs.), Univ. Ky. Fellows, Bellefonte Country Club (Ashland). Home: 121 Stoneybrooke Dr Ashland KY 41101-2159 Office: Ashland Inc PO Box 391 Ashland KY 41114

CHEN, CHING JEN, mechanical engineering educator, research scientist; b. Taipei, Taiwan, July 6, 1936; came to U.S., 1960; s. I Sung Chen and T. Yen Chen; m. Ruei-Man, Aug. 14, 1965; children—Sandra, Anthony. Diploma, Taipei Inst. Tech., 1957; M.S. in Mech. Engring., Kans. State U., 1962; Ph.D., Case Western Res. U., 1967. Design engr. Ta-Tung Grinding Co., Taipei, 1959-61; asst. prof. mech. engring. U. Iowa, Iowa City, 1967-70, assoc. prof., 1970-77, prof., 1977-82, chmn., prof. energy div., 1982-84; chmn., prof. dept. mech. engring. U. Iowa, 1982-92; sr. rsch. scientist Iowa Inst. Hydraulic Research, 1970-92; mem. exec. com. Iowa Space Grant Coll. Consortium, 1990-92; dean Coll. Engring. Fla. A&M U.-Fla. State U., Tallahassee, 1992—; cons. govtl. agys., mil. and industry. Mem. editorial bd. Altas of Visualization, 1991—; evaluator Accreditation Bd. for Engring. and Tech., 1991—; assoc. editor Jour. Engring. Mechanics, 1990-93; contbr. articles to profl. publs. Old Gold fellow Iowa Found., 1968; U.S. sr. Scientist awardee Alexander von Humboldt Fund, Fed. Republic Germany, 1974; hon. prof. Wuhan Inst. of Hydraulic and Elec. Engring, Peoples Republic of China. Fellow ASME; mem. AIAA, ASCE, Am. Soc. Engring. Edn., Internat. Hydraulic Research, Am. Phys. Soc., Soc. Theoretical and Applied Mechanics (hon.) (Taiwan), Japan Soc. Visualization, Sigma Xi. Home: 4643 High Grove Rd Tallahassee FL 32308-2974 Office: FAMU-FSU Coll Engring 2525 Pottsdamer St Tallahassee FL 32310-6046

CHEN, JAMES CHIANG-TUNG, environmental engineer; b. Taichung, Taiwan, July 1, 1940; came to U.S., 1965; m. Jane Chen, July 16, 1970; children: Anthony, Julie. BA, Northwestern Mo. State U., 1968; MA, U. Okla., 1970, PhD, 1973. Registered profl. engr. Tex. Environ. engr. Poe and Assocs., Tulsa, 1974-76; assoc. prof. Midwest Coll. Engring., Chgo., 1976-80; environ. engr. Harza Engring. Co., Chgo., 1975-80; project mgr. Dames & Moore, Chgo., 1980-81; engring. cons. Brown and Root, Inc., Houston, 1981-84; engring. mgr. Koomey Inc., Brook Shire, Tex., 1984-86, Petrolite Corp., Houston, 1986-92; environ. engring. mgr. EBC, Houston, 1992-94; pres. CTC Environ. Techs. Corp., Houston, 1994—. Contbr. to Ency. Desalination and Water Reuse, papers to profl. publs. Mem. Internat. Desalination, Internat. Found. Water Sci. and Tech., Water Pollution Control Fedn., Assn. Am. U. Profs. Home: 13323 Agarita Ln Houston TX 77083

CHEN, JAMES PAI-FUN, biology educator, researcher; b. Fengyuan, Taichung, Taiwan, May 1, 1929; came to U.S., 1952; s. Chuan and Su-wuo (Lin) C.; m. Metis Hsiu-chun Lin, Dec. 19, 1964; children: Mark Hsin-tzu, Eunice Hsin-yi, Jeremy Hsin-tao. BS, Houghton (N.Y.) Coll., 1955; MS, St. Lawrence U., 1957; PhD, Pa. State U., 1961. From instr. to assoc. prof. Houghton Coll., 1960-64; rsch. assoc. Coll. of Medicine U. Vt., Burlington, 1964-65; rsch. assoc. Sch. of Medicine SUNY, Buffalo, 1965-68; asst. prof. U. Tex. Med. Br., Galveston, 1968-75; sr. rsch. assoc. NASA/Johnson Space Ctr., Houston, 1975-76; rsch. assoc. prof. U. Tenn. Meml. Rsch. Ctr., Knoxville, 1976-78; assoc. prof. Coll. of Medicine U. Tenn., Knoxville, 1978-84, prof. Grad. Sch. of Medicine, 1984—; mem. rsch. rev. com. Tex. affiliate Am. Heart Assn., Austin, 1974-76; co-investigator Spacelab I project, Johnson Space Ctr., Houston, 1976-83; vis. prof. Trnovo Hosp. Internal Medicine, Ljubljana, Yugoslavia, 1985. Contbr. more than 40 articles to profl. jours. including Thrombosis and Haemostasis. Grantee Robert Welch Found., 1970-74, Ortho Rsch. Found., 1971-75, NIH, 1975-82, Am. Heart Assn. Tex. affiliate, 1969-72, 74-75, Am. Heart Assn. Tenn. affiliate, 1984-85, 89-90, U.S. Army Med. Rsch., 1988-91. Fellow Internat. Soc. Hematology; mem. Am. Assn. Immunologists, Am. Soc. Biochemistry and Molecular Biology, Internat. Soc. Thrombosis and Haemostasis, Internat. Fibrinogen Rsch. Soc., Internat. Soc. Fibrinolysis Thrombolysis, Am. Bd. Bioanalysis (clin. lab. dir.). Office: U Tenn Med Ctr 1924 Alcoa Hwy Knoxville TN 37920-1511

CHEN, JIANN-SHIN, biochemistry and microbiology educator; b. Chungking, Szechuan, China, May 18, 1943; came to U.S., 1968; s. Chi-Cheng and Su-Chin (Yang) C.; m. Katherine C.K. Hu Chen, May 26, 1973; 1 child, Eric H.W. BS, Nat. Taiwan U., Taipei, 1967; PhD, Purdue U., 1974. Postdoctoral assoc. Purdue U., West Lafayette, Ind., 1975-76; asst. prof. Va. Tech., Blacksburg, 1976-82, assoc. prof., 1982-90, prof. biochemistry and microbiology, 1990—; cons. Procter and Gamble Co., Cin., 1981-84, NIH, Bethesda, Md., 1984-85, USDA, Washington, 1985, 87, 89. Rsch. grantee NSF, Washington, 1979, 82, USDA, Washington, 1978—, U.S. Dept. Energy, Washington, 1985—, NESTE Oy, Finland, 1988-92. Mem. Am. Chem. Soc., Am. Soc. Biochemistry and Molecular Biology, Am. Soc. Microbiology, Orgn. Chinese Americans (treas. Va. 1991—), Sigma Xi. Office: Va Tech Dept Biochemistry Anaerobic Microbiology Blacksburg VA 24061-0308

CHEN, LINDA LI-YUEH HUANG, nutritional biochemistry educator, program director; b. Tokyo, Mar. 22, 1937; d. Chun-mu and Chiung-tein (Lin) Huang; m. Boris Yuen-jien, Dec. 23, 1961; children: Audrey Huey-wen, Lisa Min-yi. BS in Pharmacy, Nat. Taiwan U., Taipei, 1959; PhD In Biochemistry, U. Louisville, 1964. Rsch. assoc. U. Louisville, 1964-66; asst. prof. U. Ky., Lexington, 1967-72, assoc. prof., 1972-79, prof., 1979—, assoc. dean for rsch. and grad. edn., 1979-81, chmn., 1983-87, dir. multidisciplinary PhD program in nutritional scis., 1989—. Author: Nutritional Biochemistry Laboratory Methods, Experiments and Exercises, 1972; editor: Nutritional Aspects of Aging, Vol. I, Vol. II, 1986; contbr. articles to profl. jours. Mem. Am. Soc. for Clin. Nutrition, Soc. Nutritional Scis., Am. Aging Assn. Home: 531 Southbend St Lexington KY 40503-1231 Office: U Ky 204 Funkhouser Bldg Lexington KY 40506

CHEN, MICHAEL YU MEN, physician; b. Shanghai, China, Jan. 7, 1941; came to U.S., 1983; s. Shan Tong and Kun (Zhu) C.; m. Jean Y.Q. Hu, Aug. 15, 1969. MD, Shanghai Chinese Medical Sch., 1964. Radiologist Shanghai Chinese Med. Hosp., 1964-79, Shanghai Yang Poo Dist. Tumor Hosp., 1979-83; rsch. fellow Bowman Gray Sch. Medicine, Winston-Salem, N.C., 1983-87, rsch. instr., 1987-88, rsch. asst. prof., 1988-93, assoc. prof., 1993—. Editor: Radiology of the Small Bowel, 1992, Basic Radiology, 1996, Manual of Gastrointestinal Fluoroscopy, 1996; contbr. articles to profl. jours. Mem. Radiological Soc. N.Am., Soc. Gastrointestinal Radiologists. Home: 660 Limerick Ln Winston Salem NC 27104-1544 Office: Bowman Gray Sch Medicine Dept Radiology Medical Ctr Blvd Winston Salem NC 27157

CHEN, MIN-CHU, mechanical engineer; b. Hsiang-Hsiang, Hu-Nan, China, June 30, 1949; came to U.S., 1975; s. Pai-Hsun and Kua-Fan (Lee) C.; m. Yuh-Mei Chung, Aug. 1, 1975; children: Willis Fan, Thomas Li. BS, Nat. Ocean & Marine U., 1971; MS, Nat. Taiwan U., 1975; PhD, Oreg. State U., 1979. Sr. engring. Brown & Root, Inc., Houston, 1978-80; sr. rsch. engr. Exxon Prodn. Rsch. Co., Houston, 1980-81; sr. engr. Sonat Offshore Drilling Inc., Houston, 1981-85; v.p. Act Engring. Inc., Houston, 1988—; chief exec. officer C & C Internat. Svcs., Inc., Houston, 1985—; exec. v.p. Environ. Interest Inc., Houston, 1993—; bd. dir. PCtel, Inc., 1994—. Contbr. tech. articles to profl. jours. Mem. ASME, Sigma Xi.

CHEN, SHIH-FONG, pharmaceutical executive; b. Taipei, China, Sept. 28, 1949; came to U.S., 1976; s. Y.C. and T.S. (Chao) C.; m. Miau-Chin Chen, May 10, 1980; children: Vincent B., Rosemary Y. BS in Pharmacy, Nat. Taiwan U., Taipei, 1972, MS in Pharm. Scis., 1974; PhD in Pharm. Scis., U. R.I., 1980. Rsch. assoc. Brown U., Providence, 1980-83; asst. prof. Med. Scis. Brown U., 1983-84; rsch. biochemist dept. Biomed. Products E.I. du Pont de Nemours & Co. Inc., Glenolden, Pa., 1984-88, sr. rsch. biochemist dept. Med. Product, 1988-90, working group chairperson Cancer Chemotherapy Rsch. Group, 1989-91, rsch. assoc. dept. Med. Product, 1990; prin. rsch. scientist Cancer Chemotherapy Rsch. The Du Pont Merck Pharm. Co., Glenolden, Pa., 1991-92; assoc. dir. Biol. Evaluation sect. Inst. Drug Devel. Cancer Therapy and Rsch. Ctr., San Antonio, 1992-96, dir. exptl. therapeutics dept., 1996—. Patentee in field; contbr. articles to profl. jours. Mem. Am. Chem. Soc., Am. Cancer Soc., Internat. Soc. Heterocyclic Chemistry, Rho Chi. Office: Inst for Drug Devel Cancer Therapy & Rsch Ctr 14960 Omicron Dr San Antonio TX 78245-3215

CHEN, WALTER YI-CHEN, electrical engineer; b. Shanghai, Sept. 8, 1956; came to the U.S., 1980; s. Frank L. and Sally X. (Wang) C.; m. Nancy Ran Xu, May 21, 1986; children: Aaron W., Brian R. MEE, Calif. Inst. Tech., Pasadena, 1983; PhD in Elec. Engring., Poly. U., Bklyn., 1989. Mem. tech. staff AT&T Bell Labs., Holmdel, N.J., 1982-87, NYNEX Sci. and Tech., White Plains, N.Y., 1987-89, Bellcore, Morristown, N.J., 1989-95; br. mgr.

DSP R&D Ctr. Tex. Instruments, Dallas, 1995—. Contbr. articles to profl. jours. Mem. IEEE (sr.). Republican. Office: Tex Instruments 13510 North Ctrl Expressway Dallas TX 76265

CHEN, WEI-YIN, chemical engineering educator, researcher; b. Taipei, China, Apr. 5, 1950; came to U.S., 1973; s. Shao-Pong and Fong-Hwa (Tsai) C.; m. Tsuei-Ju Kao, May 18, 1987. BSChemE, Tunghai U., Taichung, Taiwan, 1973; MS in applied math., SUNY, 1975; MSChemE, Poly. Inst. N.Y., 1975; PhDChemE, CUNY, 1981. Sr. rsch. engr. Gulf South Rsch. Inst., New Orleans, La., 1981-85, mgr. fuel rsch., 1985-87; rsch. asst. prof. La. State U., Baton Rouge, 1987-90; asst. prof. U. Miss., 1990-93, assoc. prof., 1993—. Contbr. articles to profl. jours. Recipient numerous grants for rsch. in field. Mem. AIChE, Am. Chem. Soc., Combustion Inst., Am. Soc. Engring. Edn., Miss. Acad. Sci., Sigma Xi. Office: U Miss Dept Chem Engr Anderson Hall University MS 38677

CHEN, YUAN JAMES, chemical company executive; b. Keelung, Taiwan, China, June 18, 1949; came to U.S., 1975; s. Hong and Shu-chen (Cheng) C.;m. Ruey-chi Shuai, July 8, 1983; children: Eric Yen-Fu, Albert Hsin-Fu. BS in Mech. Engring., Chung-Hsing U., Taichung, Taiwan, 1971; MS in Mech. Engring., Ga. Inst. Tech., 1976, postgrad., 1976-78; postgrad., U. Houston, 1981-83. Registered profl. engr., Ala., Tex. Mech. engr. China Tech. Cons. Inc., Taipei, Taiwan, 1973-75; sr. engr. Monsanto Chems. Co., Guntersville, Ala., 1978-81; engring. specialist Monsanto Chems. Co., Texas City, Tex., 1981-86; engring. technologist Sterling Chems. Inc., Texas City, 1986—; tech. adv. com. Heat Transfer Rsch., Inc., College Station, Tex. 1986—. Mem. ASME. Home: 14218 Ridgewood Lake Ct Houston TX 77062-2349 Office: 201 Bay St S Texas City TX 77590-8779

CHEN, ZIBIN, physiologist, educator; b. Shanghai, Dec. 25, 1937; came to U.S., 1989; s. Dechi and Yezu (Zhou) C.; m. Wuhan Jiang, Feb. 9, 1964; 1 child, Lihong. MD, Shanghai First Med. Coll., 1960, PhD in Physiology, 1963; PhD in Pharmacology, Gothenburg (Sweden) U., 1993. Asst. in physiology Shanghai First Med. Coll., 1960-77, sr. instr. physiology, 1978-85; vis. asst. prof. SUNY Downstate Med. Ctr., Bklyn., 1981-83; vis. scientist George Washington U. Med. Ctr., Washington, 1982; assoc. prof. Shanghai Med. U., 1986-89; vis. prof. U. Gothenburg, 1988, Faculty St. Jerome, Marseille, France, 1988-89; vis. assoc. prof. U. N.C., Chapel Hill, 1989-90, rsch. assoc. prof., 1990—; vice chmn. dept. physiology, Shanghai Med. U., 1973-81, 84-89. Chief editor, co-author: Textbook of Physiology, 1989, Progress in Physiology of Respiratory Regulation, 1989; chpt. editor, co-author: Human Physiology, 1989; sect. editor: Physiological Technology and Methodology Series, 1979-91, Acta Physiol. Sinica, 1985-91. Recipient Internat. Exch. scholarship Chinese Edn. Ministry, 1981-83, Internat. Profl. scholarship French Edn. Ministry, 1989, Nat. Fund Natural Scis., Acad. Scis. China, 1984-86, 87-89, Rsch. Fund Med. Scis., Pub. Health Ministry China, 1986-87; named Best Tchr. Shanghai, Shanghai govt., 1987; Swedish Found. Clin. Pharmacology grantee, 1988, U. N.C. rsch. coun. grantee, 1992-93. Mem. Am. Physiol. Soc., Chinese Physiol. Soc., Soc. Shanghai Physiol. Scis., Soc. Shanghai Neuroscis., Coun. Shanghai Qigong Soc. (councilor). Home: 425 Summerwalk Cir Chapel Hill NC 27514-8683 Office: Univ of NC Dept of Physiology CB # 7545 Chapel Hill NC 27599

CHENAULT, SHIRLEY, college educator, college administrator; b. Palo Pinto County, Tex., Jan. 7, 1939; d. George Otis and Ruth Jones; m. Edwin Leon Chenault. AA, Weatherford (Tex.) Coll., 1973; BBA, Tex. Christian U., 1977; MBA, U. North Tex., 1980; EdD, East Tex. State U., 1996. Cert. profl. sec. Inst. Certifying Secs., Profl. Secs. Internat. Assn. Sec. Trinity Univ. Ins., Dallas, 1957-60, Gulf Oil Corp., Fort Worth, 1961-63; adminstrv. sec. Gen. Dynamics Corp., Fort Worth, 1963-71; career devel. coord. The Edna Gladney Ctr., Fort Worth, 1977-78; office edn. tchr. Everman (Tex.) H.S., 1978-85; instr. in office systems Weatherford Coll., 1985-93, adminstr., 1993—. Author: (book) Training Guide for Office Educator Instructors, 1983; co-author: Teacher's Microcomputer Word Processing Book, 1984; also jour. articles. Named Outstanding Woman Educator AAUW, Fort Worth, 1984, Collegiate Bus. Tchr. of Yr., Tex. Bus. Assn., Dist. XI, 1986; recipient Excellence in Tchg. award Nat. Inst. of Staff and Profl. Devel., U. Tex., 1988, Doctoral Studies scholarships, Delta Kappa Gamma, Alpha State, Austin, Tex., 1988, 90, 91. Mem. Am. Vocat. Assn. (chair resolutions com.), Nat. Assn. Classroom Tchrs. in Bus. Edn., 1989, 90, Vocational Office Edn. Tchrs. of Tex. (state pres. 1984, 85), Nat. Tech. Prep. Network, Tex. Assn. Coll. Tech. Educators, Nat. Coun. of Occupational Edn., Delta Pi Epsilon (past pres. U. N. Tex. chpt.). Republican. Disciples of Christ. Office: Weatherford Coll 308 E Park Ave Weatherford TX 76087

CHENG, CHE PING, cardiologist, researcher, educator; b. People's Republic of China, Jan. 24, 1950; came to U.S., 1982; d. Ji and Yu Zhi (Pan) C.; m. Ping Tan, Feb. 23, 1951; 1 child, Xiao Tan. MD, Nanjing (People's Republic of China) Railway Med. U., 1976; PhD, Wayne State U., 1986. Diplomate Am. Bd. Internal Medicine. Attending physician dept. cardiology First Hosp. of Harbin (People's Republic of China) Med. Sch., 1977-81; rsch. assoc. Harbin Cardiovascular Rsch. Inst., 1980-81; teaching asst. dept. pathology Wayne State U., Detroit, 1982-83, teaching asst. dept. physiology, 1983-86; postdoctoral fellow cardiology rsch. Bowman Gray Sch. Medicine, Winston-Salem, N.C., 1986-88, rsch. instr. medicine dept. internal medicine, 1989-91, asst. prof. medicine dept. internal medicine, 1991-95, assoc. prof. medicine dept. internal medicine, 1995—, assoc. physiology and pharmacology, 1991, mem. grad. faculty Ctr. Neurobiol. Investigation Drug Abuse, 1993—; lectr. in field. Author: Novel Pharmacological Interventions for Alcoholism, 1992, Diastolic Relaxation of the Heart: Modulation of Diastolic Dysfunction in the Intact Heart, 1994, Effect of Felodipine on Left Ventricular Performance in Conscious Dogs: Assessment by Left Ventricular Pressure-Volume Analysis, 1994, Left Ventricular Systolic and Diastolic Performance, 1995, Altered Ventricular and Myoyte Response to Antiotensic II in Pacing-induced Heart Failure, 1996, Response of Left Ventricular Filling to Exercise Before and After Heart Failure, 1996; contbr. articles to profl. jours. Travel grantee Internat. Soc. for Biomed. Rsch., Rsch. Soc. on Alcoholism, 1990, grantee Am. Heart Assn., 1988-94, 95-97, NIH, 1986-95, Hassle Pharm., Sweden, 1991-94, travel grantee Nat. Inst. Alcohol Abuse and Alcoholism, 1994; recipient Exptl. Biology Losartan Travel award, 1996. Mem. Am. Heart Assn. (coun.), Am. Fedn. Clin. Rsch., Am. Physiol. Soc., Internat. Soc. Biomed. Rsch. on Alcoholism, Internat. Soc. for Heart Rsch. Home: 651 Dover Dr Winston Salem NC 27104-1529 Office: Bowman Gray Sch Medicine Cardiology Dept Medical Center Blvd Winston Salem NC 27157-1045

CHENG, CHUNG PING, chemical engineer; b. Canton, China, Aug. 30, 1954; came to U.S., 1972; s. Man-Kee and Yuet-Wah (Wong) C.; m. Jennifer Chung, May 27, 1982. BS, U. Wis., 1976; PhD, U. Del., 1981. Sr. rsch. engr. Akzo (Stauffer Chem.), Dobbs Ferry, N.Y., 1981-88; sect. leader Quantum Chem., Morris, Ill., 1988-91; tech. supt. Catalyst Resources, Inc., Pasadena, Tex., 1991—. Contbr. articles to profl. jours.; patantee in field. Mem. Am. Inst. Chem. Engrs. (chmn. Tappan Zee sect. 1987, Jiolet sect. 1990). Office: Catalyst Resources Inc 10001 Chemical Rd Pasadena TX 77507-1607

CHENG, KENNETH TAT-CHIU, pharmacy educator; b. Hong Kong, Feb. 24, 1954; came to U.S., 1972; s. Shiu Fun and Alice Shiu-Wing (Leung) C.; m. Ying Hsu, Aug. 11, 1984; children: Jonathan Yee-Hang, Hannah Yee-Shing. BS in Pharmacy, SUNY, Buffalo, 1977; PhD, Purdue U., 1985. Lic. pharmacist N.Y., Ind., Kans., N.Mex., S.C.; diplomate Am. Bd. Sci. in Nuclear Scis.; cert. expert nuclear medicine tng.; cert. nuclear pharmacist. Resident in hosp. pharmacy U. Kans. Med. Ctr., Kansas City, 1978-79; research/teaching asst. Purdue U., West Lafayette, Ind., 1980-84; research fellow Harvard U. Med. Sch., Boston, 1984-85; assoc. prof. U. N.Mex., Albuquerque, 1985-88; dir. nuclear pharmacy and radiology rsch., assoc. prof. Med. U. S.C., Charleston, 1988—, assoc. prof., 1992—, tenured assoc. prof., 1995—; bd. dirs. Am. Bd. of Sci. in Nuclear Medicine. Recipient Donald E. Francke award Drug Info. Assn., 1981, Glenn E. Jenkins Qualifying Research award Purdue U., 1984; named one of Outstanding Young Men of Am., 1986; David Ross fellow Purdue U., 1982-83, research fellow Am. Cancer Soc., 1984-85. Mem. AAAS, Soc. Nuclear Medicine, Am. Soc. Hosp. Pharmacists, Am. Chem. Soc., Soc. Magnetic Resonance Imaging, Internat. Assn. Radiopharmacology, Health Physics Soc., Sigma Xi, Rho Chi, Eta Sigma Gamma. Office: Med U SC Nuclear Pharmacy Charleston SC 29425

CHENG, RICHARD TIEN-REN, computer scientist, educator; b. Nanjing, China, June 4, 1934; came to U.S., 1961; s. George T. and Elaine M. (Liu) C.; m. Nancy P. Chiang, Jan. 24, 1960; children: James S., Raymond S. BS in Edn., Taiwan Normal U., 1958; MEd, U. Wis., Menomonie, 1963; MS in Elec. Engring., U. Ill., 1969, PhD in Computer Sci., 1971. Instr. Taiwan Normal U., Taipei, 1958-60, Racine (Wis.) Tech., 1963-66; asst. prof. Stout State U., Menominie, 1966-68; rsch. asst. U. Ill., Urbana, 1968-71; asst. prof. Hunter Coll. CUNY, 1971-72; assoc. prof., chair Rochester (N.Y.) Inst. Tech., 1972-74, prof., chair, 1974-79; eminent prof., chair Old Dominion U., Norfolk, Va., 1979-85; chmn., ceo Eastern Computers, Virginia Beach, 1985—; sr. cons. Talor Instruments, Rochester, 1980-81, Ministry of Interior, Riyadh, Saudi Arabia, 1980-90; dir. Op. Smile Internat., Norfolk, 1992—; bd. dirs. Nat. Def. U., 1992—, Ctr. Innovative Tech. Va., 1993—, Signet Bank. Contbr. articles to profl. publs. Dir. Marine Sci. Mus., Virginia Beach, 1989—, foundation bd. Norfolk State U., 1992—, Navy League, Norfolk, 1991—; active Boy Scouts Am., 1990—. Recipient medal Pres. Chiang Roc, Taipei, 1961; named Nat. Minority Bus. Person of Yr., 1991, Pres. George Bush, Entrepreneur of Yr., 1992, K Peat Marwick Group, High Tech. Entrepreneur of Yr., 1992, Ernest Young, Inc. Mem. Orgn. Chinese-Am. (founder, pres. 1987-89), Def. Oriental Conf., N.Y. Acad. Sci., Cavalian Yacht & Golf Club. Home: 1536 Duke Of Windsor Rd Virginia Beach VA 23454-2504 Office: ECI Systems & Engring 596 Lynnhaven Pky Virginia Beach VA 23452-7303

CHERNAK, JERALD LEE, television executive; b. Bklyn., Nov. 7, 1942; s. Jess and Alice Kay (Kosoff) C.; m. Gail Loraine Cooper, March 26, 1967; children: Hope Ann, David. BS in Radio-TV, Indiana State U., 1965. Freelance dir., assoc. dir., asst. dir., stage mgr. N.Y.C., 1965-67; producer, dir., assoc. dir., stage mgr. ABC-TV, N.Y.C., 1967-86; exec. producer, gen. mgr. TV Nat. Shopping Club, Orlando, Fla., 1987-89; v.p., exec. producer U.C. Mktg. Group, Orlando, 1989; v.p., gen. mgr. Channel 7, Orlando, 1989-90; broadcast cons. Orlando, 1990; corp. v.p. Vision Broadcasting, Inc., Orlando, 1991-92; v.p., sta. mgr. Sta. WQBN, Tampa, Fla., 1992-93; pres. HODA Svcs., Inc., Orlando, Fla., 1993—. Post prodn. (TV news spl.) America Held Hostage ABC-TV, N.Y.C. (Emmy award 1982), 20/20 The Ump ABC-TV, N.Y.C. (Emmy nomination 1980). Bd. dirs. Children Wish Found., Orlando, 1987-88; mem. Mid. Fla. Film Coun., 1988-90. Served with USAR, 1965-70. Recipient Bronze and Silver awards Internat. Film & TV Festival, 1968-71, 82. Mem. NATAS (bd. govs. N.Y. chpt. 1976-80, 82-86), Dirs. Guils Am. (coun. rep. 1968-85, chmn. Fla. coord. com. 1988—), Soc. Profl. Journalists, Sigma Delta Chi. Home: 136 Margate Mews Longwood FL 32779-5627

CHERRY, ANDREW LAWRENCE, JR., social work educator, researcher; b. Dothan, Ala., Nov. 11, 1943; s. Andrew L. Cherry and Wyalene Cain; m. Mary Elizabeth Dillon, July 16, 1988. MSW, U. Ala., Tuscaloosa, 1974; D Social Work, Columbia U., 1986. Child welfare worker Escambia County Dept. Pensions and Securities, Brewton, Ala., 1968-72; psychiat. social worker Bryce State Hosp., Tuscaloosa, 1974-79; instr. Salisbury (Md.) State Coll., 1981-85; asst. prof. Marywood Coll. Sch. Social Work, Scranton, Pa., 1986-87; prof. Barry U. Sch. Social Work, Miami, Fla., 1987—; conf. Informed Families Dade County, Miami, 1990—, Miami Coalition for Care to Homeless, 1991-93; cons. to NAACP Minority Media and Telecomm. Coun., 1992—; with drug abuse prevention program Cath. Social Svcs., Miami, 1991—, Broward Children's Svc., Ft. Lauderdale, 1992-94, The Biscayne Inst., 1994—, St. Luke's Addiction Recovery Ctr., 1995—. Author: the Socializating Instinct: Individual, Family and Social Bonds, 1994; contbr. articles to profl. jours. Scholar NIMH, 1979. Fellow Am. Orthopsychiat. Assn.; mem. NASW, Conf. Social Work Edn., N.Y. Acad. Scis. Democrat. Office: Barry U Sch Social Work 11300 NE 2nd Ave Miami FL 33161-6628

CHERRY, BARBARA WATERMAN, speech and language pathologist, physical therapist; b. Norfolk, Va., June 25, 1949; d. Robert Bullock and Dorothy Estelle (Walsh) Waterman; m. Albert Glen Cherry, Sept. 17, 1977; 1 child, Dorothy Louise. BS in Phys. Therapy, U. Fla., 1972, MA in Speech-Lang. Pathology, 1982. Lic. phys. therapist, speech and lang. pathologist, Fla.; cert. tchr., Fla. Staff phys. therapist Retreat for the Sick Hosp., Richmond, Va., 1973-75; clin. instr. in phys. therapy Sch. of Rehab. Scis., Tehran, Iran, 1975-76; staff phys. therapist Sulmaniya Hosp., Manama, Bahrain, 1976-77, Cathedral Rehab. Ctr., Jacksonville, Fla., 1978-80; staff speech-lang. pathologist S. Allen Smith Clinic, Jacksonville, 1982-87, Mt. Herman Exceptional Child Ctr., Jacksonville, 1987-91, Duval County Sch. System, Jacksonville, 1991—. Mem. Am. Speech, Lang., and Hearing Assn., Am. Phys. Therapy Assn., Phi Kappa Phi. Episcopalian. Home: 8821 Ivey Rd Jacksonville FL 32216-3369 Office: Moncrief Elem Sch 5443 Moncrief Rd Jacksonville FL 32209-3160

CHERRY, CAROL LYNN, principal; b. Camden, N.J., Aug. 21, 1948; d. Daniel Joseph and Louise Agnes (Smith) Brown; m. Norman Reddick Cherry, Apr. 19, 1969; children: Talenthea Melaine Cherry Hollis, Aletha Renee Cherry. BS summa cum laude, N.C. AT&T State U., 1974; MEd, Savannah-Armstrong State U., 1979; EdS, U. Ga., 1989; postgrad., Ga. State U., 1992—. Cert. adminstrn. and supervision, early childhood edn., data collector. Tchr. Dept. Def., Babenhausen, West Germany, 1975-77, Chatham County Schs., Savannah, Ga., 1979-80, Clayton County Schs., Jonesboro, Ga., 1980-83, Dept. Def., Fort Buchanan, P.R., 1983-84, Beachwood and University Heights (Ohio) Schs., 1984-86, Houston County Schs., Perry, Ga., 1986-88; instrnl. coord. Houston County Schs., Perry, 1988-94, prin., 1994—; strategic planning mem. Houston County Schs., Perry, 1990-92; adv. coun. mem. Coop. Ext. Svc., Athens, Ga., 1991-94; leadership acad. Ga. Dept. Edn., Atlanta, 1992-94. Recipient J. Everette DeVaughn Outstanding Doctoral Student award Ga. State U., 1995; named to New Leaders Inst. Ga. Dept. Edn., 1995-96. Mem. NEA, Ga. ASCD, Ga. Assn. Educators, Internat. Reading Assn. (pres. Houston-Peach reading coun. 1990-91), Am. Ednl. Rsch. Assn., Ga. Assn. Elem. Sch. Prins. (sec. 3d dist. 1994-96, pres.-elect 3d dist. 1996—), Nat. Assn. Elem. Sch. Prins. Methodist. Home: 102 Cliff Ct Bonaire GA 31005-9719

CHERRY, LEON PATRICK, publisher; b. Dayton, Tenn., Jan. 18, 1955; s. J.E. and Wilma Pauline (Armstrong) C.; children: Ronald, Omega, Celeste. AA, Longview Community Coll., Kansas City, Mo., 1977; BA, M.A. Nazarene Coll., 1990; PhD, La Salle U., Mandeville, La., 1993. Computer programmer United Telephone Co., Kansas City, Kans., 1976-84; TV dir. Am. Cablevision, Kansas City, Mo., 1983-85; realtor Era McLaury Realtors, Kansas City, Mo., 1989-90; pub. Cornerstone Pub., Virginia Beach, Va., 1991—; pvt. practice therapy Virginia Beach, 1993—; adj. prof. La Salle U., 1994. Author: First Call, 1992, Heart and Soul, 1993. Mem. Am. Counseling Assn., Nat. Assn. Ind. Pubs., Black Nat. Religious Broadcasters. Office: Cornerstone Pub PO Box 2896 Virginia Beach VA 23450-2896

CHERRY, SANDRA WILSON, lawyer; b. Little Rock, Dec. 31, 1941; d. Berlin Alexander and Renna Glen (Barnes) Wilson; m. John Sandefur Cherry, Jr., Sept. 24, 1976; 1 dau., Jane Wilson. BA, U. Ark., 1962; JD, U. Ark. Sch. Law, 1975. Bar: Ark., 1975, U.S. Dist. Ct. (ea. dist.) Ark., 1979, U.S. Supreme Ct. 1979, U.S. Ct. Appeals (8th cir.) 1979. Tchr. social studies Little Rock Sch. Dist., 1966-70; chmn. social studies dept. Horace Mann Jr. High Sch., Little Rock, 1970-72; asst. U.S. atty. Dept. Justice, Little Rock, 1975-81, 83—; commr. Ark. Pub. Service Commn., Little Rock, 1981-83; adj. instr. U. Ark. at Little Rock Sch. Law, Little Rock, 1980. Contbr. case note to Ark. Law Rev., 1975. Pres. bd. dirs. Gaines House, Inc.; pres. U. Ark. at Little Rock Law Sch. Assn., 1980-81, bd. dirs., 1982; bd. dirs. Jr. League Little Rock, 1974. Recipient Gayle Pettus Pontz award U. Ark. Law Sch. Women Lawyers Assn., 1990. Mem. ABA, Ark. Bar Assn. (Ho. of Del. 1984-86, 89—, tenured del. 1994, sec., treas. 1986-89, exec. coun. chair 1995—, 8th cir. gender fairness task force), Pulaski County Bar Assn. (bd. dirs. 1989-90, 91-92, pres.-elect 1993-94, pres. 1994—), Ark. Women Lawyers Assn., Ark. Bar Assn. (Golden Gavel award 1992, com. on the status women and minorities), Little Rock C. of C. (met. coun.), Pi Beta Phi. Republican. Presbyterian. Home: 4100 S Lookout St Little Rock AR 72205-2030 Office: US Atty's Office PO Box 1229 Little Rock AR 72203-1229

CHERUNDOLO, MARY ANNE FRANCES, nurse; b. Taylor, Pa., May 24, 1944; d. Greno Paul and Nancy Madeline (Capalongo) Fumanti; m. Robert Francis Cherundolo, June 29, 1964; children—Jean Marie, Robert Francis, Joy Anne. Nursing diploma St. Joseph's Hosp., Balt., 1971. Cert. gerontol. nurse Am. Nurses Assn., 1984, 89, 94. Med.-surg. ICU nurse St. Joseph's Hosp., Balt., 1969-74; sch. health instr. Shrine Sacred Heart, Balt., 1972-74; supr. Anne Lynne Manor, Louisville, 1974, asst. dir. nursing, 1974-76; neighborhood dir. Cin. coun. Girl Scouts U.S.A., Aurora, Ind., 1976-78; office nurse V.J. Goel, Lawrenceberg, Ind., 1978; cardiac testing staff nurse J.C. Carter Co., Norwalk, Conn., 1979-80; staff nurse Courtland Gardens, Stamford, Conn., 1980, head nurse, 1981, asst. dir. nursing edn., 1981-83, dir. nursing, 1983-87; dir. nursing devel. PersonaCare, Stamford, 1987-88, dir. quality mgmt., Balt., 1988-93; corp. dir. clin. svcs. Harborside Healthcare, Clearwater, Fla., 1994—, v.p. profl. svcs., Boston, 1995—, sr. v.p. clin. svcs., 1996—. Pres., Home Sch. Assn., Shrine Sacred Heart, Balt., 1973; chmn. com. Ctrl. Catholic Home Sch., Norwalk, 1982-83; area chmn. Heart Fund Assn., Norwalk, 1981. Recipient Quality in Nursing award Am. Coll. Adminstrn., 1992. Mem. Infection Control Nurses Fairfield County, Conn. Orgn. Gerontol. Nurse Educators, Dirs. of Nurse's Council Conn. Health Care Assn., Conn. Assn. Healthcare Facilities (chmn. bd. dirs.). Roman Catholic. Club: Laurel Oak Country Club (adv. com., chmn. 1978-81). Home: 3640 Beneva Oaks Dr Sarasota FL 34238-2522

CHESLER, DORIS ADELLE, real estate professional; b. Lincoln, Ill., Sept. 23, 1924; d. Harry and Esther Pearl (Campbell) Schoth; m. Eugene Albert Aughenbaugh, May 23, 1943 (div. Sept. 1970); children: Judith C., Rodney E., Paula Sue; m. Arthur Bernard Chesler, Oct. 16, 1972. Realtor, assoc. Kilgore Real Estate, Brandon, Fla., 1969-76; broker Doris A. Chesler, Realtor, Brandon, 1976—. Den mother Cub Scouts Am., Tampa, 1961-62; leader 4-H Club, Decatur, Ill., 1956. Mem. Nat. Bd. Realtors, Fla. Assn. Realtors, Greater Tampa Assn. Realtors, Inc. Republican. Presbyterian. Office: 1104 N Parsons Ave Ste A Brandon FL 33510-3112

CHESLEY, EDDIE A., librarian, educator; b. Oak Hill, W.Va., July 10, 1946; s. Frank Luther and Eunice O'Dell (Dooley) C.; m. Donna Jean Eveland, Aug. 31, 1969; 1 child, Christopher Frank. BA, Ohio State U., 1968; MA, Marshall U., 1975; ThB, Appalachian Bible Coll., 1972; MLS, Kent State U., 1993. Assoc. prof. Appalachian Bible Coll., Bradley, W.Va., 1972-75, chmn. gen. studies, 1975-85, libr., 1987—; guest appearances, cons. Adventures in Scale Modeling, 1986—. Deacon Mt. Tabor Bapt. Ch., Beckley, W.Va., 1981—. Mem. ALA, Assn. Christian Librs., Internat. Plastic Modelers Soc./U.S.A. Republican. Baptist. Office: Appalachian Bible Coll Box ABC Bradley WV 25818

CHESNEY, THOMAS MCCOLL, pathologist; b. White Sulphur Springs, W.Va., Nov. 6, 1943; s. Jack and Helen Wallace (McColl) C.; m. Carolyn L. McIntyre, June 21, 1969; children: Catherine, Anne, Margaret, Duncan, Julia, David. AB, U. Pa., 1964; MD, Vanderbilt U., 1969. Intern Vanderbilt U. Hosp., Nashville, 1969-70; resident in pathology Mass. Gen. Hosp., Boston, 1970-74; fellow in pathology Harvard Med. Sch., Boston, 1972-74; pathologist Bapt. Meml. Hosp., Memphis, 1976—, dir. labs., 1995—; pres. Pathology Group of the Midsouth, Memphis, 1995—; clin. prof. dermatology/pathology U. Tenn., Memphis, 1988—. Lt. comdr. M.C., USNR, 1974-76. Mem. Alpha Omega Alpha. Office: Pathology Group of Midsouth 899 Madison Ave # 270 Ue Memphis TN 38103-3405

CHESNEY, W. ALLEN, journalist, travel writer; b. Knoxville, Tenn., June 13, 1951; s. Jack and Helen Wallace (McColl) C.; m. Christina Elizabeth Baker, Aug. 7, 1993. BA, U. Pa., 1974; MA, U. Va., 1976. Copy editor, arts and feature writer Chattanooga (Tenn.) Free Press, 1978—; sec. Free Press Credit Union, Chattanooga, 1995—. Editor (hist. postcard book), Chattanooga Album, 1982. Mem. So. Lit. Conf. Planning Com. Arts and Edn. Coun. Chatanooga, 1983—; mem. exec. coun. Friends of the Bicentennial Libr., Chatanooga, 1985-89; vestry mem. St. Paul's Episcopal Ch., Chattanooga, 1984-86, 89-91, 97—; bd. dirs. Sister Cities, Chatanooga, 1995—. Home: 1024 Englewood Ave Chattanooga TN 37405 Office: Chattanooga Free Press 400 E 11th St Chattanooga TN 37403-4203

CHESNUT, NONDIS LORINE, writer, consultant, former English language educator; b. South Daytona, Fla., June 29, 1941; d. Anthony Valentine and Myrtle Marie (Allen) Campbell; m. Raymond Otho Chesnut, Aug. 25, 1962; 1 child, Starlina Mintina Chesnut Kladler. BS in English and Speech, Concord Coll., 1962; postgrad., Frostburg U., 1967; MEd, Shippensburg U., 1972; postgrad., W.Va. U., 1973; Advanced Grad. Specialist Degree, U. Md., 1974; postgrad., Md. State Dept. Edn., 1976-95, Inst. Children's Lit., 1995-96. Cert. administr., secondary prin., elem. prin., reading specialist, tchr. English and speech. Tchr. English and speech Harpers Ferry (W.Va.) H.S., 1962-64; libr. Great Mills (Md.) H.S., 1968-69; tchr. English and reading North Hagerstown H.S., Hagerstown, Md., 1964-73; tchr. South Hagerstown H.S., Hagerstown, 1974-77; reading resource tchr. Woodland Way Elem. Sch., Hagerstown, 1977-83; adj. instr. grad. sch. Hood Coll., Frederick, Md., 1982-83; reading specialist Fountain Rock Elem. Sch., Hagerstown, 1983-85; tchr. Williamsport (Md.) H.S., 1985-95; reading and lang. arts cons., Md., 1973-95, Fla., 1996—; adj. instr. Daytona C.C., 1996—; spkr., presenter local, nat. and internat. workshops, 1973-95; lectr. main campus and south campus Daytona Beach C.C., 1996—; speech and debate coach. Writer for radio programs and advertisements for reading, 1986—, TV programs, 1974-78, 90-91; appeared on TV programs, 1974-78; co-editor column Beckley Post Herald, 1957-59; contbr. articles to newspapers and mags., 1964—; appeared in film Guarding Tess, 1993. Mem. debating team Concord Coll., 1961-62, mem. newspaper staff, 1959-61; mem. Washington County Network of Orgns., 1984-88; co-dir. Billy Bud, 1962; v.p. Women's Ind. Club, 1962, treas., 1961; sec.-treas. Fgn. lang. Club, 1961, Debate Club, 1961-62; treas. Meth. Youth Fellowship, 1961; pres. Tri-Hi-Y, 1959; legis. chairperson State of Md. Reading Coun., 1977-78; active Life in Spirit Group, St. Ann's Roman Cath. Ch., 1994-95, Grace United Meth. Ch., 1995, Lady of Hope Cath. Ch., 1996—. Recipient Pres.'s award State of Md. Reading Coun., 1981, Washington County Reading Coun., 1981, Voice of Democracy award VFW/Ladies Aux., 1992, Am. Heritage Writing award Williamsburg Lions Club, 1995, numerous others; W.Va. Legislature scholar, 1959-62. Mem. AAUW (ednl. chairperson 1983-85, legis. v.p. 1986-87, cmty. chairperson 1987-89), NEA (mem. publicity and scholarship coms., Washington County Tchrs. Assn., bldg. rep. 1989-95, del.), ASCD, VFW (chairperson Voice of Democracy 1989-95, VFW award 1989-95), Md. Dist. Am. Heritage Lions (Region II Lions award, Williamsport Am. Heritage Lions award 1995), State of Md. Tchrs. Assn., Md. State Tchrs. Assn., State of Md. Internat. Reading Assn. Coun. (sec. 1975-79, v.p. elect 1979-80, v.p. 1980-81, pres. 1981-82, nominating chairperson 1982-83), Washington County Tchrs. Assn., Internat. Reading Assn. (sec.-treas. sex differences in reading group 1976-77, 83-85, mem. gender differences in reading group 1985-86, mem. readability interest group, mem. mastery learning interest group, del. convs., mem. internat. rsch. com. 1976-77, 84-85, mem. disabled learners interest group 1975-82), Assn. Rsch. and Enlightenment (Guidance Helping award 1989), Coll. Reading Assn., Md. Assn. English Tchrs., United Dem. Assn., Internat. Platform Assn., Am. Legion (chairperson oratorial contest 1989-95, speech coach), Fla. Devel. Edn. Assn. Democrat. Home: 107 Old Sunbeam Dr S Daytona Beach FL 32119 Office: Daytona Beach Community College Dept Reading Bldg 14 109A 1200 W International Blvd Daytona Beach FL 32120-2811

CHESSER, BARBARA RUSSELL, human resources executive, writer; b. Portales, N.Mex., Feb. 26, 1941; d. John William Russell and Winnie L. (Deatherage) Luttrell; m. Delton Chesser, Dec. 30, 1965; 1 child, Christi. BS, Ea. N.Mex. U., 1963; MA, Mills Coll., 1965; PhD, Tex. Woman's U., 1969. Assoc. prof. U. Nev., Reno, 1965-66, Tex. Woman's U., Denton, 1966-68, U. Ark., Fayatteville, 1969-71; grad. faculty fellow, assoc. prof. U. Nev., Lincoln, 1972-81; ednl. con. African Divsn. External Affairs, Tanzania, Swaziland, Nigeria, Morocco, 1982; exec. adminstr. Baylor U., Waco, 1983-87; pres. Success Motivation, Inc., Waco, 1987—; clin. and family counselor Lincoln Pediatric Group, 1972-74; mgmt. cons. adult tng. programs U. Nebr., Lincoln, 1975-81; guest lectr. marriage enrichment program So. Bapt. Conv., Glorieta, N.Mex., 1986—. Author: Because You Care, 1987, 21 Myths That Can Wreck Your Marriage, 1991; co-author: Fatal Moments, 1991; contbr. articles to Reader's Digest Mag. Bd. dirs. Passport Success Scholarship Program, Waco, 1987—. Recipient Outstanding Alumni award Ea. N.Mex. U., 1981, The Pathfinder award Waco, Tex. YWCA, 1988. Mem. Am. Mgmt. Assn., Delta Kappa Gamma, Phi Upsilon Omicron, Sigma Xi. Baptist. Home: 2617 Regency Dr Waco TX 76710-1051 Office: Success Motivation Inc 4565 Lake Shore Dr Waco TX 76710

CHESSON, ANDREW LONG, JR., neurology educator; b. Raleigh, N.C., Nov. 29, 1948; s. Andrew L. C.; m. Linda Denise Illian, July 29, 1972; children: Andrew III, Lisa. BA, U. Tex., 1970; MD, U. Tex. Med. Sch., 1974. Lic. med. dr. Tex., La.; cert. Am. Bd. Psychiatry and Neurology, Am. Bd. Sleep Medicine; accredited Clin. Polysomnographer. Intern U. Tex. Med. Br., Galveston, 1974-75, resident in neurology, 1975-78; instr. neurology La. State U. Med. Ctr., Shreveport, 1978-79; staff neurologist VA Med. Ctr., Shreveport, 1978-85, clin. dir. dept. neurology, 1993-95; dir. neurology outpatient clinic VA Hosp., Shreveport, 1978-85; asst. prof. neurology La. State U. Med. Ctr., 1979-84, assoc. prof., 1984-93, prof., 1993—; cons. VA Med. Ctr., 1985—; dir. neurophysiology labs. La. State U. Med. Ctr., 1988—; assoc. dean for acad. affairs La. State U. Med. Ctr., Shreveport, 1994—, mem. various coms., 1978-94, acting chmn. dept. neurology, 1994-95; chief resident U. Tex. Med. Br. Dept. Neurology, 1977-78; reviewer in field; presenter in field. Contbr. chpts. to books and articles to profl. jours. Edward P. Stiles grantee, 1987. Fellow Am. Acad. Neurology (chmn. quality assurance subcom. sect. on sleep 1995—), Clin. Sleep Soc., Am. Sleep Disorders Assn. (chmn. stds. of practice com. 1995—); mem. AMA, Am. Fedn. Clin. Rsch. Office: Louisiana State University Medical Center PO Box 33932 LSUMC Shreveport LA 71130

CHESTER, FRANCIS, political science educator, lawyer; b. Bklyn., Jan. 25, 1936; s. Frank and Mary (DeFrancesco) C.; m. Diane G. Charlson, Oct. 27, 1966; children: Francis Scott, Angelique, Jennifer, Sabrina. BA in Econs., Iona Coll., 1957; JD, St. John's U., Jamaica, N.Y., 1960, MA in Polit. Sci., 1988, cert. in internat. law & diplomacy, 1988. Bar: N.Y. 1961, U.S. Dist. Ct. (ea. and so. dists.) N.Y. 1962, U.S. Ct. Claims 1964, U.S. Supreme Ct. 1964, Va. 1969, U.S. Dist. Ct. (we. dist.) Va. 1994. Sole practice Roslyn Heights, N.Y., 1961-68, East Norwich, N.Y., 1968-69, Gordonsville, Va., 1969-80, Raphine, Va., 1980-88; founder, owner Chester Farms, 1946—; pvt. practice Augusta County, Staunton, Va., 1980-92, 94—; asst. prof. polit. sci. So. Sem. Coll., Buena Vista, Va., 1989, faculty, asst. prof. polit. sci. and econs., 1989—; lectr. polit. sci. and econs. Piedmont Va. C.C., 1985-87; lectr. in sheep breeding; adj. asst. prof. govt. and econs. Blue Ridge C.C., Weyers Cave, Va., 1986-89; asst. prof. econs. and polit. sci. Christendom Coll., Front Royal, Va., 1989—, dir. politics practica program, 1989-94. Mem. Va. Bar Assn., Nat. Columbia Sheep Breeders Assn. Republican. Roman Catholic. Lodge: KC (charter grand knight, co-founder coun. 670). Home and Office: Chester Farms Rt 5 Box 115R Staunton VA 24401 Office: 11 E 2nd St Front Royal VA 22630

CHEU, HENRY WONG, physician pediatric surgery; b. Taipei, Taiwan, Sept. 30, 1959; came to U.S., 1969; s. Peter C.H., and Joan Lee C.; m. Carolyn Zimmerman; children: Margaret Victoria, Sarah Katherine, Henry Ross. BA summa cum laude, Boston U., 1983, MD summa cum laude, 1983. Diplomate Am. Bd. Surgery, Am. Bd. Pediatric Surgery, Am. Bd. Critical Care Surgery, Am. Bd. Medical Examiners. Internship surgery Wilford Hall USAF Medical Ctr., Lackland AFB, Tex., 1983-84, jr. resident in surgery, 1984-86, sr. resident in surgery, 1987-88, chief resident in surgery, 1988-89; rsch. and clinical fellow dept. pediatric surgery Children's Hosp. Pitts., 1986-87; fellow in pediatric surgery JW Riley Children's Hosp., Indpls., 1989-91; instr. in surgery Ind. U., 1989-91; clinical assoc. prof. in surgery U. Tex. Health Scis., San Antonio, 1991-94; assoc. prof., 1995—, cons. to Air Force surgeon gen. pediatric surgery, 1991—; dir. extracorporeal membrane oxygenation program Wilford Hall Medical Ctr., 1991—. Contbr. numerous articles to profl. jours. Exec. bd. dirs. San Antonio Metro Safe Kids Coalition, 1991—. With USAF, 1983—. Recipient Renssalear Polytech. Inst. Sci. award, 1976, Bausch & Lomb Sci. award, 1977, Jens G. Rosenkrantz award AAP, 1987, Clinical Surgeon's award Air Force Soc. Clinical Surgeons, 1988, 89, 90; numerous grants for rsch. in field. Fellow ACS (com. young surgeons), Am. Acad. Pediats.; mem. AMA, AAAS, Am. Pediat. Surg. Assn., Mass. Med. Soc., Soc. Air Force Clin. Surgeons (bd. govs.), San Antonio Pediat. Soc., Bexar county Med. Soc., Tex. Med. Soc., Sigma Alpha Epsilon, Phi Beta Kappa, Alpha Omega Alpha. Home: 14042 Woodstream San Antonio TX 78231-1955 Office: Wilford Hall Medical Ctr 2200 Bergquist Dr Ste 1 Lackland AFB TX 78236-5302

CHEUNG, HERBERT CHIU-CHING, biophysicist, educator. AB with honors, Rutgers U., 1954; MS in Phys. Chemistry and Physics, Cornell U., 1956; PhD in Phys. Chemistry and Physics, Rutgers U., 1961; postdoctoral studies in Biophysics, U. Calif., San Francisco, 1966-69. Asst. scientist U.S. Steel Corp., Monroeville, Pa., 1956-57; asst. instr. Rutgers U., Newark, 1958-60; rsch. chemist FMC Corp., Marcus Hook, Pa., 1960-63; lectr. in Physics evening divsn. Pa. Mil. Coll., Chester, 1961-63; rsch. chemist Allied Chem. Corp., Morristown, N.J., 1963-66; sr. fellow Cardiovascular Rsch. Inst. U. Calif., San Francisco, 1966-69; assoc. prof. engring. biophysics U. Ala. at Birmingham, Birmingham, 1969-73, assoc. prof. Biophysics dept. Biomath., 1973-74; prof., head sect. Biophysics dept. Biomath. U. Ala., Birmingham, 1974-82, prof. dept. Biostats./Biomath., prof. Biochemistry, 1982—; active NIH, 1971—; sr. scientist Comprehensive Cancer Ctr. U. Ala., Birmingham, 1976—, dir. grad. program in Biophys. Scis., 1978—, sr. scientist Cystic Fibrosis Rsch. Ctr., 1981-87, adj. prof. Physics, 1990—; with dept. Med. Biophysics Karolinska Inst., Stockholm, 1976. Contbr. articles to profl. jours. Corn Industries Rsch. Found. Predoctoral fellow, 1957-58; recipient NIH Rsch. Career Devel. award, 1971-76. Mem. Biophys. Soc., Am. Chem. Soc., The Protein Soc., Am. Soc. for Biochemistry and Molecular Biology, Cardiac Muscle Soc., Sigma Xi. Office: Univ Ala at Birmingham Dept Biochem & Molecular Genetics Birmingham AL 35294-2041

CHEUNG, WILLIAM KONG-LUNG, nuclear medicine technologist; b. Kowloon, Hong Kong, June 10, 1949; arrived in U.S., 1973; s. Norman Ping-Chean Chang and Ying Mai (Chang-Loh); divorced; 1 child, Allen Chi-Wai Cheung. BS in Biology, U. Houston, 1978; postgrad., Tex. So. U., 1979, Mt. Sinai Med. Ctr., 1984. Staff nuclear medicine technician Palmetto Gen. Hosp., Hialeah, Fla., 1984-86; supr. nuclear medicine out-patient ctr. Palmetto Gen. Hosp., Hialzah, Fla., 1986-89; staff nuclear medicine technician South Miami Hosp., 1989-90, North Shore Med. Ctr., Miami, 1990-92; contract nuclear medicine technician Health Pers. Option, Mpls., 1992-93; staff nuclear medicine technician Meth. Hosp., Lubbock, Tex., 1993-95; contract nuclear medicine tech. Imaging Temporary Inc., Houston, 1995; staff technologist Imaging Inst. Tex., Inc., Houston, 1996; supr. nuclear medicine Fannin Street imaging Inc, Houston, 1996—. Charter mem. Rep. Presdl. Task Force, Washington, 1994; col. Rep. Presdl. Legion of Merit, Washington, 1992. Home: 13914 Greenside Dr Houston TX 77083

CHEVES, HARRY LANGDON, JR., physician; b. Birmingham, Ala., Oct. 17, 1924; s. Harry Langdon and Myrtle (Churchill) C.; A.B., Mercer U., 1949; M.D., Med. Coll. Ga., 1953; m. Lois Rebecca Corry, Dec. 25, 1949; children: Rebecca Churchill, Harry Langdon III; m. 2d, Mary Agnes Moon; 1 son, Harry Michael. Intern, Univ. Hosp., Augusta, Ga., 1953-54; practice medicine, East Point, Ga.; mem. staff S. Fulton Hosp., chief of staff, 1980-81; bd. dirs. South Fulton Med. Ctr. Served with USAAF, 1942-46. Fellow Internat., Am. colls. angiology; mem. Royal Soc. Health, AMA, So. Med. Assn., Med. Assn. Atlanta, Atlanta, So. Dist. (past pres.) med. socs., Am. Geriatric Soc., Med. Assn. Ga., Ga. Heart Assn., Phi Delta Theta. Clubs: Am. Antique Automobile, Classic Car Club Am., Packard Automobile Classics, Rolls-Royce Am., Rolls-Royce Owners, Model A, Chrysler Restorers. Home: 333 Plantation Cir Riverdale GA 30296-1106 Office: 1136 Cleveland Ave Ste 400 East Point GA 30344-3618

CHIANG, KARL SY-CHERNG, interventional radiologist; b. Taipei, Taiwan, Aug. 26, 1960; arrived in U.S., 1967; s. Paul S. and Lucy (Su) C.; m. Kathy Alice Partin, Dec. 8, 1990; children: Katelyn, Austin. BS in Biology, Valdosta (Ga.) State U., 1982; MD, Med. Coll. of Ga., 1986. Diplomate Am. Bd. Radiology, Am. Bd. Vascular and Interventional Radiology. Resident in radiology Baylor Coll. Medicine, Houston, 1987-91; fellow in vascular interventional radiology Mayo Clinic, Rochester, Minn., 1991-92, staff radiologist, instr., 1992-93; staff radiologist Ea. Radiologists, Greenville, N.C., 1993—; spkr. in field. Mem. Am. Roentgen Ray Soc., Radiol. Soc. N.Am., Southeastern Angiographic Soc., Am. Coll. Radiology, Soc. Cardiovasc. and Interventional Radiology. Office: Eastern Radiologists Inc #9 Doctors Park Greenville NC 27834

CHICK, NANCY LEIGH, English language educator; b. Dallas, Feb. 28, 1968; d. Betty Jane (Leggett) C. BA summa cum laude, U. N.Mex., 1990; MA, U. Ga., 1992, postgrad., 1992—. Tutor U. N.Mex., Albuquerque, 1988-90; tchg. asst. U. Ga., Athens, 1992-96, enhanced tchg. asst., 1996—; organizer multicultural theory-pedagogy group, U. Ga., Athens, 1995-96, tchr. mentoring program, 1996—, grader Ga. Regents Exam, 1995—. Contbr. articles to profl. publs. Chief officer English Grad. Orgn., U. Ga., 1996—. Mem. MLA, Coll. Lang. Assn., Am. Lit. Assn., Nat. Women's Studies Assn., Soc. for the Study of the Multi-Ethnic Lit. of the U.S., Nat. Coun. Tchrs. English, Nat. Assn. for Ethnic Studies, Sigma Tau Delta (treas. 1995-96, v.p. 1996—). Office: Univ Ga 254 Park Hall Athens GA 30602

CHICKINSKY, ALAN, computer engineer, educator; b. Phila.; s. Irwin and Sylvia Zelda (Hunn) C.; m. Pamm Lindsay, Oct. 8, 1979; 1 child, Lindsay Sun Hwa. BSEE, N.Mex. State U., 1971; MSEE, U. Pa., 1978. From asst. to programming engr., sr. systems analyst small systems and def. and spl. systems groups Burroughs Corp./Unisys, Paoli, Pa., 1971-77; sr. network analyst, data comm. cons. worldwide data comm., info systems and control divsn. data comm. Sperry Univac/Unisys, Blue Bell, Pa., 1977-79; sr. comm. designer, spl. programming cons. Ctrl. Maine Power Co., Augusta, 1979-80; sr. project mgr. GTE Telnet Comm. Corp., Vienna, Va., 1980-81; from mem. to sr. mem. tech. staff, project mgr., advanced rsch. and devel. engr. GTE Govt. Systems, Inc., Westborough, Mass., 1981-89; sr. project mgr. EER Systems, Inc., Vienna, 1989-90; sr. project mgr., prin. engr. PRC Advanced Systems, Inc., McLean, Va., 1990-93; mem. tech. staff TASC, Reston, Va., 1993—; mem. sr. adj. faculty U. Lowell, Mass., 1982-89; sr. instr. Wentworth Inst. Tech., Boston, 1983, Northeastern U., Boston, 1983-85; instr. George Washington U., Washington, 1992—. Home: 712 Upham Pl NW Vienna VA 22180-4130 Office: TASC 12100 Sunset Hills Rd Reston VA 22090-3221

CHIEGO, WILLIAM J., museum director; b. Newark, N.J., Sept. 17, 1943; s. William Joseph and Rose Marie (Del Guercio) C.; m. Elizabeth Kimball Lee, July 3, 1971; children: Ruth Katharine, Rose Monica. BA in History with distinction, U. Va., 1965; MA in Art History, Case Western Reserve U., 1968, PhD in Art History, 1974. Asst. curator Toledo (Ohio) Mus. Art, 1973-74, assoc. curator European Paintings, 1974-76; curator Portland Art Mus., 1976-79, chief curator, 1979-82; chief curator N.C. Mus. Art, Raleigh, 1982-86; dir. Allen Meml. Art Mus. Oberlin (Ohio) Coll., 1986-91; dir. Marion Koogler McNay Art Mus., San Antonio, 1991—; regional rep. for N.C. Art Mus. Assn. of Am., 1984; mem. bd. trustees Intermuseum Conservation Assn., Oberlin, 1986-91; mem., co-chmn. mus. liaison com. Midwest Art History Soc., 1987-91; mem. exhbn. adv. com. Am. Fedn. Arts, 1988-94; mem. conservation grant panel Inst. Mus. Svcs., 1991-93; lectr. in field. Co-author, editor exhbn. catalog Sir David Wilkie of Scotland, 1987; co-organizer, author intro. to French Paintings from Tbe Chrysler Museum, 1986; coord. rsch. The N.C. Mus. Art Intro. to the Collections, 1983; author: Master Prints from the Gilkey Collection, 1980, From Oregon Private Collections, 1977; contbr. articles to profl. jours. Resident fellow Yale Ctr. for British Art, New Haven, Conn., 1982, Bingham Travel fellow Art History Case Western Reserve U., 1970-71, Univ. fellow Art History, 1969-70, Nat. Defense Edn. Act fellow Latin Am. History, 1965; Mus. Mgmt. Inst. scholar, 1981. Mem. Assn. of Art Mus. Dirs., Phi Beta Kappa. Office: Marion Koogler McNay Art Museum PO Box 6069 San Antonio TX 78209-0069

CHIEN, SUFAN, surgeon, educator; b. Zhejiang Province, China, July 20, 1938; came to U.S., 1982; s. Jiaxing and Julian (You) C.; m. Lorrain Wilson; children: Samson, Lynn. MD, Shanghai 1st Med. Coll., 1962. Resident dept. gen. surgery Zhongshan Hosp. Shanghai 1st Med. Coll., 1962-66, attending gen. surgeon, 1975-79; supr. cardiopulmonary bypass Shanghai Inst. Cardiovasc. Diseases, 1975-82, attending surgeon cardiovascular surgery, 1979-82; vis. scientist cardiovascular divsn. Mayo Clinic, Rochester, Minn., 1982-84; vis. scientist physiology and biophysics La. State U. Med. Ctr., Shreveport, 1984-85; vis. scientist surgery, physiology and biophysics U. Ky. Med. Ctr., Lexington, 1985-87, asst. prof. divsn. cardio-thoracic surgery, 1987-93, assoc. prof., 1993—; invited lectr., presenter in field; mem. sci. rev. com. study sect. NIH. Author: Hibernation Induction Trigger for Organ Preservation, 1993; editl. bd. Internat. Medicine Rev., 1979-84; author abstracts, papers in field. Grantee NIH, VA, U.S. Army, Univ. Rsch. Fellow Am. Coll. Angiology; mem. Am. Heart Assn., Chinese Med. Assn., Chinese Surg. Assn., Chinese Soc. Thoracic Surgeons, Shanghai Med. Soc., Internat. Soc. Heart and Lung Transplantation. Office: U Ky Med Ctr Surgery Lexington KY 40536-0084

CHIGER, JEFFREY STUART, banker; b. N.Y.C., July 5, 1949; s. Benjamin and Ida (Rubin) C.; m. Ruth Iris Wolnstein, Feb. 4, 1984. BBA, Pace U., 1973; MBA, Barry U., 1981. Cert. rev. appraiser, 1988; registered mortgage underwriter, 1984. Servicing mgr. Mortgage Corp. Am., North Miami, Fla., 1973-75; loan disbursement officer Housing Investment Corp., Miami, Fla., 1975-79; mortgage officer Intercontinental Bank, Miami Beach, Fla., 1979-80; asst. v.p. Sun Bank, Miami, 1980-81; v.p. Atlantic Nat. Bank, Pompano Beach, Fla., 1981-85, Midlantic Mortgage Corp., West Palm Beach, Fla., 1985-86, Citibank, Miami, 1986-94, BankAtlantic, Ft. Lauderdale, Fla., 1994—; adj. prof. Nova U., 1983—. Mem. Internat. Coun. Shopping Ctrs., Nat. Assn. Indsl. and Office Parks, Nat. Assn. Rev. Appraisers and Mortgage Underwriters. Democrat. Jewish. Office: BankAtlantic 1750 E Sunrise Blvd Fort Lauderdale FL 33304-3013

CHILCUTT, DORTHE MARGARET, art educator, artist; b. Fond du Lac, Wis., Jan. 29, 1915; d. John William and Pearl Evelyn (Burnett) Trummer. BS, U. Wis., 1940, MS, 1952; postgrad. NYU, 1975-78, Instituto Allende, Mex., summer 1958, La Romita Sch. Art, Italy, 1978-96, Schohegan Sch. Painting and Sculpture, 1959; m. Booth Chilcutt, Feb. 14, 1942; children: Karen Chilcutt Hulett, Booth, Cindy Jo Chilcutt Underhill, Debra Ann Chilcutt-Flippo. Layout artist DeVry Corp., Chgo., 1941-42; tchr. art St. Louis pub. schs., 1951-53, Monroe County Schs., Key West, Fla., 1957-62, Okeechobee Jr. High Sch. (Fla.), 1963-84, Indian River C.C., 1984-96. One woman shows Little Gallery, Key West, 1960, Martello Gallery, Key West, 1963, Ft. Pierce Art Gallery (Fla.), 1970; exhibited in group shows Jacksonville Art Mus. (Fla.), 1959, Tampa Art Mus., 1960, Norton Art Gallery, West Palm Beach, Fla., 1960, Backus Gallery, Ft. Pierce, 1977-94, St. Louis Art Mus., 1951, Wis. Salon of Art, Madison, 1947, Key West Art and Hist. Soc., 1957-90, Key West Art Ctr., 1959; represented in permanent collections Ft. Pierce Art Gallery, Martello Galleries. Recipient Best of Show awards Fla. Fedn. Art, 1974, Ft. Pierce Art Gallery, 1977, Ybor City Ann. Fiesta Day, 1980, Backus Festival, 1992, 1st pl. awards Highlands Art League 8th Ann., 1974, Jensen Beach Ann., Elliot Mus., 1974, 84, Ft. Pierce Scholarship Show, 1972-75, Four-County Art Show, Ft. Pierce, 1972-94, Tchr. of Yr. award Okeechobee County Sch. Bd., 1976, others. Mem. Fla. Watercolor Soc. (sec. 1974-84, bd. dirs. 1984-86), Gold Coast Water Color Soc., Nat. Art Edn. Assn., Fla. Art Edn. Assn. (Career Service award 1986), Miami Watercolor Soc., Treasure Coast Art Soc., Palm Beach Water Color Soc. Democrat. Contbr. articles to profl. jours. Home: 506 SW 15th St Okeechobee FL 34974-5264

CHILDERS, ANDREW AISLE, educational association administrator; b. Washington, Sept. 3, 1957; s. Herman Malcolm and Mary Louis Childers. BA in Econs., George Washington U., 1981; MS in Acctg., George Mason U., 1992. Acctg. staff Nat. Collegiate Conf. Assn., Fairfax, Va., 1982-84; assoc. exec. dir. Nat. Coll. Conf. Assn., Fairfax, Va., 1984-86, exec. dir., 1986-89, bd. dirs., 1989—, acting exec. dir., 1993. Mem. Beta Gamma Sigma. Republican. Office: 9 Oriole Dr Poughkeepsie NY 12601

CHILDERS, BOB EUGENE, educational association executive; b. Cleve., Sept. 16, 1930; s. William Nick and Allie Jeanette (Doty) C.; m. Jo Ann Roberts, May 1, 1953; children: William Frank, Robert Clayton, John Murry, Julia Ann. BA, Union U., 1953; MA, Memphis State U., 1958; EdD, U. Tenn., 1964. Cert. tchr., adminstr., Tenn. Field engr. Radio Corp. of Am., El Paso, Tex., 1955-57; instr. U.S. Navy, Memphis, 1957-60; prin. Halls High Sch., Knoxville, Tenn., 1960-61, McMinn County High Sch., Athens, Tenn., 1961-64; asst. commr. Tenn. State Dept. Edn., Nashville, 1964-66; regional dir. USOE, Vocat.-Tech. and Adult Edn., Atlanta, 1966-69; exec. dir. Commn. Occupational Edn., Atlanta, 1969-82, So. Assn. Colls. and Schs., Atlanta, 1982-92; cons. U.S. Dept. Edn., Washington, 1963-79, Fla. State Legislature, Tallahassee, 1979, Md. Values Edn. Commn., Annapolis, 1979-80. Editor SACS Procs., 1982-92. Bd. dirs. Boy Scouts Am., Atlanta, 1990-92, Ctr. for Citizenship Edn., Washington, 1978-81; bd. trustees YMCA, Nashville, 1964-66; v.p. Religious Heritage of Am., St. Louis, 1979-86; active Rotary, Atlanta, 1981-92. With U.S. Army, 1953-55. Mem. Am. Vocat. Assn. (life mem., cons.), Am. Tech. Edn. Assn. (past pres., v.p.), Am. Vocat. Rsch. Assn., Am. Soc. Assn. Execs., Phi Delta Kappa (past treas., sec.), Iota Lambda Sigma, Sigma Alpha Epsilon (pres. 1952). Democrat. Baptist. Home and Office: 960 River Rd Woodruff SC 29388

CHILDERS, NORMAN FRANKLIN, horticulture educator; b. Moscow, Idaho, Oct. 29, 1910; s. Lucius Franklin and Frances M. (Norman) C.; 4 children. BS in Horticulture, U. Mo., 1933, MS in Horticulture (Gregory scholar 1933-34), 1934; PhD in Pomology, Cornell U., 1937. Grad. asst. pomology. Cornell U., 1934-37; asst. prof. horticulture, asst. research specialist Ohio State U. and Ohio Agr. Expt. Sta., 1937-39; asso. in research Ohio Agr. Expt. Sta., 1939-44; asst. dir., sr. plant physiologist fed. expt. sta. U.S. Dept. Agr., Mayaguez, P.R., 1944-47; prof. horticulture, research specialist Rutgers U., New Brunswick, N.J., 1948-81; chmn. dept. Rutgers U., 1948-66, Maurice A. Blake distinguished prof., 1966-81, prof. emeritus, 1981—; adj. prof. U. Fla., Gainesville, 1981—. Author: Arthritis-Childers' Diet to Stop It, 5th edit., 1995; pub., co-author 10 horticulture books; rsch. author in Classic Papers in Horticultural Science, 1989; co-editor: The Peach-World Cultivars to Marketing, 1988, Modern Fruit Science, 10th edit., 1995; contbr. numerous articles to profl. jours. Councilman, Milltown, N.J., 1953-56. Recipient Best Tchr. award Alpha Zeta, Rutgers U., 1980, award Nat. Peach Coun., 1981, Disting. Svc. to Agr. award N.J. State Bd. Agr., 1982, Internat. Dwarf Fruit Tree award, 1982, Disting. Svc. award to U.S. Agr., Chevron Chem. Co., N.Am. Strawberry Growers award, 1990. Fellow Am. Soc. Hort. Sci. (recipient L.M. Ware Disting. Tchg. award 1968), Internat. Acad. Preventive Medicine (Spokesman of Yr. 1979—), Am. Acad. Neur. and Orthopaedic Surgeons, N.J. Hort. Soc. (pres. 1976); mem. Columbus Hort. Soc. (pres. 1941-43), Am. Pomology Soc. (Wilder award 1991), Pa. State Hort. Assn., Fla. State Hort. Soc. (hon. 1993, editor Procs. 1988—), N.J. Garden Club (life, Hon. Disting. award 1977). Office: U Fla Hort Scis Dept Gainesville FL 32611

CHILDERS, SHIRLEY RUTH, vocational education educator; b. Statham, Ga., Mar. 10, 1951; d. Rosevelt and Lucille (Barnette) Thurmond; children: Tyrish, Miranda. Master Lic. Cosmetology, Minosa Sch. Beauty, 1970-71; AA, Gainesville (Ga.) Coll., 1971-73; BS, Brenau Coll., 1973-75; MEd, Ga. State U., 1980-83. Cert. tchr., Ga. Owner, mgr. Shirley's Beauty Salon, Gainesville, 1971-79; vocat. tchr. Lanier Tech. Inst., Oakwood, Ga., 1977—; faculty steering com. Lanier Tech. Sch., Oakwood, 1986-91, sec. adv. bd., 1991, in-svc. com., 1992. Author: Positional Papers Hair, 1981. Chmn. AKA Cotillion, Gainesville, 1975, AKA Scholarship Com., Gainesville, 1985-90; coord. Gen. Missionary Bapt. Ch., Ga., 1980-89; pres. PTO, Gainesville, 1990; vol. Project Find, 1972 (cert.), Summer Reading Program, 1974 (cert.); active Leadership Hall County, 1992, Exec. Leadership Ga. State U., 1990-91, Coalition on Teenage Pregnancy, Hall County, 1986; v.p. Angelic Voices Choir St. John Bapt. Ch., 1971—. Recipient Cert. of Merit award Kiwanis, Gainesville, 1969, Outstanding Svc. award St. John Bapt. Ch., Gainesville, 1986, Cert. of Appreciation award Girl Scouts, Gainesville, 1987. Mem. Ga. Vocat. Assn., Cultural Ednl. Tour Inst. (pres., cons.), Alpha Kappa Alpha (Soror of Yr. 1989, 90). Democrat. Baptist. Home: 2079 Garden Rd Gainesville GA 30507-5019

CHILDRESS, WALTER DABNEY, III, insurance executive, financial planner; b. Petersburg, Va., Feb. 15, 1943; s. Walter Dabney Jr. and Myrtie Ruth (Braswell) C.; m. Patricia Nan Clark, July 2, 1969; children: Cameron Wyatt, Nora Lynn. AA, Chipola Jr. Coll., 1964; BA, Birmingham (Ala.)-So. Coll., 1969; MEd, U. Montevallo, Ala., 1973. Tchr., coach Curry Sch., Birmingham, Ala., 1969-70; tchr., coach, athletic dir. Birmingham U., 1970-72; tchr., coach Peachtree High Sch., DeKalb County, Ga., 1972-74; field rep. Guardian Life Ins. Co. Am., Atlanta, 1974—; rep. Guardian Investors Svcs. Corp., Atlanta, 1976—; owner W.D. Childress & Co., Atlanta, 1982—; investment advisor, pres. Childress Fin. Svcs., Inc., Atlanta, 1989—; bd. dirs. Atlanta Alumni chpt., Birmingham (Ala.)-So. Coll.; speaker in field. Cubmaster Pack 876 Boy Scouts Am., Stone Mountain, Ga., 1984-85, scoutmaster, 1985-90. Chipola Jr. Coll. scholar, Birmingham-So. Coll. scholar; recipient Nat. Sales Achievement, Nat. Health Quality and Nat. Quality awards, 1976—; named to Million Dollar Roundtable honor roll. Mem. Nat. Assn. Life Underwriters, Life Underwriters Polit. Action Com., Am. Assn. Chartered Life Underwriters, Internat. Assn. Fin. Planners, Lions (pres. Tucker chpt. 1984-85), Million Dollar Roundtable Found., Million Dollar Roundtable (life). Republican. Presbyterian.

CHILDS, RAND HAMPTON, data processing executive; b. Charlotte, N.C., Oct. 20, 1949; s. Wade Hampton and Francis Marion (Rand) C.; m. Anne Elizabeth Turner, Jan. 4, 1986; children: Ian Peter, Ryan Patrick. BS in Chemistry, Ga. Inst. Tech., 1971, MS in Chemistry, 1977; postgrad. Eidgenossische Technische Hochschule, Zurich, Switzerland, 1971-72. Sys. analyst computing svcs. dept. Ga. Inst. Tech., Atlanta, 1974-80, mgr. data processing computing svcs. dept., 1980-83, assoc. dir. office of computing svcs., 1983-87; v.p. Software Devel., Sirsi Corp., 1987-94, v.p. R&D, 1994—; cons. in field. World Student Fund Scholar Ga. Inst. Tech. and Swiss Govt., 1971-72. Compiler: (with Naugle and Sherry) A Concordance to the Poems of Samuel Johnson. Mem. AAAS, Am. Chem. Soc., Assn. Computing Machinery, Info. Industry Assn., VIM (6000) (Control Data Corp. User Group), Sigma Xi, Alpha Iota Delta of Chi Psi, Atlanta. Contbr. articles to profl. jours. Home: 189 Newcomb Rd Owens Cross Roads AL 35763-9752 Office: SIRSI Corp 689 Discovery Dr NW Huntsville AL 35806-2801

CHILDS, THEODORE FRANCIS, biologist, retired educator; b. Jamaica, N.Y., Feb. 17, 1921; s. Andrew W. and Maude (Thompson) C.; m. Marie Jackson; children: Ted, Sheila. BS in Biology, Shaw U., 1944, PhD (hon.), 1964; B.Phys. Therapy, State U. Iowa, 1948; MA, EdD, Columbia U., 1967. Dir. phys. theraphy VA, Bklyn., 1950-64; prof. health sci. L.I. U., Bklyn., 1964-76; chair Sch. Allied Health Tuskegee (Ala) U., 1976-81; chair dept. edn., prof. Talladage (Ala.) Coll., 1981—; dir. U.S. Com. for Ind. Rehab. Candidate for N.Y. State Senate, 1968. With U.S. Army, 1944-46, lt. col. USAR, 1946-81. Mem. Am. Phys. Therapy Assn., Athletic Trainers Assn. Episcopalian. Home: PO Box 86 Tuskegee AL 36087-0086

CHILES, LAWTON MAINOR, governor, former senator; b. Lakeland, Fl, Apr. 3, 1930; s. Lawton Mainor and Margaret (Patterson) C.; m. Rhea May Grafton, Jan. 27, 1951; children: Tandy M., Lawton Mainor III, Edward G., Rhea Gay. B.S., U. Fla., 1952; LL.B., 1955; LL.B. hon. degrees, Fla. So. Coll., Lakeland, 1971, Jacksonville U., 1971. Bar: Fla. 1955. Practiced in Lakeland, 1955-70, U.S. senator from Fla., 1971-89; gov. State of Fla., 1991—; Mem. Fla. Ho. of Reps., 1958-66, Fla. Senate, 1966-70. Trustee U. Fla. Law Center, 1968—, Fla. So. Coll., from 1971, Eckerd Coll., St. Petersburg, Fla., from 1971. Served as 1st lt. AUS, 1952-54. Mem. Phi Delta Phi, Alpha Tau Omega. Democrat. Presbyterian. Office: The Capitol Office Of Gov Tallahassee FL 32399-0001

CHILIVIS, NICKOLAS PETER, lawyer; b. Athens, Ga., Jan. 12, 1931; s. Peter Nickolas and Wessie Mae (Tanner) C.; m. Patricia Kay Tumlin, June 3, 1967; children—Taryn Tumlin, Nicole Tumlin, Nickolas Peter Tumlin. LL.B., U. Ga., Athens, 1953; LL.M., Atlanta Law Sch., Ga., 1955. Bar: Ga. 1952, U.S. Supreme Ct. 1965. Ptnr. Lester & Chilivis, Athens, Ga., 1953-58; ptnr. Erwin, Epting, Gibson & Chilivis, Athens, Ga., 1958-75; commr. of revenue State of Ga., Atlanta, 1975-77; ptnr. Powell, Goldstein, Frazer & Murphy, Atlanta, 1977-84, Chilivis & Grindler, Atlanta, 1984-95, Chilivis, Cochran, Larkins & Bever, Atlanta, 1995—; adj. prof. U. Ga. Sch. Law, Athens, 1965-75. Author: Termination Settlement, 1955. Contbr. chpts. to books, articles to profl. jours. Bd. visitors U. Ga., Athens, 1983-85; trustee Skandalakis Found., Atlanta, 1984, Found. of the Holy Apostles; former trustee U. Ga. Found.; former mem. U. Ga. Rsch. Found. Bd.; pres. and sr. warden Ch. of Apostles. With USAFR, 1953-55. Recipient Archdiocesan medal Archbishop of North and South Am., 1980. Fellow Am. Coll. Trial Lawyers, Am. Acad. Appellate Lawyers; mem. Am. Inns. of Ct. (master), Old War Horse Lawyers Club, Lawyers Club Atlanta, Commerce Club, Heritage Club, (Atlanta), Pres.'s Club (U. Ga.), Elks. Home: 854 W Paces Ferry Rd NW Atlanta GA 30327-2646 Office: Chilivis Cochran et al Chilivis Bldg 3127 Maple Dr NE Atlanta GA 30305-2503

CHIMÈNE, CALVIN ALPHONSE, oil company executive, geology consultant, writer; b. Houston, Sept. 20, 1927; s. Julius Baum and Fannie (Lipp) C.; m. Katie Virginia Allen, Aug. 31, 1952; children: Julius Baum II, Andre

Allen, Beau Calvin. BS, U. Tex., 1950; MS, U. Houston, 1952. Cert. geologist, Ark. Field geologist Que. Ministry Mines, Amos, Can., 1951; geologist Standard Oil Ohio, Tyler and Midland, Tex., 1952-56; sr. geologist Standard Oil Ohio, Houston and Lafayette, La., 1957-62, Am. Nat. Gas, Houston, 1963-64; dist. geologist Austral Oil Co., Houston, 1964-74; div. geologist Total Petroleum Co., Houston, 1974-80; v.p. exploration Fla. Exploration Co., Houston, 1980-85; pres. The Laahnz Corp., Houston, 1985—, The Laahnz Prodn. Co., Houston, 1987—; ptnr., CEO, LaGage Operation Houston, 1990—; cons. Pennzoil, Houston, 1987, Arco, Houston, 1987; spkr. in field, including Internat. Geology Congress, Washington, 1989. Contbr. articles to profl. jours. Former mem. ad hoc govt. group think tank for fgn. trade. With U.S. Army, 1946-47. Recipient cert. of appreciation U. Houston, 1985. Mem. Am. Assn. Petroleum Geologists (speaker 1974, del. 1978, 81-83), Assn. Profl. Geol. Scientists (v.p. Houston 1975-77), Soc. Econ. Paleontologists and Mineralogists, Houston Geol. Soc. (speaker 1989), U. Houston Geol. Alumni Soc. (scholastic liaison com. 1982, Tex. Exes, Sigma Gamma Epsilon. Home: 5631 Benning Dr Houston TX 77096-6135 Office: The Laahnz Corp PO Box 35992 Houston TX 77235-5992

CHIN, ALEXANDER FOSTER, electronics educator; b. Moneague, St. Ann, Jamaica, Dec. 12, 1937; s. Humphrey and Betty (Chen) C.; m. Barbara Kittner, May 18, 1974; children: Micah, Michelle. BS, Okla. State U., 1969, MS, 1974, EdD, 1983. Self-employed grocer Jamaica, 1955-62; salesman Singer Sewing Machine Co., Jamaica, 1962-64; with Bell Fibre Co., Marion, Ind., 1964-68; electronics engr. Electronic Engring. Co. of Calif., Santa Ana, 1970-71; asst. prof. electronics Tulsa C.C., 1971—; adj. prof. Okla. State U., Tulsa, 1988-89. Author: Electronic Instrument & Measurements, 1983; author numerous tech. lab. manuals. Vol. pub. sch. tchr. Monroe Middle Sch., Tulsa, 1990—. NSF grantee, 1971; Am. Inst. Fgn. Study ednl. awardee, 1981, 86, 91, Work award, Tulsa Jr. Coll., 1984. Mem. Okla. Tech. Soc. (bd. dirs. 1971—), Am. Tech. Edn. Assn., Phi Delta Kappa. Plymouth Brethren Ch. Office: Tulsa Jr Coll NE 3727 E Apache St Tulsa OK 74115-3150

CHIN, ROBERT ALLEN, engineering graphics educator; b. San Francisco, Oct. 3, 1950; s. Suey Hey and Stella (Yee) C.; m. Susan Curtis Fleming, June 18, 1976. AAS, C.C. Air Force, 1982; BA, U. No. Colo., 1974; MA in Edn., Ball State U., 1975; PhD, U. Md., 1986. Cert. sr. indstrl. technologist. Grad. teaching asst. Ball State U., Muncie, Ind., 1974-75; instr. Sioux Falls Sch. Dist., S.D., 1975-79; instr. mech. drawing U. Md., College Park, 1979-86; asst. prof. engring. graphics dept. constrn. mgmt. East Carolina U., Greenville, N.C., 1986-92, assoc. prof. engring. graphics dept. indsl. tech., 1992—, acting chmn. dept. constrn. mgmt., 1989-90; aircraft maintenance officer 113th Logistics Group DCANG, Andrews AFB, Md., 1983-95, squadron comdr. 113th Aircraft Generation Squadron, 1995—. Jour. reviewer; contbr. articles to profl. jours. Faculty advisor Disabled Student Alliance, U. Md., 1982-86. Served with USAF, 1968-72, Air N.G., 1977—. Decorated Master Aircraft Munitions and Maintenance badge USAF., Air Res. Forces Meritorious Svc. medal, Nat. Def. Svc. medal with Bronze star, Armed Forces Expeditionary medal, Armed Forces Res. medal. Mem. Air Force Assn. (chpt. sec. 1988-92, chpt. pres. 1992-94), N.G. Assn. U.S., N.G. Assn. D.C., Nat. Assn. Indsl. Tech. (region III dir. 1995—), Am. Soc. Engring Edn. (chair engring. graphics divsn. SE sect. 1993-94, vice chair instrnl. unit SE sect. 1994-95, chair 1995-96), Am. Design and Drafting Assn., Nat. Assn. Indsl. and Tech. Tchr. Educators, Coun. Tech. Tchr. Edn., Phi Kappa Phi, Epsilon Pi Tau (citation, 1991, trustee Beta Mu chpt., 1995—), Iota Lambda Sigma (v.p. Nu chpt. 1984-85, pres. Nu chpt. 1985-86). Republican. Presbyterian.

CHING, MELVIN CHUNG-HING, retired physiologist, anatomy educator, researcher; b. Honolulu, Feb. 11, 1935; s. Harry S.L. and Roseline Tam (Tom) C.; m. Jane C-A. Hsia, Aug. 21, 1965; children: Mark K-S., Mona M-L. AB, U. Nebr., 1957, MS, 1960; PhD, U. Calif., Berkeley, 1971. Instr. City Coll. San Francisco, 1964-66; instr. anatomy U. Rochester, N.Y., 1971-73, asst. prof., 1973-77; assoc. prof. Med. Coll. Va., Richmond, 1978-82; lectr. biology San Jose (Calif.) State U., 1983; sr. rsch. fellow Nat. Inst. Child Health and Human Devel., NIH, Bethesda, Md., 1983-84; asst. prof. med. anatomy Tex. A&M U., College Station, 1984-85; expert Nat. Inst. Environ. Health Scis., NIH, Research Triangle Park, N.C., 1985-89; asst. prof. vet. anatomy Ohio State U., Columbus, 1989-92; asst. prof. biology James Madison U., Harrisonburg, Va., 1992-95; ret., 1995; mem. ad hoc rsch. adv. panel Nat. Inst. Gen. Med. Scis., 1981, 92. Author 2 textbooks on physiology; referee Am. Jour. Vet. Rsch., 1991-93, Am. Vet. Med. Assn., 1992; contbr. chpts. to books, articles to profl. jours. Grantee NIH, 1977-80, Human Growth Found., 1976; NIH sr. rsch. fellow, 1983. Mem. AAAS, Endocrine Soc., Fed. Soc. Explt. Biology, Am. Assn. Anatomists (co-chmn. endocrine session 1982, 87, 92), World Assn. Vet. Anatomists, Soc. Study Reproduction, Sigma Xi. Home: 12301 Roaringbrook Ct Richmond VA 23233-2106

CHINN, MARK ALLAN, lawyer; b. Jackson, Miss., June 9, 1953; s. Rollin J. and Ann M. (Heiberg) C.; m. Cathy Hawkinson, Aug. 6, 1978; children: Courtney, Casey, Carly. BA in Polit. Sci., Iowa State U., 1975; JD, U. Miss., 1978. Bar: U.S. Dist. Ct. (no. dist.) Miss. 1978, U.S. Dist. Ct. (so. dist.) Miss. 1980; U.S. Ct. Appeals (5th and 11th cirs.) 1981; U.S. Supreme Ct. 1980. Staff atty. Miss. Senate, Jackson, 1978-79; spl. asst. Atty. Gen. Office, Jackson, 1979-80; assoc. Louis Baine, Jackson, 1980-82, Law Office William Latham, Jackson, 1982-88; atty. pvt. practice, Jackson, 1988—; adj. prof. law Miss. Coll. Sch. Law. Bd. dirs. Arts Alliance, Jackson, 1990—, Miss. Children's Home, Jackson, 1990-95; pres. Jackson Urban League Bd., 1995-97. Recipient Award of Merit, Miss. Bar Assn., 1996, Lamar Order, Miss. Bar Found. Mem. ABA, ATLA, Miss. Bar Assn. (pres. 1995-96, chmn. family law sect. 1995-96, chmn. small firm practice com. 1995-96), Miss. Trial Lawyers Assn., Hinds County Bar Assn. (dir. 1994-95, pres.-elect 1996—), Am. Inn of Ct. (master Charles Clark), Rotary, Jackson C. of C. Office: Chinn & Assocs 1675 Lakeland Dr Ste 505 Jackson MS 39216-4846

CHINULA, DONALD MCLEAN, religious studies educator; b. Bombo Mlowe, Rumphi, Malawi, Mar. 21, 1943; came to U.S., 1964; s. Assie Efron and Mairess (Mhango) C.; m. Torani Sandra Munyenyembe; children: David, Joyce, Maneno. BA, Carleton Coll., Minn., 1968; JD, U. Minn., 1976; LLM, Columbia U., 1977; MDiv, Interdenomination Theol. Ctr., Atlanta, 1985; MA, Sch. Theology, Claremont, Calif., 1991; PhD, Sch. of Theology, Claremont, Calif., 1993. Bar: Minn. 1976, Ark. 1977, D.C. 1977, Ga. 1982. Dep. dir. EEO Macalester Coll., St. Paul, 1969-73; assoc. C & W Legal Svcs., Atlanta, 1977-85; assoc. Christian edn. and youth South Hills, Northkirk and Westminster Presbyn. Chs., Ontario, Calif., 1989-94; assoc. prof. religion Stillman Coll., Tuscaloosa, Ala., 1994—; adj. prof. legal studies Ga. State U., Atlanta, 1985-94, Chaffey C.C., Alta Loma, Calif., 1989-93; mem. Coun. on Fgn. Visitors, Atlanta, 1979-82. Contbr. articles to profl. jours. Mem. Presbyn. Hunger Com., 1985-87, Self Devel. of People, L.A., 1992-94, Pastoral Care Team, Claremont, 1990-92; sec. Black Lawyers Assn., Little Rock, 1978-79; mem. permanent juc. commn. Presbytery Sheppards, Lapsley, Ala., divsn. mission Presbytery Sheppards, Lapsley, Ala. Consortium Global Edn.; faculty rep. bd. trustees Stillman Coll., assoc. chaplain. Fellow African Scholarship Program for Am. Univs., 1964-68, Weyerhauser Ednl. Found., 1976-78. Fellow Internat. Profls. of Ark. (pres. 1978), Internat. Fellows STC (pres. 1987); mem. Am. Assn. Pastoral Counselors, Ga. Bar Assn., Theta Phi. Presbyterian.

CHIPKA, STEPHEN THOMAS, telecommunications company executive; b. Owensboro, Ky., July 31, 1953; s. Walter Charles and Marion Elizabeth (McAdam) C.; m. Heather Diane Naigus, Apr. 27, 1985. BBA in Mktg., Fla. Internat. U., 1979. Nat. account mgr. Southern Bell Telephone, Miami, Fla., 1978-81; tng. mgr. Southern Bell/AT&T, Atlanta, 1981-83; nat. mktg. mgr. Communications Industries, Atlanta, 1983-85; nat. account mgr. Jarvis Corp., Atlanta, 1985; staff mgr. BellSouth Telecom. Inc., Atlanta, 1986—; pvt. practice cons., Atlanta, 1984-86. Republican. Lutheran. Office: BellSouth Telecom Inc Annex 2 1447 Northeast Wxpy NE Atlanta GA 30329-2301

CHIPMAN, DONALD EUGENE, history educator; b. Hill City, Kans.; s. Albert Cyrille and Olive Teresa (Hemmy) C.; divorced; children: Zachary Andrew, Jason Alaric. BA in History, Ft. Hays Kans. State Coll., 1955, MS in History, 1958; PhD in History, U. N.Mex., 1962. Tchr. Garfield (Kans.) Pub. Schs., 1955-57; asst. prof. Ft. Hays Kans. State Coll., 1962-64; assoc. prof. U. North Tex., Denton, 1964-67, prof., 1967—, faculty coord. for regents' faculty lecture series, 1983-86, univ. self-study com., 1979-85, univ. writing com., 1979-83, faculty rsch. com., 1971-76, arts and sci. curriculum com., 1976-79, Columbian Quincentary exec. com., 1987-92; vis. prof. U. San Francisco, 1970, U. Wash., 1962; lectr. North Tex. State U., 1980, 81, San Antonio Mus. Folk Art, 1986, U. Tex., 1988, 90, 92, 94, Witte Mus. San Antonio, 1990, Tex. Hist. Assn., 1991, 92, Las Porciones Soc., 1991, Fresno State U., 1992, Ea. Mich. U., 1992, North Harris C.C., Houston, 1992. Author: Nuño de Guzmán and the Province of Pánuco in New Spain, 1518-1533, 1967, Texas en la Epoca Colonial, 1992, Spanish Texas, 1519-1821, 1992 (1st prize Presidio La Bahia award 1992, Kate Broocks Bates award 1993, Outstanding Acad. Book award Choice mag.), (with others) Texas Through Time: Evolving Interpretations, 1991, Struggle and Survival in Colonial America, 1981, Reflections of Western Historians, 1969, Homenaje a Don José Mars289a de la Peña y Cámara, 1969, The Handbook of Victoria County, 1990; co-author: The Dallas Cowboys and the NFL, 1970; editor: (with others) Handbook of Latin American Studies, 1974; adv. editor: Handbook of Texas; contbr. articles to profl. jours. With U.S. Army, 1946-47. Fellow Tex. State State Assn., Tex. Inst. Letters; mem. So. Hist. Assn., Conf. L.Am. History, Tex. Hist. Assn., East Tex. Hist. Assn., Phi Alpha Theta, Phi Kappa Phi. Mem. So. Hist. Assn., Conf. L.Am. History, Tex. State Hist. Assn., East Tex. Hist. Assn., Phi Alpha Theta, Phi Kappa Phi. Democrat. Roman Catholic. Office: U North Tex PO Box 13735 Denton TX 76203-6735

CHIPMAN, SUSAN ELIZABETH, psychologist; b. St. Paul, Feb. 12, 1946; d. Robert Louis and Margaret Alice Fitzgerald; m. Eric George Chipman, Aug. 27, 1966. AB in Math., Harvard U., 1966, MBA, 1967, AM in Psychol., 1969, PhD in Exptl. Psychol., 1973. Asst. prof. U. Mich., Ann Arbor, 1974-75; assoc. Nat. Inst. Edn., Washington, 1976-78, asst. dir., 1979-84; sci. officer U.S. Office Naval Rsch., Arlington, Va., 1984-85, cognitive sci. program mgr., 1985—; mem. adv. bd. James S. McDonnell Found., St. Louis, 1987—. Editor, author: Thinking and Learning Skills, 1985, Women and Mathematics, 1985, Foundations of Knowledge Acquisition, 1993, Cognitively Diagnostic Assessment, 1995; contbr. articles to profl. jours. Fellow APA. Home: 2606 S Joyce St Arlington VA 22202-2214 Office: Office Naval Rsch 342 800 N Quincy St Arlington VA 22203-1906

CHIRINO, FERNANDO PORFIRIO, medical educator; b. Havana, Cuba, Sept. 15, 1918; arrived in U.S., 1960; s. Fernando Clemente and Herminia (Alonso) C.; m. Sophia Phill Flint Chirino, Mar. 21, 1940; children: Fernando, Patricia. BS, Tulane U., New Orleans, 1939; MD, 1942. Med. dir. Hershey Cuban R.R., Cuba, 1946-60; Hershey Corp., 1946-60; staff VA Hosp., New Orleans, 1960-62; asst., assoc. prof. Tulane U., New Orleans, 1962-95; prof. emeritus Tulane U. Sch. Medicine, 1993; dir. headache clinic Tulane U., 1965-80; head sect. geriatrics, 1970-84; pres. Colegio Medico, Sta. Cruz, Cuba, 1948, 50, 58, Club Cubano Prof., New Orleans, 1952; dir. med. edn. Charity Hosp., New Orleans, 1958-86; med. staff Tulane Clinic, New Orleans, 1972-91. Recipient Hon. award Liceo Cubano Jose Marti, New Orleans, 1973, Appreciation award Chairty Hosp., New Orleans, 1986; named Hon. Citizen Municipio Sta Cruz, Miami, Fla., 1984. Republican. Roman Catholic. Home: 1512 Certosa Ave Coral Gables FL 33146

CHISHOLM, TOMMY, lawyer, utility company executive; b. Baldwyn, Miss., Apr. 14, 1941; s. Thomas Vaniver and Rubel (Duncan) C.; m. Janice McClanahan, June 20, 1964; children: Mark Alan (dec.), Andrea, Stephen Thomas, Patrick Ervin. B.S.C.E., Tenn. Tech. U., 1963; J.D., Samford U., 1969; M.B.A., Ga. State U., 1984. Registered profl. engr., Ala., Ark., Del., Ga., Fla., Ky., La., N.H., Miss., N.C., Pa., Tenn., S.C., Va., W.Va. Civil engr. TVA, Knoxville, Tenn., 1963-64; design engr. So. Co. Svcs., Birmingham, Ala., 1964-69; coord. spl. projects So. Co. Svcs., Atlanta, 1969-73; sec., house counsel So. Co. Svcs., 1977-82, v.p., sec., house counsel, 1982—; asst. to pres. So. Co., Atlanta, 1973-75; sec., asst. treas. So. Co., 1977—; mgr. adminstrv. svcs. Gulf Power Co., Pensacola, Fla., 1975-77; sec. So. Energy, Inc., Atlanta, 1981-82; v.p., sec. So. Electric Internat., Atlanta, 1982—; sec. So. Devel. and Investment Group, 1985—, So. Electric Wholesale Generators, Inc., 1993—, So. Electric R.R. Co., 1993—, So. Electric Wholesale Generators, Inc., 1993—; Birchwood Devel. Corp., 1992—, SEI Birchwood, Inc., 1992—, SEI Holdings, Inc., 1993—, So. Electric Bahamas Holdings, Ltd., 1993—, So. Electric Bahamas, Ltd., 1993—; asst. sec. Freeport Power Co. Ltd., 1993—. Mem. Am. Bar Assn., State Bar Ala., Am. Soc. Corp. Secs., Am. Corp. Counsel Assn., Phi Alpha Delta, Beta Gamma Sigma. Office: The Southern Co 270 Peachtree St Ste 2200 Atlanta GA 30303

CHISHOLM, WILLIAM DEWAYNE, retired contract manager; b. Everett, Wash., Mar. 1, 1924; s. James Adam and Evelyn May (Iles) C.; m. Esther Troehler, Mar. 10, 1956; children: James Scott, Larry Alan, Brian Duane. BS in ChemE, U. Wash., 1949, BS in Indsl. Engring., 1949; MBA, Harvard U., 1955. Chemist, unit leader, tech. rep. The Coca-Cola Co., Atlanta and Los Angeles, 1949-59; contract adminstr. Honeywell Inc., Los Angeles, 1959-61, mktg. adminstr., 1961-64, contracts work dir., 1964-66, contracts mgr., Clearwater, Fla., 1966-73, contracts supr., 1973-75, sr. contract mgmt. rep., 1975-80, prin. contract mgmt. rep., work dir., 1980-82, contracts mgr., 1982-89; ret.; chmn. bd. Creative Attitudes, Inc., 1987-96; adj. faculty Fla. Inst. Tech., 1976-96. Contbr. articles to profl. jours. Trustee, John Calvin Found., 1974-82; mem. budget adv. com. City of Clearwater, 1983-85; commr. to 196th gen. assembly Presbyn. Ch. (USA), 1984; sec. bd. trustees, treas. Presbytery of Tampa Bay, 1990-96, sec. coun., 1996—, mem. rev., evaluation and planning com., 1996—, City of Clearwater rep. on the Long Ctr. Bd. Dirs., 1991—, mem. exec. com., 1992—, treas., 1992-93, v.p., 1993-95. With USN, 1944-46. Cert. profl. contracts mgr. Recipient Award of Distinction Fla. Inst. Tech. Grad. Ctr., 1987. Fellow Nat. Contract Mgmt. Assn. (chmn. S.E. region fellows 1985-87, past nat. dir., pres., v.p. Suncoast chpt.). Republican. Presbyterian (elder session mem. 1964-65, 73-76, 77-80, 81-84, 86-90, ch. treas. 1994-96). Home: 1364 S Hercules Ave Clearwater FL 34624-3748

CHISM, MARK THOMAS, computer company project leader; b. Marietta, Ga., Mar. 22, 1965; s. Arthur Black and Phyllis Arlene (Dochsteder) C.; m. Eujeana Sue Plunkette, May 20, 1989; children: Nathaniel Thomas, Aaron Charles, Ariel Yvonne. Student, Fla. State U., 1983-85. Tech. programmer AMI, Tallahassee, 1985; owner, sr. programmer Chisco Internat., Orlando, Fla., 1985-90; personal computer coord. Toshiba (Television Divsn.), Lebanon, Tenn., 1989-91; sr. tech. programmer Network Data Corp., Brentwood, Tenn., 1991; personal computer/network coord. Tridon, Inc., Smyrna, Tenn., 1991-92; project leader personal computer team Integrated Sys. Solutions Corp., Nashville, 1992—. Vol. Am. Red Cross, Rutherford County, Tenn., 1990—. Mem. IEEE Computer Soc., IEEE Comm. Soc., Assn. Computing Machinery. Republican. Mem. Ind. Baptist Ch. Home: 1011 Esquire Ct Murfreesboro TN 37130-1346 Office: ISSC 550 Metroplex Dr Nashville TN 37211-3133

CHISUM, MATTHEW EUAL, senior project scientist; b. Amarillo, Tex., Aug. 5, 1953; s. Donzell Eual and Ella Jean (Vincent) C.; m. Elizabeth Kay Neidhardt, Mar. 15, 1980; children: Brett Matthew, Kristen Marie. BS, West Tex. State U., 1975, MS, 1976. Veterinarian asst. High Plains Animal Hosp., Borger, Tex., 1976-77; instr. math. Frank Phillips Jr. Coll., Borger, 1976-77; chem. tech. Mason & Hanger Pantex Plant, Amarillo, 1977-87, sr. scientist, 1987-90; owner Chisum Cattle Co., Stinnett, 1987—, project scientist, 1990-91, sr. project scientist, 1991—; project team leader for atomic spectroscopy Pantex Plant, Amarillo, 1994—; mem. Comm. Task Force-Pantex, Amarillo, 1990-91, Emergency Spill Response-Pantex, Amarillo, 1987-92. Contbr. articles to profl. jours. Mem. Am. Chem. Soc., Soc. Applied Spectroscopy, Ducks Unltd. (chmn. Canyon chpt. 1985-86), Lions Internat. (sec. Adobe Walls 1988-95), Hutchinson County Pioneers Assn. (pres. 1994-96), Sigma Phi Epsilon (alumni chmn. Tex. Xi chpt. 1976-81, Alumnus of Yr. award 1976, 78). Home: PO Box 3338 400 Lariat St Stinnett TX 79083-3338 Office: Mason & Hanger Pantex Plant PO Box 30020 Amarillo TX 79177-0001

CHITTENDEN, STANLEY MATTHEW, municipal consultant; b. Hays, Kans., July 24, 1922; s. Stanley Stewart and Myrtle Helen (Truan) C.; m. Louise Stilwell, Nov. 30, 1947; children: John Stanley, Jill Lynn, Kimberly Kay. BSBA, Ft. Hays Kans. U., 1948; postgrad., Washburn U.; Degree in Mcpl. Mgmt., Inst. Tng. Mcpl. Adminstrn., Washington. Acct. Brown and Root Constrn. Co., Pampa, Tex., 1951-53, Celanese Chem. Corp., Pampa, 1953-59, Hill Packing Co., Pampa, 1959-63; from asst. sect. to asst. city mgr. City of Pampa, 1963—. Bd. deacons, jr. ednl. com. First Presbyn. Ch. Pampa. With USN, 1941-44. Mem. U.S. Mcpl. Fin. Officers Assn., Can. Mcpl. Fin. Officers Assn., Internat. City Mgmt. Assn., Tex. City Mgmt. Assn., Tex. Mcpl. Fin. Officers Assn., Nat. Purchasing Inst., City Clks. and City Secs. Assn. Tex., Masons, Shriners, Oasis of Isis, Kiwanis Internat., Top O'Tex. Sportsman Club (sec.-treas., chmn. bar-b-que com.), Pi Mu Alpha. Home: 2540 Christine St Pampa TX 79065-3037

CHITTY, (MARY) ELIZABETH NICKINSON, university historian; b. Balt., Apr. 27, 1920; d. Edward Phillips and Em Turner (Merritt) Nickinson; m. Arthur Benjamin Chitty, June 16, 1946; children: Arthur Benjamin, John Abercrombie, Em Turner, Nathan Harsh Brown. BA cum laude, Fla. State U., 1941, MA, 1942; DCL, U. of South, 1988. Tchr. Fla. Indsl. Sch. for Girls, Ocala, 1942-43; psychometrist neuropsychiat. dept. Sch. Aviation Medicine, Pensacola (Fla.) Naval Air Sta., 1943-46; assoc. editor Sewanee (Tenn.) Alumni News, U. of South, 1946-62; bus. mgr., mng. editor Sewanee Rev., 1962-65, dir. fin. aid and career svcs., 1970-80, assoc. univ. historiographer, 1980—; freelance editor. Editor: (with H.A. Petry) Sewanee Centennial Alumni Directory, 1954-62, (with H.A. Petry and R.Q. Dudney) Centennial Report of the Registrar of the University of the South, 1959; (with Arthur Ben Chitty) Too Black, Too White (Ely Green), 1970; author: (with Moultrie Guerry and Arthur Ben Chitty) Men Who Made Sewanee, 1981, (with A.B. Chitty and W. Givens) Ninety-Nine Iron, 1992; columnist Sewanee Mountain Messenger, 1985—. Bd. dirs. Sewanee Civic Assn., 1979-80, 86-88; CONTACT-Lifeline of Coffee and Franklin Counties, 1981-84; mem. adv. coun. St. Andrew's Sewanee Sch., 1988—. Recipient Cmty. Svc. award Sewanee Civic Assn., 1996. Mem. Assn. Preservation Tenn. Antiquities (trustee 1985-88), AAUW (pres. Sewanee br. 1975-77), Fla. State U. Alumni Assn. (dir. 1941—, permanent pres. Class of 1941), Mortar Bd., Phi Beta Kappa, Phi Kappa Phi, Phi Alpha Theta, Kappa Delta. Democrat. Episcopalian. Home: 100 South Carolina Ave Sewanee TN 37375-2045 Office: Univ of South Sewanee TN 37385-1000

CHMIELINSKI, EDWARD ALEXANDER, electronics company executive; b. Waterbury, Conn., Mar. 25, 1925; s. Stanley and Helen C.; m. Elizabeth Carew, May 30, 1946; children: Nancy, Elizabeth, Susan Jean. BS, Tulane U., 1950; postgrad. Colo. U., 1965. V.p., gen. mgr. Clifton Products, Litton Industries, Colorado Springs, Colo., 1965-67; pres. Memory Products div. Litton Industries, Beverly Hills, Calif., 1967-69, Bowmar Instruments, Can., Ottawa, Ont., 1969-73; gen. mgr. Leigh Instruments, Carleton Pl., Ont., 1973-75; pres., dir. Lewis Engring. Co., Naugatuck, Conn., 1975-85; pres., dir. Liquidometer Corp., Tampa, Fla., 1975-85; pres. Lewis div. Colt Industries, 1985-90, ret., 1990; Pres. Acad. Water Bd., 1963-65; bd. dirs. United Way, Colorado Springs, 1965-67; fellow Tulane U. Served with USN, 1943-46. Mem. Air Force Assn., Navy League.

CHO, JAI HANG, internist, hematologist, educator; b. Busan, Republic of Korea, May 1, 1942; came to U.S., 1972; s. Neung Whan and Heo Jai (Min) C.; m. Jawon Nam, Oct. 8, 1971; children: Karen, Austin. M.D., Catholic Med. Coll., Seoul, Republic of Korea, 1968. Diplomate Am. Bd. Internal Medicine. Intern, White Plains Hosp., N.Y., 1972-73; resident in internal medicine Nassau Hosp., Mineola, N.Y., 1973-76, fellow in hematology, 1976-77; fellow in hematology and oncology U. South Fla. Med. Coll., Tampa, 1977-79; practice medicine specializing in internal medicine and hematology, Tampa, 1979—; mem. staff Univ. Community Hosp.; clin. asst. prof. medicine U. South Fla. Med. Coll., 1985-92. Served to capt. Korean Army, 1968-71. Mem. AMA, ACP, Fla. Med. Assn., Hillsborough County Med. Assn. Avocation: art, antiques. Home: 16114 Ancroft Ct Tampa FL 33647-1040 Office: 13701 Bruce B Downs Blvd Tampa FL 33613-4647

CHODOSH, ROBERT IVAN, middle school educator, coach; b. Elizabeth, N.J., May 29, 1946; s. Philip Richard and Jean (Landerman) C.; m. Sharon Lynn Young, Aug. 7, 1981 (div. Apr. 1989); 1 stepson, Kevin. BS in Edn., U. Tenn., Knoxville, 1968; MEd, Fla. Tech. U., Orlando, 1975. Cert. in phys. edn., health edn. Tchr. Old Dixie Elem. Sch., Titusville, Fla., 1968-78, Surfside Elem. Sch., Satellite Beach, Fla., 1978-79; tchr., basketball and track coach Andrew Jackson Middle Sch., Titusville, 1979—; mem. comprehensive edn. com. Brevard County Schs., Melbourne, Fla., 1990-91. Com. mem. Brevard County Elementary and Secondary Physical Education Guide, 1977, 82, 85, 88. Gray leader, coach North Brevard YMCA, Titusville, 1968-78; recreation leader North Brevard Recreation Dept., 1968-78, summer program leader, 1970-75, 88; scorer, asst. coach, concession stand mgr. Indian River City Little League, 1987, 89. Recipient Tchr. of Yr. award Old Dixie Elem. Sch., Titusville, 1974, Silver Svc. award Brevard County Sch. System. Mem. AAHPERD, Am. Fed. Tchrs., Fla. Edn. Assn., Fla. Assn. for Health, Phys. Edn., Recreation, Dance and Driver's Edn., Brevard County Fed. Tchrs., U. Tenn. Alumni Assn., Andrew Jackson Mid. Sch. PTO. Democrat. Jewish. Home: 3716 Ranger St Titusville FL 32796-1575 Office: Andrew Jackson Mid Sch 1515 Knox Mcrae Dr Titusville FL 32780-5414

CHOINSKI, JOHN STANLEY, JR., biology educator, botanist; b. Southbridge, Mass., Mar. 14, 1952; s. John S. and Joyce (Butler) C.; m. Susan Cunha, June 1974; 1 child, Reed Jonathan. BS in Botany, U. Fla., 1974, MS in Botany, 1975; PhD in Botany, Ariz. State U., 1978. Rsch. asst. Ariz. State U., Tempe, 1976-78; rsch. assoc. Oreg. State U., Corvallis, 1978-79; vis. asst. prof. U. Wyo., Laramie, 1979-84; asst. prof. U. Ctrl. Ark., Conway, 1984-87, assoc. prof., 1987-93, prof., 1993—; vis. sr. lectr. plant physiology U. Zimbabwe, 1989-91; mtg. presenter Ark. Acad. Sci., 1992, Am. Soc. Plant Physiologists, 1993. Contbr. articles and abstracts to profl. and sci. publs. Grantee U. Ctrl. Ark. Rsch. Coun., 1984, 85, 91, 96, U. Zimbabwe Rsch. Bd., 1989, 90, NSF-Instrument Lab. Improvement Program, 1986, 96. Mem. Am. Soc. Plant Physiology, Am. Inst. Biol. Scis. Office: Dept Biology U Ctrl Ark Conway AR 72035

CHONIN, NEIL HARVEY, lawyer; b. Bklyn., Dec. 30, 1936; s. Morris Joseph and Shirley (Goldberg) C.; m. Lynn Barbara Weinstein (div.); children: Mitchell, David, Loree; m. Patricia Lane Perrin, Aug. 13, 1972; children: Tiffany, Jason. BA in Govt., U. Fla., 1958, LLD, 1961. Bar: Fla. 1963, U.S. Dist. Ct. (so., mid. and no. dists.) Fla. 1963, U.S. Supreme Ct. 1975, U.S. Ct. Appeals (11th cir.) 1981. Assoc. Dermer Rosen & Mofsky, Miami Beach, Fla., 1961-63; ptnr. Rosen & Chonin, Miami Beach, Fla., 1963-66, Goldstein, Franklin & Chonin, Miami Beach, Fla., 1966-72, Chonin & Sher, P.A., Coral Gables, Fla., 1972-92, Chonin, Sher & Nauvarette, Coral Gables, Fla., 1992—; lectr. on trial advocacy. Contbr. articles to profl. jours. Pres. Legal Svcs. Greater Miami, 1974-76; chmn. 3d DCA Jud. Nominating Com., Miami, 1983-87. Named Man of Yr., ACLU, 1993, 94; recipient Tobias Simon Pro Bono award, 1984. Fellow Am. Acad. Matrimonial Lawyers (bd. mgrs. 1992), Am. Bd. Civil Trial Advs.; mem. ATLA, Acad. Fla. Trial Lawyers, Family Inns of Ct. Office: Chonin Sher & Navarrete 304 Palermo Ave Coral Gables FL 33134-6608

CHONMAITREE, TASNEE, pediatrician, educator, infectious disease specialist; b. Bangkok, Thailand, Dec. 9, 1949; came to U.S., 1975; d. Surajit and Arporn (Maitong) C.; m. Somkiat Laungthaleong Pong, June 27, 1981; children: Ann L. Pong, Dan L. Pong. BS, Mahidol U., Bangkok, 1971; MD, Siriraj Med. Sch., Bangkok, 1973. Diplomate Am. Bd. Pediatrics, Am. Bd. Pediatric Infectious Diseases. Rotating intern Siriraj Hosp., Bangkok, 1973-74, resident in pediatrics, 1974-75; resident in pediatrics Lloyd Noland Hosp., U. Ala., Birmingham, 1975-78; fellow infectious disease U. Rochester (N.Y.), 1978-81; asst. prof. pediatrics U. Tex. Med. Br., Galveston, 1981-87, asst. prof. pathology, 1985-87, assoc. prof. pediatrics and pathology, 1987-94; prof. pediatrics and pathology, 1994—; assoc. dir. clin. virology lab. U. Tex. Med. Br., Galveston, 1985-92, dir. divsn. pediatric infectious disease, 1985-92. Contbr. 50 articles to profl. jours. Grantee NIH, 1994-99. Fellow Am. Acad. Pediatrics, Pediatric Infectious Diseases Soc., Infectious Diseases Soc. Am.; mem. Soc. Pediatric Rsch., European Soc. for Pediatric Rsch., Tex. Infectious Disease Soc. Buddhist. Home: 1906 Cherrytree Park Cir Houston TX 77062-2327 Office: U Tex Dept Pediatrics Med Br Ninth Street & Market Galveston TX 77555-0371

CHOPRA, ASHOK KUMAR, microbiologist, educator; b. Jallandhar City, India, Sept. 14, 1957; came to the U.S., 1984; s. D.D. and N.R. (Khanna) C.; m. V.R. Khera, June 24, 1987; 1 child, Sunayana. BSc in Biology, Dyal

Singh Coll., Karnal, India, 1976; MSc in Microbiology, Nat. Dairy Rsch. Inst., Karnal, India, 1978, PhD in Microbiology, 1982; PhD in Molecular & Cellular Biology, Czechoslovak Acad. Scis., Prague, 1984. UNESCO fellow Inst. Microbiology, Czechoslovak Acad. Scis., Prague, 1982-84; postdoctoral fellow dept. microbiology U. Tex. Med. Br., Galveston, 1984-85, McLaughlin postdoctoral fellow dept. microbiology, 1985-87, faculty assoc. dept. microbiology, 1987-90, asst. prof. dept. microbiology, 1990-95, assoc. prof. dept. microbiology, 1995—; presenter in field. Contbr. articles to profl. jours. Recipient John Sealy Recruitment grant, 1992-94; grantee NIH, 1990-93, 92-95, 95-99. Mem. Am. Soc. for Microbiology (Tex. br.), Sigma Xi. Office: Univ Tex Med Br Microbiology Immunology 11th Texas Ave Galveston TX 77555

CHOU, KAREN CHAI KWAN, civil engineering educator; research, consultant; b. Hong Kong, Dec. 10, 1955; came to U.S., 1970, naturalized 1976; d. Choi Hong and Chuen Mui (Wong) C. B.S. in Civil Engring., Tufts U., 1978; M.S., Northwestern U., 1980, Ph.D., 1983. Registered profl. engr., N.Y., Tenn. Civil engring. technician C.E., U.S. Army Waltham, Mass., 1977-78; cons. Ill. Inst. Tech. Research Inst., Chgo., summer 1979; structural engr. Harza Engring. Co., Chgo., 1979-81; research assoc. Johns Hopkins U., Balt., 1982-83; asst. prof. Syracuse U., N.Y., 1983-87; assoc. prof. civil engring., 1987-93; assoc. prof. civil engring, U. Tenn., Knoxville, 1993—; vis. assoc. prof. Univ. Minn., 1991. Contbr. articles to profl. jours. Vol. tutor Boston Tech. High Sch., 1978. Tufts U. Class of 1926 scholar, 1976-77, Tufts U. Albert Whittier scholar, 1977-78, Mass. Soc. for Univ. Edn. of Women scholar, 1977-78; AAUW fellow, 1982-83, U.S. Air Force-Universal Energy System fellow, 1985, 88; Northwestern U. grantee, 1978-79, 81-82, Johns Hopkins U. grantee, 1982-83, NSF grantee, 1984—, USAF grantee, 1986. Mem. Am. Assn. Engrs. Edn., Am. Acad. Mechanics, Am. Concrete Inst., ASCE (bd. dirs. Syracuse sect. 1984-89, newsletter editor 1984-85, sec. 1985-86, pres. 1987-88, N.Y. coun. chair, 1993), Tau Beta Pi, Chi Epsilon, Order of Engineer. Avocations: stamp collecting, volleyball, ping-pong. Office: Univ Tenn Dept Civil Engring Knoxville TN 37996

CHOUDHURY, ABDUL LATIF, physics educator; b. Dhaka, Bangladesh, Jan. 1, 1933; came to U.S., 1966; s. Abdur R. and Umme Arefa (Khatun) C.; children: Kadjol, Marcel. BSc with honors in Physics, Dhaka U., 1953, MSc in Physics, 1954; D Theoretical Physics, Free U. Berlin, 1961. Asst. to prof. physics Dhaka U., 1955; helping asst. to prof. theoretical physics Free U. Berlin, 1958-60; sr. lectr. physics Dhaka U., 1961-66, reader in physics, 1969; assoc. prof. math. and physics. Elizabeth City (N.C.) State Coll., 1966-68, assoc. prof., 1969-73, prof. physics, 1973—; cons. Nat. Bur. Standards, Washington, 1964-66; gen. sec. Dhaka U. Tchrs. Assn., 1969. Contbr. numerous articles to sci. publs. German exch. scholar DAAD, Berlin, 1955-58; rsch. fellow Fritz Haber Inst., Berlin, 1960; rsch. asst. Colombo Plan, Imperial Coll., London, 1960-61. Mem. AAUP (v.p. Elizabeth City unit 1986-87, pres. 1987-88), Am. Phys. Soc., Bangladesh Phys. Soc. (life), N.C. Acad. Sci. Home: 605 Forest Park Rd Elizabeth City NC 27909-9095 Office: Elizabeth City State Univ PO Box 886 Elizabeth City NC 27909

CHOUN, ROBERT JOSEPH, JR., religious education educator; b. Bridgeport, Conn., Aug. 17, 1948; s. Robert Joseph and Mildred Fitz C.; AA, Luther Coll., 1969; BA, Gustavus Adolphus Coll., 1971; MRE, Trinity Evang. Div. Sch., 1974; MA, Wheaton Coll., 1975; DMin, Faith Sem., 1980; postgrad. N. Tex. State U., 1978; postgrad. Dallas Theol. Sem., 1989; m. Jane Willson, July 12, 1975. Media rels. asst. Am. Bible Soc., N.Y.C., 1969-74; prof. Christian edn. Dallas Theol. Sem.; sem. leader early childhood Internat. Center Learning, Ventura, Calif., 1977—; minister edn. Pantego Bible Ch., Arlington, Tex., 1975-85; prof. edn. Dallas Theol. Sem., 1984—. Mem. bd. evaluation Pioneer Ministries, Wheaton, Ill. Mem. Nat. Assn. Dirs. Christian Edn., Christian Camping Internat., Booth Meml. Astron. Soc., Kappa Delta Phi, Phi Delta Kappa. Co-author: What the Bible Is All About, Young Explorers edit., 1987-88, Quick Reference edit., 1987-88, Directing Christian Education, 1992, The Complete Handbook for Children's Ministry, 1993; contbr. articles to profl. jours. and mags.; denominational rep., editorial cons., denom. cons., Gospel Light Publs., Ventura, Calif., nat. tng. dir. Scripture Press Publs., Wheaton, Ill., 1992—. Home: 818 Clover Park Dr Arlington TX 76013-1433 Office: 3909 Swiss Ave Dallas TX 75204-6471

CHRIS, HARRY JOSEPH, architect, architectural company executive; b. Beaumont, Tex., Sept. 13, 1938; s. Harry Adam and Lucille Helen (Junca) C.; BArch., Tulane U., 1961; MBA, Memphis State U., 1969. Registered architect, Colo., Fla., Ky., La., Mo., N.J., N.Y., Ohio, Tex. ; m. Jimmie Lea Bowen, Sept. 21, 1966; children: James, William, Mary Elizabeth, Mark, Lisa. Architect, Tex. State Bldg. Commn., Austin, 1966-68, Holiday Inn Am., Memphis, 1968-69; v.p. Club Corp. Am., Dallas, 1969-74, dir., 1972-74; pres. Architectural Designers, Inc., Dallas, 1969-74, RYA Architects, Inc., Dallas, 1974—, H.J. Chris Architects Inc., Dallas, 1978—; pres., owner Park City Club, Inc., Dallas. Lt. comdr. USNR, 1961-66. Mem. AIA, Irving C. of C., Exec. Clubs of Am., KC, Rotary, Las Colinas Country Club (Dallas). Roman Catholic. Home: 3910 Fox Glen Dr Irving TX 75062-3810 Office: 1520 W Airport Fwy Ste 200 Irving TX 75062-6101

CHRISCOE, CHRISTINE FAUST, industrial trainer; b. Atlanta, Oct. 29, 1950; d. Henry Charles and Shirley Faye (Birdwell) Faust; BA, Spring Hill Coll., 1973; postgrad. Ga. State U., 1974—; m. Ralph D. Chriscoe, June 25, 1983. Trainer, Fed. Res. Bank, Atlanta, 1973-77; project mgr., tng. dept. Coca Cola U.S.A., Atlanta, 1977-79, sr. project mgr., 1979-81, mgr. tech. tng., 1981-84, mgr. sales, mgmt. and mktg. tng., 1984-85, mgr. bottler tng., 1984-85; mgr. human resources devel., 1986-88; mgr. tng. and devel., 1988-90; pres. Christine Chriscoe and Assocs., 1990—, Ga. Pacific Corp., 1990—, dir. human resources devel., 1990-92, dir. human resources devel. and planning, 1992—, dir. strategic human resources, 1995—; speaker Best of Am. Human Resource Conf., Ga. State U., Nat. Soc. Performance Improvement. Trustee Ga. Shakespeare Festival. Mem. ASTD (speaker), Internat. TV and Video Assn., Soc. for Applied Learning Techs., Tng. Dirs.' Forum (bd. dirs.), Atlanta Human Resources Planning Soc. (bd. dirs.), The Bridge (bd. dirs.). Roman Catholic.

CHRISSOS, GEORGE, retired secondary education educator; b. Union City, N.J., July 4, 1925; s. Michael George and Helen (Theofanides) C.; m. June 10, 1951; children: Laurie Foster, Joan Chrissos Roberts. BA, CCNY, 1949; MA, Columbia U., 1957. Tchr. N.Y.C., 1955-56; tchr. Lake Ronkonkoma, N.Y., 1956-83, Bushnell, Fla., 1983-84, Winter Park, Fla., 1984-94; host Disneyworld, Kissimmee, Fla., 1995-96. Author: (book of poems) Visions and Reveries, 1996. Cpl. U.S. Army, 1943-46, ETO. Mem. Deer Run Country Club. Home: 1017 Pebble Beach Cir E Winter Springs FL 32708

CHRIST, CHRIS STEVE, lawyer; b. Canonsburg, Pa., Jan. 3, 1936; s. Michael C. and Katina (Hantzigorgis) C.; m. Lula Koutroulakis, Dec. 31, 1942; 1 child, Gina Reneè. BBA, U. Pitts., 1957; JD, Samford U., 1968. Bar: Ala., U.S. Dist. Ct. (no. dist.) Ala., U.S. Ct. Appeals (5th and 11th dists.), U.S. Supreme Ct. Sales rep. Mennen Cos., Morris Plains, N.J., 1960-62, Boston, 1962-65; sales rep. Beecham Cos., Atlanta, 1965-66; councilman City of Vestavia Hills, 1972-76; pvt. practice, Birmingham, Ala., 1968—; ptnr. Christ & McCary, Birmingham, 1988—. Pres., Jeff, Blount, St. Clair Mental Health/Mental Retardation Auth., 1981-83. Served to 1st lt. USAF, 1958-60. Mem. Ala. State Bar Assn., Birmingham Bar Assn., Nat. Assn. Criminal Defense Lawyers, Ala. Trial Lawyers Assn., Vestavia C. of C., Poinsetta's Men's Club, Masons, Shriners, Pinetree Country Club, Summit Club, The Club, Phi Alpha Delta (pres. Alumni Club 1982-88). Greek Orthodox. Office: Frank Nelson Building Birmingham AL 35203-3607

CHRISTENSEN, ALLAN ROBERT, electrical engineer, enrolled agent; b. Newton, Kans., Jan. 5, 1953; s. John Clyde and Margaret Ann (Christensen) Simpson. BSEE cum laude, Wichita (Kans.) State U., 1976; MSEE, So. Meth. U., 1981. Registered profl. engr., Tex.; enrolled agt. lic. by U.S. Treasury; accredited tax preparer, accredited tax advisor, by Accreditation Coun. for Accountancy and Taxation and Nat. Soc. Pub. Accts.; notary public, Tex.; cert. emergency care attendant, 1995; lic. Tex. Dept. Health. Draftsman, civil engring. asst. Wichita State U. State Architect's Office, 1971-72; chem. lab. asst. Wichita State U., 1973; clerk U.S. Postal Svc., Wichita, 1976; electrical engr. defense systems and elec. group, spl. guidance program Tex. Instruments, Inc., Dallas, 1977-96, jr. engr., 1977-79, engr., 1979-87, lead engr., 1987—; with spl. projects dept. Tex. Instruments, Inc., 1996—; notary public State of Tex., Dallas, 1991—; enrolled agent U.S. Treas., Dallas, 1992—; emergency care attendant, 1995—; co-facilitator semiconductor focus group Tex. Instruments Def. Systems Electronics Group, Dallas, 1993-94; ind. contbr. sr. des. engr. adv. Analog Components QIT, Dallas, 1993-94; cons. engr. to the Nat. Coun. Examiners for Engring. and Surveying, 1996. Inventor in field. Instr., cook Mormon Relief Soc., Rockwall, Tex., 1986; Christmas program com. Tex. Instruments for Hope Cottage, Dallas, 1988-89; vol. tax preparer IRS, Mesquite, Tex., 1990; fundraiser United Way, Dallas, 1990; court-appointed Spl. Advocate, Dallas CASA, 305th Dist. Ct., 1995—. Grantee in field, 1992-94; scholarship recipient; recipient Outstanding Elec. Engring. Project award IEEE, Wichita, 1976, Site Mgmt. and People's Choice award Tex. Instruments for Hope Cottage, 1989, Stretch award Tex. Instruments DSE6, 1995, 96. Mem. NSPE, Nat. Assn. Tax Practitioners (Achievers Club 1992, 93, 94, 95), Internat. Soc. Philos. Enquiry, Tex. Soc. Profl. Engrs., MENSA, Eta Kappa Nu, Tau Beta Pi. Republican. Home: 2629 Emberwood Dr Garland TX 75043-6047

CHRISTIAN, CARL FRANZ, electromechanical engineer; b. Naugatuck, Conn., May 17, 1929; s. Joseph Francis and Isabel Rose (Lizdas) C.; m. Florence Bates, May 15, 1955 (div. 1977); children: Peter Bates, Matthew Bates; m. Cynthia Belle Suntup, Apr. 15, 1977 (div. 1995). BSEE, U. Bridgeport, 1963; MS in Ocean Engring., U. R.I., 1967; MSEE, Pacific Western U., 1977, PhD in Elec. Engring., 1978. Registered profl. engr., Conn. Engr. Lewis Engring. Co., Naugatuck, Conn., 1952-64; sr. engr. electric boat div. Gen. Dynamics Co., various locations, 1964-77; systems engr. Martin Marietta Co., Cape Canaveral, Fla., 1978-87; owner, cons. C2 Engring., New London, Conn., 1987-92; ret., 1992. Mem. Elks. Home: 297 Jablo Ave Port Saint John FL 32927

CHRISTIAN, GARY IRVIN, lawyer; b. Albany, Ga., July 7, 1951; s. Rupert Irvin and Alice Amelia (Smith) C.; 1 child, Amy Margaret. BA in History, Polit. Sci., David Lipscomb Coll., 1973; MPA, U. Tenn., 1974; JD, Vanderbilt U., 1979. Bar: Fla. 1979, U.S. Dist. Ct. (no. and mid. dists.) Fla 1979. Rsch. dir. Ala. League of Mcpls., Montgomery, 1974-76; instr. in pub. adminstrn. David Lipscomb Coll., Nashville, 1977-79; assoc. Rogers, Towers, Bailey, Jones & Gay, Jacksonville, Fla., 1979-83, Foley & Lardner, Jacksonville, 1983-86; ptnr. Christian, Prom, Korn & Zehmer, Jacksonville, 1986-92, Rumph, Stoddard & Christian, Jacksonville, 1992—. Editor-in-chief Vanderbilt Jour. of Transnational Law, 1978-79. Bd. dirs. PACE Ctr. for Girls, Inc., Jacksonville, 1984—, pres., 1984-86; mem. leadership Jacksonville, 1986-87; chmn. site selection com. St. Johns County Sch. Bd., 1993-95; mem. site selection com., St. Johns County Sch. Bd., 1989-91. Mem. ABA (condominiums and planned devels. com.), Jacksonville Bar Assn. (coord. continuing edn. 1984-85, vice chmn. real property sect. 1986-87, chmn. 1987-88, chmn. corps., banking & bus. sect. 1991-92), Wavemasters Soc. (pres. 1986-87), Jacksonville C. of C. (com. 100 1986-94), Southpoint Bus. Assn. (bd. dirs. 1990—, pres. 1991-93), Oak Bridge Country Club, Seminole Club, Salt Creek Homeowners Assn. (bd. dirs. 1993—, pres. 1994-96). Republican. Mem. Ch. of Christ. Home: 1226 Salt Creek Island Dr Ponte Vedra Beach FL 32082-2541 Office: Rumph Stoddard & Christian 3100 University Blvd S Ste 101 Jacksonville FL 32216-2737

CHRISTIAN, JOHN H., librarian; b. Northport, Ala., Sept. 21, 1926; s. Levi Wilson and Zula Barringer (Abston) C.; m. Virginia Lou Stephenson, May 30, 1950; children: John M., Timothy K. AB, Samford U., 1949; MA, U. Ala., 1952; DRE, Internat. Sem., Plymouth, Fla., 1984. Minister Wadley (Ala.) Baptist Ch., 1962-74, Friendship Baptist Ch., Tallassee, Ala., 1974-76, Beulah Baptist Ch., Opelika, Ala., 1976-79, Rushenville Baptist Ch., Eclectic, Ala., 1979-82, Eagle Creek Baptist Ch., Dadeville, Ala., 1982-85, Bklyn. (Ala.) Baptist Ch., 1986-87; libr. Camden County, Woodbine, Ga., 1964-74; tchr. Wadley H.S., 1964-74. Author: Founders of St. Marys, 1989, Lesser Known Church of Paul, 1992. Served to sgt. U.S. Army, 1945-46. Mem. Rotary (archivist 1992—). Home: 413 Billyville Rd Woodbine GA 31569-9687 Office: Bryan-Lang Hist Libr PO Box 725 Woodbine GA 31569-0725

CHRISTIANSEN, LARA IRENE, journalist; b. Ridgewood, N.J., Aug. 9, 1969; d. Larry E. and Lois I. (Combs) C. BA in English and Journalism, Oral Roberts U., 1991. Pub. rels. rep. Oral Roberts U., Tulsa, 1987-91; staff writer, religion editor Broken Arrow (Okla.) Daily Ledger, 1991; staff writer, bridal editor Tulsa World, 1991—. Asst. news editor (newsletter) The Oracle, 1988-89, news editor, 1989-90, asst. features editor, 1990-91. Mem. Women in Comms., Inc., Oral Roberts U. Alumni (adv. coun.), Tulsa Press Club. Mem. Assemblies of God Ch.

CHRISTIANSON, CONRAD JOHAN, JR., retired minister, church official; b. Stoughton, Wis., Oct. 13, 1935; s. Conrad Johan and Edith Lysle (Thomas) C.; m. Eva Elisabeth Strasser, June 24, 1965; 1 child, Katrin. BA, U. Ill., 1957; BDiv, Luth. Theol. Sem., Gettysburg, Pa., 1966, STM, 1973, DMin, 1984. Ordained to ministry Luth. Ch. in Am., 1966. Min. Bethel Luth. Ch., Winchester, Va., 1966-95; retired, 1995; dean No. Valley area Luth. Ch. in Am., 1983-87; ecumenical rep. Va. Synod Evang. Luth. Ch. Am., 1988—, mem. steering com. Luth. Ecumenical Rep. Network, 1988—; mem. Va. Synod Coun., 1990-93. Bd. dirs. Cath. Charities, Winchester, 1978-81, Big Bros. Am., Winchester, 1982-89; pres. Social Svcs. Coun., Winchester, 1975, 76, Ministerial Assn./Frederick County, Va., 1982-83; chaplain W.Va. State Soc. SAR, 1983. With U.S. Army, 1958-59. Home: 580 Devland Dr Winchester VA 22603-3510

CHRISTIE, GARY FREDERICK, municipal official; b. Roanoke, Va., May 6, 1953; s. Harry Benjamin and Ruth Marie (Sutphin) C.; m. Frances Wishner, Dec. 22, 1978. BA, Hampden-Sydney Coll., 1975; MA in Spl. Studies, George Washington U., 1981. Staff asst. Rep. Ken Hechler, Washington, 1975-77; campaign mgr. Ken Hechler for Congress, Bluefield, W.Va., 1978; program mgr. Rappahannock Area Agy. on Aging, Fredericksburg, Va., 1978-79, Dist. 3 Govtl. Coop., Marion, Va., 1979-81; mgmt. analyst City of Lynchburg, Va., 1981-85, audit and analysis supr., 1985-86; city mgr. City of Princeton, W.Va., 1986-89, Town of South Boston, Va., 1989-96; exec. dir. Rappahannock-Rapidan Planning Dist. Commn., Culpeper, Va., 1996—. Mem. Rotary. Home: 503 Macoy Ave Culpeper VA 22701 Office: 211 Waters Pl Culpeper VA 22701

CHRISTIE, RICHARD GARY, plant pathologist; b. Dunedin, Fla., Aug. 24, 1934; s. William Joseph and Sibyl (Rousseau) C.; m. Elizabeth Ann Carroll, Nov. 5, 1967; children: Sibyl Carroll, Morgan Lewis. BS, U. Fla. Lab. tech. plant virus lab. U. Fla., Gainesville, prof. dept. agronomy. Auhtor monograph. With USN, 1953-54, Korea. Fellow Netherlands Ministry Agriculture, 1982. Mem. NAS, Am. Phytopathological Soc. (Ruth Allen award 1992, 93), Elks. Home: RR 2 Box 484 Alachua FL 32615-9646 Office: Univ of Florida Dept Agronomy Gainesville FL 32611

CHRISTIE, RICHARD JOEL, studio executive; b. Houston, May 14, 1962; s. Richard Joel and Winnie Jo (Jones) C.; m. Tracy Renee Taylor, Sept. 17, 1988; children: Taylor Jay, Dalton Theadore. BFA, Sam Houston State U., 1984. Sports editor TV Sta. Channel 13, Houston, 1984-85; producer, dir., dir. photography, editor Travelview Internat., Houston, 1985-88; dir. photography, editor, camera operator Studio W, Houston, 1988-92, gen. mgr., owner, 1991—; guest speaker advanced TV prodn. class Sam Houston State U., Huntsville, Tex., 990, career day Northbrook High Sch., Houston, 1982; participant Internat. Film and TV Workshops, Rockport, Maine, 1989, 90, 91. Dir. photography, editor (PBS features) A Teddy Bear Christmas, 1990 (Silver award Houston Internat. Film Festival 1990), The Heart of Things, 1990 (Bronze award Houston Internat. Film Festival 1990), Dickens-On-The-Strand, 1990 (finalist N.Y. Film Festival 1990), New Towns, 1991 (Bronze award Houston Internat. Film Festival 1991), The Joyce Gay Report, 1988—, (local cable series) Hometown Happenings, 1988—; editor (feature films) Haunted, The Hidden Jungle; numerous internat. travel documentaries, promotional videos, indsl. videos. Active Houston Livestock Show and Rodeo, 1991. Recipiant Telly award, 1990, Mercury award Nat. Media and Pub. Rels. Forum, 1989. Mem. Houston Soc. Film and Tape Profls., Tex. Film Commn., Soc. Motion Picture and TV Engrs. Republican. Methodist. Home: 5242 W Bellfort St Houston TX 77035-3030 Office: Studio W 5718 Westheimer Ste 1400 Houston TX 77057

CHRISTIE, WILLIAM GARY, finance educator; b. Toronto, Sept. 22, 1955; s. Robert Louis and Margaret Elsa (Sparling) C.; m. Kelly Maureen McNamara, July 25, 1980. B in Commerce with honors, Queen's U., Kingston, Ont., Can., 1978; MBA in Fin., U. Chgo., 1980, PhD in Fin. and Econs., 1989. Fin. analyst Hewlett-Packard (Canada) Ltd., 1980-81, Ford Motor Co. of Canada Ltd., 1981-82; rsch. asst. in statistics and fin. U. Chgo., 1983-88; asst. prof. mgmt. Vanderbilt U., Nashville, 1989-96, assoc. prof. mgmt., 1996—. Contbr. articles to profl. jours. Fellow U. Chgo., 1982-89, Social Scis. and Humanities Rsch. Coun. Can., 1982-86, Ctr. for Rsch. in Securities Prices, 1983-84; recipient Smith-Breeden award, 1995—. Mem. Am. Fin. Assn., Southwestern Fin. Assn., Western Fin. Assn., Am. Econs. Assn., European Fin. Assn. Office: Vanderbilt U Owen Grad Sch 401 21st Ave S Nashville TN 37203

CHRISTMAN, CALVIN LEE, history educator; b. Lakewood, Ohio, July 12, 1942; s. Herbert E. and Margaret R. (Burleigh) C.; m. Nina Joyce Vanderpool, Aug. 24, 1968; children: Abigail D., Alexander J. AB, Dartmouth Coll., 1964; MA and MAT, Vanderbilt U., 1966; PhD in History, Ohio State U., 1971. Instr. Middle Tenn. State U., Murfreesboro, 1966-68, Ohio State U., Columbus, 1971-72; assoc. prof. William Penn Coll., Oskaloosa, Iowa, 1972-76; prof. Mountain View Coll., Dallas, 1976-77; prof. history Cedar Valley Coll., Lancaster, Tex., 1977—; adj. assoc. prof. U. North Tex., Denton, 1991—; vis. lectr. U. Tex. at Dallas, 1978-90; vis. assoc. prof. history U. Iowa, Iowa City, spring 1976; organizer, chmn. numerous confs.; lectr. in field. Co-editor: War and the Southwest, 1992—; editl. referee Comml. and Univ. Presses, 1977—; regular book reviewer Dallas Morning News, 1977—; editl. bd. Mil. Affairs Jour., 1980-88; editor: America At War, 1995; essayist: Calculations, 1992, Guide to the Sources of United States Military History, 1975, rev. 1981; contbr. articles to profl. jours.; book reviewer Annals of Am. Acad. Polit. and Social Sci., Mid America, The Historian, Mil. Affairs, History: Reviews of New Books, Air Univ. Rev., Aerospace Historian, others. Mem. Selective Svc., Dallas, 1981—; chmn. pers. policy planning com. Dallas County Community Coll. Dist., 1979-80, chmn. history 101 competency com., 1978-79. Named Outstanding Educator of Am., 1974; Nat. Security fellow Inst. for Advanced Tech., Austin, 1991—; Franklin Roosevelt Inst. rsch. grantee, 1987, 89; Eleanor Roosevelt Inst. rsch. grantee, 1976; Ohio State U. Mershon fellow, 1968-70, doctoral fellow, 1970-71, summer rsch. grantee, 1969-70. Fellow Inter-Univ. Seminar on Armed Forces and Soc. (assoc. chmn. and southwestern regional coord. 1979—); Mem. Am. Mil. Inst. (nominating com. 1979-81, editorial adv. bd. Mil. Affairs 1980-88), Nat. Rwy. Hist. Soc., Navy League, Orgn. Am. Historians, Soc. for Historians of Am. Fgn. Rels., Soc. for Mil. History, U.S. Naval Inst., World War II Studies Assn., Phi Alpha Theta. Home: 1010 Gracelane Dr De Soto TX 75115-3302 Office: Cedar Valley Coll 3030 N Dallas Ave Lancaster TX 75134-3705

CHRISTMAS, BOBBIE JAYE, independent editor, freelance writer; b. Columbia, S.C., Sept. 18, 1944; d. Michael M. and Bernice (Mild) Rothberg; divorced, July 1983; 1 child, Sanford Lee Christmas. Student, U. S.C., 1962-64. Comm. specialist graphics dept. J.A. Jones Construction, Charlotte, N.C., 1974-76; editor Focus News, Greenville, S.C., 1976-78; account exec. Sta. WHYZ-AM, Greenville, 1978-83; supr. audio-visual dept. Leigh Mktg. Group, Greenville, 1983-84; coord. corp. comm. dept. Fluor Daniel, Greenville, 1984-87, asst. editor, reporter employee publs. dept., 1987-89, supr., editor employee publs. and media rels. dept., 1989-93; writer, editor Zebra Comm., Atlanta, 1993—; v.p., dir. S.C. Writers Workshop, Columbia, 1991-92; founder Roswell (Ga.) Writers Workshop, 1994. Contbr. articles, photography to area publs.; editor Heartbeat newsletter Greenville Cen. Area Partnership, 1988-91. Recipient 1st Pl. Writing award United Way Greenville County, 1992, 1st Pl. Nonfiction award Reader's Digest Workshop, 1991, Sandhills Writers' Conf., 1989, 1st Pl. Color award Greenville Mag., 2nd Pl. Black and White award Travelors Advisor newspaper, 1981, 2 Runners-up awards Greenville C. of C., 1989; named One of Upstate's Most Interesting People, Greenville Mag., 1986. Mem. Quest Soc. (dir. pub., rec. sec. 1989-92), Ga. Writers Inc. (bd. dirs. 1996), Women's Nat. Book Assn., Ga. Freelance Writers Assn. Office: Zebra Comm Ste 203-255 4651 Woodstock Rd Roswell GA 30075-1686

CHRISTOFF, BETH GRAVES, artist; b. Galveston, Tex., Jan. 29, 1936; d. James Warren Patterson and Wilna Margaret (Heatherly) Day; m. Lawrence D. Graves, Jr., June 22, 1954 (div. 1975); children: Jacqueline, Keith Alan, Stephen Lee; m. Nicholas Christoff, Nov. 22, 1980; 1 stepchild, Steven Gregory. Student, U. Calif., Tokyo, 1952-54, Blair Bus. Coll., Colorado Springs, Colo., 1969-70; student art, Temple Coll., 1980-84. Owner, mgr. Christoff Fashion Hideway, Belton, Tex., 1985-91; Exhibited in group shows in ctrl. Tex., 1980-96. Works exhibited in various exhbns. Ctrl. Tex., 1980-96; gallery representation The Howling Cow Gallery, Temple, Christoff Arts Studio/Gallery, Bell Fine Arts Abbey Gallery. Active Tex. Orch. Soc., Temple Civic Theatre, Friends of the Mus., Bell County Local and State Med. Auxs. Mem. Allied Artists Am. (assoc.), Pastel Soc. S.W., Am. Soc. Portrait Artists, Salado Village Artists, Bell Fine Arts, Women in the Arts, Knickerbocker Artists N.Y. (assoc.), Internat. Soc. Poets, PEO, Order Ea. Star, Rotary (Paul Harris fellow). Democrat. Methodist. Home and Studio: 312 E 22nd St Belton TX 76513-2034

CHRISTOPHER, MICHAEL MAYER, secondary education development director; b. Denver, Nov. 3, 1949; s. Charles Harry and Margaret Ann (Mayer) C.; m. Patricia A. Baldwin, Jan. 5, 1980; children: Michelle, Peter, Andrew. MusB, Cornell Coll., 1971; MA, U. Iowa, 1973; ABD, SUNY, Buffalo, 1975. Instr. music theory St. Louis (Mo.) Conservatory of Music, 1975-77, dir. admissions, registrar, 1977-84, assoc. dean, 1984-89, dir. devel., 1989-90; dir. devel. Holland Hall Sch., Tulsa, 1990—; presenter Alumni Program Coun., N.Y., 1993-94, Ind. Schs. Assn. S.W., Dallas, 1994. Composer of music. Pres. bd. dirs. Sch. Dist. of Affton, St. Louis, 1984-89; v.p. Child Abuse Network, Tulsa; pres. Mill Creek Pond Homeowners Assn., Tulsa. Mem. Coun. for Advancement and Support Edn., Nat. Soc. Fundraising Execs., LEadership Tulsa. Office: Holland Hall Sch 5666 E 81st St Tulsa OK 74137-2001

CHRISTOPHER, ROBERT PAUL, physician; b. Cleve., Apr. 27, 1932; s. Walter Matthews and Charity Marie (Roberts) C.; m. Doreen Mary O'Leary, Apr. 28, 1962; children: Robert Jr., Judith, Mark. BS, Northwestern U., 1954; MD, St. Louis U., 1959. Diplomate Am. Bd. Physical Medicine and Rehab. Chief rehab. medicine V.A. Hosp., Ann Arbor, Mich., 1963-67; asst. prof. rehab. medicine U. Mich., Ann Arbor, 1964-67; assoc. prof. rehab. medicine U. Tenn., Memphis, 1967-71, prof. rehab. medicine, 1971—; med. dirs. Les Passees Children's Rehab. Ctr., Memphis, 1976—, Le Bonheur Hosp. Rehab. Svcs., Memphis, 1981—, Regional Med. Ctr. Rehab. Svcs., Memphis, 1967—, assoc. med. dir. St. Joseph Rehab. Ctr., Memphis, 1981—. Contbg. author: Seating the Cerebral Palsey Child, 1983; author: sound/slide program Systems of Physical Therapy in Cerebral Palsy, 1971; contbr. articles to profl. jours. Pres. Mid-South Health Systems Agy., Memphis, 1980; mem. Mayor's Adv. Council for Disabled, Memphis, 1977—. Recipient Disting. Svc. Commn. on Accredited Rehab. Facilities, 1982. Fellow Am. Acad. Phys. Medicine and Rehab. (sec. 1982-88, v.p. 1992—, pres. elect 1993, pres. 1994), Am. Acad. Cerebral Palsy (pres. 1987); mem. AMA, Am. Congress Rehab. Medicine, So. Soc. Phys. Medicine and Rsch. (sec. 1976—), Am. Bd. of Phys. Medicine and Rsch. (vice chmn. 1992—), East Memphis Cath. (bd. dirs. 1969-80), K.C. (Grand Knight 1969-70). Home: 506 Thorn Ridge Cv Memphis TN 38117-3651 Office: U Tenn Coll Med 800 Madison Ave Memphis TN 38103-3400

CHRISTOPHER, THOMAS WELDON, legal educator, administrator; b. Duncan, S.C., Oct. 8, 1917; s. William Arthur and Ruby (Thomas) C.; m. Evelyn Montez Hawkins, Oct. 25, 1950 (div.); 1 son, Thomas Heflin; m. Goldie Wood Gambrell, Jan. 6, 1985. A.B., Washington and Lee U., 1939; LL.B., U. Ala., 1948; LL.M., NYU, 1950, J.S.D., 1957; LL.D., U. Ala., 1978. Bar: Ala. 1948, Ga. 1955, N.Y. 1961, N.C. 1963, N.Mex. 1968. From asst. prof. to prof. law Emory U. Law Sch., 1950-61, assoc. dean, 1954-61; atty. Corn Products Co., 1959-60; prof. law U. N.C., 1961-65; dean U. N.Mex. Law Sch., 1965-71; prof. U. Ala. Sch. Law, 1971-88; dean Sch. Law U. Ala., 1971-81, dir. Ctr. Pub. Law and Svc., 1981-85; Mem. nat. adv. food and drug council HEW, 1968-70; v.p. Food and Drug Law Found., 1974-78. Author: Poems from a Carolina Farm, 1948, (with Dunn) Special Federal Food and Drug Laws Annotated, 1951, (with others) Georgia Procedure and Practice, 1957, Constitutional Questions in Food and Drug Law, 1960, Cases and Materials on Food and Drug Law, 1966, (with Goodrich) 2d edit., 1973, Santuc-Poems, 1994. Mem. Am. Bar Assn. Club: North River Yacht. Home: 327 W Prentiss Ave Greenville SC 29605-4035 Office: U Ala Sch Law PO Box 870382 Tuscaloosa AL 35487-0382

CHRISTOPHER, WILLIAM GARTH, lawyer; b. Beaumont, Tex., Oct. 14, 1940; s. Garth Daugherty and Ollye Mittie (Harkness) C.; m. Kathleen S. Christopher; children: John William, David Noah, Michael O'Hara. BS in Engring., U.S. Mil. Acad., 1962; JD, U. Va., 1970. Bar: Va. 1970, D.C. 1970, U.S. Supreme Ct. 1975, Mich. 1977, Fla. 1988, Tex. 1989. Assoc. Steptoe & Johnson, Washington, 1970-77; ptnr. Honigman Miller Schwartz & Cohn, Detroit, 1977-94, Holland & Knight, Tampa, Fla., 1994-95, Brown Clark & Walters, P.A., Sarasota, Fla., 1995—. Contbr. articles to legal publ. Pres. Birmingham (Mich.) Hockey Assn., 1982-84; mem. Episc. Diocese of Mich. Commn. on Ministry, 1983-88, co-chmn. 1987-88, standing com., 1988. Capt. C.E. U.S. Army, 1962-67. Mem. ABA, Fed. Bar Assn., Va. Bar, D.C. Bar, Fla. Bar, Sarasota County Bar Assn., Raven Soc., Order of Coif, Phi Delta Phi. Episcopalian. Office: Brown Clark & Walters PA 1819 Main St Ste 1100 Sarasota FL 34236-5926

CHRISTOPHERSEN, DALE BJØRN, political science educator; b. Washington, Dec. 16, 1940; s. Ingolf Bjørn and Mary Elizabeth (Ducharme) C.; m. Ann Welles, Jan. 29, 1969; 1 child, Kirsten Welles. AB, Augustana Coll., Sioux Falls, S.D., 1962; MA, U. Mo., 1965; student, U. Tex., 1968; PhD, U. Mo., 1977. Rsch. asst. U. Mo., Columbia, 1962-63, teaching asst., 1963-65, 69-71; instr. polit. sci. Sul Ross State U., Alpine, Tex., 1965-68, asst. prof., 1971-77, assoc. prof., 1978-85, prof., 1985—, dir. Inst. Rsch., 1989—; bd. dirs. Westex R&D Inst., Inc., 1976-80, sec., 1977-78, pres., 1979-90; pres. Big Bend Investors, 1991; pre-law adv., 1971—. Contbr. articles to profl. jours. Del. Tex. Dem. Conv., 1974, 88, 90, 92, 94, 96; mem., vice chmn. Alpine Charter Drafting Commn., 1975-76; bd. dirs. Alpine Libr. Assn., 1981—, Hospice of the Big Bend, 1995—; chmn. Brewster County Dem. Com., 1990—. Recipient Acad. Sponsor of Yr. award Sul Ross State U., 1987. Mem. Am. Polit. Sci. Assn., N.Am. Soc. for Social Philosophy, Western Social Sci. Assn. (assoc. editor 1983-85), Western Polit. Sci. Assn., Southwestern Assn. Pre-Law Advs., Kiwanis (pres. Alpine 1980-81, sec. 1985-87, Kiwanian of Yr. award 1987), Pi Sigma Alpha, Phi Mu Alpha, Pi Kappa Delta, Phi Alpha Theta. Lutheran.

CHRISTOVICH, DANIEL JOSEPH, coast guard officer; b. Jacksonville, Fla., June 5, 1962; s. Stanley Martin and Harriet M. (Donahue) C.; m. Rebeccah Lynn Lodwick, Apr. 15, 1989; children: Heather Marie, Joshua Daniel, Zachary Joseph, Katherine Irene. BS in Ocean Engring., U.S. Coast Guard Acad., 1985. Commd. ensign USCG, Honolulu, 1985—; advanced through grades to lt. comdr. USCG, 1996; commanding officer USCG, Agana, Guam, 1987-90; officer-in-chg.law enforcement team USCG, St. Petersburg, Fla., 1990-92; staff officer USCG, Washington, 1992-95; exec. officer USCG, Mayport, Fla., 1995—. Decorated Coast Guard Commendation medal (2). Mem. Navy Mutual Aid Assn. (non-resident dir.), KC. Republican. Roman Catholic.

CHRISTY, AUDREY MEYER, public relations consultant; b. N.Y.C., Mar. 11, 1933; d. Mathias J. and Harriet Meyer; m. James R. Christy, Apr. 19, 1952; children: James R., III, Kathryn M. Smith, John T., Alysia A. Coleman, William J. BA, U. Buffalo, 1967. Pub. rels. officer Turgeon Bros., Buffalo, 1968-69; mem. pub. rels. staff Sch. Fine Arts, U. Nebr., Omaha, 1972; pub. rels. exec. Mathews & Clark Advt., Sarasota, Fla., 1974-75; profiles editor Tampa Bay mag., Tampa, Fla., 1972; pub. rels. cons. Bildex Corp., 1973-79; owner, operator Christy & Assocs., Venice, Fla., 1976—; dir. mktg. comm. Northern Trust Bank, Naples, 1994—. Trustee Big Bros./Big Sisters of Sarasota; vice chmn. Erie County March of Dimes, 1970; bd. dirs. Sarasota chpt. Am. Cancer Soc., Manasota (Pvt.) Industry Coun., 1987-89; mem. S.W. Fla. Ambulance Adv. Com., 1981; pres. Community Health Edn. Coun. Recipient various advt. awards. Mem. Pub. Rels. Soc. Am. (Outstanding Pub. Svc. award 1984), Fla. Hosp. Assn., Nat. Assn. Women Bus. Owners (charter mem. Sarasota chpt.), Sarasota County C. of C. (v.p., bd. dirs. 1990-91, vice chmn. mktg. 1984-85, 85-86, 86-87, 88-90, 90, vice chmn. 1989-90), Sarasota Manatee Press Club, LWV (editor Sarasota publ. 1978-79). Home: 216 Bayshore Cir Venice FL 34285-1407 Office: Christy & Assoc 100 W Venice Ave Ste L Venice FL 34285-1928

CHRISTY, DAVID HARDACKER, secondary school educator, music educator; b. El Reno, Okla., Sept. 4, 1955; s. Roy Myron and Mary Kathryn (Collins) C. B of Mus. Edn. summa cum laude, Southwestern Okla. State U., 1977, MEd summa cum laude, 1978. Cert. tchr., Okla., Tex. Dir. of bands Wichita County Pub. Schs., Leoti, Kans., 1978-80, Elk City (Okla.) Pub. Schs., 1980-93, Hale Ctr. Pub. Schs., 1993-95; tchr. Southeastern Okla. State U., 1995—. Mus. dir. Miss Elk City Pageant, 1981-93; dir. Elk City Concert Band Contest, 1981-93, Elk City Community Band, 1981-85, 87-93; bd. dirs. Elk City Coun. on the Arts, 1980-93, Elk City Pageant, 1986-93; dir. Hale Ctr. Music Festival, 1993-95; site chmn. Southeast Okla. Dist. Band, 1995—; bd. dirs. Western Okla. Symphony Soc., 1980-93; dir. SOSU Music Festival, 1995—. Recipient Music Dir.'s award Okla. Secondary Sch. Activities Assn., 1989, 90, 93, award Elk City C. of C., 1989. Mem. Western Okla. Symphony soc. (bd. dirs. 1980-93), Okla. Bandmasters Assn. (parliamentarian 1982-83, recording sec. 1983-84, v.p. 1984-85, pres. 1986-87), Okla. Music Educators Assn. (v.p. 1987-89), Okla. Music Adjudicators Assn. (exec. sec. 1986-93), Nat. Band Assn. (state chmn. 1985-86, rep nat. exec. bd. 1990-92, Citation of Excellence 1989, Dir. of Yr. 1989), Southwestern Okla. Band Dirs. Assn. (pres. 1983-84, Bandmaster of Yr. award 1982), Okla. Edn. Assn., Am. Sch. Band Dirs. Assn. (young band dir. of yr. 1986), Nat. Assn. Jazz Educators (Performance Cert. 1977, 78), Tex. Bandmaster's Assn., Assn. Tex. Sml. Sch. Band Dirs. (assoc.), Internat. Assn. Jazz Educators, Shortgrass Band Dirs. Assn. (pres. 1993), Music Adjudicators Assn. (exec. sec. Okla. 1986-93), Phi Beta Mu (internat. bd. dirs. 1992-94, state v.p. 1992-93), Phi Mu Alpha (Sinfonia Province Leadership award 1976), Kappa Kappa Psi (hon.). Democrat. Methodist. Home: 1201 Briarwood Ave Apt H-5 Durant OK 74701-2216 Office: Southeastern Okla State U Dept of Music Box 4047 Durant OK 74701

CHRISTY, JAMES THOMAS, public affairs executive, lawyer; b. Cin., Nov. 2, 1947; s. Thomas Perry and Mary (Vatsures) C.; m. Grace Thunborg, May 10, 1975; children: James, Diane, Caroline, Elizabeth, John, Catherine. BBA, U. Cin., 1969, JD, 1972. Legis. asst. U.S. Ho. of Reps., Washington, 1973-75, adminstrv. asst., 1975-76; pvt. practice atty. Milford, Ohio, 1976-81; counsel U.S. Ho. of Reps. Com. on Energy & Commerce, Washington, 1981-84; legis. counsel U.S. Dept. of Interior, Washington, 1984-85; mgr. fed. rels. Air Products & Chems. Inc., Washington, 1985-86, dep. dir. fed. rels., 1986-88, dir. fed. rels., 1988-93; v.p. govt. rels. TRW Inc., Arlington, Va., 1993—. Candidate 6th Congl. Dist., U.S. Congress, Ohio, 1980; chmn. bd. govs. Bryce Harlow Found. Mem. NAM (pub. affairs steering com. 1989—), Bus.-Govt. Rels. Coun., The Ohio Forum (founder), U. Cin. Coll. of Law Alumni Assn. (bd. dirs. pub. affairs coun., bd. dirs., bd. trustees). Home: 1305 Stamford Way Reston VA 20194-1315 Office: TRW Inc 1001 19th St Arlington VA 22209

CHRISTY, ROBERT ALLEN, investment broker, investment advisor; b. Butler, Pa., Feb. 22, 1956; s. Allen B. and Jane (McMinn) C.; m. Diana Lynn Hinson, June 2, 1984; children: Kenneth Robert, Ashley Lynn. BA in Econs., Grove City (Pa.) Coll., 1978. Investment broker Bache, Halsey, Stuart & Shields, Charlotte, N.C., 1982-87; v.p. investments Prudential-Bache Securities, Atlanta, 1987-90; v.p. Paine Webber, Inc., Atlanta, 1990-95, Oppenheimer & Co., Inc., 1995—; chief fin. officer Profl. Karate Assocs.; pres. North-South Ventures. Pres. Roswell Jaycees, 1990-91; chmn. North Fulton Jr. C. of C., 1991-92; Served to capt. USMC, 1978-82. Mem. Am. Mgmt. Assn., Ga. Securities Dealers Assn., N.C. Securities Dealers Assn., Internat. Assn. Fin. Planning, Ofcls. Unltd. (assoc.), Atlanta Sports Coun., Yes! Atlanta Coun., North Fulton Jr. C. of C. (chmn. 1991—), North Fulton Found. chmn. 1992), Rotary (editor Charlotte chpt. 1984-85, Paul Harris fellow 1986). Republican. Presbyterian. Office: Oppenheimer & Co Inc 1200 Monarch Plz 3414 Peachtree Rd NE Atlanta GA 30326

CHRZAN-SEELIG, PATRICIA ANN, corporate professional; b. Springfield, Mass., Mar. 3, 1954; d. Stanley Paul Jr. and Roberta Ann (Casey) Chrzan; children: H. Casey, Marguerite Andrea. BS in Human Devel., U. Mass., 1974. Dir. YWCA, Infant Day Care Ctr., Springfield, 1974-75, Tri-Cities Info. and Referral, Petersburg, Va., 1975-77; policy analyst Office of the Sec. Human Resources, Richmond, Va., 1977-78; data specialist Dept. Mental Health/Retardation, Richmond, 1978-79; programmer Sands Internat., Oakton, Va., 1979-80; owner, mgr. Preferred Custom Software, Matoaca, Va., 1980—; pres. Focused Systems, Inc., Mechanicsville, Va., 1988-93; systems engr. Pioneer-Standard Electronics, 1996—; sys. engr. Pioneer-Standard Electronics, Inc., Gaithersburg, Md., 1996—. Chmn. pack com. Crater dist. Cub Scouts Am., 1989-92; mem. St. Joseph's Sch. Bd., Petersburg, Va., 1990-95, St. Joseph Pastoral Coun., 1995-96. Mem. AAUW, NAFE. Home and Office: 9524 Eagle Cove Cir Matoaca VA 23803

CHU, LI-CHUAN, aerospace engineer, consultant; b. Chung-King, China, Feb. 8, 1949; s. Keh-Fah and Chih-Chang (Yang) C.; m. Jen-Wan Cheng, Jan 30, 1987; 1 child, Judy. Diploma engring., Taipei Inst. Tech., Taiwan, 1970; M of Engring., Old Dominion U., Norfolk, Va., 1980, PhD, 1988. Engr. Pacific Elecric Wire and Cable Corp. Ltd., Taipei, 1972-77; rsch. asst. Old Dominion U., NASA Langley Rsch. Ctr., Hampton, Va., 1978-82; engring. mgr. Systems Mgmt. Am. Corp., Norfolk, 1982-85; rsch. engr. Planning Rsch. Corp., NASA Langley Rsch. Ctr., Hampton, 1985-89; staff engr. Lockheed Engring. and Scis. Co., NASA Langley Rsch. Ctr., Hampton, 1989—; cons. Systems Mgmt. Am. Corp., Norfolk, 1985-86, C & C Technologies, Norfolk, 1989—; adj. asst. prof. Old Dominion U., Norfolk, 1988-90. Contbr. rsch. papers to profl. jours. Bd. dirs. Orgn. of Chinese Americans, Virginia Beach, Va., 1991—. With Chinese Army, 1970-72. Mem. ASME, AIAA, Soc. Mfg. Engrs. (sr.). Buddhist. Home: 1209 Botetourt Gdns Norfolk VA 23517-2201 Office: Lockheed Engring & Scis Co 144 Research Dr Hampton VA 23666-1339

CHUBBUCK, GARY MITCHELL, lawyer; b. Manhattan, Kans., Nov. 3, 1948; s. John Grafton and Syble Marie Chubbuck; m. Roberta June Lester, Aug. 9, 1975; children: John Robert, Travis Mitchell. BS, Randolph-Macon Coll., 1970; JD, U. Okla., 1975. Bar: Okla. 1975, Ill. 1978, Va. 1979, D.C. 1980. Mem. tech. staff Computer Scis. Corp., Silver Spring, Md., 1970-72; assoc. Pierce Couch Hendrickson, Oklahoma City, 1975-77, 81-82, ptnr., 1983-92; assoc. Lord, Bissell & Brook, Chgo., 1977-78, Law Offices E. Michael Paturis, Alexandria, Va., 1979-81; ptnr. Chubbuck, Bullard & Hoehner, Oklahoma City, 1992-96, Chubbuck, Chubbuck & Blew, Oklahoma City, 1996—; affiliated with Bullard & Hoehner. Mem. ABA, Okla. Bar Assn., Internat. Assn. Def. Counsel. Democrat. Home: 1709 W Irvine Dr Edmond OK 73003 Office: 3030 NW Expressway St Ste 1616 Oklahoma City OK 73112-5466

CHUDLEIGH, NORMA LANE, adult education educator, genealogy consultant; b. Houston, Aug. 13, 1938; d. Walter Harold and Elaine Bell (Painter) C. BBA, U. Houston, 1964, MEd, 1979, PhD, 1990; BS, Brigham Young U, 1971; MA, Rice U., 1981. Cert. secondary tchr., Tex.; accredited in Southern States and New Eng. Rsch. Family History Libr., Utah. Cons. family history Brigham Young U., Provo, Utah, 1968-69; br. libr. Family History Ctr., Houston, 1974-78; travel tour dir. Theil Travel, Houston, 1979-81; instr. ESL U. Houston, 1985, Houston C.C., 1986-89; v.p. Chudleigh Farms, Inc., Houston, 1990-95; propr. Genealogy Books and Consultation, Houston, 1974—; instr. Dislocated Worker Program, adult edn. United Steel Workers Am., Baytown, Tex., 1994—; mem. adv. bd. Houston C.C. Phys. Therapy, 1987-92. Author: (coloring book) Family Chase, 1981, (genogram chart) Family Patterns, 1993. Charter mem. Clayton Libr. Friends. Mem. Soc. Genealogists, Utah Geneal. Soc. (charter), Houston Geneal. Soc., Galveston County Geneal. Soc. (charter), Chaparral Geneal. Soc. (v.p. 1975-76). Republican. Mem. LDS Ch. Home: 1206 Trenton Ln Baytown TX 77520

CHUKWUMA, GODWIN NWABISI, sociology educator; b. Owerri, Imo, Nigeria, Nov. 15, 1945; came to U.S. 1979; s. Jeremiah and Benancen Ugwulo (Ozuzu) C.; m. Ada Evelyn Iboko, Aug. 13, 1983; children: Onyebuchi, Chidinma, Samuel. BS in Agrobus., Ala. A&M U., 1981, MS in Agrobus., 1983, MS in Econs., 1987; MS in Agrl. Edn., Miss. State U., 1991, PhD in Sociology, 1991. Agrl. assoc. Ministry Agr., Owerri, 1975-79; rsch. assoc. Ala. A&M U., Normal, 1982-87; asst. prof. sociology Lane Coll., Jackson, Tenn., 1992-94, Paine Coll., Augusta, Ga., 1994—. Contbr. articles to profl. publs. Usher Whole Life Ministry, Augusta, 1995—; adviser Sociology Club, Paine Coll. Augusta, 1995—; pres. African Christian Fellowship, 1995—. Mem. Am. Sociol. Assn., Mid South Sociol. Assn., Alpha Kappa Delta (pres. 1988-89). Office: Paine Coll Sociology Dept 1235 15th Street Augusta GA 30901

CHUMLEY, DONNIE ANN, business owner, consultant; b. Nacogdoches, Tex., Mar. 15, 1942; d. Vester Don and J. Erleta (Flowers) Bobo; m. Billy Warren Chumley, Aug. 23, 1958; children: Warren Don, Lanton Dan. Student, Nacogdoches Bus. Coll., 1963. Cert. fin. planner. V.p. Stone Ft. Nat. Bank, Nacogdoches, 1963-89; pres. Bobo-Chumley Lumber Co., Inc., Douglass, Tex., 1989-93, Donnie Chumley Fin. Svcs., Douglass, 1989—. Chmn. bd. Nacogdoches County Hosp. Dist., 1988-92; mem. legis. com. Atty. Gen. Child Support Enforcement, Nacogdoches, 1989-91, 93—, mem. state bd., Austin, Tex., 1990-92; bd. dirs. Nacogdoches County Aging Com., 1988—. Mem. Tex. Assn. of Bus. (workers compensation task force 1989, chmn. Pinewoods chpt.). Democrat. Baptist. Home: RR 1 Box 2975 Douglass TX 75943-9747 Office: Chumley Fin Svcs Ste 7 117 North St Nacogdoches TX 75961-5200

CHUMLEY, PHILLIP LEE, prosecutor; b. Altus, Okla., Dec. 4, 1948; s. Clyde Earl and Mildred Marie (Hamersley) C. BS, Ctrl. State U., 1976; JD, Okla. City U., 1981, MBA with honors, 1988; MA in Criminal Justice, Ctrl. Okla. U., 1987. Bar: Okla., 1980, U.S. Dist. Ct. (we. dist.) Okla. Corp. exec. S.W. Bell Telephone Co., Oklahoma City, 1970-87; pvt. practice Oklahoma City, 1987-89; social svcs. supr. Dept. of Human Svcs., Oklahoma City, 1989; staff atty. II Dept. of Human Svcs., Chickasha, Okla., 1989-91; asst. dist. atty. Dist. 23, Shawnee, Okla., 1991—. Chmn. United Way campaign, El Reno, Okla., 1976; leader Boy Scouts Am., Oklahoma City, 1982-86. Maj. USAF, 1979-83. Named Child Support Atty. of Yr. Okla. State Child Support Enforcement Assn., 1991-92. Mem. Okla. Bar Assn., Mil. Intelligence Officers Assn. Mem. Ch. of Christ. Office: Dist Atty 130 Broadway St Ste 300 Shawnee OK 74802

CHUPIK, EUGENE JERRY, business executive, financial consultant; b. Temple, Tex., Jan. 22, 1931; s. Jerry Joe and Annie E. Chupik; m. Betty Lou Fletcher, Feb. 2, 1957; children: Stephen, Donald. BBA, U. Tex., Austin, 1957. Auditor, Peat, Marwick, Mitchell & Co., Dallas, 1957-61; comptroller Vantex Enterprises, Inc., Dallas, 1961-64, v.p., 1964-66, exec. v.p., 1966—, pres., CEO, 1987—. With USN, 1949-54. Mem. Petroleum Accts. Soc., Dallas C. of C., Nat. Fedn. Ind. Bus., Real Estate Fin. Execs. Assn., Stemmons Corridor Bus. Assn. (Dallas, bd. dirs.). Republican. Methodist. Club: Northwood Country (Dallas). Home: 4500 Stanhope St Dallas TX 75205-1667 Office: Vantex Enterprises Inc 1825 W Mockingbird Ln Dallas TX 75235-5012

CHUPP, RAYMOND JEFFERY, mortgage banker; b. Rome, Ga., July 21, 1966; s. Raymond O. and Mary Ann Chupp. Student, Northside Inst., Atlanta, 1985-86. Salesman Dan Forsyth Realty, Rockmart, Ga., 1986-90; chmn. bd. dirs. R.J. Chupp & Co., Inc., Rockmart, Ga., 1990—; cons. Bait-O-Matic Corp., Jackson, Ga., 1992—, SunStates Mortgage Corp., Atlanta, 1992—. Mem. Cartersville-Bartow County C. of C. (edn. com. 1993, leadership com. 1993), Kiwanis (v.p. Rockmart 1989). Republican. Baptist. Home: 183 Springdale Rd Rockmart GA 30153-2751 Office: SunStates Mortgage Corp 3300 Northeast Expy NE Ste 7E Atlanta GA 30341-3938

CHURCH, GEORGE MILLORD, real estate executive; b. Philadelphia, Miss., Sept. 21, 1924; s. George W. and Maggie (Smith) C.; m. Ruth Green, Nov. 12, 1948; children: Ray, Gary. Diploma in acctg., So. Bus. Coll., 1947; AA with honors, Meridian (Miss.) Jr. Coll., 1954; BA in History and Polit. Sci., Coll. of Ozarks, 1957; disting. grad., U.S. Army Noncommd. Officer's Acad., 1961; grad., Realtor's Inst., 1971; postgrad., U. Miss., 1976. Boatswain's mate 1st class USN, South Pacific, 1942-46; shipfitter Ala. Dry Dock and Ship Bldg., Mobile, 1946; acct. Milton Supply Co., Meridian, 1948-50; staff sgt. USMC, Camp Pendelton, Calif., 1950-51, Meridian, 1953-54; chief acct. Meridian Grain and Elevator Co., 1951-52; cost acct. Flintkote Co., Meridian, 1952-53; enlisted U.S. Army, 1954, advanced through grades to command sgt. maj., 1968, served in Vietnam, retired, 1969; pres. Church Realty Co., Meridian, 1969—; instr. real estate, real estate math Meridain Jr. Coll. Chmn. Toys for Tots, Meridian, 1954; active Lauderdale County Planning Commn., 1980-84, past chmn.; active VFW Home for Children: charter mem. Rep. Presdl. Task Force, Washington, 1982—. Decorated 3 Bronze Star medals, Air medal, Gallantry Cross with Palm (Republic of South Vietnam), Gallantry Cross with Silver Star. Mem. Miss. Assn. Realtors (bd. dirs. 1972-73, 91, past chmn. profl. stds. com., coord. FHA and VA com.), Meridian Bd. Realtors (pres. 1972-73, 91, bd. dirs. 1972-73, 91, chmn. legis. and polit. action com., bd. congl. coord., Realtor of Yr. 1973, 89), Realtors Polit. Action Com. (life), Navy League U.S. (life, commodore), VFW (life, Nat. Home for Children), Am. Legion (life), NRA, SCV (life, comdr. Camp 1221, 1992, 93, chief of staff Miss. divsn. 1993, 94, comdr./founder Camp 1649, 1994, brigade comdr., Miss. divsn. 1995), Jefferson Davis Soc. (co-founder, sec.-treas. 1994). Baptist. Home: 4200 Pineview Dr Meridian MS 39305-3345 Office: Church Realty Co PO Box 224 Meridian MS 39302-0224

CHURCH, RANDOLPH WARNER, JR., lawyer; b. Richmond, Va., Nov. 6, 1934; s. Randolph Warner and Elizabeth Lewis (Gochnauer) C.; m. Lucy Ann Canary, July 4, 1970; children: Leslie R. Pennell, L. Weeks Kerr. BA with honors, U. Va., 1957, LLB, 1960. Bar: Va. 1960, U.S. Dist. Ct. (ea. dist.) Va. 1962, U.S. Ct. Appeals (4th cir.) 1981. Assoc. McCandlish, Lillard & Marsh, Fairfax, Va., 1960-63; ptnr. McCandlish, Lillard, Rust & Church, Fairfax, 1963-75; city atty. Fairfax, 1968-72; mng. ptnr. McCandlish, Lillard, Rust & Church, Fairfax, 1975-83; mng. ptnr. Hunton & Williams, Fairfax, 1984—, mem. exec. com., 1988-94; bd. dirs. George Mason Bank, George Mason Bankshares, Inc., George Mason Mortgage Co., 1991—, Va. Found. for Rsch. and Econ. Edn., Inc., 1994—. Author: Appellate Civil Litigation, 1984; panelist: Lawyer Professionalism: Is Change in Order? 1988, Marketing Legal Services: What's Hot and What's Not, 1990. Active Fairfax Com. of 100, 1988—, bd. dirs., 1989-92; bd. visitors George Mason U., Fairfax, 1982-90, rector, 1983-86; bd. dirs. George Mason Fund for Arts, 1987-96, Fairfax Symphony, 1991—, gen. counsel, exec. com., 1996—; bd. dirs. Va. Found. for Humanities and Pub. Policy, 1993; vice pres., exec. com. Va. Found. for Rsch. and Econ. Edn., 1996—; lectr., author Va. Continuing Edn. Program Appellate Litigation, 1985, Equity Practice, 1987-90; panelist Va. Continuing Edn. Programs; trustee George Mason U. Edn. Found., 1986-95, trustee emeritus, 1995—. Fellow Va. Law Found., Am. Bar Found.; mem. ABA, Am. Judicature Soc., Va. Bar Assn. (v.p. 1975), Tower Club, Country Club Fairfax County, U. Va. Club, Phi Beta Kappa. Episcopalian. Home: 5114 Forsgate Pl Fairfax VA 22030-4507 Office: Hunton & Williams Ste 1700 1751 Pinnacle Dr Ste 1700 Mc Lean VA 22102

CHURGIN, MICHAEL JAY, law educator; b. N.Y.C., Feb. 25, 1948; s. Raphael B. and Sylvia (Nussbaum) C. AB magna cum laude, Brown U., Providence, 1970; JD, Yale U., 1973. Bar: Conn. 1974, Tex. 1975. Supervising atty., teaching fellow Yale Law Sch., New Haven, 1973-75; asst. prof. U. Tex. Sch. Law, Austin, 1975-79, assoc. prof., 1979-81, prof., 1981-90, Raybourne Thompson prof., 1990—; bd. dirs. Legal Aid Soc. Cen. Tex., Austin; mem. adv. bd. Advocacy, Inc., Austin, 1985-90; vis. fellow Clare Hall, Cambridge, Eng., 1996; vis. fellow Wolfson Coll., Cambridge, Eng., 1992. Co-author: Toward a Just and Effective Sentencing System, 1977; author: (monograph) Analysis of the Texas Mental Health Code, 1988, 2d edit., 1994; contbr. articles to profl. jours. Mem. pub. responsibility com. Austin Travis County MHMR, 1979-85. Fellow W.K. Kellogg Nat. Found., 1980-83. Mem. Am. Soc. for Legal History (chair com. 1987—), Phi Beta Kappa. Jewish. Home: 3203 Oakmont Blvd Austin TX 78703-1345 Office: U Tex Sch Law 727 E 26th St Austin TX 78705-3224

CIANO, JAMES FRANCIS, computer systems analyst; b. Everett, Mass., Nov. 7, 1944; s. Salvatore George and Antoinette Teresa (Fraumeni) C.; m. Nancy Katherine Spriggs, Aug. 7, 1971. AA in Bus. Adminstrn., Edison C.C., 1992; postgrad., U. South Fla. Photographer Sharon Studios, Boston, 1966-84; salesman Country Living Real Estate, Salem, N.H., 1971-84; prin. N & J Realty Co., Naples, Fla., 1986-90; design analyst Computer Solutions, Naples, 1991—; founder Jim Ciano Pub. and Writer's Agy., Naples; freelance photographer, 1959-84. Active Crime Stop, Salem, 1986. Mem. Fla. Motion Picture and TV Assn., Naples Area Bd. Realtors, Masons, Scottish Rite, Shriners, Phi Theta Kappa (pres. 1991-92, named Phi Theta Kappan of Yr. 1992), Phi Beta Lambda (v.p. 1990-92, State Champion award mgmt. info. systems and bus. law 1992), Phi Sigma Omega (founding father, historian 1992). Address: 5341 6th Ave SW Naples FL 33999-2835

CIARULA, THOMAS ALAN, engineer, retired navy officer; b. Pottstown, Pa., July 6, 1948; s. Patrick Joseph and Gloria (Royal) C.; m. Nancy Ann Duruttya, Sept. 1, 1979; 1 child, Cristina Marie. BS in Aircraft Maintenance Engring., Northrop U., 1971; MS in Adminstrn., Ctrl. Mich. U., 1992. Commd. ensign USN, 1972, advanced through grades to comdr., 1987; aircraft div. officer Attack Squadron 37, NAS Cecil Field, Fla., 1973-75; maintenance control officer Naval Air Facility Kadena, Okinawa, Japan, 1975-77; line div. officer Antarctic Devel. Squadron 6, Pt Mugu Ca, Antarctica, 1977-79; maintenance control officer USS Forrestal, FPO Miami, Fla., 1979-82; wing maintenance officer Tng. Air Wing 3, NAS Chase Field, Tex., 1982-85; aircraft intermediate maintenance dept. officer Naval Air Sta., Key West, Fla., 1985-88; TASM class desk officer, cruise missiles project Navair Systems Command, Washington, 1988-89, dir. logistics, cruise missiles project, 1989-92; asst. dep. program mgr. tng. sys. PMA-205 Naval Air Systems Command, Washington, 1992-94; dep. program mgr. for software devel. PMA-270 Naval Aviation Logistics Command Mgmt. Info. Sys., Washington, Va., 1994; ret., 1994; sr. engr. HJ Ford Assocs. Inc., Arlington, Va., 1994-95; sr. supportability engr. fed. bus. unit Template Software, Inc., Arlington, 1995—. Vol. EMT, Sugarloaf Vol. Fire Dept., Sugarloaf Key, Fla., 1985-88, Burke Vol. Fire Dept., 1988-95. Republican. Roman Catholic. Home: 10924 Middlegate Dr Fairfax VA 22032-3018 Office: Template Software Inc Fed Bus Unit Ste 700 1735 Jefferson Davis Hwy Arlington VA 22202

CICALA, ROGER STEPHEN, physician, educator; b. Parkersburg, W.Va., Aug. 21, 1956; s. Edmond D. and Ann (Pettit) C.; m. Shari Lee Miller, Mar. 17, 1982 (div. Dec. 1989); children: Kristin Pettit, Paul Andrew. BS in Biology, Christian Bros. Coll., Memphis, 1978; MD, U. Tenn., Memphis, 1982. Diploamte Am. Bd. Anesthesiology, Am. Bd. Med. Examiners. Intern dept. surgery U. Tenn., 1982-83, chief resident, 1985, from instr. to asst. prof., 1987-90, assoc. prof. anesthesiology, 1990-94, dir. pain ctr., 1988-94; pvt. practice Memphis, 1986-87; med. author, illustrator, 1994—; anesthesiology staff Memphis Neuroscis. Ctr., 1986-87; dir. trauma anesthesia Elvis Presley Trauma Ctr., Memphis, 1988-92, mem. staff, 1987-94; mem. staff Meth. Hosp. Memphis, 1986-94, Eastwood Med. Ctr., Memphis, 1991-94; presenter in field. Author: (with others) Courtroom Medicine: Pain and Suffering, 1991, Geriatric Anesthesiology, 1992, Textbook of Trauma Anesthesia and Critical Care, 1992, Headache: Diagnosis and Interdisciplinary Treatment, 1992, Refresher Course in Anesthesiology, vol. 20, 1992, Handbook of Trauma Surgery, 1993, Manual of Trauma Anesthesia, 1993, The Heart Disease Handbook, 1996; editor: (with others) Textbook of Trauma Anesthesia and Critical Care, 1992, and others. Mem. AAAS, AMA, Am. Soc. Anesthesiologists, Am. Pain Soc., Internat. Soc. Study of Pain, Internat. Trauma Anesthesia and Critical Care Soc. (co-chmn. task force 1991-93), Internat. Anesthesia Rsch. Soc., Tenn. Med. Assn., Tenn. Soc. Anesthesiologists, Shely County Med. Soc., Shelby County Anesthesia Soc., Soc. Cardiovascular Anesthesiologists, Soc. Pain Practice Mgmt. (bd. dirs. 1991-94), Assn. U. Anesthesists. Home: 3080 Walnut Grove Rd Apt 401 Memphis TN 38111-3521

CICCONE, ALVIN JACOB, physician; b. Dec. 4, 1936; m. Bonnie Ciccone; children: Christopher, Grace. BS in Biology, Emory and Henry Coll., 1959; MD, Med. Coll. Va., 1964. Diplomate Am. Bd. Family Practice. Intern Norfolk Gen. Hosp., 1964-65, resident in gen. practice, 1965-66; ptnr. Hayes and Ciccone, Norfolk, 1968-75, Ciccone and Lewis, Norfolk, 1975-76; pvt. practice Norfolk, 1976-77; dir. Student Health Svc. Old Dominion U., Norfolk, 1977—; ptnr. Ciccone and Sokol, Norfolk, 1977-80, Ciccone, Sokol and Snider, Norfolk, 1980—; assoc. prof. family medicine Ea. Va. Med. Sch., Norfolk, 1984—; med. dir. family health project Sta. WVEC-TV, Norfolk, 1991—; reviewer of physicians St. Paul Ins. Co., 1982—, Va. Reciprocal Ins. Co., 1982— Doctor's Reciprocal Ins. Co., 1991—, Colonial Va. Profl. Review Orgn., 1991—; hosp. affiliations include Sentara Norfolk Gen. Hosp.,

Norfolk, Sentara Leigh Meml. Hosp., Norfolk, Children's Hosp. of Kings Daus., Norfolk, DePaul Hosp., Norfolk; mem. adv. com. state bd. nursing State Bd. Medicine Va., 1983-85, mem. several audit rev. panels, 1983—, nominated to serve state bd. medicine 1991); founding mem., bd. dirs. Traveler's Health Network, 1984—; numerous coms. Optima Health Maintenence Orgn., 1985—; pres. med. staff Sentara Norfolk Gen. Hosp., 1985-86, med. staff rep. on long range planning com., 1985—, med. staff rep. quality, 1985-91; apptd. mem. staff Sentara Leigh Meml. Hosp.; mem. Priority Health Plan, 1992—, Sentara Health Plan, 1992. Editor Housecalls newsletter, 1985—; mem. editorial bd. Pathways in Dermatology, 1993—. Team physician Norfolk Acad., 1982-85, Maury H.S., 1968-80; originator, founder Student Health Svc., Old Dominion Un., 1976-77; originator, dir. required physicals for all sports Norfolk Acad. and Old Dominion U., 1984—; lay bd. dirs. Larchmont United Meth. Ch., 1984-87, parish rels. com., 1986-91, 94-97, bd. dirs. Ch. Found., 1987-90; chmn., trustee, 1991—; asst. program dir., counselor YMCA Camp Ockinickon, Medford Lakes, N.J., 1953-60. Capt. USAF, 1966-68. Recipient Physician Recognition award AMA, 1977, Humanitarian of Yr. award, Emory and Henry Coll., 1994; named Va. Family Physician of Yr., 1988, Emory and Henry Coll. Alumnus of Yr., 1989. Fellow Am. Acad. Family Physicians (mktg. and pub. rels. com. 1990—, chmn. 1994, regional reviewer 1993); mem. AMA, Med. Soc. Va., Seabord Med. Assn. Va. and N.C. (v.p. 1988-92, pres. 1992-93), Va. Acad. Family Physicians (treas. 1982-93, treas. 1983-84, chmn. state sci. assembly 1983, v.p. 1984-85, pres. elect 1985-86, pres. 1986-87, fin. com. 1987-93, vice speaker congress dels. 1988—, chmn. pub. rels. com. 1989—), Norfolk Acad. Medicine (del. Med. Soc. Va. 1978-81, 83-86, 90—, ethics com. 1983-86, ad hoc com. workman's compensation 1988—, chmn. constn. and bilaws coms. 1989—, bd. dirs. Tidewater Physicians Assn. 1990—, bd. dirs. teenage awareness com. Hampton Rds. 1992—), Tidewater Acad. Physicians (treas. 1968-69, sec. 1969-71, v.p. 1971-72, pres. 1972-73, dir. On Call 1987—), Va. Acad. Family Physicians (chmn. membership and credentials com. 1979-83, bd. dirs. 1979-83). Office: 5205 Colley Ave Norfolk VA 23508-2043

CICET, DONALD JAMES, lawyer; b. New Orleans, May 24, 1940; s. Arthur Alphonse and Myrtle (Ress) C.; m. Iona Perry. BA, Nicholls State U., 1963; JD, Loyola U., New Orleans, 1969. Bar: La. 1969, U.S. Dist. Ct. (ea. dist.) La. 1972, U.S. Dist. Ct. (mid. dist.) La. 1978, U.S. Dist. Ct. (we. dist.) La. 1979, U.S. Ct. Appeals (5th cir.) 1972, U.S. Supreme Ct. 1972. Pvt. practice Reserve, La., 1969-88, LaPlace, La., 1988—; staff atty. La. Legis. Coun., 1972-73; legal counsel Nicholls State U. Alumni Fedn., 1974-76, 78-80; spl. counsel Pontchartrain Levee Dist., 1976—; administrv. law judge La. Dept. Civil Svc., 1981—. Mem. St. John the Bapt. Parish Emergency Planning Com., 1987—; pres. Boys' State of La. Inc., 1990-92, bd. dirs., 1988—. With AUS, 1964, USNG, 1964-70. Recipient Am. Jurisprudence award Loyola U., 1968. Fellow La. Bar Found.; mem. ABA, La. Bar Assn. (ho. dels. 1973-77, 79-85), 40th Jud. Dist. Bar Assn. (pres. 1985-87), ATLA, La. Trial Lawyers Assn., Am. Judicature Soc., Nicholls State U. Alumni Fedn. (exec. coun. 1972-76, 77-85, pres. 1982, James Lynn Powell award 1980), Am. Legion (post cmdr. 1976-77, dist. judge adv. 1975-95, judge adv. La. dept. 1990-92, 93-96, mem. La. dept. commn. on nat. security and govtl. affairs 1974-89, chmn. 1977-78, 79-81, 85-89, M.C. Gehr blue cap award 1983). Roman Catholic. Home: 116 Dave St Reserve LA 70084 Office: 197 Belle Terre Blvd PO Box 461 La Place LA 70069

CICOLANI, ANGELO GEORGE, research company executive, operating engineer; b. Norwood, Mass., Mar. 4, 1933; s. Luigi and Maria (Fossa) C.; m. Marilyn Adell Griffith, June 4, 1955 (div. 1968); children: George, Susanne, Diana; m. Patricia Anne Kirsch, Nov. 1, 1979 (dec. July 1995). Student Northeastern U., 1950; B.S., U.S. Naval Acad., Annapolis, Md., 1955; Profl. Cert., Advanced Nuclear Power Sch., 1960; B.S., Naval Postgrad. Sch., 1969. Commd. ensign U.S. Navy, 1955, advanced through grades to lt. comdr., 1975, chief reactor operator, 1958-62, exec. officer, 1963-67, systems analyst, Arlington, Va., 1969-75; cons. Arlington, 1975-77; sr. reseacher R&D Assocs., Arlington, 1977-82, program mgr., 1977-88, sr. scientist, 1982-87, tech dir. Springfield rsch. facility, 1988—. Author: The Role of Systems Analysis, 1974. Author, editor Mineral Minutes Jour., 1972 (best newsletter 1974); designer Low Speed Ram-Jet, 1954 (Inst. Aero. Scis. 1st Place award). Pres. emeritus bd. dirs. Dumbarton Concert Series, Washington, 1982—. Mem. Ops. Rsch. Soc. Am., Naval Inst., Mineral Soc. D.C. (pres. 1972-77), Ret. Officers Assn., Nature Conservancy. Office: PO Box 1220 Springfield VA 22151-0220

CILEK, JAMES EDWIN, medical and veterinary entomologist; b. Crown Point, Ind., July 1, 1952; s. Edwin James and Bernice Ruth (Burkley) C. BS, Purdue U., 1974; MS, La. State U., 1981; PhD, U. Ky., 1989. Cert. Am. Registry Profl. Entomologists. Dir. East Flagler Mosquito Control Dist., Flagler Beach, Fla., 1975-78; grad. rsch. asst. La. State U., Baton Rouge, 1979-81; pest control inspector East Baton Rouge Mosquito/Rodent Control Dist., 1981-82; grad. rsch. asst. U. Ky., Lexington, 1983-89, postdoctoral scholar, 1989-92; rsch. assoc. Southwest Kans. Rsch. Extension Ctr., Garden City, Kans., 1992-93; rsch. assoc. J.A. Mulrennan Sr. Arthropod Rsch. Lab. Fla. A&M U., Panama City, 1993—; manuscript reviewer Am. Mosquito Control Assn., Entomol. Soc. Am.; cons. Quest Engring., Inc., Lexington, 1991-94. Contbr. to profl. publs. Grantee Nat. Agrl. Pesticide Impact Assessment Program, 1988, 89, 91, 92. Mem. Entomol. Soc. Am., Am. Mosquito Control Assn., Ky. Mosquito/Vector Control Assn. (asst. editor jour.), Fla. Mosquito Control Assn. Democrat. Home: 2175 Frankford Ave Apt A202 Panama City FL 32405-2301 Office: JA Mulrennan Sr Arthropod Rsch Lab 4000 Frankford Ave Panama City FL 32405-1933

CILELLA, SALVATORE GEORGE, JR., museum director; b. Chgo., Oct. 19, 1941; s. Salvatore G. and Mary Genevieve (LaRocque) C.; m. Mary Winifred Broucek, Aug. 29, 1970; children: Salvatore G. III, Peter Dominic. BA, U. Notre Dame, 1963, MA in Am. History, 1966; MA in Hist. Mus. Tng., SUNY, Oneonta, 1971. Community amb. Experiment in Internat. Living, Iran, 1965; exec. dir. No. Ind. Hist. Soc., South Bend, 1970-72; registrar, asst. dir. N.Y. State Hist. Assn., Cooperstown, 1973-76; exec. dir. Historic Bethlehem (Pa.) Inc., 1976-79; dir. devel. and membership Old Sturbridge (Mass.) Village, 1979-81; devel. officer Smithsonian Instn., Washington, 1981-87; exec. dir. Columbia (S.C.) Mus. Art, 1987—; cons. various mus., 1979—; overseer Old Sturbridge Village, 1982-89; lectr. Seminar for Hist. Adminstrn., Williamsburg, Va., 1983—, Mus. Mgmt. Program, Boulder, Colo., 1993. Editor Collections mag.; contbr. articles to profl. jours. 1st lt. U.S. Army, 1966-69. Decorated Army commendation medal, 1969. Mem. Am. Assn. Mus. (chmn. devel. and membership com. 1984-89, bd. dirs. 1989-92), Am. Hist. Print Collectors Assn., Assn. Art Mus. Dirs., Wildewood Country Club, Rotary. Roman Catholic. Office: Columbia Mus Art 1112 Bull St Columbia SC 29201-3703

CIMA, BROOKS DEMENT, art educator; b. Pt. Arthur, Tex., Feb. 3, 1957; d. Marvin Raye and Shirley M. (Haydel) Dement; m. Dennis Louis Cima, July 11, 1987; 1 child, Caitlin Raye. BS in Dance, Lamar U., 1979, tchr. cert., 1987. Cert. tchr. art K-12, Fla., cert. tchr. art K-12, secondary dance, Tex. Instr. dance dept. Lamar U., Beaumont, Tex., 1979; tchr., owner Brooks Dement's Dance Factory, Pt. Arthur, 1979-87; dance tchr. Magnet Sch. Woodrow Wilson Mid. Sch., Pt. Arthur, 1984-87; artistic dir., founder Applause Jazz Dance Theatre, Panama City, Fla., 1987-89; art tchr. Hiland Park Elem. Bay County Ind. Sch. Dist., Panama City, 1987-89; art tchr., chair fine arts dept., drill team instr. Waller (Tex.) H.S., Waller Ind. Sch. Dist., 1989-91; art tchr. Cimarron Elem. Sch. Katy (Tex.) Ind. Sch. Dist., 1991-94, art tchr. West Meml. Elem. Sch., 1994—; dance tchr. Step in Time Studio, Katy, 1991—; bd. dirs. Bus. Growth Network, Katy; cons. Renaissance Finishes/Katy, 1991—; presenter, instr. Kindergarten Tchrs. of Tex. State Conf., Houston, 1993, Dance Troupe, Inc., 1981-85. Choreographer: (ballet) The Legend of the Lake, 1986; dir., choreographer: (opera) H.M.S. Pinafore, 1994; dir. Into the Woods, 1994; choreographer 12 shows for comty. theatre groups, 1979—. Supt. of edn. Living Word Luth. Ch., 1993-96; bd. dirs. Cimarron PTA, Katy, 1992-94; reflections chmn. Katy coun. PTA, 1994-95. Named Houston West Tchr. of Yr., Houston West C. of C., 1993-94, Outstanding Spl. Area Tchr., Assn. of Bay County Educators, 1989. Mem. Nat. Art Edn. Assn., Dance Masters Am., Tex. State Tchrs. Assn., Tex. Art Educators Assn., Houston Art Educators Assn. Lutheran.

CIMINIERI, UBALDO TOMAS, industrial engineer; b. Rasario, Argentina, Sept. 28, 1949; came to the U.S., 1966; s. Ubaldo and Nydia Esther (Ramos) C.; m. Dona Fay Clark, Mar. 4, 1972; children: Ubaldo III, Jason Ray, Jonathan Andres. BS in Physics, Washburn U., 1972; MS in Indsl. Engring., Cleve. State U., 1974. Registered profl. engr., Tex. Project engr. A.G. McKee Engring. and Constrn., Cleve., 1974-77; start-up mgr. A.G. McKee Engring. and Constrn., Pto. Ordaz, Venezuela, 1977-78; sr. project engr., engring. mgr. Davy McKee Internat., Cleve. and Mexico City, 1978-83; project mgr. The Pritchard Co., Overland, Kans., 1984-92, M.W. Kellogg Co., Houston, 1992—. Coach Udinese Soccer Club, 1985-92, Texans Soccer Club, 1992—. 1st lt. Argentinian mil., 1962-66. Mem. Project Mgmt. Inst. Home: 1630 Hoveden Dr Katy TX 77450-4902

CIMINO, RICHARD DENNIS, lawyer; b. Omaha, Nebr., June 6, 1947; s. Lewis Raymond and Louise (Monaco) C.; m. Mary Scott Reins, Feb. 12, 1977; children: John Damon, Mary Drusilla, Robert Andrew, Ann Marie. BBA, U. Notre Dame, 1969; JD, St. Louis U., 1974. Bar: Nebr. 1975, U.S. Dist. Ct. Nebr. 1975, Kans. 1989, U.S. Dist. Ct. Kans. 1989, Fla. 1994. Assoc. Kutak, Rock & Campbell, Omaha, 1975-78, ptnr., 1979; v.p., gen. counsel Silvey Refrigerated Carriers, Omaha, 1980-86, pres., 1987; ptnr. Dwyer, Pohren, Wood, Heavey & Grimm, Omaha, 1988-89; sole practice St. Marys, Kans., 1989-93; ptnr. Treadwell, Stetler, Erickson, Cimino & McElrath, Naples, Fla., 1993—. Editor St. Louis U. Law Jour., 1972-74. Bd. dirs. Bergan Mercy Hosp. Found., Omaha, 1986-87. With U.S. Army, 1969-71, Vietnam. Mem. Fla. Bar Assn., Kans. Bar Assn., Nebr. Bar Assn., Notre Dame Alumni Club (pres. Omaha chpt. 1980), Alpha Sigma Nu. Republican. Roman Catholic. Office: 4001 Tamiami Trl N Naples FL 34103-3556

CINCA, SILVIA (ROBERTA KING), writer, producer; b. Bucharest, Romania; came to U.S., 1977; d. Stephan Niculescu and Alexandrina (Mosu) Niculescu; married, Feb. 19, 1968; children: Robert, Shelby. Grad., Inst. I.L. Caragiale, Inst. Dramatic Art & Cinema, 1960, Tex. U., 1978-79, No. Va. C.C., 1979-80, Amb. Bible Coll., 1992. Editor, film critic, TV sect. Romanian Nat. Broadcasting Sys., 1960-73. Author in Romanian lang.; The Cat and The Words, 1966, Destroy the Mirrors, 1989, The Non-Stop Express, 1971, The Unseen Snow, 1973, Scream, 1989, X Ray for Love, (Romfest award Can. 1992), 1992, The Ocean, 1992, X Ray for Success, 1993 (Contact Internat. award 1993), Himera: (as Roberta King) Leaves on Route 7, 1993; author in Eng. lang.: The Night of the Rising Dead, 1985, Comrade Dracula (ARA award 1988), Homo Spiritus (ARA award 1988), 1988, Scream, Romania Ceausescu's Era, 1990, Hoot of the Owl; contbr. articles to Romanian periodicals; founder Moonfall Press. Mem. Am. Romanian Acad., Pen Am. Writers Club, LiterArt-XII Internat. Assn. Romanian Writers and Artists. Home: 7845 Glenister Dr Springfield VA 22152-2007

CINI, ANTHONY RICHARD, bookbinding craftsman; b. Johnston, R.I., May 5, 1922; s. Egisto and Raffaela (Compagnone) C.; m. Marie Dougherty, June 24, 1944 (div. 1978); children: Anthony Jr., Maryann, Robert D., Katherine, Diane. Educated, ATT La Salle Acad., Providence, 1939-41. Supr., master craftsman E. Cini Bookbinding, Providence, 1936-43, 45-47; journeyman Novelty Bindery, Phila., 1948-51, Sinneckson & Chew, Camden, N.J., 1951-53; master craftsman South Jersey Bindery, Thorofare, N.J., 1954-78, Cini Bookbinding, North Miami, Fla., 1979-87; cons. in field; lectr., condr. bookbinding demonstrations. Prin. works include restoration of rare volumes for The Vatican, Pres. H. Truman, Pres. R. Nixon, King George of Eng. VI, Walt Disney, Greek Royal Family, Queen Elizabeth II, and many more. Bd. dirs. Disabled Am. Veterans, Ft. Lauderdale, Fla.; neighborhood commr., scoutmaster Boy Scouts of Am. (40 yrs. of svc.). Served with USN, 1943-45. Recipient Cert. of Appreciation and Merit award, Jaycees, 1978, Kiwanis, 1985. Mem. DAV (life), Dante Alighieri Cultural Soc. Miami (bd. dirs.), C. of C. Lodge: K.C. Home: 18114 SE 17th St Silver Springs FL 34488-6301

CINTRON, GUILLERMO B., cardiologist, medical educator; b. San Juan, P.R., Mar. 28, 1942; s. Guillermo A. and Rosa L. (Silva) C.; children: Guillermo C. Jr., Francisco, Michael. BS in Biology cum laude, U. P.R., 1963; MD, Loyola U., 1967. Cert. Nat. Bd. Med. Examiners, Am. Bd. Internal Medicine (cardiology subspecialty). Intern George Washington U. Hosp., Washington, 1967-68; resident VA Hosp., Washington, 1970-71, Georgetown U. Hosp., Washington, 1971-72; cardiology fellow VA Hosp., Washington, 1972-74; clin. instr. medicine U. P.R. Sch. Medicine, San Juan, 1975-77, asst. prof., 1977-81, assoc. prof. medicine, 1982-83; assoc. prof. medicine/cardiology U. South Fla. Coll. Medicine, Tampa, Fla., 1983-94; prof. medicine/cardiology U. South Fla. Coll. Medicine, Tampa, 1994—, assoc. dir. divsn. cardiology dept. internal medicine, 1987—; staff cardiologist VA Hosp., San Juan, dir. coronary care unit, 1976-82; cons. in cardiology Lafayette Hosp., Arroyo, P.R., 1976-89, Roosevelt Rds. Naval Hosp., Ceiba, P.R., 1975-82; chief cardiology sect. VA Hosp., Tampa, 1983—; staff Gen. Hosp., 1983—, cardiac transplant com., 1985—, cardiology devel. com., 1989, chmn. heart transplant rsch. com., 1991-92; med. editl. cons. T. McBrian Publs. Inc., N.Y.C., 1983-89; mem. various cmty. coll. medicine U.S.F., 1986—, deans com. task force cardiovascular svcs., 1988-90, rep. faculty assn., 1991-93; mem. Working Group Cardiac Transplant Physicians, 1989—; cons. Palm Beach (Fla.) Med. Cons., 1990-94, Global Air Charter, Tampa, 1994-95; ad hoc com. Tampa Gen. Hosp., 1991—; mem. VA Nat. Organ Specific (Heart) Transplant Bd., 1992—. Reviewer: Boletin, Assoc. Medica de Puerto Rico, 1976-90, Am. Jour. Cardiology, 1986—, Circulation, 1991—, Jour. Am. Coll. Cardiology, 1993—; contbr. articles to profl. jours. Lt. comdr. USNR, 1968-70. Decorated Nat. Def. Svc. medal, 1968; grantee VA Coop Studies Program, 1976—, Ives Pharm., 1983-85, Squibb Borroughs-Wellcome, 1991, Otsuka Pharm., 1993-96; named Best Dr. in SE U.S.A., 1995. Fellow ACP (sci. com. P.R. regional meeting 1976, 82, treas. P.R. chpt. 1980-82), Am. Coll. Cardiology, Coun. Clin. Cardiology, Am. Heart Assn. (bd. dirs. P.R. chpt. 1976, chmn. prof. edn. com., long range planning 1979-80); mem. Internat. Soc. for Heart Transplant, VA Cardiology Assn. (treas. 1991-93, v.p. 1992-93), Dominican Republic Cardiology Soc. (hon.), Puerto Rican Cardiol. Soc. Office: VA Hosp Cardiol 111-A 13000 Bruce B Downs Blvd Tampa FL 33612-4745

CIPRIANO, IRENE PENA, medical technician; b. Corpus Christi, Tex.; d. Juan R. and Susie Garcia Pena; m. Reynaldo F. Cipriano, Jan. 12, 1958; 4 children. BBA in Mgmt., Tex. A&M U., 1996. Chief E.K.G. technician Physician and Surgeons Hosp., 1972-74; officer mgr., cardiologist technician Cardiopulmonary Lab., Inc., 1972-90; adj. instr. Del Mar Coll., 1990. Contbr. articles to profl. jours. Catechist tchr., vol. Saint Cyril & Methodius Cath. Ch.; bd. dirs. Nueces County Cmty. Action Agy., 1988-92, v.p. 1989-92, planning com. chmn. 1989-92, exec. com. mem., 1989-92; treas. Mex. Am. Dems., 1986-87, v.p. 1987-90, state credentials com., 1986-91, state exec. com., 1987-91, state del., 1987-89; arbitrator Better Bus. Bur., 1988-90, notary public, 1990—. Recipient Award of Gratitude Mex. Am. Dems., 1988, Appreciation award Nueces County Cmty Action Agy., 1989, 90, Cert. of Appreciation Spanish Am. Geologist Assn., 1989, Coun. Woman of Yr. Ladies LULAC Coun. #26, 1989, Dist. LULAC Woman of Yr., Nat. Woman of Yr. LULAC, 1989, Gov.'s Cert. of Vol. Svc., Gov. William P. Clemmons Jr., 1990, Govs. Cert. of Vol. Svc. Gov. Ann Richards, 1991, 92, Recognition award Pres. George Bush, 1990, 91, Founder Cert. of Merit Am. G.I. Forum of the U.S., 1992, Cert. of Commendation Mayor Mary Rhoes City of Corpus Christi, 1992; named to Texas Women's Hall of Fame, 1993. Home: 5205 Lamp Post Ln Corpus Christi TX 78415-3013

CIRAULO, STEPHEN JOSEPH, nurse, anesthetist; b. Danville, Pa., Feb. 25, 1960; s. Leonard Joseph and Mary Louise (Purpuri) C. Diploma, Geisinger Med. Ctr. Sch. Nursing, Danville, 1980; cert., Sch of Anesthesia for Nurses Univ. Health Ctr. Pitts., 1983; student, Ottawa U., 1986—. Nursing asst. Geisinger Med. Ctr., Danville, 1978-80; staff RN, part time charge RN cardiac care unit Williamsport (Pa.) Hosp., 1980-81; asst. gastroenterology research group Presbyn. Univ. Hosp., Pitts., 1982-83; staff nurse anesthetist dept. anesthesia Duke U. Med. Ctr., Durham, N.C., 1983-90; with Anesthesia Anytime, Winston-Salem, N.C., 1990, Nash Gen. Hosp., Rocky Mount, N.C., 1991-92; staff nurse anesthetist, mem. epidural analgesia svc. Nash Gen. Hosp., 1991-92; staff nurse anesthetist Wake Anesthesiology Assocs., Inc., Raleigh, N.C., 1992—; mem. coun. for nurse anesthetists dept. anesthesia Duke U. Med. Ctr., Durham, 1985-89; Wake Anesthesiology Assocs., Inc., 1992—. Charter mem. Outstanding Young Ams., 1988; mem. Duke U. Artists Series Adv. Bd., 1994—. Mem. Am. Assn. Nurse Anesthetists, N.C. Assn. Nurse Anesthetists (bylaws com. 1984-86, chmn. fin. com. 1986-88, mem. fin. com. 1988-95, fall program com. 1988, spring program speaker 1990, treas. 1991-93, pres. 1994-95), Triangle Transplant Recipient Internat. Orgn. (charter), Internat. Platform Assn. Republican. Home and Office: 1710 Falls Church Rd Raleigh NC 27609-3531

CIRCEO, LOUIS JOSEPH, JR., research center director, civil engineer; b. Everett, Mass., Aug. 31, 1934; s. Louis Joseph and Matilda (Marotta) C.; m. Brigitta H. Rockstroh, Jan. 26, 1961 (dec. 1986); children: Renata B., Craig L. BS in Engring., U.S. Mil. Acad., 1957; MS in Soils Engring., Iowa State U., 196l, PhDCE, 1963. Registered profl. civil engr., D.C. Commd. 2d lt. U.S. Army, 1957, advanced through grades to col., 1987; rsch. assoc. Lawrence Radiation Lab., Livermore, Calif., 1962-64; civil engr. Bangkok Bypass Road, Thailand, 1965-66; instr. dept. engring. and mil. sci. U.S. Army Engr. Sch., Ft. Belvoir, Va., 1966-68; civil engr. advisor Vietnamese Nat. Mil. Acad., Dalat, Vietnam, 1968-69; rsch. tech. mgr. Def. Atomic Support Agy., Washington, 1969-72; comdr. 20th Engr. Bn., Ft. Campbell, Ky., 1973-75; ops. rsch. analyst nuclear activities br. SHAPE, Mons, Belgium, 1975-79; dir. U.S. Army Constrn. Engring. Rsch. Lab., Champaign, Ill., 1979-83; dir. Nuclear Survivability, Security and Safety Directorate, Hdqrs. Def. Nuclear Agy., Washington, 1983-87; ret., 1987; prin. rsch. scientist, dir. Constrn. Rsch. Ctr., Ga. Inst. Tech., Atlanta, 1987—. Patentee recovery of fuel products from carbonaceous matter using plasma arc; in-situ soil stabilization method and apparatus, in-situ remediation and vitrification of contaminated soils, deposits and buried materials. Mem. ASCE, Soc. Am. Mil. Engrs., Assn. U.S. Army, Sigma Xi. Roman Catholic. Home: 4245 Navajo Trl NE Atlanta GA 30319-1532 Office: Ga Inst Tech Constrn Rsch Ctr Coll Architecture Atlanta GA 30332-0159

CITRON, BEATRICE SALLY, law librarian, lawyer, educator; b. Phila., May 19, 1929; d. Morris Meyer and Frances (Teplitsky) Levinson; m. Joel P. Citron, Aug. 7, 1955 (dec. Sept. 1977); children: Deborah Ann, Victor Ephraim. BA in Econs. with honors, U. Pa., 1950; MLS, Our Lady of the Lake U., 1978; JD, U. Tex., 1984. Bar: Tex. 1985; cert. all-level sch. libr., secondary level tchr., Tex. Claims examiner Social Security Adminstrn., Pa., Fla. and N.C., 1951-59; head libr. St. Mary's Hall, San Antonio, 1979-80; media, reference and rare book libr., asst. and assoc. prof. St. Mary's U. Law Libr., San Antonio, 1984-89; asst. dir. St. Thomas U. Law Libr., Miami, Fla., 1989-96, assoc. dir., 1996—, head pub. svc. Mem. ABA, Am. Assn. Law Librs. (publs. com. 1987-88, com. on rels. with info. vendors 1991-93, bylaws com. 1994-96), S.W. Assn. Law Librs. (continuing edn. com. 1986-88, chmn. local arrangements 1987-88), S.E. Assn. Law Librs. (newsletter, program and edn. coms. 1991-94), South Fla. Assn. Law Librs. (treas. 1992-94, v.p. 1994-95, pres. 1995-96). Office: St Thomas U Law Libr 16400 NE 32nd Ave Miami FL 33160

CITTONE, HENRY ARON, hotel and restaurant management educator; b. Istanbul, Turkey, May 15, 1937; s. Joseph and Debrah (Benbanaste) C.; m. Liliane Robert, Oct. 2, 1965; children: Henry Joseph, Marc Ely. BA, Coll. St. Michel, 1956; student Trade and Tech. Coll., L.A., 1971; MS, U. Houston, 1990; postgrad. in Edn. Fla. Atlantic U., Boca Raton, Fla., 1993-94. Food svc. mgr. U. So. Calif., L.A., 1971; mgr. food and beverage Sheraton Poste Inn, Cherry Hill, N.J., 1972-73; resident mgr. Aruba Caribbean Hotel, Netherlands, Antilles, 1973-74; resident mgr. Lima Sheraton Hotel (Peru), 1974-76; dir. food and beverage Bahia Mar Hotel, Ft. Lauderdale, Fla., 1978-79, Maison Dupuy, New Orleans, 1979-81, Virgin Isle Hotel, St. Thomas, 1981-84; asst. prof. hotel and restaurant mgmt. Galveston Coll. (Tex.), 1984-90; prof. Morehead (Ky.) State U., 1990-92; instr. Coll. V.I., 1983-84, Houston Community Coll., 1985-90; mem. adj. faculty N. Miami (Fla.) Johnson & Wales U., 1994. Served with Israeli Army, 1956-59. Recipient Cert. Hotel Adminstr. Designation award Ednl. Inst. AH & MA, 1986. Mem. Nat. Restaurant Assn., Am. Hotel and Motel Assn., Internat. Hotel Sales Mgmt. Assn., Internat. Soc. Food and Beverage Execs., Council on Hotel, Restaurant and Instnl. Edn., CHRIE (internat. exchange com.), Conrad Hilton Coll. Alumni Assn. (Disting. Hospitality Educator of Yr. award 1988).

CIZIK, ROBERT, manufacturing company executive; b. Scranton, Pa., Apr. 4, 1931; s. John and Anna (Paraska) C.; m. Jane Morin, Oct. 3, 1953; children: Robert Morin, Jan Catherine, Paula Jane, Gregory Alan, Peter Nicholas. BS, U. Conn., 1953; MBA, Harvard U., 1958; LLD (hon.), Kenyon Coll., 1983. Acct. Price Waterhouse & Co. (CPAs), N.Y.C., 1953-54, 56; fin. analyst Exxon U.S.A., N.J., 1958-61; exec. asst. Cooper Industries, Inc., Houston, 1961-63, treas., 1963-64, contr., 1964-67, v.p. planning, 1967-69, exec. v.p., 1969-73, pres., 1973—, COO, 1973-75, CEO, 1975-95, chmn., 1983-96; propr. Cizik Interests, Houston, 1996—; ptnr. Am. Indsl. Ptnrs., 1996—; adv. dir. Wingate Ptnrs., 1996—; bd. dirs. Harris Corp., Temple Inland, Panhandle Energy Corp., Air Products and Chems., Inc., Texans for Jud. Election Reform, 1991-95; mem. Bus. Roundtable, 1978-95; mem. host com. Houston Econ. Summit Meeting, 1990. Bd. dirs. Assocs. Harvard Bus. Sch., Boston; mem. Tex. Bus. and Edn. Coalition, 1991-94; chmn. Heartstrongs Benefit, Design Industries Found. for AIDS, 1991-92; mem. nat. adv. coun. Tex. Heart Inst.; dir. U. Tex. Houston Health Sci. Ctr. devel. bd. Recipient Gen. Maurice Hirsch award Bus. Com. for Arts, 1984, CEO of Yr. bronze award Fin. World Mag., 1987; CEO of Decade bronze award in Indsl. Equipment Cos., 1988; named Best CEO in Machinery Industry, Wall St. Transcript, 1980, 81, 83, 86, 87, 88, 89, 90-91, Internat. Exec. of Yr., Greater Houston Partnership and Houston World Trade Assn., 1990. Mem. NAM (chmn. 1992-93), Elec. Mfrs. Club (bd. govs. 1984—, pres. 1990-92), River Oaks Country Club, Forum Club Houston (founding), Houston Ctr. Office: Cizik Interests Texas Commerce Tower 600 Travis Ste 3628 Houston TX 77002

CIZZA, JOHN ANTHONY, insurance executive; b. Utica, N.Y., Oct. 22, 1952; s. Louis Pasquale and Dolores Prudence (Dieglio) C.; m. Barbara Ellen Hansen, Nov. 27, 1982. BS, Clarkson U., 1974; A in Risk Mgmt., Ins. Inst., 1979. Underwriter Utica Nat. Ins. Group, New Hartford, N.Y., 1974-77, supr. underwriter, 1977-78, supr. nat. accts., 1978-79; casualty mgr. Providence (R.I.) Wash. Ins., 1979-81, regional casualty mgr., 1981-82; underwriter Am. Re-Ins. Co., Chgo., 1982-84, sr. underwriter, 1984-86, dir. unit mgr., 1986-89, asst. v.p., 1989-92; v.p. Am-Re Mgrs., Chgo., 1992-94; v.p., regional mgr. Am-Re Mgrs., Dallas, 1994—. Roman Catholic. Office: Am-Re Mgrs 2001 Ross Ave Ste 3900 Dallas TX 75201-8001

CLAFLIN, JAMES ROBERT, pediatrician, allergist; b. Apr. 30, 1946; m. Marcee Claflin; children: James Sean (dec.), Brian Scott (dec.), Susan Nicole, Timothy Lynn. Student, Northwestern State Coll.; MD, U. Okla., 1971. Diplomate Am. Bd. Pediatrics, Am. Bd. Allergy/Immunology. Intern in pediatrics U. Tex. Med. Br., Galveston, 1971-72; advanced through grades to lt. col. USAF, 1969-84, chief pediatric svcs. Goodfellow AFB, 1972-73, 75-77; chief pediatric svcs. and hosp. svcs. RAF Upper Heyford USAF, Eng., 1977-80; chief allergy and clin. immunology Carswell AFB USAF, 1982-84; fellow allergy/immunology Lackland AFB Willford Hall USAF Med. Ctr., Tex., 1980-82; ret. USAF, 1984; clin. asst. prof. pediatrics, Oklahoma U.; presenter various programs and meetings; contbr. various publs. advisor child welfare com. Tom Green County, 1976-77; mem. child welfare com. RAF, Upper Heyford, Eng., 1978-80; mem. sch. and pub. health com. Tarrant County Med. Soc., 1984-85, chmn., 1986-87, publs. com., 1988-89, religion and meml. com., 1989; mem. quality assurance and infectious disease coms. Cook-Ft. Worth Children's Hosp., 1986-89; v.p. Brenham State Sch. Parent Assn., 1987-88; pres. Parents Assn. for the Retarded of Tex., 1987-88; chmn. cmty. conscience com. Wedgwood Bapt. Ch. Recipient Svc. award Am. Diabetes Assn., 1976. Fellow Am. Acad. Pediatrics, Am. Coll. Allergy (mem. com. on allergic rhinitis, mem. com. on adverse reactions to food 1991-96), Am. Acad. Allergy; mem. AMA, Okl. County Med. Soc. (pub. rels. com. 1991-95, ad hoc com. RBRVS conversion 1991,grievance com. 1991-94, quality of care com. 1991—) , Okla. State Med. Assn. (medicare carrier adv. com. 1992-95), Okla. Allergy Soc. Home: 750 NE 13th St Oklahoma City OK 73104-5051

CLAMON, HARLEYNE DIANNE, retired social service supervisor; b. Camden, Tex., Feb. 12, 1940; d. Harley and Ada Virginia (Handley) C. BA, Sam Houston U., 1961. Lic. master social worker, Tex. Tchr. Big Sandy Ind. Sch., Dallardsville, Tex., 1961-62; social worker Tex. Dept. Human Svcs., Tex. City, 1962-75; social service supr. Tex. Dept. Human Svcs., Galveston, 1975-79, Tex. City, 1979-80, Livingston, 1980-92. Mem. adv. com. Mental Health, Mental Retardation, Livingston, Tex., 1980-87, chmn.,

1982-87; vol. Polk County Meml. Hosp., 1982—; adult ladies Sunday sch. tchr. Leggett Bapt. Ch., 1984-95, song leader, 1994-95. Mem. AAUW (pres. Livingston 1984-86), DAR (Indian chmn. 1984-86, chaplain Livingston chpt. 1992-94), Bus. and Profl. Women (pres. Livingston 1983-85, Woman of Yr. 1982-83), Am. Pub. Welfare Assn., Tex. Pub. Employees Assn. (bd. dirs. 1970-75), Polk County Hist. Commn. (vice chmn. 1994-95, chmn. 1996—), Sam Houston State U. Alumni. Democrat. Baptist. Home: 616 W Calhoun St Livingston TX 77351-2751

CLANCE, PAULINE ROSE, psychology educator; b. Welch, W.Va., Oct. 19, 1938; d. George W. and Gladys (Riley) Rose. BS cum laude Lynchburg Coll., 1960; MS, U. Ky., 1964, PhD, 1969. Clin. psychologist G.B. Dimick Child Guidance Clinic, Lexington, Ky., 1965; psychologist Univ. Hosp. Cleve., 1966-68, Brecksville VA Hosp., 1969-71; clin. psychologist Psychol. Svcs., Oberlin Coll., 1971-74; asst. prof. Oberlin Coll., 1971-74; prof. psychology Ga. State U., Atlanta, 1974—; pvt. practice clin. psychology, Atlanta, 1974—; cons. in field. Adv. bd. Odyssey Family Svc., 1979-83; mem. Com. on Minority and Poverty Groups, Coll. Entrance Examination Bd., 1972-75; peer reviewer grants nat. Endowment for Humanities, Washington, 1972-82; reviewer curriculum materials Appalachian Ctr. for Ednl. Equity, U. Tenn., 1978. Named Feminist Foremother, Women and Therapy Assn., 1996; Oberlin Coll. leadership tng. grantee, 1973; Urban Life Ctr. grantee, 1977; others. Mem. Southeastern Psychol. Assn. (pres. 1982-83), AAUP, Assn. Women in Psychology, Am. Psychol. Assn. Author: The Impostor Phenomenon: Overcoming the Fear that Haunts Your Success, 1985; contbr. articles to profl. jours. Office: Ga State U Dept Psychology Atlanta GA 30303

CLANCY, THOMAS HANLEY, seminary administrator; b. Helena, Ark., Aug. 8, 1923; s. Thomas Hornor and Ruth (Lewis) C. AB, Spring Hill Coll., 1948; MA, Fordham U., 1950; STL, Facultes S.J., Louvain, Belgium, 1956; PhD, U. London, 1960. Joined S.J., Roman Cath. Ch., 1942, ordained priest, 1955. Instr. Spring Hill Coll., Mobile, Ala., 1950-52; assoc. editor America mag., N.Y.C., 1970-71; provincial supr. New Orleans Province S.J., 1971-77, archivist, 1977—; asst. prof. history and polit. sci. Loyola U., New Orleans, 1960-68, chmn. dept., 1966-69, v.p. acad. affairs, 1968-70, v.p. communications, 1978-89, trustee, 1966-72, 78-89; dir. Jesuit Sem. and Mission Bur., New Orleans, 1989—; lectr. on constns. and history of S.J., 1970—. Author: English Catholic Books 1641-1700: A Bibliography, 1974, An Introduction to Jesuit Life, 1976, Our Friends, 1978, 2d edit., 1989, The Conversational Word of God, 1978 (Japanese edit. 1986); contbr. articles and book revs. to profl. jours. Trustee Spring Hill Coll., 1980-89, Loyola Marymount U., L.A., 1989-94; chmn. Inst. Politics, New Orleans, 1968—. Folger Shakespeare Libr. fellow, 1961. Mem. Cath. Record Soc. Democrat. Office: 500 S Jeff Davis Pkwy New Orleans LA 70119 Home: Loyola U New Orleans LA 70118

CLANTON, JOHN CHARLES, army officer; b. Fayetteville, N.C., Feb. 20, 1960; s. Charles Tommy and Betty Ann (Green) C. BA in Music, Furman U., 1982; postgrad., So. Bapt. Theol. Sem., Louisville, 1987-89; MMus in Conducting, Eastman Sch. Music, 1994. Commd. 2d lt. U.S. Army, 1982, advanced through grades to capt., 1986; with 8th Inf. Divsn., Bad Kreuznach, Fed. Republic Germany, 1982-85; comdr. band 8th Inf. Div., Bad Kreuznach, Fed. Republic Germany, 1985-86; staff band officer 6th U.S. Army, San Francisco, 1986-87, Hdqrs. Forces Command (FORSCOM), Ft. McPherson, Ga., 1989-91; comdr. U.S. Army Ground Forces Band, 1991-93; condr. The U.S. Army Band (Pershing's Own), Washington; min. music 1st So. Bapt. Ch., Floyds Knobs, Ind., 1987-89. Contbr. articles to mags. Music dir. New Life Christian Fellowship, Greenville, S.C., 1980-82; music and youth dir. Rose Chapel, Bad Kreuznach, 1982-86; youth dir. Presidio Chapel, San Francisco, 1986-87; choir dir. First United Meth. Ch., East Point, Ga., 1992-93. Mem. NARAS, Am. Symphony Orch. League, Nat. Band Assn., Coll. Band Dirs. Assn., Condrs. Guild, Phi Mu Alpha Sinfonia (songleader 1980-82, Master Sinfonian award 1982). Home: 2250 Clarendon Blvd Apt 906 Arlington VA 22201-3339

CLAPP, ALLEN LINVILLE, electric supply and communications utility consultant, expert witness, mediator, arbitrator; b. Raleigh, N.C., Oct. 8, 1943; s. Byron Siler and Alene Linville (Hester) C.; m. Anne Stuart Calvert, Dec. 18, 1966. BS in Engring. Ops., N.C. State U., 1967, M in Econs., 1973. Registered profl. engr., N.C., N.J. Asst. engr. Booth-Jones and Assocs., Raleigh, 1965-67; assoc., 1969-71; chief ops. analysis N.C. Utilities Commn., Raleigh, 1971-77, engring. and econs. advisor to commrs., hearing examiner, 1977-82; dir. tech. assessment N.C. Alternative Energy Corp., Rsch. Triangle Park, 1982-85; pres. Clapp Rsch. Assocs. P.C., Clapp Rsch, Inc., 1985—; pvt. practice electric safety cons., Raleigh, 1971—; bd. dirs. Boling Co., 1993-96; mem. Nat. Elec. Safety Code Com., 1971—, chmn. 1984-93; lectr. in field. Author: National Electrical Safety Code Handbook, 1984, 91, 92, 96, Assembly and Testing of Aerial Mines, 1968; editor, pub. Danesc Update Newsletter; contbr. to McGraw-Hill Standard Handbook for Electrical Engineers; contbr. articles to profl. jours. Co-chmn. Brookhaven/Deblyn Park Action Com., Raleigh. Served with U.S. Army, 1967-69. Recipient cert. of Recognition and Appreciation Aerial Mine Lab., 1969. Mem. NSPE (past bd. dirs.), IEEE (mem. standards bd. 1989, 90), Profl. Engrs. N.C. (pres. 1980, Disting. Svc. award cen. Carolina chapt. 1978), N.C. Assn. Professions (pres. 1981), Power Engring. Soc., Nat. Safety Council, Am. Soc. Safety Engrs., Am. Arbitration Assn., Soc. Cable TV Engrs., Indsl. Applications Soc., Am. Nat. Standards Inst., Standard Engring. Soc. Republican. Baptist. Avocations: competitive target shooting, photography, raising orchids. Home: 3206 Queens Rd Raleigh NC 27612-6233 Office: Clapp Rsch Assocs 6112 Saint Giles St Raleigh NC 27612

CLAPP, BEVERLY BOOKER, accountant; b. Savannah, Ga., Oct. 26, 1954; d. Herschel Ray and Ida Marie (Bove) Beville; m. William L. Clapp III; 1 child, Matthew Anthony. BS in Med. Tech., Med. Coll. Ga., 1976; MS in Clin. Lab. Sci., U. Ala., Birmingham, 1977, BS in Acctg., 1989. CPA, Ala. Blood bank technologist U. Ala. Hosp., Birmingham, 1976-77; asst. supr. physiology Bapt. Med. Ctr., Montclair, Birmingham, 1977-79; rsch. chemist Nephrology Rsch. and Tng. Ctr. U. Ala., Birmingham, 1979-91; med. technologist VA Med. Ctr., Gainesville, Fla., 1991-92; CPA, mgr. J.J. Lucky & Co., Gainesville, 1992; sr. grants specialist U. Fla., Gainesville, 1992-93; accountant Beverly Booker Clapp Acctg. Svc., 1993—; treas. U. Fla. Women's Med. Guild. Treas. Boy Scouts Am. Mem. AICPA, Ala. Soc. CPAs, Am. Soc. Clin. Pathology, Fla. Inst. CPAs, Fla. Soc. Med. Tech., Alpha Aeta, Phi Kappa Phi. Roman Catholic.

CLAPP, DAVID FOSTER, library administrator; b. Birmingham, Ala., July 17, 1952; s. Merwin Bailey and Katherine Lorraine (Aderholt) C.; m. Sara Louise Stephan, Sept. 18, 1982. BA in Classical Langs., Tulane U., 1975; MS in LS, U. Ill., 1980; cert. advanced study in info. mgmt., U. Chgo., 1987. Asst. mgr. Kroch's & Brentano's Bookstore, Chgo., 1976-79; libr. I acquisitions dept. Chgo. Pub. Libr., 1980-82, libr. II, 1st asst. Walker br., 1982-83, libr. II, head Clearing br., 1983-84, libr. III, head Rogers Park br., 1984-89; asst. dir. extension svcs. Chattanooga Pub. Libr., 1989—. Recipient Outstanding Pub. Svc. award Friends Chgo. Pub. Libr., 1987; Josie B. Houchens fellow U. Ill., 1979. Mem. ALA, Pub. Libr. Assn., Libr. Adminstrn. and Mgmt. Assn., Tenn. Libr. Assn. (exec. bd. 1991-92), Chattanooga Area Libr. Assn. (pres. 1991-92), Mensa, Beta Phi Mu. Office: Chattanooga Pub Libr 1001 Broad St Chattanooga TN 37402-2620

CLARE, FOUNTAIN STEWART, III, pathologist; b. Emory, Ga., Apr. 12, 1936; s. Fountain Stewart II and Virginia (Pettigrew) C.; m. Hilda Henrietta Ramsey, June 22, 1963 (div. 1988); children: Virginia Ramsey, Aileen Pettigrew, Elizabeth King, Fountain Stewart IV; m. Elizabeth Darby Moore, Jan. 15, 1994. BS, U. S.C., 1957; MD, Med. U. of S.C., 1961. Intern in medicine U. Ala., Birmingham, 1961-62; resident in pathology Med. U. of S.C., Charleston, 1962-63, U. N.C., Chapel Hill, 1963-66; pathologist Columbia (S.C.) Hosp., 1966-69, Providence Hosp., Columbia, 1966-84, Bapt. Hosp., Columbia, 1966—; chief med. staff S.C. Bapt. Hosp., Columbia, 1982; pres. Columbia Pathologists, P.A., 1986-96; ret., 1996; clin. assoc. prof. U. S.C. Sch. Medicine, 1977-89, clin. prof. pathology, 1989—. Fellow Coll. Am. Pathologists (lab. insp.), Am. Soc. Clin. Pathologists; mem. Internat. Acad. Pathology, S.C. Soc. Pathologists (pres. 1984-85). Episcopalian. Home: 369 Alexander Cir Columbia SC 29206-4974 Office: Taylor at Marion Bapt Med Ctr Columbia SC 29220

CLARE, GEORGE, safety engineer, system safety consultant; b. N.Y.C., Apr. 8, 1930; s. George Washington and Hildegard Marie (Sommer) C.; student U. So. Calif., 1961, U. Tex., Arlington, 1963-71, U. Wash., 1980; m. Catherine Saidee Hamel, Jan. 12, 1956; children: George Christopher, Kristine René. Enlisted man U.S. Navy, 1948, advanced through grades to comdr., 1968; naval aviator, 1951-70; served in Korea; comdr. Res., 1963-70; ret., 1970; mgr. system safety LTV Missiles and Electronics Group, Missiles div., Dallas, 1963-90. Mem. Nat. Republican Com., Rep. Senatorial Com., Rep. Congl. Com., Tex. Rep. Com., Citizens for Republic. Decorated Air medal with gold star, others; cert. product safety mgr. Mem. AIAA, Am. Security Council, Internat. Soc. Air Safety Investigators, System Safety Soc., Am. Def. Preparedness Assn., Assn. Naval Aviation, Ret. Officers Assn., Air Group 7 Assn. (pres.). Roman Catholic. Home and Office: 825 Bayshore Dr Apt 500 Pensacola FL 32507-3463

CLARIDGE, RICHARD, structural engineer; b. Chgo., Feb. 22, 1932; s. Dalbert Otis and Lucille Alma (Lindquist) C.; m. Joan Elaine Powell, June 12, 1952; children: Cathy L. Jansen, Richard Allen Jr., Jaylynn P. Cook. BSBA, Fla. State U., Tallahassee, 1953; BCE, U. Fla., 1959; postgrad., U. Cen. Fla., 1972-75. Registered profl. engr. Fla., S.C. Structures engr. Douglas Aircraft Co., 1959-63, McDonnell Douglas Astro, 1963-89; ground supt. equipment, design engr. McDonnell Douglas Astro, Cape Canaveral, Fla., 1974-78; stress analyst McDonnell Douglas Astro, Titusville, Fla., 1982-89; structural cons., analyst Atlantic CADD Assocs., Titusville, 1989—; group engr. McDonnell Douglas Astro, Kennedy Space Center, 1963-74; sect. chief stress McDonnell Douglas Missile Sys., Titusville, 1983-89; structural analyst, designer Lockheed Martin Astronautics, Cape Canaveral, Fla., 1989—. Mem. Titusville Shoreline Authority, 1965. Lt. (j.g.) USNR, 1953-57. Mem. NSPE, ASCE (computer practices reviewer), AIAA, Am. Welding Soc., Fla. Engring. Soc., U.S. Naval Inst. (life), Internat. Soc. Allied Weight Engrs. Office: Atlantic CADD Assocs PO Box 386 New Smyrna Beach FL 32170-0386

CLARK, CALEB MORGAN, political scientist, educator; b. Washington, June 6, 1945; s. Tanner Morgan and Grace Amanda (Kautzmann) C.; B.A., Beloit Coll., 1966; Ph.D., U. Ill., 1973; m. Janet Morrissey Sentz, Sept. 28, 1968; children—Emily Claire, Grace Ellen, Evelyn Adair. Lectr., N.Mex. State U., Las Cruces, 1972-75, asst. prof., 1975-78, assoc. prof. govt., 1978-81; assoc. prof. polit. sci. U. Wyo., Laramie, 1981-84, prof., 1984-92, U. Auburn, 1992—, prof., head polit. sci. NDEA fellow, 1966-69; Woodrow Wilson dissertation fellow, 1969-70; grantee N.Mex. Humanities Coun., 1975, Wyo. Coun. for Humanities, 1982, U.S. Dept. Edn., 1983-85, Pacific Cultural Found., 1984-86. Am. Coun. Learned Socs., 1976, Met. Life Edn., 1978-80, NEH, 1978, NSF, 1981, Chiang Ching-Kuo Found., 1993-95. Mem. Am. Polit. Sci. Assn., Am. Assn. Chinese Studies (exec. coun. 1995-97), Western Polit. Sci. Assn., Assn. Asian Studies, Southern Polit. Sci. Assn., Internat. Studies Assn. (exec. dir. West 1981-84), Ala. Polit. Sci. Assn. (v.p. 1993-94, pres. 1994-95), Phi Beta Kappa (treas. 1983-91), Pi Eta Sigma, Phi Kappa Phi, Phi Beta Delta. Author: (with Robert L. Farlow) Comparative Patterns of Foreign Policy and Trade, 1976; (with Karl F. Johnson) Development's Influence on Yugoslav Political Values, 1976; Taiwan's Development, 1989; (with Bih-er Chou and Janet Clark) Women in Taiwan Politics, 1990; (with Steve Chan) Foresight, Flexibility and Fortuna in Taiwan's Devel., 1992; mng. editor IS Notes, 1984-92; co-editor: North/South Relations, 1983, State and Development, 1988, Polit. Stability and Economic Development, 1991, The Evolving Pacific Basin, 1992, (with K.C. Roy) Technological Change and Rurdal Development in Poor Countries, 1994; cons., assoc. editor Soviet Union, 1974-77, World Affairs, 1975-84, Social Sci. Jour., 1978-80; contbr. articles to profl. jours.

CLARK, CARTER BLUE, university administrator; b. Dallas, Jan. 11, 1946; s. Joseph Stanley and Lois (Carter) C.; m. Sheryl Susan Sullivan, Dec. 27, 1986; 1 child, Sanger Sullivan. BA, U. Okla., 1968, MA, 1970, PhD, 1976. Grant asst. adminstr. U. Utah, Salt Lake City, 1976-77; dir. Am. Indian studies Morningside Coll., Sioux City, Iowa, 1977-79; assoc. prof. Am. Indian studies San Diego State U., 1981; assoc. prof. Calif. State U., Long Beach, 1979-87, prof., 1988-92; exec. v.p. Okla. City U., 1991—; vis. assoc. prof. history UCLA, 1983; humanities scholar Okla. Found. for Humanities, Okla., 1985-88, 93—; cons., advisor Am. Ind. Sci. and Engring., Long Beach, Calif., 1990-91; advisor Red Earth, Inc., Oklahoma City, 1983—. Author: Lone Wolf v Hitchcock, 1994. Mem. The Learning Circle, U. Calif., LaJolla, 1981-88; bd. dirs. Nat. Conf. of Christians and Jews, Okla., 1993-96; cons. Cultural Diversity Com. Okla., 1987—; usher St. Paul's Episcopal Cathedral; mem. Big Cussetah Indian Meth. Ch.; sec. Episcopal Coun. on Indian Ministry, 1984-95. Fellowship Newberry Libr., 1985; recipient Okla. Hist. Soc., 1977. Mem. Western History Assn. Democrat. Office: Okla City Univ 2501 N Blackwelder Oklahoma City OK 73106

CLARK, DAVID LOUIS, education educator, author; b. Binghamton, N.Y., Nov. 14, 1929; s. Ralph Keeler and Catherine (Hartigan) C.; m. Elsie Edith Shaw, June 28, 1952; children: Patricia, Michael, Timothy, Catherine. B.A., N.Y. State Coll. Tchrs., Albany, 1951, M.A., 1952; Ed.D., Columbia Tchrs. Coll., 1954. Research asst. N.Y. State Tchrs. Assn., 1954-56; asst. to supt. Garden City (N.Y.) Pub. Schs., 1956-58; dir. coop. research program U.S. Office Edn., 1958-62; assoc. dean, prof. edn. Ohio State U., 1962-66; prof. edn. Ind. U., 1966-86; dean Ind. U. (Sch. Edn.), 1966-74; William Clay Parrish, Jr. prof. edn. U. Va., Charlottesville, 1986-90; prof. edn. U. N.C., Chapel Hill, 1991-92, Kenan prof. edn., 1992—. Author: (with John E. Hopkins) Educational Research, Development, and Diffusion Manpower, 1969, Federal Policy in Educational Research and Development, 1975, (with Egon G. Guba) The Configurational Perspective: A New View of Educational Knowledge Production and Utilization, 1974, Teacher Education Institutions as Innovators, Knowledge Producers and Change Agencies, 1977, (with Gerald Marker) The Institutionalization of American Teacher Education, 1975, (with Linda S. Lotto and Martha M. McCarthy) Secondary Source Study of Exceptionality in Urban Elementary Schs, 1980, (with McKibbin and Malkas) Alternative Perspectives for Viewing Educational Organizations, 1981, In Consideration of Goal-Free Planning: The Failure of Traditional Planning Systems in Education, 1981, (with Linda S. Lotto and Terry A. Astuto) Effective Schools and School Improvement: A Comparative Analysis of Two Lines of Inquiry, 1984; Emerging Paradigms in Organizational Theory and Research, 1985, Transforming the Structure for the Professional Preparation of Teachers, 1985, (with Terry A. Astuto) Strength of Organizational Coupling in the Instructionally Effective School, 1985; (with Terry A. Astuto) The Significance and Permanence of Changes in Federal Education Policy, 1986, Paradoxical Choice Options in Organizations, 1988, Reagan's Final Report Card, 1989; (with R.F. McNergney) Governance of Teacher Education, 1990, Leadership in Policy Development by Teacher Educators, 1992, (with Terry A. Astuto) Challenging the Limits of School Restructuring and Reform, 1992, Roots of Reform, 1994; also reports in field. Mem. Am. Ednl. Research Assn., NEA, Nat. Sci. Study of Edn., Phi Delta Kappa. Home: 207 Deepwood Rd Chapel Hill NC 27514-3205

CLARK, DAVID M., lawyer; b. Greenville, N.C., Sept. 1, 1929; s. David McKenzie and Myrtle Estelle (Brogdon) C.; m. Martha McKeller Early; children: David, Martha Dockery, Marietta Brogdon, Carolyn Elizabeth; m. Susan Summers Mullally; 1 child, McKenzie Lawrence. BA, Wake Forest Coll., 1951; LLD, NYU, 1957. Law clerk Chambers of Justice Black U.S. Supreme Court, Washington, D.C., 1957-59; assoc. Smith, Moore, Smith, Schell & Hunter, Greensboro, N.C., 1959-63; ptnr. Stern Rendleman & Clark, Greensboro, N.C., 1964-68, Clark, Wharton & Berry, Greensboro, N.C., 1968—. Mem. bd. dirs. Legal Svcs. of N.C., Raleigh, 1976-82; pres. Summit Rotary Club, Greensboro, 1967; mem. bd. trustees W. Market Street Methodist Ch., Greensboro; chmn., co-founder Greensboro Legal Aid Found., 1965-68. Mem. ABA, Am. Trial Lawyers Assn., Am. Bd. Trial Advocates, N.C. Bar Assn. (bd. govs. 1982-85), N.C. Trial Lawyers Assn., Greensboro Bar Assn. (bd. dirs.). Home: 328 E Greenway N Greensboro NC 27403 Office: Clark Wharton & Berry 125 S Elm St Ste 600 Greensboro NC 27401

CLARK, DAYLE MERITT, civil engineer; b. Lubbock, Tex., Sept. 5, 1933; s. Frank Meritt and Mamie Jewel (Huff) C.; BS, Tex. Tech. U., 1955; MS, So. Meth. U., 1967; m. Betty Ann Maples, Apr. 11, 1968; 1 dau., Alison. Registered profl. engr., registered profl. land surveyor. Field engr. Chgo. Bridge & Iron Co., 1955; mgr. L.K. Long Constrn. Co., 1958-64; faculty U. Tex., Arlington, 1964—; cons. AID, 1966, NSF, 1967-68; expert witness in court cases. Served to capt. USAF, 1955-57. Recipient Achievement award in Civil Engring., Tex. Soc. Profl. Engrs., Dallas chpt., 1995. Fellow ASCE (pres. Dallas br. 1987, pres. Tex. sect. 1992-93, Profl. Svcs. award 1991); Club: Rotary (pres. Arlington-West 1986, Paul Harris fellow, Rotarian of Yr. 1987). Editor Tex. Civil Engr., 1967-71. Contbr. papers, reports to profl. jours. Office: PO Box 185 Arlington TX 76004-0185

CLARK, DEBBIE SUZANNE, secondary school educator; b. Gainesville, Ga., May 21, 1962; d. Don Ewell and Joy Suzanne (Marlowe) C.; m. Jack Cleveland Hurt, Sept. 17, 1988 (div. Oct. 1990). Student, Gainesville Coll., 1979-81; B cum laude, U. Ga., 1983, M, 1986. Cert. tcrh., Ga. Mktg. educator Johnson High Sch., Gainesville, Ga., 1983—. Contbr. articles to newspapers and learning activity packs for marked divsn. of Ohio State U. Facilitator projects Dept. Family Children Svcs., Gainesville, Ga., 1983—, Hall County Humane Soc., 1983—; mem. Hall County Steering Com.; organizer various Red Ribbon Week activities local, county and state level schs., 1988—; organizer various Hall County bus. for reduction of shoplifting, 1983—. Apptd. Hon. Lt. Col.-Aide-de Camp-Gov.'s Office, Ga. Gov. Zell Miller, 1993. Mem. NEA, Distributive Edn. Clubs Am., Am. Vocat. Assn., Ga. Mktg. Edn. Assn. (dir.), Ga. Assn. Educators, Hall County Edn. Assn., Phi Kappa Phi, Kappa Delta Epsilon, Kappa Delta Pi. Republican. Baptist. Home: 2896 Cascade Dr Gainesville GA 30504-5702 Office: Johnson High Sch 3305 Poplar Springs Rd Gainesville GA 30507-8661

CLARK, DESMOND LAVERNE, immigration legal secretary, editor, minister; b. Omaha, May 4, 1951; d. Thomas Edward and Louise Gwendolyn (Jackson) C. BS, Tenn. State U., 1973. Sec. Atlanta (Ga.) Housing Authority, 1973, modernization asst., 1974, contract coord., 1977; word processor, proof reader Touche Ross & Co., Miami, 1981, word processing supr., 1989; asst. editor Innerself Publs., Hollywood, Fla., 1991-93; legal sec. immigration law, 1996—; editor Innerself Publs., Hollywood, Fla., 1993-96; interfaith minister Interfaith Seminary, N.Y.C., 1993—; profl. entertainer Curtain Call Prodns., Ft. Lauderdale, Fla., 1990-96. Mem. exec. com. Dem. Party, Miami, 1980-88. Mem. Asn. Interfaith Ministry. Home: 3150 NW 135th St # 1 Opa Locka FL 33054-4884 Office: TK Mahon PA 2929 E Commercial Blvd # Phe Fort Lauderdale FL 33308-4214

CLARK, EDWARD ERNEST, insurance administrator; b. San Angelo, Tex., Oct. 1, 1948; s. Jake Edward and Luda Erlene (Roberts) C.; m. Gayl Wells, Jan. 13, 1968; children: Sherry Renae, Angie Lynn. AS, Alvin (Tex.) C.C., 1987; student, U. Houston Clear Lake, 1989-92. Prodn. shift supr. E.I. DuPont de Nemours & Co., La Porte, Tex., 1969-78; process oper. specialist Arabian Am. Oil Co., Abqaiq, Saudi Arabia, 1978-80; farmer, self employed Alvin, 1980-82; loss prevention insp. The Hartford Steam Boiler Inspection & Ins. Co., Houston, 1982-92; indsl. engr., corp. safety dept. Samarec/Aramco, Jeddah, Saudi Arabia, 1992-94; sr. loss prevention cons. The Hartford Steam Boiler Inspection & Ins. Co., Danbury, Tex., 1994—. Office: Hartford Steam Boiler Inspection & Ins Co 15415 Katy Frwy Ste 300 Houston TX 77094

CLARK, EDWIN GREEN, JR., advertising agency executive; b. Roanoke Rapids, N.C., July 14, 1940; s. Edwin Green and Louise (Powell) C.; m. Emily Lamar Harris, Sept. 25, 1976; children: Jordan Pound, Benjamin Harris. AB, Davidson Coll., 1962; JD, U. N.C., 1967. Assoc. Nixon, Mudge, Rose, Guthrie, Alexander & Mitchell, N.Y.C., 1967-70; acct. exec. Benton & Bowles, Inc., N.Y.C., 1970-74; acct. supr. Cole, Henderson, Drake, Inc., Atlanta, 1975-81; pres. Lewis, CLark & Graham, Inc., Atlanta, 1982-92; chmn., CEO Warren, Clark and Graham, Atlanta, 1992—. Served as 1st lt. U.S. Army, 1962-64. Mem. Am. Mktg. Assn., Atlanta Advt. Club, Druid Hills Golf Club, Fripp Island Club. Democrat. Presbyterian. Office: 230 Peachtree St NW Ste 1700 Atlanta GA 30303-1514

CLARK, ELIZABETH ADAMS (LIZ CLARK), genealogy educator; b. Arcadia, Fla., Jan. 16, 1944; d. Calvin Emmett and Ruth Gertrude (Paxton) Adams; m. Eugene Corry Clark, Apr. 27, 1963; children: Mary Corry Clark-Cross, Walter Emmett. BS in History, Ga. Coll., 1971. Tchr. spl. reading Washington County Schs., Sandersville, Ga., 1971-72; tchr. spl. needs Adairsville (Ga.) Sch., 1973-75; instr. genealogy Blue Ridge Community Coll., Flat Rock, N.C., 1977-85; property mistress, set decorator Flat Rock Playhouse, State Theatre N.C., 1979-85; software specialist, computer cons. Fonda Corp., St. Albans, Vt., 1985-87; pub., editor Cane Break Pub., Spartanburg, S.C., 1985—; cons. in arts State Theatre N.C., 1984. Author: Cane Break Cooking, 1990; contbr. articles to profl. jours. Organizing corr. sec. Henderson County Dem. Women, 1978-80, bd. dirs., 1991—; bd. dirs. Henderson Little Theatre, 1977-85, exec. v.p., 1985; bd. dirs. Spartanburg Coalition for Choice, 1989; active NOW, 1992—, coord. Spartanburg chpt., 1992-93, treas., 1996—, coord. S.C., 1993-95; active Voters United for Equality, 1993—, Spartanburg Nat. Women's Polit. Caucus, 1992—, Fair Share, Human Rights Campaign Fund, County Dem. Party Golden Donkey Group; state legis. co-chair S.C. NOW, 1995—. Recipient S.C. NOW award, 1994, Geraldine Ferraro Woman of Yr. award, 1994; named Woman of Yr., DAR, 1974. Mem. AAUW, ACLU, VOICES (organizing mem. 1996), Carolina Alliance for Fair Employment, Corry Family Soc., Clark Family Soc. (bd. dirs., editor newsletter 1989-93). Episcopalian. Home and Office: 1009 Oak Creek Dr Spartanburg SC 29302-2981

CLARK, EMORY EUGENE, financial planning executive; b. Opelika, Ala., Jan. 24, 1931; s. Bunk Henry and Dorothy (Bolt) C.; m. Jean F. Reed, Sept. 30, 1951; children: Steven E., Michael E. Grad. pub. schs. CLU; CFP. With Mgrs. Life Ins. Co., 1956-74, agt. supr., L.A., 1956-60, mgr. Hawaii br., 1960-65, Pitts. br., 1965-68, Houston br., 1968-74; with Jefferson Standard Life Ins. Co., Fort Worth, 1974-82; fin. planner E.F. Hutton & Co., Inc., 1983-90; v.p. investments A.G. Edwards & Sons, Inc., Ft. Worth, 1990—. 1st Lt. Inf. AUS, 1950-56. Mem. Fort Worth Life Underwriters Assn., Am. Soc. Life Underwriters, Fort Worth Soc. Life Underwriters, Ft. Worth Securities Dealers Assn., Inst. Cert. Fin. Planners (cert., registered practitioner). Home: 8109 Meadowbrook Dr Fort Worth TX 76120-5309 Office: AG Edwards & Sons Inc 777 Main St Ste C-50 Fort Worth TX 76102

CLARK, ERIC C., state official; b. Smith County, Miss.; s. Mr. and Mrs. John S. C.; m. Karan C.; children: Charles, Catherine. BA in History with distinction, Millsaps Coll.; MA, U. Miss.; D in History, Miss. State U. Tchr. history and govt. Miss. Coll., 1989-95; mgr. family tree farm Smith County; sec. of state State of Miss., 1995—. Mem. Baptist Ch. Address: PO Box 136 Jackson MS 39205

CLARK, FAYE LOUISE, drama and speech educator; b. La., Oct. 9, 1936; student Centenary Coll., 1954-55; BA with honor, U. Southwestern La., 1962; MA, U. Ga., 1966; PhD, Ga. State U., 1992; m. Warren James Clark, Aug. 8, 1969; children: Roy, Kay Natalie. Tchr., Nova Exptl. Schs., Fort Lauderdale, Fla., 1963-65; faculty dept. drama and speech DeKalb C.C., Atlanta, 1967—, chmn. dept., 1977-81. Pres. Hawthorne Sch. PTA, 1983-84. Mem. Ga. Theatre Conf. (sec. 1968-69, rep. to Southeastern Theatre Conf. 1969), Ga. Psychol. Assn., Ga. Speech Assn., Atlanta Ballet Guild, Friends of the Atlanta Opera, Southeastern Theatre Conf., Atlanta Hist. Soc., Atlanta Artists Club (sec. 1981-83, dir. 1983-89), Young Women of Arts, Speech Communication Assn., Phi Kappa Phi, Pi Kappa Delta, Sigma Delta Pi, Kappa Delta Pi, Thalian-Blackfriars. Presbyterian. Club: Lake Lanier Sailing. Home: 2521 Melinda Dr NE Atlanta GA 30345-1918 Office: DeKalb Coll Humanities Divsn North Campus Dunwoody GA 30338

CLARK, GARY D., medical educator, researcher; b. Baton Rouge, June 25, 1956; s. Carrol A. and Beverly (Bacon) C.; m. Maureen Ann Rooney, June 2, 1984; children: Christopher Sean, Andrew Jonathan, Madeline Elizabeth. BS, La. State U., 1978, MD, 1982. Intern, resident Boston Children's Hosp., 1982-84; resident, neurology fellow Washington U., St. Louis, 1984-89, postdoctoral rsch. fellow, 1987-89; asst. prof. La. State U. Med. Ctr., New Orleans, 1990-94, Baylor Coll. of Medicine, Houston, 1994—. Contbr. articles to profl. jours. Mem. adv. bd. Stuart Hall Sch., New Orleans, 1993-94; com. chmn. Pack 505, 1996—. Recipient George S. Bel award Am. Heart Assn., 1991, Clinician Scientist award NIH, 1991. Fellow Am. Acad. Pediatrics, Am. Acad. Neurology; mem. Soc. Neurosci., Child Neurology Soc. (sci. selection com. 1993-95). Roman Catholic. Office:

Pediatric Neurology Clin Care Ctr #955 6621 Fannin St # Mc3 3311 Houston TX 77030-2303

CLARK, HANLEY C., state insurance commissioner; b. Huntington, W. Va.; m. Holly Hoback; 3 children. BA in History, English, Bus., Marshall U., 1972; MA in History, U. W. Va., 1974. Spl. asst. to gov. State of W. Va., Charleston, 1980-81, asst. to ins. commr., 1981-85, dep. ins. commr., 1985-88, acting ins. commr., 1988-89, ins. commr., 1989—. Mem. Nat. Assn. Ins. Commrs. (chmn s.e. zone). Office: WV Insurance Comm PO Box 50540 Charleston WV 25305-0540

CLARK, IRA C., hospital association administrator, educator. BA Gen. Sci., U. Iowa, 1959, MA honors Health and Hosp. Adminstrn., 1966; grad. Bus. Adminstrn., Rider Coll., 1963. Adminstrv. asst. divsn. Hosps. Iowa State Dept. Health, Des Moines, 1964; spl. asst. dir. planning and devel. Montefiore Hosp. and Med. Ctr., Bronx, N.Y., 1970; asst. dir. Montefiore Hosp. and Med. Ctr., Bronx, 1965-70; assoc. dir. Jersey City Med. Ctr., 1970-71, exec. dir., 1971-75; CEO Woodhull Hosp. and Mental Health Ctr., 1982-84; exec. dir. Bellevue Hosp. Ctr., 1984-85; CEO, regional adminstr. Kings County Hosp. Ctr., Bklyn., 1976-87; pres. & ceo Pub. Health Trust Jackson Meml. Hosp., 1987—; bd. dirs. Fla. Hosp. Assn., So. Fla. Hosp. Assn.; panelist Robert Wood Johnson Found. Symposium, Princeton, N.J., 1986; chmn. Coun. Exec. dirs. N.Y.C. Health and Hosps. Corp., 1978-82; chmn. com. strategic planning Coun. Exec. dirs. Counterpart com. bd. dirs.; spl. adv. panel Emergency Svcs. Act, Advanced Para-medic Tng. N.J.; adj. faculty, lectr. various Univs.; spkr. in field. Author: The History and Development of Continuing Physical Education, 1966. Recipient Disting. Svc. award Commr. Mental Health, N.Y., 1981. Mem. Am. Hosp. Assn. (house dels., charter mem. pub. gen. hosps. sect., com. nominations bd. trustees pub.-gen. hosp. sect.), Assn. Am. Med. Colls. (gen. assembly coun. teaching hosps.), N.J. Hosp. Assn. (vice chmn., chmn. coun. govt. ops. of bd. trustees, spl. com. polit. strategy). Office: Jackson Meml Hosp 1611 NW 12th Ave Miami FL 33136-1005*

CLARK, JACK, retired hospital company executive, accountant; b. Munford, Ala., Feb. 23, 1932; s. Raymond E. and Ora (Camp) C.; m. Louise Omega Lackey, Jan. 30, 1951; 1 son, Terry Wayne. BS, Springhill Coll., Mobile, Ala., 1960. Staff acct. Max E. Miller, C.P.A., Mobile, 1960-62; comptr. Mobile Gen. Hosp., 1962-67; assoc. adminstr. fin. Univ. Med. Ctr., Mobile, 1967-74; regional mgr. Humana Inc., Mobile, 1974-75, v.p., 1975-80, sr. v.p., 1980-84, exec. v.p., 1984-93; exec. v.p. Galen Health Care, Mobile, 1993-94; ret. Columbia-HCA Healthcare, 1994; trustee Mid-South region Humana hosps., 1974-87, Southwestern region, 1987-89, region IV, 1989-91, region 2, 1991-93, Regional Hosps., Columbia/HCA, 1994—. Bd. dirs. Agape S. Ala., Mobile, 1983; trustee Faulkner U., Montgomery, Ala., 1993—. Served in USAF, 1952-56, Korea. Mem. Hosp. Fin. Mgmt. Assn. (assoc.), Am. Hosp. Assn., Ala. Hosp. Assn., Ala. Hosp. Assn. Accts. (pres. so. council, dir. 1967-68), Mobile C. of C. Democrat. Mem. Ch. of Christ. Home: 6449 Cane Brake Dr Mobile AL 36695-3817

CLARK, JAMES COVINGTON, journalist, historian; b. Washington, May 22, 1947; s. William Edward and Louise (Covington) C.; children: Randall Healy, Kevin Healy. BA, Lenoir-Rhyne Coll., 1975; MA, Stetson U., 1986. Reporter UPI, Washington, 1967, Columbia (S.C.) Record, 1968; reporter AP, Charlotte, N.C., 1969-70, Phila., 1972-73; reporter Hickory (N.C.) Daily Record, 1974-75; regional editor Tampa (Fla.) Tribune, 1976-77; asst. exec. editor The Orlando (Fla.) Sentinel, 1977—; adj. prof. U. Ctrl. Fla., Orlando, 1986—. Author: Last Train South, 1984, Faded Glory: Presidents Out of Power, 1985, The Murder of James Garfield, 1994; syndicated comic writer Terry and the Pirates. Recipient George Polk award L.I. U., 1983, Gerald Loeb award, L.A., 1983, Arthur Thompson prize Fla. Hist. Soc., Gainesville, 1989. Mem. Authors Guild, Fla. Soc. Newspaper Editors (bd. dirs.), Orgn. Am. Historians, Am. Hist. Assn. Office: The Orlando Sentinel 633 N Orange Ave Orlando FL 32801-1300

CLARK, JAMES GREGORY, financial coordinator, political consultant; b. Louisville, Sept. 6, 1962; s. James Everett and Mary Louise (Adamson) C. Student, Gutenburg U., West Germany, 1985; BA in Polit. Sci., U. Louisville, 1988. Asst. campaign mgr. Mulloy for Congress, Louisville, 1984; campaign asst. mgr. Brown for Gov., Louisville, 1987; law clk. Wyatt, Tarrant & Combs, Louisville, 1987-88; policy analyst Jefferson County Govt., Louisville, 1988-89; fin. cons. trainee Shearson, Lehman, Louisville, 1989; stockbroker Stifel Nicolaus, Louisville, 1990-92; asset mgr. Dean Witter Reynolds, Louisville, 1972-93; fundraiser Dem. Leadership Coun., Washington, 1993; fin. coord. Moorhead for Md., Rockville, 1994—; fin. and fundraising asst. Clinton/Gore Presdl. Campaign, Ky., 1992; asst. campaign mgr. Paul Patton for Lt. Gov., Ky., 1991; asst. Dem. Nat. Conv., Atlanta, 1988. Sundaysch. tchr. Westport Rd. Bapt. Ch., Louisville, 1981—, deacon, 1993—; dir. Ky. Coll. Young Dems., Louisville, 1982-83. Democrat. Baptist. Home and Office: 7412 Glen Arbor Rd Louisville KY 40222-4005

CLARK, JANET EILEEN, political scientist, educator; b. Kansas City, Kans., June 5, 1940; d. Edward Francis and Mildred Lois (Mack) Morrissey; AA, Kansas City Jr. Coll., 1960; AB, George Washington U., Washington, 1962, MA, 1964; PhD, U. Ill., 1973; m. Caleb M. Clark, Sept. 28, 1968; children: Emily Claire, Grace Ellen, Evelyn Adair. Staff, U.S. Dept. Labor, Washington, 1962-64; instr. social sci. Kansas City (Kans.) Jr. Coll., 1964-67; instr. polit. sci. Parkland Coll., 1970-71; asst. prof. govt., N.Mex. State U., Las Cruces, 1971-77, assoc. prof., 1977-80; assoc. prof. polit. sci. U. Wyo., 1981-84, prof., 1984-94; prof. polit. sci., head dept. State U. West Ga., Carrollton, 1994—. Co-author: Women, Elections and Representation, 1987, The Equality State, 1988, Women in Taiwan Politics: Overcoming Barriers to Women's Participation in a Modernizing Society, 1990; editor Women & Politics, 1991—. Wolcott fellow, 1963-64, NDEA Title IV fellow, 1967-69. Mem. Internat. Soc. Polit. Psychology Gov. Coun., 1987-89. Mem. NEA (pres. chpt. 1978-79), Am. Polit. Sci. Assn., Western Polit. Sci. Assn. (exec. coun. 1984-87), Western Social Sci. Assn. (exec. coun. 1978-81, v.p. 1982, pres. 1985), Women's Caucus for Polit. Sci. (treas. 1982, pres. 1987), LWV (exec. bd. 1980-83, treas. 1986-90, pres. 1991-93), Women's Polit. Caucus, Beta Sigma Phi (v.p. chpt. 1978-79, sec. 1987-88, treas. 1988-89, v.p. 1989-90, pres. 1990-91), Phi Beta Kappa, Chi Omega (prize 1962), Phi Kappa Phi. Democrat. Lutheran. Book rev. editor Social Sci. Jour., 1982-87. Contbr. articles to profl. jours. Home: 333 Foster St # D-23 Carrollton GA 30117-2861 Office: West Ga Coll Dept Polit Sci Carrollton GA 30118

CLARK, JEANETTE MCLAIN, advertising agency executive, author; b. Pine Bluff, Ark., Nov. 11, 1946; d. William Isaiah and Grace Mae (Jones) McLain. BS, U. Ala., Tuscaloosa, 1969; MA, U. Ala., Birmingham, 1974; AA, U. Ala., 1979. Elem. tchr. Birmingham City Schs., 1970-76, Richardson (Tex.) Ind. Sch. Dist., 1976-78, Mountain Brook (Ala.) City Schs., 1978-81, Aldine (Tex.) Ind. Sch. Dist., 1981-84, Galena Park (Tex.) Ind. Sch. Dist., 1985-91; owner, pres. Poetic Sensations, Houston, 1991—; co-owner, v.p. Picturesque Thoughts, Houston, 1994—; dist. mgr. World Book Ency./World Book Ednl. Products, Houston, 1991-92; mktg. dir. Uvalde Pizza Inn, Houston, 1994-96. Author: Sometimes I Feel Like Running Away, 1995, Dazzling Daisy, 1996, Bo Boaster, 1995, Something Worth More Than Money, 1995. Vice pres. Beautification Vols., Houston, 1996; bd. dirs. Kid City USA, Houston, 1996; vol. anti-drug, anti-gang programs. Mem. Acres Homes C. of C. (corr. sec. 1996—).

CLARK, JEFF RAY, economist; b. Waynesboro, Va., Nov. 6, 1947; s. Jefferson Davis and Mildred (Cameron) C.; m. Arlene Donowitz, Dec. 17, 1988. BS, Va. Commonwealth U., 1970; MA, Va. Tech. U., Blacksburg, 1972, PhD, 1974. Assoc. dir. Joint Coun. Econ. Edn., N.Y.C., 1974-78, dir., 1978-80; chmn. econ./fin. Fairleigh Dickinson U., Madison, N.J., 1980-87; rsch. fellow Princeton (N.J.) U., 1987; Hendrix chair econs. U. Tenn., Martin, 1987-92; Probasco chair econs. U. Tenn., Chattanooga, 1992—; cons. Pew Charitable Trusts, Phila., 1987—, IT&T, Nutley, N.J., 1985, Fed. Res. Bank N.Y., N.Y.C., 1980, The Johns Hopkins U., Balt., 1984-86; disting. teaching fellow NSF, Washington, 1977, 78. Author: The Science of Cost, Benefit and Choice, 1988, 93, 96, Essentials of Economics, 1982, 86, Economics Cost and Choice, 1987, Macroeconomics for Managers, 1990. Bd. dirs. The William B. Cockroft Found., The Palmer Chitester Fund. Mem. Assn. for Pvt. Enterprise (v.p. 1991, pres. 1992, sec./treas.), Am. Econ. Assn., Ea. Econ. Assn. (bd. dirs. 1980-85), Western Econ. Assn., So. Econ. Assn. Home: 1623 Ashley Mill Dr Chattanooga TN 37421-3259 Office: U Tenn 615 Mccallie Ave Chattanooga TN 37403-2504

CLARK, JOHN GRAHAM, III, lawyer; b. Greenville, N.C., Dec. 28, 1950; s. John Graham Jr. and Ariane (Downarowicz) C. BA, U. N.C., 1973; MA, E. Carolina U., 1977; JD, Campbell U., 1984. Bar: N.C. 1984, U.S. Dist. Ct. N.C. 1988, U.S. Supreme Ct. 1988. Assoc. Nelson Taylor, III, Morehead City, N.C., 1985; asst. dist. atty. State of N.C., 1985-87; ptnr. Clark & James law firm, Greenville, 1987—. Named to Internat. Law Moot Ct. Assn. Student Internat. Law Socs., 1983. Mem. N.C. Bar Assn., N.C. Acad. Trial Lawyers, Phi Alpha Delta, Pi Sigma Alpha, Phi Alpha Theta. Office: 315 S Evans St Greenville NC 27858

CLARK, JOYCE NAOMI JOHNSON, nurse; b. Corpus Christi, Tex., Oct. 4, 1936; d. Chester Fletcher and Ermal Olita (Bailey) Johnson; m. William Boyd Clark, Jan. 4, 1958; (div. 1967); 1 child, Sherene Joyce. Student, Corpus Christi State U., 1975-77. RN, CNOR, ACLS; cert. instrument flight instr. Staff nurse Van Nuys (Calif.) Cmty. Hosp., 1963-64, U.S. Naval Hosp., Corpus Christi, 1964-68; patient care coord. Spohn Meml. Hosp. (formerly Meml. Med. Ctr.), Corpus Christi, 1968—. Leader Paisano Coun. Girl Scouts U.S.A., Corpus Christi, 1968-74; past comdr. 3rd group USAF Aux., CAP Air Search and Rescue, wing chief pilot, ret. lt. col. 1993. Recipient Charles A. Mella award Meml. Med. ctr., 1981, Paul E. Garbert award CAP, 1986, cert. of appreciation in recognition of Support Child Guard Missing Children Edn. Program Nat. Assn. Chiefs of Police, Washington, 1987, Charles E. Yeager Aerospace Edn. Achievement award, 1985, Grover Loenig Aerospace award, 1986, Cert. of World Leadership Internat. Biographical Ctr., Cambridge, Eng., 1987, Gill Robb Wilson award #1021, 1988, Merit award Drug Free Am. Through Enforcement, Edn., Intelligence Nat. Assn. Chiefs of Police, Sr. Mem. of Yr. USAF Aux., CAP Air Search and Rescue, 1986. Mem. USAF Aux., CAP Air Search and Rescue (past comdr. 3rd group, wing chief pilot, Sr. Mem. of Yr. 1986), Am. Assn. Oper. Rm. Nurses (v.p. 1969), Aircraft Owners and Pilots Assn. Home: 1001 Carmel Pky Apt 33 Corpus Christi TX 78411-2152 Office: Meml Med Ctr 4606 Hospital Blvd Corpus Christi TX 78405-1818

CLARK, KEITH COLLAR, musician, educator; b. Grand Rapids, Mich., Nov. 21, 1927; s. Harry Holt and Bethyl June (Collar) C.; m. Marjorie Ruth Park, Dec. 8, 1951; children: Nancy Joy Clark McCulley, Sandra Lynn Clark Masse, Karen Jean Clark Moore, Beth Anne Clark Barnard. Student of trumpet, Nat. Music Camp, Interlochen, Mich., 1943. 44, 45; studied under Lloyd Geisler, 1947-48, studied under Armando Ghitalla, 1974. Trumpet player Grand Rapids Symphony Orch., 1943-46; with U.S. Army, 1946, advanced through grades to master sgt., 1966; trumpet player U.S. Army Band, Washington, 1946-66; ret., 1966; assoc. prof. brass Houghton (N.Y.) Coll., 1966-80; cons., asst. project dir. Dictionary Am. Hymnology, Bethesda, Md., 1980-81; prin. trumpet S.W. Fla. Symphony Orch., Ft. Myers, 1982-86, Treasure Coast Symphony Orch., Ft. Pierce, Fla., 1989-94, Atlantic Classical Orch., Vero Beach, Fla., 1991—; adj. prof. Edison C.C., Ft. Myers, 1984-89, Indian River C.C., Ft. Pierce, 1989-94; instr. Montgomery Coll., Bethesda, 1964-66, Roberts Wesleyan Coll., Rochester, N.Y., 1969-70; condr. Houghton Coll. Symphony Orch., 1966-78, Concert Band, 1975-80; lectr. Inst. Musica Suera Mexicana, Pueblo, 1973; guest condr. Buffalo Philharm. Orch., 1969, Treasure Coast Symphony Orch., 1990. Author: A Selective Bibliography for the Study of Hymns, 1980; assoc. editor The Instrumentalist mag., 1974-76; contbr. articles to profl. publs. Music dir. Maryland Avenue Bapt. Ch., Washington, 1947-51, Cherrydale Bapt. Ch., Arlington, Va., 1953-60, Christ Meth. Ch., Arlington, 1961-65, Vero Beach Alliance Ch., 1990-93. Recipient honor awards Nat. Sch. Orch. Assn., 1976, 80. Mem. Internat. Trumpet Guild (charter, project dir. 1978-80), Hymn Soc. Am. (life, grantee 1980-81), Ch. Music Soc. (Eng.) (life), Hymn Soc. Gt. Britain and Ireland (life), Nat. Ch. Music Fellowship (pres. 1967-69), Sonneck Soc. Home: 801 Linnaen Ter NW Port Charlotte FL 33948-3616

CLARK, KEVIN ANTHONY, communications executive; b. Kansas City, Mo., Dec. 10, 1956; s. Harley Leon and Virginia Lee (Magee) C.; m. Heidi Jean Sawyer. BS, U. Tulsa, 1978. Producer, announcer Sta. KWGS-FM, Tulsa, 1976-78; assoc. communications specialist IBM Corp., Charlotte, N.C., 1979-80; communications specialist IBM Corp., Tarrytown, N.Y., 1981-82; staff communications specialist IBM Corp., White Plains, N.Y., 1983-84; corp. speak up adminstr., sr. communications specialist IBM Corp., Armonk, N.Y., 1985-87; info. rep., program adminstr. IBM Corp., White Plains, 1988-90, mgr. svcs. and mktg. media rels., 1991-93; mgr. U.S. pub. rels. IBM, 1993-94; mgr. Global Multimedia Comms., 1994-95; product mgr. global strategic mktg. mobile computing IBM PC Co., Research Triangle Park, N.C., 1995—; dir. corp. communications Okla. Intercollegiate Legislature, Oklahoma City, 1977. Author: IBM Speak Up Manual, 1986; editor: (brochure) IBM in Real Estate and Construction, 1984 (Excellence award IBM 1984, cert. Merit Printing Industries Am. 1984); author: (with others) Strategic Public Relations and Integrated Communications. Named one of Outstanding Young Men of Am., 1985. Mem. Pub. Rels. Soc. Am., Am. Mgmt. Assn., MIT Media Lab. (mem. steering com.). Home: 907 Linden Rd Chapel Hill NC 27514-7742 Office: IBM Corp 3039 Cornwallis Rd Research Triangle Park NC 27709

CLARK, LADY ELLEN MARIE, occupational health nurse, consultant; b. Jennings, La., Jan. 12, 1944; d. Henry A. and Marie Kathryn (Werner) Winters; m. Gerald L. Clark, May 12, 1990; 1 child, Eric Paul Cone; 1 foster child, Jerri Lynn Jacobs; stepchildren: Lisa Lynn Barroso, Julie Ann Rothschild. Diploma, Bapt. Hosp. Sch. Nursing, 1966; student, Lamar U., 1961-64. RN, Tex.; cert. occupational health nurse specialist, case mgr. Coord. infection control dept. Beaumont (Tex.) Med./Surg. Hosp., 1980; occupational health coord. The Goodyear Tire & Rubber Co., Beaumont Chem. Plant, Beaumont, 1981-89; supr. health svcs. Sea World of Tex., San Antonio, 1989; occupational health cons. Rehab. Ctr. of South Tex., San Antonio, 1990-91; mgr. health svcs. Pioneer Flour Mills, San Antonio, 1991—; v.p. adv. coun. Park Place Hosp., 1986-87, pres., 1987-89. Mem. steering com. and parish coun. St. Jude Thaddeus Cath. Ch., 1974-84, St. Jude's Cath. Ch., San Antonio; commn. Tex. div. Am. Cancer Soc., 1986—. Recipient Don't Get Burned award Am. Cancer Soc., 1986, Tex. State Occupational Health Schering award, 1989. Mem. Am. Assn. Occupational Health Nurses (chmn. com. local chpt. Am. Occupational Health conf. 1990), Tex. State Assn. Occupational Health Nursing (pres. 1986-90, treas. 1990-94, Sabine area chpt. 1981-84, treas. 1984, pres. 1984-87, State Occupational Health Nursing Achievement award 1986), S.E. Tex. Safety Coun. (treas. 1987-89), Sigma Theta Tau (Nat. Nursing Imagemaker award Delta Alpha chpt. 1989). Home: 310 Clubhill Dr San Antonio TX 78228-1905 Office: Pioneer Flour Mills PO Box 118 San Antonio TX 78291-0118

CLARK, LEIF MICHAEL, federal judge; b. Washington, Nov. 12, 1947; s. Charles G. and Gertrude Lyda (Zimmer) C. BA cum laude, U. Md., 1968; MDiv, Trinity Luth. Sem., Columbus, Ohio, 1972; JD cum laude, U. Houston, 1980. Bar: Tex. 1980, U.S. Dist. Ct. (we. dist.) Tex. 1981, U.S. Dist. Ct. (so. dist.) Tex. 1983, U.S. Ct. Appeals (5th cir.). 1984. Dir. Housing for Exceptional People, Detroit, 1974-75; ptnr. Cox & Smith, Inc., San Antonio, 1980-87; judge for western dist. Tex. U.S. Bankruptcy Ct., San Antonio, 1987—; prof. McGeorge Internat. Law Program, Salzburg, Austria, 1989-95; mem. adv. group U.S. Del. Working Group UNCITRAL, 1995-96; mem. adv. bd. ALI-ABA Cross Border Insolvency Project, 1995-96, USAID Jud. Tng. Project, 1995-96. Adv. bd. Insol Internat. Project, 1995. Mem. ABA, Am. Coll. Bankruptcy, Am. Bankruptcy Inst. (dir. 1991—, exec. com. 1995—), Nat. Conf. Bankruptcy Judges (planning com. 1992 ann. meeting), Comml. Law League, State Bar Tex. Lutheran. Office: PO Box 2676 San Antonio TX 78299-2676

CLARK, LINDA WILSON, educational administrator; b. Milburn, Ky., Apr. 18, 1939; d. James Oscar and Bennie Ophelia (Hayden) Wilson; m. Voris Wayne Clark, June 10, 1960; children: Angela Sharlet, John Wilson. BS, Murray State U., 1964, ME, 1970, rank I cert. in sch. adminstrn., 1972. Cert. tchr., sch. adminstr., Ky. Tchr. math. Hickman County High Sch., Clinton, Ky., 1964-68, Cen. Elem. Sch., Clinton, 1970-71; librarian Cen. Elem. Sch., 1972-78, Hickman County High Sch., 1979-87; instrnl. supr., fed. program coord. Hickman County Bd. Edn., Clinton, 1987-94; cons. Ky. Dept. Edn., Frankfort, 1975; speaker at profl. meetings. Costume designer, dir. local theater prodns., 1985—. Bd. dirs. Hickman County Pub. Libr., Clinton, 1981-93; mem. Hickman County Dem. Com., 1982. Named hon. Ky. Col., 1963, Woman of Woodcraft, 1969. Mem. ASCD, Ky. Coun. Adminstrs. Spl. Edn., West Ky. Assn. Adminstrs., West Ky. Assn. Sch. Suprs. (pres. 1991-92, sec.-treas. 1992—), West Ky. Assn. Spl. Edn. Coords., Ky. Assn. Sch. Adminstrs., First Dist. Edn. Assn., Bykota Homemakers (pres. 1980-81, v.p. 1985-86, pres., 1995—). Baptist. Home: 7391 State Rt 58 E Wingo KY 42088-9610 Office: Hickman County Bd Edn RR 3 Clinton KY 42031-9803

CLARK, MARY MACHEN, community health nurse; b. LeCompte, La., Jan. 13, 1940; d. Isaac and Louella (Snowden) Machen; m. Johnnie L. Clark, Nov. 5, 1961; 1 child, Roxane M. ADN, La. State U., 1969; BS in Nursing, Northwestern State U., 1985. Cert. med-surg. nurse, ACLS and CPR instr. Staff nurse VA Med. Ctr., Alexandria, La., 1973-90; staff nurse ob-gyn. ICU Rapids Gen. Hosp., Alexandria, 1969-73; med. nurse VA Med. Ctr., Alexandria, 1990—, community health nursing coord., 1990—; reporter Monitor Alexandria VA Med. Ctr. Newsletter, 1988-90. Mem. Rapides Parish Libr. Bd. of Control, 1989-94. Recipient Svc. award Girl Scouts U.S., 1982, Spl. Advancement for Performance award Alexandria VA Med. Ctr., 1982, 86, 91, Cert. of Appreciation Profl. Image award Dept. Veterans Affairs, 1993. Mem. ANA, La. State Nurses Assn., Alexandria Dist. Nurses Assn. (bd. dirs. 1991), Nurses Orgn. Vets. Affairs, Am. Heart Assn., Sigma Theta Tau (Nu Tau chpt.). Home: PO Box 101 Lecompte LA 71346-0101

CLARK, MICHAEL EARL, psychologist; b. Berea, Ohio, July 20, 1951; s. William Gray and Marguerite Jane (Charles) C.; m. Laura Lynn Putt, June 19, 1976 (div. Nov. 1987); 1 child, Brian Gray. BA, Kent State U., 1974, PhD, 1978. Asst. dir., chem. dependency unit N.D. State Hosp., Jamestown, N.D., 1978-79; staff psychologist VA Med. Ctr., Chillicothe, Ohio, 1979-84, Bay Pines, Fla., 1984-89; clin. dir., pain program James A. Haley Vets. Hosp., Tampa, Fla., 1989—; assoc. prof. dept. psychology U. South Fla., Tampa, 1986—, clin. asst. prof. dept. neurology Sch. Medicine, Tampa, 1991—; adj. psychologist, counseling ctr. U. South Fla.; pvt. practice program cons., Tampa, 1987—; cons. to the correctional med. authority, State of Fla., 1993—. Contbr. chpts. to Innovations in Clinical Practice, 1991, Social Psychology: A Sourcebook, 1983; contbr. articles to Biofeedback and Self-Regulation, Jour. Personality Assessment, Jour. Clin. Psychology, Jour. Dental Rsch., The Va. Practitioners, Psychol. Assessment. Vice chmn. Paint Valley Mental Health Bd., Chillicothe, 1980-84. Mem. APA, Am. Psychol. Soc. (charter), Am. Pain Soc., N.Y. Acad. Scis., Internat. Assn. for Study of Pain, Soc. for Personality Assessment, So. Pain Soc. Democrat. Home: 9645 Fox Hearst Rd Tampa FL 33647-1829 Office: Psychology Svc (116B) VAMC 13000 Bruce B Downs Blvd Tampa FL 33612-4745

CLARK, MORTON HUTCHINSON, lawyer; b. Norfolk, Va., Apr. 21, 1933; s. David Henderson and Catharine Angelica (Hutchinson) C.; m. Lynn Harrison Adams, Aug. 12, 1961; children: Allison Adams, David Henderson, Susan West, Julia Dixon. BA in English, U. Va., 1954, LLB, 1960. Bar: Va. 1960, U.S. Dist. Ct. (ea. dist.) Va. 1960, U.S. Ct. Appeals (4th cir.) 1976, U.S. Ct. Appeals (1st cir.) 1993, U.S. Supreme Ct. 1993. Assoc. Vandeventer, Black, Meredith & Martin, Norfolk, 1960-65, ptnr., 1965—. Co-editor: The Virginia Lawyer, 1991-93. Chmn. Va. Commn. for Children and Youth, Richmond. Fellow Am. Coll. Trial Lawyers, Va. Law Found.; mem. Maritime Law Assn. (exec. com. 1984-87), Hoffman I'Anson Am. Inns of Ct. (exec. com. 1993-95), The Harbor Club (pres.), Town Point Club, Princess Anne Country Club, Farmington Country Club. Episcopalian. Home: 608 Linkhorn Dr Virginia Beach VA 23452 Office: Vandeventer Black Meredith & Martin 500 World Trade Ctr Norfolk VA 23510

CLARK, OUIDA OUIJELLA, public relations executive, educator; b. Birmingham, Ala., Dec. 7, 1949; d. Fred and Johnnie (Norrington) C. BA in Spanish Edn., Dillard U., New Orleans, 1971; grad. cert. pub. relations Am. U., 1973, U. Valencia (Spain), 1974; cert. journalism NYU, 1972; postgrad. U. Chgo., 1980. Fgn. Svc. intern USIA, 1971; freelance pub. relations cons., 1972-76; tchr. English as 2d lang. Arlington (Va.) Pub. Schs., 1976-78; founder, pres. Clark Prodns., Ltd., Inc., Little Rock, 1981—; pres., founder Global Pub. Rels., Inc., Washington, 1976, and Little Rock, 1981-95, Am. Remodeling Century 21 Home Improvement, Los Angeles, Calif., 1996; multilingual free-lance pub. rels. cons.; rsch. assoc. Philander Smith Coll., 1980-81; active Africare Project, Senagal, Upper Volta, Mauritania, Niger, Chad, Sierra Leone, 1973; founder Internat. Ptnr. Sch., Vienna, Austria; Sears contractor Am. Remodeling, Little Rock, L.A., 1994-95. Recipient Pub. Rels. award Nat. Powderly Alumni Assn., 1977, NEA support funds, 1987; Ark. Endowment Humanities grantee, 1982. Musical composer, dir. Children of the 21st Century; author (radio play) Bon Voyage, Everything Has Its Place, You Just Can't Drift, Culture is Never Tasteless, various dramas for Horizons of Success series, Everything Has Its Place, On Life of James Weldon Johnson, You Just Can't Drift, Culture Is Never Tasteless, It Comes From Within Life of J.C. Penny, Controlled By the Stars The Life of the Founders of Sears and Roebuck, You Must Make a Decision Life of Mahalia Jackson, A Mixed Blessing Life of W.C. Handy, A Passion to Succeed-A Story on the Life Milton Hershey, A Vision of Tomorrow-A Story of Ralph Bunche; project dir. radio programs. Mem. Pub. Rels. Soc. Am., Am. Film Inst., Capital Press Club, Dillard U. Alumni Assn. (co-founder, Ark. chpt.). Baptist. Contbr. articles to profl. jours.; patent Nat. Directory of Music and Dance Studios, 1978, rev., 1980. Office: PO Box 583 Little Rock AR 72203-0583

CLARK, PAUL BUDDY, management information systems educator, consultant; b. Pitts., Dec. 30, 1944; s. Cecil Conrad and Joyce Agnes (Scott) C.; m. Joann Mariano, Mar. 1, 1969 (div. Mar. 1993); 1 child, Scott. BSBA, Duquesne U., 1968; MBA, Kent State U., 1979, PhD, 1992. Food svc. dir. U. Pitts., 1970, Drew U., Madison, N.J., 1970-74, Kent (Ohio) State U., 1974-80; food svc. dir. Cleve. City Sch. Dist., 1980-85, purchasing dir., 1985-86, dir. mgmt. info. sys., 1986-93; asst. prof. S.C. State U., Orangeburg, 1993—; bd. trustees Nutrition for Greater Cleve., 1980-84, pres., 1984; mgmt. seminar presenter Food Svc. Assn., Inc., Dunkirk, N.Y., 1982-86. Developer Problem Decision Support Sys. Info. sys. developer, cons. Spears for Adj. Gen. Campaign, Columbia, S.C., 1994. Sgt. U.S. Army, 1969-70, Vietnam, officer Army Nat. Guard, 1976-95. Decorated Bronze Star; recipient Rsch. grant S.C. State U., 1995. Mem. Internat. Info. Sys. Mgmt. Assn., Internat. Sch. Bus. Computing Assn., So. Mgmt. Assn., Beta Gamma Sigma. Home: 501 Pelham Dr D-103 Columbia SC 29209 Office: SC State Univ Sch of Bus Orangeburg SC 29117

CLARK, ROBERT M., JR., lawyer; b. Dallas, Mar. 7, 1948; s. Robert M. Sr. and Dorrace Helen (Schaerdel) C.; m. Kimberly Anne Kerss. BBA, U. Tex., 1972; MBA, So. Meth. U., 1978; JD, Oklahoma City U., 1982. Bar: Tex. 1982, U.S. Dist. Ct. (no. dist.) Tex. 1982, U.S. Ct. Appeals (5th cir.) 1982, U.S. Supreme Ct. 1988; cert. in civil trial law Tex. Bd. Legal Specialization. Ptnr. Eddleman, Clark & Rosen, Dallas, 1989—. Contbr. articles to profl. jours. Del. state conv. Tex. Rep. Party, 1970, 72, 74, 82, 90. Named Eagle Scout Boy Scouts Am., 1963. Fellow Soc. Antiquaries (Scot.); mem. ABA, State Bar Tex., Am. Bd. Trial Advs. (Dallas chpt.), Oak Cliff Bar Assn. (pres. 1990), Tex. Assn. Def. Counsel, Am. Soc. Legal History, Soc. of the Cin., Aztec Club, Sons Republic of Tex., Founders and Patriots Am., Knight of Order of St. John (Johanniterorden-Bailiwick of Brandenberg), Army and Navy Club (Washington), City Tavern Club (Washington), Phi Delta Phi, Phi Delta Theta. Episcopalian. Office: 4627 N Central Expy Dallas TX 75205-4022

CLARK, ROSS BERT, II, lawyer; b. Lafayette, Ind., Dec. 23, 1932; s. Ross Bert Sr. and Pauline Frances (Wilkinson) C.; m. Madge Logan Johnson, Dec. 27, 1959; 1 stepchild, George W. Johnson III. BA in History, U. of the South, 1954; JD, U. Tenn., 1960. Bar: Tenn. 1961, U.S. Dist. Ct. (we. dist.) Tenn., 1961, U.S. Dist. Ct. (no. dist.) Miss,. 1981, U.S. Dist. Ct. (ea. dist.) Ark., U.S. Ct. Appeals (6th cir.) 1962. Law clk. to presiding judge U.S. Dist. Ct. (we. dist.) Tenn., Memphis, 1961-62; assoc. Rupert & Ewing, Memphis, 1962-64, Laughlin, Watson, Garthright & Halle, Memphis, 1964-68; ptnr. Laughlin, Halle, Clark, Gibson, McBride, Memphis, 1968-84, McKnight, Hudson, Lewis, Henderson & Clark, Memphis, 1985-91, Apperson, Crump, Duzane & Maxwell, Memphis, 1991-96, Armstrong, Allen, Prewitt, Gentry, Johnston & Holmes, Memphis, 1996—; instr. med. and dental jurisprudence Coll. Health Scis., U. Tenn., Memphis, 1963-72; asst. city atty. City of Memphis, 1972-78. Chmn. bd. dirs. Memphis Heart Assn., 1971-72; mem. U. Tenn. Law Sch. Adv. Coun., 1983-90, chmn., 1986-88; trustee U. of South, 1992-95. Fellow Am. Bar Found., Tenn. Bar Found. (trustee 1989-97, chmn. 1996-97); mem. ABA, Tenn. Bar Assn. (ho. dels. 1986-88, bd. govs. 1988-94), Memphis Bar Assn. (treas. 1980, sec. 1981, v.p. 1982, pres. 1984), Rotary (sec. 1988, bd. dirs. 1988-90). Republican. Episcopalian. Office: Apperson Crump Duzane & Maxwell 1 Commerce Sq Ste 2110 Memphis TN 38103

CLARK, ROY THOMAS, JR., chemistry educator, administrator; b. Lockhart, Tex., Feb. 22, 1922; s. Roy Thomas and Ada Louise (Masur) C.; B.S. in Chemistry, S.W. Tex. State Coll., 1947, M.A. in Chemistry, 1950; m. Lavanie Anne Busby, Jan. 3, 1948; 1 son, Thomas David. Commd. 2d lt. USAAF, 1943; advanced through grades to lt. col. USAF, 1966; various assignments U.S., 1943-59; project officer propulsion br. Agena div. Directorate Space Systems, Air Force Ballistic Missile Div., Los Angeles, 1959-60; chief propulsion sect., astrovehicle br. Agena div. Office Dep. Comdr. Satellite Systems, Space Systems Div., Los Angeles, 1960-61; asst. prof. chemistry USAF Acad., Colo., 1961-63, assoc. prof., 1963-64; student Air Force Inst. Tech., Edn.-with-Industry Program, Aerojet Gen. Corp., Sacramento, 1964-65; project officer 6595th Aerospace Test Wing, Vandenberg AFB, Calif., 1965-66; chief Titan Launched Satellite Systems Office, 1966-69; ret., 1969; adminstrv. officer dept. chemistry U. Tex. at Austin, 1969-84. Decorated Air medal, Air Force Commendation medal, Meritorious Service medal. Mem. Am. Chem. Soc. Episcopalian. Home: 7711 Shadyrock Dr Austin TX 78731-1432

CLARK, SANDRA FAYE, medical technologist; b. Paducah, Ky., Oct. 21, 1954; d. Farmer Jr. ad Mildred Irene Sue (Burton) Collins; 1 child, Carla Sue Clark Cryts. BS in Biology, Murray State U., 1993. Med. technologist Columbia Regional Med. Ctr., Mayfield, Ky., 1993—. Mem. N.Y. Acad. Sci. Home: PO Box 43 West Paducah KY 42086

CLARK, SARA MOTT, retired home economics educator; b. Mahaffey, Pa., Sept. 19, 1915; d. William Benjamin and Anna Pearl (Murray) M.; m. Maximilian Steineger, Dec. 13, 1941; children: Max III, Benjamin Alan, Betsy Ann, Kathryn Louise. BS, Juniata Coll., Huntingdon, Pa., 1933-37, Ind. U. Pa., 1940-41. Dietician, Home Econ. Tchr., Internat. Porcelain Art Tchr. Dietician Adrian Hosp., Punxsutawney, Pa., 1937-40; home econs. tchr. Scio High Sch., Ohio, 1941-42, Punxsutawney (Pa.) Area Dist. Sch., 1960-77; artist, tchr. Internat. Porcelain Artist, Bradenton, Fla.; pres. N.W. Pa. Hosp. Dietetics Orgn., Punxsutawney, 1938-40; chmn. Am. Home Econs. Ctr. We. Dist., Punxsutawney, 1967-68; chmn. art com. The Shores, Bradenton, Fla. Vol. Art Display Internat. Porcelain Artist Atlanta Ga. 1986, Art in Action Festival Arts State Coll. 1981-82; Author: Various Porcelain Paintings China and Fla. 1986. Den mother Boy Scouts Am., Punxsutawney, 1951-56; Brownie leader Girl Scouts U.S., Punxsutawney, 1959; tchr. Sunday Sch. 1st Bapt. Ch., Punxsutawney, 1957-60; chmn. art com. The Shores at Bradenton Retirement Facility, 1996. Recipient Tribute to Porcelain Artist award Punxsutawney Spirit, 1987. Mem. AAUW (historian Bradenton 1991-93, chair bridge group 1993-94), Progressive Study Club (pres. 1953-54, 75-76, farewell luncheon award), Treasures of Porcelain Artists, Gulf Coast Porcelain Artists, New Floridians Club (1st v.p. 1994), The Shores (art chmn.). Republican. Home: Apt 1017 1700 3rd Ave W Bradenton FL 34205-5944

CLARK, SHELIA ROXANNE, sports association executive, legislative analyst; b. June 28, 1959; d. Milton Cornell and Mable Juanita (Grubb) C. BS in Polit. Sci., Radford U., 1983; MPA, James Madison U., Harrisonburg, Va., 1987. Dir. Black Teenage World Scholarship Program, Va., 1977-88; intern Field Found., New River Valley, Va., 1984-85, Rep. Rick Boucher, Washington, 1987; adminstrv. asst. OMB Watch, Washington, 1988; legis. asst. Nat. Community Action Found., Washington, 1988-93; exec. dir. Gary Clark's Sports Camp, 1990—; project coord. Student Coalition Against Tobacco, 1994-95; cons., asst. Nat. Children's Day Found., Washington, 1991-93. program dir. Project Unity, Va., 1984; bd. mem. VA Action, 1985, Grassroots Leadership Project, N.C., 1987; campaign worker Clinton Presdl. Campaign/Transition, Washington, 1992. Internship The Field Found., 1984-85, Congressman Rick Boucher, Washington, 1987. Mem. Nat. Council Negro Women. Home: PO Box 1865 Dublin VA 24084 Office: Gary Clarks Sports Camp 212 Broad St # C Dublin VA 24084-3203

CLARK, STEPHEN MICHAEL, information systems analyst; b. Huntsville, Ala., May 7, 1965; s. Charles Elvin Jr. and Betty Ann (Walker) C.; m. Susan Annette Gist, Jan. 3, 1987; 1 child, Christopher Michael. BS, U. North Ala., 1987. Mgr., cook, cashier KFC, Inc., Muscle Shoals, Ala., 1978-87; spreadsheet analyst Lockheed Missiles & Space Co., Huntsville, 1987; programmer SCI Systems, Inc., Huntsville, 1987-89; programmer/analyst PRC Inc., Huntsville, 1989-93; microcomputer systems analyst Athens (Ala.) State Coll., 1994—. Pub., editor: (newsletter) Hill Valley Telegraph, 1992—. Home: 1101 Cardinal Dr Madison AL 35758

CLARK, VICKY JO, artist; b. Lamesa, Tex., Sept. 14, 1937; d. John and Betty Lee (McCleskey) T.; m. Bobby Claude Clark, Jan. 2, 1960; children: John Mark, James Matthew, Ginger. Student, Abilene Christian U., 1956-59. instr. pastel workshops and pastel demonstrations. Exhibited in shows at The Pastel Soc. Am. Show, N.Y.C., 1987, 88, 89, 91, The Salmagundi Non-member Show, N.Y.C., 1988-91, The Catharine Lorillord Wolfe Show, N.Y.C., 1988-90, Shades of Pastel, Balt., 1989-90, Westcoast Pastel Soc. Show, Carmichael, Calif., 1988, 89, 91, Midwest Pastel Show, Chgo., 1989-91, Kans. Pastel Soc. Show, Wichita, 1986, 89-91, Degas Pastel Soc. Show, New Orleans, 1990, Nat. Miniature Show, La Lus, N. Mex., 1986-88, others; paintings published in the Best of Pastels Book. Recipient Southeastern Pastel Soc. Show 1st Pl. award, Atlanta, 1989, Shades of Pastel 89 Show Matthew and Mary Lou Fenton Portrait award, Balt., Nat. Miniature Show Best of Show award La Luz, N.Mex., 1987, Salmagundi-Pastel Soc. Am. NOA Mem. Show award. Mem. Pastel Soc. Am. (A&A Guffoni award), Catharine Lorillord Wolfe Art Club N.Y.C. Home: 607 SW Avenue I Seminole TX 79360-5313

CLARKE, DONALD DUHANEY, secondary education educator; b. Petersfield, Jamaica, Mar. 14, 1941; came to U.S., naturalized, 1996; m. Ann Clara Clarke, Apr. 24, 1971; children: Nova, Olivia, Gabrielle, Miranda. BS, U. West Indies, Kingston, Jamaica, 1964; BEd, Dalhousie U., Halifax, N.S., Can., 1966; Diploma in Pub. Adminstrn., Carlton U., Ottawa, Ont., Can., 1967; MA, Marquette U., 1969; MSc, U. Wis., Milw., 1970; MS, St. Thomas U., Miami, Fla., 1989; PhD, Union Inst., Ohio, 1997. Tchr. Mannings H.S., Westmoreland, Jamaica, 1964, Annapolis Royal (N.S.) Acad., 1967-68, Halifax Dept. Social Svc., 1966, St. Boniface Primary Sch., Milw., 1968-69; teaching fellow U. Wis., Milw., 1969-70; with Peace Corps, Detroit, 1970-71; tchr. Cayman Islands H.S., 1971-73, Marshalwick Sch., St. Albans, Eng., 1973-74; lectr. Coll. of the Bahamas, Nassau, 1975-80; ind. instr. hosps., Miami, Fla., 1981-84; instr. Montanari Residential Ctr., Hialeah, Fla., 1985-88; tchr. Douglas MacArthur North H.S., Hialeah, 1988—; assoc. London Inst. Edn., U. London, 1974. Mem. United Tchrs. of Dade, Pi Gamma Mu. Democrat. Home: 701 NW 186th Dr Miami FL 33169

CLARKE, J. CALVITT, JR., federal judge; b. Harrisburg, Pa., Aug. 9, 1920; s. Joseph Calvitt and Helen Caroline (Mattson) C.; m. Mary Jane Cromer, Feb. 1, 1943 (dec.1985); children: Joseph Calvitt III, Martha Tiffany; m. Betty Ann Holladay, May 29, 1986. BS in Commerce, U. Va., 1945, JD, 1945. Bar: Va. 1944. Practiced in Richmond, Va., 1944-74; partner firm Bowles, Anderson, Boyd, Clarke & Herod, 1944-60; firm Sands Anderson, Marks and Clarke, 1960-74; judge U.S. Dist. Ct. (ea. dist.) Va., 1975—; mem. 4th Circuit Judicial Conf., 1963; hon. consul for Republic of Bolivia, 1959-75. Chmn. Citizen's Advisory Com. on Joint Water System for Henrico and Hanover counties, Va., 1968-69; mem. Mayor's Freedom Train Com., 1948-50; del. Young Republican Nat. Conv., Salt Lake City, 1949, Boston, 1951; chmn. Richmond (Va.) Republican Com., 1952-54; candidate for Congress, 1954; chmn. Va. 3d Dist. Rep. Com., 1955-58, 74-75, Va. State Rep. Conv., 1958—; co-founder Young Rep. Fedn. of Va., 1950, nat. committeeman, 1950-54, chmn., 1955; chmn. 3d dist. Speakers Bur., Nixon-Lodge campaign, 1960, mem. fin. com., 1960-74; chmn. Henrico County Republican Com., 1956-58; fin. chmn. 1956; pres. Couples Sunday Sch. class Second Presbyn. Ch., Richmond, Va., 1948-50, mem. bd. deacons, 1948-61, elder, 1964—; bd. dirs. Family Service Children's Aid Soc., 1948-61, Gambles Hill Community Center, 1950-60, Christian Children's Fund, Inc., 1960-67, Children, Inc., 1967-75, Norfolk Forum, 1978-83; mem. bd. of chancellors Internat. Consular Acad., 1965-75; trustee Henrico County Pub. Library, chmn., 1971-73. Fellow Va. Law Found.; mem. Va. State Bar (mem. 3rd dist. com. 1967-70, chmn. 1969-70), Richmond Bar Assn., Norfolk-Portsmouth Bar Assn., Va. Bar Assn., Thomas Jefferson Soc. of Alumni U. Va. Lile Law Soc., McGuires U. Sch. Alumni (pres. 1995-96), Am. Judicature Soc., ABA, Va. Bar Assn. (vice chmn. com. on cooperation with fgn. bars 1960-61), Richmond Jr. C. of C. (dir. 1946-50), Windmill Point Yacht Club, Westwood Racquet Club (pres. 1961-62), Commonwealth Club, Delta Theta Phi. Office: US Dist Ct 420 US Courthouse 600 Granby St Norfolk VA 23510-1915

CLARKE, JOHN ROBERT, art history educator, art critic; b. Pitts., Jan. 25, 1945; s. John Anthony and Helena Marie (Tremontin) C. AB, Georgetown U., 1967; MA, Yale U., 1969, PhD, 1973. Lectr. Vassar Coll., Poughkeepsie, N.Y., 1972-73; asst. prof. U. Mich., Ann Arbor, 1973-74, U. Calif., San Diego, 1974-75, Yale U., New Haven, 1975-80; asst. prof. U. Tex., Austin, 1980-82, assoc. prof., 1982-88, prof. art history, 1988—, Annie Laurie Howard Regents prof., 1991—; lectr. in field. Author: Roman Black and White Figural Mosaics, 1979, Houses of Roman Italy, 1991; contbr. 25 articles to profl. jours. Fulbright-Hays grantee, Italy, 1970-71, Am. Coun. Learned Socs. grantee, Italy, 1980, 83, NEH grantee, Italy, 1989, 95, resident Am. Acad. Rome, 1995, U. Tex. rsch. grantee, 1982, 83, 86, 87, 90, Griswold Humanities Rsch. grantee, 1978, 80, U. Calif. Faculty Rsch. grantee, 1975; Yale U. fellow, 1968-69, 69-70, 71-72, Woodrow Wilson fellow, 1967-68. Mem. Coll. Art Assn. (bd. dirs., chair art history 1991-95, v.p. 1996-97), Assn. Internat. pour l'Etude de la Peinture Murale Antique (bd. dirs. 1989—), Archaeol. Inst. Am., Assn. Internat. pour l'Etude de la Mosaique Antique, Phi Kappa Phi, Phi Beta Kappa. Democrat.

CLARKE, JUANITA M. WAITERS, education educator; b. Forkland, Ala., Sept. 29, 1923; d. James Walter and Mary Ellen (McAlpine) Waiters; m. Charles Henry Clarke, Aug. 20, 1946; children: Charles Henry Jr., Charlotte Jean, Jacquelin Marie, Victoria Teresa, Carol Evangeline. BS cum laude, Xavier U., 1944; MA, U. Ala., 1967, EdS, 1974, PhD, 1979. Cert. secondary edn. tchr., Ala.; lic. profl. counselor. English tchr., counselor Holy Family High Sch., Birmingham, Ala., 1954-69; English tchr. Miles Coll., Birmingham, 1969-73, from asst. prof. edn. to assoc. prof., coord. secondary edn., 1974-86; English tchr. Lawson State Community Coll., Birmingham, 1973-74; assoc. prof. edn. Talladega (Ala.) Coll., 1987-89; asst. prof. English Ala. State U., Montgomery, 1989-91; coord. title III, dir. instl. rsch. and planning Miles Coll., Birmingham, Ala., 1992—. Author: The Right Writer, 1990. Mem. Am. Counseling Assn., Ala. Counseling Assn., Am. Assn. Individual Investors, Alpha Kappa Mu, Delta Sigma Theta. Home: 1752 Brookfield Ln Birmingham AL 35214-4820 also: PO Box 3800 Birmingham AL 35208

CLARKE, KENNETH LE ROY, telecommunications executive; b. Wichita, Kans., Mar. 22, 1957; s. Billy Earle and Carolyn Claudia (Gunnels) C. AAS, El Centro Coll., Dallas, 1981; BA in Elem. Edn., East Tex. State U., 1986. Telecomm. assoc. Sprint Corp., Dallas, 1987—. Mem. Nat. Writers Assn., Mystery Writers Am., Soc. Children's Book Writers and Illustrators, Masons. Republican. Baptist.

CLARKE, MARGARET ANNE, maternal-child nurse; b. Rockville Centre, N.Y., July 28, 1954; d. Walter Joseph and Eda Rose (Brandimarte) Meyer; m. Jeffrey Clarke, Sept. 12, 1987 (div. Nov. 1990); 1 child, Katherine Marie. BSN, Mt. St. Mary Coll., 1977. Cert. perinatal nurse specialist, ANA; cert. lactation educator, UCLA. Staff nurse, charge relief med.-surg. Scott adn White Hosp., Temple, Tex., 1977-79; staff nurse, charge relief med.-surg. nursing Community Hosp., Monterey, Calif., 1979-80; med.-surg. nurse Good Samaritan Med. Ctr., West Palm Beach, Fla., 1982-86, maternity staff nurse, charge relief, 1986-88, perinatal educator edn. dept., 1988-90; chairperson Women's Health Seminar, 1989; staff RN perinatal svcs. Good Samaritan Med. Ctr., West Palm Beach, Fla., 1990-91; staff educator New Medico, Neurol. Rehab., West Palm Beach, 1991-92; intake nurse Women's Health Svcs., West Palm Beach, 1992—; chairperson Women's Health Seminar, 1989; mem. Palm Beach County Breastfeeding Task Force, 1993—. Roman Catholic. Home: 211 Fox Tail Dr Apt B West Palm Beach FL 33415-6183

CLARKE, MARY ELIZABETH, retired army officer; b. Rochester, N.Y., Dec. 3, 1924; d. James M. and Lillian E. (Young) Kennedy. Student U. Md., 1962; D.Mil.Sci., Norwich U., Northfield, Vt., 1978. Joined U.S. Army as pvt., 1945, advanced through grades to maj. gen., 1978; exec. asst. to Chief of Plans and Policies, Office of Econ. Opportunity, 1966-67; comdr. WAC Tng. Bn., 1967-68; office dep. chief of staff for pers., 1968-71; WAC staff adviser 6th Army, 1971-72; comdr., comdt. U.S. Women's Army Corps Ctr. and Sch., 1972-74; chief WAC Adv. Office, U.S. Army Mil. Pers. Ctr., Washington, 1974-75, dir. Women's Army Corps, Washington, 1975-78; comdr. U.S. Army Mil. Police and Chem. Sch. Tng. Ctr., Ft. McClellan, Ala., 1978-80; dir. human resources devel. Office of Dep. Chief of Staff for Personnel, Washington, 1980-81, ret., 1981; hon. prof. mil. sci. Jacksonville (Ala.) State U. Mem. Def. Adv. Com. on Women in the Svcs., 1984—, vice chmn., 1986—; mem. adv. com. Women Veterans, 1989—, chmn., 1991; mem. The Presidential Commn. on the Assignment of Women in the Armed Forces. Decorated D.S.M.; recipient Toastmasters Internat. award, 1984, Nat. Veteran's award, 1994. Mem. Assn. of U.S. Army (coun. trustees), United States Automobile Assn. (bd. dirs. 1978-88), WAC Assn., WAC Mus. Found., Bus. and Profl. Women's Club. Address: 514 Fairway Dr SW Jacksonville AL 36265-3301

CLARKE, MERCER KAYE, lawyer; b. N.Y.C., Sept. 27, 1944; s. Fred Wylly and Helen Frances (Kaye) C.; m. Elizabeth Koebel (div. 1987); 1 child, James Wylly. BA in Econs., Washington and Lee U., 1966; JD, U. Fla., 1970. Bar: Fla. 1971, U.S. Dist. Ct. (so. dist.) Fla. 1971, U.S. Ct. Appeals (5th cir.) 1971, U.S. Supreme Ct. 1977, U.S. Dist. Ct. (mid. dist.) Fla. 1978, U.S. Ct. Appeals (11th cir.) 1981, U.S. Dist. Ct. (no. dist.) Fla. 1986. Assoc. Smathers & Thompson (now Kelley, Drye & Warren), Miami, Fla., 1970-75, ptnr., 1975-83, proprietary ptnr., 1983-93; ptnr. Clarke & Silverglate, 1993—. Bd. govs. Better Bus. Bur. S. Fla., Miami; trustee Beacon Council, Miami. Recipient Golden Key award City of North Miami Beach, 1988. Mem. ABA, Fla. Bar Assn., Dade County Bar Assn., Internat. Assn. Def. Counsel, Miami C. of C. (trustee), Miami City Club. Republican. Methodist. Home: 4880 Hammock Lake Dr Miami FL 33156-2218 Office: Clarke & Silverglate 100 Biscayne Blvd Ste 2401 Miami FL 33132-2306

CLARKE, ROBERT LOGAN, lawyer; b. Tulsa, Okla., June 29, 1942; s. Ralph Logan and Faye Louise (Todd) C.; m. Jean Puddin Barrow Talbert, Sept. 23, 1967; 1 child, Robert Logan Jr. BA Econs., Rice U., 1963; LLB, Harvard U., 1966. Bar: N.Mex. 1966, Tex. 1967. Legis. asst. to U.S. Senator Edwin L. Mechem Washington, 1964; assoc. Hinkle, Bondurant, Cox, Eaton & Hensley, Roswell, N.Mex., 1966; assoc. Bracewell & Patterson, Houston, 1968-73, ptnr., 1973-85, ptnr., head fin. svcs. sect., 1992—; comptr. of currency Washington, 1985-92; dir. FDIC, Washington, 1985-92, Resolution Trust Corp., Washington, 1989-92; bd. dirs. Cmty. Bancorp. N.Mex., Inc., Centex Constrn. Products, Inc., First Investors Fin. Svcs., Inc.; adv. dir. Centerville (Tex.) State Bank, 1980-85; sr. advisor to pres. Nat. Bank Poland, 1992—; advisor to bank suprs. in Ea. Europe, Mexico, Argentina, and Kazakhstan. Precinct chmn. Harris County Reps., 1970-74, 76-85, legal counsel, 1984-85; trustee Mus. N.Mex. Found., 1992—, Southwestern Grad. Sch. Banking Found., 1993—, Internat. Folk Art Found., 1995—; dist. chmn. Senatorial Dist. 15, 1978-80; del. numerous state and dist. Rep. convs., 1970-84; founding dir. Houston Rep. Club, 1982-85; bd. dirs. Houston Polit. Action Com., 1983-85; mem. adv. com. Harris County Reagan-Bush campaign, 1984; asst. scoutmaster Boy Scouts Am., Houston, 1980-85; deacon 1st Presbyn. Ch. Houston. Capt. U.S. Army, 1966-68. Recipient Disting. Svc. medal U.S. Treasury Dept., 1992, Banking Leadership award Western States Sch. Banking, Albuquerque, 1993. Mem. ABA, Houston Bar Assn., Houston Bar Found., State Bar Tex., State Bar N.Mex., Rice U. Alumni Assn. (chmn. area club com. 1984-85, mem. exec. bd. dirs. 1987-89, Disting. Alumnus award 1992), River Oaks Country Club, Chevy Chase Club, Houston Club, Coronado Club, Houston City Club, Sangre de Cristo Racquet Club (Santa Fe), Rotary (trustee student's ednl. fund Houston club 1973-85). Office: Bracewell & Patterson Pennzoil South Tower 711 Louisiana St Ste 2900 Houston TX 77002-2721

CLARKE, S. BRUCE, paper company executive; b. Wheeling, W.Va., Oct. 28, 1940; s. W. Russell and Eugenia Marie (O'Connor) C.; m. Nancy McCleary, Dec. 29, 1962 (div. Sept. 1983); children: R. Scott, S. Carter, Karen M.; stepchildren: Christine M., J. Mark; m. Marie Weaver, June 25, 1988. BA, W.Va. U., 1962. Sales mgr. Clarke Paper Co., Wheeling, 1962-72, pres., 1972-87; pres. Paper Shack, Inc., Wheeling, 1982—, Proven Papers, Inc., Wheeling, 1988—. Bd. dirs. Easter Seals Soc., Wheeling, 1980; pres. Wheeling Symphony Soc., 1983-85, mem., 1980—; pres. Symposiarchs Soc., Wheeling, 1984-85, mem., 1968—; bd. dirs. W.Va. Independence Hall Found., 1989—. Mem. Wheeling C. of C. (bd. dirs. 1983-85). Republican. Presbyterian. Home: 102 Park Pl Wheeling WV 26003-5653 Office: Proven Papers Inc 3900 Wood St # 6852 Wheeling WV 26003-4360

CLARKE, WILLIAM LINUS, pediatrics educator; b. Washington, Feb. 28, 1945; s. Linus Hamilton and Florence Marie (Thompson) C.; m. Jane Kirby Champion, June 17, 1967; children: Christopher, John. BA, Duke U., 1967; MD, Vanderbilt U., 1971. Diplomate Am. Bd. Pediatrics. Intern then resident in pediatrics Washington U., St. Louis, Mo., 1971-74, fellow in pediatric endocrinology, 1976-78; from asst. prof. to prof. pediatrics U. Va., Charlottesville, 1978—. Editor: Methods in Diabetes Clinical Research, 1986; contbr. more than 70 articles to profl. jours. Maj. USAF, 1976-78. Mem. Am. Diabetes Assn. (bd. dirs. 1989-92), Am. Acad. Pediatrics, Lawson Wilkins Pediatric Endocrine Soc., Endocrine Soc., Soc. Pediatric Rsch., Soc. Behavioral Medicine. Office: U Va Med Ctr Box 386 Charlottesville VA 22908

CLARK-SCHUBERT, DONNA LYNNE, journalism educator; b. Lineville, Ala., Dec. 29, 1964; d. James Marion and Eva Lee (Garrett) C. BA in Comm., Auburn U., 1987, MA in Comm., 1989. Pub. rels. counselor Clay County Fair Assn., 1987; pub. rels. asst. Opelika (Ala.) C. of C., 1988; grad. teaching asst. Auburn (Ala.) U., 1987-89, instr., 1989-90; asst. prof. journalism Troy (Ala.) State U., 1990—, publs. cons., 1994—. Chancellor's fellow Troy State U., 1997. Mem. Am. Advt. Fedn., Pub. Rels. Soc. Am., Troy State U. Journalism Alumni Assn. (bd. dirs.), Phi Theta Kappa, Phi Kappa Phi. Office: Troy State Univ Wallace Hall Troy AL 36082

CLARKSON, ANDREW MACBETH, retail executive; b. Glasgow, Scotland, July 9, 1937; s. Robert Gibson and Josephine Abigail (Anderson) C.; m. Carole Frances Grant, June 4, 1966; children: Jennifer Mary, William MacBeth. BA, Oxford (Eng.) U., 1960, MA, 1980; diploma in Agr., McGill U., Montreal, Que., Can., 1961; MBA, Harvard U., 1966. Various positions to asst. v.p. First Nat. Bank, Chgo., 1966-72; corp. asst. treas. Gen. Foods Corp., White Plains, N.Y., 1972-78; fin. dir. Gen. Foods Ltd., U.K., 1978-80; asst. corp. controller and controller Gen. Foods Internat., 1980-81; v.p. and treas. F.W. Woolworth co., N.Y.C., 1981-83; sr. v.p. fin. and adminstrn., dir. Malone & Hyde, Memphis, 1983-88; dir. AutoZone, Inc., Memphis, 1988—, sec., treas., 1990-94, treas., 1994-95, fin. com. chmn., 1996—; bd. dirs. Royal Furniture, Inc., Memphis, Flynn Industries, Inc., San Francisco; lectr. internat. fin. U. Conn., 1976. Treas., dir. Memphis Arts Coun., 1987-93, dir., 1995—. 2d lt. Brit. Army, 1955-57. Mem. Crescent Club (Memphis), Field Club (New Canaan), Harvard Club (N.Y.). Office: AutoZone Inc 123 S Front St Memphis TN 38103-3607

CLARKSON, CAROLE LAWRENCE, insurance company professional; b. Fredericksburg, Va., Dec. 18, 1942; d. Jerry Allen and Gladys Mae (Eubank) Lawrence; m. David Wendell Morris, Aug. 14, 1965 (div. 1977); 1 child, Peyton Lawrence; m. Lawrence Herbert Clarkson, Aug. 14, 1982. BA, Purdue U., 1965; postgrad., Ind. U., Indpls., 1970, U. Ill., 1971-73, U. Louisville Sch. of Bus., 1980-82. Pub. sch. tchr. various, Ind., Okla., Ill., N.C., Italy, 1965-75; librarian documentation U. Louisville Computing Ctr., 1980-82, IBM Corp., Austin, Tex., 1983-85; ins. mgr. Ohio State Life Ins. Co., Columbus, 1985-88, Community Life Ins. Co., Columbus, 1988-90; hosp. audit/stop loss coord. Health Adminstrn. Svcs., Houston, 1991—; supervisory mgr. Ins. Inst. of Am., 1987—. Mem. Internat. Claims Assn. (assoc. life and health claims 1987), Nat. Assn. Female Execs., Purdue U. Alumni Assn. Home: 2006 Kelona Dr Spring TX 77386-2541

CLARKSON, EDITH WEST, nursing administrator; b. Refugio, Tex., Feb. 8, 1942; d. Edward Allison and Jeannette Frances (Marsden) C. BSN, U. Tex., 1965, MSN, 1975. RN, Tex. Head nurse, staff nurse U. Tex. Med. Br., Galveston, 1965-68, 70-74; staff nurse Dr. Michael DeBakey's first heart transplant team in U.S. Meth. Hosp., Houston, 1968-70; staff nurse-surg. ICU Audie Murphy VA Hosp., San Antonio, 1976-79; quality assurance coord. VA Med Ctr., Albuquerque, 1980-81; staff nurse-surg. ICU De Tax Hosp., Victoria, Tex, 1983-84; quality assurance coord. Spohn Hosp., Corpus Christi, Tex., 1984; staff nurse med.- surg. Santa Rosa Hosp., San Antonio, 1984-86; nursing supr. Meth. Hosp., San Antonio, 1986-92; dir. patient care svcs. Refugio (Tex.) County Meml. Hosp., 1992-93; patient care coord.-hospice AIM Hospice/Home Health, Beeville, Tex., 1993-96; dir. adult psychology and chem. dependency Columbia Bayview Hosp., Corpus Christi, Tex., 1996—; clin. preceptor RN refresher program, Meth. Hosp., San Antonio, 1989-92, mem. instl. rev. bd., 1991-92; mem. bus. & industry adv. coun. San Antonio Coll., 1990-92. Bd. dirs. USDA Natural Resources Conservation Svc., Refugio, 1992-96. Mem. ANA (congl. dist. coord. 1992-96), Tex. Nurse Assn. (dist. 17 chmn. govtl. affairs com. 1992—, Tex. so. region rep. state govtl. affairs com. 1993—, dist. 17 pres.-elect 1994-95, pres. 1995-96), Sigma Theta Tau. Home: PO Box 883 Refugio TX 78377-0883 Office: Columbia Bayview Hosp 6226 Saratoga Corpus Christi TX 78414

CLARKSON, JOCELYN ADRENE, medical technologist; b. Bennettsville, S.C., July 9, 1952; d. Henry Louis and Frankie Allene (Carter) C. BA in Biology, Columbia (S.C.) Coll., 1973; cert. med. tech., Presbyn. Hosp., Charlotte, N.C., 1975. Coll. tutor of Germanic language Columbia Coll., 1970-73, switchboard operator, 1972-73; lab aide Richland Meml. Hosp., Columbia, 1974, now, med. technologist; profl. model. Appeared (TV comms.) Back Porch Restaurant and Meat Market, 1992, (film) The Chasers; author: poems, compilation, short stories, Messages from Hijac, 1989. Mem. Am. Soc. Clin. Pathologists (assoc.), Assn. for Studies of Classical African Civilization, African Am. Resource Inst. Roman Catholic. Home: 201 H L Clarkson Rd Hopkins SC 29061-9723

CLARKSON, PAMELA JEAN, elementary school educator; b. Lubbock, Tex., Apr. 1, 1952; d. Arthur L. and Lavanne (Gardener) Emery; m. Wesley Paul Clarkson, Jan. 6, 1973; children: Jeremy Paul, Jason Arthur. Student, N.Mex. State U., 1970-71; BS in Edn., U. Tex., El Paso, 1974. Cert. elem. sch. tchr., Tex., Gifted Edn. Tchr., reading, English grade 7, 8 Ft. Worth Ind. Sch. Dist., 1974-78; fgn. missionary to Spain So. Bapt. Conv.-Lang. Sch., Madrid, Vigo, Pontevedra, 1981-82, 82-84, Las Palmas, Canary Is., 1984-88; sec. Bapt. Mission Spain, Las Palmas, Canary Is., 1987-88; sec. bd. Am. Sch. Las Palmas (Spain), 1987; tchr. grade 2 Fabens (Tex.) Ind. Sch. Dist., 1988-90; tchr. grade 6 El Paso (Tex.) Ind. Sch. Dist., 1990-91, humanities tchr. grade 6, 1991—, tchr. renaissance acad. grade 7, 8, 1996. Contbr., editor: (campus newsletter) The Charger's News Line, 1994-96. Educator of the Week Herald Post, El Paso, 1995. Mem. Nat. Edn. Assn., Tex. State Tchr. Assn., El Paso Tchr. Assn., Tex. Assn. Gifted and Talented, Assn. Supervision and Curriculum Devel., Alpha Delta Kappa (corr. sec. 1996—). So. Baptist. Home: 4601 Trowbridge El Paso TX 79903 Office: H E Charles Mid Sch 4909 Trojan El Paso TX 79924

CLARKSON, PHYLLIS OWENS, early childhood educator; b. Spartanburg, S.C., Apr. 3, 1951; d. Thomas Dean and Mary Ann (Turner) Owens; m. Everett Clifford Clarkson Jr., June 6, 1970 (div. Oct. 1989); children: Stacey Danee, Trey. BA in Edn. magna cum laude, U. S.C., 1993. Substitute tchr. Spartanburg Day Sch., 1984-88, libr. aide, 1988-94; kindergarten tchr. Cedar Road Christian Acad., Chesapeake, Va., 1994-96, office mgr., 1995-96; tchr. 2d and 3d grade Cedar Rd. Christian Acad., Chesapeake, Va., 1996—. Mem. Cowpens Garden Club, 1988-94. Mem. ASCD, Assn. Childhood Edn. Internat., S.C. Edn. Assn., S.C. Assn. for Edn. of Young Children. Home: 705 Cottage Pl Chesapeake VA 23322-4621 Office: Cedar Rd Christian Acad 916 Cedar Rd Chesapeake VA 23320-7002

CLARY, RONALD GORDON, insurance agency executive; b. Moultrie, Ga., May 2, 1940; s. Ronald Ward and Hazel (Collins) C.; m. Adrian Irene Baker; children: Lynn, Beth, Lindsay, Baker. Student Young Harris Coll., 1958-60; BBA in Ins., U. Ga., 1963; LLB, Woodrow Wilson Coll. Law, 1966. Field rep. Comml. Union Ins. Cos., 1962-67; ind. ins. agt., 1967—; ins. agt., sec. of agy. Day, Reynolds & Parks, Gainesville, Ga., 1970—, pres., 1993—. Mem. Profl. Ins. Agts. Am., Ga. Assn. Ind. Ins. Agts., Gainesville Assn. Ind. Ins. Agts. (past pres.), Young Agts. Com. Ga. (past chmn.), Am. Legion. Republican. Baptist. Lodge: Elks, Rotary. Avocations: tennis, sailing. Home and Office: 730 Lindsey Baker Ct Gainesville GA 30506-1535

CLATANOFF, DORIS ANN, English language educator; b. Howells, Nebr., Jan. 29, 1932; d. Fred Rudolph Gustav and Marie Frances (Goeller) Risch; m. Duane Bernhard Clatanoff, June 8, 1952; children: Dwight (dec.), Clark, Craig. BA magna cum laude, Midland Coll., 1966; MA in Edn., Wayne State Coll., 1967; PhD English, U. Nebr., 1973. Tchr. pub. schs., Nebr., 1951-70; assoc. prof. Concordia Tchrs. Coll., Seward, Nebr., 1971-80, chmn. humanities div., 1980-85; chmn. Lang. and Lit. Dept. Tex. A&I U., Kingsville, Tex., 1985-89, dean, prof., 1991—; presenter Am. Lit. Assn. Conf. San Diego, 1990, chmn. Faculty Senate Tex. A&I U., 1990-91, mem. Tex. A&I U. "Project 30" team, 1988-91. Contbr. articles to profl. and mags. Sec.-treas. Women's Issues Tex. Faculty Assn., Austin, 1990-91; bd. trustees Midland Luth. Coll. Named Coord. Bd. Fellow Tex. Higher Edn. Coord. Bd., 1991. Mem. AAUW (pres. Nebr. divsn. 1984-85), Nat. Coun. Tchrs. English, Internat. Shakespeare Assn., Kingsville C. of C., Kingsville Rotary, Delta Kappa Gamma. Republican. Lutheran. Office: Texas A&M University Lang & Lit Dept Kingsville TX 78363

CLAUBERG, MARTIN, research scientist; b. Solingen, Germany, Oct. 4, 1964; came to U.S., 1981; s. Erich and Hannelore Gisela (Skirlo) C. BS in Biochemistry, U. Tenn., 1986, PhD of Biochemistry, 1992; postgrad., Fulde Personal Tng. Inst., Germany, 1993. Rsch., tchg. asst. U. Tenn., Knoxville, 1986-92; sr. rsch. asst., risk assessment team leader Oak Ridge (Tenn.) Nat. Lab., 1993—; cons. BCB Biotech. Consulting, Neuss, Germany, 1993; mktg. asst. Henkel Corp., Düsseldorf, Germany, 1993; freelance project analyst Umweltschutzamt Wuppertal, Germany, 1993. Contbr. articles to profl. jours. Vol. Recording for the Blind, Oak Ridge, 1994—. Fellow ADRD Conf., 1992, ORNL Ctr. for Excellence, 1986-92. Mem. AAAS, Am. Chem. Soc. Home: 3695 Brooksview Rd Lenoir City TN 37772 Office: Oak Ridge Nat Lab 1060 Commerce Park Dr # 6480 Oak Ridge TN 37830-8026

CLAUGHTON, EDWARD NAPOLEON, JR., lawyer; b. Atlanta, July 27, 1927; s. Edward Napoleon and Lillian (Corbett) C.; m. B.J. Armstrong, Dec. 22, 1951 (div. 1976); children: Jean Macrea, Lee Corbett, Edward Napoleon III; m. Lois Ann Galloway Hyatt, Nov. 12, 1976; 1 stepson, Charles Glen Hyatt. BA, Duke U., 1950; LLB, U. Fla., 1953. Bar: Fla. 1954. Pres. Claughton Co., Miami, Fla., 1939—; owner, operator Claughton Theaters, Miami, 1941-66; pres. Claughton Hotels, Inc., Miami, 1954-86; owner, operator Hound Ears Lodge and Club, Inc., Blowing Rock, N.C., 1988—; founder, dir. Elk River Devel. Corp., Banner Elk, N.C.; dir. Chgo. and East Ill. Ry. Co., 1956-58. Pres. Am. Cancer Soc., Miami, bd. dirs., 1962—; trustee Bapt. Hosp. Miami, Inc., 1983-90; com. chmn. Orange Bowl Com., Miami, 1969—. With USN, 1945-46. Mem. ABA, Fla. Bar Assn., Dade County Bar Assn., Brickell Area Assn. (bd. dirs. 1976-89), U.S. Bus. and Indsl. Coun. (bd. dirs. 1982-87), Hound Ears Club (pres., bd. dirs. 1988—), Elk River Club (pres. 1985-86, bd. dirs. 1986-90), Coral Reef Yacht Club, Miami (founder 1955—), Univ. Club (Miami) (pres. 1955-56, bd. dirs., founder), Riviera Country Club (bd. dirs., former v.p.), Kiwanis (bd. dirs. Miami chpt. 1965-75). Republican. Presbyterian. Office: 777 Brickell Ave Ste 1130 Miami FL 33131-2867

CLAUGHTON, HUGH DAWSON, SR., cruise company executive, veterinarian; b. Gadsden, Ala., June 2, 1928; s. William Posey Sr. and Anna (Dawson) C.; m. Ann Ruth Hughen, Dec. 28, 1957 (dec. Oct. 1977); children: Carol Ann, Hugh Dawson Jr., Jonathan Hughen; m. Helen Claire Hudson, Nov. 3, 1979. BS, Tulane U., 1951; DVM, Auburn U., 1956. With diagnostic lab. State of Ala., 1951-52; pvt. practice Claughton Animal Clinic, Nashville, 1956-89; pres. Belle Carol Riverboat Co., Nashville, 1969-93; pvt. practice large animal medicine and surgery Nashville, 1994-96; co-founder, sec., treas. Star of Palm Beach, Atlantic Coastal Cruises, Singer Island, Fla., 1996—; pres., founder Belle Carol of the Cumberland Excursion Co., Nashville, 1969—; diagnosis labwork State of Ala., 1951-52; v.p. River St. Riverboat Co., Savannah, Ga., 1991—. Mem. AVMA, Tenn. Vet. Med. Assn. (pub. rels. com. 1966-76, v.p. 1968-69, exec. bd. 1968-72, chmn. continuing edn. 1969-70, pres. 1971-72, Vet. of Yr. 1973), Am. Animal Hosp. Assn. (affiliate, dir. continuing edn. Tenn. 1969-70), Davidson County Acad. Vet. Med. Assn. (pres. 1965-66), Middle Tenn. Vet. Med. Assn. (pres. 1966-67), Donelson-Hermitage C. of C. (bd. dirs. 1986-88, 92—, Profl. Businessman of Yr. 1987), Nat. Assn. Passenger Vessel Owners (sec.-treas. 1983-84, pres. 1985-86, exec. bd., life), Propeller Club (bd. dirs. 1987-89, Cert. Appreciation award 1992), Omega Tau Sigma (treas. 1954-55), Zeta Club, Pi Kappa Phi. Methodist. Home: 6650 Upton Ln Nashville TN 37209-4378 Office: Belle Carol Riverboat Co 106 1st Ave S Nashville TN 37201-2102

CLAUSSEN, LOUISE KEITH, art museum director; b. Augusta, Ga., Apr. 7, 1947; d. Henry Herman and Elisabeth Winter (Bryans) C. BA, Augusta Coll., 1973. Staff writer Augusta Herald, 1968-70, women's editor, 1970-71; lively arts editor The Augusta Chronicle, 1973-77, Sunday editor, 1977-83, pub. rels. cons., 1983-88; dir. corp. fine art Morris Communications Corp., Augusta, 1988-92; acting dir. Morris Museum of Art, Augusta, 1989-92; dir. Morris Museum of Art, 1992—; editor art exhibition catalogues Morris Museum of Art, 1992-96. Mem. August-Richmond County Coliseum Authority, 1986-93; pres. Augusta Ballet Bd., 1987-88; bd. dirs. Augusta Symphony Inc., 1989-92, Historic Augusta, 1993—. Mem. Am. Assn. of Museums, Southeastern Museums Conference, Augusta Rotary. Episcopalian. Office: Morris Museum of Art One 10th St Augusta GA 30901-1134

CLAWSON, HARRY QUINTARD MOORE, business executive; b. N.Y.C., Aug. 8, 1924; s. Harry Marshall and Marguerite H. (Burgoyne) C.; m. Annemarie Korntner, Dec. 1967 (dec. 1988); m. Mary Louise Kirkland, July 1989. Student, NYU, 1951-52, New Sch. for Social Rsch., 1953. Supr. transp., liaison with U.S. Army ARC, 1945-46; asst. to dir. pers. UNESCO, Paris, 1947; resident rep. Tex. Co., Douala, French Cameroun, West Africa, 1948-50; asst. dir. overseas bus. svc. McGraw-Hill Pub. Co., 1951-58; dir. client svcs. Internat. Rsch. Assocs., N.Y.C., 1958-61; v.p., sec. Frasch Whiton Boats, Inc., 1961-63; gen. mgr. Sailboat Tng. Facility, 1961-63; pres. Harry Q.M. Clawson & Co., Inc., N.Y.C., 1961-76, Charleston, S.C., 1978—; dir. planning and adminstrn. splty. chems. div. Essex Chem. Corp., 1976-78; pres. Trident Seafarms Co., Charleston, 1980-85. Contbr. articles to profl. jours. With U.S. Army, 1943-45, ETO. Decorated Bronze Star. Mem. Ex-Mems. Assn. Squadron A., Carolina Yacht Club, Yeamans Hall Club.

CLAXTON, HARRIETT MAROY JONES, retired English language educator; b. Dublin, Ga., Aug. 27, 1930; d. Paul Jackson and Maroy Athalia (Chappell) Jones; m. Edward B. Claxton, Jr., May 27, 1953; children—E. B. III, Paula Jones. AA, Bethel Woman's Coll., 1949; AB magna cum laude, Mercer U., 1951; MEd, Ga. Coll., 1965. Social worker Laurens County Welfare Bd., Dublin, 1951-56; high sch. tchr., Dublin, 1961-66; instr. Middle Ga. Coll., Cochran, 1966-71, asst. prof. English, lit. and speech, 1971-85, assoc. prof. 1985-86; research tchr. Trinity Christian Sch., 1986, 92, sr. English tchr., 1986-87; part-time tchr., Ga. Coll., 1987, Emanuel County Jr. Coll., 1988-96, Middle Ga. Coll., 1985-96. Weekly columnist Dublin Courier Herald, 1993—; contbr. articles to profl. jours. and newspapers; editor Laurens County History, II, 1987. Pres. bd. Dublin Assn. Fine Arts, 1974-76, 82-84, Dublin Hist. Soc., 1976-78; mem. Laurens County Library Bd., 1960-68; chmn. Dublin Hist. Rev. Bd., 1980—; sec. Am. Assn. Ret. Persons, 1987-90; v.p. Dublin Cmty. Concert, 1991—. Named Woman of Yr., St. Patrick's Festival, Dublin, 1979, Most Popular tchr., Dublin Ctr., 1985, Olympic Torch Bearer 1996; recipient Outstanding Service award Cancer Soc., Dublin, 1985, 93, Ga. Coll. Outstanding Alumni award for cmty. svc., 1996. Mem. DAR (historian, regent, state, dist. and nat. awards), Sigma Mu, Alpha Delta Pi, Phi Theta Kappa, Chi Delta Phi, Delta Kappa Gamma. Democrat. Baptist. Clubs: Woman's Study (pres.), Erin Garden (pres.) (Dublin). Home: 101 Rosewood Dr Dublin GA 31021-4129

CLAY, DISKIN, classical studies educator; b. Fresno, Calif., Nov. 2, 1938; s. Norman and Florence Patricia (Diskin) C.; m. Jenny Strauss, June 21, 1963 (div. 1977); 1 child, Andreia; m. Sara Christine Clark, Oct. 28, 1978; children: Hilary, Christine. BA, Reed Coll., 1960; MA, U. Wash., 1963, PhD, 1967. Asst. prof. Reed Coll., Portland, Oreg., 1966-70; from asst. prof. to assoc. prof. Haverford (Pa.) Coll., 1970-76; prof., Francis White prof. Greek Johns Hopkins U., Balt., 1976-88; Disting. prof. Grad. Ctr. CUNY, N.Y.C., 1988-90; RJR Nabisco prof. classical studies Duke U., Durham, N.C., 1990—; Elizabeth Whitehead prof. Am. Sch. Classical Studies in Athens, 1988-89; Blegen rsch. prof. Vassar Coll., Poughkeepsie, N.Y., 1985-86. Author: Oxychynchan Poems, 1973, Sophocles, Oedipus the King, 1978, Lucretius and Epicurus, 1983, John Locke: Questions Concerning the Law of Nature, 1990, others. Fulbright fellow, Univs. Montpellier and Poitiers, France, 1960-61; Woodrow Wilson fellow, 1961-62; Am. Coun. Learned Socs., Turkey, 1975; NEH fellow, 1974-75. Mem. Am. Philol. Assn., Am. Inst. Archaeology, Dante Soc. Am., Soc. for Ancient Greek Philosophy (pres. 1991-92). Home: 204 Sierra Dr Chapel Hill NC 27514-1456 Office: Duke U Dept Classical Studies Durham NC 27708

CLAY, HARRIS AUBREY, chemical engineer; b. Hartley, Tex., Dec. 28, 1911; s. John David and Alberta (Harris) C.; m. Violette Frances Mills, June 19, 1948 (dec. 1972); m. 2d Gervice Stuart Shotwell, Apr. 28, 1973 (dec. 1989); m. Leona G. Steele, May 25, 1991. BS, U. Tulsa, 1933; MSChemE, Columbia U., 1939. Pilot plant operator Phillips Petroleum Co., Burbank, Okla., 1939-42, resident supr. Burbank pilot plants, 1942-44; process design engr. Phillips Petroleum Co., Bartlesville, Okla., 1944-45; process engring. supr. Philtex Plant, Phillips, Tex., 1946-56; tech. adviser to pilot plant mgr. Bartlesville, 1957-61, chem. engring. assoc., 1961-73; ind. cons. engr., 1974—; chmn. tech. com. Fractionation Research, Inc., 1966-71, mem. tech. com., 1972-73. Contbr. articles to profl. jours.; patentee in field. Mem. dist. commn. Boy Scouts Am. Fellow Am. Inst. Chem. Engrs.; mem. Nat. Soc. Profl. Engrs., Okla. Soc. Profl. Engrs., Am. Chem. Soc., Electrochem. Soc., Elks, Lions. Presbyterian. Home: 1723 Church Ct Bartlesville OK 74006-6401

CLAY, ORSON C., insurance company executive; b. Bountiful, Utah, July 26, 1930; s. George Phillips and Dorothy (Cliff) C.; m. Dianne Jones, June 13, 1961; children: Orson Cliff, Charles Kenneth, Elizabeth Temple. BS, Brigham Young U., 1955; MBA with distinction, Harvard U., 1959. With Continental Oil Co., various locations in, U.S.; mng. dir. Conoco A.G., Zug, Switzerland, 1962-63; dir. econs. divsn. Continental Oil Co. Ltd., London, Eng., 1964-65; gen. mgr. adminstrn. and ops. Continental Oil (U.K.) Ltd., London, 1965-66; asst. mgr. marine transp. Continental Oil, N.Y.C., 1966-68; exec. asst. fin. Pennzoil United, Inc., Houston, 1968-70; exec. v.p. fin., treas. Am. Nat. Ins. Co., Galveston, Tex., 1970-73, sr. exec. v.p., treas., 1973-76, pres., 1977-95, CEO, 1978-91, also bd. dirs., ret., 1995; bd. dirs. Stewart & Stevenson Svcs., Inc.; past mem. nat. adv. coun. mgmt. Brigham Young U. Past trustee United Way Galveston; past bd. dirs. Tex. Rsch. League; active LDS Ch., missionary in Can., 1951-53. 1st lt. USMCR, 1955-57. Donald Kirk David fellow Harvard U., 1959. Mem. Life Officers Mgmt. Assn. (bd. dirs. 1993-96). Home: 5682 169th Pl SE Bellevue WA 98006-5514

CLAY, RYBURN GLOVER, JR., resort executive; b. Atlanta, Oct. 15, 1928; s. Ryburn Glover and Catherine (Sanders) S.; m. Patricia Markwell, Nov. 10, 1951; children: Ryburn Clover III, Thomas Markwell, Zaida Sanders. BS, U.S. Mil. Acad., 1951. Commd. 2d lt. U.S. Army, 1951, advanced through grades to capt., 1955, resigned, 1955; pres. St. Simons Co., St. Simons Island, Ga., 1971-73, Sea Gate Inn, Inc., St. Simons Island, 1973—. Pres. ARC, Glynn City, Ga., 1974; vestryman Christ Ch. Frederica, St. Simons Island, 1987, sr. warden, 1988—. Decorated Silver Star, Purple Heart. Mem. St. Simons C. of C. (pres. 1972). Episcopalian. Clubs: Piedmont Driving (Atlanta), Sea Island Beach. Office: Sea Gate Inn 1014 Ocean Blvd Saint Simons GA 31522-4520

CLAYBROOK, MARJORIE ANNETTE, fiber artist; b. Corpus Christi, Tex., Aug. 13, 1940; d. Walter Bert and Nona (O'Neal) Walger; m. James Russell Claybrook, Feb. 22, 1963. BS in Organic Chemistry, U. Tex., 1962; student, Del Mar Coll., 1958-59, Toledo Mus. Sch., 1970, 76-78, Arrowmont, 1985-93. Asst. scientist U. Tex., Austin, 1961-63; assoc. scientist U. Ill., Champaign, 1966-68. Solo exhbns. include Etherridge Ctr. U. S.C., 1989, Francis Marion U., Florence, S.C., 1989, 92, Cotton Exch. Gallery, Augusta, Ga., 1990, West Ga. Coll., Carrolton, 1991, The Atrium, Augusta, 1991, Berry Coll., Rome, Ga., 1991, Colquitt Art Ctr., Moultrie, Ga., 1993, Del. Ctr. Contemporary Art, 1994; group exhbns. include Toledo Mus. Art, 1979-85, Tweed Mus., 1981, Duluth Art Inst., 1981, Am. Craft Mus. II, N.Y.C., 1983, ODC Galleries, Columbus, Ohio, 1987, Albany Mus. Art, 1990, 94, Decatur House, Washington, 1990, 91, Vanderbilt U., 1990, Miss. Mus. Art, 1991, U. Fla., 1989, Kimball Mus., Utah, 1993, others; studio artist-tchr., Augusta, 1987—; presenter workshops in field. Recipient various awards nat. exhbns., 1979-89; Ga. Arts Coun. Individual Artist grantee, 1991-92, 94-95; Arrowmont Sch. Arts and Crafts work-study fellow, 1992; Bus. and Profl. Women scholar, 1958-62. Mem Surface Design Assn., Peidmont Craftsmen Guild, Women's Caucus for Art, Jr. League, Inc. (sustaining). Republican. Jewish. Home: 3423 Walton Way Augusta GA 30909-4532

CLAYCOMB, HUGH MURRAY, lawyer, author; b. Joplin, Mo., May 19, 1931; s. Hugh and Fern (Murray) C.; m. Jeanne Cavin, May 6, 1956; children: Stephen H., Scott C. BS in Bus., U. Mo., 1953, JD, 1955; LLM, U. Miss., 1969. Bar: Mo. 1955, Ark. 1957, U.S. Tax Ct. 1956, U.S. Dist. Ct. (ea. dist.) Ark. 1957, U.S. Supreme Ct. 1979. Asst. staff judge advocate USAF, 1955-57; law clerk Ark. Supreme Ct., Little Rock, 1957-58; ptnr. Gregory & Claycomb, Pine Bluff, Ark., 1958-69; partner Haley, Claycomb, Roper & Anderson, Warren, Ark., 1969—; dir. Strong Systems, Inc., Pine Bluff, Ark., 1967—. Author: Arkansas Corporations, 1967, 82, 92. Pres. Jefferson County Bar Assn., Pine Bluff, 1969, Warren YMCA, 1973-75, S.E. Ark. Legal Inst., 1980-81, Ctrl. Ark. Estate Planning Coun., 1963-64; trustee Bradley County YMCA Found.; spl. assoc. justice Ark. Supreme Ct., 1978, 87. Lt. USAF, 1955-57. Recipient Pres.'s award Ark. Trial Lawyers Assn., 1985. Mem. Ark. Bar Found. (pres. 1990), Ark. Bar Assn. (C.E. Ransick award 1996), Warren Rotary (pres. 1972). Episcopalian.

CLAYTON, CARL A., university dean; b. Greensboro, N.C., Nov. 15; s. William A. and Mary (Moore) C.; m. Barbara F. Bennett; children—Michelle, Alan. B.S., Appalachian State Tchrs. Coll., 1967; M.A., Appalachian U., 1968; Ed.D., U. S.C., 1981. Instr. bus. and econs. U. S.C.-Florence, 1968, bus. mgr. and instr., 1969; dir. U. S.C.-Salkehatchie, Allendale, 1970—, asst. prof., 1976, prof., 1990—, now dean of univ.; CEO U.S.C.-Salkehatchie. Bd. dirs. Swallow Savannah Meth. Ch., Allendale, Bellinger Chapel Methodist Ch. Fairfax, S.C.; mem. alumni council U. S.C. Named Friend of Campus, U. S.C.-Salkehatchie, 1981. Mem. Walterboro-Colleton C. of C., Barnwell County C. of C., Allendale County Civic Assn., Bamberg County C. of C., Hampton C. of C., Nat. Conf. Regional Campus Adminstrs., Allendale C. of C.. Avocations: restoration of automobiles; hunting; fishing; tennis; swimming. Home: PO Box 27 Fairfax SC 29827-0027 Office: U SC-Salkehatchie PO Box 617 Allendale SC 29810-0617

CLAYTON, KATY, elementary education educator; b. Bellefonte, Pa., Feb. 21, 1956; d. Everette Lee and Donna June (Trowbridge) Swinney; m. Charles Edward Clayton Jr., July 15, 1977; children: Quinton, Meredith, Zachary. BS in Edn., Southwest Tex. State U., 1978, MEd in Reading, 1983. Tchr. kindergarten Lockhart (Tex.) Pub. Schs., 1978-80; owner pvt. day care San Marcos, Tex., 1980-84; tchr. 1st grade Crockett Elem. Sch., San Marcos, Tex., 1984-89, tchr. 2d grade, 1989-93, reading specialist, 1993—; dept. leader Crockett Elem. Sch., 1995—; cons. S.W. Tex. Tchr. Ctr., San Marcos, 1991-92; trainer Helping One Student to Succeed, 1995, tchr., 1996—. Bd. dirs. Little League, San Marcos, 1987-89; deacon 1st Christian Ch., San Marcos, 1988-92; presenter 23d Annual Tex. State Reading Assn. Conf., The Young Child and Literacy. Mem. Tex. Classroom Tchrs. Assn. (pres. 1990-91), Internat. Reading Assn., Reading Recovery Tchrs., Key Communicators. Democrat. Mem. Disciples of Christ. Home: 109 E Hillcrest San Marcos TX 78666-3239 Office: Crockett Elem Sch 1300 Girard St San Marcos TX 78666-2813

CLAYTON, LAWRENCE OTTO, marriage and family therapist; b. Fallon, Nev., Mar. 24, 1945; s. Lawrence Otto and Nathalie E. (Gow) C.. BS summa cum laude, Tex. Wesleyan Coll., Ft. Worth, Tex., 1976; postgrad., Emory U., Atlanta, 1976-77; MDiv, Tex. Christian U., 1978; PhD, Tex. Woman's U., 1983. Cert. alcohol and drug counselor, clin. supr. group psychotherapist, program dir. Pastor First United Meth. Ch., Maypearl, Tex., 1977-78, Godley United Meth. Ch., Tex., 1978-79, United Meth. Ch., Belton, 1979-80, Edge Park United Meth. Ch., Ft. Worth, 1980-81; exec. dir. Johnson County Mental Health Clinic, Cleburne, Tex., 1981-83; adminstr. United Meth. Counseling Svcs., 1983-88; cons. Roserock Med. Network, Oklahoma City, 1987-88; prog. coord. The Greenleaf Ctr., Oklahoma City, 1989-90; clin. dir. Fountainview Ctr., El Reno, Okla., 1990; with Systematic Orgnl. Learning Through Vital Edn., Piedmont, Okla., 1989-96; ret., 1996; cons. Great Plains Correctional Facility, Hinton, Okla., 1993—; adj. prof. Mid-Am. Bible Coll., Oklahoma City, 1991-96, Bacone Coll., Muskogee, Okla., 1992-94. Author: Assessment and Management of the Suicidal Adolescent, 1990, Coping with Depression, 1990, Coping with a Drug Abusing Parent, 1991, Coping with Being Gifted, 1991, Coping with a Learning Disability, 1992, Careers in Psychology, 1992, Coping with Sports Injuries, 1992, Designer Drugs, 1993, Barbiturates and Other Depressants, 1994, Amphetamines and Other Stimulants, 1994, The Professional Alcohol and Drug Counselor Supervisor's Handbook, 1993, All You Need to Know About Sports Injuries, 1994, Steroids, 1995, Drug Testing, 1996, Working Together Against Drug Addiction, 1996, Drugs & Drug Testing, 1996, Coping with Drug Testing, 1997, Tranquilizers, 1997, others; assoc. editor Family Perspective, 1987-95; columnist Woman's Weekly, 1991-93, Growthline, 1992-95. Sec., Okla. Coun. on Family Rels., Oklahoma City, 1985-86. With U.S. Army, 1962-68. Mem. Okla. Inst. Adult Children of Alcoholics (pres. 1987-91), Okla. Soc. for Sci. Study of Sex (pres. 1986-88), Okla. Drug and Alcohol Profl. Counselors Cert. Bd. (vice chmn. 1988-90, pres. 1990-95, counselor of yr., 1994). Republican. Home: PO Box 485 Piedmont OK 73078-0485

CLAYTON, MARVIN COURTLAND, engineering, manufacturing sourcing and health wellness consultant; b. Norwich, Conn., Feb. 19, 1938; s. Marvin C. and Peggy (Farmer) C.; children: Cheryll, Michelle, Deborah. BS in Indsl. Engring., Purdue U., 1963; MBA, U. Louisville, 1971; MPA, Penn. State U., 1986; grad., U.S. Army War Coll., 1986. Registered profl. engr., Calif., Ky., Mo., Pa.; cert. purchasing mgr., mfg. engr., mfg. mgr., profl. mgmt. cons., logistician, exec. in logistics. Mgr. shop ops. GE Appliances, Louisville, 1968-69, prog. mgr. mfg. engring., 1969-71, contracting agt. material handling and computer systems, 1973-76, program mgr., material resource systems, 1976-80, mgr., advance and indirect material purchasing, 1980-82, program mgr., purchasing programs, 1982-87, program mgr., sourcing integration, 1987-89, mgr. supplier productivity engring., 1989-93, puchasing mgr. range products bus., 1993; prin. The Clayton Group, Louisville, 1993-94; mgr. range bus. purchasing GE Appliances, Louisville, 1992-94; mgr. Strategic Sourcing, Louisville, 1994; mgr. mfg. engring. Emerson Electric Co., St. Louis, 1971-72; corp. engring. and mfg. cons. AMEDCO, Springfield, Mo., 1972-73; pres. Clayton Cons., Louisville, Ky., 1994—; prin. The Clayton Group, Global Cons., Exec. Distbrs., NuSkin, Internat., Interior Design Nutritionals, 1992—. Patentee in field. Chmn. bd. deacons Bapt. Ch., Louisville, 1975; dir. ch. choir Bapt. Ch., Arkansas City, Kans., 1963. Col. USAR, 1963-93. Named to Honorable Order of Ky. Cols. Mem. Res. Officers Assn. (exec. bd., pres. 1984, nat. councilman 1990-94), Ky. Res. Officers Assn., Inst. Indsl. Engrs., Assn. Internal Mgmt. Cons., Assn. of U.S. Army, Purdue Alumni Assn., U. Louisville Alumni Assn., Pa. State Alumni Assn., Army War Coll. Alumni Assn. Republican. Home and Office: 8215 Camberley Dr Louisville KY 40222-5534

CLAYTON, ROBERT BEVILLE, insurance and financial services professional; b. Thomasville, Ga., Feb. 9, 1948; s. B.G. and Dorothy B. Clayton; divorced; children: Robert B. Jr., Traci L. AA, U. Fla., 1968, B, 1970, MEd, 1971. CFP; cert. fund specialist. Sch. tchr. Escambia County Sch. Bd., Pensacola, Fla., 1974-77; sales mgr. Torchmark, Birmingham, Ala., 1977-84; regional v.p. United Fin. Investments, Pensacola, 1984-87; v.p., mgr. investment dept. AmSouth Bank Fla., Pensacola, 1987-90; territory mgr. Prudential Ins. and Fin. Svcs., Ft. Walton Beach, Fla., 1991-95; v.p., mgr. investment divsn. North Ctrl. Fla., SunTrust Bank, Ocala, 1995—; part-time prof. bus. dept. Pensacola Jr. Coll., 1990-95. Weekly columnist, 1987-92. 1st lt. USAF, 1972-74. Recipient Meritorious Svc. medal. Mem. Nat. Assn. Life Underwriters (Life Underwriters Tng. Coun. grad. 1978, fellow 1994; Nat. Sales Achievement award 1978, 79, 80, Nat. Quality award 1979), Inst. Cert. Fin. Planners, Internat. Assn. Registered Fin. Planners. Democrat. Methodist. Home: PO Box 6851 Ocala FL 34478 Office: SunTrust Bank 203 E Silver Springs Blvd Ocala FL 34470-5831 also: SunTrust Bank PO Box 310 Ocala FL 34478

CLAYTON, ROSE MARIE MCAFEE, journalist, writer, talent agent, television producer; b. Memphis, Dec. 18, 1939; d. John William and Florine Mary (Ransome) McAfee; m. John W. Clayton, July 18, 1964 (div. July 16, 1984). BS, Memphis State U., 1961, MA, 1962; EDs, U. Tex., 1975. Tchr., counselor Memphis City Schs., Shelby County Schs., Memphis, 1963-79; asst. to dean Coll. Comm. and Fine Arts Memphis State U., 1980-81; assoc. prodr. Entertainment Tonight Nashville bur. Paramount Pictures, Hollywood, Calif., 1982-85, field dir., prodr. Entertainment Tonight, 1988-94; spl. projects dir. Am./Poligram Records, Hollywood, 1986; pub. rels. mgr. The Peabody Hotel, Hollywood, 1987; panel prodr. Freedom Speaks Freedom Forum First Amendment Ctr., Nashville, 1995—; field dir., prodr. Access Hollywood NBC, Burbank, Calif., 1996; Memphis corr. Billboard mag., Rollingstone mag., 1979-88. Co-author, editor: Elvis Up Close: In The Words of those Who Knew Him Best, 1994; writer, prodr. (spoken word album) Interviews from the Recording Sessions of the Class of '55, 1985 (Grammy Best Spoken Word album 1986). Recipient Key to the City Mayor of Memphis, 1986, Outstanding Achievement award Music Music Industries, 1986. Mem. Nat. Acad. T.V. Arts and Scis. (Nashville, mid-south regions bd. govs. 1996), Nat. Acad. Recording Arts and Scis. (former bd. govs. Memphis 1978), Soc. Profl. Jours. (nat., mid south chpt.). Democrat. Roman Catholic. Home: 828 Neartop Dr Nashville TN 37205 Office: Freedom Forum First Amendme 2nd Fl 1207 18th Ave S Fl 2 Nashville TN 37212-2807

CLEARY, THOMAS J., social worker, administrator; b. Indpls., May 28, 1942; s. Douglas L. and June Rose (McCalip) C.; m. Kathryn Anne Beuby, Aug. 31, 1968; children: Mary Kathryn, Stephen Michael; m. Yvonne Edith Perkins, Mar. 18, 1989. BA, Marian Coll., 1964; MA, Ind. U., 1966, Midwestern State U., 1992. Cert. social worker, Tex. Psychiat. social worker Ind. State Welfare, Indpls.; psychiat. social worker U.S. Army, Ft. Riley, Kans., Ft. Sam Houston, Tex.; psychiat. social worker C.F. Menninger Meml. Hosp., Topeka; chief social work svcs. USAF, Wichita Falls, Tex.; clin. social worker Red River Hosp., Tex.; clin. social worker psychology dept. Wichita Falls Rehab. Hosp., 1995-96; pvt. practice, 1993; clin. social worker Saratoga Med. Ctr., Sheppard AFB, Tex., 1996—. Contbr. articles to various pubs. Lt. col. USAF, 1972—. Mem. Nat. Assn. Social Workers, Wichita County Mental Health Assn. (pres. 1986-87, bd. dirs. 1995—). Office: North TexasNTNS 1722 1/2 9th St. Wichita Falls TX 76301

CLECKLEY, FRANKLIN D., judge. Justice W.Va. Supreme Ct., Charleston, 1994—. Office: WVa Supreme Ct State Capitol Complex Bldg 1 Rm E 301 Charleston WV 25305

CLEGHORN, G. DEAN, university official, educator; b. Bremen, Ga., Jan. 29, 1951; s. George W. and Tillie (Axtell) C.; m. Susan M. Driver, Aug. 5, 1972 (div. 1979); m. Jo Ann Faust, July 22, 1988. BA, Lee Coll., 1973; MS, U. Tenn., 1977, EdD, 1978. Lic. psychologist. Instr. U. Tenn., Memphis, 1977-78, asst. prof., 1978-85, assoc. prof., 1985-87; asst. dean for acad. affairs U. Tenn. Coll. of Medicine, Memphis, 1982-87; exec. dir. S.C. Area Health Edn. Consortium, 1987—; assoc. prof., assoc. dean Med. U. S.C. Coll. of Medicine, Charleston, 1987—; clin. assoc. prof. dept. family medicine U. S.C., Columbia, 1989—. Mem. APA, Southeastern Psychol. Assn., S.C. Psychol. Assn., Am. Assn. Med. Colls. (regional sec. group on ednl. affairs 1988-91, co-chmn. spl. interest group on quality improvement 1995-97), So. Tchrs. Family Medicine, Nat. Rural Health Assn., Am. Soc. for Quality Control. Office: SC AHEC Med U of SC 171 Ashley Ave Charleston SC 29425-0001

CLELAND, ABBY HATCH, library administrator; b. Holden, Mass., July 27, 1945; d. David Lincoln and Mary Alice (Gies) Hatch; m. Joel Samuel Cleland, Aug. 19, 1967; children: Charles Thackston, Margaret Roper. BA, U. S.C., Columbia, 1967; MLS, 1990. Tchr. Lake Forest Elem. Sch., Wilmington, N.C., 1967-68; The Am. Sch., Tegucigalpa, Honduras, 1968-69, Lonnie B. Nelson Elem. Sch., Columbia, S.C., 1972-74; libr. Merrywood Elem. Sch., Greenwood, S.C., 1974-78; Cambridge Acad., 1984-87; dir. Children's Svcs. Greenwood (S.C.) County Libr., 1991—; facilitator Born to Read Greenwood (S.C.) County Collaboration, 1993—. Co-author: (video) Tips for Reading To Your Baby, 1994; contbr. numerous papers to profl. confs. Bd. mem. GIFT Lit. Program, Abbeville, S.C., 1991—, steering com. Success By Six, Greenwood, S.C., 1995—, task force Alliance 2020, Kellogg Found., S.C., 1995—, team mem. Act 135 Strategic Planning, Greenwood, S.C., 1994—. Recipient Cited as one of top 13 programs U.S. Dept. Edn., Washington, 1992, Com. of Yr. C. of C., Greenwood, S.C., 1993; named Champion of Reading Greenwood (S.C.) Lit. Coun., 1996; grantee Notable LSCA Grant, S.C. State Libr., Columbia, 1994. Mem. S.C. Libr. Assn. and SCYPS (pres., v.p., sec. 1992—), S.C. Assn. of Sch. Librs., S.C. State Libr. Children's Adv., The Book Group, Cateechee Study Club(pres., v.p., sec. 1975—). Episcopalian. Home: 123 W Laurel Ave Greenwood SC 29649 Office: Greenwood County Libr 106 N Main St Greenwood SC 29646

CLELLAND, ROBERT THEODORE, lawyer; b. Phila., Nov. 16, 1943; s. Robert Theodore and Elizabeth Horn (Hathaway) C.; m. Katherine Knopp, June 30, 1968 (div. 1974); children: Ted, Karyn; m. Gayle Jean Lester, Aug. 30, 1980. BS, U. Fla., 1966; JD, U. Miami, Coral Gables, Fla., 1971. Bar: Fla. 1971, D.C. 1983, Wash. 1988, U.S. Dist. Ct. (so., middle dist.) Fla., U.S. Dist. Ct. (so. dist.) Ga., U.S. Dist. Ct. (we. dist.) Wash., U.S. Ct. Appeals (11th cir.); cert. mediator Supreme Ct. of Fla., 1991—; cert. arbitrator; cert. mediator, arbitrator U.S. Dist. Ct. (so. and mid. dists.) Fla. Assoc. Fleming, O'Bryan & Fleming, Ft. Lauderdale, Fla., 1971; owner Robert T. Clelland Jr. Attys., Pompano Beach, Fla., 1971, Ft. Lauderdale, 1975, Delray Beach, Fla., 1990-91, Sebastian, Fla., 1990—, Seattle, 1990—. Fellow Fla. Bar Found.; mem. ABA (sect. litigation 1989—, constrn. law com. 1990—, com. on alt. dispute resolution 1991, com. on arbitration 1991—), Fla. Bar Assn. (real property, probate and trust law sect., constrn. law com.), Washington Bar Assn. (procurement and constrn. law com.), Am. Arbitration Assn. (arbitrator, mediator, instr.), Wash. Arbitration & Mediation Svc., Fla. Acad. Profl. Mediatros, Soc. Profls. Dispute Resolution. Democrat.

CLEM, ELIZABETH ANN STUMPF, music educator; b. San Antonio, July 9, 1945; d. David Joseph and Elizabeth Burch (Wathen) Stumpf; m. D. Bruce Clem, June 17, 1972; children: Sean David, Jeremy Andrew. BA in Music Edn., St. Mary-of-the-Woods (Ind.) Coll., 1970; MEd, Drury Coll., Springfield, Mo., 1979. Elem. tchr. St. Christopher Sch., Speedway, Ind., 1970-71; elem. and jr. high sch. tchr. Indpls. Sch. System, 1971-72; elem. tchr. Augusta (Ga.) Sch. System, 1972-73, Wabash (Ind.) Sch. System, 1976-77; pvt. practice piano tchr. Wabash, Ind., 1975-77, Honolulu, 1983-86, Burke, Va., 1986-90, Manhattan, Kans., 1990-93, Fayetteville, N.C., 1993-96; pvt. practice piano tchr. Meth. Coll. Performing Arts, Ft. Sill, Okla., 1996—, 1993-96; co-chmn. Manhattan Musicianship Auditions, 1991, chmn., 1992. Dist. fundraiser rep. Wabash chpt. Am. Cancer Soc., 1975; leadership coord. Wabash coun. Girl Scouts U.S.A., 1976; music coord. Ft. Shafter Sacred Heart Chapel, Honolulu, 1985-86; mem. exec. bd. Little Apple Invitational Soccer Tournament, 1992; vol. N.C. Symphony. Mem. Nat. Guild Piano Tchrs., Music Tchrs. Nat. Assn. (cert.), N.C. Music Tchrs. Assn. (rep. to nat. assn.), Okla. Music Tchrs. Assn., Raleigh Piano Tchrs. Assn., Fayetteville Piano Tchrs. Assn. (v.p. 1994, pres. 1995), Lawton Music Tchrs., Schubert Music Club, Lawton Piano Tchrs. Assn., Nat. Fedn. of Music Clubs. Republican. Roman Catholic.

CLEMA, JOE KOTOUC, computer scientist; b. Omaha, Sept. 23, 1938; s. Joseph Arthur and Sylva Marie (Kotouc) C.; m. Maria Estela Cobos, Apr. 1, 1960; children: Jennifer, Arta. Student, U.S. Mil. Acad., 1957-60; BS, U. Nebr., 1963; MS, U. Miami, 1969; PhD, Colo. State U., 1973. Systems analyst Gen. Electric, Louisville, 1969-70; head sci. applications Colo. State U., Ft. Collins, 1970-73; project engr. Gen. Dynamics, Ft. Worth, 1973-77; sr. mgr. Simulation Tech., Inc., Dayton, Ohio, 1977-79; program mgr. Pratt and Whitney, West Palm Beach, Fla., 1979-82; dept. mgr. CACI, Dayton, 1982-83; dir. spl. projects Systems and Applied Scis., Vienna, Va., 1983-85; chief software engr. IIT Rsch. Inst., Annapolis, Md., 1985-90; cons. to IBM with Neurosystems, Inc., Bethesda, Md., 1991-93; cons. on IRS tax system modernization TRW, Merriefield, Va., 1993-95, cons. simplified tax & wage sys., 1995—. Contbr. articles to profl. jours. Sustaining mem. Rep. Nat. Com., Washington, 1983—. Served to capt. U.S. Army, 1963-67. First Ann. Simulation Symposium Rsch. grantee, 1972; recipient Outstanding Svc. award Ann. Simulation Symposium Bd. Dirs., 1980. Mem. IEEE (sr.), ACM (nat. lectr. 1978-83), Soc. Computer Simulation (bd. dirs. , program chmn. 1988-96), Mid Atlantic Electronic Commerce Network (bd. dirs. 1995—), Spl. Interest Group on Simulation (chmn. 1979-81), Ann. Simulation Symposium (chmn. bd. dirs. 1979), Internat. Platform Assn., Armed Forces Comms. and Elec. Assn., Herndon C. of C., Hidden Creek Country Club, Worldgate Athletic Club. Republican. Home: 301 Missouri Ave Herndon VA 22070-5426 Office: Neurosystems Inc 6701 Democracy Blvd Bethesda MD 20817-1572

CLEMENS, NORA DUENAS, dietitian; b. Cardenas, Cuba, Oct. 8, 1956; d. José Antonio and Edilia (Arbide) Dueñas; m. Benjamin John Clemens, Feb. 11, 1984; children: Christina Nicole, James Carlton II. AA, Palm Beach Community Coll., 1976; BS, Fla. State U., 1979; postgrad., Emory U., 1980. Registered and licensed dietitian. Clin. dietitian JFK Meml. Hosp., Lake Worth, Fla., 1980-83; outpatient dietitian Boca Raton (Fla.) Community Hosp., 1983—; cons. dietitian West Palm Beach, Fla., 1985—. Mem. Palm Beach Dietetic Assn. (legis. chair 1993—, chair nominating com. 1992-93, pres. 1988-89). Democrat. Methodist. Home: 714 Forest Hill Blvd West Palm Beach FL 33405-4504

CLEMENT, CLARENCE CLARK, JR., petroleum engineer; b. Artesia, N.Mex., July 20, 1949; s. Clarence Clark Sr. and Virginia Maxine (Smith) C.; m. Paulette Carmen Maldonado, June 12, 1971; children: Clarence Clark III, Julie Ann. BS in chemistry, N.Mex. Highlands U., 1971. Registered profl. engr., Okla. Divsn. chemist Halliburton Svcs., Odessa, Tex., 1971-75; staff engr., region sales engr. The Western Co. of N.Am., Houston, Corpus Christi, Tex., 1975-77; HNG Oil Co. Corpus Christi, 1977-79; prodn. mgr. Robinson Bros. Production Co., Woodward, Okla., 1979-84; sr. prodn. engr., dist. engr. Sohio Petroleum/British Petroleum, Oklahoma City, Okla., 1984-88; dist. ops. supr./onshore engrng. mgr. Sohio Petroleum/British Petroleum, Houston; v.p. ops. Nu-Bore Systems, Houston, 1988-91; sr. staff drilling engr. Tex/Con Oil & Gas Co., Houston, 1991; prodn. engrng. mgr. PG&E Resources/Dalen Resources, Dallas, 1991-95; consulting petroleum engr. Brit. Petroleum, Colombia, 1995—. Contbr. articles and tech. presentations to profl. jours. Mem. Am. Assn. Drilling Engrs., Soc. Petroleum Engrs., Loyal Order of Moose. Home: 6704 Wickliff Plano TX 75023

CLEMENT, EDITH BROWN, federal judge; b. Birmingham, Ala., Apr. 29, 1948; d. Erskine John and Edith (Burrus) Brown; m. Rutledge Carter Clement Jr., Sept. 3, 1972; children: Rutledge Carter III, Catherine Lanier. BA, U. Ala., 1969; JD, Tulane U., 1972. Bar: La. 1973, U.S. Dist. Ct. (ea., mid. and we. dists.) 1973, U.S. Ct. Appeals (5th cir.) 1975, U.S. Supreme Ct. 1978, U.S. Ct. Appeals (11th cir.) 1981. Law clk. to Hon. H.W. Christenberry U.S. Dist. Ct., New Orleans, 1973-75; ptnr. Jones, Walker, Waechter, Poitevent, Carrere & Denegre, New Orleans, 1975-91; judge U.S. Dist. Ct. (ea. dist.) La., New Orleans, 1991—; speaker at seminars and profl. meetings. Life fellow La. Bar Found.; mem. Am. Law Inst., La. State Bar Assn., Maritime Law Assn. U.S., Fed. Bar Assn. (pres. New Orleans chpt. 1990-91), New Orleans Bar Assn. (v.p. 1980-81). Roman Catholic. Office: US Dist Ct 500 Camp St Rm C-455 New Orleans LA 70130-3313

CLEMENT, ROBERT LEBBY, JR., lawyer; b. Charleston, S.C., Dec. 14, 1928; s. Robert Lebby and Julia Axson (Thayer) C.; m. Helen Mathilda Lewis, Nov. 26, 1954; children: Jeanne Marie, Robert Lebby III, Thomas L.T. AB, The Citadel, 1948; JD, Duke U., 1951. Bar: N.C. 1951, S.C. 1954. Practiced in Charlotte, N.C., 1951-53; ptnr. Cornish, Clement & Horlbeck, Charleston, S.C., 1955-60, Hagood, Rivers & Young, 1960-65, Young, Clement, Rivers & Tisdale, LLP, 1965-93; of counsel, 1994—; pres. Charleston Automotive Parts, Inc., 1969-84, Charleston Mus., 1980-83; bd. dirs. Unisun (formerly Am. Mut. Fire Ins. Co.); mem. adv. bd. NationsBank; asst. city atty., Charleston, 1960; judge Mcpl. Ct., Charleston, 1961-63. Mem. Charleston County Coun., 1983-86, chmn., 1985-86. Served with JAGC, USAF, 1953-55. Mem. ABA, N.C. Bar Assn., S.C. Bar Assn., Charleston County Bar Assn. (pres. 1990-91), Rotary. Presbyterian. Office: Young Clement Rivers & Tisdale PO Box 993 Charleston SC 29402-0993

CLEMENTS, BRIAN N., English language educator; b. Memphis, Dec. 16, 1965; s. Jackie N. and Barbara Louise (McNamee) C.; m. Abbey Suzanne Waldstein, Aug. 4, 1992; 1 child, Sarah Fern. Student, Hendrix Coll., 1983-85; BA in English, So. Meth. U., 1987; MA in English, SUNY, Binghamton, 1990, PhD in English, 1993. Adj. asst. prof. SUNY, Binghamton, 1993-94; adj. lectr. Broome C.C., Binghamton, 1994; sr. lectr. U. Tex. at Dallas, Richardson, 1994—; vis. writer U. North Tex., Denton, 1995-96; coord. Share Our Strength's Writers Harvest, Dallas, 1994—; co-founding editor Rancho Loco Press, Dallas, 1996—. Author: Flesh and Wood, 1992; editor Concourse: A Jour. of Lit. & Arts, 1989-92. Mem. MLA, Associated Writing Programs, The Writers Garret (asst. dir. 1995, bd. dirs. 1995—). Office: U Tex at Dallas MS J03.1 Richardson TX 75083

CLEMENTS, JEFFREY RUSSELL, city official; b. Louisville, Oct. 24, 1959; s. John Russell and Carol Jean (Mercer) C.; m. Lee Ann Jerome, June 26, 1982; children: Jennifer Lee, Christine Elizabeth. BA, U. Va., 1981; MPA, U. S.C., 1982. Policy analyst Richland County Coun., Columbia, S.C., 1982-85; transp. planner Ctrl. Midlands Regional Planning Coun., Columbia, 1985-86; legis. analyst S.C. Adv. Commn. on Intergovernmental Rels., Columbia, 1986-89; policy analyst Jacksonville (Fla.) City Coun., 1989—; polit. sci. lectr. Jacksonville U., 1992—. Co-author: Roles and Relationships: South Carolina Government in the Year 2000, 1987, Planning for South Carolina's Future, 1989, Election Reform for Increased Voter Participation in South Carolina, 1989. Staff mem. Commn. on the Future of S.C., Columbia, 1988. Mem. Am. Soc. Pub. Adminstrn. (pres. S.C. chpt. 1988-89, pres. N.E. Fla. chpt. 1992-94, bd. dirs. S.E. Conf. for Pub. Adminstrn. 1994-96), Econ. Roundtable of Jacksonville. Roman Catholic.

CLEMMONS, BARRY WAYNE, marketing operations executive; b. Pulaski, Tenn., Dec. 10, 1949; s. Villard Thomas and Lera Mae (Blade) C.; m. Lynnette Estelle Burnside, June 4, 1982; children: Matthew H. Fulghum, Timothy M. Fulghum. Student, U. Ala., Birmingham, 1967-68, Jefferson State Jr. Coll., Birmingham, 1968-70. Asst. br. mgr. Birmingham Trust Nat. Bank, 1974-76, br. mgr., 1976-79; communications systems rep. South Cen. Bell, Birmingham, 1979, acct. exec., 1980, nat. acct. exec., 1981, asst. staff mgr., 1982; asst. staff mgr. BellSouth Svcs., Birmingham, 1983-85, staff mgr., 1989—; staff mgr. South Cen. Bell Advanced Systems, Birmingham, 1985-87, BellSouth Advanced Systems, Birmingham, 1987-89; mgr. mktg. ops. and devel. BellSouth Svcs., Inc., Birmingham, 1989—. Mem. Leadership Birmingham, 1987—; elected mem. Jefferson County Dem. Exec. Com., Birmingham, 1986; advisor to mayor, City of Birmingham, 1987; chmn. East Jefferson unit Am. Cancer Soc., Birmingham, 1987; appointed to Birmingham Libr. Bd. Birmingham City Council, 1988-90, Birmingham Bd. Edn., 1990—; v.p. Spring Lake Neighborhood Assn., 1st v.p. Voters of the Eastern Sect, 1988-90; Dem. nominee to Ala. Ho. of Reps., 1990; gov. edn. tech. liaison Govt. Ala., 1993—. Mem. Jaycees (pres. Birmingham chpt. 1976-78, state Speak Up award 1977). Baptist. Club: Toastmasters. Lodges: Kiwanis (chmn. com. Birmingham club 1986), Masons. Home: 1333 Stonehurst Dr Birmingham AL 35235-2745 Office: Bellsouth Svcs 3535 Colonnade Pky Ste S501 Birmingham AL 35243-2358

CLEMON, U. W., federal judge; b. Birmingham, Ala., Apr. 9, 1943; m. Barbara Lang; children: Herman Issac, Addine Michele. Bar: Ala. Ptnr. Adams and Clemon and predecessor, Birmingham, 1969-80; fed. judge U.S. Dist. Ct. (no. dist.) Ala., Birmingham, 1980—. Mem. Ala. Senate, 1974-80. Recipient Law and Justice award SCLC, 1980. Mem. ABA (exec. coun. 1976-79, C. Francis Stratford award 1986), Alpha Phi Alpha. Office: US Dist Ct 519 US Courthouse Birmingham AL 35203-2000

CLEMONS, GREGORY ALAN, foreign language educator; b. Milw., Aug. 30, 1963; s. Harvey Wesley and Rachel (Rivers) C. BS, U. Wis., 1985, MA, 1987; PhD, U. Fla., 1996. Teaching asst. dept. Spanish/Portuguese U. Wis., Madison, 1985-87; grad. asst. dept. romance langs. and lit. U. Fla., Gainesville, 1987-94; asst. prof. Spanish Mars Hill (N.C.) Coll., 1996—; student asst. Health Edn., Univ. Fla. Student Health Care Ctr., co-coord. Peer Edn. Programs, Student Health Care Ctr., 1992; vis. prof. Spanish Warren Wilson Coll., 1994-96. Awarded jr. year abroad in Spain, U. Wis., 1983-84; Rotary Ambassadorial scholar to Venezuela, spring 1996. Mem. MLA, South Atlantic MLA, Delta Sigma Pi. Home: 66 Chestnut Ridge Asheville NC 28804 Office: Spanish Dept Mars Hill Coll Mars Hill NC 28754

CLEMONS, JULIE PAYNE, telephone company manager; b. Attleboro, Mass., June 13, 1948; d. John Gordon and Claire (Paquin) P.; m. W. Richard Johnson, Oct. 10, 1970 (div. Oct. 1980); m. E.L. Clemons, Apr. 23, 1988. BBA, U. R.I., 1970. Svc. rep. New England Telephone, East Greenwich, R.I., 1970-71; svc. rep. So. Bell, Jacksonville, Fla., 1971-73, bus. office supr., 1973-77, bus. office mgr., 1978-84, staff mgr. assessment, 1984-86, mgr. assessment ctr., 1987-89; dir. human resource assessment State of Fla., Jacksonville, Fla., 1987-89; dir. human resource assessment Customer Svcs. Revenue Recovery Ctr., 1989-93, mgr. small bus. sales and svc., 1994-95, br. mgr. small bus. No. Fla., 1995—. Vol. Learn to Read; bd. dirs. Duval Assn. Retarded Citizens, Jacksonville, 1981-86, treas., 1983-84; mem. Leadership Jacksonville, 1996—, Leadership Jacksonville, Class of '97. Mem. NAFE, Am. Mgmt. Assn., Pioneers of Am., Jacksonville C. of C. Roman Catholic. Office: So Bell Tower 301 W Bay St Ste B1 Jacksonville FL 32202-5100

CLEMONS, MAGGIE RUTH, elementary school educator; b. Lafayette, La., Dec. 1, 1945; d. Clarence Darrell and Rita Miles; 1 child, Justina Maria Clemons. BA, So. U., 1969; MEd, Trinity Coll., Washington, 1979. Tchr. Paul Breaux Elem. Sch., Lafayette, La., 1969-70, Woodvale Elem., Lafayette, 1970-72, Myrtle Pl. Elem., Lafayette, 1972-75, Benjamin Franklin, Miami, 1975-76, Sacred Heart Sch., Washington, 1976-81, Plantation Elem., Lafayette, 1981—; Contbr. poems to books. Recipient Nat. Inventive Thinking-Winner's Tchr. Weekly Reader, 1991. Mem. NEA, La. Assn. Educators, Lafayette Parish Assn. Classroom Tchrs., La. State Poetry Soc., Alpha Kappa Alpha (new reporter 1989-92, asst. sec. 1993). Roman Catholic. Home: 815 12th St Lafayette LA 70501-6117

CLENDENIN, JOHN L., telecommunications company executive; b. El Paso, Tex., May 8, 1934; s. Maybelle Bauman; m. Margaret Ann Matthews, Aug. 30, 1954; children: Elizabeth Ann, Linda Susan, Mary Kathryn, Thomas Edward. BA, Northwestern U., 1955. With Ill. Bell Tel. Co., 1955-78, v.p., 1975-78; v.p. state region Pacific N.W. Bell, Seattle, 1978-79; v.p. ops. AT&T, 1979-81; pres., bd. dirs. So. Bell Tel. & Tel. Co., Atlanta, 1981-82, chmn. bd., 1982-83; chmn. bd., pres., CEO BellSouth Corp., Atlanta, 1984—; bd. dirs. Equifax, Inc., Providian Corp., Wachovia Corp., The Kroger Co., Coca-Cola Enterprises, Inc., RJR Nabisco Holdings Corp., RJR Nabisco, Inc., Springs Industries, Inc., N.Y. Stock Exch., Inc. Pub. rep. ARC; past nat. chmn. U.S. C. of C.; past nat. chmn. Nat. Alliance Bus.; trustee Tuskegee U.; nat. chmn. Jr. Achievement; past nat. pres. Boy Scouts Am.; chmn. bd. trustees Com. Econ. Devel. Mem. Commerce Club (bd. dir.), Cherokee Town and Country Club, Piedmont Driving Club (Atlanta), Breakers/Breakers West Club (Palm Beach, Fla.), Mid-Am. Club (Chgo.), Rotary. Presbyterian. Office: BellSouth Corp 1155 Peachtree St NE Atlanta GA 30309-3610

CLEVELAND, CHARLENE S., community health nurse; b. Haverhill, N.H., Aug. 20, 1945; d. Thomas D. and Willie E. (Smith) Sargent; children: Laura, Mary Ann. Diploma, Sylacauga Hosp. Sch. Nursing, 1967; student, Gadsden State Jr. C.C., 1979-82; BSN magna cum laude, Jacksonville State U., 1995. Staff nurse Sylacauga (Ala.) Hosp.; pub. health nurse Ala. Dept. Pub. Health, Sylacauga; staff nurse TCRC Child Devel. Ctr., Talladega, Ala.; homebound nurse Ala. Dept. Rehab., Anniston. Mem. Ala. State Nurses Assn., ARA, ASEA.

CLEVELAND, KATHLEEN CONNOR PARKER (KATHLEEN PARKER), syndicated columnist, public relations consultant; b. Winter Haven, Fla., Sept. 26, 1951; d. J. Hal Jr. and Martha Ayer (Harley) Connor; m. Sherwood McKissick Cleveland, Nov. 12, 1988; 1 child, John Connor Parker Cleveland; stepchildren: Sherwood McKissick, Jr., Samuel Henry Edmunds. BA in Spanish, Fla. State U., 1973, MA, 1976. Staff writer Charleston (S.C.) Evening Post, 1978-80, Fla. Times-Union, Jacksonville, 1980-82, Birmingham (Ala.) Post-Herald, 1982-83, San Jose (Calif.) Mercury News, 1983-87; staff writer, columnist The Orlando (Fla.) Sentinel, 1987-88; instr. journalism U. S.C. Coll. Journalism, Columbia, 1988-89; writer The Newman Partnership, Columbia, 1989-90; pres. Parker-Cleveland Inc., Columbia, 1990—; dir. written expression Buckley Sch. Pub. Speaking, Camden, S.C., 1991—. Author syndicated column Kathleen Parker, Tribune Media Svcs., 1995—; contbg. writer editl. forum USA Today, 1996—. Founder, pres. Dail Dinwiddie Safe Streets Found., Columbia, 1993—. Recipient H.L. Mencken Writing award The Balt. Sun, 1993. Office: Parker Cleveland Inc 1711 Pickens St Columbia SC 29201

CLEVELAND, LINDA JOYCE, delivery service executive; b. Ft. Worth, Aug. 31, 1948; d. Warren H. and Evelyn (Toepfer) Clason; children: Cassaundra, JoLisa, James, Andrea. Direct sales Tupperware Home Parties, Okla. City and Carthage, Mo., 1970-75; owner daycare ctr., Carthage, 1975-79; line worker Schrieber Foods, Carthage, 1979-82; mgr. quality control Shoes Too, Dallas, 1982-85; mgr. parts Maxtron, Dallas, 1985-88; owner L&W Express Delivery, Inc., Dallas, 1988—. Mem. Neuro Linguistics Programmers (master), Nat. Hypnotherapists, Dallas C. of C., Nat. Metric Assn. (cert. metrication specialist). Office: L&W Express Delivery Inc 4656 Leston St Ste 515 Dallas TX 75247-5725

CLEVELAND, MARY LOUISE, librarian, media specialist; b. Clarksdale, Miss., Dec. 4, 1922; d. George Washington and Beatrice (Orange) Jones; m. Chester Lloyd Cleveland, June 5, 1950 (div. 1973); 1 child, Ann. BS, Ala. State U., 1947; MLS, Case-Western Res. U., 1957; EdD, East Tex. State Coll., 1991. Asst. prof. libr. edn. Ala. State U., Montgomery, 1957-65; head libr. Talladaga (Ala.) Coll., 1965-66; asst. prof. Atlanta U., 1966-71; head libr. Wiley Coll., Marshall, Tex., 1971-77; assoc. prof. Ala. A&M U., Huntsville, 1977-83; dir. libr. Tex. Coll., Tyler, 1985—. So. Edn. Found. fellow, 1963, East Tex. State U. fellow, 1982-83. Democrat. Methodist. Home: 2508 Fieldcrest Dr NW Huntsville AL 35810-2122 Office: Tex Coll 2404 N Grand Ave Tyler TX 75702-1962

CLEVENSON, AARON BEN, artificial intelligence consultant; b. Laconia, N.H., Oct. 2, 1955. BS in Physics, Carnegie Mellon, 1977, MS in Measurement and Control Scis., 1978. Computer engr. E.I. DuPont, Orange, Tex., 1978-80, computer maintenance supr., 1980-83, maintenance supr., 1983-86, regional artificial intelligence coord., 1986-89; European artificial intelligence coord. E.I. DuPont, Mechelen, Belgium, 1989-90; mem. artificial intelligence task force E.I. DuPont, Orange and Kingwood, Tex., 1986—; team leader artificial intelligence task force E.I. DuPont, Kingwood, 1993—. Contbr. articles to profl. jours. Safety specialist ARC, Houston, 1985—. Recipient Clara Barton award ARC, 1989. Mem. Am. Assn. for Artificial Intelligence, FUSE, Inc. Office: EI DuPont de Nemours & Co 600 Rockmead Dr Ste 215 Kingwood TX 77339-2105

CLICK, BENNIE R., protective services official; married; 4 children. BS in Criminal Justice summa cum laude, Ariz. State U., postgrad. With Phoenix Police Dept.; chief of police Dallas Police Dept., 1993—. Active Boy Scouts Am., Greater Dallas Crime Commn., Jr. League of Dallas, Southwestern Law Enforcement Inst., Dallas Blue Found.; mem. criminal justice policy devel. com. North Ctrl. Coun. Govts.; vol. Children's Med. Ctr. of Dallas/Dallas Cowboys in multi-facted campaign to discourage possession of firearms by area youth. Mem. Internat. Assn. Chiefs of Police, Tex. Police Chiefs Assn., Nat. Law Enforcement Exec. Inst. Office: Office of Police Chief 2014 Main St Rm 506 Dallas TX 75201-5203

CLICK, DAVID FORREST, lawyer; b. Miami Beach, Fla., Dec. 17, 1947; s. David Gorman and Helen Margaret (McPhail) C.; m. Helaine London, June 2, 1974; children: Kenneth Randall, Adam Elliott. BA, Yale U., 1969, JD, 1973, MA, 1974. Bar: Conn. 1973, Md. 1983, U.S. Supreme Ct. 1983, Fla. 1984, Maine 1984. Asst. prof. Western New England Sch. Law, Springfield, Mass., 1974-77; assoc. prof. Ind. U., 1977-78, U. Md., Balt., 1978-84; assoc. Nixon, Hargrave, Devans and Doyle, Jupiter, Fla., 1984-86; sole practice Jupiter, 1986—; pres., dir. Click Farms, Inc., Clewiston, Fla. Contbr. articles to profl. jours. Mem. Christmas Cove (Maine) Improvement Assn., Palm Beach-Martin County Estate Planning Coun.; participant Leadership Palm Beach County, 1991-92. Mem. ABA, Fla. Bar Assn., Palm Beach County Bar Assn., Nat. Soc. Arts and Letters, Yale Club of the Palm Beaches (pres.), Kiwanis. Presbyterian. Home: 19216 Pinetree Dr Jupiter FL 33469-2002 Office: 810 Saturn St Ste 15 Jupiter FL 33477-4305

CLIFF, STEVEN BURRIS, engineering executive; b. Knoxville, Tenn., Mar. 30, 1952; s. Edgar Burris and Otella (Patterson) C.; m. Sharon Grace Davis, Sept. 11, 1971 ; children: Sarah Elizabeth, Susan Rebecca, Steven John. BS in Engrng. Sci., U. Tenn., 1974, MS in Engrng. Sci., 1976; postgrad., So. Sem., 1974-75. Rsch. asst. U. Tenn., Knoxville, 1972-75, asst. rsch. prof., 1975-76; program analyst Oak Ridge (Tenn.) Nat. Lab., 1976-77, rsch. engr., 1977-79; chief tech. officer Computer Concepts Corp., Knoxville, 1979-81; pres. Productive Programming Inc., Knoxville, 1981-82; v.p. R&D Control Tech. Inc., Knoxville, 1982—, corp. sec., 1991—; ptnr. Middlebrook Indsl. Properties, 1985—, Cliff Bros. Investments, 1988—. Contbr. articles to profl. jours. mem. exec. bd. Rocky Hill Parent-Tchr. Orgn., Knoxville, 1987, 91—, pres. 1994-95; deacon West Knoxville Bapt. Ch., 1984-87, Loveland Bapt. Ch., Knoxville, 1976-82; mem. tech. com. Bearden (Tenn.) Mid. Sch., 1996-97. U. Tenn. scholar, 1970. Mem. Soc. Mfgs. Engrs. (sr.), Nat. Electronic Mfg. Assn. (chmn. com. 1987-94, seminar spkr. 1988-94), Am. Assn. for Artificial Intelligence, Am. Tae Kwondo Assn. Home: 8210 Northshore Dr SW Knoxville TN 37919-8711

CLIFTON, GEORGE, design company executive. V.p. Clifton, Ezell & Clifton Design, Deltona, Fla. Office: Clifton Ezell & Clifton Design 505 Deltona Blvd Ste 201-A Deltona FL 32725

CLIFTON, GUY L., neurosurgeon, educator; b. Jacksonville, Tex., Apr. 29, 1949. BS, Tex. A&M U., 1971; MD with high honors, U. Tex., 1975. Intern in surgery U. Minn. Hosp., Mpls., 1975-76; resident in neurosurgery U. Tex. Med. Br., Galveston, 1976-80; dep. chief neurosurgical svc., dir. neurosurgical ICU Ben Taub Gen. Hosp., Houston, 1980-84; asst. prof. dept. neurosurgery Baylor Coll. Medicine, Houston, 1980-84; assoc. attending surgeon Hunter Holmes McGuire VA Med. Ctr., Richmond, Va., 1984-89, chief neurosurgery svc., 1987-90; assoc. prof. divsn. neurosurgery Med. Coll. Va., Richmond, 1984-89, interim chmn. dept. rehab. medicine, 1988-90, prof. divsn. neurosurgery, 1990; chief neurosurgery Hermann Hosp., Houston, 1990—; prof., dir. divsn. neurosurgery Health Sci. Ctr. U. Tex. Houston Med. Sch., 1990-92, prof., chmn. dept. neurosurgery Health Sci. Ctr., 1992—; mem.-at-large med. bd. Harris County Hosp. Dist., 1983-84; mem. exec. com. joint sect. on trauma Am. Assn. Neurol. Surgery/Cong. Neurol. Surgeons, 1986—; cons., reviewer NIH/NINCDS, Nat. Inst. Disability and Rehab. Rsch., Ctrs. for Disease Control; invited lectr. in field. Mem. cons. bd. editors Orthopedics, 1983-90; mem. editl. bd. Jour. Neurotrauma, 1988—; contbr. 78 articles to sci. and profl. jours., 27 chpts. to books. Recipient Roche Neurosciences award SAMA-UTMB Nat. Student Rsch. Forum, 1975; grantee Yale U., 1980-83, NIH, 1980-84, 94—, 93, 93—, Baylor Coll. Medicine, 1981-82, Mead Johnson, 1982-83, Moody Found., 1982-83, Ross Labs., 1983-84, Med. Coll. Va., 1986, Thomas F. and Kate Miller Jeffress Meml. Trust, 1986, VA, 1987-90, 90, Nat. Inst. on Disability and Rehab. Rsch., 1988-90, NIH/NINDS 1994—. Mem. AMA, ACS (Regional reidents Competition award com. on trauma, 1979), Am. Assn. Neurol. Surgeons (liason to Am. Acad. Phys. Medicine Rehab., Nat. Ctr. for Rehab. Rsch.), Am. Assn. Surgery for Trauma, Am. Spinal Injury Assn., Am. Trauma Soc., Soc. of Neurol. Surgeons, Nat. Head Injury Found. (profl. adv. bd. 1992—, Sheldon Berrol Clin. Svc. award 1993), Congress Neurol. Surgeons, Soc. Neurol. Anesthesia and Neurol. Supportive Care, Soc. Neurotrauma (founding officer, v.p. 1988, program chmn. 1991), Tex. Assn. Neurol. Surgeons (bd. dirs. 1991), Tex. med. Assn., Houston Neurol. Soc., Phi Kappa Phi, Alpha Omega Alpha. Office: U Tex Houston Med Sch Dept Neurosurgery Health Sci Ctr 6431 Fannin St Ste 7.148 Houston TX 77030-1501

CLINARD, ROBERT NOEL, lawyer; b. Welch, W.Va., Nov. 1, 1946; s. Vernon Carlos and Mary Elizabeth (Noel) C.; m. Margaret Hawthorne Higgins, May 21, 1977; children: Elizabeth Kercheval, Edward Noel, Margaret Graham Robinson, Kathryn Moir. BA, Washington & Lee U., 1968, JD, 1976. Bar: N.Y. 1977, Va. 1978, U.S. Dist. Ct. (so. dist.) N.Y. 1977, U.S. Dist. Ct. (ea. dist.) Va. 1978, U.S. Ct. Appeals (4th cir.) 1986, U.S. Supreme Ct. 1990. Assoc. Winthrop, Stimson, Putnam & Roberts, N.Y.C., 1976-78; assoc. Hunton & Williams, Richmond, Va., 1978-86, ptnr., 1986—. Sec. Va. Cultural Laureate Soc., Richmond, 1981-86, bd. dirs., 1981-90. Served to lt. USNR, 1969-72. Mem. ABA (antitrust sect., franchising and healthcare coms.), Va. State Bar (vice chmn. antitrust com. health law sect. 1985-86, chmn. 1986-87, bd. govs. antitrust sect. 1989—, vice chmn. antitrust sect. 1992, chmn. 1993), Nat. Health Lawyers Assn., Coun. of Franchise Suppliers, Internat. Franchise Assn., Order of Coif, Phi Beta Kappa, Omicron Delta Kappa. Republican. Episcopalian. Home: 6010 York Rd Richmond VA 23226-2737 Office: Hunton & Williams Riverfront Plaza East Tower 951 E Byrd St Richmond VA 23219-4040

CLINCH, NICHOLAS, assistant principal; b. Tokyo, Dec. 20, 1950; arrived in U.S., 1969; s. Harold Kenneth and Galina (Voevodina) C.; m. Carol Ann Connell, May 27, 1978; children: Michael Alan Clinch, Stephen Alexsei Clinch. BA, Davidson Coll., 1972; MA, Appalachian State U., 1973. Cert. secondary tchr., S.C. Spanish tchr. Gaffney (S.C.) H.S., 1973-74, York (S.C.) Comprehensive H.S., 1974-94; asst. prin. York Jr. H.S., 1994—; tennis coach York Comprehensive H.S., 1977-81, soccer coach, 1979-89; home-sch. coord. York County Migrant Program, 1975-81, dir., 1982. Office: York Junior High School 1280 Johnson Rd York SC 29745-2111

CLINE, ANN, artist, designer; b. Greensboro, N.C., Apr. 7, 1933; d. Grady Alton and Mae Josephine (Karsten) Merriman; scholar Cooper Union, N.Y.C., 1954, Fashion Inst. Tech., 1957, Arts Students League, 1961-62, Fine Arts Acad., 1962-63, Joachim Simon Atelier, Tel Aviv, 1962; A.B., N.E. La. U., Monroe, 1971; m. S.C. Johananoff, Mar. 9, 1959 (div. 1973); 1 child, Pamela; m. Francis X. Cline, Feb. 14, 1973. Asst. designer Adele Simpson Couture, 1959; pres. Johananoff Designs, 1967-70, Ann Cline Art Objects, Monroe, La., 1975—; pres. 165 North Properties; artist; works exhibited in group shows Haifa Mus., 1961, Am. Watercolor Soc., 1962; one person shows include: Barzansky Gallery, 1962, La. Polytech. U. Art Gallery, 1967, Mittel's Art Gallery, 1969, N.E. La. U., 1973, 71, Am. Consulate, Tel Aviv, 1962, Contemporary Gallery, Dallas, 1970, Brooks Gallery, Memphis, 1971, 14th Ann. Delta Art Exhbn. Nat. Found. Arts, 1971, Jackson Arts Ctr. Ann. Exhbn., Miss., (prize award 1971), 22d Ann. Delta Exhbn., Ark. Arts Ctr., 1972, 79, Mayor's Show, Monroe, 1979, Wesley Found. Award Show, 1979, 80, 81, Roundtree Gallery, Monroe, 1985-87, others. Bd. dirs. La. Council Performing Arts, 1974; rep. Gov.'s Conf. Arts; bd. adjustments Monroe Zoning Commn.; trustee Masur Mus., 1974-75; bd. dirs. Little Theater of Monroe, 1975-76; bd. dirs. Women of the Ch., Episcopal Ch., 1977-78, mem. Daus. of the King, 1979-82, chmn. meml. com. Recipient Young Designer competition award Fontana of Rome, 1957, 1st prize Fashion Inst. Tech., 1957, Young Designer's award Women's Wear Daily, 1960, 1st prize, Arts Students League, 1961, 2d prize, 1963, 2d prize Fine Arts Acad., 1962, 1st prize, Woodstock Gallery, 1962, 1st prize, La. Folk Art Festival, 1966, 68, 72, prize awards Temple Emmanuel Ann., Dallas, 1969, 71, 74. Mem. Internat. Butler Soc., Bayou Desiard Country Club, Little Rock Country Club, Lotus Club. Illustrator: Jessie Strikes Louisiana Gold, 1969, Rhet, the Egret. Home and Office: The Herb Soc Am Ark Unit 4909 E Crestwood Dr Little Rock AR 72207-5407

CLINE, BETH MARIE, school psychologist; b. San Diego, Apr. 21, 1959; d. Roy Donald and Betty Ruth (Gainey) Hendricks. AAS in Police Sci., Hinds Community Coll., 1979; BS in Criminal Justice, Delta State U., 1981, MEd in Sch. Psychology, 1984, EdS in Sch. Psychology, 1988, D in Edn., 1995. Sch. psychometrist Chattahoochee Flint Regional Edn. Svc. Agy., Americus, Ga., 1984-85; sch. psychometrist Clarksdale (Miss.) Mcpl. Sch. Dist., 1985-88, sch. psychologist, 1988—; sch. psychologist Clarksdale Screening Team, 1988-93; cons. trainer State Dept. of Edn., Jackson, Miss., 1988—, cons., portfolio reviewer, 1990—. Mem. adult and handbell choirs Clarksdale Bapt. Ch., 1989—, asst. Sunday sch. dir. and tchr., 1990-92, mem. Ladies Ensemble, 1994—, Sunday sch. dir., 1992-94. Mem. Nat. Assn. Sch. Psychologists, Miss. Assn. for Psychology in the Schs. (sec. 1985-87, mem.-at-large No. chpt. 1989—, pres.-elect 1991-92, pres. 1992-93, past pres. 1993-94), Ga. Assn. Sch. Psychologists (chairperson nominations com. 1985, rsch. com. 1985), Miss. Profl. Educators, Learning Disabilities Assn., Phi Delta Kappa. Baptist. Office: Clarksdale Mcpl Sch Dist PO Box 1088 Clarksdale MS 38614-1088

CLINE, CLAUDE WAYNE, technical and vocational educator, writer; b. Anniston, Ala., Jan. 26, 1945; s. Joseph Herbert and Lillian (McCoy) C. BS in Math. and Physics, Jacksonville (Ala.) State U., 1968; MA in Edn., U. Ala., 1976. Cert. in quality assurance. Math. instr. Bishop Kenny H.S., Jacksonville, 1969-70, Pub. Schs. in Ala. and Ga., 1971-77; stockbroker A.G. Edwards & Sons, Atlanta, 1978-82; license insp. Calhoun County Commn., Anniston, 1982-83; tech. editor, tech tng. instr., quality assurance adv. Def. Dept. Anniston Army Depot, 1983—. Author: Alabama Railroads, 1997. Office: Anniston Army Depot Anniston AL 36201

CLINE, JUDY BUTLER, human resources executive; b. Kodiak, Alaska, Jan. 9, 1952; d. James Rucious and Elizabeth (Strong) Butler; m. James Carter Cline, Aug. 17, 1973; children: John Wesley, James Andrew. BS in Mktg., Middle Tenn. State U., 1974; postgrad., U. Tenn., Nashville, 1974, 76. Cert. employee benefit specialist; sr. profl. in human resources. Benefits mgmt. Aladdin Industries, Inc., Nashville, 1974-83; mgr. human resources Kusan, Inc., Brentwood, Tenn., 1983-89; transition cons. Stolle Corp., Sidney, Ohio, 1989-90; dir. human resources Profl. Bags, Inc., Springfield, Tenn., 1990-91; v.p. Schroeder, Flynn & Co., Brentwood, Tenn., 1991-92; prin., part owner BenchMark Group, Inc., Brentwood, 1992-95; sr. v.p., gen. mgr. Lee Hecht Harrison, Inc., Brentwood, Tenn., 1995—; mem. Outplacement Inst. bd. dirs., 1st vice-chair Nashville Area Red Cross, 1994—; classroom cons. Jr. Achievement, 1993-94. Mem. Soc. for Human Resource Mgmt. (state coun. 1995—, bd. dirs. area II 1989-92, nat. coll. rels. com. 1987-92), Mid-Tenn. Employee Benefits Coun. (exec. com. 1981-89), Springfield-Robertson County C. of C. (bd. dirs.), Nashville Area C. of C. (employers coun.), Internat. Assn. Career Mgmt. Profls. Republican. Presbyterian. Office: Lee Hecht Harrison 155 Franklin Rd Ste 140 Brentwood TN 37027-4646

CLINE, MICHAEL PATRICK, association executive; b. Washington, Oct. 31, 1945; s. William E. and Anna (Kraynik) C.; m. Diana Cline, Dec. 31, 1989; children: Tammy, Mike, Bill, John, Terri, Nikki. AA in Bus., Cuyahoga C.C., Cleve., 1988; BA in Bus. Mgmt., Malone Coll., North Canton, Ohio, 1989. Cert. tchr., Ohio; lic. real estate, Ohio. With Phoebus Trucking, Cleve., 1967-68, Allied Delivery Sys., Cleve., 1968-86; owner M&N Auto Truck Body, Cleve., 1968-90; exec. dir. Enlisted Assn. of the N.G., Alexandria, Va., 1990—; notary pub., Va. Author: How to Improve Office Efficiency, 1989, How to Work with Congress, 1991. Pres. Homeowners Assn. Woodbridge, Va., 1993—; trustee Nat. Guard Ins. Trust, Washington, 1993—. With U.S. Army, 1963-67, Ohio N.G., 1967-92. Recipient Cert. of Merit, Mil. Coalition, Washington, 1995, Dedication/Appreciation award Medal of Honor Soc., 1992. Mem. Enlisted Assn. of N.G. (life, exec. coun.), Md. Enlisted Assn. N.G., NRA, ASAE. Methodist. Office: Enlisted Assn NG of US 1219 Prince St Alexandria VA 22314

CLINE, MICHAEL ROBERT, lawyer; b. Parkersburg, W.Va., Oct. 13, 1949; s. Robert Rader and Hazel Mae (Boice) C.; m. Carole R. Davis, Aug. 28, 1972. A.B., Morris Harvey Coll., 1972; J.D., Wake Forest U., 1975. Project coordinator Gov.'s Office Fed.-State Relations, Charleston, W.Va., 1970-72; spl. asst. W.Va. Office Econ. Opportunity, 1973; spl. asst. W.Va.-Dept. Labor, Charleston, 1974; staff asst., hearing officer, 1975-77; sole practice, Charleston, 1977—. Mem. ABA, Assn. Trial Lawyers Am., Comml. Law League Am., So. Mems. Assn. (bd. dirs.), Nat. Assn. Criminal Defense Lawyers, W.Va. Trial Lawyers Assn. (bd. dirs. 1982—, treas. 1984, v.p. 1985-86, Outstanding Mem. 1983), W.Va. State Bar (chmn. com. on econs. of law practice 1986, 91-92), Pi Kappa Delta, Phi Alpha Delta. Republican. Methodist. Lodge: Elks, Rotary. Home: 1531 Dixie St Charleston WV 25311-1903 Office: 323 Morrison Bldg Charleston WV 25301

CLINE, ROBERT THOMAS, retired land developer; b. McClave, Colo., May 31, 1925; s. John Howard and Goldie Gladys (Hiltabidel) C.; m. Martha Carolyn Erwin, Mar. 6, 1946; children: Carolyn Cline Price, Roberta Cline Colquitt. Student, Pueblo (Colo.) Jr. Coll., 1943, Wofford Coll., 1944. Real estate salesperson George H. Williams Co., Arlington, Va., 1946; real estate broker Lyon Pk. Realty Co., Arlington, 1946-48; cartographic rep. Hearne Bros. Map Co., Detroit, 1949-58; owner Aero Surveys Map Co., Marietta, Ga., 1958-65, Imperial Builders, Marietta, 1965-69; sec., treas. Personality Homes, Landmark Realty, Smyrna, Ga., 1969-78, Landmark Bldg. & Devel., Inc./Landmark Realty Co., Smyrna, 1978-96; ret., 1996. State sec. Christian Men's Fellowship Christian Ch., Ga., 1962-64; bd. dirs. Campbellstone Apts. for Elderly, Atlanta, 1980-86. With USAF, 1943-46. Republican. Home: 2665 Cold Springs Trl Marietta GA 30064-4461

CLINE, VIVIAN MELINDA, lawyer; b. Seneca, S.C., Oct. 6, 1953; d. Kenneth H. and Wanda F. (Simmons) Fuller; m. Terry S. Cline, June 15, 1974 (div. Oct. 1986); 1 child, Alicia C. BSBA, Calif. State U., Northridge, 1974; JD, Southwestern U., L.A., 1983. Bar: Calif. 1983, Tex., 1990. Paralegal Internat. House Pancakes, North Hollywood, Calif., 1976-78; assoc. Tuohey & Prasse, Santa Ana, Calif., 1983-85; paralegal Smith Internat., inc., Newport Beach, Calif., 1978-83; corp. counsel Smith Internat., inc., Houston, 1985—. Bus. cons. Jr. Achievement, Houston, 1992-94. Mem. Exec. Women's Network (sec. 1993, pres. 1994, dir. programs 1995, sec. 1996), Am. Soc. Corp. Secs. Inc. (sec. Houston chpt. 1995-96, treas. 1996—). Republican. Presbyterian. Office: Smith Internat Inc 16740 Hardy Rd Houston TX 77032-1125

CLINGERMAN, EDGAR ALLEN, SR., financial services executive; b. Wolf Lake, Ind., Dec. 27, 1934; s. Virgil Wilson and Jessie Pauline (Miller) C.; m. Betty Jean White, Dec. 9, 1966 (div. 1984); children: Tammie, Sarha, Johnny, Edgar Allen Jr. BS in Bus. Adminstrn., Ball State U., 1960; AMP, Harvard U., 1974. Mgr. Coopers & Lybrand, Fort Wayne, Ind., 1960-64; controller Joy Mfg. Co., Michigan City, Ind., 1964-67; exec. v.p. Milton Roy Co., St. Petersburg, Fla., 1967-85; sr. v.p. The Geneva Cos., Clearwater, Fla., 1985—. With USN, 1952-56. Mem. Nat. Assn. Accts., Assn. Corp. Growth, Fin. Execs. Inst. Home: 13672 Lakepoint Dr Clearwater FL 34622-2219 Office: The Geneva Cos 13535 Feather Sound Dr Clearwater FL 34622-2259

CLINKENBEARD, JAMES HOWARD, principal; b. Alexandria, Va., Apr. 1, 1950; s. Howard Samuel and Ethel Jane (Schwager) C.; m. Janelle Darlene Turner, May 27, 1972; children: Adam, Nathan, Evan. BS, Murray State U., 1977; MEd, Xavier U., 1985, postgrad., 1986-87, 89-92. Cert. tchr. and adminstr., Ky. Tchr. art Newport (Ky.) Ind. Schs., 1978-88, chief negotiator, 1985-88, asst. prin., 1988-91, 92-96, dir. Title V, 1991-92, acting prin., 1992, 94-95, prin., 1996—; freelance artist, designer Bellevue, Ky., 1977—; juror various sch. and profl. art shows; speaker pub. sch. in-service programs. Featured in Kentucky Artist and Craftsman mag., 1977; author various documents, ednl. reports. State advisor Ky. Imagination Celebration, 1984-85; bd. dirs. Kt. Citizens for the Arts in Edn., 1983-85; advisor Ky. Task Force for Comprehensive Arts, 1984, Ky. Task Force on Acad. Competition, 1985; active Ft. Thomas and Newport PTAs, Bellevue Civic Assn.; chmn. Citizens for Bellevue Schs., 1980-81, Arts Subcom., Coun. on Higher Edn., 1985-86, Ky. Foster Care Rev. Bd., 1991—; deacon First Christian Ch., Ft. Thomas, 1976—, chmn. bd., 1982-83, Sunday Sch. tchr., 1976—; mem. sel. panel Ky. Disting. Educators Program. Recipient commendation Ky. Supt. Pub. Instrn., 1984. Mem. NEA, Nat. Art Edn. Assn. (Ky. del. 1976-77, 81), Ky. art Edn. Assn. (varius orrices including pres. 1983-84, Project Art Tchr. award 1980), Ky. Edn. Assn. (svcs. com. 1985-97, del. 1986-88, mem. task force 1987-88), Newport Tchrs. Assn. (sec. 1982-83, treas. 1985-88, pres. 1988, vice chmn. polit. action com. 1984), Newport Adminstrs. Assn. (pres. 1994—), Washington Evening Star Cartoonists Guild, Ft. Thomas Swim Club (bd. dirs. 1994—, chmn. 1995—), Alpha Tau Omega (chpt. advisor 1987-91, chpt. housing corp. pres. 1993—, chpt. bd. trustees 1995—). Republican. Mem. Christian Ch. (Disciples of Christ). Home: 30 Kathy Ln Fort Thomas KY 41075-1914 Office: Newport Ind Schs 101 E 4th St Newport KY 41071-1615

CLINTON, MARY ELLEN, neurologist; b. Evanston, Ill., Feb. 15, 1950; d. Merle P. and Corinne E. (Wolf) C.; m. William J. Wade Jr. BS, Loyola/Marymount U., 1972; MD, U. So. Calif., 1976. Intern internal medicine Vanderbilt U. Hosp., Nashville, 1976-77, resident in neurology, 1979-81, chief resident, 1981-82, fellow in neuromuscular disease and electrodiagnostics, 1982-83, asst. prof. neurology, 1983-91; staff physician emergency medicine Donelson Hosp., St. Thomas Hosp., Nashville, 1977-79; asst. clin. prof. Vanderbilt U., Nashville, 1991—; dir. electrodiagnostic testing Neurosurg. Assocs., Nashville, 1991—; reviewing physician Mid South Found. for Med. Care, Inc., Memphis, 1991-94; med. expert Social Security and Disability Determination State of Tenn., 1987-95; dir. Vanderbilt Muscle Biopsy Lab., 1984-89; dir. neurodiagnostic labs. Nashville VA Hosp., 1989-91; mem. staff St. Thomas Hosp., Centennial Hosp., Nashville, So. Hills Med. Ctr.; cons. staff Bapt. Hosp., Nashville; cons. Williamson Med. Ctr., Franklin, Tenn. Contbr. articles and abstracts to profl. jours. Co-dir. Nashville br. Muscular Dystrophy Assn., 1983-91. Recipient Physician's Recognition award AMA, 1984, 88, Marymount Coll. Pres's award, 1996, Sandoz award neurology, 1993. Mem. Am. Soc. for Internal Medicine, Soc. for Neurosci., Am. Med. Women's Assn., Nashville Acad. Medicine, Tenn. Med. Assn., AMA, So. Clin. Neurol. Soc., Am. Acad. Clin. Neurophysiology, Am. Assn. for Electrodiagnostic Medicine, Am. Acad. Neurology, Kappa Gamma Pi. Office: Neurosurg Assocs 4230 Harding Rd Nashville TN 37205-2013

CLINTON, TRACY PETER, SR., financial executive, systems analyst; b. Laconia, N.H., Jan. 10, 1948; s. Francis Arthur and Jane Audrey (Ely) C.; m. Sally Carol Dedmon, Apr. 27, 1969 (div. Dec. 1975); children: Tracy Peter Jr., Christopher Mathew; m. Sheryl Ann McPherson, May 6, 1982. BBA in Banking and Fin., U. Ark., 1971. Controller Superior Air Parts, Inc., Addison, Tex., 1971-74; supr., mgr. Levi Strauss & Co., Little Rock, 1975-76; salesperson Levi Strauss & Co., Columbus, Ohio, 1977; supr. Walter E. Heller Co., Dallas, 1978-79; supr., mgr. Mary Kay Cosmetics, Inc., Dallas, 1980-92; gen. agt. Alt. Fin. Solutions, Inc., 1993; sr. bus. analyst, Tax Outsourcing Project Coord. 1st Am. Real Estate Tax Svc., Irving, Tex., 1993—. Co-chmn. Citizens for Organized Growth, Lewisville, Tex., 1983; mem. Lewisville Zoning Bd. Adjusters, 1984-86; vice chmn. Lewisville Planning and Zoning Commn., 1984-86; mem. Lewisville City Coun., 1986-92; dir. adult ministries, bd. dirs. 1st Ch. of Nazarene, Lewisville; mem. SSS Bd.; bd. dirs. Denton Ctrl. Appraisal Dist., 1992—, chmn. Mem. Am. Prodn. and Inventory Control Soc. Office: 1st Am Real Estate Tax Svc 1400 Corporate Dr Irving TX 75038-2420 Address: 1531 S Highway 121 Apt 1437 Lewisville TX 75067-5941

CLITES, ROGER MYRON, economics educator; b. Argos, Ind., Jan. 27, 1928; s. Myron Spencer and Ruth Evalena (Rogers) C.; m. Joyce Wertz Burnett, Aug. 21, 1955 (div. Nov. 1969); children: Margaret, Nina, John, Paul; m. Louise Green Griffin, Jan. 2, 1993. AB, Milligan Coll., Tenn., 1950; MA, U. Tenn., 1954. Instr. econs. U. Richmond, Va., 1956-60; asst. prof. econ. Appalachian State U., Boone, N.C.; chmn. dept. econ. and bus. adminstrn. Kans. Wesleyan U., Salina; assoc. prof. bus. econ. Clarke Coll., Dubuque, Iowa, 1981-88; assoc. prof. econ. St. Mary's U. of Minn., Winona, 1988-91, ret., 1991; fellowship nominator Found. for Econ. Edn., Irvington, N.Y., 1983-91; adv. bd. Nat. Social Sci. Assn., 1986-90, governing bd., 1990-91. Editl. bd. Nat. Social Sci. Assn. Midwest edit. jour., 1990-91; contbr. articles to profl. jours. NDEA Grad. fellow, 1960. Mem. Alpha Chi (regional v.p. 1978-80). Libertarian.

CLONINGER, DALE OWEN, finance and economics educator; b. Clearwater, Fla., Aug. 30, 1940; s. Raymond and Mary E. (Ewing) C.; m. Judy Branson Parrish, Mar. 20, 1961; children: Bret B., Eric O. BS in Indsl. Mgmt., Ga. Inst. Tech., 1962; MBA, Emory U., 1965; DBA, Fla. State U., 1973. Field engr. Gen. Telephone of Fla., 1962-64; instr. econs. U. South Fla., Tampa, 1965-68, asst. prof., 1969-74; assoc. prof. fin. and econs. U. Houston - Clear Lake, 1974-80, prof. fin. and econs., 1980—, dir. programs in acctg. and fin., 1982-85, assoc. dean Sch. Bus., 1985-87; cons. So. Bell Telephone, Atlanta, 1964-65, Fla. Fed. Savs., St. Petersburg, Fla., 1969-71, Fla. State Legislature, Tallahassee, 1967, 68, 69, various law firms, Houston, 1977—; tax and edn. cons. Fla. State Legislature, 1967-69; designer bus. and econ. activity index Fla. Fed. Savs. and Loan, 1971-74; econ. and fin. evaluator, expert testimony in civil suits of personal injury, lost profits and asset evaluations, 1977—; mem. accreditation teams So. Assn. Colls. and Schs., 1984-90; presenter in field. Author: Income, Employment and the Retired, 1967, The Economics of Crime and Law Enforcement, 1975, 2nd edit., 1980; (with Kim Q. Hill) Death on Demand, 1985, 2nd edit., 1988, 10th anniversary edit., 1994; contbr. numerous articles to profl. jours.; referee Am. Jour. Econs. and Sociology, Contemporary Policy and Issues, Fin. Rev., Jour. Applied Econs., Jour. Econ. Behavior and Orgn., Jour. Econ. Edn., Social Scis. Quar. Emory U. fellow, 1964, Am. So. Engring. Edn. fellow NASA, 1976. Mem. Am. Fin. Assn., Am. Econ. Assn., Fin. Mgmt. Assn., So. Fin. Assn., So. Econ. Assn., Beta Gamma Sigma. Methodist. Home: 1011 Live Oak Ln Taylor Lake Village TX 77586-4528 Office: U Houston Clear Lake 2700 Bay Area Blvd Houston TX 77058-1002

CLONTS, GEORGE GARY, packaging company executive; b. Alton, Ill., Mar. 22, 1940; s. George William and Fern Lorine (Miller) C.; m. Charlotte Joann Shelburn, Feb. 28, 1960; children: George Randall, Gary Deneal. Aero. engring. student, USAF, 1957-1961. Flight engr. USAF, Fairbanks, Alaska, 1957-61; prodn. worker Hoerner Boxes, Inc., Springfield, Mo., 1961-64; office mgr. Hoerner Boxes, Inc., Denver, 1964-69; sales rep. Hoerner Waldorf, Inc., Denver, 1969-72; sales rep. South West Packaging, Oklahoma City, 1972-77, gen. mgr., 1977-87; gen. mgr. Green Bay Packaging, Oklahoma City, 1987-88; pres., chief exec. officer Tech Pack, Inc., Oklahoma City, 1988—. Active Rep. Presdl. Task Force, Washington, 1982—. With USAF, 1957-61. Mem. Am. Golf Club, Petroleum Club Okla., Surrey Hills Country Club (bd. dirs. 1975-78). Home: 11729 Hackney Ln Yukon OK 73099-8130 Office: Tech Pack Inc 3801 NW 3d St Oklahoma City OK 73107-6601

CLOPINE, MARJORIE SHOWERS, librarian; b. N.Y.C., June 25, 1914; d. Ralph Walter and Angelina (Jackson) Showers; m. John Junior Clopine, June 19, 1948 (div.); m. Frank Mason Storck, Sept. 14, 1985. BA, Pa. State U., 1935; MS, Drexel U., 1936; MS, Columbia U., 1949. Gen. asst. Libr., Drexel U., Phila., 1937-42; asst. libr. Gen. Chem. Div., Allied Chem. Corp., Morristown, N.J., 1943-46; bibliographer U.S. Office Tech. Svcs., Washington, 1946; med. libr. VA Hosp., Washington, 1946-49; asst. libr. U.S. Naval Obs., Washington, 1949-52, libr., 1952-63; assoc. libr. Bethany (W.Va.) Coll., 1967-69. Alice B. Kroeger Meml. scholar Drexel U., 1935-36. Mem. AAUW, LWV, Inst. Retired Execs. and Profls., Women's Resource Ctr. of Sarasota, Friends of the Arts and Scis., Spl. Libraries Assn., Beta Phi Mu. Contbr. articles to profl. jours. Home and Office: 8400 Vamo Rd Apt 540 Sarasota FL 34231-7816

CLORE, JOHN NEWTON, endocrinologist, educator; b. Charlottesville, Va., Sept. 17, 1948; s. Jesse Newton and Thelma (Thompson) C.; m. Lydia Ellen Thomen; children: Ellen Sarah, John. Student, Washington and Lee U., 1967-71; BS, Va. Commonwealth U., 1976, MS, 1977; MD, Med. Coll. of Va., 1982. Diplomate Nat. Bd. Med. Examiners, 1983, Am. Bd. Internal Medicine, 1985, also Endocrinology and Metabolism subspecialty, 1989. Intern Med. Coll. of Va., Richmond, 1982-83, jr. asst. resident, 1983-84, asst. resident, 1984-85, endocrinology fellow, 1985-88, asst. prof. div. endocrinology and metabolism, 1988-93, assoc. prof. div. endocrinology and metabolism, 1993—; dir. gen. clin. rsch. ctr. Med. Coll. Va., 1996—; lectr. in field; mem. faculty senate Med. Coll. Va., quality assurance com., co-dir. diabetes clinic., mem. med. student rsch. project com. Holder patent in field for a method of lowering LDL cholesterol in blood; revs. in profl. jours; author numerous abstracts. Grantee NIH, 1991—. Mem. AAAS, Am. Coll. Physicians, Am. Diabetes Assn. (grantee 1988-90, bd. dirs. 1988—, del. cen. coun. 1990—, pres. Richmond chpt. 1990—, sect. Va. affiliate 1990-91, chmn. rsch. com. Va. affiliate 1991—, v.p. Va. affiliate 1991-92, pres-elect Va. affiliate 1992—), Am. Fedn. Clin. Rsch., So. Soc. Clin. Investigation, European Assn. for Study of Diabetes. Home: 8404 Valley Wood Rd Richmond VA 23229-7282 Office: Div Endocrinology & Metabolism Dept Medicine PO Box 980155 Richmond VA 23298

CLORE, LAWRENCE H., lawyer; b. Tulsa, July 31, 1944; s. Hubert Charles and Jessie Louada (Fowler) C.; m. Carol Jean Roegelein, June 3, 1967 (div. 1981); children: Robert William, James Lawrence; m. Martha Jo Lawyer; children: Kathryn Denise, Michael Hubert. BBA, Tex. Christian U., 1966; JD, U. Tex., 1969. Bar: Tex. 1969. Assoc. Fulbright & Jaworski, Houston, 1971-77, ptnr., 1977—. Capt. U.S. Army, 1969-71, Vietnam. Mem. ABA (labor and employment law sect., coun. 1990-93, vice chair 1993-94, chair 1994-95), Tex. Bar Assn. (labor and employment sect.), Indsl. Rels. Rsch. Assn., Houston Mgmt. Lawyers Forum (chmn. 1976-77). Republican. Presbyterian. Office: Fulbright & Jaworski 1301 Mckinney St Ste 5100 Houston TX 77010

CLOSE, TIMOTHY, art museum administrator. Exec. dir. Albany (Ga.) Mus. Art. Office: Albany Mus Art 311 Meadowlark Dr Albany GA 31707-4168

CLOSSER, PATRICK DENTON, radio evangelist, artist; b. San Diego, Apr. 27, 1945; s. Edward and Helen Thompson. Diploma, Am. Schs. of Cinema, 1970; hon. doctorate cinema arts, World U., Tucson, 1985. Artist Sta. KBFI-TV, Dallas, 1972-73; with Stas. KVTT and KDTX, Dallas, 1976-81, Sta. KTER and KTXO, Dallas, 1980-83; broadcaster Radio Newspaper, Panama, 1989-91; mem. Christian Film and TV Commn., Norcross, Ga., 1995—. Worked on TV commls. for Dr. Pepper, Am. Chiropractic Assn., feature movies, show Comment on Our Times, Bible's Forecast; evangelist Stas. KDTX-FM, KVTT-RM; worked on theatre trailers, network TV shows, Nelson Golf Classic, Operation Entertainment; radio evangelist Sta. Radio Africa, KXVI, WINB-shortwave, Radio Caroline, Sta. Radio East Africa Broadcasts, 1990-92, Sta. Radio Africa 2, 1991-93; spl. broadcasts Sta. KSKY-AM, Radio Africa Shortwave, 1993-94; art exhbns. St. Luke's Ch. Art Exhibit, 1987, 89, DEA Art Exhibit, 1992 (winner 1st prize, 2d prize 1991), Bachman Ctr. Art Exhibit, 1992, 93; art display/exhibit Ch. of the Ascention, 1995; contbr. articles on evangelism and learning disabilities to various mags. Mem. Coalition for Better TV CBTV, Tupelo, Miss.; mem. So. Poverty Law Ctr., Birmingham, Ala., 1981-84; spl. 1-hr. music and Christmas broadcast Radio Africa, St. Luke Episcopal Ch.. Named to Life History Ctr., Conroe, Tex., Internat. Hall of Leaders, 1988; recipient 1st place award Dallas Epilepsy Assn. Art Exhibit Contest, 1991. Mem. Coalition for Better TV CBTV, Tupelo, Miss.; mem. Amnesty Internat., 1981-83; HCJB Andex monitor, 1981-86; retainer, supporter So. Poverty Law Ctr., 1982-86. Home: PO Box 540881 Dallas TX 75220

CLOUD, BRUCE BENJAMIN, SR., construction company executive; b. Thomas, Okla., Feb. 15, 1920; s. Dudley R. and Lillian (Sanders) C.; m. Virginia Dugan, June 5, 1944; children: Sheila Marie Cloud Kiselis, Karen Susan, Bruce Benjamin, Deborah Ann Cloud McKenzie, Virginia Ann Cloud Treadwell. BCE, Tex. A. and M. U., 1940. Registered profl. engr., Tex. With H.B. Zachry Co., San Antonio, 1940-42, 55—, exec. v.p., 1963-87, pres., 1987-93, vice chmn., 1993-94, sr. corp. advisor, 1995—; also dir., partner Dudley R. Cloud & Son, constrn., San Antonio, 1946-55, also bd. dirs. Mem. adv. coun. Boysville Inc., 1978-79; bd. dirs. Tex. State Tech. Coll. Found., 1983—; mem. adv. bd. Tex. Extension Svc., 1995—. Lt. col. C.E. AUS, 1942-46, ETO. Recipient Pro Deo Et Juventute award Nat. Council Catholic Youth. Mem. AIM, NSPE, KC (3d degree), Tex. Assn. Gen. Contractors (life, dir. hwy. and heavy br. 1947-48, 72-76, pres. 1974, chmn. corps engrs. joint com. 1989-90), Am. Concrete Paving Assn. (v.p. 1970-74, bd. dirs., 1st v.p. 1975, pres. 1976), Nat. Asphalt Paving Assn., Tex. Hotmix Paving Assn. (bd. dirs. 1972), Nat. Assn. Gen. Contractors (bd. dirs. 1976-88, life dir., exec. com. 1978-79, bur. reclamaton com. 1977-97, corps engrs. com. 1986-97, equipment mgmt. com. 1978—, chmn. heavy divsn. 1979), San Antonio Livestock Assn. (life), Tex. Soc. Profl. Engrs., Tex. Good Rds.-Transp. Assn. (dir. 1974-79, exec. com. 1975-81, 85-89), Am. Mgmt. Assn., San Antonio C. of C. (chmn. better rds. task force 1978-79, 85-93, bd. dirs. 1993-94), Tex. Transp. Inst. (adv. bd. 1993—), Tex. Ext. Svc. (adv. bd. 1995—), Cons. Contractors Coun. Am. (chmn. 1989), Holy Name Soc. (v.p. 1962-63), Nocturnal Adoration Soc., Alpha Epsilon Chi. Home: 127 Cave Ln San Antonio TX 78209-2208 Office: H B Zachry Co 1100 Tower Life Bldg 310 S Saint Marys St San Antonio TX 78205-3108

CLOUD, GARY LYNN, food and nutrition services administrator; b. Knoxville, Tenn., July 14, 1945; d. Henry Kelso and Mamie Lee (Summey)

C. BS in Home Econs., Food and Nutrition, U. Tenn., 1966; MPH in Nutrition, U. N.C., 1972; postgrad., SUNY, Albany, 1988—. Lic. dietitian and pub. health nutritionist, Tenn.; registered Am. Dietetic Assn. Dietetic technician Fort Sander's Presbyn. Hosp., Knoxville, Tenn., 1966; dietetic internship N.Y. State Dept. Mental Hygiene Hudson River State Hosp., Poughkeepsie, N.Y., 1966-67; svc. systems corp. Del Monte, Inc., Bennington, Vt., 1967-70; sr. nutritionist, apprentice nutrition svc. cons., N.Y. State Dept. Health, 1970-73; assoc. nutritionist N.Y. State Bd. Social Welfare, Albany, 1973-76; playground supr. Knox County Dept. Recreation, Knoxville, 1980; chief clin. dietitian II, asst. dietary dept. dir. N.C. Dept. Human Resources, O'Berry Ctr., Goldsboro, N.C., 1980-82; nursing asst. Hillcrest North Nursing Home, Knox County, Tenn., 1988; libr. asst. U. Tenn. Libr.-Reserve Book Rm., 1990; shared facility registered dietitian Hillhaven Corp., Loudon Health Care, Tenn., 1990; regional supervising dietitian Svc. Sys. Corp., Del Monte Inc., 1967-70; dir. Bur. Nutrition Svcs. Mem. Am. Dietetic Assn., Tenn. Dietetic Assn., Knoxville Dist. Dietetic Assn., Knoxville Nutrition Coun. Home: 8500 Millertown Pike Knoxville TN 37924-1105

CLOUD, LINDA BEAL, retired secondary school educator; b. Jay, Fla., Dec. 4, 1937; d. Charles Rockwood and Agnes (Diamond) Beal; m. Robert Vincent Cloud (Aug. 15, 1959 (dec. 1985). BA, Miss. Coll., 1959; MEd, U. So. Fla., 1976; EdS, Nova U., 1982; postgrad., Walden U., 1983. Cert. tchr., Fla. Tchr. Ft. Meade (Fla.) Jr.-Sr. H.S., 1959-67, 80-89, Lake Wales (Fla.) H.S., 1967-80; pres. Cloud Aero Svcs., Inc., Babson Park, Fla., 1992—; part-time tchr. Spanish, English, Polk County Adult Schs., 1960-76; instr. Spanish Warner So. Coll., Lake Wales, 1974; instr. vocal music, drama, composition Webber Coll., Babson Park, Fla.; cons., pvt. tutor in field. Contbr. articles to profl. and equine publs.; author, dir. numerous pageants for schs. Charter mem., bd. dirs. Lake Wales Little Theatre, Inc., 1976; dir. Four Sq. swing choir; entertainer for various local orgns.; ring announcer Fla. State Fair, 1987-88; judge poetry and essay contests; bd. dirs. Defenders of Crooked Lake; mem., soloist Babson Pk. Cmty. Ch. Recipient Best Actress award Lake Wales Little Theatre, Inc., 1978-79. Mem. AAUW, Nat. Coun. Tchrs. English, Fla. Coun. Tchrs. English, Polk Coun. Tchrs. English, Polk Fgn. Lang. Assn., Babson Park Womans Club, Sassy Singers, Southeastern Peruvian Horse Club (life). Republican. Home: 1654 Seminole Rd Babson Park FL 33827-9793

CLOUD, MARINA TAYLOR, mental health counselor; b. Buawang, La Union, The Philippines, Dec. 2, 1945; came to U.S., 1947; d. Clyde and Emilia (Mazon) Blount; m. Gregory Doy Cloud, June 20, 1975 (div.). BA, U. N.C., 1978; MA, U. Fla., 1984; MEd, U. North Fla., 1989. Lic. mental health counselor, Fla. Mental health technician I Dorothea Dix Hosp., Raleigh, N.C., 1973-75; nurse's aide Wesley Long Community Hosp., Greensboro, N.C., 1976-77; community planner Guilford Native Am. Assn., Greensboro, 1979; researcher U. Fla., Gainesville, 1983-84, fin. aid evaluator Office Student Fin. Aid, 1984-85; counselor in tng. personal counsel and career devel. U. North Fla., Jacksonville, 1989-90; student aid advisor Fla. Community Coll., Jacksonville, 1986-87; employment primary counselor in stabilization unit Mental Health Ctr. Jacksonville, 1990-93, inpatient clin. svcs. mgr.; emergency svcs./inpatient clin. svcs. mgr., 1993-95; stabilization adult clin. program mgr. Mental Health Ctr., Jacksonville, 1995-96; dir. at large N.C. State U. Student Union, Raleigh, 1974; sec. U. Fla., Gainesville, 1983. Mem. ACA, Am. Mental Health Counselors Assn. Democrat. Presbyterian.

CLOUDMAN, RUTH HOWARD, museum curator; b. Oklahoma City, June 11, 1948; d. Harry Howard and Hazel Marcellus (Clay) C. BA, Washington U., St. Louis, 1970; MA, Bryn Mawr Coll., 1973. Asst. curator Joslyn Art Mus., Omaha, 1973-75, chief curator, 1975-78; guest curator Sheldon Meml. Art Gallery/U. Nebr., Lincoln, 1978-79; assoc. Newhouse Galleries, N.Y.C., 1980-84; sr. curator Portland (Oreg.) Art Mus., 1984-90; Mary and Barry Bingham, Sr. curator European and Am. Art J.B. Speed Art Mus., Louisville, 1990—, chief curator, 1990—. Author mus. catalogs and articles. Mem. Coll. Art Assn., Am. Assn. Museums. Office: JB Speed Art Mus 2035 S 3rd St Louisville KY 40208-1812

CLOUGH, LAUREN C., special education educator; b. Canton, N.Y., Mar. 17, 1924; s. Hiram William and Lena May (Ladison) C.; m. Margaret Ellen Williamson, June 8, 1951; children: David Wayne, Carol Canty (dec.). BA, U. Ala., 1947; MA in Teaching, U. Jacksonville, 1969; cert. mental retardation, U. Fla.; cert. specific LDEH, U. North Fla. Tchr. Duval County Bd. Pub. Instrn., Jacksonville, Fla., 1964-70; tchr. history Nassau County Bd. Pub. Instrn., Fernandina Beach, Fla., 1970-71, tchr. mentally retarded, 1971-73, specific learning disabled and emotionally handicapped resource tchr., 1973—; tchr. Hilliard (Fla.) Elem. Sch., 1973—; mem. Hilliard Elem. Sch. improvement co., 1991—, chmn. sch. pub. rels. com., 1993-95, mem. comm. com., 1994—, Title I com., 1994—; mem. SACS Sch. Accreditation com., 1995—. Office: Hilliard Elem 112 Ohio St Hilliard FL 32046-9451

CLOUTIER, MADISON JOSEPH, software company executive; b. Baton Rouge, La., Feb. 11, 1952; s. Joseph Jack and Madlyn (Hajek) C.; m. Leigh Ann Woodard, July 15, 1975; children: Melanie Leigh, Dustin Philip. BS in Computer Sci., Southwest Tex. State U., 1974. Programmer System Corp. Am., Houston, 1974-75; programmer, analyst Tex. Instruments, Ridgecrest, Calif. and Austin, Tex., 1975-78; system designer Columbia Scientific Industries, Austin, 1978-80; owner Travel Systems Inc., Austin, 1980-82; dir. product devel. Tymshare Travel Systems, Austin, 1982-84; mgr. product devel. McDonnel Douglas Travel Systems, Austin, 1984-86; mgr. applications devel. United Airlines Travel Systems, Austin, 1986-87; internat. mktg. mgr. Galileo Internat., Europe, 1987-90; owner, pres. Cloutier Assocs., Inc., Austin, 1990—; founder, chief ops. officer, v.p. mktg. Tower Tech. Corp., 1992—; owner Anderson Mill Travel, Austin, 1984—; mng. ptnr. Corle and Assocs., Austin, 1986-90. Recipient Eagle Scout award Boy Scouts Am., Shiner, Tex., 1967. Mem. Greater Austin C. of C., Tex. Info. Tech. Assn. (dir.), Austin-San Antonio Corridor Coun. (dir.), Austin Entrepreneurs' Coun., Austin Software Coun. (charter). Republican. Mem. Ch. of Christ. Home: 7305 Sage Oak Trl Austin TX 78759-7003 Office: Cloutier Assocs Inc 13809 Research Blvd Ste 606 Austin TX 78750-1240

CLOVER-LEE, SHEVONNE JONES, geriatrics nurse; b. Richmond, Va., Oct. 9, 1962; d. Lonnie Jr. and Ann T. (Jones) Clover; m. Larry S. Lee, Feb. 8, 1986 (dec.). Diploma in nursing, Petersburg (Va.) Gen. Hosp., 1984; student, John Tyler Community Coll., Chester, Va., 1990—. RN, Va. Cert. IV, venipuncture therapy. Pvt. duty nurse Petersburg, Va.; staff nurse John Randolph Hosp., Hopewell, Va., 1985—; charge nurse/supr. Battlefield Park Convalescent Ctr., Petersburg, Va., 1983-88, Waverly (Va.) Health Care Ctr., 1991-95.

CLOW, ELIZABETH D., academic administrator; b. Washington, Jan. 27, 1943; d. Devon E. and Mary Nelson (Powers) Dooley; m. Richard B. Clow, Aug. 19, 1967; 1 child, Martha Elizabeth. BA, U. Tenn., 1964; MEd, U. Ga., 1973, postgrad., 1993—. Tchr. Eng. & Social Studies Harford County Bd. of Edn., Belair, Md., 1965-68, Shelby County Bd. of Edn., Memphis, 1969-70, Jefferson (Ga.) City Schs., 1970-73; counselor Athens (Ga.) Acad., 1973-75; adj. instr. Dekalb Coll., Decatur, Ga., 1979-85, counselor devel. studies, 1985, coord. access ctr., 1989—. Craig E. Brandenburg scholar United Meth. Ch., 1995-96. Mem. Nat. Acad. Advising Assn. (scholar 1994), Am. Coll. Student Personnel Assn., Nat. Orientation Dirs. Assn., Nat. Assn. for Devel. Educators, Ga. Coll. Student Personnel Assn. Office: Dekalb Coll 555 N Indian Circle Clarkston GA 30021

CLOW, THOMAS JAMES, quality professional; b. Fargo, N.D., Oct. 22, 1960; s. James Oliver and Barbara Rae (Peterson) C.; m. Toni Lynn Mackenzie, Aug. 27, 1983; children: Ivan Thomas, Anders Mackenzie. BS in Indsl. Tech., Moorhead State U., 1984. Indsl. engr. Dana Corp., Roscoe, Ill., 1984-87, quality engr., 1987-92; quality mgr. Dana Corp., Lugoff, S.C., 1992—. Chmn. bd. dirs. Jr. Achievement, Kershaw County, S.C., 1993-95; campaign coord. United Way, Roscoe, 1990, 91. Mem. Am. Soc. Quality Control (cert. quality engr.). Office: Dana Corp 1235 Commerce Dr Lugoff SC 29078-9673

CLOWES, DARREL AUSTIN, education educator, retired; b. N.Y.C., Sept. 10, 1934; s. Darrel Austin and Margaret Loretta (Brennick) C.; m. June Gwendolyn Hendricks, Aug. 10, 1980 (div. July 1996); children: Jody Elizabeth, Jeffrey Sean, Darrel Austin III, Holly Doe, Collette Bailey. AB, Dartmouth Coll., 1956; MAT, Oberlin Coll., 1961; PhD, U. Tex., 1971. Faculty Turin (N.Y.) Cen. Sch. Dist., 1961-64, Jefferson C.C., Watertown, N.Y., 1964-67; regl. dir., edn. specialist U.S. Peace Corps, Korea, 1967-69; grad. asst. U. Tex., Austin, 1969-71; faculty Auburn (Ala.) U., 1971-72; assoc. dean Miami-Dade C.C., Miami, 1972-77; faculty Va. Tech., Blacksburg, 1977-96, emeritus faculty, 1996—; vis. prof. Wolverhampton Polytechnic, Eng., 1988; editor-catalyst Nat. Coun. for Comm. Svcs. and Continuing Edn, Washington, 1989-95; pres. Coun. of Univs. and Colls., Washington, 1992-93; rschr. Nat. Ctr. for Rsch. Vocat. Edn., Berkeley, Calif., 1990-95. Contbr. articles to profl. publs.; contbg. author: Higher Edn. Handbook of Theory and Practice, 1992, Handbook on Undergraduate Curriculum, 1996; editor: (monograph) Community College and Proprietary Schools, 1995. Chmn. bd. trustees Montgomery-Floyd Region Libr., Christiansburg, Va., 1985-93; pres. Sports Club, Blacksburg, Va., 1994—, Faculty Assocs./Coll. of Edn., Va. Tech., 1988-90, sen. Faculty Senate, 1990-94. Lt. USN, 1956-58. Mem. Assn. for Study of Higher Edn. (editl. bd. 1987-89), Am. Ednl. Rsch. Assn. (program divsn. J chmn. 1983-84, Svc. award 1984-85), Nat. Coun. for Continuing Edn. (bd. dirs. 1989-95, Svc. award 1990-94). Office: Coll of Human Resources/Edn Va Tech Blacksburg VA 24061-0313

CLOYD, BONITA GAIL LARGENT, rehabilitation nurse, educator; b. Paducah, Ky., Oct. 1, 1952; d. Thomas Edward and Melodean (Keeling) Largent; m. Richard Frank Cloyd, June 8, 1974; 1 child, Lawrence. ADN, Paducah C.C., 1972; BSN, Bellarmine Coll., Louisville, 1991; MSN, U. Evansville, 1994; FNP, Belmont U., 1996. RN, Ky.; cert. in enterostomal therapy. Nurse, team leader Lourdes Hosp., Paducah, 1972-74; nurse, med.-surg. team leader Suburban Hosp., Louisville, 1974-76; enterostomal therapist Western Bapt. Hosp., Paducah, 1976—. Speakers Bur. Am. Cancer Soc.; helpline vol. Chosen Children Adoption Svcs., Inc. Mem. Wound, Ostomy and Continence Nurses Soc., United Ostomy Assn. (program planner), Belmont Nurses Honor Soc. (charter), Sigma Theta Tau, Phi Theta Kappa. Home: 247 Seminole Dr Paducah KY 42001-5425

CLOYD, HELEN MARY, accountant, educator; b. Austria-Hungary, 1918; d. Valentine and Elizabeth (Kretschmar von Kienbusch) Yuhasz; came to U.S. 1922, naturalized, 1928; BS, Eastern Mich. U., 1953; MA, Wayne State U., 1956; PhD, Mich. State U., 1963; m. George S. Smith, Mar. 4, 1939 (dec.); children: George, Nora; m. Chester L. Cloyd, Apr. 16, 1960 (dec.). Pub. accounting Haskins & Sells, Detroit, 1945-53; tchr. Marine City (Mich.) High Sch., 1954-59; instr. acctg. Central Mich. U., Mt. Pleasant, 1959-60; asst. prof. Wayne State U., Detroit, 1960-61; tchr. Grosse Pointe (Mich.) High Sch., 1961-64; assoc. prof. acctg. Ball State U., Muncie, Ind., 1964-71; prof. Shepherd Coll., Shepherdstown, W.Va., 1971-76; assoc. prof. George Mason U., Fairfax, Va. Recipient McClintock Writing award CPA, Mich., Ind., W.Va. Mem. AICPA, Am. Acctg. Assn., Am. Econs. Assn., AAAS, Assn. Sch. Bus. Ofcls., Delta Pi Epsilon, Pi Omega Pi, Pi Gamma Mu. Clubs: Order Eastern Star, White Shrine. Contbr. numerous articles to publs. Home: PO Box 186 Inwood WV 25428-0186

CLOYDE, ROBERT WAYNE, social worker, clergyman; b. Tulsa, Oct. 2, 1959; s. Granville Jackson and Doris Illene (Broom) C.; m. Terri Faye Jenkins, June 4, 1983; children: Michael James, Stephen Andrew, Nicholas Lee. BA, Okla. Bapt. U., 1981; MDiv, Southwestern Bapt. Theol. Sem., Ft. Worth, 1984, DMin, 1996. Ordained to ministry Baptist Ch., 1981. Pastor First Bapt. Ch., Caney, Okla., 1981-86, Morris Meml. Bapt. Ch., Ada, Okla., 1986-92, Faith Bapt. Ch., Bokchito, Okla., 1992-94; sr. pastor Hagerman Bapt. Ch., Sherman, Tex., 1995-96; social worker Marshall Meml. Hosp., Madill, Okla., 1996—. Contbr. articles to religious mags. Named to Outstanding Young Men in Am. Office: Marshall Meml Hosp PO Box 827 Madill OK 73446

CLUBBE, JOHN LOUIS EDWIN, humanities educator; b. N.Y.C., Feb. 21, 1938; s. John and Gabrielle (Boiteux) C. AB, Columbia Coll., N.Y.C., 1959; AM, Columbia U., 1960, PhD, 1965. Lectr. U. Münster, Germany, 1965-66; asst. prof. Duke U., 1966-70, assoc. prof., 1970-75; prof. U. Ky., 1975—; vis. scholar Harvard U., 1989-90. Author: Victorian Forerunner, 1968, Cincinnati Observed: Architecture and History, 1992; co-author: English Romanticism, 1983; editor: Froude's Life of Carlyle, 1979. Fellow Nat. Endowment for Humanities, Washington, 1971-72, 83-84, John Simon Guggenheim Meml., N.Y.C., 1975-76; Vis. scholar Harvard U., 1989-90. Mem. The Byron Soc. (chmn. 1975—), Internat. Byron Soc. (joint pres. 1986—).

CLUFF, LEIGHTON EGGERTSEN, physician; b. Salt Lake City, June 10, 1923; s. Lehi Eggertsen and Lottie (Brain) C.; m. Beth Allen, Aug. 19, 1944; children: Claudia Beth, Patricia Leigh. BS, U. Utah, 1944, ScD (hon.), 1989; MD with distinction, George Washington U., 1949; ScD (hon.), Hahnemann Med. Sch., 1979, L.I. U., 1988, St. Louis U., George Washington U., 1990, U. Utah, 1990. Intern Johns Hopkins Hosp., Balt., 1949-50, asst. resident, 1951-52; asst. resident physician Duke Hosp., Durham, N.C., 1950-51; vis. investigator, asst. physician Rockefeller Inst. Med. Research, 1952-54; fellow Nat. Found. Infantile Paralysis, 1952-54; mem. faculty Johns Hopkins Sch. Medicine, Balt.; staff Johns Hopkins Hosp., Balt., 1954-66, prof. medicine, 1964-66, physician, head div. clin. immunology, allergy and infectious diseases, 1958-66; prof., chmn. dept. medicine U. Fla., Gainesville, 1966-76; VA disting. physician U. Fla., 1990-95, prof. dept. medicine, 1990—; exec. v.p. Robert Wood Johnson Found., Princeton, N.J., 1976-86, pres., 1986-90, trustee emeritus, 1990—; U.S. del. U.S.-Japan Coop. Med. Sci. Program, 1972-81; mem. council drugs AMA, 1965-67; mem. NRC-NAS Drug Research Bd., 1965-71; mem. expert adv. panel bacterial diseases (coccal infection) WHO; mem. council Nat. Inst. Allergy and Infectious Diseases, 1968-72; cons. FDA; mem. tng. grant com. NIH, 1964-68. Author, editor books on internal medicine, infectious diseases, clin. pharmacology, long-term care; contbr. articles to profl. jours. Bd. dirs. Nat. Coun. on Aging, 1995—. Recipient Ordronaux award for med. scholarship, 1949, Career Rsch. award NIH, 1962, Edward Jill award Acad. Medicine N.J., 1990, Disting. Alumnus award Duke U. Sch. Medicine, 1978, Disting. Alumnus award Johns Hopkins Sch. Med., 1992, Theobald Smith award Albany Med. Coll., 1988; Markle scholar, 1955-62; Maed-Johnson Postgrad. scholar, 1954-55. Mem. ACP (master, Fla. gov. 1975-76, Mead-Johnson postgrad. scholar 1954-55), Inst. Medicine of NAS, Assembly Life Scis. of NAS, Am. Soc. Clin. Investigation, Assn. Am. Physicians, Soc. Exptl. Biology and Medicine, Am. Assn. Immunologists, Am. Fedn. Clin. Rsch., Harvey Soc., Infectious Diseases Soc. Am. (pres. 1975-76), N.Y. Acad. Scis., So. Soc. Clin. Investigation, Am. Clin. and Climatol. Assn., Am. Social Health Assn. (bd. dirs. 1990—), Johns Hopkins U. Soc. Scholars, Alpha Omega Alpha, Sigma Theta Tau (Archon award 1992). Home: 8851 SW 45th Blvd Gainesville FL 32608-4138

CLUTTER, GAYLE ANN, radiological technologist; b. Homestead, Fla., Sept. 14, 1945; d. Henry Clay and Annabelle (Wallace) Greer; m. Richard Clutter, July 25, 1965 (div. 1973). Cert. radiol. technology, Menorah Med. Ctr., Kansas City, 1967; AS in radiol. technology, Hillsborough Community Coll., 1983; BA in Mgmt., Nat. Louis U., 1993. Staff radiol. technologist Bapt. Hosp., Kansas City, Mo., 1967-71; dir. radiation oncology Sun Coast Hosp., Largo, Fla., 1971-90, dir. cancer program, 1975-94; regional mktg. dir. ELM Svcs., Rockville, Md., 1987-90; cons. Commn. on Cancer ACoS, Chgo., 1981-84; biostats. cons. for grad. mem. edn. Sun Coast Hosp., 1993-94. Author, editor: Professional Review for Tumor Registrars, 1989; co-author: Registry Staffing Manual, Nat. Tumor Registrars Assn and Am. Coll. Surgeons, 1989. Vol. Am. Cancer Soc. Fla. Divsn. and Pinellas County, 1980—; appointee Fla. Cancer Control and Rsch. Adv. Bd., 1981-90. Recipient Life Saver award Am. Cancer Soc., Pinellas County, Fla., 1991. Mem. Fla. Tumor Registrars Assn. (profl. rev. for tumor registrars, pres. 1977-79, project dir. audio visual courses 1992), West Fla. Soc. Radiation Therapy Technicians (pres. 1987-88), Nat. Tumor Registrars Assn., Fla Soc. Radiol. Technologists. Office: Sun Coast Hosp 2025 Indian Rocks Rd S Largo FL 33774-1035

CLYBURN, JAMES E., congressman; b. Sumter, S.C., 1940; m. Emily England; children: Mignon, Jennifer, Angela. Grad., S.C. State Coll.; LHD (hon.), Winthrop Coll., 1987; DSc (hon.), Coll. of Charleston, 1992, Med. U. S.C., 1993; LHD (hon.), St. Augustine Coll., 1994; LLD (hon.), Claflin Coll., 1995; LHD (hon.), S.C. State U., 1995; LLD (hon.), Voorhees Coll., 1996. Teacher Charleston County Pub. Sch. System; counselor S.C. Employment Security Commn.; dir. Charleston County Neighborhood Youth Corps/New Careers Projects; exec. dir. S.C. Commn. Farmworkers Inc.; staffer for Gov. John C. West, Charleston, S.C., 1971-74; commr. S.C. Human Affairs Commn., Columbia, 1974-92; mem. 103rd Congress from 6th S.C. dist., D.C., 1993—; pres. Nat. Assn. Human Rights Workers, 1980-81, Internat. Assn. Official Human Rights Agys., 1985-87. Active Southern Regional Coun., Atlanta; bd. dirs. Wofford Coll., Spartanburg, Allen U., Columbia, Brookgreen Gardens Murrell's inlet, James R. Clark Sickle Cell Anemia Found., Ctr. for Cancer Treatment and Rsch., S.C. Literacy Assn. Recipient ann. award for disting. svc. to state gov. Nat. Govs. Assn.; named Pub. Adminstr. of Yr. Am. Soc. Pub. Adminstrn. S.C. chpt. Mem. NAACP (life), Masons, Shriners, Omega Psi Phi. Democrat. Office: US Ho of Reps 319 Cannon HOB Washington DC 20515

CLYMER, KENTON JAMES, history educator; b. Bklyn., Nov. 17, 1943; s. Wayne Kenton and Helen Elizabeth (Graves) C.; m. Marlee Joan Arrowsmith, Aug. 5, 1967; children: Aron Kenton, Megan Arrowsmith. AB in History with honors, Grinnell Coll., 1965; MA, U. Mich., 1966, PhD, 1970. Teaching fellow dept. history U. Mich., 1967-69, Danforth lectr., 1969-70; from asst. to assoc. prof. of history U. Tex., El Paso, 1970-82, prof., 1982—, dir. grad. studies dept. history, 1975-80, 82-84, sr. mem. grad. faculty, 1976—, asst. dean coll. liberal arts, 1980-84, interim dir. MA in interdisciplinary studies program, 1981-82, dir. religious studies program, 1983-85, 87-90, chair history dept., 1984-85, 93-96; mem. exec. com. commn. archives and history United Meth. Ch., 1976-80; Fulbright lectr. Silliman U., Dumaguete City, Philippines and Taft Ave. Consortium Univs., Manila, 1977-78, U. Indonesia, Jakarta, 1990-91; assoc. provost Tex. Internat. Edn. Consortium Program Malaysia, 1986; cons. Indochina Project, Washington, summer 1989; George Bancroft vis. prof. history U. Göttingen, Germany, 1992-93; reviewer applications NEH, Fulbright Program, Indonesia; mem. Fulbright Com., 1994—. Author: John Hay: The Gentleman as Diplomat, 1975, Protestant Missionaries in the Philippines, 1898-1916: An Inquiry into the American Colonial Mentality, 1986,Quest for Freedom: The United States and India's Independence, 1995, (with others) Reapraising an Empire: New Perspectives in Philippine American History, 1984; reviewer Pacific Hist. Rev., The Historian, Pilipinas, Meth. History, Jour. Am. History; contbr. articles to profl. jours. Mem. health planning adv. com. West Tex. Coun. Govts., 1972-76; pres. bd. dirs. Houchen Community Ctr. and Newark Maternity Hosp., El Paso, 1974-76. Grantee Univ. Rsch. Inst., 1971, 72, 73-74, 74-75, 77, 80-81, 89, Am. Philos. Soc., 1972, 76, 81, U. Tex., 1982-83, 85, NEH, 1983, 85; Rackham fellow U. Mich., hon. rsch. fellow Inst. U.S. Studies, Univ. London, 1983; rsch. fellow Indo-U.S. Subcommission Edn. and Culture, New Delhi, 1986-87; Grinnell Acad. scholar, Younker Honor scholar. Mem. Am. Hist. Assn., Orgn. Am. History, Soc. Historians Am. Fgn. Rels., Assn. Asian Studies (mem. Philippine studies group), Friars. Democrat. Presbyterian. Home: 905 McKelligon Dr El Paso TX 79902 Office: History Dept University of Texas El Paso TX 79902

CLYNE, MAUREEN ANN, fine arts consultant, artist; b. N.Y.C., Aug. 8, 1957; d. John Patrick and Sheila Mary (Doherty) Clyne; m. Richard William Clement, June 2, 1990. Student, Am. U. in Paris, 1975-76; BFA, Boston U., 1980, MFA, 1982; MBA, Georgetown U., 1992. Freelance artist, arts. mktg. Boston, N.Y.C., Washington, 1982—; acting pub. affairs officer Corcoran Gallery of Art, Washington, 1992; mktg. dir. STUDIOS, Washington, 1992-93; fine arts cons. Arlington, Va., 1993—; pres. Grad. Women in Bus. at Georgetown U., Washington, 1991-92; script cons. Nat. Found. for Women Bus. Owners, Washington, 1993. Solo exhbns. include Pastels, 1984, From the End of the World, 1986, Provincetown Dreams, 1987, Cities in Dust, 1989. The MacDowell Colony fellow Petersborough, N.H., 1984, Va. Ctr. for the Creative Arts fellow Sweet Briar, Va., 1985, N.Y. Benefit Patrons fellow Fine Arts Work Ctr., Provincetown, Mass., 1985-86. Mem. Coll. Art Assn. Office: 1400 S Barton St Apt 408 Arlington VA 22204-4845

COADY, WILLIAM FRANCIS, information services executive, consultant; b. Bklyn., June 16, 1940; s. Alexander Ignatius and Nora Monica (Dooley) C.; m. Kathleen Dolores McNerney, July 16, 1966; children: Noreen Theresa, Elizabeth Ann, Jennifer Patricia, Patricia Marie. AB in Classical Lang., St. Peters Coll., Jersey City, 1961. With IRS, 1961-88; exec. officer internal security div. IRS, Chgo., 1973-76; regional dir. internal security div. IRS, Atlanta, 1976-88; pres. Info. Svcs. Internat., Inc., Dunwoody, Ga., 1989—; cons. ethics and behavior IRS, Atlanta, 1982-88; mem. adv. coun. Info. Am., Atlanta, 1990—. Contbr. articles to bus. and profl. jours. Fellow Fed. Computer Investigation Com. (Disting. Svc. award 1989). Roman Catholic. Home and Office: 5390 Seaton Dr Atlanta GA 30338-4537

COAKER, GEORGE MACK, minister; b. McLain, Miss., Jan. 9, 1927; s. George Mack and Kate Dean (Leeke) C.; m. Catherine Sabina Pennington, Mar. 19, 1948; children: Carol Dean Coaker Brewer, JoaAnn Coaker Littlejohn, Cathy Kay Coaker Vickers. BA, Howard Coll., Birmingham, Ala., 1948; BD, New Orleans Bapt. Theol. Sem., 1951; MA, U. Miss., 1955; PhD, Vanderbilt U., 1962. Ordained to ministry, So. Bapt. Conv., 1948. Pastor Chunchula (Ala.) Bapt. Ch., 1948-51, Ecru (Miss.) Bapt. Ch., 1951-53; chaplain USAF and VA, various locations, 1953-83; pastor Milton (Tenn.) Bapt. Ch., 1983-91, Greenvale (Tenn.) Bapt. Ch., 1991—; exec. bd. Tenn. Bapt. Conv., Nashville, 1983-90. Lt. col. chaplain corps USAF, 1953-57. Mem. Res. Officers Assn., Ret. Officers Assn., Am. Legion, DAV. Home and Office: 2535 Oregon Rd Milton TN 37118

COAKER, JAMES WHITFIELD, mechanical engineer; b. Boston, Nov. 12, 1946; s. George W. and Margaret N. Coaker; m. Ruth Johnson, May 17, 1969; children—James W., John A., Stephen D. BSME, Lafayette Coll., 1968; MSB, Va. Commonwealth U., 1976. Registered profl. engr., Va. Application engr. pump and condenser div. Ingersoll-Rand Co., Richmond, Va., 1972-76; project mgr. Reco Industries, Inc., Richmond, Va., 1976-77; asst. mgr. engring. Reco Industries, Inc., Richmond, 1977-79, mgr. engring., 1979-83; systems engr., program mgr. Advanced Tech., Inc., Arlington, Va., 1983-87; program mgr. Boiler and Elevator Safety U.S. Postal Svc., Washington, 1987—; lectr. and educator in field. With USN, 1969-72; capt. USNR. Mem. ASME (past nat. chmn. plant engr. and maintenance div., chmn. elevator insps. manual com., mem. bd. profl. devel. 1990-96, v.p. elect bd. on safety codes and stds.), Nat Coun. Examiners for Engring. and Surveying (affiliate), Naval Res. Assn. (life). Home: 11675 Captain Rhett Ln Fairfax Station VA 22039-1236

COAKLEY, PATRICIA DAVIS VAUGHN, gifted education educator; b. Henderson, Ky., Feb. 22, 1941; d. Ralph Harold and Burnell (Willett) Vaughn; m. Douglas Price Coakley, June 21, 1963; children: Karen Lynn, Douglas Price. B, Murray State U., 1963, M, 1964, postgrad., 1975. Cert. elem. and secondary, gifted tchr., Ky. Grad. asst. Murray State U., 1963-64; dir. recreation Ky. Dam State Park, Gilbertsville, 1962, 64; phys. edn. Hancock Place High Sch., Lemay, Mo., 1964-65; tchr. Grand Rivers (Ky.) Sch., 1965-68; tchr. remedial program Barkley Boys Camp, Gilbertsville, 1968-69; tchr. Gilbertsville Elem., 1975-79; tchr. phys. edn. Sharpe (Ky.), Calvert City (Ky.) and Gilbertsville Elem. Schs., 1979-83; instr. Career Tng. Ctr., Calvert City, 1969-70; developer, facilitator gifted and talented program Marshall County Schs., Benton, 1982—; commr. girls Little League Softball, Calvert City, 1981; instr. insvc. Marshall County Schs., Benton, 1982—; acad. coach Marshall County High Sch., 1988—. Pres. Calvert City Swim Team, 1983-84; participant Follies Benefit, Calvert City, 1980, 81, 82; chmn. Golf Tourney for Rescue Squad, Calvert City, 1982; bd. dirs. Paducah Family History Ctr., 1986-89; music chmn., organist, pianist, tchr., 1986—; pres. Relief Soc., 1985-87, 94-96; chairperson Marshall County Found. for the Arts, 1995-96; dir. Marshall County Arts Festival, 1996. Named Nat. Presdl. Scholars Disting. Tchr., 1994. Mem. ASCD, NEA, Marshall County Edn. Assn., Ky. Edn. Assn., Commonwealth Inst. Tchrs., Ky. Assn. for Gifted Edn., Nat. Assn. for Gifted Edn., Ky. Acad. Assn. (future problem solving evaluation trainer 1989—, bd. dirs. 1995—, Kappa Delta Phi, Alpha Omicron Pi, Epsilon Sigma Alpha (chmn. benefit bike ride 1976). Democrat. Mormon. Home: 566 Maple Ave Calvert City KY 42029-8303

COALTER, MILTON J., JR., library director, educator; b. Memphis, July 5, 1949; s. Milton J. and Jewel (Mitchel) C.; m. Linda M. Block, May 20, 1973; children: Martha Claire, Siram Jacob. BA, Davidson Coll., 1971; MDiv, Princeton Theol. Sem., 1975, ThM, 1977; PhD in Religion, Princeton U., 1982. Asst. prof. Am. Religion N.C. State U., Raleigh, 1981-82; pub. svcs. libr. The Iliff Sch. Theology, Denver, 1982-84, acting libr. dir., 1984-85; libr. dir., prof. bibliography and rsch. Louisville Presbyn. Theol. Sem.,

1985—; bd. dirs. Louisville Inst. for Study Protestantism and Am. Culture, 1990-96; mem. Gen. Assembly Coun. Task Force on Ch. Membership Growth, Presbyn. Ch., Louisville, 1989-91. Author: (with John M. Mulder) The Letters of David Avery, 1979, Gilbert Tennent, Son of Thunder, 1986; (with John M. Mulder and Louis B. Weeks) The Presbyterian Presence in the Twentieth Century, 7 vols., 1989-92, Vital Signs, 1996; editor: (with Virgil Cruz) How Shall We Witness?, 1995; contbr. articles to profl. jours. Recipient Jonathan Edwards award Princeton U., 1977-80, Tchg. award Assn. Princeton Grad. Alumni, 1979-80, Francis Makemie award Presbyn. Ch. Dept. History; Lily Endowment grantee, 1987-90, N.J. Hist. Commn. grantee, 1979-80, Pew Charitable Trust grantee, 1990-93; Princeton U. Whiting fellow, 1980-81. Mem. Am. Theol. Libr. Assn., Am. Soc. Ch. History, Am. Acad. Religion, Orgn. Am. Historians. Presbyterian. Office: Louisville Presbyn Theol Sem 1044 Alta Vista Rd Louisville KY 40205-1758

COATES, FREDERICK ROSS, lawyer; b. Madison, Va., June 27, 1933; s. Fred Icer and Sarah (Hale) C.; m. Rebecca White, Nov. 25, 1959; children: Stephanie Renee Piper, Susan C. McCoy. BA, U. Richmond, 1954, JD, 1959. Bar: Va., U.S. Dist. Ct. (we. dist.) Va. 1959. Vice chmn. Madison County Rep. party, 1968-88; mem. Rescue Squad Madison County, Madison County Planning com.; commr. accounts Madison County; asst. commn. accounts Greene County, Va. Served with U.S. Army, 1954-57. Recipient Key Man award Madison Jaycees, 1962-64. Mem. ABA, Va. State Bar. Assn., Madison-Greene Bar Assn., Red Land Club, Greene Hills Club, Masons, Boosters Club, Lions, Shriners. Baptist. Home and Office: PO Box 328 Madison VA 22727-0328

COATOAM, GARY WILLIAM, periodontist; b. Cleve., June 27, 1946; s. Thomas Richard and Helen (Sadowsky) C.; m. Sharon McCoy, Nov. 25, 1967; children: Gary, Brian, Laura, Suzanne, Ellen. BS in Zoology, Ohio U., 1968; DDS, Case Western Res. U., 1972, MS in Dentistry, 1980, cert. in periodontology, 1980. Chemist Glidden Co., Strongsville, Ohio, 1967-68; lab. technician St. Johns Hosp., Cleve., 1968-72; commd. ensign USN, 1969, advanced through grades to lt., 1969; dental officer USN, Orlando, Fla., 1972; assoc. Dr. Donald Kane, Satellite Beach, Fla., 1974-75, dentist, Drs. Coatoam and Bizga, Parma, Ohio, 1975-77; asst. prof. Case Western Res. U., 1975-80, U. Fla., Gainesville, 1989—; periodontist Drs. Chace, Coatoam and Horvat, Winter Park, Fla., 1980-94, Drs. Coatoam and Krieger, Altamonte Springs, Fla., 1994—; participator World Workshop on Periodontics, Trenton, N.J., 1989. Author: Case of the Ledgewood Swingers, 1991. Festival coord. St. Mary Magdalen Ch., Maitland, Fla., 1984-89, mem. sch. bd., 1989-90. Recipient Presentation award Internat. Assn. Dental Rsch., 1982; Periodontic Rsch. fellow Case Western Res. U., 1972. Mem. ADA, Am. Acad. Periodontology (mem. profl. rels. com.), Dental Soc. Greater Orlando, So. Acad. Periodontology. Roman Catholic. Home: 110 Timbercove Cir S Longwood FL 32779-2553 Office: Dr Coatoam and Krieger 709 Douglas Ave Altamonte Springs FL 32714-2522

COATS, ANDREW MONTGOMERY, lawyer, former mayor; b. Oklahoma City, Okla., Jan. 19, 1935; s. Sanford Clarence and Mary Ola (Young) C.; m. Linda M. Zimmerman; children—Andrew, Michael, Jennifer, Sanford. B.A., U. Okla., 1957, J.D., 1963. Assoc. Crowe and Dunlevy, Oklahoma City, Okla., 1963-67, ptnr., 1967-76, sr. trial ptnr., 1980—; dist. atty. Oklahoma County, Oklahoma City, Okla., 1976-80; mayor City of Oklahoma City, 1983-87; vis. prof. law U. Okla., 1969-71; pres. Okla. Young Lawyers Conf., 1968-69; dir. Meml. Bank, N.A., Oklahoma City. Democratic nominee U.S. Senate, 1980; pres. Oklahoma County Legal Aid Soc., 1972-73 Served to lt. USN, 1960-63. Named Outstanding Lawyer in Okla., Oklahoma City U., 1977. Fellow Am. Coll. Trial Lawyers (pres. 1996-97, pres.-elect 1995-96), Am. Bd. Trial Advocates (charter pres. Okla. 1986); mem. ABA, Okla. Bar Assn. (pres. 1992-93), Oklahoma County Bar Assn. (pres. 1976-77), Order of Coif, Oklahoma City Golf and Country Club (bd. dirs. 1977-80, 93-96), Beacon Club, Petroleum Club, Phi Beta Kappa (pres. 1975), Pi Kappa Alpha (pres. 1956), Phi Delta Phi (pres. 1962). Democrat. Episcopalian. Clubs: Oklahoma City Golf and Country (bd. dirs. 1977-80), Beacon, Petroleum. Office: Crowe and Dunlevy 1800 Mid-Am Tower 20 N Broadway Ave Oklahoma City OK 73102-8202

COBB, BRIAN WAYNE, emergency physician; b. Miami, Ill., May 28, 1955; s. Harris L. and Martha (Kent) C. BA, U. S. Fla., 1979; MD, Ctrl. Tech. U., Santa Domingo, 1987. Diplomate Am. Bd. Internal Medicine. Emergency physician EMSA Ltd. Partnership, Plantation, Fla., 1987-91; med. dir. Polk Gen. Hosp., Bartow, Fla., 1991-93; emergency physician JJ&R Emergency Physicians, Port Charlotte, Fla., 1993—; mem. Polk County Emergency Svc. adv. bd., Bartow, Fla., 1974-79'; med. dir. Fla. Sheriff's Youth Villa, Bartow, 1992—, Planned Parenthood of Ctrl. Fla., Lakeland, 1993-95; mem. Human Equality Commn., Episcopal Ch., Orlando, Fla., 1993-94. Mem. ACLU, Lambda Legal Defense and Edn. Fund, Human Rights Watch. Mem. Am. Coll. Physicians, N.Y. Acad. Scis., Am. Pub. Health Assn., Physicians for Social Responsibility. Democrat. Home: 825 E Church St Bartow FL 33830

COBB, CHARLES KENCHE, lawyer, real estate broker; b. Canton, Ga., Aug. 23, 1934; s. Charlie Kench and Alice (Enloe) C.; m. Carolyn Webb, Aug. 31, 1963; children: Charlie Kenche, III, Catherine Elizabeth Fryman. BS, Ga. Tech., 1956; MBA, Harvard U., 1962; postgrad. Emory U., 1963, Georgetown U., 1959; LLD, Woodrow Wilson, 1968. Bar: Ga. 1969, Pres., C. Cobb Properties, Atlanta, 1969—, Sterling Land Co., Atlanta, 1973—, Bridgewood Properties, Stockbridge, Ga., 1983-91; dir. Canton Textile Mills, Inc., 1991—. Mem. Atlanta Area Coun.-Boy Scouts Am., 1979—; exec. com. Ga. Tech. Wesley Found., Atlanta, 1983—; former treas., sec., trustee, exec. com., Reinhardt Coll., Waleska, Ga., 1974—; lay leader Northside United Meth. Ch., Atlanta, 1978; bd. dirs. Ga. Tech. YMCA, Atlanta, 1976-89. Served to 1st lt. USAF, 1956-59, ETO. Mem. Ga Bar Assn., Atlanta Bd. Realtors (bd. dirs. 1983-90, Outstanding Transaction of Yr. award 1986), Ga. Assn. Exchangors (former pres.), Ga. Exchangor of Yr. 1971, 85, 90), Ga. Hist. Trust, Ga. Tech. Alumni Assn. (trustee 1976-79), Canton Golf Club, Buckhead 50 Club (treas., 1994, sec. 1995, v.p. 1996), Mason, Shriner. Home: 2851 Howell Mill Rd NW Atlanta GA 30327-1353 Office: One Northside 75 Ste 102 Atlanta GA 30318

COBB, HOWELL, federal judge; b. Atlanta, Dec. 7, 1922; s. Howell and Dorothy (Hart) C.; m. Torrance Chalmers (dec. 1963); children: Catherine Cobb Cook, Howell III, Mary Ann Cobb Walton; m. Amelie Suberbielle, July 3, 1965; children: Caroline Cobb Ervin, Thomas H., John L. Student, St. John's Coll., Annapolis, Md., 1940-42; LLB, U. Va., 1948. Assoc. Kelley & Ryan, Houston, 1949-51, Fountain, Cox & Gaines, Houston, 1951-54; assoc. Orgain, Bell & Tucker, Beaumont, 1954-57, ptnr., 1957-85; judge U.S. Dist. Ct. (ea. dist.) Tex., Beaumont, 1985—; mem. jud. coun. U.S. Ct. Appeals (5th cir.), 1994-96; mem. adv. com. East Tex. Legal Svcs., Beaumont. Pres. Beaumont Art Mus., 1969, bd. dirs., 1967-68; mem. vestry St. Stephens Episcopal Ch., Beaumont, 1973; mem. bd. adjustment City of Beaumont, 1972-82; trustee All Saints Episcopal Sch., Beaumont, 1972-76. 1st lt. USMC, 1942-45, PTO. Mem. ABA, State Bar Tex. (grievance com. 1970-72, chmn. 1972, admissions com. 1974—, bd. dirs. 1993-94, adv. mem.), Jefferson County Bar Assn. (sec. 1960, bd. dirs. 1960-61, 67-68), Am. Judicature Soc., Am. Bd. Trial Advs., Maritime Law Assn. U.S., Beaumont Country Club. Office: US Dist Ct 118 US Courthouse PO Box 632 Beaumont TX 77704-0632

COBB, JOHN CECIL, JR. (JACK COBB), Latin America area specialist, communications specialist and executive; b. Walton, Ky., Apr. 10, 1927; s. John Cecil and Lucy (Dean) C. B.A. in Sociology, Antioch Coll., 1950; postgrad., U. Ams., Mex., 1950; M.A. in Communication, Mich. State U., 1964. Fgn. corr., pub. exec. Vision, Inc., Rio de Janeiro, N.Y.C., 1950-55; writer Mexico City, 1956-57; dir. Antioch Coll. Program, Guanajuato, Mex., 1958-62; communication research asst. Mich. State U., East Lansing, 1962-64, mem. research staff Computer Inst. Social Sci. Research, 1964-67; Fulbright prof. U. El Salvador, San Salvador, 1967-68; cons. Peace Corps, Lima, Peru, 1968-69, San Jose, Costa Rica, 1968-69; exec. dir. Latin Am. Studies Assn., Washington, 1969-71; cons. Washington, 1972-78; pres. Human Comm. Sys., Reston, Va., 1978-93, prin., 1994—; cons. on new internat. curriculum Antioch Coll., 1990; prodn. mgr. Peace in Action mag., 1994—; cons. World Wide Web, 1996. Author: (with Howard I. Blutstein) Area Handbook of El Salvador, 1971; also monographs on land reform in El Salvador, 1980-86, study of urban family income in Bolivia, 1986, 3 software manuals on linking of electronic mail networks, 1991-92. Mem. Common Cause No. Va., 1975-77, publicity chmn., 1975-77; mem. exec. com. Washington area UN Assn., 1977-79; mem. Fairfax County Democratic Com., 1975-78. Served with USN, 1945-46. Mem. Social Sci. Computing Assn. (chair), Internat. Comm. Assn., Latin Am. Studies Assn., Inter-Am. Coun. (v.p. 1994-95, pres. 1995-96), Am. Assn. Pub. Opinion Rsch., Soc. Internat. Devel., Am. Statis. Assn., Mid-Atlantic Conf. Latin Am. Studies, Fulbright Assn., The Internet Soc.

COBB, MILLICENT AMELIA, special education educator; b. Salisbury, N.C., June 13, 1958; d. James Abernethy and Helen Millicent (Smith) C.; m. Mark Alan Cohen, Jan. 17, 1987 (div. June 1993); 1 child, Olivia Cobb Cohen. BS, Ohio State U., 1981; MS, Nova Southeastern U., 1994. Cert. K-12 tchr. spl. edn. of emotionally handicapped, Fla. Pers. asst. Lily-Tulip, Inc., Toledo, 1982-83, field sales rep., 1983-84; v.p. ops. Cobb Assocs., Inc., Toledo, 1984-87; tchr. self-conained-emotionally handicapped Duval County Schs., Jacksonville, Fla., 1994—. Troop leader Boy & Girl Scouting, Exceptional Student Edn. Students. Republican. Episcopalian.

COBB, PAULINE LANE, retired federal educational programs director; b. Dothan area, Ala., Jan. 16, 1933; d. Leon Cobb and Pansy Gertrude (Green) Griffin; m. Francis Dewitt Lane, Nov. 12, 1949 (dec. 1972); children: Larry Frank, David Dewitt; m. Ralph Gordon Tye, May 5, 1985 (dec.); m. Frank Lewis Cobb, Mar. 11, 1994. BS in Bus. Edn., Troy State U., 1965, MS in Adminstrn. and Supervision, 1966, EdS and AA in Adminstrn., Supervision, 1974; postgrad., Auburn U., 1979. Prin Madrid Jr. High Sch., Ala., 1966-67, tchr., 1965-67; tchr. Rehobeth Sch., Ala., 1968-69, Harmon Jr. High Sch., Ala., 1970-74, Wicksburg High Sch., Ala., 1974-86; asst. prin. Ashford Elem. Sch., Ala., 1986-89, dir. fed. programs chpt. I, 1989—; owner, broker Lane Realty Co., 1976-85. Mem. Wiregrass Rep. exec. com., Houston County, Ala, 1989—, nominating com. Women's Rep. Party, 1990—; supt. Coun. Ministries Big Creek United Meth. Ch., Dothan, 1989—, past jr. steward; bd. dirs. Houston County chpt. Ala. Farmers Assn. Mem. NEA, AAUW (chmn. edn. com. Dothan br. 1980), Nat. Assn. Secondary Sch. Prins., Nat. Coun. Social Studies, Ala. Edn. Assn. (del., local sec.), Ala. Coun. Sch. Adminstrn. and Supervision, Houston County Tchrs. Assn. (chair tchrs. of history in-svc. tng. meetings 1979, uniserv. rep. 1980—), Ala. Sheriff's Assn., Am. Ex-POWs (sec. 1984-85), Am. Farm Bur., Troy State U. Honors Club, Big Creek Community Club (sec., treas. 1975-79), Order Eastern Star (assoc. conductress, past matron, sec., treas. Rehobeth chpt.), Kappa Delta Pi, Phi Delta Kappa.

COBB, RONALD DAVID, pharmacist, educator; b. Louisville, May 10, 1945; s. Harry D. and Ruth (Roberts) C.; m. Patricia Lee Carroll, Sept. 4, 1964; children: Joy Ruth, Tracy Renee. BS in Pharmacy, U. Ky., 1968, PharmD, 1973. Staff pharmacist Kettering (Ohio) Meml. Hosp., 1968; pharmacist mgr. Lawrence Drugs, Inc., Lexington, Ky., 1969-70; asst. prof. Coll. Pharmacy U. Ky., Lexington, 1973-79, assoc. prof. Coll. Pharmacy, 1980—; pharmacist cons. Blue Cross/Blue Shield of Ky., Louisville, 1976-90, Market Measures, Inc., West Orange, N.J., 1976-94. Contbr. numerous articles to profl. jours. Bd. dirs. Am. Found. for Pharm. Edn., 1991—; trustee Am. Pharm. Assn. Found., 1990-93. Fellow Am. Coll. Apothecaries (assoc.); mem. Blue Grass Pharmacists Assn. (treas. 1969, exec. com. 1969-76, pres.-elect 1970, pres. 1971), Ky. Pharmacists Assn. (bd. dirs. 1972-79, chmn. 1977-78, pres.-elect 1975-76, pres. 1976-77), Am. Inst. History Pharmacy (bd. dirs. 1994—), Am. Pharm. Assn. (chmn. bd. 1989, pres. 1990, trustee 1985-91), Acad. Pharmacy Practice (pres.-elect 1982-83, pres. 1983-84, bd. dirs. 1980-86). Democrat. Baptist. Home: 1516 Pine Meadow Ct Lexington KY 40504-2310 Office: U Ky Coll Pharmacy Lexington KY 40536-0082

COBB, TERRI R. (CECI COBB), film and video producer; b. N.Y.C., Feb. 18, 1934; d. Leo Odell and Jean (Wister) Gruber; m. Ira Reamer, July 4, 1954 (div. May 1975); children: Jeff, David, Ellen; m. David G. Cobb, Aug. 2, 1975. Student, U. Miami, 1953-54, Miami Dade C.C., 1970-72. Vocalist The Girlfriends, N.Y.C., 1952-53; dental asst. Miami, Fla., 1953-56, med. asst., 1956-58; prodr., host TV talk show People and Places, Tampa, Fla., 1981—; freelance film and video prodr., prodn. coord. Encore Film & Video Prodn., Tampa, 1984—; freelance model, actress, Fla.; seminar leader Tom Kirby Assocs., Fla., 1986—; cons. U. South Fla. Dept. Edn., Tampa, 1980—. Health educator, fund raiser, speaker Fla. March of Dimes, 1974—; bd. dirs. Fla. Healthy Mother-Healthy Baby Coalition. Recipient Jone Intercable Golden Cassette award, 1989, Crystal Reel award Fla. Motion Picture & TV Assn., 1990. Mem. Fla. Perinatal Assn. (bd. dirs.), Fla. Womens' Alliance, Fla. Motion Picture and TV Assn. (bd. dirs.), Fla. Soc. Assn. Execs. (bd. dirs.). Home: 16612 Hutchinson Rd Odessa FL 33556-2327

COBBS, JAMES HAROLD, engineer, consultant; b. Bristow, Okla., Aug. 25, 1928; s. Harold Martin and Ella A. (Rountree) C.; m. Charlotte Marie Fisher, Aug. 16, 1953 (dec. June 1990); m. Mary J. Armer, May 28, 1994; children: James Harold, David Charles, Gregory Lee, Matthew Louis. BS in Petroleum Engring., U. Okla., 1949, postgrad., 1949-51; postgrad. U. Tulsa, 1955-68. Assoc. engr. Tidewater Oil Co., Midland, Tex., 1951-52; reservoir engr., Houston, 1952-55, div. reservoir engr., Tulsa, 1955-59; pvt. practice cons. engr., 1959-63; sr. engr. Fenix & Scisson Inc., Tulsa, 1963-69; pres. Cobbs Engring., Inc., cons. engrs., Tulsa, 1969—; faculty U. Wis. Extension. Various positions including scoutmaster Indian Nations coun. Boy Scouts Am., 1962-81; instr. first aid ARC, 1969-81; active Vols. in Tech. Assistance, 1978—. Registered profl. engr., 8 states; cert. of qualification Nat. Council Engring. Examiners. Mem. Petroleum Engrs., Nat. Soc. Profl. Engrs., Okla. Soc. Profl. Engrs., Inst. Shaft Drilling Tech., Nat. Acad. Forensic Engrs., World Rock Boring Assn. Republican. Mem. Christian Ch. (elder, chmn. bd. elders 1971, 79). Contbr. articles to profl. jours.; patentee in field. Home: 5144 S New Haven Ave Tulsa OK 74135-3963 Office: 5350 E 46th St Tulsa OK 74135-6601

COBERLY, PATRICIA GAIL, secondary education educator; b. Fort Smith, Ark., Jan. 7, 1962; d. Charles Joe and Marie Opal (Starling) Stracener; m. Mark Windfield Coberly, Nov. 6, 1990; children: Laura Kendrick, Christy Gail. BS, Ark. Tech. U., 1987; MEd, U. Ark., 1993, EdD, 1995. Cert. tchr., Ark. Tchr. Ozark (Ark.) Sch. Dist., 1988-96; asst. prof. Armstrong Atlantic State U., Savannah, Ga., 1996—. Contbr. articles to profl. jours. Mem. Phi Delta Kappa, Phi Kappa Phi. Office: Armstong Atlantic State U 11935 Abercorn St Savannah GA 31419

COBLE, CHARLIE GROVER, agricultural engineering educator; b. Florence, S.C., May 1, 1940; s. Charlie G. and Clara (Hutto) C.; m. Sally Elizabeth Springer, Dec. 28, 1975; children: Bradley Reed, Todd Mason. BS in Agrl. Engring., Clemson U., 1962; MS in Agrl. Engring., N.C. State U., 1965, PhD in Biol. and Agrl. Engring., 1972. Registered profl. engr., Tex. Asst. prof. agrl. engring. Tex. A&M U., College Station, 1972-77, assoc. prof., 1977-83, prof., 1983—; presenter in field. Contbr. articles to profl. jours., chpts. to books; patentee apparatus for separating clods from agrl. products. Capt. U.S. Army, 1968-70, Vietnam. Recipient Dep. Chancellor's award for team rsch. Tex. A&M U., 1989; grantee Tex. Energy Devel. Fund, 1981-83, Ctr. for Energy and Mineral Resources, 1982-86, 92-93, Gas Rsch. Inst., 1983-88, EPA, 1988-91. Mem. AAAS, NSPE, Am. Soc. Agrl. Engrs. (chmn. power and machinery div. 1991-92, Engr. of Yr. award Tex. sect. 1979), Am. Soc. for Engring. Edn., Tex. Soc. Profl. Engrs., Rotary. Republican. Lutheran. Home: 1805 Bee Creek Dr College Station TX 77840-4966 Office: Tex A&M U Agrl Engring Dept College Station TX 77843

COBLE, PAUL ISHLER, advertising agency executive; b. Indpls., Mar. 17, 1926; s. Earl and Agnes Elizabeth (Roberts) C.; A.B., Wittenberg U., 1950; postgrad. Case-Western Res. U., 1950-53; m. Marjorie M. Trentanelli, Jan. 27, 1951; children—Jeffery Mansfield, Sarah Anne Davis, Douglass Paul Coble. Reporter, Springfield (Ohio) Daily News, 1944; reporter, feature writer Rockford (Ill.) Register-Republic, 1947-48; account exec. Fuller & Smith & Ross, Inc., Cleve., 1949-57; dir. sales promotion McCann Erickson, 1957-63; dir. sales devel. Marschalk Co., 1963-65, v.p., 1965-70, sr. v.p., 1970-73; pres. Coble Group, 1973—; chmn. bd., sec.-treas. Hahn & Coble. Inc., advt., mktg. and pub. relations, 1977—; pub. Islander mag., Hilton Head Island, S.C., 1973-83; asst. prof. advt. W.Va. U., 1982-83. Chief instr. Cleve. Advt. Club Sch., 1961-73. Active fund raising drives for various charitable and youth orgns. Served with AUS, 1944-46. Mem. Sales and Marketing Internat., Assn. Indsl. Advertisers, Cleve. Advt. Club, Newcomen Soc., River Oaks Racquet Club, Sea Pines Country Club, Cleve. Rotary. Contbr. articles to profl. pubs. Home: 37 Club Course Dr Hilton Head Island SC 29928-3137

COBURN, FRANCES GULLETT, retired elementary school educator; b. Princess, Ky., Apr. 20, 1919; d. Gilbert G. and Lula (Kitchen) Gullett; m. Ralph L. Coburn, Dec. 20, 1941 (dec. Feb. 1966). BS cum laude, Morris Harvey Coll., 1950; MA in Adminstrn., Marshall U., 1952. Tchr. Braeholm (W.Va.) Elem. Sch., 1938-49; tchr. Amherstdale (W.Va.) Elem. Sch., 1949-51; prin. King Fuel Elem. Sch., Emmett, W.Va., 1951-53; tchr. Peyton Elem. Sch., Huntington, W.Va., 1953-78; supervising tchr. Marshall U., Huntington, 1953-78. Contbr. articles to profl. jours. Vol. Huntington Mus. Art; asst. with crafts at 2 Huntington nursing homes; sec. adminstrv. bd. Johnson Meml. Ch., 1981-94, sec. coun. on ministries, 1990-92; mem. Circle 7; donor rm. asst. ARC (recipient 35 yr. pin); mem. Logan County coun. Girl Scouts U.S., Logan, W.Va. Named Outstanding Elem. Tchr. of Am., 1972, Ky. Col., Gov. of Ky., 1991; recipient cert. of excellent svc. as vol. Presbyn. Manor Nursing Home, 1990-94, 35-yr. pin as vol. blood ctr. ARC, 1990, 40-yr. pin ARC, 1995. Mem. AAUW, Woman's Club Huntington, Huntington Garden Club, Women Builders of Univ. of Charleston, W.Va., Panhellenic, Delta Kappa Gamma, Kappa Delta Phi, Phi Mu. Methodist. Home: 1034 12th Ave Huntington WV 25701-3422

COBURN, LOUIS, library sciences educator, school librarian; b. N.Y.C., Aug. 13, 1915; s. Benjamin and Bertha (Smoradinsky) Cohen; m. Selma Spielman Coburn, June 25, 1950; children: Barry, Michael. BA, CCNY, 1936; BLS, Columbia U., 1937; MS in Edn., CCNY, 1941; EdD, NYU, 1961. Fellow, libr. dept. CCNY, N.Y.C., 1936-37; tchr. of libr. Samuel Gompers Vocat. Tech. H.S., N.Y.C., 1938-56, Jamaica H.S., N.Y.C., 1956-63; asst. prof., Sch. Libr. and Info. Studies Queens Coll., N.Y.C., 1963-73, assoc. prof., Sch. Libr. and Info. Studies, 1974-79. Author: Case Studies in School Library Administration, 1968, Library Media Center Problems: Case Studies, 1973, Classroom and Field: The Internship in American Library Education, 1980; contbr. articles to profl. jours. Mem. exec. br. Coconut Creek (Fla.) Dem. Club, 1993—. 1st lt., U.S. Army Air Forces, 1942-45, North Africa and Italy. Mem. ACLU, Common Cause, N.Y. Libr. Club (exec. coun. 1967-71, chmn. nominating com. 1968-69, chmn. scholarship com. 1969-71), CUNY Profl. Staff Congress (chmn. Fla. br. retirees chpt., 1990-92), NYU Alumni Assn., CCNY Alumni Assn. Democratic. Jewish. Home: 2304 Lucaya Lane Coconut Creek FL 33066

COCHRAN, CAROLYN, library director; b. Tyler, Tex., July 13, 1934; d. Sidney Allen and Eudelle (Frazier) C.; m. Guy Milford Eley, June 1, 1963 (div.). BA, Beaver Coll., 1956; MA, U. Tex., 1960; MLS, Tex. Woman's U., 1970. Libr., Canadian (Tex.) High Sch., 1970-71; rep. United Food Co., Amarillo, Tex., 1971-72; libr. Bishop Coll., Dallas, 1972-74; interviewer Tex. Employment Commn., Dallas, 1975-76; libr. St. Mary's Dominican, New Orleans, 1976-77, DeVry Inst. Tech., Irving, Tex., 1978—; with Database Searching Handicapped Individuals, Irving, 1983—; vol. bibliographer Assn. Individuals with Disabilities, Dallas, 1982-85. Mem. Am. Coalition of Citizens with Disabilities, 1982-85, Assn. Individuals with Disabilities, 1982-86, Vols. in Tech. Assistance, 1985—, Radio Amateur Satellite Corp., 1985-86; sponsor 500, Inc., 1988—. HEW fellow, 1967; honored Black History Collection, Dallas Morning News, Bishop Coll., Dallas, 1973. Mem. ALA, Spl. Libr. Assn., Am. Coun. of Blind and Coun. Citizens with Low Vision. Club: Toastmistress (pres. 1982-83) (Irving). Reviewer Library Jour., 1974, Dallas Morning News, 1972-74, Amarillo Globe-News, 1970-71. Office: DeVry Inst Tech 4801 Regent Blvd Irving TX 75063-2440

COCHRAN, GLORIA GRIMES, pediatrician, retired; b. Washington, June 24, 1924; d. Paul DeWitt and Muriel Ann (Quackenbush) Grimes; m. Winston Earle Cochran, June 10, 1950; children: Edith Ann, Winston Earle, Jr., Donald Lee, Robert Edward. BS in Zoology, Duke U., 1945; MD, 1949; MPH, Johns Hopkins Sch. Hygiene, Balt., 1979. Diplomate Nat. Bd. Med. Examiners, 1950, Am. Bd. Pediatrics, 1958. Clinic pediatrician, sch. med. advisor health dept. Montgomery County, 1955-65; assoc. dir. Child Development Clinic Baylor Med. Sch., Tex. Children's Hosp., 1966-72; dir. Northern Va. Child Devel. Field Svcs. Bur. Child Health State Health Dept. Commonwealth Va., 1972-76; coord. Handicapped Svcs. Children's Hosp. Nat. Med. Ctr., Washington, 1976-78; acting chief Divsn. of Svcs. to Children with Spl. Needs Bur. Sch. Health Svcs., Washington, 1982-89; retired, 1989; cons. Head Start Program, Md., Va., Tex., Pa., D.C., 1965-89; bd. mem. Ctrs. for Handicapped, Silver Spring, Md., 1982-89; Child Health com. Med. Soc. D.C., Washington, 1976-91. Producer, editor: (teaching film) Challenge for Habilitation: The Child with Congenital Rubella Syndrome, 1976. Steering com. Rock Days Inter-Church Camp, Washington, 1978-82; bd. mem. Open Door Cmty. Ctr., Columbus, Ga., 1993-94; co-chair curriculum com. Columbus Coll. Acad. of Life Long Learning, Columbus, 1994. Mem. Am. Assn. Mental Retardation, Am. Med. Women's Assn., Assn. for Retarded Citizens, Am. Acad. Cerebral Palsy, Am. Acad. Pediatrics, Phi Beta Kappa, Delta Omega. Democrat. Methodist. Home: 3418 N Peach Hollow Cir Pearland TX 77584

COCHRAN, JOHN MICHAEL, journalist; b. Muskogee, Okla., Dec. 25, 1936; s. Otis Fielding and Elma Catherine (Foltz) C.; m. Sondra Burson, May 30, 1959; children: John Shannon, Kendyl Beth. BA, North Tex. State Coll., 1958. Sportswriter The Denton (Tex.) Record Chronicle, 1958-59, Abilene (Tex.) Reporter-News, 1959-60; newsman AP, Dallas, 1960-61; corr. AP, Ft. Worth, 1961—. Author: Texas vs Davis, 1980, And Deliver Us From Evil, 1989. Named Star Reporter of Yr. The Headliners Club, Austin, 1983, 88, Disting. Alumnus North Tex. State U., Denton, 1988, Outstanding Centennial Alumnus U. North Tex., Denton, 1990; recipient Top Performance award AP, 1987, Stanley Walker award Tex. Inst. Letters, 1987, 91, Individual Achievement award Headliners Club, Austin, 1976, 87, 91, 92, J.B. Marryat award Outstanding Contbn. to Communications, Dallas Press Club, 1994. Mem. Soc. Profl. Journalists (v.p. 1968, bd. dirs. 1995-97), Diamond Oaks Country Club. Home and Office: AP 4509 Starlight Dr Fort Worth TX 76117-2149

COCHRAN, THAD, senator; b. Pontotoc, Miss., Dec. 7, 1937; s. William Holmes and Emma Grace (Berry) C.; m. Rose Clayton, June 6, 1964; children: Thaddeus Clayton, Katherine Holmes. BA, U. Miss., 1959, JD cum laude, 1965; postgrad. (Rotary Found. fellow), U. Dublin, Ireland, 1963-64. Bar: Miss. 1965. Practiced in Jackson, 1965-72; assoc. firm Watkins & Eager, 1965-72; mem. 93d-95th congresses from Miss., 1973-79; U.S. Senator from Miss., 1979—, chmn. Rep. conf. 104th Congress, 1995. Mem. exec. bd. Andrew Jackson council Boy Scouts Am., from 1973. Served to lt. USNR, 1959-61. Named Outstanding Young Man of Jackson, 1971, One of Three Outstanding Young Men of Miss., 1971. Mem. ABA, Miss. Bar Assn. (pres. young lawyers sect. 1972-73), Omicron Delta Kappa, Phi Kappa Phi, Pi Kappa Alpha. Republican. Baptist. Club: Rotarian. •

COCHRANE, ROBERT LOWE, biologist; b. Morgantown, W.Va., Feb. 10, 1931; s. Thomas Joseph and Isabelle Durston (Lowe) C. BA, W.Va. U., 1953; MS, U. Wis., 1954, PhD, 1961. Rsch. asst. genetics U. Wis., Madison, 1953-55, rsch. asst. zoology, 1957-60; agt. in animal husbandry U.S. Dept. Agr., Madison, Wis., 1955-61; biologist FDA, Washington, 1961-62; sr. research fellow dept. anatomy U. Birmingham (Eng.), 1962-65; project assoc. dept. physiology U. Pitts., 1965-66; sr. endocrinologist Eli Lilly & Co., Indpls., 1966-80; rsch. assoc. G.D. Searle & Co., Skokie, Ill., 1980-81; with Short's Fur Farm, Granton, Wis., 1981-83; rsch. assoc. Marshfield (Wis.) Med. Found., 1983-84; biologist Northwood Fur Farms, Inc., Cary, Ill., 1984; cons. for FAO to Wildlife Inst. India, Dehra Dun, 1985; adj. prof. div. animal and vet. sci., W.Va. U., Morgantown, 1987—; ad hoc reviewer various sci. jours.; ad hoc reviewer U.S. Dept. of Agr. Competitive Rsch. Grants. Contbr. numerous research articles and abstracts on reproduction to profl. jours.; participant Internat. Mink Show, Wis., 1976-96, W.Va. State Fox Show, Morgantown, 1989; rsch. bd. of advisors The Am. Biog. Inst., 1988-96; mem. adv. coun. Internat. Biog. Centre, 1989-96; mem. Golden Horseshoe Reunion Com., W.Va. Homecoming '96. Recipient Knight of Golden Horse Shoe award W.Va. Pub. Sch. System, 1945, W.Va. Boy's State, 1948; U. Birmingham (Eng.) sr. rsch. fellow, 1962-65. Mem. AAAS, Am. Inst. Biol. Scis., Soc. Exptl. Biology and Medicine, Soc. for Study of Fertility, Soc. Study of Reproduction, Am. Soc. Animal Sci., Endocrine Soc., N.Y. Acad. Sci., Soc. Endocrinology, Coun. Agrl. Sci. and Tech., Internat. Platform Assn., NRA (life), Sigma Xi, Pi Kappa Alpha. Achievements include major contributions to the establishment of the hormonal requirements for ova-implantation and embryonic diapause in the rat, the elucidation of the role played by prostaglandins in corpus luteum function, parturition and ductus arteriosus closure in the rat; the development of steroid synthesis inhibitors for controlling reproduction in mammals; the documentation of the timing, duration and pattern of reproductive cycles in martens; the dissemination of scientific information on fur farming to the commercial fur trade and public. Presbyterian. Home: 404 Junior Ave Morgantown WV 26505-2208

COCKERHAM, LORRIS G., radiation toxicologist; b. Denham Springs, La., Sept. 27, 1935; s. Warren Conrad and Leda Frances (Scivicque) C.; BA, La. Coll., 1957; MS, Colo. State U., 1973, PhD, 1979; m. Patricia Ann Stagg, Aug. 16, 1957; children: Michael B., Richard L., Ann E., Joseph D. Commd. 2d lt. USAF, 1961, advanced through grades to lt. col., 1977; instr. James Connelly AFB, Tex., 1963-66; squadron electronic warfare officer, Fairchild AFB, Wash., 1966-71; asst. prof. dept. chemistry and biology USAF Acad., Colo., 1973-77; wing electronic warfare officer Griffiss AFB, N.Y., 1977-78, comdr. 416 Munitions Maintenance Squadron, 1978-80, Armed Forces Radiobiology Rsch. Inst., Def. Nuclear Agy., Bethesda, Md., 1980-86; Air Force Office of Sci. Rsch., Bolling AFB, D.C., 1986-87, ret., 1987; exec. dir. NCTR-Associated Univs., Little Rock, 1988-89; pres. The Delta Agy., Little Rock, 1989-93, Phenix Cons. and Svcs. Ltd., Little Rock, 1993—; dir. Product Safety Labs., East Brunswick, N.J., 1994-95; asst. prof. physiology Sch. Medicine, Uniformed Svcs. U. Health Scis., 1981-87; assoc. prof. U. Ark. for Med. Scis., 1988-89. Troop com. chmn. Iroquois council Boy Scouts Am., 1978-80. Decorated D.F.C. (2), Airman's medal, Air medal (12), Air Force Commendation medal; Air Force Logistics Command Dioxin Research grantee, 1974-79; recipient Order of Arrow, Boy Scouts Am.; named Disting. Alumnus La. Coll., 1989. Mem. Soc. Neurosci., Internat. Brain Research Orgn., World Fedn. Neuroscientists, Soc. Toxicology, Am. Physiol. Soc., Am. Coll. Toxicology, Sigma Xi, Phi Kappa Phi. Republican. Southern Baptist.

COCKRELL, WILBURN ALLEN, archaeologist; b. Sikeston, Mo., Apr. 24, 1941; s. Wilburn Edward Cockrell and Martha Ann (Killian) Yancy; m. Rose Marie Roberson, Dec. 1961 (div. 1970); children: Padraic A., Timothy E.; m. Barbara O'Horo, 1984 (div. 1987). AB, U. Ala., Tuscaloosa, 1963; MA, Fla. State U., 1970; postgrad., Ariz. State U., 1970-72. Cert. scuba diver. Tchr. Mobile County Sch. Bd., Mobile, Ala., 1963-64, Okeechobee (Fla.) Sch. Bd., 1964-65; state hwy. archaeologist State of Fla., Tallahassee, 1966-68; tchr. Yuma (Ariz.) Sch. Bd., 1968; state underwater archaeologist State of Fla., Tallahassee, 1972-83; chief archaeologist, project dir. Warm Mineral Springs (Fla.) Archaeol. Rsch. Project, 1983-87; faculty Manatee Community Coll., 1984-87; chief archaeologist, project dir. Fla. State U., Tallahassee, 1987-92; cons. archaeologist for various orgns., 1975—; lectr. for various orgns., 1965—. Editor: In the Realms of Gold, 1980; contbr. articles to profl. jours.; author poetry; photographer for many publs.; producer videos. Bd. dirs., 1st v.p. Friends of Libr., North Port, Fla., 1987-90; com. chmn. explorer post #157 Boy Scouts Am., North Port; mem. cultural execs. com. Sarasota County Arts Coun.; co-chmn. Sarasota French Film Festival, 1989. Recipient Disting. Svc. award Ctr. for Am. Archaeology, 1983; rsch. grantee Fla. State Legis., 1984-92; recipient Resolution, Fla. Senate for achievement in sci. and history, 1979, Sigma Xi, 1993. Mem. AAAS, Soc. for Am. Archaeology, Soc. for Hist. Archaeology, Fla. Archaeol. Coun., Fla. Anthrop. Soc. (sec. 1973-74), Warm Mineral Springs Archaeol. Soc. (founder, pres. 1990-92), Am. Acad. Underwater Scis., Am. Anthrop. Assn., Archaeol. & Hist. Conservancy, Fla. Acad. Scis., Fla. Hist. Soc., Fla. Trust for Hist. Preservation, Nat. Assn. Cave Divers, Soc. for Am. Archaeology, Sigma Xi. Republican. Home: 4621 Autumn Woods Way Tallahassee FL 32303-6701

COCKRILL, SHERNA, artist; b. Chgo., Dec. 19, 1936; d. Glenn Wesley and Ruby Jean W.; m. J. Mitchell Jr., Mar. 23, 1963; 1 child, Ashley. BA, U. Ark., 1958, MA, 1966. Exhibited in one-woman shows in Okla., Ark., Tex., Ill.; exhibited in group shows at Philbrook Art Ctr., 1968, 69, Tulsa Regional 5-State Exhbn., 1968, Okla. 8-State Painting and Sculpture Exhbn., 1968, Ark. Arts Festival, 1968, 69, 70, 72, 73, Okla. Mus. Art, 1970, 71, Ozark Artists' Ann., 1969-72, Ft. Smith Art Ctr. 8-State Ann., 1972-74, Greater New Orleans Nat. Exhbn., 1973, Ark. Arts Ctr. Invitational, 1973, 74, 75, Little Rock Arts Fair Invitational Exhibit, 1973, Tex. Fine Arts Assn. Ann., 1973, 74, S.E. Ark. Arts and Sci. Ctr., 1973, Ark. Festival Arts Invitational, 1974, 75, 76, Ark. Arts, Crafts and Design Fair, 1975, 76, Gov.'s Disting. Artists Exhibit, 1976, U. Ark., 1979-86, Laguna Gloria Mus. Austin Tex., 1984, 86; represented in permanent collections Smithsonian Archives Am. Art, Mid Am. Mus., 1st Nat. Bank Little Rock, over 450 other pvt. and pub. collections. Vol. Ark. Air Mus., 1992—. Recipient 1st prize in oils Okla. Mus. Art, 1970, 1st and 2d prizes Ozark Artist's Ann., 1972, Grand prize Ft. Smith Art Ctr. 8-State Ann., 1973, Ark. State Festival Art, 1973, 1st prize in painting Little Rock Arts Fair Invitational 8-State Competition, 1973, 1st prize Ark. Arts, Crafts and Design Fair (8-State), 1974, 2d prize U. Ark. 5-State Ann. Competitive Exhibit, 1981, 84, Greater New Orleans Nat., 1986, Gov.'s Collection, State of Ark., 1994, KPMG Collection 1995, Ark. Artists Registry Invitational, 1996, Sen. Pryor's Wash. Exhibit 1996. Democrat. Episcopalian. Home: 1295 N Woodcreek Ln Fayetteville AR 72701-8881

COCOLIS, PETER KONSTANTINE, business development executive; b. Stamford, Conn., Sept. 22, 1942; s. Gus and Agnes (Vender) C.; m. Lorraine Patricia Marut, July 2, 1966; children: Peter Konstantine Jr., William Jonathan. BS in Engring., Boston U., 1964; MBA, Auburn U., 1976; cert., Def. Systems Mgmt. Coll., 1973; cert. in nat. and internat. security mgmt., Harvard U., 1996. Commd. 2d lt. USAF, 1964, advanced through grades to lt. col., 1980, ret., 1984; mktg. mgr. North Am. Aircraft Rockwell Internat., Washington, 1984-87, dir. mktg. and govt. affairs, 1987-89; dir. bus. devel. and govt. affairs Rocketdyne div. Rockwell Internat., Washington, 1989-95; sr. dir. bus. and govt. affairs N.Am. Aircraft div. Rockwell Internat., Washington, 1995—. Contbr. articles to profl. jours. Bd. dirs. Lakeforest Home Owners Assn., Springfield, Va., 1985-88; v.p. Morwood Estates Home Owners Assn.; swimming ofcl. U.S. Swimming Orgn., No. Va., 1981-91. Decorated DFC, Air medals. Mem. AIAA (sr., coun. mem., com. chmn., bd. dirs.), Am. Mgmt. Assn., Nat. Space Club, Air Force Assn., Navy League, Emeritus Found. (bd. dirs., com. chmn.), Clifton Lions. Office: Rockwell Internat 1745 Jefferson Davis Hwy Arlington VA 22202-3402

CODD, RICHARD TRENT, JR., computer scientist, educator; b. Norfolk, Va., June 1, 1945; s. Richard Trent and Mildred Joyce C.; m. Celine Marie Morisset, Aug. 10, 1968; children: Richard Trent, III, Patrick Timothy, Matthew Paul, Kevin Andrew. A.A., Miami-Dade Community Coll., 1967; B.S., U. Miami, 1970, M.A., 1974; B.S., Fla. Internat. U., 1985. Lic. tchr., ednl. adminstr. Fla. Audio technician U. Miami, Coral Gables, Fla., 1968-71; tchr. Archbishop Curley High Sch., Miami, Fla., 1972-74; tchr. St. Brendan High Sch., Miami, 1974-80, adminstr., 1980-87, asst. prin., 1981-87, dir. computer services, 1981-87; instr. St. Thomas U., Opa Locka, Fla., 1980-87, St. John Vianney Coll. Sem., Miami, 1985-87, A.C. Reynolds High Sch., Asheville, 1988-90, U. N.C., Asheville, 1988—, Advanced Edn. Ctr., Asheville, 1990-92; math. instr., computer applications programmer Haywood C.C., Clyde, N.C., 1991—; software systems developer Archdiocese of Miami, 1984-87; bd. dirs. Archdiocese of Miami Credit Union, 1979-80. Developer Master Acad. Record/Scheduling ADP System, Univ./C.C. Class Scheduling ADP System. Mem. Math. Assn. Am. Republican. Roman Catholic. Avocations: music, hiking, boating. Office: Haywood CC Freelander Dr Clyde NC 28721

CODELL, JAMES C. III, state official; m. Jeanne Achberger; 2 children. BSBA, Morehead State U. Gen. supt., then exec. v.p. Codell Constrn. Co.; dep. sec. transp. Commonwealth of Ky.; sec. transp. Commonwealth of Ky., Frankfort, 1996—; bd. dirs. adv. bd. PNC Bank. Trustee, elder First Christian Ch., Winchester, Ky.; bd. dirs. Winchester-Clark County YMCA; past pres. Clark County Hosp. Assn. Office: Ky Transp Cabinet State Office Bldg 6th Fl 501 High St Frankfort KY 40622

CODY, HIRAM SEDGWICK, JR., retired telephone company executive; b. Evanston, Ill., Nov. 1, 1915; s. Hiram Sedgwick and Harriett Mary (Collins) C.; m. Mary Vaughn Jacoby, Oct. 4, 1941; children: Margaret Vaughn, Harriett Mary, Hiram Sedgwick III, Henry Jacoby, William Collins. BS cum laude, Yale U., 1937, LLB, 1940. Bar: N.C., 1940. With Western Electric Co., Inc., 1946-71, regional mgr. engring. and installation, Chgo., 1961-64, dir. orgn. planning, N.Y.C., 1964-65, sec., treas., 1965-71; asst. treas. AT&T, N.Y.C., 1971-80. Vice pres. Morris-Sussex council Boy Scouts Am., 1970-80; vice chmn. Zoning Bd. Adjustment Mountain Lakes, 1968-80; boro councilman, Mountain Lakes, N.J., 1960-61; trustee, treas. Asheville (N.C.) Sch., 1974-84; trustee Asheville Symphony Orch., 1981-91, Asheville Community Concert Assn., 1981-91; bd. advisors Warren Wilson Coll., 1983—, chmn. 1987-90. Served USN, 1941-45, MTO, comdr. USNR 1946. N.C. State Bar, Tel. Pioneers Am. (v.p. 1969-71, treas. 1971-78), Tau Beta Pi. Home: 64 Wagon Trl Black Mountain NC 28711-2563

CODY, SARA ELIZABETH, librarian; b. St. Louis, Feb. 23, 1950; d. John Patrick and Martha Elizabeth (Brown) C. B Individualized Studies, George Mason U., 1983; MLS, N.C. Ctrl. U., 1991. Cert. libr., N.C., Ga. Libr. asst. Glencarlyn br. Arlington (Va.) Pub. Libr., 1981-84; reference dept. librarian Randolph County Pub. Libr., Asheboro, N.C., 1984-88; serials asst. Perkins Libr., Duke U., Durham, N.C., 1988-89; libr. tech. Durham Tech. C.C. Libr., 1989-91; extension librarian N.W. Ga. Regional Libr., Dalton, 1991—. Mem. ALA, Bus. and Profl. Women's Assn. (treas. 1994—). Office: NW Ga Regional Libr 310 Cappes St Dalton GA 30720

CODY, WILLIAM BERMOND, political science educator; b. Brunswick, Ga., Jan. 15, 1949; s. Bermond Hamp and Dorothy Jane (Satterfield) C.; m. Mildred Ann McInnis, Sept. 5, 1970; children: Margaret Jae, Elizabeth Joelle. AB, U. Ga., 1971, MA, 1973, JD, 1986; PhD, New Sch. Social Rsch., 1980. Bar: Ga. 1986. Student advisor New Sch. Social Rsch., N.Y.C., 1978-79; asst. to pres. Robeal Mgmt. Co., Charleston, S.C., 1983-85; assoc. Carr, Tabb & Pope, Atlanta, 1987; legal asst. Ga. Ct. Appeals, Atlanta, 1987-89; asst. prof. polit. sci. U. Ga., Athens, 1989-90; asst. prof. Oxford (Ga.) Coll. Emory U., 1990-93; assoc. prof. Oxford (Ga.) Coll. Emory U., 1993—; adj. instr. Coll. New Rochelle, N.Y., 1978-79; vis. asst. prof. Clemson (S.C.) U., 1980-83; mem. Emory U. Senate, 1995—, pres.-elect, 1996-97. Vestryman St. Bede's Episcopal Ch., Atlanta, 1988-92, jr. warden, 1990, sr. warden, 1991; bd. dirs. Interfaith, Inc., Atlanta, 1989-90. Mem. ABA, Am. Polit. Sci. Assn., Ga. Polit. Sci. Assn., So. Polit. Sci. Assn., Am. Hist. Assn., Acad. Polit. Sci., Ga. Bar Assn. Democrat. Office: Polit Sci Dept Oxford Coll Emory U Oxford GA 30267

COE, THOMAS R., police chief; m. Patty Coe, 1975; 2 children. B in Criminology, Fla. State U., M in Pub. Adminstrn.; grad., FBI Nat. Acad., Fla. Dept. Law Enforcement Chief Exec. Inst., Sr. Mgmt. Inst. Police. Cert. assessor Commn. Accreditation for Law Enforcement. Various positions Tallahassee (Fla.) Police Dept., 1972-94, chief, 1994—; chmn. criminal justice adv. bd. Tallahassee C.C.; mem. criminal justice adv. panel Fla. State U.; mem. Gov.'s Violent Crime Coun. Mem. FBI Nat. Acad. Assocs., Internat. Assn. Chiefs of Police, Fla. Police Chiefs Assn. (legis. and edn. coms.), Police Exec. Rsch. Forum. Office: 234 E 7th Ave Tallahassee FL 32303*

COENSON CROOK, BARBARA, marketing professional; b. Phila., Dec. 20, 1956; d. Martin and Rita (Cassel) Coenson; m. Steve L. Crook, Mar. 6, 1994. BS, U. Fla., 1978; M in Mgmt., Fla. Inst. Tech., 1996. Mng. editor Heritage Fla. News, Fern Park, Fla., 1978-82; freelance photographer and writer Altamonte Springs, Fla., 1982-89; campaign mgr. Pearlman for Congress, Orlando, Fla., 1990; mktg. mgr. AAA Travel Pub., Orlando, 1991-96, AAA Ptnr. Sales, Orlando, 1996—. Author: Tom and Jerry, 1989; contbr., editor articles to various pubs. Del. Fla. Rep. Conv., 1990; campaign mgr. Fla. State rep. Frank Stone, 1990; vol., advisor White House advance staff for Pres. Bush's visit to Fla., 1990. Recipient 7 Press awards Fla. Press Assn., 1980. Mem. Hadassah Club.

COFFEY, CLARENCE W., treasurer; b. New Orleans, July 10, 1946; s. Clarence W. and Kathyrn (Robinson) C.; m. Saundra Louise Goodson, Feb. 1, 1969; children: Brian, Kimberly. BBA, U. Tex., 1968; MBA, Our Lady of the Lake U., 1994. CPA, Tex. Staff acct. Freeport Sulphur Co., New Orleans, 1968-70, Tenneco Inc., Houston, 1970-73; corp. acct. First City Bankcorp., Houston, 1973-75; v.p., controller ATCO Drilling Ltd., Calgary, Alberta, Canada, 1975-81; controller Goldrus Drilling Co., Houston, 1981-86; sec. treas. Barwil Agys. NA, Inc., Houston, 1986—; bd. dirs. Barwil Agys. NA, Inc., Barwil Agys. Tex., Inc., Barwil Agys. La., Inc., New Orleans, Barber Wilhelmsen Agys., L.A. Coach Meml. Ashford Little League, Houston, 1981-89, Katy (Tex.) Little Dribblers Little League, 1985-89. Named one of Outstanding Young Men Am., 1977. Mem. AICPA, Delta Mu Delta. Home: 1106 Daria Dr Houston TX 77079-5026 Office: Barwil Agys (NA) Inc 1235 North Loop W Fl 10 Houston TX 77008

COFFEY, KEVIN T., actor; b. Lenoir, N.C., Dec. 6, 1959; s. Gary Todd and Linda Lou (Jackson) C.; m. Diane Christine Gaynor, Nov. 26, 1994. BA, U. N.C., 1982; student, Acting Studio Conservatory, Nashville. pres., owner Coffey Prodns., Marietta, Ga., 1994—. Acted at or in The Lost Colony, Manteo, N.C., 1980, Unto These Hills, Cherokee, N.C., 1981, 82-87, Tenn. Repertory Theatre, Nashville, 1987-88, Horse Cove (Ky.) Theatre, 1988, La. Repertory Theatre, Natchitoches, 1988, Nashville Acad. Theatre, 1989, Nashville Shakespeare Festival, 1989, Atlanta Shakespeare Tavern, 1994, America's Most Wanted, Atlanta, 1993. Children's ch. coord. 1st United Meth. Ch. Smyrna, Ga., 1996. Democrat.

COFFEY, LARRY B(RUCE), lawyer; b. Indpls., June 17, 1940; s. Oscar E. and Lora Kate C. BA, Wabash Coll., Crawfordsville, Ind., 1962; JD with honors, Ind. U., 1965; M of Comparative Law, U. Chgo., 1967. Bar: Ind. 1965, N.Y. 1975, N.C. 1989, U.S. Dist. Ct. (so. dist.) Ind., 1965, U.S. Dist. Ct. (we. dist.) N.C., 1989. Atty. European Community Commn., Brussels, 1967; assoc. Dewey Ballantine, N.Y.C. and Brussels, 1968-71; atty. GM, N.Y.C. and London, 1971-78; v.p. Revlon, Europe, Mid. East and Africa, Paris, 1978-83; pvt. practice Paris, 1983-89; counsel Womble, Carlyle, Sandridge & Rice, Charlotte, N.C., 1989-91; pvt. practice, 1991—. Editor: The Common Market and Common Law, 1967. Wabash Coll. scholar 1958-62, Ind. U. Law Sch. fellow, 1962-65, U. Chgo. Law Sch. fellow, 1965-67. Mem. ABA, Internat. Bar Assn., N.Y. State Bar Assn., N.C. Bar Assn., Assn. of Bar of City of N.Y., Union Internationale des Avocats. Office: 1031 S Caldwell St Charlotte NC 28203-3517

COFFIELD, KING SCOTT, urologist, educator; b. Dallas, May 22, 1944; s. Thomas Reddick and Wanda Jeanne (Williamson) C.; m. Jamie Kay Murdock, Sept. 10, 1966; children: Robert Brian, Rebekah Kate. BS in Psychology, Millsaps Coll., 1966; MD, U. Miss., 1971. Lic. to practice medicine and surgery, Tex., La. Intern surgery Baylor U. Med. Ctr., Dallas, 1971-72, resident gen. surgery, 1972-73; resident urology Univ. Med. Ctr., Jackson, Miss., 1973-76; chief urology svc. dept. surgery U.S. Army Hosp., Ft. Polk, La., 1976-78; mem. staff Baylor U. Med. Ctr., Gaston Episcopal Hosp., Parkland Meml. Hosp., Children's Med. Ctr., Dallas, 1978-80, King's Daus. Hosp., Metroplex Hosp., Temple and Killeen, Tex., 1980-81, Santa Fe Hosp., Olin E. Teague Vet.'s Ctr. Cons., Temple, 1981-91; clin. instr. U. Miss. Sch. Med., 1975-76, U. Tex. Southwestern Med. Sch., 1978-80; from assoc. prof. to prof. dept. surgery Divsn. Urology Tex. A&M U. Coll. Medicine, Temple, 1980-91; sr. staff Scott & White Meml. Hosp., Temple, 1981—; physician advisor utilization rev. com. Scott & White Meml. Hosp., 1986-91, utilization rev. com., 1987-91, social com., 1987-90, CSO bylaws subcom., 1990, fringe benefits com., 1991; asst. program dir. urology residency Scott & White Clinic, Temple, adminstrn. sr. med. student urology elective program, coord. urologic rsch., steering com. clinic staff orgn.; task force Crippled Children's Svcs., Tex. Dept. Health, 1988-89; spl. edn. subcom. Tex. chpt. So. Med. Assn., 1990. Contbr. numerous articles and papers to profl. jours. and confs. Maj. U.S. Army, 1972-79. Urologic oncology fellow U. Miss., 1969. Fellow ACS; mem. AMA, Am. Assn. Clin. Urologists, Am. Fertility Soc., Am. Urologic Assn. (AMS rsch. com. ann. meeting 1989, south cen. sect.), Tex. Med. Assn. (chmn. Bell County physician rehab. com. 1987-90), Tex. Urologic Soc., Tex. Assn. Genitourinary Surgeons, Soc. Baylor Surgeons, Bell County Med. Soc. (chmn. physician rehab. com. 1985-91), Alpha Omega Alpha. Office: Scott & White Meml Hosp 2401 S 31st St Temple TX 76508-0001

COFFIN, H(ARRIS) ALEXANDER, public relations executive, educator; b. Asheboro, N.C., Nov. 10, 1936; s. Harris A. and Parinne S. (Smith) C.; m. Sonia Kulka, Apr. 17, 1971; children: Jonathan Tristram, Anna Sloane. AB, U. N.C., 1959. Schs. city hall reporter Charlotte (N.C.) News, 1961-65; aide Rep. Charles R. Jonas Ho. of Reps., Washington, 1965-67; urban affairs reporter Atlanta Constn., 1967-76, Province, Vancouver, 1972-76; mgr. news svcs. Duke Power Co., Charlotte, 1976-85; owner Coffin Assocs./Pub. Rels., Charlotte, 1985—; prof. Queens Coll., Charlotte, 1988-91; tchr. Cen. Piedmont C.C., Charlotte, 1993-96; instr. U. N.C., Charlotte, 1995; moderator Final Edit., Sta. WTVI, Charlotte, 1979; acct. exec. Worldscape, 1996—; Carolinas rep. Info. on Hold, 1996—. Author: Brookshire and Belk, 1994; contbr. articles to profl. publs. Pres. Am. Lung Assn., Charlotte, 1990-91, Friends of U. N.C.-Charlotte, 1988-89; bd. dirs. Cmty. Sch. Arts, Charlotte, 1988-94, To Life, 1988-95, Springfest, 1987-89; elder Trinity Presbyn. Ch., 1984—. Recipient Sch. Bell award N.C. Edn. Assn., 1962. Mem. Charlotte C. of C. (v.p. 1979), Charlotte Track Club, Godiva Track Club. Democrat. Home: 1334 Cavendish Ct Charlotte NC 28211-3938 Office: Coffin Assocs/Pub Rels 1373 E Morehead St Charlotte NC 28204-2950

COFFMAN, ORENE BURTON, hotel executive; b. Fluvanna, Va., Mar. 13, 1938; d. John C. and Adele (Melton) Burton; m. John H. Emerson, Aug. 5, 1955 (div. 1972); 1 child, Norman Jay; m. Mack H. Coffman, Oct. 26, 1986. Degree in hotel and motel mgmt., Michigan State U., 1966-70. Cert. hotel mgr., Mich. State U., 1970. Telephone operator Colonial Williamsburg (Va.) Hotel, 1962-64; room clk. Colonial Williamsburg (Va.) Hotel, 1964-68; mgr. front office Colonial Williamsburg (Va.) Hotel, 1968-83; asst. mgr. Williamsburg Inn, 1983—; pres. Colonial Williamsburg Employees Fed. Credit Union, 1980-85. Mem. Am. Hotel Motel Assn. (nat. acctg. award 1970). Democrat. Baptist. Office: Williamsburg Inn PO Box 1776 Williamsburg VA 23187-3704

COFFMAN, WILMA MARTIN, women's health nurse, educator; b. Washington County, Tenn., Dec. 29, 1939; d. Oval Earnest and Buena (Light) Martin; m. Niles Lee Coffman, Aug. 26, 1961; children: Stephen Lee, Ruth Marie, Andrew William. BSN, East Tenn. State U., 1962; MS, U. Tenn., Knoxville, 1987. RN, Tenn. Staff nurse in maternal-child health Holston Valley Hosp. and Med. Ctr., Kingsport, Tenn.; instr. Kingsport City Schs., Johnson City Schs. Organist, pianist Beulah Bapt. Ch., Greenvale Bapt. Ch. Mem. Toonie Cash Evangelist Assn., Pi Lambda Theta. Home: 410 Lakeridge St Kingsport TN 37663-3760

COGAN, DENNIS CLARK, psychology educator; b. Milw., Jan. 10, 1936; s. Leo Judas and Elizabeth (Berman) C.; m. Helen Heller Noey, Dec. 27, 1994; children: Christopher, Nicholas. BS, U. Wis., Milw., 1959; MA, U. Mo., Columbia, 1966, PhD, 1966. Asst. prof. psychology Tex. Tech U., Lubbock, 1966-69, assoc. prof. psychology, 1969-83, prof. psychology, 1983—. Mem. AAAS, APS, Southwestern Psychology Assn. (pres. 1991-94). Office: Tex Tech U Dept Psychology Lubbock TX 79409

COGBURN, MAX OLIVER, lawyer; b. Canton, N.C., Mar. 21, 1927; s. Chester Amberg and Ruby Elizabeth (Davis) C.; m. Mary Heidt, Oct. 15, 1949; children: Max O. Jr., Michael David, Steven Douglas, Cynthia Diane. AB, U. N.C., 1948, LLB, 1950; LLM, Harvard U., 1951. Bar: N.C. 1950, U.S. Dist. Ct. (we. dist.) N.C. 1953, U.S. Ct. Appeals (4th cir.) 1984. Asst. dir. Inst. Govt., Chapel-Hill, N.C., 1951-52; staff mem. Atty. Gen. N.C., Raleigh, 1952-54; adminstr. asst. Chief Justice N.C., Raleigh, 1954-55; judge Gen. County Ct. Buncombe County, Asheville, N.C., 1968-70; sole practice Canton, Asheville, N.C., 1968, 1971—; ptnr. Roberts, Stevens & Cogburn, P.A., Asheville, 1986-95, Cogburn, Cogburn, Goosmann & Brazil, P.A., Ashville, 1995—. Chmn. Buncombe County Dem. Exec. Com., Asheville, 1974-76; mem. State Dem. Exec. Com., Raleigh, 1974-76. Mem. ABA, N.C. State Bar Assn., N.C. Bar Assn., 28th Judicial Dist. Bar State of N.C., Buncombe County Bar Assn. (past pres.). Roman Catholic. Home: Rt 1 Pisgah View Ranch Candler NC 28715 Office: PO Box 7647 Asheville NC 28802-7647

COGGINS, CHARLES E., transportation company executive; b. 1940. BS, U. Ala., Tuscaloosa, 1970. CPA, Ala. Acct. Deloitte, Haskins & Sells, CPA's, Birmingham and Mobile, Ala., 1970-80; with AAA Cooper Transp., Dothan, Ala., 1980—; v.p. adminstrn. and fin. Office: AAA Cooper Transp 1751 Kinsey Rd Dothan AL 36303-5877

COGGINS, GEORGE MILLER, JR., strategic planning and finance educator; b. Spartanburg, S.C., Sept. 23, 1939; s. George Miller and Inez (Caldwell) C.; m. Kathey Ann Allen, May 10, 1958; children: Rebecca, Leigh, Elisabeth, George III. BBA magna cum laude, Nat. U., 1981, MBA, 1983; D of Bus. Adminstrn., U.S. Internat. U., 1985. Mgr. logistics support B-2 div. Northrop Corp., Pico Rivera, Calif., 1985-89; prof. fin. and econs. High Point (N.C.) U., 1989—; adj. prof. Nat. U., L.A., 1983-89. Author: Excellence in the Military, 1985. Active High Point Leadership Program. Major USMC, 1956-85. Mem. High Point C. of C. Republican. Baptist. Home: 814 Hunt Rd Lexington NC 27292-6754 Office: High Point U Sch of Bus Montliew Ave Univ Sta High Point NC 27262

COGGINS, ORAN C(HALMERS), clinical counselor, addictions specialist; b. Spartanburg, S.C., Aug. 26, 1950; s. Chalmers Hadden and Geraldine Ganeva (Taylor) C.; m. Brenda Layton, July 28, 1973; children: Corrie Leigh, Brandi Elaine, Christopher Eric. AA, North Greenville Coll., 1974; BA in Religion, Gardner-Webb Coll., 1977; MA in Religious Edn., Southwestern Bapt. Sem., 1984, MA in Ch. Social Svcs., 1988. Cert. addictions counselor, criminal justice specialist and master addictions counselor. Asst. to dir. Alpha and Omega Family Ctr. Inc., Ft. Worth, 1984-88; dir. Southwayside Bapt. Ch. Family Ministry Ctr., Ft. Worth, 1987-88; clin. therapist, adminstr. Psychiatric Health Svc. of S.C., Sumter, 1988-89; clin. counselor, intensive outpatient case mgr. Cir. Park Family Counseling and Addiction Svcs., Florence, S.C., 1989—; outdoor edn. specialist, ropes course facilitator Three Oaks Adventure Ctr., 1991—; interviewer, team leader Pacific Inst. Rsch. Ctr., Berkeley, Calif., 1992—; lectr. to seminars and courses in field. Home mission intern Home Mission Bd. So. Bapt. Conv., Atlanta and Ft. Worth, 1986-88. Mem. Am. Assn. Marriage and Family Therapy (clin. mem.), Nat. Assn. Forensic Counseling (cert.), Nat. Assn. Alcoholism and Drug Abuse Counselors, S.C. Assn. Marriage and Family Therapy, S.C. Assn. Alcoholism and Drug Counselors. Home: 205 S Franklin Dr Florence SC 29501-4312 Office: Cir Park Family Counseling 601 Gregg Ave PO Box 4905 Florence SC 29502-4905

COGHE, DAVID WILLIAM, child psychiatrist; b. Pitts., May 3, 1942; s. Louis Paul and Vida Stephany (Zabric) C. BS in Chemistry magna cum laude, U. Pitts., 1963; MD, W.Va. U., 1967. Diplomate Am. Bd. Psychiatry and Neurology, Am. Bd. Child Psychiatry, Am. Bd. Addiction Psychiatry, Nat. Bd. Med. Examiners. Rotating intern Norfolk (Va.) Gen. Hosp., 1967-68; resident in gen. psychiatry, fellow in child psychiatry U. Ky. Med. Ctr., Lexington, 1970-74; pvt. practice, Lexington, 1974-85; unit dir. Oaks Treatment Ctr., Austin, Tex., 1985-94, med. dir. Amethyst program, 1986-92, assoc. med. dir., 1990, mem. adminstrv. mgmt. team and exec. com., 1990-94, co-acting med. dir., 1991-92; child psychiatrist Community Svcs., Austin State Hosp., 1994—; mem. staff Charter Ridge Hosp., 1974-85, mem. med. exec. com., 1983-86; mem. staff St. Joseph Hosp., 1974-85, Good Samaritan Hosp., 1974-85, Cardinal Hill Hosp., 1974-85, Shriners Hosp. for Crippled Children, 1974-85; presenter in field; cons. program for autistic children Fayette County Sch. Systems, Lexington, 1974-75. Capt., flight surgeon U.S. Army, 1968-70. Fellow Am. Acad. Child and Adolescent Psychiatry (substance abuse com. 1987-92); mem. Am. Psychiat. Assn., Tex. Med. Assn., Tex. Soc. Psychiat. Physicians, Tex. Soc. Child and Adolescent Psychiatry, Phi Beta Kappa. Roman Catholic. Home: 10103 Jupiter Hills Dr Austin TX 78747-1322 Office: Community Svcs Austin State Hosp 4110 Guadalupe St Austin TX 78751-4223

COGLIANO, GERARD RAYMOND, army officer; b. Canton, Mass., Dec. 30, 1956; s. Edward Sr. and Madeline (Paone) C.; m. Ruby M. Roman, May 15, 1981; children: Paula-Renee, Catherine M., Gerard R. Jr. BSBA in Acctg., Norwich U., 1978; MBA, Anna Maria Coll., Paxton, Mass., 1990. Commd. U.S. Army, 1978, advanced through grades to lt. col., 1995; comdr. HHB 7th Divsn. Arty., Monterey, Calif., 1980-81; platoon leader CBTRY 3/84th West Germany, Neckersum, 1981-82; comdr. ABTRY 3/84th West Germany, Heilbronn, 1982-85; logistical officer, comdr. HHB 26 Divarty, Rohoboth, Mass., 1985-89; adminstrv. officer, ops. 1-211th FABN, New Bedford, Mass., 1989-93; chief recruiting br. Nat. Guard Bur., Arlington, Va., 1993-95; Army N.G. liaison officer USACEC, Ft. Knox, Ky., 1995—.

Decorated Meritorious Svc. with 2 oak leaf clusters. Mem. Vets. World Wars. Office: Nat Guard Bur ARP-RE 111 S George Mason Dr Arlington VA 22204-1373

COHEN, ARTHUR DAVID, geological and marine science educator; b. Wilmington, Del., Feb. 26, 1942; s. Herman and Anna Mary (Stein) C.; m. Mary Jo Purcell, June 6, 1970; children: Benjamin M., Jonathan D. BS in Geology with honors and distinction, U. Del., 1964; PhD in Geology, Pa. State U., 1968. Rsch. asst. in coal petrology Pa. State U., 1964-68; asst. prof. U. Ga., 1968-69; assoc. prof. So. Ill. U., 1969-74; profl. geologist coal rsch. br. U.S. Geol. Survey, 1974-75; mem. staff Los Alamos (N.Mex.) Nat. Lab., 1982-88; dir. Organic Sedimentation Rsch. Ctr., U. S.C., Columbia, 1975-82, rsch. prof., 1988-90, prof. geol. and marine scis., 1990—; mem. S.C. State Alternative Energy Rsch. Subcom., 1979; cons. Pa. State U., 1969, U. Miami, 1969-74, U. Ind., 1971, Bur. Fish Rsch. Brazil, 1973, U. Ill., 1974, Shell Oil Co., 1976, U.S. Dept. Justice, 1976, 78, 82, U.S. Fish & Wildlife, 1977, Nat. Geog., 1978, U. N.C., 1979, Exxon Prodn. Rsch., 1980, Ga. Tech. U., 1982, U.S. Corps Engrs., 1982, U. N.Mex., 1983, BBC, 1984, Amoco Prodn. Co., 1987, Los Alamos Nat. Lab., 1988, U. S.W. La., 1989, Amoco, 1993, Conoco, 1993, others; regional judge Sci. Fair, 1993; invited lectr. in field. Contbr. over 250 articles, abstracts and tech. reports to sci. jourrs., chpts. to books and monographs; patentee method for in-situ removal of hydrocarbon contaminants from groundwater, method for removal of metals from groundwater using peat. Asst. den leader Cub Scout pack 301 Boy Scouts Am., 1989-91. Grantee NSF, 1969, 71, 73, 75, 77, 80, 92—, Gen. Devel. Found., 1978, U.S. Dept. Energy, 1983 (4 grants), 84, 86, U.S. A.I.D., 1985, 85-86, 87, U. S.C., 1991, S.C. Sea Grant, 1993-94, Amoco Prodn. Corp., 1993, others. Mem. ASTM (chmn. peat classification 1976-85, Standards Devel. award 1992), Geol. Sci. Am. (symposium chmn. coal divsn. 1971, symposium co-chmn., 1974, joint tech. program com. 1975, vice chmn. coal divsn. 1975, chmn. coal divsn. 1976, Gilbert H. Cady Award com. 1975-76, chair nominating com. 1976-77), Soc. for Organic Petrology (pres. 1989-90), Phi Beta Kappa, Sigma Xi, Phi Kappa Phi. Home: 1330 Raintree Dr Columbia SC 29212-1545 Office: U SC Dept Geol Scis Columbia SC 29208

COHEN, BARRY ALLAN, psychiatrist; b. N.Y.C., Sept. 16, 1939; s. Jack and Frances Cohen; m., Sherrylee McGannon, Dec. 31, 1989. BA in History, Cornell U., 1961, MD, 1965. Diplomate Am. Bd. Psychiatry and Neurology, Nat. Bd. Med. Examiners; lic. psychiatrist Fla., N.Y., Calif., N.J., D.C., Md., Va. Intern U. Miami Sch. Medicine-Jackson Meml. Hosp., 1965-66; resident in psychiatry N.Y. State Psychiat. Inst. Columbia Presbyn. Med. Ctr.-Coll. Physicians and Surgeons, N.Y.C., 1966-69; staff psychiatrist Divsn. Mental Health Svcs. NIMH, 1969-71, cons. psychiatrist Divsn. Mental Health Svs., 1971-72; psychiatrist Mt. Carmel Guild, Ridgefield Park, N.J., 1967-69; pvt. practice Boca Raton, Fla., 1969—; cons. Juvenile Svcs. Adminstrn. Annapolis, Md., 1976-79, Psychol. Svcs. Annapolis, 1976-79. Lt. commdr. USPHS, 1969-71. Lt. comdr. USPHS, 1969-71. Recipient Physicians Recognition award AMA, 1991. Mem. Am. Psychiat. Assn. (Continuing Med. Edn. award 1991), Fla. Psychiat. Soc., Palm Beach County Psychiat. Soc., Cornell U. Med. Coll. Alumni Assn., N.Y. State Psychiat. Inst.-Presbyn. Hosp. Alumni Assn. Democrat. Home and Office: 7610 Sierra Dr W Boca Raton FL 33433-3320

COHEN, BARRY MENDEL, financial executive, educator; b. Dallas, Feb. 1, 1939; s. Ben and Marjorie Joyce (Novich) C.; BA, Rice U., 1960; MA, U. Tex., 1964, PhD, 1980; postgrad. (fellow) U. Ill., summer 1974; MLS North Tex. State U., 1987; m. Rosalee Valent-Torres, July 30, 1967. Instr. history Tex. Arts and Industries U., Kingsville, 1965-67; prof. social sci. Chowan Coll., Murfreesboro, N.C., 1969-73; exec. Cohen Candy Co., Dallas, 1973-83; asso. sales mgr. McCraw Candy, 1981-83; owner BMC Brokerage, 1983—; pub. svcs. libr. Tex. Southmost Coll., 1987-90; fed. programs tutor to migrant students Porter High Sch., Brownsville, Tex., 1991-96; lectr. Richland Coll., Dallas, 1976-77, Mountain View Coll., Dallas, 1977-84, U. Tex. at Dallas, summer 1977; stringer UPI, Rio Grande Valley, 1990—; symposium speaker 14th Internat. Genetics Congress, Moscow, 1978; invited speaker John Innes Inst., Norwich, Eng., 1984; adj. prof. So. Tex. Cmty. Coll., 1996. Mem. nat. bd. advisers Ad Hoc Com. for Intellectual Freedom; mem. Cameron County Hist. Commn., 1989; bd. dirs. Kleberg County Community Action, 1966-67, Chowanoke Area Devel. Assn., 1971, City of Brownsville Pub. Libr., 1992—. Recipient Vavilov Century Bronze medallion Lenin Acad. Agrl. Scis., 1987. Mem. Am. Hist. Assn., Am. Assn. for Advancement Slavic Studies, AAUP. Democrat. Jewish. Contbr. articles to profl. jours. and newspapers. Home and Office: 239 Hibiscus Ct Brownsville TX 78520-8034

COHEN, ELIOT DORSEY, electrical engineer; b. Washington, Mar. 10, 1942; s. Walter and Clara (Goldberg) C.; m. Barbara Susan Linderman, June 22, 1968; children: Gregory, Bonnie. B of Elect. Engring., George Washington U., 1963, MS in Engring., 1966, postgrad., 1967-72. From electronics engr. to head high frequency devices sec. Naval Rsch. Lab., Washington, 1963-80; navy dir. very high speed integrated circuits program Space & Naval Welfare Systems Com., Arlington, Va., 1980-86; dep. dir. microwave & millimeter wave programs Def. Tech. Analysis Office, Arlington, Va., 1986-88; from program mgr. to dep. dir. def. mfg. office Advanced Rsch. Project Agy., Arlington, Va., 1988-91, exec. dir. microwave & millimeter wave tech., 1991-95; exec. dir. tech. ops., v.p. Palisades Inst. for Rsch. Svcs., Inc., Arlington, Va., 1995—; pres. EBCO Tech. Advising, Inc., 1995—; advisory group on electron devices Office Sec. Def., Arlington, 1971-95; mem. U.S. Govt. Sr. Exec. Svc., 1989-95; presenter in field. Contbr. articles to profl. jours. Pres. Strathmore-Bel Pre Civic Assn., Silver Spring, Md., 1980-81. Fellow IEEE; mem. Microwave Theory and Techniques Soc. Adminstrv. Com. (v.p. 1994, pres. 1995). Office: Palisades Inst Rsch Svcs Ste 500 Crystal Sq 4 1745 Jefferson Davis Hwy Arlington VA 22202

COHEN, FRANK BURTON, wholesale novelty company executive; b. Miami, Fla., Dec. 18, 1927; s. Herman and Helen Florence (Rudich) C.; BS, Emory U., 1948; m. Janis E. Stewart, Sept. 19, 1971; children: Ilene Michele, Mona Helene, Randy Stewart. With Tampa Novelty Co., Inc. (Fla.), 1948—, ptnr., 1953-72, owner, pres., 1972—. Officer Rodeph Sholom Synagogue, Tampa; mem. Am. Jewish Com.; pres. react Hillsborough County Team #4909. With USNR. Mem. Tampa C. of C., Fla. C. of C., Eagle Squadron CB Club, Classic Cadillac Convertible Club Am., Classic Thunderbird Club Am., Jewish War Vets., Nat. Fedn. Ind. Bus., Internat. Platform Assn., Fla. Sheriffs Assn., Fla. Assn. State Troopers, Internat. Buckskin Horse Assn., Am. Buckskin Horse Assn., B'nai B'rith, Masons, Moose, Appaloosa Horse, Rodeph Sholom Men's (officer), BMW Car Am., Appaloosa Cover, Cen. Fla. Appaloosa Horse. Democrat. Recipient Who's Who Worldwide Men of Achievement award; patentee center seat car tray. Home: 4934 W San Rafael St Tampa FL 33629-5404 Office: 501 S Florida Ave Tampa FL 33602-5419

COHEN, HARVEY JAY, physician, educator; b. Bklyn., Oct. 21, 1940; s. Joseph and Anne (Margolin) C.; m. Sandra Helen Levine, June 1964; children: Ian Mitchell, Pamela Robin. BS, Bklyn. Coll., 1961; MD, Downstate Med. Coll., Bklyn., 1965. Diplomate Am. Bd. Internal Medicine, Am. Bd. Hematology. Intern, then resident internal medicine Duke U. Med. Ctr., Durham, N.C., 1965-67, fellow hematology and oncology, 1969-71; chief hematology-oncology VA Med. Ctr., Durham, N.C., 1975-76, chief med. service, 1976-82, assoc. chief of staff-edn., 1982-84, now dir. geriatric research, edn. and clin. ctr.; assoc. prof. medicine Duke U. Med. Ctr., Durham, 1976-80, now prof. medicine, chief geriatric div., also dir. Ctr. for Study of Aging. Author: Medical Immunology, 1977; editor: Cancer I and II, 1987; editor Jour. Gerontology: Med. Scis., 1988-92; contbr. numerous articles to profl. jours. Served as surgeon USPHS, 1967-69. Fellow ACP, Am. Geriatrics Soc. (bd. dirs. 1987—, sec. 1991-93, ethics com. 1992—, pres. 1994-95), Gerontology Soc. Am. (clin. sect., rsch. com. 1987-92, chair 1993-94, publs. com. 1992—, program chair 1994—); mem. Am. Soc. Clin. Oncology, Am. Soc. Hematology, Am. Assn. Cancer Rsch. Home: 2811 Friendship Cir Durham NC 27705-5521 Office: Duke U Med Ctr for Study Aging & Human Devel Box 3003 Durham NC 27710-3003

COHEN, HELEN HERZ, camp owner, director; b. N.Y.C., Oct. 29, 1912; d. Fred W. and Florence (Hirsch) H.; m. Albert F. Schliefer, Sept. 22, 1933 (dec. Nov. 1941); m. Edwin S. Cohen, Aug. 31, 1944; children: Edwin C., Roger, Wendy. PhB, Brown U., 1933; MA, Columbia U., 1934; postgrad., NYU, Columbia. Counselor Camp Walden, Denmark, Maine, 1930-38, owner, 1939—; tchr. social studies Alcuin Prep. Sch., 1935; office mgr. Lewis P. Weil Importer, 1935-40; pres. The Main Idea, 1968—; founder, pres. Main Idea, Inc., 1969—. Co-author: Fabulous Foods for Fifty, 1970; author: Choosing a Camp For Your Child, 1985, Getting Your Child Ready For Camp, 1985; contbr. articles to instrnl. booklets, mags. Active alumni coun. Pembroke Coll., 1960; chmn. camp divns. Bridgton (Maine) Hosp. Fund, 1962—; trustee Fund for Advancement Camping, 1980-90. Recipient Gold Key award Columbia Scholastic Press, 1972, award Fund for Advancement of Camping Patron, 1982. Mem. Am. Camping Assn. (regional bd. dirs. 1947-50, 52-55, 56-59, 60-63, standards visitor 1957-93, chmn. pvt. camps 1961, bd. dirs. 1963—, v.p. N.Y. 1963-75, Va. sect. 1975), Pioneers of Camping, Maine Camp Dirs. Assn. (legis. com. 1960-63, bd. dirs. 1963—, Halsey Gulick award 1991), Pembroke Coll. Club (co-founder), Cosmopolitan (Westchester, N.Y.) Club, Cornell Club, Farmington Country Club, Boar's Head Sports Club. Home: Ednam Forest 104 Stuart Pl Charlottesville VA 22903-4740 Office: Camp Walden Box 3427 Charlottesville VA 22903

COHEN, IRVIN MYRON, psychiatrist; b. Birmingham, Ala., Aug. 29, 1922; s. Morris Herman and Frances (Wacholder) C.; m. Dorothy Florence Lewis, Jan. 30, 1955; children: Dannah Lynn Cohen Bonnell, David A. BA, U. Tex., 1943, MD, 1945. Diplomate in Psychiatry Am. Bd. Psychiatry and Neurology. Asst. prof. psychiatry U. Tex. Med. Br., Galveston, 1951-55, assoc. prof. psychiatry, 1955-58, clin. prof. psychiatry, 1971—; clin. assoc. prof. psychiatry Baylor Coll. of Medicine, Houston, 1958-74, clin. prof. psychiatry, 1975—; clin. prof. psychiatry U. Tex. Med. Sch., Houston, 1972—; pvt. practice in psychiatry Houston, 1958-95. Editor: Family Structure, Dynamics and Therapy, 1966; contbr. articles to profl. jours. Recipient Discovery in Biolog. Psychiatry award Taylor Manor Hosp., Balt., 1984. Fellow Am. Psychiat. Assn. (spkr. of the assembly 1987-88, bd. trustees 1986-89, Rush Gold medal award 1970, Spl. Presdl. Commendation 1995, bd. dirs. Psychiatrists' Mut. Ins. Co. 1992—), Am. Coll. Psychiatrists, So. Psychiat. Assn. (v.p. 1993-94, bd. regents 1994—); mem. Houston Psychiat. Assn. (pres. 1966-67), Tex. Soc. Psychiat. Physicians (pres. 1971-72).

COHEN, JEFFREY MICHAEL, lawyer; b. Dayton, Ohio, Nov. 13, 1940; s. H. Mort and Evelyn (Friedlob) C.; m. Betsy Z. Zimmerman, July 3, 1966; children: Meredith Sue, Seth Alan. AB, Colgate U., 1962; JD, Columbia U., 1965. Bar: Fla. 1965, U.S. Supreme Ct. 1969; cert. civil trial lawyer Fla. Bar Bd. Cert., diplomate Nat. Bd. Trial Advocacy. Asst. pub. defender Dade County (Fla.), 1968-70, asst. state's atty., 1970-72, spl. asst. state's atty., 1973; ptnr. Fromberg Fromberg Gross Cohen Shore & Berke, P.A., 1972-84, Cohen, Berke, Bernstein, Brodie, Kondell & Laszlo, P.A., Miami, Fla., 1984—; adj. prof. litigation skills U. Miami Sch. Law, 1989—, chmn. Fla. bar com. on civil trial cert. Mem. ABA, Dade County Bar Assn., Acad. Fla. Trial Lawyers, Assn. Trial Lawyers Am., Am. Judicature Soc., Nat. Inst. Trial Advocacy (chair and faculty mem.), Fla. Criminal Def. Attys. Assn. Home: 3628 Saint Gaudens Rd Miami FL 33133-6533 Office: Cohen Berke Bernstein Brodie Kondell & Laszlo PA 2601 S Bayshore Dr Fl 19 Miami FL 33133-5419

COHEN, JOY ESTHER, medical educator; b. Atlanta, Feb. 12, 1960; d. Victor Louis and Matilda (Romano) C.; m. Michael Christopher Grieb, June 7, 1986; children: Alegra, Alexandra, harrison, Anastasia. Grad., Tulane U., 1981, MD, 1985. Asst. prof. pulmonary medicine Sch. Medicine Tulane U., New Orleans, 1990-96.

COHEN, KENNETH ALLAN, chemist; b. Bklyn., Mar. 30, 1953; s. Philip and Ruth C.; m. Dory A. Cohen, Oct. 26, 1980; 1 child, Bryan M. BS, L.I. U., 1976. Chemist Coty div. Pfizer, N.Y.C., 1976, A.R. Winarick, Carlstadt, N.J., 1976-78, Cosmair Inc., Clark, N.J., 1978-80, CCM, Islip, N.Y., 1980-83, Vanity Cosmetic Labs., 1983-86, Revlon Rsch. Ctr., Edison, N.J., 1986-91; with Proctor & Gamble, Hunt Valley, Md., 1991-92; dir. R&D Maybelline Inc., Memphis, Tenn., 1992—. Mem. Soc. Cosmetic Chemists. Jewish. Office: Maybelline Inc 3030 Jackson Ave Memphis TN 38112-2020

COHEN, MELVIN LEE, pediatrician, psychiatrist, educator; b. San Antonio, Mar. 18, 1950; s. Melvin David and Elizabeth Catherine (Brown) C. BA summa cum laude, Rice U., 1972; MD, U. Va., 1977. Diplomate Am. Bd. Pediatrics, Am. Bd. Psychiatry and Neurology. Chief pediatric clinic 97th Gen. Hosp., U.S. Army, Frankfurt, Fed. Republic of Germany, 1980-83; fellow in developmental pediatrics William Beaumont Army Med. Ctr., El Paso, Tex., 1983-85; regional coord. Army exceptional family mem. program, cons. Brooke Army Med. Ctr., San Antonio, 1985-87; pvt. practice pediatrics San Antonio, 1987-89; chief of staff Bowling Green Hosp., San Antonio, 1988-89; resident in gen. and child psychiatry U. Tex. Health Sci. Ctr., San Antonio, 1989-93; pvt. practice child and adolescent psychiatry, San Antonio, 1993—; med. dir. child and adolescent partial hospitalization Laurel Ridge Hosp., San Antonio, 1992-95; clin. assoc. prof. pediats. U. Tex. Health Sci. Ctr., 1994—, clin. asst. prof. psychiatry, 1994—; mem. exec. com. Laurel Ridge Hosp., San Antonio, 1987-88, 93-94. Bd. dirs. Jewish Family Svc., 1993—, sec. bd. dirs., 1996—; mem. sci. adv. bd. WInston Sch., 1993—. Maj. U.S. Army, 1980-87, lt. col. USAR, 1987-92. Rotary Found. scholar Rice U., 1972; recipient Cert. of Appreciation, Pres. Azcona of Honduras, 1986. Fellow Am. Acad. Pediatrics; mem. Tex. Med. Assn., Tex. Med. Found., Bexar County Med. Soc., Rice U. Alumni Assn., Phi Beta Kappa. Jewish. Office: 14800 San Pedro Ave # 1110 San Antonio TX 78232-3733

COHEN, MELVYN DOUGLAS, securities company executive; b. Newtonards, Northern Ireland, Nov. 29, 1943; came to U.S., 1972; s. Arnold Ernest and Clara (Praeger Bethune) C.; m. Rosita Nahum, May 9, 1974; children: Andrew, Suzanne, Cary. AA, Miami Dade Community Coll., 1975; BBA, Fla. Internat. U., 1977, MS in Mgmt., 1981. Cert. fin. planner. With Merrill Lynch, Miami, 1977-91; v.p., mgr. sales Merrill Lynch, N.Y.C., 1986-88; v.p., resident mgr. Merrill Lynch, Coral Springs, Fla., 1988-91; divisional v.p., br. mgr. Paine Webber, Plantation, Fla., 1991-92; divsn. v.p. investments Paine Webber, Boca Raton, Fla., 1992-94; 1st v.p. Prudential Securities, Boca Raton, 1994—; fin. mgr. Donald Regan Sch. Fin. Planning. Pres. City of Parkland Homeowners Assn., 1991—; chmn. charter rev. bd. dirs. Assn. Fraternal Order of Police, City of Parkland, 1990; pres. Concerned Citizens of Cypress Head, 1990-91. Mem. Jaycees (pres. Miami chpt. 1982), Parkland Optimist Club (dir. 1990). Jewish. Office: Prudential Securities Crocker Plz 5355 Town Center Rd Ste 600 Boca Raton FL 33486-1068

COHEN, PHILIP, retired hydrogeologist; b. N.Y.C., Dec. 13, 1931; s. Isadore and Anna (Katz) C.; m. Barbara Sandler, Dec. 26, 1954; 1 son, Jeffery. B.S. cum laude, CCNY, 1954; M.S., U. Rochester, 1956. Cert. profl. geologist, Va. With U.S. Geol. Survey, 1956-94, chief Long Island program, 1968-72; assoc. chief land info. and analysis office U.S. Geol. Survey, Reston, Va., 1975-78, asst. chief hydrologist water resources div., 1978-79, chief hydrologist water resources div., 1979-94; ret., 1994. Contbr. numerous articles on geology and hydrology to profl. jours. Recipient Ward medal Coll. City, N.Y., 1954; Meritorious Ser. award Dept. Interior, 1975, Disting. Ser. award, 1979, Presdl. Meritorious Exec. Rank award, 1986, Presdl. Disting. Exec. Rank award, 1988. Fellow Geol. Soc. Am.; mem. Am. Water Resources Assn., Am. Inst. Hydrology (C.V. Theis award 1993), Sigma Xi. Office: US Geol Survey 409 Geol Survey Reston VA 22092

COHEN, RICHARD PAUL, lawyer; b. Bklyn., Nov. 18, 1945; s. Morris T. and Ida (Tepletsky) C.; m. Laura Diane Keller, July 4, 1968; 1 child, Adam Morris. BME, CCNY, 1968; JD, Fordham U., 1973. Bar: N.Y. 1974, W.Va. 1979, U.S. Ct. Appeals (2d cir.) 1974, U.S. Dist. Ct. (so. dist.) N.Y. 1974, U.S. Dist. Ct. (so. and no. dists.) W.Va. 1979, U.S. Ct. Appeals (fed. cir.) 1994, U.S. Supreme Ct. 1977, U.S. Ct. Vets Appeals 1993. Asst. counsel Waterfront Commn. N.Y. Harbor, N.Y.C., 1973-78; asst. atty. Westchester County Atty's. Office, White Plains, N.Y., 1977-78; asst. prosecutor Wetzel County Atty's. Office, New Martinsville, W.Va., 1980-82; pvt. practice law Hundred and Fairmont, W.Va., 1979-83; ptnr. Cohen, Abate & Cohen, Fairmont, W.Va., 1984—. Named One of Oustanding Young Men of Am., Outstanding Young Men of Am., 1981; recipient Meritorious Svc. award Am. Assn. Mental Dificiency, 1987. Mem. ABA, Nat. Assn. Soc. Sect. Claimants Rep, Nat. Assn. Vets. Advocates, W.Va. State Bar Assn., N.Y. State Bar Assn., N.Y. County Bar Assn., Phi Epsilon Phi. Home: 116 Lincoln Ave Morgantown WV 26505-6512 Office: Cohen Abate & Cohen Security Bank Bldg Adams St PO Box 846 Fairmont WV 26554-2822

COHEN, ROBERT, medical device manufacturing-marketing executive; b. Glen Cove, N.Y., Sept. 23, 1957; s. Alan and Selma (Grossman) C.; m. Nancy A. Arey, Jan. 17, 1981. BA, Bates Coll., 1979; JD, U. Maine, 1982. Bar: N.Y. 1983, U.S. Dist. Ct. (so. and ea.) N.Y. 1983. Atty. Pfizer Inc., N.Y.C., 1982-86; asst. corp. counsel, asst. sec. Pfizer Hosp. Products Group, Inc., N.Y.C., 1986-88; v.p. bus. devel., dir. for med. device mfr. and marketer Deknatel Inc., Fall River, Mass., 1988-92; pres., CEO GCI Med., Braintree, Mass., 1992-93; v.p. bus. devel. Sulzermedica USA, Inc., Angleton, Tex., 1993-94, group v.p., 1994—. Author: 19th Century Maine Authors, 1978. Mem. ABA, Am. Corp. Counsel Assn., Am. Mgmt. Assn., Licensing Execs. Soc. Republican. Home: 58 Heathrow Ln Sugar Land TX 77479-2500 Office: Sulzermedica 4000 Technology Dr Angleton TX 77515-2523

COHEN, STANLEY, biochemistry educator; b. Brooklyn, N.Y., Nov. 17, 1922; s. Louis and Fannie (Feitel) C.; m. Olivia Larson, 1951 (div.); children: Burt Bishop, Kenneth Larson, Cary; m. Jan Elizabeth Jordan, 1981. BA, Bklyn. Coll., 1943; MA, Oberlin Coll., 1945, PhD, 1989; PhD in Biochemistry, U. Mich., 1948; PhD, U. Chgo., 1985, Washington U., 1993. Instr. dept. biochemistry and pediatrics U. Colo., Denver, 1948-52; Am. Cancer Soc. fellow in radiology Washington U., St. Louis, 1952-53, assoc. prof. dept. zoology, 1953-59; asst. prof. biochemistry, sch. medicine Vanderbilt U., Nashville, 1959-62, assoc. prof., 1962-67, prof. biochemistry, 1967-86, disting. prof., 1986—; rsch. prof. biochemistry Am. Cancer Soc., Nashville, 1976—; Charles B. Smith vis. rsch. prof. Sloan Kettering, 1984; Feodor Lynen lectr. U. Miami, 1986, Steenbock lectr. U. Wis., 1986. Mem. editorial bd. Abstracts of Human Developmental Biology, Jour. of Cellular Physiology. Cons. Minority Rsch. Ctr. for Excellence. Recipient Research Career Devel. award NIH, 1959-69, William Thomson Wakeman award Nat. Paraplegia Found., Earl Sutherland Research Prize Vanderbilt U., 1977, Albion O. Bernstein MD award Med. Soc. State N.Y., 1978, H.P. Robertson Meml. award Nat. Acad. Sci., 1981, Lewis S. Rosentiel award Brandeis U., 1982, Alfred P. Sloan award Gen. Motors Cancer Research Found., 1982, Louisa Gross Horwitz prize Columbia U., 1983, Disting. Achievement award UCLA Lab. Biomed. and Environ. Scis., 1983, Lila Gruber Meml. Cancer Research award Am. Acad. Dermatology, 1983, Bertner award MD Anderson Hosp. U. Tex., 1983, Gairdner Found. Internat. award, 1985, Fred Conrad Koch award Endocrine Soc., 1986, Nat. Medal Sci., 1986, 89, Albert and Mary Lasker Found. Basic Med. Research award, 1986, Nobel Prize in physiology or medicine, 1986, Tennessean of Yr. award Tenn. Sports Hall of Fame, 1987, Franklin Medal, 1987, Albert A. Michaelson award Mus. Sci. and Industry, 1987. Fellow Jewish Acad. Arts and Sci.; mem. Nat. Acad. Sci., Am. Soc. Biol. Chemists, Am. Chem. Soc., AAAS, Internat. Inst. Embryology, Internat. Acad. Sci. (hon. internat. coun. for sci. devel.). Office: Vanderbilt U Sch Medicine Dept Biochemistry 607 LH Nashville TN 37232-0146*

COHEN, TED ELLIS, public relations executive, publishing executive; b. N.Y.C., Aug. 13, 1922; s. Irving and Gertrude (Cantor) C.; children: Constance, James, Ellen Farr. Grad., U.S. Naval Acad., 1947; BA, Fla. Internat. U., 1987. Pres. Ted Cohen Assocs., Miami, Fla., 1960—; exec. dir. Fla. Fashion Coun., Miami, 1967-70; pub., editor World Pageants, Inc., Miami, 1987—. Editor Internat. Dir. Pageants. Commdr. Dade County Civil Def. Police, 1960; pres. Men's Club Temple Emanuel, 1965, Greater Miami Aviation Com., 1987-89, Pres. Coun. Miami Beach, Fla., 1964-65; chmn. Conv. Svcs. Com. Miami Beach, 1967; chmn. Dade County Dem. Exec. Com., Miami, 1968-72; state rep. Fla. Leg., Tallahassee, 1972-74; chmn. marine com. Citizens Transp. Adv. Com., 1995-96. With USN, 1942-45. Recipient Disting. Svc. award U.S. Jaycees, 1959, Cooper Taylor Meml. award Fla. Jaycees, 1961, Exceptional Svc. award Civil Air Patrol nat. Bd., 1973, Leg. award United Tchrs. Dade, 1973. Mem. Elks, Williams Island Yacht Club (vice commodore 1995-96). Republican. Jewish. Home: 1000 Island Blvd Apt 3007 Aventura FL 33160 Office: World Pageants Inc 18761 W Dixie Hwy Ste 284 Miami FL 33180

COHN, ISIDORE, JR., surgeon, educator; b. New Orleans, Sept. 25, 1921; s. Isidore and Elsie (Waldhorn) C.; m. Jacqueline Heymann, July 4, 1944 (div. Aug. 1971); children: Ian Jeffrey, Lauren Kerry; m. Marianne Winter Miller, Jan. 3, 1976. MD, U. Pa., 1945; M.Med. Sci. in Surgery, 1952, DMS in Surgery, 1955; LHD (hon.), U. S.C., 1995. Diplomate Am. Bd. Surgery (bd. dirs. 1969-75). Intern Grad. Hosp. U. Pa., 1945-46, resident in surgery, 1949-52; fellow dept. surg. rsch. U. Pa., 1947-48; vis. surgeon Charity Hosp., New Orleans, 1952-62, sr. vis. surgeon, 1962—; surgeon in chief La. State U. Svc., Charity Hosp., New Orleans, 1962-89; prof. surgery La. State U. Sch. Medicine, New Orleans, 1959—; cons. surgeon VA Hosp., New Orleans, Touro Infirmary, New Orleans; instr. surgery La. State U. Sch. Medicine, New Orleans, 1952-53, asst. prof., 1953-56, assoc. prof., 1956-59, prof., 1959—, chmn. dept. surgery, 1962-89; mem. surg. rsch. rev. com. VA, Washington, 1967-68; dir. Nat. Pancreatic Cancer Project, 1975-84; mem. Soc. Surg. Chairmen, 1962-89. Mem. editl. bd. Am. Surgeon, 1963-87, Current Surgery, 1964-90, Am. Jour. Surgery, 1968—, Digestive Diseases and Scis., 1978-82, Surg. Gastroenterology, 1982—, Cancer, 1992—, Digestive Surgery, 1995—. Served to capt. M.C., AUS, 1946-47. Isidore Cohn, Jr. Professorship named in his honor at La. State U., 1987. Fellow ACS (exec. com., bd. govs. 1987-91, vice-chmn. 1989-90, chmn. 1990-91, 1st v.p. 1993-94); mem. AMA, Am. Surg. Assn., So. Surg. Assn. (1st v.p. 1979-80, treas.-recorder 1981-82, pres. 1982-83), La. Surg. Assn. (pres. 1968), So. Med. Assn., La., Orleans Parish med. socs., Soc. Univ. Surgeons, Southeastern Surg. Congress (chmn. forum on progress in surgery 1967-69, councillor for La. 1967-73, pres. 1972), Surg. Biology Club II, Assn. Acad. Surgery, James D. Rives Surg. Soc., Internat. Surg. Soc., Am. Gastroenterol. Assn., Bockus Soc. Gastroenterology, Soc. Surgery Alimentary Tract (trustee 1969-80, recorder 1973-76, pres. 1976-77, chmn. bd. 1977-78), Am. Soc. Microbiologists, Soc. Surg. Oncology, N.Y. Acad. Scis., Am. Assn. Cancer Research, Southeastern Cancer Research Assn. (pres. 1975), Collegium Internationale Chirurgiae Digestivae, Am. Cancer Soc. (vice chmn. clin. investigation adv. com. 1969, chmn. clin. investigation adv. com. 1969-73), Sigma Xi, Phi Beta Kappa, Alpha Omega Alpha, Omicron Delta Kappa. Office: La State U Med Sch New Orleans LA 70112

COHN, LAWRENCE SHERMAN, psychiatrist, educator, psychoanalyst; b. Hartford, Conn., Nov. 10, 1940; s. Lewis Eli and Anne (Radeen) C.; m. Marjorie Bass, Aug. 25, 1961 (div. Aug. 1979); m. Lynn Ellen Davis, Aug. 25, 1979; 1 child, Gary S. BS, Bates Coll., 1962; MD, U. Miami, 1966. Intern U. Miami, Fla., 1966-67; resident in psychiatry Downstate Med. Ctr., Bklyn., 1967-70; psychoanalyst Balt.-Washington Psychoanalytic Inst., Laurel, Md., 1972-78; assoc. prof. clin. psychiatry U. Miami (Fla.) Med. Sch., 1978-92, prof. clin. psychiatry, 1992—; teaching analyst Fla. Psychoanalytic Inst., Miami, 1980-95, tng. and supr. analyst, 1995—. Maj. U.S. Army, 1970-72. Fellow Am. Psychiat. Assn.; mem. Fla. Psychoanalytic Soc. (pres. 1991-93). Home: 6420 SW 134th Dr Miami FL 33156-7047 Office: 8740 N Kendall Dr Miami FL 33176-2209

COHN, LINKIE SELTZER, professional speaker, author; b. Dallas, Nov. 22, 1925; d. Nathan A. and Ann (Ravkind) Levine; m. Marcus Seltzer (dec. 1973); children: Adrienne Lithman, Cathy Brenda Negrel, Robert Michael; m. Henry Cohn, 1994. Student So. Methodist U., 1943-44, 76, U. Tex., 1944-45. Profl. dancer Starlight Operettas, Dallas, 1943-44; exec. dir. SW region Am. Friends of Hebrew U., Dallas, 1973; prin. Linkie Seltzer and The Exercise Co., Dallas, 1981; columnist Achievement Mag., 1985; profl. speaker Love in Business Makes Dollars and Sense, 1981-84; pres. Speakers Source Internat. Speakers Bur., 1989—; tchr. Dallas C.C. Sys., 1978-85. Author: (with Danny Anderson) Winners For Life-A Success Guide for Teenagers Using the Proven Power of Goal Setting; producer TV series: Covenant, 1972-73. Campaign chmn. women's div. Jewish Fedn. Dallas, 1970, pres. div., 1972-73; chmn. human rels. commn. Dallas Ind. Sch. Dist., 1968, pub. rels. Greater Dallas Cmty. Rels. Commn., 1983—. Named Campaigner of Yr., Jewish Fedn. Dallas, 1969. Mem. Internat. Group Agys. and Burs. Democrat. Office: PO Box 741414 Dallas TX 75374

COHN, MARIANNE WINTER MILLER, civic activist; b. Denver, Jan. 15, 1928; d. Henry Abraham II and Esther (Sheflan) Winter; m. Benjamin K. Miller, Dec. 29, 1948 (dec. Dec. 1972); children: Judy Ellen, Philip Henry (dec. 1996); m. Isidore Cohn Jr., Jan. 3, 1976; children: Ian Jeffrey, Lauren Kerry. Student, Colo. U., 1946-47. Mem. exec. bd. Greater New Orleans Tourist and Conv. Commn., 1985; chmn. spouse program arrangements Am. Coll. Surgeons, La., 1985; mem. exec. bd. NCCJ, New Orleans, 1987—, sec.,

1991-92, treas., 1993-94, nat. bd. dirs., 1993; bd. dirs. Jewish Endowment Found., New Orleans, 1987-88; mem. Arts Coun. of New Orleans, 1988—, v.p. devel. 1991-92, v.p. grants, exec. bd., 1995; pres. La. Mus. Found. of La. State Mus., 1989-90, bd. dirs., 1994—; mem. Sisterhood of Temple Emanuel Denver (pres. 1957-60); women's bd. dirs. Nat. Jewish Hosp. at Denver, 1951-80, pres. women's div., 1960-61, mem., sec. gov. bd., 1972-76; bd. dirs. New Orleans Symphony Aux., 1980; mem. nat. bd. Nat. Jewish Ctr., 1976—; chmn. Odyssey Ball of New Orleans Mus. Art, 1992; bd. dirs. La. Coun. for Music and Performing Arts, 1991-92; mem. exec. bd. Arts Coun. New Orleans, 1991-92, 95—; mem. governing bd. La. State Mus., 1992—; exec. bd. Arts Coun. 95' V.P. Grants, 1995-96, pres, 1997—. Recipient Edgar L. Feinberg Meml. award James D. Rives Surg. Soc., 1988, Woman of Fashion award Men of Fashion, 1989, Humanitarian award Nat. Jewish Ctr. Immunology and Respiratory Medicine, 1995. Republican.

COIL, CHARLES RAY, managed healthcare executive; b. Dallas, June 23, 1940; s. John Charles Jr. and Dixie W. (Riggs) C.; m. Sue Gail Lewis, Jan. 20, 1968; children: Christopher Ryan, Kimberly Ann. BBA, So. Meth. U., 1962. With Provident Life & Accident Ins. Co., Chattanooga, 1962-88; pres., chief exec. officer North Tex. Healthcare Network, Irving, Tex., 1988—. Republican. Methodist. Office: North Tex Healthcare 5601 N Macarthur Blvd Irving TX 75038-2616

COKE, C(HAUNCEY) EUGENE, consulting company executive, scientist, educator, author; b. Toronto, Ont., Can; s. Chauncey Eugene and Edith May (Redman) C.; m. Sally B. Tolmie, June 12, 1941. BSc with honors, U. Man., MSc magna cum laude; MA, U. Toronto; postgrad., Yale U.; PhD, U. Leeds, Eng., 1938. Dir. rsch. Courtaulds (Can.) Ltd., 1939-42; dir. R & D Guaranty Dyeing & Finishing Co., 1946-48; various exec. R & D positions Courtaulds (Can.) Ltd., Montreal, 1948-59, dir. R & D; mem. exec. com. Hart-Fibres Co., 1959-62; tech. dir. textile chem. Drew Chem. Corp., 1962-63; dir. new products fibers div. Am. Cynamid Co., 1963-68, dir. applications devel., 1968-70; pres. Coke & Assoc., Cons., Ormond Beach, Fla., 1970-78, chmn., 1978—; pres. Aqua Vista Corp. Inc., 1971-74; vis. rsch. prof. Stetson U., 1979—; internat. authority on man-made fibers; guest lectr. Sir George Williams Coll., Montreal, 1949-59; chmn. Can. adv. com. on Internat. Standards Orgn. Tech. Com. 38, 1951-58; mem. Can. Standards Assn., 1958-59; del. Textile Tech. Fedn. Can., 1948-57, bd. dirs., 1957-59. Contbr. articles to Can., U.S., Brit., Australian profl. jours. with translations into Japanese. Vice chmn. North Peninsula adv. bd. Volusia County Coun., 1975-78; mem. Halifax Area Study Commn., 1972-74, Volusia County Elections Bd., 1974-94; bd. dirs. Coun. Assns. North Peninsula, 1972-74, 76-77; pres. Greater Daytona Beach Rep. Mens Club, 1972-75; pres. Rep. Mens Club, 1972-75; pres. Rep. President's Forum, 1976-78, v.p., 1978-81. Recipient Bronze medal Can. Assn. Textile Colourists and Chemists, 1963. Fellow AAAS, Royal Soc. Chemistry (Gt. Britain, life), Soc. Dyers and Colourists (Gt. Britain), Inst. Textile Sci. (co-founder, 3d pres.), Chem. Inst. Can. (life, coun. 1958-61), Am. Inst. Chemistrs, N.J. Acad. Sci.; mem. Am. Assn. Textile Tech. (life, past pres., bronze medal), Can. Assn. Textile Colourists and Chemists (hon. life, past pres., bronz medal), N.Y. Acad. Scis. (life), U.S. Metric Assn. (life), Chemists Club. Home: 26 Aqua Vista Dr Ormond Beach FL 32176-3109 Office: Coke & Assoc Cons Ormond By The Sea Ormond Beach FL 32176

COKER, ALBERT STEINHART, JR., infectious disease consultant, physician; b. Greenville, Ala., July 4, 1939; s. Albert Steinhart and Lillian (Johnson) C.; m. Frances Marsha Whitehurst, Mar. 20, 1971; children: Jennifer, Leah, Emily. BS in Pharmacy, Auburn U., 1960; MD, Med. Coll. Ala., 1965. Diplomate Am. Bd. Internal Medicine. Intern in medicine Vanderbilt U. Hosp., Nashville, 1965-66, resident in medicine, 1966-67; sr. asst. resident in medicine U. Ala. Hosp. and Clinics, Birmingham, 1967-68, chief med. resident, 1968-69, fellow infectious diseases, 1971-73; pvt. practice Diagnostic Med. Clinic, Mobile, Ala., 1973—; chmn. medicine dept. Mobile Infirmary, 1983-86. Capt. USAF, 1969-71. Mem. ACP, AMA, Am. Soc. Microbiology, Infectious Disease Soc. Am. Methodist. Office: Diagnostic Med Clinic 1720 Springhill Ave Mobile AL 36604-1428

COKER, BERT L., principal; b. Dalton, Ga., Nov. 28, 1956; s. Gordon and Juanita (Bennett) C.; m. Joy Coker, Sept. 3, 1983; children: Brittany, Adam. BA in Music and English, Jacksonville (Ala) State U., 1978; MEd, W. Ga. Coll., 1988, DEd, 1995. Cert. tchr. music, behavior disorders, adminstrn. Tchr. Tunnel Hill Elem., Dalton, Ga., 1984-86, S.E. H.S., Dalton, Ga., 1986-88; assessment specialist Ga. Dept. Edn., Dalton, Ga., 1988-90; tchr. Child & Adolescent Ctr., Dalton, Ga., 1990-91, Eastbrook Mid. Sch., Dalton, Ga., 1990-92; asst. prin. Dawnville Elem. Sch., Dalton, Ga., 1992-95, Westside Elem., 1996—. Mem. Phi Mu Alpha, Pi Delta Kappa (historian 1989). Mem. Ch. of God. Home: 2102 Millican Ln Dalton GA 30721 Office: Whitfield County Schs Dawnville Elem Sch 1380 Dawnville Rd NE Dalton GA 30721

COKER, CHARLES WESTFIELD, diversified manufacturing company executive; b. Florence, S.C., 1933; m. Joan F. Sasser; 6 children. BA, Princeton U., 1955; MBA, Harvard U., 1957. With Sonoco Products Co., Hartsville, S.C., 1958—, v.p. adminstrn., 1961-67, v.p. gen. mgmt., corp. planning and fin., from 1967, exec. v.p., 1966-70, pres., chief exec. officer, dir., 1970-90, chmn. bd., chief exec. officer, 1990—; bd. dirs. State Capital Corp., Carolina Power and Light Co., NCNB Corp., Springs Industries Inc., Sara Lee Corp. Past pres. Hartsville Rotary Club, Pee Dee Area Coun. Boy Scouts Am. Recipient Silver Beaver award Boy Scouts Am. Mem. Palmetto Bus. Forum. 2d lt. USAR, 1957-63. Office: Sonoco Products Co 100 N. 2nd St Hartsville SC 29550-4302*

COKER, DONALD WILLIAM, economic, healthcare, valuation and banking consultant; b. Mobile, Ala., Nov. 26, 1945; s. William Mack and Gloria Antoinette (Croker) C.; m. Linda Carol Sandlin, July 12, 1969; children: Caroline Tiffany, Brittany Blaire. BA, U. Ala., 1968, postgrad., 1968; MA, Spring Hill Coll., 1996. Approved comml. arbitrator Am. Arbitration Assn. Trust mortgage officer AmSouth Bank, Mobile, 1968-72; sr. loan officer Gibraltar Savs., Houston, 1972-73; mortgage officer, asst. treas. Citicorp Real Estate, Houston, 1973-74; comml. loan officer M Bank-Houston, 1974-77; regional mgr. Comml. Credit Co., Houston, 1977-83, Ford Motor Credit, Houston, 1983-84; sr. v.p., mgr. lending and mortgage banking First Fed. Savs., San Antonio, 1984-85; exec. v.p. Home Savs., Houston, 1985-86; also bd. dirs. Home Savs.; supr. banking Tex. Savs. & Loan Dept., Houston, 1986-88; chmn. Fin. Inst. Mgmt. Svcs., Mobile, Ala., 1986—; mng. dir. Coker Consulting, Mobile, 1995—, Corp. Intelligence and Analysis, Mobile, 1994—; mng. dir. Present Value Econs., 1989—, Capstone Computer, 1990—, Capstone Ednl. Consulting, 1990—; CEO All Am. Asset Mgmt., 1988—, First Internat. Investment Bank, 1994; pres. 1st Nat. Sports Bank, 1989—; cons. Prentice-Hall Pub., IRS, FDIC, Resolution Trust Corp.; CEO All-Am. Mortgage, 1995—; cons. to fin. instns., attys., corps. and govt. agys.; legis. and govtl. cons.; nat. healthcare and profl. practice valuation cons.; expert witness on valuation, econ., fin. and banking. Author: Complete Guide to Income Property Financing, 1984, Self-Management, 1985; editor: Complete Real Estate Computer Workbook, 1986, The Complete Loan Officers' Handbook, 1997; contbr. articles to profl. jours. Trustee Katy Ind. Sch. Dist., Houston, 1987; treas. Nottingham Country Civic Club, Houston; precinct leader, del. and dep. voters registrar Rep. party. Mem. Nat. Assn. of State Savs. and Loan Suprs., Mortgage Bankers' Assn., Am. Bankers Assn., U.S. Savs. & Loan League, Houston C. of C. (bus. devel. com.). Republican. Episcopalian. Clubs: Sweetwater Country. Home and Office: PO Box 91182 Mobile AL 36691-1182

COKER, DONNA SUE, retail executive, nurse; b. Alexandria, Va., Aug. 10, 1957; d. David Stevenson and Betty Francis (Foley) Sisson; m. N. Frank Coker, Oct. 18, 1991. Diploma in nursing, Va. Bapt. Hosp., 1978; BS in Health Care Mgmt., Va. Commonwealth U., 1984. RN, Va. Critical care nurse Va. Bapt. Hosp., Lynchburg, 1978-81, 82, Dr.'s Hosp., Dallas, 1981, St. Mary's Hosp., Richmond, Va., 1982-85; supr. St. Luke's Hosp., Richmond, 1985-87; health care coord. Circuit City Stores, Inc., Richmond, 1987-88, safety coord., 1988-89, loss prevention analyst, 1989-94, loss prevention ops. supr., 1994—. Republican. Baptist. Home: PO Box 11182 Richmond VA 23230-1182 Office: Circuit City Stores Inc 9950 Mayland Dr Richmond VA 23233-1463

COKER, MARY SHANNON, surgical nurse; b. Pasadena, Tex., May 30, 1947; d. James Edward and Ruby Dee (Langford) Shannon; m. Sherman Leigh Coker, Jan. 25, 1987; children: John Lynn Brinkley, Jamie Leigh Brinkley Kelley, Amanda Renee Coker, Roy Leigh Coker. AAS, Lee Coll., Baytown, Tex., 1990. Insulator Daniel Constrn., Greenville, S.C., 1985-87; patient care attendant Humana Hosp., Baytown, 1988; staff perioperative nurse Meth. Hosp., Houston, 1989-91, Bay Coast Med. Ctr., Baytown, Tex., 1991—. Mem. Assn. Operating Room Nurses, Phi Theta Kappa. Home: 2111 Utah St Baytown TX 77520-6153

COKER, MELINDA LOUISE, counselor; b. Springfield, Mo., Apr. 28, 1946; d. Joe H. and Margaret L. (Owens) Bull; m. Richard H. Coker, Aug. 12, 1967; children: Shay, Candace, Logan. BA, Baylor U., 1968; MS, East Tex. State U., 1994. Nat. cert. counselor Nat. Bd. Counselor Cert.; lic. profl. counselor, Tex. Tchr. Houston Ind. Sch. Dist., 1968-71; owner, mgr. Greenleaves, Tyler, Tex., 1978-84; realtor Coldwell Banker, Tyler, 1989-91; counselor intern Hunt County Mental Health Mental Retardation, Greenville, Tex., 1993, Andrews Ctr., Tyler, 1994; career counselor intern Tyler (Tex.) Jr. Coll., 1994-95, spl. populations counselor, 1995—. Mem. ACA, Nat. Career Devel. Assn., Chi Sigma Iota. Home: 6701 La Costa Dr Tyler TX 75703

COKER, WILLIAM SIDNEY, historian, educator; b. Des Moines, July 18, 1924; s. William McKinnon and Myrtle (Spurgeon) C.; m. Hazel Pauline Gaskin, May 27, 1944 (dec. 1990); children: Judy, Nancy, Elizabeth, Terri; m. Frances Camferdam, April 9, 1992. BA with distinction, U. Okla., 1959, PhD, 1965; MA, U. So. Miss., 1962. From asst. to assoc. prof. U. So. Miss., Hattiesburg, 1966-69; from assoc. prof. to prof. U. West Fla., Pensacola, 1969-87, chmn. dept. history, 1987-91, prof. emeritus, 1992; dir. Papers of Panton, Leslie & Co. U. West Fla., 1973-87. Author: Spanish Censuses of Pensacola, 1981, (with others) Indian Traders of the Southeastern Spanish Borderlands, 1986 (Patrick award 1986, Phi Alpha Theta award 1986), Florida from Beginning to 1992. Recipient Rsch. award Nat. Historic Publs. and Records Commn., 1973-87. Home: 615 Bayshore Dr Apt 401 Pensacola FL 32507-3565

COLBERT-BEAVERS, ANNETTE DARCIA, silver company executive; b. Tulsa, Oct. 24, 1959; d. Buel and Bonnie Helen (Pickens) Colbert; 1 child, Siobhan Nicole. Student, Devry Inst., Dallas, 1979, Oklahoma City U., 1986. Tech. rep. Xerox Corp., Oklahoma City, 1979-80; field engr. NCR Corps., Oklahoma City, 1980; chief exec. officer Silver Mchts. Investment Trust & Holding div. Smith Co., Oklahoma City, 1981—; exec. dir., cons. Embassy, Inc., Oklahoma City, 1987—; TV producer, host Avant-Age Visage Prodn., Oklahoma City, 1988—. Fund raiser U.S. C. of C., Oklahoma City, 1985-86; project dir. Embassy Inc., Oklahoma City, 1986-87. Mem. Am. Mgmt. Assn., Am. Metal Assn., Gold and Silver Inst. Republican. Home: PO Box 780136 Oklahoma City OK 73178-0136 Office: Silver Mchts Investment Trust & Holding 6429 Hunting Hill Ln Oklahoma City OK 73116-3521

COLBORN, GENE LOUIS, anatomy educator, researcher; b. Springfield, Ill., Nov. 23, 1935; s. Adin Levi and Grace Downey (Tucker) C.; divorced; children: Robert Mark, Adrian Thomas, Lara Lee Colborn Russell; m. Sarah Ellen Crockett, Aug. 14, 1976; children: Jason Matthew, Nathan Tucker. BA with honors, Ky. Christian Coll., 1957; BS with honors, Milligan Coll., 1962; MS in Anatomy, Wake Forest U., 1964, PhD in Anatomy, 1967. Postdoctoral fellow U. N.Mex. Sch. Medicine, Albuquerque, 1967-68; asst. prof. U. Tex. Health Sci. Ctr., San Antonio, 1968-72, assoc. prof., 1972-75; assoc. prof. anatomy Med. Coll. Ga., Augusta, 1975-88, prof. anatomy, 1988—, prof. surgery, 1993—, dir. Ctr. for Clin. Anatomy, 1987—, dir. med. gross anatomy, 1975—, cons. dept. surgery, 1977—, prof. surgery, 1993—; clin. prof. surgery Emory U. Sch. Medicine; pres. Ga. State Anatomical Bd., 1983-93; cons. Eisenhower Army Med. Ctr., 1990—. Author: Practical Gross Anatomy, 1982, Surgical Anatomy, 1987, Hernias, 1988, Musculoskeletal Anatomy, 1989, Workbook of Surgical Anatomy, 1990, Clinical Gross Anatomy, 1993, Modern Hernia Repair, The Embryological and Anatomical Basis of Surgery, 1996; mem. editl. bd. Clin. Anatomy Jour.; contbr. numerous articles on cardiac conduction, nervous sys., primate anatomy, cell culture and clin. and surg. anatomy to profl. jours. Active San Antonio Symphony Mastersingers, 1970-75, Augusta Opera, 1975—, Augusta Choral Soc., 1975—; judge Regional Sci. Fairs, Augusta, 1978-90. Recipient Golden Apple award U. Tex. Health Sci. Ctr., 1975; Outstanding Med. Educator award Med. Coll. Ga., 1976, 77, 78, 82, 87, 88, 90, 91, Disting. Faculty award, 1978. Mem. AAUP, Am. Assn. Clin. Anatomists (membership chmn. 1982-86, councillor 1992-95, mem. editl. bd. Jour. Clin. Anatomy 1994—), Am. Assn. Anatomists, N.Y. Acad. Scis., KC (4th degree). Republican. Office: Med Coll Ga 15th At Laney Walker Blvd Augusta GA 30912

COLBOURN, TREVOR, retired university president, historian; b. Armidale, New South Wales, Australia, Feb. 24, 1927; came to U.S., 1948; s. Harold Arthur and Ella Mary (Henderson) C.; m. Beryl Richards Evans, Jan. 10, 1949; children—Katherine Elizabeth, Lisa Sian Elinor. B.A. with honors, U. London, 1948; M.A., Coll. William and Mary, 1949, Johns Hopkins, 1951; Ph.D., Johns Hopkins, 1953. From instr. to asst. prof. Pa. State U., 1952-59; from asst. prof. to prof. Am. history Ind. U., 1959-67; dean Grad. Sch., prof. history U. N.H., 1967-73; v.p. for acad. affairs San Diego State U., 1973-77, acting pres., 1977-78; pres. U. Central Fla., Orlando, 1978-89; Bd. dirs. Indsl. Devel. Commission Mid Fla.; bd. visitors Maxwell Air Univ. (chmn. 1985-86). Author: The Lamp of Experience, 1965, The Colonial Experience, 1966, (with others) The Americans: A Brief History, 1972, 4th edit., 1985; co-editor: (with others) The American Past in Perspective, 1970; editor: (with others) Fame and the Founding Fathers, 1974. Mem. Orgn. Am. Historians, Am. Assn. State Colls. and Univs. Office: U Cen Fla Office Pres Emeritus Orlando FL 32816

COLBY, LESTINA LARSEN, secondary education educator; b. Mt. Sterling, Ky., Apr. 19, 1937; d. Harold L. and Opal Kearney (Caudel) Larsen; m. Bruce Redfearn Colby, Dec. 28, 1962; children: Charles, Harold, Pamela. BS, U. Chgo., 1958, postgrad., 1958-62. Sci. tchr., debate coach Community High Sch., Midlothian, Ill., 1958-61; biology tchr., debate coach U. Chgo. Lab. Sch., 1961-66; sci. tchr. Springer Jr. High Sch., Wilmington, Del., 1977; biology and math. tchr. McKean High Sch., Wilmington, 1978; biology tchr., debate coach, student coun. advisor U. Liggett Sch., Grosse Pointe, Mich., 1979-93, Edsel B. Ford endowed sci. chair, 1990; biology tchr., chmn. sci. dept. Episcopal High Sch., Jacksonville, Fla., 1993—. Author: Teacher's Manual for Encyclopaedia Britannica's Evolution Unit, 1966, Plants and Animals, 1968. Mem. Nat. Assn. Biology Tchrs. (Mich. Outstanding Biology Tchr. 1990), Nat. Sci. Tchrs. Assn., Fla. Assn. Sci. Tchrs. Baptist. Office: Episcopal HS Jacksonville 4455 Atlantic Blvd Jacksonville FL 32207-2121

COLCLAZIER, JOHN WARREN, food company executive; b. Pawnee, Okla., Apr. 12, 1949; s. Clyde Stewart and Betty Ann (Woods) C.; m. Betty Ann Card, Aug. 4, 1984; 1 child, Jennifer LeAnn. Student, U. Okla., 1968-71, U. Houston. Restaurant mgr. Crystal's Pizza and Spaghetti, Oklahoma City, Ft. Worth, 1971-75; deli buyer/merchandiser Skaggs Alpha Beta, Richardson, Tex., 1975-85; nat. sales mgr. food svc. Pilgrim's Pride Corp., Dallas, 1985-89; dir. nat. accounts Hudson Foods, Inc., Rogers, Ark., 1989-90, Perdue Farms, Inc., Salisbury, Md., 1990-93; v.p. nat. accounts ConAgra Poultry Co., Birmingham, Ala., 1993-95; pres. Frisco Food Svc. Co., Louisville, 1995—. Office: Frisco Food Service Co Inc 4014 Goldstein Ln Louisville KY 40272-3062

COLDIRON, VICKI IRENE, farm owner; b. Whittier, Calif., May 1, 1945; d. Victor Ivan and Nell Eunice (Wetzel) C. BA in English, U. So. Calif., 1965. Cert. tchr. Tchr. Dept. Edn., L.A., 1965-66, Kahului, Hawaii, 1966-72; bartender Royal Lahaina (Hawaii) Hotel, 1973-90; ind. real estate speculator/developer Lahaina, 1986-90; owner/mgr. Maui Farms, Purcell, Okla., 1990—. Mem. Am. Quarter Horse Assn., Okla. Thoroughbred Assn., Tex. Thoroughbred Assn., Okla. Quarter Horse Racing Assn., Thoroughbred Owners/Breeders Assn. Democrat. Presbyterian. Home and Office: Maui Farms RR 2 Box 26 Purcell OK 73080-9609

COLDREN, SHARON LOUISE, strategic and corporate planner; b. New Castle, Pa., Aug. 7, 1951; d. Clarke Lincoln and Carol Coldren; m. Philip Jeffrey Strenger, Aug. 24, 1984; children: Maija, Diana. BA, Duke U., 1973; MSc, London Sch. of Econs., 1975. Various positions Am. Coun. on Edn., Washington, 1974-81; mgr. mktg. AT&T, N.J., 1981-84, mgr. new bus. devel., 1984-86; dir. corp. planning TSSI Inc., Ossining, N.Y., 1986-88; dir. strategic planning Pitney Bowes Inc., Stamford, Conn., 1989-90; dir. meter sys. Pitney Bowes Inc., Stamford, Conn., 1990-92. Author: The Constant Quest, 1980. Chmn. bd. Family Svc. of Westchester, White Plains, N.Y., 1991-92. Home and Office: PO Box 501197 Marathon FL 33050-1197

COLE, CHARLES DUBOSE, II, law educator; b. Monroeville, Ala., May 14, 1938. BSBA, Auburn U., 1960; JD cum laude, Samford U., 1966; LLM, NYU, 1971; D (hon.), Faculdade Marcelo Tupinamba, Sao Paulo, Brazil, 1991. Bar: Ala. 1966, U.S. Supreme Ct., 1971. Law clk., assoc. atty. Porterfield & Sch., Birmingham, Ala., 1965-66; prof. law Cumberland Sch. Law Samford U., Birmingham, 1966-75, 81—; Lucille S. Beeson prof. law and dir. internat. programs Cumberland Sch. Law, Birmingham, Ala., 1993—; dir. permanent study commn. Ala. Jud. System, 1972-74; dir. Ala. Jud. Conf. Criminal Justice Survey, 1973; dir. adv. com. Ala. jud. article implementation Ala. Dept. Ct. Mgmt., 1974-75; dir. so. regional office Nat. Ctr. for State Cts., Atlanta, 1975-79; adminstrv. dir. cts. Commonwealth of Ky., Frankfort, 1979-81; lectr. Cumberland Inst. for Continuing Legal Edn., Ala. Continuing Legal Edn., Josephson/Kluwer Bar Rev. Ctr. Am., Inc., 1967-87; law and social sci. adv. coun. Coll. Liberal Arts/Auburn U., 1991—, chmn. 1992-94; chmn. profl. adv. com. Office Advancement Auburn U., 1992-93; reporter civil justice adv. group Middle Dist. Ala., 1991-93; del. Moscow Conf. on Law and Econ. Coop., The Kremlin Palace, 1990; legal specialist (pro bono) Parliament of Ukraine, 1993; v.p. faculty Samford U., 1989-90; policy com. mem. Cumberland Sch. Law, 1989-92; mem. faculty exec. com. Samford U., 1988-89; del. U.S./Japan Bilateral Session, 1988; presenter U.S. Info Agy., Internat. Meeting Brazil/U.S., 1988; participant seminar Claremont McKenna Coll./NEH, 1986. Author: (with Brewer) Alabama Constitutional Law, 1992, (with Rulli) Comparative Constitutional Law: Brazil and the United States of America, 1996; contbr. articles to profl. jours. Named Outstanding Prof. Student Bar Assn./Cumberland Sch. Law, 1972-73, 83-84, Outstanding Alumnus Phi Alpha Delta, 1973. Mem. ABA (lectr. appellate judges seminar 1977-78), Am. Judicature Soc., Supreme Ct. Hist. Soc., Am. Trial Lawyers Assn. (faculty mem.), Ala. Bar Assn. (action group mem. 1984-85, chmn. 1985-88, reporter task force on jud. selection 1988-89, com. on the future of the profession 1990-91, task force on legal edn. 1992—, com. on judicial and legal reform 1994-95, chmn. 1995-96), Ukrainian Legal Found. (bd. fgn. advisors 1993—), Birmingham Bar Assn. Auburn U. Bar Assn. (adv. bd. 1992-94), Phi Alpha Delta. Home: 2337 Star Lake Dr Hoover AL 35226

COLE, EDITH FAE, dietitian, consultant; b. Benchley, Tex., Jan. 8, 1925; d. Horace and Bessie Mae (Seale) Cook; m. Charles Edward Cole, Feb. 12, 1979. BS, Tex. Woman's U., 1945, MA, 1947. Registered dietitian Am. Dietetic Assn. Intern Okla. A & M State U., 1946; asst. dietitian Tex. Woman's U., Denton, 1946-48; dietitian, asst. prof. U. Southwestern La., Lafayette, 1948-52; asst. dir. dietetics Hermann Hosp., Houston, 1952-55, dir. dietetics, 1955-74; pvt. practice cons. Crosby, Tex., 1974—; adj. asst. prof. U. Tex. Sch. Allied Health Sci., Houston, 1977-79. Author: Crosby's Heritage Preserved 1823-1949, 1992. Mem. Am. Dietetic Assn. (treas. 1973-75), Tex. Dietetic Assn. (pres. 1958-59, del. 1959-61, 69-71, Tex. Disting. Dietitian 1984), South Tex. Dietetic Assn. (treas. 1957-58, Disting. Dietitian of Yr. 1984), Crosby Huffman C. of C. Mem. Church of Christ. Home and Office: 1331 Hare Cook Rd Crosby TX 77532-7605

COLE, JAMES MARINER, JR., warehouse executive; b. Union, Miss., Sept. 28, 1915; s. James Mariner Sr. and Mary Corilla (Long) C.; m. Anna Lucile Ashley, July 18, 1944; children: Lucie Mae Cole Lane, James Anthony. BSBA, U. Ala., 1937. Office clk. Compress of Union, 1937-43, sec., treas., 1943-75; sec., treas. Interstate Compress & Warehouse Co., Meridian, Miss., 1943-75; pres. Interstate Mdse. Warehouse, Inc., Meridian, 1976—. Alderman Town of Union, 1949-77; pres. Newton County Cmty. Devel. Assn., Decatur, Miss., 1966-67; pres. bd. Newton County Cmty. Concert Assn., Decatur, 1983-84; mem. Choctaw Area coun. Boy Scouts Am., pres., 1956, exec. bd., 1949—; trustee Union Pub. Libr., 1973—. Recipient Silver Beaver award Choctaw Area coun. Boy Scouts Am., 1949. Mem. Miss. Cotton Compress and Cotton Warehouse Assn. (pres. 1952-54), Miss. Valley Cotton Compress and Warehouse Assn. (pres. 1954-55), Nat. Cotton Compress and Warehouse Assn. (pres. 1959-60), Miss. Econ. Coun. (bd. dirs. 1954-56, 63-65), Union C. of C. (pres. 1963-64, 82-83), Union Golf Club (pres. 1954-55), Union Lions (pres. 1946-47), Alpha Tau Omega, Phi Eta Sigma, Beta Gamma Sigma. Presbyterian. Home: 211 Peachtree St Union MS 39365-2619 Office: Interstate Mdse Warehouse Inc 1601 2nd St Meridian MS 39301

COLE, JAMES YEAGER, legal sentencing advocate, consultant; b. Cleve., Sept. 20, 1957; s. Charles and Nancy C. Cert., Blackstone Sch. Law, Dallas, 1980; JD, Elysion Coll., 1980; MA, M.C.I., London, 1981; PhD, N.W. London U., 1981. Cons. Cole Corp., Tallahassee, 1979-81; judge Inst. Advanced Law Study, Las Vegas, 1981-84; cons., sentencing advocate Cullowhee, N.C., 1984—. Recipient Presdl. medal of Merit Pres. Ronald Reagan, Washington, 1980, Knight Comdr. Royal Knights of Justice, London, 1981, Venerable Order of the Knights of Michael The Archangel Knight Chevalier. Mem. Am. Judges Assn., World Judges Assn., Am. Judicature Soc., Nat. Judges Assn., Internat. Bar Assn., N.C. Sheriff's Assn., Jackson County C. of C. Home: S Main St Waynesville NC 28786 Office: AAII PO Box 25 Waynesville NC 28786-0025

COLE, JOHN PRINCE, lawyer; b. Carrollton, Ga., Mar. 18, 1963; s. Jerry Ephraim Cole and Gloria June (Rowe) Ayers. AB, Harvard Coll., 1985; JD magna cum laude, Mercer Law Sch., 1991. Bar: Ga., U.S. Dist. Ct. (no., mid. dist.) Ga., U.S. Ct. Appeals (11th cir.). Law clerk Mitchell, Coppedge, Wester, Bisson & Miller, Dalton, Ga., 1989, Ga. Atty. Gen., Atlanta, 1990; assoc. Anderson, Walker & Reichert, Macon, Ga., 1991-94; gen. asst. to pres. Mercer U., Macon, Ga., 1994—. Trustee First Bapt. Ch., Macon, 1993—, Ga. Children's Home, 1996—; funds allocation com. United Way Ctrl. Ga., 1992-94. Capt. U.S. Army Res. Mem. ABA (labor and employement sect.), Nat. Assn. Coll. & Univ. Attys., Phi Kappa Phi. Democrat. Office: Mercer U 1400 Coleman Ave Macon GA 31207-1000

COLE, KIMBERLY ALICE, critical care and post-anesthesia care nurse; b. Mt. Pleasant, N.Y., Sept. 8, 1962; d. Elhannah and Mrytle (Tedford) C. BSN, Ea. Ky. U., 1985. RN, Ky., N.C.; cert. in ACLS, CCRN. Nurse apprentice U. Ky. Med. Ctr., Lexington; med. surgical staff nurse, post anesthesia care unit and CCU Humana U. Hosp., Louisville; staff nurse open heart unit Duke U. Med. Ctr., 1991-95; SICU/MICU Rex Health Care, Raleigh, 1996—. Mem. AACCN.

COLE, LOUIS B., retired educator; b. Amarillo, Tex., Aug. 19, 1917; s. Edward E. and Effie Mae (Daugherty) C.; m. Leona Lewis, Dec. 22, 1943; children: Kathryn, Jackie Ann, Marvine, Ginger. BBA, West Tex. State U., 1940; MEd, U. New Orleans, 1976. Cert. tchr., La. Commd. 2d lt. USAF, 1943, advanced through grades to col., ret., 1970; aerospace sci. instr. Jefferson Parish Schs., Harvey, La., 1972-89. Aerospace educator People to People, China, 1987. Decorated Legion of Merit, Air medal. Mem. World Aerospace Edn. Orgn. (dir., pres. 1983-95), Daedalians (flight rep. 1992), Phi Delta Kappa (dir., pres. U. New Orleans chpt. 1976-96), Kappa Delta Pi, Pi Kappa Pi. Home: 4500 Leo St Marrero LA 70072-3842

COLE, LUTHER FRANCIS, former state supreme court associate justice; b. Alexandria, La., Oct. 25, 1925; s. Clem and Catherine (Wiley) C.; m. Juanita Barton, Mar. 9, 1945; children: Frances Jeannette, Jeffrey Martin, Christopher Warren. Student, La. Tech. U., 1943-44; JD, La. State U., 1950. Ptnr. Cole, Mengis & Durant, Baton Rouge, 1950-66; judge 19th Jud. Dist., Baton Rouge, 1966-75, chief judge, 1975-79; judge Ct. Appeals, Baton Rouge, 1979-86; assoc. justice Supreme Ct. La., New Orleans, 1986-92; chmn. Jud. Budgetary Control Bd., 1990-92; mem. La. Bd. Ethics for Elected Ofcls., 1994—; bd. dirs. La. Lottery Corp., 1995—. Rep. La. Legis., Baton Rouge, 1964-66; v.p. Merchants Assn., Baton Rouge, 1954; chmn. awards Boy Scouts Am., Baton Rouge, 1956; mem. Civic Ctr. com., Baton Rouge, 1971-74; bd. dirs. Blundon Home, Baton Rouge, 1984-86. Served to lt. (j.g.) USN, 1943-46. Mem. ABA (ann. meeting 1991, Jury Standards award 1991), La. Bar Assn., Baton Rouge Bar Assn. (pres. 1966), La. Dist. Judges

Assn. (pres. 1972-73). Democrat. Baptist. Club: Exchange (Baton Rouge) (pres. 1954). Home: 9213 Hilltrace Ave Baton Rouge LA 70809

COLE, PATRICIA ANN, elementary school educator; b. Huntington, W.Va., Dec. 26, 1957; d. Albert James and Nancy Suzanne (Linsenmeyer) Aluise; m. Dennis Franklin Cole, Aug. 1, 1981; 1 child, Dennis Franklin Jr. BA in Elem. Edn./Math. magna cum laude, Marshall U., 1980, MA in Elem. Edn. summa cum laude, 1986. Cert. elem. tchr., math. tchr., W.Va. Bank teller First Huntington Nat. Bank, 1980; elem. and jr. H.S. tchr. Our Lady of Fatima Sch., Huntington, 1980—, tutor, math. olympiad coach and moderator, 1988—; presenter W.Va. Sci. Tchrs. Convention, Huntington, 1994. Vol. Marshall Artist Series, Huntington, 1982, W.Va. Spl. Olympics, 1988, 89, Huntington Mus. of Art, 1984, 86; sec. Ladies Guild Sacred Heart Ch., Huntington, 1988; area chmn. Heart Fund, Huntington, 1980. Grantee Diocese of Wheeling, 1991, 95. Mem. Cabell County Reading Coun., Women's Club of Huntington (com. chmn. 1984-86, treas. 1985, social chmn. 1986, 3d vice chmn. 1987, 2d vice chmn. 1988, 1st vice chmn. 1989, chmn. 1990, Outstanding Chmn. award 1984, 86, Bd. Mem. of Yr. 1987, Dist. Mem. of Yr. 1991), Gamma Beta Phi. Home: 5112 Nickel Plate Dr Huntington WV 25705-3134

COLE, SALLY ANN, critical care nurse; b. Phila., Jan. 9, 1940; d. William Joseph and Sara Erma (Jones) C.; m. Daniel Cesarini, Feb. 18, 1955 (div. Dec. 1966); children: Daniel Lee, Robert Harold, Richard Dale. Grad., North Montgomery County Area Vocational Tech. Sch., Lansdale, Pa., 1969; ASN, Univ. State N.Y., Albany, 1989. RN, Fla. Nurse North Penn Hosp., Lansdale, 1969-73; LPN St. Petersburg (Fla.) Gen. Hosp., 1974-89, ICU nurse, 1974-95, RN, 1989-95; RN, Fla.; cert. ACLS, Am. Heart Assn. Recipient Best Bedside Nursing Care award North Montgomery County Nursing Assn., 1969. Fellow AACN. Republican. Home: 4231 44th Ave N Saint Petersburg FL 33714-3548

COLE, TOM, state official; b. Shreveport, La., Apr. 28, 1949; s. John D. and Helen Gale Cole; m. Ellen Decker; children: Mason, John. BA, Grinnell Coll., 1971; MA, Yale U., 1974; PhD, U. Okla., 1984. Fellow Yale U., 1974; instr. U. Okla., 1975-78, Okla. Bapt. U., 1981; exec. dir. Okla. Rep. Com., 1980-81; dir. dist. svcs. congressman Mickey Edwards U.S. Congress, 1982-84; exec. dir. Reagan-Bush Campaign, Okla., 1984; chmn. Okla. State Rep. Party, 1985-89; pres. Cole, Hargrave, Snodgrass & Assocs., 1989—; now also sec. State of Okla.; lectr. Grinnell Coll., 1977, 79; mem. Cleve. County Rep. Exec. Com., 1979-85, Okla. County Rep. Exec. Com., 1983-85; campaign mgr. Helen Cole for State Rep., 1978, 80, 82, Helen Cole for State Senate, 1984, Ken Wilson for County Commr., 1981, Evelyn Orth for County Commr., 1981; dep. campaign mgr. Daxon for Gov., 1981-82. Fullbright fellow U. London; Watson felow Inst. Hist. Rsch., London; recipient Robert A. Taft award Okla. Rep. Party, Guardian Small Bus. award Nat. Fedn. Ind. Bus. Mem. Am. Hist. Assn., Inst. Hist. Rsch., Soc. Study Labor History, Ea. London Hist. Soc., Okla. C. of C., Phi Alpha Theta. Methodist. Office: Okla Sec State 2300 N Lincoln Blvd Rm 101 Oklahoma City OK 73105-4897*

COLEMAN, BRENDA FORBIS, gifted and talented educator; b. Dallas, May 17, 1951; d. Thomas Carlyle and Dorothy Jean (Tillerson) Forbis; m. Rufus Andrew Coleman, July 2, 1971; 1 child, Christopher Andrew. BS, Dallas Bapt. U., 1972; MEd, East Tex. State U., 1979; cert. gifted and talented, Tex. Woman's U., 1990. Elem. tchr. Plano (Tex.) Ind. Sch. Dist., 1972-79; elem. tchr. Lewisville (Tex.) Ind. Sch. Dist., 1983-86, gifted and talented facilitator, 1986-89; elem. tchr. Lake Dallas (Tex.) Ind. Sch. Dist., 1989-91, gifted and talented EXCEL program coord., 1991—; presenter in field, Univ. Interscolastic League acad. coach, 1995-96. Organizer canned food dr. Lake Dallas Families, 1989. Mem. Tex. Assn. for Gifted and Talented, Assn. of Tex. Profl. Educators, Phi Delta Kappa. Republican. Methodist. Home: 109 Woody Trl Lake Dallas TX 75065-3123 Office: Lake Dallas Ind Sch Dist 190 Falcon Dr Lake Dallas TX 75065

COLEMAN, CARL, air force noncommissioned officer; b. Yosemite, Ky., June 22, 1948; s. Dennie and Thelma (Luster) C.; m. Kum Chun Yi, Oct. 4, 1972; 1 child, Cindy Lea. Enlisted man USAF, 1967; food svc. specialist, 1967-83; corrosion controller USAF, Robins AFB, Ga., 1983-87, C-141 aircraft painter, 1987—. Author: (poetry) Come with Me to a Quiet Place, 1992, In My Eye My Best, 1995. Mem. Soc. Am. Poets (v.p. Warner Robins chpt. 1996—). Democrat. Baptist. Home: 308 Sparta St Warner Robins GA 31088

COLEMAN, H. ROBERT, food company executive; b. 1943. Grad., Allegheny Coll., 1965; grad. degree, U. South Fla., 1973. With Arthur Young, Tampa, Fla., 1973-77; with MGIC, Tampa, 1977-83, with parent co., 1983—; sr. v.p., CFO Turner Foods Corp., 1988—. With USN, 1965-70. Office: Turner Foods Corp 25450 Airport Rd Punta Gorda FL 33950-5746*

COLEMAN, JAMES EUGENE, national laboratory administrator; b. Bronx, N.Y., Sept. 6, 1945; s. James Michael and Helen Mary (Nathan) C.; m. Therese A. Carrieres, Aug. 8, 1970; 1 child, Jean Marie. BA in English, Coll. Santa Fe, 1969; MA in Pub. Adminstrn., U. N.Mex., 1971. Adminstrv. asst. to city mgr. City of Albuquerque, 1971-73; dean, asst. prof. U. Albuquerque, 1973-76; asst. dir. Tng. Ctr. ERDA, Oak Ridge, Tenn., 1976-78; assoc. dir. Exec. Seminar Ctr. CSC, U.S. Office Pers. Mgmt., Kings Point, N.Y., 1978-80; chief of staff Adminstrn. Divsn. Lawrence Berkeley Lab. U. Calif., Berkeley, 1980-84; v.p. human resources AmeriWest Fin. Corp., Albuquerque, 1984-85; assoc. dir for adminstrn. Thomas Jefferson Nat. Accelerator Facility (formerly CEBAF), Newport News, Va., 1985—; adj. instr. U. N.Mex., Albuquerque, 1975. Mem. charter revision com. City Govt. Albuquerque, 1974. With USMC, 1965-67, Vietnam. Mem. ASPA, Peninsula Track Club (pres. 1995, 96), Peninsula Triathlon Club, Peninsula Bicycling Assn., Phi Delta Kappa. Office: Jefferson Lab 12000 Jefferson Ave Newport News VA 23606-4323

COLEMAN, JAMES JULIAN, JR., lawyer, industrialist, real estate executive; b. New Orleans, May 7, 1941; s. James Julian Sr. and Dorothy Louise (Jurisich) C.; m. Carol Campbell Owen, Dec. 19, 1970 (dec. Sept. 1979); 1 child, James Owen; m. Mary Olivia Cochrane Cushing, Oct. 12, 1985. BA, Princeton U., 1963; postgrad. in law, Oxford (Eng.) U., 1963-65; JD, Tulane U., 1968. Bar: La. 1969, U.S. Supreme Ct. 1969. Chmn. Internat.-Matex Tank Terminals, New Orleans, 1969—; pres. Coleman Devel. Co., New Orleans, 1969—, IMTT, Quebec, 1993—; ptnr. Coleman, Johnson & Artigues, New Orleans, 1972—; chmn. DownTown Parking Service, New Orleans, 1978—; pres. City Ctr. Properties, New Orleans, 1980—; chmn. East Jersey R.R. and Terminal Co., 1993; trustee Loving Found., New Orleans, R.L. Blaffer Found., Houston. Author: Gilbert Antoine de St. Maxent: The Spanish Frenchman of New Orleans, 1975. Mem. Princeton U. History Coun., 1982—; mem. N.J. Commn. on Sci. and Tech., 1992—. Named H.M. Hon. Brit. Consul for La., Brit. Consulate, New Orleans, 1975—, to Order of Brit. Empire, Queen Elizabeth II, London, 1986. Mem. ABA, La. Bar Assn., N.Y. Yacht Club, N.Y. Racquet Club, Ramada Tejas Club Houston, So. Yacht Club, New Orleans Lawn Tennis Club. Republican. Mem. Ch. of Christ Scientists. Office: Coleman Johnson & Artigues 321 St Charles Ave 10th Fl New Orleans LA 70130-3145

COLEMAN, JEAN BLACK, nurse, physician assistant; b. Sharon, Pa., Jan. 11, 1925; d. Charles B. and Sue E. (Dougherty) Black; m. Donald A. Coleman, July 3, 1946; children: Sue Ann Lopez, Donald Ashley. RN, Spencer Hosp. Sch. Nursing, Meadville, Pa., 1945; student Vanderbilt U., 1952-54. Nurse, dir. nursing Bulloch Meml. Hosp., Statesboro, Ga., 1948-51, nurse supr. surgery, 1954-67, dir. nursing, 1967-71; physicians asst., nurse anesthetist to Robert H. Swint, Statesboro, 1971—; physician asst. to Dr. Earl L. Alderman, 1996—; mem. Pa. adv. com. Ga. Med. Bd., 1989—. Recipient Dean Day Smith Svc. to Mankind award, 1995; named Woman of Yr. in Med. Field, Bus. and Profl. Women, 1980. Mem. ANA, Ga. Nurses Assn., Am. Acad. Physicians Assts., Ga. Assn. Physicians Assts. (bd. dirs. 1975-79, v.p. 1979-80, pres. 1980-81), Ga. Bd. Med. Examiners (mem. physician assts. adv. com. 1987—, ex-officio mem. 1994). Democrat. Roman Catholic.

COLEMAN, JOEL LEE, literature educator; b. Bethesda, Md., Sept. 25, 1970; s. Avery Lewis and Barbara Jean (Waesche) C.; m. Michele Lee Voorhaar, Aug. 15, 1992. BA, Va. Mil. Inst., 1992; MA, U. Ga., 1994, postgrad., 1994—. Instr. English Riverside Mil. Acad., Gainesville, Ga., 1993-94; lectr. comparative lit. U. Ga., Athens, 1994—. Stuttgart Seminar fellowship U. Stuttgart, Germany, 1995; Woodward Scholarship Va. Mil. Inst., 1992, Fulbright Rsch. Scholarship U.S. Govt., 1996—; rsch. grantee Friedrich-Alexander U., Germany, 1995. Mem. Am. Comparative Lit. Assn., MLA, Pi Delta Phi, Kappa Alpha Order. Republican. Mem. LDS Ch. Office: U Ga 128 Park Hall Athens GA 30602

COLEMAN, JULIE KATHRYN, middle school educator; b. Peoria, Ill., Sept. 18, 1955; d. John Edward and Mary Ann (Koch) Birdoes Jr.; m. Richard Lee Coleman, Aug. 14, 1976; children: William Casey, Jaime Lee. BS in Edn., Ill. State U., 1977, MS in English, 1986. Cert. elem. educator, secondary English tchr., Ill., Ala., Fla. Tchr. English Norwood Sch., Peoria, Ill., 1977-85; tchr. Saint Pius X Sch., Mobile, Ala., 1985-86, Cora Castlen Elem. Sch., Grand Bay, Ala., 1986-87; tchr. Dr. W. J. Creel Elem. Sch., Melbourne, Fla., 1987-89, tchr., team chairperson, 1989-93; 7th and 9th grade lit. tchr. DeLaura Jr. High Sch., Satellite Beach, Fla., 1993—; adv. bd. Limestone Area Curriculum Adv. Com., Peoria, 1977-85; adv. com. mem. Peoria County Inst. Curriculum Com., 1982-85; presenter in field. Mem. Metro-Mobile Reading Coun., Brevard Reading Coun., Delta Kappa Gamma-Beta Sigma. Democrat. Roman Catholic. Home: 305 Park Ave Indian Harbour Beach FL 32937

COLEMAN, LESTER L., corporate lawyer. Gen. counsel, exec. v.p. Halliburton & Co., Dallas. Office: Halliburton Co 500 N Akard St Dallas TX 75201-3391*

COLEMAN, MALCOLM JAMES, JR., band director, music educator; b. Mexia, Tex., Feb. 4, 1947; s. Malcolm James and Wilma (Freeman) C. AAS, Navarro Coll., 1967; MusB, U. North Tex., 1970, M in Music Edn., 1975, PhD, 1987; MusD (hon.), London Inst. Applied Rsch., 1991, Inst. Coordinated Rsch., Australia, 1991, Acad. of Scis. Humanities U., Paris, 1991; DSc (hon.), Collegium Sancti Spiritus, Calif., 1991, The Internat. U., Bombay, 1991; Prof. (hon.), European Sci. & Ednl. Instn., Brussels, 1991; Full Accreditation (hon.), Internat. Cultural Correspondence Inst., Madras, India, 1991; MD (hon.), U. Guadalajara, Mexico, 1993. Lic. profl. counselor, Tex., cert. sch. counselor, TRT counselor. Flute player NORAD Band, Colo., 1970-73; band dir. Hubbard High Sch., Tex., 1974-75, Bremond High Sch., Tex., 1977-79; counselor Pecos-Barstow-Toyah Ind. Sch. Dist., Tex., 1979-84; band dir., flute tchr. Pharr-San Juan-Alamo I.S.D., Tex., 1985—; part time flute instr. U. Tex., Pan Am, 1995—. Flute and piccolo player, McAllen Town Band, Tex., 1985—, First Baptist Ch., Pecos, 1979-84; flute, piccolo player Rio Grande Valley Wind Symphony, 1994-95; prin. flutist Rio Grande Valley Symphony Orch., 1994-95; flute player Brownsville Cmty. Band, 1990-93. Served with U.S. Army, 1970-73. Recipient Commemorative Lifelong Achievemnt medal of Honor, 1987. Mem. NEA, Tex. Tchrs. Assn. (state del. 1981-82), Pecos-Barstow-Toyah Edn. Assn. (v.p. 1981-82, sec. 1983-84), Tex. Music Edn. Assn., Nat. Flute Assn., Tex. Bandmasters Assn., Internat. Parliament for Safety and Peace, Order KT's Jerusalem, Royal Order of Bohemian Crown (knight and baron), Assn. St. George the Martyr (knight), Holy Cross of Jerusalem (knight), Lofsenic Ursinius Order (knight and comdr.), Legion Aigle de Mer (capt.), Order of San Ciriaco (knight) (Italy), Circulo Nobiliario de los Caballeros (knight) (Spain), Ordre Souverain du Saint Sepulcre (Chevalier grand croix).

COLEMAN, MARION LESLIE, insurance company executive; b. Mobile, Ala., Mar. 20, 1925; s. Luther Woodward and Carrie (Lockler) C.; student pub. schs.; m. Joyce Kelley, Aug. 29, 1944; children: Connie Davis, Woodward L. and Franklin M. (twins). Agt., Life Ins. Co. Ga., Mobile, 1946-55, dist. mgr., El Dorado, Ark., 1955-56, Hattiesburg, Miss., 1957-60, Meridian, Miss., 1960-64; v.p., agy. dir. Nat. Preferred Life Ins. Co., Atlanta, 1964-65; v.p. tng. Found. Life Ins. Co., Atlanta, 1965—; v.p. The Triple C Real Estate and Devel. Co., 1980—; v.p. Kelley-Blakely Land Corp., Mobile; pres. Yamaha Sports World, Meridian, Melco Ltd. Custom Tailors, Meridian, Meridian Motors, Buddy Coleman Enterprises, Meridian; div. mgr. Jefferson Standard Life Ins. Co., Meridian; v.p. Merchandizers Inc. (Gibson Discount Center), Meridian; dir. Gulf Cascade Investment Properties, Inc., Long Beach, Miss. Served with USNR, 1943-46. Mem. Life Underwriters Assn., Sales and Mktg. Execs. Club. Home and Office: 2100 23rd Ave Meridian MS 39301-2137

COLEMAN, MARY STALLINGS, retired chief justice; b. Forney, Tex.; d. Leslie C. and Agnes B. (Huther) Stallings; m. Creighton R. Coleman, June 24, 1939 (dec.); children: Leslie Coleman Hagan, Carol Coleman-Steenson. B.A., U. Md., 1935; J.D., George Washington U., 1939; LL.D., Eastern Mich. U., 1974, Western Mich. U., 1974; L.H.D., Nazareth Coll., 1973; LL.D., Alma Coll., 1973, Olivet Coll., 1973, Detroit Coll. Law, 1975, Adrian Coll., 1976, U. Md., 1978, Saginaw Valley State Coll., 1979, Ferris State Coll., 1981, Hope Coll., 1981, N.Y. Law Sch., 1982; D.P.A., Albion Coll., 1982, U. Detroit, 1983, Grand Valley State Coll., 1984. Bar: D.C. 1940, Mich. 1950. Practiced in Washington, 1940-46; ptnr. Wunsch & Coleman, Battle Creek, Mich., 1950-61; probate and juvenile ct. judge Calhoun County, Mich., 1961-73; justice Mich. Supreme Ct., 1973-83; dir. K Mart Internat., Nat. Bank Detroit and NBD Bancorp, Biggs/Gilmore; adv. mem. Nat. Bank Detroit, NBD Bancorp. Contbr. articles to profl. pubs. Trustee emeritus Albion Coll.; mem. Nat. Commn. for Observance of Internat. Women's Year, 1975-76. Recipient Disting. Career award Law Sch., George Washington U., 1973, Alumni Achievement award, 1983, Disting. Alumni award U. Md., 1973, Disting. Mem. award Phi Kappa Phi, 1973, award Calhoun County Bd. Edn., 1964, award NAACP Young Adults, 1969, George award Enquirer & News, 1969, Internat. Wyman award Alpha Omicron Pi, 1975, Disting. Woman award Mich. Bus. and Profl. Women's Club, 1973, Religious Heritage of Am. award, 1974, Disting. Citizen award Mich. State U., 1977, joint resolution of commendation Mich. Legis., 1977, 82, DAR medal of honor, 1978, Disting. Svc. award Mich. Juvenile Detention Assn., 1980, Disting. Alumna award George Washington U., 1980, Award of Merit Am. Judges Assn., 1980, Disting. Vol. Leadership award March of Dimes, 1981, Disting. Jurist award Miss. State U. Pre-Law Soc., 1988; named Woman of Yr. Mich. Assn. Professions, 1976, U. Md. Hall of Fame, 1995, 1 of 10 Top Michigians of Yr., 1980, Disting. Woman Northwood U., 1981, Mich. Women's Hall of Fame, 1983. Fellow Mich. Bar Found. (founder); mem. AAUW (Disting. Svc. award Mich. 1979), PEO, Mich. Bar Assn. (Champion of Justice award 1993), Mich. Assn. Woman Lawyers, Am. Assn. Women Judges, Bus. and Profl. Women's Club, Am. Legion Aux., Jr. League (hon.), Big Sisters-Big Bros. (hon.), Altrusa Internat. (hon.), Gainesville Golf and Country Club, The Heritage Club (Gainesville), Beta Sigma Phi, Delta Kappa Gamma, Alpha Delta Kappa. Home: 415 Green Dolphin Dr S Placida FL 33946-2229 also: 2805-D214 NW 83rd St Gainesville FL 32606

COLEMAN, MICHAEL DORTCH, nephrologist; b. Jackson, Tenn., June 19, 1944; s. Ivery R. and Kathleen (Campbell) C.; children by previous marriage: Michael Dortch, Christopher Mathew; m. Stephanie Sherean Summers; 1 child, Cassandra Sherean. BA in Chemistry, U. Ark., 1966; MD, Duke U., 1970. Diplomate Am. Bd. Internal Medicine. Intern, Duke U. Med. Sch., Durham, N.C., 1970-71, resident internal medicine, 1971-72, nephrology fellow, 1972-74; practice medicine specializing in nephrology, Durham, 1972-74, Kannapolis, N.C., 1973-74, Ft. Smith, Ark., 1974—; nephrology cons. Cabarras County Hosp., Kannapolis, 1973; chief dept. nephrology Holt Krock Clinic, Ft. Smith, 1974—, dir. dialysis Holt Krock Dialysis Ctr., 1974—, Sparks Regional Med. Center, Ft. Smith, 1974—, chief medicine, 1994-96; dir. dialysis St. Edward's Mercy Med. Ctr., Ft. Smith, 1980—; assoc. prof. medicine U. Ark., Ft. Smith, 1976—; mem. med. rev. bd. Ark. Kidney Disease Commn., 1974—; nephrology cons., 1974—; mem. exec. com. and med. rev. bd. Ark.-Okla. Endstage Renal Disease Coun., 1977—. Bd. dirs. Ark. Tennis Assn., Jr. Tennis Coun., Holt Krock Clinic, Ft. Smith, Ark.; bd. dirs., mem. fin. com. Holt Krock Clinic. Mem. Internat. Soc. Nephrology, Renal Physician Assn., Am. Soc. Nephrology, Am. Heart Assn., AMA, Ark. Med. Assn., Sebastian County Med. Assn., Ft. Smith Racquet Club (bd. dirs., pres.), Town Club of Ft. Smith, Hardscrabble Country Club, Alpha Omega Alpha. Contbr. articles to med. jours. Office: 1500 Dodson Ave Fort Smith AR 72901-5128

COLEMAN, RICHARD WALTER, biology educator; b. San Francisco, Sept 10, 1922; s. John Crisp and Reta (Walter) C.; m. Mildred Bradley, Aug. 10, 1949 (dec.); 1 child, Persis C. BA, U. Calif., Berkeley, 1945, PhD, 1951. Rsch. asst. div. entomology and parasitology U. Calif., Berkeley, 1946-47, 49-50; ind. rsch., 1951-61; prof. biology, chmn. dept. Curry Coll., Milton, Mass., 1961-63; chmn. div. scis. and math. Monticello Coll., Godfrey, Ill., 1963-64; vis. prof. biology Wilberforce U., Ohio; 1964-65; prof. sci. Upper Iowa U., Fayette, 1965-89; prof. emeritus sci., 1989—; collaborator natural history div. Nat. Park Svc., 1952; spl. cons. Arctic Health Rsch. Ctr., USPHS, Alaska, 1954-62; apptd. explorer Commr. N.W. Ty., Yellowknife N.W. Ty., Can., 1966. Contbr. articles to profl. reports. Mem. AAAS, Nat. Health Fedn., Iowa Acad. Sci., Geol. Soc. Iowa (affiliate), Am. Inst. Biol. Scis., Nat. Sci. Tchrs. Assn., Ecol. Soc. Am., Am. Soc. Limnology and Oceanography, Am. Bryological and Lichenological Soc., Arctic Inst. N.Am., N.Am. Benthological Soc., Am. Malacological Union, Assn. Midwestern Coll. Biology Tchrs., The Nature Conservancy, Nat. Assn. Biology Tchrs., Fla. Auctioneers Assn., Nat. Auctioneers Assn., Sigma Xi. Methodist.

COLEMAN, ROGERS KING, insurance company executive; b. Palestine, Tex., Dec. 28, 1931; s. William Cowles and Willie (King) C.; m. Mary Lou Price, Dec. 27, 1951; children: Pamela Jean Coleman Travis, Mary Candace Ann Coleman Stroup, Christopher Clayton. BS, Tex. Christian U., 1953; MD, Baylor U., 1956. Diplomate Am. Bd. Abdominal Surgery. Intern John Peter Smith Hosp., Ft. Worth, 1956-57, resident, 1957-58; pvt. practice physician Brownwood, Tex., 1958-76; assoc. med. dir. Blue Cross & Blue Shield of Tex., Dallas, 1976-86, v.p., med. dir., 1986-88, exec. v.p., 1988-89, exec. v.p., chief operating officer, 1990, pres., chief exec. officer, 1991—. Board dirs. Juliette Fowler Homes, Dallas, 1978-86, chmn. bd. dirs., 1984-85. Recipient Exceptional Svc. award U.S. Dept. Health and Human Svcs., 1984. Mem. AMA, Tex. Med. Assn. (vice councilor, bd. councilors), Am. Soc. Abdominal Surgery, Dallas County Med. Soc. Office: Blue Cross & Blue Shield 901 S Central Expy Richardson TX 75080-7302

COLEMAN, RONALD LEE, insurance claims executive; b. Danville, Va., June 10, 1941; s. Raymond Lee and Mildred Sue (Floyd) C.; m. Stephanie Walther Barton Ewalt; children: Ronald Lee, Christopher Brent. BSBA summa cum laude, Va. Poly. Inst. and State U., 1964; BS in Pub. Adminstrn. summa cum laude, U. Richmond, 1964, postgrad., 1971; postgrad. law sch., U. Va., 1980. Pres. Johnson & Coleman, Ltd., Richmond, 1974-79, Ron Coleman & Assocs., Ltd., Richmond, 1981—; v.p. Schnell, Johnson & Coleman, Ltd., Richmond, Va., 1979-81; adj. prof. U. Tex., Austin, Pa. State U., State College; adv. coun. Pamplin Bus. Sch., Va. Tech. Author: Investigation and Handling of Aviation Claims, 1981, Presentation of Evidence in Accident Reconstruction Cases, 1989, others; editor-in-chief Claimsman mag., 1971-76; contbr. articles to profl. jours. Mem. U.S. Senatorial Bus. Adv. Bd., 1988 mem. adv. bd., of Paplin in Sch. Business, mem. bd., VA Tech Found.; mem. Rep. Presdl. Task Force, 1988; mem. Va. Rep. Com., Chesterfield County, 1984; mem. The Pres.'s Coun., 1990, Pres. Club Rep. Party. Mem. Richmond Claims Assn. (pres. 1971-72, Man of Yr. award 1971), Va. Claims Assn. (Bob Anderson Humanitarian award), Def. Law Inst., Atlanta Claims Assn., Profl. Claims Assn. Richmond, Truck Ins. Def. Assn., 1872 Soc. at Va. Poly. Inst. and State U., Assn. Lloyds Mems. (London), Ut Prosim Soc. at Va. Poly. Inst. and State U. (life, adv. coun. Pamplin Coll. of Bus.), Reform Club (London), St. James Club (London), Salisbury Country Club, Hurlingham Club (London), Sloane Club (London), Quinnipiack Club (New Haven). Methodist. Office: 1227 Mall Dr Richmond VA 23235-4737

COLEMAN, TOMMY LEE, soil science educator, researcher, laboratory director; b. Baxley, Ga., Nov. 8, 1952; s. E.C. and Lucille (Fussell) C.; m. Mildred Cross, Dec. 22, 1974 (div. 1977); m. Edna Thompson, Mar. 6, 1982; children: Sherri, Thomas, Brian. BS in Agronomy, Fort Valley State Coll., 1974; MS, U. Ga., 1977; PhD, Iowa State U., 1980. Soil scientist USDA/Soil Conservation Svc., Statesboro, Ga., 1974-77; rsch. assoc. Iowa State U., Ames, 1977-80; postdoctoral fellow in rsch. Ala. A&M U., Normal, 1981-83, asst. prof., 1983-89, assoc. prof., 1989-93, prof. soil sci. and remote sensing, 1993—, dir. remote sensing lab, 1990-95, dir. Ctr. for Hudrology, Soil Climatology and Remote Sensing, 1995—; rsch. phys. scientist USGS, Reston, Va., 1992-93; dir. Ctr. Hydrology, Soil Climatology, and Remote Sensing, 1995—; cons. Abiola Farms Ltd., Lagos, Nigeria, 1988, U.S. AID-Botswana, Gaborone, 1989-91, 1993—, INRAN-DRE and U.S. AID-Niger, Niamey, 1990. Contbr. articles to profl. jours. Mem. Am. Soc. Agronomy, Soil Sci. Soc. Am., Am. Soc. Photogrammetry and Remote Sensing, NAACP, Profl. Soil Classifiers of Ala., Minorities in Agrl., Natural Resources and Related Scis., North Ala. Golf Club (pres. Huntsville chpt. 1987-92), Omega Psi Phi (Xi Omicron chpt., chair scholarship com. Huntsville chpt. 1986-90). Democrat. Baptist. Office: Ala A&M U Dept Plant & Soil Sci PO Box 1208 Normal AL 35762-1208

COLEMAN-BIRD, VICKY, computer contractor; b. Oak Ridge, Tenn., June 9, 1955. BA in Liberal Arts, U. Tenn., 1977. Counselor State of Tenn., Knoxville, 1977-79; dir. Fed. Project, Las Vegas, 1979; programmer East Tenn. Natural Gas Co., Knoxville, 1983-84; with Fed. Deposit Ins. Corp., Knoxville, 1986-91; prin. novelties co., freelance writer Knoxville, 1991—; speaker for terminally ill children. Fundraiser for children's causes, 1995—. Home: 6100 Lillywood Ln Knoxville TN 37921-4113

COLEMAN-PORTELL, BI BI, women's health and high risk perinatal nurse; b. Columbus, Ohio, Jan. 23, 1951; d. Frederick Douglas and Rubie Anne (Jackson) Coleman; m. Joseph Philip Portell, Nov. 3, 1978; 1 child, Leslie. RN, St. Anthony Sch. Nursing, Oklahoma City, 1982; student, Ohio State U., 1973-76. RN, Okla., Fla., Tex.; cert. high risk perinatal nurse; cert. inpatient obstetric nurse; cert. gen. nursing practice. Dir. patient care coord. perinatal home care prog. Curaflex Health Svcs., Dallas, 1985; staff nurse Nursefinders, Oklahoma City, 1987-88; charge nurse-perinatal St. Anthony Hosp., Oklahoma City, 1986-87; profl. traveling nurse Nursing Projects Corp., Denver, 1989; prof. traveling nurse Univ. Hosp. Consortium, Oakbrook Terrace, Ill., 1990; asst. head nurse U. Tex. Med. Br., Galveston, 1991-92, nurse clinician IV maternal-fetal medicine, 1993-94; community health nurse Healthy Families-HRS, Tampa, 1994-95; urgent care nurse coord. Cigna Health Care, Tampa, 1994-96. Mem. ARC. Capt. USAR, 1985-96. Recipient Vincent B. Snyder award, 1981. Mem. Am. Assn. Med. Pers. (Nat. Merit award 1983), Internat. Coll. Med. Technologists (v.p. 1984-85, Disting. Citation award 1985). Home: 13801 N 37th St #202 Tampa FL 33613-5102

COLES, FELICE ANNE, foreign language educator; b. Farmington, N.Mex., Nov. 2, 1959; d. Roy Davis and Eugenia (Lauro) C. BA, La. State U., 1981; MA, U. Utah, 1983; PhD, U. Tex., 1991. Instr. Spanish Austin (Tex.) C.C., 1988-92; vis. asst. prof. linguistics U. Utah, Salt Lake City, 1992-93, U. Mont., Missoula, 1993-94; asst. prof. Spanish linguistics U. Miss., Oxford, 1994—; lang. coord. for Spanish U. Miss., 1994—. Contbr. articles to profl. jours. Mem. Linguistic Soc. Am., MLA, Nat. Assn. for Hispanic and Latino Studies (state chair Miss. 1996), AAUW, AAUP, Phi Sigma Iota. Methodist. Office: U Miss Modern Langs Bishop 312 Oxford MS 38677

COLEY, BARBARA YVONNE, computer software consultant; b. Albany, Ga., July 20, 1949; d. Leonard Earl and Hazel (Brady) C. BS in Math., U. Ga., 1971, MS in Stats., 1974. Statistician U.S. Forest Service, Athens, Ga., 1973-76; systems analyst Energy Mgmt. Assocs., Atlanta, 1976-78, product mgr., 1978-84, prin. cons., 1984—; pvt. practice cons., Atlanta, 1979—. Mem. Am. Mgmt. Assn., Phi Beta Kappa. Office: Energy Mgmt Assocs 100 Northcreek Suite 500 Atlanta GA 30327

COLEY, LINDA MARIE, secondary school educator; b. Albany, Ga., Apr. 19, 1945; d. Leonard Earl and Hazel (Brady) C. BS in Math., Piedmont Coll., 1966; MS in Math., U. Ga., 1972, postgrad. Cert. tchr., Ga. Tchr. Toccoa (Ga.) Pub. Schs., 1966-67, Hall County Sch. Dist., Gainesville, Ga., 1967-68, Clarke County Sch. Dist., Athens, Ga., 1968—. Sec., 1st v.p. Clarke County Dem. Com., Athens, 1981—. Mem. NEA, Ga. Edn. Assn., Clarke County Assn. Educators (treas., sec.), Alpha Delta Kappa (treas., sec., pres.). Democrat. Baptist. Home: 135 Ravenwood Pl Athens GA 30605-3344

COLGAN, CATHERINE CARPENTER, communications company executive; b. Shreveport, La., Sept. 10, 1930; d. John Topham and Anna Belle (Thomas) Carpenter; m. Henry Comegys Smyth, Jr., Dec. 29, 1949 (div. Jan.

1982); children: Sara Smyth Jacobs, Martha Virginia, Rebecca; m. John Gerard Colgan, July 26, 1986. Student, Randolph-Macon Women's Coll., Lynchburg, Va., 1947-48, U. Akron, 1949-50; BA, Centenary Coll., Shreveport, 1954; Cert. in Teaching, Tex. Woman's U., 1961. Dir. Dist. VII Nat. Bd. Dirs., Randolph Macon Woman's Coll. Alumnae Assn., 1978-81; cultural affairs officer U.S. Embassy USIA, Ottawa, Ont., Can., 1981-85; corp. liaison officer World Expo 88 USIA, Brisbane, Australia, 1985-88; dir. internat. programs, bd. trustees Physicians for Peace, various fgn. locations, 1988—; mem. Def. Adv. Com. on Women in the Svcs. U.S. Dept. of Def., 1989-92; ptnr. Colgan Comms., Virginia Beach, Va., 1989-93; mem. broadcast adv. com. Voice of Am., USIA, 1991-93. Contbr. articles to profl. jours. Bd. visitors U.S. Naval Acad., 1992-95; vice chmn. Rep. Party of Dallas County, 1975-79; mem. state ctrl. com. Rep. Party of Va., 1993—; nat. dir. srs. for Bush nat. voter coalition, Bush/Quayle '88 presdl. campaign Rep. Nat. Com., 1988, internat. media liaison nat. conv., 1984, 88, del.-at-large (Va.), Rep. Nat. Conv., 1992, dep. nat. chmn. Rep. Sr. Network, 1996—, Va. state coord., Srs. Network of Rep. Nat. Com., numerous other positions in Rep. Party. Mem. Tex. Fedn. Rep. Women (v.p. 1973-77, pres. 1979-81). Va. Fedn. Rep. Women, Nat. Fedn. Rep. Women (chmn., vice chmn. campaign com. 1975-79, speaker nat. conv. 1987, 89, 91, 95), Rideau Club (Can.), Capitol Hill Club (Washington), Army and Navy Club, Harbor Club of Norfolk, Va. Episcopalian. Home and Office: Colgan Comm Co 1500 Ashley Dr Virginia Beach VA 23454-1611

COLGAN, GEORGE PHILLIPS, real estate analyst; b. Tokyo, June 3, 1947; s. Jack Phillips and Kimiko (Furukawa) C.; m. Ann Elizabeth Dickerson, Sept. 1, 1968; 1 child, Matthew Seth. Student, Ga. Tech. U., 1965-66; BS in Biology, Ga. State U., 1970. Credit mgr. C&S Nat. Bank, Atlanta, 1969-74; statewide credit mgr. GE Credit Corp., Atlanta, 1974-76; regional v.p. A.L. Williams & Assocs., Atlanta and Houston, 1977-81; dir. sales and mktg. Hooker Barnes Homes, Inc., Atlanta, 1982-84, Brayson/Am. Homes, Atlanta, 1984-86; real estate markets analyst, pres. Whitehall Homes, Inc., Atlanta, 1986—. Contbr. articles to profl. jours. Asst. scoutmaster, unit commr. Troop 525 Boy Scouts Am., Norcross, Ga., 1989-94; del. So. Bapt. Conv., Atlanta, 1985; pres. Norcross H.S. Wrestling Boosters Club, 1994-96. Mem. Nat. Assn. Home Builders (Cert. of Appreciation 1986). Republican. Presbyterian. Home: 4576 Southport Crossing Norcross GA 30092 Office: Whitehall Homes Inc # 120 5380 Peachtree Indsl Blvd Norcross GA 30071

COLGATE, DORIS ELEANOR, retailer, sailing school administrator; b. Washington, May 12, 1941; d. Bernard Leonard and Frances Lillian (Goldstein) Horecker; m. Richard G. Buchanan, Sept. 6, 1959 (div. Aug. 1967); m. Stephen Colgate, Dec. 17, 1969. Student Antioch Coll., 1958-60, NYU, 1960-62. Rsch. supr. Geyer Moyer Ballard, N.Y.C., 1962-64; adminstrv. asst. Yachting Mag., N.Y.C., 1964-68; v.p. Offshore Sailing Sch. Ltd., Inc., N.Y.C., 1968-78, pres., Ft. Myers, Fla., 1978—; pres., CEO On and Offshore, Inc., Ft. Myers, 1984—; v.p. Offshore Travel, Inc., City Island, 1978-88. Author: The Bareboat Gourmet, 1983; contbr. articles to profl. jours. Mem. Royal Ocean Racing Club (London chpt.), Nat. Women's Sailing Assn. (chair nat. women's adv. bd. 1990-94, chair, 1991-94, pres. 1994—), Am. Women's Econ. Devel. Corp. (adv. bd. 1980-86, Betty Cook Meml. Lifetime Achievement award 1994, Boat/U.S. Nat. adv. coun. 1995—), Internat. Women Boating (Sail Industry Leadership award 1996). Avocations: sailing, photography, writing, cooking. Home: 1555 San Carlos Bay Dr Sanibel FL 33957-3423 Office: Offshore Inc 16731 Mcgregor Blvd Fort Myers FL 33908-3843

COLGIN, ANN BARRY, antique and arts dealer, appraiser, auctioneer; b. Waco, Tex., Apr. 5, 1958; d. Irwin Edward and Gertrude (Czajkoski) C.; m. Frederick Henry Schrader. BA in Art History, Vanderbilt U., 1980; student, Sotheby's Works of Art Course, London, 1981; MA in Arts Adminstn., NYU, 1985; certificate, Internat. Soc. Appraisers, 1989. Customer svc. rep. Christie's East, N.Y.C., 1982-85; pres. Fairchild's Fine Art, Inc., Alva, Fla., 1985—. Mem. Nat. Assn. Dealers in Antiques, Fla. Auctioneers Assn., Internat. Soc. Appraisers (cert.), Jr. League of Ft. Myers., Fla. Republican. Episcopalian. Office: Fairchild's Fine Art Inc 17301 Frank Rd Alva FL 33920-3510

COLLAZO, FRANCISCO J., company executive. Pres. Colsa Corp. Office: 6726 Odyssey Dr Huntsville AL 35801-3306*

COLLETTE, FRANCES MADELYN, retired tax consultant, lawyer; b. Yonkers, N.Y., Aug. 5, 1947; d. Morris Aaron and Esther (Gang) Volbert; m. Roger Warren Collette, Dec. 25, 1971; children: Darren Roger, Bonnie Frances. BEd summa cum laude, SUNY-Buffalo, 1969; JD, cum laude, U. Miami, 1980. Bar: Fla. 1980. Employment counselor Fla. Bur. Employment Security, Miami, 1969-73; unemployment claims adjudicator Fla. Bur. Unemployment Claims, Miami, 1973-77; Fla. unemployment tax and personnel cons.; owner Unemployment Svcs. Fla., Inc., Miami, 1977-93; lectr. in field. Mem. BBB S. Fla. (1st v.p. 1980-81, bd. govs., 2d vice chmn. 1990-91). Jewish.

COLLICHIO, STEVEN, software engineer; b. Rochester, N.Y., Apr. 14, 1962; s. James Louis and Shirley (Pilon) C. Student, Ga. Inst. Tech., 1981-82; BS in Electronics Engring. Tech., DeVry Inst. Tech., Atlanta, 1985. Field engr. Coin Fin. Systems, Norcross, Ga., 1986-87; regional support rep. Coin Fin. Systems, Boston, 1986-87; nat. tech. support specialist Barrister Info. Systems Corp., Buffalo; sr. field engr. Barrister Info. Systems Corp., Dallas, GTEX Fin. Group, Inc., Richardson, Tex., 1991; mgr. info. tech. Deloitte & Touche, Dallas, 1991—. Mem. IEEE. Roman Catholic. Office: Deloitte & Touche 2200 Ross Ave #1600 Dallas TX 75201

COLLIER, DIANA GORDON, publishing executive; b. Ottawa, Ont., Can., June 15, 1945; came to U.S., 1984; d. Edward Cecil and Vera (Lowrie) C.; m. Y. Naim, Apr. 17, 1982; 1 child, Sundiata. BA, U. B.C., 1963; MA, U. Montreal, 1975. Writer, 1972-83; editor Black Rose Books, Montreal, Que., Can., 1973-75; bus. mgr. Studies Polit. Economy, Ottawa, Ont., Can., 1980-82; pub. Clarity Press, Inc., Atlanta, 1984—; dir. communications, editor newsletter Internat. Human Rights Assn. of Am. Minorities, Chgo., 1988—. Author: Invisible Women of Washington, 1989 (Best of U.S. Small Press 1989), Minnesota Review, 1988; editor: Restructuring of America, 1991, Shelter in the Light, 1991, Israeli Peace-Palestinean Justice, 1994, A Popular Guide to Minority Rights, 1995, American Indians: Stereotypes and Realities, 1996. Bell Can. fellow, Montreal, 1973, 74; Can. Coun. grantee, Ottawa, 1975, 77. Mem. NAACP, Soc. Scholarly Pub., Pub. Mktg. Assn. Multicultural Pubs. Exch., COSMEP. Office: Clarity Press Inc 3277 Roswell Rd NE Ste 469 Atlanta GA 30305-1840

COLLIER, EVELYN MYRTLE, elementary school educator; b. Newton, Ala., Dec. 11, 1942; d. Palmer Lee and Jessie Beryl (Williams) C. BA, Samford U., 1965; M Religious Edn., Southwestern Sem., 1967; MS, Troy State U., 1977. Youth dir. Calvary Bapt. Temple, Savannah, Ga., 1967-69; tchr. Newton Elem. Sch., 1969-77, prin., 1977-94; asst. prof. elem. edn. Fla. Bapt. Theol. Coll., Graceville, Fla., 1994—. Mem. ASCD, Ala. Assn. Elem. Sch. Prins. (exec. bd. 1984-94, sec. 1985, dist. IX pres. 1983, dist. IX Disting. Prin. award 1986, 89, 92), Ala. Coun. Sch. Adminstrs. and Suprs. (bd. dirs. 1991-94), Nat. Assn. Elem. Sch. Prins., Delta Kappa Gamma (Alpha Kappa chpt., Beta state exec. bd. 1987—, pres. Ala. chpt. 1987-93, 1st v.p. 1989-91, 2d v.p. 1987-89, Golden Gift Fund award 1983, Internat. scholar 1996), Phi Delta Kappa. Baptist. Office: Fla Bapt Theol Coll 5400 College Dr Graceville FL 32440-1831

COLLIER, ROGER MALCOLM, minister; b. Richmond, Va., Nov. 10, 1950; s. Edward Malcolm and Vallie Pauline (Cuthbertson) C.; m. Sarah Catherine Carter, Apr. 5, 1980; children: Leigh Anne, Paula Kay, Edward Malcolm II. BA, U. Richmond, 1972; postgrad., Yale U. Div. Sch., 1972-73; MDiv, Southeastern Bapt. Theol. Sem., 1976; D of Ministry, Union Theol. Sem., Richmond, 1984. Ordained to ministry So. Bapt. Conv., 1975. Min. Hunton Bapt. Ch., Glen Allen, Va., 1975-85, West End Bapt. Ch., Suffolk, Va., 1985-86, Glen Allen Bapt. Ch., 1986—. Trustee Cmty. Rels. Referral Bd. Henrico County, Richmond, 1989—; pres. Glen Allen Elem. Sch. PTA, 1990-91; bd. dirs. Virginians for Integrity in Govt., 1991—; citizen mem. Va. Bd. Funeral Dirs. Named Outstanding Young Religious Leader, Glen Allen Jaycees. 1981. Mem. Bapt. Gen. Assn. Va. (chmn. Christian Life Com. 1982-85), Laurel Glen Allen Mins.' Conf. (pres. 1976, 84), Kiwanis of North Richmond (bd. dirs. 1994—), PhiBeta Kappa. Home: 2909 Susan Sheppard Ct Glen Allen VA 23060-2035 Office: Glen Allen Bapt Ch PO Box 1245 Glen Allen VA 23060-1245

COLLIER, STEVEN EDWARD, management consultant; b. Alamogordo, N.Mex., July 19, 1952; s. Homer Edward and Wanda JoAnn (Harred) C.; m. Trella Jean Wallace, May 26, 1973; children: Rachel, Joel, Lori, Ginna. BSEE, U. Houston, 1976; MSEE, Purdue U., 1977. Registered profl. engr., Okla., Tex., 1994—; Planning engr. Houston Lighting & Power Co., Houston, 1970-76; researcher Purdue Electric Power Ctr., W. Lafayette, Ind., 1976-77; analytical cons. Power Technologies, Inc., Schenectady, N.Y., 1977-79; mem. tech. staff Sandia Nat. Lab., Albuquerque, 1979-80; sr. v.p. C.H. Guernsey & Co., Oklahoma City, 1980-89; v.p. energy resources and govt. affairs Cap Rock Electric, Stanton, Tex., 1989-95; pres., CEO New West Resources, Austin, Tex., 1991-96; pres. New West Fuels, L.C., Austin, 1994-96, Detroit Tex. Gas Gathering Co., Austin, 1994-96; prin. CNG Strategy Group, Austin, 1996—; instr. NRECA MIP and Internat. Mgmt. Devel. Ctr.; speaker at confs. and convs., 1978—. Mem. editorial adv. bd. NRECA Rural Electrification Mag., 1988—, featured cover story, 1991; mem. editorial adv. bd. The Electricity Jour.; contbr. articles to profl. jours. Grad. fellow in engring. NSF, 1976. Mem. IEEE, IEEE Industry Applications Soc. (bd. dirs. 1987-90, power com. chmn. 1986-87). Republican. Office: Cap Rock Electric 807 Brazos St Ste 700 Austin TX 78701-2508

COLLIN, BRUCE EDWARD, publishing company executive; b. N.Y.C., Apr. 11, 1956; s. Robert William and Maryann (Nathan) C.; m. Sara Eskenazi, Dec. 19, 1993. BA magna cum laude, Conn.. Coll., 1978; Cert. in Spanish with highest honors, U. Salamanca, Spain, 1973. Brand asst. Procter & Gamble, Cin., 1978-80; coll. field rep. Prentice-Hall/Simon & Schuster, Englewood Cliffs, N.J., 1981-93; acquisitions editor Simon & Schuster, Plano, Tex., 1993-94; account exec. McGraw-Hill, Plano, 1995—. Cofounder, pres. Com. to Award Miss Piggy the Oscar (CAMPO), Cin., 1979-80. Mem. Phi Beta Kappa. Republican. Jewish. Home and Office: 2221 Chasefield Dr Plano TX 75023

COLLINS, CHARLES JESSE, college official, psychology educator; b. Hobbs, N.Mex., June 13, 1951; s. Albert L. and Sara Alice (Williams) C.; m. Patricia Ann Jones, Feb. 23, 1973; children: Abbey Susanne, Becky Gail, Jessi Lynn, Katie Ann. BTh, Fla. Bapt. Theol. Coll., 1987, BRE, 1987; MS in Counseling and Psychology, Troy State U., Dothan, Ala., 1994. Ordained to ministry So. Bapt. Ch., 1989. Systems loading operator Carroll Constrn. Co., Pace, Fla., 1973-76; assoc. pastor New Home Bapt. Ch., Graceville, Fla., 1986-87; pastor Poplar Head Bapt. Ch., Clarksville, Fla., 1988-89; registrar Fla. Bapt. Theol. Coll., Graceville, 1989—, adj. prof. psychology, 1994—; interim pastor Southside Bapt. Ch., Andalusia, Ala., 1991-92; pastor Gully Springs Baptist Ch., 1993-94. Staff sgt. USAF, 1976-84. Mem. Lions (bd. dirs. Graceville 1990-91, sec. 1991-94, pres. 1995-96), Am. Legion (adjutant 1995—). Home: 5374 Ceiley St Graceville FL 32440-1929 Office: Fla Bapt Theol Coll PO Box 1306 5400 College Dr Graceville FL 32440-3306

COLLINS, EARLINE BROWN, medical and surgical and nephrology nurse; b. Canton, Miss., Apr. 30, 1955; d. Oresa and Thelma Holbert (Nichols) Brown; m. James Byron Collins, Jan. 23, 1982 (div. Dec. 1995). Cert., Holmes Jr. Coll., Goodman, Miss., 1975; AAS, Shelby State C.C., Memphis, 1989. Nurse Canton Nursing Home; charge nurse Canton Manor; nurse St. Dominic, Jackson, Miss.; staff nurse nephrology med./surg. unit, 1979-90; nurse hemodialysis unit Meth. Hosp., Memphis, 1990-91, patient educator peritoneal dialysis, 1991—; clin. instr. nursing asst. program Rice Coll., 1989-90. Mem. Am. Nephrology Nurses Assn., Phi Theta Kappa. Home: 4132 Arrowhead Rd Memphis TN 38118

COLLINS, EUGENE BOYD, chemist, molecular pathologist, consultant; b. L.A., May 28, 1917; s. Harold Porter and Mina Rosannah (Eversoll) C.; m. Frances Louise File, Aug. 4, 1946 (div. May 1962); children: Dana, Diane, Eric; m. Helen Lucille Schultz, Oct. 16, 1966; 1 child, Dane. BS in Chemistry, UCLA, 1951, diploma in edn., 1962; BSChE, De Landas U., 1940, DSc (hon.), 1952; cert. advanced med. tech., Calif. State U., Dominguez Hills, 1977; MD, U. Cen. del Este, San Pedro, Dominican Republic, 1982. Lic. clin. lab. scientist, Calif.; cert. tchr., Calif. Assoc. dir. spectroscopy Union Oil Co. (Unocal), Wilmington, Calif., 1951-57; prof. chemistry Los Angeles Harbor Coll., Wilmington, 1957-74; cons. chemist Collins and Assocs., Carson, Calif., 1974-79, 83-92, Selma, Ala., 1992—; pres. Boyd Collins Co., South Gate, Calif., 1960-70; cons. Holley Carburetor Co. Research Lab., San Pedro, Calif., 1957-60; lectr. biology and clin. science Calif. State U., Dominquez Hills, 1988-92. Contbr. articles to profl. jours. Commr. Boy Scouts Am., Long Beach, Calif., 1958-59. Staff sgt. U.S. Army, 1944-46, ETO. Fellow Am. Inst. Chemists, Royal Soc. Arts; mem. AAAS, Am. Chem. Soc., Internat. Union of Pure and Applied Chemistry (affiliate), Am. Pharm. Assn., Acad. Pharm. Scis., N.Y. Acad. Scis., Am. Assn. Clin. Chemistry (molecular pathology divsn.). Office: Collins and Assoc 470 Deepwoods Dr Selma AL 36701-0467

COLLINS, G. BRYAN, JR., lawyer; b. North Wilkesboro, N.C., Sept. 13, 1960; s. George B. and Ida Maude (Black) C.; m. Donna Jarvis, Feb. 15, 1992; children: Kristy, Katie. AB cum laude, Davidson Coll., 1982; JD, U. N.C., Chapel Hill, 1985. Bar: N.C. 1985, U.S. Dist. Ct. (ea. dist.) N.C. 1985, U.S. Ct. Appeals (4th cir.) 1986. Assoc. Tharrington, Smith & Hargrove, Raleigh, N.C., 1985-89; pvt. practice Raleigh, 1989—; instr. Meredith Coll., Raleigh, 1989. Bd. dirs. Wake County Criminal Justice Partnership; mem. Gov.'s Task Force on Driving While Impaired, 1995, Raleigh Jaycees, 1990, Wake Dem. Men's Club, Raleigh, 1990, Raleigh YMCA, 1985—. Mem. N.C. Bar Assn. (exec. coun. young lawyers div. 1986), Wake County Bar Assn. (bd. dirs. 1991-92), Wake County Young Lawyers (pres. 1992), Wake County Acad. Criminal Trial Lawyers (pres. 1991). Democrat. Methodist. Home: 8601 Bensley Ct Raleigh NC 27615-3702 Office: Bryan Collins Law Offices 619 N Person St Raleigh NC 27604-1213

COLLINS, GARY ALLEN, environmental specialist; b. Seminole, Tex., Oct. 17, 1953; s. Winford Allen and Betty Lou (Rhynes) C.; m. Vicki Lynn Aycock, Mar. 17, 1982; children: David, Summer, Megan, Courtney. BS, East Ctrl. U., 1975; M in Environ. Scis., U. Okla., 1986. Registered environ. specialist. Environ. specialist I Garfield County Health Dept., Enid, Okla., 1977-81; environ. specialist II Garfield County Health Dept., Enid, 1981-82, sr. environ. specialist, 1982-89, environ. specialist supr., 1989-92; dist. sanitarian Dept. Environ. Quality, Oklahoma City Regional Program, 1992-93; dir. regional program Dept. Environ. Quality, Oklahoma City, 1993-96; asst. dir. environ. complaints and local svcs. divsn. Dept. of Environ. Quality, Oklahoma City, 1996—. Mem. Nat. Environ. Health Assn. (bd. dirs. 1992), Okla. Soc. Environ. Health Profls. (pres. elect, 1990-91, pres. 1991-92, Sanitarian of Yr. 1989). Democrat. Home: 4307 Lakewood Dr Enid OK 73703-2800 Office: Dept Environ. Quality 1000 NE 10th St Oklahoma City OK 73117-1207

COLLINS, GWENDOLYN BETH, health administrator; b. Akron, Ohio; d. Emmert Samuel and Lillice Elizabeth (Matthews) Shaffer; 1 child, Holly Marie. BA, Case Western Res. U. Exec. dir. Canton Area Regional Health Edn. Network, 1981-88; project dir. Region VII Cancer Registry, Canton, Ohio, 1984-88; program dir. Diabetes Mgmt. Ctr., St. Petersburg, Fla., 1988-89, 92-94, Pasadena Sr. Health Ctr., St. Petersburg, 1995-96; pvt. practice health program mgmt. cons. Largo, Fla., 1995—; health mgmt. cons., 1986-88, 95—; mem. continuing med. edn. com. Aultman Hosp., 1983-88; planner and evaluator Directions for Mental Health, Inc., Clearwater, Fla., 1990-92. Mem. adv. com. Camp Y-Noah, 1985-86. HHS grantee, Canton, 1986-88. Mem. Cancer Control Consortium Ohio (mem. cancer incidence mgmt. com. 1986-87). Republican. Home and Office: Unit 1410 11600 Shipwatch Dr Largo FL 33774-3737

COLLINS, HARRY DAVID, construction consultant, forensic engineering specialist, mechanical and nuclear engineer, retired army officer; b. Brownsville, Pa., Nov. 18, 1931; s. Harry Alonzo and Cecelia Victoria (Morris) C.; BS in Mech. Engring., Carnegie Mellon U., 1954; MS in Physics, U.S. Naval Postgrad. Sch., 1961; postgrad., U.S. Army Command and Gen. Staff Coll., 1970; postgrad. in exptl. physics, George Washington U., 1971-72; m. Suzanne Dylong, May 11, 1956; children: Cynthia L. Mabel, Gerard P. Commd. 2d lt. C.E., U.S. Army, 1954, advanced through grades to lt. col. 1969; comdr. 802d Heavy Engr. Constrn. Bn., Korea, 1972-73; dep. dist. engr. and acting dist. engr. Army Engr. Dist., New Orleans, 1973-75; v.p. deLaureal Engrs., Inc., New Orleans, 1975-78; v.p. Near East mktg. and project mgmt. Kidde Cons., Inc., 1978-82; dir. new bus. devel. and project mgmt. for North Africa, Middle East, Am. Middle East Co., Inc., 1982-84; sr. cons. Wagner, Hohns, Inglis, Inc., 1984-91; chief engr. bd. commrs. Orleans Levee Dist. State of La., 1991-92; pres. Harry D. Collins and Assocs., 1992—; pres. La. Security Products & QuTech, 1994—. Contbr. articles to profl. jours. Decorated Legion of Merit, Bronze Star with oak leaf cluster, Meritorious Service medal with oak leaf cluster, Joint Svc. Commendation medal, Armed Forces Expeditionary medal, Vietnam Svc. medal, Vietnam Nat. Commendation medal, Vietnam Tng. Svc. medal; registered profl. engr., Miss., La. Mem. ASME, Am. Soc. Mil. Engrs. (past pres. La Post), La. Engring. Soc., N.Y. Acad. Scis., NSPE, Am. Nuclear Soc., Am. Arbitration Assn. (panel of arbitrators and mediators), Nat. Acad. Forensic Engrs. (diplomate, cert.), Constrn. Specifications Inst. (cert. constrn. document technologist), Sigma Xi. Home: 2024 Audubon St New Orleans LA 70118-5518

COLLINS, JAMES LEE, pastor; b. Atlanta, Jan. 30, 1938; s. James Lee and Helen Era (Colston) C.; m. Sandra Bacon, Sept. 23, 1967; children: Leslie Jane, LeAnne Sandra. BA, Emory U., 1960; BD, Candler Sch. Theology, 1963; D of Ministry, Lexington Theology Sem., 1987. Ordained to ministry Christian Ch. (Disciples of Christ), 1963. Youth minister First Christian Ch., Atlanta, 1960-61; pastor First Christian Ch., Loganville, Ga., 1961-65, Brunswick, Ga., 1965-69; chaplain intern Ga. Regional Mental Hosp., Atlanta, 1969-70; pastor Ctrl. Ave. Christian Ch., Humboldt, Tenn., 1970-77; pastor First Christian Ch., Shelbyville, Ky., 1977-83, Lubbock, Tex., 1983-86; pastor Peachtree Christian Ch., Atlanta, 1986—; sec., v.p. Mission for Biblical Literacy, Athens, Ga., 1982-95; bd. dirs. Atlanta Interfaith Broadcasters, 1986-94; trustee Christian Coll. Ga., Athens, 1987-93; pres. Christian Coun. Metro Atlanta, 1988-89. Author: (manual) Christian Marriage, 1987, (Bible study) Sermon on the Mount, 1989. Mem. Am. Assn. Christian Counselors, Ministerial Assn. (pres.). Office: Peachtree Christian Ch 1580 Peachtree St Nw Atlanta GA 30309

COLLINS, JIM, artist; b. Huntington, W.Va., Sept. 12, 1934; s. Nell (Crawford) Howard; m. Debbe Hunley, May 29, 1983; children: Shawn Kathleen Collins Pittman, Jill Collins Scudder, Karen Collins Reinert. AB, Marshall U., 1957; MPH, U. Mich., 1961; MFA, Ohio U., 1966. Prof. art U. Tenn., Chattanooga, 1966-83; artist Signal Mountain, Tenn., 1983—; art cons. River Gallery Sculpture Garden, Chattanooga, 1993—. Author: Women Artists in America, 1973, Women Artists in America II, 1975; one-man shows include Hunter Mus. of Art, Chattanooga, 1978, 83, 86, Appalachian State U., Boone, N.C., 1981, Piedmont Art Gallery, Augusta, Ky., 1984, Mason County Mus., Maysville, Ky., 1984, J. Rosenthal Fine Arts, Chgo., 1991, Malton Gallery, Cin., 1992, Piedmont Gallery, Augusta, Ky., 1992, Van Cleave Gallery, St. Louis, 1994, Taylor's Conteporania Fine Arts, Hot Springs, Ariz., 1994, River Gallery, Chattanooga, Tenn., 1994, Macon & Co. Atlanta, 1995, Taylor's Contemporania Fine Arts, Hots Springs, Ariz., 1995, Bennett Galleries, Knoxville, Tenn., 1995, also numerous group shows; represented in permanent collections Am. Republic Ins. Co., Des Moines, Iowa, Huntington (W.Va.) Galleries, Berea (Ky.) Coll., Atlanta Arts Festival, Tenn. Fine Arts Ctr., Nashville, U. Tenn., Chattanooga, Wichita (Kans.) Art Assn., Inc., U. S.C., Columbia, U. of South, Sewanee, Tenn., Middle Tenn. State U., Murfreesboro, Memphis Watercolor Soc., Appalachian Corridors, Charleston, W.Va., Furman U., Greenville, S.C., Tenn. Botanical Garden and Fine Arts Ctr., Cheekwood, Nashville, Hunter Mus. of Art, Chattanooga, Brooks Mus. of Art, Memphis, Union Township Libr., Ripley, Ohio, Ripley Hist. Mus., Jones Fine Art, Maysville, Ky., also numerous pvt. collections. Named Artist-in-Residence, Assn. for Visual Artists, 1990. Mem. So. Assn. Sculptors (pres. 1970-71). Home and Office: 201 N Palisades Dr Signal Mountain TN 37377-3038

COLLINS, JUDITH CHARLENE (JUDY RHODES COLLINS), writer, poet; b. Council Bluffs, Iowa, May 14, 1947; d. L.O. Dusty and Naomi Louise (Brown) Rhodes; m. Clay G. Collins; children: Gina Watchous, Shawna Zeigler, Ronald Keithley. facilitator Wednesday Writers Night, Manion Park Studio, Tulsa, 1991, 92, 93; coord. monthly readings Mad Poets and Friends, Eclipse, Tulsa, 1991, 92, 93. Author: Naked Person; contbg. author: Special Poets Series, 2d edit., Special Poets Series, Vol. 10, Ann. Poetry Rev., Errattica; contbr. poetry to anthologies including 1989 American Poetry Annual, Another Place in Time, Dreams Live On, Visions, Expressions, The Best Poems of the 90's, Language of the Soul. Reflections, Listen with Your Heart, Garden of Thoughts; contbr. poetry to newspapers, mags. and jours. including Collinsville (Okla.) Herald, Skiatook Jour., Bumbershoot, Pegasus Rev. Recipient Poet Laureate award Verses, Nat. Authors Registry, 2 Publisher's Choice awards Watermark Press, Editor's Choice award Cader Pub., 2 Publisher's Preference awards Creative Arts and Scis. Pub., other awards nat. and internat. poetry contests. Mem. Internat. Soc. Poets (Internat. Pen award 1991), Nat. Authors Registry, Poetry Soc. Am., Tulsa Arts Coalition (founder, v.p., publicist Skiatook Lake area Arts and Humanities Coun.). Home: RR 2 Box 37-a Skiatook OK 74070-9305

COLLINS, KATHRYN SUZANNE, nurse practitioner, enterostomal therapy nurse; b. McDowell, Ky., Oct. 3, 1961; d. John Bailey and Nancy Marie (Kelley) Collins; m. Robert L. Westheimer, Feb. 14, 1992. Diploma, St. Mary's Sch. Nursing, Huntington, W.Va., 1982; BSN, Marshall U., 1988; MS, U. South Fla., 1991; postgrad., U. Fla. Cert. enterostomal therapy nurse, advanced nurse practitioner. Neonatal ICU charge nurse Cabell Huntington Hosp., Huntington; ICU staff nurse Huntington Hosp.; med. dir. Rutledge Coll., Huntington; enterostomal therapy nurse Venice (Fla.) Hosp.; nurse practitioner The Bowen Ctr for Med. Weight Loss. Mem. NOW, ANA, Fla. Nurses Assn., Internat. Assn. Enterostomal Therapists, Wound, Ostomy and Continence Nurses, Am. Acad. Nurse Practitioners, United Ostomy Assn., Am. Cancer Soc., Sigma Theta Tau. Home: 1275 Oak Tree Ln Nokomis FL 34275-2370

COLLINS, LISA DIANE, art educator; b. Long Beach, Calif., Sept. 20, 1967; d. Jimmy Royce and Cloa Mae (Westbrook) C. BS Art Edn., BA Comml. Art, Kennesaw State Coll., Marietta, Ga., 1991; student, U. Ga. Studies Abroad, Cortona, Italy, 1988, Kennesaw State Coll. Studies, San Miguel, Mex., 1989; postgrad., State U. West Ga., Carrollton. Instr. studio art for children Kennesaw State U., 1988—; art educator Josh Powell Camp, Kennesaw, 1990-92; art tchr. Floyd Middle Sch., Mableton, Ga., 1991—; freelance artist; prodn. asst. Share Mag.., Kennessaw State Coll., 1990-91, coop. tchr. to upcoming art tchrs., 1993—; dir. Floyd Celebrates Arts at Mable House Gallery, 1991—; judge Paulding County Fine Arts Assn. Exhibit, 1993. Bd. dirs. South Cobb Arts Alliance, 1996—. Named Tchr. of Yr., Floyd Mid. Sch., 1996. Mem. ASCD, Profl.. Assn. Ga. Educators., Nat. Art Edn. Assn. Home: 3800 Parks Dr Powder Springs GA 30073-2720

COLLINS, LYNN M., oncology clinical nurse specialist; b. St. Paul, Oct. 10, 1960; d. Bruce W. and Marianne (Palla) Baumann; m. Robert H. Collins Jr., Sept. 14, 1985. BSN, Winona State U., 1982; M in Nursing, UCLA, 1990. Cert. advanced oncology nurse. Staff clin. nurse II Baylor U. Med. Ctr., Dallas, supr., 1984-87; acting nurse mgr. Children's Hosp. of L.A., 1987-89; rsch. asst. UCLA Sch. Nursing; oncology clin. nurse specialist Sammons Cancer Ctr. Baylor U. Med. Ctr., Dallas, 1990—. Mem. Oncology Nursing Soc. (nat. Congress com. 1989, 90, nat. Fall inst. com. 1991, 92, chair nat. Fall inst. com. 1993), Sigma Theta Tau. Home: 6439 Westlake Ave Dallas TX 75214-3438

COLLINS, MARCUS E., SR., state agency administrator; b. Albany, Ga., Jan. 25, 1927; s. John Temple and Emma (Woodruff) C.; m. Elizabeth Ann Griffin, Nov. 21, 1948; children: Elizabeth Ann, Marcus Eugene Jr., James Edwin, David Almond, Jennifer, Rebecca. Grad. high sch., Pelham, Ga. Mem. Ho. of Reps., Mitchell County, Ga., 1961-62, 64-83; chmn. ways and means com. Ho. Appropriations Com., 1965-83; mem. agr. and consumer affairs com. Ho. of Reps., mem. house hwys. com., mem. joint house-senate legis. svc. com., mem. fiscal affairs com.; mem. house policy com., mem. met. Atlanta Rapid Transit Authority overview com., vice chmn. Ga. tax reform commn.; revenue commr. State of Ga., 1983—; bd. dirs. Met. Atlanta Rapid Transit Authority; mem. gov. econ. devel. coun.; mem. state depository bd.; chmn. State Bd. Equalization and Tax Settlement and Compromise Bd. With U.S. Army, PTO. Mem. Fedn. Tax Adminstrs. (exec. com., resolutions com.), Southeastern Assn. Tax Adminstrs. (past pres.), Internat. Assn. Assessing Ofcls., Ga. Assn. Assessing Ofcls., Am. Assn. Motor Vehicle Adminstrs., Nat. Tax Assn.-Tax Inst. Am. Democrat. Baptist. Office: Ga Revenue Dept 410 Trinity-washing Atlanta GA 30334 also: Revenue Dept 270 Washington St SW Atlanta GA 30334-9009

COLLINS, MELISSA ANN, oncological nurse; b. Wichita Falls, Tex., June 6, 1951; d. Foley D. Jr. and Pathea Jo (Thornton) C. BS, U. Tex., Austin, 1973. Cert. oncology nurse, med. radiologic technologist. Nurse technologist U. Tex. System Cancer Ctr. at M.D. Anderson Hosp., Houston; staff nurse, technologist Hermann Hosp., Houston; nurse/radiation therapist Park Plaza Hosp., Houston. Mem. Oncology Nursing Soc.

COLLINS, MICHAEL BRUCE, music educator; b. Turlock, Calif., July 26, 1930; s. Marion C. and Chrissie (Woolcock) C. BA, Stanford U., 1957, MA, 1958, PhD, 1963. Asst. prof. musicology Eastman Sch. Music, Rochester, N.Y., 1964-68; prof. musicology U. No.Tex., Denton, 1968—. Editor: Alessandro Scarlatti's Tigrane, 1983; co-editor: Opera & Vivaldi, 1984; editor: Gioachino Rossini's Otello, 1994; contbr. articles to profl. jours. Served in U.S. Army, 1951-54. Fulbright-Hays scholar, 1963. Mem. Am. Musicol. Soc. Office: Coll Music U No Tex PO Box 13887 Denton TX 76203-6887

COLLINS, PAUL STEVEN, vascular surgeon; b. Portsmouth, Ohio, July 24, 1954; s. Paul Whitney and Geralda Pearl (Hoskins) C.; m. Cathy Ann McWicker, Jan. 17, 1981; children: Lauren Elizabeth, Paul McWicker, Andrew Steven. BS, Davidson Coll., 1976; MD, U. South Fla., 1979. Diplomate Am. Bd. Surgery, spl. qualifications in gen. vascular surgery and surg. critical care; diplomate Nat. Bd. Med. Examiners; lic. surgeon, Fla., Va. Commd. 2d lt. U.S. Army, 1979, advanced through grades to lt. col., 1990; resident in gen. surgery Walter Reed Army Med. Ctr. U.S. Army, Washington, 1979-84; chief gen. surg. svc. U.S. Army, Würzburg, West Germany, 1984-86; fellow peripheral vasc. surgery Walter Reed Army Med. Ctr. U.S. Army, Washington, 1986-87; chief vascular surgery Letterman Army Med. Ctr. U.S. Army, San Francisco; resigned U.S. Army, 1992; pvt. practice St. Petersburg, Fla., 1990—; asst. clin. prof. surgery Uniformed Svcs. U. of Health Scis., Bethesda, Md., 1984—; profl. mem. Keystone, Tampa, Fla., 1993—; pres. Bay Blaza Outpatient Surgry; dir. vascular lab. St. Anthony's Hosp., St. Petersburg, 1994—; bd. dirs, trustee St. Anthony's Found. Contbr. chpts. to books, articles to med. jours. Bd. dirs. St. Anthony's Found. Recipient Physicians Recognition award AMA, 1992, Sigvaris award Camp Internat., 1987. Fellow ACS (Regional Trauma award 1984), Internat. Soc. for Cardiovascular Surgeons; mem. So. Assn. for Vascular Surgery (Pres.'s award 1992), Fla. Vascular Soc., Fla. Med. Assn., Pinellas County Med. Soc. (bd. govs.). Office: 1201 5th Ave N Ste 200 Saint Petersburg FL 33705-1410

COLLINS, PETER BARTON, international law officer; b. Cleve., May 23, 1958; s. Leo Robert and Peggy Edith (Barton) C.; m. Melinda Beymer Mack, Aug. 6, 1993; children: Macgregor Mack Collins, Keely Mack Collins. BBA, U. Miss., 1981; JD, U. Memphis, 1984; LLM, Tulane U., 1993. Cert. judge advocate. Commd. 2d lt. USMC, 1981, advanced through grades to maj., 1983; def. counsel, legal asst. atty., spl. asst. U.S. atty. U%, Camp Legeune, N.C., 1986-88; dep. staff judge advocate 4th Marine Divsn., New Orleans, 1988-92; sr. def. counsel 3rd FSSG U.S. Marine Corps, Okinawa, Japan, 1993-94; internat. law officer U.S. Ctrl. Command, MacDill AFB, Fla., 1994—. Mem. Washington State Bar Assn., Ohio State Bar Assn. Republican. Episcopalian. Home: 37540 Church Ave Dade City FL 33525 Office: US Ctrl Command 7115 S Boundary Blvd Tampa FL 33621

COLLINS, ROBERT ARNOLD, English language educator; b. Miami, Fla., Apr. 25, 1929; s. John William and Edna (Arnold) C.; m. Laura Virginia Roberts, June 3, 1960; 1 child, Judith. BA in English, U. Miami, Coral Gables, Fla., 1951; MA in English, U. Ky., 1960, PhD in English, 1968. Chair English Midway (Ky.) Jr. Coll., 1960-64; assoc. prof. English No. Ill. U., DeKalb, 1964-68, Morehead (Ky.) State U., 1968-69; from assoc. prof. to prof. English Fla. Atlantic U., Boca Raton, 1970—; founder, dir. Internat. Conf. on the Fantastic in the Arts, Ft. Lauderdale, Fla., 1980—. Author: Thomas Burnett Swann: A Critical Biography, 1980, Science Fiction and Fantasy Book Review Annual, 1987-91; editor: Scope of the Fantastic, 1985, Modes of the Fantastic, 1995; editor Fantasy Rev., 1981-87; mng. editor Jour. of the Fantastic in the Arts, 1995; contbr. articles to profl. jours. Recipient World Fantasy award World Fantasy Conv., New Haven, 1982, Balrog award Sword and Shield, 1982, 83. Home: 1320 SW 5th St Boca Raton FL 33486-4404 Office: Fla Atlantic U English Dept 500 NW 20th St Boca Raton FL 33431-6415

COLLINS, ROBERT HOWARD, JR., oncologist, internist; b. St. Louis, June 3, 1960; s. Robert Howard Sr. and Elsie (Alford) C.; m. Lynn Marie (Baumann); children: Andrew, James Michael. BA, U. Mo., 1983, MD, 1984. Diplomate Am. Bd. Internal Medicine, Am. Bd. Med. Oncology; licenced physician, Tex., Calif. Intern in internal medicine Baylor U. Med. Ctr., 1984-85, resident in internal medicine, 1985-87, asst. dir. bone marrow transplantation, 1989—, assoc. attending, 1990-96, attending, 1996—; fellow in hematology-oncology UCLA, 1987-89; assoc. Tex. Oncology, P.A., 1989-90, ptnr., 1991—; mem. com. on radiation and isotopes Baylor U. Med. Ctr., 1989-92, transfusion com., 1991—, ethics com., 1992-93, instl. rev. bd., 1992—; mem. sci. subcom. and acquired non-malignant diseases Nat. Marrow Donor Program, 1993—; presenter in field. Contbr. over 85 articles and abstracts to profl. and sci. jours. Curator's scholar U. Mo., 1979, Univ. scholar U. Mo., 1982, Flarscheim scholar; UCLA clin. oncology fellow Am. Cancer Soc., 1988. Fellow ACP; mem. AAAS, Am. Soc. Clin. Oncology, Am. Soc. Hematology, Am. Soc. for Blood and Marrow Transplantation, Tex. Soc. Med. Oncology, Dallas Med. Soc., Phi Kappa Phi. Address: 6439 Westlake Ave Dallas TX 75214-3438 Office: 3535 Worth St Dallas TX 75246-2029

COLLINS, ROBERT KEITH, health center administrator, physician; b. Aztec, N.Mex., Oct. 27, 1947; s. Clifford Calvin and Margaret Etta (Flaugh) C.; m. Pamela Cole Capps, May 28, 1972. BS in Biology, BA in Chemistry, Millsaps Coll., 1969; MD, U. Miss., 1974. Diplomate Am. Bd. Family Practice; cert. sports medicine. Resident in family practice U. Miss. Med. Ctr., Jackson, 1974-77; staff physician Miss. State U. Med. Ctr., Starkville, 1977-88; dir. John C. Longest Student Health Ctr. Miss. State U., Starkville, 1988—; mem. staff, sec., vice chief staff Oktibbeha County Hosp., Starkville, 1977-88, chief staff, 1990-92; chmn. edn. com. AIDS task force, Miss. Bd. Health, 1987-95; profl. and tech. adv. com. Ambulatory Healthcare for Joint Commn. for Accreditation Health Orgns., 1993—. Contbr. articles to med. jours. Fellow Am. Acad. Family Practice; mem. AMA, Am. Coll. Health Assn. (chmn. athletic medicine sect. 1989-90, bd. dirs. 1990-92), So. Coll. Health Assn. (pres. 1988-89), Am. Coll. Sports Medicine, Am. Med. Soc. Sports Medicine, Sigma Xi. Home: 507 N Montgomery St Starkville MS 39759-2331 Office: Miss State U John C Longest Student Health Ctr Starkville MS 39759

COLLINS, RONALD WILLIAM, psychologist, educator; b. N.Y.C., Jan. 6, 1947; s. Edward H. Collins Jr. and Estelle Lott. BA, Rutgers U., 1969; MS, Nova U., 1987; EdD, Fla. Internat. U., 1990; PhD, Saybrook Inst., 1996. Lic. profl. counselor, Mont.; LMHC, Fla. Spl. agt., ret. U.S. Secret Svc., Miami, Fla., 1971-91; adj. prof. St. Thomas U., Miami, 1990-91; asst. prof. Ea. Mont. Coll., Billings, 1991-94, Mont. State U., Billings, 1994-95; psychol. intern Inst. for Psychol. Growth, Ft. Lauderdale, Fla., 1994-95; adj. prof. counseling psychology, instrnl. analysis/design Fla. Internat. U., Ft. Lauderdale, 1995—; psychologist Ctr. Psychol. Effectiveness, Inc., Plantation, Fla., 1996—. Author: The Kabiroff Papers, 1988, Transfer of Learning, 1990; contbr. articles to profl. jours. Mem. Billings Family Violence Task Force, 1992. Mem. Am. Ednl. Rsch. Assn., Mont. Psychol. Assn., Phi Delta Kappa. Episcopalian. Home: PO Box 2053 Fort Lauderdale FL 33303 Office: Center of Psychological Effectiveness Inc 300 NW 70th Ave #302 Plantation FL 33317

COLLINS, SUSAN FORD, leadership consultant; b. N.Y.C., Dec. 8, 1939; d. Eugene Elwood and Mary Elizabeth Crighton Ford; m. Donald J. Collins, Sept. 9, 1962 (div. 1973); children: Catherine Lyn Rosenberg, Margaret Ann Chaneles. Student, Smith Coll., 1958-60; BA, U. Richmond, 1969. Rsch. psychologist NIMH, Bethesda, Md., 1962-64; rschr. success and leadership strategies Miami, Fla., 1964—; ptnr. Success Internat., Miami, 1985-86, co-dir., 1988-93; v.p. Winterstreet Corp. USA, Miami, 1986-88; pres. Our Children Are Watching, Inc., Miami, 1993—; cons. Am. Express, Digital Equipment, Kimberley-Clar, Ryder Sys., Fla. Power and Light, IBM, Levitz Furniture, Coopers and Lybrand, City of Miami, City of Seaside, Fla., Palm Beach County, Fla.; spkr. in field. Author: The Me Book: A Manual for Being Human, 1983, Our Children Are Watching: Ten Skills for Leading the Next Generation to Success, 1995, Intuition At Work, 1996; author foreword Women and Leadership, 1996; guest TV and radio shows. Fellow The Leadership Trust; mem. Nat. Spkrs. Assn., Nat. Writers Assn., Phi Beta Kappa, Psi Chi, Pi Kappa Delta, Phi Kappa Phi. address: Tech of Success Inc 12040 NE Fifth Ave Miami FL 33161

COLLINS, WHITFIELD JAMES, lawyer; b. Dallas, Aug. 26, 1918; s. Jasper and Gertrude (James) C.; m. Beth Cooper, June 5, 1951 (dec. Aug. 1980); children: Whitfield James Jr., Kay, Cooper R. AA, Kemper Mil. Sch., 1936; BA, U. Tex., 1938, JD, 1940; LLM, Harvard U., 1941. Bar: Tex. 1940, U.S. Dist. Ct. (no. dist.) Tex. 1950, U.S. Ct. Claims 1978, U.S. Tax Ct. 1949, U.S. Ct. Appeals (5th cir.) 1981. Atty. Office Gen. Counsel Treasury Dept., Washington, 1941-42, Office Chief Counsel, IRS, Washington and N.Y.C., 1946-48; assoc. Cantey, Hanger, Johnson, Scarborough & Gooch, Ft. Worth, 1949-54; ptnr. Cantey & Hanger and predecessor firms, Ft. Worth, 1954—; sec., bd. dirs. Vol. Purchasing Groups, Inc., Bonham, Tex., 1968-95; pres. Fifth Ave. Found. and C.J. Wrightsman Ednl. Fund, 1980—; bd. dirs., sec.-treas. T.J. Brown and C.A. Lupton Found., Ft. Worth; former chmn. bd. Intercultura, Inc., Ft. Worth. Contbr. articles in field to profl. jours. Bd. dirs. and past pres. Moncrief Radiation Ctr., Ft. Worth, Ft. Worth Art Assn., Arts Council Ft. Worth and Tarrant County, Ft. Worth Art Commn.; bd. dirs. Van Cliburn Found. Served to lt. commdr. USNR, 1942-46. Fellow ABA (life), State Bar Tex. (chmn. taxation sect. 1964-65); mem. Tarrant County Bar Assn. (Blackstone award 1995). Episcopalian. Home: 6732 Brants Ln Fort Worth TX 76116-7202 Office: Cantey & Hanger 801 Cherry St Ste 2100 Fort Worth TX 76102-6821

COLLINS, WILLIAM ARTHUR, III, accountant; b. Tuscaloosa, Ala., Aug. 12, 1943; s. William Arthur Jr. and Frances (Thomas) C.; m. Brenda Partin; 1 child, Elizabeth Frances. BBA in Acctg., U. Ariz., 1974. Auditor El Paso (Tex.) Natural Gas Co., 1966-69; comml. teller S.W. Nat. Bank, El Paso, 1969-72; acct., then sr. acct. Tucson (Ariz.) Electric Power, 1974-80; staff analyst acctg. Am. Arabian Oil Co., Dhahran, Saudi Arabia, 1980-82; acctg. mgr., dir. fin., v.p. fin., gen. mgr. mfg. and engring. div. Mooney Aircraft Corp., Kerrville, Tex., 1983-91; exec. v.p., chief exec. officer Reminessence, Inc., Fredricksburg, Tex., 1991-92; adminstrv. coord. Health South Rehab. Corp., San Antonio, 1992-95; gen. mgr. Far West Corp., San Antonio, 1995—; bd. dirs. RADTEK Corp., Kerrville, Mooney Sales and Fin Corp., Kerrville. Advisor Jr. Achievement, Tucson, 1980; fundraiser United Way, Tucson, 1983. Mem. Nat. Assn. Accts. Republican. Methodist. Club: Personal Computing (Kerrville). Home: 17011 Wood Canyon St San Antonio TX 78248-1413 Office: 9150 Huebner Rd San Antonio TX 78240-1545

COLLINS, WILLIAM JOSEPH, JR., lawyer, officer of marines; b. Phila., Sept. 4, 1966; s. William Joseph Sr. and Virginia T. (Dougherty) C.; m. Jill Bernice Rissmiller, Nov. 26, 1994. Student, U. Dublin, Trinity Coll., Ireland, 1987; BA, LaSalle U., 1989; JD, Widener U., 1994. Bar: Pa., U.S. Dist. Ct. (ea. dist.) Pa., U.S. Ct. Mil. Appeals. Paralegal securities litig. Berger & Montague P.C., Phila., 1989-91, atty., 1994-95; legal intern fed. divsn. Pa. Pub. Utilities Commn., Harrisburg, 1993; commd. USMCR, 1992; advanced through grades to capt. USMC, 1995, with JAG, 1995—; alumni recruiter LaSalle U., Phila., 1994—. Merit badge cons. Valley Forge Coun. Boy Scouts Am., Montgomery County, Pa., 1990—; founder Project Mercy 5K Classic Run & Walk, Harrisburg, Pa., 1993-94. Mem. Army and Navy Club, Bachelors Barge Club (rower). Republican. Roman Catholic. Home: PSC 557 Box 3621 FPO AP 96379-3621 Office: 3d FSSG FMF PAC LSSS H&S Bn Unit 38401 FPO AP 96604-8401

COLLIPP, BRUCE GARFIELD, ocean engineer, consultant; b. Niagara Falls, N.Y., Nov. 7, 1929; s. Planton G. and Audrey O. Collipp; m. Priscilla Jane Milbury, Dec. 25, 1954; children: Gary, Richard. BS, MIT, 1952, MS, 1954. Registered profl. engr., Tex.; lic. marine engr. Engring. offficer Lykes Bros., New Orleans, 1951, 53; teaching asst. MIT, Cambridge, Mass., 1954; designer, contractor Shell Oil, 1954-56, mgr. design constrn. and operation semisubmersible rig, 1956-61, prin. lectr. floating drilling and subsea completions, 1961; divsn. engr. Shell Oil, L.A., 1962-65, Lafayette, La., 1965-70; sr. staff rschr. Shell Oil, 1970-74, offshore designer Gulf of Mex., 1974-78, constrn. engr., 1978-80, project mgr., 1980-83, cheif naval architect, 1984, designer, contractor, 1985-87; cons. Shell Offshor Inc., Shell Oil Co., Exxon, World Bank, Reading and Bates Drilling C., U. of Texas, Austin, Noble Denton, PMB Systems Engring., British Petroleum, Elf Acquitaine Petroleum, Homestake Mining Inc., CBS Engring., Shell Pecten Internat., ARCO Internat., Lemle and Kelleher, 1987—; vis. prof. U. Tex., Austin, 1976—. Author: Buoyancy and Stability, 1976; contbr. over 50 tech. papers to profl. jours. Mayor Hidden Coves, Tex., 1976-86; dir. Spring Branch Meml. Sports Assn., Houston, 1972-76; mem. marine bd. Nat. Rsch. Coun., Washington, 1993—. Lt. USNR. Recipient Holley medal Am. Soc. Mech. Engrs., 1979, Gibbs Bros. medal Nat. Acad. Scis., 1991; Fulbright scholar. Mem. Nat. Acad. Engring., Soc. Naval Arch. and Marine Engring. (Blakley Smith medal 1993), Sigma Xi. Republican. Presbyterian. Home: 511 Kickerillo Dr Houston TX 77079-7428

COLLIVER, KEITH WAYNE, international program analyst; b. Anderson, Ind., Aug. 18, 1947; s. Alvin and Mildred Morene (Hymer) C.; m. Patricia Ann Gunn, May 14, 1983 (div. 1987); m. Sheryl K. Reilly, May 27, 1989; children: Jason, Aaron, Ethan. BA, Ind. U., 1969; MA, U. S.C., 1985. Commd. 2d lt. U.S. Army, 1969, advanced through grades to lt. col., 1987; reconnaissance platoon leader Strategic Tech. Directorate Adv. Team, Kontum, Pleiku, Vietnam, 1972; spl. forces detachment comdr. 10th Spl. Forces Group, Ft. Devens, Mass., 1973-75; co. comdr., supply officer, ops. & tng. officer 7th Infantry Div., Ft. Ord, Calif., 1975-79; dep. dir. spl. forces sch., chief spl. forces officer course John F. Kennedy Ctr. for Spl. Warfare, Ft. Bragg, N.C., 1980-83; chief strategic studies 4th psychol. ops. group 1st Spl. Ops. Command, Ft. Bragg, N.C., 1983-85; sr. analyst middle East Africa div. Def. Intelligence Agy., Washington, 1985-87, dep. and acting div. chief middle East Africa div., 1987-89; polit.-mil. affairs officer U.S. Arms Control and Disarmament Agy., Washington, 1989-92; ret. U.S. Army, 1992; fgn. affairs officer U.S. Arms Control and Disarmament Agy., Washington, 1992-93; sr. internat. program analyst AmerInd Inc., Arlington, Va., 1993—. Vestryman Aquia Episcopal Ch., Stafford, Va., 1994—. Decorated Purple Heart, silver star U.S. Army, Vietnam. Home: 2018 Schooner Dr Stafford VA 22554 Office: HJ Ford 1111 Jefferson Davis Hwy Arlington VA 22202

COLLUM, DANNY DUNCAN, fine arts educator; b. Greenwood, Miss., Feb. 26, 1954; s. Willie Murray and Martha Mae (Holland) C.; m. Polly Carter Duncan, Sept. 19, 1987; children: Christopher, Magdalena. Student, Miss. Coll., Clinton, 1972-77; B of Liberal Studies, Loyola U., New Orleans, 1992; MFA, George Mason U., 1995. Assoc. editor Sojourners Mag., Washington, 1980-88, columnist, 1988—; exec. dir. Abraham Lincoln Brigade Archives, Brandeis U., Waltham, Mass., 1988-93; TV critic Nat. Cath. Reporter, Kansas City, Mo., 1991-93; teaching asst. George Mason U., Fairfax, Va., 1994-95; part-time faculty Md. Inst. Coll. Art, Balt., 1995—. Author: Black and White Together, 1996; editor: African Americans in the Spanish Civil War, 1992; contbg. editor Sojourners Mag., 1988—; author articles and short story. Bd. dirs. So. Columbia Hts. Tenants Union, Washington, 1985-87; bd. govs. Abraham Lincoln Brigade Archives, 1993—; vol. Miss. Dem. Party, 1972-76, Columbia Hts. Land Trust, 1977-79; organizer Nat. Peace Pentecost Activities for Nuclear Disarmament, 1982-87. Recipient Mary Roberts Rinehart award George Mason U., 1995, Dawson Gaillard award for fiction Loyola U., 1992. Mem. MLA, Assoc. Writing Programs, Cath. Com. of the South. Home: 8 E Oak Alexandria VA 22321

COLLUM, W(ILLIAM) HAROLD, small business owner; b. Dallas, Feb. 20, 1932; s. William Mosco and Nellie Hazel (Miller) C.; m. Mattie Merelyne Stephens, Aug. 28, 1955; children: William Harold Jr., Teresa Lynn Collum Cedrone, Janice Elaine Collum Dixon, Deborah Sue Collum Condado. BA, Union Coll., 1956; postgrad., So. Meth. U., 1957-58. Mem. pension/profit sharing dept. Merc. Nat. Bank, Dallas, 1956-61, mgr. pension/profit sharing dept., until 1961; owner Collum Internat., Dallas, 1961—; dir. real estate So. Meth. U., Dallas, 1965-70; bd. chmn. Interwest Corp., Dallas, 1984-87; vice chmn. bd. Ketchum, Inc., Norwalk, Conn., 1987; chmn. Collum Internat., Dallas and Hong Kong, Hewitt Rsch. Ctr., Berrien Springs, Mich. Columnist Dallas/Ft. Worth Comml. Real Estate News. Past eagle Rep. Party, Dallas, 1983-85; candidate 3d Congl. Dist. of Tex., 1974; mem. Rep. Senatorial Inner Circle, Washington, 1991—. Cpl. U.S. Army, 1952-54, ETO. Recipient Outstanding Svc. award Hewitt Rsch. Ctr., 1972. Adventist. Office: Collum Internat PO Box 2010 Dallas TX 75221

COLLUMB, PETER JOHN, communications company executive; b. Newark, July 29, 1942; s. Peter A. and Rose M. (Coffey) C.; 1 child, Alexandra Christine. Student, East Tex. State U., 1967; postgrad in Bus. Adminstrn., U. Dallas, 1988. Registered lobbyist. Dir. pers./labor rels. Roper Corp., Chattanooga, Tenn., 1969-71; v.p. human resources Nat. Sharedata Corp., Dallas, 1971-74; dir. pers./labor Dallas Times Herald, 1975-78; dir. econ. devel. divsn. Tex. Dept. Community Affairs, Austin, 1978-80; dep. dir. Tex. Dept. Cmty. Affairs, 1978-81; legis./adminstrv. dir. U.S. Senator John G. Tower, Washington and Dallas, 1980-83; v.p. fin., sec.-treas. Diversified Packaging Co., Inc., Dallas, 1983-85; pres. N.Am. Systems, Inc., Dallas, 1981—; chmn. of bd., pres. Collumb, Hess, Navarro, Pub. Rels., Collumb, Hess, Navarro Pub. Rels., Dallas, Austin, Washington, Sacramento, 1991—; chmn., pres. Collumb Communications Co., Dallas, 1983—; chmn. Komatsu, Ashcraft and Collumb Inc.; personal envoy Ronald W. Reagan, Pres. of U.S., Washington, 1981-82; adj. prof. Bishop Coll., Dallas; bd. dirs. Tex. Housing Agy., Govs. Coms. on Aging and Migrant Affairs; guest lectr. So. Meth. U., Dallas, 1988—; chmn. bd. D.S.P. Corp., Dallas, 1985—, C.H.N. Internat., Washington, Geneva, London and Tokyo; advisor to U.S. Sec. of Labor, Houston Econ. Summit, 1990. Author: Political Process, 1982; contbr. articles to profl. publs. bd. dirs. Plano Child Guidance Ctr., Collin County Mental Health-Mental Retardation Coun., Edna Gladney Ctr., Ft. Worth, 1979—, Free Shakespeare Festival, Dallas, 1978-85, v.p. finance; bd. dirs. Outstanding Young Men Am., Atlanta, 1982—, Nat. Com. Adoption, 1986—, Bus. Continuation/Disaster Recovery Inst., 1987—, Ark. State Vocat./Tech. Schs., Ft. Worth State Sch. for the Retarded, Beautify Tex. Coun., 1980-85, Westminster Ind. Sch. Dist. Bd.; lobbyist, City of Fairview, Tex.; mem. advance staff Reagan/Bush Presdl. Campaign, Washington, 1978-85, Sam Johnson for Congress Campaign, 1991, Edwin Edward for Gov. Campaign, Bush-Quayle 1992 Presdl. Campaign; vice-chmn., dir. fin. Fair Housing Coun., 1988—; mem. community adv. coun. Coord. Bd. Tex. Colls. and Univs.; mem. Rep. Presdl. Task Force, 1984—; chmn. Fourth Border Conf. on Drug Abuse; candidate U.S. Ho. Reps., Dallas, 1982-84; del. White House Confs. on Aging, Small Bus. and the Family, Tex. Rep. Party Convs., 1984, 88, 92; pvt. advisor to Pres. U.S.: Ronald Reagan and George Bush; exec. dir., receiver Dallas County Community Action Com.; cons. U.S. Can. Free Trade Commn., Washington, 1986-87, Plano Sister Cities, Inc., others; chmn., v.p. fin., v.p. devel. Tex. World of Children; chmn. Pres.'s Adv. Coun., HUD Tech. Adv. Coun., Plano Ballet Theatre, N.E. Tex. Coun. of Svcs., Hillcrest Acad. Found., 1986-91, George Bush for Gov., 1994, Hutchinson for U.S. Senate, 1994. Named to Outstanding Young Men Am., Jaycees, 1981, Amigo Extradonaire, Govt. of Mexico, 1984. Mem. Centros de Juv Mexico (chmn. 1980-84), North Dallas C. of C. (bus. resource, internat. affairs, govt. affairs com.), Lions (v.p. Mena, Ark. chpt. 1976-77), Rotary, Lambda Chi Alpha (pres. 1967-69, chmn. Alumni control bd., pres. Alumni Assn.), Stallion Club (pres.), Tex. Sheriffs Assn. (charter), East Tex. State U. Alumni Assn. Republican. Presbyterian. Office: Collumb Communication Co 3404 Mission Ridge Rd Ste 100 Plano TX 75023-8115

COLMAN, CHARLES KINGSBURY, academic administrator, criminologist; b. Nashua, N.H., May 14, 1929; s. Charles David Colman and Lela (Bessey) Sproul; m. Marjorie Gertrude Bahe, Aug. 19, 1950; children: Charles David, Cathleen Ann. Diploma, Yale U., 1961; BA, U. Md., 1963; MEd, Stetson U., 1972; EdD, Fla. Atlantic U., 1978. Spl. agt. USAF, U.S. Army, 1947-67; asst. prin. Satellite High Sch., Satellite Beach, Fla., 1969-81, dean acad. edn., 1981-85; ctr. dir. Brevard C.C., Patrick AFB, Fla., 1985-92; provost Brevard C.C., Palm Bay, Fla., 1992-94; pres. emeritus, 1994—; Mem. Fla. State Adv. Com. on Mil. Edn., Patrick AFB, 1985—; edn. rep. Semiconductor Mfg. Tech., Dallas, 1985—. Author: Formative Years, 1970; author computer software. Co-founder Boys Club Am., Melbourne, Fla, 1968. Grantee Fla. Dept. Edn., 1987, 89, 90, 91, U.S. Dept. Edn., 1991-92; recipient Ace award Fla. Dept. Edn., 1991. Mem. Retired Officers' Assn., Assn. for Supervision and Curriculum Devel., Phi Delta Kappa (chpt. pres. 1983-84). Home: 1230 Seminole Dr Indian Harbour Beach FL 32937 Office: Brevard Community Coll Palm Bay Campus 250 Grassland Rd SE Palm Bay FL 32909-2206

COLN, DALE, pediatric surgeon, educator; b. Dallas, Dec. 23, 1934; s. Charlie Edward and Jessie Ruth (Enix) C.; m. Shirley Jane Kindberg, May 12, 1962; children: Sara, Eric, Lois, Ruth, Mary. BA, Baylor U., 1957; MD, Baylor Coll. Medicine, 1961. Intern Jefferson Davis Hosp., Houston, 1961-62; resident in surgery Parkland Meml. Hosp., Dallas, 1963-67; asst. prof. U. Tex. Southwestern Med. Ctr., Dallas, 1969-75, chmn. pediatric surgery, 1972-87, assoc. prof., 1975-93; dir. pediatric surgery Baylor U. Med. Ctr., Dallas, 1987—; rsch. fellow in surgery U. Tex. Southwestern Med. Ctr., 1962-63, prof. surgery, 1993; fellow Red Cross War Meml. Hosp., Cape Town, S. Africa, 1971-72, L.A. Children's Hosp., 1978; founder and dir. pediatric trauma unit Parkland Meml. Hosp., 1982-89. Author numerous publs. on trauma in children, fluid and electrolyte abnormalities, shock, sepsis and congenital abnormalities; contbr. numerous articles to profl. jours. Active Northwest Bible Ch., Dallas, 1972, Dallas Symphony Assn., 1984, Dallas Opera Assn., 1986. Sr surgeon USPHS, 1967-69, Sitka, Alaska. Fellow ACS, Am. Acad. Pediats., Internat. Coll. Surgeons; mem. Am. Assn. Surgery Trauma, Am. Pediat. Surg. Assn., Parkland Surg. Soc. (founding 1982, pres. 1983), Tex. Pediat. Soc. (exec. com., chmn. injury and environ. hazards com.). Evangelical. Home: 4675 Christopher Pl Dallas TX 75204-1610 Office: Baylor U Med Ctr 3600 Gaston Ave Dallas TX 75246-1800

COLÓN, PHYLLIS JANET, city official; b. Taylor, Tex., Sept. 1, 1938; d. Jack and Lydia Windmeyer; m. Henry J. Coló, Feb. 12, 1977; children: Walter N. Barnes III, Bradley H. Barnes, Mark A. Barnes. AA in Pub. Adminstrn., Del Mar Coll.; postgrad. in Acctg., Durham Jr. Coll.; BAAS in Pub. Adminstrn., Tex. A&I U., 1987; postgrad., Art Inst. Dayton. Registered profl. appraiser, Tex., assessor, Tex.; cert. tax adminstr., Tex.; lic. real estate borker, Tex. Mgr. info. Med. Arts Lab., Dayton, Ohio, 1970-73; appraiser Nueces County Appraisal Dist., Corpus Christi, 1973-82; tax assessor, collector Flour Bluff Ind. Sch. Dist., Corpus Christi, 1982, dir. spl. svcs., 1992-93; tax assessor, collector City of Laredo, Tex., 1993—; mem. profl. stds. com. Bd. Tax Profl. Examiners, 1991, vice chmn., 1992, chmn. 1994—. Mem. advance planning bd. Corpus Christi Libr.; chmn. ad hoc planning com. Del Mar Coll., 1989—. Recipient achievement award State of Tex., Hero award City of Corpus Christi. Mem. NAFE, AAUW (bd. dirs. Corpus Christi br.), Tex. Assn. Assessing Officers, Tex. Sch. Assessors Assn., Inst. Cert. Tax Adminstrs., Am. Soc. Notaries, Corpus Christi C. of C., Art Mus. South Tex., Kiwanis (treas. Corpus Christi 1989-90, pres. 1990—; 2d v.p. Laredo United Way, 1995—). Republican. Lutheran. Home: 8728 Martinique Dr Laredo TX 78045-8008 Office: City of Laredo PO Box 329 1110 Houston St Laredo TX 78040-8019

COLONEY, WAYNE HERNDON, civil engineer; b. Bradenton, Fla., Mar. 15, 1925; s. Herndon Percival and Mary Adore (Cramer) C.; m. Anne Elizabeth Benedict, June 21, 1950; 1 child, Mary Adore. B.C.E. summa cum laude, Ga. Inst. Tech., 1950. Registered profl. engr. and surveyor, Fla., Ga., Ala., N.C. Project engr. Constructora Gen. S.A., Venezuela, 1948-49, Fla. Rd. Dept., 1950-55; hwy. engr. Gibbs & Hill, Inc., Guatemala, 1955-57; project mgr. Gibbs & Hill, Inc., Tampa, Fla., 1957-59; project engr., then assoc. J.E. Greiner Co., Tampa, 1959-63; ptnr. Barrett, Daffin & Coloney, Tallahassee, 1963-70; pres. Wayne H. Coloney Co., Inc., Tallahassee, 1970-78, chmn., bd. chief exec. officer, 1978-85; pres., sec. Tesseract Corp., 1975-85; dep. chmn. Howden Airdynamics Am., Tallahassee, 1985-90; pres. Coloney Co. Cons. Engrs., Inc., 1978—; v.p., dir. Howden Coloney Inc., Tallahassee, 1985-90; prin. Coloney-Von Soosten & Assocs. Inc., Tallahassee, 1990—; chmn. adv. com. Area Vocat. Tech. Sch., 1965-78; pres. Retro Tech. Corp., 1983-93, Profl. Mgmt. Con. Group, 1983-87; pres., bd. dirs. Internat. Enterprises Inc., 1967-73; bd. dirs., exec. com. GTO, Inc., 1990—. Patentee roof framing system, dense packing external aircraft fuel tank, tile mounting structure, curler rotating device, bracket system for roof framing; contbr. articles to profl. jours. Pres. United Fund Leon County, 1971-72; bd. dirs. Springtime Tallahassee, 1970-72, pres., 1981-82; bd. dirs. Heritage Found.,

1965-71, pres., 1967; mem. Pres.'s Adv. Council on Indsl. Innovation, 1978-79; bd. dirs. LeMoyne Art Found., 1973, v.p., 1974-75; bd. dirs. Goodwill Industries, 1972-73, Tallahassee-Popoyan Friendship Commn., 1968-73; mem. Adv. Com. for Hist. and Cultural Preservation, 1969-71, Govs. Commn. for Purchase from the Blind, 1980—. Served with AUS, 1943-46. Fellow ASCE, Nat. Acad. Forensic Engrs.; mem. Am. Def. Preparedness Assn., NSPE, Fla. Engring. Soc. (sr.), Fla. Inst. Cons. Engrs., Fla. Soc. Profl. Land Surveyors, Anak, Koseme Soc., Am. Arbitration Assn., Fla. Small Bus. Assn. (pres. 1981), Gov.'s Club, Phi Kappa Phi, Omicron Delta Kappa, Sigma Alpha Epsilon, Tau Beta Pi. Episcopalian. Home: 503 McDaniel St Tallahassee FL 32303-6254 Office: Coloney Co Cons Engrs 1014 N Adams St Tallahassee FL 32303-6133

COLSKY, ANDREW EVAN, lawyer, mediator, arbitrator; b. Miami, Fla., Nov. 20, 1964; s. Jacob and Irene Vivian (Belen) C. BA, U. Fla., 1986, JD, 1989; LLM in Litigation, Emory U., 1990. Bar: Fla. 1989, Ga. 1990, D.C. 1990, U.S. Dist. Ct. (no. dist.) Ga. 1990, U.S. Dist. Ct. (so. dist.) Fla. 1990, U.S. Ct. Appeals (D.C. cir.) 1990, U.S. Ct. Appeals (11th cir.); cert. mediator Fla. Supreme Ct. Pvt. practice Miami, Fla., 1992—; pres. Mediation Assocs. Inc., Ft. Lauderdale, Fla., 1992—, Employment Risk Mgmt. Group, Ft. Lauderdale, 1996; mem. trial team U. Fla., Gainesville, 1988-89. Mem. ABA, Golden Key Honor Soc., Phi Delta Phi, Omicron Delta Kappa, Phi Kappa Phi, Alpha Lambda Chi (pres. 1985-86). Office: 110 Tower 110 SE 6th St Ste 115 Fort Lauderdale FL 33301

COLSON, WILLIAM WILDER, music theory and composition educator; b. Kansas City, Mo., July 17, 1945; s. Howard Paul and Mary (Wilder) C.; m. Barbara Joy Simpson, 1977; 1 child, John William. MusB in Composition, Oberlin Conservatory, 1967; MusM in Composition, U. Ill., 1968, MusD in Composition, 1975; student, Kursverksamheten/U. Uppsala, Sweden, 1978-79, Royal Sch. Music, Sweden, 1979, U. Ariz., 1984-85, Goethe-Inst., Germany, 1991-92, U. Heidelberg, Germany, 1992. Cellist Ft. Worth Symphony Orch., 1971-86; prof. music theory and composition Southwestern Baptist Theological Seminary, Fort Worth, 1971—, assoc. dean acad. divsn., 1990—. Author: (software) Mode Identification Drills, Interval Identification Drills, Major Key Signature Identification Drill, Chord Identification Drills, Comps. Compute, 1985, 93; editor: (book) Manual for Master's Degree Students, 1994; editorial bd. Southwestern Jour. of Theology, 1989—; editor Manual for Doctoral Students, 1990, Manual for Master's Degree Students, 1991; compiler and editor Curriculum Guide for the School of Church Music, 1993, Anthology for Sixteenth-Century Counterpoint, 1990, Anthology for Eighteenth-Century Counterpoint, 1990; gen. editor Institutional Self-Study, 1990-91. Mem. Soc. Music Theory, Tex. Soc. Music Theory, So. Baptist Ch. Music Conf., Pi Kappa Lambda. Home: 201 Grand Meadow Dr Fort Worth TX 76108-3722 Office: Southwestern Bapt Theol Sem PO Box 22000 Fort Worth TX 76122

COLSTON, FREDDIE CHARLES, political science educator; b. Gretna, Fla., Mar. 28, 1936; s. Henry Bill and Willie Mae (Taylor) C.; m. Doris Marie Suggs, Mar. 13, 1976; 1 child, Deirdre Charisse. BA, Morehouse Coll., 1959; MA, Atlanta U., 1966; PhD, Ohio State U., 1972. Instr. social sci. Ft. Valley (Ga.) State Coll., 1966-68; assoc. prof. polit. sci. So. U., Baton Rouge, 1972-73, U. Detroit, 1973-76; assoc. prof., chmn. div. social sci. Dillard U., New Orleans, 1976-78; asst. prof. polit. sci. Delta Coll., University Center, Mich., 1978-79; assoc. dir. Exec. Seminar Ctr. U.S. Office Pers. Mgmt., Oak Ridge, 1980-87; prof. Inst. of Govt. Tenn. State U., Nashville, 1987-88; prof., dir. pub. adminstrn. program N.C. Ctrl. U., Durham, 1988-91; prof. dept. history and polit. sci. Ga. Southwestern Coll., Americus, 1992—. Contbr. articles to profl. jours. Mem. bd. mgmt. Northwestern Br. YMCA, Detroit, 1976; mem. govt. subcom. Task Force 2000, City of Midland, Mich., 1979. Morehouse Coll. scholar, 1955, Atlanta U. scholar 1965, Nat. Def. Edn. Act scholar, 1964, Ford Found. Internat. Studies Summer fellow, 1967, So. Fellowships Fund fellow, 1968-71; recipient C-Span Faculty Devel. grants, 1994, 95, 96; recipient Mr. Psi award, Omegi Psi Phi, 1959, Outstanding Faculty award, Kappa Delta Sorority, Ga. SW Coll., 1995. Mem. Am. Polit. Sci. Assn., Nat. Conf. Black Polit. Scientists, Ctr. for Study of Presidency, Internat. Platform Assn., Assn. for Study of Afro-Am. Life, So. Polit. Sci. Assn., Pi Sigma Alpha, Alpha Phi Gamma. Home: 126 Hazleton Ln Oak Ridge TN 37830-7929

COLTON, SUSAN ADAMS, principal; b. Jamestown, N.Y., Sept. 26, 1950; d. Emmett Robert and Jeanne Ellen (Moynihan) Franklin; m. Charles Ira, June 30, 1990. BA in edn., Fla. Atlantic U., 1977, MEd, 1984. Tchr. grade 1 Tamarac (Fla.) Elem., 1977-79; tchr. Cresthaven Elem, Pompano Beach, Fla., 1979-84; ednl. cons. Macmillan Pub. Co., N.Y.C., 1984-86; tchr. grade 1 Maplewood Elem., Coral Springs, Fla., 1986-87; asst. prin. Coral Springs (Fla.) Elem., 1987-92; prin. Forest Hills Elem. Sch., Coral Springs, 1992; cons. Broward County Schs., Ft. Lauderdale, Fla., 1986—; adv. bd. dirs. Broward County Reading Coun., Broward City, Fla., 1990—. Active Coral Springs Edn. Task Force, 1990—; vol. Child Care Connection, Ft. Lauderdale, 1987—. Grantee Broward County Schs., 1990. Mem. ASCD, Internat. Reading Assn., Fla. Reading Assn. (Honor Coun. 1989), Broward County Reading Assn. (pres. 1988-89, Honor Coun. 1989), Nat. Assn. Elem. Sch. Prins., Fla. Assn. Elem. Sch. Prins., Phi Delta Kappa, Delta Kappa Gamma. Republican. Episcopalian. Office: Forest Hills Elem Sch 3100 NW 85th Ave Coral Springs FL 33065-4616

COLTRANE, TAMARA CARLEANE, intravenous therapy nurse; b. Greensboro, N.C., Oct. 18, 1963; d. Charles Floyd and Nancy Jane (Lemons) C. BS in Nursing, U. N.C., Greensboro, 1986. RN, N.C.; cert. in intravenous therapy. Nursing asst. (summer) Mary Field Nursing Home, High Point, N.C., 1984; med.-surgical nurse Wesley Long Cmty. Hosp., Greensboro, 1986-88, IV team nurse, 1988—; mem. nursing policy com. Wesley Long Cmty. Hosp., Greensboro, 1987-88, nursing adv. com., 1987-89, 91-93, mem. nursing edn. coun., 1996—. Mem. coun. on ministries, pianist, coord. comm. Sandy Ridge United Meth. Ch., High Point, N.C., 1990—, mem. adminstrv. bd., 1986-88, 90—; vol. worker Starmount Villa Nursing Home, Greensboro, 1984. Mem. Nat. Intravenous Nurses Soc., N.C. Intravenous Nurses Soc., Sigma Theta Tau. Office: Wesley Long Cmty Hosp 501 N Elam Ave Greensboro NC 27403-1118

COLVIN, GAYLE ANN, mental health consultant, psychotherapist, health facility administrator; b. L.A., Sept. 21, 1953; d. Robert Owen Sr. and Rachel Rebecca (Lemley) Colvin; m. Frederick Randale Phillips Sr., July 28, 1971 (div.); children: Frederick Andrew Phillips, Brian Scott Phillips. AA in Psychology, Okla. City Community Coll., Oklahoma City, 1986; BS in Sociology, Okla. State U., 1990, BS in Psychology, 1991, MS in Counseling, 1992; MSW, U. Nev., Las Vegas, 1996. Adminstr., fin. cons. Security Fin. Cons., Oklahoma City, 1980-88; case worker Big Bros./Big Sisters, Stillwater, Okla., 1988-89; counselor Payne County Family Practices, Stillwater, 1989; social worker Dept. Human Svcs. Child Welfare, Stillwater, 1990; instr. Langston (Okla.) U., 1992; counselor Payne County Dept. Guidance Clinics and Health, Stillwater and Cushing, Okla., 1992-93, Christian Counseling Assocs., Stillwater, 1993-95; clin. dir., CEO New Beginnings Clin. Svcs. Corp., Las Vegas, 1996—. Disaster vol. ARC, Oklahoma City, 1987-88, disaster injury team vol., 1995; vita site coord. IRS, Oklahoma City, 1982-84; emergency room EMT Hillcrest Hosp., Oklahoma City, 1994; EMT/intermediate paramedic Amcare Ambulance Svcs., 1994. mem. ACA, APA, NASW, Am. Assn. for Christian Counselors, Nat. Assn. Social Workers, Okla. Psychol. Assn., Okla. Assn. Counseling and Devel., Assn. for Humanist Psychology, Phi Theta Kappa, Psi Chi. Democrat. Mem. LDS Ch. Home: 5150 Spyglass Hill Dr #283 Las Vegas NV 89122 Office: Bldg 2 Ste 283 5150 Spyglass Hill Dr Apt 283 Las Vegas NV 89122-2775

COLYER, KIRK KLEIN, insurance executive, real estate investment executive; b. Fayetteville, N.C., Jan. 30, 1956; s. Joe Bill and Charlotte (Klein) C. Assoc. in Bus., SUNY, Albany, 1977; BBA in Polit. Sci., Incarnate Word Coll., 1980; student, Leonard's Tng. Sch., 1985, Tex. Crime Prevention Inst., 1985. Lic. recording agt. Councilman City of Balcones Heights, San Antonio, Tex., 1977-82, mayor, 1982-86, mayor emeritus, 1986; pres. Colyer Real Estate Investments, San Antonio, 1980—; pres., founder Colyer Ins. Agy., San Antonio, 1982—; pres. Colyer Oil Co., San Antonio, 1982—; campaign dir. Congl. Rep. nominee Carl Bill Colyer, San Antonio; campaign treas. Gerry Richkoff County Clk., Bexar County, 1994. Vice pres. Balcones C. of C., San Antonio, 1978, San Antonio Young Reps., 1991; pres. Tex. Mcpl. League Region 7, San Antonio, 1985; founder Bexar County Young Reps., 1995; bd. dirs. San Antonio March of Dimes, 1985; grad. Leadership San Antonio, 1985. Named one of Outstanding Mems. of Am., U.S. Jaycees, 1977-91; Rey Feo XLIX, 1996-97. Mem. IHIO Corridor (founder, pres. 1984-86), San Antonio Ind. Car Dealers Assn. (founder, pres. 1993—), Tex. Auto Dealers Assn. (bd. dirs. 1994—), San Antonio City Club, San Antonio Plaza Club (life), Rey Feo '97, Distributive Edn. Clubs of Am. (life), Lions (bd. dirs. Balcones chpt. 1976-78), Tex. Jaycees (dist. bd. dirs. 1978, pres. Balcones Hts. chpt. 1977, Top Recruiter 1980), San Antonio Crime Stoppers (bd. dirs. 1984—). Home: 13290 Hunters View San Antonio TX 78230 Office: Colyer Ins Agy 4311 Ihiow San Antonio TX 78201

COLYER, SHERYL LYNN, psychologist; b. Portsmouth, Va., Dec. 20, 1959; d. Joshua Clark and Lubertha (Alexander) C. BS, Howard U., 1981; MA, Columbia U., N.Y.C., 1983; EdD, George Washington U., 1996. Pers. psychologist, employee devel. specialist IRS, Washington, 1983-84; human resource devel. cons. Tech. Applications, Falls Church, Va., 1984-85; human resource devel. specialist GM, Ft. Wayne, Ind., 1985-88; tng. and devel. cons. Freddie Mac, Reston, Va., 1988-90; div. tng. mgr. PepsiCo, Hanover, Md., 1990-91, regional mgr. human resources, 1990-92; dir. human resources devel. and comm. Hechinger Co., Landover, Md., 1992-95; v.p. human resources Hardee's Food System, Inc., Rocky Mount, N.C., 1995-96. Mem. ASTD, Soc. for Indsl. and Orgnl. Psychology, Inc. chpt. APA, Pers. Testing Coun. Met. Wash., Delta Sigma Theta (pres. 1981-81). Home: 507 E Indian Spring Dr Silver Spring MD 20901-4726

COMABELLA, LUIS FERNANDO, Spanish language educator; b. Cienfuegos, Cuba, June 25, 1946; came to U.S., 1961; s. Luis Fernando and Margarita (Recio) C. BA in Modern Langs., St. Mary's Coll., Winona, Wis., 1966; MA in Spanish, U. Wis., 1967; PhD in Hispanic Langs. and Lit., UCLA, 1991. Cert. C.C. tchr., Calif., interpreter and translator, L.A., Los Angeles County. Bilingual sec. St. Mary's Coll. Press, 1963-66; Spanish tchg. asst. U. Wis., Madison, 1966-67; fgn. langs. tchr., chmn. fgn. langs. dept. Franklin Jr. H.S., San Bernardino, Calif., 1967-68; Spanish tchg. assoc. UCLA, 1968-71; Spanish interpreter, translator L.A. Superior Ct., 1985-95; Spanish instr. UCLA Extension, 1973-93; asst. prof. Spanish Loyola-Marymount U., L.A., 1993-94, Indian River C.C., Ft. Pierce, Fla., 1994-96; freelance cons., interpreter, translator, L.A., 1973-93; presenter in field; dir. L.a. Superior Ct. Interpreting Tng. Program. Editor jour. Mester, 1969-71, also contbr. poetry. Facilitator Fla. Coun. Tchrs. of English, Vero Beach, 1994; organizer, presenter Careers in Fgn. Langs., Career Day, Indian River C.C., 1994; dir. continuing edn. com. Greater L.A. chpg. Calif. Ct. Interpreters Assn. Scholar St. Mary's Coll., 1963-66L'Université Laval; Del Amo Found. fellowship grantee, 1972. Mem. AAUP, Am. Assn. Spanish and Portuguese Tchrs., Fla. Assn. C.C.'s, Fla. Fgn. Assn. Instrs. at C.C.'s (bd. dirs. 1994—), Fla. Fgn. Lang. Assn., Sigma Delta Pi (pres. UCLA chpt. 1969-71).

COMBEST, LARRY ED, congressman; b. Memphis, Tex., Mar. 20, 1945; s. Lawrence Nelson and Callie (Gunter) C.; m. Sharon McCurry, Sept. 10, 1981; children—Tonya Lee, Haydn Cudd. BBA, W. Tex. State U., 1969. Farmer, stockman Memphis, 1965-71; county trainee Dept. Agr., Graham, Tex., 1971; spl. asst. Senator John Tower, Washington, 1971-78; owner Combest Distbg., Lubbock, Tex., 1978-85; mem. 99th-103rd Congresses from 19th Tex. dist., Washington, D.C., 1985—; mem. agriculture com., chmn. intelligence select com. Recipient Santa Fe award Future Farmers Am., 1962. Republican. Methodist. Lodges: Rotary, Lions. Office: US Ho of Reps 1511 Longworth House Office Bldng Washington DC 20515-4319

COMBS, JEANNE MARIA, nurse; b. Hamilton, Ohio, Oct. 31, 1955; d. Eugene and Shirley Jean (Lattuga) Hacker Lewis; 1 child, Melinda Renee Wood, from previous marriage. AS in Nursing, Miami U., Oxford, Ohio, 1976. Cert. gerontol. nurse. Staff nurse Bethesda North Hosp., Cin., 1976-78; dir. staff devel. Mt. Pleasant Retirement Village, Monroe, Ohio, 1980-83; shift supr. Adventist Convalescent Hosp., Glendora, Calif., 1983-86; dir. nursing svcs. Colonial Manor, West Covina, Calif., 1986-88, Brethren Hillcrest Homes, La Verne, Calif., 1988-90; dir. nursing svcs., dir. human resources Cumberland Valley Dist. Health Dept., 1990-93; supr. Jackson County Home Health Program, McKee, Ky., 1990-93; dir. edn. Health Directions, Corbin, Ky., 1993—; Contbr. articles to mags. Named Woman of Yr. Trenton Ch. of God, 1983, Outstanding Dir. Nursing So. Calif. Coun. Activity Coords., 1988. Mem. Calif. Coun. Long Term Care Nurses (sec. 1986-90), Calif. Nurses Assn., Am. Soc. Aging, Calif. Assn. Health Facilities, Ky. Home Health Assn., Ky. Pub. Health Assn., Ky. Home Health Assn., West Covina C. of C. (membership com.), Covina Women's Club. Republican. Home: 895 George Mcqueen Rd Annville KY 40402-8711 Office: Health Directions PO Box 187 East Bernstadt KY 40729-0187

COMBS, JOHN RAYMOND, English literature educator; b. Stafford, Okla., Dec. 9, 1929; s. James Manuel and Floy Odessa (Cranfill) C.; m. Joyce Fay Hudson, Aug. 28, 1950 (div. 1978); children: Perry Vernon, John Cranfill, Jody Braxton; m. Vicki Elizabeth Lyle, May 10, 1980. BA, S.W. State U., Weatherford, Okla., 1951; BD, So. Meth. U., 1954; MA, Tex. A&M U., 1964; PhD, U. Tex., 1968. Pastor First Meth. Ch., Coalgate, Okla., 1954-56, Newkirk, Okla., 1956; campus min., Wesley Found. Okla. State U., Stillwater, 1956-60, Tex. A&M U., College Sta., 1960-64; asst. prof. English McMurry U., Abilene, Tex., 1967-79; prof. English Ky. Wesleyan Coll., Owensboro, 1969—; active mem. Ky. Humanities Coun., 1976—; book reviewer, Choice (pub. by ALA), 1975—. Contbr. articles and poems to profl. jours. and lit. mags. Pres. West End Daycare Ctr., Owensboro, 1971-76; vice chair, two Gov.'s commns. Inst. for Children, Commonwealth of Ky., 1974-79; mem. special projects com. United Way, Owensboro, 1990-93; editor, concert programs and newsletter, Owensboro Symphony Orch., 1972-84. Named Outstanding Prof., Ky. Wesleyan student body, 1984-85; recipient Meritorious Tcg. award Nat. Assn. United MEth. Colls. and Schs., 1972. Mem. South Atlantic MLA, Ky. Philol. Soc. Democrat. Unitarian. Home: 1205 Allen St Owensboro KY 42303 Office: Kentucky Wesleyan College 3000 Frederica St Owensboro KY 42302

COMBS, LINDA JONES, management company executive, researcher; b. Jonesboro, Ark., Apr. 12, 1948; d. Dale Jones and Neva Craig; 1 child, Nathan Isaac. BSBA, U. Ark., 1971, MBA, 1972, PhD in Bus. Adminstrn., 1983. Assoc. economist Bur. Bus. and Econ. Rsch., Fayetteville, Ark., 1973-76; pres. Combs Mgmt. Co., Springdale, Ark., 1976-83; asst. prof. fin. U. Ark., Fayetteville, 1983-87; asst. prof. fin. and mktg. Western Ill. U., Macomb, 1987-88; asst. prof. bus. adminstrn. Cen. Mo. State U., Warrensburg, 1988-89; assoc. prof. bus. adminstrn. N.E. State U., Tahlequah, Okla., 1989—; cons. in credit and polit. rsch. Fayetteville Adv. Coun., 1975-76; cons. in fin. and banking, Fayetteville, 1973-76. Contbr. articles to profl. jours. Mem. Ark. Gov.'s Inaugural Com., Little Rock, 1985; county co-chmn. Clinton for Gov., Washington County, Ark., 1984, 86, 90; bd. dirs. Shiloh Mus., Am. Cancer Soc., South Washington County, North Ark. Symphony Soc.; bd. dirs. Ark. State Hosp. Sys., sec., chmn., 1991-95; active numerous polit. campaigns for candidates and issues. Mem. Am. Mktg. Assn. (health care mktg.), Transp. Rsch. Forum. Office: Combs Mgmt Co PO Box 1452 Fayetteville AR 72702-1452

COMBS, SANDRA LYNN, state parole board official; b. Lancaster, Pa., Aug. 31, 1946; d. Clyde Robert and Violet (Sensenig) Boose; m. Allen Evans Combs, Aug. 30, 1969; children: Evan McKenzie, Leslie Ann. AAS in Nursing, Thomas Nelson C.C., Hampton, Va., 1980; BS in Psychology, Juniata Coll., 1968. RN, Va. Dir. vols. in probation Yorktown (Va.) Juvenile Ct., 1973-74; emergency nurse assoc. to pvt. practice physician Hampton, Va., 1980-82; chmn. bd. dirs., CEO Hampton Roads Gulls Profl. Hockey Team, Hampton, 1981-82; mem. sch. bd. York County Pub. Schs., Yorktown, 1985-94; vice chmn. Va. Parole Bd., Richmond, 1994—; mem. supt.'s adv. coun. York County Pub. Schs., 1984-94, mem. long range strategic planning com., 1989-94; trustee New Horizons Tech. Ctr., Gov.'s Sch., Hampton, 1991-94; mem. Va. edn. tech. adv. com. Va. Dept. Edn., 1992-95; mem. Va. Bd. Correctional Edn., 1994—, Va. Adult Basic Edn. and Literacy Adv. Coun., 1994—. Pres. Hampton Med. Soc. Aux, 1977-78, Dare Elem. PTA, York County, 1979-81, York County Coun. PTA, 1983-84; chmn. York County Rep. Com., 1984-90, 1st Dist. Rep. Congl. Com., Va., 1990-94; adviser edn. policy George Allen for Gov., Richmond, 1992-93. Capt. USAF, 1968-73, Vietnam. Decorated Bronze Star medal, Cross of Gallantry (Vietnam), Air Force Commendation medal. Mem. ASCD, VFW, Va. Sch. Bds. Assn. (bd. dirs. 1990-94, award of Excellence 1990, 91, 92), Mil. Order World Wars. Methodist. Home: 9925 Groundhog Dr Richmond VA 23235-3972 Office: Va Parole Bd 6900 Atmore Dr Richmond VA 23225-5644

COMEAUX, ELIZABETH ANNE, medical librarian; b. Austin, Tex., Feb. 17, 1951; d. William Frank and Mary (Falbo) Brown; m. Paul Julienne Comeaux, Dec. 31, 1977; children: Daniel, Madeline, Rebecca, Juliette. BA in Psychology summa cum laude, U. Tex., 1973, MLS, 1974. Libr. reference Tex. Med. Assn., Austin, 1974-77; libr. search analyst, reference U. Tex. Health Sci. Ctr., San Antonio, 1977-85, libr. sys., 1986—. Mem. Med. Libr. Assn., Phi Beta Kappa, Phi Kappa Phi. Home: 5545 Mount McKinley San Antonio TX 78251 Office: Brisco Libr U Tex Health Sci 7703 Floyd Curl Dr San Antonio TX 78284

COMER, BRAXTON BRAGG, II, entrepreneur; b. Eufaula, Ala., Aug. 5, 1951; s. Richard Johnson and Anne Laurie C.; m. Mary Anna Fay, July 22, 1972; children: Margaret Laurie, Braxton Bragg Jr. Grad., McCallie Sch., 1970; BBA, U. Tex., Austin, 1974; MBA, Vanderbilt U., 1982. Projects mgr. acctg. Avondale Mills, Sylacauga, Ala., 1978, asst. v.p., asst. contr., 1979-81, corp. contr., asst. v.p., 1981-82, v.p., contr., 1982-85; mdse. mgr. Yarn Dyes & Indigo Avondale Fabrics, 1985-89; owner, pres. CX Enterprises Inc., 1989—; bd. dirs. City Nat. Bank of Sylacauga. Bd. dirs. Sylacauga Libr., Ala. Pub. Libr. Svc., chmn., trustee; bd. advisors McCallie Sch. Mem. Sylacauga C. of C. (past bd. dirs.), Rotary (past dir., past pres.). Home: 8 Mountain Ridge Rd Sylacauga AL 35150-4641 Office: CX Enterprises PO Box 418 Sylacauga AL 35150-0418

COMER, JAMES ANDERSON, veterinary parasitologist; b. Macon, Ga., May 1, 1953; m. Lucia Marie Adams, June 5, 1982; children: Mary Anderson, Catharine Drewry. AB in Biol. Anthropology, Harvard U., 1977; MS in Forest Resources, U. Ga., 1985, PhD in Veterinary Parasitology, 1991. Rsch. technician Southeastern Coop. Wildlife Disease Study Coll. Vet. Medicine, U. Ga., Athens, 1985-86, postdoctoral assoc. dept. parasitology, 1991-95; mem. staff viral and rickettsial zoonoses br. Ctrs. for Disease Control, Atlanta, 1995—; presenter in field. Contbr. articles to profl. jours. Mem. Am. Mosquito Control Assn. (life), Am. Soc. Mammalogists (life), Am. Soc. of Tropical Medicine and Hygiene, Entomol. Soc. Am., Ga. Entomol. Soc., Soc. for Vector Ecology, Wildlife Soc., Wildlife Disease Assn., Antique Auto. Assn. Am. (life), Athens Folk Music and Dance Soc., Athens Old Cemetery Found., Ga. Alumni Soc., Ga. Trust for Hist. Preservation, Harvard Club of Ga., Athens Antique Auto Club, Phi Kappa Phi (life), Xi Sigma Pi, Gamma Sigma Delta. Home: 595 Milledge Ter Athens GA 30606 Office: U Ga College Vet Medicine SCWDS Dept Parasitology Athens GA 30602

COMER, JIMMY M., systems analyst; b. Paris, Tenn., May 31, 1958; s. James Brent and Sarah LIllian (Mizell) C.; m. Barbara Lynn Miller, Dec. 8, 1979; children: Allison Beth, Scott Allen. BS, Freed Hardman Coll., 1979. Biol. lab. technician U.S. Army Corps Engrs., Nashville, 1980-86, computer asst., 1986-90, computer specialist, 1990-96; sr. systems analyst Gresham, Smith and Ptnrs., Nashville, 1996—. Mem. Mid. Tenn. Local User's Group (chmn. 1995—). Home: 652 Vernon Ave Nashville TN 37209-1229 Office: Gresham Smith & Ptnrs 3310 West End Nashville TN 37203

COMINS, DANIEL LEE, chemistry educator, consultant; b. Chaumont, N.Y., Dec. 31, 1949; s. Harrison Eugene and Kathleen Geneva (Barth) C.; m. Carol Bailey, June 20, 1987; 1 child, Clayton Bailey Comins. BA in Chemistry, SUNY, Potsdam, 1972; PhD, U. N.H., 1977. Postdoctoral assoc. Colo. State U., Fort Collins, 1977-79; asst. prof. Utah State U., Logan, 1979-84, assoc. prof., 1984-88; prof. N.C. State U., Raleigh, 1989—; mem. various coms. Utah State U., 1981-88, N.C. State U., 1989—; cons. SmithKline, Phila., 1984-85, SmithKline Chems., Conshohocken, Pa., 1987-92, Glaxo Inc., Research Triangle Park, N.C., 1992-96, Natland Internat., Research Triangle Park, 1993-95, Research Triangle Inst., 1995—; participant numerous profl. meetings; presenter in field. Editor Jour. of Organic Chemistry, 1996—; contbr. chpts. to books and articles to profl. jours.; patentee in field. Recipient Am. Inst. Chemists award, 1972, Outstanding Rsch. award N.C. State U. Alumni Assn., 1994; U. N.H. summer fellow, 1975, 76; grantee NIH, 1988—, SmithKline Chems., 1989-91, Glaxo, Inc., 1990-95, 92-94, Lilly/DowElanco, 1990—, Rhone-Poulenc, 1990—, NSF/N.C. State U., 1992, Pfizer, Inc., 1993—, Sumitomo Chem. Co., 1993, ACS-PRF, 1994—; named to SUNY Alumni Honor Roll, 1995. Mem. AAAS, Am. Chem. Soc. (divsn. organic chemistry), Internat. Soc. Heterocyclic Chemistry, Sigma Xi, Phi Lambda Upsilon. Office: NC State Univ Dept Chemisty Raleigh NC 27695-8204

COMP, PHILIP CINNAMON, medical researcher; b. Kewanee, Ill., Feb. 28, 1945; s. Franklin Howard and Alberta (Cinnamon) C.; m. Carol Lee Winter, May 11, 1974; children: Vanessa Cinnamon, Justin Philip, Aubrie Elizabeth. BA, Reed Coll., 1967; MD, U. Wash., 1971; PhD, U. Okla., 1978. Intern, then resident U. Pa. Hosp., Phila., 1971-74; fellow allergy sect. U. Okla. Health Sci. Ctr., Oklahoma City, 1974-76, asst. prof. medicine, 1976-82, assoc. prof. medicine, 1982-88, adj. prof. pathology, 1976—, dir. thrombosis/coagulant lab., 1979—, dir. Okla. Ctr. for Molecular Medicine, 1990—; attending physician Allergy Clinic State of Okla. Teaching Hosps., Oklahoma City, 1976-89; attending physician med. svc. VA Med. Ctr., Oklahoma City, 1976—, assoc. chief of staff rsch., 1992—; dir. Adult sect. Okla. Comprehensive Hemophilia Treatment Ctr., Oklahoma City, 1980—; mem. cardiovasc. biology resident program Okla. Med. Resident Found., Oklahoma City, 1988—. Office: OK Ctr for Molecular Med BSEB-Rm 325 PO Box 26901 Oklahoma City OK 73190

COMPO, LAWRENCE JUDD, sales and marketing executive; b. Freeport, N.Y., June 18, 1955; s. Lawrence Charles and Marilyn Anne (Volz) C.; m. Lorraine Mary Schwarz, Sept. 13, 1980; children: Caitlin Laura, Dylan Lawrence. BS, Ithaca (N.Y.) Coll., 1977; MBA, St. John's U., N.Y.C., 1980. Sales and mktg. analyst Merrill Lynch, Pierce Fenner & Smith, N.Y.C., 1977-81; sr. mktg. dir. Transamerica Relocation Svc., Greenwich, Conn., 1981-85; dir. bus. devel. Coldwell Banker Relocation Mgmt., Norwalk, Conn., 1985-87; v.p., regional mgr. Assocs. Relocation Mgmt. Co., Stamford, Conn., 1987-89; sr. v.p. Assocs. Relocation Mgmt. Co., Dallas, 1989-92; v.p. Coop. Resource Svcs., Ltd., Dallas, 1992—; sr. v.p. ProSource Properties, Ltd. subsidiary of CRS, Ltd., Dallas, 1995—. Mem. Am. Mgmt. Assn., Assn. for MBA Execs., Employee Relocation Coun. (cert. relocation profl., Meritorious Svc. award), Omicron Delta Epsilon. Home: 2904 Cottonwood Ln Colleyville TX 76034-5124 Office: Coop Resource Svcs Inc PO Box 503 Colleyville TX 76034-0503

COMPTON, ASBURY CHRISTIAN, state supreme court justice; b. Portsmouth, Va., Oct. 24, 1929; s. George Pierce and Edyth Gordon Compton; m. Betty Stephenson, Nov. 17, 1953; children: Leigh Christian, Mary Bryan, Melissa Anne. BA, Washington and Lee U., 1950, LLB, 1953, LLD, 1975. Bar: Va. 1957. Mem. firm May, Garrett, Miller, Newman & Compton, Richmond, 1957-66; judge Law and Equity Ct., City of Richmond, 1966-74; justice Supreme Ct. Va., Richmond, 1974—. Trustee Collegiate Schs., Richmond, 1972-89, chmn. bd., 1978-80; former chmn. adminstrv. bd. Ginter Park United Meth. Ch., Richmond; former mem. adminstrv. bd. Trinity United Meth. Ch., Richmond; trustee Washington and Lee U., 1978-90. With USN, 1953-56, USNR, 1956-62. Decorated Letter of Commendation. Mem. Va. Bar Assn., Va. State Bar, Bar Assn. City Richmond, Washington and Lee U. Alumni Assn. (past pres., dir.), Omicron Delta Kappa, Phi Kappa Sigma, Phi Alpha Delta. Club: Country of Va. Home: 5508 Queensbury Rd Richmond VA 23226-2122 Office: Va Supreme Ct 100 N 9th St Richmond VA 23219-2335

COMPTON, JOHN CARROLL, accountant; b. Woodruff, S.C., July 3, 1941; s. Ligon Grant and Thelma (Blythe) C.; m. Monnie Digh, Jan. 7, 1967; children: Gillian Nicole, Janene Christen. BSBA in Acctg., U. N.C., 1963. CPA, N.C., Fla., S.C. Sr. acct. Peat, Marwick, Mitchell & Co., Greenville, S.C., 1963-64, supervising sr. acct., 1967-69; treas. Henderson Advt. Agy., Inc., Greenville, 1969-70; audit mgr. Cherry, Bekaert & Holland, Charlotte, N.C., 1970-71; ptnr. Cherry, Bekaert & Holland, 1971-75, resident mng. ptnr., 1975-76, 1976-78, asst. dir. acctg. and auditing, 1978-80, resident mng. ptnr., 1980-85; dir. acctg. and auditing Cherry, Bekaert & Holland, Greensboro, N.C., 1985—. Treas., mem. exec. com., chmn. fin. com. of bd. trustees All Children's Hosp.; vice-chmn., bd. dirs. All Children's Found.;

past pres., mem. exec. com., bd. dirs. Suncoast Ronald McDonald House, Inc.; sr. warden St. Thomas' Episc. Ch. Lt. (j.g.) USNR, 1963-67. Mem. AICPA (past mem. com. on banking, auditing stds. bd., ethics div. spl. taks force on firms performing govtl. grant audits, adv. bd. Nat. Sch. Banking), Fla. Inst. CPAs (practice rev. com., chmn. com. legis. policy, quality control com., pvt. cos., practice sect. com.), N.C. Assn. CPAs, Nat. Assn. Accts., Bank Adminstrn. Inst., St. Petersburg Yacht Club, Myers Pk. Country Club, Greensboro City Club. Republican. Office: 100 S Elm St Ste 500 Greensboro NC 27401-2639

COMPTON, JOHN JOSEPH, philosophy educator; b. Chgo., May 17, 1928; s. Arthur Holly and Betty Charity (McCloskey) C.; m. Marjorie Ann Yaple, July 8, 1950; children: Elizabeth Holly, Catherine Marchus, John Arthur. BA, Coll. of Wooster, 1949; MA, Yale U., 1951, PhD, 1953. Asst. prof. philosophy Vanderbilt U., Nashville, 1952-55, assoc. prof., 1955-68, prof., 1968—, chmn. or acting chmn. dept., 1966-73, 84-85, 88-89, 93-95; vis. prof. Colo. Coll., Colorado Springs, 1977, Wesleyan U., Middletown, Conn., 1984. Contbr. articles to profl. jours. and chpts. in books. Mem. bd. advisers Matchette Found., 1968—; trustee Coll. of Wooster, Ohio, 1975—. Recipient Harbison award for disting. teaching Danforth Found., 1966; fellow Belgian-Am. Edn. Found., 1956-57, sr. fellow NEH, 1974-75, fellow Ctr. for Humanities, Wesleyan U., 1974-75. Mem. AAAS, AAUP, Am. Philos. Assn. (sec. ea. div. 1970-73, v.p. 1974), Metaphys. Soc. Am. (pres. 1979), Soc. for Phenomenology and Existential Philosophy, So. Soc. for Philosophy and Psychology, Philosophy of Sci. Assn., Soc. for Values in Higher Edn. (Kent fellow 1951), Phi Beta Kappa. Democrat. Home: 3708 Whitland Ave Nashville TN 37205-2430 Office: Vanderbilt U Dept Philosophy Nashville TN 37235

COMPTON, REBECCA BAILES, interior designer; b. Ala., 1961; d. John and Mary Bailes; m. Michael Francis Compton, June 14, 1986; children: John Michael, Patrick O'Neal, Michaela Waring. BS in Interior Design, Winthrop Coll., 1983. Design asst. Carriker's Furniture & Interiors, Charlotte, N.C., 1982-83, Winthrop Coll. Campus Planning & Design, Rock Hill, S.C., 1983; interior designer B & H Kitchens & Interiors, Columbia, S.C., 1983-85, Custom Designs, Inc., Sumter, S.C., 1985-87; interior designer, ptnr. Morehouse-Compton Interiors, Sumter, 1988-90; interior designer, owner Rebecca B. Compton Interiors, Sumter, 1990—. Mem. Downtown Design Rev. Com., Sumter, 1990-95; mem. Historic Preservation Design Rev. Com., Sumter, 1996—; chmn., trustee St. Mark's United Meth. Ch., Sumter, 1991-93. Mem. Am. Soc. Interior Designers (profl. mem., nominating com. Carolinas chpt. 1993-94), Nat. Kitchen and Bath Assn. (Carolinas chpt.), S.C. Coalition of Interior Designers (chmn. pub. rels. com. 1990), Greater Sumter C. of C. Office: Rebecca B Compton Interiors PO Box 908 Sumter SC 29151-0908

COMPTON, ROBERT H., lawyer. Adminstrv. v.p., gen. counsel Ashland (Ky.) Petroleum Co., until 1988; adminstrv. v.p. Ashland Oil, Inc., Russell, Ky., 1988-92; bus. cons., atty pvt. practice, Ashland, 1992—; vice chmn. West Penn/W.Va. AAA, 1996—. Office: Ashland Oil Inc PO Box 391 1000 Ashland Dr Ashland KY 41101-7057

COMSTOCK, ROBERT DONALD, JR., real estate executive; b. Miami, Fla., Sept. 28, 1921; s. Robert Donald Sr. and Gertrude (Quigg) C.; m. Mary Evans, Oct. 12, 1949; children: Carol Frances, Robert Donald III (dec.). BS in Commerce, U. Miss., 1943. Lic. real estate broker. Acct. New Orleans Pub. Service Co., 1946-47; salesman, br. mgr. Capitol Records, Inc., New Orleans and Charlotte, N.C., 1948-51; regional v.p. Atlanta, 1952-57; owner, pres. Comstock Distbg. Co., Atlanta, 1957-74, Comstock and Assocs., Atlanta, 1968-74, Cartridge Control Corp., Atlanta, 1968-80, Comstock Properties, Atlanta, 1980—; pres. Ctr. for Rehab. Tech., Ga. Tech. U., Atlanta, 1987-91, chmn. bd., 1991—. Mem. Atlanta Arts Alliance, 1970—, Atlanta Symphony, 1970—; bd. dirs. Christian Council Met. Atlanta, 1975-77; trustee So. Ctr. for Internat. Studies; mem. Atlanta Hist. Soc. Served as lt. USN, 1943-46, PTO. Named #1 Distbr. CBS Records, Columbia Broadcasting, N.Y.C., 1965, 69, Outstanding Distbr. Columbia Phonographs, Columbia Broadcasting, 1968, 70-72. Mem. Atlanta Bd. Realtors, Capital City Club, Commerce Club, Breakfast Club (pres. 1970-71), Trinity Presbyn. Ch. Men's Club (pres. 1977, Rotary (pres. Atlanta Midtown 1978-79), Omicron Delta Kappa. Home: 3400 Ridgewood Rd NW Atlanta GA 30327-2418 Office: Ste 804 1447 Peachtree St NE Atlanta GA 30309-3031

CONDIT, LINDA FAULKNER, economist; b. Denver, May 30, 1947; d. Claude Winston and Nancy Isobel (McCallum) Faulkner; BA, U. Ark., 1969; MA, U. Wis., 1970; postgrad. U. Minn., 1974-77; m. John Michael Condit, Dec. 20, 1970; 1 child, David Devin. Economist, St. Louis Fed. Res. Bank, 1971-73; ops. analyst No. States Power Co., Mpls., 1973-76; energy economist, 1976-78; economist Pennzoil Co., Houston, 1978-79, sr. economist, 1979-81, mgr. econ. research dept., 1981-84, dir. corp. planning and econs. dept., 1984-86; dir. treasury ops., 1986-90, corp. sec., 1990—, v.p., corp. sec., 1995—; research asst. U. Wis., 1969-70; econ. cons. Jr. Achievement, 1983. Recipient Alumni award U. Ark., 1969. Mem. Internat. Assn. Energy Economists (pres., v.p., treas.), Nat. Assn. Bus. Economists, Internat. Bus. Council (v.p.), Am. Econ. Assn., N. Am. Soc. Corp. Planners, Am. Soc. Corp. Sec. (membership chmn.), Hits Theatre (bd. dirs.), Harvard Discussion Group Indsl. Economists, Phi Beta Kappa, Mortar Bd., Kappa Alpha Theta. Unitarian. Clubs: Forest, River Oaks Women's Breakfast (v.p., pres.). Home: 11822 Village Park Cir Houston TX 77024-4418 Office: Pennzoil Co PO Box 2967 Houston TX 77252-2967

CONDON, CHARLES MOLONY, state attorney general; b. Charleston, S.C., May 2, 1953; s. James Joseph and Harriet (Molony) C.; m. Emily Yarbrough, June 21, 1980; children: Charles Molony Jr., Patrick Monaghan, Doreen Yarbrough, Emily Elliot. Student, Saltzburg (Austria) Summer Sch., 1972, U. Innsbruck, Austria, 1972-73; BA, U. Notre Dame, 1975; JD, Duke U., 1978. Bar: S.C. 1978, U.S. Dist. Ct. S.C. 1978, U.S. Ct. Appeals (4th cir.) 1987, U.S. Supreme Ct. 1988. Assoc. Nexsen, Pruet, Jacobs & Pollard, Columbus, S.C., 1978-79; asst. solicitor S.C. 9th Jud. Cir., Charleston, 1979-80, solicitor, 1980-92; atty. gen. State of S.C., Columbia, 1992—; lectr. Med. U. S.C., 1982, U. S.C., 1983, Coll. Charleston, 1986, various confs.; bd. visitors com., Charleston, 1992—; panel mem. Nat. Inst. for Drug Abuse, Washington; prosecuter City of Isle Palms, S.C., 1993—; cons. Nat. Consortium for Justice Info. and Stats. profl. rep. So. Environ. Network, 1990-91. profl. rep. So. Envion. Network., 1990-91. Mem. com. Charleston County Criminal Justice Task Force; sect. chmn. govtl. divsn. United Way; bd. dirs. com. for drug free soc. Charleston County Sch. Dist., 1989, Children's Ctr., Charleston, S.C., 1990-91, S.C. Commn. on Presecution Coord., 1991-92; ex-officio mem. Friends of Charleston County Courthouse. Mem. ABA, S.C. Bar Assn., Richland County Bar Assn., Charleston Lawyers Club, S.C. Cir. Solicitors Assn. (v.p. 1987-88, pres. 1988-89), S.C. Law Enforcement Assn., Notre Dame Club, Silver Elephant Club. Republican. Home: 835 Middle St Sullivans Island SC 29482-8728 Office: Office of Attorney General PO Box 11549 Columbia SC 29211-1549

CONDON, MARIA DEL CARMEN, retired elementary school educator; b. Laredo, Tex., Aug. 31, 1929; d. Florencio and Carmen (Diaz) Briseno; m. James Robert Condon, July 24, 1967 (dec. Apr. 1978). BA, Tex. Woman's U., 1962. Tchr. Laredo Ind. Sch. Dist., 1963-9; supervising tchr. Laredo State U., 1984—. Mem. Tex. ASCD, Tex. Ret. Tchrs. Assn., Tex. Classroom Tchrs. Assn., Nat. Alumnae Assn. of Tex. Woman's U. Democrat. Roman Catholic. Home: 1514 Hibiscus Ln Laredo TX 78041-3325

CONDRA, ALLEN LEE, lawyer; b. Middlesboro, Ky., Apr. 11, 1950; s. Allen and Dorothy Dell (Douglas) C. BA, Western Ky. U., 1972; JD, No. Ky. U., 1978. Bar: Ky. 1979, U.S. Dist. Ct. (we. dist.) Ky. 1980. Staff atty. West Ky. Legal Services, Madisonville, 1979-81; dist. atty. Dept. Transp., Commonwealth of Ky., Madisonville, 1981—. Mem. Ky. Bar Assn., Hopkins County Bar Assn., Phi Alpha Delta. Democrat. Methodist. Lodge: Elks, Masons, K.T.

CONDRAY, A. L., oil industry executive. V.p. Exxon Co., Houston. Office: Exxon Company USA 800 Bell St Houston TX 77002-7426

CONDRON, GARY, company executive; b. 1955. With Holder Constrn. Co., Atlanta, 1976-87, sr. v.p., until 1987; with The Conlan Co., Marietta, Ga., 1987—, pres. Office: The Conlan Co 1800 Parkway Pl Ste 1010 Marietta GA 30067

CONE, FRANCES MCFADDEN, data processing consultant; b. Columbia, S.C., Oct. 20, 1938; d. Joseph Means and Francis (Graham) McFadden: m. Charles Cone Jr., May 1962 (div. Sept. 1964); 1 child, Deborah Ann Cone Craytor. BS, U. S.C., 1960, MEd, 1973, M Math., 1977. Systems svc. rep. IBM, 1960-62; programmer/analyst Ga. Power Co., Atlanta, 1964-68, S.C. Fin. and Data Processing, Columbia, 1968-69; instr., head dept. Midlands Tech. Coll., Columbia, 1969-75; tng. coord. S.C. Nat. Bank, Columbia, 1975-79; systems analyst S.C. Dept. Health and Environ. Control, Columbia, 1979-80; project analyst So. Co. Svcs., Atlanta, 1980-89; cons. George Martin Assocs., Atlanta, 1989-93; sr. programmer, analyst Emory U., Atlanta, Ga., 1993—; adj. prof. Golden Gate U., Sumter, S.C., 1976-80. Vol. Ga. Wildlife Found. Mem. Nat. Mgmt. Assn. (sec., treas., awards comn. 1981-89). Republican. Episcopalian. Office: Emory U Computing Ctr Atlanta GA 30322

CONE, THOMAS CONRAD, communications executive; b. Bryan, Tex., Nov. 4, 1948; s. Conrad Bryan and Monica Bonnell (Sappington) C.; m. Linda Arnold, Nov. 2, 1968 (div. 1978). BA in Journalism, Tex. A&M U., 1973; postgrad., U. Houston, 1973-75. Print, radio, TV asst. Tex. Agrl. Extension Svc., College Station, 1970-73; field rep. Rice Coun. Am., Houston, 1973-75; dir. Africa ops. Rice Council Am., Houston, 1975-80, dir. communications, 1975-81; pres. Cone Communications, Houston, 1981—; host, producer city-wide radio pub. service program, Houston, 1978-81. Sgt. USMC, 1966-69, Vietnam. Mem. Houston Jaycees (bd. dirs., advisor 1978-83, nominee one of 5 Outstanding Young Texans 1981,82), Houston Advt. Fedn. (bd. dirs. 1978-85), Houston C. of C. (named one of 5 Outstanding Young Houstonians 1981), Soc. Profl. Journalists, Rotary (bd. dirs. 1983-86). Methodist. Home: PO Box 236 Winnie TX 77665-0236

CONE, VIRGIE HORNE HYMAN, former educator, civic worker; b. Brooksville, Fla.; d. George G. and Virgie (Horne) Hyman; m. Edward Elbert Cone, Dec. 20, 1930 (dec. Feb. 1962); children: Molly Gentile (dec. Jan. 1989), Edward Elbert. BS, Fla. State Coll. Women; MEd, U. Fla., 1956. Tchr., Meml. Jr. H.S., Hillsborough County, 1929-31; tchr. Duval County Robert E. Lee Sr. H.S., Jacksonville, Fla., 1943-55, dean, 1955-70; prin. Lee High Sch. (1st woman secondary sch. prin. in county), 1971-74; owner Cone's Antiques. Chmn., ARC night vols. St. Vincent's Hosp., 1969-71; mem. task force Mayor's Community Planning Coun., 1969; pres. Hamilton County unit Am. Cancer Soc., 1974-76; v.p. Hamilton County Meml. Hosp. Aux., 1975-76; mem. adv. coun. Health and Rehab. Svcs., Dist. 3, Fla.; dir. Area Agy. on Aging, 1977-82, bd. dirs., 1982—; del. White House Conf. on Aging, 1981, 95; mem. adv. coun. Social Security; mem. state legis. com. Am. Assn. Retired Persons, 1983-87, chmn., 1986-87; mem. State Longterm Care Ombudsman Coun., 1983-87, chmn. 1985-87 mem. adv. coun. State Civil Rights Commn.; pres. North Fla. Mental Health Bd., 1978-80; mem. Hamilton County Planning Coun., Gov.'s Commn. on Status Women, 1978-80; mem. exec. bd. North Central Fla. Health Planning Coun., 1979-80; bd. dirs. Mid. Fla. Area Agy. on Aging, State Comprehensive Health Assn., State Nursing Home Adv. Com.; mem. pub. issues com. Am. Cancer Soc.; mem. Banking Sunset Task Force, Fla., 1990-91; mem. aging commn. Fla. Med. Assn., 1988-93; mem. state com. to rewrite rating scale for nursing homes; bd. dirs. United Way Suwannee Valley; adv. com. health Hamilton County Sch. Sys. Health ctr. named in her honor, Jasper, Fla., 1993. Mem. Fla. Coun. Tchrs. Math. (curriculum chmn. 1952, sec. 1949), AAUW (Jacksonville v.p. 1953), Duval Tchrs. Assn. (chmn. profl. rights and responsibilities com. 1965-66), Jacksonville Panhellenic Assn. (pres. 1959-60, mem. scholarship com. 1963-68), Duval Personnel and Guidance Assn. (organizing chmn. 1966-69), Nat. Assn. Secondary Prins., Fla. Assn. Secondary Prins., Hamilton Ret. Tchrs., Fla. Assn. Area Agy. Dirs. (pres.), Fla. Ret. Educators Assn. (state legis. chair 1990-92), Am. Assn. Ret. Persons (capitol city task force, state legis. com.), Pilot Club of Jacksonville, Suwanee Valley Country Club (dir. 1978-80), Delta Kappa Gamma (chpt. pres. 1959-61), Sigma Kappa (nat. scholarship chmn. 1963-77). Home: 3D NW St Jasper FL 32052

CONERLY, EVELYN NETTLES, educational consultant; b. Baton Rouge, Aug. 25, 1940; d. Noel Douglas and Evelyn Elsie (Pratt) Nettles; children from previous marriage: Douglas Wayne, Kelee Lynne. BS, La. State U., 1962, MEd, 1965, PhD, 1973. Tchr., East Baton Rouge Parish Pub. Schs., La., 1962-67, elem. librarian, 1967-73, prin., 1973-81, elem. library supr., 1981-83, prin., 1983-84; edn. cons., Baton Rouge, 1984—, co-owner, Acad. Learning Ctr., 1986-92; dir. Libr. Power Project, East Baton Rouge Parish, DeWitt Wallace-Reader's Digest Fund, 1992-96; vol. pub. sch.; with Nat. Libr. Power Program Network of Conss., 1996—. Co-author: Principals' Pointers for Parents, 1985. Mem. ALA, AASL, Assn. Tchr. Educators (pres. La. 1981-82), Internat. Reading Assn., La. Reading Assn., La. Ret. Tchrs. Assn., La. Libr. Assn., Inst. Reality Therapy (cert.), Phi Kappa Phi, Phi Delta Kappa, Delta Kappa Gamma. Presbyterian. Home: 3727 Woodland Ridge Blvd Baton Rouge LA 70816-2772

CONEY, ELAINE MARIE, English and foreign languages educator; b. Magnolia, Miss., Aug. 9, 1952; d. Allen Leroy and Katie Jane (McLeod) C. BA in Spanish, Millsaps Coll., 1974; MA in Spanish, U. Interam. Saltillo Coahuila, Mex., 1975, PhD, 1977; MEd, U. So. Miss., 1979. Tchr. fgn. langs. South Pike High Sch., Magnolia, Miss., 1977-91; tchr. English Amite County Schs., Liberty, Miss.; instr. Jackson (Miss.) State U.; GED instr. South Pike Schs., Magnolia, Miss.; instr. Spanish, French and English composition S.W. Miss. Community Coll., Summit, 1989—. Mem. NEA (del. conv. 1986, 88), Am. Assn. Tchrs. French, Am. Assn. Tchrs. Spanish and Portuguese, Miss. Assn. Educators (instructional profl. devel. com.), Nat. Coun. Tchrs. English, Miss. Fgn. Lang. Assn. (pres. 1991-93), SPAE (treas.). Home: PO Box 208 Magnolia MS 39652-0208

CONGER, SUE ANN, computer information systems educator; b. Akron, Ohio, Nov. 6, 1947; d. Scott Stanley and Norma Marie (Bauknecht) Summerville; m. David Boyd Conger, July 3, 1971; 1 child, Kathryn Summerville. BS, Ohio State U., 1970; MBA, Rutgers U., 1977; PhD, NYU, 1988. Programmer, analyst USDA, Washington, 1970-72; project leader Ednl. Testing Svc., Princeton, N.J., 1972-73; 2d v.p. Chase Manhattan Bank, N.Y.C., 1973-77; tech. dir. Lambda Technology, Inc., N.Y.C., 1977-80; sr. cons. Mobil Corp., N.Y.C., 1980-83; asst. prof. computer info. systems Ga. State U., Atlanta, 1988-90; asst. prof. Baruch Coll. CUNY, 1990-94; assoc. prof. So. Meth. U., Dallas, 1994—; freelance cons., educator, 1970—. Author: The New Software Engineering, 1994; contbr. articles to profl. jours. Grantee, U.S. Army Info. Systems Engrng. Command, 1989. Mem. IEEE, Assn. for Computing Machinery, Acad. of Mgmt. Office: So Meth U MIS Dept Edwin L Cox Sch Bus Dallas TX 75275

CONINO, JOSEPH ALOYSIUS, lawyer; b. Hammond, La., Aug. 17, 1920; s. Dominic and Catherine (Tamborella) C.; m. Mae Evelyn Moragas, Feb. 27, 1943; children: Joseph Aloysius Jr., Robert Carl. BBA, Tulane U., 1950; JD, Loyola U., 1961; MBA, U. Pa., 1951. Bar: La. 1961, U.S. Dist. Ct. (ea. dist.) La. 1961, U.S. Ct. Appeals (5th cir.) 1972, U.S. Supreme Ct. 1989. Pvt. practice Jefferson, La., 1961—; county judge State of La. Parish, Jefferson, 1970; del. State of La. Constnl. Conv., Baton Rouge, 1973-74; asst. atty. Parish of Jefferson, 1977—. With USN, 1942-45. Mem. La. Bar Assn. (ho. of dels. 1963-92, bd. dirs. 1981-83, 96—), Jefferson Bar Assn. (pres.), New Orleans C. of C. (bd. dirs. 1974-77), Kiwanis (pres. Metairie, La. chpt.). Office: 1920 Jefferson Hwy Jefferson LA 70121-3816

CONKEL, ROBERT DALE, lawyer, pension consultant; b. Martins Ferry, Ohio, Oct. 13, 1936; s. Chester William and Marian Matilda (Ashton) C.; m. Elizabeth A. Cargill, June 15, 1958; children: Debra Lynn Conkel McGlone, Dale William, Douglas Alan; m. Brenda Jo Myers, Aug. 2, 1980; 1 child, Chelsea Ashton. BA, Mt. Union Coll., 1958; JD cum laude, Cleve. Marshall Law Sch., 1965; LLM, Case Western Res. U., 1972. Bar: Ohio 1965, U.S. Tax Ct. 1974, U.S. Supreme Ct. 1974, Tex. 1978, U.S. Ct. Appeals (5th cir.) 1979. Supr., Social Security Adminstrn., Cleve., 1958-65; trust officer Harter Bank & Trust Co., Canton, Ohio, 1965-70; exec. v.p. Am. Actuaries, Inc., Grand Rapids, Mich., 1970-73, pension cons., southwest regional dir., Dallas, 1974-88; mgr. plans and rsch. A.S. Hansen, Inc., Dallas, 1973-74; pvt. practice, Dallas, 1973—; sr. cons., Coopers & Lybrand, Dallas, 1989; pres. Robert D. Conkel, Inc., 1989—; mem. devel. bd. Met. Nat. Bank, Richardson, Tex.; instr. Am. Mgmt. Assn., 1975, Am. Coll. Advanced Pension Planning, 1975-76. Sustaining mem. Rep. Nat. Com., 1980-88. Enrolled actuary, Joint Bd. Enrollment U.S. Depts. Labor and Treasury. Mem. ABA (employee benefit com. sect. taxation), Ohio State Bar Assn., Tex. Bar Assn., Dallas Bar Assn., Am. Soc. Pension Actuaries (dir. 1973-81), Am. Acad. Actuaries. Contbr. articles to legal publs.; editorial adv. bd. Jour. Pension Planning and Compliance, 1974-83. Office: 100 N Central Expy # 519 Richardson TX 75080

CONKLIN, GLORIA ZAMKO, artist, marketing executive; b. Detroit, Mich., Feb. 6, 1925; d. John and Lois Julia (Eager) Zamko; m. Robert Murray Conklin, Apr. 27, 1957; 1 child, Dale John. Student Am. Acad. of Art, Chicago, 1945, Art Inst. Chgo., 1946, Art Students League, N.Y., 1976; studied with Theodoros Stamos, 1971-90. Fashion illustrator, Chgo. and Detroit, 1946-49; bridal cons. Marshall Field & Co., Chgo., 1950-53; fashion coord., 1953-55; Mid-West pub. rels. and pub. rep. Celanese Corp., N.Y.C., 1955-57; artist-painter, Chappaqua, N.Y., 1971-90, Williamsburg, Va., 1990—; represented by Chasen, Sarasota, Fla.; v.p. mktg. Conklin Tech. Inc., Stratford, Conn. 1981-89. Mem. Nat. Assn. Women Artists, Nat. League Am. Pen Women, Artists Equity N.Y.

CONKLING, SARA ANN, management educator; b. Orlando, Fla., Mar. 23, 1960; d. Homer Caples Jr. and Martha Elizabeth (Fort) C. BS in Econs., U. Pa., BA in Internat. Rels.; postgrad., U. Vt. Econ. cons. pvt. practice, Phila., 1979-85; sr. cons. Future Planning Assocs., Inc., Williston, Vt., 1985-90; v.p. Hackett and Co., Inc., South Burlington, Vt., 1990-91; employee benefit cons. pvt. practice, Burlington, Vt., 1991-94; instr. Vt. Ins. Inst., 1993-94, Champlain Coll., Burlington, Vt., 1993-94; exec. dir. Brevard Ecumenical AIDS Ministry, Inc., Cocoa, Fla., 1995—; adj. instr. pub. adminstrn. U. Ctrl. Fla., Orlando, 1995—. Contbr. articles to profl. jours. Direct svc. vol. Vt. Com. AIDS Resources, Edn. and Svcs., 1990-94; counselor Camp Ta-Kum-Ta, Vt., 1992—; chair svc. to hungry and homeless com. Episcopal Diocese Pa., 1983-85; lay leader Asbury Meth. Ch., Phila., 1981-82; vestry St. Stephen's Ch., Phila., 1984-85. Grad. Teaching fellow of yr. Dept. Pub. Adminstrn., U. Vt., Burlington, 1991-92; Benjamin Franklin scholar U. Pa., 1978-82; recipient Community Svc. award United Way, 1992. Mem. Am. Soc. Pub. Adminstrn. (Vt. chpt. v.p. 1992-94, Marshall E. Dimock award 1992), Pi Alpha Alpha. Unitarian.

CONLEY, BILLY DEAN, retired protective services official; b. Clayton, Okla., Jan. 24, 1940; s. Troy Lee and Erma Louise (Jackson) C.; m. Janet L. Cobburn, Sept. 1, 1961; children: Kenneth Wayne, Timothy Craig. Student, Eastern Okla. A & M, 1958-59. Cert. Law Enforcer, Tex., Okla. Sgt. Mesquite (Tex.) Police Dept., 1962-66; master officer Tulsa (Okla.) Police Dept., 1967-87; sgt. Rogers County (Okla.) Police Dept., 1988-90, investigator, 1992-94. Contbr. poems to profl. publs. Vets. com. chmn. Elks Lodge #1230, Claremore, Okla., 1995—. Sargeant, U.S. Army, 1959-62, Korea. Mem. Fraternal Order of Police, Okla. Sheriffs & Peace Officers Assn., Internat. Soc. of Poets, Acad. of Am. Poets. Home: 13802 E 122nd St N Collinsville OK 74021

CONLEY, KATHERINE LOGAN, religious studies educator; b. Rutherford, N.C., Sept. 3, 1911; d. Claude Joseph and Mary (Beam) Logan; m. Jesse William Conley, Dec. 26, 1942. BS in Edn., Asheville (N.C.) Coll., 1936; postgrad., Presbyn. Ch. Christian Edn., Richmond, Va., 1939-40. Dir Christian edn. Presbyn. Ch., Spartanburg, S.C., 1940-41, Knoxville, 1941—; chmn. bldg. com. Seventh-Day Adventist Ch., Rutherford, N.C., 1963; lay speaker United Meth. Ch., Rutherfordton, 1973-91. Mem. Genealogical Soc., DAR (regent 1976-78), Amnesty Internat., Am. Bible Soc. (silver). Democrat. Home: 4429 US 64 Hwy Rutherfordton NC 28139-9434

CONLEY, RAYMOND LESLIE, English language educator; b. Manhattan, Kans., Feb. 25, 1923; s. Orville Ray and Goldie Gladys (Wallack) C. AB with honors, Park Coll., 1947; postgrad., Nebr. U., 1948-50; MA, Northwestern U., Evanston, Ill., 1958; postgrad., Ol Dominion U., 1968. Cert. tchr. speech, English, social scis. Dep. county clk. Nemaha County, Auburn, Nebr., 1942-45; tchr., English, speech St. Edward (Nebr.) High Sch., 1948-50, Oakland (Nebr.) High Sch., 1950-52, Nebraska City (Nebr.) High Sch., 1952-56, Galesburg (Ill.) High Sch., 1956-58, Maine Twp. High Sch. East, Park Ridge, Ill., 1958-65; asst. prof. English, speech Meth. Coll., Fayetteville, N.C., 1966-77; English prof. Campbell U., Buies Creek, N.C., 1980-83; aux. faculty Campbell U., Fort Bragg, N.C., 1978—; coach Nebr. State Debate Champs, 1951, 52; judge Iowa State Speech Contest, 1952, 53; mem. Coun. Status of Women, Fayetteville, 1965-68; aux. faculty Campbell U., Pope AFB, N.C., 1985—; speech coach, judge local and sectional contests Toastmistress Club. Actor Fort Bragg Vietnam War Tng. Films. Precinct officer Dem. party, Fayetteville, 1964-68; coord. Congrl. Dist. Common Cause, 1978, mem. state program action com., state and gov. bd. 1976-78, 95—; mem. Congress Watch/Pub. Citizen, People for the Am. Way, ACLU, N.C. ACLU; conservation coord. Sierra Club, 1978; mem. Amnesty Internat.; vol. Fayetteville Mus. Art. Recipient Am. Legion Citizenship award, 1938. Mem. NOW, AAUP, Internat. Platform Assn., Fayetteville Fgn. Film Soc. (co-founder 1967), Inst. for So. Studies, World Future Soc., Found. For Nat. Progress, N.C. Alliance For Democracy, Amnesty Internat., Ams. United for Separation Ch. and State, Lambda Chi Alpha. Presbyterian. Home: 1076 Stamper Rd Fayetteville NC 28303-4191 Office: Campbell U Bldg 284 Rm 218 Pope AFB NC 28308-2373

CONLEY, SHEILA KAY, medical/surgical nurse; b. Cullman, Ala., Oct. 1, 1950; d. Chesley Junior and Vetra Olene (Sinyard) Calvert; m. Felix Thomas Conley, Jr., June 12, 1971; children: Felix Thomas III, Crystal, Chesley. AAS, ADN, Wallace State Coll., 1989. RN, Ala. Staff/relief charge nurse orthopedic neuro trauma/pediatric Carraway Meth. Hosp., Birmingham, Ala. Active health fairs and blood pressure screenings at community ctrs., Birmingham. Carraway scholar. Mem. ANA, Ala. Nurses Assn., Nat. Assn. Orthopaedic Nurses. Home: 792 County Road 218 Bremen AL 35033-3128

CONLIN, THOMAS (BYRD), conductor; b. Arlington, Va., Jan. 29, 1944. BMus, Peabody Conservatory Music, 1966, MMus, 1967; studied with Leonard Bernstein, Erich Leinsdorf, Sir Adrian Boult. Artistic dir. Chamber Opera Soc., Balt., 1966-72; assoc. condr. N.C. Symphony Orch., 1972-74; music dir. Queens (N.Y.) Orchestral Soc., 1974-76; condr. Amarillo (Tex.) Symphony Orch., 1976-84, W.Va. Symphony Orch., 1983—; asst. prof. mus. CUNY, 1974-76. Mem. Am. Symphony Orch. League, Nat. Opera Assn., Condrs. Guild, Opera America. Office: West Va Symphony Orch 1210 Virginia St E Charleston WV 25301-2913

CONLON, PETER JOHN, JR., investment advisor; b. S.I., N.Y., Aug. 24, 1951; s. Peter John and Alice Virginia (Berk) C.; m. Tina Diane Schiller, Dec. 28, 1974 (div. 1981); m. Nancy Louise Elliott, Nov. 16, 1986. BS in Mktg., Syracuse U., 1973; MBA, U. Tex., Arlington, 1978. Registered fin. cons.; registered investment advisor. Mfrs. rep. Warner Electric/Red Lion, Ft. Worth, 1979-85; fin. cons. Shearson Lehman Bros., Ft. Worth, 1985-88; retirement planning specialist Rotan Mosle/Paine Webber, Ft. Worth, 1988-89; pres. Conlon Fin. Advisors and Assocs., Arlington, Tex., 1989—; fin. planner, investment adviser fin. planner, registered investment advisor, 1989—. Pres. Wellington Pl. Homeowners Assn., Arlington, 1981-88; bd. advisers Nat. Inst. on Fin. Issues and Svcs. for Elders). Served with USAF, 1973-79, lt. col. USAFR. Mem. Res. Officers Assn. (v.p. Ft. Worth chpt. 1987-92, pres. 1992-93), Arlington City Club (com. chmn. 1986-87), Optimists (bd. govs. North Tex. dist. 1990-91). Republican. Roman Catholic.

CONN, DAVID EDWARD, art educator; b. Jersey City, Apr. 10, 1941; s. Robert William and Evelyn (Scott) C.; m. Leslie Ann Bachran (div.); 1 child, Michael; m. Jennifer L. Cox, Feb. 19, 1984; children: Micah, Caleb. BFA, Md. Inst. Coll. of Art, 1967; MFA, U. Okla., 1970. Instr. art Tex. Christian U., Ft. Worth, 1969-87, prof. art, 1987-88, chmn. dept. art/art history, 1988-94. Ford fellow Md. Inst. Art, Balt., 1965, Visual Arts fellow NEA, 1985. Office: Tex Christian U PO Box 30793 2800 S Univ Dr Fort Worth TX 76129

CONNAWAY, ROBERT WALLACE, artist, computer programmer; b. Dothan, Ala., Nov. 5, 1956; s. Charles Earl and Ina Lee (Wallace) C.; m. Catherine Coyne. B in Info. Systems Tech., U. No. Fla., 1981; BA cum laude, Flagler Coll., 1978. Computer programmer Mgmt. Info. Systems Group, 1981-83; computer analyst/programmer Grumman St. Augustine Corp., 1985-95; flight line attendant, free-lance artist Aero Sport Inc., St. Augustine, Fla., 1978-83; founder, prin. Aviation Art Works, St. Augustine, 1978—; owner Connaway Gallery, 1996—. Ann. one-man show Profl. Artist of St. Augustine Gallery, 1988—; airshow poster art work Today Show Sta. NBC TV, 1989; commd. 6 pieces artwork St. Augustine Psychiat. Ctr., 1992. Recipient Art awards Sr. Honors Project, 1978; Honorable Mention awards Audubon Soc. Art Show, St. Augustine, 1978, 86, 87, 89, 1st Prize, 1987. Mem. St. Augustine Art Assn., Exptl. Aircraft Assn. Episcopalian. Commn.: mural St. Augustine Mcpl. Airport, 1982; exhibited Fly-In art show Exptl. Aircraft Assn., 1980. Home: 416 Arredondo Ave Saint Augustine FL 32084-3805 Office: Connaway Gallery 11 F Aviles St Saint Augustine FL 32084 also: 11 F Aviles St Saint Augustine FL 32084

CONNELL, KAREN SUE, librarian technician; b. Alva, OKla., Apr. 10, 1966; d. Robert E. and Betty Fay (Reid) Lee; m. John Dean C., July 27, 1991; 1 child, Shawn Dean. BSLS, Northwestern Okla. State U., 1988. Libr. tech. Western State Psychiat. Ctr., Ft. Supply, Okla., 1988—. Mem. Western State Psychiat. Ctr. Aux. (v.p. 1993). Methodist. Home: 2204 Maple Woodward OK 73801

CONNELLY, COLIN CHARLES, lawyer; b. Hopewell, Va., Nov. 1, 1956; s. Charles Bernell and Doris Louise (Beasley) C.; m. Stephanie Paige Lowder, May 9, 1981. AA, Richard Bland Coll., 1977; BA, Va. Commonwealth U., 1979; JD, U. Richmond, 1983. Bar: Va. 1983, U.S. Ct. Appeals (4th cir.) 1983. Assoc. Tuck, Freasier, & Herbig, Richmond, Va., 1984-87; ptnr. Tuck & Connelly Profl. Assocs., Inc., Richmond, Va., 1988-95, Connelly & Assocs., P.C., Chester, Va., 1996—; bd. dirs., v.p. Cen. Title Ins. Agy., Richmond, 1988—; agt. Chgo. Title Ins. Corp., Richmond, 1988—. Mem., assoc./counsel Home Builders Assn. South Side Va. Mem. ABA, Va. Bar Assn., Richmond Bar Assn., Southside Bd. Realtors (affiliate), Chester Jaycees, Omicron Delta Kappa, Phi Kappa Phi, Phi Alpha Delta (justice 1983-86). Baptist. Home: 14206 Masada Ct Chesterfield VA 23838-8725 Office: Connelly & Assocs. 4830 W 100 Rd Chester VA 23831 also: 4830 W Hundred Rd Chester VA 23831-1746

CONNER, ANN, artist; b. Aug. 11, 1948. MA, U. N.C., 1972, MFA in Painting, 1975. Prof. art U. N.C., Wilmington, 1972—; painter, relief print artist. Group exhbns. include U. W.V., 1995, N.C. Mus. Art, Raleigh, 1993, Dutch Internat. & Small Graphic Mus., Maastricht, Holland, 1993, Elvehjem Mus. of Art, U. Wis.-Madison, 1993, Boston U. Art Gallery, 1993, State Gallery Banska Bystrica, Slovak Republic, 1991, 93, others; solo exhbns. include Hanes Art Ctr. Gallery, U. N.C., Chapel Hill, 1991, Calif. Palace of Legion of Honor, San Francisco, 1991, Southeastern C.C., Whiteville, N.C., 1988, Waterworks Visual Arts Ctr., Salisbury, N.C., 1987, New Elements Gallery, Wilmington, N.C., 1985, Fayetteville (N.C.) Mus. Art, 1983, Danville (Va.) Mus. Fine Arts, 1982, others; represented in permanent collections Nat. Gallery of Art, Libr. of Congress, N.C. Mus. Art, IBM, Philip Morris, N.Y., Philip Morris USA, Citicorp, Citibank N.Y., ITT, RJR Nabisco, N.Y. Pub. Libr., others. Trustee Cape Fear Mus., Wilmington, 1991—. Recipient Emerging Artists grant, Arts Coun., N.C., 1990, Title III fellowship U. N.C. Wilmington, 1972, numerous univ. rsch. fellowships, 1980, 86, 88, 90-93.

CONNER, COLIN L., nursing educator; b. Denver, Feb. 4, 1955; s. William Lee and Marion Erna (Fiddelke) C. BS in Psychology, Colo. State U., 1977; BS in Nursing, U. No. Colo., 1983; MS, U. Colo., 1989. Staff nurse St. Joseph's Hosp., Phoenix; staff nurse, cons. Am. Nursing Resources, Phoenix; rsch. asst. U. Colo. Health Sci. Ctr., Denver; clin. instr. U. Colo. Sch. Nursing, Denver; cardiac transplant CNS Children's Med. Ctr., Dallas, 1990-92, Hemodialysis staff, 1992-93, team leader hemodialysis, 1993-94, clin. nurse III pediat. ICU, 1994-95; cons. Health Promotion and Wellness, Exercise Physiology, 1996—. Contbr. editorials to Pediatric Nursing. Mem. Soc. Pediatric Cardiology Nurses, Am. Heart Assn., Sigma Theta Tau.

CONNER, JEANETTE JONES, elementary school educator; b. St. Charles, Va., Nov. 29, 1934; d. Luster and Georgia (Jessee) Jones; m. Samuel Barton Conner, Aug. 3, 1966. BS in Edn., Campbellsville Coll., 1979; MA in Edn., Western Ky. U., 1980, cert. sch. psychometrist, 1980, cert. in exceptional edn. K-12, 1981, cert. reading specialist, 1984, cert. elem. sch. supr., 1985, Edn. Specialist degree, 1986. Cert. tchr., Ky. Factory worker Lee Co. Garment Factory, Pennington Gap, Va., 1956-58; receptionist Harlan (Ky.) Appalachian Hosp., 1959-67; sec. Kemper & Assoc., Louisville, 1967-69, Murray (Ky.) State U., 1970-71, Greer & Assoc., Louisville, 1971-73, Cambellsville (Ky.) Coll., 1974-76; tchr. Taylor Co. Bd. Edn., Campbellsville, 1980—. Tchr. trainer Ky. Early Learning Profile Assessment System; citizen's ambassador People to People Program Del. to Perth '94 Early Childhood Conf., 20th Trienniel Australian Early Childhood Conf.; mem. Campbellsville Woman's Club (beautification com.). Commd. Ky. Col., State of Ky., 1989. Mem. AAUW (pres. 1989-90), NEA, South Cen. Reading Coun. of the Internat. Reading Assn. (Pres. 1989-90, v.p. 1990-91), Ky. State Coun. of the Internat. Reading Assn. (bd. dirs. 1988-91), Taylor County Edn. Assn. (v.p. 1989-90, pres. 1990-91), Ky. State Reading Coun. (chair com. on parents and reading 1990-91, svc. awards for promoting reading 1989-90), Ky. Edn. Assn., Ky. Coun. New Tchr. Performance Standards, Ky. Early Childhood Task Force for Early Childhood Cert. Guidelines, Ky. Dept. Special Edn. Task Force (KEA instructional com.), Ky. Assn. Supervision and Curriculum Devel. (bd. dirs., exec. bd. dirs.), Taylor County Bus. and Profl. Women, Phi Delta Kappa. Republican. Baptist. Home: 619 Shawnee Dr Campbellsville KY 42718-1643 Office: Taylor County Elem Sch Old Lebanon Rd Campbellsville KY 42718

CONNER, PATRICIA ANN, public relations executive; b. Knoxville, Tenn., Nov. 26, 1943; d. James White Jr. and Vera Ruth (Rimmer) C. BS in Elem. Edn., U. Tenn., 1965; postgrad., Ga. State U., 1969, U. S.C., 1975-76. Tchr. 6th grade Atlanta Pub./DeKalb County Bd. Edn., 1965-70; coord. ednl. radio programming and promotion Sta. WABE-FM and Sta. WPBA-TV, Atlanta, 1970-75; mgr. instrnl. radio svcs. office instrnl. TV and radio S.C. Dept. Edn., Columbia, 1975-78; dep. dir. devel., rsch. and planning S.C. Ednl. TV Network, Columbia, 1978-81, exec. prodr., 1981-82, dep. dir. continuing edn., 1982; pres. Conner-Robison Media Mktg., N.Y.C., 1982-84; sr. account exec., acting gen. mgr. pub. rels. divsn. Bozell, Jacobs, Kenyon & Eckhardt, Atlanta, 1984-86; regional mgr. affiliate pub. rels. Home Box Office, Inc., Atlanta, 1986—. Trustee, chair pub. rels. com. Met. Atlanta Crime Commn., 1990-92; bd. dirs. Acad. Theatre. Mem. Nat. Assn. Minorities Cable, Pub. Rels. Soc. Am., Acad. TV Arts & Scis., Women Cable (bd. dirs. 1990-94, co-chair mgmt. conf. 1994, v.p. Atlanta chpt., Dedicated Svc. award Atlanta chpt., Disting. Svc. award 1988, Pres.'s award 1989, Woman of Yr. 1991, Rita Ellix Meml. Accolade nat. office 1994), Cable TV Pub. Affairs Assn. (bd. dirs. 1989-94, Beacon award 1993, 94). Democrat. Episcopalian. Office: Home Box Office Inc 3399 Peachtree Rd NE Atlanta GA 30326-1120

CONNERY, CAROL JEAN, foundation director; b. Amarillo, Tex., Oct. 22, 1948; d. William Wayne and Joyce Jean (Fenney) Connery. AA, Christian Coll., 1969; BJ, U. Tex., Austin, 1971. Asst. dir. admissions Columbia (Mo.) Coll., 1971-80; exec. dir. nat. office Teenworld Scholarship Program, Overland Park, Kan., 1980-82; account exec. Mktg. Comm., Inc., Lenexa, Kans., 1983-86; account supr. Krupp/Taylor USA, Dallas, 1986-90; mktg. cons., 1990-93; dir. devel. St. Anthony's Found., Amarillo, Tex., 1994-95; dir. devel. Am. Quarter Horse Found., Amarillo, 1995—. Trustee Columbia Coll.; mem. coun. on ministries Polk St. United Meth. Ch. Mem. Assn. Healthcare Philanthropy (mem. regional bd.), Nat. Soc. Fund Raising Execs. (mem. regional bd.), United Way, Ctr. City Bus. and Profl. Women, Zeta Tau Alpha, Phi Theta Kappa (past nat. v.p.). Home: 3507 Brennan Gardens Amarillo TX 79121

CONNOLLY, JOSEPH FRANCIS, II, defense company executive; b. Quincy, Mass., Feb. 15, 1944; s. Joseph Francis and Flora Frances C.; m. Donna M. Cameron, May 4, 1968; children: Jennifer S., Joseph F. III. BA magna cum laude, Park Coll., Parkville, Mo., 1971; LLB, Blackstone Sch. Law, Chgo., 1972, JD, 1977; postgrad., U. South Fla., 1977-79, Fla. Inst. Tech., Melbourne, Liberty U., Lynchburg, Va., Am. Mil. U., Manassas, Va.; grad., Inst. Tng. in Mcpl. Adminstrn. of Internat. City Mgmt. Assn., USAF Air Command and Staff Coll., Indsl. Coll. of the Armed Forces. Cert. EMT, firefighter and law enforcement officer, Fla. Former coord. emergency med. svcs. City of Quincy, 1971-73; former EMT Boston Ambulance Squad, 1973-74; former coord. 14-community emergency med. svcs. program, 1974; formerly safety tng. coord., lead instr. Fire Tng. Acad. Orange County Pub. Schs., Fla., 1979-82; former dir. pub. safety Poinciana, Fla., 1985-86; sr. cons. Resource, Studies, and Devel. Internat., Inc., 1988-91; CEO Connolly, Hudson, Taylor & Assocs., Orlando, Fla., 1988-91; pres. Joseph F. Connolly II, P.A., Fla., 1982-95; adj. faculty mem. Pikes Peak Community Coll., Valencia Community Coll., Fla. Inst. Tech., Nat. Fire Acad., So. Coll.; tng. counselor NRA; med. cons. State of Bahrain Def. Force; former mem. Health Planning Coun. Greater Boston. Mem. Orange County subcom. Health Systems Agy. of East Ctrl. Fla.; fire commr. Conway Fire control Dist. of Orange County, 1980-84; former combat lt., staff capt. reserve program Orange County Fire Dept.; com. chmn. Orange County Rep. Exec. Com., 1985-93; former Safety Tng. Coord. Orange County Pub. Schs., Fla., pres. Coun. of Vol. Coords., Orange County, 1987; mem. Rep. Presdl. Task Force, Natl. Rep. Senatorial Commn.; active Boy Scouts Am., 1954—; life mem. Nat. Eagle Scout Assn., ret. lt. col. CAP, 1989; operational auxiliarist USCG Aux. Master sgt. Army Spl. Forces, 1961-96. Decorated Purple Heart with two oak leaf clusters, 24 other U.S. and fgn. mil. decorations or citations, Knight Sovereign Mil. Order St. John of Jerusalem (Austria); recipient Gill Robb Wilson award CAP, Aerospace Edn. Achievement award, 1987, Resolution of Tribute award Orange County Sch. Bd., 1989; named Vietnam Vet. of the Yr., Vietnam Vets. Ctrl. Fla., Inc., 1988; named to Order Knights Templar, 1985; selected for World Martial Arts Hall of Fame, 1996. Mem. Aircraft Owners and Pilots Assn., Boat/US, Sons of the Union Vets. of the Civil War, Ducks Unltd., VFW (life), DAV (life), Nat. Fire Acad. Alumni Assn. (pres. 1984-92), Nat. Assn. of Vet. Police Officers, Internat. Assn. Counselors and Therapists, Am. Counseling Assn., Intertel, Nat. Eagle Scout Assn. (life), Legion of Frontiersmen of the British Commonwealth, Third Order St. Francis, Mil. Order of Purple Heart, Mensa, Masons, U.S. Judo Assn. (life, black belt in karate, judo, and ju jitsu), inducted into World Martial Arts Hall of Fame, 1996. Anglican Catholic. Office: PO Box 620533 Orlando FL 32862-0533

CONNOR, EDWARD HOLLIS, III, golf course architect; b. Ft. Benning, Ga., Feb. 14, 1942; s. Edward Hollis Jr. and Ann Marie (Zebroff) C.; m. Joy Kathleen Shevlin, June 24, 1960 (div. July 1973); children: Debra Kristine, Julia Diane Connor McKinney, Maureen Ann Connor Butterfield, Edward Hollis IV; m. Pamela Ann Lawlor, Sept. 10, 1987. BSCE, U. Calif., Berkeley, 1964. Lic. civil engr., gen. engrng. contractor. Asst. traffic engr. City of L.A., 1964-65; asst. project mgr. Potrero Homes Corp., Thousand Oaks, Calif., 1966-67; project engr. Boise Cascade Bldg. Corp., L.A., 1968-69; devel. mgr. McCormick Ranch/Kaiser Aetna, Scottsdale, Ariz., 1970-73; pres. Connor Irrigation Co., Palm Desert, Calif., 1974-83, Golforms, Inc., Ponce Inlet, Fla., 1984—. Developed computer terrain modeling for golf course restoration; used modern tech. to restore Pebble Beach Golf Course, Pinehurst No. 2, Seminole Golf Club, others. Mem. U.S. Golf Assn. (nat. green sect. com.), Donald Ross Soc. (scholarship com. 1987—), Golf Course Supts. Assn. Am., Nat. Golf Found. Home and Office: Data Design Labs 1270 NW 167th Place Beaverton OR 97006

CONNOR, TERENCE GREGORY, lawyer; b. Chelsea, Mass., Dec. 28, 1942; s. Joseph Gerard Sr. and Rosalie Cecilia (Ryan) C.; m. Julie Kaye Berry, Dec. 18, 1971; children: Cormac, Kristin, Etain, Brendan. AB, Georgetown U., 1964; LLB, Seton Hall U., 1967; LLM, Georgetown U., 1975. Bar: D.C. 1968, U.S. Supreme Ct. 1976, Fla. 1980. Trial atty. U.S. Dept. Justice, Washington, 1973-76; labor counsel Nat. Airlines Inc., Miami, Fla., 1976-79; practicing atty. Morgan, Lewis & Bockius, Miami, 1979-96, mng. ptnr., 1996—. Chmn. Miami: Dade citizen com. for Observance Bicentennial of U.S. Constitution, 1986. Served to capt. JAG, USAF, 1968-73. Mem. Fla. Bar Assn. (chair labor and employment law sect. 1994-95, mem. exec. coun. 1986-93), Miami C. of C. (co-chair pers. and Labor mgmt. com. 1993-94). Roman Catholic. Home: 1517 San Rafael Ave Miami FL 33134-6241 Office: Morgan Lewis & Bockius 5300 First Universal Finan Ctr 200 S Biscayne Blvd Miami FL 33131-2310

CONNORS, JOSEPH ALOYSIUS, III, lawyer; b. Washington, June 24, 1946; s. Joseph Aloysius Jr. and Charlotte Rita (Fox) C.; m. Mary Louise Bucklin, June 14, 1969. BBA, U. Southwestern La., 1970; JD, U. Tex., 1973. Bar: Tex. 1973, U.S. Dist. Ct. (so. dist.) Tex. 1975, U.S. Supreme Ct. 1976, U.S. Ct. Appeals (5th cir.) 1976, U.S. Dist. Ct. (ea., we. and no. dists.) Tex. 1981, U.S. Ct. Appeals (11th cir.) 1981, U.S. Ct. Appeals (3d, 4th, 6th, 7th, 8th, 9th, 10th and D.C. cirs.) 1986. Law clk. to assoc. justice Tex. Ct. Civil Appeals, Amarillo, 1973-74; assoc. Rankin & Kern, McAllen, Tex., 1974-76; asst. criminal dist. atty. Hidalgo County, Tex., 1976-78; pvt. practice, McAllen, 1978—; mem. faculty Criminal Trial Advocacy Inst., Huntsville, Tex., 1981-84; speaker seminars State Bar Tex., 1980-81, 84; adj. prof. Reynaldo G. Garza Sch. Law, Edinburg, Tex., 1988-89. Contbg. editor Criminal Trial Manual, Tex., 1984-95; contbr. articles to legal publs. Bd. dirs. Tex. Rural Legal Aid, 1991—, pres. bd. dirs., 1994-96. With USMCR, 1966-71. Mem. NACDL, State Bar Tex. (grievance com. 12B 1984-91, chmn. com. 1989-90), Tex. Assn. Criminal Def. Lawyers (bd. dirs. 1982-89, Excellence award 1983, 83, medal of honor 1987), Hidalgo County Bar Assn. (bd. dirs. 1981-83), Am. Soc. Writers on Legal Subjects, Hidalgo County Criminal Def. Lawyers Assn. (bd. dirs. 1991-97). Democrat. Roman Catholic. Office: PO Box 5838 Mcallen TX 78502-5838

CONNORS, MICHELE PERROTT, wholesale beverage company executive; b. Ft. Lauderdale, Fla., June 28, 1952; d. Samuel R. and Mariette (Larouche) Perrott; m. Robert Gary Connors, Apr. 14, 1973; children: Eva Marie, Colleen Elizabeth. AA, Daytona Beach Community Coll., Fla., 1972. Legal sec. Richard Krause, Ormond Beach, Fla., 1972-74; sec. S.R. Perrott, Inc., Ormond Beach, 1974-79, v.p., ops. mgr., 1979-83, pres., chief exec. officer, 1983—; prin., pres. Michele & Group Modeling Talent Agy., 1989—. Bd. dirs. Daytona Beach Easter Seals Soc., 1985—, chmn. fundraising, 1983-86; bd. dirs. Am. Cancer Soc., 1989—. Mem. Beer Industry Fla., Nat. Beer Wholesalers, Ormond Beach C. of C. (pres. 1984), Oceanside Country Club, Trails Racquet Club. Republican. Roman Catholic. Office: S R Perrott Inc PO Box 836 Ormond Beach FL 32175-0836

CONOLEY, JOANN SHIPMAN, educational administrator; b. Bartlesville, Okla., July 19, 1931; d. Joe and Frances Loomis (Wall) Shipman; m. Travis A. Conoley, Oct. 29, 1976; children by previous marriage: James F. Lane, Joe Scott Lane, Kimberly Diane Lane. BS in English and Edn., Midwestern State U., Wichita Falls, Tex., 1968, MS in English and Edn., 1971, postgrad. Tex. A&M U., 1978—. Cert. elem. and high sch. tchr., reading/language arts coord., reading cons., adminstr., supt., Tex. Tchr. 3d grade Queen of Peace Sch., Wichita Falls, 1968-69; lang. arts team leader, jr. high sch. Wichita Falls Public Schs., 1969-74; fed. programs dir., reading coordinator Rockdale (Tex.) Public Schs., 1974-78, adminstrv. asst. to supt., 1978-79, asst. supt. adminstrn. and instrn., 1979—; reading cons. ALCOA, 1977—; site cons. U.S. Dept. Edn. Secondary Sch. Recognition Program, 1987, 89; mem. secondary sch. selection panel Tex. Edn. Agy., 1989; mem. Tex. Sch. Improvement Initiative Com. Tex. Edn. Agy., 1991—. Bd. dirs. Rockdale Public Library, 1975-79, pres., 1976-77; bd. dirs. Am. Cancer Soc. Named Yellow Rose Tex. Gov. of Tex. Mem. NEA, Tex. State Tchrs. Assn., Nat. Council Tchrs. English, Internat. Reading Assn., Assn. Compensatory Edn. Tex. (exec. bd. 1977-83), Assn. Supervision and Curriculum Devel., Alpha Chi, Delta Kappa Gamma, Kappa Delta Pi. Home: 405 Bounds Ave Rockdale TX 76567-2709 Office: PO Box 632 Rockdale TX 76567-0632

CONRAD, DAVID PAUL, real estate broker, retired restaurant chain executive; b. Greensboro, N.C., Jan. 11, 1946; s. Lucas Lee and Elizabeth Gertrude (Kincaid) C.; m. Mitzi Walsh; children: Lucas Wilfong, Haley Ryanne. BSBA, East Carolina U., 1970; cert. in real estate, Forsyth Tech. Coll., 1979. From cashier to cook Libby Hill Seafood, Greensboro, N.C., 1962-64; plant mgr. Libby Hill Seafood Restaurants, Inc., Greensboro, N.C., 1970-76; mgr. Libby Hill Seafood Restaurants, Inc., Winston-Salem, N.C., 1976-85; v.p., dir. ops. Libby Hill Seafood Restaurants, Inc., Greensboro, N.C., 1985-93, also bd. dirs., 1985-93; comml. real estate broker Allied Comml. Real Estate, Kernersville, N.C., 1993—; franchise owner Swisher Maids of West Greensboro, N.C., 1994-96, regional dir., 1996—. Mem. Greensboro Jaycees, 1973-81; vol. St. Jude's Children's Rsch. Hosp. Staff sgt. N.C. N.G., 1968-74. Mem. Masons. Republican. Methodist. Office: Swisher Maids W Greensboro 319-C Westgate Dr Greensboro NC 27407

CONRAD, EDWARD CHARLES, trade shows producer; b. May 31, 1949; s. Edward Victor and Pamela (Robertson) C.; m. Tracy Ann Monroe, Feb. 16, 1985; children: Edward Tyler, Ryan Alexander. BA, Oglethorpe U., 1972. Bookkeeper/sales rep. Semco Prodns., Atlanta, 1969-72, v.p., 1972-80, pres., CEO, 1980-88, chmn., pres., CEO, 1988—; founder, chmn. Conrad Aviation Techs., Inc., 1994—. Founder Spl. Kids Ferrari Club, Atlanta, 1988—; founder, chmn. John Edward Found., Atlanta, 1989—, Internat. Health Care Devel. Assn., 1996—; bd. dirs. Ireland's Hist. Sci. Ctr., Birr, Ireland, 1991—; mem. Am. Ireland Fund, Boston, 1995—; mem. bd. advisors Pine Crest Sch., 1996—. Recipient IRV Rosenthal award Marine Retailers Assn. of Am., 1989. Mem. Nat. Assn. of Consumer Shows (pres. 1992-93), Home and Garden Show Execs. Internat. (pres. 1989-91), Soc. of Ind. Show Organizers, Nat. Assn. of Med. Equipment Supplies, Lauderdale Yacht Club, Atlanta Athletic Club. Republican. Episcopalian. Office: Semco Prodns 1130 Hightower Trail Atlanta GA 30350

CONRAD, FLAVIUS LESLIE, JR., minister; b. Hickory, N.C., May 5, 1920; s. Flavius Leslie and Mary Wilhelmina (Huffman) C.; m. Mary Elizabeth Isenhour, Nov. 4, 1944; children: Ann (Mrs. Bruce E. Meisner), Susan (Mrs. James A. Amis). AB, Lenoir Rhyne Coll., 1941; MDiv, Luth. Theol. So. Sem., 1944; MST, Temple U., 1955, STD, 1959. Ordained to ministry Evang. Luth. Ch. Am., 1944. Pastor St. Timothy Luth. Ch., Hickory, 1944-49, Holy Comforter Luth. Ch., Belmont, N.C., 1949-50; youth dir. United Luth. Ch. Am., Phila., 1950-60; pastor St. Luke's Luth. Ch., Richardson, Tex., 1960-86, pastor emeritus, 1986—; dean Dallas and East Tex. dist. Luth. Ch. Am., 1973-77, mem. publ. bd., 1974-82; del. convs. Luth. Ch. Am., 1968, 74, 76; exec. sec. Luther League Am., 1950-60; mem. exec. bd. and gen. assembly Nat. Coun. Chs. of Christ in U.S.A., 1954-60. Author: A Study of Four Non-Denominational Youth Movements, 1955, Poetic Potshots at People and Preachers, 1977; pub. sermons for The Clergy Jour., worship materials for The Minister's Annual Manual, 1996-97; contbg. editor Ch. Mgmt. mag., 1966-74; corr. The Lutheran from S.W., 1962-76; contbr. sermons, articles and poems to various mags. V.p. Piedmont (N.C.) coun. Boy Scouts Am., 1948-49. Winner Nat. Poetry Contest, 1960. Home: 1108 Pueblo Dr Richardson TX 75080-2913

CONRAD, HAROLD THEODORE, psychiatrist; b. Milw., Jan. 25, 1934; s. Theodore Herman and Alyce Barbara C.; A.B., U. Chgo., 1954, B.S., 1955, M.D., 1958; m. Elaine Marie Blaine, Sept. 1, 1962; children—Blaine, Carl, David, Erich, Rachel. Intern USPHS Hosp., San Francisco, 1958-59; commd. sr. asst. surgeon USPHS, 1958, advanced through grades to med. dir., 1967; resident in psychiatry USPHS Hosp., Lexington, Ky., 1959-61, Charity Hosp., New Orleans, 1961-62; chief of psychiatry USPHS Hosp., New Orleans, 1962-67, clin. dir., 1967; dep. dir. div. field investigations NIMH, Chevy Chase, Md., 1968; chief NIMH Clin. Research Center, Lexington, 1969-73; cons. psychiatry, region IX, USPHS, HEW, San Francisco, 1973-79; dir. adolescent unit Alaska Psychiat. Inst., Anchorage, 1979-81, supt., 1981-85; clin. assoc. prof. psychiatry U. Wash. Med. Sch., 1981-85; med. dir. Bayou Oaks Hosp., Houma, La., 1985—. Decorated Commendation medal; recipient various community awards for contbns. in field of drug abuse and equal employment opportunity for minorities. Diplomate Am. Bd. Psychiatry. Fellow Royal Soc. Health, Royal Soc. Medicine, Am. Psychiat. Assn.; mem. AMA, Alpha Omega Alpha, Alpha Delta Phi. Contbr. to publs. in field. Office: 855 Belanger St Houma LA 70360-4463

CONRAD, JOHN REGIS, lawyer; b. Bloomington, Ind., Feb. 23, 1955; s. John Francis and Patricia Ann (English) C.; m. Paula Jane Vessels, July 4, 1980; children: William Celestine Vessels, John Paul Vessels, M. Alexander Vessels, David Thomas Kelamalamalamanokeakua Vessels, Rachel Elizabeth Ho'ouluolaikealoha Vessels. AB cum laude, Harvard U., 1977; MBA, JD, Ind. U., 1981. Bar: Hawaii 1981, Fla. 1994, Tex. 1994, N.C. 1995, U.S. Dist. Ct. Hawaii 1981, U.S. Ct. Appeals (9th cir.) 1981, U.S. Ct. Claims 1981, U.S. Tax Ct. 1981. Assoc. Cades, Schutte, Fleming & Wright, Honolulu, 1981-85, 89-90, Thompson & Chan, Honolulu, 1985-89; ptnr. Cades Schutte Fleming & Wright, Honolulu, 1991-94; regional bus. mgr. Kimley-Horn and Assocs., Inc., West Palm Beach, Fla., 1994-96, regional prodn. mgr., 1996—; lectr. law Kapiolani C.C., Honolulu, 1984-86; adj. prof. law Richardson Sch. Law, U. Hawaii, 1989-90. Author: Hawaii Probate Sourcebook, 1985, rev. ed. 1986, 3d rev. ed. 1992; co-author: Beyond the Basics: Hawaii Estate Planning & Probate, 1985, Hawaii Wills & Trusts Sourcebook, 1986, Hawaii Guardianship Sourcebook, 1988; editor HICLE Fin. and Estate Planning Manual, vol. II, 1989, vol. I, 1990. Mem. planned giving com. Hawaii Heart Assn., Honolulu, 1983-86; arbitrator Hawaii Ct. Annexec Arbitration Program, 1989-94; mem. sch. bd. Star of the Sea Sch., Honolulu, 1992-94, pres., 1993-94, chair Carnival, 1992; chair Cub Scout pack Aloha coun. Boy Scouts Am., den leader Cub Scout Pack 757, Gulf Stream Coun. Fellow Am. Coll. Trust and Estate Coun.; mem. Am. Arbitration Assn., Hawaii Bar Assn. (chmn. estate and gift tax com. 1984-85, CFO probate and estate planning sect. 1989-90), Hawaii Bar Found. (bd. dirs. 1985-92, v.p. 1989, pres. 1989-91), Hawaii Estate Planning Coun. (bd. dirs. 1991-94, sec. 1993). Roman Catholic. Home: 17263 123d Terr N Jupiter Farms FL 33478 Office: Kimley-Horn and Assocs Inc 4431 Embarcardero Dr West Palm Beach FL 33407-3258

CONRAD, JUDY L., insurance company executive; b. Reading, Pa., May 22, 1952; d. Willard Martin and Mary Eleanor (Strecker) Conrad; m. Mark A. Stead, Feb. 14, 1988 (dec. 1990); stepchildren: Matthew, Mark Jr., Adrian, Angela. BS in Edn., West Chester (Pa.) U., 1974. CFP, CLU. Tchr. Auscilla Christian Acad., Monticello, Fla., 1980-82; sales agt. Alden Levin Assocs., Phila., 1977-80, John Hunt Assocs., Tallahassee, Fla., 1982-84; life and employee benefits mgr. Corp. Risk Assocs., Tallahassee, Fla., 1982-84; acct. exec. Cigna/INA Cos., Phila., 1985-86; fin. svcs. rep. The Travelers Ins. Cos., Orlando, Fla., 1986-90; fin. svcs. mgr. The Travelers Ins. Cos., Orlando and Tampa, 1990-95; regional specialist Smith Barney, Orlando, 1996—; pub. speaker, lectr. in field. With Free Fin. Clinics, Orlando Sentinel sponsored hotline 1992, local TV & radio shows St. Petersburg, Jacksonville, Orlando. Recipient Life Citation award INA/CIGNA, 1984. Mem. Am. Soc. CLU, Ctrl. Fla. Soc. ICFP (edn. dir. 1991—, v.p. 1992—, pres.-elect 1993, pres. 1994, chmn. 1995, state rep. 1996), Am. Coll. CLU & ChFC, Nat. Assn. Life Underwriters, Gen. Agts. and Mgrs. Assn., Internat. Assn. Fin. Planners. Republican. Office: Smith Barney Inc 800 N Magnolia Ave Ste 202 Orlando FL 32803-3260

CONRAD, LOUIS E., student affairs director, educator; b. St. Louis, Apr. 26, 1940; s. Eugene Louis and Elva M. (Pickard) C.; m. Linda M. Wancket, Sept. 2, 1961 (div. Feb. 15, 1984); children: Louis E. III, Lance Edward; m. Elizabeth M. Mosher, June 20, 1986. BJ, U. Mo., 1962; MS, Boston U., 1983. News writer, reporter KTIV-TV, Sioux City, Iowa, 1962-63; prodr., writer news KMOX-TV, St. Louis, 1963-69; exec. news editor WBZ-TV, Boston, 1969-79; writer, prodr. news WCVB-TV, Needham, Mass., 1979-81; owner, gen. mgr. WNRI-Radio, Woonsocket, R.I., 1981-83; lectr. journalism, mass comms. Emerson Coll., Boston, 1983-94; asst. prof. broadcast journalism Northeastern U., Boston, 1981-88, student media adv., 1988-95; asst. dir. student affairs Fla. Internat. U., Miami, 1995—. Mem. fin. com. Town of Swampscott, mass., 1983-94; mem. Swampscott Town Meeting, 1987-94, Lexington (Mass.) Town Meeting, 1971-85; music lt. Lexington Minute Men, 1974-95. Democrat. Home: 2396 SW 183rd Terr Miramar FL 33029 Office: Fla Internat U GC 210 11200 SW 8th St Miami FL 33174-2516

CONRAD, PHILIP JEFFERSON, software development engineer; b. New Iberia, La., Nov. 30, 1957; s. Karl Donovan and Dolores Beatrice (Bienvenu) C.; children: Siobhan, Turner; m. Diane Tucker, Mar. 30, 1996; stepchildren: Ryan, Ree. BSME, U. Southwestern La., 1979; postgrad., U. Okla., 1992-93. Commd. 2nd lt. USAF, 1979, advanced through grades to capt., 1983; structural engr. USAF, Dayton, Ohio, 1979-81; safety officer, investigator, specialist USAF, 1983-89; A-10 pilot USAF, Suwon AFB, Korea, 1983-84, RAF Bentwaters, U.K., 1984-87; E-3 pilot USAF, Oklahoma City, 1987-89, supv. Command Ctr., 1989-92; software engr. Texas Instruments, Dallas, 1993-96, DSC Comms. Co., Plano, Tex., 1996—. Decorated Air medal. Home: 1424 Chatsworth Lane Plano TX 75075-2570 Office: DSC Comm Corp 1000 Coit Rd MS SOFD1 Plano TX 75075-5813

CONRAD, SUZANNE LANE, marketing professional, organization administrator; b. Bitburg, Germany, Mar. 29, 1958; d. Leo Joseph Lane and Everarda (Bührs) Lane Thomas; m. Gary Lee Conrad, May 28, 1994; 1

child, Sean Thomas. BSN, U. Mass., 1981; MS in Health Care Adminstrn., Tex. Woman's U., 1992. Cert. procurement transplant coord. Am. Bd. Transplant Coords. Staff nurse Hartford (Conn.) Hosp., 1981-84, transplant coord., 1984-85; organ recovery coord. S.W. Organ Bank, Dallas, 1985-86, edn. mgr., 1986-89, mktg. mgr., 1989—; Bd. dirs. United Network for Organ Sharing, Richmond; bd. dirs. N. Am. Transplant Coord. Orgn., Lenexa, Kans., treas., 1993-94, pres., 1995-96. Contbr. article to Jour. Transplant Coord., 1991. Mem. steering com. St. Michael's and All Angels Ch., Dallas, 1991-93. Mem. Am. Coll. Health Care Execs., Assn. Organ Procurement Orgn. (chair task force 1996—), Sigma Theta Tau (Eta Omega chpt. 1981). Episcopalian. Office: SW Organ Bank 3500 Maple #800 Dallas TX 75219

CONROW, RAYMOND EUGENE, organic chemist; b. Chgo., July 26, 1953; s. Gerald Eugene and Edda Florence (Fenili) C.; m. Kimberly Ann Stampke, Dec. 30, 1989; 1 child, Adam Raymond. BA, Northeastern Ill. U., Chgo., 1977; PhD in Organic Chemistry, Northwestern U., 1983. Postdoctoral assoc. U. Minn., 1982-84, Stanford U., 1984-85; rsch. chemist synthesis sect. agrl. products dept. DuPont Co., Expt. Sta., Wilmington, Del., 1985-88; sr. scientist II medicinal chemistry dept. Alcon Labs., Inc., Ft. Worth, 1988-89, sr. scientist III, 1990-92, prin. scientist chem. preparations rsch., 1993—. Contbr. articles to profl. jours.; patentee in field. Northwestern U. fellow, 1978, NSF predoctoral fellow, 1979-82, NIH postdoctoral fellow, 1982-84. Mem. Am. Chem. Soc., Nat. Parks and Conservation Assn., Sierra Club (program chmn. Ft. Worth group 1989-93), Allman Bros. Band Fan Club. Office: Alcon Labs Inc 6201 South Fwy Fort Worth TX 76134-2001

CONSTANTINE, LYNNE MARY, writer, consultant; b. Queens, N.Y., July 29, 1953; d. Arthur Anthony and Anne Jasmine (D'Angelo) C.; partner Suzanne Scott, Nov. 15, 1980; stepchildren: Elizabeth, William, Stephanie, David. BA summa cum laude, Canisius Coll., 1973; MA, Yale U., 1975, MPhil, 1976. Asst. prof. English James Madison U., Harrisonburg, Va., 1977-80; mng. dir. Health Edn. Found., Washington, 1981-83; exec. dir. Energy Conservation Coalition, Washington, 1983-85; ptnr., creative dir. Cmty. Scribes, Arlington, Va., 1985—; cons. APA Pres.'s Commn. on Violence in the Family, Washington, 1994-95, Commn. on Violence and Youth, 1992-93, Carnegie Coun. on Adolescence, Washington, 1994-95, D.C. Area Rape Crisis Ctr., 1985-95. Co-author: Migraine: The Complete Guide, 1994; mng. editor: Woman's Monthly, 1992—, Passages award, 1995. Mem. Nat. Lesbian and Gay Journalists Assn., Nat. Soc. for Hosp. Mktg. Comm. and Pub. Rels., Washington Ind. Writers, Washington Metro Soc. for Hosp. Mktg. Comm. and Pub. Rels. Home: 4600 S Four Mile Run Dr 636 Arlington VA 22204 Office: Community Scribes 1001 N Highland St Ste PH Arlington VA 22201

CONSTANTINI, JOANN M., information management consultant, speaker; b. Danbury, Conn., July 30, 1948; d. William J. and Mathilda J. (Ressler) C. BA, Coll. White Plains, N.Y., 1970; postgrad. Central Conn. State Coll., 1977-78, U. Hartford, 1985-88, U. Jacksonville, 1991; MS, Nova Southeastern U. Sch. Psychology, 1996; Cert. records mgr., 1987; lic realtor, N.C. Psychiat. social worker N.Y. State Dept. Mental Hygiene, Wassaic, 1970-73; with Northeast Utilities, Hartford, Conn., 1973-88, methods analyst, 1979-82, records and procedures mgmt. adminstr., 1982-88; document contr., mgr. Ralph M. Parsons Co., Fairfield, Ohio, 1990-91, St. Johns River Power Park, Jacksonville, 1991—; bd. dirs. Micrographics, Inc., Gainesville, Fla.; dir. Meriden (Conn.) YWCA, 1976-77, My Sisters Place, 1984-87; mem. faculty Cen. Piedmont C.C., 1989-90, Fla. C.C., Jacksonville, 1993-95. Bd. dirs. Meriden YWCA, Conn., 1978-79; vol., 1984—, Queen City Friends, Charlotte, 1988-89; vol. Cath Charities AIDS Ministries, Jacksonville, 1996; mem. Greater Charlotte Bd. Realtors; mem. adv. coun. Clermont Coll., Cin., 1990-91, Jacksonville C.C. 1991—, Greater Hartford C.C., 1986, Vol. Catholic Charities Aids Ministries, Jacjsonville, Fla, 1996—. Mem. AAUW, Assn. Record Mgmt. and Adminstrs. (sec. 1984-85, bd. dirs., 1984-86, internat. chair industry action program 1989-93, chair industry action com. for pub. utilities, 1986-89), Assn. Image and Info. Mgmt. (dir. 1984-86), Women Bus. Owners, Assn. Configurement Data Mgmt., Electric Coun. New Eng. (chair records mgmt. com. 1985-87), Coll. White Plains Alumnae Assn., Nat. Trust for Hist. Preservation, Inst. Cert. Records Mgrs., Am. Platform Assn., Beta Sigma Phi. Democrat. Roman Catholic. Club: Northeast Utilities Women's Forum. (treas. 1983-88). Avocations: antiques, fund raising, traveling, investing. Home: 11538 Jonathan Rd Jacksonville FL 32225-1314

CONSTANTINIDES, DINOS DEMETRIOS (CONSTANTINE CONSTANTINIDES), music educator, composer, conductor; b. Ioannina, Greece, May 10, 1929; came to U.S., 1957, naturalized, 1966; s. Demetrios Constantine and Magdalini (Papastergiou) C.; m. Judith Rose Hursh, July 1, 1962; children: Lenna, John. Diploma, Greek Conservatory, Athens, 1950, 57, Juilliard Sch., 1960; MM, Ind. U., 1965; PhD, Mich. State U., 1968. 1st violinist State Orch. Athens, Radio Symphony Athens, 1952-63; concertmaster Little Orch. Athens, 1961-62; 1st violinist Indpls. Symphony, 1963-65; concertmaster Indpls. Sinfonietta, 1963-65; prin. 2d violin Lansing (Mich.) Symphony, 1965-66; guest concertmaster Kalamazoo Symphony, 1966; Boyd prof. La. State U., Baton Rouge, 1966—, chmn. Festival Contemporary Music, 1974—, dir. New Music Ensemble, 1983—; concertmaster Baton Rouge Symphony, 1966-88, Beaumont (Tex.) Civic Opera, 1966-72, Baton Rouge Gilbert and Sullivan, 1978-89, Baton Rouge Opera, 1984-87; condr., music coord. Baton Rouge Symphony Chamber Orch., 1982-90; guest composer, condr., educator People's Republic China, 1990; music dir., condr. La. Sinfonietta, 1990—. Composer: (opera) Intimations, 1975 (awards 1981, 85), (opera in 3 acts) Antigone, 1993, (works for orch.) Symphony No. 2, 1983, Hymn to the Human Spirit, 1983, China I-Shanghai for soprano, bassoon and strings, 1991; guest composer, performer U.S. Poland, Eng., France, Greece, 1966—. Mem., performer Contemporary Arts Ctr., New Orleans, 1985—. Cpl. Greek Army, 1947-51. Recipient Disting. Svc. award Am. New Music Consortium, 1985, Glen award L'Ensemble composition contest, Lifetime Achievement award Gov. La.; Greek Govt. Found. grantee, 1957-60. Mem. ASCAP (18 Standard awards 1975-93), Music Tchrs. Nat. Assn. (exec. bd. 1982-86, awards 1970, 79, 82, 88), Soc. Composers, Inc. (nat. coun. 1983-84, 88-89), Coll. Music Soc., Nat. Composers Assn. USA (nat. bd. dirs. 1991—). Democrat. Greek Orthodox. Home: 947 Daventry Dr Baton Rouge LA 70808-5830 Office: Sch Music La State U Baton Rouge LA 70803

CONTI, LOUIS THOMAS MOORE, lawyer; b. Phila., Aug. 31, 1949; s. Alexander and Yolanda (DiLorenzo) C.; m. Christina M.S. Moore, May 1, 1982; children: Charles Alexander, Whitney Caroline. BS, LaSalle Coll., 1971; MBA, Drexel U., 1972; JD, Creighton U., 1975; LLM, Temple U., 1981. Bar: U.S. Claims Ct. 1975, U.S. Tax Ct. 1975, Pa. 1975, U.S. Dist. Ct. (ea. dist.) Pa. 1978, U.S. Ct. Appeals (3d cir.) 1979, U.S. Supreme Ct. 1981, Fla. 1982, U.S. Dist. Ct. (mid. dist.) Fla. 1988. Tax atty. Office Chief Counsel IRS, Washington and Phila., 1975-81; tax mgr. Touche Ross & Co., Phila., 1981-84; assoc. Saul, Ewing, Remick & Saul, Phila., 1984-87; shareholder Swann & Haddock, P.A., Orlando, Fla., 1987-89; ptnr., chmn. corp. tax and securities dept. Holland & Knight, Orlando, 1989—. Mem. fin. com. S.E. Pa. chpt. ARC, Phila., 1984-87; advisor Vol. Lawyers for Arts, Phila., 1984-87; bd. dirs. Fla. Hosp. Found., 1989—, Ctrl. Fla. Planned Giving Coun., 1989—, Cmty. Found. Ctrl. Fla. Inc., 1993—, World Trade Ctr., Orlando, 1992-95; mem. internat. bus. adv. bd. Metro Orlando. Mem. ABA (tax and bus. law sect.), Fla. Bar Assn. (tax and corp. sect.), Orange County Bar Assn. (chmn. tax sect. 1990-91), Seminole County C. of C. (bd. dirs. 1994—), Racquet Club, Alaqua Country Club, Citrus Club. Republican. Home: 3003 Timpana Pt Longwood FL 32779-3108 Office: Holland & Knight PO Box 1526 Orlando FL 32802-1526

CONTIS, GEORGE, medical services company executive. MD, MPH. Pres. Med. Svcs. Corp. Internat. Address: 1716 Wilson Blvd Arlington VA 22209

CONTRERAS, ISRAEL, manufacturing executive; b. Dallas, Mar. 31, 1970; s. Bartolo and Elena C. Home: PO Box 541971 Dallas TX 75354-1971 Office: Bartco Concrete Inc 2614 Myrtle Springs Ave Dallas TX 75220-2515

CONWAY, JAMES DONALD, internist, educator; b. Newark, May 2, 1946; s. James M. and Dorothy (Kelly) C. BA, St. Olaf Coll., 1968; MD, U. Ill., 1972, MS, 1972. Bd. cert. internal medicine and infectious diseases. Intern Cornell Coop. Hosp., N.Y.C., 1972, resident, 1973-74; fellow infectious disease U. Mich., Ann Arbor, 1974-76; sr. resident medicine La. State U., New Orleans, 1978-79; co-dir. critical care medicine So. Md. Hosp., Clinton, 1979; assoc. prof. internal medicine, emergency medicine La. State U., 1980—; practice medicine specializing in internal medicine and infectious diseases, New Orleans, 1980—; dir. ICU Touro Hosp., 1985-86; chmn. dept medicine, dir. infection control Doctor's Hosp., ACP, 1994—; bd. dirs. Doctor's Hosp, Ponchatran IFA. Contbr. articles to profl. jours. Recipient Rsch. award U. Ill., 1973; Mich. Heart Assn. fellow rsch. award, 1974. Mem. Am. Soc. Microbiology, ACP. Home and Office: 4300 Houma Blvd Ste 205 Metairie LA 70006-2924

CONWAY, MARY MARGARET, political science educator; b. Terre Haute, Ind., May 14, 1935; d. Frank Joseph and Mary Kathryn C. BS in Econs., Purdue U., 1957; MA in Polit. Sci., U. Calif., Berkeley, 1960; PhD in Polit. Sci., Ind. U., 1965. Lectr. to prof. U. Md., College Park, Md., 1963-89; prof. U. Fla., Gainesville, Fla., 1989—. Recipient Disting. Scholar/Tchr. award U.Md., 1985. Mem. Am. Polit. Sci. Assn. (v.p. 1991-92), So. Polit. Sci. Assn. (pres. 1986-87). Office: U Fla PO Box 117325 Gainesville FL 32611-7325

COOK, ANGELA DENISE, business analyst; b. Chgo., Oct. 31, 1963; d. Mary Grey; m. Joseph Clinton Cook, Jan. 1, 1989; 1 child, Meaghan Mary. BS in Computer Sci., Northeastern U., Chgo., 1984; MBA, Northwestern U., Evanston, Ill., 1986. Quality assurance mgr. Quality Assurance Inst., Orlando, Fla., 1985—; guest speaker Harold Washington Women's Affairs com., Chgo., 1987. Counselor Rape Victim Adv., Chgo., 1984-88; bd. dirs. Rape Trauma Victim Assistance, Chgo., 1989; adv. at large Chgo. Com. on Homeless, 1988; dir. ministries homeless coun. United Meth. Ch., 1995-96. Democrat. Office: Va Power One James River Plz Richmond VA 23219

COOK, AUGUST JOSEPH, lawyer, accountant; b. Devine, Tex., Sept. 25, 1926; s. August E. and Mary H. (Schmidt) C.; m. Matie M. Brangan, July 12, 1952; children: Lisa Ann, Mary Beth, John J. BS, Trinity U., 1949; BBA, U. Tex., 1954; JD, St. Mary's U., 1960. Bar: Tex. 1960, Tenn. 1975. Bus. mgr., corp. sec. Life Enterprises, Inc. and affiliated cos., San Antonio, 1950-58, also dir.; mgr. Ernst and Whinney, San Antonio, 1960-69, ptnr. Memphis, 1970-84; ptnr. McDonnel Boyd, Memphis, 1984-91; counsel Harris, Shelton, Dunlap and Cobb, Memphis, 1991—. Author newspaper column A.J.'s Tax Fables, 1983—. Author: A.J. $ Tax Court, 1987; contbr. articles to profl. jours. Alderman City of Castle Hills, Tex., 1961-63, mayor, 1963-69; chmn. Bexar County Council Mayors, 1967-69; v.p. Tex Mcpl. League, 1968-69; bd. dirs. San Antonio Met. YMCA. Served with U.S. Army, 1945-46, PTO. Mem. AICPA, Tex. Soc. CPAs, Tex. Bar Assn., Estate Planning Council San Antonio (pres. 1967), Tenn. Soc. CPAs, Tenn. Bar Assn. (chmn. tax, probate and trust sect., 1993-95), Estate Planning Council Memphis (pres. 1983-84), Toastmasters (pres. 1963), Delta Theta Phi, Kappa Pi Sigma. Roman Catholic. Clubs: University (Memphis); Canyon Creek Country (San Antonio) (bd. dirs.); Chickasaw Country. Lodges: Optimists (bd. dirs.), Rotary (treas. 1978, bd. dirs. 1986-87). Home: 6785 Slash Pine Cv Memphis TN 38119-5617 Office: Harris Shelton Dunlap & Cobb 6445 Poplar Ste 202 Memphis TN 38119

COOK, CHARLES WILKERSON, JR., banker, former county official; b. Nashville, Sept. 10, 1934; s. Charles Wilkerson and Virginia (Jones) C.; m. Sally Randolph Frierson, June 24, 1961; children: Charles Wilkerson III, John Stephenson Frierson. B.S., Yale U., 1956; postgrad., Stonier Grad. Sch. Banking, Rutgers U., 1964-66. With Third Nat. Bank, Nashville, 1959-85, pres., 1979-83, chmn., 1983-85, also dir.; with Third Nat. Corp., Nashville, 1985-89, pres., chief exec. officer, 1985-87, chmn. bd. dirs., chief exec. officer, 1987-89, dir., 1983-90; exec. v.p. Sun Trust Banks, Inc., 1989-90; dir. fin. Met. Govt. of Nashville-Davidson County (Tenn.), Nashville, 1991-93; pres., CEO, dir. Union Planters Bank of Mid. Tenn., N.A., Nashville, 1993—; bd. dirs. Brandau Craig-Dickerson Co., Nashville Electric Power, Quality Industries, Inc., Centennial Med. Ctr. Author: History of a Bank Merger, 1969. Mem. Nashville-Davidson County Govt. Social Svcs. Commn., 1970-85; sr. warden Christ Episcopal Ch., Nashville, 1970-71; pres. Episc. Churchmen of Tenn., 1974; mem. bishop and coun. Episc. Diocese of Tenn., 1979-81; chmn., bd. dirs. United Way Nashville, 1984-85, 1993—; chmn. Project PENCIL, 1988-89, Jr. Achievement of Nashville, Bill Wilkerson Hearing and Speech Ctr., Nashville, 1970-80, Ensworth Sch., 1978-81, Better Bus. Bur. Nashville, 1980-83, Nashville Meml. Hosp., 1974-89, Tenn. Performing Arts Mgmt. Corp., 1985-89, vice-chmn., 1987-89, Tenn. State Mus. Found., 1986-89; mem. adv. bd. Salvation Army, Nashville, 1976-79; bd. dirs. Episcopal Ch. Found., 1991-92; campaign chmn. United Way Mid. Tenn., 1994. With USN, 1956-59; capt. Res., 1977-84. Mem. Nashville C. of C. (bd. govs. 1982-84, 95—), Belle Meade Country Club (bd. dirs. 1996—), Army-Navy Club (Washington), Yale Club of N.Y.C., Cumberland Club (Nashville). Office: 401 Union St Nashville TN 37219-1708

COOK, CLARK, administrator science museum. Pres. Mus. of Sci., Miami, Fla. Office: Mus of Sci 3280 South Ave Miami FL 33129

COOK, DONALD EUGENE, orthopedist; b. Cromwell, Ala., Oct. 19, 1935; s. Frances Aubrey and Ethie Francis (Nicholson) C.; m. Myrna Nell Shadow, June 20, 1959; children: Janet Lynn, Donald Scott. Student, U. Miss., 1959, MD, 1963. Extern Miss. State Hosp., Whitfield, 1962-63; intern Mobile (Ala.) Gen. Hosp., 1963-64; resident U. Miss. Med. Ctr., Jackson, 1964-68, chief resident, 1967-68; cons. physician Miss. Crippled Children's Service, Meridian, 1968-72; staff Riley Meml. Hosp., Meridian, 1968-76, Meridian Regional Hosp., 1968-89, Anderson Med. Ctr., Meridian, 1968—; pres. East. Cen. Orthopaedics, Ltd., Meridian, 1982—; CEO Astro Devel. Co., Meridian, 1986-92; pres., chief exec. officer Planetary Products, Inc., Meridian, 1986-93. Patentee. Mem. bd. dirs. ARC, Meridian, 1978-80; team physician Meredian Boxing Club, 1980-95. Served with U.S. Army, 1954-57. Mem. AMA, East Miss. Med. Assn., Miss. Orthopaedic Assn., Nat. Assn. Disability Examiners, So. Med. Assn., Miss. State Med. Assn., So. Orthopaedic Assn., Masons (32 degree), Shriners. Baptist. Home: 6485 Highway 493 Meridian MS 39305-9281 Office: East Cen Orthopaedics Ltd 5002 Highway 39 N Meridian MS 39301-1071

COOK, DORIS MARIE, accountant, educator; b. Fayetteville, Ark., June 11, 1924; d. Ira and Mettie Jewel (Dorman) C. BSBA, U. Ark., 1946, MS, 1949; PhD, U. Tex., 1968. CPA, Okla., Ark. Jr. acct. Haskins & Sells, Tulsa, 1946-47; instr. acctg. U. Ark., Fayetteville, 1947-52, asst. prof., 1952-62, assoc. prof., 1962-69, prof., 1969-88, Univ. prof. and Nolan E. Williams lectr. in acctg., 1988—; mem. Ark. State Bd. Pub. Accountancy, 1987-92, treas., 1989-91, vice chmn. 1991-92; mem. Nat. Assn. State Bds. of Accountancy, 1987-92; appointed Nolan E. Williams lectureship in acctg., 1988—. Mem. rev. bd. Ark. Bus. Rev., Jour. Managerial Issues; contbr. articles to profl. jours. Named Outstanding Grad. acctg. dept. U. Ark., 1996. Mem. AICPA, Ark. Bus. Assn. (editor newsletter 1982-85), Am. Acctg. Assn. (chmn. nat. membership 1982-83, Arthur Carter scholarship com. 1984-85, membership Ark. 1985-87), Am. Women's Soc. CPAs., Ark. Soc. CPA's (v.p. 1975-76, pres. N.W. Ark. chpt. 1980-81; sec. Student Loan Found., 1981-84, treas. 1984-92, pres. 1992—; chmn. pub. rels. 1984-88, 93-95, Outstanding Acctg. Educator award 1991), Acad. Acctg. Historians (trustee 1985-87, rev. bd. of Working Papers Series 1984-92, sec. 1992-95, pres.-elect 1995, pres. 1996), Ark. Fedn. Bus. and Profl. Women's Clubs (treas. 1979-80), Fayetteville Bus. and Profl. Women's Clubs (pres. 1973-74, 75-76, Woman of Yr. award 1977) Mortar Bd., Beta Gamma Sigma, Beta Alpha Psi (editor nat. newsletter 1973-77, nat. pres. 1977-78), Phi Gamma Nu, Alpha Lambda Delta, Delta Kappa Gamma (sec. 1976-78, pres. 1978-80, treas. 1989—), Phi Kappa Phi. Home: 1115 N Leverett Ave Fayetteville AR 72703-1622 Office: U Ark Dept Acctg Fayetteville AR 72701

COOK, EUGENE AUGUSTUS, lawyer; b. Houston, May 2, 1938; s. Eugene A. and Estelle Mary (Stiner) C.; m. Sondra Attaway, Aug. 27, 1968; children: Laurie Ann, Eugene A. BBA, U. Houston, 1961, JD, 1966; LLM, U. Va., 1992. Bar: Tex. 1966, U.S. Dist. Ct. (so. dist.) Tex. 1967, U.S. Ct. Appeals (5th cir.) 1969, U.S. Supreme Ct. 1971, U.S. Ct. Claims 1972, U.S. Tax Ct. 1974, U.S. Ct. Appeals (11th cir.) 1982, U.S. Dist. Ct. (no., we. and ea. dists.) Tex. 1983. Ptnr. Butler & Binion, Houston, 1966-85; founding ptnr. Cook, Davis & McFall, 1985-88; justice Tex. Supreme Ct., Austin, 1988-93, chmn. jud. edn. exec. com., chmn. professionalism com., 1988-92; sr. ptnr. Bracewell & Patterson, Houston, 1993—; adj. asst. prof. law U. Houston, 1971-72, 74. Editor in chief, contbg. author: Creditors Rights in Texas, 2d edit., 1981; bd. dirs. U. Houston Law Rev., 1978-79; contbr. articles to profl. jours. Vice-chmn. bd. YMCA, 1977; bd. dirs. Spl. Olympics, Tex., 1989-95, chmn. bd. dirs., 1994. Recipient Disting. Alumnus award U. Houston, 1990, Am. Inns of Ct.-Lewis F. Powell Jr. award, 1992. Fellow Am. Coll. Trial Lawyers, Am. Acad. Matrimonial Lawyers, Internat. Acad. Matrimonial Lawyers, Am. Bar Found., Tex. Bar Found. (Outstanding Pub. Svc. award 1990); mem. ABA, Am. Inns of Ct. (pres. Austin Inn 1990-91), Tex. Bar Assn. (chmn. grievance com. 1971-72, vice chmn. consumer law sect. 1976-77, chmn. consumer law sect. 1979-80, Presdl. Citation 1979, dir. family law sect. 1984-88, Presdl. Cert. Merit, 1983, 84, 86, Pres.'s award as most outstanding lawyer in Tex., 1989, chmn. pubs. com. 1981-82, Achievement award 1982, chmn. litigation sect. 1982-84, chmn. continuing legal edn., 1988-89), Houston Bar Assn. (seminar com. 1976-77, Chmn. of Yr. award, 1976-77, chmn. insts. com. 1977-78, Outstanding Service award 1977-78, chmn. continuing legal edn. com. 1978-79, Pres.'s award, 1978-79, chmn. consumer law sect. 1978-79, vice-chmn. family law sect. 1981-82, chmn. family law sect. 1982-83, Officers award 1983, chmn. staff and staffing com. 1985-86, chmn. Special Oympics Com. 1987-88, chmn. long range planning and devel. com. 1988-89, dir. 1984-86, 2d v.p. 1986-87, 1st v.p. 1987-88, pres. elect 1988-89, pres. 1989-90), Texas Bd. Legal Specialization (bd. cert.), Civil Trial and Family Law, Nat. Bd. Trial Advocacy (bd. cert. civil trial law), Tex. Assn. Cert. Civil Trial Law Lawyers, Gulf Coast Family Law Specialists Assn., Tex. Acad. Family Law Specialists, ABA, State Bar Tex., Phi Kappa Phi, Phi Theta Kappa (chmn. bd. dirs. 1966-71, 87-88, Most Disting. Alumnus in the nation award, 1988), Omicron Chi Epsilon, Omicron Delta Kappa, Phi Rho Pi. Office: Bracewell & Patterson LLP S Tower Pennzoil Pl 711 Louisiana St Ste 2900 Houston TX 77002-2721

COOK, GARY E., insurance agent; b. High Point, N.C., Jan. 19, 1932; s. Eugene Franklin and Hallie Virginia (Gardner) C.; m. Mary Ann Patton, Aug. 4, 1934; children: Gary Michael, Allison Cook Griffith. Student, U. of Md., 1958. Claims/claims mgr. Gay & Taylor, Richmond, Va., 1958-68; claims rep. Crum & Forster Group, Richmond, 1968-75; v.p. Northwestern Ins. Co., Wilkesboro, N.C., 1975-78; v.p. claims Arkwright Boston Ins., Miami, Fla., 1981; field rep. Met. Life Ins., Tampa, Fla., 1981-84; pres. Gary E. Cook Ins. Svc., Lake Worth, Fla., 1984—. Mem. Jaycees, Sertoma, Masons, Shriners, Masons. Republican. Episcopalian. Home: 1656 Grantham Dr Wellington FL 33414-8959

COOK, GARY RAYMOND, university president, clergyman; b. Little Rock, Ark., Sept. 27, 1950; s. Raymond C. and Vada (James) C.; m. Sheila Gayle Raymer, Dec. 28, 1974; children: David Daniel, Mark Andrew. BA, Baylor U., 1972; MDiv, So. Sem., Louisville, 1975; MA, U. North Tex., 1977; D in Ministry, Southwestern Sem., 1977. Pastor 1st Bapt. Ch., McGregor, Tex., 1976-78; dir. denomination and community rels. Baylor U., Waco, Tex., 1978-88; pres. Dallas Bapt. U., 1988—. Author: Retirees in Mission, 1977; co-editor: Abner McCall: One Man's Journey, 1981. Mayor pro tem City of Waco, 1983-84, mem. city coun., 1981-84; past bd. dirs. Tex. Dept. on Aging; past internat. bd. dirs. Habitat for Humanity. Recipient Humanitarian award Waco Conf. Christians and Jews, 1986. Mem. Rotary (sustaining). Home and Office: 3000 Mountain Creek Pky Dallas TX 75211-9209

COOK, GORDON F., school system administrator, educator; b. Newport, Ky., Nov. 30, 1927; s. Fred and Ella A. Cook; m. Mildred Anne Smithers, June 1, 1952; children: Timothy G., Cynthia A. Scott, Gregory E. BS, Ea. Ky. U., 1954; MEd, Miami U., Oxford, Ohio, 1959; postgrad., Ohio U., 1961, Morehead State U., 1976, Ind. U., 1978. Cert. guidance counselor. Jr. varsity basketball coach Vandalia (Ohio)-Butler High sch., 1954-57, counselor, instr., 1954-61; guidance counselor Kettering-Fairmont Sr. High Sch., Kettering, 1960-63, unit prin., 1963-64; instr. in psychology Kettering (Ohio) Adult Sch., 1961-64; prin. Fairmont Est High Sch./Summer Sch., 1964, Lee County High Sch., Beattyville, Ky., 1964-73; prep. dir. Region XII Career Edn. Project, Hazard, Ky., 1973-75; supr., instrnl. svcs. advisor Ky. Dept. of Edn., Frankfort, 1975-91; mem. adv. com. project opportunity Southern Assoc. Colls. and Schs., Atlanta, 1964-70. Mem. City og Vandalia/Ohio Planning Commn., 1959-60; pres. Beattyville Kiwanis, 1971-72; treas. Vandalia-Butler Classroom Tchrs. Assn., Vandalia, 1956-59; sec. Kettering Secondary Prins., 1962-64; liaison officer Ea. Ky. U.S. Mil. Acad., West Point, 1971-81; chmn. Lee County Home Health Adv. Com., 1966-72. Lt. col. AUS, 1944-81, ret. Mem. Masons (master 1988), Scottish Rite KCCH, Shriners (pres. Lee County club 1984-86, potentate Oleika Shrine Temple 1993, v.p. Southeastern Shrine assn.), Sons of the Am. Revolution, Phi Delta Kappa (emeritus). Episcopalian. Home: PO Box 407 Beattyville KY 41311-0407

COOK, HAROLD DALE, federal judge; b. Guthrie, Okla., Apr. 14, 1924; s. Harold Payton and Mildred Arvesta (Swanson) C.; children: Harold Dale II, Caren Irene, Randall Swanson; m. Kristen Elizabeth Ward; stepchildren: Kimberley Ward, Stephanie Ward, Erica Ward. BS in Bus., U. Okla., 1950, LLB, 1950, JD, 1970. Bar: Okla. 1950. Pvt. practice law Guthrie, Okla., 1950; county atty. Logan County, Okla., 1951-54; asst. U.S. atty. Oklahoma City, 1954-58; assoc. Butler, Rinehart and Morrison, Oklahoma City, 1958-61; ptnr. Rinehart, Morrison and Cook, 1961-63; legal counsel and adviser to Gov. State of Okla., 1963-65; ptnr. Cook & Ming, Oklahoma City, 1965, Cook, O'Toole, Ming & Tourtellotte, Oklahoma City, 1966-68, Cook, O'Toole & Tourtellotte, 1969-70, Cook & O'Toole, 1971; gen. counsel Shepherd Mall State Bank, Oklahoma City, 1967-71; pres. Shepherd Mall State Bank, 1969-71, chmn. bd., 1969-71; dir. Bur. of Hearings and Appeals, Social Security Adminstrn., HEW, 1971-74; judge U.S. Dist. Ct., Tulsa, 1974-79; chief judge U.S. Dist. Ct. (no. dist.) Okla., Tulsa, 1979-91, sr. judge, 1992; mem. legal adv. coun. Okla. Hwy. Patrol, 1969-70; mem. magistrates com. Jud. Conf. U.S., 1980-88; mem. indsl. adv. coun. Bur. Bus. and Econ.Rsch., U. Okla., 1970-71. First v.p. PTA, Sunset Elementary Sch., 1959-60; v.p. Parent-Tchrs. & Students Assn., John Marshall High Sch., Oklahoma City, 1970-71, pres., 1971; mem. Econ. Opportunity Com., Okla., 1963-65; tchr. Sunday sch. classes for coll., high sch. and adult ages Village Methodist Ch., Oklahoma City, 1959-65; mem. bd. of stewards First Meth. Ch., Guthrie, Okla., 1951-54. Served with USAAF, 1943-45. Recipient Secretary's Spl. Citation HEW, 1973. Fellow Am. Bar Found.; mem. ABA, Fed. Bar Assn., Okla. Bar Assn. (del. to state bar convs.), Oklahoma City C. of C. Republican. Clubs: So. Hills Country, Shriners, Masons, Tulsa, Order Eastern Star (past worthy patron Okla.). Office: Tulsa Fed Bldg Rm 241 224 South Boulder Tulsa OK 74103

COOK, JAMES HERMAN, estate management consultant, financial advisor; b. Valley, Ala., Oct. 13, 1927; s. James W. and Lola S. Cook; m. Minnie Brown, Oct. 1, 1953; children: James M., Debra M., George M. BS in Bus. Adminstrn., Auburn U., 1950; MS in Bus. Mgmt., Columbus Coll., 1978. Commd. 2d lt. U.S. Army, 1951, advanced through grades to col.; ret., 1976; estate mgr., fin. cons., pvt. practice Valley, Ala., 1976—, Columbus, Ga., 1976—. Decorated Air medals, Legion of Merit, Bronze Star, and others. Mem. Ret. Officers Assn., 31st Dixie Divsn. Assn., Valley Srs. Golf Assn. Protestant. Home and Office: #76 Lee Rd 778 Valley AL 36854 also: 4468 Deerfield Dr Columbus GA 31907

COOK, JAMES WINFIELD CLINTON, sales and marketing company executive; b. Camden, N.J., Nov. 23, 1908; s. Clinton and Loretta (Florence) C.; m. Isabelle Killian, Oct. 28, 1933; children: Nancy, Thomas, Barbara, Roger. AB, Dickinson Coll., 1932, DHL (hon.), 1996; postgrad., U. Pa., 1942, U. Md., 1943; DHL (hon.), Combs Coll., 1973. Supr. Wear Ever Aluminum Co., New Kensington, Pa., 1932-39; pres. Vitacraft Pa. Sales Inc., Williamsport, 1939-59, Homec Inc., Williamsport, 1959-73. Bd. dirs. Pop Warner Little Scholars, Phila., 1974—, Island Players, Long Boat Key Hist. Soc.; bd. dirs. emeritus Suburban Gen. Hosp., Norristown, Pa., 1959—; trustee Dickinson Coll., Carlisle, Pa., 1956-64, U.S. Jr. Chamber Found., 1996; cons. U.S. Jaycees Found.; pres. Nixon Clubs, Montgomery County, Pa., 1960, Island Rep. Club, Manatee, Fla., 1982; pres. bd. trustees Presbyn. Ch., Ambler, Pa., 1956-60, chmn. Manatee exec. com., 1963-66; pres. Pa. Jaycees, 1942-43. Recipient Alumni of Yr. award U.S. Jaycees, 1985; named Outstanding Former Jr. Chamber Mem., World Jaycees Internat., 1990. Mem. Sales and Mktg. Execs. Assn. (bd. dirs. 1956-57), Nat. Assn. Direct

Selling Cos. (nat. pres. 1955-57, chmn. bd. dirs.), Am. Hotel and Motel Assn., Longboat Key C. of C. (bd. dirs. 1974—, Civic Achievement award 1989-90), Union League Club (Phila.), Seaview Country Club (Absecon, N.J.), Ocean City Yacht Club, Explorers Club, Masons, Shriners. Home: 4235 Gulf Of Mexico Dr Longboat Key FL 34228-2501

COOK, JANICE ELEANOR NOLAN, elementary school educator; b. Middletown, Ohio, Nov. 22, 1936; d. Lloyd and Eleanor Lee (Caudill) Nolan; m. Kenneth J. Cook, May 16, 1980; children: Gerald W. Fultz Jr., Jana Linn Perkins, Jennylee Haines. BSEd, Miami U., 1971; MEd, reading specialist cert., Xavier U., 1982, rank 1 cert., 1987, spl. edn. cert., 1988. Tchr. pre-sch. and elem. Middletown (Ohio) Pub. Schs., 1957-58, 71-80; tchr. Boone County Schs., Florence, Ky., 1980—; resource tchr. Ky. Internship Program, 1985-95. Fellow ABI Rsch. Assn. (life); mem. NEA, Nat. Assn. Edn. Young Children, Internat. Reading Assn., Nat. Coun. Tchrs. English, Ky. Edn. Assn., Boone County Edn. Assn., Assn. Childhood Edn. Internat., Nat. Coun. Tchrs. Math. Home: 2028 W Horizon Dr Hebron KY 41048-9600 Office: New Haven Elem Sch 10854 Us Highway 42 Union KY 41091-9596

COOK, JOAN TORRIERI, marketing professional, business coach; b. Mt. Vernon, N.Y., Apr. 23, 1950; d. Carmine and Angela (Masocchi) T.; m. Jack Dale Cook, Oct. 14, 1995. BS in Music and Journalism, Ind. U., 1972; MBA, SUNY, Binghamton, 1983. Profl. musician Indpls. Symphony, 1972-73, Jalapa (Veracruz, Mex.) Symphony, 1976-80, Veracruz Symphony, 1980-81; freelance musician, various locations, 1974-76; asst. mktg. dir. Greater Miami (Fla.) Opera (now Fla. Grand Opera), 1983-85; classified mktg. mgr. Miami Herald, 1985-87, classified, gen., El Nuevo Herald mktg. mgr., 1987-89, advt. promotion mgr., 1989-92; pres. The Outsource Group, Winter Springs, Fla., 1993—; bd. dirs. Builders Assn. South Fla., Miami, 1988-90. Vol. cons. Bus. Vols. for Arts, Miami, 1986-95; mem. founding bd. dirs. Fanfare, supporters New World Symphony, 1988-89. Home and Office: 462 Dewar's Ct Winter Springs FL 32708

COOK, JOE THOMAS, retired newspaper publisher; b. Weatherford, Tex., Dec. 9, 1909; s. Thomas Milton and Martha (Glazner) C.; m. Dorothy K. McCanlies, Sept. 1, 1932; children: Joe T. Jr., Dorothy M. BA in English and Journalism cum laude, U. Tex., 1932. Editor The Daily Texan, 1931-32; editor, pub. The Mission (Tex.) Times, 1932-58; owner, editor, pub. Winston County Jour., Louisville, Miss., 1958-76; ret.; lectr. in field. Pres. Mission (Tex.) C. of C., 1950-51, Lower Rio Grande Valley (Tex.) C. of C., 1955, Louisville-Winston County (Miss.) C. of C., 1971-72; trustee U. Corpus Christi, Blue Mountain Coll., Miss.; pres., mem. bd. trustees Mission Ind. Sch. Dist.; deacon Bapt. Ch., chmn. bd. deacons, Mission and Louisville; active mem. Centennial Commn., U. Tex., 1983, others. Recipient 4 nat. 1st place awards for the Mission Times, innumerable 1st place awards for newspaper excellence in both Tex. Press Assn., Miss. Press Assn., Amos award Nat. Newspaper Assn., 1953, Herrick Editl. award, 1958, Freedom Found. George Washington Honor medals, 1968, 69, numerous others. Mem. South Tex. Press Assn. (pres. 1937-38), Tex. Press Assn. (pres. 1945-46), Nat. Newspaper Assn. (pres. 1949-50), Miss. Press Assn. (pres. 1971-72), Weekly Newspaper Reps. (pres. 1958), Rotary (pres. 1966-67), Phi Eta Sigma, Phi Beta Kappa, Sigma Delta Chi. Home: Trinity Towers Apt 603 101 N Upper Broadway St Corpus Christi TX 78401-2756

COOK, JOHN ROSCOE, JR., insurance executive; b. Houston, Apr. 17, 1943; s. John Roscoe and Ruth Mildred (Spargo) C.; m. Loxi June Gumienny, Aug. 28, 1964 (dec.); children: John T., Andrew J., Wesley A. BA, U. Houston, 1968. Pub. affairs rep Allstate Ins., Houston, 1968-72, corp. rels. rep., Northbrook, Ill., 1972-74, pub. affairs mgr., Roanoke, Va., 1974-78, Valley Forge, Pa., 1978-80, external com. mgr., Northbrook, 1980; v.p. pub. affairs Am. Ins. Assn., Washington, 1980-85; sr. v.p. Ins. Inst. for Hwy. Safety, Washington, 1985-87, exec. v.p., 1987-89; sr. v.p., chief comm. officer USAA, San Antonio, Tex., 1989—; bd. dirs. Alamo Pub. Broadcasting. Named Gold Key Lauraete Pub. Relations News, 1985, 87; bd. advisors Tex. Pub. Radio. Mem. Pub. Rels. Soc. Am.-accredited PRSA Coll. Fellows (nat. bd. dirs. 1995—, Silver Anvil award 1983, 86, 88, 91, 92, Bronze Anvil award 1993, Thoth award Nat. Capitol chpt. 1983, 86, 88), Internat. Assn. Bus. Communicators (Silver Inkwell award 1985, 87, Gold Quill award 1991, 92), Am. Soc. Assn. Execs. (Gold Circle award, 1993), Nat. Press Club, Radio TV News Dirs. Assn. Clubs: Capitol Hill (Washington), Dominion Country Club (San Antonio). Home: 206 Post Oak Way San Antonio TX 78230-5615

COOK, JUANITA KIMBELL, library director, educator; b. Pine Bluff, Ark., Aug. 25, 1948; d. Andrew Jackson and Queen Esther (Day) Kimbell; m. Curtis Lee Cook, Nov. 25, 1970; children: Melanie LaJune, Reginald, Cheryl Nicole. BS, U. Ark., Pine Bluff, 1970; MLS, Ball State U., 1972. Reference libr. Colorado Coll./Pennrose Pub., Colorado Springs, 1971, Longview Community Coll., Lee's Summit, Mo., 1973-77; dir. IMC, instr. U. Ark., Pine Bluff, 1977-80; libr. Russellville Pub. Schs., Russellville, Ark., 1981-85, Arkadelphia Pub. Schs., Arkadelphia, Ark., 1985-87; libr. dir. Learning Resources Ctr., So. Ark. U., Camden, 1987—, asst. prof., 1987-92, assoc. prof., 1992—. Pres. Ouachita-Calhoun County Literacy, Camden, 1988-89. Danforth Found. fellow, 1970, Nat. Black Studies Ins. fellow, 1989. Mem. ALA, Ark. Libr. Assn., Nat. Assn. Female Execs., Nat. Assn. Devel. Edn., Internat. Reading Assn., Zeta Phi Beta. Democrat. Apostolic. Office: So Ark U Tech Tech Sta Camden AR 71701

COOK, KELSEY DONALD, chemistry educator, consultant; b. Denver, Mar. 16, 1952; s. Harold Victor and Leanor Estelle (Stark) C. BA in Chemistry magna cum laude, Colo. Coll., 1974; PhD in Analytical Chemistry, U. Wis., 1978. Rsch. trainee dept. chemistry Colo. Coll., Colorado Springs, 1972; rsch. trainee Oak Ridge (Tenn.) Associated Univs., 1973, 74; rsch. fellow dept. chemistry U. Wis., Madison, 1974-77, rsch. asst. dept. chemistry, 1976-78; asst. prof. dept. chemistry Sch. Chem. Scis. U. Ill., Urbana, 1978-84; from asst. prof. to assoc. prof. chemistry U. Tenn., Knoxville, 1984-93, prof. dept. chemistry, 1993—; chmn. East Tenn. Mass. Spectrometry Discussion Group, 1987-89; mem. adv. bd. NSF Structural Biochemistry Ctr., U. Md., 1988-93; mem. bd. advisors NSF Mid-Atlantic Regional Mass Spectrometry Facility, Johns Hopkins U., 1986—; mem. faculty senate U. Tenn., 1989-92, mem. budget com., 1989-91, mem. rsch. coun., 1990-93; cons. Harper and Row, N.Y.C., Oak Ridge Nat. Lab., Phrasor Sci., Duarte, Calif.; condr. seminars; lectr. in field. Assoc. editor Jour. Am. Soc. for Mass Spectrometry, 1989—; mem. editorial bd. Critical Revs. in Analytical Chemsitry, 1991—; contbr. articles to profl. jours. Beckman fellow U. Ill. Ctr. for Advanced Study, 1982-83, Wis. Alumni Rsch. Found. fellow, 1974-76; Colo. Boettcher Found. scholar, 1970-74; grantee in field. Mem. Am. Chem. Soc. (chmn. local sect. 1994, chmn. nominating com. local sect. 1988, 96, program chmn. local sect. 1986, sec. local sect. 1981-83, analytical divsn. summer fellow 1977), Am. Soc. for Mass Spectrometry (nat. treas. 1986-88), Phi Beta Kappa, Sigma Xi. Office: U Tenn Dept Chemistry Knoxville TN 37996-1600

COOK, KENNETH RAY, radiologist; b. Sublette, Kans., Sept. 16, 1953; s. Curtis Carl and Carmen Madonna (Countryman) C.; m. Paula Rose Petryzyn, July 22, 1978; children: Erin Michelle, Leah Nicole, Tara Rachelle. AA, Hutchinson Community Coll., Kans., 1976; BA, U. Kans., 1979, MD, 1983. Diplomate Am. Coll. of Radiology. Resident in diagnostic radiology U. Kans. Med. Ctr., 1983-87; diagnostic radiologist Radiology Assocs., Corpus Christi, Tex., 1987—; staff radiologist Meml. Med. Ctr., Columbia Northwest, Corpus Christi, Tex., 1987—; chief radiology Bay Area Med. Ctr., 1993—, vice chmn., trustee, 1993-94, chmn., 1994-96; chief radiology Rehab. Hosp. South Tex., 1989-91; asst. clin. prof. family practice U. Tex., San Antonio; med. dir. Del Mar Coll. Ultrasound Technol. Sch. Recipient Resident Teaching award, Dept. Radiology, U. Kans., Kansas City, 1985-86, Resident Teaching award, Med. Ctr. Kans. U., 1986-87. Mem. AMA, Am. Coll. Radiology, Radiologic Soc. N. Am., Tex. Med. Soc., Tex. Radiologic Soc., Am. Inst. Ultrasound in Medicine, Nueces County Med. Soc. Republican. Roman Catholic. Office: Radiology Assocs PO Box 5608 Corpus Christi TX 78465-5608

COOK, LYNN J., nursing educator; b. Newark, Aug. 18, 1950; d. George Roy Cook and Jean Aileen (Wegner) Cook Ainsley; m. Troy Wagner Ray, Mar. 11, 1995. Diploma, Mass. Gen. Hosp. Sch. Nursing, 1971; BSN, U. Va., 1975; MPH, Boston U. Sch. Pub. Health, 1986. RN, Pa.; cert. neonatal nurse practitioner. From staff nurse newborn ICU to nursing dir. for neonatal transport and perinatal outreach edn. U. Va., Charlottesville, 1973-83, nat. coord. for the perinatal continuing edn. program, 1983—; coord. perinatal edn. for Poland/Project HOPE, Millwood, Va., Krakow, Poland, 1986-89; lectr., gen. faculty U. Va. Sch. Medicine, 1992—; staff NICU Hosp. U. Pa., Phila., 1991-93; mem. Va. Perinatal Svcs. Adv. Coun. to Va. Dept. Health, 1979-83; fellow Project HOPE, Hangzhou, China, 1985. Author: Perinatal Continuing Education Program, 1978—; contbr. articles to profl. jours. Recipient outstanding instrnl. devel. award Nat. Soc. Performance & Instrn., 1979. Mem. AWHONN, Nat. Assn. Neonatal Nurses, Nat. Perinatal Assn., Phila. Perinatal Soc., Pa. Perinatal Assn., Del. Valley Assn. Neonatal Nurses. Office: U Va Health Sci Ctr Dept Pediatrics Box 386 Perinatal Cont Edn Program Charlottesville VA 22908

COOK, MARCELLA KAY, drama educator; b. Albuquerque, Dec. 22, 1949; d. Joseph Raymond and Vivian Francis (Mullinax) Murdick; m. James Rogers Cook, Mar. 25, 1975 (dec. Aug. 1991); 1 child, Amanda Kay. BA, U. Albuquerque, 1971; MA, Eastern N.Mex. U., 1973. Prof. theatre, speech Vernon (Tex.) Regional Jr. Coll., 1973—; fine arts chair Vernon Regional Jr. Coll., 1982-87; actress, dir. Bill Fegan Attractions, Raton, N.Mex., 1974; costume designer Eastern N.Mex. Univ., Portales, 1972-73; head wardrobe mistress Cinegai Films, Rome, 1971. Recipient humanitarian svc. award Tex. Army Nat. Guard, 1979; grantee The Stokes Found., Ft. Worth. Mem. Tex. Ednl. Theatre Assn., Southwest Theatre Assn., Drama League of N.Y. Home: 4608 Leonard Vernon TX 76384 Office: Vernon Regional Jr Coll 4400 College Dr Vernon TX 76384

COOK, MARILYN JANE, elementary school educator; b. Covington, Ky., Jan. 27, 1948; d. Ralph Benjamin and Jane Elizabeth (Doddy) C.; 1 child, Elisabeth Anne Brundrett-Cook. BA, St. Andrews Presbyn. Coll., 1970; MDiv, Austin Presbyn. Theol. Sem., 1974; MS in Curriculum and Instrn., Corpus Christi State U., 1992; MS in Ednl. Adminstrn., Tex. A&M, Corpus Christi, 1996. Cert. tchr., Tex.; master tchr. Nat. Tchr. Tng. Inst. Edn. dir. Northwood Presbyn. Ch., San Antonio, 1976-77; mgr. Summer Place, Port Aransas, Tex., 1977-78; adminstrv. asst. Crisis Intervention Svc., Corpus Christi, 1978-79; mgr. Nueces County Mental Health/Mental Retardation, Corpus Christi, 1979-81; educator Sacred Heart Sch., Rockport, Tex., 1982-83, Port Aransas Sch. Dist., 1983—; mem. leadership team Project 2061, Tex., 1989-95, Tex. Ctr. Sci., Math. & Tech., 1995—; mem. manuscript and rev. panel Sci. and Children jour., Arlington, Va., 1991—, dist. and campus site based decision making teams; insvc. facilitator Tex. Elem. Sci. program; Title I sch. support team ESC region 2; adj. Tex. Essential Knowledge & Skills English/Lang. Arts. Contbr. articles to profl. jours. Troop leader Jr. Girl Scouts, Girl Scouts USA, Port Aransas, 1992—; bd. dirs. Keep Port Aransas Beautiful, 1990-93, Dewey Dreyer Cmty. Day Care, Port Aransas, 1988-90; elder Cmty. Presbyn. Ch., Port Aransas; bd. dirs. Corpus Christi Ballet, 1996—. Recipient Sadie Ray Gaff award of merit Keep Tex. Beautiful, 1990, 92. Mem. NSTA (presch./elem. program rep. area conv. 1995), AAUW, Tex. ASCD, Tex. Assn. for Environ. Edn. (bd. dirs. 1991-93), Tex. Coun. for Elem. Sci. (area dir. 1993-94, bd. dirs. 1993—, Dorothy Lohman award 1994, Dillo Press editor jour. 1995—), Coun. for Elem. Sci. Internat., Sci. Tchrs. Assn. Tex., Tex. State Reading Assn., Nat. Project Wet Crew, Orton Dyslexia Soc., Coastal Bend Art Edn. Assn., Kappa Delta Pi. Office: Port Aransas Ind Sch Dist 100 S Station St Port Aransas TX 78373

COOK, MARY GOOCH, elementary school educator; b. Columbus, Ga., May 1, 1943; d. Joe Lee and Ella Mae (Crimes) Gooch; m. Robert James Cook Sr.; children: Robert James Jr., Kevin Scott. BS, Ala. State Coll., 1965, M in Edn., reading spl., 1973; cert. in elem. edn., Tuskegee U., summer 1968; cert. reading specialist, Ga. State U., 1973; cert. edn. specialist, Troy State U., 1991. Cert. tchr., Ga. Tchr. Fox Elem. Sch., Columbus, Ga., 1973-94, Gentian Elem. Sch., Columbus, Ga., 1994—. Arbitrator BBB, Columbus, 1989-95; cmty. leader tchr. Combined Cmty. South Columbus, 1988-91; mem. voter registration com. Bd. Registration, Columbus, 1990-95; mem. support youth activities com. Columbus Cmty. Ctr., 1994. Mem. AAUW, Nat. Coun. Tchrs. Math., Internat. Reading Assn., Muscogee Assn. Educators (faculty rep. Fox Elem. Sch. 1973-94, Gentian Elem. Sch. 1994-96), Sigma Rho Sigma (pres. Montgomery, Ala. chpt. 1964—), Kappa Delta Pi. Home: 4655 Illini Dr Columbus GA 31907-6613 Office: Muscogee County Sch 6400 Forrest Rd Columbus GA 31907-1156

COOK, NEDRA JOHNSON, medical librarian; b. Texarkana, Ark., Mar. 26, 1950; d. Arthur M. and I. Nell (McClurg) Johnson; m. Christopher E. Cook, Aug. 10, 1974; children: Jamey Leigh, Steven Christopher. AA, Panola Jr. Coll., Carthage, Tex., 1970; BA in English, Bus. Edn., East Tex. State U., 1972, MS in Libr. Sci., 1973. Ref. libr., head serials Henderson State U., Arkadelphia, Ark., 1973-78; chief libr. U. Ark. for Med. Sci. Area Health Edn. Ctr., Pine Bluff, 1978-79; ref. libr. Knox County Libr. Sys., Knoxville, 1980; med./nursing libr. Ft. Sanders Health Sys., Knoxville, 1980—. Co-editor Cross Ref. newsletter, 1996—; editor Tenn. Assn. for Parents of Visually Impaired newsletter, 1985-94; contbr. articles to profl. jours. Founder, coord. East Tenn. chpt. Tenn. Assn. for Parents of Visually Impaired, Knoxville, 1985—. Named to Outstanding Young Women of Am., 1981. Mem. Acad. Health Info. Profls., Med. Libr. Assn. (Disting. Mem.), Tenn. Health Sci. Librs. Assn. (treas./sec. 1985-88), Southeastern Conf. Hosp. Librs. (treas. 1992—), Knoxville Area Health Sci. Libr. Consortium (pres. 1983-84, 96—, v.p., program chair 1995-96), West Knoxville Jaycettes (state dir. 1981, sec. 1980), Phi Theta Kappa, Alpha Chi, Sigma Tau Delta, Pi Omega Pi. Methodist. Office: Fort Sanders Health System 1915 White Ave Knoxville TN 37916-2305

COOK, NORMA BAKER, consulting company executive; b. North Wilkesboro, N.C.; d. Charles Chauncey and Mildred Baker. BA in Bus. and Econs., Meredith Coll., 1963; postgrad., Alliance Francaise, N.Y.C., 1980-83, N.Y. Sch. Interior Design, 1983-84. Cert. tchr., N.C. Pres., owner John Robert Powers Sch. Fashion Careers, Raleigh, N.C., 1971-87, NBC of Raleigh, Inc., 1979—; mem. adv. commn. N.C. Pvt. Bus., Trade and Corr. Schs., 1986; exec. distbr. NuSkin Internat., 1989—; bus. broker, 1991-93; instr. continuing edn. Meredith Coll., Raleigh, 1994—; pres. Fast Forward Concepts tm, 1996—. Author articles on fashion and success motivation for women. Established Norma Baker Cook Art Scholarship at Meredith Coll., 1989; vice chmn. Meredith Coll. Bd. Assocs., 1991-92; charter mem. Meredith Coll. Heritage Soc., Raleigh. Recipient Svc. award Am. Cancer Soc., 1978. Mem. AFTRA, The Fashion Group, Inc., Greater Raleigh C. of C. (arts com.), North Raleigh Civitans, Am. Assn. of Univ. Women. Office: 3725 National Dr Ste 118 Raleigh NC 27612

COOK, PEGGY JO, psychotherapist, consultant; b. Greenville, Miss., Jan. 2, 1931; d. Bertram R. Coffing and Mary Josephine (Rodgers) McCarthy; m. Jack Storey Cook, July 15, 1951 (div. 1969); children: Bill S., Paul K., Monte C., Carol Rose Doss. BS in Psychology, SUNY-Albany, 1979; MEd in Counseling, North Tex. State U., 1980, PhD in Counseling and Student Svcs., 1987. Co-owner, mgr. Elec. Contracting, Co., Ft. Worth, 1952-68; co-founder, dir. Family Counseling Ctr., Ctr. for Creative Living, Ft. Worth, 1968—, psychotherapist, co-dir., 1980—. Mem. ACA. Avocations: grandchildren, antiques, skiing, landscaping. Office: 2401 Oakland Blvd # 100 Fort Worth TX 76103-3291

COOK, PEGGY KRISTINE, librarian; b. Arkansas City, Kans., July 27, 1959; d. Ivan Pearl Jr. and Clara Mae (Anthis) Royster; m. Robert Charles Cook, Aug. 12, 1989. BA, Okla. Bapt. U., 1981; MLS, U. Okla., 1982. Head libr. Guthrie (Okla.) Pub. Libr., 1983-91; br. mgr. Norman (Okla.) Pub. Libr., 1991—. Mem. Norman Arts and Humanities Assn., 1991—, Crimestoppers, Norman, 1992—, PEO, Leadership Norman, 1994-95. Mem. ALA, Okla. Libr. Assn., Mountain Plains Libr. Assoc. Rep., 1996—. mem. Norman L.I.F.T., Chair Accessible Info. Task Force. Republican. Southern Baptist. Office: Norman Pub Libr 225 N Webster Ave Norman OK 73069-7133

COOK, RALPH D., judge. Former judge Ala. Cir. Ct. (10th jud. dist.); assoc. justice Ala. Supreme Ct., Montgomery. Office: 300 Dexter Ave Montgomery AL 36104-3741*

COOK, W.B., controller. V.p., contr. Exxon Corp., Irving, Tex. Office: Exxon Corp 225 E John W Carpenter Fwy Irving TX 75062-2298

COOK, WILLIAM CARLYLE, real estate appraiser; b. Dallas, Feb. 9, 1929; s. William C. and Evangeline L. (Simmons) C.; m. Bonna Lee DuBois, June 30, 1951. BBA, So. Meth. U., 1951. Cert. instr. real estate courses, Tex.; cert. gen. appraiser, Tex. Chief appraiser, dir. Am. Real Estate Corp., Beaumont, Austin, Tex.; pres. Cook & Assocs., Beaumont, 1982—. Mem. Appraisal Inst. (pres. Sabine area chpt. 1992), Soc. Real Estate Appraisers (past pres. 1974, sec. 1978-79, treas. 1980-84 chpt. 154), Beaumont Bd. Realtors (pres. 1963). Methodist. Office: 2640 Mcfaddin St Beaumont TX 77702-1621

COOK, WILLIAM LESLIE, JR., lawyer; b. Greenwood, Miss., July 1, 1949; s. William Leslie and Mary Elizabeth (Roberts) C.; m. Mary Jo Dorr, July 17, 1976; children: Leslie Patton, William Roberts, Maribeth Dorr. BA, U. Miss., 1971, JD, 1974. Bar: Miss. 1974, U.S Dist. Ct. (no. dist.) Miss. 1974, U.S. Dist. Ct. (we. dist.) Tenn. 1986. Assoc. Bailey & Trusty, Batesville, Miss., 1974-79; ptnr. Bailey, Trusty & Cook, Batesville, 1980-90, Bailey & Cook, Batesville, 1990-92, Bailey, Cook & Womble, Batesville, 1992—. Chmn., Miss. Coll. Rep. Clubs, 1973, Panola County March of Dimes, Batesville, 1976-78; Miss. chmn. Nat. Orgn. Social Security Claimants Reps., 1981-82; rep. Honor Council, U. Miss. Sch. Law, 1974; bd. dirs. N.W. Delta Arts Coun., 1995-96; bd. dirs. Northwest Miss. Arts Coun., 1995-96. Mem. ABA (torts and ins. practice sect. 1979—, vice chmn. com. on delivery of legal svcs. to the disabled Young Lawyers Div. 1983-85, gen. practice sect. 1985-86), Miss. State Bar, (state bd. bar admissions 1978-79, ethics com. 1980-83, dir. Young Lawyers Sect. 1980-83, chmn. com. on unauthorized practice of law 1983-86, workers compensation sect., com. on "Kid's Second Chance" 1992), Panola County Bar Assn. (pres. 1979-80), Assn. Trial Lawyers Am., Miss. Trial Lawyers Assn. (membership com. 1983-84), Ct. Practice Inst. (diplomate), Lawyer-Pilots Bar Assn., Lamar Soc. Internat. Law, Omicron Delta Kappa, Pi Sigma Alpha, Delta Theta Phi. Methodist. Club: Jaycees (legal counsel Batesville 1975-77). Lodges: Shriners, Masons, Rotary (pres. 1991-92, 96-97). Home: 110 Shagbark Dr Batesville MS 38606-9352 Office: Bailey Cook & Womble 357 Highway 51 N Batesville MS 38606-2346

COOKE, ALEX "TY", JR., mayor; b. Wichita, Kans., July 26, 1944; m. Judy Kay Cornelison; children: Alex K. III, Kimperly Cooke Powell. BBA, Tex. Tech. U., 1968. Commd. salesman, then officer, dir., co-owner Fields & Co., Lubbock, Tex., 1962-84; former dir., chmn. loan rev. com. and bus. devel. com. Tex. Commerce Bank, Lubbock, 1985-93; gen. ptnr. Coppercreek Land and Cattle, Lubbock; mng. ptnr. Cooke Cattle Co., Lubbock; mayor City of Lubbock; bd. dirs. State Nat. Bank; del. South Plains Assn. Govts.; pres. West Tex. Mcpl. Power Agy.; dir., pres. Tex. Pub. Power Assn.; mem. wastewater improvement com., temporary transp. adv. com. City of Lubbock; mem. pres.'s coun. Jenn-Air Corp.; mem. adv. panel GE Distbrs. Past mem. Friends of Libr. Health Scis. Bd., Tex. Tech U. Health Scis. Ctr.; past mem. found. bd. Meth. Hosp.; past dir. and pres. South Plains Childrens' Shelter; past bd. dirs. Lubbock Symphony Orch. Mem. West Tex. Home Builders Assn. (bd. dirs.), Wholesale Distbrs. Assn. (adv. com.), West Tex. Mus. Assn. (bd. dirs.), Lubbock Area Found. (founder), Lubbock Country Club (past pres.). Office: Office of Mayor PO Box 2000 Lubbock TX 79457

COOKE, CARLTON LEE, JR., mayor; b. Marion, Ala., July 12, 1944; s. Carlton Lee and Willie (Rinehart) C.; divorced; 1 child, Kimberly Ann; m. Barbara Vackar, Nov. 14, 1985. Student, U. Hawaii, 1962-65; BA, La. Tech. U., 1966; postgrad., U. Tex., 1970-72. Mfg. engr. Tex. Instruments, Austin, 1972-75, site personnel mgr., 1975-81, mktg. mgr., 1981-83; pres., chief exec. officer Austin C. of C., 1983-87; mayor City of Austin, Austin, 1988—; chmn., CEO, U.S. Med. Systems, Inc., 1992—; bd. dirs. Bill Info Concepts, Inc., U.S. Long Distance, Billing Info. Concepts, Inc., Tanisys Tech.; pres. Habitek Internat., Inc., 1991—; participant U.S. Conf. Mayors, Washington, 1991; mem. Anthony Commn., U.S.Congress;. Contbr. editor to mags. Mem. Austin City Coun., 1977-81, mayor pro tem, 1979; co-chmn. Jerry Lewis Telethon, Austin, 1986-87; chmn. United Negro Telethon, 1991, Tex. Housing Fin. Corp., 1992, Austin Charter Com., 1993-94, Tex. Walk of Stars, 1991-96. Capt. USAF, 1966-72. Decorated Bronze Star (Vietnam); recipient Carl Burnett Cmty. award, 1981, Disting. Austin Citizen's award, 1992, Excellence award Real Estate Coun. of Austin, 1992; named Jaycee of Yr. Austin Jaycees, 1976, one of Five Outstanding Young Texans Tex. Jaycees, 1979. Mem. Nat. League Cities (chair fin. steering com.), Tex. Mcpl. League (pres. 1991), Austin-San Antonio Corridor Coun. (pres. 1988, 91), VFW, Lions Club. Baptist. Home: PO Box 50442 Austin TX 78763-0442 Office: Office of Mayor 7600 Burnet Rd Ste 350 Austin TX 78757

COOKE, GLORIA GRAYSON, trust fund director; b. Smithfield, Va., Sept. 6, 1939; d. Dennis Merry Jones and Edna Ward (Gwaltney) Nash; m. Lenard Lee Cooke, June 4, 1957; children: Kelly, Karla, Lenard, Jr. Student, U. Md., Tachi Kowa, Japan, 1959-61. Cert. antiquarian book appraiser. Jr. appraiser Imperial Antiquities, Ltd., Tokyo, 1958-61; owner Millwood Rare Books, Crenshaw, Miss., 1962—, Historic Restorations, Crenshaw, Miss., 1982—; prin. Gloria Grayson Cooke, Crenshaw, Miss., 1983—. Mem. LWV, Nat. Trust for Hist. Preservation, Habitat for Humanity, Memphis Heritage, Brooks Mus. Art, Dixon Galleries, Memphis Pink Palace Mus., Friends of Miss. Libr., Tate County Hist. Soc., Am. Farm-Land Trust. Democrat. Methodist. Home: RR 1 Box 461A Crenshaw MS 38621-9762 Office: Askew House Crenshaw MS 38621

COOKE, MICHAEL THOMAS, lawyer; b. Ft. Worth, Jan. 6, 1963; s. Thomas Luke and Frances Letricia (Weir) C.; m. Pamela Ann Brossart, Sept. 30, 1989. BA with honors, Baylor U., 1985, JD, 1987. Bar: Tex. 1987, U.S. Dist. Ct. (no. dist.) Tex. 1987, U.S. Ct. Appeals (5th cir.) 1991. Assoc. Law, Snakard & Gambill, Ft. Worth, 1987-92; shareholder Friedman, Young & Suder, Ft. Worth, 1993—; speaker, seminar leader in field. Contbr. articles to profl. jours. Mem. Tarrant County Civil Trial Lawyers Assn., Tarrant County Young Lawyers Assn. Baptist. Office: Friedman Young & Suder 2000 Bank One Bldg Fort Worth TX 76102

COOKE, SARAH BELLE, health care facility professional, farmer; b. Murfreesboro, Tenn., Sept. 14, 1910; d. Robert Jesse and Mattie (Neal) C. BS, Middle Tenn. State U., 1961. Cert. tchr., Tenn. Patient funds clk. VA Med. Ctr., Murfreesboro, 1943; voucher auditor VA Med. Supply Svc., Murfreesboro, 1945-46, purchasing agt., 1946-83, contracting officer, 1984-89; now ret. Pres. VA Fed. Employees Credit Union, Murfreesboro, 1965-86. Mem. AAUW (pres. Murfreesboro chpt. 1977-79), Tenn. Credit Union League (br. pres. 1973-79). Democrat. Mem. Church of Christ. Home: 5078 Sulphur Springs Rd Murfreesboro TN 37129-7206

COOKE, STEVEN JOHN, chemical engineer, consultant, scientist; b. Grand Rapids, Mich., Oct. 1, 1954; s. Edward G. and Annette M. (Minnema) C.; m. Marguerite K. Oldenburger, June 18, 1977; children: Allison, Jonathan. BS in Chemistry, Calvin Coll., 1977; M in Chem. Enging., Ill. Inst. Tech., 1987; postgrad. in Enging., Calif. Coast U. Registered profl. engr., Ill.; cert. profl. chemist, quality engr., quality auditor. Chemist, lab. supr. Matheson Gas Products, Joliet, Ill., 1977-80; chief chemist Cardox, Countryside, Ill., 1980-85; scientist Am. Air Liquide, Countryside, 1985-92; asst. quality mgr. Alphagaz Divsn. of Liquid Air, Countryside, 1992-93; quality assurance/quality control mgr. Am. Air Liquide, Countryside, 1993-94; quality mgr. Carbonic Industries Corp., 1994—. Contbr. articles on quality systems to profl. jours. Group leader Hazardous Materials Emergency Response Team; treas. Christian Reformed Ch. Mission, Western Springs, Ill., 1982-93, Chicagoland Diaconal Task Force Bd., Palos Heights, Ill., 1989-92. Fellow Am. Inst. Chemists; mem. Fed. Analytic Chem. and Splty. Soc., Am. Soc. Quality Control, Am. Chem. Soc. (publicity chairperson indsl. and enging. chemists divsn. 1989-95). Office: Carbonic Industries Corp 3700 Crestwood Pkwy Ste 200 Duluth GA 30136-5583

COOKE, SUZANNE GAMSBY, middle school educator; b. North Hornell, N.Y., Aug. 22, 1945; d. Frank Nelson and Katherine Louise (Hildebrand) Gamsby; m. Larry D. Watson, Sept. 2, 1967 (div. 1974); m. Martin Wayne Cooke, June 23, 1984. BA, Maryville Coll., 1967; MS, U. Tenn., 1975; postgrad., State Tech. Inst. Tchr. Knox County Sch. Bd., Knoxville, Tenn., 1967—; attendee Gov.'s Acad. for Tchrs. of Writing, 1991. Recording sec. Knoxville Community Theatre, 1978-81. Recipient Meritorious Service award Knox County Juvenile Ct., 1982. Mem. Knox County Edn. Assn., East Tenn. Edn. Assn., Tenn. Edn. Assn., NEA, Tenn. Assn. Middle Schs.,

Nat. Council Tchrs. of English, E. Tenn. Assn. Tchrs of English. Baptist. Office: Halls Mid Sch 4317 E Emory Rd Knoxville TN 37938-4354

COOKE, WALTA PIPPEN, automobile dealership owner; b. Shreveport, La., Oct. 18, 1940; d. Billy Burt and Eula (Heaton) Pippen; m. John William Cooke II, Dec. 20, 1958; children: Cheryl Cooke Williams, John William III. BA, Baylor U., 1963. Co-owner, sec.-treas. Pippen Motor Co., Carthage, 1972-80, owner, sec.-treas., 1980—; dir. Sabine River Authority Tex., 1993—, v.p., sec. bd. dirs., 1996, also chmn. mgmt. and project devel. com. Pianist for sanctuary choir Ctrl. Bapt. Ch., Carthage, 1986—, children's choirs. Mem. Carthage 32 Club, Carthage Book Club (rec. sec.). Democrat. Home: 200 Timberlane Dr Carthage TX 75633-2231 Office: Pippen Motor Co 1300 W Panola St Carthage TX 75633-2346

COOL, KIM PATMORE, retail executive, needlework consultant; b. Cleve., Feb. 1, 1940; d. Herman Chester Earl and Eva (Geneau) Patmore; m. Kenneth Adams Cool Jr., Mar. 12, 1963; 1 child, Heidi Adams. BA in Econs., Sweet Briar Coll., 1962; postgrad., Case Western Reserve U., 1962-63. Test adminstr. Pradco, Cleve., 1962-63; pvt. needlework cons. Cleve., 1970-72; retail v.p., treas., custom designer And Sew On, Inc., Cleve., 1973-92, exec. v.p., treas., 1982-92; v.p. Shure Stiches Inc., 1991-92; owner Shure Stitches, Inc., Cleve., 1992-93, The Hare Necessities, Venice, Fla., Germany, 1994—, Hare Necessities Craft & Needlework Mfg., Venice, Fla.; lectr. bus. seminars Nat. Needlework Assn.; tchr. Wellesley Coll. Continuing Edn. Program, 1986; pub. Fredericktown Press, Md.; designer and mktg. assoc. Kappioe OriginalsLtd., 1988-93. Artist collector quality custom hand-painted canvases; co-author: How to Market Needlepoint--The Definitive Manual, 1988, Easy Macrame, 1990, Basic Macrame, 1990, Wearable Macrame, 1990, Playmate Dolls to Stitch, 1991, Pillows and Purses to Stitch, 1991, Needlepoint from Start to Finish, 1992, Pathway to Profit in the Needlework Industry, 1995; homes corr. Venice (Fla.) Gondolier, 1995—. Rep. committeeman Cuyahoga County, Shaker Heights, Ohio, 1964-72. Regional Curling champion, 1987-88. Mem. USFSA (competitions com., ea. vice chair precision, judges edn. tng. com., nat. vice chair for precision), Nat. Needlework Assn. (lectr. seminar on mktg. needlepoint, seminars on buying and merchandising, 1988—, charter assoc. retail), Embroiderers Guild of Cleve. (bd. dirs. 1980-82), Am. Profl. Needlework Retailers, S.E. Yarncrafters Guild (conductor merchandising seminars 1989—), Nat. Standards Coun. Am. Embroiderers, U.S. Figure Skating Assn. (nat. precision judge, sr. competition judge, gold test judge 1967—), Sweet Briar Coll. Alumnae Assn. (nat. bd. dirs., upper MW region, 1965-66, class sec. 1988-92), Cleve. Skating Club, Mayfield Country Club. Mem. United Ch. of Christ. Home and Office: The Hare Necessities 312 Shore Rd Venice FL 34285-3725

COOL, MARY L., elementary education educator; b. Buffalo, Dec. 7, 1954; d. Paul G. and Dorothy R. (O'Brien) Wailand; m. Ronald J. Cool, June 23, 1979; children: Logan Elizabeth, Colin Jeffery. BS in Elem. Edn. cum laude, SUNY, Fredonia, 1976. Cert. tchr., N.Y., Fla. Tchr. grade 1 Buffalo, N.Y., 1976-77; tchr. grade 5 Orange County, Orlando, Fla., 1979-85; tchr. grade 1, ESEA Title I head tchr. Manatee County, Myakka City, Fla., 1977-79; tchr. grade 5, media specialist Volusia County, Osteen, Fla., 1985-89; intermediate resource tchr. S.W. Volusia County, Fla., 1989-91; dist. elem. resource tchr., elem. tchr. specialist Volusia County Schs., Fla., 1991—; grade lever chair, sci. chair, reading chair, facilitative leader, coop. learning trainer, tchr. coach, tech. edn. coach, tchr. asst. coord., student success team coord. Volusia County Schs.; ednl. cons. Scholastic, Inc., Sports Illus. for Kids, Kids Discover, Marvel Comics, Miami Mus. Arts and Scis. Mem. ASCD, AAUW, Nat. Coalition for Sex Equity in Edn., Nat. Staff Devel. Coun., Kappa Delta Pi. Home: 1566 Gregory Dr Deltona FL 32738-6159 Office: PO Box 2410 Daytona Beach FL 32115-2410

COOLEY, ANDREW LYMAN, corporation executive, former army officer; b. St. Louis, Oct. 14, 1934; s. Andrew L. and Algretta R. (Carr) C.; m. Joan Lynn Wheatley, Jan. 9, 1958; children: Cathleen Wheatley, Caroline Carr. BA, George Washington U., 1964, MA, 1967; MS, U.S. Army Command and Gen. Staff Coll., 1966; postgrad., U.S. Army War Coll., 1972-73. Commd. 2d lt. U.S. Army, 1955; advanced through grades to maj. gen. U.S. Army, Continental U.S. and Hawaii, 1955-64; bn. adv. Vietnam, 1964-65; aide to chief of staff SHAPE, Belgium, 1967-69; tank bn. comdr. Germany, 1969-70; mem. staff Dept. of Army Pentagon, 1970-72; brigade comdr. and div. chief of staff Korea, 1975-77; exec. to comdr. in chief Pacific Hawaii, 1978-79; asst. div. comdr. 101st Airborne Div., 1979-81; asst. dep. dir. for politico-mil. affairs, plans and policy directorate Joint Chiefs of Staff, Washington, 1981-83; mil. adviser Habib-Draper Mission, Lebanon, 1982-83; dir. strategy, plans and policy Dept. Army, Washington, 1983-85; comdg. gen. 24th Inf. Div. (Mech.) and Fort Stewart, Hunter Army Air Field, Fort Stewart, Ga., 1985-87; chief Office Military Cooperation, Cairo, 1987-89; ret., 1989; program mgr. Vinnell Brown Root, Turkey Base Maintenance Agreement, 1989-91; project mgr. ops. and maintenance Brown and Root Svcs. Corp., Houston, 1991-94; program mgr. Project Restore Hope Somalia, 1993; ind. cons. with expertise in Africa, Croatia, Bosnia and Haiti, 1994—. Author: Diplomatic Significances of the Great White Fleet, 1966, Realistic Deterrence in NATO, 1973. Decorated Def. D.S.M. with oak leaf cluster, Legion of Merit with oak leaf cluster, Bronze Star, Air medal, others; Fed. Exec. fellow Brookings Instn., 1977-78; named to Officer Candidate Sch. Hall of Fame, 1979. Mem. Assn. U.S. Army, Armor Assn. Episcopalian. Home: 17202 De Chirico Cir Spring TX 77379

COOLEY, DENTON ARTHUR, surgeon, educator; b. Houston, Aug. 22, 1920; s. Ralph C. and Mary (Fraley) C.; m. Louise Goldsborough Thomas, Jan. 15, 1949; children: Mary, Susan, Louise, Florence, Helen. B.A., U. Tex., 1941; M.D., Johns Hopkins U., 1944; Doctorem Medicinae (hon.), U. Turin, Italy, 1969; H.H.D. (hon.), Hellenic Coll., 1984, Holy Cross Greek Orthodox Sch. of Theology, 1984; DSc honoris causa, Coll. of William and Mary, 1987. Diplomate: Am. Bd. Surgery, Am. Bd. Thoracic Surgery. Intern Johns Hopkins Sch. Medicine, Balt., 1944-45; resident surgery Johns Hopkins Sch. Medicine, 1945-50; sr. surg. registrar thoracic surgery Brompton Hosp. for Chest Diseases, London, Eng., 1950-51; assoc. prof. surgery Baylor U. Coll. Medicine, Houston, 1954-62; prof. surgery Baylor U. Coll. Medicine, 1962-69; clin. prof. surgery U. Tex. Med. Sch., Houston, 1975—; founder, surgeon-in-chief Tex. Heart Inst., 1962—. Served as capt., M.C., 1946-48. Named one of ten Outstanding Young Men in U.S., U.S. C. of C., 1955; Man of the Yr. award Kappa Sigma, 1964; Rene Leriche prize Internat. Surg. Soc., 1967; Billings Gold medal Am. Surg. Soc., 1967; Vishnevsky medal Vishnevsky Inst., USSR, 1971; Theodore Roosevelt Award, 1980; Presdl. Medal of Freedom, presented by Pres. Reagan, 1984; Gifted Tchr. award Am. Coll. Cardiology, 1987. Hon. fellow Royal Coll. Physicians and Surgeons of Glasgow, Royal Coll. Surgeons of Ireland, Royal Australasian Coll. Surgeons, Royal Coll. Surgeons of Eng.; mem. ACS, Am. Surg. Assn., Internat. Cardiovascular Soc., Am. Assn. Thoracic Surgery, Soc. Thoracic Surgery, Soc. Univ. Surgeons, Am. Coll. Cardiology, Am. Coll. Chest Physicians, Soc. Clin. Surgery, Soc. Vascular Surgery, Western Surg. Assn., Tex. Surg. Soc., Halsted Soc. Office: Tex Heart Inst PO Box 20345 Houston TX 77225-0345

COOLEY, HILARY ELIZABETH, real estate manager; b. Leesburg, Va., May 8, 1953; d. Thomas McIntyre and Helen Strong (Stringham) C. BA in Econs., U. Pitts., 1976; postgrad. in bus. adminstrn., Hood Coll., Frederick, Md., 1985-90. Mgr. Montgomery Ward, Frederick, 1976-80, merchandiser, 1980-82; asst. bus. mgr. Arundel Communications, Leesburg, 1982-84; bus. mgr. Loudoun Country Day Sch., Leesburg, 1984-85, bd. trustees, 1989-93, sec. bd. trustees, 1989-90, v.p., 1990-92; contr. Foxcroft Sch., Middleburg, Va., 1984-86, 91-92; corr. Loudoun Times Mirror, Leesburg, 1985-87; estate mgr. Delta Farm Inc., Middleburg, Va., 1988—. Area chmn. Keep Loudoun Beautiful, Middleburg, 1983-90, pres., bd. dirs. 1993-96; pres. Waterford (Va.) Citizens' Assn., 1985-86, Waterford Players, 1986-88; bd. dirs. Waterford Found., Inc., 1992-95, pres. 1995—; bd. dirs. Loudoun Hist. Soc., Leesburg, 1987, Mt. Zion Ch. Preservation Assn., 1996—. Mem. Penn Hall Alumnae Ann. (pres. 1987-92). Democrat. Episcopalian. Home and Office: Delta Farm PO Box 234 Philomont VA 20131-0234

COOLEY, LORALEE COLEMAN, professional storyteller; b. Charleston, Ill., Jan. 17, 1943; d. Leland Henry and Lorene Madge (Carpenter) C.; m. Edwin Mark Cooley, July 1, 1967; foster children: Jenni, Gail, Bridgette, Carla. BA, Ea. Ill. U., 1965; postgrad., So. Bapt. Theol. Sem., Ky., 1965-67, Ariz. State U., 1972-74; MA, Antioch U., 1994. Piano, music tchr. various schs., 1967-69; women's program dir. Sta. WDXB-AM, Chattanooga, 1969-70; tutoring svcs. coord. Newton Community Ctr., Chattanooga, 1969-71; asst. editor New Age mag., Washington, 1971-72; publicity coord. Firebird Lake/Watersports World, Phoenix, 1975; asst. libr. Casa Grande (Ariz.) Pub. Libr., 1975-77; profl. storyteller Casa Grande, 1977-78, Richmond, Va., 1978-79, Atlanta, 1979-88, Anderson, S.C., 1988-94; Pampa, Tex., 1994—; publicity dir. Callanwolde Fine Arts Ctr., Atlanta, 1987; toured Republic of Ga., Newly-Ind. States, started rsch. project on Georgian Folklore, 1989. Co-chmn. Casa Grande Bicentennial Com., 1974-76; bd. dirs. Genesis House, Pampa,1995-98, M.K. Brown Mcpl. Auditorium, Pampa, 1995-98. Named Miss Louisville, 1966 (preliminary to Miss Am. pageant). Mem. AAUW, Nat. Storytelling Assn., So. Order Storytellers (founder 1982), Pampa Fine Arts Assn. (bd., pres. 1996-97), Internat. Platform Assn., Tex. Women's Forum/Amarillo, DAR. Democrat. Presbyterian. Home and Studio: 410 Buckler Ave Pampa TX 79065-6207

COOLEY, NICOLE R., writer; b. Iowa City, Iowa, Oct. 1, 1966; d. Peter John and Jacqueline (Marks) C.; m. Alexander Laban Hinton, Jan. 9, 1994. BA, Brown U., 1988; MFA, Iowa Writers Workshop, 1990; PhD, Emory U., 1996. Teaching asst. Emory U., Atlanta, 1991-94, instr., 1994—. Author: Resurrection, 1996; poetry and fiction pub. in lit. jours. Recipient Walt Whitman award Acad. Am. Poets, 1995, Nat. Endowment for Arts grantee for fiction, 1996. Mem. MLA. Democrat. Office: Emory U Dept English Atlanta GA 30322

COOLEY, PETER JOHN, poet, educator; b. Detroit; s. Paul John and Ruth Esther (Hayhow) C.; m. Jacueline Marks, June 12, 1965; children: Nicole, Alissa, Joshua. BA, Shimer Coll., 1962; MA, U. Chgo., 1964; PhD, U. Iowa, 1970. Asst. prof. U. Wis., Green Bay, 1970-72, assoc. prof., 1972-75; asst. prof. Tulane U., New Orleans, 1975-78, assoc. prof., 1979-83, prof., 1983—. Author: The Company of Strangers, 1975, The Room Where Summer Ends, 1979, Nightseasons, 1983, The Van Gogh Notebook, 1987, The Astonished Hours, 1992; poetry editor N.Am. Rev., 1970—. Robert Frost fellow, 1981, State of La. fellow, 1982. Mem. PEN, South Ctrl. MLA, Poets and Writers. Democrat. Episcopalian. Home: 241 Harding St Jefferson LA 70121-3917 Office: Tulane U English Dept 6823 Saint Charles Ave New Orleans LA 70118-5665

COOLEY, SHEILA LEANNE, psychologist, consultant; b. Oakland, Calif., July 25, 1956; d. Philips Theadore and Helen Ellene (Newbill) C. BA, St. Leo Coll., 1979; MS, U. So. Miss., 1986; PhD, Miss. State U., 1990. Lic. psychologist, Ky. Counselor Charter Counseling Ctr., Jackson, Miss., 1988-89; staff psychologist Rivendell Psychiat. Ctr., Bowling Green, Ky., 1989-90; program dir. MidSouth Hosp., Memphis, 1990-91; resource ctr. dir. Mid-South Resource Ctr., Ridgeland, Miss., 1991-92; partial hosp. dir. Pathways Partial Hospitalization, Ridgeland, 1991-92; edn. specialist, sr. position Miss. Dept. of Edn., Bur. Spl. Svcs., Jackson, 1993-94; psychologist Western State Hosp., Hopkinsville, Ky., 1994—, Caring Connections, Hopkinsville, Ky., 1995; pvt. practice Hopkinsville, Ky., 1996—. Campaign organizer for Dem. mayor, Jackson, 1992. Mem. APA, Ky. Psychol. Assn., Phi Delta Kappa, Psi Chi, Theta Pi Sigma. Baptist. Home: 4081 Singletree Dr Hopkinsville KY 42240 Office: PO Box 2200 Hopkinsville KY 42241-2200

COOLMAN, C. DOUGLAS, company executive. Prin. Edward D. Stone, Jr. & Assocs. Address: # 110 1512 E Broward Blvd Fort Lauderdale FL 33301

COON, WILLIAM AARON, assistant principal; b. Houston, May 28, 1962; s. William Aaron Sr. and Babbett Elizabeth (Verre) C.; m. Carolyn Ruth Mishoe, July 25, 1987; 1 child, Matthew Mishoe. BS, Presby. Coll., Clinton, S.C., 1984; MA, Norwich U., 1995. Cert. tchr. social studies, secondary prin., supervision, S.C. Tchr., coach R.E. Lee Sch., Bishopville, S.C., 1985-86, Monroe Sch., Forsyth, Ga., 1987-89, Sumter (S.C.) H.S., 1989-95; asst. prin. Alice Drive Mid. Sch., Sumter, 1995—; pro-team panel mem. S.C. Ctr. Tchr. Recruitment, Rock Hill, S.C., 1996—. EIA Competitive Tchr. grantee S.C. Dept. Edn., 1995. Mem. ASCD, S.C. Assn. Sch. Adminstrs. Methodist. Office: Alice Drive Mid Sch 40 Miller Rd Sumter SC 29150

COONE, KELLY MARIE, broadcast journalist, reporter, anchorperson; b. Beaumont, Tex., Apr. 19, 1973; d. Patrick Howard Coone and Cay Dene (Willis) Melanson. BA in Journalism and Broadcast Mgmt., Baylor U., 1994. Editor, graphic artist Sta. KXXV-TV, Waco, Tex., 1994-95; photojournalist Sta. KBMT-TV, Beaumont, 1995, reporter, anchor, 1996—. Assoc. bd. dirs. Girl's Haven, Beaumont, 1996—. Mem. Soc. Profl. Journalists. Democrat. Methodist. Office: Sta KBMT-TV 525 S I-10 Beaumont TX 77701

COONEY, CHARLES HAYES, lawyer; b. Nashville, Apr. 25, 1937; s. Robert G. and Annie Lee (Hayes) C.; m. Patsy M. Cooney, Dec. 25, 1986; children: Susan, Hayes Jr. BA, Vanderbilt U., 1959, JD, 1963. Bar: Tenn. 1963. Pvt. practice Cornelius & Collins, Nashville, 1963-67; chief def. atty. gen. State of Tenn., Nashville, 1967-80; ptnr. Watkins, McGugin, McNeilly & Rowan, 1980—. Staff mem. Vanderbilt U. Law Review, 1961-62. Capt. U.S. Army, 1959. Mem. Rotary, Tenn. Bar Assn. (pres. young lawyers sect., 1961), Nashville Bar Assn. (bd. dirs. 1985-87). Presbyterian. Office: Watkins McGugin McNeilly & Rowan 214 2nd Ave N Ste 300 Nashville TN 37201-1647

COONEY, DAVID FRANCIS, lawyer; b. Chgo., Sept. 21, 1954; s. John Thomas and Margaret (Bonner) C.; m. René Marie Struzzieri, June 20, 1987; children: Lauren René, Cailin Ann. BBA in Fin. magna cum laude, U. Notre Dame, 1975, JD, 1978. Bar: Fla., U.S. Dist. Ct. (so. dist.) Fla., U.S. Ct. Appeal (5th, 8th and 11th cirs.). Assoc. Grimmett, Scherer & James, Ft. Lauderdale, Fla., 1978-82; ptnr. Conrad, Scherer & James, Ft. Lauderdale, 1982-92, Cooney, Haliczer, Mattson, Lance, Blackburn, Pettis & Richards, P.A., Ft. Lauderdale, 1992-96, Cooney Mattson, Ft. Lauderdale, 1996—. Mem. Am. Bd. Trial Advs. (assoc.). Roman Catholic. Home: 2839 NE 24th Pl Fort Lauderdale FL 33309 Office: Cooney Mattson 301 E Las Olas Blvd Fort Lauderdale FL 33301-2228

COONEY, M(URIEL) SHARON TAYLOR, medical/surgical nurse, educator; b. Edenton, N.C., Oct. 12, 1947; d. Howard Russell and Evelyn Louise (Phelps) Taylor; children: Michael James, Patrick Russell. BSN, East Carolina U., 1969; MS in Nursing, St. Louis U., 1972. Cert. orthopaedic nurse. Staff nurse Johns Hopkins Hosp., Balt., 1969-71, Barnes Hosp., St. Louis, 1971-72, Person County Meml. Hosp., 1989—; cardiovascular clin. nurse specialist Jackson Meml. Hosp., Miami, 1973-74; instr. Shepherd Coll., Shepherdstown, W.Va., 1983-84, Piedmont Community Coll., Roxboro, N.C., 1989-90, Watts Sch. Nursing, Durham, N.C., 1990—; clin. instr., lectr. Shepherd Coll.; home health care supr., mgr. Coord. Coun. for Sr. Citizens, 1985. Mem. ANA, Nat. Assn. Orthopaedic Nurses, Nat. League for Nursing, Acad. Med.-Surg. Nursing, N.C. Alliance Hosp.-Based Schs. Nursing, N.C. Nurses Assn. (coun. of clin. specialists, med.-surg. coun., chmn. coun. nurse educators). Home: 10309 S Lowell Rd Bahama NC 27503

COONEY, PATRICIA ANN, elementary school educator, secondary school educator; b. Seymour, Ind., Mar. 3, 1943; d. Omer W.H. Brandt and Lucille L. Stanfield; m. Robert Gene Cooney, Aug. 16, 1969; children: Robert P., David O., Thomas A. BS, Ball State U., 1964; MA, Mercer U., 1990. Cert. early childhood, cert. home econs. Tchr. Muncie (Ind.) Jr. H.S., 1964-65, Greece (N.Y.) H.S., 1965-71; coord. home econs. Greece (N.Y.) Sch. Dist., 1971; tchr. Faith Luth. Elem. Sch., Marietta, Ga., 1982-85, Gwinnett County Sch. Sys., Lawrenceville, Ga., 1986—; grade mgr. B.B. Harris Elem. Sch., Duluth, Ga., 1986-88; dir. sch. lunch Faith Luth., Marietta, 1982-85. Presenter in field; curriculum writer for N.Y. State, 1970, Gwinnett County Sch. Sys., 1993, Harris Elem. Sch., Duluth, 1994—. Pilot Inner-City 4-H Program, Muncie, Ind., 1963; local sch. advisor, Duluth, Ga. Mem. Phi Kappa Phi. Lutheran. Home: 2684 Kenwood Dr Duluth GA 30136 Office: BB Harris Elem Sch 3123 Clairborne Dr NW Duluth GA 30136

COONEY, WILLIAM J., lawyer; b. Augusta, Ga., July 31, 1929; s. John F. and Ellen (Joy) C.; m. Martha L. Whaley, May 1, 1971; children: William J. IV, Sarah C. BS, U. Notre Dame, 1951; JD, Georgetown U., 1954, LLM, 1955. Bar: Ga. 1963, Calif. 1961, D.C. 1954. Law clk. U.S. Ct. Appeals, Washington, 1954, U.S. Claims Ct., Washington, 1955; asst. U.S. atty. Washington, 1958-60, San Francisco, 1960-63; sole practice Augusta, 1963—. Capt. JAGC, U.S. Army, 1955-58. Mem. State Bar Ga., Spl. Master State Bar Ga., Augusta Bar Assn. (mem. exec. com., arbitrator), Am. Arbitration Assn. (arbitrator). Roman Catholic. Office: 1 Habersham Sq 3602 Wheeler Rd Augusta GA 30909-1826

COOPER, ALAN MICHAEL, psychiatrist; b. Balt., Mar. 14, 1950; s. William I. and Barbara (Stein) C.; m. Elizabeth Ann Mumper, May 31, 1980; children: William, Leigh. SB, MIT, 1972; MD, Med. Coll. of Va., 1976. Diplomate Am. Bd. Psychiatry and Neurology. Intern neurology Med. Coll. Va., 1976-77, resident psychiatry, 1977-78; resident psychiatry U. Va. Hosps., 1978-79, fellow pain clinic, 1979-80, fellow child and adolescent psychiatry, 1981; instr. psychiatry Harvard Med. Sch., Boston, 1980-81; assoc. in anesthesia (psychiatry) Brigham & Women's Hosp., Boston, 1980-81; dir. diagnostic and evaluation unit David C. Wilson Hosp., Charlottesville, Va., 1982-84; clin. adminstr. psychiatry Va. Bapt. Hosp., Lynchburg, 1984-85; chief psychiatrist Ctrl. Va. Cmty. Svcs., Lynchburg, 1985-92; cons. psychiatrist Ctrl. Va. Tng. Ctr., Lynchburg, 1992—. MIT Nat. scholar, 1968. Mem. Am. Psychiat. Assn., Am. Soc. Clin. Hypnosis, Psychiat. Soc. of Va., Lynchburg Acad. Medicine, Nat. Assn. for the Dually Diagnosed. Office: Central Virginia Tng Ctr PO Box 1098 Lynchburg VA 24505

COOPER, ALCIE LEE, JR., insurance executive; b. Gadsden, Ala., Aug. 3, 1939; s. Alcie Lee and Jettie Merle (Farabee) C.; AB, Asbury Coll., 1961; MDiv, St. Paul Sch. Theology, 1966; student. Workers Compensation Coll., 1979, Am. Inst. Property and Liability Underwriters, 1991; CPCU; m. Audrey May MacAuslan, Sept. 3, 1976. Claims adjuster Sentry Ins. A Mut. Co., St. Louis, 1967-69, claim supr., Kansas City, Kans., 1969-72, regional claims supr., Dallas, 1972-77; home office workers compensation cons. Houston Gen. Ins. Co., Ft. Worth, 1977-79, asst. claims mgr., 1979-82, worker's compensation claims mgr., 1982-85; dir. Field Claim Ctr.; asst. v.p. claims, 1986-93; ptnr. Al Cooper & Assocs., distbrs. Amway products, Ft. Worth, 1977—; mgr. br. Hammerman & Gainer, Inc., 1993—; instr. Workers Compensation Sch. 1977-85; Mem. Republican Presdl. Task Force; bd. dirs. Am. Heart Assn., Tarrant County, Tex., 1983-89. Mem. CPCU Soc. (sec. Ft. Worth chpt. 1994-95, v.p. 1995-96, pres.-elect 1996-97), Amway Distbrs. Assn. Office: 4425 W Airport Fwy Ste 210 Irving TX 75062-5832

COOPER, BARBIE PERKINS, writer; b. Columbus, Ga., Aug. 22, 1950; d. Walter W. and Sybil (Hunter) Perkins; m. Phillip R. Cooper Sr., Aug. 2, 1968; 1 child, Phillip II. Cert. in broadcasting and film prodn., Trident Tech. Coll., 1991. Adminstr. PRC Enterprises, Mt. Pleasant, S.C., 1972-86; freelance writer, screenwriter, 1984—; writer/cons. Resume Svcs., 1994—; admissions officer, adj. instr. Johnson & Wales U., Charleston, S.C., 1988—; reporter WCSC TV 5, Charleston, 1990-91. Scriptwriter: Celebrities of the Past and Present...A Stroll Down Memory Lane, 1990, Technical Colleges in America...The New Generation of Higher Education, 1990, Video Information Systems and I-T-F.S...The New Wave of Education Begins, 1990, Hugo, 1991, (feature screenplay) Child of Darkness, 1994 (2d pl. playwriting award Sandhills Writers Conf. 1995), Not My Papa, 1996 (Hon. Mention award Nat. Writers Assn. 1996), (teleplay) Signature Rapist, 1994 (America's Best Contest award Writers Found. 1994), also audio commls.; contbr. articles, editls. and poems to profl. publs.; continuity/script supr. videos. Active family support groups S.C. NG, Mt. Pleasant, 1986-88. Recipient Hon. Mention award World of Poetry, 1985, Silver Poet award, 1989, 90, Gold Poet award, 1986, 91, 92, 1st pl. screenwriting catagory Sandhills Writers Conf., Augusta, Ga., 1994. Mem. The Nat. Writers Assn., S.C. Writers Club, The Writers Workshop of L.A. Episcopalian. Home: 641 Palmetto St Mount Pleasant SC 29464-4440

COOPER, BROWN, cinematographer; b. Bryan, Tex., Dec. 5, 1957; s. James Franklin and Betty (Jamieson) C.; 1 child, Hassie Cooper; m. Janet Holmes Haws, Sept. 15, 1990; children: Katy Haws, Blair Haws, Mollie Cooper. BS with high honors, U. Tex., 1980. Owner Brown Cooper Corp., Ft. Worth, 1983—; pres. Brownie Cookie Prodns., Houston, 1980-82; co-owner, producer Americana Pictures, Houston, 1982-87; cinematographer Monkey Shine Prodns., Dallas, 1988. Dir., cinematographer, prodr. film: Suzie Stern Quintet, 1982; prodr., cinematographer: The Ride, 1986 (1st pl. comedy award Tex. Filmfest, 3rd pl. short film award Houston Internat. Film Festival); exec. prodr. TV program: The Nuclear Questions, 1982; cinematographer, creative cons.: Monkeyshine, 1988 (1st pl. short film award Houston Internat. Film Festival); dir. photography: (feature film Ice House starring Melissa Gilbert); cinematographer, camera operator award-winning commls., 1991-96. Cameraman TV pub. svc. announcements for The Family Place, Dallas, 1989, Nelson Tebedo AIDS Rsch. Found., Dallas, 1989, 90.; cinematographer "Best Buddies" Orgn., Austin Lyric Opera, 1994. Mem. Internat. Photographers Guild, Tex. Assn. Film/Tape Profls., Tex. Film Commn., Phi Kappa Phi.

COOPER, CHARLES NEILSON, lawyer; b. Norfolk, Va., July 13, 1935; s. Dudley and Mary (Miller) C.; m. Bettie Minette Switzer, June 22, 1958; children: C. Neilson Jr., Erik Switzer, Jefferson Switzer. BA in History, U. Va., 1957; LLB, Columbia U., 1962. Bar: Va. 1962, U.S. Dist. Ct. (ea. dist.) Va. 1963, U.S. Supreme Ct. 1971. Ptnr. Cooper & Cooper, Norfolk, 1963-72, sr. ptnr., 1972-78; sr. ptnr. Cooper, Kalfus & Nachman, Norfolk, 1978-79, pres., 1979-81; sr. ptnr. Cooper & North, Norfolk, 1981-85; pvt. practice law Norfolk, 1985-92; of counsel Mezzullo & McCandlish, P.C., Norfolk, 1993—; trustee Entrepreneurship & Pvt. Enterprise Ctr., 1987; sec. Greater Norfolk Corp., 1986—. Fundraiser, gen. counsel Young Audiences Va., Inc., Norfolk, 1970—; commr. Ea. Va. Med. Authority, Norfolk, 1977-79; trustee Norfolk Acad., 1983—; chmn. Greater Norfolk Corp. Downtown Revitalization Com.; mem. Mayor's Downtown Devel. Com. 1st lt. U.S. Army, 1957-65. Recipient Award of Honor, Jr. C. of C., Norfolk, 1965, Life Bravissimo award Citizens of Tidewater, Va., 1980, Cert. Appreciation of Outstanding Svc. Va. Philharm. Orch., Norfolk, 1980, Alli award for Outstanding Community Svc. Culture Alliance Greater Hampton Rds., 1989. Mem. ABA, Va. Bar Assn., Norfolk and Portsmouth Bar Assn., Tidewater Estate Planning Council. Office: Mezzullo & McCandlish PC 1160 Town Point Ctr 150 Boush St Norfolk VA 23510-1626

COOPER, CHERYL, mental health nurse; b. Paducah, Ky., Jan. 4, 1948; d. Conrad and Annie (Calhoun) Bridges; m. Richard Cooper, Apr. 22, 1967 (dec.); children: Robert, Leslie. BSN, Murray (Ky.) State U., 1989; MSN, Vanderbilt U., 1994. Mental health nurse Parthenon Pavilion, Nashville, 1992-94; psychiat. clin. specialist York VA Med. Ctr., Murfreesboro, Tenn., 1994—. Mem. Sigma Theta Tau.

COOPER, DAVID WAYNE, aerospace engineer; b. Houston, Apr. 5, 1964; s. Cary Wayne and Carolyn Kay (McDonald) C.; m. Lee Jane Hong, Apr. 30, 1994; 1 child, Cary Anthony Hong Cooper. BS, Tex. A&M U., 1988. Engr. Rockwell Space Ops. Co., Houston, 1989-96, United Space Alliance, Houston, 1996—. Mem. AIAA.

COOPER, DAVIS ALFONSO, JR., principal; b. Waycross, Ga., Aug. 7, 1950; s. Davis Alfonso Jr. and Rose Ann (Tharpe) C.; m. Felicia Cecile Harris, Sept. 4, 1974; children: Erin M., Marcellus J., Sarah Rose M. AS, South Ga. Coll., 1973; BA, West Ga. Coll., 1974, MEd, 1975; EdS, Ga. State U., 1985. Cert. social studies tchr., adminstr., supr., Ga. Resident advisor South Ga. Coll., Douglas, 1970-71; resident advisor West Ga. Coll., Carrollton, 1973-74, grad. asst., 1975; tchr., coach DeKalb Sch. System, Decatur, Ga., 1975-79, asst. prin., 1979-86, prin., 1986—. 2d v.p. Knollview Civic Club, Decatur, 1983; PTA co-pres. Rainbow Sch., Decatur, 1984-85; Boy Scouts organizer Tilson Sch., Decatur, 1990; bd. dirs. Abundant Life Ch., Lithonia, Ga., 1996. Fellow IDEA Inst., 1993-94. Mem. DeKalb Assn. Educators, Nat Sci. Tchrs. Assn., DeKalb Adminstr. Assn. DeKalb Assn. Elem. Sch. Adminstrs., ASCD, Ga. Profession Notary Pubs. Home: 3274 Rondelay Dr Lithonia GA 30038 Office: Tilson Elem Sch 2100 Bixler Circle Decatur GA 30032

COOPER, DOROTHY SUMMERS, real estate agent; b. Lee County, Ala., Aug. 8, 1918; d. Carl and Mattie Will (Thompson) Summers; m. Arthur Wiggins Cooper, July 20, 1940; children: Arthur Wiggins Jr., Mary Cooper Kitchen, Robert Wayne, Donald Summers. BS, Auburn U., 1939. Tchr. Columbus (Ga.) Jr. High Sch., 1939-40; grad. asst. Auburn (Ala.) U., 1941-42; tchr. Lee County Head Start, 1965-70; real estate agt. Stan Weber Real

Estate, New Orleans, 1972-80, Shamrock and James Grant Realty, Auburn, 1981-88; real estate exec. A&D Properties, Opelika, 1989—; lectr. Nat. Gallery Art, Washington, 1971-72; New Orleans Mus. Art, 1973-78. Treas. Auburn United Meth. Women, 1987-89. Named Honor Roll Bus., Auburn C. of C., 1990. Mem. PEO, Home Econs. Club, Sangahatchee Country Club, Delta Kappa Gamma, Green Gardeners. Democrat. Methodist. Home: 2590 Windy Hill Pl Auburn AL 36830-6408

COOPER, ELIZABETH OWNLEY, university administrator; b. Portsmouth, Va., Apr. 26, 1965; d. Robert Ellis and Lillian Ann (Carhart) Ownley; m. Michael Edwin Cooper, Oct. 23, 1993. BA in Journalism, U. N.C., 1987. Writer U. N.C. News Bur., Chapel Hill, 1986-87; reporter Suffolk (Va.) News-Herald, 1987-88, asst. editor, 1988-89; media rels. specialist Old Dominion U., Norfolk, Va., 1989-85, asst. div. univ. rels., 1995—. Co-pres. Soc. Profl. Journalists, Chapel Hill, 1986-87; care group leder Kempsville Presbyn. Ch., Virginia Beach, Va., 1992, Sunday sch. tchr., 1993, editor newsletter, 1996—. Recipient 1st Place and 3d Place awards Va. Press Assn., 1988, 1st and 2d Place awards Va. Press Assn., 1989. Mem. Pub. Rels Soc. Am., Coll. News Assn. United Daus. of Confederacy (sec. Stonewall chpt.), Coll. News Assn. Va. Republican. Home: 4951 Barn Swallow Dr Chesapeake VA 23321

COOPER, GARY ALLAN, lawyer; b. Bristol, Va., Feb. 3, 1947; s. Earl Clarence and Reba Evelyn (Jenkins) C.; m. Lynn Ellen Weir, Feb. 17, 1973; chidlren: Drew Kelsey, Gavin Morgan. BS in Journalism, U. Tenn., 1969, JD, 1972. Bar: Tenn. 1972, U.S. Dist. Ct. (ea. dist.) Tenn. 1972, U.S. Supreme Ct. 1979, Fla. 1981. Assoc. Luther, Anderson & Ruth, Chattanooga, 1972-76; ptnr. Luther, Anderson, Cleary, Luhowiak & Cooper, Chattanooga, 1976-79, Luther, Anderson, Cleary & Cooper, Chattanooga, 1979-80, Anderson, Cleary & Cooper, Chattanooga, 1981, Fleissner & Cooper, Chattanooga, 1982, Fleissner, Cooper & Marcus, Chattanooga, 1983-88, Fleissner Cooper Marcus & Steger, Chattanooga, 1988-89, Fleissner Cooper & Marcus, Chattanooga, 1990—. Author: Tennessee Forms for Trial Practice, 1977, 4th edit., 1994, Tennessee Law Office Adminstration, 1977. With USAR, 1972-79. Recipient Herman Hickman Postgrad. scholarship for Athletes U. Tenn., 1969. Mem. ABA, Chattanooga Bar Assn. (bd. dirs. 1984-86), Fla. Bar Assn. (mem. out-of-state practitioners com. 1983-86), Tenn. Bar Assn., Tenn. Def. Lawyers Assn. (chmn. amicus curiae com. 1987-89), Phi Delta Phi, Signal Mt. Golf and Country Club. Republican. Methodist. Home: 55 Carriage Hl Signal Mountain TN 37377-2331 Office: Fleissner Cooper Marcus & Quinn 800 Vine St Chattanooga TN 37403-2317

COOPER, GERALD RICE, clinical pathologist; b. Scranton, S.C., Nov. 19, 1914; s. Robert McFadden and Viola Lavender Cooper; m. Lois Corrina Painter, Mar. 9, 1946; children: Annetta, Gerald Jr., Rodney. AB, Duke U., 1936, MA, 1938, PhD, 1939, MD, 1950. Cert. Am. Bd. Clin. Chemistry. Intern Atlanta VA Hosp., 1950-51, resident, 1951-52; rsch. assoc. Duke U. Sch. Medicine, Durham, N.C., 1939-46; chief chemistry, hematology and pathology Ctrs. for Disease Control, Atlanta, 1952-72; rsch. med. officer Ctrs. for Disease Control, Nat. Ctr. Environ. Health, Atlanta, 1973—. Author (with others) books; contbr. articles to profl. jours. Col. USPHS. Decorated commendation medal, Superior Svc. award, Disting. Svc. medal, Asst. Sec. for Health award for exceptional achievement; recipient Hektoen Silver medal AMA, 1954, Fulton County Med. Achievement award, 1954, Billings Silver medal, 1956. Mem. Am. Assn. for Clin. Chemistry (pres. 1984, bd. dirs. 1975-77, chmn. bd. editors of selected methods 1967-80, bd. editors Clin. Chemistry jour. 1970-76, Fischer award 1975, Dade Internat. award 1975, N.J. Gerulat award 1979, SE Sect. Meritorious Svc. award 1989, Outstanding Contbn. Clin. Chemistry award 1992), Internat. Fedn. Clin. Chemistry (apolipoprotein expert panel 1985), Am. Soc. Clin. Pathologists (chmn. clin. chemistry coun. 1974, Continuing Edn. award 1967, 77). Methodist. Home: 2165 Bonnevit Ct NE Atlanta GA 30345-4126 Office: Ctrs for Disease Control Chamblee 17/1103 F20 4770 Buford Hwy NE Atlanta GA 30341-3717

COOPER, HENRY FRANKLYN, engineering, technology and national security affairs consultant; b. Augusta, Ga., Nov. 8, 1936; s. Henry F. and Ruby (Harris) C.; m. Barbara Kays, Aug. 17, 1958; children: Laura, Cynthia, Scott. BSME with high honors, Clemson U., 1958, MSME, 1960; PhD in Mech. Engring., NYU, 1964. Instr. engring. mechanics Clemson (S.C.) U., 1958-60; mem. tech. staff Bell Telephone Labs, Whippany, N.J., 1960-64; sci. advisor Air Force Weapons Lab., Albuquerque, 1964-71; program mgr. R&D Assocs., Rosslyn, Va. and Marina Del Rey, Calif., 1971-79; dep. asst. sec. Air Force, Washington, 1979-82; dep. dir. nuclear effects divsn. R&D Assocs., Rosslyn, 1982-83; asst. dir. U.S. Arms Control Disarmament Agy. State Dept., Washington, 1983-85; amb., chief U.S. negotiator Def. and Space Talks, Geneva, 1985-90; sr. v.p. JAYCOR, Vienna, Va., 1990; dir. strategic def. initiative Office of Sec. of Def., Washington, 1990-93; pvt. practice as cons., 1993-95; chmn. Applied Rsch. Assocs., Albuquerque, 1995—, High Frontier, Arlington, Va., 1996—; mem. bd. advisors coll. engring. Clemson U., 1985-87; adj. prof. S.W. Mo. State U., Springfield, 1992—; sr. assoc. Nat. Inst. Pub. Policy, Fairfax, Va., 1993—; advisor nat. security Empower Am., Washington, 1993—; vis. fellow Heritage Found., Washington, 1993—; mem. nat. def. panel Nat. Policy Forum, Washington, 1994—. Contbr. articles to profl. jours. 1st lt. USAF, 1964-67. Decorated Commendation medal; recipient Founders Day award NYU, 1967, Cert. of Achievement, Air Force, 1982, Superior Honor award U.S. Arms Control & Disarmament Agy., 1987, Disting. Svc. award Clemson U., 1989, Disting. Pub. Svc. medal Dept. of Def., 1993; scholar Owens Corning Fiberglass, 1957, 58. Mem. ASME, AAAS, U.S. Strategic Inst., Internat. Inst. Strategic Studies, Sigma Xi, Tau Beta Pi. Republican. Presbyterian. Office: Nat Inst Pub Policy 3031 Javier Rd Ste 300 Fairfax VA 22031-4607

COOPER, J. DANNY, state association administrator; b. Clanton, Ala., Apr. 1, 1948; s. Wiley Grady and Mary Lucile (Lowery) C.; m. Patricia Dianne Carter, Nov. 14, 1970; children: Jay Daniel, Robin Elliott. BA, U. Montevallo, Ala., 1970, MEd, 1973. Dir. vets. affairs U. Montevallo, 1973-75; tchr. Shelby County Bd. Edn., Montevallo, 1976-77; exec. dir. Ala. Rep. Party, Birmingham, 1977-80; campaign mgr. Ala. Reagan-Bush 1980, Birmingham, 1980; state dir. U.S. senator U.S. Sen. Jeremiah Denton, Birmingham, 1981-85, 86; orgnl. cons. Denton for Senate, Birmingham, 1986; v.p. Haughton & Co. Advt., Tuscaloosa, 1985; dir. Ala. State of Emergency Mgmt. Agy., Montgomery, 1987-89; exec. v.p., chief adminstrv. officer Ala. Assn. Realtors, Montgomery, 1990—; cons. McFarland for Congress, Ala., 1985; bd. dirs. Bear Creek Devel. Authority, Russellville, Ala., 1988—. Trustee Real Estate Rsch. and Edn. Ctr., U. Ala., 1995—; bd. dirs. U. Montevallo Alumni Bd., 1988—, Ala. Civil Justice Reform Commn., 1993—; mem. Ala. Emergency Response Commn., co-chmn., 1987-89; chmn. Shelby County Reps., Ala., 1976; gov.'s appointee Ala. Rapid Rail Transit Commn.; vol. Hospice of Montgomery, 1991—; commr. So. Rapid Rail Commn., 1990—; deacon Forest Pk. Bapt. Ch., Montgomery, 1988—. Mem. Am. Soc. Assn. Execs. (Ala. state legis. chairperson 1994—), Nat. Assn. Realtors (mem. polit. comm. com. 1994-97), Nat. Emergency Mgmt. Assn. (v.p. 1989—), Nat. Coord. Coun. on Emergency Mgmt., Ala. Coun. Assn. Execs. (bd. dirs. 1994—), Kiwanis, Alpha Tau Omega (Outstanding Svc. award 1970). Baptist. Home: 3438 Manchester Dr Montgomery AL 36111-2314 Office: Ala Assn Realtors 522 Washington St Montgomery AL 36104-4346

COOPER, JAMES RALPH, engineering executive; b. Muskegon, Mich., May 23, 1943; s. Earl Ralph and Henrietta Kathryn (Sebolt) C.; m. Mary Lu Geiger Marony, Jan. 13, 1962 (div. 1964); 1 child, Kenneth James; m. Kathleen Starr Walsh, Oct. 22, 1964; children: Peter, Kevin Shawn, Rhonda Reneé. BS in applied biology, Ferris State Coll., 1974, BS in vocational edn., 1987; MPA, Golden Gate U., 1983; DEd in higher edn. admin., U. Fla., 1996. Draftsman Dresser Industries, Muskegon, Mich., 1966-70; sr. engineer, public Dresser Industries, 1974-76; reliability engineer NWL Controls, Kalamazoo, 1976-78; sr. publs. mgr. Teledyne Camera Sys., Arcadia, Calif., 1978-79; sr. rsch. engineer General Dynamics Corp., San Diego, 1979-81; sr. staff engineer, admin. staff asst. Martin Marietta Corp., Denver, 1981-95; assoc. exec. dir. Cmty. Coll. Bus. Officers, Gainesville, Fla., 1995—; cons. engineer U.S. Govt. Kalamazoo, 1975-76, Rancho Cucamonga, Calif., 1984. Author: Engineering Operations Manual, 1982. Vol. probation officer Probate Ct., Traverse City, Mich. 1989-95. With U.S. Army, 1960-61. Mem. Cmty. Coll. Bus. Officers, Am. Assn. Cmty. Colls. (coun. of chairs). Republican. Lutheran. Home: 10784 SW 78th Ave Ocala FL 34476 Office: CCBO Inst Higher Edn U. Florida Gainesville FL 32611

COOPER, JEFFERY BERNARD, minister, university administrator; b. Savannah, Ga.; s. James and Idella (Goodwin) C.; m. Joanne Elizabeth Williams, Nov. 25, 1983; children: Ako, Ethan, Charity, Jeffery B. II. BA, U. Ga., 1980; Cert. in Theology, Interdenom. Theol. Ctr., 1992; D in Ministry, Grad. Theol. Found., 1996. Ordained to ministry A.M.E. Ch., 1980. Pastor St. Paul A.M.E. Ch., Siloam, Ga., 1977-79, St. Luke and Nimnoe A.M.E. Ch., Athens, Ga., 1979-80; sr. pastor Greater Bethel A.M.E. Ch., Athens, 1980-88, Trinity A.M.E. Ch., Atlanta, 1988—; chmn. Bethel Ch. Homes, Athens, 1980-88; sec. Augusta (Ga.) Ann. Conf., 1983-88; dir. minority admissions U. Ga., Athens, 1984-95; mem. gen. bd. A.M.E. Ch., Washington, 1984-88. Trustee Turner Theol. Sem., Atlanta, 1984-91; active Athens/Clarke County Ethics Bd., 1985-89; hon. dep. sheriff Fulton County, Ga., 1991. Mem. A.M.E. Mins. Union, Optimists. Office: Trinity AME Ch 604 Lynhurst Dr SW Atlanta GA 30311-2206

COOPER, JOHN BYRNE, JR., airline pilot; b. Balt., May 13, 1942; s. John Byrne and Mary Louise (Shaffer) C.; m. Virginia Johnson, Oct. 30, 1964 (div. 1974); children: John Byrne, Tracy Diane; m. Jane Marian Simpson, Apr. 1, 1977; children: Julie Allison, Scott David. B in Indsl. Engring., Ga. Inst. Tech., 1964. Pilot Delta Air Lines, Inc., Atlanta, 1970—, capt. B727, B767, 1986—, B727 line check airman, 1988-92, lead B727 line check airman, 1991-93, B767 line check airman, 1994—. Mem. exec. com. Homeowners Assn., Marietta, Ga., 1988, v.p. bd. dirs., 1995-96; soccer coach Metro North/East Cobb Soccer, Marietta, 1985-92. Decorated DFC, Air medals (23), Navy Commendation medal. Mem. U.S. Naval Inst., Assn. Naval Aviation, Naval Res. Assn., Tailhook Assn., Barefoot Sailing Club (fleet capt.), So. Sailing Club, Coronado 15 Nat. Assn. (bd. dirs. 1976), Beta Theta Pi. Lutheran.

COOPER, KENNETH STANLEY, educational administrator; b. Oxford, N.C., May 17, 1948; s. Stephen and Helen (Norman) C.; m. Nancy Robinson, June 26, 1971; children: Danielle Jamilla, Janine Kandyce. AS, Miami Dade Community Coll., 1971; BS in Criminal Justice, Fla. Internat. U., 1973, MS in Adult Edn., 1974; postgrad., Fla. Atlantic U., 1976, Ind. U., 1978. Police officer City of Miami (Fla.) Police Dept., 1971-72; tchr. Dade County Pub. Schs., Miami, 1974-76, 80-83, adminstr., asst. prin., 1983-89, prin. intern exec. tng. program, 1987-88, asst. prin., 1983-90; grad. asst. Dept. Social Studies U. Ind., Bloomington, Ind., 1976-78; pres. Cooper Williamson Auto Brokerage, Miami, 1978-80; prin. Jan Mann Opportunity Sch., Miami, Fla., 1990-92, Robert Renick Ednl. Ctr., Opa Locka, Fla., 1992-96, Pine Villa Elem. Sch., Goulds, Fla., 1996—. Guest columnist Miami Times, 1988; contbr. articles to profl. jours. Organizer, activitist Young Democrats of South Fla., 1967-68; mem. United Tchrs. of Dade County, Miami, 1974-76, 80-83; sec. bd. dirs. Cmty. Crusade Against Drugs, Miami, 1995-96. Served with U.S. Army, 1969-70. Named Adminstr. of Yr., Dade County Assn. for Counseling and Devel., 1993. Mem. NAACP. Home: 12840 SW 187th St Miami FL 33177-3000 Office: Pine Villa Elem Sch 21799 SW 117 Ct Goulds FL

COOPER, LAWRENCE ALLEN, lawyer; b. San Antonio, Feb. 1, 1948; s. Elmer E. and Sally (Tempkin) C.; 1 child, Jonathan Alexander. BA, Tulane U., 1970; JD, St. Mary's U., San Antonio, 1974; LLM, Emory U., 1980. Bar: Ga. 1975, Tex. 1975. Ptnr. Cohen & Cooper, Atlanta, 1979-88, Lawrence A. Cooper, pvt. practice law, 1989-93, Cooper, Hewitt & Katz, 1994—; pvt. practice law, 1996—; arbitrator Fulton Superior Ct.; mem. Ga. Bar fee dispute com. Mem. ABA, ATLA, Atlanta Bar Assn., Ga. Trial Lawyers Assn., Tex. Bar Assn., Ga. Trial Lawyers Assn. Home: 2460 Peach Tree Rd # 1704 Atlanta GA 30305

COOPER, MAX DALE, physician, medical educator, researcher; b. Hazelhurst, Miss., Aug. 31, 1933; s. Ottis Noah and Lily (Carpenter) C.; m. Rosalie Lazzara, Feb. 6, 1960; children: Owen Bernard, Melinda Lee Cooper Holladay, Michael Kane, Christopher Byron. Student, Holmes Jr. Coll., 1951-52, U. Miss., 1952-54; postgrad., U. Miss. Med. Sch., 1954-55; MD, Tulane U., 1957. Diplomate Am. Bd. Pediatrics. Intern Saginaw (Mich.) Gen. Hosp., 1957-58; resident dept. pediatrics Tulane Med. Sch., New Orleans, 1958-60; house officer Hosp. for Sick Children, London, 1960, rsch. asst. dept. neurophysiology, 1961; allergy fellow dept. pediatrics U. Calif. Med. Ctr., San Francisco, 1961-62; instr. Tulane Med. Sch., New Orleans, 1962-63; med. fellow specialist U. Minn., Mpls., 1963-64, instr., 1964-66; asst. prof. dept. pediats. U. Ala., Birmingham, 1967-71, assoc. prof. dept. microbiology, 1967-71, dir. rsch. Rehab. Rsch. and Tng. Ctr., 1968-70, prof. dept. microbiology, 1971—, dir. Cell. Identification Lab., 1987-90, dir. Ctr. Interdisciplinary Rsch. in Immunological Diseases, 1987-95, dir. Div. Devel./Clin. Immunology, 1987—, prof. dept. medicine, 1987—, investigator Howard Hughes Med. Inst., 1988—; sr. scientist Comprehensive Cancer Ctr. U. Ala., Birmingham, 1971—, Multipurpose Arthritis Ctr., 1979—, Cystic Fibrosis Rsch. Ctr., 1981—; dir. Cellular Immunobiology Unit of Tumor Inst. U. Ala., Birmingham, 1976-87; vis. scientist tumor immunology unit dept. zoology, U. Coll. London, 1973-74, Inst. D'Embryologie, Nogent-Sur-Marne and Inst. Pasteur, Paris, 1984-85. Co-author: Acute Hemiplegia in Childhood, 1962, Ontogeny of Immunity, 1967, Immunologic Incompetence, 1971, Immunodeficiency in Man and Animals, 1975, numerous others; mem. editl. bds. Immunology Today, 1986, Immunodeficiency Revs., 1987-94, Clin. Immunology and Immunopathology, 1987-90, Internat. Immunology, 1988—; assoc. editor Jour. Immunology, 1972-76, 77-79, Arthritis and Rheumatism, 1985-90, Jour. Clin. Immunology, 1979—; co-editor Seminars in Immunopathology, 1988-91; editor Current Topics in Microbiology and Immunology, 1981—; contbr. numerous 450 articles to profl. jours. Faculty rsch. assoc. Am. Cancer Soc., 1966-71; mem. bd. sci. advisors St. Jude Hosp., Memphis, 1981-84, 91—, Becton-Dickinson Monoclonal Antibody Ctr., 1980-90; mem. med. adv. com. Immune Deficiency Found., 1981-99; mem. bd. sci. counselors Nat. Cancer Inst., Bethesda, Md., 1982-86, Nat. Inst. Allergy and Infectious Diseases, 1978-82, 91—, Inst. Merieux, Lyons, France, 1985-90, Med. Biology Inst., La Jolla, Calif., 1986; mem. internat. sci. adv. bd. Basel (Switzerland) Inst. Immunology, 1987-91; NIH Immunobiology Study Sect., 1974-78; trustee Leukemia Soc. Am., 1983-88. Special Postdoctoral Rsch. fellow USPHS, 1964-66; recipient Teaching Traineeship award Nat. TB Assn., 1962-63, Samuel J. Meltzer Founder's award Soc Exptl. Biology and Medicine, 1966, Life Scis. award 3M, 1990, Sandoz Prize for Immunology, 1990. Mem. NAS, AAAS, AAUP, Am. Assn. Immunologists (pres. 1988-89, councilor 1983-86, chmn. mem. com. 1974-77), Am. Soc. Exptl. Pathology, Am. Soc. Clin. Investigation, Am. Assn. Cancer Rsch., Am. Acad. Pediatrics, Am. Pediatric Soc., Fedn. Am. Scientists, Med. Assn. State Ala., Internat. Soc. Devel. and Comparative Immunology, Soc. Française d'Immunologie (life Membre d'Honneur), Soc. Pediatric Rsch. (v.p. 1978), So. Soc. Pediatric Rsch. (pres. 1975), Cen. Soc. Clin. Rsch., Jefferson County Med. Assn., Clin. Immunology Soc., Am. Acad. Scis., Inst. Medicine, Am. Acad. Arts and Scis., Soc. Mucosal Immunology, Alpha Omega Alpha, Sigma Xi. Office: Howard Hughes Med Inst U Ala 1824 6th Ave S # 378 Birmingham AL 35210-2018

COOPER, PATRICIA UNTERSPAN, Spanish language educator; b. Seattle, Mar. 28, 1945; d. Ernest A. and Mary E. (Ingram) Unterspan; m. Kenneth Cooper Jr., May 29, 1967; children: Amy Cathleen, Kenneth Jack. BA, Fla. State U., 1967, postgrad., 1969; MA, La Grange Coll., 1981; PhD, U. Ky., 1990. Spanish tchr. La Grange (Ga.) H.S., 1981-86; teaching asst. U. Ky., Lexington, 1986-89, asst. coord. undergrad. program, 1989-90, microtech. faculty leader, 1989-90; assoc. prof., Spanish program coord. Georgetown (Ky.) Coll., 1990—, Spanish program dir., 1990—, faculty deve. program leader, 1992-93; adj. prof. La Grange Coll., 1986. Spanish tchr. Cmty. Continuing Edn. Program, Georgetown, 1992; English tutor Faith Bapt. Ch., Georgetown, 1992; bd. missions 1st Meth. Ch., Georgetown, 1991-93. Fellow Fulbright-Hays, 1992, NDEA, 1967-70. Mem. MLA, AAUW (treas. 1992—), Ky. Coun. on Teaching Fgn. Langs., Am. Assn. Tchrs. Spanish and Portuguese (state coord. for nat. Spanish exam. 1992-94), Am. Coun. Tchrs. Fgn. Lang., S.E. Coun. Latin Am. Studies, Phi Beta Kappa, Sigma Delta Pi. Democrat. Methodist. Office: Georgetown Coll 400 E College St # 272 Georgetown KY 40324-1628

COOPER, RALPH, environmental management consultant; b. Akron, Ohio, Mar. 23, 1947; s. James Alex and Gladys Elizabeth (Baker) C.; m. Margaret Elizabeth Cooper, Mar. 17, 1979; children: Alexis Jane, Andrew Allen. BS (hons.), Mich. State U., 1969, MA in psychology, 1971, PhD in psychology, 1974. Asst. prof. Miami U., Oxford, Ohio, 1975-77; prin. rsch. scientist Battelle Meml. Inst., Columbus, Ohio, 1978-83; dir. govt. affairs, environment and safety Sunohio, Inc., Canton, Ohio, 1984-85; prin. Cooper Assocs., San Antonio, Tex., 1985-89; pres. Am. Inst. Hazardous Material Mgmt., San Antonio, 1988-94, AMARC Inc., San Antonio, 1994—; vis. asst. prof. Loyola U., Chgo., 1974-75; program chair Hazmat Southwest Conf., Dallas, 1990-94. City council mem. City of Grandview Heights, Ohio, 1982-84. Fellow U. Mich., 1975-76, Congressional Sci. fellow U.S. Congress, Washington, 1977-78. Office: AMARC Inc Ste 1000 14307 Fox Fire Ln San Antonio TX 78231-1606

COOPER, RICHARD CASEY, lawyer; b. Tulsa, Jan. 20, 1942; s. Winston Churchill and Frances Margaret (Coppinger) C.; m. Ireen Lysbeth Evans, Nov. 24, 1965; children: Christopher Casey, Kimberly Ireen. BSBA, U. Tulsa, 1965, JD, 1967. Bar: Okla. 1967, U.S. Dist. Ct. (no., ea. and we. dists.) Okla. 1967, U.S. Ct. Mil. Appeals 1967, U.S. Ct. Appeals (10th cir.) 1972. Assoc. Boesche, McDermott & Eskridge, Tulsa, 1972-76, ptnr., 1977-92, mng. ptnr., 1990—. Editor in chief: Tulsa Law Jour., 1967. Counsel Tulsa Philharm. Orch., 1990-92; trustee Mervin Bovaird Found., Tulsa, 1991—, pres., 1995—. Lt. USNR, 1967-71, mil. judge JAGC, 1970-71. Villard Martin scholar U. Tulsa, 1967, recipient Order of the Curule Chair, 1967. Mem. ABA, Okla. Bar Assn., Tulsa County Bar Assn., So. Hills Country Club. Republican. Home: 2923 E 58th St Tulsa OK 74105-7453 Office: Boesche McDermott Eskridge 100 W 5th St Ste 800 Tulsa OK 74103-4291

COOPER, ROBERT ELBERT, state supreme court justice; b. Chattanooga, Oct. 14, 1920; s. John Thurman and Susie Inez (Hollingsworth) C.; m. Catherine Pauline Kelly, Nov. 24, 1949; children: Susan Florence Cooper Hodges, Bobbie Cooper Martin, Kelly Ann Smith, Robert Elbert Jr. B.A., U. N.C., 1946; J.D., Vanderbilt U., 1949. Bar: Tenn. 1948. Asso. Kolwyck and Clark, 1949-51; partner Cooper and Barger, 1951-53; asst. atty. gen. 6th Jud. Ct. Tenn., 1951-53; judge 6th Jud. Circuit Tenn., 1953-60; judge Tenn. Ct. Appeals, 1960-70, presiding judge Eastern div., 1970-74; justice Tenn. Supreme Ct., 1974-90, chief justice, 1976-77, 84-85; chmn. Tenn. Jud. Coun., 1967-90; chmn. Tenn. Code Commn., 1976-77, 84-85; mem. Tenn. Jud. Standards Commn., 1971-77. Mem. exec. bd. Cherokee council Boy Scouts Am., 1960-64; bd. dirs. Met. YMCA, 1956-65, St. Barnabas Nursing Home and Apts. for Aged, 1966-69. With USNR, 1941-46. Recipient Nat. Heritage award Downtown Sertoma Club, Chattanooga, 1989. Mem. Am., Tenn., Chattanooga bar assns., Conf. Chief Justices, Phi Beta Kappa, Order of Coif, Kappa Sigma, Phi Alpha Delta. Democrat. Presbyterian. Clubs: Signal Mountain Golf and Country, Masons (33 deg.), Shriners. Home and Office: 196 Woodcliff Cir Signal Mountain TN 37377-3147

COOPER, ROBERT MICHAEL, nuclear energy industry specialist; b. Little Rock, Nov. 27, 1948; s. John William and Rachel Lou Ann (Merritt) C.; m. Beverly Jean Wiles, Aug. 25, 1972; 1 child, Kristen Amanda. AA in Gen. Studies, Ark. Tech. U., 1984; BS in Indsl. Tech., So. Ill. U., 1990; MS in Ops. Mgmt., U. Ark., 1994. Electrician helper Ark. Power and Light Co., Pine Bluff, 1971-75, journeyman electrician Ark. Nuclear One, 1975-77, relay engr. Ark. Nuclear One, 1977-79; sr. quality assurance engr. Ark. Nuclear One, Russellville, 1979-90, nuclear safety and licensing specialist, 1990—. Author: Quality Surveillance Handbook, 1991; contbr. articles to Am. Nuclear Soc., Am. Soc. Quality Control. Lt. London (Ark.) Rural Vol. Fire Dept., 1985-95. Mem. Am. Nuclear Soc., Am. Soc. Quality Control (cert. quality engr. 1982, vice chair quality verification subcom., 1988-90, chair bylaws com. 1990). Baptist. Home: 780 Bowen Estates Rd Russellville AR 72801-9553

COOPER, SHARON P., epidemiologist, educator. BA in Psychology, U. Tex., 1973; MS in Quantitative Psychology, U. Okla., 1975; MS in Biostatistics/Epidemiology, Harvard Sch. Pub. Health, 1976; PhD in Epidemiology, U. Tex. Sch. Pub. Health, 1982. Rsch. asst. New Eng. Life Ins. Co., 1975; faculty assoc. dept. biometry U. Tex., Houston, 1976-79; faculty assoc. epidemiology rsch. unit U. Tex. Sch. Pub. Health, Houston, 1979-81, sr. rsch. assoc., 1983, faculty assoc. epidemiology rsch. unit, 1984-85, rsch. asst. prof. epidemiology rsch. unit, 1985-88, asst. prof. epidemiology, 1988-90; vis. scholar U. Houston, 1992-93; asst. prof. epidemiology U. Tex. Sch. Pub. Health, Houston, 1990-94, assoc. prof. epidemiology, 1995—. Contbr. numerous articles to profl. jours. Mem. nursing rsch. liaison com. U. Tex.-M.D. Anderson Cancer Ctr., 1986-88; mem. sci. adv. com. Tex. Dept. Health, 1987-88; chair rsch. com., asst. coord. Greater Houston Coalition for Safe Kids, 1989-91; mem. Human Health Risk Work Group, State of Tex. Environ. Priorities Project, 1993-94. Recipient USPHS traineeship Harvard Sch. Pub. Health, 1975-76, USPHS traineeship U. Tex., 1981-82, Harriet Cunningham citation for Meritorious Sci. Writing, 1988, 89, Outstanding Faculty award U. Tex. Health Sci. Ctr., 1992; grantee Nat. Ctr. for Health Stats., 1987-88, Nat. Heart, Lung and Blood Inst., 1989-91, Ctrs. for Disease Control, 1989-90, ICI Americas, Inc., 1990, 90-92, State of Tex. Legislature, 1992-93, Nat. Inst. Environ. Health Scis., 1929-94, Nat. Cancer Inst., 1995-96. Mem. Soc. for Epidemiologic Rsch., Am. Pub. Health Assn., Tex. Pub. Health Assn., Soc. for Pediatric Epidemiologic Rsch., Am. Statis. Assn., Soc. for Clin. Trials, Nat. Drowning Prevention Network, Houston-Galveston Area Health Promotion Consortium, Am. Coll. Epidemiology, Phi Beta Kappa, Notable Women in Tex. Office: U Tex Sch Pub Health PO Box 20186 Houston TX 77225-0186

COOPER, STEVEN MARK, law educator; b. N.Y.C., Apr. 9, 1947; s. Fred Morris and Martha (Tieger) C.; divorced. BA, NYU, 1970; MS, N.Mex. Highlands U., 1973; MA, U. Calif., Santa Barbara, 1978; JD with honors, Rutgers U., 1985; LLM, Harvard U., 1990. Bar: N.J. 1985, U.S. Dist. Ct. N.J. 1985, N.Y. 1986. Pres., chief exec. officer RT, Inc., Bronx, N.Y., 1978-86; adj. prof. law sch. We. State U., San Diego, 1986-87, Nat. U., San Diego, 1988-89; assoc. prof. Tex. Wesleyan U. Sch. Law, Irving, Tex., 1990—; corp. assoc. Paul, Weiss, Rifkind, Wharton and Garrison, N.Y.C., 1985-86. Articles editor Rutgers Computer & Tech., 1984-85; sr. editor Harvard Jour. Law and Pub. Policy, 1984-85. Sustaining mem. Rep. Nat. Com. Mem. ABA, Federalist Soc. (founder, pres. Rutgers chpt., 1984). Home: 3009 Rustic Woods Dr Bedford TX 76021-4058 Office: 2535 E Grauwyler Rd Irving TX 75061-3410

COOPER, WILLIAM JAMES, transportation executive; b. Detroit, June 16, 1951; s. Earl James and Helen Marie (Nalevanko) C.; m. Sandra Ellen DeMott, Oct. 3, 1987; 1 child, Christopher Michael. BSCE, Mich. Tech. U., 1973; MSBA, Boston U., 1977. Engr.-in-tng, Mich. Project ofcr./sr. engr. Mil. Traffic Mgmt. Command Transp. Engring. Agy., Newport News, Va., 1979-87, chief, transp. analysis br., 1987-90, chief, ops. analysis divsn., 1990-94, chief, Systems Integration Divsn., 1994—; mem. exec. coun. Army Modeling and Simulation Office, Crystal City, Va., 1996—; mem. adv. coun. Internat. Maritime, Port Logistic Mgmt. Inst., Old Dominion U., Norfolk, Va., 1993—. Asst. scoutmaster Troop 123, Boy Scouts Am., Seaford, Va., 1995—. Capt. U.S. Army, 1973-79, Europe. Decorated Army Commendation medal, Joint Svc. Commendation medal, Exceptional Civilian Svc. medal. Mem. Nat. Def. Transp. Assn. (pres. regimental chpt. 1995—), Alumni Assn. Fed. Exec. Inst., Alumni Assn. U.S. Army War Coll. Republican. Episcopalian. Home: 104 Holt Cir Seaford VA 23696 Office: Mil Traffic Mgmt Command Transp Engring Agy 720 Thimble Shoals Blvd 130 Newport News VA 23606

COOPER, WILLIAM ROBERT, pulmonary physician, health facility administrator; b. Washington, Nov. 1, 1942; s. Harold Keim and Mary Frances (Reisner) C.; m. Eileen Taliaferro Farley, June 8, 1963; children: William Harvey, Lee Taliaferro, Siobhan Farley. BA cum laude, Yale U., 1965; postgrad., St. Mary's Sch. Medicine, London, 1968; MD, U. Va., 1969. Diplomate Am. Bd. Internal Medicine, subsplty. pulmonary diseases, subsplty. critical care medicine; lic. physician Va., Ohio, Fla. Intern Cleve. Met. Gen. Hosp.-Case Western Res. U., 1969-70, resident in medicine, 1970-71; resident in medicine U. Va. Hosp., Charlottesville, 1971-72, fellow in pulmonary disease, 1972-73; fellow in pulmonary disease Mt. Sinai Med. Ctr., Miami Beach, Fla., 1973-74; med. dir. respiratory therapy and pulmonary function lab. Virginia Beach (Va.) Gen. Hosp., 1974—, chmn. dept. medicine, 1975, chief of staff, 1977, pres. med. staff, 1979; pres. Pulmonary Medicine of Va. Beach, Inc., 1976—; mem. active staff Virginia Beach (Va.) Gen. Hosp. and Sentara Bayside Hosp., Virginia Beach; med. dir. respiratory therapy course Tidewater C.C., Virginia Beach, 1979. Contbr. articles to med. jours. and profl. confs. Nat. Tuberculosis and Respiratory Diseases fellow, 1972-73. Fellow ACP, Am. Coll. Chest Physicians (mem. com. on pulmonary rehab. 1976-78); mem. AMA, Am. Thoracic Soc., Am. Soc. Internal Medicine, Med. Soc. Va., Va. Lung Assn. (past bd. dirs. Southeastern divsn.), Va. Thoracic Soc., Nat. Assn. Med. Dirs. Respiratory Care, Virginia Beach Med. Soc., Alpha Omega Alpha. Roman Catholic. Office: 1008 First Colonial Rd Ste 103 Virginia Beach VA 23454-3002

COORDSEN, KAREN GAIL, medical/surgical nurse; b. Orlando, Fla., May 27, 1946; d. Russell P. Jr. and Joyce Gwendolyn (Davis) Sullivan; m. Robert Lee Coordsen, June 27, 1984; children: Wesley Aaron Aho, Candace Yvette Aho, Michelle Lynn Coordsen, Shawn Marie Coordsen. ADN, Brevard Community Coll., Cocoa, Fla., 1973; BSN with high honors, U. Fla., 1981. Staff nurse Holmes Regional Med. Ctr., Melbourne, Fla.; staff and charge nurse Shands Teaching Hosp., Gainesville, Fla. Recipient 2-yr. scholar award U. Fla. Mem. Fla. Nurses Assn. (chmn. coms. arrangements and scholastics, conf. com.), Sigma Theta Tau (Alpha Theta chpt.), Phi Kappa Phi, Phi Theta Kappa, Golden Key. Home: 3904 SW 102nd Way Gainesville FL 32607-4658

COORE, BILL, company executive. Owner, prin. Coore & Crenshaw, Inc. Address: 1800 Nueces St Austin TX 78701

COPELAND, DAWN G., English language educator; b. Manchester, Tenn., Sept. 22, 1961; d. Cecil Horace and Florence Marie (Farrell) Gibb; 1 child, Katy. AAS, Motlow State C.C., 1981; BS, Mid. Tenn. State U., 1984, MA, 1993. Cert. tchr. Tenn. Adult edn. instr. Tullahoma (Tenn.) City Schs., 1991-92; from writing ctr. instr., dir. to English instr. Motlow State C.C., Tullahoma, 1992—. Pres. Highland Rim Alzheimer's Assn., 1994-95, bd. dirs., 1993—; mem. PTA, Tullahoma, 1990—. Mem. Nat. Hist. Preservation Soc., AAUW, AAUP, MLA, Nat. Coun. Tchrs. English, Popular Culture Assn. South, South Ctrl. Conf. on Christianity and Lit. Office: Motlow State CC Motlow Coll Rd Tullahoma TN 37388

COPELAND, JOHN DEWAYNE, law educator; b. Wichita Falls, Tex., Apr. 9, 1950; s. Howard R. and Lorene (Sharp) C.; m. Vannette Sue Thomas, July 2, 1970; children: Aaron, Seth, Sarah. BA, U. Tex., Arlington, 1971; JD, So. Meth. U., 1974; LLM, U. Ark., 1986. Bar: Tex. 1974, Ark. 1986, U.S. Dist. Ct. (no. dist.) Tex. 1974, U.S. Dist. Ct. (ea. and we. dists.) Ark. 1986, U.S. Ct. Appeals (5th cir.) 1975, U.S. Ct. Appeals (8th cir.) 1987, U.S. Supreme Ct. 1979. Ptnr. Short & Copeland, Wichita Falls, 1974-76, Helton, Copeland & Southard, Wichita Falls, 1976-78, Oldham, Copeland & Barnard, Wichita Falls, 1978-81; mem. Russell, Tate & Gowan, Wichita Falls, 1981-84; assoc. Roy & Lambert, Springdale, Ark., 1985-88; vis. asst. prof. U. Ark. Sch. Law, Fayetteville, Ark., 1988-89; dir. and rsch. prof. law Nat. Ctr. for Agrl. Law Rsch. and Info., Fayetteville, Ark., 1989—; cons. environ. com. Nat. Pork Producers Coun., Des Moines, 1991—, Am. Meat Inst., Washington, 1994—, mem. environ. compliance com. Dairy Quality Assurance Bd. Author: Understanding the Farmers Comprehensive Personal Liability Policy, 1992, Recreational Access to Private Land: Liability Issues and Solutions, 1995; author book chpts.; contbr. articles to profl. jours. Legal advisor City Charter Revision Commn., Wichita Falls, 1976-77; bd. dirs. Wichita County Bar Assn., Wichita Falls, 1976-78, treas., 1978-79, dir. lawyer referral, 1982-84. Recipient grad. fellowship U. Ark. Sch. Law, 1984. Mem. ABA (vice chair agrl. law com. 1990-91), Am. Agril. Law Assn. Baptist. Home: 232 W Cleburn Fayetteville AR 72701 Office: Univ Ark Leflar Law Ctr Fayetteville AR 72701

COPELAND, KENTON LEONARD, personal financial advisor; b. Nacogdoches, Tex., May 22, 1963; s. Earl Leonard and Dixie Ann (Queen) C.; m. Jennifer Shirley MacNaughton, June 7, 1986; children: Stephen K., Grace M. BBA cum laude, Tex. A&M U., 1985. CPA, Tex. CPA Ernst & Young, Austin, Tex., 1985-88, San Antonio, 1988-91; contr. Fairchild Aircraft Inc., San Antonio, 1991-93; pers. fin. advisor Am. Express Fin. Advisors, San Antonio, 1993—. Stewardship com. Episcopal Diocese of West Tex., 1995—; vestry St. Thomas Episcopal Ch., treas. 1992-94, Sunday sch. tchr., lay reader 1990—; bd. dirs. Respite Care of San Antonio, treas. 1990-93. Mem. AICPA, Tex. Soc. of CPAs, San Antonio Chpt. of CPAs, San Antonio A&M Club, Lupus Found. of Am. (South Tex. chpt. treas. 1996—). Home: 14715 Kinsem San Antonio TX 78248 Office: 10101 Reunion Pl Ste 100 San Antonio TX 78216

COPELAND, ROBERT MICHAEL, mechanical engineer; b. Crossette, Ark., Oct. 30, 1963; s. Robert F. and Virginia A. (Boseman) C.; m. Shana Michelle Whittington, July 11, 1987; 1 child, Taylor Michael. BSME, La. State U., 1987. Svc. tech. Hunt Engine, Inc., Harvey, La., 1979-86; design engr. McDonnell Douglas Aircraft, Long Beach, Calif., 1988-90; liaison engr. Gen. Dynamics Corp., Ft. Worth, 1990-91; chief engr. Hunt Engine, Inc., Houston, 1991—. Block capt. Sugarland (Tex.) Cmty. Assn. Crime Watch, 1993—. Mem. ASME. Office: Hunt Engine Inc 14805 Main St Houston TX 77035-6412

COPELAND, SUZANNE JOHNSON, real estate executive; b. Chgo., Aug. 1; d. John Berger and Eleanor (Dreger) Johnson; m. John Robert Copeland, Aug. 1, 1971 (div. June 1976). Assoc. French Lang. and Culture, Richland Coll., Dallas, 1974; BFA, Ill. Wesleyan U., Bloomington, 1965. Commercial artist Barney Donley Studio, Inc., Chgo., 1966-69; art dir. Levines Dept. Store, Dallas, 1970-74; creative dir. Titche-Goettinger, Inc., Dallas, 1974-78; catering mgr. Dunfey Hotel, Dallas, 1978-82; regional dir. corp. sales Lakeway/World of Tennis Resort, Austin, Tex., 1982-84; real estate sales assoc. Henry S. Miller, Dallas, 1984-86; v.p. Exclusive Properties Internat., Inc., Dallas, 1986—; cons. North Tex. Commn., Dallas, 1988. Acquisitions editor: Unser, An American Family Portrait, 1988. Mem. The Rep. Forum, Dallas, 1983-94; vol. Stars for Children, Dallas, 1988, Soc. for Prevention of Cruelty to Animals, Dallas, 1973-92, Preservation of Animal World Soc., 1986-92, Sedona Acad., 1996—, Sedona Human Soc., 1996—; charter mem. P.M. League Dallas Mus. Art. Mem. Nat. Assn. Realtors, Tex. Assn. Realtors, Greater Dallas Assn. Realtors (com. chmn., Summit award 1984, 85), North Tex. Arabian Horse Club (bd. dirs. 1975-76, Pres.'s award 1978), Dallas Zool. Soc., Humane Soc. Dallas County (v.p. 1973-74), Humane Soc. U.S./Gulf States Humane Edn. Assn. (bd. dirs. 1990-91), Am. Montessori Soc., Sedona Humane Soc., Sedona Acad., Delta Phi Delta, Phi Theta Kappa. Lutheran. Office: Exclusive Properties 5025 Capitol Ave Dallas TX 75206-6934

COPEN, MARK JAY, internist; b. N.Y.C., May 23, 1947; s. Harry and Claire (Greif) C.; m. Janet Ellen Kopp, Aug. 27, 1978; children: Harley, Howard. BA in Psychology, U. Pa., 1969; MD, SUNY-Downstate, 1973. Dir. emergency med. svcs. L.I. Jewish-Hillside Med. Ctr., New Hyde Park, N.Y., 1977-80; pvt. practice Ft. Lauderdale, Fla., 1980-96; physician specializing in primary care medicine TENET-Northridge Hosp., Ft. Lauderdale, 1993—; cons. med. quality and peer rev. State of Fla. Profl. Rev. Orgn., Ft. Lauderdale, 1985—. Mem. ACP, Am. Soc. Internal Medicine, Fla. Med. Assn., Broward County Med. Assn. Office: Northridge Hosp-TENET Healthcare 6550 N Federal Hwy Fort Lauderdale FL 33308-1404

COPLEY, EDWARD ALVIN, lawyer; b. Memphis, Jan. 17, 1936; s. Edward Alvin and Ethel Marie (Fooshee) C.; m. Connie James Patterson, Nov. 17, 1990; children: Julie, Ward, Drew, Kelly, Zeke. BA, So. Meth. U., 1957, JD, 1960. Bar: U.S. Dist. Ct. (no. dist.) Tex., U.S. Ct. Claims 1962, U.S. Supreme Ct. 1963, U.S. Tax Ct. 1966, U.S. Ct. Appeals (5th cir.) 1968. Atty. U.S. Dept. Justice, Washington, 1960-64, Ft. Worth, 1964-66; assoc. Akin, Gump, Strauss, Hauer & Feld, Dallas, 1966-67, ptnr., 1968—. Mem. ushering com., benevolence com. Highland Park Presbyn. Ch., Dallas, 1982. Fellow Am. Coll. Probate Counsel; mem. Dallas Bar Assn. (tax sect.), Dallas Estate Coun. (pres. 1975-76), So. Meth. U. Law Sch. Alumni Assn. (pres. 1978-79), Salesmanship Club (legal counsel 1984), Order of Woolsac, Barristers, Phi Alpha Delta, Dallas Petroleum Club. Clubs: Northwood Country, Dallas (pres.). Home: 3711 Shenandoah St Dallas TX 75205-2120 Office: Akin Gump Strauss Hauer & Feld 1700 Pacific Ave Dallas TX 75201-7322

COPLEY, STEPHEN JEAN, minister; b. Lawton, Okla., Oct. 13, 1961; s. Albert Jean and Mary Lou (Carnes) C.; m. Judith Ann Wallace, May 18, 1966. BA, U. Ctrl. Ark., 1984; MDiv, So. Meth. U., 1995. Minister Lamar Circuit United Meth. Ch., Barnesville, Ga., 1985-86; youth dir. Nashville (Ark) U. Meth. Ch., 1986; minister Prestwich (Eng.) Whitefield Circuit, 1986-87; youth minister Woodstock (Ga.) United Meth. Ch., 1987-88; minister Lamar/Mount Olive United Meth. Ch., 1988-89; asst. dir. Luton Indsl. Coll., Luton, Eng., 1989-92; minister Horatio (Ark.)/Winthrop United Meth. Ch., 1992—; bd. dirs. Atlanta Clerty and Laity Concerned, 1985-86, Inst. Indsl. and Comml. Ministries, 1988-89, Meth. Fedn. for Social Action, 1993; mem. Little Rock Conf.-United Meth. Ch. Bd. Global Ministries, 1993—; co-founder, dir. Ouachita Regional Enterprise Fund, 1995-96. Senator Ga. Jaycees Legislature, 1985; chair Ga. Jaycees-Multiple Sclerosis, 1985-86, Dem. Party. Com. Abroad, U.K., 1992; commr. Sevier County Housing Authority, 1993—; chaplain Little River Hist. Soc., 1992—, Sevier County Literacy Coun., 1992—, Horatio City Coun., 1995, Leadership Ark., 1995—, Ark. State Jaycees, 1993—; pres. Horatio Recreation Assn., 1993-95; bd. dirs. Little River C. of C., 1994; chmn. Horatio Parks Commn.; dep. chair Dem. Party, Ark., 1994—; mem. social affairs com. Ark. Interfaith Conf., 1996. Recipient Jaycees Young Outstanding Arkansas award, 1994; named Town and Country Pastor of Yr., United Meth. Rural Fellowship Hope Dist., 1993, 94. Mem. Am. Acad. Religion, Horatio Mchts. Assn., Sevier County C. of C., Little River C. of C., Horatio Lions Club (pres. 1994-95, zone chair 1995-97), DeQueen Rotary Club, Little Rock Civitan Club, Young Dems. of Ark. (v.p. fin.). Home: 1920 Pecan St Ashdown AR 71822

COPPENS, THOMAS ADRIAAN, retired pharmaceutical manufacturing executive; b. Rotterdam, Netherlands, Feb. 2, 1923; came to U.S., 1927; s. Philip Adriaan and Evelyn (van Capelle) C.; m. Sylvia Helen Scofield, Feb. 26, 1944; children: Laura Kathryn, Carole Elizabeth, John Philip, Barbara Helen. Student, McGill U., 1941-43, Lafayette Coll., 1944; D LL (hon.), Inst. Applied Rsch., London, 1973. Internat. rep. Sharp & Dohme, Inc., Mediterranean area, 1946-52; mng. dir. Merck, Sharp & Dohme, Manila, 1952-57; v.p. Merck & Co., Inc., Rahway, N.J., 1957-77; pres. Merck, Sharp & Dohme, BV, Haarlem, Netherlands, 1977-82; cons. Merck & Co., Inc., Rahway, 1982-84; prin. Camelot Antiques, Cooperstown, N.Y., 1984-90. Contbr. articles to profl. publs. Sr. warden St. Andrews Episcopal Ch., Harrington Park, N.J., 1958-67; bd. dirs. Hubbard Farms, Walpole, N.H., 1975-77, Walden U., Naples, Fla., 1984-96; trustee Naples Cmty. Hosp., 1988-94; mem. Collier County (Fla.) Emergency Med. Svcs. Adv. Coun., 1993-95. Decorated Purple Heart. Mem. Rotary (Paul Harris fellow), Am. C. of C. of Hague, Netherlands (bd. dirs. 1977-83). Home and Office: 6075 Pelican Bay Blvd Naples FL 34108

COPPER, MICHAEL STEVEN, computer scientist, educator; b. Winchester, Ind., Oct. 14, 1947; s. Paul Eugene and Elsie Annalee (Fischer) C.; m. Sylvia Ann Sullivan, Apr. 16, 1992; children by previous marriage: Annalee M., Richard D. BA, U. Ala., Tuscaloosa, 1977; MS, U. So. Miss., 1985. 2nd lt. U.S. Army, 1977, advanced through grades to maj., 1988; ops. officer 252D Signa Co., New Ulm, Germany, 1978-79, co. comdr., 1980-81; adjutant 69th Signal Bn., Augsburg, Germany, 1979-80; instr. 3395 TCHTG, Keesler AFB, Miss., 1981-85; retired U.S. Army, 1993; chief Pentagon Network Control The Pentagon, Washington, 1986-90; chief network surveillance control ctr. NATO, Belgium, 1990-92; info. sys. officer U.S. Army, Ft. McClellan, Ala., 1992-93; asst. prof. computer sci. U. Mobile, Ala., 1993—. Vol. Balwin County Spl. Olympics, Fairhope, Ala., 1994. Decorated Army Commendation medals, meritorious svc. medal, Air Force Commendation medal, Vietnam Cross of Gallantry, Air Force Master Instr. Mem. VFW, Ret. Officers Assn., Am. Radio Relay League, Data Processing Mgmt. Assn. (bd. dirs. 1993—), Masons, Scottish Rite. Republican. Home: 31014 Wellington Ct Spanish Fort AL 36527

COPPING, ALLEN ANTHONY, university president; b. New Orleans, Feb. 11, 1927; s. Allen J. and Marie (Burns) C.; m. Betty Hatrel, Aug. 9, 1949; children: Lisette, Cherie, Allen. DDS, Loyola U., New Orleans, 1949. Assoc. dean Sch. Dentistry La. State U., New Orleans, 1971-74; dean La. State U., 1974, chancellor Med. Ctr., 1974-85; pres. La. State Univ. System, 1985—, prof. dept. fixed prosthodontics, 1971—; pres. adv. bd. La. Health and Human Resources Adminstrn., 1973-80; bd. adminstrs. Charity Hosp., New Orleans. Served with USNR, 1949-54. Fellow Acad. Gen. Dentistry (Albert L. Borish Meml. award 1977), Internat. Coll. Dentists, Am. Coll. Dentists, Royal Soc. Health (London); mem. Am. Coll. Dentistry, ADA, New Orleans Dental Soc., Blue Key, Omicron Kappa Upsilon. Office: La State U System 3810 W Lakeshore Dr Rm 107 Baton Rouge LA 70808-4600*

COPPINGER, FRAN DONALSON, civic worker; b. Glen Rose, Tex., Apr. 25, 1938; d. Thomas Kyle and Alice Lucille (Martin) Donalson; m. Finice David Breedlove, Jr., Jan. 7, 1956 (div. 1959); m. Christopher Victor Coppinger, Oct. 11, 1970 (dec. Mar. 1995); 1 child, Celeste Elaine Coppinger Carlton. BA, U. Houston, 1975, postgrad., 1992; MA, U. Houston-Clearlake, 1986; ABD, U. Houston, 1994. Mem. Pearland (Tex.) City Coun., 1978-81; mem., v.p. Tex. Ethics Commn., Austin, 1991—; mem., past pres. mcpl. solid waste mgmt. adv. coun. Tex. Natural Resources and Conservation Commn., Austin, 1984—; bd. dirs. Keep Tex. Beautiful, Austin, 1992—; mem. adv. coun. U. Houston Environ. Inst., 1994—; v.p. Houston-Galveston Area Solid Waste Task Force; founder, bd. dirs., past pres. Clean Pearland, 1981—, Pearland Neighborhood Ctr., 1987-88; mem. Leadership Tex., 1993; also others. Named Woman of Yr., Am. Bus. Women's Assn., Pearland, 1982, Citizen of Yr., Pearland C. of C., 1984; recipient W.D. Colegrove ann. award Keep Brazoria County Beautiful Assn., 1984, outstanding vol. award United Way Brazoria County, 1988. Republican. Methodist. Home: 2111 Galveston Ave Pearland TX 77581-3423

COPULSKY, LEWIS, marketing professional; b. N.Y.C., May 22, 1958; s. William and Ruth (Brody) C.; m. Doreen Clark, Sept. 27, 1981; children: Benjamin, Daniel. BA, Bard Coll., 1979; MFA, Rutgers U., 1983. Rsch. asst. Response Analysis, Princeton, N.J., 1979-81; v.p. Jersey Cow Software, Princeton, N.J., 1982-86; ptnr. Lewis & Clark Assocs., Raleigh, N.C., 1986-90; pres. Lewis & Clark Rsch., Raleigh, N.C., 1991—. Author: (computer software) French for Computer, 1982, Spanish for Computer, 1983, Fishies, 1984, Mountains and Crustal Movement, 1986; pub. (newsletter) Jewish Ties, 1989-91. Bd. dirs. The Ctr. for Community in the Workplace, 1991-92, Jewish Community Sch. of Wake County, 1991-92. Mem. Carolina Direct Mktg. Assn. (founding bd. dirs. 1994-95), Am. Mktg. Assn. (pres. Triangle chpt. 1996). Jewish. Office: Lewis and Clark Rsch 6040 Six Forks Rd # A Raleigh NC 27609-8601

COPULSKY, WILLIAM, chemical company executive; b. Zhitomir, Ukraine, Apr. 4, 1922; s. Boris and Betty (Bruman) C.; came to U.S., 1923, naturalized, 1929; B.A., N.Y. U., 1942, Ph.D., 1957; m. Ruth B. Brody, Dec. 26, 1948; children—Stephen, Jonathan, Lewis. Chemist, Ammeco Chem. Co., Rochester, N.Y., 1942; asst. research dir. J.J. Berliner Co., N.Y.C., 1946-48; research dir. R. S. Aries and Assos., N.Y.C., 1948-51; comml. dir. W.R. Grace and Co., N.Y.C., 1951-74, v.p. operations services group, 1974-86; prof. mktg. Baruch Coll., City Univ., N.Y., 1987-92. Served with AUS, 1942-46. Mem. Am. Chem. Soc., Chemists Club, Beta Gamma Sigma. Author: Marketing Chemical Products, 1948; Forecasting Chemical Commodity Demand, 1962; Practical Sales Forecasting, 1970; Entrepreneurship and the Corporation, 1974. Home: 9520 Prince George Ln Apt B Raleigh NC 27615-2814 Office: Lewis & Clark Rsch 8711-102 Six Forks Rd Ste 123 Raleigh NC 27615-2968

CORBAT, PATRICIA LESLIE, special education educator; b. Washington, Feb. 28; d. Kenneth Lee and Stella Mary (Brey) C.; m. Noah Hughes Palmer IV, Aug. 16, 1975 (div.). BA, Coll. William and Mary, Williamsburg, Va., 1975, MEd, 1981. cert. learning disabilities/diagnostic prescriptive tchr. Learning disabilities resource/spl. edn. educator Virginia Beach (Va.) City Pub. Schs., 1981—; sec. spl. edn. eligibility com. Virginia Beach City Schs., 1981-87, chmn. gifted and talented selection com., 1985-86. Del. Va. State Dem. Conv., Norfolk, 1984, Roanoke, 1992; lobbyist Va. Gen. Assembly, Richmond, 1985; mem. Virginia Beach City Dem. Com., 1985-86; bd. dirs. Art and Company, Virginia Beach Ctr. for the Arts, 1993—, sec., 1994, treas. 1995—. Mem. Virginia Beach Reading Coun., Virginia Beach Ctr. for the Arts, Virginia Beach Edn. Assn. (rep. 1982-85, del. Va. state conv. 1983-84, city coun. contact person polit. action com. 1983-85). Office: Virginia Beach City Schs Mcpl Ctr 2512 George Mason Dr Virginia Beach VA 23456-3400

CORBETT, JAMES OTHO, industrial instrumentation company executive; b. Eustis, Fla., Dec. 31, 1945; s. Olan Dewitt and Dorothea Audrey (Davis) C.; m. Patricia Patrick (div.); 1 child, James; m. Mary Huskey (div.); 1 child, Shannon; m. Carol L. Getty, Mar. 9, 1970; children: Scott, Dolly, Darlene. Wireman Electron Michine Corp., Umatilla, Fla., 1968-69; field svc. technician Electron Machine Corp., Umatilla, Fla., 1969-70, engring. technician, 1970-71, project engr., 1971-72, prodn. mgr., 1972-73, v.p., chief engr., 1973-74, v.p. rsch. and devel., 1975—. Patentee stock consistency transmitters, concentricity gauge, carbon dioxide monitor, inventor refractometers. Mem. Instrument Soc. Am., Tech. Assn. of the Pulp & Paper Industry. Republican. Mem. Ch. of Christ. Office: Electron Machine Corp 1500 W Ocala St Umatilla FL 32784

CORBETT, LENORA MEADE, community college educator; b. Reidsville, N.C., Aug. 1, 1950; children: Kenneth Russell Johnson, Ralph Nathaniel Brown. AAS in Electromechanics, Tech. Coll. of Alamance, 1985, AAS in Electronics, 1986; BS in Indsl. Tech., Electronics, N.C. A&T State U., 1996. Cloth inspector Burlington (N.C.) Industries, 1971-74; electrician's helper Williams Electric, Greensboro, N.C., 1978, Nobility Mobile Homes, Reidsville, N.C., 1979; instr. math. and physics Alamance C.C., Graham, N.C., 1985—, chmn. learning resources, 1993. Contbr. poems to profl. publs. (Golden Poet award 1991, Merit award 1990, 92). Mem. sr. choir Jones Cross Rd. Ch., Reidsville, 1988-94, pastor's aide mem., 1988-90, jr. Sunday sch. tchr., 1989-91, asst. choir sec., 1988-94. Mem. AAUP, Alamance C.C. Alumni Assn., Golden Key. Baptist. Office: Alamance CC 1247 Jimmie Kerr Rd Graham NC 27253

CORBETT, WILLIAM PAUL, history educator, historian, consultant; b. Clarion, Pa., Nov. 19, 1948; s. Samuel Paul and Marybelle (Calhoun) C.; m. Mariam Jean Grimm, May 14, 1983; 1 child, Benjamin Chester William. BS in Edn., Clarion State Coll., 1970; MA in History, U. S.D., 1976; PhD in History, Okla. State U., 1982. Tchr. Forest Area Schs., Tionesta, Pa., 1974, Clarion-Limestone H.S., Strattanville, Pa., 1975; tutor hist. dept. U. S.D., Vermillion, 1975-76; grad. teaching fellow Okla. State U., Stillwater, 1976-80; instr. social scis. No. Okla. Coll., Tonkawa, 1980-88, dir. divsn. soc. scis., 1986-88; asst. prof. history Northeastern State U., Tahlequah, Okla., 1988-93, chair dept. history, 1990—, assoc. prof. history, 1993—. Author: Oklahoma Passage: The Telecourse Study Guide, 1991; contbr. chpts. to books and articles to profl. jours. Chmn. bldg. com. Tonkawa Pub. Libr., 1985-88, bd. dirs., 1985-88; bd. dirs. Honey Springs Battlefield Park Assn., Checotah, Okla., 1992—. With USN, 1970-74. Recipient Jefferson Davis award United Daus. of the Confederacy, 1979, Albert S. Pike Literary award Sons of Confederate Vets., 1980; Gilbert Fite scholar U. S.D., 1976, Okla. Found. for the Humanities scholar, 1982—. Mem. Okla. Hist. Soc. (bd. dirs. 1994—, chair hist. sites com. 1990—, mem. com. 1992-93, Indian heritage com. 1995—, commendation 1991, Muriel H. Wright award 1981), Okla. Assn. Profl. Historians (pres. 1995-96), Western History Assn., Kiwanis (Tonkawa, pres. 1981-82), Phi Alpha Theta. Office: Northeastern State U Dept History Tahlequah OK 74464

CORBIN, ARNOLD, marketing educator, management consultant; b. Bklyn., Feb. 16, 1911; s. Harris and Sonia (Kadish) Kowarsky; m. Claire Rothenberg, Aug. 22, 1937; children—Lee Harrison, Karen Sue. BS summa cum laude, Harvard U., 1931, MBA with distinction, 1934; PhD, NYU, 1954. Research specialist, buyer R.H. Macy & Co., N.Y.C., 1934-39; buyer, merchandiser L. Bamberger & Co., Newark, 1939-40; pres., owner Corbin Foods, N.Y.C., 1946-47; chief technologist U.S. Army Q.M.C., Inspection Service, N.Y.C., 1947-49; lectr., asst. prof. Baruch Sch. Bus. and Pub. Adminstrn., City U., N.Y.C., 1947-54; ptnr. Corbin Assocs., Delray Beach, Fla., 1949—; assoc. prof. NYU Sch. Commerce, Accounts and Finance, 1954-55, assoc. prof. Grad. Sch. Bus. Adminstrn., 1954-57, prof., 1957-76, prof. emeritus, 1976—; dir. Yardley of London, Inc., 1972-74; co-founder, dir. L.I. Comml. Rev., 1954-57; Mem. Brit. Exports Mktg. Adv. Com., 1965-68; mem. nat. mktg. adv. com. U.S. Dept. Commerce, 1967-72. Author: (with John W. Wingate) Changing Patterns in Retailing, 1956, Bibliography of Graduate Theses in Marketing, 1957, (with Hector Lazo) Management in Marketing, 1961, (with George Blagowidow and Claire Corbin) Decision Exercises in Marketing, 1964, (with Claire Corbin) Implementing the Marketing Concept, 1973; Contbr. chpts. to handbooks, textbooks, articles to encys. and profl. jours. Served with AUS, 1940-46. Frederick Sheldon traveling fellow, 1931-32; Ford Found. fellow, 1960. Mem. Am. Mktg. Assn. (dir. N.Y. chpt. 1960-63, nat. dir. 1963-65, v.p. mktg. edn. 1966-67, pres. 1975-76), NYU Grad. Sch. Bus. Alumni Assn. (dir. 1961-67), Am. Arbitration Assn., Phi Beta Kappa, Beta Gamma Sigma, Eta Mu Pi, Mu Kappa Tau, Alpha Delta Sigma. Home and Office: 6350 Timberlakes Way Delray Beach FL 33484-3576

CORBIN, CLAIRE (MRS. ARNOLD CORBIN), marketing educator; b. N.Y.C., July 16, 1913; d. Herman and Anna (Kessler) Rothenberg; m. Arnold Corbin, Aug. 22, 1937; children: Lee Harrison, Karen Sue. B.S., NYU, 1933, M.S., 1941, Ph.D., 1956, postdoctoral, 1957-60; postdoctoral, Yeshiva U., 1957-60. Sales trainee Namm Store, N.Y.C., 1929-30; mdse. trainee Macys, N.Y.C., 1930-32, buyer, 1939-40; mdse. trainee Gimbels, 1932-33; owner The Guildery gifts, N.Y.C., 1944-45; dir. sales tng. Loft Candy Corp., N.Y.C., 1945-46; ptnr. Corbin Assos., Delray Beach, Fla., 1949—; dir. promotion and tng. Decorative Fabrics Inst., N.Y.C., 1948-57; dir. Women's group activities MBS, WOR-TV, N.Y.C., 1948-58; prof. mktg. emeritus Coll. Bus. Adminstrn., Fordham U., Bronx, 1957—; mem. faculty Hofstra U., 1949-57, L.I. U., 1939-44, Baruch Sch., CUNY, 1946-49, Hunter Coll., 1946-47. Editor: Haire Publ., N.Y.C., 1933-39, Two to Six, N.Y.C., 1946-47, Today's Woman, N.Y.C., 1947-48; co-author: Principles of Retailing, 1955, Principles of Advertising, 1963, Decisions Exercises in Marketing, 1964, New Trends In American Marketing, 1965, Implementing the Marketing Concept, 1973; contbr. to: Handbook of Marketing Management, 1973. Namm scholar, 1929-33; N.Y. State Regents scholar, 1929-33. Mem. AAUP (sec.-treas. 1961-71), AAUW (chmn. mass media 1967-68), Am. Mktg. Assn. (sec.-treas. 1970-73), Am. Acad. Advt. (nat. fin. com. chmn. 1966-67), Advt. Women N.Y., Am. Soc. Interior Designers, Publ. Club N.Y., Nat. Home Fashions League (v.p. 1955-56), Beta Gamma Sigma, Eta Mu Pi, Kappa Delta Pi, Pi Lambda Theta, Gamma Alpha Chi. Home and Office: 6350 Timberlakes Way Delray Beach FL 33484-3576

CORBIN, DIB, state supreme court justice. Justice Ark. Supreme Ct., Little Rock. Office: Justice Bldg 625 Marshall Little Rock AR 72201

CORBIN, RENEE PERRY, university administrator; b. Asheville, N.C., Jan. 29, 1961; d. John Kenneth and Nancy Jane Norris Perry; m. James Edward Corbin, Oct. 20, 1979; 1 child, Courtney Elyse. BSBA, We. Carolina U., 1983, MBA, 1990. Computer programmer Western Carolina U., Cullowhee, 1984-91, coord. of undergrad. assessment, 1991—. Named to Outstanding Young Women of Am., 1986; recipient Young Careerist award Bus. and Profl. Women, Jackson County, 1987. Mem. N.C. Assn. Instl. Rsch. (treas. 1990-92), Am. Assn. Higher Edn. Office: Western Carolina Univ 570 Hfr Bldg Cullowhee NC 28723

CORBITT, DORIS ORENE, real estate agent, dietitian; b. Warrior, Ala., Oct. 25, 1929; d. Olen J. and Begie Pernie (Motte) Florence; m. Wallace R. Cornett, Nov. 29, 1952 (div. 1980); children: Wallace R. Jr., Kris J., Brett T.; m. Weldon Plant Corbitt, Jr., Apr. 21, 1984. BS in Dietetics, Maryville Coll., 1950; postgrad., Duke U., 1950-51. Registered dietitian; lic. real estate agt., Fla. Asst. dir. dietary St. Mary's Hosp., Knoxville, 1952-53; dir. dietary Soldier and Sailor Sch. for Children, Bloomington, Ill., 1966-68; tchr. Nashville Area Vocat. Sch., 1971-73; dir. dietary Westside Hosp., Nashville, 1973-79, Meml. Hosp., Tampa, Fla., 1980-85; realtor assoc. Coldwell Banker, Tampa, 1986—; Spkr. in field. Devel. original curriculum for Food Svc. Workers and Suprs., Tenn.; co-author first diet manual for Nashville Dietetic Assn.; pioneer in devel. of low-sodium programs for hypertensive patients at Westside Hosp. for outpatients, devel. of first pulmonary outpatient nutritional care program at Meml. Hosp., Tampa. Sec. Galleria Homeowners Assn., Tampa, 1986-87; Sunday sch. tchr. Recipient Internat. Citizenship award, 1995, and nobility status and title "The Honourable", 1996, both from Prince Kevin of Australia. Mem. Am. Dietetic Assn., Tampa Dietetic Assn., Tampa Bd. Realtors, Million Dollar Club. Republican. Mem. Ch. of Christ. Home: 11515 Galleria Dr Tampa FL 33624-4752 Office: Coldwell Banker Residential Real Estate Inc 14007 N Dale Mabry Hwy Tampa FL 33618-2401

CORCORAN-CRAMB, ELIZABETH HECHT, marketing and market research company executive; b. Balt., May 6, 1952; d. Alan D. and Margaret (Moses) Hecht; m. Daniel G. Corcoran, June 2, 1976 (div. June 1980); 1 child, Daniel Ted; m. Edwin R. Cramb, Apr. 27, 1989; 1 child, Andrew Alexander Cramb. BA, Northwestern U., 1973; MPH, U. Mich., 1974. Adminstr. Community Health of South Dade, Inc., Miami, Fla., 1975-77; tchr. Key Largo (Fla.) Elem. Sch., 1978-79; intern LIFELAB divsn. New World Ctr. campus Miami-Dade C.C., Miami, 1979; rsch. assoc. Ctr. Social Rsch. Aging, Coll. Arts and Scis. U. Miami, Coral Gables, Fla., 1979-86, 82-86; with biostats. divsn. dept. epidemiology and pub. health U. Miami, Miami, 1979-82; ptnr., co-founder ON TARGET SURVEYS, Miami, 1986-87; pres., owner EMITS, Inc. (Exec. Mgmt. Info. and Tech. Svcs.), Miami, 1984-92, EMITS, Inc., Clearwater, Fla., 1992—; presenter in field. Contbr. articles to profl. jours. Mem. APHA, Am. Mktg. Assn., So. Gerontol. Soc. Scientologist. Office: EMITS Inc PO Box 156 Clearwater FL 34617-0156

CORDELL, BEULAH FAYE, English language educator; b. Clifty, Ark., Mar. 5, 1939; m. Jack Cordell; children: Dennis, Kevin. B in English and Social Studies, U. Ark., 1987, M in Spl. Edn. and Reading, 1994. Cert. tchr. K-12, Ark. Tchr. Benton County Alternative Sch., Rogers, Ark., 1988-90, JTPA at Fayetteville, Ark., 1990-91, Northwest Ark. Cmty. Coll., Rogers, 1991-94; dir. spl. edn. tutoring The One-Room Sch., Springdale, 1993—; kindergarten tchr. Springdale, 1994—; tchr. ESL and GED Northwest Tech. Inst., 1996—. Mem. bd. dirs. Ozark Literacy, Inc., Fayetteville, 1984-90; pres., v.p., treas. Jones Elem. Sch. PTA, Springdale; den mother, scout coord. Boy Scouts Am., Springdale; contbg. mem. Beaver Lake Lit., Inc., Rogers, 1994—. Mem. Coun. for Exceptional Children, Am. Assn. Mentally Retarded, Poets and Writers Assn. Home: Rt 6 Box 173 Springdale AR 74764

CORDELL, FRANCIS MERRITT, instrument engineer, consultant; b. South Pittsburg, Tenn., Sept. 11, 1932; s. Lucien Hall and Sara Frances (Taliaferro) C.; m. Olivia Elizabeth West, June 17, 1950; 1 child, Francis Merritt Jr. LittB, Hamilton Coll., 1966; PhD in Physics, U. Del., 1973. Low speed code operator Dept. Army, Ft. Devens, Mass., 1949-52; materials tester TVA, Stevenson, Ala., 1952-53; instrument mechanic TVA, Stevenson, 1953-57, sr. instrument mechanic, 1957-80, instrumentation supr., 1980-86; prin. restorer, telescope and observatory project U. of the South, Sewanee, Tenn., 1982—; info. cons. South Pittsburg, 1980—; mem. Tenn. Vis. Scientists Program, Associated Univs. for the Tenn. Acad. Sci., Oak Ridge, 1989—. contbng. writer Barnard Astronomical Soc. Jour., 1973—. Recipient Llewellyn Evans award Barnard Astronomical Soc., Chattanooga, 1983. Mem. AAAS, Barnard Astronomical Soc., Instrument Soc. Am., Tenn. Acad. Sci., Astronomical Soc. Pacific. Home: Medius Lodge Dogwood Trail South Pittsburg TN 37380 Office: Info Consulting 1018 Holly Ave South Pittsburg TN 37380-1432

CORDER, BILLIE FARMER, clinical psychologist, artist; b. Dundee, Miss., Sept. 12, 1934; d. Lee Kennith and Jimmy Louise (Hawkins) Farmer; B.S., Memphis State U., 1957; M.A., Vanderbilt U., 1959; Ed.D., U. Ky., 1966; student Memphis Acad. Art, 1959, Sch. Design, N.C. State U., 1971-75; m. Robert Floyd Corder, July 11, 1961. Intern, U. Tenn. Sch. Medicine, Memphis, 1959; staff psychologist Eastern State Hosp., Lexington, Ky., 1960-65, Child Guidance Clinic, Lexington, 1965-67; asst. prof. psychology Inter-Am. U., P.R., 1967-68; dir. psychology adolescent day care Area Community Mental Health Center, Washington, 1968-70; dir. psychol. services Alcoholic Rehab. Center, Butner, N.C., 1970-71; co-dir. psychol. services in child psychiatry Dix Hosp., Raleigh, N.C., 1971—; mem. adv. bd. Raleigh Developmental Evaluation Clinic, 1976-80; adj. faculty psychology dept. N.C. State U., Raleigh, 1975—, U. N.C. Sch. Medicine, 1975—. Mem. Wake County Youth Adv. Bd., 1979-80; mem. adv. com. Raleigh Arts Commn., 1980-82; bd. dirs. Haven House for Children, 1980-85, Nazareth House for Children, 1980-85. Recipient best research award N.C. Dept. Mental Health, 1965, cert. of appreciation Washington Tchrs. Assn., 1969, Outstanding Youth Svcs. award Wake Coun., 1991; numerous awards for art, including Purchase award N.C. Mus. Art, 1976, awards N.C. Watercolor Soc., 1978, 79; numerous research grants. Mem. Am. Psychol. Assn., Southeastern Psychol. Assn., N.C. Psychol. Assn., Am. Assn. Psychiat. Services for Children (program chmn. 1976-77), Raleigh Artists Guild (pres.), Raleigh Fine Arts Soc., N.C. Art Soc., Women's Equity Action League, N.C. Women's Polit. Caucus, Durham Artists Guild, N.C. Watercolor Soc. (v.p.), Wake Visual Artists Assn. (pres.), AAUW. Democrat. Baptist. Contbr. articles to profl. jours.; dir. editorial bd. N.C. Jour. Mental Health, 1974—; adj. editorial rev. bd. Hosp. and Community Psychiatry, Quar. Jour. Studies on Alcohol, Raleigh Acad. Women, 1993. Office: Child Psychiatry Clinic Dix Hospital Raleigh NC 27611

CORDES, JAMES F., gas transmission company executive; b. 1940. BS, St. Louis U., 1963; MBA, Creighton U., 1968; MS, U. Nebr., 1976. Indsl. engr. A.E. Staley Mfg. Co., Decatur, Ill., 1963-65; ops. rsch. analyst No. Natural Gas Co., 1965-66, mgr. mgmt. systems, 1967-72, mgr. mktg. ops., 1972-77; with ANR Pipeline Co., Detroit, 1977—, now chmn., pres., chief exec. officer; also exec. v.p., pres. natural gas group The Coastal Corp., Houston, 1986. Office: Am Natural Resources Co 500 Renaissance Ctr Detroit MI 48243-1901 also: Coastal Corp 9 E Greenway Plz Houston TX 77046

CORDOVA, MARIA ASUNCION, dentist; b. Punta Arenas, Magallanes, Chile, May 14, 1941; came to U.S., 1972; d. Miguel Cordova and Maria Asucion Requena; m. Carlos F. Salinas, July 27, 1963; children: Carlos M., Claudio A., Lola. DDS, U. Chile, Santiago, 1965; DMD, Med. U. S.C., 1986. From instr. to assoc. prof. medicine U. Chile Dept. Physiology, Valparaiso, 1965-72; postdoctoral fellow Johns Hopkins U., Balt., 1972-75; from instr. to asst. prof. M.U. S.C. Dept. Physiology, Charleston, 1975-86; pvt. practice Charleston, 1987—; vis. scientist N.Y. Med. Coll., 1975. Contbr. articles to profl. jours. Program coord. Circulo Hispanic Charleston; coord. Amnesty Internat. U.S.A., Spoleto, Neighborday, Charleston, S.C.; bd. dirs. YWCA; active NOW. Mem. Charleston Women's Network (pres. 1989-90). Roman Catholic. Office: 159 Wentworth St Charleston SC 29401-1731

CORELL, ROBERT WALDEN, science administration educator; b. Detroit, Nov. 4, 1934; s. George W. and Grace (Hagland) C.; m. Billie Jo Proctor, June 16, 1956; children: Robert Walden, David Richard, Beth Anne. BSME, Case Inst. Tech., 1956; MS, MIT, 1959, PhD, 1964. Engr. GE, Cleve., 1955, program engr., Lynn, Mass., 1956-57; instr. U. N.H., 1957-58, asst. prof., 1959-60, assoc. prof., 1964-66, prof., 1966-90, chmn. dept. mech. engring., 1964-72, dir. marine program, 1975-87; asst. dir. geoscis. NSF, Arlington, Va., 1987—; rsch. engr. Huggins Hosp., Wolfeboro, N.H., 1957-60, Highland View Hosp., Cleve., 1960-64; vis. investigator Woods Hole Oceanographic Inst., 1965; rsch. assoc., vis. prof. Scripps Instn. Oceanography, 1971-72; vis. prof. U. Wash., 1985; chair U.S. Global Change Rsch. Com. of U.S. Govt., 1987—; numerous positions as chair of interagy. sci. coms. and internat. bodies. Contbr. articles to profl. jours. Founding chair Internat. Group of Funding Agencies for Global Change Rsch., 1988-90; chair Implementation Com. for Inter-Am. Inst. for Global Change Rsch., 1992—; dir. White House Conf. on Sci. and Econs. to Global Change Rsch., 1990. Mem. AAAS, Sigma Xi, Tau Beta Pi, Sigma Alpha Epsilon. Mem. AAAS, Am. Soc. Engring. Edn., IEEE, Marine Tech. Soc., Sigma Xi, Tau Beta Pi, Sigma Alpha Epsilon. Home: # 2L 7008 Channel Village Ct # 2L Annapolis MD 21403-5322 Office: NSF Geosciences 4201 Wilson Blvd Arlington VA 22203-1803

CORENFLOS, LORI COOPER, illustrator, graphic artist; b. Jonesboro, Ark., May 9, 1956; d. John Thomas and Vivian Jo (Green) Cooper; m. Jerry T. Corenflos, Aug. 16, 1987. BFA, NLU, 1978. Art dir. KTBS TV-Channel 3, Shreveport, La., 1978-81; freelance graphics/illustrator Shreveport, 1981-87, Nashville, 1987—. Author: Iris's Irises, 1995, Iris's Viruses, 1996; illustrator (book covers) Jake and the Heavenly Host, 1995, The Adventures of Lily and Her Old Fool, 1994, Oconee Dream Catcher, 1995, (cover art) The Nashville Scene, 1996; one-person shows include N.E. La. U. Art Dept., Monroe, La., 1977-78, Bastrop (La.) Nat. Bank, 1981; pet portrait artist, 1994—. Book reader La Vergne (Tenn.) Pub. Libr., 1995. Recipient Purchase prize Wesley Found., N.E. La. U., Monroe, 1978. Home: 500 Jerald Smith Ln La Vergne TN 37086

COREY, CHARLES WILLIAM, investment banker; b. Ridgewood, N.J., Mar. 23, 1952; s. William Charles and Sallie (Burns) C.; m. Beth Perry, Jan. 26, 1975 (div. Mar. 1983); children: Jordice, Trevor. BS in Mktg. and Fin. Bus., Syracuse U., 1974. Sales office prods. div., IBM, N.Y.C., 1974-76; v.p. mktg. Credit Union div., Life Investors Co. of Am., Chattanooga, 1976-83; investment banker J.C. Bradford & Co., Chattanooga, 1983—. Fund raiser PBS, Chattanooga, 1989—; co-host Children's Mirical Telethon Network, Chattanooga, 1990-91. Mem. Walden Club. Republican. Presbyterian. Office: J C Bradford & Co 701 Broad St Chattanooga TN 37402-1899

COREY, KAY JANIS, business owner, designer, nurse; b. Detroit, Aug. 22, 1942; d. Alexander Michael Corey and Lillian Emiline (Stanley) Kilborn; divorced; children: Tonya Kay, William James, Jason Ronald. Student, C.S. Mott Community Coll., 1960-62, Mich. State U., 1962-64; AA, AS in Nursing, St. Petersburg Jr. Coll., 1978; student, U. South Fla., 1985-86. RN; cert. perioperative nurse; cert. varitypist. Mgr. display Lerner Shops, Flint, Mich., 1960-62; layout artist Abdulla Advt., Flint, 1966-67; varitypist, artist City Hall Print Shop, Flint, 1967-70; nurse Suncoast Hosp., Largo, Fla., 1976-78; nurse, coord. plastic surgery svc., perioperative staff nurse Largo Med. Ctr. Hosp., 1978-81, 84—; assoc. dir. nursing Roberts Home Health Svc., Pinellas Park, Fla., 1982-84; co-owner Sand Castle Resort, White Bay, Jost Van Dyke, Brit. Virgin Island, 1990-95; perioperative nurse Columbia Golf Coast Surgery Ctr., 1996—; designer, artist K.J. Originals clothing line, 1990-95; insvc. edn. instr., dir. video edn., team leader oncology dept. Largo Med. Ctr. Hosp., 1980-81, now part-time nurse. Editor, illustrator: (book) Some Questions and Answers About Chemotherapy, 1981, Thoughts for Today, 1981; illustrator (cookbooks) Spices and Spoons, 1982, Yom Tov Essen n' Fressen, 1983; various brochures and catalogues; art work in permanent collection of C.S. Mott Jr. Coll., Flint, 1962; artist, designer of casual and hand painted clothing for children and adults. Historian Am. Businesswomen's Assn., Flint, 1968-73 (scholarship 1976); outreach chmn. Temple B'nai Israel, Clearwater, Fla., 1981-85; regional outreach coord. Union of Am. Hebrew Congregations, N.Y.C., 1983-85. Mem. Assn. of Oper. Rm. Nurses, Phi Theta Kappa. Republican. Jewish. Office: Columbia Gulf Coast Surgery 411 2nd St E Bradenton FL 34208 also: 1500 53d Ave W Palmetto FL 34221-5510

CORLEY, CAROL LEE, school nurse; b. Waco, Tex., Feb. 2, 1943; d. Henry Lee (dec.) and Irma Geraldine (King) Cranfill; m. Thomas Lane Corley, May 22, 1965; 1 child, Christopher Lyn. ADN, McLennan C.C., 1974; BSN, U. Tex.-Arlington, 1983. Staff nurse ICU Providence Health Ctr., Waco, Tex., 1974; sch. nurse Crawford (Tex.) Ind. Sch. Dist., 1975-79; coord. sch. nurse Midway Ind. Sch. Dist., Waco, 1979—. Mem. ANA, Tex. Nurses Assn. (dist. 10 pres. 1992-94, past v.p.), Tex. Assn. Sch. Nurses (dist. 12 pres. 1990), Tex. Sch. Nurses Adminstrs. Assn., Sigma Theta Tau. Home: 8930 Raven Dr Waco TX 76712-3453

CORLEY, DONNA JEAN, education educator, language arts educator; b. LaGrande, Oreg., May 23, 1950; d. Donald D. and Aria Jean (Tufford) Wattenbarger; m. Bill H. Corley, June 12, 1970; children: Jason Andrew, Seth David. AA, Tulsa Jr. Coll., 1983; BS in Elem. Edn., Northeastern State U., Tahlequah, Okla., 1985, MEd in Elem. Edn., 1987; PhD, Tex. A&M U., 1990. Cert. tchr. grades K-8, gifted and talented, Tex. Substitute tchr. Broken Aroow (Okla.) Ind. Sch. Dist., 1983-85; tchr. 5th grade Southside Elem. Sch., Broken Arrow, Okla., 1985-87; coord. microteaching Tex. A&M U., College Station, lectr., 1987-90, tchr. lang. arts methods for the elem. tchr., 1990—; with gifted programs resource div. Conroe (Tex.) Independent Sch. Dist., 1993-94; adj. prof. human growth and devel. Sam Houston State U., Huntsville, Tex., 1994—; adj. prof. Sam Huston State U., Huntsville, Tex.; apptd. task force by Tex. Edn. Agy. to devel. guidelines for edn. of gifted learners in Tex., 1996; numerous presentations and insvcs. in field. Contbr. to profl. publs. Delta Kappa Gamma scholar, 1983, 84. Mem. NEA, ASCD, Broken Arrow Edn. Assn., Okla. Edn. Assn., Okla. Reading Coun., Kappa Delta Pi, Phi Theta Kappa, Rho Theta Sigma, Alpha Chi. Home: 639 S Rivershire Dr Conroe TX 77304-4903

CORLEY, FLORENCE FLEMING, history educator; b. Augusta, Ga., Jan. 6, 1933; d. William Cornelius and Sarah Virginia (Sibley) Fleming; m. James Weaver Corley, Jr., Dec. 29, 1955; children: Florence Hart Corley Johnson, James Weaver Corley III, Mary Anne Corley Herbert, Sarah Virginia Corley, William Thomas Corley. BA, Agnes Scott Coll., 1954; MA, Emory U., 1955; PhD, Ga. State U., 1985. Cert. tchr., T-5, Ga. Alumnae rep. Agnes Scott Coll., Decatur, Ga., 1955; history tchr. The Westminster Schs., Atlanta, 1968-88, The Walker Sch., Marietta, Ga., 1989; history instr. Kennesaw State U., Marietta, Ga., 1989-91, asst. prof. history, 1991—; U.S. history cons. The Coll. Bd., N.Y.C., 1978—; reader, table leader Ednl. Testing Svc., Princeton, N.J., 1975—. Assoc. editor: American Presbyterians, Phila., 1984—, Ga. Jour. of So. Legal History, Atlanta, 1989; editor: The Landmarker, 1978-79; author: Confederate City: Augusta, Georgia 1860-65, 1960, 74, 95, 1995; contbr. articles to hist. jours.; compiler (slides/tape) Where Were the Women? 1979. Sixth grade and adult tchr. First Presbyn. Ch., Marietta, 1960—, elder, 1990—; active U.S. history contest DAR, Marietta, 1991—; cons. Girls club of Cobb/Marietta 1981; mem. Ga. Nat. Registry Rev. Bd., 1994—, chmn. 1996-97. Woodrow Wilson fellow Emory U., 1954-55; recipient fellowship in women's history NEH, Stanford U., Palo Alto, Calif., 1978-79, scholarship in classical studies, Vergilian Soc., Cumae, Italy, 1982, scholarships in medieval Eng. and Eng. today, English Speaking Union, U.K., 1979, 80. Mem. Cobb Landmarks and Hist. Soc. (charter bd. dirs., co-pres. 1985-86, 87-88), Atlanta Hist. Soc., Atlanta Civil War Round Table, Soc. Civil War Historians, Ga. Assn. Historians, Ga. Hist. Soc., So. Assn. Women Historians, So. Hist. Assn., So. Garden History Soc., Richmond County Hist. Assn., Presbyn. Hist. Soc., Phi Beta Kappa, Phi Alpha Theta. Democrat. Home: 285 Kennesaw Ave Marietta GA 30060-1671 Office: Kennesaw State Coll 1000 Chastian Rd Kennesaw GA 30144-5591

CORLEY, ROSE ANN MCAFEE, customer service representative; b. Lawton, Okla., Aug. 21, 1952; d. Claude James and Mary Margaret (Holman) McAfee; m. Gary Michael Griffin, Feb. 14, 1973 (div. Oct. 1984); m. Terry Joe Corley, July 31, 1988; stepson Troy Justin Corley. BS, Cameron U., Lawton, Okla., 1970; diploma, Army Command and Staff Coll., Ft. Leavenworth, Kans., 1989; MCJA, Oklahoma City U., 1990; cert., Army Mgmt. Staff Coll., Ft. Belvoir, Va., 1991. Cert. in Distbn. Mgt. Supply clk. Dept. of Army, Ft. Sill, Okla., 1972-80, supply mgmt. asst., 1980-82; supply systems analyst Dept. of Army, Ft. Lee, Va., 1982; supply tech. Dept. of Army, Ft. Sill, Okla., 1982-83, supr. inventory mgmt. specialist, 1983-86, manprint program mgr., 1986-91; weapon system advisor Def. Logistics Agy., San Antonio, 1991-96; customer svc. rep. Def. Logistics Agy., Robins AFB, Ga., 1996—; equal employment counselor USA Field Artillery Sch., Ft. Sill, Okla., 1976-82; mentor Fed. Women's Program, Kelly AFB, Tex., 1991-96. Recipient Cert. of Appreciation, Sec. of Def., Washington, 1984, Cert. of Appreciation, Directorate of Engring. and Housing, Ft. Sill, 1986; decorated Order of St. Barbara, U.S. Army Arty. Sch., Ft. Sill, 1991. Mem. Fed. Women's Program, Soc. Logistics Engrs., Fed. Mgrs. Assn., Kelly Mgmt. Assn., World Affairs Coun. of San Antonio, Internat. City Mgmt. Assn., Tex. Corvette Assn. Home: 325 Kibbee St Hawkinsville GA 31036 Office: Def Logistics Agy 420 2nd St Bldg 301E Robins AFB GA 31098-1640

CORLISS, SANDRA IRENE, correctional health care professional; b. Nashua, N.H., June 9, 1949; d. Robert Henry Corliss and Elizabeth Juliette (Duffina) Knowles. Diploma in Nursing, Yoville Hosp., Cambridge, Mass., 1971; postgrad., Regents Coll., 1992—. LPN, Fla.; cert. BLS, corr. health profl., IV nurse, AIDS counselor, staff tng. officer. LPN staff nurse Yoville Hosp., Cambridge, Mass., 1972-73, Huntington Gen. Hosp., Brookline, Mass., 1973-76, Riverview Nursing Home, 1976-77, Cohassett Nursing Home, 1977-78, Rosary Hill, Hawthorne, N.Y., 1982-84, Humana Hosp. Pasco, Dade City, Fla., 1984-85, Pasco County Sheriff Office, Land-o-Lakes, Fla., 1985—. Cons. Sunrise of Pasco, Dade City, 1987—, sec. bd. dirs., 1990-92, pres. bd. dirs., 1992; cons. Oaks Royal Civic Assn., Zephyrhills, Fla., 1987—, social svcs. dir. subdivsn. III; bd. advisors Sunrise Domestic Violence Shelter, Dade City. Mem. Am. Jail Assn., Am. Correctional Health Svcs. Assn., Fla. Correctional Health Svcs. Assn., Nat. League of Nursing, Fla. Jail Assn., Cert. Correctional Health Profls. Republican. Roman Catholic. Home: 36440 Malibu Way Zephyrhills FL 33541-2060 Office: Pasco County Sheriff's Office 10200 Central Blvd Land O'Lakes FL 34639-7001

CORLL, VIVIAN ANN MORGAN, secondary education educator, writer; b. Brunswick, Ga., Feb. 12, 1940; d. John Thomas and Vivian Estelle (Helmey) Morgan; m. Paul Richard Corll, Aug. 5, 1961; children: Helen Marie, Mary Elaine. BA in English, Stetson U., 1961; MA in English, Ohio U., 1966. Cert. English, gifted, ESOL tchr., Fla. Grades 6-12 tchr. Broward County (Fla.) Sch. Bd., Ft. Lauderdale, 1961-94; writer Ft. Lauderdale, 1978—; owner, pub. instrnl. materials The Information Outlet, Ft. Lauderdale, 1994—, cons., 1996—; workshop presenter 7th Nat. Creative and Inventive Thinking Conf., Ft. Lauderdale, 1993, Fla. Coun. Tchrs. of English, Sarasota and Ft. Walton Beach, 1990, 92, Broward Sch. Bd., 1993. Author: Creating the Image: A Minicourse in Creative Writing, 1994; contbr. articles to profl. jours. Vol. judge Broward County Schs. Lit. Fair, 1994, 95, 96, Internat. Trades and Endangered Species Conv., Ft. Lauderdale, 1994, Nat. Coun. Tchrs. of English, 1990, Broward County Youth Fair, 1994. Mem. Fla. Freelance Writers Assn. (1st place article essay 1988), Soc. Children's Book Writers, Broward Coun. Tchrs. of English (exec. bd. 1989—, Muse award 1993, 94). Baptist. Home: 3681 NW 17th Ter Fort Lauderdale FL 33309

CORMACK, MALCOLM, museum curator; b. Birmingham, Eng., Dec. 6, 1935; came to U.S., 1976; s. Walter James and Alice (Share) C.; m. Lynn Kaddy, Sept. 22, 1958; children: Katherine Leonie Cormack Blossom, Sarah Harriet. BA in History of Art with honors, Courtauld Inst. Art, U. London, 1959; MA, U. Cambridge (Eng.), 1965. Asst. keeper Birmingham Mus. and Art Gallery, 1959-62; asst. keeper Fitzwilliam Mus., Cambridge, 1962-68, keeper paintings and drawings, 1968-76; curator of paintings Yale Ctr. for Brit. Art, New Haven, 1976-91; Paul Mellon curator Va. Mus. Fine Arts, Richmond, 1991—; adj. prof. Va. Commonwealth U., Richmond, 1992-95. Author: The Drawings of Watteau, 1971, Constable, 1986, The Paintings of Thomas Gainsborough, 1992, others; contbr. articles to profl. jours. Office: Va Mus Fine Arts 2800 Grove Ave Richmond VA 23221

CORMAN, JACK BERNARD, lawyer, investment manager; b. Hillsboro, Tex., Nov. 16, 1926; s. Maxwell A. and Lillie (Wood) C.; children from previous marriage: Michael, Catherine, Laura; m. Annette Adler, Sept. 1991. BBA, U. Tex., 1948, LLB, 1948. Bar: Tex. 1948. Assoc. Conway & Schaff, Waco, Tex., 1948-50; lawyer Stanolind Oil & Ins. Co., Ft. Worth, 1950-52; lawyer The Brit. Am. Oil Co., Dallas, 1952-56, gen. counsel, 1958-65; assoc. Carrington Gowan Law Firm, Dallas, 1956-58; assoc. gen. counsel Tenneco, Houston, 1965-66; pres. Opco Oil & Gas. Co., Dallas, 1966-70; pvt. practice Dallas, 1970—; bd. dirs. Forum Cos., Dallas, 1970—, Forum Oil and Gas. Co., Dallas, 1970—. 1st lt. U.S. Army, 1943-44. Home: 7364 Meadow Oaks Dr Dallas TX 75230-4227 Office: 10830 N Central Expy Ste 160 Dallas TX 75231-1022

CORMIA, FRANK HOWARD, industrial engineering administrator; b. Montreal, Que., Can., Nov. 17, 1936; s. Frank Edward Cormia and Elizabeth Kulp (Hall) St. Louis; m. Mary Irene Porter, Aug. 29, 1959; children: John Howard, Carl William, Ross Michael, Judith Anne. BS in Engring., Calif. Inst. Tech., 1960. Indsl. engr. Alcoa, Vernon, Calif., 1960-64; chief indsl. engr. Warrick ops. Alcoa, Evansville, Ind., 1968-76; mgr. indsl. engring. Tenn. ops. Alcoa, 1976-95; chief indsl. engr. Wear-ever Aluminum, Chillicothe, Ohio, 1964-68. Past chmn. bd. dirs. Sch. Indsl. Sys. Engring., Ga. Inst. Tech., Atlanta; bd. dirs., past chmn. dept. indsl. sys. engring. Va. Poly. Inst. and State U., Blacksburg; chmn. long range planning com. Smoky Mountain coun. Boy Scouts Am., 1988-89. 1st lt. USAR, N.G., 1960-66. Mem. Inst. Indsl. Engrs. (sr.). Episcopalian.

CORMIER, RAYMOND, humanities educator, author; b. Bridgeport, Conn., Nov. 23, 1938; s. Alphonse Joseph and Mary Helene (Wilinich) C.; m. Patricia Picard, June 9, 1960; children: Jean-Louis Joseph, Madelaine Hélène. AB, U. Bridgeport, Conn., 1956-60; AM, Stanford U., Calif., 1960-62; PhD, Harvard U., 1967; DLitt, U. Bridgeport, Conn., 1980. Secondary French cert., Pa., N.C. Teaching asst. Stanford (Calif.) U., 1960-62; teaching fellow Harvard U., 1963-67; instr. of French Tufts U., Medford, Mass., 1965-67; asst. prof. French U. Va., Charlottesville, 1967-72; assoc. prof., full prof. Temple U., Phila., 1973-84; vis. prof. Gettysburg Coll., Dickinson Coll., 1986-88; master tchr. Dartmouth Coll., 1983-94; prof. French, Humanities, English Wilson Coll., Chambersburg, Pa., 1984-94; instr. French Ctrl. Piedmont C.C., 1994-96; vis. prof. French Longwood Coll., 1996—; co-founder Internat. Courtly Lit. Soc., 1973. Author and contbr. articles to profl. jours., 1965—. Co-founder Capitol Film Soc., Chambersburg, Pa., 1990. Fulbright Sr. Rsch. grant, Western Europe, 1983-84; Fulbright Sr. Lectureship, Barcelona, Spain, 1992; grantee Am. Philos. Soc. Rsch., Rome, Vatican Libr., 1989. Mem. MLA, Med. Acad. Am., Am. Assn. Tchrs. of French, Internat. Arthurian Soc. Republican. Home: 2664 Oakhurst Dr Rock Hill SC 29732-9027

CORNELIUS, VICKI LYNN, middle school educator; b. Greensboro, N.C., Sept. 7, 1951; d. George Rankin and Betty Jean (Thompson) C.; m. Eduardo Ramon Fernandez, Mar. 29, 1980 (div. June 1984). BS in Edn., Western Carolina U., 1973, MA in Edn., 1975; edn. specialist, U. Miami, 1984; postgrad., U. Ga., 1992-93. Cert. educator K-12 reading, elem. 1-6, math 4-9, ESOL. Loan teller Coconut Grove Bank, Miami, Fla., 1973-74; math tchr. Palm Springs Jr. High, Hialeah, Fla., 1975-76; reading, math tchr. Campbell Drive Jr. High, Homestead, Fla., 1976-79, Homestead H.S., 1979-82, Dade County Schs.-Riviera Mid. Sch., Miami, 1982-95; curriculum coord./facilitator and reading/test chairperson Riviera Mid. Sch., 1995—. Choreographer, assoc. dir. Miami Christmas Pageant, 1984—. Mem. Internat. Reading Assn., Dade Reading Coun., Fellowship of Christian Athletes. Republican. Baptist. Home: 12714 SW 96th Ter Miami FL 33186-2356

CORNELIUS, WALTER FELIX, lawyer; b. Homewood, Ala., Apr. 20, 1922; s. William Felix and Nancy Ann (Cross) C.; m. Virginia Holliman, Jan. 30, 1942, (div. Feb. 1973); children: Nancy Carol, Susan Elaine; m. Lenora Black, May 4, 1974; 1 stepchild, Kristy Ann Wells. AB, Birmingham So. U., 1949; JD, U. Ala., 1953. Bar: Ala. 1953, U.S. Dist. Ct. (no. dist.) Ala. 1953, U.S. Tax Ct. 1954. Sole practice Birmingham, Ala., 1953—; bd. dirs. numerous corps., Birmingham. Elder, teacher Presbyn. Ch., Birmingham, 1963—; chmn. bd. dirs. Brother Bryan Mission, Birmingham, 1981—; pres. bd. trustees Cahaba Valley Fire and Medical Res. Dist., Shelby County, Ala., 1984—; mem. Horizon 280 Assn., Birmingham, 1985—. Served to cpl. USAAF, 1943-46, PTO. Recipient Pacific Theater Victory Med. award, Army Air Corps, Saipan and Iwo Jima, 1946. Mem. ABA, Ala. Bar Assn., Birmingham Bar Assn., Farrah Order Jurisprudence. Home: 1101 Dunnavant Valley Rd Birmingham AL 35242-6725 Office: 210 Frank Nelson Bldg Birmingham AL 35203

CORNELIUS-RATCLIFF, CINDY LEE, newspaper editor, photographer; b. Olney, Tex., Sept. 16, 1970; d. Albert Branden and Peggy Jean (Dutton) Cornelius; m. Jeffrey Mark Ratcliff, Dec. 30, 1995. BS in Journalism, Tex. A&M U., 1993. News editor The Graham (Tex.) Leader, 1994—. Publicity chmn. Graham Area United Way, 1994-95, 96-97. Recipient 1st place award for feature writing Tex. Press Assn., 1995, West Tex. Press Assn., 1995, North and East Tex. Press Assn., 1995. Mem. Graham C. of C., Kiwanis. Home: 1326 Indiana St Graham TX 76450

CORNELL, JENNIFER A., software company executive; b. Yonkers, N.Y., June 12, 1966; d. James Austin Grenzebach and Marilynn (Wicks) DiSalvo; m. Todd Curtis Cornell, May 21, 1994. BS in Commerce, U. Va., 1988; M of Mgmt., Northwestern U., 1992. Mgmt. cons. Alpha Chi Omega, Indpls., 1988-89, McKinsey & Co., Washington, 1989-91; sr. market analyst Dun & Bradstreet Software, Atlanta, 1992-94, sr. bus. analyst, 1994-95, global edn. mgr., 1995-96, account mgr., 1996—; nat. dir. collegiate programs Alpha Chi Omega, 1990-92, nat. dir. alumnae, 1992-94, province officer, 1989-91. Mem. St. James United Meth. Ch. Chancel Choir, 1993—; mentor DeKalb County Schs., 1994-96. Mem. Am. Mktg. Assn. Home: 5090 Firelight Ln Alpharetta GA 30202-7942 Office: Dun & Bradstreet Software 66 Perimeter Center E Atlanta GA 30346-1805

CORNELL, JESS MICHAEL, vascular surgeon, physician, medical educator; b. Lubbock, Tex., Aug. 25, 1943; s. Jess Milton and Harriet Sue (Davis) C.; m. Rebecca Elizabeth Madole, Dec. 30, 1966; children: Christopher Lee, Davis Van Ness. BA in Chemistry, Tex. Tech. U., 1965; MD, U. Tex. Southwestern U., Dallas, 1969. Diplomate Am. Bd. Surgery, Am. Bd. Vascular Surgery. Intern Parkland Meml. Hosp., 1969-70, resident, 1970-74; asst. clin. prof. surgery U. Tex. Southwestern U., Dallas and San Angelo, 1976-79, assoc. clin. prof. surgery, 1980-86, clin. prof. surgery, 1986—; pres. med. staff St. John's Hosp., San Angelo, 1978, Shannon Hosp., San Angelo, 1978-86, Concho Valley Regional Hosp., San Angelo, 1992. Bd. dirs. Hospice of San Angelo, 1985, San Angelo Mus. Fine Arts, 1989-92. Fellow ACS; mem. Tex. Med. Assn. (vice councilor dist. IV 1988—), Tex. Surg. Soc., Internat. Cardiovascular Soc., Southwestern Surg. Soc., Phi Eta Sigma, Alpha Omega Alpha. Presbyterian. Office: Ste 7 2030 Pulliam St San Angelo TX 76905-5157

CORNELL, PAUL JAMES, physician, consultant; b. New Orleans, La., June 9, 1935; s. Paul James and Anne Agatha (Saha) C.; m. Joann Louise Cope, Dec. 30, 1959; children: Michael, Elizabeth, Mark. BS in chem., Tulane Univ., 1957; MD, La. State Univ., 1961. Diplomate Am. Bd. Ob-Gyn. Intern Martin Army Hosp., Ft. Benning, Ga., 1961-62; resident obgyn William Beaumont General Hosp., El Paso, Tex., 1962-65; asst. prof. Univ. Ark., Little Rock, 1969-74; pvt. practice Little Rock, 1969—; ret., 1995. Dir. Ark. Found. Med. Care, 1978-88. With U.S. Army Med. Corps., 1961-68. Fellow Am. Coll. Ob-Gyn; mem. Pulaski County Medical Soc. (pres. 1979-80). Republican.

CORNETT, GREGG, newspaper publisher, newspaper editor, computer company executive; b. Dayton, Ohio, May 12, 1954. Pres. Computer Commuter, Batesville, Ark., 1982-87, Gregg Cornett Assocs., Batesville, Bald Knob, Searcy, Ark., 1984—; pub., editor Bald Knob Banner, 1987—; CEO G.C.A. Computer Svcs., 1993—; police photographer Bald Knob Police Dept., 1988—; computer cons. Gregg Cornett Assocs., 1984—, freelance journalist, Bald Knob, 1987—. Author (booklet) Neighborhood Crime Prevention, 1989; contbr. articles to newspapers. Area coord. City Crime Prevention, Bald Knob, 1988—; assoc. KARK-TV Community Network, Little Rock, 1990—; acting city clk. City of Bald Knob, 1991; rural community cons. City of Bald Knob, 1988—; founding bd. dirs. Rsch. Internat., Aruba. Recipient Better Newspaper Advt. award Ark. Press Assn., 1988; Gregg Cornett Day proclaimed by City of Bald Knob, 1990. Fellow Rotary; mem. C. of C. (bd. dirs. 1988—).

CORNISH, CHRISTOPHER SCOTT, secondary education educator; b. Ft. Worth, Tex., Aug. 8, 1967; s. William Ross and Bobbie Lee (Miller) C. A in physics (hon.), Tarrant County Jr. Coll., Ft. Worth, 1992; BS in geology, U. Tex., Arlington, 1994. Patron asst. Ft. Worth Pub. Libr., 1991-92; circulation clerk U. Tex. at Arlington Libr., 1992; cameraman, master control operator U. Tex. at Arlington Engring. TV, 1993-94; lab tchr. geology Stephen F. Austin State U., Nacogdoches, Tex., 1995—; staff mem., spkr. S.W. Assn. of STudent Geological Socs., 1995. Author short story and play. Precinct capt. Tarrant County Dem. Party, Ft. Worth, 1988; contbr. to 1995 auction Soc. for the Prevention of Cruelty to Animals, Dallas, 1995; contbr. mem. Dem. Nat. Com., Washington, 1996, Tex. Democratic Victory Fund, 1996. Rsch. grantee Geological Soc. of Am., 1996; scholar Shreveport Geological Soc., 1996. Mem. Am. Assn. of Petroleum Geologists (v.p. Stephen F. Austin State U. chpt.) Stephen F. Austin State U. Geological Students Assn., Stephen F. Austin State U. Young Democrats (treas.), Phi Theta Kappa, Sigma Gamma Epsilon Geological Scis. Hon. Soc. (pres. Stephen F. Austin State U. chpt.). Democrat. Home: 2614 N University Dr #60 Nacogdoches TX 75961 Office: Stephen F Austin State U Dept Geology 1936 North St Nacogdoches TX 75962

CORNYN, JOHN, state supreme court justice; b. Feb. 2, 1952; married; 2 children. BA, Trinity U., 1973; JD, St. Mary's U., 1977; postgrad., U. Va. Cert. personal injury trial law Tex. Bd. Legal Specialization. Justice Tex. Supreme Ct, Austin, 1991—; assoc., ptnr. Groce, Locke & Hebdon, San Antonio, 1977-84; judge 37th Dist. Ct., Bexer County, 1985-90; presiding judge 4th Adminstrv. Jud. Region, 1989-92; justice Supreme Ct. Tex., Austin, 1991—; Tex. Supreme Ct. liaison Bd. LAw Examiners, 1991—, Gender Bias Task Force, 1993-95; lectr. CLE programs. Bd. vis. Trinity U., Pepperdine U. Sch. Law. Fellow Tex. Bar Found., San Antonio Bar Found.; mem. Am. Law Inst., William Sessions Inn of Ct. (master bencher 1988-90, pres. 1989-90), Robert W. Calvent Inn of Ct. (pres. 1994-95). Office: Tex State Supreme Ct PO Box 12248 Austin TX 78711-2248 Home: 6302 Indian Canyon Dr Austin TX 78746*

CORONADO, SANTIAGO SYBERT (JIM CORONADO), judge; b. Laredo, Tex., Nov. 12, 1951; s. Bill Gee and Lucía (Coronado) Sybert. BA cum laude, U. Tex., 1974, JD, 1978. Bar: Tex. 1978. Pvt. practice Austin, Tex., 1979-89; mcpl. judge City of Austin, 1989-91, City of Kyle, Tex., 1989-91; assoc. judge Travis County Dist. Ct., 1991—. Bd. dirs. Am. Heart Assn., Austin, 1990; state pres. Mex. Am. Bar Assn., Tex., 1988-89; pres. Capital Area Mex. Am. Lawyers, Austin, 1986-87. Mem. Hispanic Nat. Bar Assn. (regional pres. 1989-90, nat. v.p. 1991-92), Travis County Bar Assn. (dir. 1995—). Democrat. Home: 5105 Saddle Cir Austin TX 78727-6728 Office: Travis County Ct House Austin TX 78701

CORONADO, WILLIAM J., controller. Contr. Universal Corp., Richmond, Va. Office: Universal Corp PO Box 25099 Richmond VA 23260

CORRALES, PATRICK, coach, former professional baseball manager; b. Los Angeles, Mar. 20, 1941; s. David and Josephine (Rivera) C.; m. Sharon Ann Grimes, Sept. 23, 1960 (dec. July 22, 1969); children: Rena M., Michele D., Patricia A., Jason P.; m. Donna Ardene Myers, Mar. 7, 1980; 1 son, Patrick David Parker. Grad., Fresno High Sch., Calif., 1959. Signed with Phila. Phillies, 1959, profl. baseball player, 1959-78; mgr. Tex. Rangers, Arlington, 1978-80, Phila. Phillies, 1982-83, Cleve. Indians, 1983-87; coach Am. League All-Stars, Seattle, 1979, Nat. League All-Stars, Chgo., 1983; coach Am. League All-Stars, Houston, 1986, Oakland, Calif., 1987; coach N.Y. Yankees, 1989-90, Atlanta Braves, 1990—; Nat. League All-Stars, Balt., 1993; all-star coach Nat. League, Balt., 1993. Holder Am. Karate Acad. Brown Belt. Democrat. Roman Catholic.

CORRELL, ALSTON DAYTON, JR., forest products company executive; b. Brunswick, Ga., Apr. 28, 1941; s. Alston Dayton and Elizabeth (Flippo) C.; m. Ada Lee Fulford, June 23, 1963; children: Alston Dayton, Elizabeth Lee. B.S.B.A., U. Ga., 1963; M.S. in Pulp and Paper Tech., U. Maine, 1966, M.S. in Chem. Engring., 1967. Pres. paperboard div. Mead Corp., Dayton, Ohio, 1977-80, pres. paperboard group, 1980, group v.p. paperboard, 1980, group v.p. paper, 1980-81, group v.p. forest products, 1981-83, sr. v.p. forest products, 1983-88; sr. v.p. pulp and printing paper Ga.-Pacific Corp., Atlanta, 1988-89, exec. v.p. pulp and paper, 1989-91, pres., COO, 1991-93, pres., CEO, 1993, CEO, chmn. bd., 1993—; dir. Ga. Kraft Co., Rome, Brunswick Pulp & Paper Co., Ga., Northwood Pulp & Timber Ltd., Prince George, B.C., Can., B.C. Forest Products Ltd., Vancouver; pres., CEO, dir. Gr. Nd. Nekoosa Corp.; pres. Mead Tumber Co. Bd. dirs. Atlanta Symphony Orch., Miami Valley (Ohio) Boy Scouts, Nature Conservancy, Keep Am. Beautiful Inc., Ga. Rsch. Alliance; trustee U. Ga. Found., Robert W. Woodruff Arts Ctr.; chmn. United Negro Coll. Fund, vice chmn. Atlanta Campaign; mem. Atlanta Action Forum; chmn. Ctrl. Atlanta Progress; bd. councilors The Carter Ctr. Recipient Nat. Brotherhood award, 1991, Disting. Alumnus award U. Ga., Terry Coll. Bus., 1994, Inst. Human Rels. award Am. Jewish Com., 1995; named one of 100 Most Influential Georgians, Ga. Trend Mag., 1994. Mem. Ga. C. of C. (bd. dirs.), Atlanta C. of C. (bd. dirs., Forward Atlanta Policy Group), Commerce Club (Atlanta, bd. dirs.). Republican. Presbyterian. Office: Ga-Pacific Corp PO Box 105605 133 Peachtree St NE Atlanta GA 30303-1847*

CORRELL, HELEN BUTTS, botanist, researcher; b. Providence, R.I., Apr. 24, 1907; d. George Lyman and Albertine Louise (Christiansen) B.; m. Donovan Stewart Correll (dec. 1983); children: Louise, Stewart, Selena, Charles; m. William Merton Carter, Oct. 10, 1992. AB, Brown U., 1928, AM, 1929; PhD, Duke U., 1934. Instr. Smith Coll., Northampton, Mass., 1929-31, Wellesley (Mass.) Coll., 1934-39; assoc. prof. U. Md., Towson, 1956; research assoc. Tex. Research Found., Renner, 1959-65, co-investigator aquatic plant research, 1966-71; collaborator, adjunct staff Fairchild Tropical Garden, Miami, Fla., 1973-93. Co-author: Aquatic and Wetland Plants of the Southwestern United States, 1972, 2d edit. 1975, Flora of the Bahama Archipelago, 1982; editor: Wright Botanical Jour., 1959-63; contbr. articles to profl. jours. Chmn. Libr. Bd., Richardson, Tex., 1965-70; bd. dirs. East Ridge Retirement Village, 1992-94. Recipient disting. alumna citation Brown U., 1983, Marjory Stoneman Douglas award Fla. Native Plant Soc., 1985, medal for Individual Achievement in Horticulture award Fla. Fedn. Garden Clubs, Inc, 1992. Mem. Soc. Women Geographers, Friends of Fairchild (v.p. 1986-87, pres. 1987-89), Altrusa (officer 1964-71), Phi Beta Kappa, Sigma Xi. Congregationalist. Home: 216 E Ridge Village Dr Miami FL 33157-8090

CORRENTI, JOHN DAVID, steel company executive; b. Rochester, N.Y., Apr. 1, 1947; s. Nicholas William and Sara Rita (Annalora) C.; m. Dawn Jane Major, Nov. 22, 1980; 1 child, Nicholas John. BCE, Clarkson U., 1969. Supr. of contrn. U.S. Steel, Pitts., 1969-80; v.p., gen. mgr. Nucor Corp., Plymouth, Utah, 1980-87, Nucor/Yamato Steel Co., Blytheville, Ark., 1987-91; pres., vice chmn., CEO Nucor Corp., Charlotte, N.C., 1993—.

CORRIGAN, HELEN GONZÁLEZ, cytologist; b. San Diego, Tex., Sept. 30, 1922; d. Rodrigo Simon and Eva Ruby (Corrigan) Gonzalez. BS, Our Lady of Lake, San Antonio, 1943. Tchr. San Diego High Sch., 1943-45; microbiologist Nix Hosp. Profl. Lab., San Antonio, 1952-59; med. technologist Tucson Med. Ctr., 1959-60; cytologist in charge Jackson-Todd Cancer Detection Ctr., San Antonio, 1961-64; cytologist in charge cytology sect. Pathology Lab. 4th and 5th U.S. Army Ref. Area Lab., Fort Sam Houston, Tex., 1964-78; instr. trouble shooters, quality control analyst cytology sect. Brooks Med. Ctr., Fort Sam Houston, 1978-81; owner Corrigan Enterprises, San Diego, 1981-91; cytologist Waco (Tex. Med. Lab. Svc., 1988-89, Nat. Health Lab., San Antonio, 1989-90, Internat. Cancer Screening Lab., San Antonio, 1990-91; head cytologist Dr. R. Garza & Assocs., Weslaco, Tex., 1992—. Adv. bd. mem. EEO, Ft. Sam Houston, 1972-74. Mem. NAFE, Am. Soc. Clin. Pathologists (assoc.), Greater San Antonio Women's C. of C. Republican. Roman Catholic. Home: 149 Perry Ct San Antonio TX 78209-6211

CORRIGAN, JAMES JOHN, JR., pediatrician, dean; b. Pitts., Aug. 28, 1935; s. James John and Rita Mary (Grimes) C.; m. Carolyn Virginia Long, July 2, 1960; children: Jeffrey James, Nancy Carolyn. B.S., Juniata Coll., Huntingdon, Pa., 1957; M.D. with honors, U. Pitts., 1961. Diplomate: Am. Bd. Pediatrics (hematology-oncology). Intern, then resident in pediatrics U. Colo. Med. Center, 1961-64; trainee in pediatric hematology-oncology U. Ill. Med. Center, 1964-66; asso. in pediatrics Emory U. Med. Sch., 1966-67; asst. prof. Emory U. Med. Sch., Atlanta, 1967-71; mem. faculty U. Ariz. Coll. Medicine, Tucson, 1971-90; prof. pediatrics U. Ariz. Coll. Medicine, 1974-90; chief sect. pediatric hematology-ongology, also dir. Mountain States Regional Hemophilia Center, U. Ariz., Tucson, 1978-90; chief of staff U. Med. Ctr. U. Ariz., Tucson, 1984-86; prof. pediatrics, vice dean for acad. affairs Tulane U. Sch. Medicine, New Orleans, 1990-93, interim dean, 1993-94, dean, 1994—. Assoc. editor Am. Jour. Diseases of Children, 1981-89, 90-93, interim editor, 1993; contbr. numerous papers to med. jours. Grantee NIH, Mountain States Regional Hemophilia Ctr., Ga. Heart Assn., GE, Am. Cancer Soc. Mem. Am. Acad. Pediatrics, Am. Soc. Hematology, Soc. Pediatric Rsch., Western Soc. Pediatric Rsch., Am. Heart Assn. (coun. thrombosis), Internat. Soc. Thrombosis and Haemostasis, Am. Pediatric Soc., World Fedn. Hemophilia, Pima County Med. Assn. (v.p., 1986—, pres. 1988—), Alpha Omega Alpha. Republican. Roman Catholic. Office: Tulane U Sch Medicine Office of Dean 1430 Tulane Ave New Orleans LA 70112-2699

CORRIGAN, LYNDA DYANN, banker; b. Selmer, Tenn., Nov. 24, 1949; d. A. Sammuel and Eunice (Burks) Davis. BBA, Mid. Tenn. State U., 1978; MBA, U. Tenn., 1979; JD, Nashville Sch. Law, 1984. CPA, Tenn.; bar: Tenn. 1985. Sr. v.p. First Am. Corp., Nashville, 1980—; faculty Am. Inst. Banking, Nashville, 1982—; mem. Nat. Panel Consumer Arbitrators, Nashville, 1985-87. Pres. Buddies of Nashville, 1985, adv. bd., 1986—; treas. Mid.-East Tenn. Arthritis Found., Nashville, 1982-85, Floyd Cramer Celebrity Golf Tournament, Nashville, 1981-84; bd. dirs. Nashville, 1981-84; bd. dirs. Nashville Br. Arthritis Found., 1980-87. Named Instr. of Yr. Am. Inst. Banking, 1994; recipient Leadership award Mid.-East Tenn. Arthritis Found., 1985, Gold award Jr. Chamber, 1981. Mem. ABA (mem. tax com. 1987—), Nashville Bar Assn. (mem. tax com. 1986—, vice chmn. tax sect. 1989, chair tax sect. 1990), Tenn. Taxpayers and Mfrs. Assn. (mem. tax com. 1986—), Tenn. Soc. CPA's. Home: 806 Fountainhead Ct Brentwood TN 37027-5833

CORRIPIO, ARMANDO BENITO, chemical engineering educator; b. Mantua, Cuba, Mar. 6, 1941; came to U.S., 1961; s. Bernardo Manuel and Maria Teresa (Pedraja) C.; m. Consuelo Lucia Careaga, June 9, 1962; children: Consuelo T., Bernardo M., Mary A., Michael G. BChemE, La. State U., 1963, MChemE, 1967, PhD, 1970. Registered profl. engr., La. Systems engr. Dow Chem. Co., Plaquemine, La., 1963-68; instr. La. State U., Baton Rouge, 1968-70, asst. prof., 1970-74, Disting. Faculty fellow, 1974, assoc. prof., 1974-81, prof. dept. chem. engring., 1981—; pvt. cons., 1968—; vis. engr. MIT, Cambridge, 1978-79. Author: Tuning of Industrial Control Systems, 1990; co-author: Automatic Process Control, 1985; contbr. numerous articles to profl. jours. Chmn. St. George Bd. Edn., Baton Rouge, 1975-77; lector St. Aloysius Cath. Ch., Baton Rouge, 1989—. Recipient Excellence in Instrn. award Exxon Co., 1986, Excellence in Teaching award Dow Chem. Co., 1989. Fellow Am. Inst. Chem. Engrs. (instr. 1977-87, chmn. Baton Rouge sect. 1990, Charles E. Coates Meml. award with Am. Chem. Soc. 1990); mem. Instrument Soc. Am. (sr. mem.; instr. 1977—), Tau Beta Pi, Phi Lambda Upsilon, Phi Kappa Phi, Sigma Xi. Home: 9344 Bermuda Ave Baton Rouge LA 70810-1121 Office: La State Univ Dept of Chem Engring Baton Rouge LA 70803

CORRIPIO AHUMADA, ERNESTO CARDINAL, retired archbishop; b. Tampico, Mexico, June 29, 1919. Ordained priest Roman Catholic Ch., 1942. Aux. bishop, Zapara, Mex. 1953; named bishop of Tampico, 1956, of Artequera, 1967, of Puebla de los Angeles, 1976; archibishop of Mexico City, primate of Mex., 1977-94, archbishop emeritus, 1994—, created cardinal, 1979; tchr. sem., Tampico, 1945-50. Address: care Curia Arzobispal, Apdo Postal 24-433, Mexico City 06700, Mexico*

CORRY, BARBARA PRATHER, developmental center administrator; b. Jackson, Miss., Oct. 3, 1943; d. Sidney E. and Mattie (Miles) McDaniel; m. Louis G. Prather, June 24, 1961 (div. Dec. 1991); children: Lisa Prather Koencny, Michael Prather, Daniel Prather; m. Robert Steven Corry, Nov. 16, 1992; children: Michael, David, Paul. BS in Edn., U. Cin., 1974; MS in Adminstrn., Xavier U., 1978; PhD in Ednl. Leadership, U. Miss., 1996. Spl. edn. tchr. Little Miami Sch. Dist., Lebanon, Ohio, 1974-77; work-study coord. Warren County Sch. Dist., Cin., 1977-78; PhD in Ednl. Leadership U. Miss., Little Rock, 1996; exec. dir. Willowood Devel. Ctr., Jackson, 1981—; spkr., trainer State Activities for Developmentally Disabled, Miss., 1990—; Americorp nat. trainer, 1995—. Recipient Woman of Achievement award Sales and Mktg. Execs., 1992, Disting. Svc. award Nat. Coun. on Disability, 1992. Mem. Miss. Devel. Disability Planning Coun. Southern Baptist. Office: Willowood Devel Ctr 1635 Boling St Jackson MS 39213-4418

CORSERI, GARY STEVEN, writer, educator; b. N.Y.C., Mar. 31, 1946; s. Casper and Estelle (Kaplan) C.; m. Yoko Kagawa, May 28, 1982. BA cum laude, U. Fla., 1967; MAT, Harvard U., 1969; PhD, Fla. State U., 1988. English tchr. Wayland (Mass.) H.S., 1968-69, A.P. Giannini Jr. H.S., San Francisco, 1969-70; instr. English U. Fla., Gainesville, 1971-74, Atlanta Metro Coll., 1976-77; vis. poet, sr. lectr. Hokusei Gakuen Coll., Sapporo, Japan, 1978-81; lectr. in English Aoyama Gakuin U., Tokyo, 1984-86; vis. asst. prof. Ga. So. Coll., Americus, 1988-89; asst. editor Fla. Quar., Gainesville, 1966-67; poetry editor The Atlanta Gazette, 1977-78; pub. rels. cons. Japanese C. of C., Atlanta, 1990—; contbr. Contemporary Authors, Detroit, 1996. Author: (poetry) Random Descent, 1989; librettist (opera) Reverend Everyman, 1990; playwrite: None Are So Blind, Top of the Mountain; contbr. to N.Y. Times, Village Voice, Ga. Rev., City Lights Rev., Bloomsbury Rev., Poetry N.W. Recipient 1st prize Stephen Vincent Benét Narrative Poem Contest, Poet Lore, 1972, 1st prize poetry contest Fla. Arts Coun., 1975; Fla. State U. fellow, 1986, 87, 88, Ga. Poetry Circuit Reading fellow Ga. Coun. for Arts and Humanities, 1989, fellow Va. Ctr. for the Creative Arts, 1994; Tennessee Williams scholar Sewanee Writers' Conf., 1990. Mem. Assoc. Writing Programs, Phi Beta Kappa, Phi Delta Kappa. Taoist. Home: 2455 Kingsland Dr Atlanta GA 30360

CORTA, NANCY RUTH, nurse; b. Gorman, Tex., Feb. 15, 1957; d. Dale Newton and Perelene Ruth (Wright) Johnson; 1 child, Joseph Henry Johnson. BSN, Tex. Woman's U., Denton, 1980. Staff nurse Baylor U. Med. Ctr., Dallas, 1980-81; charge nurse ICU/CCU DeLeon Hosp., Tex., 1981-82; staff nurse MICU/CCU VA Med. Ctr., Phoenix, 1982-83; staff nurse Harris Hosp. Meth., Ft. Worth, 1983-84, Tex. Dept. Health, Stephenville, 1984-95; nurse Dublin Ind. Sch. Dist., 1995—. Mem. Tex. Women's U. Alumni Assn., Epsilon Sigma Alpha. Lodge: Order Eastern Star. Home: Rt 2 Box 192 De Leon TX 76444 Office: 701 Thomas Dublin TX 76446

CORTEGUERA, HOMERO JOSEPH, psychiatrist; b. Sancti Spiritus, Cuba, June 28, 1930; came to U.S., 1957; s. Joseph Maria and Natalia (Jimenez) C.; m. Sarah Dominga Villalon, Sept. 18, 1955; children: Rosemarie, Joseph Richard, Charles. MD, Havana (Cuba) U., 1954. Diplomate Am. Bd. Psychiatry and Neurology. Postgrad. fellow Menninger Clinic, Topeka, 1964-66; asst. clin. dir. Menatl Health Ctr., West Palm Beach, Fla., 1966-67; staff psychiatrist Henderson Clinic, Ft. Lauderdale, Fla., 1967-68, Sheppard-Enoch Pratt Hosp., Balt., 1968-69; chief psychiatrist North Chicago VAH, Downey, Ill., 1969-72; clin. dir. Coral Ridge Psychiat. Hosp., Ft. Lauderdale, 1972-77; clin. dir. South Fla. State Hosp., Hollywood, 1977-78, sr. psychiatrist, 1978-93; dir. psychiatry 19th St. CRISIS, Ft. Lauderdale, 1993—; clin. prof. psychiatry dept. Northwestern U. Med. Sch., Chgo., 1969-72, U. Miami (Fla.) Med. Sch., 1978—. Scholar U. Havana, 1956. Mem. AMA, Am. Psychiat. Assn., Fla. Med. Soc., Fla. Psychiat. Soc., N.Y. Acad. Scis., Broward County Med. Soc., Broward County Psychiat. Soc., Menninger Alumni Assn. Roman Catholic. Office: 204 Washingtonia Ave Fort Lauderdale FL 33308-3622

CORTEZ, MARTIN LYNN, assistant principal; b. Sept. 11, 1945; s. Alcide A. and Edna (Robichaux) C.; m. Anne Rita Bourgeois, 1971. BA, Nicholls State U., 1969, MEd in Adminstrn. and Supervision, 1978, postgrad., 1981-85, 89. Tchr. 6th grade Raceland (La.) Upper Elem. Sch., 1969-74, tchr. 8th grade, 1977-94, asst. prin., 1994; asst. prin. Bayou Blue Elem., Houma, La., 1994—; co-owner Winner's Circle Trophy Shop, Raceland, 1978—. Chmn. Lafourche Parish (La.) Social Studies Fair, 1988-93; mem. Lafourche Parish Schs. Textbook Adoption Com., 1992—; mem. Model Career Option Plan, 1992-93. Mem. Music Assn. Bayou Cajuns, Cajun French Music Assn. (past nat. pres.). Home: 225 Louise Dr Raceland LA 70394-3811 Office: Bayou Blue Elem 1916 Bayou Blue Rd Houma LA 70364-3905

CORTINA, RODOLFO JOSÉ, Spanish language educator, researcher, consultant; b. Guantanamo, Oriente, Cuba, Feb. 23, 1946; came to U.S., 1961; permanent resident, 1970; s. Rodolfo and Livia (Gomez) C.; m. Lynn E. Rice, Jan. 3, 1970; 1 child, Olivia Augusta. BA, Tex. A&M U., 1966; MA, Case Western Res. U., 1968, PhD, 1977. Univ. fellow Case Western Res. U., Cleve., 1966-67, teaching fellow, summers 1967-69, lectr., 1968; instr. Beloit (Wis.) Coll., 1969-71; asst. prof. U. Wis., Milw., 1971-77, assoc. prof., 1977-86; assoc. prof. Fla. Internat. U., Miami, 1986-88, prof., 1988-95; prof. Spanish U. Houston, 1995—; part-time instr. Cuyahoga County C.C., Cleve., 1967-69; vis. prof. Assoc. Colls. of the Midwest, San Jose, Costa Rica, fall 1978, U. Alicante, Spain, 1991. Author: Blasco Ibáñez and the Evocative Novel, 1973, Federico Garcia Lorca's Poetic Language, 1985; editor: Hispanics in the United States, 1988, Cuban American Theater, 1991, F. Varda's Jicotencal, 1995. Chair Gov.'s Spl. Commn. on Cuban Resettlement, Wis., 1980; mem. Gov.'s Hispanic Commn., Wis., 1983; bd. dirs. United Way of Greater Milw., 1981-84; mem. com. Wis. Humanities, Madison, 1978-84. Recipient Spl. award Wis. Gov., 1981, Citizen of Yr. award Lawyers in Wis., 1981, Vol. Golden Rule award J.C. Penney Co., 1983. Fellow Soc. Values in Higher Edn., Phi Sigma Iota; mem. MLA, L.Am. Studies Assn., Am. Assn. Tchrs. Spanish. Office: U Houston Dept Modern/Classical Langs 4800 Calhoun Houston TX 77204-3784

CORTS, PAUL RICHARD, college president; b. Terre Haute, Ind., Sept. 15, 1943; s. Charles H. and Hazel Corts; m. Diane Stevens, May 29, 1965; children: Kenneth Stevens, Daniel Paul, Susan Diane. BA, Georgetown Coll., 1965; MA, Ind. U., 1967, PhD, 1971. Assoc. prof. speech communication Western Ky. U., Bowling Green, 1968-78, dir. internat. edn., 1973-76, dir. univ. honors program, 1972-78, asst. dean for instrn., 1973-78, assoc. v.p. for instrn., 1978; exec. v.p., chief adminstrv. officer Okla. Bapt. U., Shawnee, 1978-83; pres. The Corts Co., Shawnee, 1983, Wingate (N.C.) Coll., 1983-91, Palm Beach Atlantic Coll., West Palm Beach, Fla., 1991—; cons. bd. govs. U. N.C., Chapel Hill, 1987-88. Co-author: Fundamentals of Effective Group Communication, 1979, Let's Talk Business, 1983. Pres. coun. pres.' Carolinas Intercollegiate Athletic Conf., 1986-88; mem. edn. com. Bapt. World Alliance, McLean, Va., 1990—; bd. dirs. United Way Cen. Carolinas, Monore and Charlotte, 1984-91. Mem. Am. Assn. Pres. Ind. Colls. and Univs. (bd. dirs.), Charlotte Area Ednl. Consortium (pres. 1987-88), Am. Coun. Edn., Williamsburg Pres. Colloquy (chmn. 1990), Palm Beach Lit. Soc. (pres. 1992—), Rotary. Office: Palm Beach Atlantic Coll Office of Pres PO Box 24708 West Palm Beach FL 33416-4708

CORTS, THOMAS EDWARD, university president; b. Terre Haute, Ind., Oct. 7, 1941; s. Charles Harold and Hazel Louise (Vernon) C.; m. Marla Ruth Haas, Feb. 15, 1964; children: Jennifer Ruth Corts Fuller, Rachel Anne Corts Wachter, Christian Haas. BA, Georgetown (Ky.) Coll., 1963; MA, Ind. U., 1968, PhD, 1972; DLitt (hon.), Georgetown Coll., 1991; DHL (hon.), Campbell U., 1995. Asst. to pres. Georgetown Coll., 1963-64, 67-69, asst. prof., 1967-69, exec. dean, 1969-73; exec. v.p. Georgetown Coll., Ky., 1973; coord. Higher Edn. Consortium, Lexington, Ky., 1973-74; pres. Wingate (N.C.) Coll., 1974-83, Samford U., Birmingham, Ala., 1983—; bd. dirs. Samford U. Found., 1990—, Found. Ind. Higher Edn., 1988-92; chmn. Ala. Commn. on Sch. Performance and Accountability. Contbr. articles to profl. jours. Bd. dirs. Birmingham chpt. ARC, 1983-89; mem. adv. bd. Salvation Army, 1987—; mem. exec. coun. Boy Scouts Am., Birmingham, 1984—; bd. dirs. Leadership Birmingham, 1984—, Birmingham Summerfest, 1984—, BBB of Birmingham, Guatemala Ptnrs., Ala. Poverty Project, Inc., Brookwood Bapt. Ch., 1984. Recipient Outstanding Alumnus award Georgetown Coll., 1987, Jefferson award Downtown Action Com., Birmingham, 1988, Outstanding Educator award Ala. Assn. Coll. and Univs.-Ala. Assn. Women, Birmingham, 1989, Good Shepherd award Assn. Bapt. for Scouting, 1990, Citizen of Yr., 1990, Most Supportive Pres. award Am. Assn. of Colls. for Tchr. Edn., 1991. Mem. Am. Assn. Pres. of Ind. Colls. and Univs. (v.p. 1990-92, pres. 1992-95), Coun. for Advancement of Pvt. Colls. in Ala. (past pres.), Ala. Assn. Ind. Colls., Nat. Fellowship Bapt. Educators (pres. 1988-89), Assn. So. Bapt. Colls. and Schs. (v.p. 1988-89, pres. 1990-91), So. Assn. Colls. and Schs. (trustee 1991—, mem. commn. on colls., vice chmn. 1991, chmn. exec. coun. 1992-94, pres. 1996), Country Club Birmingham, The Club, The Summit Club, Jefferson Club (pres. 1989—), Rotary. Democrat. Office: Samford U 800 Lakeshore Dr Birmingham AL 35229-0001

CORWIN, JOYCE ELIZABETH STEDMAN, construction company executive; b. Chgo.; d. Cresswell Edward and Elizabeth Josephine (Kimbell) Stedman; m. William Corwin, May 1, 1965; children: Robert Edmund Newman, Jillanne Elizabeth McInnis. Pres. Am. Properties, Inc., Miami, Fla., 1966-72; v.p. Stedman Constrn. Co., Miami, 1971—; owner Joy-Win Horses, Gray lady ARC, 1969-70. Guidance worker Youth Hall, 1969-70; sponsor Para Med. Group of Coral Park High Sch., 1969-70; hostess, Rep. presdl. campaign, 1968; aide Rep. Nat. Conv., 1972. Mem. Dade County Med. Aux. (chmn. directory com. 1970), Marion County Med. Aux., Fla. Psychiat. Soc. Aux., Fla. Morgan Horse Assn., Fla. Thoroughbred Breeders Assn. Clubs: Coral Gables Jr. Women's (chmn. casework com.), Golden Hills Golf and Turf, Heritage, Royal Dames of Ocala. Home: Windrift Farm 8500 NW 120th St Reddick FL 32686-4513

CORWIN, WILLIAM, psychiatrist; b. Boston, Oct. 28, 1908; M.D., Tufts Coll., 1932; m. Frances M. Wetherell (dec.) m. Joyce S. Newman, 1965. Intern Wesson Meml. Hosp., Springfield, Mass., 1932-33; physician Met. State Hosp., Waltham, Mass., 1933-37, asst. supt., 1937-42; rsrch. fellow Harvard, 1937-46; practice medicine, specializing in psychiatry, Springfield, Mass., 1946-54, Miami, Fla., 1954-88, Ocala, Fla., 1988—; mem. staff Charter Springs Hosp., Ocala., Marion Community Hosp., Ocala; instr. psychiatry Boston U., 1937-46, Tufts Coll., 1941-46; clin. assoc. prof.

psychiatry U. Miami, 1955-70, clin. prof., 1970-88. Past mem. State Fla. Adv. Com. on Mental Health; agy. ops. com. United Fund. Bd. dirs. Family and Childrens Svcs. Miami. Served to lt. col. M.C., USAAF, 1942-46. Diplomate Am. Bd. Psychiatry and Neurology, Am. Bd. Forensic Psychiatry. Fellow Am. Psychiat. Assn. (life), Am. Coll. Psychiatrists; mem. AMA, S. Fla. Psychiat. Soc. (councillor), Fla. Psychiat. Soc. Contbr. articles on physiology of schizophrenia to profl. publs. Office: 1111 NE 25th Ave Ocala FL 34470-5675

COSENZA, ARTHUR GEORGE, opera director; b. Phila., Oct. 16, 1924; s. Luigi and Maria (Piccolo) C.; m. Marietta Muhs, Sept. 16, 1950; children: Louis John, Arthur William, Maria. Student, Ornstein Sch. Music, Phila., 1946-48, Berkshire Music Festival, 1947, Am. Theater Wing, N.Y.C., 1948-50. asso. prof. Coll. Music, Loyola U. of South, 1954-84, dir. opera workshop, 1954-84; dir. Opera Program for City of New Orleans, 1955-73. Performed leading baritone roles with opera cos. throughout, U.S., Can., 1947-70; baritone, New Orleans Opera, 1954-70; producer operas, 1960-74; resident stage dir., 1965-70, gen. dir., 1970-96, artistic dir. 1996—. Served with AUS, 1943-45. Decorated Purple Heart medal; cavaliere Order Star Italian Solidarity; cavaliere Ufficiale dell' Ordine al Merito Italy; officier Ordre des Arts et des Lettres. Mem. Am. Guild Mus. Artists (hon. life), Blue Key. Home: 1720 Soniat St New Orleans LA 70115-4919 Office: New Orleans Opera Assn 333 St Charles Ave Ste 907 New Orleans LA 70130-3120

COSNER, DAVID DALE, plastics industry executive, marketing executive; b. Balt., June 24, 1955; s. Dale and Ethel Pearl (Hart) C.; m. Sept. 8, 1984; children: Anastacia C., David D. II. BA, U. Md., Balt., 1978. Contract adminstr. Environ. Elements Corp., Balt., 1978-85, Gould, Inc., Balt., 1985-86; regional mgr. Novatec, Inc., Balt., 1986-92; v.p. sales and mktg. Universal Dynamics, Inc., Woodbridge, Va., 1992-94, 1994—. Frequent presenter at plastics industry confs. Mem. Soc. Plastics Engrs. (pres. 1991-92), Soc. Plastics Industry (chmn. stats. com. 1994—, internat. trade adv. coun. 1995—, aux. stds.). Republican. Office: Universal Dynamics Inc 13600 Dabney Rd Woodbridge VA 22191-1446

COSPER, SAMMIE WAYNE, educational consultant; b. Greggton, Tex., Oct. 8, 1933; s. Sammie Hampton and Mabel Viola (Byrd) C.; m. Shirley Ann Aguillard, May 13, 1954; children: Ann Caprice, Michelle Marie, Renee Elizabeth. BS in Physics, U. Southwestern La., 1960, DSc (hon.), 1991; PhD in Nuclear Physics, Purdue U., 1965. Postdoctoral appointee Lawrence Radiation Lab. U. Calif. Berkeley, 1965-67; head Dept. Physics, dean Coll. Liberal Arts, Acad. v.p. U. Southwestern La., Lafayette, 1967-89; commr. higher edn. La. Bd. Regents, Baton Rouge, 1990-94; cons. higher edn. Lafayette, 1994—; com. mem. State Hi-Ed Exec. Officers, Denver, 1990—; sub-com. mem. La. Assn. Bus., Industry Edn. Coun., Baton Rouge, 1986—; bd. dirs. La. Coun. Econ. Edn., Baton Rouge. Contbr. articles to profl. jours. Named Communicator of Yr. La. Pub. Rels. Assn., 1993; fellow Woodrow Wilson Found., 1960. Mem. Coun. for Better La. (bd. dirs.), Krewe Gabriel Mardi Gras Assn., Krewe Triton Mardi Gras Assn. (bd. dirs.), Krewe Zeus Mardi Gras Assn. (bd. dirs.). Republican. Roman Catholic. Home: 240 Thibodeaux Dr Lafayette LA 70503

COSPOLICH, JAMES DONALD, electrical engineering executive, consultant; b. New Orleans, Dec. 19, 1944; s. Clarence James and Olga Marie C.; m. Shirley Patricia Knipper, Feb. 4, 1967; children: Brian James, Jeffery Donald, Stephen William. BEE, La. State U., 1967, MEE, 1972. Registered profl. engr., La., Calif., Tex. Geophysicist Pan Am. Petroleum Corp. subs. AMOCO, New Orleans, La., 1967; elec. engr. Waldemar S. Nelson & Co., New Orleans, 1967-74, asst. v.p., mgr. elec. engring., 1974-83, v.p., mgr. elec. engring., 1983-85, sr. v.p. ops., 1985-91, exec. v.p., 1991—; mem. Nat. Elec. Code Panel 14. Mem. Rep. Nat. Com., Washington, 1988; v.p. Ormond Civic Assn., Destrehan, La., 1985, pres., 1986; mem. representing St. Charles Parish, New Orleans Internat. Airport Noise Abatement Com. Mem. NFPA (nat. elec. code com.), IEEE, NSPE, Instrument Soc. Am. (sr., mem. various coms. 1975—), Am. Petroleum Inst. (com. recommended practice stds.), Gas Processors Assn., La. Engring. Soc., Ormond Country Club, The City Energy Club of New Orleans. Republican. Roman Catholic. Home: 61 Rosedown Dr Destrehan LA 70047-2529 Office: Waldemar S Nelson & Co Inc 1200 Saint Charles Ave New Orleans LA 70130-4334

COSSÉ, R. PAUL, realty company executive; b. Nashville, July 11, 1956; s. Xavier B. and Irene E. (Amburgey) C.; m. Benna K. Boring, Nov. 20, 1993; 1 stepchild, Nicole E. Harris; 1 child, Michelle Reneé. Student, Belmont Coll., 1974-75, Aquinas Jr. Coll., 1975-76, U. Tenn., Knoxville, 1976—, Middle Tenn. State U., 1980-81. Mktg. dir. First Tenn. Bank, Murfreesboro, Tenn., 1980-83; exec. v.p. First Federal, Columbia, Tenn., 1983-88; exec. v.p., mng. officer Security Trust Fed., Knoxville, 1988-89; pres., CEO Vol. Realty Co. Knoxville, Inc., 1989—, Mgmt. Software, Inc., Knoxville, 1991—; pres. Vol. Realty Co of Tenn., Inc., 1992—, Vol. Realty Co. Concord, Inc., 1990—, Home Mortgage Brokers, Inc., Knoxville, 1990—; pres., CEO Fin. Investor Svcs. of Tenn., Inc., Knoxville, 1992—, Ins. and Fin. Svcs. Group, Inc., Knoxville, 1992—; pres., chief exec. officer Ins. and Fin. Svcs. Group, Inc., 1992—; pres./CEO Southeastern Holdings of Tenn., Inc., 1995—; bd. dirs. YMCA, Knoxville; cons. in field. Pres. Big. Bros. and Big Sisters Maury County, Columbia, Tenn., 1987-88; bd. dirs. YMCA, Columbia, 1988; chmn. Saturn Run, Columbia, 1987-88; chmn. realtor divsn. Am. Heart Assn. and United Way, Knoxville. Mem. Tenn. League Savs. (leadership bd., publicity com.), Exch. Club. Republican. Office: Vol Realty Co 124 N Winston Rd Knoxville TN 37919-5561

COSTA, MANUEL ANTONE, recreational facility manager; b. Lawrence, Mass., Oct. 26, 1933; s. Manuel Joaquin and Mellie Theresa (Perry) C.; m. Barbara Susan Cournoyer, Dec. 2, 1967; children: David Manuel, Julia Lynn, Jeffrey David. BA in Bus., Mktg., Columbia Pacific U., San Rafael, Calif., 1983. Cert. facility exec. Dir. advt./promotions Volvo Penta of Am., Norfolk, Va., 1974-77; pres. Drummond Yachts, Inc., Dania, Fla., 1977-79; regional rep. Ga. Dept. Industry/Trade, Augusta, Ga., 1979-81; dir. Ga. Mountains Ctr., Gainesville, 1981-85, Myrtle Beach (S.C.) Conv. Ctr., 1985-88; exec. dir. Chattanooga Conv. and Trade Ctr., 1988-90; facility cons. Melbourne Beach, Fla., 1990-91; dir. Florence (S.C.) Civic Ctr., 1991-95; bd. dirs. S.C. Music and Entertainment Commn. Bd. dirs. S.C. Music & Entertainment Commn.; sec. S.C. Music & Entertainment Hall of Fame. With USMC, 1951-54. Mem. Internat. Assn. Audit Mgrs. (dist. v.p. 1987-89, bd. dirs. 1987-89, facility instr. 1990-91), Mid-Atlantic Bldg. Mgrs. Assn., Country Music Assn., Internat. Country Music Buyers Assn. Republican. Roman Catholic. Home: 154 Casseekee Trail Melbourne FL 32951

COSTA, ROBERT NICHOLAS, library director; b. Windber, Pa., Feb. 3, 1938; s. Nicholas and Clara (Buhek) C.; m. Beverley Helen Stevens, Aug. 8, 1938; children: Steven R., Scott N., Craig D., Christopher A. BA, U. Pitts., 1969, MLS, 1971. Meteorologist USN, 1956-64; research asst. U. Pitts, 1968-71; head adult services Cambria County Library System, Johnstown, Pa., 1971-74, assoc. dir., 1974-76, dir., 1976-84; city librarian Richmond, Va., 1984—; mem. Libr. Adminstrs. Devel. Program U. Md., 1985, Leadership Inst., U. Md., 1995; dir. Rotary Grill Mfg. Inc. Inventor Costa Rotary Grill; contbr. articles to profl. jours. Mgr. Little League Baseball, Windber, 1972-75; pres. Johstown YMCA Judo Club, 1972-75; v.p. Windber Pub. Library, 1973-74. Mem. ALA (legis. com. 1981-86, council com. on profl. ethics 1988-90), Va. Library Assn. (various coms. 1984—), Pa. Library Assn. (pub. relations chmn. 1982-83), Southeastern Library Assn. (mem. conf. com.), Va. Regional Literacy Com. Roman Catholic. Office: Richmond Pub Libr 101 E Franklin St Richmond VA 23219-2107*

COSTA, ROBIN LEUEEN, psychologist, counselor; b. Hackensack, N.J., Dec. 9, 1948; d. Frank G. and Hazel L. (Brown) C. BA, Colby Coll., 1970; MA in Clin. Psychology, Fairleigh Dickinson U., 1973; MBA, Fla. Atlantic U., 1984. Lic. mental health counselor, sch. psychologist, Fla.; nat. cert. sch. psychologist. Sch. psychologist Broward County Sch. Bd., Ft. Lauderdale, Fla., 1973-91; pres., chief exec. officer Silver Linings Fin. Care, Ft. Lauderdale, 1986—; pvt. practice Ft. Lauderdale, 1991—. Mem. Jung Generations Soc. (founder). Home: 3750 Galt Ocean Dr Fort Lauderdale FL 33308-7656

COSTA, TERRY ANN, educational administrator; b. Huntington, W.Va., Jan. 9, 1951; d. Hobart G. and Beatrice (Chaput) Owens; m. Joseph M. Costa, June 5, 1970; children: Carrie Lynn, Anthony Martin. BA, Marshall U., 1972, MA, 1979; EdS, Nova U., 1988. Cert. specific learning disabilities, mentally and emotionally handicapped, varying exceptionalities, ESOL, speech tchr., coach, ednl. leadership, Fla. Tchr. spl. edn. Cabell County Sch. System, Huntington, 1973-77, 80-86, coach, 1980-86; adj. instr. Marshall U., Huntington, 1979-80; tchr. spl. edn., dept. chmn. Palm Beach County Sch. Sys., West Palm Beach, Fla., 1986-94, coord. exceptional student edn., dept. chairperson, coach, 1989-94; chmn. tng. and devel. Palm Beach County Sch. System, West Palm Beach, Fla., 1988-89; asst. prin. Loggers' Run Cmty. Mid. Sch., Boca Raton, Fla., 1994—; chmn. exceptional student edn. instructional materials coun. for math. and sci. Fla. Dept. Edn., West Palm Beach, 1988, clin. educator, 1986-91. Coord., vol. Spl. Olympics, Cabell County, 1974-76; religious tchr., coord. Diocese of Wheeling-Charleston, W.Va., 1980-86; leader Girl Scouts U.S.A., W.Va., 1984-86; sch. campaign chmn. United Way, Palm Beach County, 1988-89. Mem. Nat. Assn. Secondary Sch. Prins., Coun. for Exceptional Children (sec. W.Va. 1973-74, corr. sec. 1992-93, Palm Beach County Tchr. of Yr. award chpt. 200, 1989, grantee, 1988, 89, 90, 92), Palm Beach County Sch. Adminstrs. Assn. (exec. bd. sec. 1996—). Democrat. Roman Catholic. Home: 8381 Mildred Dr W Boynton Beach FL 33437-1031 Office: Loggers' Run Cmty Mid Sch 11584 W Palmetto Park Rd Boca Raton FL 33428-2681

COSTAGLIOLA, FRANCESCO, former government official, macro operations analyst; b. Cranston, R.I., Aug. 24, 1917; s. Luigi and Rose (Lubrano) C.; m. Agnes Mary Ross, June 14, 1952; children: Francesca Gensler, Marisa Consoli, Antonia Burns, Roseanne Rubin. Student U. R.I., 1935-37; BSEE, U.S. Naval Acad., 1941; postgrad. Naval Postgrad. Sch., 1946-47, MIT, 1947-49, Cath. U. Am., 1967-71; MBA, Am. U., Washington, 1974. Commd. ensign U.S. Navy, 1941, advanced through grades to capt., 1960; served in U.S.S. Phoenix in 24 ops. PTO, 1941-46; comdg. officer U.S.S. Halsey Powell, Korea, 1951-52; various positions naval sea and shore assignments involving atomic energy, 1952-64; mil. asst. to asst. to Sec. Def., 1964-67; ret., 1968; commr. AEC, 1968-69; engr. RCA, 1974-76; staff mem. Joint Congressional Com. on Atomic Energy, Washington, 1967-68, 69-71, 76-77; staff mem. Office of Sec. of Senate, Washington, 1977-86; mem. Md. Radiation Control Adv. Bd., 1973-81. Contbr. articles to profl. jours. Decorated Legion of Merit, Bronze Star with Combat V. Mem. AAAS, Inst. Ops. Rsch. & Mgmt. Scis., Am. Nuc. Soc., U.S. Naval Inst., Pearl Harbor Survivors Assn., Naval Acad. Alumni Assn., Mil. Order World Wars, Army and Navy Club (Washington). Roman Catholic. Home: 307 Gibbon St Alexandria VA 22314-4129

COSTELLO, ALBERT JOSEPH, chemicals executive; b. N.Y.C., Sept. 4, 1935; s. John and Lena (Compiani) C.; m. Barbara Theresa Antolotti, May 31, 1958; children: Gregory A., Peter M., Albert Joseph. B.S., Fordham U., 1957; M.S., NYU, 1964. With Am. Cyanamid Co., 1957-94; asst. mng., mng. dir. Am. Cyanamid Co., Mexico City, Madrid, Spain, 1974-77; div. v.p. Am. Cyanamid Co., Wayne, N.J., 1977-82, pres. agrl. div., 1982, group v.p., 1982-83, exec. v.p., 1983-90, pres., 1990-93, chmn. bd., CEO, 1993-94; chmn., pres., CEO W.R. Grace & Co., Boca Raton, Fla., 1995—; bd. dirs. FMC Corp., Becton Dickinson and Co. Patentee in field. Trustee Fordham U., The Am. Enterprise Inst. for Pub. Policy Rsch. Mem. Chem. Mfrs. Assn. (bd. dirs. 1987—), Bus. Roundtable. Office: WR Grace & Co One Town Center Rd Boca Raton FL 33486-1010

COSTELLO, DANIEL BRIAN, lawyer, consultant; b. Arlington, Va., Apr. 23, 1950; s. James Russell and Hazel Virginia (Caudle) C.; m. Margaret Ruth Dow, June 13, 1970; children: James Brian, Rebecca Ruth, Kathleen Marie. BA, U. Va., 1972; JD, Coll. of William and Mary, 1975. Bar: Va. 1975, U.S. Dist. Ct. (ea. dist.) Va. 1979, U.S. Ct. Appeals (4th cir.) 1979, U.S. Bankruptcy Ct. (ea. dist.) Va. 1979, D.C. 1984. Reporter Globe Newspapers, Vienna, Va., 1965-68; freelance journalist Williamsburg, Va., 1972-73; news dir. Sta. WMBG, WBCI-FM, Williamsburg, 1973-76; spl. asst. atty. gen. Commonwealth of Va., Suffolk, Va., 1976-78; asst. atty. gen. Commonwealth of Va., Richmond, Va., 1978-80; ptnr. Dameron, Costello & Hubacher, Alexandria, Va., 1980-89, Costello & Hubacher, Alexandria, 1989—; press rels. cons. Va. Bar Assn., No. Va. Dem. Combined Campaign; spl. commr. in chancery Alexandria Cir. Ct. Author: Foreclosure in Virginia, 1991; co-editor, co-author The Layman's Guide to Virginia Law, 1977; editor night news Sta. WINA, 1969-72; contbr. articles to profl. jours. Mem. Va. State Bar, Alexandria Bar Assn., D.C. Bar, Soc. Alumni Coll. of William and Mary, U. Va. Alumni Soc., Rolling Hills Club. Presbyterian. Office: Costello & Hubacher 429 N Saint Asaph St Alexandria VA 22314-2317

COSTLEY, SHAWN ERIC, sales specialist; b. Ft. Dix, N.J., June 25, 1965; s. Thomas Carrollton and Anita Louise (Gladden) C. BS, Norfolk State U., 1989. Logistics mgmt. specialist Naval Air Sys. Command, Arlington, Va., 1989-93; fgn. mil. sales specialist Army Security Assistance Command, Alexandria, Va., 1993—. Contbr. articles to profl. jours. Ptnr. Chuma Investment Group, Arlington, 1993—. Mem. Toastmaster's Internat. (pub. rels.). Mem. African Methodist Episcopal Zion Ch. Home: PO Box 16201 Arlington VA 22215 Office: USASAC (AMSAC-MM/B) 5001 Eisenhower Ave Alexandria VA 22333

CÔTÉ, RICHARD NORMAN, international writer, historian, biographer; b. Waterbury, Conn., June 3, 1945; s. Norman W. and Annie Mary (Richal) C. BA, Butler U., 1965. Writer, 1981—, So. Rsch. Inst., Mt. Pleasant, S.C., 1987—; dir. micrographics S.C. Hist. Soc., Charleston, 1979-80; cons. Nat. Trust for Historic Preservation, Charleston, 1981, S.C. Hist. Soc., 1988. Author: Renegade!, 1982, Ports, Power & Trade, 1991, Love By Mail, 1991, Jewel of the Cotton Fields, 1994, Mary's World: Love War and Family Ties in Nineteenth-Century Charleston, 1996, Transits, Chains & Rattlesnakes, 1996; editor: Local and Family History in South Carolina, 1981, The Dictionary of South Carolina Biography, 1983; lit. collaborator: (with Edward Lee Howard) Safe House, 1992, (with Mischa Caplan) God's Miracle of Tears, 1996, (with Melissa Trost and Michael Vest), Under the Oi Trees, 1996, (with Dorothy Cancilla) Death by HMO, 1996, screenwriter (with Karen Mitura) Private Lives, 1996; contbr. articles on history and wine to profl. publs. Precinct chmn. Mt. Pleasant Democratic Com., 1983. Sgt. USAF, 1965-71, Vietnam. Writing grantee Post-Courier Found., 1991-94. Unitarian. Home and Office: PO Box 1898 Mount Pleasant SC 29465-1898

COTECSON, ALLAN BRUCE, systems analyst; b. Surigao del Norte, Philippines, Jan. 26, 1957; came to U.S., 1985; m. Ely Aguilar, June 25, 1983; 1 child, Elaine Dawn. BS in Civil Engring., U. So. Philippines, 1979; M in Engring., Asian Inst. Tech., 1981. Civil engr.'s aide Dept. Pub. Works, Cebu City, Philippines, 1978-79; systems engr. IBM Philippines, Manila, 1981-85; product rep. Neasi-Weber Internat., Northridge, Calif., 1985-91; sr. systems cons. Tribune Co., Chgo., 1991-92; lead systems analyst Newsday, Inc., Melville, N.Y., 1992-95; product specialist Neasi-Weber Internat., Atlanta, 1995—. Home: 160 Greenmont Cir Alpharetta GA 30201 Office: Neasi-Weber Internat 5901 Peachtree Dunwoody Rd Atlanta GA 30328

COTHRAN, PHYLLIS L., personal care industry executive; b. Charlottesville, Va., Feb. 12, 1947; d. James T. and Mary C. BS in Acctg., Va. Commonwealth U.; student, U. Va. sch. bus., Northwestern U., London Sch. Econs. Sr. acct. Blue Cross/Blue Shield Va., Richmond, 1972-74, systems acct., then sr. fin. analyst, 1974-75, adminstrv. asst. to v.p. fin., 1975-77, mgr. fin. planning and mgmt., 1977-78, corp. contr., 1978-81, v.p. fin., 1981-85, sr. v.p. fin. CHI, 1985-88, sr. v.p. fin. and planning HMC, 1988, chief. fin. officer, treas. BCBSVA, 1989, exec. v.p. ops., 1989-90, exec. v.p., chief oper. officer, then pres., chief oper. officer, 1990—; mem. audit com. Blue Cross/Blue Shield Assn., Chgo., 1990. Mem. cost rev. coun. VA Health Svcs., Richmond, 1990-91, Spl. Adv. Commn. on Mandated Health Ins. Benefits, Richmond, 1991; bd. dirs. Metro Richmond Drug Coalition, 1991, Va. Pub. Safety Found., Sci. Mus. Va. Found., Richmond Forum, Weed & Seed of Richmond, Nat. Mus. Health and Med. Found. Recipient Star award Va. Commonwealth U., 1990, YWCA Outstanding Women award. Mem. Fin. Execs. Inst., Soc. Internat. Bus. Fellows, Metro Richmond C. of C. (bd. dirs. 1991). Office: Trigon Blue Cross/Blue Shield 2015 Staples Mill Rd Richmond VA 23230-3108*

COTNEY, CAROL ANN, independent researcher; b. Huntsville, Ala., July 23, 1957; d. John Walter Sr. and Helen Maxine (Bechtold) C. BS in Family Resource Mgmt., Auburn U., 1979; BSE in Mech. Engring., U. Ala., Huntsville, 1986, MSE in Solid Mechanics, 1997; postgrad., 1996—. Clk. Jack Eckerd Drug Co., Huntsville, 1979-83; rsch. aerospace engr. U.S. Army Missile Command, RDEC, Redstone Arsenal, Ala., 1983-93; sales rep. DCA Promotions, Inc., Huntsville, 1993; substitute tchr. Madison County Bd. Edn., Huntsville, 1993—; tchg. asst. U. Ala., Huntsville, 1995—; ind. sr. researcher Huntsville, 1993—; mtkg. asst., 1996; mem. structures and mech. behavior subcom. material and properties and characterization panel, 1987-88, 93—, acting program chmn., 1987-88, profl. devel. com. originator, 1988, mem. propulsion sys. hazards subcom. cookoff hazard tech. panel, 1991—; U.S. Army rep., 1991-93; mem. cookoff workshop originator and planning com., 1991-92, mem. propulsion industry cookoff tech. long range planning com., 1991; mem. Joint Army Navy NASA Air Force Interagy. Propulsion Com., 1986—. Contbr. articles on propulsion mechanics, propulsion design, structural design, insensitive munitions, optical engring., and vehicle design to profl. jours. Internat. cook-off specialist sr. high advisor and singles coord. Covenant Presbyn. Ch., Huntsville, 1980-83; chmn. by-laws com. Christian Singles Fellowship, Huntsville, 1984, v.p., pres., 1985-86; singles coord. Hope Presbyn. Ch., Huntsville, 1984-87, trustee, 1987-88; treas. United Meth. Women, Cir. 9, Latham United Meth. Ch., Huntsville, 1991-92, mem. missions com., 1992, sec., 1992; tutor Seminole Svc. Ctr., Huntsville, 1991; mem. Friends of the Symphony, 1993—, mem. com., 1994—; mentor DOD Sci. and Engring. Apprentice Program, 1987-88; judge local, regional, state Ala. Sci. and Engring. Fair. Recipient U.S. Army Commendation 1988, 92. Fellow AIAA (assoc., U.S. Army Missle Command facility rep. Ala.-Miss. sec. 1991-92, assoc. dir. edn. 1991-92, dir. career enhancement 1992, dir. telemetry newsletter 1992, region II co-dep. dir. precoll. outreach 1992-94, nat. engrs. week planning com. region II rep. 1993, nat. precoll. outreach com. 1993-94, nat. tchr. enhancement subcom. 1993-94); mem. NAFE, ASME (region XI impromptu design contest coord. 1996, applied mechanics divsn.), Internat. Clarinet Assn. Home: 13909 Clovis Cir SW Huntsville AL 35803-2509

COTROS, CHARLES H., food products company executive; b. 1937. Exec. v.p. foodservice ops. Sysco Corp., Houston, 1989—; chmn., chief exec. officer Hardin's-Sysco Food Svcs. Inc., Memphis. Office: Sysco Corp 1390 Enclave Pky Houston TX 77077-2025*

COTTEN, CATHERYN DEON, medical center international advisor; b. Erwin, N.C., Apr. 13, 1952; d. Ben Hur and Minnie Lee (Smith) C. BS in Anthropology, Duke U., 1975. Asst. internat. advisor Med. Ctr. Duke U., Durham, N.C., 1975-76; internat. advisor Med. Ctr. Duke U., Durham, 1976—. Editor and contbr. chpt. to Advisors Manual of Federal Regulations Affecting Foreign Students and Scholars. Key vol. City of Durham, 1990-91; pres. Durham County Lit. Coun., 1992-94. Recipient Cert. Recognition So. Regional Coun. Black Am. Affairs, Atlanta, 1985. Mem. Nat. Assn. Fgn. Student Affairs: Assn. Internat. Educators (gov. regulations adv. com. 1985-96, nat. chair 1991-94, chair Southeastern region 1989-90), Altrusa Club (pres. Durham chpt. 1987-89). Office: Duke U Med Ctr PO Box 3882 Durham NC 27710

COTTER, GARY WILLIAM, financial company executive, consultant; b. White Plains, N.Y., Nov. 19, 1947; s. Edgar Richard and Frances Ray (Sturm) C.; m. Shirley Ann Pereira, Dec. 11, 1982. BA, U. Corpus Christi, 1970; MS, SUNY, 1973; postgrad., U. South Fla., 1977-78. Cert. fin. planner. Dist. mgr. IDS Fin. Svcs., St. Petersburg, Fla., 1978-81; div. mgr. IDS Fin. Svcs., Corpus Christi, Tex., 1981-83; fin. planner E.F. Hutton & Co., Inc., Corpus Christi, 1983-84; pres. Cotter & Cotter Fin. Group, Corpus Christi, 1984-89, Cotter & Cotter Fin. Cons., Inc., Corpus Christi, 1985-89, Cotter & Cotter Risk Mgmt. Corp., Corpus Christi, 1985-89; registered prin. G.A. Repple & Co., Casselberry, Fla., 1990—; pres. First Gulf Advisers, Inc., Tampa, 1991—; instr. fin. planning Rollins Coll., Winter Park, Fla., 1994; mem. Fin. Profl. Adv. Panel, 1985; fin. commentator Sta. KIII-TV, ABC, Corpus Christi, 1987-88, Sta. KEYS; panelist pers. fin. adv. Sta. WTVT-TV, CBS, Tampa, 1992-94, WFLA-TV, NBC, Tampa, 1995—; grant writer Our Lady Star of Sea Parish, Corpus Christi, 1986. Mem. fin. coun., columnist The Sun, East Bay Breeze, Carrollwood News, Town 'n' Country News, Lake Area News, South Tampa News, 1991—; contbr. articles to periodicals. Precinct del. Nueces County Rep. Conv., Corpus Christi, 1988; mem. fin. coun., lay reader Corpus Christi Cathedral. Mem. Mem. Inst. CFPs (mem. spkrs. bur. Tampa Bay Soc.), Internat. Assn. Fin. Planning (pres. Corpus Christi chpt. 1988-89, bd. dirs. 1986-87, rep. S.W. regional coun. 1987-88, sec. Tampa Bay chpt. 1992-93, bd. dirs. 1991-96, pres. 1994, chmn. 1995-96), Corpus Christi C. of C., Sun City Center Area C. of C. (bd. dirs.), Corpus Christi State U. Alumni Assn. (bd. dirs. 1983-86). Office: 5100 W Kennedy Blvd Ste 152 Tampa FL 33609

COTTER, JOHN BURLEY, ophthalmologist, corneal specialist; b. Zanesville, Ohio, Sept. 14, 1946; s. John Burley and Evelyn Virginia (Ross) C.; m. Perrine Abauzit, Aug. 17, 1977; children: Neils John, Jeremy Pierre. BA, U. Kans., 1968; med. degree, U. Kans., Kansas City, 1968-72. Ophthalmology resident U. Mo., Kansas City, 1976-79; family practice Ashland (Kans.) Hosp., 1973-74; emergency room physician Providence-St. Margaret Hosp., Kansas City, Kans., 1974-75; family orthopedic practice Mountain Med. Assocs., Vail, Colo., 1975-76; ophthalmologist, pvt. practice Duluth, Minn., 1979-82; surgeon-chief out-patient clinic King Khaled Eye Specialist Hosp., Riyadh, Saudi Arabia, 1983-90, mem. exec. com., 1985-90; asst. clin. prof. King Saud U., Riyadh, Saudi Arabia, 1985-90; corneal specialist Simel Eye Assocs., Greensboro, N.C., 1990—; seminar chmn. Status of Refractive Surgery, Riyadh, 1986; active Nat. Survey Eye Disease and Ea. Province Survey Coun., Saudi Arabia, 1984, 90. Author: (booklet) Radial Keratotomy, 1986; contbr. articles to profl. jours. Rsch. grantee Contact Lens Assn. of Ophthalmology, 1981, Lasers Steering Com. King Khalid Eye Hosp. at Hosp. Hotel Dieu, Paris, 1988; ORBIS fellow Baylor U., Houston, 1982. Fellow Am. Acad. Ophthalmology; mem. AMA, Internat. Assn. Ocular Surgeons, Internat. Soc. Refractive Keratoplasty, Societe Francaise D'Ophthalmologie, Saudi Ophthalmologisl Soc., Am. Soc. Cataract and Refractive Surgery. Independent. Office: Simel Eye Assocs 1915 Lendew St Ste 100 Greensboro NC 27408-7017

COTTER, RICHARD TIMOTHY, lawyer; b. Chgo., Sept. 2, 1948; s. Edward Timothy and Julia Maria (Kazakauskas) C.; m. Janet M. Sorrentino, Dec. 3, 1977 (div. Jan. 1993); children: Mary Julia, Carol Ann; m. Kimberly A. Morris, Sept. 11, 1993; children: Kathleen, Julia Ann. Bar: Fla. 1975, Ill. 1976, U.S. Supreme Ct. 1982. Ptnr. Echols & Cotter, Ft. Myers Beach, Fla., 1978-85, Echols, Cotter & Shenko, Ft. Myers Beach, Fla., 1985-95, Echols & Cotter, Ft. Myers Beach, 1995—; prof. Internat. Coll. Paralegal Instrn., Ft. Myers, 1992. Contbr. articles to profl. jours.; newspaper columnist Legal Eagle, 1995—. Pres. Cmty. Assn. Inst., South Gulf Coast chpt., Ft. Myers, 1984; dir. United Way of Lee County, Inc., Ft. Myers, 1990-92; dir. Chamber of S.W. Fla., Ft. Myers, 1989-91, vice-chmn. legal affairs, 1990-94; del. Fla. Democratic State Conv., 1995. Mem. Ill. Bar Assn., Fla. Bar (condo. and planned devel. com. 1993—, real property professionalism com. 1993—), Lee County Bar Assn., Fla. Assn. Realtors (local bd. attys. com. 1986-94), Ft. Myers Beach Lodge 362, Araba Shrine Temple, U.S. C. of C. (coun. mem. small bus. coun. 1994—, mem. social security com. 1995—). Office: Richard T Cotter PA 6100 Estero Blvd Fort Myers Beach FL 33931-4347

COTTINGHAM, JENNIFER JANE, city official; b. Salt Lake City, July 10, 1961; d. Miles Dixon and Ruth Eugenia (Skeen) Cottingham; m. Richard Frame Cavenaugh, July 23, 1983 (div. Apr. 1989); 1 child, John Douglas. BS in Civil Engring., So. Meth. U., 1984. Lic. profl. engr., Tex. Estimator Avery Mays Constrn., Dallas, 1981-83, project engr., 1984; owner, gen. contr. Dallas, 1985-89; asst. project mgr. Austin Comml., Dallas, 1989; ct. appointed receiver 14th Dist. Ct., State of Tex., Dallas, 1990-91; engr. asst. Dallas Water Utilities, 1990-91, project mgr., 1991-96; dir. CBC Investors, L.P., Dallas. Goodwill ambassador City of Dallas Water Utilities, 1990-92, 95-96, fin. strength com., 1991. Mem. CBC Investments (founding pres.), Dallas Symphony Orch. League, DAR (pres. jr. group 1989-92), Cotillion Book Club (founding mem.). Republican. Episcopalian. Office: City of Dallas Water Utilities 2121 Main St Ste 300 Dallas TX 75201

COTTINGHAM, STEPHEN KENT, real estate development executive, researcher; b. Denver, Dec. 28, 1951; s. Miles Dixon and Ruth (Skeen) C.; m. Susan Kay Kelfer, Aug. 11, 1984. Student, So. Oreg. Coll., 1970-71; BBA, So. Meth. U., 1974; ThM, Dallas Theol. Sem., 1984. V.p. Cottingham

Constrn. Co., Dallas, 1974-79; project mgmt. Avery Mays Constrn. Co., Dallas, 1981-82; asst. v.p. Pacific Realty Corp., Dallas, 1983-85, v.p., 1985-86, exec. v.p., 1986-88; v.p. Paragon Group, Dallas, 1988-91; regional v.p. The Prime Group Inc., San Antonio, Tex., 1991-93; pres. Brock Investment Group, Inc., San Antonio, 1993-95; chairman, pres. SKCI, Inc., San Antonio, 1995—; founder, exec. dir. Theol. Edn. Found., Internat., 1996—; adj. tchr. N.W. Bible Ch. Coll. Class, Dallas, 1981-83; student leader, counselor Young Life Internat., Dallas, 1974-76. Charter mem. Rep. Nat. Com., Washington, 1985—; tchr. Christ Episcopal Ch., San Antonio, chmn. adult edn., exec. com.; founder, pres. Theol. Edn. Foun., Internat., San Antonio, 1996—. Named one of Outstanding Young Men of Am., Montgomery, Ala., 1986; So. Meth. U. Scholar, 1972-74. Mem. Urban Land Inst. (assoc.), Evang. Theol. Soc., Phi Gamma Delta (treas.), Phi Beta Lamda.

COTTON, FRANK ALBERT, chemist, educator; b. Phila., Apr. 9, 1930; s. Albert and Helen (Taylor) C.; m. Diane Dornacher, June 13, 1959; children: Jennifer Helen, Jane Myrna. Student, Drexel Inst. Tech., 1947-49; AB, Temple U., 1951, DSc, 1963; PhD, Harvard U., 1955; Dr. rer. Nat. (hon.), Bielefeld U., 1979; DSc (hon.), Columbia U., 1980; D.Sc. (hon.), Northwestern U., 1981, U. Bordeaux, 1981, St. Joseph's U., 1982, U. Louis Pasteur, 1982, U. Valencia, 1983, Kenyon Coll., 1983, Technion-Israel Inst. Tech., 1983, U. Cambridge, 1986, Johann Wolfgang Goethe Universität, 1989, U. S.C., 1989, U. Rennes, 1992, Lomonosov U., 1992, Fujian Inst. Rsch., Chinese Acad. Scis., 1993, U. Pisa, Italy, 1994, U. Zaragoza, 1994, Cleve. State U., 1995. Instr. chemistry M.I.T., 1955-57, asst. prof., 1957-60, assoc. prof., 1960-61, prof., 1961-71; Robert A. Welch Distinguished prof. chemistry Tex. A&M U., 1971—, dir. Lab. for Molecular Stucture and Bonding, 1983—; Cons. Am. Cyanamid, Stamford, Conn., 1958-67, Union Carbide, N.Y.C., 1964—; Todd prof. U. Cambridge, 1985-86. Author: (with G. Wilkinson and P.L. Gaus) Advanced Inorganic Chemistry, 3d edit., 1995, Chemical Applications of Group Theory, 3d edit., 1989, (with L. Lynch and C. Carlington) Chemistry, An Investigative Approach; editor: Process in Inorganic Chemistry, Vols. 1-10, 1959-68, Inorganic Syntheses, Vol. 13, 1971, (with L.M. Jackman) Dynamic Nuclear Magnetic Resonance Spectroscopy, (with R.A. Walton) Multiple Bonds Between Metal Atoms, 2d edti., 1993. Recipient Michelson-Morley award Case Western Res. U., 1980, Nat. Medal Sci., 1982, Paracelsus medal Swiss Chem. Soc., 1994, Polyhedron medal, 1995; hon. fellow Robinson Coll., U. Cambridge. Mem. NAS (chmn. phys. scis. 1985-88, coun. 1991-94, gov. bd. NRC 1992-94, Cosepup 1992-94, chem. scis. bd. 1990, King Faisal Internat. prize 1990, Robert A. Welch award in chemistry 1994), Am. Soc. Biol. Chemists, Am. Chem. Soc. (awards 1962, 74, Baekeland medal N.J. sect. 1963, Nichols medal N.Y. sect. 1975, Pauling medal Oreg. and Puget Sound sect. 1976, Kirkwood medal N.Y. sect. 1978, Gibbs medal Chgo. sect. 1980, Richards medal N.E. sect. 1986, F.A. Cotton medal Tex. A&M sect. 1995), Am. Acad. Arts and Scis., N.Y. Acad. Scis. (corr.), Royal Soc. Chemistry (hon.), Royal Danish Acad. Scis. and Letters (hon.), Göttingen Acad. Scis., Societa Chimica Italiana (hon.), Indian Acad. Scis. (hon.), Indian Nat. Sci. Acad. (hon.) Royal Soc. Edinburgh (hon.), Am. Philos. Soc., Acad. Europea (hon.), Royal Soc. London (fgn.), Inst. de France (Acad. des Scis., fgn.). Home: 4101 Sand Creek Rd Bryan TX 77808-8337 Office: Tex A&M Univ Dept Of Chemistry College Station TX 77843

COTTON, LAURA LEIGH, oncology nurse; b. Colorado Springs, Colo., Apr. 25, 1965; d. John Robert and Betty Ellen (Schneider) Roeser; m. Don Ray Cotton, Aug. 9, 1987; children: Michael Austin, Kayla Marie. BSN, U. Kans., 1987. Cert. in Peripherally inserted central catheters, chemotherapy, oncology. Nurse aide U. Kans. Med. Ctr., Kansas City, 1986-87; grad. nurse Wesley Med. Ctr., Wichita, 1987; staff and relief charge nurse Brackenridge Hosp., Austin, Tex., 1987-88; head nurse Cen. Tex. Oncology Assocs., Austin, 1988-90; office nurse Stehlin Found., Houston, 1990-92; asst. dir. nursing S.W. Regional Cancer Ctr., Austin, 1992—. Mem. Sigma Theta Tau.

COTTONE, JAMES ANTHONY, dentist; b. Syracuse, N.Y., Apr. 10, 1947; s. Salvatore Anthony and Sistine (Albanese) C.; m. Linda Visciglio, Sept. 23, 1972 (div. Nov. 1979). BA, U. Pa., 1968; DMD, Tufts U., 1972; MS, Ind. U., Indpls., 1977. Diplomate Am. Bd. Oral Med., Am. Bd. Forensic Odontology. Asst. prof. U. Tex., San Antonio, 1977-81, assoc. prof., 1981-85, prof., 1985—; pvt. practice dentistry with Raymond D. Brough, DMD, Syracuse, N.Y., 1974-75; cons. in field; asst. sec. healthcare for patients with AIDS USPHS HHS, 1994; founder, dir. Johnson & Johnson Med. Inc. Postdoctoral Fellowship in Infectious Disease Control, 1992—. Author: An Outline of Forensic Dentistry, 1982, (monograph) Proceedings of a Symposium on Hepatitis B: Risk, Prevention, and the Vaccine, 1982, Dental Management of the Patient with Increased Medical Risks, 1983, A Textbook of Oral Diagnosis, Oral Medicine, and Treatment Planning, 1984, Practical Infection Control in Dentistry, 1991, Infection Control for the Dental Team, 1991, 2d edit., 1996; mem. editl. bd. Control newsletter, 1986; manuscript rev. bd. Jour. ADA, Gen. Dentistry, Calif. Dental Assn., Am. Fund for Dental Health; spkr. in field. Capt. dental corps USNR, 1964-92, ret. Named to Am. Men and Women Sci., 1986; NIH grantee, 1976, Merck, Sharp & Dohme, 1983-89, Parke-Davis Pharms., 1984, Mead-Johnson Pharms., 1984-89, Tom Russell Charitable Found., 1986-87. Fellow Acad. Gen. Dentistry, Am. Acad. Forensic Scis., Am. Coll. Dentists; mem. ADA, Am. Acad. Oral Medicine, Orgn. Tchrs. Oral Diagnosis (sec., treas. 1979-81, pres. 1982-83), Am. Assn. Dental Schs. (sect. on oral diagnosis and medicine 1983-86, adminstrv. bd. 1986-90, v.p. 1990-93), Am. Soc. Forensic Odontology (pres. 1987-88), San Antonio Dist. Dental Soc., Tex. Dental Assn., Internat. Orgn. Forensic Odonto-Stomatology, Soc. Infection Control in Dentistry (organizing com. 1984—), Acad. Internat. Dental Studies, Office Sterilization and Asepsis Procedures Rsch Found. (organizing com. 1984-85, bd. dirs. 1985—, pres. 1988-90). Roman Catholic. Office: U Tex Dental Sch 7703 Floyd Curl Dr San Antonio TX 78284-6200

COTTRELL, JEANNETTE ELIZABETH, retired librarian; b. Buffalo, Dec. 10, 1923; d. Benjamin Birch and Mary Jeannette (Ashdown) Milnes; m. William Barber Cottrell, Jan. 21, 1944 (dec.); children: Karen Jean, Susan Marie, William Milnes, Scott Barber, Stephen Ashdown. BA in Sociology, U. Tenn., 1970, MS, 1976; student, Alfred U., 1940-43. Cert. tchr. libr., Tenn. Nursery sch. tchr. Concord Meth. Ch., Knoxville, Tenn., 1964-65; libr. City Sch. System, Knoxville, Tenn., 1971-84, ret., 1984. Author: (with husband) An American Family in the 20th Century, 1987; recorder textbooks for the blind, 1983—. Libr. Concord United Meth. Ch., Knoxville, 1975—, curriculum chair spl. studies class, 1989—, reading chair Suzanna Wesley Circle. Mem. AAUW, Phi Kappa Phi, Beta Phi Mu. Republican. Methodist. Home: 308 Camelot Ct Knoxville TN 37922-2076

COTTRILL, MARY ELSIE, family nurse practitioner; b. Charleston, W. Va., Sept. 17, 1939; d. Orville Hugh and Nancy Isabell (Fletcher) C. Diploma, RN, Sch. of Nursing, Chesapeake and Ohio Hosp., Clifton Forge, Va., 1964; diploma in Christian Edn., Appalachian Bible Coll., Bradley, W. Va., 1961; diploma in Spanish, Rio Grande Bible Inst. Missionary Lang., Edinburg, Tex., 1966; family nurse practitioner, Med. Sch. Nursing, U. Miami, Fla. Nurses asst. Thomas Meml. Hosp., S. Charleston, W. Va., 1953-58; RN Emmett Meml. Hosp., Clifton Forge, Va., 1961-64, Thomas Meml. Hosp., 1964-65; med. missionary Harvesters Internat. Mission, McAllen, Texas, 1965-74; primary care nurse Jackson Meml. Hosp., Miami, Fla., 1972-75; family nurse practitioner Martin Luther King Clinic, Homestead, Fla., 1975—. Asst. scout master Boy Scouts of Am., Miami, 1983—; den leader Cub Scouts of Am., Miami, 1983—. Recipient Migrant Health Provider award Nat. Assn. of Community Health Ctrs., 1989, Wood Badge Boy Scouts Am., 1992, Dist. Award of Merit, 1989, Order of the Arrow, 1994, Dist. Chmn.'s award, 1995, Whitney Young award, 1996. Mem. Fla. Nurses Assn. Baptist. Home: 25510 SW 124th Ave Princeton FL 33032-5819

COUGHLIN, TOM, professional football coach; b. Waterloo, N.Y., Aug. 31, 1946; m. Judy Coughlin; children: Keli, Katie, Tim, Brian. BA Educ., Syracuse U.; MA Educ. Grad. asst. Syracuse U., 1969; head coach Rochester Inst. Tech., 1970-73; offensive backfield coach Syracuse U., 1974-76, offensive coord., 1977-80; offensive coord. Boston Coll., 1981-83; wide receivers coach Philadelphia Eagles, 1984-85; receivers coach Green Bay Packers, 1986-87, N.Y. Giants, 1988-90; head coach Boston Coll., 1991-93, Jacksonville Jaguars, 1994—. Office: Jacksonville Jaguars 1 Stadium Pl Jacksonville FL 32202-1928*

COULTER, ELIZABETH JACKSON, biostatistician, educator; b. Balt., Nov. 2, 1919; d. Waddie Pennington and Bessie (Gills) Jackson; m. Norman Arthur Coulter Jr., June 23, 1951; 1 child, Robert Jackson. A.B., Swarthmore Coll., 1941; A.M., Radcliffe Coll., 1946, Ph.D., 1948. Asst. dir. health study Bur. Labor Stats., San Juan, P.R., 1946; research asst. Milbank Meml. Fund, N.Y.C., 1948-51; economist Office Def. Prodn., 1951-52; research analyst Children's Bur.-HEW, 1952-53; from statistician to chief statistician Ohio Dept. Health, 1954-65; lectr. econs., then clin. asst. prof. preventive medicine Ohio State U., 1954-65; asst. clin. prof. biostats. U. Pitts. Sch. Pub. Health, 1958-62; assoc. prof. biostats. U. N.C., Chapel Hill, 1965-72, assoc. prof. econs., 1965-78, biostats. prof., 1972-90; adj. assoc. prof., hosp. adminstr. Duke U., 1972-79; assoc. dean undergrad. pub. health studies U. N.C., Chapel Hill, 1979-86, prof. biostats. emerita, 1990—. Contbr. articles to profl. jours. Mem. AAAS, AAUP, APHA (governing coun. 1970-72), Am. Econ. Assn., Am. Statis. Assn., Am. Acad. Polit. and Social Sci., Biometric Soc., Am. Evaluation Assn., Assn. for Health Svcs. Rsch., Sigma Xi, Delta Omega. Methodist. Home: 1825 N Lakeshore Dr Chapel Hill NC 27514-6734

COULTER, JOHN BREITLING, III, biochemist, educator; b. Stamford, Tex., Nov. 28, 1941; s. John Breitling and Sue Madeline (Morrow) C.; m. Brenda Kay Norman, May 27, 1966; children: Grace Kathleen, John Paul, Peter Stephen. BS, U. Tex., Arlington, 1966; PhD, Baylor U., 1970. Dir. rsch. and diagnostic labs. Scott and White Meml. Hosp. and Clinic, Temple, Tex., 1971—; assoc. prof. pathology and biochemistry Coll. Medicine Tex. A&M U., Temple, 1978—; adj. asst. prof. chemistry Baylor U., Waco, Tex., 1975-81; cons. chemist Lab. Svc., VA Ctr., Temple, 1973-90. Founder, pres. Christian Info. Coun., Inc., 1981—. With U.S. Army, 1960-63. HEW rsch. grantee, 1971-81; NDEA Title IV fellow Baylor U., 1970. Mem. AAAS, Am. Chem. Soc., Assn. for Rsch. in Vision and Ophthalmology, Am. Assn. Clin. Chemists, Sigma Xi (pres. Temple chpt. 1975). Baptist. Office: Scott & White Hosp and Clinic 2401 S 31st St Temple TX 76508-0001

COULTER, LAWRENCE P., credit union administrator; b. 1940. With So. Bell, Atlanta, 1964—; chmn. Georgia Telco Credit Union, Atlanta, 1988—. Office: Georgia Telco Credit Union 675 W Peachtree St NW Atlanta GA 30308-1952*

COULTER, MYRON LEE, retired academic administrator; b. Albany, Ind., Mar. 21, 1929; s. Mark Earl and Thelma Violet (Marks) C.; m. Barbara Bolinger, July 21, 1951; children: Nan and Benjamin (twins). BS, Ind. State Tchrs. Coll., 1951; MS, Ind. U., 1956, EdD, 1959; HLD (hon.), Coll. Idaho, 1982. Tchr. English Reading (Mich.) Pub. Schs., 1951-52; tchr. elem. grades Bloomington (Ind.) Pub. Schs., 1954-56; instr. edn. Ind. U., Bloomington, 1958-59; asst. prof. Pa. State U., 1959-64, assoc. prof., 1964-66; vis. prof. U. Alaska, Fairbanks, 1965; asso. dean edn., prof. edn. Western Mich. U., Kalamazoo, 1966-68, v.p. for adminstrn., prof. edn., 1968-76, interim pres., 1974; pres. Idaho State U., Pocatello, 1976-84; chancellor Western Carolina U., Cullowhee, N.C., 1984-94, chancellor emeritus, 1994—; del. Israeli Univs., 1976, Am. Assn. State Colls. and Univs. to People's Republic of China, 1981, Swaziland Coll. Tech., 1985, People's Republic China, 1985, 87, 88, 90, Jamaica, 1986, 89, 91, 94, Thailand, 1987, 90, The Netherlands, 1991; cons. in field. Author school textbooks. Bd. dirs. Kalamazoo C. of C., 1975-76, Pocatello Jr. Achievement; bd. dirs., chair N.C. Arboretum, 1994—; bd. dirs. WNC Pub. Radio, WNC Devel. Assn., WNC Tomorrow, Joint PVO/Univ. Rural Devel. Ctr., WNC Commn. Found.; lay leader Kalamazoo Meth. Ch., 1971-74; mem. Gov.'s Task Force on Aquaculture, 1988, N.C. Bd. Sci. and Tech., 1993—, Commn. for Competitive N.C., 1993—; chair N.C. Indian Gaming Cert. Commn., 1994—; trustee Bronson Hosp., Kalamazoo, 1975-76, N.C. Ctr. Advancement Teaching, C.J. Harris Community Hosp. With AUS, 1952-54. Named Disting. Alumnus, Ind. State U., 1975, Ind. U., 1994; recipient award Western Mich. U. Alumni Assn., 1974, resolution of tribute Mich. State Legislature, 1976. Mem. Internat. Reading Assn., Am. Assn. State Colls. and Univs. (bd. dirs. 1981-84, exec. com. 1981-84, sec.-treas. 1984-87, found. bd. dirs. 1987—, chmn. 1988-89), Nat. Soc. Study of Edn., N.C. Assn. Colls. and Univs. (bd. dirs.), Western Coll. Assn., Pocatello C. of C. (bd. dirs. 1977-80), Asheville C. of C. (bd. dirs. 1985-86), Cherokee Hist. Assn., Ind. U. Coll. Edn. Alumni Assn. (Disting. Alumnus award 1994), Phi Delta Kappa, Omicron Delta Kappa, Phi Kappa Phi, Beta Gamma Sigma. Office: Western Carolina Univ Office Chancellor Emeritus 61 Hunter Cullowhee NC 28723

COUNCIL, TERRY RAY, military officer; b. Oakley, Kans., May 1, 1953; s. Dewey Junior and Phyllis Lorene (Hosley) C.; m. Ruth Louise Newman, Dec. 27, 1974; children: Charles R., Michael S., Lisa A., David A., Johnathan R., Sarah C. BSBA, Panhandle State U., 1975; MA in Procurement and Acquistion Mgmt., Webster U., 1994. Commd. 2d lt. U.S. Army, 1975, advanced through grades to lt. col.; ops. officer 10th ADA Group, Aviation Sec., Fed. Republic Germany, 1976-79; flight instr., combat skills 1st Bat./1st Aviation Bde, Ft. Rucker, Ala., 1980-81, flight comdr., combat skills, 1981-82; co. comdr. 12th Co., 1st Bat., 1st Avn Bde, Ft. Rucker, 1982-83; avn procurement officer AHIP, Avn systems Command, St. Louis, 1984-85; chief, OH-58 Procurement Sec. Avn Systems Command, St. Louis, 1985-86; bat. exec. officer 45th Aviation Bat., Tulsa, Okla., 1986-87; co. comdr. HHC, 1st Bat./245th Avn, Tulsa, 1987-89; co. comdr. maintenance co D Co, 1st Bat./245th Avn, 1989-91; bat. exec. officer D Co, 1st Bat./245th Avn, Tulsa, 1991-92, bat. comdr., 1992-94; aviation support facility comdr. AASF #2, Tulsa, 1991-96; sr. svc. coll. fellow U. Tex., Austin, 1996—. Head usher Love and Grace Ch., Broken Arrow, 1995. Mem. Nat. Guard Assn., Army Aviation Assn. Republican. Home: 12621 Picket Rope Ln Austin TX 78727 Office: U Tex Ctr Profl Devel/Tng 4030-2 W Braker Ln Ste 200 Austin TX 78759

COUNTRYMAN, EDWARD FRANCIS, historian, educator; b. Glens Falls, N.Y., July 31, 1944; s. Edward Francis and Agnes (Alford) C.; m. Evonne von Heussen, 1987; children: Karon Samantha, Kirstein Dawn; 1 son from previous marriage, Samuel Robert. B.A., Manhattan Coll., 1966; M.A., Cornell U., Ithaca, N.Y., 1969; Ph.D., Cornell U., 1971. Lectr. in history U. Canterbury (N.Z.), 1970-74; lectr. U. Warwick (Eng.), 1975-83, sr. lectr., 1983-88, reader, 1988-91; prof. So. Meth. U., Dallas, 1991—; vis. lectr. U. Cambridge (Eng.), 1979-80; vis. scholar NYU, N.Y.C., 1980-81; Cardozo vis. prof. Yale U., spring 1989. Cons. editor: Radical History Rev., 1982—; author: A People in Revolution, 1981 (Bancroft prize 1982), The American Revolution, 1985, (video) American Independence 1776, 1989, Americans: A Collision of Histories, 1996; co-author: Who Built America, 1990. Active civil rights movement, U.S., 1965-68; spokesperson Anti-War Movement, N.Z., 1970-73; active Campaign for Nuclear Disarmament, Eng., 1981—. Woodrow Wilson fellow, 1966-67; Danforth fellow, 1966-71; Samuel Foster Haven fellow, 1983. Mem. Brit. Assn. Am. Studies. Home: 31 Radford Rd Leamington Spa, Warwicks England CV31 1NF Office: So Meth U Dept History Dallas TX 75275

COUNTS, CONNIE BROWN, executive secretary; b. Atlanta, Dec. 2, 1946; d. Fred Harold and Frances (Burdette) Brown; m. Steven Dennis Counts, Aug. 1, 1970; children: Brian Scott, Steven D. Student, Ga. State Coll., 1967. Engring. clk. AT&T, Atlanta, 1965-68; sec. Jervis B. Webb Conveyors, Atlanta, 1969-70, Associated Gen. Contractors of Am., Vero Beach, Fla., 1972-73; engr., cost analyst clk. McGregor Corp., Albany, Ga., 1970-72; tchg. assoc. Charlotte (N.C.)-Mecklenburg Schs., 1982-89, 91-94; loan coord. Squires Homes, Inc., Charlotte, 1989-90, Homes by George Steele, Inc., Charlotte, 1990-91; corp. sec. Rose Corp., Charlotte, 1994—. Vol. Habitat for Humanity, Charlotte, 1987-88; bd. dirs. Charlotte-Mecklenberg Parent Tchr. Assn., 1980-85; sec. bd. dirs. Eastway Christian Ch., Charlotte, 1982-84. Evang. chairperson Eastway Christian Ch., 1995—, sec. bd. dirs., 1996. Mem. N.C. Assn. Teaching Assocs. Democrat. Mem. Christian Ch. Home: 8329 Wilson Woods Dr Charlotte NC 28227-3540

COUNTS, MARY LOU, retired telephone company executive; b. Prescott, Ark., June 14, 1933; d. Claude L. and Katie Gertrude (Bagwell) Barker; m. Eugene Counts, June 21, 1950; children: Brenda Kay, Jeanne Lou. Operator Southwestern Bell, Dallas, 1951-52, Hot Springs, Ark., 1952-62; clk. Southwestern Bell, Hot Springs, 1962-80, supr., 1980-83; mgr. Southwestern Bell, Little Rock, 1983-88; ret., 1988; pres. Ark. Chpt. Telephone Pioneers, Little Rock, 1986-87; co-chmn. State Pioneer Assembly, Ft. Smith, Ark., 1988-89. Vol. Nat. Park Svc., Hot Springs, 1989; pres. Jones PTA, Hot Springs, 1962-63; mem. Pub. Sch. Curriculum Study, 1963-64, Friends of the Fordyce, Hot Springs, 1989; co-chmn. State Pioneer Assembly, Hot Springs, 1989-91; active Virginia Clinton Kelley Dem. Women's Club of garland County, Salvation Army Women's Aux. Named Mrs. Ark. Pioneer, 1987. Mem. Telephone Pioneers (life, rep. Ark. chpt. 1991-93, chairwoman state assembly 1994, 96), Belles Ext. Homemakers Club, Rock Gardeners Horticulture Club, Garland County Coun. Garden Clubs (sec. 1993-94), Grow and Show Garden Club, Mrs. Ark. (life). Democrat. Methodist. Home: 513 2nd St Hot Springs National Park AR 71913-3629

COUNTS, MICHAEL L., theatre educator; b. Portland, Maine, Mar. 20, 1939; s. Clifford H. and Alice E. (Stevens) C.; m. Julia F. Lomba, Nov. 22, 1986 (div. Aug. 1993); 1 child, Chanda A. Counts. BA in Theatre summa cum laude, Pace U., 1977; MA in Theatre, Hunter Coll., N.Y.C., 1979; PhD in Theatre, CUNY, 1983. Instr. theatre Mercer County Cmty. Coll., Trenton, N.J., 1979-81, Kean Coll., Union, N.J., 1981-83, Jersey City (N.J.) State Coll., 1981-84; drama dir. Bishop George Ahr H.S., Edison, N.J., 1984-87; asst. prof. theatre Ill. State U., 1987-90; adj. prof. theatre Bloomfield (N.J.) Coll., 1991-92; asst. prof., dir. theatre Lyon Coll., Batesville, Ark., 1992—; adj. prof. film Raritan Valley Cmty. Coll., N.J., summer 1992; mem. Kennedy Ctr. Am. Coll. Theatre Festival, 1993—. Author: Coming Home, 1988; contbr. author: American Playwrights 1980-1945, 1995, British Playwrights 1956-95, 1996. Bd. dirs. Batesville Cmty. Theatre. Christian Johnson fellow Lyon Coll., 1995; "A" scholar CUNY, 1981. Mem. Am. Theatre and Drama Soc., Assn. of Theatre in Higher Edn., Southwest Theatre Assn., Ark. Theatre Assn. Office: Lyon Coll PO Box 2317 Batesville AR 72503-2317

COURSON, MAXWELL TAYLOR, communication arts educator; b. Jacksonville, Fla., Sept. 8, 1936; s. Maxwell Taylor and Walton Lott (Hinson) C.; m. Mary Irene Brooks, July 3, 1965 (div. Aug. 1984); 1 child, Melinda Leigh; m. Naomi Monaray Robinson, Aug. 4, 1985. ABJ, U. Ga., 1958, MA in Journalism, 1959; PhD in Am. Studies, U. Hawaii, 1976. News dir. WGGA Radio, Gainesville, Ga., 1959-60; info. specialist U.S. Army, Ft. Benning, Ga., 1960-62; reporter UPI, Raleigh, N.C., 1963-64; pub. rels. dir. South Ga. Coll., Douglas, 1964-68; asst. dir. univ. rels., grad. student U. Hawaii, Honolulu, 1968-73, 73-75; alumni affairs dir., dir. publs. Ga. So. Coll., Statesboro, 1975-77, 77-79; univ. rels. dir. Furman U., Greenville, S.C., 1980-83; coll. fund rep. So. Educators Inc., Norcross, Ga., 1983-84; assoc. prof. mass. comm. Tenn. Wesleyan Coll., Athens, 1984-90; assoc. prof. comm. arts U. N.C., Pembroke, 1990—; Contbr. numerous articles to profl. jours. Reader for the blind S.E. N.C. Radio Reading Svc., Fayetteville, 1992—. Mem. Soc. Profl. Journalists, N.C. Collegiate Press Assn., Antique Automobile Club Am. (Ea. Carolina chpt.). Methodist. Home: 1607 Hennessy Pl Fayetteville NC 28303-3821 Office: U NC Dept Communications Pembroke NC 28372

COURTNALL, RUSS, professional hockey player; b. Victoria, B.C., Can., June 3, 1965. With Toronto Maple Leafs, 1987-88, Montreal Canadiens, 1988-92, Minn. North Stars, 1992-93; right wing Dallas Stars, 1993—; played in NHL All-Star Game, 1994. played in NHL All-Star Game, 1994. Office: Dallas Stars 901 Main St Ste 2301 Dallas TX 75202-3714*

COURTNEY, CAROLYN ANN, school librarian; b. Plainview, Tex., Aug. 1, 1937; d. John Blanton and Geneva Louise (Stovall) Ross; m. Moyland Henry Courtney, Aug. 17, 1957; 1 child, Constance Elaine. BA summa cum laude, Wayland Bapt. Coll., 1969; MEd, W. Tex. State Coll., 1976; MLS, U. North Tex., 1990. Cert. elem., secondary, libr. tchr. 5th grade tchr. Hale Ctr. (Tex.) Ind. Sch. Dist., 1970-77, libr., 1977—. Mem. LWV (bd. mem. 1970-75), DAR (Good Citizen chair 1981-85), Tex. State Tchs. Assn. (life), Tex. Classroom Tchrs. Assn. (sec. 1983-85), Tex. Libr. Assn., Delta Kappa Gamma (rsch. chair 1975-77, publs. chair 1984-86, scholarship 1975). Methodist. Home: 209 S Floydada St Plainview TX 79072-6665 Office: Hale Center Ind Sch Dist Drawer M Hale Center TX 79041

COURTNEY, CONSTANCE E., lawyer; b. Plainview, Tex., Nov. 29, 1960; d. M.H. and Carolyn Courtney. BS, U. Tex., 1982, JD, 1985. Bar: Tex., U.S. Dist. Ct. (we. and no. dists.) Tex., U.S. Dist. Ct. (we. and ea. dists.) Ark., U.S. Dist. Ct. (we. dist.) Okla., U.S. Ct. Appeals (5th cir.) Tex. Com. clk. Natural Resources Com., Tex. Ho. of Rep., 1979; legis. staff to hon. Buck Florence Tex. Ho. of Rep., 1980-82; law clk. to hon. Jerre Williams U.S. Ct. Appeals (5th cir.), 1985-86; assoc. Thompson & Knight, Dallas, 1986-92, Brown McCarroll, Dallas, 1992-94, Hutcheson & Grundy, Dallas, 1994—. Contbr. articles to profl. jours. Moderator So. Meth. U. Sch. Law Environ. Career Seminar, 1989—. Mem. ABA, State Bar Tex. (coll., chair outreach com. environ. sect. 1989—, law sch. com. 1988-89, State Bar Coll., 1995—). Office: Hutcheson & Grundy 901 Main St Ste 6200 Dallas TX 75202-3770

COURTNEY, EDWARD, classics educator; b. Belfast, Northern Ireland, Mar. 22, 1932; came to U.S., 1982; s. George and Kathleen (Nicholson) C.; m. Brenda Virginia Meek, Dec. 18, 1962; children: Richard Marcus, Adam Matthew. BA, Trinity Coll., Dublin, Ireland, 1954; MA, Oxford U., 1957. Research lectr. Christ Ch., Oxford, 1955-59; lectr. in classics King's Coll., London, 1959-70, reader in classics, 1970-77, prof. Latin, 1977-82; prof. classics Stanford U., Calif., 1982-93, Ely prof. humanities, 1986-93; Gildersleeve prof. classics U. Va., Charlottesville, Va., 1993—. Author: Commentary on the Satires of Juvenal, 1980, The Poems of Petronius, 1991, The Fragmentary Latin Poets, 1993, Musa Lapidaria, A Selection of Latin Verse Inscriptions, 1995; editor: Valerius Flaccus, Argonautica, 1970, Juvenal, The Satires, A Critical Text, 1985, Statius, Silvae, 1990; joint editor: Ovid, Fasti, 1978. Mem. Am. Philol. Assn. Office: U Va 401 New Cabell Hall Charlottesville VA 22903

COUSINS, ROLAND B., business administration and management educator; b. Peter Hannon and Helen (Hogan) C.; m. Catherine Anne Kiziuk, Sept. 4, 1982 (div. Oct. 1984). BS in Mktg., Va. Polytech. Inst., 1965, MS in Mgmt., 1966; D in Bus. Adminstrn., Ind. U., 1973. Instr. U. Southwestern La., Lafayette, 1966-69, from asst. prof. mgmt. to assoc. prof. mgmt., 1973-89; assoc. instr. Ind. U., Bloomington, 1969-73; prof. bus. adminstrn. LaGrange (Ga.) Coll., 1990—; dir. Internat. Studies LaGrange Coll., 1990—; presenter workshops in field to mfrs., gen. pub., hosps., police depts., others; designer, instr. courses for pub. through Dept. Bus. & Industry Training U. Southwestern La., 1974-89; instr. internat. summer sessions; speaker in field. Contbr. articles to profl. jours. Home: PO Box 1631 Lagrange GA 30241 Office: LaGrange Coll 601 Broad St Lagrange GA 30240

COUTU, CHARLES ARTHUR, deacon; b. Central Falls, R.I., Oct. 3, 1927; s. Charles Arthur and Aldea Alma (Laliberte) C.; m. Yvette Rhea Dery, Nov. 26, 1953. AA, Our Lady of Providence Sem., 1949; Etudes Speciales de Philosophies, Sem. Philosophy, Montreal, Que., Can., 1951; A in Casualty Claims Law, Am. Ednl. Inst. N.J., 1966. Ordained deacon Roman Cath. Ch., 1978. Master of ceremonies Bishop Tracy, Lafayette, La., 1958-59; tchr. St. Teresa's High Sch., Decatur, Ill., 1964-65, Pitts., 1964-68; tchr. Holy Family Ch., Dale City, Va., 1971—, permanent diaconate commn. mem., 1986-89; defender of the bond Tribunal, Arlington, Va., 1992; subrogation mgr. United Svcs. Automobile Assn., Reston, Va., 1976—; advocate Tribunal, Arlington, 1976—; chmn. Arbitration Com., Washington, 1975-88; mem. Diaconal Coun. Exec. Com., 1987-90; vice-chmn. Evangelization Commn., Diocese of Arlington, 1979-80. Religious emblem counselor Cath. Com. on Scouting and Campfire, 1990. Sgt. 1st class U.S. Army, 1952-55. Mem. KC. Home: 13401 Keating Dr Woodbridge VA 22193-4859 Office: US Automobile Assn 1902 Campus Commons Dr Reston VA 22091-1516

COUTURIER, GORDON WAYNE, computer information systems educator, consultant; b. Sparta, Mich., Sept. 14, 1942; s. Clifford Charles and Edith (Reyburn) C.; m. Sylvia Jean Hatch, Mar. 21, 1964; children: Andrew Scott, Laura Couturier Shepard. BSEE, Mich. State U., 1964, MSEE, 1965; PhD, Northwestern U., 1971. Mem. tech. staff Bell Telephone Labs., Naperville, Ill., 1965-72; engr. project leader ITT, Des Plaines, Ill., 1972-80; dir. engr. GTE Subscriber Equipment Group, St. Petersburg, Fla., 1980-82, Paradyne, Largo, Fla., 1982-87; cons. C & C Cons., Safety Harbor, Fla., 1987—; assoc. prof. U. Tampa, 1988—; mem. engr. adv. coun., guest U. Fla. engr. dept., 1985—; v.p. prof. devel. Am. Soc. Training & Devel., Clearwater, Fla., 1987-90. Contbr. articles to profl. jours.; inventor. Councilman City of St. Charles, Ill., 1971-75; fin. chair Heritage Meth. Ch., Clearwater, Fla., 1982-88; mem., tng. and pub. staff officer USCG Aux., Palm Harbor, Fla.,

1993—. Recipient Men of Achievement award, 1989. Mem. IEEE Computer Soc., Assn. for Computing Machinery, Decision Sci. Inst., Am. Soc. Exptl. Edn. Republican. Home: 3127 Hillside Ln Safety Harbor FL 34695-5338 Office: U Tampa 401 W Kennedy Blvd Tampa FL 33606-1450

COVER, NORMAN BERNARD, retired electronic data processing administrator; b. Ephrata, Pa., Mar. 25, 1935; s. Barney Blainey and Chelta V. (Huff) C.; student Jacksonville U., 1955; m. Violet Hurmagene Winouski, Nov. 26, 1960; children: Brian Lee, Keith Alex. Tabulator operator State Farm Fire & Casualty Co., Bloomington, Ill., 1952-53, programming operator State Farm Mut. Auto Ins. Co., Jacksonville, Fla., 1954-56, shift supr., EDP, 1957-61, asst. supt. EDP, State Farm Ins. Co., Winter Haven, Fla., 1962-67, EDP supt., 1968-78, data processing mgr., 1979-97, ret., 1997. Chmn. data processing adv. com. Polk Community Coll., 1976-1992. Sponsor Winter Haven High Sch. Cotillion Club, 1982-88. Cert. in data processing. Mem. Data Processing Mgmt. Assn. (S.E. regional treas. 1974-75, S.E. regional v.p. 1975-77, internat. v.p. 1977-78, dir. spl. interest group cert. data processors 1978-80, v.p. 1981, pres. 1982 internat. dir. Polk County chpt. 1982-83, chmn. by-laws com. 1983-97, past pres.'s com. 1970—, Individual Performance awards 1972-91), SAR. Democrat. Club: Cypress Gardens Sertoma (chmn. Stamp Out Crime com. 1975-80, dir. 1980-82, v.p. 1984, sec. 1985, pres. 1986, chmn. bd. 1987, 91), Sertoma Lake Ridge (dist. gov. 1988-89, sec. treas. 1990-91), Sertoma Camp Endeavor Inc. (dir. 1989, chmn. bd. dirs. 1997, sec. 1990, 93-95, v.p. devel. and pub. rels. 1991-92, pres. 1996—). Home: 70 Greenfield Ct Winter Haven FL 33884-1302

COVERDELL, PAUL DOUGLAS, senator; b. Jan. 20, 1939. BA in Journalism, U. Mo., 1960. m. Nancy Nally. Mem. Ga. Senate, 1970-89, minority leader, 1974-89, chmn. Fulton delegation, 1974-84; dir. Peace Corps., Washington, 1989-91; former pres., CEO Coverdell & Co., Inc., Atlanta; U.S. senator from Ga., 1993—, mem. senate fgn. rels. com., mem. senate agr. com., mem. senate small bus. com.; former pres., bd. dirs. Urban Study Inst. Ga., Ga. Health Found.; chmn. Ga. Rep. Party; former pres. Nat. Rep. Legis. Assn. Capt. USAR. Office: US Senate 200 Russell Senate Bldg Washington DC 20510-1004

COVEY, ELLEN, neurobiologist, researcher; b. Elmhurst, Ill., Sept. 26, 1947; d. Loren H. and Betty E. Covey; m. Hasmukh Doshi, 1969 (div. 1976); 1 child, Vijay; m. John H. Casseday, Jan. 1, 1981. Student, Acad. Fine Arts, Rome, 1965-67; BS in Biology, U. Houston, 1974, MS in Biology, 1976; PhD in Psychology, Duke U., 1980. Postdoctoral trainee Princeton (N.J.) U., 1980-81; rsch. assoc. Duke U. Med. Ctr., Durham, N.C., 1981-88, rsch. assoc. neurobiology, 1988-92, asst. rsch. prof. neurobiology, 1992—; vis. scientist Zoologisches Inst., U. Munich, 1985—; reviewer NSF, Nat. Inst. on Deafness and Other Comms. Disorders, NIH, Jour. Comparative Physiology A, Exptl. Brain Rsch., Brain Rsch., Jour. Neurosci., Jour. Neurophysiology. Author: (with others) Directional Hearing, 1987, Animal Sonar Systems, 1989, The Mammalian Cochlear Nuclei: Organization and Function, 1993, Handbook of Auditory Research, Vo. V: Hearing and Echolocation in Bats, 1995; contbr. articles to profl. jours. Mem. Assn. for Rsch. in Otolaryngology, Soc. for Neurosci., European Neurosci. Assn., Sigma Xi. Democrat. Office: Duke U Med Ctr Dept Neurobiology PO Box 3209 Durham NC 27710

COVEY, ROSEMARY FEIT, artist; b. Johannesburg, South Africa, July 17, 1954; d. Edward and Ruth (Morris) Feit; m. Adam Wishnow. Student printmaking, Barry Moser, 1968-72; student, Cornell U., 1972-74, Md. Inst. Coll. of Art, Balt., 1974-76. One person shows include Jane Haslem Gallery, Washington, 1992, Interlochen (Mich.) Ctr. Arts, 1992, L.A. 12th Nat. Print Exhbn., Frederick S. Wright Gallery, UCLA, 1993; group shows include Women Printmakers: 18th Century to Present, Nat. Mus. Women Arts, Washington, 1994, Fitchburg (Mass.) Art Mus., 1981, Brockton (Mass.) Art Mus., 1984; works in permanent collections at Georgetown U., Washington, The Phillips Collection, Washington, 1989; commns. include seven cover illustratoins, Washington Post/Book World, Washington, 1980-90, 90th Anniversary Print, Internat. Fedn. Metalworkers, Zurich, Switzerland, 1983, 17 illustrations World & I Mag., Washington, 1986-87, 2 wood-engravings prints GE Astro-Space, Princetoin, N.J., 1991-92; illustrator: Musical Heritage Rev., 1978, Berta Broadfoot & Pepin the Short, 1990, Shadows & Goatbones, 1992, Stark Naked on a Cold Irish Morning, 1992, Peking Street Peddlers, 1994. Recipient Torpedo Factory Artists award, 1990, 92; Nat. Printmaking grantee Alpha Delta Kappa Found., 1992. Mem. Torpedo Factory Artists Assn. (pres. Target Gallery 1993-94). Office: Torpedo Factory Art Ctr 105 N Union St Alexandria VA 22314

COVIN, CAROL LOUISE, computer consultant; b. Chgo., July 2, 1947; d. Raymond Lincoln and Elizabeth Day (Notley) Frederick; m. David William Covin, Jan. 24, 1968; children: David William Jr., Jonathan Michael. BA, George Washington U., 1972. Data base adminstr. USN, Alexandria, Va., 1973-77; cons. Data Base Mgmt., Inc., Springfield, Va., 1977-79, 82-87; pres. Covin Assocs., Falls Church, Va., 1987-90; cons. Electro-Tech. Internat., Annandale, Va., 1990-91, Abacus Tech., Chevy Chase, Md., 1991-93, Tech. Internat., Fairfax, Va., 1993-95; with Computer Products & Svcs., Inc., Fairfax, 1995—. Author: The Computer Professional's Job Guide to Washington, D.C., 1989, Covin's New England Computer Job Guide, 1991, Covin's Washington Computer Job Guide, 1993, Covin's Midwest Computer Job Guide, 1995, Covin's Southeast Computer Job Guide, 1996. Mem. Assn. Systems Mgmt. (pres. 1990-92, v.p. 1992-93, treas. 1993—), Data Adminstrn. Mgmt. Assn., Washington Apple Pi.

COVINGTON, GAIL LYNN, nurse practitioner; b. N.J., Apr. 4, 1950; d. George and Ina May (Smith) Poole; m. Alexander Palmer Covington, May 20, 1972 (div. June 1979). BS in Nursing, East Carolina U., 1972; MS in Nursing, U. N.C., 1977, postgrad., 1993. Cert. color analyst, beauty cons., ACLS provider, childbirth educator. Instr. Stuart Circle Hosp. Sch. Nursing, Richmond, Va., 1972-73; instr. Richmond Meml. Hosp. Sch. Nursing, 1973-74, relief staff nurse, 1973-74; staff nurse Rex Hosp., Raleigh, N.C., 1974-76; coordinator pediatric nursing Watts Hosp. Sch. Nursing, Durham, N.C., 1977-78; dir. clin. edn. Wake Med. Ctr., Raleigh, 1978-90; practice cons. N.C. Bd. of Nursing, Raleigh, 1990-92; family nurse practitioner Hampton & Lewis, Ob-Gyn, Oxford, N.C., 1993-95, Montgomery Women's Health Svcs., Ocracoke Health Ctr., Troy, N.C., 1995—; cons. in field. Editor: Pregnancy, 1976. Author: Post-Partum Exercises, 1977, 86. Coord. med. vols. Wake County Olympic Sports Festival, 1987; charge nurse ARC, N.C. State Fair, 1979—; bd. dirs. Friends of Elizabeth II, 1990-92, crew mem., med. officer, 1986-92; bd. dirs. Jamestown Sailing Vessels, 1991-95. Mem. NAACOG (vice chmn. 1980-82, sec.-treas. 1984-87). Home: PO Box 3171 Pinehurst NC 28374 Office: Montgomery Womens Hlth Svcs Maternity Svcs Troy NC 27371

COVINGTON, GARY WAYNE, accountant; b. Monroe, La., Dec. 21, 1956; s. William Gardner and Edith (Harris) C. BS, N.E. La. U., 1980, BBA in Acctg., 1983; MBA, La. Tech. U., 1988. CPA, cert. govt. fin. mgr. Staff acct. City of West Monroe, La., 1983-88; acctg. supr. U. Miss. Med. Ctr., Jackson, 1989; staff acct. Breazeale, Saunders & O'Neil, CPAs, Jackson, 1990; pub. accounts examiner State of Ala., Mobile, 1991-94; auditor Office of Legis. Auditor State of La., Baton Rouge, 1994-95; pvt. practice, 1996—; asst. county agt. La. State U. Ext. Svc., Columbia, 1981-82; mem. acctg. club Assn. MBA Execs., N.Y.C., 1985-89. Vol. 4-H Club, West Monroe, 1982-83; supervisory bd. mem. City of West Monroe Employees Credit Union, 1983-88. Mem. AICPA, Nat. Grants Mgmt. Assn., Assn. Govt. Accts. (cert. govt. fin. mgr.), Soc. La. CPAs, Assn. Cert. Fraud Examiners, Delta Demeter.

COVINGTON, HARRISON WALL, artist, educator; b. Plant City, Fla., Apr. 12, 1924; s. Edmund DeBerry and Maria Thomas (Gregory) C.; m. Janie Lucile Langford, June 5, 1947; children: David, Langford. BFA with honors, U. Fla., 1949, MFA with honors, 1953. Art prof. U. Fla.; chmn. art dept. U. South Fla., 1961-67, dean Coll. of Fine Arts, 1967-71, 77-82, dean emeritus, prof. emeritus, 1982—. Over 40 one-man shows; represented in permanent collections including The Nat. Gallery of Art; exhibited at Mus. of Modern Art, N.Y.C. 1st lt. Air Corps U.S. Army, 1942-46, PTO. Recipient Disting. Alumni award Coll. of Fine Arts, U. Fla., 1994-95.

COVINGTON, JAMES EDWIN, government agency administrator, psychologist; b. Wadesboro, N.C., June 26, 1943; s. James Edwin and Louise (Memory) C.; m. Linda Doreen Davis, May 31, 1971 (div. Feb. 1982); children: James Edwin III, Bradley Davis. BA, Duke U., 1965; MSc, N.C. State U., 1977, PhD, 1981. Lic. psychologist, N.C. Commd. 2d lt. U.S. Army, 1967, advanced through grades to col., 1989, served in Vietnam, ret., 1992; spl. advisor for arms control and chem. demilitarization Dept. of Def., Washington, 1993—; psychol. cons., Springfield, Va., 1992—; prof. mil. sci. Duke U., Durham, N.C., 1983; del. 1st U.S. visit to former Soviet Chem. Weapons Sites in Russia, 1990; mem. U.S. delegation for negotiation of worldwide Chem. Weapons Conv., Geneva, 1992; advisor U.S. Delegation to Chem. Weapons Preparatory Commn., The Hague, 1993. Decorated Def. Superior Svc. medal, Purple Heart with oak leaf cluster, Bronze Star, Air Medal with 7 oak leaf clusters, Army Commendation Medal with valor device, others; decorated for heroism at Hamburger Hill, Vietnam, 1969. Mem. APA, Va. Psychol. Assn. Methodist. Home: 8620 Burling Wood Dr Springfield VA 22152-2316 Office: Office of Asst to Sec of Def 2451 Crystal Dr Ste 650 Arlington VA 22202

COVINGTON, MICHAEL AARON, linguist; b. Valdosta, Ga., Sept. 14, 1957; s. Charles Gordon and Hazel (Roberts) C.; m. Melody Mauldin, July 25, 1982; children: Catherine Anne, Sharon Elizabeth. BA summa cum laude, U. Ga., 1977; MPhil, Cambridge U., 1978; PhD, Yale U., 1982. Postdoctoral fellow U. So. Calif., L.A., 1982-84; rsch. assoc. U. Ga., Athens, 1984-85, asst. rsch. scientist, 1985-90, assoc. rsch. scientist, 1990—; contbg. editor PC Technques Mag., Scottsdale, Ariz., 1990—. Author: Syntactic Theory in the High Middle Ages, 1984, Astrophotography for the Amateur, 1985, Dictionary of Computer Terms, 1986, Natural Language Processing for Prolog Programmers, 1993; contbg. editor Electronics Now Mag., Farmingdale, N.Y., 1995—; contbr. articles to profl. jours. Named U.S. Pres.'s scholar Internat. Sci. Sch., 1973; recipient First prize humanities/social scis., IBM Supercomputer Competition, 1989-90. Mem. IEEE (sr.), Assn. for Computational Linguistics, Linguistic Soc. of Am., N.Y. C.S. Lewis Soc., Am. Radio Relay League, Assn. for Logic Programming. Baptist. Office: U Ga Artificial Intelligence Ctr Athens GA 30602-7415

COVINGTON, TAMMIE WARREN, elementary education educator; b. Columbia, S.C., Dec. 20, 1960; d. Charles Larry and Betty Joyce (Collum) Warren; m. Terry Lee Covington, Dec. 22, 1979; 1 child, Matthew Lee. BA in Elem. Edn., U. S.C., 1982, M in Elem. Edn., 1989. Tchr. Ridge Spring (S.C.)-Monetta Elem. Sch., 1982-90, W. Wyman King Acad., Batesburg, S.C., 1991-92, North (S.C.) Elem. Sch., 1992-94, Batesburg (S.C.) Leesville Mid. Sch., 1994—. Mem. Delta Kappa Gamma. Home: 1204 S Lee St Batesburg SC 29006 Office: Batesburg-Leesville Mid Sch 101 W Columbia Ave Batesburg SC 29006-2124

COWAN, FREDERIC JOSEPH, lawyer; b. N.Y.C., Oct. 11, 1945; s. Frederic Joseph Sr. and Mary Virginia (Wesley) C.; m. Linda Marshall Scholle, Apr. 28, 1974; children: Elizabeth, Caroline, Allison. AB, Dartmouth Coll., 1967; JD, Harvard U., 1978. Bar: Ky. 1978, U.S. Dist. Ct. (we. dist.) Ky. 1979, U.S. Ct. Appeals (6th cir.) 1984, U.S. Supreme Ct. 1989. Vol. Peace Corps, Ethiopia, 1967-69; assoc. Brown, Todd & Heyburn, Louisville, 1979-83; ptnr. Rice, Porter, Seiller & Price, Louisville, 1983-87; atty. gen. Commonwealth of Ky., 1988-92; counsel Lynch, Cox, Gilman & Manan, 1992—; Ky. State Rep., 32d legis. dist., 1982-87; chair Ky. Child Support Enforcement Commn., 1988-91, Ky. Sexual Abuse and Exploitation Prevention Bd., 1988-91; bd. dirs. Ky. Job Tng. Coordinating Council, Frankfort, Louisville Bar Found., 1986. Vice chmn. judiciary criminal com. Ky. Ho. of Reps., 1985-87; chmn. budget com. on justice Judiciary and Corrections Ky. Ho. of Reps., 1985-87, Leadership Ky., 1985; U.S. del. election mission to Namibia Nat. Dem. Inst. for Internat. Affairs, 1989; U.S. del. dem. instns. seminar Nat. Dem. Inst. for Internat. Affairs, Slovenia, 1992; electoral supr. Orgn. for Security and Cooperation in Europe, Bosnia and Herzogovina, 1996. Mem. ABA, Ky. Bar Assn., Louisville Bar Assn., Ky. Acad. Trial Attys. Methodist. Home: 1747 Sulgrave Rd Louisville KY 40205-1643 Office: 500 Meidinger Towers Louisville KY 40202

COWAN, JAMES HOWARD, JR., fishery scientist, biological oceanographer; b. Fayetteville, N.C., Mar. 9, 1955; s. James Howard and Imelda Lee C.; m. Jean-Louise Watts, Dec. 30, 1989. BS in Biology, Old Dominion U., 1978, MS in Biol. Oceanography, 1981; PhD in Marine Sci., La. State U., 1985, MS in Exptl. Stats., 1988. Field coord. Atlantic Bluefin Tuna Rsch. Program Nat. Marine Fisheries Svc., 1979-81; rsch. asst. dept. marine sci. and coastal ecology lab. La. State U., 1981-82; fellow La. State U. Marine and Coastal Fisheries, Baton Rouge, 1983-85; rsch. assoc. La. State U. Coastal Ecology Inst., Baton Rouge, 1985-88; postdoctoral rsch. assoc. U. Md. Chesapeake Biol. Lab., Solomons, 1988-90, asst. rsch. scientist, 1990-92; rsch. assoc. Oak Ridge (Tenn.) Nat. Lab., 1990-92; sr. marine scientist Dauphin Island (Ala.) Sea Lab., 1992—; assoc. prof. U. South Ala., Mobile, 1992—; U.S. Del. Internat. Coun. for Exploration of Sea, 1991; reef fish stock assessment panel mem. Gulf Mex. Fish Mgmt. Coun., 1992—, chair, 1995—; mackerel stock assessment panel mem., 1992—; std. sci. stats. com., 1995—; ctrl. sub-sect. mem. Gulf Mex. Regional Marine Rsch. Bd., 1992—; mem. acad. rev. bd. admissions dept. marine sci. La. State U., 1984-85, rsch. and edn. program rev. com. Ctr. for Wetland Resources dept. marine sci., 1985-86; acad. coun. Ctr. for Environ. and Estuarine Studies, U. Md. Sys., 1988-91; recruitment com. dept. marine scis. U. South Ala., 1992—, chair policy and procedures com. dept. marine scis., 1992—; mem. student adv. coms. Old Dominion U., Va. Inst. Marine Scis., U. South Ala., U. Ga., U. Calif., Davis; cons. in field. Contbr. numerous articles to profl. jours. Lyle St. Amant scholar Am. Shrimp Canners Assn., 1982-83, Joseph Lipsey Meml. scholar, 1983-84, scholar Rockefeller Wildlife Refuge, 1982-85, 94, Tech. Commun. Am. Soc. Tech. Commun., Miss-Ala. Sea Grant, 1993—; La. Sea grantee, 1987, La. Fisheries Initiative grantee , 1984-85, grantee Nat. Marine Fisheries Svc., 1987-88, Va. Marine Resources Commn., 1990, Electric Power Rsch. Inst.-Oak Ridge Nat. Lab., 1990—, NSF, 1992—, Calif. Dept. Water Resources, 1991—. Mem. Am. Fisheries Soc. (pres. early life history sect. 1996—, outstanding chpt. award com. Tidewater, La. and Ala. chpt. 1995—), Am. Soc. Limnologists and Oceanographers, Estuarine Rsch. Fedn. (editl. bd. Estuaries 1994—, Gulf of Mex. Sci. 1996—). Democrat. Office: U South Ala Dauphin Island Sea Lab PO Box 369-370 Dauphin Island AL 36528

COWAN, JOHN JOSEPH, lawyer; b. Chester, Pa., Nov. 14, 1932; s. John Joseph and Helen Marie (Frame) C.; m. Hilary Ann Gregory, Dec. 29, 1960; children—Daniel, Patrick, Meg, Jennifer. A.B., LaSalle Coll., 1954; J.D. cum laude, U. Pa., 1959. Bar: D.C. 1960, Ohio 1964, W.Va. 1968, U.S. Supreme Ct. 1971. Teaching fellow Stanford U., Palo Alto, Calif., 1959-60; trial atty. civil div. U.S. Dept. Justice, Washington, 1960-63; assoc. Taft, Stettinius & Hollister, Cin., 1963-67; gen. atty. Chesapeake & Potomac Telephone Co. of W.Va., Charleston, 1968-79; ptnr. Sullivan & Cowan, Charleston, 1979-82; sole practice, Charleston, 1982—. Served to 1st lt. AUS, 1954-56. Mem. ABA. Sr. adv. editor U. Pa. Law Rev., 1958-59. Home: 2326 Windham Rd Charleston WV 25303-3021 Office: PO Box 152 Charleston WV 25321-0152

COWAN, NANCY SUE, nurse, hemodialysis technician; b. Emporia, Kans., Nov. 11, 1949; d. Paul Allen and Eva Mae (Murry) Storrer; m. J.C. Cowan, Nov. 10, 1967 (div. 1973); children: Brian Keith, Bobby Allen. Student, McNeese State U.; LPN, Sowela Tech. Inst., 1978. Nurse Lake Charles (La.) Meml. Hosp., 1978—, chmn. critical care connection, 1990-92;, 1990-93. Contbr. articles to profl. jours. Leadership vol. ARC, Lake Charles, 1978—, dir. disaster svcs., 1993-94, mem. La. field svc. team, mem. disaster svcs. team, 1990-95, chmn. KPLC-TV Cmty. Christmas, 1995-96, svc. ctr. mgr., 1995—, disaster computer operations specialist, 1995—, family svcs. coord., 1995—; den leader Boy Scouts Am., 1991-95, chmn. pack 28 com., 1993-95. Named Vol. of Yr. ARC, 1990. Office: Lake Charles Meml Hosp 1701 Oak Park Blvd Lake Charles LA 70601-8911

COWAN, RICHARD HOWARD, pediatrician; b. Harrison, Ark., Aug. 15, 1946; s. Thomas Wynne and Mary Louise (Pinkerton) C.; m. Marcia Lynn Kaplan, Sept. 3, 1972; children: Fredrick Scott, Brian Wynne. BA, Vanderbilt U., 1968; MD, U. Tenn., 1971. Diplomate Am. Bd. Pediatrics. Intern in pediatrics U. Tenn., Memphis, 1972; resident in pediatrics Children's Hosp., Birmingham, Ala., 1973-74; served in USAMC, Ft. Hood, Tex., 1975-77; fellow in pediat. nephrology U. Tenn., Memphis, 1977-78; pediatrician Jefferson Health Found., Birmingham, 1979, The Norwood Clinic, Birmingham, 1980-84, HealthAmerica/Maxicare, Birmingham, 1984-87, Brookside Pediatrics, Kingsport, Tenn., 1987-89, Miller Med. Group, Nashville, 1989-92, The Pediat. Ctr., Tullahoma, Tenn., 1992—; acting med. dir. Jefferson Health Found., Birmingham; asst. med. dir. HealthAm., 1987, chief pediatrics, 1985-87; chmn. quality assurance Miller Med. Group, 1990-92. Fellow Am. Acad. Pediatrics; mem. Coffee County Med. Soc. (pres. 1995), Kiwanis, Alpha Omega Alpha. Unitarian. Office: The Pediatric Ctr 1401 W Lincoln St Tullahoma TN 37388-5606

COWAN, THOMAS DAVID, emergency medical services professional; b. Asheville, N.C., Jan. 5, 1957; s. Richard Eugene and Mary Virginia (Jacobs) C.; m. Elaine Hyatt, June 22, 1986. AAS in Nursing, Asheville Buncombe Tech. Inst., 1977, diploma in emergency med. sci., 1982; cert. in emergency med. svc., Mgmt. Inst. U. N.C., Charlotte, 1985. RN, N.C., Tenn.; cert. paramedic, N.C. Field technician Buncombe County Emergency Med. Svc., Asheville, 1978-82, ops. supr., 1982-91; emergency med. svcs. liaison Meml. Mission Med. Ctr., Asheville, 1991-94, regional emergency med. svcs. mgr., 1994—; mem. adv. com. Emergency Sci. Med. Curriculum Asheville Buncombe Tech. Coll., 1983—. Mem. N.C. Assn. Emergency Med. Svc. Adminstrs., Am. Trauma Soc., N.C. Assn. Paramedics. Office: Meml Mission Med Ctr 509 Biltmore Ave Asheville NC 28801-4601

COWART, JOHN LAWHON, real estate company executive; b. Houston, Jan. 13, 1944; s. Lawrence and Doris (Lawhon) C.; m. Mary Elmore Kellogg, June 31, 1968 (div. Sept. 1994); children: Catherine, Robert; m. Rosemary Dowell, Nov. 25, 1994. BA, U. Tex., 1966; MDiv, Yale U., 1969. Ordained Episcopal priest, 1969, Roman Cath. Ch., 1984. Priest Episc. Ch., 1969-77; estimator Forum Masonry, Seagoville, Tex., 1977-84; priest Roman Cath. Ch., Dallas, 1984-94; file adminstr. Archon Group L.P. a subsidiary of Goldman Sach, Irving, Tex., 1994—; chaplain Fed. Bur. Prisons, Ft. Worth, 1984-90, Dallas County Jail, 1984-94. Author: The Prison Minister's Handbook, 1996, Miranda, 1995. Del. Tex. State Dem. Conv., Dallas, 1996. Democrat. Methodist. Home: 1623 W Third St Irving TX 75060 Office: J E Robert Companies 600 Las Colinas Blvd #1900 Irving TX 75039

COWART, NORTON E., SR., physician; b. Greeley, Ala., Jan. 17, 1920; s. Benjamin H. and Emily A. (Coletrane) C.; m. Lillian Lanham; children: Cynthia C. Palmer, Beverley C. Settle, Norton E. Jr., Rebecca C. Hammond, Steven L. BS, Birmingham So. Coll., 1943; MD, U. Ill., Chgo., 1946. Intern Lloyd Noland Hosp., Fairfield, Ala., 1946-47; resident in internal medicine Lloyd Noland Hosp., Fairfield, 1946-51; NSN USN, Fairfield, 1951-53; pvt. practice medicine Huntsville (Ala.) Clinic, 1950-85; pres. med. staff Huntsville Hosp., 1972-73; pres. Madison County Med. Soc.; chmn. Madison County Bd. Health; bd. dirs. Mut. Assurance, Birmingham, chmn. bd. dirs., 1987-96, ret., 1996. Organizer, bd. dirs. South Trust Bank Huntsville, 1964-85; elder Presbyn. Ch. Lt. USN, 1951-53. Mem. AMA, Ala. Med. Soc., Madison County Med. Soc. (pres. 1957), Am. Soc. Internal Medicine, Am. Diabetic Soc. Home: 2301 Covemont Dr Huntsville AL 35801-2258

COWLES, ROGER WILLIAM, federal agency administrator; b. Ft. Madison, Iowa, July 5, 1945; s. Arthur William and Enid Francis (Smith) C. BBA cum laude, Tex. Wesleyan Coll., 1968; MA, Cen. Mich. U., 1980. Cert. cost analyst, Va. Contract auditor Def. Contract Audit Agy., Ft. Worth, 1967-76; course mgr. Def. Contract Audit Inst., Memphis, 1976-78; program mgr. hdqrs. Def. Contract Audit Agy., Alexandria, Va., 1978-80, chief mgmt. info. branch, 1980-81, chief spl. audits, 1982-86; auditor dir. contract mgmt. Office of Asst. Sec. Def., 1986-88; chief audit liason div. Office Dept. Def. Compt., Washington, 1988-89, dir. for contract audit and analysis directorate, 1990—; mem. congl. staff U.S. Congress, Washington, 1981-82; head U.S. Del. for Fin. Regulations to Moscow and Kiev, Ukraine, 1994—. Creator toothpick sculpture (Spl. Merit award 1975); contbr. articles to profl. jours. Mem. adminstrv. bd. Franconia United Meth. Ch., 1989-91. Mem. Assn. Govt. Accts. (facilitator 1985-87, Tng. Program award 1981), Am. Soc. Mil. Compts. (pres. Washington chpt. 1994-95), St. Exec. Svc., Nat. Contract Mgmt. Assn., Inst. Cost Analysis, Mgmt. Devel. Program, Sr. Exec. Svc. Assn., Smithsonian Assocs., Fed. Execs. Inst. Alumni Assn., Nat. Trust for Hist. Preservation, Colonial Williamsburg Found., Nat. Cathedral Found. Republican. Methodist. Office: Office of Dept Def Compt The Pentagon Rm 3c965 Alexandria VA 22301

COWLING, DAVID EDWARD, lawyer; b. Lubbock, Tex., May 29, 1951; s. Ben Edward and Doris Patricia (Lovelace) C.; m. Amy Bosson Youngquist, Apr. 24, 1982. BA, Tex. Tech U., 1973; JD, U. Tex., 1976; LLM in Taxation, NYU, 1977. Bar: Tex. 1976, D.C. 1977, N.Y. 1979. Tax atty. Kronish, Lieb, Shainswit, Wiener & Hellman, N.Y.C., 1977-82, Jones, Day, Reavis & Pogue, Dallas, 1982—. Mem. ABA. N.Y. State Bar Assn., D.C. Bar Assn., Tex. State Bar Assn., Assn. of Bar of City of N.Y. Home: 6527 Lakehurst Ave Dallas TX 75230-5201 Office: Jones Day Reavis & Pogue 2300 Trammell Crow Ctr 2001 Ross Ave Dallas TX 75201-8001*

COX, ALBERT HARRINGTON, JR., economist; b. St. Louis, Oct. 13, 1932; s. Albert Harrington and Hildegarde (Raab) C.; m. Frances Marie French, Apr. 12, 1960; children: Cynthia, Bruce Harrington. BBA, U. Tex., 1954, MBA, 1956; PhD, U. Mich., 1965. Asst. prof. finance So. Meth. U., Dallas, 1959; economist First Nat. City Bank, N.Y.C., 1960-61; sec. research com. Am. Bankers Assn., N.Y.C., 1962-64; v.p., economist First Nat. Bank, Dallas, 1965-68; spl. asst. to chmn. Pres.'s Council Econ. Advs., Washington, 1969-70; exec. v.p., chief economist, dir. Lionel D. Edie & Co., N.Y.C., 1970-75; sr. econ. adv. Merrill Lynch, Pierce, Fenner & Smith, Inc., N.Y.C., 1970-75; pres. Merrill Lynch Econs., Inc., N.Y.C., 1976-81, chmn., 1982-84; chief economist Merrill Lynch & Co., 1976-81; mng. dir. Merrill Lynch Capital Markets Group; dir. Merrill Lynch Capital Fund; mem. econ. adv. bd. Dept. Commerce, 1974-76; dir., sr. econ. adviser BIL Trainer, Wortham Inc. (Bank in Liechtenstein, A.G.), 1985-90; sr. econ. adviser Trainer Wortham, Inc., 1991; portfolio cons. The Seibels Bruce Ins. Cos., Columbia, S.C., 1993—, dir., 1994—; dir. Atlantic Capital Corp., 1995—; mem. Pres.'s Inflation Policy Task Force, 1980; disting. lectr. in bus. and econs. U. S.C., Hilton Head, 1988-90. Author: Regulation of Interest Rates on Bank Deposits, 1966; contbg. economist Bankers Monthly mag., 1970-88; bus. columnist Hilton Head News, 1990—; contbr. articles to profl. jours. Mem. Nat. Assn. Bus. Economists (past dir.), Securities Industries Assn. (chmn. econ. adv. com. 1979-80), Am. Econ. Assn., Beta Gamma Sigma, Beta Theta Pi, Phi Eta Sigma. Republican. Mem. Reformed Ch. Home: 2002 Claudette Ct Biloxi MS 39531

COX, BARBARA CLAIRE, costume designer, educator; b. Lock Haven, Pa., Apr. 4, 1939; d. Albert Clair and June Anne (Hutchins) Shultz; m. Richard Joseph Cox, Aug. 28, 1960 (div. 1970). BA, SUNY, Albany, 1961; student, Brandeis U., 1961, Cornell U., 1961-68; MFA, Carnegie-Mellon U., 1970. Mem. faculty Stanford U., Palo Alto, Calif., 1970-73; costume dir. Utah Shakespearean Festival, Cedar City, Utah, 1970-81; costume designer Alley Theatre, Houston, 1973-76; mem. faculty dept. theatre arts Calif. State U., Long Beach, 1976-81; costume designer South Coast Repertory Theatre, Costa Mesa, Calif., 1978-82; mem. faculty dance and theatre arts U. North Tex., Denton, 1988—; costume designer Dallas Shakespeare, 1991; owner Barbara C. Cox Designs, 1978—. costume dir. Circle Theatre, Ft. Worth, 1989—. Bd. dirs. Denton Civic Ballet. Recipient Excellence in Costume Design award Los Angeles Drama Critics Circle, 1982, Costume Design awards Drama Logue, Los Angeles, 1982-88, LA Weekly, 1985-88. Mem. AAUP, AAUW, U.S. Inst. Theatre Tech., Costume Soc. Am., United Scenic Artists. Home: 65 The Retreat Denton TX 76205-2746 Office: Univ N Tex Dept Dance Theatre Arts Denton TX 76203

COX, BOBBY (ROBERT JOE COX), professional baseball manager; b. Tulsa, Okla., May 21, 1941; m. Pamela Cox; children: Kami, Keisha, Skyla. Student, Reedley Jr. Coll., Calif. Player Calif. League, Reno, Nev., 1960, Northwest League, Salem, Oreg., 1961-62, Texas League, Albuquerque, 1963-64; player Pacific Coast League, Salt Lake City, 1965, Tacoma, Wash., 1966; player Internat. League, Richmond, Va., 1967, New York Yankees, N.Y.C., 1968-69, Internat. League, Syracuse, N.Y., 1970; player Fla. State League, Ft. Lauderdale, 1971, mgr., 1971; mgr. Ea. League, West Haven, Conn., 1972, Internat. League, Syracuse, 1973-76; 1st base coach New York Yankees, N.Y.C., 1977; mgr. Atlanta Braves, 1978-81, Toronto (Ont., Can.) Blue Jays, 1982-85, Atlanta Braves, 1990—. Named Maj. League Mgr. of Yr., Baseball Writers' Assn. Am., 1985, Nat. League Mgr. of Yr., 1991; Maj. League Mgr. of Yr. Sporting News, 1985, Nat.

League Mgr. of Yr., 1991, 93. Office: care Atlanta Braves PO Box 4064 Atlanta GA 30302-4064*

COX, CAROL A., oncological nurse; b. N.C., Dec. 3, 1954. ADN, Miami (Fla.) Dade Community Coll., 1986; BSN, Fla. Internat. U., 1994. Fl. nurse Coral Reef Hosp., Miami; charge nurse, relief supr. Green Briar Nursing Ctr., Miami; charge nurse crisis unit CHI, Miami; supr. nursing Criticare Home Health, Miami; oncology staff nurse Bapt. Hosp., Miami, 1990—; nursing instr. part-time Miami Dade Cmty. Coll., 1995—.

COX, DAVID FULLEN, chemical engineering educator; b. Marietta, Ga., July 4, 1956; w. Loyd C. and Marjorie F. Cox; m. Teresa Louise Ludovici, Aug. 11, 1984; children: Lewis Michael, Abigail Lorraine. BS, U. Tenn., 1979; MS, U. Fla., 1980, PhD, 1984. NRC postdoctoral rsch. assoc. Nat. Bur. Stds., Gaithersburg, Md., 1984-86; asst. prof. chem. engring. Va. Polytechnic Inst. and State U., Blacksburg, 1986-91, assoc. prof. chem. engring., 1991—; reviewer NSF, Dept. of Energy, Petroleum Rsch. Fund., also various sci. jours. Contbr. articles to profl. jours. Recipient Rahm and Haas scholarship, 1978, 79; Shell Found. fellow, 1981, Eastman Kodak fellow, 1980. Mem. AICE (faculty advisor student chpt. 1990—), Am. Vacuum Soc. (student rsch. fellow 1983), Am. Chem. Soc., Tri-State Analysts Club. Office: Va Polytechnic Inst State U Dept Chem Engring Blacksburg VA 24061-0211

COX, EMMETT RIPLEY, federal judge; b. Cottonwood, Ala., Feb. 13, 1935; s. Emmett M. Cox, Jr. and Myra E. (Ripley) Stewart; m. Ann MacKay Haas, May 16, 1965; children: John Haas, Catherine MacKay. BA, U. Ala., 1957, JD, 1959. Bar: Ala. 1959, U.S. Ct. Appeal (5th, 8th and 11th cirs.), U.S. Supreme Ct. Assoc. Mead, Norman & Fitzpatrick, Birmingham, Ala., 1959-64; assoc. then ptnr. Gaillard, Wilkins, Smith & Cox, Mobile, Ala., 1964-69; ptnr. Nettles, Cox & Barker, 1969-81; judge U.S. Dist. Ct. (so. dist.) Ala., Mobile, 1981-88, U.S. Ct. Appeals (11th cir.), Mobile, 1988—; mem. def. svcs. com. Jud. Conf. U.S. Mem. Ala. Bar Assn., Mobile Bar Assn., Fed. Bar Assn., Maritime Law Assn. of the U.S., Omicron Delta Kappa, Phi Delta Phi, Alpha Tau Omega (past pres.). Office: US Courthouse 11th Circuit 113 Saint Joseph St Ste 433 Mobile AL 36602-3624*

COX, FRANK D. (BUDDY COX), oil company executive, exploration consultant; b. Shreveport, La., Dec. 20, 1932; s. Ohmer M. and Beulah O. (Scott) C.; m. Betty Jean Hand, June 19, 1956; children: Cynthia Dell, Carolyn Diane, Frank D. Jr. BS in Bus. Adminstrn., La. Tech. U., 1956; postgrad., Centenary Coll., 1958-59. Cert. profl. landman; lic. real estate, Fla. Various postition Exxon Corp., Houston, 1955-86, chief landman, v.p. coal resources, 1980-86; pvt. practice Houston, 1986-89; sr. v.p. Energy Exploration Mgmt. Co., Houston, 1989-94; v.p., mgr. T-Bar-X Ltd. Co., Houston, 1994—; v.p., dir. Power Exploration Internat., Houston, 1994—. Capt. USAF, 1956-58. Named disting. mil. grad. La. Tech. U., Ruston, 1955. Mem. Am. Assn. Petroleum Landmen, Houston Assn. Petroleum Landmen, W. Houston Assn. Petroleum Landmen, W. Houston Exxon Annuitant Club, 100 Club of Greater Houston, Omicron Delta Kappa. Republican. Baptist. Home: 14830 Carolcrest St Houston TX 77079-6312 Office: T-Bar-X Ltd Co 5847 San Felipe Ste 3830 Houston TX 77057

COX, GARY S., state education official; b. Sept. 21, 1944; m. Linda F. Cox; children: Dana Berliner, Allyson, Angela Hadley, Allison Jessee. BA in Polit. Sci., Morehead State U., 1966; MS in Polit. Sci., U. Ky., 1974, PhD in Polit. Sci., 1975. Dir. pub. affairs internship program Morehead State U., 1969-70, asst. prof., 1969-74; rsch. analyst Ky. Legis. Rsch. Commn., 1974, exec. asst. to dir., 1974-76, dep. dir., 1976-77; fed.-state coord. Ky. Coun. Higher Edn., 1977-78, exec. asst. to dir. govtl. affairs, 1978, dep. exec. dir. policy and govtl. affairs, 1981-86, dep. exec. dir. agy. ops. and coun. mem. rels., 1984-86, acting exec. dir., 1986-87, exec. dir., 1987—; dean sch. pub. affairs Ky. State U., 1978-80; legis. liaison Ky. Gov.'s Office, 1983-84. Author: (with others) Kentucky Government. Fellow So. Regional Tng. Program Pub. Adminstrn., 1966-67. Address: 5105 Huntington Woods Rd Frankfort KY 40601-9770 Office: Coun Higher Edn 1050 Us Highway 127 S Frankfort KY 40601-4326*

COX, GEORGE SHERWOOD, computer science educator; b. McAllen, Tex., Jan. 12, 1963; s. Jerry Alton and Eldora (Chrismier) C. BA in Communication, U. Tex. Pan Am., 1985; MA in Religious Edn., Southwestern Bapt. Theol. Sem., Ft. Worth, 1988. Lic. to ministry So. Bapt. Conv., 1985, ordained, 1990. Assoc. min. edn. South Hills Bapt. Ch., Ft. Worth, 1987-88; min. youth, assoc. pastor Trinity Bapt. Ch., McAllen, 1989-91; account exec. Christian radio Sta. KVTY, McAllen, 1991; mgr. Tex. Valley Computer, Weslaco, 1991-94; instr. computers South Tex. Vocat. Tech. Inst., McAllen, 1994—; dir. Bapt. Student Union, U. Tex., Brownsville, Bapt. Gen. Conv. Tex., Dallas, 1988-93. Republican. Home: 320 S Peking St Mcallen TX 78501

COX, GEORGE STANLEY, principal; b. Montgomery, Ala., Sept. 8, 1962; s. George Harvey and Annette (Wilson) C.; m. Kelly Marie Broom, Jan. 16, 1993; children: Wilson Marie, Benjamin Parker. BA in Psychology, Auburn U., 1984, BS in Edn., 1986; MEd, Troy State U., 1989. Tchr. Prattville (Ala.) H.S., 1986-87, Capitol Heights Jr. H.S., Montgomery, 1987-92, Baldwin Magnet Sch., Montgomery, 1992-93; asst. prin. Brewbaker Jr. H.S., Montgomery, 1993-94; prin. Georgia Washington Jr. H.S., Pike Road, Ala., 1994—; cons. State Dept. of Edn., Montgomery, 1995—. Recipient Gov.'s award Ala. Gov., 1991; named Outstanding Prin. Ala. L.D. Assn., 1995; grantee Montgomery Pub. Sch. Fund, 1996. Mem. ASCD, Montgomery Prins. Assn. (v.p. 1994—). Office: Georgia Washington Jr High Sch 696 Georgia Washington Rd Pike Road AL 36064

COX, GLENN ANDREW, JR., petroleum company executive; b. Sedalia, Mo., Aug. 6, 1929; s. Glenn Andrew and Ruth Lonsdale (Atkinson) C.; m. Veronica Cecelia Martin, Jan. 3, 1953; children: Martin Stuart, Grant Andrew, Cecelia Ruth. BBA, So. Meth. U., 1951. With Phillips Petroleum Co., Bartlesville, Okla., 1956-91; asst. to chmn. operating com. Phillips Petroleum Co., Bartlesville, 1973-74, v.p. mgmt. info. and control, 1974-80, exec. v.p., 1980-85, dir., 1982-91, pres., chief operating officer, 1985-91; bd. dirs. BOK Fin. Corp., Bank of Okla., The Williams Co.'s, Inc., Helmerich and Payne, Tulsa, Union Tex. Petroleum Holdings, Houston. Pres. Cherokee Area coun. Boy Scouts Am., 1977-82, South Ctrl. region, 1987-90, mem. nat. exec. bd., 1987-94; mem. bd. curators Ctrl. Meth. Coll., Fayette, Mo., 1984-88; trustee Philbrook Mus. Art, 1987-92, So. Meth. U., Dallas, 1988—; bd. dirs. Okla. United Meth. Found.; mem. Okla. State Regents for Higher Edn. Mem. Am. Petroleum Inst. (bd. dirs. 1982-91), Nat. Assn. Mfrs. (bd. dirs. 1985-91), Bartlesville Area C. of C. (pres. 1978), Hillcrest Country Club. Methodist. Office: Reda Bldg 401 S Dewey Ave Ste 318 Bartlesville OK 74003-3545

COX, HOUSTON ABRAHAM, JR., futures markets consultant; b. Starkville, Miss., May 21, 1918; s. Houston Abraham and Kathleen Drew (Tidmore) C.; m. Margaret Virginia Wray, June 29, 1942 (div. Mar. 1989); children: Marlys Kimbrough Cox Beetley, Kathleen McCleary Cox Burghardt, Anna Margaret Cox Gregory; m. Gloria Algarra Roca, Apr. 29, 1989; children: Maria Clara Ganley, Luis Felipe Roca. Student, Miss. State Coll., 1935-38; BA, U. Mo., 1939, BJ, 1968. News editor Sta. KPO, NBC, San Francisco, 1944-45; pres. Sta. WCLE, Clearwater (Fla.) Broadcasting Co., 1946-50; mgr. commodity dept. Merrill Lynch, Pierce, Fenner & Smith, Palm Beach, Fla., 1951-58; gen. ptnr., mgr. nat. commodity dept. Reynolds & Co., N.Y.C., 1963-71; v.p., nat. commodity dept. Reynolds Securities, Inc., N.Y.C., 1971-76; v.p. ACLI Community Svcs., Inc., N.Y.C., 1976; 1st v.p. Smith Barney Harris Upham & Co., Inc., N.Y.C., 1977-80; managed portfolio advisor Merrill Lynch Commodities, Inc., N.Y.C., 1980-85; cons. on futures markets Cox Proprietorship, Sarasota, Fla., 1985—; bd. dirs. N.Y. Coffee and Sugar Exch. N.Y., 1971-73; mem. N.Y. Cotton Exch., 1978-80; mem. Chgo. Bd. Trade, 1964-80, chmn. N.Y. membership com., 1972-80; mem. Chgo. Merc. Exch., 1964-76, Kansas City Bd. Trade, 1964-76; mem. N.Y. Cocoa Exch., 1974-80, bd. mgrs., 1974-80. Author: Common Sense Approach to Commodity Futures Trading, 1968, Concepts on Profits in Commodity Future Trading, 1972; also articles. Chmn. commodities com. Greater N.Y. coun. Boy Scouts Am., 1967-68; bd. dirs. Conn. Young Life; chmn. ofcl. bd. United Meth. Ch., Darien, Conn., 1966-69, trustee, 1966-69; mem. bd. trustees Perpetual Found., First United Meth. Ch., Sarasota, 1994-96; mem. Gulf Gate Cmty. Assn., Sarasota, 1990—. Mem. Futures Industry Assn. (bd. dirs. 1965-80, chmn. bd. 1971-73), Soc. Profl. Journalists, Swedish Colonial Soc., Blue Key, Commodity Club N.Y. (pres. 1965-67, bd. dirs. 1963-71), Kappa Sigma, Phi Eta Sigma, Sigma Delta Chi. Republican. Home and Office: 7417 Bounty Dr Sarasota FL 34231-7921

COX, JAMES D., law educator; b. 1943. J.D., U. Calif. Hastings Sch. Law, 1969; LL.M., Harvard U., 1971. Bar: Calif. 1970. Atty.-adv. Office Gen. Counsel FTC, Washington, 1969-70; teaching fellow Boston U., 1970-71; asst. prof. U. San Francisco, 1971-74; assoc. prof. U. Calif. Hastings Sch. Law, 1974-75; vis. assoc. prof. Stanford U., 1976-77; prof. U. Calif. Hastings Sch. Law, 1977-79; vis. prof. Duke U. Sch. Law, spring 1979, prof., 1979—; mem. com. on corps. State Bar Calif., N.C. bus. corp. act. draft com., N.C. nonprofit corp. draft com.; E.T. Bost rsch. prof., fall 1980. Author: Financial Information, Accounting and the Law, 1980, Sum and Substance of Corporations, 5th edit., 1988, (with Hillman and Langevoort) Securities Regulation: Cases and Materials, 1991, (with Hazen and O'Neal) Corporations, 1995. Sr. Fulbright Rsch. fellow, Australia, 1989. Mem. Am. Law Inst., Order of Coif, Phi Kappa Phi. Office: Duke U Sch Law Durham NC 27706

COX, JOHN THOMAS, JR., lawyer; b. Shreveport, La., Feb. 9, 1943; s. John Thomas and Gladys Virginia (Canterbury) C.; m. Tracey L. Tanquary, Aug. 27, 1966; children: John Thomas, III, Stephen Lewis. B.S., La. State U., 1965, J.D., 1968. Bar: La. 1968, U.S. Dist. Ct. (we., mid. and ea. dist.) La., U.S. Dist. Ct. (ea. dist.) Tex., U.S. Ct. Apls. (5th and 8th cirs.), U.S. Tax Ct., U.S. Sup. Ct. Assoc., Sanders, Miller, Downing & Keene, Baton Rouge, La., 1968-70; assoc. Blanchard, Walker, O'Quin & Roberts, Shreveport, 1970-71, ptnr., 1971—; tchr. bus. law Centenary Coll. La. Served to lt. USAR, 1963-69. Recipient Valley Forge Freedoms Found. George Washington Honor medal. Mem. ABA, La. Bar Assn., Caddo Parish Bar Assn., Am. Assn. Def. Counsel, La. Assn. Def. Counsel. Presbyterian. Club: Shreveport. Address: 555 Dunmoreland Dr Shreveport LA 71106-6124

COX, LARRY D., airport terminal executive. With Memphis Internat. Airport, Tenn., 1973-84, pres., 1984. Office: Memphis Internat Airport Memphis-Shelby County Airport Authority PO Box 30168 Memphis TN 38130-0168

COX, LYNETTA FRANCES, neonatal intensive care nurse; b. Bethlehem, Pa., Oct. 11, 1945; d. LeRoy Evan and Gloria Essie (Lee) Sell; m. Henry George Fromhartz, June 4, 1967 (div. May 1984); 1 child, Deborah Suzanne; m. Steven David Cox, Sept. 10, 1989. BS in Chemistry, Moravian Coll., 1967; diploma, Pottsville Hosp. Sch. Nursing, 1981; BSN summa cum laude, Armstrong State Coll., 1992; M Nursing in Neonatal Nurse Practitioner summa cum laude, Emory U., 1994. RN, Ga.; cert. neonatal nurse practitioner; cert. instr. BCLS and neonatal resuscitation program; cert. RN in neonatal intensive care. Rsch. chemist Water Pollution Control Dept., City of Phila., 1967-70; quality control chemist Just Born Candy Co., Bethlehem, Pa., 1971-72; neonatal staff nurse Geisinger Med. Ctr., Danville, Pa., 1981-84, Meml. Med. Ctr., Savannah, Ga., 1984-96, Egleston Children's Hosp., Atlanta, 1993-94; neonatal nurse practitioner Savannah Neonatology PC, 1995-96, Phoebe Putney Meml. Hosp., Albany, Ga., 1996—. Mem. Nat. Perinatal Assn., Ga. Perinatal Assn., Nat. Assn. Neonatal Nurses, Chattahoochee Assn. Neonatal Nurses, Sigma Theta Tau. Home: 210 Hibiscus Rd Albany GA 31705 Office: Phoebe Putney Meml Hosp Neonatal ICU 417 W 3rd Ave Albany GA 31701-1943

COX, MARY JOAN TUCKER, genealogist; b. Big Stone Gap, Va., Feb. 10, 1933; d. Thomas A. and Rosa Louise (Turner) Tucker; m. James White Cox, Nov. 6, 1953; children: Katherine D., James White. Diploma, Inst. of Jewish-Christian, Studies, Dallas, 1987; student, U. Tex., Laredo, 1963-65. Author: Breezing Through the Jones Tree: John Paul Jones and I, 1995. Vol. Contact Teleministries, Knoxville, Tenn.; past vol. Knoxville Police Dept.; dir., tchr. Sunday Sch. dept. various states, 1960-96. Recipient Scroll of Appreciation U.S. Army Europe V Corps, Germany, 1963. Home: 4116 Fulton Dr Knoxville TN 37918

COX, VICTORIA KATHLEEN, humanities educator; b. Buenos Aires, Aug. 28, 1962; d. Robert John and Maud Alice (Daverio) C. BA in Biology and Philosophy with honors, Goucher Coll., Towson, Md., 1984; MA in Philosophy, Georgetown U., 1986; MA in Spanish, CUNY, 1989; postgrad., U. Md., 1990—. Supr. college, mentor for minority students U. Md., 1993-94; instr. Spanish and Latin American lit. Presbyn. Coll., S.C., 1996—. Contbr. articles to profl. jours. Rsch. grantee CUNY, 1989. Mem. MLA, Latin American Studies Assn., Am. Assn. of Tchrs. of Spanish and Portuguese. Home: 5 South Hampton Dr Charleston SC 29407 Office: Coll of Charleston 66 George St Charleston SC 29424-0001

COX, WILLIAM JACKSON, bishop; b. Valeria, Ky., Jan. 24, 1921; s. Robert Lee and Ora Ethel (Lawson) C.; m. Betty Drake, Dec. 20, 1941; children—Sharon Lee, William Richard, Michael Colin. Student, U. Cin., 1939-40, George Washington U., Washington, 1945-46, U. Md. overseas extension, London, 1951-53, Va. Theol. Sem., Alexandria, 1957; D.Div. (hon.), Va. Theol. Sem., Alexandria, 1974, Episcopal Theol. Sem. Ky., Lexington, 1980. Ordained priest Episcopal Ch., 1957. Pres., gen. mgr. McCook Broadcasting Co., McCook, Nebr., 1947-49; rector Church of the Holy Cross, Cumberland, Md., 1957-72; suffragan bishop of Md. Episcopal Ch., Frederick, Md., 1972-80; asst. bishop Okla. Episcopal Ch., Tulsa, 1980—; pres. Appalachian Peoples Service Orgn., Blacksburg, Va., 1974-80; chmn. Standing Com. on the Church in Small Communities, N.Y.C., 1976-82. Pres., Nursing Home Bd. of Allegany County, Cumberland, Md., 1965-72; pres. Episcopal Ministries to the Aging, Balt., 1973-80. Served to lt. col. U.S. Army, 1942-46, 1949-54; ETO. Home: 6130 S Hudson Pl Tulsa OK 74136-2703 Office: Diocese of Okla 501 S Cincinnati Ave Tulsa OK 74103-4801

COX, WILLIAM WALTER, dentist; b. Abingdon, Va., Jan. 17, 1947; s. Walter Roy and Beatrice Ellen (Woodward) C.; m. Neva Duncan Herzog, Apr. 23, 1976 (div. Sept. 1985); 1 child, Lesley Ellen. BS in Chemistry, U. Richmond, 1969; DDS, Med. Coll. Va., 1973. Dentist Bisese, Kail & Cox, Inc., Portsmouth, Va., 1976—. Capt. U.S. Army, 1973-76. Settle scholar U. Richmond. Mem. Tidewater Dental Assn. (chmn. patient rels. com. 1984—), Tidewater Dental Study Club, Portsmouth-Suffolk Dental Study Club (sec.-treas. 1990-91, pres. 1991-92). Republican. Methodist. Home: 3209 Bruin Dr Chesapeake VA 23321-4601 Office: Bisese Kail & Cox 5717 Churchland Blvd Portsmouth VA 23703-3308

COX-BEAIRD, DIAN SANDERS, middle school educator; b. Murchison, Tex., Dec. 18, 1946; d. Jessie Jackson and Lola Mae (Burton) Sanders; m. Richard Lewis Cox, May 24, 1969 (div. Nov. 1993); 1 child, Stuart Scott; m. Charles A. Beaird, Dec. 1994. AA, Kilgore Jr. Coll., 1967; BA, Stephen F. Austin State U., 1969, MEd, 1983. Cert. provisional gen. elem. edn., provisional h.s. history, govt. and polit. sci. Tchr. 8th grade Am. history and 7th grade Tex. history Chapel Hill Ind. Sch. Dist., Tyler, Tex., 1970-79; tchr. 6th-7th grade regular, advanced, remedial reading Sabine Ind. Sch. Dist., Gladewater, Tex., 1981—; mem., tutor East Tex. Literacy Coun., Longview, 1992—; sec. Sabine Jr. High PTO, Gladewater, 1990-91; faculty sponsor cheerleaders Chapel Hill Ind. Sch. Dist., Tyler, 1970-73, rep. curriculum com., 1976, historian PTO, 1974; mem. anthology com. N.J. Writing Project in Tex., Kilgore, 1991; selected hostess Internat. Reading Conf., Tucson, 1992. Presenter: The Toothpaste Millionaire, 1992; contbr.: (short story) Vocies from the Heart, 1991. Leader Girl Scouts Am., Tyler, 1973; counselor Camp Natowa-Campfire Girls, Big Sandy, Tex., 1970; dir. Bible Sch., 1st Meth. Ch., Overton, Tex., 1980; sec. Young Dems., Kilgore, 1965-67; actress Gallery Theater, Jefferson, Tex.; mem. Opera House Theater and Galley Theater, 1992—. Named Outstanding Tchr. in Tex., Macmillan/McGraw Hill, 1991; Free Enterprise Forum scholar East Tex. Bapt. U., 1991. Mem. Internat. Reading Assn. (presenter 1992), Tex. Mid. Sch. Assn., Piney Woods Reading Coun., Tex. State Tchrs. Assn. (campus rep. 1990—, sec. Chapel Hill Ind. Sch. Dist. 1971-72), Laubach Literacy Action. Home: PO Box 1146 Hallsville TX 75650 Office: Sabine Jr H S RR 1 Box 189 Gladewater TX 75647-9723

COY, ELBA BOONE, real estate developer; b. Franklin, Ind., Oct. 19, 1924; s. Elba and Hazel Marie (Boone) C.; m. Maralee Thornburg, May 18, 1946 (div. 1966); children: Pamela Marie Coy Payne, Debra Diane Coy Reed, David Boone; m. Geraldine Knauff Reddick, Oct. 1, 1966; children: Steven Eugene, Kendra Joann Coy Kahn, Kristina Kay Coy Grantham, Bruce Edward. BS, Ind. U., 1949, postgrad., 1949-50; student, Purdue U., 1943-44. Assoc. prof. econs. Wharton Sch. Fin., U. Pa., Phila., 1950-51; reg. mgr. Pilgrim Life Ins. Co., Indpls., 1956-60, Tower Group Cos./Channing Funds, Boston and Battle Creek, 1960-66; dir., pres. Jackson Std. Corp., Nat. Sec. Life Assurance, Universal Mort, Indpls., 1967-69; area dir. HUD, Indpls., 1969-71; dir. Urban Nat. Devel. Co., Houston, 1971-74; dir. devel. Monesson & Co., Dallas, 1974-75; exec. dir. Harris County Community Devel./Housing Authority, Houston, 1975-76; dir. devel. Good Samaritan Luth. Home, Houston, 1976-80, Caltex, Ltd., Houston, 1980-88; cons. in field. Author: Brief History of Whiteland, Indiana, 1956. Nat. bd. dirs. U.S. Jaycees, 1955; mem. Ind. Gen. Assembly, 1961-65. With USN, 1943-46, PTO. Mem. Texas On-Site Wastewater Treatment Rsch. Coun., Am. Legion, VFW, Odd Fellows. Republican. Mem. Disciples of Christ. Address: 17602 Loring Ln Spring TX 77388-5745

COY, HOWARD LOUIS, JR., librarian; b. Monroe, La., July 16, 1945; s. Howard L. and Marie (Brown) C. BA in Advt. Design, Northeast La. U., 1969. Libr. Leesville (La.) State Sch., 1970-80; foster care worker, supr. Vernon Parish OHD/DES, Leesville, 1980-82; dir. Vernon Parish Libr., 1982—; bd. dirs. Librs. S.W., Lake Charles, La., 1989—. Treas. Dry Forks Vol. Fire Dept., 1990—; 2d vice chmn. Govt. Documents Round Table; bd. dirs. Vernon Parish Litracy Coun., Sunshine Apts., Leesville, 1988—; bd. dirs., 2d v.p. Vernon Arts Coun., 1988—. Mem. La. Libr. Assn., Librs. S.W. (bd. dirs. 1990—), Vernon Comty. Action Coun.

CRABBS, RAYMOND DOUGLAS, educational organization executive; b. Spring Valley, Ill., Jan. 5, 1947; s. Joseph Isaac and Teresa Beatrice (Levy) C.; m. Cheryl Lee Shoults, July 26, 1991; children: Brian Michael, David Christopher, Wesley Jowitt, James Jowitt, Catelyn Jowitt. BS in Agrl. Econs., Wash. State U., 1969, MA in Pub. Adminstrn., 1972. Staff assoc. Coop. Extension Svc., Everett, Wash., 1966-67; assoc. dir. Wash. State U. Found., Pullman, 1969-72; exec. dir. Wash. State 4-H Found., Puyallup, 1972-75; sr. v.p. Nat. 4-H Coun., Chevy Chase, Md., 1975-87, Quest Internat., Granville, Ohio, 1987-90; pres., CEO Nat. Soc. Fund Raising Execs., 1990; founder, pres., CEO Vision Assocs., 1990—; fund raising guest lectr., 1975—; freelance community devel. cons., Tucson, Louisville, 1984—; mem. Nat. Policy Com. on 4-H, Washington, 1979-88; dep. head mision Youth Devel. Del. to China, 1982. sst. campaign mgr. Evans for Gov. Campaign, Wash., 1968, 72; mem. Pullman City Coun., 1968-70; fund raiser St. Elizabeth's Cath. Ch., Rockville, Md., 1982-84; co-founder Nat. Coalition on Drug and Alcohol Abuse, 1982; pres. Alliance for a Drug Free Soc. (subs. Pres.'s Drug Adv. Com. 1990-94). With U.S. Army, 1969-70. W.K. Kellogg Found. fellow, 1984-87. Mem. Am. Soc. Assn. Execs., Nat. Assn. 4-H Staff, Ind. Sector, Met. Club (Chgo.). Republican. Roman Catholic. Office: 10619 Sandy Run Trail Fairfax Station VA 22039

CRABTREE, JOHN MICHAEL, college administrator, consultant; b. Fostoria, Ohio, Nov. 11, 1949; s. John Dwight and Opal Marie (Tate) C.; m. Cheryl Lynn Wallace, July 6, 1974. AA in Music Edn., Mt. Vernon Nazarene Coll., 1970; B in Mus. Edn., So. Nazarene Univ., 1972, MA in Edn., 1976; postgrad. U. Okla., 1976. Sports info. dir. So. Nazarene Univ., Okla., 1971-80, dir. pub. rels., 1974-80, assoc. dean student devel., 1974-78, dir. alumni and media rels., 1980-89, adminstrv. asst. to pres., 1989-90, dir. for Univ. Advancement, 1989, exec. dir. 1990—; adj. prof. mktg., 1979-82; bd. rsch. advisors Governing Bd. Editors and Pub. Bd. The Am. Biographical Inst. Editor The Perspective, 1981-89. Chmn. United Fund Drive, Bethany, 1983; pub. rels. dir. B.U.I.L.D. (Bethany United Improvement League Downtown); mem. exec. bd. Bethany Main St. Named Mgr. of Yr. So. Nazarene U., 1988; exec. sec. Nazerene Officers of Instl. Advancement, 1989-90—; pres. Nazarine Offices of Instl. Adv., 1996— bd. dirs. Mabel Fry Meml. Libr., Yukon, Okla., 1990-94, So. Nazarene U. Found., 1993—. Mem. Nat. Soc. Fund Raising Execs., Bethany Hist. Soc. (life), Bethany C. of C., Okla. Coll. Pub. Rels. Assn., Council for Advancement and Support of Edn., Okla. Civic Music Assn. (bd. dirs.), Okla. City Audubon Soc. (pub. rels. dir. Wildlife Film Series, 1974-93), Sports Info. Dirs. Am. (com. 1974-80, ethics com. 1978-80 job attrition bd. 1980), Oklahoma City C. of C. (pub. rels. and econ. devel. bds.), Council for the Advancement and Support of Edn., Okla. Ind. Coll. Found., Okla. Friends of the Libr., Okla. Civic Music Assn. (exec. bd. dirs.), Oklahoma City Friends of Eng. (mem. exec. bd. dirs.), Sigma Tau Delta. Republican. Club: Kiwanis. Avocations: photography, philately, antique book collector. Office: So Nazarene U 6729 NW 39th Expy Bethany OK 73008-2605

CRABTREE, YVETTE GUISLAIN, internist; b. Merriam, Kans., June 2, 1966; d. Serge Jacques and Jessamine Claire (Ewert) G.; m. Christopher Edley Crabtree, June 30, 1990; children: Madison, Yvette. Student, Kans. State U., 1988; MD, Johns Hopkins U., 1993. Internist Bapt. Hosp., Nashville, 1993—, resident, chief resident. Mem. AMA, Nashville Acad. Medicine. Home: 3549 Seasons Dr Antioch TN 37013 Office: Bapt Hosp 2000 Church St Nashville TN 37236-0001

CRAFT, CAROL ANN, librarian; b. McKinney, Tex., Mar. 2, 1942; d. Don Lee and Mattie Lee (Miller) C. BS, Tex. Woman's U., 1964, MA, 1970; MLS, U. So. Miss., 1986. Cabin counselor/tennis instr. Nakanawa Camps for Girls, Md., Tenn., 1963-73; instr. English, phys. edn. Orchard Farm (Mo.) Jr./Sr. H.S., 1964-65; instr. health, phys. edn. Graham (Tex.) Ind. Sch. Dist., 1965-66; tchr. phys. edn. Richardson (Tex.) Ind. Sch. Dist., 1969-77; libr. Our Lady of Holy Cross Coll., New Orleans, 1978-89; libr. Delgado C.C., New Orleans, 1989—, asst. prof., 1994—. Contbr. articles to newsletters; author poetry. Mem. Magnolia League Tennis Team, 1994-95, Nat. Criminal Justice Ref. Svc., 1993—. Recipient Doubles Tennis Silver medal La. Sr. Olympic Games, 1996. Mem. La. Libr. Assn. Office: Delgado Community College 615 City Park Ave New Orleans LA 70119

CRAFT, DAVID RALPH, artist, educator; b. Elberton, Ga., July 31, 1945; s. Ralph Ben and Hazel (Scott) C. BS, East Tenn. State U., 1967. Instr. Hunter Mus. Art, Chattanooga, 1974-84; tchr. art Girls Preparatory Sch., Chattanooga, 1984—. Exhibited at Smithsonian Instn., 1976, 78, 82, USIA, 1975, Nat. Mus. Am. Art, 1982, Tenn. State Mus., Nashville, 1985; one man shows include Genesis Art Gallery, Chattanooga, Tenn., 1978, Jacksonville (Ala.) State U., 1984; group shows include Greenville (S.C.) County Mus., Miss. Mus. Art, Jackson, Roanoke (Va.) Mus. Fine Arts, Birmingham (Ala.) Mus. Art, Hunter Mus. Art, Chattanooga, Nat. Mus. Am. Art, Smithsonian Inst., Washington, Gallery 210, Chattanooga, Next Door Gallery, Chattanooga, Creative Arts Guild, Dalton, Ga., Sioux City (Iowa) Art Ctr., Kalamazoo (Mich.) Inst. Arts, U. So. Colo., Pueblo, Mus. Tex. Tech. U., Lubbock, First Am. Ctr., Nashville, El Paso (Tex.) Mus. Art, Ark. Art Ctr., Little Rock, Millersville (Pa.) State Coll., Cedar Rapids (Iowa) Art Ctr., Shreveport (La.) Art Guild, Bountiful (Utah) Art Ctr., Brooks Meml. Art Gallery, Memphis; represented in permanent collections Ala. Electric, Birmingham, TVA, Knoxville, IBM, N.Y.C., Walden Club, Chattanooga, Am. Nat. Bank, Chattanooga, Hunter Mus. Art, Chattanooga, Dulin Gallery Art, Knoxville, Tenn. Arts Commn., Nashville. Mem. Assn. of Visual Artists. Office: Girls Preparatory School 200 Barton Ave Chattanooga TN 37405-4201

CRAFT, JAMES PRESSLEY, JR., educator, financial consultant; b. Louisville, Ga., Nov. 1, 1913; s. James Pressley and Edith (Galphin) C.; student Naval Postgrad. Sch., 1940-42; M.S., MIT, 1943; postgrad. Naval War Coll., 1952-53; Ph.D., U. Pa., 1969; m. Carolyn Crockett Martin, July 30, 1937; children: Carolyn Martin, James Pressley III, Frederick Galphin. Commd. ensign USN, 1934, advanced through grades to capt., 1952; head. contingency plans br. of Joint Staff of Joint Chiefs of Staff, 1960-62; comdr. U.S. Destroyers Mediterranean, 1959-60; dean men U. Pa., 1964-67, fellow, 1967-68; asst. prof. Ursinus Coll., Collegeville, Pa., 1968-69, assoc. prof. polit. sci., 1969-77, prof., 1977-80, asst. dean coll., 1970-77, exec. asst. to pres., 1977, v.p. for planning and adminstrn., 1977-80; pvt. cons., Austin, Tex., 1980—; vis. scholar U. Mich., summer 1971. Decorated Silver Star, Bronze Star with V, Purple Heart; recipient Letter of Commendation with V. NSF fellow Va. Poly. Inst. and State U., 1973. Mem. Pa. Polit. Sci. Assn.

(pres. 1978-80), Northeastern Polit. Sci. Assn. (pres.-elect 1979-80), Naval Inst. Home and Office: 7201 Montana Norte Austin TX 78731-2125

CRAFT, JANICE YVONNE, art educator; b. Palestine, Tex., Sept. 13, 1937; d. Stanley Don and Sammie Nell (Harris) C.; divorced; children: Elayne, Holly, Beth. BA, U. Houston, 1983, MA, 1984. Cert. art tchr., Ga., art and gen. tchr., Tex. Art tchr. Manvel (Tex.) Jr. High Sch., 1984-86, pvt. elem. sch., Atlanta, 1986-87, Fairplay Mid. Sch., Douglasville, Ga., 1987-89, Turner Mid. Sch., Douglasville, 1989—. Vol. art tchr. at homeless ctr. for children; mem. Douglas County Cultural ARt Ctr. Mem. Nat. Art Edn. Assn. (nat. conf. host com., dir. tours 1991, Southeastern Region Secondary Art Educator of Yr. 1992), Ga. Art Edn. Assn. (bd. dirs., dist. pres. 1991—, Mid. Sch. Art Educator of Yr. 1990). Democrat. Methodist. Home: 1799 County Line Pl Douglasville GA 30135-1187 Office: Turner Mid Sch 7101 Junior High Dr Lithia Springs GA 30057-2215*

CRAFT, JEROME WALTER, plastic surgeon, health facility administrator; b. Erie, Pa., Oct. 20, 1932; s. Walter Sion and Elizabeth Mabel (Bowen) c.; divorced; children: Jerome Robert, Christine Anne, David William. MD, Case Western Res. U., 1948. Cert. Am. Bd. Plastic and Reconstructive Surgeons. Intern gen. surgery St. Vincent's Hosp., Erie, 1949, gen. surgery preceptee, 1949-52; flight surgeon USAF, 1952-54; resident gen. surgery, 1954-56; resident, clin. instr. plastic/reconstructive/hand surgery U. Rochester, N.Y., 1956-58; fellow in head and neck surgery Roswell Pk. Cancer Inst., U. Buffalo, 1957-58; clin. practice in plastic and reconstructive surgery, head and neck surgery, surgery of hand Erie, 1958-66; chief Craft Surg. Ctr., W. Palm Beach, 1966—; pres. Craft Cosmetic Surgery Ctr., W. Palm Beach, Fla., 1974—; mem. Senator Paula Hawkins Med. Adv. Com. to U.S. Congress, Fla., 1986-87; bd. dirs. Octagon Large Wild Animal Treatment Ctr., Ft. Myers, Fla. Author: Reconstruction Hypophanynx, 1959, Burn Cardiac Arrest, 1958, Cosmetic Surgery Book, 1987; rschr. Arterial Grafts, 1957. Med. advisor Congress, Washington, 1986. Capt. USAF, 1952-54. Mem. Palm Beach County Med. Soc., Fla. Med. Soc., AMA, Am. Soc. Plastic & Reconstructive Surgeons, Am. Bd. Plastic & Reconstructive Surgeons. Republican. Office: Craft Cosmetic Surgery Ctr 535 S Flagler Dr West Palm Beach FL 33401-5903

CRAFT, JOSEPH W., III, lawyer; b. Lexington. BS, U. Ky., Lexington, 1972; JD, U. Ky., Knoxville, 1976. Counsel Falcon Coal Co., 1975-80, Diamond Shamrock, 1980; asst. gen. counsel Mapco Inc., Tulsa, 1980-82, gen. counsel, 1982-85, sr. v.p. legal and fin., 1985-86; pres. MAPCO Coal Inc., Tulsa, 1986—. Office: MAPCO Coal Inc 1717 S Boulder Ave Tulsa OK 74119-4833

CRAFT, KAY STARK, real estate broker; b. Yoakum, Tex., Oct. 15, 1945; d. Jesse James and Leona Charlotte (Manchen) Stark; m. Michael Joseph Grogan IV, May 31, 1969 (div. June 1974); 1 child, Michael Joseph V; m. Roger Dale Craft, Apr. 1, 1983. AA, Victoria (Tex.) Coll., 1964; BS, S.W. Tex. State U., 1966; Broadway Sch. Real Estate, Hot Springs, Ark., 1985. Lic. real estate broker, Ark. Tchr. Victoria Ind. Sch. Dist., 1966-68, Pasadena (Tex.) Ind. Sch. Dist., 1968-85; real estate agt. Coldwell Banker, Hot Springs Village, Ark., 1985-88; prin. broker-owner Cross Roads Realty, Inc., Hot Springs Village, Ark., 1988—, pres., bd. dirs., 1991—, v.p., 1988-91; sec., bd. dirs. Craft Classic Homes, Inc., Hot Springs Village, Ark., 1987—; v.p., bd. dirs. Coronado Homes, Inc., Hot Springs Village, Ark., 1992—. Mem. DAR, Colonial Dames of 17th Century, Nat. Soc. Magna Carta Dames, Nat. Assn. Realtors, Ark. Realtors Assn. (Million Dollar Club 1991—, Lifetime Million Dollar Prodr. award 1993, Multi Million Dollar Prodr. award 1993, 96, cert. Grad. Realtors Inst. 1992), N.W. Garland Bd. Realtors (treas. 1992, Million Dollar Prodr. award 1990, 95, 96), Woman's Coun. Realtors, Residential Sales Coun. (cert. residential specialist 1993). Republican. Methodist. Home: 45 Gerona Way Hot Springs National Park AR 71909-2762 Office: Cross Roads Realty Inc 4136 N Highway 7 Hot Springs National Park AR 71909-9564

CRAFT, LARRY, design company executive. CEO Dan Maples Design, Inc. Address: PO Box 3014 Pinehurst NC 28374

CRAFT, MARY FAYE, public relations consultant, television producer; b. Glennville, Ga., Jan. 20, 1936; d. James Levy Durrence and Mary Frances (Merritt) Thompson; widow; children: James P. Craft, Joseph A. Craft. DD, Calvary Grace Bible Inst., Rillton, Pa., 1975; cert. of journalism arts, CNS Internat., Willow Springs, Mo., 1991; D of Phil. in Film and Video, LaSalle U., Mandeville, La., 1995. Cert. tchr., Protocol Sch. of Washington, D.C., 1993. Dist. mgr. Family Record Plan, Honolulu, 1963-64; acct. exec. Heirloom Inc., Honolulu, 1964-65; pres. Durracraft Advt. and Photography, Cocoa Beach, Orlando, Fla., 1965-71; CEO Western American Corp., Orlando, 1971-73; pres. MF Craft & Assoc. Travel, Orlando, 1972-73, Mary Faye Craft & Assocs., Washington, 1977—; prodr., host FCAC Ch. 10, Fairfax, Va., 1990—; editor MFDC Rev., Springfield, Va., 1992—. Author: Poems of Perception, 1984, Gifts of Poetry, 1986, Poems by Mary Faye Craft, 1988; composer, performer music album Facets, 1989 (Mid Atlantic Contest winner 1990). Bd. dirs. Jacksonville Sister's City Assn., 1996—. Recipient three awards Civil Air Patrol, Maxwell AFB, Ala., 1982, 83, Golden Poets award, World of Poetry, Las Vegas, 1987. Mem. AAUW, Nat. Press Club, Nat. Space Club, Capitol Hill Club, Phi Theta Kappa. Republican. Roman Catholic. Office: Mary Faye Craft & Assocs PO Box 7817 Jacksonville FL 32238 also: Mary Faye Craft & Assocs PO Box 8 Glennville GA 30427

CRAFT DAVIS, AUDREY ELLEN, writer, educator; b. Vanceburg, Ky., June 9, 1926; d. James Elmer and Lula Alice (Vance) Gilkison; m. Vernon Titus Craft, Nov. 5, 1943 (dec. Aug. 1979); children: James Vernon Craft, Alice Ann Craft Schuler; m. Louis Amzie Davis, Oct. 22, 1986. PhD, Ohio U., 1964; Dr. of Metaphysics, Coll. Divine Metaphysics, 1968; DD, Ohio U., 1971; postgrad., St. Petersburg Jr. Coll., 1975. Owner beauty salon Audrey Craft Enterprises, Tampa Bay, Fla., 1970-83; owner cosmetic co. Audrey Craft Enterprises, Portsmouth, Ohio, 1958-70; owner, distbr. Nightingale Motivation, Tampa Bay, 1960—; tchr., counselor Bus. Coll. U., Tampa Bay, 1965—; ins. staff Investors Heritage & Wabash, Portsmouth, 1967-70; ins. broker Jackson Nat. & Wabash, Tampa Bay, 1971-91; pres. The Gardens 107, Inc., Tampa Bay, 1987—; travel writer, counselor Cruises/Travel & Etc., Fla., 1981—. Author: (poetry) Pathways (1 Cert. awards), 1990, Metaphysical Techniques That Really Work, 1994, Metaphysical Encounters, 1992, How to Stay Secure in a Chaotic World, 1993, Metaphysics Encounters of a Fourth Kind, 1995, How to Safeguard Your World and Avoid Becoming a Target, 1996; contbr. articles to popular mags. Bd. dirs. The Gardens Domicurculums, Cmty. Coun., 1987—; bd. dirs. State Bd. Cosmetology, Columbus, Ohio, 1962-63, Bus. and Profl. Women, Portsmouth, 1967-69, Sci. Rsch., Portsmouth, 1965-69, Tampa Bay, 1972-74. Recipient Key to Miami, Office of Mayor Claude Kirk, 1969, Million Dollar trophy Lt. Gov. John Brown Ohio; commd. Ky. Col. by Gov. Edward T. Breathitt, 1968, Gov. Wendell Ford, 1969. Mem. AARP, S.E. Writers Assn., Christian Writers Guild, Writers Digest Book Club, Nat. Assn. Retired Fed. Employees (assoc.), Am. Heart Assn. (chmn. Seminole area 1994). Democrat. Home and Office: Audacious Prodn 8039 Garden Dr Apt 204 Largo FL 33777

CRAFTON-MASTERSON, ADRIENNE, real estate executive, writer, poet; b. Providence, Mar. 6, 1926; d. John Harold and Adrienne (Fitzgerald) Crafton; m. Francis T. Masterson, May 31, 1947 (div. Jan. 1977); children: Mary Victoria Masterson Bush, Kathleen Joan, John Andrew, Barbara Lynn. Student, No. Va. Community Coll., 1971-74; A in Biblical Studies, Christ to World Bible Inst., Jacksonville, Fla., 1992; A in Pastoral Leadership, Calvary Bible Inst., Jacksonville, Fla., 1993. Mem. staff Senator T.F. Green of R.I., Washington, 1944-47, 54-60; with U.S. Senate Com. on Campaign Expenditures Senator T.F. Green of R.I., 1944-45; asst. chief clk. Ho. Govt. Ops. Com., 1948-49; clk. Ho. Campaign Expenditures Com., 1950; asst. appointment sec. Office of Pres., 1951-53; with Hubbard Realty, Alexandria, Va., 1962-67; owner, mgr. Adrienne C. Masterson Real Estate, Alexandria, 1968-82; pres. Adrienne Investment Real Estate (AIRE) Ltd., Alexandria, 1982-91; devel. staff writer Calvary Internat., Jacksonville, Fla., 1992-93; Adrienne Crafton-Masterson Real Estate, Winchester, Va., 1993-94; owner, prin., broker Adrienne Crafton-Masterson Real Estate, Haymarket, Va., 1994—; pres. AIRE-Merkli developers, 1988-92; founder AIHRE USA, Inc., 1993—. Mem. adv. panel Fairfax County (Va.) Coun. on Arts, 1987-88; founder, pres. Mt. Vernon/Lee Cultural Ctr. Found., Inc. 1984-92; life patron, life dep. gov. Am. Biog. Inst. Fellow Internat. Biog. Ctr. (dep. dir. gen.); mem. Internat. Orgn. Real Estate Appraisers (sr.), Nat. Assn. Realtors, No. Va. Assn. Realtors (chmn. comml. and indsl. com. 1982-83, cmty. revitalization com. 1983-84, pres. land. comml. indsl. mems. 1985, v.p. land comml. and indsl. mems. 1989), Greater Piedmont Area Assn. Realtors, Fairfax Affordable Housing Inc. (sec. 1990-91), Haymarket-Gainesville (Va.) Busl. and Profl. Assn. (bd. dirs. 1996—), Alexandria C. of C., Mt. Vernon/Lee C. of C., Friends of Kennedy Ctr. (founder). Office: Haymarket Profl Ctr PO Box 499 6611 Jefferson St Haymarket VA 20168-0499

CRAIG, ANNA MAYNARD, financial educator, consultant; b. Columbus, Ohio, Sept. 2, 1944; d. David Stuart and Ann (Armstrong) C.; m. John D. Hogan, Nov. 26, 1976. BA cum laude, Smith Coll., 1966; MA, U. Wis., 1970, PhD, 1972. Chartered fin. analyst; cert. fin. planner, accredited tax advisor; enrolled treasury agt. Asst. prof. U. Ill., Chgo., 1971-75; vis. asst. prof. Ohio State U., Columbus, 1974-76; asst. prof. Cen. Mich. U., Mt. Pleasant, 1976-79; cons. Am. Productivity Ctr., Houston, 1979-81; adj. prof. Houston Bapt. U., 1980-86, Jones Grad. Sch. Adminstrn., Rice U., Houston, 1984; adj. prof. dept. fin. U. Ill., Champaign-Urbana, 1987-91; adj.. faculty Goizveta Bus. Sch. Emory U., Atlanta, 1992—; faculty exec. and concentrated MBA programs Ga. State U., 1992-93; CMBA, 1995—; bd. advisors Assn. for Internat. Exch. Students in Econs. and Commerce, U. Ill., 1987-91; advisor U. Ill. FMA Nat. Honor Soc., Fin. Club. Editor: (with John D. Hogan) Dimensions of Productivity Research, Vol. 1, 1980, Vol. II, 1981. Bd. dirs. Champaign-Urbana Symphony, 1987-91; mem. trust mgmt. com. Univ. YWCA, Champaign, 1987-91. Ford fellow, U. Wis., 1970-72, NSF fellow, Stanford U., 1972; Fulbright scholar, 1966-67; named Outstanding Prof. Fin. U. Ill. Commerce Coun., 1987-88. Mem Am. Econ. Assn., Atlanta Soc. Fin. Analysts, Assn. for Investment Mgmt. and Rsch., Fin. Mgmt. Assn., Smith Coll. Alumnae Assn. (chmn. spl. gifts 1983-86, class fund agt.), Fulbright Alumni Assn., Phi Beta Kappa, Beta Gamma Sigma. Office: Emory Univ Goizueta Business School Atlanta GA 30322

CRAIG, CHRISTOPHER PATRICK, classicist, educator; b. Oklahoma City, Jan. 14, 1952; s. William Joseph and Nancy (Ryan) C.; m. Ann Elizabeth Robinson, Aug. 21, 1982; children: Sarah Elizabeth, Carolyn Ann. AB, Oberlin Coll., 1974; PhD, U. N.C., 1979. Instr. classics dept. UCLA, 1979-80; asst. prof. classics dept. U. Tenn., Knoxville, 1980-86, assoc. prof. classics dept., 1986—; Latin coord. Tenn. Gov.'s Acad. for Tchrs. Fgn. Langs., Knoxville, 1988, 91-94, cons. Stokely Inst. for Liberal Arts Edn., Knoxville, 1983-85. Author: Form as Argument in Cicero's Speeches, 1993; contbr. articles to profl. jours. Recipient Outstanding Teaching award U. Tenn. Nat. Alumni Assn., 1986. Mem. Tenn. Classical Assn. (pres. 1985-87), Vergilian Soc. Am. (trustee 1991-93, dir. summer sessions in Naples 1985, 87, 89, 93), Am. Philol. Assn., Archeol. Inst. Am., Am. Soc. for the History of Rhetoric, Internat. Soc. for History of Rhetoric, Speech Comm. Assn., Classical Assn. Middle West and South (exec. com. 1992—, pres. so. sec. 1994—), Am. Classical League. Episcopalian. Home: 1212 April Dr Knoxville TN 37919-8106 Office: U Tenn Dept Classics Knoxville TN 37996-0471

CRAIG, CYNTHIA MAE, mathematics educator; b. Brownsville, Tex., Jan. 22, 1951; d. Richard Virgil and Mae Margaret (Phillips) Cole; m. Daniel Baxter Craig, Jan. 15, 1971; children: Tammy Michele Craig Black, Heather Elizabeth Craig. BA, Augusta (Ga.) Coll., 1985, MEd, 1989, specialist in edn., 1993. Cert. devel. specialist; cert. tchr., Ga. Tchr. 5th-6th grade tchr. Blessed Sacrament Sch., El Paso, Tex., 1981-82; tchr. 4-8th grade honors math. St. Mary on the hill Cath. Sch., Augusta, Ga., 1985-87; tchr. Aquinas H.S., Augusta, 1987-88; asst. prof. of math. in devel. studies Augusta State U., 1989—; presenter in field. Mem. ASCD, Ga. Assn. of Devel. Educators, Nat. Assn. for Devel. Edn., Phi Delta Kappa (newsletter editor 1990-93, v.p. membership 1993-94, newsletter editor 1994-96, found. rep. 1996—). Office: Augusta Statet U Devel Studies 2500 Walton Way Augusta GA 30904-2200

CRAIG, DAVID CLARKE, finanacial advisor, instructor; b. Ft. Smith, Ark., Oct. 23, 1955; s. Earl Lewis Craig and Shirley Ann (Clarke) Shepherd; m. Dana Jane Thompson, Dec. 19, 1980; children: Lauren Elizabeth, Erin Jane. BBA, U. Ark., 1978, MBA, 1979; postgrad., U. Tex., 1983-88, U. Ark., 1988—. Registered fin. advisor. Mktg. officer Merchants Nat. Bank, Ft. Smith, 1979-81; instr. fin. and econs. Westark C.C., Ft. Smith, 1981—, faculty chairperson, 1987-88; asst. to pres. Richland Coll., Dallas, 1985; fin. advisor Oct. Money Mgmt., Inc., Ft. Smith, Ark., 1991—; adj. instr. John Brown U., 1995—; bd. dirs., sec. Ark. Student Loan Authority, 1989—. Pres. Am. Cancer Soc. Ft. Smith, 1988-89, co-residential chmn. 1985-87, v.p. local bd. 1987-89, active Pub. Awareness Com. Ft. Smith, 1985-91; pres. Interfaith Comty. Ctr., Ft. Smith, 1982-84; vol. Ft. Smith Art Ctr. Auction, 1987, treas. 1995—; sponsor Harding U. Invitational Bus. Games, 1986-91; bd. dirs. Old Fort Mus., 1989-91; mem. class of 1990 Leadership Ft. Smith, elder, clk. of session 1st Presbyn. Ch.; bd. ch. visitors U. Ozarks, Clarksville, Ark.; bd. dirs. Hobson Presch. and Kindergarten. Mem. Nat. Bus. Edn. Assn., Ark. Tchrs. of Bus. and Econs., Am. Inst. Banking (v.p. Ft. Smith chpt. 1981), Ark. Two Yr. Coll. Assn., Ft. Smith C. of C. (ednl. com. 1987—), Blue Key, Kappa Delta Pi, Alpha Kappa Psi 9sec. 1977-78), Phi Delta Kappa (Kappan of Month 1985), Phi Beta Lambda (co-advisor univ. ctr. 1986-95). Office: Westark CC 5210 Grand Ave Fort Smith AR 72904-7362 also: Oct Money Mgmt Inc 2220 S Waldron Rd Fort Smith AR 72903-3753

CRAIG, GEORGE DENNIS, economics educator, consultant; b. Geneva, Ill., Sept. 14, 1936; s. George S. and Alice H. (Childs) C.; m. Lelah Price, Aug. 21, 1984; children: R. Price Coyle, R. Nolan Coyle, Deborah L. Craig, W. Sean Coyle. A.B., Wheaton Coll., 1960; M.S., U. Ill., 1962, Ph.D., 1968. Asst. prof. econs. La. State U., Baton Rouge, 1965-69; assoc. prof. sch. bus. No. Ill. U., Dekalb, 1969-82; prof. econs., chmn. Oklahoma City U., 1982—; cons. AT&T, Oklahoma City, 1984—. Contbr. articles to profl. jours. Mem. Am. Econs. Assn., So. Econs. Assn. Nat. Assn. Bus. Economists, Internat. Inst. of Forecasting. Avocation: tennis. Home: 6915 Avondale Ct Oklahoma City OK 73116-5008 Office: Oklahoma City U Dept Econs NW 23rd at N Blackwelder Oklahoma City OK 73106

CRAIG, JAMES DONALD, dean; b. Nashville, Apr. 23, 1944; s. James Edwin and Lila Mai (Pentecost) C.; m. Connie Elaine Carter, Aug. 25, 1968; children: Jeffrey Donald, James Carter. BA, David Lipscomb U., 1967; MLS, Vanderbilt U., 1968. Asst. to dir. Vanderbilt U. Librs., Nashville, 1968-72; asst. libr. Mid. Tenn. State U., Murfreesboro, 1972-76, univ. libr., 1976-94, dean of libr., 1995—. Mem. Southeastern Libr. Assn., Tenn. Libr. Assn. (pres. 1986-87), Mid-State Libr. Assn. (chmn. 1969-70), Civitan (pres. West End club 1970). Mem. Ch. of Christ. Office: Mid Tenn State U U Libr Murfreesboro TN 37132

CRAIG, JAMES PAT, medical library director, consultant; b. Gould, Ark., Dec. 10, 1942; s. Hubert Eldridge and Mary Lorean (Dean) C.; m. Paula Jane Wykoff, Dec. 8, 1990. BSE, U. Ark., Monticello, 1964; MA in Libr. Sci., U. N. Tex., 1969. Tchr., libr. Gould (Ark.) Pub. Schs., 1964-69, libr. supr., 1970-73; libr. U. Ark., Fayetteville, 1969-70; libr. supr. Dumas (Ark.) Schs., 1973-75; dir. rsch. libr. Nat. Ctr. Tech. Rsch., Little Rock., Ark., 1975-82; assoc. dir. U. Tex. Southwestern Med. Sch., Dallas, 1982-85; dir. libr. svcs. U. South Fla., Tampa, 1985-87; prof., chmn. La. State U. Sch. Medicine, Shreveport, La., 1987—; dir. NLM: Regional Med. Libr. Program, Dallas, 1982-85; chmn. Tex. Libr. Consortium Alliance, Austin, 1984-85; chmn. S. Ctrl. Acad. Med. Librs., Dallas, 1992-95. Author: (MLA courses), Enhancing Role of Librarian, 1995, Information Malpractice, 1995; contbr. chpt. Encyclopedia of Libr. and Info. Sci, 1995. Mem. bd. dirs. Shreveprot Opera Assn., 1989, pres. elect, 1996—. Mem. Am. Libr. Assn., Med. Libr. Assn. (cert. instr. 1986), Spl. Libr. Assn., La. Libr. Assn., Unit 170 ACBL (pres. 1989, 93), Lions Internat. (treas. 1968-79), Elks. Republican. Methodist. Home: 630 Oak Hill Dr Shreveport LA 71106 Office: LSU Med Ctr 1501 KingsHwy Shreveport LA 71130

CRAIG, LARRY VERNON, secondary school educator; b. Cin., July 30, 1948; s. Vernon Francis and Opal Jewell (Davis) C.; m. Gwendolyn Gale Watson, July 24, 1967; children: Kimberly, David, Jonathan. BS, BA, Tenn. Temple U., 1972; MA in Bible, Ind. Bapt. Coll., Dallas, 1975; MEd, U. North Tex., 1976, PhD, 1979. Cert. tchr. English, math., spl. edn., adminstrn., supervision, Tex. Tchr. Ind. Bapt. Coll., Dallas, 1973-82; pastor First Orthodox Bapt. Ch., Ardmore, Okla., 1982-86; tchr. Irving (Tex.) Ind. Sch. Dist., 1986-91; cons. Region 10 Edn. Svc. Ctr., Richardson, Tex., 1991-92; tchr. math. and computer sci. Grand Prairie (Tex.) Ind. Sch. Dist., 1992—, computer sci. tchr., computer sci. team coach, 1994—. Mem. Assn. Tex. Profl. Educators (regional treas., membership chmn. 1991—, pres. region 10, 1993-95, pres. Grand Prairie 1994-95)), Nat. Coun. Tchrs. Math. Republican. Baptist. Home: 804 S Story Rd Irving TX 75060-3644 Office: South Grand Prairie High 301 W Warrior Trl Grand Prairie TX 75052-5718

CRAIG, NADINE KARAMARKOVICH, pharmaceutical executive; b. Sewickley, Pa., Aug. 18, 1951; d. Nicholas and Mildred (Torbica) Karamarkovich; m. Jeffrey Lynn Craig, Oct. 10, 1977; 1 child, Jacquelyn Leslie. Nursing diploma, U. Pitts., 1972. RN, Fla. Staff nurse St. Francis Hosp., Pitts., 1972-74, Orlando (Fla.) Regional Med. Ctr., 1974-75; dir. aftercare Seminole Community Mental Health Ctr., Altamonte Springs, Fla., 1975-76; sales rep. Searle Pharm., Orlando, 1976-85; sales tng. supr. Searle Pharm., Skokie, Ill., 1985-86; dist. sales mgr. Searle Pharm., New Orleans, 1986-91; prod. mgr. Searle Pharm., Skokie, Ill., 1991-92; assoc. dir. Sci. Mktg. Comm., 1992—; regional sales dir Searle Pharm., Irving, Tex., 1992-96, exec. dir. S.W.-Ctrl. Geog. Customer unit, 1996—. Office: Ste 1170 909 E Las Colinas Blvd Irving TX 75039

CRAIG, THOMAS FRANKLIN, electrical engineer; b. Indpls., Feb. 26, 1943; s. Robert Watson and Iris Evelyn (Evans) C.; BSEE (Charles M. Malott scholar), Purdue U., 1965, MSIA, 1970; m. Ester Annelle Cantrell, Aug. 3, 1968; children: Amy Delynne, Josie Leigh. Reliability engr. SCI Systems, Inc., Huntsville, 1968-71; components engr. Safeguard System Command, Huntsville, Ala., 1971-73; software engr. U.S. Army Guidance and Control Labs., Redstone Arsenal, Ala., 1973; systems engr. Pershing Project, 1974-77, comm. equipment program mgr., 1977-81, chmn. Pershing II Comm. Working Group; project engr. Stinger Project Office, 1981-82; prin. engr. Boeing Aerospace, Huntsville, Ala., 1982-89; program mgr. The EC Corp., Huntsville, Ala., 1989-91; prin. engr. space sta. program Boeing Co., Huntsville, Ala., 1991—. Asst. treas., bd. dirs., mem. adv. bd. Huntsville Depot Mus., 1976-84; chmn. bd. elders 1st Christian Ch., 1979-81, 88, chmn. ofcl. bd., 1985-86; treas., trustee Helion Temple, 1978-84; treas. Huntsville Community Ballet Assn., 1986-88, Huntsville Lit. Assn., 1994—. Served to capt. ordnance, USAR, 1965-68. Engr.-in-tng., Ind., 1965. Mem. AAAS, IEEE, Armed Forces Comm. and Electronics Assn., Am. Def. Preparedness Assn., Ala. Acad. Sci., Assn. Old Crows, Mensa. Republican. Mem. Disciples of Christ. Ch. Clubs: Mountain Springs Swim, N. Ala. R.R. Mus., Sierra. Lodges: Shriners, Masons (past master, York Rite Coll. Order of Purple Cross 1991, 33 Degree 1993). Editor The North Star, 1979—, Ala. Supplement to KT mag., 1985—. Ala. sec. Quatuor Coronati Corr. Circle, London, 1980—. Home: 1000 Lexington St SE Huntsville AL 35801-2533 Office: PO Box 240002 Huntsville AL 35824-6402

CRAIGE, DANNY DWAINE, dentist; b. Okla., Mar. 25, 1946; s. William and Ruby G. (Sinor) C.; m. Mary Ann Thompson, Dec. 22, 1970. BS in Math., Southeastern Okla. State U., 1967; MS, Okla. U., 1968, DDS, 1980. Tchr. Yuba (Okla.) Pub. Schs., 1968-69, Sherman (Tex.) Pub. Schs., 1971-73; asst. mgr. Thompson Book and Supply Co., Durant, Okla., 1973-76; pvt. practice Durant, 1980—; cons. Med. Ctr. of S.E. Okla., Durant, 1980—, Bryan County (Okla.) Nursing Homes, 1980—. Bd. dirs. Texoma chpt. Boy Scouts Am., Durant and Denison, Tex., 1983-90, chmn. sustaining membership drive, Durant, 1989, 90; bd. dirs. Durant Western Days Talent Contest, 1989, 90, 91. Capt. USNR. Okla. U. fellow, 1968. Mem. ADA, Okla. Dental Assn., Naval Res. Assn. (life), Naval Order U.S., Texoma Dental Study Club (chmn. 1980—), Lions (past chpt. pres. and bd. dirs.). Home: 601 W Pine St Durant OK 74701-3735 Office: 203 N 16th Ave Durant OK 74701-3607

CRAIN, CHRISTINA MELTON, lawyer; b. Dallas, Mar. 18, 1966; d. William Allen Sr. and Sandra (Hays) Melton. BA in Govt., U. Tex., 1988; JD, Oklahoma City U., 1991. Bar: Tex. 1992, U.S. Dist. Ct. (no. dist.) Tex. 1992, U.S. Ct. Appeals (5th cir.) 1992, U.S. Dist. Ct. (ea. dist.) Tex. 1993, U.S. Dist. Ct. (so. and we. dists.) Tex. 1994. From law clk. to assoc. Nichols, Jackson, Dillard, Hager & Smith, LLP, Dallas, 1990-93; ptnr. Kirk, Griffin & Melton, LLP (now Christina Melton Crain PC), Dallas, 1994-96; pres. Christina Melton Crain PC (formerly Kirk, Griffin & Melton), Dallas, 1996—; sr. v.p., gen. counsel Shop On Line. Chmn. Tex. Young Reps. Fedn., 1993-95, 3d v.p.; dir., auditor Pub. Affairs Luncheon Club, Dallas, 1993—; patient navigator Bridge Breast Ctr., Dallas, 1994—; vol. Twice Blessed House. Recipient U.S. Congl. Silver Medal of Honor, U.S. Congress, 1987; named 40 Under 40, The Dalls (Tex.) Bus. Jour., 1993, Outstanding Young Rep. Woman of Yr., Tex. Young Reps. Fedn., 1994, 95. Mem. Dallas Bar Assn. (co-chair memls. history com.), Dallas Assn. Young Lawyers (co-chair legal aid to elderly com.). Baptist. Office: Christina Melton Crain PC # 104 -944 5521 Greenville Ave Dallas TX 75206

CRAIN, FRANCES UTTERBACK, retired dietitian; b. Crawfordsville, Ind., Dec. 28, 1914; d. Chelsey Chalmers and Margaret Myrtle (Henderson) Utterback; m. James William Crain, Sept. 13, 1937 (div. July 1944); children: James Michael, Patrick Desmond. BA, U. Ill., 1935; postgrad., Purdue U., 1945-46. Registered dietitian. Dietetic intern Indpls. City Hosp., 1935-36, therapeutic dietitian, 1936-37; dietitian Home Lawn Mineral Springs, Martinsville, Ind., 1937-38; WPA project dietitian Ill. Soldiers & Sailors Children's Home, Normal, 1939; chief dietitian Providence Hosp., Kansas City, Kans., 1939-40, Alexian Bros. Hosp., St. Louis, 1940-41; dietitian Ill. State Dept. Pub. Welfare, Springfield, 1943-45; exec. dir. Memphis Dairy Coun., 1947-61; program cons. Nat. Dairy Coun., Chgo., 1961-68; dietitian War on Poverty Com., Memphis, 1968-69, Shelby County Hosp., Memphis, 1969-74, Shelby County Penal Farm, Memphis, 1969-80; chief dietitian Oakville Health Care Ctr., Memphis, 1974-80; dietitian feeding programs Salvation Army, 1982-93. Writer food feature column. Comml. Appeal, 1952-61; author: To Your Taste-Butter, 1957. Mem. speakers and path. coms. Memphis in May Internat. Festival, 1983, 84, 85. Named Career Women of Yr., Pilot Club of Memphis, 1955; recipient Spl. Svcs. award Salvation Army, 1983. Mem. Am. Dietetic Assn., Tenn. Dietetic Assn. (pres. 1951-52, outstanding dietitian 1977), Memphis Dist. Dietetic Assn. (pres. 1949-50, editor bull. 1958-59), Memphis Area Nutrition Coun. (pres. 1973-74), Shelby County Retirees Orgn. (pres. 1987-89). Democrat. Home: 255 N Avalon St Memphis TN 38112-5101

CRAIN, WILLIAM HENRY, retired curator; b. Victoria, Tex., July 19, 1917; s. William Henry and Margaret James (McFaddin) C. Student Tex. Mil. Inst., 1933-36; BA, U. Tex., 1940, MA, 1943, BFA, 1947, MFA, 1949, PhD, 1965. Resident playwright Artillery Lane Theatre, St. Augustine, Fla., 1950-51; dir. David G. Benjamin Inc., Austin, Tex., 1957-59 Austin Mfg. Corp., 1957-59; publicity asst. drama dept. U. Tex., Austin, 1959-60; humanities rsch. assoc. II, 1965-70; curator theater arts collections, Harry Ransom Humanities Research Ctr., U. Tex., Austin, 1970-94, ret., 1994; dir. Waterloo Press, 1971—. Writer numerous plays produced including Brains and Eggs, 1948, The Muddled Magician, 1957, Sir Marmaduke Miles, 1976, The Sweet Old Thing, 1961, The Reluctant Caesar, 1977, The Crossed Crescent, 1983. Bd. dirs. Austin Civic Theatre, 1961-64, Paramount Theatre for Performing Arts, 1976—, Friends of the Summer Musical (Dr. W.H. Deacon Crain award, 1993); adv. bd. New Texas Festival, St. Edward's U. Sch. of Humanities, Austin Gilbert & Sullivan Soc.; mem. com. curators and historians for Celebrate Broadway: 100 Yrs. in Times Sq, Drama League. Served with AUS, 1941-45. Decorated knight Holy Sepulchre, 1977, promoted knight comdr., 1982, knight comdr. with star, 1986, knight grand cross, 1992; recipient Cross of Mil. Svc., U. D.C., 1961, Jane Dunn Sibley Leadership award, 1992, Arts Week Vol. award, 1993, Philanthropist of the Year award, 1993. Mem. Assn. for Theatre in Higher Edn., Am. Soc. Theatre Rsch., U.S. Inst. for Theatre Tech. (USITT award 1996), Soc. for Theatre Rsch., Theatre Libr. Assn., Actors Fund of Am. (life), Sons Republic Tex., Serra Internat., Nat. Soc. for Arts and Letters (life), Austin Circle of Theatres (life), The Players, Phi Eta Sigma, Phi Kappa Phi, Delta Kappa Epsilon. Clubs: Serra of Austin (treas. 1978-79), The Players. Roman Catholic. Home: 2511 San Gabriel St Austin TX 78705-4321

CRAMER, BRUCE ERIC, television news director; b. St. Joseph, Mo., May 14, 1953; s. Robert Donald and Betty Jane (Leventhal) C.; m. Judy Ann Taylor, Apr. 23, 1977; children: Kerry, Kelly. BS in Broadcasting, U. Fla., 1975; M in Comms., U. West Fla., 1979. News dir. Sta. WBIA-AM,

Augusta, Ga., 1976-77; bur. chief, reporter Sta. WKRG-TV, Mobile, Ala., 1977-79; prodr., anchor Sta. WLOS-TV, Asheville, N.C., 1980-83; prodr. St. WBBH-TV, Ft. Myers, Fla., 1983-84; spl. projects prodr. Sta. WMAR-TV, Balt., 1984-89; mng. editor Sta. WCIV-TV, Charleston, S.C., 1989-92; sr. news prodr. Sta. WSMV-TV, Nashville, 1993-95; news dir. Sta. WTXL-TV, Tallahassee, 1995—. Recipient Emmy award NATAS, 1990, Award Best Overall News Coverage, 1996, Award Best New Series, 1996. Mem. Radio TV News Dirs. Assn., Soc. of Profl. Journalists. Office: Sta WTXL-TV 8927 Thomasville Rd Tallahassee FL 32312-9761

CRAMER, GAIL LATIMER, economist; b. Walla Walla, Wash., Sept. 27, 1941; s. Lawrence Theodore and Mytle Pauline (Latimer) C.; m. Marilyn Jean Karlenberg, Aug. 31, 1963; children: Karilee, Bruce. BS, Wash. State U., 1963; MS, Mich. State U., 1964; PhD, Oreg. State U., 1968. Asst. prof. Mont. State U., Bozeman, 1967-72, assoc. prof., 1972-76, prof., 1976; L.C. Carter prof. U. Ark., Fayetteville, 1987—; vis. prof. Harvard U., Cambridge, 1974-75, Winrock Internat., Morrilton, Ark., 1980-81, U. Calif. Berkeley, 1993, Ohio State U., Columbus, 1994; bd. dirs. Internat. Agrl. Mgmt. Assn. Co-author: Grain Marketing, 1993, Agricultural, Economics and Agribusiness, 1994. Bd. dirs. ARC, Bozeman, 1982-83, Bozeman Kiwanis Club, 1972-86 (Disting. Pres. 1983); mem. White House Agrl. commn. Washington. Recipient E.G. Nouse award Am. Inst. Coop., Washington, 1968, Communication award Am. Agrl. Econs. Assn., 1980, Rice Rsch. award Tech. Workers, Little Rock, 1991, Disting. Rsch. award, 1992. Home: 2381 Golden Oaks Dr Fayetteville AR 72703-3152 Office: U Ark Dept Agrl Econs Fayetteville AR 72701

CRAMER, LAURA SCHWARZ, realtor; b. St. Louis, Aug. 13, 1925; d. Frederick William and Gertrude Margaret (Kipp) Schwarz; AB, Duke U., 1947; MA, Washington U., St. Louis, 1948; m. Robert R. Cramer, Oct. 29, 1949; children: Anne Randolph, Carol Parker, Laura Forster. Model, John Robert Powers Agy., N.Y.C., 1946; grad. asst. dept. psychology Washington U., St. Louis, 1947-48, instr., 1948-49; psychometrist Clayton (Mo.) pub. schs., 1961; dir. testing Columbia Sch., Rochester, N.Y., 1964-71; asst. registrar and counselor for women students St. John Fisher Coll., Rochester, N.Y., 1971-72, registrar, dean of women, 1972-76; sales exec. Sea Pines Real Estate Co., Hilton Head Island, S.C., 1976—; registered rep. Sea Pines Securities, 1983-88. Bd. dirs. Vol. Svc. Bur., St. Louis, 1960-61, Monroe County Hosp. Aux., 1974-76, St. Louis Cmty. Music Sch., 1959-61, Vol. Ctr., Hilton Head Island, 1992—; cmty. adv. bd. Hilton Head Hosp., 1995—; bd. dirs. St. Louis Inst., chmn., 1960; bd. visitors Hilton Head Prep. Sch, 1989-93; bd. dirs. Hilton Head Coll. Ctr., 1994—, Hilton Head Island Beach and Shore Commn., 1994—. Jesse M. Barr fellow, 1947-48; named Leading Sales Exec., 1981, 84, 86, 88, Leading Listing Exec., 1982, 83, 85, 86, 87, 88, 89. Mem. Hilton Head Island Bd. Realtors (Million Dollar Club, life), Jr. League Savannah, Phi Beta Kappa, Sigma Xi. Home: 9 Brown Pelican Rd Hilton Head Island SC 29928-5615 Office: Sea Pines Plantation Co Hilton Head Island SC 29928

CRAMER, MICHAEL TODD, financial consultant; b. Knoxville, Tenn., Oct. 11, 1970; s. Richard Frederick and Linda Joyce (Key) C. BS in Acctg., Clemson U., 1992. Travel agt. Fugazy Travel, Clemson, S.C., 1988-92; activities coord. Timberline Lodge, Mt. Hood, Oreg., 1991; stockbroker Fin. Wolf & Co., Inc., Charlotte, N.C., 1992; fin. cons. Raymond James & Assocs., Greenville, S.C., 1992—. Vol. Meals on Wheels, Greenville, 1994—; vol., sr. leader Young Life, Greenville, 1993—; mem. Palmetto Soc., United Way of S.C., Greenville, 1994. Vol. Meals on Wheels, Greenville, 1994—; vol., sr. leader Young Life, Greenville, 1993—; mem. Palmetto Soc., United Way of S.C., Greenville, 1994. Recipient Best and Brightest 35 and Under award Greenville Bus. Mag., 1994. Mem. Commerce Club, Sigma Chi (chpt. adviser, pres. alumni assn.). Republican. Baptist. Office: Raymond James and Assocs 101 W Broad St Ste 100 Greenville SC 29601-2611

CRAMER, ROBERT E., JR. (BUD CRAMER), congressman; b. Huntsville, AL, Aug. 22, 1947. BA, U. Ala., Huntsville, 1969, JD, 1972. Former dist. atty.; mem. 102nd-104th Congresses from 5th Dist. Ala., 1990—; mem. transp. & infrastructure com., mem. sci. com. Democrat. Methodist. Office: US House of Reps 236 Cannon Bldg Washington DC 20515-0003*

CRANBERG, LAWRENCE, physicist, consultant; b. N.Y.C., July 4, 1917. BS in Physics, MS in Edn., City Coll. N.Y., 1937; AM in Physics, Harvard U., 1941; PhD in Physics, U. Pa., 1949. Sr. physicist, group leader optical electronics Signal Corps Engring. Labs., 1940-50; mem. staff Los Alamos Sci. Lab., 1950-63; prof. physics, founder and dir. Physics Accelerator Lab. U. Va., 1963-71; v.p. R & D Accelerators Inc., Austin, 1971-73; consulting physicist Austin, 1973—; pres. TDN, Inc., Austin, 1974—, Tex. Fireframe Co., Austin, 1974—; H. A. Wood rsch. assoc. U. Pa., 1946-49; vis. prof. physics Case Inst. Tech., 1959; Edward G. Budd lectr. Franklin Inst., 1966; editorial columnist West Austin News, 1987-89; columnist N.Y.C. Tribune, 1988-91; cons. Tex. Nuclear Corp., Atomic Energy of Japan, High Voltage Engring. Corp., Dresser-Atlas Corp., NL Industries, Subsurface Corp., Radian Corp., U.S. GAO, U. Hosp., U. Pa., Holt, Rinehart & Winston, Ency. Britannica; tech. adv. U.S. delegation 1st internat. conf. Peaceful Uses of Atomic Energy; participating scientist vis. scientists program Am. Inst. Physics, 1958-61; mem. nuclear cross sect. adv. group USAEC, 1958-61; mem. ethics com. Engring. Coun. Profl. Devel., 1968; assoc. Capitol Area Rad. and Rsch. Found., Austin, 1973-83; pub. policy expert energy, edn. and domestic policy Heritage Found., 1987—. Founder, editor Nuclear and Chem. Waste Mgmt., 1978-92; patentee in field. Founder Austin Soc. to Oppose Pseudosci., 1981—. Harrison fellow U. Pa., 1946-47, U.S. AEC predoctoral fellow, 1947-49; Guggenheim fellow Atomic Energy Rsch. Establishment, 1961-62. Fellow Am. Phys. Soc. (sr., organizer and chair secondary edn. future physicists meeting 1993); mem. AAUP (emeritus), Nat. Assn. Scholars (emeritus), Nat. Newspaper Assn., Phi Beta Kappa, Sigma Xi. Address: 1205 Constant Springs Dr Austin TX 78746-6615

CRANDALL, ROBERT LLOYD, airline executive; b. Westerly, R.I., Dec. 6, 1935; s. Lloyd Evans and Virginia (Beard) C.; m. Margaret Jan Schmults, July 6, 1957; children: Mark William, Martha Conway, Stephen Michael. Student, Coll. William and Mary, 1953-55; B.S., U. R.I., 1957; M.B.A., Wharton Sch., U. Pa., 1960. With Eastman Kodak Co., Rochester, 1960-62, Hallmark Cards, Kansas City, Mo., 1962-66; asst. treas. TWA Inc., N.Y.C., 1966-70; v.p. systems and data services TWA Inc., 1970-71, v.p., controller, 1971-72; sr. v.p., treas. Bloomingdale Bros., N.Y.C., 1972-73; sr. v.p. fin. Am. Airlines, Inc., N.Y.C., 1973-74, sr. v.p. mktg., 1974-80, pres., 1980—, chmn., chief exec. officer, 1985—, also dir., 1976—; chmn., pres., chief exec. officer AMR Corp., 1985—, also dir.; bd. dirs. Halliburton Co. Served with inf. U.S. Army, 1957. Office: AMR Corp 4333 Amon Carter Blvd Fort Worth TX 76155*

CRANDALL, SONIA JANE, medical educator; b. Quincy, Ill., Sept. 2, 1952; d. Gerald Madison and Roselma Louise (Zeiger) Syrcle; m. Edward Young Crandall, June 28, 1975. Diploma, Michael Reese Med. Ctr., Chgo., 1974; BS, Western Ill. U., 1974; MED, U. Ill., 1980; PhD, U. Okla., 1989. Med. tech. U. Mo. Med. Ctr., Columbia, 1974-75; med. tech., clin. instr. St. Johns Hosp., Springfield, Ill., 1976-81; med. tech., supr. Okla. Teaching Hosp., 1982-85, tng. officer, 1985-87; Kellog fellow U. Okla., Norman, Okla., 1987-89; asst. prof., dir. faculty devel. and edn. resources, dept. family medicine U. Okla. Health Scis. Ctr., Oklahoma City, 1989-94; asst. prof., dept. family and community medicine Bowman Gray Sch. of Medicine, Wake Forest U., 1994—. Contbr. articles to prof jours. Named one of Outstanding Young Women in Am.; elected to Women's Inner Circle of Achievement, 1995, 500 Leaders of Influence, 1993, 2,000 Notable Am. Women, 1992. Mem. Am. Edn. Rsch. Assn., Am. Assn. for Adult and Continuing Edn., Am. Soc. Clin. Pathology, Am. Acad. Physician & Patient, Soc. Tchrs. Family Medicine, Alliance for Continuing Med. Edn., World Found. of Successful Women (charter), Phi Kappa Phi. Home: 3969-E Valley Ct Winston Salem NC 27106-4379 Office: Dept Family & Cmty Medicine Bowman Gray Sch Medicine Wake Forest U Medical Center Blvd Winston Salem NC 27157

CRANE, ANGUS EDGAR, lawyer; b. Preston, Idaho, Oct. 17, 1955; s. Rex Keller and Brucia (Gordon) C.; m. Kate Russell, May 2, 1978; children: Elizabeth, Oliver, Jessamyn. AA, Ricks Coll., 1978; BA, Idaho State U., 1981; JD, SUNY, Buffalo, 1986. Bar: Idaho 1987, U.S. Ct. Appeals (5th, 9th and D.C. cirs.) 1987, U.S. Ct. Appeals (1st and 10th cirs.) 1988, U.S. Ct. Appeals (4th cir.) 1991, U. S. Supreme Ct. 1991. Caseworker Office of Sen. Frank Church, Pocatello, Idaho, 1979-80; mgr. Bell Motel, Mpls., 1981-83; jud. law clk. Idaho Supreme Ct., Boise, 1986-87; atty. Dept. Justice, Washington, 1987-90, Dickstein Shapiro & Morin, Washington, 1990-95; dir. regulatory affairs and counsel N. Am. Insultation Mfrs. Assn., Alexandria, Va., 1995—. Regional coord. Idaho for Church campaign, Boise 1980, Dem. precinct committeman Bannock, Idaho, 1978-81; various leadership roles in Mormon Ch. Harry S. Truman scholar, Idaho, 1979. Mem. ABA. Democrat. Mem. LDS Ch. Home: 24 Goodport Ct Gaithersburg MD 20878-1062 Office: N Am Insulation Mfrs Assn 44 Canal Center Plz # 310 Alexandria VA 22314

CRANE, GARY WADE, mathematician, physicist; b. Austin, Tex., Apr. 7, 1957; s. John Watson and Marjorie Lorania (Haas) C. BS, Southwest Tex. State U., 1983, MS, 1986. Engring. asst. Lower Colorado River Authority, Austin, Tex., 1975-81; teaching asst. S.W. Tex. State U., San Marcos, 1982-86; rsch. scientist assoc. III Applied Rsch. Labs., U. Tex., Austin, 1986-88; engring. technician IV Tex. Dept. Hwys. and Pub. Transp., Austin, 1988-90; actuary Tex. Dept. Human Svcs., Austin, 1990-94; statis. cons., actuary II Tex. Dept. Health, Austin, 1994; chief strategy and analysis Tex. Workers' Compensation Commn., Austin, 1991-94; statis. cons. Tex. Dept. Human Svcs., Austin, 1994—; instr. astronomy, physics and math. Austin C.C., 1993—. Home: 14902 Yellowleaf Trl Austin TX 78728-5423

CRANE, GLENDA PAULETTE, private school educator; b. Orlando, Fla., June 29, 1946; d. James Author and Elizabeth Lorine (Johnson) C. AA in Edn., Orlando Jr. Coll., 1966; BA in Elem. Edn., U. S. Fla., 1967; postgrad. So. Bapt. Theol. Sem., 1970; MEd, Rollins Coll., 1985. Tchr., Orange County Schs., Orlando, 1967-70, 79-80, Lake Highland Prep. Sch., Orlando, 1981—; tchr. Belle Glade (Fla.) Christian Sch., 1970-79, asst. prin., 1970-74, prin., 1975-79. State treas. Fla. Rainbow Girls., 1964. Mem. NEA, Fla. Edn. Assn., Fla. Council Tchrs. English, Orange County Tchrs. Assn., Assn. Supervision and Curriculum Devel., Internat. Reading Assn., Orange County Reading Council of Internat. Reading Assn., Fla. Reading Assn., Nat. Council for the Social Studies, Alumni Assn. U. South Fla., Alumni Assn. So. Bapt. Theol. Sem., Fla. Coun. Tchrs. of Math, Kappa Delta Pi. Democrat. Baptist. Clubs: Winter Park Pilot, Eastern Star, Winter Park Rainbow Girls. Home: 1705 E Harding Ave Orlando FL 32806 Office: 1919 Delaney Ave Orlando FL 32806-3005

CRANE, JONATHAN TOWNLEY, architect; b. St. Louis, Feb. 7, 1953; s. Robert Kellogg and Mildred Ellen (Price) C.; m. Lucinda Kay Sheffield, June 7, 1975; children: Robert Franklin, Christina Elizabeth. BArch, Ga. Inst. Tech., 1977. Registered architect, Fla., Ga. Intern Sheetz Assocs, Inc., Atlanta, 1978-80; architect Bradfield and Assocs, Inc., Atlanta, 1980-82; v.p. Tippett and Assocs., Inc., Atlanta, 1982-89; architect Lord, Aeck and Sargent, Inc., Atlanta, 1989—; speaker lab design Sci. Equipment and Furniture Assn., 1990, Sch. Pub. Health, Emory U., Atlanta, 1991; speaker clin. facility design Ga. Med. Group Adminstrs., 1987. Prin. works include various projects Emory U., Atlanta, Aaron Diamond AIDS Rsch. Ctr., N.Y.C., Rockdale Hosp., Conyers, Ga., various projects Sch. Medicine, Washington U., St. Louis; projects reviewed in Architecture, Facilities Planning News; co-contbr. chpt. to Laboratory Safety, Practices and Principles, Am. Soc. Microbiology, 1992. Mem. bd. trustees Counterplane Sch., Fayetteville, Ga., 1990—. Recipient Regional Energy award ASHRAE, 1986, 1st Pl. Internat. Energy award, 1987. Mem. AIA (Ga. Power/AIA Energy Design award 1984, 88), Am. Biol. Safety Assn. (speaker lab design 1991), Soc. Coll. and Univ. Planners, Constrn. Specifications Inst. (cert. constrn. specifier). Office: Lord Aeck and Sargent Inc 1201 Peachtree St NE Atlanta GA 30361-3500

CRANE, L(EO) STANLEY, retired railroad executive; b. Cin., Sept. 7, 1915; s. Leo Vincent and Blanche Gottlieb (Mitchell) C.; m. Joan McCoy, Sept. 3, 1976; children by previous marriage: Pamela Blanche, Penelope Ann. BSE, George Washington U., 1938. With So. Ry. Co., Washington, 1937-63, 65-80, engr. of tests, 1948-56, mech. rsch. engr., 1956-59, v.p. engring. and rsch., 1965-70, exec. v.p. ops., 1970-76, pres., chief adminstrv. officer, 1976-77, pres., chief exec. officer, 1977-79, chmn., 1979-80; chmn., chief exec. officer, dir. Consolidated Rail Corp. (known as Conrail), Phila., 1981-88, ret., 1988. Trustee George Washington U. Fellow ASTM (past pres.), ASME; mem. NAE, Soc. Automotive Engrs., Am. Ry. Engring. Assn., Am. Soc.. Traffic and Transp., Met. Club, Phila. Country Club, Gulph Mills Golf Club, Pine Tree Golf club. Home: 10308 St Andrews Rd Boynton Beach FL 33436-4422

CRANE, MARILYN N., homeless shelter administrator, director; b. Oreg., Mo., Oct. 18, 1930; d. Raymond Clifford and Marjorie (Evans) Nauman; m. C. Carter Crane; children: Stephen Ray, Wesley Blake, David Allen. Grad. high sch., Lawton, Okla. Exec. sec. Security Bank & Trust, Lawton, 1948-50, Officer of Pers., Ft. Sill, Okla., 1950-51, Officer of Civilian Pers., Ft. Sill, Okla., 1951-52, S.W. Bell Telephone, Lawton, 1952-60; owner Tiffanys Bakery, Oklahoma City, 1974-80, Antiques by Marilyn, Lawton, 1978-81; dir., founder Lawton Food Bank, 1985—, C. Carter Crane Shelter for Homeless, 1985—, C. Carter Crane Shelter #2, 1989—. Founder, dir. Mammography Clinic, Lawton Jr. League, 1970-72; bd. dirs. Lawton Mobile Meals, 1972-78; mem. Okla. Gov.'s Task Force for Homeless, 1987-91. Named First Lady of Lawton, Beta Sigma Phi, 1986. Mem. Human Svcs. Coun. (bd. dirs. 1985-89). Republican. Home: 12 NW 36th St Lawton OK 73505-6119 Office: C Carter Crane Shelter 1405 SW 20th St Lawton OK 73501-6940

CRANE, REGINA ANN, technical writer; b. Pine Bluff, Ark., Jan. 13, 1961; d. Lois Lynell and Lois Virginia (Martin) C. BA in Profl. & Tech. Writing, U. Ark. at Little Rock, 1983. Researcher, writer Ark. Women's History Inst., Little Rock, 1984; tech. writer UNISYS Corp., Nat. Ctr. for Toxicological Rsch., Jefferson, Ark., 1984-87; tech. editor CAE Link Corp., Jacksonville, Ark., 1988-93; assoc. tng. analyst CAE Link Corp., Jacksonville, 1993-95, Hughes Tng., Inc., Jacksonville, 1995—. Recipient Acad. Scholarship U. Ark. at Little Rock, 1979-80, Journalism Scholarship, 1982. Mem. U. Ark. at Little Rock Alumni Assn., Internat. Assn. Bus. Communicators. Office: Hughes Tng Inc PO Box 1282 Jacksonville AR 72078-1282

CRANFORD, DONNELLA BRYANT, school system administrator; b. Chgo., Feb. 2, 1950; d. Maude Devella Brown; m. Haywood Cranford, Jan. 31, 1987; 1 child, Paul Anthony. Student, Thornton Jr. Coll., 1968-69; BS, Chgo. State U., 1972; MEd, West Ga. Coll., 1984-88, cert. instrnl. leadership/supervisory, 1989; Ednl. Specialist degree, Troy State U., 1995. Tchr. Manley Elem. Sch., Chgo., 1972-74, Edward Coles Elem. Sch., Chgo., 1974-82, Cliftondal Elem. Sch., College Park, Ga., 1983-84, Cobb County/Lindley Mid. Sch., Mableton, Ga., 1984-88; instrnl. resource tchr. Conley Hills Elem. Sch., East Point, Ga., 1988-92; asst. prin. A. Philip Randolph Elem. Sch., Atlanta, 1992-94; Title 1/Chpt. 1 elem. sch. coord. Fulton County Bd. Edn., Atlanta, 1994—; cons. Fulton County Bd. Edn., East Point, 1990-93; CETA supr. Horace Mann Elem. Sch., Chgo., 1978, Edward Coles Elem. Sch., Chgo., 1979; mem. Com. Improving Curriculum, 1978-79, Textbook Inventory Com., 1984-85, Leadership Forum, 1986-87, Curriculum Writing Com., 1989-93, Ga. Compensatory Ednl. Leaders Assn., 1994; chair Student Handbook Com., 1985-86; developer Pen Pal program Fulton County Schs., 1991; trainer, facilitator Gender/Ethnic Expectation and Student Achievement, 1993—; mem. Fulton County Discipline Task Force, 1993—. Author: Adopted Just Like Jesus, Esther, Moses, 1990, Adopted Just Like Ling Pong, Abera and Jamal Andol, Gerald Ford, African American Superbowl Activity Book, 1990. Vol. Jackson for Mayor, Atlanta, 1989, Feed the Hungry, Atlanta, 1985—; active Cmty. Involvement Program, 1978-79; mem. Atlanta regional adv. bd. Just Say No, 1993—. Mem. ASCD, Internat. Reading Assn., Nat. Assn. Educators, Ga. Coun. for Social Studies (presenter 1991, 92). Methodist. Home: 3094 Dogwood Dr East Point GA 30344-3952 Office: Fulton County Bd Edn 786 Cleveland Ave SW Atlanta GA 30315-7239

CRANFORD, JAMES BLEASE, real estate executive; b. Bethune, S.C., Oct. 22, 1950; s. Colel Blease and Olivia Ardel (Adams) C.; m. Virginia Sue Black, June 24, 1972; children: Chadwick Kyle, Shaun Welborn. BSBA, Western Carolina U., 1972. Mfg. supr. Deering Milliken, Inc., Lagrange, Ga., 1972-73, mfg. tng. mgr., 1973-74; mfg. tng. mgr. Burlington Industries, Hickory, N.C., 1974; mgmt. tng. mgr. Westinghouse Electric Corp., Winston-Salem, N.C., 1974-76; real estate property mgr. Chicora Devel., Inc., Myrtle Beach, S.C., 1977-81; pres., chief exec. officer Quadrant, Inc., North Myrtle Beach, S.C., 1981—; bd. dirs. First Union Bank, 1992-95. Bd. dirs. Grand Strand YMCA, Myrtle Beach, 1986-89; area v.p. North-South High Sch. All-Star Game Com., Myrtle Beach, 1988, pres.-elect, 1989—, pres., 1990. Mem. Community Assns. Inst. (nat. trustee 1988-94, PCAM designee 1983, AMS designee 1990, Nat. Vol. of Yr. 1988, Pres. Club Hall of Fame 1989, Disting. Svc. award 1994), Cmty. Assn. Mgrs. (cert. 1996), Grand Strand Yacht Club, Tau Kappa Epsilon. Republican. Lutheran. Office: Quadrant Inc 3009 Church St Myrtle Beach SC 29577

CRANFORD, LORIN LEE, clergyman, educator; b. Perrin, Tex., Nov. 3, 1941; s. Lorinza Heath and Mary Ethlyene (Brannon) C.; m. Claire M. Allen, June 4, 1993; children: Chris, Donald, Greg, Angie, Carrie. BA, Wayland Bapt. Coll., 1964; MDiv, Southwestern Bapt. Sem., 1968, ThD, 1975; cert., Goethe Inst., 1980. Ordained to ministry Bapt. Ch., 1968. Pastor First Bapt. Ch., Graford, Tex., 1964-68, Springdale Bapt. Ch., Ft. Worth, 1968-74; prpf. N.T. Southwestern Bapt. Theol. Sem., Ft. Worth, 1974—; interim pastor First Bapt. Ch., Perrin, 1976-77, 89-90; interim pastor Arlington Hts. Bapt. Ch., Ft. Worth, 1974-75, 77-78, First Bapt. Ch., Perrin, 1976-77, 89-90, Grace Bapt. Ch., Sandhausen, Germany, 1991, others; guest prof. U. Heidelberg, 1991, U. Bonn, 1991, others. Author: Workbook for Elementary Greek, 2, vols., 1980, A Study Manual of the New Testament, 2 vols., 1981, Galatians Diagramed, 1984, James Diagrammed, 1984, A Study Guide to the Sermon on the Mount, 1985, others; editor: Theologische Auszuge zur Leseubung, 2 vols., 1984; issue editor Southwestern Jour. Theol., 1990; contbr. articles to profl. jours. Named to Outstanding Young Men of Am., 1978. Mem. Soc. Bibl. Lit., Assn. Bapt. Profs. Religion, Inst. for Bibl. Rsch., Tex. Faculty Assn. Democratic. Home: 5313 Fossil Dr Haltom City TX 76117-4568 Office: SW Bapt Theol Sem Box 22027 Fort Worth TX 76122

CRANOR, JOHN, food service executive; b. 1946. With General Mills Co., Mnpls., 1971-77, Hopkins Mfg. Co., Emporia, Kans., 1977, Pepsico, Inc., Purchase, N.Y., 1977-89; pres., CEO, corp. dir. Ky. Fried Chicken Corp., Louisville, 1989-95; pres., CEO Long John Silvers, Lexington, Ky., 1995—. Office: Long John Silvers PO Box 11988 Louisville KY 40579-1988*

CRANSTON, JOHN WELCH, historian, educator; b. Utica, N.Y., Dec. 21, 1931; s. Earl and Mildred (Welch) C.; B.A., Pomona Coll., 1953; M.A., Columbia U., 1964; Ph.D., U. Wis., 1970. Asst. prof. history W. Tex. State U., 1970-74, U. Mo., Kansas City, 1970, Rust Coll., Holly Springs, Miss., 1974-80, assoc. prof., 1980-83; historian U.S. Army Armor Ctr., Ft. Knox, Ky., 1983-95; ret., 1995; adj. prof. history and govt. Elizabethtown C.C., Ft. Knox, 1988—. Served with U.S. Army, 1953-55. Nat. Endowment for Humanities fellow, summer 1976, summer 1981. Mem. Am. Hist. Assn., Orgn. of Am. Historians. Democrat. Episcopalian. Contbr. hist. articles to profl. lit. Home: PO Box 892 Radcliff KY 40159-0892

CRANSTON, PHILIP EDWARD, foreign language professional; b. Pittsfield, Mass., Mar. 22, 1929; s. Julius Byron and Ruth Runnells (Pepin) C.; m. Mechthild Grieser-Fuerst, Oct. 12, 1938. BA, U. Ariz., 1951; MA, U. Calif., Berkeley, 1958, PhD, 1972. Asst. prof. fgn. lang. Calif. State U., Hayward, 1964-69, Western Carolina U., Cullowhee, N.C., 1971-72; from asst. to assoc. prof. French U. N.C., Asheville, 1972-92, prof. French, 1992-95; prof. emeritus, 1995; vis. assoc. prof. French Clemson (S.C.) U., 1984. Author: (poetry) Time of the Sun, 1968, Before Time, 1979; translator (poetry of J. Supervielle) Naissances/Births, 1992; contbr. articles to profl. jours. Seaman recruit to Lt. USNR, 1951-55. Grantee Ministry of Edn., Paris, 1962-64, NEH, 1976, 81. Mem. MLA, South Atlantic MLA, Am. Assn. Tchrs. French, Am. Literary Translators Assn., So. Comparative Lit. Assn., Phi Beta Kappa, Phi Kappa Phi. Democrat. Home: 113 Houston St Clemson SC 29631-1311

CRANWELL, C. RICHARD, lawyer; b. CredeKanova, W.Va., July 26, 1942; s. James Edward and Mary Elizabeth (Peters) C.; children: C. Richard Jr., Whitney Carol, James Robert, Jean Jarrett. BS, Va. Polytech. Inst., 1965; JD, U. Richmond, 1968. Assoc. Tilley & Pedigo, Roanoke, Va., 1968-70; ptnr. Pedigo & Cranwell, Roanoke, 1970-78, Cranwell, Flora, Selbe & Barbe, Roanoke, 1978-80, Gardner, Rocovich & Cranwell, Roanoke, 1980-82, Cranwell, Flora & Moore, Vinton, Va., 1982—. Del. 14th legis dist. Va. Ho. of Dels., 1972-85, chmn. fin. com., cts. of justice com., counties, cities and towns rules com., house majority leader, 1981—; past pres. Vinton Dogwood Festival, bd. dirs. 1973-75; legal advisor Vinton Rescue Squad, Mt. Pleasant Rescue Squad, Montvale Rescue Squad; bd. dirs. Roanoke Valley Juvenile Diabetes Found.; mem. Blue Ridge Develp. Coun. Named one of Outstanding Young Men in Am., U.S. Jaycees, 1970, 72; Selected Influential Young Mem. Gen. Assembly, Capital Press Corps, 1975, 77; Williams scholar. Mem. Phi Delta Phi, Vinton C. of C. (legal advisor). Democrat. Methodist. Lodge: Lions. Home: 110 W Virginia Ave Vinton VA 24179-3316 Office: PO Box 459 Vinton VA 24179-0459*

CRANWELL-BRUCE, LISA A., mental health nurse; b. Hoboken, N.J., Mar. 21, 1961; d. John J. and Arlene (Donovan) Cranwell; m. Shane T. Bruce, Oct. 14, 1984; children: John Carter, Ilaria Patricia, Olivia Dorothea, James Frederick. BSN, Coll. New Rochelle, 1983; postgrad., Ga. State U., 1995—. Cert. in psychiat.-mental health nursing. Charge nurse CPC Parkwood Hosp., Atlanta, 1986-89; nurse mgr. Laurel Hts. Hosp., Atlanta, 1989-90, acting dir. nursing, 1990, supr. nursing, 1990-94; dir. weekend svcs. Charter at Laurel Heights, 1994-96; psychiat./med. nurse, home health nurse Ctrl. Home Health Care, Lawrenceville, Ga., 1996—. Active St. Monica's circle St. Thomas More Cath. Ch., Decatur, Ga., Atlanta (Ga.) Parents of Twins Club. 1st lt. U.S. Army, 1983-85. Mem. ANA, Ga. Nurses Assn., Coll. New Rochelle Alumnae Coun., Advs. for Child Psychiat. Nursing. Home: 3283 Francine Dr Decatur GA 30033-3355 Office: Ctrl Home Health Care 1001 Hurricane Shoals Rd NE Lawrenceville GA 30243

CRAPO, GREGORY KEMPTON, furniture industry executive; b. Biloxi, Miss., Dec. 1, 1960; s. Leo Kempton and Dorothy Jean (Stewart) Crapo; m. Sandra Margaret Sentell, Apr. 3, 1993. B in Bus. Mgmt., U. South Ala., 1981; MBA, U. So. Miss., 1983; cert. interior design, Comml. Trade Inst., 1992. Furniture salesman Merchiston Hall Furniture, Biloxi, 1981-84, v.p., asst. mgr., 1984—. Mem. com. United Way Funds Allocations, 1986-96, United Way Pers. Com., 1990-92, Case Svcs. Mid. South Sight and Hearing Svc., 1991-92, United Way South Miss.; bd. dirs. Miss. Lions Sight Found., 1993—, Main St. U.S.A., Biloxi, 1995—. Recipient cert. appreciation Mayor of Biloxi, 1984; named Outstanding Young Biloxian, 1986. Fellow Melvin Jones; mem. Lions Club Internat. (Internat. Leadership award 1992, 93), Lions Club Biloxi (dir. 1981-93, bd. dirs. 1991-94, Lion of Yr. 1983, 85). Roman Catholic. Office: Merchiston Hall Furniture Galleries 918 Howard Ave Biloxi MS 39530-4118

CRASSWELLER, ROBERT DOELL, retired lawyer, writer; b. Duluth, Minn., Sept. 17, 1915; s. Arthur Hallifax and Mary Elizabeth (Doell) C.; m. Mildred Elizabeth Clarke, Mar. 21, 1942; children: Peter, Karen Farbman, Pamela Baldino. BA, Carleton Coll., 1937; LLB, Harvard U., 1941. Bar: Minn. 1941, N.Y. 1960. Pvt. practice Duluth, Minn., 1942-43; econ. warfare posts U.S. Dept. State, Washington, 1943-45; ptnr. McCabe, Gruber, Clure, Donovan & Crassweller, Duluth, Minn., 1976-51; mining exec. West Indies Mining Exec., San Juan, P.R., 1951-53; counsel Pan Am. Airways, N.Y.C., 1954-67; vis. fellow Coun. Fgn. Rels., N.Y.C., 1967-70; vis. prof. Bklyn. Coll., Sarah Lawrence, N.Y.C., 1969-70; staff atty. ITT, N.Y.C., 1970-74, gen. coun. Lat. Am., 1975-81. Author: Trujillo: Life and Times of a Caribbean Dictator, 1966, The Caribbean Community, 1972, Peron and the Enigmas of Argentina, 1986; reviewer (books) for Fgn. Affairs, 1968-81. Dir. Forum for World Affairs, Stamford, Conn., 1986-87. Mem. Internat. Assn. Torch Clubs (Chapel Hill Club v.p. 1994-95), Soc. Automotive Historians. Republican. Home: 101 York Pl Chapel Hill NC 27514

CRAVEN, ALAN ELLIOTT, English language educator, university dean; b. Kansas City, Mo., Nov. 12, 1935; m. Gloria Christine Skinner, May 13, 1989; children: Theresa, Julia, Elliott. BA, U. Kans., 1958, MA, 1963, PhD, 1965. Tchg. asst. U. Kans., Lawrence, 1958-65; asst. prof. U. Ariz., Tucson, 1965-71, Brandeis U., Waltham, Mass., 1971-72; prof. English, U. Tex., San Antonio, 1973—, dean Coll. Fine Arts and Humanities, 1995—. Contbr.

articles to profl. jours. Office: U Tex Coll Fine Arts-Humanities San Antonio TX 78249

CRAVEN, ROBERTA JILL, literature educator; b. White Plains, N.Y., Feb. 4, 1962; d. Robert James and Norma Eleanor (Page) C. BS in Math., U. N.C., 1984, postgrad., 1989—. Account systems engr. IBM Nat. Fed. Mktg., Bethesda, Md., 1984-86, account mktg. rep., 1986-89; telecomm. mktg. support rep. IBM, Research Triangle Park, N.C., 1990; instr. U. N.C., Chapel Hill, 1990—. T.J. Watson Nat. Merit scholar IBM, Armonk, N.Y., 1980, Hon. Regents scholar N.Y. Bd. Regents, 1980. Mem. MLA, Phi Beta Kappa, Phi Eta Sigma. Office: U NC Comparative Lit CB # 3150 Chapel Hill NC 27599-3150

CRAVEY, CHARLES EDWARD, minister, publisher, poet; b. Eastman, Ga., June 17, 1951; s. Carise Lee and Irene (Cooper) C.; m. Charlotte Renee Dennis, July 12, 1972; children: Angela Marie, Jonathan Edward. BS in Sociology, Ga. So. U., 1979; student, Candler Sch. Theology, 1983; M of Sacred Literature, Trinity Theol. Sem., 1989, PhD in Theology, 1991. Ordained to ministry Meth. Ch. as elder, 1987. Assoc. pastor Cochran (Ga.) Meth. Ch., 1972-73, St. Peter's United Meth. Ch., Fitzgerald, Ga., 1973-77; Newington charge pastor, 1977-79, Bartow charge pastor, 1979-82; pastor Alamo (Ga.) United Meth. Ch., 1982-86, Northview United Meth. Ch., Warner Robins, Ga., 1986-90; sr. min. 1st United Meth. Ch., Reidsville, Ga., 1991-94, Trinity United Meth. Ch., Tifton, Ga., 1994—; pres., founder In His Steps Pub. Co., Warner Robins, 1979—, The Soc. Am. Poets, Warner Robins, 1988—; chaplain Houston County Hosp., Warner Robins, 1987—. Author: 15 books on poetry and religious themes; (weekly newspaper column) Fruits from the Vineyard, Daily Prayers, 1986—; editor, pub. (quar. poetry newspaper) The Poet's Pen, also 156 books of poetry by various authors, 1988—; recorded 24 personal song albums. Bd. dirs. Warner Robins Teen Ctr., 1987—; pres. Vol. Houston County, Warner Robins, 1991. Mem. Gospel Music Assn. (nominated for 15 Dove awards 1989, 90, 91, 96), Ga. State Poetry Soc., The Soc. of Am. Poets (pres., founder), So. Poetry Assn., Warner Robins Ministerial Assn., Reidsville Ministerial Assn. (v.p. 1991—). Home and Office: Trinity United Meth Ch PO Box 85 Tifton GA 31793-0085

CRAWFORD, BOB, state commissioner; b. Bartow, Fla., Jan. 26, 1948; m. Nancy Sue Caswall; children: Robert Bruce IV, Kristin Nicole. Degree in bus., U. Miami. Rep. Fla. House, 6 yrs.; senator Fla. Senate, 8 yrs., pres., 1988-90; commr. agriculture State of Fla., 1990—. Named Most Effective State Lawmaker, Miami Herald. Baptist. Office: Agrl and Consumer Services Plz Level 10 The Capit Tallahassee FL 32399

CRAWFORD, DONNA MARIE, accounting administrator; b. Chgo., Dec. 7, 1947; d. Jack Sr. and Fannie Lou (Jones) C.; 1 foster child, Mary Ann Chee. BS, Tenn. State U., 1968; MS, U. Tenn., 1969; AS, Nashville State Tech. Inst., 1981. Registered bus. profl. educator, Tenn.; cert. govt. fin. mgr. Acct., cost acct. supr. book pubs., chem. and pharm. industry, hospitality industry, 1968-73; from sr. grants acct. to budget analyst, various depts. State of Tenn., Nashville, 1973—; acctg. mgr. State of Tenn. Dept. Corrections, Nashville, 1996—; employee rep. Tenn. State Govt. Retirement Bd., Nashville, 1986-88. Contbr. poems to: Dance on the Horizon, 1994. Participant cultural and grant activities Native Am. Indian Assn., Nashville, 1992-94. NDEA grad. sch. fellow, 1968-69. Mem. Acad. Internat. Mgmt. Office: State of Tenn Dept Corrections 3rd Fl Rachel Jackson Bldg 320 6th Ave N Nashville TN 37219-1400

CRAWFORD, E. MAC, health facilities executive; b. 1949. Grad., Auburn U., 1971. With Salem Nat. Corp., 1977-78, Arthur Young & Co., 1971-77, 78-81, GTI Ltd., 1981-85, 86, Oxylance Corp., 1985-86, Mulberry St. Investment Co., 1986-90; exec. v.p. hosp. ops. Charter Med. Corp., Atlanta, 1990-92, pres., COO, 1992—. Office: Charter Med Corp 3414 Peachtree Rd Ste 1400 Atlanta GA 30326

CRAWFORD, FRED ALLEN, JR., cardiothoracic surgeon, educator; b. Columbia, S.C., Oct. 17, 1942; s. Fred Allen and Susan Valery Floyd C.; m. Mary Jane Dantzler, June 11, 1966; children: Fred Allen, III, Mary Elizabeth. MD, Duke U., 1967. Diplomate Am. Bd. Surgery, Am. Bd. Thoracic Surgery (bd. dirs.). Intern, Duke U. Med. Ctr., Durham, N.C., 1967-68, resident in surgery, 1971-76, instr. surgery, 1975-76; asst. prof. surgery, chief div. cardiac surgery U. Miss., Med. Ctr., Jackson, 1976-79; prof. surgery pediatrics, chief div. cardiothoracic surgery Med. U. of S.C., Charleston, 1979—, chmn. dept. surgery, 1988—. Maj. U.S. Army, 1969-71. Decorated Bronze Star. Mem. ACS, Am. Surg. Assn., Charleston County Med. Soc., S.C. State Med. Assn., Soc. Thoracic Surgeons, So. Surg. Assn., So. Thoracic Surg. Assn., Am. Heart Assn., Am. Assn. Thoracic Surgery, Am. Coll. Cardiology, Phi Beta Kappa, Alpha Omega Alpha. Presbyterian. Club: Ducks Unltd. Contbr. numerous articles to profl. jours. Office: 171 Ashley Ave Charleston SC 29403

CRAWFORD, JOHN P., insurance commissioner; b. Ada, Okla., Dec. 14, 1931; s. Johnson William and Mildred Frank (Settles) C.; m. Marjorie Mae Muhs, Aug. 15, 1957; children: John P. III, Gretchen Ann. BBA, U. Okla., 1953. Chief actuary State of Okla., Oklahoma City; pvt. practice consulting actuary Oklahoma City; ins. commr. State of Okla., Oklahoma City. Candidate Fifth U.S. Congress Dist., Okla., 1992. 1st lt. U.S. Army, 1954-56. Fellow Conf. of Consulting Actuaries; mem. Am. Acad. Actuaries. Republican. Methodist. Home: 1213 Mulberry Ln Oklahoma City OK 73116

CRAWFORD, LAWRENCE ROBERT, aviation and aerospace consultant; b. Ft. Lewis, Wash., May 4, 1936; s. Richard G. and Olive O. (Ericksen) C.; m. Yvonne G. Thompson, Nov. 8, 1957; children: Scott D., Robin L., Crawford Lafrankie. BS in Indsl. Engring., Ga. Inst. Tech., 1959; MS in Mgmt., Rensselaer Poly. Inst., 1965. Lic. comml. pilot. Commd. ensign USN, 1959, advanced through grades to lt. comdr., hon. discharge, 1968; airline pilot Pan Am, San Francisco, 1968-70; dir. corp. budgets Pan Am, N.Y.C., 1970-73; dir. methods and standards Am. Airlines, N.Y.C., 1973-75, sr. dir. reservations, 1975-79; v.p. mktg. Ransome Airlines, Phila., 1979-83; sr. v.p. mktg. and planning Empire Airlines, Utica, N.Y., 1983-85; pres., CEO Avitas, Inc., Reston, Va., 1985—; mem. exec. adv. bd. EDS Fin. Corp., Dallas, 1987-90; chmn., CEO Avitas Engring. Inc., Miami, Fla., 1991—; v.p. Det Norske Veritas, Oslo, 1992—. Contbr. articles to profl. jours. Bd. dirs. Internat. Aviation Found., 1996—. Mem. AIAA, Exptl. Aircraft Assn. (builder 1987), U.S. Ultralight Flying Assn., Am. Aero. Soc., Internat. Soc. Transport Aircraft Trading, Nat. Aeronautics Inst., Soc. Sr. Aerospace Execs., Stearman Restorers Assn., Wings Club, Washington Aero Club. Republican. Methodist. Home: 10031 Scenic View Ter Vienna VA 22182 Office: Avitas Inc 1835 Alexander Bell Dr Reston VA 20191

CRAWFORD, MICHAEL WAYNE, investment company executive; b. Hampton, Va., Oct. 8, 1962; s. Oscar Lee and Buena Elizabeth (Moore) C.; m. Felicia Keene, May 23, 1987; c: Bryan Wayne, Brittany Lauren. Undergradute, Old Dominion U., 1981-83, Christopher Newport Coll., 1983-86. Branch mgr. Household Finance, Hampton, Va., 1984-86; mng. supr. Associates Financial, Springfield, Va., 1986-89; pres., CEO, chmn. Libra Investments Ltd., Reston, Va., 1989—. Mem. Am. Mgmt. Assn., U.S. C. of C., Va. C. of C., Mid-Atlantic Notary Assn. Baptist.

CRAWFORD, NORMA VIVIAN, nurse; b. Cleveland, Tex., Dec. 29, 1936; d. Ira Wesley and Lizzie Augusta (Godejohn) C.; m. Arthur B. Crawford, Sept. 20, 1956 (dec.); children: Pamela, Desiree. Lic. vis. nurse, Lee Jr. Coll., 1971-72; RN, Cumberland County Coll., 1977; BSN, U. Mary-Hardin Baylor, 1986. Charge nurse Patrick Henry Hosp., Newport News, Va., 1972-73; staff nurse Salem (N.J.) County Nursing Home, 1975-77, Nicholson Nursing Home, Penns Grove, N.J., 1977; nurse ICU, Metroplex Hosp., Killeen, Tex., 1977-79; dir. nurses Wind Crest Nursing Ctr., Copperas Cove, Tex., 1979-82; staff nurse supr., unit mgr. med./surg. unit, supr., home health nurse, dir. home health Metroplex Hosp., Killeen, Tex., 1979-87; dir. Metroplex Home Health Svcs., Killeen, Tex., 1988-91; dir. quality assurance, risk mgmt. Hill Country Home Health, Lampasas, Tex., 1991-93; clin. dir. Rollins Brook Home Health, Lampasas, 1993—. Bd. dirs. Heart of Tex. Hospice, 1990-96. Mem. Order of Eastern Star. Baptist. Home: 604 Yucca Dr Copperas Cove TX 76522-3022 Office: 1205 Central Texas Expy Lampasas TX 76550-3388

CRAWFORD, PAMELA J., critical care nurse; b. Houma, La., Aug. 10, 1957; d. Arthur Butler and Norma Vivien (Crawford) C.; children: Stephanie Pamela Cobb, Michele Anne Cobb. Assoc. of Legal Tech., Cumberland County Coll., Vineland, N.J., 1977; BSN, U. Mary Hardin-Baylor, Belton, Tex., 1987. Med. ICU-CCU staff nurse Scott and White Hosp., Temple, Tex., 1987-88; neuro ICU staff nurse Brooke Army Med. Ctr., San Antonio, 1989-91; case mgr. transplants, vendor negotiator, regional contact Traveler's Inc. Co., San Antonio, 1991-92; dir. quality control Brit-tex Home Health Svcs., 1992-94; dir. profl. svcs. Service Master Home Health, Stafford, Tex., 94—. Home Health Svcs., 1992-94; dir. Prof. Svcs., Svc. Master Home Health, Houston, 1994—. 1st lt. USAR, 1988—.

CRAWFORD, SALLY SUE, nursing educator; b. LaGrange, Ga., Nov. 17, 1944; children from previous marriage: Patricia Anne, Elizabeth Sue, James Burton Jr. AA, DeKalb Coll. Nursing, 1973; BA, Ga. State U., Atlanta, 1971, MEd, 1978; EDS, U. Ga., 1987; BSN, Clayton State Coll., 1994. RN. Sr. health educator Ga. Dept. Human Resources, Lawrenceville, 1975-88; asst. dir. staff devel. ARC, Atlanta, 1988; with Atlanta Eye Screening, 1988-89; outreach coord. Cataract Inst., Atlanta, 1989-90; tng. coord. S.E. Regional Ctr. For Drug-Free Schs. & Communities, 1990; tng. planner Atlanta Community Prevention Coalition, 1991-92; sole propr. Health Lifestyles, 1992-95; nursing instr. Griffin Tech. Sch., 1992-93; sr. nurse Clayton Ctr., Jonesboro, Ga., 1993-95; adminstrv. supr. Peachtree Regional Hosp., 1994—; clin. nursing instr. Gordon Coll. Nursing Students, 1995—; supr. Healthways, Morrow, Ga., 1995; health svcs. adminstr. Correctional Healthcare Solutions, 1996—; chmn. bd. dirs. Canine Vision, Inc. Author: 6 manuals; contbr. articles to profl. jours. Mem. NAFE, ASTD, AAPHERD, UDC (state chmn. 1988-90, nat. chmn. of pages 1989), Ga. Fedn. Profl. Health Educators, Internat. Platform Assn., Daus. of 1812 (local officer 1989—, state officer 1992-94), Continental Soc., Daus. of Indian Wars (nat. officer, state officer 1990-94), DAR (organizing regent chpt. 1982-84, nat. spkrs. staff 1986-89), Daus. Am. Colonists (chpt. regent 1988-91, state officer 1991—), Colonial Dames of XVII Century (local registrar), Ga. Soc. Magna Charta Dames (state officer 1986—), First Families of Ga., Lions (1st female mem. Atlanta club, chmn. sight and vision 1989-90, officer 1990-91), Sigma Theta Tau. Episcopalian. Home: 2305 Luther Bailey Rd Senoia GA 30276-9218 Office: Griffin Regional Youth Detention Ctr 105 Justice Blvd Griffin GA 30223

CRAWFORD, SANDRA KAY, lawyer; b. Henderson, Tex., Sept 23, 1934; d. Obie Lee and Zilpha Elizabeth (Ash) Stalcup; m. William Walsh Crawford, Dec. 21, 1968; children: Bill, Jonathan, Constance, Amelia, Patrick. BA, Wellesley Coll., 1957; LLB, U. Tex., 1960. Bar: Tex. 1960, U.S. Supreme Ct. 1965, Colo. 1967, Ill. 1974. Asst. v.p.-legal Hamilton Mgmt. Corp., Denver, 1966-68; v.p., gen. counsel, sec. Transamerica Fund Mgmt. Corp., L.A., 1968; cons. to law dept. Met. Life Ins. Co., N.Y.C., 1969-71; counsel Touche Ross & Co., Chgo., 1972-75; v.p., assoc. gen. counsel Continental Ill. Bank, Chgo., 1975-83; sr. div. counsel Motorola, Inc., Schaumburg, Ill., 1984; sr. counsel, asst. sec. Sears Roebuck & Co., 1985-90, cons., 1990—. Mem. ABA, Ill. State Bar Assn., Colo. Bar Assn., Tex. Bar Assn., Everglades Club, Beach Club (Palm Beach), River Club (N.Y.C.). Home: 100 Royal Palm Way Apt G5 Palm Beach FL 33480-4270

CRAWFORD, TIMOTHY GRAY, Old Testament and Hebrew language educator; b. Huntsville, Ala., Nov. 19, 1957; s. William Joseph and Janet (Waite) C.; m. Janet Kline, July 28, 1958. BA, Samford U., 1980; MDiv, Southwestern Bapt. Theol. Sem., Ft. Worth, 1984; PhD, So. Bapt. Theol. Sem., Louisville, 1990. Instr. O.T. interpretation So. Bapt. Theol. Sem., 1988-90; asst. prof., 1990-94; assoc. prof. Bluefield (Va.) Coll., 1994—, chair, 1991—. Author: Blessing and Curse in Syro-Palestinian Inscriptions of the Iron Age, 1992; contbg. author: Mercer Dictionary of the Bible, 1990; co-author: A Handbook to Biblical Hebrew Grammar, 1994. Mem. Soc. Bibl. Lit., Nat. Assn. Bapt. Profs. Religion, Nat. Assn. Profs. Hebrew. Office: Bluefield Coll 3000 College Dr Bluefield VA 24605-1799

CRAWFORD, VICKY CHARLENE, perinatal clinical nurse specialist; b. Waynesville, N.C., Aug. 20, 1959; d. Jerry Harrell and Geneva Pauline (Parker) C. BSN, Med. U. of S.C., 1981; MS in Maternal/Infant Nursing, Clemson U., 1991. Cert. in inpatient obstet. nursing. Staff nurse II ob Greenville (S.C.) Gen. Hosp., 1981-83; staff nurse labor and delivery Lexington County Hosp., West Columbia, S.C., 1983-84; staff RN III high risk ob-gyn Greenville Meml. Hosp., 1984-85, ob-gyn. clinician, 1985-91, ob-gyn. clin. nurse specialist, 1991-94; perinatal clin. nurse specialist Ctr. for Women's Medicine-Maternal Fetal Medicine Divsn., Greenville, 1994—; counselor, program coord. Resolve Through Sharing; developer Mother-Baby Care Cross-Tng. Program, 1989; sponsor Compassion Internat. Contbr. articles to profl. jours. Mem. Assn. Women's Health, Obstetrics and Neonatal Nursing (conv. speaker), Am. Heart Assn., Sigma Theta Tau. Home: 347 Bishop Dr Easley SC 29640-2585

CRAWFORD, WILLIAM DAVID, real estate broker, developer; b. Abbeville County, S.C., Aug. 13, 1945; s. Jesse David and Elizabeth Virginia (Ashley) C.; m. Gail Eileen Watkins, June 9, 1967 (div. Aug. 1985); 1 child, Merritt Caitlin; m. Dawn P. Lantz, June 10, 1995. BA, Wofford Coll., 1967; MS, Tex. A&M U., 1974; MBA, U. New Orleans, 1977. Lic. real estate broker, S.C., N.C., Ga., Tex., Tenn.; CCIM, CIPS; lic. comml. aircraft pilot. Gen. mgr. Ramada Inn, New Orleans, 1973-74; researcher div. bus. & econ. rsch. U. New Orleans, 1975-77; exec. asst. to pres. LaSalle Properties, New Orleans, 1977-81; v.p. Doerring Devel. Co., Austin, Tex., 1981-84; project mgr. Street-Martin Cos., Austin, 1984; pres. TriSource Corp., San Antonio, Tex., 1985-86; v.p. Merritt Properties, Inc., Greenville, S.C., 1986-87; pres. Crawford & Assocs., Greenville, 1987—. Author: Louisiana Business Survey, 1977, Application of Travel Economic Impact Model to New Orleans, 1977. Active Round Towners, Greenville, 1986—; chmn. Paris Mountain Water Dist., Greenville, 1990—. Capt. C.E., U.S. Army, 1968-71. Mem. Comml. Investment Real Estate Inst. (cert. comml. investment mem., cert. internat. property specialist internat. real estate sect.), Nat. Assn. Realtors (Internat. Real Estate sect.), Greenville Bd. Realtors, Comml. Bd. Realtors (dir.), Greenville C. of C., Urban Land Inst., Gamma Sigma Delta, Beta Gamma Sigma. Mem. Unity Ch. Home and Office: 2 Persimmon Ln Greenville SC 29609-6511

CRAWFORD, WILLIAM WALSH, retired consumer products company executive; b. Clearwater, Fla., Oct. 7, 1927; s. Francis Marion and Frances Marie (Walsh) C. B.S., Georgetown U., 1950; LL.B., Harvard, 1954. Bar: N.Y. 1955, Ill. 1972. Assoc. Sullivan & Cromwell, N.Y.C., 1954-58; counsel Esso Standard Oil, N.Y.C., 1958-60; ptnr. Alexander & Green, N.Y.C., 1960-71; v.p., gen. counsel Internat. Harvester Co., Chgo., 1971-76; v.p., gen. counsel, sec. Internat. Harvester Co., 1976-80; sr. v.p. gen. counsel Kraft, Inc., Glenview, Ill., 1980-81; sr. v.p., gen. counsel, sec. Dart & Kraft, Inc., 1981-86; sr. v.p., gen. counsel, sec. Kraft, Inc., 1986-88, sr. v.p., sec., 1988-89, ret., 1989; bd. dirs. Delchamps, Inc. Mem. ABA, Ill. Bar Assn., Assn. Bar City N.Y., Am. Judicature Soc., Am. Law Inst., Assn. Gen. Counsel, Chgo. Club, River Club (N.Y.C.), Beach Club, Everglades Club, Old Guard Soc. Palm Beach Golfers.

CREANY, CATHLEEN ANNETTE, television station executive; b. Johnstown, Pa., Jan. 14, 1950; d. Eugene Anthony and Winifred Nell (Sheridan) C. BA in Communication Arts, U. Notre Dame, 1972. Ptnr. Technivision, Inc., N.Y.C., 1972-75; producer commls. Innervision Prodns., St. Louis, 1975-76; film editor Sta. KPHO-TV, Phoenix, 1976-77, promotion asst., 1977-78, comml. and documentary photographer and producer, 1978-80; news photographer Sta. WTVH-TV, Syracuse, N.Y., 1980-81, field dir. PM Mag. show, 1981-82, exec. producer PM Mag. show, 1982-83, program dir., 1983-86, v.p., gen. mgr., 1986-92, Sta WTVH-TV, Syracuse; v.p., gen mgr. Sta. WFAA-TV, Dallas, 1993-94, pres., gen. mgr., 1994—; mem. bd. dirs. The Family Place, 1993—; Children's Med. Ctr. of Dallas, Children's Med. Found. Dallas, Better Business Bur. Dallas, adv. bd. of Jr. League, Dallas. Recipient Excellence in Photography award for PM Mag. show, 1982, Excellence in Story Producing award for PM Mag., 1983. Mem. Nat. Assn. TV Program Execs., Nat. Assn. Broadcasters, ABC TV Affiliates Assn. (mem. bd. govs.). Avocations: running, skiing, boating, gardening. Office: WFAA-TV 606 Young St Dallas TX 75202-4810

CREASEY, KATHERINE YVONNE, utilization review and surgical nurse; b. McCrory, Ark., Jan. 24, 1961; d. Earnest E. and Mary A. (Stain) Tyler; m. Earnest Leon Creasey, June 3, 1995; 1 child, Stephanie K. AS, East Ark. Community Coll., 1981; BSNtgrad., U. Ark. for Med. Scis., 1996. RN, Ark. Staff nurse Crittenden Meml. Hosp., West Memphis, Ark., 1982; nurse ICU/CCU Bapt. Meml. Hosp., Forrest City, Ark., 1981-82, 82-86, nurse gastrointestinal and non-invasive vascular labs., 1986-87, surg. nurse gastrointestinal lab., 1987-91, PRN CCU,, 1991—. Mem. AACN. Home: PO Box 986 McCrory AR 72101 Office: Bapt Meml Hosp PO Box 667 Forrest City AR 72335-0667

CREASMAN, WILLIAM PAUL, lawyer; b. Washington, Dec. 6, 1952; s. Paul and Esther B. (Tucker) C.; m. S. Teresa Deese, Aug. 18, 1973; 3 children. BA, Johns Hopkins U., 1974; JD, Wake Forest U., 1977. Bar: N.C. 1977, U.S. Dist. Ct. (mid. dist.) N.C. 1978, Ark. 1992. Asst. trust officer First Citizen's Bank & Trust Co., Raleigh, N.C., 1977-78; atty. Wrangler div. Blue Bell Inc., Greensboro, N.C. and Brussels, Belgium, 1978-83; sr. corp. atty. Hardee's div. Imasco USA Inc., Rocky Mount, N.C., 1983-84; asst. gen. counsel Imasco USA Inc., Rocky Mount, N.C., 1985-87; gen. counsel Church's Fried Chicken, San Antonio, 1984-85; sr. v.p., gen. counsel TCBY Enterprises, Inc., Little Rock, Ark., 1987—; panelist Am. Arbitration Assn., Dallas, 1988—; adj. prof. U. Ark. Sch. Law, Little Rock, . Mem. N.C. Bar Assn., Ark. Bar Assn., Pulaski County Bar Assn. Lutheran. Home: 12 Barber Dr Maumelle AR 72113-6481 Office: TCBY Enterprises Inc 1100 TCBY Tower Capitol And Broadway Little Rock AR 72201

CREASONG, JOHNNY JOE, minister; b. Middletown, Ohio, Dec. 6, 1956; s. Roy Samuel and Gladys Virginia (Davidson) C.; m. Ronda Faye Kinnard, Aug. 9, 1978; children: Jonda Lynn, Julie Darlyne, Jessica Renee, Joy Anne. BA in Ministry, Gulf Coast Bible Coll., 1979. Ordained min. Ch. of God. Pastor First Ch. of God, Farmington, N.Mex., 1979-83; assoc. pastor Redfork Ch. of God., Tulsa, Okla., 1983-85; pastor Ch. of God., Fredricktown, Mo., 1985-87, First Ch. of God, Granby, Mo., 1987-91; campus pastor, dir. coll. relations Mid.-Am. Bible Coll., Oklahoma City, 1991-94; pastor First Ch. of God, Beaumont, Tex., 1994—; dir. state youth Okla. Ch. of God., 1984-85, Mo. Ch. of God, 1986-91; bd. dirs. ministries, Mo. Ch. of God, 1986-91, sec. bd. ch. extension, 1989-91. Editor Tex. State Ch. of God Bull., 1996—. Vice chmn. Farmington Police Chaplains, 1981-83; v.p. PTA, Granby, 1988, pres., 1989-91; chmn. Eastex. Assembly of God Ch., 1995—, Eastex. Credentials Com., 1995—. Mem. S.E. Tex. Assn. of the Ch. of God (sec., exec. com. 1994—). Office: First Ch of God 4450 Crow Rd Beaumont TX 77706-6912

CREECH, DONNA LOTHEL, public relations executive; b. Nashville, Mar. 7, 1953; d. Wyman Francis and Lillie D. (Harper) C.; m. William Love Dockery, Apr. 1, 1989; children: Haley Cathryn Creech Dockery, Marshall Moses. BA, Carson-Newman Coll., 1975; MS, U. Tenn., 1983. Coord. pub. rels. State Tech. Inst., Knoxville, Tenn., 1976-81; communications rep. TRW Steering and Suspension, Sterling Heights, Mich., 1981-83; mktg. asst. St. Mary's Med. Ctr., Knoxville, 1984-85; dir. pub. rels. Bapt. Hosp., Knoxville, 1985-88; account exec. Ackermann Pub. Rels., Knoxville, 1988-90; environ. cmty. rels. specialist IT Corp., 1990-94; dir. environ. cmty. rels. SSA, Inc., Oak Ridge, Tenn., 1994—; cons. Levi Strauss Found., Knoxville, 1984-85. Chmn. Knox County Second Start, Knoxville, 1986—; publicity com. Hawkins County United Way, Rogersville, Tenn., 1982, Children's Hosp. Festival of Trees, Knoxville, 1990; bd. dirs. Knoxville Women's Ctr., 1980-81, 91-93; mem. County Regional Solid Waste Bd., 1993—. Recipient Merit award Internat. Assn. Bus. Communications, San Francisco, 1983, Addy, Knoxville Advt. Club, 1988. Mem. Women in Comm. (pres. Knoxville chpt. 1987-89, Clarion award 1987), Pub. Rels. Soc. Am. (Best External Publ. award 1987, J. Carroll Bateman award 1990), Tenn. Soc. for Hosp. Mktg. and Pub. Rels. (regional rep. 1985-87, Prism award 1985), Internat. Assn. Pub. Participation (chpt. pres. 1996—). Unitarian-Universalist. Home: 4615 Holston Hills Rd Knoxville TN 37914-5007 Office: SSA Inc 702 S Illinois Ave Ste B201 Oak Ridge TN 37830-7976

CREECY, HERBERT LEE, JR., artist; b. Norfolk, Va., Aug. 14, 1939; s. Herbert Lee and Louise (Boyce) C.; m. Charner Williams, Nov. 1961; 1 child, Herbert Lee III; m. Michelle Riendeau, Sept. 7, 1985. Student, U. Ala., 1958-60; profl. art degree, Atlanta Coll. Art, 1964; student, S.W. Hayter Atelier 17, Paris, 1964. tchr. Atlanta Coll. Art, 1969-71; lectr. U. Ga., Athens, 1980-85, U. Ga., Cortona, Italy, 1989; vis. artist U. Tenn., Knoxville, 1991. One-man shows include High Mus. Art, Atlanta, 1964, Mandola Gallery, Atlanta, 1966, Clark Coll., Atlanta, 1967, Unitarian Universalist Congregation, Atlanta, 1967, Illian Gallery, Atlanta, 1968, Image South Gallery, Atlanta, 1972, Heath Gallery, Atlanta, 1973-74, 77, 79-80, D.M. Gallery, London, 1974, Dick Jemison Gallery, Birmingham, Objects Gallery, Savannah, 1979, Cumberland Gallery, Nashville, 1981, 91, Fay Gold Gallery, Atlanta, 1984, V.N. Internat. Gallery, Alexandria, Va., 1983, Patricia Carega Gallery, Washington, 1986, Lamar Dodd Art Ctr., La Grange, Ga., 1988, Alexander Gallery, Atlanta, 1989, Novus Gallery, Inc., Atlanta, 1990, Wade Gallery, L.A., 1990-91; exhibited in group shows at Ga. Arts Show, Savannah, 1962, Calloway Gardens, Pine Mountain, Ga., 1964, 66, 67, U. Tenn., Knoxville, 1966, 1991, Am. Fedn. of Arts, Atlanta, 1970, Oglethorpe U., Atlanta, 1972, 73, New Orleans Mus. Art, 1973, High Mus. Art, Atlanta, 1976, W. Carolina U., Cullowhee, 1978, Little Rock Art Ctr., 1982, U. Ga., 1983, Ctr. Contemporary Art, Winston-Salem, N.C., 1985, Gallery 291, Atlanta, 1986, Madison (Ga.)-Morgan Cultural Ctr., 1986, Ga. Inst. Tech., 1988, Columbus (Ga.) Mus. Art, 1989, Chastain Gallery, Atlanta, 1990, 91, Chattahoochee Valley Art Mus., LaGrange, 1992, Swan Coach House Gallery, Atlanta, 1993, numerous others; represented in permanent collections Whitney Mus. Am. Art, N.Y.C., High Mus. Art, Atlanta, Akron (Ohio) Mus. Art, Indpls. Mus. Art, Norton Gallery & Sch. of Art, West Palm Beach, Ill., Cheekwood Botanical Gardens and Fine Art, Nashville, Lamar Dodd Art Ctr., Lagrange (Ga.) Coll., Herbert J. Johnson Collection Cornell U., Ithaca, N.Y., Emory U. Cannon Chapel, Atlanta, U. Ctrl. Fla. Mus. Art, Orlando. French Govt. fellow, 1964; U. Tenn. scholar, 1991; Gov.'s grantee Ga. Coun. Arts, 1988; recipient Merit award High Mus. Art, Atlanta, 1966, Lyndon House Art Ctr., Athens, 1982, Honorable Mention award, 1985, Alumni award Atlanta Coll. Art Alumni Assn., 1987. Home and Office: 27 Market St Barnesville GA 30204-1645

CREED, THOMAS G., steel company executive; b. Akron, Ohio, 1933; married. BSCE, Purdue U., 1955; postgrad., Harvard U., 1966. Project engr. Shaw Lenz & Assocs., 1957-61; estimating supr. Inland Steel Products Co., 1961-63; v.p. ops. Pollak Steel Co., 1963-71; mgr. planning Ogden Metals Inc., 1971-73; div. mgr. Tampa reinforcing steel div. Fla. Steel Corp., 1973-78, v.p. structural steel, 1978-84, v.p. mill sls, 1984-87, pres., chief oper. officer, 1987—; pres., chief oper. officer FLS Holdings, Inc., 1988—; bd. dirs. Barnett Bank Tampa. 1st lt. U.S. Army, 1955-57. Office: PO Box 31328 Tampa FL 33631-3328*

CREED, THOMAS WAYNE, retired federal agency administrator, individual investor; b. Winston-Salem, N.C., Dec. 8, 1943; s. Joseph Clunette Creed and Wilma (Walters) Peterson; m. Mary Jane Young, June 30, 1972. BS, U. Tenn., 1966; MBA, E. Tenn. State U., 1972. Instr. bus. mgmt. No. Va. Community Coll., Alexandria, 1972-74; GAO mgmt. auditor U.S. Gen. Acctg. Office, Washington, 1974-75; mgmt. analyst VA Office Planning and Program Evaluation, Washington, 1975-79; dep. dir. state cemetery grants VA Dept. Meml. Affairs, Washington, 1979-80, acting dir. state cemetery grants, 1980-81, mgmt. analyst, 1981-83; dep. dir. so. area VA Dept. Meml. Affairs, Atlanta, 1983-85, dir. so. area, 1985-94; ret., 1994. Divsn. chmn. Atlanta chpt. Combined Fed. United Way campaign, 1985, 91, 93; treas. The Village at Lenox Park Homeowners' Assn., 1994-95. Lt. USNR, 1967-70. Recipient Disting. Career award VA, 1994. Mem. Garden Hills Civic Assn. (security com. capt. 1987-88), Atlanta Assn. Fed. Execs. (exec. com. 1985-86, 1st v.p. 1986-87, pres. 1987-88), Fed. Exec. Bd. (cert. of award 1985). Methodist. Home: 1189 Village Cv NE Atlanta GA 30319-5308

CREEKMORE, DAVID DICKASON, lawyer; b. Knoxville, Tenn., Aug. 8, 1942; s. Frank Benson and Betsey (Beeler) C.; 1 child, Walton N.; divorced; 1 stepchild, Kelly L. Woody. LLB, U. Tenn., 1965, JD, 1966; grad. Judge Adv. Gen.'s Sch., 1979, U.S. Army Command Gen. Staff Sch., 1985. Bar: Tenn. 1966, U.S. Supreme Ct. 1970. Law clk. Gen. Session Ct., Knox

County, Tenn., 1963-66; asst. county atty. Knox County, 1966-70; ptnr. Creekmore, Thomson & Hollow, Knoxville, 1966-72; judge gen. sessions ct. div. II, Knox County, 1972-86; sole practice law, 1986-93; ptnr. Walter, Regan & Creekmore, Knoxville, 1993—; instr. criminal law and evidence Walters State Coll., Morristown, Tenn., 1974-80, U. Tenn., 1982—. Knox County Republican committeeman, 1970—; mcpl. judge, Town of Farragut, Tenn., 1990—; active Tenn. Hist. Assn., Blount Mansion Assn. Served to lt. col. JAGC, USAR, 1995. Mem. ABA, Tenn. Bar Assn., Knox Bar Assn., Fed. Bar Assn., Tenn. Judges Conf. (v.p. 1976-78), Res. Officers Assn. (pres. 1989-91), Am. Legion (post judge 1984-87). Methodist. Clubs: Masons, Shriners, Elks, Eagles, Lions. Home: 11824 Midhurst Dr Knoxville TN 37922-4750 Office: Burwell Bldg 9th Flr 602 S Gay St Knoxville TN 37902-1605

CREEKMORE, VERITY VEIRS, media specialist; b. Cin., May 13; d. Noble L. and Maxine (Wright) Veirs; m. Kenneth L. Creekmore, Nov. 23, 1961; 1 child, Kenneth L. Jr. BS in Edn. magna cum laude, S.C. State U., 1975; MLS, U. S.C., 1978. Cert. libr. media specialist, S.C. Media specialist John Ford High Sch., St. Matthews, S.C., 1976-77, St. John High Sch., Cameron, S.C., 1977-82, St. John Elem./Mid. Sch., Cameron, 1982-86, Sheridan Elem. Sch., Orangeburg, S.C., 1986—; directed libr. U. S.C., Columbia, 1993-94. Rep. S.C. Sci. Hub. Sys. Operator Sheridan Sch. Local Area Computer Network Trainer Laubach Literacy Program, Orangeburg, 1990—. Recipient IMAGEMAKER award SCASL, 1994. Mem. NEA, ALA, S.C. Assn. Sch. Librs., Nat. Assn. Storytelling, So. Assn. Colls. and Schs. (evaluator), S.C. Edn. Assn. (dist. rep. 1991-93, IPD rep. 1993—), Hon. Order Ky. Cols., Order Ea. Star, Alpha Kappa Mu. Home: RR 2 Box 127 Saint Matthews SC 29135-9521 Office: Sheridan Elem Sch 139 Hillsboro St NE Orangeburg SC 29115-3305

CREEKMORE, WILLIAM BROWN, construction company executive; b. Nuremburg, Fed. Republic of Germany, May 13, 1959; came to U.S. 1961; s. Billy Brown Creekmore and Marie (Puett) Howe; m. Rhonda Blaylock, Feb. 4, 1984 (div. Jan. 1990); 1 child, William Brown Jr.; m. Jane P. Jones, June 12, 1993. Student, U. No. Ala., 1977-79, U. Ga., 1979-80, Ga. State U., 1980-81. Pres. Creekmore Painting Contractors, Inc., Atlanta, 1981-83, Comml. Improvements, Inc., Dunwoody, Ga., 1983-92; v.p. Perry Realty Svcs., Atlanta, 1992—. Bd. dirs. Sandy Springs Youth Football, Morgan Falls Field, 1983. Mem. West Dekalb Rotary (bd. dirs. 1989—). Republican. Methodist. Office: Perry Realty Svcs 7740 Roswell Rd Ste 109 Atlanta GA 30350-4844

CREEL, SHARON SWENSON, bank adminstrator; b. Newburgh, N.Y., Nov. 27, 1951; d. Roy Gordon and Lois (Burres) Swenson; m. Britt Michael Barnes, Dec. 1972 (dec. 1981); m. George Charles Fray, Oct. 1982 (div. 1990); children: William George, Claire Anna, Eric Charles; m. Harold Lee Creel, Jr., May 1994. BS, U. Conn., 1977, MBA, 1979. Cert. cash mgr.; accredited ACH profl. Gen. acctg. supr. Vitramon, Monroe, Conn., 1974-77; acctg. mgr. U.S. Surg., Norwalk, Conn., 1977-79; asst. v.p., product mgr. Mfrs. Hanover Trust Co., N.Y.C., 1979-82; 2 v.p., product devel. officer Chase Manhattan Bank, N.Y.C., 1982-86; sr. analyst S.W. Fla. Water Mgmt., Brooksville, 1988-89; v.p., product mgr. First Fla. Bank, Tampa, 1989-93, Comerica Bank, Detroit, 1993-95; v.p. product devel. First Union, Charlotte, N.C., 1995—; mem. ops. com. Electronic Check Clearing House Organization, Electronic Check Coun., 1995—, Payment Solutions Network adv. bd., 1995—. Mem. Nat. Clearing House Assn., Nat. Automated Clearing Ho. (task force 1991-95), Treasury Mgmt. Assn., Mich. Automated Clearing Ho. Assn. (mktg. com. 1993-95),. Methodist. Office: First Union 301 S College St Charlotte NC 28277-0804

CREGER, DAVID L., financial planner, insurance executive; b. Bristol, Tenn., Mar. 20, 1957; s. Bobby Gene and Mary Nell (Goodman) C.; children: Joshua A., Sarah R. Student, Va. Highlands C.C., Abingdon, Va., 1976. Cert. agt./continuing edn. instr., Tenn., Va.; LUTCF. Ins. agt. Home Beneficial Life Ins. Co., Bristol, Va., 1984-85, staff sales mgr., 1985-89; personal producing gen. agt./owner The David L. Creger Co., Bristol, 1989-91; agt. and mktg. svcs. mgr. Settlers Life Ins. Co., Bristol, 1991-96; pres. Pinnacle Fin. Svcs., Inc., Bristol, 1994—; v.p., gen. mgr. Alliance Mktg. Group, Inc., Bristol, 1996—; disability income ins. course moderator Life Underwriter Tng. Coun., 1989-90; N.E. Tenn. (regional) Sales Conf. chmn. 1990; lectr. in field. Contbr. articles to profl. jours. Pres. Bristol affiliate Am. Heart Aassn., 1993-95, chmn. bd., 1995-96, chmn. Queen of Hearts Fundraiser, 1992, 93; vol. Appalachia region March of Dimes, 1992-93; account exec. United Way of Bristol, 1992-93, team capt., 1994, bd. dirs., 1995—, treas., chair fin. com., 1996. Recipient Ernest E. Cragg Amb. award Life Underwriting Tng. Coun., 1994; named to Tri-Cities Bus. Jour. Regional 40 Under Forty, 1995. Mem. Nat. Assn. Life Underwriters (polit. action com. 1989—), Tenn. Assn. Life Underwriters (N.E. Tenn. regional v.p. 1992-95, chair state profl. devel. com. 1994-95, sec. 1995-96, pres.-elect 1996—), Bristol Assn. Life Underwriters (Queen of Hearts program com. 1986—, pres. 1990, chair edn. com. 1991-93, exec. sec. 1993-94, chair state law and legis. com. 1993—, sec. 1995-96, pres.-elect 1996-97, Louis I. Dubin Pub. Svc. award, Robert L. Rose Edn. and Assn. Achievment awards), Bristol C. of C. (VA legis. com. chair 1994, fed. issues com. chair 1995, govtl. rels. coun. vice-chair 1996, bd. dirs./exec. com. 1996—), Assn. Health Ins. Agts. (charter), Internat. Assn. Fin. Planning, Inst. Cert. Fin. Planners, Internat. Platform Assn., Optimist Club. Republican. Office: Pinnacle Fin Svcs Inc 624 Lawrence Ave Bristol VA 24201-3540

CREHAN, JOSEPH EDWARD, lawyer; b. Detroit, Dec. 8, 1938; s. Owen Thomas and Marguerite (Dunn) C.; m. Sheila Anderson, Nov. 6, 1965; children: Kerry Marie, Christa Ellen. A.B., Wayne State U., Detroit, 1961; J.D., Ind. U., 1965. Bar: Ind. 1965, Mich. 1966, U.S. Supreme Ct. 1984. Pvt. practice Detroit, 1966-68; assoc. Louisell & Barris (P.C.), 1968-72; ptnr. Fenton, Nederlander, Dodge, Barris & Crehan (P.C.), 1972-74, Barris & Crehan (P.C.), 1975-88; pvt. practice Bloomfield Hills, Mich. and Naples, Fla., 1977—. Mem. Am. Trial Lawyers Assn. Roman Catholic. Home and Office: 827 Bentwood Dr Naples FL 34108-8204

CREMER, CLAUDINE PFEIFFER, landscape firm executive; b. Osaka, Japan, Nov. 3, 1951; came to U.S., 1954; d. Harry Fletcher and Victoria (Kimbell) Pfeiffer; m. Paul Kevin Cremer, Jan. 5, 1985. BA in English magna cum laude, L.I. U., 1973; cert. Horticulture Tech. summa cum laude, Haywood C.C., 1993. Social worker Butler County, Hamilton, Ohio, 1973-76; dir. Hamilton (Ohio) Appalachian People's Svc. Orgn., 1977-82, Murphy-Oakley Community Ctr., Asheville, N.C., 1982-87; congl. dist. asst. Congressman Clarke, Asheville, N.C., 1987-91; v.p., treas. Evergreen Landscaping, Inc., Weaverville, N.C., 1994—. Bd. dirs. LWV, Asheville, 1985-87, Quality Forward, Asheville, 1987-91; v.p., 1988-90, chair recycling com., 1988-91; organizer Save the Mountains, Asheville, 1985—, treas., 1988—; organizer Citizens for Clean Air, Asheville, 1988—. Mem. Natural Resources Def. Coun., Humane Soc. U.S., Nuclear Info. Resource Svc., Taxpayers Accountable Govt., Western N.C. Alliance. Democrat. Episcopalian.

CREMER, THOMAS GERHARD, music educator; b. New Brunswick, N.J., May 23, 1961; s. Gerhard Josef and Lois Elaine (Cottrell) C.; m. Eva Almira Vivanco Vargas, Feb. 8, 1986. MusB magna cum laude, U. Mass., 1983; MusM, U. Ky., 1989. Cert. music tchr., Mass., N.Y., Va., Ky., Ga. Music tchr. Athol-Royalston (Mass.) Schs., 1983-84; music tchr., band leader Am. Sch. Lima, Peru, 1984-87; instr. tuba, euphonium U. Ky., Lexington, 1988-89; hon. asst. conductor Fitchburg (Mass.) State Coll., 1989-90; dir. bands, music instr. Warwick Acad., Bermuda, 1990-95; dir. nat. band Columbia Columbia Inst. Culture, Bogota, 1995; low brass instr. Augusta State U., 1996—; music dir. Jenkins County Middle Sch. and H.S., Millen, Ga., 1996—; vis. prof. music, dir. faculty quintet Nat. Conservatory, Lima, 1985-87; tubist Nat. Symphony Peru, Lima, 1985-87; mem. Bermuda Secondary Sch. Curriculum Com., Warwick, 1991-94. Contbg. editor: Tuba Reference Guide, 1993; contbg. reviewer T.U.B.A. Jour., 1988, 94. Adv. All-City Music Fest, Lima, 1985-87. Recipient Diploma of Honor, West German Embassy in Peru, 1986; Acad. Excellence fellow U. Ky., 1988. Mem. Tubists Universal Brotherhood Assn., World Assn. Symphonic Bands Ensembles, Internat. Trombone Assn., Music Educators Nat. Conf., Masons, Phi Delta Kappa (Bermuda chpt., v.p., pres. 1992-94). Roman Catholic. Home: 706 Bay St Millen GA 30442

CREMERS, CLIFFORD JOHN, mechanical engineering educator; b. Mpls., Mar. 27, 1933; s. Christian Joseph and Marie Hildegard C.; m. Claudette May Humble, Sept. 25, 1954; children: Carla Ann, Rachel Beth, Emily Therese, Eric John, Melissa Joan. BSME, U. Minn., 1957, MSME, 1961, PhD, 1964. Rsch. fellow in mech. engring. U. Minn., 1959-61, instr. mech. engring., 1961-64; asst. prof. Ga. Inst. Tech., Atlanta, 1964-66; assoc. prof. U. Ky., Lexington, 1966-71, prof., 1971—, chmn. dept. mech. engring., 1975-84, 94-95; cons. to industry, state and fed. agys., UNESCO; vis. prof. Imperial Coll. Sci. & Tech., London, 1973; Lady Davis prof. Technion, Haifa, 1986. Contbr. articles on heat transfer to profl. jours. With USNR, 1953-55. NSF grantee, 1965, 66, 69, 71, 76, 81, 86, NASA grantee, 1967, 68, 69, 70, 71, 72, 73, 94; Trane Co. fellow U. Minn., 1959, 60. Fellow ASME (past v.p. basic engring.), AIAA (assoc.); mem. AAAS, Am. Soc. Engring. Edn., Sigma Xi. Roman Catholic. Home: 3181 Lamar Dr Lexington KY 40502-2905 Office: Univ Ky Mech Engring Dept Lexington KY 40506-0108

CREMINS, WILLIAM CARROLL, lawyer; b. Virginia Beach, Va., Nov. 13, 1957; s. James Smyth and Mary Louise (Gallagher) C.; m. Kelly Robin Knapp, July 6, 1985; children: William Carroll Jr., Robert Gallagher. BA, BJ, U. Mo., 1980; JD, St. John's U., 1984. Bar: Tenn. 1984, N.Y. 1985, U.S. Dist. Ct. (ea. dist.) Tenn., U.S. Ct. Appeals (6th cir.). Assoc. Law Offices of J.D. Lee, Knoxville, Tenn., 1984-85; pvt. practice, Knoxville, 1986—. Dep. nat. organizer Ancient Order of Hibernians in Am., Inc., Tenn., 1985; bd. dirs. Florence Crittenton Agy. of Knoxville, Inc., 1989—, pres., 1995; Little League baseball coach, 1993—, football coach, 1987, 1993-94, soccer coach, 1992, 1995. Recipient Pro Bono award Knoxville Bar Assn. Vol. Legal Assistance Program, 1992. Mem. ATLA (Advocate recognition 1994), ABA, Tenn. Bar Assn., Knoxville Bar Assn., Tenn. Trial Lawyers Assn., LeConte Club. Roman Catholic. Home: 710 Saint John Ct Knoxville TN 37922-1412 Office: 810 Henley St Knoxville TN 37902-2901

CRENSHAW, BEN, professional golfer; b. Austin, Tex., Jan. 11, 1952; m. Julie Ann; children: Katherine Vail, Claire Susan. Grad., U. Tex. Mem. U.S. World Amateur Cup Team, 1972; mem. U.S. Ryder Cup, 1981, 83, 87, 95; profl. golfer, 1973—; U.S. team capt. Kirin Cup, 1988. Winner San Antonio Open, 1973, Western Amateur open match and medal plan champion, 1973, Bing Crosby Nat. Pro-Am., Ohio Kings Island Open, Hawaiian Open, 1976, Colonial Nat. Invitational, 1977, NCAA Championship, 1971, 72, 73, Irish Open, 1976, Phoenix Open, 1979, Walt Disney World Team Championship, 1980, AnheuserOBusch Classic, 1980, Tex. State Open winner, 1980, Ryder Cup, 1981, 83, 87, Byron Nelson Classic, 1983, Masters tournament, 1984, PGA Sr. Event Jeremy Ranch Shoot-Out teameed with Miller Barber, 1985, Buick Open, 1986, Vantage Championship, 1986, USF&G, 1987, Doral Ryder Open, 1988, World Cup, 1988, Western Open, 1992, Masters winner Augusta Nat. Golf Club, 1995, Masters Tournament, 1995. Mem. Profl. Golfers Assn. Am. Office: 2905 San Gabriel St Ste 213 Austin TX 78705-3541

CRENSHAW, TENA LULA, librarian; b. Coleman, Fla., Dec. 15, 1930; d. Herbert Joseph Crenshaw and Nellie (Wicker) Cox; BS, Fla. So. Coll., 1951; postgrad. U. Fla., 1952-55; MLS (Univ. scholar), U. Okla., 1960. Tchr. pub. schs., Coleman, Fla., 1952-55, St. Petersburg, Fla., 1955-57, Houston, 1957-59; tech. librarian Army Rocket & Guided Missile Agy., Redstone Arsenal, Huntsville, Ala., 1960-61; acquisitions librarian Martin Marietta Corp., Orlando, Fla., 1961-64; reader svcs. librarian John F. Kennedy Space Center, NASA, Fla., 1964-66; rsch. info. analyst, specialist, Lockheed Missiles and Space Co., Palo Alto, Calif., 1966-68; head svcs. to pub. A.W. Calhoun Med. Library, Emory U., Atlanta, 1969-78; dep. dir. Louis Calder Meml. Library, U. Miami (Fla.) Sch. Medicine, 1979-80; head edn. library U. Fla., Gainesville, 1980-84; librarian Westinghouse Electric Corp., Orlando, 1984-86; chief librarian tech info. ctr. U. Cen. Fla., Orlando, 1986-87, librarian contracts and grants, 1987-88; library cons. Coleman, Fla., 1988-89, sch. libr., 1989-90, libr. Kennedy Space Ctr., Fla., 1990-91, libr. Patrick Air Force Base, Fla., 1992-94; chmn. Fla. State adv. Council on Libraries. Mem. Spl. Libraries Assn. (treas. S. Atlantic chpt. 1970-72, chmn. membership com. 1973, v.p. 1973-74, pres. 1974-75, mem. resolutions com. 1975-76, nominating com. biol. scis. div. 1974-75, chmn. 1977-78), Med. Library Assn. (mem. conf. planning com. So. regional group 1973-74, membership com. 1977-79 by laws rev. com. 1979-80), Southeastern (mem. new directions com. 1972-74, chmn. spl. libraries sect. 1974), Ga. (careers in librarianship com. 1974-77), Fla. Library Assns., DAR, Alpha Delta Pi, Kappa Delta Pi. Democrat. Methodist. Home: PO Box 277 Coleman FL 33521-0277

CREQUE, LINDA ANN, non-profit educational and research executive, former education commissioner; b. N.Y.C.; arrived in V.I., 1967; d. Noel and Enid Louise (Schloss) DePass; m. Leonard J. Creque, July 29, 1967; children: Leah Michelle, Michael Gregory. BS, CUNY-Queens, 1963, MS, 1969; PhD, U. Ill., 1986. Tchr. 2d grade Bd. Edn., N.Y.C., 1963, tchr. demonstrations, team tchr., 1964-65, master tchr., 1965-66; elem. tchr. P.S. 69, Jackson Hgts., N.Y., 1963-67; tchr. English Cath. U., Ponce, P.R., 1967; cmty. exch. elem. tchr. grades K-6 Ponce, 1966-67; tchr. 4th grade Dept. Edn., V.I., 1967-69, tchr. remedial reading, master tchr., 1968-69; program coord. Project HeadStart, V.I., 1969-73, coord. Inst. Developmental Studies, 1970-71, acting dir., 1972-73; prin. Thomas Jefferson Annex Primary Sch., St. Thomas, V.I., 1973-80, Joseph Sibilly Elem. Sch., St. Thomas, 1980-87; commr. edn. Dept. Edn., St. Thomas, 1987-94; founder, pres. V.I. Inst. for Tchg. and Learning, St. Thomas, 1995—; cons. Edn. Devel. Ctr., Mass. Nat. SSI Project, 1992-93, Coll. V.I., 1978; mem. exec. com., bd. overseers Regional Lab. Ednl. Improvement NE and Islands, Andover, Mass.; bd. dirs. V.I. Pub. TV; mem. exec. bd. Leadership in Edn. Adminstrv. Devel., V.I., 1989—; presenter, keynote spkr. confs. in field. Contbr. articles to profl. jours. Trustee U. V.I., 1989—; mem. V.I. Residential Task Force for Human Svcs., 1989—, V.I. Labor Coun.; bd. dirs. Nat. Urban Alliance for Effective Edn. Tchrs. Coll. Columbia U., N.Y.C., 1993—, Cultural Inst. V.I., 1989-94; mem. cultural endowment bd., V.I., 1989-94; mem. governing bd. East End Health Ctr., 1979-80; mem. Gov.'s Conf. Librs., 1978. Grantee V.I. Coun. on Arts Ceramics for Primary Children, 1974-78, Comprehensive Employment and Tng. Act, 1977, NSF, 1989-93, Carnegie Found., 1988-90; recipient award NASA, award St. Thomas-St. John Counselors Assn., 1988, Ednl. Excellence award Harvard U. Prins. Ctr. and Ill. Edn. Svc. Ctr., 1975, Outstanding Leadership award FEMA, 1990, Disting. Svc. award Edn. Commn. of U.S., 1991, Outstanding Svc. award Coun. of Chief State Sch. Officers, 1995. Mem. LWV, St. Thomas Reading Coun., Nat. Assn. Tchrs. Math., Edn. Commn. of States (commr. 1987-93, steering com. 1988-92, internal audit com. 1988, policies priority com. 1991, exec. com. 1992, alt. steering com. 1991—), Coun. Chief of State Sch. Officers (chair extra jurisdictions com., bd. dirs., task force early childhood edn., ednl. equity com., restructuring edn. com.), Phi Kappa Phi, Kappa Delta Pi, Phi Delta Kappa. Office: VI Inst for Tchg and Learning PO Box 301954 Saint Thomas VI 00803

CRESSEY, DOUGLAS B., insurance company executive; b. Red Oak, Iowa, July 9, 1946; s. William C. and Suzanne (Nelson) C.; m. Cynthia Jill Moyer, Dec. 12, 1987. BS in Social Sci., Colo. State U., 1969. Cert. ins. counselor. Pres., gen. mgr. Fulenwider Insurors, Denver, 1976-79; sr. v.p. VanGilder Ins. Corp., Denver, 1979-89; exec. v.p. Rollins Hudig Hall of Colo., Denver, 1989-91, Rolling Hudig Hall of Ga., Atlanta, 1991-94; pres. Aspen Assocs., Inc., Atlanta, 1995—; dir. risk mgmt., dir. human resources Torrey Homes, Atlanta, 1995—; mem. nat. coun. Home Ins. Co., Denver, 1986-90; mem. guest faculty Cont. Legal Edn. Colo., Denver, 1987; mem. com. govt. rels. Ind. Ins. Agents Assn., 1986-89; instr. Bldg. Owners and Mgrs. Assn., Denver, 1985-91. Contbr. articles to profl. jours. Mem. gov.'s task force, tort reform State of Colo., Denver, 1986-87. Recipient Colo. Profl. Ins. Agent of the Yr. Profl. Inst. Agents of Colo., 1986. Mem. Ind. Ins. Agents of Ga., Profl. Ins. Agents Ga., Colo. State U. Alumni (life), Alpha Tau Omega. Home: 2605 Coachmans Cir Alpharetta GA 30202 Office: Aspen Assocs Inc 3300 Highlands Pkwy #130 Smyrna GA 30082

CRESSON, DAVID HOMER, JR., pathologist; b. Danville, Va., May 23, 1955; s. David Homer and Virginia Mae (Swink) C.; m. Lisa Carol Meadors, June 23, 1979; children: Carol Christine, David William. BA in Chemistry magna cum laude, Duke U., 1977; MD, U. Tenn., 1981. Diplomate Am. Bd. Anatomic and Clin. Pathology, Dermatopathology and Cytopathology. Intern, then resident in pathology U. N.C., Chapel Hill, 1981-85, Am. Cancer Soc. surg. pathology fellow, 1985-86; fellow in dermatopathology Stanford (Calif.) U., 1986-87; pathologist, dermatopathologist Va. Bapt. Hosp.-Lynchburg Hosp., 1987—, chmn. dept. pathology, mem. exec. com. med. staff, 1991—; pathologist, dermatopathologist, cytopathologist Pathology Cons. of Cen. Va. Contbr. articles to profl. jours. Recipient Wiley Forbus Pathology Resident Rsch. award N.C. Pathology Soc., 1985. Fellow Coll. Am. Pathologists; mem. Internat. Acad. Pathology, Am. Soc. Clin. Pathologists, Am. Soc. Cytopathology, Sigma Xi, Alpha Omega Alpha. Office: Pathology Cons Cen Va 1905 Atherholt Rd Lynchburg VA 24501-1103

CRESWELL, NORMAN BRUCE, minister; b. Balt., Aug. 16, 1954; s. Norman Bruce and Ruth Lorraine (Hardin) C.; m. Carolyn Dale Main, June 9, 1979; children: Mary Elisabeth, Norman Bruce III, David Jeremiah, Gregory Frederick. Student, Balt. Sch. Bible, 1971; BA, Bob Jones U., Greenville, S.C., 1977. Ordained to ministry Ind. Bapt. Ch., 1980. Non-com leader Christian Svc. Brigade, Balt., 1969-72; asst. pastor Temple Bapt. Ch., Athens, Ga., 1974-78; tchr. Bible and U.S. history Cross Lanes Christian Sch., Charleston, W.Va., 1980-82; pastor Bellepoint Bapt. Ch., Hinton, W.Va., 1982-92; chaplain Summers County Hosp., Hinton, W.Va., 1983-92; chaplain, min. Hinton House, 1982-92; min. (local radio) Morning Light Program, 1984-89; missionary Scotland, 1985, 87, 91; pastor Faith Bible Ch., Mt. Crawford, Va., 1992—, (local radio) Gleanings From God's Word, 1993—. Bd. dirs., advisor Grace Bapt. Italian Mission. Recipient Herald of Christ award, Christian Svc. Brigade, Balt., 1972, Voice of Democracy award, VFW, 1972. Mem. Bapt. Std. Bearer Soc., Bob Jones U. Alumni Assn. Republican. Home: Rt 620 Gen Delivery Keezletown VA 22832 Office: Faith Bible Ch PO Box 206 Mount Crawford VA 22841-0206

CRETINI, BLANCHE MYERS, librarian; b. New Orleans, May 16, 1929; d. Hu Blakemore and Blanche Ethel (Davis) Myers; m. Eugene Joseph Cretini Jr., Jan. 30, 1960. BA, Newcomb Coll., 1950; MSLS, La. State U., 1961. Ref. libr. State Libr. La., Baton Rouge, 1961-70, head ref. librarian, 1970-80, coord. user svcs., 1980—, coord. La. govt. info. network, 1989—. Contbr. articles to La. Libr. Assn. bulletin. Mem. ALA, La. Libr. Assn. Episcopalian. Office: State Libr La 760 N 3rd St Baton Rouge LA 70802-5232

CRIADO-PALLARES, ENRIQUE, vascular surgeon; b. Madrid, Oct. 30, 1954; came to U.S. 1984; MD, U. Complutensis, Madrid, 1978. Asst. prof. of surgery Sch. of Medicine U. N.C., Chapel Hill, 1991—. Fellow ACS, Peripheral Vascular Surgery Soc.; mem. So. Assn. for Vascualr Surgery, Internat. Soc. for Cardiovascular Surgery (N.Am. Chpt.), Alpha Omega Alpha. Office: Univ North Carolina Dept Surgery PO Box 7210 Chapel Hill NC 27599

CRIBB, DEBORAH ANN, public relations executive; b. Florence, S.C., July 29, 1965; d. Neville Burnett and Paula Ann (Blanton) Cribb; m. Stuart Brian Cribb, May 8, 1993. BS, Clemson (S.C.) U., 1987; MA, U. Ga., 1989. Cert. tchr. secondary edn. Pub. affairs specialist U.S. Soil Conservation Svc., Columbia, S.C., 1989-93; pub. rels. mgr. Jackson-Dawson Mktg. Comm., Greenville, S.C., 1993—. Freelance newsletter editor Agr. Alumni Assn. Clemson U., 1992-93. Mem. APR, Pub. Rels. Soc. Am. Baptist. Home: 18 Summer Glen Dr Simpsonville SC 29681 Office: Jackson-Dawson Mktg Comm 37 Villa Rd #508 Greenville SC 29615

CRIBBS, JEFFREY SCOTT, SR., educational administrator; b. Meadville, Pa., Sept. 6, 1945; s. Paul and Marian Marden (Mohney) C.; m. Peggy Lynn Judy, Nov. 12, 1967; children: Jeffrey Scott Jr., Megan Lynn, Sarah Elizabeth. BGS, Chaminade U. of Honolulu, 1970; M of Commerce, U. Richmond, 1975. Material contr. Talon Div., TEXTRON, Inc., Meadville, Pa., 1966; funds mgr. USAF, Honolulu, 1966-70; budget examiner State Dept. Planning and Budget, Richmond, Va., 1970-72; coordinator fin. planning and rsch. State Coun. Higher Edn., Richmond, 1972-76; univ. budget dir. Va. Commonwealth U., Richmond, 1976-80, assoc. v.p. planning and budget, 1980-92, assoc. v.p. capital planning and real estate devel., 1992-95, assoc. v.p. capital planning and facilities mgmt., 1995-96; campus dir. Commonwealth Coll., Richmond, 1996—. Contbr. articles to profl. jours. Active Chesterfield Bus. Coun., 1988—, Chesterfield Edn. Found., 1992—, Chesterfield Cmty. in Schs. Bd., 1995—; sch. bd. vice chmn., chmn. Chesterfield County Pub. Schs., Va., 1982-88; edn. com. chmn. Va. Congress of Parents and Tchrs., 1981; pres., sec. Civic Assn., Hanover County, Va., 1974-76; bd. mem. Regional Math-Sci. Ctr., Richmond, 1983-87. Mem. Soc. for Coll. and Univ. Planning (state coordinator 1987—), Nat. Assn. Coll. and Univ. Bus. Officers, Am. Assn. Higher Edn., Am. Assn. Med. Colls., Assn. for Institutional Rsch. Methodist. Home: 1801 Hollingsworth Dr Richmond VA 23235-3915 Office: Commonwealth Coll 8141 Hull St Rd Richmond VA 23235-6411

CRICHTON, DOUGLAS BENTLEY, editor, writer; b. Petersburg, Va., Sept. 12, 1959; s. James Bentley and Marjorie Ulalier (Robertson) C.; m. Virginia Elizabeth Munsch, Sept. 5, 1981; children: Christopher Winfield, Alexander Douglas, William Perry. BA in English, U. Va., 1981. Reporter Richmond (Va.) Times-Dispatch, 1982-84; reporter, editor AP, Dallas, 1984-88; mng. editor, then editor Am. Way Mag., Dallas, 1988-93; exec. editor, then editor Cooking Light Mag., Birmingham, Ala., 1993—; judge Maggie awards Western Pub. Assn., L.A., 1989-93. Named Va. Young Journalist of Yr., UPI, 1983; recipient over 60 awards for editl. and artistic excellence Am. Way Mag.; scholar James Hay Found., 1980. Mem. Am. Soc. Mag. Editors, Western Pubs. Assn. Office: Cooking Light PO Box 1748 Birmingham AL 35201-1748

CRIDER, IRENE PERRITT, education educator, small business owner, consultant; b. Chatfield, Ark., Apr. 29, 1921; d. Dolphus France and Eula Allan (Springer) Perritt; m. Willis Jewel Crider, Aug. 3, 1945; 1 child, Larry Willis. BA, Bethel Coll., 1944; MA, Memphis State U., 1957; EdD, Fla. Atlantic U., 1977. Cert. elem., secondary tchr., adminstr., Tenn. Tchr. various schs., Tenn., 1941-57; dean girls Lake Worth (Fla.) Jr. High, 1957-65; dean women Lake Worth High Sch., 1965-73; gen. instructional supr. Palm Beach (Fla.) County Pub. Schs., 1973-75; asst. prin. Jupiter (Fla.) High Sch., 1975-76; supr. interns Fla. Atlantic U., Boca Raton, 1977-83, Palm Beach Atlantic Coll., West Palm Beach, Fla., 1982-84; cons. Paris, Tenn., 1984-87; owner, beauty sys. cons. Irene's Acad. Individual Image Improvement, 1991—; instr. edn. Bethel Coll., McKenzie, Tenn., 1987, prof. MEd Grad. Program; cons. in field. Contbr. articles to profl. jours. Founder, bd. dirs., charter mem. Palm Beach County Kidney Assn., 1973-93; chmn. citizens action com. Fla. Ch. Women United, 1982-84. Mem. Tallahassee Theatre Guild, Women's Club Tallahassee, Tallahassee Area C. of C., Zonta (Lake Worth, pres. 1969-70), Order Ea. Star, Delta Kappa Gamma (charter pres. Beta Xi-Mu 1968-70, chmn. state com., scholarship), Phi Delta Kappa, Beta Phi Mu. Democrat. Methodist. Home and Office: 1606 N Meridian Rd Tallahassee FL 32303-5644

CRIGER, NANCY S., professional society administrator; b. Ypsilanti, Mich., Apr. 16, 1951; d. Douglas D. and Edith (Nicoll) Smith; children: Amanda L. Denomme, William G. Denomme, Jr. Student, Mich. State U., 1969-71; BS in Elem. Edn., Wayne State U., 1973. Asst. v.p. Nat. Bank of Detroit, 1978-87; asst. v.p. Comerica Bank, Detroit, 1987-88, v.p. employee benefits, 1988-91; v.p. and mgr. trust adminstrn. and ops. Comerica Bank-Tex., Dallas, 1991-92; v.p. adminstrn., exec. v.p. Vis. Nurs Assn. Tex., 1992-94; pres. Continuum Healthcare Mgmt., Inc., Plano, Tex., 1994—. Asst. treas. Jr. League of Detroit, 1985-86, treas., 1986-87; treas. women's assn. Detroit Symphony Orch., 1987-89. Mem. Jr. League of Dallas, Rotary, The 500, Inc., Dallas Women's Found., Dallas Mus. of Art, DMA-PM Group, Dallas Hist. Soc., Dallas Symphony Assn., Dallas Arboretum, Dallas Zool. Soc., Dallas County Heritage Soc., Dallas Coun., Chi Omega. Home and Office: 2920 Haymeadow Ln Carrollton TX 75007

CRIM, REUBEN SIDNEY, newspaper publishing executive; b. Columbia, S.C., July 24, 1942; s. Reuben Simeon and Mattie Ione (Berry) C.; m. Phyllis James, Mar. 1, 1963 (div. Aug. 1984); children: Berry Whetstone, Jordan Bennett; m. Cathy Anderson, Oct. 17, 1986. BA in History, U. S.C., 1967. Pers. mgr. State-Record Co. Inc., Columbia, S.C., 1968-70; pers. dir. Charleston (W.Va.) Newspapers, Inc., 1970-72, asst. gen. mgr., 1972-76; v.p., gen. mgr. Beckley (W.Va.) Newspapers, Inc., 1976-81; exec. v.p., gen. mgr. State Record Co., Inc., Columbia, 1981-88, pres., gen. mgr., 1988—. Mem. adv. bd. Jr. Achievement of Greater Columbia, 1987—. Mem. So. Newspapers Pubs. Assn. Found. (trustee, treas., chmn.), Phi Beta Kappa. Home:

Bridge Pointe 100 Sunset Blvd West Columbia SC 29169-7500 Office: State-Record Co Inc 1401 Shop Rd PO Box 1333 Columbia SC 29202-1333*

CRIMM, MARCY WARE JONES, geritrics nurse, educator; b. Macon, Ga., Aug. 12, 1934; d. Paul Dewey and Evelyn Nancy (Ware) Jones; m. Carl Eugene Crimm, June 17, 1956; children: Brigetta Michelle, Carl Eugene. BA, U. Charleston, W.Va., 1956; BS, George Mason U., Fairfax, Va., 1976, MSN, 1981. Cert. gerontology nurse; cert. clin. nurse specialist in gerontology. Primary care nurse in long term care, gerontology specialist physican's office, Fairfax; lectr. George Mason U. Mem. ANA, Va. State Nurses Assn., George Mason U. Nursing Alumni Assn. (treas. 1989-90), Sigma Theta Tau (sec. chpt.).

CRIMMINS, MICHAEL THOMAS, chemistry educator; b. East St. Louis, Ill., Jan. 3, 1954; s. Thomas Carl Crimmins and Edith Pauline (Palmer) Crimmins-Sidebottom; m. Rosemary O'Mahony, Apr. 11, 1987; children: Julie Sarah, Allison Christine. BA with honors, Hendrix Coll., 1976; PhD, Duke U., 1980; postgrad., Calif. Inst. Tech., 1981. Asst. prof. U. N.C., Chapel Hill, 1981-87, assoc. prof., 1987-93, prof., 1993—; vice chmn. dept. chemistry U. N.C., 1992-93, 95—. Contbr. articles to profl. jours. Grantee NIH, 1991-94, NSF, 1994—, Petroleum Rsch. Fund, 1991-94, Rhone Poulenc; Alfred P. Sloan fellow, 1986-90, faculty fellow Am. Cyanamid, 1994; Conway Corp. scholar Hendrix Coll., 1972-76. Mem. Am. Chem. Soc. (chmn. N.C. sect. 1994, chmn.-elect 1993). Office: U NC Cb # 3290 Chapel Hill NC 27599

CRIPPEN, ROBERT LAUREL, former naval officer and astronaut; b. Beaumont, Tex., Sept. 11, 1937; s. Herbert W. and Ruth C. (Andress) C.; m. Pandora Lee Puckett, Nov. 7, 1987; children from previous marriage: Ellen Marie, Susan Lynn, Linda Ruth. BS in Aerospace Engring., U. Tex., 1960; grad., USAF Aerospace Rsch. Pilot Sch., 1965. Commd. ensign USN, 1960, advanced through grades to capt., 1980; assigned to flight tng. USN, Whiting Field, Fla., 1961, Chase Field, Beeville, Tex., 1961; attach pilot Fleet Squadron VA-72 aboard U.S.S. Independence, 1962-64; instr. USAF Aerospace Rsch. Pilot Sch., Edwards AFB, Calif., 1965-66; rsch. pilot USAF Manned Orbiting Lab. Program, L.A., 1966-69; NASA astronaut Johnson Space Ctr., Houston, 1969-87; crew mem. Skylab Med. Experiments Altitude Test, 1972; mem. astronaut support crew Skylab 2, 3 and 4 missions, Apollo-Suyez Test Project mission, 1973-74; pilot Space Shuttle Columbia STSI, 1981; comdr. Space Shuttle Challanger STS-7, STS-41C, STS-41G, 1983-84; dep. dir. Shuttle Ops. Nat. Space Transp. System Ops., NASA, Kennedy Space Ctr., Fla., 1987-89; dir. Space Shuttle, NASA, Washington, 1989-91, NASA John F. Kennedy Space Ctr., 1992-95; pres., v.p. automation Info. Systems Co., Lockheed Martin, 1995—. Recipient Exceptional Svc. medal NASA, 1972, Disting. Svc. award Dept. Defense, 1981, Achievement award Am. Astronautical Soc. Flight, 1981, Gardiner Greene Hubbard medal Nat. Geographic Soc. 1981, Disting. Svc. award FAA, 1982, Goddard Meml. trophy, Harmon trophy, 1982, 4 NASA Space Flight medals; named to Aviation Hall of Fame. Fellow Soc. Exptl. Test Pilots.

CRISCI, STEVEN, computer programmer; b. N.Y.C., Dec. 21, 1965; s. Jennie Crisci; m. Dawn Deneweth (div.). BS in Info. Systems, Va. Commonwealth U. Programmer Database Software Designs Inc, Richmond, Va. With USN, 1985-87. Mem. Cen. Va. FoxPro User Group (pres.). Home: 1113 Grove Ave #1 Richmond VA 23220 Office: Database Software Designs Inc 1113 Grove Ave #1 Richmond VA 23220

CRISCOE, ARTHUR HUGH, religious organization administrator, educator; b. Union Grove, Ala., Feb. 21, 1939. BA, Samford U., 1964; MDiv, Southwestern Seminary, Ft. Worth, 1968, M in Religious Edn., 1969, EdD, 1975. Min. New Hope Bapt. Ch., Mansfield, Tex., 1965-71; prof. Columbia (S.C.) Bible Coll., 1972-76; mgmt. support dir. Sunday Sch. Bd., Nashville, 1976—; adj. prof. Cumberland U., Lebanon, Tenn., 1988—. Author: Original, Youth Becoming Leaders, 1984, The Doctrine of the Laity Teaching Workbook, 1985, The Doctrine of Prayer Teaching Workbook, 1986, The Doctrine of the Believers Teaching Workbook, 1987, (with others) A Biblical Model for Training Leaders, 1985. Mem. World Future Soc., Assn. for Ednl. Communications, Nat. Soc. for Performance and Instrn., Nat. Assn. Profs. Christian Edn., Internat. Brotherhood Magicians, Am. Soc. Magicians. Baptist. Office: Sunday Sch Bd 127 9th Ave N Nashville TN 37203-3601

CRISP, CONNIE KING, medical/surgical nurse; b. Roanoke Rapids, N.C., Oct. 8, 1955; d. Wiley C. and Ursula (Mooring) K.; m. Horace Crisp, Sept. 1, 1990. BSN, East Carolina U., 1978. Staff nurse Pitt County Meml. Hosp., Greenville, N.C., 1978-88, nurse surgery assessment unit, 1988-91, nurse admissions testing dept., 1991—; co-chair clin. ladder com. Pitt County Meml. Hosp., 1994-96. Recipient Presdl. award Today's Women of Greenville, 1987-88, 88-89, 89-90, Most Outstanding Mem., 1988-89, 89-90. Mem. Sch. Nursing Alumni Profl. Soc. of East Carolina U. Alumni Soc., Sigma Theta Tau, Gamma Beta Phi, Phi Eta Sigma. Office: Pitt County Meml Hosp PO Box 6028 Greenville NC 27835-6028

CRISP, JENNIFER ANN CLAIR, neurosurgical nurse; b. Bangalore, India, Aug. 30, 1943; came to U.S., 1959; d. Arthur E. Cleland and Pamela M.N. Ottley Hemming; m. Fred R. Crisp; 1 child, Karyn. BSN, Greenville (Ill.) Coll., 1967. RN, Tex. Staff nurse Meth. Hosp., Ind. Sch. Nursing, Houston, 1978-80; asst. head nurse The Meth. Hosp., Houston, 1980-94, neurosurg. ICU nurse, 1994—. Home: Sea-lights PO Box 155 Gilchrist TX 77617 Office: Methodist Hosp 6565 Fannin St Houston TX 77030-2707

CRISP, POLLY LENORE, psychologist; b. Atlanta, May 20, 1952; d. John Pershing and Dorotha Amelia (Hogan) C. BA, U. Tenn., 1976; MA, Mich. State U., 1981, PhD, 1984. Psychotherapist Arbours Ctr., London, 1983-85; clin. psychologist Kennebec Valley Mental Health Ctr., Augusta, Maine, 1987-90, Overlook Mental Health Ctr., Maryville, Tenn., 1990—. Contbr. articles to profl. publs. Mem. APA (membership com. div. clin. psychology 1990—), Brit. Psychol. Soc., Soc. Psychotherapy Rsch., N.Y. Acad. Scis., Phi Beta Kappa, Phi Kappa Phi, Alpha Lambda Delta. Office: Overlook Mental Health 219 Court St Maryville TN 37804-5917

CRISP, TERRY ARTHUR, professional hockey coach; b. Parry Sound, Ont., Canada, May 28, 1943; m. Sheila Crisp; children: Tony, Jeffrey, Caley. Profl. player NHL, 1965-77; with Boston, 1965-66 season, St. Louis, 1967-72, N.Y.C., 1972-73, Phila., 1973-77; formerly coach Soo Greyhounds, Ont. Hockey League; coach Calgary Flames farm club, Moncton, 1985-87, Calgary Flames, Nat. Hockey League, Calgary, Alta., 1987-90; head coach Tampa Bay Lightning, Tampa, FL, 1992—. Named Coach of Yr. Ont. Hockey League, 1982-83, 84-85. Office: Tampa Bay Lightning 501 E Kennedy Blvd Tampa FL 33602-5200*

CRISTINA, FRANCIS MCDERMOTT (FRANK CRISTINA), corporate security company executive; b. Washington, Pa., Feb. 8, 1937; s. Fred Louis and Mary Catherine (McDermott) C.; m. Linda Kay Benson, June 12, 1959 (div. Dec. 1977); children: Mary Kay Cristina Stewart, Nancy Lynn; m. Diane Reams, Oct. 21, 1978; stepchildren: Thomas H. Eubank III, Brooke E. Eubank. BA, Juniata Coll., 1959; grad., FBI Acad., 1965. Sr. claims examiner Acacia Mut. Ins. Co., Washington, 1960-65; spl. agt. FBI, Washington, 1965-88; ret., 1988; security mgr. ADT Automotive, Nashville, 1988—. Recipient Key Man award Clarksville (Tenn.) Jr. C. of C., 1970. Mem. Soc. Former Spl. Agts. FBI (chmn.), Soc. for Preservation and Encouragement Barbershop Quartet Singing in Am. (pres., Barbershopper of Yr. award 1986), Music City Classic-T-Bird Club (pres.). Republican. Methodist. Home: 9565 In A Vale Dr Brentwood TN 37027-8222 Office: ADT Automotive 435 Metroplex Dr Nashville TN 37211-3109

CRITCHFIELD, JACK BARRON, utilities company executive; b. Rockwood, Pa., 1933. BS, Slippery Rock State Univ., 1955; postgrad., Univ. Pitts., 1968. Pres. Rollins Coll., 1969-78, Winter Pk. Telephone United Telephone, 1978-82; v.p., dir. tng. Capital Holding Co., 1982-83; v.p. Ea. and Ridge divs. Fla. Power Co., 1983-87; group v.p. energy tech. group Fla. Progress Corp., 1987-1988, pres., 1988-1990; CEO, 1990—, chmn. bd., 1991—; bd. dirs. Barnett Bank Fla., Inc., Electric Fuels Corp., Fla. Power Corp., Progress Techs. Corp. With U.S. Army, 1955-57. Home: 198-13th St E Terra Verde FL 33715 Office: Fla Progress Corp 1 Progress Plz Saint Petersburg FL 33701-4353*

CRITCHFIELD, TAMI SUE, nutrition and diabetes educator; b. Toledo, Dec. 14, 1961; d. Thomas W. and Mary L. (Patrick) Cochran; m. John R. Critchfield, July 4, 1981; children: Joshua Robert, Daniel Reece. BS in Dietetics, U. N.Mex., 1987. Cert. diabetes educator, 1993. Dietetic intern Med. Coll. Va., Richmond, 1988; clin. dietitian Richmond Meml. Hosp., 1988-91, renal nutrition support dietitian, 1991-92, chief clin. dietitian, renal dietitian, 1992; diabetes specialist dietitian Johnston-Willis Hosp., Richmond, 1992-95; renal consulting dietitian Vivra Renal Care, Richmond, 1994—; nutritionist, diabetes educator St. Mary's Hosp., Richmond, 1995—; com. em. selection dietetic internt. Med. Coll. Va., 1988, 89, 91, 92. Contbr. to newsletters and mags. Youth counselor Christ the King Luth. Ch., Richmond, Va., 1989-90; vol., profl. com. mem. Am. Cancer Soc., 1989-90; self study com. mem. Med. Coll. Va., 1989; met. coun. mem. Am. Heart Assn., Richmond, 1988-89. Recipient Kathryn Heitshu award for Potential Leadership in Dietetics, 1987. Mem. Nat. Kidney Found., Am. Assn. Diabetes Educators, Am. Dietetic Assn., Va. Dietetic Assn., Richmond Dietetic Assn. (bd. dirs., clin. nutrition rep. 1988-89). Lutheran. Office: Saint Mary's Hosp 5801 Bremo Rd Richmond VA 23226

CRITCHLOW, SUSAN MELISSA, public relations executive, advertising and printing consultant; b. Gainesville, Fla., Dec. 24, 1950; d. James Carlton and Mildred Estelle (Pringle) Barley; m. Warren Hartzell Critchlow, Jr., Aug. 18, 1973, 1 child, Suzanne Michele. BA, U. South Fla., 1972, MA in Speech Communication with honors, 1973. Asst. dir. pub. relations Goodwill Industries of N. Fla., Inc., 1973-74; dir. pub. relations St. Luke's Hosp., Jacksonville, Fla., 1974; dir. informational services Greater Orange Park Community Hosp., Orange Park, Fla., 1974-82; pres. Susan Critchlow & Assocs., New Home Life Pub., Inc.; CEO, SC&A Pub. Co., Inc., Orange Park, 1976—. Mem. bd. dirs. Children's Haven. Named N.E. Fla. Bus. Communicator of Month, 1975, 78, Outstanding Young Woman of Am. Charter mem. pub. rels. adv. coun. Coll. Journalism and Comms. U. Fla., 1978-81. Mem. Fla. Hosp. Assn. (bd. dirs. pub. rels. coun. 1976-78, Gold award 1975, Silver award 1976, 78), Jacksonville Hosp. Pub. Rels. Coun. (chmn. 1975-77), Fla. Pub. Rels. Assn. (Golden Image award 1975-86), Pub. Rels. Soc. Am., Nat. Assn. Builders, Fla. Home Builders Assn. (sold award 1991, Target award Profl. Builder Grand award 1995, Merit award 1995), N.E. Fla. Home Builders Assn. (sales and mktg. coun.), Jacksonville Advt. Fedn. (Addy award 1982-95). Republican. Episcopalian. Office: 179 Wells Rd Orange Park FL 32073-3057

CRITTENDEN, KATHERINE LUCINA, nurse; b. Newport News, Va., Aug. 16, 1957; d. James Tyler III and Lucina Nan (Titlow) C. Diploma, York Acad., 1975; student, Longwood Coll., 1975-78; Assocs., John Tyler C.C., 1984. RN, Va., Wis.; cert. ACLS, PALS, Am. Heart Assn., Trauma Nursing Care. Nurse Med. Coll. Va., Richmond, 1985-94; dir. emergency critical care svcs. Rappahannock Gen. Hosp., Kilmarnock, Va., 1994—. Dir. nursing No. Neck Free Clinic, Lancaster, Va., 1994. Mem. Jamestown Soc., Va. Nurses Assn. Mem. Philippi Christian Ch. Home: PO Box 581 Deltaville VA 23043-0581

CROCKER, BETTY CHARLOTTE, education educator; b. Jackson, Miss., Sept. 2, 1948; d. William Charlie and Virginia Frances (Cayson) C. BS, U. Tex., 1970; EdD, U. Ga., 1985. Cert. sci. edn., earth-life sci., elem. edn. Tchr. 5th grade Harlingen (Tex.) Ind. Schs., 1970-71, Am. Sch. Found., Monterrey, Mexico, 1971-74; tchr. grades 6-8, sci. chair Clear Creek Ind. Schs., Webster, Tex., 1974-83; asst. prof. edn. So. Oreg. State U., Ashland, 1985-88; asst. to assoc. prof. edn. U. North Tex., Denton, 1988—; adv. com. to state bd. edn. Tex. Environ. Edn. Adv. Com., Austin, 1991—; sci. spkr. The Edn. Ctr., Torrance, Calif., 1994-95. Author: Food for Thought, 1992, 93, 94, 95; editl. bd. mem. Jour. Elem. Sci. Edn., 1989-95; contbr. articles to profl. jours. Bd. dirs. hands-on mus. ScienceLand, Denton's (Tex.) Discovery Mus., 1994-95. Mem. S.W. Assn. Educators of Tchrs. of Sci. (sec.-treas. 1994-95, dir. elect 1995, dir. 1996-97), Sci. Tchrs. Assn. Tex. (v.p. 1990-91, pres. 1991-92, past pres. 1992-93, 94-95, Lawrence Buford award 1991), Phi Delta Kappa (sec.-treas. 1987-88, v.p. for programs 1989-90, pres. 1990-91). Office: Univ North Tex Coll Edn PO Box 13857 Denton TX 76203

CROCKER, OTTIS BRAZEL, JR., municipal judge; b. Houston, Miss., June 27, 1936; s. Ottis Brazel and Ora (Hawkins) C.; m. Kay Farris Embry, Sept. 1, 1962; children: Ottis Brazel III, Kathryn Ora. LLB, U. Miss., 1962. Bar: Miss. 1962, U.S. Dist. Ct. Miss., U.S. Tax Ct. Dir. Farmers & Merchants Bank, Bruce, Miss., 1970—; mcpl. judge City of Bruce, Miss., 1991—. County chmn. Dem. Party, Calhoun County, Miss., 1990—. With U.S. Army, 1959-65. Named Bar Commr., Miss. State Bar Assn., Jackson, 1975. Mem. Miss. Trial Lawyers Assn., Bruce Rotary Club (pres. 1974-75). Democrat. Baptist. Home and Office: PO Box 666 Bruce MS 38915-0666

CROCKETT, FELICIA DODEE FROST, brokerage firm executive; b. Oklahoma City, Oct. 19, 1956; d. Carl S. Frost and Mikki (Matheny) Marcus; m. Billy Crockett. Student So. Meth. U. Gen. mgr. Keystone Readers Svc., Dallas, 1976-80; v.p. and sr. fin. cons. Merrill Lynch pvt. client, Dallas, 1980—. Bd. dirs. North Dallas Shared Ministries, 1988-91, Mental Health Assn, adv. bd. EXCAP Ctr. for the Prevention of Child Abuse, Ronald McDonald Children's Charities, 1992—; mem. investment com. Dallas Womens Found., 1991-94. Mem. Dallas Opera (bd. dirs. 1991—), Dallas Securities Dealers Assn., Nat. Assn. Securities Dealers (gen. securities prin., mcpl. securities rulemaking bd. prin., registered options prin., bd. arbitrators), NYSE (com. mem.), Merrill Lynch Chmns. Club, Park Cities Exch. Club (charter, bd. dirs. 1991—), Chief Executive Officers Club. Republican. Office: Merrill Lynch Pierce Fenner and Smith 2000 Premier Pl 5910 N Central Expy Ste 2000 Dallas TX 75206-5152

CROCKETT, PATRICIA JO FRY, psychiatric-mental health nurse; b. Cabell Countyy, W.Va., Nov. 25, 1966; d. Roger Lee and Patricia Lee (Queen) Fry; m. Virgil LeRoy Crockett, Mar. 18, 1989; 1 child, Jennifer Lynn. Student, Marshall U., 1985-86; diploma, St. Mary's Sch. Nursing, Huntington, W.Va., 1989. RN, W.Va.; cert. CPR instr.; cert. psychiat. mental health nurse. Nurse adolescent treatment unit St. Mary's Hosp., 1989—. Home: RR 2 Box 2324 Wayne WV 25570-9755

CROCKETT-ARCHER, DEBORAH DAWN, surgeon; b. Tulsa, Dec. 11, 1959; d. Bobby Gene Mangrum and Patsy Ruth (Hembree) Priddy; m. Jerry Wayne Crockett, May 15, 1982 (div. 1989); m. Robert L. Archer, Apr. 4, 1992. BS in Physiology, Okla. State U., 1982; DO, Coll. Osteo. Medicine & Surgery, 1986. Lic. Okla.; cert. ACLS provider Am. Heart Assn., advanced trauma life support provider ACS com. on trauma. Surg. scrub technician Hillcrest Med. Ctr., Tulsa, 1976-84; intern Tulsa Regional Med. Ctr., 1986-87, resident in gen. surgery, 1987-90, chief surg. resident, 1990-91, staff gen. surgeon, 1992—; staff gen. surgeon Creek Nation Community Hosp., Okemah, Okla., 1991-92, Henryetta (Okla.) Med. Ctr., 1991-92; staff gen. surgeon Tulsa Regional Med. Ctr., 1991—, Broken Arrow (Okla.) Med. Ctr., 1992—; assoc. clin. instr. Coll. Osteo. Medicine and Surgery, Tulsa, 1988—. Recipient Clin. Rsch. award Merck, Sharp & Dohme Pharm. Co., 1989, 90; John C. Coburn Pres.'s Disting. scholar Okla. State U., 1978-82. Mem. Am. Coll. Osteo. Surgeons (Resident Achievement award 1991), Am. Osteo. Assn., Okla. Osteo. Assn., Tulsa Osteo. Med. Soc., Sigma Sigma Phi. Office: Surg Specialty Assocs 3233 E 31st St Ste 201 Tulsa OK 74105-2446

CROMLEY, ALLAN WRAY, journalist; b. Topeka, Apr. 11, 1922; s. Frank George and Elsie May (Leedom) C.; m. Marian Minor, Jan. 30, 1949; children: Kathleen, Janet, Carter. B.S. in Journalism (Summerfield scholar 1940-43, 46), U. Kans., 1948. Reporter Kansas City Kansan, 1948-49, Oklahoma City Times, 1949-53; Washington bur. chief Daily Oklahoman and Oklahoma City Times, 1953-87; sr. corr. Washington bur. Daily Oklahoman, 1987-95; ret., 1995; sec. standing com. corrs. House and Senate Galleries, 1961; nominating juror Pulitzer Prize Com., 1990. Sec. standing com. corr. House and Senate Galleries, 1961; bd. visitors U. Okla., 1970-72; active U. Okla. Found., 1994—; trustee William Allen White Found. U. Kans., 1978-90; bd. dirs. Nat. Press Found., 1987—, Population Inst., 1987-89; nominating juror Pulitzer Prize Com., 1990. With AUS, 1943-45, ETO. Mem. Soc. Profl. Journalists (dir. Washington chpt. 1984-86), Nat. Press Club (gov. 1964-68, vice chmn. bd. 1966, v.p. 1967, pres. 1968), Nat. Gridiron Club (v.p. 1977, pres. 1978, treas. 1981-88, sec. 1988-95), Omicron Delta Kappa. Home: 3320 Stoneybrae Dr Falls Church VA 22044-1222

CROMWELL, VIRGINIA PACE, communication professional; b. Oxford, Miss., Aug. 19, 1933; d. George Gibbs Pace and Virginia Sue (Dooley) Sizemore; m. Harvey Cromwell, Jr., June 26, 1955 (div. Aug. 1978); children: Harvey III, William Campbell; m. James Leslie Turrentine, July 6, 1984 (dec. May 1993). BS, Miss. U. for Women, 1955; MA, U. Miss., 1957; MS, U. So. Miss., 1970, PhD, 1984. Instr. speech dept. U. Southwestern La., 1961-66; instr. Sch. of Comm. U. So. Miss., 1966-70; instr. speech dept. U. Southwestern La., 1970-73, asst. prof. dept. comm., 1974-78, from assoc. prof., dir. grad. studies, head of pub. rels. area to prof., 1984-91; cons./prin. Strategic Comm. Mgmt., 1991—; oral comm. tchr. Memphis Oral Sch. for the Deaf, 1957-59; instr. U. Miss., 1955-56, others. Contbg. editor: Well Servicing Mag., 1979-81; U.S. Gulf Coast Editor: Drilling Contractor Mag., 1978-82; bus. editor: Lafayette Daily Advertiser, 1959-61; author: Use of Visiting Lecturers and Advisory Boards by Universities Housing PRSSA Chapters, 1988, Working with Local Media: The Foundation of Effective Public Relations, 1986, Media Handbook - A Guide for Educators on Working with Local Mass Media, 1981; contbr. articles to profl. jours. Mem. People-to People amb. to Russian and the Ukraine, 1991. Mem. Pub. Rels. Soc. Am. (accredited), Pub. Rels. Assn. La., Internat. Pers. Mgrs. Assn., Advt. Fedn. Acadiana, Acadiana Press Club.

CRONCE, DONALD THOMAS, research chemist; b. Kenosha, Wis., June 8, 1964; s. Thomas John and Beatrice Marie (Glass) C. BS, U. Wis., Milw., 1985; PhD, Pa. State U., 1991. Rsch. chemist Naval Surface Warfare Ctr., Dahlgren, Va., 1991—. Vol. in state games Spl. Olympics, University Park, Pa., 1990, 92; sci. fair judge Va. Pub. Schs., Woodbridge and King George, 1992—. Mem. AAAS, Am. Chem. Soc., N.Y. Acad. Scis., Am. Mensa, Phi Eta Sigma. Home: 5206 Magnolia Pl Fredericksburg VA 22407 Office: Naval Surface Warfare Ctr Dahlgren Divsn Code B51 Dahlgren VA 22448

CRONE, WILLIAM GERALD, hospital administrator; b. Pelzer, S.C., Jan. 27, 1932; married. BA, U. N.C., 1954. Adminstrv. res. Charlotte (N.C.) Meml. Hosp. and Med. Ctr., 1956-58, adminstrv. asst., 1958-62, asst. dir., 1962-66; adminstr. Naples (Fla.) Community Hosp., 1966-71, exec. dir., 1971-76, pres., 1976—. Contbr. articles to profl. jours. Home: 555 Mooringline Dr Naples FL 33940-4746 Office: Naples Community Hosp PO Box 413029 Naples FL 33941-3029*

CRONIN, GERARD THOMAS, community planner, negotiations specialist, writer; b. Pitts., Dec. 23, 1947; s. John Michael and Mary Veronica (White) C.; m. Frances Jeanette Thomas, Apr. 29, 1988; children: Megan Amanda, Morgan Jeanette; 1 stepchild, Veronica Shirell. BA, U. Tenn., 1969. Chief exec. officer Ind. Community Cons., Inc., Hampton, Ark., 1972—, Creative Bus. Solutions, Inc., Hampton, 1994—; chmn. search com. Nonprofit Mgmt. Assn., Mpls., 1983-84; bd. dirs. Housing Devel. Corp. So. (Hampton) Ark., Cabun Rural Health Systems, Inc., chmn. pers. com. Author, editor: Nonprofit Board Book, 1983, Personnel Matters, 1987, Guide to Arkansas Funding Sources, 1990. Justice of the Peace Calhoun County Quorum Ct., Hampton, 1990-94; chmn. county govt. budget and pers. coms.; apptd. govs. adv. coun. on minority bus. devel., 1991-94. Recipient 80 for the Eighties award Ark. Times mag., 1980. Democrat. Roman Catholic. Office: Ind Community Cons Inc PO Box 141 Hampton AR 71744-0141

CRONIN, MARY HAAG, real estate referral agent; b. Balt., June 1, 1925; d. Alfred Henry and Catherine (Hoover) Haag; m. Donald Everett Nork, Dec. 16, 1944 (div. 1958); m. John Paul Cronin, Jan. 12, 1963 (dec.). Cert. nurse asst., Sheridan Vocat. Tech. Ctr., 1975; cert. realtor, Chinelly Sch. Real Estate, 1982; cert. in eldercare, Fla. Internat. U., 1988. Nurse asst. Med. Pers. Pool, Hollywood, Fla., 1975-85; sales staff Chinelly Real Estate, Hollywood, Fla., 1982-84; referral real estate agt. Coldwell Banker Referral Network, Inc., Miami Lakes, Fla., 1991—. Patentee pot-pourri holder. Vol. nurse, Sunrise, 1988—; aux. mem. Meml. Hosp., Hollywood, 1970—. Mem. Ice Skating Club Am., Elks, Am. Legion (bd. dirs., co-dir. 1993—), Internat. Platform Assn., Inventors Soc. So. Fla., Inc., Nat. Congress Inventors Orgsn. Address: PO Box 130071 Sunrise FL 33313-0001

CRONK, DENIS STEVEN, human resources educator, researcher, writer; b. San Antonio, July 13, 1946; s. Robert Charles and Rose Anne (Fuller) C.; m. Sally Marguerite McKay, Apr. 15, 1974 (div. July 1981); children: Tonya Lyn, Billie Jo; m. Billie Jo Zick, May 6, 1988. AAS in Electronic Tech., Clark County C.C., Las Vegas, 1979; BS in Vocat.-Career Edn., U. Nev., Las Vegas, 1988; MS in Corp. Tng. and Devel., U. North Tex., 1991, postgrad., 1992—. Lic. in radiotelephone with radar endorsement, FCC. Telecom. installer/tester ITT-Systems Installations Inc., Milan, Tenn., 1970-73, Stromberg-Carlson Corp., Rochester, N.Y., 1974-75; electronics technician III Reynolds Elec. and Engring. Co., Nev., 1976-77; electronics instr. Ctrl. Telephone Co., Las Vegas, 1977-78; sr. field engr. Burroughs Corp., Las Vegas, 1978-81; pvt. practice as designer, developer, instr. Lewisville, Tex., 1991—; instr. human resources tng. and instrn. Lewisville Ind. Sch. Dist., 1992—; rschr. in field. Author: Receptive Association, 1991, The Motivation Continuum, 1994. With USMC, 1966-69, Vietnam. Mem. VFW, U. Nev. Las Vegas Alumni Assn., U. No. Tex. Alumni Assn., Phi Lambda Alpha. Republican. Home and Office: 5309 Del Monte Ave Las Vegas NV 89102-1301

CROOG, ROSLYN DEBORAH, computer systems analyst; b. New Haven, July 14, 1942; d. Herbert Bernard and Belle (Brown) Croog; m. Thomas Edward Botts; children: Bradley Jordan Paul, Katie Miriam Paul. AS, Quinnipiac Coll., 1962; BS, Fla. Internat. U., 1982. Analyst, programmer DBA Systems, Inc., Melbourne, Fla., 1982-84; system mgr. DBA Systems, Inc., Fairfax, Va., 1984-86; mem. tech. staff MRJ, Inc., Fairfax, Va., 1986—. Office: MRJ Inc 10560 Arrowhead Dr Fairfax VA 22030-7305

CROOKS, DORENA MAY (DEE CROOKS), administrative assistant, social worker; b. Center Point, W.Va., Sept. 15, 1938; d. Paul Jefferson and Ruby Catherine (Lasure) Ashcraft; m. William H.D. Crooks, June 27, 1956 (div. Nov. 1975); children: Charles Jefferson, Kimberly May, Raechelle Dee. Grad., W.Va. State Police Acad., 1977; BA, Glenville State Coll., 1992. Lic. social worker, W.Va. Legal sec. Hickel, Wilson & Hill, Attys., Parkersburg, W.Va., 1963-65, Robert T. Goldenberg, Atty., Parkersburg, W.Va., 1965-68; exec. sec. W.Va. State Rd., Parkersburg, 1968-70; dep. sheriff, sec. Wood County Sheriff Dept., Parkersburg, 1973-79; legal sec. George W. Hill, Atty., Parkersburg, 1984-88; Vista vol. Wood County Sr. Citizens Assn., Parkersburg, 1990-91, adminstrv. asst., social worker, 1991—; coord. of Widowed Persons Svc., sr. companion program and Sr. Health Ins. Network, Wood County. Office: Wood County Citizens Assn 925 Market St Parkersburg WV 26101-4736

CROOKS, JAMES BENEDICT, history educator; b. Paterson, N.J., Sept. 27, 1933; s. Archer Duryee and Rebecca Pearse (Easterbrook) C.; m. Laura Naomi Ward, July 5, 1958; children: Peter Graham, Sarah Ward. BA, Yale U., 1957; MA, Johns Hopkins U., 1962, PhD, 1964. Group pension underwriter Conn. Gen. Life Ins. Co., Hartford, 1957-59; vis. lectr. Univ. Coll., Dublin, Ireland, 1964-66; asst. prof., assoc. prof. Hollins (Va.) Coll., 1966-72; prof. history U. North Fla., Jacksonville, 1972—, chmn. dept., 1972-80, asst. dean, 1972-78, interim dean Coll. Arts and Scis., 1992-93. Author: Politics and Progress: The Rise of Urban Progressivism in Baltimore, 1968, Jacksonville After the Fire, 1901-1919: A New South City, 1991; mem. editorial bd. Fla. Hist. Quar., 1993—; contbr. articles to profl. jours. Pres. Roanoke (Va.) Valley Coun. on Human Rels., 1968-72; bd. dirs. Jacksonville Community Coun. Inc., 1988-92, 94—. Sgt. U.S. Army, 1953-55. Recipient Vol. award Vol. Jacksonville, 1986, Disting. Prof. award, 1992. Mem. Am. Hist. Assn., Orgn. Am. Historians, So. Hist. Assn., Jacksonville Hist. Soc. (historian 1991—). Democrat. Presbyterian. Office: U North Fla 4567 Saint Johns Bluff Rd S Jacksonville FL 32224-2646

CROSA, PETER JAMES, private investigator; b. Detroit, July 10, 1951; s. James R. and Adela Camelia C.; children: Robyn S., Beth A., Emile R., Michael J. Student, Miami-Dade (Fla.) Coll., 1971. Regional exec. Am. Internat. Group, Atlanta, 1978-82; br. mgr. Harold J. Smith Adjusters, Atlanta, 1982-84, Nat. Claim Svc., Atlanta, 1984-88; pres. Peter J. Crosa &

Co., Atlanta, 1988—; lic. pvt. detective. Author: Insurance Repair: Opportunities, Procedures & Methods, 1988. Mem. Atlanta Claims Assn., NRA, Nat. Speaker Assn., Ga. Speakers Assn. Office: 4135 Lavista Rd Ste 610-316 Tucker GA 30085-5003

CROSBY, JAMES EARL, newspaper publisher; b. Staunton, Va., Sept. 17, 1935; s. Lee Marvin and Mildred Lillian (Jones) C.; m. Ruth Anne Southwell, Apr. 27, 1956 (div. Mar. 1980); children: Lee Jepson, Peter William, Lynn Jeannette; m. Patsy Marie Shiflett, July 31, 1981; children: Ashley Blair, Avery Beth. Student, U. Del., 1957, U. Md., 1958. News photographer Staunton News-Leader, 1950-54, News-Jour. Co., Wilmington, Del., 1956-60; freelance photographer Unique Photo, New Castle, Del., 1960-62; devel. dir. Ocean City, Md., 1962-65; travel dir. State of Del., Dover, 1965-70, Shenandoah Valley, Inc., Staunton, 1970-71; pres. Motivation Rsch., Inc., Staunton, 1971-72; asst. to supt. Miller Sch., Va., 1973-80; pres., pub. Bulletin, Inc., Crozet, Va., 1980-94; pres. Md. Travel Coun., Annapolis, 1964-65. First aid chmn. Del. chpt. Red Cross, Wilmington, 1968-69; vice chmn. Cen. Va. chpt. Red Cross, Charlottesville, 1984; founder Western Albemarle Rescue Squad, Crozet, 1978, Albemarle County Fair, Inc., Crozet, 1981; boating instr. boating safety com. Va. Dept. Game & Inland Fisheries, Richmond, 1991—. With USN, 1954-56. Named Outstanding Citizen, City of Staunton, 1970. Mem. Soc. Profl. Journalists, USCG-Aux. (flotilla comdr. 1990-91, divsn. capt. 1994-95, Outstanding Vessel Operator 1990, Outstanding Mem. Achievement 1989, 90, 91, 92), Lake Anna Boating Safety, Inc. (pres. 1990-92), Rivanna Rifle & Pistol Club. Home and Office: 1278 Crozet Ave Crozet VA 22932-0280

CROSBY, JIM, design company executive. V.p. Planning Design Group. Address: Ste 105 5155 E 51st St Tulsa OK 74135

CROSBY, ROBERT DAVIS, property manager, consultant; b. Washington, Dec. 19, 1938; s. Jack and Mary Lou (Bogan) Foster; m. Jane Barker, Dec. 26, 1969; children: William Eugene, Robert D. Jr., John Adam. BA, Calif. State U., Sacramento, 1989. Sales rep. King Sales Co., Inc., Inglewood, Calif., 1964-66; v.p. sales Milbro Seats, Inc., Paramount, Calif., 1966-70; pres. Great Western Sales, Inc., Gardena, Calif., 1970-81, Crosby Combined Properties, Shalimar, Fla., 1967—, Echo Mktg. and Mgmt., Shalimar, 1986—; bd. dirs. Great Western Sales, Inc., 1975—; instr. Sierra Coll., Rocklin, Calif., 1988-92. Author: Guide to Big Profits in the Resume Business, 1990. Ruling elder Sierra Presbyn. Ch., Nevada City, 1982-86; bd. dirs. Sugar Bowl Nat. Ski Patrol, Norden, Calif., 1989-92; mem. Shalimar United Meth. Ch., 1992—. With USN, 1958-60. Mem. Assn. Industry Mfrs. Reps. (v.p. 1978-80). Republican. Home: 72 Marlborough Rd Shalimar FL 32579-1036

CROSKERY, RICHARD W., internist; b. Enid, Okla., May 8, 1955; s. Robert William and Beverly Ann (Fulkerson) C.; m. Andrea Jean Rosmarin, Oct. 25, 1980; children: Robin Paige, Thomas Curran. BA, U. Toledo, 1977; MD, Ohio State U., 1981. Resident in internal medicine East Carolina U., Greenville, N.C., 1981-84; ptnr. Quadrangle Med. Specialists, P.A., Greenville, 1984—; assoc. clin. prof. medicine East Carolina U. Sch. Medicine, 1985—, cons. physician Human Performance Lab., 1986—; bd. dirs. Ea. Carolina Health Orgn. (ECHO), Greenville, 1993—; plant physician Glaxo-Wellcome Co., Greenville, 1984—. Mem. exec. bd. United Way Pitt County, N.C., 1987-95, campaign chmn., 1996, physician chmn., 1986, 89, 92, 95; bd. dirs. Literacy Vols. Am., 1992—; founder, com. chmn. pack 514 Boy Scouts Am., Greenville, 1994—; mem. sessions, officer Peace Presbyn. Ch., Greenville, 1987-89, 94-96. Mem. Am. Coll. Physicians, Am. Soc. Internal Medicine, Pitt County Med. Soc. (pres. 1990), Rotary Club Greenville (pres. 1991-92). Home: 4001 Hardwick Ct Greenville NC 27834 Office: Quadrangle Med Specialists 620 S Memorial Dr Greenville SC 27834

CROSS, BETTY FELT, small business owner; b. Newcastle, Ind., Jan. 8, 1920; d. Frank Ernest and Olive (Shock) Felt; m. Paris O. Cross, July 14, 1939 (div.); children: Ernest, Betty J., Robert D., Paris, Toni, Frank; m. John B. Gatlin, 1976 (dec. Oct. 1995). Owner, mgr. Salon D'Or, Indpls., 1956-74; owner Bejon, Madison, Ind., 1974-78, Brass & Things, Madison, 1978-93; pres. Felts Mfg., Inc., 1966—, Silver City USA I, Madison, 1981—, Black Angus, Inc, 1991—, Silver City Video, Inc., Oak Grove, Ky., 1992—, Job Rock I and II, Inc., 1994—. Mem. Nashville C. of C. Avocation: collecting dolls, gold and silver coins, art objects, gold antique jewelry, silver sterling. Office: 928 Gallatin Rd S Madison TN 37115-4625

CROSS, CAROLE ANN, plastics engineer; b. Springfield, Mass., July 30, 1970; d. David Anthony and Linda Ann (Favreau) C. BS in engring. plastics, U. Lowell, 1992. Cost estimator engr. Solvay Automotive, Troy, Mich., 1993; mfg. engr. IBM Corp., Research Triangle Park, N.C., 1993-95; v.p. sales Carolina Jacobson, Sanford, N.C., 1995-96; application devel. engr. GE Plastics, Houston, 1996—. Contbr. article to profl. jours. Mem. Soc. Mfg. Engrs., Soc. Plastic Engrs., Soc. Automotive Engrs., Soc. Advancement of Materials. Roman Catholic. Home and Office: 17402 Valley Palms Dr Spring TX 77379

CROSS, DENNIS WAYNE, academic administrator; b. Bristol, Va., Apr. 18, 1955; s. Brainard C. and Genevieve Cross; m. Susan Sydney Haire, Aug. 7, 1982; children: Walker Gray, Grier Gordon, Sydney Sullivan. BA, Vanderbilt U., 1976; MDiv, Harvard U., 1979, ThM, 1982; postgrad., Vanderbilt U., 1986, Williamsburg Devel. Inst., 1987. Banking officer 1st Am. Nat. Bank, Nashville, 1982-86; dir. alumni and devel. Coll. Arts and Sci. Vanderbilt U., Nashville, 1986-92; exec. dir. Arts and Scis. Found., Inc., assoc. dean for program devel. Coll. Arts and Scis. U. N.C., Chapel Hill, 1992—. Bd. dirs. mid. Tenn. chpt. ACLU, Nashville, 1991-92; exec. com. Friends of Music, Inc., Nashville, 1987-89; mem. membership com. U. Club of Nashville, 1991-92; head edn. com. Chapel of the Cross, Chapel Hill, N.C.; vol. bicentennial campaign Coll. of Arts and Scis. U. N.C., 1992-95; bd. dirs., sec.-treas. U. N.C.-Chapel Hill Arts and Scis. Found., Inc., 1992—; mem. long-range planning com. Program in the Humanities and Human Values. Mem. Coun. for Advancement of Secondary Edn., Folk Art Soc. Am., Coun. of Friends-Tryon Palace, The Carolina Club, N.C. Triangle Vanderbilt Club (organizer), The Coll. Cabinet, The Dean's Club, Phi Beta Kappa, Delta Phi Alpha. Episcopalian. Home: 102 Juniper Ct Carrboro NC 27510-2532 Office: U NC Arts & Scis Found Inc CB # 6115 104 New West Chapel Hill NC 27599

CROSS, DOROTHY ABIGAIL, retired librarian; b. Bangor, Mich., Sept. 9, 1924; d. John Laird and Alice Estelle (Wilcox) C.; B.A., Wayne State U., 1956; M.A. in Library Sci., U. Mich., 1957. Jr. librarian Detroit Public Library, 1957-59; adminstrv. librarian U.S. Army, Braconne, France, 1959-61, Poitiers, France, 1961-63; area library supr., 1963, asst. command librarian, Kaiserslautern, Germany, 1963-67, acquisitions librarian, Aschaffenburg, Germany, 1967, Munich, Germany, 1967-69, sr. staff library specialist, Munich, 1969-72, command librarian, Stuttgart, Germany, 1972-75, dep. staff librarian, Heidelberg, Germany, 1975-77; chief librarian 18th Airborne Corps and Ft. Bragg (N.C.), 1977-79; chief ADP sect. Pentagon Library, Washington, 1979-80, chief readers services br., 1980-83, dir., 1983-91. Mem. ALA, U. Mich. Alumni assn., Delta Omicron. Methodist. Home: 6511 Delia Dr Alexandria VA 22310-2609

CROSS, ELIZABETH, nurse; b. Augusta, Ga., Dec. 10, 1956; d. Billy and Myrtle Missouri (Taylor) Keller; m. Raymond Eugene Cross, Apr. 4, 1973; children: Raymond Eugene Cross, Jr., Myrtle Elizabeth. Cert. Nursing Asst., Riley Inst., Valdosta, Ga., 1989. Cert. nursing asst. Crestwood Nursing Home, Valdosta, Ga., 1989-95, Grace More Nursing Home, 1995—; spokesperson advisor Crestwood Nursing Home, Valdosta, 1989-95. Vol. Wayne County Headstart Sch., Jesup, Ga., 1981-87. Mem. Delta Sigma Theta. Mem. Ch. of God. Home: 708 Lee St Brunswick GA 31520-7724

CROSS, GEORGE LEE, III, orthopedic surgeon; b. Bloomington, Ill., Dec. 2, 1946; s. George Lee Cross Jr. and Sara Merle (Adams) Cossé; m. Virginia Anne McKesson, Aug. 8, 1970; children: Harold Lee, Gwendolyn Diane. BS, Davidson Coll., 1969; MD, Emory U., 1973. Clin. prof. orthopedic surgery Seoul (Republic of Korea) Nat. U., 1978-79; orthopedic surgeon Ga. Bapt. Med. Ctr., Atlanta, 1980—, chmn. dept. orthopedic surgery, 1988-90. Vol. physician med. mission trips to Liberia, 1984-88, El Salvador, 1994. Maj. U.S. Army, 1978-80. Fellow Am. Acad. Orthopedic Surgeons. Baptist. Office: Atlanta Bone & Joint Surgeons 285 Boulevard Ste 310 Atlanta GA 30312

CROSS, HUGH RITCHIE, real estate broker, computer consultant; b. Portsmouth, Va., Sept. 20, 1949; s. Harry Lee Jr. and Jean (Ritchie) Cross; m. S. Lynn Bulter, Sept. 19, 1986; 1 child, Vernon C. Everwine IV. BS in Biology, N.C. Wesleyan Coll., Rocky Mount, 1972. Tchr. Nansemond County Pub. Schs., Suffolk, Va., 1972-75; real estate salesperson Harry L. Cross Jr. & Sons, Suffolk, 1975—. Chair, vice chair Suffolk Beautification Commn., 1987—; mem. policy bd. Pres.'s Task Force on Lead Hazards. Named Realtor of Yr., Suffolk Bd. Realtors, 1981. Mem. Suffolk/Franklin Assn. Realtors (pres. 1981, 82, 93, Realtor of Yr. 1987, Property Mgr. of Yr. 1987), Va. Assn. Realtors (regional v.p. 1995), Rotary Club of Suffolk (asst. sec.), Hampton Roads Realtors Assn. (dir.), Property Owners and Mgrs. Assn. (charter), Nat. Assn. Residential Property Mgrs. (Tidewater chpt.). Office: Cross Realty 1707 N Main St Suffolk VA 23434

CROSS, JOYCE ANNETTE OSCAR, newscaster; b. Chgo., July 3, 1956; d. Edward Ambrose and Gertrude (Andrews) O.; m. Jerry Wayne Cross, Sept. 8, 1990; children: Jennifer Joyce, Jeremy Oscar. BA, Western Ill. U., Macomb, 1978. Copy writer advt. Sta. WFYR/RKO, Chgo., 1978-79; video journalist Cable News Network, Atlanta, 1980; reporter, anchor Sta. WJBF-TV ABC Affiliate, Augusta, Ga., 1980-83; news anchor Sta. WDEF-TV CBS Affiliate, Chattanooga, 1983-85; news reporter Sta. WSB-TV ABC Affiliate, Atlanta, 1985—. Talent, writer, producer Spot News Report, 1983, TV reporting, rotary, 1983. Vol. March of Dimes, Atlanta, 1986-87, pub. speaker United Way Agy., Atlanta, 1986-87; com. mem. Ga. Spl. Olympics. Recipient Spot News Reporting award, UP Internat. and W. Augusta Rotary, 1983, Gavel award Ga. Bar Assn., 1990, Gavel award Atlanta Bar Assn., 1990; Unicom Ednl. TV grantee, 1975-78. Mem. Ga. Assn. Newscasters, Soc. Profl. Journalists, Sigma Delta Chi, Sigma, Sigma, Sigma. Roman Catholic. Office: Sta WSB-TV 1601 W Peachtree St NE Atlanta GA 30309-2641

CROSS, SUSAN LEE, consulting actuary; b. Abington, Pa., Mar. 10, 1960; d. James Robert and Mary Elizabeth (Schleiden) Garris; m. Kevin Michael Cross, July 15, 1979; children: Alyssa Beth, Cameron David. BS in Math., U. Md., 1981. Actuarial asst. The Wyatt Co., Washington, 1981-83; actuarial asst. Tillinghast-Towers Perrin (formerly Tillinghast), Hamilton, Bermuda, 1984-85, asst. v.p., 1985-86; cons. actuary Tillinghast-Towers Perrin (formerly Tillinghast), Arlington, Va., 1987-92, prin., 1992—. Fellow Casualty Actuarial Soc.; mem. Am. Acad. Actuaries, Soc. of Actuaries (assoc.). Republican. Home: 3051 Crosen Ct Herndon VA 22071-1538 Office: Tillinghast-Towers Perrin 1001 19th St N Rosslyn VA 22209-1722

CROSSEN, JOHN JACOB, radiologist, educator; b. Chgo., Mar. 28, 1932; s. John Shelly and Viola Catherine (Geis) C.; divorced; children: John, Pamela, Gregory, Terrence; m. Esther Aileen Cowie, Aug. 4, 1972. BS, U. Ill., 1953; MD, Loyola U., Chgo., 1957. Diplomate Am. Bd. Radiology, Nat. Bd. Med. Examiners. Intern Mercy Hosp., Buffalo, 1957-58; resident in radiology Cook County Hosp., Chgo., 1960-63; radiologist San Pedro and Long Beach, Calif., 1963-79; attending radiologist Harbor Hosp. of UCLA, Torrance, 1964-69; radiologist Tacoma, 1979-82; radiologist United Hosp. Ctr., Clarksburg, W.Va., 1982-93, dir. diagnostic radiology, 1992-93; asst. clin. prof. W.Va. U. Med. Sch., Morgantown, 1982-93; pres. Clarskburg Radiology Group Inc., 1992-94; with Columbia E Hosp. and Diagnostic Ctr., El Paso, Tex., 1993—. Capt. M.C., USAF, 1958-60. Recipient tchr. recognition Am. Acad. Family Practice, 1983-91. Fellow Am. Coll. Radiology, Internat. Coll. Surgeons, Am. Coll. Angiology; mem. AMA, Radiol. Soc. N.Am., Am. Inst. Ultrasound in Medicine, Tex. Radiology Soc., El Paso County Med. Soc., Coronado Country Club. Democrat. Roman Catholic. Home: 804 Pintada Pl El Paso TX 79912-1805

CROSSLEY, GARY EXLEY, organization executive; b. Charleston, S.C., Oct. 6, 1951; s. Gilbert Franklin and Elsie Neal (Exley) C.; m. Debra Ann Hulon, Aug. 8, 1976 (div. Nov. 1982); m. Sharon Louise Hiers, Nov. 9, 1985. BS in Mktg., U. S.C., 1973; postgrad., Coll. of Charleston. Labor market analyst S.C. Employment Security Commn., Columbia, 1973-85; labor market info. and rsch. dir. Interstate Conf. of Employment Security Agys., Inc., Washington, 1985-94; asst. dir. Charleston Naval Complex S.C. Employment Security Commn., Charleston, S.C., 1994—; cons. Army Transition Labor Market Info. Project, Washington, 1988-91. Editor, contbr. newsletter Labor Market Inform-the-Nation, 1985-94; co-editor Workforce, 1992-94; contbr. articles to profl. publs. Bd. dirs. Consortium ib Adolscent Pregnancy, Washington, 1987-90; asst. treas. St. Mark's Episcopal Ch., Washington, 1988-93. Recipient Contbr.'s award Nat. Occupational Info. Coordinating Com., 1988, Vladimir Chavrid Meml. award Interstate Conf. of Employment Security Agys., 1995. Mem. Internat. Assn. Pers. in Employment Security (bd. dirs. S.C. chpt. 1980-81, nat. bd. dirs. 1987-94, S.C. Employee of Yr. award 1982, Individual Merit award S.C. 1989), Soc. Nat. Assn. Publs., Partnership for Employment & Tng. Careers, Assn. Pub. Data Users. Democrat. Home: 314 Muirfield Pky Charleston SC 29414-6811 Office: SC Employment Security Commn CNC PO Box 70579 Charleston SC 29415-0579

CROSSMAN, STAFFORD MAC ARTHUR, agronomist, researcher; b. Basseterre, St. Kitts, W.I., Sept. 23, 1953; came to U.S., 1969; s. Arthur Crulilee Crossman and Ivy Malvina (Berkeley) Fergus; m. Lona Burnetta Austin, Apr. 27, 1985; children: Desiree Tamara, Devon Jermaine, Nicole Ashima. Diploma, Jamaica Sch. Agr., 1978; BS, Tuskegee (Ala.) U., 1981, MS, 1984. Tchr. Ministry of Edn., Basseterre, 1970-74; field asst. Nat. Agrl. Corp., Basseterre, 1975-79; field trainee Jamaica Coffee Bd., Kingston, 1978; rsch. technician Tuskegee U., 1983-84; agronomist St. Kitts Sugar Mfg. Corp., Basseterre, 1984-87; rsch. specialist U. V.I., St. Croix, 1988—; subject matter specialist U. W.I., Basseterre, 1984-87, Midwestern Univs. Consortium for Internat. Activities, 1984-87, Caribbean Agrl. Extension Project, Basseterre, 1984-87; mem. US/AID project adv. bd. Ministry of Agr., Basseterre, 1985-87; v.p. Caribbean Agrl. Tech., St. Croix, 1988—. Co-contr. articles to Jour. Hortsci., Can. Jour. Microbiology, Agronomy Jour., W.I. Sugar Technologists Procedings, Caribbean Food Crop Soc. Proceedings, Internat. Soc. Tropical Root Crops Proceedings. Class leader Bethel Meth. Ch., St. Croix, 1989-92, steward, 1991—, chapel steward, 1992—, treas., 1993—, sec., 1992—; treas. Claude O. Markoe Sch. PTA, St. Croix, 1989, 90; bd. dirs. Community United Meth. Ch., St. Croix, 1989-93, v.p., bd. dirs., 1992-93. Carver Rsch. fellow Tuskegee U., 1982-84; named Student of Yr., Jamaica Sch. Agr., 1978; recipient Cert. Food Agrl. Orgn./Internat. Atomic Energy Agy., 1986, cert. for microirrigation design and installation Internat. Irrigation Supply, 1993. Mem. Am. Soc. Hort. Scis., Am. Soc. Agronomy, Crop Sci. Soc. Am., Soil Sci. Soc. Am., Internat. Soc. Tropical Root Crops, Caribbean Food Crop Soc. (v.p. V.I. chpt. 1988-92), Internat. Herb Growers Assn. Home: PO Box 2261 Kingshill VI 00851-2261 Office: U VI RR 2 Box 10000 Kingshill VI 00850-9781

CROUCH, ARLINE PARKS, librarian; b. Corbin, Ky., Jan. 13, 1947; d. Elijah and Edna (Gibbs) Parks; m. Robert Louis Crouch, Aug. 25, 1968; children: Cara Lynn, Carlin Robert. BS, Cumberland Coll., 1967; MA, Union Coll., 1970; postgrad., U. Ky., 1973. Tchr. 3d grade Boone County Bd. of Edn., Florence, Ky., 1967-68, tchr. 2d grade, 1968-69, tchr. 3d grade, 1969-74, libr., 1975-95; libr. Crescent Springs (Ky.) Bapt. Ch., 1987-90. Mem. exec. coun. Ky. Educators Pub. Affairs Coun., Florence, 1975-78. Mem. NEA, Ky. Edn. Assn., Boone County Edn. Assn. (treas. Florence chpt. 1975-78), Ky. Sch. Librs. Assn., Boone County Sch. Libr. Assn., Phi Delta Kappa. Democrat. Home: PO Box 47 Burlington KY 41005-0047

CROUCH, DIANNE KAY, secondary school guidance counselor; b. Campbellsville, Ky., Apr. 28, 1954; d. James Edgar and Imogene (Bailey) Gabbert; m. Thomas Frederick Crouch, June 6, 1987. BA, Campbellsville Coll., 1976; MS, U. Ky., 1984, EdS, 1991. Cert. tchr. English, psychology, counselor, secondary schs., Ky. Tchr. English Grayson County High Sch., Leitchfield, Ky., 1976-78, Jessamine County Jr. High Sch., Nicholasville, Ky., 1978-83, Jessamine County High Sch., Nicholasville, 1983-89, Tates Creek Jr. High Sch., Lexington, Ky., 1989-90; guidance counselor Tates Creek High Sch., Lexington, 1990—; mem. pub. rels. com. Tates Creek H.S.; mem. task force on grouping/tracking Fayette County; selected Inst. Women in Sch. Adminstrn. Ky. Fund raiser Am. Leukemia Assn., Nicholasville, 1990-92; active Calvary Bapt. Ch., Lexington, 1991—; active Fayette County Task Force on Grouping Trucking. Named Jessamine County Tchr. of Yr., Jessamine County Bd. Edn., Nicholasville, Ky., 1986-87, Outstanding Tchr. 5th Dist., Campbellsville Coll., 1988; sponsor of Jr. High newspaper Tates Creek Clarion named 1 of top 5 in U.S Nat. Jr. Beta Club. Mem. NEA, Ky. Edn. Assn., Fayette County Edn. Assn., Ky. Assn. Secondary and Coll. Admission Counselors (sec.), Ky. Counseling Assn. (bd. dirs.), Ctrl. Ky. Assn. Counseling and Devel., Coll. Bds. Coll. Scholarship Svc. Assembly, Kappa Delta Pi. Home: 716 Keene Way Ct Nicholasville KY 40356

CROUCH, JAMES BONNEAU, JR., insurance executive; b. Winston-Salem, N.C., Oct. 28, 1948; s. James Bonneau and Hazel Elizabeth (Hall) C.; m. Janie Callahan Ryan, May 22, 1950; children: James Bonneau III, John Ryan, Adelaide Hall. BA, U. N.C., 1971. V.p. Harris, Crouch, Long, Scott & Miller, Inc., Burlington, N.C., 1972—; bd. dirs. First South Bank, Burlington, Sandhills Links, Inc., So. Pines, N.C., Bright Enterprises, Inc., Greensboro, N.C. Bd. dirs. Alamance Found., Burlington, 1990—; pres. Alamance Ednl. Found, 1993—; hon. chmn. March of Dimes Teamwalk, Burlington, 1991. Mem. Am. Bus. Club (pres. 1976), Alamance Country Club (v.p. 1982, pres. 1996). Democrat. Methodist. Home: 2529 Pineway Dr Burlington NC 27215-4439 Office: Harris Crouch Long Scott & Miller Inc 7241 Burlington Rd Whitsett NC 27377-9201

CROUCH, RICHARD W., police official, management consultant; b. Rockwood, Tenn., Nov. 15, 1950; s. Samuel Curtis and Marian (Johnson) C.; m. Mary Jean Hicks, Oct. 13, 1973; children—Allison, Bethany. B.S., Jacksonville State U., Ala., 1974, postgrad., 1975-82; MPPA Miss. State U., 1992. Cert. law enforcement officer, Ala., Miss., Ga. Police officer Anniston Police Dept., Ala., 1972-76, police sgt., 1976-77, police lt., 1977-80, police capt., 1980-82; chief of police Starkville Police Dept., Miss., 1982-87, Moultrie (Ga.) Police Dept., 1987—; guest lectr. Miss. State U., Starkville, 1983-87; accreditation assessor Commn. on Accreditation for Law Enforcement, Fairfax, Va., 1984—; instr. police tng. programs Internat. City Mgmt. Assn., 1985-91. Mem. campaign com. United Way, Starkville, 1982-84; bd. dirs. Oktibbeha County United Way, 1986-87, Colquitt County, 1991—; vol. March of Dimes, Starkville, 1983-87, Big Bros./Big Sisters, 1985-86; chmn. bd. dirs. Colquitt County chpt. ARC, 1988-90, bd. dirs., 1988-94, Colquitt County United Way, 1991—; bd. dirs. Ga. Police Accreditation Coalition, 1989-91, chmn. bd. dirs., 1989-90. Recipient Outstanding Big Brother award 1986. Mem. Internat. Assn. Chiefs Police, Ga. Assn. Chiefs of Police, Am. Soc. Pub. Adminstrn., Internat. Pers. Mgmt. Assn., Moultrie Rotary Club. Republican. Avocations: tennis, numismatics. Home: H-P PO Box 2312 Moultrie GA 31776 Office: PO Box 854 Moultrie GA 31776-0854

CROUSE, JOHN OLIVER, II, journalist, publisher; b. El Paso, Tex., Jan. 16, 1931; s. John Oliver Sr. and Helen Claire (Oliver) O.; divorced; 1 child, John Oliver III. Student, U.S. Naval Acad., 1950-51, U. Fla., 1954-56; BA, U. Miami, 1957. Sportswriter Miami (Fla.) Daily News, 1957-58, boating editor, 1958; sports editor Hollywood (Fla.) Sun Tattler, 1958; editor, pub. Key Biscayne (Fla.) Jour., 1958; owner John Crouse Assocs. Pub. Rels. Agy., Miami, 1960—; assoc. editor Powerboat Mag., Van Nuys, Calif., 1968-91; founder, owner Crouse Publs., Miami, 1969—; owner antique stores, Homestead, Fla., 1989—; dir. Homestead Auto Show, 1996—. Author: Searace: A History of Offshore Powerboat Racing, 1989. Address: 20740 SW 248th St Homestead FL 33031-1502

CROUSE, JOSEPH JOHN, marketing researcher, retired journalist; b. Cin., Nov. 10, 1924; m. Shirley Wray Henriott; 3 children. BJ, U. Mo., 1950. Reporter Cin. Post, 1951-52; reporter WHAS, Inc., Louisville, 1952-69, dir. news, 1962-69; asst. dir., sr. cons. Urban Studies Ctr. U. Louisville, 1969-71; exec. dir. Louisville Bar Assn., 1972-76; ptnr., owner The Entertainer, 1976-81, The Chronicle, Clarksville, Ind., 1980-81; chmn. bd. Cable Advt. Networks, Inc., 1981-85; exec. dir. Louisville/Jefferson County Dem. party, 1988-91; mem. Ombudsman's office Jefferson County Cir. Ct. Clk., 1991-95; pres., owner Jay Crouse & Co., Louisville, 1969-95; ret., 1995. Contbg. author: Television Station Management; contbr. articles to profl. jours. Mem. Ky. Hist. Events Celebration Com., Gov.'s Hospitality Com., Forward Thrust, Louisville; coord. Louisville Bid Com.; exec. sec. Louisville Stadium Com.; past pres. Ky.-W.Va. chpt. Cystic Fibrosis Found. With USN, 1943-46, 51-52. Mem. Radio TV News Dirs. Assn. (past pres.), Radio TV News Dirs. Found. (past pres.), Soc. Profl. Journalists (pres. Louisville profl. chpt., dir. region 5).

CROUSE, MAURICE ALFRED, history educator; b. Lincolnton, N.C., Feb. 15, 1934; s. T.M. and Essie Pauline (Goodson) C.; m. Barbara Jean Hedrick, Aug. 17, 1958; children: Melanie, Alison, Emily. BS, Davidson Coll., 1956; MA, Northwestern U., 1957, PhD, 1964; MS, U. Memphis, 1986. Asst. prof. history U. Memphis, 1962-66, assoc. prof. history, 1966-72, prof. history, 1972—. Author: The Public Treasury of Colonial South Carolina, 1977. 1st lt. U.S. Army, 1957-59. Mem. AAUP, Am. Hist. Assn., Orgn. Am. Historians, S.C. Hist. Soc. Home: 1595 Wheaton St Memphis TN 38117 Office: U Memphis Dept History Memphis TN 38152

CROUSE, TED, grocery company executive; b. 1935. With Marsh Supermarkets, Indpls., 1966-80; pres. Lewis Grocer Co., Indianola, Miss., 1980—, Jackson, Markets, Inc., Indianola, 1990—; also pres. southeast region Supervalue, Atlanta, 1995—. Office: Lewis Grocer Co Hwy 49 Indianola MS 38751-2632 Office: Supervalue PO Box 105212 Atlanta GA 30348*

CROUT, ROBERT RHODES, historian, educator; b. Augusta, Ga., Aug. 5, 1946; s. Clarence Jefferson and Rita Perry (Herring) C. BA, Augusta Coll., 1968; MA, U. Ga., 1969, PhD, 1977. Co-editor Papers of Lafayette Cornell U., Ithaca, N.Y., 1978-81; assoc. editor Papers of Jefferson Princeton (N.J.) U., 1982-83; assoc. editor Papers of James Madison U. Va., Charlottesville, 1984-87; asst. prof. history Charleston (S.C.) So. U., 1989-93, assoc. prof. history, 1993—; vis. lectr. U. S.C., Aiken, 1987-88; vis. asst. prof. Oreg. State U., Corvallis, 1988-89. Co-author: Historical Dictionary of Algeria, 1981; editor: Papers of the Marquis de Lafayette, 1981—. Sec. Am. Friends of Lafayette, 1991-94, 1st v.p., 1995-96, pres. 1996—; mem. program com. So. Hist. Assn., 1993-95. Recipient Chinard prize Soc. for French Hist. Studies, 1980; Fulbright-Hays fellow, 1973-74, NEH summer fellow, 1995. Mem. Societe d'Histoire Moderne, Am. Hist. Assn., Manuscript Soc. Episcopalian. Office: Charleston So U PO Box 118087 Charleston SC 29423-8087

CROUTHAMEL, THOMAS GROVER, SR., editor; b. Berkeley, Calif., Sept. 10, 1930; s. Martin Luther and Elizabeth (Grover) C.; m. Madalene Donati, Sept. 6, 1954; children: Thomas Grover Jr., Annalise. BS, Thiel Coll., 1953. Sr. drug investigator FDA, L.A. and Edison, N.J., 1958-81; pres. Thomas G. Crouthamel, Inc., Bradenton, Fla., 1981—; ptnr. Crouthamel & Crouthamel, Bradenton, 1983-93; treas. Crouthamel Enterprises, Inc., Liberty Hill, Tex., 1986-92; sr. editor Keystone Press, Bradenton, 1982—. Author: Auditing EtO, 1982, It's OK, 1986, A History of Trailer Estates, 1987; When the Unthinkable Happens, 1995; contbr. articles to profl. jours. Cubmaster Boy Scouts Am., Pomona, Calif., 1963, committeeman, Spotswood, N.J., 1968-76, adult adviser Explorer Post, 1976-79; trustee Spotswood Libr. Bd., 1970-79; co-leader Compassionate Friends, Sarasota, Fla., 1984-90, chpt. advisor, facilitator, Englewood, Fla., 1989-91. With U.S. Army, 1953-55. Mem. Parenteral Drug Assn., Internat. Narcotics Officers Assn., The Authors Guild, AAAS, Toastmasters (pres. 1969-71), Masons (high priest local chpt. 1967). Office: PO Box 6163 Bradenton FL 34281-6163

CROW, CHARLES DELMAR, human resources manager, consultant; b. Southerland, Nebr., Oct. 16, 1945; s. Elmer Joseph and Ruth V. (Wood) C.; m. Imalee Ruth Smith, July 1, 1967; 1 child, Annette Lynn. BA, Southern Nazarene U., Oklahoma City, 1968; D of Ministry, Nazarene Theol. Sem., 1971; DD, Phillips U., Enid, Okla., 1985. Gen. mgr. E.J. Crow Constrn. Co., Paxton, Nebr., 1971-73; adminstrv. asst. Nazarene World Hdqrs., Kansas City, Mo., 1973-76; cons. Fuller Evangelistic Assn., Pasadena, Calif., 1976-77; alumni adminstr. Southern Nazarene U., Bethany, Okla., 1977-80; cons. Specialty Resources, Oklahoma City, 1980-83; counselor, human resource devel. Bethany First Nazarene Ch., 1983-87; ops. cons. Assoc. Med. Profls., Oklahoma City, 1987—. Home: 6253 Cypress Grove Oklahoma City OK 73162-3426 Office: Assoc Med Profls 5116 N Portland Ave Oklahoma City OK 73112-2055

CROW, HAROLD EUGENE, physician, family medicine educator; b. Farber, Mo., Jan. 17, 1933; s. Leslie J. and Laura L. (Sparks) C.; m. Mary Kay Krenke, July 5, 1974; children—Janet L., Jason P. MD, U. Mo., 1963. Diplomate Am. Bd. Family Practice, Am. Bd. Med. Examiners. Intern E.W. Sparrow Hosp., Lansing, Mich., 1963-64; pvt. practice medicine specializing in family practice Lansing, 1964-70; dir. family practice residency E.W. Sparrow Hosp., Lansing, Mich., 1970-82; chmn. dept. family and community medicine Sch. Medicine U. Nev., Reno, 1982-87, dir. office Rural Health Sch. Medicine, 1984-87; med. dir. S.W. Med. Assocs., Reno, 1987-88; dir. Lynchburg (Va.) Family Practice Resident Program, 1988-96; dir. Outer Banks Project East Carolina U. Sch. of Medicine, Nags Head, N.C., 1996—; dir. Outer Banks Edn. and Program Devel. Project. Developer non-rotational residency model for family practice tng., tng. model for rural med. practice; innovator computerized health info. systems for family physicians. Numerous civic activities. With U.S. Army, 1955-57. Mem. Am. Coll. Phys. Exec., numerous profl. assns. Presbyterian. Home: 2604 Bridge Ln Nags Head NC 27959-9693

CROWDER, BONNIE WALTON, small business owner, composer; b. Lafayette, Tenn., Apr. 14, 1916; d. Edward Samuel Bailey and Nannie Elizabeth (Goad) Walton; m. Reggie Ray Crowder, Nov. 19, 1936; 1 child, Rita Faye. Grad., Nashville Beauty Coll. Owner, operator Bonnie's Beauty Salon, Tampa, Fla. Composer: A Man of Faith, 1988, This Miracle, 1988, (with Willard E. Walton) God Bless Our President, 1988, Awake, Arise America, 1989, Touching My Jesus, 1990, (with Willard E. Walton) Muscle Jerky Boogie, 1992. Mem. ch. choir, Tampa; mem. Bus. and Profl. Women's Chorus, 1960's and 70's, U. South Fla. Community Chorus, 1973-81. Mem. Beta Sigma Phi. Office: Bonnie's Beauty Salon 7230 Us Highway 301 S Riverview FL 33569-4387

CROWDER, HENRY ALVIN, military officer; b. Panama City, Fla., Aug. 30, 1953; s. Henry Ford and Margaret Ann (Bland) C.; m. Beth Marie Burlingame, Apr. 16, 1977; children: Heather Elizabeth, Jeremy Allen. Grad. high sch., Beckley, W.Va.; student, various univs., 1975-94, various mil. edn. programs. Enlisted U.S. Army, 1974, advanced through grades to chief warrant officer IV, 1995; order of battle analyst 502d Army Security Agy. Group, Augsburg, Fed. Republic Germany, 1974-75; combat intelligence analyst 856th ASA Co. 3d Armored Div., Frankfurt, Fed. Republic Germany, 1975-77; intelligence analyst, hdqrs. U.S. Army Field Artillery Ctr. and Sch., Ft. Sill, Okla., 1977-79; non-commd. officer in charge intelligence ctr. 2d M.I. 2d Inf. Div., Korea, 1979-80; team non-commd. officer in charge intelligence prodn. 504th M.I. Group III Corps, Ft. Hood, Tex., 1980-81; order of battle technician 9th Inf. Div., Ft. Lewis, Wash., 1981-84, 1st Armored Div., Ansbach, Fed. Republic Germany, 1984-87; all source intelligence technician 513th Mil. Intelligence Bridgade/3rd U.S. Army/U.S. Forces Cen. Command, Ft. Monmouth, N.J., 1987-90; sr. all source intelligence technician Ops. Desert Shield, Desert Storm U.S. Army ARCENT/U.S. Forces CENTCOM, Saudi Arabia, 1990-91; sr. all source intelligence technician 513th Intel Support Element/3d U.S. Army/U.S. Forces CENTCOM, Ft. McPherson, Ga., 1991-96; instr. U.S. Army Warrant Officer Career Ctr., Ft. Rucker, Ala., 1996—. Asst. pack leader, asst. scoutmaster, active Atlanta coun. Order of the Arrow Boy Scouts Am. Decorated Bronze Star; named Outstanding Young Man of Am. U.S. Jaycees, 1982. Mem. U.S. Army Warrant Officers Assn. (sec. Ansbach chpt. 1984-87, ways and means chmn. European region 1986-87, ways and means chmn. Jersey Shore-Ft. Monmouth chpt. 1989-91, greater Atlanta chpt. 1992-96, Ft. Rucker chpt. 1996—). Office: Commandant Attn ATZQ-WCC-GS (CW4 Crowder) 5302 Outlaw St Fort Rucker AL 36362-5000

CROWDER, JULIAN ANTHONY, optometrist; b. Asheville, N.C., May 7, 1950; s. Olfa N. and Helen (Roberts) C.; m. Paula Herda; children: Heidi Michelle, Winston Roberts. AB in Chemistry, U. N.C., 1972; OD, So. Coll. Optometry, 1978. Pvt. practice optometry Candler, N.C., 1979—; mem. Channel 13 News Med. Adv. Bd., Asheville; mem. community adv. panel BASF, Enka, N.C.; mem. adv. bd. Laser Ctr., Inc., Toronto, Can. Mem. Am. Optometric Assn., N.C. State Optometric Soc. (trustee 1990-93, v.p. 1993-94, exec. coun.), Mountain Dist. Optometric Assn. (pres. 1989-93), Southeastern Coun. Optometrists, Enka-Candler Bus. Assn. (pres. 1986). Republican. Methodist. Home: 172 Weston Rd Arden NC 28704-3109 Office: 1431 Smokey Park Hwy Candler NC 28715-8237

CROWDER, LENA BELLE, retired special education educator; b. Winston-Salem, N.C., Apr. 4, 1931; d. Henry Lee and Janie (Woods) Thomas; m. Raymond Crowder, June 12, 1954; 1 child, Rayonette Janease. BS in Edn., Winston Salem State U., 1952; MS in Edn., Agrl. and Tech. Coll., 1959. Cert. elem. edn. tchr., N.C. Tchr. 1st grade Early County Sch. System, Blakely, Ga., 1953-56; tchr. kindergarten Thomas-Anderson Kindergarten, Winston-Salem, 1956-57, 58-60, 61-62; tchr. 1st grade Beaufort (S.C.) County Schs., 1957-58; tchr. Chapel Hill (N.C.) City Sch. System, 1960-61, Forsyth County Sch. System, Winston-Salem, 1961-62, 1962-67; tchr. Winston-Salem/Forsyth County Schs., 1967-93, ret., 1993. Precinct election recorder Winston-Salem/Forsyth County Election Bd., 1961; rec. fin. sec. Mt. Zion Bapt. Ch. Adult Sunday Sch., Winston Salem, 1977, 90-91, 95—; supporter Crisis Control Ministry, Winston-Salem, 1982—; participant neighborhood watch system Winston-Salem Police Dept.; chairperson sch. involvement projects ARC, 1991-92. Mem. NEA, Nat. Assn. Univ. Women, Coun. Exceptional Children, Nat. Women of Achievement (rec. sec. 1991—), Assn. Classroom Tchrs. Democrat. Home: 1140 Rich Ave Winston Salem NC 27101-3432

CROWE, DAVID M., history educator; b. Norfolk, Va., Sept. 20, 1943; m. Kathryn Moore Crowe; children: Rebecca, John. BA, Southeastern La. Coll., 1966; MA, Miss. State U., 1967; PhD, U. Ga., 1974. Lectr. history DeKalb Coll., Atlanta, 1972-74, U. Ga., Athens, 1970-74; archivist Nat. Archives of U.S., Washington, 1974-77; prof. history Elon Coll., N.C., 1977—; cons., reader, rsch. support scheme Ctrl. European U., Prague, 1995; reader U.S. Dept. Edn., 1989-96; expert witness U.S. vs. Markovitch, Seattle, 1994. Author: Gypsies of Eastern Europe and Russia, 1995, Baltic States and Great Powers, 1993, World War I and Europe in Crisis, 1990, co-author Gypsies of Eastern Europe, 1991. Chmn. N.C. Coun. on the Holocaust, Raleigh, 1991—; mem. edn. com. U.S. Holocaust Meml. Mus., Washington, 1990—; spkrs. bur. mem. N.C. Humanities Coun., Greensboro, 1994—. Mem. Assn. for Study of Nationalities (v.p.), Assn. Advancement of Slavic Studies, Phi Kappa Phi (chpt. pres. elect 1995—), Phi Alpha Theta (treas.), Omicron Delta Kappa. Episcopalian. Home: 3505 Henderson Rd Greensboro NC 27410 Office: Dept of History Elon Coll Elon College NC 27244

CROWE, HAL SCOTT, chiropractor; b. Atlanta, Apr. 19, 1953; s. Hugh Lee and Dorothy Elizabeth (Cooke) C.; m. PiHsiou Hsu, Mar. 29, 1980; children: Hal Scott Jr., Colleen Jao. Student, Johns Hopkins U., 1971-72, Ga. State U., 1973-76, 78-80; D of Chiropractic, Life Chiropractic Coll., 1983; post D. in Chiropractic Neurology, Logan Chiropractic Coll., 1992. Diplomate Nat. Bd. Chiropractic Examiners; cert. chiropractic orthospinologist, cert. chiropractic neurologist Logan Chiropractic Coll.; cert. advance open water scuba diver, cavern diver. Radiol. technician Crowe Chiropractic Offices, College Park, Ga., 1979-83; chiropractic practitioner Crowe Chiropractic Offices, College Park and Brunswick, Ga., 1983—; clin. rschr. Sweat Found., Atlanta, 1984—; resident in neurology Am. Coll. of Chiropractic Neurology, 1989-92; mem. postgrad. faculty Life Chiropractic Coll.; interim chmn. Acad. Upper Cervical Chiropractic Orgn., 1994; preceptor faculty mem. Palmer Chiropractic Coll.; participant 4th through 12th Ann. Upper Cervical Confs., 1987-95; mem. Dolphin Project Rsch. Program. Contbr. articles to profl. jours.; 2d chair trombonist Jekyll Island Big Dance Band, 1985-94, condr., 1993-95. Host Columbus Ship Replica exhibit, 1992; missionary United Meth. Ch., Petite Goave, Haiti, 1986; mem. coun. on ministries McKendree United Meth. Ch., Brunswick, 1986-87. Recipient Appreciation award Grostic Study Club, Life Chiropractic Coll., 1985. Mem. Internat. Chiropractors Assn., Ga. Coun. Chiropractic, Soc. Chiropractic Orthospinologists (cert. doctor, instr.), Chiropractic Atlas Orthogonists, Nat. Upper Cervical Chiropractic Assn., Acad. Upper Cervical Chiropractic Orgns. Inc., Reef Environ. Edn. Found., Nat. Speleological Soc. (cave diving sect.), Lions (bd. dirs. 1986-88, Lion Tamer 1986-87, presdl. appreciation award 1986, pres. 1988-89, Tail Twister 1991), Diver's Alert Network, Ian Fleming Found. Home: 792 S Beachview Dr Jekyll Island GA 31527-0638 Office: Crowe Chiropractic Offices 2321 Parkwood Dr Brunswick GA 31520-4720

CROWELL, EDWARD BROWNING, JR., medical educator; b. Hackensack, N.J., Apr. 16, 1937; s. Edward Browning Sr. and Ruth Ellen (Rogers) C.; m. Susan Templeton Brownlee, Dec. 9, 1972; children: Jonathan Browning, Virginia Brownlee. BSChemE, MIT, 1958; MD, U. Chgo., 1962. Diplomate Am. Bd. Internal Medicine, Am. Bd. Hematology. Intern U. Chgo. Clinics, 1962-63, resident in medicine, 1963-64; resident in medicine U. Wis., Madison, 1966-67, fellow hematology, 1967-69, from instr. to asst. prof. medicine, 1969-75; prof. medicine and hematology Christian Med. Coll., Ludhiana, Punjab, India, 1976-90; assoc. prof. W.Va. U. Sch. Medicine, Morgantown, 1990—. Capt. M.C., U.S. Army, 1964-66.

CROWELL, KENNETH WAYNE, hospital materials manager; b. Ashland City, Tenn., May 19, 1939; s. Jeffery L.C. and Della Pearl (Stevens) C.; m. Sandra Katherine Gaines, Nov. 22, 1961; children: Susan Reneea, Michael Wayne,. Student, U. Tenn., 1973. Shipping clk. Anderson Hickey Co., Nashville, Tenn., 1957-65; shipping coord. E.I. DuPont, Old Hickory, Tenn., 1965-71; project coord. HCA/Shield Products Co., Nashville, 1971-73; materials mgr. HCA/Raleigh Gen. Hosp., Beckley, W.Va., 1973-75; shared materials mgr. HCA/Plantation (Fla.) Gen. and Univ. Com., 1975-76; corp. materials mgr. Gen. Care Corp., Nashville, 1976-78; materials mgr. HCA Univ. Community Hosp., Tamarac, Fla., 1978-79; dir., materials mgr. Nashville Meml. Hosp., Madison, Tenn., 1980—. Chmn. sustaining membership enrollment Boy Scouts Am., Nashville, 1987-89. Mem. Tenn. Hosp. Assn. Materials Mgrs. (pres. 1986), Southeastern Hosp. Conf. Materials Mgrs. (pres. 1989), Rotary (Paul Harris fellow). Office: Nashville Meml Hosp 612 W Due West Ave Madison TN 37115-4402

CROWELL, LORENZO MAYO, historian, educator; b. Milw., June 24, 1943; s. Lorenzo Mayo and Auslaug Odella (Birkestrand) C.; m. Marianne McGrane, Dec. 31, 1973; children: Anna, Ruth, Lorenzo, James. BS in History, Air Force Acad., 1965; MA in History, Duke U., 1973, PhD in History, 1982. Commd. USAF, 1965, advanced through grades to lt. col., 1988; assoc. prof. USAF Air War Coll. USAF, Maxwell AFB, Ala., 1983-87; ret. USAF, 1988; asst. prof. Miss. State U., Mississippi State, 1988-91; assoc. prof., 1991—; adj. prof., mem. grad. faculty U. Ala., Tuscaloosa, 1984-88; adj. prof. Troy State U., Montgomery, Ala., 1987-88; lectr. in field; conf. participant. Author: Just Cause: "The Forces Involved, the Adequacy of Intelligence and Its Success as a Joint Operation", 1990; contbr. articles to profl. jours. Atlantic coun. academic assoc. NATO Discussion Series in Brussels, 1987; academic assoc. Atlantic Coun. U.S., 1986, 87. Fellow USAF, 1971-72; faculty rsch. and lecture awards Air War Coll., 1983-84; recipient Miss. State U. Provost's Spl. Teaching Project award, 1992. Mem. Am. Hist. Assn., Soc. for Mil. History, Assn. Asian Studies, Orgn. Am. Historians, Inter-Univ. Seminar on Armed Forces and Soc., So. Hist. Assn., Miss. Hist. Soc., Phi Kappa Phi, Phi Alpha Theta. Home: 1576 Pine Top St Starkville MS 39759-8255 Office: Miss State U Dept History Box H Mississippi State MS 39762

CROWELL, SHERRY DIEGEL, clinical psychologist; b. Colorado City, Tex., Oct. 19, 1951; d. Charles Ambrose and Jo Ellen (Elliot) Diegel; 1 child, Charles Michael. BA, Tex. Tech U., 1983, MA, 1985, PhD, 1992. Lic. psychologist, Tex. Sr. dir. Psychol. Clinic, Lubbock, Tex., 1987-89; psychometrist Med.-Surg. Neurology Clinic, Lubbock, 1987-89; assoc. clin. psychologist Big Spring (Tex.) State Hosp., 1987-89; psychology intern Austin (Tex.) State Hosp., 1989-90; pvt. practice psychotherapy Abilene, Tex., 1990-93; clin. psychologist Abilene Regional Mental Health Mental Retardation Ctr., 1991-93; pvt. practice psychology Abilene; cons. and chief psychologist Young County Family Resource & Advocacy Ctr., Child Advocacy of Tex., 1996—; adj. prof. psychology McMurry U., 1994—; chair symposium Tex. Assn. on Mental Retardation, 1992; presenter in field. Contbr. rsch. articles to profl. publs. Mem. adv. bd. Big Country AIDS Support Group, Abilene, 1992—; mem. Lubbock AIDS Health Care Planning Group, Lubbock, 1987-89; founding mem., trustee West Tex. AIDS Found., Lubbock, 1986-89, mentoring program, 1995—. Mem. APA, Tex. Psychol. Assn. (chair symposium 1987, 88, 92-93, Alexander award for Rsch. Excellence in Psychobiologic Field 1992), Abilene Philharmonic. Home: 1217 Ross Ave Abilene TX 79605-4230 Office: 3301 N 3rd St Ste 113 Abilene TX 79603-7033

CROWLEY, JAMES WORTHINGTON, retired lawyer, business consultant, investor; b. Cookville, Tenn., Feb. 18, 1930; s. Worth and Jessie (Officer) C.; m. Laura June Bauserman, Jan. 27, 1951; children: James Kenneth, Laura Cynthia; m. Joyce A. Goode, Jan. 15, 1966; children: John Worthington, Noelle Virginia; m. Carol Golden, Sept. 4, 1981. BA, George Washington U., 1950, LLB, 1953. Bar: D.C. 1954. Underwriter, spl. agt. Am. Surety Co. of N.Y., Washington, 1953-56; adminstrv. asst., contract adminstr. Atlantic Rsch. Corp., Alexandria, Va., 1956-59; mgr. legal dept., asst. sec., counsel Atlantic Rsch. Corp., 1959-65, sec., legal mgr., counsel, 1965-67; sec., legal mgr., counsel Susquehanna Corp. (merger with Atlantic Rsch. Corp.), 1967-70; pres., dir. Gen. Communication Co., Boston, 1962-70; v.p., gen. counsel E-Systems, Inc., 1970-95, sec., 1976-95; ret., 1995; ind. cons. bus. and fin., investor Dallas, 1995—; v.p., asst. sec., dir. Cemco, Inc.; v.p., dir. TAI, Inc., Serv-air, Inc., Greenville, Tex., Engring. Rsch. Assocs., Inc., Vienna, Va., HRB Systems, Inc., State Coll., Pa.; mem. adv. bd. sec. Internat. and Comparative Law Ctr.; v.p., sec., dir. Advanced Video Products, 1992-95; v.p., sec., gen. counsel E-Systems Med. Electronics, Inc., 1992-95. Mem. Am. Soc. Corp. Secs. (pres. Dallas regional group 1988-89, nat. dir. 1989-92), Inf. Mus. Assn., Nat. Security Indsl. Assn., Mfrs.' Alliance for Productivity and Innovation (mem. law coun.), Omicron Delta Kappa, Alpha Chi Sigma, Phi Sigma Kappa. Republican. Baptist. Home and Office: 16203 Spring Creek Rd Dallas TX 75248-3116

CROWLEY, JOHN FRANCIS, III, university dean; b. New Haven, Jan. 29, 1945; s. John Francis Jr. and Anna Cecil (Elliott) C.; m. Alice Ann Kennedy, Dec. 26, 1970; children: John Francis IV, Sarah Ann. BA in History, Art History, U. Okla., 1970, MA in Regional and City Planning, 1973, PhD in Urban Geography, 1977. Planner Lawton Urban Renewal Authority, Okla., 1971-72; dir. planning City of Seminole, Okla., 1972-73; chief planner Okla. Divsn. State Parks, Oklahoma City, 1973-74; asst. prof. environ. design U. Ga., Athens, 1974-78; exec. dir. Tulsa Metro Area Planning Commn., 1978-80; v.p., devel. Williams Realty Corp., Tulsa, 1980-87; pres. Urbantech Inc., Tulsa, 1987—; dir. Okla. Dept. of Transp., Oklahoma City, 1993-95. Mem. Tulsa County Bd. Adjustment, Tulsa, 1981-83; bd. dirs. Downtown Tulsa Unltd., 1983-89; chmn. Sales Tax Overview Com., Tulsa, 1988-90; sec. bd. trustees Tulsa County Pub. Facilities Authority, 1983-96. 1st lt. U.S. Army, 1965-69. Sara Moss faculty fellow U. Ga., 1976. Mem. Am. Inst. Cert. Planners, Am. Planning Assn., Nature Conservancy. Democrat. Roman Catholic. Home: 333 Crystal Ct Athens GA 30606

CROWLL, JOHN LEE, intelligence research specialist; b. Youngstown, Ohio, Apr. 16, 1954; s. John and Irene (Nagy) C.; m. Cynthia Ann Hasler, Apr. 29, 1995. AAS summa cum laude in Computer Info. Systems, Piedmont Va. Community Coll., 1993. Intelligence rsch. specialist U.S. Nat. Ground Intelligence Ctr., Charlottesville, Va., 1976—. Mem. Rep. Nat. Com., 1986—; assoc. mem. Va. Sheriff's Inst., 1988—. With U.S. Army, 1972-79. Decorated Commendation medal; recipient Spl. Act award Dept. of Army, 1991, Spl. Svc. award Dept. of Army Civilian Awards, 1987. Mem. Am. Def. Preparedness Assn., Assn. of Old Crows, U.S. Chess Fedn., Am. Legion. Republican. Office: Natl Ground Intelligence Ctr 220 7th St NE Charlottesville VA 22902-5307

CROWN, NANCY ELIZABETH, lawyer; b. Bronx, N.Y., Mar. 27, 1955; d. Paul and Joanne Barbara (Newman) C.; children: Rebecca, Adam. BA, Barnard Coll., 1977, MA, 1978; MEd, Columbia U., 1983; JD cum laude, Nova Law Sch., 1992. Cert. tchr.; Bar: Fla. 1992. Tchr. Sachem Sch. Dist., Holbrook, N.Y., 1978-82; v.p. mail order dept. Haber-Klein, Inc., Hicksville, N.Y., 1984-88; mgr. mdse., dir. ops. Sure Card Inc., Pompano Beach, Fla., 1988-89; legal intern Office U.S. Trustee/Dept. Justice, 1992; assoc. John T. Kinsey, P.A., Boca Raton, Fla., 1993-95; pvt. practice Nancy E. Crown, P.A., Boca Raton, Fla., 1995—. Recipient West Pub. award for acad. achievement, 1992. Mem. ABA, NAFE, Fla. Bar Assn., South Palm Beach County Women's Exec. Club, Phi Alpha Delta. Democrat. Jewish.

CROWTHER, ANN ROLLINS, dean, political science educator; b. Zanesville, Ohio, Aug. 29, 1950; d. Walter Edmund and Norma Lucille (Rollins) C. BA in English, Rollins Coll., 1972; M, EdS, U. Fla., 1975; D in Pub. Adminstrn., U. Ga., 1988. Dir. residence hall Ga. Southern U., Statesboro, 1975-78; asst. to head personnel and staff devel. dept. coop. ext. svc. U. Ga., 1978-80, acad. advisor Franklin Coll. Arts & Scis., 1980-81, grad. teaching asst. dept. polit. sci., 1981-84, instr. evening classes program, 1982-85, coord. acad. advising Franklin Coll. Arts & Scis., 1984-89, asst. dean, adj. asst. prof. polit. sci. Franklin Coll. Arts & Scis., 1989-93, assoc. dean, adj. asst. prof. polit. sci. Franklin Coll. Arts & Scis., 1993—. Mem. Am. Polit. Sci. Assn., Am. Soc. Pub. Adminstrn., Ga. Assn. Women in Edn., Nat. Acad. Advising Assn., Nat. Assn. Women in Edn., Nat. Assn. Acad. Affairs Afminstrs. Home: 270 Snapfinger Dr Athens GA 30605-4433 Office: Univ Ga Franklin Coll Arts & Scis 212 New College Athens GA 30601-1853

CROXALL, MARK Y., II, advertising executive; b. 1941. Student, Tenn. Tech. U., Cookeville, 1965-69. With Burlington Industries, N.Y.C., 1967-69, Charles Tombras & Assocs., Inc., Knoxville, Tenn., 1969-71, McDonald, Cardin, Cherry & Terrell, Nashville, 1971-73; pres. Croxall & Assocs., Inc., Chattanooga, 1973—. With U.S. Air Force, 1961-65. Office: Croxall & Assoc Inc 11777 Katy Fwy Ste 495 Houston TX 77079-1704*

CROZIER, RICHARD LEWIS, artist, educator; b. Honolulu, Dec. 28, 1944; s. Donald Orrie and Ruth (Canaday) C.; m. Marjorie Ann Pingel, July 23, 1980. BFA, U. Wash., 1968; MFA, U. Calif., Davis, 1974. Prof. fine arts U. Va., Charlottesville, 1974—. Co-author: Inventing the Landscape, 1989; paintings in permanent collections at J.B. Speed Mus., Louisville, Greenville (N.C.) Art Mus. Served with U.S. Army, 1969-70, Korea.

CRUGER, THOMAS WAYNE, chemistry educator; b. Washington, Jan. 18, 1949; s. Raymond Leslie and Glenadene (Sutton) C.; m. Jeanne Marie Reina, Aug. 3, 1983; children: Katherine Marie, Elizabeth Ann. BA in Chemistry, U. Colo., 1980; MS in Chemistry, George Mason U., 1994. Plant maintenance tech. Foliage Plant Systems, Washington, 1975-76; asst. tchr. Auraria Childcare Ctr., Denver, 1977; lab. tech. U. Colo., Denver, 1977-80; supr. Camp Dresser and McKee, Wheatridge, Colo., 1980; chemist Vitreous State Lab., Washington, 1980-81; rsch. asst. Am. Mgmt. Systems, Arlington, Va., 1981-86; tchr. chemistry, sci. dept. chmn. Arlington Pub. Schs., 1986—; track and field coach Wakefield High Sch., Arlington, 1991—, chess team sponsor, 1987—. Patient care vol. Hospice of Northern Va., Arlington, 1987-92. With U.S. Army, 1971-75. Rsch. grantee George Mason U., Naval Rsch. Lab., 1992. Mem. Nat. Sci. Tchrs. Assn., Va. High Sch. Coaches Assn. Republican. Roman Catholic. Home: 12607 Colby Dr Woodbridge VA 22192-2108 Office: Wakefield High Sch 4901 S Chesterfield Rd Arlington VA 22206-1018

CRUIKSHANK, THOMAS HENRY, energy services and engineering executive; b. Lake Charles, La., Nov. 3, 1931; s. Louis James and Helene L. (Little) C.; m. Ann Coe, Nov. 17, 1955; children: Thomas Henry, Kate Martin, Stuart Coe. B.A., Rice U., 1952; postgrad., U. Tex. Law Sch., 1952-53, U. Houston Law Sch., 1953-55. Bar: Tex.; C.P.A., Tex. Accountant Arthur Andersen & Co., Houston, 1953-55, 58-60; mem. firm Vinson & Elkins, Houston, 1961-69; v.p. Halliburton Co., Dallas, 1969-72, sr. v.p., 1972-80, exec. v.p., 1980, pres., chief exec. officer subs. Otis Engring. Corp., 1980-81, pres., 1981-83, pres., chief exec. officer, 1983-89, chmn., CEO, 1989-95, dir., 1977-95; bd. dirs. Goodyear Tire & Rubber Co., Williams Cos., Inc., Ctrl. and Southwest Corp., Seagull Energy, Inc., Lehman Bros. Holdings Inc.; former mem. Nat. Petroleum Coun., policy com. Bus. Roundtable. Pres. Jr. Achievement, Dallas, 1974-76, chmn., 1976-78, mem. nat. bd. dirs., 1976-95, chmn. 1989-90; bd. dirs. Up With People; trustee Caiif. Inst. Tech. Lt. (j.g.) USNR, 1955-58. Mem. ABA, Tex. Bar Assn., Am. Petroleum Inst., Dallas Country Club (bd. govs. 1977-79, 86-88), River Oaks Country Club (Houston), Pine Valley Golf Club (N.J.), Haig Point Country Club (S.C.), Preston Trail Golf Club, Peninsula Club (N.C.), Grandfather Golf and Country Club (N.C.), Eldorado Country Club (Calif.). Home: 3508 Marquette St Dallas TX 75225-5015 Office: Sterling Plz Ste 860 5949 Sherry Ln Dallas TX 75225

CRUMB, DUANE JAMES, organization executive; b. Watertown, N.Y., Dec. 10, 1945; s. Donald Jacob and Helen (Coulter) C.; m. Joyce Elaine Harmon, May 11, 1974; children: Danita Jo, Danae Joy. AA, Pasadena City Coll., 1965; BA, U. Redlands, 1968. Asst. v.p. United Calif. Bank, L.A., 1970-73; asst. v.p., br. mgr. Riverside (Calif.) Nat. Bank, 1973-77; adminstr. Harvest Christian Fellowship, Riverside, 1977-85; press sec. U.S. Ho. of Reps., Washington, 1985-87; exec. dir. Am. Inst. for Teen AIDS Prevention, Ft. Worth, 1987—; pres. Teen Choices, Inc., Ft. Worth, 1995—; presenter numerous parent seminars and tchr. tng. programs; tchr. on AIDS, STD/pregnancy prevention pub. schs., Ho Chi Minh City, Vietnam, tchr. trainer, curriculum writer, summer 1996. Author: Positive HIV/AIDS Education, 1993, Developing Your Church AIDS Policy, 1994; prodr., spkr. video It's Your Choice, 1990, 92, 95. Bd. dirs., chmn. Manna Ministries, 1988-92; bd. dirs., v.p. Christian AIDS Svcs. Alliance, 1989—; bd. dirs., sec., treas. Celebrate Kids, Inc., 1991—; bd. dirs. Found. Pharmacists for AIDS Edn., 1992-96; trustee Echoing Hills Village, Ohio, 1995—. Mem. Internat. Soc. for AIDS Edn. Office: Teen Choices PO Box 136116 Fort Worth TX 76136

CRUMBLEY, ARTHUR JACKSON, III, cardiothoracic surgeon; b. Atlanta, Oct. 24, 1948; s. Arthur Jackson Jr. and Virginia Elizabeth (Locherer) C.; m. Anne Bryce Grand, Oct. 26, 1976 (div. 1982); m. Patricia Ellen Turner, June 26, 1991; 1 child, Arthur Jackson IV. BS cum laude, Davidson Coll., 1970; MD, Washington U., 1974. Intern Duke U. Med. Ctr., Durham, N.C., 1974-75, resident in surgery, 1975-76; resident in surgery U. Minn., Mpls., 1979-86; assoc. prof. surgery Med. U. S.C., Charleston, 1986—, dir. cardiac transplantation, 1987—, dir. thoracic organ transplantation, 1992—; cardiothoracic surgeon Ralph H. Johnson Va Med. Ctr., Charleston, 1986—. Contbr. articles to profl. jours. Capt. U.S. Army, 1976-79. Cardiovascular and Thoracic Surgery fellow U. Minn., 1984-86, Cardiac Transplantation fellow, 1986. Fellow ACS; mem. Soc. Thoracic Surgeons, So. Thoracic Surg. Assn., Internat. Soc. for Heart and Lung Transplantation, Am. Heart Assn. (basic sci. coun.), Assn. for Acad. Surgery, S.C. Surg. Soc., AMA, Charleston County Med. Soc., S.C. Med. Soc., Alpha Epsilon Delta, Gamma Sigma Epsilon, Scabbard and Blade, Phi Beta Kappa, Alpha Omega Alpha, Phi Kappa Phi. Presbyterian. Office: Med U SC 171 Ashley Ave Charleston SC 29425-0001

CRUMBLEY, DEIDRE HELEN, anthropology educator; b. Phila., Dec. 12, 1947; d. Joseph Jr. and Bernice Beverly (Nicholson) C. BA magna cum laude, Temple U., 1970; M of Theol. Studies, Harvard U., 1978; MA in Anthropology, Northwestern U., 1984, PhD in Anthropology, 1989. Jr. rsch. fellow Inst. African Studies U. Ibadan, 1982-84, asst. lectr. dept. archeology and anthropology, 1984-86; asst. prof., coord. African and African-Am. studies Rollins Coll., 1988-91; prof. dept. anthropology U. Fla., Gainesville, 1991—. Pres.'s scholar Temple U., 1970, Harvard U. scholar, 1976; Lilly fellow, 1979, Fulbright Hays Dissertation fellow, 1985, Ford Found. postdoctoral fellow , 1991-92, Carter G. Woodson affiliate, U. Va., 1996-97. Mem. Am. Anthrop. Assn., Am. Acad. Religion, Assn. Black Anthropologists, Nat. Coun. for Black Studies, Fulbright Assn., African Assn. for Study of Religion, N.Am. Soc. for African and African Diaspera Philosophy and Studies. Office: U Fla Dept African Studies Gainesville FL 32605

CRUMBLEY, ESTHER HELEN KENDRICK, realtor, retired secondary education educator; b. Okeechobee, Fla., Oct. 3, 1928; d. James A. and Corrine (Burney) Kendrick; m. Chandler Jackson, Oct. 24, 1949; children: Pamela E., Chandler A., William J. BS in Math. Edn., Ga. So. Coll., 1966; M in Math., Jacksonville (Fla.) U., 1979. Cert. secondary edn. tchr., Ga. Secondary edn. tchr. Camden County Bd. Edn., St. Mary's, Ga., 1958-92, ret.; realtor Watson Realty, St. Mary's, 1985—; valedictorian H.S., 1946, dept. chairperson Camden H.S., St. Mary's, 1966-72; pres., sec., treas. Camden GMA, St. Mary's, 1976-78. Area contact person Max Cleand Sec. of State, Atlanta, 1982—; councilwoman City of St. Mary's, 1979-86, mayor pro tem, 1981-86. Named Star Tchr., 1972, Camden GMA, 1979-88. Mem. Camden Ga. Assn. Educators (pres. 1976, sec.-treas. 1977-78, star tchr. 1972), PAGE (biog. com. rep. 1984-92, 1992 retired, named outstanding 8th dist. bldg. rep.), Camden Gen. Mcpl. Assn. (pres., sec.-treas. 1979-88), fin. and budget coms.), Math. Assn., Internat. Platform Assn. Internat. Dictionary Ctr., ABI. Republican. Baptist. Home: RR 3 Box 810 Folkston GA 31537-9729

CRUMLEY, JOHN WALTER, lawyer; b. Ft. Worth, July 20, 1944; s. Frank E. and Mary Cecilia (Gaudin) C.; m. Paulette Gavin, July 25, 1970; children: John Gavin, Brian Christopher. BS, Springhill Coll., 1967; JD, So. Meth. U., 1970, M of Comparative Law, 1973. Bar: Tex. 1970, U.S. Dist. Ct. (no. dist.) Tex. 1976, U.S. Ct. Appeals (5th cir.) 1981, U.S. Tax Ct. 1988. Assoc. McBryde & Bogel, Ft. Worth, 1973-75; ptnr. Crumley, Murphy & Shrull, Inc., Ft. Worth, 1975-85, Tracy, Crumley & Holland, Ft. Worth, 1985-92; prin. John W. Crumley, P.C., Ft. Worth, 1992—; mem. bd. dirs. Goodrich Ctr. for the Deaf, 1995—; vice chair Bingo Advisor Com., 1995-96. Mem. steering com. Tarrant County Vol. Guardianship, Ft. Worth, 1986-87; bd. dirs. Camp Fire, Ft. Worth, 1985-87, Cath. Social Svcs., Ft. Worth, 1985-86. Capt. U.S. Army, 1970-72. Mem. State Bar Tex., Tarrant County Bar Assn., Tex. Assn. Def. Counsel, Tex. Assn. Diocesan Attys., U.S. Conf. Diocesan Attys. Assn., Serra Club (pres. Ft. Worth club 1985-86), KC (state adv. 1986-91, 95—). Office: 316 University Ctr 1300 S University Dr Fort Worth TX 76107-5735

CRUNDEN, ROBERT MORSE, history educator; b. Jersey City, Dec. 23, 1940; s. Allan Bernard and Marjorie (Morse) C.; children: Evelyn Anne, Rebecca Jane. BA magna cum laude, Yale U., 1962; PhD, Harvard U., 1967. From asst. to full prof. history and Am. studies U. Tex., Austin, 1967—; dir. Am. Studies Rsch. Ctr., Hyderabad, India, 1982-84; dir. program in Am. studies U. Tex., Austin, 1985-90; guest prof. dept. English, U. Würzburg, Germany, 1979, 82; sr. Fulbright lectr. dept. history La Trobe U., Australia, 1978; bicentennial prof. Am. studies U. Helsinki, Finland, 1976-77, 91-92; lectr. in field. Editor: The Superfluous Men: Conservative Critics of American Culture, 1900-1945, 1977, Traffic of Ideas Between India and America, 1985; editor Indian Jour. of Am. Studies, 1982-84; author: The Mind and Art of Albert Jay Nock, 1964, A Hero in Spite of Himself: Brand Whitlock in Art, Politics and War, 1969, From Self to Society 1919-1941, 1972, Ministers of Reform: The Progressives' Achievement in American Civilization, 1889-1920, A Brief History of American Culture, 1990, American Salons: Encounters with European Modernism, 1885-1917, 1993; contbr. articles to profl. jours. Recipient H.G. Porthan prize Finnish Hist. Soc., 1991, OHIOANA award for best biography of an Ohio figure, 1970. Mem. Soc. Am. Historians, Western History Assn. (award of merit 1974). Office: Univ of Texas Dept History Austin TX 78712

CRUSE, IRMA BELLE RUSSELL, writer; b. Hackneyville, Ala., May 3, 1911; d. Charles Henry and Nellie Dunn (Ledbetter) Russell; m. Jesse Clyde Cruse, Dec. 22, 1931; children: Allan Baird, Howard Russell. Student, Birmingham So. Coll., 1927-28; corr. student, U. Chgo., U. Wis., U. Minn., intermittently 1958-68; AB, U. Ala., 1976; MA in English, Samford U., 1981, MA in History, 1984. With So. Bell and successor South Cen. Bell, Birmingham, Ala., 1928-44, 54-76, pub. rels. supr., 1965-68, rate supr., 1968-76; free lance writer, 1956—. Editor: The Ala. Bapt. Historian, 1986-89; contbr. articles to various publs. Bd. dirs. Festival of Arts, Birmingham, 1970-73, Birmingham Council Christian Edn.; v.p. Birmingham Council Clubs, 1973-74; pres. Jefferson County Radio and TV Council, 1971-72; mem. Gov.'s Commn. Employment of Handicapped; chmn. oral history program Ala. Bapt. Hist. Commn., 1985-89; clk. Mt. Brook Bapt. Ch., 1986-88. Recipient numerous awards including Freedoms Found., 1967-69, Silver Bowl for Lit. award Birmingham Festival of Arts, 1988; named Beautiful Activist, 1972; named to Ala. Voter Hall of Fame, 1986, Ala. Bapt. Historian of Yr., 1990; named Outstanding Alumna U. Ala., 1990-91. Mem. AAUW (chmn. women's work/women's worth Birmingham chpt. 1987-89), Birmingham Bus. Communicators, Ala. Writers' Conclave (pres. 1973-74), Met. Bus. and Profl. Women (pres. 1970-71, woman of achievement 1970-71), Women in Communications (pres. 1970-71), Birmingham Bus. Communicators (pres. 1968-69), Telephone Pioneers Am. (editor newsletter 1970-74, pres. Birmingham South Life Mem. Club 1986-87, historian Ala. chpt. 1987-90), Ala. State Poetry Soc. (program chmn. 1972-74, editor newsletter 1976-78), Women's C. of C. (2d v.p. 1978-79), Ala. Bapt. Hist. Commn., Freedoms Found. of Valley Forge, Birmingham Geneal. Soc., Salvation Army Women's Aux. (chaplain 1988-89), Women's C. of C., Nat. League Am. Pen Women (1st v.p. programs Birmingham chpt. 1990-91, historian 1991-92), Arlington Hist. Assn., Quota Club of Birmingham (pres. 1976-77), Sigma Tau Delta, Phi Kappa Phi, Phi Alpha Theta. Home: 702 27th Pl S Birmingham AL 35233-3410

CRUSE, JULIUS MAJOR, JR., pathologist, educator; b. New Albany, Miss., Feb. 15, 1937; s. Julius Major and Effie (Davis) C. BA, BS with honors, U. Miss., 1958; D.Microbiology with honors (Fulbright fellow), U. Graz, Austria, 1960; MD, U. Tenn., 1964, Ph.D. in Pathology (USPHS fellow), 1966, USPHS postdoctoral fellow, 1964-67. Mem. faculty U. Miss. Med. Sch., 1967—; prof. immunology, biology Grad. Sch., 1967-74, prof. pathology, 1974—, asso. prof. microbiology, 1974—, dir. grad. studies program in pathology, 1974—, dir. clin. immunopathology, 1978—, dir. immunopathology sect., 1978—, dir. tissue typing lab., 1980—, assoc. prof. medicine, 1989—; lectr. pathology U. Tenn. Coll. Medicine, 1967-74; aj. prof. immunology Miss. Coll., 1977—; mem. sci. adv. bd. Immuno Tech. Corp., L.A.; active FDA Expert Panel on Alternatives to Silicone Breast Implants, 1994—. Author: Immunology Examination Review Book, 1971, rev. edit., 1975, Introduction to Immunology, 1977, Principles of Immunopathology, 1979; editor-in-chief Immunologic Research, 1981—, Pathology and Immunopathology Research, 1982-90, Concepts in Immunopathology, 1985—, The Year in Immunology, 1984—, Pathobiology: Jour. Immunopathology, 1990—, Molecular and Cellular Biology, 1990, Transgenics: Biological Analysis Through DNA Transfer; contbns. to Microbiology and Immunology; editor Immunomodulation of Neoplasia, Antigenic Variation: Molecular and Genetic Mechanisms of Relapsing Disease, 1987, Autoimmunoregulation and Autoimmune Disease, 1987; The Year in Immunology, vol. 1, 1984-85, vol. 2, 1985-86, The Year in Immunology, vol. 3, 1987, The Year in Immunology, vols. 4, 5, 1988, vol. 6, 1989-90, Genetic Basis of Autoimmune Disease, 1988, Cellular Aspects of Autoimmunity, 1988, Therapy of Autoimmune Diseases, 1989, B Lymphocytes: Function and Regulation, Conjugate Vaccines, 1989, Molecules and Cells of Immunity, 1990, Immunoregulation and Autoimmunity, 1986, Organ-Based Autoimmune Diseases, 1985, Autoimmunity: Basic Concepts, Systematic and Selected Organ-Specific Diseases, 1985, Clinical and Molecular Aspects of Autoimmune Diseases, 1990, Immunoregulatory Cyrokines and Cell Growth, 1989, Complement Profiles, 1992; author chpts. to books on immunology; co-editor: Self-Nonself Discrimination in the Immune System, 1992, Complement Profiles, vol. 1, 1992, Illustrated Dictionary of Immunology, 1995, Atlas of Immunology, 1996-97; contbr. articles to profl. jours. Recipient Pathologists award in continuing edn. Coll. Am. Pathologists-Am. Soc. Clin. Pathologists, 1976; Julius M. Cruse collection in immunology established in his honor Middleton Med. Libr., U. Wis., Madison, 1979, Julius M. Cruse Modern Lit. collection, Gen. Theol. Sem. (Episcopal), N.Y.C.; Wilson Found. grantee, 1990-95, 93-94. Fellow AAAS, Royal Soc. Promotion Health, Am. Acad. Microbiology, Am. Soc. for Histocompatibility and Immunogenetics (chmn. publs. com. 1987-95), Intercontinental Biog. Assn.; mem. AMA (Physicians Recognition award 196-75), Clin. Immunology Soc., Am. Inst. Biol. Scis., Am. Soc. Clin. Pathologists, Can. Soc. Microbiologists, N.Y. Acad. Scis. Exptl. Biology and Medicine, Soc. Francaise d'Immunologie, Reticuloendothelial Soc., Transplantation Soc., Electron Microscopy Soc. Am., Am. Assn. History Medicine, The Paul Ehrlich Soc., Am. Assn. Pathologists, Am. Chem. Soc., Brit. Soc. Immunology, Can. Soc. Immunology, Am. Soc. Microbiology, Internat. Acad. Pathology, Am. Assn. Immunologists (historian 1990—), Sigma Xi, Phi Kappa Phi, Phi Eta Sigma, Alpha Epsilon Delta, Gamma Sigma Epsilon, Beta Beta Beta. Episcopalian. Office: U Miss Med Ctr Dept Pathology 2500 N State St Jackson MS 39216-4500

CRUSE, REX BEACH, JR., lawyer; b. Sherman, Tex., July 2, 1941; s. Rex Beach and Mary Ellen (Sim) C.; m. Maebeth Ann Brock, Mar. 19, 1958 (div. 1975); 1 child, Vicki Ann.; m. Carol A. Schaller, July 14, 1977 (div. 1983). BBA highest honors, U. Tex., 1962, PhD in Bus. Adminstrn., 1973; JD, St. Mary's U., San Antonio, 1988. Bar: Tex. 1989, N.Y. 1989, D.C. 1991, U.S. Dist. Ct. (we. dist.) Tex. 1990, U.S. Tax Ct. 1990, U.S. Bankruptcy Ct. 1990, U.S. Ct. Internat. Trade 1993, U.S. Ct. Fed. Claims 1996; CFP; CPA. Various Am. Inst. CPA's, N.Y., 1964-75, mng. dir., 1976-83; dean Sch. Accountancy U. Hawaii, Honolulu, 1983-84; pvt. practice acctg. San Antonio, 1985-89, pvt. practice law, 1989-96; assoc. Duncan, Ulman, Weakley, Glass & Bressler, Inc., San Antonio, 1996—. Pres. San Antonio Coun. on Alcohol and Drug Abuse, 1994-96; bd. dirs. Unicorn Ctrs., Inc., 1994-96; sec. Start Found. Mem. ABA, AICPA (cert. spl. merit 1992), Nat. Health Lawyers Assn., State Bar Tex. (The Coll. of the State of Bar of Tex.), Barra de Abogados de Mex. y Tex., Tex. Soc. CPAs (Outstanding com. chmn. 1993-94), San Antonio Bar Assn. (med.-legal liaison com.). Republican. Methodist. Home: 8401 N New Braunfels # 106 San Antonio TX 78209-1110 Office: Duncan Ulman Weakley Glass & Bressler 600 Navarro Ste 1000 San Antonio TX 78205-1838

CRUSEMANN, F(REDERICK) ROSS, advertising agency official; b. Ft. Worth, Nov. 9, 1953; s. Frederick Ross and Louise (Russell) C. BA, Austin Coll., 1975; MBA, Tex. Christian U., 1977. Supr. Ben E. Keith Co., Ft. Worth, 1977-78; project dir. Parmer Cos., Ft. Worth, 1978-80; mktg. mgr. Shoreline Products, Ft. Worth, 1980-85; mktg. cons. Dallas, 1986; mgr. programs visibility FW divsn. Gen. Dynamics, Ft. Worth, 1986-89; dir. mktg. Motel 6, Dallas, 1989-94; mgmt. supr. Peter H. Mayer Advt., Baton Rouge, 1994—. Sponsor Spl. Olympics Internat., Washington, 1992—, Dallas Symphony Assn., 1992—, Sta. KERA-PBS Affiliation, Dallas, 1993—. Recipient Commendation award Radio Advt. Bur., N.Y.C., 1993. Mem. Am. Mktg. Assn. (Tomy award 1989), Assn. Nat. Advertisers (com. chmn. 1989—), Travel Industry Assn. (com. mem. 1992—, nat. conf. planning com. 1992—, POW WOW internat. planning com. 1993—), Am. Hotel and Motel Assn. (comms. com. 1991—), Hotel Sales and Mktg. Assn. Internat. (Adrian award 1989—). Home: 6403 Ellsworth Ave Dallas TX 75214-2723 Office: Peter H Mayer Advt 5757 Corporate Blvd Ste 300 Baton Rouge LA 70808

CRUSIUS, TIMOTHY WOOD, English language educator; b. Ft. Worth, Feb. 9, 1950; s. Milton Wood and Lois Lorraine (Lovell) C.; m. Elizabeth Ann Smith, Oct. 16, 1986; children: Micah Wood, Rachel Elizabeth. BA, U. Houston, 1972, MA, 1974; PhD, U. So. Calif., L.A., 1978. Asst. prof. U. N.C., Greensboro, 1978-80; asst./assoc. prof. Tex. A&M U., College Station, 1980-90; asst. prof. English So. Meth. U., Dallas, 1990—. Author: Discourse: A Critique and Synthesis of Recent Theories, 1989, A Teacher's Introduction to Philosophical Hermeneutics, 1991, The Aims of Argument, 1994. Mem. Nat. Coun. Tchrs. English. Democrat. Methodist. Home: 9452 Angleridge Rd Dallas TX 75238 Office: Southern Methodist Univ Dept English Dallas TX 75275

CRUTCHER, DIMETREC ARTEZ, electronics technician; b. Gallatin, Tenn., June 27, 1964; s. James Davis and Lavenia Ann (Turner) C.; m. Kimolin Gilbert, Aug. 1, 1992; 1 child, Dimitria Kim. AS in Electronic Engring., ITT Tech. Inst., 1984. Audio-visual specialist Allied Audio-Visual Svcs., Nashville, 1985-88; field svc. tech. Spectradyne Inc., Nashville, 1988-94; field svc. supr. Spectradyne Inc., Louisville, Ky., 1990-94; co-owner Urbannetic Comms., 1994—; spl. profl. Granada Electronic Svcs. Group; co-owner Urbannet Comm.; audio-visual cons., engr. Key Meth. Ch., Gallatin, 1988—. Recipient 1st Place award Queen City Bodybldg. Championship, 1985, Southeastern Bodybldg. Championship, 1987, 3d Place award Music City Regional Championship, 1986, 2d Place award Tri-Counties Bodybldg. Championship, 1985. Mem. Nat. Physique Com. Democrat. Methodist. Home: 887 Green Wave Dr Gallatin TN 37066-3685

CRUTCHFIELD, CAROLYN ANN, physical therapy educator; b. New Castle, Colo., Apr. 2, 1942; d. Leland Arnold and Josephine Kathyrn (Leppink) C. BA, Western State Coll., 1964; cert. phys. therapy, Duke U., 1965; MS in Anatomy, West Va. U., 1970, EdD, 1976. Lic. phys. therapist, Ga. Dir. Rockingham Crippled Children's Ctr., Harrisonburg, Va., 1967-68; staff therapist Woodrow Wilson Rehab. Ctr., Fisherville, Va., 1966-67, West Va. U. Hosp., Morgantown, Va., 1968-70; asst. prof., asst. dir. Dept. Phys. Therapy, West Va. Sch. Medicine, Morgantown, 1970-75, assoc. prof., dir., 1975-78, prof., acting chair, 1978-80; prof., dir. grad. studies Dept. Phys. Therapy, Ga. State U., Atlanta, 1980—; chair Am. Bd. Phys. Therapy Specialties, Alexandria, Va., 1978-90; sec. Soc. for Behavioral Kinesiology, 1977-79. Author: The Muscle Spindle, 1972, Reflexes in Motor Development, 1978, Patient at Home, 1970, 84, Reflex and Vestibular Aspects of Motor Control, Motor Learning, Motor Development, 1990, Peripheral Components of Motor Control, 1984, Motor Control and Motor Learning in Rehabilitation, 1993, others; contbr. numerous chpts. to book and articles to jours. Chair ushers North Decatur Presbyn. Ch., Decatur, Ga., 1990, co-treas., 1991—. Recipient Cert. of Merit award Am. Bd. Phys. Therapy Specialties, 1990. Mem. Am. Phys. Therapy Assn. (chair neurology sect. 1983-85, treas. 1989-91, pres. West Va. chpt. 1978-79, Baethke-Carlin Teaching award 1984, Lucy Blair Svc. award 1991, Catherine Worthingtham fellow 1996), Assn. Clin. Electrophysiology. Home: 3127 W Roxboro Rd NE Atlanta GA 30324-2541

CRUTCHFIELD, EDWARD ELLIOTT, JR., banking executive; b. Detroit, July 14, 1941; s. Edward Elliott and Katherine (Sikes) C.; m. Nancy Glass Kizer, July 27, 1963; children: Edward Elliott, III, Sarah Palmer. BA, Davidson Coll., 1963; MBA, U. Pa., 1965. With First Union Nat. Bank, Charlotte, N.C., 1965—, head retail bank services group, 1970-72, exec. v.p. gen. adminstrn., 1972-73, pres., 1973-84, vice chmn., from 1984; pres. First Union Corp. (parent), Charlotte, 1983-86, chief exec. officer, 1984—, now also chmn., bd. dirs.; bd. dirs. Bernhardt Industries, Inc., Charlotte, 1983—. Bd. deacons Myers Park Presbyn. Ch.; bd. dirs. United Community Services, Salvation Army, Charlotte Bd., Charlotte Latin Sch.; trustee Mint Mus. Art, N.C. Nature Conservancy; bd. mgrs. Charlotte Meml. Hosp.; bd. visitors Davidson Coll. Mem. Charlotte C. of C., Assn. Res. City Bankers, Am., N.C. bankers assns., Am. Textile Mfrs. Assn., Young Pres.'s Orgn. Clubs: Charlotte City, Charlotte Country, Linville (N.C.) Golf. Office: 1st Union Corp 301 S Tryon St Charlotte NC 28288*

CRUVER, SUZANNE LEE, communications consultant, writer; b. Indpls., Mar. 24, 1942; d. William Edward and Margaret Rosetta (McArtor) Ozzard; m. Donald Richard Cruver, June 9, 1963 (div. Feb. 1989); children: Donald Scott, Kimberly Sue, Brian Richard. BA in English, Rutgers U., 1964; postgrad., Rice U., 1990—. Asst. dir. pub. rels. dept. Upsala Coll., East Orange, N.J., 1964-65; asst. planner, pub. editor N.J. Divsn. State & Regional Planning, Trenton, 1967-68; realtor Vonnie Cobb Realtors, Houston, 1979-81; owner Sugar Land Comm., 1980-94; exec. v.p., mktg. mgr. Photoflight Aviation Corp., Sugar Land, Tex., 1982; exec. v.p., artist mgr. H. McMillan Orgn., Inc., Sugar Land, 1983-85; account exec. Mel Anderson Comm., Inc., Houston, 1986; exec. dir. Ft. Bend Arts Coun., Sugar Land, 1986-87; dir. resource devel., vol. svcs., pub. info. Richmond (Tex.) State Sch., Tex. Dept. Mental Health/Mental Retardation, 1987-93; dir. corp. and found. giving Meml. Found., Meml. Healthcare Sys., Houston, 1993-94; owner SLC Comms., Houston, 1994—; mem. adv. bd. Ft. Bend Regional Coun. on Alcoholism and Drug Abuse, Rosenburg, Tex., 1989—. Writer, editor: PATCH Handbook: A Parent to Parent Guide to Texas Children's Hospital, 1983, Ft. Bend mag., 1985-86; book editor: Fort Bend County, Texas - A Pictorial History. Pres. Ft. Bend Arts Coun., Ft. Bend County, Tex., 1987-89; founding dir. PATCH, Tex. Children's Hosp., Houston, 1982; mem. adv. bd. Challenger Ctr. of Ft. Bend. Mem. NAFE, Nat. Soc. Fundraising Execs., Women in Comm., Ft. Bend Profl. Women, Pub. Rels. Soc. Am., Houston World Trade Assn., Ft. Bend C. of C., Rosenberg/Rich C. of C., Leadership Tex. Alumni Assn., Exch. Club of Sugar Land. Republican. Presbyterian.

CRUZ, DAVID RAMIREZ, priest; b. Lubbock, Tex., Feb. 6, 1961; s. Florentino and Margarita (Ramirez) C. Student, Immaculate Heart Sem., Santa Fe, 1979-82; BA in History, Coll. Santa Fe, 1982; M in Religious Studies, U. Louvain, Leuven, Belgium, 1986; Major in Sem., Am. Coll., Leuven, Belgium, 1986. Ordained priest Roman Cath. Ch., 1986. Assoc. pastor Christ the King Cathedral, Lubbock, 1986-87, Sacred Heart Ch., Lubbock, 1987-88; adminstr. St. Theresa's Ch., Lubbock, 1988—; assoc. dir. Office of Renew, Lubbock, 1987-89; exec. dir. Christian Renewal Ctr., Lubbock, 1989—; dir. Cursillo Movement, Lubbock, 1989—. Exec. dir. West Tex. Community Orgn., Lubbock, 1988—. Mem. KC (hon.). Office: Assumption Seminary 2600 W Woodlawn San Antonio TX 78228

CRUZ, NESTOR ENRIQUE, lawyer; b. Havana, Cuba, June 29, 1945; came to U.S., 1960; s. Carlos and Teresa (Gavalda) C.; m. Margarita Maza, Dec. 23, 1969; children: Augustine, Mariana. BA, Villanova U., 1966; MBA, Cornell U., 1969, JD, 1970. Bar: Fla. 1972, D.C. 1975, Va. 1993. Corp. exec. Rohm and Haas Co., Phila., 1970-74; atty. NLRB, Washington, 1974-77, counsel, 1988-91; assoc. Muller & Mintz, Miami, Fla., 1977; atty. City of Miami, Miami, 1978-79; dir., Office of Review and Appeals EEOC, Washington, 1979-82, assoc. legal counsel, 1982-84, counsel, 1984-88; pvt. practice law Annandale, Va., 1988—; pres. St. George's Assocs. Contbr. numerous articles to jours. Mem. ABA, Am. Econ. Assn., Sleepy Hollow Club. Home: 3902 Moss Dr Annandale VA 22003-1920

CRUZAN, CLARAH CATHERINE, dietitian; b. Cushing, Okla., Mar. 17, 1913; d. Ulysses Grant and Mamie Amanda (Montgomery) C. BS, Okla. State U., 1941; MS, U. Iowa, 1942. Lic. dietitian, Okla., 1984. Instr. household sci. Okla. State U., Stillwater, 1942-43, instr. home econs. edn., 1947-49; cons. dietitian Rest Haven Nursing Home, Cushing, Okla., 1967-91. Sec. Cushing Sr. Citizens Steering Coun., 1972-91; reporter Okla. Pioneer club, Cushing, 1973-85; precinct election judge, 1989-94. 1st lt. U.S. Army, 1943-46, ETO. Decorated Bronze Star. Mem. AAUW (life, treas. 1970-72, pres. 1974-75), Am. Dietetic Assn., Okla. Heritage Assn., Iris Garden Club (pres. 1971-73), Eastside Garden Club (reporter 1970-75), Omicron Nu, Phi Kappa Phi. Republican. Presbyterian. Home: RR 4 Box 2445 Cushing OK 74023-9123

CRYMES, MARY COOPER, secondary school educator; b. Abilene, Tex., Oct. 27, 1950; d. James Travis and Mary Francis (Chapple) Cooper; m. David Stuart Crymes, Dec. 25, 1970. BS, U. Tex., 1974. Tchr. govt. Midland (Tex.) Ind. Sch. Dist., 1974-80, Abilene (Tex.) Ind. Sch. Dist., 1980—. Author: (poem) Young America Sings, 1970; co-author: County Records Inventory, 1974. Recipient Teaching Excellence in Free Enterprise 1st prize award West Tex. C. of C., 1980, Martha Washington medal SAR, 1990; named Taft Sr. fellow Taft Inst., 1993. Mem. NEA, Tex. State Tchrs. Assn., Abilene Educators Assn., Nat. Coun. for Social Studies, Tex. Coun. for Social Studies, Abilene Coun. for Social Studies (pres. 1984-86), Daus. of Republic of Tex. (treas. 1990-95, v.p. 1995—), West Tex. Geneal. Soc. Office: Abilene High Sch 2800 N 6th St Abilene TX 79603-7125

CRYSTAL, CHARLOTTE HELEN, journalist; b. Berkeley, Calif., Jan. 29, 1955; d. Bruce William and Roxbury Maclay (Hyde) C.; m. David Bruce Mattern, June 30, 1979; 1 child, Benjamin Maclay. AB in Internat. Rels., Brown U., 1977; MA in Internat. Affairs, Columbia U., 1983. Analyst U.S. AID, Dire, Mali, 1979-81; asst. editor Corp. Fin. Week, N.Y.C., 1984; bus. and edn. reporter The Middletown (Conn.) Press, 1985-87; fin. reporter Richmond (Va.) Bus. Jour., 1988; fin. bus. reporter Richmond News Leader, 1988-91; sr. editor, trade Internat. Bus. mag., Harrison, N.Y., 1992; freelance reporter Charlottesville, Va., 1992—. Contbg. author: Guide to International Reporting: Europe, 1992, Great Events from History II: Business and Commerce, 1994. Vol. U.S. Peace Corps, Mali, 1977-79, Byrd Elem. Sch., Goochland County, Va., 1993, Recording for the Blind and Dyslexic, Charlottesville, 1987-88, Hospice of the Piedmont, Charlottesville, 1987-88. Internat. fellow Columbia U., 1981-82; jr. fellow Harriman Inst., 1981-82. Mem. Soc. Am. Bus. Editors and Writers, Va. Press Women (high sch. journalism contest dir. 1992-94), Richmond Export-Import Club, Soc. Profl. Journalists. Jewish. Home: 1874 Field Rd Charlottesville VA 22903

CRYSTAL, JONATHAN ANDREW, executive recruiter; b. New Rochelle, N.Y., May 18, 1943; s. Robert Garrison and Luella (Peters) C.; m. Pamela Paterson, July 31, 1965; children: Alexandra, Laura, Elizabeth, Matthew. BS in Bus., Northwestern U., 1965; MBA in Fin., Columbia U., 1971. Mktg. rep. Texaco, Inc., 1965-66; trainee Chase Manhattan Bank, 1971; assoc. corp. fin. Drexel Burnham & Lambert, Inc., 1971-73; acct. officer Citicorp, N.Y.C., 1973-77, asst. v.p., 1975-77; v.p., regional treas. mgr. Citicorp, Houston, 1977-80; prin. Russell Reynolds & Assocs., Houston, 1980-88, SpencerStuart, Houston, 1988—; speaker numerous trade convs., 1980—. Contbr. articles to profl. jours. Lt. (j.g.) USN, 1966-69. Named one of Top 200 Recruiters in the U.S. The Career Makers, 1990. Mem. Houston Forum (bd. govs. 1992—), Spring Branch Edn. Found. (bd. dirs. 1993—), Univ. Club. Home: 14419 Broadgreen Dr Houston TX 77079-6635

CUBIT, WILLIAM ALOYSIUS, lawyer; b. Phila., Aug. 7, 1930; s. William C. and Sophie (Kelly) Cubit Levey; m. Loretta E. Brooks, Feb. 12, 1952; children: William, Mark John, Dennis, Phyllis, Christine, Thomas. BSBA, St. Joseph's U., 1959; JD, Widener Law Sch., 1988. Bar: N.J. 1989, U.S. Supreme Ct. 1989, U.S. Dist. Ct. (ea. and we. dists.) Pa. 1989, U.S. Ct. Appeals (D.C. dir.) 1990, Fla. 1993, U.S. Dist. Ct. (so. dist.) Fla. 1993. Claims adjuster Home Ins., Phila., 1957-63, Wilmington, Del., 1957-63; claims adjuster Nationwire Ins., Phila., 1963-69, claims mgr., 1969-77; claims mgr. Nationwire Ins., Wilkes Barr, 1969-77; claims negotiator Chubb Ins. Group, Phila., 1977-89, atty., 1989—. Pres. S.E. Delco Sch. Bd., Folcroft, Pa., 1972-74; v.p. Sharon Hill (Pa.) Sch. Bd., 1968-70. Staff sgt. USMC, 1948-52, Korea. Mem. ABA, CPCU, Pa. Trial Lawyers Assn. Republican. Roman Catholic. Home: 1301 Woodland Ave Sharon Hill PA 19079-2121 Office: 727 NE 3rd Ave Fort Lauderdale FL 33304-2646

CUDDY, BRIAN GERARD, neurosurgeon; b. Syracuse, N.Y., July 13, 1959; s. Edward Michael and Mary Elizabeth (O'Brien) C. BS in Biology, SUNY, Albany, 1981; MS in Physiology, Albany Med. Coll., 1983, MD, 1987. Asst. prof. neurosurgery Med. U. S.C., 1994—, Med. Coll. Wis., 1993-94. Contbr. articles to profl. jours. Mem. Am. Assn. Neurol. Surgeons, Sigma Xi. Roman Catholic. Office: Med U of SC Dept Neurosurgery 171 Ashley Ave Charleston SC 29425-0001

CUELLAR, TERRENCE MICHAEL, pediatrics nurse; b. Des Moines, Jan. 10, 1964; s. John and Peggy Cuellar. BSN, U. Mo., 1988; MN Pediatric Nurse Practitioner, U. Fla., 1994. RN, Fla., Mo.; cert. BLS, pediatric advanced life support, BLS instr. Pediatrics staff nurse Univ. Hosp. and Clinics, Columbia, Mo., 1988-90; nurse Camp Winadu, Pittsfield, Mass., 1989; adolescent unit nurse Univ. Hosp. and Clinics, Columbia, 1990-91; pediatrics staff nurse Shands Hosp. U. Fla., Gainesville, 1991—; nurse Alachua Regional Juvenile Detention Ctr., Gainesbille, Fla. (student asst.), 1992; instr. Nursing Simulated Lab., Santa Fe C.C. Nursing Programs, Gainesville, 1993-95, pediat. clin. instr. ADN program, 1994-95. Vol. nurse Camp Quality, Columbia, 1991, Big Bros./Big Sisters, Columbia, 1983-86; vol. height/weight screener for children Health Fair, Columbia Mall, 1991. Staff scholar Univ. Hosp. and Clinics, 1987, scholar Fla. chpt. Nat. Assn. Pediatric Nurse Assocs. and Practitioners, 1991; grantee HHS, 1991, 92; recipient U.S. Achievement Acad. Nat. award. Mem. ANA, Fla. Nurses Assn., NAPNAP, Sigma Theta Tau. Home: 2370 SW Archer Rd Apt 49 Gainesville FL 32608-1056

CUELLAR, VIRGINIA ADRIEN, art historian and consultant; b. Dallas, Jan. 11, 1967; d. Frank Xavier Jr. and Marcia Nell (Stiles) C. BA in Art History, So. Meth. U., 1988, MA in Art History, 1993. Art cons. Omni Art, Dallas, 1985-86, rsch. asst., 1988; art historian and cons. cuellART, Inc., Dallas, 1988—; mus. edn. tchr. Meadows Mus., So. Meth. U., Dallas, 1991-93, Dallas Mus. of Art, 1992; art history and art appreciation instr. North Lake Cmty. Coll., Dallas, 1993—. Arts adminstr. The Ft. Worth Classic Guitar Soc., 1994—. Named to The Nat. Dean's List, 1983-84. Mem. Phi Beta Kappa. Republican. Roman Catholic. Office: cuellART Inc 655 N Park Blvd Apt 199 Grapevine TX 76051-6966

CUFFE, ROBIN JEAN, nursing educator; b. Frankfurt, Sept. 8, 1951; d. Russell Bates and Jean May (Clark) Preuit; m. Ronald Frederick Cuffe, Mar. 9, 1974; 1 child, Matthew David. Diploma, Richmond Meml. Hosp., 1973; BSN, Marymount U., 1982; MS in Edn., Va. Technol. and State U., 1990. RNC; cert. in cardiac rehab. nursing AACN; cert. health edn. specialist. Staff nurse Fairfax Hosp., Falls Church, Va., 1973-75; asst. head nurse, staff nurse, supr. ICU Arlington (Va.) Hosp., 1975-78, asst. coord. cardiac rehab., 1978-81, coord. cardiopulmonary rehab., 1981—. Bd. dirs. Am. Heart Assn., Northern, Va., 1982-91; jr. high youth group leader Ch. of the Holy Comforter, Vienna, Va., 1988-90, mem. adult edn. commn., 1990—. Fellow Am. Assn. Cardiovascular and Pulmonary Rehab. (chair stds. and reimbursement com. 1991—, pres.-elect 1994-95, pres. 1995-96, treas. 1996—), Sigma Theta Tau (pres. chpt. 1984-86). Episcopalian. Home: 1804 Cloverlawn Ct Mc Lean VA 22101

CULLAR, CAROL LEE, visual arts educator; b. Shamrock, Tex., July 7, 1944; d. James Ernest and Martha Nell (Darnell) Payne; children: Starla Robin Barrier-Reese, Thédra Jolie Cullar-Ledford. BA in Fine Art, Hardin-Simmons U., Abilene, Tex., 1969; MFA in Crafts, Instituto Allende, San

Miguel de Allende, Mexico, 1971. Art instr. Western Tex. Coll., Snyder, Tex., 1970-72, Cisco (Tex.) Jr. Coll., 1972-74; gallery mgr. Johnson Galleries, Santa Fe, N.Mex., 1974; art instr. Colegio Americano, Mexico City, 1977-79, Eagle Pass (Tex.) Ind. Sch. Dist., 1979—; editor The Maverick Press, Eagle Pass, 1989—; dir. Rio Bravo Lit. Arts Coun., Eagle Pass, 1985-96; editor The Maverick Press, 1989-96, S.W. Poets' Series, Eagle Pass, 1992-96. Author: Inexplicable Burnings, 1992, Haiku, 1992, This Hunger, 1993, Life and Death, Mostly, 1994; contbg. author: (anthologies) Texas in Poetry, 1994, Texas Short Fiction, 1994, 96, Superstition, Myth & Magik-The MacGuffin, 1996, The Gun Beneath the Bed, 1996; contbr. articles to lit. jours. Recipient honorable mention Salmon Run Press Nat. Poetry Book Award, 1995. Mem. Acad. Am. Poets, Tex. Assn. Creative Writing Tchrs., Tex. State Tchrs. Assn. Home and Office: Rt 2 Box 4915 Eagle Pass TX 78852-9605

CULLEN, WILLIAM ZACHARY, lawyer; b. Stamford, Conn., Feb. 15, 1955; s. John Cornelius and Ann D. (Woytowicz) C. BA, U. Conn., 1977; JD, New Eng. Sch. Law, 1980. Bar: Ala. 1989, U.S. Dist. Ct. (no. dist.) Ala. 1989, U.S. Ct. Appeals (11th cir.) 1989. Legal asst. Birmingham (Ala.) Legal Svcs., 1980-82; legal asst. Cooper, Mitch, Crawford, Kuykendall & Whatley, Birmingham, 1983-89, atty., 1989—. Office: Cooper Mitch Crawford Kuykendall & Whatley 505 20th St N Birmingham AL 35203-2605

CULLER, ROBERT RANSOM, furniture designing and product development company executive; b. High Point, N.C., Nov. 16, 1950; s. Roy Braxton and Dorthey Faye (Pegram) C.; m. Heidi Miller Maas, Feb. 24, 1969; children: Robert Ransom, John Byron, Kathrine Marie. Profl. degree in furniture design and interior design Kendall Sch. Design, Grand Rapids, Mich., 1974. Head of design La-Z-Boy Chair Co., Monroe, Mich., 1974-76; pres. R.R. Culler Assoc., High Point, 1976—, RCR Devel. Corp., High Point, 1978—; dir. The Color Works, Greensboro, N.C. Mem. Am. Furnitire Designers Assn., Am. Soc. Interior Designers. Democrat. Baptist. Club: Triad World Trade. Avocation: scuba diving. Office: RCR Devel Corp 1009 Finch Ave High Point NC 27263-1625

CULLINGFORD, HATICE SADAN, chemical engineer; b. Konya, Turkey, June 10, 1945; came to U.S., 1966; d. Ahmet and Emine (Kadayifcioglu) Harmanci. Student, Mid. East Tech. U., 1962-66; BS in Chem. Engring. with high honors, N.C. State U., 1969, Engring. Honors Cert., 1969, PhD, 1974. Registered profl. engr., Tex.; cert. mgr. Statis. clk. Rsch. Triangle Inst., 1966; reactor engr. AEC, Washington, 1973-75; spl. asst. ERDA, Washington, 1975; mech. engr. U.S. Dept. Energy, Washington, 1975-78; staff mem. Los Alamos (N.Mex.) Nat. Lab., 1978-82; sci. cons. Houston, 1982-84; environ. control and life support systems test bed mgr. Johnson Space Ctr., NASA, Houston, 1984-85, sr. project engr. advanced tech. dept., 1985-86, sr. staff engr. divsn. solar system exploration, 1986-88, asst. divsn. advanced devel., 1988-90; sr. system engr. Exploration Programs Office NASA, Houston, 1990-92; engring. and mgmt. cons. Houston, 1992—; founder Peace U., 1993; mem. internal adv. com. Ctr. for Nonlinear Studies Los Alamos Nat. Lab., 1981; organizer tech. workshops, sessions at soc. meetings; lectr. in field; docent Mus. Fine Arts, Houston. Editor, author tech. reports; contbr. articles to profl. jours.; patentee in field. Mem. curriculum rev. com. U. N.Mex., Los Alamos, 1980. Recipient Woman's badge Tau Beta Pi, 1968, ERDA Spl. Achievement award, 1976, Inventor award Los Alamos Nat. Lab., 1982, Group Achievement award NASA Johnson Space Ctr., 1987, Outstanding Performance award NASA Johnson Space Ctr., 1987, 89, Superior Performance award NASA Johnson Space Ctr., 1987, 89, Cert. of Recognition for Inventions, NASA, 1988, 89, 90, 92, 93. Mem. AIAA (organizer, 1st chmn. human support com. Houston chpt. 1988-93), AIChE (organizer, 1st chmn. No. N.Mex. club 1980-81, organizer and chmn. low-pressure processes and tech. 1981-89), Am. Nuclear Soc. (sec.-treas. fusion energy divsn. 1982-84, vice chmn. South Tex. sect. 1984-86, mem. local sects. com. 1986-88), Am. Chem. Soc., Soc. for Risk Analysis (organizer, sec. Lone Star chpt. 1986-88, chmn. soc. publicity 1990-93), No. N.Mex. Chem. Engrs. Club, Engrs. Coun. Houston (councilor, sec. energy com.), Sierra Club, Houston Orienteering Club, Phi Kappa Phi, Pi Mu Epsilon.

CULP, BARBARA JUNE, secondary school educator; b. Hallettsville, Tex., Nov. 1, 1944; d. Arthur William and Marion A. (Vick) Clark; m. Charles Linden Culp, Aug. 27, 1966; children: John David, Brian Clark. BS in Biology, Psychology and Math., Stephen F. Austin State U., Nacogdoches, Tex., 1966, MS in Biology, 1969, cert. mid-mgmt., 1985. Tchr. Horace Mann Jr. High, Baytown, Tex., 1966-80; tchr. gifted Cedar Bayou Jr. High, Baytown, 1980-82; tchr., dept. chmn. Gentry Jr. High, Baytown, 1982-85; tchr. Ross S. Sterling High Sch., Baytown, 1985—; Lee Coll., Baytown, 1992—; mem. Goose Creek Consol. Ind. Sch. Dist. Recovery Com. for Dropouts; mem. gifted and talented adv. coun. GATE program for Goose Creek Consol. Ind. Sch. Dist., 1980-82, math./sci. fair coord., 1983-84, ednl. adv. coun., 1987-89, TAAS math. coord., 1994—; state textbook advisor Tex. State Textbook Com., Baytown, 1984, 89; number sense and math. coach U. Interscholastic League R.S. Sterling H.S., 1984—, sponsor student coun., 1992—. Pres., treas. Tri-Cities DeMolay Mothers Club, Baytown, 1983-88; youth educator Grace United Meth. Ch., Baytown, 1978-79; mem. Caring Adults Reaching Everyone team R.S. Sterling High Sch., 1989. Nominee for Presdl. Award of Excellence for Math. Teaching, 1990. Mem. NEA, Nat. Coun. Tchrs. Math. (conf. presenter 1991, 92), Tex. State Tchrs. Assn., Tex. Classroom Tchrs. Assn. (com. chmn., conv. del. 1980-84), Tex. State Tchrs. Math., Baytown Edn. Assn. (treas., com. chair 1980-84), Baytown Classroom Tchrs. Assn. (chmn., Tchr. of Yr. 1985), Tex. State Tchrs. Math., San Jacinto Coun. Tchrs. Math., Delta Kappa Gamma (pres. 1990-92). Methodist. Home: 4905 Saint Andrews Dr Baytown TX 77521-3017 Office: 300 W Baker Rd Baytown TX 77521-2301

CULP, JOE C(ARL), electronics executive; b. Little Rock, July 23, 1933; s. Charles Carl and Doris Evelyn (Jackson) C.; m. Norma Carol Kennan, Jan. 26, 1954; 1 dau., Karen Gay Culp Ashorn. BSEE, U. Ark., 1955. Staff asst. to exec. v.p. Collins Radio, Dallas, 1967-68; with Rockwell Internat., Dallas, 1968-88, dir. data systems mktg., 1968-71, dir. mktg. trans systems div., 1971-78, v.p. Latin Am., 1978-80, v.p., gen. mgr. trans systems div., 1980-82, pres. telecomm. group, 1982-88; pres., CEO Lightnet, Rockville, Md., 1988-89; exec. v.p. Comm. Transmission, Inc., Austin, Tex., 1989-90; pres. Culp Comm. Assocs., Inc., Austin, Tex., 1990—; bd. dirs. IXC Comms., Inc., Crosskeys Corp, Multimedia Access Corp.; mem. chmn. exec. coun. Newbridge Networks Corp. Chmn. engring. bd. U. Tex., Arlington, 1984; bd. advisors Coll. Engring. U. Ark., Fayetteville, 1982. Named Disting. Grad., Coll. Engring. U. Ark., 1981, Disting. Engr., U. Tex., Arlington, 1984. Mem. Electronic Industry Assn. (bd. govs. 1984-88), U.S. Telephone Suppliers Assn. (dir. 1984-88), Ind. Telephone Pioneers. Republican. Methodist. Office: Culp Communications Assocs Inc 5 Hedge Ln Austin TX 78746-3208

CULPEPPER, RICHARD ALAN, religious studies educator; b. Little Rock, Mar. 2, 1946; s. Hugo H. and Ruth (Cochrane) C.; m. Jacquelyn McClain, June 24, 1967; children: Erin Lynn, Rodney Alan. BA, Baylor U., 1967; MDiv, So. Bapt. Theol. Sem., 1970; PhD, Duke U., 1974. Prof. N.T. So. Bapt. Theol. Sem., Louisville, 1974-91; prof. religion Baylor U., Waco, Tex., 1991-95; dean Mercer Sch. of Theology, Atlanta, 1995—. Author: The Johannine School, 1975, Anatomy of the Fourth Gospel, 1983, 1, 2, 3 John, 1985, John, The Son of Zebedee: The Life of a Legend, 1994, Luke New Interpreter's Bible, vol. 9, 1996; editor Rev. and Expositor, 1982-91; assoc. editor Perspectives in Religious Studies, 1991-93, editor, 1993—; co-editor Bibl. Interpretation Series, 1993—. Mem. Soc. N.T. Studies, Soc. Bibl. Lit., Nat. Assn. Bapt. Profs. of Religion, Westar Inst. Baptist. Home: 1871 Chedworth Ct Stone Mountain GA 30087 Office: Mercer Sch Theology Atlanta GA 30341-4415

CULTER, RAY MICHAEL, conservation executive; b. Flushing, N.Y., Aug. 20, 1945; s. Ray William and Louise (Hewitt) C.; m. Paulette Ruth Wuerth, Nov. 4, 1967; children: Paul Alan, Tina Ann. BSCP, U. Cin., 1968. Planner Hamilton County Planning Com., Cin., 1967-68; exec. dir. Little Miami, Inc., Lebanon, Ohio, 1968-73; v.p., dir. stewardship The Nature Conservancy, Arlington, Va., 1973-81, v.p., dir. trade lands, 1981-88, v.p., dep. dir. resources, 1988-91, v.p., dir. adminstrn. and trade lands dispositions, 1991—. Exec. dir. Internat. Leadership Coun.; judge Navy Cons. Awards, Dept. Navy, Washington, 1989, 90, 91, 93. Recipient Letter of Commendation, Pres. of U.S., Gulf Oil Conservation award Gulf Oil Corp., 1982, Natural Resources Conservation award Sec. of Navy, 1990. Mem. Am. Rivers (bd. dirs., chmn. devel. com. 1990-92, chmn. bd. 1992-95, chmn. bd. governance and nominating com.), Holmes Run Area Rec. Assn. (bd. dirs. 1985-86, 89-90, pres. 1990), Little Miami (bd. dirs., ex-officio 1988-92). Office: The Nature Conservancy 1815 N Lynn St Arlington VA 22209-2003

CULVER, DAN LOUIS, federal agency administrator; b. Savannah, Ga., Dec. 7, 1957; s. Louis Harry and Jean Marie (Snow) C. BS in Mktg., U. Tenn., 1981; postgrad., Air Force Acad., 1982, Cornell U., 1985; D. in Bus. Admstrn. (hon.), London Sch. Applied Rsch., 1992; BS in Edn. and Tng., U. West Fla., 1995. Lic. realtor; cert. tchr., Fla. Hotel gen. mgr. U.S. Govt., Ft. Walton Beach, Fla., 1982-85, asst. dir. food and lodging, 1985-86; mgmt. assoc. Barnett Bank, Ft. Walton Beach, 1987-89; loan officer SBA, Atlanta, 1989—; bus. cons. Ft. Walton Beach, Fla., 1990—; diplomatic envoy UN, N.Y.C., 1992—; promoter, program coord. for profl. entertainers, speakers, models and authors, 1994—; advisor to leaders in bus., govt. and edn.; bd. dirs. several bus. and non-profit orgns. Pioneered automation of air force support ops., 1982-84. Vol. disaster relief for victims of Hurricane Hugo, Charleston, S.C., 1989, Hurricane Andrew, Miami, Fla., 1992, Miss. River flood, 1993, L.A. earthquake, 1994; fund raiser, promoter spl. events for non-profit orgns. With USAF, 1982-86. Recipient Commander-in-Chief's Spl. Recognition for Excellence award, Pres. of U.S. Mem. ASTD, Internat. Parliament for Safety and Peace, Maison Internat. des Intellectuels, Lofsensic Ursinius, Internat. Platform Assn., Am. Inst. Banking, U. Tenn. Alumni Assn., Fairfield Cmty. Country Club, Asia Soc., Sigma Phi Epsilon, Phi Kappa Phi. Office: PO Box 5453 Fort Walton Beach FL 32549-5453

CULVER, JOHN BLAINE, minister; b. Urbana, Ill., Nov. 3, 1938; s. Lawson Blaine and Sunray Lillian (Cooper) C.; m. Rosa Bertha Diaz-Mori, Feb. 28, 1970; children: Janice Lillian, John Manuel, Edward Blaine. BA, U. Ill., 1962, MA, 1964; MDiv cum laude, Chgo. Theol. Sem., 1972; postgrad., Escuela de Idiomas, Sociedad de Santiago Apostol, Pontifical U., Lima, Peru, 1969-70. Ordained to ministry United Ch. of Christ, 1973. Pastor, adminstr. Winnebago Indian Mission, United Ch. of Christ, Black River Falls, Wis., 1972-75; pastor Bethany United Ch. of Christ, San Antonio, 1975-78, Bethany Congl. Ch., San Antonio, 1978-96 (ret.); interim pastor Pilgrim Congl. Ch., San Antonio, 1978, Iglesia Unida de Cristo Betania, San Antonio, 1982-83; part-time instr. San Antonio Coll., 1978-96; bd. dirs. South Ctrl. Conf. United Ch. of Christ, Austin, Tex., 1982, 84-87, 90-92, gen. synod del., 1997—; mem. exec. com., sec.-registrar South Tex. Assn. United Ch. of Christ, 1982-90, 94-96, moderator, 1982, 90-92. Bd. dirs., program chmn. Illini Young Reps., Urbana, Ill., 1963; bd. dirs. Greater San Antonio Community of Chs., 1976-80, San Antonio Urban Coun., 1984-86, 88; sec. Tobin Hill Neighborhood Assn., San Antonio, 1978-79. Mem. Masons (chaplain 1981-82, 90-92, tiler 1980-81, 84-85). Home: 102 Shadywood Ln San Antonio TX 78216-7334

CULVERN, JULIAN BREWER, retired chemist, educator; b. July 23, 1919; m. Shirley Bowman, 1946; children: Janine Amelia, David Bowman, Linda Hazel. BS, N.C. State U., 1942; MSc, Ohio State U., 1948; postgrad., U. Tenn., 1970-72. Assay chemist Haile Gold Mine, 1940-41; asst. mgr. Chem. & Microscopical Lab., 1949-61; sr. process engr. Am. Enka Corp., Lowland, Tenn., 1961-69; instr. gen. chemistry, earth and space sci., environ. sci. Morristown (Tenn.) Coll., 1969-76, chmn. div. natural sci., 1969-73.; conducted libr. rsch. in field sci. and religion Templeton Found., 1970; chemist atomic bomb project Corps of Engrs., Manhattan Dist., Oak Ridge, Tenn. Columnist Daily Gazette-Mail, Morristown, 1960-74; contbr. articles to Sci. of Mind mag., others. Chmn. Cherokee dist. Boy Scouts Am.; ruling elder 1st Presbyn. Ch., Morristown, Tenn., Marshall, N.C. With U.S. Army, 1944-46. Mem. AAUP, Am. Chem. Soc., Tenn. Acad. Scis., Gamma Sigma Epsilon, Phi Lambda Upsilon. Home: Birdsong Hill 2832 Indian Trl Morristown TN 37814-5824

CUMBO, LAWRENCE JAMES, JR., economics and business educator, consultant; b. Saltville, Va., June 22, 1947; s. Lawrence James and Mary (Martin) C.; m. Mary Lee Tuggle, Nov. 27, 1970; children: Tori Jill, Kolbi Lee, Benjamin James. BS, E. Tenn. State U., 1970; MBA, Coll. William and Mary, 1975; PhD, Va. Polytech. Inst. and State U., 1981. Acct. Mason and Dixon Lines, Inc., Kingsport, Tenn., 1970-72; asst. bus. mgr. King Coll., Bristol, Tenn., 1972-74; acct. Appalachian Broadcasting Corp. Bristol, Va., 1974; prof. econs. and bus. Emory and Henry Coll., Emory, Va., 1975—, chmn. social sci. div., 1987—; pres. Cumbo and Assoc., Inc., Emory, 1979—; cons., 1977—. Contbr. articles to profl. jours.; book reviewer Choice mag.; author software packages. Bd. dirs. William King Found., Abingdon, Va., 1987-89. Recipient Excellence in Tchg. award Emory and Henry Coll., 1982, Hull Chair of Bus., 1984. Mem. Va. Assn. Economists, So. Mgmt. Assn., S.E. Decision Scis. Inst. Democrat. Presbyterian. Avocations: alpine skiing, tennis, golf. Home: Drawer QQ Emory VA 24327 Office: Dept Economics Emory and Henry Coll Emory VA 24327

CUMMING, CATHLEEN MARY, dietitian/nutritionist; b. St. Paul, July 14, 1955; d. John Frederick and Celia Frances (Lanphear) C. AA, Normandale Coll., 1975; BA, U. Minn., 1978, BS, 1978; MS, James Madison U., 1990. Registered dietitian; cert. diabetes educator. Clin. nutritionist U. Va. Hosp., Charlottesville, 1986—. Contbr. articles to profl. jours. Dietetic intern scholarship U. Va. Hosp., 1985. Mem. Am. Dietetic Assn. (Recognized Young Dietitian 1991), Va. Dietetic Assn. (Profl. Devel. award 1993, scholarship 1989), Blue Ridge Dietetic Assn. (pres. 1988-89), Am. Diabetes Assn. (bd. dirs. 1986-88), Am. Heart Assn. (nutrition com.). Democrat. Office: U Va Hosp PO Box 273-59 Charlottesville VA 22908

CUMMINGS, ANTHONY WILLIAM, lawyer, educator; b. Port Jefferson, N.Y., Dec. 3, 1962; s. Leonard and Annie (Earl) C. Student, Tulane U., 1980-81; BS in Applied Econs., Hofstra U., 1985, JD, 1988; postgrad., U. N.C., 1995—. Bar: N.Y. 1988, D.C. 1990, U.S. Dist. Ct. (ea. and so. dists.) N.Y. 1990, U.S. Ct. Mil. Appeals 1990, U.S. Ct. Appeals (2d, 11th and fed. cirs.) 1991, U.S. Tax Ct. 1991, U.S. Supreme Ct. 1992, N.C. 1995. Assoc. Ronald J. Rosenberg, Garden City, N.Y., 1988-89; of counsel Costa & Bernsten, Hauppauge, N.Y., 1989-92; contract atty. Bernsten & Newman, Hauppauge, 1990-93; pvt. practice, Patchogue, N.Y., 1990-94, Raleigh, N.C., 1994—; adj. instr. law Suffolk County C.C., Selden, N.Y., 1992-94; coord. adminstrv. svcs. N.C. Biotech. Ctr., Research Triangle Park, N.C., 1994-95; adj. instr. bus. Wake Tech. C.C., Raleigh, 1995—; coord., lectr. CLE programs Suffolk Acad. Law. 1989-94; co-chmn. appellate practice com. Suffolk County Bar Assn.; judge Jessup Internat. Law Moot Ct. Competition, 1990-91. Editor-in-chief Hofstra Property Law Jour., 1988; assoc. editor Jour. Suffolk Acad. Law, 1992-94. Mem. adv. bd. Bellport (N.Y.) Found., 1994—. Recipient award of recognition Suffolk County Bar Assn., 1991, cert. of disting. merit Suffolk Acad. Law, 1991. Mem. ABA, N.C. Acad. Trial Lawyers, N.C. State Bar Assn., D.C. Bar Assn., Hofstra U. Alumni Orgn. (exec. coun. 1990-94), Scabbard and Blade, Phi Eta Sigma. Office: 6014 Duraleigh Rd 2nd Fl Raleigh NC 27612

CUMMINGS, NORMAN ALLEN, rheumatologist, educator; b. N.Y.C., Mar. 26, 1935; s. Maurice and Bertha (Daniels) C.; m. Elaine Gaffin, Sept. 11, 1960; children: Marshall Bruce, Lisa Ellen. AB, NYU, 1955; MD, SUNY, Buffalo, 1959. Diplomate Am. Bd. Internal Medicine; lic. physician, N.Y., Tex., Md., Ky. Intern in medicine Jewish Hosp. Bklyn., 1959-60, resident in internal medicine, 1960-61; resident in internal medicine Univ. Hosp.-U. Mich., 1961-62; fellow Rackham Arthritis Rsch. Unit dept. biophysics U. Mich. Med. Ctr., 1962-64; vis. fellow in rheumatology NYU-Bellevue Med. Ctr., 1962; rsch. assoc. dept. medicine U. Mich. Med. Ctr., 1963-64; rsch. assoc. lab. biochemistry Nat. Cancer Inst.-NIH-USPHS, 1964-66; asst. prof. medicine Baylor U. Coll. Medicine, 1966-67; attending staff Ben Taub and Houston VA Hosps., 1966-67; med. officer, head connective tissue disease program Oral Medicine and Surgery br. Nat. Inst. Dental Rsch.-NIH, 1967-74; dir. arthritis ctr., chief clin. immunology and connective tissue disease sect., assoc. prof. dept. medicine U. Louisville, 1974-78, prof. medicine, 1974-78, clin. prof. medicine, 1983—; mem. attending staff internal medicine Louisville Gen. Hosp. (now named Univ. Hosp.), 1974—; pvt. practice rheumatology Louisville, 1983—; clin. rsch. com. Nat. Inst. Dental Rsch., 1973-74, cons. 1974; cons. Jewish Hosp., Louisville, NIH, Norton-Children's Hosp, 1974; chmn. Baylor Med. Rsch. Seminars; mem. program com. Nat. Arthritis Found., 1975; mem. med. and sci. com. Ky. chpt. Arthritis Found., 1975; rsch. contract rev. com. Nat. Inst. Dental Rsch.-NIH Lab. Reorgn. Com., det. medicine U. Louisville Sch. Medicine, 1977, curriculum com. dept. medicine, 1978, subcom. grad. edn. dept. medicine, 1978, ad hoc com. merit rev. dept. medicine, 1978, dean's rev. com. for chmn. dept. physiology and biophysics, 1979; med. adv. bd. Lupus Found. Kentuckiana, Inc., 1980—; phys. therapy com. Jewish Hosp., 1980; phys. therapy com. St. Anthony's Med. Ctr., 1985—, chmn. dept. medicine, exec. com., quality assessment com., 1988-90; phys. therapy com. Jewish Hosp., 1990. Mem. editorial bd. Louisville Medicine, 1980. Exhibits sub-com. Nat. Arthritis Found., 1980. Fellow ACP (founding, co-dir. med knowledge self-assessment program V 1980); mem. Am. Rheumatism Assn. (exhibits com.), Rheumatism Soc. D.C. (med. adv. com. 1971-74, chmn. subcom. clinic site visits 1972, chmn. membership com. 1971-72), Ky. Med. Assn., Jefferson County Med. Soc., Louisville Soc. Internists, Univ. Mich. Rsch. Soc., Phi Beta Kappa, Sigma Xi. Home: 7301 Fox Harbor Rd Prospect KY 40059-9329 Office: 801 Barret Ave Ste 224 Louisville KY 40204-1733

CUMMINGS, PATRICK HENRY, manufacturing executive; b. Cleve., May 3, 1941; s. Henry Patrick and Ruth (Farrell) C.; m. Sharon Lynn Slama; children: Dawn, Kelly, Patrick. BS in Indsl. Engring., GMI Engring. and Mgmt. Inst., 1964. Prodn. analyst Euclid (Ohio) Div. Gen. Motors Corp., 1964-65; methods engr. Euclid Div. Gen. Motors Corp., Hudson, Ohio, 1965-68, supr. parts, methods and warehouse Terex div., 1968-71, gen. supr., prodn. planning Terex div., 1972; parts mgr. Lorain div. Koehring Co., Chattanooga, 1973-74, material control mgr. Lorain div., 1974-77; materials mgr. Robbins div. Joy Mfg. Co., Birmingham, Ala., 1977-80; materials mgr. Unit Rig and Equipment Co., Tulsa, 1980-85; data processing mgr. Kendavis Holding Co., Ft. Worth, 1985-87; info. svcs. mgr. Stratoflex Aerospace & Mil. Connectors div. Parker Hannifin, Ft. Worth, 1987-89, materials mgr., 1990—. Republican. Roman Catholic. Home: 5716 Guadalajara Dr Fort Worth TX 76180-6122 Office: Parker Hannifin Stratoflex Aero/Mil Connecters Div PO Box 10398 Fort Worth TX 76114

CUMMINGS, PETER THOMAS, chemical engineering educator; b. Wingham, New South Wales, Australia, Feb. 10, 1954; came to U.S., 1981; s. Henry St.John and Mary Clarence (McLeod) C.; m. Elizabeth June Way, May 17, 1975. B.Math. with 1st class honors, U. Newcastle, Australia, 1975; Ph.D., U. Melbourne, Australia, 1980. Postdoctoral research fellow dept. physics U. Guelph, Ont., Can., 1980; research assoc. dept. mech. engring. and chemistry SUNY-Stony Brook, 1981-83; asst. prof. dept. chem. engring. U. Va., Charlottesville, 1983-87, assoc. prof., 1987-91, prof. 1991-93; disting. prof. dept. chem. engring. U. Tenn., 1994—, disting. scientist chem. tech. divsn. Oak Ridge Nat. Lab., 1994—. Contbr. articles to profl. jours. Commonwealth Sci. and Indsl. Research Orgn. fellow, 1980; grantee Dreyfus Found., 1983, NSF, 1984—, DOE, 1987—, Petroleum Research Fund, 1984. Mem. Am. Inst. Chem. Engrs., Am. Chem. Soc., Am. Phys. Soc., Sigma Xi. Presbyterian. Office: Dept Chem Engring U Tenn 419 Dougherty Engring Knoxville TN 37996

CUMMINGS, VIRGINIA (JEANNE), former real estate company executive; b. Greenwood, S.C., June 24, 1923; d. Samuel Barksdale and Alma Virginia (Davis) Jones; m. John W. Cummings, Nov. 7, 1938; children: John W., Martha Jean Wells. Student, U. Miami; PhD (hon.), Colo. State Christian Coll., 1973. Sec. Pine Crest Pvt. Sch., Ft. Lauderdale, Fla., 1956-59; real estate broker Am. Realty, Ft. Lauderdale, 1959-62; pres., founder Cummings Realty Inc., Ft. Lauderdale, 1962-85; v.p. Magic Carpet Travel, Ft. Lauderdale, 1975-89; pres. Women's Coun. Ft. Lauderdale Bd. Realtors, 1961; freelance writer. Feature writer Fla. Living Mag., 1969-74; contbr. articles to profl. jours. Bd. dirs., past chmn. Ch. of Religious Sci., Ft. Lauderdale. Mem. Nat. Bd. Realtors, Ft. Lauderdale Area Bd. Realtors, DAR. Democrat. Home: 4300 N Ocean Blvd Apt 19A-B Fort Lauderdale FL 33308

CUMMINS, DELMER DUANE, academic administrator, historian; b. Dawson, Nebr., June 4, 1935; s. Delmer H. and Ina Z. (Arnold) C.; m. Darla Sue Beard, Oct. 6, 1957; children: Stephen Duane, Cristi Sue, Caroline Renee. BS, Phillips U., Enid, Okla., 1957; MA, U. Denver, 1965; PhD, U. Okla., 1974; LLD, Williams Woods Coll., 1979; HHD (hon.), Phillips U., 1983; DLitt (hon.), Chapman U., 1996. Tchr., Jefferson County Pub. Schs., Denver, 1956-67; mem. faculty Oklahoma City U., 1967-77, Darbeth-Whitten prof. history, 1974-77, curator George Shirk Collection, 1977; chmn. dept. history Oklahoma City U., 1969-72; dir. Robert A. Taft Inst. Govt., 1972-77; pres. div. higher edn. Christian Ch., 1978-88; pres. Bethany (W.Va.) Coll., 1988—; bd. dirs. Wesbanco Bank and Trust. Author: The American Frontier, 1968, 3d edit., 1978, Origins of the Civil War, 1971, 2d edit., 1978, The American Revolution, 1968, 3d edit., 1978, Contrasting Decades, 1920's and 1930's, 1972, 2d edit., 1978, Consensus and Turmoil, 1972, William R. Leigh: Biography of a Western Artist, 1980, A Handbook for Today's Disciples, 1981, 2d edit., 1991, (with D. Hohweller) An Enlisted Soldier's View of the Civil War, 1981, (with others) Seeking God's Peace in a Nuclear Age, 1985, The Disciples Colleges: A History, 1987, The Search for Indentity, Disciples Of Christ-The Restructure Years, 1987; editor The Disciples Theol. Digest, 1986-88; contbr. articles to profl. jours. Trustee Culver-Stockton Coll., 1978-88, Tougaloo Coll., 1978-88, vice chmn., 1985-88, W.Va. Ind. Coll. Found., 1988—; Danforth assoc., 1976-78; moderator, active multiple nat. bds. and task forces Christian Ch., 1993-95; mem. Pitts. Opera Bd., 1996—; bd. dirs. West Bend, 1991—. Mem. Okla. Council Humanities (grantee 1974), Phillips U. Alumni Assn. (pres. 1975-76), Nat. Assn. Ind. Colls. and Univs. (secretariat, policy commn. 1990-94), chair pres.'s athletic conf. 1990-92), W.Va. Assn. Ind. Colls. (chair 1994-97). Home: Bethany Coll Pendleton Heights Bethany WV 26032 Office: Bethany Coll Old Main Bethany WV 26032

CUMMINS, JAMES DUANE, correspondant, media executive; b. Cedar Rapids, Iowa, Mar. 11, 1945; s. Dewey Homer and Dorothy Marie (Colgan) C.; m. Constance Marie Driscoll, July 27, 1968; children: Kimberly, Christine, Douglas, John, Molly, Bill. BS in journalism, Northwestern U., 1967, MS in journalism, 1968. News reporter Sta. KGLO-TV, Mason City, Iowa, 1969-70, Sta. WOOD-TV, Grand Rapids, Mich., 1970-73, Sta. WTMJ-TV, Milw., 1973-75, Sta. WMAQ-TV, Chgo., 1975-78; corr. NBC News, Chgo., 1978-89; corr./bur. chief NBC News, Dallas, 1989—. Corr. (news reports) Civil War-El Salvador, 1981, Korean Airline Disaster, 1983, Hurricane Hugo, 1989, Waco Standoff, 1993, Calif. Earthquake, 1994, Okla. City Bombing, 1995. Recipient Nat. News Emmy award for "Floods", 1993, Emmy award Chgo. TV Acad., 1976. Mem. Northwestern U. Sch. Journalism Alumni Assn., Northwestern U. N Men's Club, Sigma Delta Chi (journalism soc.). Roman Catholic. Home: 5815 Flintshire Ln Dallas TX 75252-5132 Office: NBC News 3100 Mckinnon St Dallas TX 75201-7003

CUNDIFF, LOU WILLIE, artist, sculptor, writer; b. Nashville, Mar. 20, 1926; d. John Melvin and Bertha Agnes (Johnson) Gibson; m. James Howard Cundiff, Sept. 16, 1944; children: Billie June, James Howard, Jr., Michael Douglas. Diploma, Howard H.S., Nashville. Typist clk. City of Nashville Ct., 1944; sales asst. mgr. Spartan Dept. Store, Nashville, 1966-70; credit clk. Woolco Credit Office, 1970-72; sec. H.D. Lee, Nashville, 1972-75; exec. sec. Red Kap Industries, Nashville, 1972-75; vol.; art judge AT&T Pioneers of Am., Nashville, 1990, Cheatham County H.S., Ashland City, Tenn., 1993, 94, 95. Maury County, Columbia, Tenn., 1994; Tenn. Art League Sch. Auctions, Tenn. Art League Gallery, Nashville, 1990-96. Author, illustrator: Miss Cundiff Speaking, 1975; editor, illustrator: Tennessee Art League Cookbook, 1995-96; compiler, illustrator: Word and Image Guild Manual, 1995-96; writer, compiler, illustrator: Steps of Time Chapbook, 1995. Speaker, artist 55 Health Fair Symposiums, Two Rivers Bapt. Ch., 1991; sec., scrapbook host Christian Women Club, Internat. Soc. Poets, Nashville; TV interview CT 39 TV, Murfreesboro, Tenn., 1993, WAGG Channel 3, Franklin, Tenn., 1987-90. Recipient 1st Oil 1982, 85, 92, Tenn. State Fair, Nashville, CASE Parthenon Ctrl. South Art Exhbn., Nashville, 1991, Solo 1992 Show Cheekwood Art Ctr., Pineapple Rm., Nashville, 1992, Ornament 1991 Trees nat. Mus. Women in Arts, Washington, 1991. Tenn. Art League Gallery, Tenn. Art League Gallery, Word and Image Guild, Friends of Tenn. Art League Gallery, Hendersonville Artists Guild. Mem. Two Rivers Baptist Ch. Home: 909 Drummond Dr Nashville TN 37211

CUNNINGHAM, BRENTON JON, marketing educator; b. Gadsden, Ala., July 22, 1965; s. Billy Wayne and Delores Ann (Tolleson) C.; m. Dana Joy Shaw, May 9, 1987; children: Brenton Jon II, Garrison Shaw. BS, U. Tenn.,

Martin, 1985; BS in Mktg., Jacksonville State U., 1987; MA in Mktg., U. Ala., Tuscaloosa, 1990; postgrad., U. Miss., Oxford, 1993—. Appliance mgr. K-Mart Corp., Union City, Tenn., 1982-84; supr. Goodyear Tire and Rubber, Union City, 1984; sales rep. Bennett's Inc., Union City, 1984-86, Noxell Corp., Hunt Valley, Md., 1987-88; teaching asst. U. Ala., Tuscaloosa, 1988-90; instr. mktg. Union U., Jackson, Tenn., 1990-93, asst. prof. mktg., 1993—, MBA dir., 1994-95. Leader Northbrook Bapt. Ch., Jackson, 1993—; advisor Students in Free Enterprise, Jackson, 1993—. Named Outstanding Young Educator, Jackson Jaycees, 1992. Mem. Am. Mktg. Assn., So. Mktg. Assn., Southwestern Mktg. Assn., Christian Bus. Faculty Assn., Phi Beta Lambda (treas., v.p., faculty advisor 1986—, Outstanding Officer award 1986), Mu Kappa Tau, Sigma Tau Delta (treas. 1986-87). Office: Union U 2447 Us Highway 45 Byp Jackson TN 38305-2002

CUNNINGHAM, DAVID COLEMAN, career officer; b. Chgo., Sept. 4, 1950; s. David Christopher and Ruth Beatrice (Fike) C.; m. Mary Lee Brock, Oct. 7, 1971; 1 child, Caleb Brock Cunningham. BA in Speech, Harding U., 1973; MTh, Harding U., Memphis, 1984; grad., Air Command Staff Coll., Montgomery, Ala., 1991. Master navigator; cert. clin. hypnotherapist. Commd. USAF, 1974, advanced through grades to lt. col., 1995; navigator tng. (disting. grad.) USAF, Mather AFB, Calif., 1974-75; fighter tng. AT-38, F-4E USAF, Homestead AFB, Fla., 1975-76; weapons sys. operator F-4D 493rd Tactical Fighter Squadron USAF, Lakenheath RAFB, Eng., 1976-77, F-4E 10th Tactical Fighter Squadron USAF, Hahn AFB, Germany, 1977-80; navigator C-130A 155th Tactical Airlift Squadron Tenn. Air Nat. Guard, Memphis, 1981-84; navigator technician 164th Airlift Group/Wing Tenn. Air Nat. Guard, Memphis, 1984—; tactics officer-navigator 164th Airlift Group/Wing USAF, Memphis, 1984-90; chief of tactics 164th Ops. Support Flight Tenn. Air Nat. Guard, Memphis, 1990-95; comdr. 164th Ops. Support Flight Tenn. Air N.G., Memphis, 1995—; inspector gen. Tenn. Air and Army Nat. Guard, 1994—; chief exercise evaluation team 164th Airlift Wing, 1995—; comdr. 164th Ops. Support Flight, Tenn. Air Nat. Guard, Memphis, 1995—. Editor: Air National Guard Long Range Plan, 1988-89; chief editor, author: Air National Guard Long Range Plan, 1990; chief author, editor: 164th Unit Self Evaluation, 1995. Mem. adv. bd. Harding U. Grad. Sch. Religion, Memphis, 1994. 95. 96; organizer Fire Four Miler (race), Harding U., 1994. Recipient Meritorious Svc. medal, Air Force Commendation medal with oak leaf cluster, Air Force Achievement medal with oak leaf cluster, Humanitarian Svc. medal. Mem. Nat. Guard Assn. U.S., Nat. Guard Assn. Tenn., Memphis Runners Track Club. Mem. Ch. of Christ. Home: 6794 Robin Perch Cove Memphis TN 38119-6728 Office: 164th Airlift Wing Ops Support Flight Tenn Air Nat Guard 2815 Democrat Rd Memphis TN 38118-1510

CUNNINGHAM, DON RODGER, English language educator, researcher; b. Indpls., Jan. 30, 1948; s. Don N. and Mary Katherine (Chapman) C.; m. Deborah Rae Cornn, Sept. 27, 1992; 1 child, Jessica Spring. BA in English, Marshall U., 1968; MA in Letters, Ind. U., 1972, PhD in Comparative Lit., 1980. Instr. Sue Bennett Coll., London, Ky., 1984-88, assoc. prof., 1988-94, prof., 1994—. Author: Apples on the Flood, 1987 (W. D. Weatherford award 1987). With U.S. Army, 1969-71. Named Woodrow Wilson Designate, Woodrow Wilson Found., 1968; recipient James Still fellowship Mellon Found., 1989. Mem. Am. Studies Assn., Appalachian Studies Assn., Nat. Coun. Tchrs. English, Melus, South Atlantic Modern Lang. Assn. Office: Sue Bennett Coll English Dept London KY 40741

CUNNINGHAM, JACK WAYNE, lawyer; b. Odessa, Tex., July 13, 1962; s. James D. and Florimel (Campbell) C. Cert. of tech., Tex. A&M Inst. Electronic Sci., 1982; BA in Bus. and Polit. Sci., Houston Bapt. U., 1991; JD/MBA, Tex. Tech. U., 1994. Electronics research technician Baroid Corp., Houston, 1982-87, Tideland Signal Corp., Houston, 1987-88; assoc. Law Offices of Forest D. Cook, Austin, Tex., 1994—. State del. Rep. Party Tex., Dallas, 1986. Baptist. Home: 13005 Heinemann Dr Apt 1001 Austin TX 78727-6978

CUNNINGHAM, JAMES WILLIAM, literacy education educator, researcher; b. Chattanooga, Jan. 22, 1947; s. Ernest James and Ann Louise Katherine (Martin) C.; m. Patricia M. Cunningham, Aug. 24, 1974; 1 child, David Ernest. BA in English, U. Va., 1970; MA in Reading Edn., U. Ga., 1973, PhD in Reading Edn., 1975. Classroom tchr. South Pittsburg (Tenn.) Elem. Sch., 1970-72; project coord. Right-to-Read Project, Athens, Ga., 1972-74; asst. prof. edn. U. N.C., Chapel Hill, 1975-80, assoc. prof., 1980-93, prof., 1993—. Contbr. numerous articles to profl. jours; co-author 7 textbooks, including: Developing Readers and Writers in the Content Areas: K-12, 2nd edit., Reading and Writing in Elementary Classrooms, 3rd edit. Mem. Internat. Reading Assn., Nat. Reading Conf., Nat. Conf. on Rsch. in Lang. and Literacy (fellow). Home: 811 Leigh Dr Gibsonville NC 27249-2734 Office: 304 Peabody Hall Cb 3500 U Nc Chapel Hill NC 27599

CUNNINGHAM, JOHN THOMAS, medicine educator, gastroenterologist; b. Washington, May 11, 1944; s. Edward J. and Henrietta (Ellis) C.; 1 child, Sean M. BS in Biology, Va. Poly. Inst. and State U., 1966; MD, Med. Coll. Va., 1970. Diplomate Am. Bd. Internal Medicine, Am. Bd. Gastroenterology. Intern Washington Hosp. Ctr., 1970-71; resident internal medicine Med. U. S.C., 1973-75, chief resident, 1974-75, fellow gastroenterology, 1975-77; asst. prof. medicine Med. U. S.C., Charleston, 1977-82, assoc. prof., 1982—, chief gastrointestinal endoscopy, 1980-94, prof. medicine, 1996—. Exhibited in group show Am. Physician Artists Assn., 1993 (2d pl. award), 1994 (1st pl. award). Fellow ACP, Am. Coll. Gastroenterology (bd. govs. 1986-92); mem. Am. Gastroenterology Assn., Charleston Yacht Club (commodore 1984-85). Home: 8 Jasper St Charleston SC 29403-6006 Office: Med U SC Digestive Disease Ctr 171 Ashley Ave Charleston SC 29425-0001

CUNNINGHAM, JUDY MARIE, lawyer; b. Durant, Okla., Sept. 7, 1944; d. Rowe Edwin and Margaret (Arnott) C. BA, U. Tex., 1967, JD, 1971; postgrad., Schiller Coll., Heidelberg, Fed. Republic Germany, 1976. Bar: Tex. 1972. Quizmaster U. Tex. Law Sch., Austin, 1969-71; researcher Tex. Law Rev., Washington, 1970; staff atty. Tex. Legis. Coun., Austin, 1972-75; adminstrv. law judge, dir. sales tax div., assoc. counsel Comptroller of Pub. Accounts, Austin, 1975-85; owner, editor J.C. Law Publs., Austin, 1986—; pvt. practice Austin, 1986—. Author: (with others) Texas Tax Service, 1985; pub., editor, contbr. (newsletter) Tex. State Tax Update, 1986—; contbr. articles to Revenue Adminstrn.; assoc. editor Tex. Law Rev., 1968-71. State del. Dem. Party, Ft. Worth, 1990, county del., Austin, 1972, 88, 90, 92; vol. numerous Dem. campaigns, Austin, 1972-90; mem. North Austin Dems., Austin, 1986—. Mem. Industry Practitioners Liaison Group (comptr. pub. accts.), State Bar Tex. (taxation sect.), Travis County Bar (bus. corp. and taxation sect.), Tex. Taxpayers and Rsch. Assn. Office: 4905 W Park Dr Austin TX 78731-5535

CUNNINGHAM, KAREN JEAN, humanities educator; b. Woonsocket, R.I., Oct. 9, 1946; d. William Harvey and Ethel Mae (Graham) C.; m. Gary Jay Karasik. BA in English with honors, Sacramento State Coll., Calif., 1969; MA in English with honors, San Francisco State Coll., 1972; PhD in English, U. Calif., Santa Barbara, 1985. Cert. adult edn. tchr., Calif. Mgr. mgmt. achievement program Pacific Telephone, San Francisco, 1972-73; instr. ESL Berlitz Lang. Schs., San Francisco, 1973-74; libr. asst. City of Daly City, Calif., 1974-77; lectr. dept. of English U. Calif., Santa Barbara, 1985-86; asst. prof. English Fla. State U., Tallahassee, 1987-93, assoc. prof. English, 1993—. Contbr. articles to profl. jours. Income tax assistance vol. V.I.T.A., San Francisco, 1972-73; election precinct vol. City and County of San Francisco, 1973-76; commr. Fla. Commn. on the Status of Women, Tallahassee, 1995—. Rsch. fellowship S.C. Davis Ctr. for Hist. Rsch., Princeton U., 1993, U. Calif., 1981-82; grantee Folger, Shakespeare Inst. and NEH,. Mem. AAUW, MLA, Marlowe Soc. of Am., Renaissance Soc. of Am., Shakespeare Assn. of Am., Soc. for the Study of Early Modern Women, South Atlantic MLA (women's caucus). Democrat. Office: Fla State Univ English Dept Tallahassee FL 32306-1036

CUNNINGHAM, NANCY SCHIEFFELIN, business educator; b. Mobile, Ala., Sept. 14, 1951; d. William Orville and Burline (Liningston) Schieffelin; m. Donald Frank Cunningham, Aug. 18, 1975; children: Benjamin Grant, Paige Allison. BA magna cum laude, U. North Tex., Denton, 1975; MA, Ohio State U., 1982. Cert. Myers Briggs Type Indicator adminstr. Mem. English faculty Franklin U., Columbus, Ohio; English curriculum coord. Ctr. for Unique Learners, Rockville, Mo.; mem. English faculty McClennan Community Coll., Waco, Tex.; coord. bus. writing Baylor U., Waco. Contbr. articles to profl. jours.; created and administers a writing proficiency exam. for bus. students. Baylor U. summer rsch. grantee. Mem. MLA, Assn. for Bus. Communication (rep.), Nat. Coun. Tchrs. English, Soc. for Tech. Communications.

CUNNINGHAM, PAUL RAYMOND GOLDWYN, surgery educator; b. Jamaica, July 28, 1949; came to U.S., 1974; s. Winston Pommells and Sylvia Fenella (Marsh) C.; m. Bridget Ann Mulvany, 1974 (div. 1985); children: Rachel Louise, Lucinda Jane; m. Sydney Louise Keniston, Feb. 14, 1987. MB, BS, Univ. West Indies, Jamaica, 1972. Diplomate Am. Bd. Surgery. Commd. maj. U.S. Army Res. Med. Corp., 1990; resident surgeon Mt. Sinai Hosp., N.Y.C., 1974-78, chief resident surgery, 1978-79, clin. instr., 1978-81; asst. dir. surgery and joint diseases North Gen. Hosp., N.Y.C., 1979-81, instr., 1981-84; attending surgeon Bertie County Meml. Hosp., Windsor, N.C., 1981-84, vice chief of staff, 1981-84; clin. instr. surgery East Carolina U. Sch. Medicine, Greenville, N.C., 1981-84, asst. prof. surgery Dept. Surgery, 1984-89, assoc. prof. and tenure, 1989-93, prof., 1993—; med. dir. Pitt County Meml. Hosp. Trauma Svc., Greenville, 1986—, chief of staff, 1991, various coms.; mem. N.C. Com. on Trauma, 1985—; cons., mem. Bertie County Dept. Health, Windsor, 1982-84. Contbr. articles to profl. jours. Mem. AMA, Am. Coun. on Transplantation, N.C. Med. Soc., Pitt County Med. Soc. A. Trauma Soc. (pres. N.C. chpt. 1989-91). Office: Pitt County Meml Hosp PO Box 6028 Greenville NC 27835-6028

CUNNINGHAM, R. WALTER, venture capitalist; b. Creston, Iowa, Mar. 16, 1932; s. Walter Wilfred and Gladys (Backen) C.; children: Brian Keith, Kimberly Ann. B.S. in Physics, UCLA, 1960, M.A., 1961; advanced mgmt. program, Harvard Grad. Sch. Bus., 1974. Research asst. Planning Research Corp., Westwood, Calif., 1959-60; physicist RAND Corp., Santa Monica, Calif., 1960-64; astronaut NASA, 1964-71; crew member of first manned Apollo spacecraft Apollo 7; sr. v.p. Century Devel., 1971-74; pres. Hydrotech Devel. Co., Houston, 1974-76; sr. v.p. 3D/Internat., Houston, 1976-79; founder The Capital Group, Houston, 1979-86; mng. ptnr. Genesis Fund, 1986—; bd. dirs. numerous tech. based cos. Author: The All American Boys, 1977. Judge Rolex awards for enterprise, 1984. With USNR, 1951-52, fighter pilot USMCR, 1952-74, col. ret. Recipient NASA Exceptional Service medal, also Haley Astronautics award; Profl. Achievement award U. Calif. at Los Angeles Alumni, 1969; Spl. Trustee award Nat. Acad. Television Arts and Scis., 1969; medal of valor Am. Legion, 1975; Outstanding Am. award Am. Conservative Union, 1975; named to Internat. Space Hall of Fame, Houston Hall of Fame. Fellow Am. Astronautical Soc.; mem. Soc. Exptl. Test Pilots, Am. Inst. Aeros. and Astronautics, Assn. Space Explorers-U.S.A., Am. Geophys. Union, Sigma Pi Sigma. Office: Genesis Venture Ptnrs 520 Post Oak Blvd Ste 130 Houston TX 77027-9405

CUNNINGHAM, THOMAS CRAIG, human resources professional; b. Lincoln, Nebr., Aug. 6, 1941; s. Thomas Clelland Cunningham and Helen Estelle (Rouse) Harrell. BA in Edn., Nebr. Wesleyan U., 1963; postgrad., U. Wyo., 1962, 63. Various human resource mgmt. positions Xerox Corp., until 1976; corp. pers. mgr. Loral Vought Sys. and Lockheed Martin Vought Sys., Grand Prairie, Tex., 1976-77; pers. dir. Wilson Food Co. subs. Loral Vought Systems Corp. div. Loral Corp., Grand Prairie, Tex., 1977-79, dir. pers. resources, 1979-84, dir. human resources missiles div., 1984-86, v.p. human resources, 1986—; mem. adv. bd. Ctr. for Human Resources Mgmt., Tex. A&M U.; mem. adv. bd. Student Work Consortium, U. Tex., Arlington. Mem. Phi Kappa Tau (nat. pres. 1979-81, bd. dirs. Found., Alumnus of Yr. award 1975). Office: Loral Vought Systems Corp PO Box 539002 Grand Prairie TX 75053-9002

CUNNINGHAM, WILLIAM HUGHES, academic administrator, marketing educator; b. Detroit, Jan. 5, 1944; married; 1 child. B.A., Mich. State U., 1966, M.B.A., 1967, Ph.D., 1971, LLD (hon.), 1993. Mem. faculty U. Tex., Austin, 1971—, assoc. prof. mktg., 1973-79, prof., 1979—, assoc. dean grad. programs, 1976-82, Foley/Sanger Harris prof. retail merchandising, 1982-83, acting dean Coll. Bus. Adminstrn. and Grad. Sch. Bus., 1982-83, dean, 1983-85, pres., 1985-92, Centennial Chair Bus. Edn. Leadership, 1983-85, Regents Chair Higher Edn. Leadership, 1985-92, Lee Hage and Joseph D. Jamail Regents Chair Higher Edn. Leadership, 1992—, James L. Bayless Chair for Free Enterprise, 1988—; chancellor U. Tex. System, Austin, 1992—; bd. dirs. La Quinta Motor Inns, Inc., Jefferson-Pilot Corp., John Hancock Funds; mem. Corp. of the Conf. Bd. Author: (with W.J.E. Crissy and I.C.M. Cunningham) Selling: The Personal Force in Marketing, 1977, 2d edit. (with D.W. Jackson and Cunningham), 1988, Effective Selling, 1977, Spanish edit., 1980, (with S. Lopreato) Consumers' Energy Attitudes and Behavior, 1977, (with Cunningham) Marketing: A Managerial Approach, 1981, 2d edit. (with Cunningham and C. Swift), 1988, (with R. Aldag and C. Swift) Introduction to Business, 1984, 3d edit. (with R. Aldag and S. Block), 1992, 4th edit. (with R. Aldag and M. Stone), 1995, (with B. Verhage and Cunningham) Grondslagen van het Marketing Management, 1984, (with R. Aldag and S. Block) Business in a Changing World, 1992, also monographs and articles; editor Jour. Mktg., 1981-84. Bd. dirs. Houston Area Rsch. Coun., 1984; mem. Mental Health/Mental Retardation Legis. Oversight Com., 1984; mem. adv. bd. Found. for Cultural Exch./The Netherlands-U.S.A.; bd. dirs. Lyndon Baines Johnson Found. Recipient Teaching Excellence award Coll. Bus. Adminstrn., U. Tex., 1972, Alpha Kappa Psi, 1975, Hank and Mary Harkins Found., 1978, Disting. Scholastic Contbn. award Coll. Bus. Adminstrn. Found. Adv. Council, 1982, Disting. Alumnus award Coll. and Grad. Sch. Bus., Mich. State U., 1983, 93, Tree of Life award Jewish Nat. Fund, 1992; named among top 20 profs. Utmost Mag., 1982; research grantee Univ. Research Inst., 1971, 72-73, Latin Am. Inst., 1972, So. Union Gas Energy, 1975-76, ERDA, 1976. Mem. Am. Inst. for Decision Scis., Am. Mktg. Assn., Assn. Consumer Research, So. Mktg. Assn., S.W. Social Sci. Assn., Phi Kappa Phi, Omicron Delta Kappa. Office: U TX System Office 601 Colorado St Austin TX 78701-2904*

CUNTZ, MANFRED ADOLF, astrophysicist, researcher; b. Landau, Rheinland-Pfalz, Fed. Republic Germany, Apr. 21, 1958; came to U.S., 1988; s. Gerhard Hermann and Irene Emma (Messerschmitt) C.; m. Anne-Gret Vera Friedrich, Sept. 19, 1988; 1 child, Heiko Benjamin. Diplom in Physics, U. Heidelberg, Fed. Republic of Germany, 1985, PhD in Astronomy, 1988. Postdoctoral, rsch. assoc. Joint Inst. Lab. Astrophysics-U. Colo., Boulder, 1989-91; postdoctoral, rsch. assoc. High Altitude Obs. div. Nat. Ctr. Atmospheric Rsch., Boulder, 1992-94; habilitation in astronomy U. Heidelberg, Germany, 1995; staff rsch. scientist dept. mech. engring. Ctr. Space Plasma & Aeronomic Rsch., U. Ala., Huntsville, 1996—. Contbr. articles to Astrophys. Jour., Astronom. Jour., Astronomy and Astrophysics. Grantee German Rsch. Found., NASA, NSF, Dutch Nat. Sci. Orgn. Mem. Internat. Astron. Union (com. 36), Am. Astron. Soc., Deutsche Astronomische Gesellschaft, Deutsche Physikalische Gesellschaft, Vereinigung der Sternfreunde. Office: Ctr Space Plasma Aeronomic Rsch Univ Alabama Huntsville AL 35899

CUPP, ROBERT ERHARD, golf course designer, land use planner; b. Lewistown, Pa., Dec. 27, 1939; s. Foster Wilson and Elizabeth (Erhard) C.; m. Glenda Dell, Aug. 26, 1962 (div. 1983); children: Robert E. II, Caren E., Laura G.; m. Pamela Patricia Amy, Dec. 27, 1986. BA, U. Miami, Coral Gables, Fla., 1962; MA, U.S. Army, Anchorage, 1966. Art dir. Jefferson, Inc., Miami, 1966-67; golf profl. Colonial Palms Country Club, Miami, 1967-68, Crooked Creek Country Club, Miami, 1968-69; pvt. practice golf course architect Miami, 1969-72; golf course architect Golden Bear Enterprises, North Palm Beach, Fla., 1972-84; pvt. practice golf course architect Atlanta, 1984—; sr. designer Jack Nicklaus Design, North Palm Beach, 1972-84; pres. Cupp Design, Inc., Atlanta, 1984—. Designed East Sussex (Eng.) Nat. Golf Club, site of 1993-94 European Open Championship (Best New Golf Course, Golf Monthly), Pumpkin Ridge Golf Club, Portland, Oreg., Greystone Country Club, Birminham, Ala., permanent site of Bruno Meml. Classic, PGA Tours Seniors, Old Waverly Golf Club, West Point, Miss. (Top 100 Golf Course in U.S., Golf Digest), Settindown Creek Golf Club, Atlanta, permanent site of U.S. Nike Tour Ann. Championship, Pumpkin Ridge, Ghost Creek, 1992 (Best New Course, Golf Digest), Western Gales, Osceola, Mich., 1993, Indianwood, Lake Orion, Mich., 1988 (Runner up Best New Course, Golf Digest), Pumpkin Ridge, Witch Hollow, Portland, 1992, Old Waverly, West Point, 1989, Big Sky Country Club, Pemberton, B.C., Can., 1994. Served to capt. U.S. Army, 1963-66. Named Golf World/Golf Digest Designer of Yr., 1992. Office: Cupp Design Inc Two Piedmont Ctr Ste 504 Atlanta GA 30305

CURBOY, ROBERT EDWARD, aviation safety consultant; b. Southbridge, Mass., Jan. 4, 1928; s. William Joseph and Rosetta (Lariviere) C.; m. Dawn Lorraine Kirkness, June 6, 1968. BS, St. Louis U., 1952; MS, Embry-Riddle, Daytona Beach, Fla., 1987. Cert. FAA airman. Aviation safety rep. North Am. Aviation, Inc., Columbus, Ohio, 1955-57; Pacific area rep. North Am. Aviation, Inc., Kaneohe, Hawaii, 1957-59; test program dir. North Am. Aviation, Inc., Columbus, Ohio, 1960-63; team leader North Am. Aviation, Inc., Sanford, Fla., 1963-67; base mgr. Rockwell Internat. Corp., Sanford and Key West, 1967-78; Middle East rep. Rockwell, Sabreliner Div., Amman, Jordan, 1978-79; Southeastern U.S. regional rep. Rockwell, Sabreliner Div., Ft. Lauderdale, Fla., 1979-83; project mgr. Rockwell Internat. Corp., El Segundo, Calif., 1983-89; cons., owner Aviation Safety Sci., Lake Mary, Fla., 1989—; adj. prof. Embry-Riddle Aero. U., Riverside, Calif., 1987-89, alumni corp. rep., 1988-89; citizen ambassador People to People, Peoples Rep. of China, 1988. Contbr. articles to profl. jours.; editor: (tng. manual) Aircraft Systems, 1953. Dir. Home Owners Assn., Key West, 1974-76; pres. Home Owners Assn., Lake Mary, Fla., 1995—; pres. Condo Owners Assn., Winter Springs Ctr. Recipient Boss of Yr. award, City of Albany, Ga., 1973. Mem. AIAA, Am. Soc. Safety Engrs., Internat. Soc. Air Safety Investigators (mem. standards and policy rev. bd. 1991—), Nat. Space Soc., Exptl. Aircrafts Assn. (bd. dirs. chpt. 949, 1992—), Ret. Naval Officers Assn. (bd. dirs. Sanford area 1991—), People to People Internat., Phi Alpha Chi (pres. St. Louis chpt. 1951-52). Home and Office: Aviation Safety Sci 807 Whittingham Ct Lake Mary FL 32746-6301

CURETON, CLAUDETTE HAZEL CHAPMAN, biology educator; b. Greenville, S.C., May 3, 1932; d. John H. and Beatrice (Washington) Chapman; m. Stewart Cleveland, Dec. 27, 1954; children: Ruthye, Stewart II, S. Charles, Samuel. AB, Spelman Coll., 1951; MA, Fisk U., 1966; DHum (hon.), Morris Coll., Sumter, S.C., 1996. Tchr. North Warren High Sch., Wise, N.C., 1952-60; tchr. Sterling High Sch., Greenville, 1960-66, Wade Hampton High Sch., Greenville, 1967-73; instr. Greenville Tech. Coll., 1973-95, ret., 1995; bd. dirs. State Heritage Trust, 1978-91; commr. Basic Skills Adv. Program, Columbia, 1990—; mem. adv. bd. Am. Fed. Bank, NCNB Bank, Greenville, 1991—. Mem. Greenville Urban League, NAACP, S.C. Curriculum Congress; v.p. Bapt. E.& M. Conv. of S.C.; mem. S.C. Commn. on Higher Edn. Com. for Selection of the 1995 Gov.'s Prof. of the Yr. Recipient Presdl. award Morris Coll., 1987, 91, Svc. award S.C. Wildlife and Marine Dept., 1986, Outstanding Jack and Jill of Am. citation, 1986, Excellence in Tchg. award Nat. Inst. for Staff and Orgnl. Devel., U. Tex., Austin, 1992-93, Educator of Yr. award Greenville chpt. Am. Cancer Soc., 1994, Outstanding Svc. award Best Chance Network/Am. Cancer Soc., 1994, Citation S.C. House of Reps., 1995. Mem. AAAS, AAUW, Nat. Assn. Biology Tchrs., S.C. Curriculum Congress, Nat. Coun. Negro Women, Inc., Higher Edn. S.C. Com. for Selection Prof. of Yr. 1995, Delta Sigma Theta (past v.p. Greenville chpt. alumnae). Home: 501 Mary Knob Greenville SC 29607-5242

CURL, SAMUEL EVERETT, university dean, agricultural scientist; b. Ft. Worth, Dec. 26, 1937; s. Henry Clay and Mary Elva (Watson) C.; m. Betty Doris Savage, June 6, 1957 (div.); children: Jane Ellen, Julia Kathleen, Karen Elizabeth; m. Mary Behrends Reeves, Sept. 11, 1993; stepchildren: Ryan Andrew, Shelly Lyn. Student, Tarleton State Coll., 1955-57; BS, Sam Houston State U., 1959; MS, U. Mo., 1961; PhD, Tex. A&M U., 1963. Mem. faculty Tex. Tech U., Lubbock, 1961, 63-76, 79—, tchr., researcher animal physiology and genetics, 1963-76, asst., assoc. and interim dean Coll. Agrl. Sci., 1968-73, assoc. v.p. acad. affairs, 1973-76, dean Coll. Agrl. Scis., prof., 1979—; pres. Phillips U., Enid, Okla., 1976-79; agrl. cons., 1964—; bd. dirs. Agrl. Workers Mut. Auto Ins. Co.; mem. Gov.'s Task Force on Agrl. Devel. in Tex., 1982-83, 88; chmn. Tex. Fire Ant Adv. Bd., 1993—; mem. Tex. Crop and Livestock Adv. Com., 1985-91; mem. Tex. Agrl. Resources Protection Authority, 1989—, Tex. Agribus. Rsch. Promotion Coun., 1995—; del. Eisenhower Consortium for Western Environ. Forestry Rsch., 1979-84; mgmt. com. S.W. Consortium on Plant Genetics and Water Resources, 1984—, chmn., 1989—; mem. USDA Nat. Planning Com. on Hispanic Minority Recruitment, 1988-93; trustee Consortium for Internat. Devel., mem. exec. com., 1981-84, 86-87, 89-90; mem. High Plains Rsch. Coord. Bd.; former mem. So. Regional Coun., U.S. Joint Coun. Food and Agrl. Scis.; former trustee Water Inc.; chmn. agrl. and natural resources program rev. task force Sam Houston State U., 1982-83; mem. adv. com. Sch. Agr. Angelo State U., 1989—; mem. 1995 farm bill task force Tex. Dept. Agr., 1994-95. Author: (with others) Progress and Change in the Agricultural Industry, 1974, Food and Fiber for a Changing World, 1976, 2d edit., 1982; contbr. 95 articles to profl. jours. Pres. Lubbock Econ. Coun., 1982; bd. dirs. Market Lubbock Econ. Devel. Corp.; former mem. bd. overseers Ranching Heritage Assn.; mem. Goals for Lubbock: A Vision into the 21st Century Com.; elder Westminster Presbyn. Ch., Lubbock. 2d lt. U.S. Army, 1959, capt. USAR. Danforth Assn. fellow, 1964-76, Am. Coun. Edn. fellow, 1972-73; recipient Disting. Alumnus award, Faculty-Alumni Gold medal U. Mo., 1975, Outstanding Agr. Alumnus award Sam Houston State U., 1986, Disting. Alumnus award, 1993, Tex. Citation for Outstanding Svc. award Tex. 4-H Found., 1987, Tex. 4-H Alumni award, 1993, Disting. Svc. award Vocational Agrl. Tchrs. Assn. Tex., 1987, Blue and Gold Meritorious Svc. award Tex. Future Farmers of Am., 1988, Tex. State degree Future Farmers Am., 1988, Area Disting. Svc. award Vocat. Agr. Tchrs., 1987. Mem. Am. Soc. Animal Sci. (program com. Biennial Symposium on Animal Reprodn. 1972-76, reviewer Jour. Animal Sci.), Am. Assn. Univ. Agrl. Adminstrs., Assn. U.S. Univ. Dirs. Internat. Agrl. Programs, So. Assn. Agrl. Scientists, Nat. Assn. State Univs. and Land-Grant Colls. (exec. com. bd. agr. 1994—), Coun. Adminstrv. Heads of Agr., Tex. Agrl. Lifetime Leadership Adv. Coun., Profl. Agrl. Workers Tex. (bd. dirs., Disting. Svc. to Tex. Agr. award 1984), Tex. Tech. Ex-Students Assn. Century Club, West Tex. C. of C. (bd. dirs., chmn. agrl. and ranching com.), Lubbock C. of C. (bd. dirs. 1988-92, chmn. agr. task force, chmn. rsch. com. 1981-86, water com., legis. affairs com., agr. com., gubernatorial appointments task force), Rotary (bd. dirs., 1st. v.p. Lubbock club), Farmhouse Frat. (assoc.), Omicron Delta Kappa, Sigma Xi, Phi Kappa Phi, Gamma Sigma Delta. Home: 5613 83rd Ln Lubbock TX 79424-4627 Office: Office Dean Agrl Scis Tex Tech U Lubbock TX 79409

CURLE, ROBIN LEA, computer software industry executive; b. Denver, Feb. 23, 1950; d. Fred Warren and Claudia Jean (Harding) C.; m. Lucien Ray Reed, Feb. 23, 1981 (div. Oct. 1984). BS, U. Ky., 1972. Systems analyst 1st Nat. BAnk, Lexington, Ky., 1972-73, SW BancShares, Houston, 1973-77; sales rep. Software Internat., Houston, 1977-80; dist. mgr. Uccell, Dallas, 1980-82; v.p. Info. Sci., Atlanta, 1982-83; v.p. sales TesserAct, San Francisco, 1983-86, Foothill Rsch., San Francisco, 1986-89; pres., founder Curle Cons. Group, San Francisco, 1987-89; mgr. strategic mktg. MCC, Austin, Tex., 1989-90; founder, exec. v.p. Evolutionary Tech., Inc., Austin, 1991—. Mem. U. Ky. Alumni Assn., Delta Gamma (pres. 1969). Republican. Home: 7009 Quill Leaf Cove Austin TX 78750

CURLEE, DOROTHY SUMNER, social worker; b. Coleman, Tex., July 31, 1921; d. Thaddeus Pickett and Lena (Pierson) Sumner; B.A., Howard Payne Coll., 1942; postgrad. Tulane U., 1944; M.S. in Social Work, Columbia U., 1963; 1 child, Lenae. Supr. child welfare Tex. Dept. Human Resources, 1944-54, 59-60; dir. adoptions Hope Cottage Children's Bur., Dallas, 1961-69; cons. Adoption Resource Exchange N.Am., Child Welfare League Am., 1969-70; asso. dir. Children's Home Soc. N.C., Greensboro, 1970-72; med. psychiat. social worker Tex. Dept. Mental Health and Mental Retardation, Denton, 1972-78; program mgr. crippled children's div. Tex. Dept. Health, Abilene, 1978-87; field instr. social work U. Tex., 1950-52, 69, 86.

CURLEE, ROBERT GLEN, JR., special education educator; b. Wetumpka, Ala., July 19, 1951; s. Robert Glen and Betty Jean (Poston) C.; m. Cherie Bowick, Apr. 3, 1981; children: Emily, Amy, Christian. BEd in Elem. and Spl. Edn., Auburn U., Montgomery, Ala., 1974; MEd in Adminstrn. and Supervision, Troy State U., Montgomery, 1976. Cert. tchr., Ala. Tchr. Elmore County Headstart, Wetumpka, 1978, supr. of ctr., 1979; elem., jr. and sr. high sch. spl. edn. tchr. of homebound Elmore County Bd. Edn., Wetumpka, 1974—. Mem. Wetumpka Civitan Club (v.p. 1989-91).

Democrat. Methodist. Home: 57 1st Pl Wetumpka AL 36092-8715 Office: Elmore County Spl Edn Annex Broad St Wetumpka AL 36092

CURLEY, JOHN J., diversified media company executive; b. Dec. 31, 1938; m. Ann Conser; two sons. BA, Dickinson Coll., 1960; MS, Columbia Univ., 1963. Reporter, editor AP, 1961-66; with Gannett Co., Inc., Arlington, Va., 1969—; pres. Mid-Atlantic newspaper group Gannett Co., Inc., Washington, 1980-82; sr. v.p. Gannett Co., Inc., Washington, 1983-84, pres., 1984—, chief operating officer, 1984-86, chief exec. officer, 1986—, chmn., 1989—, also bd. dirs. Lt. U.S. Army, 1960-62. Office: Gannett Co Inc 1100 Wilson Blvd Arlington VA 22209-2297

CURLEY, THOMAS, newspaper executive; b. Easton, Pa., July 6, 1948; s. John Joseph and Emily Dixon (Sprague) C.; m. Marsha Stanley, Sept. 14, 1974; children: Laura Stanley, Melinda Burke. BA in Polit. Sci., La Salle U., 1970; MBA, Rochester Inst. Tech., 1977. Reporter The News Tribune, Woodbridge, N.J., 1967, 68, reporter, copy editor, 1970-72; night city/suburban editor The Times-Tribune, Rochester, N.Y., 1972-76; dir. info. Gannett Co., Inc., Rochester, 1976-80, dir. research, 1980-82; editor Norwich (Conn.) Bulletin, 1982-83; pub. The Courier-News, Bridgewater, N.J., 1983-85; exec. v.p. USA Today, Washington, 1985-86, pres., 1986-89, pres., chief operating officer, from 1989, now pres., pub.; trustee La Salle U., Phila., 1987—; trustee Rochester Inst. Tech. Pres. Ctrl. Jersey C. of C., Plainfield, N.J., 1984-85; exec. v.p. United Way Somerset Valley, Bridgewater, 1985; bd. dirs. Assn. for Retarded Citizens, Manville, N.J., 1983-85. Pub. Opinion Rsch. fellow Northwestern U., 1976; recipient Alumnus of Yr. award Rochester Inst. Tech., 1986. Office: USA Today 1000 Wilson Blvd Arlington VA 22229

CURNES, JOHN TAYLOR, neuroradiologist; b. South Charleston, W.Va., Dec. 8, 1954; s. George Carl and Grace Beatrice (Taylor) C.; m. Cheryl Anne Viglione, June 17, 1984; children: Anthony, Laurie, John, Nicole, Natalie. BS in Chemistry summa cum laude, Hampden-Sydney Coll., 1974; MD, Tulane U., 1978. Diplomate Am. Bd. Radiology. Intern surgery U. N.C. Hosps., Chapel Hill, 1978-79, resident neurosurgery, 1979-81, resident radiology, 1981-84, asst. prof. neuroradiology, 1985-87; instr. neuroradiology Bowman Gray Sch. Medicine, Winston-Salem, N.C., 1984-85; asst. prof. neuroradiology Duke U. Med. Ctr., Durham, N.C., 1987-88; dir. neuroradiology Moses Cone Hosp., Greensboro, N.C., 1988—; clin. asst. prof. U. N.C. Hosps., Chapel Hill, 1990—. Mem. editorial rev. bd. Am. Jour. Neuroradiology, 1990—; contbr. articles to profl. jours. Recipient Award for Outstanding Undergrad. majoring in chemistry Am. Inst. Chemists. Mem. Am. Soc. Neuroradiology (sr. mem.), Am. Coll. Radiology, Radiol. Soc. N.Am., Southeastern Neuroradiology Soc., Southeastern Angiographic Soc., Starmount Forest Country Club. Home: 119 Staunton Dr Greensboro NC 27410-6064 Office: Greensboro Radiology Assocs 1302 Carolina St # A Greensboro NC 27401-1002

CUROL, HELEN RUTH, librarian, English language educator; b. Grayson, La., May 30, 1944; d. Alfred John and Ethel Lea (McDaniel) Broussard; m. Kenneth Arthur Curol, June 25, 1967 (div. 1988); children: Edward, Bryan. BA, McNeese State U., 1966; postgrad., L.I. U., 1969-70; MLS, La. State U., 1987. Tchr., libr. Cameron Parish Schs., Grand Lake, La., 1966-67; media specialist Brentwood (N.Y.) Sch. Dist., 1967-69; sch. libr. Patchogue (N.Y.) H.S., 1969-70;, 1976-95; reference libr., mgr. circulation dept. McNeese State U., Lake Charles, La., 1976-96; test adminstr. Edn. Testing Svc., Princeton, N.J., 1987-95; asst. prof. McNeese U., 1989-95; owner Creative Concepts Cons., Lake Charles, 1995—; head adult svcs. Laman Pub. Libr., North Little Rock, Ark., 1996—; rschr. Boise Cascade, DeRidder, La., 1987-88, Vidtron, Dallas, 1990-92, Nat. Archives, Washington, 1989; cons. Cmty. Housing Resource Bd., Lake Charles, 1988-93, Boyce Internat. Engrs., Houston, 1988-89, La. Pub. Broadcasting, Baton Rouge, 1989; devel. cons. Calcasieu Women's Shelter, 1988-92; reference cons. Calcasieu Parish Pub. Libr., 1990-95; presenter conf. at Tulane U., South Ctrl. Women's Assn., 1994. Sr. arbitrator Better Bus. Bur., Lake Charles, 1986-95; local facilitator La. Com. for Fiscal Reform, Lake Charles, 1988; state bd. dirs. PTA, Baton Rouge, 1981-83, LWV La., Baton Rouge, 1983-85; chairperson budget panel com. United Way S.W. La., Lake Charles, 1992-94, bd. dirs., 1995-96; judge La. region IV Social Studies Fair, 1979-89; program spkr. region IV tng. conf. HUD, El Paso, 1992. Named Citizen of the Day, Sta. KLOU, 1978; grantee La. Endowment for Humanities, 1987, La. Divsn. Arts, 1989, Fair Housing Initiative Program, 1990, HUD, 1992, La. Ctr. Women and Govt. of Nicholls State U., 1993. Mem. ALA (sec. coun. 1988-90, chairperson coun. 1990-91), AAUW (chairperson intellectual freedom com. 1988-89), La. Libr. Assn. (chairperson reference group 1988-90), La. Assn. Coll. and Rsch. Librs. (chairperson 1995-96), Ark. Libr. Assn., McNeese U. Alumni Assn., S.W. La. C. of C. (mem. legis. com. 1992), Krewe du Feteurs (Mardi Gras Ct. Duchess 1992), Beta Sigma Phi (pres. Lake Charles chpt. 1983-84), Beta Phi Mu. Democrat. Lutheran. Office: Laman Pub Libr 2801 Orange St North Little Rock AR 72114

CURRAN, CHRISTOPHER, economics educator; b. Washington, Nov. 5, 1943; s. Charles Daniel and Virginia (Wray) C.; m. Nannette Carter, June 10, 1978; children: John Fredrick, Christianne Michelle. BA in History, Rice U., 1967; MS in Econs., Purdue U., 1969, PhD in Econs., 1972. Grad. instr. econs. Purdue U., 1967-70; asst. prof. econs. Emory U., Atlanta, 1970-77, sr. acad. assoc. Law and Econs. Ctr., 1983-86, sr. acad. assoc. law and econs., 1986—, assoc. prof. econs., 1977—, dir. undergrad. studies, 1994-96; Fulbright lectr., Peru, 1976. Contbr. articles and book revs. to profl. jours. Bd. mem. Lullwater Sch., Atlanta, 1975; v.p. Virginia Hill Condo Assn., Atlanta, 1993, pres. 1994, treas. 1995. Krannert rsch. grantee, 1969-70, grantee Emory U., 1972, 75, 79, Emory Bus. Sch., 1978-80, 82. Mem. Am. Econ. Assn., So. Econ. Assn., Am. Law and Econs. Assn., European Assn. Law and Econs. (assoc.). Home: 587 Virginia Ave NE Apt 603 Atlanta GA 30306-3697 Office: Emory U Dept Econs 1641 N Decatur Rd NE Atlanta GA 30307-1009

CURRAN, DAVID BERNARD, JR., real estate executive; b. New Haven, June 6, 1959; s. David Bernard Sr. and Helen Rita (Healey) C.; m. Nancy Manier Nickey, Mar. 19, 1988; children: David Bernard III, George Nickey, Sarah Elizabeth. BBA, So. Meth. U., 1981. Ptnr., exec. v.p. Fults Realty Corp., Dallas, 1981—; bd. trustees bldgs. and grounds com. So. Meth. U. Fundraiser Am. Heart Assn., Dallas, 1982—, Boy Scouts Am., Dallas, 1983; vol. Big Bros. Dallas, 1985. Mem. North Tex. Comml. Assn. of Realtors, Northwood Country Club. Republican. Roman Catholic. Home: 3541 Colgate Ave Dallas TX 75225-5010 Office: Fults Realty Corp 9400 N Central Expy Fl 5 Dallas TX 75231

CURRAN, DIAN BEARD, physicist, consultant; b. Woodland, Calif., Aug. 8, 1956; d. David Breed and Eileen Mona (Hersey) Beard; m. Terrence Antony Whelan, June 28, 1985 (div. June, 1990). BS in Physics, U. Kans., 1983; MS in Physics, U. Iowa, 1987. Cons. S.W. Rsch. Inst., San Antonio, 1988-93; rsch. asst. astronomy dept. U. Tex., Austin, 1992—; mem. Am. Indian Resource and Edn. Coalition, 1991-94. Contbr. articles to Jour. Geophys. Rsch., Geophys. Rsch. Letters, Mercury, Radio Sci. Mem. San Antonio Coun. Native Ams., 1989-93, bd. dirs., 1991-93; Dem. del. to Iowa State Conv., 1984, 88; bd. dirs. Pet Helpers, Austin, 1992-93. Travel fellow NASA, 1987, 91. Mem. Am. Geophys. Union, Am. Astron. Soc. (jr. mem.). Democrat. Home: 314 Craigmont Dr # B Austin TX 78745-4456 Office: U Tex Astronomy Dept Austin TX 78712

CURRIE, CAMERON MCGOWAN, judge; b. 1948. BA, U. S.C., 1970; JD with honors, George Washington U., 1975. Tchr. Moultrie H.S., Mt. Pleasant; law clk. to magistrate judge Hon. Arthur L. Burnett U.S. Dist. Ct. D.C., 1973-74; atty. Arent, Fox, Kintner, Plotkin & Kahn, Washington, 1975-78; asst. U.S. Atty. Office U.S. Atty., Washington, 1978-80, Columbia, S.C., 1980-84; magistrate judge U.S. Dist. Ct. S.C., Columbia, 1984-86; pvt. practice Columbia, 1986-89; chief dep. atty. gen. Office Atty. Gen., State of S.C., Columbia, 1989-94; judge U.S. Dist. Ct. S.C., Florence, 1994—; adj. prof. in trial advocacy Sch. Law U. S.C., 1986-89. Assoc. editor SEC No Action Letters Index, 1972-73. Bd. dirs. Wings, Inc., 1986-94, sec., 1992-94. Mem. ABA, S.C. Bar, D.C. Bar, S.C. Bar Assn., S.C. Women Lawyers Assn. Office: US Dist Ct PO Box 2617 Florence SC 29503-2617

CURRIE, JOHN THORNTON (JACK CURRIE), retired investment banker; b. Houston, Aug. 4, 1928; s. John Felix and Irma Lillian (Haxthausen) C.; m. Dorothy Lee Peek, May 30, 1959; children: Harriss Thornton, Laura Tucker. BA, U. Tex., 1949, BBA, 1950. Salesman Harris, Upham & Co., N.Y.C. and Houston, 1950-52; ptnr. Moreland, Brandenberger & Currie, Galveston, Tex., 1955-60; pres., bd. dirs. Moroney, Beissner & Co., Inc., Houston, 1960-74; sr. v.p., bd. dirs. Rotan Mosle Inc., Houston, 1974-81, chmn., 1981-83; vice chmn. Rotan Mosle Fin. Corp., Houston, 1984; mng. dir. Mason Best Co., Houston, 1984-86; bd. dirs. Stewart & Stevenson Svcs., Inc., Houston, Am. Nat. Growth Fund, Am. Nat. Income Fund, Triflex Fund, Galveston, Am. Indemnity Fin. Corp., Galveston; Internat. Exec. Svc. Corps rep. Muslim Comml. Bank, Karachi, Pakistan, 1992, Govt. of Lithuania, Vilnius, 1993. Trustee Holly Hall, Hosuton, 1968-73, Harris and Eliza Kempner Fund, Galveston, Tex., 1975—; mem. devel. bd. U. Tex. Health Sci. Ctr., Houston, 1978-89, U. Tex. Med. Br., Galveston, 1992—; mem. chancellor's coun. U. Tex. System; established Mary Tucker Currie Professorship, Tex. A&M u. 1st lt. U.S. Army, 1952-54. Mem. Houston Country Club, Galveston Artillery Club, Krewe of Momus Galveston (pres. 1990-91), The Yacht Club (Galveston). Republican. Episcopalian. Home: 323 Longwoods Ln Houston TX 77024-5615 Office: 515 Post Oak Blvd Ste 750 Houston TX 77027-9408

CURRIER, SUSAN ANNE, computer software company executive; b. Melbourne, Victoria, Australia, Nov. 20, 1949; d. David Eric and Irene Hazel (Baker) Bruce-Smith; m. Kenneth Palmer Currier, Feb. 16, 1974. Student, Melbourne U., 1967-70. Fashion model Eileen Ford Model Agy., N.Y.C., 1971-74, Wilhelmina Models, N.Y.C., 1974-82; owner Softsync Inc., N.Y.C., 1981-91; pres. Expert Software, Coral Gables, Fla., 1989—. Home: 201 Crandon Blvd Apt 1141 Key Biscayne FL 33149-1520 Office: Expert Software Exec Tower 800 S Douglas Rd Coral Gables FL 33134-3125

CURRY, DONALD ROBERT, lawyer, oil company executive; b. Pampa, Tex., Aug. 7, 1943; s. Robert Ward and Alleith Elizabeth (Elliston) C.; m. Carolyn Sue Boland, Apr. 17, 1965; 1 son, James Ward. BS, West Tex. State U., 1965; JD, U. Tex., 1968. Bar: Tex. 1968, U.S. Dist. Ct. (no. dist.) Tex. 1970, U.S. Tax Ct. 1973. Assoc., Day & Gandy, Ft. Worth, 1968-69, ptnr., 1970-72; pvt. practice, Ft. Worth, 1972—; mng. ptnr. Curry & Thornton Oil, 1981—; lectr. in field. Bd. regents West Tex. State U., Canyon, 1969-77, sec., mem. exec. com., 1972-75; mem. exec. bd. Longhorn council Boy Scouts Am., 1970—, dist. chmn., 1970-75 (recipient Silver Beaver award 1994); precinct chmn. Tarrant County (Tex.) Democratic Party, 1982—, election judge, 1982-94; mem. aviation adv. bd. City of Ft. Worth, 1990-95, vice chmn. bd., chmn. bd. dirs., 1994-95. Fellow Tex. Bar Found.; mem. State Bar Tex., ABA, Fort Worth-Tarrant County Bar Assn., Ft. Worth Bus. and Estate Council, Tex. Ind. Producers and Royalty Owners Assn., Phi Alpha Delta, Phi Delta Theta. Methodist. Clubs: YMCA Century, Ft. Worth, Petroleum of Fort Worth. Home: 3800 Tulsa Way Fort Worth TX 76107-3346 Office: 905 Ft Worth Clb Bldg Fort Worth TX 76102-4911

CURRY, EDWARD THOMAS, JR., tire dealership executive; b. Phila., May 23, 1926; s. Edward Thomas and Ethel Vincent (Reeve) C.; m. Kathleen Wiegand, June 1950 (div. July 1971); children: Reeve, Michael; m. Violet O'Daniel, July 16, 1971; children: Rosalind, Ann, Edgar, Richard. BSBA, Rutgers U., 1950. With mktg. Standard Oil Indiana, Madison, Wis., 1951-52, Sun Oil Co., Camden, N.J., 1952-55, Atlantic Richfield, Charlotte, N.C., 1956-64; pres. Hub City Oil Co., Inc., Hickory, N.C., 1964-69, Ind. Enterprises, Inc., Greensboro, N.C., 1970—; arbitrator Am. Arbitration Assn., Greensboro, 1990—, Ford Consumers Appeal Bd., 1987-90; bd. arbitrators Nat. Assn. Security Dealers, 1991—; panel arbitrators N.Y. Stock Exch., 1991—. Bd. dirs. Adult Ctr. for Enrichment, 1994—. Mem. BBB Cen. N.C. (Arbitrator of Yr. 1991), Mediation Svc. of Guilford County (bd. chmn. 1986-89, 94—, cert. N.C. mediator mediated settlement conf. pilot program 1994), Forest Oaks Country Club. Republican. Presbyterian.

CURRY, LINDA JEAN, social studies educator; b. Logan, W.Va., Aug. 12, 1947; d. Jack Curry and Jean (Chafin) Hunt; children: Celeste Holley Henderson, Martin McTyeire Holley. BA, U. S.C., 1969; MA, Appalachian State U., 1983; PhD, Tex. A&M U., 1990. Cert. tchr., S.C., Tex. Instr. Tex. A&M U., College Station, 1988-90; asst. prof. social studies, supr. student tchrs. Clemson (S.C.) U., 1990—; Montessori tchr. Dallas Ind. Sch. Sys., 1993—. Editor The Clemson Kappan, 1993—; contbr. articles to profl. jours. Advisor Head Start, Anderson, S.C., 1994—; mem. adv. bd. L.L. Hotchkiss Montessori Acad., Dallas, 1997-98. Mem. Internat. Reading Assn. (Foothills chpt. membership chmn. 1991-92), Phi Delta Kappa (Clemson chpt. v.p. 1991-93, pres. 1993—, Outstanding Achievement award in higher edn. 1993). Democrat. Home: Lake Hartwell Anderson SC 29625 Office: Clemson Univ 405 Tillman Hall Clemson SC 29634-0709

CURRY, NANCY LYNNE STILES, radiologist, educator; b. Rochester, N.Y., Jan. 11, 1947; d. Melvin Stuart and Alvina Christine (Scherer) S.; m. Robert Wilker Curry, Aug. 16, 1979; children: Scott, Ryan, Laurel. BA, U. Rochester, 1968; MD, Med. Coll. Pa., 1972. Diplomate Am. Bd. Radiology. Internal medicine intern Med. Coll. Pa., Phila., 1972-73, resident in internal medicine, 1973-74; pvt. practice Oak Orchard Community Health Ctr., Rochester, 1974-76; resident in radiology U. Rochester, 1976-79; fellow in uroradiology UCLA, 1979-80; asst. prof. radiology Med. U. S.C., Charleston, 1980-86, assoc. prof. radiology, 1986-95, prof. radiology, 1995—. Contbr. chpts. to 11 books, 44 articles to profl. jours. Fellow Am. Coll. Radiology; mem. S.C. Radiol. Soc. (pres. 1994-95). Office: Med U SC Dept Radiology 171 Ashley Ave Charleston SC 29425-0001

CURRY, NANCY MADDOX, elementary education educator; b. Fayetteville, Tenn., July 18, 1947; d. Alton Madison and Dorothy Alene (McGinnis) Griffin; m. Horace David Maddox, Sep. 8, 1968 (div. Aug. 1978); 1 child, Chad David Maddox; m. William Larry Curry, Dec. 16, 1995; stepchildren: Patrick Curry, Shannon Stovall, Shea Curry. BS, Middle Tenn. State U., 1968, MEd, 1970; ednl. specialist, Tenn. State U., 1990, DEd, 1992. Cert. elem. tchr., Tenn., elem. adminstrn. and supervision, Tenn. First grade tchr. Highland Rim Elem. Sch., Fayetteville, 1970—; sales assoc. Castner-Knott Co., Huntsville, Ala., 1992-95; adult edn. tchr. Fayetteville, Lincoln County, 1990-93; coll. adj. faculty Tenn. State U., 1995—; career Ladder educator Career Ladder of Tenn., Fayetteville, 1985—. Com. chair Democratic Women, Fayetteville, 1985—; com. mem. Ptnrs. in Edn., Fayetteville, 1987-90; mem. planning com. Intermediate Conf. Tenn. State Dept. Edn., 1991; mem. negotiating team Lincoln County Edn. Assn., Fayetteville, 1987-91; adult leader Boy Scouts of Am., Fayetteville, 1981-86; mem. Highland Rim PTA, 1970—. Named Educator of the Yr., Fayetteville C. of C., 1988, Innovatice Tchr. of Yr., Optimist Club, Fayetteville, 1989, 92, 94. Mem. NEA, Mid South Ednl. Rsch. Assn., Tenn. Edn. Assn., Lincoln County Edn. Assn. (various offices 1970—, Lincoln County Tchr. of Yr. 1988), Phi Delta Kappa, Delta Kappa Gamma (various offices 1980—, Maycie K. Southall scholar 1989). Democrat. Presbyterian. Home: 216 Edgar Gooch Rd Hazel Green AL 35750 Office: Highland Rim Elem Sch 111 Highland Rim Rd Fayetteville TN 37334-6077

CURRY, RICHARD GILBERT, JR., information systems specialist; b. Wheeling, W.Va., Dec. 25, 1948; s. Richard G. Sr. and Mary L. (Harshman) C.; m. Barbara A. Stover, Dec. 20, 1980; children: Christopher R., Nicholas A. A in Applied Bus., Columbus (Ohio) Tech. Inst., 1978; BSBA, Franklin U., 1980. Cert. data processing, systems profl., computing profl., OS/2 engr., OS/2 LAN server adminstr. Computer programmer Columbus (Ohio) Gas Sys. Svc. Corp., 1979-80; systems analyst Shoe Corps. of Am., Columbus, 1980-84; micro computer systems mgr. JC Penney Casualty Ins. Co., Westerville, Ohio, 1984-89; micro computer systems mgr. JC Penney Co., Dallas, 1989-94, remote systems mgmt. mgr., 1994—; pres. Pro*Tree Bus. Svcs., Columbus, 1983-84; evening instr. Columbus Tech. Inst., 1982-88. Coach Plano (Tex.) Baseball Assn. Little League, 1993-95. With U.S. Army, 1969-72. Office: JC Penney Co Inc 12700 Park Central Pl Dallas TX 75251

CURRY, TONI GRIFFIN, counseling center executive, consultant; b. Langdale, Ala., June 23, 1938; d. Robert Alton and Elsie (Dodson) Griffin; m. Ronald William Curry, June 13, 1959 (div. 1972); children: Christopher, Catherine, Angela. BA, Ga. State U., 1962; MSW, U. Ga., 1981. Lic. clin. therapist; cert. addictions counselor. Tchr. DeKalb County Bd. Edn., Atlanta, 1962-63; counselor Charter Peachford Hosp., Atlanta, 1974-79; dir. aftercare, 1976-79; dir. aftercare and occupational services Ridgeview Inst., Atlanta, 1979-82; owner, dir., adminstr., counselor Toni Curry and Assocs., Inc., Atlanta, 1982—; founder, bd. dirs. Anchor Hosp., 1985-93; cons., lectr. to numerous cos. and orgns.; mem. adv. bd. Peachford Hosp., Atlanta, 1982-87, Rockdale House, Conyers, Ga., 1981—, Outpatient Addictions Clinics Am., 1983-85; bd. dirs. Employee Assistance Programs Inst.; lectr. local, nat. and internat. confs. Cloud's House, Wilshire, Eng., 1986; founder Internat. Recovery Ctr., Cannes, France, 1990; seminars on addiction in Italy and Switzerland; pres., mem. exec. bd. Ga. Employee Assistance Programs Forum, Atlanta, 1981-86; appointed to Gov.'s Advisory Council on Mental Health, Mental Retardation and Substance Abuse, 1984, Gov.'s Commn. on Drug Awareness and Prevention, 1986; chairperson Ga. Gov.'s Driving Under Influence of Alcohol Assessment Task Force; adv. bd. Hawthorne House; presenter European Conf. Drugs and Alcohol, Edinburgh, Scotland. Mem. Nat. Assn. Social Workers, Ga. Addiction Counselors Assn. (dir. 1982-86), Ga. Citizens Council Alcoholism, Employee Assistance Programs Assn., Assn. Behavioral Therapists, Nat. Assn. Alcoholism and Drug Abuse Counselors, Mems. Guild of High Mus. Art, Kappa Alpha Theta. Home: 7245 Chattahoochee Bluff Dr Atlanta GA 30350-1071 Office: 4546-D Barclay Dr Atlanta GA 30338

CURTIN, RICHARD BRENDAN, research institute executive; b. N.Y.C., Mar. 29, 1940; s. Richard B. and Margaret (Lynch) C. BEE, Manhattan Coll., 1961; ME, Yale U., 1962; MS in Bus. Adminstrn., Trinity U., San Antonio, 1967. Exec. v.p. S.W. Rsch. Inst., San Antonio, 1965—. 1st lt. USAF, 1962-65.

CURTIS, ALBERT BRADLEY, II, financial planner, tax specialist; b. Oklahoma City, Dec. 17, 1957; s. William Clyde Jr. and Ava Rene (Sewell) C.; m. Patricia Rae Curtis; children: A. Bradley III, Patrick Troy, Michael Gabel, Lori Gabel. BS in Bus., Oklahoma City U., 1981. CPA, Okla. Cost acct. Macklangurg-Duncan Corp., Oklahoma City, 1976-81; sr. auditor, tax acct. Ephraim, Sureck & Miller, CPA's, Oklahoma City, 1981-83; tax mgr., mem. joint com. Ward Petroleum Corp. & Associated Entities, Enid, Okla., 1983-90; asst. treas. Dewey F. Bartlett Ctr., Inc., Oklahoma City, 1989—; prin. A. Bradley Curtis II, CPA, Oklahoma City, 1990—; asst. sec./treas. TNT Resources, Inc., 1990—. Fundraiser profl. div. United Way, Oklahoma City, 1981-83, 86-88; registrar Enid Voter Registration Campaign, 1986. Mem. AICPA, Ind. Petroleum Assn. Am. (tax com. 1995—), Okla. Soc. CPA's. Home: 301 Dogwood Ln Enid OK 73703-3620 Office: 502 S Fillmore St Enid OK 73703-5703

CURTIS, CAROLINE A. S., community health and oncology nurse; b. Salem, Mass., June 7, 1941; d. Lawrence A. and Celestine L. (Wyman) Sager; m. John S. Curtis, July 31, 1981; children: Richard H. Smith, Craig A. Smith. Diploma, Lynn (Mass.) Hosp., 1962. Cert. oncology nurse. Head nurse, developer inpatient oncology unit Atlanticare Med. Ctr., Lynn, 1981-86; hospice nurse Greater Lynn Vis. Nurses Assn., Lynn, 1986-87; case manager Bon Secours Home Health, Englewood, Fla., 1988—; terminal care coord., oncology & pain cons., 1992—, terminal care coord.; bd. dirs., guest spkr. support group Am. Cancer Soc.; mem. pain mgmt. task force Bon Secours health Sys., 1996—. Mem. Oncology Nursing Soc., Internat. Soc. Nurses in Cancer Care, Home Health Nursing Assn., Am. Pain Soc.. Home: 328 Eden Dr Englewood FL 34223-1963

CURTIS, JOYCELYN, social worker; b. Mobile, Ala., Nov. 2, 1956; d. Albert Earl and Barbara Faye (Maye) Autry; m. Wayne Curtis, June 19, 1982; 1 child, Imari Solomon Curtis. BA in Polit. Sci., U. South Ala., 1979; postgrad., Clark Atlanta U. Credit investigator Sears, Mobile, 1978-80; catalog sales rep. Sears, Carlsbad, Calif., 1982-83; social worker Dept. Human Resources State of Ala., Mobile, 1980-82; counselor, facilitator, intern Ga. Coun. on Child Abuse, Atlanta, 1993; counselor First Steps, Atlanta, 1993—; intern Families First, Atlanta, 1994—; Rapha therapist, 1995—. Poll taker U. South Ala., 1977; nursing home ministry coord., Portsmouth, Va., 1989-91. Mem. NASW, Nat. Assn. Black Social Workers. Baptist. Home and Office: 6050 Colt Ridge Trl Mableton GA 30059-5712

CURTIS, LISA MARGARET, biological scientist; b. Gulfport, Miss., Feb. 23, 1963; d. Wakeman Byron Sr. and Martha Genevieve (Wolfe) Curtis. AA, St. Petersburg Jr. Coll., 1983; BS, U. Fla., 1988, U. Fla., 1990; postgrad., U. Fla., 1996—. Biol. scientist U. Fla., Gainesville, 1990-93; sr. biol. scientist U. Fla., 1993-95. Contbr. articles to profl. jours. Office: U Fla Health Sci Center Dept Anatomy & Cell Biology PO Box 100235 Gainesville FL 32610

CURTIS, MARY ANN CARTER, English language educator; b. Waynesboro, Tenn., Aug. 17, 1937; d. Everett Earl and Lou Ella (Merriman) Carter; m. Bobby Dean Curtis, Aug. 18, 1956; children: Mary Beth, Maxwell Carter, Suzanne Elise. BA magna cum laude, Mid. Tenn. State U., 1984, MA, 1989; postgrad., Cambridge (Eng.) U., 1984, 90, St. Meinrad Sch. Theology, 1993. Teaching fellow English Mid. Tenn. State U., Murfreesboro, 1987-88, adj. faculty, 1989, 92-93, instr., 1989-92, 94—. Peck scholar Mid. Tenn. State U., 1987-88, 88-89. Mem. MLA, Tenn. Philol. Assn., Phi Kappa Phi, Sigma Tau Delta. Office: Mid Tenn State U English Dept Box 70 Murfreesboro TN 37132

CURTIS, MICHAELA SCHMITT, emergency and maternal/fetal nurse, educator; b. Bludenz, Austria, Oct. 28, 1963; came to U.S., 1964; d. Frank Henry and Maria (Mayer) Schmitt; m. Alex K. Curtis; children: Christina, Bradley, Matthew, Jonathan. AAS, Fayetteville Tech. Inst., 1987; postgrad., Hawaii Pacific U., 1991. ž̌N, N.C., Hawaii, Tex., Ala.; cert. BLS for healthcare providers; cert. health, safety and nursing instr. ARC; cert. BLS-HCP instr., Am. Heart Assn. Maternal-fetal nurse Sierra Med. Ctr., El Paso, 1987-88; medical-surg. nurse Berlin MEDDAC, 1988-90; nursing coord. ARC, 1988-90; nursing chmn. ARC, Hickam AFB, Hawaii, 1990-93; emergency room nurse 15th Med. Group, Hickam AFB, Hawaii, 1990-92; staff ob-gyn. Kaiser Med. Ctr., 1992-93; birthing instr., ob-gyn. patient counselor; instr. BLS, first aid, advanced first aid, preparation for parenthood Frei U. Berlin, 1988-90; owner Options and Answers; pvt. duty hom health care nurse, high risk prenatal care nurse; pvt. bus. cons. OSHA; lactation cons.; early instrn. counsel. Author: (booklet) Better Birthing, 1990. Active Spl. Parents Info. Network, Honolulu, 1991—, Hawaii Blood Bank, ARC. Named Vol. of Yr., ARC, Berlin, 1989. Mem. ARC, Am. Cancer Soc., Am. Heart Assn., Am. Soc. Labor Assts., Hawaii Nurses Union. Roman Catholic. Home: 20 Cypress Pointe Demopolis AL 36732-3171

CURTIS, PHILIP KERRY, real estate developer; b. Mineola, N.Y., Nov. 6, 1945; s. William Kerry and Cherry (Smith) C.; m. Janet McDowell, Sept. 9, 1970; 1 child, Kerry Bowen. AB, Dartmouth Coll., 1968; JD, Harvard U., 1971, MBA, 1974. Bar: N.Y. 1971, Ga. 1974. Assoc. White & Case, N.Y.C., 1971-72, Hansell & Post, Atlanta, 1975-76; counsel, asst. to pres. Wiggins & Assocs., Atlanta, 1976-82; exec. v.p. Coers, Steinemann & Co., Atlanta, 1982-84; exec. v.p., ptnr. Western Devel. S.E., Atlanta, 1984-87; ptnr., sr. v.p. Charter Properties, Inc., Atlanta, 1987-93; exec. v.p. JDN Realty Corp., 1994—; vis. lectr. real estate Kennesaw Coll. Grad. Bus. Sch., 1992-93. Elder Peachtree Presbyn. Ch., Atlanta, 1983-86; dir. Met. Arts Found., Atlanta, 1983-87. 1st lt. U.S. Army, 1971-78. Mem. German Club (pres. 1986), Harvard Club of Ga., Cherokee Town & Country Club, Buckhead Rotary, Dartmouth Club of Ga. (pres. 1982-84, Club of the Yr. 1984), Harvard Bus. Sch. Club of Atlanta (pres. 1982-83), Sons Am. Revolution, Sigma Chi Club Atlanta (dir. 1985-86). Republican. Home: 3111 Arden Rd NW Atlanta GA 30305-1916 Office: 3340 Peachtree Rd NE Ste 1530 Atlanta GA 30326-1078

CURTIS, VERNA P., reading educator; b. Jackson, Miss., Mar. 20, 1940; d. William Grady Polk and Mary Ann Gray; m. Edward L. Curtis, Apr. 12, 1968; 1 child, Vera. BS cum laude, Jackson State U., 1962; MEd, Boston U., 1968; EdS, Jackson State U., 1987; postgrad., Cornell U.; EdD, Jackson State U., 1991. Reading specialist/reading facilitator Jackson Pub. Schs., tchr.; reading instr. Jackson State U.; instr., advisor for second chance careers program Tougaloo Coll. Recipient fellowship. Mem. ASCD, Jackson Area Reading, IRA, MSCD, Miss. Reading Assn. Home: 114 Waylawn Ct Jackson MS 39206-2305

CURTIS, WILLIAM ROGER, JR., media specialist; b. Hiawassee, Ga., Oct. 6, 1952; s. Roger William and Mary Wanda (Long) C.; m. Rhonda Lee Carvalho, July 14, 1979; children: Zachary William, Cody James Robert. BA, U. N.C., Chapel Hill, 1975; MEd, Western Carolina U., 1987. Tech. dir. WLOS-TV, Asheville, N.C., 1978-80; media specialist Blue Ridge C.C., Flat Rock, N.C., 1980—. Prodr. (video) Western North Carolina-The Beginning, 1986. Recipient Vol. award U.S. Park Svc., 1991. Office: Blue Ridge CC College Dr Flat Rock NC 28731

CURTISS, JEFFERY STEVEN, management consultant; b. Victoria, Tex., Oct. 18, 1958; s. Gary Oran and Mary Elizabeth (Haschke) C.; m. Annette Fay Hyatt, Nov. 19, 1983. B of Mus. Edn. cum laude, Oral Roberts U., 1981; MA summa cum laude, Regent U., 1983; PhD, U. South Fla., 1994. Cert. K-12 adminstr., K-12 music tchr. Asst. adminstr. Glade Valley (N.C.), 1983-84; adminstr. Good Shepherd Sch., Owensboro, Ky., 1984-86, Faith Acad., Orlando, Fla., 1986-90; pers. adminstr. Winter Park (Fla.) Meml. Hosp., 1991-92; found. assoc. Orlando Regional Healthcare Found., 1994-95; Mercer U., 1995—. Vol. Give Kids the World, Kissimmee, Fla., 1993, Orlando Regional Healthcare Found., 1993. Mem. Nat. Soc. Fundraising Execs., Phi Kappa Phi. Republican. Home: 624 Chastain Pl Marietta GA 30066

CUSIMANO, CHERYLL ANN, nursing administrator; b. New Orleans, Oct. 5, 1946; d. Raymond M. and Bernadette R. (Rich) Schroeder; m. Richard C. Cusimano, Aug. 27, 1967; children: Richard C. Jr., Beth Ann, Mark Allen. Diploma, Mercy Hosp. Sch. Nursing, New Orleans, 1967; cert. vocat. tchr., La. State U., 1979; student, U. New Orleans. RN, La.; cert. in ACLS, med. surg. nursing ANCC. Various nursing positions, 1967-76; asst. head nurse pediatric unit East Jefferson Hosp., 1976-77; instr. allied health field Jefferson Parish Vocat.-Tech. Sch., 1977-79; instr. med.-surg. nursing Charity Hosp., New Orleans, 1979-80; dir. operating room Marion County Gen. Hosp., Columbia, Miss., 1981; night house supr. Children's Hosp., New Orleans, 1984; asst. supr. progressive care unit Northshore Regional Med. Ctr., Slidell, La., 1985-87; pediatric staff nurse pediatric unit Touro Infirmary, New Orleans, 1982-85, charge nurse med.-surg. unit, 1987-91; nursing supr. Touro Infirmary Ctr. Chronic Pain, Rehab., New Orleans, 1992-94, program coord., 1994—. Mem. nursing com. East Jefferson chpt. ARC; ; former vol. classroom asst. Roudolph Matas Elem. Sch.; former mem. adv. bd. Project Head Start; guest speaker Am. Cancer Soc.; bd. dirs. Northshore Hospice, 1986-87, Charity Hosp. Sch. Surg. Tech., 1980. Nursing scholar Am. Legion. Mem. Am. Soc. Pain Mgmt. Nurses. Office: Touro Infirmary Chronic Pain Unit 1401 Foucher St New Orleans LA 70115-3515

CUTCHER, JEFFREY LEE, electrical engineer; b. Toledo, Ohio, June 14, 1969; s. Robert and Kathleen (Kovacs) C. ET, DeVry Inst. Tech., Woodbridge, N.J., 1989; BSEE, N.J. Inst. Tech., Newark, 1994, MSEE, 1995. Engrng. asst. N.J. Steel Corp., Sayreville, 1989-95; intern elec. engrng. IBM, Boca Raton, Fla., 1992-93; with Motorola, Inc., Ft. Lauderdale, Fla., 1995—. Mem. IEEE, Tau Beta Pi, Eta Kappa Nu. Roman Catholic. Home: 163 SW 96th Ter Plantation FL 33324

CUTCHINS, CLIFFORD ARMSTRONG, III, banker; b. Southampton County, Va., July 12, 1923; s. Clifford Armstrong Jr. and Sarah (Vaughan) C.; m. Ann Woods, June 21, 1947; children: Clifford Armstrong IV, William Witherspoon, Cecil Vaughan. BSBA, Va. Poly. Inst. and State U., 1947; grad., Stonier Grad. Sch. Banking, 1953. From asst. cashier to pres., dir. Vaughan & Co. Bankers, Franklin, Va., 1947-62; pres., cashier dir. Tidewater Bank & Trust Co., Franklin, 1962-63; sr. v.p., bd. dirs. Tidewater Bank & Trust Co. (merged with Va. Nat. Bank 1963), Norfolk, 1963-65; exec. v.p. Va. Nat. Bank, Norfolk, 1965-69, pres., 1969-80, chmn. bd., CEO, dir., 1980-83; chmn. bd., CEO, dir. Sovran Bank, N.A., Norfolk, 1983-86; CEO, dir. Sovran Fin. Corp., Norfolk, 1983-90, chmn. bd., 1983-89, ret. chmn. bd., 1989; rector Va. Poly. Inst. and State U., 1989-91; dir. Franklin Equipment Co., bd. dirs. RF&P Corp. Bd. dirs. Camp Found., Franklin, 1962—, Tidewater Scholarship Found., Nat. Maritime Ctr. Found.; bd. dirs., trustee Sentra Health System, Va. Retirement System; bd. visitors Va. Poly. Inst. and State U., 1965-70, 87-91; chmn. Future of Hampton Rds., Inc.; bd. dirs. Greater Norfolk Corp., The Norfolk Forum, Olympia Devel. Corp., German Club Alumni Found., Inc., Va. Tech. Found.; trustee The Nature Conservancy, Va. chpt.; mem. devel. com. Ea. Va. Med. Found.; mem. adv. coun. Va. Tech. Bus. Coun.; active Va. Inst. Marine Sci. and Marine Sci. Devel. Coun. Mem. Va. Tech. Alumni Assn. (hon. bd. dirs.). Presbyterian. Home: 5906 Ocean Front Virginia Beach VA 23451-2137 Office: NationsBank Ctr 6th Fl 1 Commercial Pl Norfolk VA 23510-2100

CUTERI, FRANK R., JR., automotive executive; married; 2 children. BA cum laude, Waynesburg Coll., 1975. Auto. sales rep. North Hills Chrysler-Plymouth, Inc., Pitts., 1974-75; dist. sales mgr. Chrysler Corp., 1975-77; gen. sales mgr. Dodge City Inc., Morgantown, W.Va., 1977-80, Ted McWilliams Volkswagen, Monroeville, W.Va., 1980-83; gen. mgr. Ted McWilliams Porsche-Audi-Toyota, Monroeville, W.Va., 1983-86, West Hills Motors, Inc. Pontiac-Nissan-Jeep Eagle, Coroapolis, W.Va., 1986-91; pres., gen. mgr. Brown's Volvo-Subaru-Hyundai, Alexandria, Va., 1991-92, Brown's Fairfax (Va.) Nissan, 1992; exec. v.p. sales ops. Mid-Atlantic Cars, 1992-95; pres. Mid-Atlantic Cars, Fairfax, 1996—. Office: Mid-Atlantic Cars 20245 Ordinary Pl Ashburn VA 22011

CUTLER, MALCOLM RUPERT, environmentalist; b. Plymouth, Mich., Oct. 28, 1933; s. Edward Malcolm and Gladys Victoria (Bayler) C.; m. Gladys Frances Rothenbecker, Mar. 23, 1956; children: Richard E. (dec.), Philip W.; 1 stepchild, Mona Re Thaxton. BS in Wildlife Mgmt., U. Mich., 1955; MS in Resource Devel., Mich. State U., 1971, PhD of Resource Devel., 1972. Cert. assn. exec. Chief edn. divsn. Va. Dept. Game and Inland Fisheries, Richmond, 1958-62; mng. editor Nat. Wildlife Nat. Wildlife Fedn., Washington, 1962-65; asst. exec. dir. Wilderness Soc., Washington, 1965-69; asst. prof. resource devel. Mich. State U., East Lansing, 1972-77; asst. sec. USDA, Washington, 1977-80; sr. v.p. programs Nat. Audubon Soc., N.Y.C., 1980-84; exec. dir. Population-Environment Balance, Washington, 1984-88; pres., CEO Defenders of Wildlife, Washington, 1988-90; exec. dir. Va.'s Explore Park, Roanoke, 1990—. Mem. Wildlife Soc., Soc. Am. Foresters. Home: 2865 S Jefferson St Roanoke VA 24014 Office: Virginia's Explore Park PO Box 8508 Roanoke VA 24014

CUTLIP, RANDALL BROWER, retired psychologist, college president emeritus; b. Clarksburg, W.Va., Oct. 1, 1916; s. M.N. and Mildred (Brower) C.; m. Virginia White, Apr. 21, 1951; children: Raymond Bennett, Catherine Baumgarten. AB, Bethany Coll., 1940; cert. indsl. personnel mgmt., So. Meth. U., 1944; M.A., East Tex. U., 1949; Ed.D., U. Houston, 1953; LL.D., Bethany Coll., 1965, Columbia Coll., 1980; L.H.D., Drury Coll., 1975; Sc.D., S.W. Bapt. U., 1978; Litt.D., William Woods U., 1981. Tchr. adminstr. Tex. pub. schs., 1947-50; dir. tchr. placement U. Houston, 1950-51, supr. counselling, 1951-53; dean students Atlantic Christian Coll., Wilson, N.C., 1953-56, dean, 1956-58; dean personnel, dir. grad. div. Chapman U., Orange, Calif., 1958-60; pres. William Woods Coll., Fulton, Mo., 1960-81, pres. emeritus, 1981—; trustee William Woods U., Fulton, Mo., 1981-85, 92—; chmn. bd. dirs. Mo. Colls. Fund, 1973-75; chmn. Mid-Mo. Assn. Colls., 1972-76; bd. dirs. Marina del Sol, bd. pres., 1985-90, 92—. chmn. bd. dirs. Mo. Colls. Fund, 1973-75; chmn. Mid-Mo. Assn. Colls., 1972-76; bd. dirs. Marina del Sol, bd. pres., 1985-90, 92-95. Mem. visitors' bd. Mo. Mil. Acad., 1966-90, chmn., 1968-72; trustee Shreiner Coll., Kerrville, Tex., 1983-92, Amy Shelton McNutt Charitable Trust, 1983—, Permanent Endowment Fund, Scholarship Found. and Res. Fund of Christian Ch.; bd. dirs. Univ. of the Americas, 1984—, exec. v.p., 1985—; bd. dirs. Tex. State Aquarium, 1994; elder Life Christian Ch. Recipient McCubbin award, 1968, Delta Beta Xi award, 1959. Mem. Am. Personnel and Guidance Assn., Alpha Sigma Phi, Phi Delta Kappa, Kappa Delta Pi, Alpha Chi. Address: 1400 Ocean Dr Corpus Christi TX 78404-2109

CUTSHALL, JON TYLER, aerospace engineer, researcher; b. Texas City, Tex., July 15, 1964; s. Gerald Clayton and Susan Florine (Davis) C.; m. Wiede Marie Koop, July 1, 1989. BS in Aerospace Engrng., U. Tex., 1988. Registered profl. engr. Rsch. asst. U. Tex., Austin, 1986-88; engr. The Dee Howard Co., San Antonio, 1988-89; rsch. engr. S.W. Rsch. Inst., San Antonio, 1989—. Mem. AIAA, NSPE, Am. Helicopter Soc. Home: 7207 W Beverly Mae Dr San Antonio TX 78229-4945 Office: SW Rsch Inst 6220 Culebra Rd San Antonio TX 78238-5166

CUTTER, PORTIA LYNETTE, mathematics educator; b. N.Y.C., Dec. 28, 1938; d. JeRoyd Wiley and Portia Mae (Russell) Greene; m. James Allen Cutter Sr., Mar. 3, 1962; children: James Allen Jr., Michelle Denise. Student, Long Beach State Coll., 1962-63, Morgan State Coll., 1955-57; BA, CUNY, 1961; MS in Teaching, Memphis State U., 1972, postgrad., 1980-83. cert. math. educator, Tenn. Tchr. 7th grade Del Norte Elem. Sch., West Covina, Calif., 1961-62; tchr. algebra Vanguard Jr. High Sch., Compton, Calif., 1963-64; tchr. 7th grade math Klondike Elem. Sch., Memphis, 1965; tchr. 7th grade sci. Humboldt (Tenn.) Jr. High. Sch., 1966-68; tchr. 7th and 8th grade math Georgian Hills Jr. High Sch., Memphis, 1968-71; math. tchr. Kingsbury Jr. High Sch., Memphis, 1971-95, chair math dept., 1982-95; Kingsbury H.S., Memphis, 1995—. Fin. sec. Greater Faith Baptist Ch., 1975—. Office: Kingsbury Jr High Sch 1276 N Graham St Memphis TN 38122-1511

CYMROT, DONALD JAY, economist, researcher; b. Queens, N.Y., Apr. 20, 1950; s. Irwin M. and Anne (Kipnis) C.; m. Deborah Newhouse, Aug. 8, 1971; 1 child, Avigael. BS, Lehigh U., 1972; AM, Brown U., 1973, PhD, 1978. Vis. asst. prof. U. N.C., Chapel Hill, 1976-78; asst. prof. Miami U. of Ohio, Oxford, 1978-82, assoc. prof., 1982-85; mem. rsch. staff Ctr. for Naval Analyses, Alexandria, Va., 1985-92, dir. manpower and med. program, 1992—. Author: Working Through Microeconomics, 1988; contbr. articles to profl. jours. Mem. Am. Econ. Assn., Phi Beta Kappa. Jewish. Office: Ctr for Naval Analyses 4401 Ford Ave Alexandria VA 22302-1432

CYR, ELLIE R., retired geologist, educator; b. Cambridge, Mass., Jan. 21, 1942; d. Philip and Pauline (Nemser) Raab; m. Guy A. Cyr, Sept. 1, 1968 (div. June 1980); children: Barry, Gary. BA in Philosophy cum laude, Clark U., 1963; postgrad., U. Mass., 1965; MS in Geology, Lehigh U., 1967. Cert. geolog. scientist, sewage enforcement officer; reg. profl. geologist, S.C. City geologist Dept. Pub. Works, Bethlehem, Pa., 1966-68; geologist Rosdor Constrn., Ardsley, N.Y., 1968-69; tchr. Jewish Day Sch., Allentown, Pa., 1970-74; owner, v.p. M&E Sewerage Specialists, Inc., Nazareth, Pa., 1974-78; geologist R&G Engrng. Co., Inc., Bethlehem, Pa., 1977-78; cons. geologist Macungie Pa. and Durham N.C., 1979-94. Zoning officer Bushkill Township, Nazareth, 1974-76; planner Bushkill Planning Commn., 1975-78; vol. firefighter Macungie Fire Dept., 1980-86; pres. Woodwinds Homeowners Assn., 1989-91; master gardener N.C. Agr. Ext. Svc., 1990-94. Recipient Cert. of Merit, Nat. Assn. Home Builders, 1982; Chester Kingsley fellow, 1965. Mem. Geol. Soc. Am., Am. Inst. Profl. Geologists, Fireman's Relief Assn. (treas. 1981-85), Phi Beta Kappa, Sigma Gamma Epsilon. Democrat. Jewish. Home: 18 Forest View Way Ormond Beach FL 32174-6757

CYRAN, WILLIAM JOHN, marketing professional; b. Stevens Point, Wis., June 13, 1954; s. James Alfred and Eleanor Frances Cyran. BSBA, U. Tex., 1986; MBA, U. Dallas, 1990. Accredited airport exec. Am. Assn. Airport Execs. Store mgr. Towne Jewelers, Wisconsin Rapids, 1973-80; salesman wholesale and retail Dallas, 1980-83; computer programmer U. Tex.-Dallas, Richardson, 1983-87; tng. adminstr. DFW Internat. Airport, Dallas, 1987-88, mktg. mgr., 1989-94; dir. mktg. and pub. rels. Reno/Tahoe Internat. Airport, 1994-95; asst. v.p. market rsch. Bank One Tex., Dallas, 1996—. Vol. ARC, Dallas, 1973—; mem. vestry All Saints Episcopal Ch., Dallas, 1985, jr. warden, 1985; mem.-at-large City of Stevens Point Airport Commn., 1976. Mem. Am. Assn. Airport Execs., Aircraft Owner's and Pilot's Assn., Stevens Point Pilot's Assn. (founding pres., charter), Tex. Econ. and Demographics Assn., Travel and Tourism Rsch. Assn. Office: Bank One Tex 1717 Main St Dallas TX 75201

CZARLINSKY, RANDALL GREGG, organization executive; b. Nashville, Jan. 29, 1954; s. Robert Gary and Sandra Elaine (Friedman) C. BS in Journalism, U. Kans., 1976; MSW in Social Strategy, U. Md., Balt., 1979. Assoc. Jewish Fedn. Greater Seattle, 1979-80; asst. dir. Am. Jewish Com., Chgo., 1980-82; dir. Am. Jewish Com., St. Louis, 1982-84; media specialist Am. Jewish Com., N.Y.C., 1984-85; asst. dir. Springfield (Mass.) Jewish Fedn., 1985-88; assoc. exec. dir. Jewish Community Rels. Coun., Boston, 1988-90; dir. community rels. Jewish Fedn. Greater Houston, 1990—; mem. adminstrv. and steering coms. 8th Nat. Workshop on Christian-Jewish Rels., 1983; mem. exec. com. Ecumedia News Svc., N.Y.C., 1984-85; lectr., panelist; former mem. staff synagogue coun. Am. Inst. for Jewish Policy, Planning and Rsch., Jewish Cmty. Coun. Greater Washington; mem. Leadership Houston, Class 14, 1995-96. Founding mem. editl. bd. MOSAIC (Honston's first interfaith monthly newspaper), 1994—; contbr. articles to various publs. Co-founder Com. on Decent Umbiased Campaign Tactics, St. Louis, 1984, Am. Forum on Religion and Politics, N.Y.C., 1985; organizer, mem. Greater Springfield Black-Jewish Dialogue, 1985; former mem. Task Force on Soviet Resettlement, Washington; active various congl. campaigns; founding mem. Loan Fund for Affordable Housing Western Mass.; facilitator S.W. Houston 2000, Inc., fighting crime and drug traffic; mem. Mayor's Commn. on Cmty., 1992-94, co-chair commns. pub. rels. com., 1992-94. Inst. for Jewish Policy, Planning and Rsch. grantee, 1978. Mem. Assn. Jewish Community Rels. Workers, Assn. Jewish Communal Workers. Democrat. Office: 5603 S Braeswood Blvd Houston TX 77096-3907

DAANE, MARY CONSTANCE, English language educator; b. Sheboygan, Wis.; d. Julian Winfred and Julia Constance (Westermeyer) D.; m. William Robert Kicklighter, Feb. 17, 1990; children: Peter Cirasella, Jill Cirasella. BA in English cum laude, Upsala Coll., 1969; MA Edn., Seton Hall U., 1979; PhD, NYU, 1990. Preceptor NYU, 1984-86; adj. instr. Union County Coll., 1979-83, 86, 88; instr. Sch. Gen. Studies Am. Lang. Program Columbia U., summer 1989; asst. prof. devel. reading, writing and coll. English Union County Coll., 1982-83, 90-91; assoc. prof. devel. English and reading Waycross (Ga.) Coll., 1991—, chair div. devel. studies, 1992—. Bd. dirs. WARE 2000, Waycross, 1994—. Mem. MLA, GAWE, Coll. English Assn., Internat. Reading Assn. (pres. Ofefenokee coun. 1994-95), Nat. Assn. Devel. Educators, Nat. Coun. Tchrs. English, So. Conf. English in Two-Yr. Colls., Kiwanis Internat. Office: Waycross Coll 2001 Francis St Waycross GA 31503-9248

DABBS, JEANNE MCCLUER KERNODLE, retired public relations executive; b. Corsicana, Tex., 1922; d. Robert and Anne (Forrest) McCluer; m. John David Kernodle, June 27, 1942 (dec. 1968); 1 child, Elizabeth Kernodle Cabell; m. Jack Autrey Dabbs, Feb. 14, 1981 (dec. 1993). BS in Sociology, Tex. Woman's U., 1970. Supr., writer pub. rels. St. Paul's Hosp., Dallas, 1974-76; dir., v.p. mktg. svcs. Fidelity Union Life Ins. Co., Dallas, 1976-81, ret., 1981. Author poetry book and greeting cards. Mem. comm. com. Mental Health Assn., Austin, Tex., 1991—; pres. aux. Seton Med. Ctr., Austin, 1985-86; mem. Dallas Civic Chorus, Austin Choral Union. Recipient Editorial medal Freedoms Found. Valley Forge, 1973, Eddy award Internat. Assn. Bus. Communicators, 1974, 76, 79, Matrix award Women in Comm., Inc., 1975, Best of Show award Life Ins. Advts. Assn., 1980, Sr. Vol. award Retirees Coordinating Bd., 1989. Mem. Tex. Women's U. Alumnae Assn. (pres. Capital Area chpt. 1987-89), Tuesday Book Club Austin (pres. 1986), Austin Poetry Soc. Methodist. Home: 2301 Lawnmont Ave Apt 11 Austin TX 78756-1939

DABDOUB, PAUL OSCAR, academic administrator; b. La Lima, Honduras, July 7, 1946; came to U.S., 1955; s. Jacob Abraham and Helen (McNabb) D.; m. Lorrie Suzanne Shell, Aug. 9, 1993; children by previous marriage: Desiree, John Kelly, Paul Jacob. B of Bible, Open Bible Coll., 1983; student, Liberty U., 1979. Fin. mgr. 3d Nat. Bank, Nashville, 1973-78; min. Mooring Bapt. Ch., Tiptonville, Tenn., 1978-79, Kinfolks Ridge Bapt. Ch., Caruthersville, Mo., 1979-80; min., founder Victory Bapt. Ch., Caruthersville, 1980-91; min. Victory Bapt. Ch., Caruthersville, Mo., 1980-91; adminstr., founder Victory Bapt. Acad., Caruthersville, 1984-91; min. Victory Bapt. Ch., Caruthersville, Mo., 1980-91, Victory Bapt. Acad., Caruthersville, 1984-91, Ridge Meml. Bapt. Ch., Slidell, La., 1991—; sci. instr. Northlake Christian Sch., Covington, La., 1991; founder, pres., instr. Slidell Bible Coll., 1994—. Home and Office: PO Box 7 Slidell LA 70459-0007

DACK, CHRISTOPHER EDWARD HUGHES, lawyer; b. Huntingdon, Eng., Jan. 12, 1942; came to U.S., 1948; s. Edward Harold and Nora Gwendolyn (Hughes) D.; 1 child, Hilary Gail; m. Gail Merel, May 30, 1987. BA, U. Southwestern La., 1964; JD, U. Tex., 1970. Bar: Tex. 1970. Ptnr. Fulbright & Jaworski, Houston, 1970-77, 82—, London, 1977-82. Served to capt. USAF, 1964-68. Mem. ABA, Internat. Bar Assn. Office: Fulbright & Jaworski 1301 Mckinney St Houston TX 77010

DACUS, EDWIN CURTIS, mental health services professional, minister; b. Greer, S.C., Aug. 31, 1934; s. William Doyle and Margaret Gladys (Holland) D.; m. Martha Ellen Barnette, Jan. 21, 1967; children: Michael Edwin, Reba Ellen. BA, Furman U., 1961; MDiv, Southeastern Theol. Sem., 1968. Cert. substance abuse profl., N.C., substance abuse residential facility dir., N.C., substance abuse counselor, clin. supr., internationally cert. substance abuse counselor, case presentation method evaluator; ordained to ministry Bapt. Ch., 1960. Tchr., athletic coach Evans High Sch., Appling, Ga., 1961-64; pastoral min. New Hope Bapt. Ch., Lincolnton, Ga., 1960-64, Ebenezer Bapt. Ch., Washington, Ga., 1960-64; assoc. min. First Bapt. Ch., Clayton, N.C., 1965-67; clin. pastoral edn. resident S.C. State Hosp., Columbia, 1968-69; substance abuse program dir. Roanoke-Chowan Human Svcs. Ctr., Ahoskie, N.C., 1970—; pastoral min. Roberts Chapel Bapt. Ch., Pendleton, N.C., 1973-80, Holy Grove Bapt. Ch., Ahoskie, 1985—; interim and supply pastor, Murfreesboro, N.C., 1970-73, Ahoskie, 1980-85; program rules com. N.C. Divsn. Mental Health Devel. Disabilities, Substance Abuse, Raleigh, 1990-93. Contbr. articles to profl. jours. Coach Little League Baseball, 1982-84; active Parent Involvement Coun., Hertford County Bd. Edn., 1987—, Rotary, 1971-80; pres. R.L. Vann Pub. Sch. PTA, Ahoskie, 1982-83. With U.S. Army, 1957-59, Korea. Recipient Cert. of Appreciation, State of N.C., Gov. James G. Martin, 1988, Outstanding Substance Abuse Program award Ea. Region N.C., Divsn. Mental Health, Developmentally Disabled, and Substance Abuse Svcs., 1992; named Citizen of the Week News-Herald, Ahoskie, 1985; elected to Greer High Sch. Athletic Hall of Fame, 1992. Mem. Internat. Platform Assn., Addictions Profls. N.C. Baptist. Office: Roanoke-Chowan Human Svcs RR 3 Box 22A Ahoskie NC 27910-9320

DADDIO, PETER MICHAEL, chiropractor; b. Mineola, N.Y., June 9, 1958; s. Carmine and Philomena Daddio; m. Gina Marie Antosca, Dec. 3, 1982; children: Kyle, Stephanie, Kelsey, Christopher. BS in Edn., SUNY, Cortland, 1980; D in Chiropractic, N.Y. Chiropractic Coll., 1985. Cert. chiropractic sports physician. sports medicine cons. various high schs., N.Y., Va., 1982—. N.Y. State Chiropractic Assn. scholar, 1984, Gennaro scholar N.Y. Chiropractic Coll., 1985. Mem. Am. Chiropractic Assn., Coun. on Sports Injuries and Phys. Fitness, Fedn. Internat. Sports Chiropractors. Office: 21 E Fort Evans Rd NE Leesburg VA 22075

DADE, JOANN, critical care nurse, small business owner; b. Dewitt, Ark., June 27, 1948; d. Roosevelt and Ersylene (Ledbetter) Shorter; m. Paul Dade; children: Marvin, Marcus. ADN, U. Ark., 1980. RN, Ga.; cert. critical care nurse; cert. BLS instr./trainer, ACLS provider. Staff nurse Bapt. Med. Ctr., Little Rock, 1968-78; plant nurse Timex Corp., Little Rock, 1978-80; staff nurse Cen. Ark. Home Health Agy., Little Rock, 1980-86, VA Med. Ctr., Atlanta, 1986—; pres. Dade Enterprise, Decatur, Ga., 1994—. Mem. There is Hope-Ministries, Decatur, Ga., 1992, Arthritis Found., Atlanta, 1992, Dekalb County Concerned Citizens, Decatur, 1991—. Recipient Outstanding Nurse award Ga. Hosp. Assn., 1993. Mem. ANA (cert. med.-surg.), ACA, Ga. Nursing Assn. Pentecostal. Home: 2621 Rainwater Ct Decatur GA 30034-2249

DADISMAN, J. CARROL, publishing executive; b. 1934. With Marietta Ga. Daily Jour., 1966-72; with parent co., 1972-80; pres. Tallahassee (Fla.) Dem., 1980—. Office: Tallahassee Dem PO Box 990 Tallahassee FL 32302-0990

DAESCHNER, WILLIAM EDWARD, retired government official; b. Preston, Nebr., Nov. 1, 1939; s. William Edward Suess and Kathryn Carolyn (Nanninga) D.; m. Alice Colburn Grimes, May 31, 1963; children: Deborah Lee Hughes, Michael William. BA, U. Kans., 1961; MS, Naval Postgrad. Sch., 1968, PhD, 1975. Sr. analyst shore systems Navy Fleet Material Support Office, Mechanicsburg, Pa., 1975-76, dir. supply systems performance evaluation, 1976-78; dir. ops. and inventory analysis staff Naval Supply Systems Command Hdqrs., Arlington, Va., 1978-81; dir. stock control divsn. Navy Ships Parts Control Ctr., Mechanicsburg, 1981-83, dir. plans and info. svcs., 1983-85; commanding officer Navy Fin. Ctr., Cleve., 1985-88; asst. comptroller fin. mgmt. systems Dept of Navy, Arlington, Va., 1988-90, spl. asst. to asst. sec. fin. mgmt., 1990-91; dep. dir. info. mgmt. Def. Fin & Acctg. Svc., Arlington, 1991-95. Creator (inventory model) Navy Retail Range Model, 1978. Mem. Inst. for Ops. Rsch. and the Mgmt. Scis., Assn. Govt. Accts., Am. Soc. Mil. Comptrollers, Am. Soc. Computing Machinery, Sigma Pi Sigma, Pi Mu Epsilon. Methodist.

DAFFRON, MARTHA, retired education educator; b. Fairburn, Ga., Apr. 10, 1919; d. William D. and Sarah Jane (Cochran) Duggan; children: Patricia Ruth Daffron Kelly, Doris Vesta Daffron Dodson, Billy Wayne. B in Edn., Miss. State U., 1963, MEd, 1966, PhD, 1971. Lang. arts cons. Office of Dr. Joe Owens, Lincolnton, Ga., 1971-72; lab. asst. Midlands Tech., Columbia, S.C., 1975-76, speed reading tchr., 1976-78; prof. Morris Coll., Sumter, S.C., 1972-91, ret.; rschr. in field; presenter at various reading confs. Contbr. articles to profl. jours. Mem. Internat. Reading Assn., NEA, S.C. Edn. Assn., SEAOPP, SCCSP, Delta Kappa Gamma, Phi Kappa Phi, Kappa Delta Pi. Home: 2328 E Pass Rd Gulfport MS 39507-3807

DAGENHART, BETTY JANE MAHAFFEY, nursing educator, administrator; b. Welch, W.Va.; d. Charley F. and Edith L. (Lucas) Mahaffey; divorced; 1 child, Cynthia Leigh. BA in Health Care Adminstrn., Mary Baldwin, Staunton, Va., 1991; postgrad., St. Joseph's Coll. RN, Va.; cert. nursing adminstr., ANA. Nurse mgr. ortho. and emergency svcs. Cmty. Hosp. of Roanoke (Va.) Valley, 1967-77, asst. dir. nursing svcs., 1977-83, coord. quality mgmt., dir. occupl. health svcs., dir. emergency svcs., 1983-92, dir. med./surg. nursing, 1992-94; dir. nursing edn. City of Salem (Va.) Sch. Sys., 1994—; mem. disaster planning coun. City of Roanoke, 1980-90, prehosp. care providers, 1982-88, chmn. pers. com.; organized free standing clinic Cmty. Hosp. Roanoke, 1986. Bd. dirs. Emergency Med. Svcs. Western Va., 1979-92; mem. pers. com. Cave Spring Bapt. Ch., Roanoke, 1991-92. Mem. ANA, Va. Orgn. Nurse Execs., Exec. Females, Health Occupation Educators. Home: 2638 Southwoods Dr Roanoke VA 24018-2523 Office: Salem HS 400 Spartan Dr Salem VA 24153-3202

DAGG, MIKE, business executive. Exec. dir. La. U. Marine Consortium, Chauvin. Office: La U Marine Consortium 8124 Hwy 56 Chauvin LA 70344

D'AGNESE, HELEN JEAN, artist; b. N.Y.C.; d. Leonardo and Rose (Redavid) De Santis; m. John J. D'Agnese, Oct. 29, 1942; children: John, Linda, Diane, Michele, Helen, Gina, Paul. Student CUNY, 1940-42; student Atlanta Coll. Art, 1972-76. One-woman shows: Maude Sullivan Gallery, El Paso, 1964, John Wanamaker Gallery, Phila., 1966, U. N.Mex., 1967, Karo Manducci Gallery, San Francisco, 1968, Tuskegee Inst. Carver Mus., 1968, Lord & Taylor Gallery, N.Y.C., 1969, Harmon Gallery, Naples, Fla., 1970, Fountainbleau, Miami, 1970, Reflections Gallery, Atlanta, 1972, Williams Gallery, Atlanta, 1973, Atlanta Coll. of Art, 1976-80, Americana Gallery, Mineola, Tex., 1977, E. M. Howard Gallery, Amelia Island, Fla., 1978, Haitian Primitives Gallery, 1981, Highland Gallery, Atlanta, 1987, Edge of the World Gallery, 1996, others; donated painting to Fernandiana Beach High Sch., 1991; group shows: Musseo des Artes, Juárez, México, 1968, Benedictine Art Show, N.Y.C., 1967, Southeast Contemporary Art Show, Atlanta, 1968, Atlanta U., 1969, Red Piano Gallery, Hilton Head, S.C., Terrace Gallery, Atlanta, Ann. Bible Heritage Art Exhibit, Marietta, Ga., 1976, Nat. Judaic Theme Exhbn., Atlanta, 1976, Crystal Britton Gallery, Atlanta, Odyssey Collection Gallery, Mich., 1988, Artist Gallery, Atlanta, 1991, Pompono Beach, Fla., Ft. Lauderdale, 1992; represented in permanent collections: Carter Pres. Ctr., Atlanta, Juarez (Mexico) Art Mus., Vatican Mus., Rome, Nassau (Fla.) County Pub. Library. Judge art show Mt. Loretto Acad., El Paso, 1967; commd. sculptor of Bob Marley in Limestone, 1985; art demonstration and lectr. Margaret Harris Sch., Atlanta, 1970; artist-in-residence Montessori Sch., Atlanta, 1978-79. Recipient Gold medal Accademia Italia delle Arti, Italy, 1979, Calvatone, 1982, Golden Flame award, 1986; 1st place sculpture award Tybee Island Art Festival, 1982, Golden Flame award Parliamento U.S.A., 1987, Golden Palette award Academia Europea, 1986, 87, Gold medal Internat. Parliament for the Arts, 1982. Mem. Nat. Mus. of Women in the Arts (chartered), Arts Alliance

Amelia Island. Home: 3240 S Fletcher Ave Apt 557 Fernandina Beach FL 32034-4321 Office: D'Agnese Studio & Fine Art Gallery 14 1/2 N 4th St Fernandina Beach FL 32034-4124

D'AGNESE, JOHN JOSEPH, sanitation and pest management consultant; b. N.Y.C., Apr. 2, 1920; s. Michele and Liberata (Cucolo) D'A.; m. Helen DeSantis, Oct. 29, 1942; children: John Jr., Linda, Diane, Michele, Helen, Gina, Paul. BS, CCNY, 1946; student, U. San Francisco, 1953-54. Lic. pest mgmt., Fla., Ga.; lic. chief purser USCG. Chief purser U.S. Merchant Marine, 1942-46; commd. officer USPHS, 1946; quarantine officer USPHS, Staten Island, N.Y., 1946-53; supervisory quarantine officer USPHS, San Francisco, 1953-62; Mexican border supervisory quarantine officer USPHS, El Paso, Tex., 1962-68; chief program ops. quarantine div. Ctr. Disease Control USPHS, Atlanta, 1968-80, dir. quarantine div., 1980-81; ret. USPHS, 1981; dir. Cruise Ship Consultation Svc., Fernandina Beach, Fla., 1981—. Contbr. sci. and health-related articles to nat. mags. and jours. including Pest Control Tech., Jour. Environ. Health, Jour. Milk Food Tech., Pest Control Jour. Mag. Bd. dirs. Nat. Coun. Aging, 1986-90. Recipient United Fund Leadership award El Paso Tex., 1966-67. Fellow Nat. Sanitation Found.; mem. Am. Pub. Health Assn., Fla. Pest Control Assn., Ga. Pest Control Assn., Nat. Assn. Fed. Ret. Employees. Democrat. Roman Catholic. Home: 3240 S Fletcher Ave Fernandina Beach FL 32034

DAGNON, JAMES BERNARD, human resources executive; b. St. Paul, Jan. 31, 1940; s. James Lavern and Margaret Elizabeth (Coughlin) D.; m. Sandra Ann McGinley, June 4, 1960; children: Sheri T. Dagnon Tice, Terry J., Laurie M., Diana L. BS in Bus. with distinction, U. Minn., St. Paul, 1979, cert. in indsl. rels., 1978. Various clerical positions No. Pacific Ry. Co., St. Paul, 1957-70; supr., then mgr. pers. rsch. and stats. Burlington No. R.R. Co., St. Paul, 1970, mgr. manpower planning, 1970-78, dir. compensation and organizational planning, 1978-81; asst. v.p. compensation and benefits Burlington No. Inc., Seattle, 1981-84; from v.p. labor rels. to exec. v.p. employee rels. Burlington No. Santa Fe Ry Co., Ft. Worth, 1984-95; sr. v.p. employee rels. Burlington No. Santa Fe Ry Co., Ft. Worth, 1995—; bd. dirs. Electro-No. Inc., Ft. Worth, Inroads Inc. Pres. Cath. Evang. Outreach, Seattle, 1981-84; chmn. Corp. Champions, Ft. Worth, 1994-96; bd. trustees Cook-Ft. Worth Children's Med. Ctr., 1995—; bd. dirs. United Way Met. Tarrant County, 1995—. Capt. USAR, 1957-70. Mem. Ft. Worth Petroleum Club, River Crest Country Club, Mira Vista Country Club, Beta Gamma Sigma. Republican. Home: 6409 Forest Highlands Dr Fort Worth TX 76132-4440 Office: Burlington No Santa Fe 2650 Lou Menk Dr Fort Worth TX 76131-6000

D'AGUSTO, KAREN ROSE, lawyer; b. Phila., Jan. 4, 1952; d. Les and Anne (Masciarelli) Heilenman; m. Stephen Joseph Bernasconi, Aug. 21, 1976; children: Lesley Anne D. Bernasconi, Stephanie Kalena D. Bernasconi. BA in History cum laude, Immaculata Coll., 1974; JD, U. San Diego, 1977; postgrad. U. So. Calif., 1983—. Bar: Conn. 1977, Hawaii 1978, S.C. 1986. Tng. coord. Protection and Advocacy, Honolulu, 1978, adv. coord., 1979, staff atty., 1980-81, assoc. dir., 1982, project dir., 1983—; regional coord. S.C. Protection & Adv. System, 1986-88; dep. dir. Hawaii Protection and Advocacy, 1989-91; pvt. practice law, Mililani, Hawaii, 1980—; instr. Hawaii Pacific Coll., Honolulu, 1982; atty. Mil. Montessori Sch., Honolulu, 1982-84; dir. Harmon-Johnson Inst., Honolulu, 1983—. Author: Legal Rights of Handicapped, 1980. Author, editor curriculum Vol. I Guardians Ad. Litem, 1983. Pres. Cen. Oahu Mental Health Ctr., Pearl City, Hawaii, 1981-82; officer Kings Grant Assn. Summerville, S.C., 1988; rep. St. Andrews Priory Parent-Tchr. Fellowship Bd., 1990-91; mem. John B. Dey PTA, mem. bd. dirs., chair legis. com.; leader Girl Scouts Am., svc. unit mgr., trainer, cons. Cape Henry Svc. unit, Colonial Coast coun.; mem. PTA legis. com.; vol. Great Neck Mid. Sch. Recipient Exceptional Achievement award, 1989-90, Disting. Contbn. to Civil Rights of Persons with Disabilities award, 1991, Outstanding Svc. to Hawaiis Disabled Citizens award, 1982, Outstanding Vol. of Yr. award Colonial Coast coun. Girl Scouts U.S., 1995, Vol. of Yr. award Great Neck Middle Sch., 1996; named Outstanding Adv., 1985. Mem. ABA, Hawaii State Bar Assn., S.C. Bar Assn., Hawaii Lawyers Care, Am. Assn. Counsel for Children Counsel, Wimbledon on the Bay Homeowners Assn. (v.p. 1992-93, chair by-laws com. 1993-94). Editor: Jour. Comparative Legis. Analysis of Protection and Advocacy System, 1991.

DAHL, SHIRLEY ANN WISE, education educator; b. Oklahoma City, Apr. 30, 1941; d. T.W. and Edith F. Wise; m. Ralph L. Dahl, Oct. 7, 1983; children: Chandler S. Fulton, Stephane R. Ready. BA, So. Ark. U., 1968; MEd in Reading, East Tex. State U., 1975, PhD in Elem. Edn. and Reading, 1977; cert., Stephen F. Austin State U., 1987. Cert. diagnostician, Tex., reading specialist, English/Spanish, elem., secondary tchr., profl. supr. Cons. Region VII Edn. Svc. Ctr., Kilgore, Tex.; adj. prof. Kilgore Coll., East Tex. State U., Texarkana; prof. East Tex. Bapt. U., Marshall; exch. lectr. Guandong (China) Fgn. Lang. Normal Sch., summer 1991; mem. task force write outcomes tchr. prepration Tex.'s Instns. Tchr. Edn., 1992-93; tex. tchr. appraiser; cons. in field; pres. Faculty Assembly, 1987. Author: The Teaching of High School Reading, 1918-1972: Objectives as Stated in eriodical Literature, 1977, The Childcare professional Training Program, Semester I and II, Applied Learning Experiences in Child Care (APP-L-E), 1991; editor, contbr. articles Ednl. Resources and Techniques, 1980, Centerpoint, 1991, Forum, 1993; co-editor: Tex. Tchr. Educator Forum, 1995-96. Bd. dirs. Tex. Coop. Tchr. Ctr., 1980—. Recipient Pres. Svc. award Tex. Coop. Tchr. Ctr., 1989-90; Piper Prof. award, 1996, Ted Booker award, 1996. Mem. Tex. Assn. Tchr. Educators, Tex. Tchrs. Educators, Assn. Tchr. Educators, Consortium State Orgns. Tchr. Edn. (bd. dirs.), Tex. Soc. Coll. Tchrs. Edn. (pres. 1991-93, Svc. award 1993), Internat. Reading Assn., Tex. Reading Assn., Optimist (Marshall chpt. pres. 1995-96, lt. gov. Zone 15, 1996-97), Piney Woods Reading Coun., Phi Delta Kappa (historian found. rep. 1995—, pres. 1983-84, Svc. award 1984), Alpha Upsilon Alpha, Sigma Tau Delta, Delta Kappa Gamma. Home: 114 Caddo St Marshall TX 75670-2704 Office: East Tex Bapt U 1209 N Grove St Marshall TX 75670-1423

DAHLBERG, ALFRED WILLIAM, electric company executive; b. Atlanta, 1940. Grad., Ga. State U., 1970. Chmn., pres., CEO Southern Co., Atlanta; bd. dirs. So. Co., So. Co. Svcs., Inc., So. Electric Generating Co., Protective Life Corp., Electric Power Rsch. Inst., Trust Co. Ga., Trust Co. Bank; pres., dir. Piedmont-Forrest Corp.; mem. Southeastern Electric Exch., Edison Electric Inst. Office: Southern Co 270 Peachtree St Ste 2200 Atlanta GA 30303

DAHLBERG, CARL FREDRICK, JR., entrepreneur; b. New Orleans, Aug. 20, 1936; s. Carl Fredrick and Nancey Erwin (Jones) D.; m. Constance Weston, Dec. 30, 1961; children: Kirsten Erwin Dahlberg Turner, Catherine Morgan. BSCE, Tulane U., 1958; MBA, Harvard U., 1964. Registered profl. engr., La.; registered land surveyer, La. Regional mgr. bond dept. E.F. Hutton & Co., Inc., New Orleans, 1965-67; chmn. exec. com. Dahlberg, Kelly & Wisdom, Inc., New Orleans, 1967-71; pres. St. Mary Galvanizing Co., Inc., New Orleans, 1971—; co-organizer, dir. Charter Med. Corp., 1969-72; adv. dir. Rathborne Cos., 1985-91; Internat. Trade Mart, 1974-89, mem. exec. com. 1981-84, treas., 1983-84; consul gen. of Monaco, New Orleans, 1981—; treas. Counsul Corps of New Orleans, 1990-94. Trustee, Metairie Park Country Day Sch., New Orleans, 1976-85; treas., 1980-82, chmn., 1982-84; trustee, Eye, Ear, Nose and Throat Hosp., New Orleans, 1980-96, mem. exec. com., 1980-83; trustee Eye, Ear, Nose and Throat Found., 1980-83, U. of South, Sewanee, Tenn., 1984-90; bd. dirs. New Orleans Tech. Coun., 1993—; vestryman Christ Ch. Cathedral, New Orleans, 1981-85. Served with U.S. Army, 1958-59. Mem. ASCE, Am. Soc. Venerable Order Hosp. of St. John of Jerusalem, Mil. and Hospitaller Order St. Lazarus, Order of Merit of Italian Republic. Republican. Episcopalian. Clubs: New Orleans Country Club, Pickwick Club. Co-author: Hydrochloric Acid Pickling, 1979. Home: 199 Audubon Blvd New Orleans LA 70118-5538 Office: 1618 Highway 182 E Morgan City LA 70380-5331

DAHLFUES, DONALD MICHAEL, accountant; b. Bronx, N.Y., Oct. 21, 1939; s. John Axel and Rose Mary (Romash) D.; m. Virginia Eleanor Paulsen, June 2, 1962 (div. June 1974); children: Sharon Lee, John Edwin, Michael Edward; m. Barbara Lynn Elliott Gourley, Aug. 24, 1974. BA in Bus., William Jewell Coll., Liberty, Mo., 1961; BBA in Acctg., Hofstra U., 1965. CPA, N.Y., Fla. Audit supr. Peat, Marwick, Mitchell, N.Y.C. and Garden City, N.Y., 1965-72; CFO U. Hosp. of Jacksonville, Fla., 1972-74, Coral Gables (Fla.) Hosp., 1974-77; S.E. regional ptnr. Laventhol & Horwath, Coral Gables, 1977-90; prin. Millward & Co., Ft. Lauderdale, Fla., 1991-92; shareholder, owner Donald M. Dahlfues, P.A., Miami, Fla., 1992—; keynote spkr. Am. Assn. Inhalation Therapy, Miami, 1981. Contbr. articles to profl. jours. Dir., treas. Retirement Housing Coun., Tallahassee, Fla., 1981-93; chmn. golf com. Jr. Orange Bowl Com., Coral Gables, 1988—; mem. Litigation Support Soc., Miami, 1986-94. Mem. AICPA, Fla. Inst. CPAs, Hosp. Fin. Mgmt. Assn., Fla. Assn. Homes for Aged, Homestead C. of C., Dinner Key Crusiing Club (past commodore, pres, 1982-83), Fleet-Country Club of Coral Gables (past commodore, pres. 1987-88), Redlands Golf and Country Club (dir., treas. 1995), Miami Elks (charity com. 1992—), Masons (chaplain 1985—), Shriners. Republican. Methodist. Home and Office: 14525 SW 84th Ct Miami FL 33158

DAHM, LAWRENCE JOHN, pathologist; b. Dallas, May 10, 1950; s. Cornelius George and Georgene Maryann (Schuessler) D.; m. Charlotte Faye Talbot, June 14, 1975; children: Andrew, Christopher, Theresa. BA in Biochemistry, Rice U., 1972; MD, U. Tex. Southwestern, 1976. Bd. cert. in anatomic/clin. pathology Am. Bd. Pathology. Resident physician in pathology U. Tex. Southwestern Med. Sch., Dallas, 1976-80; attending physician Dolly Vinsant Meml. Hosp., San Benito, Tex., 1980—; attending physician Valley Bapt. Med. Ctr., Harlingen, Tex., 1980—, med. dir. labs., 1990—; med. dir. United Blood Svcs.-Rio Grande Valley, McAllen, Tex., 1988—. Welch Found. fellow Rice U., 1970-71, Chilton Found. fellow U. Tex. Southwestern Med. Sch., 1972-73. Fellow Coll. Am. Pathologists, Am. Soc. Clin. Pathologists; mem. AMA, Harlingen Rotary. Office: Valley Bapt Med Ctr 2101 Pease St Harlingen TX 78550-8307

DAHOTRE, NARENDRA BAPURAO, materials scientist, researcher, educator; b. Poona, India, Dec. 2, 1956; came to U.S., 1981; s. Bapurao B. and Latika B. Dahotre; m. Anita Thangan, Dec. 6, 1984; children: Shreyas, Shruti, Sanket. BS in Metall. Engrng., U. Poona, 1980; MS in Metallurgy, Mich. State U., 1983, PhD in Materials Sci., 1987. Instr. metallurgy and materials sci. Mich. State U., East Lansing, 1985-86; postdoctoral fellow, instr. materials sci. U. Wis., Milw., 1987-88; rsch. metallurgist U. Tenn. Space Inst., Tullahoma, 1988-91, adj. asst. prof. engrng. sci. and mechanics, 1991-95, adj. asst. prof. materials sci. and engrng., 1995-96; rsch. assoc. prof. materials sci. and engrng., 1996—; vis. rsch. fellow Electrotech. Lab., Agy. Indsl. Sci. and Tech., Ministry Internat. Trade and Industry, Tsukuba, 1995. Prin. editor: Elevated Temperature Coatings: Science and Technology-I, 1995; mem. internat. editl. bd. Indsl. Laser Handbook, 1992-94; reviewer Jour. Metall. Transactions, 1991—, Jour. Materials and Mfg. Processes, 1991—; contbr. articles to profl. jours. and conf. procs. Rsch. grantee Internat. Lead Zinc Rsch. Orgn., 1990-91, Energy Conversion Program, U. Tenn. Space Inst., 1992—, NASA Marshal Flight Ctr., 1990-91, NASA Godard, 1994—, Dept. Energy, 1993—, Dept. Defense, 1994—. Mem. Am. Soc. for Metals, The Metall. Soc. of AIME, Laser Inst. Am. Materials Rsch. Soc., Am. Ceramic Soc., Soc. Mfg. Engrs., Sigma Xi. Office: U Tenn Space Inst BH Goethert Pkwy Tullahoma TN 37388

DAICOFF, GEORGE RONALD, surgeon, educator; b. Granite City, Ill., Nov. 10, 1930. BA, Ind. U., 1953, MD, 1956. Diplomate Am. Bd. Surgery, Am. Bd. Thoracic Surgery. Extern Sunnyside Sanitorium, Indpls., 1954-56; intern U. Chgo., 1956-57, jr. asst. res. surgery, 1957-58, sr. asst. res. surgery, 1958-59, res. in surgery, 1959-60, sr. res., instr. surgery, 1960-61, instr., sr. res. surgery, 1961-62, chief res., instr. gen. surgery, 1962, chief res. in thoracic and cardiovascular surgery, instr., 1963, asst. prof., 1963-67; assoc. prof. U. Fla., 1967-70, prof., 1970-77, chief thoracic and cardiovascular surgery, 1977-82, clin. prof. dept. surgery, 1982—; chief cardiac surgery All Children's Hosp., 1977-80, 86-88; attending surgeon Bayfront Med. Ctr., 1977—; mem. bd. dirs. Rogers Heart Found., trustee, 1981; mem. critical care unit com. Bayfront Med. Ctr., mem. med. proficiency com.; vis. colleague Postgrad. Med. Sch. London, 1965; mem. adv. bd. Assn. Physician Assts. in Cardiovscular Surgery; mem. children's adv. com. Divsn. Children's Med. Svcs. Recipient Cardiovascular Surg. fellow Mayo Clinic, 1966, Rsch. fellow Schweppe Found., 1963-66. mem. AMA, Am. Heart Assn. (mem. rsch. com. Suncoast chpt., mem. profl. edn. com., exec. coun. on cardiopulmonary disease), Am. Coll. Surgeons, Am. Coll. Chest Physicians, Am. Coll. Cardiology, Am. Assn. Thoracic Surgery, Am. Thoracic Soc., West Coast Acad. Cardiology (pres. 1979-80), So. Thoracic Surgical Assn., Ill. Soc. Med. Rsch., Fla. Med. Soc., Fla. Heart Assn., Fla. Soc. Thoracic and Cardiovascular Surgeons, Fla. Physicians Assn., Inc., Chgo. Surgical Soc., Pinellas County Med. Soc. (past program chmn.), Internat. Cardiovascular Soc., Assn. Advancement Med. Instrumentation, Soc. Thoracic Surgeons, Sigma Xi, Alpha Epsilon Delta. Office: 603 7th St S Ste 450 Saint Petersburg FL 33701-4704

DAIGLE, SHARON ROGER, auditor; b. Thibodaux, La., July 25, 1952; d. Freddie A. and Lucy (Bourgeois) Roger; m. Ronald P. Daigle, Nov. 17, 1978; 1 child, Fredi M. BS in acctg., Nicholls State U., 1986. Account clerk Nicholls State U., Thibodaux, 1978-86; acctg. sys. controller Nicholls State U., 1986-88, payroll, grants coord., 1988-90, internal compliance auditor, 1990-92, internal auditor dir., 1992—; v.p. Nicholls Fed. Credit Union, Thibodaux, 1990—; treas. Krewe of Ambrossia, Thibodaux, 1990—; bd. dirs. Nicholls State U. Dyslexia Ctr., Thibodaux, 1995—. Lector/commentator St. Genevieve Catholic Ch., 1988—; parent vol. E.D. White Catholic H.S., 1994—. Mem. E.D. White Mothers' Club. Home: 319 W Thibodaux Bypass Thibodaux LA 70301 Office: Nicholls State U PO Box 2001 Thibodaux LA 70301

DAIL, HILDA LEE, psychotherapist; b. Franklin Springs, Ga., Aug. 23, 1920; d. Ransom Harvey and Mattie (Gray) Lee; m. Francis Roderick Dail, Dec. 27, 1941; children: Janice Sylvia, Roderick Lee. BA, Piedmont Coll., 1941; PhD, The Union Inst., 1979. Cert. expressive therapist. Tchr. pub. schs. N.C., Tenn. and Ga., 1939-54; assoc. sec. Bd. of Missions, Methodist Ch., New York, 1954-60; dir. pub. rels. and tchr. Leonard Theol. Coll., Jabalpur, India, 1960-64; editor lit. Bd. of Missions, United Meth. Ch., N.Y.C., 1964-70; exec. dir. Int. Found. Ewha Women's Univ., Seoul, Republic of Korea, 1970-71; dir. devel. Ch. Women United, 1971-73; dir. resources cen. nat. bd. YWCA, 1973-75; pres. Hilda Lee Dail & Assoc. Internat., N.Y.C., 1975-83, Myrtle Beach, S.C., 1983—; mem. adj. faculty Coastal Carolina U., Conway, 1981-95, Webster U., Myrtle Beach, 1981—; bd. dirs. Enablement Inc., Boston, 1975-89, Assn. Coop. Agys. Asian Women's Coll., 1971-85; founder, pres. Internat. Ctr. for Creativity and Consciousness, 1989—; mem. Horry County Human Rels. Coun., 1994—. Author: Decision and Destiny, 1957, Encounters Extraordinary, 1969, Let's Try a Workshop With Teen Women, 1974, The Lotus and the Pool, 1983, How to Create Your Own Career, 1989. Dir. Citizens Against Spouse Abuse, Myrtle Beach, 1982-88, pres. Gotham Bus. and Prof. Women's Club, N.Y., 1978, dir. Green Chimney Sch., N.Y., 1978-83, v.p., Zonta Internat., N.Y., 1976-84. Fellow Nat. Expressive Therapy Assn. (speaker 1983-89); mem. ASTD (bd. dirs. 1972-89), Mental Health Assn. (bd. dirs., pres. 1988-89). Democrat. United Methodist. Home and Office: Briarcliffe Acres 154 Pine Tree Ln Myrtle Beach SC 29572-5641

DAILEY, KATHLEEN MARIE, city official; b. Port Clinton, Ohio, May 23, 1964; d. James Edgar and Louise Ann (Orosz) D. BA in Comm., Bowling Green (Ohio) State U., 1986, MA in Pub. Adminstrn., 1988. Rschr./cons. Ohio Rural Univs. Program, Bowling Green, 1986-88; grad. intern City of Defiance, Ohio, 1987-88; mgmt. intern city of Kissimmee, Fla., 1988-89; asst. city mgr. City of Venice, Fla., 1989—. Ex-officio mem. Econ. Devel. Adv. Bd., Venice, 1993—, Handicapped Accessibility Adv. Com., Venice, 1990; capital campaign capt. The Salvation Army, Venice, 1996; Heart Walk Industry leader Am. Heart Assn., Venice, 1996; grad./alumni Leadership Sarasota. Mem. Internat. City/County Mgmt. Assn., Fla. City and County Mgmt. Assn. (co-chair assts. com. 1986—), Am. Soc. Pub. Adminstrn., Sertoma of Venice (v.p. 1993—), Rotary Internat. (mem. group study exch. to Eng. 1996—). Roman Catholic. Home: 927 Capri Isles Blvd # 8 Venice FL 34292 Office: City of Venice 401 W Venice Ave Venice FL 34285

DAILY, ELLEN WILMOTH MATTHEWS, technical publications specialist; b. Marfa, Tex., Aug. 13, 1949; d. Lynn Henry Sr. and Wilmoth Hamilton (Cox) Matthews; m. John Scott Daily Sr., Mar. 21, 1970; children: John Scott Jr., Kristen Michelle. BS in Physics, U. Tex., El Paso, 1971; postgrad., George Mason U., Fairfax, Va., 1980; continuing edn., North Lake Coll., Irving, Tex., 1996—. House dir., activity counselor Southwestern Children's Home, El Paso, Tex., 1965-68; analyst Schellenger Research Found. Labs, El Paso, 1968-70; computer operator, supr. keypunch El Paso Nat. Bank, 1970-73; supr., progam analyst El Paso Sand Products, 1973-74; tech. rep. Xerox Corp., Jackson, Miss., 1975-77; product tech. specialist Xerox Corp., Jackson, 1977-79; tech. trainer Xerox Corp., Leesburg, Va., 1979-82; sr. tech. writer, tng. analyst Xerox Corp., Lewisville, Tex., 1982-95; technical publs. specialist RFMonolithics, Inc., Dallas, 1995-96; group rep. Xerox Corp., various cities, 1975-90; co-owner Triple "D" Enterprises, 1994—; owner Daily Delight Cattery, Chantilly, Va. and Carrollton, Tex., 1979-89; co-owner J & M Answering Svc., Dallas, 1983-84. Co-author: (electronic Bible verse) Verse of the Day, 1987-92. Team and divsn. mgr. Chantilly Youth Assn., 1980-82; bd. dirs., swim team dir. Brookfield Swim Club, Chantilly, 1980-82; vol. Metrocrest Svc. Ctr., Carrollton, 1986-89; elder Nor'Kirk Presbyn. Ch., Carrollton, 1989-91; founding mem. United We Stand Am., 1993—; vol. Catherine the Great, 1992. Mem. Internat. Platform Assn. (mem. red carpet com. 1994—), U. Tex. El Paso Cannoneers Club (sec.-treas. 1967-71), Xerox Bowling League (pres. 1988-89), Sigma Pi Sigma, Kappa Delta (social svc. dir. 1969-70). Home: 3701 Grassmere Dr Carrollton TX 75007-2616 Office: RF Monolithics Inc 4347 Sigma Rd Dallas TX 75244

DAILY, LOUIS, ophthalmologist; b. Houston, Apr. 23, 1919; s. Louis and Ray (Karchmer) D.; B.S., Harvard U., 1940; M.D., U. Tex. at Galveston, 1943; Ph.D., U. Minn., 1950; m. LaVerl Daily, Apr. 5, 1958; children: Evan Ray, Collin Derek (dec.). Intern, Jefferson Davis Hosp., Houston, 1943-44; resident in ophthalmology Jefferson Davis Hosp., 1944-45, Mayo Found., Rochester, Minn., 1947-50; individual practice medicine, specializing in ophthalmology, Houston, 1950—; clin. assoc. prof. ophthalmology U. Tex-Houston, 1972-86, Baylor Med. Sch., Houston, 1950—. Vice pres. bd. dirs. Mus. Med. Sci., 1973-85, pres., 1980-82. Served as lt. (j.g.) USNR, 1945-46. Diplomate Am. Bd. Ophthalmology. Fellow A.C.S., Internat. Coll. Surgeons; mem. Soc. Prevention of Blindness (med. chmn. Tex. 1968-70), Contact Lens Assn. Ophthalmologists (exec. bd. 1976-78), Tex. Ophthal. Assn. (pres. 1963-64), Houston Ophthal. Soc. (pres. 1970-71), numerous other med. socs., Sigma Xi, Alpha Omega Alpha. Jewish. Clubs: Doctors, Harvard (dir. 1965-66) (Houston). Editorial bd. Jour. Pediatric Ophthalmology, 1964-68; asso. editor Eye, Ear, Nose and Throat Monthly, 1962-65, Jour. Ophthalmic Surgery, 1970; contbr. numerous articles to profl. publs., also contbr. to books. Home: 2523 Maroneal St Houston TX 77030-3117 Office: 1517 Med Towers 1709 Dryden Rd Houston TX 77030-2400

DAKE, CYNTHIA LEWIS (CINDY DAKE), editor, freelance writer; b. Wichita Falls, Tex., Jan. 17, 1962; d. Fred Eugene and Sandra Ann (Rauch) Lewis; m. Edward Finis Dake, Dec. 31, 1988. BA in Journalism, Midwestern State U., 1984; MA in Comm., Southwestern Bapt. Theol. Sem., 1987. Media asst. Travis Ave. Bapt. Ch., Ft. Worth, 1987-91, min. media, 1990-91; traffic coord. Sta. KCBI-FM, Arlington, Tex., 1991; editor Contempo Mag. Woman's Missionary Union, Birmingham, Ala., 1991-93, mng. editor Contempo and Royal Svc. Mags., 1993-95; editor Missions Mosaic mag., 1995—. Office: Woman's Missionary Union 100 Missionary Ridge Dr Birmingham AL 35242-5236

DALE, CYNTHIA LYNN ARPKE, educational administrator; b. Plymouth, Wis., Jan. 11, 1942; sd. BS, Wis. State U., Oshkosh, 1964; M degree, U. Ctrl. Fla. Cert. tchr., Wis., Fla. Tchr. Omro (Wis.) Sch. Sys., 1964-68, West Allis (Wis.) Sch. Sys., 1973-77; substitute tchr. Brevard County Sch. Sys., Melbourne, Fla., 1981-88; early edn. tchr. various schs. Melbourne, Fla., 1988-92; supr. site coord. for S. Brevard County Sch. Sys. Child Care Assn., Melbourne, Fla. Contbg. author: (poetry) A Far Out Place, 1994 (merit award), Forgetfulness, 1995 (merit award), Ickey Poo, A Special Birthday and Beth, 1996. Mem. PTA various schs. sys.; mem. choir, Christian edn. com., Sunday sch. tchr. Palmdale Presbyn. Ch., Melbourne; cub scout den mother Boy Scouts Am., Melbourne; soccer mother, coach, asst. Little League, Melbourne, swimming instr.; mem. homeowner's assn. Groveland Mobile Home Park, Melbourne. Mem. AARP, ASCD, Audubon Soc., Internat. Soc. Poets. Republican. Home: 4651 W Eau Gallie Blvd # 98 Melbourne FL 32934

DALE, JUDY RIES, religious organization administrator; b. Memphis, Dec. 13, 1944; d. James Lorigan and Julia Marie (Schwinn) Ries; m. Eddie Melvin Ashmore, July 12, 1969 (div. Dec. 1983). BA, Rhodes Coll., 1966; M in Religious Edn., So. Bapt. Theol. Sem., 1969, Grad. Specialist in Religious Edn., 1969. Cert. tchr. educable mentally handicapped, secondary English, adminstrn. and supervision in spl. edn. EMH tchr., curriculum writer, tchr. trainer Jefferson County Bd. Edn., Louisville, 1969-88, ednl. cons., 1988-90; dist. coord. Gt. Lakes dist. Universal Fellowship Met. Community Chs., Louisville, 1990—; lectr. Jefferson C.C., Louisville, 1987-93, U. Louisville, 1976-77, 87-90; mem. faculty Samaritan Inst. for Religious Studies, 1992—; mem. program adv. com. Internat. Conf. Spl. Edn., Beijing, 1987-88. Editor, writer: (handbook) Handbook for Beginning Teachers, 1989, A Manual of Instructional Strategies, 1985; author: (kit) Math Activities Cards, 1978. Bd. sec. Com. of Ten, Inc., Louisville, 1987-91; active Greater Louisville Human Rights Commn., 1985-90, Ky. Civil Liberties Union, 1986—; v.p. GLUE, 1988-92, pres., 1992-94; mem. Universal Fellowship of Met. Cmty. Chs., programs and budget divsn., mem. gen. coun., core team, 1990—, active Women's Secretariat steering com., 1991-95; mem. membership com. Cmty. Health Trust, 1991-94; trustee Samaritan Inst. Religious Studies, 1992—, chair acad. affairs com., 1996—. Recipient Honorable Order of Ky. Cols., 1976; named Outstanding Elem. Tchr. Am., 1975. Mem. AAUW, NOW, Coun. Exceptional Children (keynote speaker 1984-88, internat. pres. 1986-87, exec. com. 1984-88, bd. govs. 1981-88), Ky. Coun. Exceptional Children (bd. dirs. 1976-90, Mem. of Yr. 1987), Internat. Platform Assn., Women's Alliance, Phi Delta Kappa. Democrat. Home and Office: 1300 Ambridge Dr Louisville KY 40207-2410

DALE, KATHY GAIL, rehabilitation rheumatology nurse; b. Evansville, Ind., Sept. 28, 1954; d. Albert Joseph and Doris Maxine (Dunning) D. ADN, U. Evansville, 1975, BSN, 1986; MS in Health Svcs. Adminstrn., Coll. of St. Francis, Joliet, Ill., 1992. RN, Tenn., Ind.; cert. rehab. registered nurse. Staff nurse St. Mary's Med. Ctr., Evansville, Ind., 1975-86, Vanderbilt Med. Ctr., Nashville, 1986-87; head nurse St. Thomas Hosp., Nashville, 1987-89; referral coord. Edgefield Rehab. Ctr., Nashville, 1989-90; nurse educator Arthritis and Osteoporosis Care Ctr. at Bapt. Hosp., Nashville, 1990—. Contbr. articles to profl. jours. Mem. Assn. Rehab. Nurses, Tenn. Assn. Rehab. Nurses (pres.-elect 1990, 94, pres. 1991, 95, bd. dirs. 1992, 96), Am. Assn. Neurosci. Nurses. Home: 865 Bellevue Rd Apt D-18 Nashville TN 37221-2759 Office: Arthritis and Osteoporosis Care Ctr Bapt Hosp-Med Office Bldg 300 20th Ave N Ste G-1 Nashville TN 37203-2115

D'ALEMBERTE, TALBOT (SANDY D'ALEMBERTE), academic administrator, lawyer; b. Tallahassee, June 1, 1933; m. Patsy Palmer; children: Gabrielle Lynn, Joshua Talbot. BA in Polit. Sci. with honors, U. South, 1955; postgrad., London Sch. Econs. and Polit. Sci., U. London, 1958-59; JD with honors, U. Fla., 1962. Assoc. Steel Hector & Davis, Miami, Fla., 1962-65, ptnr., 1965-84, 89-93; prof. Fla. State U., 1984—, dean, 1984-89, pres., 1994—; lectr. U. Miami Coll. Law, 1969-71, adj. prof., 1974-76; reader Fla. Bd. Bar Examiners, 1965-67; mem. jud. nominating commn. Fla. Supreme Ct., 1975-78; chief counsel Ho. Select Com. for Impeachment of Certain Justices, 1975; mem. Fla. Law Revision Coun., 1968-74; chmn. Fla. Constl. Revision Commn., 197-778. Contbr. articles to profl. jours.; articles editor U. Fla. Law Rev. Mem. Fla. Ho. Reps., 1966-72, chmn. com. on ad valorem taxation, 1969-70, chmn. judiciary com., 1971-72, mem. various coms.; chmn. Fla. Commn. on Ethics, 1974-75; trustee Miami-Dade Community Coll., 1976-84. Served with USN, 1955-58; to lt. USNR. Recipient award Fla. Acad. Trial Lawyers, 1972, 93, Fla. Patriots award Fla. Bicentennial Commn., 1976, Disting. Alumnus award U. Fla., 1977, Nelson Poynter award Fla. Civil Liberties Union, 1984, Gov.'s Emmy award Nat. Acad. TV Arts and Scis., 1985, 1st Amendment award Nat. Sigma Delta Chi/Soc. Profl. Journalists, 1986, Medal of Honor award Fla. Bar Found., 1987; named Outstanding First Term House Mem., 1967, Most Outstanding Mem. of House, Capital Press Corps; Rotary Found. fellowship. Mem. ABA (pres. 1991-92, chmn. spl. com. on election reform 1973-76, chmn. spl. com. on resolution of minor disputes 1976-79, chmn. spl. com. on med. malpractice 1985-86, state del. from Fla. 1980-89, commn. on governance 1983-84, rules and calender com. ho. of dels. 1982-84, individual rights and responsibilities com., co-founder Ctrl. and East European Law Initiative), Fla. Bar Assn. (bd. govs. 1974-82), Dade County Bar Assn. (pres. young lawyers sect. 1965-66, bd. dirs.), Am. Judicature Soc. (pres. 1982-84), U. Fla. Law Ctr. Assn. (trustee 1967—), Order of Coif, Omicron Delta Kappa, Phi Beta Kappa. Office: Office of Pres Fla State U 211 Westcott Bldg Tallahassee FL 32306-1037

DALEUSKI, EDWARD JOSEPH, principal; b. Jackson, Calif., Feb. 5, 1931; s. John Glen Daleuski and Blanche (Rampelburg) Ferretti; m. Janet C. Claus, Sept. 17, 1958; children: Susan, Diane, Nancy. BS, U. Nebr., 1967; MS, Nova U., 1987, EdD, 1992. Commd. 2d lt. U.S. Army, 1951, advanced through grades to lt. col., 1975, ret., 1975; co. exec. Aluminum Cos., 1976-85; asst. prin. Gilchrist County Schs., Trenton, Fla., 1986-89, elem. sch. prin., 1989—; mid. sch. prin., North Miami, Fla., 1992—. Cons. PTO, Bell, Fla., 1986-92, Kindergarten to 6th Grade, Bell, 1988-92, Math. and Sci. Club, Bell, 1988-92, North Miami Mid. Sch., 1992. Decorated Silver Star, Bronze Star. Mem. Pen and Sword Soc., Am. Ednl. Rsch. Assn., Nat. Assn. of Secondary Sch. Prins., Civitan, Am. Legion. Home: 5329 SW 79th Ter Gainesville FL 32608-4483

DALEY, DENNIS MICHAEL, political science educator; b. Great Falls, Mont., May 29, 1949; s. Thomas Cornelius and Frances Louise (Taleff) D. BA in Govt., Montana State U., 1972, BA in History, 1972; MA in Polit. Sci., U. Montana, 1974; PhD in Polit. Sci., Wash. State U., 1980. Instr. Mankato (Minn.) State U., 1977-78; instr., then asst. prof. Iowa State U., Ames, 1978-83; asst., then assoc. prof. U. Miss., Oxford, 1983-88; assoc. prof. N.C. State U., Raleigh, 1988—; dir. MPA program U. Miss., 1985-88, N.C. State U., 1988-90. Author: Performance Appraisal in Public Sector, 1992. Mem. Am. Soc. Pub. Adminstrn. (chpt. exec. coun., pres. sect. on pers. and labor rels. exec. coun.), Am. Polit. Sci. assn., Internat. Pers. Mgmt. Assn., Soc. Human Resource Mgmt., Acad. Mgmt. Democrat. Mem. Unitarian Ch. Home: 5566 Hamstead Crossing Dr Raleigh NC 27612-7016 Office: NC State U Dept Political Sci Raleigh NC 27695-8102

DALGLISH, MEREDITH RENNELS, artist, educator; b. Bryn Mawr, Pa., Apr. 15, 1941; d. James Garven and Esther Jane (Parsons) D.; m. Thorsten Horton, July 27, 1970 (div. June 1976); m. William G. Beebe, Mar. 23, 1985. BA, Goddard Coll., 1967; postgrad., U. Wis., 1970-72; MFA, Claremont (Calif.) Grad. Sch., 1983. Dir. Ormond Art Mus., Ormond Beach, Fla., 1986-87; adj. prof. Daytona Beach C.C., 1988-90; art specialist Volusia County Schs., Daytona, Fla., 1990-91; adj. prof. Miami (Fla.) Dade C.C., 1991-93; founder, dir. Women's Inst. for Creativity, Inc., Miami, 1992—; adj. prof. Fla. Internat. U., Miami, 1993—; mem. adv. bd. Volusia County Arts Commn., Daytona, 1990-91, Women's Caucus for Art, Miami, 1993-95; dir. of bd. Women's Inst. for Creativity, Inc., Miami, 1992—; vis. artist Volksogschool, Bergen, Holland, China, Japan, 1976, 77, Isle of Eigg, Scotland, 1977; guest artist U. So. Calif., Idyllwild, 1982, Orange County (Calif.) Arts Festival, 1985, Stetson U., DeLand, Fla., 1986, Orlando (Fla.) Mus. Art, 1987; artist in residence Project Leap, Palm Beach County, Fla., 1996—, Arts in Medicine Program, U. Miami, 1996; lectr. in field. One-woman shows include MIEL Ctr., Miami, 1994, 1st Union Bank, Ft. Lauderdale, Fla., 1995; exhibited in group shows Polk C.C., Winter Haven, Fla., 1987, Zanesville (Ohio) Mus., 1987, Stetson U., 1988, Nat. Assn. Women Artists Centennial Anniversary Exhibit, N.Y.C., 1989, Fla. Ctr. for Contemporary Art, Tampa, 1989, Ceramic League of Miami, 1990 (award), Earthday Celebration St. Thomas U., Miami, 1995, juried exhbn., 1995, numerous others; represented in permanent collections including Ralph Rudin Designs, L.A., 1980, Hyatt-Regency Hotel, Orlando, 1983, Sheraton Hotel, Naples, Fla., 1984, Marriott Hotel, Washington, 1984, Ramada Inn Hotel, Beverly Hills, Calif., 1985, Sheraton-Scottsdale (Ariz.) Hotel, 1985, Gallery Contemporanea, Jacksonville, Fla., 1986, Exec. Suites Holiday Inn, Schenectady, N.Y., 1990, IBM Corp., Miami, 1990, Adminstrv. Suites Omni Internat. Hotel, Miami, 1995, Hilton Hotel, Atlanta, 1995, numerous pvt. collections; prin. works include San Francisco Mus. Art, 1980, Barnsdall Mcpl. Art Mus., L.A., 1980, Claremont Grad. Sch., 1981, 83, U. So. Calif., Idyllwild, 1982, Orlando Mus. Art, 1986, DeLand Mus., 1986, Stetson U., DeLand, 1986, Dayton Beach C.C., 1988; documented in book The Dinner Party (Judy Chicago), 1979; documented in film Right Out of History-The Making of The Dinner Party, 1979; prodr.: (video) Earthwing, 1988; TV appearances, live performances. Vol. The Dinner Party Feminist Art Installation, 1977; pres.-elect Women's Caucus for Art, Miami, 1994. Grantee Ruth Chenven Found., N.Y.C., 1990; recipient Elizabeth Kittrell award Kittrell Found., 1969, award Dade Cmty. Found., Miami, 1993. Mem. Layerist Soc., Transformative Art, Nat. Assn. Women Artists, Coll. Art Assn. Office: Women's Inst for Creativity Inc PO Box 164243 Miami FL 33116

DALHOUSE, WARNER NORRIS, banker; b. Roanoke, Va., June 4, 1934; s. Jefferson William and Gay-Nell (Henley) D.; m. Barbara Ann Dalhouse, Dec. 27, 1984. Student, Roanoke Coll., 1952-54; BS in Commerce, U. Va., 1956. Vice pres. 1st Nat. Exchange Bank, Roanoke, Va., 1967-69, sr. v.p., 1969-73, exec. v.p., 1973-77, pres., chief adminstrv. officer, 1977-81; exec. v.p., chief adminstrv. officer Dominion Bankshares Corp., Roanoke, Va., 1977-81, pres., CEO, 1981-89; chmn. bd., CEO Dominion Bankshares Corp., Roanoke, 1989-93; CEO First Union Nat. Bank Va., Roanoke, 1993—, chmn. bd., 1995—; bd. dirs. Shenandoah Life Ins. Co., Roanoke, Apple Ridge Farm, Copper Hill, Va. Pres. Roanoke (Va.) Pub. Libr. Found.; bd. dirs. Carilion Health Sys. Roanoke; mem. Va. Gov.'s Econ. Adv. Coun.; mem. bd. visitors U. Va.; mem. exec. com. Partnership for Urban Va. Office: First Union Nat Bank Va PO Box 13327 Roanoke VA 24040-7200

DALKE, BARBARA HELEN, elementary school educator; b. Ft. Worth, Mar. 1, 1946; d. Arthur Lee and Annie Rowena (Hinton) Benson; m. Michael Francis Dalke, July 10, 1947; children: Suzanne Christine, Kelly Lynn. AA, Alvin (Tex.) Community Coll., 1966; student, U. Houston, 1966-68. Cert. elem. tchr., Tex. Tchr. Houston Ind. Schs., 1968-69, Pearland (Tex.) Ind. Schs., 1969-71; tchr. Clear Creek Ind. Schs., League City, Tex., 1971-73, Webster, Tex., 1979—; tchr. Mark Twain Elem. Sch, Alvin, Tex., 1975-79, Alvin Ind. Schs., 1976-79; chmn. 4th grade level McWhirter Elem. Sch., Webster, Tex., 1980-81, 86-87, 5th grade level chairperson, 1994-95, multiple sch. com., 1993-94; book adoption com. Clear Creek Schs., League City, 1989-90, math. conf. rep., 1983-84; presider Conf. for Advancement Math. Teaching, Houston, 1988; mem. Challenge Team of Educators Clear Creek Sch. Dist., 1990-94; participant Gov.'s Conf. Sci. Tech. and Math. Edn., 1990; McWhirter Elem. rep. on Clear Creek Sch. Dist.'s Districtwide Ednl. Improvement Coun. com., 1995-97, sec. Districtwide Ednl. Improvement com., 1995-97. Active Webster Sesquicentennial com., 1985-86; vol. Lunar Rendezvous Antique Sale, Clear Lake City, Tex., 1985-86; team mom Friendswood (Tex.) Soccer Club, 1984-85, 86-87; pres. Women's Club Night Cir., Meth. Ch., Friendswood, 1984-85, ch. sec., 1984-85, 86-87; mem. 1992 Fourth of July Parade com., Friendswood, Lang. Arts Book Adoption Com. for Clear Creek Dist., 1989-90; mgr. Girls' Softball Assn., 1988—; mem. dist. ednl. improvement coun. Clear Creek Sch. Dist., 1996—; mem. facilities planning com. Friendswood Ind. Sch. Dist., 1995-96. Mem. NEA, Tex. State Tchrs. Assn. Home: 1901 San Jose St Friendswood TX 77546-5984 Office: McWhirter Elem Sch 300 Pennsylvania St Webster TX 77598-5231

DALL, PETER ANDREW, management and organizational consultant; b. Nashville, Dec. 5, 1951; s. David George and Agnes Mariah (Suggs) D.; m. Mary Lou Boudrie, Apr. 26, 1980; 1 child, David George II. BS in Edn., Tenn.-Wesleyan Coll., 1976. Cert. power exec. Gen. mgr. VIP Placement & Counseling Svc., Hixson, Tenn., 1978-79; dir. edn., tng. and conf. Tenn. Valley Pub. Power Assn., Chattanooga, 1979-87; dep. chief mgmt. tng. and devel. TVA, Chattanooga, 1987-88; asst. to pres.-chief exec. officer Cobb Electric Membership Corp., Marietta, Ga., 1988-92; nat. sales mgr. John-Michaels Enterprises, Inc., 1992—; bd. dirs. Greater Atlanta Electric League. Active Chattanooga Big Bors. and Big Sisters Assn., 1980-84, 86-88; mem. state tech. com. Ga. Bd. Tech. and Adult Edn., Atlanta, 1989-90, state v.p.; asst scoutmaster Troop 172, Boy Scouts Am., 1994—. Mem. Nat. Safety Mgmt. Soc. (state v.p.), Nat. Utility Tng. and Safety Edn. Assn., Internat. Assn. for Continuing Edn. and Tng. (pres. 1990-92, bd. dirs.), N.Am. Hunting Club, Highland Sportsman Club (bd. dirs. 1987-88), Rotary (pres. North Cobb chpt. 1990-91). Presbyterian. Home: Tall Pines Estates Box 16 9218 Dayton Pike Soddy Daisy TN 37379-4825

DALLMAN, MARK JAY, veterinarian; b. Cleve., Jan. 13, 1941; s. Edwin W. and Viola M. (Klein) D.; m. Carol R. Ehrhardt, Aug. 20, 1960; children: Karen B., Kris R., Kurt M. BS, U. Wis., 1964; MS, U. Mo., 1967, DVM, 1970, PhD, 1981. Vet. clinician Vet. Clinic of Joliet (Ill.), 1970-75; instr. Coll. Vet. Medicine U. Mo., Columbia, 1975-81, asst. prof., 1981-83; asst. prof. Va. Md. Regional Coll. Vet. Medicine, Blacksburg, 1983-90; clinician, owner North Main Small Animal Clinic, Blacksburg, 1990—. Bd. dirs. Humane Soc. Montgomery County, Blacksburg, 1993; treas. Blacksburg Master Chorale, 1989—; asst. scoutmaster, sponsor liason Troop 152, Boy Scouts Am., Blacksburg, 1983—. Mem. Am. Vet. Med. Assn., World Assn. Vet. Anatomists, Va. Vet. Med. Assn., S.W. Va. Vet. Med. Assn. (treas. 1993-95, v.p. 1995-96), Ruritan (bd. dirs. 1995—), Phi Zeta. Methodist. Office: N Main Small Animal Clinic 1407 N Main St Blacksburg VA 24060-2563

DALRYMPLE, CHRISTOPHER GUY, chiropractor; b. Beaumont, Tex., Sept. 2, 1958; s. Guy H. and Betty Jane (Williams) D.; m. Angela Hackley, Dec. 15, 1979; children: Sarah E., William C., Clayton G. Student, Baylor U., 1976-78; D. in Chiropractic Medicine, Tex. Chiropractic Coll., 1982. Diplomate Nat. Bd. Chiropractic Examiners, Tex. Bd. Chiropractic Examiners; ordained Baptist Deacon, 1988. Chiropractor Brassard Chiropractic Clinic, Beaumont, 1982-85; chiropractic physician, adminstr. Brenham (Tex.) Chiropractic Clinic, 1985—; host Back Talk, 1987-88; cons., lectr. in field. Author: Brenham & Masonry ... 150 Years Together, 1995; contbr. articles to profl. jours. Team chiropractor track team Blinn Coll., Brenham, 1987-94, Tex. track and field participants Olympics, 1992; sunday sch. dir. First Baptist, 1986-87, 90-93, sunday sch. tchr., 1987-89, bd. trustees Calvary Baptist Ch., Brenham, 1992-94, sunday sch. tchr. youth, 1993-94, actor, playwrite ch. pagents, 1993, 94, 96, deacon, chmn., 1994—, chmn. personnel com., 1995—, chmn. long range planning com., 1995—, adult sunday sch. tchr., 1995—; treas. Brenham Ind. Sch. Devel.-PAC, 1994; participant Health Occupation Students of Am. Program, Brenham H.S., 1992-96. State Sweepstakes Winner "Jake", Tex. Jaycees, 1984, Outstanding Officer, 1984. Mem. Tex. Chiropractic Assn. (mem. state com., labor rels. 1983, membership com. 1994-95, dist. 9 sec. 1983-84, chmn. publ. com. 1987—, editor-in-chief 1987—, dist. 8 state dir. 1996—), Christian Chiropractors Assn., Tex. Chiropractic Coll. Alumni Assn., Baylor Alumni Assn. (life), Royal Arch, Gideons Internat. (bible chmn. 1994—), Graham Masonic Lodge (various offices), Delta Sigma Chi (sec. 1981, bd. dirs. 1982). Republican. Baptist. Office: Brenham Chiropractic Clinic PO Box 2350 Brenham TX 77834-2350

DALTON, ANNE, lawyer; b. Pitts., Dec. 6, 1951; d. Thomas John and Mary Olive (Paul) D.; m. Oliver E. Martin, Dec. 26, 1987. BA in Polit. Sci., NYU, 1973; JD, Fordham U., 1977. Bar: N.Y. 1978, U.S. Dist. Ct. (so. and ea. dists.) N.Y. 1979, Pa. 1987, Fla. 1990. Assoc. Mendes & Mount, N.Y.C., 1979-80; atty. news div. ABC, N.Y.C., 1980-85; TV news producer ABC Network, N.Y.C., 1985-86; sr. atty. Radio City Music Hall Prodns., Inc., N.Y.C., 1986-87; pvt. practice Stroudsburg, Pa., 1987-91; asst. county att., asst. port authority atty. Lee County, Ft. Myers, Fla., 1991-94; pvt. practice Ft. Myers, 1994—; family law mediator Fla., 1994—, cir. civil mediator, 1995—; spl. hearing master 20th Jud. Cir., Fla., 1991—, ct. Commr., gen. master family and probate divsn., 1995—; adj. prof. Edison C.C., Ft. Myers, Barry U., Ft. Myers; cir. civil mediator, 1995. Recipient Clio award Internat. Clio Award Com., 1978. Mem. Pa. Bar Assn., Fla. Bar Assn., N.Y. Bar Assn., Lee County Bar Assn. Roman Catholic. Office: 2044 Bayside Pkwy Fort Myers FL 33901-3102

DALTON, HARRY JIROU, JR., public relations executive; b. San Antonio, Feb. 7, 1927; s. Harry Jirou and Dorothy Bess (black) D.; m. Marion Packard Hume Dalton, Aug. 21, 1954; children: Cynthia Kay, Robert Hume, Steven Jirou. BBA in Advt., U. Tex., 1949, postgrad., 1949-50; postgrad., Boston U., 1958, U. Nebr., Omaha, 1958-60. Commd. 2d lt. USAF, 1950, advanced through grades to brigadier gen., 1975; from assoc. to dir. corp. com. EDS Corp., Dallas, 1980-84; mgr. corp. comm. The LTV Corp., Dallas, 1984-92, Vought Aircraft Co., Dallas, 1992-93; pvt. practice as pub. rels. counsel Dallas, 1994—; adv. coun. U. Tex. Coll. Comm., Austin, 1983-89; adj. prof. Defp. Def. Info. Sch., Ft. Meade, Md., 1992—; comm. advisor to pres. Air Force Assn., Washington, 1992—. Bd. Trustees Air Force Hist. Found., Washington, 1980—. Named Outstanding Govt. Pub. Info. Officer Aviation/Space Writers Assn., Washington, 1974. Fellow Pub. Rels Soc. Am. (pres. 1990); mem. Air Force Pub. Affairs Alumni Assn., Tex. Pub. Rels. Assn. (bd. dirs. 1974—, Outstanding Pub. REls. Practitioner in Tex. award 1989, Silver Spur award 1991), Omaha Press Club. Presbyterian. Home and Office: 6411 Laurel Valley Rd Dallas TX 75248-3904

DALTON, JAMES CARROLL, market research professional; b. Davenport, Iowa, Apr. 27, 1936; s. Carroll Dale and Camilla (Kendall) D.; m. Judith Kay Hill, Apr. 27, 1959; children: Christina, Wendy. BA, Macalester Coll., 1960; BDiv, U. Chgo., 1963; MBA, U. St. Thomas, 1976. Advt. copywriter Spiegel Inc., Chgo., 1963-64; asst. advt., sales promotion mgr. Hon Industries, Muscatine, Iowa, 1964-65; overseas advt. agy. and media coord. Deere & Co., Moline, Ill., 1965-68; rsch. mgr. St. Paul (Minn.) Pioneer Press, 1968-77, Atlanta Jour. & Constitution, 1977-83, BellSouth Telecomms., Atlanta, 1983-95. Mem. Am. Mktg. Assn. Congregationalist. Home: 5212 Biffle Rd Stone Mountain GA 30088-3801 Office: Dalton Rsch Inc 5212 Biffle Rd Stone Mountain GA 30088-3801

DALTON, JENNIFER FAYE, accountant; b. Maryville, Tenn., May 1, 1959; d. James Theodore Teffeteller and Melody (Potts) Allison; m. Robert Byron Dalton, Dec. 15, 1979. Student, U. Tenn., 1977-79, Coastal Carolina Community Coll., 1980-81, 84-86; BS in Mgmt., Golden Gate U., Camp Lejeune, N.C., 1982. Bookkeeper, with accounts payable dept. McMar Too, Inc., Jacksonville, N.C., 1980-83; acctg. technician City of Jacksonville, 1983-89; acctg. mgr., corp. sec. treas. Bankers Mortgage Corp., Louisville, 1989-92; sr. acct., payroll officer City of Louisville, 1992-96; sr. acct. Louisville Zoo, 1996—. Alcoa Found. scholar, 1977. Mem. Amateur Radio Transmitting Soc., Inst. Mgmt. Accts., Gamma Beta Phi. Republican. Baptist. Home: 827 Markham Ln Louisville KY 40207-4444

DALTON, ROBERT ISSAC, JR., textile executive, consultant, researcher; b. Charlotte, N.C., Apr. 2, 1921; s. Robert I. and Edith (Gossett) D.; m. Gwin Barnwell, Nov. 16, 1946; children—Millie, Edith. B.S. in Textile Engring., N.C. State U. Vice pres. sales Whitin Machine Works, Whitinsville, Mass., 1946-67; pres. Cocker Machine and Foundry, Gastonia, N.C., 1967-70, Tech-Tex Inc., Charlotte, 1970—, Gossett-Dalton Co., Charlotte, 1973—, dir., 1955—; bd. dir. Cadmus Communication Co., Richmond, Va., 1983—, Am.-Truetzschler, Charlotte, 1976—, N.C. Nat. Bank, Charlotte, 1962-94. Pres. Charlotte Symphony Orch., 1979-80; mem. bd. edn. Mecklenburg County, Charlotte, 1957-58; chmn. nat. bd. dirs. Handicapped Orgn. Women, Inc., 1986; chmn. bd. trustees Brevard Coll, 1987-93. Served to maj. U.S. Army, 1943-46, ETO. Mem. Phi Psi. Methodist. Clubs: Charlotte City (pres. 1980-81), Charlotte Country. Avocations: tennis; photography. Home: 318 N Canterbury Rd Charlotte NC 28211-1426

DALY, STEPHEN JEFFREY, art educator; b. Governor's Island, N.Y., July 4, 1942; s. Doris (Leanord) Daly; m. Sharon Jane Able, Aug. 24, 1964; 1 child, Sabina. BA in Art, San Jose State U., 1964; MFA in Sculpture, Cranbrook Acad. Art, 1967. Instr. U. Minn., Mpls., 1967-69; asst. prof. Humboldt State U., Arcata, Calif., 1969-73, assoc. prof., 1975-79; asst. prof. U. Tex., San Antonio, 1979-81; asst. prof. U. Tex., Austin, 1981-86, assoc. prof., 1986-91, prof. art, 1992—; vis. artist, U. Hawaii, Manoa, Honolulu, 1983, U. Ohio Sch. Art, Athens, 1984, So. Ill. U., Carbondale, 1985, U. Wash., Seattle, 1988, U. Okla. Sch. Art, Norman, 1992, etc.; art and architecture panel Tex. Commn. on Arts, 1980-82; curator Patrick Gallery, 4th Tex. Sculpture Symposium, Austin, 1983, San Antonio Art Inst., 1985. One-man shows include Am. Acad. in Rome, 1975, Triton Mus., Santa Clara, Calif., 1977, Graham Gallery, Houston, 1983, William Campbell Contemporary Art, Ft. Worth, 1986, 87, 89, 93, others; exhibited in group shows Hooks-Epstein Gallery, Houston, 1993, Ramapo Coll., Mahwah, N.J., 1994, Foothills Art Ctr., Golden, Colo., 1995, Grounds for Sculpture, Hamilton, N.J., 1995; represented in pub. collections Oakland (Calif.) Art Mus., Bank of San Antonio, others. Recipient Rome prize in sculpture Am. Acad. Rome, 1973-75, Louis Comfort Tiffany award in sculpture Tiffany Found., 1977-78, Summer Rsch. award U. Rsch. Inst., U. Tex., Austin, 1984; Reinhart fellow in sculpture Am. Acad. Rome, Md. Inst. Art, 1974-75, Grace Milam Centennial fellow in fine arts Coll. Fine Arts, U. Tex., 1984-85, 1990-91, Foxworth Centennial fellow, 1988-89; Rsch. grantee U. Rsch. Inst., U. Tex., 1984. Democrat. Home: 40000 N RR 12 # 101 Dripping Springs TX 78620 Office: U Tex Dept Art and History Austin TX 78712-1285

DAME, WILLIAM KARL, technical training professional; b. Chgo., Aug. 16, 1967; s. Karl and Christine (Teppo) D.; m. Kathleen Lisa Litz, Sept. 30, 1995. BA, Rutgers U., 1989; MBA, U. Va., 1993. Rsch. asst. Nova Link Co., Falls Church, Va., 1989-91; tech. trainer Werik Assocs. Inc., Fairfax, Va., 1992—. Mem. Rotary. Office: Werik Assocs Inc 10720 Main St Ste 303 Fairfax VA 22030-3712

DAME-BRAYTON, LAUREEN EVA, nursing administrator; b. Framingham, Mass., Mar. 15, 1947; d. Irving Lawrence and Cora Justina (Wells) Dame; children: Daryl Lawrence, Jeffrey Lee. Diploma, Dartmouth-Hickock Med. Ctr., Hanover N.H., 1968; BSN, Clayton State Coll., Morrow, Ga., 1996; postgrad., Emory U., 1996—. RN, Ga. Staff nurse, charge nurse, team leader maternity and surgical nursing various hosps., N.H., Boston, St. Louis, 1968-69, 80-83; sch. nurse practitioner Dept. Pub. Health, Bedford, Mass., 1983-85; perioperative nurse, 1st asst. South Fulton Hosp., East Point, Ga., 1985-86; nurse, first asst., plastic surgery John Munna M.D., Atlanta, 1986-90; resource nurse, intake coord. Shallowford Hosp., Atlanta, 1989-91; staff educator, quality assurance coord. dept. surgical svcs. Shallowford Hosp., Atlanta, 1991-92; quality improvement coord., nursing South Fulton Med. Ctr., East Point, Ga., 1992; nurse coord. quality assurance Kaiser Permanente, Atlanta, 1992-93, dir. quality assurance, 1993-95; mgr. coord. care Egleston Children's Hosp., Emory U., Atlanta, 1995-96; mgr. quality mgmt. Egleston Pediat. Group, Decatur, Ga., 1996—. Mem. NAACOG (charter; chmn. steering com. 1972), AORN (chmn. hospitality com. 1992, mem. workshop and publicity coms. 1983), NAFE, Am. Soc. Plastic and Reconstructive Surg. Nurses, Nat. Assn. Quality Profls., Ga. Assn. Quality Profls., Ga. North Ctrl. Dsit. Quality Profls., Am. Acad. Disting. Students, Am. Needlepoint Guild and Embroiderers Guld of Am. (life), Sigma Theta Tau. Lutheran. Home: 8726 Twin Oaks Dr Jonesboro GA 30236-5152 Office: Egleston Pediat Group 125 Clairmont Rd Ste 520 Decatur GA 30033

DAMERON, JOHN PRESTON, postal worker; b. Danville, Va., July 21, 1944; s. Russell O. and Eva C. (Searcy) D.; m. Edna Ogle, May 8, 1976; children: John Christopher, Tara Marissa, Philip James. Student, U. Va., 1962-65; AA, Danville C.C., 1969; BA in English, Averett Coll., Danville, 1971; student, U. West Fla., 1972. Tchr. Hargrave Mil. Acad., Chatham, Va., 1972; window clerk & mail distributer U.S. Postal Svc., Danville, 1973-95, window svc. tech., 1995—. Editor: Piedmont Lit. Rev., 1978-81. Commr. Dan River Dist., Danville, 1975-77; leader cub pack Boy Scouts Am., 1987-84; mem. Danville Jaycees, 1971—; bd. dirs., steward Trinity United Meth. Ch., 1982-88; v.p. Tunstall H.S. Acad. Booster, 1994—. Mem. Am. Postal Workers Union (pres. Danville chpt. 1978, 1987-90, 1993—), Dan River Philatelic Soc. (v.p. 1995—). Home: 1932 Orphanage Rd Danville VA 24540 Office: US Postal Svc 700 Main St Danville VA 24541

DAMMANN, WILLIAM PAUL, oceanographer; b. Melbourne, Fla., Aug. 19, 1953; s. Earl Roy and Helen Marie (Wheeler) D.; m. Jacqueline Sue Kennedy, May 10, 1986; children: Laura Christine, Holly Frances. AAS, Miami-Dade Jr. Coll., 1973; AA, Miami-Dade C.C., 1977; BS, Fla. Atlantic U., 1979; MS, U. Miami, 1991. From phys. scis. aide to rsch. oceanographer U.S. Dept. Commerce, Miami, 1973—; tech. adv. com. S.E. Fla. Outfall Experiment, Miami, 1987—. Pres-sch. com. chair Perrine Peters United Meth. Ch., Miami, 1994, trustee, Sunday sch. tchr., 1994—, adminstrv. coun. chair, 1996-97. Mem. Am. Geophysical Union, Acoustical Soc. Am., U.S. Naval Inst. Home: 9960 Broad Channel Dr Miami FL 33157-6925 Office: US Dept Commerce NOAA/AOML 4301 Rickenbacker Causeway Miami FL 33149

DAMON, GENE **See GRIER, BARBARA G.**

DAMPIER, HAROLD DEAN, JR., lawyer; b. Raleigh, N.C., Feb. 28, 1962; s. Harold Dean and Janie D. Student, Am. U., 1983; BA, U. Okla., 1984; JD, South Tex. Coll. Law, 1987. Bar: Tex. 1989, U.S. Dist. Ct. (no., so., ea. and we. dists.) Tex. 1991, 92. Assoc. Law Office of Ray McQuarry, Houston, 1989; assoc. Gerald J. Goodwin & Assocs., Houston, 1989-91; ptnr. Dampier & Watson, Houston, 1991-95; pvt. practice Law Offices of Harold D. Dampier, Jr., 1995—. Recipient Washington semester scholarship U. Okla., 1983; named Outstanding Freshman Sen. Okla. Intercollegiate Legislature, 1984. Mem. Assn. Trial Lawyers Am., Tex. Bar Assn., Tex. Trial Lawyers Assn. (bd. dirs.), Houston Bar Assn. (moderator 1990—), Houston Trial Lawyers Assn. (bd. dirs.), Houston Young Lawyers Assn. Office: 811 Dallas St Ste 1001 Houston TX 77002

DAMUTH, JOHN ERWIN, marine geologist; b. Dayton, Ohio, Nov. 22, 1942; s. Jason Donald and Sarah Maxine (Simpson) D.; m. Patricia Jane Keenan, Oct. 8, 1971 (div. July 1990). BS in Geology, Ohio State U., 1965; MA in Geology, Columbia U., 1968, PhD in Geology, 1973. Grad. rsch. asst. Lamont-Doherty Geol. Obs., Columbia U., 1965-73, rsch. scientist, 1973-74, rsch. assoc., 1974-82, sr. rsch. assoc., 1982-83; rsch. geologist Dallas Rsch. Lab. Dallas Rsch. Lab., Mobil R & D Corp., 1983-84, sr. rsch. geologist, 1984-92; sr. rsch. scientist Earth Rsch. and Environ. Ctr., U. Tex., Arlington, 1992—; adj. prof. dept. geology U. Tex., Arlington, 1996—; adj. rsch. scientist Lamont-Doherty Geol. Obs., Columbia U., 1983-91; instr. ecology adult edn. N.J. H.S., 1977-83; mem. Nat. Site Assessment Com. Subseabed Disposal High-Level Nuc. Waste, 1978-83; cons. crustal evolution project Nat. Assn. Geology Tchrs., 1978; lectr. in field. Contbr. articles to profl. jours. Texaco scholar, 1964-65; Eugene Higgins fellow, 1965-66, Pan Am. Oil Co. fellow, 1967, Pres.'s fellow, 1968-69, Nat. Lord Britton fellow, 1967-68. Fellow Geol. Soc. Am.; mem. Am. Assn. Petroleum Geologists, Soc. Econ. Paleontologists and Mineralogists, Am. Geohphys. Union, Sigma Xi. Office: Univ Tex Dept Geology PO Box 19049 Arlington TX 76019

DANAHAR, DAVID C., academic administrator, history educator; b. Dobbs Ferry, N.Y., Sept. 29, 1941; s. Walter Vincent and Catherine Marie (Charles) D.; m. Cecelia Upritchard, Aug. 24, 1985; children: Deirdre, Rebecca, Michael. BA, Manhattan Coll., Bronx, N.Y., 1963; MA, U. Mass., 1965, PhD, 1970. Instr. U. Mass., Amherst, 1969-70; asst. prof. SUNY, Oswego, 1970-73, assoc. prof., 1973-84, prof., 1984-85; dean Coll. Arts and Scis., prof. history Fairfield (Conn.) U., 1985-92; provost, acad. v.p. Loyola U., New Orleans, 1992—; vis. prof. U. Pisa, Italy, 1971-72. Contbr. articles on Habsburg and Austrian history to profl. jours. Mem. Fairfield 2000, 1985-88; bd. trustees New Orleans Mus. of Art, 1992—. Univ. fellow U. Mass., 1966-69, rsch. fellow Am. Coun. Learned Socs., 1975-76; grantee SUNY Rsch. Found., 1971-73, NEH, 1983-88, also numerous others from U.S. Govt., Founds. and Corps. including Hilton Found., Monroe Found., HUD, DOE, Culpeper Found., Keck Found., IBM, GE, 1985—. Mem. Am. Hist. Assn., Am. Conf. Acad. Deans, Coun. Colls. Arts and Scis., Conf. on Cen. European History, Am. Assn. Higher Edn. Office: Loyola U Marquette 221C Box 007 6363 Saint Charles Ave New Orleans LA 70118-6143

DANBURG, JEROME SAMUEL, oil company executive; b. Houston, Dec. 21, 1940; s. August and Rosalie (Bornstein) D.; m. Gudrun Ella Ernestine Scholz, Sept. 8, 1965; children: Aron Ralf, Andrea Leda, Sylvia Freia, Sonja Rebecca. BS in Physics, MIT, 1962; Diplom in Physics, Freie Universität Berlin, 1964; PhD in Physics, U. Calif., Berkeley, 1969. Assoc. physicist Brookhaven Nat. Lab., Upton, N.Y., 1969-72; sr. rsch. geophysicist Shell Devel. Co., Houston, 1973-81, rsch. mgr., 1981-86, rsch. dir., 1992-93; mgr. Shell Oil Co., Houston, 1986-92, 93-94, Shell E&P Tech Co, Houston, 1994—; physics dept. vis. com. mem. U. Tex., Austin, 1990—. Contbr. articles to profl. jours. Fulbright scholar, Freie Universität Berlin. Mem. Am. Phys. Soc., Soc. Exploration Geophysicists, Fulbright Alumni Assn. Home: 7611 Burning Hills Dr Houston TX 77071-1413 Office: Shell E&P Tech Co PO Box 481 Houston TX 77001-0481

DANCE, ROBERT BARTLETT, artist; b. Tokyo, May 31, 1934; came to U.S., 1940; s. Stuart Lee and Dorothy Bell (Stuart) D.; widowed, 1991; children: Scott B., Mark C., Stuart S. Grad., Phila. Mus. Coll. Art, 1956. Painting Hatteras Standing featured on 1st Nat. Pk. admission stamp, 1988; one-man shows include Mint Mus. Art, Charlotte, N.C., 1978, N.C. Maritime Mus., Beaufort, 1985; 20-yr. retrospective at Southea. Ctr. Contemporary Art, Winston-Salem, N.C., 1991; exhibited in group shows at Watercolor Soc. N.C., 1973 (award), 74 (award), 76, 77 (award), Southea. Ctr. Contemporary Art, 1974, 75, 76, 77, 78, 81, 88, Northwestern Bank, Winston-Salem, 1974 (award), R.J. Reynolds Industries Collection, Winston-Salem, 1977, Collectors Gallery, N.C. Mus. Art, Releigh, 1977, Miss. Mus. Art, Jackson, 1979, High Point (N.C.) Arts Coun. Theatre Art Galleries, 1979, 80, Asheville (N.C.) Mus. Art, 1979, Mystic (Conn.) Seaport Gallery, annually 1986-96, Smithsonian Instn., Washington, 1987 (Arts for the Pks. award); contbr. articles to Am. Artist, The Artist, Today's Art, paintings to Maine Boats and Harbors, Seafood Bus., Yankee Mag., Woodenboat Mag., Nat. Fisherman Yearbook, Nat. Fisherman (cover), Va. Wildlife, Wildlife in N.C., So. World, others; profiled in various publs., including Chesapeake Bay Mag., Midwest Art, The State, others. Top award recipient Easton (Md.) Waterfowl Festival, 1987; presented to U.S. Pres. George Bush. Home and Studio: 320 Anita Dr Winston Salem NC 27104

DANDALIDES, STEVEN MICHAEL, gastroenterologist, educator; b. Akron, Ohio, June 9, 1956; s. George and Des (Alatis) D.; m. Linda Ann McNeill, May 29, 1983; children: Jaeson Eugene, Michael George, Alexis Despina. BA, Oberlin Coll., 1978; MD, Vanderbilt U., 1982. Diplomate Am. Bd. Internal Medicine, Am. Bd. Gastroenterology. Intern and resident in internal medicine U. Calif., San Diego, 1982-85; fellow in gastroenterology Cleve. Clinic, 1985-87; pvt. practice, Norfolk, Va., 1987—; clin. instr. internal medicine Ea. Va. Med. Sch., Norfolk, 1987—. Contbr. articles and abstracts to med. jours. Fellow ACP, Am. Coll. Gastroenterology (edn. affairs com. 1993-96, pub. rels. com. 1996—); mem. Am. Soc. for Gastrointestinal Endoscopy, Am. Gastroent. Assn. (pub. policy com. 1993-96), Norfolk Acad. Medicine. Home: 2349 Haversham Close Virginia Beach VA 23454-1154 Office: Gastroenterology Assocs Tidewater PC 160 Kingsley Ln Ste 200 Norfolk VA 23505-4600

D'ANDREA, MARK, radiation oncologist; b. Palos Park, Ill., May 24, 1960; s. Anthony E. and Adriene (Boka) D'A. BA in Chemistry, Religion, and Biology, Luther Coll., 1981; MD, Ponce (P.R.) Sch. Medicine, 1985. Diplomate Am. Acad. Pain Mgmt., Am. Bd. Radiology in Radiation Oncology. Resident in internal medicine Cabrini Med. Ctr., N.Y.C., 1985-86; resident in radiation oncology Meth. Hosp., Bklyn., 1986-89; radiation oncologist East Tex. Cancer Ctr., Tyler, 1989-94, Mother Frances Hosp., Tyler, Med. Ctr. Hosp., Tyler, U. Tex. Health Ctr., Tyler, St. Josephs Hosp., Paris, Tex., McCuistion Hosp., Paris, Tex., Longview (Tex.) Radiation Oncology Ctr.; resident U. Tex. Med. Branch, Galveston, 1991-92; dir. radiation oncology Bayshore Hosp., Pasadena, Tex., 1994—; prin. investigator R.T.O.G., Bayshore Cancer Ctr., 1995—; prof. radiation biology Tyler Jr. Coll., 1990-91; chief resident in radiation oncology Meth. Hosp., Bklyn., 1988-89; cons. Longview Regional, Good Shepherd Hosp., 1989-94, pres., chmn. bd. Danhul Corp., 1992. Patentee diagnostic marking catheter system for use in radiation diagnosis procedures. Chmn. Com. Pub. health Kings and Bklyn. County, N.Y., 1988-89. Named One of Outstanding Young Men Am., 1987; recipient Outstanding award Ill. Jr. Acad. Sci., 1978. Fellow Am. and Internat. Coll. Angiology, InterAm. Coll. Physicians and Surgeons; mem. Am. Inst. Chemists (ethics com.), Am. Chem. Soc., Am. Soc. Clin. Oncology, Am. Soc. Therapeutic Radiology and Oncology, AMA, Radiol. Soc. N.Am., Med. Soc. N.Y. State, Kings County Med. Soc., Acad. Medicine Bklyn., Smith County Med. Soc., Tex. Med. Assn., Circilo de Radioterapeutas ibero Latino Americanos. Office: Bayshore Hosp Ctr Dept Radiation Oncology 4000 Spencer Hwy Pasadena TX 77504-1221

DANDRIDGE, WILLIAM SHELTON, orthopedic surgeon; b. Atoka, Okla., May 21, 1914; s. Theodore Oscar and Estelle (Shelton) D.; m. Pearl Sessions, Feb. 3, 1941; children: Diana Dawn, James Rutledge. B.A., U. Okla., 1935; M.D., U. Ark., 1939; M.S., Baylor U., 1950. Intern, St. Paul's Hosp., Dallas, 1939-40; surg. residence Med. Arts Hosp., Dallas, 1940; commd. 1st lt. USAF, advanced through grades to lt. col., 1950; chief reconditioning svc. and reconstructive surgery Ashburn Gen. Hosp., McKinney, Tex., 1945-46; neurosurg. resident Brooke Army Med. Center, San Antonio, 1946-47; orthopedic surg. resident, 1947-50; chief orthopedic svc. and gen. surgery Francis E. Warren AFB, Cheyenne, Wyo., Travis AFB, Susan, Calif., 1950-51; chief orthopedic svc. and gen. surgery Shepherd AFB, 1951-52; comdg. officer, chief orthopedic svc., chief gen. surgery Craig AFB Hosp., Selma, Ala., 1952-53; pvt. practice medicine specializing in orthopedic surgery, Muskogee, Okla., 1954-69, 72-94; courtesy staff Muskegon Gen. Hosp.; orthopedic cons. McAlester (Okla.) Gen. Hosp., VA Hosp., Muskogee. Exec. mem. Eastern Okla. council Boy Scouts Am. Fellow ACS, Internat. Coll. Surgeons; mem. Am. Fracture Assn., Nat. Found. (adviser 1958-61), N.Y. Acad. Scis., Okla. State, Pan-Am., So., Aerospace Med. Assns., AMA, So. Orthopaedic Assn., Garfield County Med. Soc., S.W. Surg. Congress, Am. Rheumatology Soc., Air Force Assn. (life). Republican. Methodist. Masons, K.T. Shriners, Jesters, Lions, Club of Enid. Contbr. articles to profl. jours.; research and evaluation of various uses of refrigerated homogenous bone. Home: 802 S Hayes St Apt 13 Enid OK 73703-6655

DANFORTH, ARTHUR EDWARDS, finance executive; b. Cleve., Jan. 23, 1925; s. Arthur Edwards and Jane (Hillyard) D.; m. Elizabeth Wagley, Mar. 17, 1956; children: Hillyard Raible, Nicholas Edwards (dec.), Jonathan Ingersoll, Elizabeth Wagley, Michael Stowe. B.A., Yale, 1949. With Hayden Miller Co., Cleve., 1949-54, First Nat. City Bank (predecessor to Citibank N.A.), N.Y.C., 1954-63; asst. mgr. Buenos Aires office First Nat. City Bank (predecessor to Citibank N.A.), 1959-61; treas. Bunge Corp., N.Y.C., 1963-65; sr. v.p., treas. Colonial Bank & Trust Co., Waterbury, Conn., 1965-70; chmn., chief exec. officer Farmers Bank of Del., Wilmington, 1970-76; prin. Danforth Group, New Canaan, Conn., 1976—. Former bd. dirs. United Way of Del., Boys Club of Wilmington, Grand Opera House Inc. of Del., NCCJ, Audubon Soc. Conn., Greater Wilmington Devel. Council. Served as ensign USNR, 1945-46. Mem. Sankety Head Golf Club, Nantucket Yacht Club, Yale Club, Jonathan's Landing Golf Club. Home: 1664 SE Colony Way Jupiter FL 33478-8305

DANFORTH, LOUIS FREMONT, banker, educator; b. L.A., Nov. 15, 1913; s. Louis F. and Louise (Bauerle) D.; m. Leota V. Schwulst, Sept. 8, 1944; children—David Louis, Victoria Leota. Grad., Columbia U., 1934; postgrad., N.Y. U., 1952; D.B.A., Oklahoma City U., 1982. With Guaranty Trust Co., N.Y.C., 1946-55; economist, chief fin. officer, sr. v.p., treas. Liberty Nat. Bank & Trust Co., Oklahoma City, 1955-79; cons. Liberty Nat. Corp., 1979—; prof. econs., MBA and MLA programs Oklahoma City U., 1973—; bd. dirs. Credit Adjustment, Investors Trust Co., Duncan, Okla.; dir. St. Gregory's Coll. Past pres., bd. dirs. Better Bus. Bur.; past pres. Cmty. Coun. Ctrl. Okla., Ctrl. Okla. Coun. for Children with Learning Disabilities; bd. dirs., past pres. Sunbeam Home and Family Svc.; bd. dirs. Assn. Industries Okla., Okla. Coun. on Econ. Edn., Okla. State U., Okla. Lung Rsch. Program, Am. Heart Assn.; bd. dirs., past pres. Cmty. Coun.; past pres., trustee United Appeal Greater Oklahoma City Area; mem. adv. coun. Bus. Rsch. Ctr., Oklahoma City U., bd. dirs. Grad. Sch. Cmty. Bank; chmn. bd. commrs. Oklahoma City Pub. Housing Authority; past pres. Oklahoma County Mental Health Assn., 1983; chmn. Alcohol, Drug Abuse and Cmty. Health Planning and Coordination Bd., State of Okla.; dir. St. Gregory's Coll., Shawnee, Okla. Mem. Econ. Club Okla. (past pres.), Okla. Soc. Financial Analysts (past pres.), Okla. Financial Analysts Fedn. (past regional v.p.), Nat. Assn. Bus. Economists, Men's Dinner Club, Petroleum Club. Republican. Episcopalian. Home: 1404 NW 122nd St Apt 410 Oklahoma City OK 73114-8034 Office: Liberty National Corp PO Box 61027 Oklahoma City OK 73146-1027

DANG, JAMES BAC, business planner, educator; b. Bac Ninh, Vietnam, Jan. 10, 1953; came to U.S., 1979; s. Chinh Van and Ut Thi Dang; m. Nguyen Luong, Oct. 17, 1978; children: Tien, Tiffany, Tina, Theresa, Tracy. BS in Agrl. Engring., Saigon (Vietnam) U., 1978; BS in Computer Sci., U. Ctrl. Okla., 1983, MEd in Math., 1985, MS in Applied Physics, 1989; BSEE, Okla. Christian U., 1988; MS in Applied Maths., Oklahoma City U., 1995, MBA in MIS, 1994; BSEE, Okla. U., 1989; postgrad., Walden U., 1993—. Planner mgmt. specialist AT&T Tech. Co., Oklahoma City, 1983—; adj. instr. Okla. State U., Oklahoma City, 1987-91, Langston (Okla.) U., 1988—, Oklahoma City U., 1990—, Park Coll., Oklahoma City, 1992—, Oklahoma City C.C., 1995—. V.p. Vietnamese Cath. Cmty., Oklahoma City, 1993-96. Mem. Sigma Pi Sigma. Home: 6527 Eastbourne Ln Oklahoma City OK 73132-2006

DANIEL, ARLIE VERL, speech education educator; b. Spencer, Iowa, May 15, 1943; s. Arlie Verl and Eleanor Marie (Grover) D. AA, Iowa Lakes C.C., 1963; BA, Morningside Coll., 1965; MA, U. Iowa, 1978; PhD, U. Nebr., 1981. High sch. tchr. Missouri Valley (Iowa) Pub. Schs., 1965-68, Clinton (Iowa) Pub. Schs., 1971-78; dir. speech edn. East Cen. U., Ada, Okla., 1981—. Co-author: Project Text for Public Speaking, 6th edit., 1991; co-author chpt. in Basic Communications Course Annual, 1994; editor: Activities Integrating Oral Communication Skills for Students in Grades K-8, 1992; contbr. chpt. to Teaching and Directing the Basic Communication Course, 1993. 1st lt. U.S. Army, 1968-71. Mem. AAUP, Assn. Tchrs. Educators, Internat. Comm. Assn., Okla. Speech Theatre Comm. Assn. (pres. 1986-87, exec. sec. 1989-92, Outstanding Comm. Educator award 1985, Josh Lee Svc. award 1992, Spl. award for Contbns. to Profession 1994), Ctrl. States Comm. Assn. (life, exec. sec. 1994—, Outstanding Young Speech Tchr. award 1985), Speech Comm. Assn. (life), Rotary Internat. (chairperson youth com. Ada chpt. 1994—, Dist. 5770 1995-97), Pi Kappa Delta. Democrat. Methodist. Home: RR 6 Box 1395 Ada OK 74820-9216 Office: East Cen U Dept Speech Education Ada OK 74820-6899

DANIEL, CATHY BROOKS, tutor, educational consultant; b. Nashville, Sept. 1, 1946; d. Conway William and Alliene Marie (Gilliam) B.; m. James Newton Daniel Jr., Dec. 29, 1967 (div. July 1988; children: Laura Marie, James Newton III. Student, Memphis State U., 1964-66; BS, George Peabody Coll., 1968, MA, 1971. Cert. elem. tchr., special edn. tchr., learning disabilities and behavior disorders. Tchr. Fairview (Tenn.) Elem. Sch., 1968-69; special edn. tchr. Ross Elem. Sch., Nashville, 1969-70, Rosebank Elem. Sch., Nashville, 1970-71, Graymar Elem. Sch., Nashville, 1971-73, Norman Binkley Elem. Sch., Nashville, 1973-74; cons. ednl. and family counseling, ednl. testing Franklin, Tenn., 1976—. Methodist. Home and Office: 2203 Springdale Dr Franklin TN 37064-4962

DANIEL, COLDWELL, III, economist, educator; b. New Orleans; s. Coldwell Jr. and Josephine Agnes (Weick) D.; children: Anne Alexis, Coldwell IV. BBA, Tulane U., 1949; MBA, Ind. U., 1950; PhD, U. Va., 1959; postdoctoral, U. Chgo., 1964-65. Instr. stats. U. Va., 1955-56; instr. econs. Pomona Coll., 1956-57; prof. econs., dept. chmn. U. So. Miss., 1958-65; prof. econs. U. Houston, 1965-70, U. Memphis, 1970—; rsch. coord. So. Calif. Rsch. Coun., 1956-57; vis. prof. La. State U., 1959; sr. Fulbright prof. econs. Dacca U., Bangladesh, 1961-62; project dir. Miss. Test Facility Econ. Impact Study NASA, 1963; prin. The Anwell Co., Memphis, 1974—. Author: Mathematical Models in Microeconomics, 1970; reader Jour. Econ. and Bus., 1991—, Social Sci. Jour., 1988—, Am. Jour. Econs. and Sociology, 1990—; founder, chmn. bd. editors, The Southern Quarterly, 1962-64; co-founder and manuscript review editor Jour. Econs. and Fin., 1977-91, mem. editl. bd., 1991-94; assoc. editor for econs. Social Sci. Quarterly, 1968-70, mem. editl. bd., 1972-84; contbbr. articles to profl. jours. Trustee Christ United Meth. Ch. With USAF, 1945-46; 1st lt. U.S. Army, 1951-53. NSF Sci. Faculty fellow, 1964-66. Mem. Am. Econ. Assn., Pakistan Econ. Assn. (life), Southwestern Econs. Assn., Acad. Econs. and Fin. (co-founder, pres. 1977-78, area coord. Indsl. Orgn. and pub. Policy, 1990-94, Disting. Svc. award 1979, Cert. Appreciation 1981), Mo. Valley Econs. Assn. (pres. 1984-85, Meritorious Svc. award 1986), So. Econ. Assn., Atlantic Econ. Soc. (exec. com. 1991-94, area coord. Indsl. Orgn. and Pub. Policy 1989-94), The Raven Soc., Beta Gamma Sigma, Omicron Delta Kappa, Pi Kappa Pi, Omicron Delta Epsilon, Pi Gamma Mu, Delta Tau Kappa, Pi Sigma Epsilon, Delta Sigma Pi. Office: U Memphis Dept Econs Memphis TN 38152

DANIEL, DOROTHY ISOM, nurse specialist, consultant; b. El Paso, Tex., Aug. 13, 1943; d. Charles Dandridge Isom Jr. and Joyce Marie (Mayo) Fisher; m. Marshall E. Daniel Jr., June 20, 1987; children: Michael P. Taylor, Julia D. Taylor, Laura A., Keith R., Craig C. BSN, U. N.C., 1965. RN, Va., Mo., N.C.; cert. diabetes educator, med.-surg. nursing, cardiopulmonary resuscitation. Staff nurse maternal-child health Rex Hosp., Raleigh, N.C., 1974-78; staff nurse rehab. unit St. John's Mercy Med. Ctr., St. Louis, 1983-84; staff nurse med.-surg., diabetes resource nurse Alexandria (Va.) Hosp., 1980-83, 84-87, diabetes nurse specialist, 1987—; expert witness; developer, educator tng. diabetes care and mgmt.; diabetes case mgr. for inpatients and outpatients; cons. diabetes edn. programs; lectr. in field; mentor 1st Internat. Diabetes Edn. Mentor Program, 1993; adv. bd. Eli Lilly Lispro, 1994-96. Chair advanced practice coun. Alexandria Hosp., 1991-92. Mem. Am. Assn. Diabetes Educators (exec. bd. 1987-91, treas. 1989-91, pres. 1992-93, past pres. 1993-95, ADA liaison 1995—, hon. chpt. Diabetes Educator of Yr., 1995-96, No. Va. chpt. James M. Moss award 1996), Sigma Theta Tau. Home: 5245 Pumphrey Dr Fairfax VA 22032-2627 Office: Alexandria Hosp 4320 Seminary Rd Alexandria VA 22304-1500

DANIEL, J. REESE, lawyer; b. Sanford, N.C., Dec. 24, 1924. AB, U. S.C., 1949, JD cum laude, 1956. Bar: S.C. 1955, U.S. Dist. Ct. S.C. 1956, U.S. Tax Ct. 1959, U.S. Cr. Appeals (4th cir.) 1959. Ptnr. Thomas, Wyndham, Daniel & Dial; sr. ptnr. Daniel & Daniel, Litchfield, S.C.; mem. S.C. Supreme Ct. Bd. Commrs. on Grievances and Discipline, 1970-73, Columbia Zoning Bd. of Adjustment, 1970-79. Contbg. author 7 South Carolina Law Quarterly; contbr. articles to profl. jours. With USNR, 1943-46. Mem. ABA, S.C. Bar Assn. (assoc. editor S.C. Bar Assn. News Bull. 1957, editor 1958-59), Phi Delta Phi. Office: Daniel & Daniel PO Box 857 10B Pawleys Sta Hwy 175 Pawleys Island SC 29585

DANIEL, MARGARET HAGEN, music and voice educator; b. Eau Claire, Wis., Sept. 9, 1949; d. Harold Odin and Genevieve (Kjendalen) Hagen; m. Douglas Vaughn Daniel, Aug. 9, 1975; children: Nathan Elliot, Adam Stuart, Jason Christopher (dec.). MusB in Voice, Wis. State U., Eau Claire, 1971; postgrad., Boston U., 1971; MusM in Voice, U. Wis., 1973; pvt. studies in piano and voice. Pvt. instr. piano, 1965-71; instr. music, voice U. Southwestern La., Lafayette, 1973-80, asst. prof. music, voice, class piano and music fundamentals, 1980-93, assoc. prof. music, voice, diction, pedagogy, 1993—; asst. to dir. Sch. Music, U. Southwestern La., 1991-95; guest faculty summer music symposium Kansas State U., 1994; adjudicator mus. competitions and auditions, 1974—; presenter vocal clinics Grace Presbyn. Ch., Lafayette, 1983, 85, Chorale Acadienne, Lafayette, 1985, 86, First Bapt. Ch., Lafayette, 1989, Cantors of St. Joseph Ch., Milton, La., 1991; guest artist Luther Northwestern Theo. Sem., St. Paul, 1991, McNeese State U., Lake Charles, La., 1993, Troy (Ala.) State U., 1993, Nicholls State U., Thibodaux, La., 1994-95, New Orleans, 1995, Houston, 1996, Monroe, La., 1996, Shreveport, La., 1997; lectr./recital performer So. Chpt. Coll. Mus. Soc., 1993, 95, 96, La. Music Tchrs. Assn., 1993, 95, La. Music Educators Assn., 1994, 95. Performer operas, including Roméo et Juliette, 1973, Rigoletto, 1974, La Traviata, 1978, others; oratorios include Handel's Messiah, 1980, Haydn's The Creation, 1982, Brahms' Ein Deutsches Requiem, 1989, Mendelssohn's Elijah, 1992, others; contbr. articles to profl. publs. Dir. music summer bible sch. Grace Presbyn. Ch., 1986-90, dir. children's choir, 1987-88; mem. cultural arts com. Plantation Elem. PTO, 1991-93; team coord. Cajun Sports Assn., 1991-93, Lafayette Youth Soccer Assn., 1991-93; active L.J. Alleman Mid. Sch. PTO, 1992; guest soloist numerous chs., 1966—. Recipient Cert. of Appreciation, Coun. Devel. of French in La., 1975, Plantation Elem. Sch., 1989, 90, 91, 92; music scholar U. Wis., Eau Claire, 1967-71. Mem. AAUP, Nat. Assn. Tchrs. of Singing (v.p. South La. chpt. 1988-90, pres. 1990-92), Music Educators Nat. Conf., La. Music Tchrs. Assn., Music Tchrs. Nat. Assn. (nat. cert.), Coll. Music Soc., Sigma Alpha Iota (life, pres. 1978-80, 87-88, editor 1983-85, faculty advisor 1980—, Sword of Honor 1982), Pi Kappa Lambda (pres. 1990-92), Phi Kappa Phi. Office: U Southwestern La PO Box 41207 # U Lafayette LA 70504-1207

DANIEL, MARILYN JANE, journalist; b. Birmingham, Ala., Nov. 14, 1969; d. William Howard and Mary Frances (McAnally) D. BA in journalism, U. Ala., 1994. Announcer/engineer WJSR Radio, Birmingham, 1989-91, pub. svc. dir., 1990-91; announcer/tech. asst. WBHM Radio, Birmingham, 1992—; staff writer Kaleidscope, Birmingham, 1993, news editor, 1994; editor, pub. No. Shelby News, Birmingham, 1994—; producer "The Fine Line" WERC-AM Radio, 1995—; writer Pioneer, 1991. Vol. Radio Reading Svc. for Print in Panel, Birmingham, 1992—, Firehouse Shelter, Birmingham, 1992. Mem. Soc. Profl. Journalists (pres. 1994, v.p. 1993), WJSR Radio Club (sec. 1990-91). Baptist. Home: 708 Huckleberry Ln Hoover AL 35226 Office: North Sherby News 2481 Valleydale Rd Ste C Birmingham AL 35244-2017

DANIELL, HENRY, molecular genetics educator; b. Salem, Nov. 9, 1950; s. Christian and Leela Henry. BS, U. Madras, 1969, MS, 1971; PhD, Madurai Kamaraj U., 1980. Postdoctoral rsch. assoc. U. Ill., Champaign-Urbana, 1980-83; asst. prof. biochemistry, adj. assoc. prof. Wash. State U., Pullman, 1983-91; assoc. prof. biol. scis. U. Idaho, Moscow, 1986-91; assoc. prof. molecular genetics Auburn (Ala.) U., 1991—; mem. vis. faculty Harvard U., Cambridge, 1988; cons. UN Indsl. Devel. Orgn., 1989, 91; dir. Internat. Workshop on Molecular Strategies for Crop Improvement, 1991; chmn. NATO Workshop, Italy, 1993; ad hoc reviewer NIH, NSF, USDA; lectr. in field; judge numerous sci. olympiad presentations; appeared on CBS, NBC, ABC, and in more than 70 newspapers in U.S., 1995. Patentee in field; author: Recombinant DNA Volume 217, 1993, Methods in Molecular Biology, Vols. 62, 63, 1996; assoc. editor Scandinavian Jour. Devel. Alternat., 1986-91; contbr. numerous articles to profl. and sci. jours. Recipient Environ. Program award UN Greece, 1980, Environ. award, Belgrade, 1980, UNESCO award Argentina, 1988, Sci. and Tech. award Govt. India, Brussels, 1983, Auburn Univ. Alumni award and Auburn Univ. Sigma Xi Rsch. award, 1994. Mem. AAAS, Am. Soc. Plant Physiology, Internat. Soc. Plant Molecular Biology. Methodist. Home: 400 Kimberly Dr Auburn AL 36830-6718 Office: Auburn U 101 Life Scis Bldg Auburn AL 36849-5407

DANIELS, ELREA MAE, retired elementary and special education educator; b. Havana, Fla., May 16, 1913; d. Emanuel and Polly Ann (Wester) Curtis (dec.); widowed. BS, Fla. A&M U., 1945, MEd, 1954. Tchr. Jackson County Elem. Sch., Jackson County Sch. Bd., Marianna, Fla., 1939-76, ret., 1976; chairperson Patrol Girls, tchr. Majorettes, Jackson County Elem. Sch., 1954-60. Steward, class leader, mem. choir, mem. missionary soc. St. James A.M.E. Ch. Recipient Outstanding Contbn. to Youth award Jackson County Guidance Clinic Bd., 1977-82, Recignition for outstanding accomplishments in edn. and cmty. svcs. Delta Sigma Theta, 1996, Recognitionand Honor for positive significant outstanding svc. in Black Cmty., Black Women's Program Com. of Pope Chapel AME Ch., 1996; named Outstanding Citizen, Chipola Svcs. Orgn., 1980. Mem. NAACP, Coun. Exceptional Children (life), Nat. Ret. Tchrs. Orgn., Fla. Ret. Tchrs. Orgn., Jackson County Educators Orgn., Order Ea. Star (treas. R. W. Whitehurst chpt. 1975-90). Democrat. Home: 4281 Oak St Marianna FL 32448-4223

DANIELS, FRANK ARTHUR, JR., newspaper publisher; b. Raleigh, N.C., Sept. 7, 1931; s. Frank Arthur and Ruth (Aunspaugh) D.; m. Julia Bryan Jones, June 4, 1954; children: Frank Arthur III, Julia Graham Nowell. A.B., U. N.C., 1953. With News and Observer Pub. Co., Raleigh, 1953—; pres., pub. News and Observer Pub. Co., 1971—; trustee Commonwealth Fund, N.Y.C., 1994—; chmn. Associated Press, 1992—; bd. dirs. Landmark Comm. Bd. dirs., mem. exec. com., campaign chmn. Triangle United Way, 1964, pres., 1974-75; bd. dirs. Greater Triangle Community Found.; former trustee Peace Coll., St. Mary's Coll.; former chmn. Rex. Hosp.; chmn., former pres. Am. Newspaper Pub. Assn. Found.; former mem. Raleigh-Durham Airport Authority; past trustee Woodberry Forest Sch.; past bd. visitors U. N.C. Served with USAF, 1954-55; bd. dirs. Smithsonian Inst., 1996—; campaign chmn. Triangle United Way, 1996. Named Outstanding Young Man of Yr. Raleigh Jaycees, 1963. Mem. So. Newspaper Pubs. Assn. (chmn. bd. 1973-74, pres. 1972-73, dir.), Am. Newspaper Pubs. Assn. (past bd. dirs., treas.), N.C. Press Assn. (past pres.), Greater Raleigh C. of C. (bd. dirs.), Carolina Motor Club (dir.), Delta Kappa Epsilon. Democrat. Presbyn. Clubs: Kiwanian. (Raleigh), Capital City (Raleigh), Carolina Country (Raleigh), Sphinx (Raleigh); University (N.Y.C.); Coral Beach (Bermuda). Office: News & Observer Pub Co 215 S Mcdowell St Raleigh NC 27601-1331

DANIELS, IRISH C., principal; b. Miami, Fla.; children: Irisha, Jessica. BS, Fla. A&M U., 1964, MEd, 1974; postgrad., Fla. State U., 1978. cert. adminstrn., supervision, early childhood, elem. edn., reading gifted edn., health. Tchr. Gadsden County Sch. Bd., Quincy, Fla.; tchr. Leon County Sch. Bd., Tallahassee, asst. prin.; grade level chmn.; sch. SACS chmn.; originator, coord. vocat. incentive program Hartsfield Sch., 1988-90; establisher, coord. Help Ctr. for grades 3-5, 1991; organizer, coord. Parent Tutorial Program, 1993-94; presenter AACTE Conv., 1994, ATE Conv., 1996. Named Disting. Black Educator from Hartsfield, 1991, Disting. Educator of Minorities, 1992. Mem. Asst. Prins. Facilitator or Sch. Improvement (chair), Phi Delta Kappa, Kappa Delta Pi. Home: 2605 Vence Dr Tallahassee FL 32312-3239

DANIELS, JAMES DOUGLAS, academic administrator; b. Harmony, N.C., Nov. 14, 1935; m. Marie Brown, Oct. 6, 1957; children: Christopher James, Gregory John, Susan Marie. AB, Davidson Coll., 1957; MA, U. N.C., 1962, PhD, 1968. Exec. tng. program Deering-Milliken Textile Corp., Gainesville, Ga., 1957-58; history instr. Hargrave Military Acad., Chatham, Va., 1961-62, chmn., div. social sci., 1962-65, dean students, summer sch., 1964-65; asst. prof. history Valdosta (Ga.) State Coll., 1968-71, assoc. prof. history, 1971-78, history prof., 1978, dean, sch. arts, sci., 1970-80; pres., prof. history Coker Coll., Hartsville, S.C., 1981—; bd. dirs. Byerly Hosp., 1981-85; Sunday sch. tchr. First Presbyn. Ch. Hartsville, 1981—. Adv. bd. Nations Bank, 1988—, Pee Dee Heritage, 1982—, Darlington County Mental Health Citizens, 1987—; mins. search com. First Presbyn. Ch. Hartsville, 1984-85; com. on ministry Pee Dee Presbytery of S.C., 1985—, moderator, 1985. With U.S. Army, 1958-60. NDEA fellow, U. N.C., 1966-68; recipient Man and Boy award Valdosta Boys' Club Bd. Dirs., 1970. Mem. Greater Hartsville C. of C. (bd. dirs. 1982-88, v.p. 1986, pres. 1987, chmn. bd. 1988), Hartsville High Sch. Acad. Boosters Club and Band Boosters, Rotary (bd. dirs. 1982—, Citizen of Yr. award 1989), Omicron Delta Kappa. Presbyterian. Home: 222 E Home Ave Hartsville SC 29550-3714 Office: Coker Coll E College Ave Hartsville SC 29550

DANIELS, JOSEPH HOWARD, II, broadcast engineer; b. Cin., May 20, 1954; s. Joseph I and Sadie (Rice) D.; m. Shelita Daniels, Feb. 14, 1992; 1 child, Nicole Pratt. BS in Music Edn., Winston-Salem State U., 1972. Edn. leader Columbus County Schs., Hallsboro, N.C., 1976-77; counselor Forsyth County Workshop, Winston-Salem, N.C., 1977-79; keyboardist, arranger Amani Euritha Players, Paris, 1979-80; prodn. asst. WXII-TV 12 (NBC), Winston-Salem, 1980-85; satellite technician Va. Tech., Falls Church, 1987-88, U. Va., Falls Church, 1988-90; choir dir. Duval High Sch., Greenbelt, Md., 1987-88; band dir. Kettering Mid. Sch., Upper Marlboro, Md., 1988-90; producer, dir. Black Coll. Satellite Network, Washington, 1990-91; chief engr. radio/TV Winston-Salem State U., 1991—. Recipient Outstanding Svc. awards Hallsboro Gospel Choir, 1977, Delta Sigma Theta, 1984, Duval High Sch., 1988, Winston-Salem State U. Marching Band, 1992. Mem. Assn. Computing Machinery, Soc. Broadcast Engrs. Home: Ste 102 5603 B W Friendly Ave Greensboro NC 27410

DANIELS, MICHAEL ALAN, lawyer; b. Cape Girardeau, Mo., Mar. 6, 1946. BS in Speech, Northwestern U., 1968, MA in Polit. Sci., 1969; JD, U. Mo., 1973. Bar: Fla. 1974, U. S. Supreme Ct. 1983. Spl. asst. for polit. sci. research Office Naval Research, Washington, 1969-71; legal aid Edwards, Seigfried, Runge and Hodge, Mexico, Mo., 1972-73; corp. atty. CACI, Inc., Washington, 1974-77; exec. v.p. gen. counsel Datex, Inc., Washington, 1977-78; chmn. bd., pres. Internat. Pub. Policy Research Corp., Falls Church, Va., 1978-86; sect. v.p. Sci. Applications Internat. Corp., Mc Lean, Va., 1986—; pres. U.S. Global Strategy Council, Washington, 1986-94; chmn. bd. Network Solutions, Inc., 1995—. Mem. Republican Nat. Com., Internat. Affairs Council, Nat. Security Adv. Council; mem. investment policy adv. com. Office U.S. Trade Rep., 1982-87. Recipient Outstanding Fed. Securities Law Student award U. Mo., 1973. Mem. ABA (chmn. working group on law, nat. security and tech., standing com. law and nat. security 1984-92), Fla. Bar Assn., Fed. Bar Assn. (chmn. internat. law com. 1979-86), Internat. Studies Assn. Office: SAIC 1710 Goodridge Dr Mc Lean VA 22102-3701

DANIELS, ROBERT SANFORD, psychiatrist, administrator; b. Indpls., Aug. 12, 1927; s. Harry H. and Mary (Bassett) D.; m. Vikki Ashley; children: Stephen, Allen, Lynn, Judith. BS, U. Cin., 1948, MD, 1951. Intern Cin. Gen. Hosp., 1951; resident U. Cin. Hosp., 1954-57; mem. faculty U. Chgo., 1957-71, dir. psychiat. consultation svc., 1961-63, asso. prof. psychiatry, acting chmn. dept., 1963-66, clin. dir., 1966-68, asso. dean community and social medicine, 1968-71, prof. psychiatry and social medicine, 1970-71; dir. Center Health Adminstrn. Studies, Grad. Sch. Bus., 1970-71; dir. dept. psychiatry U. Cin., 1971-75; interim dean U. Cin. (Coll. Medicine), 1972-75; dean Coll. Medicine, U. Cin., 1975-86, also sr. v.p., 1982-86; dean La. State

U. Sch. Medicine, New Orleans, 1986-95, exec. asst. to chancellor, 1995—; chief staff Cin. Gen. Hosp., 1972-86, Holmes Hosp., 1972-86; vis. prof. social medicine and clin. epidemiology St. Thomas' Hosp. Med. Coll., London, Eng.; sci. exchange visitor Ministry Health, Moscow, USSR; vis. scholar King Edward VII Hosp. Fund, London, 1977; cons. Cook County Hosp., Ill. State Psychiat. Inst.; spl. research community and group psychiatry, health planning, community health, 1967-69; Chmn. Ill. Mental Health Planning Bd.; mem., chmn. rev. com., psychiatry edn. br. Health Services and Mental Health Adminstrn., 1971-75; mem. nat. mental health adv. bd. NIMH, 1975-79; bd. dirs. Hamilton County Bd. Mental Health and Retardation, 1974-78. Asso. editor: Social Psychiatry. Bd. dirs. Central Ohio River Valley Planning Authority, 1979—. Served with AUS, 1946-47; Served with USAF, 1952-54. Recipient Stella Feis Hoffheimer award U. Cin., 1951. Mem. AMA, Am. Psychiat. Assn., Am. Group Psychotherapy Assn., Assn. Am. Med. Colls. (exec. coun. 1982-87, psychiatry residency rev. coun. 1990—, Daniel Drake medal 1988), Ill. Group Psychotherapy Soc. (pres. 1965-66), Ill. Psychiat. Soc. (pres. 1967), Phi Beta Kappa, Alpha Omega Alpha. Office: La State U Sch Medicine Office of the Chancellor 433 Bolivar St Rm 820 New Orleans LA 70112

DANIELS, ROY MELVIN, elementary school principal; b. St. Charles, Ark., Apr. 27, 1952; s. Willie and Norvella (Marina) D.; m. Gloria Dean People, Sept. 16, 1978 (div. Aug. 1980); m. Shirley Ann Buschanon, Mar. 21, 1982; 1 child, Roy Melvin. BA in Social Sci., Ark. Bapt. U., Little Rock, 1979; MSE in Sch. Adminstrn., U. Ctrl. Ark., Conway, 1993. Cert. in adminstrn. and social studies, Ark., Tenn. Women's basketball coach Ark. Bapt. Coll., 1979-89; coach, tchr., prin. Humnoke (Ark.) Sch. Dist., 1989-95; elem. prin. Cotton Plant (Ark.) Elem. Sch., 1995—. V.p. Developmental Club, Cotton Plant. Mem. ASCD, Ark. Assn. Elem. Sch. Prins., Nat. Assn. Secondary Sch. Prins., U. Ctrl. Ark. Alumni Assn. Baptist. Home: 5401 Timberland Dr Little Rock AR 72204 Office: Cotton Plant Elem Sch Martin Luther King Dr Little Rock AR 72204

DANILOW, DEBORAH MARIE, rancher, musician, bondsman; b. Mineral Wells, Tex., Dec. 9, 1947; d. Stanton Byron and Irval Leona (Vanhoosier) D.; m. William Paul Cook Jr., June 1965 (div. Oct. 1967); m. Chance Gentry, Oct. 1971 (div. May 1974); m. Ellis Elmer Aldridge, Dec. 3, 1977 (div. Nov. 1984); children: Chandra Desiree, Anthony Ellis; m. Carl Graham Quisenberry, Feb. 7, 1992. Student, Brantley Draughon Bus. Coll., Ft. Worth, 1965-66, Tex. Christian U., 1965-67, U. Ariz., 1967-69. Asst. to pres. Hollywood Video Ctr., L.A., 1969-72; producer Western Inst. TV, L.A., 1972-77; owner Chanelde Ranch, Weatherford, Tex., 1977-84; band musician Bonnie Raitt, Malibu, Calif., 1984, Mick Fleetwood, Malibu, 1984; lead musician Jazz Talk, Ft. Worth, 1985—; owner Brazos Valley Ranch Inc., Seymour, Tex., 1987—, AAA Bail Bonds, Seymour, 1990—; lead musician Soul Full O' Jazz, 1996—. Composer numerous pub. songs, 1969—; lead musician Debbie Danilow and Soul Full o' Jazz, 1996—. Active Sheriffs Assn. Tex., Seymour, 1991—, North Tex. Taxpayers League, Wichita Falls, Tex., 1991—, Tex. State Notary Bd., Austin, 1990—. Mem. NAFE, NRA, Okla. Game Breeders Assn., United Game Breeders Assn., Tex. Game Breeders Assn., Tex. Limousin Assn., Tex. Southwestern Cattle Raisers Assn., Tex. Cattlewomen's Assn., Am. Quarter Horse Assn. (life), Dallas-Ft. Worth Profl. Musicians Assn., Ft. Worth Jazz Soc. (sec. 1987-89), N.Am. Limousin Found. (life), Australian Shepherd Club Am., Internat. Platform Assn., Marchigiana Cattle Assn. (life), N.Am. Fishing Club. Baptist. Office: Brazos Valley Ranch Inc 111 S Main St Seymour TX 76380-2528

DANJCZEK, DAVID WILLIAM, manufacturing company executive; b. Phillipsburg, N.J., Sept. 29, 1951; s. William Emil and Erna (Lob) D. BSFS, Georgetown U., 1973; postgrad. Waseda U., 1973-74, Loyola U., Los Angeles, 1977-78. Contract adminstr. Aero Products, Woodland Hills, Calif., 1974-76, sr. contract adminstr., 1976-78; dir. internat. ops. Litton Industries, Washington, 1978-90, v.p. internat. bus., 1990-93; v.p. govt. and internat. affairs Western Atlas Inc., 1993—; adj. prof. Georgetown U. Vice chair industry sector adv. com. U.S. Dept. Commerce; bd. dirs. Exec. Coun. on Diplomacy. Mem. Mfrs. Alliance Productivity and Innovation (vice chmn. internat. ops. coun.). Republican. Roman Catholic. Clubs: University, Internat. Aviation. Avocations: squash, bridge. Home: 1300 Crystal Dr Arlington VA 22202-3234 Office: Western Atlas Inc 1725 Jefferson Davis Hwy Arlington VA 22202

DANKO, PATRICIA ST. JOHN, visual artist, writer, educator; b. Orange, Tex., Aug. 7, 1944; d. George Milton and Rebecca Alice (McCoppin) Solomon; m. Jim Danko, Aug. 19, 1973 (dec. 1983). BA, Dominican Coll., Houston, 1965; postgrad. U. Ibero-Americana, Mexico, 1965, Mich. State U., 1965, Mus. Fine Arts Sch., Houston, 1972; BFA, U. Houston, 1979, MEd in Second Lang. Edn., 1992. Tchg. asst. Mich. State U., East Lansing, 1965; vol. Peace Corps, Chile, 1965-68; silkscreen apprentice, printer Atelier Zárate, Buenos Aires, 1969; tchr. h.s. Orange Ind. Sch. Dist. (Tex.), 1971, Houston Ind. Sch. Dist., 1973; instr. English, English Lang. Svcs., Houston, 1973-75; instr. English, Spanish, Inlingua Lang. Schs., 1976; instr. Art League Houston, 1978-81; performance art writer Houston Art Scene, 1979-84, editor, 1981-84, mng. editor, 1982-83, exec. editor, 1983-84; acting Tex. editor New Art Examiner, 1985-86; contbg. editor Tex. New Art Examiner, 1986-88; curriculum writer Houston Ind. Sch. Dist., 1990-91; tchr. Caminos Bilingües al Exito Fed. Title VII Grants program Burbank Middle Sch., Houston, 1996—; ind. art hist. rschr., writer; freelance writer, 1979-85; Visual artist, pub. collections: Nat. Mus. Women in Arts, Washington, Libr. and Rsch. Archives, Washington, N.Y. Feminist Art Inst., Equinox Theatre, Houston, Chomo Uri Collective, U. Mass., Memphis-Brooks Mus. Art, Several Dancers Core Sch., Atlanta, McGlothlin Ins. Agy., Houston, Cameron Petroleum Co., Houston, Emdyne, Inc., Women's Studio Workshop, N.Y. Designer numerous art therapeutic programs for children; designer and mask-maker numerous artistic and theatrical performances; exhbns. of artistic work to numerous museums and cultural instns. throughout U.S., Mex. and China; designer, writer Bilingual Sci. Curriculum Houston Zoo, 1994. Jesse H. Jones Found. scholar, 1961-65; recipient Presdl. Commendation by Pres. Johnson for Service to U.S. and Chile, 1968; named Outstanding Young Woman of Am., OYWA Press, Chgo., 1970; Sum Arts grantee for sculpture The Matriarch as Phoenix, 1981; Shell Found. grantee for performance of Thanatopsis, 1983, grantee Ruth Chevon Found., Inc., 1987, Change, Inc., N.Y.C., 1987, Adolph and Esther Gottlieb Found., 1988; Lamar Found. grantee, 1989; Impact II Developer grantee, 1990-91; Bus. Com. for Ednl. Excellence grantee, 1991-92, 94-96; Title VII Edn. Project grantee U. Houston, 1991-92; endowed chair to design and implement program for immigrant and refugee children, I Have a Dream Found., 1991-92, endowed chair to continue program for immigrant & refugee children Mid. Sch. Initiative Funds, Houston Ind. Sch. Dist., 1992-96; tchr., curriculum writer Fed. Title VII grants program Burbank Mid. Sch., Houston, 1996—. Mem. Artists Equity Assn., Contemporary Arts Mus. (Houston). Roman Catholic. Address: 2112 Dunlavy St Houston TX 77006-1704

DANN, OLIVER TOWNSEND, psychoanalyst, psychiatrist, educator; b. Mansfield, Ohio, Aug. 10, 1935; s. Edward William and Mary Virginia (Townsend) D.; m. Linda Marie Schweers, July 15, 1961; children: Sara Katharine, Jonathan William Jenner, Luke Nathan Townsend, Jesse Charles. AB, Columbia U., 1958; MD, Yale U., 1962. Diplomate Am. Bd. Psychiatry and Neurology. Resident in psychiatry Yale U. Sch. Medicine, New Haven, 1963-67, asst., assoc. prof. psychiatry, 1967-79; clin. prof. psychiatry U. Miami (Fla.) Sch. Medicine, 1980—; pvt. practice, Miami, 1979—. Contbr. articles to profl. jours. Fellow APA; mem. Am. Psychoanalytic Assn., Internat. Psychoanalytic Assn., Western New England Inst. Soc. Psychoanalysis, Balt.-Washington Inst. Soc. Psychoanalysis, Fla. Psychanalytic Inst. Soc. Found., Phi Beta Kappa, others. Home and Office: 4550 SW 74 St Miami FL 33143-6271

DANNER, RICHARD ALLEN, law educator, dean; b. Marshfield, Wis., Aug. 26, 1947; s. Reuben Mathias and Evelyn (Fischer) D.; m. Cheryl Clark Sanford, Jan. 27, 1973; children—Zachary Allen, Katherine Elizabeth. B.A., U. Wis., 1969, M.S., 1975, J.D., 1979; postgrad., MIT, 1973. Bar: Wis. 1979. Environ. law librarian U. Wis. Law Library, Madison, 1975-79; assoc. law librarian Duke U. Sch. Law, Durham, N.C., 1979-80, acting law librarian, instr., 1980-81, dir. law libr., 1981-93, asst. prof. law, 1981-82, assoc. prof., 1982-85, prof., 1985—, assoc. dean, 1993—; dir. Triangle Research Libraries Network, 1984—. Author: Legal Research in Wisconsin, 1980, Strategic Planning: A Law Library Management Tool, 1991; editor Law Library Management Tool, 1991, Law Libr. Jour., 1984-94; co-editor: Introduction to Foreign Legal Systems, 1994; contbr. articles to profl. jours. With U.S. Army, 1969-71. Decorated Bronze Star. Mem. Am. Assn. Law Librs. (pres. 1989-90), ALA, State Bar Wis. Home: 2419 Tryon Rd Durham NC 27705-5511 Office: Duke U Sch Law Libr PO Box 90361 Durham NC 27708-0361

DANNHEISSER, BERTRAM VIVIAN, JR., dentist; b. Pensacola, Fla., Aug. 2, 1927; s. Bertram Vivian Sr. and Frieda (Goodman) Dannheisser; m. Joyce Ann Schulein; children: Bertram V. III, Thomas Victor, Matthew Edward. Student, Tulane U., New Orleans, 1946-47, Emory U., Atlanta, 1947-48; DDS, Washington U., St. Louis, 1952. Pvt. practice Pensacola, Fla., 1954—; staff mem. Bapt. Hosp., Sacred Hosp., Univ. Hosp., 1954—; past dir. Fla. Dental Svcs. Inc.; orgnl. com. chmn., past chmn. adv. com. Pensacola Jr. Coll. Dental Assts. Sch.; coun. mem. Fla. Panhandle Health Systems Agy. Editor Fla. Dental Jour., 1978—. Past pres. Temple Beth-El, Reform Judaism, past pres. Men's Club; past dir. Pensacola Little Theater; past pres. Learning Disorder of Greater Pensacola; past dir., v.p. Escambia County Cmty. Coun.; past pres. Workman Jr. High PTA; past dir. Excambia County Tb Assn.; past instl. rep. Boy Scouts Am.; past dir., past sec.-treas. Jr. Achievement; charter mem. Washington H.S. Adv. Com.; dist. 1 former rep. State of Fla. Coun. on Aging. Fellow Am. Coll. Dentists, Fla. Acad. Dental Practice Adminstrn.; mem. ADA (del. 1972-84), Fla. Dental Assn. (past trustee, past pres., mem. long range planning com., past dir. polit. action com.), N.W. Dist. Dental Assn. (past pres.), Escamb-Santa Rosa Dental Assn. (past pres.), Pierre Fauchard Acad., Am. Soc. Preventive Dentistry (past pres. Fla. chpt.), So. Acad. Clin. Nutrition, Acad. Gen. Dentistry, Fla. Dental Health Found. (dir.), U. Fla. Coll. Dentistry Acad. 100 (past pres.), Am. Assn. Dental Editors (past pres.), Washington U. Sch. Dentistry Alumni Assn. (trustee), Pensacola Kiwanis (past pres.), Pensacola C. of C. (chmn. edn. task force, dir. 1982—), Scenic Hills Country Club (past pres.), Gulf Coast Econs. Club (dir.), Alpha Omega. Home: 781 Gerhardt Dr Pensacola FL 32503 Office: 14 W Jordan St Ste 2G Pensacola FL 32501-1735

DANTONE, W. BRYAN, real estate investor, principal; b. Hammond, La., Sept. 4, 1951; s. Joseph Dominic and Regina Marjorie (Brelsford) D.; m. Liz Burkholder, Sept. 21, 1985. BA in Econs./Pre-Law, U. St. Thomas, 1977. Acct. mgr. Wilson Internat., Houston, 1977-79; mktg. rep. C.E.-VETCO, New Orleans, 1979-81, Houston, 1981-84; spl. products Knapp Specialties, Houston, 1984-85; investor Dantone & Burkholder, Houston, 1985-89, prin., 1989—. Mem. Neartown Civic Assn., Houston, 1985—, Houston Mus. Fine Arts, Mus. Natural Scis.; co-founder W.A.M.M. Civic Assn., Houston, 1990. Mem. Audobon Pl. Assn., Roseland Estates Assn., F.M.C. Assn. Republican. Episcopalian. Office: Dantone and Burkholder 4318 Stanford St Houston TX 77006-5930

D'ANTONI, DAVID J., chemicals executive. Pres. Ashland Chems. Office: Ashland Oil Inc PO Box 391 Ashland KY 41105-0391 also: Ashland Chem Co 5200 Blazer Memorial Pky Dublin OH 43017-5309

DANTZLER, J.A., business executive; b. 1926. Farmer, 1950-84; pres. Elloree (S.C.) Gin & Co. Office: Elloree Gin Co 645 Snider St Elloree SC 39047

DANZIG, SHEILA RING, marketing and direct mail executive; b. N.Y.C., Mar. 18, 1948; d. David and Yetta Ring; m. William Harold Danzig, Aug. 11, 1968; children: David Scott, Gregory Charles. BS, CUNY, 1968; PhD, Am. Coastline U., 1996. Tchr. N.Y.C. Bd. Edn., 1968-71; treas. Nat. Success Mktg. Inc., Sunrise, Fla., 1969—; pres. Innovative Comm. Market Cons., Plantation, Fla., 1984-87; cons. Crush Softball Team, Hollywood, Fla., 1986-87, The Eye Ctr., Sunrise, 1986-87, Bus. Expo., Plantation, 1987. Author: You Deserve to be Rich, 1972, A Free Press, 1990, A Better Medical Practice, 1986; author, pub.: Turn Your Computer Into A Money Machine, 1994; contbr. articles to profl. jours. Coord. Day Out program Mills Boys' Shelter, Ft. Lauderdale, Fla., 1985, 87, Put Seat Belts on Sch. Buses program Broward County Sch. Bd., 1986; vol. Miami Children's Hosp.; campaign dir. Help the Handicapped Keep Their Parking Spots, 1987. Mem. Mail Order Bus. Bd., Am. Med. Writers Assn., Plantation Bus. and Profl. Women's Assn., MADD, Speechcrafters. Office: Nat Success Mktg 2574 N University Dr Fort Lauderdale FL 33322-3045

DANZIG, WILLIAM HAROLD, marketing executive; b. Bklyn., Feb. 24, 1947; s. Sidney and Beatrice (Reiss) D.; m. Sheila Ring, Aug. 11, 1968; children: David Scott, Gregory Charles. BS in Acctg., Baruch Coll., 1969; MS in Edn., Long Island U., 1971; PhD, Am. Coastline U., 1996. Acct. JK Lasser, N.Y.C., 1972; tchr. N.Y.C. Bd. Edn., Queens, 1969-74; pres. Nat. Success Mktg. Inc., Ft. Lauderdale, Fla., 1969—; sponsor Coop. Bus. Edn., Broward County, Fla., 1986; participant Bus. Expo, Ft. Lauderdale, 1985; cons. Mail Market Monitor, Ft. Lauderdale, 1988—, Gulfstream Pub., Ft. Lauderdale, 1988—. Co-author: You Deserve to be Rich, 1975, Play to Win, 1982; publisher (computer program) Turn Your Computer Into A Money Machine, 1994. Mem. Mail Order Bus. Bd., Greater Ft. Lauderdale C. of C., B'nai Brith (chpt. bd. dirs. 1976). Republican. Jewish. Office: Nat Success Mktg Inc 2574 N University Dr Ste 201 Fort Lauderdale FL 33322-3045

DANZIGER, TERRY LEBLANG, public relations and marketing consultant; b. Jan. 20, 1933; d. Leon Leventhal and Dorothy Leblang; m. Arthur Lewis Danziger, Mar. 29, 1953; children: Robin Danziger-Ross, Stephen. Student, Syracuse U., 1950-52, C.W. Post Coll., 1962-66; BA in Psychology, Empire State Coll., 1974. Advt. copywriter, account exec. Grey Adv., Foote, Cone & Belding, Kaplan & Bruck, and others, N.Y.C., 1952-55; editorial writer Syosset (N.Y.) Tribune, 1956-62; pres. Mail Arts Co., Syosset, 1962-68; exec. dir. Nassau Easter Seal Soc., Crippled Children and Adults, Inc., Albertson, N.Y., 1968-74; pres. TLD Enterprises, Syosset, Bethpage, N.Y., 1974-77; regional dir. Telequin Ltd., N.Y.C., 1977-78; state pub. rels. dir., regional campaign dir. Arthritis Found. Fla., Miami, Ft. Lauderdale, 1978-79; pub. rels. dir. FPA Corp., Pompano Beach, Fla., 1979-81; pres. PR Mktg. Concepts, Boca Raton, Fla., 1980—. Adv. coun. NCCJ. Mem. Am. Mktg. Assn. (bd. dirs.), Pub. Rels. Soc. Am. (counselors acad.), Am. Bus. Women's Assn., Pub. Rels. Soc. Fla. (v.p.), Profl. Resource Network, Psi Chi. Office: PR Mktg Concepts 1280 S Powerline Rd Ste 120 Pompano Beach FL 33069

DAOUD, ABRAHAM JOSEPH, IV, funeral director, former police officer; b. Miami Beach, Fla., Jan. 19, 1957; 1 child, Joseph Abraham. AS in Funeral Services, Miami Dade Community Coll., 1980, cert. police officer, 1980; cert. crime prevention, S.W. Tex. State U., 1981; BS, Barry U. Cert. police officer; lic. funeral dir., Fla., N.C., Tex. Pres. Daoud's, Inc., Miami Beach, Fla., 1974-76; coordinator Fed. CETA Program, Miami Beach, 1978; aux. police officer Miami Beach Police Dept., 1976-79, police officer, 1979-86; v.p. Daoud Med. Ctr., Miami Beach, 1982-84; crime prevention officer Miami Beach Police Dept., 1980-82; funeral dir. Riverside Meml. Chapels, Miami Beach, 1981-86; with Guardian Plan Inc., 1986-88; regional mgr. Osiris Corp., 1988-95; asst. regional v.p. S.E. U.S. Loewen Group; coord. Aux. Police, Miami Beach, 1981. Recipient cert. of appreciation Dade County Pharm. Assn., 1974, citation of appreciation Am. Legion, 1984, Outstanding Citizen award Miami Beach Taxpayers, 1986, Disting. Citizen award City of Miami Beach, 1986. Mem. Miami Beach Police Athletic League (exec. dir. 1982-86, Fla. state pres. 1985, nat. v.p. 1986-87, 9 Svc. awards, Police Athletic League Recreation Hall dedication 1986), Fla. Police Athletic League (pres. 1983-87), Jaycees (pres. Miami Beach club 1984, mgmt. v.p. 1982, 83, Appreciation award 1984), Fraternal Order of Police, Internat. Assn. Chiefs of Police, Internat. Assn. Chiefs of Police, Gemological Internat. Assn., Miami Beach C. of C. Democrat. Roman Catholic. Lodges: Elks (Miami Beach) (trustee, Exalted Ruler 1985), Masons, Shriners, Optimists, Rotary. Office: 3434 W Flagler St Miami FL 33135-1026

DAR, MOHAMMAD SAEED, pharmacologist, educator; b. Lahore, Pakistan, Dec. 10, 1937; came to U.S., 1979; s. Mohammad Usaf and Amir Begum (Amir) D.; m. Parveen Saeed, Mar. 16, 1969; children: Mohammed Mujtaba, Moahad Saeed. MS in Pharmacy, U. Med. Scis., Bangkok, 1966; PhD in Pharmacology, Med. Coll. Va., 1970. Rsch. assoc. Rockefeller Found., Bangkok, 1970-72; asst. prof., then assoc. prof. Shiraz (Iran) U. Med. Sch., 1972-79, acting chmn., 1977-79; asst. prof. dept. pharmacology East Carolina U. Sch. Medicine, Greenville, N.C., 1979-85, assoc. prof., 1985-90, prof. pharmacology, 1990—. Contbr. rsch. articles to sci. jours. Mem. Am. Soc. Pharmacology and Exptl. Therapeutics, Soc. Neurosci., Rsch. Soc. Alcoholism, N.Y. Acad. Scis., Internat. Soc. Biomed. Rsch. on Alcoholism. Home: 115 Heritage St Greenville NC 27858-6730 Office: East Carolina U Sch Medicine Greenville NC 27858

DARBY, JOHN PRESTON, internist; b. Columbia, S.C., Oct. 21, 1930; s. John Preston and Mary Lunsford (Hayne) D.; m. Audrey Anne Graham, Dec. 18, 1953 (div. 1974); children; John Preston, Steven Graham (dec.), Catherine Hayne; m. Pamela Brook Wescott, Apr. 16, 1982; children; Hayne Thomson, Mary Preston, Sarah Galbraith. BS, U. S.C., 1950; MD, Med. Coll. S.C., 1954. Diplomate Am. Bd. Internal Medicine. Intern Meth. Hosp., Gary, Ind., 1954-55; commd. 1st lt. USAF, 1955; resident Brooke Army Med. Ctr., San Antonio, 1957-60; fellow Walter Reed Army Inst. Rsch., Washington, 1960-61; advanced through grades to major USAF, ret., 1964; staff internist Malone and Hogan Clinic, Big Spring, Tex., 1964-69; pvt. practice San Angelo, Tex., 1969-86; internist West Tex. Med. Assocs., 1987—; chief of medicine Angelo Cmty. Hosp., San Angelo, 1988, St. John's Hosp., San Angelo, 1972-78, chief of staff, 1971-72. Active Good Shepherd Episc. Ch.; pres. Internat. Orphan Care, L.A., 1992—. Named Disting. Alumnus Med. U. S.C., 1987, Algernon Sydney Sullivan award U. S.C., 1995. Fellow ACP, Am. Coll. Chest Physicians; mem. Tex. Med. Assn., Tex. Acad. Internal Medicine, Tom Green Eight County Med. Soc., Am. Geriatric Soc., MENSA. Republican. Home: 6486 Callison Rd San Angelo TX 76904 Office: West Tex Med Assocs 3555 Knickerbocker Rd San Angelo TX 76904-7610

DARBY, MARIANNE TALLEY, elementary school educator; b. Adel, Ga., Nov. 8, 1937; d. William Giles and Mary (McGlamry) Talley; m. Roy Copeland Darby, Apr. 2, 1958; children: Susan, Leslie, Allison Darby Davis. Student, Emory U., 1955-57; BS in Early Childhood Edn., Valdosta (Ga.) State Coll., 1973. Cert. early childhood and elem. edn. tchr., Ga. Tchr. 2d grade Adel Elem. Sch., spring 1973, tchr. 1st grade, 1973—. Pres. Cook County Jaycettes, Adel, 1962. Mem. Internat. Reading Assn. (South Cen. Ga. coun.), Profl. Assn. Ga. Educators, Adel Garden Club, Alpha Epsilon Upsilon, Alpha Delta Kappa (sec. 1980-82), Sigma Alpha Chi, Alpha Chi, Kappa Alpha Theta. Republican. Methodist. Home: 710 S Forrest Ave Adel GA 31620-3523

D'ARCY, THOMAS JOSEPH, engineering consultant; b. Chgo., Feb. 14, 1933; s. Charles L. D'Arcy and Mary Hermanek; m. Marie Margaret Brzoska, Apr. 7, 1956; children: Karen Ann D'Arcy Dumdei, Lauren Ann D'Arcy Simpson, Susan Ann D'Arcy Mannas, Thomas Joseph Jr. BSCE, U. Ill., 1955. Registered profl. engr., Ariz., Ark., Colo., Conn., Del., Fla., Ill., Kans., La., Mass., Miss., N.J., N.Mex., N.C., N.Y., Okla., Pa., Tenn., Tex., Va. Design engr. Hazelet and Erdal, Chgo., 1955-60; tech. dir. Prestressed Concrete Inst., Chgo., 1960-64; sales engr. Concrete Material, Inc., Charlotte, 1964-67; sales mgr. Concrete Material, Inc., Atlanta, 1967-69; dir. engring. and promotion San Vel Corp., Littleton, Mass., 1969-72; pres. Rocky Mountain Prestress, Denver, 1972-79; mktg. mgr. Stanley Precast, San Antonio, 1979-82; pres. Cons. Engrs. Group, Inc., San Antonio, 1982—. Dinner chair benefit Sta. KLRN-TV, 1991. Fellow ASCE, NSPE; mem. Am. Concrete Inst., Prestressed Concrete Inst. (com. chmn., bd. dirs., merit award 1988-90), Nat. Parking Assn. (chmn. cons. coun., bd. dirs. Bernard Dutch Meml. award). Office: Cons Engrs Group 2455 NE Loop 410 Ste 125 San Antonio TX 78217-5650

DARDEN, EDGAR BASCOMB, JR., consultant, retired biophysicist; b. Raleigh, N.C., Jan. 23, 1920; s. Edgar Bascomb and Willie Harllee (Pugh) D.; m. Ruth Lee Dossett, Dec. 13, 1969; 1 stepchild, Glenn Leinart. BS, Coll. William and Mary, 1941; postgrad., U. Va., 1946-47; MS, U. N.C., 1950; PhD, U. Tenn., Knoxville, 1957. Physicist's aide USN, Norfolk, Va., 1941; instr. physics Coll. William and Mary, Williamsburg, Va., 1941-42; jr. biologist Oak Ridge (Tenn.) Nat. Lab., 1949-55; rschr. Oak Ridge (Tenn.) Inst. Nuclear Studies, 1955-56; biologist Oak Ridge (Tenn.) Nat. Lab., 1956-73; prof., head radiation safety Comparative Animal Rsch. Lab., U. Tenn., Oak Ridge, 1973-81; radiation safety officer Oak Ridge Assoc. Univs., 1981-87; ret., 1987; cons. FAA, Oklahoma City, 1990—; reviewer Radiation Rsch., Charlottesville. Contbr. articles to sci. jours. Mem., pres., mgr. Oak Ridge Cmty. Chorus, 1949-52; vol. Ecumenical Storehouse, Oak Ridge, 1980—; vol. Habitat for Humanity, East Tenn., 1985—. 1st Lt. U.S. Army, 1942-46, PTO. Mem. Am. Phys. Soc. (emeritus), Health Physics Soc. (emeritus, coun. East Tenn. chpt. 1978-80), Sigma Xi, Sigma Pi Sigma, Phi Beta Kappa. Democrat. Episcopalian. Home: 105 Orchard Ln Oak Ridge TN 37830

D'AREZZO, KAREN WILLIAMS, science writer; b. Royal Oak, Mich., Mar. 29, 1950; d. Winston Conway and Margaret Jane (Wilcox) Williams; m. Alfred John D'Arezzo Jr., Aug. 28, 1971; children: Andrew Williams, James John, Daniel Wilkin. Student, U. Wis., 1968-71; BS in Comms., U. Tenn., 1972. Cert. editor in the life scis. Assoc. campus dir. Campus Crusade for Christ, Johnson City, Tex., 1972-74, Austin, Tex., 1974-75, Boston, 1975-77; sr. editor devel. office Trinity Coll., Chgo., 1977-81; tech. writer Oak Ridge (Tenn.) Nat. Lab., 1982-87; sr. med. writer Biotech. Svcs. Inc., Little Rock, 1990-92; cons. med. writer U. Ark. for Med. Scis., Little Rock, 1992—, sr. med. writer, 1993-94; dir. of grants and sci. publs. Ark. Cancer Rsch. Ctr., Little Rock, 1994—. Mem. Am. Med. Writers Assn. Presbyterian. Office: 4301 W Markham Slot 752 Little Rock AR 72205

DARGAN, PAMELA ANN, systems/software engineer; b. Norfolk, Va.; d. Thomas J. and Stana E. (Verich) Piazza; m. W. Scott Dargan, Dec., 1990. BS in Math., Va. Polytech. & State U., 1979; MS in Computer Sci., George Mason U., 1993. Tech. staff BDM Corp., Mc Lean, Va., 1981, TRW Fed. Sys. Group, Mc Lean, Va., 1981-87; dep. program mgr. Mystech, Inc., Alexandria, Va., 1987-89; lead engr. MITRE Corp., Mc Lean, 1989—; program chair East Coast Artificial Intelligence Work Sta. Users Group, 1984-85. Contbr. articles to profl. jours. Mem. IEEE, Assn. Computing Machinery. Office: MITRE Corp 1820 Dolley Madison Blvd Mc Lean VA 22102

DARLING, SHANNON FERGUSON, special education educator; b. Spokane, Wash., Feb. 25, 1968; d. Carl Frederick Jr. and Roberta Ernestine (Phelps) Ferguson; m. Paul Garner Darling, Jan. 9, 1988. BA in Elem. and Spl. Edn., La. State U., Shreveport, 1991. Cert. tchr., spl. edn. tchr., La., respite caregiver for handicapped foster children. Tchr. autistic spl. edn. Meadowview Elem. Sch., Bossier City, La., 1991—; spl. edn. com. to develop spl. edn. alternative program curriculum Bossier Parish, 1994-95, spl. edn. adv. coun., 1994—, sec., 1994—, coun. exceptional children, 1988-95. Vol. Com. for Spl. Arts Festival and Sports Day, 1993-94; vol. tutor Bossier Parish, 1992—; asst. dir. Camp Rainman: Autistic Camp, 1994—; vol. Alternat. Family Care Foster Svcs., 1985—, Caddo-Bossier Assn. Retarded Citizens, 1980-85; active Meadowview PTA, 1991—. Recipient Spl. Edn. Tchr. of Yr., Bossier Parish, 1994; grantee Optimist Club, summer 1992, 93, 95, Isle of Capri Casino, summer 1994, 96, Nightmares: Charity Fundraising Com., fall 1995; grantee Horseshoe Casino, summer 1996. Mem. Autism Soc. (sec., rep. to bd. dirs. mtgs. 1994—, pres. 1996—). Methodist. Home: 1275 Moran St Haughton LA 71037-8622 Office: Meadowview Elem Sch 4315 Shed Rd Bossier City LA 71111-5222

DARLING, STEPHEN EDWARD, lawyer; b. Columbia, S.C., Apr. 12, 1949; s. Norman Rushton and Elizabeth (Clarkson) D.; m. Denise Howell, June 30, 1979; children: Julia Hanley, Edward McCrady, Elizabeth Rushton. BS in Banking, Fin., Real Estate, Ins., U. S.C., 1971, JD, 1974. Bar: S.C. 1974, U.S. Dist. Ct. S.C. 1975, U.S. Ct. Appeals (4th cir.) 1975, U.S. Ct. Appeals (5th cir.) 1976, U.S. Supreme Ct. 1982. From assoc. to ptnr. Sinkler, Gibbs & Simons, Charleston, S.C., 1974-87; ptnr. Sinkler & Boyd, Charleston, 1987—. Mem. ABA, S.C. Bar Assn., S.C. Def. Trial Attys. Assn. (exec. com. 1994—), Charleston County Bar Assn. (exec. com. 1989-90, 92-93), Internat. Assn. Def. Counsel, Southeastern Admiralty Law Inst., Met. Exch. Club (Charleston) (sec. 1980). Episcopalian. Home: 63 E Bay St Charleston SC 29401-2546 Office: Sinkler & Boyd 160 E Bay St Charleston SC 29401-2120

DARLINGTON, FRANK, industrial engraving company executive, retired, i; b. Manchester, Eng., Mar. 2, 1928; came to U.S., 1955; s. Harry and

Louisa Ann (Aikin) D.; m. Ivy Waite, Jan. 28, 1950; children: Peter Barrie, Pamela Darlington Duval. Student in Photo Engraving Processes, Manchester Coll. of Tech., 1946-50. Apprentice engraver Lockett Crossland Co., Manchester, 1943-49; sketch maker Std. Engraving, Eccles, Eng., 1950-53; artist, photo engraver Roll Phot Engravers, Manchester, 1953-55; head sketch making dept. Consolidated Engravers, Charlotte, N.C., 1955-59, plant prodn. control, 1959-63, v.p. sales and prodn., 1963-67, dir., part owner, 1967-70, pres., 1970-89; CEO Consolidated Group, Charlotte, N.C., 1989-91; ret., 1991; founding dir. First Charlotte Bank and Trust, 1983-93; chmn. graphic arts bd. Clemson (S.C.) U., 1985-94; city bd. dirs. Centura Bank, Charlotte. Mem. adv. bd. Boy Scouts of Am., Charlotte, 1991—. Mormon. Home and Office: Darlington Investments 7302 Baltusrol Ln Charlotte NC 28210

DARNELL, DONALD GENE, English language professional; b. Galveston, Tex., Mar. 10, 1932; s. Marvin William and Dorothy (Cross) D.; m. Janella Holloway, Dec. 22, 1953; 1 child, Sally. BS in Petroleum Geology, Tex. Technol. Coll., 1953; MA in English, U. Okla., 1962; PhD in English, U. Tex., 1964. Geologist Gen. Geophys. Co., Houston, 1953-56; instr. English dept. U. Wichita, Kans., 1957-60; from instr. to assoc. prof. English dept. U. N.C., Greensboro, 1964-77, prof. English dept., 1977—. Author: William Hickling Prescott, 1975, James Fenimore Cooper: Novelist of Manners, 1993; contbr. articles to profl. jours. Mem. MLA, South Atlantic MLA, James Fenimore Cooper Soc. Democrat. Episcopalian. Home: 5006 Lancaster Rd Greensboro NC 27410-4307

DARNELL, RILEY CARLISLE, state government executive, lawyer; b. Clarksville, Tenn., May 13, 1940; s. Elliott Sinclair and Mary Anita (Whitefield) D., married, 5 children; BS, Austin Peay State U., 1962; JD, Vanderbilt U., 1965; m. Mary Penelope Crockarell, June 2, 1963; children: Neil Whitefield, Duncan Edward, Mary Eve, Penelope Joy, Dawson Riley. Bar: Tenn. 1965. Gen. practice, Clarksville, 1965-66, 69—; mem. Tenn. Ho. of Reps. from 67th Dist., 1971-80, treas. house-senate caucus, 1971-86, sec. house com. ways and means, chmn. joint house-senate fiscal rev. com., 1975-80; mem. Tenn. State Senate, 1980-92, chmn. transp. com., 1982-86, chmn. joint com. children and youth, 1987-89; senate majority leader, 1988-92; sec. of state State of Tenn., Nashville, 1993—. Served to capt. JAGC, USAF, 1966-69. Democrat. Fellow Tenn. Bar Found.; mem. ABA, Montgomery County Bar Assn., Tenn. Trial Lawyers, Tenn. Bar Assn., Nat. Conf. State Legislators (jud. task force), So. Legis. Conf. (mem. fiscal affairs com.), Clarksville C. of C., Moose, Clarksville Downtown Civitan Club. Mem. Ch. of Christ. Home: 603 Waterloo Dr Clarksville TN 37043-6014 Office: State Capital Fl 1 Nashville TN 37243-0305

DARNELL, TIMOTHY HOYT, journalist; b. Atlanta, May 15, 1961; s. Lonnie Kinglsey and Amy Carolyn (Howard) D.; m. Susan Kay Herman, Oct. 29, 1994. BA in political sci., Ga. State Univ., 1983. Reporter Neighbor Newspaper, Atlanta, 1985-87; editor Communication Channels, Atlanta, 1987-92, Network Communications, Atlanta, 1992-94, Shore Communications, Atlanta, 1994; industry focus editor Atlanta Bus. Chronicle, Atlanta, 1996—. Editor: Southern Yankees, 1995. Vol. The Peach Bowl Atlanta C. of C., 1988—, Hands on Atlanta, 1989—; newsletter editor Drew Valley Civic Assn., 1995—. Recipient Best Editorial Commentary award Magazine Assn. of Ga., 1994. Mem. Chamblee Lodge 444 F&AM, (master). Democrat. Baptist. Home: 2364 Poplar Springs Dr NE Atlanta GA 30319-3942

DARR, JAMES EARL, JR., lawyer; b. Ann Arbor, Mich., July 12, 1943; s. J. Earl and Nora M. (Patton) D.; m. Marcia Edwards Darr, Feb. 21, 1982; children: James E. III, Carolyn. BSBA, U. Ark., 1966, JD, 1971. Bar: Ark. 1971, U.S. Supreme Ct., U.S. Tax Ct. Ptnr. Eichenbaum, Scott, Miller, Crockett, Darr & Hawk, PA, Little Rock, 1971-85; sr. v.p., sec., gen. counsel Dillard Dept. Stores Inc., Little Rock, 1985—. Mem. ABA, Ark. Bar Assn., Pulaski County Bar Assn. Office: Dillard Dept Stores Inc 1600 Cantrell Rd Little Rock AR 72201-1110

DARTEZ, LOUIS AVERY, rancher, typographer; b. Lafayette, La., Dec. 12, 1925; s. Joseph Avery and Marie (LeBlanc) D.; student in Journalism and Bus. Adminstrn., U. Houston, 1956-59, 62-63; m. Barbara Ann Jackson, Oct. 13, 1951. Engring. clk. Stone & Webster Engring. Corp., Houston, 1946-48; supr. non-tech. sect. Mathieson Chem. Co., Balt., 1949-52; adminstrv. asst. to v.p. dept. engring. Tellepsen Constrn. Co., Houston, 1952-59; founder, owner, operator Dart Type Co., Houston, 1959—; rancher Round Top Farm, Houston; owner Dart Aircraft Leasing & Chartering, Houston, Am. Manor Apts., Houston; partner Greenlea Land Devel., Houston; speaker on small bus. mgmt., typography and communications to sch. groups. Served with USAAF, 1943-46, USAF, 1948-49. Mem. Printing Industries Assn. Houston (pres. 1970-71, award of appreciation and recognition 1974), Nat., Houston (pres. 1974) composition assns., Printing Craftsmen Club, Houston Litho Club, Gen. Aviation Pilots Assn., Attakapas Hist. Soc. Republican. Roman Catholic. Contbr. articles on typography to tech. publs., newspapers; author copyfitting charts; contbr. editor Graphics S.W. Mag., 1968-70; geneal. research, including extensive travel, 1956—. Office: 3313 Damico St Houston TX 77019-1905

DAS, KAMALENDU, chemist; b. Sylhet, Bangladesh, Feb. 2, 1944; came to U.S. 1971; s. Kailash and Prabhashini Das; m. Shyamali Chowdhury, Dec. 6, 1969; children: Mrinal Kanti, Sampa. BSc with honors, U. Dhaka, 1964, MSc, 1966; PhD, U. Houston, 1975. Asst. prof. Women's Coll. & Tolaram Coll., Bangladesh, 1966-71; postdoctoral instr. U. Houston, 1976-78; rsch. scientist, group leader Baker Sand Control, Houston, 1979-85; rsch. chemist, physical scientist, project mgr. U.S. Dept. Energy, Morgantown, W.Va., 1985—; Contbr. articles to profl. jours. Tennis com. chmn. Homeowners Assn., Houston, 1982-84. Pres. Mountaineer Toastmasters Club 8538, 1994-95, v.p. edn., 1995-96. Fellow Am. Inst. Chemists; mem. Am. Chem. Soc., Soc. Petroleum Engrs., Internat. Union Pure and Applied Chemistry. Hindu. Home: 465 Lawnview Dr Morgantown WV 26505-2130 Office: US Dept of Energy-METC MS C05 PO Box 880 Morgantown WV 26507-0880

DAS, SAJAL KUMAR, computer science educator, researcher; b. Dainhat, India, Jan. 3, 1960; came to U.S., 1985; s. Baidya Nath and Bimala (Dhani) D.; m. Nandini Dutta, Dec. 15, 1989; 1 child, Somak. BS in Physics with honors, Calcutta U., 1980, B in Tech., 1983; MS in Computer Sci., Indian Inst. Sci., 1984; PhD in Computer Sci., U. Ctrl. Fla., 1988. Teaching asst. computer sci. dept. Wash. State U., Pullman, 1985-86; rsch. asst. dept. computer sci. U. Ctrl. Fla., Orlando, 1986-88; asst. prof. dept. computer sci. U. North Tex., Denton, 1988-92, assoc. prof., 1995—, dir. Ctr. for Rsch. in Parallel and Distributed Computing, 1990—; faculty advisor U. North Tex. Badminton Club, Denton, 1989-90; founding advisor India Student Assn. of U. North Tex., Denton, 1990-93; mem. steering com. Internat. Conf. on Computing and Info., Can., 1992; vis. prof. Bell No. Rsch., Dallas, 1993-94; mem. program coms. and adv. coms. several internat. confs.; speaker and presenter in field. Mem. editorial bd. Parallel Processing Letters, 1991—, Jour. Parallel Algorithms and Applications, 1992—; contbr. articles to profl. jours.; more than 70 refereed papers. Summer Rsch. fellow U. North Tex., 1990, Honor Profl. award U. North Tex., 1991; Rsch. grantee Higher Edn. Coordinating Bd., Tex., 1991—, Travel grantee Goethe U., Germany, 1992, grantee Bell. No. Rsch., Dallas, 1993-94; Leonardo Fibinacci Inst. scholar, 1993. Mem. IEEE Computer Soc. (jour. reviewer, tech. sessions chair), Assn. for Computing Machinery (sponsoring faculty student chpt. U. North Tex.), N.Y. Acad. Scis., Sigma Xi. Office: Univ North Tex Dept Computer Sci PO Box 13886 Denton TX 76203-6886

DAS, SUMAN KUMAR, plastic surgeon, researcher; b. Calcutta, India, May 6, 1944; came to U.S., 1980; s. Bisweswar and Devi Rani (Ghosh) D.; m. Carole Ellen Simmons, July 10, 1976 (div. Apr. 1984); children: Louise Angelique, Natalie Krishna; m. Rosyln Tanner, Mar. 22, 1991. B of Medicine and Surgery, Calcutta (India) U., 1967; MD, Ednl. Commn. Fgn. Med. Grad., 1981. Diplomate Am. Bd. Plastic Surgery. Intern R.G. Kar Med. Coll. and Hosp., Calcatta, 1966-67, resident in gen. surgery, house officer, 1967-68; sr. house officer in accident and emergency, orthopaedics Royal Infirmary, Bolton, Lancs, Eng., 1968-69, house surgeon in gen. surgery, 1969-70; sr. house officer in gen. surgery Royal United Hosp., St. Martins's Hosp., Bath, Eng., 1970-72; house officer in medicine Whiston Hosp., Prescot, Liverpool, Eng., 1970; registrar in gen. surgery Frenchay Hosp., Bristol, Eng., 1972-73, sr. house officer in plastic surgery, 1973-74; registrar in plastic surgery Frenchay Hosp., Bristol, Eng., 1974, Royal Victoria Infirmary, Fleming Meml. Children's Hosp., Newcastle-Upon-Tyne, Eng., 1974-77; fellow in plastic and reconstructive surgery Hosp. for Sick Children, Toronto, Ont., Can., 1978; fellow in micro and hand surgery St. Vincent's Hosp., Melbourne, Australia, 1979-80, asst. plastic surgeon, 1979-80; rsch. assoc. in plastic surgery UCLA Med. Ctr., 1980-82; co-dir. microsurgery tng. program Harbor/UCLA Med. Ctr., 1980-82; dir. plastic surgery rsch. VA Wadsworth Med. Ctr., L.A., 1980-82; resident in plastic surgery U. Miss. Med. Ctr., Jackson, 1982-83, sr. and chief resident in plastic surgery, 1983-84; pvt. practice Jackson, 1984-86; chief and asst. prof. div. plastic surgery U. Miss. Med. Ctr., Jackson, 1986-87, chief and assoc. prof. div. plastic surgery, 1987-90, prof. plastic surgery, chief div. plastic surgery, chief, 1990-95, clin. prof. plastic surgery, 1995—; cons. plastic surgery Meth. Hosp., Miss. Bapt. Med. Ctr., River Oaks Hosp.; attending Meth. Rehab. Ctr., U. Miss. Med. Ctr., River Oaks East Hosp., Parkview Hosp., Vicksburg, Miss.; vis. prof. dept. surgery divsn. plastic surgery U. Calif., San Francisco, 1981, U. Ala., 1992; mem. patient care com. U. Miss., Jackson, 1990—; presenter and exhibitor in field at numerous profl. meetings. Author: (with others) Manual of Operative Plastic and Reconstructive Surgery, 1980, Textbook of Surgery, 2nd edit., 1988, Ency. of Flaps, 1990; mem. editorial bd. So. Med. Jour., 1993—; contbr. articles to Brit. Jour. Surgery, Brit. Jour. Plastic Surgery, Indian Jour. Dermatology, Hand, Plastic Surgery Forum, Jour. Singapore Acad. Sci., Jour. Oral Surgery, Plastic Reconstrn. Surgery, Acta Anatomica, Jour. Clin. Pathology, others; inventor turmeric on wound healing. Donor Miss. Symphony Orch., Jackson, 1991, Indian Assn., 1991; archangel New Stage Theatre, 1991. Recipient prize North Eng. Surg. Soc., 1977, Plastic Surgery Ednl. Found. Rsch. grant 1983-84, other grants Eli Lilly 1989, Tyra, 1989, Collagen Corp. 1989, 90-91, NIH, 1989, Am. Soc. Aesthetic Plastic Surgery, 1990, 91. Fellow ACS, Royal Coll. Surgeons London, Royal Coll. Surgeons Edinburgh (traveling scholarship 1976); mem. AMA, AAAS, Am. Fedn. for Clin. Rsch., Am. Assn. Hand Surgery (rsch. grant com. 1990-91, chmn. rsch. grant com. 1992), Am. Assn. Acad. Plastic Surgeons (fellowship com. 1990), Am. Soc. Plastic and Reconstructive Surgeons, Am. Assn. Plastic Surgeons, Internat. Soc. Burn Injuries, Internat. Soc. Reconstructive Microsurgery, Internat. Soc. Surgery, Internat. Soc. Emergency Medicine and Critical Care (charter), Brit. Assn. Plastic Surgeons (best prize and cert. 1967), Brit. Soc. Surgery of Hands (European traveling scholarship 1977), Soc. N.Am. Skull Base Surgery (founding), Miss. State Med. Assn., Plastic Surgery Rsch. Coun., N.Y. Acad. Sci., S.E. Soc. Plastic and Reconstructive Surgeons (program com. 1990—), Miss. Acad. Scis. (chmn. 1992), Acad. Surgical Rsch., Assn. for Acad. Surgery, Southeastern Surgical Congress, Internat. Fedn. Surgical Colls., Southern Med. Assn. (chmn. elect 1991, chmn. 1992), Sigma Xi. Home: 242 Highland Hills Ln Flora MS 39071 Office: 764 Lakeland Dr Ste 306 Jackson MS 39216-4617

DASO, DIK ALAN, military officer, history educator; b. Cleve., Aug. 4, 1959; s. Richard Paul and Patricia Ellen (Grady) D.; children: Lindsey Ryan, Taylor Jean. BS, USAF Acad., 1981; MA, U. S.C., 1992, PhD, 1996. Commd. 2d lt. USAF, 1981, advanced through grades to maj.; T-38 instr. pilot USAF, Laughlin AFB, 1982-86; RF-4C air combat tng. instr. pilot, flight commdr. USAF, Shaw AFB, S.C., 1986-89; flight examiner, RF-4C air combat tng. instr. pilot USAF, Taegu AFB, Korea, 1989-90; F-15A RTU USAF, Tyndall AFB, Fla., 1990-91; squadron life support officer USAF, Holloman AFB, N.Mex., 1991; history instr. USAF Acad., 1992; historian USAF Sci. Adv. Bd., 1994-95; chief USAF Doctrine Br. The Pentagon, Washington, 1995—. Author: Architects of Air Supremacy, 1996; editor, contbr.: The Aspen World History Handbook, 1993; contbr. proceedings S.C. Hist. Soc. ann. meeting, 1994; contbr. revs. to profl. jours. Air Force Hist. Rsch. Ctr. rsch. assoc., 1993-94. Mem. Air Force Assn., World History Assn., Order of Daedalians (adjutant 1987-89), Phi Alpha Theta. Republican. Protestant.

DATTA, RAMA D., education educator; d. Amulya K. and Ruby Jyotsna (DasGupta) Das; m. Bishnu P. Datta. BA with honors, Presidency Coll., Calcutta, India, 1962; MA, Calcutta U., 1967, Syracuse U., 1979; PhD, Syracuse U., 1983. Lectr. Serampore Missionary Coll., 1967-68; tenured prof. B.K.C. Govt. Sponsored Coll., Calcutta, 1967-74; tchg. asst. Syracuse U., N.Y., 1974-78; lectr. Francis Marion U., Florence, S.C., 1980-86, Meth. Coll., Fayetteville, N.C., 1989-90; assoc. prof. Fayetteville State U., 1990—. Author: Indus Valley Civilization, 1996. Contbr. articles to profl. jours. and publs. Vol. Am. Cancer Soc., Fayetteville, 1994, Am. Diabetes Assn., Fayetteville, 1995. Mem. Am. Philos. Assn., Am. Acad. Religion, Aristotelian Soc., Assn. Asian Studies, Soc. for Comparative Philosophy, Indian Philosophy Congress and Indian Acad. of Philosophy. Office: Fayetteville State Univ Fayetteville NC

DAUB, S. SPENCER, computer engineer, consultant; b. N.Y.C., Feb. 12, 1927; s. Jerome Augustus and Susan (Schneider) D.; m. Annette Denise Teller, Feb. 1, 1946 (dec. Mar. 1951); children: (twins) Doron Allen (dec.) and Karen Andrea (dec.). BA in Math., U. Miami, 1961. Various positions, prior to 1971; v.p. engring. Terrarobotics Co., Miami, Fla., 1971-82; pres. S. Spencer Daub Cons., Miami, 1982—. Contbr. articles to profl. jours. Mem. IEEE, Computer Soc. of IEEE, Assn. for Computing Machinery, Am. Math. Soc., Armed Forces Comm. and Electronics Assn., Soc. Mfg. Engrs., N.Y. Acad. Scis., Mensa. Republican. Roman Catholic. Office: PO Box 694237 Miami FL 33269-1237

DAUFFENBACH, ROBERT C., economic and management administrator, educator; b. Albuquerque, May 25, 1946; s. Robert C. Sr. and Faye C. (Carson) D.; m. Mary C. Shapland, July 16, 1977; children: Hugh Ross, Thomas Shapland. BA, Wichita State U., 1968, MA, 1969; PhD, U. Ill., 1973. Prof. econ. Wayne State U., Detroit, 1973-75; rsch. economist U. Ill., Urbana, 1976-77; prof. Okla. State U., Stillwater, 1977-90, dir. Bus. and Econ. Rsch., 1985-90; prof., dir. Econ. and Mgmt. Rsch. U. Okla., Norman, 1990—; bd. dirs. Okla. Acad. for State Goals, Oklahoma City; advisor State of Okla., 1985—, Sci. Resource Studies, NSF. Recipient grant NSF, 1976-94. Home: 3841 Waverly Ct Norman OK 73072-3218 Office: Univ Oklahoma 307 W Brooks St Norman OK 73069-8822

DAUGHDRILL, JAMES HAROLD, JR., academic administrator; b. LaGrange, Ga., Apr. 25, 1934; s. James Harold and Louisa Coffee (Dozier) D.; m. Elizabeth Anne Gay, June 26, 1954; children: James Harold III, Louisa Rish Daughdrill Hoover, Elizabeth Gay Daughdrill Boyd. Student, Davidson Coll., 1952-54, D.D., 1974; A.B., Emory U., 1956; B.D., Columbia Theol. Sem., 1967, M.Div., 1969. Ordained to ministry Presbyn. Ch., 1967. Pres. Kingston Mills, Inc., Cartersville, Ga., 1956-64; minister St. Andrews Presbyn. Ch., Little Rock, 1967-70; sec. of stewardship Presbyn. Ch. in U.S., Atlanta, 1970-73; pres. Rhodes Coll., 1973—; past chmn. Nat. Adv. Com. on Instl. Quality and Integrity, Dept. Edn.; past chair Assn. Am. Colls.; past dir. Am. Coun. on Edn. Author: Man Talk, 1972; co-author: New Directions for Higher Education Source Book. Past chmn. Tenn. Coun. Pvt. Colls.; past pres. Coll. Athletic Conf.; past chmn. bd. So. Coll. Univ. Union; past trustee Memphis-Brooks Art Gallery, Hutchinson Sch.; past bd. dirs. Tenn. Ind. Colls., Liberty Bowl, Chickasaw coun. Boy Scouts Am., Memphis U. Sch., Memphis Ptnrs.; mem. exec. bd. Dixon Gallery and Gardens. Named Educator of Yr. Greater Memphis State, Memphis Planner of Yr., Pillar of Memphis Jewish Nat. Fund; recipient Spirit of Life award City of Hope, Svc. award Rotary Club Memphis Community, 1987, McCallie Sch. Alumnus of Yr. award 1978, Disting. Nat. Eagle Scout award, 1991. Mem. NCJJ (nat. trustee), Assn. Presbyn. Colls. and Univs. (bd. dirs.), World Bus. Coun. (young pres.' orgn., Young Man of Yr. 1961), Chief Execs. Orgn. (past), Memphis C. of C. (past bd. dir.), Univ. Club (N.Y.C.), Phi Delta Theta, Omicron Delta Kappa. Home: 91 Morningside Park Memphis TN 38104-3037 Office: Rhodes Coll 2000 N Parkway Office Pres Memphis TN 38112-1690

DAUGHERTY, FREDERICK ALVIN, federal judge; b. Oklahoma City, Aug. 18, 1914; s. Charles Lemuel and Felicia (Mitchell) D.; m. Marjorie E. Green, Mar. 15, 1947 (dec. Feb. 1964); m. Betsy F. Amis, Dec. 15, 1965. LL.B., Cumberland U., 1933; postgrad., Oklahoma City U., 1934-35, LL.B. (hon.), 1974; postgrad., Okla. U., 1936-37; HHD (hon.), Okla. Christian Coll., 1976. Bar: Okla. 1937. Practiced Oklahoma City, 1937-40; mem. firm Ames, Ames & Daugherty, Oklahoma City, 1946-50, Ames, Daugherty, Bynum & Black, Oklahoma City, 1952-55; judge 7th Jud. Dist. Ct., Okla., 1955-61; U.S. dist. judge Western, Eastern and No. Dists. Okla., 1961—; chief judge Western Dist. Okla., Okla., 1972-82; mem. Fgn. Intelligence Surveillance Ct., 1981-88, Temporary Emergency Ct. Appeals, 1983-93, Multi dist. Litigation panel, 1980-90; mem. codes of conduct com. U.S. Jud. Conf., 1980-87. Active local ARC, 1956—, chmn., 1958-60, nat. bd. govs., 1963-69, 3d nat. vice chmn., 1968-69; active United Fund Greater Oklahoma City, 1957—, pres., 1961, trustee, 1963—; pres. Community Coun. Oklahoma City and County, 1967-69; exec. com. Okla. Med. Rsch. Found., 1966-69. With AUS, 1940-45, 50-52. Decorated Legion of Merit with 2 oak leaf clusters, Bronze Star with oak leaf cluster, Combat Infantrymans badge; recipient award to mankind Okla. City Sertoma Club, 1962, Outstanding Citizen award Okla. City Jr. C. ofC., 1965, Disting. Alumni citation Samford U., 1974, Disting. Svc. citation Okla. U., 1973, Constn. award Rogers State Coll., 1988, Pathmakers award Oklahoma County Hist. Soc., 1991; named to Okla. Hall of Fame, 1969. Mem. Fed. Bar Assn., Okla. Bar Assn., Am. Bar Found., Sigma Alpha Epsilon, Phi Delta Phi, Men's Dinner Club (Oklahoma City) (pres. 1966-69), Kiwanis (pres. 1957, lt. gov. 1959), Masons (33 degree, sovereign grand insp. gen. in Okla. 1982-86), Shriners, Jesters. Episcopalian (sr. warden 1957).

DAUGHERTY, J(AMES) PATRICK, oncologist; b. Athens, Tenn., May 17, 1948; s. James Larson and Dorothy Mae D.; m. Rebecca Poteet, Sept. 6, 1969; children: Lori, Andrea, Amy. BS in Natural Sci. cum laude, Lee Coll., 1969; postgrad., U. Chattanooga, 1967, Cleve. State C.C., 1968, E. Tenn. State U., 1969-70; PhD, U. Tenn., 1975; MD, U. Ala., 1981. Diplomate Am. Bd. Internal Medicine. Intern, resident Carraway Meth. Med. Ctr., Birmingham, Ala., 1982-84; fellow med. oncology Fox Chase Cancer Ctr., Phila., 1985-87; staff physican Med. Ctr. Shoals, Muscle Shoals, Ala., 1987—; founder, dir., physician N.W. Ala. Cancer Ctr., Muscle Shoals, Florence, 1987—; staff physician Helen Keller Meml. Hosp., Sheffield, Ala., 1988—; staff physician Eliza Coffee Meml. Hosp., Florence, 1987—, Florence Hosp., 1987—; med. dir. Cumberland Valley Cancer Ctr., 1995—, North Ctrl. Ala. Cancer Ctr., 1996—; cons. physician Northwest Ala. Med. Ctr., Russellville, 1996; adj. prof. biomed. sci., co-dir. Lab. Applied Tech., U. North Ala.; grad. tech. asst. East Tenn. State U., Johnson City, 1969-70, U. Tenn., Knoxville, 1973-74; postdoctoral investigator Oak Ridge Grad. Sch. med. Sci. and Biology divsn. Oak Ridge Nat. Lab., 1974-76; vis. lectr. Lee Coll., Cleveland, Tenn., 1976-77; rsch. assoc. Lab. Molecular Biology, U. Ala., Birmingham, 1976-80, assoc. scientist Comprehensive Cancer Ctr., Newtown, 1980-84; mem. dir. Chandler Hall Hospice, Newton, Pa., 1986-87; mem., chmn. several coms. Florence Hosp., ECM Hosp., Med. Ctr. Shoals, Helen Keller Meml. Hosp. Contbr. numerous articles to profl. jours. Bd. dirs. Lauderdale County chpt. Am. Cancer Soc., 1987—, pres., 1992—; bd. dirs. R&D coun. Riverbend Mental Health Ctr., Florence, 1992—, United Way of the Shoals, 1990—, Shoals Area C. of C., exec. com., vice chair pub. policy; chmn. bd. trustees Woodmont Christian Sch., Florence, 1994—; deacon Woodmont Bapt. Ch., 1994—; pres. cabinet U. No. Ala.; bd. dirs., investment com. U. No. Ala. Found.; steering com. Conf. Spiritual Renewal. Named Disting. Alumnus Lee Coll., Cleveland Tenn., 1992, Small Bus. of Yr. Shoals Area C. of C., 1994; NDEA fellow, 1971-73. Mem. ACP,AMA, Am. Soc. Internal Medicine, Am. Assn. Cancer Rsch., Am. Soc. Clin. Oncology, So. Assn. Oncology, Med. Assn. Ala. (alt. del 1989, del 1992), Lauderdale County Med. Soc., Colbert County Med. Soc., So. Med. Assn., Ala. Cattleman's Assn., Shoals Area C. of C. (bd. dirs., exec. com., vice chmn. pub. policy), Christian Booksellers Assn., Rotary, Sigma Xi. Home: 1960 Jackson Rd Florence AL 35630-1007 also: NW Ala Cancer Ctr 302 W Dr Hicks Blvd Florence AL 35630 also: 101 WH Blake Jr Dr Muscle Shoals AL 35661

DAUGHERTY, WILLIAM JAMES, military officer, intelligence officer, educator; b. Tulsa, Okla., Aug. 31, 1947; s. Charles Hines and Ann Robertson (Burti) D.; m. Monelle Bernadette Huffman, Sept. 26, 1986. BA, U. Calif., Irvine, 1976; PhD, Claremont (Calif.) Grad. Sch., 1979. Commd. 2d lt. USMC, 1966, advanced through grades to capt., resigned, 1974, air traffic controller, 1966-69; aviator USMC, Vietnam, 1969-74; intelligence officer CIA, Washington, 1979-96. Decorated Medal of Valor U.S. State Dept., Iran, 1979-81, Exceptional Svc. medalCIA, Iran, 1979-81, W. Averill Harriman award Fgn. Svc. Assn., Iran, 1981, Exceptional Performance awards (2) CIA, Washington, 1989, 95; named Man of Yr. Claremont Colls., 1981. Methodist. Home: 373 Foxfield Ln Fairfax VA 22033

DAUGHTREY, MARTHA CRAIG, federal judge; b. Covington, Ky., July 21, 1942; d. Spence E. Kerkow and Martha E. (Craig) Piatt; m. Larry G. Daughtrey, Dec. 28, 1962; 1 child, Carran. BA, Vanderbilt U., 1964, JD, 1968. Bar: Tenn. 1968. Pvt. practice Nashville, 1968, asst. U.S. atty., 1968-69, asst. dist. atty., 1969-72; asst. prof. law Vanderbilt U., Nashville, 1972-75; judge Tenn. Ct. Appeals, Nashville, 1975-90; assoc. justice Tenn. Supreme Ct., Nashville, 1990-93; circuit judge U.S. Ct. Appeals (6th cir.), Nashville, 1993—; lectr. law Vanderbilt Law Sch., Nashville, 1975-82, adj. prof., 1988-90; mem. faculty NYU Appellate Judges Seminar, N.Y.C., 1977-90, 94—. Mem. bd. editors ABA Jour., 1995—; contbr. articles to profl. jours. Pres. Women Judges Fund for Justice, 1984-85, 1986-87; active various civic orgns. Recipient Athena award Nat. Athena Program, 1991. Mem. ABA (chmn. appellate judges conf. 1985-86, jud. adminstrv. div. 1989-90, ho. of dels. 1988-91, standing com. on continuing edn. of bar 1992-94, commn. on women in the profession 1994—, bd. editors ABA Jour. 1995—), Tenn. Bar Assn., Nashville Bar Assn. (bd. dirs. 1988-90), Am. Judicature Soc. (bd. dirs. 1988-92), Nat. Assn. Women Judges (pres. 1985-86), Lawyers Assn. for Women (pres. Nashville 1986-87). Office: US Ct Appeals 304 Customs House 701 Broadway Nashville TN 37203-3944

DAULTON, MARIETTA, education educator; b. Fleming County, Ky., Dec. 6, 1950; d. Elbert Clifton and Elsie (Ratliff) D. BS, Morehead State U., 1971; MS, U. Ky., 1982, EdD, 1987. Cert. tchr., Ky., Tex. Tchr. Fleming County Schs. Flemingsburg, 1971-72, Rhein-Main AFB, Fed. Republic Germany, 1977, Lexington (Ky.) Christian Sch., 1981-82; substitute tchr. Randolph Pvt. Sch., Huntsville, Ala., 1972, Lawton (Okla.) Pub. Schs., 1972-73; gen. edn. devel. tchr. Babenhausen (Fed. Republic Germany) Edn. Ctr., 1977; program dir. Dairy and Food Nutrition Coun., Lexington, 1979-81; teaching asst., instr. U. Ky., Lexington, 1982-85; asst. prof. vocat. home econs. Carson-Newman Coll., Jefferson City, Tenn., 1985-94; asst. prof. leadership and secondary edn. Morehead (Ky.) State U., 1994—; active Ky. Edn. Reform Act Grant, Ky. Inst. Edn. Rsch. Grant, Goals 2000 project; presenter in field. Active Future Homemakers Am., Home Econs. Related Occupations. Grantee PEW. Mem. Assn. Tchr. Educators, Assn. Supr. and Curriculum Devel., Am. Vocat. Assn., Am. Home Econs. Assn. (cert.), Tenn. Home Econs. Assn. (state advisor 1989-90, chmn. dist. D, 1990-91), Nat. Assn. for Educators Vocat. Home Econs., Panasophic (pres. 1988-89), Phi Upsilon Omicron, Kappa Omicron Phi. Office: Morehead State U 503 Ginger Hall Morehead KY 40351

DAUPHIN, SUE, writer, producer; b. Balt., Sept. 1, 1928; d. William Goll and Elsie Elizabeth (Lipps) Helfrich; m. Vernon Mayfield Dauphin, Feb. 7, 1959; children: William Mayfield, Katie Dauphin Collins. BA cum laude, U. Houston, 1976, MA, 1979; Cert., Boston Mus. Sch. Fine Arts. Exec. prodr. and writer videos: LAMPS Light: A Support Group Profile, 1993, Safe Handling of Sharps, 1991, Safe Cytotoxics, 1990, Beyond Apothecary: The Pharmacists in Today's Hospital, 1989; writer radio drama broadcast by KUHF, Psyche and the Pskyscraper, 1985; prodr., writer, host Sue Dauphin's Curtain Call weekly radio program, KUHF-FM, Houston, 1975-87, Diversions, weekly radio program KLYX-FM, Houston, 1974-75. Author: Understanding Sjogren's Syndrome, 1993 (Japanese transl. 1994), Parkinson's Disease: The Mystery, the Search, and the Promise, 1992 (Japanese transl. 1995), Sjogren's Syndrome: The Sneaky "Arthritis", 1988 (Japanese transl. 1990), Houston by Stages, A History of Theatre in Houston, 1981; contbr. theatre revs. to Miami Herald, 1987-88, Palm Beach Post, 1992—; contbr. articles to profl. jours.; prodr. play: Transit, 1983. Mem. The Am. Theatre Critics Assn., Internat. Theatre Critics Assn., Internat. Assn. Ind. Pubs., Nat. Sjogren's Syndrome Assn. (pres., bd. dirs.), Palm Beach Macintosh Users Group, Fla. Motion Picture and TV Assn. (State Crystal Reel award for documentary scriptwriting 1990, 91, 92, for documentary prodn. 1992). Office: DauphinArts PO Box 3151 Tequesta FL 33469-0151

DAUS, ARTHUR STEVEN, neurological surgeon; b. Louisville, Feb. 6, 1957; s. Arthur Theodore Daus Jr. and Marilyn Ann (McCord) Hanish; m. Victoria Lynn Schilla, July 10, 1982; children: Arthur S. Jr., Haley N. BS in

Physics magna cum laude, Vanderbilt U., 1977; MD, St. Louis U., 1981. Diplomate Nat. Bd. Med. Examiners, Am. Bd. Neurol. Surgery; lic. physician, Ky., N.Mex., Ariz., Mo., Calif. Rotating intern in surgery U. Ky. Med. Ctr., Lexington, 1981-82, resident neurosurgeon, 1982-88; pvt. practice Midwest Neurosurgery Ctr., Joplin, Mo., 1988—; instr. cervical spine instrumentation A.M.E. Med. Co., Kansas City, Mo., 1992. Mem. Nat. Coalition of Physicians Against Family Violence, Chgo., 1994—. Named Ky. Col. State of Ky., 1985—. Mem. AMA (Physician's Recognition award 1990-94, Physician's Recognition award with spl. commendation 1993—), So. Med. Assn., Jasper-Newton County Med. Soc., So. Neurosurg. Soc., Congress of Neurol. Surgeons, Am. Assn. Neurol. Surgeons (continuing edn. award 1990-92), Nat. Audubon Soc., Phi Beta Kappa. Republican. Roman Catholic. Home: 5 Teal Dr Joplin MO 64804 Office: Midwest Neurosurgery Ctr Ste 101 1020 McIntosh Circle Dr Joplin MO 64804

DAUS, ARTHUR THEADORE, JR., pain medicine physician, psychiatrist; b. Louisville, Aug. 26, 1934; s. Arthur Theadore and Rose Antoinette (Weaver)D.; m. Marilyn McCord (div. 1963); children: Arthur Steven, Kevin Michael; m. Jo-Ann Freeman Ryan, Aug. 14, 1965 (div. 1995); 1 child, Arthur Theadore III. BA in Chemistry, U. Louisville, 1956, MD, 1960. Diplomate Am. Acad. Pain Mgmt. Intern Brooke Gen. Hosp., San Antonio, 1960-61; resident in neuropsychiatry Walter Reed Gen. Hosp., Washington, 1961-62; staff psychiatrist Mental Hygiene Clinic, Ft. Myer, Va., 1962-63; resident in psychiatry U. Louisville Sch. Medicine, 1963-65; pvt. practice, Louisville, 1965—; mem. S.W. Spinal Pain Clinic, Louisville, 1980—; physician cons. ski jumping team U.S. Olympic Com., 1990-92, sport psychology registrant and rsch., 1992; on-site ind. reviewer pain faculty accreditation Am. Acad. Pain Mgmt., 1992—, mem. pain program adv. com., 1992—; assoc. clin. prof. vol. faculty U. Ky. Coll. Allied Health Professions, Lexington, 1981—; chmn. med. adv. bd. Spencerian Coll., Louisville, 1981—; psychiatr. cons. U.S. Atty.'s Office for Western Dist. Ky., Louisville, 1983—. Contbg. author: The Physical and Emotional Aspects of Sports, 1993; columnist Hi-Tech Coaching and Tng. mag., 1991-95, Ky. HOOPS mag., 1992—; contbr. articles to med. jours. Capt. U.S. Army, 1960-63. Fellow Am. Soc. Group Psychotherapy and Psychodrama, Acad. Psychosomatic Medicine (exec. coun. 1985-92), Am. Soc. Psychoanalytic Physicians; mem. AMA (Physician Recognition award for continuing med. edn. 1969—), Wildwood Country Club (bd. dirs. 1979-81, chmn. com. 1979—). Democrat. Roman Catholic. Home: 1202 N Wellington Pl Louisville KY 40207-2239 Office: 1169 Eastern Pkwy Louisville KY 40217-1417

DAUSER, KIMBERLY ANN, physician assistant; b. Detroit, Nov. 20, 1947; d. George Leonard and Jeanne (Austin) Wilkie; m. Steven Kent Dauser, Nov. 10, 1983; 1 child, Aaron Thomas. AA, Pensacola Jr. Coll., 1971; BS in Medicine, physician's asst. cert. in medicine, U. Ala., Birmingham, 1976; cert. in mgmt., Am. Mgmt. Assn., 1989; postgrad., U. West Fla., 1995—. Cert. physician's asst. Asst. mgr. Christo's, Gulf Breeze, Fla., 1966-67; teller, bookkeeper loan dept. Bank Gulf Breeze, 1967-72; med. tech. aide USN Hosp., Pensacola, 1972, physician's asst., 1972-73; physician's asst. John Kingsley, MD, Pensacola, 1976, Mountain Comprehensive Health Corp., Whitesburg, Ky., 1976-78; physician's asst. N.W. Fla. Nephrology, Pensacola, 1978-87, med. adminstr., 1987-95; med. adminstr. Nephrology Ctr. of Pensacola, Fla., 1987-95; COO Nephrology Ctr. Inc., Crestview, Pensacola, 1995—, Nephrology Ctr., Inc., Crestview, Pensacola, 1995-96, Nephrology Ctr. Assocs., Pensacola, 1995-96; regional COO Renal Care Group Inc., Pensacola, Fla., 1996—; regional chief ops. ofcr Nephrology Ctr., Inc./Renal Care Group, Inc., Pensacola, 1996—. Fellow Am. Acad. Physician's Assts. (del. nat. mtg. 1978-95), Nat. Commn. on Cert. Physician's Assts., Fla. Acad. Physician's Assts. (mem. jud. com. 1979-80), Natural Wildlife Assn. Republican. Roman Catholic. Office: Nephrology Ctr Inc 1717 N E St Ste 501 Pensacola FL 32501-6337

DAVENPORT, ANN ADELE MAYFIELD, home health agency administrator; b. New Orleans, Nov. 12, 1941; d. Henry Louis and Myrtie Iola (Cason) Mayfield; m. John Wayne Davenport, June 18, 1966; children: Steven Lyle, Daniel Ryan, Elaine Adele. BA, Southeastern La. Coll., 1963; MA in Edn., George Peabody C., 1965; MA in Sociology, Tex. Tech. U., 1971. Tchr. various schs., 1963-70; instr. of sociology Tex. Tech. U., Lubbock, 1970-74, James Madison U., Harrisonburg, Va., 1981-82, Ga. So. Coll., Statesboro, 1982-84; 5th grade tchr. Bulloch county Schs., Statesboro, Ga., 1985-87; gerontology project coord. Dept. of Nursing Ga. So. Coll., 1987-88; project dir. Sr. Companion Program Ctr. for Rural Health and Rsch., Ga. So. U., Statesboro, 1988-93; instr. dept. health sci. edn. Ga. So. Coll., Statesboro, 1993-95; exec. dir. Ogeechee Home Health Agy., Statesboro, 1995—. Editor various newsletters, 1987—. Bd. dirs. Citizens Against Violence, Statesboro, 1987-88, Habitat for Humanity, 1990—; pres. Coun. on Children and Parents, Statesboro, 1988-89, 93-94; mem. steering com. Bulloch County Commn. on Human Svcs., 1989—; mem. adminstrv. bd. dirs., coun. on ministries, nominating com. Pittman Park United Meth. Ch.; pres. Ogeechee Wellness Coun., 1992—; bd. dirs. Ogeechee Home Health Agy., 1989-93. Mem. Ga. Rural Health Assn. (sec. 1988-89, editor state newsletter 1989—), So. Sociol. Soc., Ga. Gerontol. Assn., Ga. Sociol. Assn., AAUW (newsletter editor Statesboro 1987-89), Am. Soc. on Aging, Nat. Coun. on the Aging, Am. Rural Health Assn. Home: 1 Greenwood Ave Statesboro GA 30458-5845

DAVENPORT, CHRISTIAN, political scientist, educator; b. N.Y.C., June 4, 1965; s. Donn and Juliet (Davenport) C. BA, Clark U., 1987; MA, Binghampton U., 1990, PhD, 1992. From asst. prof. to assoc. prof. U. Houston, 1992—; adv. bd. African Am. Studies, Houston, 1992-96, Inst. for African Am. Rsch., Hston, 1992-96; adv. bd., editl. bd. Am. Jour. Polit. Sci., 1994—; guest spkr. Ryan Mid. Sch., Houston, 1994-95. Instr. Shade Cultural Ctr., Houston, 1993-96, West Dallas Detention Ctr., Houston, 1995. Named Leader of Tomorrow Ebony Mag., 1995. Mem. Am. Polit. Sci. Assn., Nat. Coalition of Blacks for Reparations in Am., Amnesty Internat., Midwest Polit. Sci. Assn., Southwest Polit. Sci. Assn. Office: U Houston Dept Polit Sci Houston TX 77204-3474

DAVENPORT, FOUNTAIN ST. CLAIR, electronic engineer; b. Harmony, N.C., Jan. 16, 1914; s. Dennis F. and Margaret E. (Winfield) D.; m. Jane Helena Hermann, June 11, 1948 (dec. Sept. 1973); 1 child, Sylvia Jane; m. Joyce Allen Huff, Mar. 16, 1974 (dec. 1983); m. Florence Cereceda Ryan, May 19, 1985. BEE, U. Miami, 1950, postgrad., U. Balt.; MS, Fla. Inst. Tech., 1970. Engr., Bendix Aviation Corp., Towson, Md., 1951-53; project engr. Vitro Labs., Eglin AFB, Fla., 1953-55; engr. A, RCA Missile Test Project, Patrick AFB, Fla., 1955-60; supr. radar engring., guided missiles range div. Pan Am. World Airways, Inc., Patrick AFB, Fla., 1960-65, sr. systems engr. Aerospace Services Div., 1965-77; pvt. practice cons. engring., 1977-82; pres. Davenport Enterprises, Inc., 1982-88. Cons. N.R.C., Churchill Research Range, Man., Can., 1966-67; faculty Fla. Inst. Tech., 1958-60, 62-63, mem. edn. com., 1964, adj. faculty physics and aerospace scis., 1979-85. With USN, 1934-37; with Res., 1942-45. Life mem. Friends Melbourne Library. Mem. IEEE (life), Am. Defense Preparedness Assn. (life), Amnesty Internat. Lodge: Mason (32 deg.). Home: 371 Coconut Dr Indialantic FL 32903-3843

DAVENPORT, GERALD BRUCE, lawyer; b. Adrian, Mich., May 17, 1949; s. Bruce Nelson and Mildred Louise (Avis) D.; m. RoxAnn Ferguson, Dec. 27, 1975; children: Jonathan Gerald, Christopher Bruce, Timothy Charles. AB, U. Mich., 1971; JD, U. Tex., 1975. Bar: Tex. 1975, Okla. 1993. Pvt. practice Law Office of Gerald B. Davenport, Cedar Park, Tex., 1975-77; atty. Milchem Inc., Houston, 1977-81, Baker Hughes Prodn. Tools Inc., Houston, 1981-87; sr. atty. Baker Hughes Inc., Houston, 1987-88; gen. atty. environ. law Tex. Ea. Corp., Houston, 1988; atty. Browning-Ferris Industries, Houston, 1988-89, mgr. environ. law sect., 1989-92; asst. gen. counsel environ. law Mapco Inc., Tulsa, 1992-94; of counsel McKinney, Stringer & Webster, P.C., Tulsa, 1994-95; dir. Davenport & Williams, P.C., Tulsa, 1995-96; shareholder Hall, Estill, Hardwick, Gable, Golden & Nelson, P.C., Tulsa, 1996—. Contbr. articles to profl. jours. Mem. ABA, State Bar Tex. (environ. law sect.), Okla. Bar Assn. (environ. law sect.), Houston Bar Assn. (chmn. environ. law sect. 1992). Republican. Office: Hall Estill Hardwick Gable Golden & Nelson PC 320 S Boston Ave Ste 400 Tulsa OK 74103

DAVENPORT, JAMES GUYTHON, minister; b. Columbia, N.C., Sept. 15, 1932; s. Llewellyn Harrison and Lillian Mae (Brickhouse) D.; m. Bethany Lavinia Sawyer, Nov. 23, 1956 (div. July 1983); 1 child, Kathleen Nina Davenport Ingram; m. Jacqueline Ann Wilson, Aug. 5, 1983; children: Daniel, Jeffrey, Jack, Jerry. AA, Chowan Coll., 1963; BA, Miss. Coll., 1965; MDiv, Southeastern Bapt. Theol. Sem., 1968; Clin. Pastoral Edn. Cert., Cen. State Hosp., Milledgeville, Ga., 1971; DD, Bethany Theol. Sem., 1991. Ordained to ministry So. Bapt. Conv., 1963; cert. hosp., instnl., mil. chaplain. Pastor Holy Grove Bapt. Ch., Powellsville, N.C., 1963, Siloam Bapt. Ch., Windsor, NC., 1965-68, Fellowship Bapt. Ch., Ettrick, Va., 1968-70, 71-83, Dinwiddie (Va.) Bapt. Ch., 1983-85, McKenney (Va.) Bapt. Ch., 1983-95; ret.; substitute tchr. Dinwiddie County Sch. Bd., 1985-95; chaplain CAP, Hopewell, Va., 1969-83, Ellrick-Matoaca rescue Squad, 1973-74, Petersburg (Va.) Correctional Ctr., 1974-83; staff counselor Southside Area Counseling Svc., Petersburg, 1968-91. Vol. fireman St. Brides Fire Dept., Chesapeake, Va., 1959-61; mem. Ettrick-Matoaca Rescue Squad, 1968-74, Planning Commn., McKenney, 1989-94; mem. electorial bd. Dinwiddie County, 1985-95; chaplain Petersburg FOP, 1975-80 (Outstanding Svc. plaque 1977); mem. elector bd. Buckingham County, 1996. Mem. Petersburg Bapt. Assn. (sec. 1974). Home: Rt 1 Box 5160 Dillwyn VA 23936-9633

DAVENPORT, JOHN WAYNE, education educator; b. Jackson, Tenn., Nov. 1, 1938; s. John Heron and Mary Margaret (Troutt) D.; m. Ann Adele Mayfield; children: Steven, Dan, Elaine. BS, Union U., 1960; MS, U. Miss., 1964; PhD, Tex. Tech. U., 1974; MS, U. S.C., 1987. Claims rep. Social Security Adminstrn., Tupelo, Miss., 1960-62; mathematician Texaco Rsch. Lab., Houston, 1964-67; instr. Stephen F. Austin U., Nacogdoches, Tex., 1968-70; asst. prof. James Madison U., Harrisonburg, Va., 1974-82; prof. Ga. So. U., Statesboro, 1982—. Author: Calculus Labs Using Mathematica, 1993, Calculus Labs Using Maple V, 1994; contbr. articles to profl. jours. Mem. IEEE, Assn. for Computing Machinery, Math. Assn. Am., Pi Mu Epsilon. Office: Georgia Southern Univ PO Box 8093 Statesboro GA 30460

DAVENPORT, PAMELA BEAVER, rancher, small business owner; b. Big Spring, Tex., Nov. 18, 1948; d. Frank Jones and Doris Glynn (Wills) Beaver; m. Robert Sampson Davenport, Feb. 2, 1982; 1 child, Danielle. BS in Mktg. and Textiles, Tex. Tech U., 1969, MS, 1970; cert. in spinal orthotics, Northwestern U., 1976. Adminstrv. asst. Tex-Togs, Inc., El Paso, 1971-75; dir. edn. Camp Internat., Jackson, Mich., 1975-79; realtor Tom Carpenter, Realtor, San Angelo, Tex., 1979-83; retailer Davenport Barber & Beauty, San Angelo, 1985-95; owner, mgr. The Little Gym, San Antonio, Tex., 1995—. Copntbr. articles to profl. jours. Vice chmn. adv. bd. San Angelo Recreation Dept., 1987-88; chmn. adv. bd. Recreation Dept., River Stage, 1990; chmn. Tom Green County Adult Literacy Coun., 1989-90; publicity chmn. San Angelo Cultural Affairs Coun., 1986; treas. San Angelo Commun. Hosp. Aux., 1980-82; publicity chmn. Christmas at Old Fort Concho, 1986; mem. Leadership San Angelo. Mem. AAUW (cultural chmn. Tex. bd. 1988-89, pres. 1986-88, chmn. conv. 1984-86). Methodist. Home: 107 Longsford San Antonio TX 78209

DAVENPORT, RAY CHARLES, artist, lithographer; b. Rockville Center, L.I., N.Y., May 5, 1926; s. Raymond Forbes D.; m. Lula Kate Chatham, Dec. 28, 1946; children: Louise, Raymond, Susan. Student in Advt. Design, Pratt Inst., Bklyn., 1948; student in Lithography, U. S.C., 1980. Draftsman B.L. Montague Co. Inc., Sumter, S.C., 1951-57; comml. artist Sumter, S.C.; illustrator 9th Air Force, Shaw AFB, S.C., 1959-61; advt. mgr. B.L. Montague Co. Inc., Sumter, 1961-65; mgr. printing dept. Osteen-Davis Printing Co., Sumter, 1965-75; artist, lithographer Sumter, 1975—. Chmn. Sumter County Cultural Commn., 1977; chmn., bd. dirs. Sumter Gallery of Art, 1980; mem. acquisitions com. S.C. Arts Commn., Columbia, 1981. Sgt. U.S. Army Air Corps, 1944-45. Recipient Best in Show award S.C. State Fair Art Dept., 1992, 1st place award Sumter Gallery Art, 1991, Nat. Merit award Mod. Maturity Mag., 1990, 1st place award S.C. Festival Flowers, 1989. Mem. Nat. Soc. Painters in Casein and Acrylic (Ralph Fabri award 1973, Mordecai Newman award 1995), Allied Artists Am. (Atto Newer award 1983, Gloria Benson Stacks award 1985), S.C. Watercolor Soc. (Winsor and Newton award 1981), Artists Guild Columbia (Best in Show award 1981), Sumter Artists Guild (1st place award 1978), Guild S.C. Artists (pres. 1989).

DAVES, DON MICHAEL, minister; b. Wichita Falls, Tex., Mar. 4, 1938; s. Floyd Lee and Johnnie Majorie (Dunn) D.; m. Patricia N. McLean, Aug. 29, 1958; children: Paul Lee, Donna Michelle. BA, Midwestern U., 1959; ThM, So. Meth. U., 1963; D. Humanities (hon.), Southwestern Coll., 1971. Ordained to ministry Meth. Ch., 1963. Pastor 1st Meth. Ch., Holliday, Tex., 1963-66, Prarie Heights Meth. Ch., Grand Prairie, Tex., 1966-72; minister to soc. North Tex. Conf. United Meth. Ch., 1972-77; pastor Meml. United Meth. Ch., Dallas, 1977-78; assoc. pastor Preston Hollow United Meth. Ch., Dallas, 1978-81, 1st United Meth. Ch., Duncanville, Tex., 1981-85; pastor 1st United Meth. Ch., Cedar Hill, Tex., 1985-91; assoc. pastor Walnut Hill United Meth. Ch., Dallas, 1992-95; pastor First United Meth. Ch., VanAlstyne, Tex., 1995—; mem. North Tex. Conf., United Meth. Ch.; trustee Charlton Meth. Hosp., Dallas, 1986-95. Author: Devotional Talks for Children, 1961, Famous Hymns & Their Writers, 1962, Sermon Outlines on Romans, 1962, Meditations on Early Christian Symbols, 1963, Come with Faith, 1964, Young Readers Book of Christian Symbolism, 1967, Advent: A Calendar of Devotions, 1971, Joy is Now, 1988. Named for Best Children's Book by a Tex. Author, Tex. Inst. Letters, 1968. Mem. Am. Assn. Pastoral Counselors, Rotary, Order of St. Luke. Home: 39 Preakness Pl Van Alstyne TX 75495 Office: Box 125 Van Alstyne TX 75495

DAVES, JADA LEDFORD, secondary education educator, motivational speaker; b. Cleveland, Tenn., Apr. 15, 1970; d. William Donald and Wilby Jean (Lively) Ledford; m. Kevin Edward Daves, Apr. 2, 1994. BS in Secondary Education, U. Tenn., Chattanooga, 1991. Cert. secondary tchr., Tenn. Nutritionist I Hamilton County Health Dept., Chattanooga, 1991-92; substitute tchr. Hamilton County and Chattanooga City Schs., 1992; life skills coord. summer youth program Cleveland State C.C., 1992; tchr. Marion County Dept. Edn., Jasper, Tenn., 1992-93, Hamilton County Dept. Edn., Chattanooga, 1993-95; cons., motivational spkr., owner Positive Results, Chattanooga, 1995—. Author: ...And the Tardy Bell Rings, 1995. Advisor Future Homemakers of Am., Ooltewah H.S., 1993-95. Mem. NEA, Tenn. Edn. Assn., Publishers Assn. of the South, Southeastern Booksellers Assn., Nat. Speakers Assn., Chattanooga Area Home Econs. Assn., Kappa Delta Pi. Baptist. Office: Positive Results PO Box 25644 Chattanooga TN 37422

DAVID, CANDACE HEIDERICH, educational consultant; b. Balt., Feb. 13, 1947; d. John Elvin and Margaret (Roberts) Heiderich; m. C. Herbert Pund III (div. 1987); children: Whitney Carol Pund, Jennifer Leigh Pund; m. Ronald B. David, July 1, 1989; stepchildren: Bryan David, Beth Kurtz, Susan Soueidan, Tom David. BS in Edn., U. Cin., 1969; M in Edn., Copin State Coll., Balt., 1973. Cert. profl. tchr., Va. 2d grade tchr., specialist Howard County, Md., 1970-71; learning disability resource tchr. various elementary schs., Md., 1972-78, Henrico County, Va., 1978-84; ednl. cons. Children's Neurolog. Svcs., Richmond, Va., 1984—; dir. devel. testing svc. Va. Found. for Exceptional Child and Adolescent, Richmond, Va., 1985—; adj. instr. U. Richmond, 1993; program cons. The Greater Richmond Area Family Support Project, 1986—. Presenter, lectr. in field of Attention Deficit Disorder and edn. Pres. Learning Disability Coun., Richmond. Mem. Orton Dyslexia Soc. (v.p. Va. br.). Home and Office: 1825 Monument Ave Richmond VA 23220

DAVID, J(AMES) BARRY, equine veterinarian; b. Ft. Collins, Colo., July 5, 1957; s. James T. and Shirley A. (Cahill) D.; m. Amanda Hamilton, May 31, 1994. BS, Colo. State U., 1983, DVM, 1987. Intern veterinarian Hagyard-Davidson-McGee Assocs., Lexington, Ky., 1987-88, assoc. veterinarian, 1988-91; assoc. veterinarian Georgetown Equine Hosp., Charlottesville, Va., 1992-94, Dubai (United Arab Emirates) Equine Hosp., 1994; resident in large animal internal medicine Tex. A&M U., College Station, 1994—. Recipient clin. resident award Tex. Vet. Med. Assn. Aux., 1996. Mem. Am. Vet. Med. Assn., Am. Assn. Equine Practitioners. Office: Tex A&M U Dept Large Animal Med-Surg College Station TX 77803

DAVID, JOSEPH RAYMOND, JR., writer, periodical editor; b. Chgo., July 9, 1936; s. Joseph R. Sr. and Elsie (Sarakhan) D. BA, Lake Forest Coll., 1957. Freelance writer various pubs., 1970—; editor Education in Focus, Alexandria, Va., 1990—; cons. Annenberg CPB Math & Sci. Project, 1993. Author: The Fire Within, 1981, Glad You Asked!, 1986, Teacher of the Year, 1996. Mem. Washington Press Club. Home: PO Box 2 Alexandria VA 22313

DAVID, MARTHA LENA HUFFAKER, real estate agent, former educator; b. Susie, Ky., Feb. 7, 1925; d. Andrew Michael and Nora Marie (Cook) Huffaker; m. William Edward David, June 24, 1952 (div. Jan. 1986); children: Edward Garry, William Andrew, Carolyn Ann, Robert Cook. AB in Music magna cum laude, Georgetown (Ky.) Coll., 1947; postgrad., Vanderbilt U., 1957-58; Spanish cert., Lang. Sch., Costa Rica, 1959; MEd, U. Ga., 1972. Elem. tchr. Wayne County Bd. Edn., Spann, Ky., 1944-45; music tchr. Mason County, Mayslick, Ky., 1947-49, Hikes Grade Sch., Buechel, Ky., 1949-53; English and Spanish tchr. Jefferson (Ga.) High Sch., 1961-63; music and English tchr. Athens (Ga.) Acad., 1967-71; music tchr. Barrow County Bd. Edn., Winder, Ga., 1971-88; real estate agt. South Best Realty, Athens, 1986—; data collector Regional Ednl. Svcs. Agy., Athens and Winder, 19176-78; tchr. music Union Theol. Sem., Buenos Aires, 1957-60. Author: (poems) Parcels of Love, 1980; composer (music plays) The B.B.'s, The Missing Tune, A Dream Come True, The Stars Who Creep Out of Orbit, 1976-86. Active cultural affairs orgns., Athens, 1962—; entertainer nursing homes and civic orgns., Athens, 1962; chmn. cancer drives, heart fund drive United Way, March of Dimes, Athens, 1962—; elder, pianist Christian Ch. Winner regional piano competition Ky. Philharm. Orch., 1946; nominated Tchrs. Hall of Fame, Barrow County, 1981. Mem. Ret. Tchrs. Assn., Writer's Group, Ga. Music Tchrs., Nat. Music Tchrs. Assn., Athens Music Tchrs. Assn. (pres. recital chmn.), Ga. World Orgn. China Painters, Athens Area Porcelain Artists, Women's Mus. Arts (assoc.), Women's Mus. Art (Washington), Touchdown Club, Band Boosters, Alpha Delta Kappa, Delta Omicron (life, scholar 1944). Republican. Mem. Christian Ch. Home: 105 Nassau Ln Athens GA 30607-1456

DAVID, ROBERT JEFFERSON, lawyer; b. New Roads, La., Aug. 10, 1943; s. Joseph Jefferson and Doris Marie (Olinde) D.; m. Stella Marie Scott, Jan. 21, 1967; children: Robert J. Jr., Richard M. BA, Southeastern La. U., 1966; JD, Loyola U., New Orleans, 1969. Bar: U.S. Dist. Ct. (ea. dist.) La. 1969, U.S. Dist. Ct. (mid. dist.) La. 1969, U.S. Dist. Ct. (we. dist.) La. 1975. Assoc. Gainsburgh, Benjamin, Fallon, David, New Orleans, 1969-74; ptnr. Gainsburgh, Benjamin, Fallon, David & Ates, New Orleans, 1974—; adj. faculty mem. Tulane U. Sch. Law, New Orleans, 1982-84; pres. Arden Cahill Acad. PTL, New Orleans, 1979-80, lectr., speaker continuing legal edn. seminars. Staff mem. Loyola U. Law Rev., 1967-69. Reader, recorder for La. Blind and Handicapped, 1986-91; charter mem. Lawyers for Alliance for Nuclear Arms Control, New Orleans, 1986—. Named Best Lawyers In Am., 1995. Mem. ABA (malpractice com.), ATLA, Nat. Bd. Trial Advocacy, Am. Bd. Profl. Liability Attys., La. State Bar Assn. (asst. examiner commn. on bar admissions 1974-93, spl. ins. commn. 1974-82, med. legal interprofl. com. 1987—, co-chmn. 1991-94, contbr. Bar Assn. Jour. column on Profl. Liability 1989—), La. Bar Found., La. Trial Lawyers Assn. (bd. govs. 1981-83, 95—, exec. com. 1996—, contbg. editor Civil Trial Tactics manual 1981, chmn. sect. med. malpractice 92-94, legis. com.), Kappa Sigma, Phi Alpha Delta. Home: 2559 Eton St New Orleans LA 70131-3837 Office: Gainsburgh Benjamin Fallon David & Ates 2800 Energy Ctr New Orleans LA 70163

DAVID, YADIN B., biomedical engineer, health care technology consultant; b. Haifa, Israel, Nov. 25, 1946; came to U.S., 1972, naturalized, 1982; s. Bezalel and Ziona (Kovalsky) D.; m. Becky Lask, Jan. 23, 1968; children: Tal, Daniel. BS, W.Va. U., 1974, MS, 1975, PhD, 1983. Registered profl. engr., cert. clin. engr., Tex. Dir. biomed. engring. W.Va. U. Hosp., Morgantown, 1976-82, asst. prof., 1979-82; pres. TALDAN Cons., Houston, 1976—; dir. biomed. engring. St. Luke's Episc. Hosp., Tex. Children's Hosp., Tex. Heart Inst., Houston, 1982—; adj. assoc. prof. anesthesia dept. U. Tex. Med. Sci. Ctr., Houston, 1984—; adj. assoc. prof. Baylor Coll. Medicine, 1987—; tech. dir. TeleHealth Ctr., 1993—; pres. Ctr. Telemedicine Law, 1995—; program chmn. Clin. Engring. Symposium ann. confs., 1983-87. Contbr. chpts. to books, articles to tech. jours. Advisor B'nai B'rith Youth Orgn., Morgantown, 1981-82. Grantee W.Va. U., 1976. Mem. IEEE (rep. to standards com. 1978-94, health care engring. policy com. 1984-95), Am. Inst. Med. and Biol. Engring. (founding fellow), Am. Coll. Clin. Engring. (past pres. 1993), Engring. in Medicine and Biology (chmn. clin. engring. com. 1983-86), Assn. Advancement Med. Instrumentation (mem. edn. com. 1985-87), Eta Kappa Nu. Office: Tex Childrens Hosp Biomed Engring Dept 6621 Fannin St Houston TX 77030

DAVIDS, ROBERT NORMAN, petroleum exploration geologist; b. Elizabeth, N.J., Apr. 27, 1938; s. William Scheible and Anna Elizabeth (Backhaus) D.; AB in Geology, U. Va., 1960; MS, Rutgers U., 1963, PhD, 1966; m. Carol Ann Landauer, Apr. 20, 1957; 1 child, Robert Norman. With Exxon Co. USA, 1966—, micropaleontologist, New Orleans, 1965-71, uranium geologist, Denver, 1971-72, Albuquerque, 1972-78, supervisory geologist Tex. area exploration, Corpus Christi, 1978-80, N.W. area supr., 1981, dist. geologist so. dist., New Orleans, 1981-84, div. exploration tng. coord., spl. trades unit geologist, 1984-86, geol. tng. advisor, Houston, 1986-89; rsch. geologist Exxon Prodn. Rsch. Co., 1989-92; exploration geologist Exxon Exploration Co., 1992—. Formerly active local Little League Baseball, Jr. Achievement. NSF grad. fellow, 1964-65. Mem. Geol. Soc. Am., AIME, Soc. Econ. Paleontologists and Mineralogists (treas. Gulf Coast sect. 1971), Am. Assn. Petroleum Geologists, Explorers Club, Krewe of Endymion, Sigma Xi, Beta Theta Pi. Author papers. Home: 173 Golden Shadow Cir Spring TX 77381-4162 Office: PO Box 4778 Houston TX 77210-4778

DAVIDSON, CHANDLER, sociologist, educator; b. May 13, 1936; m. Sharon Lavonne Plummer, Nov. 1, 1986. BA, U. Tex., 1961; PhD, Princeton U., 1969. Prof. sociology Rice U., Houston, 1966—; co-prin. investigator NSF, 1988-92, Rockefeller Found., 1990. Author: Biracial Politics, 1972, Minority Vote Dilution, 1984, Race and Class in Texas Politics, 1990, Controversies in Minority Voting, 1992, Quiet Revolution in the South, 1994. Fulbright scholar, 1961-62; Woodrow Wilson fellow, 1963-64, rsch. fellow Nat. Endowment for Humanities, 1976-77; recipient Gustavus Myers Ctr. for Study of Human Rights award for outstanding book on human rights, 1993. Mem. Am. Sociol. Assn., Am. Polit. Sci. Assn. (Fenno prize 1995), Phi Beta Kappa. Office: Rice U PO Box 1892 6100 South Main St Houston TX 77251

DAVIDSON, CHARLES, design company executive. Dir. bus. devel. Gary Roger Baird Design. Address: Ste 301 2505 Hillsboro Rd Nashville TN 37212

DAVIDSON, CLAYTON LESLIE, chemical engineer; b. Kingsford, Mich., July 21, 1930; s. James William and Fern Una (Shambeau) D.; m. Alice Mae Mitchell, Mar. 15, 1952; children: Richard L., Scott M., Jeff A. BSChemE, Mich. Tech. U., 1951; postgrad., Ind. U., 1976. Registered profl. engr., Mich. Chem. engr. Dow Corning, Midland, Mich., 1953-58, bldg. supt., 1958-63; prodn. supt. Dow Corning, Elizabethtown, Ky., 1963-69; plant mgr. Dow Corning Europe, Seneffe, Belgium, 1969-73, Dow Corning, Carrollton, Ky., 1973-75; tech. mgr. Dow Corning, Midland, 1975-80; plant mgr. Dow Corning, Campinas, Brazil, 1980-83; mfg. mgr. Dow Corning Interam., Midland, 1983-86; dir. supt. Silinor (Dow Corning JV), Salvador, Brazil, 1986-89; internat. cons. Lucky DC, Seoul, Republic of Korea, 1989-92; mfg. cons. Dow Corning, Munich, Chiba, Japan, 1968-73. Cubmaster, scoutmaster Boy Scouts Am., Midland, Brussels, 1955-73; pres. PTA, Midland, 1958-63; vol. Internat. Exec. Svc. Corp., 1992—; bd. dirs. Hendersonville Little Theater, 1995—. 1st lt. U.S. Army, 1951-53. Decorated Bronze Star, Purple Heart; recipient Citoyan do Honor (Seneffe), Belgium, 1972, Native Son award Iron Mountain Rotary, 1991. Mem. AIChe, Dow Corning Retirees Club (v.p. 1991-93), Kiwanis (pres. 1981-82). Republican. Methodist. Home: 111 Continental Dr Flat Rock NC 28731-8521

DAVIDSON, DEBRA ANN, medical and surgical, diabetes, critical care nurse; b. Dayton, Ohio, June 18, 1956; d. Charles E. and Daisy I. (Waterhouse) Badders. BSN magna cum laude, Wright State U., Dayton, 1978, MS in Nursing summa cum laude, 1987. RN, Ohio, Fla.; cert. diabetes educator. Primary nurse I and II Miami Valley Hosp., Dayton, 1979-84, clin. nurse specialist in endocrinology, 1984-93, primary nurse II, ICU, diabetes cons., 1993; diabetes clin. nurse specialist, diabetes program coord.

Florida Hosp., Orlando, Fla., 1993—; cons. in insulin pump therapy Fla. Hosp., Miami Valley Hosp.; cons. diabetes program devel.; developer, coord. profl. diabetes workshop; presenter, nat. known spkr. on diabetes and other endocrine disorder to various orgns.; coord. various inpatient and outpatient diabetes programs; charter mem. Miami Valley Hosp. nursing coun., com. mem. clin. ladder and case mgmt.; mem. diabetes collaborative practice and diabetes med. adv. com. Fla. Hosp.; adj. faculty mem. Valencia C.C., Orlando, Fla. Author: Diabetes: Making It Part of Your Lifestyle; rsch. in field. Recipient award Recognition, Ohio Dept. Health; scholar Advanced Studies Inst. Diabetes Edn. Mem. Am. Assn. Diabetes Educators (past pres. Western Ohio chpt.), Ctrl. Fla. Assn. Diabetes Educators, Am. Diabetes Assn. (Nat. Recognition for Miami Valley Hosp. Diabetes Patient Edn. Program 1992), Diabetes Assn. Dayton Area (past bd. dirs.). Office: Fla Hosp Diabetes Program 601 E Rollins St Orlando FL 32803-1248

DAVIDSON, EVELYNE MONIQUE, internist; b. Knoxville, Tenn., Apr. 5, 1961; d. Elvyn Verone and Esther M. (Johnson) D. BS, Vanderbilt U., 1983; MD, Ea. Tenn. State U., 1987. Intern New Hanover Meml. Hosp., Wilmington, N.C., 1987-88, resident in internal medicine, 1988-90; pvt. practice, Knoxville, 1990-94; physician Bapt. Primary Care System, 1994—; med. dir. east office Housecall Home Health, Knoxville, 1990—. Mem. AMA, Nat. Med. Assn., Am. Soc. Internal Medicine. Office: 710 N Cherry St Knoxville TN 37914-5254

DAVIDSON, GLEN HARRIS, federal judge; b. Pontotoc, Miss., Nov. 20, 1941; s. M. Glen and Lora (Harris) D.; m. Bonnie Payne, Apr. 25, 1973; children: Glen III, Gregory P. B.A., U. Miss, 1962, J.D., 1965. Bar: Miss. 1965, U.S. Ct. Appeals (5th cir.) 1965, U.S. Supreme Ct. 1971. Asst. dist. atty. First Jud. Dist., Tupelo, Miss., 1969-74; dist. atty. First Jud. Dist., 1975; U.S. atty. U.S. Dist. Ct. (no. dist.) Miss., Oxford, 1981-85; U.S. district judge U.S. Ct. House, Aberdeen, Miss., 1985—; atty. Lee County Sch. Bd., Miss., 1974-81. Bd. dirs. Community Devel. Found., Tupelo, 1976-81; mem. exec. bd. Yocona Council Boy Scouts Am., 1972—. Served to maj. USAF, 1966-69. Mem. Fed. Bar Assn. (v.p. 1984), Miss. Bar Found., Lee County Bar Assn. (pres. 1974), Assn. Trial Lawyers Am., Miss. Prosecutors Assn. Presbyterian. Lodge: Kiwanis (pres. Tupelo 1978). Office: US Dist Ct PO Box 767 Aberdeen MS 39730-0767

DAVIDSON, MARC LEON, journalist, fine arts consultant; b. Daytona Beach, Fla., July 7, 1954; s. Herbert Marc Jr. and Josephine (Rosenfield) D.; m. Karen McLellan, Apr. 16, 1988 (div. Aug. 1989); m. Joanne Keyland, Apr. 18, 1991; 1 stepchild, Lise Forte. BA in Asian Studies, Fla. State U., 1976. Computer programmer News-Jour. Corp., Daytona Beach, 1973-79, copy editor, 1988-90, reporter, 1990-94, editor News Jour. Ctr., 1994—; dealer rare coins PMV, Inc., Daytona Beach, 1979-87; owner Davidson Gallery, Daytona Beach, 1984-88; bd. dirs. News Jour. Corp.; bd. dirs., gen. mgr. PMV, Inc., Daytona Beach. Author, editor Classical Coin Newsletter, 1985-87. Trustee Daytona Beach Mus. Arts and Scis., 1991; bd. dirs. Family Welfare Assn., Daytona Beach, 1991-95; officer Volusia County Dem. Exec. Com., 1993—. Mem. Am. Numismatic Assn. (life), Fla. United Numismatists (life), C. of C. Democrat. Office: News-Jour Corp 901 6th St Daytona Beach FL 32117-3352

DAVIDSON, NORMA LEWIS, concert violinist, composer, music educator, psychologist; b. Provo, Utah, Oct. 12, 1929; d. Arthur and Mary (Mortimer) Lewis; m. William James Davidson, Dec. 29, 1949; children: Kevin James, Nathanael Arthur. Artist's diploma, Juilliard Sch., N.Y.C., 1950; BS, North Tex. State U., 1962, MS, 1965; MusM, So. Meth. U., 1970. Prof. violin and chamber music Mannes Coll. Music, N.Y.C., 1950-54; prof., artist-in-residence Tex. Womans U., Denton, 1961—; vis. prof. North Tex. State U., Denton, 1968-69; violinist Dallas Symphony Orch., 1955—; violinist, soloist Utah Symphony, Salt Lake City, Ft. Worth Symphony Orch., New Symphony Orch. of N.Y., Richardson Symphony, Wichita Falls Symphony, San Antonio Symphony; assoc. concertmaster Graz (Austria) Symphony, 1990—; soloist movie documentary, Eng., 1987. Numerous concert tours in U.S., Europe, Asia, Mex., Can., 1945—; composer numerous works for voice, violin, viola, string quartet, and chamber music; contbr. articles to profl. jours. Recipient cert. of merit Federated Music Clubs, 1978, 1st prize for composition, 1984; 1st prize for composition Tex. Composers Guild, 1980; rsch. grantee Tex. Womans U., 1979. Mem. APA (assoc.), Am. String Tchrs. Assn., Phi Kappa Phi (internat. rep. for arts, pres. Tex. Womans U. chpt. 1991-93), Sigma Alpha Iota (arts assoc. 1980—), Phi Kappa Phi (nat. rep. for arts 1989-91, editorial bd. Nat. Forum 1994—). Office: Tex Womans U Dept Performing Arts Denton TX 76204

DAVIDSON, PAUL, political economics educator, consultant; b. N.Y.C., Oct. 23, 1930; s. Charles and Lillian (Janow) D.; m. Louise Tattenbaum, Dec. 27, 1952; children: Robert Alan, Diane Carole, Greg Stuart. BS, Bklyn. Coll., 1950; MBA, CUNY, 1955; PhD, U. Pa., 1958. With U. Pa., Phila., 1951-52, asst. prof., 1961-63, assoc. prof. econs., 1963-66; asst. prof. Rutgers U., 1958-60, prof. econs., assoc. dir. bur. econ. rsch., 1966-86, chair dep. econs. and allied scis. bur. econ. rsch., 1975-78, prof. econs., assoc. dir. bur. econ. rsch., 1966-86; J.F. Holly chair of excellence in polit. economy U. Tenn., Knoxville, 1987—; vis. lectr. U. Bristol, Eng., 1964-65; sr. visitor Cambridge (Eng.) U., 1970-71; vis. prof. Inst. for Advanced Studies, Vienna, 1980, 84, U. Strasburg, France, 1986; prof. Internat. Summer Sch., Centro di Studi Economici Avanzati, Trieste, 1980—; George Miller disting. lectr. U. Ill., Urbana, 1972; Bernardin disting. vis. lectr. U. Mo., 1979. Author: Theories of Aggregate Income Distribution, 1960, Aggregate Supply and Demand Analysis, 1966, The Demand and Supply of Outdoor Recreation, 1969, Money and the Real World, 1972, 2d edit., 1980, Milton Friedman's Monetary Theory: A Debate with his Critics, 1974, Japanese edit., 1978, International Money and the Real World, 1982, 2d edit., 1991, Economics for a Civilized Society, 1988, 2d edit., 1996, Controversies in Post Keynesian Economics, 1991, Post Keynesian Macroeconomic Theory, 1994; contbr. numerous articles to profl. jours. Recipient Lindbeck award, 1976; Rutgers U. fellow, 1980. Democrat. Jewish. Office: U Tenn Jour Post Keynesian Econs # 508 Smc Knoxville TN 37996

DAVIDSON, ROY GRADY, JR., dentist; b. Birmingham, Ala., Apr. 16, 1922; s. Roy Grady and Lois Rada (Glass) D.; m. Betty Travis, July 26, 1945; children: Denise Annette, Jennifer Jo, Frederic Grady, Cecilia Marie. DDS, U. Tenn., Memphis, 1950; B in Gen. Studies (hon.), Samford U., 1980. Lic. dentist, Ala. Pvt. practice Birmingham, Ala., 1950—. 1st lt. U.S. Air Corps, 1942-45. Fellow Am. Coll. Dentists, Internat. Coll. Dentists, Birmingham Dist. Dental Soc. (pres. 1970-71), Ala. Dental Assn. (pres. 1981); mem. ADA, Am. Equilibration Soc., Birmingham Dist. Dental Soc., Birmingham Dental Study Group (charter), Pierre Fauchard Hon. Dental Assn., U. Tenn. Dental Alumni (chmn. bd. trustees 1992),U.T. Dean's Hon. Odontological Soc., OKU Nat. Dental Honor Soc. Methodist. Home: 2224 Gay Way Birmingham AL 35216-3309 Office: 3351 Montgomery Hwy Birmingham AL 35209-5601

DAVIDSON, (EMILY) SUZANNE, performing arts association administrator; b. Stephenville, Tex., Oct. 5, 1947; d. Jimmy Hale and Vanita Mae (Browning) D.; m. David Warren Chitwood, Aug. 24, 1967 (div. May 1983). BSE, Henderson State U., 1969, MSE, 1980. Tchr. Arkadelphia (Ark.) Pub. Schs., 1969-82; bus. owner Mary & Martha's Gifts and Flowers, Arkadelphia, 1982-86; registered rep. IDS Fin. Svcs., Little Rock, 1986; dir. programs Ark. Arts Coun., Little Rock, 1987-89; gen. mgr. Dallas Classic Guitar Soc., 1989-94; arts consulting various nonprofit orgns., Dallas, 1989—. Sec., bd. dirs. Tex. Arts Mktg. Network, Dallas, 1990—; bd. dirs. Dallas Coalition for Arts, Dallas, 1994—, Henderson State U. Alliance for Excellence in Edn., 1993—; pres. Partnership for Arts, Culture and Edn., Dallas, 1994—.

DAVIDSON, VAN MICHAEL, JR., lawyer; b. Baton Rouge, Nov. 26, 1945; s. Van Michael Sr. and Elizabeth Lamoine (Arnold) D.; m. Judith Ann Begue, Aug. 5, 1967; children: Van Michael III, Catherine Annette, Mary Elizabeth. BA in History, La. State U., 1968; JD, U. Miss., 1973; judge adv. gen.'s postgrad. course, 1978. Bar: Miss. 1973, U.S. Dist. Ct. (no. dist.) Miss. 1973, U.S. Ct. Mil. Appeals 1974, U.S. Supreme Ct. 1978, U.S. Ct. Claims 1979, U.S. Tax Ct. 1980, U.S. Ct. Appeals (5th cir.) 1981, La. 1982, U.S. Dist. Ct. (we. and mid. dists.) La. 1982, U.S. Dist. Ct. (no. dist.) Tex. 1982, U.S. Ct. Appeals (Fed. cir.) 1982, U.S. Dist. Ct. (so. dist.) Miss. 1985, U.S. Dist. Ct. (ea. dist.) La. 1985, D.C., 1987. Commd. 2d lt. U.S. Army, 1968, advanced through grades to maj., 1980; forward observer U.S. Army, Ft. Bragg, N.C., 1968; battery battalion officer U.S. Army, Ft. Bliss, Tex., 1968-69, battery comdr., 1969-70; command spokesman IV U.S. Army, Vietnam, 1970-71; trial counsel U.S. Army, New Ulm, Fed. Republic Germany, 1974-77; trial atty. contact appeals div. U.S. Army, Washington, 1978-81; resigned U.S. Army, 1981; ptnr. Carmouche, Gray & Hoffman, Lake Charles, La., 1981-87; sole practice Lake Charles, 1987-94; gen. counsel Stapp Towing Co. Inc., Lake Charles, 1994—; chmn. bd. dirs. Southwest Legl Services Agy., Lake Charles. Contbr. articles to profl. jours. Lt. col. USAR, 1987. Decorated Bronze Star, Army Commendation medal, Meritorious Svc. medal with one oak leaf cluster. Mem. ABA, Fed. Bar Assn., Assn. Trial Lawyers Am., Bd. of Contract Appeals Bar Assn., Phi Delta Phi. Republican. Presbyterian. Home: 1525 N Greenfield Cir Lake Charles LA 70605-5307

DAVIES, GORDON K., state agency administrator; b. N.Y.C., Aug. 8, 1938; m. Elizabeth Brinson; children: Sarah, Benjamin, Valerie, Oscar. BA in English, Yale U., 1959, MA in Philosophy of Religion, 1963, PhD, 1967; LHD (hon.), Averett Coll., 1988; LLD (hon.), Bridgewater Coll., 1989; LHD (hon.), Mary Washington Coll., 1993, Shenandoah U., 1995. Dir. Harvard-Yale-Columbia Intensive Summer Studies Program, 1969-71; dean acad. devel. Richard Stockton State Coll., N.J., 1971-73; assoc. dir. State Coun. Higher Edn. Va., Richmond, 1973-77, dir., 1977—. Contbr. articles to profl. jours. Lt. USN, 1959-61. Mem. Commn. Univ. 21st Century, State Higher Edn. Exec. Officers, So. Regional Edn. Bd. Office: State Coun Higher Edn 101 N 14th St Richmond VA 23219-3684

DÁVILA, MARITZA, artist, educator; b. Santurce, Puerto Rico, Apr. 18, 1952; came to U.S., 1975; d. Ramón Dávila-Cruz and Dolores Irizarry Vanentín; m. Jon W. Sparks, Nov. 23, 1979; children: Joshua R. Sparks-Sávila, Jaqueline Luisa MarÍa Sparks-Dávila. BA in Art Edn. with honors, U. P.R., 1974; MFA, Pratt Inst., 1977. Cert. fine arts tchr., P.R., N.Y. Asst. Pratt Graphics Ctr., N.Y.C., 1974; art tchr. Ramon Power H.S., San Juan, 1975; tchr. painting dept. Glass Masters, N.Y.C., 1977-78; bilingual tchr. N.Y.C. Bd. Edn., 1978-79, elem. sch. substutite tchr., 1979-80, artist-in-residence, 1980; mus. instr, coord. elem. and jr. high program Am. Mus. Natural History, 1979-81; printmaking instr. Memphis Coll. Art, 1982—; vis. artist Robert Blackburn Printmaking Workshop, N.Y.C., 1986, Delta State U., Cleveland, Miss., 1991, San Jose (Calif.) State U., 1991; spkr., lectr. in field; judge Helen Keller Arts and Crafts Fair, Tuscumbia, Ala., 1992, Arts in the Park Fine Arts Festival Children's Exhbn., Memphis, 1995; juror Jr. Mid-South Scholastic Art Awards, Memphis Brooks Mus. Art, 1993; represented by Normandy Gallery, San Juan, Dorothy Solomon and Assocs., Water Mill, N.Y., Botello Gallery, P.R. One and two-person exhbns. at Casa Alcaldia, San Juan, 1975, Pratt Inst., 1977, Art 4 Gallery, N.Y.C., 1979, Serial Fed. Savs. Bank, N.Y.C., 1980, Coabey Gallery, San Juan, 1980, NYU, 1980, Lowenstein Libr. Gallery, Fordham U., N.Y.C., 1981, Vodra and Courtney Galleries, Jersey City State U., 1981, Germantown (Tenn.) Cumberland Presbyn. Ch., 1982, Cayman Gallery, N.Y.C., 1983, Memphis Acad. Arts, 1983, Liga de Estudiantes de Arte, San Juan, 1984, Playhouse on the Sq., Memphia, 1985, Memphis Pub. Co., 1985, La Casa Amarilla, San Juan, 1985, Hostos C.C., Bronx, N.Y., 1986, Albers Fine Arts Gallery, Memphis, 1987, 90, Clough-Hansen Gallery, Rhodes Coll., Memphis, 1988, Mus. No. Ala., Florence, 1989, Museo del Grabado, Instituto de Cultura Puertorriqueña, San Juan, 1989, Delta State U. Gallery, Cleveland, 1991, Maine Coll. Art, Portland, 1993, Satellite Gallery for Museo de Arte Contemporáneo de Puerto Rico, San Juan, 1996, Mountain Empire C.C., Va., 1996; exhibited in numerous group shows including Memphis Coll. Art, 1992, 93, 94, 95, 97, Santa Monica (Calif.) Coll., 1992, Memphis State U., 1993, Brand Libr. Art Galleries, Glendale, Calif., 1993, Vincent Visceglia Arts Ctr., Caldwell, N.Y., 1993, Instituto de Cultura Puertorriqueña, 1993, Charleston (S.C.) Arts Gallery, 1994, Parthenon Galleries, Nashville, 1994, Ga. Coll., Milledgeville, 1994, Southeastern La. U., Hammond, 1995, Askew Nixon Fergudon Architects Gallery, Memphis, 1995, 96, U. Nebr., Lincoln, 1995, Museo de Arte Moderno, Santo Domingo, 1995, XXXIV Salon Internat. Del Val D'or, Orval, France, 1996 (prix de sessin et Gravure 1996), XXI Salon Internat. De Buxieres Les Mines, France, 1996, others. Panelist Tenn. Nat. Civil Rights Mus., 1993; mentor Girl Scouts U.S., Memphis, 1986—. Recipient Printmaking medal of honor Nat. Assn. Women Artists, 1987, Action Auction Art Competition award WKNO, 1988, 90, Merit award WKNO-TV, 1991, Best of Show award WKNO-TV, 1992, Outstanding Hispanic of Yr. in Art and Culture, Somos Latinos, 1993, mentor award Screen Printing Assn. Internat., 1993; Memphis Coll. Art travel grantee, 1985, 86, 91, 97, Pratt Graphics Ctr. grant, 1976. Mem. SECAC, Nat. Assn. Women Artists, L.A. Printmaking Soc., So. Graphic Coun., Tenn. Assn. Crafts Artists, Asociación Difusora Obra Gráfica Internacional, Print Club of U. Memphis, Phila. Print Club, U. Tenn. Print Club. Home and Office: 3233 N Waynoka Cir Memphis TN 38111

DAVILA, NORMA, developmental psychologist and program evaluator; b. Rio Piedras, P.R., Dec. 17, 1962; d. Fernando and Ana (Maldonado) D. BA in Psychology, Yale U., 1985; MA in Behavioral Sci., U. Chgo., 1988, PhD in Psychology, 1991. Asst. edn. coord. Head Start, New Haven, 1984-85; rsch. asst. Disengagement of Talent Project, Chgo., 1985-86; rsch. asst. Chgo. Stress Project, 1986-87, project coord., 1987; sr. pro-analyst Rsch. Pros, Chgo., 1988-89; instr. dept. psychology St. Xavier Coll., Chgo., 1988-89, 90, Roosevelt U., Chgo., 1990-91; asst. prof. dept. psychology U. P.R., Rio Piedras, 1991-96; dir. evaluation PR-SSI Project, Rio Piedras, 1993-95, dir. evaln. and assessment, 1996—; career counselor and career devel. instr. Women Employed, Chgo., 1991. Recipient Trustee's Fellowship U. Chgo., 1985-86, Minority Grad. Incentive Program Fellowship, State of Ill., 1986-89, Dissertation of Yr. Fellowship, Dorothy Danforth Compton Found., 1990-91. Mem. APA, Psychol. Assn. of P.R., Am. Ednl. Rsch. Assn., Am. Evaluators Assn. Office: Dept Psychology U Puerto Rico Rio Piedras PR 00936

DAVIS, A. DANO, grocery store chain executive; b. 1945. Student, Stetson U. With Winn-Dixie Stores Inc., Jacksonville, Fla., 1968—, corp. v.p., mgr. Jacksonville div., 1978-80, sr. v.p. and regional dir. Jacksonville and Orlando (Fla.) and Atlanta divs., 1980-82, pres., 1982-88, chmn., CEO, also bd. dirs., 1988—. Office: Winn-Dixie Stores Inc 5050 Edgewood Ct Jacksonville FL 32254-3601*

DAVIS, ANN GRAY, nurse, consultant; b. Phila., Jan. 18, 1932; d. Joseph Edward and Elaine (Wheaton) Gray; m. Herbert Paul Davis, Oct. 21, 1950 (div. June 1976); children: Debra Davis Gianni, Paul, Derek, Megan Davis Alekson; m. Wallace Franklin Tallant, June 26, 1988. BS, Roberts Wesleyan Coll., 1974; M in Nursing, Emory U., 1978. Cert. clin. specialist adult psychiat. mental health nursing. Nurse, St. John's Home, Rochester, N.Y., 1974-75; instr. nursing Roberts Wesleyan Coll., Rochester, 1975-77; instr. nursing Lenoir-Rhyne Coll., Hickory, N.C., 1978-79, acting chmn. dept. nursing, 1979-80; psychiat. nurse clinician Glenn R. Frye Hosp., Hickory, N.C., 1980-81, dir. staff devel., 1981-82, asst. dir. nursing cons., assessment, research and evaluation, 1982-84, clin. specialist psychiatry, 1984-87; nurse specialist Broughton Hosp., Morganton, N.C., 1987-89, asst. dir. nursing acute divs., 1989—; guest faculty Lenoir-Rhyne Coll. and Northstate Acad., 1981-84; adj. faculty N.C. U., Greensboro, 1985—; psychiat. nursing cons. Sec. treas. Catawba Valley Health Planning Coun., 1978-82; mem. adv. coun. Health Occupations Edn., 1981-82; mem. Task Force on Edn., Catawba County, 1982-88; mem. Family Life Task Force, Catawba County, 1982-88; mem. Rape Task Force, N.C. Coun. on Status of Women, 1981-88. NIMH grantee, 1977-78. Mem. Am. Nurses' Assn. (cert. clin. specialist in adult psychiat. nursing, mem. coun. specialists in psychiat./mental health nursing), N.C. State Nurses' Assn., Catawba County C. of C. (health com. 1986-88), Sigma Theta Tau, Alpha Kappa Sigma. Democrat. Episcopalian. Office: Broughton Hosp Cen Nursing Office 1000 S Sterling St Morganton NC 28655-3938

DAVIS, ANNALEE C., clinical social worker; b. Bentonville, Ark., July 8, 1944; d. Lloyd Milton and Jesse Alberta (Robe) Conyers; m. Rushton Eric Davis, Aug. 26, 1967 (div. Apr. 1980); children: Michelle Leigh, Rushton Kendrick. BA, Hendrix Coll., 1966; MSW, U. Okla., 1982. Internat. cert. alcohol and drug counselor; diplomate Internat. Acad. Behavioral Medicine, Counseling and Psychotherapy; lic. marriage and family therapist, Okla.; lic. clin. social worker, Okla.; diplomate in clin. social work. Psychiat. intern Tulsa Psychiat. Ctr., 1980-82, postgrad. intern, 1982-83; clin. social worker New Choice, Inc., Tulsa, 1983-85; pvt. practice Tulsa, 1985—; bd. dirs. Associated Ctrs. for Therapy. Head edn. com. Sunbelt Alliance, Tulsa, 1978-80; mem. Fgn. Policy Study Group, Tulsa, 1980-88, LWV, Tulsa, 1978—; mem., tchr. Meth. Ch., Tulsa, 1967-90; bd. dirs. Ctr. Christian Counseling, 1978-88. Mem. NASW (diplomate), Acad. Cert. Social Workers, Am. Assn. Marriage and Family Therapists, Okla. Assn. Social Workers, Okla. Assn. Profl. Counselors, Okla. Assn. Alcohol and Drug Abuse. Democrat. Methodist. Home: 6714 E 76th St Tulsa OK 74133-3422

DAVIS, BARBARA JEAN SIEMENS, service company executive; b. Louisville, Nov. 12, 1931; d. Gustav Adolph Siemens and Alberta Jeanette (McAdams) Simon; m. Donald Elmore Davis, Aug. 4, 1950; children: Dale Montgomery, Gale Sue Davis Beaty. Mktg. and personnel mgr. Kelly Svcs., Louisville, 1962-65; tchr. asst. TV English, Jefferson County Schs., Louisville, 1965-70; wedding and floral designer Wedding Ring, Louisville, 1971-73; owner, designer Nook Flowers and Gifts, Memphis, 1973-75; cons. pub. rels. Dixie Rents, Memphis, 1975-79; div. mgr. pres. Party Concepts, Inc., Memphis, 1980-88; pres. Siemens-Davis Assoc., Cordova, Tenn., 1989-91; cons. Leon Loard, 1992; ficilitator/trainer Motivational Concepts Internat. 1993; pres., CEO, Siemens-Davis Assoc., 1993-94; cons., INTERIM personnel, Montgomery, Ala., 1994-95; chmn. bd. dirs. sdb Greenscape, Fla., 1996—. Author: Wedding Workshop Brides Work Book, 1984., Wedding Party Consultants Certification Program, 1984, Wedding Directors & Party Consultant Program, 1995. Mem. Sales and Mktg. Execs., Am. Rental Assn. (mem. party coun. 1985-88), Nat. Assn. Wedding Cons. (pres. 1983-87); NAFE dir. (Memphis Network, mem. Internat. Platform Assn.). Republican. Presbyterian.

DAVIS, BARBARA LANGFORD, financial planner; b. Newberry, S.C., Jan. 2, 1957; d. Ella Mae (Harp) Langford; m. G. Bernard Davis, Aug. 8, 1981; children: Bryant Mckenzie, Brandan Langford. BA in Sociology, Newberry Coll., 1979. CFP. Customer svc. mgr. Riegel Textile Co., Johnston, S.C., 1979-80; knitwear dept. mgr. Riegel Textile Co., Johnston, 1980-82; fin. advisor Am. Express Fin. Advisors Inc., Columbia, S.C., 1982-96. Mem. Nat. Coun. Negro Women, 1990-94; bd. dirs. Family Shelter, Columbia Forum, Leadership Columbia, Leadership S.C., Midlands Tech. Coll. Found. Mem. Internat. Assn. Fin. Planners, Newberry Coll. Lettermen's Club (bd. dirs.), Newberry Coll. Indian Club (bd. dirs.), Inst. Cert. Fin. Planners, S.C. Soc. Cert. Fin. Planners, Greater Columbia C. of C. (bd. dirs.), Am. Bu. Women's Assn. Home: 2 Cardigan Ct Columbia SC 29210-6112 Office: Am Express Fin Advisors Inc 140 Stoneridge Dr Ste 650 Columbia SC 29210-8200

DAVIS, BARRY ROBERT, biostatistician, physician; b. N.Y.C., June 2, 1952; s. Hyman Israel Davis and Judith Estelle (Ahrend) Block; m. Wallis Ann Lowenthal, June 30, 1974; children: Hillel Asher, Rachel Shira. MD, U. Calif., San Diego, 1977; PhD, Brown U., 1982. Diplomate Am. Bd. Preventive Medicine. Asst. prof. applied math. & medicine Brown U., Providence, 1982-83; asst. prof. biometry U. Tex. Sch. Pub. Health, Houston, 1983-87, assoc. prof. biometry, 1987-92, prof. biometry, 1992—; cons. NIH, Bethesda, Md., 1985—; com. mem. Nat. Inst. Allergy and Infectious Disease, Bethesda, 1990-94; mem. adv. bd. Va. New Haven, 1991—. Contbr. articles to profl. jours. Coach Odyssey of the Mind, Sugar Land, Tex., 1992-93. Mem. Dean's Tchg. Excellence List, U. Tex., 1987. Fellow Am. Coll. Preventive Medicine, Am. Heart Assn. (coun. on epidemiology, chair com. on criteria and methods 1988-91), Am. Statis. Assn. (rep. 1992—); mem. Biometric Soc. (reg. com. 1995—), Soc. Clin. Trials (bd. dirs. 1993—). Democrat. Jewish. Office: U Tex Sch Pub Health 1200 Hermann Pressler Dr Houston TX 77030-3900

DAVIS, BILLIE JOHNSTON, school counselor; b. Charleston, W.Va., Sept. 24, 1933; d. William Andrew, Jr. and Garnet Macil (Johnston) D. BS, Morris Harvey Coll., Charleston, W.Va., 1954; MA, W.Va. U., 1959. Tchr. math. Kanawha County schs., Charleston, 1954-59, counselor, 1959—; mem. public edn. study commn. W.Va. Legislature, 1980. Mem. W.Va. Commn. on Juvenile Law, 1982—; bd. dirs. W.Va. Com. for Prevention Child Abuse, W.Va. Sch. Health Adv. Com.; appointed W.Va. rep. at Tchr.'s Inaugural Experience for Inauguration of Pres. George Bush by Gov. of W.Va., 1989; mem. subcom. W.Va. Health Care Task Force, 1992; bd. trustees W.Va. Youth Advocate Program, 1993-95, Nat. Youth Adv. Program, 1994-95; mem. oversite com. W.Va. Juvenile Predisposition Plan, 1993—. Recipient Anne Maynard award W.Va. Sch. Counselor Assn., 1986; named Am. mid./jr. high Sch. Counselor of Yr. Am. Sch. Counselors Assn., 1987, Citizen of the Yr., Dunbar Lions Club, 1987. Mem. Am. Assn. Counseling and Develop. (Spl. Recognition award 1991), W.Va. Assn. Counseling and Devel. (pres. 1964-66, legis. chmn., 1974—; spl. award legis. svcs. 1981), W.Va. Edn. Assn. (past legis. chmn.), Kanawha County Sch. Counselors Assn. (pres., legis. chmn. 1974—), W.Va. Sch. Counselors Assn. (chmn. gov. rels., parliamentarian), Alpha Delta Kappa (past chpt. pres.), Phi Delta Kappa. Democrat. Baptist. Home: 12 Warren Pl Charleston WV 25302-3613 Office: Ben Franklin Career & Tech Edn Ctr 500 28th St Dunbar WV 25064-1622

DAVIS, BRUCE GORDON, retired principal; b. Fulton, Tex., Sept. 2, 1922; s. Arthur Lee and Clara Katherine (Rouquette) D.; B.A., U. Tex., 1950; M.Ed., U. Houston, 1965; m. Mary Virginia Jackson, Aug. 31, 1946; children—Ford Rouquette, Barton Bolling, Katherine Norvell Davis McLendon. Tchr., Edison Jr. High Sch., Houston, 1951; tchr. Sidney Lanier Jr. High Sch., Houston, 1957-60, asst. prin., 1966-74, prin., 1974-83; tchr. Johnston Jr. High Sch., Houston, 1960-66; prin. Sidney Lanier Vanguard Sch., Houston, 1974-82; ret., 1983. Served with USMC, 1942-45; with U.S. Army, 1951-57. Mem. Nat. Assn. Secondary Sch. Prins., Tex. Assn. Secondary Sch. Prins., Houston Profl. Adminstrs., U.S. Army Officers Res. Assn., Houston Congress Tchrs., Am. Legion. Republican. Presbyterian. Club: Masons. Home: 6614 Sharpview Dr Houston TX 77074-6338

DAVIS, CAROL LYN, research consultant, office assistant; b. West Palm Beach, Fla., Oct. 22, 1953; d. Robert Lee and Barbara Jean (Collett) D. BFA, Tex. Christian U., Ft. Worth, 1975, MA in Am. Studies, 1977. R & D product line designer Am. Handicrafts/Merribee Needlearts, Ft. Worth, 1977-81; ceramics/china sales cons. Dillard's, Ft. Worth, 1981-82; dept. mgr. Stripling-Cox, Ft. Worth, 1982-83; freelance ceramic and string art designer, 1982-83; with phase III, IV, V hist. sites inventory of Tarrant County for Hist. Preservation Coun. for Tarrant County (Tex.) and Page, Anderson & Turnbull, Inc., San Francisco, 1983-86; rep. Tarrant County Greater Ft. Worth Housing Starts, Texas Update, Inc., 1987-94, M/PF Rsch., Inc., Dallas, 1989-94; sales office clk. Summer Creek-Hulen Bend subdivsns. Perry Homes, Inc., A Joint Venture, Ft. Worth, 1994—; Mem. mgmt. adv. panel Chem. Week, 1981; alternative precinct election judge Dem. Party, 1994—. Author Pamphlets in field. Mem. Royal Over-Seas League. Democrat. Episcopalian. Home: 7800 Garza Ave Fort Worth TX 76116-7717

DAVIS, CHARLES RAYMOND, political scientist, educator; b. Hampton, Va., Jan. 16, 1945; s. Cecil Raymond and Fronda Gail (Bradshaw) D.; m. Terry Lorraine Barr, Oct. 1, 1963 (div. July 1979); children: Kimberly Dawn Ingram, Charles Robert; m. Raymonda Carolyn Mays, Feb. 12, 1982. BA in Polit. Sci., U. Louisville, 1974; MA in Polit. Sci., U. Ky., 1975, PhD of Polit. Sci., 1985. Instr. Jefferson Community Coll., Louisville, 1976; claims rep. Aetna Casualty, Madisonville, Ky., 1977-78; rsch. asst. U. Louisville, 1979-80; rsch. analyst Ky. Health Svcs., Frankfort, 1981-85; asst. prof., masters degree program coord. U. So. Miss., Long Beach, 1986-89; asst. prof. U. So. Miss., Hattiesburg, 1989, assoc. prof., 1991—; policy analyst Ky. Gov's. Coalition on Health Costs, Frankfort, 1982; acting dir. grad. studies, U. So. Miss., Hattiesburg, 1990. Author: Organization Theories and Public Administration, 1996; contbr. articles to profl. jours. Mem. ASPA, Am. Polit. Sci. Assn., So. Polit. Sci. Assn., Northeastern Polit Sci. Assn., Miss. Polit. Sci. Assn., Miss. chpt. ASPA. Mem. Ch. of Christ. Home: 417 Browns Bridge Rd Hattiesburg MS 39401 Office: U So Miss Dept Polit Sci Southern Sta # 5108 Hattiesburg MS 39406

DAVIS, CHERYL SUZANNE, critical care nurse; b. Ft. Worth, Aug. 9, 1946; d. James Theodore and Christine Lenora (Wells) Harper; m. Charles F. Davis, June 29, 1969; children: James, Michael, Chris. AD, Nicholls State U., 1984. RN, La.; CCRN; ACLS, PALS. Staff nurse ICU Leonard Chabert Med. Ctr., Houma; home health and pool nurse Med. Team, New Orleans; primary care and charge nurse emergency rm. Terrebonne Gen.

Med. Ctr., Houma; primary care nurse Med Force Internat., New Orleans. Mem. AACN, Sigma Theta Tau, Phi Eta Sigma. Home: 200 Midland Dr Houma LA 70360-6232

DAVIS, CINDY ANN, military officer, nursing educator; b. Phila., Feb. 8, 1955; d. John Mostyn and Darthy K. Davis. BS in Nursing, Pa. State U., 1977; MS in Psychology, Fla. State U., 1989. Intensiv care oncology nurse, Bone Marrow Transplant Unit The Cancer Ctr., Johns Hopkins Hosp., Balt., 1977-78; staff nurse, operating rm. Johns Hopkins Hosp., Balt., 1978-80; commd. officer USAF, 1979, advanced through grades to maj., 1989; staff nurse, oper. rm. USAF Med. Ctr., Keesler AFB, Miss., 1980-83, OIC Cen. Sterilization & Distbn., USAF Reg. Hosp., RAF Lakenheath, U.K., 1983-86; staff nurse, asst. supr., officer in charge Cen. Processing & Sterilization, 325th Med. Group, Tyndall AFB, Fla., 1986-88; supr. operation rm. svcs. 325th Med. Group, Tyndall AFB, 1988-90; chief nurse recruiting br. 3546th USAFRSQ, Houston, 1990-91; nurse flt. commdr. 341st USAF Recruiting Squadron, Lackland AFB, Tex., 1991-94; supr. oper. rm. edn. and tng. 59th med. wing Wilford Hall Med. Ctr., San Antonio, 1994—. Decorated Meritorious Svc. medal with one oak leaf cluster, Air Force Achievement medal, Air Force Commendation medal, Navy Meritorious Unit Commendation medal. Mem. Assn. Operating Rm. Nurses (cert. clin. nurse operating rm., exec. bd. mem. local chpt. 1988, chpt. pres. Gulf Coast chpt. 1983-84), Air Force Assn., Am. Mil. Surgeons of the U.S., Fedn. Houston Profl. Women, Pa. State Nursing Alumni Assn. Republican. Baptist. Home: 1134 Dwyerbrook San Antonio TX 78253-6100 Office: Operating Room Ste Wilford Hall Med Ctr Lackland AFB TX 78236

DAVIS, CLARICE MCDONALD, lawyer; b. New Orleans, Jan. 20, 1941; d. James A. and Helen J. (Ross) McDonald. BA, U. Tex., 1962, MA, 1964; JD, So. Meth. U., 1968. Bar: Tex. 1969, U.S. Dist. Ct. (no. dist.) Tex. 1970, U.S. Ct. Appeals (5th cir.) 1971, U.S. Supreme Ct. 1973. Law clk. to presiding justice U.S. Ct. Appeals (5th cir.), Dallas, 1969-71; from assoc. to ptnr. Akin, Gump, Strauss, Hauer & Feld, Dallas, 1971—; comments editor Southwestern Law Jour., 1967-68; instr. Southern Methodist Univ. Sch. of Law, 1968-69. Bd. visitors So. Meth. U., Dallas, 1979-82, v.p. Law Sch. Alumni Adv. Coun., 1992, pres. 1993-94, mem. bd. govs., 1995—. Home: 6317 Churchill Way Dallas TX 75230-1807 Office: Akin Gump Strauss Hauer & Feld 1700 Pacific Ave Ste 4100 Dallas TX 75201-4624

DAVIS, CLAUDE HARRISON, II, accountant; b. Mooresville, N.C., Oct. 20, 1933; s. Claude Harrison Sr. and Eutrilla (York) D.; m. Mae Frances Toney, Nov. 22, 1956; children: Claude Harrison III, Joseph Wesley. Diploma in Acctg., Comml. Tech. Inst., Little Falls, N.J., 1984; Diploma in Fed. Income Tax, Nat. Tax Tng. Sch., Monsey, N.Y., 1979. Ins. salesman N.C. Mut. I.C., Winston-Salem, N.C., 1955-68, ins. sales mgr., 1968-84; tax acct. Davis Tax & Notary Svc., Winston-Salem, 1965—; asst. chmn. Customer Adv. Counsel Vol., Winston-Salem, 1993-96. With USMC, 1952. Mem. Am. Soc. Notaries, Nat. Soc. Tax Profls. Democrat.

DAVIS, CLAUDE-LEONARD, lawyer, educational administrator; b. Augusta, Ga., Feb. 16, 1944; s. James Isaac and Mary Emma (Crawford) D.; m. Margaret Earle Crowley, Dec. 30, 1965; 1 child, Margaret Michelle. BA in Journalism, U. Ga., 1966, JD, 1974. Bar: Ga. 1974. Broadcaster Sta. WKLE Radio, Washington, Ga., 1958-62; realtor Assocs. Realty, Athens, Ga., 1963-66; bus. cons. Palm Beach, Fla., 1970-71; asst. to dir. Ga. Coop. Extension Svc., Athens, 1974-81; atty. U. Ga., Athens, 1981—; mem. faculty, regent Ga. Athletics Inst., 1988—; cons. numerous agrl. chem. industry groups nationwide, 1977—, Congl. Office Tech. Assessment, Washington, 1978-79, USDA, Washington, 1979-80; del. Kellogg Nat. Leadership Conf., Pullman, Wash., 1980. Editor and contbr. Ga. Jour. of Internat. and Comparative Law, 1972-74; contbr. articles on agr. and fin. planning to profl. jours.; author and editor: DAWGFOOD: The Bulldog Cookbook, 1981, Touchdown Tailgates, 1986. Del. So. Leader Forum, Rock Eagle Ctr., Ga., 1976—; trainer Ga. 4-H Vol. Leader Assn., 1979—; vol. Athens United Way, 1980—; coordinator U. Ga. Equestrian Team, Athens, 1985-87; mem. Clarke County Sheriff's Posse, 1985—. Capt. U.S. Army, 1966-70. Chi Psi Scholar, 1965; Recipient Outstanding Alumnus award Chi Psi, 1972, Service to World Community award Chi Psi, 1975. Mem. ABA, Nat. Assn. Coll. and Univ. Attys., NRA, Disabled Am. Vets., Poets Soc., Nat. Football Found. (Hall of Fame 1991), Rotary, The President's Club (Athens), Gridiron Secret Soc., Chi Psi (advisor and bd. dirs. 1974). Baptist. Home: 365 Westview Dr Athens GA 30606-4635 Office: U Ga Peabody Hall Ste 3 Athens GA 30602

DAVIS, CONNIE WATERS, public relations and marketing executive, fashion consultant; b. Gainesville, Ga., July 3, 1948; d. Starling Randolph and Evelyn Jeanette (Bonds) Waters; m. John W. Davis, Jr., Sept. 24, 1971; 1 son, John Christopher. AA, Gainesville Jr. Coll., 1968; BA in Human Resource Mgmt., Brenau U., 1988, postgrad.; student Evaluation Inst. of Washington, 1988, U. Ga., 1972-73, 1985—. Project evaluator Model Cities Program, Gainesville, 1970-74; personnel dir. Lanier Park Hosp., Gainesville, 1977-79; asst. dir. Ga. Mountains Ctr., Gainesville, 1979-83; owner, CEO Models by Davis and Davis, Gainesville, 1979—; dir. pub. rels. and sales Ramada Hotel, Gainesville, 1985—; dir. corp. devel. Chestatee Reg. Hosp.; dir. Fashion Works, Gainesville; pres. Davis Consulting; cons. pub. rels. and mktg. Contbr. articles to mags. and newsletters; writer nat. poulty industry publ., 1990, 95. Publicity chmn. Cancer Soc., 1982, 83, 85; mem. Theatre Wings and Arts Coun.; bd. dirs., mem. mktg. com. Gainesville Jr. Coll., 1985—, trustee, 1995—; bd. dirs. ARC, 1978-79. Recipient Peach award Lions Club, 1979; Vol. award ARC, 1978; various modeling awards So. Models Assn., 1983; 2 silver shovel awards 1993, 94; state vol. award, 1995; named Best Dressed Woman, Fashion Tour Group, 1984. Mem. Am. Heart Assn. (pres. 1995-96), Am. Lung Assn. (state bd. dirs.), Greater Hall C. of C. (bd. dirs.), Gainesville C. of C., Gainesville Coll. Exec. Coun., Tourism & Conv. Bur. (chmn. 1983-84), Northeast Ga. Advt. Club, Personnel Adminstrs. Group, Ga. Hospitality and Travel Assn., Phoenix Soc., Rotary, Beta Sigma Phi. Baptist. Club: Fashion (bd. dirs.). Avocations: exercising, skiing, boating, jogging, writing. Home: 1214 Chestatee Rd Gainesville GA 30501-2816

DAVIS, CRAIG CARLTON, aerospace company executive; b. Gulfport, Miss., Dec. 14, 1919; s. Craig Carlton and Helen Lizette (Houppert) D.; B.S., Ga. Inst. Tech., 1941; J.D., Harvard U., 1949; children: Kimberly Patricia, Craig Carlton. Instr. aeros. Escola Tecnica de Aviacao, Sao Paulo, Brazil, 1946; contract adminstr. Convair, Fort Worth, 1949-51; mgr. contracts and pricing, atomics internat. and autonetics divs. N.Am. Aviation, Anaheim, Calif., 1954-62, asst. corp. dir. contracts and proposals, El Segundo, Calif., 1963-70; dir. contracts Aerojet Electro Systems Co., Azusa, Calif., 1971-81, v.p., 1982-86; pvt. law practice, Washington and Dallas, 1987-92. Served with AUS, 1941-45; USAF, 1951-53, to col. res., 1953-66. Mem. ABA, Fed. Bar Assn., D.C. Bar Assn., Res. Officers Assn., Harvard U. Alumni Assn., Ga. Tech. Alumni Assn. Republican. Episcopalian. Club: Harvard. Home: 4343 Westside Dr Dallas TX 75209-6515

DAVIS, CRESWELL DEAN, lawyer, consultant; b. Abilene, Tex., Sept. 12, 1932; s. Emmett Dean and Marye (Creswell) D.; m. Mollie Villeret, Aug. 9, 1958; children: Addison Dean Davis, Kevin Tucker Davis. BA with honors, U. North Tex., 1953; JD, U. Tex., 1958. Bar: Tex. 1958. Asst. atty. gen. State of Tex., Austin, 1958-61; sr., mng. ptnr. Davis & Davis, P.C., Austin, 1961—; dir. Tex. Jr. Bar Conf., 1964-65. Author: Texas Legal and Consent Manual for Texas Hospitals, 1967-90; contbr. articles to profl. jours. Mem. U. North Tex. bd. regents, 1967-88, chmn., 1988; mem. U. North Tex. Health Sci. Ctr. and Tex. Coll. Osteopathic Medicine, 1967-88, chmn. 1988; adj. prof. hosp. law, Trinity U., San Antonio, 1967-90; adj. prof. pharmacy jurisprudence, U. Tex., 1969—. Recipient Disting. Svc. award Tex. Pharm. Assn., 1973, Outstanding Achievement award Tex. Assn. Life Underwriters, 1986, Outstanding Svc. award Tex. Assn. Child Care Facilities, 1984, Disting. Alumnus award U. North Tex., 1990. Mem. Rotary, Masons, Phi Alpha Delta. Episcopalian. Office: Davis & Davis PC 9442 N Capital of Texas Hwy Austin TX 78759-7262

DAVIS, CYNTHIA MARIE, medical writer; b. Atlanta, Jan. 31, 1964; d. Dorsey Kytle and Frances Marie (Childers) D.; m. Ben Edwin Brown, Nov. 19, 1989; 1 child, Lindsey Marie. BA cum laude, Meredith Coll., 1986; PhD, Georgetown Univ., 1990. Biological aide Nat. Inst. Environ. Health Scis., Research Triangle Park, N.C., 1985-86; grad. fellow Georgetown Univ., Washington, 1986-90; postdoctoral fellow Glaxo Inc. Rsch. Inst., Research Triangle Park, N.C., 1990-92, sr. medical communications assoc., 1992-95, project mgr., 1995—. Recipient Am. Soc. Cell Biology travel award, 1989, CEO award, 1994. Mem. Am. Medical Writers Assn., Am. Soc. Cell Biology, Am. Assn. Advancement of Sci. Office: Glaxo Wellcome Inc 5 Moore Dr Research Triangle Park NC 27709

DAVIS, DAISY SIDNEY, history educator; b. Bay City, Tex., Nov. 7, 1944; d. Alex. C. and Alice M. (Edison) Sidney; m. John Dee Davis, Apr. 17, 1968; children: Anaca Michelle, Lowell Kent. BS, Bishop Coll., 1966; MS, East Tex. State U., 1971; MEd, Prairie View A&M, 1980. Cert. profl. lifetime secondary tchr., Tex.; mid-mgmt. adminstr. Tchr., Dallas pub. schs., 1966—; instr. Am. History El Centro Coll., 1991—; adv. Am. history telecourse Dallas Cournty C.C. dist. Coord. Get Out the Vote campaign, Dallas, 1972, 80, 84, 88, 92, 94, 96. Recipient Outstanding Tchr. award Dallas pub. schs., 1980, Jack Lowe award for ednl. excellence, 1982; Free Enterprise scholar So. Meth. U., 1987; Constl. fellow U. Dallas, 1988; named to Hall of Fame, Holmes Acad., 1979. Mem. NEA, Tex. State Tchrs. Assn., Classroom Tchrs. Dallas (faculty rep. 1971-77), Dallas County History Tchrs., Afro-Am. Daus. Republicof Tex. (founder), Zeta Phi Beta. Democrat. Baptist. Club: Jack & Jill, (Dallas) (rec. sec., v.p., chair Beautillion Ball, pres.). Home: 1302 Mill Stream Dr Dallas TX 75232-4604 Office: 3000 Martin Luther King Jr Dallas TX 75215-5525

DAVIS, DEMPSIE AUGUSTUS, former air force officer, educator; b. Roebuck, S.C., Oct. 11, 1929; s. Dempsie Augustus and Hontas (Frey) D.; m. Sally Frey, Mar. 5, 1956; children: Elizabeth, Peggy, Dempsie. BS, U.S. Mil. Acad., 1955; Edn. with Industry, A.F. Inst. Tech., 1961; MS in Bus. Econ., Clairmont Coll., 1969; diploma in nat. security mgmt., Indsl. Coll., 1973. Commd. 2d lt. USAF, 1955, advanced through grades to col., 1978; served as maintenance officer and test support pilot USAF Spl. Weapons Detachment, Nev., 1967-69; project officer Sci. Advisors Office, Mil. Assistance Command Vietnam, Saigon, Vietnam, 1969-70; systems mgr. USAF Air Logistics Ctr., Warner Robins AFB, Ga., 1970-72; chief F-15 logistics evaluation USAF, Edwards AFB, Calif., 1972-75, dir. flight test evaluation, 1975-77; dir. Joint Acquisition Logistics, Eglin AFB, Fla., 1977-79; ret. USAF, 1979; sr. engrng. mgr. Westinghouse, Balt., 1981-82; fin. cons., prof. U. S.C., Spartanburg, S.C., 1982-90; tchr., video producer River Bend Sports Resort, Spartanburg, 1990-93. Decorated Legion of Merit, Bronze Star, Meritorious Service medal, Air medal, Joint Svcs. Commendation medal, Air Force Commendation medal; recipient Leading Skeet award Nat. Skeet Shooting Assn., San Antonio, 1958. Mem. Nat. Sporting Clays Assn. (life), NRA (life, Disting. Expert 1964), Quail Unltd. (charter), Ducks Unltd., Masons (32 degree). Office: Foothills Video Prodns 1884 E Main St Spartanburg SC 29307-2306

DAVIS, DEREK HAMILTON, law educator; b. Laredo, Tex., July 14, 1949; s. David Keithley and Wanda Jean (Martin) D.; m. Kimberly Ann Jordan, July 25, 1970; children: Jeffrey Jordan, Melanie D'Ann. BA, Baylor U., 1971, JD, 1973, MA in Ch.-State Studies, 1988; PhD in History of Ideas, U. Tex., Dallas, 1993. Bar: Tex., U.S. Dist. Ct. (ea. dist.) Tex., U.S. Ct. Claims, U.S. Tax Ct., 1973. Assoc. Kendrick, Kendrick & Bradley, Dallas, 1973-75; ptnr. Dawson, Sodd, Davis & Moe, Corsicana, Tex., 1975-90; assoc. dir. J.M. Dawson Inst. Ch.-State Studies Baylor U., Waco, Tex., 1990-95, dir., 1995—. Editor: Jour. Ch. and State, 1994—, The Separation of Church and State Defended: Selected Writings of James E. Wood, Jr., 1995; author: Original Intent: Chief Justice Rehnquist and the Course of American Church-State Relations, 1991; co-editor: The Role of Religion in the Making of Public Policy, 1991, The Role of Government in Monitoring and Regulating Religion in Public Life, 1992, Legal Deskbook for Administrators of Independent Colleges and Universities, 1994, Problems and Conflicts Between Law and Morality in a Free Society, 1993; contbr. articles to profl. jours.; articles editor: Baylor Law Rev., 1972. Past pres. Navarro County Child Welfare Bd., Navarro County Boy Scouts Assn. Fellow Internat. Acad. Freedom of Religion and Belief; mem. Nat. Coun. Chs. (religious liberty coun. 1995—), ABA, Tex. Bar Assn., Waco Bar Assn., Rotary, Omicron Delta Kappa. Home: 10017 Lost Oak Ridge Waco TX 76712 Office: Baylor U PO Box 97311 Waco TX 76798

DAVIS, DONALD EUGENE, real estate management executive; b. Huntington, W.Va., July 18, 1931; s. James and Madge Elizabeth (Queen) D.; m. Elba Natalia Philippi, Sept. 3, 1955; children: Jeannette Natalia, James Edward. Student, Marshall U., 1949-51, Cameron U., 1979. Cert. Supervisory Air Traffic Control Specialist. Sales rep. Nabisco, Parkersburg, W.Va., 1955-56; with air traffice control FAA, San Juan, P.R., 1956-64, Miami, Fla., 1964-68, Huntington, W.Va., 1968-82; co-owner Davis & Philippi, Inc., Hato Rey, P.R., 1982-94; pres. CAA Caribe Fed. Credit Union, San Juan, 1961-63. Inventor USN adopted wheelhouse damage control plotting chart. Instn. rep. Cub Scouts of Am., Miami, 1965-66; vol. VA Med. Ctr., Huntington, 1986-88. With USN, 1951-55, Korea. Mem. Internat. Platform Assn., Am. Legion, Masons, Rotary. Democrat. Home: # 2 907 9th Ave Huntington WV 25701-2841 Office: Woodwinds Corp 1108 11th Ave Ste 2 Huntington WV 25701-3568

DAVIS, DONNA JO, English language educator; b. Miami, Fla., Nov. 27, 1955; d. Joseph Anderson and Shirley Willene (Jones) Crenshaw; m. Richard Keith Davis, Dec. 20, 1976; children: Michael Keith, Emilee Elisabeth. BA, U. Ctrl. Fla., 1992. Cert. tchr. Fla. Assn. of Christian Colls. and Schs. English/advanced placement tchr. Altamonte Christian Sch., Altamonte Springs, Fla., 1988—; workshop leader FACCS Tchrs.' Conv., Orlando, Fla., 1995-96. Free-lance reporter Sanford (Fla.) Herald, 1991. Sign lang. interpreter Palm Springs Dr. Bapt., Altamonte Springs, 1985-96, ch. pianist, 1987-96. Mem. MLA, Mother's Aux. of Ballet Guild of Sanford. Democrat. Baptist. Home: 210 Clear Lake Cir Sanford FL 32773 Office: Altamonte Christian Sch 601 Palm Springs Dr Altamonte Springs FL 32701-7840

DAVIS, EDWARD BERTRAND, federal judge; b. W. Palm Beach, Fla., Feb. 10, 1933; s. Edward Bertrand and Mattie Mae (Walker) D.; m. Patricia Lee Klein, Apr. 5, 1958; children: Diana Lee Davis, Traci Russell, Edward Bertrand, III. JD, U. Fla., 1960; LLM in Taxation, N.Y. U., 1961. Bar: Fla. 1960. Pvt. practice Miami, 1961-79; counsel High, Stack, Lazenby & Bender, 1978-79; U.S. dist. judge So. Dist. Fla., 1979—. Served with AUS, 1953-55. Mem. Fla. Bar Assn., Dade County Bar Assn. Office: US Dist Ct 301 N Miami Ave Miami FL 33128-7702

DAVIS, EDWARD BRAXTON, III, political science educator; b. Dinwiddie County, Va., Jan. 6, 1938; s. Edward Braxton Jr. and Edith Virginia (Browder) D.; m. Sheila McClarren, June 15, 1963; children: John Edward, James Andrew. BA, Va. Mil. Inst., 1960; PhD, U. Va., 1970. From instr. to asst. prof. dept. history and polit. sci. Va. Mil. Inst., Lexington, 1965-71; asst. prof. dept. polit. sci. Roanoke Coll., Salem, Va., 1971-74; from asst. prof. to prof. dept. polit. sci. The Citadel, Charleston, S.C., 1974—. Contbr. chpts. to books. Commr. Boy Scouts Am., Charleston, 1974—. 1st lt. USAR, 1963-65, from capt., 1978-90, lt. col., 1990-91. NDEA fellow, 1960-63. Fellow Inter-Univ. Seminar on Armed Forces and Soc., Internat. Inst. for Strategic Studies (London); mem. AAUP, Internat. Studies Assn., Am. Polit. Sci. Assn., Assn. U.S. Army, Pi Sigma Alpha, Phi Alpha Theta, Sigma Iota Rho. Episcopalian. Office: The Citadel Dept Polit Sci Charleston SC 29409

DAVIS, ELISE MILLER (MRS. LEO M. DAVIS), writer; b. Corsicana, Tex., Oct. 12, 1915; d. Moses Myre and Rachelle (Daniels) Miller; student U. Tex., 1930-31; m. Jay Albert Davis, June 27, 1937 (dec. June 1973); 1 dau., Rayna Miller (Mrs. Michael Edwin Loeb); m. 2d, Leo M. Davis, Aug. 23, 1974. Freelance writer, 1945—; merchandiser and dir. Jay Davis, Inc., Amarillo, Tex., 1956-73; instr. mag. writing U. Tex., Dallas, 1978; lectr. creative writing Baylor U., Waco, Tex., 1980, 81, 83. Mem. Am. Soc. Journalists and Authors (bd. dirs. 1985-91). Author: The Answer Is God: The Personal Story of Dale Evans and Roy Rogers, 1955; articles to periodicals including Reader's Digest, Woman's Day, Nation's Business, others. Home: 7838 Caruth Ct Dallas TX 75225-8123

DAVIS, ELIZABETH EMILY LOUISE THORPE, vision psychophysicist, psychologist; b. Grosse Pointe Farms, Mich., Aug. 11, 1948; d. Jack and Mary Alvina (McCarron) Thorpe; student U. Calif.-Irvine, 1966-69; BS, U. Ala., 1972; MA, Columbia U., 1975, MPhil, 1976, PhD in Exptl. Psychology, 1979, MS in Computer Sci., 1987; m. Ronald Wilson Davis, May 16, 1969. Lectr. Am. Lit. and English composition Nei Ming Inst., Lamtin, Hong Kong, 1969-71; research fellow Columbia U., 1973-77; postdoctoral fellow N.Y.U., 1979-81, adj. asst. prof., 1981; asst. prof. exptl. psychology Oberlin (Ohio) Coll., 1981-82; rsch. asst. prof., mem. grad. faculty Inst. for Vision Rsch., SUNY Coll. Optometry, 1983-87; assoc. prof. dept. visual scis., 1987-90; assoc. prof. sch. psychology Ga. Inst. Tech., 1990—, co-assoc. dir. in internal activities of graphics visualisation and usability ctr., 1994-96, mem. exec. com., Sch. of Psychology, 1996—. Recipient Nat. Rsch. Svcs. award; fellow Hertz Found., 1983; NIH grantee, 1979-81, 84-90; grantee Sigma Xi, 1977, Oberlin Coll., 1981. Mem. AAAS, APA, Assn. Rsch. Vision and Ophthalmology, Soc. Neurosci., Optical Soc. Am. (co-feature editor jour. 1987, session chair 1984), N.Y. Acad. Scis., Psychonomic Soc. (session chair 1988), Human Factors and Ergonomics Soc., Soc. Photo-Optical Instrumentation Engrs., Sigma Xi, Pi Mu Epsilon. Author papers and book chpts. in field. Office: Ga Inst Tech Sch Psychology Atlanta GA 30332-0170

DAVIS, ELIZABETH HAWK, English language educator; b. Ft. Smith, Ark., Sept. 6, 1945; d. Arthur Carlton and Lolitta (Poe) Hawk; m. Leo Carson Davis, Aug. 31, 1968. BA, U. Ark., 1967, BM, 1967, MA, 1969; EdD, East Tex. State U., 1989. Classroom tchr. Springdale (Ark.) Pub. Schs., 1967-68; lectr. U. Md., Heidelberg, Fed. Republic Germany, 1978-79; from instr. to asst. prof. performing arts So. Ark. U., Magnolia, 1981-92, assoc. prof., 1992-96, chair English and fgn. langs. dept., 1993—, prof., 1996—. Contbr. articles to profl. jours. Organist First Presbyn. Ch., Magnolia, 1984—. Mem. MLA, Nat. Coun. of Tchrs. of English, Ark. Tchrs. of Coll. English, Ark. Philol. Assn., Phi Beta Kappa. Office: So Ark U PO Box 1356 Magnolia AR 71753

DAVIS, ELLA DELORES, special education educator, elementary school educator; b. Quitman, La., July 19, 1957; d. Gencie Lee and Bessie (J.) D. BA, La. Tech. U., 1979; MS, Grambling State U., 1989. Tchr. lang. arts, social studies and leisure time activities Jackson Parish Sch. Bd., Jonesboro, La., 1982—; mem. Spl. Edn. Coun. Jonesboro, 1991-93. Author: The Power of Jesus--An Enlightening Story of Incidences That Happened in My Life and How Jesus Interceded, 1989, Behavior Booklet, 1992, A Complete Guide to Setting Up a Special Education Program, 1992, Special Education Lesson Plan Booklet, 1992, My Math Fact Booklet, 1992, My Word Booklet, 1993; inventor health and beauty aid products, variety other products. Mem. exec. bd. NAACP, Jonesboro, 1992—; mem. 5th Dist. Black Caucus, Monroe, La., 1990—, Jonesboro Beautification Bd., 1993—. Mem. La. Assn. Educators. Democrat. Baptist. Home: 271 Sugar Creek Rd Quitman LA 71268-1313

DAVIS, ERNESTINE BADY, nurse educator; b. Atlanta, Apr. 8, 1943; d. Henry Benjamin and Martha (Shropshire) Bady; m. Luther Davis Jr., Aug. 14, 1965; children: Luther III, Ella Michelle. BSN, Tuskegee U., 1965; MSN, Med. Coll. Ga., 1973; EdD, U. Ala., 1979. Instr. Tuskegee (Ala.) U., 1971-77; asst. prof. U. Ala. Weekend Coll., Tuscaloosa, Ala., 1977-80, Capstone Coll. Nursing, Tuscaloosa, Ala.; prof. U. North Ala., Florence. Contbr. articles to profl. jours. Named Outstanding Young Women of Am., Zeta Woman of Yr.; recipient Lillian Harvey award, 2000 Notable Am. Women award. Mem. Am. Cancer Soc., Delta Sigma Theta, Phi Kappa Phi. Home: 110 Colonial Dr Florence AL 35633-1456

DAVIS, FERD LEARY, JR., law educator, lawyer, consultant; b. Zebulon, N.C., Dec. 4, 1941; s. Ferd L. and Selma Ann (Harris) D.; m. Joy Baker Davis, Jan. 25, 1963; children: Ferd Leary III, James Benjamin, Elizabeth Joy. BA, Wake Forest U., 1964, JD, 1967; LLM, Columbia U., 1984. Bar: N.C. 1967. Editor Zebulon (N.C.) Record, 1958; tchr. Davidson County Schs., Wallburg, N.C., 1966; ptnr. Davis & Davis and related law firms, Zebulon and Raleigh, N.C., 1967-76; asst. prosecutor Wake County Dist. Ct., Raleigh, 1968-69; town atty., Town of Zebulon, 1969-76; founding dean Campbell U. Sch. Law, Buies Creek, N.C., 1975-86, prof. law, 1975—; dir. Inst. to Study Practice of Law and Socioecon. Devel., 1985—; chmn. The Davis Cons. Group, Inc., Buies Creek, 1987—; pres. LAWLEAD, 1995—; cons. U. Charleston, W.Va., 1979; vis. scholar Ctr. for Creative Leadership, 1993. Assoc. editor Wake Forest U. Law Rev. Trustee Wake County Pub. Libraries, 1971-75, Olivia Raney Trust, 1969-71; mem. N.C. State Dem. Exec. Com., 1970-72; mem. N.C. Gen. Statutes Commn., 1977-79. 1st Lt. USAR, 1959-66. Babcock scholar Wake Forest U., 1963-67; Dayton Hudson fellow Columbia U., 1982-83. Fellow Coll. Law Practice Mgmt.; mem. ABA, N.C. Bar Assn., N.C. State Bar, Phi Delta Phi, Delta Theta Phi, Omicron Delta Kappa. Democrat. Baptist. Office: Campbell U Sch of Law PO Box 279 Buies Creek NC 27506-0158 also: The Davis Cons Group Inc PO Box 279 Buies Creek NC 27506-0279

DAVIS, FRANK TRADEWELL, JR., lawyer; b. Atlanta, Feb. 2, 1938; s. Frank T. and Sue (Burnett) D.; m. Winifred Storey, June 23, 1961; children: Frank, Frederick, Gordon. A.B., Princeton U., 1960; J.D., George Washington U., 1963; LL.M., Harvard U., 1964. Bar: Ga. 1963, D.C. 1966, U.S. Ct. Appeals (5th cir.) 1963, U.S. Ct. Appeals (11th cir.) 1982, U.S. Supreme Ct. 1968. Assoc. Hansell, Post Brandon & Dorsey, Atlanta, 1964-67; ptnr. Hansell & Post, Atlanta, 1968-77, 79-86, Long, Aldridge & Norman, Atlanta, 1986—; ptnr., gen. counsel Pres.'s Reorgn. Project Office of Pres., 1977-79; vis. instr. U. Ga. Law Sch., 1964-66, Ga. State U. Law Sch., 1988-90; vis. prof. Emory U. Law Sch., 1992—. Author: Business Acquisitions, 1977, (2d edit.), 1982; contbr. articles to legal jours. Bd. dirs. Nat. Inst. Justice, 1980-81, Westminster Schs., 1969—, chmn. bd. dirs., 1984-89; sr. warden All Saints' Episcopal Ch., 1982; bd. dirs. Va. Sem., 1980-94, exec. com., 1985-89; mem. Atlanta Charter Commn.; chmn. Atlanta Crime Commn., 1977; mem. bd. councilors Carter Presdl. Ctr., 1988—; chmn. Rotary Ednl. Found. Atlanta. Lt. USNR, 1960-62. Mem. Am. Law Inst., Atlanta C. of C. (bd. dirs. 1975-77), Piedmont Driving Club (Atlanta), Chevy Chase Club (Md.), Rotary (pres. Atlanta chpt. 1990-91, bd. dirs., sec. 1988-89, chmn. bd., 1991-92). Home: 9 Nacoochee Pl NW Atlanta GA 30305-4164 Office: 303 Peachtree St NE Ste 5300 Atlanta GA 30308-3201

DAVIS, FRANK WILLIAM, JR., elementary and secondary school educator; b. Balt., Aug. 12, 1945; s. Frank William and Pauline (Gales) D.; m. Ruth McMillian, Aug. 15, 1971; 1 child, William Derval. BA, Livingstone Coll., Salisbury, N.C., 1967; MDiv., Hood Sem., Salisbury, 1973; postgrad., A&T U., Greensboro, N.C., Gardner Webb Coll., Boiling Springs, N.C.; DDiv, Belmont, N.C., 1994. Sunday Sch. tchr., pastor Shiloh AME Zion Ch., Mt. Holly, N.C.; tchr. Forest Hts. Elem. Sch., Gastonia, N.C.; pastor Wright's Chapel Amezion, Lowell, N.C. 1st lt. U.S. Army, 1968-71, mem. Res. Decorated Air medal. Mem. NAACP (life), NEA, N.C. Edn. Assn., N.C. So. Assn. Accreditation, Alphi Phi Alpha. Office: Wright's Chapel Amezion 701 Cobb St Lowell NC 28098

DAVIS, FRED, columnist, educator; b. Columbia, S.C., Feb. 14, 1947; s. Nathaniel Lewis Sr. and Arneatha Pearl (Robinson) D.; m. Joan Sineta Walker, Jan. 14, 1967; children: Alex LaMar, Kevin Alexander. BS in English Edn., N.C. A&T State U., 1969. City/coun. reporter WFMY-TV/CBS, Greensboro, N.C., 1969-70; govtl. reporter WJRT-TV/ABC, 1970-74, dir. documentaries and pub. affairs, 1974-75; anchor-reporter WMAL-TV (WJLA-TV/ABC), Washington, 1975; various positions in field to reporter, news editor WRC-TV/NBC News, Washington, 1975; gen. assignment, news program svc. reporter KNBC-TV/NBC News, Burbank, Calif., 1976; writer/reporter KHJ-TV/Ind., Hollywood, Calif., 1976-78; anchor/editor WIS-TV/NBC, Columbia, S.C., 1978-80; asst. news dir., sr. producer WJXT-TV/CBS, Jacksonville, Fla., 1980-81; staff writer Jacksonville Jour./Fla. Pub. Co., 1981; news dir. ABC Direction Radio Network/ABC News, N.Y.C., 1981-88; weekly commentator CBS-owned radio stas., 1992; self-syndicated columnist S.C. newspapers, 1992—; Disting. prof. mass media mgmt. Wash. State U., Pullman, 1995—; columnist The Seattle Times, The Spokesman-Rev., 1996—; owner media svcs./broadcast news consultancy, 1989—; vis. lectr. Benedict Coll., Columbia, 1979-80, 90, Coll. of Journalism U. S.C., 1987; with Journalism and Mass Comm. del. to China, Citizens Ambassador Program, 1996. Contbr. articles to USA Today; provider news commentaries for CBS-owned radio stas. in N.Y., L.A., Chgo., Phila., San Francisco, Detroit, Mpls. Bd. visitors, N.C. A&T State U., Greensboro, 1988—. Recipient awards Leadership Flint (Mich.), 1973, Internat. Radio Festival of N.Y., 1983-88, Ohio State award ABC Radio, 1986, Nat. Press Club award, 1984, 85, Comm. Excellence to Black Audiences award of distinction ABC

Dir./Radio Network, 1987, b'nai b'rith Edward R. Murrow Brotherhood award, 1986, Disting. Alumni award Nat. Assn. for Equal Opportunity in Higher Edn., 1988. Mem. Internat. Platform Assn., Radio-TV News Dirs. Assn., Am. Fedn. TV and Radio Artists, Acad. TV Arts and Scis., Nat. Assn. Black Journalists, Soc. Profl. Journalists, S.C. Press Assn., Assn. for Edn. in Journalism and Mass Comm., Broadcast Edn. Assn., Alpha Phi Alpha. Baptist. Office: Wash State Univ Edward R Murrow Sch Comm Pullman WA 99164

DAVIS, FRED DONALD, JR., optometrist; b. Greenville, S.C., Oct. 16, 1959; s. Barbara Ann (Poteet) D.; m. Barbara Carol Howell, Dec. 20, 1979; children: Julie Marie, Daniel Jesse. Student, Columbia (Tenn.) State Coll., 1980; BS, David Lipscomb U., 1984; OD, So. Coll. Optometry, 1988. Optician Bob Petty Optical, Nashville, 1978-84; lab. asst. Donelson Hosp., Nashville, 1977-84; optometrist Eye Specs Unltd., Old Hickory, Tenn., 1988—. Mem. Gideon, Wilson County, Tenn, 1990—. Recipient Low Vision award Noir Technologies, 1988. Mem. Am. Optometric Assn. (low vision sect., contact lens sect.), Tenn. Optometric Assn., Middle Tenn. Optometric Soc., Tenn. Soc. to Prevent Blindness, Lions. Mem. Ch. of Christ. Home and Office: Eye Specs Unltd 4961 Lebanon Rd Old Hickory TN 37138-4103

DAVIS, FREDERICK BENJAMIN, law educator; b. Bklyn., Aug. 21, 1926; s. Clifford Howard and Anne Frances (Forbes) D.; m. Mary Ellen Saecker, Apr. 21, 1956; children: Judith, Robert, James, Mary. AB, Yale U., 1948; JD, Cornell U., 1953; LLM with honors, Victoria U. of Wellington (N.Z.), 1955. Bar: N.Y. 1953, Mo. 1970, Ohio 1981. Assoc. Engel Judge & Miller, N.Y.C., 1953-54; instr. U. Pa. Law Sch., 1955-56; asst. prof. NYU, 1956-57; asst. prof. U. S.D., 1957-60, assoc. prof., 1960-62; assoc. prof. Emory U., 1962-63, prof., 1963-66; prof. U. Mo.-Columbia, 1966-70, Edward W. Hinton prof. law, 1970-81, Edward W. Hinton prof. emeritus, 1981—; dean, prof. law U. Dayton Sch. Law, 1981-86; vis. prof. Wake Forest U. Sch. Law, 1980, 86-87; dean, prof. Memphis State U., 1987-92, prof. 1992—; cons. adminstrv. procedure Mo. Senate, 1974-77; vis. prof. U. Wis., 1960, George Washington U., 1965, Tulane U., 1966, U. Mo.-Kansas City, 1973, U. Ky., 1977. Contbr. numerous articles, comments, revs., notes to profl. jours. Served with USNR, 1944-46. Mem. ABA (council sect. adminstrv. law 1969-75), Am. Law Inst., Memphis South Rotary Club, Summit Club, River Terrace Yacht Club. Republican. Episcopalian. Home: 2019 Quail Creek Cv Memphis TN 38119-6410 Office: U Memphis Sch Law Memphis TN 38152

DAVIS, G. REUBEN, lawyer; b. Muskogee, Okla., Nov. 5, 1943; s. Glenn Reuben and Margaret Elizabeth (Linebaugh) D.; m. D. Candace Jensen, June 17, 1967; children: Clay Reuben, Hayden Jensen. BA, Westminster Coll., 1966; JD, U. Okla., 1973. Bar: Okla. 1973, U.S. Dist. Ct. (no. dist.) Okla. 1973, U.S. Ct. Appeals (10th cir.) 1973, U.S. Supreme Ct. 1988. Assoc. Boone, Smith, Davis, Hurst & Dickman, Tulsa, 1973-78, ptnr., 1978—. Past pres. Tulsa Cystic Fibrosis Found., bd. dirs., 1976—; trustee Hillcrest Med. Ctr., Inc., Tulsa, 1979, Alexander Trust, Tulsa Found.; v.p., bd. dirs. Indian Nations coun. Boy Scouts Am., 1987—. Mem. ABA, Am. Inns Ct., Okla. Bar Assn., Tulsa County Bar Assn. (v.p. 1986-87, pres. 1988-89), Order of Coif. Republican. Methodist. Office: Boone Smith Davis Hurst & Dickman 100 W 5th St Ste 500 Tulsa OK 74103-4288

DAVIS, GEORGE EDWARD, industrial designer; b. Hugo, Okla., July 3, 1928; s. Silas William and Florence Elva (White) D.; m. Betty Sue Walker, July 21, 1951; children: Susan Elizabeth, Laura Ellen. student U. Tex., 1946-49; BA, Art Ctr. Coll. of Design, L.A., 1956. Registered interior designer, Tex. Staff designer Friedrich Refrigeration Co., San Antonio, 1957; design dir. comml. div. Woodarts Co., Houston, 1958-59; staff designer Brede, Inc., Houston, 1960-61; designer, co-founder Concept Planners and Designers, Houston, 1962-64; mgr. archtl. dept. Lockheed-Calif. Co., NASA Manned Spacecraft Ctr., Clear Lake, Tex., 1965-66; staff designer Litton Industries, office products div., Austin, San Antonio, 1967-68; staff designer Clegg Design Group, San Antonio, 1969-76; ind. design cons., San Antonio, 1977—; interior designer for USAA, San Antonio, 1991—; dir. Systemics, Inc., San Antonio, Christian Bookmark, Inc., San Antonio, 1972-88. Trustee, San Antonio Christian Sch., 1973-82, chmn. bd., 1979-80; bd. elders Christ Presbyterian Ch., San Antonio, 1982-85; mem. Zoning Commn., City of Castle Hills, 1983-93, councilman City Coun., 1993-94, Architectural Rev. Com., 1995—. Served with USAF, 1950-54. Decorated D.F.C., Air medal with 3 oak leaf clusters. Mem. AIA (profl. affiliate), Tex. Soc. Architects (profl. affiliate, award of merit 1968). Home: 205 Wisteria Dr Castle Hills TX 78213-2109 Office: PO Box 13385 San Antonio TX 78213-0385

DAVIS, GILLIAN FRANCES, dance educator; b. Westcliffe-on-Sea, Essex, Eng., Mar. 30, 1936; came to the U.S., 1956; d. Joseph and Cecilia Wimbourne; m. Richard Beattie Davis, Mar. 26, 1983; 1 stepson, Christopher. Student, Arts Ednl. Sch., Hertfordshire, England, 1945-54. Proprietor, prin. Miss Gillian's Sch. of Dancing, Dollis Hill, London, 1954-56; tchr. Imperial Studios, Palm Beach, Fla., 1956-57; proprietor, prin. Miss Gillian's Boynton Beach (Fla.) Dance Acad., 1957-83; tchr. various recreation depts., Palm Beach County, 1958-59; tchr., choreographer Gulf Stream Sch., Palm Beach County, 1989—; tchr. of cotillion Sailfish Club, Palm Beach, 1957-58; choreographer exhbn. ballroom dancing, Miami Beach, Fla., 1956; co-organizer exhbns. 19th century Russian and German music publs. Great Britain-USSR Assn., London, 1986, Barbican Ctr., London, 1987, Schwabach (Germany) Town Coun., 1989; music composer, choreographer children's musical Jezebel, Vinehall Sch., Robertsbridge, Eng., 1996. Composer, choreographer children's musical Jezebel, 1996. Selector Arts in Abundance, Palm Beach County, 1987; mem. County Coun. of Arts, Palm Beach County, 1980; vol. fundraiser local pub. radio and TV, Palm Beach County, 1973-94. Recipient Golden Mike award Sta. WHRS-FM, 1983. Mem. Imperial Soc. Tchrs. Dancing (life), Royal Acad. Dancing. Home: 1037 Coral Dr Boynton Beach FL 33426-3520

DAVIS, GLORIA J., gerontology clinical specialist; b. Victoria, Va., Oct. 27, 1949; d. James and Hattie (Ruffin) Davis; m. Babafemi Elufiede, 1980; 5 children. AA, Morris Harvey Coll., Charleston, W.Va., 1971; BA in Sociology and Psychology, U. Charleston, 1979; MA in Gerontology and Sociology, Fisk U., Nashville, 1985. Charge nurse Kanawha Valley Hosp., Charleston, W.Va., 1971-72; community nurse ACTION/V.I.S.T.A., Washington, 1972-74; geriatric nurse Riverside Nursing & Convalescent Home, St. Albans, W.Va., 1977-78; nurse mgr. St. Francis Hosp., Charleston, 1974-81; mem. Crossroads Africa, Kenya, East Africa, 1980-81; substance abuse specialist, nurse/counselor Shawnee Hills Treatment Ctr., St. Albans, 1981-83; nurse therapist Psychogeriatric unit Parkview Med. Ctr., Nashville, 1984-85; gerontology clin. specialist West Paces Ferry Hosp., Atlanta, 1987-88; asst. dir. nursing, clin. specialist Glenwood Manor Nursing Home, Decatur, Ga., 1988-89; dir. nursing, asst. adminstr. Glenwood Manor Nursing Home, 1989-92, gerontology clin. specialist, 1994—; healthcare coord. Care & Share Adult Day Care, 1992-94; dir. rehab. svcs. Providence Convalescence; gerontology clin. specialist cons.; long-term care specialist; instr. C.P. C.C., Charlotte, N.C., 1995—. Mem. Gerontol. Soc. Am., Am. Soc. of Aging, ARC, So. Gerontol. Soc., Ga. Nurses for Long Term Care, Nat. Assn. Dirs. Nursing Admininstrn., Long Term Care, Adult Day Care Assn.

DAVIS, H. ALAN, retired airline captain, consultant; b. Knoxville, Tenn., Apr. 24, 1932; s. Fred Edwin Davis and Rose Lee (Perrin) Davis Williams; m. Betty Jean Carter, June 11, 1951; children: Cynthia Lynn Davis Roper, Linda Susan Davis Williamson, Scott Alan. BS, Jackson Coll., Honolulu, 1965; disting. grad., Indsl. Coll. of Armed Forces, 1970; M of Arts in Teaching, Rollins Coll., 1972; EdD, Nova U., 1980. Cert. FAA in airline transport. Commd. 1st sgt. USAF, 1951, advanced through grades to maj., 1972; dir. ops., chief pilot Sky Safari Air Travel Club, Orlando, Fla., 1972-73; co. check airman, capt. Rich Internat. Airways, Miami, Fla., 1979-85; dept. chmn., tchr. Maynard Evans High Sch., Orlando, 1973-85; co. check airman, line capt. Trans Air Link Corp., Miami, 1985-92; with ops. dept. Walt Disney World, Orlando, Fla., 1992-94; chief pilot Hemisphere Internat. Airlines, Miami, 1994—; Air Santo Domingo line capt. APA Internat., 1992-93. Recipient Nat. Achievement award, Am. Soc. Aerospace Edn., 1980. Mem. Aircraft Owners and Pilots Assn., Retired Officers Assn., Shriners, Masons, Quiet Birdmen. Republican. Home: 8208 Banyan Blvd Orlando FL 32819-4145

DAVIS, HELEN GORDON, former state senator; b. N.Y.C., Dec. 25; m. Gene Davis; children: Stephanie, Karen, Gordon. BA, Bklyn. Coll.; post-grad., U. South Fla., 1967-70. Tchr., High Sch. Commerce, N.Y.C., Hillsborough High Sch., Tampa, Fla.; grad. asst. U. South Fla., 1968; mem. Fla. Ho. of Reps. (1st woman to be elected in 1974 from Hills Co., 1st woman to chair the legis. delegation), 1974-88, state senator, 1988-92; mem. Fla Supreme Ct. Commn. on Gender Bias in the Cts., 1988-90; mem. Fla. Supreme Ct. Commn. on Mediation and Arbitration, 1987—. chmn. senate appropriations subcom. human svcs., mem. rules com., internat. trade and econ. devel. com., health and rehab. svcs. com. Jud. chmn. Local Govt. Study Commn. Hillsborough County (Fla.), 1964; mem. Tampa Commn. on Juvenile Delinquency, 1966-69, Mayor's Citizens Adv. Com., 1966-69, Quality Edn. Commn., 1966-68, Gov.'s Citizen Com. for Ct. Reform, 1972, Hillsborough County Planning Commn., 1973-74; mem. Gov.'s Commn. on Jud. Reform, 1976; mem. employment com. Commn. Community Relations, 1966-69; by-laws chmn. Arts Coun. Tampa, 1971-74; 1st v.p. Tampa Symphony Guild, 1974; bd. dirs. U. South Fla. Found., 1968-74, Stop Rape, 1973-74; founder Ctr. for Women, Tampa, 1978; past pres. PTA; active adv. commn. Nat. Child Care Action Campaign, Nat. Ctr. for Crime and Delinquency; chair Hillsborough County Dem. Party. Recipient U. South Fla. Young Democrats Humanitarian award, 1974, Diana award NOW, 1975, Woman of Achievement in Arts award Tampa, 1975, Tampa Human Rels. award, 1976, Hannah G. Solomon Citizen of Yr. award, 1980, St. Petersburg Times/Fla. Civil Liberties award, 1980, Friend of Edn. award, 1981, Fla. Alliance for Responsible Parenting award, 1981, Humanitarian award Judeo-Christian Clinic, 1984, Fla. Network of Runaway Youth award, 1985, Ctr. for Women Leader-advocate Friend award, 1985, Nat. Assn. Juvenile Ct. Judges Appreciation award 1986, Legis. Leadership appreciation Centre for Women, 1986, Children's Crisis Ctr. Leadership award, 1987, AAUW leadership award, 1987, Hillsborough County Halfway House appreciation, 1988, Martin Luther King award City of Tampa, 1988, Nat. Fedn. Dem. Women appreciation, 1989, Dept. Legal Affairs appreciation, 1990, Superwoman award Mus. Sci. and Industry, 1990, Nat. Childcare Merit award Nat. Assn. Sch. Psychologists, 1992, Am. Judicature award Am. Judicature Assn., 1993; named. Fla. Motion Picture and TV Outstanding Legislator, 1990, others. Mem. LWV (pres. Hillsborough County 1966-69, lobbyist, Fla. adminstrn. of justice chmn. 1969-74), Temple Guild Sisterhood (past pres.), Am. Arbitration Assn. Home: 45 Adalia Ave Tampa FL 33606-3301

DAVIS, HERBERT OWEN, lawyer; b. D.C., June 11, 1935; s. Owen Steir and Claudie Lea (Pointer) D.; children: Herbert O. Jr., Ann P., Paul B. BA, U. N.C., 1957; JD, Duke U., 1960. Bar: N.C. 1960, U.S. Dist. Ct. (mid. dist.) N.C. 1960. Assoc. Smith Moore Smith Schell & Hunter, Greensboro, N.C., 1960-66, ptnr., 1966-86; ptnr. Smith Helms Mulliss & Moore, Greensboro, 1986—; bd. dirs. Custom Industries, Inc., Greensboro. Editor in chief Duke Law Jour., 1959-60. Mem. ABA, N.C. Bar Assn., Greensboro Country Club, Greensboro City Club (bd. dirs.), The Carolina Club, Phi Beta Kappa. Home: 2303 Danbury Rd Greensboro NC 27408-5123 Office: Smith Helms Mulliss & Moore 300 N Greene St Ste 1400 Greensboro NC 27401-2167

DAVIS, JACK WAYNE, JR., newspaper publisher; b. Toledo, Ohio, May 21, 1947; s. Jack Wayne and Virginia (Moore) D.; m. Amélie Claiborne Matthews, June 24, 1977; 1 child, Claiborne Levering. Grad., Harvard Coll., 1969. Mng. editor Figaro, New Orleans, 1972-73; reporter, columnist, asst. city editor, city editor Item, New Orleans, 1973-80; metro editor The Times - Picayune, New Orleans, 1980-83; assoc. metro editor, night metro editor, metro editor The Chgo. Tribune, 1983-87; editor, v.p. Daily Press, Newport News, Va., 1987-94; pres., pub., CEO Daily Press, Newport News, 1994—. Mem. adv. bd. William and Mary Law Sch. Bill of Rights Law Inst., Williamsburg, Va., 1991—, Norfolk (Va.) State U. Journalism Dept., 1991—; bd. dirs. Va. Peninsula Econ. Devel. Coun., 1994—, Peninsula Advanced Technology Ctr., 1995—, United Way of the Va. Peninsula, 1995—, Hampton Rds. Partnership, 1996—. Frank Knox fellow U. Rajasthan, India, 1971, Profl. Journalism fellow Stanford U., 1977-78. Mem. Am. Soc. Newspaper Editors. Office: The Daily Press Inc 7505 Warwick Blvd Newport News VA 23607-1517

DAVIS, JAMES ANDREW, newspaper reporter; b. Tacoma, Wash., Jan. 6, 1961; s. Renzo Delk and Lois (Allen) D.; m. Victoria Delaine Arnett, Mar. 30, 1991; 1child, Melody; stepchildren: Adam, Nicole, Jeremy. BA, Davidson (N.C.) Coll., 1984. Reporter, news editor The Press-Sentinel, Jesup, Ga., 1985—. Chmn. culture subcom. Wayne County Growth Strategies Planning, Jesup, 1993; mem. Wayne County Friends of the Libr.; publicity chmn. Wayne County divsn. Am. Heart Assn., 1989-96. Named Exchangite of Yr. Wayne County Exch. Club, 1989; recipient Silver Gavel award Ga. Bar Assn., 1990, Media Achievement awards (7), Ga. Affiliate Am. Heart Assn., 1990-96. Mem. Wayne County Optimist Club (bd. dirs. 1993-95, 2d v.p. 1995-96), Altamaha Cmty. Concert Assn. (publicity chmn.). Democrat. Home: 1016 Seven Oaks Rd Jesup GA 31546-5530 Office: The Press Sentinel PO Box 607 Jesup GA 31545-0607

DAVIS, JAMES ARNOLD, academic administrator; b. Apr. 18, 1945; m. Janet Copple; children: Barclay, Andrew, Stephanie. AA, Ferrum Coll., 1965; BA in History, Randolph-Macon Coll., 1967; MA in History, Va. Polytechnic Inst. and State U., 1969; PhD in Coll. Adminstrn., Fla. State U., 1972. Cert. lay spkr., United Meth. Ch. Asst. prof. history Ferrum Coll., 1968-71, chmn. social sci. div., assoc. prof. history, 1971-72, acad. dean, 1972-76, dean of coll., 1976-80, sr. v.p., dean of coll., 1980-82; pres. Shenandoah U., 1982—; mem. supt.'s adv. com. Franklin County Schs.; elected to commn. on Colls. of the So. Assn. of Colls. and Schs., 1987-90. Pres. Franklin County United Fund; founding mem. Franklin County Bicentennial Com.; vice-chmn. Patrick Henry Dist. Boy Scouts of Am., mem. Shenandoah area coun. ; bd. dirs. Jefferson Nat. Bank, No. region; elected Bd. of Higher Edn. United Meth. Ch. by Southeast Jurisdiction, 1988; mem. Corp. Winchester Med. Ctr., 1984—; lay leader Winchester Dist. United Meth. Ch.; bd. dirs. Toll Rd. Corp. Va., 1989—; elected to Va. Gen. Assembly Ho. of Del., 1978, 79, 81; active Gen. Assembly Com.; apptd. by gov. to spl. com. on Selection of Gov.'s awards for the Arts , Commonwealth of Va., 1984;apptd. by gov. to Waste Mgmt. Bd. for Commonwealth, 1985, chmn., 1985-88, Hist. Commn. to study Preservation in Va., 1987-89; elected bd. dirs. Washington-Dulles Task Force, 1986-89. Recipient Outstanding Citizen award Woodmen of the World, 1984; named Adminstr. of Yr. Greater Madison Found., 1988. Mem. Frederick County Hist. Soc., Rotary (Winchester chpt.), Phi Beta Kappa, Phi Theta Kappa (outstanding alumnus in U.S. 1980), Omicron Delta Kappa. Office: Shenandoah U Office of President 1460 University Dr Winchester VA 22601

DAVIS, JAMES CARL, retired government official, government consultant; b. St. Louis, Jan. 13, 1945; m. Linda L. Coston, Dec. 22, 1976. AA, St. Leo, Fla., 1977; BS, U. State of N.Y., Albany, 1989. Cert. pilot. Commd. 2d. lt. U.S. Army, 1963, advanced through grades to maj., 1980, ret., 1984; pres. Knights of Malta Found., New Orleans, 1984-86; adminstrn. cons. McTernan, Parr & Rumage, New Orleans, 1986-87; spl. asst. to the comdg. gen. Hdqrs. D.C. N.G., Washington, 1987-90; cons. local and U.S. govt., 1990-95; cons. internat. ops., bus. mgr. Alton F. Doody Co., 1995-96. Author: Where's My Award, 1982. Decorated two Bronze stars, two Purple Hearts. Mem. NRA, Res. Officers Assn., The Ret. Officers Assn. Home: 2897 Burnt Bridge Rd Picayune MS 39466

DAVIS, JAMES RANDALL, real estate developer; b. Seward, Alaska, Oct. 29, 1959; s. Jamed Edmund and Margerat Bernice (Bowie) D.; m. Lisa Bell, June 29, 1985; 1 child, Jamie Megan. BBA, U. Miss., 1981. Internal rev. auditor Alaska N.G., Anchorage, 1985-87; owner Davis Duplexes, Davis Devel., Osford, Miss., 1993—; cons. Bethel Native Corp. Exec. mem. Lafayette County Reps., Oxford, 1996. Capt. Alaska N.G., 1987-89, Miss. N.G., 1989-93. Mem. N.G. Assn. U.S. (rep. Area IV 1991-93), Airplane Owners and Pilots Assn. Methodist. Home and Office: Davis Devel/Duplexes 137 Anchorage Oxford MS 38655

DAVIS, JEFF See DAVIS, JOHN ALLEN, JR.

DAVIS, JESSIE PAVY, secondary English educator; b. Opelousas, La., Jan. 25, 1946; d. Edmond Estillette and Mina (Duncan) Pavy; m. Dewey Hamilton Davis II, June 21, 1969; children: Glen Talbot, Gregory Pavy. BS, La. State U., 1967; MEd, U. So. La., 1991. Tchr. Northwood H.S., Shreveport, La., 1967-70, Sunset (La.) H.S., 1985-91, Beau Chene H.S., Arnaudville, La., 1990—; tchr., cons. La. Writing Project, Baton Rouge, 1990, 92, Nat. Writing Project of Acadiana, Lafayette, 1990—. Sunday sch. tchr. Epiphany Episcopal ch., Opelousas, 1985-95, vacation bible sch. dir., 1986-89, ch. vestry, 1993-96. Mem. Nat. Coun. of Tchrs. of English, La. Coun. of Tchrs. of English, Acadiana Coun. of Tchrs. of English, Delta Kappa Gamma (2d v.p. 1994-96, pres. 1996—). Home: Rt 7 Box 12 Opelousas LA 70570 Office: Beau Chene High Sch 7076 Hwy 93 Arnaudville LA 70512

DAVIS, JIMMIE MAE CLAYBORN, elementary school educator; b. Longview, Tex., May 11, 1930; d. Cain Clayborn and Effie (Jackson) Clayborn Smith; m. Comoses Delano Davis, Nov. 1953; children: Denise Del, Wanda Yvette, Kelly Van. BS, Prairie View A&M U., 1952; MEd in Elem. Supervision, Stephen F. Austin U., 1969, MEd in Mgmt., Adminstrn., 1978. Sec. Citizen's Funeral Home, Longview, Tex., 1952-53; tchr. elem. sch. Danville Sch. Dist., Kilgore, Tex., 1953-58; home-bound tchr. Kilgore Ind. Sch. Dist., 1958-59; elem. tchr. Longview Ind. Sch. Dist., 1961—; cons. Mary Kay Cosmetics, Longview, 1984—; adviser Tex. State Textbook Com.; mem. textbook selection com. Tex. Edn. Agy., 1984. Bd. dirs. East Tex. Educators Rsch. Coun., 1983-85, ARC, Longview, 1987-91, Longview Commn. of Women, 1988—, Cmty. Outreach Mission, Longview, 1990—; mem. Tex. Congress PTA, 1991; pres. Bethel Missionary Soc., 1992. Mem. NAACP, NEA, AAUW (pres. 1979-81, dist. dir.), Tex. State Tchrs. Assn. (local pres., dist. chmn.), Nat. Coun. Negro Women, Ch. Women United, Gamma Rho Sigma, Sigma Gamma Rho, Alpha Gamma Sigma. Baptist. Home: 2308 Lilly St Longview TX 75602-3700

DAVIS, JIMMY FRANK, lawyer; b. Lubbock, Tex., June 14, 1945; s. Jack and Fern Lisemby D.; m. Joyce Zelma Hart, Nov. 6, 1976; children: Jayme Leigh, Julee Ellen. B.S. in Edn., Tex. Tech. U., 1968; J.D. U. Tex., 1972. Bar: Tex. 1972, U.S. Supreme Ct. 1975, U.S. Dist. (no. dist.) Tex. 1976, U.S. Ct. Appeals (5th cir.) 1976, U.S. Ct. Appeals (11 cir.) 1981. Asst. criminal dist. atty. Lubbock County, Tex., 1973-77, adminstrv. asst. for office, 1976-77; county and dist. atty. Castro County, Tex., 1977-92, asst. Atty Gen. of Tex., 1993—. Mem. State Bar of Tex. (com. admissions dist. 16 1974-78, dist. 13 1983-92, govt. lawyers sect., coun. mem. 1991-92), Tex. Dist. and County Attys. Assn., Lubbock County Jr. Bar Assn. (pres. 1977), Tex. Tech. Ex Students Assn. (dist. rep. 1981-84, bd. dirs, 1985-90), Coll. of State Bar of Tex. (continuing legal edn. 1984-93), Kiwanis of Lubbock (pres. 1977), Kiwanis of Dimmitt (pres. 1981), Delta Theta Phi. Baptist. Office: 1208 14th St Ste 800 Lubbock TX 79408-2747

DAVIS, JINNIE YEH, librarian; b. Sian, China, Dec. 1, 1945; came to U.S., 1957; d. Woo and Wujen (Wang) Yeh; m. Jerry Mallory Davis, Sept. 21, 1968; 1 child, Emily Davis. AB, U. Mich., 1967, AMLS, 1968; MHS, Auburn U., 1974; PhD, Ind. U., 1980. Asst. libr. Freer Gallery of Art, Washington, 1968-69; Spanish cataloger Ohio State U. Librs., Columbus, 1969-73; order libr., acquisitions dept. Auburn (Ala.) U., 1974-75; asst. head, serials dept. U. Librs., Raleigh, N.C., 1980-81, asst. head, monographic cataloging dept., 1981-85; asst. dir., planning and rsch. N.C. State U. Librs., Raleigh, 1985—. Mem. editl. bd. Libr. Quarterly, Chgo., 1995—, Coll. and rsch. Librs., Chgo., 1993—; editor: Academic Librarianship, 1989, Calligraphy, 1982; author: Monographic Searching on the OCLC Terminal, 1981; contbr. articles to profl. jours. Adv. bd. Raleigh Dance Theatre, 1990-94. Recipient Margaret Mann award U. Mich., Ann Arbor, 1968. Mem. ALA, N.C. Libr. Assn., Acad. and Coll. Rsch. Librs., Libr. Adminstrn. and Mgmt. Assn., Phi Kappa Phi, Sigma Delta Pi, Beta Phi Mu. Office: N C State Univ Librs Box 7111 Raleigh NC 27695

DAVIS, JOAN CARROLL, museum director; b. Binghamton, N.Y., Sept. 20, 1931; s. Homer Leslie and Ruby Isabelle (Stone) G.; m. Frederic E. Davis, Aug. 22, 1953; children—Timothy, Terri, Tami, Traci, Todd, Tricia. Student Bob Jones U., 1949-52. Supr. Day Care Ctr. Bob Jones U., Greenville, 1953-63; docent Univ. Art Gallery, Greenville, 1964-73, dir., 1974—. Republican. Baptist. Office: Bob Jones Univ 1700 Wade Hampton Blvd Greenville SC 29614-1000

DAVIS, JOHN ALLEN, JR. (JEFF DAVIS), financial planner; b. Canton, Ohio, Apr. 9, 1952; s. John Allen and Esther Marie (Falcone) D.; m. Donna Z. Davis, Dec. 5, 1981; children: John III, NIcholas, Rachel. BSJM, U. Fla., 1975. CFP, 1990. Asst. wrestling coach U. Fla. Athletic Assn., Gainesville, 1975-79; assoc. gen. agt, unit mgr. Ky. Cen. Life, Gainesville, 1979-83; assoc. Jack McGriff & Assocs., Gainesville, 1983-88; ptnr. Bowling, Whitaker & Davis, Gainesville, 1988-90; pvt. practice Gainesville, 1990—; pres. Falcon Fin. Mgmt., Gainesville, Fla., 1994; guest speaker on fringe benefits U. Fla., 1988—, Nat. Wrestling Coaches Assn., Palm Beach, Fla., 1991; pres. and chief investment officer Falcon Fin. Mgmt., Inc. Columnist Gainesville Sun. Commr. Gainesville Sport Organizing Com., 1990-94; event dir. USA Wrestling, Gainesville, 1990-93, Nat. Espoir Wrestling Championships, 1991, 92; staff wrestling, athlete escort, tng. site supr. Centennial Olympic Games; mem. Holy Faith Cath. Ch. Mem. Inst. of CFP's, Registry Fin. Planners, Registry CFP Practioners, Estate Planning Coun. Gainsville, Gainesville C. of C., Pres.'s Coun. U. Fla., UAA Letterman's Club, Kiwanis (com. chmn., bd. dirs. Gainesville). Office: Falcon Fin Mgmt Inc 2631 NW 41st St Gainesville FL 32606-7470

DAVIS, JOHN HOWARD, English language educator; b. Bessemer, Ala., Dec. 5, 1942; s. John Howard and Zelphia Katherine (Riley) D.; m. Sarah McCaa Winborn, Mar. 16, 1969; children: Sarah Tarah, Hugh Howard. BA with honors, Ala. Coll., Montevallo, 1967; MA, Auburn (Ala.) U., 1970, PhD, 1975. Grad. teaching asst. Auburn U., 1969-75, instr., 1975; asst. prof. Talladega (Ala.) Coll., 1975-81; instr. lit. and composition Chowan Coll., Murfreesboro, N.C., 1981-92, assoc. prof. English and Lit., 1992-96, full prof. English, 1996—; conf. presenter in field. Contbr. articles to Mark Twain Encyclopedia, and profl. jours. With U.S. Army Res., 1968-74. NDEA fellow Auburn U. Grad. Sch., 1967-70, Carnegie-Mellon fellow Vanderbilt U., 1981. Mem. MLA, Popular Culture Assn. in South, Mark Twain Cir. (charter), South Atlantic MLA, N.C.-Va. Coll. English Assn., Philol. Assn. Carolinas, Phi Alpha Theta, Sigma Tau Delta (faculty sponsor Chowan Coll.). Office: Chowan Coll Div English Murfreesboro NC 27855

DAVIS, JOHN WESLEY, III, health facility administrator; b. Fayetteville, N.C., Aug. 29, 1940; s. John Wesley Jr. and Helen Elizabeth (Edge) D.; m. Sandra Kay Schuette, May 14, 1977; children: John Wesley IV, Kelly Kay Fahrenkrug, Elizabeth Kay, John Richard. BA in Gen. Studies, U. Nebr., 1971; MA, U. Okla., 1974. Commd. 2d. lt. USAF, 1961, advanced through grades to col., 1990; ret., 1990; prof., chmn. dept. aerospace studies Fla. State U., Tallahassee, 1986-88; dir., donor recruitment South Tex. Blood and Tissue Ctr., San Antonio, Tex., 1990—; com. mem. South Ctrl. Assn. of Blood Banks, 1994—. Mem. Order of Daedalians (flight capt. 1984-85), Air Force Assn., Am. Assn. of Blood Banks. Lutheran. Home: 6130 Grand Point San Antonio TX 78239 Office: South Tex Blood/Tissue Ctr 6211 IH-10 West San Antonio TX 78201

DAVIS, KAREN BARNETT, special education educator; b. Mobile, Ala., June 24, 1956; d. Morrison C. and Ruth W. (Bazzell) Barnett; m. Robert Alan Davis, Jan. 8, 1988; children: Whitney, Jordan, Joel. BS in Edn., U. South Ala., 1978; MEd, Jacksonville (Ala.) State U., 1989, EdS, 1993. Cert. in mental retardation, learning disabilities, behavior disorders, tchr. support. Mental retardation tchr. Horace B. Slaughter Elem. Sch., Louisville, 1978-80, McEachern H.S., Powder Springs, Ga., 1984-90; interrelated resource tchr. Dowell Elem. Sch., Marietta, Ga., 1990—; mem. remedial adv. com. State of Ga., Atlanta, 1995; mem. Cobb County Bd. Educators, State of Ga., 1994—; mem. spl. edn. revision com. Cobb Bd. Edn., Marietta, 1995. Sunday sch. tchr. singles First Bapt. Ch., Powder Springs, 1994—; mem. legis. contact Cobb County Bd. Educators, Marietta, 1996; active in ch. and children's PTA groups. Mem. ASCD, Woodmen of the World, Ga. Assn. Educators. Republican. Home: 4842 W McEachern Woods Dr Powder Springs GA 30073

DAVIS, KATHRYN LOUISE, physical educator; b. Hartselle, Ala., Oct. 12, 1956; d. Samuel Jackson and Elizabeth Louise (Thomas) D. BSPE, U. N.C., Greensboro, 1978; MA Tchg., U. N.C., Chapel Hill, 1983. Cert. tchr. K-12 health and physical edn. Physical edn. tchr., coach Fayetteville (N.C.)

Acad., 1978-82; from lectr. phys. edn. to assoc. prof. phys. edn. N.C. State U., 1983—; presenter AIESEP World Congress, Netanya, Israel, 1995, Women in Sports Delegation, Shenyang, China, 1994. Author: The Art of Sports Officiating, 1995, Volleyball, 3d edit., 1996, Advanced Volleyball Everyone, 1992, Fitness Walling Everyone, 1996; contbr. articles to profl. jours. Grantee N.C. Amateur Sports, 1994. i. Mem. AAHPERD, Nat. Assn. Girls & Women in Sports, Nat. Assn. for Sport & Phys. Edn., N.C. Alliance for Health, Physical Edn., Recreation, and Dance, Women's Sports Found., Volleyball Ofcls. Assn. Democrat. Office: NC State U Box 8111 Carmichael Gym Raleigh NC 27695-8111

DAVIS, KENNETH BRUCE, JR., biologist; b. Texarkana, Ark., Mar. 13, 1940; s. Kenneth Bruce and Dorothy Ennis (Cross) D.; m. Clara Ann Brister, 1969 (div. 1975); m. Mary Anna Suttle, June 6, 1987; 1 child, Kenneth Bruce III. BA, U. Ark., 1963, MS, 1965; PhD, La. State U., 1970. Instr. La. State U., Baton Rouge, 1968-69; from asst. prof. to prof. Memphis State U., 1969—; physiology sect. head U.S. Fish & Wildlife Svc., Marion, Ala., 1978-79. Contbr. articles to profl. jours. Office: U Memphis Dept Biology Memphis TN 38152

DAVIS, KIM MCALISTER, real estate sales executive, real estate broker; b. Woodruff, S.C., Dec. 30, 1958; d. James Calhoun and Nancy (Caldwell) McAlister; m. Robert James Godfrey (div.); 1 child, Lindsey Paige; m. Don Brigham Davis. BA in Elem. Edn., U. S.C., 1982, MBA, 1983—. Cert. tchr., S.C.; lic. real estate, Fla. Adminstrv. asst. to pvt. physician, Woodruff, 1977-78; sales rep. Reimer's Dept. Store, Woodruff, 1978-80; tchr. Spartanburg County Sch. Dist., Woodruff, 1981-82; pres., owner Godfrey Carpets, Inc., Woodruff, 1983-88; pharm. sales rep. Parke-Davis Pharm. Co., Ponte Vedra Beach, Fla., 1989-90. Mem. decorating com. 1st Bapt. Ch., Woodruff, 1984-87; chmn. bd. dirs. Small Towns Program, Woodruff, 1987-88; Rep. candidate for Spartanburg County Coun., 1987; mem. S.C. Rep. Com.; sustaining mem. S.C. Rep. Party; chmn. Nat. Bus. Women's Week, 1984; bd. dirs., pres. 1991-93, Ponte Vedra-Palm Valley Elem. Sch. Parent Tchr. Student Orgn.; sustaining mem. Fla. Rep. Party; bd. dirs. St. Johns Pub. Edn. Found., St. Johns County Edn. Found.; mem. human resources strategic planning com. St. Johns County Pub. Schs.; Rep. candidate St. Johns County Sch. Bd., 1994. Named Young Careerist of the Yr., Nat. Bus. and Profl. Women, 1984. Mem. Nat. Fedn. Ind. Bus., Greater Woodruff Area C. of C. (pub. spkr., bd. dirs. 1985-87, pres. 1986), Bus. and Profl. Women (v.p. 1985), Woodruff Jr. Women's Club, Ponte Vedra Assn. Realtors, Disting. Million Dollar Club, St. John's County C. of C. (Ponte Vedra coun., exec. bd.). Home: 8160 Seven Mile Dr Ponte Vedra Beach FL 32082-3004 Office: 270 Solano Rd Ponte Vedra Beach FL 32082-2234

DAVIS, LILA ROSS, public health officer; b. Balt., June 16, 1941; d. Robert P. and Lila (Norfleet) D. BA in Psychology, Mary Washington Coll., 1963; cert. in med. record adminstrn., USPHS Sch. for Med. Record Adminstrs., 1964. Chief med. record dept. DePaul Hosp., Norfolk, Va., 1964-66, Kings Daughters Children's Hosp., Norfolk, 1966-69; research analyst Norfolk Gen. Hosp., 1969-73; commd. officer USPHS, 1973, advanced through grades to capt., 1983; dep. chief med. record dept. USPHS Hosp., Norfolk, 1973-74; chief USPHS Hosp., 1974-79; chief med. record dept. USPHS Hosp., San Francisco, 1979-81; dep. dir. USPHS Health Data Ctr., Lanham, Md., 1981-83, dir., 1983-86; dir. USPHS Health Data Ctr., GWL Hansen's Disease Ctr., Carville, La., 1986—; cons. Fed. Bur. Prisons; participant, cons. disaster med. assistance program Bur. Health Care and Delivery, Rockville, Md., 1983-86. Mem. Am. Med. Record Assn., La. Med. Record Assn., Commd. Officer Assn. USPHS, Assn. Mil. Surgeons U.S. Presbyterian. Lodge: Zonta. Office: GWL Hansens Disease Ctr Carville LA 70721

DAVIS, LOUIS POISSON, JR., lawyer, consultant; b. Washington, July 17, 1919; s. Louis Poisson and Edna (Shethar) D.; m. Emily Elizabeth Carl, Mar. 9, 1922; 1 dau., Cynthia. B.Sc., U.S. Naval Acad., 1941; postgrad. Princeton U., 1947-48; J.D., Rutgers U., 1953. Bar: N.Y. 1954, Ill. 1963, U.S. Supreme Ct. 1964, U.S. Dist. Ct. (so. dist.) N.Y. 1956, U.S. Dist. Ct. (no. dist.) Ill. 1965. Mgr. engring. Esso Standard Oil, Linden, N.J., 1946-57; sr. economist, head econs. and market research dept. Internat. Petroleum Co., Lima, Peru, 1957-60; asst. overseas ops. AMF Internat, N.Y.C., 1961-62; sr. atty. Internat. Abbott Labs., North Chicago, Ill., 1962-65; gen. mgr. Far East ops. Ralston Purina Co., pres. Ralston Purina Eastern, Hong Kong, 1966-71; dir. internat. devel. Archer Daniels Midland Co., v.p. Archer Daniels Midland Internat., Decatur, Ill., 1972-74; lectr., researcher internat. law and mgmt., N.Y.C., 1974-76; corp. rep. Europe, Mid East, Africa, Alexander & Baldwin Agribus., Inc., Abidjan, Ivory Coast, 1976, Madrid, Spain, 1977; internat. atty., cons., Sarasota, Fla., 1978—; cons. Sarasota County Office of Sci. Advisor, 1985-86, Office of Gen. Counsel, 1989-91; vol. income tax assistance program IRS, 1983—; cons., seminar leader ChipSoft Inc., 1989-90; vol. atty. Gulfcoast Legal Svcs., 1987-91; instr. Sarasota Tech. Inst., 1990—; cert. cons. Capsoft Dev. Corp. Legal Automation Software, 1991; gen. counsel Manasota Industry Council Inc., 1984-89; bd. dirs. Exxon Annutant Club of Sarasota-Manatee Counties, Inc., 1986-89, also v.p.; bd. dirs. Siesta Key Assn., 1989-95, v.p. 1993-94. Lt. comdr. USN, 1937-46. Recipient Pres. Bonus, Ralston Purina Co., 1969, 70. Mem. Am. Bar Assn., Hong Kong Country Club, Oaks Club (Sarasota). Republican. Episcopalian. Home and Office: 620 Mangrove Point Rd Sarasota FL 34242-1230

DAVIS, LOURIE IRENE BELL, computer education and sytems specialist; b. Las Vegas, N.Mex., Apr. 8, 1930; d. Currie Oscar and Minnie I. (Rodgers) Bell; m. Robert Eugene Davis, Aug. 21, 1950; children: Judith Anne, Robert Patrick, (adopted) Jaime Alleyn, Flint Christopher. BS, West Tex. U., 1959; student Ea. N.Mex. U., 1947-49. Cert. systems profl.; cert. data processing profl. Programmer/analyst Blue Cross/Blue Shield Okla., Tulsa, 1972-75, mgr. systems, 1977-81, dir. info. systems, 1981-82, mgr. project control, 1982-83, mgr. info. ctr., 1984-85, mgr. profl. cons. and tng., 1985-87; faculty devel. coord. CAID Okla. State U., Okmulgee, 1987-90; computer bus. and edn. cons. Davis Cons., 1991—; adminstrv. officer Intertel, Inc., 1991-95, pres., CEO, 1995—; systems curriculum coord., computer sci. instr. Tulsa Jr. Coll., 1975-76, mem. computer sci. adv. bd., 1976-83; mem. steering com. U.S. Senate bus. adv. bd., 1981; ind. cons., Tulsa, 1987; lectr. computer assisted instruction success League of Innovation Conf., St. Louis, 1989, Music Users Group Conf., U. Tenn., Chattanooga, 1989, Pres's. Day Des Moines Area C.C., 1990. Mem. budget panel United Way Tulsa, 1981-87, Allocations Exec. Com. Appreciation award, 1987; mem. U.S. Rep. Presdl. Task Force, 1982-93; mem. Holy Family Sch. Bd., 1991-95, nominating com. chair, 1993, sec., 1993-95. Winner League of Innovation for C.C.s. Competition, IBM, 1989. Mem. Assn. Systems Mgmt. (regional dir. 1985-86, chpt. membership chair 1982-84; internat. awards 1980, 84), NAFE, AAUW, Tulsa Area Systems Edn. Assn. (recorder 1980-81), Higher Edn. Acad. Coun. of Okla., Sierra Club, Alpha Chi, Mensa, Intertel (nat. acceptance com. chair 1978, dir. region VIII 1987-91, membership officer 1991-92, chmn. bd. 1995—, pub. Integra 1992—). Republican. Mem. Unity Ch. of Christianity. Home and Office: Davis Cons 2403 W Oklahoma St Tulsa OK 74127-3027

DAVIS, LYNN HAMBRIGHT, culinary arts educator; b. Gaffney, S.C., Aug. 7, 1950; d. Samuel Anderson and Elizabeth (Nolen) Hambright; m. Ronnie Dale Davis, Aug. 10, 1969; children: Marty, Jennifer. BS in Home Econs. Edn., Winthrop Coll., 1972, MS in Home Econs. Edn., 1982, EDS, 1996. Cert. secondary home econs. edn. tchr., early childhood edn., N.C., S.C. Tchr. Crest Sr. High, Shelby, N.C., 1975-76; dietitian Cleveland Meml. Hosp., Shelby, 1977-78; tchr. culinary arts Cherokee Tech. Ctr., Gaffney, 1978—; chairperson Staff Devel. Com. and Culinary Arts Craft Coun., Gaffney, 1978—; advisor Future Homemakers Am., Gaffney, 1978—. Mem. Am. Vocat. Assn. (region II policy com. 1992-95, state rep. region II 1992-95), S.C. Vocat. Assn. (v.p. 1991-92), Nat. Assn. Vocat. Home Econs. Tchrs., S.C. Assn. Vocat. Home Econs. Tchrs. (pres. 1991-92, advisor 1992-93, Tchr. of Yr. 1995), Am. Home Econs. Assn., S.C. Home Econs. Assn. (sec. food svc. adminstrs. com. 1991-92, Tchr. of Yr. 1993), Home Econs. Edn. Assn. Democrat. Baptist. Home: 2100 Albert Blanton Rd Shelby NC 28152-8151 Office: Cherokee Tech Ctr 3206 Cherokee Ave Gaffney SC 29340-3564

DAVIS, M. G., lawyer; b. Concho County, Tex., Nov. 11, 1930; s. Zack and Olive (Clifton) D.; m. Jeanne Focke, Feb. 7, 1959; children: Linda Jeanne, Lisbeth Dianne. BBA, Tex. Tech. U., 1952; JD, U. Tex., 1958. Bar: Tex., 1957, U.S. Supreme Ct., 1964; atty. Gen. Land Office, Austin, Tex., 1959-60, firm Smith, Porter & Caston, Longview, Tex., 1960-61; v.p. Am. Title Co. Dallas, 1961-67; owner, operator Security Land Title Co., Amarillo, Tex., 1967-69; pres. Dallas Title Co., Houston, 1969-70, Guardian Title, Houston, 1970-72, Collin County Title Co., Plano, Tex., 1972-87; pvt. practice, Plano, 1972-82; ptnr. firm Davis & Davis, Dallas, 1982-93, Davis & Sallinger, L.L.P., Dallas, 1993—; guest lectr. U. Houston, Richland Jr. Coll. Chmn. Selective Service Bd. 46, 1982-92; mem. legis. task force, employer support for guard and reserve affairs TNGA. 1st lt. USAF, 1952-54; Korea. Recipient Involved Citizen award Dallas Morning News, 1980. Mem. State Bar Tex., Dallas Bar Assn., Coll. State Bar of Tex., Sons Republic Tex., Tex. Land Title Assn. (v.p. 1970-71), Tex. Tech. Ex-Students Assn. (dir. 1961-63), Collin County Title Assn. (pres. 1977), Dallas Mortgage Bankers Assn., Collin County U. Tex. Ex-Students Assn. (pres. 1980), U. Tex. Ex-Students (exec. council 1983-86), Alpha Tau Omega. Democrat. Episcopalian. Home: 3708 Canoncita Ln Plano TX 75023-6001 Office: Ste 350 5520 Lyndon B Johnson Fwy Dallas TX 75240-6209

DAVIS, MAGGIE (MARIE HILL), writer; b. Norfolk, Va.; d. George Blair and Dorothy Austin (Mason) Hill; children: Stuart, Richard, David, Cambren. Advt. copywriter Young and Rubicam, N.Y.C.; asst. in rsch. to chmn. dept. psychology Yale U., New Haven; instr. creative writing courses Yale U.; guest writer/artist Internat. Cultural Ctr., Hammamet, Tunisia. Author: The Far Side of Home, 1992, Daggers of Gold, 1993, Moonlight and Listletoe, 1993, The Amethyst Crown, 1994, Blood Red Roses, 1991 (named Best Medieval Novel by Romantic Times mag.), A Christmas Romance, 1991 (dramatized as CBS Sunday Night Movie 1994), Eagles, 1980, The Sheik, 1977, Rommel's Gold, 1971; feature writer Atlanta Jour. Constn.; contbr. articles and short stories to Ga. Rev., Cosmopolitan, Ladies Home Jour., Good Housekeeping, Holiday, Venture mags. Named Ga. Author of Yr., 1963; recipient Silver Pen award Affaire de Coeur Mag., 1987, Lifetime Achievement award in romantic comedy Romantic Times Mag., 1987. Mem. Medieval Acad. Am., Authors Guild, Romance Writers of Am., Pub. Rels. Soc. Am., Acad. Am. Poets, Women's Polit. Caucus, Caledonian Club. Democrat. Soc. of Friends. Home and Office: 1149 Tarpon Ave Sarasota FL 34237-3744

DAVIS, MARGUERITE HERR, judge; b. Washington, Nov. 12, 1947; d. Norman Phillip and Margaretha Joanna (Dewaard) Herr; m. James Riley Davis, June 20, 1970; children: Amy Marguerite, Christine Riley. AA with honors, St. Petersburg J. Coll., Clearwater, Fla., 1966; BA with honors, U. of South Fla., 1968; JD with honors, Fla. State U., 1971. Bar: Fla. 1971, U.S. Dist. Ct. (no. dist.) Fla. 1971, U.S. Dist. Ct. (mid. dist.) Md. 1985, U.S. Ct. Appeals (11th cir.) 1985, U.S. Supreme Ct. 1986. Atty. workers compensation div. U.S. Dept. Labor, Tallahassee, 1971; sr. legal aide Fla. Supreme Ct., Tallahassee, 1971-85, exec. asst. to Hon. Chief Justice Alderman, 1982-84; ptnr. Swann & Haddock, Tallahassee, 1985-87, Katz, Kutler, Haigler, Alderman, Davis & Marks, Tallahassee, 1987-93; judge U.S. Dist. Ct. of Appeal, 1st Dist., Tallahassee, 1993—. Mem. editl. bd. Trial Advocate Quar., 1991-93; contbr. chpts. to books. Mem. ABA, Fla. Bar Assn. (Tallahassee chpt., appellate ct. rules com. 1985—, grievance com., disciplinary rev. com., chmn. supreme ct. local rules adv. com., jud. cir. grievance com., rules of jud. adminstrn. 1995—, jud. evaluation com. 1995—, exec. coun. appellate advocacy sect.), Fla. State Fed. Jud. Coun. (exec. dir. 1985—), Tallahassee Women Lawyers, Fla. Def. Lawyers Assn. (amicus curiae com.), Fla. Supreme Ct. Hist. Soc., Am. Arbitration Assn. (ad hoc com. stds. for appellate practice certification), Altrusa Club of Tallahassee (treas. 1971-76), Fla. State U. Alumni Assn. (bd. dirs. 1975-76), Phi Theta Kappa. Methodist.

DAVIS, MARIA TERESA, architect; b. Galveston, Tex., May 3, 1961; d. John Thomas and Mary Frances (Purcell) D. B of Environ. Design, Tex. A&M U., 1982, MArch, 1984. Registered architect, Tex. Grad. asst. Tex. A&M U., College Station, 1984; interior architect Group 4 Architects, Bryan, Tex., 1984-85; assoc. HKS, Inc., Dallas, 1984—. Mem. AIA, Tex. Soc. of Architects. Office: Harwood K Smith & Partners 1111 Plaza of the Americas N Dallas TX 75201

DAVIS, MARIAN BLOODWORTH, secondary school educator; b. Decatur, Ala., Apr. 7, 1933; d. Benjamin McGowan and Marguerite Maud (Nelson) Bloodworth; m. Judson Ervill Davis, Jr., June 6, 1958; children: Katheryne, Judson Ervill III, James Alexander Bloodworth. BA, U. Ala., Tuscaloosa, 1957; MA, U. North Ala., 1989. Cert. tchr., Ala. Social worker State of Ala., Decatur, 1957-58; tchr. Decatur City Schs., 1979—. Treas., bd. dirs. Jr. League Morgan County, Decatur, 1966-72; area coord. The Close Up Found., Washington, 1990—; mem. Morgan County Reps., 1990—. Mem. NEA, Ala. Edn. Assn., Decatur Edn. Assn., Nat. Coun. Social Studies, Ala. Coun. Social Studies (dist. dir. 1990-94, pres. 1994-95), Nat. Trust Historic Preservation, Ala. Hist. Soc., Nat. Alumni Assn. U. Ala., Delta Kappa Gamma (sec. 1996—), Kappa Delta. Republican. Baptist. Home: 2326 Quince Dr SE Decatur AL 35601-6138 Office: Decatur High Sch 1011 Prospect Dr SE Decatur AL 35601-3229

DAVIS, MARK WARDEN, lawyer; b. Greenville, Miss., Sept. 17, 1958; s. Joseph Warden and Ruby Nell (Alford) D.; m. Angela Leigh Perry, Apr. 8, 1989; children: Ashleigh Elizabeth, Autumn Arissa. BS, Delta State U., 1980; JD, U. Miss., 1984. Bar: Miss. 1984, U.S. Dist. Ct. (no. and so. dist.) 1984, U.S. Ct. Appeals (5th cir.) 1984. Assoc. Hopkins, Logan, Vaughn & Anderson, Gulfport, Miss., 1984-87; ptnr. Davis & Emil, Gulfport, 1988—; speaker in field. Mem. nat. com. Miss. Young Reps., 1984-88; chmn. Gulf Coast Young Reps., 1984-88. Mem. ABA, Miss. Bar Assn., Harrison County Bar Assn., Harrison County Young Lawyers Assn. (del.), Am. Trial Lawyers Assn., Miss. Trial Lawyers Assn., Gulf Coast C. of C., Ducks Unltd., Bayou Bluff Tennis Club, Windance Country Club, Gulfport Jaycees. Presbyterian.

DAVIS, MARTHA ALGENITA SCOTT, lawyer; b. Houston, Oct. 1, 1950; d. C.B. Scott and Althea (Lewis) Scott Renfro; m. John Whittaker Davis, III, Aug. 21, 1976; children: Marthea, John IV. BBA, Howard U., 1971, JD, 1974. Bar: Tex. 1974, U.S. Dist. Ct. (so. dist.) Tex. 1975, U.S. Ct. Appeals (5th cir.) 1976, U.S. Supreme Ct. 1980. Tax atty. Shell Oil Co., Houston, 1974-79; counsel Port of Houston Authority, 1979-89; sr. v.p., community affairs officer Tex. Commerce Bancshares, 1989—; ptnr. Burney, Edwards, Hall, Hartsfield & Scott, Houston, 1975-78; bd. dirs. Unity Nat. Bank. Bd. dirs. Houston Citizens Chamber, 1980-90, Neighborhood Ednl. Ctr., Houston, 1983-87, Peoples' Workshop to Performing Arts; coordinator Operation Big Vote, Washington, 1984-85; mem. planning commn. City of Houston, 1987-91; founding chair Houston Downtown Mgmt. Corp., 1991-92; nat. parliamentarian, The Links, Inc., 1994—. Pres. Greater Houston Women's Found., 1996. Recipient Achievement award Greek Council, Houston, 1973; Houston's Most Influential Black Women award Black Experience Mag., Five Young Outstanding Houstonians award Houston Jr. C. of C., 1989; named one of Houston Ten Women of Distinction, Chrones and Colitis Found. and The Houston Press, 1993, one of Women on the Move, Houston Post, 1994. Mem. Nat. Bar Assn. (pres. 1990-91, sec. 1983-88, chmn. voter edn./registration com. 1985-86, pres. award 1993, 94), Black Women Lawyers Assn. (vice chair 1983-84, profl. achievement award 1984), Houston Lawyers Assn. (bd. dirs. 1977-78, 85-89, pres. 1988-89). Baptist. Club: Links (Nat. we. area parliamentarian, Houston parliamentarian). Office: Tex Commerce Bancshares MS 26 TCBE 45 PO Box 2558 Houston TX 77252

DAVIS, MARVIN ARNOLD, manufacturing company executive; b. St. Louis, Nov. 16, 1937; s. Sam and Pauline (Neuman) D.; m. Trudy Brenda Rein, Aug. 11, 1968; children: Julie, Jeffrey. BS in Chem. Engring., Washington U., St. Louis, 1959; MBA in Fin.and Mktg., Washington U., 1966. Lead engr. Standard Oil Calif., San Francisco, 1962-64; product mgr. Shell Chem. Co., N.Y.C., 1966-69; group controller Pfizer, Inc., N.Y.C., 1969-75; exec. v.p. Good Hope Industries, New Orleans, 1975-77; pres., chief exec. officer Reed Industries, Inc., Stone Mountain, Ga., 1978—; pres. Sentrex Ltd., Atlanta, 1977-82; v.p. Sentry Ins., 1982-84; cons. Grisanti Galef Goldress, 1984—, pres., 1991—; chmn., CEO Petrowax PA, Inc., 1992-94, Signal Apparel Corp., 1993-94; chmn. Folger Adams Corp., Simplicity Pattern Co., Pandick Press; instr. Farleigh Dickinson U., 1968-71; lectr. Washington U., 1966, 77; cons. in field; bd. dirs. Wherehouse Enterntainment Corp., Fairlanes Bowling Corp., Celluland Corp., Northwest Pipe and Casing Co., Empty Corp., Turn Around Mgmt. Assn., Cherokee Corp.; pres. AMA Fund, Inc. Author: The Profit Prescription, 1985, Turnaround, 1987. Active Seville Recreation Assn. Served to lt. USNR, 1959-62. Recipient scholarship Washington U., 1959, fellow, 1968. Mem. DeKalb C. of C., Beta Gamma Sigma, Alpha Chi Sigma. Jewish. Club: Horseshoe Bend Country. Office: 80 Seville Chase Atlanta GA 30328

DAVIS, MARY BYRD, conservationist, researcher; b. Cardiff, Wales; came to U.S., 1947; d. John Dymond and Joanna Inger (Falconer) Byrd; m. Robert Minard Davis; children: Carol, John. BA, Agnes Scott Coll., 1958; MA, U. Wis., 1968, PhD, 1972; MLS, Simmons Coll., 1974. Acquisitions libr. No. Mich. U., Marquette, 1974-75; asst. libr. Georgetown (Ky.) Coll., 1975-78; libr. U. Ky., Lexington, 1978-83; freelance writer and editor Georgetown, 1983-90, 93—; staff writer, office mgr. Earth First Jour., Canton, N.Y., 1990; co-founder and pub. Wild Earth, Canton, N.Y., 1991-92; assoc. editor Wild Earth, Richmond, Vt., 1993—; dir. Ygdrasil Inst., Georgetown, Ky., 1994—. Author: The Military Civilian Nuclear Link, 1988, Guide de L'Industrie Nucleaire Francaise, 1988, The Green Guide to France, 1990, Going Off the Beaten Path: An Untraditional Travel Guide to the U.S., 1991, Old Growth in the East: A Survey, 1993; co-author: Les Déchets nucléaires militaires Français, 1994; editor: Eastern Old-Growth Forests: Prospects for Rediscovery and Recovery, 1996. Bd. dirs. Centre de Documentation et de Recherche sur la Paix et les Conflits, Lyon, France, 1989—. Mem. Sierra Club (editor energy report 1986-87, exec. com. Cumberland chpt. 1982-84), Phi Beta Kappa.

DAVIS, MARY VIRGINIA, medical and surgical nurse; b. Sumter County, Ala., Nov. 17, 1956; d. Coleman and Eliza Mae (Chambers) Danner; m. Iris Davis, Dec. 25, 1986. Cert. in geriatric nursing, U. Ala., Tuscaloosa, 1979, BSN, 1981; MS in Nursing, Miss. U. for Women, 1990. RN, Ala.; cert. adult nurse practitioner, ANA. Staff nurse Druid City Hosp. Regional Med. Ctr., Tuscaloosa, 1981-85, asst. head nurse, 1985-1990, head nurse, 1990-92; adult nurse practitioner Tuscaloosa County Health Dept., 1992, Bibb Med. Ctr., Centreville, Ala., 1992—. Home: 5607 34th Pl Tuscaloosa AL 35401-6273

DAVIS, MICHAEL, engineering company executive. Pres. NKF Engring., Inc., Arlington, Va. Office: NKF Engring Inc 4200 Wilson Blvd Ste 900 Arlington VA 22203-1800

DAVIS, MICHAEL JORDAN, civil engineer, natural gas company executive; b. Hudson, N.Y., Aug. 30, 1957; s. Ronald James and Virginia Ann (Jordan) D.; m. Camellia Jane Poland, Dec. 24, 1984; children: Kelly Dewayne, Elizabeth Ann. BSCE, Syracuse U., 1980. Field engr. Tenn. Gas Pipeline, Lafayette, La., 1980-85; divsn. engr. supr. Tenn. Gas Pipeline, Enfield, Conn., 1989-91; engr. Tenneco Gas, Houston, 1985-86, pipeline engr., 1986-89, mgr. drafting, 1991-94; dist. supt. Tenn. Gas Pipeline, Houma, La., 1994—. Mem. Houma-Terrebonne Arts and Humanities Coun. Mem. So. Gas Assn., Gulf Coast Conservation Assn. Republican. Methodist. Home: 133 Presque Isle Dr Houma LA 70363-3827 Office: Tenn Gas Pipeline 224 Aviation Rd Houma LA 70363-5491

DAVIS, PATRICIA M., literacy educator; b. Lloydminster, Alberta, Can., Nov. 16, 1932; d. George E. and Edith May (Kent) McKerihan; m. Harold M. Davis, Dec. 17, 1958 (dec. Dec. 24, 1971); children: Harold Neal, Rosemary Anne. BA, Dallas Bapt. Coll., 1981; MA, U. Tex., 1988, PhD, 1994. From grass roots worker to materials cons., tchr. trainer Summer Inst. Linguistics/Min. Edn., Peruvian Amazon region, 1963-84; literacy trainer Summer Inst. Linguistics, England, 1985-88; internat. literacy and edn. cons. Summer Inst. Linguistics, Dallas, 1995—. Author: Cognition and Learning, 1991; co-author: Bilingual Education: An Experience in Peruvian Amazonia, 1979. Mem. Internat. Reading Assn., Comparative and Internat. Edn. Soc., Alpha Chi, Kappa Delta Pi, Phi Kappa Phi. Office: Summer Inst Linguistics 7500 W Camp Wisdom Rd Dallas TX 75236

DAVIS, PAUL B., mechanical engineer, civil engineer, retired; b. N.Y.C., Jan. 20, 1909; s. Samuel and Esther (Schwartz) D.; m. Sally Vogel (dec.), Nov. 24, 1932; children: Gerald Joseph, Audrey Thea Coll. Student, Bklyn. Poly. Inst., 1928. Engring. draftsman Mcpl. Pub. Works, N.Y.C., 1929-41; asst. engr. Bd. Water Supply, N.Y.C., 1941-42; sr. designer to asst. supt. design Ebasco Svcs., Inc., N.Y.C., 1942-66; mgr. Spanish projects Ebasco Overseas Corp., Madrid, 1966-72; project engring. mgr. Burns & Roe, Hempstead, N.Y., 1973-76; ednl. coord. Argonne Nat. Lab., Argonne, Ill., 1977. Dir. Poinciana Condominium Assn., Lake Worth, Fla., 1979-86. Mem. NSPE (life), N.Y. State Soc. Profl. Engrs., Sierra Club, Zionist Orgn. Am., World Jewish Congress, Nat. Wildlife Fedn., B'nai B'rith, Poinciana Country Club. Home: 3755 Poinciana Dr Apt 412 Lake Worth FL 33467-2828

DAVIS, PAUL ESTILL, environmental executive; b. Nashville, May 13, 1949; s. Allan D. and Grace Wilson (Estill) D.; m. Marjorie Jean McCormick, July 24, 1993. MS in Water Resources, U. Tenn., 1971, BS in Engring. Sci., 1973. Registered profl. engr. Tenn. Environ. engr. Water Pollution Control, Knoxville, Tenn., 1974-78; chief compliance sect. Water Pollution Control, Knoxville, 1978-80, mgr. permits sect., 1980-85, dep. dir., 1985-88, dir., 1988—; grad. Tenn. Govt. Exec. Inst., Nashville, 1989. Mem. Assn. State and Interstate Water Pollution Control Adminstrs. (bd. mem. 1987-94), Ky.-Tenn. Water Environ. Assn. (sec.-treas. 1987-94, Bedell award 1993), Environ. Action Fund (bd. mem., treas. 1989-94). Home: 45 Burris Ct Mount Juliet TN 37122-2001 Office: Tenn Dept Environ Conserv 6th Fl L & C Annex 401 Church St Nashville TN 37219-2213

DAVIS, PAUL MICHAEL, sales executive; b. Burlington, N.C., Apr. 18, 1940; s. Paul P. and Margaret (Mebane) D.; m. Sarah Gillon, Aug. 11, 1963; children: Paul Michael Jr., Jennifer Lynn. BSBA, U. N.C., 1962. Terminal mgr. McLean Trucking Co., various locations, 1964-86; asst. to v.p. McLean Trucking Co., Indpls., 1971-72, dist. mgr., 1972-79; v.p. McLean Trucking Co., Kearny, N.J., 1979-81, Memphis, 1981-86; sr. v.p. sales, mktg. Builders Transport, Inc., Camden, S.C., 1986—; v.p. dedicated fleet div. Builders Transport, Inc., Camden, 1989—. Republican. Lutheran. Lodge: Sertoma (Nashville). Office: Builders Transport Inc 2029 W DeKalb St PO Box 7005 Camden SC 29020

DAVIS, PAUL MILTON, television news administrator; b. Effingham, Ill., Dec. 21, 1938; s. Plaford Milton and Zona Matilda (Buchholz) D.; m. Marilynne Bohne, Aug. 26, 1961; children: Paul Mark, Glenn Stokes, Marinell Kathryn. Student, Georgetown (Ky.) Coll., 1956-58, Baylor U., 1958-60; BA, U. Ill., 1963. Anchor-reporter news dept. WCIA-TV, Champaign, Ill., 1960-67, news dir., 1967-80; news dir. WGN-AM and TV, Chgo., 1980-83, WGN-TV, Chgo., 1983-93; pres. Tribune Broadcasting News Network, Inc., Chgo., 1990-91, cons., 1993—; news dir. WLVI-TV, Boston, 1994-96; pres. The Paul Davis Co., 1994—; v.p. First Amendment Congress, 1979-87; mem. World Press Freedom Com.; chmn. UPI Broadcast Adv. Bd., 1983-88, mem. editorial rev. com., 1987; mem. nat. adv. com. Ctr. for Info. Law, John Marshall Law Sch.; mem. nat. adv. bd. Wharton Sch. Broadcast Mgmt. Programs, U. Pa., 1978-81; underwriter RTND Found. Directory of Minority Resources, 1996. Co-author Jane Pauley Task Force Report on State of Broadcast Journalism Edn., 1996; contbr. articles to profl. jours. Founding bd. mem., pres. Boys Club, Champaign/Urbana, 1968-71; pres. bd. Family Svc. Champaign County, 1969-72; nat. treas. Family Svc. Assn. Am., N.Y.C., 1975-77; chmn. Ill. Dept. Pub. Aid Title XX Adv. Coun., Springfield, Ill., 1977-79; v.p., founder United Way Ill., 1975-79; mem. adv. bd. Ill. Dept. Children and Family Svcs., 1968-70. Named Citizen of Yr., NASW, Champaign County, 1969; recipient award Nat. Ctr. Freedom of Info. Studies, Loyola U., Columbia-Dupont Citation, numerous reporting awards from wire svc. and profl. assns. Mem. NATAS (bd. govs., Gov.'s award Chgo. chpt. TV Acad. 1993), Radio-TV News Dirs. Assn. (pres. 1979, chmn. EEO com., disting. svc. award), Soc. Profl. Journalists (pres. 1989), Ill. News Broadcasters Assn. (pres. 1966, Illinoisan of Yr. 1993), Ill. State Bar Assn. (past chmn. media law com., mem. subcom. on cameras in the ct.), ABA (mem. media-law com. 1992—), Headline Club Chgo. (mem. bd. 1982-87, mem. long range planning com.), Ill. Freedom of Info. Coun.

DAVIS, RALPH PAUL, software developer; b. Bklyn., Oct. 31, 1947; s. Bertram Hylton and Ruth Austin (Benedict) D.; m. Jan Yvonne Sharrer,

June 4, 1983; 1 child, Lauren Michelle. BA, Columbia U., 1972. Jazz pianist, composer, 1971-85; software support technician Ashton-Tate, L.A., 1985-86; software developer L.A., 1986-87; sr. cons. Ori Calculon, Rockville, Md., 1987-89; software developer Stafford, Va., 1989—. Author: Windows NT Network Programming, 1994, Windows Network Programming, 1993, Netware/386 Programmers Guide, 1992; author (software) App Meter, 1992. mem. Dem. Nat. Com., Washington, 1994-95. Home: 3206 Titanic Dr Stafford VA 22554 Office: Davis Software Prodns 3206 Titanic Dr Stafford VA 22554

DAVIS, REBECCA ANNETTE, elementary educator; b. Las Vegas, Nev., Sept. 8, 1967; d. Timothy E. and Judith Marie (McBrayer) McGuire; m. Allan Paul Davis, July 8, 1995. BS in Elem. Edn., Auburn U., 1995. Cert. elem. tchr., Ga. Owner, pres. Confetti, Birmingham, Ala., 1987—; intern Auburn (Ala.) City Schs., 1994; tchr. Ga. Sch. Sys., Atlanta, 1995—. Vol. Family Violence Ctr., 1988—; chmn. Univ. Program Coun., 1992. Mem. NEA, Ala. Edn. Assn., Phi Mu. Republican. Home: 700 W Magnolia Ave Auburn AL 35830

DAVIS, RICHARD WATERS, lawyer; b. Rocky Mount, Va., July 9, 1931; s. Beverly Andrew and Julia (Waters) D.; m. Mary Alice Woods; children: Debra, Julie, Richard Jr., Bob, Bev. B, Hampden-Sydney Coll., 1951; LLB, U. Richmond, 1959. Bar: Va. 1959. Pvt. practice Radford, Va., 1959—; dist. judge City of Radford, 1962-80; mem. Pub. Defenders Commn. Va., 1993—; mem. Va. State Bar Coun., 1989-95; assoc. prof. bus. law Radford U.; lectr. Va. Trial Lawyers Assn. Fellow Am. Coll. Trial Lawyers, Am. Bar Found., Va. Law Found. Coun.; mem. ABA, Va. Bar Assn. Home: 101 5th St Radford VA 24141-2401 Office: PO Box 3448 Radford VA 24143-3448

DAVIS, ROBERT ALDINE, academic administrator; b. Broxton, Ga., June 15, 1928; s. Robert Aldine and Leda Estelle (Palmer) D.; m. Phyllis Clough, Aug. 5, 1955; children: Robert Aldine III, Phyllis Blaine, Palmer Clough. B.B.A., U. Ga., 1949; M.Div., Emory U., 1952; S.T.M., Yale U., 1959; D.D., Pfeiffer Coll., N.C., 1970; L.H.D., Westmar Coll., 1977. Ordained to ministry United Methodist Ch., 1952; dir. Wesley Found., Va. Poly. Inst., Blacksburg, 1952-59, Ga. Inst. Tech., Atlanta, 1959-62; assoc. dir. bd. higher edn. United Meth. Ch., Nashville, 1962-69; pres. Brevard (N.C.) Coll., 1969-76; pres. Fla. So. Coll., Lakeland, 1976-94, pres. emeritus, 1994—; mem. univ. senate United Meth. Ch.; pres. Fla. Ind. Colls. Fund., 1978-80; mem. adv. com. bd. govs. U. N.C., 1972-76; sec. N.C. Assn. Ind. Coll., 1970-74; mem. 2d Dist. Ct. Appeal Jud. Nominating Com., 1982-86. Pres. Brevard United Way, 1970, Brevard C. of C., 1975; bd. dirs. Lakeland YMCA, 1976-79; mem. Fla. R&D Com., World Meth. Coun. Edn. Com., 1992—, World Meth. Coun., 1996—; mem. Fla. Coun. of 100, 1993—; trustee Polk Mus. Art, 1986; mem. adv. bd. Lakeland Imperial Symphony Orch., 1990—; trustee Meth. Found. for Higher Edn., 1994—; chmn. Imperial Symphony Adv. Bd., 1996—. Danforth scholar, 1958-59; named Young Man of Yr., Blacksburg C. of C., 1957, mem. Fla. Coun. of 100, 1979—; recipient Outstanding Svc. award Brevard C. of C., 1975, Abraham Flexner award for contbn. to excellence in med. edn. Watson Clinic Found., 1994. Mem. Nat. Assn. Ind. Colls. and Univs., Ind. Colls. and Univs. Fla. (pres. 1980-82), Fla. Assn. Colls. and Univs. (pres. 1985-87), Internat. Assn. Univ. Pres. (bd. dirs. N.Am. coun.), Nat. Assn. Schs. and Colls. of United Meth. Ch. (pres. 1989-90), Lakeland C. of C. (bd. dirs. 1977-86), Ednl. and Instl. Ins. Adminstrs. Inc. (chmn.), Omicron Delta Kappa, Phi Kappa Phi, Beta Gamma Sigma. Club: Rotary (past pres. Brevard).

DAVIS, ROBERT LEE, small business owner; b. New Orleans, July 12, 1928; s. Bemiss North and Hazel (Pettit) D.; m. Sue Vanderford, Feb. 5, 1977; children: Carey Pettit, Andrew Calder. BS in Civil Engring., La. State U., 1949; MS in Civil Engring., Northwestern U., 1951. Foundation engr. Skidmore, Owings & Merrill, Camp Kue, Okinawa, 1953-54; sales engr. CECO Steel Products, New Orleans, 1954-56; mfg. rep. Manufacturers Svc. of So., High Point, N.C., 1956-61; pres., chmn. Coll. Suppliers, Ridgeland, Miss., 1962—. Contbr. article to profl. jour. Trustee Nat. Assn. Coll. Stores, Oberlin, Ohio, 1970-71, Coll. Stores Rsch. & Ednl. Found., 1989-92. Served with U.S. Army, 1951-53. Republican. Presbyterian. Office: Coll Suppliers Co 642 Ridgewood Rd Ridgeland MS 39157-3906

DAVIS, RUSSELL HADEN, association executive, pastoral psychotherapist; b. Washington, Nov. 26, 1940; s. Walter Haden Davis and Virginia (Russell) Edge; m. Iva Lee Crocker, 1964; children: Brandon Denise, Haden Arnold. BA, U. Va., 1962; MDiv, Union Theol. Sem., N.Y.C., 1965; ThM, So. Bapt. Theol. Sem., Louisville, 1966; STM, Union Theol. Sem., N.Y.C., 1978, PhD, 1986. Ordained to ministry So. Bapt. Ch., 1961. Clin. chaplain Ky. State Reformatory, LaGrange, 1966-71, Ctrl. State Hosp., Milledgeville, Ga., 1971-77; assoc. minister The Riverside Ch., N.Y.C., 1977-86; asst. prof. psychiatry and religion Union Theol. Sem., N.Y.C., 1986-91; mem. faculty Blanton-Peale Gard. Inst. Pastoral Psychotherapy, N.Y.C., 1989-91; dir. Psy-Law, N.Y.C., 1989-91; asst. prof. U. Va., 1994, assoc. prof., 1994-95; pvt. practice pastoral psychotherapy, 1974—; asst. prof. Union Theol. Sem., 1981-83; exec. dir. Assn. for Clin. Pastoral Edn., Inc., Decatur, Ga., 1995—. Author: Freud's Concept of Passivity, 1993; also articles. Bd. dirs. Inst. for Relationship Therapy, N.Y., 1981-88, Counseling Ctr., Riverside Ch., 1978-82. Named Ky. Col., State of Ky., 1970; fellow Union Theol. Sem., 1979-81, rsch. grantee, 1987-90; fellow Oaklawn Found., 1980. Fellow Coll. Chaplains (bd. cert.), Commonwealth Ctr. Lit. and Cultural Change (assoc.); mem. Assn. Clin. Pastoral Edn. (cert. supr.), Am. Assn. Pastoral Counselors.

DAVIS, RUTH MARGARET (MRS. BENJAMIN FRANKLIN LOHR), technology management executive; b. Sharpsville, Pa., Oct. 19, 1928; d. W. George and Mary Anna (Ackermann) D.; m. Benjamin F. Lohr, Apr. 29, 1961. BA, Am. U., 1950; MA, U. Md., 1952, PhD, 1955. Statistician FAO, UN, Washington, 1946-49; mathematician Nat. Bur. Standards, 1950-51; head ops. rsch. div. David Taylor Model Basin, 1955-61; staff asst. Office Dir. Def. Rsch. and Engring. Dept. Def., 1961-67; asso. dir. rsch. and devel. Nat. Libr. Medicine, 1967-68; dir. Lister Hill Nat. Center for Biomed. Communications, 1968-70; dir. Inst. for Computer Scis. and Tech. Nat. Bur. Standards, 1970-77; dep. undersec. def. for rsch. and engring., 1977-79; asst. sec. resource applications U.S. Dept. Energy, 1979-81; pres., CEO Pymatuning Group Inc., 1981—; chmn. Aerospace Corp.; bd. dirs. Ceridian Inc., Sprint Corp., Air Products and Chems., Varian Assocs., BTG, Inc., SSDS, Inc., Premark Internat., Inc., Prin. Fin. Group, Inc., Tupperware Inc., Giddings and Lewis Inc.; trustee Consol. Edison Co. of N.Y.; lectr. U. Md., 1955-57, Am. U., 1957-58; vis. prof. computer sci. U. Pa., 1969-72; adj. prof. U. Pitts.; cons. Office Naval Rsch., Washington, 1957-58; mem. Md. Gov.'s Sci. Adv. Coun., 1971-77; chmn. nat. adv. coun. Elec. Power Rsch. Inst., 1975-76. Contbr. articles to profl. jours. Trustee Inst. Def. Analysis; bd. visitors Cath. U. Am. Recipient Rockefeller Tech. Mgmt. award 1973, Fed. Woman of the Yr. award, 1973, Systems Profl. of Yr. award, 1979, Disting. Svc. medal U.S. Dept. Def., 1979, Disting. Svc. medal U.S. Dept. Energy, 1981, Gold medal, 1981, Ada A. Lovelace award, 1984, Disting. Alumnus award U. Md., 1993; inducted into Computer News Hall of Fame, 1988. Fellow AIAA, Soc. for Info. Display; mem. AAAS, Am. Math. Soc., Math. Assn. Am., Nat. Acad. Engring., Nat. Acad. Pub. Adminstrn., Nat. Acad. Arts and Scis., Washington Philos. Soc., Phi Kappa Phi, Sigma Pi Sigma, Tau Beta Pi. Office: Pymatuning Group Inc 4900 Seminary Rd Ste 570 Alexandria VA 22311-1811

DAVIS, SARA LEA, pharmacist; b. Knoxville, Tenn., Aug. 1, 1951; d. Horace William and Margaret Jewel (Hill) D. BS in Liberal Arts, U. Tenn., 1973; BS in Pharmacy, U. Tenn., Memphis, 1976, PharmD, 1977. Asst. mgr. Pharmaco Nuclear, Inc., Chgo., 1977-79; nuclear pharmacist Kansas City, Mo., 1979, Bapt. Meml. Hosp., Memphis, 1979-83; asst. mgr. Syncor, Inc., Washington, 1983-84; staff pharmacist Rite Aid Corp., Knoxville, 1984-87, pharmacist-in-charge, 1987—; rep. 3d High Country Nuclear Medicine Conf., Vail, Colo., 1983; mem. adv. bd. V.I.P. Home Nursing & Rehab., Knoxville, 1985-86. Active Leconte Exec. Women's Coun. Mem. Am. Pharm. Assn., Acad. Pharm. Sci. (sect. nuclear pharmacy), Soc. Nuclear Medicine, Memphis Bus. and Profl. Women's Assn. (bd. dirs. 1982-83), Club Leconte, U. Tenn. Century Club, Mortar Bd., Phi Beta Kappa, Phi Kappa Phi, Rho Chi, Alpha Lambda Delta. Baptist. Office: Rite Aid Pharmacy 508 E Tri County Blvd Oliver Springs TN 37840-2018

DAVIS, SARAH IRWIN, retired English language educator; b. Louisburg, N.C., Nov. 17, 1923; d. M. Stuart and May Amanda (Holmes) D.; m. Charles B. Goodrich, Nov. 18, 1949 (div. 1953). AB, U. N.C., 1944, AM, 1945; PhD, NYU, 1953. Teaching asst. English dept. NYU, 1948-51; tchr. English Elizabeth Irwin High Sch., N.Y.C., 1951-53; editor coll. texts Henry Holt, N.Y.C., 1953-55; editor coll. texts, enclopedias McGraw-Hill, N.Y.C., Rome, 1953-60; asst. prof. English Louisburg (N.C.) Coll., 1960-63; asst. prof. English Randolph-Macon Woman's Coll., Lynchburg, Va., 1963-70, assoc. prof. English, 1970-75, chairperson Am. studies, 1971-87, prof. English and Am. studies, 1975-87, ret., 1987. Contbr. articles to profl. jours. Mem. MLA, Am. Studies Assn., N.C.-Va. Coll. English Assn. (various coms.), Franklin County Hist. Soc. (pres. 1989—). Home: PO Box 246 Louisburg NC 27549-0246 also: PO Box 998 Chapel Hill NC 27514-0998

DAVIS, SHARON DENISE (SHERRY DAVIS), editor; b. Nashville, Mar. 19, 1961; d. Kenneth W. and Barbara J. (Brewer) D. BS in Edn., Tenn. Technol. U., 1986; postgrad., U. Tenn., 1993, MS in Comm., 1995. Tchr. Van Buren County Schs., Spencer, Tenn., 1986-88, Knox County Schs., Knoxville, Tenn., 1989-90; pres. Davis Comm., Waynesboro, Tenn., 1990—; editor Ind. Appeal, 1996—. Editor: The Report-Student Press Law Center, 1994; reporter The Daily Beacon, 1992;. Chairperson acad. scholarships Tenn. Tech. Alumni Assn., Knox County, 1992-93. Mem. Tenn. Rep. Women Fedn., Tenn. Young Rep. Fedn., Nat. Newspaper Orgn. Mem. Church of Christ. Home: PO Box 47 Waynesboro TN 38485

DAVIS, SHIRLEY HARRIET, social worker, editor; b. Brookline, Mass., June 27, 1922; d. Jacob and Matilda (Goldberg) Freedman; m. Edward H. Davis, Nov. 11, 1943; children: Anita Maureen Davis Winn, Lawrence Paul. AB, Calvin Coolidge Coll., 1944; postgrad., Simmons Sch. of Social Work, 1944-45. Social worker Travelers Aid of N.Y., N.Y.C., 1944-48; dir. Community Svc. Workshop of Woodmere (N.Y.) Acad., 1966-70; v.p. for program and membership West End Aux. Peninsula Hosp. Ctr., Edgemere, N.Y., 1973-80; dir. Family Practice Playroom Coll. Medicine, Downstate Med. Ctr., Bklyn., 1977-83; officer mgr. Edward H. Davis, M.D., Loxahatchee, Fla., 1983-93; dir. publicity and pub. rels. Fla. Atlantic Region of Hadassah, 1994—. Editor: Hadassah of Wellington Fla., 1990-93. V.p. membership Hadassah of Wellington, 1992-94, bulletin bus. mgr.; dir. publicity and pub. rels., bd. dirs. Fla. Atlantic Region of Hadassah, 1994—; chair Fla. Atlantic Region of Hadassah Women's Health Symposium, 1996. Wellingtn chpt. honoree Fla. Atlantic Region of Hadassah ann. Woman of Valor awards, 1996; recipient Nat. Hadassah Love of a Lifetime award, 1996. Republican. Jewish. Home: 13604 Firewood Ct West Palm Beach FL 33414-8522

DAVIS, STEWART THORPE, accountant; b. Houston, Aug. 28, 1951; s. Robert Lee and Winifred (Freeman) d.; m. Heather Sutherland, Aug. 26, 1973; children: Stewart, Jared, Corey, Lindsay, Austin, Jayce. AA, Schreiner Coll., 1972; BS in Bus. Adminstrn., Trinity U., 1975; postgrad., U. Tex., San Antonio. CPA, Tex. Staff acct. Pressler Thompson & Co., Kerrville, Tex., 1975-78; acct. Daryl Beach, Kerrville, 1978-79; ptnr. Davis & Mathis, Kerrville, 1979-83, Davis, Klein & Spies, Kerrville, 1983-84; pvt. practice in acctg. Kerrville, 1984—; pres. Stewart T. Davis & Co., Kerrville, 1989—; instr. Schreiner Coll., Kerrville, 1984—; chief fin. officer Communication Solutions, Pitts., 1985—; mng. ptnr. BJS Investments. Income tax commentator daily radio broadcast, 1989, syndicated broadcast, 1990; contbr. articles to profl. jours. Chmn. Kerrville City Coun. Goals for the 80s com., 1981, mem. Kerrville City Coun. Goals for the 90s com.; hon. chmn. March of Dimes, Kerrville, 1980; bd. dirs. Kerrville Little League, 1970-84; bd. dirs. Hill County Youth Soccer, Kerrville, 1980-81, Kerr County Hospice, 1988-92; scoutmaster and cubmaster Boy Scouts of Am.; pres. Tex. State Govs. Cup Gymnastic Invitational, 1995—. Mem. AICPA, Tex. Soc. CPAs (San Antonio chpt.). Republican. Mormon. Office: 222 Sidney Baker St S Ste 430 Kerrville TX 78028-5900

DAVIS, T. WAYNE, executive of golf course management company. Grad., Baylor Sch., Chatanooga, Tenn.; JD, U. Ala. Bar: Ala., Fla. Vice chmn. Riverside Golf Group, Inc., Jacksonville, Fla.; also bd. dirs. Riverside Golf Group, Inc., Jacksonville; bd. dirs. Winn-Dixie Stores, Russell Security Svcs., Enterprise Nat. Bank; chmn. of bd. Gen. Parcel Svc;. Mem. bd. trustees Bolles Sch., Jacksonville Art Mus., Jacksonville Wolfson Children's Hosp., Jacksonville Symphony Orch., WJCT Channel 7, St. Vincent's Hosp. Found. Capt. U.S. Army. Office: Riverside Golf Group Inc 111 Riverside Ave Ste 330 Jacksonville FL 32202-4929

DAVIS, TAMMIE LYNETTE, music educator, director; b. Kingsport, Tenn., Jan. 17, 1961; d. James T. and Gertrude (Bridges) D. BS in Music Edn., Tenn. Technol. U., 1983; MEd in Ednl. Leadership, East Tenn. State U., 1992. Cert. tchr., Tenn. Chorus and orchestra director John Sevier Mid. Sch., Kingsport, 1983—; chmn. dept. fine arts John Sevier Mid. Sch., 1987, 91-93, chmn. adv. bd., 1991-93; participant Music Educators Nat. Conf., 1981—, Tenn. Arts Acad., 1993. Violist Kingsport Symphony Orch., 1979-89, 92—, bd. dirs., 1987-89; mem. (hammered dulcimer folk group) Wire Kwire, Kingsport, 1986—. Designated Career Ladder Tchr. II, State of Tenn., 1992; named one of Outstanding Music Educators, Gov.'s Sch. for Arts, Tenn., 1990. Mem. NEA, ASCD, Tenn. Edn. Assn., Nat. Sch. Orch. Assn., Am. Choral Dirs. Assn., Am. String Tchrs. Assn., East Tenn. Vocal Assn., East Tenn. Sch. Band and Orch. Assn. (orch. chmn. 1992-94), Kingsport Edn. Assn. (treas. 1992-94, pres.-elect 1994—). Nat. Assn. for Preservation and Perpetuation of Storytelling, Tenn. Assn. for Preservation and Perpetuation of Storytelling, Bays Mountain Dulcimer Soc. (pres. 1988-90). Home: 2021 Pendragon Rd Kingsport TN 37660-3432 Office: John Sevier Mid Sch 1200 Wateree St Kingsport TN 37660-4550

DAVIS, THOMAS HILL, JR., lawyer; b. Raleigh, N.C., June 11, 1951; s. Thomas Hill and Margie Wayne (Perry) D.; m. Julia Dee Wilson, May 31, 1980; children: Thomas Hill III, Alexander Erwin, Julia Hadley, Hunter McDowell. BA, N.C. State U., 1973; JD, Wake Forest U., 1976. Bar: N.C. 1976, U.S. Dist. Ct. (ea. and middle dist.) N.C. 1976, U.S. Ct. Appeals (11th cir.) 1982, U.S. Ct. Appeals (4th cir.) 1986, U.S. Supreme Ct. 1979. Reporter Winston-Salem (N.C.) Jour., 1974-76; staff asst. atty. N.C. Dept. Justice, Raleigh, 1976-88; gen. ptnr. Poyner & Spruill, Raleigh, 1988—; arbitrator Am. Arbitration Assn., Charlotte, N.C., 1990—; lectr. Campbell U. Sch. Law, Buies Creek, N.C., 1992—. Supplement editor: Construction Litigation, 1992; contbg. author: Public & Private Contracting in North Carolina, 1985, North Carolina Adminstrative Law, 1996; contbr. articles to profl. jours. Mem. N.C. R.R. Legis. Study Commn., Raleigh, 1985-87; legal counsel N.C. Aeronautics Coun., Raleigh, 1981-88. Capt. N.C. State Def. Militia, 1993—. Mem. ABA, N.C. Bar Assn. (Appreciation award 1989), Wake County Bar Assn. (VLP award 1995), North Hills Club, Lions. Democrat. Presbyterian. Home: 608 Blenheim Pl Raleigh NC 27612-4943 Office: Poyner & Spruill 3600 Glenwood Ave Raleigh NC 27612-4945

DAVIS, THOMAS M., III, congressman; b. Minot, N.D., Jan. 5, 1949; m. Peggy Davis; 3 children. BA in Polit. Sci., Amherst Coll., 1971; JD, U. Va., 1975. Page U.S. Senate, 1964-67; pvt. practice, 1975-79; v.p., gen. counsel Advanced Techs., 1979-90; mem. Mason Dist., 1979-91; chmn. Fairfax County Bd. Suprs., 1992—; gen. counsel PRC, Inc., 1990-94; mem. 104th Congress from 11th Va. dist., 1995—. Republican. Office: US House Reps 415 Cannon Washington DC 20515-4311

DAVIS, THOMAS PINKNEY, secondary school educator; b. Seminole, Okla., Oct. 10, 1956; s. George Pinkney and Flora Elizabeth (Bollinger) D.; m. Leslie Anne Workman, Jan. 26, 1990; children: Brianna Elizabeth, Mary Katherine, James Pinkney; stepchildren: Christopher Lee, Jennifer Dawn, Matthew Joseph, Daniel Jacob, Joshua Issiac Beene. BS with Honors, East Cen. U., Ada, Okla., 1979, BA with Honors, 1979. Dir. math. lab. East Cen. U., 1991-92; tchr., chair math. dept. Roosevelt (Okla.) High Sch., 1992-93; tchr. math., chair math. dept. Keota (Okla.) High Sch., 1993—; book reviewer Jour. Assn. of Lunar and Planetary Observers/The Strolling Astronomer. Reviewer Sci. Books and Films, 1986—; contbr. book revs. to Jour. of Assn. of Lunar and Planetary Observers/The Strolling Astronomer. Fellow Brit. Interplanetary Soc.; mem. AIAA, Am. Astronautical Soc., Assn. Lunar and Planetary Observers, Nat. Coun. Tchrs. Math., Okla. Coun. Tchrs. Math., Alpha Chi, Pi Gamma Mu. Republican. Episcopalian. Home: RR 2 Box 4117 Stigler OK 74462-9633 Office: Keota High Sch PO Box 160 Keota OK 74941-0160

DAVIS, TOM IVEY, II, management executive; b. New Bern, N.C., Feb. 14, 1946; s. Tom Ivey and Carrie Best (Tyson) D.; m. Linda Ann Sawyer, Mar. 9, 1968; children: Tom Ivey III, Matthew Curtis. BS, BA, East Carolina U., 1976. CPA, N.C. Bus. mgr. Davis Oil Co., New Bern, 1973-76; acct. to supr. sr. acct. Peat Marwick Mitchell & Co, CPA, Raleigh, N.C., 1976-80; chief fin. officer HCM, Inc., Virginia Beach, Va., 1980-82, ATC Petroleum, Inc., Wilmington, N.C., 1982-83; v.p. fin., chief fin. officer Brian Ctr. Mgmt. Corp., Hickory, N.C., 1983-84, exec. v.p., chief oper. officer, 1984-95; pres. T.J. Ivey & Co., Hickory, 1996—; bd. dirs. BB&T, Hickory. Bd. dirs. Luth. Nursing Homes, Inc., 1995—, Catawba Valley chpt. ARC, 1994—; mem. bd. visitors Lenoir-Rhyne Coll., 1995—. With USNR, 1973-94. Mem. AICPA, Nat. Assn. Accts., N.C. Assn. CPAs, N.C. Health Care Facilities Assn. (multi-facility v.p., co-chmn. provider rels. coun. 1990-92, chmn. consumer rels. com. 1992-94, chmn. rsch. and date com. 1994—), Ga. Health Care Assn. (various coms.), N.C. Uniform Billing (com. 1988-90), Catawaba County C. of C. (small bus. adv. coun. 1989). Republican. Lutheran. Office: 34 2d St NW Hickory NC 28601

DAVIS, WALLACE EDMOND, JR., university administrator, educator; b. Olney, Tex., Jan. 20, 1932; s. Wallace Edmond and Sara Mildred (Douglas) D.; m. Helen Janis Smith, Aug. 20, 1955; children: Scott, Melanie Williams. BA, Baylor U., 1951, MS, 1955; PhD, U. Tex., 1971. Tchr. Iowa Park (Tex.) Ind. Sch. Dist., 1952-53; high sch. tchr. Corpus Christi (Tex.) Ind. Sch. Dist., 1953-55, elem. tchr., 1955-59, prin., 1959-64, asst. dir. elem. edn., 1964-66, dir. elem. edn., 1966-67, asst. supt. instr., 1967-73; dean of edn. Corpus Christi (Tex.) State U., 1973-89; v.p. acad. affairs Tex. A&M U. at Corpus Christi, 1989-91; pres. Wayland Bapt. U., Plainview, Tex., 1991—; mem. incentive and initiative formula study com. Tex. Higher Edn., coord. bd., 1989—; tchr. edn. Contbr. articles to profl. jours. With U.S. Army, 1952-54, Korea. Mem. Tex. Tchr. Ctr. Network (induction yr. com.). Home: 1307 W 6th St Plainview TX 79072-7811 Office: Wayland Bapt U 1900 W 7th St Plainview TX 79072-6900

DAVIS, WAYNE T., oil company and insurance agency executive; b. La., June 28, 1929; s. Jimmie T. and Ethel (Nealy) D.; m. JoAnne Norris, Mar. 9, 1951; children: Pamela, Gregory, Philip. BS in Agr. Edn., La. State U., 1950; postgrad., Northwestern State Coll., Centenary Coll., 1955-65, U. Southwestern La., 1967-68. Tchr. agr. Bossier Parish Sch. System, La., 1950-53; with Sunray DX Oil Corp., 1953-68; acctg. Shreveport (La.) dist., 1956-67; dist. prodn. office mgr. Lafayette, La., 1967-68, in charge budgets, safety dir., 1967-68; with Doles Ins. Agy., Plain Dealing, La., 1969—; pres. Discus Oil Corp., Plain Dealing, 1969—; cattle farmer, Plain Dealing. Mem. Greater Bossier Econ. Devel. Found., Bossier Pub. Trust Financing Authority, Indsl. Devel. Bd. Parish of Bossier Inc.; pres. Plain Dealing Devel. Assn.; mem., pres. Caddo Bossier Port commn. Recipient Rueben White award for outstanding svc. in vol. econ. devel. Coordinating and Devel. Coun., 1989. Mem. Nat. Assn. Ind. Ins. Agts., La. Assn. Ind. Ins. Agts. (legis. com.), Shreveport-Bossier Ind. Ins. Agts. (bd. dirs., legis. com.), Profl. Ins. Agts. La., La State U. Alumni Assn. (chmn. local grass roots group to contact local legislators where help needed for favorable legis. to La. State U.), Bossier Cattlemen assn. (past pres.), Bossier Farm Bur. (past pres.), Lions (past pres. Plain Dealing, Lion of Yr. award 1991). Home and Office: PO Box 368 Plain Dealing LA 71064-0368

DAVIS, WENDELL EUGENE, English language educator; b. Toledo, Sept. 30, 1934; s. George Addison and Grace Wilma (Nussuer) D.; m. Shirley McCallum, July 7, 1962; children: Thomas, Rebecca. BA, Bowling Green State U., 1956, MA, 1958; PhD, Case Western Res. U., 1962. Asst. prof. Thiel Coll., Greenville, Pa., 1961-63, Purdue U., West Lafayette, Ind., 1963-71; assoc. prof. Purdue U., West Lafayette, 1972—; dir. study abroad program Hamburg Univ., Germany, 1976-77. Author: The Celebrated Case of Esther Waters, 1984, Hardy: An Annotated Secondary Bibliography, 1983, co-author Vol. I, II, 1973; co-author: The Transitional Age, 1973; mem. editl. adv. bd. Eng. Lit. in Transition, 1964—. Recipient Fulbright Faculty award U.S. Govt., 1969-70. Democrat. Presbyterian. Home: 7202 Burtonwood Dr Alexandria VA 22307 Office: Purdue Univ Heavilon Hall West Lafayette IN 47907

DAVIS, WILLIAM EUGENE, federal judge; b. Winfield, Ala., Aug. 18, 1936; s. A.L. and Addie Lee (Lenahan) D.; m. Celia Chalaron, Oct. 3, 1963. J.D., Tulane U., 1960. Bar: La. 1960. Assoc. Phelps Dunbar Marks Claverie & Sims, New Orleans, 1960-64; ptnr. Caffery Duhe & Davis, New Iberia, La., 1964-76; judge U.S. Dist. Ct., Lafayette, La., 1976-83, U.S. Ct. Appeals (5th Cir.), Lafayette, 1983—. Mem. ABA, La. Bar Assn., Maritime Assn. U.S. Republican. Office: US Ct Appeals 556 Jefferson St Ste 300 Lafayette LA 70501-6972

DAVIS, WILLIAM HOWARD, lawyer; b. Monmouth, Ill., May 24, 1951; s. Orville Francis and Alice Gertrude (Hennenfent) D.; m. Susan Claire Parris, April 11, 1981; children: Benjamin Patrick, Jackson Mitchell, Claire Marie. BA with honors, U. South Fla., 1974; JD with high honors, Fla. State U., 1977. Bar: Fla. 1977, U.S. Dist. Ct. (no. dist.) Fla. 1977, U.S. Dist. Ct. (mid. dist.) Fla. 1986, U.S. Ct. Appeals (11th cir.) 1986, U.S. Supreme Ct. 1993. Assoc. Thompson, Wadsworth, Messer & Rhodes, Tallahassee, 1977-80; ptnr. Wadsworth & Davis, P.A., Tallahassee, 1980—; instr. law Fla. State U., 1976-77. Editor notes and comments Fla. State U. Law Rev., 1976-77. Bd. dirs. Legal Aid Found., Inc., 1980-81, Fla. Legal Svcs., Inc., 1988-96, pres., 1993; pres. student govt., chmn., state coun. student body pres. U. South Fla.; chmn. student ct. Fla. State U. Mem. ATLA, Fla. Bar Assn. (2d cir. judge nominations commn. 1986-90, chmn. 2d cir. jud. grievance com. 1988-90), Fla. Bar Found. (bd. dirs. 1993-94, legal assistance to poor com. 1993—), Tallahassee Bar Assn. (bd. dirs. 1982-88, pres. 1986-87), Tallahassee Assn. Criminal Def. Lawyers, Am. Inns of Ct. (master of bench, exec. com. Tallahassee 1994—), Amnesty Internat., Civil Justice Found. (founder), Cath. Social Svcs. (bd. dirs. Tallahassee region 1995—), Fla. Supreme Ct. Hist. Soc., Exch. Club, Gulf Winds Track Club, Capital Tiger Bay Club, Omicron Delta Kappa, Phi Sigma Alpha. Democrat. Home: 914 Mimosa Dr Tallahassee FL 32312-3012 Office: Wadsworth & Davis PA 203 N Gadsden St Ste 1 Tallahassee FL 32301-7633

DAVIS, WILLIAM (WALTER), recruiter, trainer; b. Pewee Valley, Ky., Jan. 5, 1946; s. B.E. Garvey and Clara Virginia (Gordon) D. Student, Ky. So. Coll., 1964-67; BA, U. Louisville, 1967. Vol. community devel. U.S. Peace Corps, Colombia, 1967-69; edn. staff Encampment for Citizenship, N.Y.C. and Louisville, 1969; researcher, editor radio program The Bible People CBC, Winnipeg, Man., Can., 1973; office mgr. Opportunities for Youth, Toronto, Ont., Can., 1974-75; field worker, pub. participation planner Earl Berger Ltd., Toronto, 1975-76; sr. clk. Man. Rent Rev. Commn., Winnipeg, 1976-78; coord. Man. region Can. Univ. Svcs. Overseas, Winnipeg, 1978-79, nat. bd. dirs., 1979; devel. educator Sask. Cross-Cultural Centre, Inc., Saskatoon, Can., 1979-88; trainer So. Empowerment Project, Inc., Maryville, Tenn., 1988—; pres. local 543 Can. Union Pub. Employees, Winnipeg, 1976-78, local 3012, Sask., 1984-85, pres. dist. coun., 1986-87; bd. dirs. steering com. Cmty. Link Bd., Washington, 1991-92; founding mem. Nat. Organizers Alliance, Washington, 1992. Co-editor One Sky Reports jour., 1979-88; contbg. writer Appalachian Reader, 1988-93; mem. editl. com. NOA's Ark, 1994—; contbr. articles to profl. jours. Mem. Save Our Cumberland Mountains, Lake City, Tenn., 1988—, Kentuckians for the Commonwealth, London, Ky., 1988—; chmn. nat. youth svc. program Saskatoon Katimavik, 1986-87; mem. adv. bd. Nat. Coalition Bldg. Inst. East Tenn., 1996—. Named Ky. Col., 1967. Home: 1525 Barbra Estates Dr Seymour TN 37865-3637 Office: So Empowerment Project Inc 343 Ellis Ave Maryville TN 37804-5824

DAVIS, WILLIAM WOOTTON, JR., insurance executive; b. Lexington, Ky., Apr. 30, 1933; s. William Wootton and Gilberta (Knight) D.; m. Mary Ann Smith, Nov. 22, 1959; 1 child, Hannah Logan Davis Emig. AB, Washington & Lee U., 1955. Agt Ky. Ins. Agy., Lexington, 1959-61; exec. v.p. Tobacco Warehouse Ins. Service, Lexington, 1961-67, Security Planning Inc., Lexington, 1967-72, Mktg. Ins. Specialists, Lexington, 1972-76; chmn., chief exec. officer Equity Ins. Mgrs. Inc., Lexington, 1976—. Contbr. articles to profl. jours. Served to lt. (j.g.) USN, 1955-59. Mem. Am. Assn. Mng. Gen. Agts., Nat. Assn. Profl. Surplus Lines Offices, USA Alliance (pres. 1986-87, 87-88), Rotary, Lexington Club. Democrat. Mem. Christian Ch. Home: 407 Adair Rd Lexington KY 40502-2424 Office: Equity Ins Mgrs Inc PO Box 14032 3201 Nicholasville Rd 600 Lexington KY 40512-4032

DAVIS, YOLETTE MARIE TOUSSAINT, critical care, flight, orthopedic and surgical nurse; b. Port-au-Prince, Haiti, May 8, 1956; d. Edner Casimir and Ursule (Lamour) Toussaint; children: Jacques Edner, Noelle Lorraine. BSN, Incarnate Word Coll., San Antonio, 1985; cert. flight nurse, Sch. Aerospace Medicine, San Antonio, 1988; cert. in basic critical care, U. Tex., San Antonio, 1989; cert. in battlefield nursing, Sch. Aerospace Medicine, San Antonio, 1989; postgrad., Incarnate Word Coll. RN, N.Y., Calif., Ohio, Fla., Tex.; cert. ACLS. Staff nurse pediatrics unit Humana Hosp. San Antonio; staff-charge nurse surg. ICU, Humana Hosp. Met., San Antonio; pvt. practice nurse San Antonio; staff nurse Wilford Hall Med. Ctr.; enlisted as capt. USAF, 1991; asst. DON Avalon Pl., Alamo Height Health and Rehab. Ctr., San Antonio; DON Pearsall (Tex.) Manor Health & Rehab. Ctr., 1995; asst. dir. nursing, wound care mgr. Silver Creek Manor, San Antonio, Tex., 1995—. Capt. USAF Reserve 433d Contingency Hosp., Wilford Med. Ctr., Tex. Mem. NAFE, Nat. Assn. Orthopedic Nursing, Women in Bus., Wound Ostomy and Continence Nurses Soc. Home: 6102 Prince Charles San Antonio TX 78240-1949 Office: Silver Creek Manor 9014 Timberpath San Antonio TX 78250

DAVIS-FLOYD, ROBBIE ELIZABETH, anthropologist, educator; b. Casper, Wyo., Apr. 26, 1951; d. Walter Gray and Robbie Elizabeth (Peyton) Davis; m. Robert Newton Floyd, June 30, 1978; children: Peyton Elizabeth, Jason Phillip. BA summa cum laude with spl. honors, U. Tex., 1972, MA in Anthropology/Folklore, 1974, PhD in Anthropology/Folklore, 1986. Tchr. h.s. St. Mary's Hall, San Antonio, 1977-79; teaching asst. dept. anthropology U. Tex., Austin, 1979; adj. asst. prof. dept. sociology/anthropology U. Tenn., Chattanooga, 1980-83; asst. prof. dept. anthropology Trinity U., San Antonio, 1987-89; vis. lectr. dept. anthropology Rice U., Houston, 1993-96, rsch. assoc. dept. anthropology, 1994-96; rsch. fellow dept. anthropology U. Tex., Austin, 1994-96; lectr. and presenter in field. Author: Birth as an American Rite of Passage, 1992; editor: Birth in Four Cultures, 1993; mem. editl. bd. Jour. Pre-and Perinatal Psychology; contbr. chpts. to books, revs. to jour. and orgns., articles to peer-reviewed profl. publs. Recipient Fetzer Inst. award, 1994; faculty devel. grantee Trinity U., 1988-89, NEH grantee, 1980; rsch. fellow U. Tex. Mem. APHA, Am. Anthropol. Assn., Soc. for Social Study of Sci., Soc. for Med. Anthropology, Assn. for Feminist Anthropology, Am. Holistic Med. Assn., Am. Ethnol. Soc., Am. Folklore Soc., Assn. for Pre- and Perinatal Psychology and Health (bd. dirs.), Coun. on Anthropology and Reprodn., Internat. Childbirth Edn. Assn., Midwive's Alliance of N.Am., Social Neurosci. Network, Phi Beta Kappa, Phi Kappa Phi. Democrat. Home: 804 Crystal Creek Dr Austin TX 78746-4706 Office: B128 1301 Capital of Texas Hwy Austin TX 78746

DAVIS-IMHOF, NANCY LOUISE, elementary school educator; b. Stamford, Conn., Feb. 17, 1940; d. Ernest A. and Margaret (Carlson) Davis; m. William A. Imhof, Nov. 17, 1962 (div. Dec. 1989); children: Samuel, Jacqueline, Susan. BA, Barnard Coll., 1962; MEd, George Mason U., 1975. Cert. tchr., Va. Tchr. Arlington (Va.) Pub. Schs., 1975—; freelance photographer. Mem. family life edn. com., Arlington Pub. Schs., 1990-91; mem. ad hoc com. on future of T.J. Community Ctr., 1991; mem. vestry St. Georges Episcopal Ch., Arlington, 1987-90. Arlington Sch. System grantee, 1988-89. Mem. NEA, Va. Edn. Assn., Arlington Edn. Assn. (sch. rep. 1989, 90). Democrat. Home: 894 N Ohio St Arlington VA 22205-1530 Office: Arlington Traditional Sch 855 N Edison St Arlington VA 22205

DAVIS-LEWIS, BETTYE, nursing educator; b. Egypt, Tex., Sept. 19, 1939; d. Henry Sr. and Eliza (Baylock) Davis; divorced; children: Kim Michelle, Roderick Trevor. BS, Prarie View A&M U., 1959; BA in Psychology, U. Houston, 1972; MEd, Tex. Southern U., 1974, EdD, 1982. Dir. edn. Houston Internat. Hosp., 1987—; dir. nurses Mental Health & Mental Retardation Auth. Harris County, Houston, 1982-87, Riverside Gen. Hosp., Houston; CEO, owner Diversified Health Care Systems, Inc., Houston, 1985—; asst. clin. prof. psychiatric nursing U. Tex., 1988—; asst. prof. allied health sci. Tes. Southern U., Houton, 1989—; adj. prof. Coll. Nursing, Prairie View (Tex.) A&M U., 1986—; lectr. in field; leadership extern. Mem. Harris County Coun. Orgns., 1987—; mem. polit. action com. Coalition 100 Black Women, 1988—; founder, mem. Hattie White aux. br. NAACP, 1988; mem. grievance com. State Bar Tex., 1988—; chmn. S.W. Regional Nat. Black Leadership Initiative on Cancer, 1988—; grad. Leadership Tex. Recipient Disting. Rsch. award Internat. Soc. Hypertension; fellow Am. Leadership Forum. ellow Internat. Soc. Hypertension in Blacks; mem. Nat. Black Nurses Assn. (bd. d irs.), Sigma Theta Tau, Chi Eta Phi. Home: 9114 Mcafee Dr Houston TX 77031-1104

DAVISON, E. HOLLY O., home economics educator; b. Kingsport, Tenn., Oct. 29, 1953; d. Joe and Mary Elizabeth (Holly) Osborne; m. Timothy Mark Davison, June 23, 1973. AA, Hiwassee Jr. Coll., 1973; BS, E. Tenn. State U., 1977, MA, 1980, postgrad.; cert. in supervision and adminstrn., 1989. Mayor City of Watauga, Tenn., 1983-85; orientation isntr. JTPA Summer Youth Program, Johnson City, Tenn.; tchr. home econs., occupl. food svc. Science Hill H.S., Johnson City Schs.; presenter many local, state, and nat. presentations. Mem. Gender Fairness commn. Tenn. Supreme Ct., 1994-96; bd. dirs. N.E. Tenn. Women's Polit. Caucus. Recipient Freedom of Info. Citizen award, 1983, Program of Excellence award Tenn. Sch. Bd. Assn., 1990, 91, Program of Excellence award Nat. Sch. Bd. Assn., 1996; EXCEL scholar, 1986. Mem. NEA, AAUW, Nat. Assn. Vocat.-Tech. Edn. Commn. (4 nat. program awards 1989-91), Am. Vocat. Assn. (equity cons. region 2), Tenn. Edn. Assn. (equity cons. region 2), Tenn. Edn. Assn. (status of women com. 1990-92, Susan B. Anthony award 1990), Tenn. Vocat. Assn., Tenn. Mcpl. League (bd. dirs. 1984-85, Women in Govt. pres. 1984-85), Internat. Platform Assn., Johnson City Edn. Assn. (bldg. rep. 1980-81, 88-89, chmn. social com. TEA del. 1981, 83, 84, PACE Coun. 1982-86, 95-96, co-pres. 1993-94, Disting. Tchr. of Yr. 1988, 95), Phi Kappa Phi, Alpha Delta Kappa, Delta Kappa Gamma, Phi Delta Kappa. Home: 221 E 4th Ave Watauga TN 37694-3043

DAVISON, ELIZABETH JANE LINTON, education educator; b. Las Cruces, N.Mex., Mar. 9, 1931; d. Melvy Edgar Linton and Clara Virginia Hale; m. Curwood Lyman Davison, Jan. 29, 1954; 1 child, Lawrence. BS, N.Mex. State U., 1957; postgrad., U. N.Mex.; Grad., Norris Sch. Real Estate, Albuquerque, 1984. Cert. tchr., N.Mex., Oreg.; cert. real estate agt., N.Mex., appraiser. Sec., treas. C.L. Davison, Md., Pa., 1975-88, Clovis, N.Mex., 1975-88; ind. real estate contractor Century 21, Las Cruces, 1984-85; ret. Albuquerque Pub. Schs., 1957-60, 64-68; pres. Sun Dial Enterprises, 1984-95; tchr. Beaverton Pub. Schs., 1960-64. Mem. NEA, Legis. Coun., N.Mex. Albuquerque Classroom Tchrs. Inter-City Coun. (v.p.), AAUW, Phi Delta Kappa (Svc. key). Home: 3013 Cumberland Dr San Angelo TX 76904-6108

DAVISON, FREDERICK CORBET, foundation executive; b. Atlanta, Sept. 3, 1929; s. Frederick Collins and Gladys (Carsley) D.; m. Dianne Castle, Sept. 3, 1952; children—Frederick Corbet, William Castle, Anne Harper. D.V.M., U. Ga., 1952; Ph.D., Iowa State U., 1963; H.H.D. (hon.), Presbyn. Coll., 1977; LL.D. (hon.), Mercer U., 1979; hon. degree, U. N.B., Can., 1985. Pvt. practice veterinary medicine Marietta, Ga., 1952-58; rsch. assoc. Iowa State U., Ames, 1958-60, asst. prof., 1960-63; assoc. Inst. Atomic Research, Ames, 1960-63; asst. dir. dept. sci. activities AVMA, Chgo., 1963-64; dean sch. vet. medicine U. Ga., Athens, 1964-66; vice chancellor Univ. System Ga., 1966-67, pres., 1967-86; pres. U. Ga., Athens, 1967-86, prof. vet. medicine, Fred C. Davison chair Sch. Vet. Medicine, 1986-88; pres., chief exec. officer Nat. Sci. Ctr. Found., Inc., Augusta, Ga., 1988—; bd. dirs. 1st Union Nat. Bank Ga., So. Ctr. for Internat. Studies; bd. trustees Presbyn. Coll. Contbr. articles to profl. jours. Mem. NE Ga. commn. Boy Scouts Am., past pres. Area 5; hon. mem. bd. counselors Oxford Coll. Recipient Disting. Achievement award Iowa State U., 1979, Disting. Svc. award Univ. Ga., 1975, Appreciation award, 1976; named Georgian of Yr. Ga. Assn. Broadcasters, 1980. Mem. Am., Ga. vet. med. assns., Sigma Xi, Phi Kappa Phi, Sigma Alpha Epsilon, Omega Tau Sigma, Alpha Zeta, Phi Zeta, Gamma Sigma Delta. Office: Nat Sci Ctr Found Inc PO Box 15577 Augusta GA 30919-1577

DAVISON, LISA MICHELE, religious educator; b. Radford, Va., May 18, 1966; d. Barnie Allen and Peggy Ann (Graham) Wilson; m. Michael Andrew Davison, Jr., Oct. 14, 1989. BA, Lynchburg (Va.) Coll., 1988; MDiv, Brite Div. Sch., Ft. Worth, 1991; MA, Vanderbilt U., 1996, postgrad., 1996—. Ordained to ministry Christian Ch., 1991. Interim assoc. minister Hurstbourne Christian Ch., Louisville, 1992-93; coll. chaplain Culver-Stockton Coll., Canton, Mo., 1995-96; assoc. prof. O.T. Lexington (Ky.) Theol. Sem., 1996—; campus ministry cons. Christian Ch. in Ky., Lexington, 1992-95. Co-author: (study guide) Pocket Bible Guides, 1996, (curriculum) Journey Through the Bible, 1996. Mem. Canton Coun. Chs., 1995-96. Sommerville scholar, 1987-88; recipient Colby D. Hall award Brite Div. Sch., 1991. Mem. Am. Acad. Religiion, Assn. Christian Ch. Educators, Soc. Bibl. Lit. Office: Lexington Theological Seminary 631 S Limestone St Lexington KY 40508-3218

DAVISON, MICHAEL SHANNON, retired military officer; b. San Francisco, Mar. 21, 1917; s. Paul Root and Gladys Marie (Hamm) D.; m. Jean Helen Miller, June 22, 1940 (dec. Dec. 1983); children: Michael S. Davison, Mrs. C. Clifton Hill III, Donald A Davison; m. Helen Walker Beals, Feb. 2, 1985. BS, U.S. Mil. Acad., 1939; MPA, Harvard U., 1951; LLD (hon.), U. Md. Commd. 2d lt. U.S. Army, 1939, advanced through grades to gen., 1971; intelligence officer 45th Infantry Divsn., North Africa and Italy, 1942-44; lt. col., comdr. Divsn. Infantry Batt., 1944; staff officer Hdqrs. VI Corps., 1944; promoted to col. U.S. Army, 1945; served in variety of staff and command positions, 1945-61; corps chief of staff, then to brig. gen. U.S. Army, Europe, 1962; comdt. of cadets U.S. Mil. Acad., 1963-65; maj. gen. The Pentagon; lt. gen., dep. comdr.-in-chief U.S. Army Pacific, 1968-70; comdr.-in-chief Field Force, Vietnam, 1970-71; gen., comdr.-in-chief U.S. Army Europe, 1971-75; comdr. Ctrl. Army Group, NATO, 1971-75; v.p. devel. Joseph R. Loring & Assocs., 1975-84; mem. world bd. dirs. USO, 1975-91, pres., 1975-78; pres. Shannon Enterprises, Ltd., 1981-89. Decorated Legion of Honor, Croix de Guerre (France); Grand Cross of Merit, Bavarian Grand Cross of Merit (Germany); knight 1st class Royal Order of King of Thailand; DSM with 2 oak leaf clusters, Silver Star, Legion of Merit with oak leaf cluster, Bronze Star with V and oak leaf cluster, Air medal with 8 oak leaf clusters, Purple Heart with oak leaf cluster. Mem. Assn. Grads. U.S. Mil. Acad. (pres. 1983-89), Army-Navy Country Club (chmn. bd. govs. 1990-93), German Am. Bus. Assn. (chmn. bd. advisors), U.S. Cavalry Assn. (chmn. bd. dirs. 1992-94), Army and Air Force Mut. Aid Assn. (chmn. fin. com., vice chmn. bd. dirs.). Home: 2331 S Queen St Arlington VA 22202-1550

DAVISON, PAUL SIOUSSA, lawyer; b. Wright-Patterson AFB, Ohio, Nov. 14, 1955; s. Ralph Scroggs and Aimee (McCormick) D.; m. Pamela Ann Randolph, Dec. 28, 1979 (div. Nov. 1980); m. Georgia Ann Mayfield, Jan. 8, 1982; children: Melinda Marie, Christopher Paul. BA in Polit. Sci., U. Ala., Tuscaloosa, 1977, JD, 1980. Bar: Ala., Ill., Ga. Staff atty. USAF, Altus AFB, Okla., 1980-84; dep. dist. atty., dir. Montgomery (Ala.) County Child Support Enforcement Office, 1984-85; atty. advisor San Antonio Air Logistics Ctr. USAF, Kelly AFB, Tex., 1986—; res. legal advisor San Antonio Contracting Ctr. USAF, Ft. Sam Houston, Tex., 1986-89, Lackland AFB (Tex.) Tng. Ctr., 1989-94, Human Systems Ctr. Brooks AFB, Tex., 1994—. Author: ATC Lawyers Guide to Base Contracting, 1987. Capt. USAF, 1980-84; adv. to major USAFR, 1991—. Mem. ABA, Fed. Bar Assn., Ala. State Bar, State Bar of Ga., Ill. State Bar Assn., Pi Sigma Alpha, Phi Alpha Delta. Republican. Episcopalian. Office: San Antonio Air Logistics Ctr Attn: JAN 204 Lombard Dr San Antonio TX 78241-5609

DAVISON, VICTORIA DILLON, real estate executive; b. Ada, Okla., Jan. 11, 1949; d. Wiliam Jackson Jr. and Helen Lucille (Cate) Dillon; m. Charles Alton Jewett, July 7, 1973 (div.); m. Denver Norris Davison, May 31 1985; stepchildren: Shaun, Malia, Denver II. BFA, Tulane U., 1970. Exec. sec. ITT Corp., Washington, 1970-71; adminstrv. asst. Berens Associated, Washington, 1972-73; real estate trainee Equitable Life Assurance Soc. Comml. Real Estate, Washington, 1974-75, real estate analyst, sr. appraiser, 1976-82; v.p. Am. Security Corp., Washington, 1983-85; exec. v.p. Ada Shopping Ctr., Inc., 1985—; pres. Victoria Properties, Ltd., Ada, 1989—; bd. dirs. W.J. Dillon Co., Inc., Ada, Ada Shopping Ctr. Inc. Jr. warden and vestry St. Luke's Episcopal Ch., Ada, 1990-91. Mem. Ada Area C. of C. (bd. dirs. 1990, co-chmn. area retail 1990-92), Appraisal Inst. (MAI), Edn. for Ministry (award 1992), Ada Music Club, Tanti, Leadership Ada. Republican. Home: 825 W Kings Rd Ada OK 74820-8045 Office: Victoria Properties Ltd 902 Arlington Ctr Ste 196 Ada OK 74820-2883

DAWES, ROBERT LEO, research company executive; b. Big Spring, Tex., Mar. 5, 1945; s. William Robert and Josephine Melloo (Duflot) D.; m. Rosemary Mae Nelson, Oct. 10, 1970; children: Sara Michelle, Karen Melissa. BS in Math., Tex. Tech U., 1966, MS in Math., 1968; PhD in Math., U. Tex., 1977. Mem. tech. staff Tex. Instruments, Inc., Dallas, 1975-81; sr. specialist E-Systems, Inc., Garland, Tex., 1981-85; pres. Martingale Rsch. Corp., Allen, Tex., 1985-94; founder, chair Metroplex Inst. Neural Dynamics, Dallas, 1986-90. Mem. city coun. City of Parker (Tex.), 1988—. Lt. USNR, 1968-71. Mem. IEEE (chmn. Dallas chpt., Acoustics, Speech and Signal Processing Soc. 1988), Internat. Neural Network (chair math. and theory spl. interest group 1990-92). Home: 4308 Sycamore Ln Parker TX 75002-5908 Office: Martingale Rsch Corp 100 Allentown Pky Ste 211 Allen TX 75002-4200

DAWKINS, DAVID MICHAEL, data processing executive; b. Royston, Ga., Mar. 27, 1948; s. Hugh Erwin and Dorothy Nell (David) D.; m.Gloria Anne Robinson, June 27, 1970; children: David Michael Robinson. Student, Anderson Coll., S.C., 1968, Furman U., 1975, C. Wesleyan U., 1993. Programmer M. Lowenstein, Anderson, S.C., 1969-72; software/programmer Steel Heddle Mfg. Co., Greenville, S.C., 1972-76; project mgr. Riegel Textile/Mt. Vernon, Greenville, 1976-87; communication/info. ctr./ops. supr. Hoechst Celanese Corp., Greer, S.C., 1987—; cons. in field; bd. dirs. Robinson & Dawkins, Greenville, 1970—; sound/light engr. First Presbyn. Ch., Greenville, 1988—. Vol. Greenville County Schs., 1987—, Pelmountco Community Club, 1975—. Mem. Assn. for System Mgmt., C. of C. Greenville (launch dir. 1988—), Pelmountco Swim and Racquet Club, Golf Club. Home: 4588 Coach Hill Dr Greenville SC 29615-3804 Office: Hoechst Celanese Hood Rd Greer SC 29651

DAWKINS, DIANTHA DEE, librarian; b. McCamey, Tex., Oct. 6, 1942; d. Kirby Walls and Lucille (Watson) D. BA U. Tex., 1966, MLS, 1971. Cert. sch. librarian. Asst. librarian Lee High Sch., Midland, Tex., 1966-70; asst. librarian, media coord. Midland High Sch., 1970-73; librarian Austin Freshman Sch., Midland, 1973-79; librarian, media coord. Lee Freshman High, 1979—; lead librarian Midland ISD, 1994—. Editor Communication Report, 1980-81. Bd. dirs. Meml. Christian Ch., Midland, 1980-82, sec. bd., 1982. Treas. Lee Freshman PTA, 1985-86, mailing chmn., 1986-93, life mem.; mem. MISD Comms. Com., 1988-95, 96—, Ednl. Improvement Coun., 1991—. Mem. ALA, Tex. Library Assn. (life; coms. 1981-89, 91-94, 95—, coun. 1984-86 dist. chmn. elect 1985-86, 95-96, chmn. 1986-87, 96—), Am. Assn. Sch. Librarians (affiliate assembly 1979, 82), Tex. Assn. Sch. Librarians (chmn. 1979-80, coun. 1978-86, dist. workshop coord. 1989—), Tex. Classroom Tchrs. Assn., Midland Classroom Tchrs. (dir. 1976-84, 86-88, pres. 1979-80), Tex. State Tchrs. Assn. (life; dir. ex-officio 1979-80), Grad. Sch. Library and Info. Sci. U. Tex. (life), U. Tex. Ex-Students (life), Freedom to Read Found., Tex. Hist. Assn., Delta Kappa Gamma., Epsilon Eta (first v.p. 1988-90, pres. 1990-92). Mem. Disciples of Christ Ch. Home: PO Box 80459 Midland TX 79708-0459 Office: Lee Freshman Sch Libr 1400 E Oak Ave Midland TX 79705-6899

DAWLEY, WILLIAM RILEY, society administrator; b. Abilene, Tex., July 23, 1959; s. James Harvey and Margie Anelle (Sullivan) D.; m. Virginia Lois Wilhelm, Oct. 10, 1987; 1 child, William Harrison. BBA in Mktg., Tex. A&M U., 1984. Cert. assoc. in fidelity and surety bonding, Ins. Inst. Am. Supt. U.S. Home Corp., Dallas, 1985-86, Tom Cooper Homes, Dallas, 1986; contract rep. SAFECO Ins. Cos., Dallas, 1986-90; br. mgr. Amwest Surety Ins. Co., San Antonio, 1990-91, Atlanta, 1991; br. mgr. Universal Surety of Am., San Antonio, 1991—. Mem. Nat. Assn. Surety Bond Prodrs. (affiliate), Am. Subcontractors Assn. (San Antonio chpt.), Surety Assn. South Tex. (pres. 1992-93), Builders Exch. Tex., Tex. A&M U. Assn. of Former Students, Woodlake Country Club. Office: Universal Surety Am 404 E Ramsey Rd Ste 106 San Antonio TX 78216-4665

DAWN, FREDERIC SAMUEL, chemical and textile engineer; b. Shanghai, Republic of China, Nov. 24, 1916; s. Keith Frederic and Paula (Yui) D.; m. Marie Dunn; children: Robert, William, Victoria. BS in Chemistry summa cum laude, China Inst. Tech., 1936; MS in Textile Engring., U. Lowell and N.C. State U., 1938, 39; PhD in Chemistry, Nat. Inst. Tech., 1948; DSc in Chemistry with honors, China Inst. Tech., 1967. Prof. China Inst. Tech., Shanghai, 1939-49; dir. rsch. China Textile Ind., Inc., Shanghai, 1945-49; postdoctoral rsch. fellow and assoc. U. Wis., Madison, 1950-55; dir. rsch. Decar Plastic Corp., Madison, 1955-60; supervisory rsch. engr. USAF, Aeronautical Systems Div., Wright Patterson AFB, 1960-62; chief matls. rsch. lab. NASA Manned Spacecraft Ctr., Houston, 1962-76; dir. adv. matls. rsch. and devel. NASA Johnson Space Ctr., Houston, 1976-89, chief engr., sr. exec. svc. Fed. Govt., 1989—; adv. bd. Nat. Elec. Mfrs. Assn., N.Y.C., 1956-60. Tech. adv. com. Jour. Indsl. Fabrics, 1985-87; contbr. articles to profl. jours. Bd. dirs. Houston Sister City Soc., 1970—; mem. Presdl. Task Force, Washington, 1982—; mem. bd. regents Liberty U., Lynchburg, Va., 1995—. Decorated Legion of Merit; named to Space Tech. Hall of Fame, U.S. Space Found., 1989; recipient Exceptional Engring. Achievement medal NASA, 1984, Sci. medal, 1991, Tech. award, 1991, Presdl. Medal Legion of Merit, 1994, numerous awards from NASA and other govt., agy., profl. and community orgns. Fellow NSPE, AIAA, Am. Inst. Chemists; mem. Am. Chem. Soc. (sr. mem.), Phi Lambda. Home: 2823 Timber Briar Cir Houston TX 77059-2904

DAWSON, EARL BLISS, obstetrics and gynecology educator; b. Perry, Fla., Feb. 1, 1930; s. Bliss and Linnie (Calliham) D.; BA, U. Kans., 1955; student Bowman Gray Sch. Medicine, 1955-57; MA, U. Mo., 1960; PhD, Tex. A&M U., 1964; m. Winnie Ruth Isbell, Apr. 10, 1951; children: Barbara Gail, Patricia Ann, Robert Earl, Diana Lynn. Rsch. instr. dept. ob-gyn. U. Tex. Med. br., Galveston, 1963-65, rsch. asst. prof., 1965-68, rsch. assoc. prof., 1968-89, assoc. prof. dept. ob-gyn., 1989—; cons. Interdeptl. Com. on Nutrition for Nat. Def., 1965-68; cons. Nat. Nutrition Survey, 1968-69. Scoutmaster Boy Scouts Am., 1969—. With USNR, 1951-52. Nutrition Rsch. fellow, 1960-61; NSF scholar, 1961-62; NIH Rsch. fellow, 1962-63. Mem. Tex., N.Y. Acads. Scis., Am. Fert. Soc. Am. Inst. Nutrition, Am. Soc. Clin. Nutrition, Am. Coll. Nutrition, Am. Fertility Soc., Soc. Exptl. Biology and Medicine, Soc. Environ. Geochemistry and Health, Sigma Xi, Phi Rho Sigma. Baptist. Mason. Club: Mic-O-Say (Kansas City, Mo.). Author: Effect of Water Borne Nitrites on the Environment of Man; contbr. numerous articles to profl. jours., chpts. to books. Achievements include research on prenatal nutrition, male fertility, epidemiology of lithium in Tex., biochemical changes associated with pre-menstrual syndrome. Home: 15 Chimney Corners Dr La Marque TX 77568-5274 Office: U Tex Med Br Dept Ob-Gyn Galveston TX 77550

DAWSON, GARY JOHN, defense firm analyst; b. Niagara Falls, N.Y., Jan. 26, 1962; s. Jack Ernawld and Dorothy Florence (Bowen) D. BA, Buffalo State Coll., 1984; MA, George Washington U., 1987. Writer Def. and Fgn. Affairs, Washington, 1986-87; nat. security analyst Sys. Planning Corp., Arlington, Va., 1987-95; energy mgmt. specialist Titan Sys. Group, Reston, Va., 1995—. Contbg. author Defense and Foreign Affairs Handbook, 1987-88. N.Y. State Bd. Regents scholar, 1980, SUNY Washington Semester scholar, 1983; named for Outstanding Svc. in Polit. Sci. Buffalo State Coll., 1984. Mem. Pi Sigma Alpha. Independent. Roman Catholic. Office: Titan Sys Corp 1900 Campus Commons Dr Reston VA 22091

DAWSON, GERALD LEE, engineering company executive; b. Santa Ana, Calif., July 6, 1933; s. Harold Guy and Violet Jean (Swanson) D.; m. Shirley Jean Webb, Dec. 28, 1966; children: Debbi Lynn, John Guy. Grad. high sch., Santa Ana. Technician Beckman Instruments, Costa Mesa, Calif., 1954-55, mgr. quality control, 1955-57; mgr. Nat. Theaters, Santa Ana, 1958-59; customer engr. IBM Corp., Santa Monica, Calif., 1959-63; engring. specialist IBM Corp., Lexington, Ky., 1963-65, engr., 1965-70, engring. mgr., 1970-75, prodn. engr., 1975-82, sr. engr., 1982-89; pres. MAS-HAMILTON Group/MAS-HAMILTON Security Internat., Lexington, 1990—, chief tech. officer, 1994—. Patentee electronic keyboard, 9 electronic combination locks, access control systems. Bus. chmn. United Way, Calif., 1958; chmn. Rep. campaign, Calif., 1957. Mem. Robotics Internat., Soc. Mfg. Engrs., Elks, Moose (prelate 1969-70).

DAWSON, JAMES DOYNE, historian, educator; b. Cape Girardeau, Mo., Nov. 27, 1941; s. Ralph Purdy and Velma Inez (Parrish) D. BA in History, U. Minn., 1964; PhD, Princeton U., 1974. Asst. prof. humanities Reed Coll., Portland, Oreg., 1968-73, chm. dept. history, 1970-72; editor Sage Publs., Beverly Hills, Calif., 1975-77; sr. lectr. in history Boston U., 1980-88; lectr. in history Mount Ida Coll., Newton, Mass., 1990; adj. assoc. prof. Mass. Coll. Pharmacy and Allied Health Scis., Boston, 1990-91; vis. lectr. High Point (N.C.) U., 1992-94; instr. N.C. A&T State U., 1994—; asst. prof. Elon Coll., N.C., 1994—; adj. faculty Mass. Bay C. C., 1984-91; instr. in history Emerson Coll. Boston, 1989-90; adj. faculty Middlesex C.C., Bedford, Mass., 1988; instr. mil. history MIT, Cambridge, 1986-87; lectr. Northeastern U., Boston, 1984-87; assoc. dir. Higgins Armory Mus., Worcester, Mass., 1983-84; cons., rsch. assoc. MIT Mus., 1984-86; cons. Michael Sands, Inc., 1988, Charles River Mus. of Industry, Waltham, Mass., 1988. Author: Cities of the Gods: Communist Utopias in Greek Thought, 1992, The Origins of Western Warfare: Militarism and Morality in the Ancient World, 1996; contbr. articles and book revs. to profl. jours. Mem. adv. bd. on peace and fgn. policy, coord. arms control Citizens for Participation in Polit. Action, Boston, 1984-90; active Boston Working Group for Common Security, 1988-90; vol. Boston Regional United Campuses Against Nuclear War, 1988-90. Grantee NEH, 1994, U.S. Army, 1983, Medieval Acad. Am., 1972, Am. Coun. Learned Soc., 1975. Home: 4908 Golden Acres Rd Greensboro NC 27409-9509

DAWSON, LEWIS EDWARD, minister, retired military officer; b. Louisville, Oct. 26, 1933; s. Lewis Harper and Zelma Ruth (Hocutt) D.; m. Margaret Ellen Poor, July 29, 1956; children: Edward Rhodes, David Harper, Deborah Louise, Virginia Ruth. BA, Baylor U., 1954; MDiv, So. Bapt. Sem., 1960; postgrad., Presbyn. Sch. Christian Edn., 1977—. Ordained to ministry So. Bapt. Conv., 1960. Pastor Fincastle (Va.) Bapt. Ch. and Zion Hill Bapt. Ch., 1960-63, First So. Bapt. Ch., Great Falls, Mont., 1963-67; commd. capt. USAF, 1967, advanced through grades to col., 1983; chaplain McCoy AFB, 1967-69, Vietnam, 1969-70, Sheppard AFB, 1971-73, RAF, Chicksands, Eng., 1973-76, Keesler AFB, 1977-79; sr. chaplain Ankara (Turkey) Air Sta., 1979-81; mem. USAF Chaplain Res. Bd. Maxwell AFB, 1981-84; sr. chaplain Wright-Patterson AFB, 1984-87; sr. chaplain Elmendorf AFB, Alaska, 1987-89, ret., 1989; assoc. dir. mil. chaplaincy Home Mission Bd., Atlanta, Ga., 1989-93; assoc. to dir. chaplaincy divsn. Home Mission Bd., So. Bapt. Conv., Alpharetta, Ga., 1994—; clk. Triangle Bapt. Assn., 1965-66; chmn. Mont. Indian mission com. Mont. So. Bapt. Fellowship, 1965-66, treas., 1965-66. Mem. exec. coun. Save the Children Fund, Shefford, Eng., 1973-76. Decorated Bronze Star, Meritorious Svc. medal with 4 oak leaf cluster, Legion of Merit, Air Force Commendation medal. Home: 1926 Coventry Way Jonesboro GA 30236-2688 Office: Home Mission Bd 4200 N Point Pkwy Alpharetta GA 30202-4174

DAWSON, SYLVIA ETORA, government employee, vocalist, writer; b. Richmond, Va., June 5, 1955; d. Randolph and Catherine (Greene) Jones; m. Donald Lee Dawson, Nov. 1, 1979; children: Terri, Donald, Summerlyn, Lori. Student, Va. State Coll., 1974-77, St. Leo Coll., Fla., 1982-87. Waitress, hostess Tuesday Restaurant, Petersburg, Va., 1974-76, Gene's Restaurant, Petersburg, 1976-77; billing clk. Wilson Trucking Co., Richmond, 1977; clk. USN Police Dept., Norfolk (Va.) Naval Base, 1985-86; word processing technician Navy Mgmt. Engring. Ctr., 1986; mil. pers. clk., manpower specialist U.S. Army Tng. and Doctrine Command, Ft. Monroe, Va., 1986—. Writer songs. Sgt. USAF, 1978-84. Home: 715 Keppel Dr Newport News VA 23608

DAWSON, WILLIAM STONE See TAZEWELL, CALVERT WALKE

DAY, AFTON J., elementary school educator, administrator; b. Murray, Utah, Feb. 11, 1938; d. Hans C. and Eunice (Greenwood) Jensen; m. Sherman R. Day, Dec. 28, 1960; children: Kristin Day Lester, Brad, Sandra Day Barnes. BS, Brigham Young U., 1960; MEd, U. Ga., 1966; EdS, Ga. State U., 1994. Instr. U. Ga., Athens, 1967; instr., supr. Ga. State U., Atlanta, 1968-69; founder The Day Sch. Pre-Sch. and Kindergarten, 1970; tchr., learner support coord. King Springs Elem., Smyrna, Ga., 1975-86, adminstrv. asst., 1986-93; learner support strategist Bryant Elem. Sch., Mableton, Ga., 1993-94; tchr. Brumby Elem. Sch., 1994—; co-founder Smart Kids. Author four books; contbr. articles to profl. publs.; developer ednl.

program for children Eliminate Your Self Defeating Behaviors. Named Reader's Digest Am. Hero in Edn., 1993. Mem. Internat. Reading Assn., Ga. Assn. Educators, Nat. Assn. Educators, Delta Kappa Gamma. Office: Brumby Elem Sch Powers Ferry Rd Marietta GA 30061

DAY, ANGELA RIDDLE, occupational health nurse, educator; b. Greenville, S.C., Oct. 23, 1963; d. Earl C. and Sandra (Grooms) Riddle; m. Herbert Day, May 26, 1984; 2 children. BSN, Clemson U., 1985. RN, S.C.; cert. occupational health nurse; cert. occupational hearing conservationist, pulmonary function technician, CPR, first aid instr. Staff nurse St. Francis Hosp., Greenville, 1985-86; dir. occupational health nursing, ednl. coord. North Hills Med. Ctr., Greenville, 1986-94; occupational health nrse BMW Mfg. Corp., Greer, S.C., 1994—. Mem. Am. Assn. Occupational Health Nurses, S.C. State Assn. Occupational Health Nurses (com. chmn.). Office: BMW Mfg Corp PO Box 11000 Spartanburg SC 29304-4100

DAY, CHARLES ROGER, JR., editor-in-chief; b. Cleve., Jan. 17, 1947; s. Charles Roger Sr. and Dorothy Jane (Hauselman) D.; m. Judith Ann Babyak, Sept. 11, 1971; children: Christopher M., Margarita M., Gretchen L. (dec.). BA in History, Albion Coll., Mich., 1969. Sports writer The Cleve. Press, 1969-76; asst. editor Industry Week Mag., Cleve., 1976-79, assoc. editor, 1979-81, news editor, 1981-82; editor Modern Office Tech. Mag., Cleve., 1982-84; assoc. editor Industry Week Mag., Cleve., 1984-86, mng. editor, 1986-89, editor, 1989-91, editor in chief, 1991-95; editor Sports Trend Mag., Atlanta, 1995—. Contbr. articles to profl. jours. Bd. dirs. Lakewood (Ohio) City Schs., 1978-93, v.p., 1979, 85, 90, pres., 1980, 86, 91; eucharistic minister, lectr. St. Luke's Ch., Lakewood, 1983—. Mem. City Club (Cleve.), Rotary (Lakewood, v.p. 1982-83, pres. 1983-84). Republican. Roman Catholic. Office: Shore Varrone Inc 6255 Barfield Rd Atlanta GA 30328

DAY, DAVID OWEN, lawyer; b. Long Beach, Calif., Apr. 3, 1958; s. Robert Owen and Linda Sue (Weaver) D.; m. Vicki Temple Butler, Sept. 24, 1980; children: Candi, Chad, Charles, Chase, Catelyn. BA magna cum laude, E. Tenn. State U., 1980; JD with high honors, U. Tenn., 1984. Bar: Tenn. 1984, U.S. Dist. Ct. (mid. dist.) Tenn. 1984, U.S. Ct. Appeals (6th cir.) 1990, U.S. Supreme Ct. 1990. Assoc. Law Office of Donald G. Dickerson, Cookeville, Tenn., 1984-87; ptnr. Dickerson and Day Attys. at Law, Cookeville, 1987-90; pvt. practice Cookeville, Tenn., 1990—. Asst. editor Tennessee Law Review, 1982-83. Frederick T. Bonham scholar U. Tenn., 1981, Harold C. Warner scholar U. Tenn., 1982, Carl W. Miller scholar U. Tenn., 1983. Mem. ABA, Assn. Trial Lawyers Am., Tenn. Trial Lawyers Assn., Putnam County Bar Assn., Tenn. Bar Assn., Phi Kappa Phi, Alpha Lambda Delta. Ch. of Jesus Christ of Latter-day Saints. Home: PO Box 704 Cookeville TN 38503-0704 Office: 19 S Jefferson Ave Cookeville TN 38501-3307

DAY, JANETH NORFLEETE, religious studies educator; b. Birmingham, Ala., Sept. 14, 1945; d. Herschel Harold and Edith Louise (Sanders) D. BA, Samford U., 1967; MLS, U. Ala., 1975; MDiv, Samford U., 1993; postgrad., Baylor U., 1993—. Personnel officer U.S. Navy, Mountain View, Calif., 1969-71; libr. asst. U. Ala., Birmingham, Tuscaloosa, 1971-75; from catalog libr. to assoc. dir. Birmingham Pub. Libr., 1975-90; bus., officer mgr. Birmingham Area Libr. Svc., 1990-93; from adj. prof. to instr. Samford U., Birmingham, 1992—. Mem. Ala. Libr. Assn. (pres. tech. svc. round table), Jefferson County Librs. Assn., Sigma Tau Delta, Pi Gamma Mu, Kappa Delta Epsilon, Phi Alpha Theta, Beta Phi Mu. Baptist. Office: Samford U Beeson Div Sch 800 Lakeshore Dr Birmingham AL 35229-0001

DAY, KATHLEEN PATRICIA, financial planner; b. West Palm Beach, Fla., Nov. 16, 1947; d. John I. and Lorraine A. (Risavy) Simmons; m. Bryan Patrick Day, Sept. 20, 1969; children: Kevin Kristopher, Amy Teresa. BS in Med. Tech., U. Fla., 1969; MBA, Fla. Internat. U., 1980. Cert. Fin. Planner; Chartered Fin. Analyst. Credit analyst corp. lending Southeast Bank NA, Miami, Fla., 1981-83; fin. cons. in pvt. practice Miami, 1983-87; pres. Integrated Asset Mgmt. Inc., Miami, 1987-88; fin. planner Raymond James & Assocs., Miami, 1988; rep. Royal Alliance Assocs., N.Y.C., 1989—; pres. Kathleen Day & Assoc. Inc., Miami, 1989—; guest lectr. Miami Dade Community Coll., Miami, 1988-89, Barry U., 1989. Controller, bd. dirs. Delphi Found., Miami, 1985-88. Mem. Inst. Cert. Fin. Planners, Assn. Investment Mgmt. & Rsch. Office: Kathleen Day and Assocs 7355 SW 87th Ave Ste 300 Miami FL 33173-3565

DAY, RICHARD EARL, lawyer, educator; b. St. Joseph, Mo., Nov. 2, 1929; s. William E. and Geneva C. (Miller) D.; m. Melissa W. Blair, Feb. 2, 1951; children: William E., Thomas E. BS, U. Pa., 1951; JD with distinction, U. Mich., 1957. Bar: Ill. 1957, D.C. 1959, S.C. 1980. Assoc. Kirkland & Ellis, Chgo., 1957-58, Howrey Simon Baker & Murchison, Washington, 1958-61; asst. prof. law U. N.C., Chapel Hill, 1961-64; assoc. prof. Ohio State U., Columbus, 1964-66, prof. 1966-75; prof. U. S.C., Columbia, 1975-76, 80-86, dean, 1977-80, John William Thurmond chair prof. of law, 1986—; cons. U.S. Office Edn., 1964-66; course dir. Ohio Legal Ctr. Inst., Columbus, 1970-75; vis. prof. law U. Southampton (Eng.), fall 1988. Author: The Intensified Course in Antitrust Law, 1972, rev. edit., 1974; book rev. editor Antitrust Bull., 1968-71, adv. bd., 1971—; adv. bd. Antitrust and Trade Regulation Report, 1973-76, Jour. Reprints for Antitrust Law and Econs., 1974—. Ohio commr. Nat. Conf. on Uniform State Laws, 1967-75, S.C. commr., 1977-80; mem. Ohio Gov.'s Adv. Council Internat. Trade, 1972-74, S.C. Jud. Council, 1977-80; chmn. S.C. Appellate Def. Council, 1977-80, S.C. Com. Intellectual Property and Unfair Trade Practices Law, 1981-87. Named John William Thurmond Disting. Prof. Law. Served to lt. USNR, 1952-55. Mem. ABA, S.C. Bar Assn. (bd. govs. 1977-80), Am. Law Inst., Am. Intellectual Property Law Assn. Methodist. Home: 204 Saint James St Columbia SC 29205-3002 Office: U SC Law Ctr Main and Green Sts Columbia SC 29208

DAY, ROBERT MICHAEL, oil company executive; b. Winnfield, La., Jan. 28, 1950; s. Robert Neal and Virginia Ruth (Franklin) D.; m. Noelie Barron, Dec. 20, 1975; children: Robert Michael Jr., Brionne. BS, La. State U., 1976; MBA, U. Houston-Clear Lake, 1989. Roustabout, floorman Global Marine Drilling Co., Houston, 1976-77; sales engr. NL Baroid Petroleum Svcs., Houston, 1977-78; drilling technician East Tex. div. Exxon Co., USA, Houston, 1978-79; sr. drilling technician Southeastern div. Exxon Co., USA, New Orleans, 1979-81, drilling supt., 1981-84; drilling supt. hdqrs. Exxon Co., USA, Houston, 1984-89; drilling supt. Offshore div. Exxon Co., USA, New Orleans, 1989-91; ops. supr. hdqrs. drilling Exxon Co., Internat., Houston, 1991—. Contbr. articles to profl. jours. Ruling elder Clear Lake Presbyn. Ch., Houston, 1987-88. With U.S. Army, 1969-73. Mem. Soc. Petroleum Engrs., Soc. of the 1st Inf. Divsn., Masons, Sigma Pi. Republican. Home: 20730 Chappell Knoll Dr Cypress TX 77429-5510

DAYS, RONALD JEROME, financial professional, consultant; b. Mobile, Ala., Apr. 9, 1956; s. Ramon Nathaniel and Hattie Mae (Marks) D.; m. Esther LeVond Williams, Feb. 14, 1981; 1 child, Sherron Nakia. BS in Math., Morehouse Coll., 1979; BS in Civil Engring., Ga. Tech., 1979; MBA, Savannah State Coll., 1983; M in Fin., Ga. State U., 1991. CFA. Engr. engring. dept. So. Bell, Savannah, Ga., 1979-86; mgr. regulatory BellSouth Corp., Atlanta, 1986-90, mgr. corp. budget, 1990-94; bus. plan cons., 1994—. Dir. Atlanta (Ga.) Jaycees, 1988-91. Named Outstanding Young Man of Am., 1983, 89. Mem. Atlanta Fin. Soc., BellSouth Fin. Soc. (dir. 1991—), Toastmasters (v.p.), Beta Gamma Sigma, Math. Honor Soc., Physics Honor Soc., Sci. Honor Soc. Home: 5608 Treemountain Pkwy Stone Mountain GA 30083 Office: Bellsouth Telecom 23G57 SBC 675 W Peachtree St Atlanta GA 30375

DAYTON, DEANE KRAYBILL, computer company executive; b. Marion, Ind., May 24, 1949; s. Wilber Thomas and Donna Irene (Fisher) D.; m. Carol Mae Noggle, June 2, 1969; 1 child, Christopher Thomas. BA in Chemistry Edn., Ind. Wesleyan U., 1970; MS in Teaching, Randolph-Macon U., 1974; MS in Instrnl. Tech., 1976, PhD in Instrnl. Tech., 1976. Sci. tchr., chair sci. dept. Jessamine County Jr. High Sch., Nicholasville, Ky., 1970-73; asst. prof. instructional tech. sch. edn. U. Va., Charlottesville, 1976-77; grad. asst., teaching asst. Ind. U., Bloomington, 1973-76, asst. prof. instrnl. tech. Sch. Edn., 1977-83, dir. prodn. svcs. audio-visual ctr., 1979-83; dir. media div. CDC, Atlanta, 1981; v.p. cons. svcs. Ednl. Techs., Inc., Charlotte, N.C., 1983-85; exec. mgr. documentation and lang. transl. Intergraph Corp., Huntsville, Ala., 1985—; cons. trainer George Meany Ctr. Labor Studies, Silver Spring, 1978-82; cons., developer Discover Pl., Charlotte, 1984-86; tng. developer First Union Bank, Charlotte, 1982-85, United Carolina Bank, Monroe, N.C., 1984; cons. Anacomp, Sarasota, Fla., 1982-84. Co-author: Planning and Producing Instructional Media, 1985; producer (film) Computer Graphics for Communication, 1982; contbr. articles to profl. jours. Chairperson exhibits com. North Ala. Sci. Ctr., Inc., Huntsville, 1990-92. Recipient Young Scholar award AV Comm. Rev./Ednl. Resources Info. Ctr., 1977. Mem. ASTD, Nat. Soc. for Performance and Instrn., Soc. for Tech. Comm., Assn. for Ednl. Comm. and Tech. (pres. media design and prodn. divsn. 1982, James W. Brown award 1986). Home: 301 Lincoln St SE Huntsville AL 35801-3144 Office: Intergraph Corp Huntsville AL 35894-0001

D'CRUZ, OSMOND JEROME, research scientist, educator; b. Mangalore, Karnataka, India, Sept. 27, 1953; s. Francis Salvadore and Juliana Angelina (Pinto) D'C.; m. Ruby Lynne Waters, Jan. 4, 1985; 1 child, Lauren Allison. BSc, U. Mysore, India, 1973, MSc, 1975; PhD, Indian Inst. Sci., 1982. Faculty instr. U. Okla. Health Sci. Ctr., Oklahoma City, 1990-92, asst. prof., 1992—. Author: Iwanami Immunology Series, 1985, Insect Immunity, 1992; co-author: Antisperm Antibodies, 1995; contbr. articles to profl. jours. including Immunology, Orgyn-Internat. Prin. investigator Rockefeller Found., 1993—. Mem. AAAS, Am. Soc. for Reproductive Medicine (ad hoc reviewer 1993—), Am. Soc. for Reproductive Immunology (New Investigator award 1990), Soc. for Biology of Reproduction. Roman Catholic. Home: 1416 Mary St Oklahoma City OK 73127 Office: U Okla HSC 920 S L Young Blvd Oklahoma City OK 73190

DEAHL, ROBERT WALDO, retired music educator, trombonist; b. Pitts., Oct. 9, 1928; s. Kenneth Joshua and W. Ruth (Jones) D.; m. Gertrude Hlobil Kreuzer, Oct. 1, 1965 (div. Nov. 1972); m. Lora Gay Ching, Aug. 27, 1974; 1 child, Erica Sachiyo. MusB, Oberlin Coll., 1950, MusM, 1952; student, Acad. Mozarteum, Salzburg, Austria, 1963-64. Instr. music Oberlin (Ohio) Coll. Conservatory, 1956-58; dir. Salzburg Divsn. Oberlin Coll. Conservatory, Salzburg, Austria, 1959-64; instr. music Texas Tech, Lubbock, 1958-59, prof. and assoc. dir. sch. music, 1964-94. 1st trombone Lubbock Symphony Orch., 1958-59, 70-90, Midland Odessa (Tex.) Symphony Orch., 1970-76, Roswell (N.M.) Symphony Orch., 1976-91. Dir. choir St. John's United Meth. Ch., Lubbock, 1964-70. With USAF, 1952-56. Mem. Internat. Trombone Assn., Tex. Music Educators Assn. Home: 3212 25th St Lubbock TX 79410

DEAL, ERNEST LINWOOD, JR., banker; b. Florence, Ala., Jan. 5, 1929; s. Ernest Linwood and Nell W. (Willingham) D.; m. Mary Cooper, Dec. 27, 1952; children: Theresa Lynn, Sarah Street, Matthew Cooper, Jennifer Willingham. Student, Florence State Coll., 1947-49; BS, U. Ala., 1952; postgrad., Southwestern Grad. Sch. Banking, So. Meth. U., 1961. V.p. Tex. Commerce Bank, Houston, 1956-65; sr. v.p. Capital Nat. Bank, Houston, 1965-71; pres., CEO Fannin Bank, Houston, 1971-82, chmn., CEO, 1982; chmn., chief exec. officer InterFirst Bank, Houston, 1983, First City Nat. Bank (name changed to First City Tex.), Houston, 1984-88; sr. chmn. First City Tex., Dallas, 1988-91; chmn. bd. dirs., pres., CEO First City Tex., Austin, 1991-92; chmn. adv. bd. Frost Nat. Bank-Austin, 1993—; bd. dirs. Houston Trust Co., United Med. Care, Houston. Bd. visitors M.D. Anderson Hosp., Houston, 1971—; bd. dirs. Phi Gamma Delta Ednl. Found., 1996—; past chmn. Houston Pks. Bd., Houston Aviation Com.; chmn. local organizing com. U.S. Olympic Festival, 1986; Tex. state chmn. U.S. Olympic Com., 1989-93, S.W. regional chmn., 1993—, nat. fin. com.; past chmn. bd. trustees, life trustee Kinkaid Sch.; trustee Southwestern Grad. Sch. Banking. Lt. USNR, 1952-55. Mem. U. Ala. Alumni Assn., Houston C. of C. (bd. dirs., exec. com.), Am. Bankers Assn. (governing coun., state v.p., govt. rels. coun. 1977-82, v.p. 1978-79), Tex. Bankers Assn. (bd. dirs.), Assn. Res. City Bankers (chmn. golf com.), Houston Country Club, Preston Trail Golf Club (Dallas), Austin Country Club, Phi Gamma Delta (bd. trustees 1990-96), Delta Sigma Pi, Omicron Delta Kappa. Republican. Presbyterian. Office: Frost Nat Bank-Austin PO Box 1727 816 Congress Ave Austin TX 78701-2435

DEAL, NATHAN J., congressman, lawyer; b. Aug. 25, 1942; m. Sandra Dunagan; children: Jason, Mary Emily, Carrie, Katie. BA, Mercer U., 1964, JD, 1966. Atty., 1968—; asst. dist. atty. N.E. cir. Hall County, Ga., 1970-71, judge, juvenile court, 1971-72; mem. Ga. State Senate, 1980-93; pres. Pro Tempore, 1991-92; mem. 103d Congress from 9th Ga. Dist., 1993—, 105th Congress from 9th Ga. Dist., 1996—; mem. com. on commerce, subcoms. on energy and power, telecomm. and fin., commerce, trade and hazardous materials. Capt. JAGC, U.S. Army, 1966-68. Republican. Office: US Ho Reps 1406 Longworth HOB Washington DC 20515-1009

DEAL, ROBIN SINK, women's health nurse; b. Lexington, N.C., Jan. 10, 1956; d. Robert Wade and Helen Louise (Younts) Sink; m. Stuart Craig Deal, Jan. 5, 1980; children: Adam Wade, Sarah Elizabeth. BSN, U. N.C., Charlotte, 1979. RN, N.C.; cert. CCE, BCLS instr. Staff nurse labor and delivery Lexington Meml. Hosp., 1979-80; head nurse Davidson Family Practice, Lexington, 1980-81; staff nurse Rex Hosp., Raleigh, N.C., 1982-85; head nurse Mid-Carolina Ob.-Gyn., Raleigh, 1985-91; perinatal educator Rex Hosp., Raleigh, 1991—. Recipient Edith Brocker Alumni award U. N.C.-Charlotte, 1979. Mem. Am. Soc. Psychoprophylaxis in Obstetrics-Lamaze, N.C. Bapt. Nursing Fellowship, Sigma Theta Tau. Democrat. Baptist.

DE ALESSI, LOUIS, economist, educator; b. Turin, Italy, June 29, 1932; came to U.S., 1947; s. Lawrence and Viola (Giaiminietti) DeA.; m. Helen Peak, May 9, 1959; 1 child, Michael L. BA, UCLA, 1954, MA, 1955, PhD, 1961. Asst. prof. Duke U., Durham, N.C., 1961-65, assoc. prof., 1965-68; prof. George Washington U., Washington, 1968-76, U. Miami, Coral Gables, Fla., 1976—; cons. in field. Contbr. articles to profl. publs. Lt. U.S. Army, 1955-57. Fulbright Rsch. grantee, 1959-60, NSF Rsch. grantee, 1971-74, ICER Rsch. grantee, 1992. Mem. Am. Econ. Assn., So. Econs. Assn., We. Econ. Assn., Pub. Choice Soc., Mt. Pelerin Soc., Phi Beta Kappa. Home: 13057 Nevada St Coral Gables FL 33156-6433 Office: U Miami Dept Econs PO Box 248126 Coral Gables FL 33124-8126

DE ALVARÉ, ANA MARIA, systems engineer; b. Havana, Cuba, Mar. 7, 1961; came to U.S., 1961; d. Humberto De Alvaré and Ana Maria Arenas; children: Jessica Maria Thomas, Joanna Maria Thomas. BS in Computer Sci. cum laude, Calif. State U., Hayward, 1984; BS in Math. cum laude, Calif. State U., 1984; MS in Computer Sci., U. Calif., Davis. Computer scientist Lawrence Livermore (Calif.) Nat. lab., 1984-90; tech. staff SGI, Mt. View, Calif., 1990-92; system engr. SGI, Ft. Lauderdale, Fla., 1992—; computer security stds. IEEE-POSIX Std., 1989-92; consulting for security issues Lawrence Livermore (Calif.) Lab., 1990-91; Silicon Studio trainer, course developer, specialist on visual simulation, animation, spl. effects for film and TV, film and TV digital prodn. issues, 1991—. Author: How to Select a Better Password, 1990, A Framework for Password Selection, 1991. Mem. IEEE, Assn. for Computing Machinery, USENIX Assn., Uniforum Assn. Roman Catholic. Home: 866 SW 12th Ave Boca Raton FL 33486-8428 Office: SGI 100 W Cypress Creek Rd Ste 975 Fort Lauderdale FL 33309-2115

DEALY, WILLIAM AUSTIN, JR., federal agency administrator, consultant; b. Florence, Ala., Feb. 1, 1945; s. William Austin Sr. and Emma Louise (Hoffman) D.; m. Linda Kovach, Feb. 1, 1973; 1 child, Tyrone Christopher. BS, Fla. Atlantic U., Boca Raton, 1968; MEd, Fla. Atlantic U., 1973. Cert. in arbitration and mediation. Tchr./counselor/spl. asst. to supt. edn. Broward County Pub. Schs., Ft. Lauderdale, Fla., 1969-73; sr. pers. mgmt. advisor U.S. Office Pers. Mgmt., Atlanta, 1974-78; regional pers. advisor, Employment and Tng. Adminstrn. U.S. Dept. Labor, Atlanta, 1978-83, regional mgmt. analyst, Employment and Tng. Adminstrn., 1983—; cons. in human resources mgmt., 1981-90. Author: (economic report) Looking to the Year 2000: A View From the SE, 1987, The SE 21st Challenge Atlanta 2000, 1987, Challege 21, 1990; contbr. articles to profl. jours. With U.S. Army, 1963-67. Nominated Disting. Performance Nat. Alliance of Bus., Atlanta, 1988, Fed. Profl./Scientific Employee of Yr., Atlanta, 1988. Mem. ASPA, Internat. Pers. Mgmt. Assn., Metro Atlanta Exec. Coun. for Pers. and Human Resources Mgmt., Indsl. Rels. Rsch. Assn. Democrat. Methodist.

DEAN, BEALE, lawyer; b. Ft. Worth, Feb. 26, 1922; s. Ben J. and Helen (Beale) D.; m. Margaret Ann Webster, Sept. 3, 1948; children: Webster Beale, Giselle Liseanne. B.A., U. Tex., Austin, 1943, LL.B., 1947. Bar: Tex. 1946. Asst. dist. atty. Dallas, 1947-48; assoc. Martin, Moore & Brewster, Ft. Worth, 1948-50; mem. Martin, Moore, Brewster & Dean, 1950-51, Pannell, Dean, Pannell & Kerry (and predecessor firms), 1951-65; ptnr. Brown, Herman, Scott, Young & Dean, Ft. Worth, 1965-71, Brown, Herman, Scott, Dean & Miles, 1971—. Regent Nat. Coll. Dist. Attys., 1985—. With AUS, 1942-45, ETO. Recipient Blackstone award, 1991. Mem. ABA, Ft. Worth-Tarrant County Bar Assn. (past v.p., dir., pres. 1971-72, Blackstone award 1991), Am. Coll. Trial Lawyers, State Bar Tex. (dir. 1973-75), Am. Bar Found., Tex. Bar Found. (charter mem.). Presbyterian. Clubs: Ft. Worth Boat, Ridglea Country, Fort Worth. Office: 200 Ft Worth Club Bldg Fort Worth TX 76102-4905

DEAN, BILL VERLIN, JR., lawyer; b. Oklahoma City, Jan. 11, 1957; s. Bill V. and Mary Lou (Dorman) D.; m. Christine Potter; children: Bill V. III, Mary Megan. BS, Cen. State U., 1978; JD, Oklahoma City U., 1981. Bar: Okla. 1982, U.S. Dist. Ct. (we. dist.) Okla. 1983, (no. dist.) Okla. 1986, (ea. dist.) Okla. 1987, Tex. 1990, N.Y. 1992; lic. real estate broker and ins. agt. Second dep. assessor Okla. County Assessor, Oklahoma City, 1978-80; atty. Struthers Oil and Gas Corp., Oklahoma City, 1980-82; cons. Bill Dean & Co., Jones, Okla., 1978—; ptnr. Dean & Assocs., Jones, Okla., 1982—. Mem. Okla. County Bar Assn., Okla. Bar Assn., Tex. Bar Assn., N.Y. Bar Assn., Shriners. Methodist. Home: 200 Cherokee St Jones OK 73049-7709 Office: Dean & Assocs PO Box 1060 110 W Main St Jones OK 73049-1060

DEAN, DAVID ALLEN, lawyer; b. Chattanooga, Tenn., Jan. 14, 1948; s. William Berry and Elizabeth (Connor) D.; 1 child, Hillary Diane. BBA, So. Meth. U., 1969; JD, U. Tex.-Austin, 1973. Bar: Tex. 1973. Asst. dir. Tex. Office Comprehensive Health Planning, Austin, 1973; adminstrv. asst. Gov. Tex., Austin, 1974; legal counsel Gov. Briscoe, State of Tex., Austin, 1975-78, to Gov. Clements, 1979-81; sec. state State of Tex., Austin, 1981-83; ptnr. Winstead, McGuire, Sechrest & Minick, Dallas, (now Winstead, Sechrest & Minick) 1983-93, chmn. pub. law sect., PAC com., bus. devel. com., also bd. dirs., 1994—; shareholder David A. Dean & Assocs., P.C., Dallas, 1994—; pres. Transp. Strategies, Inc., Dallas; pres., CEO Dean Internat., Inc., Dallas, 1994—, Innovative Transp. Strategies, Dallas, 1994—; lectr. in field. Editor: Texas Campaign and Financial Disclosure Manual, 1984; Election Study of Fifty States, 1982. Author: Gubernatorial Parole Policies, 1980. Contbr. articles to Tex. Bus. and Comml. Quar., 1981-83, Dallas Bus. and Profl. Rev. Exec. dir. Gov.'s Criminal Justice Div., Austin, 1980-81, Crime Stoppers Adv. Council, 1979-81; chmn. State Fed. Voter Fraud Task Force, 1982; chmn. Gov.'s Task Force on Health and Human Services, 1975-79, Nat. Gov.'s Health Consortium, 1977-78; trustee Dean Learning Ctr., Dallas, 1970—, mem. exec. com., chmn. nominating com., 1970—; bd. dirs. Girlstown U.S.A., 1973-85, Greater Dallas Crime Commn., 1983—, chmn., 1985-88, former mem. exec. com., past chmn. legis. com.; mem. Interstate Oil Compact Commn., Austin, 1979-83, State Bd. Canvassers, Austin, 1981-83; mem. spl. interim com. Criminal Justice System Tex., Austin, 1981; co-chmn., mem., chmn. subcom. pub. disclosure, polit. funds, and lobby regulations Pub. Servant Stds. Conduct Adv. Com., Austin, 1981-83; v.p., mem. Dallas Challenge Task Force, bd. dirs., 1983-88, mem. exec. com., 1983-88; mem. long-range planning com. St. Mark's Sch. Tex., Dallas, 1983-84; mem. exec. com. bd. dirs., chair pub. policy Nat. Crime Prevention Coun., Washington, 1984—; co-chmn., chmn. legis. com., mem. exec. com. Mayor's Criminal Justice Task Force, City of Dallas, 1985-88; mem. Greater Dallas Ahead, Inc., 1985-86, U.S Marshall Selection Com., 1986-87; mem. exec. com. Tex. Criminal Justice Task Force, Austin, 1986-90, vice-chmn., chmn. legis. com., 1986-90; mem. Citizen's Adv. Com. Long-Range Water Supply Study, City of Dallas, 1988-90; mem. Task Force Pub. Utility Regulation, State of Tex., Austin, 1989-90; mem. adv. bd. Dallas United, 1990-92; commr. Pres.'s Commn. Model State Drug Laws, Washington, 1992-93; co-chair Dallas host com. N.Am. Free Trade Agreement Negotiations, 1992; subcom. chmn. fin. com. Ursuline Acad. Dallas, 1992—, mem. bd. of dad's club, 1992—; co-chmn. Dallas Meml. Ctr. Holocaust Studies, Dallas, 1993; mem. mktg. com. Dallas/Ft. Worth Internat. Airport, 1994—; trustee Meth. Med. Ctr., Dallas, 1992, mem. quality rev. com., 1992, mem. long range planning com., 1992; bd. dirs. Swiss Ave. Ctr. Pastoral Care and Family Counseling, Dallas, 1983-88, Cotton Bowl Coun., Dallas, 1984-89, Tex. Bus. Hall of Fame, Dallas, 1988-90, Dallas Summer Musicals, 1992, Nat. Alliance Model State Drug Laws, 1993, mem. exec. com., 1993; sec. bd. dirs. St. Paul Hosp. Found., Dallas, 1985-88. Served with Tex. Air N.G., 1975. Recipient Spl. Recognition award Dallas City Coun., Mayor of Dallas, 1992. Mem. Am. Prosecutors Rsch. Inst., Tex. Bar Assn. (mem., chmn. spl. com. study Tex. election laws 1982-83), ABA, Dallas Bar Assn., Ctrl. Dallas Assn. (mem. exec. com. bd. dirs., mem. govtl. and legal affairs com.), Ducks Unltd., Am. Quarter Horse Assn., Greater Dallas C. of C. (chmn. N.Am. Free Trade Agreement initiatives, former chmn. pub. affairs divsn., past chmn. state govtl. affairs com., former bd. dirs., past mem. exec. com.), U. Tex. Ex-Students Assn. (life), Sigma Alpha Epsilon. Methodist. Clubs: Idlewild, Terpsichorean, Rainbo lake, Tower, Salesmanship Club (Dallas). Office: David A Dean & Assocs PC 750 N Saint Paul St Ste 1000 Dallas TX 75201-3922

DEAN, EDWIN BECTON, government official; b. Danville, Va., Feb. 7, 1940; s. Edwin Becton and Lois (Campbell) D.; m. Deirdre Anne Jacovides, Aug. 16, 1964; children: Jennifer E., Kristin R., Brian N. BS in Physics, Va. Poly. Inst. and State U., 1963, MS in Math., 1965; postgrad in ops. rsch., George Washington U., 1974-77. Technician, assoc. engr. Johns Hopkins U. Applied Physics Lab., Laurel, Md., 1959-64; physicist, mathematician, electronic engr., and ops. rsch. analyst Naval Surface Warfare Ctr., Silver Spring, Md., 1964-79; owner, mgr. Gen. Bus. Svcs. and Beta Systems, Virginia Beach, Gen. Bus. Services and Beta Systems, 1979-84; Virginia Beach Communique Inc., Virginia Beach, Va., 1980-81; registered rep. First Investors Corp., Arlington, Va., 1971-85; dir. Tips Club of Virginia Beach (Va.), Inc., 1980-82; computer specialist Naval Supply Systems Command, Norfolk, Va., 1982-83; head cost estimating office NASA Langley Rsch. Ctr., Hampton, Va., 1983-90; tech. resource mgr. Space Exploration Initiative Office NASA Langley Rsch. Ctr., 1990-94, sr. rsch. engr. multidisciplinary design optimization br., 1994—. Author numerous sci. articles; presenter in field. NASA fellow, 1963-65. Mem. IEEE, AIAA, Assn. for Computing Machinery, Internat. Soc. Parametric Analysts (past chmn. bd. dirs.), Inst. for Ops. Rsch. and Mgmt. Scis., Am. Statis. Assn., Am. Soc. for Quality Control, Am. Assn. Cost Engrs., Internat. Neural Network Soc., Internat. Coun. Sys. Engrs., Soc. for Indsl. and Applied Math., Am. Math. Soc., N.Y. Acad. Scis., QFD Inst., Sigma Pi Sigma, Pi Mu Epsilon, Phi Kappa Phi. Office: NASA-Langley Rsch Ctr Ms # 159 Hampton VA 23665

DEAN, GARY NEAL, artist, architect; b. Alexandria, Va., Sept. 19, 1953; s. Louie Franklin Dean. BS in Architecture, U. Ill., 1977. Registered architect, Calif., Tex., Ill., N.Y., Fla., Vt., N.C., Wis., Iowa, Ark, Ga., Md.; cert. Nat. Coun. Archtl. Registration Bds.; registered interior designer, Ill., Tex. Designer, draftsman SRGF, Inc. Architects, Springfield, Ill., 1977-79; project mgr. Sarti-Huff Archtl. Group, Inc., Springfield, 1979-82; architect Henningson, Durham & Richardson, Inc., Dallas, 1982-84; prodn. mgr. Bogard, Guthrie & Ptnrs., Inc., Dallas, 1984-85; mgr., project architect Archtl. Designers, Inc., Dallas, 1985-87; pvt. practice architecture Dallas, 1987—; prin. Kaiser Gochnauer Ltd., 1987—; v.p., ptnr. Designhaus, Inc., 1989-94; project arch. Hard Rock Cafe Internat., Inc., Orlando, Fla., 1994—; pvt. practice Orlando, 1995—; v.p., ptnr. Designhaus, Inc., 1989-94; project arch. Hard Rock Cafe Internat., Inc., Orlando, Fla., 1994-95. Prin. works include State of Ill. Capitol, LaCima Club, Las Colinas, Tex., Hackberry Creek Country Club, Las Colinas, Renaissance Club, Phoenix, Creve Coeur Club, Peoria, Ill., Hard Rock Cafe Retail Store, N.Y.C., Hard Rock Cafe, Singapore, Atlanta, Miami, Fla., Madrid, Nashville, San Antonio, N.Y.C., Copenhagen, Myrtle Beach, S.C. Home: 4872 Cypress Woods Dr Apt 124 Orlando FL 32811-3751

DEAN, JAMES WENDELL, military officer, nurse; b. Hamtramck, Mich., Apr. 29, 1948; s. Albert Jack and Kathleen Elizabeth (Freeman) D.; m. Iris Viola Rankine, Sept. 10, 1971; children: James W. Jr., Christopher N., Veronica V. AS in nursing, Wayne County Community Coll., Detroit, 1975; BSN, Madonna Coll., Livonia, Mich., 1980, B in Natural Sci., 1980. RN, Pulmonary Function tech., audiometric tech. Charge nurse Lakeside Gen. Hosp., Detroit, 1975-76, Detroit Gen. Hosp., 1976-77; nursing instr. Automated Acad., Detroit, 1976-77; occupl. health nurse GM-Cadillac Motor

Co., Detroit, 1977-83, Walt Disney World, Orlando, 1983-84; supr. occupl. health nurse Dept. of Def., USN, Orlando, 1984-87; occupl. health nurse VA, Orlando, 1987—; commd. capt. USAF, 1990, advanced through grades to maj., 1992. Crime watch patrolman Buena Ventura Lakes Crimewatch, Kissimmee, Fla., 1986. Maj. USAF, 1989—. Recipient sustained superior performance award Dept. Def., Orlando, 1985, 86, presdl. unit citation USAF, Wurtsmith AFB, Mich., 1968. Mem. ANA, Fla. Nurses Assn., Nurses Orgn. Va. (chpt. rep. 1988—), Cen. Fla. Occupational Health Nurses Assn. (v.p. 1985-86), Res. Officers Assn., AMVETS Post #30, Am. Legion, VFW. Democrat. Baptist. Home: 612 Redwood Ct Kissimmee FL 34743-9028

DEAN, JEAN BEVERLY, artist; b. South Paris, Maine, Aug. 23, 1928; d. Henry Dyer and Doris Filena (Judd) Small; m. Samuel Lester Dean. AS, Becker Coll., Worcester, Mass., 1948; AA, Edison Coll., Ft. Myers, Fla., 1980. Artist Ft. Myers, 1963—. One person shows include Edison C.C. Gallery, Ft. Myers, Joan Ling Gallery, Gainesville, Fla., Berry Coll., Mt. Berry, Ga., Gallery 10, Asheville, N.C., Cape Coral (Fla.) Arts Studio, Barbara B. Mann Performing Arts Hall, Ft. Myers, 1992, Sanibel (Fla.) Gallery, 1993, Barrier Island Group for the Arts, Sanibel, 1994, 96, Sanibel Gallery, 1995, Gallery Mido, Belleview Mido Resort, Belleair, Fla., 1996, No. Trust Bank, Ft. Myers, 1996, Lee County Alliance of the Arts, Ft. Myers, 1996, Art League of Manatee County, Fla., 1996; exhibited in group shows at S.E. Painting and Sculpture Exhbn., Jacksonville, Fla., Southeastern Ctr. for Contemporary Art, Ybor City, Park Shore Gallery, Naples, Fla., 1991, S.W. Fla. Internat. Airport, 1991, 95, Ctr. Art Show, St. Petersburg, Fla., 1991, Lee County Alliance of Arts, Ft. Myers, 1991, Ridge Juried Art Show, Winter Haven, Fla., 1992, Fla. Artists Group, Sarasota, 1992, Women's Caucus for Art, Sarasota, 1993, Polk Mus., Lakeland, Fla., 1993, Barrier Island Group for Arts, Sanibel, 1994, Daytona (Fla.) Mus., 1994, Women's Caucus Art Nat. Show, San Antonio, 1995, Capitol Gallery, Tallahassee, Fla., 1995, Women's Caucus Art State Show, Sarasota, 1995 , Women's Caucus for Art, Miami, 1996, Lee County Alliance of the Arts, Fla., 1996, Fla. Artist Group, Winter Haven, 1996; represented in permanent collections U.S. Embassy, Madrid, Edison Coll., First Fed. Savs. and Loan, Ft. Myers and Naples, Fla., NCNB Bank, Tampa, HealthPark, Ft. Myers, Clara Barton House, Washington, Hirshhorn Collection. Mem. Lee County Alliance for Arts, 1994, 95, 96; chair invitational com. Barrier Island Group for Arts, Sanibel, 1994, 95, 96.; founder Open Doors Lee County Alliance of the Arts, Fla., 1990—. Recipient more than 100 awards. Mem. Nat. Mus. Women in the Arts (charter mem.), Maine Coast Artists, Women's Caucus for Art, Fla. Artists Group. Democrat. Unitarian. Home: 17643 Captiva Island Ln Fort Myers FL 33908-6115

DEAN, LYDIA MARGARET CARTER (MRS. HALSEY ALBERT DEAN), nutrition coordinator, author, consultant; b. Bedford, Va., July 11, 1919; d. Christopher C. and Hettie (Gross) Carter; m. Halsey Albert Dean; children: Halsey Albert Jr., John Carter, Lydia Margerae. Grad., Averett Coll.; BS, Madison Coll., 1941; MS, Va. Poly. Inst. and State U., 1951; postgrad., U. Va., Mich. State U.; PhD, D Nutrition Sci., UCLA, 1985. Cert. nutrition specialist Am. Coll. Bd. Nutrition, 1994. Dietetic intern, clin. dietitian St. Vincent de Paul Hosp., Norfolk, Va., 1942; jr. physicist U.S. Naval Op. Base, Norfolk, 1943-45; clin. dietitian Roanoke Meml. Hosps., 1946-51; assoc. prof. Va. Poly. Inst. and State U., 1946-53; community nutritionist Roanoke, Va., 1953-60; dir. dept. nutrition and dietetics Southwestern Va. Med. Ctr., Roanoke, 1960-67; food and nutrition cons. Nat. Hdqs. ARC, Washington, 1967—; staff and vol. Nat. Hdqs. ARC, 1973—; nutrition scientist, cons. Dept. Army, Washington, 1973—, Dept. Agr., 1973—; pres. Dean Assocs.; cons., assoc. dir. Am. Dietetic Assn., 1975—; coord. new degree program U. Hawaii, 1974-75; dir., nutrition coord. pub. health HHS, Washington, 1973-95, vol., 1996; mem. task force White House Conf. Food and Nutrition, 1969—; chmn. fed. com. Interagy. Com. on Nutrition Edn., 1970-71; tech. rep. to AID and State Dept.; chmn. Crusade for Nutrition Edn., Washington, 1970—; participant, cons. Nat. Nutrition Policy Conf., 1974. Author: (with Virginia McMasters) Community Emergency Feeding, 1972, Help My Child How to Eat Right, 1963, rev. edit., 1978, The Complete Gourmet Nutrition Cookbook: The Joy of Eating Well and Right, 1978, rev. edit., 1982, The Stress Foodbook, 1980; contbr. articles to profl. jours. Trustee World U., 1987—; apptd. rsch. bd. advisors Am. Biog. Inst., 1990. Named Women's Inner Cir. of Achievement N.Am., 1990. Fellow APHA, Internat. Inst. Cmty. Svc.; mem. AAUW (Hall of Fame 1992), Am. Dietetic Assn., Bus. and Profl. Women's Club (cons. 1970—, pres. 1981-82), Am. Home Econs. Assn. (rep. and treas. joint congl. com.), Inst. Food Technologists (blue ribbon spkr. 1972). Home: 7816 Birnam Wood Dr Mc Lean VA 22102-2709

DEAN, MARILYN FERWERDA, nursing consultant and administrator; b. Oak Park, Ill., Oct. 5, 1938; m. Frank Dean; children by previous marriage: Cathy Cree Denisco, Cliff Cree; stepchildren: Derek, Jeff Dean. BSN, U. Miami (Fla.), 1960; MPH, U. Mich., 1963. With Broward County Health Dept., Fort Lauderdale, Fla., 1960-65, supr., 1963-65; with Med. Pers. Pool, Fort Lauderdale, 1971-78; dir. nursing svc. North Beach Med. Ctr., Ft. Lauderdale, 1978-79, regional dir. Med. Pers. Pool, 1979-82, nat. dir. profl. and consumer affairs, 1982-85, nat. dir., health care svcs., 1985-92; Interim Health Care Nat. Dir. Health Care Svcs., 1992—; instr. Broward Community Coll., 1975-78. Mem. editl. bd. Home Health Care Nurse mag., 1996—. Bd. dirs. Luth. High Sch., 1980-83. Mem. ANA (bd. dirs.), Nat. League Nursing, Am. Assn. Continuity of Care, Inservice Educators S. Fla. (pres. 1977-78), Assn. Care of Children's Health, Nat. Hospice Orgn. Lutheran. Home: 5521 NE 19th Ave Fort Lauderdale FL 33308-3104 Office: 2050 Spectrum Blvd Fort Lauderdale FL 33309-3008

DEAN, PAMELA LEE, journalist; b. Chgo., Apr. 25, 1959; d. Floyd Andrew and Ruby Lee (Shipp) Jefferson; m. Marc E. Dean, Aug. 23, 1983 (div. 1987); children: Nicholas C., Lea N., Megan A. BA in journalism, Columbia Coll., 1985. Cert. FCC Restricted Radio Telephone Operator. Editl. asst., asst. editor H.H. Backer Assocs., Chgo., 1988; religion editor, investigative reporter Chgo. Daily Defender, 1988-89, asst. editor, night editor, 1990-92; radio announcer, producer Sta: SOUTH 106, Columbus, Ga., 1995-96; radio announcer Sta: FOXIE 105/WOKS, Columbus, 1996—; mentor Urban Journalism Workshop Youth Communication Chgo. Ctr., 1989-92; judge communication scholars Archdiocese Chgo., 1989. Author: (play) Ressurection at Daybreak, 1994. Walk coordinator Nat. Multiple Sclerosis Soc. Ga. chpt., Columbus, 1996. Named Woman of Yr. God Never Fails Ministries, Chgo, 1989; honorable mention Reporting Women in Communications, Chgo., 1989. Mem. Nat. Multiple Sclerosis Soc. (Ga. chpt.). Democrat. Roman Catholic. Home: 4202 Swann St Columbus GA 31903

DEAN, RALPH ADRIAN, plant pathologist, educator; b. Huddersfield, Eng., Sept. 21, 1958; came to U.S., 1980; s. Peter Allan and Eileen (Cleary) D.; m. Nancy Sue Doubrava, July 12, 1987; children: Graham, Julia. BS in Botany with honors, U. London, 1980; PhD in Plant Pathology, U. Ky., 1986; postgrad., U. Ga., 1989. Asst. prof. plant pathology Clemson (S.C.) U., 1990-95, assoc. prof., 1996—. Sr. editor Phytophtology; contbr. articles to profl. jours. Mem. AAAS, Am. Soc. Microbiology, Am. Phytopathol. Soc., Phytochem. Soc. N.Am., Sigma Gamma Delta. Home: 214 Hunter Ave Clemson SC 29631 Office: Clemson Univ Dept Plant Pathology Clemson SC 29534

DEAN, ROBERT FRANKLIN, insurance company executive; b. Houston, Nov. 1, 1942; s. Claude Nathan and Nellie Gladis (Davis) D.; m. Kathy Copeland, Aug. 16, 1963 (div. Jan. 1970); 1 child, Robert Franklin Jr.; m. Betsy Ellen Kniehl, Sept. 20, 1975 (dec. Jan. 1994); children: James, Kyle, Courtney Elizabeth; m. Charlene Harmon Sailors, Feb. 25, 1995. BBA in Bus. Mgmt., U. Houston, 1968. Cert. safety profl. Safety engr. Gulf Ins. Group, Houston, 1968-69, Indsl. Indemnity Ins., Houston, 1969-75; loss control mgr. Crum & Forester Ins. Group, Houston, 1975-78; sr. mktg. cons. Aetna Ins. Co., Houston, 1978-80; v.p. mktg. div. Stanley Ins., Houston, 1980-81; pres., chief exec. officer Drew, Dean & Vaughan Ins. Agy. Inc., Houston, 1981—. Head football coach Alief Youth Assn., Houston, 1975-81; mem. steering com. Rep. Party, Houston, 1988; bd. trustees Harris County Impact Political Action Com., 1991-96. Recipient Cert. of Appreciation, Spring Br. Sch. Dist., 1985, Outstanding Svc. award Tex. Automotive Assn., 1985. Mem. Am. Soc. Safety Engrs. (cert. com. on edn. Houston chpt. 1975-76), Houston Gemini Automation Group (bd. dirs. Houston chpt. 1989-90, pres. 1990-92), Ind. Ins. Agts. of Am. (bd. dirs. Houston chpt. 1991-96), Houston Assn. of Ins. Agts. (legis. com. 1993-94, mem. recreation com., charitable events bd. liaison, bd. dirs. charitable found.), Gemini User of Am.; trustee Harris County Impact Com., 1991—. Republican. Episcopalian. Office: Drew Dean & Vaughan Ins Agy 11011 Richmond Ave Ste 333 Houston TX 77042-6707

DEAN, TAD, research laboratory executive. Dir. R&D So. Testing & Rsch. Labs., Wilson, N.C. Office: 3809 Airport Dr Wilson NC 27890

DEAN, VIRGINIA AGEE, principal; b. Duff, Tenn., Oct. 15, 1945; d. Jack Harris and Edna Virginia Agee; m. Herman Ronald Dean, July 10, 1965; children: Virginia Renée, Ronald Craig. BEdin Elem. Edn., Lander Coll., 1967; MEd, Clemson U., 1974. 7th grade reading and maths. tchr. Ellen Woodside Elem. Sch., Pelzer, S.C., asst. prin.; head of guidance dept. Beck Mid. Sch., Greenville, S.C.; prin. Blythe Elem. Sch., Greenville, S.C., Fork Shoals Elem. Sch., Pelzer, S.C., Oakview Elem. Sch., Simpsonville, S.C.; curriculum cons. Greenville Sch. Dist., S.C.; proprietor, mgr. Basquettes, Inc., Greenville, S.C., cons., 1989, 90; spkr., cons. SCORE, Greenville, 1989, 90; mem. supt. adv. bd. Sch. Dist. Greenville County, 1975, 76. Recipient Small Bus. award of yr. Greenville SCORE chpt., 1985. Mem. S.C. DAR (Outstanding jr. mem. 1980). Home: 596 Reedy Fork Rd Piedmont SC 29673 Office: Oakview Elem Sch 515 Godfrey Rd Simpsonville SC 29681

DEAN, WILLIAM GROMER, insurance company executive; b. Kansas City, Mo., Sept. 6, 1933; s. William David and Lulu (Gromer) D.; m. Myra Kennerly Houser, Feb. 7, 1958 (dec. Feb. 16, 1994); 1 child, Myra Lou. BS, U. S.C., 1957. Cert. Profl. Ins. Agent. With Dean Ins. Assocs., Inc., Matthews, N.C., 1958—, pres., 1994—, chmn., 1987—; pres. Indep. Ins. Agents Charlotte (N.C.), 1976-77; dir. United Carolina Bank, Matthews, 1964-92. Pres. Matthews Rotary, 1987-88, Alpha Phi Omega, Columbia, 1954; adjutant Matthews Am. Legion, 1961; sec. Red Fez Club, Charlotte, 1971. With U.S. Army, 1954-56. Mem. River Hills Lions Club, Shrine Bowl of the Carolinas (chmn. ins. com.), Oasis Temple Aaonms (ins. com.), South Atlantic Shrine Assn. (ins. com.), River Hills Country Club, Phi Kappa Alpha. Methodist. Home: 34 Quayside Ct Lake Wylie SC 29710-9248 Office: Dean Ins Assocs Inc 301 W John St Matthews NC 28105-5356

DEANDA, JAMES, retired federal judge; b. Houston, Tex., Aug. 21, 1925; s. Javier and Mary Louise DeAnda; m. Joyce Anita DeAnda. BA, Tex. A&M U.; LLB, U. Tex., 1950. Bar: Tex. Pvt. practice Houston, 1951-54, Corpus Christi, 1955-57, 66-68; mem. McDonald, Spann & DeAnda, Corpus Christi, 1957-62, Edwards & DeAnda, 1962-66, 69-74, Flores, Sanchez, De-Anda & Vidaurri,, McAllen, 1974-79; judge, then chief judge U.S. Dist. Ct. (so. dist.) Tex., Houston, 1979-92; pvt. practice Houston, 1992—. Mem. ABA, Am. Judicature Soc. Roman Catholic. Office: Transco Tower 2800 Post Oak Blvd Ste 6400 Houston TX 77056-6106

DEANE, SILAS EDWARD, II, marketing executive; b. Lexington, Ky., Dec. 21, 1965; s. Silas E. and Ann (Weaver) D.; m. Angela Ray, Oct. 28, 1991. BS in Econs., U. Ky., 1989; MPA, U. Pa., 1996. With Ky. State Auditor, Frankfort, 1989; with profl. staff Sen. Al Gore Jr., Washington, 1989-91; spokesperson Nat. Bill of Rights Tour, N.Y.C., 1991-92; legis. advisor, press dir. U.S. Rep. Bob Clement, Washington, 1992-94; dir. mktg./devel. The Microelectronics Soc., Reston, Va., 1994—. Editor: Advancing Microelectronics, 1995-96. Mem. Alumni bd. Coll. Dems. Am., Washington; chmn. Fels PAC U. Pa., Phila. Mem. Am. Mgmt. Assn., Assn. for Assn. Execs. Methodist. Home: 2043 Approach Ln Reston VA 22091

DEARDEN, ROBERT JAMES, retired pharmacist; b. Phila., Sept. 25, 1932; s. Raymond Francis and Genevieve (Hendershot) D.; m. Marie Elizabeth Harrell, Aug. 21, 1954; children: Cherylanne, James, Jeanette, Denise. BS in Pharmacy, Temple U., 1955. Registered community pharmacist, Fla., N.J., Pa. Pharmacist, mgr. Merck Sharp and Dohme, Phila., 1955-57, Roman Pharmacy, Phila., 1957-63; pharmacist Phila. Polio Immunization Drive, 1963; pharmacist, pres. Barclay Pharm. Surg. Corp., Cherry Hill, N.J., 1964-83; pharmacist, mgr. Eckerd Drug Corp., Clearwater, Fla., 1983-95; ret., 1995; preceptor Fla. State Bd. Intern Program, Sarasota, 1986-95. V.p., treas. Wedgewood Lakes Condo. Assn. Mem. Am. Pharm. Assn., Fla. Pharm. Assn., Nat. Audubon Soc., Kappa Psi. Republican. Roman Catholic. Home: 5202 Wedgewood Ln Sarasota FL 34235-7020

DEARING, REINHARD JOSEF, city official; b. Bamberg, Fed. Republic of Germany, May 1, 1947; came to U.S., 1960; m. Michele Jack, Feb. 14, 1967 (div. Oct. 1980); 1 child, Lauren; m. Patricia Lee Pollack, Jan. 2, 1982; 1 child, Bradford. AA, La. State U., Baton Rouge, 1968, BA, 1975, MA, 1977, ABD, 1979. Cert. pub. mgr. Adminstrv. officer La. Nat. Bank, Baton Rouge, 1972-75; teaching asst. La. State U., 1975-79; adj. asst. prof. U. So. Miss., Natchez, 1977-79; chief of staff City of Slidell, La., 1979—; cons. La. Mcpl. Assn., Baton Rouge, 1985-87. Author: The Waffen-SS: A Representative Study, 1977; contbr. articles to profl. jours. Coach Slidell Youth Baseball Club, Slidell Youth Football Club; mem. La. State Arts Coun., 1988—; commr. St. Tammany Parish Parks and Recreation Dist., 1989—. With U.S. Army, 1968-72. Decorated Silver Star; named Hon. State Senator, La. Mem. La. Mcpl. Assn., Nat. League Cities, St. Tammany Mcpl. Assn., Am. Pub. Works Assn., La. State U. Alumni Assn. (dir. 1985-87), Assn. U.S. Army, Am. Legion, La. Airport Mgrs. Assn., Internat. City Mgrs. Assn., Lions. Republican. Office: City of Slidell PO Box 828 Slidell LA 70459-0828

DEARMON, THOMAS ALFRED, automotive industry financial executive, life insurance executive; b. Montgomery, Ala., Dec. 28, 1937; s. Thomas A. and Rose (Giardina) D.; m. Leigh Caroline Smith, Dec. 28, 1963 (dec. May 1989); children: Jacob Thomas, Joshua Carter; m. Betty Marie Anderson, June 22, 1991. BBA, U. Okla, 1961; JD, Oklahoma City U., 1968. Bar: Okla. 1968; CPA, Okla. Audit mgr. Arthur Andersen & Co., Oklahoma City, 1961-68; account exec. F.I. DuPont, Oklahoma City, 1968-73; sr. v.p., CFO Fred Jones Auto Group Inc., and Fred Jones Cos., 1973-94, now bd. dirs.; pres., dir. Century Holdings, Inc. and subs., Century Life Assurance, Century Property and Casualty Ins., Century Mgmt. Co., 1983—; sec., dir. emeritus Hist. Preservation Inc., Oklahoma City; bd. dirs. Oklahoma City Philharmonic Orch., 1989—, pres., 1994-95, Okla. City Econs. Club, Men's Dinner Club. With U.S. Army, 1963. Mem. Okla. Bar Assn., Okla. Soc. CPAs, Fin. Execs. Inst., Downtown Lions (pres. 1985-86), Downtown YMCA (bd. mgmt. 1992—). Democrat. Methodist. Office: 123 S Hudson Ave Oklahoma City OK 73102-5020

DEASY, WILLIAM JOHN, construction, marine dredging, engineering and mining company executive; b. N.Y.C., June 22, 1937; s. Jeremiah and Margaret (Quinn) D.; m. Carol Ellyn Lemmons, Feb. 1, 1963; children: Cameron, Kimberly. BS in Civil Engring, Cooper Union, 1958; LLB, U. Wash., 1963. With Morrison Knudsen Corp., Boise, Idaho, 1964-88, v.p. N.W. region, 1972-75, v.p. mining, 1975-78, group v.p. mining, 1978-83, exec. v.p. mining, shipbuilding and mfg., 1983-84, pres., chief operating officer, 1984-85, pres., chief exec. officer, bd. dirs., 1985-88; vice chair, pres., CEO, bd. dirs. T.L. James & Co., New Orleans, 1991—; bd. dirs. Constrn. Industry Pres.'s Forum, Bus. Coun. New Orleans; mem. Jefferson Parish Bus. Coun., New Orleans. Mem. La. Com. of 100. Mem. Beavers, Moles. Home: 2427 Camp St Apt C New Orleans LA 70130-5645 Office: T L James & Co Inc PO Box 20115 New Orleans LA 70141-0115

DEATON, CHERYL DAVIS, school system administrator; b. Montgomery, Ala., Feb. 22, 1951; d. William Lee and Lucile (Spencer) Davis; m. William Lynn Deaton, Aug. 3, 1978; children: William Davis Deaton, Celia Lee Deaton. BS in Elem. Edn., Auburn U., 1973, MEd in Elem. Edn., 1974, EdD in Adminstrn. and Supervision, 1978, 6th yr. cert., 1979. Intern Collegio Pan Am. Sch., Bucaramanga, Columbia, 1973; teaching asst. dept. ednl. media Auburn (Ala.) U., 1973-74; tchr. Westview Elem. Sch., Phenix City, Ala., 1974-75; tchr. English and journalism Monrovia Mid. Sch., Huntsville, Ala., 1975-76; prin. summer program Harvest Sch., Madison County, Ala., 1976; asst. prin. Hazel Green Sch., Huntsville, 1976-77; rsch. asst. Internat. Paper Co. Found., Auburn U., 1977-78; tchr. Carver Elem. Sch., Opelika, Ala., 1978-81; prin. Pepperell Intermediate Sch., Opelika, 1981-92, West Forest Intermediate Sch., Opelika, 1992-94; chief officer for ednl. improvement Montgomery County (Ala.) Bd. of Edn., 1994—; tchr. rep. Ala. Edn. Assn., Phenix City, 1974-75; sponsor and faculty advisor The Hawksville Times student newspaper Monrovia Mid. Sch., 1975-76; co-chairperson Coun. Elem. and Secondary Sch. Adminstrs., Madison County, Ala., 1976-77. Mid. Sch. Task Force Study Comsn., Madison County, 1976-77; pres. dist. VII Ala. Assn. Elem. Prins., 1983-84, dist. rep. (2 terms), 1984-88; mem. Gov.'s Task Force Tchr. Cert., 1984; rev. com. So. Assn. Colls. and Schs., Montgomery County, 1987, 92, Ala. reform comsn. appraisal rev. com. Task Force to Rev. Career Ladder Evaluation Instruments, 1985; evaluator trained and cert. N.C. Teaching Performance Assessment System, 1985; program head and asst. prof. sch. adminstrn. program Troy State U. Montgomery, 1990-91; vis. asst. prof. coll. edn. Auburn U., 1991-94; dir. project SPACE Pepperell Intermediate Sch./West Forest Intermediate Sch., 1991-94; state coord. 1st Ann. Ala. Elem. Sch. Student Coun. Workshop, 1990; appointed to Ala. Commn. on Sch. Performance Standards and Accountability; presenter in field. Editor (3 terms, jour.) The Ala. Elem. Sch. Adminstr., 1983-86; mem. editorial bd. The Profl. Educator, 1991—, Social Studies and the Young Learner, 1991—; appeared on Nat. Pub. Radio show Talk of the Nation, 1993; contbr. numerous articles to profl. jours. Rsch. grantee Auburn U., 1986; grantee Opelika Kiwanis, 1986-87, Ala. Dept. Econ. and Community Affairs, 1989, E. Ala. Regional In-Svc. Ctr., 1991, AmSouth Bancorporation, 1991-92, RJR Nabisco Found. Next Century Schs. Program, 1991—, Nike Corp., 1993, numerous others; named Program Presenter LEAD Acad., 1993; subject of Ala. Pub. TV prodn. The Principal of the Thing, 1992. Mem. ASCD, Am. Assn. Sch. Adminstrn., Nat. Assn. Elem. Sch. Prins. (evaluator annual conv. 1984, del. 1986, 87), Nat. PTA, Internat. Reading Assn. (editor Reading Today Goes to Class 1991-92), Mid-South Ednl. Rsch. Assn., So. Regional Coun. Ednl. Adminstrn., Ala. Assn. Elem. Sch. Adminstrs. (fall conf. com. chairperson 1981-82, mem. exec. com. 1983-91, chairperson and mem. state elections com. 1988-92, chairperson state nominating com. 1990-91, Disting. Prin. award dist. VII 1992), Ala. Coun. Sch. Adminstrs. and Suprs. (bd. dirs. 1983-87, Leadership award dist. VII 1987, 88), Ala. Coun. Tchrs. Social Studies, Ala. PTA, Phi Delta Kappa (founds. rep. 1985-86), Kappa Delta Pi, Delta Kappa Gamma (sec. 1984-86). Office: Montgomery County Bd Edn PO Box 1991 307 S Decator St Montgomery AL 36102-1991

DEATS, JAMES LAWTON, retail executive; b. Austin, Tex., Nov. 14, 1948; s. Fred G. Jr. and Ellen (Lukas) D.; m. Carolyn Sue Wiler, Feb. 12, 1970; children: Phillip, Gregory. BS in Math., East Tex. State U., 1970. Applications programmer Tex. Power & Light Co., Dallas, 1976-77; dir. applications devel. Sanger Harris, Dallas, 1977-85; v.p. systems Federated Dept. Stores, Atlanta, 1985-90; v.p. info. tech. Pier 1 Imports, Inc., Ft. Worth, 1990—. Capt. USAF, 1970-76. Office: Pier 1 Imports 301 Commerce St Fort Worth TX 76102-4140

DEAVENPORT, EARNEST W., JR., chemical executive. Chmn., CEO Eastman Chem., Kingsport, Tenn. Office: Eastman Chem Co 100 N Eastman Rd Kingsport TN 37662

DEAVER, PETE EUGENE, civil engineer; b. Ft. Worth, Mar. 8, 1936; s. Elmer Jack and Mattie Alline (Kelley) D.; m. Birdie Jo Foster, Apr. 30, 1954; children: Pete Eugene, Jr., Stephen Lewis, Mickey Jo, Robert. BS in Civil Engring., Cramwell Inst., 1957, BS in Geology, 1964; student, U. Tex., Arlington, 1954-61; MS in Engring. Mgmt., Pacific Western U., 1992, PhD in Mgmt., 1994. Aircraft engr. Gen. Dynamics Corp., Ft. Worth, 1957-61; project engr. ejection seat studies Kirk Engring. Co., Bethpage, N.Y., 1961-64; sr. engr. Ling Tempco Vought Aeros., Dallas, 1964-65; stress engr. Boeing Aircraft Co., Seattle, 1965-66; sr. aero. engr. Gen. Dynamics Corp., Albuquerque, 1966-74; owner, operator Deaver Engring. Co., Midland, Tex., 1974-84; cons. constrn. and petroleum industry. Served with USNR, 1952-54. Registered profl. engr., N.Mex., Tex. Mem. Tex. Water Pollution Control Assn., Soc. Exploration Geophysicists, Tex., Nat. socs. profl. engrs. Baptist. Club: Masons (32 deg.). Author: Basic Stress Analysis for Engineers and Draftsmen, 1967; Drilling Manual for Rotary Drilling, 1981, Rock Bit Design and Evaluation, 1992, Factors Affecting Rock Bit Penetration Rate, 1992, Solids Control in Drilling Muds, 1992, Drilling Management, 1994. Home: 2200 Sharpshire Ln Arlington TX 76014-3526

DEAVERS, JAMES FREDERICK, optometrist; b. St. Augustine, Fla., Apr. 23, 1947; s. James Lonnie and Gwen Eula (Fields) D.; m. Janet Allen, Jan. 1, 1995; children: Samuel, Chris, Marie. BS, So. Coll. of Optometry, Memphis, 1979, OD, 1978. Optometrist Berkeley Eyecare Ctr., Inc., Moncks Corner, S.C., 1979-95, Cmty. Eyecare, Moncks Corner, 1995—. Staff sgt. USAF, 1965-69. Recipient Air Force Commendation Republic Vietnam, 1967. Mem. Am. Optometric Assn., Coll. of Optometrist Vision Devel. (assoc.), Rotary Internat. Republican. Mem. Christian Fellowship Ch. Office: Cmty Eyecare 118-B Cumbie Plaza Moncks Corner SC 29461

DEBAKEY, LOIS, science communications educator, writer, editor; b. Lake Charles, La.; d. S. M. and Raheeja (Zorba) DeBakey. BA in Math., Tulane U., MA in Lit. and Linguistics, 1959, PhD in Lit. and Linguistics, 1963. Asst. prof. English Tulane U., 1963-64; asst. prof. sci. communication Tulane U. Med. Sch., 1963-65, assoc. prof. sci. communication, 1965-67, prof. sci. comm., 1967-68, lectr., 1968-80, adj. prof., 1981-92; prof. sci. comm. Baylor Coll. Medicine, Houston, 1968—; mem. biomed. libr. rev. com. Nat. Libr. Medicine, Bethesda, Md., 1973-77, bd. regents, 1981-86, cons., 1986—, co-chmn. permanent paper task force, 1987—, lit. selection tech. rev. com., 1988-93, chmn., 1992-93, outreach planning panel, 1988-89; dir. courses in med. comm. ACS and other orgns.; bd. trustees DeBakey Med. Found.; exec. coun. Commn. on Colls. So. Assn. Colls. and Schs., 1975-80; mem. nat. adv. coun. U. Soc. Calif. Ctr. Continuing Med. Edn., 1981, steering com. Plain English Forum, 1984, founding bd. dirs. Friends Nat. Libr. Medicine, 1985—, chmn. med. media award of excellence com. FNLM, 1992—, adv. com. Soc. for Preservation English Lang. Literature, 1986, Nat. Adv. Bd. John Muir Med. Film Festival, 1990-92, The Internat. Health and Med. Film Festival, Acad. of Judges, 1992-93; mem. adv. coun. U. Tex. at Austin Sch. Nursing Found., 1993—; cons. legal writing com. cons. ABA, 1983—; former cons. Nat. Assn. Std. Med. Vocabulary; pioneered instruction in sci. communication in meds. schs. Sr. author: The Scientific Journal: Editorial Policies and Practices, 1976; co-author: Medicine: Preserving the Passion, 1987; mem editorial bd.: Tulane Studies in English, 1966-68, Cardiovascular Research Center Bull., 1971-83, Health Communications and Informatics, 1975-80, Forum on Medicine, 1977-80, Grants Mag, 1978-81, Internat. Jour. Cardiology, 1981-86, Excerpta Medica's Core Jours. in Cardiology, 1981—, Health Comm. and Biopsychosocial Health, 1981-82, Internat. Angiology, 1985—, Jour. AMA, 1988—; mem. usage panel: Am. Heritage Dictionary, 1980—; cons. Webster's Medical Desk Dictionary, 1986; contbd. articles on biomed. communication and sci. writing, literacy, also other subjects to profl. jours., books, encys., and pub. press. Active Found. for Advanced Edn. in Sci., 1977—; trustee DeBakey Med. Found., 1995—. Recipient Disting. Svc. award Am. Med. Writers Assn., 1970, Bausch & Lomb Sci. award, 1st John P. McGovern award Med. Libr. Assn., 1983, Outstanding Alumna award Newcomb Coll., 1994; fellow Am. Coll. Med. Informatics, 1990, Royal Soc. for Encouragement of Arts Mfrs. and Commerce, 1991. Fellow Am. Coll. Med. Informatics; mem. Internat. Soc. Gen. Semantics, Med. Libr. Assn. (hon.), Coun. Biology Editors (dir. 1973-77, chmn. com. on editl. policy 1971-75), Coun. Basic Edn. (spl. com. writing 1977-79), Assn. Tchrs. Tech. Writing, Dictionary Soc. N.Am., Nat. Assn. Sci. Writers, Soc. for Health and Human Values, Com. of Thousand for Better Health Regulations, Golden Key, Phi Beta Kappa. Office: Baylor Coll Medicine One Baylor Plz Houston TX 77030-3498

DEBAKEY, MICHAEL ELLIS, cardiovascular surgeon, educator, scientist; b. Lake Charles, La., Sept. 7, 1908; s. Shaker Morris and Raheeja (Zorba) DeB.; m. Diana Cooper, Oct. 15, 1936; children: Michael Maurice, Ernest Ochsner, Barry Edward, Denis Alton, Olga Katerina; m. Katrin Fehlhaber, July 1975. BS, Tulane U., 1930, MD, 1932, MS, 1935, LLD (hon.), 1965; Docteur Honoris Causa, U. Lyon, France, 1961, U. Brussels, 1962, U. Ghent, Belgium, 1964, U. Athens, 1964; DHC, U. Turin, Italy, 1965, U. Belgrade, Yugoslavia, 1967; LLD, Lafayette Coll., 1965; MD (hon.), Aristotelean U. of Thessaloniki, Greece, 1972; DSc, Hahnemann Med. Coll., 1973; Docteur honoris causa, U. Louis Pasteur, Paris, 1991; D Mil. Medicine & Surgery, Uniformed Svc. U. Health Scis., 1996; D Letters in Medicine (hon.), Baylor U., 1996. Diplomate Nat. Bd. Med. Examiners, Am. Bd. Surgery, Am. Bd. Thoracic Surgery. Intern Charity Hosp., New Orleans, 1932-33, asst. surgery, 1933-35; asst. surgery U. Strasbourg, France, 1935-36,

U. Heidelberg, Fed. Republic of Germany, 1936; instr. surgery Tulane U., New Orleans, 1937-40, asst. prof., 1940-46, assoc. prof., 1946-48; prof., chmn. dept. surgery Baylor Coll. Medicine, 1948-93, Disting. svc. prof., 1968—, v.p. med. affairs, 1968-69, CEO, 1968-69, pres., 1969-79, Olga Keith Weiss prof. of surgery, 1981—, Olga Keith Weiss prof. of surgery, chancellor, 1978-96; chancellor emeritus, 1996—; pres. The DeBakey Med. Found., 1961—; dir. Nat. Heart Blood Vessel Rsch. Demonstration Ctr. Baylor Coll. Medicine, Tex., 1975-85; dir. DeBakey Heart Ctr., Baylor Coll. Medicine, 1985—; chancellor emeritus Baylor Coll. Medicine, 1996—; surgeon-in-chief Ben Taub Gen. Hosp., 1963-93; sr. attending surgeon Meth. Hosp.; clin. prof. surgery U. Tex. Dental Br., Houston; cons. surgery VA Hosp., St. Elizabeth's Hosp., U. Tex., M.D. Anderson Hosp., St. Luke's Hosp., Tex. Children's Hosp., Tex. Inst. Rehab. and Rsch. Brooke Gen. Hosp., Brooke Army Med. Ctr., Ft. Sam Houston, Tex., Walter Reed Army Hosp., Washington, D.C.; mem. med. adv. com. Office Sec. Def., 1984-50, Ams. for Substance Abuse Prevention, 1984; mem. med. adv. bd. Internat. Brotherhood Teamsters, 1985—; chmn. com. surgery NRC, 1953, mem. exec. com. 1953; mem. com. med. svcs. Hoover Commn.; founding bd. dirs.Friends of Nat. Libr. of Medicine, 1985—, mem. bd. regents Nat. Libr. Medicine, 1994-60, chmn., 1959-63, 94—; past mem. nat. adv. heart coun. NIH; mem. Nat. Adv. Health Coun., 1961-65, Nat. Adv. Coun. Regional Med. Programs, 1965—, Nat. Adv. Gen. Med. Scis. Coun., 1965, Program Planning Com., Com. Tng., Nat. Heart Inst., 1961—; mem. civilian health and med. adv. coun. Office Asst. Sec. Def.; chmn. Pres.'s Commn. Heart Disease, Cancer and Stroke, 1964; mem. adv. coun. Nat. Heart Lung and Blood Inst., 1982-87; mem. Tex. Sci. and Tech. Coun., 1984-86; chmn. Found. Biomed. Rsch., 1988—, Physicians for Health in the Middle East, 1991—; trustee, v.p. Baylor Med. Found.; chmn., med. adv. bd. The DeBakey Heart Ctr. Health Letter; adv. bd. Family Cir.; internat. sci. coun. Fondation Cardiologique Princesse Liliane; adv. Dag Hammarskjöld Med. Sci. Prize Com.; mem. bd. visitors Uniformed Svcs. U. Health Scis., U. Calif.-Davis Sch. Medicine. Author: (with Robert A. Kilduffe) Blood Transfusion, 1942; (with Gilbert W. Beebe) Battle Casualties, 1952; (with Alton Ochsner) Textbook of Minor Surgery, 1955; (with T. Whayne) Cold Injury, Ground Type, 1958, A Surgeon's Visit to China, 1974, The Living Heart, 1977, The Living Heart Diet, 1985, The Living Heart Brand Name Shopper's Guide, 1992, The Living Heart Guide to Eating Out, 1993, The New Living Heart Diet, 1996; editor: Yearbook of Surgery, 1958-70; chmn. adv. editl. bd. Medical History of World War II; founding editor Jour. Vascular Surgery, 1984-88; contbr. over 1500 articles to med. jours. Mem. Tex. Constl. Revision Commn., 1973. Col. Office Surgeon Gen., AUS, 1942-46; now Col. Res.; cons. to Surgeon Gen., 1946—; disting. mem. U.S. Army Med. Dept. Rgt., 1989. Decorated Legion of Merit, 1946, Independence of Jordan medal 1st Class, Merit order of Republic 1st Class Egypt, comdr. Cross of Merit Pro Utiliate Hominum Sovereign Order Knights of Hosp. of St. John of Jerusalem in Denmark; recipient Rudolph Matas award, 1954, Internat. Soc. Surgery Disting. Svc. award, 1958, Modern Medicine award, 1957, Leriche award Internat. Soc. Surgery, 1959, Great medallion U. Ghent, 1961, Grand Cross, Order Leopold Belgium, 1962, Albert Lasker award for clin. research, 1963, Order of Merit Chile, 1964, St. Vincent prize med. scis. U. Turin, 1965, Orden del Libertador Gen. San Martin Argentina, 1965, Centennial medal Albert Einstein Med. Ctr., 1966, Gold Scalpel award Internat. Cardiology Found., 1966, Baylor Alumni Disting. Faculty award, 1973, Eleanor Roosevelt Humanities award, 1969, Meritorious Civilian Service medal Office Sec. Def., 1970, USSR Acad. Sci. 50th Anniversary Jubilee medal, 1973, Phi Delta Epsilon Disting. Service award, 1974, La Madonnina award, 1974, 30 Yr. Service award Harris County Hosp. Dist., 1978, Knights Humanity award honoris causa Internat. Register Chivalry, Milan, 1978, diploma de Merito Caja Costarricense de Seguro Social, San Jose, Costa Rica, 1979, Disting. Service plaque Tex. Bd. Edn., 1979, Britannica Achievement in Life award, 1979, Medal of Freedom with Distinction Presdl. award, 1969, Disting. Service award Internat. Soc. Atherosclerosis, 1979, Centennial award ASME, 1980, Marian Health Care award St. Mary's U., 1981, Inst. Med. Nat. Acad. Sci., 1981, Soc. Biomaterials award for clin. rsch. in biomaterials Clemson U. and Soc. Biomaterials, 1983, Humana Heart Inst. award, 1985, Theodore E. Cummings award, 1987, Nat. Med. of Sci. award 1987, Presdl. Medal Sci., 1987, Markowitz award Acad. Surg. Rsch., 1988, Assn. Am. Med. Colls. award 1988, George Crile award Internat. Platform Assn., 1988, Thomas Alva Edison Found. award, 1988, first issue Michael DeBakey medal ASME, 1989, Inaugural award Scripps Clinic and Rsch. Found., 1989, DeBakey-Bard Chair in Surgery, Baylor Coll. of Medicine, 1990, Disting. Svc. award Am. Legion, 1990, Lifetime Achievement award Found. for Biomed. Rsch., 1991, Jacobs award Am. Task Force for Lebanon, 1991, Maxwell Finland award Nat. Found. for Infectious Diseases, 1992, Lifetime Achievement award Acad. Med. Films, 1992, Order of Independence First Class medal United Arab Emirates, 1992, Academy of Athens award, 1992, Cmdrs. Cross Order of Merit (Fed. Germany), 1992, Pres. Disting. Svc. award Baylor Coll. Medicine, 1992, Gibbon award Am. Soc. Extracorporeal Tech., 1993, named in his honor Michael E. DeBakey Libr., Svc. Outreach award Friends of the Nat. Libr. Medicine, 1993, Alton Ochsner award relating smoking to health, 1993, Thomas Jefferson award AIA, 1993, Ellis Island Medal of Honor, 1993, Lifetime Achievement award Am. Heart Assn., 1994, Caring Spirit award Inst. Religion Tex. Med. Ctr., 1994, Samaritan Living Legend award Women's Internat. Ctr., 1994, Giovanni Lorenzini Med. Fedn. prize for basic biomed. rsch., 1994, Disting. Svc. award Tex. Soc. Biomedical Rsch., 1994, Heart Saver award Save A Heart Found., Cedars-Sinai Med. Ctr., 1994, Honor award United Meth. Assn. Health & Welfare Ministries, 1995, Michael E. DeBakey chair in Pharm. Baylor Coll. Med., 1995, Nat. Order of Vasco Nunez de Balboa (Panama), 1995, Health Care Hall of Fame Modern Healthcare, 1996, Sci. Rschr. of XX Century award govt. of Argentine Republic, 1996, others; named Dr. of Yr., Med. World News, 1965, Med. Man of Yr., 1966, Disting. Service Prof., Baylor U., 1968, Humanitarian Father of Yr., 1974, Tulane U. Alumnus of Yr., 1974, Tex. Scientist of Yr., Tex. Acad. Sci., 1979; Michael E. DeBakey Heart Inst. Wis. named in his honor Kenosha Hosp. and Med. Ctr., 1992; Michael E. DeBakey, M.D. award for Excellence in Visual Edn. named in his honor, 1993; DeBakey Scholar in Cardiovasc. Scis. MD-PhD Program named in his honor Baylor Coll. Medicine, 1994; Michael E. DeBakey, MD Excellence in Rsch. award named in his honor Baylor Coll. Medicine, 1994, dedication of Northwestern U. Med. Sch. book, 1995. Fellow ACS (Ann. award Southwestern Pa. chpt. 1973), Inst. of Medicine Chgo. (hon.), Royal Coll. Physicians and Surgeons of U.S. (hon., disting. fellow 1992), Am. Inst. Med. and Biol. Engring. (founding fellow 1993), Biomaterials Sci. and Engr., Soc. Biomaterials, Am. Coll. Cardiology (hon.), Am. Coll. Health Care Execs. (hon.); mem. AAAS, Royal Soc. Medicine, Halsted Soc., Am. Heart Assn., So. Soc. Clin. Rsch., Southwestern Surg. Congress (pres. 1952), Soc. Vascular Surgery (pres. 1954), Soc. Vascular Surg. Lifeline Found. (pres. 1989), AMA (Disting. Svc. award 1959, Hektoen Gold medal 1954, 70), Am. Surg. Assn. (Disting. Svc. award 1981, pres. 1989), So. Surg. Assn. (pres. 1989-90, chmn. coun. 1995—), Western Surg. Assn., Am. Assn. Thoracic Surgery (pres. 1959), Internat. Cardiovascular Soc. (pres. 1958, pres. N.Am. chpt. 1964), Assn. Internat. Vascular Surgeons (pres. 1983), Mex. Acad. Surgery (hon.), Soc. Clin. Surgery, Nat. Acads. Practice Medicine, Soc. Univ. Surgeons, Internat. Soc. Surgery, Soc. Exptl. Biology and Medicine, Hellenic Surg. Soc. (hon.), Bio-med. Engring. Soc. (bd. dirs. 1968), Houston Heart Assn. (mem. adv. coun. 1966-69), Soc. Nacional de Cirugia (hon., Cuba), Japanese Assn. Thoracic Surgery (first fgn. hon. mem. 1989), Assn. Française de Chirurgie (hon.), University Club (Washington), Acad. of Athens, Sigma Xi (William Procter prize for scientific achievement 1995), Alpha Omega Alpha. Office: Baylor Coll Medicine 1 Baylor Plz Houston TX 77030-3498 also: Tex Med Ctr 6535 Fannin St Houston TX 77030-3498

DEBAKEY, SELMA, science communications educator, writer, editor, lecturer; b. Lake Charles, La.. BA, Newcomb Coll., Tulane U., New Orleans, postgrad. Dir. dept. med. communication Ochsner Clinic and Alton Ochsner Med. Found., New Orleans, 1942-68; prof. sci. communication Baylor Coll. Medicine, Houston, 1968—; editor Cardiovascular Research Ctr. Bull., 1970-84; mem. panel judges Internat. Health and Med. Film Festival, 1992. Author: (with A. Segaloff and K. Meyer) Current Concepts in Breast Cancer, 1967; past editor Ochsner Clinic Reports, Selected Writings from the Ochsner Clinic; contbr. numerous articles to sci. jours., chpts. to books. Mem. AAAS, Soc. Tech. Communication, Assn. Tchrs. Tech. Writing, Am. Med. Writers Assn. (past bd. dirs.; publ., nominating, fellowship, constn., bylaws, awards, and edn. coms.), Council Biol. Editors (past mem. trn. in sci. writing com.), Soc. Health and Human Values, Modern Med. Monograph Awards Com., Nat. Assn. Standard Med. Vocabulary (former cons.). Office: Baylor Coll Medicine 1 Baylor Plz Houston TX 77030-3498

DEBANTO, JOHN ROBERT, internist; b. Dayton, Ohio, Dec. 15, 1965; s. Thomas Charles and Janet Louise (Schaefer) DeB.; m. Wendy Elizabeth Atkins, Oct. 7, 1995. BS, U. Dayton, 1988; MD, Wright State U., Dayton, 1992. Diplomate Am. Bd. Internal Medicine. Resident in internal medicine Med. U. S.C., Charleston, 1992-95, chief resident, 1995-96. Mem. AMA, So. Med. Assn., Order of Omega, Phi Rho Sigma, Sigma Chi. Roman Catholic. Home: 1110 Winborn Dr Charleston SC 29412 Office: Med U SC 171 Ashley Ave Charleston SC 29425

DEBOLD, CYNTHIA ANN, sculptor; b. Lexington, Ky., June 12, 1950; d. Louis Bryan and Consuelo (Lopez) Skaggs; m. William Frank Debold, Nov. 16, 1974 (div. July 1989); children: James Patrick, Casey Louis. AA, Orange Coast Coll., 1971, Art Ctr. Coll. of Design, 1973. instr. in field. Exhibited in numerous nat. juried art shows. Mem. Internat. Sculpture Ctr., Tex. Soc. Sculptors (chmn. Sculptfest 1993, pres. 1993-95), Tex. Sculpture Assn., Tex. Fine Arts Assn., Austin Visual Arts Assn., Austin C. of C. (bus. com. for the arts 1993-95). Studio: 1117 W 5th St # D Austin TX 78703-5301

DEBOLT, JOSEPH WAYNE, JR., editorial assistant; b. Ravenna, Ohio, Oct. 17, 1962; s. Joseph Wayne and Beverly Denise (Gallagher) DeB. BA, Kalamazoo Coll., 1984; MA, Ctrl. Mich. U., 1988. Circulation asst. Am. Spectator, Arlington, Va., 1989-90, subscription mgr., 1990-93; customer svc. rep. Franklin Mortgage Capital Corp., Falls Church, Va., 1993-94; customer svc. rep. Comm. Briefings, Alexandria, Va., 1994-96, editl. asst., 1996—. Chmn. ch. coun. Comty. Ch. of God, Arlington, 1992-93, 96—, mem. bus. bd., 1994-95. State of Mich. scholar, 1980. Home: 9903 Kingsbridge Dr Fairfax VA 22031 Office: Comms Briefings Ste 110 1101 King St Alexandria VA 22314

DE BREMAECKER, JEAN-CLAUDE, geophysics educator; b. Antwerp, Belgium, Sept. 2, 1923; came to U.S., 1948, naturalized, 1963; s. Paul J.C. and Berthe (Bouché) De B.; m. Arlene Ann Parker, Nov. 29, 1952; children—Christine, Suzanne. M.S. in Mining Engring, U. Louvain, Belgium, 1948; M.S. in Geology, La. State U., 1950; Ph.D. in Geophysics, U. Cal. at Berkeley, 1952. Research scientist, sr. research scientist Inst. pour la Recherche Sci. en Afrique Centrale, Bukavu, Congo, 1952-58; Boese postdoctoral fellow Columbia, 1955-56; postdoctoral fellow Harvard, 1958-59; faculty Rice U., Houston, 1959—; prof. geophysics Rice U., 1965-94, prof. emeritus, 1994; research asso. U. Calif., Berkeley, 1966; vis. mem. Tex. Inst. for Computational Mechanics, U. Tex., Austin, 1977; vis. prof. U. Paris, 1980-81. Author: Geophysics, the Earth's Interior, 1985. Chmn. Citizens for McCarthy, Houston, 1968. Served with Belgian Army, 1944-45. Mem. AAUP, Am. Geophys. Union, Fedn. Am. Scientists, Internat. Assn. Seismology and Physics of Earth's Interior (assoc. sec. gen. 1963-71, sec. gen. 1971-79). Home: 7490 Brompton St Apt 382 Houston TX 77025-2211 Office: Rice U Dept Geology and Geophysics 6100 Main St Houston TX 77005-1892

DECHMAN, THOMAS ALEXANDER, II, gifted education educator; b. Atlanta, Nov. 17, 1945; s. Thomas Alexander Dechman and Mary Grace (Arbour) Dechman Miller; 1 child, Thomas Alexander, III. BS, La. State U., 971; LLB, John Marshall Law Sch., Atlanta, 1975; MEd, Ga. State U., 1978. Cert. speech and lang. pathology, gifted speech tchr., Ga. Supr. mid. and h.s. gifted curriculum and instrn. Cobb County Pub. Schs., Marietta, Ga.; dean of students Ga. Gov.'s Honors Program. Author: (play) Odie, 1988, One More Time, 1989, Dream A Little Dream, 1991. Named Star Tchr., 1974, 79, 80, 84, 85, 87, 7th Congl. Dist. Star Tchr., 1979, 87, Tchr. of Yr., 1974, 87. Mem. Nat. Assn. Gifted Children, Ga. Assn. for Gifted Children, Nat. Chess Assn. (life). Office: PO Box 1088 Marietta GA 30061-1088

DECHURCH, FRANCES ELIZABETH, physician; b. Mt. Holly, N.J., Nov. 21, 1958; d. Daniel and Sarita Lee (Bingaman) DeC.; m. Hugh Erskine Fraser, III, June 14, 1980; children: Katherine, Clair, Benjamin, Ian. Student, U. Richmond, 1977-79; BA, Wake Forest U., 1982, MD, 1986. Diplomate Am. Bd. Internal Medicine. Resident in internal medicine Geisinger Med. Ctr., Danville, Pa., 1987-90, ambulatory care physician, 1990-91, dir. inpatient medicine svc., 1991-93; pvt. practice internal medicine Anne Penn Hosp., Reidsville, N.C., 1993—; med. dir. subacute svcs. Vencor Hosp., Greensboro, N.C., 1995—; med. dir. Britthaven of Madium, N.C., 1994—. Mem. ACP, AMA. Episcopalian. Office: Vencor Greensboro 2401 S Side Blvd Greensboro NC 27406

DECKER, BARBARA COOPER, education educator; b. San Antonio, Jan. 29, 1935; d. Eugene Nataly and Lola Dell (Mead) Berato; m. Willis McLain Cooper, Dec. 19, 1952 (div. May 1973); children: Kathryn Cooper Van Gilder, Michael Eugene; m. David Weston Cooper, July 27, 1979. BS in Edn., U. Ark., 1968, MEd, 1970, EdD, 1973. 5th grade tchr. Huntsville (Ala.) Pub. Schs., 1967-69; edn. dir. child study ctr. U. Ark., Little Rock, 1973-77; asst. prof. U. Cen. Ark, Conway, 1977-79; asst. prof. La. State U., Shreveport, 1979-82, assoc. prof., 1982-87, prof., 1987-94, asst. dean, 1991-94; dean Sch. Edn. and Behavioral Scis., dir. tchr. edn. Southeastern Okla. State U., Durant, 1994—; ind. ednl. cons., 1973-94; owner The Reading Ctr., Inc., Shreveport, 1981-84; pvt. practice as clin. reading specialist, Shreveport, 1984-94. Treas. Okla. Assn. Colls. of Tchr. Edn., 1994-95, pres.-elect, 1996-97; v.p. Red River Arts Council. Mem. Am. Assn. Coll. Tchr. Edn., La. Reading Assn. (named Coll. Tchr. of Yr. 1986, 88, pres. 1979), La. Coll. Tchr. Reading (pres. 1980), Phi Delta Kappa (pres. 1985-86), Kappa Delta Pi (pres. 1987-88), Pi Delta Kappa. Office: Southeastern Okla State U Sch Edn and Behavioral Sci Durant OK 74701

DECKER, JOSEPHINE I., clinic administrator; b. Barling, Ark., May 24, 1933; d. Ralph and Ada A. (Claborn) Snider; BS in Health Mgmt., Kennedy Western U., 1986, MS in Bus. Adminstrn., 1987; m. William Arlen Decker, Feb. 4, 1952; 1 son, Peter A. With Southwestern Bell Telephone Co., Ft. Smith, Ark., 1951-52; with Holt Krock Clinic, Ft. Smith, 1952—, bus. adminstr., 1970—. Bd. dirs. Sparks Credit Union, Adv. Council Northside and Southside high schs., Ft. Smith, Ft. Smith Girls Shelter, Ft. Smith Credit Bur. Mem. Credit Women Internat., Soc. Cert. Consumer Credit Execs. Office: Holt Krock Clinic 1500 Dodson Ave Fort Smith AR 72901-5128

DECKER, MICHAEL LYNN, lawyer, judge; b. Oklahoma City, May 5, 1953; s. Leroy Melvin and Yvonne (Baird) D.; m. Robin Strom, July 25, 1987. BA, Oklahoma City U., 1975, JD, 1978; grad., Nat. Jud. Coll., U. Nev., Reno, 1990. Bar: Okla. 1978, U.S. Ct. Appeals (10th cir.) 1979, U.S. Dist. Ct. (we. dist.) Okla. 1985, U.S. Supreme Ct. 1994. Assoc. Bay, Hamilton, Lees, Spears, and Verity, Oklahoma City, 1978-80; assoc. dir. devel. Oklahoma City U., 1980-81, asst. dean, Sch. of Law, 1981-82; sr. oil and gas adminstrv. law judge Okla. Corp. Commn., Oklahoma City, 1982-92, sr. asst. gen. counsel oil and gas conservation, 1992-95, deputy gen. counsel oil and gas conservation, 1995—; campaign staff intern U.S. Senator Henry Bellmon's Re-election Campaign, 1974; mem. Civil Arbitration Panel, U.S. Dist. Ct. (we. dist.) Okla., 1985—; seminar spkr. Am. Inst. Profl. Geologists (Okla. sect.), 1985; mem. dean's adv. com. Oklahoma City U. Law Sch., 1986; mem. sys. rev. bd. Okla. Corp. Commn., 1990-93, mem. process mgmt. rev. team, 1995—; lectr. adminstrv. law Vanderbilt U. Sch. Law, 1993. Trustee Oklahoma City U., 1989-91, mem. alumni bd. dirs., 1988-95, also mem. devel. com., long range planning com. and adminstrv. liaison com.; mem. com. of twenty Oklahoma City Art Mus., 1987-95, co-chair omelette party, 1990; vol. Contact Teleminster, Oklahoma City, 1986-91, bd. dirs., 1987-90; mem. rev. bd. Okla. Corp. Commn., 1990; mem. adminstrv. bd. St. Luke's United Meth. Ch., 1988-92, chair missions com., 1993-94; bd. dirs. March of Dimes, Western Okla., 1990-93; mem. Class XI Leadership Oklahoma City, 1993; area rep. Okla. Mozart Fest., Bartlesville, 1988—. Mem. Okla. Bar Assn. (mineral law sect., environ. law sect.), Okla. County Bar Assn. (exec. com. young lawyers sect. 1978-82, mem. law day com. 1979-88, chmn. law day luncheon spkr. com. 1985-88), Oklahoma City Mineral Lawyers Soc., Lions, Phi Alpha Delta, Lambda Chi Alpha (treas. bldg. corp. 1984-89, pres. 1989-91, Outstanding Alumnus award 1983), Oklahoma City Dinner Club. Republican. Home: 2008 NW 44th St Oklahoma City OK 73118-1902 Office: Okla Corp Commn State Capitol Complex Jim Thorpe Bldg Oklahoma City OK 73116

DECKER, NORMAN, psychiatrist, educator; b. June 12, 1936. AB, Columbia U., 1957, MD, 1961. Diplomate Am. Bd. Psychiatry and Neurology, Diplomate in Psychiatry. Internship King County Hosp., Seattle, 1961-62; residency Mt. Sinai Hosp., N.Y.C., 1962-65; pvt. psychiat. practice N.Y.C., 1967-74, Houston, 1974—; staff psychiatrist U.S. VA Med. Ctr., Houston, 1974-84, chief, psychiat. liaison svc., 1975-84; clin. asst. prof., asst. prof. psychiatry Baylor Coll. Medicine, Houston, 1974-75, 75-84, clin. asst. prof. family practice, 1976-82, asst. prof. family practice, assoc. prof. clin. psychiatry, 1982-85, 84-86, clin. assoc. prof. psychiatry, 1986—. Contbr. articles to profl. jours. Pres. PTA, River Oaks Sch., 1976; counselor Cancer Counseling, Inc., Houston, 1984—, chmn. bd. dirs., 1984-85, bd. dirs., 1983-85, 86-95, med. adv. bd., 1983—. Mem. AMA, Am. Psychiat. Assn. (elected fellow 1979, com. on spl. benefits 1984-92), Houston Psychiat. Soc. (v.p., program chmn. 1978-79, pres.-elect 1979-80, pres. 1981, chmn. pub. info. com. 1990-92), N.Y. Psychoanalytic Soc., Houston/Galveston Psychoanalytic Soc. (sec.-treas. 1986-88), Am. Psychoanalytic Assn., Tex. Med. Assn., Houston County Med. Soc., Multiple Personality and Dissociative Disorder Study Group (Houston), Internat. Soc. for Study of Dissociation. Office: 5300 San Jacinto St Ste 170 Houston TX 77004-6841

DECKERT, MYRNA JEAN, executive director; b. McPherson, Kans., Nov. 4, 1936; d. Francis J. and Grace (Killion) George; m. Ray A. Deckert, Sept. 29, 1957; children: Rachelle, Kimberly, Charles, Michael. AA, Coll. of Sequoias, 1956; BBA, U. Beverly Hills, 1983, MBA, 1984. Youth dir. Asbury Meth. Ch., El Paso, Tex., 1960-63; teen program dir. YWCA, El Paso, 1963-69, assoc. exec. dir., 1969-70, exec. dir., 1970—; chair strategic planning com. Tex. Dept. Pub. and Regulatory Svcs., 1994—. Exec. forum, pres., 1991-92; bd. dirs. Tex. Commerce Bank, El Paso; chmn. Tex. State Title XX DayCare Providers, 1987-89; commr. Housing Authority City of El Paso, 1989-92; chair bd. trustees Columbia Med. Ctr. East, Tex. Tech. Med. Found. Bd.; trustee Dues/High Tower Found.; chair Leadership EP, 1994-95; trustee Unite El Paso. Recipient Hannah Soloman Cmty. Svc. award Nat. Coun. Jewish Women, Sertoma Club award Svc. to Mankind, 1974, Cmty. Svc. award League United L.Am. Citizens, 1980, Humanitarian award, 1994, Vol. Svc. award Vol. Bur., 1984, Merit award Adalante Mujer, 1986, Social Svc. award KVIA/Sunturians, 1986, Excellence award Nat. Assn. YWCA Execs., 1990, Racial Justice award YWCA of the U.S.A., 1991; named Woman of Yr., AAUW, 1975, Dir. of Yr., United Way El Paso County, 1985, First Lady of El Paso, Beta Sigma Phi, 1991, One of 10 Most Influential Women, El Paso Times, 1995, Citizen of Yr., Mil. Order of World Wars, 1996; inducted into El Paso Women's Hall of Fame, 1990, El Paso Hist. Soc. Hall of Honor, 1995. Mem. Coun. of Agy. Execs., Rotary (Club of El Paso, v.p. 1990-93). Methodist. Home: 4276 Canterbury Dr El Paso TX 79902-1352

DECOTIS, JOHN DECIO, school administrator; b. Utica, N.Y., Sept. 16, 1953; s. Alfonso P. and Carmella B. (Pitrel) Dec.; m. Concetta Josephine Carzo, July 21, 1984; children: Johanna, John Paul, Maria. BSE, SUNY, Cortland, 1975; MEd, Springfield (Mass.) Coll., 1979; EdS, Ga. State U., 1986; EdD, U. Ga., 1993. Tchr. Lourdes Sch., Utica, N.Y., 1975-78; grad. asst. Springfield Coll., 1978-79; tchr. Fayette County Schs., Fayetteville, Ga., 1979-81, asst. prin., 1981-84, prin., 1984-88, elem. dir., 1988-94, exec. dir. edn., 1994—; pres. regional orgn. Griffin RESA GACIS, Griffin, Ga., 1992-93. Author: Ensuring A Quality Education for Your Children: A Guide to Parents, 1995; contbr. articles to profl. jours. Chmn. bd. dirs. YMCA, Fayetteville, 1990-95. Named Adminstr. of Yr., Phi Delta Kappa, 1993, Disting. Adminstr., Ga. Pre-Sch. Assn., Atlatna, 1994. Mem. ASCD, Am. Assn. Sch. Adminstrs., Ga. Assn. Ednl. Leaders, KC, Toastmasters Internat. (pres. 1991-94), Delta Kappa Pi. Home: 185 Ridge Way Fayetteville GA 30215 Office: Fayette County Bd Edn 210 Stonewall Ave Fayetteville GA 30214

DECRESCENZO, JAME MELISSE, insurance company executive; b. Midland, Tex., June 19, 1955; d. James Edward and Hari Jean (Jackson) Hanks; m. Michael Harry DeCrescenzo; children: Alexandra, Andrew. BA, U. Md., Spain, 1975; BSN, Tex. Women's U., 1980; MA magna cum laude, U. Tex., 1984. RN. Dir. spl. accounts Dey Labs., Dallas, 1978-80; salesman SMI, Dallas, 1980-83; ind. oil and gas investor Dallas, 1983-88; with Am. Gen. Ins. Co., 1988; dir. devel. Travelers Ins. Co., Richardson, Tex., 1990-94; dir. provider devel. Found. Health, A Tex. Health Plan, Dallas, 1994—. Republican. Roman Catholic.

DECUIR, ALFRED FREDERICK, JR., financial executive; b. East Orange, N.J., Oct. 11, 1950; s. Alfred F. Sr. and Virginia A. (Thorn) DeC. BA in Math. Econ., Brown U., 1972; MBA in Fin. and Acctg., U. Chgo., 1974. Credit analyst to banking officer Nat. Bank North Am. (name changed to Nat. Westminster USA), N.Y.C., 1974-79; asst. v.p. to group head v.p. Credit Suisse, N.Y.C., 1979-83; mgr. fin. markets and treasury analysis Allied Corp., Morristown, N.J., 1983-84; v.p., treas. EF Hutton Credit Corp. (name changed to Chrysler Capital Corp.), Greenwich, Conn., 1984-86; mng. dir. JW Charles Capital Corp., Boca Raton, Fla., 1986-88; pvt. practice Boca Raton, 1985-87; chief fin. officer Krypton Corp and Cons., Boca Raton, 1987-90, 1990—. Mem. Fin. Execs. Inst. Home and Office: 2707 N Ocean Blvd Apt D208 Boca Raton FL 33431-7128

DE DATTA, SURAJIT KUMAR, soil scientist, agronomist, educator; b. Shwebo, Upper Burma, Burma, Aug. 1, 1936; came to U.S., 1991; s. Dinanath and Birahini De Datta; m. Vijayalakshmi L., April 20, 1967; 1 child Raj Kumar De Datta. BS in Agrl., Banaras Hindu U., 1956; MS Soil Sci. and Agrl. Chem., Indian Agrl. Rsch. Inst., New Delhi, India, 1958; PhD Soil Sci., U. Hawaii, 1962. Postdoctoral agrl. experiment station Ohio State U., Columbus, 1962-63; prof. agronomy and soil sci. U. Philippines, Los Banos, Philippines, 1964-91; assoc. agronomist Internat. Rice Rsch. Inst., Manila, Philippines, 1964-69, agronomist, 1969-85, radiological health and safety officer, 1967-78, acting head dept. soil chem., 1975-76, dept. head, agronomy, 1967-89, principle scientist, 1986-91, program leader, 1990-91; dir., office internat. rsch. and devel. Va. Tech., Blacksburg, Va., 1991—, assoc. dean internat. agrl., 1993—, prof. crop and soil environ. sciences, 1991—, chair, 1996-97; bd. dirs. S.E. Consrotium for Internat. Devel., Washington; prin. investigator IPM CRSP Project (USAID), Va. Tech.; vis. prof. Purdue U., 1971-72, Kasetsart U., Thailand, 1984-91, Ctrl. Luzon State U., Nueva Ecija, Philippines, 1983-91; vis. scientist U. Calif., Davis, 1978-79. Author: Principles and Practices of Rice Production, 1981; consulting editor: Fertilizer Rsch. Jour. 1978-96; contbr. numerous articles to profl. jours. Recipient Internat. Soil Sci. award Soil Sci. Soc. Am., 1986, Best Paper award Weed Sci. Pest Control Coun. Philippines, 1986, Eminence award Bureau of Plant Industry, Philippines, 1987, Best Paper award Asian-Pacific Weed Sci. Soc., Taiwan, 1987, Second Best Paper award Asian-Pacific Weed Sci. Soc., Korea, 1989, Agronomic Rsch. award Am. Soc. Agronomy, 1990, Norman Borlaug award Coramandal, New Delhi, India, 1992. Fellow Am. Soc. Agronomy (chmn. internat. agronomy divsn. 1982-83), Soil Sci. Soc. Am., Indian Soc. Soil Sci., Internat. Svc. in Agronomy, Nat. Acad. Agrl. Scis. (India); mem. Crop Sci. Soc. Am., Internat. Soil Sci. Soc., Soil Sci. Soc. Japan, Crop Sci. Soc. Philippines, Weed Sci. Soc. Philippines, Indian Soc. Weed Sci., Asian-Pacific Weed Sci. Soc., Internat. Weed Sci. Soc., Pakistan Weed Sci. Soc. Hindu. Home: 512 Floyd St Blacksburg VA 24060-5071 Office: Office Internat Rsch & Devel Virginia Tech 1060 Litton Reaves Hall Blacksburg VA 24061

DEDE, J. ANTHONY, obstetrician, gynecologist; b. N.Y.C., July 12, 1933; s. Frank Paul and Clara (Curcio) D.; m. Cynthia Ann McNally, Aug. 14, 1969 (div. Oct. 1981); children: Kevin Darryl, Kisten Liese Elliott, Keith Randall Sean, Kathleen Andrea Rosi; m. Jean Price Lazzer, Feb. 11, 1984. AB, NYU, 1953; MD, Columbia U., 1957. Diplomate Am. Bd. Ob-Gyn. Surg. intern N.Y.U.-Cornell, N.Y.C., 1957-58; resident Sloan Hosp. for Women, Columbia Med. Ctr., 1961-64; rsch. fellow dept. ob-gyn. Columbia Sch. of Medicine, N.Y.C., 1964-66; ptnr. Rose-Besser-Dede, Princeton, N.J., 1966-77; pres. J. Anthony Dede MD PA, Princeton, 1977-79; ptnr. Havre (Mont.) Clinic, 1979-84; asst. clin. prof. U. South Fla., Daytona Beach, 1984-90; pres. J. Anthony Dede MD PC, Jesup, Ga., 1991—; instr. Columbia U., N.Y.C., 1965-68, Rutgers U., New Brunswick, N.J., 1968-73. Mem. Social Awareness Coun., Princeton, 1976-78; bd. dirs. All Saints Ch., Princeton, 1975-78, Rape Coun., Daytona Beach, Fla., 1988-90. Col. U.S. Army, 1990-91. Decorated Commendation medal; recipient commendation Am. Cancer Soc., Princeton, 1974, Jesup, 1995. Mem. Am. Cancer Soc. (med. dir. Jesup), Kiwanis. Home: 1033 Bennett Crossing Jesup GA 31545 also: 928 S First St Jesup GA 31545

DEDLOW, (EDNA) ROSELLEN, pediatric nurse practitioner; b. West Palm Beach, Fla., July 24, 1958; d. Robert Eugene and Mary Margaret (Danner) D. AS in Nursing, Indian River Community Coll., 1978, AA, 1989; BSN, U. Fla., 1990, MSN Child Health, Pediatric Primary Care, 1992. RN, Fla.; cert. ARNP, BLS, pediatric ALS, Am. Heart Assn. Staff nurse Martin Meml. Hosp., Stuart, Fla., 1978-85; nursing fellow Pediatric Pulmonary Ctr. U. Fla. Coll. Medicine, Gainesville, 1991-92; pediatric nurse practitioner/clin. nurse specialist Multihandicapped Splty. Clinics, U. Fla., Gainesville, 1992—; summer camp nurse Muscular Dystrophy Assn., Palm Beach, Fla., 1979-81, Am. Lung Assn., State of Fla., 1982, 84, 90, 92, 94; crisis care/foster care provider Div. Youth Svcs., Martin County Health and Rehab. Svcs., Fla., 1981-83, U. Fla. Family Camp, 1993-94, Fla. Claft Palate Craniofacial Assn. Family Camp, 1995. Mem. ANA (cert. pediat. nurse practitioner), Am. Acad. Nurse Practitioners, Fla. Nurses Assn., Spina Bifida Assn. Am., Fla. Cleft Palate/Craniofacial Assn., Sigma Theta Tau, Phi Kappa Phi, Phi Theta Kappa. Office: U Fla Coll Medicine Dept Pediatrics PO Box 100296 Gainesville FL 32610

DEEB, LARRY CHARLES, pediatric endocrinologist, epidemiologist; b. Tallahassee, Fla., July 2, 1947; s. Charles Hobeica and Carol Anna (Goll) D.; m. Josephine Marie Sutter, Oct. 7, 1978; children: Michael Larry, Laura Elzabeth. BA, Emory U., 1969, MD, 1973. Diplomate Am. Bd. Pediatrics. Pediatric resident U. Minn., Mpls., 1973-75, endocrine fellow, 1975-77; epidemiologist Ctrs. for Disease Control, Atlanta, 1977-80; pediatric endocrinology Childrens Clinic, Tallahassee, Fla., 1980—; epidemiologist cons. State of Fla., Tallahassee, 1980—; clin. prof. U. Fla., Gainesville, 1980—; med. dir. Diabetes Ctr. at Tallahassee; epidemiologist NIH, Bethesda, Md., 1988-93; bd. dirs. Fla. Camp for Children and Youth with Diabetes. Mem. editl. bd. practical Diabetes, 1987—, Clin. Diabetes, 1988-92, 96—, Meml. Rey Med. Ctr., 1992—, Diabetes Spectra, 1992; contbr. articles to profl. jours. Lt. comdr. USPHS, 1965-77. Fellow Am. Acad. Pediatrics, Lawson Wilkins Pediatric Endocrinology Soc., Internat. Soc. Pediatric and Adolescent Diabetes, Am. Assn. Clin. Endocrinologists; mem. Am. Diabetes Assn. (Fla. chpt. bd. dirs. 1981—), Internat. Diabetes Fedn. (life), Rotary. Episcopalian. Home: 2307 Trescott Dr Tallahassee FL 32312-3429 Office: Children's Clinic 2416 E Plaza Dr Tallahassee FL 32308-5301

DEEDS, ROBERT CREIGH, lawyer, state legislator; b. Richmond, Va., Jan. 4, 1958; s. Robert Livingston Deeds Jr. and Emma Lewis (Tyree) Hicklin; m. Pamela Kay Miller, Feb. 10, 1981; children: Amanda Jane, Rebecca Lewis, Austin Creigh, Susannah Kemper. BA, Concord Coll., Athens, W.Va., 1980; JD, Wake Forest U., 1984. Bar: Va. 1984, U.S. Dist. Ct. (we. dist.) Va. 1988. Assoc. Carter, Craig & Bass, P.C., Danville, Va., 1984-85, John C. Singleton, Warm Springs, Va., 1985-87; ptnr. Singleton & Deeds, Warm Springs, Va., 1988—; mem. Va. Ho. of Dels., 1992—; Commonwealth atty. Bath County, Va., 1988-92. Bd. dirs. Va. Mus. Frontier Culture. Mem. Va. State Bar, Alleghany-Bath Bar Assn., Va. Trial Lawyers Assn., Va. Assn. Commonwealth's Attys. (bd. dirs. 1989-91). Democrat. Presbyterian. Office: PO Box 116 Warm Springs VA 24484-0116

DEEGEN, UWE FREDERICK, marine biologist; b. Freising, Germany, Mar. 27, 1948; came to U.S., 1953; s. Friedrich Rudolf and Maria Magdalena (Dyrda) D.; m. Barbara Lynn Cannon, Aug. 7, 1982; 1 child, Jennifer Marie. BS, U. So. Miss., 1970, MS, 1972; PhD, U. Tex., 1979. Cert. fed. grants adminstr. Dept. Commerce, shellfish sanitarian FDA. Grad. rsch. assoc. U. So. Miss., Hattiesburg, 1970-72; instr. biology. Biloxi (Miss.) Sr. High Sch., 1972-73; instr. biology Pensacola (Fla.) Jr. Coll., 1973-74; grad. fellow U. Tex., Austin, 1974-76; staff scientist Miss. Marine Resources Coun., Long Beach, 1976-80; chief saltwater fisheries Miss. Bur. Marine Resources, Long Beach, 1980-89; sr. systems analyst Miss. Dept. Wildlife, Fisheries, and Parks, Biloxi, 1989-95; chief marine fisheries Miss. Dept. Marine Resources, Biloxi, 1995-96, dep. dir. Dept., 1995—; mem. Gulf Mex. Fishery Mgmt. Coun., Tampa, Fla., 1980-89; mem. tech. rev. com. U.S./Israel Binat. Agrl. R&D Fund, 1980-86; vice chmn. statis. subcom., chmn. rec. fisheries com. Gulf States Fisheries Commn., Ocean Springs, 1983-87; mem. freshwater inflow adv. com. EPA/Gulf Mex. Program, 1990—. Author: Mathematical Modeling of Oxygen Distribution in Streams, 1972; columnist Coastal Fishing, 1983—; contbr. articles to profl. jours. Tournament weightmaster Miss. Trout Invitational Tournament, Pass Christian, 1985—, Long Beach Jaycees Fishing Tournament, 1989—. Recipient King Neptune award Miss. Deep Sea Fishing Rodeo Bd. Dirs., Gulfport, Miss., 1991. Mem. Am. Fisheries Soc. (cert., mem. estuarine and marine resources com. 1993—), Estuarine Rsch. Fedn., Internat. Gamefish Assn., Kappa Mu Epsilon, Beta Beta Beta. Lutheran. Home: 121 E 4th St Long Beach MS 39560-6107 Office: Miss Dept Marine Resources 152 Gateway Dr Biloxi MS 39531-4409

DEEKENS, ELIZABETH TUPMAN, writer; b. Washington, Aug. 25, 1926; d. William Spencer Tupman and Isabelle McNeil Roberts; m. William Carter Deekens, July 30, 1955 (dec. 1988); children: Arthur Carter, Christine Deekens Old, Catherine Deekens Ward. Student, George Washington U., 1945-49. parish sec. All Souls Episcopal Ch., Washington, 1951-52; Washington corres. The Living Ch., Mpls., 1951-52; woman's editor Episcopal Churchnews, Richmond, Va., 1952-57; mem. Episcopal Churchwomen Bd., Diocese of Va., Richmond, 1968; mem. Bishop's Liturgical Commn., Diocese of Va., 1975; newsletter editor Vestry, Ch. of Epiphany, Richmond, 1974-82; editor, layreader St. Martin's Ch., Richmond, 1983—. Contbr. articles to mags. including Seventeen, Good Housekeeping, features to various newspapers. Mem. publicity staff First Mills Godwin Gubernatorial Campaign, 1965; v.p. corp. comms. Va. Hosp. Assn., 1968-88. Recipient numerous state and nat. writing awards. Fellow Am. Soc. Hosp. Mktg. and Pub. Rels.; mem. Va. Hosp. Mktg. and Pub. Rels. (a founder, bd. dirs. 1969-88, treas. 1975-85), Richmond Pub. Rels. Assn. (prs. 1983-84), Va. Press. Women, Internat. Order of St. Luke the Physicians (sec.-teas. 1989-91, convenor Richmond chpt. 1996—), Stephen Minister Lay Pastoral Care Ministry. Home: 9711 Royerton Dr Richmond VA 23228-1217

DEEL, GEORGE MOSES, elementary school educator; b. Haysi, Va., Apr. 9, 1938; s. Emory Floyd and Nancy Jane Deel. BS, Emory (Va.) & Henry Coll., 1961; MEd, Radford (Va.) U., 1965. Cert. tchr. Tchr. math. and gen. sci. Grundy (Va.) Jr. High Sch., 1961-79; resource tchr. gifted and academically talented Vansant (Va.) Elem. Sch., 1979-91; ret., 1991; cons. on gifted and talented Vansant (Va.) Elem. Sch., 1991—. Mem. NEA, Assn. Supervision and Curriculum Devel., Va. Edn. Assn., Buchanan Edn. Assn. Home and Office: RR 2 Box 168 Haysi VA 24256

DEEPAK, ADARSH, meteorologist, aerospace engineer, atmospheric scientist; b. Sialkot, India, Nov. 13, 1936. BS, Delhi U., 1956, MS, 1959; PhD in Aerospace Engr., U. Fla., 1969. Lectr. physics DB & KM Cols., Delhi U., 1959-63; instr. phys. sci. U. Fla., 1965-68, rsch. assoc. aerospace engring., 1970-71; fellow Nat. Rsch. Coun. Marshall Space Flight Ctr., NASA, 1972-74; rsch. assoc. prof. physics & geophys. sci. Old Dominion U., 1974-77; pres. Inst. Atmospheric Optics & Remote Sensing, Hampton, Va., 1977-84, 93—, Sci. & Tech. Corp., Hampton, Va., 1979—; rsch. assoc. U. Fla. and Wayne State U., 1970-72; mem. panel remote sensing & data acquisition NASA/ODAT Technol. Workshop, 1975; NSF travel grant to visit Indian insts., 1976; adj. prof. physics Coll. William & Mary, 1979-80; leader U.S. Del. Internat. Workshop Appln. Remote Sensing Rice Prod., India, 1981. Recipient U.S. SBA Minority Small Businessperson of Yr. award Richmond Dist., 1990. Mem. Am. Assn. for Aerosol Rsch., AAAS, Optical Soc. Am., Am. Meteorol. Soc., Am. Chem. Soc., Am. Geophys. Union, Soc. Environ. Toxicology and Chemistry. Office: Sci & Tech Corp 101 Research Dr PO Box 7390 Hampton VA 23666

DEERING, BRENDA FLORINE, secondary education educator; b. Porterville, Calif., July 25, 1953; d. Kenneth Henry Rogers and Barbara Oleta (Herron) Ledbetter; m. Robert Edward Deering, Feb. 14, 1975; children: David James, Duane Jason. BS in Psychology, Tex. Wesleyan U., 1989, MS in Edn., 1993. Lic. alcohol and drug abuse counselor. Substitute tchr. Birdville Ind. Sch. Dist., Haltom City, Tex., 1984-94; counselor pvt. practice, Bedford, Tex., 1991—, Residential Treatment Ctr., Bedford, Tex., 1990-91; tchr. secondary sch. Bridville Ind. Sch. Dist., 1994—; counseling affiliate Tarrant Bapt. Assn., Ft. Worth, 1992-94; tchr. ESOL Bedford Pub. Libr., 1993-94. Named Vol. of Yr. City of Bedford, 1993. Mem. NEA, Nat. Coun. Tchrs. English, Tex. Assn. Alcohol and Drug Abuse Counselors (edn. com. 1990—), Internat. Reading Assn., Sigma Tau Delta (Creative Writing award 1992), Pi Lambda Theta (corr. sec. 1993—), Kappa Delta Pi. Home: 3721 Windomere Dr Bedford TX 76021-2327 Office: Haltom Mid Sch 5000 Hires Ln Haltom City TX 76117

DEES, MORRIS S., lawyer. BA, U. Ala., 1958, LLB, 1960; JD (hon.), Whittier Coll., 1990, Providence Coll., 1990, Howard U., 1991, Wesleyan U., 1992, U. San Diego, 1993. Bar: Ala. Pres. Book Publ. Complex merged with L.A. Times, 1960-70; ptnr. Dees and Fuller P.A., Montgomery, Ala., 1960-64, Levin and Dees P.A., Montgomery, 1969-71; lawyer co-founder, chief trial counsel So. Poverty Law Ctr., Montgomery, 1971—; instr. Jones Law Sch. 1960-62; vis. instr. John F. Kennedy Sch. of Govt., Harvard Coll., 1972-76. Contbr. articles to profl. jours. Named one of 10 Outstanding Young Men of Am., U.S. Jaycees, 1966, hon. fellow of Law Sch., U. Pa., 1988; recipient Human Rights Outstanding Svc. award, Tuskegee Inst., 1976, Ala. Civil LIberties Union, 1981, Young Lawyers Disting. Svc. award ABA, 1987, Pub. Svc. Achievement award Common Cause, 1988, Roger Baldwin award, ACLU, 1989, Martin Luther King Jr. Meml. award NEA, 1990, Humanitarian award, Dir. Mktg. Day, N.Y., 1991, Barbara Jordan award Hollywood Women's Polit. Com., 1991, William O. Douglas award, Public Counsel, 1992, Oleander Peacemaker award, 1992, Humanitarian award U. Ala., 1993, Found. for Improvement of Justice award 1994, Justice Michael A. Musmanno award, Phila. Trial Lawyers, 1994, W.E. Chilton Leadership Lectr. award W. Va. Grad. Coll. Found., 1995. Office: PO Box 2087 400 Washington Ave Montgomery AL 36102

DEES, SANDRA KAY MARTIN, psychologist, research consultant; b. Omaha, Apr. 18, 1944; d. Leslie B. and Ruth Lillian (May) Martin; m. Doyce B. Dees; BA magna cum laude, Tex. Christian U., 1965, MA, 1972, PhD, 1989. Adminstrv. asst./rsch. coord. Hosp. Improvement Project, Wichita Falls (Tex.) State Hosp., 1968-69; caseworker adoptions Edna Gladney Home, Ft. Worth, Tex., 1970-71; psychologist Mexia (Tex.) State Sch., 1971-72; sch. psychologist Ft. Worth Ind. Sch. Dist., 1971-78, program evaluator, 1978-86; pvt. counselor, 1986-88; assoc. rsch. scientist Tex. Christian U., 1989—; mem. adj. faculty, 1991-92, grad. faculty, 1994—; bd. dirs Because We Care, Ft. Worth, 1988—, Hill Sch., 1994—. Dallas TCU Women's Club creative writing scholar, 1962-64, Virginia Alpha scholar, 1963; NASA research asst., 1965-67; USPHS trainee, 1967-68; cert. Am. Montessori Soc., 1977. Mem. APA, Am. Ednl. Rsch. Assn., Mental Health Assn., Mortar Bd., Mensa, Alpha Chi, Phi Alpha Theta, Psi Chi, Phi Delta Kappa. Contbr. articles to profl. publs. Home: 29 Bounty Rd W Fort Worth TX 76132-1003 Office: Tex Christian U Dept Psychology Fort Worth TX 76129

DEES, TOM MOORE, internist; b. Dallas, Mar. 4, 1931; s. Tom Hawkins and Maida Elizabeth (Board) D.; m. Suzanne Settle, Feb. 20, 1971; children: Tom Moore III, David Walsh. BA, Johns Hopkins U., 1952; MD, Southwestern Med. Sch., 1956. Intern Bellevue Hosp., N.Y.C., 1957, resident, 1958-59; rsch. fellow in cardiology Southwestern Med. Sch., Dallas, 1961; internist, ptnr. pvt. practice med. office Dallas, 1962—; dir. and mng. ptnr. Swiss Ave. Med. Bldg., Dallas, 1984—; clin. asst. prof. medicine Southwestern Med. Sch., Dallas, 1962—; assoc. attending physician Baylor Med. Ctr., Dallas, 1962—. Mem. dist. commn. Boy Scouts Am., Dallas, 1963-72; mem. ofcl. bd. Highland Park Meth. Ch., Dallas, 1963-72. Capt. USAF, 1959-61. Mem. ACP (life), AMA, Am. Soc. Internal Medicine, Johns Hopkins U. Alumni Assn. (pres. North Tex. chpt 1964-68), Tex. Club of Internists (pres. 1992-93). Republican. Home: 3649 Stratford Ave Dallas TX 75205-2810 Office: 3434 Swiss Ave Ste 420 Dallas TX 75204-6239

DEFELICE, SOFIA, real estate broker, owner; b. Naples, Italy, Aug. 20, 1945; d. Antonio and Anna (Gambardella) DeFelice; children: Timothy J. Noreika, Steven P. Noreika. Student, Greater Hartford Community Coll., 1970-71; real estate sales lic., U. Conn., 1980, diploma in real estate appraisal, 1985; diploma in real estate finance, 1988. Lic. real estate broker Conn., 1989, Fla., 1993, N.C. Hostess Holiday Season Restaurant, Waterbury, Conn., 1974-79; owner Sofia Tops Plus, Woodbury, Conn., 1979-84; realtor RE/MAX Properties Unltd., Southbury, Conn., 1984-88; owner Action Realty, Watertown, Conn., 1988-93, DeFelice Art Gallery, 1992—; community sales mgr. Davis Homes, 1993; owner RE/MAX Ctrl. Realty, Virginia Beach, Va., 1996—; land developer, Watertown, 1987; dir. Multiple Listing Svc. Greater Waterbury, Inc., 1990—. Den mother Boy Scouts Am., Bethlehem, Conn., 1980-83; vol. Bethlehem Elem. Sch., 1980-85; fund raiser Little League Baseball, Bethlehem, 1983-85, United Way, 1989; sponsor Miss Greater Watertown, 1989; dir. Multiple Listing Svc. of Greater Waterbury, Inc., 1990—. Mem. Waterbury Bd. Realtors, Nat. Assn. Realtors, Conn. Assn. Realtors, Multiple Listing Svc., RE/MAX Hundred Percent Club, RE/MAX Internat. Referral Network, Va. Realtors, Sons of Italy. Republican. Roman Catholic. Home: 1130 Toler Pl Norfolk VA 23503

DEFOOR, J. ALLISON, II, lawyer; b. Coral Gables, Fla., Dec. 6, 1953; s. James Allison Sr. and Marjorie (Keen) DeF.; m. Terry Ann White, June 24, 1977; children: Melissa Anne, Mary Katherine, James Allison III. BA, U. So. Fla., 1976; JD, Stetson U., 1979; MA, U. So. Fla., 1979; postgrad., Harvard U., 1989, So. Fla. Ctr. Theol. Studies, 1994—. Bar: Fla. 1979, U.S. Dist. Ct. (so. dist.) Fla. 1980, U.S. Ct. Appeals (5th cir.) 1981, U.S. Ct. Appeals (11th cir.) 1982. Asst. pub. defender, 1979-80; asst. state's atty. 16th Cir., Key West, Fla., 1980-83, dir. narcotics task force, 1981-83; judge Monroe County, Plantation Key, Fla., 1983-87; assoc. Cunningham, Albritton, Lenzi, Warner, Bragg & Miller, Plantation Key, 1987-89; sheriff Monroe County, Fla., 1989-90; sr. v.p. CEO Wackenut Monitoring Systems Inc., Coral Gables, Fla., 1991-92; gen. counsel, sec. HEM Pharm. Corp., Phila. and Key Largo, 1992-93; ptnr. Hershoff, Lupino DeFoor & Gregg, Tavernier, Fla., 1993—; bd. dirs. PCS, Inc., Tavernier, Fla.; adj. faculty St. Leo Coll., Key West, 1980-81, U. So. Fla., Ft. Myers, 1981-82, Fla. Internat. U., Miami, 1985, U. Miami Law Sch., 1985-90, 91—; faculty Nat. Jud. Coll., Reno, Nev., 1985-86; trustee U. of the South, Sewanee, Tenn., 1983-92; trustee So. Fla. Ctr. for Theol. Studies, 1992—, vice chair, 1995-96, chair, 1996—; mem. Fla. Humanities Coun., 1992-95; trustee Fla. Hist. Soc., 1996—, So. Fla. Jail Ministries, 1996—, Fla. Chamber Found., 1991-95; mem. adv. com. Fla. Keys Nat. Marine Sanctuary, 1992—, vice chair. Editor U. Miami Law Rev., 1985; author: DeFoor & Schultz, Fla. Civil Procedure Forum with Practice Commentary, 1989. Pres. Fla. Keys Land Trust, 1985-90, Mariners Hosp., 1988; chmn. Monroe County Rep. Exec. Com., 1987-88, 94, state committeeman, 1994—; mem. Fla. Rep. Exec. Com., 1995-96; del. Rep. Nat. Conv., 1992; Rep. nominee for Lt. Gov. of Fla., 1990; trustee So. Fla. Jail Ministries, Fla. Hist. Soc. Named one of Five Outstanding Young Men in Fla., Jaycees, 1984, Ten Outstanding Young Men in Am., Jaycees, 1985; recipient Merit award Fla. Crime Prevention Commn., 1982, Leadership Fla. Class V. Mem. ABA, Fla. Bar (bd. govs. 1995—), Monroe County Bar Assn., Mensa, Fla. Keys Bar Assn., Ocean Reef Club (Key Largo, Fla.), Key West Yacht Club, Explorer's Club (New York), Fla. Hist. Soc. (bd. trustees), South Fla. Jail Ministries. Republican. Episcopalian.

DEFOOR, WILLIAM ROBERT, minister; b. Atlanta, Dec. 2, 1941; s. Joseph T. and Mary Louise (Sheriff) DeF.; m. Sandra Bailey, June 22, 1962; children: Jennifer Louise, W. Robert, Stephanie Ruth. BA, Baylor U., 1964; MDiv, So. Bapt. Theol. Sem., Louisville, 1968, D in Ministry, 1975. Ordained to ministry So. Bapt. Conv., 1965. Pastor Mt. Moriah Bapt. Ch, Boston, Ky., 1965-68, Gilead Bapt. Ch., Glendale, Ky., 1969-73; assoc. pastor Druid Hills Bapt. Ch., Atlanta, 1973-75, pastor, 1976-79; pastor Harrodsburg (Ky.) Bapt. Ch., 1979—; evangelist So. Bapt. Home Mission Bd, Atlanta, 1977-83, 85, 88; pres. Ga. Bapt. Pastor's Conf., 1978-79; dir. Western Recorder, Middletown, Ky, 1983—; mem. exec. bd, Ky. Bapt. Conv., 1985-1988, 1st v.p., 1994; field supr. So. Bapt. Theol. Sem. 1987—; pres. Ky. Bapt. Fellowship, 1997—. Author: Sunday sch. lessons for religious publs. Coach Harrodsburg Little League, 1980-83; mem. Harrodsburg Bd. Edn., 1982-87; bd. dirs. Harrodsburg YMCA, 1983-86, United Way, 1988; trustee Georgetown Coll., 1993—. Mem. Mercer Ministerial Assn. (pres. 1981-83), Rotary (bd. dirs. 1984, pres. 1990, Rotarian of Yr. 1983). Democrat. Home: 815 Southgate Dr Harrodsburg KY 40330-2125 Office: Harrodsburg Bapt Ch Main at Office St Harrodsburg KY 40330

DEFOORE, JOHN NORRIS, management consultant; b. Sidon, Miss., June 12, 1919; s. George Gray and Ann Judson (Smith) DeF.; m. Zola Estella DeFoore, Sept. 5, 1945; children: John Norris, William G., Richard G., Marney W. BS, Miss. Coll., 1947; ThM, So. Seminary, 1951; postgrad., U. Edinburgh, 1957-59, Jungian Inst., Zurich. Exec. dir. Pastoral Care and Counseling, Boerne, Tex.; mgmt. cons. Promus Corp., Memphis; therapist in pvt. practice. Maj. U.S. Army, 1940-45. Mem. LMFT. Home: RR 1 Box 245B Comfort TX 78013-9801

DEFRANCESCO, GERRY, broadcasting company executive. Pres. Gannett Radio. Office: Gannett Co Inc 1100 Wilson Blvd Arlington VA 22234

D'EGIDIO, CONNIE SUE, contracts specialist; b. Effingham, Ill., Aug. 15, 1950; d. Vernon Cecil and Mabel Marie (Griffith) Swager; m. Anthony George D'Egidio, May 15, 1983. AS, U. Ky., Henderson, 1970; BS, U. Ky., Lexington, 1972. Quality assurance mgr. Bristol-Myers Co., Evansville, Ind., 1972-74, purchasing mgr., 1974-79; corp. purchasing mgr. Bristol-Myers Co., N.Y.C., 1979-1982; mfg. engr. IBM, Fishkill, N.Y., 1982-86, electronic industry competitive analyst, 1986-90, semiconductor mfg. tech. staff, 1990-93; market analyst IBM, Boca Raton, Fla., 1993-95, product announcement planner, 1995-96, sr. contract adminstr. software devel., 1996—. Advisory mem. Nat. Minority Purchasing Coun., N.Y.C. and Washington, 1979-82. Recipient Purchasing Excellence award Rutgers U. Sch. of Purchasing, 1982. Mem. IEEE (gen. program com. internat. electronics mfg. tech. conf. 1992-95, gen. program com. electronic component and tech. conf. 1992-94, asst. nat. program chmn. electronic component and tech. conf. 1995-96, nat. program chmn. electronic component and tech. conf. 1996—). Home: 9092 Villa Portofino Cir Boca Raton FL 33496

DE GRAVES, FRED JOHN, veterinarian, educator; b. Shelby, Mich., July 12, 1955; s. Fred John and Doris Edna (Apel) DeG. BS, Mich. State U., 1978, DVM, 1983; PhD, N.C. State U., 1991. Dairy practioner Dairyland Animal Health Inc., Weyauwega, Wis., 1983-87; asst. prof. Auburn (Ala.) U., 1991—. Contbr. articles to profl. jours. Mem. Am. Assn. Bovine Practitioners, Nat. Mastitis Coun., Am. Vet. Med. Assn., Am. Dairy Sci. Assn., Mammary Gland Physiology and Pathol. Soc., Soc. for Theriogenology.

DE GRAW, DARREL GARVIN, criminal justice educator; b. Mitchell, Nebr., July 12, 1934; s. Frederick and Faye (Catron) De G.; m. Shirley May Hand, Sept. 22, 1957; children: Diane Lynne, Debra Sue, Denise Rae, Douglas Gregg. MA, U. Nebr., Lincoln, 1967; EdS, U. Nebr., 1974; BS in Criminal Justice, U. Nebr., Lincoln, 1975, PhD, 1984; MBA, Kearney State Coll., 1978; MSEd, U. Dayton, 1982; BS, SUNY, 1982; MS, Am. Tech. U., 1988; MSHR, U. Cen. Tex., 1989; BA, Ind. U., 1990, Bemidji State U., 1990; MS in Criminal Justice, U. Ala., 1993; MA, Ctrl. Mo. State U., 1995. Tchr. Lincoln (Nebr.) Pub. Schs., 1960-72; minister Christian Ch., Beaver Crossing, Nebr., 1966-76; instr. in criminal justice Kearney (Nebr.) State Coll., 1976-80; asst. prof. in criminal justice U. Dayton, Ohio, 1980-83, Bemidji (Minn.) State U., 1984-85, Mohave C.C., Kingman, Ariz., 1986; assoc. prof. in criminal justice Am. Technol. U., Killeen, Tex., 1986—; dir. criminal justice program U. Cen. Tex., Killeen, 1987-93, Mo. Valley Coll., Marshall, 1993—; adj. faculty Wilmington Coll. Ohio, 1983. Contbr. booklets, aticles to popular mags., profl. jours. Bd. dirs. Police Hall of Fame and Mus., Miami. Mem. Acad. Criminal Justice Scis., Rotary, Phi Theta Kappa, Phi Delta Kappa, Delta Psi Omega, Alpha Phi Sigma, Pi Gamma Mu, Tau Kappa Epsilon, Psi Beta. Home: 500 E College St Marshall MO 65340-3109

DEGRILLA, ROBERT J., real estate executive; b. San Francisco, July 29, 1942; s. Robert M. and Josephine B. DeGrilla; m. Barbara Ann Gibson; children: Angela, Sean, Nicole. BBA in Real Estate, Calif. State U., San Francisco, 1965. Mgr. Coldwell Banker & Co., San Jose, Calif., 1967-72; v.p. IDC Real Estate, Houston, 1972-75, Wells Fargo Realty Advisors, Marina del Rey, Calif., 1975-78; pres. Wells Fargo Asset Mgmt. Co., Marina del Rey, 1978-83; exec. v.p., COO, Wynne/Jackson Inc., Dallas, 1983-92, pres., 1986-92; pres., CEO, Wynne Jackson Advisors, Dallas, 1985-92; pres. Wynne/Jackson Brokerage, 1988-92; mng. dir. Faison, Orlando, Fla., 1993—. Sgt. U.S. Army and USMC, 1965-67. Mem. Nat. Assn. Real Estate Investment Trusts, Nat. Assn. Corp. Real Estate Execs., Urban Land Inst., Bldg. Owners and Mgrs., Internat. Coun. Shopping Ctrs., Nat. Assn. Indsl. and Office Parks. Republican. Office: 225 E Robinson St Ste 500 Orlando FL 32801-4326

DEHAN, RODNEY SAMUEL, environmental scientist, researcher; b. London, Eng., June 19, 1945; came to U.S., 1968; s. Jean-Claud B. and Elizabeth Anne (McLeod) DeH.; m. Katherine Marion Houston, Oct. 24, 1984; 1 child, Kristin Whitney. DVM, U. Edinburgh, Scotland, 1967; MS, Kans. State U., 1969; PhD, Fla. State U., 1973. Chief microbiologist Trinity Luth. Hosp., Kansas City, Mo., 1968-70; microbiologist U. Kans. Med. Ctr., Kansas City, Mo., 1968-70; mem. rsch. faculty Fla. State U., Tallahassee, 1973-80; environ. specialist Dept. Environ. Regulation, Tallahassee, 1974-81, environ. adminstr., 1981-85, asst. chief, 1985—; cons. Congl. Office Tech. Assessment, Washington, 1984; cons. adv. coms. EPA, Washington, 1984-89. Contbr. articles to profl. jours. Recipient Cert. Appreciation EPA, 1985, 90, Nat. Environ. Health Assn., 1989. Mem. Nat. Water Well Assn. (regulatory ofcls. com. 1985—), Nat. Groundwater Assn. (pres.-elect groundwater protection coun., Groundwater Advocate award 1993), Underground Injection Practices Coun. (bd. dirs. 1988—, Cert. Appreciation 1990), Fla. Defenders of the Environment. Office: Dept Environ Protection 2600 Blairstone Rd Tallahassee FL 32399-6516

DEHART, ARNOLD O'DELL, engineering and design consultant; b. Davy, W.Va., May 8, 1926; s. William Guy and Sallie Ellen (Cock) DeH.; m. Wilma Joyce Jackson, June 24, 1951; children: Barry Dell, Thomas Edward, Ronald Allan. BSME, W.Va. U., 1950; postgrad., Wayne State U., 1952. Supr. Bur. of Census Dept. of Commerce, Welch, W.Va., 1950; jr. rsch. engr. Rsch. Labs. GM, Detroit, 1951-53, rsch. engr. Rsch. Labs., 1953-56, sr. rsch. engr. Rsch. Labs., 1956-62, sr. engr. Rsch. Labs., 1962-63, supervisory rsch. engr. Rsch. Labs., 1963-76, sr. staff rsch. engr. Rsch. Labs., 1976-81, prin. rsch. engr. Rsch. Labs., 1981-87; cons. Bearing Systems Tech., Naples, Fla., 1987-88; engring. and design cons. Naples, 1988—; chmn. guidance and evaluation panel ECUT Tribology program Dept. Energy, 1987-88. Contbr. numerous articles to profl. jours.; patentee in field. Pres. Pine Ridge Civic Orgn., 1995-96; mem. adv. com. Naples (Fla.) Mcpl. Airport, 1995-96. Cadet U.S. Air Corps, 1944-45. Recipient Nat. Silver medal in vet. class bicycling, 1988, Fla. Gold medal in vet. class, 1989, 90, 91, 93, 94, 95, Gold medal Fla. Sr. Games, 1992, Clifford Steadman prize Inst. of Mech. Engrs., 1986. Mem. Am. Soc. Lubrication Engrs., Soc. Tribologists and Lubrication Engrs. (past mem. bearing and lubrication com., lectr. sliding surface bear ednl. courses), Soc. Automotive Engrs. (mem. bearing materials subcom., past chmn. bearing subcom., past chmn. bearing materials subcom., Arch T. Colwell Merit award 1984, Ralph R. Teetor Indsl. lectr. 1985), Plain Bearing Stds. Assn., U.S. Cycling Fedn., Pi Tau Sigma, Tau Beta Pi. Home and Office: 7000 Trail Blvd Naples FL 33963-2655

DEHAVEN-SMITH, WESTI JO, academic administrator; b. Pensacola, Fla., Oct. 21, 1947; d. Joseph Burnes and Doris Rae (Stoneman) deHaven; m. Jeffrey E. Zink, June 19, 1970 (div. 1977); 1 child, Matthew Edward; m. Lance Michael deHaven-Smith, Oct. 9, 1980; 1 child, Joseph Michael, 1 stepchild, Erin C. Smith. BA, Kent State U., 1970; MPA, Fla. Atlantic U., 1986. Program specialist Ohio Appalaachian Child Devel. Program, 1970-73; social svcs. dir. Stark Met. Housing Authority, 1973-75; planner Brona, Inc.; project mgr. Urbanistics, Inc.; researcher econs., planning and policy analysis dept. Battelle Meml. Inst., Columbus, Ohio, 1979-81; dir. publs. FAU-FIU Joint Ctr. for Environ. and Urban Problems, external rels./rsch. coord. coll. engring., asst. to v.p. for univ. rels., 1982—. Contbr. articles and monograph to profl. jours.; editor: Environ. and Urban Issues, 1982-89. Mem. steering com. Greater Boca Raton Vision 2002, 1992—; mem. exec. com., chair vol. com. Meet Me Downtown, Boca Raton, 1993, 92; mem. sch. improvement team mem. Country Hills Elem. Sch., Broward County, Fla., 1992-93; pres. Children's Learning Ctr. Boca Raton, Inc., 1990-92; bd. mem. Unitarian Universalist Fellowship Boca Raton, 1989-91, Columbus Day Care Cooperative, 1978-80, Ohio Citizen's Coun. for Health and Welfare, 1976-78, Stark County Presch. and Day Care Program, 1973-75, others. Recipient Miklos award for acad. excellence; named to Outstanding Young Women of Am., 1974. Mem. Phi Kappa Phi, Pi Alpha Alpha. Democrat. Home: 3429 Welwyn Way Tallahassee FL 32308 Office: Fla Atlantic U 500 NW 20th St Boca Raton FL 33431-6415

DEHAY, JERRY MARVIN, business educator; b. Brownwood, Tex., Nov. 21, 1939; s. Marvin Edward and Willie Marie (Daniell) DeH.; m. Dana Lea Laxson, May 29, 1960 (div. June 30, 1973); children: David, Deanna; m. Marilyn Ann Lethco, July 28, 1973; children: Colin, Beva, Sue. BBA, A&M Coll. Tex., 1962; MBA, Tex. A&M U, 1966; PhD, North Tex. State U., 1978. Sales mgr. Procter and Gamble, Corpus Christi, Tex., 1962-65; instr., mktg. Tex. A&M U., College Station, 1966-69; asst. prof. bus. Howard Payne U., Brownwood, Tex., 1969-73; coord. food mktg. Tarrant County Jr. Coll. N.E., Hurst, Tex., 1973-75; instr. math. Brownwood State Sch., 1976-77; asst. prof. mktg. East Tex. State U., Commerce, 1977-78, prof., 1979-83; assoc. prof. bus. Hardin Simmons U., Abilene, Tex., 1978-79; dean Coll. Bus. Adminstrn. Tarleton State U., Stephenville, Tex., 1983-94; CEO JMD Cons., Brownwood, Tex., 1994—j; co-owner Recollections Antiques and Collectibles, Early, Tex., 1996—; dir. continuing edn. Howard Payne U., 1971-73, SBI East Tex. State U., 1979-83, SBI Tarleton State U., 1983-87, SBDC, 1987-89; mem. Tex. State U. Agribus. Incubator Adv. Bd., SBDC adv. bd. Co-author: Supervision, 1984; author, presenter PBS TV series Business File, 1985. Sec. bd. trustees Brownwood Ind. Sch. Dist., 1972; trustee Mullin (Tex.) Ind. Sch. Dist. 1979; chmn. regional adv. bd. SBA. Named Outstandinf educator of Am., 1973, 74, 75, Outstanding Am. of Bi-Centennial Era, 1976. Mem. Sales and Mktg. Execs. Ft. Worth (educator mem.), Delta Sigma Pi, Mu Kappa Tau, Pi Sigma Epsilon (educator v.p. 1984-85, adminstrv. v.p. 1985-86, nat. pres. 1987, Top Faculty Advisor award 1983). Baptist. Home and Office: 801 Quail Run Brownwood TX 76801-6314

DEICHMANN, RICHARD E., internal medicine physician; b. Mar. 23, 1957; m. Cecile L. Many; children: Elizabeth, Claire, Paige. Student, Harvard U., 1976, U. Calif., Berkeley, 1978; BS cum laude, Tulane U., 1980, MD, 1982. Diplomate in internal medicine and geriatrics Am. Bd. Internal Medicine. Intern Med. Coll. Va., 1982-83; resident internal medicine U. N.C., Chapel Hill, 1983-85, clin. instr., chief resident in medicine, 1985-86; physician Mahorner Clinic, New Orleans, 1986-92; co-founder, physician Audubon Internal Medicine, New Orleans, 1992—; bldg. com. Mahorner Clinic, New Orleans, 1987-89, mktg. com., 1988-92, chmn. quality assurance program, 1989-92, risk mgmt. com., 1989-92; staff So. Bapt. Hosp., New Orleans, 1986—, chmn. grand rounds com., 1988-91, med. adviser Home Health Svcs. Agy., 1992—; staff Tulane U. Hosp., New Orleans, 1986—, Charity Hosp. New Orleans, 1986—, Touro Infirmary, New Orleans, 1987-93, East Jefferson Gen. Hosp., 1991—; clin. instr. U. N.C. Sch. Medicine, 1985-86; clin. asst. prof. Tulane U., 1986—; others. Bd. dirs. New Orleans Symphony, 1988-89; dir. Physicians' Symphony Fund, 1988-89. Recipient Kappa Alpha scholarship cert. Fellow ACP; mem. AMA, Orleans Parish Med. Soc. (bd. govs. 1992—, orgnl. restructuring task force 1993—), La. State Med. Soc. (del. 1989, 92, med.-legal interprofl. com. 1992—), Am. Soc. Internal Medicine, Physicians for Social Responsibility, Am. Coll. Home Care Physicians, New Orleans Acad. Internal Medicine, Am. Geriatrics Soc., Phi Beta Kappa, Phi Eta Sigma, Alpha Epsilon Delta, Omicron Delta Kappa. Office: Audubon Internal Medicine 2820 Napoleon Ave New Orleans LA 70115-6916

DEIDAN, CECILIA THERESA, neuropsychologist; b. N.Y.C., Oct. 24, 1964. BA Biology, Spanish, Psychology, St. Louis U., 1985; MEd in Counseling Psychology, U. Mo., 1987, PhD in Counseling Psychology, 1992. Lic. psychologist, Fla., sch. psychol. examiner, Mo. Counselor, detoxification asst. McCambridge Ctr. for Women, Columbia, Mo., 1986-88; shc. psychol. examiner Columbia Pub. Schs., 1988-90; geriatric neuropsychology postdoctoral fellow U. Miami Sch. Med., 1992-93; pvt. practice Pembroke Pines, Fla., 1993—; adj. prof. Fla. Internat. U., Miami, 1993—. Mem. ACA, NAN, APA, Kappa Delta Pi, Psi Chi, Sigma Delta Pi, Alpha Sigma Nu, Beta Beta Beta.

DEISENHOFER, JOHANN, biochemistry educator, researcher; b. Zusamaltheim, Bavaria, Germany, Sept. 30, 1943; came to U.S., 1988; s. Johann and Thekla (Magg) D.; m. Kirsten Fischer-Lindahl, June 19, 1989. Diploma in Physics, Technische U., Munich, 1971, PhD, 1974, Doctor habilis, 1987. Postdoctoral fellow Max-Planck Inst. Biochemie, Martinsried, Fed. Republic of Germany, 1974-76, staff scientist, 1976-88; investigator Howard Hughes Med. Inst., Dallas, 1988—; prof. biochemistry U. Tex., Dallas, 1988—. Contbr. over 50 sci. papers to profl. pubis. Recipient Nobel prize for chemistry, 1988; co-recipient Biol. Physics prize Am. Phys. Soc., 1986, Otto Bayer prize, 1988; decorated The Knight Commader's Cross (Badge and Star) Of the Order of Merit of Germany, 1990, Bavarian Order of Merit, 1992. Mem. AAAS, Am. Crystallographic Assn., German Biophys. Soc., The Protein Soc., Biophysical Soc., Academia Europaea.

DEITCH, D. GREGORY, meteorologist; b. Gettysburg, Pa., Aug. 22, 1953; s. Druid Cassatt and Betty Jane (Ridinger) D.; m. Judith Arline Brown, Sept. 1, 1990; 1 stepchild, Kevin Miller. BS in Astronomy, Villanova U., 1975; BS in Meteorology, U. Utah, 1978, MS in Meteorology, 1981. Meteorologist intern Nat. Earth Satellite Svc., Anchorage, 1979, Honolulu, 1980; meteorologist at Amundsen-Scott South Pole Sta. ITT Antarctic Svcs., 1981-82; operational and ballistics meteorologist U.S. Army Atmospheric Scis. Lab., White Sands Missile Range, N.Mex., 1982-90; rsch. meteorologist in climatology Dept. Air Force, Asheville, N.C., 1990—; team chief Ft. Huachuca (Ariz.) Meteorl. Team, 1985. Mem. Am. Meteorol. Soc. Republican. Home: 44 Foxfire Dr #C Asheville NC 28803-3152

DEJEAN, BETTY L., county administrator; b. Bklyn., Feb. 1, 1946. MBA, Barry U., 1989. Catalog sales, credit sales mgr. Sears, Roebuck & Co., L.A., Hollywood and Miami, Fla., 1964-76; bus. mgr. Quisqueya Christian Sch., Port-au-Prince, Haiti, 1979-83; credit supr., salary adminstr., info. sys. officer Barnett Bank S. Fla., Hallandale and Miami, 1983-89; spl. project coord., adminstrv. mgr., asst. to dept. dir. Broward County Govt., Ft. Lauderdale; asst. to dir. community svcs. dept. Broward County Govt., Ft. Lauderdale, Fla., 1989—. Mem. Am. Soc. Pub. Adminstrs. Office: Community Svcs Dept Broward County 115 S Andrews Ave Ste 427 Fort Lauderdale FL 33301-1801

DEKAY, GARY EARL, non-profit organization executive; b. Utica, N.Y., Nov. 11, 1946; s. Carl Bernard and Mary Francis (Schafer) DeK.; m. Karen Elizabeth Centro; 1 child, Kimmerly Mildred DeKay Moore. BS, Embry-Riddle Aero. U., Daytona Beach, Fla., 1980, MBA, 1982. Commd. 1st lt. U.S. Army, 1965, advanced through grades to col., 1996; now in res.; aviation officer Ala. Army N.G., Mobile, 1975-94; logistic mgmt. officer Ala. Army N.G., Birmingham, 1985-95; logistics mgmt. cons. Mobile, 1995-96; exec. dir. Bay Area Food Bank, Mobile, 1996—; mem. dist. 1 Employer Support of Guard and Res., Mobile, 1995—. Exec. v.p. Mobile Area Vets. Day Commn., Mobile, 1995—. Decorated Meritorious Svc. medal, Bronze Star medal, Air medal with 24 oak leaf clusters. Mem. Air Force Assn. (v.p. aerospace edn. Mobile chpt. 1994—, pres. 1996), Army Aviation Assn. Am., Vietnam Helicopter Pilots Asn., N.G. Assn. U.S. Baptist. Home: 134 Lake Shore Dr Daphne AL 36526 Office: Bay Area Food Bank 551-C Western Dr Mobile AL 36670

DEKU, AFRIKADZATA, African-Centric Pan-African language educator, consultant; b. Kadjebi, Ghana, Dec. 13, 1949; m. Yayra Deku; children: Mawunyo, Aku Sika, Mawulolo. BA with honors, U. Cape Coast, Ghana, 1977; MSc, U. Ife, Nigeria, 1981; diploma, Inst. Internat. D'Adminstrn. Pub., Paris, 1983; MPhil, U. Paris XI, Sorbonne, 1983, PhD, 1985. Lic. mediator, arbitrator, negotiator. Ind. post-doctoral rsch. scholar U. Denver, 1986-87; founder, chief exec., prof. pan-Afrikan studies Afrikan Culture Inst., 1987—; vis. assoc. prof. African history Clark Atlanta U., 1990-91; vis. assoc. prof. African studies Morris Brown Coll., Atlanta, 1990; assoc. prof. Afrikan culture dept. continuing edn. Ga. State U., 1990; pub. The Afrikan Truth, 1994—; vis. prof. French and African lit. Wofford Coll., Spartanburg, S.C., 1988-89, Converse Coll., Spartanburg, 1989; lectr., spkr. and cons. in field. Author: (poetry) We Are All Continental Afrikans, 1991, Sacred Verses For My Afrikan Queen, 1992, Sacred Afrikan Spiritual Power From Within, 1993, Agbenoxevie Menye, Ablodesafui, Agbedefu (Ewe poetry), Courage, Mere Afrique, Cris de Tonnerre, Coups de Marteau, A Toi le Paradis de Ma Langue (Afrikan Poetry in French); (plays) No Where is Heaven, Breaking the Bloody Sword of Apartheid, (rsch. books) L'Union Continentale Africaine, vols. 1-3, 1986, Continentale Afrikan Power Now, 1987, The Afrikan-Centric Perspective of the Afrikan World Crisis, 1988, Continental Afrikan Manifesto, 1990, Continental Afrikan Power in Figures, 1989, The Afrikan Gospel of Total Happiness Now and Always, 1991, The Power of Afrikan-Centricity, 1992, AFRIKAMAWUNYA or the Holy Afrikan Bible, 1993, Continental Afrika: From Two Hundred Million Seasons to the Present, 1994, The Power and Benefits of Continental Afrikan Culture, 1994, How to Be A Continental Afrikan Again, 1994, Positive Self-Knowledge Technology, 1994, Positive Goal Achievement Technology, 1994, Positive Problem-Solving Technology, 1996, Positive Decision-Making Technology, 1994, Positive Financial Security Technology, 1994, I Want to Tell You Why, 1995, From Eagle to Chicken, 1995, Behold: The Continental Afrikan Savior is Born, 1996, Le Rastafari ou le Retour en Afrique, 1996, La Negritude Radicale et Moderee, 1996, Socialist/Communist Practices by USA Governments Past and Present, 1995. Founder Afrikan-Centricity Movement, Continental Afrikan Govt. Orgn., Continental Afrikan Found., Continental Afrikan Devel. Authority. Grantee S.C. Arts Commn., 1990-91; scholar Ghana Govt., 1970-72, 73-77, Commonwealth, 1975, 77, 78, French Govt., 1982-85; recipient OYO State Bursary award, 1980-81, Spartanburg, S.C. Arts Coun. award, 1989-90. Mem. ABA, Am. Arbitration Assn., S.C. Coun. for Mediation and Alternative Dispute Resolution, Internat. Biog. Assn., Internat. Platform Assn., French PhD Holders Assn., African Studies Assn., African Heritage Studies Assn., Am. Polit. Sci. Assn. Home: 182 Stribling Cir Spartanburg SC 29301-1651 also: Box 209, Dansoman-Accra Ghana

DELAFOUNTAINE, CHARLES RANDALL, security company official; b. Bloomington, Ind., Sept. 18, 1964; s. Charles Francis LaFountaine and Rosalee Harris. Student, U. North Fla., 1995—. Cert. security officer, Fla. Various positions, Bloomington, 1983-91; security officer Security Svcs., Inc., Pitts., 1991-92, Pinkerton Security, Inc., Jacksonville, Fla., 1993; office adminstr. Christ Cmty. Ch., State College, Pa., 1992; security officer Gray's Security, Inc., Jacksonville, 1995—. Contbr. poetry to anthologies. Vol. Rep. presdl. campaigns, 1984, 88, 92, 96; candidate for Monroe County (Ind.) Cmty. Sch. Corp., 1986; mem. Fla. and Duval County Rep. coms., 1993—. Home: 5201 Atlantic Blvd Apt 192 Jacksonville FL 32207

DELAFUENTE, JEFFREY CHARLES, pharmacy educator; b. Cleve., Mar. 1, 1950; s. Morris H. and Judith D. (Roller) D. BS in Pharmacy, U. Fla., 1973, MS in Pharmacy, 1976. Rsch. fellow dept. of medicine U. Fla., Gainesville, 1976-79, asst. prof., 1984-87, assoc. prof., 1987-94, assoc. chmn., 1990—, prof., 1994—; asst. prof. St. Louis U., 1979-84. Editor: Therapeutics in the Elderly, 1988, 2d edit., 1995, Pharmacotherpy Self-Assessment, 1996; editl. bd. Annals of Pharmacotherapy, Cin., 1989—. Fellow Am. Coll. Clin. Pharmacy; mem. Am. Assn. of Colls. of Pharmacy, Am. Pharm. Assn., Am. Assn. of Asthma Allergy and Immunology, Fla. Pharmacy Assn., Am. Soc. of Health System Pharmacists, Rho Pi Phi. Office: Univ Fla PO Box 100486 Gainesville FL 32610-0486

DE LA GARZA, JOEL SANTIAGO, assistant principal; b. San Benito, Tex., Jan. 18, 1952; s. Jose and Esther (Noyola) D.; m. erica Cathlene Whitinger, Aug. 14, 1976; 1 child, Joel Santiago II. AA, Tex. Southmost Coll., Brownsville, 1972; BEd, Pan Am. U., 1979; MEd, U. Tex., Edinburg, 1995. Cert. tchr., Tex. Tchr. Harlingen (Tex.) Consol. Ind. Sch. Dist., 1980-94, asst. prin., 1994—; inclusiveness cons. Tex. State PTA, Austin, 1993-94. Bd. dirs. San Benito Pub. Libr., 1983-87, Tex. State PTA, Austin, 1991-94, HomeFest, Inc., San Benito, 1995—; bd. advisor Literacy Ctr., San Benito, 1992-94; coach, bd. dirs. San Benito Youth Baseball, 1974-84; Region I site-based adv. bd. Region I Svc. Ctr., Edinburg, 1992-96; adv. mem. U.I.L., Austin, 1994; treas. Harlingen South Band Boosters, 1994-96. Named Coach of the Yr., Harlingen Boys Club, 1986, 88, 91. Mem. Tex. Elem. Prins. and Suprs., Tex. PTA (life), Nat. PTA (life). Democrat. Roman Catholic. Home: 255 Hidalgo St San Benito TX 78586 Office: Harlingen Consolidated Ind Sch Dist 309 Madeley Combes TX 78535

DE LA GARZA, KIKA (ELIGIO DE LA GARZA), congressman; b. Mercedes, Tex., Sept. 22, 1927; s. Dario and Elisa (Villarreal) de la G.; m. Lucille Alamia, May 29, 1953; children: Jorge Luis, Michael Alberto, Angela Dolores. Student, Pan Am. Coll., Edinburg, Tex., 1947-48; LLB, St. Mary's U., San Antonio, 1951; LLD (hon.), Lincoln U. of Mo., 1982, U. Md., 1985, Hanyang U., Seoul. Bar: Tex. 1951. Mem. from Hidalgo County Tex. Ho. of Reps., 1953-64; mem. 89th-104th Congresses from 15th Tex. dist., Washington, 1965-96. With USNR, World War II; with AUS, Korea. Democrat.

DELAGI, EDWARD FRANCIS, physician; b. N.Y.C., Nov. 4, 1911; s. Michael Nicholas and Angela (Ciani) D.; m. Westa Vespa, Feb. 16, 1941; children—West Ann (Mrs. Richard Hanafin), Edwina (Mrs. Donald Askew). B.S., Fordham U., 1934; M.D., Hahnemann Med. Coll., 1938. Intern Fordham Hosp., Bronx, N.Y., 1938-40; resident Bronx VA Hosp., 1951-54, chief ward sect. phys. medicine and rehab., 1954-56; dir. phys. medicine and rehab. Misericordia Hosp., Bronx, 1958-65; attending physician Bronx Municipal Hosp. Ctr., 1956-85; cons. phys. med. and rehabilitation No. Westchester Hosp., Misericordia Hosp., Bronx, St. Joseph's Hosp., Yonkers, N.Y.; asst. prof. dept. rehab. medicine Albert Einstein Coll. Med., Bronx, 1950-55, assoc. prof., 1959, 64, prof., 1964-85, prof. emeritus, 1985—. Served with AUS, 1941-45. Decorated Bronze Star. Fellow ACP, Am. Acad. Phys. Medicine and Rehab., N.Y. Acad. Medicine; mem. AAAS, Am. Congress Phys. Medicine. Home: 6178 SE Riverboat Dr Stuart FL 34997-1527

DELAHANTY, EDWARD LAWRENCE, management consultant; b. South Bend, Ind., Feb. 17, 1942; s. Edward Lawrence and Rosemary Margaret (DeVreese) D.; m. Rebecca A. Paczesny, June 22, 1963; children: David Edward, Debra Ann. BS in Math., U. Notre Dame, 1963. Enrolled actuary. Asst. actuary Aetna Life & Casualty Co., Hartford, Conn., 1963-70; mng. ptnr. Hewitt Assocs., Mpls., 1971-85, mem. exec. com., 1981-87, 90-95; southeast region mng. prin., Hewitt Assocs., L.L.C., Atlanta, 1986—; v.p., sec.-treas., bd. dirs. CMI Stores Inc., 1983-85; bd. dirs. Brandt Barringmann Inc., 1981-84; bd. dirs. United Telco, Inc., 1992-95; Fellow Soc. Actuaries; mem. Am. Acad. Actuaries, Enrolled Actuary, Am. Compensation Assn., Atlanta Area Compensation Assn., So. Employee Benefits Conf., Atlanta Nat. Golf Club, Peachtree Club, Ravinia Club, Buckhead Club, 191 Club. Home: 86 Blackland Ct NW Atlanta GA 30342-4434 Office: 2100 Riveredge Pky NW # 900 Atlanta GA 30328-4656

DELAHANTY, REBECCA ANN, school system administrator; b. South Bend, Ind., Oct. 18, 1941; d. Raymond F. and Ann Marie (Batsleer) Paczesny; m. Edward Delahanty, June 22, 1963; children; David, Debbie. BA, Coll. of St. Catherine, Minn., 1977; MA, Coll. St. Thomas, Minn., 1983; PhD, Ga. State U., 1994. Cert. in adminstrn. and supervision, Ga. Initiator, tchr. gifted kindergarten Dist. 284 Sch., Wayzata, Minn., 1977-83; gifted kindergarten coord. St. Barts Sch., Wayzata, 1983-85; prin. Dabbs Loomis Sch., Dunwoody, Ga., 1987-91; asst. to supt. Buford (Ga.) City Schs., 1993—; mem. staff devel. adv. coun. Ga. Contbr. article to profl. publ. Mem. ASCD, Am. Ednl. Rsch. Assn., Nat. Assn. Gifted Children, Minn. Coun. Gifted and Talented, Phi Delta Kappa, Omicron Gamma.

DE LAMA, ALBERTO, artist; b. Havana, Cuba; s. Victorio and Carmen (Pena) de L.; m. June Rose Milazzo de Lama, Mar. 11, 1961. AA, Am. Acad. Art, Chgo., 1965. Tchr. Am. Acad. Art, Chgo., 1969-75; pres. Graphic Direction, Tampa, Fla., 1982—. Works exhibited in various shows including Wis. Tourist Office, Chgo., Welna Gallery, Chgo., Galeria Sans Souci, Caracas, Venezuela, Talisman Gallery, Bartlesville, Okla., LeBlanc's Wildlife Gallery, Minocqua, Wis., Publicidad STOP, Caracas, Tamiami Hall, Miami, Fla., Omni Ctr., Miami, Univ. Club Tampa, Fla., Galeria Vanidades, Miami; represented in permanent collections Fla. Eye Ctr., Tampa, Pullman Bank, Chgo., Talman Home Fed. Savs., Chgo., Jim Walter Corp., Tampa, Delta Airlines, Atlanta, The Celotex Corp., Tampa, Uniroyal Corp., N.Y.C., Galeria Vanidades, Miami. Adv. bd. Salvation Army, Tampa, Fla., 1990—. Recipient 1st prize Carnival Poster Competition, Havana, Cuba, 1959, Diamond medal 1970-71, Gold medal, 1972-75 Palette and Chisel Acad.m Chgo., 3rd prize Mucpl. Art League, Chgo., 1974, Harriett Bitterly Meml. award, Chgo., 1976. Home: 3005 Horatio St Tampa FL 33609

DELAMATER, THOMAS ROBERT, public relations and fundraising executive; b. Cleve., June 30, 1957; s. Charles Edward and Evelyn Marie (Bower) D.; m. Doreen Joan Stansbury, Sept. 28, 1982; children: Jaclyn Renae, John Charles, Joseph Ryan. BA, Amb. U., 1984; MA, U. Tex., Tyler, 1988. Assoc. creative dir. Annie's Attic, Inc., Big Sandy, Tex., 1984-85; advt. cons. Tyler, 1986-87; account exec. Design Strategy, Tyler, 1988; chair mass comm. Ambassador U., Big Sandy, 1988-89, dir. instnl. advancement, 1990—. Mem. Upshur County Econ. Devel. Com., Gilmer, Tex., 1993—. Mem. Nat. Soc. Fund Raising Execs., Pub. Rels. Soc. Am. (nat. exec. com. for edn. and cultural orgns. sect. 1994—), Big Sandy C. of C. (bd. dirs., pres. 1995—). Office: Ambassador Univ Instnl Advancement Dept Hwy 80 E Big Sandy TX 75755

DELANEY, ANDREW, retired insurance company executive, consultant; b. Vienna, Ohio, Aug. 2, 1920; s. John David and Elizabeth L. (Wurstner) D.; m. Wynelle Shellhouse, Apr. 5, 1947; 1 dau., Janet Lynn; m. Pauline Mills, July 31, 1982. B.A., Oberlin Coll., 1942; B.S., NYU, 1942. Actuarial trainee Equitable Life Assurance Co., N.Y.C., 1946-49; asst. actuary Union Central Life Ins. Co., Cin., 1949-54; v.p. actuary Am. Gen. Life Ins. Co., Houston, 1954-68, sr. v.p., 1968-76, sr. v.p., chief investment officer, 1976-82, vice chmn. bd., chief investment officer, 1982-85; ret., 1985. Life bd. dirs. Big Bros., Houston, 1969—; trustee Found. for Retarded, 1982—; past chmn., bd. trustees Emerson Unitarian Ch., Houston. Capt. USAF, 1942-46. Fellow Soc. Actuaries (bd. govs.); mem. Houston Racquet Club, Ramada Club, River Oaks Country Club, Horshoe Bay Club, The Forest Club. Republican. Home: 2205 Pelham Dr Houston TX 77019-3530 Office: 2727 Allen Pky Ste 460 Houston TX 77019-2100

DELANEY, HERBIE See **BRYANT, HERBERT MCCOY, JR.**

DELANEY, ROBERT ANTHONY, clinical pharmacist, researcher; b. Jersey City, July 8, 1947; s. Robert Thomas and Katherine Florence (Blumetti) D.; m. Arlene June Lewczak, Feb. 19, 1972; children: Jennifer Suzanne, Meghan Elizabeth. BS, Columbia U., 1970; MA, U. No. Colo., 1974; PharmD, Phila. Coll. Pharmacy, 1977. Pharmacy intern Jersey City Med. Ctr., 1970; chief pharmacy svc. USAF Hosp., Ellsworth AFB, S.D., 1971-76, Little Rock AFB, 1977-80; assoc. dir. pharm. svcs. William Thompson Hosp., Ft. Worth, 1980-85; dir. pharm. svcs. Clark Air Base, The Philippines, 1985-88; dir. clin. rsch. lab. USAF Kessler AFB, Biloxi, Miss., 1988-91; clin. mgr. Our Lady of the Med. Ctr., Baton Rouge, 1991-92; area clin. mgr. Owen Healthcare, Hammond, La., 1992—; clin. cons. to surgeon gen. Pacific Forces, Hickam AFB, 1985-89. Contbr. numerous articles to profl. jours. Staff officer Coast Guard Aux., 1991—. Rsch. grantee Surgeon Gen. USAF, 1989, 91. Mem. Am. Soc. Hosp. Pharmacists, Am. Coll. Clin. Pharmacists, Am. Radio Relay League, S.E. Soc. Hosp. Pharmacists (co-editor jour. 1990—), Ocean Springs (Miss.) C. of C., 1991. Roman Catholic.

DELANO, KENNETH JAMES, JR., air force officer; b. Anchorage, Feb. 15, 1963; s. Kenneth James and Evelina Gladys (Ramirez) D.; m. Deborah Jean Molina, Dec. 17, 1983; children: Cynthia Ann, Michael Joseph. BSEE, Tex. A&M U., 1984; MS in Tech. Mgmt., U. Md., 1993. Registered cryptologic engr. Commd. 2d lt. USAF, 1985—, advanced through grades to maj., 1996; satellite program mgr. space divsn. USAF, L.A., 1985-89; global positioning sys. mgr. Nat. Security Agy., Ft. Meade, Md., 1989-93; engring. br. chief human sys. divsn. USAF, San Antonio, 1993-96, chief C4I project sect. edn./tng. command, 1996—.

DE LA PIEDRA, JORGE, orthopedic surgeon; b. Peru, Feb. 11, 1923; came to U.S., 1960; naturalized, 1963; s. Luis G. and Rosa M. (Quinones) de la P.; m. June M. Daugherty, May 1, 1955; children: Ana Maria, Jorge Antonio, James Michael. grad. Facultad de Ciencias, Universidad de San Marcos, Lima, Peru, 1942, Facultad de Medicina, MD, 1950. Diplomate Am. Bd. Orthopedic Surgery, Am. Bd. Profl. Disability Cons. Intern, Army Hosp., Lima, 1951-52; rotating intern Augustana Hosp., Chgo., 1952-53; resident in orthopedic surgery St. Francis Hosp., Peoria, Ill., 1953-54, Charlotte (N.C.) Meml. Hosp., 1954-57; fellow in orthop. divsn. Duke U. Hosp., 1956-57; acting chief orthopedic dept. Social Security Adminstrn. Hosp. #1, Lima, 1958-59; orthopedic Surgeon Mullens (W.Va.) Hosp., 1960-66; practice medicine specializing in orthopedic surgery, Princeton, W.Va., 1966—; mem. staff Princeton Community Hosp., 1966—, dir., 1974—. Served with Peruvian Army, 1951-52. Recipient award Disting. Physicians of Am. Fellow Internat. Coll. Surgeons, Am. Acad. Disability Evaluating Physicians; mem. AMA (physician's award 1969, 72-74, 77, 80, 84), W.Va. State Med. Assn., Mercer County Med. Soc., Am. Fracture Assn., So. Med. Soc., Latin Am. Soc. Orthopedic Surgeons, Orthopedic Rsch. and Edn. Found. (life), Peruvian Acad. of Surgery. So. Orthopedic Soc., W.Va. Orthopedic Soc., Peruvian Am. Med. Soc., Nat. Assn. Disability Evaluating Physicians (charter). Roman Catholic. Lodge: K.C. Office: Morrison Dr Princeton WV 24740-2322

DELARUE, LOUIS C(HARLES), priest; b. Orange, Tex., Mar. 24, 1939; s. Garrett Louis and Ethel Marie (Walker) D. Student, St. Joseph Sem., Washington; BS in Secondary Edn., Lamar U.; postgrad., U. St. Thomas; MDiv, St. Mary's Sem., 1978. Ordained priest Roman Cath. Ch., 1976. Assoc. pastor St. Mary's Ch., Port Arthur, Tex., 1976-77, pastor, 1978-83; pastor Our Lady of Lourdes, Chireno, 1983-85; assoc. pastor St. Anne's Ch., Beaumont, Tex., 1985-86; deacon Diocese of Beaumont, Port Arthur, 1978-79; assoc. pastor St. Mary's Cath. Ch., Port Arthur, 1979-80; pastoral adminstr. St. Mary Ch., Port Arthur, 1980-81; campus minister Stephen F. Austin U., Nacogdoches, Tex., 1983-86; pastor St. Therese, Orange and St. Maurice Mission, Mauriceville, Tex., 1986—; del. Nat. Fedn. Presbyn. Couns., Hosp. Ministry; spiritual asst. Secular Franciscan and other assns.; chaplain Cath. Student Ctr., Stephen F. Austin U., Nacogdoches, Lamar U., Beaumont, 1985; ecumenical dir. Diocese Beaumont, Tex. Cath. Conf.; spiritual dir. Parish Afro-Am. Ecumenical Dance Group Henderson Sch. Dance; cons. Afro-Am. Diocesan Cath. Commn., Diocese Beaumont, 1987-91; pres. Diocesan Presbyteral Coun., Diocese of Beaumont, 1991-92; adminstr. St. Maurice Cath. Ch. Mission, Mauriceville. Recipient Outstanding Preacher award Black Preachers Assn., 1980. Mem. NAACP, Canon Law Soc., Nat. Black Seminarian Assn., Nat. Black Clergy Caucus, Assn. Pastoral Counseling, Interfaith Groups, Nat. Assn. Cath. Ecumenical Dirs., Nat. Black Cath. Clergy Caucus, Tex. Cath. Campus Ministry Assn., Nat. Cath. Campus Ministry Assn., Assn. Spiritual Dirs., Toastmasters, Kiwanis, KC. Home and Office: Saint Maurice Ch RR 12 Box 1335 Orange TX 77632-9812

DELASHMET, GORDON BARTLETT, newsprint executive; b. Moss Point, Miss., Dec. 19, 1928; s. Thomas Lewis and Ione (Broome) DeL.; m. Barbara Harris, Sept. 11, 1971 (div.); 1 child, Katherine Casey; m. Lois Ross, Nov. 20, 1994; children by previous marriage: Gordon Bartlett Jr., W. Pemble. BA, U. Miss., 1950. Salesman Internat. Paper, Montreal, Que., Can., 1955-63, regional mgr., Atlanta, 1963-68; exec. v.p. Claredon Paper Sales, Atlanta, 1968-73; v.p. sales Abitibi Newsprint Corp., Atlanta, 1973-77; sr. v.p. Abitibi-Price Sales Corp., N.Y.C., 1977-80, exec. v.p., 1980-88; asst. to pres. Southeast Paper Mfg. Co., Marietta, Ga., 1989—; pres. S.E. Paper Newsprint Sales, Marietta, Ga., 1991—; bd. dirs. Resource Center. Patron South Africa Air Force Mus. Capt. U.S. Army, 1950-53, prisoner of war, Korea. Pres. Korean POW Assn. (Camp 2), 1995—. Named to ROTC Hall of Fame. Mem. Am. Forest and Paper Assn., Sigma Chi (Award of Excellence 1983, Significant Sig 1987, Constantine Sig 1990), Commerce Club, Capital City Club, Tournament Players Club, Cavalry and Guards Club (London), Masons (Knight Comdr. Ct. of Honor 1987), Rotary (Fred Hoyt award Atlanta chpt. 1976). Republican. Avocations: golfing, goose and duck hunting, salmon fishing. Home: 2856 Kingsland Ct NW Atlanta GA 30339-4253

DE LA TEJA, JESÚS FRANCISCO, historian, educator; b. Cienfuegos, Cuba, July 17, 1956; came to U.S., 1963; s. Francisco R. de la Teja and Julia M. (Irimia) Castellano; m. Magdalena H. de la Teja, Aug. 6, 1983; children: Eduardo, Julia. BA in Polit. Sci., Seton Hall U., 1979, MA in Latin Am. History, 1981; PhD in Colonial Latin Am. History, U. Tex., 1988. Grad. asst. history dept. Seton Hall U., 1979-81; rsch. asst. U. Tex., Austin, 1982-84; adj. instr. Austin C.C., 1988-90; asst. archivist Tex. Gen. Land Office, Austin, 1985-89, archivist, 1989-90, dir. archives and records, 1990-91; asst. prof. history S.W. Tex. State U., San Marcos, 1991-96, assoc. prof., 1996—; judge Presidio La Bahia award Sons of Republic of Tex., 1988, Summerfield G. Roberts award, 1992-94, T.R. Fehrenbach Book award Tex. Hist. Commn., 1993-95; pres. Castlewood-Oak Valley Neighborhood Assn., 1995-97. Author: San Antonio de Béxar: A Community on New Spain's Northern Frontier, 1995; mng. editor: The Land Commissioners of Texas: 150 Years of the General Land Office, 1986, Guide to Spanish and Mexican Land Grants in South Texas, 1988, Jour. Tex. Cath. History and Culture, 1990—; tech. editor Soc. S.W. Archivists Guide to Archival and Manuscript Repositories, 1993; adv. editor Handbook of Tex., 1989-96; editor, compiler; A Revolution Remembered: The Memoirs and Selected Correspondence of Juan N. Segin, 1991; newsletter editor Castlewood-Oak Valley Neighborhood Assn., 1991-95; mem. editl. bd. Southwestern Hist. Quar., 1996—; contbr. articles to profl. jours. Mem. adv. com. Cath. Archives Tex., 1989—; bd. dirs. Tex. Conservation Fund, 1991—. Recipient Presidio La Bahia award, 1995, book citation San Antonio Conservation Soc., 1996; fellow U. Tex., 1981-82, 84-85; grantee John D. and Catherine T. MacArthur Found., 1991-92, Sons Republic of Tex., 1992. Mem. Am. Hist. Assn., Conf. Latin Am. History (demographic history and hist. stats. com. 1989-91), Tex. Cath. Hist. Soc., Soc. S.W. Archivists (program com. 1989 ann. meeting 1988-89), S.W. Coun. on Latin Am. Studies (life), Western History Assn., Tex. State Hist. Assn. (life, chair program com. 1994 ann. meeting 1993-94, program com. 1993 ann. meeting 1992-93), Austin Libr. Commn. Office: SW Tex State U Dept History San Marcos TX 78666

DE LA TORRE, JORGE, psychiatrist, psychoanalyst, educator, physician; b. Camaguey, Cuba, Sept. 6, 1934; came to U.S., 1960; s. Diego A. and Esther (Puentes) de la T.; m. Julia Rose McDermott, June 23, 1962; children: Jorge Ignacio, Martin John, Julia Maria, Cristina Maria. MD BS, Havana U., Cuba. Diplomate Am. Bd. Psychiatry. Asst. dir. outpatient clinic Topeka State Hosp., 1966-68; tchr. Menninger Sch. Psychiatry, 1968-76, Topeka Inst. Psychoanalysis, 1974-76; sr. cons. Menninger Clinic, 1974-76; dir. diagnostic svc. C. F. Menninger Meml. Hosp., Topeka, 1973-76; dir. psychiat. clinic Baylor Coll. Medicine, Houston, 1976-78; pvt. practice psychiatry, psychoanalysis Houston, 1978—; trng., supervising analyst Houston-Galveston (Tex.) Psychiat. Inst., 1980—. Contbr. articles to profl. jours. Fellow APA (cert. bd. prof. stds. 1976); mem. Am. Psychoanalytic Assn., Internat. Psychoanalytic Assn., Tex. Med. Assn., Harris County Med. Soc. Office: 5300 San Jacinto St Ste 140 Houston TX 77004-6841

DELAVALLADE, MICHAEL LYNDON, videographer; b. Gary, Ind., May 11, 1959; s. Annette Dorthy deLavallade. Student, N.C. Sch. Arts, 1977-79. Various positions Sta. KOA-TV, Denver, 1980-83, N.Y.C., 1991—; dir., videographer, actor Atlanta; sports camera operator Turner Broadcasting, Atlanta; videographer World Series, Baseball Network, 1995, Olympics, World Feed, 1996; condr. internat. film and TV workshops, Rockport, Maine. Performed in off-Broadway prodns. including The Erudite, 1984, and films including Beat Street; prodr., dir. one-act plays including Cabin 12 and the Death of Bessie Smith, 1985; assoc. prodr., 1st asst. dir. film Blue Plate, 1989; 1st asst. dir., dir., actor film The Three Muscatels, 1990; harmonica player and singer The Blues Barons. Home and Office: 471 Glenwood Ave SE # A Atlanta GA 30312-3220

DE LEON, JOHN LOUIS, lawyer; b. North Miami, Fla., Feb. 14, 1962; s. Leon Juan and Lydia (Diaz Cruz) de L. AB cum laude, U. Miami, 1983; JD, Georgetown U., 1986; M in Internat. Affairs, Columbia U., 1992. Bar: Fla. 1987. V.p. Bristol Investment Group, Coral Gables, Fla., 1982-85; jud. intern to Judge Francis Bason Fed. Bankruptcy Ct., Washington, 1986; asst. pub. defender Office Pub. Defender for 11th Jud. Cir., Miami, 1987—; law clk. Geiger, Riggs & Freud, P.A., Miami, Fla., 1986-87; mem. bd. arbitrators Nat. Assn. Security Dealers, N.Y.C., 1989; press officer, intern. Delegation of the Commn. of the European Communities, UN, N.Y.C., 1990; mem. steering com. Georgetown Criminal Justice Clinic, Georgetown U. Law Ctr. Bd. dirs. Citykids, Inc., Miami, 1986; steering com. Georgetown U. Law Ctr. Criminal Justice Clinic, 1992; mem. adv. bd. Douglas MacArthur Sr. H.S., Miami; mem. audience devel. commn. Mus. Contemporary Arts, North Miami, Fla. Mem. ABA, Cuban Am. Bar Assn., Nat. Assn. Criminal Def. Lawyers, Am. Civil Liberties Union, Fla. Assn. Pub. Defenders, Amnesty Internat., Golden Key, Phi Delta Phi, Phi Kappa Phi, Pi Sigma Alpha. Roman Catholic. Home: 1805 Ixora Rd Miami FL 33181-2309 Office: Pub Defender Svc 1320 NW 14th St Miami FL 33125-1609

DELERY, ALFRED ALBERT, priest, physician; b. Cambridge, Mass., Jan. 2, 1919; s. Louis Arnold and Albertine (Vezina) D. AB, Boston Coll., 1941; MD, Tufts U., 1944. Ordained Roman Catholic priest Cistercians of the Strict Observance, 1954; diplomate Am. Bd. Internal Medicine. Intern internal medicine Boston (Mass.) City Hosp., 1944-45, resident internal medicine, 1947-49; pvt. practice internal medicine Medford, Mass., 1949-54; monastery physician St. Joseph's Abbey, Spencer, Mass., 1954-81, Holy Cross Abbey, Berryville, Va., 1981—; Abbot Holy Cross Abbey, Berryville, 1984-90; instr. medicine Tufts Med. Sch. Contbr. articles to profl. jours. Capt. U.S. Army, 1945-47. Recipient Disting. Alumni award Boston Coll. Alumni Assn., 1991. Fellow ACP; mem. Boston Coll. Gold Key Soc. Home: RR 2 Box 3870 Berryville VA 22611-9526 Office: Holy Cross Abbey Infirmary RR 2 Box 3870 Berryville VA 22611-9526

DELFINO, JOSEPH JOHN, environmental engineering sciences educator; b. Port Chester, N.Y., Oct. 6, 1941; s. John J. and Frances C. (Santoro) D.; m. Dorothy Delfino; children: Janelle, Justin. BS in Chemistry, Holy Cross Coll., 1963; MS in Chemistry, U. Idaho, 1965; PhD in Civil and Environ. Engrng. & Water Chemistry, U. Wis., 1968. From instr. to assoc. prof. chemistry USAF Acad., Colorado Springs, Colo., 1968-72; Sect. head, tech. mgr. IBT & Nalco Environ. Sci., Northbrook, Ill., 1972-74; sect. head environ. scis. Wis. State Lab. Hygiene, Madison, 1974-82; from asst. prof. to assoc. prof. U. Wis., Madison, 1974-80; assoc. dir. water resources ctr. U. Wis., 1977-78, prof. civil and environ. engring., 1980-82; prof. environ. engring. sci. U. Fla., Gainesville, 1982—, affiliate prof. chemistry, 1990—, chmn. dept. environ. engring. sci., 1990—; affiliate prof. natural resources and environment U. Fla., 1994—; interim dir. Ctr. for Wetlands and Water Resources U. Fla., Gainesville, 1995; mem. state univ. sys. Fla. adv. bd. Fla. Ctr. for Solid and Hazardous Waste Mgmt., 1996—; mem. adj. faculty U. Colo., Colorado Springs, 1969-71, Ill. Inst. Tech., Chgo., 1973; mem. adv. bd. Fla. State U. Sys. Ctr. for Solid and Hazardous Waste Mgmt., 1996—, Fla. State U. Sys. Ctr. for Environ. Studies, 1996—. Writer, co-originator documentary Fla. Water Story, Sta. WEDU-TV, Tampa, Fla.; contbr. articles on water chemistry and environ. scis. to profl. publs. Mem. Citizens Environ. Quality Coun., Northbrook, 1972-74; mem. Mercury Tech. Adv. Com., State of Fla., 1991-93. Capt. USAF, 1968-72. Recipient Pub. Svc. award Univs. Coun. on Water Resources, 1990. Fellow AAAS; mem. Am. Chem. Soc. (mem. exec. com. environ. chem. divsn. 1973-76, editor Envirofacs environ. chem. divsn. 1973-76, student awards com. environ. chem. divsn. 1995—, Cert. of Merit environ. chem. divsn. 1991), Assn. Environ. Engring. Profs., Am. Soc. Engring. Edn. Office: U Fla Dept Environ Engring Sci 217 Black Hall Gainesville FL 32611-2013

DEL FOSSE, CLAUDE MARIE, aerospace software executive; b. Paris, June 27, 1940; came to the U.S., 1963; s. Guy and Gabrielle (Bouyges) D.F.; m. Genevieve Juliette Des Devises, Dec. 23, 1971; children: Laurent Fabrice, Olivier Andre, Oriane Gabrielle. Diploma in Enging. Ecole Nat. Supérieure, d'Arts et Métiers, Paris, 1963; MS, Calif. Inst. Tech., 1964; MBA, U. Paris, 1966. Software engr. Soc. d'Info. Appliquée, Paris, 1964-67, Control Data Corp., L.A., 1968-69; sr. tech. staff CACI, Inc., L.A., Washington, 1969-78; v.p., div. mgr. CACI, Inc., Washington, 1979-84; cons., chief scientist Bite, Inc., Washington, 1984-86; mgr. program devel. Software Productivity Consortium, Reston, Va., 1986-89; v.p. tech. transfer Software Productivity Consortium, Herndon, Va., 1989—; bd. dirs. Winter Simulation Conf., 1979-82, gen. chmn., 1981. Bd. dirs. Lincolnia Park Recreational Club, Alexandria, Va., 1981, 82, 88. NATO fellow, 1964, Fulbright fellow, 1964. Mem. AFCEA, AIAA, Tech. Transfer Soc. Home: 5229 Chippewa Pl Alexandria VA 22312-2023

DELGADO, ERIC DIRK, optometrist; b. San Antonio, Jan. 26, 1963; s. Richard Toscano and Irma Lillian (Lopez) D. Student, San Antonio Coll., 1981-83, U. Houston, 1983-86; BS, So. Coll. Optometry, 1989, OD, 1990. Primary collector Doctors Collection Agency, San Antonio, 1981-82; chmn. PreOptometry Soc. U. Houston, 1983-84, U. Houston Sports Com., 1985; asst. mgr. Tex. State Optical, San Antonio, 1985-86; v.p. Phi Theta Upsilon Internat., Memphis, 1987-88; pres. Tex. Club So. Coll. Optometry, Memphis, 1988-90; v.p. ILD Ranches Inc., San Antonio, 1987—, Sr. Cabinet So. Coll. Optometry, Memphis, 1989-90; optometrist Delgado Eye Care Ctrs., San Antonio, 1990—. Dr., examiner Save Your Vision Week, Memphis, 1988-90, San Antonio, 1990-91; vol. March of Dimes, San Antonio, 1990. Named Outstanding Sr. Clinician, Deans' List So. Coll. Optometry, Optometric Honor Soc. Gold Key Internat., Outstanding Mem. of Yr., Phi Theta Upsilon Internat. Mem. Tex. Assn. Optometrists, Tex. Optometric Assn., Am. Optometric Assn., U.S. Golf Assn. Republican. Roman Catholic. Home: 207 Furr Dr San Antonio TX 78201-4414 Office: Delgado Eye Care Centers 803 Castroville Rd Ste 129 San Antonio TX 78237-3148 also: Master Eye Assocs 7900 N Ih 35 Ste N731 San Antonio TX 78218-2215

DELGADO, GLORIA ENEIDA, medical nurse; d. Francisca Benitez; children: Daniel, Othoniel. AAS in Nursing, Bronx Community Coll., 1977; BS in Behavioral Sci., Mercy Coll., 1983. Staff nurse Montifiori Hosp. Ctr., N.Y.C.; case mgr., health practitioner, RN Multi-Purpose Sr. Svcs. Program, L.A.; staff nurse U. Community Hosp., Tampa, Fla.; RN specialist State of Fla., Tampa.

DELGADO, JOSE ANTONIO, retired air force officer, history educator; b. San Juan, P.R., Aug. 15, 1939; s. Jose Ferdinand and Rosa (Perea) D.; m. Elsa Luisa Boyd, Sep. 30, 1962; children: Elsa Lizette, Nelson Jose. BA magna cum laude, U. P.R., 1962; MA, St. Mary's U., San Antonio, 1975; PhD, U. Tex., Arlington, 1995. Commd. 2d lt. USAF, 1962; advanced through grades to lt. col., 1978; 1st lt, capt., missle launch officer Vandenberg AFB, Calif., 1964-68; maj., personnel officer Clark Air Base, The Phillipines, 1971-73; maj., lt. col., behavioral scientist USAF, Tex., 1975-79; lt. col., vice commdr. svc. sch. Albrook AFB, Panama, 1979-82; lt. col., personnel dir. Torrejon AFB, Spain, 1982-85; lt. col., personnel dir. Altus AFB, Okla., 1985-90, ret., 1990; vis. prof. history U. North Tex., Denton, 1995-97. Mem. Soc. for the History of Discovery (essay award 1994). Republican. Home: 2209 Baltic Ave Arlington TX 76011

DELGADO-RODRIGUEZ, MANUEL, secondary school educator; b. Caguas, P.R., Dec. 15, 1932; s. Manuel Delgado-Planas and Angelina Rodriguez-Andaluz. MA in Edn. and History, U. P.R., 1969. Tchr. English Juncos (P.R.) H.S., 1962; social studies/Spanish tchr. Ponce de Leon Jr. H.S., Humacao, P.R., 1962; tchr. history Univ. H.S., Rio Piedras, P.R., 1963-65, 67—; mem. curriculum com. Univ. H.S., Rio Piedras, coord. presdl. classroom for young Ams., 1970—. Mem. ASCD, P.R. Assn. Historians, Nat. Coun. for Social Studies. Home: PO Box 461 Humacao PR 00792-0461

DELING, ELAINE MARIE, special education educator; b. Miami, Apr. 4, 1969. BS, Fla. Internat. U., 1991, MS, 1995. Cert. Fla. Spl. edn. tchr. Dade County Pub. Schs., Miami, 1991—. Mem. Autistic Soc. Am., Coun. Exceptional Edn., Autism Rsch. Rev. Internat. Home: 6890 SW 26th Terr Miami FL 33155

DELISIO, SHARON KAY, secondary school educator, school administrator; b. Kansas City, Kans., May 7, 1943; d. Bernard James and Bernice Marie (Hansen) Hansen; m. Louis Charles Delisio, 1963; children: Lisa, Annette, Louis. BA summa cum laude, SUNY, Albany, 1974, MS in Reading, 1975, MS in Spl. Edn., 1980. Cert. reading, English, ESOL, varying exceptionalities. English tchr. Charlton Sch., Burnt Hills, N.Y., 1975-78; dir. edn., sch. prin. Charlton Sch., Burnt Hills, 1978-89; English/reading tchr. Lyndon B. Johnson Jr. High Sch., Melbourne, Fla., 1989-95, tchr., asst. principal, 1995—; N.Y. del. Internat. Conf. on Spl. Edn., Beijing, Republic of China, 1988; bldg. rep., mem. Brevard Fedn. of Tchrs., 1993-94; coun. mem. Tchr. Edn. Ctr. Coun., 1994-96; mem. capital planning team Brevard County Schs., 1994; tchr. of yr. selection com. and mgmt. plan Devel. Team; mem. improvement com. Johnson Jr. H.S., 1992-96. Mem. Melbourne Civic Theatre, Melbourne, 1992-94; mem. supporter Brevard County Zoo, Melbourne, 1993-96. Mem. AAUW (book sale vol. 1992-94), Nat. Coun. of Tchrs. of English (presenter Nat. Conv. at Orlando 1994), Brevard Coun. of Tchrs. of English, Internat. Reading Assn., Secondary Reading Coun. of Fla., Delta Kappa Gamma. Roman Catholic. Office: Lyndon B Johnson Jr HS 2155 Croton Rd Melbourne FL 32935-3337

DE LISSER, ROBERT MEDCALFE, naval officer; b. New Rochelle, N.Y., Jan. 7, 1933; s. Austin Medcalfe and Gertrude Kenaugh (Noble) De L. BA, Middlebury Coll., 1955; MD, Temple U., 1959. Bd. cert. in gen. surgery. Intern U.S. Naval Hosp., Newport, R.I., 1959-60; gen. med. officer U.S. Naval Hosp., Portsmouth, N.H., 1961-63; resident U.S. Naval Hosp., Phila., 1963-67; commd. 2d lt. USN, 1959, advanced through grades to capt., 1973, retired, 1988. Republican. Lutheran. Home: 100 Redwood Cir Pensacola FL 32506

DELK, FAY LOUISE, journalist; b. Columbia, Tenn., Oct. 24, 1952; d. Allen Freed and Mary Mildred (Overbey) D. AS, Columbia State C.C., 1972; BA in English, Psychology, Mid. Tenn. State U., 1974; MA in Mass Comm., U. N.C., Chapel Hill, 1992. Tchr. West Side Mid. Sch., Dalton, Ga., 1974-75; jr. social counselor Tenn. Dept. Human Svcs., Columbia, 1975-78, 79; adminstrv./rsch. asst. Tenn. Hunger Coalition, Nashville, 1980-83; info. svcs. coord. Coun. of Cmty. Svcs., Nashville, 1983-87; directory coord. Parents Anonymous, Nashville, 1987, 88; with Vanderbilt U., Nashville, 1988-89; reporter/staff writer The Columbia Times, 1990; free-lance writer Durham-Herald Sun, Chapel Hill, 1989-91, Closeup - The Tennessean, Nashville, 1993; reporter The Daily Herald, Columbia, 1993-94, city editor, 1994-96; instr. dept. journalism Coll. Mass. Comm., Mid. Tenn. State U., Murfreesboro, 1996—. Editor: Directory of Community Service, 1984; co-editor: Parent Resource Directory - Tennessee, 1987. Bd. dirs., com. chair, fund-raising world hunger task force Manna Inc.-Anti-Hunger Agy., Nashville, 1986-89; host family Internat. English Inst., Nashville, 9177-89; Spring benefit pub. chair Neighborhood Edn. Project, Nashville, 1988; participant, fundraiser Crop Walk, Chapel Hill, 1991. Mem. Soc. Profl. Journalists, Mac Interested Computer User Group. Home: PO Box 52 4147 Hampshire Pike Hampshire TN 38461

DELL, MICHAEL S., manufacturing executive; b. Houston, 1965; s. Alexander and Lorraine D.; m. Susan Lieberman, Oct. 23, 1989; children: Kira, Alexa. Student, U. Tex., 1983-84. Founder Dell Computer Corp. (formerly PC's Ltd.), Austin, 1984—, now chmn., CEO. Recipient Entrepreneur of Yr. award Inc. Mag., 1990, Customer Satisfaction award JD Power, 1991, 93; named CEO of Yr. Fin. World Mag., 1993. Office: Dell Computer Corp 2214 W Bracker Ln Ste D Austin TX 78758

DELL, WILLIE JONES, social services executive, educator; b. Rocky Mt., N.C., May 8, 1930; d. Willie Aikens and Emma Mae (Anderson) Grant; m. James A. Jones; 1 child, Wayne; m. Nathan Dell, June 19, 1967. BA, St. Augustine Coll., 1952; MSW, Coll. William & Mary, 1961. Lic. social worker, Va. Tchr. Enfield (N.C.) Sch. System, 1955-56; case worker Va. Dept. Welfare, Richmond, 1956-59; student advisor Va. Union U., Richmond, 1964-65; chief med. social worker Med. Coll. Va., Richmond, 1961-67, Pub. Health Dept., Richmond, 1967-69; asst. prof. Va. Commonwealth U., Richmond, 1969-74; assoc. prof. U. Richmond, 1974-95; exec. dir. Richmond Cmty. Sr. Ctr., 1976-94. Contbr. articles to profl. jours. Elected mem. city coun. City of Richmond, 1973-82; v.p. Richmond Crusade Voters, 1983; pres. Richmond chpt. Nat. Caucus Black Aged, 1987, Human Resources, Inc., Richmond, 1987—; bd. dirs. St. Joseph's Home for Boys, Port Au Prive, Haiti, Heifer Project Internat. Recipient Good Govt. award Delta Sigma Theta, 1982; named Outstanding Woman in Govt., YWCA, 1982, Outstanding Vol., Powhattan Correctional Ctr., 1988. Mem. NAACP (life), Nat. Black Presbyn. Caucus (pres. 1986-91). Democrat. Home: 2923 Hawthorne Ave Richmond VA 23222-3524 Office: Assoc Prof U Richmond Richmond VA 23173

DELLAPA, GARY J., airport terminal executive. Dir. of internat. aviation Miami Internat. Airport. Office: Miami Intl Airport PO Box 59-2075 Am Miami FL 33159-2075

DELLINGER, CHARLES WADE, minister; b. Lincolnton, N.C., Feb. 25, 1949; s. Coy Hillard Dellinger and Lorene (Russ) Harbinson; m. Sarah Lynn Baxter, July 20, 1969; children: Sarah Beth, Charles Matthew. AA, Gardner-Webb Coll., 1969, BA cum laude, 1971; MDiv, S.E. Bapt. Sem., 1975, D of Ministry, 1983. Ordained to ministry Bapt. Ch., 1969. Pastor Roseland Bapt. Ch., Lincolnton, N.C., 1969-71; assoc. pastor, pastor Temple Bapt. Ch., Gastoma, N.C., 1971-74; pastor Mulls Meml. Bapt. Ch., Shelby, N.C., 1975-87; sr. pastor Old Town Bapt. Ch., Winston-Salem, N.C., 1987—; bd. dirs. Gardner-Webb Coll., Bolling Springs, N.C., 1980-84, 86-90; assoc. chaplain Cleveland Meml. Hosp., Shelby, 1985-87. Author: Personal Moments, 1990. Bd. dirs. Boy Scouts Am., Winston-Salem, 1989—, dist. advancement chmn., 1990—; moderator Kings Mountain Bapt. Assn., Shelby, 1985-87; chmn. ministry coun., Bapt. State Conv., Raleigh, 1987-88. Recipient Disting. Citizen award State of N.C., 1973. Mem. Am. Family Counselors, Am. Assn. Christian Counselors (charter). Democrat. Baptist. Home: 1625 Turfwood Dr Pfafftown NC 27040-9513

DELOACH, HARRIS E(UGENE), JR., lawyer, manufacturing company executive; b. Columbia, S.C., Aug. 7, 1944; s. Harris Eugene and Julia (Murdock) DeL.; m. Louise Hawes, June 12, 1969; children: Harris Eugene III, John Wilson Malloy, Jeanette Hawes. BBA, U.S.C., 1966; JD, 1969. Bar: S.C. 1969, U. S.Dist. Ct. S.C. 1969, U.S. Ct. Appeals (4th cir.) 1974. Ptnr., Wilmeth & DeLoach, Hartsville, S.C., 1972-85; v.p., gen. counsel Sonoco Products Co., Hartsville, 1986-90, exec. v.p. 1996—; v.p. HDFP, 1990-92; bd. dirs. Bank of Hartsville, Coker's Pedigreed Seed Co., Hartsville. Trustee Coker Coll., Hartsville, 1974-79, vice chmn., 1979; chmn. bd. trustees Byerly Hosp., Hartsville, 1976-79; chmn. bd. dirs. Thomas Hart Acad., Hartsville, 1984. Served to capt. USAF, 1969-72. Recipient Algernon Sydney Sullivan award Coker Coll., 1985. Mem. ABA, S.C. Bar Assn., 4th Jud. Cir. Assn. S.C. (v.p. 1974-78), Darlington County Bar Assn. (pres. 1984), Hartsville C. of C. (pres. 1977). Presbyterian. Lodge: Rotary (pres. Hartsville club 1977, Citizen of Yr. of Hartsville club 1980). Home: 329 Kenwood St Hartsville SC 29550-3227 Office: Sonoco Products Co 2D N St Hartsville SC 29550

DELOACH, ROBERT EARL, II, civil and environmental engineer, consultant; b. Jacksonville, Fla., Nov. 18, 1937; s. Robert Earl Sr. and Wyolen Lavina (Sweat) DeL.; m. Patricia Ann Baird, Apr. 9, 1960 (div. Feb. 1974); 1 child, Alison Jeanne; m Charlene Elizabeth Kinney, Oct. 21, 1978; children: Kenneth Jefferson Wiggins, Christine Elizabeth. AA, U. Fla., 1962, B in Civil Engring., 1965; M in Sanitary Engring., Ga. Inst. Tech., 1968. mgmt. cons. City of Warner Robins (Ga.), 1986—.; lic. profl. land surveyor, Fla., Ga.; lic. profl. engr., Fla., Ga., Ala., Tenn. Pub. health engr. Ga. Water Quality Control Bd., Atlanta, 1965-66, water quality control engr., 1966-68, chief ops. sect., 1968-69; assoc. Flood & Assocs., Inc., Jacksonville, Fla., 1969-77; presdl. exch. exec. The White House, Washington, 1977-79; v.p. Flood Engrs. Architects Planners, Inc., Atlanta, 1979-80, sr. v.p., 1980-82; sr. v.p. Flood Engrs. Architects Planners, Inc., Macon, Ga., 1982-91, Flood Engrs., Inc., Macon, 1991-93; prin. DeLoach Engring. Cons., Macon, 1993—; cons. City of Warner Robins, Ga., 1986-93. Officer Jacksonville Jaycees, 1969-77. Inducted in U. Fla. Hall of Fame, 1964. Mem. Am. Water Works Assn., Water Environment Fedn., Fla. Blue Key, Delta Sigma Phi (pres. Gainesville chpt. 1957-58). Democrat. Baptist. Home: 719 Forest Ridge Dr W Macon GA 31204-1511 Office: DeLoach Engring Cons PO Box 6116 Macon GA 31208-6116

DE LOS SANTOS, GILBERTO, marketing educator; b. El Moral, Mex., Sept. 2, 1941; came to U.S., 1946; s. Jose and Guadalupe (Jiminez) De Los S.; m. Nora Oralia Benavides, Aug. 4, 1965 (div. Aug. 1981); children: Michael, Robert, Marisa, Cristal; m. Juanita Ayala, Oct. 16, 1982. AA, S.W. Tex. Jr. Coll., 1963; BBA cum laude, U. Houston, 1965; MBA, Tex. A&I U., 1967; PhD, U. Tex., 1972. Prodn. supr. A.C. Nielsen Co., Laredo, Tex., 1965-66; instr. S.W. Tex. Jr. Coll., Uvalde, 1967-70; dean of instrn. El Paso (Tex.) C.C., 1972-76; v.p. for instrn. Pikes Peak C.C., Colorado Springs, Colo., 1976-77; dean of students & inst. svcs. U. Tex.-Pan Am., Edinburg, 1977-83, prof. mktg., 1983—; cons. U. Tex., Austin, 1970-72, also numerous corps., Rio Grande Valley, 1985—; dir. doctoral program Nova U., El Paso, 1974-76; clin. asst. prof. U. Tex. Health Sci. Ctr., San Antonio, 1993—. Editor: The Borderlands Jour., 1986; contbr. articles and monographs to profl. jours. Chmn. bd. dirs. Trinity Opportunities Ctr., El Paso, 1974-76, Edinburg Tchrs. Credit U., 1987-88, La Luz Cultural Ctr., El Paso, 1974-76. Named Jaycees Outstanding Young Man Am., 1973. Mem. Am. Mktg. Assn. (faculty advisor U. Tex.-Pan Am. chpt. 1992—), Am. Acad. Scis., Bus. Assn. Latin Am. Studies, Tex. Assn. Coll. Tchrs., S.W. Mktg. Assn. Home: 1802 W Smith St Edinburg TX 78539-2202 Office: U Tex-Pan Am 1201 W University Dr Edinburg TX 78539-2909

DELOZIER, MAYNARD WAYNE, marketing educator; b. Newport News, Va., Apr. 21, 1945; s. Raymond Leo and Jean (Burton) D. PhD, U. N.C., 1971. Lectr., U. N.C.-Greensboro, 1969-70; asst. prof. Va. Poly. Inst. and State U., 1970-71; asst. prof. Wright State U., 1971-73; assoc. prof. U. S.C., Columbia, 1976-87; disting prof. mktg. Nicholls State U., 1987—. Mem. Am. Mktg. Assn., Acad. Mktg. Sci. (gov.), Am. Acad. Advt., So. Mktg. Assn., Southwestern Mktg. Assn. Author: The Marketing Communications Process, 1976, Consumer Behavior Dynamics, 1977, Experimental Learning Exercises in Marketing, 1977, Marketing Management, 1978, Retailing, 1982, Retailing Casebook, 1982, Retailing Workbook, 1982, Promotion Management and Marketing Communications, 1986, Retailing: Principles and Practices, 1986, Retailing: Principles and Practices (with instructors textbank and discussion question manual), 1986, Study Guide to Retailing: Principles and Practices, 1986, Retailing Principles and Practices 3rd edit. (instructors textbank and discussion question manual), 1989, Study Guide to Retailing: Principles and Practices, 1989. Home: 302 Marcello Blvd Thibodaux LA 70301-6922 Office: Coll Bus Adminstrn Nicholls State U Thibodaux LA 70310

DEL RÍO, LOURDES R., journalist; b. Mayagüez, P.R., Oct. 20, 1964; d. Rafael A. Del Río and Ilia M. Cruz; m. Carlos R. Calvo, Dec. 17, 1988. Student in polit. scis., U. P.R., 1982-84; B in Pub. Comm. magna cum laude, U. P.R., Río Piedras, 1986; M in Comm. Arts, Barry U., 1995. Anchorwoman Sta. WORA-TV, Mayagüez, 1982-84; reporter, anchorwoman Sta. WSJN-TV, Hato Rey, P.R., 1986-87, Sta. WAPA-TV, Guaynabo, P.R., 1987-91; reporter Sta. WSCV-TV, Hialeah, Fla., 1992—; freelance corr. Univision, San Juan, P.R., 1989; feelance reporter CNN Spanish, Miami, 1993-94. Recipient Journalist of Yr. award P.R. Mayors Assn., 1988, Disting. Journalist award Hogares CREA, 1989, TV Reporter of Yr. award Agueybaná, 1990. Roman Catholic. Office: WSCV Channel 51 2340 W 8th Ave Hialeah FL 33010-2019

DEL RUSSO, ALESSANDRA LUINI, law educator; b. Milan, Italy, Jan. 2, 1916; d. Avvocato Umberto and Candita (Recio) Luini; m. Carl R. del Russo, Apr. 12, 1947; children: Carl Luini, Alexander David. PhD in History with honors, Royal U., Milan, 1939; SJD summa cum laude, Royal U., Pavia, Italy, 1943; LLM in Comparative Law, George Washington U., Washington, 1949. Bar: Md. 1956, Md. Ct. Appeals, Ct. of Appeals (Milano) 1947, U.S. Ct. Appeals (D.C. cir.) 1950, U.S. Supreme Ct. 1955. Legal adviser Allied Mil. Govt. and Ct., Milan, 1945-46, U.S. Consulate Gen., Milan, 1946-47; pvt. practice Washington, Bethesda, Md., 1950-58; atty. adviser Legis. Ref. Libr. of Congress, Washington, 1958-59; atty. U.S. Commn. on Civil Rights, Washington, 1959-61; prof. Howard U. Sch. Law, Washington, 1961-81, dir. grad. program, 1972-74; prof. emerita Howard U. Sch. Law, 1981—; adj. prof. Stetson U. Coll. Law, St. Petersburg, Fla., 1980-95, prof. emerita, 1995—; professorial lectr. George Washington U. Law Ctr., 1970-80; mem. legal cons. com. U.S. Commn. on Status of P.R., Washington, 1965-66; lectr. in field. Author: International Protection of Human Rights, 1971; editor and chmn. of symposium on International Law of Human Rights, 1965; contbr. numerous articles to internat. and Am. profl. jours. Rsch. grant Howard U., 1963. Mem. ABA, Br. Inst. Internat. and Comparative Law, Am. Soc. Internat. Law. Republican. Roman Catholic. Home: 400 Ocean Trail Way Apt 908 Jupiter FL 33477-5527

DELTA, BASIL GEORGE, physician; b. Istanbul, Turkey, Mar. 4, 1927; came to U.S., 1958.; s. George and Katina (Karayannides) D.; m. Helen L. Murray (dec.), Jan. 9, 1960. MD, U. Istanbul, 1952; MPH, Johns Hopkins U., 1975. Diplomate Am. Bd. Pediat., Am. Bd. Preventive Medicine. Dir. ambulatory svcs. Childrens' Hosp., Milw., 1965-66; dir. pediat. Kern Med. Ctr., Bakersfield, Calif., 1967-69; dir. med. edn. rsch. Queen of Angels Hosp., L.A., 1969-71; chief med. svcs. Dept. Human Resources, Arlington County, Va., 1972-74; deputy health dir. Prince George's County (Md.) Health Dept., 1975-79; health dir. Mecklenburg County Health Dept., Charlotte, N.C., 1979-89; adj. prof. U. N.C., Charlotte and Chapel Hill, 1980-90; clin. assoc. prof. Georgetown U., Washington, 1990—; vis. prof. U. Istanbul, 1993—. Contbr. numerous articles to profl. jours. Maj. U.S. Army, 1963-65. Grantee Am. Cancer Soc., 1965-68, USPHS, 1974-75; recipient AMA Physicians' Recognition award for CME, 1969, 72, 76, 79, 82, 85, 88, 91, 95, Nat. Assn. of Counties Achievement award, 1982, 84, 85, 87 (two), 88. Fellow ACP, Am. Acad. Pediatrics, Am. Coll. Preventive Medicine; mem. APHA, AAAS, Internat. Health Soc., Nat. Assn. County Health Officers,

Am. Hellenic Edn. Progressive Assn., John Hopkins U. Alumni Assn., Am. Legion. Independent. Greek Orthodox. Home: 1221 N Roosevelt St Arlington VA 22205

DEL TORO, ILIA, retired education educator; b. Ponce, P.R., July 17, 1918; d. Gerardo Gabriel and Angela (Robledo) del T.; m. Claudino Santiago. BA, U. P.R., Rio Piedras, 1940; MA in Edn., NYU, Rio Piedras, 1958. Elem. tchr. State Dept. Instrn., 1941-44, tchr. high sch. social studies, 1944-57; instr. high sch. social studies Coll. Edn. U. P.R., Rio Piedras, 1957-59, officer external resources, 1975-76, assoc. prof., 1979-86, coord. student teaching, 1979-86, supr. student teaching, methods in high sch. social studies, edn. sociology, elem. edn. in social studies, curriculum and teaching dept., 1959-71, coord. Inst. Family Fin., 1962-69; coord. EPDA/U.S. Project, 1970-75. Author: The Acts of the Cabildo of Ponce, Puerto Rico: 1812-23, 1993; author papers in field. Puerto Rican del. to Edith Macy Girl Scout Camp, 1947; v.p. Liceo Ponceño North Zone Ex Alumnae and Friends Chpt.; mem. lady aux. Salvation Army, 1990-91, v.p. P.R. chpt.; bd. dirs. ex alumnae Ponce High Sch. '36. Mem. NEA, Assn. Supervision and Curriculum Devel. (nat. bd.), Assn. Tchr. Educators, Nat. Coun. Social Studies, P.R. Tchr. Assn., Assn. Ret. Profs. (bd. dirs.), Assn. Tchr. Educators (pres. Puerto Rican chpt.), Future World Soc., Smithsonian Instn., Phi Delta Kappa (pres. of ceremonials, 1978, 84-85, Outstanding Educator, San Juan chpt. Diamond Jubilee, 1981), Friends of Ponce, AARP, Delta Kappa Gamma (state founder, 1976, chpt. pres., 1978-80, state pres. 1983-85, Golden Gift Fund scholar Leadership/Mgmt. seminar Exec. Devel. Ctr. U. Ill. 1983-85, mem. internat. exec. com., mem. state bd. 1987—, bd. dirs. state and Alpha chpt. P.R. internat. soc.), Soc. Puerto Rican Genealogy. Roman Catholic. Home: 506 Parque De Las Fuentes San Juan PR 00918

DELUCCA, GREGORY JAMES, wine industry executive; b. Milw., June 2, 1937; s. Anthony James and Irene Eleanor (Linski) DeL.; BS in Chem. Engring., U. Wis., 1959, MBA, 1962. m. Carol L. Enrico, Apr. 8, 1967; children: Alison, Ashley. Mgr. mktg. Pacific Coca-Cola Bottling Co., Seattle, 1967-71, mgr. ops. Western area Coca-Cola U.S.A., Burlingame, Calif., 1971-73, mgr. ops. engring. The Coca Cola Co., Atlanta, 1973-77; v.p., gen. mgr. Sterling Vineyards, Calistoga, Calif., 1977-82, pres., 1982-84; owner Gregory J. DeLucca Co. Wine Cons., 1985; pres. Lyeth Vineyard and Winery, Ltd., 1985-87, Chateau St. Jean Vineyards and Winery, 1987-90, Cru Industries, 1990-92, owner Gregory J. DeLucca Wine Consulting Co., 1992-93; mgr. equipment and systems purchasing The Coca-Cola Co., 1993-95, global purchases mgr. production equipment The Coca-Cola Co., 1995—. Served to capt. USAR, 1959-67. Mem. Napa Valley Vintners (pres.), Sonoma County Wineries Assn. (bd. dirs.). Republican. Roman Catholic. Home: 235 Lachaize Cir NW Atlanta GA 30327-4346 Office: The Coca-Cola Co 1 Coca Cola Plz NW Atlanta GA 30313-2420

DELZELL, CHARLES NEAL, mathematics educator; b. Nashville, Nov. 19, 1953; s. Charles F. and Eugenia M. (Robertson) D.; m. Brigitte Assfalg, Aug. 24, 1985. BS in Math with honors, Vanderbilt U., 1974; MS in Math, Stanford U., 1980, PhD in Math, 1980. Teaching asst. dept. math Stanford U., 1974-76, 77-80; asst. prof. math La. State U., Baton Rouge, 1980-85, assoc. prof. math, 1986-94, prof. math., 1994—; vis. asst. prof. Maharishi Internat. U., Fairfield, Iowa, 1981; vis. scholar U. Calif., Berkeley, 1990, vis. assoc. prof. math, 1991. Contbr. articles to profl. jours. Rsch. grantee NSF, 1981, 82, 87, 91, 94, 95, 96, Nat. Security Agy.'s Math. Scis. Program, 1996. Mem. Am. Math. Soc. Libertarian. Office: La State U Dept Of Math Baton Rouge LA 70803

DEMA, ROBERT JOHN, public school system administrator; b. Astoria, N.Y., Apr. 30, 1933; s. D. Lawrence and Mary Elizabeth (Gara) D.; m. Joan Muriel Farrell, May 1, 1954; children—James, Lawrence. B.B.A., Hofstra U., 1957, M.Ed., 1968. Cert. tchr., adminstr. N.Y., Conn.; cert. asbestos abatement investigator. Tchr., Brentwood pub. schs., N.Y., 1961-63, Elmont pub. schs., 1963-69; bus. adminstr. Newtown pub. schs., Conn., 1969-72; asst. supt. bus. Union Free Sch. Dist., Tarrytown, N.Y., 1972-78, Garden City pub. schs., N.Y., 1978-85, dep. supt., 1985-89, supt., 1989-93; founder, attorney-in-fact, dir. N.Y. State Ins. Reciprocal; career counselor Hofstra U., 1984-87, hearing officer on teachers facing disciplinary charges, N.Y. State Edn. Dept., 1987-93, master instr. food service accountability and mdse. N.Y. State Edn. Dept., 1987-93. trainer doctoral candidate Columbia U., 1976-77. Author-editor: How to Do Business With Our Schools, 1970. Dir. Open Door Club for Midwestern Conn. Mental Health Assn., 1969-71, day camp and recreation programs, West Nassau Y.M.C.A., 1963-69; founder, past pres. Pocantico Lake Civic Assn., 1978-90; chmn. audit com. Westchester County United Way, 1967-69; past commander Garden City Post AMVETS, 1960's, asst. scoutmaster Stewart Manor Troop Boy Scouts Am., 1960's; vol. fireman, 1960's; dir. Am. Cancer Soc., 1990-93; active Hilton Head Archeol. Soc., 1993—; vol. S.C. Eye Bank, 1993—; active Coast Guard Aux., 1994—; dir., scholarship com. chmn. UNICO, 1994—. Served to acting sgt. U.S. Army, 1951-53, Korea. Recipient Presdl. Citation, Korean Govt., 1952, decorated Bronze Star, U.S. Army. Mem. Am. Assn. Sch. Adminstrs., Assn. Sch. Curriculum Dirs., Assn. Sch. Athletic Dirs., Internat. Assn. Sch. Bus. Adminstrs., N.Y. State Assn. Sch. Bus. Adminstrs., Nassau Assn. Sch. Bus. Adminstrs. Roman Catholic. Avocations: sport fishing, horses, bowling.

DE MARCO, NATALIE ANNE, sales and marketing executive; b. Easton, Pa., Feb. 9, 1961; d. Lawrence Adriano and Donna Louise (Gordon) De M. Student, Indiana U. Pa., 1979-81, Northampton Community Coll., 1982, Broward Community Coll., 1986. Mgr. Louise's Contourella, Easton, 1982-83; sales rep. Wainwright's Travel, Bethlehem, Pa., 1983-84; sec. Benthor-Sanijura Inc., North Miami Beach, Fla., 1984, pres., treas., corp. officer, 1984-89; br. mgr. ADIA Pers. Svcs., Miami, Fla., 1989-90; regional mktg. mgr. Romac Profl. Temporaries, Ft. Lauderdale, Fla., 1990-93; new bus. devel. dir. Citibank, F.S.B., Miami, Fla., 1994-95; asst. v.p. Citibank, F.S.B., Miami, 1995—. Mem. Beacon Coun., 1994. Mem. Inst. Mgmt. Accts. (Miami chpt. v.p. memberships 1993—), Japan Soc. South Fla., Asian-Am. C. of C. (bus. devel. com. 1996—). Roman Catholic.

DEMAREE, ROBERT GLENN, psychologist, educator; b. Rockford, Ill., Sept. 20, 1920; s. Glenn and Ethel Mae (Champion) D.; BS, U. Ill., 1941, MA, 1948, PhD (univ. fellow 1949-50), 1950; m. Alyce Anisia Jones, Sept. 4, 1948; children— Dee Anne, Marta, James, David. Chief performance br. Pers. and Tng. Rsch. Ctr., Lowry AFB, Denver, 1951-57; dir. human factors Martin Space Flight div. Bell Aircraft Corp., Balt., 1958-60; dir. programs Matrix Corp., Arlington, Va., 1960-61; dir. office instructional rsch. U. Ill., 1961-63; projects dir. Life Scis., Inc., Hurst, Tex., 1963-66; mem. faculty Tex. Christian U., Ft. Worth, 1966-85, prof. psychology, prof. Inst. Behavioral Rsch., 1970-85, emeritus, 1985—; cons., 1985—. Served with AUS, 1941-46. Mem. APA, Am. Statis. Assn., Psychometric Soc., Soc. Multivariate Exptl. Psychology, Sigma Xi. Home: 4813 Eldorado Dr Fort Worth TX 76180-7227

DEMAREST, SYLVIA M., lawyer; b. Lake Charles, La., Aug. 16, 1944; d. Edmand and Emily (Meyers) D.; m. James A. Johnston, Jr., Oct. 31, 1975 (div. Dec. 1979). Student U. S.W. La., 1963-66; J.D., U. Tex., 1969. Bar: Tex. 1969, U.S. Supreme Ct. 1973, U.S. Ct. Appeals (5th cir.) 1970, U.S. Ct. Appeals (7th cir.) 1979, U.S. Ct. Appeals (11th cir.) 1980, U.S. Dist. Ct. (no. dist.) Tex. 1970, U.S. Dist. Ct. (ea. dist.) Tex. 1970, U.S. Dist. Ct. (so. dist.) Tex. 1972. Reginald H. Smith Community Lawyer fellow, Corpus Christi and Dallas, 1969-71; house counsel Tex. Inst. Ednl. Devel., San Antonio, 1972-73; staff atty. Dallas Legal Services Found., Inc., 1973, exec. dir., 1973-76; sole practice, Dallas, 1977-78; mgr. product litigation, dir. Windle Turley, P.C., Dallas, 1978-83; sole practice, 1983-85; ptnr. Demarest & Smith, 1985—; mem. faculty trial advocacy program So. Meth. U Law Sch., 1984; lectr. Contbr. articles to profl. jours. Mem. ABA, State Bar Tex., Assn. Trial Lawyers Am., Dallas Bar Assn., Dallas Trial Lawyers Assn. (past pres.), Dallas Inn of Ct. (master of the bar 1989—). Democrat. Roman Catholic. Home: 1812 Atlantic St Dallas TX 75208-3002 Office: 2305 Cedar Springs Rd Ste 350 Dallas TX 75201-7807

DEMARIA, MICHAEL BRANT, psychologist; b. Norwalk, Conn., Apr. 23, 1962; s. Francesco and Jacqueline (Campbell) DeM.; m. Kathleen Jean Kies, July 4, 1982; 1 child, Danielle. BA in Psychology magna cum laude, U. West Fla., 1982, BA in Philosophy magna cum laude, 1982; MA in Psychology, Duquesne U., Pitts., 1983, PhD in Clin. Psychology, 1987. Lic. clin. psychologist, Fla.; registered play therapist; diplomate in expressive therapy. Doctoral intern Bapt. Hosp. and Lakeview Ctr., Pensacola, Fla., 1985-86; resident Clin. Psychology Assn., Pensacola, 1986-88, clin. psychologist, 1988-89; clin. psychologist, pres., clin. dir. DeMaria and Assoc., Pensacola, 1989—; therapist Counseling Ctr. Point Park Coll., Pitts., 1983-84, Ctr. Tng. and Rsch. in Psychology Duquesne U., 1983-86, instr. Psychology Dept., 1983-85, rsch. asst., 1983-85; faculty assoc. U. West Fla., 1985—; cons. Adolescent Stress Ctr. Bapt. Hosp., Pensacola, 1985-89, IMPACT Program, 1986-88, Child Protection Team, 1986-89; cons./expert witness State Atty. Office, Pensacola, Renascence Recovery Ctr., Anchorage Counseling Svcs., Community Drug & Alcohol Commn., Rivendale Hosp.; speaker in field. Author: Horns and Halos: Towards the Blessing of Darkness, 1992; contbr. articles to The Humanistic Psychologist, Internat. Journey of Play Therapy, The Arts in Psychotherapy: An International Jour. Mem. Fla. Legis. Task Force on Child Abuse and Neglect Reports, 1988—. Recipient Merit scholarship Dept. Psychology, Dept. Philosophy U. West Fla., Alumni Found. scholarship. Mem. APA, Soc. for Personality Assessment, Assn. for Play Therapy, Southeastern Psychol. Assn., Fla. Psychol. Assn. (treas. 1989—), Psi Chi, Phi Kappa Phi. Office: 512 E Zarragossa St Pensacola FL 32501-6155

DEMARK-WAHNEFRIED, WENDY, nutritionist, researcher; b. Detroit, Jan. 31, 1956; d. Rudolph and Helen Demark; m. Gene Arthur Wahnefried, Feb. 16, 1980; children: Nicholas Jay, Petra Justine. BS, U. Mich., 1978; MS, Tex. Women's U., 1980; PhD, Syracuse U., 1988. Reg. dietitian; lic. dietitian/nutritionist. Supervising dietitian Interstate United Corp., Syracuse, N.Y., 1980; dir. outpatient nutritional svcs. SUNY Med. Ctr., Syracuse, 1980-84; pvt. practice nutritionist Syracuse, 1986-91; adj. faculty mem. Syracuse U., 1980-91, SUNY, Syracuse, 1981-91, SUNY Cortland, Durham, N.C., 1989-91; cons. Food Communications, Inc., Chgo, 1990-91, Johnston County Cholesterol Lowering Project, Raleigh, N.C., 1991; rsch. specialist cancer control rsch. Duke U. Med. Ctr., Durham, N.C., 1991-92; asst. prof., asst. dir. Stedman Ctr. Nutritional Studies, 1993—; N.C. Dept. Agriculture, Raleigh, 1992—, Tristate Appalacian Leadership Initiative on Cancer, Raleigh, 1992—. Contbr. articles to profl. jours. Grantee Nat. Cancer Inst., 1993; recipient investigator award Cancer Rsch. Found. Am., 1993, instnl. award Am. Cancer Soc., 1993. Mem. Am. Dietetic Assn. (named Young Dietitian Yr. 1983, reviewer 1980—, control study sect. 1994—), Am. Soc. Preventive Oncology, Nutrition Rsch. & Edn. Practice Group (awards com. 1992—), Sports & Cardiovascular Nutritionists Group. Home: 105 Birkhaven Dr Cary NC 27511-8942 Office: Duke U Med Ctr Stedman Ctr Nutri Studies Box 3487 Durham NC 27705-4640

DEMARTINI, EDWARD JOHN, lawyer, real estate investor; b. New Orleans, May 30, 1932; s. John and Ethel (McNulty) DeM.; m. Patricia Morgan, Oct. 3, 1953; children: Edward Jr., Margaret S., John, JoAnn. BS, Tulane U., 1953, LLB, 1967; MBA, U. Mich., 1962. Bar: La. 1967, U.S. Dist. Ct. (so. and ctrl. dist.) 1967, U.S. Ct. Appeals (5th cir.) 1968. Officer U.S. Navy, 1953-63; pres. Edsa, Inc., Kenner, La., 1964—; ptnr. Duplantier & DeMartini, New Orleans, 1968-74; sr. ptnr. DeMartini & LeBlanc, Kenner, La., 1974—. Commdr. USNR, 1963-73. Mem. Rotary Club, Elks Club, Am. Judicature Soc., Assn. Naval Aviation, Tailhook. Office: DeMartini & LeBlanc 3329 Florida Ave Kenner LA 70065-3644

DEMBO, RICHARD, criminology educator; b. N.Y.C., Jan. 4, 1940; s. Louis and Rose Dembo; m. Enid Betsy Pullman, Sept. 24, 1967; children: Julie Beth, Gareth Scott. BA, NYU, 1961, PhD, 1970; MA, Columbia U., 1965. Parole officer N.Y. State Div. of Parole, N.Y.C., 1966-69; rsch. scientist, sr. rsch. scientist N.Y. State Narcotic Addiction Control Commn., N.Y.C., 1969-70; rsch. officer U. Leicester (England) Mass Communication Rsch. Ctr., 1970-73; assoc. rsch. scientist N.Y. State Drug Abuse Control Commn., N.Y.C., 1973-76; assoc. prof. sociology Clarkson (N.Y.) Coll. Tech., 1976-78; dir. Colo. criminal justice system study Colo. Div. Criminal Justice, Denver, 1978-79; sr. rsch. assoc. Mental Health Systems Evaluation Project, U. Denver, 1979-81; from assoc. prof. to prof. dept. criminology U. South Fla., Tampa, 1981—; cons. Nat. Inst. Drug Abuse, Rockville, Md., 1986—, Office Juvenile Justice and Delinquency Prevention, Washington, 1991—, Nat. Inst. Justice, Washington, 1992—, Ctr. for Substance Abuse Treatment, Rockville, 1992—, NSF, 1995—, NIMH, 1995—. Editor: Drugs and Crime, 1993; editor spl. issue Internat. Jour. Drug Addictions, 1991, Jour. Drug Issues, 1985-86, 91, 94. Vice-chmn., mem. Hillsborough County Anti-Drug Alliance, Tampa, 1991—; exec. com. mem. Juvenile Justice Coun. Hillsborough County, Tampa, 1994—. Lt. U.S. Army, 1965-71. Grantee Nat. Inst. Justice, Office of Juvenile Justice Delinquency Prevention, Nat. Inst. Drug Abuse, Fla. Dept. Health and Rehab. Svcs., Fla. Dept. Juvenile Justice. Mem. Am. Soc. Criminology, Am. Sociol. Assn., Acad. Criminal Justice Scis. Office: U South Fla Criminology Dept 4202 E Fowler Ave Tampa FL 33620-9900

DEMENCHONOK, EDWARD VASILEVICH, philosopher, linguist, researcher, educator; b. Vitebsk, Belarus, Jan. 1, 1942; came to U.S., 1992; s. Vasiliy Ivanovich Demenchonok and Olga Stanislavovna Plovinskaya; m. Sondra Marisa Franceil, July 1, 1993; children: Anna, Leonid. BA in Music, Mus. Coll., Minsk, Belarus, 1961; MA in Russian and Spanish, Moscow State U. Lomonosov, 1969; PhD, Russian Acad. Scis., Moscow, 1977. Rschr., then sr. rschr. Inst. Philosophy Russian Acad. Scis., 1970-95; assoc. prof. Moscow State U. Lomonosov, 1982-84; prof. Moscow State Pedagogic U., 1991-92; prof. Spanish Am. dept. Acad. Slavic Culture, Moscow, 1991-92; assoc. prof. Spanish Brewton-Parker Coll., Mt. Vernon, Ga., 1994-95; assoc. prof. fgn. langs. Ft. Valley (Ga.) State U., 1995—; vis. rschr. Acad. Scis. Cuba, 1978, 79, 83; vis. prof. U. INCCA Colombia, Bogota, 1988-90; vis. prof. Spanish U. Ga., Athens, 1992-93; lectr. literature Spanish Am. thought and philosophy at various instns., including U. Cordoba, Argentina, 1987, Inst. Missionary Theology, Bogota, 1990, Nat. Inst. Sci. Rsch. Coord. Colombia, Bogota, 1989, 90, Inst. Faith and Secularity, Madrid, Spain, 1992, U. Complutense Madrid, 1992, others; participant profl. confs., most recently Internat. Congress of L.Am. Philosophy: Ethics in L.Am., Bogota, 1990, Internat. Congress: East and West, Dialogue of Cultures in Contemporary World, Moscow, 1992, 9th Internat. Congress in Galicia: Philosophy and Nation, Pontevedra, Spain, 1992, 2nd Internat. Congress L.Am. Philosophy, San Juan, P.R., 1993, 93rd Ann. Meeting Am. Philos. Assn., Chgo., 1995. Author: Contemporary Technocratic Thought in the U.S.A., 1984; (in Spanish) América Latina en la Época de la Revolución Científico-Téchnica, 1990, Filosofía en el Mundo Contemporaneo, 1990, Filosofía Latinoamericana: Problemas y Tendencias, 1990; editor: Problems of Philosophy and Culture in Latin America, 1983, Contemporary Catholic Philosophy, 1985, New Tendencies in Western Social Philosophy, 1988; contbr. articles to profl. jours., chpts. to books. Mem. MLA (participant convs. 1992, 93), L.Am. Studies Assn. (participant XVIII congress 1994), Assn. Cultural Rschrs. Russia, Assn. for Philosophy and Liberation. Russian Orthodox.

DE MENT, IRA, judge; b. Birmingham, Ala., Dec. 21, 1931; s. Ira Jr. and Helen (Sparks) DeM.; m. Ruth Lester Posey; 1 child, Charles Posey. AS, Marion Mil. Inst., 1951; AB, U. Ala., 1953, LLB, 1958, JD, 1969. Bar: Ala. 1958, U.S. Dist. Ct. (mid. dist.) Ala. 1958, U.S. Ct. Appeals (5th cir.) 1958, U.S. Supreme Ct. 1966, U.S. Dist. Ct. (so. dist.) Ala. 1967, U.S. Dist. Ct. D.C. 1972, U.S. Ct. Appeals (D.C.) 1972, U.S. Tax Ct. 1972, U.S. Customs and Patents Appeals 1976, U.S. Dist. Ct. (no. dist.) Ala. 1977. U.S. Ct. Appeals (11th cir.), 1981, U.S. Ct. Mil. Appeal 1972. Law clk. Sup. Ct. Ala., 1958-59; asst. atty. gen. State of Ala., 1959, spl. asst. atty. gen., 1966-69, 81-92; asst. U.S. atty., Montgomery, Ala., 1959-61; pvt. practice Montgomery, 1961-69, 77-92; U.S. dist. judge (mid. dist.) Ala., 1992—;acting U.S. atty. Mid. Dist. Ala. 1969, U.S. atty., 1969-77; asst. atty., legal advisor to police and fire depts. City of Montgomery, 1965-69; instr. Jones Law Sch., 1962-64; instr. Montgomery Police Acad. 1964-77; lectr. constl. law Ala. Police Acad., 1971-75; instr. law enforcement U. Ala., 1967, mem. adj. faculty New Coll., 1974-75, adj. prof. psychology, 1975-92; spl. counsel to Gov. State Ala., 1980-88, gen. counsel Commn. on Aging, 1980-82. Lt. col. USAR, 1953-74; maj. gen. USAFR ret. Recipient Disting. Service award Internat. Assn. Firefighters, 1975; Rockefeller Pub. Service award, Woodrow Wilson Sch. Pub. and Internat. Affairs Princeton U., 1976; named Alumnus of Yr. Marion Mil. Inst., 1988. Mem. ABA, Fed. Bar Assn., D.C. Bar Assn., Ala. Bar Assn. (mem. editorial adv. bd. The Alabama Lawyer 1966-72), Am. Judicature Soc.,Nat. Assn. Former U.S. Attys., Phi Alpha Delta. Republican. United Methodist. Clubs: Masons, Shriners. Address: PO Box 2149 Montgomery AL 36102-2149

DE MENT, JAMES ALDERSON, soil scientist; b. Haughton, La., Dec. 22, 1920; s. Ben Alderson and Myrtle Inez (Rounsavall) De M.; m. Ruby Mae Weaver, June 2, 1941; children: James Alderson Jr., David W. BS, La. State U., 1941; PhD, Cornell U., 1962. Soil scientist Soil Conservation Svc., Okla., 1941-48, La., 1948-56; grad. asst. Cornell U., Ithaca, N.Y., 1956-62; rsch. soil scientist Soil Conservation Svc., Lincoln, Nebr., 1962-65; soil scientist Soil Conservation Svc., Ft. Worth, Tex., 1965-77; ret.; cons. Lockheed Electronics, Clear Lake, Tex., 1977-78, Espey-Huston, Dallas, 1978-84, De Ment & Assocs., Haughton, 1984—. Lt. col. USAF, 1942-45; 1951-52. Recipient 3 Certs. of Merit, Soil Conservation Svc. Mem. Soil and Water Conservation Soc., Am. Soc. Agronomy (cert. profl. soil scientist), Sigma Xi, Alpha Zeta (chancellor 1940-41). Home: 2476 Bellevue Rd Haughton LA 71037-9999

DEMERAU, SCOTT, business executive; b. 1961. Grad., Ferris State U., 1985. With Fantasy Golf Devel. Inc., Norcross, Ga., 1985-91; pres. Malibu Grand Prix Corp., Alpharetta, Ga., 1991—. Office: Malibu Grand Prix Corp 5859 Windward Pky 220 Alpharetta GA 30202

DE MERE-DWYER, LEONA, medical artist; b. Memphis, May 1, 1928; d. Clifton and Leona (McCarthy) De M. BA, Rhodes Coll., Memphis, 1949; MSc, U. Memphis, 1984; PhD, Kennedy-Western U., 1990. Lic. embalmer, funeral dir.; m. John Thomas Dwyer, May 10, 1952; children: John, DeMere, Patrice, Brian, Anne-Clifton DeMere Dwyer, McCarthy-DeMere Dwyer. Med. artist for McCarthy DeMere, Memphis, 1950-80; pres. Aesthetic Med. & Forensic Art, 1984—; speech therapist, Memphis, 1950-82; lectr. on med. art univs., conf., assns.; cons. in prostheses Vocat. Rehab. Svcs.; elected expert witness in funeralization Nat. Forensic Ctr. Author: AIDS; Care of Health Care Workers in the Workplace. Bereavement counselor, organizer Ladies of St. Jude, Memphis, 1960; active Brooks Art Gallery League of Memphis; mem. God's Unfinished Bus. com. Temple Israel; vice dir. Tellico Hist. Found., 1980-80; mem. exec. bd. Chickasaw council Boy Scouts Am.; active Rep. campaign coms.; mem. com. God's Unfinished Bus. Temple Israel Congregation. Recipient Disting. Svc. award Gupton-Jones Coll. Mortuary Sci., 1981, Silver medal Sons of the Am. Revolution medal, 1985, Martha Washington medal. Mem. Nat. Foresic Ctr. (expert witness funeralization 1991—), Fedn. Internat. de'Automobile (internat. car racing 1972, lic.), Assn. Med. Illustrators, Am. Assn. Med. Assts., Emergency Dept. Nurses Assn., Am. Physicians Nurses Assn., Am. Soc. Plastic and Reconstructive Surgeons Found. (guest mem., cons.), Women in Law (chmn. assocs.), Exec. Women Am., Brandeis U. Women, DAR (1st v.p. regent 1980), UDC (pres. Nathan Bedford Forrest chpt.), Cotton Carnival Assn. (chairperson children's ct. 1968-70), Pi Sigma Eta, Kappa Delta (adv.), Kappa Delta Pi. Clubs: Tenn., Royal Matron Amaranth (Faith Ct.), Sertoma (1st female mem. Memphis, elected pres. 1989-90) (Memphis). Author: Aids: Care of Healthcare Workers in the Workplace, 1990; contbr. articles to profl. jours. Home: 1000 Murray Hill Ln # 304 Memphis TN 38120-2665

DEMING, KATHEY S., medical nurse; b. Austell, Ga., Feb. 4, 1948; d. Claude L. and Edith C. (Bell) Smith; m. Jon P. Deming, Feb. 17, 1967; children: Tracy L. Deming Joseph, Jon Thomas. LPN, Carroll Tech. Nurse HCA Parkway Hosp., Lithia Springs, Ga., 1980-87; office mgr. Cobb Nephrology, Austell, Ga., 1988—; trainer peritoneal dialysis patients. Baptist. Home: 1165 Huey Rd Douglasville GA 30134 Office: Cobb Nephrology 1810 Mulkey Rd Ste 103 Austell GA 30001

DEMIRIS, CHRIS H., medical manufacturing diagnostics administrator; b. Astoria, N.Y., Mar. 3, 1961; s. Harry Chris and Kalliopi (Constantine) D.; m. Caroline C. Peters, Oct. 26, 1986; children: Angelica, Theodore. BS, SUNY, 1983; MBA, Adelphi U., 1991. Sales rep. Bio-Rad Labs., N.Y.C., 1985-87, Beckman Industries, N.Y.C., 1987-91; from acct. mgr. to nat. svc. product mgr. Coulter, N.Y.C., Miami, 1991—. Mem. Am. Mgmt. Assn., Clin. Lab. Mgmt. Assn. Republican. Greek Orthodox. Home: 1182 Maghoney Ln Fort Lauderdale FL 33327 Office: Coulter Corp 11800 SW 147th Ave Miami FL 33196-2500

DEMLING, ANN MARIE, theatre educator; b. Ft. Sill, Okla., Aug. 19, 1954; d. Martin Andrew and Marie Elizabeth (Hatter) D. BA, Okla. State U., 1976, MA, 1978; PhD, La. State U., 1983. Tchg. asst. Okla. State U., Stillwater, 1976-78, La. State U., Baton Rouge, 1978-83; assoc. prof. speech/theatre No. Montana Coll., Havre, Mont., 1983-92; assoc. prof. theatre Brenau U., Gainesville, Ga., 1992—; dir. theatre No. Montana Coll., 1984-92, Brenau U., 1992—. Mem. Assn. Theatre in Higher Edn., Speech Comm. Assn., Southeast Theatre Conf. Democrat. Roman Catholic. Home: 371 Woodland Dr Gainesville GA 30501 Office: Brenau U One Centennial Cir Gainesville GA 30501

DEMONSABERT, WINSTON RUSSEL, chemist, consultant; b. New Orleans, June 12, 1915; s. Joseph Francis and Davida Elizabeth (Gullett) deM.; m. Eleanor Ray Ranson, Aug. 8, 1955; 1 child, Winston Russel. BS in Chemistry, Loyola U., New Orleans, 1937; MA in Edn., Tulane U., 1945, PhD in Chemistry, 1952. Asst. prof. Loyola U., New Orleans, 1948-49, assoc. prof., 1949-55, prof., 1955-66; chief chemist Nat. Center for Disease Control, Dept. Health and Human Services, Atlanta, 1966-69, chief contract liaison br. Nat. Center for Health Services Research, 1969-73, chief extramural programs Bur. Drugs, FDA, Rockville, Md., 1973-79, scientist adminstr. office of interagy sci. coordination, office of commr. FDA, after 1979; now cons., govt. liaison environ. chemistry and toxicology; assoc. prof. Tulane U., 1957-58; research chemist Am. Cyanamid Co., 1957-58; vice-chmn. Interagy. Testing Com., 1982. Committeeman Boy Scouts Am., New Orleans and Atlanta; mem. curriculum coms. New Orleans Pub. Sch. Bd., 1965. Fellow AAAS, Am. Inst. Chemists (chmn. La. chpt. 1958-60, chmn. Ga. chpt. 1968-69, pres. D.C. chpt. 1982-83); mem. Am. Chem. Soc. (past chmn. La. sect.). Roman Catholic. Contbr. to Ency. Americana, Ency. Chemistry, also profl. jours. Achievements include research in environmental effects (detection, prevention and treatment) of toxic wastes, pesticides and air pollution, and zirconium chemistry. Home and Office: 4317 Lake Trail Dr Kenner LA 70065-1541

DEMOTT, DEBORAH ANN, lawyer, educator; b. Collingswood, N.J., July 21, 1948; d. Lyle J. and Frances F. (Cummings) DeMott. BA, Swarthmore Coll., 1970; JD, NYU, 1973. Bar: N.Y. 1974. Law clk. U.S. Dist. Ct. (so. dist.) N.Y., 1973; assoc. Simpson, Thacher & Bartlett, N.Y.C., 1974-75; vis. asst. prof. U. Tex., Austin, 1977-78; asst. prof. Duke U., Durham, N.C., 1975-78, assoc. prof., 1978-80, prof. law, 1980—, Bost rsch. prof. law, 1981; vis. prof. U. Calif. Hastings Coll. Law, 1986, U. Colo., 1989, U. San Diego, 1991; James L. Lewtas vis. prof. law Osgoode Hall Law Sch., Toronto, Ont., Can., 1991; vis. fellow U. Melbourne, 1993, 95; Huber C. Hurst Eminent vis. scholar U. Fla. Coll. Law, 1996. Author: Shareholder Derivative Actions, 1987, Fiduciary Obligation Agency and Partnership, 1991; editor: Corporations at the Crossroads: Governance and Reform; contbr. articles to profl. jours.; bd. advisors Jour. Legal Edn., 1983-86. Trustee Law Sch. Admission Council, 1984-88; mem. N.C. Gen. Statutes Commn., 1990—; mem. selection com. Coif Book award, 1988-90. Recipient Pomeroy prize, NYU Sch. Law, 1971-73 ; AAUW fellow, 1972-73; Fulbright Sr. scholar Sydney U. and Monash (Australia) U, 1986. Mem. ABA, Am. Law Inst. (reporter restatement of agy. 1995—). Office: Duke U Law Sch PO Box 90360 Durham NC 27708-0360

DEMPSEY, BERNARD HAYDEN, JR., lawyer; b. Evanston, Ill., Mar. 29, 1942; s. Bernard H. and Margaret C. (Gallagher) D.; m. Cynthia T.; children: Bernard H. III, Matthew B., Kathleen N., Rose Maureen G., Alexandra C., Anastasia M. BS, Coll. Holy Cross, 1964; JD, Georgetown U., 1967. Bar: Fla. 1968, D.C. 1979. Law clk. to chief judge U.S. Dist. Ct. (mid. dist.) Fla., 1967-69; asst. U.S. atty. Mid. Dist. Fla., 1969-73; assoc. Dixon, Shear, Brown & Stephenson, Orlando, Fla., 1973-75; sr. ptnr. Dempsey & Kelly, Orlando, 1975-77, Dempsey & Slaughter, P.A., 1977-84, Dempsey & Goldsmith, P.A., 1984-90, Dempsey & Assocs., P.A., 1990—; lectr. trial tactics seminars. Recipient John Marshall award U.S. Dept. Justice, 1973, Outstanding Performance award, 1972. Mem. Fla. Bar Found., ABA, Fed. Bar Assn., Assn. Trial Lawyers Am., Am. Judicature Soc., Nat. Health Lawyers Assn., Nat. Assn. of Criminal Def. Lawyers, Delta Theta Phi. Republican. Roman Catholic. Clubs: Univ. (Orlando); Winter Park (Fla.) Racquet. Contbr. articles to legal jours. Home: 1132 Country Club Dr Orlando FL 32804-6714 Office: Dempsey & Assocs PA PO Box 1980 Orlando FL 32802-1980

DEMPSEY, BUCKLEY KINARD, cardiologist; b. Memphis, Nov. 27, 1944; s. Edmond Noel and Cora (Conner) D.; m. Margaret Elaine Jones, Dec. 19, 1969; children: Buckley Kinard, Jason Matthew, Anna Ward. BS, Memphis State U., 1966; MD, U. Tenn., 1969. Diplomate Am. Bd. Internal Medicine, Am. Bd. Cardiology. Intern Tulane div. Charity Hosp., New Orleans, 1970; resident in internal medicine U. Tenn. Coll. Medicine, Memphis, 1971-73, fellow in cardiology, 1982-84; cardiologist in pvt. practice Memphis, 1984—. Fellow Am. Coll. Cardiology; mem. ACP. Methodist. Office: 6005 Park Ave Ste 910 Memphis TN 38119-5219

DEMPSEY, FREDERICK GERARD (TERRY), JR., association management executive, consultant; b. Ft. Bliss, Tex., June 17, 1949; s. Frederick G. and Rosalie L. (Esser) D.; m. Diann Page Vicars, Aug. 28, 1971; children: James P., David M. BBA with high distinction, U. Ky., 1971; MBA, Ga. State U., 1977. Asst. exec. dir. Med. Assn. Atlanta, 1977-85; gen. mgr., pres. Med. Soc. Svcs., Inc., 1977-85; pres. Dempsey Mgmt. Svcs., Stone Mountain, Ga., 1985—, Ga. Industry Assn., Stone Mountain, 1996—; exec. v.p. Am. Fence Assn., Stone Mountain, 1988—; mem. adv. bd. Consumer Credit Counseling Svc., Atlanta, 1981-84; bd. dirs., mem. exec. com. Med.-Dental-Hosp. Burs. Am., Chgo., 1981-86. Asst. scoutmaster troop 19 Boy Scouts Am., Redan, Ga., 1982-88; pres. Redan PTA, 1985-86. Capt. U.S. Army, 1971-77. Recipient Disting. Svc. award Med.-Dental-Hosp. Burs. Am., 1984, President's award Internat. Fence Industry Assn., 1991, Army Commendation medal with oak leaf cluster. Mem. Am. Soc. Assn. Execs. (cert.), Ga. Soc. Assn. Execs. (pres. 1985-86, Clifford M. Clarke award 1988), Beta Gamma Sigma. Presbyterian. Office: 5300 Memorial Dr Ste 116 Stone Mountain GA 30083

DEMPSEY, JOSEPH PAGE, retired minister, counselor; b. Nashville, N.C., Mar. 8, 1930; s. Sidney Hilliard and Irene Alice (Vick) D.; m. Evelyntyne Humphrey, May 31, 1958; children: Denise P., Joseph T., Eric H., Kathy D. BS, Fayetteville State U., 1958; MDiv, Shaw Div. Sch., 1964; MA, N.C. Ctrl. U., 1971; D Ministry, Faith Luth. Sem., 1988; ThD, Jacksonville Theol. Sem., 1992. Grammer tchr. C.E. Perry H.S., Roseboro, N.C., 1958-61, B.F. Person H.S., Franklin, N.C., 1964-67, Apex (N.C.) Consol. H.S., 1967-71; boys' dir. YMCA, Raleigh, N.C., 1961-67; pastor Oberlin Bapt. Ch., Raleigh, 1964-80, Cir. of Faith Bapt. Ch., Raleigh, 1980-84; assoc. dir. Counseling Ctr. N.C. Ctrl. U., Durham, 1971-91; ret., 1991. Baptist. Home: 1409 E Martin St Raleigh NC 27610-2611

DENABURG, CHARLES ROBERT, metallurgical engineer, retired government official; b. Birmingham, Ala., Apr. 23, 1935; s. Simon and Mary E. Denaburg; m. Sara Rose Lepp, Aug. 12, 1956; children: Elisa Jan, Cheryl Lyn, Daniel A. BS in Metall. Engring., U. Ala., 1959. Registered profl. engr., Ala. Extraction metallurgist U.S. Bur. Mines, U. Ala., Tuscaloosa, 1959; metall. engr. Lazarov Surplus, Memphis, 1959-60; aerospace technologist for materials Marshall Space Flight Ctr.-NASA, Huntsville, Ala., 1960-61, 62-67; aerospace technologist for materials Kennedy Space Ctr. (Fla.)-NASA, 1967-83, chief malfunction analysis br., 1983-90, ret., 1990; chief exec. officer C.R. Denaburg & Assocs., Inc., Indian Harbour Beach, Fla., 1978—; mem. materials and processes working group NASA, Washington, 1987—, mem. space shuttle tech. steering group, 1969-81, mem. wind tunnel evaluation team, 1986. Contbr. articles to profl. publs. Mem. Indian Harbour Beach Planning and Zoning Bd., 1973-74, Windward Cove (Fla.) Archtl. Rev. Bd., 1989—. With U.S. Army, 1961-62. Recipient cert. of commendation Kennedy Space Ctr., 1973, NASA Exceptional Svc. medal, 1986; Snoopy award NASA Astronaut Office, 1970. Mem. Aircraft Owners and Pilots Assn., Internat. Soc. on Air Safety Internat., Am. Soc. for Metals (editing team on corrosion failures Metals Handbook 1972-73, exec. com. Ctrl. Fla. chpt. 1974-76), Am. Ceramic Soc., Nat. Mgmt. Assn., B'nai B'rith (chpt. rec. sec. 1993-96, pres. 1996-97). Home and Office: 140 Windward Way Melbourne FL 32937

DENHAM, CAROLINE VIRGINIA, retired college official; b. Detroit, June 22, 1937; d. Athel Fredric Denham and Emma Virginia (Franck) Kuhns. B.Mus., U. S.C., 1973. Sec. Shawnee Press, Inc., Delaware Water Gap, Pa., 1958-61, editorial asst., 1961-68; clk. typist U. S.C., Columbia, 1969-72, rsch. asst., 1972-76, dir. instnl. rsch., 1976-93; ret., 1994; libr. Columbia Philharm. Orch., 1970-82, pers. mgr., 1972-82; pers. mgr. S.C. Philharmonic Orch. Assn., Columbia, 1982—. Mem. S.C. State Employees Assn., S.C. Assn. for Instl. Rsch. (emeritus, treas. 1987-91, pres. 1992-93), Assn. for Instl. Rsch., emeritus, , So. Assn. Instl. Rsch., emeritus, Pi Kappa Lambda, Delta Omicron.

DENHAM, VERNON ROBERT, JR., lawyer; b. Atlanta, Apr. 18, 1948; s. Vernon Robert and Sara Elizabeth (Robertson) D.; m. Susan Elizabeth Willis, Mar. 19, 1974; children: Whitney Willis, Tyler Willis. Student, Rensselaer Poly. Inst., 1966-68; BSE, U. Mich., 1970, MSE, 1972; JD with honors, U. Fla., 1979. Bar: Fla. 1979, Ga. 1979, U.S. Dist. Ct. (no. dist.) Ga. 1979, U.S. Ct. Appeals (11th cir.) 1981. Engr. Ford Motor Co., Dearborn, Mich., 1972-73; assoc. Powell, Goldstein, Frazer & Murphy, Atlanta, 1979-86, ptnr., 1986—; mem. case notes com. U.S. Dist. Ct. (no. dist.) Ga., Atlanta, 1980-86, mem. magistrate merit selection panel, 1983. Lt. USNR, 1973-76. Mem. ABA (natural resources law sect., litigation sec., corp. and bus. sect.), Am. Chem. Soc., Internat. Soc. Regulatory Toxicology and Pharmacology, Fla. Bar (gen. practice trial sect., environ. and land use law sect.), State Bar Ga. (litigation and environ. sects.), Atlanta Bar Assn. (litigation, environ. sects., vice chair environ. sect. 1992-93, chair 1993-94), Order of Coif, Tau Beta Pi. Home: 1433 Sheridan Walk NE Atlanta GA 30324-3253 Office: Powell Goldstein Frazer & Murphy 191 Peachtree St NE Fl 16 Atlanta GA 30303-1741

DENHAM, WILLIAM ERNEST, JR., minister, counselor; b. Louisville, Oct. 8, 1911; s. William E. and Myrtle (Lane) D.; m. Priscilla Kelley, June 27, 1941 (dec.); children: William Ernest III, James Kelley, Priscilla, Elizabeth Denham Thompson; m. 2d, Louise D. Yelvington, Nov. 23, 1974. AB, Washington U., 1933; ThM, So. Bapt. Theol. Sem., 1940, PhD, 1944; postgrad. U. Tex., Austin, 1971-73. Lic. profl. counselor, Tex., marriage and family counselor, Tex. Sec. Bapt. Student Union, Mo. Baptist Conv., 1933-35, Atlanta, 1935-37; pastor Silas Bapt. Ch., Bourbon County, Ky., 1938-43, Oakland Bapt. Ch., Oklahoma City, 1940-43, 1st. Bapt. Ch., Newport, Tenn., 1944-47, Macon, Ga., 1947-52, River Oaks Bapt. Ch., Houston, 1952-64, 1st. Bapt. Ch., Austin, 1964-75; founder, dir. Counseling and Pastoral Care Ctr., Austin, 1975-93, dir. spiritual growth, 1987—; mem. bd. Bapt. Radio Commn., So. Bapt. Conv.; exec. com. mem. Bapt. Gen. Conv., Tex.; founding bd. chmn. Houston Bapt. U.; founding sponsor Amigos de las Americas; Protestant chaplain gen. Boy Scouts Am., 1969. Mem. Family Mediation Assn. (cert.), Am. Assn. Marriage and Family Therapists, Am. Assn. Sex Educators, Counselors and Therapists, Am. Assn. Pastoral Counselors (diplomate), Omicron Delta Kappa. Democrat. Lodges: Rotary, Kiwanis. Contbr. articles to profl. jours. Address: Counseling and Pastoral Care Ctr 5425A Burnet Rd Austin TX 78756-1627

DE NIGRIS, ANNA MARIA THERESA, middle school educator; b. N.Y.C., Oct. 18, 1947; d. Salvatore and Rosaria (Colletti) Insalaco; m. Michael Peter De Nigris, July 12, 1969; children: Jenniffer Ann, Tamara Alicia. AA in Langs., Bronx C.C., 1968; BA in English and Langs., CCNY, 1969; MA in English Linguistics, George Mason U., 1988. Cert. lang. profl., secondary tchr., Va. Tchr. Spanish and core subjects St. John's, Rubidoux, Calif., 1969-70; ESL specialist Sunset Hills Elem. Sch., San Diego, 1980; tchr. Sunrise Acres Elem. Sch., Las Vegas, Nev., 1984-85; tchr. 1st grade Talent House Pvt. Elem. Sch., Fairfax, Va., 1987-88; tchr. ESL Hammond Jr. High Sch., Alexandria, Va., 1988-90, Washington Irving Intermediate Sch., Springfield, Va., 1990-91; tchr. ESL 6th grade Ellen Glassgow Mid. Sch., Alexandria, 1991-92; tchr. ESL and English 7th grade Cooper Mid. Sch., McLean, Va., 1992-93; tchr. ESL Poe Mid. Sch., Annandale, Va., 1993-94; tchr. ESL and social studies Longfellow Mid. Sch., Falls Church, Va., 1994-95; tchr. ESL Herndon (Va.) Mid. Sch., 1995—; tchr. adult ESL, George Mason H.S., Falls Church, Va., 1988-89; chmn. for multicultural forum Coun. for Applied R & D, George Mason U., 1990-94; mem. steering com., faculty adv. com. Herndon Mid. Sch., 1995—; presenter in field; mem. sch. adoption com. Va. Dept. Transp., 1991, human rels com., 1990-91, ESL Portfolio Assessment com., 1993—; sch.-based mem. for minority achievement in prin.'s cabinet F.C. Hammond Jr. H.S., Alexandria, 1989-90. Vol. Family Svcs., Wright Patterson AFB, Ohio, 1971-72, ARC, Ohio and S.C., 1971-73; leader Girl Scouts U.S., 1980-87. Mem. Va. Edn. Assn. (del. 1990—), Nat. Assn. Bilingual Edn., Southwestern Conf. Lang. Tchrs., ESL Multi-Cultural Conv. (presenter, facilitator 1989), Tchrs. ESL, Washington Tchrs. ESL, Calif. Tchrs. ESL, Va. Assn. Tchrs. English, Fairfax Edn. Assn. (sch. rep., del. Va. Edn. Assn. 1991—). Roman Catholic. Home: 8814 Hayload Ct Springfield VA 22153-1213

DENISON, JOHN G., airline executive; b. 1945. BA, Oakland U., 1967; MBA, Wayne State U., 1975. Mgr. corp. financing and corp. studies Chrysler Corp., 1969-80; asst. treas. LTV Corp., Dallas, 1980-86; v.p. fin., CFO S.W. Airlines Co., 1986—, exec. v.p., 1989, exec. v.p. corp. svcs., 1994—. Office: SW Airlines Co Box 36611 2702 Love Field Dr Dallas TX 75235*

DENISON, LLOYD WILLIAM, retired mechanical engineer; b. Springfield, Mass., Sept. 2, 1923; s. Lloyd W. and Lillian Denison; married; children: Susannah Denison Rouse, Charles S. Student, The Citadel; BSME, Va. Poly. Inst. Gen. mgr. sales Yarway Corp., Phila., 1951-69; owner, v.p. mktg. Crosby Valve, Wrentham, Mass., 1969-82. Lt. U.S. Army, 1942-45. Mem. Martin Downs Country Club, Monarch Country Club. Home: 2230 Whitemarsh Way Palm City FL 34990 also: 12443 Bradford Ct Fishers IN 46038

DE NITTO, JOHN FRANCIS, human resources administrator, medical researcher; b. Passaic, N.J., July 26, 1953; s. Bruno and Mary (Yawlak) De N.; m. Kathleen Sharon Hey Mahady, Apr. 29, 1978 (div. Mar. 1988). AAS, Essex Coll., 1975. Lic. comml. fire insp.; cert. healthcare safety profl., healthcare hazard comms. compliance officer. Regional mgr. Alert/N.J. Pvt. Investigations Bur. Svcs., Hackensack, N.J., 1973-75; dir. comms. and safety St. Mary's Hosp., Passaic, 1975-89; exec. dir. Orgn. Healthcare Hazard Communications Compliance Officers, Passaic, 1989-90; loss control program cons. State of Fla., Lakeland, 1990-91; corp. dir. human resources Ctrl. Fla. Investments, Orlando, 1991-95; pres. Antique Mall, Winter Haven, Fla., 1995—; host, writer satellite ednl. TV healthcare info., Princeton, N.J., 1986-88. Author: An Intensely Personal Matter, 1993; contbr. articles to profl. jours. Campaign mgr. Joseph P. Lazur for City Coun., Passaic, 1987; bd. dirs. Poinciana (Fla.) Villages Bd., 1990-93; mem. constrn. bd. appeals City of Passaic, 1988-89. Mem. N.J. Hosp. Dirs. Assn. (life, pres. 1983-85, Safety Mgr. of Yr. 1989), Orgn. Healthcare Hazard Comms. Compliance Officers (exec. bd. dirs. 1987-91). Republican. Roman Catholic. Home: 564 Koala Dr Poinciana FL 34759-4210 Office: Antique Malls USA 3170 US Hwy 17 Winter Haven FL 33881

DENIUS, FRANKLIN WOFFORD, lawyer; b. Athens, Tex., Jan. 4, 1925; s. S.F. and Frances (Cain) D.; m. Charmaine Hooper, Nov. 19, 1949; children: Frank Wofford, Charmaine. B.B.A., LL.B., U. Tex. Bar: Tex. 1949. Practiced in Austin, 1949—; past sec.-treas., dir. Telcom Corp.; past pres., chief exec. officer, chmn. bd., dir. So. Union Co.; dir. Tex. Commerce Bank-Austin; past legal counsel Austin Better Bus. Bur. Chmn. spl. schs. div. United Fund, 1960, Pacesetters div., 1961, Schs. div., 1964; 1st v.p. United Fund; chmn. steering com. sch. bond campaign, past trustee Austin Ind. Sch. Dist., 1964; past pres. Young Men's Bus. League Austin; past pres., exec. council Austin Ex-Students Assn. U. Tex.; past co-chmn. LBJ U Tex. Library Found.; mem. chancellor's council, pres.'s assos. U. Tex.; bd. dirs. Tex. Research League; advisory trustee Schreiner Coll. Decorated Silver Star medal with 3 oak leaf clusters, Purple Heart; recipient Outstanding Young Man of Austin award Jr. C. of C., 1959; named Disting. Alumnus U. Tex. Ex-Students Assn., 1991. Mem. ABA, Tex. Bar Assn., Travis County Bar Assn., Tex. Philos. Soc., Longhorn Club (past pres.), West Austin Optimists (past dir.), Headliners (pres., sec. bd. trustees, exec. com.), Masons. Presbyterian (deacon, elder). Home: 3703 Meadowbank Dr Austin TX 78703-1025 Office: Tex Commerce Bank Bldg 700 Lavaca St Ste 700 Austin TX 78701-3102

DENMARK, KATHY BRYANT, critical care and medical/surgical nurse; b. Clinton, La., June 1, 1960; d. William Nickless and Eunice (Stroud) Bryant; m. Steven Bryan Denmark, July 7, 1984; children: Nicholas Bryan, Justin Ryan, Trey Aidan. ADN, Alcorn State U., Natchez, Miss., 1982. RN, La.; CCRN; registered cardiovasc. technician; cert. ACLS, BLS, BLS instr. Weekend charge nurse SICU, nurse preceptor Baton Rouge Gen. Med. Ctr., 1982-92; nurse, heart catheterization lab. Our Lady of the Lake Regional Med. Ctr., Baton Rouge, 1992—. Mem. ANA, AACN, La. State Nurses Assn.

DENNEHY, LEISA JEANOTTA, company executive; b. Fairfield, Ohio, May 30, 1961; d. Will Robert and Rethel Jeanotta (Russell) Fights. BA in Chemistry, Miami U., Oxford, Ohio, 1982; BS in Med. Tech., Miami U., 1983; MBA, Duke U., 1991. Registered med. technologist. Med. technologist Mercy Hosp., Hamilton, Ohio, 1982-85; analytical chemist Procter & Gamble Co., Cin., 1985-87, products rsch. chemist, 1987-88; new products anlyst GlaxoWellcome, Research Triangle, N.C., 1988-90; internat. product mgr.-dermatology GlaxoWellcome, Research Triangle Park, N.C., 1990-91, mgr. new product market devel., 1991-95, sr. product mgr., 1995-96, internat. comml. strategy mgr., 1996—. Co-author: Supercritical Fluid Extraction and Chromatography, 1988; contbr. articles to profl. jours. Named Women of the Day, 1979; recipient many acad. scholarships, 1980-82. mem. Am. Soc. Med. Tech., Am. Soc. Clin. Pathology. Home: 130 Marquette Dr Cary NC 27513-3488

DENNEY, LAURA FALIN, insurance company executive; b. Knoxville, Tenn., Sept. 23, 1948; d. Jack Gordon and Marilyn Frances (Ramsey) Falin; m. Richard Earl Buchannan, Feb. 14, 1970 (dec. Oct. 1972); m. Peter Michael Denney, Sept. 6, 1978. BS, East Tenn. State U., 1970. Underwriting asst. Safeco Ins. Co., Atlanta, 1971-73, underwriter, 1973-79, mgr. area underwriting, 1979-90, mgr. personal lines underwriting, 1990—. Counselor St. Patrick's Episc. Ch., Dunwoody, Ga., 1983-86. Republican. Mem. Ch. of God. Office: Safeco Ins Co 1551 Juliette Dr Stone Mountain GA 30083-1509

DENNEY, ROBERT BLAKE, public relations specialist; b. Mason City, Iowa, Aug. 31, 1951; s. Robert Benjamin and Kathryn Ann (Blake) D. BA, U. Iowa, 1973, MA, 1979. Asst. sports editor Burlington (Iowa) Hawk Eye, 1973-77; staff writer Cedar Rapids (Iowa) Gazette, 1980-92; pub. rels. writer PGA of Am., Palm Beach Gardens, Fla., 1992—. Author, editor: 1994-95 Guide to the PGA Championships. Roman Catholic. Office: PGA of America 100 Avenue Of Champions Palm Beach Gardens FL 33418

DENNIS, BARRY LEE, timber company executive; b. DeRidder, La., Jan. 1, 1952; s. Orville Lee and Geraldine (Hebert) D.; m. Donna Arlene Bowen, June 3, 1972; 1 child, Angela Michelle. A, Ea. Okla. State Coll., 1973. Procurement forester Ga.-Pacific, Crossett, Ark., 1973-74; procurement/asst. logging supr. Ga.-Pacific, Stamps, Ark., 1974-76; asst. gen. mgr. Ward-English Pulpwood Co., Stamps, 1976-80; timber broker, owner Dennis Forestry Svcs., Stamps, 1980-93; owner/mgr. Dennis Trucking Svcs., Inc., Waldo, Ark., 1993-94; timber broker/owner/mgr. Dennis Trucking Svcs., Inc., Waldo, 1994—; cons. (720 acres timberland) Dennis Forestry Svcs., Waldo, 1976—; mgr./pres. Timberjack Deer Club, Lewisville, 1976—. Pres. Ducks Unlimited, Stamps, 1981-82; mgr., co-operator Acres for Wildlife (Ark. Game and Fish Commn.), Lewisville, 1976—. Mem. NRA. Mem. Ch. of Christ. Home: 1520 Highway 344 Waldo AR 71770-9096 Office: Dennis Trucking Svcs Inc 1520 Highway 344 Waldo AR 71770-9096

DENNIS, GORDON SCOTT, secondary school educator; b. Dallas, June 5, 1962; s. J.G. and Gwndolyn Ann (Burkholder) D. BA, U. Tex., 1989. Cert. tchr., Tex. Tchr., advisor Refugio (Tex.) H.S., 1990-92, Burbank H.S., San Antonio, Tex., 1992—; on air personality KSLR Radio, San Antonio, 1992—; talent coord. Today's Walk TV Show, San Antonio, 1992—.

DENNIS-HOLLIS, ROBBIE SMAGULA, marketing communications executive; b. Dover, Del., Oct. 15, 1957; d. Thomas David and Billie Jo (Talkington) Smagula; m. Mark Steven Dennis, May 26, 1979 (div. May 1982); 1 child, Gregory Steven; m. Stuart D. B. Hollis, Nov. 18, 1989; children: Hanna Joellen, Rachael Nicole. BS in Marine Biology, Tex. A&M U., 1978. Tech. writer Tex. Trans. Inst., College Station, Tex., 1978-80; documentation coord. Genentech, Inc., South San Francisco, Calif., 1980-82; sr. tech. writer Cen. & South West Svcs., Inc., Dallas, 1982-88; sales promotion mgr. Computer Assocs. (formerly UCCEL Corp.), Dallas, 1984-88; with corp. communications J. Driscoll & Assocs., Dallas, 1988-89; mgr. mktg. communications ANTRIM Corp., Plano, Tex., 1989-94; mgr. Hogan Corp. Comms., Dallas, 1994—. Mem. Soc. Tech. Communication (Best of Show and Excellence Achievement award 1985, 86), Internat. Assn. Bus. Communicators, NAFE.

DENNISON, RAMONA POLLAN, special education educator; b. Floydada, Tex., Jan. 19, 1938; d. William C. and Anne M. (Tivis) Pollan; m. Bob Dennison, Oct. 12, 1956; 1 child, Tajquah. BS, MEd, E. Cen. U., 1972, cert. in psychometry, 1974, lic. in profl. counseling, 1975. Lic. psychometrist, profl. counselor. Tchr. Konawa (Okla.) Pub. Sch., 1972—. Mem. NEA, Okla. Edn. Assn., Okla. Assn. Children of Learning Disabilities, Konana Edn. Assn., Lic. Profl. Counselor Assn., Nat. Assn. Children Learning Disabilities, E. Cen. Alumni Assn., Tanti Study Club, Oak Hills Country Club, Delta Kappa Gamma, Phi Delta Kappa. Democrat. Baptist. Home: RR 4 Box 568 Ada OK 74820-9443

DENNY, DWIGHT D., rental company executive; b. 1943. BBA, U. N.C. Various mgmt. and exec. positions Ryder Truck Rental Inc., 1969—, exec. v.p., gen. mgr. comml. leasing and svcs., 1991, pres. comml. leasing and svcs., 1992-95; exec. v.p. devel. Ryder Sys. Inc., 1995—. Office: Rider Truck Rental Inc 3600 NW 82nd Ave Miami FL 33166-6623

DENNY, FRANK WILLIAM, county clerk; b. Moody, Tex., Nov. 12, 1909; s. William Robert and Hallie Harriet (Harding) D.; m. June 24, 1932; 1 child, Hallie Ann Gaffney. BBA, Baylor U., 1932. Mgr. of family bus. Moody, 1939-68; county clk. McLennan County, Waco, Tex., 1969—. Mayor Moody, Tex., 1950-58; mem. childrens activity com. Waco, 1969-85. Mem. Masons, York Rie, Scottish Rite. Democrat. Baptist.

DENNY, J(AMES) WILLIAM, utility company executive; b. Nashville, Aug. 25, 1935; s. James R. and Margaret (Osment) D.; m. June Ralls, Aug. 31, 1957; children: Kevin, Steven, Jennifer. Student, Vanderbilt U., 1953-57. Road mgr. Phillip Morris Country Music Show, 1957-58; account exec. McDonald & Alsup Advt. Agy., 1958-69; mgmt. trainee Third Nat. Bank, Nashville, 1959-61; pres. So. Star Investors Assocs., 1960; mgr. Columbia Records Rec. Studio, Columbia Records Custom Prodns., 1961-63; exec. v.p. Sta. WSNT, Sanderville, Ga., 1963-67; pres. Cedarwood Pub. Co., Inc., Nashville, 1963-83; pres., dir. Nashville Gas div. Tenn. Natural Inc., 1983-85; v.p. Piedmont Natural Gas, 1985—; ptnr. Hatch Show Print, 1964-83, Nat. Tape Corp., 1980—; bd. dirs. Dominion Bank of Middle Tenn., Tenn. Natural Gas Lines, Inc., Nashville City Bank, First Union Bank, Background Am., Inc., Leadership Music. Mem. Met. Nashville Auditorium Commn., 1977-82; chmn. bd. Country Music Found., 1967, pres., 1968; pres. Leadership Nashville Alumni Assn., 1977-78; bd. dirs. Nashville Cancer Soc., 1967-69, Brentwood Acad., 1971-80, Nashville Children's Hosp., 1978-81; bd. dirs. Crimestoppers of Nashville, 1983, chmn., 1987; mem. adv. bd. Salvation Army, 1983—, chmn., 1988; mem. Nashville Century III Com., 1978079; trustee Wilkerson Speech and Hearing Ctr., 1975-79; bd. dirs. Leadership Music, 1990, treas., 1990—. Recipient Spl. Achievement award Record World mag., 1967; named Country Music Pub. of Year Music Bus. mag., 1964. Mem. Am. Gas Assn. (bd. dirs. 1984-86, labs. bd. 1984—), So. Gas Assn. (bd. dirs. 1984-87), Southeastern Gas Assn. (bd. dirs. 1984-87), Better Bus. Bur. (bd. dirs. 1984, chmn. 1988), NARAS (trustee 1965-82, pres. 1977-79), Chef's Club Nashville, Nashville Jaycees (gov., Man of Year award 1967), C. of C. (chmn. sch. bd. task force 1990—), Copyright Soc. of South (chmn. bd. 1990—), Sigma Alpha Epsilon, Alpha Phi Omega. Mehtodist (dir. ch. 1967—). Home: 917 Tyne Blvd Nashville TN 37220-1506 Office: Nashville Gas Co 665 Mainstream Dr Nashville TN 37228-1203

DENNY, MARY CRAVER, state legislator, rancher; b. Houston, July 9, 1948; d. Kenneth and Lois (Skiles) Craver; m. Henry William Denny, Jan. 26, 1969 (div. Aug. 1990); 1 child, Bryan William. Student, U. Tex., 1966-70; BS in Elem. Edn. magna cum laude, U. North Tex., 1973. Cert. tchr., Tex. Owner, mgr. Craver Ranch, Aubrey, Tex., 1973—; mem. Tex. Ho. of Reps., Austin, 1993—. Vol. Tex. Rep. Com., 1964—; chmn. Denton County Rep. Com., Denton, Tex., 1983-91; bd. dirs. Tex. Com. for Humanities, 1990, YMCA, Denton, 1985—, Tex. Fedn. Rep. Women, 1988-92, 94-96; life mem. president's coun. U. North Tex., Denton, 1974—, chmn., 1983; del. state and nat. Rep. convs., 1972—; mem. Denton Benefit League, 1976—, Denton Arts Coun., 1986—; member numerous other civic orgns. Named Outstanding Rep. Vol., Denton County Rep. Com., 1985, One of 10 Outstanding Rep. Women, Tex. Fedn. Rep. Women, 1991, Outstanding Alumna in Edn., U. North Tex. Coll. Edn., 1993. Mem. Am. Legis. Exch. Coun., Nat. Conf. State Legislatures, Ariel Club, Delta Zeta. Episcopalian. Address: 6637 FM 2153 Aubrey TX 76227-8732 Office: PO Box 2910 Austin TX 78768-2910 also: 416 W University Dr Ste 200 Denton TX 76201-1842

DENNY, OTWAY B., JR., lawyer; b. Shreveport, La., Sept. 26, 1949; s. Otway B. and Mary Alice (Oakmail) D.; m. Bonnie Burris, Aug. 14, 1971; children: Amy, Lisa, Stacey. BA, Tex. A&M U., 1971; JD, Baylor U., 1973. Bar: Tex. 1973, U.S. Dist. Ct. (so. dist.) Tex. 1974. Ptnr. Fulbright & Jaworski, Houston, 1973—. Author: Survey of Insurance, 1984; contbr. (chpt. in book) Texas Torts and Remedies-General Settlements, 1987. 2nd lt. U.S. Army, 1974. Mem. Am. Bd. Trial Advocates (advocate), Houston Bar Assn. (pres. 1992-93), Houston Young Lawyers Assn. (pres. 1981-82). Office: Fulbright & Jaworski 1301 Mckinney St Houston TX 77010

DENNY, WILLIAM FRANCIS, computer science educator; b. Shreveport, La., Feb. 14, 1946; s. William F. and Ouida Marie (Harris) D.; m. Jerry Ann Daughtry, Dec. 17, 1983; 1 child, William G. BS, La. Tech. U., 1968; MA, U. Okla., 1970, PhD, 1974; PhD, U. Southwestern La., 1988. Asst. prof. McNeese State U., Lake Charles, La., 1975-82, assoc. prof., 1982-88, prof., 1988—; cons. in field. Mem. IEEE, Assn. Computing Machinery, Soc. Indsl. and Applied Math. Home: 602 N Lake Ct Dr Lake Charles LA 70605 Office: McNeese State U PO Box 92340 Lake Charles LA 70609

DENSMORE, DOUGLAS WARREN, lawyer; b. Jan. 30, 1948; s. Warren Orson and Lois Martha (Ery) D.; m. Janet Roberta Broadley, Oct. 26, 1973; children: Bradley Wythe, Andrew Fitz Douglas. AB, Coll. of William and Mary, Williamsburg, Va., 1970; JD cum laude, U. Toledo, 1975. Bar: Ohio 1976, U.S. Dist. Ct. (no. dist.) Ohio 1976, Va. 1980, U.S. Dist. Ct. (ea. and we. dists.) Va. 1980, U.S. Ct. Appeals (4th cir.) 1980. Assoc. Gertner, Barkan & Robon, Toledo, 1975-77, Shumaker, Loop & Kendrick, Toledo, 1977-79; corp. counsel Dominion Bankshares Corp., Roanoke, Va., 1979-80; assoc. Woods, Rogers, Muse, Walker & Thornton, Roanoke, Va., 1980-84; ptnr. Woods, Rogers & Hazlegrove, Roanoke, Va., 1984-96, Flippin, Densmore, Morse, Rutherford and Jessee, Roanoke, Va., 1996—. Co-author: Examining the Increase in Federal Regulatory Requirements and Penalties: Is Banking Facing Another Troubled Decade?, 1995; contbr. articles to profl. jours. Bd. dirs. Orgn. Aiding Rehab., Roanoke, 1983-88; chmn. lawyer's sect. Cancer Crusade, Roanoke, 1984; v.p. Blue Ridge Highlands Scottish Festival, Roanoke, 1988-91, pres., 1992. 2d lt. U.S. Army N.G., 1970-76. Decorated knight Order of St. John, knight grand cross Order of St. Catherine, first class Order of Polonia Restituta, knight grand officer Order of the Temple, knight comdr. Order of Crown of Thorns, knight grand cross Order of St. Michael and St. George, knight grand cross Orthodox of Order St. John, knight grand cross Order of Holy Cross of Jerusalem, knight grand cross with collar Order of St. Gregory, knight grand cross Order of St. Stephen, knight Royal Ukranian Order of St. Vladimir the Great, knight grand cross Greek Order of St. Denis of Zante. Mem. ABA (banking law com. 1988—, uniform comml. code com. 1988—), Va. Bar Assn. (corp. code com. 1984—), Scottish Soc. Va. Highlands (v.p. 1994-95, pres. 1995—), Brit. Manorial Soc., English Speaking Union, Kiwanis Internat., Masons (32 degree, master, jr. deacon 1992), Shriners, Shenandoah Club (Roanoke, Va.), Roanoke Country Club, Farmington Country Club (Charlottesville, Va.), Hunting Hills Country Club (Roanoke). Episcopalian. Office: Flippin Densmore et al Rutherford & Jessee 2625 S Jefferson Roanoke VA 24014

DENT, EDWARD DWAIN, lawyer; b. Ft. Worth, Dec. 23, 1950. BA, Tex. Christian U., 1973; JD, St. Mary's U., Tex., 1976. Bar: Tex., U.S. Dist. Ct. (no. and so. dists.) Tex., U.S. Supreme Ct. Atty., ptnr. Kugle, Stewart, Dent, Frederick, Ft. Worth, 1979-89; atty., founder Dent Law Firm, Ft. Worth, Harlingen, Dallas, 1990—. Bd. dirs. Greater Boys/Girls Clubs, Ft. Worth, 1989—. Recipient Hist. Preservation award Tarrant County Hist.

Coun., 1992. Mem. Am. Trial Lawyers Assn., U.S. Supreme Ct. Hist. Soc., Tex. Trial Lawyers (bd. dirs. 1989—), Tarrant County Trial Lawyers (bd. dirs. 1988-89, officer 1989), Ft. Worth Club, Colonial Country Club. Democrat. Office: Dent Law Firm 1300 Summit Ave Ste 700 Fort Worth TX 76102-4424 also: Ste 203 2302 S 77 Sunshine Strip Harlingen TX 78550

DENT, LEANNA GAIL, art educator; b. Manhattan, Kans., Oct. 21, 1949; d. William Charles and Maxine Madeline (Kackley) Payne; children: Laura Michelle, Jeffery Aaron. BS in Edn., U. Houston, 1973; postgrad., U. Tex., 1975-76; MS in Edn., Okla. State U., 1988. Cert. elementary and secondary art tchr., Okla., Tex. Tchr. art Popham Elem. Sch., Del Valle, Tex., 1973-77; graphic artist Conoco, Inc., Ponca City, Okla., 1987-88; tchr. art Garfiled Elem. Sch., Ponca City, Okla., 1988-91, Reed Elem. Sch., Houston, 1991-92, Copeland Elem. Sch., Houston, 1992-94, Campbell Jr. High Sch., Houston, 1994—; cons. and specialist in field. Author: Using Synectics to Enhance the Evaluation of Works of Art, 1988. Vol. 1st Luth. Day Sch., Ponca City, 1977-91, Ponca City Inds. Sch. Dist., 1987-91; work com. Cy-Fair Ind. Sch. Dist., Houston, 1991-94. Acad. and Mem. scholar Okla. State U., 1986-88; named Spotlight Tchr. Yr., 1992-93. Mem. Nat. Art Edn., Tex. Art Edn. Assn. (judges commendation 1993), Assn. Tex. Profl. Educators, Houston Art Edn. Assn. (v.p. 1992-93, pres.-elect 1993-95, pres. 1995—), Phi Delta Kappa, Phi Kappa Phi. Republican. Lutheran. Office: Campbell Jr High Sch 11415 Bobcat Rd Houston TX 77064-3001

DENTISTE, PAUL GEORGE, city and regional planning executive; b. Tacoma, Oct. 31, 1930; s. George and Mary (Orphanides) D.; m. Mary Catherine Lucas, Feb. 27, 1971; children: Michele Louise. AB in Sociology, Guilford Coll., 1955; M of City Planning, U. Pa., 1959. Planning intern Dept. Planning City Raleigh, N.C., summer 1957; acting dir. planning, planning intern Dept. Planning City of Pensacola, Raleigh, Fla., 1958; asst. dir. planning Dept. Planning City Durham, N.C., 1959-62; urban planner mil. installations Planning div. Dist. Pub. Works Office, 4th Naval Dist., Phila., 1962-64; asst. to dir. planning, head comprehensive planning Dept. Planning New Castle County, Newark, Del., 1964-80; exec. dir. Birmingham (Ala.) Regional Planning Commn., 1980-95; team leader planning and zoning specialists and adminstrs. SBA, Inc., Birmingham, 1995—; bd. dirs. Horizon 280 Assn., Neighborhood Comml. Devel. Corp.; mem. Gov.'s Internat. Airport Adv. Com., 1991—. Mem. Gov.'s The Ala. Reunion Celebration Com., 1987-88, Gov.'s Regional Econ. Devel. Adv. Bd., 1987-93, Design Ala., 1988—, U. Pa. Student Screening Com., 1985—, Downtown Action Com., 1985—, Tenn-Tom Waterway Devel. Coun., 1984-95, Phase III Devel. Campaign, Birmingham-Southern Coll., 1983-95, Gov.'s Regional Employment and Tng. Adv. Coun., 1983-86, River Run Neighborhood Civic Assn., 1982—, Cmty. Chest-United Way, 1982-95, Gov.'s Task Force Concerning Marine Recreation, 1978-80, Gov.'s Del. Tomorrow Commn. Study, 1974-75; bd. dirs., Vol. and Info. Ctr. for Greater Birmingham, Inc., 1981-85, Operation New Birmingham, 1980—. Recipient 100% Sec.'s award Pike Creek Valley Lions, 1976, Pres. and Leadership awards Appalachian Regional Commn., 1986, Bronze Medallion, 1985, awards and honors Devel. Dist. Assn. of Appalachia, U.S Dept. Def., 1995, CAWACO RC and D Coun., 1995; named hon. Lt. Col. ADC, Ala. State Militia, 1987. Mem. So. Growth Policies Bd., SE US/Japan Assn., Southeastern States Regional Couns. Assn., Internat. Assn. City Mgrs., Ala. Assn. Regional Couns. (pres., v.p. 1980-82, Citation 1983-95, v.p. 1991-92), Nat. Assn. Devel. Orgns. (chmn. J. Roy Fogle award com. 1982), Nat. Assn. Regional Couns., Urban Land Inst. (book reviewer 1978-80), UN Roster of Planning Experts, Am. Planning Assn. (pres. Del. chpt. 1978-79, Citation from Del. chpt. 1979), U. Pa. Gen. Alumni Assn. (organizing chmn. Planners Alumni Assn. 1963), Guilford Coll. Gen. Alumni Assn. and numerous other memberships. Democrat. Greek Orthodox. Lodges: Kiwanis, Lions (charter mem. Pike Creek Valley club). Home: 3919 S River Cir Birmingham AL 35243-4717 Office: SBA Inc 631 Beacon Pkwy W Ste 103 Birmingham AL 35209-3130

DENTON, CAROL FORSBERG, training systems designer; b. Boston, Mar. 5, 1937; d. Algot Oscar and Isabelle Marie (Flynn) Forsberg; m. Earle Lewis Denton; children: Susan E., Kathleen E. Denton Pierson. BS in Geology, U. Okla., 1959; MA in Teaching Counseling, Rollins Coll., Winter Park, Fla., 1970, postgrad., 1971. Cert. sci. tchr., counselor, Fla. Counselor U. Okla., Norman, 1958-59; sci. tchr. Lee County Bd. Pub. Instruction, Ft. Myers, Fla., 1960-61; counselor U. Fla., Gainsville, 1961-62; tchr. Seminole County bd. Instruction, Sanford, Fla., 1965-69; pers. mgmt. specialist Naval Tng. Device Ctr., Orlando, Fla., 1969-73, ednl. specialist, 1973-93; head instrn. systems br. surface/undersea systems Naval Air Warface Ctr. Tng. Sys. Divsn., Orlando, Fla., 1993—, Dept. of Navy Aquisition Profl. Cmty., 1995—; Mission pilot, observer, tchr. Civil Air Patrol, Orlando, 1965-75; mem. Joint Svc. Action Group ICW, Pentagon, Washington, 1986—; steering com. Intersvc./Industry Tng. Sys. and Edn. Conf., Orlando, 1991-94, chair, 1994; mem. Navy Adv. Group, Interactive Courseware, Washington, 1986—. Contbr. articles to profl. jours. Human rels. commn. City of Orlando, 1972-75; bd. dirs. Fairwinds Fed. Credit Union, Orlando, 1987—; apptd. Army Arlington Ladies personal rep. for Army Chief of Staff, Washington, 1984-86. Recipient Civilian Exemplary Svc. award, 1995. Mem. Ctrl. Fla. Human Factors Soc. (pres., bd. dirs. 1978-80), Altrusa Internat. (pres. Orlando chpt. 1978-82), Sigma Xi, Kappa Delta Pi. Republican. Presbyterian. Home: 1017 Gran Paseo Dr Orlando FL 32825 Office: Naval Air Warfare Ctr Tng Sys Divsn Code 4972 12350 Research Pkwy Orlando FL 32826-3261

DENTON, JESSE LESLIE, JR., fire protection professional; b. Grenada, Miss., Feb. 1, 1946; s. Jesse Leslie and Virginia (Phillips) D.; m. Barbara Rhodes Haven, Jan. 27, 1967; children: Jesse Michael, Lesley Michelle. BS, Miss. State U., 1968. Registered environ. property assessor. Loss prevention cons. Indsl. Risk Insurers, Atlanta, 1968-86; fire protection mgr. Holiday Inn Worldwide, Memphis, Atlanta, 1986-94; sr. cons. Zurich Am. Ins., Schaumburg, Ill., 1994—. Author, editor video Hotel Fire Protection, 1989. Staff sgt. Army N.G., 1968-91. Mem. Environ. Info. Assn., Nat. Safety Coun. (slips and falls prevention com.), Nat. Fire Protection Assn. (com. on initiating devices of nat. fire alarm code). Republican. Baptist. Office: Zurich Am Ins 1400 American Ln Schaumburg IL 60196-5452

DENTON, MICHAEL DAVID, JR., lawyer; b. Oklahoma City, Okla., Sept. 21, 1963; s. Michael David and Nancy Marie (Boone) D.; m. Kristin Marie Drea; 1 child, Michael David III. BSBA, Southwestern Okla. State U., 1987; JD, U. Okla., 1990. Bar: Okla. 1991, U.S. Dist. Ct. (no., ea. and we. dists.) Okla. 1991. Law clk., intern, assoc. Edmonds Cole Hargrave Givens & Witzke, Oklahoma City, 1989-92; assoc. Hammons & Taylor, Oklahoma City, 1992, A. Scott Johnson & Assoc., Oklahoma City, 1992-95, Huddleston, Pike & Assoc., 1995-96; Hiltgen & Brewers, P.C., 1996—. Mem. First Bapt. Ch., Mustang, Okla., 1980—. With U.S. Army, 1985-87. Mem. ABA, ATLA, Okla. Trial Lawyers Assn., Okla. Bar Assn., Okla. County Bar Assn. (chmn. athletic com., 1994—, exec. dir. young lawyer divsn 1992—), Sigma Tau Gamma (chpt. advisor 1991-92, chpt. counselor 1991—, Outstanding Athlete award, 1987, Super Sig Tau 1987). Republican. Office: Hiltgen & Brewer PC 117 Park Ave 3rd Fl Oklahoma City OK 73102

DENTON, ROBERT WILLIAM (PETE DENTON), financial executive; b. Wilmington, Del., May 27, 1944; s. William R. and Margaret L. (Mitchell) D.; m. Donna Hughes, Dec. 20, 1978; children: Dyanna, Rhett, Whitney. BBA, U. S.C., 1966, M in Accountancy, 1973, EdD, 1980; postgrad., U. Ky., 1975, Harvard U., 1985; MBA, U. S.C., 1967. Registered real estate broker, S.C.. With U. S.C., Columbia, 1967—, asst. v.p. fin., 1976-77, v.p. fin., 1977-81, system v.p. fiscal affairs, 1981-83, sr. v.p. bus. and fin., 1983-88, treas., exec. v.p. bus. and fin., 1988-94, spl. asst. to pres., 1994—; bd. dirs. Faculty House Carolina, Columbia, Dominion Fin. Svcs. Corp., Columbia, Outsource, Inc. Conn.; lectr. Coll. Bus. Adminstrn., 1994—; ptnr. Lockhart Car Wash Chain, S.C. Author: A Study Guide for use with Financial Accounting: A Basic Approach, 1980, (monograph) The Shopping Mall on Campus: A Guide for Planning, Implementing, and Administering, 1993; co-author: Current Issues in College and University Human Resources, 1993; contbr. articles to profl. jours. Bd. dirs. U. S.C. Aux. Svc. Found.; mem., past chmn. bd. dirs. Better Bus. Bur., Inc., mem. exec. com., Com. of Admiral in Tex. Navy, Order of the Palmetto for State of S.C. Named Ky. Col. Mem. Nat. Assn. Coll. and Univ. Bus. Officers (pres., bd. dirs., past chair profl. devel. com.), Nat. Assn. State Univs. and Land Grant Colls., So. Assn. Coll. and Univ. Bus. Officers (past pres., mem. bd. dirs., mem. exec. com., past chair program com., profl. devel. com., audit com., past editor newsletter), So. Assn. Colls. and Schs. (criteria and review com., vis. accreditation com.), Nat. Assn. Coll. Aux. Svcs., Southeastern Mfg. Tech. Ctr. (bd. dirs.), S.C. Student Loan Corp. (bd. dirs.), S.C. Pub. Colls. and Univs., Univ. Assocs., U. S.C. Alumni Assn., Ducks Unltd., Beta Alpha Psi, Beta Gamma Sigma, Omicron Delta Epsilon, Omicron Delta Kappa. Home: 109 Old Arms Ct Columbia SC 29212-1832 Office: U SC System 332 BA Bldg Columbia SC 29208

DENUR, JACK BOAZ, scientific researcher, scientific consultant; b. N.Y.C., Sept. 12, 1951; s. Amnon Denur and Gail Levin. AS, El Centro Jr. Coll., Dallas, 1971; BS in Chemistry, U. Tex., Arlington, 1975; MS in Chemistry, Tex. A&M U., 1976; MS in Physics, U. North Tex., 1988. Scientific cons. Comml. Tech., Inc., Dallas, 1980—, Electric & Gas Tech., Inc., Dallas, 1980—, Atmospheric & Magnetics Tech., Inc., Dallas, 1996—. Mem. AAAS, Am. Phys. Soc., Am. Assn. Physics Tchrs., Am. Assn. Weather Observers, Tex. Severe Storms Assn. Democrat. Jewish. Home: 5045 Royal Ln Dallas TX 75229-4310 Office: Comml Tech Inc 13636 Neutron Rd Dallas TX 75244-4410 also: Electric and Gas Tech Inc 13636 Neutron Rd Dallas TX 75244-4410

DENYES, JAMES RICHARD, industrial engineer; b. Detroit, Oct. 9, 1948; s. Heyward Thornton and Rosalie (Blair) D.; BS in Indsl. Engring. and Ops. Research, Va. Poly. Inst. and State U., 1970; m. Pamela Brothers, Jan. 1, 1994; children: Amy Cheryne, Laura Michelle. Indsl. engr., prodn. control engr., distbn. foreman Allied Chem. Corp., Moncure, N.C., 1970-72; quality control engr. Duke Construction. Co., Norfolk, Va., 1972-75; command indsl. engr., staff indsl. engr. Navy Manpower and Material Analysis Center, Atlantic, Norfolk, 1975-84, head mgmt. engring. dept., 1981-84; dir. Navy Sch. Work Study, Navy Manpower Engring. Ctr., Norfolk, 1984-88; mgr. indl. engring. Navy Manpower Analysis Ctr., Chesapeake, 1988-89, dir. Navy Sch. Manpower Mgmt., 1989-94; tng. adminstr. Navy Occupational Health and Safety and Environ. Tng. Ctr., 1994—; co-founder Idea Assocs., 1983-94. Author: Work Smarter Not Harder - Methods Improvement Workbook, 1991; leadership staff Work Simplication Confs., 1992. Treas. Va. Orgn. To Keep Abortion Legal, 1977-79, bd. dirs., 1979-81; fin. adv. NOW, 1975-76; pres. B.M. Williams Elem. Sch. PTA, 1982-83, 1st v.p., 1983-84, 1st v.p./pres., 1984-85; mem. stds. of quality planning coun. Chesapeake pub. schs., 1982-83; pres. Crestwood Elem. Sch. PTA, 1986-87;. Mem. Am. Inst. Indsl. Engrs. (sr., bd. dirs. 1977-91, pres. Southeastern Va. chpt. 1980-81, 88-89), Am. Soc. Tng. and Devel. (dir. Southeastern Va. chpt., 1992-93, exec. v.p. 1993-94, pres. 1995), Improvement Inst. (trustee 1982-85, 86-88, pres. 1989-92, Pres.'s Cup 1985), Creative Problem Solving Inst. (leadership staff 1985—), Va. Congress of Parents and Tchrs. (hon. life mem.); bd. dirs. Hampton Roads quality mgmt. coun. 1989-91, Pi Delta Epsilon. Home: 2248 Bayberry St Virginia Beach VA 23451 Office: NAVOSHENVTRACEN Norfolk VA 23511

DEO, MARJOREE NEE, painter; b. Escanaba, Mich., Aug. 27, 1907; d. Coleman and Margaret (Glavin) Nee; m. M. Robert Deo, Nov. 9, 1934; children: Jane, Mary Nee. BA, U. Wis.; studies with Jack Tworkov, Boris Margo, Am. U.; studies with Karl Knaths, Phillips Gallery; studies with Philip Guston, James Brooks, Marca Relli, New Coll. Inst. Fine Arts. Numerous one-woman shows in N.H., Fla., N.C., Washington D.C., U. Wis., Mich., Chgo., spanning 1942—; exhibited in group shows at Corcoran Biennial, 1963, Ringling Mus., 1953, 59, 60, Balt. Mus., 1962, Pa. Acad., 1960, Detroit Inst., 1960, Washington Water Color Nat., 1962, Mus. Fine Arts, Boston, 1954, and others; traveling exhbns. include U.S. Art in Embassies Program, Europe, South Am., Cairo, USIA, Europe, 1959, 60, Corcoran Gallery, Washington, 1960, 61, and others. Recipient awards Art Forms Women's Juried, 1991, Fla. Artist Group, 1969, 73, 84, Sarasota Visual Arts Ctr., 1952, 53, 65, 77, 83, St. Boniface, 1983, Festival of States, Fla., 1969, Soc. Washington Artists, 1955, 57, 63, Del. Art Mus., 1959, 62, Washington Water Color Nat., 1962, Corcoran Gallery, Washington, 1947, 51, 59, St. John's Coll., Annapolis, Md., 1958, Terry Mus., Miami, 1952. Republican. Roman Catholic. Home: 700 John Ringling Blvd Apt 503 Sarasota FL 34236-1505

DE PADRO GAINEY, ANNE MICHELLE, banker, accountant, trust tax officer; b. Fort Lauderdale, Fla., Sept. 7, 1963; d. Michael Anthony and Anne Carroll (Tetaz) De P. BS in Bus. Adminstrn., Auburn U., 1986; postgrad Acctg., U. Ala., Birmingham, 1987-88. Trust tax acct. AmSouth Bancorp., Birmingham, Ala., 1989-91; trust tax officer SunBank/South Fla., Fort Lauderdale, 1991—. Bd. dirs. Broward Friends of Miami City Ballet, 1993—, Camerata, 1993—, Hospice Hundred, Jr. Alliance for Bonnett House, 1995—, pres., 1995—; bd. dirs. Young Profls. for Covenant House, 1993—, Jr. League of Fort Lauderdale, 1993—, Jr. Philharmonic Guild; loaned exec. United Way; mem. Hospice Hundred, Bonnet House Jr. Alliance; bd. dirs. Jr. Philharmonic Guild, 1992—; mem. com. Festival of the Trees, Easter Lily Ball, Promenade in the Park, Art a la Carte. Mem. Inst. of Mgmt. Accts. (bd. dirs.). Office: SunBank South Fla NA 501 E Las Olas Blvd Fort Lauderdale FL 33301-2232

DEPAOLO, ROSEMARY, college dean; b. Bklyn., July 17, 1947; d. Nunzio and Edith (Spano) DeP.; m. Dennis B. Smith, 1977 (div. 1983); m. T. Frederick Wharton, 1984. BA, CUNY, Flushing, 1970; MA, Rutgers U., 1974, PhD, 1979. Asst. prof. to prof., dir. Ctr. for Humanities Augusta (Ga.) Coll., 1975-90; asst. dean coll. Arts & Sci. Ga. So. U., Statesboro, 1990-93; dean coll. Arts & Scis. Western Carolina U., Cullowhee, N.C., 1993—; mem. exec. bd. So. Humanities Coun., 1989—; bd. advisors Highlands (N.C.) Biol. Ctr., 1993—; mem. policy bd. Kellogg Ctr. for Craft, Creativity and Design, Hand Made in Am., 1995—. Woodrow Wilson Found. fellow, 1970. Office: Western Carolina U Coll Arts & Scis Cullowhee NC 28723

DEPERSIO, RICHARD JOHN, otolaryngologist, plastic surgeon; b. Oak Ridge, Tenn., July 10, 1949; s. John Dominick DePersio and Genevieve (Kellerman) Weinberg; m. Melissa Eddleman, Nov. 23, 1994; children: Lauren Elizabeth, Katherine Genevieve, Gerard Edward. BS with honors, U. Tenn., Knoxville, 1971; MD, U. Tenn., Memphis, 1974. Diplomate Am. Bd. Facial, Plastic and Reconstructive Surgery, Am. Bd. Otolaryngology. Intern City of Memphis Hosps., 1975; surgery resident Meth. Hosp., Memphis, 1976-77; otolaryngology resident U. Tenn., Memphis, 1977-80; pvt. practice Knoxville Otolaryngology Facial Surgery Clinic, 1980—; clin. asst. prof., U. Tenn. Dept. Surgery, Knoxville, 1980—. Fellow ACS, Am. Acad. Cosmetic Surgery, Am. Acad. Facial, Plastic and Reconstructive Surgery, Am. Acad. Otolarygology-Head and Neck Surgery, Am. Rhinologic Soc., Am. Acad. Aesthetic and Restorative Surgery, Am. Soc. TMJ Surgeons, Am. Soc. Laser Surgery and Medicine. Roman Catholic. Home: 7841 Embercrest Trl Knoxville TN 37938-3404 Office: Knoxville Otolaryngology 930 E Emerald Ave Knoxville TN 37917-4539

DE PLANQUE, EMILE, III, computer consultant; b. Providence, Dec. 15, 1942; s. Emile de Planque Jr. and Dorothy M. (Rainalter) Baker; m. Rosanna Kathleen Bowden, Nov. 11, 1966; children: Suzanne Brigitte, Ian Christopher, Thomas James. Student, U. Va., 1960-65, Georgetown U., 1965; BA in English, George Mason U., 1969, postgrad., 1970-71, 88-89. Purchasing agent York Corrugating Co., Washington, 1965-66; comml. rep. C&P Telephone Co., Washington, 1966-70; staff assoc. C&P Telephone Co., Silver Spring, Md., 1970-77, staff analyst, 1977-81; mem. program staff AT&T, Oakton, Va., 1981-83; mgr. AT&T, Fairfax, Va., 1983-85; info. mgmt. specialist AT&T, Herndon, Va., 1985-89; sr. cons. Mindbank Cons. Group, Vienna, Va., 1990—; sec., treas. Kona Corp., Manassas, Va., 1979-83, bd. dirs., 1979—, v.p., 1984—; owner Innovation, Fairfax, 1984-91; prin. Presssmont Creative Enterprises, Fairfax, 1994—. Treas. Greenbriar West PTA, Fairfax, 1975-77, 80, v.p., 1978. Mem. Am. Assn. for Articifical Intelligence, Internat. Town and Country Club (nominating com. 1989). Home: 13210 Pressmont Ln Fairfax VA 22033-3008 Office: Mindbank Cons Group 7800 Leesburg Pike Vienna VA 22182

DEPLONTY, DUANE EARL, builder, real estate developer; b. Saginaw, Mich., June 1, 1923; s. Earl Edward and Ruth (Bond) DeP.; m. Larraine Sue Kerr, Nov. 23, 1962 (div. 1969); 1 dau., Stacey Sue; m. 2d, Joan Julia Wacker, Jan. 23, 1970; children: Ronald, David, Mary Ann. LLB, LaSalle U., 1951; AA, Delta Coll., 1968. Cert. gen. contractor. Pres., DePlonty Constrn., Inc., Punta Gorda, Fla., 1973—, DePlonty Realty, Punta Gorda, 1976—; dir., chmn. Heating, Air Conditioning, Refrigeration and Ventilation Bd., Charlotte County, 1976; mem. Charlotte County Bldg. Bd., 1976-78; pres. Olean Plaza Owners Assn., Port Charlotte, Fla., 1979-83, Sunshine Villas Owners Assn., Port Charlotte, 1977-81. Mem. Nat. Assn. Homebuilders, C. of C., John and Mable Ringling Mus. Art, Oaks Club. Republican. Presbyterian. Clubs: Kiwanis, Rotary, Elks, Sarasota Country (dir. 1982-83), Sarasota Yacht, Charlotte Harbour Yacht, Punta Gorda Country. Home: 937 Blue Heron Overlook Osprey FL 34229 Office: Villas del Sol - DePlonty Constrn Inc 5656 Bermont Rd Punta Gorda FL 33950

DE RAAD, BERNARD RUTH, food and ingredient broker, researcher, consultant; b. Utrecht, The Netherlands, Apr. 7, 1957; came to U.S., 1989; s. Markus and Hendrika Catharina (van de Brink) De R.; m. Vivian L. Dubberly, Oct. 24, 1985. BBA, Nijenrode U., Breukelen, The Netherlands. CEO, exec. pres. De Raad Bakeries, Utrecht, The Netherlands; CEO food brokerage, mgmt. cons. Vintage Internat., St. Augustine, Fla.; pres. South A1A Apparel and Sportswear, St. Augustine.

DERBES, ALBERT JOSEPH, III, lawyer, accountant; b. New Orleans, Mar. 18, 1940; s. Albert Joseph Jr. and Marcelle (Jourdan) D.; m. Shirley Brown, June 8, 1963; children: Albert Joseph IV, Eric Joseph. BBA, Tulane U., 1963, JD, 1966. Bar: La.; CPA, La., Miss., Ga., Fla. Ptnr. Derbes & Derbes, CPA's, New Orleans, 1964-69, Trahan, Kernion, & Derbes, CPA's, New Orleans, 1970-78, Hurdman & Cranston, CPA's, New Orleans, 1978-79, Main, Hurdman, CPA's, New Orleans, 1979-82, Windhorst, Pastorek & Gaundry, Attys. at Law, Harvey, La., 1982-88, Derbes & Co., CPA's, Metairie, La., 1982—; pvt. practice law Metairie, 1988—. Served to capt. USAF, 1966-69. Mem. ABA, AICPAs, La. State Bar Assn., La. Soc. CPAs, Miss. Soc. CPAs, Nat. Assn. State Bds. of Accountancy (bd. dirs. 1983-84, v.p. 1984-85, pres. 1986-87). Republican. Roman Catholic. Office: 3027 Ridgelake Dr PO Box 8176 Metairie LA 70011

DERICK, KENNETH, engineering executive; b. 1952. BSCE, Ga. Inst. Tech., 1975, M in Civil Engring., 1977. V.p. Universal Engring., Orlando, Fla. Office: Universal Engring Scis 3532 Maggie Blvd Orlando FL 32811-6697

DE RIEMER, DANIEL LOUIS, leasing company executive; b. San Antonio, Jan. 10, 1950; s. Sydney Daniel and Loraine (Neugebauer) De R.; m. Laura Rosen, Nov. 6, 1993. BS, U. Mo., Rolla, 1972. Engr. Cen. Soya Co., Chattanooga, 1976-78, Mark Controls Corp., Overland Park, Kans., 1978; gen. mgr. Pye Nissan, Inc., Dalton, Ga., 1978-82; pres. Total Leasing Systems, Inc., Chattanooga, 1982—. Editor Tennhorn newsletter, 1984-85. Bd. dirs. Chattanooga Riverbend Festival, 1990, 91, supr., 1992; mem. vol. staff 1996 Centennial Olympic Games, Atlanta, 1996' vol. Atlanta Com. for Olympic Games, 1996. Mem. Nat. Vehicle Leasing Assn., Nat. Vehicle Leasing Corp., Porsche Club Am. (treas. Tenn. chpt. 1982-84, pres. 1986-87, 89, membership chmn. 1992, Peach State Region co-chair Concours de Elegance 1996), Lions (sec. 1987-88, 2d v.p. 1991, 1st v.p. 1992, pres. 1993). Home: 735 Ashcreek Ct Roswell GA 30075-1385 Office: Total Leasing Systems Inc 1 Northgate Park Ste 304 Chattanooga TN 37415-6913

DERISE, NELLIE LOUISE, nutritionist, educator, researcher; b. Jeanerette, La., Aug. 9, 1937; d. O'Niell Paul and Anita (Savoy) D. BS, U. Southwestern La., 1962; MS, U. Ala., 1964; PhD, Va. Poly. Inst., 1973. Grad. asst. U. Ala., Tuscaloosa, 1962-64; asst. prof. Iowa State U., Ames, 1968-70; asst. prof. U. Southwestern La., Lafayette, 1964-68, assoc. prof., 1973-81, prof. home econs., 1981-94; ret., 1994; Chmn La. State Nutrition Council, 1977-78. Contbr. articles to profl. jours. Mem. Am. Home Econs. Assn., Am. Dietetic Assn., U.S. Metric Assn., Soc. Nutrition Edn., La. Home Econs. Assn. (bd. dirs. 1973-75), La. Dietetic Assn. (bd. dirs. 1982-86), Inst. Food Tech., Sigma Xi. Democrat. Roman Catholic. Home: 1108 Highway 668 Jeanerette LA 70544-8611

DERITA, THOMAS, JR., automobile company executive; b. Providence, Sept. 4, 1943; s. Thomas Sr. and Lena (Zinno) DeR.; m. Barbara G. Costanzo, Jan. 22, 1966; children: David T., Brian T. Student, Roger Williams Jr. Coll., Providence, 1962-63, Johnson & Wales Coll., Providence, 1963-65, U. R.I., 1965-66, Rutgers U., 1968-70. Cert. automotive cons. Mktg. mgr. Hoffman LaRoche Inc., Nutley, N.J., 1966-72; auto dealer, pres. DeRita/Kuzon Pontiac Saab, Palmer, Mass., 1972-74; dealer delv. mgr. Ford Mt. Co., Boston, 1974-77; gen. mgr. Fla. Chrysler Plymouth, West Palm Beach, 1977-78; gen. sales mgr. River Oaks Chrysler Plymouth, Houston, 1978-82; auto dealer, pres. North Point Assn., Houston, 1982-86; COO Cuillo Enterprises, West Palm Beach, 1986-92; auto dealer, v.p. Stuart (Fla.) Nissan/Suzuki, 1992—; vice chmn. nat. dealer coun. Chrysler Corp., 1983-85; cons. Northwood U., West Palm Beach, 1987—. Vice pres. child abuse and neglect Children's Place-Conners Nursery, West Palm Beach, 1987—; mem. adv. bd. Adam Walsh Found., West Palm Beach, 1991—; bd. dirs. Assn. Retarded Citizens, West Palm Beach, 1991-93; mem. speakers bur. Northwood U., also chmn. Martin County challenge of 90's bldg. campaign; chmn. for Dodge, Spl. Olympics, Austin. Mem. Am. Internat. Automobile Dealers Assn. (dir. involvement com. 1993, dir. contracts 1993), Fla. New Car Dealers Assn., Palm City C. of C., Stuart C. of C., Rotary (Rotarian of Yr. award 1986, achievement award 1991, Paul Harris fellow). Republican. Roman Catholic. Home: 5770 Whirlaway Rd Palm Beach Gardens FL 33418 Office: Stuart Nissan Suzuki 2755 S Federal Hwy Stuart FL 34994-4536

DEROSA, DONALD V., academic administrator. CEO U. N.C., Greensboro. Office: U NC Greensboro Office of Provost Greensboro NC 27412-5001 also: Weatherspoon Art Gallery Spring Garden Tate St Greensboro NC 27412

DE ROSA, GUY PAUL, orthopedic surgery educator; b. Napoleon, Ohio, Oct. 25, 1939; married. BS, Notre Dame U., 1961; MD, Ind. U., 1965. Diplomate Am. Bd. Orthopedic Surgery (oral examiner 1983—, site investigator residency rev. com. 1983—, bd. dirs. 1990—, mem. credentials com. 1990-93, mem. oral examinations com. 1990—, mem. grad. edn. com. 1990—, chmn. 1995-97, mem. oral recertification examination com. 1992-93, mem. practice audit com. 1992-93, ABMS rep. alt. 1992-93, ACS adv. coun. 1992-94, sec. 1993-94, mem. exec. com. 1993-94, mem. cert. renewal com. 1993-94, mem. fin. com. 1993-94, vice chmn. residency rev. com. 1994—). Resident in gen. surgery Sch. Medicine, Ind. U., Indpls., 1965-66, resident in orthopedic surgery, 1966-70; fellow in pediat. orthopedics Hosp. for Sick Children, London, 1969-70; asst. prof. orthopedic surgery Sch. Medicine, Ind. U., Indpls., 1970-76, assoc. prof., 1976-82, dir. undergrad. edn. dept. orthopedic surgery, 1972—, chief neuromuscular disease, 1972—, coord. Garceau-Wayu Lectureships dept. orthopedic surgery, 1975—, dir. Cerebral Palsy Clinic, 1978-88, orthopedic cons. Hemophilia Clinic, 1978-91, prof. orthopedic surgery, 1981—, orthopedic cons. Rheumato-Orthopedic Clinic, 1984—, chmn. dept. orthopedic surgery, 1986-95; attending physician Wishard Meml. Hosp., Indpls., 1970-95, Ind. U. Med. Ctr., Indpls., 1970-95, James Whitcomb Riley Hosp. for Children, Indpls., 1970-95; coord. Ctrl. Ind. and So. Ind. State Bd. Health Programs, Scoliosis and Sch. Screening, 1977; mem. orthopedic surgery steering com. Children's Cancer Study Group, 1990; mem. residency rev. com. for orthopedic surgery Accreditation Coun. for Grad. Med. Edn., 1990—; vis. prof. Children's Hosp., Columbus, Ohio, 1977, St. Joseph Hosp., Ft. Wayne, Ind., 1977, Miami Valley Hosp., Dayton, Ohio, 1978, 82, 85, 86, Deaconess Hosp., Evansville, Ind., 1980, Bloomington (Ind.) Hosp., 1982, U. Tex., Galveston, 1982, U. Mo. Med. Ctr., Columbia, 1983, Southwestern Mich. Area Health Edn. Ctr., Kalamazoo, 1985, Newington (Conn.) Children's Hosp., 1988, Children's Hosp. Med. Ctr., Akron, Ohio, 1992, and numerous others; active Hemophilia Med. Adv. Coun., 1978—; presenter in field. Contbr. numerous articles to profl. jours. Bd. dirs. United Cerebral Palsy, 1973-85, Hemophilia Found., 1978—, New Hope of Ind., 1984-86, also mem. long range planning com. 1984-85, mem. task force on serving brain injured 1988, Ind. Found. Hand Surg. Rsch. and Edn., 1989-95; mem. adv. bd. Head Injury Found., 1983-95, Children's Limb Found., 1992—; mem. pub. rels. and promotion com. Ind. Gov. Coun. on Phys. Fitness and Sports Medicine, 1986-92, mem. promotion com. 1988-92; dir. State of Ind. Orthop. Rsch. and Edn. Found., 1993, bd. trustees, 1994. Maj. USAF, 1970-72. Grantee in field; recipient Ensminger award for rsch. in trauma, 1967, Willis Gatch award, 1968. Mem. AMA, Am. Orthop. Assn. (mem. nominating com. 1988-89, del.-at-large exec. com. 1988-89, mem. com. on N.Am. travelling fellowship 1989-

93, mem. com. planning and devel. 1991—, 2nd pres.-elect 1994—), Am. Fracture Assn. (Wellmerling award 1982), Am. Acad. Pediats., Am. Acad. Orthop. Surgeons (mem. com. undergrad. edn. 1976-83, chmn. 1979-83, mem. com. pediat. orthopedics 1988-94, mem. subcom. on spine 1990, mem. subcom. on pediats program com. 1992, mem. coun. clin. resources 1993-94), Am. Acad. Cerebral Palsy and Devel. Medicine, Am. Orthop. Foot and Ankle Soc. (mem. com. biomechanics 1982-84, mem. program com. 1985—), Ind. Orthop. Soc. (mem. exec. com. 1986-95), Ind. State Med. Soc., Assn. Orthop. Chmn., Clin. Orthop. Soc., Acad. Orthop. Soc. (mem. undergrad. edn. com. 1983-87), Little Orthop. Club, Marion County Med. Soc., Mid-Am. Orthop. Assn. (chmn. program com. 1986-87, bd. dirs. 1986—, sec. 1990-93, 2nd v.p. 1993-94, 1st v.p. 1994—), Orthop. Letters Club, Pediat. Orthop. Soc. N.Am. (mem. com. on fellowships 1986-92, bd. dirs. 1990-92, 2nd v.p. 1994, 1st v.p. 1995, pres. 1996), Russell Hibbs Soc., Scoliosis Rsch. Soc. (mem. edn. com. 1985—), Internat. Soc. Orthop. Surgery and Traumatology, Spectators Orthop. Letters Club, 20th Century Orthop. Assn., Alpha Omega Alpha, Alpha Epsilon Delta. Office: ABOS 400 Silver Cedar Ct Chapel Hill NC 27514

DE ROSA, THOM VINCENT, luthier, musician, recording technician; b. N.Y.C., May 5, 1949; s. Angelo William and Laura Rose (Paganone) De R. AA, Middlesex County Coll., 1969. Musician, rec. technician Atco Studios, N.Y.C., L.A. and Seattle, 1972-78; electronic and guitar technician Fender Mus. Instruments, Seattle and Homosassa, Fla., 1976—, Gibson Guitar Co., Homosassa, 1992—; owner OmniBop Prodns. Shoppe, 1975, The Shoppe divsn. OmniBop Prodns. Shoppe, 1989; prodr., engr. Citrus Recording, Homosassa, 1993—; cons. in field, 1990—; prodr. Citrus Jazz Soc., Crystal River, Fla.,1 992—. With U.S. Army, 1969-71, Vietnam. Recipient cert. Crystal River Police Dept., 1993. Mem. Guild of Am. Luthiers, NFIB, Homosassa C. of C., Better Bus. Found. Office: The Shoppe 7990 W Homosassa Trl Homosassa FL 34448-2855

DEROUEN, SIDNEY MARC, animal sciences researcher; b. Baton Rouge, Feb. 23, 1956; s. Thomas Marc and Lela Rita DeRouen; m. Rose Mary Richardson, Dec. 11, 1981; 1 child, Chloe Marie. BS, La. State U., 1979, MS, 1983, PhD, 1990. Rsch. assoc. La. State U., Baton Rouge, 1979-81, 84-87; asst. prof. La. State U., Homer, La., 1991-95, assoc. prof., 1995—; standing mem. Beef Rsch. Adv. Com., Baton Rouge, 1991—. Mem. Am. Soc. of Animal Sci. (breeding and genetics com. so. sect. 1994—), Am. Registry of Profl. Animal Scientists, Sigma Xi, Gamma Sigma Delta. Democrat. Roman Catholic. Home: Rte 1 Box 5A Homer LA 71040 Office: La State U Hill Farm Rsch Sta Rte 1 Box 10 Homer LA 71040

DEROUNIAN, STEVEN BOGHOS, lawyer, retired judge; b. Sofia, Bulgaria, Apr. 6, 1918; came to U.S., 1921; s. Boghos and Eliza (Aprahamian) D.; m. Emily Ann Kennard, Aug. 20, 1947; children: Ann Ashby, Eleanor Kennard, Steven Blake. A.B., N.Y. U., 1938; LL.B., Fordham U., 1942. Bar: N.Y. 1942, D.C. 1959, Tex. 1981. Practiced in Mineola, N.Y., Garden City, N.Y., also Washington; former mem. law firm Derounian, Candee, Guardino Murphy; mem. 83d-87th U.S. Congresses, 2d Dist. N.Y., 88th Congress 3d Dist. N.Y.; mem. com. on ways and means; now ret. justice Supreme Ct. State of N.Y.; Councilman, mem. bd., Town of North Hempstead, N.Y., 1948-52. Served to capt. inf., 103rd Div. AUS, 1942-46; maj. Res. Decorated Purple Heart, Bronze Star with cluster, Combat Infantryman's badge. Mem. Am., Travis County bar assns., V.F.W., Am. Legion, Delta Theta Pi. Republican. Clubs: Chowder and Marching (Washington). Lodges: Masons; Elks. Home: 3103 Pleasant Run Pl Austin TX 78703-1152

DERRICK, GARY WAYNE, lawyer; b. Enid, Okla., Nov. 3, 1953; s. John Henry and Leota Elaine (Glenn) D.; m. Susan Adele Goodwin, Dec. 22, 1979 (div. June 1981); m. Francys Hollis Johnson, May 3, 1986; children: Meghan, Drew, Jane. BA in History, English, Okla. State U., 1976; JD, U. Okla., 1979. Bar: Okla. 1979. Assoc. Andrews, Davis, Legg, Bixler, Milsten & Price, Oklahoma City, 1979-84, ptnr., 1985-90; of counsel McKinney, Stringer & Webster, P.C., Oklahoma City, 1990-93; ptnr. Derrick & Briggs, Oklahoma City, 1994—; active Securities Law and Acctg. Group, Oklahoma City, 1979—; chmn. Gen. Corp. Act Commn., Okla., 1984—, chmn. Securities Liaison Com., Okla., 1985-86; lectr. sem. Okla. Corp. Act, 1986—. Conbg. author: Oklahoma Business Organizations. Mem. Okla. State U. Found., Stillwater, 1983-89, U. Okla. Found., Norman, 1982—; mem. condr.'s circle Okla. Symphony Orch., 1981-88; bd. dirs. Hist. Preservation, Inc., 1990—. Mem. ABA (taxation and corp. sect., banking and bus. law sect.), Okla. Bar Assn. (chmn. bus. assn. sect. 1985-87), Oklahoma County Bar Assn. (bd. govs. young lawyers div. 1981-82), Am. Soc. Corp. Secs. (pres. Okla.-Ark. chpt. 1994-95), Oklahoma City Boat Club. Republican. Episcopalian. Home: 500 NW 15th St Oklahoma City OK 73103-2102 Office: Derrick & Briggs Liberty Tower 20th Fl 100 N Broadway Ave Oklahoma City OK 73102-8606

DERRICKSON, DENISE ANN, secondary school educator; b. Seaford, Del., Sept. 20, 1956; d. William Hudson and Patricia Ann (Adkins) D. BS, James Madison U., 1978; MEd in Counseling and Human Devel., George Mason U., 1990, MEd in Curriculum & Instrn., 1994. Social studies instr. Brentsville Dist. High Sch., Nokesville, Va., 1978-91, Woodbridge (Va.) Sr. High Sch., 1991—; faculty liaison Parent-Tchr. Action Coun., 1990-91; prin.'s adv. coun., 1994-96. Vol. Childrens Hosp., Washington, 1983-86, Action in the Community through Svc., Inc.-Helpline, Manassas, Va., 1988-92. Recipient Cert. Appreciation Prince William County Sch. Bd., 1989, Outstanding Educator award Va. Govs. Sch., 1990, ACTS-Helpline Outstanding Vol. Svc. award, 1990. Mem. NEA, AAUW, ASCD, Am. Assn. Curriculum Devel., Nat. Soc. for Study of Edn., Va. Edn. Assn., Va. Assn. Supervision and Curriculum Devel., Prince William Edn. Assn., Internat. Platform Assn., Kappa Delta Phi, Phi Delta Kappa. Office: Woodbridge Sr High Sch 3001 Old Bridge Rd Lakeridge VA 22192-3221

DERUBERTIS, PATRICIA SANDRA, software company executive; b. Bayonne, N.J., July 10, 1950; d. George Joseph and Veronica (Lukaszewich) Uhl; m. Michael DeRubertis, 1986. BS, U. Md., 1972. Account rep. GE, San Francisco, 1975-77; tech. rep. Computer Scis. Corp., San Francisco, 1977-78; cons., pres. Uhl Assocs., Tiburon, Calif., 1978-81; cons. mgr. Ross Sys., Palo Alto, Calif., 1981-83; COO, exec. v.p. Distributed Planning Sys., Calabasas, Calif., 1983-92; pres. DeRubertis & Assocs., Thousand Oaks, Calif., 1992-94, DeRubertis Software Sys., Inc., Jensen Beach, Fla., 1995—. Author: Rose Gardening By Color, 1994. Troop leader San Francisco coun. Girl Scouts Am., 1974; participant Woman On Water, Marina Del Rey, Calif., 1983; vol. Martin County Coun. for the Arts, 1995. Mem. AAUW, NAFE, Delta Delta Delta. Democrat. Office: 3300 Eventide Pl Stuart FL 34994

DERVARTANIAN, DANIEL VARTAN, biochemistry educator; b. Boston, July 16, 1933; s. Donabed and Nevart (Ouzounian) DerV.; m. Marie Elizabeth Ypma, May 15, 1964; children: Merle, Adrienne. AA, Boston U., 1953, BA, 1956; MS, Northeastern U., 1959; ScD, U. Amsterdam, The Netherlands, 1965. Wetenschappelijke medewerker U. Amsterdam, 1961-65; rsch. assoc. U. Wis., Madison, 1965-68; asst. prof. U. Ga., Athens, 1968-73, assoc. prof., 1973-78, prof. biochemistry, 1978—, assoc. dir. Sch. Chem. Scis., 1985-91, chmn. divsn. biol. scis., 1991—. Contbr. numerous articles to profl. jours.; editl. bd. Jour. Bioenergetics and Biomembranes, Boston, 1976-85, Jour. Bacteriology, Washington, 1980-82, Biochimica Et Biophysica Acta, Amsterdam, 1988-95. With U.S. Army, 1959-60. Recipient Rsch. Career award NIH, Bethesda, 1971-76; Rsch. grantee NSF, Washington, 1969-72, 84-87, 90-93, NIH, Bethesda, 1971-81, 85-95. Mem. Am. Soc. Microbiology, Am. Soc. Biochemistry and Molecular Biology. Armenian Gregorian (apostolic). Office: Univ Ga Divsn Biol Scis Biol Scis Bldg Rm 400 Athens GA 30602

DESAI, MANUBHAI HARIBHAI, surgeon; b. Kosamba, Bulsar, India, Aug. 21, 1933; came to U.S., 1976; m. Sudha. Nathubhai; 3 children. MBBS, U. Bombay, 1957, M in Surgery, 1962. Lic. surgeon, Tex., Mass., N.Y., N.J.; cert. Edn. Coun. for Fgn. Med. Students, Fed. Licensing Exam. Bd. Intern Grant Med. Coll., Allied J.J. Group Teaching Hosps., Bombay, 1958; resident house surgeon in gen. surgery Allied J.J. Group Teaching Hosps., Bombay, 1959, resident house surgeon in ENT, 1959-60, resident surg. registrar in gen. surgery, 1960-62; locum thoracic registrar in exptl. thoracic surgery J.J. Group Teaching Hosps., Bombay, 1962; resident surg. registrar Bombay Hosp., 1962-63; govt. med. officer Ministry of Health, Zambia, 1963-64; surg. specialist Kitwe Cen. Hosp., Zambia, 1965-72; chief surgeon Comml. and Indsl. Med. Aid Hosps., Kitwe, Ndola, Zambia, 1972-75; clin. fellow Cornell Med. Ctr., 1977-78; assoc. dir. critical care svcs. Baystate Med. Ctr., Springfield, Mass., 1978-83; assoc. prof. surgery divsn. gen. surgery U. Tex. Med. Br., Galveston, 1983-91, prof., 1992—, dir. Blocker Burn Ctr., 1992—; asst. chief of staff Shriners Burns Inst., Galveston, 1983—; cons. surgeon to Nchanga Consolidated Group of Copper Mind Hosps., Rokana divsn., Zambia, 1972-75; guest speaker in field; prin. investigator rsch. U. Tex. Med. Br., 1989—, Baystate Med. Ctr., Springfield, Mass., 1982-84. Author: (with others) Art and Science of Burn Care, 1987; contbr. articles to Med. Jour. Zambia, Maharashtra Med. Jour., Current Med Practice (Bombay), Arch. Surg., Nutritional Support Svcs., Cancer Treatment Reports, Am. Surgeon, Jour. Burn Care Rehab., Critical Care Quar., Jour. Trauma, Pediatric Clinics in N.Am., Emergency Care Quar., Surg. Forum, Annals of Surgery, Metabolism, Emergency Medicine, Jour. Pediatric Surgery, Postgrad. Medicine, Burns, Surg. Gynecology and Obstetrics. Recipient Appreciation placque Critical Care Founders Circle, 1989; grantee Shriners Hosps. for Crippled Children, 1986-89; HHS grantee Baystate Med. Ctr., 1982-84. Fellow ACS, Am. Coll. Critical Care Medicine, Internat. Coll. Surgeons, East African Assn. Surgeons, Royal Coll. Surgeons of Edinburgh; mem. AMA (Physician Recognition award 1982-84-90), Surg. Infection Soc., Galveston County Med. Soc., Tex. Med. Assn., Singleton Surg. Soc., Pan Am. Med. Assn., Am. Trauma Soc., Soc. Critical Care Medicine, Mass. Med. Soc., Internat. Soc. for Burn Injuries, Hampden Dist. Med. Soc., Assn. for Acad. Surgery, Am. Burn Assn., Zambia Med. Assn., East African Assn. Surgeons, Rotary. Office: Shriners Burns Inst 815 Market St Galveston TX 77550-2725

DESHA, DORIS HOLLINGSWORTH, elementary education educator; b. Pleasanton, Tex., Sept. 7, 1927; d. Carl and Sallie Jane (Burmeister) Hollingsworth; m. George K. Desha, Jr., May 12, 1951 (dec. Nov. 1993); children: Paul Alan, George K. III. Student U. Tex., 1944-46, 47-48, Sam Houston U., 1949, Tarleton U., 1961-62; BS, U. N.Mex., 1969, postgrad., 1971-72; MEd, Tex. Christian U., 1980. Tchr., Jourdanton, Tex., 1946-47, Leming, Tex., 1949-50, Cost, Tex., 1951; substitute tchr., Big Spring, Tex., Albuquerque, Crowley, Tex., 1964-66, 76-77; substitute tchr., Crowley, Tex., 1991-92; tchr. McCollum Elem. Sch., Albuquerque, 1969-75, S.W. Christian Sch., Ft. Worth, 1975-76, 91, 92; elem. tchr. St. Andrews Interparochial Sch., Ft. Worth, 1977-91, also reading coord. kindergarten through 4th grade, substitute tchr. St. Andrew's, 1991-92; substitute tchr. Ft. Worth, 1992-95; ret.; vol. libr. storyteller, 1995-96, tutor in elem. reading and math. Mem. Soil Conservation Svc. Alumni, Am. Assn. Ret. Persons, Alpha Delta Kappa. Democrat. Mem. Ch. of Christ. Home: 1501 Linwood Ln Fort Worth TX 76134-2851

DESIDERIO, DOMINIC MORSE, JR., chemistry and neurochemistry educator; b. McKees Rocks, Pa., Jan. 11, 1941; s. Dominic Morse and Jewell Aline (Hull) D.; m. Julie Marie Thomas, Oct. 9, 1965; children—Annette Marie, Dominic Michael. B.A., U. Pitts., 1961; S.M., MIT, 1964, Ph.D., 1965. Organic control chemist Pitts. Coke and Chem. Co., 1958-60; research chemist U. Pitts., 1960-61; teaching asst. MIT, Cambridge, 1961-62, research asst., 1962-65; research chemist Am. Cyanamid Co., Stamford, Conn., 1966-67; asst. prof. chemistry Baylor Coll. Medicine, Houston, 1967-71, assoc. prof. chemistry and biochemistry, 1971-78; prof. neurology (chemistry) and biochemistry, dir. U. Tenn., Memphis, 1978—; exch. student Internat. Assn. Exch. Students for Tech. Experience; polymer chemist Badische Anilin and Sodafabrik, Germany, summer 1962. Author and editor of books, chpts. in books and articles including Analysis of Neuropeptides by Liquid Chromatography and Mass Spectrometry, 1984, Mass Spectrometry of Peptides, 1990, Mass Spectrometry: Clinical and Biomedical Applications, vol. I, 1992, vol. II, 1994; co-editor Mass. Spectrometry Revs., 1993—. Recipient 1st Ann. Internat. award Mass Spectrometry in Biochemistry and Medicine, Alghero, Italy, 1975; Intra-Sci. Research Found. fellow, 1971-75. Mem. Am. Soc. Biol. Chemistry, Am. Chem. Soc., Am. Soc. Mass Spectrometry, AAAS, Soc. for Neurosci., Memphis Neurosci. Soc. (pres. 1984-85), NIH (Metallobiochemistry study sect. 1985-89). Office: U Tenn Memphis Stout Neurosci Mass Spectrometry Lab 800 Madison Ave Memphis TN 38103-3400

DESILVEY, DENNIS LEE, cardiologist, educator, university administrator; b. May 17, 1942; m. Kathleen Selkirk, Aug. 28, 1965; children: Ethan Selkirk, Caitlin O'Brian, Sarah Candace Shaw. BA in History and Religion magna cum laude, Yale U., 1964; MD, Columbia U., 1968. Lic. Vt., Va.; cert. Advanced Trauma Life Support instr. Intern medicine Cornell Med. Ctr., N.Y.C., 1968-69, resident medicine, 1969-71, resident medicine, cardiology, 1971; chief med. resident medicine North Shore U. Hosp., Manhasset, N.Y., 1972-73; instr. medicine North Shore U. Hosp., Manhasset, 1972-73; mem. staff Rancocas Valley Hosp., Willingboro, N.J., 1973-75; cardiologist Brachfeld Med. Assocs., Willingboro, N.J., 1974-75, Castleton (Vt.) Med. Assocs., 1975-77; attending physician Rutland Regional Med. Ctr., Rutland, Vt., 1975—; pvt. practice Rutland, Vt., 1977-92; adj. asst. prof. clin. medicine Dartmouth Hitchcock Med. Ctr., Hanover, N.H., 1979-92; asst. prof. medicine U. Vt., Burlington, 1983-92; mem. staff Dwight David Eisenhower Med. Ctr., Ft. Gordon, Ga., 1991; dir. ambulatory cardiology, dir. cardiology consult svc., mem. clin. faculty cardiovascular divsn., dept. medicine Health Scis. Ctr. U. Va., Charlottesville, 1992—, assoc. prof. medicine Health Scis. Ctr., 1992—; cons. Southwestern Vt. Med. Ctr., Bennington, 1986—, Kellwer U.S. Army Hosp., West Point, N.Y., 1985—, internal medicine Veteran Affairs Med. Ctr., Salem, Va., 1993—; mem. critical care com. Rutland Regional Med. Ctr., pharmacy and therapeutics com., investigational review bd., ethics com.; mem. pharmacy and therapeutics com. Health Scis. Ctr. U. Va., nutrition com., health care evaluation com., ambulatory policy com.; bd. dirs., mem. profl. affairs com., mem. bylaws com. Blue Cross/Blue Shield Vt.; bd. dirs., founding mem. Vt. Cardiac Network; presenter New Eng. regional meeting Am. Coll. Physicians, Hanover, N.H., 1976, Advanced Concepts Shock and Trauma, Woodstock (Vt.) Inn, 1982. Contbr. articles to profl. jours. Med. advisor skiing svcs. Killington Ski Area, 1975-92, Smokey House Found., 1975-80, Farm and Wilderness Camps, 1975-85; mem. steering com. Vt. Med. Practice Variation Assessment Program, 1988; mem. cardiology study sect. Vt. Program Quality Care, 1988-92, Vt. Gov.'s Coun. Phys. Fitness, 1985-88; vestry Trinity Episcopal Ch., 1986-89; bd. dirs. Vermont Diabetes Assn., 1975-79, Rutland Mental Health Svc., 1975-82, Rutland Area Vis. Nurses Assn., 1975-77, chmn. profl. affairs com., mem. utilization review com.; bd. dirs. Barstow Sch., 1986-90; town health officer Wallingford, Vt., 1975-80. Maj. U.S. Army, 1973-75; col. USAR, 1985—. Decorated Nat. Def. Svc. medal, Reserve Achievement medal, Army Commendation medal; recipient Physician Recognition award Am. Med. Assn., Exceptional Svc. award, Spiritual Aims award Kiwanis Club Am., 1983, U. Va. Pres.'s Report award, 1992. Fellow Am. Coll. Physicians, Am. Coll. Cardiology, N.Am. Soc. Pacing and Electrophysiology; mem. Am. Heart Assn. (ACLS instr., BCLS instr., nat. faculty ACLS Vt., mem. mil. tng. network ACLS, Advanced Trauma Life Support; bd. dirs. 1978-80, bd. dirs., at large appointee 1988-93, agenda planning com. 1986-89, affiliate relations com. 1986-88, sci. pub. com. 1989-93, "heart and stroke" planning com. 1989-90, participant edn. and inf. group heart guide consumer health and info. program, 1989-91, chmn. task force mission to elderly 1989-90; v.p.-elect New Eng. region 1986-87, regional v.p. 1987-88, fellow coun. clin. cardiology, bd. dirs. Charlottesville divsn. 1992—, bd. dirs. Va. affiliate 1992—, bd. dirs. Rutland, Vt. divsn. 1986-92, program coun. 1986-92, bd. dirs. Vt. affiliate 1975-92, exec. com. 1978-92, pres.-elect 1982-83, pres. 1983-85, co-chair capital campaign 1988-90, nominating com. 1984-86, cardiac rehab. com. 1982-85, program coun. 1978-90, ACLS com. 1978-90, cardiac critical care com. 1978-82, hypertension com. 1975-82, chmn. emergency cardiac care com. region V 1976-80, bd. dirs. N.J. affiliate 1973-75, BCLS com. 1973-75, mem. greater N.Y. affiliate 1966-72, BCLS instr. 1968-72, del. N.E. regional heart com. 1985-91, reaffiliation com. 1987-89, nominating com. 1987-88, Pysician of Yr. award 1992), Am. Soc. Echocardiology, N.Y. Acad. Scis., Vt. Cardiac Network (vice chmn. 1982-86), Phi Beta Kappa. Home: 410 Altamont Cir Charlottesville VA 22902-4618 Office: U Va Cardiovascular Dept Medicine Box 158 Health Scis Ctr Charlottesville VA 22908

DESJARDINS, DANIEL DEE, poet, translator and playwright; b. Miami, Fla., May 27, 1954; s. Ulysses John-Joseph (Peter) and Regine Madelaine (Copus) D. BS in Chemistry, Fla. State U., 1977; BSEE, U. N.Mex., 1984; student, Am. Coll. Paris, 1973-74, Boston U., 1975-76. Chemist Fla. Dept. Agrl., Ft. Lauderdale, 1978; Commd. 2d lt. USAF, 1982, advanced through grades to maj., 1996, retired, 1992; maj. USAR, 1996. Poet: Ode to Stoicism (World Poetry Golden Poet award 1992), Love's Tragedy (World Poetry Golden Poet award 1993), To Lord Acton and His Democratic Consorts, The Condensed Tale Beowolf and Grendel in Modern English Prosody (semi finalist 1995, North Am. Open Poetry contest, Nat. Libr. Poetry), By The Wiskers of William Wallace (pub. in Best Poems of 1996, Nat. Libr. Poetry), To A Tender Gaoler (semi finalist 1996 N.Am. Open Poetry Contest, Nat. Libr. Poetry); translator: A View of Hitler and the 1935 Reichsparteitag by a Member of the Acadèmie Française, 1992, playwright: Der Anschluss, 1994, Young Man of Promise, 1995. Mem. Nat. Geographic Soc., Smithsonian Inst., Inst. Hist. Rev. (translator French 1993). Independent. Roman Catholic.

DE SNYDER, SOAMI SANTIAGO, audiologist; b. Phila., Feb. 4, 1963; d. Angel Luis and Julia Maria (Santiago) Santiago; m. Victor Abram Snyder, July 2, 1988. BS, U. P.R., Mayaguez, 1983; MS, Med. Sci. Sch., San Juan, P.R., 1985; postgrad., Ohio State U., 1989—. Audiology intern VA Hosp., Pitts., 1987-88; audiologist Menonnite Gen. Hosp., Aibonito, P.R., 1986-87; with Coll. Health Related Professions U. P.R. Med. Sci. Campus, San Juan, 1989; tchr. assoc. Ohio State U., Columbus, 1989. Contbr. articles to El Nuero Dia Newspaper. Mem. Pro-Life Orgn., San Juan, 1983, Orgn. Speech Pathology and Audiology P.R. student corps, San Juan, 1983. Recipient Student Clin. Excellence award OPPHLA-P.R., 1985. Mem. Am. Auditory Soc., ASHA, OPPHLA of P.R., Am. Acad. Audiology, Alexander Graham Bell Assn. for the Deaf, Ohio Coun. Audiology, Acoustic Soc. Am., P.R. Acad. Audiology (founder), Mich. Acad. Audiology, Tri-Beta. Home: Calle 5 N 18 Reina de Los Angeles Gurabo PR 00778 Office: Coll Health Related Professions Med Scis Campus Audiology Program PO Box 365067 San Juan PR 00936

DE SOFI, OLIVER JULIUS, data processing executive; b. Havana, Cuba, Dec. 26, 1929; came to U.S., 1956; naturalized, 1961; s. Julius A. and Edith H. (Zsuffa) DeS. B.S. in Math. and Physics, Ernst Lehman Coll., 1950; postgrad. in agronomy U. Havana, 1952, B.S. in Aero. Engring., 1956; m. Phyllis H. Dumich, Feb. 14, 1971; children: Richard D., Stephen R., Kerri L. Dir. EDP tech. svcs. and planning Am. Airlines, N.Y.C., 1968-70; dir. Sabre II, Tulsa, 1970-72; v.p. data processing and communications Nat. Bank of N. Am., Huntington Station, N.Y., 1972-76, sr. v.p. data processing and communications, 1976-78, sr. v.p. systems and ops., 1978-79, sr. v.p. adminstrn., N.Y.C., 1979-80, exec. v.p. adminstrn. group, 1980-83; exec. v.p. data processing methodologies and architecture Anacomp, Inc., Ft. Lee, N.J. and Sarasota, Fla., 1983-84; v.p. corp. devel. Computer Horizons Corp., N.Y.C., 1984-86; pres., CEO Coast to Coast Computers Inc., Sarasota, 1986—, CEO, 1993-94; chief data processing cons. Arab Nat. Bank, Riyadh, Kingdom of Saudi Arabia, 1991-92; CEO, ; bd. dirs. The Bentley Group, San Francisco, Innovative Mgmt. Systems, Inc., Sarasota, Doks Enterprises, Inc., Carson City, C.C. Lawn Care, Inc., Sarasota; lectr. program for women Adelphi Coll. Mem. Data Processing Mgmt. Assn., Computer Exec. Round Table, Am. Mgmt. Assn., Sales Execs. Club, Bank Adminstrn. Inst., AAAS, Internat. Platform Assn., Nat. Rifle Assn. Republican. Club: Masons (Havana).

DE SOUSA, BYRON NAGIB, physician, anesthesiologist, clinical pharmacologist, educator; b. Goiania, Goias, Brazil, Jan. 15, 1949; came to the U.S., 1972; s. Lazaro Jose and Zarife (Chaul) de; m. Ana Maria Soares, Nov. 15, 1991; stepchildren: Thiago M., Thais Martins; children: Daniela N., Elisabeth L. BS in Biology, U. Brasilia, Brazil, 1970, BS in Biology Edn., 1971, MD, 1973; PhD in Physiol. Chemistry, Ohio State U., 1976. Prin. CASEB & CSL biology tchr. Adult Sr. H.S., Brazil, 1969-71; instr. biochemistry U. Goias, Brazil, 1972; rsch. asst. prof. neurology UCLA-Wadsworth V.A. Med. Ctr., L.A., 1978-79; cons. physician Brentwood V.A. Med. Ctr., L.A., 1979-80; intern Wadsorth-Brentwood V.A. Med. Ctr., L.A., 1980-81; resident in Anesthesiology U. So. Calif. Med. Ctr., L.A., 1981-83; anesthesiologist Simi Valley Presbyn. Hosp., Calif., 1983-85, Simi Valley Community Hosp., Calif., 1983-85, Rio Hondo Meml. Hosp., L.A., 1983-85, Kaiser Permanente Med. Ctr., Orange County, Calif., 1983-84, Hollywood Presbyn. Med. Ctr., L.A., 1983-84, Pacoima Community Hosp., L.A., 1984; assoc. prof. biochemistry, pharmacology Fed. U. Goias, 1986-89; adj. prof. pharmacology U. North Tex. Health Sci. Ctr., Ft. Worth, 1993; anesthesiologist UTSMC affiliated hosps., Dallas, 1993; vis. prof. pharmacology, med. microbiology and immunology U. North Tex. Health Sci. Ctr., Ft. Worth. Author, editor (book) Arts of Politics: Thoughts and Quotations, 1988; reviewer sci./clin. jours.; contbr. over 60 articles to sci. jours.; inventor in field. NIA postdoctoral fellow Med. Coll. Pa., 1976-77, postdoctoral fellow U. Wis., 1977-78, Internal Medicine fellow UCLA Med. Ctr., 1979-80. Fellow Am. Coll. Internat. Physicians (trustee, pres. Dallas-Ft. Worth chpt.); mem. AAAS, AMA, Am. Soc. Anesthesiologists, Am. Soc. Neurochemistry, Western U.S.A. Pain Soc., Calif. Med. Assn., Calif. Soc. Anesthesiologists, Tex. Med. Assn., Tarrant County Med. Soc. Orange County Anesthesiology Soc., L.A. County Soc. Anesthesiologists, L.A. County Med. Soc., Internat. Anesthesia Rsch. Soc., Internat. Soc. Neurochemistry, European Brain and Behavior Soc., European Soc. Regional Anesthesia, Brazilian Coun. Ophthalmology, British Brain Rsch. Assn., Gerontological Soc., Soc. Neurosci. Office: U North Tex Health Sci Ctr Dept Pharmacology 3500 Camp Bowie Blvd Fort Worth TX 76107-2699

DESSEN, ALAN CHARLES, English language educator; b. Balt., Nov. 16, 1935; s. Maurice M. and Shirley (Kaplan) D.; m. Cynthia Sheldon, Aug. 4, 1963; children: Michael Joel, Sarah Elizabeth. BA magna cum laude, Harvard U., 1957; MA, Johns Hopkins U., 1961, PhD, 1963. From instr. to assoc. prof. English U. Wis., Madison, 1963-69; assoc. prof. English Northwestern U., Evanston, Ill., 1969-73; prof. English U. N.C., Chapel Hill, 1973—, Peter G. Phialas prof. English, 1994—, dir. ACTER, 1994—. Author: Jonson's Moral Comedy, 1971, Elizabethan Drama and the Viewer's Eye, 1977, Elizabethan Stage Conventions and Modern Interpreters, 1984, Shakespeare and the Late Moral Plays, 1986, Titus Andronicus, 1989, Recovering Shakespeare's Theatrical Vocabulary, 1995; mem. editorial bd. Studies in Philology, 1974—, Shakespeare Quar., 1975—, Renaissance Drama, 1976—. NEH fellow, 1976-77, 91. Mem. MLA, Shakespeare Assn. of Am. (trustee 1987-90), The Malone Soc., Phi Beta Kappa. Home: 1100 Willow Dr Chapel Hill NC 27514-2924 Office: U NC Dept English Chapel Hill NC 27599

DESSLER, GARY S., business educator, author, consultant, administrator; b. N.Y.C., June 8, 1942; s. Alexander and Laura D.; m. Claudia Gloria (Offman), Mar. 19, 1970; 1 child, Derek Carter. BSc, N.Y.U., 1966; MSc, Rensselaer Polytech, 1967; PhD, City U. N.Y., 1973. Asst., assoc. prof. bus. Fla. Internat. U., Miami, 1971-78, assoc. dean coll. bus., 1971-79, prof. bus., 1979—, chmn. mgmt. and internat. bus. dept., 1992—; cons. and corp. dir.; pres. Relsed Pub. Co., Inc., 1979—; columnist Miami Herald, 1979-91. Author: Human Behavior--Improving Performance at Work, 1980, Organization and Management, 1982, Applied Human Relations, 1983, Improving Productivity at Work, 1983, Management Fundamentals, 1985, Organization Theory, 1986, Human Resource Management, 7th edit., 1996 (also Spanish and internat. edit.); co-author: Introduction to Business, 7th edit., 1994, Winning Commitment, 1994, Managing Organizations in an Era of Change, 1995; contbr. articles to profl. jours. Mem. Acad. Mgmt., Authors Guild. Office: Fla Internat U Coll of Bus Tamiami Trail Miami FL 33199-0001

DETTMAR, KEVIN JOHN HOFFMANN, English language educator; b. Burbank, Calif., Dec. 24, 1958; s. Wilbur George and Joan Elizabeth (Fiddis) D.; m. Robyn Hoffmann, Aug. 15, 1981; children: Emily Susan, Audrey Elizabeth, Esther Katherine, Colin Adam. BA in English and Psychology, U. Calif., Davis, 1981; postgrad. diploma, Trinity Coll., Dublin, Ireland, 1982; MA in English, UCLA, 1988, PhD in English, 1990. Teaching asst., assoc. fellow dept. English UCLA, 1984-90; vis. asst. prof. dept. English Loyola Marymount U., 1990-91; asst. prof. English Clemson U., S.C., 1991-94, assoc. prof., asst. head dept. English, 1994—; presenter in field. Author: The Illicit Joyce of Postmodernism: Reading Against the Grain, 1996; co-editor: Marketing Modernisms: Self-Promotion, Canonization, Rereading, 1996; editor, contbr. Rereading the New: A Backward Glance at Modernism, 1992; contbr. articles to profl. publs.; cons. reader Mosaic: A Jour. for the Interdisciplinary Study of Literature, 1991—. NEH travel grantee, 1992-93; NEH summer stipend, 1994; fellow U.S. Dept. Edn., 1986-87, Jacob K. Javits fellow U.S. Dept. Edn., 1987-88, 88-89, 89-90. Mem. AAUP, MLA (mem. del. assembly 1993-95), James Joyce Found., South Atlantic MLA, Soc. for Study of Narrative Lit. Home: 111 Pleasant View Dr Clemson SC 29631-1782 Office: Clemson U Dept English PO Box 341503 Clemson SC 29634-1503

DEUTSCH, HUNTING FOLGER, banker; b. Miami, Fla., Sept. 18, 1952; s. William Lee and Julia Ann (Fales) D.; m. Mary Elisabeth Brassil, Oct. 4, 1975; children: Patrick MacGregor, Stephen Lloyd Fales. Student, Harvard U., 1972; BA, U. N.H., 1974; MBA, U. Miami, 1982; postgrad., U. Pa. With S.E. First Nat. Bank of Miami, 1971-78, asst. v.p., adminstrv. services, 1978-79, asst. v.p., corp. ops., 1980-81; v.p., account services Flagship Nat. Bank of Miami, 1981-83; v.p. account and bus. services Sun Bank Service Corp., Miami, 1983-84; sr. v.p. and cashier, ops. div. Sun Bank Miami N.A., 1984-87; exec. v.p. trust and investment mgmt. divsn. Sun Bank/Miami N.A. subs. SunTrust Banks, Inc., Miami, 1987-93; exec. v.p. Fla. Trust and Investment Svcs., Sun Trust Bank of Fla. Inc., Orlando, Fla., 1993—; exec. v.p. trust and investment svcs. Sun Trust Bank, Orlando, 1993—; pres. Sun Trust Annuities, Inc.; treas., bd. dirs. south Fla. chpt. Bank Adminstrn. Inst., Miami, 1978-85, pres., 1982-83, adv. com., 1992. Mem. campaign cabinet, chmn. real estate cultivation group United Way of Dade, Miami, 1986, 88, 90; mem. Com. of 100; trustee New World Symphony, Dade Cmty. Found., St. Francis Med. Found., 1987—, Performing Arts Ctr.; bd. dirs. Ctrl. Fla. Cmty. Found., Winter Park Hosp. Found.; active Leadership Fla.; mem. U. of Miami Pres. Coun., 1996; bd. advisors ABD Nat. Trust Schs. of Northwestern U.; mayors com. for devel. New Performing Arts Ctr.; bd. trustees Winter Park Health Endowment; vice chmn. Cmty. Found. of Ctrl. Fla. Mem. Bus. Network, Beacon Coun. (cmty. agenda com., internal mgmt. com.), Greater Miami C. of C. (West Dade banking fin. com. 1986), Bath Club, U. Miami Alumi Assn. (adv. bd.), Biscayne Bay Yacht Club, Interlacken Country Club, Citrus Club. Republican. Office: Sun Trust Bank of Fla Inc 200 S Orange Ave Fl 8 Orlando FL 32801-3410 Office: Sun Trust Banks of Fla Inc 200 S Orange Ave Orlando FL 32801-3410

DEUTSCH, LAWRENCE IRA, minister; b. Bklyn., June 17, 1939; s. Meyer Irving and Lillian (Ilkovitz) D.; m. Carolyn Ann Beaton, June 2, 1960 (div. Oct. 1986); children: Michael Keith, Eric Scott; m. Karol White, Dec. 31, 1987; stepchildren: Sharlotte Lester, Jason Lester. AAS, Bklyn. Coll., 1961; BTh, Calvary Bible Coll., Lake Charles, La., 1990; MA, Cornerstone U., 1991; Dr.Religious Edn., Moody Theol. Sem., 1992. Ordained to ministry Bapt. Ch., 1982. Pastor Congregation Beth Ha'Shem, Houston, 1988—; chaplain T.D.C. & Houston Downtown Med. Ctr., 1981—; bd. dirs. Jesus the Messiah Sem., 1990—, Beth Ha'Shem Christian Counseling Ctr. Author: (poetry) various publs. (silver award 1986, golden award 1987-89). Pub. rels. officer to mayor Gulfport, Miss., 1968-69. With USMC, 1958-64. Mem. So. Bapt. Messianic Alliance, Messianic Jewish Alliance Am., Internat. Writers Alive (v.p. 1990—). Republican. Mem. Messianic Ch. Home and Office: 3510 Greenwood Pl Deer Park TX 77536-5700

DEVANE, DENIS JAMES, health care company executive; b. N.Y.C., Feb. 11, 1938; s. Eugene and Deborah (Courtney) D.; m. Margaret Mary Walsh, Oct. 14, 1961; children: Denise, Daniel, Deborah, Tara. BS, Fordham U., 1959. Asst. v.p. nat. sales mgr. C.I.T. Bldgs. Corp., N.Y.C., 1971-72, v.p., gen. mgr., 1973-74, pres., 1974-75; v.p. Lifemark Corp., Houston, 1975-80, sr. v.p., 1980-84; pres. Hosp. div. Health Group, Inc., Nashville, 1984; pres., chief operating officer Healthdyne, Inc., Marietta, Ga., 1985-86; pres., chief exec. officer Am. Rehab. Services Inc., Atlanta, 1987-88; chmn., CEO Rebound, Inc., Hendersonville, Tenn., 1989-92; exec. v.p. Healthsouth Corp., Birmingham, Ala., 1993-95. Mem. Summit Club, Greystone Golf Club. Home: 1097 Greymoor Rd Birmingham AL 35242-7211

DE VARGAS, CECILIA CORDOBA, psychiatrist; b. Obando, Valle, Colombia, Nov. 26, 1940; came to U.S., 1972; d. Miguel and Susana (Ortiz) Cordoba; children: Juanita, Daniel. MD, Universidad Del Valle, Cali, Colombia, 1966. Resident in psychiatry Universidad Del Valle, 1967-70; resident in child and adolescent psychiatry Coll. Medicine Baylor U., Houston, 1972-74; resident in psychiatry Sch. of Medicine Creighton U., Omaha, 1974-76; assoc. prof. U. N.Mex., Albuquerque, 1977-78; med. dir. El Paso (Tex.) Child Guidance Ctr., 1978—; med. dir. St. Margaret's Ctr. for Children, El Paso, 1978-81; med. dir. adolescent and children's unit Sun Valley Regional Hosp., El Paso, 1986-92. Mem. Am. Acad. Child and Adolescent Psychiatry, Colombian Med. Assn. Roman Catholic. Office: El Paso Child Guidance Ctr 2710 E Yandell Dr El Paso TX 79903-3727 also: 1810 Murchison Dr Ste 302 El Paso TX 79902-2906

DEVAULT, JOHN LEE, oil company executive, geophysicist; b. Kansas City, Mo., Aug. 4, 1937; s. Isaac Henderson and Evelyn Margaret (Rowell) DeV.; m. Janet Ann Miller, Sept. 11, 1968; children: Bryan Charles, Chris Lee. B Chem. Engring., Case Inst. Tech., Cleve., 1959; BS, MacMurray Coll., Jacksonville, Ill., 1961; MS, U. Houston, 1975. Lic. geophysicist, Calif., Am. Assn. Petroleum Geologists, Am. Inst. Profl. Geologists, Soc. Ind. Profl. Earth Scientists. Geophysicist United Geophys., Europe, Africa, Middle East, Australia-Asia, Alaska and Houston, 1961-74; pres. Sercel Inc., Houston, 1974-88; chmn. Jade Corp., Houston, 1988—. Contbr. articles to Oil and Gas Jour. Dir. Jaycees, Springfield, Ill., 1960; downstate v.p. Young Rep. Club, Springfield, 1960; bd. mem. Honors Coll., U. Houston, 1990—; trustee Culver Legion-Culver Academies. Mem. Geophys. Soc. Houston (hon. life, pres. 1987), Soc. Exploration Geophysics (1st v.p. 1993). Mem. Disciples of Christ Ch. Home: 703 Queensmill Ct Houston TX 77079 Office: Jade Corp PO Box 218567 Houston TX 77079

DEVAULT, WILLIAM LEONARD, orthopaedic surgeon; b. Elizabethton, Tenn., Dec. 4, 1950; s. Robert Moulton and Betty (Cloyd) DeV.; m. Anna Lee Homewood, Apr. 12, 1986; children: Jonathan, Elizabeth. BS in Chemistry, Birmingham-So. Coll., 1979; MD, Wake Forest U., 1983. Diplomate Nat. Bd. Med. Examiners, Am. Bd. Orthpaedic Surgery. Resident in orthopaedic surgery U. S.C., Columbia, 1983-88; pvt. practice, Beaufort, S.C., 1988-89, Fredericksburg, Va., 1989-91, Clemson, S.C., 1992—; fellow in sports medicine and reconstructive surgery Jewett Orthopaedic Clinic, Orlando, Fla., 1991-92. Mem. Am. Acad. Orthopaedic Surgeons, Am. Assn. Sports Medicine, Arthroscopy Assn. N.Am. Baptist.

DE VECIANA, MARGARITA, obstetrician, gynecologist; b. Paris, Nov. 13, 1958; came to the U.S., 1979.; d. Antonio and Brynhild May (Anderson) D. BS with honors, Sussex U., 1979; MS in Biol. Scis., Stanford U., 1980; MD, Cornell U., 1988. Ob-gyn. resident U. Calif., Irvine, 1988-92, maternal fetal medicine fellowship, 1992-94; asst. prof. ob-gyn. Ea. VA Med. Sch., Norfolk, Va., 1994—; dir. diabetes in pregnancy program Ea. VA Med. Sch., Norfolk, 1994—. Mem. ACOG (jr. fellow), Soc. for Perinatal Obstetricians (pres. assoc. membership 1995-96), Am. Diabetes Assn. Office: Ea Va Med Sch Ob Gyn 825 Fairfax Ave Ste 310 Norfolk VA 23507

DEVENNY, LILLIAN NICKELL, trophy company executive; b. Chesapeake, Ohio; d. Hayes Basil and Alice Irene (Noble) Nickell; m. John Paul DeVenny Jr., Dec. 31, 1955; children: Carrie DeVenny Paganini (dec.), John Hayes. Student, Covington Bus. Sch., 1954-55, Norfolk Coll., 1980-81. Office mgr., bookkeeper Nickell Electric Co., Covington, Va., 1950-55; exec. Nickell Electric Co., 1960-62; sec. 5th Naval Dist. Hdqtrs., Norfolk, Va., 1955-58, Profl. Realty, Va. Beach, 1971; pub. relations corp. sec. Hobby Industries, Va. Beach, 1973-74; owner, mgr., instr., sec.-treas. Deste Corp. t/a Hobby Assoc., Va. Beach, 1974—; singer, actress Tidewater Dinner Theater, Norfolk, part-time, 1971-75; involved numerous continuing edn. units. Writer coloumn on Va. travel, 1978-79; editor news letter, 1972-73. Founding mem., chmn. bd. dirs. Va. Opposing Drunk Driving, 1981—, state v.p., 1981-86, state pres., 1986—; mem. adv. bd. Va. Commn. on Alcohol Safety, 1987-91, 95-97; participant Va. Assembly on Future of Va.'s Cts., U. Va., Commn. Pub. Svc., 1989; mem. spl. White House briefing on ways to combat tragedy of drunk driving, 1989; mem. Va. Civilian-Mil. Comty. Safety Com., 1988; mem. Va. Alcohol Safety Action Program Commn., 1991—; co-chmn. Va. Coalition Against Drunk Driving, 1989—; contbr. passage Omnibus Alcohol Safety Act, Va. Gen. Assembly, 1994. Recipient Community Svc. award J.C. Penney Co., 1985, Hometown Hero, Sta. WVEC-TV, 1986. Mem. Internat. Ceramists Assn., Modern Woodmen Am. (regional sec. 1954), Beta Sigma Phi (mem.-at-large). Episcopalian. Office: Deste Corp t/a Hobby Assocs 5004 Cleveland St Virginia Beach VA 23462-2504

DEVENPORT, JOHN THOMAS, JR., public relations professional; b. Jacksonville, Tex., Sept. 1, 1961; s. John T. and Virginia Nash D.; m. Amy Branson, May 8, 1993. BS, U. Tex., 1984. Coord. comm. Tex. Vet. Med. Assn., Austin, Tex., 1984-90; v.p. comm. Tex. Automobile Dealers Assn., Austin, Tex., 1990—. Editor Tex. Vet. Med. Jour., 1987-90, Dealer's Choice, 1990—. Print media rels. com. United Way/Capital Area, Austin, 1993-94; mem. editorial task force Boy Scouts of Am./Capital Area Coun., Austin, 1988-90; mem. regional scholarship com. Nat. Eagle Scout Assn., 1988-89; chmn. pub. rels. com. Austin Jr. C. of C., 1987-88. Recipient Best of Austin award Internat. Assn. Bus. Comm./Austin Chpt., 1987, 88, 92, 95, 1st Pl. Single Project award for Pub. Rels., Tex. Jaycees, 1988. Mem. Pub. Rels. Soc. Am. (membership chair 1995, treas. 1996, accredited in pub. rels., Rising Star award Austin chpt. 1995, pres.-elect 1997), Am. Soc. Assn. Execs. (cert. in comm.), Tex. Soc. Assn. Execs. (chmn. ad hoc comm. task force 1993-94, chmn. editl. adv. com. 1993, mem. editl. adv. com. 1994—), Internat. Assn. Bus. Comm. (Austin chpt. pres. 1990-91), Tex.-Based Task Force for Older Drivers (dealership industry rep. 1991-92), Tex. Coalition for Safety Belts (rep. 1990-91). Office: Tex Automobile Dealers Assn 1108 Lavaca St Austin TX 78701-2125

DEVEREUX, MARIE P., pediatrics nurse; b. Eros, La., Oct. 1, 1923; d. Daniel Lee and Minnie Oler (Phillips) Peterson; m. Michael R. Devereux Sr., Oct. 11, 1947; children: Sheila Cochran, Michael R. Jr., Daniel. Diploma, St. Francis Sanitarium, 1946; student, N.E. La. U., 1985-87. RN, La. Lab. technician St. Francis Sanitarium, Monroe, La.; head nurse Children's Clinic; nurse Monroe City Sch. Bd., ret. With N.C., U.S. Army, 1944-46. Home: 1506 University Ave Monroe LA 71203-3551

DEVICTOR, D. J., landscape architect. BS in Landscape Architecture, Ohio State U., 1977. Registered landscape arch., Ga., Tenn. Dir. planning and devel. Fairfield Communities Inc. Resort/Golf Course Devel. Co.; arch. Bill Oliphant & Assocs., Knoxville, Tenn., Beighley' Krause, PC, Portland, Oreg., Arthur Hills and Assocs., Toledo, Ohio; prin. DeVictor Langham, Roswell, Ga.; active City of Roswell (Ga.) Design Rev. Bd. Mem. long range planning com. Fellowship Christian Acad. Mem. USGA, Am. Soc. Landscape Archs., Nat. Golf Found. Office: DeVictor Langham Inc 45 W Crossville Rd Ste 502 Roswell GA 30075-2964

DEVIGNE, KAREN COOKE, retired amateur athletics executive; b. Phila., July 31, 1943; d. Paul and Matilda (Rich) Cooke; m. Jules Lloyd Devigne, June 26, 1965; children: Jules Paul, Denise Paige, Paul Michael. AA, Centenary Coll., Hackettstown, 1963; student, Northwestern U., 1963-65; BA, Ramapo Coll., Mahwah, 1976; MA, Emory U., Atlanta, 1989. Founder GYMSET, Marietta, Ga., 1981—. Cons. Girls Club Am. Marietta, 1989; vol. Cobb County Gymnastic Ctr., Marietta, 1976-95, Ga. Youth Soccer Assn., Atlanta, 1976-95; fundraiser Scottish Rite Children's Hosp., Atlanta, 1989. Recipient recognition awards from various youth groups, Atlanta, 1976—; named Nominee Woman of Yr. ABC News, Atlanta, 1984. Home: 3701 Clubland Dr Marietta GA 30068-4006 also: 445 White Cloud Breckenridge CO 80424

DEVILLA, LUCENA M., home healthcare nurse, administrator, business owner; b. Naujan, Oriental Mindoro, The Philippines, May 30, 1950; came to U.S., 1975, naturalized, 1986; d. Potenciano and Nazaria (Maramot) De Villa; divorced; children: Rommel John, Christina Michelle, Abigail Anne. BSN, U. Santo Tomas, Manila, The Philippines, 1972; MS in Nursing, Tex. Woman's U., Houston, 1992. RN; Cert. med.-surg. nurse, critical care nurse, oncology nurse, home infusion therapy nurse. Agy. nurse Houston, 1983-84; emergency room nurse St. Joseph Hosp., Houston, 1984-85; dir. nurses surgicare Medi-Plex of Houston, Inc., Channelview, 1985-86; recovery room nurse, critical care nurse, head nurse VA Hosp., Houston, 1986-88; owner, adminstr. Med. Insights & Care Unltd. Inc., Home Health Agy. & Nursing Agy., Houston, 1986—. Mem. ANA, Tex. Nurses Assn., Philippine Nurses Assn. (life), Tex. Assn. Home Health Agys., Exec. Woman's Network, Houston Philippine-Am Lions Club (sec., named Mrs. Phillipines of Houston, 1992, chairperson Mrs. Philippines of Houston, 1994, 95), North Channel C. of C. (operation rainbow), Philippine-Am. C. of C., North Channel Philippine-Am Assn. (pres.), U.S. C. of C. Address: PO Box 96711 Houston TX 77213-6711 Office: 8200 Wednesbury Ln Ste 270 Houston TX 77074

DEVILLE, DONALD CHARLES, accountant; b. New Roads, La., Sept. 18, 1953; s. Sterling Joseph and Barbara J. (Beaud) DeV.; m. Michelle L. Rinaudo, Apr. 14, 1984; children: Ariel Elizabeth, Stewart Charles. BS in Acctg., La. State U., 1976. CPA, La. Auditor State of La., Baton Rouge, 1976-78; mgr. Hawthorn Waymouth & Carroll, Baton Rouge, 1978-89; pvt. practice acct. Baton Rouge, 1989—. Pres. Baton Rouge Work Exch., 1988; publicity dir. Baton Rouge Opera, 1989-90, treas., 1991—; liturg. min St. George Cath. Ch., Baton Rouge, 1987—; bd. dirs. Capital Area Safety Coun. La., treas., 1994-95; bd. dirs. Baton Rouge Boys Club. Recipient Freedom award La. Farm Bur. Mem. AICPA, La. Soc. CPAs, SAR (sec. 1990-93, pres. 1994, La. Meritorious Svc. award). Republican. Roman Catholic. Home: 8925 Orleans Dr Baton Rouge LA 70810-2165

DEVINE, MICHAEL JOSEPH, construction executive; b. Cleve., June 17, 1952; s. James Thomas Jr. and Helen (Langa) D.; m. Donna Jo Muntz, Mar. 17, 1974; children: Jeremy Michael, Kristin Helen. BBA, U. Toledo, 1974. Estimator AC&S Inc., Tampa, Fla., 1975-77; pres., chief exec. officer Comml. Insulation Co., Inc., Jacksonville, Fla., 1977—; pres. Environ. Safety, Inc., Jacksonville, 1986-88, Northeast Fla. Enterprises, Inc., 1987—. Inventor in field. Bd. dirs. West Jacksonville C. of C., 1986-88, Great Western coun. Boy Scouts Am., 1988. Recipient Blue Chip Enterprise U.S. C. of C. Mem. S.E. Insulation Contractors Assn., Am. Water Works Assn., Am. Soc. San. Engrs., Kiwanis (treas. West Jacksonville chpt. 1986—, Kiwanian of Yr. 1987-88, Group Vol. award 1990-91). Democrat. Roman Catholic. Office: Comml Insulation Co Inc 250 Lane Ave N Jacksonville FL 32254-2815

DEVINEY, MARVIN LEE, JR., research institute scientist, program manager; b. Kingsville, Tex., Dec. 5, 1929; s. Marvin Lee and Esther Lee (Gambrell) D.; m. Marie Carole Massey, June 7, 1975; children: Marvin Lee III, John H., Ann-Marie K. BS in Chemistry and Math., S.W. Tex. State U., San Marcos, 1949; MA in Phys. Chemistry, U. Tex., Austin, 1952, PhD in Phys. Chemistry, 1956. Cert. profl. chemist. Devel. chemist Celanese Chem. Co., Bishop, Tex., 1956-58; rsch. chemist Shell Chem. Co., Deer Park, Tex., 1958-66; sr. scientist, head group phys. and radio-chemistry Ashland Chem. Co., Houston, 1966-68, mgr. sect. phys. and analytical chemistry, 1968-71; mgr. sect. phys. chemistry div. rsch. and devel. Ashland Chem. Co., Columbus, Ohio, 1971-78; rsch. assoc., supr. applied surface chemistry Ashland Ventures Rsch. and Devel., Columbus, 1978-84, supr. electron microscopy, advanced aerospace composites, govt. contracts, 1984-90; inst. scientist, mem. internal R & D com. SW Rsch. Inst., San Antonio, Tex., 1990—; adj. prof. U. Tex., San Antonio, 1973-75, Ohio State U., 1990-91; mem. sci. adv. bd. Am. Petroleum Inst. Rsch. Project 60, 1968-74. Contbr. numerous articles to profl. jours.; patentee in field. Mem. ednl. adv. com. Columbus Tech. Inst., 1974-84, Cen. Ohio Tech. Coll., 1975-82, Hocking Tech. Coll., 1989-91. Lt. col., USAR, retired. Humble Oil Rsch. fellow, 1954. Fellow Am. Inst. Chemists (pres. Ohio Inst. 1978-82); mem. Tex. Acad. Sci., Am. Def. Preparedness Assn., Electron Microscopy Soc. Am., Materials Rsch. Soc., SAMPE Composite Soc., N.Am. Catalysis Soc., Am. Soc. Composites, Soc. Plastics Engrs., Soc. Automotive Engrs., Am. Chem. Soc. (chmn. chpt. exec. bd. 1969, bus. mgr. nat. div. Petroleum Chemistry, 1986-90, Best Paper award rubber div. 1967, 70, Hon. Mention awards 1968, 69, 73, symposia co-chmn., co-editor books on catalysis-surface chemistry 1985, carbon-graphite chemistry 1975), Engr.'s Coun. Houston (sr. councilor 1970-71), Sigma Xi, Phi Lambda Upsilon, Alpha Chi, Sigma Pi Sigma. Methodist. Home: 15934 Alsace San Antonio TX 78232-2790 Office: SW Rsch Inst PO Box 28510 San Antonio TX 78228

DEVITO, TERESA MARIE, artist; b. Bangoli del Tigino, Italy, June 11, 1920; came to U.S., 1924, naturalized, 1926; d. Bartolomeo and Santo Donatello Cimaglia; m. Americao DeVito; children: Richard (dec.), Sandra Ann DeVito King. BA inEdn., Fairmont State Coll., 1960; MA, W.Va. U., 1964; postgrad., Wagner Coll., 1968; D (hon.), Minsitry Fgn. Affairs of Malta. Tchr. East Fairmont (W.Va.) High Sch., 1960-68, Miller Jr. High Sch., Rivesville, W.Va., 1969-70; instr. art Fairview H.S., 1970-86, Barrockville H.S., Farmington H.S. One-woman shows include Lynn Katler Gallery, N.y.C., 1975; exhibited at group shows at Morgantown Art Assn. Exhbn., 1960; commd. work includes paintings on cloth at Immaculate Conception Ch., Fairmont, Fairmont Bowling Ctr., 1988, Disney World. Recipient Internat. Statue of Victory, Einstein Peace Medal, Rhodeodendron Festival award, Honoris Causea, Internat. Found., 1987. Mem. AAUW, NEA, Nat. Art Edn. Assn., Tole Painters Am., W.Va. Art Assn., W.Va. Artist and Craftsman Guild, Artists Equity, League Ind. Artists (past v.p.), Village Garden Club, Cath. Daus. Am. Roman Catholic. Home: 417 Newton St Fairmont WV 26554-5218

DEVOL, SKIP, entertainer; b. Chgo., July 19, 1948; s. Earl Lon and Bernice G. (Olsen) DeV.; m. Johanna Diane Jultak, Aug. 22, 1993. Student, U. Kans., 1966-69. Mus. dir. Summer Theatre, Lake of the Ozarks, Mo., 1970. Performed with USO tour, Vietnam, 1969, Landmark Hotel Main Showroom, 1975-77, Royal Caribbean Cruise Line, 1977—, Holland Am. Cruises, 1980—, Queen Elizabeth Cunard Line, 1983—, Crystal Cruises, 1992—; actor various voice over and on-camera radio and TV advt., 1976— (Gold Medal award nat. competition 1989); co-producer, performer recordings including Ultra Banjo, 1980, World Class, 1989; concert entertainer many U.S. corps., 1980—; featured artist in-flight programming Eastern Airlines, summer 1986; regular guest appearance Arthur Godfrey Show, 1969-71, The Nashville Network, 1983-86, (T.V. show) Country Tonite, 1993; performer The Tonight Show, 1974, The Merv Griffin Show, 1976, Kennedy Ctr. Concert Hall, 1990; writer, musical arranger live performances, 1975—; on air radio personality Sta. KHUB-AM, 1964; composer, arranger Warp Speed, 1978, guest artist Boca Pops Symphony Orch., 1992, Aurora (Colo.) Symphony Pops, 1994; guest artist Wildwood Festival Theatre Inaugural Gala, Litte Rock, Ark., 1996; guest performer Nat. Anthem, Minn. Twins, 88, 89, Colo. Rockies Innaugural Year, 1995; host (highlights video) Grand Nat. and World Championship Morgan Horse Show, 1996. Writer, producer, performer TV and radio advt. United Way So. Nev., 1976; guest artist Easter Seals Telethon (nat.), L.A., 1977; host local segments Jerry Lewis Muscular Dystrophy, Las Vegas, 1977-78; participant Celebrity Pro-Am. golf tournaments. Recipient John Philip Sousa band award, 1966, Promoting Patriotism through Performance award Gage Park (Ill.) Civic Bd., 1969, Golden Crutch award Hejaz Shrine, Spartanburg, S.C., 1990—; named Ky. Col., 1990, Adm. Nebr. Navy, 1990; U. Kans. Sch. Fine Arts scholar, 1966-67. Mem. ASCAP (writer/composer), Am. Fedn. Musicians, Internat. Platform Assn., Phi Mu Alpha (Xi chpt.). Republican. Office: Gary Mann Prodns PO Box 368 Mount Prospect IL 60056-0368

DEVORE, KIMBERLY K., sales executive; b. Louisville., June 19, 1947; d. Wendell O. and Shirley F. DeV.; student, Xavier U., 1972-76; AA, Coll. Mt. St. Joseph, 1979. Patient registration supr. St. Francis Hosp., Cin., 1974-76; cons., bus. mgr. Family Health Care Found., Cin., 1976-77; exec. dir. Hospice of Cin., Inc., 1977-80; pres. Micro Med, 1979-86; v.p. Sycamore Profl. Assn., 1979-86; ptnr. Enchanted House, 1979-86, sec., 1979-80, treas. 1980-83; dist. sales rep. Control-O-Fax, 1986, br. sales mgr., 1987, nat. dealer devel. rep., 1987—, computer specialist, 1987, nat. computer field sales trainer, 1987-90; pres. U.S. Exec. Leasing and U.S. Med. Leasing, Inc., 1991—, Accu Svcs., Inc., 1993—, U.S. Med. Mgmt., Inc., 1994—, U.S. Med. Mgmt. of Ga., Inc., 1994—; pres. Saddle Creek Homeowners Assn., Inc., 1992-95, parliamentarian, 1995-96; membership chairperson Smith Plantation City of Roswell, 1996—; pres. Roswell Citizen's Police Acad., Inc., 1994—; mem. North Fulton Civic League, Inc., 1995-96; bd. dirs. Nat. Hospice Orgn., 1979-82, chmn. long-term planning com., fin. com., ann. meeting com., 1979-82, sec., 1980-81. treas., 1981-82; bd. dirs. Hospice of Miami Valley, Inc., 1982-86, also chmn. pers. com., by-laws com.; mem. med. dist. com. City Roswell, 1995—; bd. dirs. Smith Plantation, 1996—, membership chmn., 1996—. Mem. Greater Cin. Soc. Fund Raisers, Better Housing League; Mem. service and rehab. com. Hamilton County Unit, Am. Cancer Soc., 1977-78; chair road com. Saddle Creek Homeowners Assn., 1991-92. Mem. Ohio Hospice Assn. (co-founder, state chmn., pres., 1978-83), Nat. League for Nursing, Ohio Hosp. Assn., Nat. Fedn. Bus. and Profl. Women's Clubs, Ohio Fedn. Bus. and Profl. Women's Clubs, Cin. Bus. and Profl. Women's Clubs (pres. 1973-75).

DE VRIES, ROBBIE RAY PARSONS, author, illustrator, international consultant; b. Idabel, Okla., Sept. 11, 1929; d. General Forrest Sr. and Jessie Demma (Burch-Oldham) Parsons; m. Douwe de Vries, Apr. 2, 1953; children: Jessica Joan de Vries Kij, Peter Douwe. BS in Bus. Adminstrn. and Journalism, Okla. State U., 1952; postgrad., U. Houston, 1987, 88, Rice U., 1988, 89. Sec. to mgr. drafting and survey Shell Oil Co., Houston, 1952-53; sub. tchr. Spring Br. Ind. Sch. Dist., Houston, 1989-92; pres., owner Robbie P. de Vries Interests, Houston, 1983—, author, illustrator, pub., 1989—; mem. governing bd. Oilfield Systems, Inc., Houston, 1981—; bd. dirs. Friends of Okla. State U. Libr., Stillwater; mem. Friends of U. Houston Libr., 1981—; bd. dirs., cons. Ctr. for Internat. Trade, Okla. State U., Stillwater, 1990—; invited guest Peoples Republic of China/U.S. State Dept., China, 1992. Columnist Conroe, Tex. Daily Courier, 1988-89; editor Idabel Warrior newspaper (Gold medal), 1947, Houston Symphony League newspaper, 1974-75; author, illustrator, pub.: A Cultural Exchange: American and Chinese Weddings, 1993, Chinese edit., 1995; author, pub.: Regional Study of Russian and the Eurasian States, 1996. Vol cultural and internat. areas, New Orleans, 1960-69, Houston, 1969—; bd. dirs. New Orleans C. of C., 1964-69; bd. dirs. Houston Symphony Soc. and League, 1972—, Inst. Internat. Edn., Houston, 1969—; home host internat. youth exch./The Netherlands, 1978; grand jury mem. Harris County Tex., 1986-87; patron Jr. League, Houston, 1970—; docent Mus. Fine Arts, Houston, 1974—; mem., yearbook cover designer Tuesday Music Club, Houston, 1975—; mem. Forum Club Houston, 1980—; co-chmn. Houston-Baku, Azerbaijan, USSR Sister City, 1979-89; bd. dirs. Boy Scouts, Houston, 1985—; bd. dirs., chair Internat. Conf. YWCA, Houston, 1986-87; mem. magic cir. Rep. Women of Houston, 1989—; mem. donor Baylor Med. Sch. Devel., 1990—. Recipient Ann. Fund Silver Tray award Houston Symphony League, 1972, Miss Ima Hogg Orchid award Houston Symphony Soc., 1975, Gen. Maurice Hirsch Leaf and Letter award Symphony Soc., 1980, 81, 82, Tex. Mother of Yr., Alpha Delta Pi, 1982, Mayor's award Baku, Azerbaijan USSR, 1979, 83, 87, 89, U.S. State Dept. pin, 1986, 10-Yr. Leadership award Mayor of Baku, 1988, U. Houston Ball Merit/Honor, 1991, Merit award Boy Scouts of Am., 1993, 10-Yr. Svc. award, 1995; named Acting First Lady of Houston for goodwill trip to Baku, Azerbaijan, USSR, by Mayor of Houston Jim McConn, 1979; named Hon. Dep. Sheriff, Harris County Sheriff Johnny Klevenhagen, 1986, Harris County Sheriff Tommy B. Thomas, 1996; feature Honor Villages mag., 1994. Mem. AAUW (past pres.), Tex. Fine Arts Assn., Inspirational Writers, Houston Coun. Writers, Nat. Women's Hall of Fame, Étoffe Littéraire (founder, Founder's award 1985), Tex.-Netherlands Bus. Assn., Nat. Mus. Women in the Arts (charter), Mu Kappa Tau. Republican. Presbyterian. Home and Office: Robbie P de Vries Interests 802 Piney Point Rd Houston TX 77024-2725

DEWBERRY, BETTY BAUMAN, retired law librarian; b. Dallas, Jan. 18, 1930; d. William Allen Bauman and Julia Ella (Owen) Hurt; m. James A. Dewberry Jr., Mar. 22, 1952 (div. Apr. 1976); children: Mary Julienne, Jennifer Camille, Robert Bruce. BA, U. Tex., 1951; MLS, Tex. Women's U., 1982. Asst. librarian Johnson & Swanson, Dallas, 1979-85; dir. librs. Johnson & Gibbs, Dallas, 1985-94; retired, 1994. Mem. Am. Assn. Law Libraries, Dallas Assn. Law Librarians, Women's Nat. Book Assn., Lakeside Browning Club, Zeta Tau Alpha. Democrat. Methodist.

DEWEY, ANNE ELIZABETH MARIE, lawyer; b. Balt., Mar. 16, 1951; d. George Daniel and Elizabeth Patricia (Mohan) D.; children: Brendan M., Andrew P., Meghan E. BA, Mich. State U., 1972; JD, U. Chgo., 1975; grad., Stonier Grad. Sch. Banking, East Brunswick, N.J., 1983. Bar: D.C. 1976. Legal clk. and atty. FTC, Washington, 1975-78; atty. and sr. atty. Comptr. of Currency, Dallas and Washington, 1978-86; assoc. gen. counsel, gen. counsel, spl. counsel Farm Credit Adminstrn., McLean, Va., 1986-92, FDIC counsel, closed bank litig. and policy sect., 1993-94; gen. counsel Office of Fed. Housing Enterprise Oversight, HUD, 1994—. Mem. ABA (bus. law sect., mem. banking law com.), FBA (bd. dirs. D.C. chpt. 1988-91), Women in Housing and Fin. (bd. dirs. 1982-83, gen counsel 1991-93), D.C. Bar Assn. Roman Catholic.

DEWITT, CHARLES BENJAMIN, III, lawyer, educator; b. Glendale, Calif., Nov. 29, 1952; s. Charles Benjamin Jr. and Lucille Ann (Johnston)

DeW.; m. Karen Denise Blackwood, Dec. 29, 1979. BA magna cum laude, Pacific Union Coll., 1973; JD, U. So. Calif., 1976; MA, U. Memphis, 1995. Bar: Tenn. 1984, U.S. Dist. Ct. (we. dist.) Tenn. 1984, D.C. 1989. Atty., agy. mgr., v.p. SAFECO/Chgo. Title Ins., Memphis, 1980-87, 89-91; regional underwriting counsel Commonwealth Land Title Ins. Co., 1991-93; asst. prof., instr. U. Memphis, 1986—, asst. dean, 1993—. Author numerous poems; contbr. articles to profl. jours. Registrar gen. Washington Family Descendants;. Mem. Memphis Bar Assn., Tenn. Land Title Assn. (sec.-treas. 1983-87), U. S.C. Alumni Assn. (life), Order Crown of Charlemagne, Kiwanis, Mensa, Phi Alpha Theta, Phi Kappa Phi. Home: 2488 Cedarwood Dr Germantown TN 38138 Office: U Memphis Sch Law Memphis TN 38152

DEWOLFE, MARTHA ROSE, singer, songwriter, publisher; b. Arlington, Tex., Nov. 30, 1959; d. Homer C. and Grace R. DeWolfe. Student, N. Tex. State U., 1978-79, Larimer County Vocat.-Tech., Ft. Collins, Colo., 1983; cert. peace officer, Tarrant County Jr. Coll., Euless, Tex., 1984; student, North Central Tex. Coun. Govts., 1984-94, Southwestern Law Enforcement Sch. of Police Supervision. Police officer Grand Prairie (Tex.) Police Dept., 1984-94, sgt., 1989-94, supr. crime prevention unit, 1991-92; mem. Police Employee Rels. Bd., 1990-91; BMI assoc.; estabished Maui Records, 1992, Midnight Tiger Music, BMI, 1994. Albums include That Flame Keeps Burning, Take Good Care of My Heart; songs include Adrianna, Worse Than Being Lonely, All the Blue, Patsy Come Home, River of Tears, Take Good Care of My Heart, If You Don't Want Us, Insomniac in a Cadillac; acting credits include Paramount's "Denton County Massacre", 1993, and commercials. Sec. Grand Prairie Police Assn., 1985-86. Recipient 1st place Tex. Comml. Art Skill Speed Competition, 1977-78. Mem. NAFE, Nat. Assn. Women Police, Tex. Assn. Women Police, Tex. Police Assn., Fraternal Order Police, Grand Prairie Police Assn., Tex. Assn. Vet. Police Officers, Country Music Assn., Nashville Songwriter's Assn. Internat., Mensa, Leo Club (sec. 1976-78). Home: PO Box 2132 Hendersonville TN 37077

DE WREE, EUGENE ERNEST, manufacturing company executive; b. Fairbanks, Alaska, June 26, 1930; s. Henry Joseph and Bertha Agnes DeWree; m. Shirley May Russo, Apr. 16, 1955 (dec. Sept. 1990); children: Angela Kathryn, Mary Rebecca, Thomas Albert Babette Gabrielle, Jane Elizabeth; m. Jean Stanley Mack, Sept. 4, 1993; children: John Currie, Brigget Currie. BSME Cogswell Engrng. Coll., 1955; MBA Stanford U., 1979. Project engr. Heat & Control Co., San Francisco, 1955-59; chief applications engr., then market mgr. Wesix Electric Heater Co., San Francisco, 1959-65; account mgr. Fisher Controls, San Francisco, 1965-76; market and sales mgr. TRW Mission, Houston, 1976-80; v.p. mktg.-sales Houston Heat Exchange, 1980-82; mktg. mgr. Anderson, Greenwood & Co., 1982—; sr. partner Affiliated Products Inc.; pres. DeWree Enterprises, DeWree Rental Properties; ptnr., dir. Constrn. Info. Services, Cismap, TVMP; sr. v.p. Indsl. Market Rsch.; dir. Creative Capers, San Francisco and Houston. Mem. Belmont (Calif.) Personnel Bd., 1965; com. chmn. Boy Scouts Am., 1970; elected to bd. dirs. Cypress Forest Pub. Utility Dist. of Harris County, Tex., 1981, 83, 85, 86-90, 92-96, Harris County Regional Water Supply; pres. Water Bd. Served to capt., arty. U.S. Army, 1951-53; Korea. Named Outstanding Jaycee of Yr., 1966. Mem. Am. Mgmt. Assn., Am. Nuclear Soc., Valve Mfg. Assn., Instrument Soc. Am. (sr.), Assn. Water Bd. Dirs., Water Pollution Control Fedn., Sales and Mktg. Execs., Housing Econ. and Scientific Soc., KC (3d degree, dep. Grand Knight, 4th degree trustee), Inner Circle, Houston Engrng. and Sci. Soc. Republican. Roman Catholic. Clubs: Pine Forest Country, Plaza; Engrs. (San Francisco). Home and Office: Unit # 110 13231 Champion Forest Dr Houston TX 77069-2600

DEWS, CARLOS LEE, English language educator, writer; b. Nacogdoches, Tex., Sept. 26, 1963. BA, U. Tex., 1987; MA, U. Minn., 1992, PhD, 1994. Prof. Am. lit. U. West Fla., Pensacola, 1994—. Office: U West Fla Dept English 11000 University Pky Pensacola FL 32514

DEXTER, DEIRDRE O'NEIL ELIZABETH, lawyer; b. Stillwater, Okla., Apr. 15, 1956; d. Robert N. and Paula E. (Robinson) Maddox; m. Terry E. Dexter, May 14, 1977; children: Daniel M. II, David Maddox. Student, Okla. State U., 1974-77; BS cum laude, Phillips U., 1981; JD with highest honors, U. Okla., 1984. Bar: Okla., U.S. Dist. Ct. (no. and ea. dists.) Okla. 1985, U.S. Dist. Ct. (we. dist.) Okla. 1987, U.S. Ct. Appeals (10th cir.) 1987; grad. Nat. Inst. Trial Advocacy Advanced Trial seminar, 1990. Jud. intern Supreme Ct. Okla., Oklahoma City, summer 1983; assoc. Conner & Winters, Tulsa, 1984-90, ptnr., 1991, shareholder, 1991—. Article editor Okla. U. Law Rev., 1982-84. U. Okla. scholar, 1983. Mem. ABA, Okla. Bar Assn. (advising atty. state champion H.S. mock trial team competition 1992), Tulsa County Bar Assn., Order of Barristers, Order of Coif, Am. Inns of Ct. (barrister), Delta Theta Phi. Republican. Episcopalian. Office: Conner & Winters 2400 First Place Tower 15 E 5th St Tulsa OK 74103

DEXTER, HELEN LOUISE, dermatologist, consultant; b. Cin., July 28, 1908; d. William Jordan and Katherine (Weston) Taylor; AB, Bryn Mawr Coll., 1930; MD, Columbia U., 1937; postgrad. U. Cin. Coll. Medicine, 1948-50; m. Morrie W. Dexter, Jan. 27, 1937; children: Katharine, Helen Dexter Dalzell, Elizabeth Taylor, William Taylor. Intern, Jersey City Med. Center, 1938-39; internist Cin. Babies Milk Fund, Maternal Health Clinic, 1938-45; clinician U. Cin. Med. Sch., 1938-48, lectr. dept. dermatology, 1948-53; practice medicine specializing in dermatology, Clearwater, Fla., 1954—; dermatology cons. VA, 1955—; investigation of carcinogenic effects of shale oil U.S. Bur. Mines, Rifle, Colo., 1950. Mem. Clearwater Power Squadron Aux.; commr. Town of Belleair, 1980. Recipient Ina Clay trophy Intercollegiate Ski Champion, 1928-30. Mem. AMA, Soc. Investigation Dermatology, Am. Acad. Dermatology, S.E. Dermatol. Assn. (v.p. 1963-64), Fla. Dermatol. Soc. (pres. 1959), Fla. Soc. Dermatology (pres.), Noah Worcester Dermatol. Soc., Am. Archaeol. Soc., Pan-Am. Dermatol. Soc., Soc. Tropical Dermatology. Presbyterian. Club: Clearwater Yacht Carlouel Yacht. Contbr. articles to profl. jours. Address: 409 Bayview Dr Belleair FL 34616

DEYO, STEVE, small business owner, professional speaker; b. Columbus, Ohio, July 26, 1949; s. Harold McKinley and Martha Louise (Brown) D.; m. Graciela Olivia Guerrero, Feb. 15, 1975 (div. June m1994); children: Kevin, Robin, Stephen. BA, Miami U., 1971. Sales rep. Rocky Mountain Mktg., Denver, 1971-72; tax agt. Ohio Dept. of Taxation, Columbus, 1972-75; claims rep. Nationwide Ins., Atlanta, 1975-78; sales mgr. Azrock Industries, Atlanta, 1978-86; acct. exec. Mercer Plastics, Atlanta, 1986-87; acct. mgr. Computer Assocs., Atlanta, 1987-88; editor La Vista de Mexico, Atlanta, 1988—; founder Deyo Comm., Lilburn, 1991—; CEO Aventura Prodns., Duluth, Ga., 1994—. Mem. Internat. Platform Assn., Nat. Spkrs. Assn., Toastmasters Internat. (Gwinnett County pres. 1987-88, Outstanding Spkr. award 1985, 88), Beta Theta Pi. Republican. Roman Catholic. Home and Office: 740 Kenilworth Cir Ste 102 Heathrow FL 32746

DEYOUNG, BILLIE SCHAEFER, medical clinic administrator; b. Shreveport, La., Dec. 3, 1936; d. William Henry and Catherine (Russell) Schaefer; widowed; children, Dennis Ray, Denette D. Johnson. Student, La. State U., Shreveport, 1972. Cert. adminstrv. med. asst. Career registry sec. La. State U. Med. Ctr., Shreveport, 1956-60; adminstr. The Diagnostic Clinic, Shreveport, 1961-94; clinic mgr. Schumpert Internal Medicine Specialists, Shreveport, 1994—; clin. instr. La. Tech. U., Ruston, 1981—. Mem. Caddo-Bossier Med. Assts. (pres. 1964), Am. Assn. Med. Assts., La. State Assn. Med. Assts., La. Med. Group Mgmt. Assn., Shreveport C. of C. Office: Schumpert Internal Medcine 1534 Elizabeth St Shreveport LA 71101

DEZARN, GUY DAVID, English language educator; b. Corona, Calif., Nov. 15, 1956; s. Joseph Gordon and Mary Forbes (Bergman) DeZ.; m. Maryam Samad; children: Monique, Zahra. BA in English, George Mason U., 1981; JD cum laude, Am. U., 1995. Tchr. Congrl. Sch. Va., Falls Church, 1981-85, Alexandria City (Va.) Pub. Schs., 1985—; legal intern U.S. Pub. Interest Group, Washington, 1992-95, rschr., 1995—; adj. prof. Washington Coll. Law, 1996—; prof. legal studies No. Va. C.C., 1996—. Mentor tchr. Alexandria Pub. Schs., 1990-91; dir. Early Adolescent Helper Program Ctr. Advanced Studies in Group Edn,. 1992-93; founder And Clothing for All, Alexandria, 1988—. Home: 200 N Pickett St Alexandria VA 22304-2120 Office: Alexandria City Pub Schs 5700 Sanger Ave Alexandria VA 22311-5602

DEZFULIAN, MANOUCHER, microbiology educator; m. Guity Dezfulian; children: Cameron, Kevin. BS in Pharmacy, Tehran U., 1959; MS in Microbiology, U. Ill., 1961; PhD in Bacteriology, U. Calif., Berkeley, 1966. Asst. prof. Pahlavi U., Shiraz, Iran, 1967-68; postdoctoral fellow Wistar Inst., Phila., 1968-69; from assoc. prof. to prof., chair microbiology, dir. Landmark Clin. Labs., Nat. U., Tehran, Iran, 1969-78; rsch. scientist CDC, Atlanta, 1978-80; rsch. scientist, mem. faculty Johns Hopkins U. Sch. Medicine, Balt., 1980-87; clin. microbiology scholar and rsch. cons. UCLA Med. Ctr./VA Wadsworth Med. Ctr., 1987-88; assoc. prof. microbiology Fla. Internat. U., Miami, 1988—. Contbr. numerous articles to profl. jours. U. Calif. scholar, U. Ill. scholar; fellow U. Pa.; rsch. awardee NIH, U.S. Army, Johns Hopkins Ctr. for Alternatives to Animal Testing, Fla. Internat. U., others. Mem. AAAS, Am. Soc. Clin. Pathologists, Am. Soc. for Microbiology. Office: Florida Internat Univ Dept Med Lab Sci College Of Health Miami FL 33199

D'GABRIEL, CARLOS LEONARDO, travel executive; b. Havana, Cuba, Mar. 10, 1930; came to U.S., 1955; s. Zeidel and Hana (Schneider) D'G.; m. Judith Lobel, June 24, 1950 (div. 1971); children: Alexander P., Michelle E. D'Gabriel Killian; m. Prudence Saig, Dec. 4, 1971. Grad., Ga. Mil. Acad., 1944. Mgr. Shipairland Travel, Havana, 1945-50; corp. exec. Skycoach Internat. Airline, N.Y.C., 1950-55; mgr. Pan Am. World Airways, N.Y.C., 1955-62; v.p. Cophresi Travel Bur. Corp., N.Y.C., 1962-68; pres. Carber Travel Bur. Inc., N.Y.C., 1968-70, Superior Travel Bur., Inc., Miami Beach, Fla., 1970-95; regional v.p. Fla. Superior Travel, Miami Beach, 1995—. Recipient Shalom award Israel Ministry of Tourism, 1977, Willy Prestergard Meml. award Travel Industry Assn. Fla., 1980, Great Am. Traditions award B'nai B'rith Found. of U.S., 1993. Mem. Am. Soc. Travel Agts. (v.p. 1982), Inst. Cert. Travel Counselors, Assn. Retail Travel Agts. (bd. dirs. 1969), Williams Island Club, Skal Club Internat. Republican. Jewish. Home: 3762 NE 167th St Miami FL 33160-3538 Office: Travelogue Inc 521 Lincoln Rd Miami Beach FL 33139-2913

DHARWADKER, APARNA, English studies educator; b. Jaipur, Rajasthan, India, June 14, 1955; came to U.s., 1981; d. Deoki Nandan and Sarla Bhargava; m. Vinay Dharwadker, July 10, 1976; children: Aneesha, Sachin. BA, U. Rajasthan, Jaipur, 1975; MA, U. Delhi, 1977; PhD, Pa. State U., 1990. English lectr. Hindu Coll. U. Delhi, 1977-81; English lectr. U. Ill., Chgo., 1987-89; English instr. U. Ga., Athens, 1989-91; asst. prof. English U. Okla., Norman, 1991—. Translator Tri-Quar. Jour., 1990, New Eng. Rev., 1985, Chgo. Rev., 1992; contbr. articles to profl. jours. Fellow Folger Shakespeare Libr., 1984, Newberry Libr., 1988; grantee Okla. Found. for the Humanities, 1993, U. Okla., 1992-95. Mem. MLA, Am. Soc. for Eigtheenth-Century Studies. Office: U Okla Dept English Gittinger Hall # 113 Norman OK 73019

DHOOPER, SURJIT SINGH, social work educator; b. Kartarpur, Punjab, India, May 8, 1934; s. Bachint Singh and Kartar Kaur (Wasson) D.; m. Harpal Kaur Dhooper; children: Amrit Kaur, Devinder Singh, Manjot Kaur, Nimrat Kaur. MA in Polit. Sci., Agra U., India, 1961; MSW, Delhi U., India, 1963; PhD, Case Western Res. U., 1982. Social work supr. Cleve. Metro Gen. Hosp., Cleve.; sr. lectr. Visva Bharati U., Shantiniketan, India; edn. officer Delhi Maternity Hosp., New Delhi; prof. social work U. Ky., Lexington. Author: (books) Social Work and Transplantation of Human Organs, 1994, Social Work in Health Care in the 21st Century, 1996; editor Asian Am. Social Work Educators Newsletter; mem. editl. bd. Jour. Social Work Edn., Health and Social Work, Jour. Gerontol. Social Work, Araté, Adult Residential Care Jour.; book reviewer. Mem. NASW, Ky. Assn. Social Work Educators, Coun. Social Work Edn. Home: 660 Halifax Dr Lexington KY 40503-4227

DHOPLE, ARVIND MADHAV, microbiologist; b. Ankola, Canara, India, June 13, 1937; came to U.S., 1969; s. Madhav Keshav and Kamala Madhav (Savitri) D.;m. Padmini Arvind, Dec. 26, 1966; children: Anita, Anil. BSc, U. Bombay, 1957, MSc, 1959, PhD, 1963. Rsch. asst. Acworth Leprosy Hosp., Bombay, 1962-63; post-doctoral fellow Johns Hopkins U., Balt., 1963-66; rsch. officer Cen. Leprosy Rsch. Inst., Chinglepu, India, 1966-69; rsch. assoc. Johns Hopkins U., Balt., 1970-75, asst. prof., 1975-80; rsch. prof. Fla. Inst. Tech., Melbourne, 1980—; vis. prof. Japan Soc. for Promotion of Rsch., Kurume, Japan, 1977, Chinese Acad. Med. Scis., Nanjing, People's Republic China, 1985. Contbr. articles to sci. jours. Mem. City of Satellite Beach (Fla.) Comprehensive Planning, 1988—; sec. troop 301 Boy Scouts Am., Satellite Beach, 1986—; mem. Brevard County Sch. Adv. Com., Satellite Beach, 1983—. Mem. Internat. Leprosy Assn., Am. Soc. for Microbiology, Indian Leprosy Assn., Chinese Acad. Med. Scis. (hon.), Fla. Acad. Scis., Sigma Xi. Home: PO Box 372274 Melbourne FL 32937-0274 Office: Fla Inst Tech 150 W University Blvd Melbourne FL 32901-6982

DIAMOND, DAVID ARTHUR, manufacturing company executive; b. Miami Beach, Fla., July 15, 1960; s. Harvey Jerome and Betty Lou (Ball) D.; m. Deborah Heiens, May 26, 1986. BA cum laude, U. Miami, 1982, MBA, 1984; JD, U. N.C., 1986. Bar: N.Y. 1986. Trust officer Morgan Guaranty Trust Co. N.Y., N.Y.C., 1986-89; trust officer, v.p. J.P. Morgan Fla., Palm Beach, Fla., 1989-96; pres. Plasti-Vac, Inc., Charlotte, N.C., 1996—. Pres. bd. dirs. Easter Seals of Palm Beach County, West Palm Beach, Fla. Mem. ABA, Fla. Bankers Assn. (trust and comm. com.), East Coast Estate Planning Coun. Office: Plasti-Vac Inc 214 Dalton Ave Charlotte NC 28206

DIAMOND, HARVEY JEROME, machinery manufacturing company executive; b. Charlotte, N.C., Dec. 7, 1928; s. Harry B. and Jeanette (Davis) D.; m. Betty L. Ball, May 22, 1953 (dec. Nov. 1988); children: Michael, Beth, David Abby; m. Miriam Letey, 1989. BS, U. N.C., 1952. Sales mgr. Dixie Neon Supply House, Charlotte, 1950-61; pres., gen. mgr., chmn. bd., CEO Plasti-Vac, Inc., Charlotte, 1961—; pres., gen. mgr. Diamond Supply, Inc., 1971-84, chmn. bd. dirs., 1984—; pres. Plastic Prodn., Inc., 1973—, PVI Internat. Corp., 1980—; mem. dist. export coun. Dept. Commerce, 1979-93; del. White House Conf. on small Bus., 1980; bd. dirs. U.S. Free Trade Zone No. 57, 1983. Author: (manual) Introduction to Vacuum Forming, 1976; patentee inverted clamping frame system for vacuum forming machines, process of vacuum forming plastics with vertical oven. Chmn. Mecklenburg Dem. Party, 1974-75, treas., 1972-74; del. Dem. Nat. Conv., 1972; bd. advisors Pfeiffer Coll., Misenheimer, N.C., 1977-89; participant White House conf. on Small Bus., 1978, White House Conf. on Anti-Inflation Initiatives, 1978; bd. dirs. U.S. Com. for Sports in Israel, 1993—. Recipient award for Activity in U.S. Trade Mission to S.Am., Dept. Commerce, 1967, March of Dimes award, 1966, Excellence in Exporting award N.C. Trade Club, 1981. Mem. Soc. Plastics Engrs., Soc. Plastics Industries, So. States Sign Assn. (bd. dirs. 1983-87), Southeastern States Sign Assn. (bd. dirs. 1991), Nat. Electric Sign Assn., Metrolina World Trade Assn. (v.p. 1982-83), Metrolina World Trade Club (pres. 1983-84), N.C. World Trade Assn. (bd. dirs. 1983-86, gen. chmn. ann. conv. 1984), Masons, Shriners. Jewish. Home: 9400 White Hemlock Ln Charlotte NC 28270-4403 Office: PO Box 5543 Charlotte NC 28225-5543

DIAMOND, PAUL CRAIG, family practice physician; b. Bklyn., Nov. 16, 1949; s. Louis and Pearl (Goldberg) D.; married 1979; 3 children. AB in Biol. Sci., Rutgers U., 1971; DO, Coll. Osteo. Med. and Surgery, Des Moines, 1976. Diplomate Am. Bd. Family Practice; cert. Nat. Bd. Osteo. Examiners. Intern Zeiger/Botsford Hosps., Detroit, 1976-77; resident in family practice Wayne State U., Harper Hosp., Detroit, 1977-80; pvt. practice Shelby, Mich., 1980-81, Boca Raton, Fla., 1982—; bd. dirs. So. Fla. Healthcare Assocs., Boca Raton; team physician U.S. Swimming, 1987—. Reviewer Patient Care jour., 1986—. Fellow Am. Acad. Family Physicians; mem. Am. Osteo. Assn., Am. Heart Assn., Am. Osteo. Acad. Sports Medicine, Am. Coll. Osteo. Gen. Practitioners, Fla. Acad. Family Physicians, Fla. Osteo. Med. Assn. Office: West Boca Family Care Ctr 9960 Central Park Blvd N Boca Raton FL 33428-1759

DIANA, JOHN NICHOLAS, physiologist; b. Lake Placid, N.Y., Dec. 19, 1930; s. Alphonse Walton and Dolores (Mirto) D.; m. Anita Louise Harris, May 8, 1966; children: Gina Sue, Lisa Ann, John Nicholas. B.A., Norwich U., 1952; Ph.D., U. Louisville, 1965. Asst. prof. physiology Mich. State U. Med. Sch., 1966-68; assoc. prof., then prof. U. Iowa Med. Sch., 1969-78; prof. physiology, chmn. dept. La. State U. Med. Center, Shreveport, 1978-85; dir. cardiovascular research ctr. U. Ky., 1985-87, assoc. dean research and basic sci., 1987-88; dir. T&H Rsch. Inst., 1988—; cons. Nat. Inst. Neurol. Diseases and Stroke, 1973-75, Nat. Heart, Lung and Blood Inst., 1974—, mem. cardiovascular and renal study sect., 1980-85, mem. clin. scis. study sect., 1986-91, chmn. 1989-91; rsch. com. Iowa Heart Assn., 1974-77, bd. dirs., 1977-79; mem. cardiovascular study sect. Am. Heart Assn., 1981-84. Author papers, abstracts in field. Served with AUS, 1952-54; Served with USAR, 1961-62. NIH postdoctoral fellow, 1965-67. Mem. Am. Fedn. Clin. Research, Am. Physiol. Soc. (editorial bd. jour. 1974-78), Microcirculation Soc. (pres. 1977-78, editorial bd. jour. 1979-85), Am. Heart Assn. (fellow council circulation), N.Y. Acad. Scis., La. Heart Assn. (dir. 1979-81, research com. 1978-82), Sigma Xi. Democrat. Home: 3656 Eleuthera Ct Lexington KY 40509-9525 Office: U Ky Coll Medicine Dean's Office 900 Rose St Rm MN140D Lexington KY 40546

DIAZ, GUSTAVO ADOLFO, computer integrated manufacturing engineer; b. Barranquilla, Colombia, Feb. 4, 1951; came to U.S., 1978; s. Odilon and Gladys (Poveda) D.; m. Anabelle Rudin, Dec. 7, 1978; 1 child, Ana-Laura. BSChemE, U. Costa Rica, San Jose, 1972, BS in Indsl. Engring., MS in MIS, 1974; MS in Indsl. Engrng. and Ops. Rsch., Pa. State U., 1980, MA in Applied Math., 1982. Simulation engr. Systems Modeling Corp., State College, Pa., 1980-87; mgr. expert sys. Am. Express Travel-Related Svcs. Co., Plantation, Fla., 1989-93; sr. indsl. engr. Racal-Datacom Corp., Sunrise, Fla., 1987-89, mgr. computer integrated mfg., 1993—; adj. instr. math. Pa. State U., University Park, 1982-87; adj. instr. indsl. engring. U. Miami, Fla., 1992-93; adj. instr. bus. Nova U., Davie, Fla., 1993-84, dir. master quality and tech., 1993-94; session chmn. 1993 Winter Simulation Conf., L.A., 1993. Editor: Simulation Practice Using Siman, 1981. Vice pres. West Pine Mid. Sch. PTA, Sunrise, 1993-94. Mem. Inst. Indsl. Engrs. (sr., pres. Ft. Lauderdale 1992-93, bd. dirs. 1993-94), Ops. Rsch. Soc. Am./The Inst. Mgmt. Sci. Office: Racal-Datacom Corp H-225 1601 Harrison Pky Sunrise FL 33323-2802

DIAZ, RAFAEL JOSÉ, electrical engineer, communications engineer, consultant; b. San Juan de los Morros, Venezuela, Oct. 25, 1956; came to U.S., 1984; s. Rafael E. Diaz-Garcia and Olga C. (Nieves-Croes) Diaz; m. Alba M. Aleman, Mar. 23, 1990. Grad. in Electronics Engring., U. Simon Bolivar, Caracas, Venezuela, 1980; MEE, George Washington U., 1985, PhD in Elec. Engring., 1994. Sr. engr. Venezuelan Comm. Div., Caracas, 1980-83; rsch. asst. Cybercom Corp., Arlington, Va., 1986-88; mem. tech. staff GTE Lab./Contel Tech. Ctr., Chantilly, Va., 1990-91; grad. teaching asst. George Washington U., Washington, 1985-91; dir. RF planning and tech. strategy EON Corp., Reston, Va., 1992-96; v.p. tech. strategy AirLink Tech., Inc., Chantilly, Va., 1996—; cons. Pan Am. Health Orgn., Washington, 1989, Qualcomm, Washington, 1991. Editor Interactive Source newsletter, 1992—. Treas. Bolivarian Soc., Washington, 1989-91; mem. Latin Am. Student Assn., Washington, 1988-89, Casa Cuba, Arlington, Va., 1990—. Recipient scholarship Guarico State, Venezuela, 1975, Fundacion Gran Mariscal de Ayacucho, Venezuela, 1983. Mem. IEEE, AAAS, Assn. for Computing Machinery, Colegio de Ingenieros de Venezuela, Phi Beta Delta. Home: 14703 Virginia Infantry Rd Centreville VA 20120-2592 Office: EON Corp 1941 Roland Clarke Pl Reston VA 22091-1405

DIAZ, RAUL, psychologist; b. Phila., Aug. 23, 1957; s. Raul and Ofelia (Perez) D.; m. Connie M. Parsons, Jan. 17, 1957; children: Benjamin R., Samuel Alan, Natalie Lynn. BS, U. Fla., 1979; MA, Bowling Green (Ohio) State U., 1983, PhD, 1985. Lic. psychologist, Fla.; registered Nat. Register Health Svc. Providers in Psychology. Clin. psychology intern U. South Fla., Tampa, 1984-85; dir. psychol. svcs. Lake Hosp. of the Palm Beaches, Lake Worth, Fla., 1985-89; clin. leader adult psychiat. unit Humana Hosp.—Palm Beaches, West Palm Beach, Fla., 1989-90; pres., co-dir. Woodlake Psychol. Assocs., P.A., Greenacres, Fla., 1990—; psychol. cons. to various police depts. including Office of Palm Beach County Sheriff, West Palm Beach, 1989—; area clinician Drug Enforcement Adminstrn. U.S. Dept. Justice, Employee Assistance Program, 1994—. Named Hijo Predilecto, Municipio de Candelaria, 1989. Mem. APA (divsns. Am. psychology-law soc., psychologists in pub. svc. police and pub. safety sect., divsn. clin. neuropsychology, divsn. psychologists in ind. practice and divsn. of psychotherapy), Fla. Psychol. Assn. (neuropsychol. interest divsn.), Coun. Police Psychol. Svcs. Office: Woodlake Psychol Assocs PA 3900 Woodlake Blvd Ste 211 Greenacres FL 33463-3045

DIAZ-ARRASTIA, GEORGE RAVELO, lawyer; b. Havana, Cuba, Aug. 20, 1959; came to U.S., 1968; s. Ramon Fuentes and Elihut (Ravelo) D.-A.; m. Maria del Carmen Gomez, Aug. 6, 1983. BA in History, Rice U., 1980; JD, U. Chgo., 1983. Bar: Tex. 1983, U.S. Dist. Ct. (so. dist.) Tex. 1985, U.S. Ct. Appeals (5th and D.C. cirs.) 1985, U.S. Supreme Ct. 1992, U.S. Dist. Ct. (no., we. and ea. dists.) Tex. 1994. Assoc. Baker & Botts, Houston, 1983-88, Deaton & Briggs (formerly Deaton, Briggs & McCain), Houston, 1988-90; ptnr. Gilpin, Paxson & Bersch, Houston, 1991—. Fellow Tex. Bar Found., Houston Bar Found.; mem. ABA, Am. Judicature Soc., Am. Soc. Internat. Law, State Bar of Tex., Houston Bar Assn. Republican. Roman Catholic. Home: 3794 Drake St Houston TX 77005-1118 Office: Gilpin Paxson & Bersch 1900 West Loop S Ste 2000 Houston TX 77027-3208

DIAZ-BALART, LINCOLN, congressman; b. Havana, Cuba, Aug. 13, 1954; m. Cristina Fernandez; children: Lincoln Gabriel, Daniel. BA in Internat. Rels., New Coll. of U. So. Fla., 1976; diploma in Brit. Politics, Cambridge U.; JD, Case Western Reserve U., 1979. Lawyer Legal Svcs. of Greater Miami, Fla.; pros. atty. State of Fla.; mem. Fla. Ho. of Reps.from 110th Dist., 1986-89, Fla. State Senate from Dist. 34, 1989-92, 103d Congress from 21st Fla. Dist., 1993—; mem. hpuse oversight com., rules com., chmn. task force on Latin Am. and Caribbean affairs, Rep. rsch. com. Mem. Dade County Assn. Retarded Citizens, Reps. of Fla.; exec. com. Congl. Human Rights Caucus; vice chmn. Nat. Rep. Congl. Com. Mem. ABA, Fla. Bar Assn., Dade County Bar Assn., Cuban-Am. Bar Assn., Rep. Nat. Lawyers Assn., Lions. Republican. Roman Catholic. Office: US Ho of Reps Office of Ho Mems 431 Cannon Washington DC 20515

DÍAZ DE GONZALEZ, ANA MARÍA, psychologist, educator; b. San Juan, P.R., July 26, 1945; d. Esteban Díaz-González and Petra (Guadalupe) De Díaz; m. Jorge Gonzalez Monclova, Jan. 7, 1968; children: Ana Teresa, Jorge, Julio Esteban. BS, U. P.R., Río Piedras, 1965, MEd, 1973; MS, Caribbean Ctr. Advanced Study, San Juan, 1982, PhD, 1983. Lic. psychologist, P.R. Home economist U. P.R., Fajardo and San Juan, 1965-82; specialist in human devel. and gerontology U. P.R., San Juan, 1983—. Mem. APA, Assn. Economists Hogar (pres. 1965-92, Disting. Svc. award 1973), Assn. Specialists SEA (pres. 1982-93), Assn. Psychology P.R., Epsilon Sigma Phi (sec. 1970—), Gamma Sigma Delta. Roman Catholic. Home: 1325 Calle 23 San Juan PR 00924-5249 Office: U PR Svc Extension Agr Terrenos Estacion Exptl Río Piedras San Juan PR 00928

DÍAZ SALDAÑA, MANUEL, Puerto Rican government official; b. San Juan, Puerto Rico, Jan. 10, 1949; s. José J. Díaz and Josefina Saldaña; me. Elba E. Negrón, July 17, 1970; children: Francisco Díaz-Negrón, Elba M. Díaz-Negrón, Gabriel Díaz-Negrón. BS in Bus. Adminstrn., U. P.R., Río Piedras, 1970. Auditor Arthur Andersen & Co., Hato Rey, P.R., 1970-72; internal auditor Empresas García Comml., Río Piedras, 1972-73; auditor, field supr. Peat Marwick & Co., Hato Rey, 1973-74; audit supr. Pedro Galarza & Co., Hato Rey, 1974-75; ptnr. Díaz Saldaña, Rivera Marrero & Co., Hato Rey, 1978-92; sec. treasury Treasury Dept., San Juan, 1996—; pres. fin. bd. Govt. Retirement Sys.; pres. bd. dirs. Govtl. Devel. Bank; pres. P.R. Soc. CPAs, 1984-85. Office: Dept of Treasury PO Box 9024140 San Juan PR 00902-4140

DIAZ-VERSON, SALVADOR, JR., investment advisor; b. Havana, Cuba, Dec. 31, 1951; s. Salvador and Metodia Diaz-V.; m. Patricia Dianne Floyd, Apr. 24, 1976; children: Salvador III, Patricia Elizabeth. BA in Fin., Fla. State U., Tallahassee, 1973. Chief investment officer Am. Family Life Assurance, Columbus, Ga., 1977-79; exec. v.p. Am. Family Corp., Columbus, 1980-83, pres., 1983-91, also dir.; pres. Diaz-Verson Capital Investment, 1991—; bd. dirs. Columbus Bank and Trust, Total System Svcs., Synouous Fin., Clemente Capital; pres., CEO Diaz-Verson Capital Investment Inc., 1992. Trsutee St. Francis Hosp., Fund Am. Studies; bd. dirs. United Way, Columbus, 1983—. Mem. Columbus C. of C. (bd. dirs. 1983—, chair 1989), Green Island Country Club, Country Club of Columbus. Roman Catholic. Office: Diaz-Verson Capital Investment Ste 105 1200 Brookstone Centre Pky Columbus GA 31904-2954

DIBLASI, PHILIP JAMES, archaeologist; b. Syracuse, N.Y., May 6, 1954; s. Philip A. and Ann Marie (Gorczyca) D.; m. Jan Marie Hemberger, June 12, 1992. BA, U. Louisville, 1976, MS, 1981. Staff archaeologist U. Louisville, 1982—; adj. curator Louisville Mus. History and Sci., 1979—, Portland Mus., Louisville, 1982—; cons. Filson Club Mus., Louisville, 1982-86, U. Louisville Alumni Assn. Author ann. report, 1984, newsletter, 1985; co-editor Procs. of Ohio Valley Urban and History Archaeology, 1984-89; contbr. articles to profl. jours. Bd. dirs. Cave Rsch. Found., 1994—; pres., mem. Hist. Preservation Commn. Jefferson Co., Ky.; pres. Cave Rsch. Found. Mem. Am. Assn. Phys. Anthropologists, Nat. Speological Soc. (life), Ky. Orgn. Profl. Archaeologists, Am. Cave Conservation Assn., Assn. Field Archaeology, Soc. Am. Archaeologists, Soc. Hist. Archaeology, S.E. Archeol. Conf. (life), Tenn. Anthrop. Assn. (life). Office: U Louisville Dept Archaeology Louisville KY 40292

DICARLO, SUSANNE HELEN, financial analyst; b. Greensburg, Pa., Nov. 24, 1956; d. Wayne Larry and Clara Emogene (Weaver) Gower; m. John Joseph DiCarlo, June 21, 1980; children: Sarah Rose, Kristen Marie. BS in Acctg., Va. Poly. Inst. and State U., 1978. Auditor U.S. Army Audit Agy., Ft. Monroe, Va., 1978-79; acct. technician Fleet Combat Tng. Ctr., Virginia Beach, Va., 1980-82, supervisory auditor, 1982-83; fin. analyst Comml. Activity Mgmt. Team, Norfolk, Va., 1983—; fed. women's program mgr. Fleet Combat Tng. Ctr., 1980-83. Creator newsletter Fed. Women's Program Manager, 1980-83. Mem. Am. Soc. Mil. Comptrollers. Club: Seaside Mountaineers (Va. Beach) (treas. 1986-88). Home: 4013 Dillaway Ct Virginia Beach VA 23456-1257

DICE, BRUCE BURTON, retired exploration company executive; b. Grand Rapids, Mich., Dec. 24, 1926; s. William and Wilma (Rose) D.; children: Karen, Kevin, Kirk. BS in Geology, U. Mich., 1950; MS in Geology, Mich. State U., 1956. With El Paso Natural Gas, 1956-62, Drilling and Exploration Co., 1962-63, Ocean Drilling and Exploration, New Orleans, 1963-75; pres. Transco Exploration Co., Houston, 1975-82, Dice Exploration Co., Inc., Houston, 1982-95; ret., 1995; cons. in field. Mem. Republican Com., Houston; active Houston Symphony, Sante Fe Opera, Shepherd Soc. at Rice U., Carmel Music Soc. Mem. Am. Assn. Petroleum Geologists, Houston Geol. Soc., Forum Club (Houston). Home: 1907 Grand Valley Dr Houston TX 77090-1052 Office: Wadi Petroleum Inc 14405 Walters Rd Houston TX 77014-1337 also: PO Box 73507 Houston TX 77273-3507

DICHARRY, JAMES PAUL, company official, retired air force officer; b. Burnside, La., June 29, 1953; s. Donald Joseph Sr. Dicharry and Rae Marie (Bourgeois) Dicharry-Tuttle; m. Debra Ann Hoagland, May 27, 1971 (div. Aug. 1973); 1 child, Eric Raymond; m. Betty May Hare, June 21, 1975; children: Charlotte Rene, Douglas Paul. BA cum laude in Acctg., Tex. Luth. Coll., 1978; MMA in Bus., Troy State U., 1985. Enlisted man USAF, 1973-79, commd. 2d lt., 1979, advanced through grades to maj., 1990; pers. specialist 27th Combat Support Group, Cannon AFB, N.Mex., 1973-75; pers. specialist hdqs. mil. pers. ctr. USAF, San Antonio, 1975-79, budget officer hdqs. officer tng. sch., 1979-81, budget analyst hdqs. air tng. command, 1981-82; chief budget br. 32d Tactical Fighter Squadron, The Netherlands, 1982-84; chief cost and mgmt. analysis br. USAF, The Netherlands, 1984-85; intern banker devel. United Bank Denver, 1985-86; air staff banking officer hdqs. acctg. and fin. ctr. USAF, Denver, 1986-87, exec. to commdr. acctg. and fin. ctr., 1987-89; fin. analyst Army and Air Force Exch. Svc., Dallas, 1989-93; ret., 1993; mgr. cash mgmt. dept. FootAction USA, 1993-94; pres. South Pork Ranch Miniatures, De Soto, Tex., 1993-95; owner, operator Southpork Ranch; v.p. Tint 'n More, Inc., Joplin, Mo., 1995—; past mem. and vice chmn. bd. dirs. Space Age Fed. Credit Union, Denver. Drive adminstr. South Tex. Regional Blood Bank, San Antonio, 1981; asst. coach, coach various recreation depts., The Netherlands, Aurora, Colo., De Soto, 1983-92; asst. scoutmaster Boy Scouts Am., Aurora, Duncanville, Tex., 1985-91. Named one of Outstanding Young Men of Am., Jaycees, 1989. Mem. Am. Legion, Rotary Internat. Home: 2012 S Jackson Ave Joplin MO 64804 Office: 300 N Main Miami OK 74354 also: 2230 Main Joplin MO 64804

DICK, JAMES CORDELL, concert pianist; b. Hutchinson, Kans., June 29, 1940; s. George Gerhard and Dorothy Lois (Ulsh) D. 1958-63; Studied with, Dalies Frantz; MusB with spl. honors, U. Tex., 1963; studied with Sir Clifford Curzon, 1963-65; postgrad., Royal Acad. Music, London, 1963-65. Concert pianist Sol Hurok Presents, N.Y.C., 1968-70, Shaw Concerts, N.Y.C., 1970-75, Columbia Artists, N.Y.C., 1975-89, A.G. Declert and Assocs., Round Top, Tex., 1989—; founder, artistic dir. Internat. Festival-Inst., Round Top, 1971—; judge internat. recording competition Nat. Guild Piano Tchrs., 1970-71; nat. cons. music com. Inst. Internat. Edn., N.Y.C., 1971-72; mem. internat. jury Tschaikovsky Competition, Moscow, 1974, Van Cliburn Competition, Ft. Worth, 1975, 78; chmn. Fulbright Panel in Music, N.Y.C., 1978. Commd. (Am. piano concerto) Shiva's Drum, (nominated Pulitzer Prize in music), 1994. Recipient First Prize award Shreveport Symphony Competition, 1958-60, San Angelo Symphony Competition, 1958-60, Dallas Symphony, 1961-62, Nat. Guild Piano Tchrs., 1961-62, Tschaikovsky Internat. Competition, 1965-66, Leventritt Piano Competition, 1965-66, Busoni Internat. Piano Competition, 1965-66, Citation cert. Tex. Ho. Reps., 1975, award Japan Soc. Houston, 1975, Presdl. citation Nat. Fedn. Music Clubs, 1979, Round Top award Gov. William. P. Clements, Tex., 1980, Headliner of Yr. award Headliners Club, 1983; honoree Pres. Lyndon B. Johnson, 1965-66; nominee Pulitzer Prize in Music, 1974; commd. Ambassador of Goodwill, State of Tex., 1978; named Hon. Texan, Gov. Dolph Briscoe, 1978, Chevalier des Arts et Lettres French Ministry Culture, 1994; Fulbright scholar, Tobias Matthay fellow, Royal Acad. Music, Hon assoc., 1969, recipient Merit cert., 1965, Beethoven prize, Recital medal, Chevalier des Arts et Lettres, French Ministry of Cult., 1994. Mem. English Speaking Union, Philos. Soc. Tex. (treas. 1976—), Tex. Fedn. Music Clubs (hon. life), Tex. Lyceum Assn. (adv. dir. 1978—), Tuesday Mus. Club (hon.), Rotary Internat. (hon. life), Bohemians Club (N.Y.C.). Office: Festival Hill Hwy 237 and Jaster Rd Round Top TX 78954

DICKENS, CHARLES ALLEN, petroleum company executive; b. Mount Gilead, N.C., Nov. 26, 1932; s. Alonzo Newton and Elizabeth Ann (Haywood) D.; BS, N.C. State U., 1954; m. Helen Theresia Baudendistel, Jan. 4, 1958; children: Karen Ann, Constance Lynn, Pamela Jean, Kimberly Susan. Asst. chem. engr., chem. engr., sr. chem. engr., project chem. engr. Texaco, Inc., Beacon, N.Y., Port Arthur, Tex., 1954-63, sr. engr., London, 1963-65, project engr., Brussels, 1965-67, mgr. additive sales, Brussels, 1967-69, asst. sales mgr., additive div., Chgo., 1969-72, Houston, 1972-84, v.p. mktg. and tech. South Coast Terminals Inc., Houston, 1984-96, cons., 1996—; ptnr. Chearlens Assocs., 1996—. Served with USAF, 1955-57. Fellow British Inst. Petroleum; mem. Am. Inst. Chem. Engrs., Am. Soc. Lubrication Engrs., Am. Mgmt. Assn., Soc. Automotive Engrs., Scabbard & Blade, Sigma Xi, Tau Beta Pi. Republican. Club: Westador Residents.

DICKENS, CHARLES HENDERSON, retired social scientist, consultant; b. Thomasville, N.C., Nov. 22, 1934; s. Argie Marshall and Edna (Sullivan) D.; m. Jane McClung, Aug. 27, 1965; children: Martha Jane, Anne Elizabeth. BS, Duke U., 1957, MEd, 1964, ED, 1966. Asst. prof. Wake Forest U., Winston-Salem, N.C., 1965-67; planning specialist NSF, Washington, 1967-69, assoc. program dir. undergrad. instrnl. studies group, 1969-73, study dir. sci. edn. studies group, 1973-83, sect. head scientific and tech. pers. studies sect., 1983-86, sect. head surveys and analysis sect., 1986-90; sr. policy analyst Fed. Coordinating Coun. for Sci., Engring., and Tech., Washington, 1990-92, exec. sec., 1992-93, ret., 1993; mem. adv. bd. Am. Men and Women of Sci., New Providence, N.J., 1991—, C.C. Cameron Applied Rsch. Ctr. U. N.C., Charlotte, 1994—. With U.S. Army, 1958-59. Recipient Angier B. Duke prize Duke U., 1953-57; Woodrow Wilson fellowship Woodrow Wilson Fellowship Found., 1963, James B. Duke fellowship Duke U., 1963, 64. Mem. AAAS, Nat. Assn. Ret. Fed. Employees (mem. chpt. 156, v.p. 1995-96, pres. 1996-97), N.Y. Acad. Scis. Republican. Presbyterian. Home: One Arrow Pl Asheville NC 28805-9748

DICKENS, JUSTIN KIRK, nuclear physicist; b. Syracuse, N.Y., Nov. 2, 1931; s. Milton Clifford and Jennette Martin (Holmes) D.; m. Marcay Cosette Jordan, Dec. 21, 1957; children: Alan Russell, Leonard Raymond, Steven Kenneth, Michael Loren. AB in Physics, U. So. Calif., L.A., 1955, PhD in Physics, 1962; MS in Physics, U. Chgo., 1956. Engring. assoc. Collins Radio Co., Burbank, Calif., 1955; electronic technician Enrico Fermi Inst. for Nuclear Studies, Chgo., 1956-57; grad. teaching asst. U. So. Calif., L.A., 1957-61, rsch. assoc., 1961-62; rsch. staff mem. Oak Ridge (Tenn.) Nat. Lab., 1962-78, sr. rsch. staff mem., 1978-94; private cons., 1995; rsch. prof. physics U. Tenn., Knoxville, 1996—; gen. chmn. Internat. Conf. on Nuclear Data for Sci. and Tech., Gatlinburg, Tenn., 1994. Co-author (tech. standard) Am. Nat. Standard on Decay Heat; contbr. 200 articles to profl. jours. Bd. dirs. Oak Ridge Community Playhouse, 1972, 85. With U.S. Army, 1950-52. Mem. Am. Phys. Soc., Am. Nuclear Soc., Phi Beta Kappa, Sigma Xi. Office: Ctr of Exec Bldg 6010 Inst Heavy Ion Rsch MS 6354 Oak Ridge TN 37831-6354

DICKERSON, GEORGIE JULIAN, writer, artist; b. Greenville, S.C., Mar. 17, 1934; d. George Washington and Mamie Sue (Reeves) Julian; m. William T. Dickerson, May 11, 1952; children: Dan William, Joseph Scott, Jeffery David, Namie Sue White, Andrew Lee. BS in Edn., Lander U., Greenwood, S.C., 1971; MEd in Counseling, U. S.C., 1975. Cert. tchr., S.C. Tchr., counselor Spartanburg Dist. 7 Schs., Spartanburg Dist. # 3, Spartanburg, S.C., 1971-78, Spartanburg Dist. 7 Schs., Pacolet, S.C., 1978-82. Author: (children's books) Mouse, Potatoes, Kitty and Me, 1990, Kiss the Ears of a Horse, 1992; (poetry book) Trill the Blue Whistle, 1995, (book) The Haunting and Healing of Anna, 1994. Spartanburg Art Mus. Exhbn. County Fair, 1990-95. Mem. Spartanburg Artists Guild (1st pl. pastel portraits, several yrs., 90-95). Republican. Baptist. Home: 244 Chapman Rd Pacolet SC 29372

DICKERSON, JAMES L., writer, photographer, consultant; b. Greenwood, Miss., Sept. 14, 1945; s. James Luther and Emily Juanita (Turner) D.; divorced; 1 child, Jonathan Turner. BA, U. Miss., 1968. Reporter Delta Democrat-Times, Greenville, Miss., 1977, Greenwood (Miss.) Commonwealth, 1977-78, Tallahassee Democrat, 1978-79; editorial page editor Jackson (Miss.) Daily News, 1979-82; editorial writer The Comml. Appeal, Memphis, 1982-86; editor, pub. Nine-O-One Mag., Memphis, 1986-88; exec. prodr. Pulsebeat Prodns., Memphis, 1987-89; freelance writer, photographer Memphis, 1989—; book critic Toronto Star, Balt. Sun, 1974-75; columnist Facing South, 1977-78; panelist Nat. Entertainment Journalists Assn., 1987. Author: Coming Home: 21 Conversations about Memphis Music, 1986, (screenplay) Dazzle, 1993, Dark Remembrance, 1993, (with Rachel E. Dwyer) The Gambit, 1994, Goin' Back to Memphis, 1996, Country Music's Most Embarrassing Moments, 1996; contbr. short story Cimarron Rev., 1973, articles to mags., profl. jours., poetry to mags., anthologies. Recipient first place in editorial writing, AP, 1981.

DICKERSON, MARIE HARVISON, nurse anesthetist; b. Leaf, Miss., Oct. 14, 1946; d. Thurman C. and Mary C. (Jarrell) Harvison; m. George T. Dickerson, Sept. 2, 1978; children: George H., Kathryn Marie. AA, Jones County Jr. Coll., 1967; BS, U. Ottawa, Kansas City, Kans., 1976; MEd, U. S. Ala., 1978. RN; cert. registered nurse anesthetist. Oper. rm. supr. George County Hosp., Lucedale, Miss., 1967-70; dir. Sch. Anesthesia, Mobile, Ala., 1972-79; chief anesthesia Wayne Gen. Hosp., Waynesboro, Miss., 1979-84; pres. Wayne Anesthesia, P.A., Waynesboro, 1984—. Maj. USAR. Mem. ANA, Miss. Nurses Assn. (dist. pres. 1983), Am. Assn. for Counseling and Devel., Miss. Assn. Nurse Anesthetists (bd. dirs.), Miss Counseling Assn. Baptist. Club: Waynesboro Home and Garden. Avocations: piano; voice; computers; antiques. Home: 824 Pou Dr Waynesboro MS 39367-2532

DICKERSON, MILDRED THORNHILL, public school educator; b. Lynchburg, Va., Aug. 10, 1951; d. Norman Nemrod and Ruby (Brown) Thornhill. BS in Edn., Elizabeth City State U., 1973; postgrad., U. Va., 1974-82, U. Tex., 1986-87; M in Ednl. Adminstr., U. North Tex., 1994. Cert. tchr., Va., Tex. Tchr. Campbell County Pub. Sch., Rustburg, Va., 1973-84; leader recreation City Lynchburg, Va., 1976-77; tchr. Dallas Ind. Sch. Dist., 1984—; dir. Dealey After Sch. Tutoring Program. Officer NAACP, Campbell County, Va., 1980-84; sch. coord. March of Dimes; mem. Task Force Excellence in Edn., Richmond, 1982-84; charter mem. leadership edn. com. S.W. Edn. Devel. Labs., Austin, 1985-86; dir. youth dept. devel. programs Bethany Bapt. Ch., 1974-83; chaplain, tchr. Missionary Soc.-1st Bapt. Ch., Hamilton Park; adult leader Campbell County 4-H Clubs, 1973-83; appointee Tex. Edn. Agy. Grant Reader Rev. Com. Named Outstanding Young Woman Am., 1981. Mem. NEA, Classroom Tchrs. Dallas (minority affairs chair, black caucus chair, instrnl. and profl. devel. chair, v.p. region 19 exec. bd.), Va. Edn. Assn., Campbell County Edn. Assn. (pres. 1982-83), Tex. State Tchrs. Assn. (cert. trainer for profl. staff devel. 1984—, campus coord. Project Early Options, regional rep. to instrnl. advocacy com.), Elks, Zeta Phi Beta. Baptist. Home: 7222 Fair Oaks Ave Dallas TX 75231 Office: Dealey Montessori Academy 6501 Royal Ln Dallas TX 75230-4174

DICKERSON, MONAR STEPHEN, city official, newspaper reporter; b. El Reno, Okla., Jan. 26, 1947; s. Monar Frank and Grace Elizabeth (Hooper) D.; m. Jean Rollins, May 16, 1969; 1 child, Kelli Leigh. Student, Oklahoma City U., 1965-69, Miss. Gulfcoast Jr. Coll., 1973-74; BS in Psychology, U. So. Miss., 1990. Asst. news dir. WVMI/WQID Radio, Biloxi, Miss., 1973-74, ops. mgr., 1974-75; mgr. purchasing and inventory Nacol Jewelers, Biloxi, 1975-76; news anchor, reporter WLOX-TV, Biloxi, 1976-81; asst. to mayor City of Gulfport (Miss.), 1981-84; employee benefits specialist Stewart, Sneed, Hewes Inc., Gulfport, 1984-87; program specialist Area Agy. on Aging of So. Miss., Gulfport, 1987-90; bus. reporter Sun-Herald newspaper, Gulfport, 1990-93; asst. to mayor, pub. affairs mgr. City of Gulfport, 1993—. Vice chmn. Miss. March of Dimes, 1987-88, chmn. Magnolia div., 1984-90; bd. dirs. Long Beach Dixie Youth/Babe Ruth Baseball, 1986-88; pres. Harrison County Rep. Club, 1982-84; charter mem. strategic planning team Gulfport Sch. Dist., co-chair facilities planning com.; mem. devel. adv. com. U. So. Miss., Gulfport. With USAF, 1969-73. Named Alumni of Yr., 4-H Club, 1977, Vol. of Yr., March of Dimes, 1985, 86, 87. Mem. Gulf Coast C. of C. (youth svcs. com.), Hera Kings Club, Kiwanis. Methodist. Home: 16 Independence Dr Gulfport MS 39507-1944

DICKERSON, VERA M., artist, educator; b. July 28, 1946. BAF, Radford Coll., 1968; MFA in Painting, Am. U., 1970; studied with Charles Reid, 1975, studied with A.B. Jackson, 1977, studied with Daniel Green, 1986, studied with Katherine Liu, 1993. Teaching fellow Am. U., Washington, 1969; instr. in art Keuka Coll., Keuka, N.Y., 1970-72; asst. prof. art Va. Western Community Coll., Roanoke, Va., 1972-81, chmn. art dept., 1978-91; instr. Roanoke Mus. Fine Arts, 1974, 76, 79-80, 85-86; artist in residence Va. Mus., Richmond, Va., 1983-84; co-founder The Studio Sch., Roanoke, Va., 1990—; instr. in art Radford Coll., Radford, Va., spring, 1970, summer, 1971; instr. papermaking workshops Longwood Coll., Norfolk Acad., New River Fine Arts Ctr., Lynchburg Fine Arts Ctr., Roanoke City Schs., Roanoke Mus. Fine Arts, Va. Dept. Edn. Arts Tchrs. Workshop. One women shows include Danville Mus. of Art and History, 1976, 84, Roanoke Mus. Fine Arts, Va., 1976, Lynchburg Fine Arts Ctr., Va., 1978, William Dale Gallery, New Orleans, 1978, North Close Sch., Roanoke, Va., 1978, 84, Emory and Henry Coll., 1980; exhibited in group shows Va. Mus., Richmond, Va. (juror's choice 1976), Lauren Rodgers Meml., Laurel, Miss. (purchase award 1979), SECCA Drawing and Print Show, Winston-Salem, N.C., (purchase award 1973), Lynchburg Fine Arts Ctr., (best in show 1981, 82), Miller and Main Gallery, Blacksburg, Va., 1986, 94, Bath Regional Art Competition (best in show 1994); represented in permanent collections First Union Bank, Shenandoah Life Ins., Roanoke Mus. Fine Arts, Miller Brewing Co., Nations Bank, Bank of Va., Gannett Publishing Co., Marriott Inns, Clarion Hotels; published work includes (catalog) Over the Blue Ridge, 1981, More Than Land or Sky, 1981; (book) A Treasury of Southern Art and Literature, 1993. Grantee Va. Commn. for Art and Humanities, 1978. Home: 3232 W Arrowhead Ct Troutville VA 24175-3900 Office: The Studio Sch Jefferson Center 541 Luck Ave Roanoke VA 24016

DICKERSON, WILLIAM JOSEPH, bank executive; b. Flint, Mich., Mar. 20, 1927; s. Frank Lewis D.; m. Marianne L. Pierce, Sept. 17, 1951; children: Jerolyn, Angelique, William J. II, Dawn, Erin (dec.); m. Ardene Louise Maria Heim, Oct. 28, 1979. BS, BA, Kans. State U., 1955. With Security Pacific Nat. Bank, L.A., 1957-69; pres. Broadway Nat. Bank, Kansas City, 1969-74; chmn., pres. Capital City State Bank & Trust, Topeka, 1974-77, Northgate Nat. Bank, Hutchinson, Kans., 1978-81, First State Bank, Thayer, Kans., 1981-84; cons. Farmers Home Adminstrn., Southeast, Kans., 1985-86; pres., chief operating officer, CLO First Nat. Bank & Trust Co., Cushing, Okla., 1986-88; chmn., pres. First Nat. Bank, Pawhuska, Okla., 1989—; trustee Livestock Mktg. Inst., Kansas City, Mo., 1972-84; bd. dirs. First Nat. Bank, Pawhuska, Okla., 1989—. Dist. commdr. The Am. Legion, Manhattan, Kans.; advisory trustee U. Calif., Northridge, 1971-72; pres. Father's, Inc., Hutchinson, Kans., 1980; Sgt. USMC, 1942-47. Named Citizen of Yr. L.A. City Coun., 1972, Bd. of Suprs. L.A. County, 1973. Mem. Northridge C. of C. (pres. 1972, Businessman of Yr. 1970), Pawhuska C. of C. (chmn. bd. 1989-91), Rotary (Pawhuska chpt. pres. 1990-92), Kiwanis (pres. Northridge chpt. 1970-71, Man of Yr. 1973). Office: First Nat Bank PO Box 809 Pawhuska OK 74056

DICKERT, LINDA GOING, computer science educator; b. Asheville, N.C., Aug. 6, 1942; d. Harold and Wilma (Rathburn) Going; m. Kendall J. Dickert, Dec. 21, 1962; 1 child, Linda Delene. BA, U. S.C., 1964; MEd, Clemson U., 1975. Coord. Greenwood (S.C.) Heart Assn., 1977-78; sci. and math. instr. Emerald Jr. High Sch., Greenwood, 1978-82; profl. rep. Hoechst-Roussel Pharms., 1982-88; med. rep. Summit divsn. Ciba-Geigy Pharms., 1988-90; computer trainer Summit Pharms., Atlanta, 1988-90; computer instr. Lowcountry Tech. Coll., Beaufort, S.C., 1990—; cons. Lindata Computer Consultants, Beaufort, 1990—; computer specialist Beaufort Meml. Hosp., 1996—; bd. dirs. Beaufort County Humane Assn., JCL Computer Task Force; dir. tng. MicroAge Computer Corp. Set designer Greenwood Little Theatre, 1974-76; fundraiser Greenwood Art Coun., 1976; mem. task force for instructional tech. edn. Beaufort County Sch. Dist., 1992. Named County Tchr. of the Yr., Greenwood, S.C., 1972. Mem. Zonta Internat. (bd. dirs. Beaufort chpt. 1994, mem. exec. women), Beaufort C. of C., Trident and Beaufort Literacy Assn. (cert. instr.), Lander Coll. Senators Club (bd. dirs. 1977-80), S.C. Lung Assn. (fund raising chmn. 1975-77, Vol. of Yr.). Home and Office: PO Box 973 Saint Helena Island SC 29920

DICKEY, DAVID HERSCHEL, lawyer, accountant; b. Savannah, Ga., Dec. 31, 1951; s. Grady Lee and Sara (Leon) D.; m. Carolyn Amanda Brooks, June 11, 1983; children: David Bradford, Carolyn Amanda. BBA in Acctg. and Fin., Armstrong State Coll., 1974; M in Accountancy, U. Ga., 1977, JD, 1977. Bar: Ga. 1978, U.S. Dist. Ct. (so. dist.) Ga. 1978, U.S. Dist. Ct. (no. dist.) Ga. 1980, U.S. Ct. Claims 1978, U.S. Tax Ct. 1978, U.S. Ct. Appeals (5th and 11th cirs.) 1978, U.S. Supreme Ct. 1981; CPA, Ga.; accredited estate planner. Assoc., acct. Thompson and Benken, Attys., Savannah, 1977-79; pub. acct. Arthur Andersen & Co., Atlanta, 1979-81; assoc. Oliver Maner & Gray, Attys., Savannah, 1981-82, ptnr., 1982—; pres. Savannah Estate Planning Coun., 1986-87, chmn. bd., 1987-88; bd. dirs. Chatham-Savannah Citizen's Advocacy; mem. legal adv. bd. Small Bus. Coun. Am., Inc., 1989—; pres. Seminar Group, Inc., 1989—, Hist. Investment Properties, Inc., 1991—. Mem. staff Ga. Law Rev., 1975. Bd. dirs. Savannah Theatre Co., 1984, Savannah chpt. Am. Cancer Soc., 1986-91, Hist. Savannah Found., Inc., 1988-94; chmn., trustee Armstrong State Coll. Alumni Endowment Fund, Inc., 1991; chmn. lawyers div. Chatham County United Way, 1992. Recipient Outstanding Svc. award Am. Cancer Soc., 1987, Outstanding Alumni Svc. award Armstrong State Coll., 1992; named to Leadership Savannah, Savannah C. of C., 1984-86. Mem. AICPA, ABA (estate and gift tax com. taxation sect. 1990—), Ga. Bar Assn., Savannah Bar Assn., Ga. Soc. CPAs, Am. Assn. Atty.-CPAs, First City Club (bd. dirs. Savannah 1987-90), Chatham Club. Home: 4 Springfield Pl Savannah GA 31411-2132 Office: Oliver Maner & Gray 218 W State St Savannah GA 31401-3232

DICKEY, JOHN HARWELL, lawyer, public defender; b. Huntsville, Ala., Feb. 22, 1944; s. Gilbert McClain and Marjorie Loucille (Harwell) D.; m. Nancy Margaret Eagar, Nov. 24, 1984; children: Marjorie Ruth, Gilbert Charles. BA, Samford U., 1966; JD, Cumberland Sch. of Law, 1969. Bar: Tenn. 1971, U.S. Dist. Ct. (ea. dist.) Tenn. 1972. Adminstrv. asst. Dist. Atty.'s Office, Huntsville, 1969-70; law clerk domestic and juvenile divsn. Cir. Ct., Huntsville, 1970-72; trial lawyer Legal Aid Soc., Chattanooga, 1972-75; pvt. practice Chattanooga, 1975-77, Fayetteville, Tenn., 1977-89; dist. pub. defender 17th jud. cir. State of Tenn., Fayetteville, 1989—; mem. continuing edn. com. Pub. Defenders Conf., Tenn., 1990-92, mem. long range planning com., 1991-93, mem. legis. com., 1990-93, mem. exec. com., Mid. Tenn. rep., 1993-94. Lectr. Fayetteville-Lincoln County Leadership Tng. Program, 1989—; mem. adv. bd. Community Correction South Ctrl. Tenn., Fayetteville, 1989—; mem. Bedford County Dem. Club, 1989—. Mem. Nat. Assn. Criminal Def. Lawyers, Tenn. Bar Assn., Tenn. Assn. Criminal Def. Lawyers (membership com. 1989—, juvenile law com. 1988—), Marshall County Bar Assn., Fayetteville-Lincoln County Bar Assn. (treas. 1977, sec. 1978, v.p. 1979, pres. 1980), Fayetteville-Lincoln County C. of C., Elks, Masons (jr. steward 1991, sr. steward 1992, jr. deacon 1993, jr. warden 1994, sr. warden 1995, worshipful master 1996), York Rite Mason, Scottish Rite Mason (32 degree), Shriners (sgt.-at-arms 1993, v.p. 1994, dir. pub. rels. 1994, 96, pres. 1995), Internat. Platform Assn., Order of Ea. Star (chaplain 1993-94). Democrat. Methodist. Home: 122 Brookmeade Dr Fayetteville TN 37334-2046 Office: 17th Jud Dist Pub Defender 105 Main Ave S Fayetteville TN 37334-3057

DICKEY, LORRAINE ARLENE, air force officer, neonatologist; b. Redmond, Oreg., Dec. 17, 1961; d. LeRoy Anthony Roberts Sr. and Patricia Ann Kelley; m. Douglas Allen Dickey, Sept. 17, 1983; children: Benjamin Franklin, Anna Leigh, John Patrick. BS, U.S. Air Force Acad., 1983; MD, U. Nebr., Omaha, 1987. Diplomate Am. Acad. Pediatrics, Am. Acad. Gen. Pediatrics. Commd. 2d lt. USAF, 1983, advanced through grades to major, 1993-94; intern in pediatrics U. Nebr. Med. Ctr., 1987-88; resident in pediatrics Wright-Patterson USAF Med. Ctr., Dayton, 1988-91; fellow in neonatology Wilford Hall Med. Ctr., San Antonio, 1991-94. Candidate fellow Am. Acad. Pediatrics; mem. AMA, Am. Med. Women's Assn. Presbyterian. Office: U Nebr Med Ctr UNMC/CUMC Joint Div Newborn 42nd Dewey Ave Omaha NE 68198

DICKEY, PATRICE JANE, public relations executive, sales educator; b. Evanston, Ill., Sept. 24, 1955; d. Joseph Merrel and Mary Elizabeth (Mauntel) D. BA in Journalism and English, U. N.C., 1977. Regional program adminstr. Am. Mgmt. Assn., Atlanta, 1977-79; cons Donor Resources divsn. ARC, Atlanta, 1979-80; tng. specialist Dale Carnegie Inst., Atlanta, 1980-83; dir. corp. sales and pub. rels. Downtown & Lenox Athletic Clubs, Atlanta, 1983-84; dir. spl. events Atlanta C. of C., 1984-85; account exec. Tom Deardorff Assocs., Atlanta, 1985-87; account supr. Anderson, Eilers & Blumberg, Atlanta, 1987-89; owner, pres. PD Comm., Atlanta, 1989—; instr. sales course Dale Carnegie Inst., 1986—. Contbr. articles to profl. publs. Mem. U. N.C. Alumni Assn., Union Concerned Scientists, Peace Action, GARAL, Planned Parenthood, Ga. Conservancy, NARAL, Journalism Alumni and Friends Assn., Soc. Profl. Journalists, Kiwanis (1st female pres. N.W. Atlanta chpt. 1991-92, Disting. Pres. award, Outstanding Kiwanian, 1991. 92), Kappa Kappa Gamma. Presbyterian.

DICKEY, RICHARD ALLEN, endocrinologist; b. Kankakee, Ill., Aug. 21, 1937; s. Clarence Richard and Catherine Marie (Eilers) D.; m. Margaret Niederberger, June 22, 1963; children: Kirsten Lynn, James Richard, Kurt Haywood. AB, Kenyon Coll., 1959; MD, Columbia U., 1963. Diplomate Nat. Bd. Med. Examiners, Am. Bd. Internal Medicine. Intern in internal medicine Ind. U. Med. Ctr., Indpls., 1963-64; flight surgeon, capt. USAF, Altus AFB, Okla., 1964-66; resident in internal medicine Ind. U. Med. Ctr., 1966-68, fellow in endocrinology, 1968-69; pvt. practice Farmington, Conn., 1969-73; group practice Davis Hosp., Statesville, N.C., 1973-74; pharm. rsch. Hoffman LaRoche Inc., Nutley, N.J., 1974-81, Am. Cyanamid/Lederle, Pearl River, N.Y., 1981-82; fellow in endocrinology U. Conn. Health Ctr., Farmington, 1982-83; pvt. practice endocrinology Hickory, N.C., 1983—. Author: Intensive Management of Diabetes Mellitus, 1994. Fellow Am. Coll. Physicians, Am. Coll. Endocrinology (trustee 1994—); mem. AMA (adv. com. 1994—), Am. Assn. Clin. Endocrinologists (bd. dirs., sec. treas. 1991—), Catawba County Med. Soc. (pres. 1995-96). Republican. Episcopalian. Home: 262 Harbor Town Dr Taylorsville NC 28681 Office: 415 N Center St Ste 203 Hickory NC 28601

DICKINSON, CATHERINE SCHATZ, retired microbiologist; b. Cin., Jan. 6, 1927; d. Ralph Marvin and Mabel (Dare) Schatz; student U. Cin., 1944-46, postgrad. 1952; A.B., Miami U., Oxford, Ohio, 1948; m. Willard C. Dickinson, Jr., June 23, 1956; children—Kellie Dare, Bradley Clark. Supr., Bacteriology Lab., Children's Hosp., Cin., 1948-53; supr., sect. head Microbiology Lab., Ochsner Found. Hosp., New Orleans, 1953-95, ret., 1995; lectr. in field. Mem. New Orleans Area Soc. for Microbiology (pres.

1979), Am. Soc. Microbiology, Am. Soc. Clin. Pathologists (specialist in microbiology), New Orleans Soc. Microbiology, Nat. Registry for Microbiologists, Delta Zeta. Episcopalian. Club: Order Eastern Star. Home: 10001 Hyde Pl New Orleans LA 70123-1521

DICKINSON, TEMPLE, lawyer; b. Glasgow, Ky., Mar. 13, 1956; s. Lewis and Selma (Goodman) D.; m. Jan Marie Wussow, Oct. 7, 1995. AB, Transylvania U., 1978; JD, Harvard U., 1984. Bar: Mass. 1985, N.Y. 1990, Ky. 1995, U.S. Dist. Ct. Mass. 1985, U.S. Ct. Appeals (1st cir.) 1988. Assoc. Casner, Edwards & Roseman, Boston, 1984-88; asst. dist. atty. Atty.'s Office Kings County, Bklyn., 1988-95; ptner. Gillenwater, Hampton and Dickinson, Glasgow, Ky., 1995—. Democrat. Mem. Disciples of Christ. Office: Gillenwater Hampton et al 103 E Main St Glasgow KY 42141-2835

DICKS, JACK WILLIAM, lawyer; b. Tampa, Fla., Sept. 12, 1949; s. James R. and June (Simmons) D.; m. Linda Edmunds, Apr. 29, 1972; children: Jennifer, Lindsay. BSc, U. Fla., 1971; JD, George Mason U., 1980. Bar: Va. 1980, Fla. 1981. Ptnr. Pino & Dicks, Orlando, Fla., 1987—; pres. Fin. Talk Network, Inc., 1990-92; pres. Delta First Fin., Inc.; nat. lectr. on real estate and fin. topics; instr. Nat. Assn. Relators, Chgo., 1982-86, Real Estate Securities and Syndication Inst., Chgo., 1982-87; pres. Delta Capital Properties; v.p. Delta Capital Devel. Corp. Author: Cash Management, 1984, Real Estate Forms, 1985, Questions and Answers on Real Estate, 1980, Syndicating Real Estate, 1985, Equity Sharing Solutions, 1985, The Option Strategy, 1984, Riches in Real Estate, 1980, Divorce and Money, 1989, Starting Out or Starting Over, 1989, The Other Side of Everyday, 1990, The Financial Success System, 1990, The Florida Investor, 1994, The Entrepreneur Legal Companion, 1994, (newsletter) Entrepreneur 2000, 1991—, The Mut. Fund Letter, 1987—, The Strategies Report, 1983-86; monthly columnist Forecast and Strategies, Fin. Digest; contbr. articles to publs. Mem. Nat. Assn. Realtors, Nat. Assn. Securities Dealers, Sigma Chi (v.p. 1970-71). Republican. Office: Pino & Dicks 520 Crown Oak Centre Dr Longwood FL 32750-6187

DICKSON, JOHN J., soft drink company executive; b. N.Y., June 17, 1957. BA in Acctg., U. Houston, 1980; MBA, Harvard U., 1990. CPA, Tex. Sr. auditor Arthur Andersen & Co., Houston, 1980-83; internat. prin. auditor The Coca-Cola Co., internat. locations, 1983-88; corp. fin. exec. MMG Patricof & Co., Madrid, 1990-91; exec. v.p. corp. fin. Intermediaciones & Finanzas, SA, Madrid, 1991-93; bus. devel. mgr. The Coca-Cola Co., Atlanta, 1993—. Office: The Coca Cola Co PO Box 1734 Atlanta GA 30301-1734

DICKSON, MARKHAM ALLEN, wholesale company executive; b. Shreveport, La., June 10, 1922; s. Claudius Markham and Marjorie (Fields) D.; m. Margaret Shaffer, Sept. 4, 1943 (div. Mar. 1981); m. June Baldwin Dickson, Apr. 19, 1981; children: Louise Dickson Cravens, Claudius Markham, Markham Allen, Paul Meade. BS, MIT, 1947; MS, Calif. Inst. Tech., 1952, DD, Cranmer Theol. House Sem., 1996. Registered profl. engr., La.; ordained priest Episcopal Ch., 1973. Prodn. engr. Brewster Co., Shreveport, 1948-51; pres. Shreveport Druggists, 1951-52, Morris & Dickson Co. Ltd., Shreveport, 1952-95, also chmn. 1995—. Trustee Cranmer Theol. House Sem. Served to capt. USAAF, 1941-46. Recipient Conservationist of Yr. award DAR. Mem. Nat. Wholesale Druggists Assn. (Tech. award 1991). La Wholesale Drug Distbrs. (pres. 1981-90), La. Bd. Wholesale Drug Distbrs. (chmn. bd. 1988-92), Kappa Alpha, Shreveport Club, Masons. Office: Morris & Dickson Co Ltd 410 Kay Ln Shreveport LA 71115-3604

DICKSON, RUSH STUART, holding company executive; b. Charlotte, N.C., Aug. 18, 1929; s. Rush Smith and Lake (Simpson) D.; m. Joanne Shoemaker, Oct. 12, 1951; children: Rush Stuart, Thomas Walter, John Alexander, Laura Lake. Grad., Davidson Coll., 1951. With Am. & Efird Mills, Mt. Holly, N.C., 1951, Goldman, Sachs & Co., N.Y.C., 1951-52; pres. R. S. Dickson & Co., Charlotte, 1952-68; chmn. bd. Ruddick Corp., Charlotte, 1968-94, chmn. exec. com., 1994—; bd. dirs. Am. & Efird Mills, Harris-Teester Supermarkets, PCa Internat., Inc., Textron Inc., 1st Union Corp., United Dominion Industries Ltd., Dimon Inc. Chmn. Charlotte-Mecklenburg Hosp. Authority; chmn. bd. dirs. The Dickson Found., Found. U. N.C., Charlotte, Found. for Carolinas; trustee Arts and Sci. Coun., Heineman Found., Davidson Coll., Queens Coll. With USAR. Mem. Charlotte C. of C., Newcomen Soc. N.C., Boston Club, Charlotte City Club, Charlotte Country Club, Quail Hollow Country Club, Capital City Club, Country Club N.C., Linville (N.C.) Country Club, Oakland Club, Tower Club, Wachesaw Plantation Club. Democrat. Office: Ruddick Corp 2000 Two First Union Ctr Charlotte NC 28282

DICLAUDIO, JANET ALBERTA, health information administrator; b. Monroeville, Pa., June 17, 1940; d. Frank and Pearl Alberta (Wolfgang) DiC. Cert. in Med. Rsch. Libr. Sci., Luth Med. Ctr., 1962; BA, Thiel Coll., 1975; MS, SUNY, Buffalo, 1978. Registered record adminstr. Dir. med. records Bashline Hosp., Grove City, Pa., 1962, St. Clair Meml. Hosp., Pitts., 1963-73; asst. prof. Ill. State U., Normal, 1976-81; corp. dir. med. records Buffalo Gen. Hosp., 1981-85; dir. med. records Candler Hosp., Savannah, Ga., 1985-94, med. records analyst, 1994—; med. record cons. White Cliff Nursing Home, Greenville, Pa., 1973-75; mgmt. cons. Gifford W. Lorenz MD, Savannah, 1992-94. Contbr. articles to periodicals. Bd. dirs. Mid-Ill. Areawide Health Planning Corp., Normal, 1979-81. Mem. Am. Health Info. Mgmt. Assn., Ga. Health Info. Mgmt. Assn. Office: Candler Hosp 5353 Reynolds St Savannah GA 31405-6005

DICROCE, DEBORAH MARIE, college president; b. Portsmouth, Va., Apr. 8, 1952; d. Quirino Gerry and Margaret (Yanalavage) DiC. BA, Old Dominion U., 1974, MA, 1975; EdD, Coll. William and Mary, 1984. Asst. editor Old Dominion U., Norfolk, Va., 1974-75; prof. English, Tidewater C.C., Portsmouth, Va., 1976-80; chmn. humanities div. Tidewater C.C., Virginia Beach, Va., 1980-85, campus provost, 1985-89; pres. Piedmont Va. C.C., Charlottesville, 1989—; mem., chmn. numerous statewide coms. on edn., 1984—; adj. vis. prof. higher edn.Coll. William and Mary, Williamsburg, Va., 1985—, U. Va., Charlottesville, 1994—; vis. coms. Commn. on Colls.; trustee Endowment Assn. of Coll. William and Mary, 1995—. Contbr. articles on higher edn. and lang. to profl. publs. Mem. Virginia Beach Arts and Humanities Commn., 1983-86, Portsmouth Partnership, 1985-89; bd. dirs. Friends of Women's Studies, Norfolk, 1985-89, Jr. Achievement Greater Hampton Rds., Norfolk, 1986-89; chmn. Virginia Beach Archtl. Design Awards Com., 1985, Portsmouth Vocat. Edn. Adv. Coun., 1988; chmn. cmty. campaign United Way, Portsmouth, 1988, Charlottesville, 1994; bd. dirs. Jefferson Area United Way, 1989—, Thomas Jefferson chpt. Am. Heart Assn., 1990-92, Piedmont Coun. of the Arts, 1989-92, First Va. Bank Ctrl., 1990-94, Ash-Lawn Highland Adv. Bd., 1993—; leadership coun. Martha Jefferson Hosp., 1991-95, Jefferson Nat. Bank, 1994—. Mem. AAUW, Am. Assn. Higher Edn., Assn. for Study Higher Edn., So. Assn. Colls. and Schs. (vis. com. 1987—, commn. on colls. 1990-96, trustee 1996—), Rotary (bd. dirs. Portsmouth 1988-89, Charlottesville 1994-96). Roman Catholic. Office: Piedmont Va CC 501 College Dr Charlottesville VA 22902-9806

DICUS, BRIAN GEORGE, lawyer; b. Kansas City, Mo., Oct. 29, 1961; s. Clarence Howard and Edith Helen (George) D.; m. Vali Ann Venner, Dec. 14, 1985; children: Brian George, Cady Alyssa. BA, So. Meth. U., 1984, JD, 1987. Bar: Tex. 1987, U.S. Dist. Ct. (no. dist.) Tex. 1988; bd. cert. estate planning and probate law Tex. Bd. Legal Specialization. Assoc. Thorp & Sorenson, Dallas, 1987-89, Joseph E. Ashmore Jr., P.C., Dallas, 1989-92; pvt. practice Dallas, 1992—. Chmn. local alumni student recruiting program So. Meth. U., Dallas, 1989-90. Fellow Tex. Bar Found.; mem. Tex. Bar Assn., Dallas Bar Assn., Phi Alpha Delta, Pi Sigma Alpha. Home: 2336 Serenity Ln Heath TX 75087-1922 Office: Ste 260 5910 N Central Expy Dallas TX 75206

DIDLAKE, RALPH HUNTER, JR., surgeon; b. Albuquerque, Sept. 9, 1953; s. Ralph Hunter Sr. and Lorraine (McLaurin) D.; m. Millie Faith McDonald, Nov. 12, 1983; children: James Daniel, Jennifer Claire, Sarah Hunter. BS in Zoology with honors, U. Miss., 1975; MD, U. Miss., Jackson, 1979. Diplomate Am. Bd. of Surgery; lic. Miss. Gen. surgery resident U. Miss. Med. Ctr., Jackson, 1979-81, 83-84, resident in transplantation rsch. Exptl. Surgery Lab, 1981-83, chief resident in gen. surgery, 1984-85; transplantion fellow, instr. surgery U. Tex. Health Sci. Ctr., Houston, 1985-87; asst. prof. surgery U. Miss. Sch. Medicine, Jackson, 1987-90, assoc. prof., 1990—; mem. staff Hermann Hosp., Houston, 1985-87, Univ. Hosp., Jackson, 1987—, (also cons.) Med. Ctr., Jackson, 1987—, Miss. Meth. Rehab. Ctr., Jackson, 1987—; bd. dirs. ESRD Network 8, Inc., 1988—, med. rev. bd. mem., 1988-90; mem. teaching faculty, Geriatric Edn. Ctr.; mem. adv. com. Hinds Community Coll., Raymond, Miss.; invited lectr. Dept. Surgery, Ottawa (Ont., Can.) Civic Hosp., 1988; vis. prof., Dept. Surgery, Abington (Pa.), Meml. Hosp., 1990; presenter in field, internat. and U.S. Co-contbr. over 45 articles and 35 abstracts to sci. publs. Co-grantee NIH, 1984-89, Nat. Lung Inst., 1986-91; grantee Biomed. Rsch. Support, 1987-88, 89-90, Merck, Sharp and Dome, 1990-91. Fellow ACS (applicants com. 1990); mem. AMA, Acad. Surg. Rsch. (bd. dirs. 1990-91), Am. Soc. Transplant Surgeons, Soc. Am. Gastrointestinal Endoscopic Surgeons, Assn. Acad. Surgery, Am. Heart Assn. (Basic Sci. Coun.), Am. Soc. Gastrointestinal Endoscopy, Soc. for Leukocyte Biology, The Microcirculatory Soc., Miss. Med. Assn. (House Dels. 1990), Miss. Acad. Sci. (chmn. Health Sci. div. 1984), Southeastern Surg. Congress, Cen. Med. Soc., Transplantation Soc., Miss. Gerontol. Soc., Sigma Xi. Office: U Miss Med Sch 2500 N State St Jackson MS 39216-4500

DIECKMANN, MERWIN RICHARD, retired physician; b. Clarksville, Iowa, Nov. 30, 1928; s. Louis Frederick and Esther Clara (Nordmeyer) D.; m. Betty Jane Baker, Sept. 9, 1950; children: Mark Lee, Ann Lee, David Lee, Nancy Lee, Jane Lee. BS, Iowa State U., 1950; MD, U. Iowa, 1954. Physician, ptnr. Drs. Waterbury, Loomis, Buckles, and Dieckmann, Waterloo, Iowa, 1957-63; pvt. practice Waterloo, Iowa, 1963-76; assoc. prof. Coll. Medicine East Tenn. State U., Johnson City, 1976-82, East Carolina U., Greenville, N.C., 1982-88; med. dir., physician W. Carteret Med. Ctr., Cape Carteret, N.C., 1988-93; physician, ret. Topsail Beach, N.C., 1993—. Bd. dirs. Bremwood, Waverly, Iowa, 1972-76; airport commr. Waterloo Mcpl. Airport, 1974-76; presdl. elector 3d dist. Iowa Rep. Ctrl. Com., sec. Black Hawk County, 1970-71. Capt. USNR, ret. Black Hypertension Study grantee CIBA, 1986-88. Mem. AMA, Am. Acad. Family Physicians, N.C. Acad. Family Physicians, N.C. Med. Soc. Lutheran. Home and Office: 607 N Anderson Blvd Holly Ridge NC 28445-6845

DIEDERICH, J(OHN) WILLIAM, financial consultant; b. Ladysmith, Wis., Aug. 30, 1929; s. Joseph Charles and Alice Florence (Yost) D.; m. Mary Theresa Klein, Nov. 25, 1950; children: Mary Theresa Diederich Evans, Robert Douglas, Charles Stuart, Michael Mark, Patricia Anne Diederich Irelan, Donna Maureen (dec.), Denise Brendan, Carol Lynn Diederich Weaver, Barbara Gail, Brian Donald, Tracy Maureen, Theodora Bernadette Diederich Davidson, Tamara Alice, Lorraine Angela. PhB, Marquette U., Milw., 1951; MBA with high distinction, Harvard U., 1955. With Landmark Comm., Inc., Norfolk, Va., 1955-90, v.p., treas., 1965-73, exec. v.p. fin., 1973-78, exec. v.p. community newspapers, 1978-82, exec. v.p., CFO, 1982-90, fin. cons., 1990—; chmn. bd. dirs. Landmark Cmty. Newspapers, Inc., 1977-88; pres. Exec. Productivity Sys., Inc., 1982-88, LCI Credit Corp., 1991-93, Landmark TV Inc., 1991—, LTM Investments, Inc., 1991—; v.p., treas., KLAS, Inc., 1994-95; v.p. Internet Express, Inc., 1994-96; pres., bd. dirs. Wide World Web Internat., 1995—, TWC Holdings, Inc., 1996—; instr. Boston U., 1954, Old Dominion U., 1955-59. Lt. col. USMC, 1951-53, USMCR, 1953-71. Baker scholar Harvard U., 1955. Mem. SAR, Nat. Assn. Accts., Am. Numismatic Assn., Nat. Geneal. Soc., Wis. Geneal. Soc., Pa. Geneal. Soc., Sigma Delta Chi. Roman Catholic. Home and Office: PO Box 7677 1466 Glarus Ct Incline Village NV 89452-7677

DIEGO, MANUEL ROXAS, production engineer; b. Cabantuan, Nueva Ecija, The Philippines, Nov. 20, 1955; came to U.S., 1977; s. Hermogenes M. and Josefa Consolacion Diego; m. Lina Ladanan Alvizo, June 1, 1982; children: Amanda Josefa, Kathryn. BS, U. Santo Tomas, Manila, 1977; BS in Indsl. Engring., Lama U., 1980; MS, S.W. Tex. State U., 1993. Engr., estimator Beaumont Well Works, Houston, 1980-81, Triten Ops., Houston, 1981-82; engr. in tng. Gas Turbine Engine br. Kelly AFB, San Antonio, 1988-91, lead engr. Aircraft/Engine Accessories br., 1991-93; gen. engr. Air Force Non-Destructive Inspection Program Office, 1993—. Mem. S.W. Ind. Sch. Dist. Mentoring Program. Roman Catholic. Home: 5651 Timberhurst San Antonio TX 78250-4148 Office: Kelly AFB SA-ALC/LDTBE SA-ALC/LDN Bldg 1562 San Antonio TX 78241

DIEM, DEBRA R., elementary school educator; b. Ronceverte, W.Va., Dec. 31, 1956; d. Aubrey Wayne and Nancy E. (Feamster) Rickman; m. Dennis Keith Diem, Mar. 15, 1980; children: Laura, Nicole. BS in Elem. Edn. cum laude, Bluefield (W.Va.) State Coll., 1984; BS in Learning Disabilities, W.Va. Coll. Grad. Studies, Institute; AAS, Greenbrier Community Coll., Lewisburg, W.Va., 1977; MA in Learning Disabilities, U. W.Va., 1991. Tchr. 2d grade Greenbrier County Schs., Lewisburg. Mem. W.Va. Edn. Assn., Greenbrier County Edn. Assn., Greenbrier County Reading Assn. Home: HC 30 Box 106 Caldwell WV 24925-9708

DIEM, RICHARD A., college educator, educational consultant; b. Kansas City, Mo., Dec. 13, 1945; s. William M. and Rose (Chawkin) D.; m. Roberta Ann Lewin, July 12, 1970; children: Joshua, Sarah. BS, Bradley U., 1967; MS, So. Ill. U., 1969; MA, Colo. State U., 1971; PhD, Northwestern U., 1975. Cert. tchr. Tex., Mo., Colo., Ill. Tchr. Maine North High Sch., Des Plaines, Ill., 1971-75; clin. prof. No. Ill. U., DeKalb, 1974-75; prof. U. Tex., San Antonio, 1975—. Contbr. articles to profl. jours.

DIEMER, ARTHUR WILLIAM, real estate executive; b. Queens County, N.Y., Nov. 5, 1925; s. John and Elizabeth (Bernhard) D.; m. Opal Louise Droddy, Mar. 25, 1950; children: Paul A., Liddia E. Student, CCNY, 1943, St. Lawrence Univ., Canton, N.Y., 1944; BS, Dartmouth Coll., 1947; MS, Thayer Sch. of Engring., Hanover, N.H., 1948. Civil engr. Union Carbide, S. Charleston, W.Va., 1948-56; bldg. mgr. Union Carbide Realty Div., N.Y.C., 1960-67; v.p., pres. Cabot & Forbes Property Mgmt. Co., Boston, 1967-75; pres. Renaissance Ctr. Mgmt. Co., Detroit, 1975-77; co-founder, v.p. Renaissance Properties, Inc., Charlotte, N.C., 1977-84; pres. The Realty Evaluation Group, Inc., Charlotte, N.C., 1985—; Founder, pres. Discovery Assocs., Charlotte 1985—; mem. adv. commn. Ctr. for Bldg. Tech., U.S. Commerce Dept. Washington 1975-76, ad hoc com. U.S. Dept. Energy, Washington, 1974. Author articles in profl. jours. Incorporated Village of Bellerose, N.Y. commr. of parks, commr. of pub. works, elected trustee; bd. dirs. Lutheran Social Svcs., Detroit, 1976-77, Family Housing Svcs., Charlotte 1979-81. Mem. Internat. Grapho Analysis Soc., Dartmouth Club of Charlotte (pres. 1993-94). Republican. Lutheran. Home and Office: 4337 Silo Ln Charlotte NC 28226-5504

DIERCKS, FREDERICK OTTO, government official; b. Rainy River, Ont., Can., Sept. 8, 1912; s. Otto Herman and Lucy (Plunkett) D.; m. Kathryn Frances Transue, Sept. 1, 1937; children: Frederick William, Lucy Helena. B.S., U.S. Mil. Acad., 1937; M.S. in Civil Engring., MIT, 1939; M.S. in Photogrammetry, Syracuse U., 1950. Registered profl. engr., D.C. Commd. 2d lt. U.S. Army Corps Engrs., 1937; advanced through grades to col. U.S. Army, 1952; comdg. officer 656th Engr. Topographic Battalion, France and Germany, 1944-45, U.S. Army Map Service, Washington, 1957-61; asst. dir. mapping, charting, and geodesy Def. Intelligence Agy., 1961-63; dep. engr. 8th U.S. Army, Korea, 1963-64; dir. U.S. Army Coastal Engring. Research Ctr., 1964-67; ret., 1967; assoc. dir. U.S. Coast and Geodetic Survey, Rockville, Md., 1967-74; U.S. mem. commn. on cartography Pan Am. Inst. Geography and History, OAS, 1961-67, alt. U.S. mem. directing council, 1970-74, exec. sec. U.S. sect., 1975-87. Decorated Legion of Merit (U.S.), Grand Cross Order of King George II (Greece), Comdr. Most Exalted Order of White Elephant (Thailand), Bronze medal U.S. Dept. Commerce. Fellow ASCE, Soc. Am. Mil. Engrs. (Colbert medal); mem. Am. Soc. Photogrammetry (hon. mem., pres. 1970-71, Luis Struck award), Am. Congress on Surveying and Mapping, N.Y. Acad. Scis., Sigma Xi. Republican. Presbyterian. Clubs: Army-Navy, Cosmos (Washington). Lodge: Hancock Lodge 311, A.F. and A.M. (Fort Leavenworth, Kans.). Home: 9120 Belvoir Woods Pky Apt 216 Fort Belvoir VA 22060-2724

DIERKS, RICHARD ERNEST, veterinarian, educational administrator; b. Flandreau, S.D., Mar. 11, 1934; s. Martin and Lillian Ester (Benedict) D.; m. Eveline Carol Amundson, July 20, 1956; children—Jeffrey Scott, Steven Eric, Joel Richard. Student, S.D. State U., 1952-55; BS, U. Minn., 1957, DVM, 1959, MPH, 1964, PhD, 1964; MBA, U. Ill., 1985. Diplomate Am. Coll. Vet. Microbiologists, Am. Coll. Vet. Preventive Medicine. Supervisory microbiologist Communicable Disease Ctr., Atlanta, 1964-68; prof. coll. veterinary medicine Iowa State U., Ames, 1968-74; head dept. veterinary sci. Mont. State U., Bozeman, 1974-76; dean Coll. Veterinary Medicine U. Ill., Urbana, 1976-89; dean Coll. Veterinary Medicine U. Fla., Gainesville, 1989-97, prof., dean emeritus, 1997—; mem. tng. grant rev. com. Nat. Inst. Allergy and Infectious Diseases, 1973-74. Contbr. articles on virology, immunology and epidemiology to profl. jours. Served with USPHS, 1964-67. Career Devel. awardee Nat. Inst. Allergy and Infectious Diseases, 1969-74, Nat. Acad. Practitioners, 1995. Mem. Am. Vet. Medicine Assn., Am. Soc. Virology, Am. Soc. Microbiologists, Am. Assn. Immunologists, Am. Assn. Vet. Lab. Diagnosis, Colo. Vet. Medicine Assn., Fla. Vet. Medicine Assn., Soc. Exptl. Biology and Medicine, Gamma Sigma Delta, Phi Kappa Phi, Phi Zeta. Republican. Lutheran. Club: Rotary. Office: U Fla Coll Vet Medicine Health Sci Ctr PO Box 100125 Gainesville FL 32610-0125

DIETEL, WILLIAM MOORE, former foundation executive; b. Islip, N.Y., Aug. 14, 1927; s. Frederick William and Zillah Yolanda (Vannuccini) D.; m. Linda Remington, June 16, 1951; children: Elizabeth Lynn, Cynthia Lyon, Lisa Remington, John Frederick, Victoria Moore. AB, Princeton U., 1950; MA, Yale U., 1952, PhD, 1959; postgrad., London U. Inst. Hist. Research, 1953-54. Instr. history U. Mass., Amherst, 1954-59; asst. dean of coll., asst. prof. humanities Amherst Coll., 1959-61; prin. Emma Willard Sch., Troy, N.Y., 1961-70; pres. Rockefeller Bros. Fund, N.Y.C., 1975-87; dir. Va. Ea. Shore Corp., Belle Haven, Va., TEAM, Plc, London. Chmn. Nat. Ctr. for Non-Profit Bds., Washington; pres. Pierson-Lovelace Found., L.A. Trust, Idyllwild (Calif.) Arts, Am. Farmland Trust, Washington. Fellow World Acad. Art & Sci. Fellow World Acad. Art and Sci.; mem. Brain Mapping Med. Rsch. Orgn. (bd. dirs.). Clubs: Univ., (N.Y.C.), Cosmos (Washington). Office: PO Box 309 Flint Hill VA 22627-0309

DIETHELM, ARNOLD GILLESPIE, surgeon; b. Balt., Jan. 13, 1932; s. Oskar Arnold and Grace (Gillespie) D.; m. Nancy Lee Lane, June 21, 1951; children: Nancy Elizabeth, Linda Lane, Eugene Arnold (dec.), Ellen Jeanette, Richard Gillespie. A.B., Wash. State U., 1953; M.D., Cornell U., 1958. Intern, then resident in surgery N.Y. Hosp., 1958-65; asst. in surgery, research fellow Peter Bent Brigham Hosp., Boston, 1965-66; research fellow surgery Harvard U. Med. Sch., 1966-67; instr. Cornell U. Med. Sch., 1964-65; mem. faculty U. Ala. Med. Center, Birmingham, 1967—; prof. surgery U. Ala. Med. Center, 1973—, vice chmn. dept., 1973-82, chmn. dept. surgery, 1982—. Contbr. articles med. jours. Mem. AAAS, ACS, AMA, Am. Soc. Nephrology, Am. Soc. Transplant Surgeons, Am. Surg. Assn., Am. Bd. Surgery (dir. 1987-93), Assn. Acad. Surgery, Transplantation Soc., So. Surg. Assn. Home: 3248 Sterling Rd Birmingham AL 35213-3508 Office: U Ala Hosp Dept Surgery 619 19th St S Birmingham AL 35233-1924

DIETLINDE, AGNES JULIANE See KATRITZKY, LINDE

DIETZ, ARTHUR TOWNSEND, investment counseling company executive; b. Mt. Vernon, N.Y., Oct. 30, 1923; s. William Arthur and Adele Townsend (Dods) D.; m. Mary Archer, June 29, 1947 (dec. 1980); children: Adele Archer Dietz, Laura Townsend Stamm, Amelia Edmunds Williams; m. Mary Laura Peavy, Sept. 16, 1982 (dec. 1992); m. Margie Nell Lee Baghose, Oct. 4, 1992. AB, Wesleyan U., Middletown, Conn., 1946; MA, Princeton U., 1948, PhD, 1953. Instr. Princeton U., 1948-49; asst. prof. Wesleyan U., 1949-54; Mills Bee Lane prof. fin. and banking, dir. MBA program Emory U., Atlanta, 1959-77; dir. Alpha Funds, Atlanta, 1972-85, Enterprise Funds, Atlanta, 1985—, Enterprise Accumulation Trust, 1995—; pres. ATD Adv. Corp., 1996—. Author books; contbr. articles to profl. jours. Pres. Fernbank PTA, DeKalb County, Ga., 1959-60; mem. DeKalb County Devel. Authority, 1980-84; Retirement Facility for Elderly Authority, DeKalb County, 1982-84. Sgt. AUS, 1942-45, ETO. Recipient Emory Williams Disting. Teaching award Emory U., 1983; Woodrow Wilson fellow, 1946. Fellow Fin. Analysts Soc.; mem. Phi Beta Kappa (pres. Gamma chpt. 1964-65). Methodist. Office: ATD Adv 1917 Chamdun Way Atlanta GA 30341

DIETZ, ROBERT LEE, lawyer; b. Miami, Fla., Apr. 28, 1958; s. Edward William and Anna C. D.; m. Laura Sanders, May 8, 1982; children: John Edward, Stephanie Elizabeth. BA with honors, Eckerd Coll., St. Petersburg, Fla., 1979; JD, Vanderbilt U., 1982. Bar: Fla. 1984; cert. workers' compensation, 1992; Supreme Ct. cert. cir. civil mediator, 1995. Atty. Zimmerman, Shuffield, Kiser & Sutcliffe, P.A., Orlando, Fla., 1984—. Contbr. articles to profl. jours. Vice chair S.E. region bd. dirs. Canine Companions for Independence, Orlando, 1991-93; alumni bd. dirs., chair alumni capital campaign Eckerd Coll., 1992—. Recipient McArthur Alumni award Eckerd Coll., 1993. Mem. ABA (nat. chair ABA Tips, workers compensation and employer liability com. 1995-96), Fla. Bar Assn. (workers compensation rules com. 1988-91), Orange County Bar Assn. (chmn. workers compensation com. 1996—, Guardian ad Litem of the Yr. 1996), Fla. Def. Lawyers Assn. (bd. dirs. 1991-95, chair workers compensation com. 1989—), Civitan Internat. (Disting. gov. 1993-94, internat. mem. mktg. com. 1994-96, Club Honor key East Orlando club 1994, Dist. Honor key Sunshine dist. 1994). Home: 1879 Bristol Ct Maitland FL 32751-3460 Office: Zimmerman Shuffield Kiser & Sutcliffe PA 315 E Robinson St Ste 600 Orlando FL 32801-4328

DIFFENBAUGH, JOHN NICHOLAS, architect; b. Chambersburg, Pa., June 18, 1954; s. Richard Max and Jean Elizabeth (Gruver) D.; m. Ruth Cartledge, July 14, 1984. BArch, Clemson U., 1976; MArch, Washington U., St. Louis, 1979. Registered architect NCARB, S.C., Va., Pa., N.Y. Intern Nat. Trust for Hist. Preservation, 1976; architect Kennedy, Brown & Assocs., Indpls., 1979-81, Lucas, Stubbs, Pascullis, Powell & Penney Ltd., Charleston, S.C., 1981-83; assoc. Karl E. Kohler & Assocs., Vienna, Va., 1983-89; prin. Nicholas Diffenbaugh Architect, P.C., Fairfax Station, Va., 1989—.

DIFFILY, DEBORAH LYNN, early childhood education educator; b. San Bernardino, Calif., July 23, 1955; d. J.W. and Bobbye Dale (Funkhouser) Titsworth; m. David Thomas Hawkins, Feb. 1, 1983; 1 child, Michael Spear Hawkins; m. James Patrick Diffily, Aug. 3, 1991. BA, Oral Roberts U., 1976; MA, Tex. Wesleyan U., 1989; PhD, U. North Tex., 1994. Pre-kindergarten tchr. The White Lake Sch., Ft. Worth, 1988-90; kindergarten and 1st grade tchr. Ft. Worth Ind. Sch. Dist., 1990-96; faculty Tex. Wesleyan U., 1996—; teaching fellow U. North Tex., Denton, 1993; tchr., lectr. Tex. Christian U., Ft. Worth, 1993-95; adj. prof. Tex. Wesleyan U., Ft. Worth, 1995—. Co-author: Early Childhood Education: An Introduction, 1997; editor: Helping Parents Understand: Newsletter Articles on Early Childhood Issues, 1995; co-editor: Family Friendly Communication in Early Childhood Programs; contbr. articles to profl. jours. Trustee St. Luke's Episc. Sch., Ft. Worth, 1990-93; mem task force Ft. Worth Mus. Sci. and History, Ft. Worth, 1992; mem. alumni leadership coun. Tex. Wesleyan U., Ft. Worth, 1991-93; mem. renovation com. Fossil Rim Wildlife Ctr., Granbury, Tex., 1994. Community Fund grantee, 1993-94; Velma E. Schmidt scholar, 1993; Lauream Christian Robertson fellow, 1993. Mem. ASCD, Ft. Worth Area Assn. for Edn. of Young Children (pres. 1993-94), Tex. Assn. for Edn. of Young Children, So. Early Childhood Assn., Nat. Assn. for Edn. of Young Children, Phi Delta Kappa. Home: 3905 Sanguinet St Fort Worth TX 76107-7237

DI GIROLAMO, MICHAEL, airport executive. Dep. exec. dir. airport ops. Dallas/Ft. Worth Internat. Airport.

DIKET, MARY READ M., academic administrator, educator; b. Oak Ridge, Tenn., Aug. 2, 1944; d. Edmund Warren and Jeanne (Howie) Montgomery; m. Merrill Edward Diket, Feb. 12, 1966; children: Cameron, Melissa, Tally. B in Art Edn., U. Miss., 1965; M in Art Edn., U. So. Miss., 1988; PhD in Art, U. Ga., Athens, 1991. Art and English instr. Murrah High Sch., Jackson, Miss., 1965-66; art instr. St. John's Day Sch., Laurel, Miss., 1971-73, 86; ptnr. Art Assocs. Studio, 1987-89; grad. teaching asst. U. So. Miss., 1987-89; grad. teaching asst. U. Ga., 1989-90, rsch. affiliate, 1991-92; dir. creativity workshop William Carey Coll., Laurel, Miss., 1992—, dir. honors program, 1992—, assoc. prof. art and edn., 1992—; prodr., instr. workshops U. Ga. Family Housing, 1989; humanities instr. and testing cons. creative scholars program Lamar U., Beaumont, Tex., 1990-93; adj. prof. William Carey Coll., 1992; vis. prof. art dept. U. So. Miss., 1992; reviewer Am. Edn. Rsch. Assn., 1992, 93, 94; dir. Apple Edn. Seed Grant, 1995-96;

presenter papers Nat. Art Edn. Assn., 1990-96, Fla. State Art History Grad. Symposium, 1991, Am. Ednl. Rsch. Assn., 1992-95, Nat. Assn. Gifted Children, Atlanta, Salt Lake City, 1993-96. Co-editor: Trends in Art Education From Diverse Cultures, 1995; editor: Miss. Assn. for Gifted Children, 1993; contbr. articles to profl. jours.; exhbns. U. Miss., 1964-65, Protective Paint Co. Jackson, Miss., 1965, McComb Juried Art Show, 1966, Jones County Jr. Coll., 1987, YWCA, Laurel, Miss., 1988, U. So. Miss., 1988, U. Ga., 1990; costume designer, set designer for 10 plays Laurel Little Theatre, 1981-87; cartoonist: (campus newspaper) Mississippian, 1963. Recipient Nat. Historian award Delta Delta Delta, 1984, Faculty Excellence award William Carey Coll., 1993; grantee Task Force for Edn. Govt. Elect Kirk Fordice, 1991, Lauren Rogers Mus., 1986. Mem. Internat. Soc. Edn. Through Art, Am. Ednl. Rsch. Assn. (co-chmn. arts and learning 1993, 94, editor arts and learning rsch. 1995, 96), Nat. Art Edn. Assn., Miss. Art Edn. Assn., Nat. Assn. for Gifted, Miss. Assn. for Gifted Children, Laurel Arts League, Phi Delta Kappa, Alpha Chi. Home: 805 N 6th Ave Laurel MS 39440-2710 Office: William Carey Coll 498 Tuscan Ave Hattiesburg MS 39401-5461

DILCHER, CHARLES F., JR., holding company executive; b. Chgo., May 14, 1932; s. Charles F. and Joan R. Dilcher; m. Virginia May Llewellyn, Mar. 1953; children: Rebecca Joan, Charles Llewellyn. BSME, Purdue U., 1954. Engr. Sunbeam Corp., Chgo., 1954-56, sales engr., 1956-57; chief engr. Pneutrol Corp., Bellwood, Ill., 1957; asst. chief engr. Sunbeam Equipment Corp., Meadville, Pa., 1958-60; pres. Dilcher Engring. Co. Inc., Atlanta, 1960—, So. Lab. Supply, Atlanta, 1983—, So. Calibration & Svc., Atlanta, 1983—, Llewellyn/So. Co., Atlanta, 1983—. Mem. ASTM, Am. Soc. for Materials, Capitol City Country Club, Keowee Key Country Club, Phi Kappa Psi. Republican. Presbyterian. Home: 229 Lake Forrest Ln NE Atlanta GA 30342-3211 Office: Llewellyn/So Co Inc 460 Plasamour Dr NE Atlanta GA 30324-4006

DILGER, ROBERT JAY, political scientist; b. Waterbury, Conn., Mar. 20, 1954; s. Franklin Jay and Marie Claire (Lalonde) D.; m. Gloria Jean Fugate, Mar. 10, 1973; children: Anne Elizabeth, Alexander Jay. BA, Johns Hopkins U., 1976; PhD, Brandeis U., 1981. Rsch. fellow Brookings Instn., Washington, 1979-80; asst. prof. Marshall U., Huntington, W.Va., 1980-81, Wittenberg U., Springfield, Ohio, 1981-83; rsch. fellow Adv. Commn. on Intergovtl. Rels., Washington, 1983-84; Lincoln Govt. fellow Nat. League of Cities, Washington, 1984-85; assoc. prof. U. Redlands, Calif., 1985-90; dir., prof. W.Va. U., Morgantown, 1990—. Author: The Sunbelt/Snowbelt Controversy, 1982, American Intergovernmental Relations Today, 1986, National Intergovernmental Programs, 1989, Neighborhood Politics, 1992; co-author: West Virginia Politics and Government, 1996, West Virginia in the 1990s, 1993; contbr. articles to profl. jours. Mem. Am. Polit. Sci. Assn. (exec. coun. sect. on federalism and intergovtl. rels. 1990-96). Office: Inst for Pub Affairs W Va U PO Box 6317 Morgantown WV 26506

DILKS, SATTARIA S., mental health nurse, therapist; b. Iola, Kans., Oct. 12, 1955; d. Paul J. and Janice E. (McHenry) Smith; m. Lawrence S. Dilks, Feb. 24, 1990; children: Jason Kaine Alexander, Cameron Gray Alexander, Russell Morris Alexander, Michelle Elizabeth Dilks. BSN, West Tex. State U., 1978; MA in Psychology, McNeese State U., 1988. Cert. psychiat./mental health nurse; lic. profl. counselor, La. Mental health technician Killgore Children's Psychiat. Hosp., Amarillo, Tex.; nurse mgr. psychiat. unit St. Patrick Hosp., Lake Charles, La.; DON, clin. coord. Charter Hosp. of Lake Charles, adolescent svcs. program adminstr.; pvt. practice mental health counseling and consultation. Pres. adv. bd. Lake Charles Mental Health Ctr., 1990; active Girl Scouts U.S. Mem. La. Counseling Assn., La. Mental Health Counseling Assn., Girl Scouts U.S., Sigma Theta Tau. Home: 1901 E Rosedown Dr Lake Charles LA 70605 Office: 2829 4th Ave Ste 150 Lake Charles LA 70605

DILLABER, PHILIP ARTHUR, budget and resource analyst, economist, consultant; b. Springfield, Mass., Aug. 24, 1922; s. Ralph E. and Grace (Holman) D.; m. Jacqueline M. Bertin, July 16, 1946; children: Anne Erline (Mrs. Donald Youngblood), Katherine Marie, John Philip, Patricia Elizabeth (Mrs. Joseph Mickley). BA, Am. Internat. Coll., 1949; MBA, Ind. U., 1950; postgrad., U. Mich., Ind. U., 1950-54; PhD, Pacific Western U., 1985. Cert. govt. fin. mgr. Clk. rsch. and devel. div. Springfield Armory, 1946-47; rsch. asst. dept. econs. Ind. U., 1951, lectr. econs., 1955-57; orgn. and methods examiner USAF, Gulfport, Miss., 1952-53; mgmt. analyst 5th U.S. Army, Chgo., 1954-61; program progress and resources mgmt. analyst Continental Army Command, Ft. Monroe, Va., 1962-66; adminstrv. officer U.S. Army NIKE-X System Office, Alexandria, Va., 1967; program analyst Office Asst. Chief Staff Force Devel. Dept. Army, Washington, 1967-71, budget analyst Office Dep. Chief Staff Logistics, 1971-74; budget analyst Office Dep. Chief Staff Rsch., Devel. and Acquisition, Washington, 1974-80; sr. analyst Info. Spectrum, Inc., Arlington, Va., 1980-87; mem. Nat. Def. Exec. Reserve, Washington, 1985—; cons. Profl. Group, Inc., 1992—; del. Citizen Amb. Program Pub. Budgeting and Fin. Mgmt., People's Republic of China, 1995; guest lectr. econs. Purdue U., 1959-61. Decorated Commendation medal Regional Coun., Normandy, France, 1994, Wall of Liberty Meml. Mus., Caen, France, 1994; mem. Exceptional WWII Fin. Unit displayed U.S. Army Fin. Corps Mus., Ft. Jackson, S.C. Mem. ASPA, SAR, Am. Econ. Assn., Nat. Contract Mgmt. Assn., Am. Def. Preparedness Assn., Performance Mgmt. Assn., Am. Assn. Budget Program Analysis, Project Mgmt. Inst., Assn. Govt. Accts. (cert. govt. fin. mgr.), Beta Gamma Sigma. Home: 3003 Arkendale St Woodbridge VA 22193-1223

DILLAHA, THEO A., III, environmental engineer, educator, consultant; b. Little Rock, Apr. 5, 1952; s. Theo A. Jr. and Mary Ann (Davis) D.; m. Rebecca L. Caldwell, Aug. 9, 1977; children: Kristine A. Miller, Essra D. BE, Vanderbilt U., 1974, MS Environ. and Water Resources Engring., 1976; PhD in Engring., Purdue U., 1981. Registered profl. engr., Va. EPA grad. fellow Vanderbilt U., Nashville, 1974-75; environ. engr. WAPORA, Inc., Bethesda, Md., 1975-77; san. engr. U.S. Peace Corps, Agadir, Morocco, 1976-77; grad. asst. U. Ark., Fayetteville, 1977-78; grad. rsch. instr. Purdue U., West Lafayette, Ind., 1978-81; asst. prof. U. Guam, Manigalo, 1981-83; asst. prof. Va. Poly. Inst. and State U., Blacksburg, 1983-90, assoc. prof. biol. systems engring., 1990—. Contbr. articles to profl. jours. Mem. Dem. Nat. Com., 1993—; treas. Blacksburg New Sch., 1988-90. Recipient Nat. Pollution Prevention award U.S. EPA, 1992; Fulbright scholar program Coun. for Internat. Exch. of Scholars, Mauritius, 1994-95. Mem. ASCE (Wesley W. Horner award 1990), Am. Soc. Agrl. Engrs., Water Environment Fedn., Soil and Water Conservation Soc. (pres. Va. chpt. 1992), Sierra Club, Tau Beta Pi, Gamma Sigma Delta, Alpha Epsilon. Office: Biol Systems Engring Dept Va Poly Inst & State U Blacksburg VA 24061-0303

DILLAHUNTY, WILBUR HARRIS, lawyer; b. Memphis, June 30, 1928; s. Joseph S. and Octavia M. (Jones) D.; 1 child, Sharon K. JD, U. Ark., 1954. Bar: Ark. 1954. City atty. West Memphis, Ark., 1958-68; U.S. atty. (ea. dist.) Little Rock, 1968-79; exec. asst. adminstr. SBA, Washington, 1979-80; prin. Dillahunty Law Firm, Little Rock, 1980—; chancery and probate judge 6th Jud. Dist., 6th Divsn., Little Rock, 1997—. Served to lt. U.S. Army, 1945-48, ETO. Mem. ABA, Pulaski Bar Assn., Nat. Assn. Former U.S. Attys. (pres. 1991—), Am. Inns of Ct. (pres. William R. Overton chpt. 1989-90). Home: 9710 Catskill Rd Little Rock AR 72227-5562 Office: Pulaski County Courthouse # 360 Little Rock AR 72201

DILLARD, ALEX, executive. Offfice: Dillard Department Stores Inc 1600 Cantrell Rd Little Rock AR 72201-1110

DILLARD, BETTY LYNN, English language educator; b. Ft. Worth, Mar. 15, 1952; d. Robert Allan and Laura Margaret (Cann) D. Student, U. Aberdeen, 1970; BA in Journalism, Baylor U., 1973; MA in English, Counseling, Sul Ross State U., 1992. Freelance journalist Dallas, 1975-78; editor Soc. Prof. Engrs., Dallas, 1978-80; assoc. editor Tex. Homes Mag., Dallas, 1980-85; editor, co-owner Big Bend Sentinel, Marfa, Tex., 1986-88; edit. asst. Sul Ross State U., Alpine, Tex., 1988-91, adj. instr., 1991—; advisor Non-Traditional Students Orgn., Alpine, 1990—. Author: The Grand Homes of Texas, 1982; contbr. articles to newspapers and jours. Bd. dirs. Rio-Pecos Family Crisis Ctr., Alpine, 1988-891 judge Univ. Interscolastic League, Alpine, 1987—, Coll. Bowl Tournament, Alpine, 1989—. Mem. MLA, DAR, Nat. Coun. Tchrs. English, Tex. Assn. Coll. and Univ. Student Pers. Adminstrs., Soc. Profl. Journalists, Sigma Tau Delta (advisor), Alpha Omega. Home: 307 E Sul Ross Ave Alpine TX 79830-4723 Office: Ctr for Big Bend Studies PO Box C-210 Alpine TX 79832

DILLARD, GEORGE STEWART, III, minister; b. Jacksonville, Fla., Dec. 17, 1958; s. George Stewart II and Carolyn Faye (Brown) D.; m. Reneé Cheryl Barnes, Mar. 26, 1988; children: Tiffany Reneé, Alexis Nichole. BS, Atlanta Christian Coll., 1983; postgrad., Emmanuel Sch. Religion, 1983-85; M in Ministry magna cum laude, Evang. Theol. Sem. Ordained to ministry Christian Ch., 1980. Min. Countyline Christian Ch., Brooks, Ga., 1980-82, New Hope Christian Ch., Rogersville, Tenn., 1983-85; sr. min. 1st Christian Ch., Rincon, Ga., 1985-93; min. preaching, Evangelism Peachtree City (Ga.) Christian Ch., 1993—; pres. Min. Asst., Christian Ch., Savannah, Ga., 1986-88; v.p., treas., bd. dirs. Bd. Coastal Empire Christian Camp, Sylvania, Ga., 1986-93; com. mem. Ga. Christian Youth Conv., Atlanta, 1987, Ga. Christian Missionary Rally, Atlanta, 1989-93; chaplain Effingham County (Ga.) Sheriffs Dept., 1986-93, Effingham County High Sch. Football, 1986-93. Author column Mins. Thoughts, 1985-93. Chmn. com. George Bush for Pres., 1988; chmn. Victims/Witness Asistance Program, Effingham County, 1989-93; mem. Tidelands Coun. Prevention of Drug Abuse, Effingham County, 1989-93; pres. Effingham County Athletic Booster Club, 1990-93. Recipient Outstanding Young Mins. award N.Am. Christian Conv., Louisville, Ky., 1990; named one of Outstanding Young Men in Am., 1996. Mem. Rotary (bd. dirs. 1989-91, co-chmn. tel. dir.), Peachtree Christian Conv. (founder, chmn. 1992). Home: 335 Little Creek Dr Sharpsburg GA 30277-9556 Office: Peachtree City Christian Ch Wisdom Rd Peachtree City GA 30269

DILLARD, JOHN ROBERT, lawyer; b. Sylva, N.C., Mar. 14, 1955; s. George Washington and Ethel Thomasine (Freeman) D. BSBA cum laude, Western Carolina U., 1977; JD, Samford U., 1980; postgrad., Western Carolina U., 1986-88; PhD in Bus. Adminstr. with honors, S.W. U., 1989. Bar: N.C. 1980, U.S. Dist. Ct. (we. dist.) N.C. 1981. Sole practice Cashiers, N.C., 1980-81; ptnr. Alley, Killian, Kersten & Dillard, Waynesville, N.C., 1981-85; sr. v.p., atty. Commonwealth Land Title Co., Asheville, N.C., 1985-93; pres., state mgr. Stewart Title of N.C., Asheville, 1993—; legal counsel Woodmen of World Ins., Waynesville, 1982-85, bd. dirs.; sec. Beta-Zeta Ltd., Waynesville, 1982-84, bd. dirs.; cons. Nereus Inc., Greenville, Tenn., 1986-88; adj. faculty Asheville-Buncome Tech. Coll., 1990-93, Mars Hill Coll., 1992; instr. Nat. Bus. Inst., 1996. Legal counsel, bd. dirs. Lambda Chi Alpha, Cullowhee, N.C., 1983-85; adv. Jr. Achievement, Clyde, N.C., 1984. Recipient Unsung Brother award, Lambda Chi Alpha, 1974. Mem. ABA (cert. arbitrator), ATLA, N.C. Acad. Trial Lawyers, N.C. State Bar (mem. constl. law com. 1996—), N.C. Coll. Advocacy, Am. Land Title Assn., N.C. Real Property Assn., Masons, Woodmen (trustee 1982—). Democrat. Episcopalian. Home: 4 Wagner Branch Dr Asheville NC 28804 Office: Stewart Title of NC 9 S Pack Square Ste 301 Asheville NC 28801

DILLARD, MARY KATHERINE, secondary education educator; m. Weldon Dillard; children: Lyn Brown, Laurie Reasons. BA, Baylor U., 1954; MA, Tex. Woman's U., 1968. Permanent tchg. cert. Tchr. West (Tex.) Ind. Sch. Dist., 1953-54, Louisville Ind. Sch. Dist., 1954-57; legal sec. Hunt Oil Co., Dallas, 1963-64; tchr. Highland Park Jr. H.S., Dallas, 1965-70, Highland Park H.S., Dallas, 1970-96; learning dir. Secrets to Success, Dallas, 1996—; cons. Coll. Bd., Austin, Tex., 1985-96. Author (study guide) The Great Gatsby, 1994. Mem. Altrusa Club, Dallas, 1965-70; past pres. Greater Dallas Coun. Tchrs. English, 1980-81. Named Tchr. of the Week, Minyard's and Radio Sta., Dallas, 1993, Highland Park H.S., 1990, 92. Mem. Nat. Coun. Tchrs. English (liaison 1981-82), Tex. Coun. Tchrs. English. Baptist. Home: 5206 Miller Heights Rowlett TX 75088 Office: Highland Park High Sch 4220 Emerson Dallas TX 75205

DILLARD, MIKE, executive. Office: Dillard Department Stores Inc 1600 Cantrell Rd Little Rock AR 72201-1110

DILLARD, ROBERT PERKINS, pediatrician, educator; b. Ft. Benjamin Harrison, Ind., June 7, 1941; s. Harry Knight and Anna Frances (Perkins) D.; children: Robert Perkins, Ann Michele, Christopher Stevens, Catherine Colleen; m. Roberta L. Schaffner, Oct. 20, 1991; 1 child, Toby. AB, Transylvania U., 1963; MD, U. Ky., Lexington, 1967. Diplomate Am. Bd. Pediatrics, subbd. pediatric gastroenterology; lic. physician, Ky., Fla., N.C. Rotating intern U. Okla. Med. Ctr., Oklahoma City, 1967-68; resident in pediat. Children's Meml. Hosp., U. Okla. Med. Ctr., Oklahoma City, 1968-71; fellow pediatric gastroenterology and nutrition Children's Hosp. Med. ctr., Cin., 1989-90; clin. asst. prof. pediatrics U. South Fla. Coll. Medicine, Tampa, 1975-77; asst. prof. pediatric medicine, assoc. dir. ambulatory peds. East Carolina U., Greenville, N.C., 1977-83, dir. pediatric nutrition support svcs., 1981-83; assoc. prof. pediatrics U. Ky. Coll. Medicine, Lexington, 1983, dir. level I nursery, asst. dir. gen. pediatrics, 1983-89, assoc. prof., dir. pediatric gastroenterology and nutrition, 1990-94, assoc. prof. multidisciplinary PhD program, 1993-94; dir. pediatric gastroenterology and nutrition Sacred Heart Children's Hosp., 1994—; cons. pediatrician Children's Hosp. at Sacred Heart, Pensacola, Fla., 1971-73; attending physician St. Joseph's Hosp., Tampa Gen. Hosp., Women's Hosp., Tampa, 1973-77, Pitt County Meml. Hosp., Greenville, 1977-83, U. Ky. Med. Ctr., Lexington, 1983-94, Children's Hosp. at Sacred Heart, 1994—; pvt. practice, Tampa, 1973-77; rsch. asst. dept. animal pathology U. Ky., 1959-62, dept. anatomy, 1963, summer rsch. fellow dept. ob/gyn., 1964; extern Ctrl. Bapt. Hosp., Lexington, 1965; sr. aviation med. examiner FAA, Lexington, 1983-94, Pensacola, 1994—. Author: Newborn Care Manual, 1981, Parent's Guide to Newborn Care, 1986, Parent's Guide to Newborn Care/Resident and Student Handbook, 1986; (videotape) Care of the Newborn, 1980; author exam questions subbd. pediat. gastroenterology Am. Bd. Pediatrics; contbr. articles to profl. jours., chpts. to books. With USN, 1971-73, capt. Res. Grantee Ross Labs., 1981-82, Mead-Johnson, 1982, Children's Miracle Network, 1990, 92, 94-96, Nat. Dairy Coun., 1984, 87. Fellow Am. Acad. Pediat., N.Am. Soc. Pediat. Gastroenterology and Nutrition; mem. NRA, Sons Confederate Vets., Am. Gastroenterology Assn., Aerospace Med. Assn., Soc. USN Flight Surgeons, U. Ky. Coll. Medicine Alumni Assn., So. Gut Club. Republican. Office: Sacred Heart Childrens Hosp W C Payne Bldg 5149 N 9th Ave Ste 308 Pensacola FL 32504-8755

DILLARD, WILLIAM, II, department store chain executive; b. 1945; married. Grad., U. Ark.; MBA, Harvard U. With Dillard Dept. Stores, Little Rock, 1967—, exec. v.p., 1973-77, pres. and chief oper. officer, 1977—, also dir., now chmn.,CEO. Office: Dillard Dept Stores Inc 1600 Cantrell Rd Little Rock AR 72201-1110*

DILLEN, MARK EDMUND, diplomat; b. Detroit, July 11, 1951; s. John Thomas and Evelyn Dillen; m. Anne Marie Chermak, July 23, 1977; children: Vanessa, Nicholas. BA, U. Mich., 1973; MS, Columbia U., 1974; PhD (hon.), U. Nat. and World Economy, 1994. Press attaché U.S. Embassy, Rome, 1985-89; pub. affairs officer U.S. Embassy, Sofia, Bulgaria, 1991-94; sr. cultural attaché U.S. Embassy, Bonn, Berlin, Germany, 1996—; dir. press office U.S. Dept. State, Washington, 1989-91; sr. policy officer U.S. Info. Agy., Washington, 1994-96. Hon. judge We the People Civic Edn. Competition, Washington, 1995-96. Diplomat-in-residence Am. Inst. for Contemporary German Studies, 1996. Mem. U. Mich. Alumni Assn., Am. Fgn. Svc. Assn. Office: US Embassy Bonn PSC 117 Box 215 APO AE 09080

DILLER, MARCELLA MARY, middle school educator; b. Sherman County, Tex., July 23, 1932; d. Marvin S. and Frances Christina (Husmann) D. BA in English, Mt. St. Scholastica Coll., Atchison, Kans., 1960; MA, U. Notre Dame, 1966. Cert. secondary sch. tchr., Tex. Tchr. Kans. Cath. schs., various locations, 1951-68; tchr. English Mullen H.S., Denver, 1968-76, Met. State Coll., Denver, 1976; tchg. asst. Colo. U., Boulder, 1977-78; tchr. English Nat. Coll. Bus., Denver, 1976-77; book buyer Daleiden Co., Denver, 1977-78; tchr. English St. Mary of the Plains, Garden City, Kans., 1980; pers. dir. St. Catherine Hosp., Garden City, 1978-82; tchr. Pampa (Tex.) Mid. Sch., 1983—. Bd. dirs. St. Catherine Hosp., Garden City, 1979-81; counselor ct. probation Jefferson County, Golden, Colo., 1969-76; mem. St. Vincent Sch. Bd., Pampa, 1984-86; tchr. Laubach Literacy Program, Pampa, 1985—; judge, coach Odessey of the Mind, Pampa, 1986, 89, 96; mem. ch. women's coun. U. Colo. fellow, 1977-78. Mem. Kans. Hosp. Pers. Dirs. Assn. (treas. 1980-81). Republican. Roman Catholic. Home: 1105 Charles Pampa TX 79065 Office: Pampa Middle School 2401 Charles St Pampa TX 79065

DILLEY, CAROL ANN, association executive; b. Ft. Worth; d. Jimmy Brierton and Evelyn B. (Hanchey) D.; m. Jerry Dilley; children: Trey D., Cassandra K. Student, Ft. Worth Sch. Bus., Tarrant County Jr. Coll., Ft. Worth, Tex. Office supv., acct. Dyman Indsl., Ft. Worth, 1980-91; event coord. Tex. Longhorn Breeders Assn. Am., Ft. Worth, 1991-93; exec. dir., 1993—; past officer, bd. mem. N. Tex. Longhorn Breeders Assn., 1988-92; TLBAA rep. Nat. Cattleman's Beef Assn., 1993—; bd. mem. U.S. Beef Breeds Coun., 1993—; dir. Tarrant County Agrl. Extension Svc., 1995-98. Recipient Appreciation awards Tex. Longhorn Breeders of Tomorrow, 1988-95, Mountains and Plains Tex. Longhorn Assn., 1995. Office: PO Box 4430 Fort Worth TX 76106

DILLINGHAM, JOHNNY ROY, materials manager; b. Corinth, Miss., Apr. 18, 1960; s. Roy C. and W. Vadine (Hodum) D.; m. Gwendolyn B. Skinner, May 29, 1980; children: John Robert, Joshua Ryan. BBA, Memphis State U., 1985, MBA, 1989. Prodn. planner Dover Elevator Sys., Inc., Middleton, Tenn., 1980-86; internat. materials mgr. Wright Med. Tech., Inc., Arlington, Tenn., 1986—; master scheduler Dow Corning Wright, Arlington, Tenn., 1986-89, ops. mgr., silicone products, 1989-90. treas. County Line Bapt. Ch., Walnut, Miss., 1982, deacon, 1984, chmn. deacons, 1993. Home: 3575 Stonehenge Cv S Bartlett TN 38135-3087 Office: Wright Med Tech PO Box 100 Arlington TN 38002-0100

DILLINGHAM, MARJORIE CARTER, foreign language educator; b. Bicknell, Ind., Aug. 20, 1915; m. William Pyrle Dillingham, (dec. 1981); children: William Pyrle (dec.), Robert Carter, Sharon Dillingham Martin. PhD in Spanish (Delta Kappa Gamma scholar and fellow), Fla. State U., 1970. High sch. tchr. Fla.; former instr. St. George's Sch., Havana; former mem. faculty Panama Canal Zone Coll., Fla. State U., Duke U., Univ. Ga.; dir. traveling Spanish conversation classes in Spain, Ctrl. and S. Am.; U.S. rep. (with husband) Hemispheric Conf. on Taxation, Rosario, Argentina. Named to Putnam County Hall of Fame, 1986. Mem. Am. Assn. Tchrs. Spanish and Portuguese (past pres. Fla. chpt.), Fla. Edn. Assn. (past pres. fgn. lang. div.), La Sociedad Honoraria Hispanica (past nat. pres.), Fgn. Lang. Tchrs. Leon County, Fla. (pres.), Delta Kappa Gamma (pres.), Phi Kappa Phi, Sigma Delta Pi (pres.), Beta Pi Theta, Kappa Delta Pi, Alpha Omicron Pi, Delta Kappa Gamma. Home: 2109 Trescott Dr Tallahassee FL 32312-3331

DILLON, CYRUS IRVINE, librarian; b. Roanoke, Va., Sept. 23, 1949; s. Cyrus I. Jr. and Muriel (Leedy) D.; children: James E., Ann English. BA, Washington & Lee U., 1971; MA, Ariz. State U., 1976, PhD, 1979. Tchr., coach Henry County Pub. Schs., Martinsville, Va., 1971-72; learning lab. coord. Floyd (Va.) County Pub. Schs., 1972-74; teaching asst. and assoc., instr. English Ariz. State U., Tempe, 1975-79; dir. alternative edn. Danville (Va.) City Schs., 1979-80; prin. Fieldale-Collinsville High Sch., Martinsville, 1980-81; assoc. dean Ferrum (Va.) Coll., 1981-85, libr. dir., 1985—. Editor Va. Librs. Grantee Appalachian Regional Commn., 1972-75, U.S. Dept. Edn., 1979-80, Va. State Libr., 1991-93. Mem. S.W. Info. Network (pres.-elect 1993-94, pres. 1994-95), Va. Pvt. Coll. Librs. (sec. 1985-93), Roanoke Valley Libr. Assn. Democrat. Office: Ferrum Coll Stanley Library Ferrum VA 24088

DILLON, DAVID ANTHONY, journalist, lecturer; b. Fitchburg, Mass., Aug. 24, 1947; s. John Joseph and Lauretta Irene (Morris) D.; m. Sally Ann Hall, June 5, 1971; children: Christopher, Catherine. BA, Boston Coll., 1963; MA, Harvard U., 1965, PhD, 1970. Asst. prof. So. Meth. U., Dallas, 1970-77; mag. editor D Mag., Dallas, 1978-81; archtl. editor Dallas Morning News, 1981—. Author: Experience and Expression, 1976, Dallas Architecture, 1986; contbg. editor: Texas Architect, Architecture, 1982—, Landscape Architecture, 1982—, So. Accents, 1982—. Loeb fellow Harvard U., 1986-87; NEA Critic's grantee, 1980; recipient AP award for criticism, 1988, 90, 91. Democrat. Roman Catholic. Home: 7123 Dalewood Ln Dallas TX 75214-1812 Office: The Dallas Morning News 508 Young St Dallas TX 75202-4808

DILLON, JANIE, nurse; b. Burtonwood AFB, Lancashire, Eng., Jan. 21, 1956; d. Charles Jasper and Mary Elizabeth (Miller) D. BSN, Radford Coll., 1978. RN, Va., N.C., S.C., CCRN, CEN, EMT-cardiac tech. instr.; ACLS provider/instr.; emergency nurses pediat. course instr. Commd. 2d lt. USAF, 1984, advanced through grades to capt./charge nurse, 1988-90; charge/staff nurse Med. U. S.C., Charleston, 1978-79, Johns Hopkins Hosp., Balt., 1980-83, Orlando Regional Med. Ctr., Fla., 1983-84, Univ. Hosp., Charlotte, 1990-91; ER supr. Twin County Regional Hosp., Galax, Va., 1991—; speaker, instr. in field; cons. to chief nurse, Wilford Hall USAF Med. Ctr. on intra-aortic balloon pumps. Mem. ENA, AACN, Res. Officers Assn. Home: RR 1 Box 147 Max Meadows VA 24360-9735

DILLON, JOHN AMBROSE, journalist; b. Rockford, Ill., Dec. 4, 1947; s. John Donald and Joan Marie (Nappi) D.; m. Janet Dale Clement, Nov. 11, 1972; children: Regan E., Erin M. BA, Creighton U., Omaha, Nebr., 1969; MA, U. Minn., 1974. With Richmond (Va.) Times-Dispatch, 1975—, dep. mng. editor, 1994—; mem. adv. bd. Va. Commonwealth U. Sch. Mass. Comm., Richmond, 1990—. Pres. Richmond Cmty. High Sch. PTA, 1992-93. 1st lt. U.S. Army, 1970-73. Mem. Va. Press Assn., Soc. Profl. Journalists (chpt. pres. 1992-93). Office: Richmond Times-Dispatch PO Box 85333 Richmond VA 23293-5333

DILLON, RAY WILLIAM, engineering technician; b. China Lake, Calif., Aug. 8, 1954; s. Duane L. and Audrey J. (Amende) D.; m. Kathy M. Shrum, Sept. 3, 1980; 1 child, Stephanie. Student, U. Okla., 1976-78, Oklahoma City Comm. Coll., 1986; BA, So. Nazarene U., Bethany, Okla., 1987; MBA, Oklahoma City U., 1997. Cert. level IV Nat. Inst. for Certification in Engring. Techs. Technician B&B Fire Protection, Oklahoma City, 1977-78; lead technician Grinell Fire Protection Systems, Oklahoma City, 1978-80; gen. mgr. A.L. Fire Protection, Inc., Oklahoma City, 1980-87, exec. v.p., 1989-90; store mgr. Master Systems Ltd., Oklahoma City, 1987-89; region mgr. Casteel Automatic Fire Protection, Oklahoma City, 1990-92; gen. mgr. Allied Rubber & Gasket Co., Dillon, Colo., 1992-93; design mgr. Al Fire Protection, Inc., Oklahoma City, 1994—; instr. Okla. State U., 1990-91. Mem. Nat. Inst. Cert. Engring. Technicians (cert.), Oklahoma City IBM-PC Users Group, Okla. Fire Protection Contractors Assn. (sec. 1986-87, chmn. 1987, sec. 1990-91), Nat. Fire Protection Assn., Soc. of Fire Protection Engrs. Republican. Baptist. Home: PO Box 990154 Yukon OK 73099-0001 Office: AL Fire Protection 9617 NW 4th St Oklahoma City OK 73127-2951

DILLON, RODNEY LEE, lawyer; b. Vincennes, Ind., Feb. 25, 1938; s. Ray E. and Jeanne E. (O'Conner) D.; m. N. Swarts (div. May 1975); children: Vicki, Terri, Jacki, Kelli; m. Rebecca Boyer, Mar. 28, 1981. BA in Econs., U. Cin., 1960; JD, U. Louisville, 1972. Bar: Fla. 1973, U.S. Dist. Ct. (mid. dist.) Fla. 1973, U.S. Ct. Appeals (5th cir.) 1977, U.S. Supreme Ct. 1977, U.S. Ct. Appeals (11th cir.) 1988; bd. cert. consumer bankruptcy law. Pvt. practice, Sarasota, Fla., 1973—. Recipient awards of appreciation Lawyers Referral Svc., Sarasota County Bar Assn. Mem. ABA, Fla. Bar Assn. (lawyer referral svc. 1994-95), Am. Bankruptcy Inst., Tampa Bay Bankruptcy Bar Assn., Sarasota County Bar Assn., Columbus Assn. (pres. 1978-80), Sarasota Outboard Club (commodore 1991-92), Eagles, Elks, KC (adv. 1983-89). Republican. Roman Catholic. Office: 2831 Ringling Blvd Ste 210D Sarasota FL 34237-5352

DILORENZO, CARRIE LUCAS, research scientist, medical illustrator; b. Taunton, Mass., June 12, 1957; d. Ronald Eugene and Bernadette Marie (Lucas) DiL.; m. Alan Charles Jeffries, June 25, 1988. Student, St. Louis U., 1973-75; BA, Oberlin Coll., 1979; postgrad., U. Mich., 1981, Washtenaw C.C., Ann Arbor, Mich., 1981-84, No. Va. C.C., Annandale, 1985-86, George Washington U., 1986, Augusta Coll., 1991; MS in Med. Illustration, Med. Coll. Ga., 1989. Cert. med. illustrator. Grad. rsch. asst. sci. illustration Mus. Natural History, U. Mich., Ann Arbor, 1981-83; freelance illustrator sci. illustration and design Performance Network Stes., Ann Arbor, 1983-85; grad. student teaching asst. Med. Coll. Ga., Augusta, 1987-89;

student intern Med. Illustration Studio, Bethesda, Md., 1988; instr. computer graphics dept. med. illustration Med. Coll. Ga., Augusta, 1989—, med. illustrator med. illustration and design svcs., 1989-92, computer graphics cons. Sch. Allied Health Scis., 1989-92, Apple Computer resource support coord., 1992—, asst. rsch. scientist sect. neurosurgery dept. surgery, 1992—; graphic arts coord. Appalachia-Sci. in the Pub. Interest, Corbin, Ky., 1977; exhbn. com. chairperson ann. meeting Guild Natural Sci. Illustrators, Ann Arbor, 1982-83, sec.-treas. Mich. chpt., 1982-84; med. illustrator SOURCEBOOK Editl. Bd., 1988—; presenter in field. Contbr. articles to profl. jours. Mem. Assn. Computing Machinery (mem. spl. interest group in computer graphics), Assn. Med. Illustrators (mem. ethics com. 1991—, mem. publicity com. 1991-95, mem. Vesalius trust bd. 1994—). Home: 306 S Center St Zearing IA 50278 Office: Engring Animation Inc 2625 N Loop Dr Ames IA 50010-8615

DILWORTH, HAL CONN, JR., lawyer, military educator; b. Ruston, La., Sept. 17, 1943; s. Hal Conn ad Grace Margaret (Trussell) D.; m. Margaret May Nee, Aug. 15, 1970; children: Kathryn Frances, Heather Jean, Pamela Ann. BA in Speech, History, U. Miss., 1965, JD, 1973. Bar: Miss. 1973, U.S. Ct. Mil. Appeals 1973, U.S. Ct. Fed. Claims 1996. Advt. rep. Proctor and Gamble, Cin., 1966-67; commd. 2d lt. U.S. Army, 1967, advanced through grades to lt. col., 1987; with 3392 USARF Sch., Vietnam, 1969-70; Army trial judge adv. 3d Infantry Div., Wurzburg, Fed. Republic of Germany, 1973-76; Army trial judge adv. U.S. Army Missile Command, Redstone Arsenal, Ala., 1977-79, patriot missile project counsel, 1979-86, tow missile project counsel, 1986-89, sr. adversary proceedings, 1989—. Pres. PTA, Weatherly Sch., 1980; mem. Civilian Welfare Fund Coun., Redstone Arsenal, 1989—. Decorated Bronze Star. Mem. Miss. State Bar, Redstone Arsenal Flying Club (pres. 1979—). Republic. Episcopalian.

DIMARIA, ROSE ANN, nursing educator; b. Bronx, N.Y., Nov. 14, 1964; d. Angelo and Julia (Ingenito) DiM. BSN cum laude, Hunter Coll., 1986, MS in Nursing, 1990; postgrad., NYU, 1991—. RN, N.Y.; cert. nutrition support nurse. Staff nurse gen. surgery unit Bronx Mcpl. Hosp. Ctr., 1986-87, staff nurse SICU/burn unit, 1987-89, nutrition nurse clinician, 1989-93, asst. DON surg. critical care, 1993-95; lectr. Sch. Nursing W.Va. U., 1995—. Mem. AACN, Am. Soc. Parenteral and Enteral Nutrition, N.Y. State Nurses Assn., W.Va. State Nurse Assn., W.Va. Soc. for Parenteral and Enteral Nutrition, N.Y. Acad. Sci., N.Y.C. Soc. Parenteral and Enteral Nutrition (pres. 1992-93),.

DI MEDIO, GREGORY LAWRENCE, English language educator, writer; b. Columbus, Ohio, Nov. 17, 1963; s. Gabriel Silvio and Patricia Ann (Kennedy) Di M.; m. Rebecca Westmoreland Brown, Mar. 22, 1991. BA in English, U. Colo., 1987; MA in English, U. S.C., 1994. Instr. English Nationalities Svcs. Ctr., United Way, Phila., 1987; with Ctr. Rsch. in Human Devel. and Edn. Temple U., Phila., 1987-88; tech. writer/editor Ctr. Rsch. in Human Devel. and Edn., Temple U., Phila., 1988-91; freelance computer cons. U. S.C., Columbia, 1991-93; adj. mem. faculty dept. arts and scis. Midlands Tech. Coll., Columbia, 1992-94, writing ctr. coord., 1993-94; prof. English dept. arts and scis. Denmark (S.C.) Tech. Coll., 1994—; chairperson computer com. Ctr. Rsch. in Human Devel. and Edn., Temple U., Phila., 1988-91; grants cons. Am. Poetry Ctr., Phila., 1990; writing ctr. tutor U. S.C., Columbia, 1993. Contbr. articles to profl. jours. Mem. MLA, Nat. Writing Ctrs. Assn., Nat. Coun. Tchrs. of English, Sierra Club (newsletter editor 1986-87, freelance editor 1989-91, lobbyist 1990-91), Sigma Tau Delta, Alpha Phi Gamma. Democrat. Home: 14 4th St Pittsburgh PA 15215 Office: Denmark Tech Coll Dept Arts and Scis PO Box 327 Denmark SC 29042-0327

DIMIT, ROBERT LESLIE, petroleum engineer; b. Dallas, Feb. 4, 1959; s. Richard O. and Margaret (Perkins) D.; m. Kimberly Dann Pulse, Oct. 10, 1992. BS in Petroleum Engring., Colo. Sch. Mines, 1983; MS in Petroleum Mgmt., U. Kans., 1987. Registered profl. engr., Tex. Cons. petroleum engr. E. Ralph Green & Assoc., Midland, Tex., 1983-84; sr. petroleum engr. Henry Petroleum Corp., Midland, Tex., 1984-95; dir. bus. devel. Arco-Permian, Midland, Tex., 1995—; owner, ptnr. Mardim Co., Midland, 1992—. Recipient Ednl. Found. award Phi Gamma Delta Frat., 1978. Mem. Nat. Gas Producers Assn. (pres. 1992—), Soc. Petroleum Engrs. (bd. dirs. 1983—), Soc. Profl. Engrs., Permian Basin Petroleum Assn., Green Tree Country Club (bd. dirs. 1993—). Republican. Methodist. Home: 4100 Stratton Midland TX 79707

DIMITRY, THEODORE GEORGE, lawyer; b. New Orleans, Jan. 15, 1937; s. Theodore Joseph and Ouida Marion (Seiler) D.; m. S. Elizabeth Warren; children—Mary Elizabeth, Theodore Warren. B.S., Tulane U., 1958, J.D., 1960. Bar: La. 1960, Tex. 1964. Assoc. firm Phelps, Dunbar, Marks, Claverie & Sims, New Orleans, 1965-69, ptnr., 1969-75; ptnr. firm Vinson & Elkins, Houston, 1975—; research fellow Southwestern Legal Found., Dallas, 1973—; speaker on maritime law, offshore contracting, ins. and resource devel. at profl. seminars, 1975—. Contbr. articles to profl. jours. Mem. permanent adv. bd. Tulane U. Admiralty Law Inst., 1985—. Served with USN, 1960-64. Mem. Maritime Law Assn. U.S., Southeastern Admiralty Law Inst., Am. Soc. Internat. Law, ABA. Office: Vinson & Elkins 2300 First City Tower 1001 Fannin St Houston TX 77002

DINCULESCU, ANTONIE, chemical engineer, researcher; b. Bucharest, Romania, Mar. 29, 1941; came to U.S., 1991; s. Antonie and Maria (Negruse) D.; m. Elefteria Arnautu, Dec. 15, 1965; 1 child, Astra. M-SChemE, Polytech. U., Bucharest, 1965, PhD in Organic Chemistry, 1980. Registered chemical engr., Bucharest. From rsch. scientist to dept. head Chem. Pharm. Rsch. Inst., Bucharest, 1965-91; sci. advisor Ortho-Cycle Co., Hollywood, Fla., 1991-92; sr. rsch. scientist, group leader Pharmos Corp., Alachua, Fla., 1992—. Author: Pyrylium Salts, 1982, Solar Energy Storage, 1991; contbr. articles to Jour. Chem. Rsch., Jour. Pharm. Sci., Pharm. Rsch., Romanian Jour. Physics, Talanta, Tetrahedron, Heterocycles, Chemica Scripta. Mem. AAAS, Am. Chem. Soc., N.Y. Acad. Sci. Office: Pharmos Corp 2 Innovation Dr Alachua FL 32615-9585

DINDINGER, JACK WILSON, military officer; b. Omaha, Mar. 26, 1924; s. John Wilson and Gladys Elizabeth (Crook) D.; m. Patricia Elizabeth Bracken, Mar. 15, 1950; children: Gail K., Heidi J., Leigh A., John W., Thomas A. BS, U. Md., 1959. Commd. 2d lt. USMC, 1945, advanced through grades to col., ret., 1975; long range group mem. Mil Ops. Rsch. Symposium, Washington, 1966-73. Ch. sch. tchr. 8th grade Lakeside Presbyn. Ch., Duluth, Minn., 1961-62, jr. h.s. youth group leader, 1961-62; elder Oceanside Presbyn. Ch., 1964; chmn. by-laws and nominations com. Homeowners Assn., Staunton, Va., 1991—. Decorated Legion of Merit (U.S.): Order of Hwarang (Korea). Mem. NRA, Am. Legion, Marine Corps Assn., Retired Officers Assn. Republican. Home: 204 Yardley Square Staunton VA 24401

DI NICOLO, ROBERTO, allergist; b. Trieste, Italy, Mar. 29, 1958; s. Michele and Maria (Universo) Di N.; m. Lisa Joy Goetz, Sept. 1, 1984; 1 child, Calvin Alexander. Grad., Superior Sch. Sci., Trieste, Italy, 1977; MD, U. Trieste, 1985. Diplomate Am. Bd. Pediats., Am. Bd. Internal Medicine, Am. Bd. Allergy and Immunology. Intern SUNY, Winthrop Univ. Hosp., Stony Brook, N.Y., 1986-87; resident dept. pediats. All Children's Hosp., U. South Fla., 1987-89; clin. fellow adult and pediat. allergy and immunology U. South Fla. Tchg. Hosps., St. Petersburg and Tampa, Fla., 1989-91; pvt. practice allergy and immunology Volusia Asthma and Allergy Specialists, Ormond Beach, Fla., 1991-93, The Asthma, Allergy and Sinus Clinic, Daytona Beach, Fla., 1993—; part-time emergency room physician Bayfront Med. Ctr., St. Petersburg, Fla., 1990-91; part-time pvt. practice allergy and immunology Drs. W. Schmid and R. Doyle, St. Petersburg, 1990-91. Med. columnist Daytona Beach (Fla.) News Jour., 1992—. Recipient McCarthy award Halifax Med. Ctr., 1991. Fellow Am. Acad. Pediats.; mem. Am. Coll. Allergy and Immunology, Fla. Med. Assn. (Physician Communicator of Yr. 1994), Volusia County Med. Soc. Home: 86 Hollow Branch Xing Ormond Beach FL 32174-4814 Office: The Asthma Allergy & Sinus Clinic 600 N Clyde Morris Blvd Ste 2 Daytona Beach FL 32114-2322

DINKINS, CAROL EGGERT, lawyer; b. Corpus Christi, Tex., Nov. 9, 1945; d. Edgar H. Jr. and Evelyn S. (Scheel) Eggert; children: Anne, Amy. BS, U. Tex., 1968; JD, U. Houston, 1971. Bar: Tex. 1971. Prin. assoc. Tex. Law Inst. Coastal and Marine Resources, Coll. Law U. Houston, Tex., 1971-73; assoc., ptnr. Vinson & Elkins, Houston, 1973-81, 83-84, 85—, mem. mgmt. com., 1991—; asst. atty. gen. environ. and natural resources Dept. Justice, 1981-83, U.S. dep. atty. gen., 1984-85; chmn. Pres.'s Task Force on Legal Equity for Women, 1981-83; mem. Hawaiian Native Study Commn., 1981-83; dir. Nat. Consumer Coop. Banks Bd., 1981. Author articles in field. Chmn. Tex. Gov.'s Flood Control Action Group, 1980-81; bd. dirs. The Nature Conservancy, 1996—, Oryx Energy Co., 1990-95, U. Houston Law Ctr. Found., 1985-89, 96—, Environ. and Energy Study Inst., 1986—, Houston Mus. Natural Sci.l, 1986—, Tex. Nature Conservancy, 1985—, chair, 1996—. Mem. ABA (ho. of dels., past chmn. state and local govt. sect., chair-elect sect. nat. resources, energy, and environ. law 1995-96), Fed. Bar Assn. (bd. dirs. Houston chpt. 1986), State Bar Tex., Houston Bar Assn., Tex. Water Conservation Assn., Houston Law Rev. Assn. (bd. dirs. 1978). Republican. Lutheran. Office: Vinson & Elkins 3300 First City Tower 1001 Fannin St Houston TX 77002

DINKLER, LEONARD RONALD, engineering consultant; b. Mabscott, W.Va., Sept. 22, 1925; s. Emil Leonard and Almeda Nancy (Jarrett) D.; m. Elizabeth Jordan Outlaw, June 2, 1957; children: Karl Leonard, Hugh Daniel, Paul Ronald. BS in Mech. Engring., Duke U., 1950; basic electronic cert., Guilford Coll., 1957; student, U. Fla., 1969. Engr. Western Electric Co., Burlington, N.C., 1951-57; prodn. engr. Vick Chem. Co., Greensboro, N.C., 1957-58; sr. engr. Sperry Microwave Electronics Co., divsn. Sperry Rand Corp., Clearwater, Fla., 1958-63; v.p. Tech. Enterprises, Inc., Largo, Fla., 1963-64; mech. engr. Apollo Support Dept. GE, Cape Canaveral, Fla., 1964-66; mgr. NiCd vented cell engring. battery bus. dept. GE, Gainesville, Fla., 1966-86; engring. cons. Gainesville, 1986—. Patentee in field. With Air Corps USN, 1943-46. Mem. ASME. Home and Office: 1536 NW 7th Ave Gainesville FL 32603-1206

DINNING, WOODFORD WYNDHAM, JR., lawyer; b. Demopolis, Ala., Aug. 15, 1954; s. Woodford W. and Gladys (Brown) D.; m. Tammy E. Cannon, May 27, 1994. AS, U. Ala., 1976, JD, 1979. Bar: Ala. 1979, U.S. Dist. Ct. (so. dist.) Ala. 1980. Judge City of Demopolis, 1980-93; ptnr. Lloyd, Dinning, Boggs & Dinning, Demopolis, 1979—; pres. and bd. dirs. Tenn. Tom Motel, Inc.; atty. Marengo County Commn. and City of Linden, Ala. Mem. U. Ala. Alumni Assn. (chmn. 1985-86). Office: Lloyd Dinning Boggs & Dinning PO Drawer Z Demopolis AL 36732

DINSMOOR, ROBERT DAVIDSON, judge; b. El Paso, Tex., May 19, 1955; s. William Bell Jr. and Mary (Higgins) D. BA in Polit. Sci., Brigham Young U., 1979, JD, 1982. Bar: Tex. 1983, U.S. Dist. Ct. (we. dist.) Tex. 1985, U.S. Ct. Appeals (5th cir.) 1986, U.S. Supreme Ct. 1987. Rsch. assoc. J. Reuben Clark Law Sch., Brigham Young U., Provo, Utah, 1981-82; asst. dist. atty. El Paso (Tex.) Dist. Atty., 1983-90; dist. ct. judge State of Tex., El Paso, 1991—; speaker Tex. County Judges Assn., 1992, 1992 Ann. Mex. Am. Bar Assn. of Tex. Conf., 1992, also various h.s. and mid. schs., El Paso, 1988—; co-founder El Paso Criminal Law Study Group. Contbr. articles to profl. jours. Bd. dirs. S.W. Repertory Orgn., El Paso, 1994-95; Sunday Sch. pres. Latter Day Saints Ch., 5th ward, El Paso, 1993-95; exec. sec. to bishop, 1995—. Recipient Outstanding Achievement award El Paso Young Lawyers Assn., 1990. Mem. State Bar Tex. (mem. indigent representation com. 1994—, victim/witness com. 1992-95), El Paso Bar Assn. (mem. legal bar com., libr. com., criminal law com., others 1980—, bd. dirs. 1993-96, sec. 1996—). Democrat. Office: 120th Dist Ct County Bldg Rm 605 500 E San Antonio Ave El Paso TX 79901-2419

DINWOODIE, ROXAN EMMERT, marketing consultant; b. Lancaster, Pa., Feb. 15, 1955; d. Joseph Wellington Emmert and Mary Ann Sherrard; m. Winston Olivier Dinwoodie, Apr. 24, 1983. BA with honors, Eckerd Coll., 1976; MS in Mktg., Ga. State U., 1985. Prin. Via Nova Consulting, Atlanta, 1982—; planning dir. Ga. Rehab. Svcs., Atlanta, 1987-91; asst. staff mgr. Privatization Task Force Gov's Commn. on Effectiveness & Economy in Govt., Atlanta, 1991-92. vol. Citizen's Democracy Corps, Czech Rep., 1993, 94; active East Point Involved Citizens; bd. dirs. Advs. for Self Govt., Inc. Recipient Dimensions of Excellence Leadership award, 1988. Mem. Am. Mktg. Assn., Inst. Mgmt. Cons., Alpha Mu Alpha. Libertarian. Episcopalian. Home and Office: 1228 Winburn Dr East Point GA 30344-2750

DIOMEDE, MATTHEW, English language educator, author; b. Yonkers, N.Y., June 8, 1940; s. Frank and Josephine D.; m. Barbara R. Diomede, June 29, 1968. BA, Fordham U., 1962, MS, 1965; MA, Long Island U., 1975; PhD, St. Louis U., 1992. Cert. secondary sch. tchr. English, prin., supr., N.Y., tchr. English, Latin, Italian, Conn. Tchr. English, Latin U. S. Fla., Tampa, Conn., NY, 1962-79; lectr., coord. comm. U. Mo., St. Louis, 1979-82; asst. prof. English Parks Coll. St. Louis U., Cahokia, Ill., 1982-92; tchg. fellow English Harris-Stowe State Coll., St. Louis, 1984-85; English instr. St. Louis C.C., 1992-95, U. Tampa, Fla., 1995—, U. S. Fla., Tampa, 1995—; mem. several coms. at Parks Coll., St. Louis U. and at the U. including Acad. Affairs com., Student Devel., Student Life Coun., Course Substitution Com. Author: (book) Pietro Di Donato, The Master Builder, 1995; also articles, fiction, poetry in over 50 periodicals; translator Salvatore Quasimodo's Italian Poem A Winter Past. in The Apalachee Quarterly; presenter of poetry to various U.S. groups, 1975-92. With USMCR, 1959-65. Finalist Va. Commonwealth Univ. Contemporary Poetry Series, 1975; recipient Poetry scholarship Rope Walk Writers Retreat, U. So. Ind. at Evansville, 1990. Mem. MLA, Nat. Coun. Tchrs. of English, Fordham U. Spiked Shoe Club (v.p., chmn. of bd.). Nat. Assn. Remedial/Developmental Postsecondary Edn. Conf., St. Louis, Mo. (chmn. evaluation com.). Home: 125 10th St E Tierra Verde FL 33715-2206

DIPAOLO, PETER THOMAS, engineering executive, educator; b. Phila., Sept. 4, 1937; s. Peter T. and Erma (Palestini) DiP.; m. Josephine M. Mercurio, Apr. 28, 1962; children: Louis Joseph, Michael Louis. BSME, Villanova U., 1971; MBA, Nova U., 1980, D of Bus. Adminstrn., 1987. Mech. designer RCA Corp., Camden, N.J., 1955-66; project engr. Boeing Corp., Morton, Pa., 1966-68; mech. engr. Burroughs Corp., Paoli, Pa., 1968-70; sect. mgr. Gould-Systems Engring. Labs, Ft. Lauderdale, Fla., 1970-76; corp. fellow Modular Computer Systems, Ft. Lauderdale, 1976-86; sr. dir. hardware engring. Datapoint, Inc., San Antonio, 1986-88; pres. Sanford Rose Assocs., Ft. Lauderdale, 1988—, Integrated Consulting Internat., Ft. Lauderdale, 1990—; prof. mgmt. grad. sch. Nova U., Ft. Lauderdale, 1981—. Patentee in field. Served to cpl. USMCR, 1959-65. Mem. Fin. Execs. Inst. (Award for Excellence 1985), Epsilon Tau Lambda. Republican. Roman Catholic. Home and Office: Integrated Cons Internat 7337 SW 9th Ct Fort Lauderdale FL 33317-4138

DIPIANTI, ROBERT, religious association executive. Pres. Soc. Traditional Roman Caths. Address: PO Box 13173 Charlotte NC 28270-0077

DIROSA, LINDA MARY, education specialist, diagnostic company executive; b. New Orleans, Mar. 23, 1951; d. Frank Jr. and Emilie Olympe (Ory) DiR. BS, S.W. Tex. State U., 1973; MEd, Lamar U., 1978. Cert. ednl. diagnostician, K-12 prin., mid-mgmt. Tchr. Houston Ind. Sch. Dist., 1974-79, ednl. diagnostician, 1979-83; tchr., prin. designee Fairbanks (Alaska) North Star Borough Sch. Dist., 1983-90, tchr., adminstrv. intern, 1990-92; edn. specialist Tex. Edn. Agy., Austin, 1993-94; pres., CEO Diagnostic/Learning, Austin, 1994—; mem. state mgmt. team Tex. Edn. Agy., Austin, 1993-94. Fellow World Found. of Successful Women; mem. AAUW, NAFE, Am. Ednl. Rsch. Assn., Nat. Assn. Ednl. Therapists (profl. registry), Tex. Profl. Ednl. Diagnostician (profl. registry), Learning Disabilities Assn. Roman Catholic. Address: 13411 Balcrest Dr Houston TX 77070

DISANTO, VINSON MICHAEL, osteopath; b. Phila., June 15, 1956; s. Vinson James and Dolores (Lyons) DiS. BS in Biology, Widener U., Chester, Pa., 1981; DO, Phila. Coll. Osteo. Medicine, 1986; cert. Bau-Biology, Inst. Bau-Biologie, Germany, 1993; DSc, Medicina Alternativa, Sri Lanka, 1992, PhD, 1992. Resident Phoenix General Hospital, 1986-87; family practice medicine Phoenix, 1987-88, San Diego, 1988-89; environ. physician Bio Tox Inc., San Diego, 1989-90; dir. emergency medicine Villa View Hosp., San Diego, 1990-91; dir. occupational medicine H.O.E.M., Eureka, Calif., 1991-92; mini residency, Occupational/Environmental Med. Univ. Ca. S.F., 1991-92; med. dir. Pacific Urgent Care, Vista, Calif., 1993; clin. dir. U.S. Penitentary, Atlanta, 1993—; clin. dir. Bur. Prisons, Atlanta, 1993—; dir. Health Svcs. Acad., City of Phila., 1983. Tchr., spokesman Henry George Sch., Phila., 1981—. 1st lt. Air Guard, 1984-86. Recipient Action Achievement award Dept. Edn., Phila., 1981. Mem. Am. Osteo. Assn., Inst. Bau-Biologie, Oriental Medicine Inst., Am. Coll. Occupl. and Environ. Medicine. Republican. Home: 3078 Clairmont Rd # 6312 Atlanta GA 30329 Office: US Penitentary Atlanta GA 30329

DISMUKES, CAROL JAEHNE, county official; b. Giddings, Tex., July 17, 1938; d. Herbert Emil and Ruby (Alexander) Jaehne; m. Harold Charles Schumann, Feb. 7, 1959 (div. May 1970); children: Timothy, Michael, Keith, Gregory; m. Milton Brown Dismukes, Mar. 19, 1971. Student Tex. Lutheran Coll., 1958. Dep. Lee County Clk., Giddings, Tex., 1970-74, chief dep., 1975-77; accounts receivable clk. Invader Inc., Giddings, 1977-79; prodn. sec. Humble Exploration, Giddings, 1979-80; county clk. Lee County, Giddings, 1980—. Mem., Dime Box Ind. Sch. Dist. Trustees, Tex., 1972-80, pres., 1977-80; v.p. St. Johns Lutheran Ch. Council, 1982-84; chmn. Dime Box Homecoming and Mini-Marathon, 1978—; chmn. scholar com. Lee Co. Jr. Livestock Show, 1982—; sec. St. John's Luth. Ch., 1986, treas., 1987-89; chmn. St. John's Luth. Ch., 1991-93. Mem. County and Dist. Clks Assn. Tex. Democrat. Avocations: reading; sewing. Office: Lee County Clk PO Box 419 Giddings TX 78942-0419

DISON, CHARLOTTE ANNE, nursing administrator; b. Staunton, Va., July 26, 1931; d. Robert Clayton and Alice Clare (Eppard) Comer; m. Jack L. Dison, Nov. 6, 1954; 1 child, Jack Ross. Diploma, Lynchburg Gen. Hosp., 1953; BS in Nursing, Fla. State U., 1963; MA, Columbia U., 1966; postgrad., U. Pa. Wharton Sch. Bus., 1989. RN, Fla., Va.; cert. nursing adminstr., advanced. Staff nurse Norton (Va.) Community Hosp., 1953-55; asst. dir. nursing svcs. Miners Meml. Hosp. Assn., Wise, Va., 1956-64; nursing supr. Beekman-Downtown Hosp., N.Y.C., 1965-66; dir. nursing Bapt. Hosp. of Miami, 1966-79, assoc. adminstr. for patient care svcs., 1979-86, v.p. for patient care svcs., 1986—; mem. nursing coun. Sun Health Corp., 1992—. Contbr. articles to profl. jours. co-chair nursing manpower task force Commn. on Future of Nursing in Fla., 1988-91, nurse exec. rep. state commn., 1987-90, rec. sec., 1987-90; co-chiar FNA-FMA Task Force on Nursing Shortage, 1991—. Recipient Inaugural Leadership award Am. Orgn. Nurse Execs., 1995; Miami-Dade Coll. and Bapt. Hosp. grantee, 1987-88, 94. Mem. ACHE (diplomate, ad hoc com. on nurse execs.), Fla. Nurses Assn. (long-range planning com. 1988—, bd. dirs. dist. 5 1991—, mem. nursing adv. coun. 1991—, Employer of Yr. 1986, 87, 88, 90, Nurse Exec. of Yr. 1989, 90), Fla. Orgn. Nurse Execs. (pres. 1988-89, mktg. com. 1989—, chair search com. for exec. dir. 1989—), South Fla. Orgn. Nurse Execs. (pres. 1985-86, bd. dirs. 1980-82).

DISTELHORST, CRAIG TIPTON, savings and loan executive; b. Pitts., Nov. 3, 1941; s. Carl Frederick and Josephine Harris (Smith) D.; m. Judith Ann Harrill, Oct. 6, 1979. BS, Washington and Lee U., 1963; JD, George Washington U., 1963, George Washington U., 1966. Bar: N.Y. 1969, D.C., 1967. Sr. v.p., sec. Home Fed. Savs., Greensboro, N.C., 1976-79; v.p. Mortgage Guaranty Ins. Corp., Milw., 1979-82; exec. v.p., chief operating officer Benjamin Franklin Savs. and Loan, Houston, 1982-84, pres., 1984-85, chmn. exec. com., 1985-86; pres., chief exec. officer Village Savs. and Loan, Houston, 1986-89, chmn. bd., 1988; pres., chief exec. officer Murray Fed. Savs. and Loan, Dallas, 1989—; chmn. bd. dirs, chief exec. officer Murray Mortgage Corp.; vice chmn., chief exec. officer Murray Realty; pres., chief exec. officer Murray Devel. Corp.; exec. v.p. Murray Ins.; bd. dirs. Security Capital Credit Corp. Hartford, Conn., Foster Ins. Mgrs., Inc., Houston, Lloyds Mgmt. Corp., Houston, Security Capital Lloyds, Houston. Mem. corp. bd. dirs. Milw. Sch. Engring., 1980—; vol. steering com. United Craftsman, Bedford-Stuyvesant, N.Y., 1968-69; chmn. support program, George Washington U. Law Sch., 1969; mem. Mo. Rep. State Com., 1972-74; adv. Ret. Sr. Citizens Vol. Program, Nevada, Mo., 1975-76; vol. Juvenile Probation Officer, Nevada, 1974-76; bd. dirs. Mo.-Kans. Regional council Boy Scouts Am., 1975-76; bd. dirs. Greater Greensboro Housing Found., N.C., 1978-79; state fin. chmn. for election Gov. Kit Bond of Mo., 1972; chmn. Vernon County United Fund, Nevada, 1975, Nevada City Planning Commn., 1973-75, Mo. Mcpl. Bond Com., 1978-79; vice chmn., bd. dirs. United Arts Council Greensboro, 1979; mem. Nevada City Council, 1975-76; mem. 25th anniversary class reunion com. Washington and Lee U., 1987-88. Mem. Kingwood Country Club, Elks, Rotary (bd. dirs. 1975-76, chmn. program 1974-76), Phi Delta Phi. Presbyterian. Home: 7791 Tangier Dr Springfield VA 22153-2327 Office: United Savings Assn Ste 109 5550 Lyndon B Johnson Fwy Dallas TX 75240-6264

DITMANN, LAURENT, French language educator; b. Paris, Apr. 9, 1962; came to U.S., 1986; s. Marcel and Suzanne (Bercu) D.; m. Mary R. Johnson, June 29, 1990. Student, U. Paris X, Nanterre, France, 1988; MA in English, Portland State U., 1988; agregation, Ecole Normale Superieure, St. Cloud, France, 1989; PhD in French, Brown U., 1991. Libr. Mil. Staff Coll., Paris, 1984-85; eleve prof. Ecole Normale Superieure, 1985-89; instr. in French Portland (Oreg.) State U., 1986-88; grad. teaching asst. Brown U., Providence, 1989-91; asst. prof. French Spelman Coll., Atlanta, 1991-96, assoc. prof. French, 1996—; mem. faculty coun. Univ. Ctr. in Ga., Atlanta, 1993—. Mem. MLA, Coll. Lang. Assn., Mil. Hist. Assn. Office: Spelman Coll Box 797 350 Spelman Ln SW Atlanta GA 30314-4398

DITTO, (JOHN) KANE, mayor; b. Bowling Green, Ky., May 18, 1944; m. Betsy Martin. BA, Duke Univ.; JD, Vanderbilt Univ. State rep. from. dist. 66 Miss., 1988-89; atty. and real estate developer; mayor City of Jackson, Miss., 1989—. Mem. ABA, Miss. Econ. Coun., C. of C., Miss. and Hinds County Bar Assn., Nat. Civic League. Baptist. Address: Office of the Mayor PO Box 17 Jackson MS 39205-0017 also: 219 S President St 3rd Fl Jackson MS 39201-4312

DIVISH, MARGARET MARY, physician; b. Camden, N.J., May 25, 1964; d. William Joseph and Patricia Ann (Dolan) D.; m. Edward Beman McMillan, Sept. 17, 1994. BS, Xavier Univ., 1986; MD, Albert Einstein Coll. Medicine, 1991. Diplomate Am. Bd. Internal Medicine. Intern, resident Johns Hopkins Med. Inst., Balt., 1991-94; physician Naval Primary Care Clinic, Quantico, Va., 1994-96, Charlotte (N.C.) Med. Clinic, 1996—. Nat. Merit scholar Internat. Bricklayers Union, 1982-86, Rev. Joseph Peters scholar Xavier Univ., 1984; Howard Hughes fellow NIH, 1989-90. Mem. ACP, Airplane Owners Pilots Assn. Office: Charlotte Med Clinic Inc 7810 Providence Rd Ste 103 Charlotte NC 28226

DIXON, ALBERT KING, II, university administrator; b. Savannah, Ga., Dec. 28, 1936; s. Albert King and Katharine Blanchard (Simmons) D.; m. Augusta Lee Mason, Mar. 27, 1959; children: Albert King III, Augustus Mason, Lee Simmons. BA in Polit. Sci. cum laude, U. S.C., 1959; postgrad., Furman U., 1984, U. Okla., 1985, Am. Inst. Banking, 1984-85. Commd. 2d lt. USMC, 1959, advanced through grades to lt. col., 1975; exec. officer USMC, Camp Pendleton, Calif., 1961, Okinawa, Japan, 1961-62; series officer Recruit Depot, athletic officer, head football coach USMC, San Diego, 1962-65; commdg. officer USMC, Vietnam, 1966-67; instr., Marine Corps Devel. and Edn. Commd., head platoon tactics sect. Basic Sch. USMC, Quantico, Va., 1967-70; schs. officer, staff sec. to commdg. gen. Pacific Fleet Marine Force USMC, Camp Smith, Hawaii, 1970-73; head football coach Quantico Marines, 1968; ops. and ground tng. officer USMC, Okinawa, 1973-74; officer in charge recruiting sta. USMC, Oklahoma City, 1974-77; ground support tng. and equipment officer Hdqs. Marine Corps USMC, Washington, 1977-81, retired, 1981; exec. dir. Laurens (S.C.) Family YMCA, 1981-83; v.p., city exec. Palmetto Bank, Laurens, 1983-88; assoc. v.p. alumni affairs U. S.C., Columbia, 1988, dir. athletics, 1988-92, spl. asst. to pres. for univ. promotion and leadership devel, 1993—. Active Boy Scouts Am.; Sunday Sch. tchr., elder, mem. com. various Presbyn. chs., Hawaii, Okla., S.C., Va.; Chmn. capital campaign Laurens County Libr., 1987-88; past pres. Laurens Dist. H.S. Booster Club, Laurens County Touchdown Club; past bd. visitors Lander Coll.; past mem. U. S.C. Edn. Found.; past mem. found. bd. Piedmont Tech.; bd. dirs. Dixie Youth Baseball, 1987, vice chmn., player agt., bd. dirs., Laurens, 1982-88; bd. dirs. Upper Savannah Coun. Govts., 1988; pres. Laurens 100 Club, 1984, 88; vice chmn. Laurens County Hist. Soc., 1985-87, Laurens County Bicentennial Com., 1985-86, Palmetto Partnership, Found. for Drug Abuse, Columbia, 1989-91; mem. study com. City of Columbia Baseball Stadium, 1989-90; mem. adv. bd. Midlands chpt. Nat. Football Found. and Hall of Fame; mem. steering com. Future Group Richland County; gov. Rotary Dist. 7750., 1987-88. Recipient Dist. award of Merit, Silver Beaver award and Scoutmaster of Yr. award Boy Scouts Am.; named to U. S.C. Athletic Hall of Fame, State of S.C. Athletic Hall of

Fame. Mem. S.C. Assn. Regional Couns. (bd. dirs. 1992—, pres. 1995), So. Ind. Collegiate Ofcls. Assn. (athletic dirs. representative 1989-90), Greater Columbia C. of C. (mem. coun. on edn.), Coll. Football Assn. Athletic Dirs. (mem. com. 1989-90), VFW, Am. Legion, Laurens 100 Club (pres. 1984, 88), Masons, Shriners, Rotary Club of Five Points (dist. 7750 gov. 1987-88), Phi Beta Kappa, Sigma Alpha Pi, Omicron Delta Kappa (past pres.), Kappa Sigma Kappa (past pres.), Kappa Alpha. Home: RR 3 Box 205 Laurens SC 29360-9510 Office: U SC Carolina Plz Ste 1522 Columbia SC 29208

DIXON, DANIEL ROBERTS, JR., tax lawyer; b. Rocky Mount, N.C., Feb. 22, 1911; s. Daniel Roberts and Ida Louise (Mason) D.; children: Daniel Roberts III, Carolyn Roy Dixon Dyess. AB, Coll. William and Mary, 1937; JD, Duke U., 1941; LLM in Taxation, NYU, 1951. CPA, N.C.; bar: N.C. Atty. Hamel, Park & Saunders, Washington, 1951-52; asst. prof. N.C. State U., Raleigh, 1954-76; pvt. practice Raleigh, 1953—. Author: Graphic Guide Fundamental Accounting; inventor building block; contbr. articles to profl. jours. Mem., judge advocate NLUS-Triangle Coun., Wake County, N.C.; mem. Internat. Visitors Coun., Raleigh, N.C. Capt. U.S. Air Corps., 1942-46. Mem. Navy League of U.S. (judge advocate 1990-96), N.C. Triangle Coun., N.C. Bar Assn., Wake County Bar Assn., Phi Beta Kappa (pres. Wake county). Home: 1022 Shelley Rd Raleigh NC 27609 Office: Dixon & Hunt 7 N Bloodworth St Raleigh NC 27601

DIXON, ERNEST THOMAS, JR., retired bishop; b. San Antonio, Oct. 13, 1922; s. Ernest Thomas and Ethel Louise (Reese) D.; m. Lois F. Brown, July 20, 1943 (dec. 1977); children: Freddie Brown, Ernest Reese (dec. 1990), Muriel Jean, Leona Louise; m. Ernestine Gray Clark, May 18, 1979; 1 child, Sherryl D. Clark. B.A. magna cum laude, Samuel Huston Coll., 1943; B.D., Drew Theol. Sem., 1945; D.D. (hon.), Huston-Tillotson Coll., 1962; L.H.D. (hon.), Southwestern Coll., Winfield, Kans., 1973; LL.D. (hon.), Baker U., 1973; Litt.D. (hon.), Westmar Coll., 1978; H.H.D. (hon.), Kans. Wesleyan Coll., 1980. Ordained to ministry Methodist Ch., 1946, consecrated bishop, 1972. Pastor Methodist Ch., Brackettville, Tex., 1943; asst. pastor East Calvary Meth. Ch., Harlem, N.Y., 1943-44, Wallace Chapel, A.M.E. Zion Ch., Summit, N.J., 1944-45; dir. religious extension service Tuskegee Inst., Ala., 1945-51; exec. sec. West Tex. Conf. Bd. Edn., 1951-52; staff mem. Div. Local Ch. Bd. Edn., Meth. Ch., 1952-64; pres. Philander Smith Coll., Little Rock, 1965-69; asst. gen. sec. div. coordination, research and planning Program Council United Meth. Ch., 1969-72, bishop Kans. area, 1972-80; bishop San Antonio area United Meth. Ch., Tex., 1980-92; ret., 1992; pres. Council of Bishops, 1988-89; pres. bd. dirs. Bethlehem Ctr., Nashville, 1953-64; del. gen. conf. Meth. and United Meth. Chs., 1964-72; pres. Gen. Bd. Higher Edn. and Ministry, United Meth. Ch., 1972-76; Ala. del. Midcentury White House Conf. Children and Youth, 1950. Citizens adv. com. Gov. Ark., 1967-69; bd. dirs. Little Rock C. of C., 1967-69; pres. Tex. Conf. Chs., 1984-86; trustee Mt. Sequoyah Assembly, Fayetteville, Ark., 1972-92, Gammon Theol. Sem., Atlanta, 1978-92, Gulfside Assembly, Waveland, Miss., 1978—, pres. bd. dirs. 1978-92, Huston-Tillotson Coll., Austin, Tex., 1978—, Lydia Patterson Inst., El Paso, 1980-92, Mission Home, San Antonio, 1980-92, Meth. Home, Waco, Tex., 1980—, Morningside Manor, 1980-92, Southwestern U., Georgetown, Tex., 1980-92, S.W. Tex. Meth. Hosp., San Antonio, 1980—, others. Mem. Alpha Phi Alpha, Sigma Pi Phi.

DIXON, GILES H., engineering manager; b. Greensboro, N.C., July 24, 1951; s. Charles M. and Frances (Schuler) D.; m. Jallene Perry, Oct. 27, 1973; children: Jeremy, Mackenzie. AS in Architecture, Guilford County C.C., Jamestown, N.C., 1972. Draftsman Varco Pruden United Dominion, 1972-76, drafting systems mgr., 1976-85, systems mgr., 1989-91, sales systems mgr., 1991-93; R&D and systems mgr. Strian Bldgs., 1985-89; R&D dir. Am. Bldgs., Eufaula, Ala., 1993-95; dir. engring. svcs. Am. Bldgs., Eufaula, 1995—. Office: Am Bldgs State Docks Rd Eufaula AL 36027

DIXON, JEROME WAYNE, lawyer; b. Shreveport, La., July 7, 1955; s. Huey P. and Myrtle (Martin) D. BA, U. Calif., Santa Cruz, 1981; JD, So. U., Baton Rouge, La., 1986. Bar: La. 1988, U.S. Dist. Ct. (mid. dist.) La. 1988, U.S. Dist. Ct. (ea. dist.) La. 1989, U.S. Dist. Ct. (we. dist.) La. 1989, U.S. Dist. Ct. (no. dist.) Calif., 1989, U.S. Ct. Appeals (5th cir.) 1989. Pvt. practice Baton Rouge, 1988—; staff atty. Legis. Bur. Senate, Baton Rouge, 1988—; La. State Senate atty. for rsch. svcs., 1991. Coach Baker Brownfield Athletic Assn., Baton Rouge, 1990, Glen Oaks Athletics, Baton Rouge, 1989. Mem. ABA, Assn. Trial Lawyers Am., La. Trial Lawyers Assn., Baton Rouge Bar Assn., Kiwanis (v.p. 1989). Office: 842 East Blvd Baton Rouge LA 70802-6308

DIXON, JOHN SPENCER, international executive; b. London, Apr. 23, 1957; s. Richard Kennedy and Elizabeth Ann (Flaxman) D.; m. Karen Beth Swanson, Aug. 18, 1984; children: Katherine Elizabeth, John Spencer Jr. BA with honors, Oxford U., 1979, MA, 1985; MBA, Harvard U., 1982. Supply exec. Hi-Tec Sports Ltd., Essex, England, 1982-86; pres. Hi-Tec Internat. Ltd., Taichung, Taiwan, 1983-84; founder, ptnr. Transatlantic Mktg. Co., Essex, England, 1985—; exec. v.p. Decipher, Inc., Norfolk, Va., 1988-90; pres. Waller Whittemore & Co., Virginia Beach, Va., 1992—. Mem. Brit. Toy and Hobby Mfrs. Assn. Presbyterian. Home: 4829 Berrywood Rd Virginia Beach VA 23464-5874 Office: 1060 Laskin Rd Ste 22B Virginia Beach VA 23451-6365

DIXON, JUDY E(ARLENE), management and marketing executive, consultant; b. Sweetwater, Tex., July 19, 1950; d. Robert E. Stewart and Verna May (Brown) Kirkpatrick; children: Tammy Taylor, Tara R. Taylor. Cert., U. Houston, 1986; BA in Mktg. and Mgmt. with honors, Ctr. Degree Study, Pa., 1992. Ops. mgr. Retail Investment Group, Odessa, Tex., 1981-82; sales cons. Rupert Advt., Odessa, Tex., 1982-83; dir. training Paisano Girl Scout Coun., Corpus Christi, Tex., 1979; owner Gingerbread Bakery, Odessa, 1981-83; exec. dir. Nat. Multiple Sclerosis Soc., Midland, Tex., 1983-86; mktg. dir. Melvin, Simin & Assocs., Midland, Tex., 1986-87; exec. dir. West Tex. Rural Health Edn. Ctr., Odessa, 1987-91; owner Creative Svcs., Odessa, 1991—; cons. small bus. mktg., 1984—. Editor, pub. West Tex. Health Prospective mag., 1989-90; contbr. articles to profl. jours. Recipient Writing grant Ector County Ind. Sch. Dist., 1990-91, Nat. Vice Chmn.'s award Nat. Multiple Sclerosis Soc., Cmty. Involvement award N.W. Civic League, 1979, Silver Appreciation award United Way, 1977. Republican. Home and Office: Creative Svcs 8418 NE 131st Pl Kirkland WA 98034

DIXON, MARY OLETTA, special education educator; b. Franklin, N.C., June 17, 1950; d. Frederick June Penland and Lacy Lee (Chavis) Penland Scott; m. Howard Julius Dixon, Jan.1, 1974; 1 child, Mersadies Denise. AA, Ga. Mil. Coll., 1980; BS, Ga. Coll., 1991. Health svc. technician Ctrl. State Hosp., Milledgeville, Ga., 1974-79; correctional officer Men's Correctional Inst., Hardwick, Ga., 1979-82; libr. asst. dept. corrections Men's Correctional Inst., Hardwick, 1982-91; spl. edn. tchr. Baldwin H.S., Milledgeville, 1991—; activity leader Ctrl. State Hosp., Milledgeville, 1977-79. Mem. Ga. Assn. Educators. Democrat. Baptist. Home: 149 A Minor Rd NE Milledgeville GA 31061 Office: Baldwin HS 155 Hwy 49 West Milledgeville GA 31061

DIXON, NANCY POWELL, educational research administrator; b. Villa Rica, Ga., Oct. 22, 1943; d. Jack Wheeler and Myra (Lowry) Powell; children: Peter George, Susan Powell. BS in Edn., U. Ga., 1965, MEd, 1966; EdD, Okla. State U., 1975, postgrad., 1983-85. Spl. edn. tchr. Clarke County Pub. Schs., Athens, Ga., 1966-67, Putnam County Pub. Schs., Cookeville, Tenn., 1967-68; remedial reading tchr. Daniel Arthur Rehab. Ctr., Oak Ridge, Tenn., 1968-70, Morrison (Okla.) Pub. Schs., 1973-76; assoc. prof. spl. edn. Western Carolina U., Cullowhee, N.C., 1976-83; assoc. dir. exptl. program to stimulate competitive rsch. Okla. State Regents for Higher Edn., Stillwater, 1985—; mem. state adv. com. exptl. program to stimulate competitive rsch., 1991—; mem. Okla. Space Grant Consortium. Author: Children of Poverty With Handicapping Conditions: How Teachers Can Cope Humanistically, 1981. V.p. Friends of the Libr., Stillwater, 1988-92. Mem. Alliance for Invitational Edn., Okla. State U. Women's Coun., Phi Kappa Phi, Phi Delta Kappa. Democrat. Baptist. Office: Okla EPSCoR Oklahoma State U 001B Life Sciences E Stillwater OK 74078

DIXON, RICHARD ARTHUR, botany educator, researcher; b. Capetown, South Africa, Dec. 29, 1951; came to U.S., 1988; s. Arthur and Ena (Parrott) D.; m. Rachel Corfield, Aug. 5, 1978; children: Lois Mary, Arthur Malcolm. BA in Biochemistry, Oxford (Eng.) U., 1973, MA, 1976, DPhil in Botany, 1976. Postdoctoral fellow in biochemistry Cambridge (Eng.) U., 1976-78; biochemistry lectr. U. London, 1978-85, reader in plant biochemistry, 1985-88; dir. plant biology Samuel Roberts Noble Found., Ardmore, Okla., 1988—; adj. prof. biochemistry Okla. State U., Stillwater, 1988—; adj. prof. botany U. Tex., Austin, 1993—; adj. prof. botany and microbiology U. Okla., Norman, 1993—; mem. adv. panel on cellular biochemistry NSF, Washington, 1990-93; mem. adv. bd. botany vis. com. U. Tex., Austin, 1990—, mem. adv. bd. Plant Jour., 1990—; mem. applied rsch. com. Okla. Ctr. for Advancement Sci. and Tech., Oklahoma City, 1992—. Editor: Plant Cell Culture: A Practical Approach, 1985, Biotechnology for Aridland Plants, 1993, Transgenic Rsch., 1991—; assoc. editor: Plant Mol. Biol., 1994—; mem. editl. bd. Archives of Biochemistry and Biophysics, 1991—. Grantee Agr. and Food Rsch. Coun., Eng., 1979-88, Sci. and Engring. Rsch. Coun., Eng., 1982-88. Mem. Am. Soc. Plant Physiologists (publs. com. 1991—), Internat. Soc. for Plant Molecular Biology, Phytochem. Soc. N.Am., Phytochem. Soc. Europe (com. 1983-86). Office: Samuel Roberts Noble Found 2510 Highway 199 E Ardmore OK 73401

DIXON, SHIRLEY JUANITA, restaurant owner; b. Canton, N.C., June 29, 1935; d. Willard Luther and Bessie Eugenia (Scroggs) Clark; m. Clinton Matthew Dixon, Jan. 3, 1953; children: Elizabeth Swanger, Hugh Monroe III, Cynthia Owen, Sharon Fouts. BS, Wayne State U., 1956; postgrad., Mary Baldwin Coll., 1958, U. N.C., 1977. Acct. Standard Oil Co., Detroit, 1955-57; asst. dining room mgr. Statler Hilton, Detroit, 1958-60; bookkeeper Osborne Lumber Co., Canton, N.C., 1960-61; bus. owner, pres. Dixon's Restaurant, Canton, 1961—; judge N.C. Assn. Distributive Edn. Assn., state and dist., 1982—; owner Halbert's Family Heritage Ctr., Canton. Past Pres. Haywood County Assn. Retarded Citizens Bd., 1985-94, past v.p., chmn. bd. dirs.; bd. commrs. Haywood Vocats. Opportunities, 1985-94, treas. bd. dirs.; Haywood Sr. Leadership Council; dist. dir. 11th Congl. Dist. Dem. Women, 1982-85; state Teen-Dem. advisor State Dem. party, 1985-90; del. 1988 Dem. Nat. Conv., Atlanta; alderwoman Town of Canton, N.C.; vice-chair Gov.'s. Adv. Coun. on Aging, State N.C., 1982-89; 1st v.p. crime prevention Community Watch Bd., State N.C., 1985, 86; mem. Criminal Justice Bd., N.C. Assembly on Women and the Economy; chair Western N.C. Epilepsy Assn., Haywood County N.C. Mus. History, 1987—; co-chair Haywood County Commn. on the Bi-Centennial of Constn., 1987-92; Haywood County Econ. Strategy Commn.; v.p., bd. dirs. Haywood County Retirement Coun., Region A Coun. on Aging; bd. dirs. Haywood County Sr. Housing, C.B.C. United Way (mem. chair); chair bd. Canton Sr. Citizen's Ctr.; mem. Haywood County Ease Retirement Com.; pres., chairwoman bd. Haywood County Assn. Retarded Citizens; pres. N.C. coun. Alzheimer's Disease and Related Disorders Assn.; bd. dirs. Canton Recreation Dept., Western N.C. Alzheimer's Disease and Related Disorders Assn., 1987-91, v.p., C.B; bd. dirs. Haywood Literary Coun., Haywood Sr. Leadership Coun., W.N.C. Econ. Devel. Com., United Way, 1991—, drive chmn.; mem. legis. subcom. Alzheimer's-State of N.C.; bd. dirs. N.C. Conf. for Social Svcs., 1987-91; v.p. bd. Western N.C. Alzheimer's Assn., 1987-91; pres. State Coun. on Alzheimer's; apptd. mem. Legis. Study Com. on Alzheimer's; apptd. mem. State of N.C. Adv. Bd. on Community Care and Health; mem. Habitat for Humanity Haywood County; bd. chair Pigeon Valley Optimist Club; apptd. by Senate Western N.C. Econ. Devel. Commn.; appointee Haywood County Econ. Devel. Commn., Canton Hist. Commn.; judge U.S. Olympic Torch Bearers. Recipient Outstanding Svc. award Crime Prevention from Gov., 1982, Gov.'s Spl. Vol. award, 1983, Outstanding Svc. award N.C. Cmty. Watch Assn., 1984, Cmty. Svc. award to Handicapped, 1983-84, Outstanding Svc. award ARC, 1988; named Employer of Yr. for Hiring Handicapped N.C. Assn. for Retarded Citizens, 1985, Cmty. Person of Yr. Kiwanis Club, 1991, Citizen of Yr. in Western N.C., 1995; Rec. Outstanding award Haywood Co. Sr. Games, 1992. Mem. AAUW, NAFE, Women's Polit. Caucus, Internat. Platform Assn., Women's Forum N.C., Nat. Bd. Alzheimers Assn. (regional del.), Canton Bus. and Profl. Assn. (pres. 1974-79, Woman of Yr. 1984), Altrusa (Woman of Yr. in N.C. 1989). Democrat. Episcopalian. Home: 104 Skyland Ter Canton NC 28716-3718 Office: Dixons Restaurant 30 N Main St Canton NC 28716-3805

DIXON-GAYLE, PAMELA EVE, reporter, journalist; b. El Paso, Tex., July 14, 1966; d. William Cecil and Mary Diane (Flanigan) D.; m. Troy William Gayle, June 22, 1991; children: Aaron William, Alexander Andrew. Student, Lamar U., 1984-88, McNeese State U., 1988-89. Copywriter, announcer KBIU Radio, Lake Charles, La., 1983-84; news asst. KPLC TV, Lake Charles, La., 1984, asst. prodr., 1988-89, anchor, reporter, 1990—; news asst. KBMT TV, Beaumont, Tex., 1984-86; prodn. asst. KFDM TV, Beaumont, Tex., 1986-88; reporter FOX 29, Lake Charles, La., 1989-90; bur. chief reporter KJAC TV, Beaumont, Port Arthur, Tex., 1990; copywriter tv., radio, print Ann Lee Advtsg., Beaumont, Tex., 1985-86. Mem. Jr. League Lake Charles (bd. dirs. 1996—). Roman Catholic. Office: KPLC TV 320 Division St Lake Charles LA 70601

DJINN See LEWIS, CARL EDWIN

DOAN, PATRICIA NAN, librarian; b. Fayetteville, Ark., Oct. 27, 1930; d. William Rader and Olga (White) Rogers; B.A., U. Ark., 1951; m. John Cannon Doan, Apr. 2, 1950; children—William Curtis, Sarah Cannon, Mary Virginia. Librarian, Okmulgee (Okla.) Public Library, 1967-94. Treas. Okmulgee Art Guild, 1969-71; sec. Okmulgee County Devel. Council, 1971—, Creek Nation Council House Bd., 1975-93. Mem. Okmulgee Meml. Hosp. Found.; mem. Okmulgee Task Force, county chmn. Okmulgee County History Book Com.; bd. dirs., mem. adv. bd. Okmulgee Main Street, 1987-94. Mem. ALA, Okla. Library Assn. (sec. public library div. 1970), Okmulgee County Geneal. Soc. (v.p. 1970), Sigma Alpha Iota, Zeta Tau Alpha. Democrat. Episcopalian. Compiler: Index of the 1907 Census of Okmulgee, Oklahoma, 1971. Home: Rt 4 Box 51 Okmulgee OK 74447

DOANE, THOMAS ROY, environmental toxicologist; b. Warsaw, N.Y., Feb. 8, 1947; s. Howard John and Janice Leanora (Whipple) D.; m. Donna Marguerite Felix, July 20, 1968. BS, Oneonta State U., 1969; MS, Cornell U., 1971; MA, U. Tex., 1979; PhD, Va. Poly. Inst., 1984. Cert. sr. ecologist. Commd. 1st lt. USAF, 1974, advanced through grades to lt. col., 1989; environ. technician USAF Environ. Health Lab., McClellan AFB, Calif., 1971-74; environ. cons. USAF Environ. Health Lab., Kelly AFB, Tex., 1974-77, AF Occupation & Environ. Health Lab., Brooks AFB, Tex., 1977-81; chief ecology functions AF Occupation & Environ. Health Lab., Brooks AFB, 1984-87; dir. environ. protection Hdqrs. Human Systems divsn., Brooks AFB, 1974; assoc. dir. ops. Battelle Meml. Inst., San Antonio, 1991-95, dir. San Antonio ops., 1995—; cons. Toxeco Consultants Inc., San Antonio, 1987-91. Author (book chpt.): Fresh Water Biological Monitoring, 1984; contbr. articles to N.Y. Fish and Game Jour., Procs. of 11th Conf. on Toxicology, Internat. Jour. Environ. Analytical Chemistry; editor: Land Based Environmental Monitoring-Herbicide Orange, 1980. Recipient Regent scholarship N.Y. State, 1965-69; grantee U.S. EPA, 1969. Fellow ASTM (award of merit 1995); mem. Soc. Environ. Chemistry and Toxicology, Ecol. Soc. Am., Air Force Assn., Phi Theta Kappa, Phi Kappa Phi, Sigma Xi. Home: RR 1 Box 62H Cibolo TX 78108-9601 Office: Battelle Meml Inst 4414 Centerview Ste 260 San Antonio TX 78228-1405

DOBBIN, MARJORIE WILCOX, English language educator; b. Elmira, N.Y., July 31, 1934; d. Stephen LeRoy and Florence L. (Sawyer) Wilcox. BA in English, SUNY, Fredonia, 1975, MA in Am. Lit., 1977; PhD in Medieval Lit., U. Ga., 1987. Freelance newspaper writer Westfield Rep., N.Y., 1970-73; prof. English Ctrl. Wesleyan Coll., Central, S.C., 1979-80; teaching asst. U. Ga., Athens, 1980-84, 85-86, instr. English, 1986-87; prof. English Emmanuel Coll., Franklin Springs, Ga., 1984-85, Brewton-Parker Coll., Mt. Vernon, Ga., 1987—. Office: Brewton-Parker Coll Rt 280 Mount Vernon GA 30445

DOBBINS, AUSTIN C., retired English language educator; b. Nashville, Oct. 14, 1919; s. Gaines Stanley and May Virginia (Riley) D.; m. Mary Denmead Willis; children: Mary Virginia, Elizabeth Anne. BA, Miss. Coll., 1941; MA, U. N.C., 1948, PhD, 1950. From asst. prof. to head English dept. Samford U., Birmingham, Ala., 1950-90, Disting. prof. English, 1986—. Author: Dean Percy Pratt Burns, 1957, Milton and the Book of Revelation, 1975, Gaines S. Dobbins: Pioneer in Religious Education, 1981, Grandfather's Journal, Company B, Sixteenth Mississippi Infantry, 1988; contbr. articles to profl. jours. Sgt. U.S. Army, 1943-45, CBI. Mem. So. Atlantic MLA, Phi Kappa Phi (pres. 1988), Sigma Tau Delta, Alpha Phi Omega, Omicron Delta Kappa. Baptist. Home: 1113 S Shadesview Terr Birmingham AL 35209

DOBBINS, JAMES TALMAGE, JR., analytical chemist, researcher; b. Chapel Hill, N.C., June 13, 1926; s. James Talmage and Lila (Shore) D.; m. Jacqueleene Bowen, Dec. 22, 1951; children: James Talmage III, Steven Earl. BS in Chemistry, U. N.C., 1947, PhD in Analytical Chemistry, 1958. Chief indsl. hygiene sect. Med. Gen. Lab., Tokyo, 1953-55, head dept. chemistry, 1955-6; rsch. chemist II R.J. Reynolds Tobacco Co., Winston-Salem, N.C., 1958-65; rsch. sect. head II R.J. Reynolds Tobacco Co., Winston-Salem, 1965-72; mgr. analytical rsch. div. R.J. Reynolds Industries, Winston-Salem, 1972-75; master scientist RJR Nabisco, Winston-Salem, 1975-83; master chemist Bowman Gray Tech. Ctr., Winston-Salem, 1983-89; retired, 1989. Contbr. articles to Jour. Assn. Official Agrl. Chemists, Jour. Assn. Official Analytical Chemists, Spectroscopy, Encyclopedia Ind. Chem. Analysis. Fellow Am. Inst. Chemists; mem. AAAS, Soc. for Applied Spectroscopy, N.Y. Acad. Sci., N.C. Acad. Sci., Am. Chem. Soc. (sec., chmn. elect and chmn. ctrl. N.C. sect. 1964, 65, 66), Sigma Xi (sec. Wake Forest chpt. 1986-90). Democrat. Baptist. Home: 2838 Bartram Rd Winston Salem NC 27106-5105

DOBBS, ELWYN HAROLD, food service executive; b. Huntsville, Ala., Feb. 21, 1935; s. Chester Dee and Edith (Tucker) D.; m. Patricia Anne Dunn, Sept. 28, 1956; children: Elwyn Harold Jr., Wendy Carlyn. Student, U. Ala., 1954-57. With Equifax, Atlanta, 1957-77; various positions Hardee's Food System Inc., Atlanta and Rocky Mt., N.C., 1977-89; franchise owner Hardee's Food System Inc., Rocky Mt., 1992—; dir. ops. Drain Enterprises, Scottsboro, 1989-90; owner Hardees of Hazel Green, Ala., 1990—, Hardee's of Waverly, Tenn., 1994—; ptnr. Advantage Elec. Svc., Buford, Ga., 1993—, Hardee's of Hodgenville, Ky., 1993-95; pres. Bluegrass Mgmt. Svcs. Inc. (BP Convenience Store), Hodgenville, Ky., 1995—. Home and Office: 7611 Teal Dr SW Huntsville AL 35802-2836

DOBBS, GEORGE ALBERT, funeral director, embalmer; b. Atlanta, Oct. 16, 1943; s. Albert F. and Ruby Lee (Haynes) D. Student Fla. Bapt. Theol. Coll., 1963-67; BA, Cornell U., 1974; AA in Mortuary Sci. and Adminstrn., John A. Gupton Coll., 1990. Cert. funeral svc. practitioner.' Retail store mgr. Alterman Foods, Atlanta, 1962-74; ind. mng. agt. George A. Dobbs & Assocs., Decatur, Ga., 1974-78, motivational spkr., Hermitage, Tenn., 1992—; retail mgr. K-Mart Corp., Decatur, 1978-91; funeral dir., embalmer, SCI Nashville Group, , 1991—. Named Small Bus. Mgr. of Year, Dekalb Businessman's Assn., 1974, 76. Mem. Ga. Lodge of Rsch., Scottish Rite Rsch. Soc., Mo. Lodge of Rsch., Capital City Club, Mason (past master Ga. and Tenn.), Grotto, Knights of Mecca, Shriner. So. Bapt. Republican. Address: 108 Thistle Ln Hermitage TN 37076-2724 Office: Woodlawn Funeral Home 660 Thompson Ln Nashville TN 37204-3608

DOBBS, RITA MARIE, travel company executive; b. Chgo., May 12, 1965; d. Frank R. and Mary Ann (Kalata) D. BA in French, U. Houston, 1992, postgrad., 1992—. Assoc. Macy's, Houston, 1984-91; travel assistance coord. Am. Internat. Assistance Svcs., Houston, 1992—. Pi Delta Phi scholar, 1987. Mem. MLA, Am. Translators Assn., L'Alliance Francaise Houston, Tex. Fgn. Lang. Assn., Russian Studies Club, Pi Delta Pi (sec. 1987). Home: 12115 Leafy Arbor Dr Houston TX 77070-5212 Office: Am Internat Assistance Svc 675 Bering Dr Ste 100 Houston TX 77057-2128

DOBER, STANLEY, pediatrician; b. Bridgeport, Conn., May 21, 1942; s. Max and Goldie (Weinstein) D.; m. Joan Sharon Krommel, May 30, 1965; children: Eve Lynne, Marc Steven, Craig Scott. BA, U. Vt., 1963; MD, Albert Einstein Coll., 1967. Diplomate Am. Bd. Pediatrics. Intern U. Calif., San Francisco, 1967-68, resident in pediat., 1968-69; resident in pediat. U. Miami Med. Ctr., 1971-72; pediatrician Children's Clinic, Lake Worth, Fla., 1972—; chief pediat. John F. Kennep Hosp., Atlantis, Fla., 1980-82; chief gen. pediat. Good Samaritan Hosp., West Palm Beach, Fla., 1989-92. Maj. U.S. Army, 1969-71, Vietnam. Mem. AMA, Am. Acad. Pediat., Fla. Pediat. Soc., Fla. Med. Assn., Palm Beach County Med. Soc. Democrat. Jewish. Office: Childrens Clinic 1718 N Federal Hwy Lake Worth FL 33460-6643

DOBRZYN, JANET ELAINE, quality management professional; b. Allentown, Pa., Oct. 9, 1956; d. Frank John and Doris (Ross) D. Diploma, Pottsville Hosp. Sch. Nursing, 1977; AA, L.A. Valley Coll., 1984; BSN, Calif. State Coll., Long Beach, 1985; MSN, Azusa (Calif.) Pacific U., 1991. RN, Calif., Okla., Pa., Ky.; cert. profl. healthcare quality. Charge nurse evenings Allentown (Pa.) Osteo. hosp., 1977-80; charge nurse relief Encino (Calif.) Hosp., 1980-81; registry nurse Profl. Staffing, Northridge, Calif., 1981-82; clin. nurse II pediatric ICU Childrens Hosp. of L.A., 1982-86, clin. info. specialist, 1986-89; quality mgmt. specialist PacifiCare of Calif., Cypress, 1989-91, quality mgmt. spl. projects coord., 1991-92; mgr. quality mgmt. PacifiCare of Okla., Tulsa, 1992-93, sr. project specialist quality mgmt., 1993-95; accreditation facilitator Humana, Louisville, Ky., 1995-96; mgr. quality mgmt. Healthwise of Ky., Lexington, 1996—; guest lectr. Spaulding U., U. Louisville; cons., reviewer of prototype pub. Commerce Clearing House, Inc., Riverwoods, Ill., 1993; mem. ANA/GHAA task force to develop nursing curriculum in managed care for nursing students, 1994; speaker in field. Camp nurse vol. Forest Home Conf. Ctr., San Bernardino, Calif., 1988. Mem. Nat. Assn. for Healthcare Quality, Sigma Theta Tau (newsletter editor). Republican. Home: 207 Rolling Ridge Way Simpsonville KY 40067 Office: Healthwise of Kentucky 2409 Hamodsburg Rd Lexington KY 40504

DOBSON, BRIDGET MCCOLL HURSLEY, television executive and writer; b. Milw., Sept. 1, 1938; d. Franklin McColl and Doris (Berger) Hursley; m. Jerome John Dobson, June 16, 1961; children: Mary McColl, Andrew Carmichael. BA, Stanford U., 1960, MA, 1964; CBA, Harvard U., 1961. Assoc. writer General Hospital ABC-TV, 1965-73, head writer General Hospital, 1973-75; producer Friendly Road Sta. KIXE-TV, Redding, Calif., 1972; head writer Guiding Light CBS-TV, 1975-80, head writer As the World Turns, 1980-83; creator, co-owner Santa Barbara NBC-TV, 1983—, head writer Santa Barbara, 1983-86, 91, exec. producer Santa Barbara, 1986-87, 91, creative prodn. exec. Santa Barbara, 1990-91; pres. Dobson Global Entertainment, L.A., 1994—. Author, co-lyricist: Slings and Eros, 1993; prodr. Confessions of a Nightingale, 1994. Recipient Emmy award, 1988. Mem. Nat. Acad. TV Arts and Scis. (com. on substance abuse 1986-88), Writers Guild Am. (award for Guiding Light 1977, for Santa Barbara 1991), Am. Film Inst. (mem. TV com. 1986-88). Office: 3490 Piedmont Rd NW Ste 1206 Atlanta GA 30305

DOBSON, ROBERT ALBERTUS, III, lawyer, investment manager, lay minister, volunteer; b. Greenville, S.C., Nov. 27, 1938; s. Robert A. Jr. and Dorothy (Leonard) D.; m. Linda Josephine Bryant, Nov. 18, 1956; children: Robert, William, Michael, Daniel, Jonathan, Laura (dec.); m. Catherine Elizabeth Cornmesser, Sept. 17, 1983; children: Andrew, Thomas. BS in Acctg. summa cum laude, U. S.C., 1960, JD magna cum laude, 1962. Asst. dean of students U. S.C., 1960-62; pvt. practice pub. acctg. Greenville, 1962-64; ptnr. Dobson & Dobson, Greenville, 1964-93; pres. Dobson Mgmt. Corp., Greenville, 1993—; chmn., bd. trustees Limestone Coll., 1987-89. Contbr. articles on tax and acctg. to profl. jours. Lay minister St. Francis Episcopal Ch., Greenville; chmn. bd. Dobson Tape Ministry, Homeless Children Internat., Inc.; bd. dirs. A Child's Haven, Inc., Found. for the Multihandicapped, Deaf and Blind, Spartanburg, S.C.; mem. adv. bd. Salvation Army, Greenville. Mem. ABA, S.C. Bar Assn., AICPAs, Am. Assn. Attys. and CPAs, S.C. Assn. CPAs, S.C. Assn. Pub. Accts., Block C Assn. The Group, U. S.C. Alumni Assn. (cir. v.p.), Kappa Sigma (chmn. legal com. 1989-93, dist. grand master 1971—, constn. bylaws and rules chmn. 1975—, Nat. Dist. Grand Master of the Yr. 1986), Phi Beta Kappa. Episcopalian. Lodges: Sertoma Internat. (dist. treas.), Sertoma Sunrisers (pres. Greenville club). Home: 1207 Pelham Rd Greenville SC 29615-3643 Office: 1306 S Church St Greenville SC 29605-3814

DOBSON, ROBERT ALBERTUS, IV, corporate executive; b. Greenville, S.C., June 16, 1957; s. Robert Albertus III and Linda (Bryant) D.; m. Belinda Joy Jolly, July 21, 1984; children: Robert Albertus V, Jourdan

Marie, Lauren Priscilla. BS in Mgmt., U. S.C., 1981. Gen. mgr. Winners Corp., Greenville, 1984-87; pres., chief exec. officer Foothills Family Properties Inc., Greenville, 1987—. Republican. Episcopalian. Office: Foothills Family Properties 100 Pelham Rd Greenville SC 29615-2173

DOBY, JANICE KAY, elementary education educator; b. Hamlet, N.C., Dec. 4, 1953; d. James Robert and Marguerite (Greene) D. B Music Edn., Lee Coll., Cleveland, Tenn., 1978; MS in Elem. Edn., Nova U., 1992; EdD, Fla. Atlantic U., 1996. Elem. tchr. Palm Springs (Fla.) Bapt. Sch., 1981-82; tchr. music, chmn. fine arts Mil. Trail Elem. Sch., West Palm Beach, Fla., 1982-89; tchr. music Seminole Trails Elem. Sch., West Palm Beach, 1989—; tchr. music potentially gifted minority student project Palm Beach County Schs., West Palm Beach, summer 1989; mem. adj. faculty elem. and mid. sch. sci. methods Fla. Atlantic U., Boca Raton, 1994—, rsch. asst. 1995—; math./sci. specialist West Rivera Math./Sci./Tech. Magnet Sch., 1995—; dir. music Marantha Ch., Palm Beach Gardens, Fla., Family Worship Ctr., West Palm Beach, Bethel Temple Assembly of God, Lake Worth, Fla.; regional teen talent adjudicator Assemblies of God, Lake Worth, 1982-85; state teen talent adjudicator Ch. of God, Palm Beach Gardens, 1990; judge Local and Dist. Science and Engring. Fairs, 1995—. Contbg. author, editor: IDEAS Handbook for Teachers, 1995. Recipient citation Palm Beach County Sheriff's Dept., 1989. Mem. ASCD, Fla. Ednl. Rsch. Assn., Fla. Assn. Sci. Tchrs., Nat. Assn. for Rsch. in Sci. Teaching, Higher Edn. Consortium., Kappa Delta Pi.

DOBYNS, LLOYD (ALLEN), free-lance journalist; b. Newport News, Va., Mar. 12, 1936; s. Lloyd A. and L. Helen (Stokes) D.; m. Patricia Louise Parker, Mar. 16, 1957; children: Denise, Brian, Alison Dobyns-Aycock, Kenneth. B.A., Washington and Lee U., 1957; PhD in Humane Letters (hon.), U. N.C., Asheville, 1992. Reporter WDBJ-AM/TV, Roanoke, Va., 1957-58; news dir. WCUM-AM, Cumberland, Md., 1960; reporter WAVY-AM/TV, Norfolk, Va., 1960-63, news dir., 1963-68; mng. editor WNEW-TV, N.Y.C., 1968-69; asst. news dir. WNBC-TV, N.Y.C., 1969-70; news dir. WMAQ-TV, Chgo., 1970-72; corr. NBC, Paris, 1972-74; prin. writer-reporter Weekend, NBC, N.Y.C., 1974-79; corr. NBC, N.Y.C., 1979-82, prin. writer, co-anchor NBC News Overnight, 1982, prin. writer, anchor, editor Monitor/First Camera, 1983-84; Asia corr. and Tokyo bur. chief NBC News, 1984-86; freelance journalist, 1986—; writer, narrator The Deming Libr. Co-author: Quality or Else, 1991, Thinking About Quality, 1994. Served with U.S. Army, 1958-60. Recipient Christopher award for writing-reporting NBC News TV documentary If Thats a Gnome, This Must Be Zurich, 1974, Christopher award for writing-reporting for NBC White Paper: Gambling, 1980; George Foster Peabody Broadcasting award for Weekend, 1976; TV award Am. Inst. Indsl. Engrs.; Martin R. Gainsburgh award; Dupont-Columbia award; Nat. Headliners award for writing-reporting NBC White Paper: If Japan Can, Why Can't We, 1980; Aviation and Space Writers award; Nat. Soc. Profl. Engrs. award for NBC Reports; Janus award; San Francisco Film Festival award, Gabriel award, Golden Eagle award for NBC Reports: Bataan, The Forgotten Hell, 1982, Work Worth Doing, 1987. Office: 7640 White Oak Rd Garner NC 27529-8805*

DOCKERY, DAVID SAMUEL, theology educator, editor; b. Tuscaloosa, Ala., Oct. 28, 1952; s. Samuel Wesley and Pansye (Pierson) D.; m. Lanese Huckeba, June 14, 1975; children: Jonathan Samuel, Benjamin Paul, Timothy David. BS, U. Ala., 1975; MDiv magna cum laude, Grace Theol. Sem., Winona Lake, Ind., 1979; MDiv, Southwestern Bapt. Theol. Sem., Ft. Worth, 1981; MA, Tex. Christian U., 1986; PhD, U. Tex., Arlington, 1988. Ordained to ministry So. Bapt. Conv., 1982. Pastor Met. Bapt. Ch., Bklyn., 1981-84; prof. theology Criswell Coll., Dallas, 1984-88; asst. prof. N.T., So. Bapt. Sem., Louisville, 1988—; gen. editor Broadman Press, Nashville, 1990—; bd. dirs. Billy Graham Ctr., Louisville, 1989-91. Author: Doctrine of the Bible, 1991; editor: Baptist Theologians, 1990, People of God, 1991, New Testament Criticism and Interpretation, 1991; gen. editor The New American Cmmentary, 1991—. Bd. advisors Alternative Pregnancy Ctr., Louisville, 1990. Fellow Inst. Bibl. Rsch.; mem. Evang. Theol. Soc., Soc. Bible Lit., Am. Acad. Religion, Nat. Assn. Bapt. Profs. Religion. Office: Broadman Press 127 9th Ave N Nashville TN 37203-3601 Address: 801 Foxfire Dr Louisville KY 40223-2781

DODD, ANITA ADREON, oil company executive; b. L.A., Feb. 28, 1946; d. John R. and Elizabeth (Bruner) Vines; 1 child, John Marshall Dodd. Student, U. Southwestern La., Lafayette, 1963-65. Geol. sec. Amerada Petroleum, Lafayette, 1968-69; receptionist Amerada-Hess Oil Co., Corpus Christi, Tex., 1970-71; sec. to pres. Amer. Bank, Corpus Christi, 1971-72; TV/comml. model Corpus Christi, 1971-72; sales rep. Superior Chem., Lafayette, 1972-74; sales rep. Internat. Chem. & Cons., Lafayette, 1974, Houston, 1974-76; pres./owner Dodd Internat., Inc., Houston, 1976—. Patentee spherical glass bead to reduce torque, drag and sticking in oil well drilling; contbr. articles to profl. jours. Mem. Soc. Petroleum Engrs. Republican. Methodxist. Home: 2907 Stetson Ln Houston TX 77043-1323 Office: Dodd Internat Inc 10222 Hammerly Blvd # 610 Houston TX 77043-2100

DODDRIDGE, ROCK EDWARD, pastor, educator; b. N.Y.C., Apr. 16, 1949; s. Rodney Kolb and Dorothy Jane (Williams) D.; m. Suzanne Edwards, June 14, 1970; children: Jonathan, Ryan, Lindsey. BA, U. Fla., 1971, MEd, 1976; MDiv, Fuller Theol. Sem., 1976, DMin, 1982; MA in Religious Edn., North Park Theol. Sem., 1983; PhD, Loyola U., Chgo., 1986. Ordained minister Evangelical Covenant Ch., 1984. Dean of students, bible instr. Bayshore Christian Sch., Tampa, Fla., 1971-73; youth dir. First United Meth. Ch., Colorado Springs, Colo., 1976-78; assoc. dir. program devel. Christian Marriage Encounter Internat., Colorado Springs, Colo., 1980-81; dir. coll. ministries North Park Covenant Ch., Chgo., 1981-83; assoc. prof. psychology Marymount Coll., Kans., 1986-89; assoc. pastor of edn. First Covenant Ch., Salina, Kans., 1983-90; sr. pastor First Covenant Ch., St. Petersburg, Fla., 1990—. Author: Small Group Leadership, 1981; contbr. articles to profl. jours. Parent edn. trainer Active Parenting, Kans., Fla., 1983-96; bd. dirs. Coalition for the Prevention of Child Abuse, Salina, Kans., 1983-90; trainer of preventing male violence various chs. and Marymount Coll., Kans., Fla., 1983-96; anger mgmt. cons. various chs. and schs., Kans., Fla., 1983-96; chmn. adult edn. com. Midwest Conf. Bd. Edn., 1988-90; mem. exec. bd. SE conf. Evangelical Covenant Ch., 1991—, chmn. com. on ministerial standing, 1993-95, mem. nominations com., 1993-95, chmn.; cons., spkr. Evangelical Covenant Ch. Planting Com., 1995; mem. Nat. Stewardship com., 1995—. Mem. Nat. Assn. Evangelicals, St. Petersburg Ministerial Assn. Office: Faith Covenant Ch 150 62nd Ave NE Saint Petersburg FL 33702

DODGE, R(ALPH) EDWARD, family physician; b. Salamanca, N.Y., Jan. 14, 1936; s. Ralph Edward and Eunice Elvira (Davis) D.; m. Nancy Lou De Lay, Aug. 14, 1957; children: Randall, Jeffrey, Amy. BA, Taylor U., 1958; MD, Ind. U., 1962; MPH, Johns Hopkins U., 1967. Diplomate Am. Bd. Preventive Medicine, Am. Bd. Family Practice. Rotating intern L.A. County Gen. Hosp., 1962-63; resident gen. preventive medicine sch. hygiene & pub. health Johns Hopkins U., 1966-69; asst. prof. pub. health Haile Sellassie U., Gondar, Ethiopia, 1967-69; staff physician Frontier Nursing Svc., Hyden, Ky., 1970-71; med. dir. Citrus-Levy County Health Dept., Inverness, Fla., 1971-74; physician emergency dept. Waterman Meml. Hosp., Eustis, Fla., 1974-75; pvt. practice Inverness, 1975-96; med. dir. Citrus Primary Care Network, 1994-96; clin. asst. prof. U. Fla., 1994—. Contbr. articles to med. jours.; editor Fla. Family Physician, 1991-95; newspaper columnist: Health Simplicity, 1988-90, Life and Health, 1990—. Bd. dirs. Marion-Citrus Mental Health Ctrs., Ocala, Fla., 1972-74, North Cen. Fla. Health Planning Commn., Gainesville, 1979-80, Fla. div. Am. Cancer Soc., 1988-90, Citrus Meml. Health Found., Inverness, 1988-94. Lt. comdr. USPHS, 1964-66. Recipient Disting. Svc. award Fla. Assn. Emergency Med. Technicians, 1976, Community Svc. award Seventh Day Adventist Ch., Inverness, 1978, Citizen of Yr. award Citrus County Chronicle, 1987. Mem. AMA, Am. Coll. Preventive Medicine, Am. Acad. Family Physicians, Fla. Acad. Family Physicians (bd. dirs. 1994-96), Fla. Med. Assn., Citrus County Med. Soc. (pres. 1977, sec.-treas. 1981-86), Citrus County C. of C. (Outstanding Comty. Svc. award 1972). Democrat. Office: Citrus Primary Care 511 W Highland Blvd Inverness FL 34452-4719

DODSON, GEORGE W., computer company executive, consultant; b. Danville, Ill., Jan. 21, 1937; s. Maurice Keith and Marjorie Ruth (Ingalsbe) D.; m. Evandra May Mendenhall, Aug. 4, 1957; children: Michael, Curtis, Janet. BS in Math., U. Ill., 1966; MS in Ops. Rsch., Union Coll., 1970. Statis. mgr. U. Ill., Urbana, 1960-66; sr. performance anayst IBM Corp., Poughkeepsie, N.Y., 1966-70, performance mgr., 1970-79; lab. performance mgr. IBM Corp., Tucson, 1979-85; program mgr. IBM Corp., Roanoke, Tex., 1987-91, prin. info. systems mgmt. cons., 1991-93; prin. info. systems mgmt. cons. IBM Consulting Group, Dallas, 1994—; dir. tech. svcs. Morino Assocs., Vienna, Va., 1985-86; dir. performance products UCCEL Corp., Dallas, 1986-87. Mem. Computer Measurement Group (chmn. 1983, 89, pres. 1983-85, bd. dirs. 1985-89, treas. 1990—). Office: IBM Cons Group 20-07-7081 1605 Lyndon B. Johnson Fwy Dallas TX 75234-6062

DODSON, LOUIS RAYMOND, computer systems engineer; b. N.Y.C., Aug. 10, 1953; s. Marcelo and Maria Luisa (Maldonado) Diaz; m. Helayne Ivy Cornfield Dodson, June 18, 1978; children: Justin, Alana. AAS in Data Processing, No. Va. C.C., Annandale, 1985; BBA in Mktg., George Washington U., 1979; MA in Orgnl. Mgmt., U. Phoenix, San Francisco, 1993. Computer specialist Sontag and Annis, Inc., Rockville, Md., 1985-86; programmer CRC Systems Inc., a divsn. Network Mgmt. Inc., Fairfax, Va., 1986-89; sr. programmer/analyst Pinkerton Computer Cons., Inc., Rosslyn, Va., 1989-91; computer sys. engr. Lockheed Martin Corp., Springfield, Va., 1991-95, supr. computer software engring., 1995; sr. computer sys. engr. Sci. Applications Internat. Corp., Reston, Va., 1995—. Home: 7705 Lakeloft Ct Fairfax Station VA 22039-2956 Office: Sci Applications Internat 1953 Gallows Rd Vienna VA 22182

DOE, PATRICIA LOUISE, industrial engineer; b. Hazelton, Pa., Mar. 8, 1948; d. Thomas Victor and Dorothy Eleanor (Kimmel) McLaughlin; m. Lawrence Whittier Doe, Dec. 27, 1969; children: Lawrence Whittier Jr., Christopher Thomas. BA in Math., Newark State Coll., 1970; MS in Indsl. Engring., Lehigh U., 1987. Sr. tech. analyst Bell Telephone Labs, N. Andover, Mass., 1970-72; math tchr. St. Maria Goretti High Sch., Hagerstown, Md., 1976-77, 80-81; programer analyst Air Products & Chems., Inc., Allentown, Pa., 1981-83; sr. programmer analyst Air Products & Chems., Inc., Allentown, 1983-84, tech. support analyst, 1984-85, sr. tech. support analyst, 1985-88, prin. tech. analyst, 1988-91, prin. tech. assessment analyst, 1991-92, prin. info. tech. analyst applied tech., 1992-94; mgr. client/server tech. svcs. The Vanguard Group, Valley Forge, Pa., 1994-95; prin. Laredo Assocs., Boca Raton, Fla., 1995—; dir. ops. Alliance Entertainment Corp., Coral Springs, Fla., 1996—. Asst. treas. Washington County (Md.) PTA, 1980-81; fin. sec. Faith Presbyn. Ch., Emmaus, Pa., 1982-84; dir. bell choir St. Andrews Presbyn. Ch., Williamsport, Md., 1978-81. Mem. Kappa Delta Pi. Republican. Home: 19243 Cloister Lake Ln Boca Raton FL 33498 Office: Laredo Techs 19243 Cloister Lake Ln Boca Raton FL 33498-4857 also: Alliance Entertainment Corp 4250 Coral Ridge Dr Coral Springs FL 33065

DOENECKE, JUSTUS DREW, history educator; b. Bklyn., Mar. 5, 1938; s. Justus Christian and Eleanore (Smith) D.; m. Carol Anne Soukup, Mar. 21, 1970. BA, Colgate U., 1960; MA, Princeton U., 1962, PhD, 1966. Instr. Colgate U., Hamilton, N.Y., 1963-64; instr., then asst. prof. Ohio Wesleyan U., Delaware, 1965-69; asst. prof., assoc. prof., now prof. history New Coll. of U. South Fla., Sarasota, 1969—; editl. bd. Anglican and Episc. History, 1987—; manuscript reader, various mags. and presses; book rev. editor USA Today mag., 1980-81. Author: Not to the Swift: The Old Isolationists in the Cold War Era, 1979, The Presidencies of James A. Garfield and Chester A. Arthur, 1981, The Diplomacy of Frustration, 1983, When the Wicked Rise: American Opinion-Makers and the Manchurian Crisis, 1931-33, 1984, Anti-Intervention: A Bibliographical Introduction to Isolationism and Pacifism from World War I to the Early Cold War, 1987, In Danger Undaunted: The Anti-Interventionist Movement of 1940-41 as Revealed in the Papers of the America First Committee, 1990, (with John Wilz) From Isolation to War—1391-1941, 1991, The Battle Against Intervention, 1939-1941. Vestryman St. Mary's Episcopal Ch., Palmetto, Fla., 1983-84; trustee St. Stephen's Episcopal Sch., Bradenton, Fla., 1989-92. Danforth fellow, 1960, Woodrow Wilson Nat. fellow, 1960. Mem. Conf. on Peace Rsch. in History (coun. 1975-89), Soc. Historians of Am. Fgn. Rels. (program co-chair 1986, Arthur S. Link award for documentary editing 1991), Phi Beta Kappa. Home: 3943 Riverview Blvd W Bradenton FL 34209-2000 Office: New Coll U South Fla 5700 N Tamiami Trl Sarasota FL 34243-2146

DOEPPNER, THOMAS WALTER, electrical engineer, consultant; b. Berlin, May 22, 1920; came to U.S., 1939; s. August Friedrich and Ella Judith (Fraustädter) D.; m. Marjorie Ann Sloan, Sept. 16, 1944; children: Thomas Walter Jr., Ronald Sloan. Student, McPherson Coll., 1939-41; BSEE, Kans. State U., 1944; MSEE, U. Calif., Berkeley, 1959. Enlisted U.S. Army, 1944, advanced through grades to col., 1973, radio officer, 1945-65; program mgr. Def. Dept. Adv. Rsch. Proj. Agy., Washington, 1965-69; dir. electronics directorate U.S. Army, Washington, 1969-73; communications rsch. dir. Gen. Rsch. Corp., McLean, Va., 1973-76, dir. logistics engring. ops., 1976-84; prof. Def. Systems Mgmt. Coll., Ft. Belvoir, Va., 1984-86; cons. Alexandria, Va., 1986—; v.p. Washington Acad. Scis., 1991-94; asst. prof. mil. sci. U. Calif., Berkeley, 1955-59; instr. math. U. Md., College Park, 1967-69. Contbr. numerous articles to profl. publs. Decorated Legion of Merit (2), Bronze Star; Medal of Honor (Republic of Vietnam); recipient Sr. Engr. of Yr. award D.C. Coun. of Engring. and Archtl. Socs. Inc., 1994. Fellow IEEE (life, Patron award 1982, Centennial medal 1984, George Abraham Meml. award 1996, Regional Profl. award 1996), Washington Acad. Scis. (life). Home and Office: 8323 Orange Ct Alexandria VA 22309-2166

DOERR, BARBARA ANN, health facility director; b. Poteet, Tex., Apr. 2, 1951; d. William Ira and Margaret Sophia (Lozano) Potts; m. Michael F. Doerr, Aug. 19, 1984; 1 child, Jennifer. BSN, U. Tex., 1975. RN, Tex.; cert. nursing adminstr. Nursing house supr. Brackenridge Hosp., Austin, Tex., 1980-84, clin. coord., 1984-87, dir. med./surg. nursing, 1987-93, acting asst. adminstr., 1989-90, dir. nursing adminstrn., 1993—. Mem. ANA, Tex. Nurses Assn. (dist. V, Nurse of Yr. 1990-91), U. Tex.-Austin Sch. Nursing Alumni Assn. (pres.), Tex. Orgn. of Nurse Execs., Sigma Theta Tau (Epsilon chpt.). Home: 4139 Bee Creek Rd Spicewood TX 78669

DOGGETT, LLOYD, congressman, former state supreme court justice; b. Austin, Tex., Oct. 6, 1946; s. Lloyd A. and Alyce (Freydenfeldt) D.; m. Elizabeth Belk, 1969; children: Lisa, Catherine. BBA in Bus., U. Tex., 1967, JD with honors, 1970. Bar: Tex. 1971, U.S. Ct. Appeals (5th cir.) 1972, U.S. Dist. Ct. (we. dist.) Tex. 1972. Mem. Tex. State Senate, Dist. 14, 1973-85; ptnr. Doggett and Jacks, Austin, 1975-88; justice Tex. Supreme Ct., Austin, 1989-94; mem. 104th U.S. Congress from 10th Tex. dist., Washington, DC, 1995—; mem. various coms. U.S. Ho. of Reps., including budget com., sci. com. and subcom con basic rsch., Dem. caucus task force on crime, Dem. caucus parliamentary group, co-chair Dem. caucus task force on budget; adj. prof. U. Tex. Sch. of Law, 1989-94; chair Supreme Ct. Task Force on Jud. Ethics, 1992-94. Named one of Five Outstanding Young Texans Tex. Jaycees, 1977, Outstanding Young Lawyer of Austin, 1978, one of Best Legislators, Tex. Monthly, 1979, 81, Outstanding State Senator, Common Cause, 1980, Disting. Alumnus, Bus. Adminstrn. Honors program U. Tex., 1989, Outstanding Jurist in Tex., Mex. Am. Bar Assn., 1993; recipient James Madison award Freedom of Info. Found. Tex., 1990, First Amendment award Nat. Soc. Profl. Journalists, 1990, Arthur B. DeWitty award for outstanding achievement in human rights Austin NAACP, others. Mem. Consumers Union U.S. (bd. dirs. 1976-79, 80-81, 86-89), Tex. Consumer Assn. (pres. 1973). Methodist. Office: US House Reps 126 Cannon House Office Bldg Washington DC 20515-4310

DOHERTY, COLLEEN ANN, critical care nurse; b. Cin., Mar. 22, 1961; d. William Martin and Marian Louise (Smith) D. Diploma in nursing, Jewish Hosp. Sch. Nursing, 1983; BSN, Xavier U., Cin., 1988; MSN, U. Cin., 1993. RN, Ohio. Staff nurse med./surg. oncology Jewish Hosp., Cin., 1983-85, asst. nurse mgr. cardiac med. surg. unit, 1985-87, clin. nurse I, mem. critical care float pool, 1987-91, clin. nurse III ICU, critical care unit, 1991-92, clin. nurse specialist in cardiology, 1992-94; clin. nurse specialist critical care St. Elizabeth Med. Ctr., Edgewood, Ky., 1994—. Mem. AACN, Ohio Nurses Assn., Sigma Theta Tau. Office: St Elizabeth Med Ctr One Med Village Dr Edgewood KY 41017

DOHERTY, JAMES EDWARD, III, physician, educator; b. Newport, Ark., Nov. 22, 1923; s. James Edward D.; children: Richard Edward, Margaret Elise. B.S. Medicine, U. Ark., 1944, M.D., 1946. Diplomate: Am. Bd. Internal Medicine (cardiovascular disease). Intern Columbus (Ga.) City Hosp., 1946-47; resident internal medicine U. Ark. Sch. Medicine, 1949-52, instr. medicine, 1952-53, asst. prof., 1953-61, assoc. prof., 1962-68, prof., 1968—, dir. cardiology div., 1969-77, dir. cardiovascular research, 1977—, dir. continuing med. edn., 1977—; chief cardiology sect. VA Hosp., Little Rock, 1956-68; del. U.S. Pharmacopeial Conv., 1970, 85; mem. so. regional research and adv. com. Am. Heart Assn., 1969-70. Contbr. articles to profl. publs. Bd. dirs. Ark. Heart Assn., 1960-70, sec., 1955-56, pres., 1959-60. Served with AUS, 1943-46; with USAF, 1947-49. Recipient Casimir Funk award, 1975, Abernathy award, 1985, Disting. Faculty award U. Ark. Coll. Medicine, 1986. Fellow Am. Coll. Chest Physicians (com. on cardiology 1992—, treas. Coun. on Geriatric Cardiology 1991-92); mem. Am. Coll. Cardiology (gov. Ark. 1962-65, 68-71), ACP (Ark. gov. 1979-82), Soc. Nuclear Medicine, N.Y. Acad. Scis., So. Soc. Clin. Investigation, Assn. Univ. Cardiologists (sec. 1984-86, v.p. 1987-88, pres. 1988-89), Med. Ctr. Camera Club, Raquet Club, Med. Ctr. Scuba Club (v.p. 1983-84, pres. 1984-85), Masons, Sigma Xi, Alpha Omega Alpha, Alpha Epsilon Delta, Sigma Chi. Office: 4300 W 7th St Little Rock AR 72205-5411

DOHERTY, REBECCA FEENEY, federal judge; b. Ft. Worth, June 3, 1952; d. Charles Edwin Feeney and Annabelle (Knight) Smith; divorced; 1 child, George Jason. BA, Northwestern State U., 1973, MA, 1975; JD, La. State U., 1981. Bar: La. 1981, U.S. Dist. Ct. (mid., ea. and we. dists.) La. 1981, U.S. Ct. Appeals (5th cir.) 1981, U.S. Dist. Ct. (so. dist.) Tex. 1986, U.S. Dist. Ct. (ea. dist.) Tex. 1989. Assoc. Onebane, Donohoe, Bernard, Torian, Diaz, McNamara & Abell, Lafayette, La., 1981-84, ptnr., 1985-91; U.S. dist. ct. judge We. Dist. La., Lafayette, 1991—; adj. instr. Northwestern State U., Natchitoches, La., 1975; co-dir. secondary level gifted and talented program Webster Parish, La., 1978. Contbr. articles to profl. jours.; mem. La. Law Rev., 1980, 81. Recipient Am. Jurisprudence award Lawyers Coop. Pub. Co., 1980, Career Achievement award 1991; inducted into La. State U. Law Ctr. Hall of Fame, 1987. Mem. ABA, La. Bar Assn., La. Assn. Def. Counsel, La. Assn. Trial Lawyers, Acadian Assn. Women Attys., Order of Coif. Office: US Dist Ct 705 Jefferson St Ste 200 Lafayette LA 70501-6936

DOHERTY, ROBERT CUNNINGHAM, advertising executive; b. N.Y.C., Sept. 30, 1930; s. Francis Joseph and Helen (Utley) D.; m. Brucie Rial (div. 1961); children: Michael Bruce, Robert Kelly; m. Kerstin Brigetta Karlsson; children: Andrew Seger, Thomas Nils. BA, Princeton U., 1952. Account exec. Needham Harper Steers, N.Y.C., 1958-62, v.p., account supr., 1962-65; exec. v.p. John Rockwell and Assocs., N.Y.C., 1965-73, ptnr., chmn. bd., 1973-75; v.p. mgmt. group Wells, Rich & Greene, N.Y.C., 1975-79; sr. v.p. McKinney & Silver, Raleigh, N.C., 1979-83, exec. v.p., 1983-87, pres., 1987-90, chief exec. officer, 1991—; chmn., 1993—; guest lectr. U. N.C. Bus. Sch., 1982—, Duke U. Fuqua Sch. Bus., 1987—. Trustee N.C. Symphony, 1991—. Served to 1st lt. USMC, 1952-54, Korea. Mem. Figure Eight Yacht Club (Wilmington, N.C.), Princeton Club (N.Y.C.), Ivy Club (Princeton, N.J.), Windermere Island Club (Eleuthera, Bahamas). Episcopalian. Office: McKinney & Silver 333 Fayetteville Street Mall Raleigh NC 27601-1738

DOHLMAN, DENNIS RAYE, oil company executive; b. Iowa Falls, Iowa, Mar. 16, 1946; s. Lowell L. and Harmina (Ploeger) D.; m. Mary Ilene Ontjes, Sept. 2, 1966; children: John Bradley, Rebecca Ralene. BSChemE, Iowa State U., 1968. Process engr. No. Petrochem. Co., Morris, Ill., 1968-70, maintenance engr., 1970-72, utility area asst. supt., 1972-74, utility area supt., 1974-76; plant supt. Aminoil U.S.A., Inc., Tioga, N.D., 1976-79; project engr. Fenix & Scisson Inc., Casper, Wyo., 1979-80; sr. gas engr. ARCO Oil & Gas Co., Crane, Tex., 1980-81, ops. supr., 1981-84, sr. plant engr., 1984-90; sr. mech. engr., 1990—. Trustee Crane Ind. Sch. Bd., 1989—, pres., 1995—. Mem. AIChE, Permian Basin Sch. Bd. Assn. (v.p. 1994-95, pres. 1995—), Lions (Lion of Yr. award Crane 1992). Home: 300 E 19th St Crane TX 79731-4404 Office: ARCO Oil & Gas Co FM1601 HC-65 Box 55 Crane TX 79731-9801

DOHNAL, WILLIAM EDWARD, retired steel company executive, consultant, accountant; b. Cleve., May 25, 1912; s. Frank and Anna (Florian) D.; children: David, Dennis. Student Western Res. U., 1940. CPA, Ohio. Auditor, Lybrand, Ross Bros. and Montgomery, 1942-45; acting auditor Cleveland-Cliffs Iron Co., Cleve., 1946-47, auditor, 1947-53, asst. treas., 1953-58, compt., 1958-63, v.p., compt., 1963-64, v.p. internat., 1964-73, sr. v.p., from 1973, now ret.; internat. bus. cons. Mem. Coun. World Affairs. Mem. Am. Soc. CPA's, Ohio Soc. CPA's, Weld Club (Perth, Australia). Address: 1710 Lake Cypress Dr Safety Harbor FL 34695-4503

DOJAHN, JULIE GOODMAN, secondary school educator; b. Beech Grove, Ind., May 9, 1956; d. Earl Luke and Patricia (Williamson) Goodman; m. William Herbert Dojahn, July 21, 1984. BA in Chemistry, Ind. State U., 1977; MEd in Secondary Edn., U. Houston, 1986, MS in Chemistry, 1994. Undergrad. teaching/rsch. asst. Ind. State U., Terre Haute, 1974-77; lab. technician Pillsbury Co., Inc., Seelyville, Ind., 1977-78; sr. lab. technician Pillsbury Co., Inc., Seelyville, 1978-79; quality assurance supr. Chgo. area Foremost-McKesson, Inc., San Francisco, 1979-81; divsn. quality control mgr. Hunt-Wesson, Inc., Valparaiso, Ind., 1981-82; quality assurance supr. Houston Riviana Foods, Inc., Houston, 1982-84; chemistry chair Alvin (Tex.) H.S., 1988—; cons. Amoco Chem. Co., Alvin, 1989-94; adj., rsch. assoc. U. Houston, Clear Lake, 1995—. Author: (textbook) Fundamentals of Chemistry, 1990, 2d edit., 1991. Active Partnerships Between Bus. and Edn., Alvin, 1989-94; mem. Cmty. Adv. Panel, 1996—. Recipient Honors scholarship Ind. State U., Terre Haute, 1974, Zeon fellowship U. Houston, Tex., 1993, 94. Mem. NEA, Am. Chem. Soc., Tex. State Tchrs. Assn., Sci. Tchrs. Assn. Tex., Phi Kappa Phi, Alpha Lambda Delta, Sigma Delta Epsilon. Lutheran. Office: Alvin High Sch Chemistry 802 S Johnson St Alvin TX 77511-3300

DOKES, GENEVA, secondary school educator; b. Little Rock, Apr. 14, 1946; d. James Arthur and Vernice (Casey) Streeter; m. Calvin Dokes; children: Amielia, Felicia, Andra, Calvin Jr., Anthony, Tyus. BA, U. Ark., 1982. Rsch. asst. V.A., Little Rock, 1982-89; social sci. rsch. interviewer Nat. Opinion Rsch. Ctr. U. Chgo., 1983-90; tchr. English Alternative Learning Ctr., Scott, Ark., 1989—. Recipient Humanitarian Award McAlmont Ch. of Christ, 1986, 90, 94. Mem. NAACP, Browser Associated Women for Svc. (sec. 1975). Democrat. Mem. Ch. of Christ. Home: 304 Smart St Jacksonville AR 72076

DOKSON, JOEL STEVEN, neurologist; b. Miami, Fla., June 19, 1942; s. Edward Oscar and Marriet (Siegel) D.; m. Marian Segel, Sept. 28, 1969; 1 child, Matthew. MS, U. Miami, 1967. Diplomate Am. Bd. Psychiatry and Neurology. Intern Mt. Sinai Hosp., N.Y.C., 1967-68, resident, 1968-71; Neurologist pvt. practice, Miami Beach, Fla., 1973—; co-chief of neurology Mt. Sinai Med. Ctr., Miami Beach, 1986—. Maj. USAF, 1971-73. Office: 4302 Alton Rd Ste 680 Miami FL 33140-2877

DOLAN, DENNIS JOSEPH, airline pilot, lawyer; b. St. Louis, Mar. 19, 1946; s. Robert Glennon and Lucille Anne (Stanley) D.; m. Aura Maritza Vargas, June 8, 1974; children: Dennis J. Jr., Rebecca and Robert (twins). BSC, Spring Hill Coll., Mobile, Ala., 1967; JD cum laude, St. Louis U., 1985. Bar: Mo., 1985, U.S. Dist. Ct. (ea. dist.) Mo. 1987. Commd. 2d lt. USMC, 1967, advanced through grades to capt., 1970, resigned, 1976; served to maj. USMCR; airline pilot Western Air Lines, L.A., 1976-87, Delta Air Lines, Inc., Atlanta, 1987—; pvt. practice law Clayton, Mo., 1985-88. Mem. ABA, Assn. Trial Lawyers Am., Airline Pilots Assn. (bd. dirs. 1992-94, exec. v.p. 1994-96, chmn. Delta Master exec. coun. 1996—). Roman Catholic. Home: 13065 Addison Rd Roswell GA 30075-6305

DOLAN, RONALD VINCENT, insurance company executive; b. Charleroi, Pa., Aug. 27, 1942; s. James L. and Kathryn (Stopp) D.; m. MaryJane Tousignant, 1978; children: Gina, Ronalee, Mark, Craig, Samantha. B.A., St. Vincent Coll., Latrobe, Pa., 1964. Mgr. El Bent Supply, Pa., 1964-67; actuarial assoc. Penn Mut. Ins., Phila., 1967-72; pres., chief exec. officer First Colony Life, Lynchburg, Va., 1973—, also bd. dirs.; bd. dirs. Ctrl. Fidelity Bank, Richmond, Va., Am. Mayflower Life, N.Y., Ethyl Corp., 1st Colony Corp. Chmn. Ctrl. Va. C.C. Found.; bd. dirs. Randolph Macon Women's Coll., United Way of Ctrl. Va. Mem. Soc. Actuaries (assoc.), Am. Acad.

Actuaries. Home: RR 1 Box 9 Wingina VA 24599-9701 Office: 1st Colony Life Ins Co PO Box 1280 Lynchburg VA 24504-1280

DOLAN, TIMOTHY EMMETT, political scientist, educator; b. Wichita, Kans., July 21, 1952; s. Robert Emmett and Geraldine (Thompson) D.; m. Choon Geum Park, Feb. 18, 1981; children: Will Emmett, Aurora Ki'i-aka. BA, San Diego State U., 1975; MA, U. Hawaii, 1978, PhD, 1991. Lectr. in polit. sci. U. Hawaii, Honolulu, 1984-88; instr. Catholic Charities, Honolulu, 1989-90; asst. prof. polit. sci. U. Hawaii, Hilo, 1990-93, U. Tex., Tyler, 1993—; lectr. West Oahu Coll., Honolulu, 1988, U. Hawaii, Manoa, 1986-90, Hawaii Pacific Coll., Honolulu, 1989, Honolulu C.C., 1990. Mem. Am. Youth Soccer Assn. (coach), Nat. Assn. Svc. and Conservation Corps, Am. Polit. Sci. Assn., U.S. Amateur Soccer Assn. Roman Catholic. Office: U Tex 3900 University Blvd Tyler TX 75799

DOLEN, WILLIAM KENNEDY, allergist, immunologist, pediatrician, educator; b. Memphis, Oct. 16, 1952; s. William Smith and Dorothy DeWitt (Kennedy) D.; m. Carolyn Canon, Dec. 21, 1974; children: John William, Susan Elizabeth. BS in Biology with distinction and honors, Rhodes Coll., 1974; MD, U. Tenn., 1977. Cert. Nat. Bd. Med. Examiners, Am. Bd. Pediatrics, Am. Bd. Allergy and Immunology. Commd. 2d lt. U.S. Army, 1974, advanced through grades to maj., 1982; intern in pediatrics U. Tenn. Hosp., Knoxville, 1977-78; med. officer SHAPE Med. Ctr., Belgium, 1978-79; commdr. U.S. Army NATO Health Clinic, Belgium, 1979-80; resident in pediatrics Letterman Army Med. Ctr., San Francisco, 1980-82; pediatrician Bassett Army Community Hosp., Ft. Wainwright, Alaska, 1982-84; fellow allergy and clin. immunology Fitzsimons Army Med. Ctr., Aurora, Colo., 1984-86; clin. instr. pediatrics F. Edward Hébert Sch. Medicine Uniformed Svcs. U. Health Scis., Bethesda, Md., 1986-87, clin. asst. prof. pediatrics, 1988-89; allergist, immunologist Ochsner Clinic, New Orleans, 1988-89, Allergy Respiratory Inst. Colo., Denver, 1989-92; chief pediatric allergy sect. allergy-immunology svc. Fitzsimons Army Med. Ctr., Aurora, Colo., 1986-88; clin. assoc. prof. medicine Ctr. for Health Scis. U. Colo., Denver, 1990-92; assoc. prof. pediatrics and medicine Med. Coll. Ga., Augusta, 1992—; chair subcom. on allergen selection, practice parameters task force Joint Coun. Allergy and Immunology, 1992—; presenter in field. Author: (with others) Rhinolaryngoscopy, 2d edit., 1989, Rhinitis, 2d edit., 1991; mem. editl. bd. Annals of Allergy, 1993—, ad hoc reviewer, 1990-93; author (audiovisual programs) Allergy Case Studies, 1992, The Upper Airway, 1992, Asthma is an Allergic Disease, 1994; contbr. articles to profl. jours. Fellow Am. Coll. Allergy, Asthma and Immunology (bd. regents, 1993—, chair comm. coun. 1993—, chair workshop com. 1990—, mem. ann. program com. 1986-87, 90—, CME com. 1988—, chair Rhinitis com. 1988-93, workshop com. 1989-90), Am. Acad. Allergy and Immunology (chair com. on in vivo testing 1991—, com. computers and tech. 1994—, workshop com. 1993—); mem. AMA, Ga. Soc. Allergy and Immunology, European Acad. Allergology and Clin. Immunology (subcom. skin testing 1992—). Episcopalian. Office: Sect Allergy Immunology Med Coll GA Augusta GA 30912

DOLEZAL, LEO THOMAS, telecommunications executive; b. Perry, Okla., Aug. 3, 1944; s. Leo Frank and Evalena Augusta (Pursley) D.; m. Derrla Mae Lawhon, Oct. 21, 1963 (dec.); children: Corinna, Rohmona, Consuela, Derral, Kyle; m. Lynda M. Manley, Nov. 11, 1994. AS in Electronics, No. Okla. Coll., 1964. Licensed gen. radiotelephone operator; registered EMT. Aircraft radio technician Serv Air Inc., Enid, Okla., 1964-69; frame attendant S.W. Bell Tel., Enid, 1969-70, comm. technician, 1970-74; combination technician S.W. Bell Tel., Billings, Okla., 1974-78, Ponca City, Okla., 1978-80; mgr. network ops. S.W. Bell Tel., Enid, 1980—; mem. O.T. Autry Vo-Tech Tech. Electronics Adv. Com., Enid, 1987—. Vol. emergency med. tech. and fireman Billings Fire Dept., 1978—; pres. Billings Housing Authority, 1990-94. Lt. col. USAR, ret. Mem. NRA (life), Res. Officers Assn., Emergency Med. Tech. Assn., Lions (pres. 1977, 90-92), Billings Rotary (pres. 1978, 92, sec. 1991-92), Masons (past master Billings lodge), Billings C. of C. Republican. Mem. Ch. of The Brethren. Office: PO Box 392 Enid OK 73702-0392

DOLT, FREDERICK CORRANCE, lawyer; b. Louisville, Oct. 10, 1929; s. O. Frederick and Margaret A. (Corrance) D.; m. Lucy M. Voelker, Dec. 8, 1960; 1 child, Frederick C. Jr. JD, U. Louisville, 1952. Bar: Ky. 1952, U.S. Ct. Appeals (6th cir.) 1965, U.S. Supreme Ct. 1972, La. 1982. Assoc. Morris & Garlove, Louisville, 1955-59; sole practice Louisville, 1959-70, 79—; ptnr. Leibson, Dolt & McCarthy, Louisville, 1970-73. Mem. Inner Circle Advocates, 1981. Served with U.S. Army, 1953-55. Mem. ABA, Ky. Bar Assn. (chmn. ins. negligence sect. 1968-70, mem. Ho. of Dels. 1970-80), Assn. Trial Lawyers Am. (state del. 1965-70), Ky. Trial Lawyers Assn. (pres. 1970). Republican. Presbyterian. Home: 19634 Lost Creek Dr Fort Myers FL 33912-5539 Office: 310 Starks Bldg Louisville KY 40202

DOMBRO, RICHARD, financial planner; b. Phila., Dec. 12, 1927; s. William and Sadie (Cornfield) D.; m. Dorothy Moxie, Apr. 10, 1955 (div. 1989); m. Mary Ann Blizard, Sept. 2, 1989; children: Janice, Beverly, Barbara, Jeanne, Stephanie, Jamie, Jeffery. BA, Pa. State U., 1946; postgrad., U. Denver, 1976. Notary pub., Fla.; grad. Coll. for Fin. Planning, 1976. Mgr., agent, rep. Universal Marion Corp., Orlando, Fla., 1950-60; broker, prin., mgr. Hardy Hardy Assocs., Sarasota, Fla., 1960-65; broker, prin. Walston & Co., Sarasota, 1965-70; prin. Prudential Bache (formerly Bache), Sarasota, 1970-81; owner, operator, broker Commodity Exch., Sarasota, 1981-97; bd. regents, trustees Coll. for Fin. Planning, 1971-72; pres. Pvt. Realty Inc., Sarasota, 1978-85, Pvt. Bourse Inc., Sarasota, 1978-85; bd. chmn. United Energy Techs., Scottsdale, Ariz., 1985-88. Author: The Financial Planner, 1972, Financial Planning for the Retired Investor, 1976, Black Jack (21) The Card Game, 1996, Black Jack for Winners, 1996. Mem. Young Reps., Washington, 1950-97; sponsor, mem. Fla. Sheriffs Assn., Tallahassee, 1960-97; bd. chmn. Sarasota YMCA, 1972-74. Staff sgt. U.S. Army, 1946-48, Japan. Recipient Trustee Cert. award Fla. State Elks Assn., 1976. Fellow Internat. Assn. Fin. Planners; mem. Am. Assn. Ret. Persons, Am. Numismatic Assn., Fla. United Numismatists Inc., Internat. Platform Assn., Am. Legion, Ky. Col., S.W. Blood Bank (donor, club chmn. 1951-94), 10 Gallon Donor. Roman Catholic. Office: Commodity Exchange 1918 Bay Rd Sarasota FL 34239-6908

DOMINGUE, DEBORAH GAIL, tax preparer, bookkeeper; b. Longview, Tex., Oct. 29, 1955; d. Grady L. Marshall and Earnestine (Bonner) Stephens; m. Joseph L. Domingue, Jan. 3, 1977 (div. Apr. 1981); 1 child, Demetrius T. Assoc. degree, Ft. Worth Bus. Coll., 1985; postgrad., Control Data Inst., 1986; cert., Federated Tax Svc. Sch., 1994. Cert. tax preparer. Clerical asst. Pers. Pool, Inc., Ft. Worth, 1975-93; acctg. asst. Robert Half Accountemps, Ft. Worth, 1985-93; 10 key operator Contract Dataflo, Inc., Dallas, 1985-93; bookkeeper, tax preparer Domingue, Inc., Bedford, Tex., 1985—. With U.S.M.C., 1978. Mem. NASE. Democrat. Mem. Church of Christ. Home: 1970 C Shadyrest Ct Bedford TX 76021

DOMINGUEZ, FRANK A., language educator. BA, Hobart Coll., 1967; MA, U. Mich., 1968, PhD, 1973. Asst. prof. U. N.C., Chapel Hill, 1974-79, assoc. prof., 1979-90, prof., 1990—, chair Romance langs., 1995—; cons. Nat. Endowment Humanities, Washington, 1993—; mem. IAT adv. bd., Raleigh, Durham, N.C., 1989-94. Author: Cancionero de Obras de Burlas, 1979, The Mediaval Argonautica, 1979 (Choice award 1979), Love and Remembrance: The Poetry of Jorge Manrique, 1989 (Choice award 1989), (software) Spanish Microtutoer, 1989, (software) !Atajo!, 1993, (software) Mundos Hispanos, 1996; mem. editl. bd. Hispania, 1992-95. Fellow Nat. Endowment for the Humanities Inst., 1982, 92; Office of Internat. Edn. rsch. grant Dept. Edn., 1985-87, 87-88, 93-95. Mem. MLA (com. on emerging technologies 1994—). Office: UNC Dept Romance Langs CB #3170 Dey 014A Chapel Hill NC 27599

DOMINGUEZ, MURIEL FARLEY, writer, consultant, educator; b. N.Y.C., Feb. 15, 1943; d. James Joseph and Muriel (Ross) Farley; m. José Dominguez-Urosa, Dec. 27, 1970; children: Maria, Ruth. MAT in French and Edn., Wells Coll., 1964; MAT in Lang. Arts and Endl. Psychology, Wesleyan U., 1965; diploma in French studies, l'Université de Paris, 1966; MA in French Studies, Middlebury Grad. Sch., France, 1966; PhD in Romance Langs. and Lits., Harvard U., 1978. Tchr. French Glastonbury (Conn.) High Sch., 1965, Scarsdale (N.Y.) High Sch., 1966-68; teaching fellow Harvard U., Cambridge, Mass., 1969-70, 72-73; tchr. ESL World Bank, 1977-78; lectr. French Georgetown U., Washington, 1978-87; rsch. assoc. sch. advanced internat. studies Johns Hopkins U., Washington, 1987-88; assoc. prof. fgn. langs. Marymount U., Arlington, Va., 1991—; mem. Arlington County Adv. Coun. Instrn., 1982-83, Arlington County Fgn. Langs. Adv. Com., 1983-85; vis. scholar Sch. Advanced Internat. Studies Johns Hopkins U., Balt., 1989. Author: (with others) The Art of the Proustian Novel Reconsidered, 1979; contbr. articles to profl. jours.; prodr. (video) Séjour dans le Lot-et-Garonne, 1992, others. Faculty Rsch. grantee Que. Ministry Internat. Rels., 1988, 92; fellow Middlebury-Wesleyan Program France, 1966, Govt. of France, 1990. Mem. MLA, Am. Assn. Tchrs. French, Am. Assn. Can. Studies, Am. Coun. Que. Studies, Harvard Club (Washington). Home: 2428 N Tuckahoe St Arlington VA 22205-1949

DOMINGUEZ, ROBERTO ALFONSO, psychiatrist; b. Santiago de Cuba, Cuba, Aug. 2, 1948; s. Roberto Felix and Zoila Altagracia (Gonzalez) D.; m. Penny Holtzclaw, Aug. 15, 1971; 1 child, Maria Cristina. BA, Western Ky. U., 1970; MD, U. Louisville, 1974. Diplomate Am. Bd. Psychiatry and Neurology; lic. MD, Fla., Ky., Calif. Resident psychiatry U. Louisville Affiliated Hosps., 1974-77; fellow in psychopharmacology U. Louisville Sch. Medicine, 1977-78; attending psychiatrist, staff psychiatrist VA Med. Ctr., Louisville, 1977-78, 78-80; clin. instr. U. Louisville Sch. Medicine, 1977-79, asst. prof., 1979-80; asst. prof. U. Miami (Fla.) Sch. Medicine, 1980-85, assoc. prof., 1985—, med. dir. psychopharmacological clinic, 1980-93, dir. psychopharmacology program, 1993—; cons. in psychiatry and rsch. divsn. clin. pharmacology U. Miami, 1980-91; sci. adv. com. U. Miami Sch. Medicine, 1988-90; cons. in psychiatry South Fla. Bioavailability Clinic, Miami, 1991—; treatment and assessment com. NIH, Washington, 1991—. Co-author: Review Course: Fundamental and Clinical Aspects of Internal Medicine, 1983, 86; contbr. numerous articles to profl. jours. Guest lectr. local or regional mental health support orgsn.; mem. Obsessive Compulsive Disorder Found.; founder South Fla. Obsessive-Compulsive Disorder Support Group. Recipient Spafford S. Ackerly award for Outstanding Work in Psychiatry, U. Louisville, 1973, Henry P. Laughlin award Nat. Psychiat. Endowment Fund, 1977, Physicians Recognition award for Continued Med. Edn., AMA, 1977-79, 82, 85, 88; nominee for Sol W. Ginsburg fellowship, 1974, for the Falk Residency fellowship, 1975. Fellow Am. Psychiat. Assn., Am. Coll. Clin. Pharmacology; mem. AMA, Fla. Med. Assn., Ky. Med. Assn., Ky. Psychiat. Assn., Jefferson County Med. Soc., South Fla. Psychiat. Soc., Dade County Med. Assn., Southeastern Pharmacology Soc., Assn. for Acad. Psychiatry, Am. Soc. Clin. Psychopharmacology. Roman Catholic. Office: Jackson Meml Hosp Dept Psychiatry (D-29) 1611 NW 12th Ave Miami FL 33136-1005

DOMINIK, JACK EDWARD, lawyer; b. Chgo., July 9, 1924; s. Ewald Arthur and Gertrude Alene (Crotzer) D.; children: Paul, David, Georgia Lee, Elizabeth, Sarah, Clare. BSME with distinction, Purdue U., 1947; JD, Northwestern U., 1950. Bar: Ill. 1950, U.S. Patent Office 1953, Wis. 1959, Fla. 1964, U.S. Dist. Ct. (ea. dist.) Wis. 1959, U.S. Supreme Ct. 1965, U.S. Dist. Ct. (no. dist.) Ohio 1962, U.S. Dist. Ct. (so. dist.) Ill. 1965, U.S. Ct. Appeals (7th and 9th cirs.) 1965, U.S. Ct. Appeals (4th cir.) 1973, U.S. Dist. Ct. (so. dist.) Fla. 1974, U.S. Ct. Appeals (5th cir.) 1977, U.S. Dist. Ct. (mid. dist.) Fla. 1979, U.S. Ct. Appeals (fed. cir.) 1983, U.S. Ct. Appeals (11th cir.) 1984, U.S. Ct. Appeals (2d cir.) 1987. Assoc. Carlson, Pitzner, Hubbard & Wolfe, Chgo., 1950-54; ptnr. Ooms and Dominik, Chgo., 1954-59, White & Hirshboeck, Milw., 1959-62, Dominik, Knechtel, Godula & DeMeur, Chgo., 1962-78, Dominik & Stein, Miami, 1978—. Served to 1st lt., C.E. AUS, 1943-46, ETO. Mem. ABA, Wis. Bar Assn., Fla. Bar Assn., Chgo. Bar Assn., Am. Patent Law Assn., Chgo. Patent Law Assn. (chmn. taxation com. 1966, 69-70), Milw. Patent Law Assn., Patent Law Assn. So. Fla. (founder, dir. 1982—), Chgo. Yacht Club, Union League Club. Home: 14751 Lewis Rd Miami Lakes FL 33014-2731 Office: 6175 NW 153rd St Hialeah FL 33014-2435

DONADIO, BEVERLY ROSE, writer; b. Winston-Salem, N.C., Dec. 28, 1930; d. Lawson Francis and Katherine Lucille (Thrift) Ivester; m. Karl G. Smith (div.); children: Vickie Lee, Karl Gregor, Theodore Francis; m. Joseph Donadio, Dec. 21, 1968 (dec. May 1987); 1 child, Joseph Christopher. Student, Greensboro Coll., N.C., Ringling Sch. of Art, Sarasota, Fla. Interior designer N.C., Fla.; writer, illustrator Rosebrier Pub. Co., Laurel Pub. Co., Inc., Charleston, S.C., 1996—. Author: (children's books) The Rabbit Family, 1989 (Best Illustrated Book 1989).

DONAHOO, ANN ROCHELLE, elementary education educator; b. Dallas, Oct. 9, 1966; d. Hayden Rodney and Janis Estell (Joseph) Denison. BS magna cum laude, U. North Tex., 1990, MEd, 1990. Cert. elem. tchr., Tex. Head instr. Gymnastics Plus, Southlake, Tex., 1983-90; tchr. 2d grade Lewisville (Tex.) Ind. Sch. Dist., 1990—. Author and presentor workshops on child abuse, 1989. Meadows Found. grantee, 1990. Mem. Nat. Assn. Edn. of Young Children, Southern Assn. Children Under Six, Denton Assn. Edn. Young Children; Golden Key, Phi Kappa Phi, Phi Delta Kappa, Kappa Delta Pi. Republican. Baptist. Home: 7875 Creekview Rd Frisco TX 75034

DONAHOO, MELVIN LAWRENCE, aerospace management consultant, industrial engineer; b. Balt., Dec. 28, 1930; s. Lawrence E. and Margaret Donahoo; m. Charlene Bruce; children: Patricia Ann, Joseph, Teresa, Melvin Lawrence Jr. BS, U. Balt., 1954, MBA, 1974; postgrad., Am. Univ., 1964-67, George Washington U., 1969-71. Cons., v.p. L.E. Donahoo & Assoc., Phila., 1954-58; chief indsl. engring. Martin Marietta Corp., Balt. and Orlando, Fla., 1958-63; program mgr. NASA Goddard Space Flight Ctr., Greenbelt, Md., 1963-90; dir. ops. Idea, Inc., 1990-92; pvt. aerospace cons., 1992—; instr. indsl. mgmt. Author: Aircraft Learning Curves, 1959, Project Planning Handbook, 1970; also research papers. With USN. Mem. Soc. Mfg. Engrs. (sr., life, mem. coms.), Inst. Indsl. Engrs. (sr., life, mem. coms.), Am. Legion (post comdr. Md. 1983, county comdr. 1984-86), Kent Island Yacht Club, Naval Airship Assn., Patrick AFB Officers Club, Missile-Space and Range Pioneers Assn.

DONAHUE, KATHERINE MARY, sales executive; b. Worcester, Mass., Dec. 3, 1950; d. Richard Francis and Theresa Marie Eva (Choiniere) D. A.A. in Allied Health, L.A. C.C., Republic of the Philippines, 1977; AA in Pre-Liberal Arts, Hillsborough C.C., 1978; BA, U. South Fla., 1981; MBA, Doctoral Candidate, Nova U., 1991, 92—. RN. Sales rep. Vestal Labs., St. Louis, 1981-82; profl. sales rep. Hoechst-Roussel Pharms. Inc., Somerville, N.J., 1992-95, sr. sales rep., 1995—. Vol. nurse Good Samaritan Clinic, Holiday, Fla., 1993—; vol. Big Bros./Big Sisters, Pinellas County, Fla., 1993—; speaker Am. Heart Assn., New Port Richey, Fla., 1993—. 1st lt. USAF, 1975-78; capt. USAFR, 1978-81. Mem. AAUW, NAFE, Acad. Mgmt., Am. Mktg. Assn., Exec. Women in Sales and Mktg., Tampa Bay Sales Profls. (rec. sec.), U. South Fla. Alumnae Assn., Worcester Hahnemann Hosp. Alumnae Assn., Pinellas IBM PC Users Group, Palm Harbor IBM Users Group, Sierra Club. Home: 6732 298th Ave N Clearwater FL 34621-1621

DONAHUE, PATRICIA TOOTHAKER, retired social worker, administrator; b. Alamo, Tex., Sept. 6, 1922; d. Henry Tull and Minnie Elizabeth (Scott) Toothaker; m. Hayden Hackney Donahue, Feb. 22, 1947; children: Erin Kathleen, Kerry Shannon, Patricia Marie. BA, U. Okla., 1977, MSW, 1978. Lic. social worker with specialty in clin. social work, Okla. Clin. social worker Cen. Okla. Community Mental Health Ctr., Norman, 1979-91; participant VII World Congress Mental Health, Vienna, Austria, 1983; adj. asst. prof. U. Okla. Sch. Social Work, Norman, 1989—. Vol. counselor Woman's Resource Ctr., Norman, 1978-79; active Cleve. County Aging Svcs. Adv. Coun., 1988-91, pres., 1991. Mem. Nat. Alliance for Mentally Ill, Cleve. County Mental Health Assn., Cleve. County Med. Aux. (pres. 1970-71), Reviewers Club Norman (pres. 1970). Democrat. Methodist. Home: 1109 Westbrooke Ter Norman OK 73072-6308

DONALDSON, ARTHUR JOSEPH, lawyer; b. N.Y.C., Mar. 29, 1938; s. Francis Leo and Mabel J. (Erckert) D.; children: Sheelagh, Shannon, Sean, Seamus; m. Nancy Donaldson. BA, Cath. U. Am., Washington, 1960, JD, 1963. Bar: D.C. 1965, N.C. 1966, U.S. Dist. Ct. (mid. dist.) N.C. 1967, U.S. Ct. Appeals (4th cir.) 1968, U.S. Supreme Ct. 1974. Spl. agt. FBI, 1963-67; pvt. practice law Salisbury, N.C., 1967-88; ptnr. Donaldson & Horsley, Greensboro, N.C., 1988—. Contbr. articles to profl. jours. Candidate N.C. Supreme Ct., 1986, 88. Mem. Nat. Lawyers Assn., Rep. Nat. Lawyers Assn., N.C. Rep. Lawyers Assn. (pres., founder 1981). Roman Catholic. Home: 1806 Northbay Dr Browns Summit NC 27214 Office: Donaldson & Horsley PA 208 W Wendover Ave Greensboro NC 27401-1307

DONALDSON, ROBERT HERSCHEL, university administrator, educator; b. Houston, June 14, 1943; s. Herschel Arthur and Vera Edith (True) D.; m. Judy Carol Johnston, June 27, 1964 (div. Apr. 30, 1984); children: Jennifer Gwynne, John Andrew; m. Sally S. Abravanel, Mar. 31, 1985; children: Mark Elliot, Ryan Scott. A.B., Harvard U., 1964, A.M., 1966, Ph.D., 1969. Prof. polit. sci. Vanderbilt U., 1968-81, assoc. dean Coll. Arts and Sci., 1975-81; provost, v.p. acad. affairs, prof. polit. sci. Herbert H. Lehman Coll. CUNY, 1981-84; pres. Fairleigh Dickinson U., Rutherford, N.J., 1984-90, U. Tulsa, 1990-96; vis. research prof. U.S. Army War Coll., 1978-79. Author: Stasis and Change in Revolutionary Elites, 1971, Soviet Policy toward India, 1974, The Soviet-Indian Alliance: Quest for Influence, 1979, The Soviet Union in the Third World: Successes and Failures, 1981, Soviet Foreign Policy since World War II, 1981, 85, 88, 92. Council Fgn. Relations fellow, 1973-74. Mem. Coun. on Fgn. Rels., Phi Beta Kappa. Republican. Methodist. Home: 6449 S Richmond Ave Tulsa OK 74136-1669 Office: Univ Tulsa Office of President 600 S College Ave Tulsa OK 74104-3126

DONALDSON, WILLIS LYLE, research institute administrator; b. Cleburne, Tex., May 1, 1915; s. Charles Lyle and Anna (Bell) D.; m. Frances Virginia Donnell, Aug. 20, 1938; children: Sarah Donaldson Seaberg, Susan Donaldson Pollock, Sylvia Donaldson Nelson, Anthony Lyle. B.S., Tex. Tech. U., 1938. Registered profl. engr., Pa., Tex. Distbn. engr. Tex. Electric Service Co., 1938-42, supervisory engr., 1945-46; asst. prof. elec. engring. Lehigh U., 1946-51, assoc. prof., 1953-54; with S.W. Research Inst., San Antonio, 1954—; v.p. S.W. Research Inst., 1964-72, v.p. planning and program devel., 1972-74, sr. v.p. planning and program devel., 1974-85, sr. cons., 1985—. Bd. dirs. San Antonio Chamber Music Soc., pres., 1962-72, 87-93, mem., 1954—. Capt. USNR, 1942-45, 51-53. Named Disting. Engr. Tex. Tech. U., 1969. Fellow IEEE, Am. Soc. Nondestructive Testing; mem. Armed Forces Communications and Electronics Assn. (disting. life), Sigma Xi, Tau Beta Pi, Eta Kappa Nu, Alpha Chi. Home: PO Box 160218 San Antonio TX 78280-2418 Office: 6220 Culebra Rd San Antonio TX 78238-5166

DONALLEY, JUDITH D., education educator; b. Charleston, W.Va., Nov. 29, 1938; d. James R. DeBoard and Charlotte R. (Nebbergall) DeBoard Jarvis; m. Kenneth G. Donnalley Sr., Apr. 24, 1973 (dec. May 1978); 1 child, Jason. BS, U. Charleston, 1960; MLS, U. Pitts., 1966. Tchr. Anne Arundel County, Annapolis, Md., 1960-63; libr. asst. W.Va. Libr. Commn., Charleston, 1964; tchr. U. Pitts., 1965; asst. cataloger Kanawha County Pub. Libr., Charleston, 1965-66; asst. prof. U. Charleston, 1966-69; assoc. prof. East Carolina U., Greenville, 1969—. Author: Families in Tradition: An Annotated Bibliography, 1988; contbr. articles to profl. jours. Democrat. Home: PO Box 2943 Greenville NC 27836-0943 Office: Dept Library Studies Sch Edn East Carolina U Greenville SC 27858

DONATH, JANET SUE, hospice and home health care nurse; b. Columbus, Ohio, Jan. 30, 1945; d. Samuel Joseph and Lola Mae (Marshall) Glines; m. Monroe Jefferson Donath, Jr., Dec. 10, 1966; children: Joseph Jefferson, James Monroe. Cert. vocat. nursing, Rosebud Sch. Vocat. Nursing, 1979; ADN, McLennan Community Coll., 1982; BSN, U. Tex., Arlington, 1990. RN, Tex. From nurse's aide to floor nurse Rosebud Community Hosp., 1977-81; patient care nurse Hillcrest Bapt. Med. Ctr., Waco, Tex., 1981-83; from charge nurse to home health dir. Rosebud Community Hosp., 1983-88; dir. hospice and home health svcs. Hillcrest Bapt. Med. Ctr., Waco, 1988-93; dir. home health, hospice and community outreach St. Joseph Hosp., 1993-95; dir. VNA Hospice, Vis. Nurse Assn. Houston, Inc., 1995-96; cons. home health and hospice VNA Hospice, Houston, 1996—. With USN, 1963-66. Mem. ANA, Nat. Nurses Assn., Tex. Nurses Assn. (rec. sec. 1991-92, 92-93), Tex. Hospice Orgn. Home: 11326 Meadowchase Dr Houston TX 77065-4923

DONEHOO, SHEILA ROWAN, engineering educator; b. Oakland, Calif., Oct. 20, 1960; d. Lawrence Gilbert and Barbara June (Harris) Rowan; m. Ronald James Flora, Jan. 16, 1988 (div. 1989); m. Ralph Scott Donehoo, May 25, 1991; 1 child, Scott. BS, U. N.C., Chapel Hill, 1987; postgrad., N.C. State U., 1987-88, So. Coll. Tech., 1992—. Dog obedience instr. Orange County Animal Protection Soc., Chapel Hill, 1987-89, asst. mgr., 1988-89; rschr. N.C. State U., Raleigh, 1987-88, Emory U., Atlanta, 1989-92; instr. So. Coll. Tech., Marietta, Ga., 1993—. Mem. Women in Electronics, IEEE. Republican. Baptist. Home: PO Box 453 Roswell GA 30077 Office: So Coll Tech 1100 S Marietta Pkwy Marietta GA 30060

DONG, QUAN, ecologist, educator; b. Beijing, China, July 18, 1954; came to U.S., 1986; s. Chung Cai and Duan Fang (Jiang) D. MS, Duke U., 1992; PhD, Vanderbilt U., 1994. Rsch. asst. Inst. Zoology, Chinese Acad. Scis., Beijing, 1974-77, rsch. fellow, 1982-85; vis. scholar Can. Wildlife Svc., Edmonton, Alta., 1985-86; rsch. asst., teaching asst. Sch. of the Environment, Duke U., Durham, N.C., 1986-89; hon. fellow U. Wis., Madison, 1991; fellow Electric Power Rsch. Inst., 1991-93; teaching asst. Vanderbilt U., Nashville, 1993-95; rsch. assoc. U. Miami, Fla., 1995—. Writer TV sci. documentary Ctrl. TV Sta. of China, 1983 (Milky Way award 1984); editor Chinese Jour. Applied Ecology, 1996; contbr. chpt. to book, articles to profl. jours. Gen. sec., chief editor newsletter Sino-Eco Club, 1994, pres., 1995. Recipient Tng. award World Univ. Svc. of Can., 1985-86. Mem. Ecol. Soc. Am., Ecol. Soc. China (coun. mem. 1995). Office: DIMAS/RSMAS U Miama Miami FL 33149

DONIE, SCOTT, Olympic athlete, platform diver; b. Vicenza, Italy, Oct. 10, 1968. BA in communication/advt., So. Meth. U., 1990. Olympic platform diver Barcelona, Spain, 1992; Olympic springboard diver Atlanta, 1996. Recipient Silver medal platform diving Olympics, Barcelona, 1992, 4th place medal springboard diving Olympics, Atlanta, 1996. Home: 13315 Apple Tree Rd Houston TX 77079-7107

DONLON, WILLIAM JAMES, lawyer; b. Colorado Springs, Colo., Apr. 22, 1924; s. John Andrew and Kathleen M. Donlon; m. Josephine A. Janssen, July 19, 1946; children—William James, Gregory A., Michele, Dru Ann Gazelle. Student Colo. Coll., 1941-43; B.S., U. Denver, 1949, J.D., 1950. Bar: Colo. 1950, Ohio 1964, Ill. 1969, U.S. Dist. Ct. Colo. 1956 (no. dist.) Ill. 1974, U.S. Ct. Apls. (10th cir.) 1957, U.S. Ct. Apls. (5th cir.) 1970, U.S. Ct. Apls. (7th cir.) 1974, U.S. Ct. Apls. D.C. 1979, U.S. Supreme Ct. 1965. Dep. clk. U.S. Dist. Ct. Denver, 1949-50; solo practice, Denver, 1953-63; gen. counsel Brotherhood Ry., Airline and S.S. Clks., Freight Handlers, Express and Sta. Employees, Rosemont, Ill., 1963-84, Rockville, Md., 1963-86; instr. labor U. Ill., 1972-78. Served with USAAF, 1942-45. Decorated Air medal with 2 oak leaf clusters. Mem. ABA (council sect. labor and employment law 1977-86), Ill. Bar Assn., D.C. Bar Assn., Am. Legion, VFW, KC (Grand Knights coun. 10329 1991-93), Phi Alpha Delta, Phi Delta Theta. Democrat. Roman Catholic.

DONNELLAN, BARBARA MCCARTHY, tax specialist; b. Plainfield, N.J., July 17, 1957; d. Edward Daniel and Mary Gloria (Burrell) McCarthy; m. Kevin J. Donnellan, Sept. 24, 1983. BA, St. John's U., Jamaica, N.Y., 1979, MA, 1981. Cert. mgmt. trainer, DDI Corp. Sr. budget analyst City of N.Y., 1980-83; sr. metro analyst Arlington (Va.) County, 1983-88, asst. to dir. cmty. planning, housing devel., 1988, adminstrv. svcs. divsn. chief, 1988-94, acting dir. librs., 1995-96, sr. tax policy coord., 1995—. Advance rep. Rep. Geraldine A. Ferraro Ireland Tour, 1985; asst. dir. of fundraising Dem. Nat. Conv., San Francisco, 1984; vol. Ferraro for Congress, N.Y.C., 1978, 80, 82; vol. Meals on Wheels, Arlington, 1994—. Mem. ALA. Democrat. Roman Catholic. Office: Arlington County 2100 Clarendon Blvd Arlington VA 22201

DONNELLY, BARBARA SCHETTLER, medical technologist; b. Sweetwater, Tenn., Dec. 2, 1933; d. Clarence G. and Irene Elizabeth (Brown) Schettler; A.A., Tenn. Wesleyan Coll., 1952; B.S., U. Tenn., 1954; cert. med. tech., Erlanger Hosp. Sch. Med. Tech., 1954; postgrad. So. Meth. U., 1980-81; children—Linda Ann, Richard Michael. Med. technologist Erlanger Hosp., Chattanooga, 1953-57, St. Luke's Episcopal Hosp., Tex. Med. Ctr., Houston, 1957-58, 1962; engring. R &D SCI Systems Inc., Huntsville, Ala.,

1974-76; cons. hematology systems Abbott Labs., Dallas, 1976-77, hematology specialist, Dallas, Irving, Tex., 1977-81, tech. specialist microbiology systems, Irving, 1981-83, coord. tech. svc. clin. chemistry systems, 1983-84, coord. customer tng. clin. chemistry systems, 1984-87, supr. clin. chemistry tech. svcs., 1987-88, supr. clin. chemistry customer support ctr., 1988-93, supr. clin. chemistry and x-systems customer support ctr., 1993—. Mem. Am. Soc. Clin. Pathologists (cert. med. technologist), Am. Soc. Microbiology, Nat. Assn. Female Execs., U. Tenn. Alumni Assn., Chi Omega. Contbr. articles on cytology to profl. jours. Republican. Methodist. Home: 204 Greenbriar Ln Bedford TX 76021-2006 Office: 1921 Hurd Dr Irving TX 75038-4313

DONNELLY, MICHAEL JOSEPH, management consultant; b. Montreal, Quebec, Can., Dec. 28, 1951; s. Terrence James and Beatrice Miriam (Faloon) D.; m. Barbara Lynne Webb. BA in Commerce, Simon Fraser U., 1976. Chartered acct. Acct. Campbell, Sharp, Chartered Accts., Victoria, B.C., Can., 1973-76, Peat Marwick Thorne, Victoria, 1976-79; controller Park Pacific Group of Cos., Victoria, 1979-80; gen. mgr. Indsl. Plastics (A subs. of the Park Pacific Group of Cos.), Victoria, 1980-83; chief fin. officer Action Group of Cos., Ft. Lauderdale, 1984-85; pres. Beacon Mgmt. Group, Inc., Pompano Beach, Fla., 1985—; trustee, mem. bd. trade PAC Inc., 1990-95; dir. Enterprise Amb. Program, 1991, chmn. adv. bd., 1995—. Contbr. articles to profl. jours. Chmn. Uptown Bus. Coun., 1996; chmn. adv. bd. Fla. Atlantic U. Small Bus. Devel. Ctr., 1993-96. Mem. Nat. Assn. Accts. (bd. dirs. Ft. Lauderdale chpt. 1988-90), Inst. Chartered Accts. B.C., Can. Am. Bus. Alliance South Fla. (pres. 1989-95), Fla. Small Bus. Devel. Ctr. Network (adv. bd. 1990—, chmn. 1995—), Turnaround Mgmt. Assn., Assn. Insolvency Accts., Uptown Bus. Assn. (pres. 1989-90, chmn. CEO adv. coun. 1991-94, chmn. Uptown Bus. Coun. 1996), Greater Ft. Lauderdale C. of C. (bd. govs. 1995-96, bd. dirs. 1996). Office: Beacon Mgmt Group Inc 1000 W Mcnab Rd Pompano Beach FL 33069-4719

DONOGHUE, WILLIAM THOMAS, antiques executive, gemologist; b. Houston, Nov. 13, 1932; s. Gerald Thomas and Louise (Huggins) D.; m. Christa Neidhardt, Apr. 6, 1957; children: Charlotte Luisa, Hilary. BA in Econs., U. Va., 1954; grad. Gemological Inst. Am., 1991. Ptnr., Christy Donoghue Antiques, Bad Nauheim, W. Ger., 1957-61, Victoria, Tex., 1961-69, pres., Victoria, 1969—. Bd. dirs. Victorial Regional Mus. Assn., 1970-80. Served to 1st lt. U.S. Army, 1954-57; ETO. Mem. Gemological Inst. Am., Alumni Assn. Avocations: ranching, hunting. Home and Office: Christy Donoghue Antiques Inc PO Box 3790 Victoria TX 77903-3790

DONOHO, TIM MARK, insurance and publishing executive; b. St. Louis, Sept. 25, 1955; s. James O. and Jean (Dace) D.; m. Deborah Ann Peeples, Feb. 28, 1981; children: Drew Morgan, Jourdan Alexis. BABA, Columbia Coll., 1979. Editor U.S. Army, Okinawa, Japan, 1973-77; sales mgr. Unival Investments, Okinawa, 1975-77; nat. dir. mktg. Pyramid Life Ins. Co., Springfield, Mo., 1978-82; chmn., owner Ins. Mktg. Group, Springfield, 1982-90; pres., owner Am. Dental Program, Inc., Ft. Lauderdale, Fla., 1984—, Donoho Gruppe Cos., Ft. Lauderdale, 1985—; owner Advantage Dental Health Plans, Ft. Lauderdale, Fla., 1984—; pub., editor, owner Prime Years News Mag., Ft. Lauderdale, 1985-95, Investors Consortium, Ft. Lauderdale, 1988-95. Designer "Signal Activity", 1975 (Army Svc. Award 1976). Bd. dirs. So. Fla. chpt. Nat. Multiple Sclerosis Soc., 1996—; founder, chmn. bd. dirs. Pastors Closet, 1989—. With U.S. Army, 1973-77. Mem. Nat. Assn. Dental Plans (chmn. bd. dirs. 1988—). Republican. Baptist. Home: 1075 Hillsboro Mile Hillsboro Beach FL 33062 Office: Donoho Gruppe Cos 8100 N University Dr Fort Lauderdale FL 33321-1717

DONOHUE, EDITH M., human resources specialist, consultant; b. Balt., Nov. 10, 1938; d. Edward Anthony and Beatrice (Jones) McParland; m. Salvatore R. Donohue, Aug. 23, 1960; children: Kathleen, Deborah. BA, Coll. Notre Dame, Balt., 1960; MS, Johns Hopkins U., 1981, CASE, 1985, PhD in Human Resources, 1990. Dir. pub. relations Coll. Notre Dame, Balt., 1970-71, asst. dir. continuing edn., 1978-81, dir. continuing edn., 1981-86; coord. program bus. and industry Catonsville C.C., Baltimore County, Md., 1986-88; mgr. tng. and devel. Sheppard Pratt Hosp., Balt., 1988-90; assoc. prof. Barry U., advisor grad. program, 1993—; adj. faculty Loyola Coll. Grad. Studies Program, Fla. Inst. Tech., Indian River C.C. Co-author: Communicate Like a Manager, 1989; co-editor, contbg. author career devel. workshop manual, 1985; contbr. articles to profl. jours. Pres. Cathedral Sch. Parents Assn., 1972-74; asst. treas., treas. Md. Gen. Hosp. Aux., 1975-78; dir. Homeland Assn., 1978-81; regional rep., leader Girl Scouts Cen. Md., 1975-76; dir. sect. Exec. Women's Network, Balt., 1983-85; adv. bd. Mayor's Com. on Aging, 1981-86; dir. Md. Assn. Higher Edn., 1985-88; vol. trainer United Way Martin County, co-chair campaign, 1994—; mem. steering com. Chautaugua South. Recipient Mayor's Citation, City of Balt. Council, 1985. Mem. Am. Assn. Tng. and Devel (bd. dirs.), Am. Counseling Assn., AAUW (dir., v.p. 1980-83), Soc. Human Resources Mgmt., Martin County Personnel Mgt. Assn. (edn. chmn. 1991-94), Martin County C. of C. (edn. com. 1991-94), Friends of Lyric (bd. dirs., chmn., strategic planning, pres.), Chi Sigma Iota (pres.), Phi Delta Kappa. Republican. Roman Catholic. Avocations: tennis, performing arts, reading, wellness. Home: Ste 3103 144 NE Edgewater Dr Apt 3103 Stuart FL 34996-4477 Office: Barry U 590 NW Peacock Loop Ste 5 Port Saint Lucie FL 34986-2213

DONOHUE, MAUREEN ANN, nursing administrator, operating room nurse; b. Buffalo, Oct. 26, 1956; d. Robert J. and Helen Patricia (Yauger) D. AAS in Nursing, Trocaire Coll., Buffalo, 1976; student, D'Youville Coll., Buffalo, St. Joseph's Coll., Windham, Maine. RN, N.Y., Va., Ohio, Fla.; cert. CNOR, healthcare risk mgr. Staff nurse burn treatment ctr. Sheehan Meml. Emergency Hosp., Buffalo, 1976-77; asst. head nurse oper. rm. Buffalo Gen. Hosp., 1977-82; staff nurse surg. and diagnostic unit Norfolk (Va.) Gen. Hosp., 1982-83; staff nurse operating room Ohio State U. Hosps., Columbus, 1983-87, HCA Bayonet Point/Hudson Med. Ctr., Hudson, Fla., 1987-88; supr. operating room Suncoast Eye Ctr., Hudson, 1988-90; nurse mgr. HHI Hernando Healthcare Inc.-The Surgery Ctr. at Pinebrook, Brooksville, Fla., 1991-92; nurse mgr. surg. svcs. HHI Hernando Healthcare Inc.-Spring Hill Regional Hosp., Fla., 1991-92; dir. nursing, adminstrv. dir. Urology Health Ctr., New Port Richey, Fla., 1992—. Nursing scholar. Mem. NAFE, Assn. Oper. Rm. Nurses (cert., voting del. nat. congress 1980), Career Assocs. (pub. rels. chmn. 1992-93, backstage vol. Fla. orch. 1991—), Am. Urol. Assn. Allied, Inc. (spkr. seminar Waterworks 1993), Fla. Soc. Ambulatory Surgery Ctrs.

DONOVAN, GERARD KEVIN, pediatrician; b. Tulsa, May 23, 1948; m. Mary Powers. AB, U. Notre Dame, 1970; MD, U. Okla., 1974, MA, 1994. Diplomate Am. Bd. Pediatrics, Sub-bd. Pediatric Gastroenterology; lic. physician, 1975. Resident in pediatrics Baylor Coll. Medicine, Houston, 1974-77; fellow in pediatric gastroenterology U. Okla., Oklahoma City, 1977-79; staff fellow developmental gastroenterology, nutrition sect., neonatal and pediatric medicine br. NIH, Bethesda, Md., 1979-80; clin. assoc. Nat. Inst. Child Health and Human Devel., NIH, Bethesda, 1979-80; asst. prof. dept. pediatrics Baylor Coll. Medicine, Houston, 1980-82; asst. prof. dept. pediatrics U. Okla. Coll. Medicine, Tulsa, 1982-88, assoc. prof. dept. pediatrics, 1988-96, prof. dept. pediatrics, 1996—; dir. pediatric gastroenterology and nutrition U. Okla.-Coll. Medicine, Tulsa, 1982—, dir. Warren program in bioethics, 1990-95; dir. Okla. Bioethics Ctr., 1995—; pres. St. Luke Soc. Physician's Guild, 1988-90, 95, exec. com., 1992—; cons. Hissom State Sch., 1986-90; mem. pediatric quality attainment com. St. Francis Hosp., 1983-87, endoscopy com., 1983—, chmn. med. ethics com., 1986-88, mem. nutritional support, 1988—, pediatric ethics com., inst. ethics com., 1990—, ethics com. Laureate Psychiat. Clinic and Hosp., 1990, pres. institutional rev. bd., 1995; sci. adv. bd. Am. Liver Found., 1984—, Okla. chpt. Nat. Found. for Ileitis and Colitis, 1982-88; bd. dirs. Okla. Organ Sharing Network; chmn. med. adv. com. Okla. chpt. Crohn's and Colitis Found., 1990-94, bd. trustees, 1992—; bd. dirs. pediatric divsn. Tulsa Med. Edn. Found., 1984—; search com. chmn. dept. pediatrics OUCMT Faculty, 1984, 85; chmn. com. on medical ethics OUCMT, 1991—; bd. dirs. Okla. Assoc. Healthcare Ethics. Reviewer Acad. Medicine, 1992—, Jour. Pediatric Gastroenterology and Nutrition, 1986-91; contbr. articles and papers to profl. jours. Vol. Neighbor-for-Neighbor Free Clinic, 1982—; civil surgeon U.S. Immigration & Naturalization Svc., 1988-90; mem. bd. rev. Indian Nations coun. County Boy Scouts; instr. sex edn. St. Mary's Elem. Sch., 1986-87; mem. med. adv. com. Senator Don Nickles, 1984—; vol. Am. Acad. Pediatrics, 1983-84. With USPHS, 1973-74. Bioethics fellow Kennedy Inst. of Ethics, Washington, 1989-90. Fellow Am. Acad. Pediatrics (sect. gastroenterology, chmn. sect. on bioethics 1995-96); mem. AMA, N.Am. Soc. Pediatric Gastroenterology, Am. Gastroenterol. Assn., Soc. for Parenteral and Enteral Nutrition, Am. Soc. Law, Medicine and Ethics, Okla. State Med. Assn., Tulsa County Med. Soc. (appearance on Call the Doctor TV program 1983, 94), Soc. for Health and Human Values. Home: 2917 E 75th Ct Tulsa OK 74136-5640 Office: U Okla Dept Pediatrics 2815 S Sheridan Rd Tulsa OK 74129-1045

DONOVAN, LOWAVA DENISE, data processing administrator; b. Galesburg, Ill., Mar. 27, 1958; d. Richard Eugene and Lowava Jeanine (Squire) Corbin; m. James Dean Rutledge, June 17, 1977 (div. May 1981); 1 child, Tiffany Michelle; m. Neal Edwin Donovan, July 9, 1983. Computer operator cert., Carl Sandburg Coll., 1977, student, 1976-86; student, IBM Edn., Chgo., 1979-87. Keypunch operator Fin. Industry Systems, Galesburg, Ill., 1977-79; computer operator Solution Assocs., Peoria, Ill., 1979-80; programmer, data processing mgr. May Co., Galesburg, 1980-81; programmer Kirkendall Gen. Offices, Galesburg, 1981-82; programmer, data processing mgr. Munson Transp., Monmouth, Ill., 1982-85, programmer/analyst, dir. data processing, 1985-87, dir. mgmt. info. systems, 1987-89; ind. contract programmer analyst Oklahoma City, Okla., 1989-92; product line mgr. Innovative Computing Corp., 1992-94; sr. programmer analyst, dir. info. resources Freymiller Trucking, Inc., Oklahoma City, 1994-96; ptnr. D&D Computers and Comm., 1996—. Mem. Ch. of God.

DONOVAN, MARION CONRAN, school social worker; b. Quincy, Mass., Oct. 11, 1926; d. Joseph and Ellen (Fitzgerald) Conran; m. Francis Joseph Donovan, Nov. 22, 1952; children: Jeanne Francis Jr., Darilyn, Judith, Kenneth, Brian, David. AB, Emmanuel Coll., 1948; MSW, Boston Coll., 1950. Lic. social worker. Family caseworker Newark Family Svc., 1953; family svc. worker Boston Family Svc., 1950-52, 54; sch. social worker Plainville (Mass.) Pub. Sch. System, 1977-78; sch. social worker Needham (Mass.) Pub. Schs., 1978-91, ret., 1991. Chmn. child abuse study LWV, 1989-90; founding pres. St. Elizabeth's Hosp. Aux., Brighton, Mass., 1969—; bd. dirs. Tufts Med. Sch. Faculty Wives, 1968-75, Mass. Hosp. Assn. Aux., 1970-73. Mem. NEA, LWV, Nat. Assn. Social Workers, Mass. Tchrs. Assn. Roman Catholic.

DOODY, BARBARA PETTETT, computer specialist; b. Cin., Sept. 18, 1938; d. Philip Wayne and Virginia Bird (Handley) P.; 1 child, Daniel Frederick Reasor Jr. Attended Sinclair Coll., Tulane U., 1973-74. Owner, mgr. Honeysuckle Pet Shop, Tipp City, Ohio, 1970-76; office mgr. Doody & Doody, CPAs, New Orleans, 1976-77; computer ops. mgr. Doody & Doody, CPAs, 1979—; office mgr. San Diego Yacht Club, 1977-79; owner Hope Chest Linens, Ltd., 1994—. Mem. DAR, UDC, Jamestown Soc., Magna Charta, So. Dames, Colonial Dames of 17th Century, Nat. Soc. Daus. of 1812, Daus. Am. Colonists, Dames Ct. Honor, Colonial Order of the Crown, Societe Huguenot Nouvelle-Orleans, Huguenot Soc. Manakin, Soc. Knights of the Garter, Americans of Royal Descent, Plantaget Soc. Republican. Lutheran. Home: 36 Cypress Rd Covington LA 70433-4306 Office: 2525 Lakeway III 3838 N Causeway Blvd Metairie LA 70002-1767

DOODY, LOUIS CLARENCE, JR., accountant; b. New Orleans, Feb. 5, 1940; s. Louis Clarence and Elsie Clair (Connors) D.; BCS, Tulane U., 1963; m. Barbara Virginia Pettett, Oct. 9, 1982; children by previous marriage: Dana Lori, Mary Lyn, Kathleen Louise. Accountant, Louis C. Doody, C.P.A., 1963-68, partner Doody and Doody, C.P.A.'s, 1969—. C.P.A., La., Tex., Miss. Mem. AICPA, La. Soc. C.P.A.'s. Home: 36 Cypress Rd Covington LA 70433-4306 Office: Ste 2525 3838 N Causeway Blvd Metairie LA 70002-1767

DOODY, MARGARET ANNE, English language educator; b. St. John, N.B., Can., Sept. 21, 1939; came to U.S., 1976; d. Hubert and Anne Ruth (Cornwall) D. B.A., Dalhousie U., Can., 1960; B.A. with 1st class hons., Lady Margaret Hall-Oxford U., Eng., 1962, M.A., 1965, D.Phil., 1968; LLD (hon.), Dalhousie U., 1985. Instr. English U. Victoria (B.C., Can.), 1962-64, asst. prof. English, 1968-69; lectr. Univ. Coll. Swansea, Wales, 1969-76; assoc. prof. English U. Calif.-Berkeley, 1976-80; prof. English dept. Princeton U., N.J., 1980-89; Andrew W. Mellon prof. humanities, prof. English Vanderbilt U., Nashville, 1989—, dir. comparative lit. program, 1992—. Author: A Natural Passion: A Study of the Novels of Samuel Richardson, 1974; (novels) Aristotle Detective, 1978, The Alchemists, 1980; (play) (with F. Stuber) Clarissa, 1984; The Daring Muse: Augustan Poetry Reconsidered, 1985; Frances Burney: The Life in the Works, 1988, The True Story of the Novel, 1996; editor: (with Peter Sabor) Samuel Richardson Tercentenary Essays, 1989, The True Story of the Novel, 1996; co-editor: (with Douglas Murray) Catharine and Other Writings by Jane Austen, 1993. Guggenheim postdoctoral fellow, 1979; recipient Rose Mary Crawshay award Brit. Acad., 1986. Episcopalian. Office: Vanderbilt U English Dept Nashville TN 37235

DOOLEY, THOMAS PATRICK, molecular biologist; b. Atchison, Kans., May 3, 1959; s. Thomas Edward and Wilma Rosa (Sauer) D.; m. Laura Lynnette Anderson, May 30, 1981; children: Isaac, Catherine, Jeannette, Thomas S. BS in Cell Biology, U. Kans., 1981; PhD in Molecular Biology, Ind. U., 1986. Helen Hay Whitney postdoctoral fellow Imperial Cancer Rsch. Fund, London, 1986-88; rsch. scientist II Upjohn Co., Kalamazoo, 1988-91; asst. prof. U. Tex. Health Sci. Ctr., San Antonio, 1991-94, assoc. prof., 1994-95; asst. scientist dept. genetics S.W. Found. for Biomed. Rsch., San Antonio, 1991-94, assoc. scientist, 1994-95; dir. molecular pharmacology, Ala. Power endowed chair So. Rsch. Inst., Birmingham, 1995—; cons. in field. Contbr. over 40 articles to profl. jours.; patentee in field. Grantee U.S. Army, NIH, many others. Mem. Am. Soc. Microbiology (Raymond Sarber award 1985, Garner award 1984), Am. Assn. Cancer Rsch., Soc. Investigative Dermatology. Office: So Rsch Inst 2000 9th Ave S Birmingham AL 35205-2708

DOOLEY, VINCENT JOSEPH, college athletics administrator; b. Mobile, Ala., Sept. 4, 1932; s. William Vincent and Nellie Agnes (Stauter) D.; m. Barbara Anne Meshad, Mar. 19, 1960; children: Deanna, Daniel, Denise, Derek. B.S. in Bus. Adminstrn., Auburn U., 1954, M.A. in History, 1963. Asst. football coach Auburn U. (Ala.), 1960, head freshman football coach, 1961-63; head football coach, U. Ga., Athens, 1964-92, athletic dir., 1979—. Chmn. Ga. State Easter Seals Soc. Served to 2d lt. USMC, 1954-56, capt. res. Named NCAA Coach of Yr., 1980, S.E. Conf. Coach of Yr., U. Ga., 1964, 66, 68, 76, 78, 80, 81; named to Ga. Sports Hall of Fame, 1978, Ala. Sports Hall of Fame, 1984, Nat. Football Found. Hall of Fame, 1994; winner nat. championship, 1980. Mem. Am. Football Coaches Assn. (trustee, past chmn. ethics com., past pres.). Office: Univ of Ga Athletic Dept PO Box 1472 Athens GA 30603-1472

DOOLEY-HANSON, BARBARA ANN, special education educator; b. Vici, Okla., Feb. 16, 1948; d. Loitz Eldon and Cora Lee (Morgan) Myers; m. Donald R. Hanson, Sept. 25, 1993; children: Lisa M. White, James B. Dooley. BS in Spl. Edn., Ctrl. State U., 1989, MEd in Spl. Edn., 1992. Cert. tchr., Okla. Tchr. Ctrl. City Bapt. Acad., Oklahoma City, 1975-76; spl. edn. tchr. Seminole (Okla.) Pub. Schs., 1977-78; tchr. Jones (Okla.) Pub. Schs., 1978-79; spl. edn. tchr. Midwest City-Del City Pub. Schs., 1979-95; spl. edn. coord. II State Dept. Edn., 1995—; adj. prof. U. Ctrl. Okla., fall 1995. Co-author: Doorway-Transition to the Real World, 1993. Mem. Citizens for a Safe Environ., Edmond, Okla., 1994; soccer coach Edmond Soccer Assn., 1985, 88. Mem. Learning Disabilities Assn., Kappa Delta Pi (v.p., pres., exec. bd. dirs. 1989—), Spl. Edn. Vocat. Edn. Assn. (mem. adv. bd. 1993, 95). Baptist. Home: 13205 Golden Eagle Dr Edmond OK 73013-7406 Office: State Dept Edn Spl Edn Sect 2500 N Lincoln Oklahoma City OK 73105

DOOLITTLE, BETH D., librarian; b. St. Croix Falls, Wis., Jan. 31, 1964; d. Duane Charles and Charlotte Lynn D. BA, Bethel Coll., 1986; MLS, U. Wis., 1990. Catalog libr. Montgomery County Libr. Sys., Conroe, Tex., 1991-93; tech. svcs. mgr. Montgomery County Libr. Sys., Conroe, 1993—. Mem. ALA. Office: Montgomery County Libr 104 I-45 N Conroe TX 77301

DOONE, MICHELE MARIE, chiropractor; b. Oak Park, Ill., Oct. 3, 1942; d. Robert Emmett and Tana Josephine (Alioto) D. Cert., Valley Coll. of Med. and Dental Careers, 1962; student, L.A. Valley Coll., 1960-63, Dallas County Community Coll., 1983-84; D in Chiropractic summa cum laude, Parker Coll. of Chiropractic, 1986. Lic. chiropractic, Calif., Tex.; cert. Nat. Bd. Chiropractic Examiners, impairment rater; diplomate Am. Acad. Pain Mgmt.; bd. eligible chiropractic orthopedist. Med. asst. William Orlando M.D., Edwin Crost, M.D., 1962-65; nursing supr., chief radiologic technologist Vanowen Med. Group, North Hollywood, Calif., 1965-76; radiologic technologist/purchasing agt. Lanier-Brown Clinic, Dallas, 1976-83; faculty mem./ chief radiologic technologist Parker Coll. of Chiropractic, Irving, Tex., 1983-85; exam and X-Ray doctor Margolies Chiropractic Ctr., Richardson, Tex., 1986; clinic staff doctor, assoc. prof. Parker Coll. of Chiropractic, Irving, Tex., 1986-87; doctor/ mgr. contractor Accident Ctrs. of Am., Garland, Tex., 1987; clinic dir. Back Pain Chiropractic, Carrollton, Tex., 1988-91; assoc. in group practice Mullican Chiropractic Ctr., Addison, Tex., 1991—; adviser health-related matters Inner Devel. Inst., Dallas, 1977—; seminar com. Back Pain Chiropractic, Inc., Metairie, La., 1989-91, clinic dir., 1988-91. Mem. Tex. Chiropractic Assn. (radiology com. chmn. 1990-94, practice protocols and parameters com. 1992-94), Metroplex Neurospinal Diagnostic Med. and Surg. Group (med. adv. com. 1989-95), Parker Chiropractic Rsch. Found., Parker Coll. Alumni Assn. (bd. dirs. 1988-90, 93-94, 95—, Dr. of Yr. 1990), Pi Tau Delta. Home: 4837 Cedar Springs Rd Apt 216 Dallas TX 75219-1280 Office: Mullican Chiropractic Ctr 4021 Belt Line Rd Ste 201 Dallas TX 75244-2330

DORAISWAMY, DEEPAK, chemical engineer; b. Coimbatore, Tamilnadu, India, Apr. 10, 1961; came to U.S., 1982; s. Laxmangudi and Rajam D. BChemE, Bombay U., 1982; MChemE, U. Del., 1985, PhD, 1987. Postdoctoral rsch. fellow ceramics dept. Rutgers U., Piscataway, N.J., 1987-88; rsch. engr. DuPont Ctr. R&D, Wilmington, Del., 1988-92; sr. rsch. engr. DuPont Ctrl. R&D, Wilmington, Del., 1992—. Guest editor: (festschrift issue) Indsl. and Engring. Chem. Rsch. Jour., 1994; contbg. author: CRC Engineering Handbook, 1995. Nat. Merit scholar Govt. India, 1977; recipient Scholar's award U. Del., 1987. Mem. AIChE (chmn. mixing session San Francisco 1994), Poly. Proc. Soc. (chmn. mixing session 1992), Soc. Rheology, Sigma Xi. Home: 5718 Maple Brook Dr Midlothian VA 23112 Office: DuPont Adv Fib Sys Spruance Plant PO Box 27001 Richmond VA 23261

DORAN, DAVID STEPHEN, music educator; b. Jan. 29, 1942; s. Irwin Julius and Evelyn (Previs) D.; m. Karole Anne Kindig, May 30, 1969. BM, U. Louisville, 1964, MM, 1965; D Humanities (hon.), London Inst. Applied Rsch., 1993. Nat. cert. music tchr. Music educator, now prof. U. Ky. at Jefferson C.C., Louisville, 1968—, coord. of music, 1982-95; nat. lectr. on Biblical topics. Composer music for harpsichord. Named Ky. Col., Gov. of Ky., 1983. Mem. Music Tchrs. Nat. Assn., Ky. Music Tchrs. Assn. (past pres.), Louisville Composers Alliance (pres.), Greater Louisville Music Tchrs. Assn. (past pres.), Southeastern Hist. Keyboard Soc. Office: Jefferson Coll/ U Ky 109 E Broadway Louisville KY 40202-2005

DORAN, MARK RICHARD, real estate financial executive; b. Chgo., June 17, 1954; s. Paul George and Mae (Olson) D.; m. Wendy Carole Beckham, Dec. 17, 1977; children: Blake, Barrett, Hayley. BBA in Acctg., Baylor U., 1975, MBA, 1976. From asst. acct. to supr. Peat, Marwick, Mitchell & Co., Dallas, 1977-81; sr. v.p. fin. Lincoln Property Co., Dallas, 1982-89; exec. v.p. treas. Prentiss Properties Ltd. Inc., Dallas, 1990—. Deacon Park Cities Bapt. Ch., Dallas, 1988—. Mem. Nat. Assn. Industrial and Office Pks., The Urban Land Inst., The Real Estate Council, Univ. Park Dads Club, Baylor U. Alumni Assn., Las Colinas Sports Club. Office: Prentiss Properties Ltd Inc 1717 Main St Ste 5000 Dallas TX 75201-7364

DOREMUS, OGDEN, lawyer; b. Atlanta, Apr. 23, 1921; s. C. Estes and Mary (McAdory) D.; m. Carolyn Wooten Greene, Aug. 30, 1947 (dec. Aug. 1989); children: Celia Jane, Frank O., Dale Marie Doremus; m. Linda Parker, Dec. 4, 1992. BA, Emory U., 1946, JD, 1949. Bar: Ga. 1947. Asst. solicitor gen. Atlanta, 1947-49; ptnr. firm Smith Field Doremus & Ringel, Atlanta, 1949-60, Falligant, Doremus and Karsman, Savannah, Ga., 1960-72, Doremus, Jones & Smith, P.C., Metter, Ga., 1972-94; of counsel Karsman, Brooks & Callaway, 1994—; prof. Woodrow Wilson Sch. Law, Atlanta, 1948-50; judge State Ct. Candler County, Ga.,1985—; pres. Ga. Coun. State Ct. Judges, 1990-91; mem. Jud. Coun. State of Ga., 1989-91. Mem. editorial adv. bd. Environ. Law, Reporter, 1969-80. Mem. Atlanta City Coun., 1950-53; mem. Savannah Govtl. Reorgn. Commn., 1960-61, Ga. Ct. Futures Commn., 1991-93; adv. com. Nat. Coastal Zone Mgmt. Coun., 1978-86; trustee Ga. Conservancy; bd. dirs. Legal Environ. Assistance Found., 1983-86, Ga. Hazardous Waste Authority, 1989—, Chatham Environ. Forum, 1990-93; mem. strategic planning com. Coun. State Cts. Ga., 1996—. Served with USAAC, 1942-46, ETO. Named Young Man of Yr. Atlanta, 1951; recipient Thomas H. gignilliat award Cultural Progress of Savannah, 1969, Tradition of Excellence award Ga. State Bar, 1988, 1st Ann. Coun. of State Cts. award named Ogden Doremus in his honor, 1993. Mem. ABA (chmn. environ. law com., gen. practice 1976-77), State Bar Ga. (chmn. ins. law sect. 1963-67, 77-83), Savannah Bar Assn., Ga. Inst. Trial Advocacy (chmn. 1984-89), Izaak Walton league (founder Ga. chpt. 1950), Sierra Club (exec. com. Chattahoochee chpt. 1965-75, Lifetime Achievement Ga. environ. coun. Citizenship award), Chatham Club, Chatham Tennis Club, Willow Lake Country Club, Atlanta Soc. Home: RR 2 Box 188A Metter GA 30439-9570 Office: Doremus and Assocs Courthouse Sq PO Box 702 Metter GA 30439

DOREN, ARNOLD TILDEN, photography educator; b. Chgo., July 29, 1935. AAS, Rochester Inst. Tech., 1959, BFA, 1961. Asst. prof. art dept. U. N.C., Greensboro, 1978-83; assoc. prof. U. N.C., 1983—. Work represented in collections including George Eastman House of Photography, Rochester, Mus. of Modern Art, N.Y.C., MIT, Mus. of R.I. Sch. of Design, Providence, Dallas Mus. of Art; one-man exhbns. include Oswego State Tchrs. Coll., 1961, Osaka (Japan) U., 1961, The Studio, N.Y.C., 1979-80, Durham (N.C.) Arts Coun., 1981, Duke U., 1987, Meridian (Miss.) Art Mus., 1990, Photography Circle, Athens, 1990, The Photographic Ctr. of Athens, 1990, Holt-McPherson Gallery, High Point, N.C., 1994; juried exhbns. include Photo Educators 1995-Internat. Exhbn., 1995, 45th Internat. Exhbn. of Photography, Del Mar, Calif. Fair, 1994 (honorable mention), Northwest Internat. Exhbn. of Photography, Puyallup, Wash., 1988 (1st prize), Unfair, Cologne, Germany, 1993. With USN, 1953-57. Mentioned The Photograph Collector's Guide, 1982, An Index to American Collections, 1983, Encyclopedia of Photographic Artists, 1983. Home: 314 N Elam Greensboro NC 27403 Office: Art Dept University North Carolina Greensboro NC 27412

DORIO, MARTIN MATTHEW, material handling company executive; b. Bklyn., Nov. 12, 1945; s. Martin M. and Josephine V. (Marsala) D.; m. Gayle M. Morris, June 16, 1968; children: Paul, Jay. BS, SUNY, Stony Brook, 1967; PhD, U. Mass., 1975. Rsch. chemist Diamond Shamrock Corp., Painesville, Ohio, 1975-76; group leader Diamond Shamrock Corp., Painesville, 1977-79; venture mgr. Gen. Electric Lighting Bus., Cleve., 1979-81, quality and mfg. tech. mgr., 1981-87; dir. quality and productivity FMC Corp., Chgo., 1987-90; v.p. worldwide product mgmt. and market strategy Case Corp., Racine, Wis., 1990-91; v.p. corp. planning and devel. J.I. Case Corp., Racine, Wis., 1992-95; pres., CEO, dir. Clark Material Handling Co., Lexington, Ky., 1995—; mem. adv. com. Dept. Energy, Washington, 1977-79, Am. Productivity and Quality Ctr., Houston, 1988-90; mem. adv. com. on quality Ency. Brittanica, 1988-90; mem. bd. examiners Nat. Inst. Sci. and Tech., 1988-90. Author: Multiple Electron Resonance Spectroscopy, 1979; contbr. articles to profl. jours.; patentee in field. Coach Little League Ball, Mentor, Ohio, 1982-84; pres. Homeowners Assn., 1983-85. Capt. USAF, 1968-71. Recipient Nat. Quality award Nat. Inst. Sci. and Tech., 1988-90. Mem. Am. Soc. Quality Control (exec. com. 1984-85), Am. Mgmt. Assn., Assn. Mfg. Excellence, World Future Soc., Planetary Soc. Home: 2105 Wiltshire Pl Lexington KY 40515 Office: Clark Material Handling Co 172 Trade St Lexington KY 40511-2607

DORION, ROBERT CHARLES, entrepreneur, investor; b. N.Y.C., Dec. 28, 1926; s. William J. and Adelaide (Bacardi) D.; m. Ana Maria Ferber, Nov. 26, 1954; children: Robert Patrick, Marianne Michelle, Nicholas Christian, Kristel Alexia. Student, Columbia U., 1943-44; B of Naval Scis., Dartmouth Coll., 1946. Buyer Balfour, Guthrie and Co. Ltd., 1948-49; capt. M/V Assault Shark Industries div. Borden & Co., 1950-51; pres. Dorion,

Rubio and Cia, 1952-57; mgr., ins., mining and chem. dept. Grace & Co., 1954-59; sales mgr. Gen. Tires, Guatemala, 1960-61; chmn. El Salto, S.A., 1962-78; pres. Tecnios En Seguros, S.A., 1979—, Marcas Mundiales, S.A.; dir. Bacardi Ltd., Bermuda, Marcas Mundiales S.A., Industrias Rio Dulce S.A.; trustee USN Meml. Found. Contbr. articles to profl. jours. Friend Am. Mus. of Nat. History, N.Y.C.; bd. dirs. Marine Resources Found., Key Largo, Fla., field assoc. Fla. Mus., Gainesville, Mote Marine Lab., Sarasota, Fla. Fellow Internat. Oceanographic Found. (life); mem. Rotary (Paul Harris fellow), World Scout Orgn. (Baden-Powell fellow), U.S. Naval Inst., Audubon Soc., Internat. Wildlife Soc., Order of The Bronze Wolf. Office: care Bacardi Imports Inc 2100 Biscayne Blvd Miami FL 33137-5014 also: Kristel SA, Apt 195A, Guatemala City Guatemala

DORLAND, JOHN HOWARD, international management consultant; b. Washington, July 23, 1940; s. Gilbert Meding and Lillian (Okkerse) D.; m. Harriet Etter, June 12, 1965; children—John Henry, Howard Etter. BS, USMA, 1963; MS, U. So. Miss., 1968; MBA, U. Tenn., 1978. Commd. 2d lt. U.S. Army, 1963, advanced through grades to maj., 1973, ret. col., USAR, 1985; exec. v.p. Commerce Union Bank, Nashville, Tenn., 1973-81, FCB/FCBI, Pompano Beach, Fla., 1981-82; pres. Fla. Coast Bank, Pompano Beach, 1982-84; pres., CEO Hollywood (Fla.) Bank, 1984-90; CEO interim Suburban Bankshares, Inc., 1993-94; prin. Gemini Cons., 1994-95; pres. Dorland & Assocs., 1990—; dir. FCCS, Margate, Fla., FCB, Pompano Beach. Author: Duty, Honor, Company-West Point Fundamentals for Business Success, 1992. Commr. Mid. Tenn. coun. Boy Scouts Am., 1979; with Leadership Nashville, 1979; bd. dirs. YMCA, Ft. Lauderdale, 1983-89, Honda Golf Classics, Broward Econ. Devel., Com. of 100, United Way of Broward County. Decorated Bronze Star with 5 oak leaf clusters, Air medal with 5 oak leaf clusters, Purple Heart. Mem. Am. Bankers Assn., BEDC Broward County, Fla. Bankers Assn. (bd. dirs.), Fla. League Fin. Instns., Hollywood C. of C. Republican. Episcopalian. Home: 2828 Old Hickory Blvd #1411 Nashville TN 37209 Office: Dorland & Assocs 233 Oceola Ave Ste 206 Nashville TN 37209

DORMINEY, HENRY CLAYTON, JR., allergist; b. Tifton, Ga., May 15, 1949; s. Henry Clayton and Virginia (Petty) D.; m. Diane Louise Thiel, Sept. 29, 1978. BS, Davidson Coll., 1971; MD, U. Iowa, 1975. Diplomate Am. Bd. Internal Medicine, Am. Bd. Allergy and Immunology; lic. physician, Ky., Iowa, Ga. Med. intern, U. Iowa Hosps. and Clinics, Iowa City, 1975-76, med. resident, 1976-78, allergy and immunology fellow, 1978-80; practice medicine specializing in allergy and clin. immunology Allergy and Dermatology Assocs. P.C., Tifton, Ga., 1981—; mem. staff Tifton Gen. Hosp.; bd. dirs. Brumby's Crossing, Dorminey Enterprises; chmn. and founder Tifton Mus. Arts and Heritage, 1991. Assoc. editor, contbg. author Vital Signs, 1969-71. Bd. dirs. Tift County Found. Ednl. Excellence, Tifton Heritage Found., pres., 1992. Recipient Physician's Recognition award AMA, 1979, 85, Lee Willingham III trophy Davidson Coll., 1987; VA grantee, 1978-80, Am. Coll. Allergy grantee, 1980. Mem. ACP, Am. Acad. Allergy (travel grantee 1980), Allergy & Dermatology Assn. Tifton, Tift County Med. Soc. (sec., treas. 1983-84, v.p. 1984-85, pres. 1985-86), Med. Assn. Ga., Forward Tifton, Tifton C. of C. Democrat. Lodge: Rotary (Spl. Merit award, founder Tifton Directory, bd. dirs. 1988-93, pres.-elect 1989-90, pres. 1990-91, Paul Harris fellow 1993). Home: 1001 N Ridge Ave Tifton GA 31794-3953 Office: 820 Love Ave Tifton GA 31794-4000

DORN, SAMUEL O., endodontist; b. N.Y.C., Jan. 1, 1946; s. Benjamin and Mae (Baylin) D.; m. Linda Frances Neuger, Dec. 23, 1984; children: Lanelle, Brian, Adam, Dawn. BA, Queens Coll., 1966; DDS, Fairleigh Dickinson U., 1970; cert., Nassau County Med. Ctr., 1976. Diplomate Am. Bd. Endodontics (bd. dirs.). Capt. USAF, Washington, 1970-72; assoc. Dr. Moodnik, Greenfield & Atkinson, Forest Hills, N.Y., 1972-76; pvt. practice Ft. Lauderdale, Fla., 1976—; clin. instr. Fairleigh Dickinson U. Dental Sch., Hackensack, N.J., 1973-74; cons. in field; chmn. advanced endodontics Dade County Dental Rsch. Clinic, Miami, 1977-93; clin. assoc. prof. U. Fla. Sch. Dentistry; clin. asst. prof. U. Miami Sch. Medicine, 1977-93; dir., treas. Am. bd. Endodontics; dir. Post-Grad. Endodontics Nova Southeastern U. Sch. Dental Medicine; lectr. in field. Trustee Endowment & Meml. Found., Chgo., 1987-88. Named Dentist of the Year East Coast Dental Soc., 1987. Fellow Am. Coll. Dentists, Internat. Coll. Dentists; mem. Am. Assn. Endodontists (bd. dirs. 1988-91), Fla. Assn. Endodontists (pres. 1990-92), Greater Hollywood Dental Soc. (pres. 1988-89), South Fla. Endodontic Soc. (pres. 1982-83), East Coast Dist. Dental Soc. (pres.), Am. Assn. Dental Rsch. Jewish. Home: 1031 SW 91st Ave Fort Lauderdale FL 33324-3817 Office: 8200 W Sunrise Blvd Fort Lauderdale FL 33322-5426 also: 2213 N University Dr Pembroke Pines FL 33024

DORNAN, JOHN NEILL, public policy center professional; b. Canonsburg, Pa., July 20, 1944; s. Carl Edward and Kathryn (Neill) D.; m. Jacquelin Riggs (div. 1971); children: Jodie Lynn, John Neill; m. Carol Michaels (div. 1976); m. Anne Marie Deegan (div. 1993). BA, Ind. (Pa.) U., 1966; postgrad., U. Pitts., 1966-68. English tchr. Moon Twp., Coraopolis, Pa., 1966-69; field rep. NEA, Harrisburg, Pa., 1969-70; media rep. NEA, San Francisco, 1970-71; asst. exec. dir. Ill. Edn. Assn., Springfield, Ill., 1970-74; asst. to pres. AFSCME, Washington, 1974-75; assoc. exec. dir. Coalition of Am. Pub. Employees, Washington, 1975-76, N.Y. Edn. Assn., Albany, 1976-82; exec. sec. N.C. Assn. Educators, Raleigh, 1982-86; pres. Pub. Sch. Forum, Raleigh, 1986—; cons. in field; adj. faculty Cornell U., Albany, 1981-82, Appalachian U., Boone, N.C., 1987-88, N.C. Prin's. Exec. Program, 1986-90. Contbr. numerous articles to profl. jours. Treas. N.C. Non-Profit Assn. Ctr.; bd. dirs. Gov.'s Commn. on Workforce Preparedness, Leadership N.C., Wake Edn. Ptnrship., N.C. Goals 2000 Panel; mem. nat. bd. dirs. Parents for Pub. Schs., The Columbia Group, N.C. Pub. Affairs. Mem. ASCD, NEA Pub. Rels Coun. (pres. 1981-82), Raleigh C. of C. Democrat. Presbyterian. Home: 105 Thorncliff Cir Cary NC 27513-4709 Office: Koger Ctr Cumberland Bldg 3739 National Dr Ste 210 Raleigh NC 27612-4844

DORNING, JOHN JOSEPH, nuclear engineering, engineering physics and applied mathematics educator; b. Bronx, N.Y., Apr. 17, 1938; s. John Joseph and Sarrah Cathrine (McCormack) D.; m. Helen Marie Driscoll, July 27, 1963; children: Michael, James, Denise. B.S. in Marine Engring., U.S. Mcht. Marine Acad., 1959; M.S. (AEC fellow), Columbia U., 1963, Ph.D. (AEC fellow), 1967. Marine engr. U.S. Mcht. Marine, 1960-62; asst. physicist Brookhaven Nat. Lab., Upton, N.Y., 1967-69, assoc. physicist, group leader, 1969-70; assoc. prof. nuclear engring. U. Ill., Urbana, 1970-75, prof., 1975-84; Whitney Stone prof. nuclear engring., engring. physics and applied math. U. Va., Charlottesville, 1984—; NRC vis. prof. math. physics U. Bologna, Italy, 1975-76, 81, 85, 87; internat. prof. nuclear engring. Italian Ministry of Edn., 1983, 84, 86; physicist plasma theory group, div. magnetic fusion energy Lawrence Livermore (Calif.) Nat. Lab., 1977-78; cons. to U.S. nat. labs. and indsl. research labs., 1970—. Contbr. articles to various publs. Served as ensign USN, 1959-60. Recipient Ernest O. Lawrence award U.S. Dept. Energy, 1990. Fellow AAAS, Am. Phys. Soc., Am. Nuclear Soc. (Mark Mills award 1967); mem. Am. Soc. for Engring. Edn., (Glenn Murphy award 1988), Soc. Indsl. and Applied Math., N.Y. Acad. Scis., Sigma Xi. Office: U Va Reactor Facility Thornton Hall Charlottesville VA 22903-2442

DORRIS, CARLOS EUGENE, chemicals executive; b. Sugarland, Tex., Aug. 25, 1935; s. T.J. and Laura Mae D.; m. Karen Ruth Wood, Aug. 17, 1969; children: Twanda, Kristen, Anthony, Jeffery, Thomas. BS, U. Tex., 1959. Chemist Dow Chem. Co., Freeport, Tex., 1959-63; from chemist to corp. mgr. Jones Blair Co., Dallas, 1963—. Mem. Nat. Paint & Coating Assn., Soc. Coatings Tech. (pres. 1986-87), Dallas Soc. Coatings Tech. (pres.). Office: Jones Blair Co 2728 Empire Central Dallas TX 75235-4409

DORSETT, CHARLES IRVIN, mathematics educator; b. Lufkin, Tex., Sept. 25, 1945; s. C.B. and Dorothy Alice (Smith) D. BS, Stephen F. Austin State U., Nacogdoches, Tex., 1967, MS, 1968; PhD, N. Tex. State U., 1976. Cert. secondary sch. tchr., Tex. Teaching fellow Stephen F. Austin State U., 1967-68, instr., 1968-71; teaching fellow North Tex. State U., Denton, 1971-76, lectr., 1976-77, 78-79; asst. prof. La. Tech U., Ruston, 1977-78, assoc. prof., 1982-90, prof., 1990—; lectr. Tex. A&M U., College Station, 1979-82; reviewer Zentralblatt Für Mathematik und Ihre Grenzgebrite, 1983—; referee Indian Jour. Pure and Applied Math., 1986—, Indian Jour. Math., 1986—, Bull. of the Faculty of Sci., Assiut Univ.; Physics and Math., 1986—, Glasnik Matematicki, 1988—, Bull. of the Malaysian Math. Soc., 1989—; mem. bd. editors Pure Mathematics Manuscript, 1987—. Contbr. articles to profl. publs. Recipient Cert. for Excellence in Rsch., La. Tech U., 1984-85, La. Tech. Sigma Xi Rsch. award, 1987. Mem. Indian Acad. Math., Bharata Ganita Parisad, Sigma Xi. Baptist. Avocations: mathematical rsch., farming. Home: 402 W Arizona Ave Lot 20 Ruston LA 71270-4372 Office: La Tech U Dept Math and Stats Ruston LA 71272

DORSETT, PATRICIA JEAN POOLE, business consultant; b. New Castle, Ind., May 26, 1935; d. George Meredith and Margaret (Bryan) Poole; m. Carroll Edwin Cleek, Jan. 8, 1954 (div. 1976); children: Cynthia Anne Cleek, Patricia Jill Cleek, Deborah Susan Cleek, David Carroll Cleek; m. John Ford Dorsett, Feb. 11, 1978. BS in Edn. cum laude, Ga. State U., 1982, MS in English Edn., 1986. Cert. tchr., Ga. Pres. Direct Systems Corp., Orchard Park, N.Y., 1969-72; coordinator reservations and travel Ciba-Geigy Corp., Greensboro, N.C., 1975-78; pvt. practice travel cons. Conyers, Ga., 1979-81; cons. property mgmt. and bus. P&J Assocs., Conyers, 1980—; sec.-treas. Dorsett & Hightower (formerly P&J Assocs.), Conyers, 1979—; tchr. language arts Cousins Mid. Sch., Covington, Ga., 1983-93, staff devel. chair, 1987-89; part-time English instr. DeKalb C.C., Rockdale County, Ga., 1993—. Editor: (newsletter) St. Mark's Caller, 1964-69, The Voter, 1982-87, Direct Systems Corp. Mail Order Catalog, 1969-72. Pres. Coop. Nursery Sch., Orchard Park, 1961-62; leader 4-H Club, Orchard park, 1964-74; active Atlanta Post-polio Assn., 1990—. Mem. LWV (1st pres. Rockdale County chpt. 1982-83, fin. chmn. 1984-85, sec. 1986-87, adminstrv. v.p. 1987-89, chmn. natural resources 1987-89, bd. dirs. Ga., 1987-89, Outstanding Svc. award 1986), Nat. Fedn. Women's Club (chmn. scholarship fund 1974-75). Episcopalian. Home: 2090 Lost Forest Ln SW Conyers GA 30207-6173 Office: Dorsett & Hightower 954 Main St NE Conyers GA 30207-4577

DORSEY, DONNA BAGLEY, insurance agent; b. Macon, Ga., May 26, 1952; d. Clarence Henry and Sybil Audrey (Phillips) Bagley; m. David M. Lewis, June 14, 1969 (div. May 1979); children: Scott D., Jeffrey A.; m. J. Larry Dorsey, July 1, 1980. Grad. high sch., Macon, Ga. Cert. ins. counselor; cert. profl. ins. woman. Rating clk. Bibb Underwriters Ins., Macon, 1977-80; book-keeper Wilson Typewriter, Macon, 1980-85; customer svc. rep. Ga. Ins. Agy., Macon, 1985; agt., customer svc. rep. Johnson and Johnson Ins., Inc., Macon, 1985—. Recipient Outstanding Customer Svc. Rep. Ga. award Ind. Ins. Agts. Ga., 1993; Ruth Dupree Meml. scholar, 1987, Safeco Ins. Achievement award, 1995. Mem. Profl. Ins. Agts. Ga. (bd. dirs. 1990-93, Eagle award 1989), Young Profl. Coun. Ga. (chmn. 1991-92), Ins. Women Macon (treas. 1991-92, v.p. 1992-93, pres. elect 1993-94, pres. 1994-95, Macon Ins. Woman of Yr. 1994, Ga. Ins. Woman of Yr. 1994, President's Vol. award 1994, Macon Ins. Profl. of Yr. 1995, Indivdual Edn. Achievement award 1996). Office: Johnson and Johnson Ins Inc 420 Rogers Ave Macon GA 31204-2042

DORSEY, HATTIE, community economic development executive; b. Teachey, N.C., May 31, 1939; d. Edward Henry and Gladys (Alderman) Dorsey; m. James F. Harlow, Nov. 1, 1979 (div.); m. Kenneth Samuel Hudson, Nov. 3, 1990 (div.); 1 child, Victoria Michelle Dorsey. Student, Clark Coll., 1957-61. Exec. dir. Stanford Mid-Peninsula Urban Coalition, Stanford, Calif., 1979-81; program officer Edna McConnell Clark Found., Calif., 1982-84; v.p. Atlanta Econ. Devel. Corp., 1985-91; pres. Atlanta Neighborhood Devel. Partnership, Inc., Atlanta, 1991—; cons. Spartanburg (N.C.) Devel. Coun., 1991, Econ. Devel. Alternatives, Washington, 1984. V.p. Young Dems., Washington, 1965-66; founding pres., organizer Metro Atlanta Coalition 100 Black Women, Atlanta, 1986-91; v.p. Nat. Coalition 100 Black Women, N.Y.C., 1987-92, pres., 1995—; dir. Nat. Assn. Housing Ptnr. Mem. Spelman Coll. Corp. Roundtable; exec. comm. and bd. mdm. of Nat. Housing Conf; mem. Buckhead/Cascade Chpt. of Links, Inc.; chair, GRAPEVINE (polit. action comm.). Democrat. Methodist. Office: Atlanta Neighborhood Devel Partnership 57 Forsyth St NW Ste 1250 Atlanta GA 30303-2210

DORSEY, RICHARD NEAL, minister; b. Madison, Ind., Apr. 21, 1953; s. Jack Weldon and Ruth Elizabeth (McKnight) D.; m. Susan Ann Williams, Oct. 13, 1990. BS, Eastern N.Mex. U., 1975; M of Church Music, So. Bapt. Theol. Sem., 1978, MA in Christian Edn., 1986. Music, youth min. Elsmere (Ky.) Bapt. Ch., 1976-78, Westgate Bapt. Ch., Columbus, Ohio, 1978-79, Coronado Bapt. Ch., El Paso, Tex., 1979-80, Green Valley (Ariz.) Bapt. Ch., 1982-84; music min. Calvary Bapt. Ch., Madison, Ind., 1984-87; music, edn. min. United Love Bapt. Ch., Midland, N.C., 1987-90; music min. Arlington (Va.) Bapt. Ch., 1990-94; with chaplaincy program Med. Coll. Va., Richmond, 1994-95; chaplain resident St. Luke's Hosp., Chesterfield, Mo., 1995—; discipleship tng. dir. Cabarrus Bapt. Assn., Concord, N.C., 1988-90. Mem. No. Va. C.C. Band, Alexandria, 1993-94. Music scholar Eastern N.Mex. U., 1971. Democrat. Home: 3400H Princess Grace Ct Richmond VA 23223-1623

DORST, MARY CROWE, artist; b. Milw., June 5, 1927; d. Neal Francis and Ruth Barker Crowe; m. Claire Vanderhoof; children: Sherry, Neal, Robin. AA, Bradford Jr. Coll., Mass., 1947; BA, Beloit Coll., 1949; MA, No. Ill. U., 1966. Dir. gallery Fla. Atlantic U., Boca Raton, 1973-76; art critic Boca Raton News, 1975-76, 85-86; dir. Palmetto Gallery Gulfstream Bank to NCNB, South Palm Beach County, 1976-84; adj. instr. Fla. Atlantic U., Boca Raton, 1967, 87-91, Broward C.C., Pompano Beach, 1974-76, Palm Beach C.C., Boca Raton, 1979-84; mem. adv. bd. Morikami Mus., Delray Beach, 1976-86; founding pres. Arts Alliance of Boca Raton, 1976; founding com. mem. Palm Beach County Coun. of Arts; del. World Crafts Conf., Japan, 1978. Exhibited work at Harvest Festival, Lake Worth, 1995 (3rd award), Soc. of Four Arts, 1995, 1996, Soc. of Experimental Artists Nat. 1994, Included in Best of Colored Pencil III, Soc. Am., 1995, Women in Visual Arts, 1996 (hon. mention). Scholarship U. Wis., 1962-63. Mem. Am. Crafts Coun., Colored Pencil Soc. Am., Palm Beach Watercolor Soc. (hon., pres., show chair 1990-92, 93), Fla. Craftsmen (hon., area dir.), Surface Design Assn. Congregationalist. Home: 618 High St Boca Raton FL 33432

DORTCH, ALICE JEAN, supervisory visual information specialist; b. Greenville, Miss., Sept. 21, 1947; d. Davis Andrew Jr. and Jean Eloise (Wait) Whitfield; m. Mark Stephen Dortch, May 2, 1969; children: Margaret Alison, Stephen Wesley. BA in Comml. Art, Miss. State U. for Women, 1969. Illustrator engring. divsn. U.S. Army Corps Engrs., Vicksburg, Miss., 1979-86, chief visual info. sect. info. mgmt. office, 1986—. Participant in art shows locally and statewide; painter airbrush and oil paintings on consignment. Recipient numerous awards including Best of Show award Magnolia Fine Arts Competition, Jackson, Miss., 1995, 96. Mem. Vicksburg Art Assn., Vicksburg Nat. Hist. Preservation Soc., Federally Employed Women, Inc. Methodist. Office: US Army Corps Engrs 2101 N Frontage Rd Vicksburg MS 39180-5182

DORTON, TRUDA LOU, medical/surgical and geriatrics nurse; b. Elkhorn Creek, Ky., Aug. 26, 1949; d. Earl D. and Joyce (Kidd) Marshall; m. Eugene Anderson, Nov. 26, 1966 (dec. Apr. 1971); children: Gena Lynn, Richard Eugene; m. Leon Dorton, Dec. 15, 1972; children: Leondra Michelle, Jerald Thomas, Jonathan Layne. AS, Pikeville Coll., 1993, student, 1993. RN, Ky. Instr. computer usage Lookout (Ky.) Elem. Sch., 1983; water/sewage technician McCoy & McCoy Environ. Cons., Pikeville, Ky., 1984; owner Signs of the Times, Elkhorn City, Ky., 1979-89; sec.'s asst. humanities and social scis. divsns. Pikeville Coll., 1989-92; nurse aide Mud Creek Clinic, Grethel, Ky., 1992-93; charge nurse Jenkins (Ky.) Community Hosp., 1993-94; case mix coord. Parkview Manor Nursing Home, 1994-95, minimum data set and nursing care plan coord., 1995; staff nurse Harrison Meml. Hosp., Cynthiana, Ky., 1996—; vol. nurse aide Mud Creek Clinic, Grethel, 1989-92. Founder free blood pressure clinic H.E.L.P.S. Community Action Program, Hellier, Ky., 1983; co-founder H.E.L.P.S. Community Action Group, Hellier, 1983; mem. Ellis Island Centennial Commn., N.Y., 1986. Appalachian Honors scholar Pikeville Coll., 1989-92. Mem. Nat. Geog. Soc., Ky. Nursing Assn., Order Ky. Cols. (Honorable Ky. Col. 1989), Smithsonian Inst., Pikeville Coll. Alumni Assn. Democrat. Mem. Worldwide Ch. of God. Home: 503 W Pleasant St Cynthiana KY 41031-8950 Office: Harrison Meml Hosp South Wing 150 Millersburg Pike Cynthiana KY 41031

DOSSIN, STEVEN CHARLES, statistician, consultant, educator; b. Ft. Worth, Tex., May 29, 1954; s. Harry Alver and Betsy Drusilla (Hill) D.; m. Margaret Henabray Butler, Jan. 1, 1982 (div. Nov. 1989); m. Anita Claire Roth, Dec. 1990. BA in Math., Austin Coll., 1976; MS in Statistics, So. Meth. U., 1978; PhD in Statistics, So. Meth. U., Dallas, 1981. Programmer analyst Lincoln Property Co., Dallas, 1975-77; instr. So. Meth. U., Dallas, 1978-79; cons. Dallas, 1978-80; dir. adminstrv. svcs. The Leo J. Schindler Co., Inc., Dallas, 1980-85; mgr. info. sys. Schnee-Morehead, Inc., Irving, Tex., 1985-87, dir. fin. and adminstrn., 1987-91; co-author, owner Living the Abundant Life Ministry, Carrollton, Tex., 1992—; cons. Dossin Bus. Solutions, Carrollton, 1991—; adj. prof. U. Tex., Dallas, 1992-93, So. Meth. U., 1991-93, U. Dallas, 1990-95; adj. prof. Dallas Christian Coll., 1993—, Le Tournea U., 1994—. Author in field. Elder Lord of Life Luth. Ch., Plano, Tex., 1992-95; stewardship com. Tex. Dist. Luth. Ch., Mo. Synod, Austin, 1992—. Mem. Am. Statis. Assn. (North Tex. chpt., program chmn. 1985-86, v.p. 1986-87, pres. 1987-88). Republican. Lutheran. Office: Dossin Bus Solutions 2613 Winterlake Dr Carrollton TX 75006-2707

DOSTER, DANIEL HARRIS, counselor, minister; b. Moultrie, Ga., Dec. 15, 1934; s. Percy James and Juanita (Huff) D.; m. Robin Baker, Mar. 29, 1964; children: Christopher Robin Eagy, Sally Sheppard Powell. BA, Fla. State U., 1961; MS, Ft. Valley State Coll., 1984. Ordained minister, 1980. Min., deacon Christ Episcopal Ch., Dublin, Ga., 1980—; counselor Dodge Correctional Instn., Chester, Ga., 1984-87, Community Mental Health Ctr. Mid. Ga., Dublin, 1987-96; ret., 1996; pres. Ga. Retail Bakers Assn., Atlanta, 1964-65; chaplain Parkside Lodge Dublin, 1984-92, Al Sihah Shrine Temple, Macon, 1991—. Pres. Cmty. Concert Assn., Dublin, 1985, 86, 87, bd. dirs., 1984—; membership chmn. Al Sihah Shrine Temple, 1993—, chaplain, 1992—. Mem. Kiwanis (pres. Dublin-Shamrock Club 1981, Kiwanian of Yr. 1981), Masons, Shriners, Laurens Shrine Club (Dublin, Ga., sec. 1992-93), Fla. State U. Mid. Ga. Seminole Club (bd. dirs. 1993, v.p. acad. affairs 1994), Kappa Alpha. Republican. Home: 724 Victoria Cir Dublin GA 31021-5542 Office: Community Mental Health Ctr 2121A Bellevue Rd Dublin GA 31021-2952

DOSTER, JUNE MARKEN, minister; b. Des Moines, June 10, 1930; d. DeLoss Irving and Helen (Roberts) Marken; m. Harold Charles Doster, June 19, 1955; children: Deborah, Diana, Donald, Denise. BA magna cum laude, State U. Iowa, 1952; MRE, Yale U., 1957. Ordained to ministry Christian Ch. (Disciples of Christ), 1982. Instr. sociology Bethany Coll., W.Va., 1961-62; dir. religious edn. Meml. Christian Ch., Ann Arbor, Mich., 1966-68; min. ch. edn. First Christian Ch., Wilson, N.C., 1981-83; assoc. regional min. Christian Ch., Macon, Ga., 1984—; mem. cabinet Ch. Women Fellowship, Canton, Mo., 1975-77, Wilson, 1979-83, mem. exec. com., Indpls., 1985-90. Author: Major Prophets; Major Messages, 1985, To Speak or Not to Speak, 1991, God is Love: I John, 1993; author retreat, jr. camp curriculum Christian Ch. in N.C. Leader Girl Scouts U.S., Ky., W.Va., 1968-73, treas. neighborhood coun. Wilson, N.C., 1978-83; bd. dirs. Wilson Concerts, 1981-83, Parents Anonymous, Wilson, 1982-83; mem. adv. bd. Villa Internat., 1985-90, Christmount Christian Assembly, 1985—. Sr. woman scholar Iowa State U., 1951. Mem. PEO, Gen. Fedn. Women (Keyser, W.Va. and Canton chpts.), Wilson Women's Club, Phi Beta Kappa, Alpha Xi Delta. Republican. Home: 275 Power Point Rd Milledgeville GA 31061 Office: Christian Ch in Ga 2370 Vineville Ave Macon GA 31204-3118

DOTSON, ALLEN CLARK, physics and mathematics educator; b. Badin, N.C., Mar. 21, 1938; s. William Grady and Nell Elizabeth (Smith) D. BS in Physics, Wake Forest Coll., 1960; PhD in Physics, U. N.C., Chapel Hill, 1964. Asst. prof. physics Western Mich. U., Kalamazoo, 1964-67, assoc. prof., 1967-81; assoc. prof. St. Andrews Presbyn. Coll., Laurinburg, N.C., 1981-91, prof. physics, 1991-95, prof. math. and physics, 1995—, chmn. dept. chemistry and physics, 1993-94, chmn. divsn. math., natural and health scis., 1985-88. Contbr. articles to profl. jours. Mem. Am. Assn. Physics Tchrs., Sigma Xi. Democrat. Methodist. Home: 702 McNeill Dr Laurinburg NC 28352 Office: St Andrews Presbyn Coll Dept Math Scis 1700 Dogwood Mile Laurinburg NC 28352

DOTSON, VICKY LYNN, special education educator; b. Stuttgart, Ark., Feb. 3, 1953; d. William John and Maxine (McDowell) Schott; m. Robert Earl Dotson, May 15, 1976; children: Robert Daniel, Shannon Lynn. B in Music Edn., U. Cen. Ark., 1976; postgrad., Longwood Coll., 1991—. Cert. music tchr., Va.; cert X-Ray technician. Music lab. operator U. Cen. Ark., Conway, 1972-75; computer operator, X-Ray technican Dr. Earl Dotson, Dental Practice, Richmond, Va., 1976-88; music, learning disabled tchr. Fuqua Sch., Farmville, Va., 1989—; bd. dirs. Fuqua Sch., Farmville. Choir dir. Oakwood United Meth. Ch., Columbia, Va., 1979—, bd. trustees, 1988—, Sunday sch. treas., 1991—, tone chime dir.; dental asst. Goochland Women's Correctional Inst., 1986-88; pres., treas. Tiny Tots Nursery Bd., Columbia, 1989-92; mem. Band Boosters Fuqua Sch., 1992—, ATP. Mem. ASCD, Nat. Assn. Music Educators, Va. Music Educators Assn., Assn. Va. Acads., Am. Choral Dirs. Assn., Lioness Club (pres. Richmond 1979-81), Alpha Chi, Gamma Beta Phi. Republican. Home: 1155 Ampthill Rd Columbia VA 23038-2807 Office: Fuqua Sch PO Box 328 Farmville VA 23901-0328

DOTT, GREGORY ALAN, physician; b. Chgo., Aug. 5, 1957; s. Raymond Neil and Elsie Marie (Overgaard) D.; m. Cynthia Sue Tinsley, June 26, 1982; children: Timothy Alan, Erica Sue. BS in Biology, Tex. Luth. Coll., 1978; DO, U. North Tex., 1984. Diplomate Am. Osteo. Bd. Family Physicians, Am. Osteo. Bd. Spl. Proficiency in Osteo. Manipulative Medicine, Am. Acad. Pain Mgmt.; lic. physician, Maine, Tex. Intern Osteo. Hosp. Maine, Inc., Portland, 1984-85; resident in family practice Dallas Meml. Hosp., 1985-86; dir., physician Main St. Med. Clinic, Grapevine, Tex., 1986-88; preceptor, physician dept. family practice Tex. Coll. Osteo. Med., Ft. Worth, 1986-88, instr. dept. manipulative medicine, 1988-89, asst. prof. dept. manipulative medicine, 1989-94, assoc. prof. dept. manipulative medicine, 1994-96; clin. assoc. prof. manipulative medicine NFL's Dallas Cowboys, 1996—, cons. physician, 1994—; staff physician Beltline Minor Emergency Clinic, Irving, Tex., 1986-88; teaching asst. dept. osteo. philosophy principles and practice Tex. Coll. Osteo. Medicine, 1981-82, co-dir. R&D dept. manipulative medicine, 1988-91, course coord. manipulative medicine yr 1, 1989-91, course dir. osteo. manipulative medicine, 1991-95; faculty The Sutherland Cranial Teaching Found., Inc., Ft. Worth, 1989-94; clin. dir. undergrad. teaching fellow program U. North Tex. Health Sci. Ctr., 1992-94; mem. numerous profl. coms.; lectr., presenter in field; consulting physician NFL's Dallas Cowboys, 1994—. Pres. Undergrad. Am. Acad. Osteopathy, Tex., 1980-82; active YMCA Indian Guides, 1992—; team physician Dallas City League Softball, 1985-89, Richardson (Tex.) City League Softball, 1990, Dallas Ch. Softball Assn., 1991—; team physician, asst. coach Lake Highlands Soccer Assn., 1992-93, YMCA T-Ball, 1993-94; first aid physician Ft. Worth Symphony at the Botanical Gardens, 1991. Student scholar Am. Acad. Osteopathy, 1982; Tex. Coll. Osteo. Medicine grantee, 1983. Fellow Am. Acad. Osteopathy; mem. Am. Osteo. Assn., Tex. Osteo. Med. Assn. (sec. Dist. V 1992-93, v.p. 1993-94, prs. 1995-96), Am. Coll. Osteo. Family Physicians, Tex. State Soc. Am. Coll. Osteo. Family Physicians, Cranial Acad., Am. Acad. Pain Mgmt., Tex. Med. Assn., Dallas County Med. Soc., Tex. Acad. Osteopathy (pres. 1992-95), Tex. Coll. Osteo. Medicine Alumni Assn. (life), Beta Beta Beta. Office: Family Clinic 6780 Abrams Rd # 211 Dallas TX 75231

DOTTIN, ERSKINE S., education educator; b. St. Michael, Barbados, July 21, 1940; s. Grafton Howard and Beryl Dottin; m. Cynthia E. Dottin, Apr. 25, 1970; 1 child, Farrell S. BS, U. West Fla., 1973, MEd, 1974; PhD, Miami U., Oxford, Ohio, 1976; AA, Pensacola (Fla.) Jr. Coll., 1972. Tchr. Pensacola Sch. Liberal Arts; from instructional specialist to assoc. prof. edn. U. West Fla., Pensacola, 1977-92; prof. Fla. Internat. U., 1992—. Author: Thinking About Education, 1989, Teaching as Enchancing Human Effectiveness, 1994. Mem. ASCD, Global Alliance for Transformation of Edn., Am. Ednl. Rsch. Assn., Am. Ednl. Studies Assn., S.E. Philosophy Edn. Soc., Fla. Founds. Edn. Soc. (past pres.), NCATE Bd. Examiners, Coun. Learned Socs. in Edn. (v.p.), Phi Kappa Phi, Phi Delta Kappa. Home: 14810 SW 149th Ave Miami FL 33196-2334 Office: Fla Internat Univ Coll Edn Dept Founds University Park Miami FL 33199

DOTY, GRESDNA ANN, education educator; b. Oelwein, Iowa, Feb. 22, 1931; d. James William and Gresdna (Wood) D.; m. James G. Traynham, Nov. 28, 1980. AA, Monticello Coll., Alton, Ill., 1951; BA, U. No. Iowa, 1953; MA, U. Fla., 1957; PhD, Ind. U., 1967. Instr. S.W. Tex. State U., San Marcos, 1957-61, asst. prof., 1964-65; asst. prof. La. State U., Baton Rouge, 1967-73, assoc. prof., 1973-79, dir. theatre, 1973-77, 81-91, prof., 1979-84, alumni prof., 1984—, chair dept. theatre, 1991-93. Author: Anne Brunton Merry in the American Theatre, 1971; co-editor: (with Billy J. Harbin) Inside the Royal Court Theatre, 1956-81: Artists Talk, 1990; contbr. articles to profl. jours. Bd. dirs. Arts Coun. Greater Baton Rouge, 1987—, pres., 1990-91. Rsch. grantee Nat. Endowment Humanities, 1981, Exxon Edn. Found., 1981. Fellow S.W. Theatre Assn.; mem. Am. Theatre Assn. (bd. dirs. 1977-80), Am. Coll. Theatre Festival (nat. chmn. 1976-79), Am. Soc. Theatre Rsch. (mem. exec. com. 1988-91, v.p. 1994-97), Nat. Theatre Conf., Assn. Theatre Higher Edn., Coll. of Fellow of Am. Theatre. Home: 628 Polytech Dr Baton Rouge LA 70808-4755 Office: La State U Theatre 217 Da Bldg M Baton Rouge LA 70803

DOUBLEDAY, CHARLES WILLIAM, dermatologist, educator; b. Houston, Oct. 1, 1954; s. Leonard Charles and Margaret (Walker) D.; m. Verlinde Van den Berge Hill, June 22, 1985; children: George Marchant, Julia Van den Berge, Walker Hill. BA with honors, U. Tex., Austin, 1976; MD, U. Tex., Houston, 1981. Diplomate Am. Bd. Dermatology, 1987. Rotating intern John Peter Smith Hosp., Ft. Worth, 1981-82; resident in dermatology U. Tex. Med. Sch., 1982-83, 85-87, fellow in dermatology, 1985, clin. asst. prof. dermatology, 1988—; pvt. practice, Houston, 1987—. Contbr. articles to med. jours. Recipient high sci. quality award Soc. for Investigative Dermatology, 1986; rsch. fellow Dermatology Found., 1985. Fellow Am. Acad. Dermatology; mem. Tex. Med. Assn., Harris County Med. Soc., Tex. Dermatol. Soc., Houston Dermatol. Soc., U. Tex. Home Health Sci. Ctr. (devel. coun., 1994—), Houston Country Club. Republican. Episcopalian. Office: Sage Pla 515 Post Oak Blvd Ste 535 Houston TX 77027

DOUGAN, DEBORAH RAE, neuropsychology professional; b. Urbana, Ill., Jan. 22, 1952; d. Francis William and Barbara Belle (Ash) D. BA in Psychology, U. Ill., 1973; MA in Counseling, Gov.'s State U., 1978; PhD in Neuropsychology, Oreg. State U., 1982. Lic. psychol. assoc., Tex. Staff therapist Ozark Community Mental Health, Joplin, Mo., 1982-85; neuropsychol. cons. Tex. Commn. for the Blind, Austin, 1985-87; psychol. assoc. Warm Springs Rehab. Hosp., Gonzales, Tex., 1987-88, Rehab. Hosp. South Tex., Corpus Christi, 1988-89; psychosocial dir. New Medico Rehab. Ctr., Lindale, Tex., 1989-90; clin. coord. Rainbow Rehab. Ctrs., Ft. Worth, 1991-93; neuropsychology profl. Cypress Creek Rehab. Ctr., Houston, 1993-95; coord. stategic stress mgmt. seminars Cypress Creek Rehab. Ctr., 1996—; predoctoral intern State Hosp., Vinita, Okla., 1981-82. Mem. APA, Tex. Head Injury Assn. (North Ctrl. chpt. bd. dirs., survivors coun. liaision 1991-93, survivors group leader Corpus Christi head injury chpt. 1988-89, Tyler (Tex.) head injury chpt. 1989-90, survivors group leader Ft. Worth head injury chpt. 1991-93, vice chair chpt. rels. state orgn. 1994-96, bd. dirs., sec. Houston chpt. 1995-96), Toastmasters Internat. Home: PO Box 73642 Houston TX 77273

DOUGHERTY, DANA DEAN LESLEY, television producer, educator; b. Birmingham, Ala.; d. Paul Russell and Daisy Dean (Dunham) Lesley; m. Floyd Wallace Dougherty; 1 child, Lesley Dean. BS in Secondary and Bus. Edn., Speech Therapy, Drama, Auburn U., 1968. Cert. elem. tchr., Ala. Tchr. speech, drama, computer typing, shorthand, acctg., bus. law Jefferson State Jr. Coll., Birmingham, 1968-73; office mgr. Baker, McDaniel & Hall, Birmingham, 1973-78; tchr. Mountain Brook Bd. Edn., Birmingham, 1979—; producer, dir. drama and music TV show Dean and Company, Birmingham, 1980—; corp. sec. F.W. Dougherty Engrs. and Assocs. Inc., 1987—. Composer various songs. Mem. Arlington Hist. Soc.; mem. women's com. Ala. Ballet. Recipient numerous awards Birmingham Cable TV, 1981-89, Cable TV Vulcan award, 1989-90, 90-91, World Poetry Golden Poet award, 1990, 91, Silver poet award, 1991. Mem. ALA, Poetry Soc., Actors and Theatre Guild, So. Bus. Edn. Assn., Ala. Assn. Legal Secs., Ala. Theater Orgn. Soc., Nat. Theater Orgn. Soc., Jr. Women's C. of C., Thalian Lit. Club (Woman of Yr. award 1994—), Arlington Hist. Soc., Nat. Bus. Edn. Assn., Quill Club (libr. award, libr. writing award), Beta Sigma Phi. Baptist. Office: Dean and Co 2441 Old Springville Rd Birmingham AL 35215-4053

DOUGHERTY, DAVID EDWARD, agricultural research scientist; b. Canton, Ohio, Nov. 4, 1946; s. Cyril Edward and Gladys Helene (Bennett) D.; m. Jenelle Louise Shover, Dec. 30, 1977 (div. July, 1989). B.A., Denison U., 1968; M.S., Ohio State U., 1973; Ph.D., U. Ga., 1976. Asst. plant pathologist U. Fla., Immokalee, 1977-80; field rsch. scientist BASF Corp., Raleigh, N.C., 1980-86, agrl. rsch. assoc., 1986—. Contbr. articles to profl. jours. With U.S. Army, 1968-71. Mem. Am. Phytopathol. Soc. (new fungicides com., sect. editor of fungicide and nematicide test reports 1988-92), So. Weed Sci. Soc., Am. Peanut Rsch. & Edn. Soc., U.S. Jr. C. of C. (pres. 1979-80). Lodge: Rotary (Immokalee, Cary-Kildaire). Avocations: gardening, computers. Home: 7005 Orchard Knoll Dr Apex NC 27502-9773 Office: BASF Corp PO Box 13528 Durham NC 27709-3528

DOUGHERTY, F(RANCIS) KELLY, data processing executive; b. Lubbock, Tex., May 15, 1953; s. Francis Kelly and Mary Ann (Odell) D.; m. Bonnie Lee Burch, June 14, 1975; children: Anne Katherine, Margaret Erin, Mary Bridget, Kerry Meaghan, Frances Cara. BA in Math. and Physics summa cum laude, U. Dallas, 1975; cert. assoc. customer svc. Life Office Mgmt. Inst., 1992. CLU; cert. computing profl.; chartered fin. cons.; cert. Microsoft profl. Actuarial trainee Ranger Nat. Life Ins., Houston, 1976-77; mgr. time sharing services Phila. Life Ins. Co., Houston, 1977-81; systems engr. Electronic Data Systems, Dallas, 1981-85; technical specialist J.C. Penney Life Ins. Co., Plano, Tex., 1985—. U. Dallas scholar, 1971-75; Rice U. fellow, 1975-76. Pres. St. Elizabeth Seton Parish Bd. Edn., 1989-92. Fellow Life Mgmt. Inst. (master); mem. KC. Republican. Roman Catholic. Home: 2713 S Cypress Cir Plano TX 75075-3154 Office: JC Penney Life Ins Co 2700 W Plano Pky Plano TX 75075-8205

DOUGHERTY, JOHN CHRYSOSTOM, III, lawyer; b. Beeville, Tex., May 3, 1915; s. John Chrysostom and Mary V. (Henderson) D.; m. Mary Ireland Graves, Apr. 18, 1942 (dec. July 1977); children: Mary Ireland, John Chrysostom IV; m. Bea Ann Smith, June 1978 (div. 1981); m. Sarah B. Randle, 1981. BA, U. Tex., 1937; LLB, Harvard, 1940; diploma, Inter-Am. Acad. Internat. and Comparative Law, Havana, Cuba, 1948. Bar: Tex. 1940. Atty. Hewit & Dougherty, Beeville, 1940-41; ptnr. Graves & Dougherty, Austin, Tex., 1946-50, Graves, Dougherty & Greenhill, Austin, 1950-57, Graves, Dougherty & Gee, Austin, 1957-60, Graves, Dougherty, Gee & Hearon, Austin, 1961-66, Graves, Dougherty, Gee, Hearon, Moody & Garwood, Austin, 1966-73, Graves, Dougherty, Hearon, Moody & Garwood, Austin, 1973-79; ptnr. Graves, Dougherty, Hearon & Moody, Austin, 1979-93, sr. counsel, 1993—; spl. asst. atty. gen., 1949-50; Hon. French Consul, Austin, 1971-86; lectr. on tax, estate planning, probate code, community property problems; mem. Tex. Submerged Lands Adv. Com., 1963-72, Tex. Bus. and Commerce Code Adv. Com., 1964-66, Gov.'s Com. on Marine Resources, 1970-71, Gov.'s Planning Com. on Colorado River Basin Water Quality Mgmt. Study, 1972-73, Tex. Legis. Property Tax Com., 1973-75. Co-editor: Texas Appellate Practice, 1964, 2d edit., 1977; contbr. Bowe, Estate Planning and Taxation, 1957, 65; Texas Lawyers Practice Guide, 1967, 71, How to Live and Die with Texas Probate, 1968, 7th edit., 1995, Texas Estate Administration, 1975, 78; mem. bd. editors: Appellate Procedure in Tex., 1964, 2d edit., 1982; contbr. articles to legal jours. Bd. dirs. Tex. Beta Students Aid Fund, 1949-84, Grenville Clark Fund at Dartmouth Coll., 1976-90, Umlauf Sculpture Gardens, Inc., 1990-91, New Life Inst., 1993—; past bd. dirs. Advanced Religious Study Found., Holy Cross Hosp., Sea Arama, Inc., Nat. Pollution Control Found., Austin Nat. Bank; trustee St. Stephen's Episcopal Sch., Austin, 1969-83, Tex. Equal Access to Justice Found., 1986-90, U. Tex. Law Sch. Found., 1974—; mem. adv. com. Legal Assts. Tng. Inst., U. Tex., 1990—; mem. vis. com. Harvard Law Sch., 1983-87. Capt. C.I.C., AUS, 1941-44, JAGC, 1944-46, maj. USAR. Decorated Medaille Française France, Medaille d'honneur en Argent des Affairs Etrangeres France, chevalier, L'Ordre Nat. du Merite. Fellow Am. Bar Found., Tex. Bar Found., Am. Coll. Trust and Estate Counsel, Am. Coll. Tax Counsel; mem. ABA (ho. of dels. 1982-88, standing com. on lawyers pub. responsibility 1983-85, mem. spl. com. on delivery legal svcs. 1987-91), Am. Arbitration Assn. (nat. panel arbitrators 1958-90), Inter-Am. Bar Assn., Travis County Bar Assn. (pres. 1979-80), Internat. Acad. Estate and Trust Law (exec. coun. 1988-90), State Bar Tex. (chmn. sect. taxation 1965-66, pres. 1979-80, com. legal svcs. to the poor 1986-94), Am. Judicature Soc. (bd. dirs. 1985-87), Internat. Law Assn., Am. Fgn. Law Assn., Am. Law Inst. (adv. com. project law governing lawyers 1990—), Tex. Supreme Ct. Hist. Soc. (trustee), Philos. Soc. Tex. (pres. 1989, bd. dirs. 1989-96), Harvard Law Sch. Assn. (mem. com. on pub. svc. law 1990—, chmn. 1990-95, coun. 1991-95, exec. com. 1992-95), Rotary. Presbyterian. Home: 6 Green Ln Austin TX 78703-2515 Office: 515 Congress Ave Ste 2300 Austin TX 78701-3503 also: PO Box 98 Austin TX 78767-0098

DOUGHERTY, MICHAEL JOHN, social sciences educator; b. Savannah, Ga., Dec. 17, 1963; s. William C. and Rose Marie B. D. BA in Govt., Coll. of William & Mary, 1985; M of Urban Affairs, Va. Polytech. Inst., 1989, PhD in Planning, 1995. Staff writer Daily Press Inc., Newport News, Va., 1983-87; editl. asst., writer Roanoke (Va.) Times, 1987-95; asst. prof. divsn. cmty. & econ. devel. West Va. U., 1995—. Mem. First Night Planning Com., Morgantown, Va., 1996—; v.p. for individual devel. Morgantown Jaycees, 1996—. Mem. ASPA, Assn. on Budget and Fin. Mgmt. (mem. World Wide Web task force 1995—), Toastmasters (pres.-elect 1996—). Roman Catholic. Home: 181 Fairmor Dr Westover WV 26505 Office: WVU-ES CED PO Box 6031 Morgantown WV 26506

DOUGHERTY, MOLLY IRELAND, organization executive; b. Austin, Tex., Oct. 3, 1949; d. John Chrysostom and Mary Ireland (Graves) D. Student, Stanford U., 1968-71, Grad. Theol. Union, Berkeley, 1976; BA, Antioch U., 1980. Tchr., fundraiser Oakland Community Sch., Calif., 1973-77; assoc. producer, asst. editor film Nicaragua: These Same Hands, Palo Alto, Calif., 1980; free-lance journalist, translator, Nicaragua, 1981; assoc. producer, film: Short Circuit: Inside the Death Squads; exec. dir. Vecinos, A Tex. Inter-Am. Initiative, Austin, Tex., 1984—; cons. Magee & Magee Assocs., 1991—. Spanish lang. tutor St. Stephen's Episcopal Sch., Austin, 1988-89. Bd. dirs. Nat. Immigration Refugee and Citizenship Forum, Washington, 1985-88; speaker, fund-raiser Salvadoran Assn. for Rural Health, 1986—; lectr. St. Stephen's Episcopal Sch., 1989. Home: 1100 Claire Ave Austin TX 78703-2502 Office: Vecinos Inter-Am Initiative PO Box 4562 Austin TX 78765-4562

DOUGHERTY, ROBERT JAMES, safety consultant; b. Bartlesville, Okla., Aug. 31, 1923; s. Charles Francis and Isabelle Frances (Meder) D.; m. Margaret Rita Cullen, Nov. 27, 1946 (div. 1974); children: Robert Jr., Kathleen, Deborah, Dennis, Laurie, Maureen; m. Frances Munoz Tart, Oct. 1, 1974; stepchildren: Robert, Sheila, George, Amanda, James Tart. Student, St. Charles Seminary, Carthagena, Ohio, 1941-44. Cert. safety profl. Corp. safety dir. Stearns Roger Corp., Denver, 1953-69; civil svc. safety officer U.S. Bur. Mines, Denver, 1969-70; safety mgr. U.S. Army Adv. Team, Vietnam, 1970-73, U.S. Civil Svc., Fort Sam Houston, Tex., 1973-83; safety cons., advisor San Antonio, 1983—; mem. Colo. Dept. Edn. ad hoc com. safety edn. curriculum, 1966; guest speaker Nat. and Internat. Safety Confs. Contbr. articles to profl. jours. Vice chmn. Alamo Field Fed. Health and Safety Coun., San Antonio, 1980; mem. sch. bd. dist. 50, Westminster, Colo., 1969-70; mem. gov.'s hwy. safety commn., Denver, 1968-75; group safety officer maj. Civil Air Patrol, Denver. Decorated Medal of Honor (1st class, Vietnam), Medal for U.S.A. Civil Svc. in Vietnam. Mem. Am. Soc. Safety Engrs. (regional v.p., bd. dirs. 1960-62, past pres. Colo. chpt.), Vets. Safety Internat. (bd. dirs. 1964-65, regional v.p. 1964-65), Nat. Safety Coun. (past safety program cons., past editor Constrn. newsletter), Colo. Soc. Engrs. (life). Home and Office: 4951 Grey Hawk St San Antonio TX 78217-1218

DOUGHTY, MICHAEL DEAN, insurance agent; b. Oklahoma City, Nov. 7, 1947; s. Charles Dean and Francis Jean (Schumpert) D.; m. Sherrie Lynn Perkins, May 30, 1970; children: Steven Kyle, Brian Edward. BS in Edn., Okla. State U., 1971; postgrad., Command Sgts. Maj. Acad.; Assoc. in Risk Mgmt., Ins. Inst. Am., 1993. Accredited advisor in ins. Ins. Inst. Am.; cert. ins. counselor; cert. profl. ins. agt., 1996. Tchr., coach Perry (Okla.) Pub. Schs., 1971-80; asst. v.p., field agt. Coaches Ins. Assn. Am., Memphis, 1980-84; v.p., officer mgr. Albright Ins. Agy., Inc., Perry, Okla., 1984-88; producer Holt Ins. Agy., Perry, 1988—, co-owner, 1992—; instr. Indian-Meridian Voc. Tech., Stillwater, Okla., 1985, new ins. edn. program Excellence in Svc., Ava, Moa., 1996—; faculty instr. Cert. Ins. Svcs. Rep. Program, Soc. Cert. Ins. Couns., 1992—, Excellence in Svc. Comml. Ins. courses, 1996—. Bd. dirs. United Fund Perry, 1983-86, 94-96, 97-99; youth sports cons. Noble County Family YMCA, Perry, 1985; active vocat. bus. adv. bd. Perry H.S., 1990-95; mem. fin. adv. com. on taxes Noble County, 1993; mem. bus. devel. com. Perry Devel. Coalition. Command sgt. maj. Okla. Army N.G., 1970-96, ret. 1996. Mem. Okla. Assn. Ins. Agts. (pub. rels. com. 1988-91, chmn. 1990-91, group discussion leader 1988), Ind. Ins. Agts. Am., Profl. Ind. Ins. Agts. Okla. (rural and small agts. com. 1992-93), Ins. Inst. Assn. (assoc. risk mgmt.), Internat. Platform Assn., Stillwater Life Underwriters Assn. (pres. 1982-83), Jaycees (past chpt. pres. 1992-93), Perry C. of C. (bd. dirs. 1993-96, v.p. 1994, pres. 1995, 96), Am. Legion, N.G. Assn. Okla. (life), Non-Commd. Officers Assn., Assn. U.S. Army, Perry Quarterback Club (pres. 1990-92), Perry Diamond Club (v.p. 1990-91), Elks (chmn. Americanism 1989-94), Perry C. of C. (v.p. 1993-94, pres. 1994-96). Democrat. Baptist. Home: 915 Jackson St Perry OK 73077-3012 Office: Holt Ins Agy 718 Delaware St Perry OK 73077-6425

DOUGLAS, ANDREW, rehabilitation nurse, consultant; b. N.Y., Mar. 27, 1948; s. Lloyd James and Paula (Levine) D.; m. Lauren Gail Gentile, Aug. 6, 1988. AS in Nursing, Coll. of the Desert, 1976; Ryan teaching credential, Calif. State U., 1979, MA in Bioethics, 1985; BS in Health Sci., Health Care, Redlands U., 1982. CRRN, CIRS, CCM, ACLS instr., RN. Orderly ER Desert Hosp., Palm Springs, Calif., 1972-74; charge nurse CCU, founder terminal illness program Desert Hosp., 1974-78; head nurse ICU, shock unit cardiac lab. Weil & Shubin Hollywood Presbyn. Med. Ctr., U. So. Calif. Med. Ctr., L.A., 1978-83; critical care instr. ethics com. Queen of Angels Hosp., L.A., 1983-84; pres., owner Med. Systems Designs, L.A., 1984-89; case mgr. Nancy Sapp & Assocs., Orlando, Fla., 1989-93, Resource Opportunities, Orlando, 1992-93, Med. Mgmt. & Re-Employment, Orlando, 1993—; pres., owner, med.-legal expert Health Care Adv. Cons., Boca Raton, Fla., 1989—; founder, cons., speaker Profls. Assisting the Dying, L.A., 1988-89; educator AACN, FARN, 1983—; cons. brain injuries Goodwill Industries, West Palm Beach, Fla., 1994—; cons. adv. bd. Pinecrest Rehab. Hosp., Delray Beach, Fla., 1993-94. Author: (books) Socialization, Sexism & Stereotyping, 1982, Stress and Bioethics in Critical Care Units, 1985; contbr. articles to jours. in field. Speaker Greiving Parents, Boca Raton, Fla., 1992—, Profls. Assisting the Dying, L.A., 1984-89. Mem. AACN, Assn. Rehab. Nurses, Assn. & Soc. of Law and Medicine, Individual Cas Mgmt. Assn., Hastings Ctr. for Human Ethics, Thanatology Soc. Home: 3199 NE 8th Ave Boca Raton FL 33431-6912

DOUGLAS, CLARENCE JAMES, JR., corporation executive, management consultant; b. Corry, Pa., May 9, 1924; s. Clarence James and Pearl Vivian (Rager) D.; m. Barbara M. Creighton, Jan. 30, 1949; children: Stephen, James, Jeffrey, Shawn Lynn, Robert, Heather. BBA magna cum laude, U. Pitts., 1958; postgrad., Indsl. Coll. of Armed Forces, Washington, 1965; MBA, George Washington U., 1966. Commd. 2d lt. U.S. Army Air Corps., 1944; advanced through grades to brig. gen. USAF, 1970, ret., 1975; successively navigator, radar observer U.S. Army Air Corps; sr. pilot USAF, 1943-66, dir. programs def. comm. planning group DCA, 1966-70, chief of staff U.S. Taiwan Def. Command, 1970-72, comdr. 1st Composite Wing, 1972-75; program dir Decisions and Designs Inc., McLean, Va., 1975-85; asst. to pres. PSC, Inc., Fairfax, Va., 1985-86; CEO Carr Techs. Inc., Oklahoma City, 1988-91; sr. mgmt. cons., 1986—; pres. J3 Investment Group, Herndon, Va., 1988-91; sec., bd. dirs. Seamast, Inc., Fairfax, PSC, Inc., 1988—. Internat. Video Broadcasts, Inc., Fairfax, 1988-94; founder., sec., bd. dirs. Internat. Privatization Enterprises, 1994-96; sec., bd. dirs. The Adler Cos., 1992—. Pres. PTA, Colton, Calif., 1963; deacon Presbyn. Ch., Erie, Pa., 1940. Decorated Disting. Svc. medal USAF, 2 Legions of Merit, Medal of Cloud and Banner Govt. Republic of China; named Disting. Citizen State of Md., 1974. Mem. DAV (life), Ret. Officers Assn., Air Force Assn., Army Navy Country Club (Arlington Va.), Evergreen Country Club (Haymarket, Va.), Am. Legion, Beta Gamma Sigma. Home: 3518 Woolman Dr Haymarket VA 20169-1821

DOUGLAS, DARCY, special education educator; b. Ft. Belvoir, Va., Apr. 17, 1950; d. James Shepard and Jeanne Marie (Dupré) D.; m. John H. Carpenter, Sept. 27, 1975 (div. June 1980); children: Troy Douglas, Angela. BS in Spl. Edn. summa cum laude, James Madison U., 1972; MA in Edn. summa cum laude, George Washington U., 1975. Cert. mental retardation tchr., interrelated tchr. Multi-handicapped tchr. Martinsburg, W.Va., 1972-74; resource tchr. Md., 1975; edn. dir. Pearl St. House, Framingham, Mass., 1976; nursery worker YMCA, Cin., 1977-78; day care dir. Atlanta, 1980; staff devel., mgmt., tchr. Ga. Retardation Ctr., Atlanta, 1980-88; resource tchr., tchr. self-contained learning disabilities Cobb County Pub. Schs., Marietta, Ga., 1988—. Fellow State of W.Va., 1974-75, Washington, 1974-75. Mem. Coun. Exceptional Children, Benton Mackaye Trail Assn. (treas. 1985-86, pres. 1987-89, newsletter editor 1989-91, Maintenance 1991-94), Appalachian Trail Club, Nature Conservancy. Home: 3233 Rangers Gate Dr Marietta GA 30062-1472 Office: Sope Creek Elem Sch Cobb County Pub Schs Marietta GA 30060

DOUGLAS, JOHN HAROLD, manufacturing executive; b. Canton, Ohio, July 30, 1931; s. Constantine George and Penelope (Peroulakis) Maragakes; m. Ann Hatzidakis, Sept. 16, 1956 (div. 1979); children: Constant, Penelope, George, Michael, Thomas, Andreas; m. Sherry Babic, 1980; 1 child, Stephen. BS, Bowling Green State U., 1953; postgrad. Georgetown U., 1956-58. Pres. Am. Learning Systems, Inc., N.Y.C., 1969, Ednl. Scis. Program, N.Y.C., 1970; v.p., gen. mgr. CBSEdnl. Svcs., 1970; group v.p. CBS Ednl. Pub. Group, 1971-74; pres. Gen. Ednl. Svcs. Corp., 1974-76, United Electronics, Pompano Beach, Fla., 1977-81; pres., owner Bank Security Camera Mfg. Co., Louisville, 1982-84, Rodanis Corp., Boca Raton, Fla., 1984-86; pres. San Andreas Mgmt. Corp., 1982-88; exec. v.p. Paragon Water Systems, Clearwater, Fla., 1989—; bd. dirs. Morality in Media, Inc. Dem. candidate U.S. Congress, 6th dist., Md., 1962; committeeman Nassau County coun. N.Y. coun. Boy Scouts Am.; mem. Nat. Archdiocese Com. on Spiritual Renewal, N.Y.C., 1973-90, Greek Orthodox Archdiocesan Coun.; mem. pub. bd. Orthodox Observer. Lt. (j.g.) USN, 1953-55. Fellow Am. Soc. Psychical Rsch.; mem. Mensa, Army-Navy Club (Washington), N.Y. Athletic Club. Home: 1000 Cove Cay Dr Clearwater FL 34620 Office: Paragon Water Systems 14001 63rd Way N Clearwater FL 34620-3619

DOUGLAS, JOHN PAUL, lawyer, mediator, arbitrator; b. Louisville, Jan. 6, 1939; s. John Sammuel and Margaret Mary (Wagner) D.; m. Laura Christine Welborn, Feb. 17, 1968; children: Constance, John, Robert, D. Bear. AB, Regis U., Denver, 1968; JD, No. Ky. U., 1976. Bar: Ohio 1976, Tex. 1981, U.S. Supreme Ct. 1982. Program officer Cath. Relief Svcs., India, 1968-70; adminstr. Hamilton County, Cin., 1970-76, trial atty., 1976-80; gen. counsel Gen. Exploration Co., Dallas, 1980-86; pvt. practice Douglas & Assocs., Dallas, 1989-60, 92—; pres. Legal Mgmt. Assn., Dallas, 1995—; adj. prof. law U. Dallas, 1989-91; mem. Bede Griffiths Internat. Trust, Big Sur, Calif., 1994—. Contbr. articles to various publs. Pres. Maria Kannon Zen Ctr., Dallas, 1996. With USN, 1957-62, 90-92, capt. Res. Mem. Am. Arbitration Assn. (arbitrator 1990—), Hindu-Christian Soc., Buddhist-Christian Soc., Order of St. Benedict (Camaldolese Oblate 1994—). Roman Catholic. Home: 1723 Barclay Dr Richardson TX 75081 Office: Legal Mgmt Assn PO Box 851521 Richardson TX 75085-1521

DOUGLAS, KATHLEEN MARY HARRIGAN, psychotherapist, educator; b. Boston, Apr. 24, 1950; d. John Joseph and Kathleen Margaret (Connolly) Harrigan; m. Dr. Robert E. Douglas, Feb. 24, 1977; children: David, Pamela, Elizabeth. Student, Uxbridge, England; BA in Psychology, Sophia U., Tokyo, 1972; MA in Counseling Psychology, Chapman U., Orange, Calif., 1983; PhD in Counselor Edn., U. Fla., 1990. Elem tchr. Marymount Prep Sch., Palos Verdes, Calif., 1973-75; pvt. practice Orlando, Fla., 1985-95; psychology prof. Valencia C.C., Orlando, Fla., 1989-93; prof. Fla. Inst. Tech., 1990-94; asst. prof., acad. advisor, clin. internship supr. Troy State U., Orlando, Fla., 1993—; software developer of clinically oriented software Troy State U., 1994—; drug/alcohol counselor Ft. Belvoir, Va., 1981-82; counselor Orange County Mental Health Ctr., Winter Park, Fla., 1982-83; child abuse therapist Thee Door, Orlando, 1983-84; presenter in field. Author: The Therapeutic Superhighway, 1995. Counselor Winter Park Towers Nursing Home, 1985; vol. group counselor Hillcrest Halfway House, Orlando, 1985. 1st Lt. U.S. Army, 1976-80. Recipient Marion medal Cath. Ch., Boston, 1966, Civic award Spouse Abuse, Inc., Orlando, 1984. Mem. Am. Assn. for Counseling and Devel., Kappa Delta Phi, Pi Lambda Theta, Chi Sigma Iota. Roman Catholic. Home: 1781 Lake Berry Dr Winter Park FL 32789-5911

DOUGLAS, KENNETH DALE, artist; b. Fulton, Mo., Mar. 29, 1943; s. G. Louis and Lois Dean (Self) D.; m. Ruby Mae Bushnell, May 30, 1971; children: Kimberly Marie, Joanna Leigh. BA, U. Mo., 1971, MA, 1973. Artist, engraver Silver Products, Memphis, Tenn., 1974-75; freelance artist, engraver Olive Branch, Miss., 1975—. Mem. Am. Medallic Sculpture Assn., Fedn. Internat. Médaille. Home: 8940 Deer Creek Ln Olive Branch MS 38654-5985

DOUGLAS, MICHELE THERESA, communications executive; b. Forest Hills, N.Y., Nov. 25, 1955; d. Frederick Rochlitz Claus and Jean Michele (Deutsch) Smith; m. Scott Allan Douglas, June 18, 1988; 1 child, Andrea Jean. B, Bellarmine Univ., 1994. Language specialist U.S. Army Security Agy., Seoul, Korea, 1974-78; computer mktg. Software Source, Lousiville, Ky., 1983-85; paralegal Conlifte, Sandmann, Gorman, Sullivan, Louisville, Ky., 1985-89; communication specialist Brown-Forman Corp., Louisville, Ky., 1990-94. Author, editor: Trip to Italy, 1995. Mem. Internat. Assn. Bus. Communicators, Bus. Profl. Woman, Soc. Profl. Journalists. Episcopalian. Home and Office: Brown Forman Corp 850 Dixie Hwy Louisville KY 40210-1038

DOUGLAS, ROBERT ROY, journalist educator; b. Kensett, Ark., Oct. 4, 1924; s. Roy Elmer and Marie Foster D.; m. Mary Young, Aug. 1950 (div.); children: Angela, Sharon; m. Martha Leslie, Apr. 17, 1954; children: Bruce, Alan, Leslie. BA, U. Ark., 1948. Reporter Ark. Gazette, Little Rock, 1948-50; news editor Kark Radio, Little Rock, 1950, Asheville (N.C.) Citizen, 1950-52; copy editor, telegraph editor, news editor, mng. editor Ark. Gazette, Little Rock, 1952-81; journalism prof., dept. chmn. U. Ark., Fayetteville, 1981-91; columnist N.W. Ark. Times, Fayetteville, 1993—. Recipient Freedom of Info. award Soc. Profl. Journalists, 1974, Pres.'s award Ark. Broadcasters Assn., 1990, Journalism Edn. award Ark. Press Assn., 1991, Disting. Svc. award Golden 50 Newspaper Sc. award, 1994. Home: 1224 Hillcrest Ave Fayetteville AR 72703-1922

DOUGLAS, WILLIAM ERNEST, retired government official; b. Charleston, S.C., Nov. 26, 1930; s. William Ernest and Helen A. (Fortune) D.; m. Nancy Anne Gibson, July 18, 1980. A.B., The Citadel, 1956; postgrad., U. S.C., 1956-59. Asst. dist. dir. Jackson dist. IRS, Miss., 1972-73, Atlanta dist. IRS, 1973-74; asst. regional commr. S.E. region IRS, Atlanta, 1974-78, dir. Regional Service Ctr., 1978-80; commr. Fin. Mgmt. Svc. U.S. Treasury Dept., Washington, 1980-91. Served with U.S. Army, 1948-52. Home: 205 Settlers Rd Saint Simons GA 31522

DOUGLASS, FRANK RUSSELL, lawyer; b. Dallas, May 29, 1933; s. Claire Allen and Caroline (Score) D.; m. Carita Calkins, Feb. 5, 1955 (div. 1983); children: Russell, Tom, Andrew, Cathy; m. Betty Elwanda Richards, Dec. 31, 1983. BBA, Southwestern U., 1953; LLB, U. Tex., 1958. Bar: Tex. 1957, U.S. Dist. Ct. (we. dist.) Tex. 1960, U.S. Dist. Ct. (so. dist.) Tex. 1981, U.S. Dist. Ct. (no. dist.) Tex. 1985, U.S. Dist. Ct. (ea. dist.) Tex. 1987, U.S. Supreme Ct. 1964, U.S. Ct. Appeals (5th cir.) 1985; cert. in civil trial law, and oil, gas and mineral law. Various positions to ptnr. McGinnis, Lochridge & Kilgore, Austin, Tex., 1957-76; sr. ptnr. Scott, Douglass, Luton & McConnico, Austin, 1976—; bd. dirs. Mallon Resources, Denver, Rio Petroleum Co., Amarillo, Tex; trustee Southwestern U., Georgetown, Tex. Contbr. articles to profl. jours. City atty., Westlake Hills, Tex., 1968. Served as airman USAF, 1953-55. Fellow Am. Coll. Trial Lawyers; mem. ABA (natural resources law sect., coun. 1987-90, litig. sect.), Am. Inns of Ct., State Bar of Tex., Tex. Bar Found., The Tex. Ctr. for Legal Ethics and Professionalism (founding), Dallas Bar Assn., The Littlefield Soc. U. Tex. (charter). Home: 10424 Woodford Dr Dallas TX 75229-6317 Office: Scott Douglass et al PO Box 803541 Dallas TX 75380-3541

DOUGLASS, GUS RUBEN, state agency administrator; b. Leon, W.Va., Feb. 22, 1927; s. Gus Rodney and Fannie Elizabeth (Grimm) D.; m. Anna Lee Roush, Oct. 23, 1947; children: Steve, Thomas, Mary Lee, Cynthia. BA, W.Va. U., 1985. Asst. commr. agr. W.Va. Dept. Agr., 1957, commr. agr., 1964-88, 92—; bd. dirs. Citizens Nat. Bank, Bank One Point Pleasant; trustee Pleasant Valley Hosp.; trustee, adminstr. W. Va. Rural Rehab. Loan

Fund; chmn. so. regional com. Food and Agr. under Pres. Jimmy Carter; pres. So. U.S. Trade Assn.; mem. adv. com. fgn. animal and poultry diseases U.S. Sec.; mem., past chmn. W.Va. Rural Devel. Coun.; chmn. State Soil Conservation Com.; past chmn. W.Va. Air Pollution Control Commn., State Forestry Commn.; mem. W.Va. Housing Devel. Fund; co-operator 400 acre beef and grain farm. Gubernatorial candidate W.Va., 1988; bd. dirs. State Farm Mus., State Fair W.Va.; mem. Leon Bapt. Ch. Recipient Disting. Svc. award Gamma Sigma Delta, Man of Yr. award Progressive Farmer Mag.; named to Agriculture and Forestry Hall of Fame, 1990. Mem. Future Farmers Am. (state and nat. pres.), Nat. Future Farmers Am. Alumni Assn. (past pres.), Nat. Assn. State Depts. Agriculture (past. pres.), So. Assn. State Depts. Agriculture (past pres.), Farm Bureau (county pres.), Poultry Assn., Livestock Assn., Masons, Shriners. Democrat. Office: WVa Dept Agriculture Rm 28 State Capitol Charleston WV 25305

DOUGLASS, HARRY ROBERT, architect, health care consultant, educator; b. McCook, Nebr., Mar. 27, 1937; s. Harry William and Irma Ruth Douglass; 1 child from previous marriage, William Robert; m. Darlene Thompson. BArch, U. Nebr., 1963; MArch in Hosp. Planning, U. Minn., 1966; grad. owner/pres./mgmt. program, Harvard U. Bus. Sch., 1983; M in Design Studies, Harvard Grad. Sch. Design, 1992; D of Design, Harvard U., 1994. Assoc., design leader Leo A. Daly Co., Omaha, 1964-68; v.p. health facilities div. Caudill Rowlett Scott, Houston, 1968-71; v.p., dir. architecture CE Maguire Inc., Boston, 1971-73; chmn., CEO Robert Douglass Assocs. Inc., Hosp. Cons., Houston, 1973-88; ptnr. Deloitte & Touche, Houston, 1988-91; ptnr.-in-charge Douglass Group of Deloitte & Touche, Houston, 1988-91; pvt. practice Cambridge, Mass., 1991-94, Houston, 1994-95; tchg. fellow Harvard U., Cambridge, 1992-94; architect Watkins Carter Hamilton, Houston, 1995—; assoc. prof., dir. grad. program Rice U. Sch. Architecture, Houston, 1973-76, U. Tex. Sch. Pub. Health, Houston, 1973-76; mem. practice curriculum com. Harvard Grad. Sch. design, 1993-95. Author, editor: Managing the Health Facility Devel. Process, 1988, Assn. U. Programs in Healthcare Adminstrn., Aspen Manual for Health Svcs. Mgmt., Facilities Planning and Constrn., 1992; editor Jour. of Acad. of Arch. for Health, 1996—; guest editor med. facilities issue Progressive Arch. mag., 1992, guest editor hosps. issue, 1971; mem. edit. bd. Jour. Health Adminstrn. Edn., 1980-91, CITE mag., 1990; contbr. articles to profl. jours. Mem. adv. bd. Health Environments Inst., U. Houston Coll. Architecture, 1988—; chmn. profl. adv. coun. U. Nebr. Coll. Architecture, 1987-88, contbr. Douglass Chair in Architecture, 1991—; established the Douglass Scholarship in Health Care Adminstrn., U. Minn., 1983—. Recipient Presdl. Silver medal for Charles River Project, Boston, 1984; AIA-Am. Hosp. Assn. fellow 1964-66. Fellow AIA (nat. com. on architecture for health, chmn. fellowship com. 1991); mem. Am. Assn. Hosp. Planning (bd. dirs. 1975-80), Am. Coll. Healthcare Execs., Soc. Hosp. Planners. Episcopalian.

DOUGLASS, JAMES, academic administrator. Pres. Tex. So. U., Houston. Office: Tex So U 3100 Cleburne St Houston TX 77004

DOUGLASS, JAMES FREDERICK, business administration educator; b. Detroit, Sept. 17, 1934; s. Samuel Henry and Edith Rachel (Day) D.; m. Dorrine Marie Harma; children: James Lloyd, Marie Rachel. BA in Social Scis., Mich. State U., 1957; MBA, U. Ala., 1973; advanced cert., Coll. William and Mary, 1977, postgrad. in higher edn. Enlisted man U.S. Army, 1957-59; new bus. rep. Consumer's Power Co., Jackson, Mich., 1959-63; commd. 2d lt. USAF, 1963, advanced through grades to lt. col., 1967; sr. Air Force advisor 6146th Adv. Group, Camp Humphrys, Republic of Korea, 1969-70; assigned to Hdqrs. Tactical Communications Div., Langley AFB, Va., 1971-75; ret. USAFR, 1991; adminstr. Fla. Inst. Tech., Melbourne, 1975-79; assoc. prof. grad. bus. adminstrn., acad. advisor Embry Riddle Aero U., Langley AFB, 1979—; edn. specialist Dept. Army, Ft. Eustis, Va., 1979-88. Chpt. pres. Protestant Men of Chapel, Fed. Repulic Germany and Japan, 1958-65; deacon Presbyn. Ch., Detroit, 1961-63. Mem. ASTD (editor Southeastern Va. chpt. jour. 1983-84), Armed Forces Communications and Electronics Assn., Ret. Officers Assn. (pres. Ft. Eustis chpt. 1980). Democrat. Home: 22 Bayview Dr Poquoson VA 23662-1034 Office: Embry-Riddle Aero U PO Box 816 Hampton VA 23665-0816

DOUGLASS, KENNETH HARMON, physicist; b. Rochester, N.Y., Oct. 27, 1942; s. Pritchard C. and Elizabeth Harmon D.; m. Nancy Ann Hess, July 24, 1965; 1 child, Melanie Joy. BS, U. Rochester, 1964; MS, Carnegie-Mellon U., 1966, PhD, 1970. Diplomate Am. Bd. Sci. in Nuclear Medicine, Am. Bd. Radiology. Asst. prof. Pa. State U., Schuylkill Haven, 1969-71; rsch. fellow Case Western Res. U., Cleve., summers 1970-71; postdoctoral fellow dept. biophysics Johns Hopkins U., Balt., 1971-74, instr. Sch. of Medicine, 1974-84, asst. prof., 1984-88; assoc. prof. Sch. of Medicine W.Va. U., Morgantown, 1988-96, dir. radiation safety, adj. prof. radiology, 1996—. Contbr. articles to profl. jours.; author abstracts in field. Mem. Soc. Nuclear Medicine, Am. Assn. Physicists in Medicine, Am. Coll. Radiology. Office: W Va Univ Sch Medicine Dept Radiology Morgantown WV 26506-9235

DOUGLASS, LEE, state insurance commissioner; m. Mauri Thomas; children: Keri, Jay. BA in Polit. Sci./Criminal Justice, U. Ark., JD. Bar: Ark., U.S. Dist. Ct. Ark., U.S. Ct. Appeals (8th cir.). Dep. prosecuting atty. Pulaski County (Ark.) 6th Jud. Dist., 1980-88; asst. commr./chief counsel Ark. Ins. Dept., 1988-89, dep. ins. commr., 1989-90, ins. commr., 1990—. Mem. Nat. Assn. Ins. Commrs. (v.p. 1994, pres. 1995). •

DOUGLASS, WILFORD DAVID, corporate executive; b. Titusville, Pa., July 3, 1927; s. Wilfred Earl Douglass and Madelon Creecraft (Bly) Arthur; m. Audrey Lois Smith, Dec. 28, 1950 (dec. 1973); children: Diane Noel Delio, Patricia Ann Swalm, Erin Marie Douglass Fish; m. Nitaya Tsumjamroon, Sept. 19, 1989. BA, Tulane U., 1958. Enlisted USMC, 1945, commd., 1951, advanced through grades to colonel/chief of staff, 1971, retired, 1975; real estate salesman Evans Realty Inc., Willingboro, N.J., 1975-76; mng. dir. Aeromaritime Internat. Mgmt. Services Ltd., Lagos, Nigeria, 1976-78; v.p. Aeromaritime Internat. Corp. and Aeromaritime Internat. Mgmt. Services Ltd., Washington, 1978-80; pres., chief exec. officer Aeromaritime Investment Co., Fairfax, Va., 1980-92, Acre Ltd., Mass, Inc., Fairfax, 1982-92; dir. Aeromaritime Consolidated Real Estate, Woodbridge, Va., 1993—; bd. dirs. Marinvest Transport Svcs. Ltd., Rio de Janeiro, Environ. Products Corp., Fairfax, Belgian Overseas Shipping, Antwerp, Belgium; pres. Aeromaritime (Brazil) Ltd., Rio de Janeiro, 1985-91; vice chmn. bd. Dicon Salt PLC, Lagos.; dir. AIMS, Channel Islands; chmn. Cross Group Holdings, AIMS, Liberia, Aeromaritime Investment Co. Decorated Legion of Merit with combat V, Meritorious Service medal, Navy Commendation medal; made African Chief of Otun Olorogun by King of Lagos, 1991. Mem. Lagos Caledonian Soc., Lagos Assn. Titled Chieftains. Republican. Clubs: Beachland Boat Lagos. Lodges: Masons, Tyrian. Home: Beachland Estates, 1 Clinic Close Kiri Kiri Wharf, Apapa Lagos PMB 1193, Nigeria Office: Aeromaritime Consolidated Real Estate 1515 Davis Ford Rd Ste 3 Woodbridge VA 22192-2740

DOUGLAS WANZA, ISABEL, foundation administrator; b. Denison, Tex.; d. Eldorado Anderson and Minnie Mae D. BBA in Acctg. cum laude, Prairie View (Tex.) A&M Univ., 1982. Found. adminstr. United Way Texas Gulf, Houston, Tex. Office: United Way Tex Gulf 2200 N Loop W Houston TX 77018

DOUIDAR, SAMIR MOHAMAD, pediatrics educator; b. Tanta, Egypt, Dec. 29, 1948; came to U.S., 1980; s. Mohamad Ahmad and Zenab Ahmad Douidar; m. Abla Mahmoud Zayed, Nov. 22, 1993; children: Yasmine, Shaddy. MB ChB, Tanta (Egypt) Coll. Medicine, 1973, MS in Pediatrics, 1977; PhD, U. Tex., 1985. Diplomate Am. Bd. Pediat.; lic. physician, Va., Tex., Fla., Egypt. Mandatory rotating intern Tanta U. Hosps., 1974-75; resident dept. pediatrics Tanta Coll. Medicine, 1975-78, asst. instr. dept. pediatrics, 1978-80; postdoctoral fellow U. Tex. Med.Br., Galveston, 1980-82, resident dept. pediatrics, 1985-87, fellow divsn. clin. pharmacology & toxicology, 1988-89; asst. prof. dept. pediatrics and dept. pharmacology Tex. Tech. U. Health Scis. Ctr., Amarillo, 1990-94, asst. prof. dept. internal medicine, 1992-94, dir. pediatric residency program, 1993-94, dir. divsn. clin. pharmacology and toxicology, 1993-94; dir. pediat. emergency care ctr. Univ. Cmty. Hosp., Tampa, 1994—; cons. poisoning and overdose cases Tex. Tech. U. Health Scis. Ctr., Amarillo, 1990-94; mem. staff N.W. Tex. Hosp., Amarillo, High Plains Bapt. Hosp., Amarillo. Contbr. articles to profl. jours. Recipient Physicians' Recognition award AMA, 1985, 88, 92, 95, Outstanding Teaching award Pediatric Residents, Amarillo, 1992; grantee AID, 1982, Tex. Tech U. Health Scis. Ctr., 1992, Proctor and Gamble-Richardson-Vicks Inc., 1992, Alcon Labs., Inc., 1993. Mem. Am. Soc. Clin. Pharmacology and Therapeutics, Am. Acad. Pediatrics, So. Soc. Pediatric Rsch., Tex. Med. Assn., Tex. Pediatric Soc. (Essay Contest award 1996), Potter Randall County Med. Soc. Office: Pediatric Emergency Care Ctr U Community Hosp 3100 E Fletcher Ave Tampa FL 33613-4613

DOUMAR, ROBERT GEORGE, judge; b. 1930; m. Dorothy Ann Mundy; children: Robert G., Charles C. BA, U. Va., 1951, LLB, 1953, LLM, 1988. Assoc. firm Venable, Parsons, Kyle & Hylton, 1955-58; sr. ptnr. Doumar, Pincus, Knight & Harlan, 1958-81; U.S. dist. judge Eastern Va., Norfolk, 1981—. Office: US Dist Ct 183 US Courthouse 600 Granby St Norfolk VA 23510-1915

DOUMLELE, RUTH HAILEY, communications company executive, broadcast accounting consultant; b. Charlotte County, Va., Nov. 6, 1925; d. Clarrie Robert Hailey and Virginia Susan (Slaughter) Ferguson; m. John Antony Doumlele, May 8, 1943; children: John Antony, Suzanne Denise Doumlele Owen. Cert. in commerce, U. Richmond, 1968; BA, Mary Baldwin Coll., 1982. Sta. acct. WLEE-Radio, Richmond, Va., 1965-67, bus. mgr., 1967-73; area bus. mgr. Nationwide Communications Inc., Richmond, 1973-75; corp. bus. mgr., Neighborhood Communications Corp., Inc., Richmond, 1978-86, asst. v.p., 1981-86; owner Broadcast Acctg. Cons., Midlothian, Va., 1986-95; treas., dir. Guests of Honor, Ltd., Richmond, 1984-89; sec., Inner Light, Inc., 1984-96. Contbr. articles to profl. jours.; mem. editorial rev. bd. The Woman C.P.A., 1980—. Mem. Am. Soc. Women Accts. (chpt. pres. 1974-76, contbg. editor The Coord. 1990, Chgo., Woman of Achievement award 1991), Broadcast Fin. Mgmt. Assn., Nat. League Am. Pen Women (br. pres. 1984-86), Am. Fedn. Astrologers, Va. Assn. Amateur Athletic Union (records chmn. 1959-62), Women's Club of Powhatan, Selective Svc. System Local Bd., Powhatan Hist. Soc. Episcopalian. Avocations: salt water fishing, Civil War history, travel, astrology. Home and Office: 2510 Chastain Ln Midlothian VA 23113-9400

DOUTHITT, SHIRLEY ANN, insurance agent; b. Mexia, Tex., Feb. 21, 1947; d. Othello Young and Hazel Lorene (Corley) Thompson; m. A. Dwane Douthitt, Nov. 24, 1966; 1 child, Steven Dwane. Student, Leonard's Tng Sch., Houston, 1979; student Tex. local recording agts. licensing course, Austin, Tex., 1980; student farmers ins. group tng. program, Austin, 1980; student life underwriters trng course, Tyler, Tex., 1987. Lic. ins. agt. Sec. Lindsey & Newsom Ins. Adjusters, Palestine, Tex., 1965-73, J. Herrington Ins. Agy., Palestine, 1973-76, Ramsey Ins. Agy., Palestine, 1976-79; agt. Farmers Ins. Group, Palestine, 1979—. Recipient Bus. Woman of Yr. Palestine Profl. Bus. Women, 1983. Mem. NAFE, Women's Club. Office: Shirley Douthitt Ins Agy 101 7th St PO Box 7000 Palestine TX 75802

DOVE, LORRAINE FAYE, gerontology nurse; b. West Reading, Pa., Feb. 20, 1960; d. Blaine Hoye Sr. and Faye Louise (Heisey) D. Diploma, Reading Hosp. Sch. of Nursing, 1982. RN, Fla., Pa., Ga.; cert. gerontol. nurse. Asst. dir. nursing Leader Nursing and Rehab. Ctr., Lebanon, Pa., 1983-84; dir. nursing Sunrise Manor, Ft. Pierce, Fla., 1986-88, Vero Beach (Fla.) Care Ctr., 1988-92, Okeechobee (Fla.) Health Care Facility, 1992-94; regional nurse cons. Patient Care Pharmacy, Pompano Beach, Fla., 1994-95; CQI/RA coord. Colonial Palms East, Pompano Beach, 1995; DON, Atlantis, Lantana, Fla., 1995—; past mem. FHCA AIDS task force, Health and Human Svcs. Bd., Aging and Adult Com., AIDS Consortium of the Treasure Coast. Mem. Nat. Assn. Dirs. Nursing Adminstrn., Fla. Assn. Dirs. Nursing Adminstrn., Intravenous Nurses Soc.

DOVE, RITA FRANCES, poet, English language educator; b. Akron, Ohio, Aug. 28, 1952; d. Ray A. and Elvira E. (Hord) D.; m. Fred Viebahn, Mar. 23, 1979; 1 child, Aviva Chantal Tamu Dove-Viebahn. BA summa cum laude, Miami U., Oxford, Ohio, 1973; postgrad., Universität Tübingen, Fed. Republic Germany, 1974-75; MFA, U. Iowa, 1977; LLD (hon.), Miami U., Oxford, Ohio, 1988, Knox Coll., 1989, Tuskegee U., 1994, U. Miami, Fla., 1994, Washington U., St. Louis, 1994, Case Western Res. U., 1994, U. Akron, 1994, Ariz. State U., 1995, Boston Coll., 1995, Dartmouth Coll., 1995, Spelman Coll., 1996, U. Pa., 1996. Asst. prof. English Ariz. State U., Tempe, 1981-84, assoc. prof., 1984-87, prof., 1987-89; prof. U. Va., Charlottesville, 1989-93, Commonwealth prof. English, 1993—; U.S. poet laureate/cons. in poetry Libr. of Congress, Washington, 1993-95; writer-in-residence Tuskegee (Ala.) Inst., 1982; lit. panelist Nat. Endowment for Arts, Washington, 1984-86, chmn. poetry grants panel, 1985; judge Walt Whitman award Acad. Am. Poets, 1990, Pulitzer prize in poetry, 1991, Ruth Lilly prize 1991, Nat. Book award in poetry 1991, Anisfield-Wolf Book awards, 1992—. Author: (poetry) Ten Poems, 1977, The Only Dark Spot in the Sky, 1980, The Yellow House on the Corner, 1980, Mandolin, 1982, Museum, 1983, Thomas and the Beulah, 1986 (Pulitzer Prize in poetry 1987), The Other Side of the House, 1988, Grace Notes, 1989 (Ohioana award 1990), Selected Poems, 1993 (Ohioana award 1994), Lady Freedom Among Us, 1994, Mother Love, 1995; (verse drama) The Darker Face of the Earth, 1994; (novel) Through the Ivory Gate, 1992 (Va. Coll. Stores Book award 1993); (short stories) Fifth Sunday, 1985 (Callaloo award 1986); (essays) The Poet's World, 1995; mem. editorial bd. Nat. Forum, 1984—, Iris, 1989—; mem. adv. bd. Ploughshares, 1992—, N.C. Writers Network, 1992—, Civilization, 1994—; assoc. editor Callaloo, 1986—; adv. and contbg. editor Gettysburg Rev., 1987—, TriQuarterly, 1988—, Ga. Review, 1994—. Commr. The Schomburg Ctr. for Rsch. in Black Culture, N.Y. Pub. Libr., 1987—; mem. Renaissance Forum Folger Shakespeare Libr., 1993—, Coun. of Scholars Libr. of Congress, 1994—; mem. nat. launch com. AmeriCorps, 1994; mem. awards coun. Am. Acad. Achievement, 1994—. Presdl. scholar, 1970, Nat. Achievement scholar, 1970-73; Fulbright/Hays fellow, 1974-75, rsch. fellow U. Iowa, 1975, teaching/writing fellow U. Iowa, 1976-77, Guggenheim Found. fellow, 1983-84, Mellon sr. fellow Nat. Humanities Ctr., 1988-89, fellow Ctr. for Advanced Studies, U. Va., 1989-92; grantee NEA, 1978, 89; recipient Lavan Younger Poet award Acad. Am. Poets, 1986, GE Found. award, 1987, Bellagio (Italy) residency Rockefeller Found., 1988, Ohio Gov.'s award 1988, Literary Lion citation N.Y. Pub. Libr., 1991, Women of Yr. award Glamour Mag., 1993, NAACP Great Am. Artist award, 1993, Golden Plate award Am. Acad. Achievement, 1994, Disting. Achievement medal Miami U. Alumni Assn., 1994, Renaissance Forum award for leadership in the literary arts Folger Shakespeare Libr., 1994, Carl Sandburg award Internat. Platform Assn., 1994; inducted Ohio Women's Hall of Fame, 1991; named Phi Beta Kappa poet Harvard U., 1993. Mem. PEN, Poetry Soc. Am., Associated Writing Programs (bd. dirs. 1985-88, pres. 1986-87), Am. Acad. Achievement (mem. golden plate awards coun. 1994—), Phi Beta Kappa (senator 1994—), Phi Kappa Phi. Office: U Va Dept English Wilson Hall Charlottesville VA 22903

DOWBEN, CARLA LURIE, lawyer, educator; b. Chgo., Jan. 22, 1932; d. Harold H. and Gertrude (Geitner) Lurie; m. Robert Dowben, June 20, 1950; children: Peter Arnold, Jonathan Stuart, Susan Laurie. AB, U. Chgo., 1950; JD, Temple U., 1955; cert., Brandeis U., 1968. Bar: Ill. 1957, Mass. 1963, Tex. 1974, U.S. Supreme Ct., 1974. Assoc. Conrad and Verges, Chgo., 1957-62; exec. officer MIT, Cambridge, Mass., 1963-64; legal planner, Mass. Health Planning Project, Boston, 1964-69; assoc. prof. Life Scis. Inst., Brown U., Providence, 1970-72; asst. prof. health law U. Tex. Health Sci. Ctr., Dallas, 1973-78, assoc. prof., 1978-93; ptnr. Choate & Lilly, Dallas, 1989-92; head health law section Looper, Reed, Mark and McGraw, 1992-95; of counsel, 1995—; adj. assoc. prof. health law U. Tex., 1993-95; cons. to bd. dirs. Mental Health Assn., 1958-86, Ft. Worth Assn. Retarded Citizens, 1980-90, Advocacy, Inc., 1981-85; dir. Nova Health Systems, 1975—, Tockwotton Home, 1994—. Contbr. articles to profl. jours.; active in drafting health and mental health legis., agy. regulations in several states and local govts. Mem. vis. com. sch. law Te mple U., 1992—. Mem. ABA, Tex. Bar Assn., Dallas Bar Assn., Nat. Health Lawyers Assn., Hastings Inst. Ethics, Tex. Family Planning Assn. Soc. of Friends. Office: Looper Reed Mark & McGraw 1601 Elm St 4100 Thanksgiving Tower Dallas TX 75201

DOWD, BRIAN JOHN, healthcare executive; b. Hartford, Conn., Dec. 9, 1948; s. John Hugh and Mary Ann Dowd; m. Nora Alice Walker, June 9, 1973; 1 child, Trevor Walker. AB in English, Georgetown U., 1970; DDS, Emory U., 1974. V.p., Chief Info. Officer Dentfirst, P.C., Norcross, Ga., 1982—; v.p. Avcor, Inc., Norcross, 1989—, Dentcore, Inc., Norcross, 1992—; software cons., 1990—. Adult leader Boy Scouts Am., Duluth, Ga., 1993. Lt. USN, 1974-76. Fellow Acad. Gen. Dentistry; mem. Emory Alumni Assn. (class rep. 1979-89, chmn. staff, parish com. 1987-88). Methodist.

DOWD, JACK HENRY, sculptor; b. N.Y.C., Mar. 23, 1938; s. Charles A. and Elizabeth R. (Homier) D.; m. Jill, May 19, 1962; children: Jayne, Jonathan, Jacquelyn, Joshua. BFA, Adelphi Coll., 1963. exhbns. reviewed, work featured in various newspapers, mags., TV programs; artwork featured in (movie) Aspen Extreme, and (TV program) B. L. Stryker. One-man shows include Fall Intellectual & Cultural Events, Adelphi U., Garden City, N.Y., 1990, One World Gallery, Las Vegas, 1995, Elaine Horwitch Gallery, Santa Fe, 1990, North Gallery, Sarasota, Fla., 1991, Loretta Goodwin Gallery, Birmingham, Ala., 1995, Ziegenfuss Gallery, Sarasota, 1995, Lee County Alliance for the Arts, Ft. Myers, Fla., 1993; exhibited in group shows at Boca Raton (Fla.) Mus. Art, 1992, Montgomery (Ala.) Mus. Fine Art, 1992, Brevard Art Ctr. & Mus., Melbourne, Paradise Gallery, Boca Grand, Fla., 1996. Chmn. Sarasota County Art in Pub. Spaces, 1991-92. Recipient 1st Place Sculpture award Coconut Grove Arts Festival, Miami, 1990-91, Best of Show award Artstravaganza, Chattanooga, 1991, 2d Place award Clara Kott Von Storch Gallery, Dexter, Mich., 1992, Helen Gapen Oehler award Allied Artists Show, N.Y.C., 1993; named Artist of the Yr., Sarasota Art Assn., 1992. Office: Jack Dowd Studios 1269 1st St Ste 7 Sarasota FL 34236-5518

DOWD, WILLIAM TIMOTHY, lawyer, energy association executive; b. Muskogee, Okla., May 3, 1927; s. Timothy J. and Nelle (McCune) D.; m. Charlotte H. Engelkamp, Dec. 1, 1951; children: Timothy C., Terence R., Nancy C. Perry, Kathryn H. Lund; m. Maria Revelis, June 4, 1966; children: William J., Ellen M. AB, Xavier U., 1951; LLB, U. Tulsa, 1957. Bar: Okla. 1957, U.S. Supreme Ct. 1967. Assoc. Landrith & McGee, Tulsa, 1957-63; ptnr. Landrith, McGee & Dowd, Tulsa, 1963-65, McGee & Dowd, Tulsa, 1965-66; pub. defender Tulsa County, 1958; mem. Okla. Ho. of Reps., 1963-64; chief legal officer to Gov. of Okla., 1967-69; exec. dir. Interstate Oil and Gas Compact Commn., Oklahoma City, 1969-93. Mem. Okla. Gov.'s Energy Adv. Council, 1975-79, Nat. Petroleum Council Com. on Enhanced Recovery, 1976-77, Fed. Power Commn. Natural Gas Survey, 1971-72, U.S. Nat. Com. World Energy Conf., 1972-75, Task Force on Underground Injection Control Programs, EPA, 1975-85; mem. adv. com. on minerals accountability Dept. of Interior, 1982-83; mem. royalty mgmt. adv. com. U.S. Dept. Interior, 1986-90; chmn. petroleum tech. adv. com. to People's Republic of China, 1984. Served with U.S. Army, 1945-47. Mem. ABA, Okla. Bar Assn., Fed. Energy Bar Assn., Assn. Petroleum Writers. Republican. Roman Catholic. Club: Oklahoma City Petroleum.

DOWDELL, MICHAEL FRANCIS, critical care and anesthesia nurse practitioner; b. Cleve., June 5, 1949; s. Harry William and Dorothy May (McGivney) D.; 1 child, Michael Patrick. BSN, Ohio State U., 1975; MA in Counseling, Nat. U., San Diego, 1981; MSN, Calif. State U., Long Beach, 1991; diploma in nursing anesthesia, Kaiser Sch. Anesthesia, L.A., 1991; postgrad., Case Western Res. U., 1996—. CCRN, CRNA, ARNP; cert. ACLS instr; cert. community coll. instr., Calif. Enlisted USN, 1968, commd. ensign, 1974, advanced through grades to lt. comdr., 1984, ret., 1988; resident nurse anesthesist Kaiser Sch. Anesthesia for Nurses, 1989-91; staff nurse anesthetist Kaiser Hosp., Panorama City, Calif., 1991-92, HCA Med. Ctr., Largo, Fla., 1992-93, Meml. Mission Hosp., Asheville, N.C., 1993—; vis. lectr. dept. anesthesia Makerere U., Kampala Uganda, 1995. Decorated Navy Achievement medal. Mem. AACN, NRA, Am. Assn. Nurse Anesthetists, Assn. Mil. Surgeons U.S., Ret. Officers Assn., Fleet Res. Assn., Am. Legion, Nat. Muzzle-Loading Rifle Assn., North-South Skirmish Assn. Republican. Home: 2 White Pine Cir Arden NC 28704-9553

DOWDY, CECELIA YOUNG, critical care and medical/surgical nurse; b. Altavista, Va., Sept. 27, 1947; d. Willie Audry and Mary Briley (Coffey) Young; m. Warren Stephens Dowdy, Sept. 28, 1968; children: Warren Stephens II, William Andrew, Samuel Mark. Student, Danville (Va.) Community Coll.; diploma, Meml. Hosp. Sch. Nursing, Danville, 1988. RN, Va.; cert. EMT, ACLS; CCRN. Staff-charge nurse critical care unit Danville Regional Med. Ctr., 1988, 90—; intravenous therapist Meml. Hosp. Danville, 1990. Home: 1719 Buckhorn Dr Danville VA 24540-5119

DOWDY, DOROTHY WILLIAMS, political science educator; b. Limon, Colo., June 11, 1939; d. Thomas Edwin and Rachel Mae (Henry) Williams; m. Thomas William Dowdy, Feb. 28, 1963; children: Jessica, Laura, Thomas. AA, George Washington U., 1958; BA, George Washington U, 1961; MA in Polit. Sci., Tulane U., 1965. Cert. secondary educator in social studies and history, Va. Analyst CIA, Washington, 1961-62; govt. tchr. Fairfax (Va.) County Pub. Schs., 1964-69, 83-96; co-owner, mgr. Buckingham Springs Stables, Fairfax Station, Va., 1973-96; tchr. advanced placement U.S. govt. polit. and comparative politics Chantilly (Va.) H.S., 1987—; coach Nat. Acad. Decathlon, Chantilly, 1989-90, "Its Academci Team", Chantilly, 1985-96; del. Russian-Am. Joint Conf. on Edn., Moscow, 1994; presenter U.S.-Russian Educators Moscow COnf., 1994. Pres. Fairfax Lawyers Wives, 1976; co-founder Fairfax 4-H Therapeutic Riding Program, 1978; pres. Burke (Va.) Elem. Sch. PTA, 1982-84; mem. Fairfax Com. of 100, 1988-90, St. Georges United Meth. Ch., 1984-96. Named Tchr. of Yr., Chantilly High Sch., 1989, Tchr.-Leader, People to People Soviet Union Friendship Caravan, 1989; recipient Disting. Svc. award Fairfax 4-H Ext. Svc., 1988. Mem. Topical Symposia Nat. Def. U. Methodist. Office: Chantilly HS 4201 Stringfellow Rd Chantilly VA 22021-2600

DOWDY, FREDELLA MAE, secondary school educator; b. Granby, Mo., Feb. 2, 1943; d. Arthur Clem and Helen Margaret (Davis) Rinehart; m. David Sherman Dowdy, Aug. 31, 1962; children: Ingrid Cara, Eric Davis. BS in Edn. summa cum laude, Cen. State Coll., Edmond, Okla., 1964; MEd, Cen. State U., Edmond, 1975. Cert. tchr., Okla. Tchr. Hayes County High Sch., Hayes Center, Nebr., 1964-65; sec. Masonic Homes of Okla., Guthrie, 1965-66, 68-73; tchr. Guthrie Pub. Schs., 1966-68, 73—, chmn. dept. bus., 1987-89, 90—, chmn. bus./vocat. dept., 1989-90. Swim instr. aide Logan County Red Cross, Guthrie, 1982-88; accompanist children's choir First So. Bapt. Ch., Guthrie, 1980-83; brownie leader Redlands council Girl Scouts Am., 1977-79. Mem. NEA, Okla. Edn. Assn., Guthrie Asn. Classroom Tchrs. (sec. 1975-76), Cen. State U. Alumni Assn., Okla. Found. for Excellence. Republican. Baptist. Home: 1119 Pin Oak Dr Guthrie OK 73044-2017 Office: Guthrie High Sch 200 Crooks Dr Guthrie OK 73044-3927

DOWELL, EARL HUGH, university dean, aerospace and mechanical engineering educator; b. Macomb, Ill., Nov. 16, 1937; s. Earl S. and Edna Bernice (Dean) D.; m. Lynn M. Cary, July 31, 1981; children: Marla Lorraine, Janice Lynelle, Michael Hugh. B.S., U. Ill., 1959; S.M., Mass. Inst. Tech., 1961, Sc.D., 1964. Rsch. engr. Boeing Co., 1962-63; rsch. asst. MIT, 1963-64, rsch. engr., 1964, asst. prof., 1964-65; asst. prof. aerospace and mech. engring. Princeton U., 1964-68, assoc. prof., 1968-72, prof., 1972-83, assoc. chmn., 1975-77, acting chmn., 1979; dean Sch. Engring. Duke U., Durham, N.C., 1983—; cons. to industry and govt.; mem. sci. adv. bd. USAF; mem. bd. visitors Office of Naval Rsch. Author: Aeroelasticity of Plates and Shells, 1974, A Modern Course in Aeroelasticity, 1978, 3rd edit., 1995, Nonlinear Studies in Aeroelasticity, 1988; assoc. editor: AIAA Jour., 1969-72, Jour. Sound and Vibration, 1988—, Jour. Fluids and Structures, 1987—, Jour. Nonlinear Dynamics, 1990—; contbr. articles to profl. jours. Chmn. N.J. Noise Control Council, 1972-76. Named outstanding young alumnus U. Ill. Sch. Aero. and Astronautical Engring., 1973, disting. alumnus, 1975; recipient Alumni Honor award Coll. Engring. U. Ill. Fellow AIAA (Structures, Structural Dynamics and Material award 1980, v.p. publs. 1981-83), ASME, Am. Acad. Mechs. (pres. 1991, Disting. Svc. award 1994); mem. NAE, Acoustical Soc. Am., Am. Helicopter Soc. Home: 2207 Chase St Durham NC 27707-2228 Office: Duke U Sch Engring Durham NC 27706

DOWELL, RICHARD PATRICK, computer company executive; b. Washington, Apr. 21, 1934; s. Cassius McClellan and Mary Barbara (McHenry) D.; m. Eleanor Craddock Halley, Dec. 23, 1957 (div. Sept. 1973); children: Richard Patrick Jr., Robert Paul, Christopher Lee; m. Sandra Susan Humm, June 16, 1974; children: Ethan Leslie Smith, Allison Courtney Smith. BS, U.S. Mil. Acad., 1956; MA, Stanford U., 1961, postgrad., 1962; postgrad., The Am. U., 1971-80; grad., The Nat. War Coll., 1975. Commd. 2d lt.

USAF, 1956, advanced through grades to lt. col., 1974, ret., 1976; mgr. The BDM Corp., Fairfax, Va., 1977-79; sr. analyst Anser, Inc. (formerly, Analytic Svcs., Inc.), Arlington, Va., 1979-81, div. mgr., 1981-84, v.p., 1984-91; cons. Anser, Inc. (formerly, Analytic Svcs., Inc.), 1991; sr. staff MITRE Corp., Arlington, 1991-92; program dir. The Oakland Corp., Silver Spring, Md., 1992-93; pres., CEO Software Valley Corp., Morgantown, W.Va., 1993—; chmn. Software Valley Found. Contr. articles to profl. jours. Pres. Alexandria (Va.) Taxpayer's Alliance, 1983. Decorated Bronze star, Air medal with 13 oak leaf clusters, D.F.C. with one oak leaf cluster. Mem. Nat. War Coll. Alumni Assn., Navy League, Air Force Assn. Republican. Episcopalian. Home: 41 Hasell St Charleston SC 29401-1604

DOWIE, WILLIAM JOHN, JR., English language educator; b. New Orleans, Nov. 21, 1940; s. William John and Ruth Alice (Kent) D.; m. Alba Dolores Taylor, Jan. 9, 1994. BA in English/Classics, Spring Hill Coll., 1964, MA in Philosophy, 1965; PhD in English, Brandeis U., 1970; MDiv in Theology, Weston Coll., 1973. Lectr. Loyola U., New Orleans, 1973-74; asst. prof. Southeastern La. U., Hammond, 1974, assoc. prof., 1980, prof., 1987—, dir. English grad. program, 1989—. Author: (book) Peter Matthiessen, 1991; contbr. articles/essays to profl. jours. and publs. Woodrow Wilson fellow, 1965-66. Mem. MLA, Nat. Assn. Tchrs. of English, Phi Beta Kappa. Office: Southeastern La Univ PO Box 700 Hammond LA 70402

DOWNER, RICHARD FENTON, insurance agency executive; b. Washington, Apr. 26, 1940; s. Reuben Fenton and Alice Jane Elize (Scheibel) D.; m. Linda L. Downer; children: Douglas G., Debra W. Downer Vigotsky, Doreen A. Meadows. BS in Commerce, U. Va., 1962. Cert. ins. counselor. Restaurant mgr. Marriott Corp., Washington, 1962-65; field underwriter N.Y. Life Ins. Co., Arlington, Va., 1965-67; ins. agt., owner, pres. HRI Assocs./Herndon Reston Ins., Herndon, Va., 1967—. Bd. dirs., treas. The Elden St. Players, 1994—. Recipient outstanding citizen award Greater Herndon Jaycees, 1982, citizen of yr. award, 1984, 95, Outstanding Alumni award 1996; named among most influential people in Herndon, The Reston Times Newspaper, 1984, The Connection Newspaper, 1987. Mem. Soc. Cert. Ins. Counselors, Ind. Ins. Agts. of Am., Ind. Ins. Agts. Va., Profl. Ins. Agts. Va. and D.C., Herndon C. of C. (bd. dirs. 1980-83), Rotary (bd. dirs. 1986-89). Republican. Methodist. Home: 1049 Nicklaus Ct Herndon VA 20170-3449 Office: HRI Assocs 505 Huntmar Park Dr #220 Herndon VA 20170-5138

DOWNEY, DOROTHY JEAN, health and physical education educator; b. Riverton, Wyo., Apr. 22, 1933; d. William Kenneth Downey and Marguerite Harriott (Chapin) Manning. BA, Bellarmine-Ursuline, Louisville, 1963; MA, Western Ky. U., 1973; PhD, Ohio State U., 1981. Cert. health edn. specialist. Elem. tchr. Ursuline Soc. and Acad. Edn., Louisville, 1954-64; jr. high sch. tchr. Palm Desert (Calif.) Unified Sch. Dist., 1968-70; teaching asst. We. Ky. U., Bowling Green, 1972-73; dept. head health and theology Angela Merici High Sch., Louisville, 1975-78; high sch. tchr. Ursuline Soc. and Acad. Edn., Louisville, 1964-68, 70-78; teaching assoc. Ohio State U., Columbus, 1978-81; asst. prof. U. Tenn., Knoxville, 1981-82, West Tex. A&M U., Canyon, 1982-94; ret., 1994; with Hrycyk Fin., Amarillo, Tex., 1994—; health edn. coord. Dept. Health, Phys. Edn., Canyon, 1982—; del. People's Republic of China Am. Sch. Health Assn., Kent, Ohio, 1987. Juror Potter County, Amarillo, Tex., 1984—; vol. ARC, Amarillo, 1972—. Recipient PACE award Am. Cancer Soc., Tex., 1984. Mem. AAHPER (award 1988), NEA, Am. Sch. Health Assn., Tex. Faculty Assn., Tex. Edn. Assn., Phi Delta Kappa. Democrat. Roman Catholic. Home: 1531 S Alabama St Amarillo TX 79102-2226 Office: Hrycyk Fin Amarillo TX 79100

DOWNING, DIANE VIRGINIA, public health nurse; b. Cin., Dec. 18, 1948; d. Edward Patrick and Virginia Agnes (Heis) D. BSN, U. Va., 1971, MSN, 1981; cert. psychiatric nurse clin. specialist, San Francisco Army Med. Ctr., 1972. RN, Va., N.Y. Commd. lt. Nurse Corps U.S. Army, 1967; lt. col. USAR, 1975; chief nurse 343d Combat Support Hosp., Ft. Hamilton, N.Y., 1992-94; sudden infant death syndrome project coord. Ind. State Bd. Health, Indpls., 1981-85, dir. local health stds., 1985-87, dir. maternal and child health div., 1987-90; asst. commr. nursing and quality assurance N.Y.C. Dept. Health, 1990-92; dir. policy rsch. Pub. Health Found., Washington, 1992-93; nurse mgr. Arlington County Health Svcs. Divsn., Dept. Human Svcs., Arlington, Va., 1993—; tng. officer combat stress control 531st Med. Co., N.Y.C.; tng. officer 531st Med. Co., Balt., 1995—. Vol. Big Sisters-Little Sisters, Indpls., 1982-89. Lt. col. USAR, 1988. Mem. APHA (governing coun. representing pub. health nursing sect. 1992-95, chair elect pub. health nursing sect. 1996), ANA, Pub. Health Assn. N.Y.C., Ind. Pub. Health Assn. (treas. 1987, v.p. 1988, pres. 1989), Nat. Sudden Infant Death Syndrome Found. (chair Greater Indpls. chpt. 1983-85, Outstanding Contbn. award 1986). Office: Arlington County Health Svc Dept Human Svcs 1800 N Edison St Arlington VA 22207-1938

DOWNING, MARGARET MARY, newspaper editor; b. Altoona, Pa., June 3, 1952; d. Irvine William and Iva Ann (Regan) D.; m. Gary Beaver; children: Ian Downing-Beaver, Timothy Downing-Beaver, Abby Downing-Beaver. BA magna cum laude, Tex. Christian U., 1974. Reporting intern Corpus Christi Caller Times, 1973; reporter, bur. chief Beaumont Enterprise & Jour. (Tex.), 1974-76, Dallas Times Herald, 1976-80; from reporter, asst. city editor, asst. bus. and met. editor to mng. editor Houston Post, 1980-93; mng. editor Jackson (Miss.) Clarion-Ledger, 1993—; jurist Pulitzer Prize Awards 1992, 93; bd. dirs. News Media Credit Union, 1993, Santa's Helpers, 1992-93; respite foster parent vol. Harris County Children's Protective Svcs., 1993; chmn. landscape com. Windsor Hills Homeowners Assn.; active PTA Madison Sta. Elem., 1993—. Mem. AP Mng. Editor's Assn. (2d v.p. La./Miss. chpt. 1995-96, 1st v.p. 1996—), YMCA (runners club 1994, activities adv bd. 1994, youth soccer & t-ball coach), Soc. Profl. Journalists, Press Club of Houston (pres. 1984, bd. dirs. 1982-85), Quota Club (bd. mem. 1996—), Leadership Jackson (bd. dirs. 1996-97). Episcopalian. Home: 114 Windsor Hills Dr Madison MS 39110-8563 Office: The Clarion Ledger 311 E Pearl St Jackson MS 39201-3407

DOWNS, HARTLEY H., III, chemist; b. Ridgewood, N.J., Oct. 21, 1949; s. Hartley Harrison and Jennie Mae (Smith) D.; m. Cindy Marie Millen, June 19, 1976; children: Kathryn Marie, Jennifer Anne, Susanna Jayne. BS, Grove City Coll., 1971; MS, Indiana U. of Pa., 1973; PhD, W. Va. U., 1978; postgrad., U. Colo., 1976-77. Postdoctoral rsch. assoc. chemistry dept. U. So. Calif., L.A., 1977-78; staff chemist corp. rsch. labs. Exxon Rsch. and Engrng. Co., Linden, N.J., 1978-81, Houston, 1981-83, Annandale, N.J., 1983-86; rsch. scientist, surface chemistry and corrosion sci. group supr. Baker Performance Chems., Houston, 1986-91, rsch. mgr., 1991-92, tech. dir., 1992—. Contbr. articles to profl. jours., chpt. to book; patentee in field. Recipient Award for Grad. Rsch., Sigma Xi, 1973, Union Carbide award W.Va. U., 1975, Stan Gillman award U. Colo., 1977, Tech. Merit award Baker-Hughes, 1989, 91, 93. Mem. Am. Chem. Soc., Soc. Petroleum Engrs., Offshore Operators Com. (task force on environ. sci.), Nat. Assn. Corrosion Engrs., Phi Lambda Upsilon. Presbyterian. Office: Baker Performance Chems Inc PO Box 27714 Houston TX 77227-7714

DOWNS, JON FRANKLIN, drama educator, director; b. Bartow, Fla., Sept. 15, 1938; s. Clarence Curtis and Frankie (Morgan) D.; student Ga. State Coll., 1956-58; BFA, U. Ga., 1960, MFA, 1969. Drama dir. DeKalb Coll., Clarkston, Ga., 1969—. Dir., author The Beastly Purple Forest (marionettes) U. Ga., 1968, Dracula: A Horrible Musical, DeKalb Coll., 1971; dir. A Streetcar Named Desire, DeKalb, 1974, Brigadoon, DeKalb, 1981, West Side Story, 1983, Amadeus, 1984, Noises Off, 1986, The Three Musketeers, 1988, A Midsummer Night's Dream, 1990, A Little Night Music, 1991, Hamlet, 1993, over 200 others; actor Wedding in Japan, N.Y.C., 1960, Dark at the Top of the Stairs, N.Y.C. and tour, 1961, A Life in the Theatre, DeKalb Coll., 1981, numerous others; designer Sweeney Todd, DeKalb Coll., 1970, Romulus, 1971, Grass Harp, 1972, many others; writer, dir. plays Tokalitta, Gold!, The Vigil; on tour of Ga., summers 1973, 74, 75, 76. Ga. Dept. Planning and Budget arts sect. grantee, 1973, 74. State and Nat. Bicentennial Commn. grantee, 1975. Mem. Southeastern Theatre Conf. (state rep. 1971-73), Ga. Theatre Conf. (exec. bd. 1970-73 79-82). Author: The Illusionist, 1979; film reviewer: Southernflair Mag., 1994—. Home: 1124 Forrest Blvd Decatur GA 30030-4736 Office: Dept Fine Arts DeKalb Coll Clarkston GA 30021

DOWRIDGE, DONALD LEE, JR., motivational speaker; b. Balt.; 1 child, Donald L. III. Student, Monterey Peninsula Jr. Coll., Calif., 1982; AS in Mktg. Mgmt., Tampa (Fla.) Coll., 1995. Mail processor U.S. Postal Svc., Tampa, 1985—; motivational spkr. drug awareness, alcoholism, self-esteem Tampa, 1990—; owner, founder, CEO D.L.D. Enterprise (Determine to Learn and Develop), Tampa. Author: Truth in the Poem, 1992, The Key: Coping with a Better Self, 1995, The Power of Being of W-I-N-N-E-R, 1996; author 110 poems; features on several radio talk shows and TV shows including Upfront and the N.O.W. show. Gov. Fla. Victory Award, 1992; bd. dirs. Drugs Destroy Dreams and The 3R Project. Office: PO Box 22722 Tampa FL 33622-2722

DOYLE, DELORES MARIE, elementary education educator; b. Madison, S.D., July 24, 1939; d. Martin N. and Pearl M. (Anderson) Berkelo; m. Patrick J. Doyle; children: Kathleen, Shawn, Tamara, Timothy. AS, Dakota State Coll., Madison, 1959; BS, Mid. Tenn. State U., 1966, MEd, 1968, EdS, 1975; PhD, Peabody/Vanderbilt U., 1980. Cert. career ladder III tchr. Tchr. 4th grade Meriden-Cleghorn Schs., Meriden, Iowa, 1960-62; tchr. 1st grade Hanover (Ill.) Sch., 1963-66; tchr. 2d grade Hobgood Sch., Murfreesboro, Tenn., 1969-70; tchr. 1st grade Reeves-Rogers Sch., Murfreesboro, 1972-80, tchr. 2d grade, 1981—; summer sch. dir. Murfreesboro City Schs., 1986-89; lead project tutor Reeves-Rogers Sch., 1987-90; cooperating tchr. Mid. Tenn. State U. Student Tchrs., Murfreesboro, 1972—. Bd. dirs. Grace Luth. Ch., Murfreesboro, 1991-93, mem. choir, 1975-95; active Edn. 2000 Com. Murfreesboro C. of C., 1993, task force on edn. Mid. Tenn. State U., 1992-93; trustee Mid. Tenn. State U. Found., 1995—. Named Career Ladder III Tchr., Dept. Edn., Nashville, 1984; recipient Tenn. Tech. of Yr. award State Dept. Edn., Nashville, 1992, Murfreesboro City Tchr. of Yr. award Murfreesboro City Schs., 1991, Mid-Cumberland Dist. Tchr. of Yr. award Dist. Dept. Edn., 1991, Trailblazer award 1995; Creative Tchg. grantee State Dept. Edn., 1992, 93. Mem. NEA, Nat. State Tchr. of Yr. Orgn., Tenn. Edn. Assn. (Disting. Classroom Tchr. award 1991), Tenn. Reading Assn., Murfreesboro Edn. Assn. (pres. 1981-82), Delta Kappa Gamma (2d v.p.), Kappa Delta Pi. Democrat. Home: 1710 Sutton Pl Murfreesboro TN 37129-6513 Office: Reeves-Rogers Sch 1807 Greenland Dr Murfreesboro TN 37130-3119

DOYLE, ESTHER PIAZZA, critical care nurse, educator; b. Birmingham, Ala., Apr. 8, 1952; d. Vincent and Dorothy Virginia (Danforth) Piazza; m. James Patrick Doyle III, Sept. 14, 1974. ADN, Jefferson State Coll., Birmingham, 1976; BSN magna cum laude, Spalding U., Louisville, 1988. RN, Ky. Post-op cardiac care Cleve. Clinic Ohio, 1976-77; level I trauma staff nurse surg. ICU Hermann Hosp.-U. Tex., Houston, 1977-79; SICU level I trauma, MICU, burn unit profl. nurse recruiter, trauma clin. coord., utilization rev. coord. Humana-U. Louisville, 1979-90; ICU and CCU nurse Presbyn. Hosp., Charlotte, N.C., 1991—; conducted trauma awareness seminars. Author: Family Guide to Critical Care. Bd. dirs., sec.-treas. Neighborhood Assn. Mem. ANA, N.C. Nurses Assn., Internat. Honor Soc. Nursing, Sigma Theta Tau. Home: 6016 Mallard Grove Rd Charlotte NC 28269-1389

DOYLE, IRENE ELIZABETH, electronic sales executive, nurse; b. West Point, Iowa, Oct. 5, 1920; d. Joseph Deidrich and Mary Adelaide (Groene) Schulte; m. William Joseph Doyle, Feb. 3, 1956. RN, Mercy Hosp., 1941. Courier nurse Santa Fe R.R., Chgo., 1947-50; indsl. nurse Montgomery Ward, Chgo., 1950-54; rep. Hornblower & Weeks, Chgo., 1954-56; v.p. William J. Doyle Co., Chgo., 1956-80, Ormond Beach, Fla., 1980-88. Served with M.C., U.S. Army, 1942-46. Mem. Electronic Reps. Assn. Republican. Roman Catholic. Club: Oceanside Country (Ormond Beach).

DOYLE, JOHN ROBERT, JR., writer; b. Dinwiddie County, Va., Jan. 22, 1910; s. John Robert and Marian Stickley (Binford) D.; m. Clarice Alise Slate, June 13, 1942; 1 child, Gwendolen Binford Doyle Hurst. B.A., Randolph-Macon Coll., 1932; M.A., U. Va., 1937, Bread Loaf Sch. English, 1941; postgrad., U. N.C., 1944-45. Head dept. English Dinwiddie High Sch., Va., 1932-40; instr. English Clemson U., 1940-41; asst. prof. English The Citadel, 1941-44, 46-57, assoc. prof., 1957-63, prof., 1963-75, prof. emeritus, 1975—, dir. Fine Art Series, 1965-75; lectr. in physics U. N.C., 1944-45; lectr. lit. Stephens Coll., 1945-46; vis. prof. Am. lit. Univs. Cape Town and the Witwatersrand, 1958. Author books including: The Poetry of Robert Frost, 1962; William Plomer, 1969; Francis Carey Slater, 1971; Thomas Pringle, 1972; Arthur Shearly Cripps, 1975; William Charles Scully, 1978. Founding editor The Citadel Monograph Series. Contbr. articles and essays to periodicals. Pres., Charleston Civic Ballet, 1963-65; chmn. fine arts events S.C. Tri-Centennial, 1970. Recipient Smith-Mundt grant to South Africa, 1958, Daniel Disting. Teaching award, 1968, Algernon Sidney Sullivan award The Citadel, 1971, Disting. Alumnus award Randolph-Macon Coll., 1993. Mem. Poetry Soc. S.C. (past pres., dir. writing group 1947-75, award of merit 1971), MLA (chmn. conf. So. lit. 1965, world lit. written in English 1967), Am. Studies Assn. (past dir.), Coll. English Assn., Va. Writers Club, Phi Beta Kappa. Home and Office: 10633 Rives Ave Mc Kenney VA 23872

DOYLE, JOSEPH FRANCIS, III, art educator; b. Boston, Jan. 20, 1960; s. Joseph Francis Jr. and Ellen Mary (Hayes) D.; m. Ginger Leigh Davis, Dec. 18, 1993. BFA, Tex. Tech U., 1983, M of Edn., 1990. Coord. elem. art Round Rock (Tex.) Ind. Sch. Dist., 1983-84; art educator Ctrl. High Sch., San Angelo, Tex., 1985-86; art educator, art dept. chmn. Aldine Jr. High Sch., Houston, 1986-92; art educator MacArthur Sr. High, Houston, 1992—; tchr. night high sch. continuing edn. Aldine Ind. Sch. Dist., 1988, chmn. dist. youth art month, sponsor nat. jr. art honor soc., 1989-91, chmn. textbook selection com. elem. art, 1989, chmn. textbook selection com. sr. high art, 1995, mem. dist. tchr. of yr. selection com., 1992-93; insvc. trainer Tex. Arts Coun., Austin, 1991-93; presenter in field. Exhibited in group show Tex. Art Edn. Assn., 1988, 89, Tex. Trends Art Edn., 1989, Nat. Art Edn. Assn., 1990. vol. graphic arts Tex. Spl. Olympics, Houston, 1988-90. Recipient Vol. in People award Sta. K-Lite-FM, 1990; named Houston Post Tchr. of Week, 1992; Disting. Alumnus award Texas Tech. U., 1992. Mem. Nat. Art Edn. Assn. (nat. conv. evaluator jr. high concerns, 1988, Western Region Art Educator of Yr., 1992, Nat. Jr. Art Hon. Soc. Sponcer of the Year, 1993), Tex. Art Edn. Assn. (v.p. youth arts month 1993-95, long range task force com., region VI rep., chmn. reps., insvc. presenter 1985-92, Rising Sun award 1983, Excellence in Art award 1990, Outstanding Art Educator jr. high/mid. sch. divsn. 1991, v.p. youth art month 1992-94), North Houston Art Edn. Assn. (pres. 1989-92). Roman Catholic. Home: 1402 Plumwood Dr Houston TX 77014-2608

DOYLE, MICHAEL O'BRIEN, retail executive; b. Alpena, Mich., Dec. 13, 1948; s. Patrick Reed and Joyce Patricia (Bezotte) D.; m. Ruth Ann Gamage, May 21, 1971. BBA, Cen. Mich. U., 1973. With Hickory Farms of Ohio, Inc., Maumee, 1973-80, dir. career and profl. devel., 1979-80; pres. Am. Splty. Foods, Inc., Augusta, Ga., 1980-83; pres. O'Brien Stationers, Inc., Augusta, 1983—, also bd. dirs. Served as sgt. U.S. Army, 1968-70. Mem. Nat. Office Products Assn., Ga. Office Products Assn., Augusta Mall Mchts. Assn. (v.p. 1984-86), Regency Mall Mchts. Assn. (bd. dirs. 1981-83). Roman Catholic. Home: 3246 Skinner Mill Rd Augusta GA 30909-1917 Office: O'Brien Stationers Inc 1028 Augusta Mall Augusta GA 30909

DOYLE, MICHAEL PATRICK, food microbiologist, educator, administrator; b. Madison, Wis., Oct. 3, 1949; s. Donald Vincent and Evelyn (Bauer) D.; m. Annette Marie Ripple, Dec. 27, 1971; children: Michael Patrick, Patrick Matthew, Kristen Anne. BS in Bacteriology, U. Wis., 1973, MS in Food Microbiology, 1975, PhD in Food Microbiology, 1977. Sr. project leader Ralston Purina Co., St. Louis, 1977-80; asst. prof. U. Wis., Madison, 1980-84, assoc. prof., 1984-88, prof., 1988-91; prof., dir. U. Ga., Griffin, 1991—; dept. head U. Ga., Athens, 1993—; mem. food and nutrition bd. Inst. Medicine, NAS, 1991—; mem. nat. adv. com. on microbiol. criteria for foods USDA, Washington, 1988-90, 94—; trustee Internat. Life Scis. Inst.-N.Am., Washington, 1992—, sci. advisor, 1987—; mem. Internat. Commn. on Microbiol. Specifications for Foods, 1989—;Wis. disting. prof. bd. regents U. Wis., Madison, 1988-91; James M. Craig meml. lectr. Oreg. State U., Corvallis, 1990; sci. lectr. Am. Soc. Microbiology Found., 1991-93; Peter J. Shields lectr. U. Calif., Davis, 1993; G. Malcolm Trout vis. scholar Mich. State U., Lansing, 1994. Editor: Foodborne Bacterial Pathogens, 1989; contbr. articles to Applied and Environ. Microbiology, Jour. Food Protection, Internat. Jour. Food Microbiology, Jour. Clin. Microbiology. Recipient Am. Agrl. Econs. Assn. award for profl. excellence, 1992. Fellow Am. Acad. Microbiology; mem. Internat. Assn. Milk, Food and Environ. Sanitarians (pres. 1992-93, Norbert F. Sherman article excellence award 1993), Am. Soc. for Microbiology (chmn. food microbiology divsn. 1987-89, P.R. Edwards award for outstanding career achievements 1994), Inst. Food Technologists (Fred. W. Tanner lectr. 1986, sci. lectr. 1987-90, Samuel Cate Prescott award for rsch. 1987, Nicholas Appert award for preeminence in and contbns. to field of food tech. 1996), Phi Kappa Phi, Gamma Sigma Delta. Roman Catholic. Office: U Ga Ctr Food Safety Quality Enhancement Ga Expt Sta 1109 Experiment St Griffin GA 30223

DOYLE, NELL MEADOWS, program director; b. Pine Bluff, Ark., Aug. 15, 1949; d. Bobby Emmanuel and Patricia Ann (Doyle) Meadows; m. Jimmie Lyle Rorie, June 3, 1970 (div. 1985); m. Robert Gardner Shoemaker, July 27, 1991. BA, Hendrix Coll., 1971. Officeworker Boston U. Sch. of Theology, 1971-73; office mgr. U. Mo., Kansas City, 1973-75, U. Ark., Little Rock, 1975-80; rsch. analyst Bur. of Legislative Rsch., State Legislature, Little Rock, 1980-88; assoc. dir. Murphy Fedn./Hendrix Coll., Conway, Ark., 1988—. Office: Hendrix Coll 1600 Washington Ave Conway AR 72032

DOYLE, SALLY A., controller; b. Somerville, N.J., Jan. 19, 1956; d. Edward L. and Sarah M. (Wenrich) Padrazas; married. BA in Bus., Coll. of St. Elizabeth, Convent Station, N.J., 1989. CPA, Ga.; cert. mgmt. acct. Payroll clk. Ethicon, Somerville, 1974-78, asst. supr. payroll, 1978-81, payroll supr., 1981-86; payroll supr. J & J Advanced Materials Co., New Brunswick, N.J., 1986-89; gen. acctg. supr. J & J Advanced Materials Co., New Brunswick, 1989-90; sr. acct. J & J Advanced Materials Co., Gainesville, Ga., 1990-92, plant acctg. mgr., 1992-94; regional plant controller J & J Advanced Materials Co., Benson, N.C., 1994-95; regional contr. Chicopee, Inc., Benson, 1995-96; divsn. contr. PGI Non-Wovens/Chicopee Inc., Benson, 1996—. Mem. AICPA, Inst. Mgmt. Accts. Office: Chicopee Inc PO Box 308 Benson NC 27504-0308

DOYLE, WILLIAM LYNN, non-profit management specialist; b. Lanette, Ala., Feb. 1, 1941; s. Leon Hurston and Olla Belle (DeMoss) D.; m. Helen Ruth Reedy, June 16, 1960; children: Dondi Karen, Jay Allen. BA, U. Ark., 1970; grad., Nat. Planned Giving Inst., Memphis, 1990, Exec. Leadership Inst., Indpls., 1991. Owner private business, Little Rock, Ark., 1962-76; regional dir. March of Dimes, Little Rock, 1976-82; sr. cons. CSB, Inc., Dallas, 1982-88; pres. Holston Valley Heath Care Found., Kingsport, Tenn., 1988-93; exec. dir. Candler Hosp. Found., Savannah, Ga., 1994-96; with Nat. Diabetes Trust Fund, 1996—; lectr., seminars Am. Fund Raising Inst., Estate Planning Coun., NSFRE; served on many bds. for seniors, children, various disadvantaged. Contbr. articles to profl. jours. With USAF, 1958-62. Named Outstanding Local Pres. Ark. Jaycees, Sherwood, 1976; Harris fellow Rotary Internat. Mem. Assn. Healthcare Philanthropy (1st place awards 1989-91). Roman Catholic. Office: Diabetes Trust Fund Ste 154 9220 A-1 Parkway East #104 Birmingham AL 35206

DOZIER, GLENN JOSEPH, medical, surgical products distribution executive; b. Lexington, Ky., Apr. 7, 1950; s. Emmitt and Henrietta Elsie (Geisler) D.; m. Paula Jean Cook, June 3, 1974; children: Laura Jean, Diana Leigh. BS in Indsl. Engring. and Ops. Rsch., Va. Poly. Inst., 1972; MBA, U. Va., 1975. Mfg. engr. Tex. Instruments, Dallas, 1972-73; fin. analyst Dravo Corp., Pitts., 1975-76, mgr. corp. fin. analysis, 1976-79, dir. corp. devel., 1980-82, dir. corp. planning and devel., 1982-83; v.p. fin. Dravo Constructors, Inc., Pitts., 1983-87; chief fin. officer, treas., asst. sec. AMF Bowling Internat. Inc. and AMF Bowling, Inc., Richmond, Va., 1987-90; v.p., chief fin. officer, treas. Owens and Minor, Inc., Richmond, 1990-93, sr. v.p. ops. and systems, chief fin. officer, 1991-92, sr. v.p. fin., chief fin. officer, 1992—. Author: Economic Development Finance, 1986. Mem. Colonies Civic Assn. Mem. Nat. Assn. Accts., Colonies Swim and Tennis Club, Phi Eta Sigma, Alpha Pi Mu, Phi Kappa Phi, Tau Beta Pi. Republican. Methodist.

DOZIER, L(AWRENCE) DOW, public relations executive; b. Heavener, Okla., May 23, 1934; s. Lorenzo Dow and Nena (Stewart) D.; m. U. Carolyn Cooper, Aug. 28, 1955; children: Lauri C. Reeg, Lisa D. Holder, Drew C. BA in Journalism, U. Okla., 1957. Gen. mgr. Lake Eufaula FUN, McAlester, Okla., 1964-66; advt. dir. The News-Capital, McAlester, 1966-69; editor co. publs. Okla. Gas & Electric Co., Oklahoma City, 1969-73, info. supr., 1973-75, news editor, 1975-77; dist. mgr. Okla. Gas & Electric Co., Alva, Okla., 1977-80, Woodward, Okla., 1980-82; mgr. corp. comm. Okla. Gas & Electric Co., Oklahoma City, 1982-90; assoc. dir. corp. comm. Kerr-McGee Corp., Oklahoma City, 1990-94, dir. corp. comm., 1994—; pres. Okla. U. Jour. Alumni Assn., Oklahoma City, 1994. Recipient George Washington Honor medal Freedoms Found. at Valley Forge, Pa., 1972, 73, Silver medal for lifetime achievement Am. Advt. Fedn., Oklahoma City, 1994, Disting. Alumni award U. Okla. Sch. of Journalism and Mass Comm., 1996. Mem. Pub. Rels. Soc. Am. (treas. 1993), Oklahoma City Ad Club. Democrat. Methodist. Home: 6805 Waterwood Way Oklahoma City OK 73132-6526 Office: Kerr-McGee Corp 123 Robert S Kerr Ave Oklahoma City OK 73102-6425

DOZIER, NANCY KERNS, retired geriatrics nurse; b. Akron, Ohio, May 31, 1930; d. Guy F. and Alma Jane (Good) Kerns; 1 child, Frederick A. Dietz. AAA, Prince George C.C., 1972; student, Catonsville (Md.) Coll., 1976, Catonsville (Md.) Coll., 1978. RN, Ohio, Fla., Md.; cert. in basic and advanced coronary care. Med.-surg., orthopedic staff nurse Childrens Hosp., Balt., 1973-74; nurse med. surg. flr. Bon Secours Hosp., Balt., 1974-76; staff nurse Md. State Maximum Security Penal Inst., Jessup, 1974-75, Bonifay (Fla.) Nursing Home, 1985-86; staff float nurse UpJohn Health Care Svcs. U. Md. Hosp. Balt., 1979-81; charge, treatment nurse Monticello (Fla.) Nursing Home, 1983; supr. Estes Nursing Home (Beverly Enterprises), Tallahassee, 1984, Ponce De Leon Care Ctr., St. Augustine, Fla., 1987-88; charge nurse Graceville (Fla.) Hosp., 1984; charge, patients care plans nurse U. Nursing Care Ctr., Gainesville, Fla., 1989-90.

DOZIER, RUSSELL WILLIAM, JR., actuarial consultant, pension consultant; b. Oklahoma City, Feb. 11, 1927; s. Russell W. Sr. and Irene (Ware) D.; m. Margaret Cunningham (div. July 1974); children: Russell W. III, Charles Raymond; m. Bette Ann Ray, Jan. 14, 1977. Student, Tex. Tech U., 1944, N.C. State U., 1945, U. Okla., 1947-48; LLB, U. Okla., 1953. CLU. Life ins. agt. Mass. Mut. Life Ins. Co., Oklahoma City, 1947-62; pres. The Dozier Co., Oklahoma City, 1962-90; chmn. bd. dirs. emeritus Fringe Benefits Design, Inc., Oklahoma City, 1990-94; bd. dirs. Shawnee Milling Co., Actuarial Edn. and Rsch. Found., 1988-91; actuarial rep. Employee Retirement Income Security Act adv. com., 1991-94. 1st lt. U.S. Army, 1944-52, Korea. Decorated Bronze Star; named Outstanding Life Underwriter, Okla. City Assn. Life Underwriters, 1961. Fellow Am. Soc. Pension Actuaries (bd. dirs. 1965-87, pres. 1987); mem. Am. Acad. Actuaries (mem. ethics com.), Am. Soc. CLUs (bd. mem. 1959-62, local pres. 1961). Republican. Office: Fringe Benefits Design 9400 N Broadway Ext Oklahoma City OK 73114-7401

DOZIER, WILLIAM EVERETT, JR., newspaper editor and publisher; b. Delhi, La., June 12, 1922; s. William Everett and Harriet E. (Miles) D.; m. Eleanor Ruth Roye, Sept. 1, 1944; children: Martha Carolyn Dozier Hunnicutt (dec. July 1995), Sarah Rebecca. BA in Journalism, La. Tech. U., 1943. Assoc. editor Delhi Dispatch, 1936-39; reporter, state editor New Orleans Times-Picayune, 1946-50; editor Courier-Times-Telegraph, Tyler, Tex., 1952-65; pres., editor, pub. Kerrville (Tex.) Daily Times, 1965-88; pres. Hills o'Texas Publs., Inc., 1982-92; gen. ptnr. Frio-Nueces Publs., Ltd., 1976—. V.p., Kerrville Music Found. and Performing Arts Soc., 1978-84, also bd. dirs.; bd. dirs. Adm. Nimitz Ctr. Found., Fredericksburg, Tex., 1976—; chmn. United Fund campaign, Kerrville, 1967; mem. adv. bd. Salvation Army, 1967—; v.p. Tex. State Arts & Crafts Fair Assn., 1980-90, also bd. dirs., 1972-92; trustee Schreiner Coll., 1987-96, Sid Peterson Meml. Hosp., 1989—. Served with USN, 1943-46, 50-52; ret. comdr., 1973. Lay leader First United Meth. Ch., Kerrville, 1984-86, past chmn. bd. trustees, chmn. adminstrv. bd. Mem. Am. Soc. Newspaper Editors, Am. Newspaper Pubs. Assn., Nat. Newspaper Assn., Tex. AP Mng. Editors Assn. (pres. 1964-65), Tex. Press Assn. (pres. 1979-80), Tex. Daily Newspaper Assn. (dir. 1984-87), Tex. Press Found. (pres. 1982-92), So. Newspaper Pubs. Assn. (chmn. smaller newspaper com. 1983-84, dir. 1984-87), Kerr County C. of

C. (pres. 1973-74), W. Tex. C. of C. (regional v.p. 1981-84, pres. 1985-86), Tex. C. of C. (founding dir. 1987-90), Sigma Delta Chi. Lodges: Masons (Tyler); Kiwanis (lt. gov. div. 5 Tex.-Okla. dist. 1974, pres. Kerrville 1973; Disting. Club Pres. 1973, Disting. Lt. Gov. 1974). Home: 376 Englewood Dr Kerrville TX 78028-6411 Office: 815 Jefferson St Ste A Kerrville TX 78028-4581

DRACOS, THEODORE MICHAEL, journalist, television producer; b. Boston, June 30, 1945; s. Harry M. and Helen C. (Dore) D.; m. Mary Jill Moore, Oct. 28, 1969 (div. June 1979); 1 child, Erin. BA in History, U. Wis., 1969. Radio host WMFM-Radio, Madison, Wis., 1970-72; founder, CEO, dir. Small Planet Rsch. Assocs., Seattle, 1973-76; contbg. writer Seattle Weekly Mag., 1977-80; investigative reporter Harte-Hanks TV, San Antonio, 1980-82; dir. investigative reporting Gannett Broadcast Group, Mpls., 1983; investigative reporter/prodr. McGraw-Hill TV, San Diego, 1984-89; S.W. bur. chief Orion Nat. Telepictures, San Antonio, 1990; journalism instr. Incarnate Word Coll., San Antonio, 1991; editl. commentator Harte-Hanks TV, San Antonio, 1992-93; docementary prodr./writer San Antonio, 1994—. Writer, prodr. (documentary) One Moment of Madness, 1981 (Best Nat. Reporting award Nat. Headliners 1982, Charles Green Best Feature award Tex. Headliners 1982), Poisoning Paradise, 1987, Johnny Massingale, 1986, Stanley Stress, 1985. Mem. Exec. com. Puget Sount Sierra Club, Seattle, 1974-76; citizen activity coord. U.S. EPA Region 10, Seattle, 1974-75; med. dir. Jimmy Carter Presdl. Campaign, Washington, 1976; vol. Child Advocates of San Antonio, 1993. Recipient Golden medallion for best legal reporting Calif. State Bar, 1986.

DRAFTS, JAMES PICKENS, III, financial and actuarial examiner; b. Batesburg, S.C., Jan. 24, 1938; s. James Pickens, Jr. and Ella Catherine (Shealy) D. BA summa cum laude, Newberry Coll., 1960; postgrad., U. S.C., 1964-65. Cert. fin. examiner, ins. examiner. Tchr. Cochran (Ga.) High Sch., 1961-64, Aiken (S.C.) Sr. High Sch., 1965; asst. coord. continuing edn. U. S.C., Columbia, 1967-68; pers. dir. Colonial Life & Accident Ins. Co., Columbia, 1968-71; actuarial examiner S.C. Dept. Ins., Columbia, 1971-90; fin. and actuarial contract examiner self-employed, Batesburg, Leesville, S.C., 1990—. Mem. Pres.'s Club of Newberry Coll., 1989—. Recipient Gaver Math. award Newberry Coll., 1958; Woodrow Wilson fellow Woodrow Wilson Fellowship Found., 1960; named Star Tchr., Ga. C. of C., 1963, Outstanding Young Man of Am., 1970; cited by Gov. Carroll B. Campbell for Svcs. Rendered to S.C. during Hurrican Hugo, 1989-90. Mem. Soc. Fin. Examiners, Ins. Regulatory Examiners Soc. (bd. govs. 1990-92). Republican. Lutheran. Home and Office: 309 Bates St Batesburg SC 29006

DRAGO, EDMUND LEON, history educator; b. Chgo., Oct. 16, 1942; s. Rosario Charles and Margaret (Burke) D.; m. Cheyle Choi, Dec. 20, 1970. BA, Santa Clara U., 1964; MA, U. Calif., Berkeley, 1966, PhD, 1975. Prof. history Coll. Charleston, S.C., 1975—; adv. bd. S.C. Hist. Records, 1991—. Author: Black Politicians and Reconstruction in Georgia: A Splendid Failure, 1981, Initiative, Paternalism and Race Relations: Charleston's Avery Normal Institute, 1990, Broke By the War: The Letters of a Slave Trader, 1991. Capt. U.S. Army, 1969-72, Vietnam. NEH fellow, 1981; Fulbright scholar, 1994. Mem. AAUP, Am. Hist. Assn., So. Hist. Assn., Orgn. Am. Historians. Office: Coll Charleston Dept Hist 66 George St Charleston SC 29424

DRAGOO, CHRISTINE WORTHINGTON, editor; b. St. Helens, Gt. Britain, Nov. 5, 1942; came to U.S., 1977; d. Stanley and Beatrice (Ball) Worthington; m. Don W. Dragoo, Aug. 23, 1971 (wid. Aug. 1988). BA with honors, U. Western Australia, 1965; Diploma of Librarianship, U. NSW, Sydney, 1966. Pictorial libr. Nat. Libr. of Australia, Canberra, 1967, map libr., 1968-71; film and photograph libr. Australian War Meml., Canberra, 1971; rsch. assoc. Carnegie Mus. of Natural History, Pitts., 1973-77, Environment Cons., Inc., Dallas, 1977-80; sr. assoc. Inst. for Human History, Gloucester, Va., 1980—; editor Chesopiean Mag. Inst. for Human History, Gloucester, 1992—. Contbr. articles to profl. jours. Mem. Ky. Cols., King's Daus., Gloucester Woman's Club (pres. 1986-88), Eastern States Archaeol. Fedn. Office: PO Box 648 Gloucester VA 23061

DRAHOVZAL, JAMES ALAN, geologist; b. Cedar Rapids, Iowa, Feb. 13, 1939; s. John Blahoslav and Anna Elizabeth (Kucera) D.; m. Rebecca Lee Barels, Aug. 17, 1963; children: Robert John, Elizabeth Marie, Sarah Ann. BA, U. Iowa, 1957-61, MS, 1961-63, PhD, 1963-66. Registered Profl. Geologist, Ky. Geologist Pan Am. Petroleum Corp., New Orleans, 1965-66; geologist Geol. Survey of Ala., Tuscaloosa, 1966-76, asst. state geologist, dir., 1976-78; sr. rsch. geologist Gulf Rsch. and Devel. Corp., Pitts., 1978-84; rsch. assoc. Arco Oil and Gas Co., Plano, Tex., 1984-88; geologist and head petroleum and stratigraphy Ky. Geol. Survey, Lexington, Ky., 1989—; cons. geologist LaMoreaux and Assocs., Tuscaloosa, 1974-78; lectr. geology U. Ala., Tuscaloosa, 1970; mem. geosat com. Coyanosa (Tex.) Test Site Team, 1979-81; adj. assoc. prof. geology U. Ky., Lexington, 1991—. Author in field. Elder Presbyn. Ch., Iowa City, Plano, Tuscaloosa, Lexington, 1963—. Teaching Asst. fellow NSF, 1965, Travel grantee Prague, Czechoslovakia, 1968. Fellow Geol. Soc. Am. (hdqs. com. mem. 1983-85, 92, nominating com. 1994); mem. Am. Assn. Petroleum Geologists (del. from Pa., 1983, Ky. 1991—, chmn. membership com. for Ea. sect., mem. rsch. com.), Ala. Geol. Soc. (pres. 1973-74), Eastern Oil Shale Symposium (adv. bd., session chmn. 1989-91). Democrat. Presbyterian. Office: U Ky Ky Geological Survey 228 MMRB Lexington KY 40506

DRAIN, EVELYN LOUISE, telecommunications specialist; d. Dernard DuBose and Fannie Bell (DuBose) Molton; widowed, Nov. 1966; 1 child, Pherow L. VIII. Degree in System Sci., Bus. Adminstrn. Mgmt., Troy State U., 1989; student, Pensacola Jr. Coll., 1979, Learning Tree, Data Tech Comm. Inst., 1993. Key punch operator Naval Regional Data Automation Ctr. USN, Pensacola, Fla., 1969-71; lead key punch operator NARDAC, Navy, Pensacola, Fla., 1971-72, mainframe computer operator, 1972-73, sr. computer mainframe operator, 1973-78, supr. computer operator, 1978-86, computer specialist, 1986-87, telecomm. specialist, 1987—. CHIPS therapeutic parent Lakeview, Center Pensacola, 1988—. Recipient Letter of Recognition for outstanding community svc. Lakeview CHIPS Dept., 1990, 92, 93, Computer and Telecomms. Sta./Comdg. Officer, Pensacola, 1993, Halo award for oustanding community svc., 1992; Retailer of Yr. award Wal-Mart, 1989; named to Outstanding Young Women of Am., 1982. Mem. Federally Employed Women Orgn. (officer), Nat. Coalition of 100 Black Women (founding mem. Pensacola chpt., fin. sec. 1993—, fund raising chair 1993-94), Ladies of Distinction Federated Orgn. (officer). Home: 5633 Esperanto Dr Pensacola FL 32526-2204

DRAKE, DAVID LEE, electronics engineer; b. Campton, Ky., Mar. 15, 1960; s. Dudley and Sarah Ellen (Combs) D.; m. Bitha Mae Turner, June 10, 1983; children: Thomas Shelton, Rachel Leann. AAS, Morehead State U., 1981, BS, 1983. Electronics lab. technician Morehead (Ky.) State U., 1979-81; quality control technician Computer Peripherals, Campton, 1981; robotics rsch. engr. Morehead State U., 1981-83; personal computer test technician Campton Electronics, 1984-86; chief engr. Automation Svcs., Lexington, Ky., 1986—. Contbr. articles to profl. jours. Mem. IEEE, Sigma Tau Epsilon (parliamentarian 1982-83). Democrat. Home: PO Box 533 Campton KY 41301-0533 Office: Automation Svcs Inc 2549 Richmond Rd Ste 400 Lexington KY 40509-1595

DRAKE, EDWARD JUNIUS, lawyer; b. Dallas, Feb. 7, 1924; s. Edward Junius Drake and Nettie Wallace (Brown) Hamman; m. Donda Dodson, Jan. 2, 1954; children: Edward J. III, Diane Drake Burns, Carol Drake Fletcher. BBA, U. Tex., 1947, JD, 1949. Bar: Tex. Assoc. atty. Biggers, Baker, Lloyd & Carver, Dallas, 1949-50; ptnr. Brady, Drake & Wilson, Dallas, 1950-77; sr. mem. Vineyard, Drake and Miller, Dallas, 1977-88; of counsel Jordon, Dunlap & Prather, Dallas, 1989-92; pvt. practice Dallas, 1992—. Pres. The Sci. Place, Dallas, 1961-63; exec. com. So. Bapt. Conv., Nashville, 1982-90; mayor City of Univ. Park, Tex., 1984-86; mem. Tex. Adv. Commn. on Intergovtl. Rels., Austin, 1979-86; pres. Nat. Easter Seal Soc., Chgo., 1974-75. Named One of Five Outstanding Young Texans Tex. Jaycees, 1956, Justinian award Dallas Lawyers Aux., 1993. Mem. Dallas Arboretum & Botanical Soc., Dallas Christian Leadership. Home: 6930 Turtle Creek Blvd Dallas TX 75205

DRAKE, STEPHEN DOUGLAS, clinical psychologist, health facility administrator; b. Iola, Kans., Sept. 8, 1947; s. Harry Francis and Emojean (Price) D.; m. Rebecca Gonzalez, June 1, 1968; 1 child, Michael Paul. BA, U. Tex., 1970; PhD, U. North Tex., 1987. Lic. psychologist. Mental health worker Austin (Tex.) State Hosp., 1970-73; claims rep. Social Security Adminstrn., Galveston, Tex., 1974-77; ops. supr. Social Security Adminstrn., Dallas, 1977-79, staff asst., 1979-80; clin. psychologist Terrell (Tex.) State Hosp., 1987-89, Austin (Tex.) State Hosp., 1989-90; program dir. Austin State Hosp., 1990-92; cons. Tex. Rehab. Commn., 1992—. Contbr. articles to profl. jours. Vice-Chmn. bd. dirs. Galveston (Tex.) Island Mental Health/Mental Retardation Ctr., 1977; v.p. Grad. Assn. Students in Psychology U. North Tex., 1984, grad. rep. exec. com., 1984. Mem. APA, Assn. Advancement Behavior Therapy, Mensa, Phi Kappa Phi. Office: Tex Rehab Commn 6102 Oltorf St Austin TX 78704-1206

DRAKE, VAUGHN PARIS, JR., electrical engineer, retired telephone company executive; b. Winchester, Ky., Nov. 6, 1918; s. Vaughn Paris and Margaret Turney (Willis) D.; student U. Ky., 1936-41; m. Lina Louise Wilson, May 5, 1946; 1 son, Samuel Willis. With Gen. Telephone Co. Ky., Lexington, 1945-81, asst. engr., 1945-50, field engr., 1950-54, dist. engr., 1954-56, div. engr., 1956-57, depreciation engr., 1957-62, gen. valuation and cost engr., 1962-81. Mem. profl. adv. bd. Zoning Commn., Lexington and Fayette County (Ky.), 1955-57. Served with AUS, 1941-45. Decorated Pearl Harbor Commemorative medal, 1991. Registered profl. engr., Ky. Mem. Nat., Ky. (chmn. engrs. in industry sect. 1967-68, Outstanding Engr. in Industry award 1979) socs. profl. engrs., IEEE (sr.), Ind. Telephone Pioneer Assn. (life), Ky. Hist. Soc. Author: (manual) Conduit Engineering for Telephone Engineers, 1958. Home and Office: 633 Portland Dr Lexington KY 40503-2161

DRANGE, THEODORE MICHAEL, philosophy educator; b. N.Y.C., Mar. 14, 1934; s. Louis M. and Enni Maria (Seppa) D.; m. Annette Rose LeeSoy, Aug. 12, 1959; children: Susan, Michael. BA, Bklyn. Coll., 1955; postgrad., Yale U., 1955-56; PhD, Cornell U., 1963. Lectr. Bklyn. Coll., 1960-62; instr. U. Oreg., Eugene, 1962-63, asst. prof., 1963-65; asst. prof. Idaho State U., Pocatello, 1965-66; asst. prof. W. Va. U., Morgantown, 1966-67, assoc. prof., 1967-74, prof., 1974—. Author: Type Crossings, 1966; contbr. articles to jours. Fellow NSF, Stanford (Calif.) U., 1967, NEH, U. Calif., Irvine, 1971. Mem. Am. Philos. Assn., W. Va. Philos. Soc. (pres. 1970-71, 82-83, treas. 1982—). Home: 521 Meridan St Morgantown WV 26505 Office: W Va U PO Box 6312 Morgantown WV 26506

DRAPER, EVERETT T., JR., publishing executive, educator; b. Lochapoka, Ala., Jan. 23, 1939; s. Everett Turner and Susie A. (Wilson) D.; m. Emma Jeanette Smith, 1 child, Evangeline Hope. BA in Nat. Sci. and Math., Miles Coll., 1960; MEd, North Adams State Coll., 1969. Tchr. Cornwall Acad., Great Barrington, Mass., 1960-63, Housatonic Valley Regional H.S., Falls Village, Conn., 1963-69; asst. editor Harcourt Brace Jovanovich, Inc., N.Y.C., 1969-71; exec. editor Am. Book Co., N.Y.C., 1971-78; mng. editor Holt Rinehart and Winston Pubs., N.Y.C., 1979-86; exec. editor Prentice Hall, Inc., Englewood Cliffs, N.J., 1986-89, product mgr., 1989-94; pres. Academics Svcs., San Antonio, Tex., 1994—; math. cons. South-Western Ednl. Pub., 1996—; adj. lectr. LaGuardia C.C., Long Island City, N.Y., 1974—. Author: Metric Guide for Educational Materials, 1977, Math Power: Volumes 1 and 2, 1983, 90; co-author: The Volume Library Algebra, 1980. Mem. Nat. Coun. Tchrs. Math., Nat. Coun. Suprs. Math., Nat. Alliance Black Sch. Educators. Presbyterian. Home: 3630 Richwood Dr San Antonio TX 78230-2326 Office: Academic Svcs San Antonio TX 78230

DRAPER, J(OSIAH) EVERETT, artist, author, educator; b. East Orange, N.J., Oct. 17, 1915; s. Harold Walcott and Anna Frederika (Petersen) D.; m. Evelyn Ruth Wehlau, Sept. 25, 1943; children: Pamela Ruth Draper Whyte, Richard Everett. Grad. in Advt. Design, Pratt Inst., Bklyn.; student Illustration (Harvey Dunn), Grand Ctrl. Sch. of Art, N.Y.C. Art dir. Prudential Ins. Co., Newark and Jacksonville, N.J., Fla., 1935-72; pres. J.E. Draper AWS, Inc., Ponte Vedra, Fla., 1972—; adj. instr. art and design Newark Sch. Fine and Indsl. Att, 1947-51; instr. water color workshops internationally, 1972—. Author: Putting People in Your Painting, 1986, People Painting Scrapbook, 1989; artist: paintings in many one man shows, over 400 corp., govt. and privat collections, world wide, permanent collections of several museums and univs.; twice seclected for Am. Watercolor Soc. travelling exhbns. Pres. St. Augustine (Fla.) Art Assn., 1973-76. Master sgt. U.S. Army Intelligence, 1941-45. Mem. Am. Watercolor Soc. (Carolyn Stern award 1967), Fla. Watercolor Soc. (past pres.), Salmagundi Club, Ponte Vedra Club, Whiskey Painters of Am. Episcopalian. Home and Office: JE Draper AWS Inc PO Box 12 Ponte Vedra Beach FL 32004-0012

DRAPER, STEPHEN ELLIOT, engineer, lawyer; b. Columbus, Ga., Mar. 17, 1942; s. Philip Henry and Ethel Illges (Woodruff) D.; m. Lucy Leila Hargrett, June 20, 1970; 1 child, Jessie Roxanne. BS, U.S. Mil. Acad., 1964; MBA, C.W. Post/L.I. U., 1976; JD, Ga. State U., 1992; MSCE, PhD, Ga. Inst. Tech., 1971, 81. Registered profl. engr., Ga., Fla. Commd. 2d. lt. U.S. Army, 1964, advanced through grades to col., retired, 1984; forensic engr. Atlanta, 1984-86; pres. and tech. dir. Draper Engrng. Rsch., Atlanta, 1986-93, The Draper Group, Atlanta, 1993—. Contbr. articles to profl. jours. Bd. dirs. J.W. & E.I. Woodruff Found., Columbus, Ga., 1991—, Met. Boys Club, Columbus, 1981-84; mem. long-range planning com. Atlanta Area Coun., Boys Scouts Am., 1972; trustee the Foxcroft Sch., Middleburg, Va., 1994-97. Decorated Gallantry Cross with Silver Star, Legion of Merit, Bronze Star (2), Soldier's medal, Purple Heart (3), Air medal (2), Army Commendation medal (4), others; recipient Am. Jurisprudence award Ga. State U., 1992, Spl. Actions award Women's Equity Action League, 1976. Mem. ABA, Am. Soc. Civil Engrs., Am. Water Resources Assn., Am. Water Works Assn., Nat. Acad. Forensic Engrs., Nat. Soc. Profl. Engrs., The Capital City Club, The Commerce Club. Office: The Draper Group 1401 Peachtree St NE Ste 500 Atlanta GA 30309

DRAPKIN, ROBERT LOUIS, medical oncologist; b. Albany, N.Y., Sept. 22, 1944; s. Isadore and Frances Drapkin; m. Chitranee Mary Kumeraperu, June 25, 1978; children: Julia Kumari, Jessica Kumari. BS, Union Coll., Schenectady, 1966; MS, Rensselaer Poly. Inst., 1967; MD, Wayne State U., 1971. Diplomate Am. Bd. Internal Medicine, Am. Bd. Med. Oncology. Instr. medicine U. Ill., Chgo., 1975; fellow in oncology Sloan-Kettering Cancer Ctr., N.Y.C., 1975-78; attending physician Roswell Park Inst., Buffalo, 1978-79; instr. oncology SUNY, Buffalo, 1979; pvt. practice, Clearwater, Fla., 1979—; clin. attending physician U. South Fla., Tampa, 1980—; staff physician Mease Hosp., Dunedin, Fla., 1979—, Morton Plant Hosp., Clearwater, 1979—. Contbr. articles to med. jours., chpt. to book. Trustee Mus. Fine Arts, St. Petersburg, 1985-93. Fellow ACP; mem. Am. Soc. Clin. Oncology. Office: 3890 Tampa Rd Ste 406 Palm Harbor FL 34684-3675

DRAPO, PEGGY JEAN, community health, pediatric, mental health nurse; b. Wichita Falls, Tex., Apr. 22, 1928; d. Glen Evans and Sally Enola (Williams) Brooks; m. Charles F. Drapo, June 10, 1950; children: Charles J., Jody Drapo Thomas. ASN, Niagara County Community Coll., Sanborne, N.Y., 1968; BSN, SUNY, Buffalo, 1974; MSN, SUNY, 1975; PhD, U. N. Tex., 1983. Staff nurse Degraff Meml. Hosp., North Tonawanda, N.Y., 1968-76; nurse clinician United Cerebral Palsy Assn., Buffalo, 1974-76; prof. nursing Tex. Woman's U., Denton, 1976-95, prof. emerita, 1995—, dir. nurse managed care ctr., 1989-95. Contbr. articles to profl. jours.and chpt. to nursing textbooks. U.S. Dept. Health and Human Svcs./USPHS grantee, 1989-95. Mem. ANA, Am. Assn. Pub. Health, Nat. League Nursing, Sigma Theta Tau (Beta Beta chpt.). Home: 1008 Abbots Ln Denton TX 76205-8046 Office: Tex Woman's U Coll Nursing PO Box 23026 Denton TX 76204-1026

DRAUGHON, FRANCES ANN, microbiology educator; b. Tazewell, Va., Apr. 30, 1952; d. Raymond Jefferson Moore and Helen Frances (Johnson) Fox; m. Kenneth Earl Draughon, Dec. 15, 1973 (dec. Mar. 1988); children: William Bradford, Andrew Kenneth. BS in Microbiology, U. Tenn., 1973, MS in Food Sci., 1976; PhD in Food Sci., U. Ga., 1979. Asst. prof. microbiology U. Tenn., Knoxville, 1979-83, Roddy Rsch. assoc. prof., 1983-89, prof., 1989—. Chairperson Inst. Agr. Adv. Coun., U. Tenn., 1988-90. Mem. So. Assn. Agrl. Scientists (chairperson food sci. sect. 1988, Devel. Scientist award 1978, Grad. Scientist award 1979, Profl. Scientists award 1993), Inst. Food Technologists (program com. 1990-93), Am. Soc. Microbiology, Internat. Assn. Milk Food and Env. Sanitarians (v.p. 1993-94, program chair 1993, pres. 1995—), Tenn. Assn. Milk and Food Protection (pres. 1994) Sigma Xi (sec. 1981-84), Phi Kappa Phi (sec. 1981-84), Phi Tau Sigma (pres. 1983-84). Democrat. Presbyterian. Office: U Tenn Po Box 1071 Food Tech and Sci Knoxville TN 37901-1071

DRAUGHON, SCOTT WILSON, lawyer, social worker; b. Muskogee, Okla., June 17, 1952; s. Arthur Eugene and Helen Carrie (Vanhooser) D. AA, Tulsa Jr. Coll., 1972; BA, Okla. State U., 1974; JD, U. Tulsa, 1977; postgrad., Oxford U., Eng., 1978; MSW, U. Okla, 1992. Bar: Okla. 1979, U.S. Dist. Ct. (no. dist.) Okla. 1980, U.S. Claims Ct., U.S. Tax Ct. 1979, U.S. Ct. Appeals (10th cir.) 1984, U.S. Supreme Ct. 1984. Lic. social worker with clin. specialty cert. Sole law practice Tulsa, 1979—; stockbroker, 1983-93; pvt. practice fin. planning Tulsa, 1984—; aftercare dept. coord. Tulsa Boys' Home, 1992-94; pvt. practice social worker, 1994—; med. social worker Americare of Okla., Inc., 1995—; legal counsel Tulsa City County Health Dept., 1996—; clin. social worker Cushing (Okla.) Regional Hosp., 1996—; founder, exec. dir. The Fin. Hotline, Tulsa, 1984—; adj. faculty Tulsa Jr. Coll., 1986-87; student intern, social work dept. Laureate Psychiat. Clinic and Hosp., summer 1991; v.p. govtl. and pub. affairs Okla. Credit Union League, Inc., 1988-90, dir. rsch./info. Okla. Credit Union League Affiliates, 1991. Mem. grad. program com. Leadership Okla., Inc., 1995—; active Indian Affairs Commn. City of Tulsa, 1989-91, 20th Anniversary Com. Leadership Tulsa, Inc., 1992—, class IX grad.; mem. exec. bd. Tulsa Assn. Vol. Adminstrs., 1994—; bd. dris. Arts and Humanities Coun., Tulsa, 1982-83, Ea. Okla. chpt. March of Dimes, 1989-90, Internat. Coun. Tulsa, 1987-91, Tulsa County Regional Planning Coord. Bd. Svcs. to Children and Youth, 1992—; mem. exec. com. Corp. Vol. Coun. Greater Tulsa, 1990; chmn. pub. rels. com., exec. com. Tulsa Human Rights Commn., 1987-88; registered lobbyist Okla. Credit Union League Affilliate, 1988-90; student intern Social Svcs. Dept. St. Frances Hosp., 1992. Mem. NASW (treas. Okla. chpt. 1992-94), Assoc. mem., Okla. Assn. of Mcpl. Atty. (assoc.), Okla. Bar Assn., Tulsa Area Human Resources Assn. (v.p. cmty. rels. com. 1990-91), Masons, Shriners, Phi Delta Phi (life). Republican. Methodist. Office: Cushing Regional Hosp 1027 E Cherry Cushing PO Box 1409 Cushing OK 74023

DRAVIS, JACQUELIN DENISE, editor; b. Kingston, N.Y., Mar. 10, 1973; d. John Michael Dravis and Judith Ann (Beabes) Frampton; m. Robert Walls Boutwell, Aug. 27, 1994 (div. Aug. 1996). BA, Wesleyan Coll., Macon, Ga., 1994. Cert. secondary edn. tchr., Ga. Student tchr. Ctrl. H.S., Macon, 1993-94; sales assoc. Belk Matthews, Macon, 1994—; asst. children's educator Smyth & Helwys Publ., Macon, 1993—. Asst. editor Formations, 1993-95, FaithSteps, 1996; author (poetry) Silhoutte, 1990. Tutor Project Read, Macon, 1990-94. Methodist. Office: Smyth & Helwys Publ 6316 Peake Rd Macon GA 31210-3960

DRECHSEL, CHARLES NICKLOS, private school educator, horticulturist; b. Bklyn., Aug. 10, 1936; s. Karl Oswald and Elise Drechsel; m. Karen rose Altman, Aug. 1, 1971; children: Maria Hannalore, Marta Ingalotte, Kurt Karl. BME, NYU, 1957; MEd in Natural Sci., Worcester State Coll., 1981; AAS in Crop Prodn., Jefferson State Coll., Birmingham, Ala., 1996. Engr./rschr. NASA-Lewis Rsch. Ctr., 1957-62; self-employed in bldg. maint. N.Y.C., Queens, 1962-65; bldg. cons. Greater N.Y. Conf. SDA, Nassau County, 1965-70, Greater N.Y. Acad., Woodside, 1970-73, Sunnydale Acad., Centralia, Mo., 1973-77; bldg. maint. cons. Pioneer Valley Acad., New Braintree, Mass., 1977-81; adminstr., devel. dir. West African Union of SDA, Yele, Sierra Leone, Ghana, West Africa, 1981-87; tchr., adminstr. Union Springs (N.Y.) Acad., 1987-91, Gulf State Conf. of SDA, Pell City, Ala., 1991—. Named Alumnus of Yr., Greater N.Y. Acad., 1973, 91. Mem. ASME, Nat. Sci. Tchrs. Assn., Nat. Coun. Tchrs. Math. Mem. SDA. Home: 3785 Pop Stone Cir Trussville AL 35173-1993 Office: Gulf State Conf of SDA 925 Academy Cir Pell City AL 35125-4951

DRECKSHAGE, BRIAN JEFFREY, materials manager; b. St. Louis, Dec. 30, 1955; s. George Gerald and Anna Ruth (Hubbard) D.; m. Suzanne Watson, June 30, 1990. BS, S.W. Mo. State U., 1982; MBA in Internat. Bus. with honors, Okla. City U., 1993. Proj. mgr. A.P.C. Skills Co., Palm Beach, Fla., 1982-84; supv. cons. Mgmt. Alternatives, Ltd., Detroit, 1984-86; prin. Tng. Resources, St. Louis, 1986-87; sr. cons. Inst. Mgmt. Resources, Westlake Village, Calif., 1987-90; materials mgr. Fred Jones Mfg. Co., Oklahoma City, 1990-94; purchasing and materials mgr. Ctrl. Sales Promotions, Inc., Oklahoma City, 1994-95; sr. functional analyst Lockheed Martin Tech. Svcs., Dayton, Ohio, 1995—. Fellow Am. Prodn. and Inventory Control Soc. Office: Lockheed Martin Tech Svcs 1374-A N Fairfield Rd Dayton OH 45432-2644

DRENNEN, JEAN COBBLE, retired public relations executive, linguist; b. Rome, Ga., Sept. 30, 1924; d. James Ernest and Vorus Frost (Ware) Cobble; m. Gaston Cliff Drennen, Nov. 21, 1948 (dec. Sep. 1994); 1 child, Cheryl Jen. BA, U. Tenn., 1946, MA, 1965. Publicist Curt Weinberg Assoc., N.Y.C., 1946-47; freelance columnist N.Y.C., 1947-49; ad copywriter Miller's Inc., Knoxville, Tenn., 1949-51; pub. rels. dir. United Fund, Knoxville, Tenn., 1955-58; instr. dialect studies Knox County Schs., Knoxville, Tenn., 1961-66; copy dir. Lavidge Assocs., Knoxville, Tenn., 1967-73; program devel dir. Medic Regional Blood Ctr., Knoxville, Tenn., 1974-89. Author, prodr. (video, poster) What Good Is A Blood Donor, 1984 (10th anniversary choice of Am. Blood Commn. 1985); (book, audio tape) Speaking English: A Sound Approach, 1965; author book: The Company Blood Drive Coordinator's Guidebook, 1987; contbr. articles to profl. jours. Adv. United Way; mem. nat. pub. rels. bd. United Funds of Am., 1956—. Recipient 36 1st place awards for TV and newspaper ads Greater Knox Ad Club, 1970-73. Mem. Am. Assn. Blood Banks (nat. pub. rels. bd. 1985—). Home: 1600 Ebenezer Rd Knoxville TN 37922-6332

DRENNEN, WILLIAM MILLER, JR., cultural administrator, film executive, producer, director, mineral resource executive; b. Charleston, W.Va., Nov. 5, 1942; s. William Miller and Margaret (Morton) D.; m. Sarah Polk Wilson, Nov. 27, 1969; children: Zachary Polk, Samuel Boyd. BArch., Yale U., 1964; postgrad., George Washington U., 1977, U. Charleston, 1978, W.Va. Grad. Coll., 1989-92; MA in Humanities, W.Va. Grad. Coll., 1993. Freelance writer, film maker, 1967-69; v.p. Communication Corps, Inc., Washington, 1969-79; freelance writer, film maker The Aerial Image, Charleston, 1979; pres. Briar Mountain Coal and Coke Co., Charleston, 1980-89; founder, pres. Max Media, Inc., Charleston, 1984-89; commr. culture and history State of W.Va., 1989—; mng. gen. ptnr. C&D Enterprises, 1981—; past pres. Cox Morton Co., 1980-89; past pres., founder W.Va. Internat. Film Festival, Charleston, 1986-89; bd. dirs. Charleston Milling Co.; bd. advisers Alliance Petroleum Corp. Cameraman (film) Evolving Environment, 1972 (Cine Golden Eagle award); editor (film) River of Life, 1975 (U.S. Film Festival award); patentee computerized optical system. Founder, pres. W.Va. Youth Soccer Assn., 1979-84; bd. dirs. Sunrise Mus., charleston, 1983-86, Renaissance Com., Charleston, 1984-89; trustee U. Charleston, 1985-89; pres. Mountain Arts Found.; founder W.Va. Assn. Mus., 1990; chmn. Capital Bldg. Commn.; state hist. preservation officer; v.p., sec. W.Va. History Film Project, Inc., 1991—; bd. dirs. W.Va. Rural Devel. Coun.; mem. adv. com. W.Va. Byways and Backways; mem. adv. panel Edn. First. Decorated Bronze Star; recipient 2 Cine Eagle awards, cert. Excellence for documentary film work, award Hist. Landmarks Commn. Kanawha County. Mem. Film Arts Guild W.Va. (pres. 1981-87), Cosmos Club, Cress Creek Golf & Country Club. Democrat. Episcopalian. Office: The Cultural Ctr Capitol Complex Charleston WV 25305

DRESCHER, JUDITH ALTMAN, library director; b. Greensburg, Pa., July 6, 1946; d. Joseph Grier and Sarah Margaret (Hewitt) Altman; m. Robert A. Drescher, Aug. 10, 1968 (div. 1980); m. David G. Lindstrom, Jan. 10, 1981. AB, Grove City Coll., 1968; MLS, U. Pitts., 1971. Tchr. Hempfield Sch. Dist., Greensburg, 1968-71; children's libr. Cin. Pub. Libr., 1971-72; br. mgr. Cin. Pub. LIbrary, 1972-74; dir. Rolling Meadows (Ill.) Pub. Libr., 1974-79, Champaign (Ill.) Pub. Libr., 1979-85, Memphis/Shelby County Pub. Libr. and Info. Ctr., 1985—; cons. Providence Assocs., Dallas, 1986-94; Tenn. del. White House Conf. on Librs. and Info. Svcs. Task Force, 1991-92; mem. Tenn. Sec. of State's Commn. on Tech. and Resource Sharing, 1991, 93, steering com. Tenn. Info. and Infrastructure, 1994—, nat. adv. panel for assessment of role of sch. and pub. librs. U.S. Dept. Edn., 1995—.

Mem. Rhodes Coll. Commn. on 21st Century, Memphis, 1986-88, presdl. adv. com. Rhodes Coll., 1992—; mem. Leadership Memphis, 1987—, selection com., 1992-96; mem. Memphis Arts Coun., 1989-94; bd. dirs. Literacy Coun., 1986-91, Memphis NCCJ, 1989-93, Memphis Grants Info. Ctr., 1992—, sec., 1993—; bd. dirs. Memphis Literacy Found., 1988-92, v.p., 1989-90; bd. dirs. Goals for Memphis, 1988-93, chair edn. com., 1989-91, chair nominating com., 1992; mem. exec. adv. bd. Children's Mus., 1988-94, exec. adv. coun. U. Memphis, 1989—; mem. allocations subcom. United Way, 1989-91, allocations com. Memphis Arts Coun., 100 for the Arts, 1989-91, Libr. Self-study Com. U. Memphis; pres. adv. coun. Lemoyne Coll. Recipient Govt. Leader award U. Ill. YWCA, 1981; Communicator of Yr. award Pub. Rels. Soc. of Am., 1992. Mem. ALA (chmn. intellectual freedom com. 1986-87, coun. 1992—), Tenn. Libr. Assn., Memphis Libr. Coun., Pub. Libr. Assn. (v.p., pres. 1994-95), Rotary (bd. dirs. 1992-94, sec. 1993-94, chair mem. devel. com. 1994-95), Beta Phi Mu. Home: 1505 Vance Ave Memphis TN 38104-3810 Office: Memphis Shelby County Pub Libr & Info Ctr 1850 Peabody Ave Memphis TN 38104-4021

DRESKIN, JEANET STECKLER, painter, medical artist, educator; b. New Orleans, Sept. 29, 1921; d. William Steckler and Beate Bertha (Burgas) Steckler Gureasko; m. E. Arthur Dreskin, May 9, 1943; children: Richard Burgas, Stephen Charles, Jeanet Dreskin Haig, Rena Dreskin Schoenberg. BFA, Newcomb Coll., 1942; grad. cert. in med. art Johns Hopkins U., 1943; MFA, Clemson U., 1973; postgrad., Art Students League, N.Y.C., Art Inst. Chgo., 1946, Balt. Mus. Fine Art, 1943. Cert. med. illustrator. Staff artist Am. Mus. Natural History, N.Y.C., 1943-45, U. Chgo. Med. Sch., 1945-50; mem. faculty Mus. Sch. Art, Greenville, S.C., 1950-52, 62—, dir., 1968-75; adj. prof. art U. S.C. at Mus. Sch. Art, 1973—; mem. faculty Govs. Sch. for Arts, Greenville, 1980—; condr. workshops, lectr. in art edn., 1970-93; mem. arts adv. bd. S.C. State Mus., Columbia, 1984-90; workshop leader art dept. U. Ga., 1985; rep. by Fay Gold, Atlanta, Hampton III, Taylors, S.C., also by Art South Gallery, Washington. Group shows Butler Inst. Am. Art, Youngstown, Ohio, 1974, 83, Chataugua exhbn. Am. Art, N.Y., 1970, Nat. Mus. Illustrators, N.Y.C., 1986; represented in permanent collections Nat. Mus. Am. Art, Washington, S.C. State Art Collection, Columbia, Ga. Mus. Art, Athens, Greenville County Mus. Art, Guild Hall Mus., East Hampton, N.Y., Gibbes Mus., Charleston, S.C., Columbia Mus. Art, Tex. Fine Art Assn., Sunrise Valley Mus., Charleston, W.Va., Beaufort Mus., S.C., Kate Shipworth Mus. at U. Miss., McDonald Corp. Coll., Chgo., N.C. Nat. Bank Coll., Asheville (N.C.) Mus. Art, Fed. Res. Bank, Richmond, Va., C & S Collection, Columbia, S.C., U. Ala. Mus.; exhibited at Butler Inst. Am. Art, 1974, 83, Nat. Mus. of Ill., N.Y.C., 1986, Nat. Print and Drawing, Clemson U., 1987-89, 93, Mid.-Am. Arts Alliance, Emporia, Kans., 1989-91, 93, 94, Broome St. Gallery, N.Y.C, 1995-96, Am. Contemporary Artists, 1994, traveling invitational exhbns. of so. graphics, 1990—, numerous others; Contbr. med. drawings to various publs. Mem. Cmty. Found. Greenville, 1968-84, chmn. projects com., 1968-76; historian, hon. mem. Rose Ball, Greenville, 1972—; bd. dirs. Charity Ball, Greenville, 1971—. Recipient Kaplan award Nat. Assn. Painters in Casein, 1969, 71, Keenen award Am. Contemporary Exhbn., Palm Beach, Fla., 1970. Mem. Guild S.C. Artists (pres. 1970-71, bd. dirs. 1981-86, numerous awards 1965, 67, 68, 71, 73, 84), S.C. Watercolor Soc. (pres. 1983-84, bd. dirs. 1985—), So. Watercolor (So. Watercolor-Mabry award 1981, 85, 88, numerous other awards), So. Graphics Coun. (invitational exhibits 1975-77, 88, v.p. 81-83, treas. 1988—), Nat. Assn. Women Artists (S.C. membership chmn. 1970—), Nat. Assn. Med. Illustrators, Am. Contemporary Artist N.Y.C., Greenville Artists Guild (pres. 1956-58, 63, bd. dirs. 1954-83). Avocation: sailing. Home: 60 Lake Forest Dr Greenville SC 29609-5038 Office: Mus Sch Art 420 College St Greenville SC 29601-2017

DRESSLER, ROBERT A., lawyer; b. Fort Lauderdale, Fla., Aug. 20, 1945; s. R. Philip and Elisabeth (Anthony) D.; m. Patricia Kate Toth, Nov. 7, 1981; chidlren: James Philip, Kathryn S. AB cum laude, Dartmouth Coll., 1967; JD cum laude, Harvard U., 1973. Bar: Mass. 1973, Fla. 1974, D.C. 1980, U.S. Dist. Ct. (so. dist.) Fla., U.S. Dist. Ct. Mass., U.S. Ct. Appeals (1st cir.), U.S. Ct. Appeals (5th cir.), U.S. Supreme Ct. Assoc. Goodwin, Proctor & Hoar, Boston, 1973-75; ptnr. Dressler & Dressler, Ft. Lauderdale, 1975-82; mayor City of Ft. Lauderdale, 1982-86; pvt. practice law Ft. Lauderdale, 1982—. Vice chmn. Broward Tng. and Employment Adminstrn., 1982-86; bd. dirs. Broward County League of Cities, 1985-86; nat. committeeman Fla. Fedn. Young Reps., 1981-83; bd. regents State Univ. System, 1987-93; mem. bd. govs. Nova Law Sch., 1988; mem. Estate Planning Coun. Broward County; adv. com. Fla. Atlantic U., Broward, 1989—; exec. com. Tchr. Edn. Alliance, 1991—; chmn. Seflin Free-Net Adv. Bd., 1994—. Capt. USMC, 1969-72. Named Person of Yr. Fla. Atlantic U., 1993. Mem. ABA, Greater Ft. Lauderdale C.of C. (bd. govs. 1982-89), Broward County Bar Assn., Fla. Bar Assn., D.C. Bar Assn., Vietnam Vets. Am., Tower Forum (bd. govs. 1983-86), Phi Beta Kappa. Presbyterian. Home: 1608 NE 6th St Fort Lauderdale FL 33304-2976 Office: PO Box 2425 Fort Lauderdale FL 33303-2425

DRESSNER, PAUL ROBERT, outside sales and customer service representative; b. Chester, Pa., Feb. 1, 1955; s. Robert Lodge and Mary Louise (Rutt) D.; m. Donna Ellen Smith, June 1, 1980 (div. Feb. 1990); children: Robert Warren, Christopher Ryan. BS in Hotel and Restaurant Mgmt., U. Wis., Stout, 1977. Asst. mgr. Morrisons Cafeteria, Columbia, S.C., 1977-79, Florence, S.C., 1979-80, Wilmington, N.C., 1980-83; night mgr. ARA Svcs., Greensboro, N.C., 1983-84; food svc. dir. ARA Svcs., Sewanee, Tenn., 1984-86, Americus, Ga., 1986, Frankfort, Ky., 1987, Cleveland, Tenn., 1987-88, Wilmington, N.C., 1988-89; mgr. Dressner's Village Cafe, St. Simons Island, Ga., 1989-90; customer svc. rep., svc. mgr. Island Automotive, St. Simons Island, 1990-95; outside salesman Brooks Auto Parts, Brunswick, Ga., 1995—. Named one of Outstanding Young Men of Am., 1985. Mem. Brunswick Civic Orch. Home: PO Box 24206 Saint Simons GA 31522-7206

DREW, HORACE RAINSFORD, JR., lawyer; b. Jacksonville, Fla., Jan. 1, 1918; s. Horace Rainsford and Margaret Louise (Phillips) D.; B.S. in Bus. Adminstrn., U. Fla., 1940, LL.B., 1941, J.D., 1967; m. Rae Berger, Oct. 28, 1944; children: Shelley Louise, Robert Fairbanks, Horace Rainsford III. Bar: Fla. 1941. Estate tax examiner Office Internal Revenue Agt. in Charge, Jacksonville, 1946-50; practice law, Jacksonville, 1951—; ptnr. Buck, Drew, Ross & Short, 1951-84, Buck, Drew & Ross, 1985-90, Hand, Drew, Showalter, Mercier, Kelly & McCaulie, P.A., 1991-94, of counsel, 1994—. Bd. dirs. Childrens Home Soc. Fla., 1962-71; founder, trustee Episcopal High Sch., Jacksonville; founding mem. So. Acad. Letters, Arts and Scis. Served to maj. F.A., AUS, 1941-45; ETO; lt. col. JAGD Res. (ret.). Mem. Fla. Bar (chmn. estate and gift tax com. 1956-58, chmn. tax sect. 1959-60, chmn. spl. liaison tax com. Southeastern region 1962-63), Jacksonville Bar Assn. (chmn. com. on taxation 1955-56, 64-65) Am. Judicature Soc., Sons of Confederate Vets., Fairbanks Family in Am. (life), Internat. Order Blue Gavel, Phi Delta Phi, Sigma Alpha Epsilon. Episcopalian. Clubs: San Jose Country, San Jose Yacht (commodore 1978); Officers U.S. Naval Air Sta. (Jacksonville). Home: 861 Waterman Rd Jacksonville FL 32207 Office: 1020 Sun Life Bldg 200 W Forsyth St Jacksonville FL 32202-4349

DREW, K, financial advisor, management consultant; b. Freeport, N.Y.; d. Harry P. and Kathleen (Isdal) Barton; m. Peter Pantazes; children: Karen, Donna. BA, U. Ga., 1960; postgrad., U. Ill., 1961. Dir. YWCA, Corpus Christi, Tex., 1969-72, Dwoskin Nat. Wallcovering Co., Atlanta, 1974-76; dep. asst. fin. presdl. campaign, 1976-77; dir. fin. Presdl. Inaugural, Washington, 1976; dep. adv. for small bus. SBA, Washington, 1977-80, asst. to adminstr., 1980-82; v.p. Alpha Systems, Inc., Washington and Athens, Greece, 1980-85; human resource cons. MBA Mgmt., Inc., McLean, Va., 1982-84; bus. cons. Drew Cons., McLean, 1984—; cons. assoc. Walling, June & Assocs., Old Town Alexandria, Va., 1986-89; fin. advisor The Family Extended, Washington, 1990—; bus. rep. Nikken, Inc., Washington, 1996, KareMor Internat., Inc., Washington, 1996; fin. advisor SAKA, Inc., Merrifield, Va., 1991—, Warrenton, Va., 1991-92, DeLeoand Assocs., McLean, Va., 1991-92; fin. dir. Disting. Environments, Reston, Va., 1992-94. State rep. poverty program and suicide prevention bds. Corpus Christi Bus. Coun., 1969-71; bd. dirs. YWCA, Washington, 1983-85; head speaker's bur. Fairfax Symphony, 1979-85, mem. exec. devel. com., 1979-86; mem. Mental Health Exec. Bd. Dirs., Washington, 1983-88; deacon Nat. Presbyn. Ch., Washington, 1988-90; asst. to exec. dir. T. Monk Found., Jazzs Sch., Duke U., 1987-89; event dir. Easter Seal Soc., 1990-91; mem. Youth for Tomorrow devel. com. Joe Gibbs Charities, Washington, 1990-92; presdl. campaing team captain Va. and Ga. Inaugural Com., 1993; Ga. Ball host, Washington, 1993; host Presdl. Inaugural Gala, Washingotn, 1993; In Kind Svcs. to White House Advance Office of Pres., 1993—, In Kind Svcs., 1993-95, Washington Greetings Office, 1995; bus. cons. Bethany House for Battered Women, 1994. State rep. poverty program and suicide prevention bds. Corpus Christi Bus. Coun., 1969-71; bd. dirs. YWCA, Washington, 1983-85; head speaker's bur. Fairfax Symphony, 1979-85, mem. exec. devel. com., 1979-86; mem. Mental Health Exec. Bd. dirs., Washington, 1983-88; deacon Nat. Presbyn. Ch., Washington, 1988-90; asst. to exec. dir. T. Monk Found., Jazz Sch., Duke U., 1987-89; event dir. Easter Seal Soc., 1990-91; mem. Youth for Tomorrow devel. com. Joe Gibbs Charities, Washington, 1990-92; presdl. campaign team captain Va. and Ga. Inaugural Com., 1993; Ga. Ball host, Washington, 1993; host Presdl. Inaugural Gala, Washington, 1993; In Kind Svc. to White House Advance Office of Pres., 1993—; cons. advisor Battered Spouses & Their Children, Washington, 1995—. Mem. Nat. League Am. Pen Women (v.p., pres. Washington Capital chpt. 1987-89, nat. bd. dirs. 1987-90, nat. roster chmn. 1989—), Bus. and Profl. Women Washington, Nat. Platform Assn., Alpha Gamma Delta. Office: Ste 1-121 8350 Greensboro Dr Mc Lean VA 22102

DREW, NANCY MCLAURIN SHANNON, counselor, consultant; b. Meridian, Miss., Apr. 29, 1934; d Julian Caldwell and Emma Katherine (Sanders) Shannon; m. Thomas Champion III, Feb. 11, 1956; children: Thomas Champion IV, Julian C. Shannon. BA, Furman U., 1956; MEd, N.C. State U., 1968. Cert. sch. counselor; cert. supr. curriculum and instrn., N.C. Rsch. asst. N.C. State U., Raleigh, 1957-59; tchr. English Raleigh City Schs., 1959-60; dir. guidance program Millbrook Sr. High/Wake County Schs., Raleigh, 1969-77; guidance chmn. Daniels Middle Sch./Wake County Schs., Raleigh, 1977-84, guidance info. specialist, 1984-85; guidance supr. Wake County Pub. Schs., Raleigh, 1985-88; coord. model dropout prevention program Wake County Pub. Sch./State Dept. Pub. Inst., Raleigh, 1985-88; counseling chmn. Garner Middle Sch., Raleigh, 1988-96; presenter, cons. 1st and 2d Nat. Dropout Prevention Confs., Winston-Salem, N.C., 1986-87, Raleigh, 1986-88, N.C. Sch. Counselors Conf., Raleigh, 1986-88, Am. Pers. and Guidance Assn., 1976; presenter career workshops ParentScope 1996, speakers' staff ParentScope 1995-96. Contbr. articles to profl. jours. Vice chmn. bd. trustees Crossnore (N.C.) Sch., 1977—; mem. adv. bd. Tamassee DAR Sch., 1994—; sec., bd. dirs. Wake Teen Med. Svcs., Raleigh, 1978-88, Garner Edn. Found., 1991-95; mem. Wake County Bus. and Edn. Leadership Coun., 1992-96. Mem. AACD, NEA, DAR (area rep. spkrs. staff N.C. 1975-78, chmn. state DAR sch. com. 1985-88, state editor DAR News 1989-91, 94—, chpt. regent 1992-95, nat. house com. 1992-94, nat. vice chmn. spl. svcs., state officer 1989-91, dir. dist. VI N.C. State DAR, N.C. Outstanding Jr. Mem. 1970), N.C. Edn. Assn., Am. Sch. Counselors Assn., N.C. Sch. Counselors Assn., Phi Delta Kappa, Delta Kappa Gamma (pres. chpt. 1985-88, state chmn. 1991-93, state com. chmn. 1994—). Democrat. Methodist. Home: 6000 Winthrop Dr Raleigh NC 27612-2142

DREWRY, LYMAN AUBREY, economics educator; b. Richmond, Va., Feb. 25, 1934; s. Lyman Aubrey and Evelyn (Hawthorne) D.; m. Elizabeth Stebbing-Allen, Oct. 14, 1967; children: Timothy Allen, Jonathan Hawthorne. BS in Commerce, U. Va., 1954, MA in Econs., 1956, PhD, 1960. Prof. fin. U. Ga., Athens, 1960-69; dean Sch. Bus. Western Carolina U., Cullowhee, N.C., 1969-73; dean Coll. Bus. Marshall U., Huntington, W.Va., 1973-77; prof. bus. Birmingham (Ala.)-So. Coll., 1977—; Fulbright lectr. U. Malta, 1982; Fulbright prof. U. Ceylon, 1960-61; prof. U. Pitts., 1987; participant Salzburg (Austria) Seminar, 1982. Editor: Money, the Market and the State, 1967. Home: 320 N Burbank Dr Birmingham AL 35226-1608 Office: Birmingham-So Coll 900 Arkadelphia Rd Birmingham AL 35254-0001

DREYER, WILLIAM JEFFREY, pediatrician, researcher; b. St. Petersburg, Fla., July 16, 1955; s. William R. and Constance Lurayne (Socks) D.; m. ZoAnn Eckert, Sept. 7, 1986; 1 child, Taylor Manchester. BS magna cum laude, Furman U., 1977; MD, U. Fla., 1981. Diplomate Am. Bd. Pediatrics, subs. Bd. Pediatric Cardiology. Pediatric intern Vanderbilt U. Hosps., Nashville, 1981-82; resident in pediatrics U. Calif., San Francisco, 1982-84; fellow in pediatric cardiology Baylor Coll. Medicine, Houston, 1984-88, asst. prof. depts. pediatrics and internal medicine, 1988—. Mem. adv. editorial bd. Jour. Thoracic and Cardiovascular Surgery, 1993; contbr. articles to profl. jours. Grantee NIH, 1990—, 91-96, Am. Heart Assn., 1991-93, 96—. Fellow Am. Acad. Pediats., Am. Coll. Cardiology, Am. Heart Assn. (coun. on basic sci 1989, coun. on cardiovasc. disease in the young 1993), Tex. Med. Soc., Harris County Med. Soc., Phi Beta Kappa, Alpha Omega Alpha. Episcopalian. Office: Tex Children's Hosp 6621 Fannin St Houston TX 77030-2303

DREZ, DAVID JACOB, JR., orthopedic surgeon, educator; b. Lake Charles, La., Aug. 21, 1938; s. David Jacob and Hester Adele (Bingham) D.; m. Judith Diane Wolfe, June 5, 1963; children: Susan Drez Joseph, Catherine Ann Self, David Jacob III. BS, Tulane U., 1959, MD, 1963. Diplomate Am. Bd. Surgery, Am. Bd. Orthopaedic Surgery. Intern Charity Hosp., New Orleans, 1963-64, resident in gen. surgery, 1964-68, resident in orthopaedic surgery, 1968-71; resident Scottish Rite Hosp., Atlanta, 1969, USPHS Hosp., New Orleans, 1970; pvt. practice Orthopaedic Assocs., Lake Charles, 1971-82; pvt. practice Orthopaedic and Sports Injury Clinic Knee and Sports Medicine Ctr., Lake Charles, 1982-94; pvt. practice Ctr. for Orthopaedics, Lake Charles, 1994—; staff Lake Charles Meml. Hosp., 1973—, bd. trustees, 1973, 80-82, sec.-treas., 1977, pres., 1981, chief surgery, 1984, 85; med. staff dept. orthopaedics Children's Hosp., New Orleans, 1988; La. state chmn. Orthopaedic Rsch. and Edn. Found., 1987, 90-92; network of orthopedic surgeons U.S. Gymnastics Fedn., 1988—; physician U.S. Soccer Assn., 1988—; examiner Am. Bd. Orthopaedic Surgery, 1989, 91, 92, bd. dirs.; vis. prof. numerous hosps. and univs.; speaker in field. Author: (with R. D'Ambrosia) Prevention and Treatment of Running Injuries, 1982, Prevention and Treatment of Running Injuries, 2d edit., 1989, (with D.W. Jackson) The Anterior Cruciate Deficient Knee-New Concepts in Ligament Repair, 1986, Orthopaedic Sports Medicine: Principles and Practice , 1994 (with Jesse DeLee); author 8 chpts. in books; editor Am. Jour. Sports Medicine, 1988—, Jour. Orthopaedic Techniques, 1993—; co-editor Operative Techniques in Sports Medicine jour., 1993—; mem. editorial bd. Orthopaedics, 1983—, Arthroscopy, 1984-89, Sports Medicine News, 1989—; author 5 video tapes, audio tape; mem. adv. bd. Clin. Update, Sports Medicine, 1983—, Clin. Orthopaedics and Related Rsch., 1987-93; con. rev. bd. Jour. Bone and Joint Surgeons, 1989—; contbr. over 35 articles to profl. jours. Team orthopaedist athletic dept. McNeese State U., Lake Charles, 1974—, pres. 100 Club, 1979; co-dir. Runner's Clinic, La. State U. Sch. Medicine, New Orleans, 1978-81; chief physician NAAU Boxing Championship, Lake Charles, 1979; mem. Gov.'s Coun. on Phys. Fitness and Sports, 1981; bd. dirs. Lake Area Runners, 1989-92. Maj. La. N.G., 1963-71. Named to La. Athletic Trainers Assn. Hall of Fame, 1989, McNeese State U. Hall of Honors, 1990. Mem. Acad. Orthopaedic Soc., Am. Acad. Orthopaedic Surgeons, Am. Acad. Sports Physicians, Am. Coll. Sports Medicine, Am. Coll. Surgeons, Am. Orthopaedic Assn., Am. Orthopaedic Foot Soc., Am. Orthopaedic Foot and Ankle Soc., Am. Orthopaedic Soc. Sports Medicine, Arthroscopy Assn. N.Am., Assn. Bone and Joint Surgeons, Assn. Sports Medicine Fellowship Dirs., Mid. Am. Orthopaedic Assn., Assn. Arthritic Hip and Knee Surgery, Australian-Am. Orthopaedic Soc., Calcasieu Parish Med. Soc., Clin. Orthopaedic Soc., European Soc. Knee Surgery and Arthroscopy, Herodicus Sports Medicine Soc. (past sec., v.p., pres.), Internat. Arthroscopy Assn., Internat. Soc. Knee, La. Orthopaedic Assn. (pres. 1992), La. State Med. Assn., Oscar Creech Surg. Soc., Orthopaedic Rsch. Soc., Soc. Internat. Chirurgie Orthopedique Traumatologie, Soc. Internat. Recherche Orthopedique Tramatologie. Office: Ctr for Orthopaedics 3rd Fl 1717 Oak Park Blvd Fl 3 Lake Charles LA 70601-8990

DREZNER, MARC KENNETH, endocrinologist; b. Newark, Oct. 27, 1945; s. Murray Harold and Rose (Levine) D.; m. Sherree Ann Merenstein, June 18, 1967; children: Todd Eric, Jody Michelle. BS magna cum laude, U. Pitts., 1966, MD cum laude, 1970. Diplomate Am. Bd. Internal Medicine. From assoc. in medicine to prof. Duke U. Med. Ctr., Durham, N.C., 1975—; sr. fellow ctr. for aging Duke U. Med. Ctr., 1983—, dir. sec. bone and mineral metabolism, 1983-91, chief divsn. endocrinology, 1991—, dir. Stedman Nutrition Ctr., 1991—, med. dir. EndoMet Lab., 1991—; med. review bd. Vet. Adminstrn., 1982-85; chmn. gen. medicine & study sect. NIH, 1987-89. Mem. Am. Fedn. Clin. Rsch., Am. Soc. Bone and Mineral Rsch., Am. Soc. Clin. Investigation, Am. Assn. Physicians, Endocrine Soc., Sigma Xi. Office: Duke U Med Ctr Rsch Park I Rm 107A Durham NC 27710

DRIES, ALICE EMERITA, horticulturist, educator; b. Danville, Ill., Dec. 16, 1920; d. Joseph and Theresa M. (Steger) Fazekas; widowed; 1 child, Joseph M. BS in Ornamental Horticulture, U. Ill., 1954, MS, 1965, postgrad., 1991—; attended, Hixson Sch. Design, Cleve., 1975, Boomer Sch. Design, Hawaii, 1982. Cert. in floral design, landscaping, interiorscaping, floral judging, botany, Rosarian and agriculture. Founder ornamental horticultural program Danville Area Community Coll., 1965, instr. ornamental horticulture, 1965-91; owner flower shop, profl. floral designer, judge Danville; designer, judge Danville; judge at various flower shows throughout U.S., 1970—; lectr., commentator program designer for garden clubs, tchrs. seminars, civic orgns., 1965—; tchr. master gardener classes Extension Ctr. U. N.C. Columnist; contbr. articles on floriculture to profl. jours. Mem. coun. of aging Sr. Citizen of McDowell County. Recipient awards Ill. State Garden Club, 1990, Ill. Assn. Community Coll. 1972, Agriculture Instrs., 1980, Ill. Assn. Community Coll., 1966, Tchrs., Danville Area Community Coll., Holiday Workshop, 1991, Nat. Coun. of State Garden Clubs, 1990, Head Start, 1986-88, Men's Garden Club of Am., 1989. Mem. AAUW, Florist Profl. Orgn., Ill Assn. Agriculture Tchrs., Exec. Club, Roselawn Garden Club, Ill. State Garden Club, Rose Soc., State Flower Club (mem. coun.), Danville Women's Club, Toastmasters, Altar and Rosary Soc., Delta Kappa Gamma. Home: RR 1 Box 22214 Old Fort NC 28762-9801

DRIMMER, BERNARD E., research physicist; b. N.Y.C., July 31, 1917; s. David and Rebecca (Kupferschmidt) D.; m. Mary E. Bauckman Edwards, Sept. 3, 1966 (div. Sept. 1984); m. Anne R. Yumkas Gordon, Dec. 1, 1993. BS in Chemistry, CCNY, 1938. Clerical positions, 1938-41; analytical chemist Washington Navy Yard, Washington, 1941-42, U.S. Bur. Mines, College Park, Md., 1942-44; gaseous diffusion engr. Columbia U., N.Y.C., 1944, Carbide & Carbon Corp., Oak Ridge, Tenn., 1944-46; explosives rsch. physicist U.S. Naval Ordnance Lab., Indian Head & White Oak, Md., 1946-50; project engr. explosives U.S. Army Office of Chief of Ordnance, Washington, 1950-52; prodn. engr. U.S. Atomic Energy Com., Washington, 1952-53; Brussels rep. USN Ordnance Tech. Office, Brussels, 1953-56; explosives rsch. br. head U.S. Naval Ordnance Lab., White Oak, Md., 1956-63; rsch. dir. explosives and propellants USN Bur. Naval Weapons, Washington, 1963-66; rsch. dir. explosives, propellants and batteries U.S. Naval Ordnance Sys. Command, Washington and Arlington, Va., 1966-74; pvt. practice cons. explosives and rockets various corps., Arlington & Silver Spring, Va., Md., 1974-79; explosives engr. VSE Corp., Alexandria, Va., 1979-90; cons. explosives VSE Corp., Arlington, 1990—. Author: (5 vols.) Navy Bank of Explosives Data, 1983; contbr. articles to profl. jours.; patentee in field. Mem. AAAS, Am. Phys. Soc., Washington Philos. Soc., N.Y. Acad. Sci., Nat. Geographic Soc., Sigma Xi. Home: 5341 Bodega Pl Delray Beach FL 33484-6665

DRINNON, JANIS BOLTON, volunteer; b. Pineville, Ky., July 28, 1922; d. Clyde Herman and Violet Ethiele (Hendrickson) Bolton; m. Kenneth Cleveland Drinnon, June 13, 1948; 1 child, Dena Daryl. Student, Lincoln Meml. U., Harrogate, Tenn., 1947-48; cert., Art Instrn. Sch., Mpls., 1968. Organizer, prodr., dir. religious plays drama dept. Alice Bell Bapt. Ch., Knoxville, Tenn. Republican. Home: 7434 Hodges Ferry Rd Knoxville TN 37920-9731

DRISCOLL, BARBARA HAMPTON, special education educator; b. Natchitoches, La., July 25, 1949; d. Rick Hampton and Frances (Lovell) Davis; m. Charles M. Driscoll, Mar. 5, 1973; children: Kelli Anne, Christopher Mark. BS, Northwestern State U., 1970; MEd in Adminstrn., U. Miss., Oxford, 1977; EdS, Northwestern State U., 1988. Prin. Proprietary Bus. Sch., Shreveport, La., 1979-80; curriculum cons. St. John Berchman's Sch., Shreveport, 1987-88; tchr. severely emotionally disturbed adolescents Caddo Parish Pub. Schs., Shreveport, 1983-87, 1983-87, juvenile delinquency residential facility tchr., 1987—; pvt. cons. for exceptional children, 1987—; tchr. Boyce (La.) High Sch., 1970-71, John H, Martyn Vocat.-Tech. High Sch., New Orleans, 1971-73, Northwestern State U., Natchitoches, 1977-78. Mem. bd. deaconesses Kings Hwy. Christian Ch., Shreveport, 1987-91; vol. Hospitality House, Shreveport, 1985-88; active local campaigns, Shreveport, 1980; vol., leader Girl Scouts U.S., Shreveport, 1986-89; asst., vol. Boy Scouts Am., Shreveport, leader, 1986—. Mem. Coun. for Exceptional Children, Coun. for Children with Behavioral Disorders. Mem. Christian Ch. (Disciples of Christ). Home: 202 Ockley Dr Shreveport LA 71105-3025 Office: Rutherford House 1707 Line Ave Shreveport LA 71101-4609

DRISCOLL, GARRETT BATES, telecommunications executive; b. Terre Haute, Ind., July 10, 1932; s. James Edgar and Lorraine Emma (Simmons) D.; m. Suzanne Keder O'Reilly, Apr. 30, 1960 (div. Sept. 1984); children: Garrett Edward, Lorraine Elizabeth Driscoll Veltri; m. Ivy Juanita Bryant, Sept. 24, 1985 (div. Aug. 1995); children: Jennifer Louise, Caroline Margaret; m. Janice Patterson Buckalew, Oct. 25, 1996. AA, Broward C.C., Ft. Lauderdale, Fla., 1973; BA, Fla. Atlantic U., Boca Raton, 1979. Tech. supr. TRT Telecom. Corp., Ft. Lauderdale, 1972-80; asst. mgr. N.Y. ops. TRT Telecom. Corp., N.Y.C., 1980-82; asst. v.p. telecom. 1st Am. Bank, Lake Worth, Fla., 1983-86; dir. telecom. R&D John Alden Sys. Co., Miami, Fla., 1986—; lectr. U. Miami, 1988—. With USAF, 1951-71. Lutheran. Office: John Alden Sys Co 7300 Corporate Center Dr Miami FL 33126-1232

DRISCOLL, JAMES JOSEPH, JR., advertising executive; b. La Jolla, Calif., June 8, 1943; s. James Joseph and Wanda Mae (Brown) D.; m. Mary Louise Steuterman, Dec. 24, 1975 (dec. Dec. 1990); children: James Joseph III, Mary Alison. BA in History, U. N.C., 1970. Journalist radio and TV stas., N.C., 1970-73; exec. editor Davis Newspapers/Willows (Calif.) Daily Jour., 1973-75; pub. rels./advt. exec. CP Nat. Corp., San Francisco, 1975-79, Kaiser Aluminum & Chem. Corp., Oakland, Calif., 1979-80; publ., editor Round Valley News, Covelo, Calif., 1980-84; advt. agy. exec. John Malmo Advt., Memphis, 1984-87, Bozell, Atlanta, 1987-90, GTPD Advt., Memphis, 1990-92; co-founder, pres. IDEX Creative Mktg., Memphis, 1992-95; founder, pres. Driscoll & Assoc. Advt., Memphis, 1995. Capt. U.S. Army, 1964-68, Vietnam. Mem. Pub. Rels. Soc. Am., Memphis Advt. Fedn., Train Collectors Am., Lionel Collectors Club Am., Grand Krewe of Ennead. Episcopalian. Office: IDEX Creative Mktg 860 Ridge Lake Blvd Ste 377 Memphis TN 38120-9423

DRISCOLL, JOSEPH FRANCIS, real estate executive; b. Louisville, Apr. 23, 1943; s. Francis Xavier and Elizabeth (Brisse) D.; m. Joann Heskamp, Dec. 27, 1967 (dec. Apr. 1979); 1 child, Michael; m. Margaret Rebecca Thomas, Sept. 24, 1982. BA in Edn., Bellarmine Coll., Louisville, 1965. Lic. real estate salesperson, Tenn.; cert. tchr., Tenn. Real estate agt. Baker Harwell, Joel Riggs Better Homes & Gardens, Nashville, 1984-89, Beck & Beck Real Estate, Nashville, 1989-91, Folk-Jordan Better Homes & Gardens, Nashville, 1991—; cons. Sovran Bank/Ctrl. South, Nashville, 1991-92; citizen mem. bd. Regions Bank. Editor, author: Joe's Notes, 1993-95. Candidate U.S. Congress from 5th Dist. Tenn., 1987-88; candidate Mayor of Nashville, 1991; pres. Snap Housing, South Nashville Action People, 1986-92; mem. Low-income Housing Forum, 1986-93; tchr. Holy Rosary Ch., 1992-93. Served with U.S. Army, 1967-69, Vietnam. Decorated Purple Heart. Mem. Nat. Bd. Realtors, Donelson-Hermitage Chamber (bd. dirs. 1987-88). Democrat. Roman Catholic. Home: 811 Redwood Dr Nashville TN 37220-1810 Office: Folk-Jordan Better Homes 486 Bell Rd Nashville TN 37217-3823

DRIVER, JOE L., state legislator, insurance agent; b. Rockwall, Tex., Sept. 29, 1946; s. Marshall Laguin and Alice Elizabeth (Patillo) D.; m. S. DeAnne Browning, Nov. 20, 1993; stepchildren: Eric Browning, Lynsey Browning. BBA, U. North Tex., 1971; grad., Garland Citizen's Police Acad., 1993. With Steak & Ale Restauants, Dallas, 1971-73; law instr. Garland (Tex.) Ind. Sch. Dist., 1972; mgr. Marshall Driver Ins., Garland, 1972-73; trainee State Farm Ins. Cos., Dallas, 1973-75, mem. regional advt. bd., 1978-82; owner, agt. Joe Driver Ins.-State Farm, Garland, Tex., 1975—; mem. Tex. Ho. of Reps., 1993—, mem. energy resources com., 1993-95, mem. ins. com., 1993—, mem. pub. safety com., 1995—. Pres. Christian Singles Unltd., Garland, 1979; bd. dirs. First United Meth. Ch., Garland, 1979-81, Garland Econ. and Devel. Authority, 1986, Garland Crimestoppers, 1985-88, 93—, Am. Heart Assn., 1991-93; bd. dirs. New Beginning Family and Violence Prevention Ctr., 1988-91, v.p., 1990-91; chmn. SITE Found. of Garland,

Inc., 1991-92; mem. bd. mgmt. Garland YMCA, 1983-85; fundraising chmn. YWCA, 1992; mem. long-range planning com. City of Garland, 1986-88; mem. devel. coun. Baylor Med. Ctr., Garland, 1991—; mem. Downtown Citizen Rev. Com., 1991-92; active Tex. Conservative Coalition, 1993—, Rep. Caucus Tex. Ho. of Reps., 1993—. Recipient Human Relations award Dale Carnegie Cos., 1978. Mem. Nat. Assn. Life Underwriters (Nat. Quality award 1978-83, 86-92), Dallas Assn. Life Underwriters, Garland C. of C. (bd. dirs. 1983-87, chmn. 1986, corp. coun. 1988-90), Rowlett C. of C., Sachse C. of C., Tex. Dist. Exch. Clubs (dist. dir. 1984, Outstanding Dist. Dir. award 1985, Pres.'s award 1986), Noon Exch. Club Garland (bd. dirs. 1982-86, 90-91, pres. 1983, 90, Outstanding Svc. award 1986-87), Leadership Garland Alumni Assn. (bd. dirs. 1990-91), U. North Tex. Alumni Assn., Republican Forum, Lambda Chi Alpha (pres. 1971). Office: 201 S Glenbrook Dr Garland TX 75040-6227

DRIVER, JUDY ANNE, home health consultant; b. Bowdon, Ga., Sept. 2, 1946; d. Robert Eual and Verdie Louise (Whitman) Jeter; m. Louis Edward Driver, Mar. 7, 1965; children: Wendy Leigh-Anne, Stefanie Robyn. ADN, West Ga. Coll., 1978. Staff nurse to asst. dir. nursing Bowdon (Ga.) Area Hosp., 1978-82; edn. coord. Higgins Gen. Hosp., Bremen, Ga., 1982-91; standards surveyor Ga. Dept. Human Resources, Office of Regulatory Svcs., Atlanta, 1991; clin. dir. Liberty Home Health, Carrollton, Ga., 1992; cons. Family Home Health, Inc., Carrollton, 1992; regulatory cons. Cen. Health Svcs., Atlanta, 1992-96, Simione Ctrl., Inc., 1996—; PROBE chmn. for West Ga., Ga. Soc. Healthcare Edn. and Tng., 1988-89. Svc. and rehab. chmn. Am. Cancer Soc., Haralson County, Ga., 1986-91; profl. edn. chmn. Am. Heart Assn., Haralson County, 1987-91; dist. bd. dirs. Am. Lung Assn., 1982-85; coord. Lifeline Emergency Sys., Haralson County, 1983-91. Republican. Baptist. Home: 205 Hidden Lakes Dr Carrollton GA 30116

DRIVER, LOTTIE ELIZABETH, librarian; b. Newport News, Va., Dec. 6, 1918; d. James W. and Lottie (Williams) D. Student, Averett Coll., 1936-37; B.S., Mary Washington Coll. of U. Va., 1939; A.B.L.S., Coll. William and Mary, 1944. Band instr. Hampton (Va.) Sch. System, 1939-41; asst. librarian Newport News Pub. Library, 1941-47, librarian, 1947-69; asst. dir. Newport News Pub. Library System, 1969, dir., 1977-81; author book rev. column in Daily Press; library news reporter radio sta. WGH, 1959. Author articles for library supply house. Active United Fund. Recipient Community Service certificate Kiwanis Clubs Newport News, 1970; named Outstanding City Employee, 1970. Mem. ALA, Southeastern, Va. library assns., AAUW, P.E.O., DAR, Phi Theta Kappa, Alpha Phi Sigma. Baptist.

DRODDY, JESSE DARYL, education educator; b. Call, Tex., Jan. 24, 1944; s. Jesse Pershing Droddy and Sue Frances (Jones) Wells; m. Judith Anne Wright, July 16, 1966 (div. May 1981); 1 child, Melissa Jane; m. Judith Darlene Frank Droddy, Feb. 19, 1983. BS, Stephen F. Austin State Coll., 1966; MBA, U. N.D., 1973; JD, Harvard Law Sch., 1989; MA, U. Ky., 1995, PhD, 1996. Bar: Oreg., 1989, Colo., 1990, Ky., 1991. Assoc. Stoel, Rives, Boley, Jones & Grey, Portland, Oreg., 1989-90, Stites & Harbison, Louisville, 1991-93; asst. prof. of govt. Western Ky. U., Bowling Green, 1996—; vis. asst. prof. of law, Lewis & Clark Sch. of Law, Portland, 1990-91. Bd. govs. Goodwill Industries, Louisville, 1992-93. Lt. col. USAF, 1966-86. Mem. Mensa, Ctr. for Study of the Presidency, Supreme Ct. Hist. Soc., Am. Soc. Pub. Adminstrn., Am. Polit. Sci. Assn. Republican. Home: 220 Brandywood Ct Bowling Green KY 42101-3911 Office: Western Ky Univ Dept Govt 1 Big Red Way Bowling Green KY 42101

DROESSLER, EARL GEORGE, geophysicist educator; b. Dubuque, Iowa, Jan. 14, 1920; married; 5 children. AB, Loras College, Dubuque, Iowa, 1942, ScD (hon.), 1958; MS in Meteorology, U.S. Naval Postgraduate Sch, Annapolis, Md., 1944. Meteorologist Office of Naval Rsch., 1956-50, head geophys. br., 1950; exec. sec. coord. com. gen. sci. Office of Asst. Sec. Def. for R&D, 1954-58; program dir. atmospheric sci. NSF, 1958-1966; prof. atmospheric sci. SUNY, Albany, 1966-1971; prof. geoscis. N.C. State U., 1971-79, prof. emeritus geosciences, 1979—; dir. univ. affairs Nat. Oceanic & Atmospheric Adminstrn., 1979-83; asst. sec. natural resources N.C. Dept. Natural Resources & Cmty. Devel., 1983-85; former head atmospheric scis. divsn. NSF; mem. Adv. Com. Weather Control, 1953-57, U.S. Nat. Com. Internat. Geophys. Year, 1955-64, N.C. Commn. Sci. & Tech., 1971-79; bd. govs. Rsch. Triangle Inst., N.C., 1973-79, exec. com., 1975-79. Fellow Am. Geophys. Union (Waldo E. Smith medal 1993), Am. Meteorol. Soc. (pres. 1983, Charles Franklin Brooks medal 1976, Cleveland Abbe award 1992). Home: 1305 Glen Eden Dr Raleigh NC 27612-4750 Office: NC State U Dept Marine and Atmospheric Scis Raleigh NC 27650

DROKE, ROSE MARY, university administrator; b. Tecumseh, Mo., July 3, 1935; d. Lonnie Vesta and Madge Elizabeth (Clark) White; m. William Joseph Droke, Jan. 9, 1954; children: Susan, Julia, Rebecca, David, Timothy, Nancy, Kathleen, Daniel. AA, San Antonio Jr. Coll., 1954. Collection corr. Richard Gill Cos., San Antonio, 1952-55; sales assoc. Joske's of Tex., San Antonio, 1956-58; specifications designer Wallace Thomas, Architect, San Antonio, 1960-64; pvt. investigator Rhode's Dept. Store, San Antonio, 1970-72; with St. Mary's U., San Antonio, 1970—, placement coordinator, 1973-74, dir. career planning and placement, 1974-94, dir. employee rels., 1994—; presenter HACU Conf., Washington, 1992. Vol. San Antonio State Hosp., 1955-60; active St. Dominic's Ch., San Antonio; mem. Alamo bd. Pvt. Industry Coun. 1990-93. Recipient cert. recognition, San Antonio Women's Hall of Fame, 1986, Nat. Assn. of Colleges and Employer, award of excellence for ednl. programming, 1996. Mem. Tex. Assn. Sch., Coll. and Univ. Staffing (sec. 1978, treas. 1979, cert. of appreciation 1979), SW Placement Assn. (sec. 1979-80, treas. 1981-82, pres. 1985, bd. govs. 1989, program chair ann. conf. 1993, achievement award 1986, John M. Brooks award 1990), Am. Soc. Pers. Adminstrs., San Antonio Pers. and Mgmt. Assn. (pres. 1981-84, award 1984), Coll. Placement Coun. (bd. govs. 1986-91, chmn. nat meeting 1989, chair, exec. dir. search com. 1991-92, Warren Kaufman award 1992), Women's Assn., Alcoholic Beverage Industry, Phi Kappa. Republican. Roman Catholic. Office: Saint Mary's U 1 Camino Santa Maria St San Antonio TX 78228-5433

DROLSHAGEN, LEO FRANCIS, III, radiologist, physician; b. Detroit, June 9, 1956; s. Leo Francis Jr. and Janet Marie (Phillppart) D.; m. Barbara Sharon Ritchie, June 29, 1979; children: Leo VI, Colin, Eric. BA English magna cum laude, U. Detroit, 1977; MD, Wayne State U., 1981; postgrad., Armed Forces Inst. of Pathology, Washington, 1985. Diplomate Am. Bd. Radiology, Nat. Bd. Med. Examiners; lic. Tenn., Mich., Ark. Resident in radiology Henry Ford Hosp., Detroit, 1981-85; fellow Vanderbilt U. Hosp. Sch. of Medicine, Nashville, Tenn., 1985-86; radiologist Radiologist P.A., Ft Smith, Ark., 1986—; med. dir., magnetic resonance imaging St. Edward Mercy Med. Ctr., Ft Smith, 1986-90; chief, dept. radiology St. Edward Mercy Med. Ctr., 1988-91, vice chief of med. staff elect, 1991-92; v.p. Radiologist P.A., Ft. Smith, 1991—; chief of staff St. Edward Mercy Med. Ctr., 1992—; clinical asst. prof. of Magnetic Resonance Imaging U. Ark., St. Edward Mercy Med. Ctr. Author: (with others) Magnetic Resonance Imaging of the Normal and Abnormal Female Pelvis, 1986, The Pelvis, 1986, Critical Diagnostic Pathways in Radiology, 1987; contbr. articles to profl. jours. Recipient Tchr. of the Year in Sonography award Vanderbilt U. Med. Ctr., 1985-86, Howard Walsh Meml. award U. Detroit, 1977. Mem. AMA, Am. Coll. Radiology, Radiologic Soc. N.Am., Am. Inst. Ultrasound in Medicine, Am. Coll. Radiology, Soc. Magnetic Resonance Imaging in Medicine, Sebastian County Med. Soc., Mensa, Ft. Smith C. of C., Ducks Unlimited, Bonsai Club. Home: 7500 Westminister Pl Fort Smith AR 72903-4253 Office: Radiologist PA PO Box 3887 1501 S Waldron Rd Ste 109 Fort Smith AR 72903-2592 also: St Edward Mercy Med Hosp Dept Radiology Fort Smith AR 72903

DRONEBURG, NANCY MARIE, geriatrics nurse; b. Frederick, Md., Jan. 29, 1953; d. John G. and Marie K. (Stone) D. AA, St. Phillip's Coll., San Antonio, 1979; BSN, U. Tex., San Antonio, 1983. RN, Tex.; cert. geriatrics, med./surg. Staff nurse Audie L. Murphy VA Hosp., San Antonio, 1983—. With U.S. Army, 1972-79. Home: 513 Mesquite St Converse TX 78109-1313

DRONET, VIRGIE MAE, secondary education educator; b. Kaplan, La., Mar. 17, 1941; d. Percy Joseph and Zula Mae (Harrington) D.; B.S., U. Southwestern La., 1963, M.Ed., 1970; Ed.S., McNeese State U., 1976; Ed.D., E. Tex. State U., 1979. Tchr. sci.-math., Lake Arthur, La., 1962-89; asst. instr. Center Ednl. Media and Tech., E. Tex. State U., 1977-78; with photog. prodn. lab., 1977-78; ; tchr. physics, chemistry, biology, lgebra, computer scis. Lake Arthur High Sch. 1962-88; assoc. prof. McNeese State U., 1989—; vis. lectr. McNeese State U., 1982-88; mem. Internat. Scholarship Com., 1980-82; chmn. Internat. Rsch. Com., 1982-84; chmn. Internat. Nom. Com., 1992; mem. Internat. Leadership Devel. Com., 1992-94, Internat. Constitution com., 1996-98. Delta Kappa Gamma scholar, 1973, 77; NSF grantee, 1967; La. grantee, 1990, 96. Mem. NEA, Assn. Ednl. Communications and Tech., Nat. Council Tchrs. Math., Assn. Supervision and Curriculum Devel., La. Assn. Educators, La. Assn. Ednl. Communications and Tech., La. Assn. Supervision and Curriculum Devel., Jefferson Davis Assn. Educators, Catholic Daus. Am., Delta Kappa Gamma (participant leadership seminar Baylor U. 1982), Phi Delta Kappa, Kappa Delta Pi, Kappa Mu Epsilon, Alpha Omega, Delta Kappa Gamma (state pres. 1989-91). Democrat. Author articles in field; editor La. Deltion, 1981-87. Home: PO Box 674 Lake Arthur LA 70549-0674 Office: McNeese State U Coll Edn PO Box 91815 Lake Charles LA 70609-1815

DROWOTA, FRANK F., III, state supreme court justice; b. Williamsburg, Ky., July 7, 1938; married; 2 children. B.A., Vanderbilt U., 1960, J.D., 1965. Bar: Tenn. 1965, U.S. Dist. Ct. Tenn. 1965. Sole practice, 1965-70; chancellor Tenn. Chancery Ct. Div. 7, 1970-74; judge Tenn. Ct. Appeals, Middle Tenn. Div., 1974-80; assoc. justice Tenn. Supreme Ct., Nashville, 1980-89, chief justice, 1989-93, assoc. justice, 1993—. Served with USN, 1960-62. Office: Tenn Supreme Ct 318 Supreme Ct Bldg 401 7th Ave N Nashville TN 37219-1406*

DRUCKENMILLER, JOHN CHARLES, newspaper editor; b. Barberton, Ohio, Nov. 1, 1954; s. Morris F. Jr. and Dorothy Ann (Brown) D.; m. Jean Wilkening, Oct. 19, 1996. AA, Brevard C.C., Cocoa, Fla., 1975; BS in Journalism, U. Fla., 1977. Reporter The Ledger, Lakeland, Fla., 1978-81; reporter, asst. city editor News-Press, Fort Myers, Fla., 1981-83; city editor, asst. mgr., editor Fla. Today, Cocoa, 1983-86; editor, reporter USA Today, Arlington, Va., 1987; editor Charlotte Co. News-Press, Port Charlotte, Fla., 1987-88; exec. metro News-Press, Fort Myers, 1988-90; mng. editor The Times, Gainesville, Ga., 1990—; guest prof. U. Fla., Gainesville, 1984; lectr. Brenau U., Gainesville, Ga., 1990—, Am. Press Inst., Reston, Va., 1994-95. Weekly columnist The Times, 1990—. Mem. adv. coun. Ga. AP Assn., 1990-93. Recipient Liberty Bell award Gainesville (Ga.)-N.E. Bar Assn., 1996. Mem. Rotary Club South Hall (program dir. 1995—). Roman Catholic. Home: 2202 Colonial Cir Gainesville GA 30501 Office: The Times 345 Green St NW Gainesville GA 30501

DRUCKER, DANIEL CHARLES, engineer, educator; b. N.Y.C., June 3, 1918; s. Moses Abraham and Henrietta (Weinstein) D.; m. Ann Bodin, Aug. 19, 1939; children: R. David, Mady Drucker Upham. BS, Columbia U., 1937, MCE, 1938, PhD, 1940; D Engring. (hon.), Lehigh U., 1976; DSc in Tech. (hon.), Technion, Israel Inst. Tech., 1983; DSc (hon.), Brown U., 1984, Northwestern U., 1985, U. Ill., 1992. Instr. Cornell U., 1940-43; supr. Armour Rsch. Found., Chgo., 1943-45; asst. prof. Ill. Inst. Tech., 1946-47; assoc. prof. Brown U., Providence, 1947-50, prof., 1950-64, L. Herbert Ballou Univ. prof., 1964-68, chmn. div. engring., 1953-59, chmn. phys. scis. coun., 1960-63; dean Coll. Engring. U. Ill., Urbana, 1968-84; grad. rsch. prof. engring. scis. U. Fla., Gainesville, 1984-94, prof. emeritus, 1994—; Marburg lectr. ASTM, 1966; mem., past chmn. U.S. Nat. Com. on Theoretical and Applied Mechanics; past chmn. adv. com. for engring. NSF; mem. Nat. Sci. Bd., 1988-94; hon. chmn. 3d SESA Internat. Congress on Exptl. Mechanics; rsch. in stress-strain rels., finite plasticity, stability, fracture and flow on macroscale and microscale. Author: Introduction to Mechanics of Deformable Solids, 1967; contbr. chpts. to tech. books, papers to mech. and sci. jours. Recipient Gustave Trasenster medal U. Liège, Belgium, 1979, Thomas Egleston medal Columbia U. Sch. Engring and Applied Sci., 1978, John Fritz medal Founder Engring. Socs., 1985, Nat. Medal of Sci., 1988, ASME medal, 1992; Guggenheim fellow, 1960-61; NATO Sr. Sci. fellow, 1968; Fulbright Travel grantee, 1968. Fellow AAAS (past chmn. sect. engring., past mem. coun.), AIAA (assoc.), ASME (hon. mem., chmn. applied mechanics div. 1963-64, v.p. policy bd. communications 1969-71, pres. 1973-74, Timoshenko medal 1983, Thurston lectr. 1986, Disting. lectr. 1987-89), ASCE (von Karman medal 1966, past pres. New Eng. coun., past pres. Providence sect., past chmn. exec. com. engring mechanics div.), Am. Acad. Mechanics (past pres.), Am. Acad. Arts and Scis. (past mem. membership com.); mem. NSPE, Ill. Soc. Profl. Engrs. (hon.), Soc. Exptl. Stress Analysis (hon.; past pres., W.M. Murray lectr. 1967, M.M. Frocht award 1971), Am. Technion Soc. (past pres. So. N.E. chpt.), Soc. Rheology, Am. Soc. Engring. Edn. (charter fellow mem., past 1st v.p., past chmn. engring. coll. coun., dir., pres. 1981-82, Lamme award 1967, Disting. Educator, Mechanics div. 1985, named to Hall of Fame 1993), NAE (mem. com. on pub. engring. policy 1972-75, chmn. membership policy com. 1982-85), Soc. Engring. Sci. (William Prager medal 1982), Polish Acad. Scis. (fgn. mem.), Internat. Union Theoretical and Applied Mechanics (treas. 1972-80, pres. 1980-84, v.p. 1984-88, personal mem. Gen. Assembly 1988—), Internat. Coun. Sci. Unions (past mem. gen. com.), Sigma Xi (past pres. Brown U. chpt.), Phi Kappa Phi (past pres. U. Fla. chpt.), Tau Beta Pi, Pi Tau Sigma, Chi Epsilon, Sigma Tau. Office: U Fla 231 Aerospace Engring Bldg Gainesville FL 32611-6250

DRUM, JOAN MARIE MCFARLAND, federal agency administrator; b. Waseca, Minn., Mar. 31, 1932; d. Leo Joseph and Bergetthe (Anderson) McFarland; m. William Merritt Drum, June 13, 1954; children: Melissa, Eric. BA in Journalism, U. Minn., 1962; MEd, Coll. William and Mary, 1975, postgrad., 1984-85. Govt. ofcl. fgn. claims br. Social Security Adminstrn., Balt., 1962-64; freelance writer Polyndrum Publs., Newport News, Va., 1967-73; tchr. Newport News (Va.) Pub. Schs., 1975-79; writer, cons. Drum Enterprises, Williamsburg, Va., 1980-82; developer, trainer communicative skills U.S. Army Transp. Sch., Ft. Eustis, Va., 1982-86; govt. ofcl. test assistance div. U.S. Army Tng. Ctr., Ft. Eustis, 1986, course devel. coord. distributed tng. office, 1992; adj. faculty English dept. St. Leo Area Coll., Ft. Eustis, 1975-78; del. Communicative Skills Conf., Ft. Leavenworth, Kans., 1983; mem. Army Self-Devel. Test Task Force, 1991-92; task force mem. U.S. Army Tng. FAA; program developer multi-media electronic delivery prototype. Author: Ghosts of Fort Monroe, 1972, Travel for Children in Tidewater, 1974, Galaxy of Ghosts, 1992; editor: army newsletter for families, 1968-73, Social Services Resource Reference, 1970; contbr. articles to profl. jours. Chmn. Girl Scouts U.S., Tokyo, 1964-66, Army Cmty. Svc., Ft. Monroe, Va., 1967-68; chmn. publicity Hist. Home Tours, Ft. Monroe, 1971-73; chmn. adv. bd. James City County Social Svcs., 1989-95, chmn. adult svcs., 1989-90; mem. James City County Leadership Devel. Program Bd. Recipient numerous civic awards including North Shore Cmty. Svc. award, Hialeah, Hawaii, 1966, Home Bur. Svc. award, 1975, Svc. award Girl Scouts U.S., Tokyo, 1965, Comdrs. award for civilian svc., 1995. Mem. Nat. Soc. for Performance Instrn. (v.p. adminstrn. Tidewater chpt.), Va. Writers Club, Kappa Delta Pi. Home: 9 Bray Wood Rd Williamsburg VA 23185-5504 Office: Ind Tng Support Directorate US Army Tng Ctr Newport News VA 23604

DRUMMOND, CAROL CRAMER, voice educator, singer, artist, writer; b. Indpls., Mar. 5, 1933; adopted d. Burr Ostin and L. Ruth Welch; m. Roscoe Drummond, 1978 (dec. 1983). Student, Butler U., 1951-53; studied with Todd Duncan, Rosa Ponselle,, John Bullock and Dr. Peter, Herman Adler.; studied with, Frances Yeend, James Benner, W.Va.; studied drama with, Washington. Original performer Starlite Musicals, Indpls., 1951; singer Am. Light Opera Co., Washington, Seagle Opera Colony, Schroon Lake, N.Y., 1963, 64, Noyes Flude, Lufkin, Tex., 1965; soloist St. John's Episcopal Ch., Lafayette Sq., Washington, 5th Ch. of Christ, Scientist, Washington, 1963-78, St. John's Episc. Ch., Washington; performer Concerts in Schs. Program, Washington Performing Arts Soc., 1967—; soloist with Luke AFB band ofcl. opening Boswell Meml. Hosp, Sun City, Ariz., 1970; painter, artist, 1980—; pvt. tchr. voice and speech Mt. Desert Island, Maine, 1986—; voice tchr. Mt. Desert Island High Sch., 1986—; soloist numerous oratorio socs., appearances with symphony orchs. including Nat. Symphony Orch., Fairfax (Va.) Symphony Orch., 1970, 71, Buffalo Philharm. Orch. Concerts in the Pk., Arlington Opera Co., Lake George Opera Co., Glen Falls, N.Y., Noyes Flood, Lufkin, Tex., 1965, Washington Opera; voiceover radio and TV commls., 1965-84, U.S. Govt. host The Sounding Bd., Sta. WGTS-FM, Washington, 1972-78; dir. ensembles, music/voice cons. Summer Festival of the Arts, S.W. Harbor, Maine, 1992-95; dir. Amahl and the Night Visitors, 1992; vocal solo concert, The Smithsonian Instn., 1980. Former columnist Animal Crackers; writer newspaper and mag. articles and stories; exhibited in art group shows; one-woman shows in painting, oil and acrylics at Maine Med. Ctr., Bangor, 1995; one-woman shows Lemon Tree,, Bangor, 1995, 96, Grand Theater, Ellsworth, Maine, 1995, two-woman shows The Cosmos Club, Washington, 1996, Members Art Show, The Arts Club, Washington, 1997. Bd. dirs. Washington Sch. Ballet, 1978; life bd. dirs. Internat. Soundex Reunion Registry, Carson City, Nev. Recipient 1st pl. women's divsn. Internat. Printers Ink Contest, 1951. Mem. Nat. League Am. Pen Women, Am. Art League, Nat. Press Club (Washington), Arts Club of Washington, Maine State Soc. (life), Kappa Kappa Gamma. Republican. Episcopalian. Home: Dream Come True 79 Clark Pt Rd PO Box 791 Southwest Harbor ME 04679 Office: 1350 Beverly Rd Ste 115-135 Mc Lean VA 22101-3924

DRUMMOND, NEIL HIDEN, retired secondary school educator; b. Newport News, Va., Sept. 6, 1940; s. Milton Dwight and Ethel Virginia (Hiden) D. BS, Coll. William and Mary, 1962, MA in Math., 1964. Cert. tchr., Va. Math. tchr. Warwick High Sch., Newport News, 1962-65, chmn. math. dept., 1966-91; ret., 1991; treas., exec. bd. Newport News Edn. Assn., 1965-72; chmn. City Textbook Adoption Com., Newport News, 1965-91; mem. State Textbook Adoption Com., Richmond, VA., 1968; speaker State Math. Conf., Alexandria, Va., 1969; exec. bd. Newport News Retired Tchrs. Assn., 1993-94. sponsor Mu Alpha Theta, Newport News, 1965-91, Sr. Class Warwick High Sch., Newport News, 1966-67, Hi-Y and Jr. Hi-Y, Newport News, 1965-71; mem. Nat. Honor Soc. Com., Newport News, 1976-91; fin. com. First United Meth. Ch., Newport News, 1987-91. Mem. NEA, Nat. Coun. Tchrs. Math., Am. Swedish Hist. Soc., Va. Edn. Assn., Evaluating Teams of High Sch. in Va., Vasa Order of Am. Drott Lodge. Home: 27 Nutmeg Quarter Pl Newport News VA 23606-3911

DRUMMOND BORG, LESLEY MARGARET, clinical geneticist; b. Wellington, New Zealand, Oct. 26, 1948; came to U.S., 1986; d. Grant Allen and Yolanda Drummond; m. Kenneth Irvin Borg; children: Marc, Kyle. MBChB, Otago Med. Sch., New Zealand, 1971, MD, 1983; BSc, Auckland U., New Zealand, 1976. Diplomate Am. Bd. Pediatrics, Am. Bd. Med. Genetics; cert. clin. geneticist. Fellow in clin. genetics U. Auckland Med. Sch., 1974-77, med. geneticist, 1977-79; pediatric resident Hosp. Sick Children, Toronto, Ont., Can., 1980-82; gen. practitioner ARAMCO, Saudi Arabia, 1983-86; sr. fellow med. genetics U. Wash., Seattle, 1986-88; clin. geneticist Genetic Screening and Counseling Svc., Denton, Tex., 1988-95; dir., genetics divsn. Tex. Dept. of Health, Austin, Tex., 1995—; clin. asst. prof. Tex. A&M U., College Station, 1991—; cons. staff Odessa (Tex.) Women's Children's Hosp., 1991—, Cook/Ft. Worth Children's Med. Ctr., 1991—. Contbr. articles to profl. jours. Fellow Am. Acad. Pediatrics, Am. Coll. Med. Genetics (founder); mem. AMA, Am. Soc. Human Genetics. Office: Genetic Divsn Tex Dept of Health 1100 W 49th St Austin TX 78746

DRURY, JOHN E., retired waste management company executive; b. 1944; married. Owner, ptnr. Lakeville Sanitary Svc., 1964-68; with Atlas Disposal Svc., 1967-70; bought by Browning-Ferris Industries Inc., 1970; with Browning-Ferris Industries, Inc., Houston, 1970—, exec. v.p. waste systems div. and mem. mgmt. com., 1972-83, pres., chief oper. officer, 1983-91, also dir.; CEO, chmn. bd. USA Waste Svcs., Inc., Dallas, 1994—; pvt. investor, 1991—. Office: USA Waste 5400 LBJ Frwy Ste 300 Dallas TX 75240

DRVAR, MARGARET ADAMS, vocational education educator; b. Morgantown, W.Va., Dec. 22, 1953; d. Lester Morris and Daun Collette (Benson) Adams; m. Marvin Lynn Drvar, July 29, 1978; children: Jacob Elias, Jared Nathaniel. BS in Family Resources, W.Va. U., 1977, MS in Family Resources, 1982. Cert. tchr., vocat. home econs. tchr., W.Va. Substitute tchr. Monongalia County Bd. Edn., Morgantown, 1983-86; tchr. vocat. home econs. Clay Battelle Jr.-Sr. H.S., Blacksville, W.Va., 1986-89, 91-92, South Jr. H.S., Morgantown, 1992—; instr. culinary arts Monongalia County Tech. Edn. Ctr., Morgantown, 1989-91; youth group adv. Future Homemakers of Am., 1986—. V.p. United Meth. Women, Brookhaven, W.Va., 1985-92; sec. bd. trustees Brookhaven United Meth. Ch., 1989—; bd. dirs., sec. Morgantown AES Fed. Credit Union, 1989—; vol. 4-H leader Brookhaven Bulls 4-H Club, 1992—; mem. Monongalia County 4-H Leaders Assn., sec., 1995—. Named Master Advisor, Am. Assn. FHA/HERO and W.Va. Assn. FHA/HERO, 1996, Outstanding 4-H Leader in Monongalia County, W.Va. 4-H Assn., 1996; recipient Golden Apple Achiever award Ashland Oil Co., 1996. Mem. NEA, Am. Assn. Family and Consumer Scis. (cert.), W.Va. Edn. Assn., Monongalia County Edn. Assn., W.Va. Assn. Family and Consumer Scis., Monongalia County Assn. of Family and Consumer Scis., Am. Vocat. Assn., W.Va. Vocat. Assn., W.Va. Vocat. Assn. (historian family and consumer sci. divsn. 1995-96), Alpha Upsilon Omicron, Gamma Phi Beta. Home: 3307 Darrah Ave Morgantown WV 26505 Office: Monongalia County Schs South Jr High Sch 500 E Parkway St Morgantown WV 26505-6839

DRYE, JERRY LIPE, SR., librarian; b. Albemarle, N.C., Sept. 8, 1941; s. James Lipe and Sarah Edith (Smith) D.; m. Shirley Marie Harrell, Apr. 1966 (div. Oct. 1994); children: Leigh Ayn Drye Henderson, Jerry L. Jr., Stuart Tracy (dec.). BS in Elem. Edn., Old Dominion U., 1965; MLS, Emory U., 1968. 5th grade tchr. Bayside Elem. Sch., Virginia Beach, Va., 1965-67; reference librarian Norfolk (Va.) Pub. Libr., 1968-70, br. librarian, 1970-72, head bus., tech. and social scis. dept., 1973—. Mem. ALA, Va. Libr. Assn., Sunrise Optimist Club (pres. 1995). Methodist. Home: 4601 Mayflower Rd 8-H Norfolk VA 23508 Office: Norfolk Pub Libr 301 E City Hall Ave Norfolk VA 23510

D'SOUZA, ALAN S., tax consultant, real estate agent, pianist, writer; b. Calcutta, India, Jan. 11, 1954; came to U.S., 1967; s. Anthony C. and Irene E. (Azavedo) D'S.; m. Mary Ann Conanan, Aug. 6, 1985; children: Angela Bernadette, Anna Maria. BS in Physics, N.E. Mo. State U., 1974; postgrad. in Bus. Adminstrn., U. New Orleans, 1985; diploma in Real Estate, Bob Brooks Sch. of Real Estate, Baton Rouge, 1996. Bus. and estate cons. Hinsdale-Oakbrook (Ill.) Assoc., 1979-82; pianist Marriott Hotels, Lake of the Ozarks and Canal St., New Orleans, 1982-84; revenue officer IRS, Baton Rouge, 1985-89; tax cons., pianist, writer Baton Rouge, 1989—; vol. income tax assistance IRS, Baton Rouge, 1985—. Author: (series) Latin Jazz, 1995-96; author customer svc. manual Beckley Candy Co., 1974-79; author: (with others) DSK Favorites: Our Best Home Cooking, 1996; featured performer (pianist) Beyond Category: The Musical Genius of Duke Ellington, 1996; contbr. articles to profl. jours. Mem. Soc. Profl. Journalists, Acad. Polit. Sci., Jazz Soc. Baton Rouge (founding bd. dirs. 1990—, author newsletter 1992-96, editl. advisor newsletter 1995—), Baton Rouge C. of C. (founding mem. internat. trade coun. 1990—), Smithsonian Instn., Libr. of Congress Assocs. (assoc.). Democrat. Roman Catholic. Home: 15728 Council Ave Baton Rouge LA 70817 Office: DSK Inc Realtors 37338 Perkins Rd Prairieville LA 70769

D'SPAIN, SUZANNE LANCASTER, mental health therapist; b. Schenectady, N.Y., Oct. 7, 1947; d. H. Carroll and Tommie (Spence) Lancaster; children: Michael F., Shera C. BS, Abilene Christian U., 1969; MEd, U. Okla., 1988. Lic. profl. counselor, Okla., Marital and Family Therapist, Okla. Clerical supr. Tex. Dept. Human Svcs., Austin, Tex., 1970-72; psychol. asst. Taliaferro Community Mental Health Ctr., Duncan, Okla., 1988-91; therapist Christian Family Counseling Ctr., Lawton, Okla., 1991-93; pvt. practice, 1993—. Vol. Bible class tchr. for children and adults, Meals on Wheels, children's camp music tchr., children's day sch. ch. program, Girl Scouts USA, 1972-86; sec. bd. dirs. Duncan, 1990—, bd. dirs., 1991-92; newsletter chmn. Duncan Little Theater, 1993—. Recipient Acting Excellence award Okla. Community Theater Assn., 1989. Mem. Okla. Assn. Counseling and Devel., Am. Assn. Christian Counselors, Chi Sigma Iota Internat. Office: Christian Counseling Ctr 1206 N Highway 81 Duncan OK 73533-1760

DUARTE, PATRICIA M., real estate and insurance broker; b. Truro, Mass., Feb. 23, 1938; d. Antone Jr. and Marjorie (Beckley) Duarte. Grad. high sch., Provincetown, Mass. Lic. ins. and real estate broker; constrn. supt. Sec. various ins. agys., Amherst, Mass., 1957-60; ins. and real estate agt. Duarte Ins. & Real Estate, Truro, 1960-66, owner, prin. agt., 1966-78; ins. risk mgr. J.L. Marshall & Sons, Inc., Pawtucket, R.I., 1979-92; owner, mgr. Patricia-Duarte Real Estate, Rockport, Maine, 1988—; restorer antique homes New Eng., Mass., 1979—. Mem., sec. Truro Planning Bd., 1965-72, chmn., 1974-78; mem. exec. com. Cape Cod Planning and Econ. Devel. Com., 1971-76; mem. Reelect Brawn for Senate Com., Camden, Maine, 1988; mem. Rockport Planning Bd., 1991-94, Rockport Comprehensive Plan Implementation Com., 1991-94; co-chmn. Rockport Capital Improvement Com., 1991—; bd. dirs. Cape Cod chpt. Am. Heart Assn., 1963-70; mem. Opera House Commn., 1992-94. Mem. Penobscot Bay Bd. Realtors, Profl. Ins. Agts. New Eng. (bd. dirs. 1974-76), Gen. Fedn. Women's Clubs (2d v.p. Camden chpt. 1989), Hist. Preservation Assn. St. Thomas. Republican. Roman Catholic. Home and Office: 46 Pascal Ave Rockport ME 04856-5918 also: The Anchorage 6600 Estate Nazareth # 55 Saint Thomas VI 00802

DUBAY, STEPHEN NEWTON, hospital administrator; b. Atlanta, Dec. 12, 1941; s. Charles Merrill and Katherine Cushing (Shultis) D.; m. Gloria Elizabeth Carver, July 16, 1972; children: Stephen Newton Jr., Sonya. BA in English, Clemson (S.C.) U., 1969; MPH, U. N.C., 1992. Asst. adminstr. Roanoke Rapids (N.C.) Hosp., 1971-72; assoc. adminstr. Huntersville (N.C.) Hosp., 1972-77, adminstr., 1977-81; assoc. dir. Charlotte (N.C.) Rehab. Hosp., 1982-83; adminstr. McCain (N.C.) Hosp., 1984-96; managed care mgr., health svcs. sect. N.C. Dept. Correction, Raleigh, 1996—. Bd. dirs. West Charlotte Rotary Club, 1982-83; chmn. Nursing Home Adv. Com., Mecklenburg County, N.C., 1983. With U.S. Army, 1962-65. Recipient Vigil Honor, Boy Scouts Am., 1968, Silver Beaver award, 1984. Mem. Am. Coll. Healthcare Execs. Democrat. Episcopalian. Home: PO Box 1275 Southern Pines NC 28388-1275 Office: NC Dept Correction 831 W Morgan St Raleigh NC 28000

DUBE, WILLIAM JOHN, III, dean; b. Houston, Apr. 2, 1946; s. William John and Kathryn (Townlin) D. BA, Baylor U., 1968, MBA, 1972. Auditor Ernst & Ernst, Dallas, 1972-73; assoc. dir. Baylor U., Waco, Tex., 1973-79, asst. v.p., dir. student fin. aid, 1979-84; pres., owner Dube's Inc., Katy, Tex., 1984-90; asst. v.p. Baylor U., 1986-89, dean admissions, acad. sch. fin. aid, 1989-96, dean acad. sch. fin. aid, 1996—; Baylor U. rep. to Coll. Bd. Assembly. Pres. St. Paul Luth Ch., Waco, 1990—, Katy Bus. Assocs., 1984-86. Named Outstanding Young Man Am., Jaycees, 1980; recipient Chpt. Adv. of Yr. award, Alpha Tau Omea, 1989. Mem. Nat. Assn. Student Fin. Aid Adminstrs., Nat. Assn. Coll. Admissions Counselors, Tex. Assn. Coll. Admissions Counselors, Tex. Assn. Student Fin. Aid Adminstrs., S.W. Assn. Student Fin. Aid Adminstrs., Tex. Assn. Coll. and Univ. Student Pers. Adminstrs., Katy C. of C. (bd. dirs. 1984-86). Lutheran. Office: Baylor U PO Box 97028 Waco TX 76798-7028

DUBEL, DORIS GERALDINE COTTRELL, gerontology nurse; b. Bedford, Va., May 21, 1924; d. Roy Owen and Eunice (Johnson) Cottrell; m. Arthur T. Dubel, Jan. 28, 1945; children: Dolores Dubel Fletcher, Ronald A. Diploma, Lewis Gale Hosp., 1945; student, Duquesne U., 1974, U. Pitts., 1977, 78, St. Petersburg (Fla.) Jr. Coll, 1979, 90. RN, Pitts., Fla. With Salk Polio Team, Pitts.; mem. polio and rubella innoculation team Allegheny County, Pitts., 1960-65; fair nurse Allegheny County Fair, Pitts., 1960-70; pvt. duty nurse Nurses Profl. Registry, Pitts., 1974-78; disaster team nurse Greater Pitts. Airport, 1957-72; staff nurse St. Francis Hosp., Pitts., 1945; nurse Mt. Mercy Coll., Pitts., 1974; staff nurse Mercy Hosp., Pitts., 1957-72; staff vis. nurse Roberts Home Health, Pinellas Park, Fla., 1990-95; staff nurse Univ. Gen. Hosp., Seminole, Fla., 1979; participant health study Harvard U. Med. Sch., 1976—, Arthritis Rsch. Inst. Am. Study, 1988—, Womens Antioxidant Cardiovascular study Harvard U. Med. Sch., 1996. With U.S. Army, 1944-45. Recipient DAR award, Florence Nightingale award; NIH grantee U. Pitts. Mem. ANA, Am. Nurses Found., Fla. Nurses Assn., Gerontology Coun. Fla., St. Petersburg Writers Club, Suncoast Christian Writers Club, Fla. State Poets Assn. (pres. prime time poetry), Nat. League Am. Pen Women. Home and Office: 11099 100th Ave N Seminole FL 33772

DUBINA, JOEL FREDRICK, federal judge; b. 1947. BS, U. Ala., 1970; JD, Cumberland Sch. Law, 1973. Pvt. practice law Jones, Murray, Stewart & Yarbrough, 1974-83; law clk. to presiding judge U.S. Dist. Ct. (mid. dist.) Ala., Montgomery, 1973-74, U.S. magistrate, 1983-86, U.S. Dist. judge, 1986-90; judge U.S. Ct. Appeals (11th cir.), 1990—. Mem. FBA (pres. Montgomery chpt. 1982-83), Nat. Coun. U.S. Magistrate Judges, Fed. Judges Assn. (bd. dirs.), Supreme Ct. Hist. Soc., Ala. State Bar Assn., 11th Cir. Hist. Soc., Montgomery County Bar Assn. (chmn. Law Day com. 1975, constrn. and bylaws com. 1977-80, grievance com. 1981-83), Cumberland Sch. Law Alumni Assn., Lions, Phi Delta Phi. Office: US Cir Ct Appeals 11th Cir PO Box 867 Montgomery AL 36101-0867

DUBOIS, JULES EDWARD, security firm executive, consultant; b. Panama, Panama, Feb. 18, 1940; (parents Am. citizens); s. Jules Dubois and Maria Lucilla de la Guardia; m. Ann M. Lambert, Aug. 16, 1963; children: Shawn Mitchell, Bettina Lucille, Michelle Ann. BA in Mass Comm., U. Miami, 1962; postgrad., Boston U., 1968; student, USAF Squadron Officer Sch., 1974, Air Command and Staff Coll.; postgrad., Okla. U., 1980. Commd. 2d lt. USAF, 1963, advanced through grades to lt. col., dir. pub. affairs, ret., 1983; pvt. practice cons. San Antonio, 1984-85; dir. corp. community rels. Wackenhut Svcs. Inc., Aiken, S.C., 1985-87; area mgr. Wackenhut, San Antonio, 1987-90, dist. mgr. Tex., 1990-93, regional v.p. ops., 1994-95; dir. Latin Am. ops. Pinkerton Security and Investigations, San Antonio, 1995—. Former mem. indsl. I com. commerce, urban affairs com. Aiken United Way; lay eucharistic min.; mem. Fiesta San Antonio com., San Antonio Armed Forces Pub. Affairs Coun. Decorated Bronze Star; recipient gallantry cross with palm Republic of Vietnam, Peruvian Cross Military Merit, Defense Meritorious Svc. medal, Air Force Meritorious Svc. medal, Air Force Commendation medals (2), Expeditionary Forces medal. Mem. Am. Soc. Indsl. Security, Tex. Pub. Rels. Assn., Air Force Assn. (life), Ret. Officers Assn. (life), Air Force Sergeants Assn., Rotary, Sigma Chi (life, Gamma Chi chpt.). Office: 25823 Whata View San Antonio TX 78258

DUBOIS, NANCY Q., elementary school educator; b. St. Petersburg, Fla., June 6, 1960; d. Thomas Malcolm and Barbara Jean (Leitner) Quehl; m. Donald F. Dubois, Nov. 27, 1981; children: Jacquelyn Nicole, Justin Jared. BA, U. South Fla., Tampa, 1983; MEd, U. Fla., 1993. Cert. tchr., Fla., N.Mex., Tex. Tchr. St. Patricks Sch., Fayetteville, N.C., 1984-85, The Most Holy Name Sch., Gulfport, Fla., 1985-88, Kirtland Elem. Sch., Albuquerque, 1988-91; field advisor Coll. Edn., U. Fla., Gainesville, 1991-93; 4th grade tchr. Schulze Elem. Sch., San Antonio, 1993—. Mem. ASCD, Fla. Coun. Tchrs. of Math., Kappa Delta Pi. Republican. Roman Catholic.

DU BOISE, KIM REES, artist, art educator; b. Hattiesburg, Miss., Apr. 7, 1953; d. Samernie and Margaret J. (Mitchell) R.; m. Michael Lynn Du Boise, Feb. 23, 1974; children: Timothy L., M. Ashley. BA, U. So. Miss., 1986, M of Art Edn., 1988; postgrad., U. Ala., 1994-95. Art tchr. grades 7-12 Columbia (Miss.) Acad., 1975-76; owner, buyer Fashion Alley, Columbia, 1978-79; with prodn./ad design Columbian-Progress/Sunday Mirror (News), Columbia, 1980-81; with advt. design/prodn. Washington Parish ERA-Leader (newspaper), Franklinton, La., 1981; art tchr. grades kindergarten-12 Hattiesburg Prep. Sch., 1984-85; instr. art Pearl River C.C., Poplarville, Miss., 1987-94; artist/photographer Dogwood Studios, 1988—; festival coord. Very Spl. Arts Festival, SE Dist., Poplarville, Miss., 1989-94; art show juror Lamar County Home Extension Art Show, Lumberton, Miss., 1988; fine art juror Pearl River County Fair Competition, Poplarville, 1989; juror Picayune PTA Competition and Annual Art Competition-Picayune Meml. High Sch., 1990; participant regional round-Table on discipline based art edn. Getty Ctr. for Edn. in Arts, Tulsa, 1988. Sculptor Ann. Student Juried Exhibit, 1986; artist, weaver fine crafts (tapestry) Ann. Student Juried Exhibit, 1996, Ann. Bi-State Competition, 1986; group exhbn. MSC/JCAIA Art Exhbn., 1991, Miss. Cmty. Jr. Coll. Art, 1991-92, Art by Art Tchrs. MAEA, 1992, mixed media/photography Ann. Juried Art Student League Exhibit, 1995, photography Black Warrior 10 Exhibit, U. N.Mex., 1995, others. Chmn. troop 21 Dixie Com. Boy Scouts Am., Hattiesburg, 1989-93; mem. Miss. Jaycettes/Marion County Jaycettes, Columbia, 1976-84, U.S. Jaycee Women, 1976-84. Named one of Outstanding Young Women of Am., 1981-84, First Lady #83 (Life Mem.) Miss. Jaycettes, 1982, Winner Speak-Up Competition, Miss. Jaycettes, 1981. Mem. Miss. Art Edn. Assn., Nat. Art Edn. Assn., New Orleans Mus. of Art (assoc.), Nat. Mus. of Women in the Arts (charter), Am. Crafts Coun., Miss. Community/Jr. Coll. Art Instr. Assn., Nat. Conservancy, U. So. Miss. Alumni Assn., Walter Anderson Mus. Art, Kappa Delta Pi. Episcopalian. Home: 245 Rogers Rd Hattiesburg MS 39401-9372

DUBOSE, DOROTHY, educator, publishing consultant; b. Nicholls, Ga., Sept. 10, 1931; d. Charlie Norman and Lelia Mae (Solomon) DuB. BA in English and Edn. summa cum laude, Berry Coll., 1952; MA, Tchrs. Coll. Columbia U., 1969; postgrad., Vanderbilt U., Emory U., Columbia U. Editorial dir., product devel. Macmillian Pub. Co., 1970-86; dir.. Scholars Pub., 1990—; English instr. Clayton State Coll., Morrow, Ga., 1987-96; on site degree program coord., instr. The Union Inst., Atlanta, 1990-93; coord. Ctr. for Acad. Devel., Nat-Louis U., 1990—; editor Learning Power, 1996—; lang. arts cons. Appleton Century Pub. Co. Author: Gulliver's Travels Booknotes, What Is It?; editor Theshold Early Learning Libr., Learning Abilities, Scholastic Elem. Tchr., N.J. Edn. Assn. Rev., The Tenn. Tchr. Vol. tutor N.Y.C. Literacy Vols., 1986; mem. publs. planning com. New Readers Press, 1986, leader tutor tng. workshops, 1987-91; pres. Macmillan Women's Group, 1974-75, 76-77. Named Outstanding Vol. Clayton County, United Way, 1991. Mem. MLA, Nat. Assn. Devel. Edn., Women's Nat. Book Assn. N.Y.C. bd. dirs. 1980-86). Home: 1105 Clairemont Ave # B Decatur GA 30030-1256

DUBOSE, ELIZABETH, community health nurse; b. Ozark, Ala., Nov. 11, 1930; d. Samuel D. and Mattie Victoria (Harrell) Preston; m. Charles Raymond Hudson, Jul. 31, 1949; 1 child, Julianne Hudson Adams; m. John Calvin DuBose, Jul. 15, 1978. AD nursing, Columbus Coll. Sch. Nursing, 1973, BSN, 1977. Lab tech. II Ala. Bureau of Labs., Dothan, Ala., 1951-62; student nurse CCU St. Francis Hosp., Columbus, Ga., 1972-73; charge nurse The Medical Ctr., Columbus, Ga., 1973-75, infection control nurse, 1975-78; charge nurse The Bradley Ctr., Columbus, Ga., 1974-78; clinical instr. RN Columbus Coll., Columbus, Ga., 1977-78; dir. nursing Oakview Manor Nursing Home, Ozark, Ala., 1979-84; patient care coord. Wiregrass Home Health Agy., 13 Counties in SE Ala., 1984-86; home health coord. Ala. Pub. Health Dept., Abbeville, Ala., 1986-90; home health nurse Dale Co. Health Dept., Ozark, Ala., 1990—; libr. com. mem. The Medical Ctr., Columbus, Ga., 1974-77; chmn. adv bd. Oakview Manor, Ozark, 1980-84. Mem. adv. bd. Henry Co. Health Dept., Abbeville, 1986-88, chmn. adv. bd., 1988-90. Republican. Protestant. Home: RR 1 Box 68 Ariton AL 36311-9718 Office: Ala State Health Dept Dale Co Ala Home Health Deese Rd Ozark AL 36360

DUCA, JOHN VINCENT, economist, researcher; b. Bklyn., Apr. 12, 1960; s. Settimo Z. and Angela (Puleo) D.; m. Therese Annette Palmer, Aug. 24, 1986; 1 child, Evan Thomas. BA in Econs. summa cum laude, Yale U., 1982; PhD in Econs., Princeton U., 1986. Staff economist Fed. Res. Bd., Washington, 1986-91; sr. economist, policy advisor Fed. Res. Bank, Dallas, 1991-93, rsch. officer, 1994—; part-time lectr. U. Md., College Park, 1991. Contbr. articles to profl. jours. Social Sci. Found. fellow Princeton U., 1985. Mem. Am. Econ. Assn., NOW (treas. Arlington chpt. 1988-89), Western Econ. Assn., Phi Beta Kappa. Office: Fed Res Bank of Dallas 2200 N Pearl St Dallas TX 75201-2216

DUCHATELET, MARTINE, economics educator; b. Liege, Belgium, Apr. 4, 1949; came to U.S., 1972; d. Louis Fernand Francois and Marie Claire (Firket) D.; m. Eric Vincent Moore, Apr. 24, 1976; children: Frederic, Peter, Anne. BA in Econs., U. Brussels, 1971, MA in Econs., 1972; PhD in Econs., Stanford U., 1977. Asst. prof. econs. U. Va., 1977-79; assoc. prof. fin. and econs. CUNY, Hunter Coll., 1982-87; assoc. prof. econs., internat. bus. and fin. Barry U., Andreas Sch. Bus., Miami, Fla., 1989—; vis. asst. prof. bus. econs. Columbia U., 1979-82, vis. asst., assoc. prof., 1982-88; vis. assoc. prof. fin. Fordham U., 1987-88. Contbr. papers to profl. jours. Harkness fellow Common Wealth Fund N.Y., 1973-75. Mem. Delta Sigma Kappa. Office: Barry U 11300 NE 3rd Ave Miami FL 33161-6606

DUCKWORTH, JERRELL JAMES, electrical engineer; b. Ft. Payne, Ala., July 22, 1940; s. James K. and Maggie Lee (Hartline) D.; m. Yvonne Cheryl Jones, Nov. 2, 1974; one child, Shelby Elizabeth. AAS in Elec. Engring., DeVry Inst. Tech., 1963. Gen. engr. McDonnell Aircraft Corp., St. Louis, 1963-66; sr. assoc. engr. IBM Corp. Space Systems Ctr., Huntsville, Ala., 1966-72; chief engr. Electric Systems Inc., Chattanooga, 1972-80; dir. elec. engring. Chattanooga Corp., 1980-91; dir. engring. Chattanooga Group Inc., 1991-95; v.p. of engring. GoPro, Inc., Hendersonville, Tenn., 1995—. Served with U.S. Army, 1958-61. Recipient Apollo 8 medallion NASA, 1968, Apollo 11 medallion, 1969, Apollo Achievement award, 1970. Mem. IEEE, Engring. in Medicine and Biology Soc., Assn. for the Advancement of Med. Instrumentation, Instrument Soc. Am., U.S. Space Found. Mem. Ch. of God. Home: 7916 Shallowmeade Ln Chattanooga TN 37421-1930 Office: GoPro Inc 4295 Cromwell Rd Chattanooga TN 37421

DUCKWORTH, JOSEPH CLYDE, manufacturing technician, writer; b. Parkersburg, W.Va., July 4, 1950; s. Clyde and Virginia Hope (O'Dell) D.; m. Patricia Ann, Jan. 25, 1986. BA, W.Va. Inst. Tech., 1977. Installment loans dept. Charleston (W.Va.) Nat. Bank, 1972-74; corp. quality assurance supr. McJunkin Corp., Charleston, 1974-85; lab. tech. A.B. Chance Co., Parkersburg, 1986-89; project tech. Corning, Inc., Parkersburg, 1989-93; Pres. Duckworth Manuscript Svcs., Davisville, W.Va., 1993. Author: Turn of the Century Missionary, 1992; author and dir: Crosses and Crowns, 1994; writer short stories. Lay leader Kanawha United Meth. Ch., 1992-94. Mem. Eastwood Lions Club (pres. 1981, 85, 86, treas. 1982, sec. 1992, 93). Republican. Home: RR 1 Box 51-b Davisville WV 26142-9801 Office: Duckworth Manuscript Svcs RR 1 Box 51-b Davisville WV 26142-9801

DUCKWORTH, PAULA OLIVER, secondary school educator, freelance artist, writer, photographer; b. Dallas, Aug. 5, 1940; d. Allen Oliver and Minnie Lila (Paul) D. BA, U. Tex., 1963; MA, So. Meth. U., 1968; postgrad., U. London, 1972, R.I. Sch. Design, 1983, U. North Tex., 1985—. Tchr. English San Antonio Ind. Sch. Dist., 1963-65; tchr. art and English Highland Pk. Ind. Sch. Dist., Dallas, 1965—; seminarian Perkins Sch. of Theology, So. Meth. U. Illustrator: A Cotton Feast, 1982; paintings exhibited in several shows and pvt. collections. Patron, Kimball Art Mus., Ft. Worth, Dallas Zool. Soc. Mem. So. Meth. U. Alumni Assn., Soc. Children's Book Writers and Illustrators, Kappa Alpha Theta, Delta Kappa Gamma (Sim Green scholar 1973). Democrat. Presbyterian. Office: Highland Pk High Sch 4220 Emerson Ave Dallas TX 75205-4620

DUDIK, ROLLIE M., healthcare executive; b. Hartford, Conn., Sept. 29, 1935; s. Martin and Iola Maxine (Hamilton) D.; m. Nancy A. Slicner. PhD, Am. U., 1981. Gen. mgr. Freedman Artcraft Engring., Charlevoix, Mich., 1970-73; exec. v.p. Harrison Community Hosp., Cadiz, Ohio, 1973-77; dir. instl. rev. Dade Monroe PSRO, Miami, Fla., 1977-78; exec. dir. Fla. Keys Meml. Hosp., Key West, 1978-82; exec. v.p. Eisenhower Hosp., Colorado Springs, 1982-83; v.p. South Fla. Med. Mgmt., Inc., Miami, 1982—, Doctor's Health Systems Mgmt. Corp., Coral Gables, Fla., 1985-96, About Health, Inc., Rockville, Md., 1996—; pres. R.M. Dudik & Assocs., Inc., Miami, 1983—, Sydney, Australia, 1988—; med. projects cons. Orah Wall Med. Enterprises, Inc., San Antonio, 1985—; pres. Caribbean Diagnostic Ctrs., Inc., Coral Gables, 1986—; chief fin. officer Forenpsych Assocs., Inc., Coral Gables, 1990—. Served with U.S. Army, 1956-62. Mem. Am. Inst. Indsl. Engrs., Am. Acad. Med. Adminstrs., Am. Coll. Healthcare Executives, Hosp. Fin. Mgmt. Assn., Hosp. Mgmt. Systems Soc., Am. Soc. Law and Medicine, Nat. Assn. Flight Instrs., Nat. Assn. Accts., Nat. Counter-intelligence Corps Assn., Assn. Former Intelligence Officers, Australian Intelligence Assn., Aerospace and Environ. Medicine Assn., Rotary, Kiwanis. Address: 2308 Floral Park Rd Clinton MD 20735-9657

DUDLEY, BROOKE FITZHUGH, educational consultant; b. East Orange, N.J., Oct. 22, 1942; s. Benjamin William and Jean (Peeples) D.; AB in Econs., Colgate U., 1966; m. Elizabeth Slater; 1 child, Catherine Sanford. Sales mgr. De La Rue Instruments, Phila., 1968-71; comml. banker Bankers Trust Co., N.Y.C., 1966-68, Provident Nat. Bank, Phila., 1972-74; dir. admissions/fin. aid St. Stephen's Episc. Sch., Austin, Tex., 1974-78; exec. dir. U. Tex. Law Sch. Found., Austin, 1978-85; ednl. cons., 1982—; founding ptnr. The Edn. Group Southwest, Inc., 1989-92; exec. dir. San Antonio Art Inst., 1992-93. Chmn. bd. trustees Austin Evaluation Ctr.; trustee Austin Repertory Theater; chmn. bd. dirs. All Saints Episc. Day Sch., Austin; bd. dirs. Symphony Sq., Austin Child Guidance and Evaluation Ctr.; advisory trustee Winston Sch., San Antonio; Republican campaign mgr., N.Y.C., 1966-68. Served with U.S. Army, 1962-64. Mem. Ind. Ednl. Cons. Assn. Found. (chmn. bd. trustees), Hill Sch. Alumni Assn. (mem. exec. com. 1968-71), Edna Gladney Austin Aux. (past pres.). Episcopalian. Office: 359 E Hildebrand Ave San Antonio TX 78212-2412

DUDLEY, DELORES INGRAM, secondary education educator, poet, writer; b. Portsmouth, Va., Oct. 9, 1948. BA in English, Norfolk State U., 1971, MA in Comm., 1990; postgrad., U. Va., 1981-84, Old Dominion U., Va. State Coll., U. S.C. Tchr. English Ctrl. Jr. High Sch., Charlotte, Va., 1972-78, Cradock High Sch., Portsmouth, 1982-92; tchr. English and pub. speaking Manor High Sch., Portsmouth, 1992-94; columnist Citizens Press, 1985-87; faculty corr., columnist Portsmouth Times, 1992; guest columnist Va. Pilot Ledger-Star Newspaper. Author: A Collection of Poems, 1993. Directress Baptist Tng. Union Third Bapt. Ch., 1995—, past ch. activities include sec. youth assembly, 1st v.p. youth assembly, pres. youth assembly, mem. sr. choir, tchr. vacation bible sch., dir. vacation bible sch., co-dir. vacation bible sch., adult city-wide summer missionary, dir. tng. union; vol. Salvation Army, Feed the Hungry Program. Recipient Higher Edn. fellowship State Coun., Gov.'s Physical Fitness award, 1989. Mem. NEA, Nat. Assn. Tchrs. English, Nat. Assn. Univ. Women (sec. Portsmouth br.), Portsmouth Edn. Assn., Southeastern Va. Arts Assn. (contbr. articles to monthly newsletter). Home: 907 Tazewell St Portsmouth VA 23701-3229

DUDLEY, ELIZABETH HYMER, retired security executive; b. Hibbing, Minn., Mar. 12, 1937; d. Howard Golden and Esther Juliette (Wanner) Hymer; m. Richard Walter Dudley, 1962. BA Brown U., 1959; postgrad. U. Calif., Berkeley. With AT&T Bell Labs., Murray Hill, N.J., 1959-89, systems programmer, personnel info., 1965-67, systems analyst, personnel info., 1967-71, sr. systems analyst, mgmt. info. and adminstrv. systems, 1971-77, applications systems coordinator mgmt. info. and adminstrv. systems, 1977-78, group supr. affirmative action compliance and reports, 1978-81, group supr. service ops. system support group, 1982-84, mgr. security, 1984-85, mgr. govt. security, 1986-89; ret., 1989. Bd. dirs. Boca Ballet Theatre Co., 1994—; treas. Fla. Atlantic U. Vol. League, 1993-94; chmn. boutique Boca Ballet Guild, 1994, pres. 1994—. Mem. Humanitarian Society, Brown Nat. Alumni Sch. Program, Nat. Security Indsl. Assn., Women's Rights Assn. (treas. 1977, v.p. 1978), Am. Soc. Indsl. Security, Nat. Classification Mgmt. Soc., Brown Network, Royal Palm Improvement Assn. (bd. govs., chair. environ. inspection 1993-94, v.p., 1994, pres. 1994-96, chair security 1994), Friends of the Boca Pops (mem. governing coun.). Club: Pembroke Coll. of N.J. (publicity chmn. 1965-69, v.p. 1969-70).

DUDLEY, EVERETT HASKELL, JR., lawyer; b. Fitchburg, Mass., June 2, 1930; s. Everett H. Sr. and Marguerite I. (Connors) D.; m. Joyce Pettapiece, Aug. 23, 1952; children: Everett H. III, Lisa R. McKim. AA, Boston U., 1950, BS, 1954; JD, U. Miami, 1960. Bar: Mass. 1961, Fla. 1960, U.S. Dist. Ct. (so. dist.) Fla. 1961, U.S. Supreme Ct. 1964. Assoc. Sams, Anderson, Alper, Meadows & Spencer, Miami, Fla., 1960-61; ptnr. Stamey, Kravitz & Dudley, Hialeah, Fla., 1961-63, Kravitz, Dudley & Dean, Hialeah, Fla., 1963-69, Kravitz, Dudley & Duckworth, Hialeah, Fla., 1972-79, Weinbtraub, Weintraub, Seiden, Dudley & Press, Miami, Fla., 1979-85; judge Criminal Ct. of Record, Miami, Fla., 1969-71, City of Miami Springs, Fla., 1971-73; pres., prin. Everett H. Dudley Jr., P.A., Ft. Lauderdale, Fla., 1985-89; ptnr. Keeley, Hayes, Dudley, Johnson, Roberts, Keeley, Hayes & Dudley, Boca Raton, Fla., 1989-95, Keeley, Hayes, Dudley, Cappeller & Meeker, Boca Raton, 1995—. Founder, pres. Coun. on Drug Edn., Miami, 1970-72; chmn. Nat. Cancer Cytology Ctr., 1961-79, Miami Springs Charter Bd., 1974, Miami Springs Code Rev. Bd., 1975; cons. Dade County Drug Abuse Adv. Bd., 1971-75; mem. Dade County Secretariat on Crime and Law Enforcement, 1971-72; bd. dirs. Dade County Crime Commn., 1971-81. With USMC, 1953-56. Recipient Citizen of Yr. award Op. Self-Help, 1970, Disting. Svc. award City of Miami Springs, 1974; commd. Ky. Col., Commonwealth of Ky., 1990. Mem. ABA, Assn. Trial Lawyers Am., Am. Judicature Soc., Mass. Bar Assn., Fla. Bar Assn., Am. Arbitration Assn., Navy League of U.S. (judge adv. Delray Beach coun. 1990—), Masons, Shriners, Delta Theta Phi, Sigma Alpha Epsilon. Office: Keeley Hayes et al 2424 N Federal Hwy Boca Raton FL 33431-7735

DUDLEY, GARY ALTON, exercise science educator; b. Huntington, W.Va., Aug. 13, 1952; s. Glenn and JoAnn (Boley) D.; m. Tammie Leigh, Dec. 20, 1975; children: Kara, Jared, Joshua, Kristen. BA, Marshall U., 1974; MA, Ohio State U., 1975, PhD, 1978. Teaching asst. phys. edn. Ohio State U., Columbus, 1974-75; instr. Ctrl. Ohio Nautilus, Columbus, 1976; physiology tutor dept. physiology Ohio State U., Columbus, 1977; postdoctoral rsch. asst. physiology SUNY Upstate Med. Ctr., Syracuse, 1978-80; asst. prof. dept. zool. and biomed. scis. Ohio U. Coll. Osteo. Medicine, Athens, 1980-86, assoc. prof. dept. zool. and biomed. scis., 1986-87; environ. muscle physiologist Bionetics Corp., Kennedy Space Ctr., Fla., 1987-91; sr. rsch. physiologist NASA, Kennedy Space Ctr., Fla., 1991-92; dir. muscle biology lab. Sport Sci. and Wellness Inst. Marshall U., Huntington, 1993; assoc. prof. exercise sci. U. Ga., Athens, 1993-96, prof. exercise sci., 1996—; mem. sci. adv. com. U.S. Olympic Com., 1986-88; grantee reviewer; vis. scientist Univ. Space Rsch. Assocs., Houston, 1993. Reviewer Jour. Applied Physiol., Med. Sci. Sports Exercise, Clin. Physiol., Jour. Applied Sport Sci. Rsch., Microvascular Rsch., Phys. Sport Medicine, Sports Medicine, Internat. Jour. Sports Medicine, Am. Jour. Cardiology; sr. assoc. editor Jour. Strength and Conditioning Rsch., 1992—; mem. editorial bd. Jour. Applied Physiology, 1993—; contbr. over 85 articles to profl. jours. Recipient numerous grants, 1982—, Faculty Devel. award Ohio U., 1983. Fellow Am. Coll. Sports Medicine (rsch. awards com. 1989—, chair 1994—, Vis. Scholar award 1983); mem. Am. Physiol. Soc., Nat. Strength and Conditioning Assn. (cert., rsch. com. 1981-91, CSCS Cert. com. 1982-85, assoc. editor NSCA Jour. 1982—, Pres.'s award 1986, Outstanding Sport Scientist award 1996), Nat. Strength and Conditioning Specialist Agy. (CSCS exam. com. 1993—, NSCA-CPT exam. devel. com. 1993-95, exec. coun. 1993), Am. Orthopaedic Soc. Sports Medicine (task force 1985). Methodist. Office: Univ Ga Dept Exercise Sci Athens GA 30602

DUDLEY, GARY EDWARD, clinical psychologist; b. Columbus, Ohio, July 19, 1947; s. Ray Leonard and Mary Virginia (Russi) D.; BS, Ohio State U., 1969; MS (NIMH fellow, 1971, VA fellow, 1971), U. Miami, 1972, PhD (NIMH fellow, 1973), 1975; m. Linda Jean Patterson, June 21, 1969; children: Michelle Denise, Karen Elizabeth. Tchr. Columbus (Ohio) pub. schs., 1969-70; intern in clin. psychology Mt. Zion Hosp. and Med. Center, San Francisco, 1972-73; clin. psychologist Met. Dade County Jail, Miami, Fla., 1974-76, Southeast Inst. Criminal Justice, Miami, 1974-76, Ga. So. Coll., Statesboro, 1976-80; pvt. practice clin. psychology, Marietta, Ga., 1980—; cons. Child Devel. Ctr., Ga. Psycho-Ednl. Network, Atlanta. Lic. psychologist, Ga., Fla. Mem. Am. Psychol. Assn., Nat. Acad. Neuropsychologists, Am. Bd. Med. Psychotherapists, Southeastern Psychol. Assn., Ga. Psychol. Assn., Nat. Honor Soc. in Psychology, Atlanta Area Psychological Assocs., P.C. (dir. svcs.), Accurate Assessment Svcs. of Atlanta, Inc. (pres.), Sigma Xi. Contbr. articles to profl. jours. Home: 592 Cupelo Dr Marietta GA 30064-1120 Office: Doctors Bldg/Windy Hill 2520 Windy Hill Rd Ste 203 Marietta GA 30067-8650

DUDLEY, GEORGE ELLSWORTH, lawyer; b. Earlington, Ky., July 14, 1922; s. Ralph Emerson and Camille (Lackey) D.; m. Barbara J. Muir, June 28, 1950 (dec. Feb. 1995); children: Bruce K., Camille Dudley McNutt, Nancy S., Elizabeth Dudley Stephens. BS in Commerce, U. Ky., 1947; JD, U. Mich., 1950. Bar: Ky. 1950, D.C. 1951, U.S. Dist. Ct. (we. dist.) Ky. 1962, U.S. Ct. Appeals (6th cir.) 1987. Assoc. Gordon, Gordon & Moore, Madisonville, Ky., 1950-51; pvt. practice law Louisville, 1952-59; ptnr. Brown, Ardery, Todd & Dudley, Louisville, 1959-72; ptnr. Brown, Todd & Heyburn, Louisville, 1972-92, of counsel, 1992—, mem. mgmt. com., 1972-90, chmn., 1989-90. Pres. Ky. Easter Seal Soc., Louisville, 1971-72; treas. Ky. Dem. Party, Frankfort, 1971-74; bd. dirs. Alliant Adult Health Svcs., Louisville, 1976—; 1st v.p. Nat. Easter Seal Soc., Chgo., 1981. Capt. inf. U.S. Army, 1943-46, ETO; capt. JAGC, U.S. Army, 1951-52. Mem. ABA, Ky. Bar Assn., Louisville Bar Assn., U.S. 6th Cir. Jud. Conf. (life), Harmony Landing Country Club (pres. 1978-79), Tavern Club, Barristers Soc., Omicron Delta Kappa. Presbyterian. Home: 1905 Crossgate Ln Louisville KY 40222-6405 Office: Brown Todd & Heyburn 3200 Providian Louisville KY 40202

DUDLEY, PERRY, JR., business executive; b. New Haven, June 5, 1928; s. Perry and Ella (Leach) D.; m. June Ungar, Feb. 13, 1993; children: Bruce Lawrence, Virginia Barbara (from previous marriage). BSEE, Purdue U.,

1952; MBA, U. Santa Clara, 1966. Sales engr. Reliance Electric Co., Cleve. and Los Angeles, 1952-60, GTE Sylvania, Burlingame, Calif., 1960-65; sr. applications engr. Varian Assocs., Palo Alto, Calif., 1965-68; product mgr. Ampex Corp., Redwood City, Calif., 1968-70; program mgr. Genesys Systems, Inc., 1972-73; indsl. real estate broker, salesman, 1974-80; program mgr. Dalmo Victor Ops., Bell Aerospace Div., Textron, 1980-85; mktg. and program mgr. Loral Data Systems, San Diego, 1986-88; mgmt. cons. San Diego, 1989-94; real estate agent Prudential Atlanta Realty, 1995-96; program mgr. EMS Sys., Norcross, Ga., 1996—; instr. mktg. and mgmt. San Francisco State U., 1982, West Coast U., 1990-94. Pres. Young Rep. Club, Pasadena, Calif., 1959; precinct capt. Menlo Park (Calif.) Rep. Com., 1961-72; elder Presbyn. Ch. With USN, 1946-48. Mem. Nat. Assn. of Mgmt., Assn. of Old Crows, North Fulton County Rep. Club, Purdue Alumni Club (pres. 1959), Mensa, Phi Gamma Delta. Home: 1030 Taylor Knoll Close Roswell GA 30076

DUDRICK, STANLEY JOHN, surgeon, scientist, educator; b. Nanticoke, Pa., Apr. 9, 1935; s. Stanley Francis and Stephania Mary (Jachimczak) D.; m. Theresa M. Keen, June 14, 1958; children: Susan Marie, Paul Stanley, Carolyn Mary, Stanley Jonathan, Holly Anne, Anne Theresa. B.S. cum laude, Franklin and Marshall Coll., 1957; M.D., U. Pa., 1961. Diplomate Am. Bd. Surgery. Intern Hosp. of U. Pa., Phila., 1961-62, resident in gen. surgery, 1962-67; acad. practice specializing in surgery Phila., 1967-72, 88-90; pvt. practice specializing in surgery Houston, 1972-88, 90-94; chief surg. svcs. Hermann Hosp., Houston, 1972-80, surgeon in chief, dir. Ctr. Cardiovascular Disease, dir. nutritional support svcs., dir. Nutritional Sci. Ctr., 1990-94; prof. surgery U. Tex. Med. Sch., Houston, 1972-82, clin. prof. surgery, 1982-95, chmn. dept. surgery, 1972-80; cons. in surgery M.D. Anderson Hosp. and Tumor Inst., 1973-88, clin. prof. surgery, cons. to pres., 1982-88; sr. cons. surgery and medicine Tex. Inst. for Rehab. and Rsch., 1974-88; mem. Anatomical Bd., State of Tex., 1973-78; examiner Am. Bd. Surgery, 1974-78, bd. dirs., 1978-84, sr. mem. 1984—, also mem. and chmn. various coms.; chmn. sci. adv. com. Tex. Med. Ctr. Libr., 1974; mem. food and nutrition bd. NRC-Nat. Acad. Scis., 1973-75; mem. sci. adv. com. Nat. Found. for Ileitis and Colitis; mem. surgery, anesthesia and trauma study sect. NIH, 1982-86; chmn. dept. surgery Pa. Hosp., Phila., 1988-90, surgeon in chief, 1988-91, hon. surgery staff, 1991—; clin. prof. surgery U. Pa., 1988-93; assoc. chmn. deptt surgery, 1994—, dir. surgery program, 1994—, Assoc. chmn, dept. surg., 1944—, dir.. Med. Edn., 1995—, St. Mary's Hosp., Waterbury, Conn., 1994—; clin. prof. surgery, Yale, New Haven, Conn., 1995—. Editor: Manual of Surgical Nutrition, 1975, Manual of Preoperative and Postoperative Care, 1983, Current Strategies in Surgical Nutrition, 1991, Practical Handbook of Nutrition in Clinical Practice, 1994, Surgical Nutrition: Strategies in Critically Ill Patients, 1995; assoc. editor Nutrition in Medicine, 1975—; editorial bd. Annals of Surgery, 1975—, Infusion, 1978—, Nutrition and Cancer, 1980—, Nutrition Support Services, 1980-86, Jour. Clin. Surgery, 1980-83, Nutrition Research, 1981—, Intermed. Communications Nursing Services, 1981—, Postgraduate General Surgery, 1992—; others; contbr. chpts. to books, articles to profl. jours.; inventor of new technique of intravenous feeding and anti-cholesterol therapy. Bd. dirs. Found. for Children, Houston, Harris County unit Am. Cancer Soc., Phila. chpt., 1988-90; trustee Franklin and Marshall Coll., 1985—, mem. student life and trusteeship coms., 1986—, mem. overseers bd., 1986—, exec. com. 1986—, alumni programs and devel. com., 1991—, pres. regional adv. coun., 1992—, vice chmn. 1994—, John Marshall Soc., 1993—. Decorated knight Order St. John of Jerusalem Knights Hopitalier; recipient VA citation for significant contbn. to med. care, 1970; Mead Johnson award for rsch. in hosp. pharmacy, 1972; Seale Harris medal So. Med. Assn., 1973; AMA-Brookdale award in medicine, 1975; Great Texan award Nat. Found. Ileitis and Colitis, 1975; Modern Medicine award, 1977; Disting. Alumnus citation Franklin and Marshall Coll., 1980; WHO, Houston, 1980; Stinchfield award Am. Acad. Orthopedic Surgery, 1981; Bernstein award Med. Soc. State of N.Y., 1986, Alumni Svc. award U. Pa. Med. Sch., 1996; numerous others. Fellow ACS (vice chmn. pre and post operative com. 1975, gov. 1979-85, com. on med. motion pictures 1981-90, SESAP com. 1990—, co-chmn. multiple choice com. 1993—, mem. Conn. chpt.), Philippine Coll. Surgeons (hon.), Coll. Medicine and Surgery of Costa Rica (hon.), Am. Coll. Nutrition (Grace A. Goldsmith award 1982); mem. AMA (council on food and nutrition 1971-76, exec. com. 1975-76, council on sci. affairs 1976-81, Goldberger award in clin. nutrition 1970), AAAS, AAUP, Am. Surg. Assn., Am. Acad. Pediatrics (hon., Ladd medal 1988), Am. Pediatric Surg. Assn. (hon.), Am. Sc. Nutritional Support Services (bd. dirs. 1982-87, pres. 1984, Outstanding Humanitarian award 1984) Soc. Univ. Surgeons (exec. council 1974-78), Assn. for Acad. Surgery (founders group), Internat. Soc. Surg., Internat. Fedn. Surg. Colls., Internat. Soc. Parenteral Nutrition (exec. council 1975—, pres. 1978-81), Internat. Fedn. Surgery Soc., So. Med. Assn. (chmn. surgery sect. 1984-85), Houston Gastroent. Soc., Houston Surg. Soc., Tex. Surg. Soc., Tex. Med. Assn. (com. nutrition and food resources), Tex. Med. Found., Harris County Med. Soc., New Haven (Conn.) County Med. Soc., Conn. Soc. Am. Bd. Surgeons, Am. Radium Soc., Am. Soc. Clin. Oncology, Am. Soc. Parenteral and Enteral Nutrition (pres. 1977, bd. advs. 1978—, chmn. bd. advisers 1978, Vars award 1982, Rhoads lectr. 1985, Dudrick Rsch. Scholar award named in his honor), Penn. Nutritionists Soc. (pres. 1985), Am. Gastroent. Assn., Soc. Surg. Oncology, James Ewing Soc., Ravdin-Rhoads Surg. Assn., Excelsior Surg. Soc. (Edward D. Churchill lectr. 1981), Soc. Laparoendoscopic Surgery, Soc. Surg. Chairmen, So. Surg. Assn., Southwestern Surg. Congress, Southeastern Surg. Congress, Surg. Biology Club II, Surg. Infection Soc. (chmn. membership com. 1987-90), Western Surg. Soc., Halsted Soc., Allen O. Whipple Surg. Soc., Am. Inst. Nutrition, Soc. Clin. Surgery, Am. Soc. Clin. Investigation, Soc. for Surgery of Alimentary Tract, Am. Trauma Soc. (founders group), Am. Assn. for Surgery of Trauma, Soc. Clin. Surgery, Am. Soc. Clin. Nutrition, Fedn. Am. Soc. Exp. Biology, Am. Burn Assn., John Marshall Soc., Coll. Physicians Phila., Phila. Acad. Surgeons, George Hermann Soc., Union League Phila., Med. Club Phila., Franklin Club Phila., Houston Doctors Club (gov. 1973-76), Nat. Alumni Coun. U. Pa. Med. Sch. (chmn. 1994—), Conn. United for Rsch. Excellence (bd. dirs. 1995—), Cosmos Club, Athenaeum, The Penn Club (charter), Phi Beta Kappa, Phi Beta Kappa Assocs., Sigma Xi, Alpha Omega Alpha. (sec.-treas. Houston chpt. 1982-83),. Home: 3050 Locke Ln Houston TX 77019-6202 Office: St Mary's Hosp Dept Surgery 56 Franklin St Waterbury CT 06706-1501

DUDUIT, J(AMES) MICHAEL, clergyman, public relations executive, university official; b. Sandwich, Ill., Aug. 18, 1954; s. James Loren and Sarah Lee (baker) D.; m. Laura Ann Niemann, Jan. 11, 1986. BA, Stetson U., 1975; MDiv, So. Bapt. Sem., 1979; PhD in Humanities, Fla. State U., 1983. Ordained minister Bapt. Ch.; cert. fund raising exec. accreditation. Pastor Union Flatrock Bapt. Ch., Osgood, Ind., 1976-78; news dir. So. Bapt. Sem., Louisville, 1975-78, dir. communications, 1984-87; dir. pub. affairs Palm Beach Atlantic Coll., West Palm Beach, Fla., 1978-80; asst. to pres. Cuneo Advt., Inc., Tallahassee, 1980-81; assoc. campus minister Bapt. Campus Ministry, Tallahassee, 1981-83; assoc. pastor Immanuel Bapt. Ch., Tallahassee, 1982-84; pres. Preaching Resources, Inc., Jacksonville, Fla., 1985—; dir. devel. Samford U., Birmingham, 1987-93; exec. dir. Am. Acad. of Ministry, Louisville, 1993-96; exec. v.p. Union U., Jackson, Tenn., 1996—. Author: Joy in Ministry: Messages From Second Corinthians, 1989; editor: Great Preaching, 1990, A Handbook of Contemporary Preaching, 1992, Communicate With Power, 1996; pub. Preaching jour., 1990; contbr. articles to profl. jours. Mem. Bapt. Pub. Rels. Soc. (newsletter editor 1977-78), Bapt. Pub. Rels. Assn. (pres. 1992-93), Homewood C. of C. (v.p. 1988-89), Religious Conf. Mgmt. Assn., Religious Speech Comm. Assn., Nat. Conf. on Preaching (bd. dirs.), Acad. Homiletics. Republican. Home: 61 Torrey Pines Jackson TN 38305 Office: PO Box 369 Jackson TN 38302-0369

DUER, ELLEN ANN DAGON, anesthesiologist; b. Balt., Feb. 3, 1936; d. Emmett Paul and Annie (Sollers) Dagon; m. Lyle Jordan Millan IV, Dec. 21, 1963; children: Lyle Jordan V, Elizabeth Lyle, Ann Sheridan Worthington.; m. T. Marshall Duer, Jr., Aug. 23, 1985. AB, George Washington U., 1959; MD, U. Md., 1964; postgrad., Johns Hopkins U., 1965-68. Intern Union Meml. Hosp., Balt., 1964-65; resident anesthesiology Johns Hopkins Hosp., Balt., 1965-68, fellow in surgery, 1965-68; practice medicine specializing in anesthesiology Balt., 1968—; faculty Church Home and Hosp., Balt., 1969—; attending staff Union Meml. Hosp., Church Home and Hosp., Frankling Sq. Hosp., Children's Hosp., James Lawrence Kernan Hosp., Balt., 1982-94; co-chief anesthesiology James Kernan Hosp., 1983-94, med. dir. out-patient surgery dept., 1987-94; mem. med. exec. com. Kernan Hosp., 1988-94; affiliate cons. emergency room Church Home and Hosp., Balt., 1969—, mem. med. audit and utilizaions com., 1970-72, mem. emergency and ambulatory care com., 1973-74, chief emergency dept., 1973-74; cons. anesthesiologist Md. State Penitentiary, 1971; fellow in critical care medicine Md. Inst. Emergency Medicine, 1975-76; mem. infection control com. U. Md. Hosp., 1975—; instr. anesthesiology U. Md. Sch. Medicine, 1975—; staff anesthesiologist Mercy Hosp., 1978—, audit com., 1979-80, 82; asst. prof. anesthegiology U. Md. Med. Sch., 1989-94; mem. med. exec. com. Kernan Hosp., 1990-94, v.p. 1990, chief of staff, 1992—; mem. Tappahannock Family Practice, 1994-96, Rappahannock Gen. Hosp. Family Practice, 1996—; active staff Rappahannock Gen. Hosp., 1996—; med. examiner No. Neck of Va., 1996—; mem. Commonwealth of Va. Med. Bd. Mem. AMA, Am. Coll. Emergency Physicians, Met. Emergency Dept. Heads Am., Md. Soc. Anesthesiologists, Balt. County Med. Soc., Mid. Peninsula Med. Soc., No. Neck Med. Soc., Med. Soc. Va., Med. and Choir Faculty Med., Chirurgical Soc., Internat. Congress Anaesthesiologists, Internat. Anesthesia Rsch. Soc., Am. L'Hirondelle Club, Annapolis Yacht Club, Chesapeake Bay Yacht Racing Assn, Rappahannock River Yacht Club. Episcopalian. Address: Deep Creek Farm House RR 3 Box 463 Lancaster VA 22503-9803

DUERR, DAVID, civil engineer; b. Newark, July 4, 1953; s. Warren August and Dorothy (Lanzillo) D.; m. Roberta Kay Apolant, Oct. 12, 1991. B of Engring., Pratt Inst., 1975; MS, U. Houston, 1985. Registered profl. engr. Project engr. Hoffman Internat., Pt. Newark, N.J., 1974-76; chief engr. Williams Crane & Rigging, Richmond, Va., 1976-79; sr. structural engr. Hudson Engring. Corp., Houston, 1980-86; pres. 2DM Assocs., Inc., Houston, 1986—; frequent lectr. constrn. industry seminars. Contbr. tech. papers to profl. jours. Mem. ASCE, Am. Cons. Engrs. Coun., Soc. Automotive Engrs., Soc. Naval Architects and Marine Engrs. Home: 8439 Hunters Creek Dr Houston TX 77024-3204 Office: 2DM Assocs Inc 7322 Southwest Fwy Houston TX 77074-2010

DUES, THEODORE ROOSEVELT, JR., lawyer; b. Montgomery, W.Va., June 23, 1953; s. Theodore Roosevelt and Mary Lucille (White) D.; m. Mona Lisa Day, Aug. 25, 1979; children: Theodore Roosevelt III, Ryah Leigh. BBA, W.Va. U., 1975, JD, 1978. Bar: W.Va. 1978, U.S. Dist. Ct. (no. and so. dist.) W.Va. 1978, U.S. Ct. Appeals (4th cir.) 1978. Pvt. practice, Fayetteville, W.Va., 1978-79, Charleston, W.Va., 1979-81; sr. ptnr. Dues, Tyree & Hicks, Charleston, 1981-83, Dues & Tyre, Charleston, 1983-85; sole practice, Charleston, 1985—, hearing examiner W.Va. Human Rights Commn., Charleston, 1981-90; mem. bd. govs. W.Va. State Bar, 1985—. Bd. dirs. Family Svcs. United Way Agy., Charleston, 1983—, Appalachian Rsch. and Def. Fund, Charleston, 1979-83, Legal Aid Soc., 1981-84; commr. Kanawha County Dep. sheriffs, 1984—, City of Charleston Fire Dept., 1987—; pres. Kanawha County Civil Svc. Commn., 1987-90; trustee, supt. Sunday sch. First Bapt. Ch. London, 1991—; mem. Gov.'s Task Force on Pers., 1992—; bd. dirs. Adult Basic Edn., 1991—; appointed chair Martin Luther King, Jr. Holiday Commn., 1995. Named Most Outstanding Black Atty., Black Am. Law Students, 1982. Mem. NAACP (W.Va. legal redress com. 1978—, chmn. Charleston legal redress com. 1983—), Mountain State Bar Assn. (pres. 1988-90, chmn. bd. dirs. 1990—), W.Va. State Bar Assn. (jud. improvement com. 1983—). Office: Daniel Boone Bldg 405 Capitol St Charleston WV 25301-1727

DUETT, EDWIN HAROLD, finance and economics educator; b. Phila., Jan. 1, 1956; s. Edwin H. Sr. and Martha Beatrice (Moore) D.; m. Margaret Ann Taylor, Nov. 6, 1977; children: Nicholas Edwin, Joshua Kyle. BS, Miss. State U., 1977, MBA, 1980; PhD in Fin., U. Ga., 1987. Instr. Copiah-Lincoln Jr. Coll., Natchez, Miss., 1980-82; asst. prof. fin. and econs. U. So. Miss., Natchez, 1982-83; grad. asst. U. Ga., Athens, 1983-86; asst. prof. corp. fin. U. North Tex., Denton, 1986-87; assoc. prof. dept. fin. and econs. Miss. State U., Starkville, 1987—; mem. panel Southwestern Bus. Symposium, 1986; program leader continuing edn. series Profl. Devel. Inst.; discussion leader Microcomputers in Banking, 1986, Ga. Banking Sch.; researcher in field. Author: REMICS and the Secondary Mortgage Market, 1990; chief assoc. editor Jour. Fin. & Strategic Decision Making; mem. editorial bd. Jour. Econs. and Fin.; book reviewer Harper & Row, West Pub.; ad hoc reviewer Jour. Econs. and Bus., Jour. Fin. Rsch., Jour. Real Estate Rsch., Jour. Ins. Issues; contbr. articles to profl. jours., chpts. to books, also presentations and procs. in field. Recipient Rsch. Initiation grant U. North Tex., 1987, Pres.' Faculty Excellent. Mem. So. Fin. Assn. (discussant 1986, 89, 90, 91), Southwestern Fin. Assn., Fin. Mgmt. Assn. (program com. 1989, session chmn. 1990), Mid-South Assn. Econs. and Fin., Midwest Fin. Assn., Am. Fin. Assn., Fin. Analysts Fedn., Midsouth Econs. and Fin. Assn., Beta Gamma Sigma. Home: 1764 Lisa Lane Starkville MS 39759-9802

DUFALLO, RICHARD JOHN, conductor; b. East Chicago, Ind., Jan. 30, 1933; s. John William and Olga (Lesak) D.; m. Zaidee Parkinson, Oct. 15, 1966 (div. 1985); children: Basil, Cornelius; m. Pamela Mia Paul, June 19, 1988. MusB, Am. Conservatory Music, 1953; BA, UCLA, 1956, MA, 1958; studies with William Steinberg, N.Y.C. Lectr. music, assoc. condr. UCLA Symphony, 1959-62; festival coord. Ojai (Calif.) Festival, 1961-63; assoc. condr. Buffalo Philharm., 1962-67; instr. SUNY, Buffalo, 1963-67; condr. Ctr. Creative and Performing Arts, Buffalo, 1964-67; artistic dir., condr. Conf. Contemporary Music Aspen (Colo.) Music Festival, 1970-85; prin. condr., artistic advisor Met. Opera Mini-Met, N.Y.C., 1972-74; music dir., condr. Juilliard Theatre Lincoln Ctr., N.Y.C., 1972-79; asst. condr. N.Y. Philharm., N.Y.C., 1973-74; artistic advisor Het Gelders Orkest, Arnhem, Netherlands, 1980-81, season 1982, permanent guest condr.; acting dir. Aspen Inst. Italia, Rome, 1984-85; internat. guest condr. Orchestre National de O.R.T.F. Paris (European debut), 1970, Concertgebouw Orch., Rotterdam (Holland) Philharm., Berlin Philharm., London Symphony, Royal Philharm., more than 70 major orchs. and festivals in N.Am., Austria, Belgium, Denmark, England, France, Germany, Holland, Italy, Spain, Poland, Portugal and Yugoslavia. Author: Trackings, 1989; condr. (TV prodns.) Bill Moyers Journal, WNET, N.Y., Meeting Mr. Ives, NOS TV, Holland, Guest Artists Series, NOS TV, Holland, The Lighthouse (world premiere), Scottish TV, (recordings) Festival Chamber Orch., Columbia Records, Red Seal, Concerto for Two Pianos, RCA London, Works of Isao Matsushita, Fontec Records, St. Thomas Wake, Louisville First Editions, Nederlands Blazers Ensemble, Chandos Records, and others. Lt. (j.g.) USN, 1953-55.

DUFF, DORIS EILEEN (SHULL), critical care nurse; b. Va., Feb. 23, 1960; d. Harley Ray and Eloise (Whitmer) Shull; m. William DeLaney Duff, Feb. 1, 1992; 1 child, William D. II. BS in Gen. Sci., Radford (Va.) U., 1983; diploma in nursing, Roanoke (Va.) Meml. Hosps., 1985. RN, Va. Med.-surg. nurse Roanoke Meml. Hosp., 1985-87, nurse emergency-trauma dept., 1987—. Mem. Emergency Nurses Assn. (pres. Roanoke chpt. 1995), Roanoke Meml. Hosps. Sch. Nursing Alumni Assn. (pres. 1996). Office: Roanoke Meml Hosp Belleview at Jefferson Sts Roanoke VA 24033

DUFF, ERNEST ARTHUR, political scientist, educator; b. Charlottesville, Va., Dec. 27, 1929; s. Ernest Ragland and Emma Ruth (Bennett) D.; m. Barbara Ellen Jones, Aug. 30, 1955; children: Ernest A. Jr., Melanie Duff Badesch, Cameron John, Valerie. BA, U. Va., 1952, MA, 1957, PhD, 1964. Fgn. svc. officer Dept. of State, Havana, Cuba, 1957-60, Washington, 1960-62, Bogota, Colombia, 1962-63; prof. Randolph-Macon Woman's Coll., Lynchburg, Va., 1964—, Charles Dana prof., 1986; spl. field rep. Rockefeller Found., Cali, Colombia, 1966-67; vis. Fulbright prof. U. of Mexico, Mexico City, 1979-80. Author: Agrarian Reform in Colombia, 1968, Violence and Repression in Latin America, 1974, Leader and Party in Latin America, 1984. Polit. analyst WSET-TV, Lynchburg, Va., 1987—. Lt. USN, 1952-55, Korea. NROTC scholar USN and U. Va., 1948-52; Helen Wessell fellow, U. Va., 1963-64, NEH summer fellow, Brown U., Providence, 1990. Mem. Latin Am. Studies Assn., So. Polit. Sci. Assn., Southeastern Coun. Latin Am. Studies, Va. Polit. Sci. Assn. Baptist. Home: 1633 Dogwood Ln Lynchburg VA 24503-1923 Office: Randolph Macon Woman's Coll 2500 Rivermont Ave Lynchburg VA 24503-1555

DUFF, MICHAEL JAMES, physicist; b. Manchester, Jan. 28, 1949; s. Edward and Elizabeth (Kaylor) D.; m. Lesley Yearling, 1984; children: Jessica, Matthew. BS, Queen Mary Coll., U. London, 1969; PhD, Imperial Coll., U. London, 1972. Postdoctoral fellow in theoretical physics Internat. Ctr. Theoretical Physics, Trieste, Italy, Oxford (Eng.) U., U. London, Brandeis U., Waltham, Mass., 1972-79; faculty mem. Imperial Coll., 1979-88; sr. physicist CERN, Geneva, 1984-87; prof. physics Tex. A&M Univ., College Station, 1988-92, Disting. prof. physics, 1992—. Contbr. articles to profl. jours. Fellow Am. Phys. Soc. Home: Southwood Forest 907 Carmel Pl College Station TX 77845 Office: Tex A&M U Dept Physics College Station TX 77843

DUFF, WILLIAM GRIERSON, electrical engineer; b. Alexandria, Va., Dec. 16, 1936; s. Johnnie Douglas and Annetta Osceola (Rind) D.; BEE, George Washington U., 1959, postgrad., 1959-72; MS, Syracuse U., 1969; DSc in Elec. Engring., Clayton U., 1977; m. Sandra K. Via, June 25, 1983; children: Warren David, Valerie Lynn, Dawn Elizabeth, Deborah Arleen, Kelly Juanita. Chief engr. systems engring. div. Computer Scis. Corp., Springfield, Va., 1959—; asst. prof. Capitol Inst. Tech., Greenbelt, Md., 1972—; instr. Interference Control Technologies, Don White Cons., Inc., Gainesville, Va. Counselor, Meth. Sr. High Youth Group, 1965-73. Recipient Good Citizenship award DAR, 1955; Math. award George Washington High Sch., Alexandria, 1955. Fellow IEEE (pres. EMC Soc., assoc. editor group newsletter 1970—); mem. AIEE (Best Paper award 1961), George Washington U. Engring. Alumni Assn. (pres. 1963-64, Engring. Alumni Svc. award 1980), Springfield Golf and Country Club, Occoquan Water Ski Club (pres. 1976), Sigma Tau, Theta Tau. Author: EMI Handbook, vol. 5, EMI Prediction and Analysis Techniques, 1972; Mobile Communications, 1976, Fundamentals of EMC, 1988, EMC in Telecommunications, 1988; contbr. articles to profl. jours. Home: 7601 S Valley Dr Fairfax VA 22039-2965 Office: Computer Scis Corp 5501 Backlick Rd Ste 300 Springfield VA 22151-3940

DUFFEY, WILLIAM SIMON, JR., lawyer; b. Phila., May 9, 1952; s. William Simon and Elinor (Daniluk) D.; m. Betsy Byars, Dec. 17, 1977; children: Charles, Scott. BA in English, honors, Drake U., 1973; JD cum laude, U. S.C., 1977. Bar: S.C. 1977, Ga. 1982, U.S. Dist. Ct. (no., mid. and so. dists.) Ga. 1982, U.S. Ct. Appeals (llth cir.) 1983, U.S. Supreme Ct., 1992. Atty. Nexson, Pruet, Jacobs & Pollard, Columbia, S.C., 1977-78, King & Spalding, Atlanta, 1982-94; dep. ind. counsel Office of the Ind. Counsel, Little Rock, 1994-95; ptnr. King & Spalding, Atlanta, 1995—. Articles editor S.C. Lawyer, 1990-94. Pres. Pine Hills Civic Assn., Atlanta, 1984-88; trustee Drake U.; mem. Atlanta Task Force Neighborhood Buyouts, 1986, Ga. Rep. Found.; bd. dirs. Ga. Wilderness Inst., 1992—; mem. Peachtree Rd. Race Com., 1993—, chmn. Ga. Good Govt. Com. Mem. Altanta Bar Assn. (chmn. alt. dispute resolution com. 1984-88), Lawyers Club, Atlanta Track Club (gen. counsel 1993—), Nat. Practitioners Advisory Coun. The Fed. Soc. Republican. Home: 4825 Franklin Pond Rd Atlanta GA 30342 Office: King & Spalding 191 Peachtree St Atlanta GA 30303

DUFFIE, VIRGIL WHATLEY, JR., state agency administrator; b. Greenwood, S.C., Sept. 10, 1935; s. Virgil Whatley and Lorena (Ouzts) D.; m. Mary Hartzog, Oct. 6, 1962; children: Rebecca Louise, Mary Page, Virgil W. III. BA, U. S.C., 1957, JD, 1959. Bar: S.C. 1959. Trust officer Bankers Trust S.C., Columbia, 1959-67, sr. trust officer, 1967-70, sr. v.p., 1970-73, exec. v.p., 1973-84, 1st exec. v.p., 1984-86; sr.v.p., trust officer NCNB S.C., Columbia, 1986; sr. v.p. Interstate Securities Corp., Columbia, 1987-88; dir. spl. gifts U. S.C., Columbia, 1988-89; apptd. commr. S.C. Dept. Labor, Columbia, 1989-94, appt. dir. labor, licencing and regulations, 1994-95, dept. dir. labor, licensing and regulations, 1995—; bd. dirs. Index-Pub. Co., Greenwood, Stier Supply Co., Columbia, George W. Park Seed Co., Greenwood. Bd. dirs. Palmetto Boys State, Charleston, S.C., 1954-74; chmn. bd. Carolina Children's Home, Columbia, 1976; sec. bd. dirs. Richland Meml. Hosp., Columbia, 1970-73. Mem. ABA, S.C. Bar Assn., S.C. Bankers Assn. Home: 34 Quinine Hill Rd Columbia SC 29204-3414 Office: SC Dept Labor PO Box 11329 Columbia SC 29211-1329

DUFFLEY, PATRICIA FRANCES, rehabilitation counselor; b. Tampa, Fla., Mar. 29, 1955. BA in Acad. Psychology, U. Tenn., Knoxville, 1986, MS in Safety Edn., 1993, MS in Rehab. Counseling, 1995. Cert. rehab. counselor; registered med. asst., hearing conservationist, med. lab. technician. Med. corpsman/med. sect. supr. U.S. Army, 1973-81; with Ft. Sanders Regional Med. Ctr., 1981-82; lab. technician, med. asst. Knoxville Family Practice Group, 1982-83; health technician, lab. technician Mil. Entrance Processing Sta., 1983-85; subcontractor U. Tenn., 1991-92; clk. U.S. Postal Svc., 1985-96; transition care mgr. Knox County (Tenn.) Schs./Vocat. Rehab., 1996; v.p. or rehab. Goodwill Industries, Knoxville, 1996—. Home: PO Box 1203 Norris TN 37828

DUFFY, MARGARET MCLAUGHLIN, nephrology nurse, educator; b. N.Y.C., Feb. 5, 1939; d. Paul Anthony and Margaret Doris (Thorne) McLaughlin; children: William, Paul, Eileen. BSN, Villanova U., 1960; MA, Columbia U., 1966; EdD, U. S.C., 1989. Cert. nephrology nurse; cert. case mgr. Instr. nursing Salve Regina Coll., Newport, R.I., 1970-72; asst. prof. nursing Bristol C.C., Fall River, Mass., 1973-75, Grossmont C.C., El Cajon, Calif., 1976-77; assoc. prof. nursing Med. U. S.C., Charleston, 1978—, case mgr. renal transplant svc., 1990-94, clin. educator, 1994—. Contbr. articles to profl. jours. Lt. comdr. USN, 1960-69; lt. col. USAR, 1983—. Sandoz Pharms. clin. practice fellow, 1989; Amgen Ednl. scholar, 1990; U.S. Army 9A designation. Mem. ANA, Trident Nurses Assn. (pres.), Am. Nephrology Nurses Assn. (pre. Palmetto chpt., chair continuing edn.), Nat. Kidney Found. (chmn. resource devel. com.), Sigma Theta Tau. Home: 304 Stratford Dr Summerville SC 29485-8667

DUFFY, SALLY M., psychologist; b. Charleston, S.C., Mar. 16, 1953; d. Edward Baker and Mary Jane (Hutchins) D. BA, U. S.C., 1976; MS, Ea. Ky. U., 1979; PhD, U. Ky., 1989. Diplomate Am. Acad. Pain Mgmt. Psychologist, dir. Partial Hospitalization Program, Stanton, Ky., 1979-80; staff psychologist Frazier Rehab. Ctr., Louisville, 1981-84; psychologist Comprehensive Med. Rehab. Ctr., Lexington, Ky., 1987-89; postdoctoral fellow Med. U. S.C., Charleston, 1989; psychology svcs. coord. Carolinas Spine & Rehab. Ctr./HealthSouth, Charlotte, N.C., 1990-92; health psychologist The Rehab. Ctr., Charlotte, 1992—; adj. prof. psychology Georgetown Coll., 1988-89; lectr. in field. Contbr. articles to profl. jours. Mem. OneVoice Chorus, Charlotte, 1991—. NIMH traineeship, 1985-86, 86-87; Counseling Psychology Departmental merit fellow U. Ky., 1984-85. Mem. APA (div. 17 counseling psychology of women), Am. Bd. Med. Psychotherapists, Ky. Psychol. Assn., N.C. Psychol. Assn., Southeastern Psychol. Assn., Am. Pain Soc. Democrat. Office: The Rehab Ctr 2610 E 7th St Charlotte NC 28204-4375

DUFRECHOU, CARLTON FRANCIS, foundation administrator; b. New Orleans, Mar. 19, 1956; s. Leo Francis and Beverly Joyce (Heim) D. BSCE, Tulane U., 1978, MS in Environ. Engring., 1993. Cert. planner. Civil engr. Walter Blessey, Engr., New Orleans, 1978-79, L.F. Dufrechou, Architects, New Orleans, 1979-82; developer Dufrechou & Assocs., New Orleans, 1982-86; planner U.S. Army Corps of Engrs., New Orleans, 1986-91, project mgr., 1991-92; dir. Lake Pontchartrain Basin Found., New Orleans, 1992—. Dir. emergency svcs. La. Wing CAP, New Orleans, 1990-92, chief of staff, 1994—; environ. dir. Metairie (La.) Sunrise Rotary, 1992—, treas., 1995-96. With USMCR, 1976-78. Mem. ASME, ASCE, NSPE, Am. Planning Assn., La. Engrs. Soc., Soc. Tulane Engrs. Republican. Roman Catholic. Home: 6316 Fontainebleau Dr New Orleans LA 70125-4239 Office: Lake Pontchartrain Found 3500 N Causeway Blvd Ste 821 Metairie LA 70002-3527

DUFRESNE, ELIZABETH JAMISON, lawyer; b. Winter Haven, Fla., July 29, 1942; d. John W. and Thelma M. (Kinney) Jamison; 1 child, Brennan. BA, Vanderbilt U., 1964; JD, U. Fla., 1966. Bar: U.S. Dist. Ct. (so. dist.) Fla. 1967, U.S. Dist. Ct. (mid. dist.) Fla. 1968, U.S. Ct. Appeals (5th cir.) 1968, U.S. Supreme Ct. 1969, U.S. Ct. Appeals (11th cir.) 1981. Atty. So. Fla. Migrant Legal Svc., Miami, 1967-69; law reform chief Greater Miami Legal Svc., Miami, 1969-71; assoc. Tobias Simon P.A., Miami, 1971; ptnr. Tobias Simon & Elizabeth duFresne, P.A., Miami, 1971-77; sr. ptnr. duFresne & duFresne, P.A., Miami, 1977-82, duFresne & Bradley, P.A., Miami, 1982-86; equity ptnr. Steel, Hector & Davis, Miami, 1986—; bd. dirs., chmn. labor law divsn. Steele, Hector & Davis, Miami; adj. prof. law U. Miami, Coral Gables, Fla., 1977-93; mem. Civil Justice Adv. Group USDC, S.D. Fla., 1990—. Recipient Award of Honor ACLU, Dade, 1969, Award of Merit ACLU, Fla., 1970, 73. Mem. ABA, Fla. Bar Assn. (Pioneer award 1977), Dade County Bar Assn., Fed. Bar Assn., Assn. Trial Lawyers Am., Assn. Trial Lawyers Fla., Fla. Assn. Women Lawyers. Democrat. Roman Catholic. Office: 200 S Biscayne Blvd Miami FL 33131-2310

DUFRESNE, JOHN LOUIS, English language educator; b. Worcester, Mass., Jan. 30, 1948; s. Bernard Vincent and Doris Maud (Berard) D.; m. Marilyn Marie Virbasius, Apr. 30, 1971 (div. Oct. 1978); m. Cynthia Claire Chinelly, May 18, 1985; 1 child, Tristan. BA, Worcester State Coll., 1970; MFA, U. Ark., 1984. Instr. N.E. La. U., Monroe, 1984-87, Augusta (Ga.) Coll., 1988-89; asst. prof. Fla. Internat. U., Miami, 1989-94, assoc. prof., 1994—. Author: The Way That Water Enters Stone, 1991, Louisiana Power and Light, 1994, Lethe, Cupid, Time and Love, 1994, Love Warps the Mind a Little, 1997. Recipient Syndicated Fiction award PEN, N.Y., 1984, Fiction award Yankee Mag., N.H., 1989; named Notable Book of Yr., N.Y. Times, 1994. Mem. MLA, Nat. Writers Union, Nat. Coun. Tchrs. English, Author's Guild, Associated Writing Programs. Home: 1299 SE 7th Ave Dania FL 33004 Office: Fla Internat Univ N Miami Campus North Miami FL 33181

DUFUR, BILL, utility field supervisor; b. Caddo, Okla., June 30, 1939; s. Sherman D. and Jettie Opal (Cole) D.; m. Tommie Louise Collum, Nov. 5, 1960 (div. Mar. 1995); children: Marc Wayne, Gregory Brent, Todd Mitchell, Patrick Thomas; m. Brenda Nell DePauw, May 1, 1995. AAS, Texas A&M U., 1958, Eastern N.M. U., 1981, Wayland Bapt. Coll., 1982, Amarillo (Tex.) Coll., 1984. Truck driver Red Ball Motor Freight, Denver, 1958-60, Denver Climax Truck Lines, 1960-70, Curry Motor Freight, Amarillo, Tex., 1970-76; field supr. Southwestern Pub. Svc., Amarillo, Tex., 1976-87, Utility Engring. Corp., Amarillo, Tex., 1987—. Republican. Mem. Christian Ch. of God. Home: 1502 S Kentucky Amarillo TX 79102

DUGAN, CHARLES CLARK, physician, surgeon; b. Penn Yan, N.Y., Jan. 24, 1921; s. Charles Emanual and Wilhemia May (Clark) D.; m. Eugenie Alice Pounds, Aug. 12, 1944 (div. 1963); children: Charles Clark II, Douglas Craig, Timothy Gene; m. Ruth Louise Fugh, Dec. 3, 1965 (dec. 1983); adopted children: Dain Walters, Carl Jay. AA, Wentworth Mil. Jr. Coll., 1940; AB, Cornell U., 1942; MD, Jefferson Med. Coll., 1946; MPH, Naval Med. Sch. & Johns Hopkin, 1956. Diplomate Am. Bd. Dermatology, Am. Bd. Allergy and Immunology, Spl. Bd. Dermatopathology, Am. Bd. Cosmetic Plastic Surgery, Am. Bd. Preventive Medicine, Aviation Medicine and Pub. Health, Nat. Bd. Med. Examiners. Resident in psychiatry Pa. Psychiat. Hosp., Phila., 1945-46; rotating intern extended in gen. surgery Harrisburg (Pa.) Gen. Hosp., 1946-47; resident in dermatology U. Colo. Med. Ctr., Denver, 1956-57; resident in dermatology and allergy Henry Ford Hosp., Detroit, 1957-59; pvt. practice dermatology, allergy, cosmetic plastic surgery West Palm Beach, Fla., 1959—; physician mem. bd. Palm Beach County Environ. Control Hearing Bd., West Palm Beach, 1981-94; active staff Palm Beach Gardens (Fla.) Cmty. Hosp., Good Samaritan Hosp., West Palm Beach, St. Mary's Hosp., West Palm Beach; mem. Wellington Regional Med. Ctr., West Palm Beach; active staff Good Samaritan Hosp., West Palm Beach. Contbr. articles to profl. jours. Lt. col. USAF, 1947-56, ret. Recipient Cert. of Svc., Am. Cancer Soc., West Palm Beach, 1961; named Surgeon of Yr., Fla. Soc. Dematol. Surgeons, 1991. Fellow AMA, FMA, PBCOMS, Am. Acad. Dermatology, Am. Coll. Preventive Medicine, Am. Coll. Allergy, Asthma and Immunology, Am. Acad. Allergy, Asthma and Immunology, Internat. Acad. Cosmetic Surgery, Am. Acad. Facial Plastic and Reconstructive Surgery, Am. Acad. Cosmetic Surgery, Am. Soc. Dermatol. Surgery (bd. dirs. 1980-83), Am. Soc. Dematopathology, Am. Soc. Cryosurgeons, Am. Soc. Cert. Allergists, Internat. Soc. Dematopathology, Noah Webster Dermatol. Soc., Fla. Soc. Dermatology (pres. 1973-74, Practitioner of Yr. award 1993), Fla. Soc. Dermatol. Surgeons (pres. 1980-83), numerous others. Republican. Presbyterian. Office: M D Center 2600 Broadway West Palm Beach FL 33407-5431

DUGGAN, ANN CLEEK, medical/surgical and critical care nurse; b. Sullivan County, Tenn., June 6, 1940; d. Elmer and Elizabeth Louise (Loyd) Cleek; children: Jamie Michele, Jennifer Ann. Diploma, Baroness Erlanger Hosp., Chattanooga, 1961. Staff nurse Erlanger Hosp., 1961-65; scrub nurse, office nurse to physician, Chattanooga, 1965; staff nurse Combustion Engring., Chattanooga, 1966-67; part time office nurse, 1974-82; charge nurse Meml. Hosp., Chattanooga, 1983—. Home: 4001 Dodson Ave Chattanooga TN 37406-1413

DUGGAN, CAROL COOK, research director; b. Conway, S.C., May 25, 1946; d. Pierce Embree and Lillian Watkins (Eller) Cook; m. Kevin Duggan, Dec. 29, 1973. BA, Columbia Coll., 1968; MS, U. Ky., 1970. Reference asst. Richland County Pub. Libr., Columbia, S.C., 1968-69, asst. to dir., 1970, chief adult svcs., 1971-82; dir. Maris Rsch., Columbia, 1982—; lectr., mem. Friends of Richland County Pub. Libr., 1977—, Greater Columbia (S.C.) Literacy Coun., 1973—; mem. worship com. Washington St. United Meth. Ch., Columbia, 1985-86, mem. staff-parish relations com., 1986-91, mem. history and archives com., 1988—, mem. adminstrv. bd., 1992—, chair staff-parish relations com., 1993, trustee 1995—; mem. exec. bd. United Meth. Women 1983—, treas. unit 7, 1989-91, pres. unit 7, 1992—. Recipient Sternheimer award, 1968; treas. Friends S.C. Librs. Mem. ALA (councilor 1980-82, chmn. state membership com. 1979-83), S.C. Libr. Assn. (sec. 1976, exec. bd. 1976, 78-82), S.C. Pub. Libr. Assn. (pres. 1980-81), Friends of S.C. Libr. (treas. 1995—), Columbia Coll. Alumnae Assn. Coun. (spl. events com. 1996—), Beta Phi Mu. Methodist. Club: PEO (pres. 1983-85, chmn. amendments and recommendations com. 1983-85, historian 1986-87, 90—, treas. State conv., 1987-88), Columbia Coll. Afternoon of S.C. Home: 2101 Woodmere Dr Columbia SC 29204-4341

DUGGAN, KEVIN, data processor; b. St. Louis, Feb. 29, 1944; s. Leo Patrick and Jean Claire (McHenry) D.; BA, U. S.C., 1977, MA, Webster U., 1988; m. Lillian Carol Cook, Dec. 29, 1973. With S.C. Nat. Bank, Columbia, 1970-79, mgr. tech. support, 1978-79; dir. info. sci. tech., Midlands Tech. Coll., Columbia, 1979—; cons. electronic data processing. Mem. Richland County Friends of Library, Literacy Council S.C., chmn. fin. com., 1987-90; chmn. stewardship com., 1982-86; mem. evangelism and membership coms., 1982-86; mem. council on ministries, 1982—; mem. exec. com., 1987—; mem. adminstrv. bd. Washington St. United Meth. Ch., lay leader, 1992—. Served with USMC, 1963-67. Decorated Bronze Star (3). Mem. Assn. Systems Mgr., IBM Users Group, Data Processing Mgmt. Assn., Palmetto Fencing Soc., Amateur Fencing League Am. Methodist. Lodge: Rotary. Office: PO Box 2408 Columbia SC 29202-2408

DUGGER, WILLIAM MAYFIELD, economics educator; b. Garden City, Kans., Nov. 7, 1947; s. Charles B. and Mary Genevieve (Cline) D.; m. Pauline June Laddusaw, Mar. 24, 1967. BS, U Tulsa, 1970; PhD, U. Tex., Austin, 1974. Asst. prof. econs. North Tex. State U., Denton, 1974-79, assoc. prof., 1980-81; assoc. prof. DePaul U., Chgo., 1981-84, prof., 1985-93; prof. Econs. U. Tulsa (Okla.), 1993—; Cochran-Hersh meml. lectr. U. North Tex., Denton, 1988. Author: Alternative to Retrenchment, 1984, Corporate Hegemony, 1989, Underground Economics, 1991; editor: Radical Institutionalism, 1989, Inequality, 1996; co-editor: (with William Waller) The Stratified State, 1992. Vol. Com. in Solidarity with People of El Salvador, Chgo., 1985—; contbr. Jesse Jackson Presdl. Campaign, Chgo., 1987. Mem. AAUP (pres. DePaul U. chpt. 1991—), Assn. Social Econs. (pres. 1984-85, exec. coun. 1980-82), Assn. Evolutionary Econ. (bd. dirs. 1990—), Assn. Instl. Thought (pres. 1987-88), Union Radical Polit. Econs., Am. Econ. Assn., Western Social Sci. Assn. Democrat. Office: Dept Economics U Tulsa Tulsa OK 74104-3189

DUGGIN, NANCY YOUREE, primary school educator; b. Murfreesboro, Tenn., Sept. 15, 1952; d. James Hall Jr. and Annie Ruth (Harney) Youree; m. Ivan Emerson Duggin, Oct. 27, 1973; children: Mark Emerson, Emily Elizabeth. BS, Mid. Tenn. State U., 1974, MEd, 1976, EdS in Curriculum and Instrn., 1996. Cert. edn. specialist, adminstrn. and supervision, Mid. Tenn. State U., 1991, cert. learning styles trainer. Tchr. kindergarten Murfreesboro City Schs., 1974-77, elem. tchr., 1977—, insvc. presenter, 1984—; insvc. presenter Lincoln, Maury and Williamson counties schs., Oak Ridge City Schs., 1984—, She;by Co., Blount Co.; presenter Tenn. Dept. Edn., 1988—; tele-conf. presenter U. Tenn., Knoxville, 1990; mem. Tenn. Tchr.'s Study Coun.; developer, coord. Teaching, Learning, Caring Parent Program, 1991—, New Tchr. Handbook and Staff Devel.; study group mem. Appalachia Edn. Lab. Conflict Resolution, 1992—; regional trainer Peace Edn. Found., Miami, Fla. Lectr. in field. Bd. dirs. Bus.-Edn. Partnership, Murfreesboro, 1989—; dir. presch. div. lst Bapt. Ch., Murfreesboro, 1983-87, chmn. presch. edn. com., 1984-86, dir. adult III Sunday sch., 1988-90, chmn. family enrichment com., 1990; co-chair Rutherford 2000 Pub. Rels. Com. Jennings and Rebecca Jones Found. grantee, 1989, Bus. Edn. Partnership grantee, 1993; named Disting. Classroom Tchr., Northfield Elem. Sch., 1990-91. Mem. NEA, Internat. Reading Assn., Nat. Assn. Yr.-Round Edn., Tenn. Assn. for Sch. Supervision and Adminstrn., Tenn. Edn. Assn. (Disting. Classroom Tchr.'s award 1991), Tenn. Reading Assn. (presenter 1987-90), Murfreesboro Edn. Assn. (newsletter editor, sec. 1986-87, chmn. instruction and profl. devel. com. 1985—), MaryTom Berry Reading Coun. (newsletter editor), Rutherford County C. of C., Kappa Delta Pi, Phi Delta Kappa, Delta Kappa Gamma (newsletter editor Delta chpt. 1988-90, pres. 1990—, scholar 1990, participant state leadership sch. 1990, advanced leadership sch. 1991). Office: Murfreesboro City Schs 400 N Maple St Murfreesboro TN 37130-2832

DUHAIME, RICKY EDWARD, music educator, woodwind specialist; b. Rochester, N.H., Jan. 3, 1953; s. Edward Francis and Ruth Frances (Lyons) D. BA, BS, U. N.H., 1976; MusM, U. Ill., 1978; D Musical Arts, U. North Tex., 1986. Lectr. U. N.H., Durham, 1976; grad. asst. U. Ill., Urbana, 1976-78; instr. music Austin Coll., Sherman, Tex., 1978-80, prof., 1980—, dir., performer instrumental ensembles, 1978—, chmn. dept. music, 1992—; Mildred S. Mosher prof. of music Austin Coll., 1993—; vis. prof. Haydn Konservatorium, Austria, 1996; prin. clarinet mid-Am. Tour Am. Wind Symphony Orch., 1978, Latin Am. Tour U. Ill.-U.S. Dept. State, 1977, Sherman Symphony Orch., 1978— Am. Chamber Winds, 1991, Austrian Classical Music Seminar Festival, Vienna, 1992—; guest soloist Walden String Quartet, 1977, Galliard String Quartet, 1986; concerto soloist Sherman Symphony Orch., 1978, 85, 91, 93, U. N.H. Wind Symphony, 1988; founding dir., performer Grand Avenue Trio, 1989—. Editor modern edits. 18th century woodwind concerti; contbr. articles and revs. to profl. jours. Mem. Nat. Assn. Coll. Wind and Percussion Instrs., Internat. Clarinet Soc., Phi Kappa Phi, Pi Kappa Lambda. Office: Austin Coll 900 N Grand Ave Sherman TX 75090-4440

DUHE, JOHN MALCOLM, JR., judge; b. Iberia Parish, La., Apr. 7, 1933; s. J. Malcolm and Rita (Arnandez) D.; children: Kim Duhe Holleman, Jeanne Duhe Sinitier, Edward M., M. Bofill. BBA, Tulane U., 1955, LLB, 1957. Atty. Helm, Simon, Caffery & Duhe, New Iberia, La., 1957-78; dist. judge State of La., New Iberia, 1979-84; judge U.S. Dist. Ct. (we. dist.) La., Lafayette, 1984-88; cir. judge, U.S. Ct. Appeals (5th cir.), Lafayette, 1988—. Office: US Ct Appeals 556 Jefferson St Ste 200 Lafayette LA 70501-6972

DUKE, GARY JAMES, electronics executive; b. Norman, Ark., Aug. 3, 1947; s. Arley Matthew and Evelyn Ethia (Cogburn) D.; m. Evonne Pearson, Oct. 7, 1966; children: Arlon Matthew, Anton Lee, Angela Michelle. Student, U. Ark., Little Rock, 1969-70. With Diebold Inc., 1970—; dist. mgr. Diebold Inc., San Antonio, 1974-75, Charleston, W.Va., 1975-76; area tech. specialist Diebold Inc., Little Rock, 1976; tech. mgr. south cen. area Diebold Inc., Memphis, 1977-87; tech. mgr. southwestern area Diebold Inc., Dallas, 1988; tech. mgr. so. div. Diebold Inc., Atlanta, 1988-90; customer svc. mgr. Diebold Inc., Memphis, 1990—; mem. gen. adv. coun. State Tech. Inst. at Memphis, 1984-86; mem. Tenn. Gov.'s Task Force, 1984; v.p.-employer Tenn. Coll. Placement Assn., 1985. Contbr. articles to various publs. Brotherhood dir. lst Bapt. Ch., Collierville, Tenn., 1985-88, Shelby Bapt. Assn., Memphis, 1987-88; v.p. Bapt. Men, Tenn. Bapt. Brotherood, 1987-88. Sgt. USMC, 1965-69. Recipient honor award Armed Forces Communications and Electronics Assn., 1966, Exceptional Svc. award State Tech. Inst. at Memphis, 1985. Home: 1213 Greenview Rd Collierville TN 38017-1161 Office: Diebold Inc 5425 E Raines Rd Ste 10 Memphis TN 38115-6701

DUKE, STEPHEN OSCAR, physiologist, researcher; b. Battle Creek, Mich., Oct. 9, 1944; s. Oscar and Azalee Rosa (Tallant) D.; m. Barbara Alice Rowe, June 2, 1967; children: Gregory Ivan, Robin Anne. BS, Henderson State U., 1966; MS, U. Ark., 1969; PhD, Duke U., 1975. Plant physiologist So. Weed Sci. Lab. USDA, Stoneville, Miss., 1975-84; research leader USDA, Stoneville, 1984-87, lab. dir., 1987—; adj. prof. Miss. State U., Starkville, 1978—. Co-author: Physiology of Herbicide Action, 1993; editor: Weed Physiology, 2 vols., 1985, Pest Control with Enhanced Environmental Safety, 1993, Porphyric Pesticides, 1994, Herbicide Resistant Crops, 1995; contbr. articles to profl. jours. Head referee Greenville Youth Soccer Assn. (Miss.), 1982—; soccer coach Washington Sch., Greenville, 1986-88. Served to 1st lt. U.S. Army, 1968-70, Vietnam. Decorated Bronze Star; recipient Edminster award USDA, 1986, Disting. Alumnus award Henderson State U., 1989, CIBA-GEIGY/Weed Sci. Soc. Am. award CIBA-GEIGY Corp., 1990. Fellow AAAS, Weed Sci. Soc. Am. (assoc. editor 1978-83, pres. 1996, Outstanding Young Scientist award 1984, Outstanding Article award 1984, Rsch. award 1990); mem. Am. Soc. Plant Physiology (chmn. so. sect. 1985-86), Coun. for Agrl. Sci. and Tech. (bd. dirs. 1993-94), Am. Chem. Soc., Scandinavian Soc. Plant Physiology, So. Weed Soc. (pres. 1995). Home: 1741 W Azalea Dr Greenville MS 38701-7508

DUKE, WINSTON WAYNE, auditor; b. Tyler, Tex., May 17, 1952. BA, U. Tex., 1974, MBA, 1979. CPA, Tex. Internal auditor Curtis Mathis Corp., Athens, Tex., 1980-81; analyst/acct. Sherwin-Williams, Garland, Tex., 1981-83; with Am. Plan Corp., Plano, Tex., 1983-84; realtor/acct. Dallas, 1984-88; auditor Henderson County, Athens, 1988—. Actor Athens Little Theater, 1989-93, treas., 1990-93. Mem. Rotary. Office: Henderson County County Courthouse Athens TX 75751

DUKES, EDMOND CRAIG, physicist, educator; b. Dayton, Ohio, Oct. 27, 1953; s. Ernest Franklin Jr. and Marie-Anne (Doos) D.; m. Catherine Anne Rivers, July 11, 1992. BS, Coll. of William and Mary, 1975; PhD, U. Mich., 1984. Fellow CERN, Geneva, 1985-87; rsch. fellow U. Mich., Ann Arbor, 1987-89; prof. physics U. Va., Charlottesville, 1989—; guest scientist SSC, Dallas, 1992-93; co-organizer in field, Snowmass, Colo., 1993; spokesperson HyperCP experiment Fermilab, Chgo. Recipient Cert. of Recognition, Sigma Xi, 1992. Mem. AAAS, IEEE, Am. Phys. Soc., N.Y. Acad. Scis., Phi Beta Kappa, Sigma Chi. Roman Catholic. Home: 1246 Clifden Greene Charlottesville VA 22901-8922 Office: U Va Physics Dept Charlottesville VA 22901

DUKES, MELINDA SHAW, elementary school educator; b. Lexington, Ky., June 7, 1971; d. James Carlton and Julia Shaw Dukes. BA in Edn., U. Fla., 1993, MEd, 1994. Cert. reading, elem. tchr., Fla. Tchr. Gardendale Elem. Magnet Sch., Merritt Island, Fla., 1994—. Guardian ad litem Guardian ad Litem, Gainesville, 1994—; leader Girl Scouts U.S., Gainesville, 1991-94. Recipient Outstanding Vol. award Guardian ad Litem, 1994, Girl Scouts U.S., 1992. Office: Gardendale Elem Magnet Sch 301 Grove Blvd Merritt Island FL 32953

DULA, BOBBY, writer, poet; b. High Point, N.C., Feb. 12, 1973; s. Frances Mae D. Free lance writer High Point, N.C., 1992—. Author: (poetry books) Volume I: A Cross with Langston Hughes, 1993, Stephen is King, 1994; (books) Dr. Seuss, 1993, Where Did Uncle Jo Jo Go?, 1994. With U.S. Air Force, 1992-93. Recipient State Achievement award, N.C. 47th Ann. Career Devel. Conf., Winston-Salem, 1991, Accomplishment of Merit, Creative Arts and Sci. Enterprises, 1992, Golden Poet trophy World of Poetry, Sacramento, Calif., 1992, Humanitarian award USA Today, 1994. Home and Office: The Imitator 702 B E Kearns Ave High Point NC 27260

DULA, ROSA LUCILE NOELL, retired secondary education educator; b. Hillsborough, N.C., May 18, 1914; d. Frederick Young and Mary Rebecca (Lloyd) Noell; m. Thomas Hershaw Dula (dec.); children: Thomas Hunter, Harry Sutton, Frederick Lloyd (dec.). BA, East Carolina U., 1934; MEd, Duke U., 1951. English and algebra tchr. Hillsborough High Sch., 1935-36; English and history tchr. Aberdeen (N.C.) High Sch., 1937, Hillsborough High Sch., 1937-40; English tchr. Garner (N.C.) High Sch., 1942-43; tchr. Caldwell High Sch., Rougemont, N.C., 1943-44, Elon College (N.C.) High Sch., 1944-45; English and history tchr. Aycock High Sch., Cedar Grove, N.C., 1945-48; English Tchr. Burlington (N.C.) High Sch., 1948-51; English, speech and advanced composition tchr. Walter Williams High Sch., Burlington, 1951-74; speech events coach Burlington High Sch., Williams High Sch., 1948-74; mem. com. readers N.C. English Tchrs., 1960-84. Author: Pelican Guide to Hillsborough, 1979, rev. edit., 1989, Morsels for Miscellaneous Moments, 1986; contbr. prose, fiction, poems to lit. publs. Editor newsletter St. Matthew's Episcopal Ch., Hillsborough, 1983, lay reader, 1982-85, 95—; judge local speech events; speaker to schs., civic and religious groups; lay reader St. Matthew's Episcopal Ch.; v.p. Orange County Retired Sch. Pers., 1994-96. Recipient Commendations for high sch. Voice of Democracy participation VFW, 1959-61, Degree of Distinction, Nat. Forensic League, 1957, Honor plaques Freedom's Found. Valley Forge, 1969-72, Extraordinary Woman of N.C. award Lady Stetson div. Coty, 1987, light verse awards Idaho Writers League, 1988, N.C. Poetry Soc., 1989, Valley Forge Tchrs. award, 1974; Nat. Coun. Tchrs. of English grantee English Inst., Duke U., summer 1962, Purdue Speech Workshop, summer, 1969. Mem. AAUW, Am. Assn. Ret. Persons, Acad. Am. Poets, N.C. Poetry Soc., Hillsborough Hist. Soc., N.C. Ret. Tchrs. Assn., Orange County Rep. Sch. Pers. (v.p. 1994—), Am. Legion Aux., Kappa Delta Pi. Democrat. Home: PO Box 222 Hillsborough NC 27278-0222

DULANEY, WILLIAM MARVIN, history educator, curator; b. Troy, Ala., July 21, 1950; s. Willie Frank and Pauline Dulaney; m. Carol Ann Simmons, June 6, 1973; 1 child, Malik Hashim. BA, Ctrl. State U., 1972; MA, Ohio State U., 1974, PhD, 1984. Career counselor Wittenberg U., Springfield, Ohio, 1978-81; intercultural affairs advisor Tex. Christian U., Fort Worth, 1981-83; asst. dir. U. Tex., Arlington, 1983-85, asst. prof., 1986—; asst. prof. St. Olaf Coll., Northfield, Minn., 1985-86; curator of history African-Am. Mus., Dallas, Tex., 1986—; exec. dir. African-Am. Rsch. Assocs., Dallas, 1992—; dir. Avery Rsch. Ctr. Coll. Charleston, 1994—. Author: Black Police in America, 1996; editor: Essays on American Civil Rights, 1993. Chmn. bd. dirs. Our Brothers' Keeper NDUGU, Dallas, 1993—. Recipient Carter G. Woodson award African Am. Cultural Ctr., Dallas, 1989, Urban League svc. award Urban League Young Adult Coun., 1991. Mem. Assn. Study of Afro-Am. Life and History, Orgn. Am. Historians, So. Conf. Afro-Am. Studies (v.p.), Tex. State Hist. Assn. Office: Avery Rsch Ctr 125 Bull St Charleston SC 29401-1247

DULIN, TERESA DIANNE, primary school educator; b. Winchester, Ky., Oct. 18, 1955; d. Elmer Noland and Dorothy Jean (Chism) Wall; m. Freddie Mitchell Dulin, Jan. 9, 1975; 1 child, Adam Mitchell. BA, Morehead State U., 1979; MA, Ea. Ky. U., 1987. Kindergarten tchr. Emmanuel Episc. Day Sch., Winchester, Ky., 1979-80; tchr. 4th and 5th grades Clark County Bd. Edn., Winchester, 1980-85, 87-88, kindergarten tchr., 1988-95, tchr. primary (grades 2-3), 1995—. Mem. NEA, Phi Kappa Phi. Home: 9797 Irvine Rd Winchester KY 40391-9332 Office: Trapp Elem Sch 11400 Irvine Rd Winchester KY 40391-9334

DUMAN, BARRY LANCE, economics educator; b. Jan. 6, 1943; m. Sofia L. Baurch, Dec. 26, 1965 (div. Oct. 1974); m. Dyana Patterson; children: Laura, Jeffrey. AA in Liberal Arts, George Washington U., 1962, BA in Govt. and Econs., 1964; MA in Econs., U. Del., 1966; PhD in Econs., U. So. Calif., 1971. Asst. prof. econs. Northrop Inst. Tech., 1968; inst. L.A. Trade Tech. Coll., 1968-69; asst. prof. econs. West Tex. A&M U., Canyon, 1969-73, assoc. prof. econs., 1973-78, prof. econs., 1978—, head dept. bus. analysis, 1980-86, head dept. acctg., econs. and fin., 1986—. Contbr. articles to profl. jours. Emma K.Carr scholar, 1963-64; faculty fellow U. Del., 1964-65, Calif. State fellow, 1968-69; faculty grantee West Tex. A&M U., 1974, 76, 78, 80, 82. Mem. Am. Econs. Assn., Nat. Assn. Forensic Economists, S.W. Social Sci. Assn., S.W. Fedn. Adminstrv. Disciplines, Soc. for Advancement Behavioral Econs., Congress Polit. Economists, Mortar Bd., mem. bd., Harrington Regional Med Ctr. Inc., Omictron Delta Epsilon, Phi Beta Delta, Sigma Delta Pi. Home: 6516 Arroyo Vista Pl Amarillo TX 79124-1202 Office: West Tex A&M U Dept Acctg Econs and Fin T Boone Pickens Coll Bus Canyon TX 79016

DUMENY, MARCEL JACQUE, lawyer; b. Teaneck, N.J., Oct. 25, 1950; s. Marcel Lawrence and Mary Jane Elizabeth (White) D.; m. Kathryn Paulette Smith, Apr. 29, 1979; children: Marcel Ryan, Riva Collette. Student, Eastbourne Coll., Sussex, Eng., 1968-69; BS, U. Pa., 1972, JD, 1975. Bar: Ohio 1975, Tex. 1986. Of counsel Diamond Shamrock Chems. Co., Cleve., 1975-80, sr. counsel, 1980-83; gen. counsel Diamond Shamrock Chems. Co., Irving, Tex., 1983-86; v.p., gen. counsel Diamond Shamrock Chems. Co., Irving, 1985-86; sr. v.p. law and devel. Fairfield Communities, Inc., Little Rock, 1987-89, sr. v.p., gen. counsel, 1989—. Eastbourne Coll. scholar, 1968, English Speaking Union scholar, 1968. Mem. ABA. Office: Fairfield Communities Inc 2800 Cantrell Rd Little Rock AR 72202-2040

DUMIT, EDWARD SALIM, communications educator; b. Tulsa, Aug. 14, 1929; s. Salim Jacob and Anisa Dumit. BA in Speech, U. Tulsa, 1951, MA in Speech, 1957; postgrad., Northwestern U., 1957-66, U. Okla., 1967-69. Radio announcer, newscaster, classical music commentator KWON, Bartlesville, Okla., 1949, KMUS, Muskogee, Okla., 1951-52, KFMJ, Tulsa, 1952-55; from instr. to assoc. prof. comm. U. Tulsa, 1955-93, assoc. prof. emeritus comm., 1993—; mgr. KWGS-FM U. Tulsa pub. radio sta., 1955-72, program dir., 1984-89, arts prodr., 1989-93; pvt. voice, diction and interview coach for beauty pageant contestants, broadcast announcers and new reporters; broadcast prodr. and commentator Okla. Mozart Internat. Festival, 1986—, Tulsa Philharm. Orch., 1983—. Co-author: (with Ben Henneke) The Announcer's Handbook, 1959; prodr. recording and booklet Say It Right!, 1959; reader audiocassette of book An Angel in My House (by Tobias Palmer), 1975. Elder 1st Presbyn. Ch. of Tulsa, 1970—, mem. chancel choir, 1968—; actor and singer U. Tulsa Theatre, Theatre Tulsa, Gilbert and Sullivan Soc., 1949—; bd. dirs. ConcerTime, Tulsa, 1950's, 96—, Theatre Tulsa, 1970's, Recording Vols. for the Blind, 1980—, Tulsa Alliance for Classical Theatre, 1980's. Recipient Katie Westby Harwelden award for lifetime contbn. to arts and Humanities Coun. of Tulsa, 1990, Gov.'s Arts award Gov. of Okla., 1993. Mem. AAUP, Phi Mu Alpha Sinfonia, Phi Gamma Kappa (pres., v.p., sec.), Phi Kappa Phi, Alpha Epsilon Rho, Theta Alpha Phi. Home: 1560 S Gillette Ave Tulsa OK 74104-4906

DUMONT, EDWARD ABDO, intern architect, registered interior designer; b. Bklyn., July 4, 1961. AA, Miami Dade Community Coll.; BArch, U. Fla., 1984. Designer Paul, Paul and Madrid Architects, Houston, 1984-87; project mgr. William Crosskey and Assocs. Architects, Hartford, Conn., 1987-89, Brand Allen Architects, Houston, 1989—. Mem. Nat. Trust Historic Preservation, Colonial Williamsburg Found., Mus. of Fine Arts Houston, U. Fla. nat. Alumni Assn. Home: 4412 Effie St Bellaire TX 77401-5617 Office: Brand Allen Architects 1400 Post Oak Blvd Ste 200 Houston TX 77056-3005

DUNAGAN, WALTER BENTON, lawyer, educator; b. Midland, Tex., Dec. 11, 1937; s. Clinton McCormick and Allie Mae (Stout) D.; m. Tera Childress, Feb. 1, 1969; children: Elysha, Sandi. BA, U. Tex., 1963, JD, 1965, postgrad., 1965-68. Bar: Tex. 1965, Fla. 1970, U.S. Dist. Ct. (mid. dist.) Fla. 1971, U.S. Ct. Appeals (11th cir.) 1982. Corp. atty. Gulf Oil, New Orleans, 1968-69, Getty Oil Co., L.A., 1969—, Westinghouse/Econocar, Internat., Daytona Beach, Fla., 1969-72; assoc. Becks & Becks, Daytona Beach, 1973-75; prin. Walter B. Dunagan, Daytona Beach, 1975—; cons. Bermuda Villas Motel, Daytona Beach, Buccanneer Motel, Daytona Beach, Pelican Cove West Homeowners Assn., Edgewater, Fla. Organizer Interfaith Coffee House, New Orleans; tchr., song leader various chs.; chief Indian guide/princess program YMCA, Daytona Beach; bd. dirs. Legal Aid, Daytona Beach. Lance cpl. USMC. Mem. Volusia County Bar Assn., Lawyers Title Guaranty Fund, Phi Delta Phi. Home: 180 Willow Run Ormond Beach FL 32174-8432 Address: 1141 S Ridgewood Ave Daytona Beach FL 32114-6149

DUNBAR, BURDETT SHERIDAN, anesthesiologist, pediatrician, educator; b. Kewanee, Ill., Dec. 6, 1938; s. C. Marion and Marjorie LaVonne (Sweat) D.; m. Kathleen C. Empsucha, Aug. 12, 1989; children: Michael Eugene, Brian Randal, Alex Seaton, Bradley Hughes. BS cum laude, U. Ill., 1960, MD, 1963. Diplomate Am. Bd. Anesthesiology, Nat. Bd. Med. Examiners; lic. physician, Pa., Ill., D.C., Va., Tex. Intern Springfield (Ohio) City Hosp., 1963-64; resident U. Pa. Hosp., Phila., 1964-66; NIH fellow U. Pa., Phila., 1966-67; clin. asst. prof. anesthesiology U. Tex., San Antonio, 1968-69, prof. anesthesiology, 1986-89; asst. prof. U. Chgo., 1969-71; from asst. prof. to assoc. prof. anesthesiology George Washington U. Med. Ctr., Washington, 1974-80, prof., 1980-86; prof. anesthesiology and pediatrics Baylor Coll. Medicine, Houston, 1989—; clin. cons. Bexar County Hosp. Dist., San Antonio, 1968-69; assoc. attending physician Michael Reese Hosp. & Med. Ctr., Chgo., 1969-71; assoc. dir. spl. care unit George Washington U. Hosp., Washington, 1971-74, attending staff, 1971-86; assoc. chmn. anesthesiology Children's Hosp. Nat. Med. Ctr., Washington, 1974-83, acting chmn., 1983-85, sr. attending staff, 1974-86; attending staff Hermann Hosp., Houston, 1987-89; chief pediatric anesthesiology svc. Tex. Children's Hosp., Houston, 1989—. Author: (with others) Surgical Diseases of the Chest,

1974, The Practice of Clinical Engineering, 1977, Pediatric Trauma Surgery, 1979; contbr. numerous articles and abstracts to profl. jours. and newsletters. Emergency med. svcs. D.C. Dept. Health and Human Svcs., Washington, 1975-81, transp. safety com. 1981-84, vice-chmn. pub. info. com. 1983-85. Capt. USAF, 1967-69. Fellow Am. Coll. Anesthesiologists, Am. Acad. Pediatrics; mem. AMA, AAAS, AAUP, Am. Soc. Anesthesiologists (del. Ho. of Dels. 1979-85, alt. dir. 1985-86), Am. Bd. Anesthesiology (sr. assoc. examiner 1987—), Am. Soc. Anesthesiolgoists, Md./D.C. Anesthesiology Soc. (pres. 1985-86), Tex. Gulf Coast Anesthesia Soc., Tex. Med. Soc., Internat. Anesthesia Rsch. Soc., Harris County Med. Soc., Soc. Critical Care Medicine, Soc. Edn. Anesthesia, Soc. Ambulatory Anesthesia, Soc. Pediatric Anesthesia. Office: Tex Childrens Hosp 6621 Fannin Mc 2 # 1495 Houston TX 77030

DUNBAR, DAVID WESLEY, bank executive; b. New Haven, June 23, 1952; s. Carl Owen and Ann Harris (Peck) D; m. Cynthia Susan Minnick, Mar. 8, 1980. BS in Fin., Acctg., Fla. State U., 1974; Cert. Comml. Lender in Comml. Lending and Fin., U. Okla., 1977; cert. in banking and fin., La. State U., 1982. Legis. analyst Fla. State Ho. of Reps., Tallahassee, 1973-74; mgmt. trainee S.E. Banking Corp., Miami, 1975; asst. v.p. S.E. Bank of St. Petersburg (Fla.), 1976; v.p. S.E. Bank of Pinellas, Largo, Fla., 1977-80; v.p. regional S.E. Banking Corp., Tampa, Fla., 1980-81; pres., CEO Republic Bank, Clearwater, Fla., 1981-88, 91-93; pres. Dunbar Corp., Palm Harbor, Fla., 1989—; exec. v.p., bd. dirs. People's State Bank, New Port Richey, Fla., 1993-95; chmn., CEO, founder Peoples Bank, Palm Harbor, Fla., 1995—; chmn. Fla. Bankpac Fla. Bankers Assn., Tallahassee, 1985-87. Treas. Morton Plant-Mease Hosp. Found., Clearwater, 1986-88, 94-96; mem. Donald Roebling Soc., dress circle Performing Arts Ctr. Theater; fin. com. for Congressman Michael Bilirakis, dist. 9, Fla., 1986, 88, 90, 92, 94, 96; bd. dirs. Retarded Citizens Found., Clearwater, 1982-90, Pinellas County Edn. Found., Largo, 1986-92, Pinellas County Arts Coun., 1984-86; gov.'s appointee as commr. to Taxation and Budget Reform Commn. State of Fla., 1990—; mem. state fin. com. Gov. Bob Martinez, Fla., 1990; fin. chmn. State Senator Jack Latvala, 1994, 96; campaign treas. Rep. Sandy Safley, 1992, 94, 96; trustee Morton Plant-Mease Hosp., 1997—. Named one of Outstanding Young Men of Am., U.S. Jaycees, 1980, Fla. Advance Team Mem., U.S. White House, 1980. Mem. Fla. State U. Found. (Pres.'s Club), Innisbrook Hilton Resort. Office: Peoples Bank 32845 Us Highway 19 N Palm Harbor FL 34684-3123

DUNBAR, GEORGIA LEE, educator; b. Rochester, Pa., May 21, 1948; d. Gerald G. and Grace Ellen (Schuller) Buser; m. Thomas Michael Dunbar, Aug. 2; children: Michael, Kristin. BS, Kennesaw (Ga.) State Coll., 1989; MEd, Brenau U., 1992; ednl. specialist, U. Ala., 1994. Tchr. Cobb County Bd. Edn., Marietta, Ga., 1989—; trainer, staff devel. Newton County Faculty, Covington; instr. Cobb County Paraprofls., Marietta, Ga. Faculty rep. Citizen's Adv. com., Marietta, 1989-95. Mem. ASCD, Internat. Reading Assn., Phi Delta Kappa. Roman Catholic. Home: 3281 Hampton Ridge Dr Marietta GA 30066 Office: Cobb County Bd Edn 2400 Rocky Mountain Rd Marietta GA 30066

DUNBAR, JACOB ROSS, III, toxicologist; b. Erwin, Tenn., Sept. 17, 1952; s. Jacob Ross Dunbar, Jr. and Dorothy Carolyn (Tucker) Peoples; m. Deborah Jean Collette, June 8, 1974; children: Rebecca Anne, Sara Collette. BS in Biology, E. Tenn. State U., 1975, MS in Biology, 1977, PhD in Biomed. Sci., 1987. Rsch. technician dept. surgery Quillen Coll. Medicine, E. Tenn. State U., Johnson City, 1977-78; advanced rsch. technician dept. surgery Quillen Coll. Medicine, E. Tenn. State U., 1978-81, sr. med. rsch. tech. dept. surgery, 1981-87, clin. asst. prof., dir. div. exptl. surgery dept. surgery, 1987-88; sect. head bioanalytical chemistry Beecham Labs., Bristol, Tenn., 1988-90; mgr. analytical chemistry pharm. devel. new product pharm. support svcs. SmithKline Beecham Pharms., Bristol, 1990-93, leader devel. team pharm. techs., 1993—; adj. faculty dept. pharmacology Quillen Coll. Medicine, E. Tenn. State U., Johnson City, 1988—, alternate mem. instutional review bd., 1991—. Contbr. articles to profl. jours. Mem. Soc. Toxicology (councillor Southeastern chpt. 1988-90), Am. Assn. Pharm. Scis., Sigma Xi. Home: 500 Steeplechase Dr Johnson City TN 37601-2927 Office: SmithKline Beecham Pharms Bristol Industrial Pk Weaver Pike Bristol TN 37620

DUNBAR, JAMES REGINALD, II, insurance agent, Baptist minister; b. Hendersonville, N.C., July 11, 1954; s. James and Lula Mae Love (Cash) Dunbar-Ragland; m. Ernestine Kennedy, June 15, 1974 (div. Sept. 1978); 1 child, Babydoll Kennedy. Student in Polit. Sci., Austi Peay State U., Clarksville, Tenn., 1974-75; student in Bus. Adminstrn., Tenn. State U. Pres., CEO Dunbar Ins., Fin. Svcs., Atlanta, 1978—; Bd. dirs., founding pastor Love Ctr. Ch., Atlanta, 1996. Mem. Young Dems., Hendersonville, N.C.; attendee Washington Workshops and Congrl. Seminars, Hendersonville, N.C. With U.S. Army, 1972-77. Mem. Alpha Phi Alpha, Thomas A Simms Jr., Lodge #170. Home and Office: Dunbar Ins Fin Svcs PO Box 92512 Atlanta GA 30314-0512

DUNBAR, JAMES V., JR., lawyer, educator, real estate broker, broadcaster, business consultant; b. Union, S.C., June 4, 1937; s. James V. and Hatten (Crawford) D.; children: Nancy Phillips, Katherine Crawford. BS in Bus., U. S.C., 1959; JD, U. Va., 1965. Bar: S.C. 1965, Va. 1965, Colo. 1965, U.S. Supreme Ct. 1980. Assoc. Holme, Roberts & Owen, Denver, 1965-68; v.p. Cosmos Broadcasting Corp., Columbia, S.C., 1969-74; founding ptnr. Berry Dunbar & Woods, Columbia, 1974-86; ptnr. Berry, Dunbar, Daniel, O'Connor, Jordan, Eslinger, 1986—; pres. Mid-Carolina Communications, Inc., 1978—, Selected Brokerage Realty, 1975—, Internat. Bus. Devel. Inc., 1988—; grad. prof. U. S.C.; lectr. corp. structure and immigration, U.S. and abroad. Author: Foreign Business in South Carolina: A Legal Overview, 1993. Chmn. S.C. Lawyers for Reagan, 1980; pres. Columbia Philharm. Orch., 1981-82, Trinity Cathedral Men's Club, 1979-80, Mid-Carolina Council on Alcohol and Drug Abuse, 1974-78; gen. counsel S.C. Broadcasters Assn. Col. USMCR, 1959—. Named Young Man of Year, S.C. Jaycees, 1970. Mem. ABA, Colo. Bar Assn., S.C. Bar Assn., Va. Bar Assn., Fed. Communications Bar Assn., Am. Immigration Lawyers Assn., Kappa Alpha Order, Phi Alpha Delta. Episcopalian. Clubs: Forest Lake Country, Belle Isle, Summit, Kiwanis, World Trade Club. Contbr. articles to profl. publs.; lectr. in field. Office: Berry Dunbar et al 1200 Main St Columbia SC 29211-1695

DUNCAN, DOUGLAS RONALD, JR., golf company executive; b. Augusta, Ga., Dec. 21, 1962; s. Douglas R. and Frances (Clark) D.; m. Jean Hopkins, Jan. 23, 1988; children: Douglas Ronald III, Charles Milledge, Molly Anne. BBA in Mktg., Augusta Coll., 1985. Pres., CEO, Golf Augusta Pro Shops, Inc., 1994—. Past moderator bd. deacons Reid Meml. Ch., Augusta; trustee Augusta Coll. Found., 1992—; mem. bus. coun. Am. Lung Assn., 1993—; chmn. Ralph Hudgens for Congress, 1994, Guy Miller for U.S. Senate, 1996; trustee Univ. Hosp. Found., 1994—; chmn. renovation com. Maxwell House; chmn. study coun. Columbia County Inc.; mem. presdl. search com. Ga. Bd. Regents; chmn. Augusta Coll. President's Club; mem. alumni bd. Augusta Coll., com. chmn., 1990—, pres., 1992-94; outreach chmn. Christian Bus. Men's Com., 1988-93. Mem. Augusta C. of C. (chmn. govt. affairs com.), West Lake Country Club, Augusta Country Club, Rotary (bd. dirs. Augusta club 1991). Republican. Presbyterian. Home: 3518 Pebble Beach Dr Augusta GA 30907-9520 Office: Golf Augusta Pro Shops 3515A Walton Way Ext Augusta GA 30909

DUNCAN, ELAINE HERMOINE, reading educator; b. Bethel, Okla., Feb. 19, 1922; d. Herbert Lee and Vera Ethel (Standridge) Wright; children: Barbara, Helen Barner, James W. BS, U. So. Miss., Hattiesburg, 1964, MS, 1967. Tchr. 3d grade Biloxi (Miss.) Pub. Schs., 1963-65, spl. reading tchr., 1965-67; instr. reading Miss. Gulf Coast Jr. Coll., Jefferson Davis campus, Gulfport, 1967-91; chairperson devel. studies, 1974-91. Author: The Little Street Gets Big, 1986; contbr. articles to religious publs. Pres. Gulf Coast Rescue Mission, Biloxi, 1986-89. Mem. AAUW, Internat. Reading Assn., Seashore Reading Coun., Nat Assn. Educators, Miss. Assn. Educators (pres. chpt. 1990—), Miss. Assn. Devel. Educators, Miss. Reading Assn. (sec.), Phi Delta Kappa. Baptist. Home: 349 Popps Ferry Rd Biloxi MS 39531-2220

DUNCAN, ERNEST LOUIS, JR., lawyer; b. Roscoe, Tex.; s. Ernest Louis and Velma Fern (Carll) D.; m. Sheila Darlene Mc Dougal, May 29, 1965; children—Andrew Louis, Elizabeth Diane. Student, Tex. Tech. Coll., 1961-64; J.D. cum laude, Baylor U., 1967. Bar: Tex., 1967, Fla., 1972. Briefing atty. Sup. Ct. Tex., 1967-68; assoc. Smith, Hulsey, Schwalbe & Nichols, Jacksonville, Fla., 1972-77, Branscomb & Miller, Corpus Christi, 1978-81, Barnhart, Mallia, Cochran & Luther, Corpus Christi, 1982-86, Luther & Duncan, Corpus Christi, 1987-87; of counsel Meredith, Donnell & Abernethy, 1989—. Lt. JAGC, USNR, 1968-72. Mem. ABA, Nueces County Bar Assn., Phi Gamma Delta, Phi Alpha Delta. Methodist. Home: 214 Palmetto St Corpus Christi TX 78412-2736 Office: 1500 One Shoreine Pla PO Box 2624 Corpus Christi TX 78403-2624

DUNCAN, FRANCES MURPHY, retired special education educator; b. Utica, N.Y., June 23, 1920; d. Edward Simon and Elizabeth Myers (Stack) Murphy; m. Lee C. Duncan, June 23, 1947 (div. June 1969); children: Lee C., Edward M., Paul H., Elizabeth B., Nancy R., Richard L. BA, Columbia U., 1942; MEd, Auburn U., 1963, EdD, 1969. Head sci. dept. Arnold Jr. H.S., Columbus, Ga., 1960-63; tchr. physiology, Spanish, Jordan H.S., Columbus, 1963-64; tchr. spl. edn. mentally retarded Muscogee County Sch. System, Columbus, 1964-65; instr. spl. edn. Auburn (Ala.) U., 1966-69; assoc. dir. Douglas Sch. for Learning Disabilities, Columbus, 1969-70; prof. edn. and spl. edn. Columbus Coll., 1970-85; ret., 1985. Past dir. Columbus Devel. Ctr.; dir. Columbus Regional Chartered Coun. Child Abuse-first steps/TRUST programs. Past sec. exec. bd. Muscular Dystrophy Assn., 1968-70; 73-74; mem. Gov.'s Commn. on Disabled Georgians; past trustee Listening Eyes Sch. for Deaf; past mem. Mayor's Com. on Handicapped; mem. team for evaluation and placement of exceptional children Columbus Pub. Schs. Fellow Am. Assn. Mental Retardation; mem. AAUP, AAUW (pres. 1973-75, div. rec. sec. 1975—), Council Exceptional Children (legis. chmn. 1973-74), Psi Chi, Phi Delta Kappa. Roman Catholic. Home: 1811 Alta Vista Dr Columbus GA 31907-3210

DUNCAN, GWENDOLYN MCCURRY, elementary education educator; b. Walhalla, S.C., Feb. 24, 1943; d. Benjamin Harrison and Lucy Rosa (Quarles) McCurry; m. Harold Edward Duncan, July 29, 1962; children: Gregory Scott, Michael Lane. BA in Elem. Edn., Clemson (S.C.) U., 1984. Tchr. Westminster (S.C.) Elem. Sch., 1984—. Sunday sch. tchr. Mountain View Bapt. Ch., Walhalla, 1968—; mem. Westminster Elem. PTA, 1984—. Mem. NEA, Oconee County Edn. Assn., S.C. Edn. Assn., S.C. Tchrs. of Math., Nat. Coun. of Tchrs. of Math., Kappa Delta Pi. Baptist. Home: 389 Fowler Rd West Union SC 29696-3122 Office: Westminster Elem Sch 206 Hamilton Dr Westminster SC 29693-1541

DUNCAN, JANICE MARIE, education educator; b. Rolla, Mo., May 5, 1945; d. Oscar Lloyd and Alice Mae Duncan. BS, U. Mo., 1967; MA, U. Miss., 1969; PhD, U. Nebr., 1991. Cert. lifetime tchr. Asst. prof. SW Bapt. U., Bolivar, Mo., 1969-84; grad. tchg. asst. U. Nebr., Lincoln, 1984-91; asst. prof. Northeastern State U., Tahlequah, Okla., 1994—; adj. prof. U. Nebr., 1992; com. work Southwest Bapt. U., 1969-84, U. Nebr., 1986-90. Recipient MICEFA award U. Paris, 1987. Mem. MLA, Am. Assn. Tchrs. of French, Delta Kappa Gamma Soc. Internat. (v.p., state scholar recipient 1984-86, author play 1976). Baptist. Office: Northeastern State U Arts & Letters Tahlequah OK 74464

DUNCAN, JOHN J., JR., congressman; b. Lebanon, Tenn., July 21, 1947; m. Lynn Hawkins; children: Tara, Whitney, John J. III, Zane. BS, U. Tenn., 1969; JD, George Washington U., 1973. Pvt. practice Knoxville, Tenn., 1973-81; state trial judge, 1981-88; mem. 100th-104th Congresses from 2nd Tenn. dist., Washington, 1988—; mem. pub. works and transp. com., mem. natural resources com. Bd. dirs. or past bd. dirs. ARC, YWCA, Sunshine Ctr. for Mentally Retarded, Beck Black Heritage Ctr., Knoxville Union Rescue Mission, St. Citizens Home Aid Svc., Knoxville Girls Club, others; active elder Eastminster Presbyn. Ch. Capt. U.S. N.G. and Res. Mem. Am. Legion, Elks, Sertoma Club, 40&8, Masons, Shriners. Office: US Ho of Reps 2400 Rayburn Washington DC 20515

DUNCAN, KENNETH, state treasurer. Treas. State of La., Baton Rouge. Office: Office State Treas 2837 Lydia Ave Baton Rouge LA 70000

DUNCAN, MARTHA GRACE, law educator; b. Little Rock; d. Richard Forrester Jr. and Elizabeth Louise (Kramer) D. BA summa cum laude, Occidental Coll., 1967; MA, Columbia U., 1969, PhD, 1976; postgrad., NYU, 1977-79; JD, Yale U., 1983. Instr. Columbia U., 1976-77; adj. asst. prof. Cooper Union for the Advancement of Sci. and Art, 1976-77; asst. prof. polit. sci. Wagner Coll., S.I., N.Y., 1977-80; jud. clk. U.S. Ct. Appeals, Washington, 1983-84; assoc. Covington & Burling, 1985-86; asst. prof. law Emory U., Atlanta, 1986-89, assoc. prof. law, 1989-96, prof. law, 1996—. Author: Romantic Outlaws, Beloved Prisons, 1996; articles editor Yale Law Jour., 1982-83; contbr. articles to profl. jours. Woodrow Wilson fellow Woodrow Wilson Soc., 1967, fellow of the faculty of pub. law and govt. Columbia U., 1968-72, Pres.'s fellow Columbia U., 1973. Mem. MLA, ABA, Internat. Soc. Polit. Psychology, Law and Humanities Inst., Phi Beta Kappa. Office: Emory Univ Sch Law 1301 Clifton Rd Atlanta GA 30322

DUNCAN, MAURICE GREER, accountant, consultant; b. Marshall, Mo., July 16, 1928; s. Carl I. and Marguerite (Greer) D.; m. Sara Bangert, Aug. 29, 1959; children: Nancy L., Guerry M., Barbara D. BSBA, U. Okla., 1950. CPA, Okla. Staff acct. Amoco Corp., Houston, 1951-52; staff acct. B.W. Vetter & Co., CPAs, Tulsa, 1953-58, ptnr., 1959-73; ptnr. Hurdman & Cranston, CPAs, Tulsa, 1974-79; mng. ptnr. Main Hurdman, CPAs, Tulsa, 1979-87; ptnr. KPMG Peat Marwick, CPAs, Tulsa, 1987-88; cons. Maurice G. Duncan, CPA, Tulsa, 1988—; mem. Tulsa Estate Planning Forum, 1978-88, pres. 1981. With USNR, 1950-59. Mem. AICPAs, Okla. Soc. CPAs, Tulsa Execs. Assn. (pres. 1985), Kiwanis. Republican. Methodist. Home and Office: 4325 E 87th St Tulsa OK 74137-2726

DUNCAN, RALPH V., JR., computer scientist, consultant; b. Feb. 15, 1951. BA, U. Mich., 1973; MA, U. Calif., Berkeley, 1977; MS, Ga. Inst. Tech., 1982. Grad. rsch. asst. Ga. Tech. Rsch. Inst./EES, 1979-81; rschr., software designer Control Data corp./Ceridian, 1981-93; cons., 1993—; reviewer, referee NSF; lectr. in field. Contbg. author: Advances in Computers, 1992, Handbook of Parallel and Distributed Computing, 1996, Parallel Computing: Paradigms and Applications, 1996; contbr. articles to profl. jours, conf. proceeding pubs. Mem. IEEE (sr. mem., referee, reviewer Computer, Transactions on Parallel and Distributed Systems, Transactions on Systems, Man and Cybernetics), Phi Beta Kappa. Office: PO Box 451227 Atlanta GA 31145-9227

DUNCAN, ROBERT MICHAEL, banker, lawyer; b. Oneida, Tenn., Apr. 14, 1951; s. Robert C. and Barbara (Taylor) D.; m. Joanne Kirk, June 3, 1972; children: Robert Michael. BA, Cumberland Coll., 1971; JD, U. Ky., 1974; postgrad., U. Wis., 1977-80; LLD (hon.), Cumberland Coll., 1990; owner pres. mgmt. program, Harvard U., 1990. Cert. lener-bus. banking, 1994. V.p. Inez (Ky.) Deposit Bank, 1974-77, exec. v.p., 1977-81, chmn., 1981—; chmn. Community Holding Co., Inez, 1983—; with First Nat. Bank, Louisa, Ky., 1984—; dir. Cin. Br. of Cleve. Fed. Res. Bank, 1987-90; chmn. Morehead State U., 1985-86; trustee, chmn. Alice Lloyd Coll., Pippa Passes, Ky., 1978—, acting pres., 1993-94; ptnr. Kirk Ins. Agy., 1978—; mem. class XX Pres.'s Commn. on Exec. Exchange assigned to White House Office Pub. Liaison as asst. dir.; dir. Christian Appalachian Project, 1995—. Del. Rep. Nat. Conv., 1972, 76, 92, 96; Rep. Nat. Com. mem. from Ky., 1992—; chmn. Rep. Party Ky., 1995; trustee Highlands Regional Med. Ctr., 1977—; active Govt. Rels. Coun., White House Conf. on Small Bus., 1995; chmn. Govs. Scholars, 1995, chmn. East Ky. Corp., 1996; vice-chmn. Ctr. for Rural Devel.; bd. dirs. Christian Appalachian Project, 1996—. Named Cumberland Coll. Outstanding Alumnus, 1976, Outstanding Young Man, Ky. Jaycees, 1982; U. Ky. fellow, 1978, White House fellow finalist, 1989. Mem. Am. Bankers Assn., Ky. Bankers Assn. (pres. 1985-86, dir.), ABA, Ky. Bar Assn., Ky. C. of C. (dir.), Kiwanis (lt. gov. 1983-84). Baptist. Home: PO Box 331 Inez KY 41224-0331 Office: PO Box 365 Main St Inez KY 41224

DUNCAN, STEPHEN MACK, lawyer; b. Oklahoma City, Mar. 28, 1941; s. Marion Claude and Helen Colleen (Stone) D.; m. Luella S. Rinehart, Mar. 13, 1965 (dec. Aug. 1996); children: Kelly Lue, Paige Anne. BS, U.S. Naval Acad., 1963; AM in Govt., Dartmouth Coll., 1969; JD, U. Colo., 1971. Bar: Colo. 1972, U.S. Dist. Ct. Colo. 1972, U.S. Ct. Appeals (10th cir.) 1972, U.S. Ct. Mil. Appeals 1973, U.S. Supreme Ct. 1975, Va. 1993. Asst. U.S. atty. U.S. Attys. Office, Denver, 1972-73; pvt. practice Denver, 1973-82; ptnr. Hopper, Kanouff, Smith, Peryam, Terry and Duncan, Denver, 1982-87; asst. sec. of def. for res. affairs Dept. Def., Washington, 1987-93, coord. for drug enforcement policy and support, 1989-93; of counsel Mays & Valentine, McLean, Va., 1993—; mem. faculty U. Va. Trial Adv. Inst., Charlottesville, 1986—, Nat. Inst. Trial Adv., Boulder, Colo., 1981; mem. adv. bd. RAND Drug Policy Rsch. Ctr. Author: Citizen Warriors: America's National Guard and Reserve Forces and the Politics of National Security, 1996; contbr. articles to profl. jours. Mem. adv. bd. RAND Corp. Drug Policy Rsch. Ctr.; nominee for atty. gen. Colo., 1978; elder Presbyn. ch. Served as lt. USN, 1963-69; capt. USNR, 1969—. Decorated Vietnam Navy Commendation medal with V device, Cross of Gallantry, Republic of Vietnam; recipient medal and 2 awards for Disting. Pub. Svc., Dept. Def., 1989, 93, William J. Brennan Advocacy award U. Va. Sch. Law, 1992; adj. fellow Strategic and Internat. Studies. Fellow Internat. Soc. Barristers; mem. Colo. Bar Assn. (vice chmn. litigation coun. 1984-85, mem. bd. govs. 1979-81), Denver Bar Assn. (mem. bd. trustees 1984-87), Res. Officers Assn., U.S. Naval Inst., Army-Navy Club. Republican. Office: Mays & Valentine Tysons Corner 8201 Greensboro Dr Ste 800 Mc Lean VA 22102

DUNCAN, SYLVIA LORENA, gifted education educator; b. Henderson, Tex., Dec. 19, 1949; d. William Presley and Sylvia Lorena (Cherry) Bumpass; m. Barry Patrick Duncan, Apr. 13, 1981. AA, Kilgore (Tex.) Jr. Coll., 1969; BS, North Tex. State U., 1971, MEd, 1975. Cert. tchr. generic spl. edn., elem. edn., elem. English, psychology, tchr. mentally retarded, Tex. Spl. edn. tchr. Henderson Ind. Sch. Dist., 1971-72; spl. edn. tchr. Mesquite (Tex.) Ind. Sch. Dist., 1972-85, tchr. 2nd grade, 1985-88, tchr. of gifted/talented, 1988-95; faculty rep. Mesquite Ind. Sch. Dist., 1974-76, vice chairperson admission, rev. and dismissal com., 1979-85, chairperson spl. edn. referral, 1990—. Contbr. editor (newspaper) News at 10, 1976. Zoo parent Dallas Zool. Soc.; sustaining mem. Dallas Mus. Art, Dallas Symphony Assn.; active Assn. Retarded Citizens, Dallas and Richardson, Tex. Mem. Tex. Assn. for Gifted and Talented, Mesquite Edn. Assn., Smithsonian Assocs., Nat. Mus. Women in Arts (charter).

DUNCAN-SIMON, JO DEE, chemist, research and development specialist; b. Orange, Tex., Nov. 29, 1960; d. Kelly Jim and Barbara (DeFore) D. BS in Chemistry, Southwest Tex. State U., 1984; PhD, U. Mo., 1991. Lab instr. analytical chemistry S.W. Tex. State U., San Marcos, 1982-84; tchg. asst. freshman chem. Tex. Tech. U., Lubbock, 1986-87; tchg. asst. phys. chem. U. Mo., Rolla, 1987-88, rsch. asst., 1988-91; postdoct. environ. engr. lab. U. Tex., Austin, 1992; lectr., lab. instr. organic chemistry Austin C.C., 1992; scientist R & D chemistry DPT Labs., San Antonio, 1993, lab coord. R & D chemistry, 1996—; tchg. asst. chital chromatography short course, St. Louis, 1989-90; presenter in field. Contbr. articles to profl. jours.; exhibited Local Women Scientist Exhibit Witte Mus., San Antonio, 1995. Mem. sci. adv. bd. Witte Mus., San Antonio, 1994—, vol., spkr., demonstrator Seek Out Sci. program, 1994—; presenter Chemistry Camp Hoelscher Elem. Sch., San Antonio, 1995—; mem. San Antonio Equal Rights Caucus, 1995—. Expanding Your Horizons Appreciation scholar U. Tex., 1995, 96. Mem. Am. Chemistry Soc., AAAS. Home: 8642 Serene Ridge San Antonio TX 78239 Office: DPT Labs 318 McCullough San Antonio TX 78215

DUNCANSON, HARRY RICHARD, accountant, financial executive; b. San Diego, Mar. 10, 1947; s. Howard Milton Duncanson and Claire Marie (Ouellette) Wolfert; m. Carole Lynn Brame; children: Lisa, Sheree, Amber. Student, Miami (Fla.) Dade Jr. Coll., 1967; BBA, U. Miami, 1972. CPA, Fla. Asst. shortage contr. Burdine's Dept. Stores, Miami, 1967-68; contr. Dukane Press, Inc., Hollywood, Fla., 1968-71; staff acct. Stanley Cohen and Co., CPA, North Miami Beach, Fla., 1972; v.p. fin. Dynacolor Graphics, Inc., Miami, 1973—; ptnr. Duncanson & Sheinfeld P.A., CPAs, Hollywood, 1990—; cons. in field; arbitrator Am. Arbitration Assn., Miami, 1982—; del. White House Conf. on Small Bus., Washington, 1986; bd. dirs. Hollywood Econ. Growth Corp. Mem. Broward Rep. Exec. Com., Ft. Lauderdale, 1981—; chmn. adv. com. acctg. and bus. Miami-Dade Cmty. Coll., 1984-87; treas. Fla. Fedn. Young Reps., 1986-87; del. gov.'s conf. on Small Bus., 1988; mem. bd. commrs. South Broward Hosp. Dist.; apptd. by Gov. to Bd. of Coms., So. Broward Hosp. Dist., 1988, 92, 96, vice chmn., 1988-89, chmn., 1989-91; bd. dirs. Broward Ambulatory Ctr., 1991-95; guardian Nat. Fedn. Ind. Bus. of Fla., 1987—; mem. Broward County Alcohol, Drug Abuse and Mental Health Coun.; mem. So. Broward unit Am. Cancer Soc., 1989—. Mem. AICPAs, Fla. Soc. CPAs (bd. dirs. Dade County chpt. 1981-83), Hollywood C. of C. (bd. dirs. 1991—, pres. 1994, Inaugural Presdl. award 1995), Rotary (treas. Miami-Norland chpt. 1986-88), Beta Alpha Psi. Roman Catholic. Office: 1182 NW 159th Dr Miami FL 33169-5808 also: 2131 Hollywood Blvd Ste 507 Hollywood FL 33020-6753

DUNDON, MARGO ELAINE, museum director; b. Cleve., July 3, 1950; d. Elmer Edward and Ruth Ann (Dreger) Buckeye. BS in Communications cum laude, Ohio U., 1972; postgrad. in Mus. Studies, U. Okla, 1987. Mem. gen. staff Grout Mus. History and Sci., Waterloo, Iowa, 1974-75; coordinator edn. Grout Mus. History and Sci., Waterloo, 1976-78, co-dir., 1979-87, dir., 1988-90; exec. dir. Mus. Sci. and History, Jacksonville, Fla., 1990—. Chairperson Waterloo Hist. Preservation Commn., 1987-88; cultural com. Visitors and Conv. Bur., Waterloo, 1988-90, My Waterloo Days, 1982, 93; mem. Jacksonville Women's Network, Non-Profit Execs. Round Table, 1990-95; bd. dirs. Resource Plus, Waterloo-Cedar Falls, Iowa, 1986-88; mem. Jacksonville C. of C., 1990—; bd. dirs. CJI; bd. dirs. Girls Inc. of Jacksonville, 1994-95. Am. Law Inst.-ABA scholar, 1979, 86; recipient Mayor's Vol. Performance award, Waterloo, 1983, Vol. award Gov. of Iowa, 1990. Mem. Am. Assn. Mus. (site surveyor ant. assessment program 1982—, site examiner ant. accreditation commn. 1987-90, regional councilor 1988-90), Midwest Mus. Conf. (pres. 1988-90), S.E. Mus. Conf., Fla. Assn. Mus. (pres. 1995—), Iowa Mus. Assn. (pres. 1984-86), Rotary, Quota Club (pres. 1982). Office: Mus Sci & History 1025 Museum Cir Jacksonville FL 32207-9006

DUNFORD, JUNIUS EARLE, JR., retired newspaper editor and journalism instructor; b. Richmond, Va., Aug. 28, 1926; s. Junius Earle and Mary (Lightfoot) D.; m. Jane Carroll Redd, Oct. 17, 1953; children: Lucie Garnett, Catherine Montague. BA, U. Richmond, 1948. Asst. exec. sec., asst. editor Fraternity Phi Gamma Delta, Washington, 1948-50; asst. editor U.S. C. of C., Washington, 1951-52; reporter, asst. city editor Richmond (Va.) Times-Dispatch, 1952-69, city editor, 1969-88; adj. lectr. in journalism U. Richmond, 1969-96. Author: (book) Richmond Times-Dispatch--The Story of a Newspaper, 1995. Staff sgt. U.S. Army, 1944-46, Italy. Episcopalian. Home: 42 Willway Ave Richmond VA 23226

DUNGAN, WILLIAM JOSEPH, JR., insurance broker, economics educator; b. New London, Conn., Mar. 19, 1956; s. William Joseph and Alpha (Combs) D.; m. Janet Dudek, May 28, 1983. BS in Biology, Old Dominion U., 1978, postgrad. in Econs., 1978-80; postgrad., U. Pa., 1984-85, Coll. for Fin. Planners, 1983-84; MS in Fin. Svcs., Am. Coll., 1988, MS in Mgmt., 1990. CLU; chartered fin. cons., cert. fund. specialist,. Rep. Prudential Ins. Co., Norfolk, Va., 1979-80; assoc. Russ Gills and Assocs., Virginia Beach, Va., 1980-88; instr. Tidewater C.C., Virginia Beach, Va., 1979-86; v.p. life and employee benefits Henderson & Phillips Inc., Norfolk, Va., 1988—; founding pres. First Fin. Resources, 1987—; instr. employee benefits and econs. Inst. Mgmt., Old Dominion U., 1988—, chmn. cert. employee benefit specialists adv. bd. Bd. dirs. Epilepsy Assn. Va.; trustee Old Dominion U. Ednl. Found., 1991—; v.p. Epilepsy Assn. of Va. Mem. Internat. Assn. Fin. Planning (pres. Hampton Rds. chpt.), Nat. Assn. Life Underwriters, Assn. for Advanced Life Underwriting, Inst. Cert. Fin. Planners, Inst. Cert. Employee Benefits Specialists, Am. Soc. CLUs, Norfolk Assn. Life Underwriters (bd. dirs.), Monarch Bus. Soc., Old Dominion Univ.'s Ins. and Fin. Svcs. Ctr., Epilepsy Assn. Va. (bd. dirs.), Million Dollar Round Table. Republican. Home: 4201 Mercedes Ct Virginia Beach VA 23455-5649 Office: Henderson & Phillips Inc 235 E Plume St Norfolk VA 23510-1706

DUNHAM, GREGORY MARK, obstetrician, gynecologist; b. Trenton, N.J., Feb. 11, 1958; s. Robert Latham and Nancy Ann (Duncan) D.; m. Sarita Fawn Pennington, July 10, 1982; children: Taylor Erin, Seth Ian, Kambri Leigh. BS, Abilene Christian U., 1978; MD, U. Tex. Southwestern, 1983. Diplomate Am. Bd. Ob-Gyn. Intern St. Joseph Hosp., Denver, 1983-84, resident, 1984-86, chief resident, 1986-87; ob-gyn. Shannon Clinic (formerly Angelo Clinic Assn.), San Angelo, Tex., 1987—; advisor Home Econs. Adv. Coun., San Angelo, 1987—; med. dir. Child Advocacy Ctr., San

Angelo, 1991—, Sexual Assault Nurse Examiner Program, San Angelo, 1992-94; chmn. dept. ob-gyn. Shannon Med. Ctr., San Angelo, 1993-94, chmn. div. Women's and Children's Health, 1994-96, mem. med. bd., 1992-96. Bd. dirs. Angelo Clin. Assn., 1992-95; med. dir. Shannon Clinic, 1995—; deacon Johnson St. Ch. of Christ, San Angelo, 1989—. Recipient Physician's Recognition award AMA, 1986, 92, 96. Fellow ACOG; mem. Soc. Laparoendoscopic Surgeons, Am. Coll. Physician Execs., Tex. Assn. Ob-Gyn., N.Am. Soc. for Pediat. and Adolescent Gynecology, Tex. Physician Resource Coun. (exec. bd. 1994-96). Republican. Office: Shannon Clinic PO Box 22000 San Angelo TX 76903-5919

DUNKELBERGER, JOHN EDWARD, sociology educator; b. Sunbury, Pa., Feb. 11, 1935; s. Marlin Frederick and Evelyn (Binkley) D.; m. Jane M. Eckman, Aug. 31, 1957; children: Cathy Jane, Cindy Jean Dunkelberger-Edmiston. AB, Franklin and Marshall Coll., 1957; MS, Pa. State U., 1959; PhD, Miss. State U., 1965. Instr. Miss. State U., Starkville, 1959-62; from asst. prof. to prof. sociology Auburn (Ala.) U., 1962—. Mem. Am. Sociol. Assn., Rural Sociol. Soc. (sec.-treas.), So. Rural Sociol. Assn. (sec., pres.), So. Sociol. Soc., Mid-South Sociol. Assn. (exec. com.), Ala.-Miss. Sociol. Assn. (coun., pres., charter mem.), Ala. Acad. Scis. Home: 111 Laurel Dr Auburn AL 36830 Office: Dept Agrl Econs/Rural Sociology 306A Comer Hall Auburn AL 36849

DUNKLY, JAMES WARREN, theological librarian; b. Alexandria, La., Aug. 1, 1942; s. James Warren and Frances Estelle (Jones) D.; m. Nancy Rose; children: Margaret Rose, Michael Benjamin. BA, Tex. Christian U., 1963; diploma in Theology, Oxford U., Eng., 1964; MA, Vanderbilt U., 1968, PhD, 1982. Grad. fellow, tutor Episcopal Theol. Sch., Cambridge, Mass., 1969-71; libr. Nashotah (Wis.) House, 1975-83; dir. librs. Episcopal Div. Sch., Weston Sch. Theology, Cambridge, 1983-92; libr. Sch. Theology U. of the South, Sewanee, Tenn., 1993—; assoc. libr. U. of the South, Sewanee, 1995—; instr. Inst. Christian Studies, Milw., 1975-83, Wis. asst. editor N.T. Abstracts, 1971-72, mng. editor, 1972-75; mem. corp. for Anglican Theol. Rev., 1976-95, asst. editor for N.T., 1976-84, editor, 1984-88; mem. bd. Sewanee Theol. Rev., 1994—; contbr. articles to profl. jours. Conant Fund grantee, Episcopal Ch., 1981-82; Henry fellow, Oxford U., 1963-64, Vanderbilt U. teaching fellow, 1967-69, Rockefeller doctoral fellow, 1969-70; Vanderbilt U. scholar, 1966-67. Mem. Soc. Bibl. Lit., Cath. Bibl. Assn., Am. Theol. Libr. Assn. (publs. com. 1977-83, bd. dirs. 1980-83, task force on structure, 1981, index bd. 1985-89, exec. com. index and preservation bds. 1988-89, v.p. 1989-90, pres. 1990-92), Anglican Assn. Biblical Scholars. Home: PO Box 3206 Sewanee TN 37375-3206 Office: U of the South du Pont Libr Sewanee TN 37383-1000

DUNLAP, ALBERT JOHN, venture capitalist; b. Hoboken, N.J., July 26, 1937; s. Albert Joseph and Mildred Veronica (O'Toole) D.; m. Judith Ann Stringer, Mar. 30, 1968. BS, U.S. Mil. Acad., 1960; LLD (hon.), Stetson U.; DEng (hon.), Stevens Inst. Tech. Various positions forest products, packaging and consumer products industries, 1963-77; sr. v.p., corp. mgmt. exec. com. Am. Can Com., Greenwich, Conn., 1977-82; sr. v.p. Manville Corp., 1982-83; chmn., chief exec. officer Lily-Tulip, Inc., Toledo, Augusta (Ga.), 1983-86, Sir James Goldsmith, 1986-89, Anglo Group PLC, London, 1989-91, Gyrestar Inc., 1991—; CEO, mng. dir. Consol. Press Holdings, Sydney, Australia, 1992-94; chmn. bd., CEO Scott Paper Co., Phila., 1994-95, Sunbeam Corp., Ft. Lauderdale, Fla., 1996—; commr. blue ribbon commn. dir. compensation Nat. Assn. Corp. Dirs.; spkr. in field. Author: Mean Business: How I Save Bad Companies and Make Good Companies Great, 1996. Trustee Talladega (Ala.) Coll., 1995—. With U.S. Army, 1960-63. Named CEO of Yr., Fin. World mag., 1994. Republican.

DUNLAP, STANTON PARKS, risk assessment and loss control consultant; b. San Diego, Sept. 18, 1934; s. Stanton Baldwin and Abby V. (Parks) D.; m. Dorothy Joan Denon, June 22, 1957; children—Stanton P., Christopher D. B.S.M.E., U.S. Naval Acad., 1957; M.S.S., U. So. Calif., 1983; Ph.D., Calif. Western U., 1985. Cert. hazard control mgr.; cert. profl. safety cons. Commd. ensign U.S. Navy, advanced through grades to capt., 1979; ops. officer, exec. officer Reconnaissance Attack Squadron 3, 1971-73; comdg. officer Tng. Squadron 86, 1973-74; safety officer USS America, 1974-77; force safety officer Naval Air Force-Atlantic Fleet, 1977-80; dir. naval aviation safety programs Naval Safety Ctr., Norfolk, Va., 1980-87, ret., 1987; cons., lectr. in field, 1987—. Contbr. articles to profl. jours. Mgr., coach, umpire Little League, 1969-75; scoutmaster Boy Scouts Am., 1969-75. Decorated Legion of Merit with oak leaf cluster, Meritorious Service medal, Air medal with 4 clusters, others. Mem. Am. Soc. Safety Engrs., Nat. Safety Mgmt. Soc., System Safety Soc., Naval Inst., Naval Acad. Alumni Assn. (v.p. 1982-83). Republican. Lodges: Masons, Shriners. Avocations: woodworking, gardening, boating, cycling.

DUNMAN, LEONARD JOE, III, trucking company executive; b. Louisville, June 8, 1952; s. Leonard Joe Jr. and Betty (Moody) D.; m. Carol Ann Heckel, Aug. 10, 1974 (div. Sept. 1990); children: Leonard Joe IV, Jacob Martin, Kathryn Elaine; m. Bridgette Denise Posante, Sept. 10, 1994; 1 child, Logan Tyler Dunman; 1 stepchild, Jordan Scott Hinton. BS in Bus., Murray State U., 1974. Supr. Philip Morris USA, Louisville, 1974-75, Boone Box Co., Louisville, 1975-77; mgr. sales Atlas Concrete Co., Louisville, 1977-81, East & Westbrook Concrete Constrn., Buckner, Ky., 1981-82; mgr. Mercer Transp. Co., Louisville, 1982—; instr., Nat. Safety Coun., Indpls., 1984-89; expert witness on trucking matters, various law firms in Louisville area, 1986-87. Pres. Crescent Hill Community Coun., Louisville, 1987-89; v.p. Louisville Inter-Neighborhood Coalition, 1988-90; pres. Peterson-Dumesnil Found., Louisville, 1989-90, sec., 1992-93; asst. cub pack leader Louisville area Boy Scouts Am., 1988-90; bd. dirs. Jefferson County Pub. Schs., 1990—; chmn. Crescent Hill Libr. Task Force, 1990-91; mem. strategic planning and fin. com. Louisville-Jefferson County Met. Sewer Dist., 1992—. Mem. Am. Mgmt. Assn., Internat. Facility Mgmt. Assn. Democrat. Home: 3626 Echo Valley Circle LaGrange KY 40031 Office: Mercer Transp Co PO Box 35610 Louisville KY 40232-5610

DUNN, ADOLPHUS WILLIAM, orthopedic surgeon; b. Eden, N.C., Nov. 23, 1922; s. Adolphus William and Sally Grey (Ivie) D.; m. Doris Margery Nash, June 23, 1945 (div. 1975); children: John B.R., Adolphus W. III; m. Clara Delores Kelly, Sept. 3, 1977. BS, Wake Forest Coll., 1942; MD, Duke U., 1945. Diplomate Am. Bd. Orthopaedic Surgery. Commd. ensign USN, 1943, advanced through grades to capt., 1959, ret., 1965; intern Yale U. Hosp., New Haven, Conn., 1945; resident U.S. Navy Hosp., San Diego, 1948, Bethesda, Md., 1952-53; resident Children's Hosp., Boston, 1954; chmn. dept. orthopaedic surgery Ochsner Med. Instns., New Orleans, 1965-88; clin. prof. dept. orthopaedics sch. medicine Tulane U., New Orleans, 1965-88; ret., 1988. Contbr. numerous articles to profl. jours. Fellow Am. Acad. Orthopaedic Surgeons (emeritus); mem. Am. Orthopaedic Assn. (emeritus), Phi Beta Kappa. Republican. Home: One Kingfisher Cove Saint Helena Island SC 29920

DUNN, BERNARD DANIEL, former naval officer, consultant; b. Providence, Feb. 10, 1934; s. Alexander Gerard and Mary Alice (Fitzpatrick) D.; m. Hilda Hughes Tunney, Jan. 4, 1958; children: Bernard Daniel Jr., Brian Lindsay, Mary Catherine, J. Alexander. BS in Econs., Villanova U., 1956; MBA in Transp., Mich. State U., 1971. Commd. ensign USN, 1956, advanced through grades to capt.; asst. supply officer USS Rushmore, Norfolk, Va., 1957-58; asst. material divsn. officer, stock control divsn. officer Sub Base New London, Groton, Conn., 1958-61; material and fiscal divsn. supt. Ship Repair Facility, Guam, 1961-63; nuclear weapons material divsn. officer Naval Supply Ctr., Oakland, Calif., 1963-64; supply ops. officer Nuc. Weapons Supply Annex, Oakland, Calif., 1964-65; commn. supply officer USS Fox, 1965-68; project officer Naval Supply Sys. Command, Washington, 1968-70; asst. for sea transp. Office Chief Naval Ops., Washington, 1971-73; sr. mem. Mobile Tng. Team, Bogota, Colombia, 1973; dir. warehousing/transp. Def. Depot, Tracy, Calif., 1973-76; dep. project mgr., Navy rep. Joint Container Steering Group Office of Sec. of Def., Washington, 1976-77; dir. transp. field ops. divsn. Naval Supply Sys. Command, Washington, 1977-78; head transp. mgmt. and policy br. Office Chief Naval Ops., Washington, 1978-83; comptr./dir. supply Naval Edn. and Tng. Command, Newport, R.I., 1983-85; A-76 program officer Mil. Sealift Command, Washington, 1985; dir./chief staff Merchant Marine and Def., Alexandria, Va., 1985-88; bd. dirs., corp. sec. Greenwich Ctr., Inc., East Greenwich, R.I., 1988—; cons., Alexandria, 1988-91; chief program analyst Resource Cons., Inc., Vienna, Va., 1991-94. Life mem. East Greenwich (R.I.) Fire Dept., 1953—. Decorated Def. Meritorious Svc. medal, Meritorious Svc. medal, Joint Svc. Commendation medal with oak leaf cluster, Navy Meritorious Unit commendation, Air Force Outstanding Unit award, Humanitarian medal, Nat. Def. Svc. medal, Vietnam Svc. medal with one bronze star, Rep. of Vietnam Campaign medal. Mem. U.S. Naval Inst., Nat. Def. Transp. Assn. (pres. San Joaquin chpt. 1974-75), USCG Acad. Found., East Greenwich Vets. fireman Assn., Ret. Officers Assn., Washington Area Supply Corps. Assn., Naval Submarine League, USS Rushmore Assn. (founder and charter mem., assoc. treas.). Roman Catholic. Home: 5817 Shalott Ct Alexandria VA 22310-1427

DUNN, CHARLES DEWITT, retired academic administrator; b. Magnolia, Ark., Dec. 2, 1945; s. Charles Edward and Nora Lucille (Bailey) D.; m. Donna Jane Parsons, Apr. 9, 1966; children: Aimee, James, Joseph, Mary Elizabeth. BA, So. Ark. U., 1967; MA, North Tex. State U., 1970; PhD, So. Ill. U., 1973; cert. inst. ednl. mgmt., Harvard U., 1991. Instr. polit. sci. U. Ark., Monticello, 1969-72, asst. prof., 1972-75; assoc. prof. U. Central Ark., Conway, 1975-80, prof., from 1980, chmn. dept. polit. sci., 1976-82, dir. govt. rels., 1982-86; pres., Henderson State U., Arkadelphia, Ark., 1986—. Chmn. Commn. for Ark.'s Future, 1989-93; chmn. Ark. Higher Edn. Coun., 1992-96. Mem. Am. Polit. Sci. Assn., Am. Assn. State Coll. and Univs., NCAA (pres.'s commn. 1996—), Ark. Polit. Sci. Assn. (pres. 1976-77), Conway C. of C. (bd. dirs. 1984-85, v.p. 1985-86), Arkadelphia C. of C. (bd. dirs. 1987-91), Rotary. Methodist. Office: Henderson State U PO Box 7532 1100 Henderson St Arkadelphia AR 71999-0001

DUNN, DAVID JOHN, human resources executive; b. New Hartford, N.Y., May 24, 1943; s. Leslie Sherwood and Mary Frances (Spreaker) D. BS, Rensselaer Polytech. Inst., 1965; MBA, U. Mo., 1976. Dir. bus. placement U. Mo., Columbia, 1973-76; pres. Am. Med. Mgmt., Inc., Columbia, Mo., 1979-81; v.p. mgmt. services Med. Corp. Am., Kansas City, Mo., 1981-82; dir. corp. devel. Forum Group, Inc., Indpls., 1982-84; v.p. fin. DRG, Inc., Kansas City, 1984-86; v.p. devel. Inst. Tech. Devel. Living Systems div., Oxford, Miss., 1986-87; pres., gen. mgr. Mgmt. Recruiters of Columbia, 1988-94; v.p. Drake Beam Morin Inc., Memphis, 1994-95; mng. dir., sr. v.p. Russell, Montgomery & Assocs., Memphis, 1995—. Ward committeeman Boone County Rep. Cen. Com., 1985-86. Served to capt. USAF, 1967-73. Recipient NASA Achievement award Apollo Mission Control, 1969; Regents scholar, 1961-65; faculty fellow U. Mo., 1973. Mem. Soc. for Human Resources Mgmt. Roman Catholic. Home: 6554 Kirby Gate Cv Memphis TN 38119-8203 Office: Russell Montgomery & Assocs 1355 Lynnfield Rd Ste 184 Memphis TN 38119-5883

DUNN, DEAN ALAN, oceanographer, geologist, educator; b. Groton, Conn., Nov. 11, 1954; s. Edward Daniel Jr. and Margaret Elizabeth (Smillie) D.; m. Jana Marie Adams, May 24, 1986; 1 child, Michael Sean. BS in Biology cum laude, U. So. Calif., 1976, BS in Geology, 1977; PhD in Oceanography, U. R.I., 1982. Lab. technician geology dept. U. So. Calif., L.A., 1975-77; geophys. asst. Union Oil Co., Santa Fe Springs, Calif., 1976; grad. teaching asst. geology dept. Fla. State U., Tallahassee, 1977-78; grad. rsch. asst. oceanography U. R.I., Kingston, 1978-82; staff scientist deep sea drilling project U. Calif., San Diego, 1983-86; asst. prof. geology U. So. Miss., Hattiesburg, 1983-86, assoc. prof., 1986-93, prof., 1993—, vis. assoc. prof. Ctr. Marine Sci., 1987; summer faculty fellow U.S. Naval Oceanographic Office, Bay St. Louis, Miss., 1988-92; cruise scientist oceanography cruises U. So. Calif., 1976-77; shipboard scientist oceanography cruises U. R.I., 1979; shipboard sedimentologist deep sea drilling project, 1982; shipboard sci. rep., sedimentologist, 1983; lead scientist oceanography cruises, 1988, shipboard scientist, oceanographic surveys, 1989-90, Naval Oceanographic office. Author: (with others) Initial Reports of the Deep Sea Drilling Project, vol. 85, 1985; co-editor, author vol. 93, 1987; textbook reviewer John Wiley & Sons, Inc., Macmillan Pubs., W.H. Freeman, 1988-89, 91-94; contbg. author: Magill's Survey of Earth Science, 1990; contbr. articles to profl. jours. Named Nat. Merit scholar, 1972-77, Trustee scholar U. So. Calif, 1972-77, Dolphin scholar U.S. Navy, 1973-77. Mem. Am. Assn. Petroleum Geologists, Geol. Soc. Am., Am. Geophys. Union, Soc. for Sedimentary Geology, Mensa, Sigma Xi, Sigma Gamma Epsilon. Presbyterian. Avocations: photography, bicycling, racquetball, reading, music. Home: PO Box 8506 Hattiesburg MS 39406-8506 Office: U So Miss Dept Geology PO Box 5044 Hattiesburg MS 39406-5044

DUNN, DELMER DELANO, political science educator; b. Sentinel, Okla., Oct. 31, 1941; s. Robert Patrick and Mildred Marion (Morris) D.; m. Ann Gregg Swinford, May 15, 1971; children—John Swinford, Kielly McKee. B.A., Okla. State U., 1963; M.S., U. Wis., 1964, Ph.D., 1967. Asst. prof. polit. sci. U. Ga., Athens, 1967-71, assoc. prof., 1971-77, prof., 1977-82, Regents prof., 1982—, dir. Inst. Govt., 1973-82, acting head dept. polit. sci., 1987-88, assoc. v.p. acad. affairs, 1988-91; rsch. assoc. The Brookings Instn., Washington, 1969-70; vis. fellow dept. polit. sci. faculty of arts The Australian Nat. U., Canberra, 1992. Author: Public Officials and the Press, 1969, Financing Presidential Campaigns, 1972; mem. editl. bd. Social Sci. quar., 1988-94; contrbr. articles to profl. jours. Trustee Leadership Ga., 1976-82; pres. Clarke/Oconee unit Am. Cancer Soc., 1981-82, chmn., 1982-83. Mem. AAAS, Am. Polit. Sci. Assn. (Congl. fellow, 1968-69), So. Polit. Sci. Assn., Nat. Assn. Schs. of Pub. Affairs and Adminstrn. (pres. 1987-88), Am. Soc. Pub. Adminstrn., Pi Alpha Alpha (nat. pres. 1983-85). Presbyterian. Office: Univ Ga Dept Polit Sci Athens GA 30602

DUNN, GLENNIS MAE, writer, lyricist; b. Montevideo, Minn., Sept. 11, 1938; d. James Arnold and Mabel Helmina (Anderson) Haugernd; m. Edward Henry Roske, Mar. 19, 1956 (div. Mar. 1975); children: Daniel Edward, Deborrah Kay Roske Hawthorne, Judith Ann Roske Rinker, Kristine Jean Roske Harbeson, James William, William Benjamin; m. George Maurice Dunn, Sept. 1, 1984 (dec. Dec. 1992). Grad., Montevideo High Sch. Cert. pvt.-instrument pilot, basic ground flight instr. Comml.-instrument ground instr. Sawyer Aviation, Phoenix, 1976-78; pvt.-instrument pilot West Air Flight Club, Phoenix, 1976—; sales telemarketer Lone Star Performing Arts, 1994—, group sales rep., 1996; entrepreneur, 1996; security pub. adminstrn. officer Star of Tex., Galveston, 1994; flight program specialist Embery Riddle Aero. U., Daytona Beach, Fla., 1980-83. Author: You Never Need to Worry-If You Forget to Grow Up, 1985, Someday Darling, Under My Wings We'll Fly, 1993; author, lyricist (song) A Vet's Song, 1992, My Red, White and Blue, 1993, Little Crystal Town, 1993, Riverwalk Christmas, 1993, Santa Keeps an Eye on Me, 1993, One for the Duck, One for Mother, 1993, Texas Auction at the Wheel, 1993, Love your Irish Blue Eyes, 1994. Named to Tex. Hall of Fame, 1996. Mem. Nat. FAA Pilot Assn. (radio operator), Internat. Platform Assn., Am. Legion Aux., Fraternal Order Eagles Aus. Republican. Home: PO Box 1643 12 Seadrift Rd Crystal Beach TX 77650

DUNN, JAMES EARL, psychotherapist; b. Watertown, N.Y., Jan. 31, 1945; s. John Owen and Eleanor (Bradley) D. BA in Psychology, SUNY, Potsdam, 1967; MEd in Counseling and Counselor Edn., St. Lawrence U., 1969; EdD in Counseling and Counselor Edn., Okla. State U., 1976. Cert. tchr. K-6, N.Y. Elem. sch. tchr. Knox Meml. Ctrl. Sch., Russell, N.Y., 1968-71; teaching asst. dept. ednl. psychology Okla. State U., Stillwater, 1971-73, 75-76; stress counselor, psychotherapist Counseling Ctr. SUNY, Oneonta, 1973-75; asst. dir. office of spl. programs and minority affairs SUNY, Oswego, 1976-78; dir. Preventive Ednl. Substance Abuse Svcs., Fulton, N.Y., 1978-79; dir., psychotherapist, stress counselor Human Potential Specialists, Fulton, 1979-80, Aquarius Stress Counseling and Human Devel. Ctr., Myrtle Beach, 1981—. Author: Communication Alternatives for Parents and Couples Planning on Becoming Parents, 1992, Adolescents: Their Attitudes & Behaviors, 1993, The Aquarian Technique, Combining Biofeedback and Meditation, Producing Dramatic Physical Symptom Relief of Headaches, 1993, Stress Counseling: How I See It, 1994, (books) Communications for Couples & Singles & Anyone with Young Children, America in the 21st Century, 1994, Marriage: Making It Work, 1994, Your Mental Well-Being, 1995, (tchg. manual) Communication Alternatives for Parents, 1992 (facilitators manual). Mem. Horry S.C. Bd. Edn., 1988-92. Grantee Divsn. Substance Abuse Svcs. Mem. Am. Counseling Assn., S.C. Counseling Assn., Lions, Masons, Toastmasters, Phi Delta Kappa. Home: PO Box 111 Little River SC 29566 Office: 4405 Socastee Plz Socastee Blvd Myrtle Beach SC 29575

DUNN, JAMES RANDOLPH, chief financial officer; b. Newport News, Va., June 23, 1948; s. Joseph Thomas Jr. and Nancy C. (Hall) D.; m. Muriel Word, Mar. 17, 1978; children: Emily Muriel, Allison Margaret. BSBA in Acctg., Old Dominion U., 1970; postgrad., Fairleigh Dickinson U., 1973. CPA, Tex., Md. Operational auditing Exxon Co. U.S.A., Md., N.J. and Houston, 1970-82; v.p., CFO Modern Furniture Rentals, Houston, 1982-84, Tex. Pipe and Supply Co., Inc., Houston, 1984—; pub. acctg. James R. Dunn, CPA, Houston, 1980-82; spkr. in field. Mgr. Little League Baseball, Md. Sgt. USMCR, 1970-76. Recipient Life Flight Man of Yr. award Hermann Hosp., Houston, 1994. Mem. AICPA, Tex. Soc. CPA (Houston chpt.), Md. Assn. CPA, Alpha Kappa Psi (life, chaplain). Republican. Episcopalian. Home: 6921 Cutten Pky Houston TX 77069 Office: Tex Pipe and Supply Co Inc 2330 Holmes Rd Houston TX 77051

DUNN, JIM EDWARD, sales executive; b. Ft. Belvoir, Va., Feb. 22, 1948; s. James Edward and Alice Jane (Dunlap) D.; m. Karen Lorraine Dunn (div. Nov. 1974); m. Mary Margaret McElroy; children: Dana Leigh, Erica Ann. Student, Southwestern State Coll., Weatherford, Okla., 1966-67, U. Md., 1969-70, Abilene Christian Coll., 1970-71; BS, West Tex. State U., 1975. Warehouse asst., deliveryman Bamco, Inc., Amarillo, Tex., 1971-73; inside sales Bamco, Inc., Amarillo, 1973-75, purchasing agt., 1975-77, outside sales, 1977-82, br. mgr., 1982-85; dist. mgr. Kaman Bearing & Supply Co., Amarillo, 1985—; ptnr. KDS Sales, ISR Filtration, 1990—; sales coord. Johnson Filtration Products, Inc., Amarillo, 1991-93, sales mgr., 1993—. Served to sgt. USAF, 1967-71, Vietnam. Waukika High Sch. scholar, 1966. Mem. Am. Bus. Clubs, Panhandle Purchasing Assn. (chmn. membership 1975-81, bd. dirs. 1981-83, v.p. 1983-84, Curtis Barrett award 1982). Republican. Clubs: Pioneer Gun (Claude, Tex.), Amarillo S.W. Optimist. Lodges: Shriners, 1330 San Jacinto, Masons. Home: 6610 Drexel Rd Amarillo TX 79109-6917

DUNN, JOHN CLINTON, writer, editor; b. Little Rock, Mar. 12, 1942; s. Eugene William and Clara Ava (Samuel) D.; m. Wanda Padgett, Aug. 29, 1970; children: Jonathan Victor, Gene Stephen, Samuel Padgett. Student, U. Ala., 1961-64; BA in English, Columbus (Ga.) Coll., 1974. Reporter, city editor, state editor The Columbus Enquirer, 1967-75; dir. pub. rels. LaGrange (Ga.) Coll., 1975-78; editor News/Daily of Clayton County, Jonesboro, Ga., 1978-80; dir. pubs. Ga. Tech. Alumni Assn., Atlanta, 1980—. Editor Ga. Tech. Alumni Mag., Tech. Topics alumni newspaper. With U.S. Army, 1964-67. Recipient Profl. Devel. award Ga. Tech. Found., 1989. Home: 9450 Brown Rd Jonesboro GA 30236 Office: Georgia Tech Alumni Assn 225 North Ave Atlanta GA 30332

DUNN, JOSEPH RICHARD, psychologist; b. Murray, Ky., July 13, 1948; s. Joe Lee and Rosebud D.; 1 child, Jonathan. BA, David Lipscomb Univ., Nashville, 1969; MA, Harding Grad. Sch. Religion, Memphis, 1970; MS, U. Memphis, 1971; PhD, Miss. State U., 1975. Prof. Wesley Coll., Dover, Del., 1971-74; dir. sch. psychology, counseling Greenville (S.C.) County Sch. Dist., 1976; dir. clin. svcs. Mental Health Ctr., Brookhaven, Miss., 1977-78; prof. Christian Bros. Coll., Memphis, 1978-80; dir. outpatient svcs. Mental Health Ctr., Vicksburg, Miss., 1980-83; pvt. practice Jackson, Miss., 1983—; exec. dir. Humor & Health Inst., Jackson, 1995—. Editor Christian Jour. Psychology & Counseling, 1986-91, pub., editor jour., 1992—. Mem. Am. Assn. Christian Counselors (founder, exec. dir. 1986-91, adv. bd. 1991—). Republican. Office: Humor & Health Inst PO Box 16814 Jackson MS 39236

DUNN, MARGARET ANN, religious studies educator, administrator, minister; b. Marshall, Mich., Nov. 18, 1953; d. Lee Donald and Hazel Lucille (Boehmer) D. BS cum laude, Alma Coll., 1975; MDiv, Asbury Theol. Sem., 1983; MA, Ball State U., 1989; EdD, U. Houston, 1995. Lic. minister Ch. of God (Anderson, Ind.), 1989, ordained, 1996. Tchr. Lydia Patterson Inst., El Paso, Tex., 1976-79; campus affiliate InterVarsity Christian Fellowship, Richmond, Ky., 1980-81; teaching asst. Asbury Theol. Sem., Wilmore, Ky., 1981-83; tchr. Southwood Christian Acad., Indpls., 1984-85, Liberty Christian Sch., Anderson, 1985-86; libr. clk. Anderson Sch. Theology, 1986-88; prof. religious studies, registrar, dir. admissions Bay Ridge Christian Coll., Kendleton, Tex., 1988—, registrar, 1993—; vis. lectr. Asbury Theol. Sem., 1983; min. Christian edn. Rosenberg (Tex.) 1st Ch. God, 1991-92, coord. women in ministry-mission Ch. of God, Anderson, Ind., 1992-94; dir. student ministries Bay Ridge Christian Coll., 1992-93, 94—; mem. Sunday Sch. TEAM Bd. of Christian Edn., Ch. of God. 1993—; adj. prof. U. Houston, Victoria, Tex., 1995—. Co-author: Framework of Our Faith, 1983. Chairperson South East Tex. Ministerial Assembly Christian Edn. Com. Mem. ASCD, Southwest Ednl. Rsch. Assn., Nat. Assn. Fgn. Student Advisors, Assn. Internat. Educators, Gamma Delta Alpha, Omicron Delta Kappa. Office: PO Box 58 East Bernard TX 77435-0058

DUNN, MÁRIA BACH, writer, researcher, translator; b. Kleinbettange, Luxembourg, Feb. 6, 1910; came to U.S., 1946; naturalized, 1950.; d. Dominique and Marie (Müller) Bach; m. James Taylor Dunn, Dec. 23, 1946. Student, Institut Ste Anne Soeurs du Sacré Coeur, Hougaerde, Belgium, 1926-28, Lycée Esch-Alzette, Luxembourg, 1922-26. interpreter, translator, negotiator hist. documents, 1967-71; translator ednl. program Voice Am., N.Y. State Hist. Assn., Cooperstown, 1953; initiator, sponsor Bibliotheque Luxemburgiana, St. Thomas U., St. Paul, 1993; active Mária Bach Dunn scholarship Miami U. European Ctr., Luxembourg Program, Oxford, Ohio, 1992. Contbg. editor: Luxembourg News Am., 1959—. Vol. Mary Imogene Bassett Hosp., Cooperstown, 1950-55; contbg. mem. Luxembourg Heritage Soc. Inc.; charter mem. U.S. Holocaust Mus.; sponsor Maria Bach Dunn scholarship Miami U. Dolibois European Ctr., Luxembourg, 1993—. Recipient Nat. Medal of Merit, Luxembourg Govt., 1993, award of merit regional chpt. Nat. Red Cross Am., 1950, 52. Mem. NOW, ACLU. Democrat. Roman Catholic.

DUNN, RONALD HOLLAND, civil engineer, management executive, railway consultant, forensic engineer; b. Balt., Sept. 15, 1937; s. Delmas Joseph and Edna Grace (Holland) D.; m. Verona Lucille Lambert, Aug. 17, 1958; children: Ronald H., Jr. (dec.), David R., Brian W. Student U. S.C., 1956-58; BS in Engring., Johns Hopkins U., 1969. Registered profl. engr., Va., D.C. Diplomate forensic engr. Field engr. Balt. & Ohio R.R., Balt., 1958-66; chief engr. yards, shops, trackwork DeLeuw, Cather & Co., Washington, 1966-73; mgr. engring. support Parsons-Brinckerhoff-Tudor-Bechtel, Atlanta, 1973-76; dir. railroad engring. Morrison-Knudsen Co., Inc., Boise, Idaho, 1976-78; v.p. Parsons Brinckerhoff-Centec, Inc., McLean, Va., 1978-83; v.p., area mgr., tech. dir. engring., profl. assoc. Parsons Brinckerhoff Quade & Douglas, Inc., McLean and Pitts., 1983-84; dir. transp. engring. R.L. Banks & Assocs., Inc., Washington, 1984; pres. R.H. Dunn & Assocs., Inc., Fairfax, Va., 1984-91, Williamsburg, Va., 1991—; insp., rail transit facilities, Europe, 1980, 82, 84, China and Hong Kong, 1985; involved in engring. of 18 railroads and 17 rail transit systems throughout N. Am., in over 35 states, Washington, D.C., and 6 provinces; guest Japan Railway Civil Engring. Assn., 1972, French Nat. Railroads and Paris Transport Authority, 1988; mem. adv. com. track engrs. U.S. Dept. Transp., 1968-71. Chmn. Cub Scout Pack, Boy Scouts Am., 1972-73, committeeman, 1973-75, troop committeeman, 1979-85. Fellow ASCE, Inst. Transp. Engrs., Nat. Acad. Forensic Engrs.; mem. Am. Arbitration Assn., Am. Mgmt. Assn., Am. Ry. Engring. Assn., Am. Public Transit Assn., Soc. Am. Mil. Engrs., Roadmasters and Maintenance of Way Assn. of Am., Am. Ry. Bridge and Bldg. Assn., Constrn. Specifications Inst., Nat. Soc. Profl. Engrs., Transp. Research Bd., Nat. Assn. R.R. Safety Cons. and Investigators, Can. Soc. Civil Engring., Va. Soc. Profl. Engrs., Can. Urban Transit Assn., Ry. Tie Assn., Inst. of Rapid Transit, Phi Kappa Sigma. Methodist. Office: PO Box 3106 Williamsburg VA 23187-3106

DUNN, SALLY SKEEHAN, school system administrator; b. Pitts., Feb. 22, 1947; d. Thomas Francis and Mary (Costello) Skeehan; m. James Edward Dunn, Jr., June 6, 1970; children: Meghan, Mark. BA in English, Carnegie-Mellon U., 1969, MA in English, 1970. Tchr. English Gateway High Sch., Pitts., 1970-72; devel. dir. Holmes Regional Med. Ctr., Melbourne, Fla., 1980-86, Ga. Coun. Child Abuse, Atlanta, 1986-87; dir. devel. and pub. rels. Marist Sch., Atlanta, 1987—. Bd. trustees Holy Trinity Episcopal Sch., 1984-87. Mem. Nat. Soc. Fundraising Execs. (v.p. 1987—), Coun. for Advancement and Support of Edn., Ga. Planned Giving Coun., Jr. League DeKalb County. Roman Catholic.

DUNN ARNOFF, REBECCA DIANE, human resources specialist; b. Roanoke, Ala., May 8, 1948; d. Avery Moore and Iva Delle (Brewer) Cunningham; m. R. Neal Arnoff; children: Elizabeth, Catherine. Student, Jacksonville (Ala.) State U., 1968; BS in Mgmt. of Human Resources, Faulkner U., Montgomery, Ala. Pvt. practice piano tchr. Alexander City, Ala., 1971-85; mfg. interviewer personnel Russell Corp., Alexander City, 1985-87; cons. Horizons for Learning Russell Corp., Alexander City, Ala., 1983-86; supr. clerical dept. and hourly employees Russell Corp., Alexander City, 1987-89; personnel mgr. Corporate Svcs., 1989-91, mgr. ednl. svcs., 1991—; corp. rep. Adult Basic Edn. Adv. Bd., Alexander City, 1986-92, v.p., 1992-93, pres., 1993-94; chmn. bus. edn. craft com. Area Vocat. Tng. Ctr., Alexander City, 1987-93, pres. adv. bd., 1994-95; mem. adv. coun. Sch.-to-Work Transition, Tallapoosa, Elmore, and Butler counties, Ala., 1996-97, chair coun., Elmore County; chmn. edn. com. Russell Corp. Mem. Ala. Textile Mfrs. Assn. (chmn. edn. com.), Laubach Literacy Action. Baptist. Office: Russell Corp PO Box 272 755 Lee St Alexander City AL 35010

DUNNAVANT, BETSY R., elementary school educator; b. Henderson, Tex., Jan. 13, 1942; d. Jack and Imogene Ross; m. Jack Dunnavant, Sept. 7, 1961; children: Steven, Michael, Clay. AS, Kilgore (Tex.) Coll., 1967; BS, U. Tex., Tyler, 1985. Tchr. Gilmer (Tex.) Ind. Sch. Dist., 1985-86, Spring Hill Ind. Sch. Dist., Longview, Tex., 1986-89, Pine Tree Ind. Sch. Dist., Longview, 1989—. Pres. Pine Tree PTA, 1977-78. Named Tchr. of Yr. Pine Tree Mid. Campus, 1990; recipient Pine Tree Ind. Sch. Dist. Bravo award, 1992. Mem. Nat. Coun. Tchrs. Math., Internat. REading Assn., Tex. Coun. Tchrs. Math., Tex. Coun. for Gifted and Talented, Assn. Tex. Profl. Educators, Tex. PTA (life), Alpha Chi Honor Soc. Home: NI-28 Lake Cherokee Longview TX 75603 Office: Pine Tree Mid Sch 5/6 PO Box 5878 Longview TX 75608-5878

DUNNE, JAMES ROBERT, academic administrator, management consultant, business educator; b. Cleve., July 8, 1929; s. Carroll Joseph and Wilma Agnes (Sutmore) D.; m. Nancy Anne McSween, Oct. 28, 1952; children: James Jr., Stephen. BA, Albion Coll., 1951; MA, SUNY, Albany, 1964, PhD, 1972. Sect. mgr. news bur. GE, Schenectady, N.Y., 1955-63; asst. to chancelor SUNY, Albany, 1963-68; dir. pub. affairs N.Y. State Office Gen. Svcs., Albany, 1968-73; v.p. mktg. N.Y. State Higher Edn. Assistance Corp., Albany, 1973-76; exec. on loan N.Y. State U.S. Office Edn., 1976-78; pres. J.R. Dunne, Inc., Orlando, Fla., 1978-94; program mgr. Eagle Tech., Inc., Orlando, 1983-85; asst. prof. mgmt., acad. program chmn. Fla. Inst. Tech., Orlando, 1985-89; sr. mgmt. analyst Star Mountain, Inc., 1989-90; regional dir. Webster U., Orlando, Fla., 1990—; adj. prof. Schenectady C.C., 1968-76, SUNY, Brockport, 1970-72; adj. instr. Valencia C.C., Orlando, 1980-94, Fla. So. Coll., Orlando, 1980-81, Brevard C.C., Titusville, Fla., 1979-80, Columbia Coll., Orlando, 1980-94; mem. nat. faculty Nova U., Ft. Lauderdale, Fla., 1980-91; acad. assoc. Atlantic Coun., 1982—; advisor doctoral dissertation Nova U., 1988—. With USN, 1952-55, capt. USNR, 1985, ret. 1989. Paul Harris fellow, 1989. Mem. Rotary (chmn. dist. youth exch. 1981-91, mem. Paul Harris Sch. com. 1988—, Rotarian of Yr. Altamonte Springs chpt. 1981, 83, 85). Republican. Roman Catholic. Home: 102 Hickory Dr Longwood FL 32779-2420

DUNNIGAN, T. KEVIN, electrical and electronics manufacturing company executive; b. Montreal, Que., Can., Jan. 31, 1938; s. John George and Olive Mary (Brophy) D.; m. Beverley Alice Laramee, Apr. 11, 1960 (div. June 1980); children: David, Kathleen; m. Leah Anne Merlo. BA in Commerce, Loyola U., 1971. With Can. Elec. Distbg. Co., prior to 1962; salesman No. Telecom, Montreal, 1956-60; purchasing agt. Black-MacDonald, Montreal, 1960-62; salesman Thomas & Betts Corp., Iberville, Que., 1962-67, v.p. sales, 1967-70, pres., 1970-73; div. pres. Thomas & Betts Corp., Bridgewater, N.J., 1974-78, corp. exec. v.p. electronics, 1978-80, pres., 1980—, chief oper. officer, 1980-85, chief exec. officer, 1985—, chmn. bd., 1992—; bd. dirs. Lukens Steel Corp., Elsag-Bailey, N.V., C.R. Bard Inc. Office: Thomas & Betts Corp 1555 Lynnfield Rd Memphis TN 38119-7290

DUNNIHOO, DALE RUSSELL, physician, medical educator; b. Dayton, Ohio, June 8, 1928; s. John Russell and Hazel Nora (Roth) D.; m. Betty Lu Patterson, Sept. 1, 1950; children: Diana Lynn, John Russell, Dale Russell, Brian Michael, Janet Elizabeth. BS in Biology, Gannon U., 1949; MS in Zoology, U. Mich., 1950; MD cum laude, Washington U., St. Louis, 1956; PhD in Physiology, U. So. Calif., 1972. Diplomate Am. Bd. Obstetrics and Gynecology; lic. in medicine, Mo., Alaska, Calif., Miss., La. Asst. prof. biology Millsaps Coll., Jackson, Miss., 1950-52; intern straight medicine, resident in ob-gyn Washington U./Barnes Hosp., St. Louis, 1956-58, 61-63, fellow in oncology, 1963-64; commd. USAF, 1958, advanced through grades to col., 1978; fellow in maternal-fetal medicine U. So. Calif., L.A., 1969-72; dir. ob.-gyn. E.A. Conway Meml. Hosp., Monroe, La., 1980-88; prof. ob-gyn., prof. family medicine and comprehensive care La. State U., Shreveport, 1980-94, vice chmn. dept. ob-gyn, 1988-92; clin. prof. ob.-gyn. U. La. Med. Sch., Shreveport, 1994—; cons. to USAF Surgeon Gen., 1973-78; clin. asoc. prof. Tulane U., 1973-78; cons. Am. Jour. Ob-Gyn., 1980, 90-92, 95, 96, Ob-Gyn. Jour., 1990; cons. in Ob-gyn. Risk Mgmt. Divsn. State of La., 1994—; dept. chmn. and residency program dir. Keesler USAF Hosp., Biloxi, Miss., 1972-78, interim dep. commdr., 1975, 78; sec. med. staff E. A. Conway Meml. Hosp., 1984-85, vice chief of staff, 1985-86, chief of staff, 1986-87; adv. panel on ob-gyn. U.S. Pharmacopeial Conv., 1985-90; USAF reg. cons. Keesler USAF Med. Ctr., 1987-91; rep. to Assn. Am. Med. Colls., 1990-94. Author: Fundamentals of Gynecology and Obstetrics, 1990, 2d edit. 1992; contbr. numerous articles to profl. jours. Recipient tchr. of family practice award Am. Acad. Family Physicians, 1980-88, disting. alumni award Gannon U., 1990; named hon. citizen New Orleans, 1977, Admiral in L.A. Navy, 1977; decorated meritorious svc. medal USAF, 1978; Jackson-Johnson scholar Washington U., 1955, 56. Fellow Am. Coll. Ob-Gyn. (chmn. Armed Forces dist. 1974-77, Appreciation award 1973, 77, 79, Kermit Krantz Cons. award Armed Forces dist. 1992, exec. bd. 1974-77, Continuing Med. Edn. award 1984-87, 87-90, 90-93, 93-96), ACS, Royal Soc. Medicine (London), Internat. Coll. Surgeons; mem. AMA (Physician's Recognition award 1984-87, 87-90, 90-93, 93-96), AAAS, Assn. Profs. Ob-Gyns., Gulf Coast Ob-Gyn. Soc. (founder, 1st pres.), So. Perinatal Assn., Soc. Air Force Clin. Surgeons, Miss. Ob-Gyn. Soc., Ctrl. Assn. of Ob-Gyns., La. Med. Soc., U.S. Power Squadron, St. Louis Gynecologic Soc., San Antonio Ob-Gyn. Soc., Am. Soc. Psychosomatic Ob-Gyn, Ouachita Parish Med. Soc., Masons, Shreveport Med. Soc., Lambda Chi Alpha (Hall of Fame 1996), Alpha Epsilon Delta, Phi Beta Pi. Episcopalian. Home: 1701 Parks Rd Benton LA 71006-4224

DUNSFORD, DEBORAH WILLIAMS, English language, journalism educator; b. Sedalia, Mo., Dec. 17, 1956; d. Clyde Marion and Oleta Jean (Hoard) Williams; m. Bart Roberts Dunsford, May 24, 1980. BS in Agrl., Kans. State U., 1979; MA in English, Tex. A&M U., 1987, PhD, 1993. Asst. editor, reporter Ag Press Publ., Manhattan, Kans., 1978-80; editorial asst. High Plains Jour., Dodge City, Kans., 1980-82; adminstrv. clk., customer svc. rep. Gen. Tele. Co. the S.W., Bryan, Tex., 1982-85; asst. editor Tex. Real Estate Rsch. Ctr., College Station, 1985-86; instr. English, journalism Tex. A&M U., College Station, 1987-91; lectr. English, journalism Old Dominion U., Norfolk, Va., 1991; lectr. English, study skills Mt. St. Clair Coll., Clinton, Iowa, 1992-93; asst. editor, ext. N.C. State U., Raleigh, 1993-94; asst. prof. agrl. journalism Tex. A&M U., College Station, 1994—; instr. Wake Tech. C.C., Raleigh, 1993, Ctrl. Carolina C.C., Sanford, N.C., 1993, Clinton (Iowa) C.C., 1992-93, Blinn C.C., College Station, 1989-90; tech. writer Computer Data Systems, Inc., Norfolk, Va., 1991; comm. specialist, ext. Tex. A&M U., College Station, summers, 1986-91, grad. teaching asst., 1987, 89-90; freelance writer Fayetteville (N.C.) Observer-Times, 1993, Raleigh News & Observer, 1993. Contbr. articles to local newspapers. Vice-chair Clinton County Dem. Party, 1993; vol. campaign worker Brazos County, 1988; sec.-treas. Internat. Assn. Bus. Communicators, 1986-87, Brazos bravo com. 1987-88; Tex. A&M Conf. on lang. and lit. com. English Grad. Students Assn., 1989-90; dir. Bryan-College Station Jaycees, 1985-86. Recipient Brazos Bravo award Internat. Assn. Bus. Communicators, Bryan, 1986, Future Farmers Am. awards, Kans., 1974-75. Mem. MLA, Nat. Coun. Tchrs. English, Assn. for Edn. in Journalism and Mass Comm., Assn. for Advanced Composition, Eighteenth Century Soc., Gold Key Nat. Honor Soc. Democrat. Office: Tex A&M U Dept Journalism Reed Mcdonald Bldg College Station TX 77843

DUNSTAN, WILLIAM EDWARD, historian; b. Elizabeth City, N.C., Sept. 25, 1939; s. William Edward and Ida Powell (Fuller) D. BA in Religion and Polit. Sci., U. N.C., 1962, MACT, 1969; MA in Religious Studies, U. Tulsa, 1966; DA in History, Carnegie Mellon U., 1975; postgrad., Harvard U., 1985; cert., Adminstrs.' Leadership Inst., N.C. State U., 1987. Archivist Va. State Archives, Richmond, 1969; editor Virginia Cavalcade, 1969-70; instr. history Carnegie Mellon U., Pitts., 1973; editor Nat. Archives, 1976-77; instr. history U. N.C., Asheville, 1979; assoc. prof. history Brevard Coll., 1980-86; dir. coll. transfer program Durham (N.C.) Tech. C.C., 1986-88; vis. asst. prof. N.C. State U., Raleigh, 1988—; vis. scholar in history U. N.C., Chapel Hill, 1988—; pres.'s adv. com. Carnegie Mellon U., 1974; presented travelogues Brevard Coll., 1983-86; conduccted European Tours, 1982-84; pub. lectr. series in field, 1985. Author: sixteen publs. including The Ancient Near East, 1997, Ancient Greece, 1997, Ancient Rome, 1997. U. Tulsa Grad. scholar, 1962-63; recipient Citation and award U.S. Dept. Treasury, Washington, 1976. Mem. Assn. Ancient Historians, Am. Hist. Assn., Carolinas Symposium on British Studies, Coll. Art Assn., Phi Alpha Theta. Home: 111 Pinegate Cir Apt 10 Chapel Hill NC 27514-2258 Office: Univ NC Dept History Chapel Hill NC 27599-3195

DUNTON, JAMES GERALD, association executive; b. Circleville, Ohio, Nov. 10, 1899; s. Oscar Howard and Florence (Nightengale) D.; A.B., Harvard U., 1923, M.Ed., 1928; m. Dorothy Winfough, Oct. 10, 1944. Freelance author, 1925-34; Fed. Projects dir., Ohio, 1935-37; spl. rep. Fed. N.W. Ter. Sesquicentennial Commn., 1938; editor Ohio Democracy, 1939-40; Ohio field rep. Office Govt. Reports, Exec. Office of Pres., 1940-41; dir. spl. activities Office Sec. Def., 1950-61; exec. dir. Va. Health Care Assn., 1965-75, spl. rep., 1975—; Washington rep. Am. Chess Found., 1962-81; adv. council Oliver Wendell Holmes Assn., 1966—. Mem. vets. com. Presdl. Inaugurations, 1965, 69, 77; pres. Nat. Capital USO, Washington, 1966-67, mem. nat. council, 1966—; mem. Va. State Adv. Com. Adult Services, 1972; disting. sponsor 100th Anniversary 1st Battle of Bull Run, 1961. Served with Ambulance Corps, A.E.F., U.S. Army, 1918-19, to maj. AUS, World War II, Korea. Recipient cert. of appreciation Nat. Press Club, 1955, Commendation award Pres.'s Com. on Employment of Handicapped, 1963, mem. Pickaway Co. Historical Soc.(life), (; decorated Army Commendation medal, VHCA highest hon., James C. Dunton disting. svc. award; hon. fellow Truman Library Inst. Mem. Nat. Assn. Execs., U.S. Army Hon. Ret. Res., SAR, Am. Legion (Nat. Comdr.'s award 1975), Vets. World War I, DAV, VFW, U.S. Army Ambulance Service Assn., Mil. Order World Wars, Ohio Soc. Washington, Soc. of Va. (pres. 1984—). Presbyterian (elder). Club: Harvard (Washington). Author: Wild Asses, 1925; Murders in Lovers Lane, 1927; Maid and a Million Men, 1928; Counterfeit Wife, 1930; Honey's Money, 1933; Queen's Harem, 1933; (anthology) C'est La Guerre, 1927. Contbr. articles to mags., newspapers. Address: 2820 Bisvey Dr Falls Church VA 22042-1701

DUPLANTIER, ADRIAN GUY, federal judge; b. New Orleans, Mar. 5, 1929; s. F. Robert and Amelie (Rivet) D.; m. Sally Thomas, July 15, 1951; children: Adrian G., David L., Thomas, Jeanne M., Louise M., John C. J.D. cum laude, Loyola U., New Orleans, 1949; LLM, U. Va., 1988. Bar: La. 1950, U.S. Supreme Ct. 1954. Pvt. practice law New Orleans, 1950-74; judge Civil Dist. Ct. Parish of Orleans, 1974-78, U.S. Dist. Ct., New Orleans, 1978—; part-time prof. code of civil procedure Loyola U., 1951—, lectr. dental jurisprudence, 1960-67, lectr. English dept., 1948-50, chmn. law sch. vis. com., 1993—; mem. La. State Senate, 1960-74; 1st asst. dist. atty. New Orleans, 1954-56. Editorial bd.: Loyola Law Rev, 1947-48; editor-in-chief, 1948-49. Del. Democratic Nat. Conv., 1964; pres. Associated Cath. Charities New Orleans, Social Welfare Planning Council Greater New Orleans; mem. adv. bd. St. Mary's Dominican Coll., 1970-71, Ursuline Acad., 1968-73, Mt. Carmel Acad., 1965-69; chmn. pres.'s adv. council Jesuit High Sch., 1979—, Boys Hope, 1980—; active Assn. Retarded Children. Recipient Meritorious award New Orleans Assn. Retarded Children, 1965; Gov.'s Cert. of Merit, 1970. Mem. ABA (award 1960), La. Bar Assn., New Orleans Bar Assn., Jud. Conf. of U.S., Order of Coif, Alpha Sigma Nu. Office: US Dist Ct C-205 US Courthouse 500 Camp St New Orleans LA 70130-3313

DUPLANTIER, CHANTLER WAYNE, telecommunications engineer; b. Baton Rouge, May 31, 1968; s. Willie James and Jacqueline Marie (Handy) D. BS in Computer Sci., Baylor U., 1990. Sys. programmer S.W. Bell Tel. Co., St. Louis, 1990-91; mgr. computer ops. and corp. telecom. S.W. Bell Tel. Co., Dallas, 1991-92; product mgr. data comm. S.W. Bell Telcom., St. Louis, 1992-93; corp. mgr. tech. support S.W. Bell Telcom., Dallas, 1993-95, corp. mgr., tech. supt. product mgmt., 1995-96; dir. mktg. S.W. Bell Comm. Svcs., Dallas, 1996—. Vol. United Way, 1990-96; chair S.W. Bell Telecom United Way, 1994, 95. Office: SW Bell 1651 N Collins Ste 300 Richardson TX 75080

DUPLANTIER, DAWN ELIZABETH, communications director; b. New Orleans, May 1, 1970; d. Dennis Paul and Judith Dawn (Hepburn) D. BBA, U. Tex., 1991, MA in Journalism/Pub. Rels., 1994. Pub. rels. asst. Nat. Wildflower Rsch. Ctr., Austin, Tex., 1993; comms. dir. Travis County Bar Assn., Austin, 1993-95, Tex. Bankers Assn., Austin, 1995—; mem. Austin Postal Customer Coun., 1992-95. Editor: (mags.) Austin Lawyer, 1993-95, Tex. Banking, 1995—. Vol. Am. Heart Assn., Austin, 1995, Goodwill Industries, Austin, 1995. Scholar Nat. Assn. Bar Execs. Mem. Women in Comms., Am. Soc. Assn. Execs., Soc. Profl. Journalists, Phi Kappa Phi. Office: Tex Bankers Assn 203 W 10th St Austin TX 78701

DUPLANTIER RHEA, BÉATRICE MARIE CHARLOTTE, international art consultant, interior decorator; b. Bayonne, France, Oct. 10, 1942; came to U.S., 1960; d. Jean Pierre Marie Ferdinand Duplantier and Odile Marie Mathilde (Guilhot) de Spens d'Estignols; m. Edward Jenkins Rhea, July 13, 1964 (div. Aug. 1989); children: Alexander, William (dec.), Jean-Edwin, Kenneth. BA in Langs., Ecole Supérieure Interprêtes Traducteurs, Paris, 1964; BA in Russian, Ecole Nat. Langs. Orientales, Paris, 1971. Restorer old farms and manors, St.-Sever-sur-Adour, France, 1966-76, old apts., Paris, 1966-76; interpreter Ministry Fgn. Affairs, Paris, 1979-81; cons. art, entertainment Bread Oven Restaurants, Washington, 1982-86; cons., decorator various cities, 1986—; internat. art agt., cons. Four Winds Designs, Winter Park, Fla., 1986—; coord. cultural visits for tourists St.-Sever-sur-Adour, Landes, France, 1962-64; agt. internat. artists, 1986—; coord. art. and cultural visits for guests of French govt., Paris, 1979-81; exhbn. cons. Orlando (Fla.) Mus. Art, 1991; cons. exhibitions Boca Raton Hotel Club, 1990-95, Museum Montaut-en-Chalosse, France, 1991, 92, 93, 94, French Embassy, N.Y.C., 1992, Alliance Francaise, Miami, 1994. Mem. Friends of Olney Theatre, 1982-93, Allied Bd. Trade, 1989-93, Cornell Fine Art Mus., Maitland Art Mus., Nat. Mus. Women in the Arts, Enzian Theatre, Friends of Vielles Maisons Françaises, Musée de Montaut-en-Chalosse, Washington Design. Ctr., Design. Ctr. Ams., Atlanta Decorative Ctr. Am. Field Svc. scholar, 1960. Mem. Design Ctr. of the Ams., Washington Design Ctr., Minority Bus. Women Enterprise (cert. Orange County 1990, Orlando 1991), Friends Vieilles Maisons Francaises (coord. art confs., Atlanta, 1990), Winter Park C. of C., Greater Orlando C. of C., Hispanic C. of C. Roman Catholic. Home: 1645 N Park Ave Winter Park FL 32789-2436 Office: Four Winds Designs Internat Art 1645 N Park Ave Winter Park FL 32789-2436

DUPLECHAIN, RHYN LOUIS, parish assessor; b. Mar. 29, 1938; s. Warren and Rena (Chautin) D.; m. Glenda Rita Joubert, Aug. 8, 1964; children: Garett, Deonne, Christine. Student, U. Southwestern La., 1957-59. Cert. assessor, La. Supr. Canal Refining Co., La., 1966-82; city councilman Opelousas, La., 1974-86; parish assessor St. Landry Parish, Opelousas, La., 1986—. Scout master Troop 32, Opelousas, 1972-73; bd. dirs. St. Landry Preservationsists, Opelousas, 1982—, Opelousas Doctors' Hosp., 1982-89; With Army Nat. Guard, 1958-64. Mem. Internat. Assn. Assessing Officers, La. Assessors' Assn., Opelousas Kiwanis Club (past pres. 1990), St. Landry C. of C., St. Landry Farm Bur. and Cattlemens' Assn. Democrat. Roman Catholic. Home: 1902 Alonzo St Opelousas LA 70570-4764 Office: Saint Landry Parish Assessor P O Drawer C Opelousas LA 70571

DUPONT, NANCY MCKENZIE, broadcast journalism educator; b. Gulfport, Miss., June 20, 1952; d. Joseph David and Clarice (Scarborough) McKenzie; m. Joseph Cyrille Dupont III, Nov. 30, 1991. BA, Loyola Univ., New Orleans, 1974, MA, 1994. News reporter WLOX-TV, Biloxi, Miss., 1974-76, WCBD-TV, Charleston, S.C., 1976-77, WTVC, Chattanooga, Tenn., 1977-80; exec. prodr. WEAR-TV, Pensacola, Fla., 1980-81; news prodr. KPNX-TV, Phoenix, 1981-82; exec. prodr. WSOC-TV, Charlotte, N.C., 1982-89, WDSU-TV, New Orleans, 1989-91; instr. Loyola U., New Orleans, 1993—; presenter in field. Editor Tattoo, New Orleans, 1995—. Comm. co-chair Cath. Conf. Ctr. Capitol Campaign, Charlotte, 1987; mem. Jr. League New Orleans, 1991—. Grantee La. Endowment for Humanities, 1993. Office: Loyola Univ Box 201 6363 Saint Charles Ave New Orleans LA 70118

DUPRE, JUDITH ANN NEIL, real estate agent, interior decorator; b. Houma, La., May 7, 1945; d. Herbert Joseph and Doris Mae (LeBouef) Neil; m. Michael Anthony Dupre, Jan. 7, 1962 (div. Aug. 1987); children: Arienne Danielle, Travis Lance. BA in Psychology, Southeast Okla. State U., 1982. Fin. mgr., supr. Gen. Fin. Loan Co., La., Colo., 1960-69; exec. sec. Progressive Bank & Trust Co., Houma, La., 1973-74; health coordinator Spring Cypress Cultural & Recreation Ctr., 1974-75; bus. mgr., buyer June Morris Boutique, Ardmore, Okla., 1978-79; actress, model David Payne Agy., Dallas, 1985—; real estate agt. Vonnie Cobb Inc. Realtors, Sugar Land, Tex., 1986-91, Raymond Jepta Daniel, Jr., 1991—; nat. mktg. asst. North American Mortgage Co. (subs. MONY Mut. N.Y.), Houston, 1987-88; mgr., care coord. Sanus N.Y. Life, Inc., 1988-89; mgr. PPO Am. Health Network, 1989—; dir. admissions and bus. devel. The Transitional Learning Community, Galveston, Tex., 1990-92; owner Paradigm Health Care, 1993—; exec. dir. Rehab. Svcs. Network, Inc.; workers compensation cons. ETHIX S.E.; owner, pres. Summit Internat. Cons., Charlotte, N.C., Houston, 1991—, Ams. With Disabilities Act, Charlotte, 1991, JD Enterprises Internat., Inc., 1994—; adminstr. Ea. Carolina Med. Assn., Florence, S.C., 1995—, Coastal Physicians Org., LLC, Conway, S.W., 1995—. Active Strake Jesuit-Mothers' Club, Houston, 1985-87, St. Agnes Acad. Women's Club, Houston, 1985-87, Ft. Bend Republican Women, Sugar Land, 1985-86, Charlotte Philharm., 1994—, mem. CAST, 1994—; chmn. Texans War on Drugs, Sugar Land, 1985-86; bd. dirs. MUD (Dist. 6), Sugar Land, 1986-92. Mem. Cath. Daus. of the Americas, Nat. Assn. Realtors, Tex. Assn. Realtors, Bal Harbour Homeowners Assn., Assn. Profl. Mortgage Women, Lake Wylie Homeowners Assn., Sweetwater Ladies Golf Assn. Club, Sweetwater Country Club (Sugar Land), Assn. River Hills Country Club, Ladies Assn., Alpha Chi. Roman Catholic. Avocations: tennis, golf, fishing, boating, dancing. Home: 106 Timbelake Dr Florence SC 29501

DUPUY, ARNOLD CHRISTIAN, publisher, military historian; b. Ft. Belvoir, Va., May 22, 1962; s. Trevor N. and Christine (Geissbuhler) D.; m. Linda Cleary, May 25, 1996; children: Alexander Davis, Jeffrey Chamberlain. BA in History, George Mason U., Fairfax, Va., 1988, MA in Internat. Trans., 1994. Analyst Data Memory Systems, Inc., Fairfax, 1981-91; mgr. HERO Books, Fairfax, 1991-92; pres. NOVA Publs., Falls Church, Va., 1993—. Co-author: How to Defeat Saddam Hussein, 1991; contbr. articles to profl. jours. Home and Office: 7342 Lee Hwy # 201 Falls Church VA 22046

DURAND, ALAIN-PHILIPPE, French language educator; b. Marseilles, France, Apr. 25, 1968; came to U.S., 1988; s. Alain André and Josiane Paule (Clautrier) D.; m. Sherri Michelle Stafford, June 6, 1992. BA in French, Spanish and Bus. cum laude, Emporia State U., 1992; MA in French Lit. with honors, U. Kans., 1994, MA in L.Am. Studies, 1995; postgrad., U. N.C., 1995—. Grad. tchg. asst. U. Kans., Lawrence, 1992-95, coord. grad. tchg. assts., 1993-95, mem. scholarship bd. dept. French and Italian, 1992-93; grad. tchg. asst. dept. Romance langs. U. N.C., Chapel Hill, 1995—, coord. grad. tchg. assts., 1996-97; co-coord. 3d Ann. Carolina Conf. on Romance Lits., Chapel Hill, 1996-97; editl. asst. N.C. Studies in Romance Langs. and Lits. Editor-in-chief Chimères, Jour. French Lit., 1992-95; contbr. articles to profl. jours. With paratroopers French Army, 1992. Grad. sch. fellow U. Kans., 1994, Fgn. Lang. Area Studies scholar, 1995; conf. grantee U. N.C., 1996. Mem. MLA, Am. Assn. Tchrs. French, Am. Portuguese Studies Assn. Office: U NC Dept Romance Langs Chapel Hill NC 27599-3170

DURANT, JOHN RIDGEWAY, physician; b. Ann Arbor, Mich., July 29, 1930; s. Thomas Morton and Jean Margaret (deVries) D.; m. Mary Sue Avery Dillon, Jan. 13, 1990; children by previous marriage: Christine Joy, Thomas Arthur, Michele Grace, Jennifer Margaret. B.A., Swarthmore (Pa.) Coll., 1952; MD, Temple U., Phila., 1956; hon. degree, U. Ala., 1993. Diplomate: Am. Bd. Internal Medicine. Intern, then jr. asst. resident in medicine Hartford (Conn.) Hosp., 1956-58; resident in medicine Temple U. Med. Center, 1960-62; spl. fellow med. neoplasia Meml. Hosp. for Cancer and Allied Diseases, N.Y.C., 1962-63; Am. Cancer Soc. advanced clin. fellow Temple U. Health Scis. Center, 1964-67, instr., then asst. prof. medicine, 1963-67; clin. assoc. chemotherapy Moss Rehab. Hosp., Phila., 1964-67; research assoc. Fels Research Inst., Phila., 1965-67; mem. faculty U. Ala. Med. Center, Birmingham, 1968-82; prof. medicine, dir. comprehensive cancer center U. Ala. Med. Center, 1970-82, prof. radiation oncology, 1978-82, chmn. Southeastern coop. cancer study group at univ., 1975-82, Disting. faculty lectr., 1980; pres. Fox Chase Cancer Ctr., Phila., 1982-88; sr. v.p. health affairs and dir. med. ctr. U. Ala., Birmingham, 1988-95; exec. v.p. Am. Soc. Clin. Oncology, Birmingham, 1995—; chmn. coop. group exec. com. Nat. Cancer Inst., NIH, 1977-82, chmn. coop. group chairmen, 1979-82; cons. VA Hosp., Tuskegee, Ala., 1970-82; exec. com. Birmingham chpt. ARC, 1972-77; mem. Nat. Cancer Adv. Bd., 1986-92. Mem. editorial bd. Cancer Clin. Trials, 1979-82, assoc. editor, 1982—; editorial bd. Med. and Pediatric Oncology News, 1975-90; assoc. editor Cancer, 1984-92; contbr. numerous articles to med. jours. Served as officer M.C. USNR, 1958-60. Named Temple U. Med. Sch. Alumnus Yr., 1982. Fellow ACP, Coll. Physicians Phila.; mem. Am. Cancer Soc. (vice chmn. advanced clin. fellowship com. 1974-76, 85-87, mem. instl. rsch. grant com. 1979-82, pres. Ala. divsn. 1973-75, 77-79), Am. Assn. Cancer Rsch., Am. Radium Soc. (pres. 1984), Am. Bd. Int. Med. Oncology (subcom. 1979-85, chmn. 1983-85), Assn. Am. Cancer Insts. (dir. 1978—, pres. 1982-83), Assn. Cmty. Cancer Ctrs. (dir. 1979-81), Am. Soc. Clin. Oncology (chmn. pub. rels. com. 1976-79, bd. dirs. 1979-82, 84-87, pres. 1985-86), among others. Methodist.

DURDEN, ROBERT J., state commissioner, lawyer; b. Atlanta, Nov. 2, 1947; s. Raymond Robert and Annie Maude (Woodcock) D.; m. Donna Morgan, Dec. 18, 1976; children: Courtney, Kathleen. BA, Emory U., 1970, MA in Polit. Sci., 1973, JD, 1979. Bar: Ga. 1980, U.S. Dist. Cts. (no. dist., mid. dist.) Ga. 1980, U.S. Ct. Appeals (11th cir.) 1980, U.S. Supreme Ct. 1983. Instr. Emory U., Atlanta, 1973-76; assoc. Greene, Buckley, DeRieux & Jones, Atlanta, 1979-82; pvt. practice Atlanta, 1982-90; pub. svc. commr. State of Ga., Atlanta, 1991—, chmn. Ga. Pub. Svc. Commn., 1991—. Active Gwinnett County Dem. Exec. Com., 1986—, state com. 1991—. Sgt. USMC, 1969-75. Mem. State Bar Ga., Pi Sigma Alpha. Baptist. Office: 244 Washington St SW Atlanta GA 30334-9007

DUREN, MICHAEL, cardiologist; b. Galveston, Tex., Nov. 16, 1939; s. Norman and Edwina M. Duren; m. Esther Louise Lutzweiler, July 27, 1979; children: Tracy Norman, Lara Michelle; stepchildren: Royce, Jennifer, Timothy Bane. BA, U. Tex., 1962; MD, U. Tex. Med. Br., 1966. Diplomate Am. Bd. Internal Medicine. Intern Meth. Hosp. Dallas, 1966-67; resident in internal medicine Meth. Hosp. of Dallas, 1969-70, 71-72; fellow in cardiology Cardiopulmonary Inst. Meth. Hosp. Dallas-Tex. and Southwestern Med. Sch., 1970-71; pvt. practice Baylor Med. Ctr., Garland, Tex., 1972—, chief of medicine, 1990—, chief of ICU, 1990-93, chief of cardiology, 1990-94, med. advisor cardiac rehab. program, 1989—; bd. dirs. Cardiovascular Ctr. of Excellence, Humana Med. City Hosp., Dallas, Med. City Hosp. Dallas. Mem. adv. bd. to editors: Am. Jour. Sports Medicine; contbr. articles to med. jours. Bd. dirs. Health Occupations Students Am. program Garland Ind. Sch. Dist.; bd. dirs. Garland Civic Theater. Capt. M.C., USAF, 1967-69. Fellow ACP, Am. Coll. Sports Medicine (speakers bur.); mem. Am. Coll. Cardiology, Am. Soc. Echocardiography, Am. Soc. Internal Medicine, Am. Heart Assn. (bd. dirs., speakers bur.), Am. Profl. Practice Assn., Tex. Med. Assn., Dallas County Med. Soc. Home: 540 Buckingham Rd Apt 517 Richardson TX 75081-5663 Office: 700 Walter Reed Blvd Ste 206 Garland TX 75042-5743

DURGIN, DIANE, lawyer; b. Albany, N.Y., May 17, 1946; d. Leslie P. and Shirley A. (Albright) D. BA, Wellesley Coll., 1970; JD magna cum laude, Boston Coll., 1974. Assoc. Shearman & Sterling, N.Y.C., 1974-83; corp. sec. Ga.-Pacific Corp., Atlanta, 1983-92, v.p. law, dep. gen. counsel, 1986-89, sr. v.p. law, gen. counsel, 1989-93; arbitrator, mediator Atlanta, 1993—; dep. exec. dir. legal and non-profit affairs Atlanta Housing Authority, 1994—; bd. dirs. Am. Arbitration Assn. Bd. dirs. Atlanta Symphony Orch., 1991—,

Met. Atlanta chpt. ARC, 1988-94; bd. dirs., mem. exec. com. Alliance Theatre Co., 1985—; mem. bd. sponsors Georgian Chamber Players, Inc., 1986-92. Mem. ABA, Am. Corp. Counsel Assn., N.Y. State Bar Assn., Ga. State Bar, Am. Law Inst., Nature Conservancy (bd. dirs. Ga. chpt. 1989-96), Order of Coif, Ga. Exec. Women's Network, Commerce Club Atlanta.

DURHAM, BILL GEORGE, safety consultant company executive; b. Goose Creek, Tex., May 5, 1943; s. Dolton Doyal Durham and Mozell (Walker) Franklin; m. Anita Thompson, Nov. 22, 1969; 1 child, Sonja Niki-a. Assoc., Texarkana (Tex.) Jr. Coll., 1964; student, Texas A&I U., 1964-66, U. Houston, Clear Lake, 1984-87; B in Safety Mgmt., St. Edwards U., 1987; postgrad., La Salle U., 1993—. Bd. cert. Forensic Examiner; cert. Vets. of Safety Internat. safety exec., safety mgr., occupl. health and safety tech., Tex. Workers Compensation Commn./field svc. rep., profl. source for safety cons., accident investigator. Supr. Penn Mutual Ins. Co., Dallas, 1969-71; supr. safety Braswell Motor Freight, Dallas, 1971-73; regional mgr. loss prevention Transport Ins. Co., Dallas, Birmingham, Ala., 1973-77; mgr. loss prevention Eck Miller Transp. Co., Owensboro, Ky., 1977-78; mgr. safety and compliance Conalco Contract Carrier, Inc., Jackson, Tenn., 1978-81; surp. driving safety Houston Lighting & Power, 1981-92; pres. Combined Accident Reduction Efforts, Inc., 1992—; chmn. Houston Coun. Safety Profls., 1987-88, Safety Coun. of Greater Houston, 1989-92, Bus & Truck Transp. Legis. Edn., Houston, 1990-92; pres. Gulf Coast Fleet Maintenance Coun., Houston, 1990-92. Author: (manuals) Hazardous Communication, 1987, Texas Safety Compliance, 1989, (video) What To Do in Case of An Accident, 1988. Active Transp. Club of Houston; lobbyist State of Tex., notary pub.; mem. Gospel Quartet-Master's Vessels; trustee Tex. Safety Found.; pres. Houston Traffic Safety Awareness Task Force, 1991—. Recipient Appreciation award City of Houston, 1983, Sec.'s Award for Excellence, U.S. Dept. Health and Human Svcs., 1988; names Safety Profl. of the Yr., Houston Coun. of Safety Profls., 1988; named 70% Plus Honor Roll participant Pres. Bush's Office, Washington, 1990. Mem Am. Soc. Safety Engrs. (profl.), Nat. Safety Coun. (speaker, 1990), World Safety Org. (profl.), Houston Lighting & Power Speaker Bur. (lectr. 1989-92), Vets. Safety Internat., Tex. Safety Assn. (exec. bd. dirs. 1989—, chmn. strategic planning com., chmn. motor transp. com., Excellence award 1990-91), Disabled Vets. Am., Tex. Motor Transp. Assn. (bd. dirs., membership chmn., 1989-92, pres. club, 1989-90), U. Houston Alumni Assn., Masons. Republican. Baptist. Home and Office: 16007 Capistrano Falls Dr Friendswood TX 77546-2443

DURHAM, CAROLYN RICHARDSON, foreign language and literature educator; b. Bklyn., Jan. 13, 1947; d. Herbert Nathaniel and Fannie Elaine (Franklin) Richardson; m. Edward Cassell Durham; children: Diana Kristine, Dara Marie. BA, Drew U., Madison, N.J., 1968; MA, Rutgers U., 1972, PhD, 1987. Rsch. analyst Equitable Life Assurance Soc., N.Y.C., 1968-69; instr. Hampton (Va.) U., 1972-76, asst. prof. fgn. lang. and lit., 1976-91, coordinator modern fgn. lang., 1981-91; assoc. prof. Tex. Christian U., Ft. Worth, 1991—; cons. Archdiocese of N.Y. Schs., N.Y.C., 1982, U.S. Dept. Edn., 1992, 95, NEH, 1992. Author: Finally Us: Contemporary Black Brazilian Women Writers; contbr. articles to profl. jours. Bd. dirs. Adv. Bd. on Black Adoptions, Va., 1983-85; interpreter ARC, Yorktown, Va., 1981—; del. nominating conv. Dem. Party, 1984, 86. Ford Found. fellow, 1990; Fulbright-Hays awardee, 1989; NEH seminar award, 1989; Russell fellow, 1972; recipient Cert. of Recognition, State of Va., 1984, TCU Rsch. award 1991, 94, 96, TCU Edn. in a Global Soc. award 1993. Mem. MLA, Afro-Latin Am. Rsch. Assn., Am. Coun. on Tchg. and Fgn. Lang., Am. Assn. Tchrs. Spanish and Portuguese, Coll. Lang. Assn., South Ctrl. MLA, Assn. Acad. Programs in Latin Am. and the Caribbean, Feministas Unidas, Phi Sigma Iota, Sigma Delta Pi. Democrat. AME Zion Ch. Home: 5808 Highland Park Dr Apt 1093 Fort Worth TX 76132-2717 Office: Tex Christian U Fort Worth TX 76129

DURHAM, DIANA LOUISE, cardiovascular nurse; b. Indpls., Nov. 10, 1952; d. Jack Lee and Joan (Lamb) D. BSN, Ind. State U., 1975; postgrad., Southeastern La. U., 1989, McNeese State U., 1989. RN, Ind., Okla., Tex., La., Ga.; cert. cardiovascularnurse specialist; CCRN; cert. BLS. Staff nurse Community Hosp., Indpls., 1976-77, St. Anthony's Hosp., Oklahoma City, 1977-78; cardiovascular specialist Meth. Hosp., Houston, 1978-79; critical care clin. specialist, instr. Baton Rouge Gen. Med. Ctr., 1980-93, part-time instr. Sch. Nursing, 1992; clin. edn. specialist Meml. Med. Ctr. Inc., Savannah, Ga.; cardiovasc. nurse specialist Rsch. Med. Ctr., 1994-95; clin. edn. specialist Charlotte Regional Med. Ctr., Punta Gorda, Fla., 1995—; cons. Genentech, Baton Rouge, 1987—,. Vol. Am. Heart Assn., Baton Rouge, 1980—. Mem. AACN (pres. Greater Baton Rouge chpt. 1989-90, pres.-elect 1988-89, founder 1982, sec. 1982-84), Soc. Critical Care Medicine. Mem. Christian Ch. (Disciples of Christ). Home: # 7C8 175 Kings Hwy Punta Gorda FL 33983 Office: Charlotte Regional Med Ctr 809 E Marion Ave Punta Gorda FL 33950-3819

DURHAM, DONALD LEE, oceanographer; b. McKenney, Ky., May 1, 1942; s. Russell E. and Nina J. Durham; m. Nancy G. Durham, July 29, 1967; children: Kimberly Elizabeth, Russell Graves. BS in Physics and Math., Centre Coll., 1964; MS in Oceanography, Tex. A&M U., 1967, PhD in Phys. Oceanography, 1972. Rsch. oceanographer Waterways Expt. Sta., Vicksburg, Miss., 1972-78; oceanographer NORDA, Stennis Space Center, Miss., 1978-81, head mapping, charting & geodesy divsn., 1981-86; asst. chief of staff integration program COMNAVMETOCCOM, Stennis Space Center, Miss., 1986-88, tech., dept. dir., 1988—; v.p. Miss. Sci. & Tech. Commn., Jackson; mem. U.S. v.p. Gore's Environ. Task Force; mem. Miss. External Rsch. Adv. Coun. Guest editor Marine Tech. Soc. Jour., 1992, 96. Recipient U.S. Presdl. commendation, 1976, Navy Spl. Achievement commendation, 1979, Def. Mapping Agy. R & D award, 1986, Disting. Civilian Svc. award Dept. of Navy, 1994. Mem. Am. Hydrographic Soc., Am. Soc. Oceanography/ Marine Tech. Soc., Miss. Acad. Scis., Internat. Hydrographic Soc., Geophys. Union, Sigma Xi. Office: COMNAVMETOCCOM Code OT 1020 Balch Blvd Bay Saint Louis MS 39529-5050

DURHAM, G. ROBERT, diversified manufacturing company executive; b. 1929. BS, Purdue U., 1951. With Phelps Dodge Corp., Phoenix, 1967-89, exec. v.p. Philps Dodge Aluminum Corp. div., 1967-69; chmn. Phelps Dodge Internat. Corp., N.Y.C., 1977-80, corp. v.p., 1980-82, sr. v.p., 1982-85, pres., COO, 1985-87, chmn., pres., CEO, 1987-89, ret.,, 1989; exec. v.p. Consol. Aluminum Corp., N.Y.C., 1969-72, pres., CEO, 1972-75; ret. Phelps Dodge Corp., N.Y.C., Fla., 1989; pres., CEO Walter Industries, Inc., 1991-95, chmn., CEO, 1995—.

DURHAM, JAMES MICHAEL, SR., marketing consultant; b. Shreveport, La., May 27, 1937; s. Judson Burney and Edith Eloise (Whittington) D.; m. Constance Manuela Alvarez, June 4, 1960; children: Jennifer Paige Esperanza, James Michael Jr., Christopher Jon, David Bradley, Matthew Craig. BS in Math., Centenary Coll. La., 1959; MSME, N.Mex. State U., 1963; MS in Sys. Mgmt., U. So. Calif., 1981; MBA, Mich. State U., 1988. Commd. 2d lt. U.S. Army, 1959, advanced through grades to col., 1979, mgmt. analyst Office Chief of Staff, 1972-74; command and staff positions 3d Infantry Div. U.S. Army, Wurzburg, Germany, 1974-77; student U.S. Army War Coll., Carlisle Barracks, Pa., 1977-78; product mgr. U.S. Army Tank-Automotive Materiel Readiness Command, Warren, Mich., 1978-80; commander Mainz Army Depot, Mainz, Germany, 1980-83; exec. officer to deputy commanding gen. U.S. Army Devel. and Readiness Command, Alexandria, Va., 1983; program mgr., tactical vehicles U.S. Army Tank Automotive Command, Warren, Mich., 1984-86, ret., 1986; dir. tank automotive programs Cypress Internat., Troy, Mich., 1986-89; v.p. govt. business Cummins Engine Co., Inc., Columbus, Ind., 1989-92, v.p. govt. products, 1992-95; retired, 1995; ret. Cummins Engine Co., Inc., Columbus, Ind., 1995; pres. Cummins Mil. Sys. Co., Inc., Columbus, 1992-93, JD Interests Inc., Farnham, Va., 1995—. Chmn. Bartholomew County Solid Waste Mgmt. Dist. Citizens Adv. Com., 1991-95, Bartholomew County Solid Waste Mgmt. Authority, 1993-95, Bartholomew County Landfill Site Selection Com., 1993; co-chmn. Project Water, Columbus, 1990-95; chmn. bd. dirs. Am. Youth Activities Assn., Mainz, Germany, 1980-83, pres. Am. Youth Activities Assn., Kitzingen, Germany, 1975-77; bd. dirs. Indpls. Mus. Art-Columbus Gallery, 1995; chmn. devel. com. Richmond County (Va.) Habitat for Humanity, 1996—. Decorated Legion of Merit with oak leaf cluster, Bronze Star, Vietnam campaign medal with 60 device, Vietnamese Cross of Gallantry with palm. Mem. ASME, Am. Def. Preparedness assn. (exec. bd. tank and automotive sys. divsn. 1991—, steering com. combat vehicle sys. divsn. 1988—, chmn. 1991-95, steering com. tactical vehicle sys. sect. 1986-95), Assn. U.S. Army, Soc. Mfg. Engrs., Soc. Automotive Engrs., Retired Officers Assn., Ordnance Assn., Armor Assn., Pi Kappa Alpha. Republican. Home: 2494 Simonson Rd Farnham VA 22460-2212

DURHAM, J(OSEPH) PORTER, JR., lawyer, educator; b. Nashville, May 11, 1961. AB in Polit. Sci. and History cum laude, Duke U., 1982, JD, 1985. Bar: Tenn. 1985, Md. 1988. Assoc. Piper & Marbury, Balt., 1988-90; assoc. Miller & Martin, Chattanooga, 1985-88, ptnr., 1990—; adj. prof. dept. acctg. and fin. U. Tenn., Chattanooga, 1992—. Editor Duke Law Mag., 1984-85; contbr. articles to legal publs. Mem. Balt. Citizens Planning and Housing Assn., 1988-90; career edn. spkr. Explorer Scout program Boy Scouts Am., 1985, 88, 90-92; mem., v.p. bd. dirs., chmn. fin. com. Waxter Ctr. Found., 1989-91; mem., sec. bd. dirs. Assn. for Visual Artists, 1993-96; trustee Good Shepherd Sch., 1992-93; chmn. spl. mgmt. com. Nashville Rehab. Hosp., 1995; trail maintenance vol. U.S. Pk. Svc., 1993-95; mem. adv. com. Chattanooga State Tech. C.C. Recipient Outstanding Svc. award Waxter Ctr. Found., 1991. Mem. ABA, Tenn. Bar Assn., Md. Bar Assn., Duke U. Law Sch. Alumni Assn. (bd. dirs. 1994-97), Duke U. Gen. Alumni Assn. (bd. dirs. 1986-92, exec. com. 1989-92). Home: 600 W Brow Rd Lookout Mountain TN 37350 Office: Miller & Martin 1000 Volunteer Bldg Chattanooga TN 37402-2291

DURHAM, RICHARD MONROE, lawyer; b. Winston-Salem, N.C., July 7, 1954; s. George Washington and Martha Rebecca (Teague) D.; m. Tina Marie Tunks, Dec. 1, 1984; children: Eric Patrick, Sarah Kathryn. BA with honors, U. N.C., 1976, JD, 1979. Bar: N.C. 1982, U.S. Dist. Ct. (ea. and mid. dists.) N.C., 1982, U.S. Ct. Appeals (4th cir.) 1983, U.S. Supreme Ct. 1986, U.S. Dist. Ct. (we. dist.) N.C., 1992. Legal asst. Robert A. Ades & Assocs., PC, Springfield, Va., 1980-82; assoc. H. Weldon Lloyd, Esq., Henderson, N.C., 1982-83, Jenkins, Lucas, Babb and Rabil, Winston-Salem, 1983-85, James J. Booker, PA, Winston-Salem, 1985-87; sole practice Winston-Salem, 1987—. V.p. Cancer Svcs., Inc.; bd. trustees Home Moravian Ch. Mem. N.C. Bar Assn., N.C. Acad. of Trial Lawyers, N.C. Coll. of Advocacy, Ardmore Comty. Club, U. N.C.-Charlotte Alumni Assn. (bd. govs.), Phi Delta Phi (exchequer 1977-79). Democrat. Home: 2313 Walker Ave Winston Salem NC 27103-4331 Office: 8 W 3rd St Winston Salem NC 27101-3923

DURIE, JACK FREDERICK, JR., lawyer; b. Lexington, Ky., Jan. 25, 1944. BS, U. Ky., 1966, JD, 1969. Bar: Ky. 1969, Fla. 1969, U.S. Ct. Mil. Appeals 1970, U.S. Dist. Ct. (so. dist.) Fla. 1974, U.S. Ct. Appeals (5th cir.) 1974, U.S. Dist. Ct. (mid. dist.) Fla. 1978, U.S. Ct. Appeals (11th cir.) 1982, U.S. Supreme Ct. 1975; bd. cert. civil trial lawyer, Fla., also Nat. Bd. Trial Advocacy; cert. mil. judge 1971. Pvt. practice Orlando, Fla., 1979—. Capt. JAGC, USAF, 1970-74. Mem. ABA, Ky. Bar Assn., Fla. Bar Assn. (chmn. aviation and space law com. 1978-79, vice chmn. 1980-81), Orange County Bar Assn., Dade County Bar Assn. (bd. dirs. 1976-78, pres. young lawyers sect. 1978-79), Assn. Trial Lawyers Am., Acad. Fla. Trial Lawyers, Lawyer-Pilots Bar Assn., Lances, Beta Alpha Psi, Sigma Chi, Phi Delta Phi. Office: 1000 E Robinson St Orlando FL 32801-2024

DURIEUX, MARCEL ELOY, anesthesiology educator, researcher; b. Krommenie, The Netherlands, Nov. 11, 1959; came to U.S., 1986; s. Johannes and Adriana (Butterman) D.; m. Marijke Elvira Van der Sterre, June 25, 1983; children: David Marcel, Renée Claire. Vis. student, Washington & Lee U., 1978-79; MD cum laude, U. Leiden, The Netherlands, 1986; vis. rsch. student, U. Va., 1982. Diplomate Am. Bd. Anesthesiology; ACLS. Rsch. assoc. U. Va., Charlottesville, 1986-87, anesthesiology resident, 1988-91; anesthesiology rsch. fellow U. Va., Charlottesville, 1991-93, asst. prof. anesthesiology, 1994-95; asst. prof. anesthesiology and neurosurgery U. Va., Charlottesville, 1995-96, asst. prof. anesthesiology, pharmacology, and neurosurgery, 1996—; transitional resident Roanoke (Va.) Meml. Hosps., 1987-88; instr. Advanced Pediatric Life Support, Advanced Trauma Life Support; lectr. in field. Co-author: (with E.W. Kruyt and J.D. Laird) Introduction to Measuring in Medicine, 1984, Lysophosphatidate Signaling, Cellular Effects and Molecular Mechanisms, 1995; contbr. articles to profl. jours. Grantee Am. Heart Assn., 1993, NIH, 1994, Am. Cancer Soc., 1994. Mem. Royal Netherlands Soc. for the Advancement of Medicine, Am. Soc. Anesthesiologists, Internat. Anesthesia Rsch. Soc. Office: U Va Dept Anesthesiology PO Box 238 Charlottesville VA 22908

DURIO, WILLIAM HENRY, lawyer; b. Crowley, La., May 15, 1947; s. Lennard Edwin and Helen Hazel (Miller) D.; m. Rita Jane Putch, June 6, 1971; children: Matthew, Caroline. BS, U. Southwestern La., 1970; JD, La. State U., 1975. Sole practice Lafayette, La., 1976-78, 83-89; ptnr. Hughes Durio & Grant, Lafayette, 1978-83; gen. counsel Global Industries Ltd., Maurice, La., 1990-91; sole practice Lafayette, 1991—; adj. prof. mineral law U. Southwestern La., Lafayette, 1983-84. With U.S. Army, 1970-72. Mem. La. State Bar Assn., Lafayette Town House Club, Order of Troubadours. Office: 803 Coolidge Blvd Lafayette LA 70503

DURIZCH, MARY LOU, radiology educator; b. Sayre, Pa., July 1, 1939; d. Ralph Elwood and Mary Louise (Inman) Goble; m. Frank Durizch, July 7, 1956 (div. Sept. 1960); children: Terry Ann, John Alex; m. Jesse Littleton III, Mar. 25, 1995. Radiologic Technologist, Robert Packer Hosp., Sayre, Pa., 1960-63; AS, Mansfield (Pa.) U., 1975; BS, Springhill Coll., Mobile, Ala., 1980; MBA, U. South Ala., Mobile, 1986. Cert. radiologic technologist. Staff radiologic technologist Robert Packer Hosp. and Guthrie Clinic, Sayre, 1963-64, dir. tomographic tech., 1964-77, co-chief radiologic technologist, 1974-77; tech. clin. and rsch. asst. dept. radiology U. South Ala. Coll. Medicine, Mobile, 1977-82, lectr., 1983-92, instr., 1992-93, asst. prof., 1994—; cons., radiographic equipment developer, presenter, exhibitor; mem. admissions com. Sch. Radiologic Tech., U. South Ala., Mobile, 1981—, Robert Packer Hosp. Sch. Radiologic Tech., Sayre, 1974-77; radiology rep. to med. staff quality assurance com., 1991—. Mem. editl. bd. Applied Radiology, 1988-89; contbg. author: Learning the Principles of Tomography: A Programmed Learning Workbook, 1975; author: Technical Aspects of Tomography, 1977, Traumex-TRX5: Quick Reference Instruction Manual, 1987, (with J. T. Littleton and W.C. Lim) Chest Atlas: Radiographically Correlated Thin-Section Anatomy in Five Planes, 1994; editor: (with J.T. Littleton) Sectional Imaging Methods: A Comparison, 1983; contbr. articles to profl. jours. Bd. dirs. Eichold-Heustis Med. Mus., Mobile, 1990. Mem. Am. Soc. Radiologic Technologists, Ala. Soc. Radiologic Technologists (program com. chmn. 38th ann. meeting 1985), Acad. Health Svcs. Mktg. of Am. Mktg. Assn. Methodist. Office: U South Ala Med Ctr 2451 Fillingim St Mobile AL 36617-2238

DURKEE, JOE WORTHINGTON, JR., nuclear engineer; b. Albuquerque, Mar. 10, 1956; s. Joe Worthington Sr. and Hallie Mae (Payne) D. BS, Tex. A&M U., 1978, ME, 1981, PhD, 1983. Staff mem. Los Alamos (N.Mex.) Nat. Lab., 1983-95; asst. prof. radiology U. Tex. Southwestern Med. Sch., Dallas, 1995—; rsch. proposal reviewer LANL, 1986-87, Dept. Energy/ER Nuc. Engr. Proposal Rev. Panel, 1988-94. Invited resch. paper reviewer Jour. Nuclear Tech., 1987, Jour. Biomech. Engr., 1991; contbr. articles to Jour. Physics in Medicine and Biology, Progress in Nuclear Energy, Annuals Nuclear Energy, Jour. Nuclear Tech. Mem. Am. Nuclear Soc. (admissions com. 1986—, chair 1990—), Tex. A&M Former Student Assn., Nat. Space Soc. Office: Univ of Texas Southwestern Medical Ctr 5323 Harry Hines Blvd Dallas TX 75235-9058

DURKEE, KAREN MARIE, marketing professional; b. Baton Rouge, La., May 1, 1961; d. Henry Merlin and Cindy Lou (Muskarella) Hugo; m. John David Durkee, Nov. 20, 1987; 1 child, Kendall John Durkee. AA in Bus. Adminstrn., San Jacinto Coll., Pasadena, Tex., 1982; BS in Mktg., U. Evansville, 1984. Cert. meeting profl. Sales rep. Modern Bus. Systems, Evansville, 1984-85; monitor med. data Searle Pharms., Skokie, Ill., 1985-87; dir. mktg. programs Future HealthCare, Inc., Cin., 1987; mgr. spl. events Cystic Fibrosis Found., Cin., 1988; mktg. cons. various, Atlanta, 1989-90; events planner Sprint, Atlanta, 1990-93; program mgmt. Durkee & Assocs., Atlanta, 1993—. Mem. Am. Mktg. Assn. (v.p. Atlanta Vol. of Yr. programs, v.p. ops., Atlanta, asst. v.p. mktg. awards, Atlanta, v.p. mem. involvement, Cin., asst. v.p. reservations, Cin., collegiate chpt. sec., Evansville), Meeting Planners Internat. (dir. programs, Atlanta, cert. meeting profl.). Office: Durkee & Assocs 4274 Edgewater Dr Kennesaw GA 30144-1371

DURRENCE, JAMES LARRY, state executive, history educator; b. Glennville, Ga., Aug. 22, 1939; s. James Levy and Iona Bell (Groover) D.; children: April Denise, Jeffrey Marshall. BA, Fla. So. Coll., 1966; MA, U. Ga., 1968, PhD, 1971. Sales, inventory control staff Hammond Electronics, Inc., Lakeland, Fla., 1959-66; instr. history Stetson U., DeLand, Fla., 1969-70; asst. prof. Fla. So. Coll., Lakeland, 1970-78, assoc. prof., 1978-85, prof., 1985-90; exec. dir. Taxpayers League of Polk County, Bartow, Fla., 1980; city commr. City of Lakeland, 1981-89; exec. dir. Fla. taxation and budget reform commn. Fla. Ctr. Pub. Mgmt. Fla. State U., 1990-92; taxpayer rights and intergovtl. rels. advocate Fla. Dept. Revenue, 1992—; reader, assoc. prof. Am. History Ednl. Testing Svc., Princeton, N.J., 1985-90. Contbr. book revs. to Fla. Hist. Quarterly jour., 1980, Jour. of So. History, 1980, also articles to profl. jours. Mayor City of Lakeland, 1982, 86; pres. Fla. League of Cities, Tallahassee, 1987-88; mem. Fla. Adv. Council on Intergov. Relations, Tallahassee, 1987-88, State Job Tng. Coordinating Council, Tallahassee, 1984-87, Crime Prevention and Law Enforcement Study Commn., Tallahassee, 1988-89, Fin., Adminstrn., and Intergovtl. Relations Steering Com., Nat. League of Cities, Washington, 1988, Com. for Study Substate Dist. Boundaries, Tallahassee, 1986-87, Fla. Coordinating Coun. on Radon Protection, Tallahassee, 1988-90, Cen. Fla. Regional Planning Council, Bartow, 1986-88; bd. dirs. Fla. Downtown Devel. Assn., Tallahassee, 1985-88, Fla. Bapt. Hist. Assn., DeLand, 1975-78, Fla. League of Cities, 1985-88, Fla. Trust for Hist. Preservation, Tallahassee, 1988-91, Girls Club of Lakeland, 1983-86, Vols. Service to Elderly, 1986-90, Tax Watch Inc., Tallahassee, 1980-84; bd. dirs. Lakeland Chamber of Commerce, 1982-85, Spl. Olympics Polk County, 1986-87, bd. dirs. Lakeland Econ. Devel. Coun., 1986-88. Mem. Fla. Hist. Soc. (mem. fin. com. 1988-90, bd. dirs. 1989—, v.p. 1992-94, pres. 1996—), So. Hist. Assn. (mem. membership com. 1986), Fla. Polit. Sci. Assn., Ridge League Mcpls. (pres. 1983), Ridge League Cities, Inc. (exec. dir. 1989-90), Fla. Mcpl. Utilities Assn. (mem. legis. com. 1983), 1000 Friends of Fla. (bd. dirs. Tallahassee chpt. 1989-90), Fla. Coll. Tchrs. of History (v.p. 1989, pres. 1990), Southeastern Assn. of Tax Adminstrs. (fin. com. chair 1995, policy com. 1995—), Fla. Supreme Ct. (steering com. on family law 1996—). Democrat. Methodist. Office: Fla Dept Revenue Carlton Building Rm 104 Tallahassee FL 32399

DURRICK, GEORGE THOMAS, elementary school educator; b. Troy, N.Y., Sept. 14, 1951; s. George Joseph and Irene Marie (O'Konski) D. BS, Coll. St. Rose, 1974; postgrad. in Music Edn., U. South Fla., 1978-81; M in Ch. Music, Fairfax U., 1990; PhD in Music Therapy Edn., The Union Inst., 1994. Cert. tchr., N.Y., Fla.; cert. facilitative leader, 1993; cert. music therapist, 1994. Tchr. Music Stillwater (N.Y.) Ctrl. Sch. System, 1974-76; substitute tchr. Music Gloversville (N.Y) Pub. Schs., 1976-77; tchr. music Hillsborough County Schs., Tampa, Fla., 1978—; mem. com. for screen of new asst. prins., Hillsborough County Pub. Schs., 1996. Dir. music, choirmaster St. Matthew's Episc. Ch., 1988-92, St. Anne of Grace Episc. Ch., Seminole, Fla., 1992-94; site rep. Hillsborough Classroom Tchrs. Assn., Tampa, 1993—; founder, coord. Pinellas County Ecumenical Choir. Named Tchr. of Yr. Hillsborough County Pub. Schs., 1995-96. Mem. Am. Guild of Organists (dean St. Petersburg chpt. 1990—), Music Educators Nat. Conf., Fla. Music Educators Conf., Am. Guild of English Handbell Ringers, Nat. Assn. for Music Therapists, Am. Assn. Music Therapists. Home: 6565 Exeter Ct Seminole FL 34642-6509

DURSHIMER, MARGO ELLEN GILBERT, freelance writer; b. Miami, Fla., Oct. 29, 1962; d. Stanley Raymond Gilbert and Roberta (Riesman) Berkan; m. Arthur Henry Durshimer III, July 10, 1993; children: Jacob Allen, Benjamin Gilbert. BS in Journalism, Boston U., 1984; MA in Mass. Comm., U. South Fla., 1993. Reporter Saugus (Mass.) Advertiser, 1984-85; reporter, asst. editor Belmont (Mass.) Citizen, 1985-86; assoc. editor South Dade News Leader, Homestead, Fla., 1986-88; news editor South Dade News Leader, Homestead, 1988-89; asst. news editor Bradenton (Fla.) Herald, 1989-92; copy editor Sarasota (Fla.) Herald Tribune, 1993-95. Recipient 3d pl. contest Fla. Press Club, 1988, 2d pl. Fla. Soc. Newspaper Editors, 1989. Jewish.

DURSUM, BRIAN A., museum curator, art educator. BA in History, La Salle Coll., 1970; MA in East Asian History and Culture, U. Pitts., 1974. Instr. English Taiwan Normal U., Taipei, 1971-73; clk. Otto G. Richter Libr., U. Miami, Coral Gables, Fla., 1973, account clk., 1974-75; teaching asst. in history U. Pitts., 1973-74; account clk. Lowe Art Mus., U. Miami, Coral Gables, 1975-76, asst. to dir., 1976-82, acting chief adminstr., 1978, curator Oriental art, 1978—, registrar, 1982-90, acting dir., 1989-90, dir., 1990—; lectr. art dept. U. Miami, 1992—; rschr. in field. Contbr. articles to profl. jours. Grantee Southeast Banking Corp., 1979, Wilder Found., 1979, 80, Ryder Sys., Inc., 1981, 83, Sun Glass Hut, Inc., 1989, Stiefel Labs., Inc., 1989, Federated Dept. Stores, Inc., 1989, 90, 92, MegaBank, Inc., 1989, Alma Jennings Found., 1989, 90, Manny and Ruthy Cohen Found., 1992. Mem. Am. Assn. Muss., Assn. Art Mus. Dirs., Phi Alpha Theta. Home: 1249 Mariana Coral Gables FL 33134 Office: 1301 Stanford Dr Miami FL 33146*

DURYEE, WILLIAM RANKIN, retired cell physiology educator, consultant; b. Saranac Lake, N.Y., Nov. 11, 1905; s. George Van Waganen and Margaret Van Nest (Smith) D.; m. June 30, 1931 (dec. Jan. 1983); 1 child, Sanford Huntington. BA in Biology, Yale U., 1927, PhD in Zoology and Anatomy, 1933. Instr. Northwestern U., Evanston, Ill., 1937-40; chief med. publs. Office Surgeon Gen., Washington, 1944-45; with NRC, Washington, 1945-46; sr. fellow Nat. Cancer Inst., NIH, Bethesda, Md., 1948-55; head cell physiology unit WCI, Bethesda, 1950-55; prof. cell physiology George Washington U., Washington, 1955-60, prof. emeritus pathology, 1960—; cons. in biology rsch., Arlington, Va., 1960—; guest lectr. U. Pa. Bicentennial Conf., Phila., 1941; mem. sci. adv. coun. Damon Runyon Meml. Fund, N.Y.C., 1961-68; profl. assoc. com. on growth NRC, 1946-48. Mem. editl. bd. Jour. Nat. Cancer Inst.; contbr. articles to sci. jours., including Biol. Bull, Sci., Anat. Record, Annals N.Y. Acad. Sci. Maj. Med. Adminstrv. Corps, U.S. Army, 1939-45. Fellow N.Y. Acad. Scis. (hon.); mem. AAAS (coun. 1958-64), Am. Inst. Biol. Scis. (co-founder, governing bd. 1953-57), Royal Soc. Medicine (affiliate, London), Am. Soc. Physiology, Biophysics Soc. (charter), Washington Acad. Medicine, Philos. Soc. Washington, Cosmos Club (chmn. libr. com.). Episcopalian. Home: 3241 N Woodrow St Arlington VA 22207

DUSANEK, LINDA SUE, municipal housing official; b. Ottumwa, Iowa, Oct. 24, 1942; d. Walter Carol and Mildred Mozelle (Gharrett) Edmund; m. Donald Allen Carlson, Dec. 30, 1962 (div. May 1980); children: Lisa, John, Jeffrey; m. Robert John Dusanek, June 28, 1987; children: Michelle, Christine, Kendra, Andrea, Jonathan. Student, Black Hawk Coll., 1981, Marycrest U., 1988; cert. property mgmt., Inst. Real Estate Mgmt., 1989. Cert. property mgr., housing quality inspector. Asst. exec. dir. Housing Authority City of Rock Island, Ill., 1974-91; dir. of adminstrn. Housing Authority City of Ft. Pierce, Fla., 1991-96, exec. dir., 1996—. Charter mem. Rock Island Clean and Beautiful, 1980-91; grad. St. Lucie County Leadership Bd., 1993, 94; campaign supporter Friends of Senator Bob Graham, Fla., 1992; mem. exec. bd., chair human resource com. Boys & Girls Club St. Lucie County, v.p. ops., 1996; bd. dirs. Restoration Ho., Hospice of St. Lucie County. Mem. Nat. Assn. Housing and Redevel. Ofcls. (cert. pub. housing mgr. 1980), Adminstrn. Mgmt. Soc. (treas. Quad-Cities 1989-91), Bi-State Housing Assn. (pres., founder Iowa and Ill. chpts. 1987-91), No. Ill. Coun. Housing Assn. (sec.-treas. 1986-91), St. Lucie Pers. Assn. (sec. 1992, pres. 1994, 95), Soc. Human Resource Mgmt. (mem. state coun. 1994, 95), Pub. Housing Dirs. Assn., St. Lucie County Exec. Round Table Shared Svcs. Network. Lutheran. Home: 4103 Smokey Pines Ct Fort Pierce FL 34951-3341 Office: Housing Authority Ft Pierce 707 N 7th St Fort Pierce FL 34950-3131

DU TOIT, BRIAN MURRAY, anthropology educator; b. Bloemfontein, South Africa, Mar. 2, 1935; s. John Murray and Nada (Stevens) Du T.; m. Sona Van Rooyen, Mar. 15, 1958; children: Helene Murray, Desiree Murray, John Murray. BA, U. Pretoria, South Africa, 1956, MA, 1961; PhD, U. Oreg., 1963. Lectr. U. Stellenbosch, South Africa, 1964-66, U. Cape Town, South Africa, 1966; asst. prof. U. Fla., Gainesville, 1966-69, assoc. prof., 1969-75, prof. anthropology, 1975—; rschr. Nat. Inst. on Drug Abuse, Am.

Philos. Soc. Author: Beperkte Lidmaatskap: 'n Antropologies Westenskaplike Studie van Geheime Organisasies, 1965, People of the Valley: Life in an Isolated Afrikaner Community, South Africa, 1974, Akuna- A New Guinea Village Community, 1975, Migration and Urbanization, 1975, Migration and Development, 1975, Ethnicity in Modern Africa, 1978, African Healing Strategies, 1985, Aging and Menopause Among Indian South African Women, 1990, Boer Settlers in the Southwest, 1995, Colonia Boer: An Afrikaner Settlement in Chubut, Argentina, 1995; others; author monographs and chpts. in books; contbr. articles to jours. U. Fla. Pres.'s scholar, 1976-77. Fellow Am. Anthropol. Assn., Soc. for Applied Anthropology; mem. Current Anthropology (assoc.), Sigma Xi, Phi Kappa Phi. Republican. Methodist. Home: 3300 NW 29th Ter Gainesville FL 32605-2114 Office: Univ of Florida Dept Anthropology Gainesville FL 32611

DUTT, KAMLA, medical educator; b. Lahore, Punjab, India; came to U.S., 1969; d. Gulzari Lal and Raj Bansi Dutt. BS with honors, Panjab U., Chandigarh, India, 1961, MS in Zoology with honors, 1962, PhD, 1970. Rsch. assoc. Harvard Med. Sch. Sidney Farber Cancer Ctr., Boston, Mass., 1972-76; rsch. assoc. Eye Inst. Retinal Fedn., Boston, 1977-80; sr. rsch. assoc. Yale Med. Ctr., New Haven, 1980-81, Emory U., Atlanta, 1981-82; asst. prof. Morehouse Sch. Medicine, Atlanta, 1983-89, assoc. prof., 1989—. Contbr. numerous articles to sci. jours.; author short stories (in Hindi); prodr., actor 3 maj. plays, Atlanta; actor 11 maj. plays, India. Bd. dirs. VSEI (vol. fundraising orgn. for edn. in India), 1973-78; v.p. Indian Am. Cultural Assn., 1985; podium spkr., participant King Week, 1990, 91, 93; spkr. Gandhi Day Celebration, 1984, 85; key participant Intercultural Conf., 1990; main participant joint document Women's Perspective; active human rights issues; stake holder Vision 20/20 Collaborative State of Ga., diversity and edn. coms., 1995. Hindu. Office: Morehouse Sch Medicine 720 Westview Dr SW Atlanta GA 30310-1458

DUTTON, CLARENCE BENJAMIN, lawyer; b. Pitts., May 31, 1917; s. Clarence Benjamin and Lillian (King) D.; m. Marian Jane Stevens, June 21, 1941; children: Victoria Lynn Dutton Sheehan, Barbara King Dutton. BS with distinction, Ind. U., 1938, JD with high distinction, 1940, LLD, 1970. Bar: Ind. 1940. Instr. bus. law Ind. U. Sch. Bus., 1940-41; atty. E.I. duPont de Nemours & Co., Inc., Wilmington, Del., 1941-43; asst. prof. law Ind. U. Sch. Law, 1946-47; pvt. practice, Indpls., 1947—; bd. dirs. Sarkes Tarzian, Inc., The Hunt Corp.; mem. Ind. Jud. Study Commn., 1965-74; regional adv. group Ind. U. Sch. Medicine, 1966-75; mem., sec. Ind. Civil Code Study Commn., 1967-73; mem. Ind. Commn. on Uniform State Laws, 1970—, chmn., 1980-91, life mem., 1991. Author: (bus. law sect.) Chemical Business Handbook, 1954; contbr. articles to profl. jours. Bd. dirs. Found. Ind. U. Sch. Bus., Found. Econ. and Bus. Studies; mem. bd. visitors Ind. U. Sch. Law, 1971—, chmn., 1974-75; bd. dirs. Soc. for Advanced Study, Ind. U., 1984-95, pres., 1985-87; mem. Acad. Alumni Fellows, Ind. U. Sch. Law, 1988. Comdr. USNR, 1943-45. Recipient Ind. Bar Found. 50-Yr. award, 1992, Ind. U. Disting. Alumni Svc. award, 1995. Mem. ABA (ho. of dels. 1960-62, state del. 1967-72, bd. govs. 1971-74, chmn. gen. practice sect. 1971-72), Ind. State Bar Assn. (bd. mgrs. 1957-63, pres. 1961-62), Indpls. Bar Assn. (v.p. 1957), Ind. Soc. Chgo., Lawyers Club (pres. 1959-60), Indpls. Country Club (pres. 1955), Columbia Club, Woodstock Club, Wilderness Country Club (Naples, Fla., dir. 1991-94). Republican. Presbyterian. Home: # 3101 100 Tall Pine Ln Naples FL 34105-2614

DUTTON, FRANK ELROY, data processing executive; b. Warren, Ohio, Nov. 16, 1946; s. Robert Wade and Ann Victoria (Sessions) D.; m. Nancy June Gephart, Nov. 6, 1965 (div. 1981); children: Cynthia, Frank, Robert; m. Margaret Elizabeth Sessions, Dec. 16, 1981 (div. Dec. 1987); m. Paula Kay Gately, Feb. 14, 1992 (div. Sept. 1994). With sales dept. Zylco Cutlery Rena Ware Distrs., Warren, 1964-68; advt. salesman Directory Dept. Ohio Bell Telephone Co., Cuyahoga Falls, 1968-69; pvt. practice residential constrn. Warren and Hammond (La.), 1970-74; technician J. Ray McDermott & Co., New Orleans, 1974-83, McDermott Internat., Antwerp, Belgium, 1975, McDermott SE Asia, Singapore, 1981-83; owner Computer Time, Inc., Hammond, 1983-85; mgr. tech. services Industry Programs, Inc., Houston, 1985-86; owner Affordable Automation, Houston, 1987-89; program, analyst The Phillips Group, Stafford, Tex., 1989-92; ptnr., software and hardware integrator IHMS Software Support, Onalaska, Tex., 1992—; cons. in computer communications Southmark Industries, Houston, 1986-87, Crown Broadcasting, Hammond, La., 1987-89, Bee-Line Delivery Svc., Houston, 1986-89. Author, designer various computer games, utility software programs, computer software for radio stas., Turbo Pascal Toolbox, 1988 (award of disting. tech. communication 1989, award of excellence Internat. Soc. Tech. Communication 1989), French transl., 1988, Portuguese trans., 1990, French trans., 1990; contbr. articles to profl. jours. Served with USAR, 1966-72. Mem. Am. Mensa Soc. Home and Office: PO Box 68 Onalaska TX 77360-0068

DUTTON, MARK ANTHONY, lawyer; b. Moulton, Ala., Jan. 24, 1964; s. William B. and Judith C. (Barrett) D. BA, Huntingdon Coll., Montgomery, Ala., 1987; JD, Samford U., 1990. Bar: Ala. 1991, U.S. Dist. Ct. (no. dist.) Ala. 1991, U.S. Ct. Appeals (11th cir.) 1991. Pvt. practice Moulton, Ala., 1991—. Exec. committeeman Dem. Party, Lawrence County, Ala., 1993—. Mem. Ala. Bar Assn., Ala. Trial Lawyers Assn., Masons. Democrat. Baptist. Home: 14220 Market St Moulton AL 35650 Office: 714 East St Moulton AL 35650-1668

DUTTON, SHARON GAIL, elementary school educator; b. Greenville, S.C., Jan. 5, 1947; d. Melvin Thornton and Bessie Mae (Whitmire) B. BS in Elem. Edn., E. Tenn. State U., 1969; MA in Early Childhood Edn., Western Carolina U., 1976, EdS in Early Childhood Edn., 1983. Cert. tchr. N.C. elem, secondary, sch. adminstrn., early childhood. Tchr. grade 4 Brevard (N.C.) Elem. Sch., 1970; tchr. grade 3 Rosman (N.C.) Elem. Sch., 1970, tchr. grade 2, 1970-72, tchr. reading, 1972-73, tchr. grades 2, 3, 1973-87, tchr. grade 4, 1987-89; tchr. Headstart Rosman Elem. Sch. 1971, summer sch., 1972; lead tchr. Teacher Corps Grade 2 Western Carolina U., Cullowhee, N.C., Rosman, 1974-76; clin. practicum and reading conf. Western Carolina U., VA Ctr., Oteen, N.C., summer 1976. Organist, pianist, East Fork Bapt. Ch., Brevard, N.C. Mem. NEA, ASCD, Am. Fedn. Tchrs., N.C. Assn. Edn., Transylvania County Assn. Edn. Democrat. Home: PO Box 422 Rosman NC 28772-0422

DU VALL, BRENKA LYNN, telemetry nurse; b. Douglas, Ga., Oct. 31, 1953; d. Freddie La Vare and Ruby Lee (Walsh) Du V. BS in Elem. Edn., U. Ga., 1975; BSN, Ga. Coll., 1989, postgrad., 1990—. Cert. BLS, ACLS. Tchr. Laurens County Schs., East Laurens, Ga., 1975-76; supr. small display advt. Greensheet Advt. Paper, Houston, 1976-78; sec. BMC Software, Mobil Oil Corp., Houston, 1978-86; nurse USAFR, Warner Robins, Ga., 1989-92; telemetry nurse Oconee Regional Med. Ctr., 1992-93; gyn. nurse South Fulton Med. Ctr., Atlanta, 1993-95; psychiat. nurse Ga. Mental Health Inst., Atlanta, 1993-96. With USAFR, 1989-92. Whitehall scholar Whitehall Found., 1988-89; recipient Air Force Commendation medal. Mem. Nightingale Honor Soc., Sigma Theta Tau. Republican. Home: 3425-M North David Hills Rd Decatur GA 30033

DUVALL, DAVID GARLAND, real estate company executive, accountant; b. Franklin, N.C., Apr. 21, 1949; s. Fred Garland and Margaret Louise Murray D.; m. Margaret Ann Holbrook, June 20, 1971; children: David Christopher, Amanda Leigh. BSBA, Western Carolina U., 1971. CPA, S.C. Staff acct. J.W. Hunt and Co., Columbia, S.C., 1972-80; chief fin. officer Columbia Mgmt. Corp., Columbia, 1980-82, L.P. Cox Co., Sanford, N.C., 1983-86; chief fin. officer U.S. Capital Corp., Columbia, 1980-83, exec. v.p., 1986-90; CFO, Am. Capital Holdings, Inc., Columbia, 1989—; pvt. practice acctg., 1992. Mem. AICPA, S.C. Assn. CPA's, Alpha Kappa Psi. Home and Office: 2116 Ohara Ct Columbia SC 29204-4319

DUVALL, JACK, television executive, fund raiser, speechwriter; b. San Diego, July 10, 1946; s. John William and Margaret (Clark) DuV. AB cum laude, Colgate U., 1968. Mgmt. cons. Ohio Bell, Cleve., 1969; spl. agt. Air Force Office of Spl. Investigations, 1969-72; compliance officer Price Commn. U.S., Washington, 1972-73; chief industry compliance br. Cost Living Council, Exec. Office Pres. U.S., Washington, 1973-74; dir. pub. affairs Nat. Soybean Processors Assn., Hearing Industries Assn., Nat. Assn. Child Devel. Edn., and Food Protein Council, Washington, 1975-80; dir. corp. relations U. Chgo., 1980-85; v.p. program resources WETA TV/Radio, Washington, 1985-89; prin. Mars Hill, Alexandria, Va., 1989—; cons. Albert Einstein Peace Prize Found., Chgo., 1983-84; advisor-cons. Mil. Reform Inst., Washington, 1984-87, Sta. KCET-TV, 1989-91, Sta. WTVS-TV, 1990-92, The Learning Channel, 1990-92, Vision Interfaith Satellite Network, 1990-95, Jefferson Energy Found., 1990-91, Nat. Found. for People with Disabilities, 1990-91, Compass Films, Ltd., 1990-91, NOVA Child Devel. Ctrs., 1989-90, Hr Prodns., 1991-92, Nat. Park Trust, 1992, Lifetime Med. TV., 1991-92, Boston Ballet, 1992-93, Maritime Heritage Prints Video, 1992-93, Mind Ext. U., 1992-93, Jefferson Ctr. New Dem. Processes, 1993, Brit. Consulate Gen. L.A., 1990-95, Sta. WLIW-TV, 1992-93, Sta. WBGU-TV, 1992-93, Com. on Constitutional Sys., 1990-94, Colonial Williamsburg Fd., 1993-94, Child Welfare League Am., 1994, Christian Sci. Monitor, 1994, Nat. Video Comms., 1994-95, Tele-Comm. Inc., 1995-96, Md. Pub. TV, 1995-96, Turner Broadcasting Sys., 1995-96, S.C. Ednl. TV, 1996—, First Ch. of Christ Scientist, 1996—, Hedrick Smith Prodns., 1995-96; coord. Working Group on Ednl. Tech. and Programing, 1992-93. Author: (with others) Historical Working Papers of the Economic Stabilization Program, 1975; exec. prodr. TV series Economic life, 1993, Learning About Democracy, 1993, People Power, 1996; contbr. poems and articles to various publs. Speechwriter Sen. Adlai Stevenson Ill. gov. campaign, 1982; Ill. spokesman Sen. Gary Hart pres. campaign, 1983-84; mem. Nat. Dem. Platform Com., Washington, 1984, Social Services Adv. Bd., Alexandria, 1986-87, mem. bd. advisors Ctr. for A New Democracy, Washington, 1985-87; issues, speech advisor presdl. campaign Gov. Michael S. Dukakis, 1987-88; mem., bd. dirs. Arlington Inst., 1991—. Capt. USAF, 1969-72. Mem. Delta Sigma Rho, Phi Beta Kappa, Phi Alpha Theta. Office: Mars Hill PO Box 707 Alexandria VA 22313-0707

DUVALL, LORRAINE, recreation center owner; b. Hamilton, Ohio, Jan. 31, 1925; d. Saul and Martha Jane (Huff) Baker; m. Ray DuVall, June 12, 1951; children: Sharon DuVall Keese, Deborah D. Velchoff, Steve, Annette. BA, U. Cin., 1951; MA, Tex. A&I U., 1963; postgrad. Miami U., Oxford, Ohio, 1958, U. Toledo, 1959, U. Tex.-Austin, 1968. Elem. tchr. Larkmoor, Lorain, Ohio, 1956-60; tchr. math. Incarnate Word High Sch., Corpus Christi, 1964-70; owner, instr. Aerobic Fitness, Corpus Christi, 1973-93; owner, coach Corpus Christi Marlin Swim Team, 1972—; mgr. Corpus Christi Country Club Pool, 1973-88; pres., mgr. Club Estates Pool Chems., Corpus Christi, 1980-89, Club Estates Recreation, Corpus Christi, 1977—. Vol. psychiat. ward Meml. Hosp., Corpus Christi, 1966-70, U.S. Swimming Club Devel., 1993—; harpist First Bapt. Ch. Orch., 1995—; adminstrv. vice-chair South Tex. Swimming, 1996; liaison to U.S. Swimming Club Devel. Com., 1995; bd. dirs. vol. YWCA, Corpus Christi, 1970-77; water safety trainer ARC, Corpus Christi, 1975-82; CPR instr. Am. Heart Assn., Corpus Christi, 1980-84; vol. children's choir dir. St. John Methodist Ch., Corpus Christi, 1966-78, Asbury United Meth. Ch., 1980-93; vol. harpist 1st Bapt. Ch., 1995. NSF grantee U. Tex.-Austin, 1968. Mem. Am. Swim Coaches Assn., Am. Harp Soc. Avocations: music, swimming, tennis, skiing, backpacking. Home: 6709 Pintail Dr Corpus Christi TX 78413-2337 Office: 4902 Snowgoose Dr Corpus Christi TX 78413-2328

DUVALL, WALLACE LEE, management educator, consultant; b. Charleston, Ark., Mar. 10, 1926; s. Marion Oscar and Clara Ann (Jackson) D.; m. Bonnie Frances Moore, May 23, 1948; children: Ronald L., Nancy L. BS in Edn., Ark. Tchrs. Coll., 1949; MS, U. Ark., 1950; MHA, Baylor U., 1961; PhD, North Tex. State U., 1981. Enlisted U.S. Army, 1944, advanced through grades to lt. col., 1968; served with med. services corp. U.S. Army, Korea and Vietnam; ret. U.S. Army, 1968; assoc. prof. Trinity U., San Antonio, 1968-71; asst. adminstr. S.W. Tex. Med. Hosp., San Antonio, 1971-74; adminstr. Flow Meml. Hosp., Denton, Tex., 1974-78; prof. mgmt., dir. grad. program in health care adminstrn. Tex. Woman's U., Denton, 1978-81; assoc. Arnold Assocs., Denton, 1981-82; pres. Wallace L. Duvall Health Care Mgmt. Cons., Denton, 1982—; spl. adj. prof. North Tex. State U., Denton, 1984-86; prof., chmn. div. bus., acting v.p., dir. grad. studies Wayland Bapt. U., Plainview, Tex., 1986. Chmn. Denton County Health Planning Council, Denton, 1976-78; mem. North Tex. Area Planning Bd., Arlington, 1976-79. Decorated Silver Star. Fellow Am. Coll. Health Care Execs. (advancement examiner); mem. Am. Hosp. Assn., Nat. Assn. Realtors, Tex. Hosp. Assn. (del., chmn. comprehensive health care council), Tex. Assn. Realtors, Denton Bd. Realtors (mem. fin. com.). Baptist. Home: 2100 Sauls Ln Denton TX 76201 Office: Dir Grad Studies Wayland Bapt U Plainview TX 79072-9801

DUVO, MECHELLE LOUISE, oil company executive, consultant; b. East Stroudsburg, Pa., Apr. 25, 1962; d. Nicholas and Arlene Birdie (Mack) D. AS, Lehigh County Community Coll., 1982. Rehab. counselor Phoenix Project, Bakersfield, Calif., 1982-84; nat. sales mgr. Olympia Advt., L.A., 1984-85; oil exploration cons. Cimmaron Mgmt., Nashville, 1985-86; exec. sec. Pueblo Resources Corp., Bowling Green, Ky., 1986-87; nat. oil cons. El Toro, Inc., Bowling Green, 1986-87; founder, pres. and CEO Majestic Mgmt. Corp., Albany, Ky., 1987—; nat. oil cons. Impact Oil, Inc., Bowling Green, 1987—; lease procurator El Toro, Inc., 1986-87; spkr. Nat. Investment Seminars, 1994—. Editor, pub.: (newsletter) The Majestic Field Copy, 1994—. Fundraiser Am. Cancer Soc., L.A., 1984-85; vol. Humane Soc., Nashville, 1985-86, Humane Soc., Bowling Green, 1986—; counselor Salvation Army, Bakersfield, 1982-84. Mem. NAFE (exec. program), AAUW, Internat. Platform Assn., Ky. Oil & Gas Assn. Home and Office: Majestic Mgmt Corp 1202 S Green St Glasgow KY 42141-2014

DVORETZKY, EDWARD, German language educator; b. Houston, Dec. 29, 1930; s. Max and Anna Lea (Greenfield) D.; m. Charlotte Silversteen, Aug. 1, 1953; 1 child, Toban. BA, Rice U., Houston, 1953; AM, Harvard U., 1956, PhD, 1959. Tchg. fellow in German Harvard U., Cambridge, Mass., 1954-56; instr. German Rice U., Houston, 1956-59, asst. prof. German, 1959-64, assoc. prof., 1964-67; prof. German U. Iowa, Iowa City, 1967-92, chmn. dept. German, 1969-79; mem. Ford Com. and Danforth Fellowship Selection Com., Rice U., 1965; mem. Fulbright Selection Com., U. Iowa, 1971, 89; project proposal cons. Nat. Endowment for Humanities, 1987; resident tutor Modern Lang. Ctr., Harvard U., 1954-55. Translator: (dramas) Emilia Galotti, 1962, Miss Sara Sampson, 1977, Philotas, 1979; author: (books) The Enigma of Emilia Galotti, 1963, The Eighteenth-Century English Translations of Emilia Galotti, 1966, Der Teufel und sein Advokat, 1981, Tief im Herbstwald, 1983; co-author: Koscher Hanswürste made in USA, 1981, Windfüsse-The Feet of the Wind, 1984, Im Osten wie im Westen (Both East and West), 1987, Fische, Hühnerschlachtlieder und die Leidenschaften, 1989; editor: Lessing, Dokumente zur Wirkungsgeschichte 1755-1968, 2 vols., 1971, 72, Lessing Heute-Beiträge zur Wirkungsgeschichte, 1981; compiler: Lessing Yearbook Index to Volumes I-XX and the Supplements, 1994; author: (poetry) in Tränen im Schweigen, 1988, Das Dritte Buch der Renga-Dichtung/The Third Book of Renga Poetry, 1989, Kleine Graphikum-Phonothek, 25 Jahre Internationaler Autorenkreis Plesse-Vorstellung und Texte, 1989, Crossings-Kreuzungen: Festschrift for Helmut Kreuzer, 1990, Hans-Joachim Haecker-80 Jahre, 1990, Im Raschelnden Laub, 1990, Im Wechsel der Jahre, 1990, Poetic Mosaics in 1989, 1990, Die Lieder der Quelle, 1990, In der Eulenflucht, 1990, Nicht nur in Märzwind, 1990, Das Grosse Buch der Haiku-Dichtung/The Great Book of Haiku Poetry, 1990, Cooking Lions 1990, 1991, Wohnungen, 1991, Das Grosse Buch der Senku-Dichtung/The Great Book of Senku Poetry, 1992, Carl Heinz Kurz-70 Jahre, 1992, Haikai Anthology, If Mozart had produced Haikai, 1991, 92, others; contbr. articles to profl. jours. Pres. Agudas Achim Congregation, Iowa City, 1971-72. Fulbright fellow, 1953, 58, Old Gold summer faculty rsch. fellow U. Iowa, 1969; recipient gen. edn. bd. scholarship Rockefeller Found., 1953. Mem. MLA (sec., chmn. South-Ctrl. German II sect. 1960-62), Midwest MLA (sec. German II sect. 1970-71, chmn. 1970-71, nominating com. 1971), Lessing Soc., Internat. PEN, Die Neue Avantgarde des Surrealismus, Autorenkreis Plesse/API, Phi Beta Kappa (v.p., pres. Beta of Tex. 1964-65, 65-66, mem. senate 1966-67), Delta Phi Alpha. Home: 1314 Nails Creek Dr Sugar Land TX 77478

DWIGGINS, CLAUDIUS WILLIAM, JR., chemist; b. Amity, Ark., May 11, 1933; s. Claudius William and Lillian (Scott) D.; B.S., U. Ark., 1954, M.S., 1956, Ph.D. (Am. Oil Co. fellow, Coulter-Jones scholar), 1958. With U.S. Dept. of Energy, Bartlesville (Okla.) Tech. Center, 1958-83, chemist, 1958-60, project leader surface physics project, 1960-65, project leader petroleum composition research project, 1965-80, supervisory research chemist, thermodynamics div., 1980-83; sr. chemist Nat. Inst. Petroleum and Energy Research, 1983-84; cons., 1984—. Mem. Am. Chem. Soc., N.Y. Acad. Scis., AAAS, Am. Crystallographic Assn., Am. Inst. Physics, Sigma Xi (sec. 1966-67), Alpha Chi Sigma, Delta Sigma Phi (treas. 1952). Contbr. articles to profl. jours. Home: 1211 S Keeler Ave Bartlesville OK 74003-4756

DWIGHT, KENNETH HARLAN, metallurgical engineer; b. Pampa, Tex., Nov. 10, 1949; m. Joyce A. Schwebke, June 7, 1975; 1 child, Brad T. AS, Frank Phillips Coll., 1970; BS in Metall. Engring., U. Tex., El Paso, 1973. Registered profl. engr., Tex. Jr. metall. engr. Phelps-Dodge Copper Refinery, El Paso, 1973-79; reservoir engr. El Paso Natural Gas Co., 1979-81, sr. reservoir engr., 1981-85, cons. reservoir engr., 1985-92, mgr. bus. devel., reservoir engr., 1992—. Adult leader 4-H, El Paso, 1989—. Named Disting. Adult Leader 4-H Dist. 6 Tex., 1993. Mem. NSPE, AIME (assoc.), Potential Gas Com. (chmn. mid-continent 1986—, bd. dirs., editl. com.), El Paso Geol. Soc. Home: 4229 Boy Scout Ln El Paso TX 79922-2346 Office: El Paso Natural Gas Co 100 N Stanton St El Paso TX 79901-1442

DWORKIN, DANIEL MARTIN, government official, environmentalist; b. Providence, Mar. 10, 1923; s. Isadore and Rose Irene (Fradin) D.; m. Dorothea Barbara Kumin, June 16, 1946; children: Judith, Barbara Conteh, Ida. BA, Clark U., 1948, MA, 1973, PhD, 1974. Scientist Holcomb Rsch. Inst., Indpls., 1974-78; asst. prof. U. So. Ill., Carbondale, 1978-80; adj. assoc. prof. Clark U., Worcester, Mass., 1980-83; internat. advisor Iris Internat., Phoenix, 1983-87; sr. scientist U. Ariz., Tuscon, 1987-91; environ. advisor U.S. AID, Arlington, Va., 1991—. Staff sgt. U.S. Army, 1942-46. Home: 4141 N Henderson Rd Apt 905 Arlington VA 22203 Office: AID 1111 19th St N Arlington VA 22209-1704

DWORSKY, CLARA WEINER, merchandise brokerage executive, lawyer; b. N.Y.C., Apr. 28, 1918; d. Charles and Rebecca (Becker) Weiner; m. Bernard Ezra Dworsky, Jan. 2, 1944; 1 child, Barbara G. Goodman. BS, St. John's U., N.Y.C., 1937, LLB, 1939, JD, 1968. Bar: N.Y. 1939, U.S. Dist. Ct. (ea. dist.) N.Y. 1942, U.S. Dist. Ct. (so. dist.) Tex. 1993, U.S. Ct. Appeals (9th cir.), 1994, U.S. Ct. Appeals (5th cir.) 1996. Pvt. practice, N.Y.C., 1939-51; assoc. Bessie Farberman, N.Y.C., 1942; clk., sec. U.S. Armed Forces, Camp Carson, Colo., Camp Claiborne, La., 1944-45; abstractor, dir. Realty Title, Rockville, Md., 1954-55; v.p. Kelley & Dworsky Inc., Houston, 1960—; appeals agt. Gasoline Rationing Apls. Bd., N.Y.C., 1942; bd. dir. Southlan Sales Assocs., Houston. Vol. ARC, N.Y.C.; vice chmn. War Bond pledge drive, Bklyn.; vol. Houston Legal Found., 1972-73; pres. Women's Aux. Washington Hebrew Acad., 1958-60, v.p. bd. trustees, 1959-60; co-founder, v.p. S. Tex. Hebrew Acad. (now Hebrew Acad.) Houston, 1970-75, hon. pres. women's div., 1973. Recipient Cert. award Treas. of U.S., 1943; Commendation Office of Chief Magistrate of City N.Y., 1948; Pietas medal St. Johns U., 1985. Mem. ABA (chmn. social security com., sr. lawyers divsn. 1989-93, 95—, chair subcom. 1993-95, mem. sr. lawyers divsn. coun. 1989-95), N.Y. State Bar Assn., Fed. Bar Assn. (vice-chair for programs, sr. lawyers divsn. 1994-96, dep. chairperson 1996—), Houston Bar Assn. (sec. social security sect. 1995-96), Nat. Assn. Women Lawyers (chmn. organizer Juvenile Delinquency Clinic N.Y. 1948-51), St. Johns U. Alumni Assn. (coord. Houston chpt. 1983—, pres. 1986), Delphians Past Pres.'s Club, Amit Women Club, Hadassah. Jewish. Home: 9726 Cliffwood Dr Houston TX 77096-4406

DWYER, DENNIS GRANT, food broker executive; b. Erie, Pa., June 23, 1947; s. Paul V. and Ethel (Grant) D.; children: Ennis II, Kathleen, Melissa. Student, John Carroll U., 1965-66, U. Pitts., Fla., 1971-72, U. Miami, 1973-74; Masters Lic., USCG, 1996. Asst. v.p. sales Firch Baking Co., Erie, 1963-66; sales mgr. Northern-Haserot, Cleve., 1975-76; regional sales mgr. Readi-Bake, Inc., Grand Rapids, Mich., 1977-79; pres. Dwyer Foods, Inc. (formerly Food Brokers Ga., Inc.), Altanta, 1979—; exec. bd. Idaho Fresh Pak, Inc., Lewisville, 1987-88; nat. sales broker Griffith Packing Plant, Inc., Demopolis, Ala., 1991—. Vol. Big Bros. Atlanta, 1978-81; little league coach McDonough Youth Assn., 1992; bd. dirs. Newton County Bd. Family and Children Svcs., Covington, Ga., 1980-86. Capt. USMC, 1966-71, Vietnam. Capt. USMC, 1966-71, Vietnam. Mem. Food Svc. Brokers Am., Nat. Food Brokers Assn., Ga. Sch. Food Svc. Assn. (adv. bd. 1983-86), Atlanta Food Brokers Assn., K.C., Eastlake Country Club, Eagles Landing Country Club. Republican. Roman Catholic. Office: Paddys Lanter Princess Inc 6917 Holiday Rd Buford GA 30518

DWYER, GERALD PAUL, JR., economics educator, consultant; b. Pittsfield, Mass., July 9, 1947; s. Gerald Paul and Mary Frances (Weir) D.; m. Katherine Marie Lepiane, Jan. 15, 1966; children: Tamara K., Gerald P. III, Angela M., Michael J.L., Terence F. BBA, U. Wash., 1969; MA in Econs., U. Tenn., 1973; PhD in Econs., U. Chgo., 1979. Economist Fed. Res. Bank, St. Louis, 1972-74, vis. scholar, 1987-89; economist Fed. Res. Bank, Chgo., 1976-77; asst. prof. Tex. A&M U., College Station, 1977-81, Emory U., Atlanta, 1981-84; assoc. prof. U. Houston, 1984-89; prof. Clemson (S.C.) U., 1989—; acting head Dept. Economics, Clemson U., 1992-93; sr. rsch. assoc. Law and Econ. Ctr. Emory U., Atlanta, 1982-84; vis. scholar Fed. Res. Bank, Atlanta, 1982-84, 94—; cons. FTC, Washington, 1983-84, Arthur Bros., Corpus Christi, Tex., 1980-81, Amerigas, Houston, 1985, Western Container Corp., 1987, Metrica, Inc., Bryan, Tex., 1989—; vis. fin. economist Commodity Futures Trading Commn., Washington, 1990; vis. scholar Fed. Reserve Bank of Mpls., 1995. Contbr. articles to profl. jours. NSF trainee U. Tenn., 1970-72; Weaver fellow Intercollegiate Studies Inst., 1974-75, Earhart Found. fellow 1975-77; rsch. grantee NSF, Earhart Found. Mem. Am. Econ. Assn., Am. Stats. Assn., Econometric Soc., Econ. History Assn., We. Econ. Assn., So. Econ. Assn., Beta Gamma Sigma, Phi Kappa Phi. Avocation: computers.

DWYER, JOHN JAMES, mechanical engineer; b. Jersey City, Mar. 1, 1928; s. John J. and Margaret (Casey) D.; m. Joan Catherine Hyde, June 26, 1954 (div. Jan. 1984); children: William J., Kathleen M., Barbara A.; m. JoAnna Mary Kuta, Feb. 4, 1989. BS, N.J. Inst. Tech., 1957; MBA, Lehigh U., 1972. Registered profl. engr., Pa., Tex. Machinery engr. Air Products and Chems., Inc., Allentown, Pa., 1957-63, mgr. machinery engring., 1963-83; cons. Houston, 1983—. Sgt. U.S. Army, 1950-52, Korea. Mem. ASME (mem. performance test code for centrifugal compressors com. 1975—), NSPE, Tex. Soc. Profl. Engrs. Roman Catholic. Home and Office: 8346 Silvan Wind Ln Houston TX 77040-1412

DWYER, MARY JO, medical librarian; b. Chgo., Mar. 19, 1941; d. William Michael and Helen Lucille (Ramsden) D.; m. James Thomas Miller, Aug. 19, 1977. BA, St Xavier Coll., 1963; MALS, Rosary Coll., 1976. Papal vol. Latin Am. Colegio Monte María, Guatemala City, 1964-68; rsch. assoc. AMA, Chgo., 1968-76, reference libr., 1976-82, assoc. dir. reference, 1982-84; circuit libr. Victoria (Tex.) Coll., U. Houston, 1985-89; circuit libr. U. Tex. Health Sci. Ctr., San Antonio, 1989—, sr. circuit libr., 1995—; bd. dirs. Nat. Network Librs. of Medicine/South Ctrl. Region, Houston, 1991-92. Presenter, producer (video) Library Video Magazine, 1989. Recipient DeBakey Libr. Svcs. Outreach award Friends, Nat. Libr. of Medicine, Washington, 1993. Mem. Am. Libr. Assn., Med. Libr. Assn. (hosp. librs. sect. govt. rels. com., s. ctrl. chpt. govt. rels. com.). Democrat. Roman Catholic. Office: U Tex Health Sci Ctr 7703 Floyd Curl Dr San Antonio TX 78284

DWYER, RALPH DANIEL, JR., lawyer; b. New Orleans, Apr. 23, 1924; s. Ralph Daniel Sr. and Carolyn (Nolting) D.; m. Gwendolyn Betpouey, Feb. 12, 1955; children: Ralph, Bridget Mary, Frederick Henry, Patrick Rees, John Betpouey, Timothy Paul, Kathleen Mary, Mary Megan, Pegeen Mary. BS in Econs., Loyola U., New Orleans, 1943; Japanese area and lang. program, U. Chgo., U. Mich., 1943-45; JD, Loyola U., New Orleans, 1950; grad., Army War Coll., 1976. Bar: La. 1950. Law clk. to judge Civil Dist. Ct., Parish Orleans, 1950-51; pvt. practice New Orleans, 1950—. Mem. La. Civil Service League, 1968—, bd. govs., 1984—; past pres. Japanese Soc. New Orleans. Served to col. AUS, La. N.G., 1978, ret. Awarded Order of Sacred Treasure, Japanese Govt., 1973, Order of Medallion of St. Louis, Archdiocese of New Orleans, 1982; recipient Monte M. Lemann award La. Civil Svc. League, 1982, 84. Mem. La. State Bar Assn. (com. on law reform 1971-82, ho. of dels. 1975-77), New Orleans Bar Assn. (3d v.p. 1968-69), St. Thomas More Cath. Lawyers Assn. (pres. 1968-70). Democrat. Roman Catholic. Home and Office: 1622 Cadiz St New Orleans LA 70115-4816

DWYER, REX ALLEN, computer scientist; b. Muncie, Ind., Mar. 13, 1959; s. Wayne Wendell and Lois Roberta (Hamilton) D.; m. Vicki Coleen Leary, Sept. 12, 1992; m. Nancy Liesta Mamlin, June 20, 1981 (div. May

1988). AB in Germanic Langs., Ind. U., 1979, MS in Computer Sci., 1981; PhD in Computer Sci., Carnegie-Mellon U., 1988. Mem. tech. staff Hewlett-Packard Co., Cupertino, Calif., 1981-83; rsch. asst. Carnegie-Mellon U., Pitts., 1982-88; asst. prof. N.C. State U., Raleigh, 1988-95, assoc. prof., dir. grad. program, 1995—. Contbr. articles to jours. Algorithmica, Discrete and Computational Geometry, Probability Theory and Related Fields, Advances in Applied Probability. Mem. Assn. for Computing Machinery, Soc. Indsl. and Applied Math., Phi Beta Kappa, Sigma Xi. Democrat. Methodist. Office: NC State U Box 8206 Raleigh NC 27695

DYBELL, ELIZABETH ANNE SLEDDEN, clinical psychologist; b. Buffalo, Sept. 25, 1958; d. Richard Edward and Angela Brigid (Scimone) Sledden; m. David Joseph Dybell, Nov. 30, 1985. BA in Psychology summa cum laude, U. St. Thomas, Houston, 1980; PhD in Psychology, Tex. Tech. U., 1986. Lic. clinical psychologist, Tex. Rsch. asst. health sci. ctr. Tex. Tech. U., Lubbock, 1983-84, psychol. cons. health sci. ctr. neurology dept., 1982-84; psychology intern U. N.Mex. Med. Sch., Albuquerque, 1984-85; psychotherapist Katz & Assocs. P.C., Houston, 1985-88, Meyer Ctr. for Devel. Pediatrics Tex. Children's Hosp., Houston, 1988-92; pvt. practice Houston, 1990—. Author: (monograph) When Will Life Be Normal?, 1989; contbr. articles to numerous publs. choir mem. St. Thomas More Ch., Houston, 1974-87. Mem. Am. Psychol. Assn., Assn. for the Care of Childrens Health, Nat. Ctr. Clin. Infant Programs, Soc. Pediatric Psychology, Southwestern Psychol. Assn., Tex. Psychol. Assn., Houston Psychol. Assn., Am. Psychol. Soc. (charter). Roman Catholic. Office: 6001 Savoy Dr Ste 208 Houston TX 77036-3322

DYCHE, KATHIE LOUISE, secondary school educator; b. Waynoka, Okla., Sept. 8, 1949; d. Loren Neil and Bessie Louise (Wait) Callaway; m. Steven Lee Dyche, July 5, 1969; children: Cherilyn Nettie, Bradley Callaway. BA in Edn. in Art, Northwestern Okla. State U., 1972; postgrad., Southwestern Okla. State U., 1975, 78, Phillips U., 1981, 83-85; MEd, U. Cen. Okla., 1993. Cert. art, Am. history and democracy tchr., Okla. Tchr. art Fairview (Okla.) Pub. Schs., 1973-81, cons., 1973-76; asst. to handicapped Glenwood Elem. Sch., Enid, Okla., 1982-83; reading and math. asst. Longfellow Jr. High Sch., Enid, 1983-84; tchr. art Emerson Jr. High Sch., Enid, 1984—; freelance artist Gaslight Theater, Okla. Small Bus. Devel. Ctr., also others; represented by Dean Lively Gallery, Edmond, Okla. Exhibited in group shows Amarillo (Tex.) Artists' Studio, 1975, Kallistos Invitational Show, 1985, Dean Lively Gallery, Edmond, Okla., Art Educators as Artists exhibit Philbrook, Tulsa, 1994, 96. Pres., v.p., sec., historian, reporter Gamma Mother's Club, Fairview, 1973-80; co-chmn. Fairview Show of Arts, 1979, 80; art vol. Glenlwood Elem. Sch., 1981-82; pres., historian, parlimentarian Delta Child Study Club, Enid, 1981-84. Recipient Okla. Fall Arts Inst. Honor award, 1992, 94, 95, 96; Northwestern Okla. State U. scholar, 1968. Mem. NEA, Nat. Art Edn. Assn., Okla. Art Edn. Assn., Okla. Edn. Assn., Cardinal Key, Kappa Delta Pi, Delta Kappa Gamma (sec. 1986-88, scholar 1993, 2d v.p. 1994-96), Phi Delta Kappa (historian 1995-96). Episcopalian. Office: Emerson Jr High Sch 700 W Elm Ave Enid OK 73701-3082

DYE, BRADFORD JOHNSON, JR., lawyer, former state official; b. Tallahatchie County, Miss., Dec. 20, 1933; married; 3 children. BBA, LLB, U. Miss. Bar: Miss. 1959. Practiced law Grenada, Miss., 1959-61, later in Jackson, Miss.; mem. Miss. Ho. of Reps., 1960-64, Miss. Senate, 1964-68; dir. Agrl. and Indsl. Bd., 1968-71; treas. State of Miss., 1972-76; lt. gov. State of Miss., 1980-92; ptnr. Pyle, Dreher, Mills & Dye PA, 1992—; bd. dirs. Fed. Home Loan Bank, Dallas; southeastern adv. bd. Alexander Proudfoot Productivity Mgmt. Co.; formerly served with U.S. Senate Judiciary Com. Staff; pres. Jackson Fed. Savs. Assn., 1976-79; charter pres. Bus. Sch. Alumni Assn. Univ. of Miss. Charter v.p. Grenada Jaycees; former mem. adv. bd. Miss. State U. Sch. Bus. and Industry; bd. dirs. Jr. Achievement; active state heart fund drive, ARC, United Way, Cancer Drive, YMCA Youth Sports; del. Dem. Nat. Conv., 1980, 84. Mem. U. Miss. Bus. Alumni Assn. (charter pres.), Masons, Shriners, Pi Kappa Alpha. Methodist. Office: Pyle Dreher Mills & Dye 775 Woodlands Pky Ste 100 Ridgeland MS 39157-5212

DYE, CARL MELVYN, academic administrator, educational association executive, insurance consultant; b. Cedar Rapids, Iowa, Oct. 7, 1940; s. Floyd Carmen and Inger Marie (Johansen) D.; BA, Parsons Coll., 1962; MSEd, No. Ill. U., 1967. Cert. ins. rehab. specialist; cert. case mgr. Dir. admissions counselors Parsons Coll., Fairfield, Iowa, 1962-68; acad. dean Bryant and Stratton Coll., Milw., 1968-69; pres. Coll. of the South, Pascagoula, Miss., 1969-70; acad. dean Massey Jr. Coll., Atlanta, 1970-71; pres. Am. Schs. Assn., Chgo., 1967—; dir., founder The Job Group, 1982—. Served with U.S. Army, 1963-64. Mem. ASTD, Nat. Assn. Rehab. Profls. Pvt. Sector, Ga. Assn. Rehab. Nurses, Am. Cons. League, Phi Kappa Phi. Home: 424 G W Armitage Ave Chicago IL 60614

DYE, DAVID RAY, tax accountant, financial advisor; b. Hobart, Ind., Aug. 4, 1951; s. Clifford C. and Lola May (Garrett) D.; m. Claudia Ann Forrester, June 20, 1974; children: Jason Charles, Eric David, Heather Ann. BBA in Acctg., Valparaiso U., 1973. CPA, Va., Ill., Ind.; lic. securities series 7 and health and life, Va., Ohio, N.C., Ind.; registered Renaissance advisor. From staff mem. to sr. mgr. Peat, Marwick, Mitchell, Chgo., 1973-81; dir. tax ops. Touche, Ross & Co., Richmond, Va., 1982-85; ptnr., prin. Womacke & Burke, Richmond, 1986-88; exec. v.p. Deaton Fin. Svcs., Inc., Richmond, 1988—; pres. DRD, Inc., Richmond, 1985—; assoc. Strategic Assets, Inc., Richmond, 1990—, 1996—; pres. Paradigma for Client's, Inc.; registered advisor Renaissance, Inc.; founder Fin. Solutions. Mem. Rep. congl., nat. and life rep. orgns. and precinct coms., Hobart, Inc., 1978-83; mem. Save the Bay, Arbor Found., Neighborhood Housing Svcs. Bd. of Richmond. Named River Conservationist of Yr., Va. Wildlife Fedn., 1995. Mem. AICPA (tax com., personal fin. planning com.), Va. Soc. CPAs, Inc. Soc. CPAs, Ill. Soc. CPAs, Nat. Planned Giving Execs., Econ. Soc. Va. Planned Giving Study Group, U.S. Jaycees, Wilderness Soc., Audubon Soc., Lions, Omicron Epsilon, Sigma Tau Gamma. Home: 8009 Dulles Dr Richmond VA 23235-6711 Office: DRD Inc 8009 Dulles Dr Richmond VA 23285 also: Fin Solutions 2911 Turner Rd Ste A-2 Richmond VA 23224

DYE, KEN, chemical company executive. Pres. Finger Dye Spann, Inc. Office: Finger Dye Spann Inc Ste 50 1001 S Dairy Ashford St Houston TX 77077-2341

DYE, WILLIAM DAVID, pension plan administrator; b. Columbia, S.C., Nov. 24, 1961; s. James Madison and Frances Anne (Smith) D.; m. Mary Scott Sims, May 24, 1986; 1 child, William Sims. BS, U. S.C., 1984. Registered rep. IRS Ctrl. Authorized File. Acct. Select Bus. Equipment, Inc., Columbia, 1985-86; ops. mgr. Capital Wine and Beverage Distbrs. Co. Columbia, Inc., 1986-88; dir. pension svcs. McCain and Assocs., Inc., Columbia, 1989-91; pvt. practice Asheville, N.C., 1992-94; plan adminstr. Sovereign Benefits Adminstrn., Asheville, N.C., 1994—. Mem. Nat. Inst. Pension Adminstrs., Nat. Assn. Accts., Kiwanis (youth svcs. chmn. Richland club 1989-90, sec. 1990-91, treas. project com. 1991-92), Friday Lunch Group (sec. 1989—), U. S.C. Gamecock Club, Kappa Alpha. Republican. Lutheran. Office: PO Box 1430 Asheville NC 28802-1430

DYER, DAVID HARRISON, clergyman; b. Munich, July 22, 1948; came to U.S., 1949; s. Vernard Craft and Isabell Maxine (Laflin) D.; m. Marian Louise Erdman, Sept. 5, 1971; children: Jennifer Lee Dyer Ross, Lucy Elizabeth. AB, King Coll., Bristol, Tenn., 1970; D Min., Union Theol. Sem. in Va., Richmond, 1974. Ordained to ministry Presbyn. Ch., 1974. Pastor Village Presbyn. Ch., Richmond, Va., 1974-76, Oaks Presbyn. Ch., Houston, 1978-86, Westover Hills Presbyn. Ch., Little Rock, 1986-93; asst. prof. philosophy and religion Philander Smith Coll., Little Rock, 1994; interim assoc. exec. Presbyter Presbytery of Ark., Little Rock, 1995; area III instr. Ark. Gov.'s Sch., Conway, 1993-95. Contbr.: Book of Common Worship, 1994. Home: 19 Coolwood Little Rock AR 72202 Office: Presbytery of Ark 2200 S Gaines St Little Rock AR 72206

DYER, DAVID WILLIAM, federal judge; b. Columbus, Ohio, June 28, 1910; s. Joseph H. and Nelle (Peters) C.; m. Helen Hannah., June 28, 1932 (dec.); children—David William, Hannah; m. Mary Elsie Ring, Apr. 29, 1978. Student, Ohio State U., 1932; LL.B., John B. Stetson Coll. Law, 1933. Bar: Fla bar 1933. Ptnr. firm Batchelor & Dyer, 1934-42, Smathers, Thompson & Dyer, 1945-61; judge U.S. Dist. Ct., So. Dist. Fla., 1961-66, chief judge, 1962-66; judge U.S. Court of Appeals, 5th Circuit, 1966-80; judge U.S. Court of Appeals, 11th Circuit, 1980—, sr. judge, 1976—. Served to maj., judge adv. gen. dept. AUS, 1942-45. Mem. Fla. Bar (exec. com. 1957-59), Maritime Law Assn. U.S. (exec. com. 1957-59), Dade County Bar Assn. (pres. 1955-56), Sigma Chi. Home: 200 Ocean Lane Dr Key Biscayne FL 33149-1461 Office: US Ct Appeals 11th cir Fed Justice Bldg 99 NE 4th St Rm 1245 Miami FL 33132-2140

DYER, JAMES HAROLD, JR., English language educator; b. Christiansburg, Va., Mar. 23, 1946; s. James Harold and Dorothy Louise (Bennett) D. BA in English, Augusta Coll., 1970; MEd in English Edn., Ga. State U., 1975, EdS in English Edn., 1978; PhD in Brit. Lit., U. S.C., Columbia, 1992. Cert. secondary sch. tchr., S.C. English tchr. Aiken (S.C.) High Sch., 1975-79; prof. English Ga. Mil. Coll., Ft. Gordon, 1979—; grad. teaching asst. U. S.C., Columbia, 1982-83. Mem. MLA, The Dickens Fellowship, Lambda Iota Tau (Saul Bellow hon. pres). Office: Ga Mil Coll Dept English 38804 Academic Dr Fort Gordon GA 30905-0258

DYESS, JEFFREY ALAN, investment representative; b. Dallas, Nov. 25, 1966; s. George Curtis and Shirley Avon (Haddock) D. BS in Polit. Sci., Tex. A&M U., 1990. Messenger Tex. State Senate, Austin, 1991; elections specialist Travis County Elections, Austin, 1991-92, bus. names clk., 1992, micrographics technician, 1992-94; svcs. rep. Fidelity Investments, Irving, Tex., 1994—. Sec. Aggie Dems., College Station, Tex., 1988-90; mem. Polit. Forum, College Station, 1989-90; contbg. mem. Dem. Nat. Com., Washington, 1990—; precinct coord. Travis County Dem. Party, Austin, 1992; invited attendee Presdl. Inauguration, Washington, 1993; active Epilepsy Found. Am., 1993—. Mem. Tex. A&M Century Club (contbg. mem.), So. Poverty Law Ctr. (contbr.). Home: Apt 2065 3126 W Northgate Dr Irving TX 75062 Office: Fidelity Investments 433 E Las Colinas Blvd Irving TX 75039-5579

DYKEMAN, WILMA, writer, educator; b. Asheville, N.C., May 20, 1920; d. Willard J. and Bonnie (Cole) Dykeman; m. James R. Stokely Jr., Oct. 12, 1940; children: Dykeman Cole, James R. III. BS inSpeech, Northwestern U., 1940; LittD, Maryville Coll., 1974; LHD, Tenn. Wesleyan Coll., 1978. Lectr. English dept. U. Tenn., Knoxville, 1975-95, adj. prof., 1985—; columnist Knoxville News-Sentinel, 1962—; historian State of Tenn., 1980—; nat. lectr. in field; bd. dirs. First Union Bank. Author 16 books including: The French Broad: A Rivers of America Volume, 1955, The Tall Woman, 1962, Seeds of Southern Change, 1962, The Far Family, 1966, Return the Innocent Earth, 1973; co-author: Neither Black Nor White, 1957, Tennessee: A Bicentennial History, 1976, Tennessee Women: An Infinite Variety, 1993, Explorations, a collection of essays, 1984; contbr. articles to nat. mags. and Ency. Brit. Trustee Berea Coll., 1971—, Phelps Stokes Fund, 1981—, U. N.C.-Asheville, 1985—; active Friends of Great Smokies Nat. Park. Guggenheim fellow, 1956-57, NEH fellow, 1976-77; recipient Hillman award, 1957, Disting. So. Writers award So. Festival of Books, 1989; N.C. Gold medal for Contbn. to Am. letters, 1985. Mem. PEN, Authors Guild, So. Hist. Assn., Cosmos Club, Phi Beta Kappa, Delta Kappa Gamma. Home: 282 Clifton Heights Rd Newport TN 37821-2402 also: 189 Lynn Cove Rd Asheville NC 28804-1910

DYKES, ARCHIE REECE, financial services executive; b. Rogersville, Tenn., Jan. 20, 1931; s. Claude Reed and Rose (Quillen) D.; m. Nancy Jane Haun, May 29, 1953; children: John Reece, Thomas Mack. BS cum laude, East Tenn. State U., 1952; MA, E. Tenn. State U., 1956; EdD, U. Tenn., 1959. Prin., Church Hill (Tenn.) High Sch., 1955-58; supt. Greeneville (Tenn.) Schs., 1959-62; prof. edn., dir. U. Tenn. Ctr. for Advanced Grad. Study in Edn., Memphis State U., 1962-66; chancellor U. Tenn. at Martin, 1967-71, at Knoxville, 1971-73; chancellor U. Kans., 1973-80; chmn., pres., chief exec. officer Security Benefit Group of Cos., Topeka, 1980-88; chmn. Capital City Holdings Inc., 1988—; bd. dirs. Whitman Corp., Chgo., Bradford Capital Ptnrs., Nashville, Fleming Cos., Inc., Oklahoma City, Manville Corp., Denver, Pet, Inc., St. Louis, Riverwood Internat. Corp., Atlanta; trustee Keen Industries Trust, N.Y.C., Kans. U. Endowment Assn. Author: School Board and Superintendent, 1965, Faculty Participation in Academic Decision Making, 1968. Vice chmn. Commn. on Operation U.S. Senate, 1975-76; mem. Nat. Adv. Coun. Edn. Professions Devel., 1975-76; trustee Truman Libr. Inst., 1973-80, Menninger Found., 1982-88, Nelson Art Gallery, 1973-80, Dole Found., William Allen White Found.; chmn. bd. trustees U. Mid-Am., 1978-79; mem. adv. commn. U.S. Army Command and Gen. Staff Coll., 1974-79, chmn., 1978-79; mem. consultative bd. regents U. Qatar, 1979-80; mem. bd. regents State of Kans., 1982-86. Ford Found. fellow, 1957-59; Am. Council on Edn. postdoctoral fellow U. Ill., 1966-67; named Outstanding Alumnus, E. Tenn. State U., 1970. Mem. Tenn. Coll. Assn. (pres. 1969-70), Am. Coun. Life Ins. (dir. 1981-86), Nat. Assn. State Univs. and Land Grant Colls. (coun. pres. 1971-80), Newcomen Soc. N.Am., Kans. Assn. Commerce and Industry (dir. 1975-82), Phi Kappa Phi. Home: 506 Belgrave Park Nashville TN 37215-2450

DYKES, OSBORNE JEFFERSON, III, lawyer; b. L.A., Dec. 3, 1944; s. Osborne J. Jr. and Frances (Fox) D.; m. Ann Dennis, Dec. 29, 1973; children: Barbara Nell, Osborne J. IV. BA, Stanford U., 1966, MA, 1968; JD, U. Tex., 1972. Bar: Tex. 1973, U.S. Supreme Ct. 1977, U.S. Ct. Appeals (5th cir.) 1973, U.S. Ct. Appeals (11th cir.) 1981, U.S. Dist. Ct. (so. dist.) Tex. 1975, U.S. Dist. Ct. (ea. dist.) Tex. 1976. Law clk. to Hon. Homer Thornberry U.S. Ct. Appeals 5th Cir., Austin, Tex., 1972-73; ptnr. Fulbright & Jaworski, Houston, 1973—. Contbr. articles to profl. pubs. With U.S. Army, 1969-71. Fellow Am. Bar Found., Tex. Bar Found. (life); mem. ABA (chmn. property ins. law com. 1983-84, tort and ins. practice sect.), Tex. Assn. Civil Trial Specialists (pres. 1982-83, bd. dirs. 1984—), Fedn. Ins. and Corp. Counsel. Republican. Episcopalian. Home: 5135 Holly Terrace Houston TX 77056 Office: Fulbright & Jaworski 1301 Mckinney St Houston TX 77010

DYKES, VIRGINIA CHANDLER, occupational therapist, educator; b. Evanston, Ill., Jan. 10, 1930; d. Daniel Guy and Helen (Schneider) Goodman; children: Ron Lee, Chuck Lee Chandler, James R. Jr. BA in Art and Psychology, So. Methodist U., 1951; postgrad. in occupational therapy Tex. Women's U., 1953. Occupational therapist Beverly Hills Sanitarium, Dallas, 1953-55; dir. occupational and recreational therapy Baylor U. Med. Ctr., Dallas, 1956-60, 68-89; pvt. practice, Dallas, 1989-92; dir. occupational and recreational therapy Fla. Hosp., Orlando, 1962-65; staff therapist Parkland Meml. Hosp., Dallas, 1965-68; cons. Arthritis Found., 1974-89, benefactor; Fanny B. Vanderkodi lectr. Tex. Women's U., 1993—. Mem. coordinating bd. allied health adv. com. Tex. Coll. and Univ. System, 1980-88; bd. dirs. Tex. Arthritis Found., chmn. patient svcs. com., 1985-89, exec. bd. sec.; sponsor Kimball Art Mus.; bd. dirs. Dallas Opera, also women's bd., CPA Wives, Theatre Ctr. Guild; women's bd. Dallas Arboretum; pres. Diana Dean Head Injury Guild, 1992-93. Named Tex. Occupational Therapist of Yr., 1985. Mem. Tex. Occupational Therapy Assn. (life mem. award), Am. Occupational Therapy Assn. (del. Fla. 1964, Tex. 1980-88), World Fedn. Occupational Therapists (participant 8th Internat. Congress, Hamburg, Germany, 1982, del. to 10th European Congress on Rheumatology, Moscow 1983), Chi Omega. Clubs: Boomerang (dir. 1971-88), Les Femmes du Monde, Pierian Lit. Club. Author: (manual) Lightcast II Splints, 1976; Adult Visual Perceptual Evaluation, 1981; contbr. articles to profl. jours. Home: 3203 Alderson St Dallas TX 75214-3059

DYSART, BENJAMIN CLAY, III, consultant, conservationist, engineer; b. Columbia, Tenn., Feb. 12, 1940; s. Benjamin Clay and Kathryne Virginia (Thompson) D.; m. Nancy Elizabeth McDonald, Dec. 28, 1991. BE, Vanderbilt U., 1961, MS in San. Engring., 1964; PhD in Civil Engring., Ga. Inst. Tech., 1969. Staff engr. Union Carbide Corp., 1961-62, 64-65; from asst. prof. to prof. Clemson U., 1968-90, McQueen Quattlebaum prof. engring., 1982-83, dir. S.C. Water Resources Rsch. Inst., 1968-75, dir. water resources engring. grad. program, 1972-75, adj. prof., 1990-93; facility devel. mgr. Chem. Waste Mgmt., Inc., Marietta, Ga., 1990-91; regional facility devel. mgr. Chem. Waste Mgmt., Inc., Memphis, 1991; dir. project planning and integration WMX Technologies, Inc., Washington, 1991-92; pres. Dysart & Assocs., Inc., Atlanta, 1992—; sci. advisor Office Sec. of Army, Washington, 1975-76; mem. EPA Sci. Adv. Bd., from 1983; sr. fellow The Conservation Found., 1985—; mem. adv. coun. Electric Power Rsch. Inst., 1989-95; mem., chief of engrs. environ. adv. bd. U.S. Army Corps Engrs., 1988-92; mem. Glacier Nat. Park Sci. Coun., Nat. Park Svc., 1988-91; mem. S.C. Gov.'s Wetlands Forum, 1989-90; sec. appointee Outer Continental Shelf Adv. Bd. and OCS Sci. Com. Dept. Interior, 1979-82; mem. S.C. Environ. Quality Control Adv. Com., 1980-90, chmn., 1980-81; mem. Sci. Panel to Rev. Interagy. Rsch. on Impact of Oil Pollution NOAA, Dept. Commerce, 1980; mem. Nuclear Energy Ctr. Environ. Task Force Dept. Energy-So. States Energy Bd., 1978-81; mem. Nonpoint Source Pollutant Task Force EPA, 1979-80; mem. civil works adv. com. Office Sec. Army-Young Pres.'s Orgn., 1975-76; mem. S.C. Heritage Adv. Bd., 1974-76; cons. on strategic environ. mgmt., corp. environ. leadership programs and stakeholder involvement matters to industry and govt. agys. Editor: (with Marion Clawson) Managing Public Lands in the Public Interest, 1988, Public Interest in the Use of Private Lands, 1989; contbr. articles on math. modeling in water quality and environ. mgmt. and pub. involvement to profl. jours.; author numerous profl. papers, reports. Trustee Rene Dubos Ctr. for Human Environs., 1985-94, vice chmn., mem. exec. com., 1988-94; bd. visitors Kanuga Episcopal Conf. Ctr., 1988—. Recipient Tribute of Appreciation for Disting. Svc. EPA, 1981, 86, McQueen Quattlebaum Engring. Faculty Achievement award Clemson U., 1982, Order of Palmetto Gov. S.C., 1984; named Hon. Ky. Col., 1976. Mem. ASCE, Trout Unltd. (bd. trustees 1990-94), Nat. Wildlife Fedn. (bd. dirs. 1974-90, v.p. 1978-83, pres., chmn. bd. dirs. 1983-85), Am. Geophys. Union, Assn. Environ. Engring. Profs. (bd. dirs. 1978-83, pres., chmn. bd. dirs. 1981-82), Water Environ. Fedn. (hon., bd. dirs. Rsch. Found. 1989-91), S.C. Wildlife Fedn. (bd. dirs. 1969—, pres., chmn. bd. dirs. 1973-74, S.C. Wildlife Conservationist Yr.), The Ga. Conservancy (bd. trustees 1994—), Cosmos Club (Washington), Sigma Xi, Tau Beta Pi, Phi Kappa Phi, Chi Epsilon, Omega Rho, Sigma Nu. Episcopalian. Office: Dysart & Associates Inc 224 Broadland Ct NW Atlanta GA 30342-3601

DYSART, DIANA BARCELONA, school system administrator; b. New Orleans, Oct. 14, 1955; d. Anthony and Mildred (Schroeder) Barcelona; m. Daniel Lee Dysart, Aug. 12, 1978; children: Cori, Katie, Daniel J., Christopher. BA in Elem. Edn., U. Southwestern La., 1976; MEd in Supervision and Adminstrn., La. State U., 1977. Mem. St. Bernard Parish Sch. Bd., Chalmette, 1983—, v.p., 1985-88, pres., 1988—; with Nat. Sch. Bds. Assn., La. Sch. Bds. Assn. Chmn. Mothers March, March of Dimes, 1985-91, bd. dirs., 1985—; bd. dirs. Nunez Community Coll. Found., Chalmette, 1990-94, Am. Heart Assn., 1994; mem. Ednl. Excellence Com., Chalmette, La.; booth chmn. St. Mark Fair; active St. Bernard Beautification Com.; co-chair St. Bernard Cleanest Parish Com.; bd. dirs. Discovery Festival, YWCA. Mem. aAUW, Internat. Reading Assn., Just Between Friends Homemakers Assn., C. of C. (mem. exec. com.), KOC (women's aux.), Serra Internat. Democrat. Roman Catholic. Office: Saint Bernard Sch Bd 57 E Chalmette Cir Chalmette LA 70043-4522

DYSINGER, PAUL WILLIAM, physician, educator, health consultant; b. Burns, Tenn., May 24, 1927; s. Paul Clair and Mary Edith (Martin) D.; m. Yvonne Minchin, May 11, 1958; children: Edwin, Wayne, John, Janelle. B.A., So. Missionary Coll., 1951; M.D., Coll. Med. Evangelists, 1955; M.P.H., Harvard, 1962. Diplomate Nat. Bd. Med. Examiners, Am. Bd. Preventive Medicine. Intern Washington, 1955-56; sr. asst. surgeon USPHS; with Blackfeet Indians in Mont., Navajos of Ariz., 1956-58; physician, med. adviser Am. embassy, PhnomPenh, Cambodia, 1958-60; rsch. assoc. dept. preventive medicine Loma Linda (Calif.) U. (formerly Coll. Med. Evangelists), 1960-62, dir. field sta. Western Tanganyika, 1962-64, adminstrv. asst. div. pub. health, 1964-67, asst. to dean, chmn. dept. tropical health Sch. Pub. Health, 1967-69, asst. dean for acad. affairs and internat. health Sch. Pub. Health, 1969-71, assoc. dean for acad. affairs, 1971-79, dir. preventive med. residency Sch. of Medicine, 1983-88; pres., CEO, sr. health advisor Devel. Svc. Internat., Williamsport, Tenn., 1992—; med. cons. dept. Vocat. Rehab., Riverside, Calif., 1964-88; mother and child health cons. Ministry of Health, Tanzania, 1978-80; med. dir. Village Health Program, Punjab, Pakistan, 1980-81, tchr., cons., S.Am. and Caribbean, 1981-83; chief preventive medicine Pettis Meml. VA Hosp., Loma Linda, 1986-88; sr. health advisor Adventist Devel. and Relief Agy., 1988-92. Contbr. articles to med. publs. WHO fellow, Somalia, Ethiopia, India, Nepal and Burma, 1969. Fellow Royal Soc. Tropical Medicine and Hygiene, Am. Pub. Health Assn., Am. Coll. Preventive Medicine, Internat. Health Soc. (pres.); mem. AMA, Nat. Council for Internat. Health, Adventist Internat. Med. Soc. (pres. 1983-84), Delta Omega (nat. pres. 1977-78). Adventist. Home and Office: 684 Dry Prong Rd PO Box 210 Williamsport TN 38487-0210

EADDY, PAULA JOHNSON, women's health nurse; b. Raleigh, N.C., June 9, 1965; d. Jack R. and Alice Faye (Paul) Johnson; m. Joseph Marion Eaddy III, June 3, 1995. Student, East Carolina U., Greenville, 1983-85; AAS, Ctrl. Carolina C.C., Sanford, 1987; AAS in Nursing, Wake Tech. C.C., Raleigh, 1990. RN, N.C.; BLS; cert. neonatal resusitation. Vet. med. technician N.C. State U., Raleigh, 1987-88; nurse technician II Wake Med. Ctr., Raleigh, 1988-90, maternal/child staff nurse II, staff nurse III, 1990—. Active United Way of N.C., Raleigh. Mem. Tarheel Triangle Cat Fanciers (past pres.). Baptist. Office: 3000 New Bern Ave Raleigh NC 27610-1215

EADS, ALBERT E., JR., school administrator; b. Chgo., Aug. 30, 1937; s. Albert E. and Pauline (White) E.; m. Margaret Oliver, Dec. 31, 1957; children: Rosemarie, Albert E. III, Randy, David, Ellen. BS, The Citadel, Charleston, S.C., 1959; MEd, Duke U., 1964; advanced cert., U. S.C., 1973, PhD, 1974. Cert. English, social sudies, gen. sci., elem. reading tchr., reading supr., elem. and secondary prin., supt., S.C. Prin. Riverland Terr. Elem. Sch., 1960-63, Stiles Point Elem. Sch., Charleston, S.C., 1963-66, St. John's High Sch., Darlington, S.C., 1976-84, Gaffney (S.C.) High Sch., 1984-86; supt. schs. Hampton Dist. 2, Estill, S.C., 1988-96; exec. dir. S.C. Assn. for Rural Edn., Goose Creek, S.C., 1996—. Contbr. articles to profl. publs. Recipient numerous civic awards; fellow NDEA. Mem. ASCD, Am. Assn. Sch. Adminstrs. (S.C. Supt. Yr. 1994), Nat. Assn. Secondary Sch. Prins., Internat. Reading Assn., S.C. Optimists (past gov.), Phi Delta Kappa, Kappa Delta Pi.

EADS, JOHN A., accountant; b. Dallas, Feb. 6, 1939; s. Arver A. and Nettie Mae (Dawson) E.; m. Joanna Y. Eads, Aug. 12, 1967; children: Leslie, Ashley, John Jr. BBA, U. Tex., 1966. CPA, Tex. Pvt. CPA practice, 1974-81; pres., mng. shareholder Eads, Hunter & Co., P.C., Dallas, 1981—; pres. Practice Mgmt. Group, Dallas, 1981; sec.-treas. Haemachem Rsch. Assocs., Inc., Dallas, 1983—. Author: Practice Continuation Agreements, 1992. Trustee Charlton Meth. Hosp., Dallas, 1988—, pres., chmn. bd. dirs., 1990; treas., bd. dirs. Citizens Devel. Ctr., Dallas, 1990-95; adv. coun. Dallas Meth. Hosp. Found., 1991—, Cmtys. Found. of Tex., 1988—. Served with USAF, 1960-66. Recipient Disting. Pub. Svc. Award for CPA, White House Office of Pvt. Sector Initiatives, 1987. Mem. AICPA (Pub. Svc. award 1995), Tex. Soc. CPAs (bd. dirs. 1981—, treas. 1991, pres. 1996, pres. Dallas chpt. 1989-90, Outstanding Chpt. Pres. award, CPA of Yr. 1988), Dallas Estate Planning Coun. (bd. govs.), Internat. Assn. Lions Clubs (gov. 1985-86, state coun. chmn. 1986-87). Republican. Methodist. Office: Eads Hunter & Co PC 2777 N Stemmons Fwy Ste 1659 Dallas TX 75207-2229

EADS, LYLE WILLIS, retired government inspector; b. Ida Grove, Iowa, June 29, 1916; s. David J. and Bertha E. (McGonigle) E.; m. Betty Boles, Dec. 22, 1946 (dec. Feb. 1996); children: Diane, Mary Ellen. Enlisted U.S. Navy, 1934, advanced through grades to comdr., ret., 1964; asst. inspector gen. Naval Sea Systems Command, Washington, 1966-84, ret., 1984—. Author: Survival Amidst the Ashes, 1978. Decorated Merito Naval Degree of Knight, Republic of Brazil, Rio de Janeiro. Mem. DAV, Confederation Chivalry, Am. Legion, Mil. Order of Purple Heart, Am. Ex-Prisoners of War, Inc., Ret. Officers Assn., Nat. Adv. Bd., Am. Security Coun., Internat. Platform Assn., Masons. Methodist. Home: 1561 Valley Forge Ln Melbourne FL 32940-6741

EADS, ORA WILBERT, clergyman, church official; b. Mill Spring, Mo., Jan. 2, 1914; s. John Harrison and Effie Ellen (Borders) E.; m. Mary Ivaree Cochran, Mar. 25, 1944; children—Ora Wilbert, Wayne B., Carol Vernice, Janet Karen and Janice Inez (twins). J.D., John Marshall Law Sch., Atlanta, 1940, LL.M., 1941; postgrad., Sch. Theology, St. Lawrence U., Canton, N.Y., 1947-48. Bar: Ga. bar 1940. Practiced in Atlanta, 1940-46; ordained to ministry Christian Congregation, Inc., 1946; parish minister Sampson County, N.C., 1948-52; evangelist Charlotte, N.C., 1952-61; gen. supt. Christian Congregation, Inc., 1961—. Author numerous books of poetry, 1967—. Office: Christian Congregation Inc 804 W Hemlock St La Follette TN 37766-3947

EADS, RONALD PRESTON, management consultant; b. Greensboro, N.C., Oct. 17, 1948; s. Wayne Oather and Marcella (Tatarski) E.; m. Gail Senn, Feb. 8, 1975; children: Tanya, Michael, Shannon, Kevin. BBA, Roanoke Coll., 1970. Mgmt. trainee GE, Salem, Va., 1970-71; dept. mgr. Mauney Hosiery, Kings Mountain, N.C., 1971-72; v.p. Eads Mgmt. Devel. Assocs., Gastonia, N.C., 1972-82; pres. Eads Mgmt. Devel. Assocs., 1982—. Co-author: Let's Plan Management Future, 1983. Deacon, First Presbyn. Ch., Gastonia, 1986-88, elder, 1990—. Republican. Home: 3548 Gardner Park Dr Gastonia NC 28054-4946 Office: Eads Mgmt Devel Assocs 3017 Redbud Dr Gastonia NC 28056-8441

EADY, CHARLOTTE KING, elementary education educator; b. Waycross, Ga., Dec. 27, 1950; d. Giles William and Jeannette Evelyn (Howard) K.; m. Isreal Lee Eady Jr., July 9, 1971; children: Isreal III, Maya LaRah, Giles King. BS, Albany State Coll., 1972; MEd, Ga. State U., 1977; specialist in edn., Ga. Southwestern Coll., 1987. Tchr. supprort specialist Ga. Dept. Edn. Tchr. C.A. Gray Elem., Moultrie, Ga., 1972-74, North Elem. Sch., Pelham, Ga., 1975-77, Mitchell County Elem., Camilla, Ga., 1977-81, Mitchell County Middle, Camilla, 1981-90, Fourth Ward Elem., Griffin, 1990-91, Taylor St. Middle Sch., Griffin, 1991—; presenter Internat. Conf. on Critical Thinking, Sonoma, Calif., 1993; mem. Adv. Bd. for Critical Thinking, Ga., 1994. Co-author: (manual) A Novel-Based Manual of Critical Thinking Application, 1990. Pres. Taylor St. Middle PTSO, Griffin, 1993; mem., bd. of deaconness Mt. Zion Bapt. Ch. Mem. NEA (local pres. 1984), Internat. Reading Assn., Jack & Jill of Am., Inc. (Pen Pal chmn. 1995), Phi Delta Kappa, Alpha Kappa Alpha Sorority Inc. (Black Family award 1995). Home: 1466 Gloria St Griffin GA 30223 Office: Taylor St Middle Sch 234 E Taylor St Griffin GA 30223

EAGAN, CLAIRE VERONICA, lawyer; b. Bronx, N.Y., Oct. 9, 1950; d. Joseph Thomas and Margaret (Lynch) E.; m. M. Stephen Barrett, Aug. 25, 1978 (div. 1984); m. Anthony J. Loretti, Jr., Feb. 13, 1988. Student, U. Fribourg, Switzerland, 1971-72; BA, Trinity Coll., Washington, 1972; postgrad., U. Paris, 1972-73; JD, Fordham U., 1976. Bar: N.Y. 1977, Okla. 1977, U.S. Dist. Ct. (no. dist.) Okla. 1977, U.S. Ct. Appeals (10th cir.) 1978, U.S. Dist. Ct. (we. dist.) Okla. 1981, U.S. Ct. Appeals (5th cir.) 1982, U.S. Dist. Ct. (ea. dist.) Okla. 1988, U.S. Ct. Appeals (Fed. cir.) 1990, U.S. Supreme Ct. Mem. Hall, Estill, Hardwick, Gable, Golden & Nelson, Tulsa, 1978—, shareholder, 1981—; also bd. dirs., exec. com. Editor Fordham Law Rev., 1975-76. Bd. dirs. Cath. Charities, Tulsa, 1983—, Cystic Fibrosis Found., Tulsa, 1982-84; mem. Jr. League Tulsa, Inc., 1983—; bd. trustees Gannon U., Erie, Pa., 1995—; bd. dirs. Okla. Sinfonia, Tulsa, 1982-86; adj. settlement judge, Tulsa County, 1990—. Mem. Tulsa County Bar Assn., 10th Cir. Jud. Conf., Am. Inns of Ct. Republican. Roman Catholic. Office: Hall Estill Hardwick Gable Golden & Nelson 320 S Boston Ave Ste 400 Tulsa OK 74103-3704

EAGAN, WILLIAM LEON, lawyer; b. Tampa, Fla., Feb. 10, 1928; s. John Robert and Margaret (Williams) E.; m. Marjorie Young, Mar. 6, 1949; children—Barbara Anne, Rebecca Elizabeth, Laurel Lea. Student U. Tampa, 1959, LL.B., U. Fla., 1961. Bar: Fla. 1961, U.S. Dist. Ct. (mid. dist.) Fla. 1959, U.S. Dist. Ct. (so. dist.) Fla. 1962, U.S. Ct. Appeals (5th cir.) 1972; bd. cert. civil trial lawyer, Fla. Assoc. Dexter, Conlee & Bissell, Sarasota, Fla., 1961-62; ptnr., v.p. Arnold, Matheny & Eagan, P.A., Orlando, 1962—; mem. Fla. Bar Ninth Circuit Grievance Com., 1982-84; mediator Family Law Mediation Program. Articles editor U. Fla. Law Rev., 1961. Chmn. bd. trustees First Baptist Ch. Winter Park, Fla., 1970-72, chmn. bd. deacons, 1967-69; active Indsl. Devel. Commn. Mid-Fla., Orlando, 1979-84. Served to seaman 2d class USN, 1945-46. Mem. Acad. Fla. Trial Lawyers, Am. Trial Lawyers Assn., Lawyers Title Guaranty Assn., Orange County Bar Assn. (exec. council), Order of Coif, Phi Alpha Delta, Phi Kappa Phi. Republican. Baptist and Methodist. Clubs: University, Citrus (Orlando). Office: Arnold Matheny & Eagan PA 801 N Magnolia Ave Ste 201 Orlando FL 32803-3842

EAGAR, STEPHEN WADE, television news anchor/reporter; b. Lompoc, Calif., Sept. 5, 1962; s. David Melvin and Judith Lynn (Chippendale) E.; m. Michele Lisa Salmon, Sept. 18, 1985; children: Camden Clarke, Kelsey Nicole, Kyle David. Student, Utah Tech. Coll., 1980-82; BA, Brigham Young U., 1987. Profl. baseball player Detroit Tigers, 1984-86; news anchor/reporter Sta. KYMA-TV, Yuma, Ariz., 1987-89, Sta. KVBC-TV, Las Vegas, 1989-91, Sta. KSL-TV, Salt Lake City, 1991-95, Sta. KDFW-TV, Dallas, 1995—. Adv. bd. mem. Easter Seal Soc., Plano, Tex., 1996—, Caring for Children, Collin County, Tex., 1996—. Recipient Best Newscast, Best Series Reporting award Ariz. Assoc. Press, Yuma, 1988; Best TV Spot News Story award Utah Broadcasters Assn., Salt Lake City, 1992, 93. Mem. Profl. Baseball Players Alumni Assn., Soc. of Profl. Journalists (chpt. pres. 1987, Best TV Spot News Story 1992), Radio & TV News Directors Assn. (Edward R. Murrow award Best News Series 1995). Mem. LDS Ch. Office: KDFW-TV 400 N Griffin Dallas TX 75202

EAKIN, RICHARD RONALD, academic administrator, mathematics educator; b. New Castle, Pa., Aug. 6, 1938; s. Everett Glenn and Mildred May (Hammerschmidt) E.; m. Jo Ann McGeehan, Aug. 23, 1960; children: Matthew Glenn, Maridy Lynn. AB in Math., Geneva Coll., Beaver Falls, Pa., 1960; MA in Math., Washington State U., 1962, PhD in Math., 1964. Asst. prof. math. Bowling Green (Ohio) State U., 1964-68, assoc. prof. math., 1968-87, asst. dean grad. sch., 1969-72, vice-provost student affairs, 1972-80, vice-provost instl. planning, 1979-80, exec. vice-provost budgeting and planning, 1980-83, v.p. budgeting and planning, 1983-87; chancellor, prof. math. East Carolina U., Greenville, N.C., 1987—. Editor revs. and evaluations sect. (jour.) The Math. Tchr., 1968-70. V.p. and mem. bd. dirs. Nat. Hemophilia Found., N.Y.C., 1983-84, chmn. bd., v.p. adminstrn. and fin., 1984-87. NDEA fellow Wash. State U., Pullman, 1960-63, NSF fellow, 1963-64. Mem. Math. Assn. Am., So. Assn. Colls. and Schs. (commn. on colls.), Sigma Xi, Phi Kappa Phi, Omicron Delta Kappa. Office: East Carolina U Office of Chancellor Greenville NC 27858

EALEY, CHRYSTA LEA, medical/surgical nurse; b. Paris, Tex., Mar. 19, 1949; d. Herschel Albert and Shirley Louise (Linthicum) Lynch; m. Robert Michael Johnson, Aug. 30, 1969 (div.); children: Judy Lea, Robert Thomas; m. Bobby Lewis Ealey, Jr., May 9, 1992. Student, Tex. Womans U., 1967-69; Assoc. in Nursing, Cook County Coll., 1974. RN, Tex. Head nurse of surg. fl. Flow Meml. Hosp., Denton, Tex., 1974-79; nursing dir. First Tex. Med. Clinic, Denton, 1979-81; head nurse surg. fl. Denton (Tex.) Regional Med. Ctr., 1981-90; office nurse and surg. nurse F. Jeffery Charney, M.D., Denton, 1990—; Charter mem. Am. Acad. Ambulatory Nurses Assn., 1981; part time nursing supr. Denton Regional Med. Ctr., 1991—. Mem. Am. Heart Assn. (bd. dirs. 1988—, v.p. 1995, pres. 1996, chmn. health site com. 1997, CPR instr. 1977—, CPR instr. trainer 1989—), Confederate Air Force Med. Detachment (col. 1987—). Republican. Episcopalian. Home: 2805 Wildwood St Denton TX 76205-3591

EARHART, CHARLES FRANKLIN, JR., microbiology educator; b. Melrose Park, Ill., Oct. 26, 1941; s. Charles Franklin and Katherine (Laho) E. BA with honors, Knox Coll., 1962; PhD, Purdue U., 1967. Rsch. asst. Argonne (Ill.) Nat. Lab., 1961-62; NIH trainee Purdue U., Lafayette, Ind., 1962-63, NIH predoctoral fellow, 1963-66, postdoctoral fellow, 1966-67, NIH postdoctoral fellow, 1967-68; NIH postdoctoral fellow Tufts U. Sch. Medicine, Boston, 1967-68; faculty assoc. U. Tex., Austin, 1968-70, asst. prof. microbiology, 1970-77, assoc. prof., 1977-83, prof., 1983—; mem. rev. panel on prokaryotic genetics NSF, 1985; symposium secretariat Internat. Symposium on Iron, 1990. Mem. editorial bd. Jour. Bacteriology, 1979-84, Biology of Metals, 1988-92, BioMetals, 1992—; contbr. more than 40 articles to profl. jours. Grantee NSF, NIH, Welch Found. and Rsch. Corp. Mem. AAAS, Am. Soc. for Microbiology (lectr. Found. for Microbiology 1988), Genetics Soc. Am., Sigma Xi, Phi Lambda Upsilon. Office: U Tex ESB # 519 Austin TX 78712-1095

EARL, DENNIS CHARLES, audiologist; b. Pitts., Apr. 20, 1955; s. Charles W. and Doris B. Earl; m. Patricia Wojciak, Aug. 27, 1983; children: Christine, Lucas. BA, U. Ala., 1979; MA, U. Tenn., 1983, PhD, 1987. Dir. audiology Knoxville (Tenn.) Otolaryngology, 1980—. Bd. dirs. Old North Knoxville, Inc., 1993—. Fellow Am. Acad. Audiology, Am. Auditory Soc., Acad. Dispensing Audiologists; mem. Am. Speech and Hearing Assn., Acoustical Soc. Am. Office: Knoxville Otolaryngology 930 E Emerald Ave Ste 713 Knoxville TN 37917-4561

EARL, LYN See HUMPHREYS-MUSSELMAN, CAROLYN EARL

EARP, JAMES FRANCY, civil engineer; b. Spencer, W.Va., Feb. 11, 1935; s. Fogle Francy and Hettie Catherine (Langford) E.; m. Alice Sue Moon; children: James Kevin, Gregory Allen, Jennifer Lynn, Leslie Allen Whitfield. BSCE, W.Va. U., 1958. Sec., mgr. F.F. Earp & Son, Inc., Fairmont, W.Va., 1958-60; pres. Laurel Materials & Engring., Inc., Fairmont, 1960-65; engr. Anderson's Black Rock, Inc., Charleston, W.Va., 1965-68, Polk County Engring. Dept., Bartow, Fla., 1969-70; owner J.F. Earp Assocs., cons. engrs., Lakeland, Fla., 1970-80, P.R.M. Sales, Lakeland, 1971-89; internat. mktg. cons. PRMS Internat., Inc., Lakeland, 1980—; cons. transactional analysis, 1973—; profl. image cons., 1986—; past tchr. adult continuing edn. Polk Community Coll., Winter Haven, Fla.; also freelance writer and photographer. Mem. NSPE, Internat. Transactional Analysis Assn. Methodist. Home and Office: 4855 Ferney Ln Lakeland FL 33810-3512

EASH, JIMMIE RUTH, accountant; b. Smithville, Tex., Nov. 23, 1934; d. James Reid and Ruth (Tolleson) Dunham; m. Richard L. Eash, Oct, 3, 1953; children: Ellen Ruth, Richard L. Jr. Student, San Antonio Coll., 1951-52, Tex. A&I, 1952-53, N. Tex. State U., 1963-64. Supply clk., purchasing and contract clk. Lackland AFB U.S. Govt., San Antonio, 1951-54; asst. to city mgr. City of San Antonio, 1955-57; co-owner, mgr. Tex. Paper Rolls, San Antonio, 1976-92; account mgr. Am. Rolls, Inc., San Antonio, 1993—. Author: Golding Family, 1990; editor: Revolutionary War Soldiers Buried in Texas, 1976; author, compiler (textbook) Texas History for 5th grade - Christian Schs. Mem. DAR (organizing regent Atascosa chpt., state chmn. 1983-94, regent 1981-83), Capt. Augustus Chpt. Daus. of 1812 (pres., state officers, nat. chmn.), Daus. of Republic of Tex. (Alamo Missions and Alamo Heroes Chpt.), United Daus. of Confederacy. Baptist. Home and Office: 2550 Oak Island Dr San Antonio TX 78264-3507

EASLEY, CHRISTA BIRGIT, nurse, researcher; b. Berlin, Apr. 30, 1941; came to U.S., 1966; d. Albert and Marianne (Uhlmann) Baldauf; m. Loyd Allen Easley, Oct. 23, 1964 (widowed Dec. 1993). Degree in nursing, Pawlow Coll. of Nursing, Aue, Fed. Republic of Germany, 1959; BS, NYU, Albany, 1978; MBA, Cen. Mich. U., 1979; EDS, Ctrl. Mo. U., 1983; PhD, Kensington U., Glensdale, Calif., 1983. With placement sect. Sembach, A.B., Fed. Republic of Germany, 1972-73, suggestion program mgr., 1973-74; adminstrv. clk. Lajes Field, A.B., Terceira, Acores, Portugal, 1975-78, incentive awards and suggestion program mgr., 1978-79; intern Cen. Mo. State U., Warrensburg, 1980-81; instr. in bus. overseas campus Cen. Tex. Coll../Yokota, A.B., Japan, 1983; instr. Tokyo Ctr. for Lang. and Culture, 1981-83; tchr. dept. of def. Yokota Dept. of Def., Yokota AFB, Japan, 1981-84; tax examiner IRS, Austin, Tex., 1984-86; clin. rsch. coord. HealthQuest Rsch., Austin, 1987-94; v.p. Austin Clin. Rsch., 1994—. Treas. Am. Sch. System PTA, Acores, 1978-79; precinct chmn. Austin Rep. Com., 1988—. Mem. Assocs. of Clin. Pharmacology, Am. Assn. Translators, AAUW, Sigma Tau Delta. Methodist. Home: 12422 Deer Trak Austin TX 78727-5746 Office: Austin Clin Rsch Inc Creek Plaza # 202 8705 Shoal Creek Austin TX 78757

EASLEY, JUNE ELLEN PRICE, genealogist; b. Chgo., June 7, 1924; d. Fred E. and Bernadette (Mailloux) Price; m. Raymond Dale Easley, Dec. 24, 1945. Student, McCormack Sch. Commerce, Englewood Jr. Coll., Chgo. Lic. genealogist Assn. Profl. Genealogists. Statis. clk. Arthur Andersen & Co., Chgo., 1968-74; corr. sec. ICG R.R., Chgo., 1974-86; self-employed genealogist-computers Arlington Heights, Ill., 1986-94, Mountain Home, Ark., 1994—; editor, typist genealogical books, 1996—. Contbr. religion articles to Daily Herald, 1991; editor romance stories, 1990—. Mem. DAR (auditor-treas. Chgo. chpt. 1981-82, rec. sec. Chgo. chpt. 1982-88, Mountain Home 1995—, publicity chmn. 1996—), Huguenot Soc., Nat. Soc. R.R. Bus. Women (newsletter editor 1991—), Northwest Suburban Coun. Genealogists (pres. 1988-90, corr. sec. 1990-94), Clean Water Club (sec. 1996—), Daus. of War of 1812. Republican. Methodist. Home and Office: 1601 Franklin Ave Mountain Home AR 72653-2041

EASLEY, MICHAEL F., state attorney general; b. Rocky Mount, N.C., 1950; m. Mary Pipines; 1 child, Michael F., Jr. BA in Polit. Sci. cum laude, U. N.C., 1972; JD cum laude, N.C. Ctrl. U. Dist. atty. 13th Dist., N.C., 1982-91; pvt. practice Southport, N.C., 1991-93; atty. gen. N.C., 1993—. Contbr. numerous articles in field. Recipient Pub. Svc. award U.S. Dept. Justice, 1984. Pres. N.C. Conf. Dist. Attys.; mem. N.C. Dist. Attys. Assn. (past pres., legis. chmn.). Office: PO Box 629 Raleigh NC 27602-0629

EASLEY, PATSY FLETCHER, interior designer; b. Amarillo, Tex., Jan. 7, 1931; d. Lowery Thurman Fletcher and Winnie Ozella (Hart) Leverett; m. Jack Wayne Easley, June 7, 1948; 1 child, James William. Student, Nicholls State U., Thibodaux, La., 1974-76, Nicholls State U., Thibodaux, La., 1974-76; B in Interior Design, La. State U., 1990. Lic. real estate salesperson, La.; registered interior designer Tex., La. Co-owner, treas., designer Easley's Fabrics/Interiors, Morgan City, La., 1964-72; owner, designer Pat Easley-Interior Designer, Morgan City, 1973-90, New Orleans, 1990—; real estate agt. Gertrude Gardner Realtors, New Orleans, 1993—; mgr., dir. Leah Norman Schreier Community Ctr., Morgan City, 1986-88. A designer Am. Soc. Interior Designers showcase Cityscapes, Fed. Fiber Mills Bldg., New Orleans, 1986. Bd. dirs. Morgan City Community Concert Assn., 1966-72; mem. St. Mary Arts and Humanities Coun., 1984-88, Preservation Resource Ctr., New Orleans, 1986—; mgr., bd. dirs. Leah Norman Schreier Community Ctr., Morgan City, 1986-88. Named Laywoman of the Yr. First Bapt. Ch., Patterson, La., 1979. Mem. AAUW, Am. Soc. Interior Designers, Nat. Trust for Hist. Preservation (assoc.), Constrn. Specifications Inst., New Orleans Met. Assn. Realtors, New Orleans Mus. of Art (assoc.), Wives of U.S. Submarine Vets. WWII, Ladies Petroleum Club (Morgan City pres. 1981-92), Order Ea. Star, Lakeshore Garden Club, Lakeshore Woman's Club. Baptist. Home and Office: 814 Amethyst St New Orleans LA 70124-3604

EASON, MARCIA JEAN, lawyer; b. Dallas, Aug. 31, 1953; d. John Keller and Sara Marguerite (Prindle) McCarron; m. S. Lee Meredith, Sept. 12, 1981 (div. Oct. 1989); m. David O. Eason, Aug. 21, 1993; stepchildren: Chelsea, Shannon, Valerie. BA, Trinity U., 1975; JD, U. Houston, 1979. Bar: Tex. 1978, U.S. Dist. Ct. (so. dist.) Tex. 1978, U.S. Ct. Appeals (5th cir.) 1979, Tenn. 1985, U.S. Dist. Ct. (ea. dist.) Tenn. 1985, U.S. Supreme Ct. 1985, U.S. Ct. Appeals (6th cir.) 1986, U.S. Ct. Appeals (4th cir.) 1994. Ptnr. Byrnes & Martin, Houston, 1984-85, Miller & Martin, Chattanooga, 1987—. Pres., bd. mem. Chattanooga's (Tenn.) Kids on the Block, 1987—; bd. mem. AIM Ctr, Chattanooga, 1993—; campaign chair, attys. divsn. United Way, Chattanooga, 1994. Mem. ABA, Tenn. Bar Assn., Chattanooga Bar Assn. (com. chair 1985—), Tenn. Lawyers Assn. for Women (co-chair com. 1994, treas. 1995—). Home: 33 Rock Crest Dr Signal Mountain TN 37377-2326 Office: Miller & Martin 832 Georgia Ave Ste 1000 Chattanooga TN 37402-2291

EAST, CHARLES E., JR., advertising and public relations executive; b. Baton Rouge, La., Dec. 5, 1949; s. Charles Elmo and Sarah (Simmons) E.; m. Laura Gaddy Durrett, June 15, 1996; BA in Journalism, La. State U., 1971; children: Rachel Elizabeth, Catherine Mae. Successively state desk copy editor, gen. assignment reporter, edn. writer Times-Picayune, New Orleans, 1971-73; co-founder, editor Gris-Gris, Baton Rouge, 1973; successively advt. and pub. rels. copywriter Weill/Strother, Inc., Baton Rouge, 1973-74, exec. v.p., 1974-79; ptnr. Weill/Strother/East, Inc., 1979-81; ptnr. Weill & East, Inc., 1981-88 , pres., 1984-88; pres. The East Agy., 1988-89; advt. pub. rels. cons., 1989-90; pres. East Advt. and Pub. Rels., Inc., 1990—. Recipient Journalism awards La. State U., 1969, 70, 71, Hodding Carter award, 1971, Mpls. Star award, 1970, Telly award, 1991, 94, 96, Pres. of Yr. award 7th Dist. Am. Advt. Fedn., 1994, Pete Goldsby award, 1996. Mem. Am. Advt. Assn. (treas. 7th dist. 1996—), La. Assn. Advt. Agys. (dir. 1983, v.p. 1984, pres. 1985), Advt. Fedn. of Greater Baton Rouge (bd. dirs. 1991—, v.p. 1992-93, pres. 1993-94), Rotary. Democrat. Home: 4436 Broussard St Baton Rouge LA 70808-1209 Office: Ste 2B 5800 One Perkins Place Dr Baton Rouge LA 70808-9114

EAST, JACK MILTON, rehabilitation counselor, administrator, social worker; b. Little Rock, Jan. 7, 1950; s. James M. and Virginia (Price) E.; m. Nan Ellen Dickinson, May 27, 1979; step-children: Tyndall, Lee Butler, Edward. Student, U. Ark., Little Rock, 1969-72, 79-82; BS in Edn. and Rehab. Counseling, S.W. U., New Orleans, 1985, MA in Rehab. Counseling, 1988, postgrad., 1988—. Lic. social worker. Pres., founder Am. Amputee Found., Little Rock, 1975-77, exec. dir., 1977—; founder Life Care Mgmt. and Planning, 1985—; pres. Life Care Mgmt. and Planning, Little Rock, 1985—; del. Ark. Conf. on Disabled, White House Conf. on Disabled; adv. Ark. Rehab. Act of 1973; mem. planning com. and panel Atty. Gen.'s Conf. on Laws and Rights of Handicapped. Editor Nat. Resource Dir. for Amputees, 1984—, Ark. amputees referral program law, pub. sch. system drivers edn. program for handicapped, also articles and manuals; producer, dir. One Step at a Time, You're Not Alone; producer Winners, Arkansas Government: Close-Up, Hunger, Here and Now, That's A Good Boy, Ritchie, 12 Steps of Alcoholics Anonymous, Technologies for the Disabled in the 90's. Founder Am. Drug Abuse Prevention Found., Little Rock, 1980, Ark. Handicapped Athletic Assn. Rollin Razorbacks, 1980; co-founder Ark. Environ. Barriers Coun., Little Rock, 1980's; vol. Ark. Coalition for Handicapped, Am. Coalition for Citizens with Disabilities, Archtl. Barriers com. and Consumer Adv. coun. Ark. Spinal Cord Commn., Adv. coun. Ark. Div. Rehab., Nat. Orgn. Disability (chmn. Ark. chpt.). Recipient Gov.'s Vol. Activist award, Nat. Vol. Activist award, Citation award; named Outstanding Young Man of Am. Jaycees. Mem. Nat. Rehab. Assn., Nat. Rehab. Adminstrs. Assn., Internat. Soc. Prosthetist and Orthotist, Nat. Orgn. Disability, Nat. Spinal Cord Injury Assn., Rehab. Engring. Soc. N.Am. Republican. Methodist. Home: 11 Tanglewood Ln Little Rock AR 72202-1518 Office: Am Amputee Found Inc PO Box 250218 Little Rock AR 72225-0218

EAST, NANCY MCKINLEY, private primary music educator; b. Harlan, Ky., Mar. 5, 1935; d. John H. and Nina (Howard) McKinley; children: Marie, Sandy, John, Nancy Elizabeth. BS, U. Ky., 1957, Kennesaw State Coll., 1984. Cert. piano tchr., Ga. Home svc. dir. Green River Rural Electric, Owensboro, Ky., 1972—; pvt. practice tchr. piano, kindermusik Marietta, Ga., 1989—. Past pres. Guild of the Cobb Symphony Orch., Hickory Walk Home Owners Assn.; pres. Episcopal Ch. women St. James Episcopal Ch.; Marietta convocation rep. Atlanta Diocese. Mem. Cobb County Music Tchrs. Assn. (past pres., program chmn.), Ga. Music Tchrs. Assn. (v.p.), Greater Atlanta Music Alliance (sec.), Am. Matthay Assn., Phi Upsilon Omicron, Sigma Alpha Iota (Outstanding Chpt. Mem. award). Home and Office: 360 Hickory Walk Marietta GA 30064-3090

EASTER, PETER, trade association administrator, lobbyist; b. Chgo., Jan. 3, 1938; s. Donald Woodward and Virginia (Follett) E.; m. Carol Osborne, Aug. 28, 1959; children: Deborah, Douglas, Brooke. BA, Dartmouth Coll., 1960. With Peoples Bank, Charlottesville, Va., 1961-63; dir. printed product sales Acme Visible records, Crozet, Va., 1963-67; dir. sales Janssen Products Corp., Charlottesville, 1967-68; dist. mgr. Commonwealth Propane, Charlottesville, 1968-75; v.p. Va. Bankers Assn., Richmond, 1975-76; pres. Easter Assocs., Inc., Charlottesville, 1976—; owner Springhaven Farm, Charlottesville, 1962—. Mem. Albemarle County Plan Com., Charlottesville, 1973-77, chmn., 1978. 1st lt. U.S. Army, 1960. Mem. Am. Soc. Assn. Execs. (cert.), Inst. Assn. Mgmt. Cos. (bd. dirs. 1984-87), Va. Soc. Assn. Execs., Va. C. of C., Va. Hunting Preserve Assn., Farmington Country Club. Episcopalian. Home: 2679 Free Union Rd Charlottesville VA 22901 Office: Easter Associates Inc 630 Country Green Ln Charlottesville VA 22902

EASTERLING, CHARLES ARMO, lawyer; b. Hamilton, Tex., July 22, 1920; s. William Hamby and Jennie (Arilla) E.; m. Irene A. Easterling, Apr. 25, 1943; children: Charles David, Danny Karl, Jan Easterling Petty. BBA, Baylor U., 1951, LLB, 1951, JD 1969. Bar: Tex. 1950, U.S. Supreme Ct. 1954. Sr. asst. city atty. City of Houston, 1952-64; sole practice, Houston, 1964-70; city atty. Pasadena (Tex.), 1970-82; of counsel Easterling and Easterling, Houston, 1982—; instr. So. Tex. Coll. Law, 1954-69. Served to lt. col. (ret.) USAFR. Mem. Houston-Harris County Bar Assn., Phi Alpha Delta. Democrat. Methodist. Clubs: Masons (33d deg.; insp. gen. hon.), Shriners, Arabia Temple Shrine (past potentate), Red Cross Constantine, Jesters.

EASTMAN, CAROLINE MERRIAM, computer science educator; b. Columbus, Ohio, Dec. 25, 1946; d. Robert Merriam and Kathryn Parmelee (Benedict) E.; m. Robin Michael Carter, Mar. 31, 1968. AB magna cum laude, Radcliffe Coll., 1968; MS in Computer Sci., U. N.C., 1974, PhD in Computer Sci., 1977. Asst. prof. dept. math. and computer sci. Fla. State U., Tallahassee, 1977-82; asst. prof. dept. computer sci. and engring. So. Meth. U., Dallas, 1982-84, assoc. prof., 1984-85; program dir. NSF, Washington, 1984-85; assoc. prof. dept. computer sci. U. S.C., Columbia, 1986-91, prof., 1991—. Contbr. articles to profl. jours. Rsch. grantee NSF, Fla. State U., 1980-82, So. Meth. U., 1982-84, Air Force Office Sci. Rsch., Fla. State U., 1981-82. Mem. AAAS (nominating com. electorate 1987-90, mem.-at-large sect. 1993-97), Assn. Computing Machinery (v.p. N.W. Fla. chpt. 1978-79), Assn. Women in Computing (bd. dirs.-at-large 1979-83), Am. Soc. Info. Sci. Office: Dept Computer Sci Univ of South Carolina Columbia SC 29206-2846

EASTMAN, EDWARD SHIRRELL, JR., clinical psychologist; b. Petersburg, Va., Nov. 1, 1951; s. Edward S. Sr. and Vera Marie (Davis) E.; m. Christine Moorhead, Apr. 21, 1979 (div. 1992); 1 child, Seth Alden. BA in Psychology, U. Va., 1974; MS in Counseling Psychology, Va. Commonwealth U., 1979; D in Clin. Psychology, Va. Consortium Profl. Psycholo, Norfolk, Va., 1988. Lic. profl. counselor, 1984, clin. psychologist, 1990. Psychologist Barrow Geriatric Treatment Ctr., Petersburg, 1979-82; crisis mental health counselor Norfolk (Va.) Cmty. Mental Health Svcs., 1983-85; with Ea. Va. Med. Sch., Norfolk, intern in clin. psychology, 1985-86; fellow in family therapy Coll. William & Mary, 1986-87; sr. psychologist Ctrl. State Hosp., Petersburg, Va., 1987-91, clin. psychologist supr., 1991-95, forensic clin. psychologist, 1995—; clin. psychology cons. Cmty. Meml. Pavilion, South Hill, Va., 1994—. Contbr. articles to profl. jours. Mem. Va. Psychol. Assn., Va. Acad. Clin. Psychologists (legis. network), Am. Psychol. Assn. Home: 4172 Creek Way Chester VA 23831-4647 Office: Ctrl State Hosp Forensics PO Box 4030 Petersburg VA 23831

EASTMAN, JAMES CLIFFORD, investment management consultant; b. Bridgeton, Maine, Apr. 21, 1954; s. Robert Hawley and Mary Catherine (Chapman) E.; m. Lynne Walker Jones, June 14, 1975; children: Jamin Paul, Devin James, Megan Leslie. BS in Acctg. with highest honors, Bentley Coll., Waltham, Mass., 1976. CPA, Conn., Mass., Fla.; cert. personal fin. specialist. Acct. Ernst & Ernst, New Haven, Conn., 1976-81; sr. fin. analyst Polaroid Corp., Cambridge, Mass., 1981-87; acct. Wentzel, Berry & Swope, Naples, Fla., 1987-91; investment officer Robert W. Baird & Co., Milw., 1991-93; founder, sr. investment mgmt. cons. Pvt. Investment Counsel, Milw., 1993—. Pres. Collier County Young Reps., Naples, 1991, 92; mem. gubernatorial com. Jim Smith for Gov., Naples, 1994; mem. fin. com. St. Johns Episcopal Ch., Naples, 1987-93; mem. coun. Boy Scouts Am., Naples, 1988-90; mem. Rep. Exec. Com., Collier County, 1992—. Mem. AICPA (personal fin. planning div. 1987—), Fla. Inst. CPAs, Naples Estate Planning Coun., Pelican Bay Bus. Assn. (co-founder 1992). Office: Robert W Baird & Co 5811 Pelican Bay Blvd Naples FL 34108-2752

EASTON, GLENN HANSON, JR., management and insurance consultant, federal official, naval officer; b. N.Y.C., Mar. 11; s. Glenn Herman and Cornelia Blanchard (Hanson) E.; m. Jeanne Milhall, June 15, 1944; children: Jeanne, Glenn Hanson III, Michelle, Carol. Assoc. in Bus. Adminstrn., U. Pa., 1949, B.A. in Econs., 1950; M.B.A., NYU, 1959. USCG lic. as 3d asst. engr. steam vessels of any horsepower, as 3d mate of steam and motor vessels of any gross tons upon the waters of oceans; CLU. Various positions to asst. traffic mgr. Keystone Shipping Co., Phila., 1940-54, Phila. Jr. C. of C., 1946-54; various positions to mgr. transp. econs. div. Standard-Vacuum Oil Co., White Plains, N.Y., 1954-59; various positions to cons. to pres. S.R. Guggenheim Found., N.Y.C., 1959-84; pres. Glenn Easton & Assocs. (mgmt. and ins. cons.), Port Chester, N.Y., 1970—; emeritus spl. agent Northwestern Mutual Life Ins. Co., 1974—; polit. appointee U.S. Dept. Labor, Washington, 1982-88; emeritus spl. agt. Northwestern Mut. Life Ins. Co., 1974—; assoc. prof. mgmt. L.I. U., Brookville, N.Y., 1971-72. Rep. candidate for congressman, N.Y., 1972, 74, 80; pres. local Rep. Club, 1973-74; mem.

Westchester County Rep. Com., 1972-83; Rep., Conservative and Ind. candidate for supr. Town of Rye, N.Y., 1973, 75, 79, 81, Rep. Candidate for councilman, 1977; vice chmn. Ind. Conservative Caucus, Westchester, 1977-83; exec. v.p. bd. trustees N.Y.-Phoenix Schs. Design, 1968-74; Eagle Scout with 4 Silver Palms. With Maine N.G., 1936-38; served to comdr. USN, 1938-40, 43-46, 50-54, 70, PTO, ret., 1979. Mem. Soc. Naval Archs. and Marine Engrs. (life, Golden award), Navy Athletic Assn., Fed. Exec. Inst., Ret. Officers' Assn., C. of C., Am. Mgmt. Assn., Naval Res. Assn. (life, v.p. Westchester chpt.), Militia Assn. N.Y. (life), Westchester Organ Soc. (v.p.), Met. Organ Soc. Va., No. Va. Ragtime Soc., Am. Theatre Organ Soc., U.S. Capitol Hist. Soc., The Conservative Network (life), Am. Legion, Masons, Shriners, Kiwanis, Elks, Pi Gamma Mu, Sigma Kappa Phi, Phi Delta Theta (Golden Legionnaire). Home: 1385 Old Quincy Ln Reston VA 20194-1309 Office: 1537 Inlet Ct Reston VA 20090-4423

EASTON, ROBERT MORRELL, JR., optometric physician; b. Miami, Fla., Sept. 23, 1954; s. Robert Morrell Easton Sr. and Joan (Saxon) Faust; m. Gloria Rocio Flores, Mar. 19, 1983; children: Robert Morrell Easton III, Linda Easton. AA, Broward Community Coll., 1974; BS in Chemistry, U. Cen. Fla., 1977; OD, U. Houston, 1982. Cert. Optometric physician, Fla. Extern Bascom Palmer Eye Inst., Miami; pvt. practice Ft. Lauderdale, 1982—. Mem. Victory 88 Campaign-Bush-Quayle, 1988, Victory 90 Campaign Gov. Bob Martinez, 1989-90. Recipient Up & Comer's award for Health Care South Fla. Mag., 1993; named One of Top Optometrists in U.S., 20/20 mag., 1991. Mem. Fla. Optometric Assn. (pres.-elect 1992-93, pres. 1993-94), Am. Optometric Assn. (state rep. 1987—, polit. action, profl. rels. com. 1994—, bd. dirs. AOA-PAC 1994—), Fla. Pub. Health Assn. (charter, chmn. vision care sect. 1992-93), Broward County Optometric Assn. (past pres., Optometrist of Yr. 1985), Rotary Club of Ft. Lauderdale (bd. dirs. 1986-89, Svc. award 1989), Tower Forum (v.p. 1994-95). Republican. Presbyterian. Office: 2708 E Oakland Park Blvd Fort Lauderdale FL 33306-1605

EASTRIDGE, MICHAEL DWAYNE, clinical psychologist; b. Martinsville, Va., June 14, 1956; s. James Edward Eastridge and Ann Marie (Stone) Beechum; m. Joyce Gayle Helms, Sept. 9, 1978; children: Philip Michael, Abigail Joyce. BA, Averett Coll., 1978; MS, Va. Tech., 1981, PhD, 1983. Diplomate Am. Acad. Pain Mgmt., Am. Bd. Profl. Disability Cons., Am. Bd. Vocat. Neuropsychology. Staff psychologist New River Valley Mental Health Svcs., Pulaski, Va., 1981-82; asst. prof., cons. Fla. Mental Health Inst., U. South Fla., Tampa, 1983-86; staff psychologist Humana Regional Pain Clinic, St. Petersburg, Fla., 1987-88; cons. Ctr. for Anxiety and Depressive Disorders, Largo, Fla., 1989-90, Recovery Bridge, Largo, 1990-91; dir. Fla. Neurobehavioral Inst., St. Petersburg, 1986-89, Biobehavioral Svcs., St. Petersburg, 1987—; pvt. practice psychology St. Petersburg, 1983—; dir. Fla. Neurobehavioral Inst., St. Petersburg, 1986-91; guest lectr. Pineallas County Profl. Guardian Assn., 1989-91, Am. Lung Assn., Pinellas County, 1990-91; vol. free svcs. for poor children 1989-91, free support groups for parents and handicapped children, St. Petersburg, 1990-91. Editor Ember, 1977; author various workshops stress, assertiveness, work efficiency, 1983-91. Mem. APA, Soc. Behavior Medicine, Fla. Psychol. Assn., Biofeedback Cert. Inst. Am., Alpha Chi, Omicron Delta Kappa. Home: 214 S Trask St Tampa FL 33609-2537 Office: 9455 Koger Blvd N Ste 104 Saint Petersburg FL 33702-2431

EATON, DOREL, elementary school educator; b. Atlantic City, N.J., Sept. 8; d. Ethel Donovan Joyce; divorced; 1 child, Melissa Elizabeth Eaton-Midgley. BA in Edn., U. Fla.; MS, Barry U., 1973; Design degree, Sch. for Interior Design, Miami Shores, Fla., 1976. Cert. guidance counseling, elem. educator, Fla. Elem. edn. tchr. Dade County Pub. Sch., Miami. Art displayed in numerous galleries including The Curzon Art Gallery of Boca Raton (Fla.) Country Club, Bill Nessen's Showroom/Design Ctr. of the Americas, Dania, Fla.; contbr. Book Nat. Coalition Against Pornography. Named Outstanding Alumnus Barry U., 1996. Mem. MADD, Nat. Coalition for Protection of Children and Families, Concerned Women of Am., U.S. Holocaust Meml. Mus. (charter mem.), Morality in Media, Inc., Am. Fedn. for Decency, Prison Fellowship, Design Ctr. of the Ams., People for the Ethical Treatment of Animals, Enough is Enough, Physicians Com. for Responsible Medicine, Fla. Right to Life.

EATON, GORDON PRYOR, geologist, research director; b. Dayton, Ohio, Mar. 9, 1929; s. Colman and Dorothy (Pryor) E.; m. Virginia Anne Gregory, June 12, 1951; children: Gretchen Maria, Gregory Mathieu. BA, Wesleyan U., 1951; MS, Calif. Inst. Tech., 1953, PhD, 1957. Instr. geology Wesleyan U., Middletown, Conn., 1955-57, asst. prof., 1957-59; asst. prof. U. Calif., Riverside, 1959-63, assoc. prof., 1963-67, chmn. dept. geol. sci., 1965-67; with U.S. Geol. Survey, 1963-65, 67-81; dep. chief Office Geochemistry and Geophysics, Washington, 1972-74; project chief geothermal geophysics Office Geochemistry Geophysics, Denver, 1974-76; scientist-in-charge Hawaiian Volcano Obs., 1976-78; assoc. chief geologist Reston, Va., 1978-81; dean Coll. Geoscis. Tex. A&M U., 1981-83, provost, v.p. acad. affairs, 1983-86; pres. Iowa State U., Ames, 1986-90; dir. Lamont-Doherty Earth Obs. Columbia U., Palisades, N.Y., 1990-94, U.S. Geol. Survey, Reston, Va., 1994—; mem. Commn. on Internat. Edn., Am. Coun. Edn.; mem. coun. advisors World Food Prize; mem. bd. earth scis. and resources; ocean studies bd., and com. on formation of nat. biol. survey NRC, also mem. geophysics study com.; bd. dirs. Midwest Resources, Inc., Bankers Trust; mem., chair adv. com. U.S. Army Command and Gen. Staff Coll. Mem. editl. bd. Jour. Volcanology and Geothermal Rsch., 1976-78; contbr. articles to profl. jours. Trustee Wesleyan U.; pres., bd. dirs. Iowa 4-H Found., 1986-90; mem. U.S. del. sci. & tech. com. Gore-Chernomyrdin Commn., 1996—. Standard Oil fellow Calif. Inst. Tech., 1953; NSF grantee, 1955-59. Fellow Geol. Soc. Am., AAAS; mem. NSF (mem., chair earth scis. adv. com., mem. Alan T. Waterman award com., mem. del. sci. & tech. com. Gore-Chernomyrdiu commn.), Am. Geophys. Union, Hawaii Natural History Assn. (bd. dir. 1976-78). Home: 1334 Garden Wall Ct # B Reston VA 22094-2025 Office: Office US Geol Survey MS100 12201 Sunrise Valley Dr Reston VA 22091-3401

EATON, JOE OSCAR, federal judge; b. Monticello, Fla., Apr. 2, 1920; s. Robert Lewis and Mamie (Gireadeau) E. AB, Presbyn. Coll., 1941, LLD (hon.), 1979; LLB, U. Fla., 1948. Pvt. practice law Miami, Fla., 1948-51, 55-59; asst. state atty. Dade County, Fla., 1953; circuit judge Miami, 1954-55, 59-67; mem. Fla. Senate, 1956-59; mem. law firm Eaton & Achor, Miami, 1955-58, Sams, Anderson, Eaton & Alper, Miami, 1958-59; judge U.S. Dist. Ct. (so. dist.) Fla., 1967—, chief judge, from 1983, now sr. judge; Instr. law U. Miami Coll. Law, 1954-56. Served with USAAF, 1941-45; Served with USAF, 1951-52. Decorated D.F.C., Air medal. Methodist. Club: Kiwanian.

EATON, MICHAEL WILLIAM, lawyer, educator; b. Dallas, July 28, 1958; s. Charles H. and Helen Gilbough (Miller) E. BS in Polit. Sci., So. Meth. U., 1980, JD, 1984; MPA, U. Tex., Dallas, 1996. Bar: Tex. 1984, U.S. Dist. Ct. (no. dist.) Tex. 1985, U.S. Ct. Appeals (5th cir.) 1986, U.S. Supreme Ct. 1988. Asst. gen. counsel Kirby Petroleum, Inc., Dallas, 1984-85; ptnr. Leonard & Eaton, Dallas, 1985-86; assoc. Page & Addison, P.C., Dallas, 1986-87; pvt. practice Dallas, 1987—; pres. San Jacinto Investments Group, 1992—; lectr. in econs. El Centro (Tex.) Coll., 1995—; lectr. in constl. law U. Tex., Dallas, 1996—. Co-author: Expert Witnesses in The Courtroom, 1996; reviewer Am. Jour. of Polit. Sci., 1994—. Vol. Texans for Bush/Quayle, Dallas, 1988; del. John Connolly for Pres. Campaign, Dallas, New Orleans, 1980; north Tex. youth coord. William P. Clements for Gov. Campaign, Dallas, Ft. Worth, Denton, 1978; So. Meth. U. re-election chmn. John Tower for U.S. Senate Campaign, Dallas, 1978. Mem. State Bar Tex., Tex. Young Lawyers Assn., Dallas Assn. Young Lawyers, Assn. Trial Lawyers Am., Phi Alpha Delta, Ancient Order of Hibernians. Republican. Roman Catholic. Office: 4151 Beltline Rd Ste 124 Dallas TX 75244-2323

EATON, TIMOTHY WALTER, college dean, minister; b. Joplin, Mo., Mar. 5, 1953; s. Walter Willis and Lillie Dean (Hutchings) E.; m. Marthajane Evinger, Aug. 10, 1973; children: Tara Marie, Leah Nicole, Hope Elizabeth. ThB, Hillsdale Coll., Moore, Okla., 1975; MDiv, Southwestern bapt. Theol. Sem., Ft. Worth, 1979. Sr. pastor Free Will bapt. Ch., Mo., 1979-89; v.p. acad. affairs Hillsdale Coll., Moore, 1989—; ednl. cons. David C. Cook Pub., Chgo., 1980-84. Mem. Okla. Assn. C.C. Instrnl. Adminstrs., Okla. Assn. Collegiate Registrars and Admissions Officers. Republican. Home: 1416 E Main St Moore OK 73160 Office: Hillsdale Free Will Baptist College PO Box 7208 Moore OK 73153

EATON, WAYNE CARL, chiropractic physician; b. Albuquerque, Nov. 18, 1937; s. Alvin Wayne and Yvonne G. Eaton. AA, South Oklahoma City Jr. Coll., 1972; DC, Logan Coll. of Chiropractic, St. Louis, 1977. Diplomate Nat. Bd. Chiropractic Examiners; lic. in Fla., Okla. Chiropractic physician Eaton Chiropractic Clinic, PA, High Springs, Fla., 1977—; examiner Fla. Bd. Chiropractor Examiners and Dept. of Profl. Regulations for State of Fla. Bd. Examiners, 1992, 93, 94; creator first Chiropractic Assts. Assn. in State of Fla., 1992. All sports team physician Santa Fe High Sch., Alachua, Fla., 1986—; examining physician Pop Warner Football, High Springs, Alachua and Newberry, 1988—; com. mem. High Springs Nursing Facility, 1991; mem. Fla.'s Suwannee Valley Pvt. Industry Coun., 1991. Recipient Heritage award Found. for Chiropractic Edn.and Rsch., 1993, Pres.'s Coun. award, 1992, 93. Mem. Am. Chiropractic Assn. (coun. on sports injuries and phys. fitness, coun. on roentgenology), Fla. Chiropractic Assn. (coun. on orthopedics), Logan Coll. Chiropractic Alumni (ethics com. chmn. 1990-91, 92-94), Mid-Fla. Chiropractic Soc. (pres. 1992-93). Office: Eaton Chiropractic Clinic PA Box 886 High Springs FL 32643

EAVES, SANDRA AUSTRA, social worker; b. Chgo., Aug. 30, 1960; d. Maris and Ilze (Kursulis) Muiznieks; m. Gerald Eaves, Oct. 7, 1989. BA, Northwestern U., 1982; MSW, Loyola U., Chgo., 1984. Social worker Chgo. Pub. Schs., 1982-83, Cook County Hosp., Chgo., 1983-84; pvt. practice Dr. Harry A. Croft & Assoc., PA, San Antonio, 1990—; social worker VA, San Antonio, 1984-91. Mem. NASW, Tex. Soc. fon Clin. Social Work, Coun. Nephrology Social Workers. Lutheran. Office: Dr Harry A Croft & Assoc 8038 Wurzbach Ste 570 San Antonio TX 78229-3539

EBBERS, FRANCES ANN, librarian; b. Cleve., July 24, 1936; d. Paul and Adele (Brazaitis) Mancino; m. Allen F. Ebbers, Dec. 26, 1959; children: Christopher, Kenneth, Carolyn. AB, Ohio U., 1958; MLS, U. Tex., 1986. Instr. English Reading (Ohio) H.S., 1958-59, Dept. of Def., Hanau, Germany, 1973-75, Libertyville (Ill.) H.S., 1977-81; adminstrv. asst. Southwestern U., Georgetown, Tex., 1982-84; instr. English, libr., curriculum dir. St. Michael's Acad., Austin, Tex., 1984-88; libr. St. Edward's U., Austin, 1988—; instr. English New Coll. St. Edward's U., Austin, 1995—, U. Tex. Ind. Learning, Austin, 1993—. Co-author: English 1A, English 1B, 1993, Supervisor/Student Teacher, 1992, Information Literacy, 1991, American Literature, V. 1, V. 2, 1990. Com. mem. Main, Met. Austin Interactive Network, 1992—. Mem. Nat. Coun. Tchrs. English (instrl. tech. com. 1994-97), Internat. Sirsi Users Group (treas. 1994-96), Tex. Libr. Assn. (sec./treas. Reference Round Table 1995-97), Ctrl. Tex. Coun. Tchrs. English (v.p. 1995—), Kappa Delta Pi. Home: 4700 Indian Wells Dr Austin TX 78747 Office: Saint Edward's Univ Libr 3001 S Congress Ave Austin TX 78704

EBERLE, DAVID EUGENE, gastroenterologist; b. Quantico, Va., June 24, 1946; s. Harry Eugene Eberle and Dorothy Marie (Burger) Jones; m. Jennifer Pate Bagley; children: Deanna Renee, Lorri Christine. BS cum laude, Ga. Tech. U., 1969; MD, U. Tenn., 1974. Diplomate Am. Bd. Internal Medicine; bd. cert. gastroenterology. Assoc. prof. medicine UCLA Med. Sch., L.A., 1980-81; gastroenterologist Acad. Gastroenterology, Inc., Chattanooga, Tenn., 1981—; chief medicine Hutcheson Tri-County Hosp., Ft. Oglethorpe, Ga., 1983-85, Downtown Gen. Hosp., Chattanooga, 1987-88, chief of staff, 1988-89. Med. dir. Hospice, Chattanooga, 1986-90, pres., 1994; vestry Good Shepard Episc. Ch., Lookout Mountain, Tenn., 1990-93; pres. New Life Home for Boys, Chattanooga, 1994. Fellow ACP, Am. Coll. Gastroenterology; mem. Am. Gastroenterology Assn., Am. ssn. Study Liver Diseases, Acad. Hospice Physicians (bd. mem. 1994). Office: Am Gastroenterology Inc Ste 512 White Hall Med Bldg 960 E 3rd St Chattanooga TN 37403-2104

EBERT, ROBERT ANTHONY, agricultural educator; b. Manhattan, Kans., Apr. 14, 1947; s. Kenneth R. and Dorothy L. (Weixelman) E.; m. Patricia Ann McLean, July 23, 1977 (div. Aug. 1984); children: A.J., Robin; m. Carol Ann Marston, Dec. 23, 1988; children: Pam, Jennifer, Beth. BS, Kans. State U., 1970; MEd, Auburn U., 1992. Farm mgr. Kittiwake Farms, Jasper, Ala., 1970-85; unit mgr. Auburn (Ala.) U., 1985-95, extension specialist, 1995—. Vice chmn. Walker Farmers' Coop., Jasper, 1978-85. Named Hon. State Farmer Ala. FFA Found., 1976. Mem. Walker County Cattleman Assn. (pres. 1981-85), Ala. Polled Hereford Assn. (pres. 1984-86), KC (state youth dir. 1990-92, grand knight Auburn U. coun. 1990-92).

EBIEFUNG, ANIEKAN ASUKWO, mathematics educator and researcher; b. Nto Mbadum, Akwaibom State, Nigeria, Nov. 10, 1958; came to U.S., 1985; s. Asukwo Thomas and Florence Asukwo (Udofa) E.; m. Anne Aniekan Ekon, Jan. 2, 1989; children: Ediobong, Uduak. BS in Math. and Statistics 1st honors, U. Calabar, Nigeria, 1982; MS in Math., Howard U., 1987; PhD in Math. Scis., Clemson U., 1991. Instr. math. Federal U. of tech., Owerri, Nigeria, 1982-83, U. Cross River State, Uyo, Nigeria, 1983-85, U. D.C. Lorton (Va.) Prison Coll. Program, 1987-88, Howard U., Washington, 1985-88; teaching asst. Clemson U., 1988-91; asst. prof. math. U. Tenn., Chattanooga, 1991—; prof. math. U.C. Found., 1994; lectr. in field; ctr. chmn. Tenn. Math. tchrs. Assn. state-wide math contest, U. Tenn., Chattanooga, 1992—. Contbr. articles to profl. jours.; editor NASM Bull., 1980-81. Grantee Ctr. of Excellence for Computer Applications, 1993, scholar, 1995-96; grantee Oak Ridge Assoc. Univs., 1993, UC Found., 1993, Tenn. Higher Edn. Commn., 1994-95. Mem. Math. Assn. Am., Am. Math. Soc., Ops. Rsch. Soc. Am., Chattanooga Area Math. Tchrs. Assn., Internat. Linear Algebra Soc. Office: Univ of Tenn 615 Mccallie Ave Chattanooga TN 37403-2504

EBISUZAKI, YUKIKO, chemistry educator; b. Mission City, B.C., Can., July 25, 1930; came to U.S., 1957; d. Masuzo and Shige (Kusumoto) E. BS with honors, U. Western Ont., London, Can., 1956, MS, 1957; PhD, Ind. U., 1962. Postdoctoral U. Pa., Phila., 1962-63; faculty rsch. assoc. Ariz. State U., Tempe, 1963-67; acting asst. prof. UCLA, 1967-75; assoc. prof. N.C. State U., Raleigh, 1975—. Contbr. articles to profl. jours. Ont. Rsch. Found. fellow Ont. Rsch. Coun., 1957-60, Gerry fellow Sigma Delta Epsilon, 1977-78. Mem. AAUW, Am. Chem. Soc., Am. Phys. Soc., Sigma Xi. Office: NC State Univ Dept Chemistry Clb # 8204 Raleigh NC 27695

EBITZ, DAVID MACKINNON, art historian, museum director; b. Hyannis, Mass., Oct. 5, 1947; s. Robert White Creeley and Ann (MacKinnon) Kucera; m. Mary Ann Stankiewicz, Jan. 1, 1983; children: Rebecca Aemilia, Cecilia Charlotte. BA, Williams Coll., 1969; AM, Harvard U., 1973, PhD, 1979. Teaching fellow, then head teaching fellow dept. fine arts Harvard U., Cambridge, Mass., 1975-78; asst. prof., then assoc. prof. dept. art U. Maine, Orono, 1978-87, interim dir. galleries, curator univ. art collection, 1986-87; head dept. edn. and acad. affairs J. Paul Getty Mus., Santa Monica, Calif., 1987-92; dir. John and Mable Ringling Mus. Art, Sarasota, Fla., 1992—; vis. faculty Bangor (Maine) Theol. Sem., 1981; lectr. in field; presenter workshops. Author exhbn. revs., book revs.; contbr. articles to arts publs., exhbn. catalogues. Heritage Found. fellow, 1968. Mem. Assn. Art Mus. Dirs., Coll. Art Assn., Nat. Art Edn. Assn., Am. Assn. Museums (mus. edn. com.), Medieval Acad. Am., Internat. Ctr. Medieval Art, Phi Beta Kappa. Office: John & Mable Ringling Mus of Art 5401 Bay Shore Rd Sarasota FL 34243-2161

EBY, PATRICIA LYNN, plastic surgeon; b. Gordonville, Pa., July 13, 1956; d. Donald S. and Marian E. (Thomas) Eby; m. Peter A. Aldea, June 6, 1993. BA, Georgetown U., 1978; MD, Washington U., St. Louis, 1982. Diplomate Am. Bd. Surgery; lic. surgeon, Tex., Mass., Fla., N.C., Tenn. Tng. in surgery Baylor Coll. Medicine, Houston, 1982-86; chief resident in surgery Berkshire Med. Ctr., Pittsfield, Mass., 1988-89; rsch. fellow in microsurgery St. Joseph Hosp., Houston, 1989-90; rsch. fellow in nerve regeneration Lahey Clinic, Burlington, Mass., 1990-91, resident in plastic surgery, 1991-93; pvt. practice plastic surgery Memphis, 1994—. Contbr. articles to profl. jours.; presenter in field. Mem. ACS, Am. Soc. Plastic and Reconstructive Surgery. Home: 80 Humphreys Center Ste 300 Memphis TN 38120

EBY, THOMAS LEE, neuro-otologist, educator; b. Milw., Aug. 7, 1953; s. Lee George and Lorna S. (Smith) E.; m. Mary Margaret O'Donoghue, Apr. 19, 1982; children: Margaret, Brendan, Conor. BS, Stanford U., 1975; MD, U. Wis., 1979; postgrad., U. Minn., 1979-81. Diplomate Am. Bd. Otolaryngology. Fellow, resident Harvard U., Boston, 1981-85; fellow in neurotology U. Hosp. Zürich, Switzerland, 1986-87; asst. prof. in surgery U. Ala., Birmingham, 1987-92, assoc. prof. in surgery, 1992—; chief otolaryngology VA Hosp., Birmingham, 1990—. Contbr. articles to med. jours. Fellow ACS, Am. Acad. Otolaryngology, Harold Schuknecht Soc.; mem. AMA, Am. Neurology Soc., Am. Otological Soc., Triologic Soc. Home: 3146 Pine Ridge Rd Birmingham AL 35213-3906 Office: U Ala Divsn Otolaryngology 1501 5th Ave S Birmingham AL 35233-1614

ECCLES, STEPHEN DAVID, retired international banker; b. Mold, Wales, Feb. 10, 1938; came to U.S., 1966; s. Bertie Harold and Anne (Shann) E.; m. Magdalena Josefa Pita, May 7, 1964; children: Maria Magdalena Eccles Free, Ana Maria, Stephen Thomas Pita. BA in Math., Cambridge (Eng.) U., 1959, MA in Math., 1965. With Brit. Fgn. Office, London, Madrid, Havana, Cuba, 1961-64; asst. res. rep. UN Tech. Assistance Bd., Mexico City, 1964-66; jr. positions World Bank, Washington, 1966-76, divsn. chief Ea. Africa agr., 1977-82, asst. projects dir. Western Africa region, 1982-87, dep. treas., dir. fin. ops., 1987-90, v.p., contr., 1990-94; ret., 1994; chmn. adv. coun. Internat. Acctg. Stds. Com., London, 1995—. Treas., bd. dirs. BirdLife Internat. (formerly Internat. Coun. for Bird Preservation), Cambridge, 1990—, Am. Bird Conservancy, Washington, 1994—; chmn. parents giving campaign Northeastern U., Boston, 1995—. 2d lt. Brit. Army, 1959-61. Mem. Am. Numismatics Assn., United Oxford and Cambridge U. Club (London). Home: 8904 Narem Pl Annandale VA 22003

ECHEVARRIA, ALVARADO ANA H., clinical psychologist, criminologist; b. Ponce, P.R.; s. Fauto Echevarria and Luisa Alvarado. BA in Social Sci., Cath. U., Ponce, 1965; MA in Criminal Justice summa cum laude, Interamerican U., Santurce, P.R., 1981; MS in Clin. Psychology magna cum laude, Caribbean Ctr., Santurce, 1988; PhD candidate, Caribbean Ctr., 1989. Tchr. Ednl. Dept., Juana Diaz, P.R., 1966; with social svc. techniques Dept. Social Svc., San Juan, P.R., 1967-81; exec. functionary Dept. Social Svc., 1981-82, exec. dir., 1982-85; prof. psychology Internamerican U., San Juan, 1986—; clin. psychologist Ednl. Therapy Ctr., Ednl. Svc. Inst., Carolina-Bayamón, P.R., 1985—; dir. Psychol. and Ednl. Met. Ctr., Inc., 1986—; clin. psychologist Ednl. and Psychol. Svcs., Carolina-Bayamón, 1986; pres. Psychol. and Ednl. Therapy Ctr., 1990—; cons. svcs. lectr. Learning Disabilities Children. Mem. Am. Assn. Counseling Devel., Internat. Soc. Community Devel., Learning Disabilities and Handicapped Children Orgn., Mental Health Assn.

ECHOLS, M. EILEEN, judge; b. Oklahoma City, Mar. 16, 1951; d. O.C. Steve and Eileen E. (Carter) Dodson; m. David W. Echols, Aug. 12, 1977; children: Matthew, Jonathan, Meridith. BS, Cen. State U., Edmond, Okla., 1974; MEd, Cen. State U., 1975; JD, Oklahoma City U., 1979. Bar: Okla. 1979, U.S. Dist. Ct. (we. dist.) Okla. Tchr. mentally handicapped students Oklahoma City pub. schs., tchr./coordinator; pvt. practice law Oklahoma City; judge Oklahoma County Spl. Dist. Ct., Oklahoma City, 1989—; mem. Med. Licensure and Supervision Bd., State of Okla., 1994—. Contbr. articles to profl. jours. Recipient Outstanding Family Law Judge award State of Okla., 1991, 93. Mem. Okla. Bar Assn. (past chair family law sect., chairperson jud. com., family rels. sect.), Okla. County Bar Assn.(chairperson family law div., 1990-91), Lions Internat. Home: 8501 S Pennsylvania Ave Oklahoma City OK 73159-5206

ECHOLS, ROBERT L., federal judge; b. 1941. BA, Rhodes Coll., 1962; JD, U. Tenn., 1964. Law clk. to Hon. Marion S. Boyd U.S. Dist. Ct. (we. dist.) Tenn., Nashville, 1965-66; legis. asst. Congressman Dan Kuykendall, 1967-69; ptnr. Baily, Ewing, Dale & Conner, Nashville, 1969-72, Dearborn & Ewing, Nashville, 1972-92; fed. judge U.S. Dist. Ct. (mid. dist.) Tenn., Nashville, 1992—. With U.S. Army, 1966; col. Tenn. Army NG, 1969—. Mem. ABA, Am. Bar Found., Am. Coll. Mortgage Attys., Fed. Judges Assn., Tenn. State-Fed. Jud. Coun., Am. Judicature Soc. (chair alternate dispute resolution com. U.S. Dist. Ct. (mid. dist.) Tenn.), Tenn. Bar Found., Tenn. Bar Assn., Nashville Bar Assn., Phi Delta Phi. Office: US Dist Ct 801 Broadway Ste A820 Nashville TN 37203-3815

ECK, DAVID WILSON, minister; b. Pitts., Apr. 7, 1962; s. Herbert Walter Eck and Linda Joan (Pitrusu) Butera. BS in Chemistry, U. Pitts., 1984; MDiv, Luth. Theol. Sem., Gettysburg, Pa., 1988. Ordained to ministry Evang. Luth. Ch. in Am., 1988. Assoc. pastor Mt. Zion Luth. Ch., Conover, N.C., 1988-93; pastor Abiding Savior Luth. Ch., Asheville, N.C., 1993—; mem. young adult com. N.C. Synod, Salisbury, 1989-90, mem. worship and mus. com. N.c. Synod, 1993-95, mem. AIDS Taskforce N.C. Synod, 1992, N.C. Synod Coun., 1995—; bd. dirs. Coop Christian Ministry, Hickory, N.C., 1989; owner Twelvestring Pub., 1995—. Mem. editl. adv. bd. Soli Deo Gloria, 1990—, also contbr. articles, poetry and music; singer, songwriter, music pub. Recipient cert. of achievement Billboard Songwriting Contest, 1990. Democrat. Home: 110 Coleman Ave Asheville NC 28801-1304 Office: Abiding Savior Luth Ch 801 Charlotte Hwy Fairview NC 28730-9782

ECK, KENNETH FRANK, pharmacist; b. Alma, Kans., Feb. 4, 1917; s. Clarence Joseph and Rosa Barbara (Noller) E.; m. Ouida Susie Landon, July 2, 1938 (dec. Sept. 1986); children: Alan Grantland, Mark Warren, Dana Landon; m. Lorraine B. Wooster Rubottom, Apr. 14, 1989. BS in Pharmacy summa cum laude, Southwestern Okla. State U., 1950. Ptnr., mgr. Taylor Drug Store, Healdton, Okla., 1950-51, Taylor-Eck Drug Store, Healdton, 1951-59, Johnson-Eck Drug Store, Healdton, 1959-72; pres. Eck Drug Co., Inc., Healdton, 1972-87, cons., relief pharmacist, 1987—; cons., relief pharmacist Eck Drug and Gift, Waurika, Okla., 1987—; affiliate instr. pharmacy Southwestern Okla. State U., Weatherford, 1970-87, mem. dean's adv. com. Sch. of Pharmacy, early 1980's; bd. dirs. med. adv. bd. Dept. Human Svcs. Okla., Oklahoma City, 1990-91. Past mem. governing bd. Healdton Mcpl. Hosp.; mem. Okla. Profl. Responsibilty Tribunal of Okla. Bar Assn., 1983-88, vice chief master, 1988; past mem. bd. dirs. Carter County chpt. ARC, Ardmore, Okla.; bd. dirs. Healdton Oil Mus., 1993—; pres. bd. dirs. Okla. Pharmacy Heritage Found., 1994-95; mem. fin. com. Healdton br. Chickasaw Libr., 1993; bd. dirs. Healdton Econ. Devel., 1993-95; deacon Ch. of Christ, 1945—. With USN, 1942-45, PTO. Recipient Achievement award Merck Sharp & Dohme, 1991, Bowl of Hygeia, 1985, outstanding svc. award Okla. Profl. Responsibility Tribunal of Okla. State Bar Assn., citation State of Okla. Ho. of Reps., 1996; named to Hall of Fame, Okla. Pharmacy Heritage Found., 1996. Mem. VFW (post comdr. Healdton 1974-78), Okla. Pharm. Assn. (pres. 1990-91, plaque 1991) Healdton C. of C. (bd. dirs. 1975—, pres. 1984-85), So. Okla. Devel. Assn. (coun. area agy. on aging adv. bd. 1987—, 1st v.p. 1994-95, pres. 1995-96), Nat. Assn. Retail Druggists (profl. affairs com. 1990-91), Am. Legion (post comdr. Healdton 1985—), Lions (eye bank bd. 1993-95, coord. campaign first sight 1993-94, pres. Healdton 1994-95). Democrat. Home: 1033 E Texas St Healdton OK 73438-3017

ECK, RONALD WARREN, civil engineer, educator; b. Allentown, Pa., May 11, 1949; s. Warren Edgar and Viola (Ruth) E.; m. Deborah Lynn Gregory, Oct. 14, 1989. BSCE, Clemson (S.C.) U., 1971, PhD, 1975. Registered profl. engr., W.Va. Asst. prof. civil engring. W.Va. U., Morgantown, 1975-80; assoc. prof. civil engring. W.Va. U., 1980-84, prof. civil engring., 1984—, dir. rsch. coll. engring., 1994-96; cons. in field. Contbr. articles to profl. jours. Chmn. City Traffic Commn., Morgantown, 1989—; mem. Region 3, U.S. DOT, Nat. Def. Exec. Res., 1982-94. Recipient Dow Outstanding Young Faculty award Am. Soc. Engring. Edn., 1980, W.Va. U. Found. Outstanding Tchr. award, 1988, others. Mem. NSPE, Am. Soc. Engring. Edn. (v.p., profl. interest coun., 1987-88), ASCE (pres. W.Va. sect. 1980), Inst. Transp. Engrs. (chmn. dept. 2 1987-90), Transp. Rsch. Bd. (chmn. com. on low volume rds. 1990-96), Am. Soc. Safety Engrs. Home: 609 Valley View St Morgantown WV 26505-2412 Office: West Virginia U PO Box 6103 Morgantown WV 26506-6103

ECKART, GABRIELE RUTH, German language educator; b. Falkenstein, Germany, Mar. 23, 1954; came to U.S., 1987; d. Siegfried and Ruth (Reuter) e.; m. Harry Winter, May 23, 1988 (div. 1993). MA, Humboldt U., 1976; PhD, U. Minn., 1993. Freelance writer Berlin, 1976-87; writer-in-residence U. Tex., Austin, 1988; tchg. asst. U. Minn., Mpls., 1988-93; asst. prof. Spring Hill Coll., Mobile, Ala., 1994—. Author: So sehe ick die Sache, 1984, Der gute fremde Blick, 1992, Hitchhiking, 1992, Sprachtraumata in den Texten Wolfgang Hilbigs, 1996. Mem. MLA, Am. Assn. Tchrs. of German,

German Studies Assn. Home: 111 Macy Pl Mobile AL 36604 Office: Spring Hill Coll Dauphin St Mobile AL 36604

ECKBERT, WILLIAM FOX, author, psychiatrist; b. Balt., Jan. 3, 1940; s. William Fox and Sarah Ann (Wilson) E.; m. Angeline Ellen Stadler, June 20, 1964; children: Ashley Ann, John Haden. AB, Davidson Coll., 1960; MD, Emory U., 1965. Diplomate Am. Bd. Psychiatry and Neurology. Pvt. practice psychiatry Winter Pk., Fla., 1971-90, author, 1990—. Author: Victory in Vietnam, 1994. Maj. U.S. Army, 1969-71. Republican. Office: Old Court Press PO Box 1387 Winter Park FL 32790-1387

ECKELSON, ROBERT ALAN, orthodontist; b. Cleve., Feb. 2, 1947; s. Sam Robert and Frances (Kaplan) E.; m. Linda Goldstine, July 23, 1984. DDS, Ohio State U., 1971; postgrad., U. Ill., Chgo., 1971-73. Diplomate Am. Bd. Orthodontists. Pvt. practice Boca Raton, Fla., 1973—; mem. staff Boca Raton Community Hosp., 1978—. Bd. dirs. Boca Forum, Boca Raton, 1988-93, pres., 1992-93. Mem. So. Assn. Orthodontists, Fla. Dental Assn., Boca Raton Roundtable (pres. 1993-95), Rotary (pres. Boca Raton 1996-97). Office: 951 NW 13th St Ste 3B Boca Raton FL 33486-2337

ECKERLIN, RALPH PETER, biology educator; b. N.Y.C., Feb. 10, 1938; s. John George and Anna Maria (Suhr) E.; m. Joyce Mary Koepper, Nov. 29, 1958 (dec. June 1968); children: Laura Sue, Linda Sue; m. Mary Kristina Peay, June 30, 1979. BA in Biol. Scis., Rutgers U., 1960; MS in Zoology, U. Miami, 1962; PhD in Zoology and Parasitology, U. Conn., 1975. Lab. asst. dept. biology Rutgers U., New Brunswick, N.J., 1958-59; lab. technician Microbiology Lab., E.R. Squibb and Sons, New Brunswick, 1959-60; grad. rsch. asst. biology dept. U. Miami, Coral Gables, Fla., 1960-62; rsch. biologist parasitology dept. Lederle Labs. div. Am. Cyanamid Co., Pearl River, N.Y., 1962-66; grad. teaching asst. biol. scis. group U. Conn., Storrs, 1966-67, 69-70; rsch. biology div. marine scis. U. Conn., Noank, 1970; instr. U. Conn., Waterbury, 1970-71; prof. biology No. Va. C.C., Annandale, 1971—; professorial lectr. biology and parasitology George Washington U., Washington, fall 1980—. Author: The Biology Experience, 1978; contbr. articles to sci. jours. Parasitology tng. grantee NIH, Costa Rica, 1961-62; Am. Cynamid Co. ednl. fellow U. Conn., 1967-69. Mem. Am. Soc. Parasitologists, Entomol. Soc. Washington (membership chmn. 1992-93, pres. 1995-96), Helminthological Soc. Washington (pres. 1986, editor Jour. 1989-93), Tropical Medicine Assn. Washington (pres. 1983), Va. Acad. Sci. (treas. 1992-93), Va. Assn. for Biol. Edn. (bd. dirs. 1991-93, pres. 1995), Am. Soc. Tropical Medicine and Hygiene, Assn. for Tropical Biology, Internat. Soc. for Med. and Applied Malacology, Southeastern Soc. Parasitologists, Wildlife Disease Assn. Home: 4955 Roslyn Rd Annandale VA 22003-5126 Office: No Va CC 8333 Little River Tpke Annandale VA 22003-3743

ECKERT, CHARLES ALAN, chemical engineering educator; b. St. Louis, Dec. 13, 1938; s. Clarence Theodore and Mildred Hortense (Potlitzer) E.; divorced; children: Carolyn Helen, Theodore James. S.B., MIT, 1960, S.M., 1961; Ph.D., U. Calif.-Berkeley, 1964. Postdoctoral fellow CNRS, Paris, 1964-65; asst. prof. U. Ill., Urbana, 1965-69, assoc. prof., 1969-73, prof., 1973-89, head dept. chem. engring., 1980-86; J. Erskine Love prof. engring. Ga. Inst. Tech., Atlanta, 1989—, Inst. prof., 1994; cons. numerous cos. Author several books, instructional computer programs. Fellow NATO, 1964, Guggenheim Found., 1971. Mem. NAE, AIChE (Allan Colburn award 1973), Internat. Soc. for Advancement of Supercritical Fluids (v.p.) Am. Chem. Soc. (Ipatieff prize 1977, Murphree award 1995), Am. Soc. Engring. Edn. Home: 1053 St James Crossing Atlanta GA 30319 Office: Ga Inst Tech Sch Chem Engring Atlanta GA 30332-0100

ECKERT, CHARLES ARTHUR, accountant; b. Oakland County, Mich., Oct. 3, 1926; s. Albert August and Margaret Stella (Lockman) E.; m. Wenonah Marie Smith, Nov. 22, 1952 (dec. Jan. 1980); 1 child, Charles Arthur Jr.; m. Bonnie Jean McClanahan Martindale, Apr. 25, 1987; children: Charles C. Martindale, David D. Martindale, George A. Martindale. Car, U. Detroit, 1952; postgrad., U. Mich., Oakland U., Wayne State U., U. Va. CPA, Mich. Acct. Kingsworthy, McGraw & Wright, CPAs, Detroit, 1952-54, Schmultz & Reick, CPAs, Detroit, 1954-64; owner, mgr. Charles A. Eckert, CPA, Grosse Pointe Woods, Mich., 1964—, Zephyrhills, Fla., 1990—; substitute tchr. Grosse Pointe Pub. Schs., 1968-70; officer Cloyd Container Corp., Detroit, 1970, Boxcraft Corp., Detroit, 1970. Treas. PTA, Grosse Pointe Woods, 1967-68, pres., 1968-69. With USN, 1945-46. Mem. AICPA, Mich. Soc. CPA's, Elks. Home and Office: 36813 Hibiscus Ct Zephyrhills FL 33541

ECKHARDT, ROBERT FUESS, safety and environmental director; b. Ft. Worth, Aug. 19, 1949; s. Guss Fuess and Mary Elizabeth (Fatherree) E.; m. Karen Boyce Eckhardt, Jan. 3, 1981. BS, Angelo State U., San Angelo, Tex., 1974, MS, 1975. Cert. safety profl., environ. profl. Sr. environ. engr. Dresser Industries, Houston, 1975-79; environ. cons. Eckhardt Environ. Cons., Austin, Tex., 1980-83; safety and pers. mgr. Justin Industries, Austin, 1983-85; safety and environ. dir. Hydro Conduit Corp., Houston, 1986—. Mem. Am. Soc. Safety Engrs. (officer 1989-94), Am. Concrete Pipe Assn. (mem. safety com.), Tex. Safety Assn. (bd. dirs. 1994—), Beta Beta Beta. Home: 4018 Valley Haven Dr Kingwood TX 77339-1902 Office: Hydro Conduit Corp PO Box 60297 Houston TX 77205-0297

ECKL, WILLIAM WRAY, lawyer; b. Florence, Ala., Dec. 2, 1936; s. Louis Arnold and Patricia Barclift (Dowd) E.; m. Mary Lynn McGough, June 29, 1963; children—Eric Dowd, Lynn Lacey. B.A., U. Notre Dame, 1959, LL.B., U. Va., 1962. Bar: Va. 1962, Ala. 1962, Ga. 1964. Law clk. Supreme Ct. of Ala., 1962; ptnr. Gambrell, Harlan, Russell & Moye, Atlanta, 1965-68, Swift, Currie, McGhee & Hiers, Atlanta, 1968-82, Drew, Eckl & Farnham, Atlanta, 1983—. Served to capt. JAGC, USAR, 1962-65. Mem. Def. Research Inst., State Bar of Ga. Roman Catholic. Clubs: Lawyers of Atlanta, Brookwood Hills. Home: 348 Camden Rd NE Atlanta GA 30309-1513 Office: Drew Eckl & Farnham 880 W Peachtree St PO Box 7600 Atlanta GA 30309

ECKMAN, DAVID WALTER, lawyer; b. Ogden, Utah, Oct. 23, 1942; s. Walter and Ann-Marie Pauline (Nelson) E.; m. Laurie Alden Waters, Aug. 28, 1965; children: Christian Davidson, Catherine Marie. Student, Rice U., 1960-61; B.A. with honors, U. Tex., Austin, 1964, J.D. (Sam D. Hanna scholar), 1967. Bar: Tex. 1967, Calif. 1976, U.S Ct. Appeals (5th cir.) 1983. With Exxon Co., U.S.A. div. Exxon Corp., 1967-78; mem. Prudhoe Bay Law Task Force Exxon Co., U.S.A. div. Exxon Corp., Houston and Los Angeles, 1974-75; counsel Pacific Region Exxon Co., U.S.A. div. Exxon Corp., Los Angeles, 1975-77; counsel hdqrs. Exxon Co., U.S.A. div. Exxon Corp., Houston, 1977-78; gen. counsel Natomas N.Am. Inc., Houston, 1978; v.p.-legal, corp. chief legal counsel Natomas N.Am. Inc., 1978-82; sole practice Houston, 1982—. Vestryman, dir. Christian edn. All Sts. Episcopal Ch., Corpus Christi, 1968-70; leader adult study St. Mark's Episcopal Ch., Houston, 1971-74; v.p. St. Mark's Sch. PTO, 1981-82; vol. Bible Study tchr., one-on-one counseling Tex. Dept. Criminal Justice, Houston, 1983-94; lay reader St. John the Divine Episc. Ch., Houston, 1982—, leader adult study, 1983-86, 94—; mem. St. Patrick's Sch. Bd., Thousand Oaks, Calif., 1976-77; pres. Houston Youth Soccer Assn., 1979-81, bd. dirs., 1979-83; pres. Neartown Soccer Club, 1980-83; v.p. Old Braeswood Civic Assn., 1982-85; bd. dirs. Friends of Pyramid House, Inc., 1985-95. Recipient Am. Jurisprudence award in antitrust law U. Tex., 1967. Mem. ABA, Tex. State Bar, Calif. State Bar, Houston Bar Assn., Full Gospel Bus. Men's Fellowship Internat. (v.p. downtown Houston chpt. 1985-89), Lambda Chi Alpha, Phi Delta Phi. Office: 6800 W Loop S Ste 425 Bellaire TX 77401-4523

ECONOMIDES, CHRISTOPHER GEORGE, pathologist; b. Alexandria, Egypt, Dec. 25, 1940; came to U.S., 1967; s. George and Tina E. MD, Alexandria U., 1966. Diplomate Am. Bd. Anatomic Pathology, Am. Bd. Clin. Pathology, Am. Bd. Cytopathology. Intern Alexandria U. Hosps., 1965-66, Balt. City Hosps., 1967-68; resident in anatomic pathology, then chief resident Jackson Meml. Hosp., U. Miami, Fla., 1968-70, resident in clin. pathology, 1970-71, 73-74, resident in ob-gyn., 1971-72, resident in anatomic pathology, 1972-73; pathologist Hialeah (Fla.) Hosp., 1974, chief dept. pathology, 1975—; officer med. bd. Hialeah Hosp., 1975—, chief of staff, chmn. med. bd., 1980, 81, trustee, 1989—, mem. numerous coms.; med. and surg. clerkships Alexandria U. Hosp., Victoria Hosp., Scotland, Royal Salop Infirmary, England; mem. family planning program Broward County Health Dept., Fla., 1972-77; mem. courtesy staff North Shore Hosp., Miami, 1975, Palmetto Gen. Hosp., Hialeah, 1979-90; clin. asst. prof. pathology U. Miami, 1980-85; med. dir. SmithKline-Beechman Clin. Labs., 1983-92; bd. dirs. Immunopathology Labs., 1987-92, Ambulatory Ctr. of Hialeah, 1987—, Dimension Health-PHO, 1993—. Trustee The Hialeah Found., 1989-91, Dade Community Found., 1992—. Recipient Physician Recognition award AMA, 1971—, St. Marks Cross from His Holiness Patriarch Nicholaus I, 1981. Fellow Am. Soc. Clin. Pathologists, Coll. Am. Pathologists, Internat. Coll. Surgeons; mem. Am. Soc. Cytology, Internat. Acad. Pathology, Internat. Acad. Cytology, Fla. Med. Assn., Fla. Soc. Pathologists, South Fla. Soc. Pathology (pres. 1983, 84), Dade County Med. Assn., N.Y. Acad. Sci., Fisher Island Club (charter). Office: Hialeah Hosp 651 E 25th St Hialeah FL 33013-3814

ECONOMIDES, NICHOLAS GEORGE, plastic surgeon; b. Alexandria, Egypt, July 8, 1949; came to U.S. 1974; s. George P. and Sophia N. (Mikalis) E.; m. Linda M. Economides; children: George, Celia, Constantine. BS, Athens U., Greece, 1970; MD, Athens U., 1973. Resident in gen. surgery U. Tenn., Memphis, 1974-79; resident in plastic surgery U. Tenn., 1979-81; plastic surgeon Plastic Surgery Group, Memphis, 1985-91, Plastic and Reconstrv. Inst. of Memphis, P.C., 1992—, Page Clinic Inc., Memphis, 1981-85; dir. Memphis Pharmacotherapy and Clin. Research Ctr., Memphis, 1986—; chmn. Bapt. Meml. Hosp. dept. plastic surgery, 1985—; designer Med. Engring. Corp., 1985. Recipient spl. dilligence awards, U. Athens, 1970-73. Fellow ACS; mem. AMA, Am. Soc. Plastic and Reconstructive Surgery, So. Med. Assn. Greek Orthodox. Office: Plastics/Reconstrv Inst 80 Humphreys Ctr Ste 300 Memphis TN 38120-2352

EDDINGS, JAMES DEAN, data processing executive; b. Gastonia, N.C., Aug. 2, 1956; s. James Clyde and Dorothy (Rhyne) E.; m. Charlotte Shupe, Nov. 24, 1990; children: Dorothy Caroline, James Barton. BA, U. N.C., 1979. Announcer Sta. WGNC-AM & FM, Gastonia, 1973-76; engr. Sta. WCHL and Village Broadcasting, Chapel Hill, N.C., 1976-79; programmer, analyst Jefferson Data Systems, Charlotte, N.C., 1979-81; data processing mgr. Ithaca Industries, Inc., Gastonia, 1981-92; dir. info. sys. Acme Svcs., Inc., Gastonia, 1992—; ptnr. E & E Properties, Gastonia, 1989—; pres. BEP and Assocs., Inc., Lexington, 1989-93. Composer Musical Flickers, 1985. Pres., bd. dirs. Southwood Arms Homeowner's Assn., Belmont, N.C., 1988—. Recipient Best Dir. of Small Chorus award Region 14, Sweet Adelines, Internat., 1985, 86, 88, Music Man of Decade award Little Theater Gastonia, 1990. Mem. Nat. Space Soc., Planetary Soc., Soc. Preservation and Encouragement Barbershop Quartet Singing in Am. (dir. Greater Gaston chpt. 1991—), U. N.C. Alumni Assn. (life). Home: 629 Torrence Dr Gastonia NC 28054-4032 Office: Acme Svcs Inc 543 Cox Rd Gastonia NC 28054-0628

EDDINS, JAMES WILLIAM, JR., marketing executive; b. Wadesboro, N.C., Dec. 22, 1944; s. James William and Mildred Ruth Eddins; m. Barbara Ann Nelson, Oct. 2, 1965 (div. 1986); 1 child, Christopher; m. Ann Manley McAdams, Sept. 25, 1988; 1 stepchild, Keith. AB, Pfeiffer Coll., 1966; M.Pub. Sch. Adminstrn., Appalachian State U., Boone, N.C., 1968; postgrad., U. N.C., 1969. Prin. Stanly County Bd. Edn., Albemarle, N.C., 1966-70; gen. sales mgr. ITT Continental Baking Co., Tampa, Fla., 1970-75; reg. sales mgr. Sunshine Biscuit Co., Tampa, 1975-81; nat. sales mgr. Beatrice Foods, Bakery div., Augusta, Ga., 1981-83; dir. sales/mktg. Bensons, Inc., Athens, Ga., 1983-86; reg. sales mgr. Sunshine Biscuit Co., Greenville, S.C., 1986-87; dir. sales, nat. accts. Christie-Brown and Co., Burlington, N.C., 1987—; dir., v.p. Atlas Mktg.-Food Broker, Charlotte, N.C., 1996—; cons. in field. Active in past various charitable orgns. Named Oustanding Prin., Stanly County Bd. Edn., 1970. Mem. Biscuit Cracker Distbrs. Assn., Nat. Food Distbrs. Assn. Republican. Methodist. Home: 3230 Ardmore St Burlington NC 27215-8109 Office: Christie-Brown & Co PO Box 994 Burlington NC 27216-0994

EDDOWES, E(LIZABETH) ANNE, early childhood education specialist; b. Sandusky, Ohio, Nov. 23, 1931; d. Carl Emerson and Helen Ruth (Sutter) Evans; m. Edward Everett, June 17, 1956; children: Andrew Wayne, Scott Edward. BS, Ohio State U., Columbus, 1953; MEd, U. Mo., St. Louis, 1969; PhD, Ariz. State U., Tempe, 1977. Tchr. Sandusky (Ohio) Pub. Schs., 1954-56, Alachua County Pub. Schs., Gainesville, Fla., 1957-59; dir. Florissant (Mo.) Coop. Nursery Sch., 1967-70; instr. Florissant Valley Community Coll., Ferguson, Mo., 1970-73; grad. and faculty assoc. Ariz. State U., Tempe, 1974-78, coord. student teaching, 1979-84; child devel. assoc. rep. Coun. for Early Childhood Profl. Recognition, Washington, 1978—; asst. prof. U. Ala., Birmingham, 1985-91, assoc. prof., 1991—; validator Nat. Assn. Edn. Young Children, Washington, 1986—; cons. Southside Bapt. Child Devel. Ctr., Brookwood Forest Child Devel. Ctr., Mountain Brook, 1986-92. Contbr. articles to profl. jours. Pres., v.p. Family Resource Ctr., Tempe, 1977-79, children's ctr. bd. Desert Palm United Ch. of Christ, Tempe, 1978-84. Recipient Outstanding Svc. award Ariz. State U., 1984. Mem. Orgn. Mondiale pour Edn. Prescolaire, Ala. Assn. on Young Children (pres. 1989-90), Ala. Assn. Early Childhood Tchrs., Jefferson County Assn. Young Children, Phi Delta Kappa, Alpha Phi. Office: U Ala Dept Curriculum & Instrn University Sta Birmingham AL 35294

EDDY, ROBERT, English language educator, author; b. Winchester, Mass., Sept. 10, 1948; s. Alanson Gayton and Mary Eve (Ferrara) E.; m. Ann Jang, July 27, 1981; children: Eileen, Serena. BA, Boston U., 1971; MPhil, U. Nottingham, Eng., 1974; PhD, U. Durham, Eng., 1983. English tutor U. Nottingham, 1972-74; instr. English No. essex C.C., Haverhill, Mass., 1974-76; lectr. in extra-mural studies U. Durham, 1976-78; lectr. English Taichung U., Taiwan, China, 1978-81, U. Alexandria, Egypt, 1981-84; asst. prof. English U. Lowell, Mass., 1984-87; asst. prof. rhetoric Boston U., 1987-92; assoc. prof. English Fayetteville (N.C.) State U., 1992—. Author: Reflections on Multiculturalism, 1996, Writing Across Cultures, 1996. Mem. MLA, Soc. for Multiculturalism, Soc. Border Crossings, Rhetoric Soc. Am., Coll. Composition and Comm., Soc. for Values in Higher Edn. Office: Fayetteville State University 1200 Murchison Rd Fayetteville NC 28301

EDE, FRED OKOTCHY, marketing educator; b. Nigeria, May 6, 1949; came to U.S., 1979; s. Philemon Okeke and Mabel Uzo (Okochi) E.; 1 child, Fred Jr. BS in Mktg., U. Nigeria, 1977; MBA, U. Detroit, 1980; PhD, U. S.C., 1985. Asst. lectr. dept. mktg. Inst. Mgmt. and Tech., Enugu, Nigeria, 1978-79; grad. rsch. asst. U. S.C., 1980-85; asst. prof. dept. bus. adminstrn. Allen U., 1982-85; asst. prof. S.C. State U., 1983-85; asst. prof. dept. fin. and mktg. Norfolk State U., 1985—; chmn. bus. fin. and investment session 28th Internat. Atlantic Econ. Conf., Montreal, 1989, chmn. mktg. session, 1989; reviewer mktg. communications track Acad. Bus. Adminstrn. Conf., 1991—. Contbr. articles to profl. jours. Fellow Acad. Mktg. Sci.; mem. Am. Mktg. Assn., Nigerian Inst. Mktg., Alpha Mu Alpha. Home: 3936 Landvale Rd Virginia Beach VA 23456-1738

EDE, JOYCE KINLAW, counselor, marketing executive; b. Lumberton, N.C., Aug. 9, 1936; d. Neil Archibald and Myrtle Carolyn (Kinlaw) Kinlaw; m. William L. Schmid, Sept. 17, 1954 (dec. Nov. 1956); 1 child, Cheryl Ann; m. Archie L. Phillips, Jr., Nov. 11, 1960 (div. July 1973); children: Archie L. III, Michael Bartley, John Wade; m. Kenneth Russell Ede, Dec. 27, 1984. Certs. Lake Sumter Community Coll., 1976, 77, 79, Volusia Community Coll., 1977, Ocala Jr. Coll., 1979, Univ. Central, Orlando, Fla., 1980, Triton Coll., 1981. Counselor, social worker Epilepsy Assn. Cen. Fla.-Lake County, 1973-76; social worker Lake Sumter Community Mental Health, Med. Social Svcs., Leesburg, Fla., 1976-79; counselor, social worker Epilepsy Assn. Cen. Fla.-Lake County, 1979-81; mktg. coord. Friendship Village, Schaumburg, Ill., 1981-84; retirement counselor Health Care Assocs., Winter Haven, Fla., 1984-85; in mktg. Cambridge Park Manor, Wheaton, Ill., 1985-88; dir. women and children Pacific Garden Mission, Chgo., 1990-92; pres. Lake County Svcs. Coun., Leesburg, 1978-79; del. central Fla. Nat. Conf. on Epilepsy, Washington, 1975; mem. State Conf. on Epilepsy, Tampa, Fla., 1977-81; dir. Lake County, Epilepsy Job Tng., Tavares, Fla., 1979-81; mem., advocate Lake/Sumter County Geriatric Program, 1979; chairperson Epilepsy Bd. Fla., Tavares, 1974-75. Contbr. articles on epilepsy to profl. jours. Mem. Lake County PTA, Leesburg, 1970-76; mem. Parents Adv. Coun., Lake County, Leesburg, 1977-80; mem. Parents Coun., Dixie Youth Baseball League, Fruitland Park, Fla., 1980. Recipient Certs. Epilepsy Assn. Central Fla., Orlando, 1980, Kiwanis Clubs, Leesburg and Mt. Dora, Fla., 1974, Rotary Clubs, Leesburg, Mt. Dora, Groveland, Fla., 1974, Lions Clubs, Leesburg, Mt. Dora, Tavares, 1974-75. Mem. NAFE, Am. Bus. Women's Assn. (hosp. chairperson 1979-80), Concerned Women for Am. Avocations: reading, sports, art, music, cooking, crafts, visiting library, playing piano. Home: 604 Orange St Fruitland Park FL 34731

EDEKI, TIMI IMOAFIJE, medical educator; b. Edo, Nigeria, Mar. 28, 1960; came to the U.S., 1989; s. Imevbore and Femi (Koyenikan) E. MD, U. Lagos, Nigeria, 1982; PhD in Pharmacology, U. London, Eng., 1989. Diplomate Am. Bd. Clin. Pharmacology. Intern U. Lagos (Nigeria) Teaching Hosp., 1982, U. Benin (Nigeria) Teaching Hosp., 1982-83; nat. youth svc. corp. mem. U. Lagos, Nigeria, 1983-84; rsch. fellow II, lectr. U. Lagos, 1984-85; exch. scientist U. Bonn (Germany) Teaching Hosp., 1985-86; commonwealth scholar U. London, Eng., 1986-89; rsch. fellow Vanderbilt U., Nashville, 1989-91; asst. prof. Meharry Med. Coll., Nashville, 1991—, dir. clin. pharmacology tng. program, dept. pharmacology, 1991—. Bd. dirs. Clergy and Laity Concerned, Nashville, 1993—. Recipient Exch. fellow award Deutsche Akademische Auslandaustauch Dienst, 1985, Commonwealth scholar Assn. Commonwealth U., 1985, Devel. grante clin. pharmacol. units Pharmacol. Mfrs. Assn., 1992. Fellow Am. Coll. Clin. Pharmacology; mem. AAAS, Am. Soc. for Clin. Pharmacology, Am. Fedn. Clin. Rsch. Office: Pharmacology Med Coll 1005 D B Todd Blvd Nashville TN 37208

EDELSTEIN, PAUL RAY, artist, art dealer; b. Marion, Ky., Nov. 21, 1955; s. Samuel Bernard and Eline (Lefkowitz) E.; 1 child, Polly Rose. BA in Russian Lang., U. Memphis; BFA, Cranbrook Acad. Artist Memphis, Tenn., 1970—; art gallery dir. Paul Edelstein Gallery, Memphis, 1989—; art agt. Edelstein/Dattel Art Investments, Memphis, 1985-89; sustainer Memphis Brooks Mus., 1980—, Dixon Gallery and Gardens, Memphis, 1981—, Mcpl. Art Gallery, Jackson, Miss., 1985-90; friend Art Today, Memphis, 1985—. Exhibited in group shows at Memphis Internat. Airport, 1996, Madison Ave. Gallery, Memphis, 1996; contbr. articles to profl. jours. Art donor LeBonheur Hosp., Memphis, 1980-87, Memphis Brooks Mus. Gala, 1986-90; counselor Suicide and Crisis Intervention, Memphis, 1974-81, Rape Crisis Ctr., Memphis, 1974-81. Recipient Hon. Mention award Mid South Fair, Memphis, 1977, Sta. WKND, PBS, Memphis Orpheum Theatre, award Meridian Mus. of Art, Miss., 1979. Mem. Russian Honor Soc. (cert. Merit 1980). Democrat. Jewish. Home: 519 N Highland St Memphis TN 38122-4521 Office: Paul Edelstein Gallery 519 N Highland St Memphis TN 38122-4521

EDEN, NATHAN E., lawyer; b. Key West, Fla., Mar. 24, 1944; s. Delmar M. and Lois (Archer) E.; m. Cindy Pike, Jan. 4, 1964 (div. Mar. 1984); 1 child, Jennifer S. BA, U. Fla., 1966; JD magna cum laude, Stetson U., 1969. Bar: Fla. 1969, U.S. Dist. Ct. (so. and mid. dists.) Fla. 1969, U.S. Ct. Appeals (5th cir.) 1969, U.S. Ct. Appeals (11th cir.) 1982. Assoc. Nelson, Stinnett, Surfus, et al, Sarasota, Fla., 1969; ptnr. Feldman & Eden & predecessors, Key West, 1970-84; sole practice Key West, 1984—; of counsel Lazzara and Paul, P.A., Tampa, 1982—; bd. atty. Utility Bd. of Key West, 1974—; asst. pub. defender State of Fla., Key West, 1970, county solicitor State of Fla., Key West, 1970-72; chief asst. state atty State of Fla., Key West, 1972-74; U.S. magistrate, U.S. Dist. Ct. (so. dist.) Fla., 1974-78. Mem. jud. nominating com. 16th Jud. Cir. State of Fla., 1995. Mem. Acad. Trial Lawyers, Fla. Acad. Trial Lawyers, Nat. Assn. Criminal Def. Lawyers, Fla. Bar Assn. (bd. govs. 1976-80), North Am. Hunt Club, NRA. Democrat. Office: 417 Eaton St Key West FL 33040-6511 also: Lazzara and Paul PA Ste 2001 606 Madison St Tampa FL 33602-4017

EDEN, NOBLE KEITH, career officer; b. Bryan, Tex., July 15, 1956; s. Noble Wilmer Jr. and Faye (Franklin) E.; m. Pamela Elizabeth Bordelon, Aug. 5, 1978; children: Brandyn Morgan, Jonathan Noble. BS in Bus. Adminstrn., La. State U., 1978; MBA, Webster U., 1987. Commd. 2d lt. USAF, 1978, advanced through grades to maj., 1990; missile launch officer Strategic Missile Wing, Little Rock, Ark., 1979-83; sr. instr. Vandenberg AFB, Calif., 1983-85; budget officer Air Refueling Wing, Wichita, Kans., 1985-87; controller staff officer Air Refueling Wing, Warner Robins, Ga., 1987-89; controller Air Base Group, Izmir, Turkey, 1989-91; chief policies and procedures Air Force Special Operations, Ft Walton Beach, Fla., 1991-95; chief oper. and maintenance U.S. Ctrl. Command, Tampa, Fla., 1995—. Mem. Am. Soc. Mil. Comptrollers. Home: 2406 Kenwick Dr Valrico FL 33594

EDGAR, R(OBERT) ALLAN, federal judge; b. Munising, Mich., Oct. 6, 1940; s. Robert Richard and Jean Lillian (Hansen) E.; m. Frances Gail Martin, Mar. 30, 1968; children: Amy Elizabeth, Laura Anne. BA, Davidson Coll., 1962; LLB, Duke U., 1965. Bar: Tenn. 1965. From assoc. to ptnr. Miller & Martin, Chattanooga, 1967-85; judge U.S. Dist. Ct. (ea. dist.) Tenn., Chattanooga, 1985—. Mem. Tenn. Ho. of Reps., Nashville, 1970-72, Tenn. Wildlife Resources Commn., Nashville, 1979-85. Served to capt. U.S. Army, 1966-67, Vietnam. Decorated Bronze Star, 1967. Mem. Fed. Bar Assn., Chattanooga Bar Assn. Episcopalian. Office: US Dist Ct PO Box 1748 Chattanooga TN 37401-1748

EDGE, DONALD RICHARD, architect, planner; b. Detroit, Jan. 25, 1927; s. Ernest R. and Grace Louise (Beymer) E.; m. Alice Nan Divine, June 2, 1956; children: Barbara Carol, Karl Richard, Nancy Lynn. BArch, U. Mich., 1951. Registered arch., Fla.; cert. Nat. Coun. Archtl. Registration Bds. Assoc. King & Edge, Archs., West Palm Beach, Fla., 1956-58; ptnr. Plockelman, Powell & Edge, Palm Beach, Fla., 1958-60, Maass, Edge & Willson, Palm Beach, 1964-66; owner, prin. Donald R. Edge, Arch., Palm Beach, 1960-64; pres. Powell & Edge, Palm Beach, 1966-76, Edge Group, P.A., West Palm Beach, 1976—; mem. Joint Commn. on Accreditation Healthcare Orgns. and Health Care Safety, Chgo., 1979-86. With USN, 1945-46. Mem. AIA (com. chmn. 1973-74), Nat. Fire Protection Assn. (life safety code com. 1976-89). Republican. Episcopalian. Office: 444 Bunker Rd West Palm Beach FL 33405-3639

EDGE, JEFF LYNN, physical education educator; b. Potosi, Mo., Oct. 10, 1970; s. James Edward and Shirley Jean (Martin) Hahn; m. Jacqueline Dawn Simpson, June 20, 1992. BS in Edn. cum laude, S.W. Bapt. U., 1994; postgrad., U. Ark., 1994—. Cert. phys. edn., health, social sci. and adapted phys. edn. tchr., Ark. Asst. women's basketball coach S.W. Bapt. U., Boliver, Mo., 1991-94; phys. edn. tchr. Gene George Elem. Sch., Springdale, Ark., 1994—; basketball camp instr., supr. Camp of Champions, Bolivar, 1992-94; phys. edn. tchr. Bolivar Elem. Sch., summer 1994. Vol. coach, mem. staff Area III Spl. Olympics, N.W. Ark., 1994—; vol. basketball coach Show-Me State Games, Warsaw, Mo., 1991-93, Nat. Nat. Assn. Youth Sports Coaches, Bolivar, 1991-92; youth pastor, dir. Overcoming Christian Ctr., Warsaw, 1990-91. Mem. AAHPERD, Nat. Assn. Sport and Phys. Edn., Assn. for Excellence in Health Edn., Ark. Assn. Health, Phys. Edn., Recreation and Dance, Mo. Assn. Health, Phys. Edn. Recreation and Dance, Women's Basketball Coaches Assn. Republican. Home: 1211 N Leverett Apt # 12 Fayetteville AR 72703

EDGELL, KARIN JANE, reading specialist, special education educator; b. Rockford, Ill., July 17, 1937; d. Donald Rickard and Leona Marquerite (Villard) Williams; m. George Paul Edgell III, May 6, 1960; 1 child, Scott. Student, Rollins Coll., 1955-57; BS, U. Ill., 1960, MEd, 1966; MA, Roosevelt U., 1989. Tchr. Alexandria (Va.) City Pub. Schs., 1963-79; asst. to dir. Reading Ctr. George Washington U., Washington, 1979-80; tchr. Winnetka (Ill.) Pub. Schs., 1982-89, Arlington County (Va.) Pub. Schs., 1989—. Mem. NEA, ASCD, Nat. Coun. Tchrs. Eng., Internat. Reading Assn., Va. Edn. Assn., Va. Reading Assn., Greater Washington Reading Coun., Coun. Exceptional Children, Phi Delta Kappa. Home: 6275 Chaucer View Cir Alexandria VA 22304-3546

EDGELL, STEPHEN EDWARD, psychology educator, statistical consultant; b. Inglewood, Calif., June 20, 1947; s. Stephen F. and Evelyn L. (Humborg) E.; m. Donna M. Grassello, Aug. 17, 1974. AA in Math., El Camino Jr. Coll., Gardena, Calif., 1968; AB in Psychology, Calif. State U., Long Beach, 1970; PhD in Math. Psychology, Ind. U., 1974; MA in Math., U. Louisville, 1987. Tchg. and rsch. asst. Ind. U., Bloomington, 1971-72, rsch. asst., computer sys. programmer, 1972, fellow, 1972-73, assoc. instr., 1973-74; asst. prof. psychology U. Louisville, 1974-80, assoc. prof., 1980-85, prof., 1985—, dir. exptl. psychology program, 1983, 88-91; mgr. software devel. Shelton Metrology Lab., Paducah, Ky., summer 1979; cons. on statis.

analysis and exptl. design, product design, customer profile analysis, discrimination, computer software sys.; presenter in field at confs. and profl. meetings. Contbr. articles to profl. jours. Fellow NIMH, 1970-71. Mem. Soc. for Judgment and Decision Making (sec.-treas. 1986-89), Soc. for Math. Psychology, Am. Statis. Assn., Psychometric Soc., Psychonomic Soc., Sigma Xi. Home: 10604 Grassy Ct Louisville KY 40241-2011 Office: U Louisville Dept Psychology Louisville KY 40292

EDGERTON, RICHARD, restaurant and hotel owner; b. Haverford, Pa., May 2, 1911; s. Charles and Ida (Bonner) E.; m. Marie Lytle Page, Oct. 24, 1936; children: Leila, Margaret, Carol. LLD (hon.), Berry Coll., Mt. Berry, Ga. Pres./owner Lakeside Inn Properties, Inc., Mt. Dora, Fla., 1935-80; pres. emeritus Twoton Inc.; owner 35 Burger King restaurants, Pa., 1967—; gen. mgr., pres. Buck Hill Falls (Pa.) Co., 1961-65; pres., CEO Eustis Sand Co., Mt. Dora, Fla., 1961—; founding dir. Fla. Service Corp., Tampa; v.p., dir. 1st Nat. Bank, Mt. Dora. Mem. Gov.'s Little Cabinet, Fla. Hotel & Restaurant Commmr., 1955-61. Trustee emeritus Berry Coll.; bd. dirs. Mt. Dora Cmty. Trust Fund; past. mem. Lake County Fla. Indsl. Devel. Commn.; trutee Lake Sumter Mental Health Ctr. Found.; trustee emeritus Lake Sumter C.C. Served to lt. USNR, 1944-46; ETO. Named to Mid-Fla. Bus. Hall of Fame, 1994. Mem. Am. (dir.), Fla. (hon., past pres.) hotel and motel assns., N.H. Hotel Assn. (past pres.), Newcomen Soc., Welcome Soc., Pa. Soc. Clubs: Mt. Dora Yacht, Mt. Dora Golf. Lodge: Mt. Dora Kiwanis (past pres.). Home: PO Box 175 Mount Dora FL 32757 Office: 234 W 3rd Ave Mount Dora FL 32757-5562

EDIC-CRAWFORD, DARLENE MARIE, AIDS nurse; b. Las Vegas, Aug. 18, 1967; d. Robert Franklin and Belinda Lee (Brunning) E.; m. Robin Patrick Crawford, Dec. 1, 1990. BSN, U. Fla., 1990; MSN, U. Miami, 1996. Clin. nurse II in-patient AIDS unit Jackson Meml. Hosp., Miami, 1990-92; unit mgr. sub-acute AIDS unit Human Resources Health Ctr., Miami, 1992-95; adminstr. Jackson Meml. Hosp., Miami, 1995—. Mem. ANA (congl. dist. coord. 1991—), Fla. Nurses Assn. (state bd. dirs. 1995—), trustee PAC 1989—, pres. dist. 1993-96, newsletter editor 1991-96), Nat. League for Nursing, Fla. League for Nursing, Assn. Nurses in AIDS Care (nat. bylaws com. 1993—, treas. Miami chpt. 1993-94, pres. Miami chpt. 1995—). Republican. Home: 3057 E Rd Loxahatchee FL 33470 Office: Jackson Meml Hosp West Wing 105 1611 NW 12th Ave Miami FL 33136-1005

EDLIN, JOHN CHARLES, pediatrician; b. Wilmington, Del., June 16, 1943; s. Frank Edward and Eleanor Laura (Frederick) E.; m. Mailand Lorenda Stevens, Aug. 23, 1969; children: Mark Steven, Scott Charles, Matthew Shawn. BS in Psychology, Duke U., 1965; MD, U. Tenn., 1968. Diplomate Am. Bd. Pediatrics; lic. physician, Tex. Asst. prof., dir. divsn. adolescent medicine U. Tex. Southwestern Med. Sch., Dallas, 1973-81, clin. asst. prof. dept. pediatrics, 1981—; pvt. practice, pres. Adolescent Health Assocs., P.A., Dallas, 1981—; mem. admissions com. Southwestern Med. Sch., Dallas, 1978-93; med. dir. Bridgeway Day Hosp., Dallas, 1988-91; med. cons. North Tex. Job Corps, McKinney, 1991—. Contbr. articles to profl. jours. Elder Canyon Creek Presbyn. Ch., Richardson, 1994—. Recipient Region 8, Adolescent Health Tng. Project grant Dept. HEW, 1976-81. Fellow Soc. Adolescent Medicine (exec. coun. 1978-81), Am. Acad. Pediats.; mem. Tex. Pediat. Soc., Dallas County Med. Soc., Greater Dallas Pediat. Soc., Tex. Med. Assn. Home: 6702 Robin Willow Ct Dallas TX 75248 Office: Adolescent Health Associates 12800 Hillcrest #216 Dallas TX 75230

EDLOE, LEONARD LEVI, pharmacist; b. Richmond, Va., July 10, 1947; s. Leonard Lacy and Lucille (Harris) E.; m. Serita V. Hamilton, Jan. 16, 1988; 1 child, Leonard Lenisse. BS in Pharmacy, Howard U., 1970. Ptnr. Harrington's Pharmacy, Richmond, Va., 1970-72; pres. Leonard L. Edloe Corp., Richmond, 1973—; chmn. bd., chief exec. officer Pharmaceutical Assocs., Inc., Richmond, 1985—. Bd. dirs. Richmond Renaissance, Richmond Conv. and Visitors Bur., chmn. bd., 1990-91; chmn. bd. dirs. Alcohol and Drug Abuse Prevention and Tng. Services; pres. Churchill Model Cities, 1973, Richmond Urban League, 1975-78. Named one of Outstanding Young Men Am. U.S. Jaycees, 1983, Practitioner of Yr. Assn. Black Hosps., 1984, Alumnus of Yr. Howard U. Coll. Pharmacy, 1985, Pharmacist of Yr. Old Dominion Pharmaceutical Assn., 1989. Mem. Am. Pharm. Assn. (trustee), Nat. Pharm. Assn., Am. Assn. Colls. Pharmacy, Va. Pharm. Assn. (Cert. Merit 19820, Richmond Pharm. Assn., Met. Richmond C. of C. (bd. dirs.), Retail Merchants Assn. Great Richmond (bd. dirs., Disting. Retailer of Yr. 1993). Baptist. Home: 6523 Foxbernie Dr Mechanicsville VA 23111-5646 Office: 1124 N 25th St Richmond VA 23223-5256

EDMARK, DAVID STANLEY, communications director; b. Oklahoma City, Aug. 2, 1951; s. Carl Bernard and Dorothy (Stacy) E. BJ, U. Mo., 1973; MA, U. Ark., 1993. Reporter Springdale (Ark.) News, 1974-78, State Jour.-Register, Springfield, Ill., 1978-79, Ark. Gazette, Little Rock, 1979-81; asst. dir. info. U. Ark., Fayetteville, 1981-84; city editor The Morning News, Springdale, Ark., 1984-95; comm. dir. Food Safety Consortium, U. Ark., 1995—. Mem. Coun. for Advancement and Support of Edn., 1981-84; bd. dirs. Fayetteville Open Channel TV, 1986-90, pres. bd., 1988. Named Ark. Journalist of Yr., Council for Advancement and Support of Edn., 1989. Mem. Sigma Delta Chi Soc. Profl. Journalists (pres. Ozarks chpt. 1977. 82), Agrl. Communicators in Edn. Presbyterian. Home: 220 E Cleburn St Fayetteville AR 72701-2109 Office: U Ark 110 Agriculture Bldg Fayetteville AR 72701

EDMISTON, MARILYN, clinical psychologist; b. Lewiston, Maine, Dec. 9, 1934; d. Lewis Walter and Anne Mary (Nezol) Burgess; m. John Laing Edmiston (div. May 1969); children: John Laing, Eric James. BA, Fla. Atlantic U., 1967, MA, 1969; PhD, U. Ga., 1973. Lic. ind. practice psychologist, Calif., Fla. Staff psychologist children and adolescent unit Cen. Ga. Regional Hosp., Milledgeville, 1973-74, chief psychologist, 1974-75; clin. psychologist South Fla. State Hosp., Pembroke Pines, 1976-77; state psychol. cons. Office Vocat. Rehab., Fla. Dept. Health and Rehab. Svcs., Tallahassee, 1977-83; sr. psychologist forensic svcs. Fla. State Hosp., Chattahoochee, 1983-96, pres.-elect, pres. profl. clin. staff, 1990-94; pvt. practice Tallahassee, 1996—; expert witness Fla. cts., 1983—. Mem. APA, Am. Bd. Forensic Examiners (diplomate), Nat. Register Health Svc. Providers in Psychology, World Fedn. for Mental Health, Internat. Coun. Psychologists. Democrat. Home and Office: 2161 Shangri La Ln Tallahassee FL 32303-2360

EDMISTON, WILLIAM F., foreign language educator; b. Lock Haven, Pa., Aug. 30, 1948; s. Fredrick K. and Bernice C. (Kester) E. BA in French, Pa. State U., 1970; MA in French Lit., Ind. U., 1972, PhD in French Lit., 1978. Assoc. instr. Ind. U., Bloomington, 1970-74, 76-77, Univ. fellow, 1975-76; vis. asst. prof. U. S.C., Columbia, 1978-79, asst. prof., 1979-85, assoc. prof., 1985-92, prof., 1992—, chair dept. French and classics, 1994—; instr. English Lycée Henri Moissan, Meaux, France, 1974-75; referee tenure and promotion U. N.Mex., 1987, Wake Forest U., 1992, U. Del., 1993; presenter numerous confs., seminars. Author: Diderot and the Family: A Conflict of Nature and Law, 1985, Hindsight and Insight: Focalization in Four Eighteenth-Century French Novels, 1991, (with Annie Duménil) La France contemporaine, 1993; referee manuscripts Univ. N.C. Studies Romance Langs. and Lits., 1985, Diderot Studies, 1985—, Eighteenth-Century Life, 1990, Eighteenth-Century Fiction, 1991, South Atlantic Review, 1991—, Studies in Eighteenth-Century Culture, 1991—, Can. Review Comparative Lit., 1994; contbr. articles, reviews to profl. jours. Recipient Excellence in Teaching award Mortar Bd., 1991; grantee U.S. Dept. Edn., 1984, Carolina Venture Fund, 1985, 90, U. S.C., 1986, S.C. Dept. Edn., 1987, 91, Folger Inst., 1991. Mem. MLA (bibliographer MLA Internat. Bibliography 1978-90), Am. Soc. Eighteenth-Century Studies, Am. Assn. Tchrs. French, South Atlantic Modern Lang. Assn. (sec. French II sect. 1982-83, chair 1983-84), Philol. Assn. Carolinas (manuscript referee 1983-86, chair sect. narratol. approaches to French lit. 1984, sec.-treas. 1984-86), Société Diderot. Office: U SC Dept French and Classics Columbia SC 29208

EDMONDS, GRAYDON PRESTON, mathematics educator; b. Houston, July 18, 1949; s. Mildred Dee (Land) E. AA, Tyler Jr. Coll., 1969; BS, Tex. A&M, 1971; MEd, SFA, 1988. Engr. Dresser Atlas, Houston, 1972-84; tchr. Grand Saline (Tex.) Ind. Sch. Dist., 1984—. Mem. Tex. Math. Tchrs., Tex. Counseling Assn., Tex. Profl. Educators, Former Student Assn. Tex. A&M. Baptist. Home: 2015 Belmont Dr Tyler TX 75701-4328

EDMONDS, MAX EARL, secondary education educator; b. Marshall, N.C., Jan. 6, 1943; s. Ernest Earl and Bessie Bernece (Sprinkle) E.; m. Wanda Ruth Baldwin, Apr. 16, 1967; children: Rebecca, David. Welding diploma, Asheville Bus. Tech. Coll., 1962. Cert. tchr. N.C. Welding tchr. Buncombe County Pub. Schs., Asheville, N.C., 1988—; apprentice pipe welder Local Union 487, Asheville, 1961-66; journeyman pipe fitter Plumbers and Pipefitters, Asheville, 1966-85. With U.S. Army, 1963-65. Named Welding Instr. of Yr. State Tchrs. Assn., 1995, 96. Fellow Am. Welding Soc., N.C. Vocat. Assn. Baptist. Home: 701 White Oak Rd Mars Hills NC 28754 Office: 175 Bingham Rd Asheville NC 28806

EDMONDS, MICHAEL DARNELL, music educator; b. May 19, 1960; s. William Thomas and Virginia (Haskins) E.; m. Janet Denise Wyche. BS, Norfolk State U., 1987. Minister of music Christian Charities Deliverance, Wakefield, Va., 1980-92; sale specialist B.D. Laderberg and Son, Inc., Suffolk, Va., 1989-91; sales specialist T.J. Maxx, Chesapeake, Va., 1991—; reporter Maxxline for T.J. Maxx, Chesapeake, 1991—; music dir. First Calvary Handbell Choir, Norfolk, Va., 1982-83, Norfolk State U. Gospel Choir, 1984-85, Little Gilfield Bapt. Ch. Gospel Choir, Irov, Va., 1988; music min. Full Gospel Ch. of Deliverance, Norfolk, 1986-87; singer with I. Sherman Greene Chorale, Norfolk, 1984-88, Covenant Presbyn. Choir, 1984-85, 87-88, The Brown Delegation of Ivor, 1987-89; mem. Norfolk State U. Concert Choir and Chamber Emsemble, 1983-87; mus. dir. pageant Shiloh Bapt. Ch., Zuni, 1988; founder, dir. Interdenominational Singers, Norfolk, 1984-85, New Horizon Singers of Ivor, 1987-89; choir, vocal coach, tchr. piano Ctr. State Theatre, Norfolk, 1985-87; performer sixth ann. Am. Negro Spiritual Festival; tchg. asst. Jr. Music Program Norfolk State U., 1983-84; sales specialist So. Food Stores, Windsor, Va., 1988-89; tchr. asst. specialist Southampton Sch. Sys., 1987-89; customer svc. rep. T.J. Maxx, Janaf and Norfolk, Va., 1985-87. Editor Chrisitn Charity Newsletter, Wakefield, 1980-90, composer choral gospel arrangements. Mem. Choir of Joy, Suffolk, Va., 1991; mem. Crusade choir St. Mark Ch. of Deliverance, Portsmouth, Va., 1993, sr. sunday sch. asst. tchr., 1991-92, club staff mem., praise and worship leader. Mem. Music Educators Nat. Conf., Intercollegiate Music Assn. Home: 1038 Cherokee Rd Apt H Portsmouth VA 23701-1858 Office: APAC Telesvcs 11008 Warick Rd Newport News VA 23601

EDMONDS, RICHARD RADCLIFFE, editor, writer, public policy consultant; b. Mpls., Aug. 14, 1947; s. Peter Robert and Elizabeth Knox (Donovan) E.; m. Marianne Fiermark, Dec. 21, 1971; children: Leslie, Jenny. BA in Am. History and Lit. magna cum laude, Harvard U., 1969. Editorial asst. to James Reston Washington Bur. N.Y. Times, 1969-70; editorial writer, asst. city editor, reporter Winston-Salem (N.C.) Jour., 1970-77; editor, reporter Phila. Inquirer, 1977-82; editor Fla. Trend St. Petersburg Times, 1982-85, editor, pub. Fla. Trend, 1985-90, exec. v.p. Fla. Trend, Ga. Trend, Ariz. Trend, 1986-90, exec. v.p. Governing, Congl. Quar., 1990, dir. affiliates, 1990-91, mng. editor Tampa, 1991-93; editor, writer, consultant, 1993—; cons. comm., orgn. Fla. Coun. 100, Tampa, 1993—, Fla. C. of C., Tallahassee, 1993, Leadership Fla., 1993—; editor Fla. Humanities Coun. Forum, Tampa, 1994—; staff dir. Bus./Higher Edn. Partnership, 1995—; co-dir. Gov.'s Commn. on Higher Edn., 1996—. Columnist Fla. affairs Fla. Trend Mag., 1982-90, Media, 1996—. Mem. bd. regents Leadership Fla., 1983-93, internat. affairs Coun. Fgn. Rels. Recipient Al Burt award for best writing on growth mgmt. 1000 Friends of Fla., 1990; finalist Pulitzer Prize for Nat. Reporting, 1982; John Knox fellow Essex U., Eng., 1971-72. Democrat. Home and Office: 1344 Pleasant Way S Saint Petersburg FL 33705-6131

EDMONDS, THOMAS LEON, lawyer, management consultant; b. Borger, Tex., May 10, 1932; s. Cline Azel and Flora (Love) E.; m. Virginia Marguerite Leon, June 20, 1960; 1 child, Stephanie Lynn. BS in Chem. Engring., Tex. Tech. U., 1953, JD, 1973. Bar: Tex. 1974, U.S. Tax Ct. 1975, U.S. Ct. Appeals (5th cir.) 1975, U.S. Dist. Ct. (no. dist.) Tex. 1976, U.S. Supreme Ct. 1996. Registered profl. engr., Tex. Engr. computers-exec. dept. Phillips Petroleum, Bartlesville, Okla., 1953-67; mktg. specialist Control Data, Dallas, 1967-68; exec. v.p. CUI, Austin, Tex., 1968-70; mgmt. cons. Mcauto, St. Louis, 1970-71; sr. ptnr. Edmonds & Assocs., Borger, 1973—; city atty. Borger, Stinnett, Fritch, Tex., 1991—; treas., dir. Ram Biochemicals, Inc.; bd. dirs., pres. council Tex. Tech. U.; bd. dirs. Can. River Mcpl. Water Authority, Hutchinson County Tex. Hist. Commn., chmn. Mem. Tex. Soc. Profl. Engrs. Club: Borger Country. Home: 210 Broadmoor St Borger TX 79007-8210 Office: PO Box 985 Borger TX 79008-0985

EDMONDS, VELMA MCINNIS, nursing educator; b. N.Y.C., Feb. 17, 1940; d. Walter Lee and Eva Doris (Grant) McInnis; children: Stephen Clay, Michelle Louise. Diploma, Charity Hosp. Sch. Nursing, New Orleans, 1961; BSN, Med. Coll. Ga., 1968; MSN, U. Ala., Birmingham, 1980; postgrad. in doctoral nursing sci., La. State U., 1994—. Staff nurse Ochsner Found. Hosp., New Orleans, 1961-63, 1987—, clin. educator, 1987-89; staff nurse Suburban Hosp., Bethesda, Md., 1963-65; asst. DON svc., dir. staff devel. Providence Hosp., Mobile, Ala., 1967-70; staff nurse MICU U. So. Ala. Med. Ctr., Mobile, 1980-82, clin. nurse specialist, nutrition/metabolic support, 1982-84; instr., coord., BSN completion program Northwestern State Univ., Coll. Nursing, Natchitoches, La., 1984-86; head nurse So. Bapt. Hosp., New Orleans, 1986-87; instr. of nursing La. State U.Med. Ctr., New Orleans, 1989-91, asst. prof. nursing, 1991—; clin. coord. Transitional Hosp. Corp., 1994-95; gov.-apptd. mem. La. State Bd. Examiners in Dietetics and Nutrition, 1990—, sec.-treas. State Bd. of Examiners, 1996—. Gov.'s appointee La. State Bd. Examiners in Dietetics and Nutrtion, sec.-treas. Recipient Excellence in Nursing group award Ochsner Fedn. Hosp., New Orleans, 1987, cert. Merit Tuberculosis Assn. Greater New Orleans, 1961. Mem. ANA, Nat. Soc. Nutrition Edn., La. State Nurses' Assn. (dist. 7), Am. Soc. Parenteral and Enteral Nutrition, La. State Soc. Parenteral and Enteral Nutrition (program and edn. coms.), Assn. La. State Soc. Parenteral and Enteral Nutrition, Mobile Area Nonvolitional Nutrition Support Assn. (past pres.), Sigma Theta Tau.

EDMONDSON, DREW, attorney general. Atty. gen. State of Okla., Oklahoma City. Office: Off of Atty Gen 112 State Capitol Bldg Oklahoma City OK 73105*

EDMONDSON, JERRY HOLLIS, clergyman; b. Newellton, La., Sept. 13, 1933; s. Frank and Opal (Colvin) E.; m. Patsy C. Pippen, Dec. 16, 1962; 1 child, Eric F. BS, La. Tech. U., 1955; BDiv, New Orleans Theol. Sem., 1964; ThD, Luther Rice Sem., 1971; DDiv (hons.), United Theol. Sem., 1984. Pastor, missionary La. Bapt. Conv., 1964-66; pastor Mooringsport (La.) Bapt. Ch., 1966-70, Fair Park Bapt. Ch., West Monroe, La., 1970-78; dir. missions La. Bapt. Conv., Monroe, La., 1978—; chmn. bd. Ouachita Pastoral Counseling Orgn., Monroe, 1993-95. Col. USAF, 1955-58, with Res. 1959-85. Mem. Rotary (pres.). Home: 302 Tupawek Dr West Monroe LA 71291 Office: La Bapt Conv 308 Pine St West Monroe LA 71291

EDMONDSON, LINDA LOUISE, optometrist; b. Wyandotte, Mich., Dec. 11, 1947; d. Richard Eugene and Mildred Louise (Horste) Weaver; m. William Edmondson II, June 1, 1969. BA, Ohio Wesleyan U., 1969; AM, Ind. U., 1971; BS, Pa. Coll. Optometry, 1975, OD, 1977. Assoc. instr. Ind. U., Bloomington, 1967-72; editor biol. abstracts Biosis Info. Svcs., Phila., 1972-73; optometrist pvt. practice, Bluefield, W.Va., 1977-84; prof. Northeastern State U. Coll. Optometry, Tahlequah, Okla., 1984—; jour. referee Jour. of Am. Optometric Assn., 1988—, Optometry and Vision Sci., 1990—. Editor: Eye and Vision Conditions in the American Indian, 1990; contbr. articles to profl. jours. Asst. dir. Heart O'The Hills Chpt., Sweet Adelines, Tahlequah, Okla., 1989—. Mem. AAUW, Am. Acad. Optometry, Am. Optometric Assn., Okla. Profl. Country Dance Assn., Cherokee County Soc. for Prevention of Cruelty to Animals, Beta Sigma Kappa. Home: PO Box 871 Tahlequah OK 74465-0871 Office: NSU Coll of Optometry Tahlequah OK 74464

EDMONDSON, MICHAEL HERMAN, secondary school educator; b. Lafayette, Ala., Aug. 9, 1954; s. Herman L. and M. Ruth (Hurley) E. BS in Chemistry, Edn., Columbus (Ga.) Coll., 1978, MS in Gen. Sci., 1986, Specialist in Edn., Sci., 1990. Cert. tchr. sci. edn. T-6, chemistry, tchr. support specialist. Tchr. sci., chemistry, physics William H. Spencer H.S., 1980-94; tchr. phys. sci., chemistry, physics Hardaway H.S., Columbus, Ga., 1994—; lead tchr. sci. tech. Carver High Sch.; lead flight dir. Ga. Space Sci. Ctr.; staff devel. instr. computer courses Muscogee County Sch. Dist., 1987-90; part-time lab. instr. Columbus Coll., summers, 1988, 89, organizer, tchr. summer chemistry program for h.s. students, summer 1989, part-time instr., 1990-93, Ext. in LaGrange, 1994; instr. Columbus Coll. Youth Acad., 1993; instr. KIDS Club, Ga. Inst. Tech., 1993, Workshop for Middle Sch. Tchrs., Auburn U., 1993, 94; project reviewer chemistry and physics edn. NSF, Washington, 1990; head tchr. sci./tech. Magnet Sch. Program, Carver H.S. Planning Team, 1991; advisor sci., math., integrated tech. magnet sch. program Dimon Elem. Sch., 1993; developer chemistry camp ages 11-14 Columbus Coll. Continuing Edn. Ctr., 1994; tchr. rep. Muscogee County Sch. Dist. Co-author: Atomic Structure and the Periodic Table: A Resource Book for Teachers, 1987, Chemistry for the Health Sciences, Part 1: Inorganic chemistry, 1988, Part 2: Organic Chemistry, 1988; contbr. numerous articles to profl. jours.; writer numerous sci. curriculums; contbr. to America Online Edn. Librs., Compuserve's Education+ and Science/Math+ Forums' Librs., FCClient Bull. Bd. Svc.: Education, Debates and Hypercard Librs., 1994; lectr. in field. Vol. Ft Benning Inf. Mus., 1984; reader's adv. coun. Ledger-Enquirer newspapers, 19089, chmn., 1986-89; bd. dirs. Springer Theater Co., 1986-87, 88-90, Springer Children's Theatre, 1986-89, sec., 1987-89, mailing list organizer, 1986-89, nominating com., 1988; mem. Met. Columbus Urban League; participant Alzheimer's Memory Walk, 1994; originator Christmas Stocking and Coloring Book project for Housing Project Day Care Ctr. Children, Easter Egg project; actor Springer Theatre. Recipient cert. of excellence NSF Summer Inst., 1985, cert. of appreciation Nat. Honor Soc. Spencer H.S., 1988, 89, 92, Gov.'s tech. award for Muscogee County, 1988, cert. of recognition Key Club Spencer H.S., 1989, Outstanding Southeastern Educator award Optical Soc. Am., 1989, Presdl. award for excellence in sci. and math. tchr., Ga., 1989, Outstanding Physics Tchr. award Am. Assn. Physics Tchrs., 1990, Swift Textiles Outstanding Educator award, 1990, Tchr. of Yr. award Muscogee County Sch. Dist., 1990, Ga. Secondary Schs., 1989; Tandy Tech. scholar, 1990; grantee NSF, Muscogee County Sch. Dist.; sci.-math. fellow Coun. for Basic Edn., 1995. Mem. Nat. Sci. Tchrs. Assn., Ga. Sci. Tchrs. Assn. (Dist. VI Sci. Tchr. Yr. 1989, Ga. Secondary Schs. Sci. Tchr. of Yr. 1989), Am. Chem. Soc., Valley Area Sci. Tchrs. (v.p. 1989, Valley Area Sci. Tchrs. pres. 1993-94), Optical Soc. Am., Assn. Presdl. Awardees for Excellence in Sci. Teaching, Math. Assn. Am., Soc. Indsl. and Applied Math., ASCD, Nat. Sci. Tchrs. Assn., Phi Delta Kappa (Secondary Schs. Tchr. of Yr. 1993), Kappa Delta Pi. Home: 4913 River Rd Columbus GA 31904-5836 Office: Coca-Cola Space Sci Ctr 701 Front Ave Columbus GA 31901

EDMONDSON, W. A. DREW, state attorney general; b. Washington, Oct. 12, 1946; m. Linda Larason; children: Mary Elizabeth, Robert Andrew. BA in Speech Edn., Northeastern State U., Tahlequah, Okla., 1968; JD, U. Tulsa, 1978. Mem. Okla. Legislature, 1974-76; intern Office Dist. Atty., Muskogee, Okla., 1978—, asst. dist. atty., 1979, chief prosecutor, 1982—, dist. attorney, 1982-92; pvt. practice atty. Muskogee, 1979-82, Edmondson & Green, 1992-94; atty. gen. State of Okla., 1994—. With U.S. Navy, 1968-72. Named Outstanding Dist. Atty., State of Okla., 1985. Mem. Okla. Bar Assn. (bd. govs. 1982—), Okla. Dist. Attys. Assn. (pres. 1983—), Assn. Govt. Attys. Engaged in Capital Litigation. Office: Office Atty Gen 2300 N Lincoln Blvd Rm 112 Oklahoma City OK 73105-4802

EDMONSON, THOMAS L(OFTON), JR., city-county health district administrator; b. Tyler, Tex., Nov. 1, 1934; s. Thomas Lofton Sr. and Catherine Elizabeth (Kennedy) E.; m. Billie Yvonne Emery, June 14, 1963; 1 child, Lori Lynn. Student, West Tex. State U., 1954; BBA, Midwestern U., 1961; postgrad., Tex. Tech U., 1967, Midwestern State U., 1969, 74, 75. Sanitarian I City of Wichita Falls (Tex.) Health Dept., 1963-64; sanitarian I and III, chief and sanitarian V Wichita Falls-Wichita County Health Dept., 1964-85, dist. mgr., 1985—, dir. of health, 1993—; pres. Tex. Mosquito Control Assn., 1979-80; mem. coun. pub. health cons. NSF, 1995—; mem. cmty. adv. com. Wichita Falls Rehab. Hosp., 1996—. Author, editor: We're the Talk of the Town, 1983, TAS/TEHA's First Thirty Years, 1986. Loaned exec. United Way, 1988-89; life mem. Tex. Health Found., 1993—; bd. dirs. Pub. Health Mus. Tex., 1995—; pres. Wichita Falls Fed. Credit Union, 1992-95, Wichita Falls Crime Stoppers, Inc., 1992; chmn. Wichita Falls chpt. Rocky Mountain Elk Found., 1994; grad. Citizen Police Acad., 1995. Recipient Disting. Vol. Service award Tex. Gov. Mark White, 1984. Fellow Tex. Pub. Health Assn. (hon. life mem., chmn. sanitarian sect. 1982-83); mem. Tex. Assn. Mcpl. Health Ofcls. (sec.-treas. 1986-88, pres. 1989-90), Nat. Environ Health Assn (regional v.p. 1982-87), Tex. Environ. Health Assn. (pres. 1984-85, exec. sec. 1987-90, 93—, I.E. Scott award 1987), Am. Pub. Health Assn. (environ. health com.), Buckaroo Club, Leadership Wichita Falls. Home: 4207 Seymour Rd Wichita Falls TX 76309-3517 Office: Wichita Falls-Wichita County Health Dist 1700 3rd St Wichita Falls TX 76301-2113

EDSON, HERBERT ROBBINS, foundation and hospital executive; b. Upper Darby, Pa., Dec. 26, 1931; s. Merritt Austin and Ethel Winifred (Robbins) E.; m. Constance Anne Lowell, May 20, 1961 (div. Nov. 8, 1967); m. Rose Anne McGowan, July 25, 1970; children: Patricia Anne, David William, Merritt Austin III, Herbert Robbins Jr. BA, Tufts U., 1955; MBA, U. Pa., 1972. Commd. 2d lt. USMC, 1955, advanced through grades to major, 1967, adminstr., mgr., supr. various orgns., 1955-72; controller III Marine Amphibious Force and 3d Marine Div. USMC, Camp Butler, Japan, 1972-73; dir. acctg. Marine Corps Supply Activity USMC, Phila., 1973-75; ret. USMC, 1975; cons. acctg. Ardmore, Pa., 1975-77; CFO Mercy Meml. Hosp. Corp., Monroe, Mich., 1977-92, Mercy Meml. Hosp. Found., Monroe, 1986-92, Monroe Health Ventures Inc., 1986-92, Monroe Community Health Svcs., 1989-92, Byerly Hosp., Hartsville, S.C., 1992-95, Byerly Found., Hartsville, S.C., 1995—; assoc. Quorum Health Resources, Inc., Brentwood, Tenn., 1992-95. Co-pres. Custer Elem. Sch. Parent Tchr. Orgn., Monroe, 1985-87; v.p., trustee Christ Evang. Luth. Ch., Monroe, 1981-86; treas., chmn. Taylor Endowment Fund com. St. Paul's Evang. Luth. Ch., Ardmore, Pa., 1974-76, trustee, chmn. property com., 1976. Decorated Purple Heart, Navy Commendation medal, Combat Action ribbon. Mem. Am. Hosp. Assn., Healthcare Fin. Mgmt. Assn., Inst. Mgmt. Accts., Monroe County C. of C. (bd. dirs. 1982-84), NRA (life), U.S. Naval Inst. (life), Marine Corps Assn. (life), 1st Marine Div. Assn. (life), Edson's Raiders Assn. (hon. life 1st Marine Raider Bn.), Ret. Officers Assn. (life), Am. Assn. Ret. Persons, Nat. Geog. Soc., Edson Geneal. Assn., Marines Meml. Club, Hartsville Country Club, Army and Navy Club. Republican. Lutheran. Home: 1121 Pinelake Dr Hartsville SC 29550-7990 Office: Byerly Foundation PO Drawer 1925 Hartsville SC 29551-1925

EDWARD, DAVID ANDREW, environmental engineer; b. Sierra Vista, Ariz., Nov. 24, 1962; s. Edmond Stricklan and Jeanne Clark (Herbert) E.; m. Paula Elizabeth Woods; children: Paul David, Stephen Seth. BS in Petroleum Engring., West Va. U., Morgantown, 1986; MBA, U. Louisville, 1991. Registered profl. engr., Ky. Commd. 2nd. lt. U.S. Army, 1985; advanced through grades to capt., 1992; exec. officer A Co. 3/81st Armor Regiment, Ft. Knox, Ky., 1987-88; asst. adjutant 1st Armor Tng. Brigade, Ft. Knox, Ky., 1988-89; adj. 4/13th Armor Regiment, Ft. Knox, Ky., 1989-90; platoon leader, exec. officer A Troop 5/12 Cavalry Regiment, Ft. Knox, 1990; ops. mgr. Earth Sci. Techs., Inc., Louisville, 1990-92; project engr. Commonwealth Tech., Inc., Lexington, Ky., 1992-93; project mgr., 1993—. Chmn. various coms. Alpha Phi Omega Svc. Fraternity, W.Va. U., Morgantown, 1981-86; post mgr. Army Emergency Relief Fund Drive, Ft. Knox, 1988; Sunday sch. tchr. Beulah Presbyn. Ch., Louisville, 1988, 92; com. mem. Goals for Greater Louisville, 1992; mem. citizens adv. com. Jefferson County (Ky.) Pub. Schs., 1992; mem. Bluegrass Tomorrow Regional Devel. Com., 1992; mem. adv. com. Ohio River Corridor Master Plan, 1994; mem. Jefferson County Comprehensive Land Use Adv. Com., 1994; mem. Ky. Profl. Engrs. Disaster Response Com., 1993, 94. Named Ky. Col., State of Ky., 1989. Mem. ASCE, NSPE, Am. Acad. Environ. Engrs., Soc. Petroleum Engrs., Soc. Am. Mil. Engrs., Hazardous Materials Mgrs. (Ky. chpt.), Nat. Ground Water Assn., Am. Assn. Cost Engrs., Air and Waste Mgmt. Assn., U. Louisville Alumni Assn., Scottish-Am. Mil. Soc., W.Va. U. Alumni Assn., Nat. Eagle Scout Assn., Tau Beta Pi. Home: 10913 Oak Harbor Dr Louisville KY 40299-4254

EDWARDS, BARRY MICHAEL, English language educator; b. Memphis, Oct. 30, 1948; s. Billy Matt and Martiel Evelyn (Austin) e.; m. Jacqueline Sue Caughron, Nov. 7, 1969; children: Emily Katherine, Anna Elizabeth. BA in English, U. of the South, 1972; MA in English, U. Va., 1973; PhD in English, U. Miss., 1989. English tchr. Montgomery Bell Acad., Nashville, 1976-80; pres. Human Potential Inst., Nashville, 1980-81;

ops. dept. head U.S. Navy, Seattle, 1981-85; instr. English U. Miss., 1985-87, coord. univ. writing ctr., 1987-89; asst. prof. English Embry-Riddle Aeronautical U., Daytona Beach, Fla., 1989-91; dir. composition U. West Fla., Pensacola, 1991-92; dir. writing across the curriculum U. West Fla., 1992-94; instr. English Santa Fe C.C., Gainesville, Fla., 1994—. Author: Wordsworth's Preface, 1989; contbr. articles to profl. publs. Mem. MLA, Nat. Coun. Tchrs. of English, Conf. on Coll. Composition & Comm., Fla. Coll. English Assn., Nat. Network of Writing-across-the-curriculum Programs. Republican.

EDWARDS, BLAINE DOUGLASS, lawyer; b. Borger, Tex., Sept. 30, 1961; s. Charles Afton and Harriett (Hauser) E.; m. Jill Summers Hendrickson. Sept. 1, 1984; children: Audrey Summers, Cole Douglass. BBA in Acctg. and Fin., Tex. A&M U., 1984; JD magna cum laude, St. Mary's U., 1990. Bar: Tex. 1990, U.S. Dist. Ct. (so., no., ea. and we. dists.) Tex. 1991, 96, U.S. Ct. Appeals (5th cir.) 1992. Oil and gas/real estate lending officer InterFirst Bank, San Antonio, 1984-87; participating assoc. Fulbright & Jaworski, LLP, Houston, 1990-95, Shook, Hardy & Bacon, LLP, Houston, 1995—. Co-author: Texas Environmental Law Handbook, 1990, 92; editor St. Mary's Law Jour., 1989-90; contbr. articles to profl. jours. Mem. Phi Delta Phi. Office: Shook Hardy & Bacon 600 Travis Ste 2000 Houston TX 77010

EDWARDS, BRENDA FAYE, counselor; b. Hattiesburg, Miss., Apr. 3, 1945; d. Jack Howell and Annie C. (Sullivan) Zeigler; m. James A. Edwards Jr., June 5, 1962. BA, U. So. Miss., 1968; MEd, U. Ga., 1977. Registered catastropic rehab. supplier; lic. profl. counselor; cert. ins. rehab. specialist. Various positions Miss., 1968-70; tchr. Brunswick (Ga.) Coll., 1970-71; tng. coord. Coastal Ga. Regional Devel. Ctr., Brunswick, 1971-72; tchr. Glynn County Bd. Edn., Adult Edn. Ctr., Brunswick, 1972; social work tech. Gateway Ctr. for Human Devel., Brunswick, 1973; coord. consultation edn. and tng. Coastal Area Community Mental Health Ctr., Brunswick, 1979; rehab. counselor Div. Rehab. Svcs., Dept. Human Resources, Brunswick, 1973-78; supr. basic edn. dept. Brunswick Job Corp. Ctr., 1979-80; rehab. specialist Intracorp, Savannah, Ga., 1980-83; counselor, owner Southeastern Rehab. Svcs., St. Simons Island, Ga., 1983—. Pres. Citizens for Humane Animal Treatment, Brunswick, 1987-90, v.p. 1990-91; sec. Glynn County Animal Control Adv. Bd., Brunswick, 1987-88. Mem. ACA, Am. Mental Health Counselors Assn., Nat. Rehab. Assn., Ga. Rehab. Assn., Lic. Profl. Counselors Assn. Ga., Employee Assistance Profls. Assn., Brunswick Golden Isles C. of C. (chmn. drugs don't work com. 1995—), Internat. Coachmen Caravan, South Ga. Puddle Jumpers. Home: 135 Saint Clair Dr Saint Simons GA 31522-1036 Office: Southeastern Rehab Svcs 2483 Demere Rd Ste 103 Saint Simons GA 31522

EDWARDS, BRUCE WALTON, JR., auditor; b. Ft. Lauderdale, Fla., Jan. 10, 1960; s. Bruce Walton and Betty Jean (Shinholster) E.; m. Alice Marie Brown, Nov. 28, 1992; 1 stepchild, Rachel Nicole Cooper. BS in Indsl. Mgmt., Ga. Inst. Tech., 1982. Proprietor, auctioneer Quasar Comics & Collectibles, various locations, 1982—; gen. mgr. Cobb Coin and Stamp, Atlanta, 1982-84, Fantasyland Records, Atlanta, 1984-86; trainer field adminstrn. Providian Corp., Orlando, Fla., 1986-89; staff auditor Providian Corp., Louisville, 1989-92, sr. auditor, 1992—; sr. advisor Overstreet Pubs., Timonium, Md., 1991—; advisor Krause Pubs., Iola, Wis., 1991—. Pub./editor: Incredible Tales of Adventure, 1982-84, The Wooden Nickel, 1974-76. Grad. asst. instr. Jr. Achievement, Jacksonville, Fla., 1976. Fellow Life Mgmt. Inst. (assoc. customer svc.); mem. Am. Assn. Comic Book Collectors (evaluating and grading com. 1993—), Am. Soc. CLUs. Home: PO Box 2227 Louisville KY 40201 Office: Providian Corporation 400 W Market St Louisville KY 40202-3346

EDWARDS, CHARLES ARCHIBALD, lawyer; b. Lumberton, N.C., Sept. 19, 1945; s. Charles Edwin and Elizabeth Gertrude (Gooden) E.; m. Judy Carol Griffin, Aug. 14, 1966; children: Lee McNeill, Caroline Averitt. AB, Davidson Coll., 1967; JD, U. N.C., 1970. Bar: Ga. 1970, U.S. Supreme Ct. 1974, D.C. 1981, N.C. 1987. Assoc. Connerat, Dunn, Hunter, Houlihan, Maclean & Exley, Savannah, Ga., 1970-71, ptnr., 1972-76; ptnr. Constangy, Brooks & Smith, Atlanta, Ga., 1976-82, Greene, Buckley, Derieux & Jones, Atlanta, 1982-86, Graham & James, Raleigh, N.C., 1986-94, Womble Carlyle Sandridge & Rice, PLLC, Raleigh, 1994—. Author: Georgia Employment Law, 1983; contbr. articles to profl. publs. Mem. N.C. Bar Assn., Fed. Bar Assn., Atlanta Bar Assn. (chmn. labor law sect. 1983-84). Republican. Episcopalian. Office: Womble Carlyle Sandridge & Rice PO Box 831 2100 1st Union Capitol Ctr Raleigh NC 27602

EDWARDS, D. M., retail, wholesale distribution and commercial real estate investment executive; b. Tyler, Tex., Apr. 12, 1953; s. Welby Clell and Davida (Mount) E.; m. Susan Alicia Pappas, 1984 (div. 1986). AA cum laude, Tyler Jr. Coll., 1974; BBA, Baylor U., 1976. Corp. coord. Dillard Dept. Stores, Inc., Ft. Worth, 1976-77; exec. v.p. W.C. Supply Co., Tyler, 1977-83; pres., owner Walker Auto Spring, Inc., Shreveport, La., 1978-88, Edwards & Assocs., Inc., 1984-96; v.p. W.C. Square, Inc., 1976-92; chmn. bd. dirs., CEO Pruitt Co. Inc., Houston, 1988—; chmn. bd., CEO Odessa Spring Brake & Axle, Inc., 1991—; comml. real estate investor, Shreveport, La., Houston, Odessa, and Tyler Tex; gen. ptnr. ESE Properties, Tyler, 1991—; mng. gen. ptnr. Heritage Dr. Plz. Office Stes., 1992-95. Mem. planning com. Tyler Heritage Tour, 1982-83; originator Designer Show-Case, Tyler, 1983; founder, chmn. Rose Garden Trust Fund, 1981-87; bd. dirs. Carnegie History Ctr., 1984-85; chmn. merger com. Smith County Hist. Soc. and Carnegie History Ctr. merger, 1993-94; pres. East Tex. Baylor Club, 1986-87, Smith County Youth Found., 1986-87, mem., bd. dirs., 1984-91; pres. East Tex. State Fair, 1991-94; bd. assocs. East Tex. Bapt. U., Marshall, 1988—, v.p. bd. assocs., 1990-91, pres. bd. assocs., 1991-93; bd. trustees East Tex. Bapt. U., Marshall, 1995—, mem. exec. com., East Texas State Fair, 1990; v.p. Camp Fannin Assn., Tyler, 1992—; trustee Timberline Bapt. Camp and Conf. Ctr., 1987-90, treas., 1989-90; mem. Smith County Hist. Commn, 1984-85, 91—; chmn. stewardship com. First Bapt. Ch. Tyler, 1995-96. Mem. Tyler Area C. of C., Smith County Hist. Soc. (chmn. bd. govs. 1984-85, 87-88, pres. 1984-85, bd. govs. 1991-94), Hist. Tyler, Inc., Tyler Jaycees (v.p. 1982-83, bd. dir. 1981-85), Nat. Trust for Hist. Preservation, SCV (treas. camp 124, 1979-83). Baptist. Clubs: Tyler Petroleum, Willow Brook Country (Tyler). Home: 3102 Bracken Dr Tyler TX 75701 Office: WC Sq PO Drawer 929 Tyler TX 75710 also: Mountwood Ranch RR 17 Box 30 Tyler TX 75704-9817

EDWARDS, DAVID NESBIT, JR., university administrator; b. Winston Salem, N.C., May 26, 1939; s. David Nesbit and Sadye Victoria (Ripple) E.; m. Marcia Jene Baldwin, Dec. 30, 1972; children: Lisa Lynn, Holly Ann. BA, Davidson Coll., 1961; JD, Duke U., 1964. Bar: N.C. Law clk. Womble, Carlyle, Sandridge & Rice, Winston Salem, 1966-67; assoc. atty. Surratt & Early, Winston Salem, N.C., 1967-68; dir. field experience Elmira (N.Y.) Coll., 1968-71; assoc. dir. N.C. Internship Office, Raleigh, N.C., 1971-73; spl. asst. to pres. U. N.C., Chapel Hill, N.C., 1973—; negotiation team mem. ACE-NACUBO Music Licensing, Washington, 1980—. Author: (with others) Legal Deskbook for Adminstrators of Independent Colleges and Universities, 1982; contbr. articles to profl. jours. Pres. Gideons Internat. Durham South Camp., 1996—; elder Presbyn. Ch., Durham. Mem. N.C. Bar Assn., State Bar N.C., Am. Canal Soc. (life.). Home: 2 Breton Place Durham NC 27707 Office: U N C General Adminstrn 910 Raleigh Rd Chapel Hill NC 27514

EDWARDS, DON RAYMOND, computer programmer; b. Lafayette, Ind., May 26, 1955; s. William Clark and Rozalia (Szyrwiel) E. BA, St. Johns Coll., 1978; PhD, Brown U., 1984; MS in Engring., Johns Hopkins U., 1996. Classicist Depauw U., Greencastle, Ind., 1983-84; liberal artist Ky. State U., Frankfort, Ky., 1984-86; computer programmer MFI Inc., Lanham, Md., 1987-89, VSE, Inc., Alexandria, Va., 1989-91, CACI, Inc., Arlington, Va., 1990—; classicist George Mason U., Fairfax, Va., 1991-95. Office: CACI Inc 1100 N Glebe Rd Arlington VA 22201-4798

EDWARDS, DONNA REED, nurse; b. Pine Bluff, Ark., Jan. 12, 1955; d. Ray and LaVerne (Domon) Reed; m. Ralph L. Edwards; 1 child, Christopher Michael; stepson, Andrew Romac. ADN, U. Ark., Monticello, 1975; BSN, SUNY, Albany, Albany; postgrad., Webster U. RN, ARk.; CCRN, AACN; cert. in BCLS, ACLS. Staff nurse med. stepdown Little Rock VA Med. Ctr., 1977-79, charge nurse surg. ICU, 1980-84; staff nurse post anesthesia care unit John L. McClellan Meml. VA Med. Ctr., Little Rock, 1984-86, head nurse, 1986-92; med. clin. coord. John L. McClellan VA Med. Ctr., 1992-93, asst. chief nurse for medicine, 1993—. Contbr. articles to profl. jours. Mem. AACCN, Nurses Orgn. of VA, Am. Heart Assn. Mem. Assembly of God Ch. Office: JL McClellan Meml VA Med Ctr Nursing Svc 4300 W 7th St Little Rock AR 72205-5411

EDWARDS, GEORGE CHARLES, III, political science educator, writer; b. Rochester, N.Y., Jan. 3, 1947; s. George Charles Jr. and Mary Elizabeth (Laing) E.; m. Carmella Rose Pierce, May 22, 1981; 1 child, Jeffrey Allan. BA, Stetson U., 1969; MA, U. Wis., 1970, PhD, 1973. Asst. prof. polit. sci. Tulane U., New Orleans, 1973-78; assoc. prof. polit. sci. Tex. A&M U., College Station, 1978-81, prof., 1981-90, disting. prof., 1990—, Jordan prof. in liberal arts, 1991—, dir. Ctr. for Presdl. Studies, 1991—; vis. asst. prof. U. Wis.-Madison, 1976; vis. prof. U.S. Mil. Acad., West Point, N.Y., 1985-88, Peking U., Beijing, 1993; pres. Presidency Rsch. Group, 1984-85; lectr. U.S. Info. Svc., Europe, 1985, 89, U.S., 1988, 92, Brazil, 1988; cons. NSF, Washington, 1977—, Internat. Republican Inst., Moscow, 1994, Ctr. for Strategic and Internat. Studies, Washington, 1990-91, Nat. Acad. Pub. Adminstrn., Washington, 1987-88. Author: Presidential Approval, 1990, At the Margins, 1989, Government in America, 1989, 91, 94, 96, Presidential Leadership, 1985, 90, 94, The Public Presidency, 1983, Presidential Influence In Congress, 1980, Implementing Public Policy, 1980, The Policy Predicament, 1978; editor: Researching the Presidency, 1993, National Security and the U.S. Constitution, 1988, The Presidency and Public Policy Making, 1985, Studying The Presidency, 1983, Public Policy Implementation, 1984, Perspectives on Public Policy-Making, 1975; mem. editl. bd. Am. Jour. Polit. Sci., 1985-87, 94—, Am. Politics Quar. 1981-87, Presdl. Studies Quar., 1978—, Congress and the Presidency, 1981—, Policy Studies Jour., 1981-83, Am. Rev. Politics, 1994—; contbr. articles to profl. jours. Pres., Greenfield Plaza Condominium Assn., Bryan, Tex., 1980-81; mem. East Tex. 2000 Commn., 1980-81. Served to capt. USAR, 1971-79. Decorated for Disting. Civilian Svc. U.S. Army, 1988; Woodrow Wilson fellow 1969-70, Ford Fellow 1970-73. Mem. Am. Polit. Sci. Assn. (sect. pres. 1984-85), Am. Assn. Pub. Opinion Rsch., So. Polit. Sci. Assn., Midwest Polit. Sci. Assn., Policy Studies Orgn., Ctr. Study of Presidency (bd. dirs. 1978—), Phi Beta Kappa, Pi Sigma Alpha, Phi Alpha Theta, Pi Alpha Alpha, Phi Kappa Phi. Avocations: collecting art, skiing, tennis, scuba diving, travel. Home: 2910 Coronado Dr College Station TX 77845 Office: Tex A&M U The Ctr for Presdl Studies College Station TX 77843-4348

EDWARDS, HARRY LAFOY, lawyer; b. Greenville, S.C., July 29, 1936; s. George Belton and Mary Olive (Jones) E.; m. Suzanne Copeland, June 16, 1956; 1 child, Margaret Peden. LLB, U. S.C., 1963, JD, 1970. Bar: S.C. 1963, U.S. dist. Ct. S.C. 1975, U.S. Ct. Apls. (4th cir.) 1974. Assoc. Edwards and Edmunds, Greenville, 1963; v.p., sec., dir. Edwards Co., Inc., Greenville, 1963-65; atty. investment legal dept. Liberty Life Ins. Co., Greenville, 1965-67, asst. sec., asst. v.p., head investment legal dept., 1967-70; asst. sec. Liberty Corp., 1970-75; asst. v.p. Liberty Life Ins. Co., 1970-75; sec. Bent Tree Corp., CEL, Inc., 1970-75; sec., dir. Westchester Mall, Inc., 1970-75; asst. sect. Libco, Inc., Liberty Properties, Inc., 1970-75; pvt. practice Greenville, 1975—. Editor U. S.C. Law Rev., 1963. Com. mem. Hipp Fund Spl. Edn., Greenville County Sch. System; mem. Boyd C. Hipp II Scholarship Com., Wofford Coll. Spartanburg, S.C.; mem. scholarship com. Liberty Scholars, U. S.C., 1984, 86-96. With USAFR, 1957-63. Mem. ABA, S.C. Bar Assn., Greenville County Bar Assn., Phi Delta Phi, Greenville Lawyers, Poinsett Club (Greenville). Baptist. Home: 106 Ridgeland Dr Greenville SC 29601-3017 Office: PO Box 10350 Greenville SC 29603-0350

EDWARDS, JACK, former congressman, lawyer; b. Birmingham, Ala., Sept. 20, 1928; s. William Jackson and Sue (Fuhrman) E.; m. Jolane Vander Sys, Jan. 30, 1954; children: Mrs. Richard Weavil, Richard Arnold. BS in Commerce and Bus. Adminstrn., U. Ala., 1952, LLB, 1954. Bar: Ala. 1954, D.C. 1983. Practice Mobile, 1954-64; mem. 89th-98th Congresses from 1st Dist. Ala., 1965-85; mem. com. appropriations; mem. def. and transp. subcom.; vice chmn. Ho. Rep. Conf.; with Hand Arendall L.L.C., Mobile, Ala., 1985—; bd. dirs. The Southern Co., Holnam Inc., Northrop Grumman Corp., QMS, Inc. Trustee U. Ala. Served with USMC, 1946-48, 50-51. Mem. ABA, Ala. Bar Assn., Mobile Bar Assn. (sec. 1956), Mobile Jr. Bar Assn. (pres. 1957), D.C. Bar Assn., Mobile Area C. of C. (chmn. bd. 1986), Kappa Alpha (pres. 1951-53), Omicron Delta Kappa. Presbyterian. (elder). Office: First Nat Bank Bldg Ste 3000 Mobile AL 36601

EDWARDS, JAMES BENJAMIN, accountant, educator; b. Atlanta, Apr. 27, 1935; s. James T. and Frances L. (McEachern) E.; m. Virginia Ann Reagin, Feb. 21, 1958; children: James Benjamin II, Chad Reagin, Calli Ann, Judy Clair. BBA in Fin., U. Ga., 1958, MBA, 1962, PhD in Bus. Adminstrn., 1971. CPA Tenn., Ga., S.C.; cert. mgmt. acct.; cert. internal auditor; cert. in data processing; cert. cost analyst. Contr. Better Maid Dairy Products, Inc., Athens, Ga., 1958-62; staff acct. Max M. Cuba & Co., Atlanta, 1962-63; mng. ptnr. Wilson, Edwards and Swang, accts., Nashville, 1964-66; ptnr. Q.F. Lester & Co., Athens, 1967-68; v.p., chmn. bd. dirs. Gen. Data Svc. Inc., Athens, Ga., 1970-71; internal cons. J.W. Hunt and Co., CPAs, Columbia, 1983-84; v.p. Integrated Cost Mgmt. Systems Inc., Arlington, Tex., 1990-91; instr. David Lipscomb Coll., Nashville, 1963-66; instr. Nashville Ctr. U. Tenn., 1964-66; instr. acctg. U. Ga., Athens, 1966-71; asst. prof. U. S.C., Columbia, S.C., 1971-73, assoc. prof., 1973-77, prof., 1977—, fellow Bus. Partnership Found., 1977-90; William W. Bruner Disting. Faculty fellow U. S.C., Columbia, 1990—; instr. staff tng. program local C.P.A. firms, Nashville, 1963-66. Contbr. articles on mgmt. acctg. to profl publs. Coach Little League Baseball, Columbia, 1972-76; bd. dirs. Atlanta Bible Camp, Inc.; bd. dirs. Ga. Christian Found., Inc., pres., 1968-69; bd. dirs. Spring Valley End. Found., 1983-93, v.p., 1983-85, treas., 1985-93. Recipient 8 nat. awards for contbns. to acctg. lit. Mem. Am. Acctg. Assn., Am. Inst. CPAs, Inst. Internal Auditors, Planning Execs. Isnt. (asst. editor nat. mag. 1971-77), Am. Inst. Decision Scis. (v.p. Southeastern sect. 1975-76), Nat. Assn. Accts. (pres. Columbia chpt. 1973-74, nat. rsch. com. 1974-75, nat. edn. com. 1977-80, 95—, nat. dir. 1975-77, pres. Carolinas coun. 1976, nat. v.p. 1980-81), S.C. Soc. CPAs, S.C. Assn. Acctg. Instrs. (founding pres. 1972-73), Omicron Delta Epsilon, Beta Alpha Psi, Delta Sigma Pi, Sigma Chi. Mem. Ch. of Christ. Clubs: Five Points Optimist of Athens, Spring Valley Band Boosters. Home: 38 E Branch Ct Columbia SC 29223-6809 Office: U SC Coll Bus Adminstrn Columbia SC 29208

EDWARDS, JAMES EDWIN, lawyer; b. Clarkesville, Ga., July 29, 1914; s. Gus Calloway and Mary Clara (McKinney) E.; m. Frances Lillian Stanley, Nov. 22, 1948; children: Robin Anne Edwards Kaylor, James Christopher, Clare Edwards Weber. Student U. Tex. 1931-33; B.A., George Washington U., 1935, J.D. cum laude, 1946. Bar: Fla. 1938, Va 1987. Practice law, Cocoa, Fla., 1938-42; hearing and exam. officer USCG, 1943-45; div. asst. State Dept., Washington, 1945-50; practice law Ft. Lauderdale, Fla., 1951-55, 59-77; mem. firm Bell, Edwards, Coker, Carlon & Amsden, Ft. Lauderdale, 1956-59; sole practice, Coral Springs, Fla., 1977-81, 84-85; asst. city atty. Fort Lauderdale, 1961, 63-65; mem. firm. Edwards & Leary, Coral Springs, 1981-84; mem. panel Am. Arbitration Assn., 1984—; sole practice, Albemarle County, Va., 1987-88, Charlottesville, Va., 1988—. Author: Myths About Guns, 1978. Commr., Coral Springs, 1970-76, mayor, 1972-74; mem. bd. suprs. Sunshine Water Mgmt. Dist., 1976-80; chmn. Ft. Lauderdale for Eisenhower, 1952; pres. Fla. Conservative Union, Broward County, 1976. Served to lt. USCGR, 1943-45, to lt. col. JAG, USAFR, 1950-68. Recipient 50-Yr. award Fla. Bar, 1988. Mem. SAR, English Speaking Union Club (Charlottesville), The Ret. Officers Assn., Rotary. Office: Commonwealth Ctr 300 Preston Ave Ste 312 Charlottesville VA 22902-5044

EDWARDS, JOE MICHAEL, journalist; b. Crawfordsville, Ind., May 25, 1947; s. Donald H. and Betty Louise (McKinney) E.; m. Karen Ruth Branscome, Sept. 6, 1969 (divsn. June 1989); 1 child, Melissa Kristine; m. Sandra Loventhal, Apr. 20, 1991. BA, Ea. Ky. U., 1971. Journalist AP, Nashville, 1970—; commentator The Nashville Network, 1987. Rec. sec. Redeemer Luth. Ch., Nashville, 1988. Mem. So What Club (v.p., pres. 1980-81). Office: AP Ste 110 215 Centerview Dr Brentwood TN 37027

EDWARDS, JOHN SAUL, lawyer; b. Roanoke, Va., Oct. 6, 1943; s. Richard Thomas and Augusta Elizabeth (Saul) E.; m. Catherine Dabney, July 8, 1972; children: John Jr., Dabney, Catherine. AB cum laude, Princeton U., 1966; postgrad., Union Theol. Sem., 1966-67; JD, U. Va., 1970. Bar: Va. 1970, D.C. 1974, U.S. Ct. Mil. Appeals 1971, U.S. Dist. Ct. D.C. 1974, U.S. Ct. Appeals (4th and D.C. cirs.) 1975, U.S. Dist. Ct. (we. dist.) Va. 1976, U.S. Supreme Ct. 1976. Assoc. Sidley & Austin, Washington, 1970, 74-76, Gentry, Locke, Rakes & Moore, Roanoke, 1976-80; U.S. atty. western dist. State of Va., Roanoke, 1980-81; ptnr. Martin, Hopkins, Lemon & Carter, P.C., Roanoke, 1981-90, Martin, Hopkins, Lemon & Edwards, P.C., 1990-92; pvt. practice, Roanoke, 1993—. Mem. Va. Dem. Ctrl. Com., 1978-80, 85-93; chmn. Roanoke City Dem. Com., 1983-85, 6th Dist. Dem. Com., 1987-93; chmn. Va. Luth. Homes, Inc., Roanoke, 1985—; trustee Roanoke Valley United Way, 1982-88; mem. Roanoke City Civic Ctr. Commn., 1985-93, chmn., 1990-92; mem. Roanoke City Coun., 1993-95, vice mayor, 1994-95; mem. Senate of Va., 1996—. Rockefeller Bros. Theol. fellow, 1966-67. Mem. ABA, Va. Bar Assn. (chmn. criminal law com. 1987-91), Roanoke Bar Assn. (bd. dirs. 1986-88), Assn. Trial Lawyers Am., Va. Trial Lawyers Assn., Nat. Assn. Former U.S. Attys., Omicron Delta Kappa, Raven Soc. Lodge: Kiwanis. Home: 3745 Forest Rd SW Roanoke VA 24015-4509 Office: PO Box 1179 725 Crestar Plz Roanoke VA 24006-1179

EDWARDS, LANCE A., engineering executive; b. Lakeland, Fla., Oct. 2, 1961; s. Arthur Tillis Edwards and Judith Ann (Porter) Wiley; m. Eri Takemura, June 25, 1988; 1 child, Stephanie Erica. BSChE, U. Houston, 1984; MSChE, U. Notre Dame, 1985. Profl. engr. Tex. From project engr. to mgr. bus. devel. Aspen Tech., Inc., Houston, 1985—. Mem. AIChE, Instrument Soc. Am., Entrepreneurial Soc. Office: Aspen Tech Inc 14701 Saint Marys Ln Houston TX 77079-2905

EDWARDS, LEONARD, police officer. BA, U. Memphis, 1976. Sgt. Memphis Police Dept., 1973—; exec. dir. Commn. on Missing and Exploited Children, Memphis, 1991—. 7. Vice chair Vol. Support Com. Svc., Memphis, Nat. Organ Transplant Fund, Memphis; mem. Shelby County Truancy Initiative, Memphis, County Cmty. Coun., Memphis. Recipient Golden Deed award Exch. Club of Memphis, 1995, Memphis Underwriters Assn. Officer of Month, 1995, Youth Svc. award Kiwanis Clubs of Memphis, 1994, 95. Office: Commn on Missing and Exploited Children 616 Adams Rm 102 Memphis TN 38105

EDWARDS, LINDA SUE, bookkeeper; b. Winchester, Tenn., Nov. 4, 1947; d. Charlie John and Cora (Dola) Glasner; m. William Douglas Edwards, Oct. 10, 1966; children: Kevin, Thomas, Charles. Grad. H.S., Winchester, 1966. Cafeteria worker North Jr. H.S., Decherd, Tenn., 1983-89; bookkeeper Edwards Constrn. Co., Winchester, 1989—. Author: (poetry) Rhythms and Rhyms for These Hard Times, 1994. Republican. Mem. Ch. of Christ. Home: 1112 Williams Cove Rd Winchester TN 37398-2739

EDWARDS, MARGARET MCRAE, college administrator, lawyer; b. Wadesboro, N.C., July 2, 1931; d. Martin Alexander and Margaret Ashe (Redfearn) McRae; m. Sterling J. Edwards, June 30, 1953; children: Martin, Robert, Lee, Elizabeth. BA cum laude, Agnes Scott Coll., 1953; JD cum laude, Cumberland Law Sch., 1979. Bar: N.C. 1979, Ala. 1980, Fla. 1981. Asst. to alumnae dir. Mt. Vernon Coll., Washington, 1961-64; devel. staff S.E. Inst., Chapel Hill, N.C., 1973-75; law clk. U.S. Dist. Ct., Birmingham, 1979-80; atty. Carlton, Fields, Tampa, Fla., 1980-82; pvt. practice Birmingham, 1983-85; dir. planned giving Birmingham-So. Coll., 1985-90, assoc. v.p. for endowment and planned giving, 1991—; cons. Blackbaud Planned Giving Conf., Charleston, S.C., 1991—, Planned Giving, Philanthropic Action Coun., Tampa, 1980-82, Am. Philanthropy Group, Birmingham, 1983-88; prof. bus. law Samford U., Birmingham, 1984. Index editor: Manual for Complex Litigation, 1985. Bd. dirs. Girls Club, Birmingham, 1984-90, Ala. Planned Giving Coun., 1991-94, Ala. divsn. Am. Cancer Soc., co-chair major gifts, 1991—; speakers bur. Nat. Com. on Planned Giving. Recipient Achievement award in Planned Giving, Coun. for Achievement and Support of Edn., 1992, Will/Tax award Young Lawyers Assn., 1979, Estate Planning award Am. Jurisprudence, 1979. Mem. Am. Arbitration Assn. (arbitrator 1985—), Audubon Soc. (bd. dirs.), Agnes Scott Alumnae (pres. Birmingham 1967-69, Charleston, S.C. 1954-55). Presbyterian. Home: 4239 Chickamauga Rd Birmingham AL 35213-1811 Office: Birmingham-So Coll Arkadelphia Rd Birmingham AL 35254

EDWARDS, MARVIN RAYMOND, investment counselor, economic consultant; b. N.Y.C., June 29, 1921; s. Albert H. and Blanche (Gans) E.; m. Helene C. Sirota, Mar. 20, 1955; children: Jeffrey Randall, Douglas Lee, Carolyn Beth. BS, NYU, 1947. Pres. White Star Sales Corp., Jacksonville, Fla., 1947-58; pres. Edwards & Edwards, Inc., Jacksonville, 1958—. Interviews on investments and the economy have appeared in numerous publs. including Bus. Week, Scrap Age, Miami Herald, Tampa Tribune, The Market Chronicle, others; subject of interview ABC World News Tonight, 1993, 94. Exec. v.p., bd. dirs. Greater Jacksonville Taxpayers Assn., 1965-71; pres., bd. dirs. Better Schs. Citizens Com, Jacksonville, 1959-65, Community Service Planning Council, Jacksonville, 1955-58; v.p., b.d dirs. Jacksonville Humane Soc., 1953-56, Jacksonville Safety Council, 1948-50; bd. dirs. North East Fla. Kidney Found., Jacksonville, 1971-73. Lt. USAF, 1943-46, ETO. Decorated Air medal; recipient Outspoken Citizen's award Jacksonville Southside Bus. Men's Club, 1993. Mem. Jacksonville Fin. Analysts Soc. (pres., bd. dirs. 1977-78, 87-88), Econ. Roundtable Jacksonville (pres., bd. dirs. 1975-77, 90-91), Assn. for Investment Mgmt. and Rsch., Nat. Assn. bus. Economists, Nat. Economists Club, Soc. Profl. Journalists, Nat. Press Club of Washington, Vets. of the Office of Strategic Svcs. Home: 1345 Riverbirch Ln Jacksonville FL 32207-7540 Office: Edwards & Edwards Inc PO Box 33 Jacksonville FL 32201-0033

EDWARDS, PAUL BEVERLY, retired science and engineering educator; b. Ridge Spring, S.C., Nov. 12, 1915; s. Paul Bee and Chloe Agnes (Watson) E.; m. Sarah Dee Barnes, Apr. 10, 1943; 1 child, Susan Dee Edwards Von Suskil. BS, U. Tampa, 1937; EdM, Harvard U., 1958; EdD, George Washington U., 1972. Owner, operator Edwards' Hobbies, Tampa, Fla., 1938-54; tchr. math. Hillsborough High Sch., Tampa, 1955-60; head dept. math. King High Sch., Tampa, 1960-63; coord. Grad. Ctr., supr. edn. and tng. Johns Hopkins U. and Applied Physics Lab., Balt. and Laurel, Md., 1963-75; dir. Grad. Ctr., supr. edn. and tng. Johns Hopkins U. and Applied Physics Lab., Balt. and Laurel, 1975-81. Contbr. articles to profl. jours. Mem. Sun City Ctr. Voters League, 1989—, Community Assn., Sun City Ctr., 1987—; mem. Greenbriar Property Owners Assn., Sun City Ctr., 1987—. Lt. comdr. USNR, 1942-46. Named Meritorious Tchr., State of Fla., 1962; recipient various fellowships. Mem. Ret. Officers Assn., Naval Res. Assn. Home: 1843 Wolf Laurel Dr Sun City Center FL 33573-6422

EDWARDS, PHILLIP MILTON, import-export company executive; b. Borger, Tex., Feb. 24, 1933; s. Aaron Moses and Ada Elsie (Feist) E.; m. Mildred M. L. Weber, Aug. 18, 1956. BA, Okla. U., 1958. Polit. officer U.S. Embassy, Jedda, Saudi Arabia, 1961-64; vice consul U.S. Consulate Gen., Dhahran, Saudi Arabia, 1965-67; sr. advisor Dept. of Army, Vinh Long, Vietnam, 1968-70; publs. mgr. DOT Systems, Incorp., Vienna, Va., 1971-77; v.p. Transcontinental Trade Corp., Washington, 1978-81, Security Support Svcs., Washington, 1981-92; mem. profl. staff Alderson Reporting Co., Washington, 1992—. Contbr. articles to profl. jours. Recipient Silver medal SAR, 1979. Presbyterian. Home: 1917 Aubrey Place Ct Vienna VA 22182-1976 Office: Security Support Svcs 695 Old Hunt Way Herndon VA 22070-3159

EDWARDS, ROY ALVIN, physician, psychiatrist, educator; b. Huntington, W.Va., June 23, 1921; s. Roy Alvin and Willie Hazel (Stanley) E.; m. Dorothea Frances Brodtrick, June 16, 1943 (div. Aug. 1973); children: Madalin Ann, Mary Margaret, John Brodtrick; m. Wanda Jean Ferrell, Nov. 30, 1973. BS, Marshall U., 1942; MD, Med. Coll. Va., 1948. Diplomate Am. Bd. Psychiatry and Neurology. Rotating intern Med. Coll. Va. Hosps., Richmond, 1948-49; resident in internal medicine C&O Hosp., Huntington, W.Va., 1949-50; resident in psychiatry Columbus (Ohio) State Hosp., 1950-52, Cleve. Receiving Hosp., 1952-53; supt. Western State Hosp., Hopkinsville, Ky., 1953-56; pvt. practice psychiatry Huntington, 1956-86; mem. med. staff Huntington State Hosp., 1986—, clin. dir., 1986-95; clin. prof. Marshall U. Med. Sch., Huntington, 1986-94; clin. prof. Marshall U. Med. Sch., Huntington, 1986-94; dir. Christian County Mental Health Clinic, Hopkinsville, 1953-56; psychiat. cons. Outwood (Ky.) VA Hosp., 1954-56; mem. courtesy staff St. Mary's Hosp., Huntington, 1956—. Contbr. articles to med. jours. Mem. W.Va. Ho. of Dels., Charleston, 1973-75; mem., chmn. numerous civic orgns., 1957-80. With AUS, 1943-46. Named Ky. Col.,

1975. Fellow Am. Psychiat. Assn. (life); mem. AMA, So. Med. Assn., W.Va. Med. Assn., W.Va. Psychiat. Assn. (pres. 1961, 68), Guyam Golf and Country Club. Republican. Methodist. Home: 25 Parkway Dr Huntington WV 25705-2716

EDWARDS, SAMUEL LEE, religious organization executive; b. Waynesville, N.C., June 18, 1954; s. James Roy and June Elise (Settle) E.; m. Dorinda Kay Waddell, June 9, 1979; children: David Thomas, Rachel Karen. Diploma, Brevard (N.C.) Coll., 1974; BA magna cum laude, Am. U., Washington, 1976; MDiv cum laude, Nashotah (Wis.) House, 1979. Ordained Anglican deacon, 1979, priest, 1980. Curate St. Timothy's Episcopal Ch., Ft. Worth, Tex., 1979-81, rector, 1989-93; vicar St. Laurence Episcopal Ch., Grapevine, Tex., 1980-81; instr. Anglican Sch. Theology, Irving, Tex., 1980-87; theol. cons. Schs. of Spirituality, Dallas, 1981—; curate St. Francis Episcopal Ch., Dallas, 1981-87; vicar St. Patrick's Episcopal Ch., Bowie, Tex., 1987-89, Trinity Episcopal Ch., Henrietta, Tex., 1987-89; exec. dir. Episcopal Synod of Am., Ft. Worth, 1993—; priest/assoc. Cmty. of St. Mary, 1982—. Editl. bd.: The Anglican Service Book, 1990; features editor The Evangelical Catholic, 1985-89; contbr. articles to profl. jours. Mem. Sons of Confederate Vets. (camp chaplain 1993-96), Mil. Order of the Stars and Bars, Soc. of King Charles the Martyr. Republican. Office: Episcopal Synod of America 6300 Ridglea Pl Ste 910 Fort Worth TX 76116-5735

EDWARDS, THOMAS HENRY, JR., retired construction company executive; b. Montgomery, Ala., Feb. 16, 1918; s. Thomas Henry and Florence Virginia (Cameron) E.; m. Marilyn Rae Myers, Nov. 18, 1943; children: Thomas Henry III, Mary Lynn Edwards Angell. BS in Civil Engring., Auburn U., 1939; postgrad. U. Mich., 1940-41. Registered profl. engr. and land surveyor, Ala. San. engr. W.K. Kellogg Found., Battle Creek, Mich., 1939-40; estimator Algernon Blair Constrn. Co., Montgomery, 1946-47; engr. Tenn. Coal and Iron div. U.S. Steel Corp., Birmingham, Ala., 1947-53; project mgr. Sullivan, Long, Hagerty, Birmingham, 1953-73, v.p., 1973-83; ret., 1993. Served with U.S. Army, 1942-45. Mem. Sigma Nu. Republican. Methodist. Lodge: Lions. Home: 4333 Wilderness Rd Birmingham AL 35213-2211

EDWARDS, VIRGINIA DAVIS, music educator, concert pianist; b. Syracuse, N.Y., Jan. 8, 1927; d. Leslie Martz and Elsie (Gannon) Davis; m. William B. Edwards, Jan. 12, 1954. BA magna cum laude, Marshall U., 1948; MusB, Cin. Conservatory of Music, 1950, MusM, 1950; postgrad., U. Chgo., 1950-56, U. Calif., Berkeley, 1963. Pianist, young artists series Conservatory of Music, Cin., 1949-50; piano instr. Conservatory of Music, Evanston, Ill., 1955-56; music instr. Harvard Sch. for Boys, Chgo., 1954-55; pianist Opera Studios of Dimitri Onofrei/Bianca Saroya, Chgo., 1957-61; piano instr. Community Music Ctr., San Francisco, 1962-63; v.p. Gold Rush Gun Shop, Benet Arms Co. Imports, San Francisco, 1963-68, Afton, Va., 1968—; pvt. practice Afton, Va., 1978—; instr. piano Mary Baldwin Coll., Staunton, Va., 1988—. Soloist Marshall U. Symphony Orch., 1948, Chgo. Pops Concert Orch., Duluth, Minn., 1961; recitalist Curtis Hall, Chgo., 1961, Legion of Honor, San Francisco, 1966, Sta. WRFK-FM, Richmond, Va., 1979; prodr., performer Presbyn. Hunger Program series, 1984-87, St. John's Cath. Ch., Waynesboro, Va., 1985, Basic Meth. Ch., 1989, Augusta Hosp. Corp. Benefit, 1989; author: Conspiracy of 30 -- Their Misuse of Music from Aristotle to Onassis, 1994. Mem. AAUW, DAR, Va. Museum Soc. Unitarian. Home: PO Box 87 Waynesboro VA 22980-0066

EDWARDS, VIVIAN, retired humanities educator; b. Bklyn., May 19, 1915; d. L. James and Helen Louise (Gaynor) Joseph; m. Seth Carlyle Edwards, June 21, 1943; children: Seth Carlyle Jr., Jeanne. AB, Bklyn. Coll.-CCNY, 1936; MA, Columbia U., N.Y.C., 1937, EdD, 1959. Instr. English Barber-Scotia Jr. Coll., Concord, N.C., 1937-44; head dept. English Cuttington Coll. (now Cuttington U. Coll.), Suakoko, Liberia, 1949-60, chairperson, 1972-79; head dept. English U. Liberia, Monrovia, 1962-68; dir. freshman English Hampton (Va.) Inst./U., 1969-72; English head divsn. humanities St. Augustine's Coll., Raleigh, N.C., 1979-96; ret., 1996; sponsor English honor soc. publs.-faculty jour. U. Liberia, 1963-68; mem. faculty jour. staff St. Augustine's Coll., 1985. United Negro Coll. Fund grantee, 1984; recipient poetry award Internat. Soc. Poets, 1994, 95, John Winters award St. Augustine's Coll., 1988. Mem. Sigma Tau Delta (sponsor LambdaLambda chpt. 1979—, medal 1996). Democrat. Home: 712 Delany Dr Raleigh NC 27610 Office: Saint Augustines Coll Divsn Humanities Raleigh NC 27611

EDWARDS, WILLIAM HAWKINS, surgeon, educator; b. Nashville, Mar. 16, 1927; s. Leonard Wright and Mary (Hawkins) E.; m. Frances Nuckols McGaughy, Dec. 27, 1952; children: William Jr., Mary Frances, Norton M., Sarah Elizabeth. BA, Vanderbilt U., 1949, MD, 1953. Intern Vanderbilt U., 1953-54, resident, 1954-56, 57-59; resident UCLA, 1956-57; vascular fellow Baylor Coll. Medicine, 1959-60; clin. prof. surgery Vanderbilt U. Med. Ctr., Nashville, 1981-91, H. William Scott Jr. prof. surgery, 1991-95, prof. surgery emeritus, 1995; pres. State Vol. Mut. Ins. Co., Brentwood, Tenn., 1983-94. Contbr. articles to med. jours. Seaman 2nd class USN, 1945-47. Mem. ACS (pres. Tenn. chpt. 1977-78, bd. govs. 1984-87), So. Med. Assn. (pres. sect. surgery 1984-85), Nashville Surg. Soc. (pres. 1989-90), Southeastern Surg. Congress (councilor), Vanderbilt U. Med. Alumni (pres. 1980-81), So. Vascular Assn. (bd. dirs. 1990-93, pres.-elect so. assn. 1995, pres. 1996), Belle Meade Country Club. Home: 50 Concord Park E Nashville TN 37205-4705

EDWARDS, W.L. JACK, retired physician; b. Dallas, Sept. 21, 1926; s. William Leslie and Martha Effie (Caldwell) E.; m. Patsy Margaret Hayes, Mar. 15, 1947; children: Patricia E. Hight, Dana E. Nearburg, William L. Student, Harvard Coll., 1943-44; MD, Southwestern Med. Sch., Dallas, 1948. Diplomate Am. Bd. Internal Medicine. Pathology intern Peter Bent Brigham Hosp., Boston, 1948-49; med. intern Mass. Meml. Hosp., Boston, 1949-50; resident in medicine Parkland Hosp., Dallas, 1950-52, Univ. Hosp., Birmingham, Ala., 1952-53; trainee Nat. Heart Inst., Birmingham, 1953-54; staff physician Baylor U. Med. Ctr., Dallas, 1955—, Parkland Hosp., Dallas, 1955—, Presbyn. Hosp., Dallas, 1966-77; clin. instr. pathology Harvard Med. Sch., Boston, 1948-49; clin. instr. medicine Boston U. Sch. Medicine, 1949-50, U. Ala., Birmingham, 1952-54; from clin. asst. prof. to clin. prof. medicine Southwestern Med. Coll., Dallas, 1954—. Author med. papers. Served to lt. USNR, 1950-52, U.S. and Japan. Fellow ACP; mem. AMA, Tex. Med. Assn., County Med. Soc., Tex. Heart Assn. (bd. dirs. 1972-75), Tex. Club of Internists, Dallas Heart Assn. (pres. 1971-72), Southwestern Alumni Assn. Presbyterian. Home: 3521 Rosedale Ave Dallas TX 75205-1225

EFAW, FRITZ, economics educator; b. Stillwater, Okla., Dec. 10, 1946; s. Forrest Clark and Leonah Ernestine (Damme) E.; 1 child, Julianne Anastasia. BS, MIT, 1968; AA, The Archtl. Assn., 1975; MA, Rutgers U., 1983, PhD, 1987. Rsch. asst. Air Force Cambridge Rsch. Lab., Bedford, Mass., 1967-68; programmer, analyst London U. Computer Svcs., 1969-73; planning cons. Thalis Argyropoulos & Assocs., London, 1975-76; project coord. Nat. Amnesty Coun., N.Y.C., 1976-77; rsch. analyst Mathematica, Inc., Princeton, N.J., 1978-81; instr. Rutgers U., New Brunswick, N.J., 1981-87; prof. econs. U. Tenn., Chattanooga, 1988—; vis. prof. econs. Vanderbilt U., Nashville, 1987-88; bd. dirs. Arts and Edn. Coun., Chattanooga. Nominated v.p. Dem. Nat. Conv., N.Y.C., 1976; del. nat. conv. Dem. Party, London & N.Y.C., 1976, pres., founder Union Am. Exiles Britain, London, 1969-76. Recipient Lifetime Achievement award Nat. Multple Sclerosis Soc., 1992. Mem. Am. Econ. Assn., Union Radical Polit. Econs., History Econs. Soc. Democrat. Office: U Tenn Econs Dept 615 Mccallie Ave Chattanooga TN 37403-2504

EFAW, SUZANNE HALL, elementary school educator; b. Cherry Point, N.C., June 29, 1956; d. Raymond James Hall and Janet Anne (Bender) Dean; m. Fritz William Efaw, Aug. 15, 1992; 1 child, Julianne Anastasia. BS in Elem. Edn. cum laude, U. Tenn., Chattanooga, 1993. Pvt. acad. tutor Signal Mountain, Tenn., 1994—. Vol. Multiple Sclerosis Soc., Chattanooga, 1990—; ESL tchr. READ of Chattanooga, 1994—. Mem. NEA, ASCD, Tenn. Edn. Assn., Tenn. Reading Assn., U. Tenn. Adult Scholars (v.p. 190-93), Golden Key Nat. Honor Soc., Kappa Delta Pi. Democrat. Congregational. Home: 502 Signal Mountain Blvd Signal Mountain TN 37377

EFESOA-MOKOSSO, HENRY (TEDDY), social sciences educator. BA in History, U. Lagos, Nigeria, 1967; MA in History, Howard U., 1987, PhD in History, 1987; Cert. in Cons., Cath. U. Am., 1980. Inspector secondary edn. Edn. Hdqrs., Buea, West Cameroon, 1968-70; prin. Govt. Tchr.Tng. Coll., Kumba, West Cameroon, 1970-72, Royal Poly. Coll., Lagos, Nigeria, 1972-75; lectr. history Xavier U., New Orleans, 1981-83; teaching asst. Howard U., Washington, 1976-79, 84-87; adj. asst. prof. history Loyola U. La., 1990; asst. prof. history Southern U., New Orleans, 1989-91, assoc. prof. history, 1992—, chmn. dept. social scis., 1993—; external reader PhD Dissertation Com., U. New Orleans, 1992; rsch. asst. Rockville Cons., Inc., Washington, summer 1979, Inst. of Urban Affairs, Howard U., Washington, summer 1980; lectr. in field. Editorial adv. bd. World Civilization, Collegiate Press, Aeta Loma, Calif., 1993; author: My First Pair of Shoes and the Little Altar Boy: A Pair of Childhood Memories, 1991, A Guide for History Student Teachers, 1973; contbr. articles to profl. jours. Adv. bd. Ctr. for african and African Am. Studies, So. U., New Orleans, 1989—; judge 1993 Regional Social Studies Fair, Jefferson Parish Schs. 1991 Region IX Social Studies Fair, 1990 Region IX Social Studies Fair, New Orleans Sch. System. Mem. African Studies Assn., Soc. for Children Book Writers, Am. Black Writers Assn., Mayor of New Orleans Coun. of Internat. Trade, 1994; chmn. Lyceum Comm. So.U. New Orleans, 1995. Home: 4170 Old Gentilly Rd Apt 313 New Orleans LA 70126-4945

EFFIONG, PHILIP U., English language educator; b. Kaduna, Nigeria, Nov. 5, 1960; came to U.S., 1988; s. Philip A. and Josephine L. (Abbott) E.; children: Noah, Ini, Lawrence. BA in English/Lit. with honors, U. Calabar, Nigeria, 1982, MA in English/Lit., 1985; PhD in Theatre/Drama, U. Wis., 1994. Grad. asst. U. Calabar, 1983-85, asst. lectr., 1985-88; part-time prof. U. Wis., Madison, 1992-94; asst. prof. English U. Tenn., Martin, 1994—; faculty cons. Coll. Bd. and ETS, 1995. Contbr.: (books) Nigeria: The People and Their Cult, 1987, Issues and Identities in Literature, 1996; contbr. (dictionary): Dictionary of 20th Century Culture, 1996. Named Outstanding Prof. U. Tenn.-Martin Older Students assn., 1996; Fulbright scholar, 1988-92, U. Calabar Grad. scholar, 1983-85. Mem. MLA, African Studies Assn., Tenn. Philol. Assn., Tenn. Writers Alliance. Office: University of Tennessee 131 Humanities Martin TN 38238

EFFRON, SETH ALAN, journalist; b. Stamford, Conn., July 23, 1952; s. Marshall Roven and Marion Nancy (Glickman) E.; m. Nancy G. Thomas, May 30, 1982; children: Rebecca Ann, Eve Margo. BA in Polit. Sci. with honors, U. N.C., 1974. Reporter Fayetteville (N.C.) Times, 1974-77, Tallahassee (Fla.) Dem., 1977-80, Wichita Eagle-Beacon, 1980-85; govt. and polit. reporter Greensboro (N.C.) News & Record, 1985-93; founder, editor The Insider, Raleigh, N.C., 1993—; exec. editor Nando.net, Raleigh, 1995—. Editor: Old Jess, Jesse Helms Quoted, 1994, CoachSpeak, 1995, North Carolina Almanac of Government and Politics, 1995, (mag.) Jacob's Fans Guide to ACC Basketball 1996, 1995. V.p., pres. Fred A. Olds Elem. Sch. PTA, Raleigh, 1994-96; mem. adv. panel Z Smith Reynolds Found., Winston-Salem, N.C., 1986-89. Nieman fellow Harvard U., 1991-92. Jewish. Home: 308 Dixie Tr Raleigh NC 27607 Office: Nando net/New Media 127 W Hargett Ste 406 Raleigh NC 27601

EFIRD, JAMES MICHAEL, theology educator; b. Kannapolis, N.C., May 30, 1932; s. James Rufus and I. Z. (Christy) E.; m. Vivian Lee Poythress, Mar. 7, 1975; 1 child, Whitney Michelle; 1 stepchild, Anthony Kevin Crumpler. AB, Davidson Coll., 1954; MDiv, Louisville Presbyn. Theo. Sem., 1958; PhD, Duke U., 1962. Ordained to ministry Presbyn. Ch. (U.S.A.), 1958. Asst. prof. Duke Div. Sch., Durham, N.C., 1962-68, assoc. prof., 1958-85, prof., 1985—, dir. acad. affairs, 1971-75; interim min. Glenwood Presbyn. Ch., Greensboro, N.C., 1989-91, Mebane Meml. Presbyn. Ch., Roxboro, N.C., 1991-92, Hillsborough Presbyn. Ch., 1993, Little River Presbyn. Ch., 1995-96. Author: How To Interpret the Bible, 1984, Marriage and Divorce, 1985, End-Times: Rapture, Anti-Christ, and Millennium, 1986, Revelation for Today, 1989, A Grammar For New Testament Greek, 1990. Duke U. scholar, 1958-62. Mem. Soc. Bibl. Lit., Phi Beta Kappa. Home: 2609 Heatherglen Dr Durham NC 27712-1027 Office: Duke Div Sch Durham NC 27708-0967

EFLAND, SIMPSON LINDSAY, entrepreneur; b. Efland, N.C., May 5, 1913; s. Mack Paul Sr. and Mary Estelle (Forrest) E. AB in Edn., Univ. N.C., 1935; postgrad., U. Ala., 1940; BS in Engring., U. Tenn., 1942, profl. cert., 1942. Lic. real estate broker. TVA-safety/health engr. Tenn. Valley Authority, Knoxville, 1935-42; head coach boxing, track, wrestling, cross-country U. Tenn., Knoxville, 1939-42, asst. coach football, 1939-42; safety engr. Dupont Corp., St. Paul, 1942; owner, organizer, exec. Orange Hosiery Mills, Inc., Efland, 1946-94; engr., exec. Sinclair Refining, B. P., ARCO, Atlanta, 1971-76; cattleman, realtor, entrepreneur, corp. owner, lessor, 1976—; organizer, dir. N.C. Cattleman's Assn., Raleigh, 1946, N.C. Cattleman's Found., Inc., 1980; artificial inseminator, breeder Am. Breeder Svc., Wis., 1970. County commr. Orange County, Hillsborough, N.C., 1950-56; dir. N.C. Ednl. Found., Chapel Hill, 1950; various offices N.C. Dem. Party, Raleigh, 1946-80, Orange County Dem. Party, Hillsborough, 1946-80; organizer Efland Vets. Housing Assn., 1947, Efland Town Coun., Efland, 1941-47, Orange County Fire Dept., Hillsborough, 1952; chmn. Orange County Voiture 1266 40 & 8 Nursing Tng. Program, Chapel Hill, 1951—; organizer, dir., treas. Orange County Med. Found., Inc., Hillsborough, 1974—; organizer, dir Efland Cheek Multi-Purpose Ctr., 1965; mem. N.C. Country Squire, Raleigh, 1952, United Fund-Orange County Budget Com., Hillsborough, 1966; mem., officer YMCA, 1936-42, WILDLIFE, 1985—; life mem. Boy Scouts Am., 1925-35; pres., dir. Hillsborough Legion Meml. Hut, Inc., 1988—; mem. inter-frat. coun. U. Tenn., 1941-42. Lt. Comdr. USN, 1942-46. Recipient various campaign ribbons. Mem. NRA, Am. Assn. Ret. Persons, Am. Legion, Peter Tare, Inc. (organizer, dir.), N.C. Farm Bur., Gen. Francis Nash Vets, Legion Brigade (comdr.), U. N.C. Alumni Assn. (life), U. N.C. Living Legends (organizer), U. N.C. Monogram Club, PT Boats, Inc. (organizer, dir.), Sons of Confederacy, Century Club U. Tenn., Moose (charter, 1st gov., organizer), Delta Sigma Phi (pres. 1940-42), Omicron Delta Kappa. Democrat. Methodist. Home: PO Box 64 3416 Southern Dr Efland NC 27243-9704

EGALON, CLAUDIO OLIVEIRA, physicist, researcher; b. Volta Redonda, Rio de Janeiro, Brazil, Aug. 16, 1963; came to U.S., 1985; s. Irany and Marlene Oliveira Egalon. BS, Fed. U. of Rio de Janeiro, 1984; MSc, Coll. of William & Mary, 1988, PhD, 1990. Rsch. scientist NASA Langley Rsch. Ctr., Hampton, Va., 1990—. Mem. AIAA, IEEE, NSS, APS, Challenger Ctr. (founder). Home: 2658 N Armistead Ave Apt 2B Hampton VA 23666-1530 Office: NASA Langley Rsch Ctr Ms # 231 Hampton VA 23681

EGAN, MARTHA AVALEEN, history educator, archivist; b. Kingsport, Tenn., Feb. 26, 1956; d. Jack E. and Opal (Pugh) E. BS in Comms., U. Tenn., 1978; MA in History, East Tenn. State U., 1986; postgrad., U. Ky., 1986-89, Milligan Coll., 1990. Cert. tchr., Tenn. News reporter, anchor WJCW-AM/WQUT-FM, Johnson City, Tenn., 1980-82; staff asst. 1st Dist. Office U.S. Senator Jim Sasser, Blountville, Tenn., 1982-84; instr. history East Tenn. State U., Johnson City, 1984-86; teaching asst. dept. history U. Ky., Lexington, 1986-89; teaching intern Dobyns-Bennett High Sch., Kingsport, Tenn., 1990; researcher history project Eastman Chem. Co., Kingsport, 1991; adj. faculty history Northeast State Tech. C.C., Blountville, 1992-93; archivist Kingsport Pub. Libr. and Archives, 1993—; adj. asst. prof. history King Coll., Bristol, Tenn., 1994—. Researcher: Eastman Chemical Company: Years of Glory, Times of Change, 1991. Vice chair Sullivan County Dem. Party, 1992-93; rec. sec. Sullivan County Dem. Women's Club, 1992, corr. sec., 1994; mem. Kingsport Tomorrow Exploritorium Task Force; mem. Kingsport Symphony Chorus, sec.-treas., 1994-95; mem. East Tenn. Camerata, Kingsport Cmty. Band. Mem. AAUW (Kingsport chpt.), Orgn. Am. Historians, Nat. Coun. Social Studies, Soc. Am. Archivists, Tenn. Archivists, Kingsport Music Club (corr. sec. 1995—), Phi Alpha Theta, Pi Gamma Mu, Sigma Delta Chi. Episcopalian. Home: PO Box 481 Kingsport TN 37662-0481 Office: Kingsport Pub Libr/Archives 400 Broad St Kingsport TN 37660-4208

EGAN, MICHAEL JOSEPH, lawyer; b. Savannah, Ga., Aug. 8, 1926; s. Michael Joseph and Elise (Robider) E.; m. Donna Cole, Apr. 14, 1951; children: Moira Elizabeth, Michael Joseph, Donna, Cole, Roby, John Patrick. B.A., Yale U., 1950; LL.B., Harvard U., 1955. Bar: Ga., D.C. Assoc. Sutherland, Asbill & Brennan, Atlanta, 1955-61; ptnr. Sutherland, Asbill & Brennan, 1961-77, 79—; mem. Ga. Ho. of Reps., 1966-77, minority leader, 1971-77; assoc. atty. gen. U.S. Dept. Justice, Washington, 1977-79; mem. Ga. Senate, 1989—. Served with U.S. Army, 1945-47, 50-52. Mem. ABA, Atlanta Bar Assn., State Bar Ga., Am. Law Inst., Am. Coll. Trust and Estate Counsel, Atlanta Lawyers Club. Republican. Roman Catholic. Home: 97 Brighton Rd NE Atlanta GA 30309-1518 Office: Sutherland Asbill & Brennan 999 Peachtree St NE Fl 24 Atlanta GA 30309-3964 also: 1275 Pennsylvania Ave NW Washington DC 20004-2404

EGAN, SHIRLEY ANNE, nursing educator, retired; b. Haverill, Mass.; d. Rush B. and Beatrice (Bengle) Willard. Diploma, St. Joseph's Hosp. Sch. Nursing, Nashua, N.H., 1945; B.S. in Nursing Edn., Boston U., 1949, M.S., 1954. Instr. sci. Sturdy Meml. Hosp. Sch. Nursing, Attleboro, Mass., 1949-51; instr. sci. Peter Bent Brigham Hosp. Sch. Nursing, Boston, 1951-53, ednl. dir., 1953-55, assoc. dir. Sch. Nursing, 1955-59, med. surg. coord., 1971-73, assoc. dir. Sch. Nursing, 1973-79, dir., 1979-85; cons. North Country Hosp., 1985-86; infection control practitioner, 1986-87; contract instr. Natchitohes Area Tech. Inst., 1988-90, Sabine Valley Tech Inst., 1990-91; coord. quality assurance Evangeline Health Care Ctr., 1991-92, asst. dir. nursing, 1992-93; coord. quality assurance Evangeline Health Care Ctr., Natchitoches, La., 1994-96, retired, 1996; nurse edn. adviser AID (formerly ICA), Karachi, Pakistan, 1959-67; prin. Coll. Nursing, Karachi, 1959-67; dir. Vis. Nurse Service, Nashua, N.H., 1967-70; cons. nursing edn. Pakistan Ministry of Health, Labour and Social Welfare, 1959-67; adviser to editor Pakistan Nursing and Health Rev., 1959-67; exec. bd. Nat. Health Edn. Com., Pakistan; WHO short-term cons. U. W.I., Jamaica, 1970-71; mem. Greater Nashua Health Planning Council. Contbr. articles to profl. publs. Bd. dirs. Matthew Thornton health Ctr., Nashua, Nashua Child Care Ctr.; vol. ombudsman N.H. Council on Aging; mem. Nashua Service League. Served as 1st lt., Army Nurse Corps., 1945-47. Mem. Trained Nurses Assn. Pakistan, Nat. League for Nursing, Assn. for Preservation Hist. Natchitoches, St. Joseph's Sch. Nursing Alumnae Assn., Boston U. Alumnae Assn., Brit. Soc. Health Edn., Cath. Daus. Am. (vice regent ct. Bishop Malloy), Statis. Study Grads. Karachi Coll. Nursing, Sigma Theta Tau. Home: 729 Royal St Natchitoches LA 71457-5716

EGAN, THOMAS MICHAEL, surgeon, educator; b. Toronto, July 15, 1952; came to the U.S., 1988; MD, U. Toronto, 1976, MSc, 1984. Diplomate Am. Bd. Surgery, Am. Bd. Thoracic Surgery; lic. surgeon, N.C. Intern York-Finch Gen. Hosp., Toronto, 1976-77; resident U. Toronto, 1980-82, 84-88, rsch. fellow thoracic surgery, 1982-84; instr. surgery Washington U., St. Louis, 1988-89; asst. prof. surgery U. N.C., Chapel Hill, 1989-93, assoc. prof. surgery, 1993—, assoc. chief divsn. chief for gen. thoracic surgery, 1996—. Mem. editl. bd. Jour. Heart and Lung Transplantation: contbr. chpts. to books and articles and abstracts to publs. Med. officer, flight surgeon Can. Forces Base Chatham, New Brunswick, Can., 1977-80. Faculty scholarship St. Michael's Coll., 1970, Gulf Oil can. Ltd. scholar, 1970-74; fellowship Can. Lung Assn., 1983-84, faculty fellow Washington U., 1988-89; grantee Am. Lung Assn., 1990-91, Cystic Fibrosis Found., 1991-93. Fellow ACS, Am. Coll. Chest Physicians; mem. AMA, Am. Assn. Thoracic Surgery, Am. Soc. Artificial Internal Organs, Am. Thoracic Surgery, Assn. Acad. Surgery, Gen. Thoracic Surg. Club, Internat. Soc. Heart and Lung Transplantation (founding co-chair coun. on pulmonary transplantation), N.C. Med. Soc., N.C. Thoracic Soc., Nathan A. Womack Surg. Soc., Soc. Thoracic Surgeons, Soc. Univ. Surgeons, So. Thoracic Surg. Assn. Office: U NC CB # 7065 Chapel Hill NC 27599

EGGAN, HUGH MELFORD, accountant; b. Velva, N.D., Feb. 24, 1930; s. Elmer M. and Esther (Guernsey) E.; B.A. magna cum laude, U. Wash., 1956; m. Dorothy L. Rowland, June 3, 1949; children—Kathleen Eggan Davis, Gary, Laurie Eggan Berry Ward. Mem. staff Deloitte Haskins & Sells, Seattle, (now Deloitte & Touche), 1956-64, mem. staff, Washington, 1964-67, ptnr., 1967-68, with exec. office, N.Y.C., 1968-72, ptnr. in charge, Cleve., 1972-78, ptnr. in charge So. region, Atlanta, 1978-85, retired 1985. Contbr. to Jour. Accountancy. Former chmn. Pacific (Wash.) Town Planning Comm.; former officer Calvary Luth. Ch., Federal Way, Wash.; former bd. trustees Citizens League Cleve.; adminstrv. sec., council mem., pres. Emmanuel Luth. Ch., Washington; former bd. trustees Luth. Planning Council Met. Washington; treas., bd. dirs. D.C. Inst. Mental Hygiene, 3d St. Music Sch., N.Y.C.; former bd. dirs. Goodwill Industries, Atlanta. CPA, Wash., N.C. Mem. AICPA, Country Club of Asheville, Phi Beta Kappa, Beta Alpha Psi.

EGGEMEYER, ALICIA ANN, elementary education educator; b. Morgan City, La., Aug. 27, 1971. BA in English, U. Tex., 1994; Cert., Edn. Svc. Ctr. Region XIII, Austin, 1995. Presch. tchr. Grace Temple Child Devel. Ctr., San Angelo, Tex., summer 1991, Jackie's Performing Arts Presch., Austin, Tex., 1991-92; pre-kindergarten lead tchr. Elsass Acad., Austin, 1992-93; substitute tchr. Eanes Ind. Sch. Dist., Austin, 1993-94, Austin Ind. Sch. Dist., 1994—; camp counselor Crenshaw Athletic Club, Austin, summer 1994. Pub. rels. vol. Mexic-Arte Mus., Austin, 1993. Carr acad. scholar Angelo State U., 1989-90. Mem. ASCD, Nat. Assn. for Edn. of Young Children.

EGGLAND, ELLEN THOMAS, community health nurse, consultant; b. Canton, Ohio, Nov. 2, 1947; d. John Marron and Mary Mernabelle (Miller) Thomas; m. Gregory Hugh Eggland, Sept. 9, 1972; children: Karen, Ryan. BSN, Georgetown U., 1969; MN, Emory U., 1972. Staff nurse Cleve. Clinic Hosp., 1969-71; nurse clinician Univ. Hosps., Cleve., 1972-73; dir. nursing Med. Personnel Pool, Cleve., 1975-83; v.p. Healthcare Pers., Inc., Naples, Fla., 1984—; nursing cons., Ohio, Fla., 1983—; v.p. MedPad, Atlanta, 1991-93; mem. adv. bd. Springhouse (Pa.) Skillbuilder Series, 1991-92; vis. lectr. symposium Fla. Gulf Coast U., 1996; vis. lectr. U. South Fla., 1996. Author: Nursing Documentation Resource Guide, 1993, Nursing Documentation: Charting, Reporting and Recording, 1994; contbg. author: Better Documentation, 1992, Managing the Nursing Shortage, 1989, Community and Home Health Care Plans, 1990; contbr. articles to profl. nursing jours.; design inventor computerized clin. record. Chmn. St. William Respect Life/Sr. Citizens, Naples, 1985-86; mem. health com. Naples C. of C., 1985-86; sec. Pelican Bay Incorporation Study Com., Naples, 1990-91; bd. dirs. Prevent A Care, Naples, 1986-87; bd. dirs., sec. Pelican Bay Found., Naples, 1993-96; bd. vis. Georgetown U. Sch. Nursing, 1993-96. Fed. grantee for edn. U.S. Govt., 1971; recipient Involved Mem. of Yr. award Greater Cleve. Nurses Assn., 1978, 5th Ann. Author's award U. South Fla., 1995. Mem. ANA, Fla. Nurses Assn., Nat. League Nursing, Master's Group, Greater Cleve. Hosp. Assn. (info. tech. and nursing com. 1991-95), Sigma Theta Tau. Democrat. Roman Catholic. Office: Healthcare Personnel Inc 2335 Tamiami Trl N Ste 407 Naples FL 34103-4459

EGGLESTON, G(EORGE) DUDLEY, management consultant, publisher; b. Buffalo, June 11, 1936; s. George Staub and Betty (Ball) E.; m. Susan Michaels, June 4, 1960 (div. Sept. 1987); children: George Dudley Jr., M. Blair; m. Linda Stephens, Mar. 31, 1990 (div. 1996). BE, Vanderbilt U., 1960; MBA, Ga. State U., 1979. Product mgr. Exxon Chem., N.Y.C., 1960-71; real estate agt. Woodward & Assocs., Atlanta, 1971-74; v.p. JFK Land Co., Atlanta, 1974-75; pres. Dudley Eggleston Co., Atlanta, 1975—, Maids Unique, Atlanta, 1976-81, Eggleston Cons. Internat., Atlanta, 1981—. Capt. USMC, 1960-63. Mem. Urban Land Inst., Internat. Coun. Shopping Ctrs., Nat. Assn. Real Estate Investment Trusts. Republican. Episcopalian.

EHLE, JOHN MARSDEN, JR., writer; b. Asheville, N.C., Dec. 13, 1925; s. John M. and Gladys (Starnes) E.; m. Gail Oliver, Aug. 30, 1952 (div. Apr. 1967); m. Rosemary Harris, Oct. 22, 1967; 1 child, Jennifer Anne. BA, U. N.C., 1949; DFA (hon.), N.C. Sch. Arts, 1981; LHD (hon.), Berea Coll., 1986, U. N.C., Asheville, 1987; DLitt (hon.), U. N.C., Chapel Hill, 1990. Faculty U. N.C., Chapel Hill, 1951-63; spl. asst. to Gov. Terry Sanford, Raleigh, N.C., 1963-64; program officer Ford Found., N.Y.C., 1964-65; spl. cons. Duke U., 1976-80; founder N.C. Sch. Arts, N.C. Gov.'s Sch., N.C. Sch. Sci. and Math. Author: (novels) Move Over, Mountain, 1957, Kingstree Island, 1959, Lion on the Hearth, 1961, The Land Breakers, 1964, The Road, 1967, Time of Drums, 1970, The Journey of August King, 1971, The Changing of the Guard, 1975, The Winter People, 1981, Last One Home, 1983, The Widows Trial, 1989, (biographies) The Free Men, 1965 (Mayflower Soc. cup), The Survivor, 1968, Shepherd of the Streets, 1960, Dr. Frank, Living with Frank Porter Graham, 1993, (non-fiction) The Cheeses and Wines of England and France, with Notes on Irish Whiskey, 1972, Trail of Tears: The Rise and Fall of the Cherokee Nation, 1988; pub. also in several fgn. countries; (screenplay) The Journey of August King, 1995. Mem. White House Group for Domestic Affairs, 1964-66, Nat. Coun. Humanities, 1966-70; mem. exec. com. Nat. Book Com., N.Y.C., 1972-75, N.C. Sch. Arts Found., Winston-Salem, 1970-75; mem. awards commn. State of N.C., 1982-93, Mary Reynolds Babcock Found., Winston-Salem, 1985-89. With AUS, 1944-46. Recipient Walter Raleigh prize for fiction N.C. Dept. Cultural Affairs, 1964, 67, 70, 75, 84, State of N.C. award for Lit., 1972, Gov.'s award for Disting. Meritorious Svc., 1978, Lillian Smith prize Southern Regional Coun., 1982, Disting. Alumnus award U N.C., Chapel Hill, 1984, Thomas Wolfe Meml. award Western N.C. Hist. Assn., 1984, W.D. Weatherford award Berea Coll., 1985, Caldwell award N.C. Humanities Coun., 1995. Mem. PEN, Authors League, Century Club (N.Y.C.). Democrat. Methodist. Home: 125 Westview Dr NW Winston Salem NC 27104-1947

EHLEN, MARTIN RICHARD, state agency administrator, management analyst; b. Highland Park, Ill., Dec. 28, 1953; s. Martin Henry and Marilyn Lucille (Tomtingen) E. BA in Polit. Sci., Western Ill. U., 1976; MA in Pub. Adminstrn., Norwich U., 1993. Mktg. and sales exec. Reedy Industries, Inc., Glenview, Ill., 1978-86; owner, CEO San Diego Pub. Rels. and Advt. Co., San Diego, 1986-88; non commd. officer U.S. Army, 1988-91; grad. student Norwich U., Montpelier, Vt., 1992-93; records adminstr. Dept. Hwy. Safety and Motor Vehicle, Fla., 1994-95; sr. mgmt. analyst Dept. Revenue, Fla., 1995—; cons. San Diego Pub. Rels. and Mktg., Calif., Ill., Fla., 1986-88; mem. ASPA Washington, Fla., 1991—, Acad. Polit. Sci., Washington, 1995—. Mem. governing bd. Assoc. Students of Polit. Sci., Western Ill. U., 1974-76. With U.S. Army, 1988-91. Recipient Mil. Commendation Nat. Def. and Achievement medals, U.S. Army, 1990, 91. Mem. ASPA, Toastmasters Internat. Home: 3733 Sutor Ct Tallahassee FL 32311-4071 Office: State of Fla Dept Revenue 12th Fl Rm 1256A 325 W Gaines St Tallahassee FL 32399-3150

EHLINGER, JANET ANN DOWLING, elementary school educator; b. Des Moines, Mar. 1, 1955; d. Joseph Patrick and Sadie Agnes (Klein) Dowling; m. Steven Mark Ehlinger, July 22, 1989; children: Bridget Ann, Brian Mark. BS, Benedictine Coll., Atchison, Kans., 1977; MEd, U. St. Thomas, Houston, 1985. Cert. tchr., Tex. Tchr. English, sci. Our Lady Mt. Carmel, Houston, 1977-78; tchr. social studies, history, religion St. Michael's Sch., Houston, 1978-82; tchr. social studies and history Kinkaid Sch., Houston, 1982-90. Mem. Mus. Fine Arts, Houston, 1992, Children's Mus. of Houston, 1993-96; bd. dirs. St. Cyril of Alexandria Ladies Guild, Houston, 1992. Mem. Nat. Coun. Social Studies, Tex. State Hist. Assn., Houston Zool. Soc., Kappa Delta Pi (rep.-at-large Pi Lambda chpt. 1985-86, sec. 1987-89). Home: 6111 Cheena Dr Houston TX 77096-4614

EHLONAN, JEFFREY D., writer, educator; b. Houston, Nov. 3, 1954; d. Shawn and Theresa (Krawiecki) E.; m. Maria Alpert, Dec. 31, 1978; children: Elizabeth Anne Shirley, Nicholas. BA in English, U. Tex., 1976. adj. prof. creative writing U. Va., 1991—; cons. Werik Pub. Co., Arlington, Va., 1990—. Author: (children's books) Elizabeth and Her Baby Brother, 1986, Rebecca Finds a Cat, 1987, Little Big Socks, 1987, Rebecca Gets a Christmas Tree, 1988, Tara and Rebecca, 1989, Tara Moves In, 1990, Tara Gets a Ring, 1991, Tara and the Fish, 1992, Tara and Brian, 1992, Stephanie Moves In, 1992, Tracey Bumps Her Head, 1993, Tracey Falls Asleep, 1993, Greg-Chuck Takes a Nap, 1994, Sharon Goes to New York, 1994, Stephanie Goes to Disney World, 1994, Hazel Catches a Cold, 1995, Rock and Bowl, 1995, Harriet the Tiger, 1995, Rebecca's Spots, 1996, Elyse Takes a Break, 1996, Kevin Gets Away, 1996, Sam Says So, 1996, Rebecca Goes to School, 1996; (novels) Better Nate Than Lever, 1987, Time's Fun When You're Havin' Flies, 1990, Creative Writing 101: A Guide for Students of Literature, 1996; contbr. stories to literary jours. Vol. Project Literacy, Dallas, 1990-94. Mem. ASCAP, International Assn. Amusement Parks and Attractions, Juvenile Lit. Soc., U. Tex. Alumni Assn., Children Book Writers Soc. Presbyterian.

EHRHARDT, CHARLES WINTON, law educator; b. Elkader, Iowa, Oct. 24, 1940. BS, Iowa State U., 1962; JD with high honors, U. Iowa, 1964. Bar: Iowa 1964, Fla. 1972. Law clk. to judge U.S. Ct. Appeals (8th cir.), 1964-65; asst. U.S. atty. no. dist. Iowa, 1965-67; asst. prof. Fla. State U., 1967-70, assoc. prof., 1970-74, prof., 1974-77, Ladd prof. of evidence, 1977—; co-dir. advanced seminar in Anglo-Am. Jurisprudence Wadham Coll. Oxford U., 1994, 91, 88, 86; dir. summer program in law Oxford U., 1975-76; faculty Fed. Jud. Ctr., Washington, 1985—, Nat. Jud. Coll., Reno, 1983—; lectr. in field; mem. Fla. Law Rev. Coun., 1975-76; mem. legal staff Gov.'s Com. to Study Capital Punishment, 1972; chair athletic dir. search and screening com. Fla. State U., 1989, 94-95, chair athletic bd. 1984—). Author: Florida Evidence, 1995, 94, 93, 92, Florida Trial Objections, 1993, Florida Evidence, 2d edit., 1984, Loth's Iowa Civil Procedure Forms, 2 vols., 1977, 76, 75, 74, 73, West's Florida Practice Forms, 4 vols., 1979, 75; comtbr. articles to profl. jours.; bd. editors: Iowa Law Rev. Mem. NCAA (chair faculty athletics reps. assn. 1989-91, mem. pres. commn. liaison com. 1993—, mem. eligibility com. 1994—, mem. spl. com. to review NCAA enforcement and infractions process 1991, faculty rep. 1984—), Atlantic Coast Conf. (v.p. 1994—, sec.-treas. 1994-95), Coll. Football Assn. (chair acad. evaluation com. 1993-94, mem. monitoring com. 1989-91). Home: 606 Middlebrooks Circle Tallahassee FL 32312 Office: Fla State U Coll Law Tallahassee FL 32312

EHRLICH, GERALDINE ELIZABETH, food service management consultant; b. Phila., Nov. 28, 1939; d. Joseph Vincent and Agnes Barbara (Campbell) McKenna; m. S. Paul Ehrlich, Jr., June 20, 1959; children: Susan Patricia, Paula Jeanne, Jill Marie. BS, Drexel Inst. Tech. Nutrition cons., hypertension rsch. team U. Calif. Micronesia, 1970; regional sales dir. Marriott Corp., Bethesda, Md., 1976-78; dir. sales and profl. svcs. Coll. and Health Care div. Macke Co., Cheverly, Md., 1978, gen. mgr., 1978-79; v.p. ops., div., 1979-80, pres. Health Care div., 1980-81; regional v.p. Custom Mgmt. Corp., Alexandria, Va., 1981-83, v.p. mktg., 1983-87; v.p. mktg. and healthcare sales Morrison's Custom Mgmt., Mobile, Ala., 1987-88; v.p. sales ARA Svcs., Phila., 1988-93; v.p. bus. devel., ARAMARK, Phila., 1993-96; pres. Mktg. Matrix, 1996—; cons. mktg. The Green House, Tokyo, 1987-88; chmn. bd. Mktg. Matrix, Falls Church, Va., 1984—. Mem. Health Systems Agy. No. Va., 1976-77; chmn. Health Care Adv. Bd. Fairfax County Va., 1973-77; vice chmn. Fairfax County Cmty. Action Com., 1973-77; treas. Fairfax County Dem. Com., 1969-73; trustee Fairfax Hosp., 1973-77; bd. dirs. Tennis Patrons, Washington, 1984-88, Phila. Singers, 1993—, Physicians for Peace, 1994—. Mem. AAUW, Internat. Women's Assn., Am. Mgmt. Assn., Nat. Assn. Female Execs., Soc. Mktg. Profls. Home and Office: 6512 Lakeview Dr Falls Church VA 22041-1102

EHRLICH, JEFFREY, data processing company executive; married; 1 child. BSEE, U. R.I.; MS in Tech. Mgmt. and Computer Sci., Rensselaer Polytechnic Inst.; postgrad., GE Mgmt. Inst., Crotonville, N.Y. Formerly CIO GE Med. Syss. Bus., Milw.; chief technology officer Nat. Data Corp., Atlanta. Designer on-line database transaction sys. for GE Capital. Office: National Data Plz Atlanta GA 30329-2010

EHRLICH, JOHN GUNTHER, writer; b. Berlin, Apr. 6, 1930; s. Walter Frederick and Henrietta (Fletch) E.; m. Frances Hendrika Vernon, Nov. 17, 1952 (div. Nov. 1978); children: Timothy Walter, Lisa Frances Gamble; m. Karen Ann Carr, Dec. 31, 1982. BJ, Syracuse U., 1952; JD, Bklyn. Law Sch., 1962. Bar: N.Y. 1962; Federal, 1962; U.S. Dist. Ct. (so. dist., ea. dist.), 1962. Reporter Newsday, Huntington, N.Y., 1955-60; exec. asst. Suffolk County Rep. Com., Blue Point, N.Y., 1960-63; bur. chief Suffolk County Dist. Atty., Hauppauge, N.Y., 1963-90; writer Little River, S.C., 1990—. Author: Revenge, 1959, Court Martial, 1960, Parole, 1961, Slow Burn, 1961, Cry, Baby, 1962, The Girl Cage, 1967, Close Combat, 1969, The Drowning, 1970, The Chatham Killing, 1976, The Fastest Gun in the Pulpit, (German, French, Swedish transl., movie script from novel), 1972, Bloody Vengeance, 1973, The Laramie River Crossing, 1973, Rebellion at Cripple Creek, 1979; contbr. short stories, non-fiction articles to mags. Capt. USAF, 1952-54. Recipient Investigative Reporting award Nat. Home Builders, 1958, Edgar Allan Poe award Mystery Writers, N.Y.C., 1970, Cert. Appreciation, Suffolk County Police Benevolent Assn., 1989. Republican. Episcopalian. Office: PO Box 62 Little River SC 29566-0062 also: Theron Raines 71 Park Ave # 4A New York NY 10016-2507

EHRLICH, MARGARET ISABELLA GORLEY, systems engineer, mathematics educator, consultant; b. Eatonton, Ga., Nov. 12, 1950; d. Frank Griffith and Edith Roy (Beall) Gorley; m. Jonathan Steven Ehrlich. BS in Math., U. Ga., 1972; MEd, Ga. State U., 1977, EdS, 1982, PhD, 1987; postgrad. Woodrow Wilson Coll. of Law, 1977-78. Cert. secondary tchr., Ga. Tchr. DeKalb County Bd. Edn., Decatur, Ga., 1972-83; chmn. dept. math. Columbia H.S., Decatur, 1978-83; with product devel. Chalkboard Co., Atlanta, 1983-84; math instr. Ga. State U., Atlanta, 1983-92; pres. Testing and Tech. Svcs., Atlanta, 1983—; course specialist Ga. Pacific Co., Atlanta, 1984-86; sys. engr. Lotus Devel. Corp., 1986-89; rsch. assoc. SUNY-Stony Brook, 1976; modeling instr. Barbizon Modeling Sch., Atlanta, 1991; instr. Ga. State Coll. for Kids, 1984-85; team leader guest svcs. ACOG; test-taking cons., hon. mem. Comm. Workers of Am. Local 3204, Atlanta, 1985—. Author: (software user manual) Micro Maestro, 1983, Music Math, 1984, (test manual) The Telephone Company Test, 1991, AMI Pro Advanced Courseware, 1992, A Study Guide for the Sales and Service Representative Test, 1993, A Study Guide for the Technical Services Test, 1995; mem. editl. bd. CPA Computer Report, Atlanta, 1984-85. Active Atlanta Preservation Soc., 1985, Planned Parenthood; tchr. St. Phillips Ch. Sch., Atlanta, 1981-88; vol. Joel Chandler Harris Assn., Atlanta, 1984-87; mem. St. Phillips welcome com., 1988-94, drug and alcohol counseling HOPE, 1988-94; sponsor Fair Test 1991—, Ctr. Fair and Open Testing; mem. parish choir St. Phillips Ch., 1995—; team leader guest svcs. Atlanta Com. Olympic Games. Named STAR Tchr. DeKalb County Bd. Edn., 1979, 80, 81, Most Outstanding Tchr., Barbizon Schs. of Modeling, 1980, Colo. Outward Bound, 1985, Disting. Educator, Ga. State U., 1987. Mem. LWV, Math. Assn. Am., Nat. Coun. Tchrs. Math., Ga. Coun. Tchrs. Math., Math. Assn. Am., Assn. Women in Math. (del. to China Sci. and Tech. Exch., 1989-90), Am. Soc. Tng. and Devel. Greater Atlanta, Ga. Hist. Soc., DeKalb Personal Computer Instr. Assn. (pres. 1984), Aux. Med. Assn. Ga., Daus. of Confederacy, Atlanta Track Club, N.Y.C. Track Club. Democrat. Episcopalian. Avocations: piano, jogging, fashion modeling, skiing, bonsai. Home: 240 Cliff Overlook Atlanta GA 30350-2601 Office: PO Box 500173 Atlanta GA 31150-0173

EHRLICH, RICHARD, electrical engineer, researcher; b. N.Y.C., Mar. 14, 1925; s. Benjiman M. and Paula (Nilva) E.; m. Bennette Sonya Mann, May 9, 1948; children: Michael Barry, Candice Jo, Alyson Tracy. BSEE, U. Miami, 1949. Comm. tech. civil aeronautics U.S. Govt., Guantanamo Bay, Cuba, 1945-48, field engr., 1949-50; field engr. Western Union, Miami, Fla., 1952-76; rsch. devel. Atmospheric Water, Miami, 1976—; cons. Atmospheric Water, Miami, 1976—. Patentee in field. With USAF, 1942-45, CBI. Home: 175 NW 121 St Miami FL 33168

EHRMAN, MADELINE ELIZABETH, federal agency administrator; b. N.Y.C., July 4, 1942; d. Donald McKinley and Marie Madeleine (Brandeis) Ehrman. BA summa cum laude Brown U., 1964, MA, 1965; M of Philosophy, Yale U., 1967; PhD, The Union Inst., 1989. Sci. linguist U.S. Dept. State, Washington, 1969-73, regional lang. supr. U.S. Embassy, Bangkok, Thailand, 1973-75, lang. tng. supr. U.S. Dept. State, Washington, 1975-84, curriculum and tng. specialist, 1984-85, acting chmn. dept. Asian and African Langs., 1985, chmn. dept. Asian and African Langs., 1986-88, acting assoc. dean Sch. Lang. Studies, 1987-88, dir. rsch., evaluation and devel., 1989—. Author: The Meanings of the Modals in Present Day American English, 1966, Contemporary Cambodian, 1975, Indonesian Fast Course, 1982, Communicative Japanese Materials, 1984, Ants and Grasshoppers, Badgers and Butterflies: Qualitative and Quantitative Exploration of Adult Language Learning Styles and Strategies, 1989, Understanding Second Language Learning Difficulties, 1996; mem. editorial bd. Jour. Psychol. Type, 1991—. Mem., ESOL/HILT Citizen's Adv. Coun., Arlington County, Va., 1985-89; psychotherapist Meyer Treatment Ctr. Washington Sch. Psychiatry, 1989-94. Woodrow Wilson Found. fellow, 1964; NSF fellow, 1964-69; recipient Meritorious Honor award U.S. Dept. State, 1972, 83. Mem. Am. Psychol. Assn., Tchrs. of English to Speakers of Other Langs., Am. Assn. Asian Studies, Assn. for Psychol. Type, Am. Orthopsychiat. Soc., Phi Beta Kappa, Psi Chi. Avocations: reading, bicycling, gardening. Office: Fgn Svc Inst 4000 Arlington Blvd Arlington VA 22204-1586

EICHBERG, RODOLFO DAVID, physician, educator; b. Pforzheim, Germany, July 26, 1937; came to the U.S., 1965; s. Julio and Ilse (Schonfarber) E.; m. Yvette Salama, May 21, 1965; children: William Amadeo, Matias David. Baccalaureate, St. Andrews Scots Sch., Argentina, 1955; MD, U. Buenos Aires, 1963. Intern, resident Grace Hosp. Wayne State U., Detroit, 1965-67; orthopedic surgeon Mar Del Plata, Argentina, 1968-73; resident physical medicine NYU, 1973-75; pvt. practice Rehab. and Electro Diagnosis Assocs., P.C., Tampa, 1975—; prof. U. So. Fla., Tampa, 1975-93, clin. assoc. prof., 1994—; chief spinal cord injury rehab. Tampa Gen. Hosp., 1984—; mem. state adv. coun. Head Spinal Cord Injuries, Tallahassee, 1976—. Contbr. articles to profl. jours. Bd. trustees Congregation Schaaraizedek, Tampa, 1980-82. Recipient Honors award City of La Paz, Bolivia, 1994. Mem. AMA, Am. Acad. Phys. Medicine Rehab. (health policy legis. com. 1990-95), Am. Spinal Injury Assn. (internat. rels. rep. S.C. 1990—), Am. Congress Rehab. Medicine, Assn. Med. Latino Americana de Rehab., Colombian Phys. Medicine Rehab. Soc. (corr.), Argentine Soc. Rehab. Medicine (corr.), Fla. Med. Assn., Fla. Soc. Phys. Medicine Rehab. (pres. 1994-96), Hillsborough County Med. Soc. (bd. censors 1975—). Jewish. Office: 2914 North Blvd Tampa FL 33602-1208

EICHELBERGER, JERRY WAYNE, computer engineer; b. Sacramento, Calif., Dec. 21, 1964; s. Hayward Wayne and Helen Jean (Mooney) E.; m. Jeannie Kaye Merritt, July 9, 1994. BS in Computer Engring., U. So. Miss., 1989. Computer technician Sverdup Tech/NASA, Stennis Space Ctr., Miss., 1989-91; computer engr. U.S. Dept. Justice, Jackson, Miss., 1991—; with Law Net Com., Inc., Brandon, Miss., 1994—. Chair 5th jud. circuit office Automation Conference, 1995. Col. Confederate Air Force, 1993—. With USN, 1985-89. Methodist. Home: 111 Long Branch Dr Brandon MS 39042 Office: US Cts 234 E Capitol St Ste 100 Jackson MS 39201-2410

EIGENBRODT, MARSHA LILLIAN, internal medicine educator, epidemiologist; b. Ruston, La., Mar. 9, 1952; d. James and Martha Evelyn (Rives) Richardson; married, Oct. 11, 1980; children: Stanton Paul, Edwin Parker. Student, La. Tech. U., 1970-73; MD, La. State U., 1977; MPH, U. Tex., 1995. Diplomate Am. Bd. Pathology. Resident in pathology Parkland Meml. Hosp./U. Tex. Southwestern Med. Sch., Dallas, 1977-81; anatomic and clin. pathologist Irving (Tex.) Cmty. Hosp., 1981-82; asst. prof. pathology U. Tex. Southwestern Med. Ctr./VA Med. Ctr., Dallas, 1983-89; asst. prof. pathology and lab. medicine U. Tex. Health Sci. Ctr., Houston, 1990-94; asst. prof. internal medicine, clin. epidemiologist U. Miss. Med. Sch., Jackson, 1996—. Contbr. articles to profl. jours. Lewis Gotlieb scholar La. State U., 1977, John Freeman Tchg. award, 1996. Mem. Alpha Omega Alpha. Mem. Ch. of Christ. Office: U Miss Med Sch Dept Internal Medicine 2500 N State St Jackson MS 39216-4500

EILAND, GARY WAYNE, lawyer; b. Houston, Apr. 25, 1951; s. William N. and Louise A. (Foltin) E.; m. Sandra K. Streetman, Aug. 4, 1973; children: Trina L., Peter T. BBA, U. Tex., 1973, JD, 1976. Bar: Tex. 1976, U.S. Ct. Claims 1977, U.S. Ct. Appeals (5th cir.) 1978, U.S. Ct. Appeals (11th cir.) 1981, U.S. Supreme Ct. 1989. Assoc. Wood, Lucksinger & Epstein, Houston, 1976-81, ptnr., 1981-91; ptnr. Vinson & Elkins L.L.P., Houston, 1991—; co-chair health industry group, 1996—; lectr. Aspen Health Care Industry seminars, Aspen Pubs., Inc., Rockville, Md., 1978-89, HLO Health Care seminars, 1990-91. Mem. Tex. Bar Assn. (chmn. health law sect. 1991-92), Am. Acad. Healthcare Attys. (bd. dirs. 1991—, pres. 1996—), Nat. Health Lawyers Assn., Healthcare Fin. Mgmt. Assn. Region 9 chpt. liaison rep. 1994-95), Assn. Am. Med. Colls., Houston Ctr. Club, Bentwater Country Club. Home: 23319 Holly Hollow Tomball TX 77375-3684 Office: Vinson & Elkins LLP 1001 Fannin St Ste 2300 Houston TX 77002

EILERS, MARLENE ANNA LOUISE, librarian, gealogist; b. Teaneck, N.J., June 14, 1954; d. Thomas Theodore and Gertrude Clara (Last) E.; m. William Allen Koenig, Nov. 25, 1995. BA in Eng., William Paterson Coll. of N.J., 1976; MLS, SUNY, Albany, 1981. News libr. Assoc. Press, N.Y.C., 1981-89; libr. mgr. CNN, Washington, 1989-94. Author: Queen Victoria's Descendants, 1987; co-editor: A Romanov Diary, 1989; pub. Royal Book News, 1985—; contbr. articles to mags. Republican. Lutheran. Home: 5590 Jowett Ct Alexandria VA 22315

EILTS, MICHAEL DEAN, research meteorologist, manager; b. La Chapelle, France, Aug. 22, 1959; (parents Am. citizens); s. Leonard Gene and Arlys Mamie (Ziegler) E. BS in Meteorology, U. Okla., 1981, MS in Meteorology, 1983, MBA in Fin. and Human Resource Mgmt., 1991. Rsch. asst., rsch. meteorologist Coop. Inst. for Mesoscale Meteorol. Studies, Norman, Okla., 1981-84; rsch. meteorologist Nat. Severe Storms Lab., Norman, 1984-87, mgr. weather hazards to aviation project, 1987-91, chief forecast applications rsch. group, 1991-93, asst. dir., chief stormscale rsch. and applications divsn., 1993—; mem. exptl. forecast facility mgmt. group, 1991—; mem. Cleveland County YMCA Program Com., 1991-93; spl. mem. adj. faculty U. Okla. Sch. Meteorology, Norman, 1989—; mem. Okla. Mesonet Steering Com.; coun. mem., fellow Coop. Inst. Mesoscale Meteorol. Studies. Contbr. articles to profl. jours. Grantee FAA, 1987-96, NASA, 1990-91, 96, Nat. Weather Svc., 1991-96; recipient Dist. Authorship award Environ. Rsch. Labs., 1991. Mem. Am. Meteorol. Soc. Lutheran. Home: 3405 S Bryant Ave Moore OK 73160-8401 Office: Nat Severe Storms Lab 1313 Halley Cir Norman OK 73069-8480

EINSPRUCH, BURTON CYRIL, Psychiatrist; b. N.Y.C., June 27, 1935; s. Adolph and Mala (Goldblatt) E.; B.A., So. Meth. U., 1956, Sc.B., 1958; M.D., Southwestern Med. Sch., Dallas, 1960; m. Barbara Standen Traeger, Oct. 9, 1960; children: Julia Moat, Alexander Louis, Robert Sands. Intern, Montefiore Hosp., N.Y.C., 1960-61; resident Nat. Hosp. Inst. Neurology, London, 1962, U. Tex., Dallas, 1961-64 (also fellow); sr. resident Parkland Meml. Hosp., Dallas, 1964; instr. psychiatry U. Pa., 1964-66; pvt. practice psychiatry, Dallas, 1966—; mem. staff Presbyn. and Parkland hosps., Timberlawn Psychiat. Hosp.; clin. asst. prof. U. Tex., Health Sci. Center, Dallas, 1966-70, dir. psychiat. div. Student Health Service, 1966-72, clin. assoc. prof., 1970—; dir. Southwestern Adult Psychiat. Clinic, Dallas, 1966-74; dir. psychiat. service Dallas Home for Jewish Aged, 1966-82, now cons. staff dir. Dallas Nat. Bank; research cons. Dallas Geriatric Research Inst., 1974-80; adj. prof. sociology N. Tex. State U., Denton, 1975-82; cons. staff Baylor U. Hosp., Golden Acres Hosp.; clin. assoc. prof. psychiatry U. Tex. Health Scis. Ctr., Dallas, 1971—; assoc. prof. psychiatry U. Tex. Southwestern Med. Ctr., Dallas, 1971—; clin. assoc. prof. psychiatry NYU Med. Ctr., N.Y.C., 1990; chmn., bd. dirs. Planned Behavioral Health Care, Inc., Dallas; affiliate Tex. Inst. Rsch. and Edn. on Aging, Health Sci. Ctr. Fort Worth; Mem. editorial bd. Tex. Medicine. Bd. dirs. Mental Health Assn. Dallas, 1960-69, Jewish Family Service, 1969-71, 73-75. Trustee Evans Fedn., N.Y.C., 1986—, St. Mark's Sch. Tex., 1987—, Jaffe Collection McDermott Libr., U. Tex., Dallas, 1987—; mem. exec. bd. libr. So. Meth. U., 1992—; adv. dir. Leonhardt Fedn., N.Y.C., 1990, Children of Alcoholics Fedn., 1991; arbitrator, N.Y. and Am. Exchs., N.Y.C., 1884—. Served to lt. comdr. M.C., USNR, 1964-66. Diplomate Am. Bd. Psychiatry and Neurology (examiner, 1974—). Fellow Am. Psychiat. Assn., Am. Coll. Psychiatrists, Am. Soc. Adolescent Psychiatry, N. Tex. Soc. Adolescent Psychiatry (past pres.); mem. Royal Coll. Psychiatry London, AMA, Tex. Med. Assn. Contbr. profl. jours. Home: 5411 Meaders Ln Dallas TX 75229-6651 Office: 8330 Meadow Rd Ste 117 Dallas TX 75231-3750

EINSTEIN, ALBERT B., JR., health facility administrator, oncologist, educator; b. Balt., Nov. 17, 1941; s. Albert Brooks and Janet Emaline Einstein; m. Margery Andersen; children: William, Matthew, Christina, Brooks. AB cum laude, Princeton U., 1963; MD, Cornell U., 1967. Diplomate Am. Bd. Med. Examiners, Am. Bd. Internal Medicine, Am. Bd. Med. Oncology; lic. oncologist, Md. 1971, Wash. 1972, Calif. 1973, Fla. 1993. Intern Johns Hopkins Hosp., Balt., 1967-68, resident, 1968-69; resident U. Wash. Sch. Medicine, Seattle, 1971-72; clin. assoc. immunology br. Nat. Cancer Inst., Bethesda, Md., 1969-71; sr. fellow in medicine, divsn. oncology U. Wash., 1972-74, asst. prof. medicine, divsn. oncology, 1974-75; pvt. practice internal medicine, hematology and med. oncology Virginia Mason Clinic, Seattle, 1976-93; assoc. ctr. dir. clin. affairs H. Lee Moffitt Cancer Ctr. and Rsch. Inst., Tampa, Fla., 1993—; prof. medicine U. S. Fla., 1993—, med. oncologist genitourinary cancer program, 1993—; clin. asst. prof. dept. medicine U. Wash., 1976-79, clin. assoc. prof., 1979-93; med. dir. Virginia Mason Cancer Ctr., 1989-92, pres., 1990-92; affiliate investigator Fred Hutchinson Cancer Rsch. Ctr., Seattle, 1991-92; med. dir. Wash. State Cancer Pain Initiative; rschr. in field. Author: (with others) Pain Management and Care of the Terminal Patient, 1992; contbr. numerous articles to profl. jours. Recipient Nat. Found. Rsch. award 1979. Fellow Am. Coll. Physicians; mem. AMA, Am. Fedn. Clin. Rsch., Am. Assn. Cancer Rsch., Am. Soc. Clin. Oncology (nominating com. 1987, clin. practices com. 1990-93), Am. Coll. Physician Execs., Am. Cancer Soc. (King County unit bd. dirs. 1985, profl. edn. com. 1985, Tampa Bay unit bd. dirs. 1993—, pub. affairs com. 1993—, Jr. Clin. Faculty fellowship 1973-75), Assn. Community Cancer Ctrs. (various positions and coms.), Fla. Assn. Clin. Oncology, King County Med. Soc., Hillsborough County Med. Soc. Episcopalian. Office: H Lee Moffitt Cancer Ctr/Rsch Inst 12902 Magnolia Dr Tampa FL 33612-9416

EISELE, GARNETT THOMAS, federal judge; b. Hot Springs, Ark., Nov. 3, 1923; s. Garnett Martin and Mary (Martin) E.; m. Kathryn Freygang, June 24, 1950; children: Wendell A., Garnett Martin II, Kathryn M., Jean E. Student, U. Fla., 1940-42, Ind. U., 1942-43; AB, Washington U., 1947; LLB, Harvard U., 1950, LLM, 1951. Bar: Ark. 1951. Practiced in Hot Springs, 1951-52, Little Rock, 1953-69; assoc. Wootten, Land and Matthews, 1951-52, Owens, McHaney, Lofton & McHaney, 1956-60; asst. U.S. atty. Little Rock, 1953-55; pvt. practice law, 1961-69; judge U.S. Dist. Ct. (ea. dist.) Ark., 1970—, chief judge, 1975-91, sr. judge, 1991—; legal adviser to gov. Ark., 1966-69. Del. Ark. 7th Constl. Conv., 1969-70; trustee U. Ark., 1969-70. Served with AUS, 1943-46, ETO. Mem. ABA, Ark. Bar Assn., Pulaski County Bar Assn., Am. Judicature Soc., Am. Law Inst. Office: US Dist Ct PO Box 3684 Little Rock AR 72203-3684

EISELE, WILLIAM DAVID, insurance agency executive; b. Iron Mountain, Mich., July 31, 1927; s. David Christian and Muriel Elizabeth (Ockstadt) E.; B.S., U. Mich., 1950; m. Helen Jeanne Holmberg, Dec. 27, 1953; children—David, Meg. Ins. agt. Employers Mut. of Wausau, Milw., 1951, West Bend, Wis., 1952-53, Watertown, Wis., 1953-56, Orlando, Fla., 1957, Tampa, Fla., 1958; pres. William D. Eisele & Co., Clearwater, Fla., 1959—. Charter pres. Heritage Presbyn. Housing Project, 1971-72; town commr., Belleair Shore, Fla.; elder Presbyn. Ch. Recipient disting. alumni service award U. Mich., 1975. Mem. Fla. Assn. Ins. Agts., Clearwater-Largo-Dunedin Insurors (past pres.), U. Mich. Alumni Assn. (dir., v.p.). Clubs: Clearwater Rotary; U. Mich. (organizer, past pres. Pinellas County, Fla.). Office: 13080 Belcher Rd S Largo FL 33773-1658

EISENBERG, ROBIN LEDGIN, religious education administrator; b. Passaic, N.J., Jan. 10, 1951; d. Morris and Ruth (Miller) Ledgin. BS, West Chester State U., 1973; M Edn., Kutztown State U., 1977. Administrv. asst. Keneseth Israel, Allentown, Pa., 1973-77; dir. edn. Cong. Schaarai Zedek, Tampa, Fla., 1977-79, Kehilath Israel, Pacific Palisades, Calif., 1979-80, Temple Beth El, Boca Raton, Fla., 1980—. Contbr. Learning Together, 1987, Bar/Bat Mizvah Education: A Sourcebook, 1993, The New Jewish Teachers Handbook, 1994. Chmn. edn. info., Planned Parenthood, Boca Raton Fla. 1989. Recipient Kamiker Camp award Nat. Assn. Temple Educators, Pres.'s award for adminstrn., 1990. Mem. Nat. Assn. Temple Educators (pres. 1990-92), Coalition Advancement of Jewish Edn. Home: 5692 Santiago Cir Boca Raton FL 33433-7297 Office: Temple Beth El 333 SW 4th Ave Boca Raton FL 33432-5709

EISENBRAUN, EDMUND JULIUS, chemist educator; b. Wewela, S.D., Dec. 10, 1920; s. Julius and Elizabeth (Herrmann) E.; m. Joyce Marie Abrahamson, Aug. 20, 1949; children: Ellen, Greta, Ann. BS in Chemistry, U. Wis., 1949, MS in Chemistry, 1951, PhD of Organic Chemistry, 1955. Rsch. chemist Monsanto Chem. Co., Dayton, Ohio, 1955-56; rsch. fellow Wayne State U., Detroit, 1956-59; rsch. assoc. Stanford (Calif.) U., 1959-60, sr. rsch. assoc., 1960-61; dir. rsch. Aldrich Chem. Co., Milw., 1961-62; assoc. prof. Okla. State U., Stillwater, 1962-68, prof., 1968-75, regents prof., 1976—. Contbr. articles to profl. jours. Served with AUS, 1941-46. Recipient Merit for Outstanding Scientist award Okla. Acad. Scis., 1982, Okla. Chemist award Am. Chem. Soc., 1983. Republican. Office: Okla State U Dept Chemistry Stillwater OK 74078

EISNER, JEROME ALLAN, trade association executive; b. Sheboygan, Wis., July 6, 1945; s. Harold Frederick and Frieda (Diener) E.; m. Eileen Ann Dixon, Aug. 17, 1968; children: Elizabeth Ann, Kimberly Jinmee. B.S., U.Wis.-Oshkosh, 1968; Edn. Cert. Alverno Coll., 1970; cert. Grad. Builder Inst., assoc. exec. Tchr. Pius XI High Sch., Milw., 1968-71; sales rep. R.L. Polk & Co., Kansas City, Mo., 1971-72; mem. sales, mktg. staff 3M Co., St. Paul, 1972-78; program developer Golle & Holmes, Minnetonka, Minn., 1978-82; exec. dir. U.S. Jaycees, Tulsa, Okla., 1983; pres., owner Servpro of So. Hills, Tulsa, 1983-86, exec. v.p. Builders Assn. of Met. Tulsa, 1986-91; exec. v.p. Builders Assn. Ft. Worth, 1991—; sec. Nat. Found. for Volunteerism, Tulsa, 1982-83; mem. nat. adv. bd. Am. Family Soc., Washington, 1983. Author: Member's Guide to Speak Up, 1976; You Can Be Whatever You Want to Be, 1978. Bd. dirs. Project Concern, Minn., 1980-82; bd. dirs. Minnesota Jaycees, 1977-82, pres., 1980-81; bd. dirs. Minn. Jaycees Charitable Found., 1980-82, vice chmn. United Way Tulsa. Named Jaycees Internat. Senator, 1980, U.S. Jaycees Ambassador, 1982, Minn. Jaycees Statesman, 1981, Outstanding Young Men of Am., 1978, 79, 81, one of 10 Outstanding Sr. Men, 1968; recipient Clayton Frost Meml. award U.S. Jaycees, 1981, Cert. Merit award 3M Chmn. of Bd., 1975; Greek Man of Yr. award, 1968. Mem. Personal Dynamics Assn., Am. Soc. Assn. Execs., Tulsa Soc. Assn. Execs. (membership chmn., pres. 1986—), Tex. Soc. Assn. Execs., Dallas-Ft. Worth Soc. Assn., Exec. Officers Council, Nat. Assn. Homebuilders (bd. dirs. 1990—, David G. Lloyd Meml. award 1988, sec.-treas. 1994, v.p. 1995, pres. 1996, seminar dean 1992), Tulsa Pvt. Industry Tng. Council (bd. dirs.), Tulsa C. of C. (chmn. east area council), Broken Arrow C. of C., Ft. Worth C. of C., Pi Kappa Delta, Alpha Epsilon Rho. Club: St. Benedicts Men's (Broken Arrow, Okla.). Roman Catholic. Lodge: KC (advocate 3rd degree). Avocations: reading; weightlifting; karate. Home: 900 Tennison Dr Euless TX 76039

EISS, NORMAN SMITH, JR., mechanical engineering educator; b. Buffalo, Mar. 13, 1931; s. Norman Smith and Elizabeth Charlotte (Hengerer) Eiss; m. Carol Mae Siegel, Aug. 17, 1957 (div. Mar. 1975); children: Martin E., Christine C., Jennifer L. Voland; m. Nancy Jean Siegrist, Mar. 27, 1975. B in Mech. Engring., Rensselaer Polytech. Inst., 1953; MS, Cornell U., 1959, PhD, 1961. Mech. process engr. duPont Rayon Plant, Buffalo, 1953-54; asst. mech. engr. Cornell Aero. Lab., 1956-58, rsch. mech. engr., 1961-66; assoc. prof. Va. Poly. Inst., Blacksburg, 1966-77, prof., 1977-88, George G. Goodson prof. mech. engring., 1988—; cons. Litton Systems, Blacksburg, 1966-70, 71—, GM, Lockport N.Y., 1973, N.J. Inst. Tech., Newark, 1975, Harris Corp., Melbourne, Fla., 1976, Dun-Donnelly Pub. Corp., N.Y.C., 1976, 77, Borg Warner Corp., Des Plaines, Ill., 1977, Johnson and Johnson, East Windsor, N.J., 1978, 80, Fairmont (Minn.) Railway Motors, 1979, Inland Motors, Radford, Va., 1979—, Dept. Transp., Washington, 1979, Tenn. Eastman Co., Kingsport, 1980, Ecton Corp., Dayton, Ohio, 1981, Bendix Advanced Tech. Ctr., Columbia, Md., 1982, Cummins Engine, Columbus, Ind., 1982, James Brincefield, Richmond, Va., 1982, Owings Corning Fiberglass, Granville, Ohio, 1982, Armstrong World Industries, Lancaster, Pa., Worthington Pump, Moutainside, N.J., 1984, Thoratec Labs, Berkeley, Calif., 1984, Synertech Inc., Richmond, 1984, Am. Hoechst Corp., Greer, S.C., 1984, IBM, Tucson, 1984, Eastman Kodak, Rochester, N.Y., 1985-87, 90, WESTVACO Rsch. Lab., Laurel, Md., 1985, Tech. Adv. Svcs. for Attys., Ft. Washington, Pa., 1985, Air Products and Chemicals, Allentown, 1988, DuPont, Wilmington, Del., 1988, Ford Motor Co., Dearborn, Mich., 1988, Am. Rsch. Corp. Va., Radford, 1988, Gates Rubber Co., Denver, 1990, GenCorp, Akron, Ohio, 1991, Prince Corp., Holland, Mich., 1992, Beloit Corp., Clarks Summit, Pa., 1993, Genicom Corp., Waynesboro, Va., 1994, Dow Chem., Freeport, Tex., 1994; rschr. 3M Co., St. Paul, 1969, Inland Motors, Radford, 1981; proposal reviewer U.S. Army Rsch. Office, 1972—; presenter, chmn., speaker numerous confs., symposia. Co-editor: Tribology and Mechanics of Magnetic Storage Systems, vol. I, 1984, vol. II, 1985, vol. III, 1986, vol. IV, 1987, vol. V, 1988, vol. VI, 1989; editor numerous meeting proceedings; contbr. articles to profl. jours. Bd. dirs. YMCA, Blacksburg, 1994—. 1st. lt. USAF, 1954-56, Libya. Grantee Wood and Books Co., 1957-58, Abrasive Grain Assn., 1961-65, S.S. White Co., 1966, USAROD, 1973-76, 77-80, GM, 1974, Va. Hwy. Safety Divsn., 1977, 78, Litton Sys., 1977, Alumnium Co. Am., 1978, USARO, 1980-83, Alcoa Found., 1980-82, Office Naval Rsch., 1982-86, 96-97, NASA, 1982-88, U.S. Army Rsch. Office, 1983-87, Inst. Computer Aided Engring., 1984, Reynolds Metals Co., 1985, Ford Motor Co., 1988-92, 94-97, Va. Inst. Material Sys., 1988-92, NSF Sci. and Tech. Ctr., 1989-92, Windward Internat. Inc., 1988-90; Office of Naval Rsch., 1996-98. Fellow STLE (chmn. edn. com. 1969-70, 71-73, edit. rev. com., wear control com. 1973-75, co-chmn. advanced seminar 1976, assoc. editor Tribology Trans. 1976-80, 81-89, chmn. wear tech. com. 1978-79, vice chair 1979-81, joint conf. planning com. 1979-83, chmn. 1981-82, vice chmn. 1982-83, co-organizer symposium 1984-89, STLE Nat. award 1991, Hunt Best Paper award 1994-95); mem. ASEE, ASME (engring. accreditation com. 1993-97), ASTM (G-2 com. 1972—, chmn. polymer wear task group 1978-82), Am. Soc. Lubrication Engrs. (edit. rev. com. 1972—, assoc. editor Transactions 1976-80, 81-89, bd. dirs. 1986-92), Sigma Xi, Phi Kappa Phi, Pi Tau Sigma, Tau Beta Pi. Office: Va Polytech Inst Dept Mech Engring Blacksburg VA 24061

EISSLER, VEDA ALICIA, middle school educator, musician; b. Houston, Feb. 19, 1960; d. William Eugene and Veda Mae (Greb) E. MusB, U. Houston, 1982, MusM, 1986, student, 1989—. Actress, singer and musician The Lone Star Hist. Drama, Galveston, Tex., 1977; music and fine arts instr. Fleming Fine Arts Acad., 1982-86; head orch. dir. and fgn. lang. instr. Strack Intermediate Sch., Klein, Tex., 1986—; violinist and violist Houston Instrumental Ensemble, 1976-81, Summer Arts Festival Orch., San Luis Potosi, Mex., 1982; violinist Houston Luth. Chorale, 1991—. Co-author: Headstart to Spanish, 1989, Headstart to French, 1989, Headstart to German, 1989. Bicentennial courier Am. Bicentennial Commn., Montevideo, Uruguay, 1976; dir. handbell choir Meml. Drive Presbyn. Ch., 1986-87; rep. Dem. Precinct Conv., Houston, 1978, Rep. Precinct Conv., 1980, Rep. Congl. Dist. Conv., 1980, Rep. State Conv., 1980. Mem. Music Educators' Nat. Conf., Am. String Tchr. Assn., Tex. Music Educators' Assn., Tex. Orch. Dir. Assn., Tex. State Tchr. Assn. Home: 9527 Meadowcroft Dr Houston TX 77063-3814 Office: Strack Intermediate Sch 18027S Kuykendahl Rd Spring TX 77379-8116

EISSMANN, ROBERT FRED, manufacturing engineer; b. Bklyn., Jan. 17, 1924; s. Fred Arno and Katherine Elizabeth (Petersohn) E.; m. June I. Vreeland, Dec. 29, 1950; 1 child, Roy Norman. Student, Pratt Inst., 1942-43, 46. Wireman, Western Electric Co., Kearney, N.J., 1946-49; assembler Indsl. TV, Clifton, N.J., 1949-51; leadman Bogue Electric, Paterson, N.J., 1951-60, 65-68; wireman, engring. asst. Kearfott, Gen. Precion, West Paterson, N.J., 1960-65; assembler-wireman Henderson Industries, Fairfield, N.J., 1968-72; prodn. mgr. Mipco Inc., West Caldwell, N.J., 1972-80, plant mgr., Fairfield, N.J., 1980-84, product support mgr., 1984-85, value engr., 1985-86; advance product design engr., 1986-87, design engr. indsl., elec. products. Amerace Corp., 1987-90, ret., 1990; staff mem. Russellstoll div. Midland Ross Corp., Livingston, N.J., 1980-83. Mem. freight container standards com. Elec. Task Force. With Signal Corps, U.S. Army, 1943-46. Methodist.

EJIMOFOR, CORNELIUS OGU, political scientist, educator; b. Owerri, Nigeria, Oct. 10, 1940; came to U.S., 1963; s. Osuji and Helen Domaonu (Atashia) E.; m. Priscilla Loveth Amaugo, Mar. 10, 1966; children: Cornelia, Caroline, Cornelius Jr., Priscilla, Ebere. AA, Warren Wilson Coll., 1965; BA in Polit. Sci., Wilberforce U., 1966; MPA, U. Dayton, 1967; MA, PhD, U. Okla., 1971. Tchr. Cath. Mission Schs., Emekuku, Nigeria, 1959-63; rsch. asst. U. Dayton, Ohio, 1966-67; instr. polit. sci. Edward Waters Coll., Jacksonville, Fla., 1967-68, prof. polit. sci., 1992—; grad. asst. U. Okla., Norman, 1968-70; asst. prof. William Paterson Coll., Wayne, N.J., 1970-72; from assoc. prof. to prof. Tuskegee (Ala.) U., 1972-80, dept. head polit. sci., 1972-77; sr. lectr., reader U. Nigeria, Nsukka, 1980-91, prof. polit. sci., 1991-92; coord., head, prof. sub-dept. pub. adminstrn. and local govt. U. Nigeria, 1990-92, coord. local govt. tng. programs, 1990-92. Author: British Colonia Objectives and Policies in Nigeria, 1987, Management of Human Resources: A Generic Approach, 1992. Mem. Am. Soc. for Pub. Adminstrn. (state coun. mem. Ala. 1976-78), Am. Polit. Sci. Assn., Nigerian Polit. Sci. Assn., AAUP. Democrat. Roman Catholic. Home: 5723-2 Holly Bell Dr Jacksonville FL 32277

EKDAHL, RICHARD WILLIAM, educational association executive; b. Worcester, Mass., Feb. 25, 1930; s. Harold Gustavus and Hildur Marianne (Nordlander) E.; BMus, Boston U., 1951, AM, 1954; EdD, U. Houston, 1970; m. Mary Edgerton Hazard, Nov. 22, 1956; 1 child, Lauren Lee. Choral dir. St. Bernard's Sch., Gladstone, N.J., 1954-55, Cushing Acad., Ashburnham, Mass., 1955-57; tchr., asst. dean St. John's Sch., Houston, 1957-68; tchr., dir. admissions Holland Hall Sch., Tulsa, 1968-72; exec. dir. Ind. Schs. Assn. Southwest, Tulsa, 1965-95; chmn. Okla. Pvt. Sch. Accreditation Commn.; trustee, treas., vice chmn. trustees Town and Country Sch., Tulsa; trustee, sec. Inst. Study Pvt. Schs., L.A., Tex. Assn. Nonpub. Schs. Treas., Concertime, Inc., Tulsa; trustee Winston Sch., Dallas, Coun. for Religion in Ind. Schs., Washington; chmn. Tex. Pvt. Sch. Accreditation Commn. Mem. ASCD, Assocs. for Rsch. Pvt. Edn. (trustee), Am. Ednl. Rsch. Assn., Nat. Coun. Tchrs. Math. Episcopalian. Home: 3632 S Yorktown Pl Tulsa OK 74105-3452 Office: PO Box 52297 Tulsa OK 74152

EKERY, ADRIANA TERESA, healthcare administrator, oncology nurse; b. Terrell, Tex., Feb. 15, 1957; d. Fernando V. and Josefina (Quintero) Rodriguez; m. Alan D. Ekery, Sept. 23, 1989. Assoc. in Nursing, McLennan Community Coll., 1979; BSN, U. Tex., Arlington, 1983. Nurse administrator Caremark Home Care, El Paso, Tex., 1988; Medicare coord./supr. Mission Health Care Svcs., El Paso, 1989-93; DON (2 brs.) Columbia Health Care Svcs. (formerly Mission Health Care Svcs.), 1993—; adminstr., dir. nursing Home Health Svc., Inc., 1992—; profl. in establishing home health aide competency test for all HHA's, City of El Paso. Mem. Am. Soc. Parenteral and Enteral Nutrition, Oncology Nursing Soc., Intravenous Nurses Soc., El Paso Home Health Assocs. (rec. sec.).

EKPO, EFREMFON FRANK, physicist, educator; b. Uyo, Nov. 29, 1944; came to U.S., 1974; s. Frank and Arit Udo Ekpo; m. Inyang Effiong Asukwo, July 11, 1974; children: Ubong, Eme-Obong, Anyanime, Inemesit. BS, U. Lagos, Nigeria, 1970; MS, Va. State U., 1976; postgrad., George Washington U., 1981; PhD, Howard U., 1986. Registered profl. engr., Md. Asst. prof. physics U. D.C., 1986-92; assoc. prof., dir. physics maj. program Bethune-Cookman Coll., Daytona Beach, Fla., 1993—. Contbr. articles to profl. publs. Environ. careers awareness program grantee WMX Techs., Inc., 1996. Mem. AAAS, IEEE, NSPE, Nat. Soc. Black Physicists, Nat. Sci. Tchrs. Assn., N.Y. Acad. Scis. Democrat. Office: Bethune-Cookman Coll Physics Dept 640 Dr MM Bethune Blvd Daytona Beach FL 32114-3099

EKWEM, ROBERTSON M., lawyer; b. Lagos, Nigeria, Oct. 16, 1962; s. Chief B.N. and Lolo Briget (Oforha) E. BBA in Banking and Fin., Tex. So. U., Houston, 1987; JD, Thurgood Marshall Sch. Law, Houston, 1994. Bar: Tex. 1994, U.S. Dist. Ct. (so. and ea. dists.) Tex. 1995, U.S. Ct. Appeals (5th cir.) 1995. Pvt. practice Houston, 1994—. Mem. ABA, Houston Bar Assn., Assn. Trial Lawyers Am., Houston Young Lawyers Assn., NAACP, Harris County Criminal Lawyers Assn., Tex. Trial Lawyers Assn., Phi Alpha Delta. Roman Catholic. Home: 6601 Sandspoint Dr Unit 55 Houston TX 77074 Office: 8323 Southwest Fwy 555 Houston TX 77074

ELAM, ANDREW GREGORY, II, conventions and visitors bureau company executive; b. Winchester, Va., Feb. 6, 1932; s. Andrew Gregory and Frances Clayton (Gold) E.; m. Rebecca Rhea Cole, Oct. 26, 1958; children: Andrew Gregory III, Philip Cole, Dawna Frances. AB, Presbyn. Coll., 1955. Adminstrv. asst. Citizen's and So. Nat. Bank, Columbia, S.C., 1955-56; nat. exec. dir. Pi Kappa Phi, Sumter, S.C., 1956-59; pres. Carolina Potato Co., Inc., West Columbia, S.C., 1959-61; mem. pub. relations staff Kendavis Industries Internat., Inc., Ft. Worth, 1961-63; dir. sales promotion Pioneer Am. Ins. Co., Ft. Worth, 1963-64, dir. pub. rels. and sales promotion, 1964-66; asst. v.p., 1966-68, v.p., mem. exec. com., 1968-71, bd. dirs., 1970-71; v.p. pub. relations and sales promotion Gt. Am. Res. Ins. Co., Dallas, 1972-89, J.C. Penney Life Ins. Co., Dallas, 1972-89; owner Solution House, 1989—; v.p. communications, meeting profl. in residence Dallas Conv. and Visitors Bur., 1989—; Mem. pub. relations adv. council Am. Council of Life Ins., Washington, 1971-89; mem. pub. relations com. Tex. Life Conv., 1970-82. Mem. public info. adv. com. Am. Cancer Soc., Tex. div., 1969-80, chmn., 1972-78, exec. com., bd. dirs., 1972-78; vice-chmn. pub. relations com. Tarrant County United Fund, 1967; campaign leader Community Pride Campaign Performing Arts, 1969. Bd. dirs., treas., vice-chmn. Tarrant County unit Am. Cancer Soc., 1963-71, bd. dirs. Dallas County unit, 1972-93, sec., 1977-78; bd. dirs. Ft. Worth Community Theatre, 1971-72, Baylor U. Med. Ctr. Found., Dallas, 1980-95; mem. adv. bd. Sammons Cancer Ctr., Dallas, 1980-86; deacon Presbyn. Ch., Dallas, 1966-68, ruling elder, 1969-71, 81-84, 95—; mem. adv. com. Dallas Conv. and Visitors Bur., 1987-89. Mem. Life Ins. Communicators Assn. (dir. communications workshop 1970-71, exec. com. 1973-74, chmn. So. Round Table 1972, chair ann. meeting arrangements com. 1986), Pub. Relations Soc. Am., Tex. Pub. Relations Assn. (bd. dirs. 1966), Indsl. Editors Ft. Worth (pres. 1968), Ft. Worth C. of C. (chmn. publ. com. 1970), Dallas Advt. League, Dallas Ins. Club, Meeting Planners Inst. (pres. Dallas chpt. 1980, internat. dir. 1981-83, 86-87, Dallas chpt. Planner of Yr. 1985-86, Internat. Planner of Yr. 1987), Soc. Preservation and Encouragement of Barbershop Quartet Singing in Am. (chpt. pres. 1978, chpt. barbershopper of yr., 1976), Southwestern dist. Barbershopper of Yr. 1982, treas. Southwestern dist. 1983-85, exec. v.p. 1986-87, pres. 1988-89, Hall of Fame, 1992, internat. bd. 1990-91, mem. internat. com. logopedics and svcs. 1985-90, chmn. internat. mem. devel. com. 1990-92, chmn. 50th anniversary million dollar fund drive 1988), Life Ins. Mktg. Rsch. Assn. (mktg. and communications com. 1985, vice chmn. 1986-87, chmn. 1987-89). Presbyterian. Home: 7730 Chattington Dr Dallas TX 75248-5306 Office: 1201 Elm St Ste 2000 Dallas TX 75270-2114

ELAM, CRAIG STEPHEN, medical librarian; b. Cheyenne, Wyo., Sept. 6, 1946; s. Edgar J. and Jean F. (Edgecombe) E.; m. Elizabeth Ann O'Neil, Sept. 9, 1972; children: Sean Michael, Christopher Ryan. AA, Menlo Coll., Menlo Park, Calif., 1966; AB, Stanford U., 1968; MLS, U. Calif., Berkeley, 1972; cert. med. librarianship, UCLA, 1973. Libr. asst. NASA Ames Rsch. Ctr., Moffett Field, Calif., 1969-71; intern UCLA, 1972-73; serials cataloger U. Wis., Madison, 1973-78, coord. tech. svcs., 1976-78; assoc. dir. tech. svcs. U. North Tex. Health Sci. Ctr., Fort Worth, 1978—; cons. Parker Coll. Chiropractic, Dallas, 1989; manuscript reviewer Med. Libr. Assn., 1995. Mem. Med. Libr. Assn., Acad. Health Info. Profls. (disting. mem.), Osteo. Librs. Spl. Interest Group (convenor 1992—), Osteo. Librs. Sect. (chmn. 1985-86). Office: U North Tex Health Sci Ctr Lewis Health Sci Libr 3500 Camp Bowie Blvd Fort Worth TX 76107

ELBEIN, ALAN DAVID, medical science educator; b. Lynn, Mass., Mar. 20, 1933; s. Gersh and Golda (Stryer) E.; m. Elaine J. Brooks, June 21, 1953; children: Steven Conrad, Bradley Martin, Richard Craig. AB, Clark U., 1954; MS, U. Ariz., 1956; PhD, Purdue U., 1960. Rsch. assoc. in biochemistry Med. Sch. U. Mich., Ann Arbor, 1960-63; rsch. assoc. in biochemistry U. Calif., Berkeley, 1963-64; asst. prof., then assoc. prof. biology Rice U., Houston, 1964-69; prof. Health Sci. Ctr. U. Tex., San Antonio, 1969-90; prof., chmn. biochemistry dept. U. Ark. Med. Sci., Little Rock, 1991—; mem. study sect. NSF, 1972-75, NIH, 1983-87, 93—; mem. editl. bd. Jour. Biol. Chemistry, Arch. Biochem. Biophysics, Plant Physiology, Glycobiology, Jour. Bacteriology, Eur. Jour. Biochem. Editor: Swainsonine; contbr. articles, revs. to profl. jours. Mem. Am. Chem. Soc., Am. Soc. Plant Physiology, Am. Soc. Biol. Chem. and Molecular Biology. Jewish. Home: 23 Fontenay Cir Little Rock AR 72211-9569 Office: U Ark Med Scis Dept Biochem & Mol Biology 4301 W Markham St Little Rock AR 72205-7101

ELBERRY, ZAINAB ABDELHALIEM, insurance company executive; b. Alexandria, Egypt, Sept. 30, 1948; came to U.S., 1973; d. Abelhaliem Elberry and Nazieha Ahmed (Ezzat) E.; m. Mohammed Nour Naciri, Aug. 7, 1975; 1 child, Nadeam El Shami. BA, Ain Shams U., Cairo, 1971; MA, Am. U., Cairo, 1975. Cataloger Vanderbilt Joint U. Librs., Nashville, 1976-77; sales rep. Equitable Life Assurance Soc., 1977-80; with Met. Life Ins., Nashville, 1980—, account rep., 1981—, mgr., 1984; mem. adv. bd. Parkview Surgery Ctr., 1983-84. Chmn. com., bd. dirs. Nashville Internat. Cultural Heritage, 1983—, also bd. dirs.; chmn. Internat. Women Nashville Fair, 1977-78; bd. dirs. YWCA, Coun. for Nat. Interest; fundraiser Peace Links, 1989, YMCA Internat. House, 1987-89, Nashville Animal Shelter, 1979, Nashville League Hearing Impaired, 1976-81; mem. adv. bd. Nashville celebration Internat. Yr. of Disabled Persons; pres. Internat. Women Nashville. Recipient Spl. Contbn. award U.S. Coun. Internat. Disabled Persons, 1981. Mem. Nat. Assn. Life Underwriters, Nat. Assn. Profl. Saleswomen (Recognition award 1986), Gen. Agy. Mgrs. Assn., UN Assn. (bd. dirs. Nashville chpt.), Altrusa Club. Islam. Home: 5600 Kendall Dr # B Nashville TN 37209-4548

ELBERT, JAMES PEAK, independent insurance agent, minister; b. Pampa, Tex., Feb. 5, 1937; s. James Monteen and Nannie Pearle (Harwell) E.; m. Jean Coburn, June 25, 1960 (div. Jan., 1983); children: James Michael, Steven Lawrence; m. Ann English Smith, Apr. 23, 1983; 1 child, Jennifer English Aberle. BA, Southwestern U., Georgetown, Tex., 1959; MDiv, So. Meth. U., 1962. Minister First Meth. Ch., Glen Flora, Tex., 1962-65, Falvey Meml. Meth. Ch., Wells, Tex., 1965-67; assoc. minister First United Meth. Ch., Orange, Tex., 1967-69; minister of edn. Trinity United Meth. Ch., Beaumont, Tex., 1969-70; minister First United Meth. Ch., Murchiston, Tex., 1970-71; campus minister Henderson County Jr. Coll., Athens, Tex., 1970-71; v.p., owner Elbert Insur. Agy., Lake Jackson, Tex., 1971-76, Bennett-Elbert Co., Lake Jackson, 1976-83; v.p., gen. mgr. Jahn-Austin Insur., Galveston, Tex., 1983—; pres. Galveston Ins. Bd., 1986-88, Elbert Ins. Agy., Lake Jackson, Tex., 1995—; apptd. to Windstorm Study com. Tex. Dept. Ins., 1992, liaison to Tex. Dept. Ins. bldg. code study com., 1992—; supernumerary Tex. Conf. United Meth. Ch.; campus minister Henderson County Jr. Coll., Athens, Tex., 1970-71. Bd. dirs. Jr. Achievement of Brazoria County, 1980-81; active Lake Jackson Little League, 1974-77, Lake Jackson Teenage League, 1978-79, Lake Jackson Babe Ruth League, 1980; sec. Galveston Windstorm Action Com., 1988—; pres. Galveston Housing Fin. Corp., 1983-95, City of Galveston Property Fin. Authority, Inc., 1993-95; v.p. Bay Area coun. Boy Scouts Am., 1988—; pres. Ball H.S. Band Boosters, Galveston, 1991-92; mem. Mayor's Roundtable on Housing, City of Galveston, 1993-95; chmn. com. on ministries Moody Meml. First United Meth. Ch., 1994-95. Recipient Dist. award of Merit Bay Area Coun. Boy Scouts Am. Quintana Dist., Lake Jackson, 1979, Silver Beaver Bay Area Coun. Boy Scouts Am., Galveston, 1985. Mem. Cert. Ins. Counselors (cert., pres. Tex. chpt. 1992), Ind. Ins. Agts. Tex. (chmn. com. 1991-95), Tex. Assn. Ins. Agts. (liaison to Tex. windstorm pool 1993-95, bd. dirs. 1995—, Chmn. of the Yr. 1993-94), Galveston C. of C. (bd. dirs. 1992-95), Rotary of Galveston Island (pres. 1993-94, Rotarian of Yr., Paul Harris fellow 1990, Bd. Mem. of Yr. 1991), Brazosport C. of C. (mem. bd. 1980-81), Phi Delta Theta. Home: 7754 Beaudelaire Cir Galveston TX 77551-1625 Office: Elbert Ins Agy 127 Circle Way Ste C Lake Jackson TX 77566 also: Jahn-Austin Insurance 6025 Heards Lane Galveston TX 77552

ELBL, FRANCISCO, pediatrician, educator; b. Madrid, Aug. 23, 1935; came to U.S., 1963; s. Francisco and Rosa Micaela (Puertas) E.; m. Carmen Milagros Nieves, June 7, 1968; children: Maria Selima, Tamara Adriana, Francisco Jose, Frederico Alejandro. BS, Nat. U. Buenos Aires, 1954; MD, U. Buenos Aires, 1962. Intern McLaren Gen. Hosp., Flint, Mich., 1963-64; pediatric resident Children's Hosp., U. Louisville, 1964-66, pediatric cardiology fellow, 1968-70, asst. prof. pediatrics and pediatric cardiology, 1970-77, assoc. prof. pediatrics and pediatric cardiology, 1977—, co-dir. pediatric cardiology, dir. pediatric cardiac lab., 1977—; pediatric cardiology fellow Montefiore Hosp. and Med. Ctr., N.Y.C., 1966-68. Fellow Am. Coll. Cardiology; mem. Am. Heart Assn., Ky. Med. Assn., Jefferson County Med. Assn., Argentinian Coll. Cardiology. Home: 6414 Lime Ridge Pl Louisville KY 40222 Office: Pediatric Cardiology Assocs 601 S Floyd St Louisville KY 40202-1835

ELDER, BESSIE RUTH, pharmacist; b. Ovalo, Tex., June 28, 1935; d. William Kinsalow and Ima Ruth (Carter) Griffing; m. George Davis Elder, Sept. 15, 1950 (dec. Nov. 1991); children: Michael Davis, Linda Sue Elder Claborn. BS in Pharmacy, Southwestern Okla. U., 1989. Staff pharmacist Coleman Pharmacy, Dimmitt, Tex., 1989-90, United Pharmacy, Lubbock, Tex., 1990—, St. Mary's Hosp. Pharmacy, Lubbock, 1992-95, Albertsons Pharmacy, 1996—. Home: 5902 86th St Lubbock TX 79424

ELDER, JAMES CARL, lawyer; b. Detroit, Mar. 11, 1947; s. Carl W. and Alta M. (Bradley) E.; m. Margaret Ford, Apr. 6, 1974; children: James B., William J., Michael L., Samuel F. BA, U. Okla, 1969, JD, 1972. Bar: Okla. 1972, U.S. Dist. Ct. (we. dist.) Okla. 1972. Atty, ptnr., dir. Crowe & Dunlevy, Oklahoma City, 1972-82; atty., dir. Mock, Schwabe, Waldo, Elder, Reeves & Bryant, Oklahoma City, 1982-96; atty., ptnr. Gable Gotwals Mack Schwabe, 1996—. Nat. coun. rep., pres. elect Last Frontier Coun. Boy Scouts Am.; trustee Norman (Okla.) Pub. Sch. Found., 1989—, pres., 1995-97; elder Meml. Presbyn. Ch., Norman, clk. of session, 1992-96. Recipient Silver Beaver award Boy Scouts Am., Oklahoma City, 1988. Fellow Okla. Bar Found. (life), Baden Powell World Fellowship; mem. ABA (mem. title ins. com. real property, probate and trust law sect. 1993—, chair closing issues subcom. 1995—), Beta Theta Pi Corp. of Okla. (trustee, v.p., chpt. counselor 1975-85, pres. 1995—). Office: Gable Gotwals Mock Schwabe 211 N Robinson 1 Leadership Sq 15th Fl Oklahoma City OK 73102

ELDER, JOHN BLANTON, psychologist, clergyman; b. Dallas, Dec. 27, 1926; s. Arthur Blanton and Inez (Staub) E.; m. Jeanine Copeland, June 9, 1950 (div. 1971); children: Nancy, Arthur, Jeanne; m. Thersia Dost, Sept. 21, 1974; 1 child, John Eric. BS, U. Tex., 1946; MDiv, Austin Sem., 1951; MA, U. Tex., 1966; PhD, U. Houston, 1974. Ordained to ministry Presbyterian Ch., 1951. Pastor Presbyn. chs., various locations, 1951-69; lectr. U. Md., College Park, 1976-88; clin. psychologist VA Med. Ctr., Grand Island, Nebr., 1989-90; clin. dir. Dept. of Army, Ft. Hood, Tex., 1990-91; pvt. practice Georgetown, Tex., 1991—; min. Leander (Tex.) Presbyn. Ch. Moderator Brazos Presbytery, Houston, 1969; bd. dirs. Nebraskans for Ind. Living, 1989. Lt. (j.g.) USN, 1944-47. Mem. APA. Home and Office: 1204 Power Rd Georgetown TX 78628-3145

ELDER, JOHN FLETCHER, IV, science educator, researcher; b. Seoul, Republic of Korea, Sept. 18, 1961; s. John Fletcher III and Carlyn Marie (Lang) E.; m. Elizabeth Hinson, Dec. 22, 1984; children: Catherine Jean, John Fletcher V, Anna Ruth, Rebecca Grace. BSEE, Rice U., 1983, MEE, 1984; PhD in Systems Engring., U. Va., 1993. Intern Smithsonian Instn., Washington, summer 1978; jr. fellow U.S. Geol. Survey, Vienna, Va., summer 1979; programmer Adaptronics, Inc., McLean, Va., summer 1980-82; rsch. scientist Barron Assocs., Inc., Standardsville, Va., 1984-89; dir. rsch. Delta Fin., Inc., Virginia Beach, Va., 1989-92; rsch. asst. U. Va., Charlottesville, 1989-93; rsch. scientist dept. computational and applied math. Rice U., Houston, 1993-95; adj. faculty U. Va., Charlottesville, 1996—; cons. Security Capital Mgmt., Inc., Stamford, Conn., 1993, Rosemont Mgmt., Charlottesville, Va., 1994—; chief scientist Vantage Consulting, 1995—. Author: (book chpts.) Advances in Control Networks, 1994, Knowledge Discovery in Databases, 1996, Artificial Intelligence and Statistics, 1996; reviewer various jours., 1992—; contbr. articles to profl. jours. and confs. Camp counselor Boy Scouts Am., Goshen, Va., summer 1977; mem. missions com., dir. internat. ministry Trinity Presbyn. Ch., Charlottesville, 1988-93; adminstrv. bd. dirs. 1st United Meth., Houston, 1993-95. Recipient assistantship NSF, 1993-95, Marie Alexander Leadership award Hanszen Coll., 1980; Nat. Merit scholar, 1979, G. Dobelman scholar, 1979-80, Brown scholar, 1983, Soroptimists scholar, NSPE scholar, 1979-84. Mem. IEEE (tech. chair sys., man and cybernetics soc., adaptive learning sys. group 1995—), Am. Statis. Assn., Order of Penguin. Home and Office: 1006 Wildmere Pl Charlottesville VA 22901

ELDER, NANCY HELM, patient care attendant, author; b. Louisville, Sept. 6, 1945; d. George Crosby and Dorothy Elizabeth (Myatt) Helm; m. Jerry Nall Elder, Feb. 10, 1968; 1 child, Carrie Ann. Student, Spencerian Bus. Coll., Louisville, 1965, U. Louisville, 1986-87. Sr. ops. asst. First Ky. Trust Co., Louisville, 1965-91; mem. customer resource team in micrographics Capital Initiatives Corp., Louisville, 1991-92; unit coord. Columbia Healthcare Corp./Suburban Med. Ctr., Louisville, 1993—; home health aide Caretenders, Louisville, 1993—. Author, illustrator 21 children's books including Animal Village Series, 1985-91, distributed free to charities; compiler 5 books for sr. citizens, 1990-94, 2 books for troops in Persian Gulf, 1989; 6 poems pub. in assorted books, 1988-90. Vol. St. Joseph Children's Home, Louisville, 1982-87, Area IV Spl. Olympics, Louisville, 1987—, Humana Hosp.-Suburban, Louisville, 1991-93, Channel 15 Super-Auction, Louisville, 1988-92, others. Recipient Letter of Commendation for Cmty. Svc. Pres. Bush, 1990, award for outstanding vol. First Ky. Nat. Corp., Spirit of Louisville Found., 1989. Mem. Ky. State Poetry Soc. Democrat. Roman Catholic. Home: 2810 Goose Creek Rd Louisville KY 40242-2202 Office: Suburban Med Ctr 4001 Dutchmans Ln Louisville KY 40207-4714

ELDREDGE, BRUCE BEARD, museum director; b. Van Wert, Ohio, July 1, 1952; s. Thomas Harte and Barbara Louise (Beard) E.; m. Janet Duncan Roth, May 17, 1975; children: Lindsay Katherine, Barbara Roth. BA, Ohio

Wesleyan U., 1974; MA, Tex. Tech U., 1976; postgrad., SUNY, 1980-81. Dir. Geneva (N.Y.) Hist. Soc. and Mus., 1976-78, Schenectady (N.Y.) Mus., 1978-80; coord. art and humanities Capital Dist. Humanities Program, SUNY, Albany, 1980-81; exec. dir. Frederic Remington Art Mus., Ogdensburg, N.Y., 1981-84; dir. Muskegon (Mich.) Mus. Art, 1984-87, Tucson Mus. Art, 1987-89, Portsmouth (Va.) Mus's., 1990-92, Stark Mus. Art, Orange, Tex., 1992-96, Mus. of the Horse, Ruidoso Downs, N.Mex., 1996—; presenter Gov.'s Conf. on Tourism, Phoenix, 1989; mem. coun. Midwest Mus. Assn., Chgo., 1986-87, chmn. program ann. meeting, Grand Rapids, Mich., 1987. Vice pres. Schenectady County count. Boy Scouts Am., 1979-81, Seaway Valley coun., Canton, N.Y., 1982-84, West Mich. Shores coun., Grand Rapids, 1985-87, dist. com. Three Rivers coun., 1992—, v.p. Three Rivers coun., 1995-96; bd. dirs. Orange Cmty. Concer Assn., 1995—. Mem. Am. Assn. Mus., Tex. Assn. Mus. (sourcebook editor 1993-96), S.E. Tex. Assn. Mus. (officer-at-large 1993-94), Adirondack League Club, Alto Lakes Country Club, Rotary. Republican. Presbyterian. Home: PO Box 1998 Ruidoso Downs NM 88346-1998 Office: Mus of the Horse PO Box 40 Ruidoso Downs NM 88346-0040

ELDREDGE, LINDA GAILE, psychologist; b. Lubbock, Tex., Apr. 3, 1959; d. Jerry Greever and Madge (Harshbarger) Eldredge. BS, Howard Payne U., 1980; MA, Tex. Woman's U., 1981; EdD, Baylor U., 1989. Lic. psychologist, chem. dependency counselor, Tex.; cert. tchr. hearing impaired, sch. counselor, spl. edn. counselor, Tex.; lic. marriage and family therapist; cert. verbal self def. trainer; cert. eye movement desensitization and reprocessing. Tchr. hearing impaired Waco (Tex.) Ind. Sch. Dist., 1982-85, spl. edn. sch. counselor, cons. hearing impaired, 1986-87; doctoral teaching fellow Baylor U., Waco, 1985-87; dir. regional alcohol and drug abuse svcs. Heart of Tex. Coun. Govts., Waco, 1987; psychotherapist Houston, Tex., 1989-91; psychologist Houston, 1991-93; pvt. practice psychology Austin, 1993—; psychologist Tex. Sch. for the Deaf, Austin, 1993-95. Mem. APA, Nat. Assn. Alcoholism and Drug Abuse Counselors, Am. Deafness and Rehab. Assn., Am. Assn. of the Deaf-Blind, Gentle Art of Verbal Self-Defense Trainers Network, Tex. Assn. Alcoholism and Drug Abuse Counselors (sec.-treas. Waco chpt. 1988-89). Office: 5806 Mesa Ste 220 Austin TX 78731-3742

ELDRETH, JOHN PAUL, systems analyst; b. Bluefield, W.Va., Sept. 13, 1958; s. William Bruce and Thelma Azella (Hall) E.; m. Michelle Debra Parent, June 28, 1987. BS in Computer Sci., Va. Inst. Tech. and State U., 1980; MS in Computer Sci., George Mason U., 1992. Computer programmer Naval Aviation Logistics Ctr., Lexington Park, Md., 1980-82, Computer Scis. Corp., Falls Church, Va., 1982-83; software engrng. specialist I ICL, Inc., Reston, Va., 1983-93; prin. systems analyst PRC, Inc., Reston, 1993-95; software developer Am. Online, 1996—. Home: 15120 Philip Lee Rd Chantilly VA 20151-1305

ELDRIDGE, DARYL ROGER, religious educator, dean; b. Clinton, Mo., Aug. 2, 1951; s. D'Wayne Logan and Venita Ruth (Harris) E.; m. Carole Ruth Compton, Sept. 29, 1973; children: Melinda, Mark. BA, Drury Coll., Springfield, Mo., 1973; MRE, Southwestern Sem., Ft. Worth, Tex., 1977, PhD, 1985. Minister of youth and music First Bapt. Ch., Republic, Mo., 1971-72; minister youth/edn. First Bapt. Ch., Branson, Mo., 1972-73, Boulevard Bapt. Ch., Springfield, Mo., 1973-75, Parkview Bapt. Ch., Arlington, Tex., 1977-80; minister edn. Tate Springs Bapt. Ch., Arlington, 1980-84; prof., dean Sch. Religious Edn. Southwestern Bapt. Theol. Sem., Ft. Worth, 1984—; minister edn. Hurst (Tex.) Bapt. Ch., 1991-96. Editor: Teaching Ministery of the Church, 1995; contbr.: (book) Sociological Framework of the Contemporary Family, 1996; contbr. articles to profl. jours. Recipient J.M. Price award Southwestern Bapt. Theol. Sem., 1977, Albert G. Marsh award, 1982. Mem. So. Bapt. Religious Edn. Assn. (bd. dirs. 1996—), N.Am. Profs. of Christian Edn. (v.p. 1995—), Bapt. Religious Edn. Assn. of S.W. (pres. 1995), Tarrant Bapt. Religious Edn. Assn. (v.p. 1994), Rotary. Office: southwestern Bapt Theol Seminary Box 22000 Fort Worth TX 76122

ELDRIDGE, RICHARD MARK, lawyer; b. Okmulgee, Okla., June 20, 1951; s. H.G. and Marcheta (Barnes) E.; m. Nellene Jane Mark, Aug. 20, 1971; children: Richard Mark Jr. (dec.), Christopher Bryan, Ryan Matthew, Michael Jonathan. BA, Okla. State U., 1973; JD, U. Tulsa, 1975. Bar: Okla. 1976; U.S. Dist. Ct. (no. dist.) Okla. 1976, U.S. Dist. Ct. (ea. dist.) Okla. 1989; U.S. Ct. Appeals (10th cir.) 1977, U.S. Dist. Ct. (we. dist.) Okla. 1991. Ptnr. Jacobus, Green & Eldridge, Tulsa, 1976-78; spl. judge Dist. Ct., Tulsa, 1979-82; ptnr. Rhodes, Hieronymus, Jones, Tucker & Gable, Tulsa, 1982—; adj. prof. Oral Roberts U., Tulsa, 1985. Tchr. Couples for Christ, Asbury United Meth. Ch., Tulsa, 1979—; pres., sec. Christian Businessmen's Com., Tulsa, 1981-93; chmn. Asbury Presch. Bd., Tulsa, 1985-90. Recipient Cert. of Achievement, Am. Acad. Jud. Edn., 1979. Mem. Okla. Bar Assn., Tulsa County Bar Assn. Democrat. Home: 2916 E 88th St Tulsa OK 74137-2507 Office: Rhodes Hieronymus et al One OK Plz Ste 400 100 W 5th St Tulsa OK 74103-4287

ELDRIDGE, ROBERT COULTER, retired telephone company executive; b. Chattanooga, Tenn., July 20, 1917; s. David McGill and Eugenia (Coulter) E.; m. Helen Francis Brannum, May 29, 1941 (dec. 1974); children: Robert C. Jr., Richard H.; m. Anna Yvonne Glass, Aug. 1, 1975; 1 child, Jason Von Mayfield. BS in Bus., U. Tenn.1, 1941. Lineman, engr., then installer So. Bell, Knoxville, Tenn., 1941-42, 46-50; dist. constrn. supr. So. Bell, Chattanooga, 1952-56; div. plant supr. So. Bell, Memphis, 1956-58; dist. plant mgr. South Cen. Bell, Knoxville, 1958-72, div. plant supr., 1972, dist. engr., 1972-73; engr., then gen. mgr. Concord Telephone Exch., Knoxville, 1973-86, pres., 1986-93; also bd. dirs. Concord Telephone Exch.; ret., 1993; dist. plant mgr., AT&T Co., N.Y.C., 1965. With U. Tenn. football team at Orange Bowl game, 1938, Rose Bowl game, 1939, Sugar Bowl game, 1940; bd. dirs., East Tenn. Nat. Football Hall of Fame, 1964—, East Tenn. Children's Hosp., Knoxville, 1985-86; mem. exec. bd. Knoxville area Boy Scouts Am., 1987—. Capt. U.S. Army, 1942-46, ETO, maj., 1950-52, Korea. Mem. E-911, Sertoma, Kiwanis, Elks. Home: 1157 Laurel Hill Rd Knoxville TN 37923-2051

ELEQUIN, CLETO, JR., retired physician; b. Antique, Philippines, Oct. 18, 1933; s. Cleto and Enriqueta (Tengonciang) E.; m. Nancy Johnson, May 14, 1958; children: Tracy, Thomas Kyle, Stuart Scott. M.D., Far Eastern U., Philippines, 1957. Rotating intern Good Samaritan Hosp., Lexington, Ky., 1957-58; gen. practice resident Central Bapt. Hosp., Lexington, 1958-59; psychiat. resident State Hosp., Danville, Pa., 1959-60, 61-62; psychiat. resident with child psychiatry State Hosp., New Castle, Del., 1962-63; staff physician Eastern State Hosp., Lexington, 1960-61, dir. Fayette County Project, dir. intensive treatment service, 1964-67, supt., 1969-71; dep. commr. Dept. Mental Health, State Ky., 1967-69; practice medicine, specializing in family practice Pecos, Tex., 1971-72, Austin, Tex., 1974-89; ret.; cons. psychiatrist Texas Youth Commn., Peyote, Tex., Permian Basin Cmty. Mental Health-Mental Retardation, Odessa, Tex., Prude Ranch for Emotionally Disturbed Children and Adolescents, Ft. Davis, Tex., Dept. Mental Health-Mental Retardation State of Tex.; vis. lectr. in medicine and psychiatry Am. U. of the Caribbean, Plymouth, Montserrat; asst. dep. commr. Tex. Dept. Mental Health and Mental Retardation, Austin, 1973-74, dep. commr. mental health, 1974; pvt. practice family therapy and psychiatry, Austin, 1974-85; mem. attending staff Brackenridge Hosp., St. David Med. Ctr., Seton Med. Ctr., Shoal Creek Hosp.; med. dir. Mary Lee Sch. and Found., 1974-80, bd. trustees, 1980-85; attending psychiatrist U. Ky. Med. Ctr., 1964-71, Good Samaritan Hosp., 1969-71, Ctrl. Bapt. Hosp., 1966-71; cons. psychiatrist U. Ky. Student Health Svc., 1965-71, Peace Corps, 1966-68, Bur. Rehab. State Ky., 1965-71, Blue Grass Cmty. Care Ctr., 1967-71, Covington (Ky.) Cmty. Care Ctr., 1969-71, Hazard Cmty. Care Ctr., 1969-71, Danville (Ky.) Cmty. Ctr., 1969-71, Maysville (Ky.) Cmty. Care Ctr., 1969-71; clin. instr., asst. clin. prof. dept. psychiatry U. Ky. Med. Ctr., 1964-69, assoc. clin. prof., 1969-71; cons. psychiatrist Tex. Youth Commn. Tex. Dept. of MH-MR, State of Tex.; pvt. practice in psychiatry, Austin, 1974-85; mem. attending staff Brackenridge Hosp., St. David Med. Ctr., Seton Med. Ctr., Shoal Creek Hosp.; med. dir. Mary Lee Sch. and Found., 1974-80, mem. bd. trustees, 1980-85. Mem. Profl. Adv. Coun. Community Mental Health-Retardation Ctr., Lexington, 1967-71; mem. Lexington Hosp. Coun., 1969-71. Mem. AMA, Am. Psychiat. Assn., Am. Acad. Family Physicians (life), Assn. Med. Supts. Mental Hosps., Tex. Med. Assn., Travis County Med. Soc., Austin Psychiat. Soc. Home: 10101 Jupiter Hills Dr Austin TX 78747-1322

ELEUTERIUS, DAVID WAYNE, journalist, graphic designer; b. Gulfport, Miss., Feb. 22, 1970; s. Wayne Atlas and Lollie Connie (Fucich) E. BA in Comm., La. State U., 1996. Sports graphic designer The Times, Shreveport, La., 1994-95. Author, guest columnist Shreveport Times, 1996. Mem. Soc. Profl. Journalists (v.p. 1995-96). Home: 7000 Fern Ave #28 Shreveport LA 71105

ELFERVIG, LUCIE THERESA SAVOIE, ophthalmic nursing consultant; b. Donaldsonville, La., Oct. 15, 1948; d. Charles Clarence Sr. and Ursula Marie (Prados) Savoie; m. John Lars Elfervig, May 19, 1972; children: John Lars II (dec.), Martye Elizabeth, Michelle Karene, Taylor Anders. BSN, U. Southwestern La., 1972, postgrad., 1979-80; MSN, Northwestern State U., 1975; D Nursing Sci., La. State U. Med. Ctr., 1993—. RN, Utah, Ga., Ark., Ariz., Miss., Tenn., La., Mo.; cert. ophthalmic nurse, advanced practice RN, CNS, Tenn., La., Utah, Mo., Miss., Ga. Nurse's aide St. Elizabeth's Hosp., Paincourtville, La., 1969, Charity Hosp., New Orleans, 1971; staff nurse Confederate Meml. Med. Ctr., Shreveport, La., 1972-73; staff nurse med./surg. dept. Dr.'s Hosp., Shreveport, 1973; pediatric clin. nurse specialist La. State U. Med. Ctr., Shreveport, 1975-76; instr. in nursing U. Southwestern La., Lafayette, 1980; pediatric clin. nurse specialist, emergency staff nurse LeBonheur Children's Med. Ctr., Memphis, 1984-85; pediatric clin. nurse specialist, agy. nurse emergency dept. So. Health Sys., Profl. Health Care, Memphis, 1985-90; ophthalmic clin. nurse specialist Hamilton Eye Clinic, Memphis, 1990-91; ind. ophthalmic cons. Memphis, 1992—; pediatric instr. Stanley Kaplan Ednl. Ctr., Memphis, 1986; ophthalmic clin. nurse specialist Mid-South Retina Assocs., Memphis, summer 1988, Albany (Ga.) Retinal Eye Ctr., summer 1989; cons. Rea & Assocs., Inc., Med. Mgmt. and Fin. Svcs., Memphis, 1992-94, Vitreo-Retinal Found., Memphis, Van Dyck Eye Ctr., Paris, Tenn., So. Eye Assocs., Jonesboro, Ark., Ridge Lake Ambulatory Surgery Ctr., Memphis, 1992—; lectr., cons., ophthalmic clin. nurse cons. People to People Citizen Ambassador Program. Contbr. articles to profl. publs. Vol. blood pressure screening program La. Heart Assn., Shreveport, 1974; vol. Holy Rosary Sch., Memphis, 1981-92; math. tchr. Head Start of Memphis, 1986; track meet ofcl. Germantown (Tenn.) Track Club, 1988-92; vol. ophthalmic nurse specialist South Am. Mission/World Lens Project, Pupalla, Peru, 1991, Marantha Mission, Cadereyta, Mex., 1993; campaign vol. Gov.-Elect Don Sundquist, 1994; team leader silent auction bldg. fund benefit Christian Bros. H.S., Memphis, 1993, 94. Recipient Endowment, Rep. Congl. Order of Liberty, 1993, Congl. Cert. of Appreciation U.S. Congress, 1993; advanced ednl. scholar Akorm-Metico, 1996. Mem. ANA (coun. nurses in advanced practice), Am. Soc. Ophthalmic RNS (mem. peer rev. com. jour. 1994—, Honor award 1996), Tenn. Nurses Assn., NLN (coun. for nursing practice), West Tenn. League Nurses (chpt. chaor 1994-95), Am. Nurses Found., Nat. Assn. Pro-Life Nurses, Mid. Tenn. Advanced Practice Nurses, Sigma Theta Tau. Office: Vitreo-Retinal Found 825 Ridge Lake Blvd Ste 310 Memphis TN 38120-9411

ELFMAN, DOUGLAS SAYRE, journalist; b. San Francisco, Feb. 18, 1967; s. Bradley Sayre and Julia Anne (Youngblood) E. BA in Journalism, La. State U., 1990. Staff writer Daily Reveille, Baton Rouge, 1988-90, mng. editor, 1989-90; staff writer Times-Picayune, New Orleans, 1990, News Star, Monroe, La., 1990-91, Daily Times, Maryville, Tenn., 1991-93; features editor News Herald, Panama City, Fla., 1994-96, Daytona Beach (Fla.) News Jour., 1996—. Vol. bell-ringer coord. Salvation Army, Panama City, 1995-96; chmn. protocol Soc. Profl. Journalists, Baton Rouge, 1989-90. Recipient 2d pl. editl. writing award Soc. Profl. Journalists, 1989, 3d pl. editl. writing award Southwestern Journalism Congress, 1990, 1st pl. writing award Southwestern Journalism Congress, 1991, 2d pl. investigative reporting award Soc. Profl. Journalists, 1993. Office: News Jour 111 S Alabama Ave Deland FL 32724

ELGART, LARRY JOSEPH, orchestra leader; b. New London, Conn., Mar. 20, 1922; s. Arthur M. and Bessie (Aisman) E.; m. Lynn Walzer, June 28, 1963; children by previous marriage: Brock, Brad. Altosaxophonist, formed Les and Larry Elgart Orch., 1947, rec. artist for Decca, RCA, Victor, MGM, Columbia labels. Recipient Billboard award, 1959, Downbeat Most Played Band award Disc Jockey poll, 1959, Downbeat, Cashbox and Billboards awards in popularity polls, Gold record album for Hooked on Swing, 1982, Platinum, 1984.

ELGAVISH, ADA, molecular, cellular biologist; b. Cluj, Romania, Jan. 23, 1946; came to U.S. 1979; d. David and Malca (Neuman) Simchas; m. Gabriel A. Elgavish, Dec. 28, 1968; children: Rotem, Eynav. BSc, Tel-Aviv U., 1969, MSc, 1972; PhD, Weizmann Inst. Sci., Rehovot, Israel, 1978. Postdoctoral vis. fellow NIH, Balt., 1979-81; instr. U. Ala. Sch. Medicine, Birmingham, 1981-82, rsch. assoc., 1982-84, rsch. asst. prof., 1984-89, asst. prof. comparative medicine, 1989-92, assoc. prof., 1992—; assoc. scientist Cystic Fibrosis Ctr., Birmingham, 1984-90; scientist Cell Adhesion and Matrix Rsch. Ctr., Birmingham, 1995—. Grantee Cystic Fibrosis Found., 1986-90, Am. Lung Assn., 1987-92, NIH, 1989—. Mem. AAAS, Am. Physiol. Soc., Am. Urol. Assn., N.Y. Acad. Sci., Ala. Acad. Sci., Soc. for Basic Urol. Rsch., Am. Thoracic Soc., Sigma Xi. Home: 1737 Valpar Dr Birmingham AL 35226-2343 Office: U Ala Sch Medicine Dept Comparative Medicine Birmingham AL 35294

ELGAVISH, GABRIEL ANDREAS, physical biochemistry educator; b. Budapest, Hungary, July 29, 1942; arrived in Israel, 1957, came to U.S., 1979; s. László and Katalin Barbara (Szentmiklóssy) Schwarcz; m. Ada Stephanie Simcas, Dec. 28, 1967; children: Rotem László Abraham, Eynav Elgavish. BSc, Hebrew U., Jerusalem, 1967; MSc, Tel-Aviv U., 1972; PhD, Weizmann Inst. of Sci., 1978. Vis. fellow NIH, Balt., 1979-81; asst. prof. U. Ala., Birmingham, 1981-87, assoc. prof., 1987-95, prof., 1995—. 1st lt. Israeli Army, 1961-64. Mem. Am. Chem. Soc., Am. Soc. for Biochemistry and Molecular Biology, Am. Heart Assn./Basic Sci., Soc. Magnetic Resonance in Medicine. Jewish. Office: U Ala THT 336 1900 University Blvd Birmingham AL 35233-2008

ELIASOPH, JEFFREY PAUL, television news anchor; b. N.Y.C., July 29, 1956; s. Ira Ingram E. and Ann Patricia (Levy) Klein; m. Elisa Robin Malinovitz, Aug. 8, 1988; children: Vivien Norma, Hannah Ida. BA in Polit. Sci., Johns Hopkins U., 1978. Reporter Sta. KCBQ-AM, San Diego, 1979-80; sports reporter Mutual Broadcasting, San Diego, 1980-81; features editor Copley News Svc., San Diego, 1982; reporter, anchor Sta. KGBT-TV, Harlingen, Tex., 1983-85; news anchor Tex. State Network, Dallas, 1986; reporter, anchor Sta. KTBS-TV, Shreveport, La., 1986-88; morning news anchor Sta. KXAS-TV, Dallas, 1989—; media cons. Dallas Jewish Coaliton for the Homeless, 1992—. Speaker and presenter in field. Master of ceremonies Fort Worth (Tex.) Clean City, 1993—, Tarrant County (Tex.) Employee's Day, 1993—; spokesman Tex. Red Ribbon Anti-drug Campaign, Dallas, 1991—; vol. Dallas Jewish Coalition for the Homeless, Vogel Family Alcove. Recipient Spot News Excellence award Tex. AP, 1991, Planned Event Coverage 1st Place award La. AP, 1987, Spot News Story award, 1986, Exceptional Vol. Svc. award Tex. Gov. Mark White, 1984. Mem. NAACP, Soc. Profl. Journalists, So. Poverty Law Ctr. Office: KXAS TV 5 3900 Barnett St Fort Worth TX 76103-1400

ELION, GERTRUDE BELLE, research scientist, pharmacology educator; b. N.Y.C., Jan. 23, 1918; d. Robert and Bertha (Cohen) E. AB, Hunter Coll., 1937; MS, NYU, 1941; DSc (hon.), Hunter Coll., 1989, NYU, 1989; DMS (hon.), Brown U., 1969; DSc (hon.), U. Mich., 1983, N.C. State U., 1989, Ohio State U., 1989, Poly. U., 1989, U. N.C., Chapel Hill, 1990, Russell Sage Coll., 1990, Duke U., 1991, MacMaster U., 1992, SUNY, Stony Brook, 1992, George Washington U., 1969, Columbia U., 1992, Washington Coll., 1993, U. South Fla., 1993, U. Wis., 1993, East Carolina U., 1993, Wake Forest U., 1994, Utah State U., 1994; MD (hon.), U. Chieti, Italy, 1995; DHL (hon.), Rochester Inst. Tech., 1996; DSc (hon.), Phila. Coll. Pharmacy, 1996, Albany Coll. Pharmacy, 1996, Rensselaer Polytech. Inst., 1996. Lab. asst. biochemistry N.Y. Hosp. Sch. Nursing, 1937; rsch. asst. in organic chemistry Denver Chem. Mfg. Co., N.Y.C., 1938-39; tchr. chemistry and physics N.Y.C. secondary schs., 1940-42; food analyst Quaker Maid Co., Bklyn., 1942-43; rsch. asst. in organic synthesis Johnson & Johnson, New Brunswick, N.J., 1943-44; biochemist Wellcome Rsch. Labs., Tuckahoe, N.Y., 1944-50; sr. rsch. chemist Wellcome Rsch. Labs., 1950-55, asst. to assoc. rsch. dir., 1955-62, asst. to the rsch. dir., 1963-66, head exptl. therapy, 1966-83, sci. emeritus, 1983—; adj. prof. pharmacology and exptl. medicine Duke U., 1970, rsch. prof. pharmacology, 1983—; adj. prof. pharmacology U. N.C., Chapel Hill, 1973; chmn. Gordon Conf. on Coenzymes and Metabolic Pathways, 1966; mem. bd. sci. counselors Nat. Cancer Inst., 1980-84; mem. coun. Am. Cancer Soc., 1983-86; mem. Nat. Cancer Adv. Bd., 1984-91. Contbr. articles to profl. jours.; patentee in field. Recipient Garvan medal, 1968, Pres.'s medal Hunter Coll., 1970, Medal of Honor Am. Cancer Soc., 1990; Disting. Chemist award N.C. Inst. Chemists, 1981, Judd award Meml. Sloan-Kettering Cancer Ctr., 1983, Bertner award M.D. Anderson Hosp., 1989, Third Century award Fedn. for Creative Am., 1990, Discoverers award Pharm. Mfg. Assn., 1990, City of Medicine award Durham, N.C., 1990; co-recipient Nobel prize in medicine, 1988, Nat. Medal of Sci. NSF, 1991; inductee Hunter Coll. Hall of Fame, 1973, Nat. Inventors Hall of Fame, 1991, Nat. Women's Hall of Fame, 1991, Engrng. and Sci. Hall of Fame, 1992; named Dame, Order of St. John of Jerusalem Ecumenical Found. (Knights of Malta) 1992. Fellow N.Y. Acad. Scis.; mem. AAAS, NAS (coun. 1994-97), Royal Soc. (fgn. mem.), Am. Chem. Soc., Am. Acad. Arts and Scis., Inst. of Medicine, Chem. Soc. London, Am. Soc. Biol. Chemists, Am. Assn. Cancer Rsch. (bd. dirs. 1981, 83, pres. 1983-84, Cain award 1984), Am. Soc. Hematology, Transplantation Soc., Am. Soc. Pharmacology and Exptl. Therapeutics. Home: 1 Banbury Ln Chapel Hill NC 27514-2504 Office: Glaxo Wellcome Inc 5 Moore Dr Research Triangle Park NC 27709

ELISH, HERBERT, retired manufacturing company executive; b. Bklyn., 1933; married. Student, Williams Coll.; LLB, Harvard U., 1957. Formerly commr. sanitation City of New York; then v.p. Citibank; then exec. dir. Mcpl. Assistance Corp., N.Y.C.; then v.p. Internat. Paper Co., then sr. v.p. adminstrn.; then sr. v.p. Dreyfus Corp.; with Weirton Steel Corp., chmn., pres., CEO, 1987-95; ret., 1995. Office: 400 Three Springs Dr Weirton WV 26062-4950

ELISHA, WALTER Y., textile manufacturing company executive; b. 1932; married. Student, Wabash (Ind.) Coll., Harvard U. Sch. Bus. Vice chmn. bd., dir. Jewel Cos., 1965-80; chmn., CEO Springs Industries Inc., Ft. Mill, S.C.; bd. dirs. AT&T, Cummins Engine. Office: Springs Industries Inc PO Box 70 205 N White St Fort Mill SC 29716*

EL-KEIB, ABDURRAHIM A., electrical engineering educator, consultant; b. Tripoli, Libya, Aug. 8, 1950; came to U.S., 1973; s. Abdulhafiz Ali and Fatima A. (Ahmed) El-K.; m. Mawia Bakri Kaddoura, July 21, 1977. BSEE with honors, U. Tripoli, 1973; MSEE, U. So. Calif., 1976; PhD in Elec. Engrng., N.C. State U., 1984. Tchg. asst. U. Tripoli, 1973-74; rsch. and tchg. asst. N.C. State U., Raleigh, 1980-84; lectr. U. Tripoli, 1982; from asst. prof. to assoc. prof. U. Ala., Tuscaloosa, 1990-96, prof., 1996—; cons. So. Co. Svcs., Birmingham, 1990—, Ala. Power Co., Birmingham, 1987-88, Nat. Investment Co., Tripoli, 1978. Contbr. chpts. to The Encyclopedia of Support Systems; contbr. papers and articles to profl. jours. Chmn. of bd. IST, Tuscaloosa, Ala., 1993—. Recipient NSF Rsch. Initiation award, 1989-90. Mem. IEEE (sr., 1st pl. award tech. paper prize competition Ala. sect. 1996, 2d pl. award 1995, 3d pl. award 1986), Power Engrng. Soc., Edn. Soc., Am. Soc. Engrng. Edn., Internat. Assn. Sci. and Tech. for Devel., Eta Kappa Nu, Sigma Xi. Home: 2420 Brandon Pkwy Tuscaloosa AL 35406 Office: U Ala Dept Elec Engrng Box 870286 Tuscaloosa AL 35487-0286

ELKINS, JAMES ANDERSON, JR., banker; b. Galveston, Tex., Mar. 24, 1919; s. James Anderson and Isabel (Mitchell) E.; m. Margaret Wiess, Nov. 24, 1945; children—Elise, James Anderson III, Leslie K. B.A., Princeton U., 1941. With First City Nat. Bank, Houston, 1941—, v.p., 1946-50, pres. then chmn. bd., 1950-82; dir. First City Bancorp., Houston, 1982-88; bd. dirs. Freeport-McMoran Inc., New Orleans, 1970-91, Am. Gen. Cos., Houston, 1973-92. Bd. dirs. Houston Grand Opera; trustee Tex. Children's Hosp., Tex. Med. Ctr., 1991; chmn. bd. trustees Baylor Coll. Medicine, 1970—. Episcopalian. Address: 1001 Fannin St Ste 1166 Houston TX 77002-6708

ELKINS, JAMES ANDERSON, III, banker; b. Houston, May 21, 1952; s. James Anderson Jr. and Margaret K. (Wiess) E.; m. Mary Virginia Arnold, Dec. 8, 1984; children: Margaret Wiess, James Anderson IV, Buck Arnold, John Caldwell, Harry Carothers, Samuel Hill. BA, Princeton U., 1974; MBA, U. Tex., 1976. Asst. treas. Morgan Guaranty Trust Co., N.Y.C., 1976-79; exec. v.p. First City Tex., Houston, 1979-93; chmn. Houston Trust Co., 1994—. Bd. govs. Rice U., Houston, 1982—; trustee Tex. Children's Hosp., Houston, 1989—, Children's Mus., Houston, 1988—, Houston Mus. Natural Sci., 1993—, Houston Zool. Soc., 1993—; bd. advisors U. Tex. Health Sci. Ctr., Houston, 1990; adv. bd. Salvation Army, 1990—; bd. trustees Houston Parks Bd. Mem. Am. Bankers Assn. (exec. bd. corp. council), Houston Club, Robert Morris Assocs., Tex. Bankers Assn., Forum Club. Methodist. Office: Houston Trust Co 1001 Fannin St Ste 1500 Houston TX 77002-6714

ELKINS, ROBERT NEAL, lawyer; b. Tampa, Fla., Dec. 11, 1944. BA, Vanderbilt U., 1967; MBA, U. So. Miss., 1972; JD, U. Ga., 1976. Bar: Ga. 1976, Fla. 1976, U.S. Dist. Ct. (mid. and no. dists.) Ga. With Las Vegas City Attys. Office, 1976-77; asst. dist. atty. Office of Dist. Atty., Athens, Ga., 1978-83; ptnr. Fortson Bentley & Griffin, Athens, 1983—; mem. adv. com. Athens Tech. Paralegal Studies, 1983—. Bd. dirs. Athens Clark Libr., 1980—, Clark County unit Am. Cancer Soc., 1980—; mem. Leadership Athens, 1983. Capt. USAF, 1968-73. Mem. Western Cir. Bar Assn. Office: Fortson Bentley & Griffin 440 College Ave Ste 220 PO Box 1744 Athens GA 30601

ELKINS, THOMAS EDWARD, obstetrician-gynecologist; b. Corpus Christi, Tex., Dec. 23, 1949; s. Novis Noble and Laura Kathryn (Ellison) E.; m. Carolyn Ethel Link, Aug. 1, 1970; children: Jeffrey, Ginny, John. BA in Religion magna cum laude, Baylor U., 1972, MD with honors, 1975; MA in Religion, Harding U., 1983. Diplomate Am. Bd. Ob-Gyn; lic. physician Tex., Tenn., Ark., Miss., Mich., La. Intern in family practice Naval Regional Med. Ctr., Portsmouth, Va., 1976-80; resident in ob-gyn. Naval Regional Med. Ctr., Portsmouth, 1977-80; clin. instr. dept. ob-gyn. U. Tenn. Coll. Medicine, Memphis, 1980-83, asst. prof. dept. ob-gyn., 1983-85; asst. prof., chief divsn. gynecology U. Mich. Med. Sch., Ann Arbor, 1985-87; assoc. prof., chief divsn. gynecology U. Mich. Med. Sch., 1987-92; prof., chmn., co-dir. urogynecology and pelvic floor surgery La. State U. Med. Sch., New Orleans, 1992-96; adj. prof. dept. tropical medicine Tulane U. Sch. Pub. Health and Tropical Medicine, New Orleans, 1993—; Carnegie-sponsored cons. to Ghana for postgrad. tng., vis. prof. Accra and Kumasi and Nalerigu, Ghana, 1988, 89, 90, 91, 92, 93, 94, 95, 96; external examiner West Africa Coll. Surgeons Ob-gyn. sect., Ibadan, Nigeria, 1989, 90, external cons. Korle Bu Tchg. Hosp., Accra, 1992; vis. prof. Addis Ababa Fistula Hosp., Ethiopia, 1995; oral bd. examiner Am. Bd. Ob-Gyn., 1990-95; mem. nat. adv. bd. Ethics in Reprodn., 1991-95; mem. family physicians adv. coun. Focus on the Family, 1993-95; mem. Coun. on Aid for Impaired Med. Students U. Tenn. Coll. Medicine, 1984-85, steering com. and adv. bd. Contraception Immersion Studies Program, La. State U. Med. Ctr. Inst. Profl. Edn., 1994; spkr. numerous confs. in field. Author: (with D. Brown) Faith for Troubled, 1988, (with J.P. Edwards) Just Between Us. A Social Sexual Guide for Parents and Professionals with Concerns for Persons with Developmental Disabilities, 1988, (monograph) On The Need for More Careful Consideration by Gynecologists of Sex Education Programs in Public Schools, 1989; contbr. numerous articles to profl. jours.; prodr. ednl. videos; mem. editl. bd., spl. reviewer Am. Jour. Ob-gyn., Obstetrics and Gynecology, Internat. Jour. Gynecology and Obstetrics, Down Syndrome Quar., Jour. Urology. Deacon Bapt. Ch., Portsmouth, Va., 1978-80, Memphis, 1982-85, Ann Arbor, 1986-91, New Orleans, 1994-96; mem. Nat. Down Syndrome Congress, bd. dirs., 1984-92, chmn. profl. adv. com., 1986-91; mem. Am. Assn. on Mental Deficiency, Mich. Assn. for Retarded Citizens; pack master Cub Scouts, Ann Arbor, 1986-89, 91; coach Norman Recreation Ctr., New Orleans, 1993-94; prof. advisor Downs Parents of Memphis, 1982-84; mem. infant care rev. com. task force Am. Acad. Pediat., 1984, nat. ethics commn. Christian Med. Soc., 1986-87; vol. physiican So. Bapt. Fgn. Mission Bd., Eku (Nigeria) Bapt. Hosp., 1975, 76, 83, Sanyati (Zimbabwe) Bapt. Med. Ctr., 1976, Nalerigu (Ghana) Bapt. Med. Ctr., 1978-83, 85-86, 87, Komfo Anokye Tchg. Hosp., Kumasi, Ghana, 1986, 87. Grantee DeRoy Found., 1987-89,

90, 91, Carnegie Corp., Ghana, 1988-91, 91-93, 94-95, Mich. Mental Health Dept., 1988-91, La. Dept. Health, 1994; recipient Outstanding Young Alumnus award Baylor U., Waco, Tex., 1986; named Citizen of Yr., Washtenaw County Assn. Retarded Citizens, 1987. Fellow ACOG (adv. coun. Mich. sect. 1988-92, com. on bioethics 1983-88, cons. to arrange post-grad. tng. program, London, Accra, Ghana 1987, prologue task force in gynecology 1992-93, com. on internat. affairs 1996—, adv. coun. La. sect. 1992-96, 1st prize for audiovisual programs 1989); mem. AMA, Am. Gynecology and Obstetrics Soc., Soc. for Gynecologic Surgeons, Am. Uro-Gyneologic Soc., Am. Profs. Gynecology and Obstetrics (task force on tchg. of law in residencies 1991, 92, 93), N.Am. Soc. Pediatric and Adolescent Gynecology (bd. dirs. 1988-89, v.p., chmn. membership com. 1990, membership com. 1991-92), Soc. Health and Human Values, Soc. Pelvic Reconstructive Surgeons, Am. Soc. Law and Medicine, Ctrl. Assn. Obstetrics and Gynecology, Am. Colposcopy Soc., Bapt. Med. and Dental Fellowship, Am. Assn. Maternal and Neonatal Health, Christian Med. and Dental Soc. (student faculty advisor U. Tenn. Med. Sch. 984-85, U. Mich. Med. Sch. 1989-91, La. State U. Med. Sch. 1994-95), Jacobs Inst. Women's Health Soc., Greater New Orleans Ob-gyn. Soc., Norman Miller Soc., Washtenaw County Ob-gyn. Soc., Phi Eta Sigma, Alpha Chi, Omicron Delta Kappa. Baptist. Office: La State U Med Sch 1542 Tulane Ave New Orleans LA 70112-2822

ELKINS, TONI MARCUS, artist, art association administrator; b. Tifton, Ga., Feb. 22, 1946; m. Samuel M. Elkins, 1968; children: Stephanie Elkins Sims, Eric Marcus. Student, Boston U., 1965; ABJ, U. Ga., 1968; postgrad., Columbia (S.C.) Coll., Athens, 1980-82; postgrad. photography/silk screening, Columbia (S.C.) Coll. Owner, designer Designs by Elkins, Columbia, 1986—; water color artist, 1983—; supt. fine art S.C. State Fair Art Exhbn., 1987-96. Works include watercolors All American Things, And the Good Ones Look Alike, And the Good Ones with Lace. Auction chair The Elegant Egg McKissick Mus., Columbia, 1994; bd. dir. Trustus Theatre, 1994—. Recipient Best of Show award 18th Internat. Dogwood Festival, 1991, So. Water Color Assn. Pres.'s award, 1992, Purchase award Anderson County Arts Coun. 17th Ann. Exhibit, 1992, Meyer Hardware award Rocky Mountain National, 1992, Howard B. Smith award S.C. Watercolor Ann., 1992. Mem. Nat. Watercolor Soc., Watercolor U.S.A., S.C. Watercolor Soc., Nat. Watercolor Okla., Penn. Watercolor Soc., Ga. Watercolor Soc., Rocky Mountain Nat. Watercolor Soc., Cultural Coun. of Richland & Lexington Counties (exec. bd. sec. 1990-93), Southeastern Art and Craft Expn. (adv. bd. 1993-94). Home and Studio: 1511 Adger Rd Columbia SC 29205-1407

ELLENBROOK, EDWARD CHARLES, county government social services administrator; b. Lawton, Okla., Aug. 12, 1938; s. Edward Charles Ellenbrook and Lera Belle (Pair) Becker; m. Carolyn Kay Baker, Apr. 13, 1968; 1 child, Margaret Elizabeth. BA, Okla. Bapt. U., 1964. Social worker Dept. Human Svcs., Lawton, 1964-73; dir. Comanche County Juvenile Bur., Lawton, 1973—; author, owner, pub. In-The-Valley-Of-The-Wichitas, Lawton, 1983—. Author: Outdoor & Trail Guide to the Wichita Mountains, 1983, Endless Encounters, 1988; outdoors/nature columnist Lawton-Constitution-Wichita Mountains Field Notes newspaper, 1989. Bd. dirs. Lawton Heritage Assn., 1989, Southwestern Okla. Hist. Soc., Lawton, 1970, Okla. Ornithol. Soc., Ada, Okla., 1990, Friends of the Wichitas, Lawton, 1989, City of Lawton's Model Cities Com., 1968, Mus. of the Great Plains; mem. Cameron U. Criminal Adv. Bd.; bd. dirs. Teen Ct., Inc. With U.S. Army, 1962-64. Mem. Book Pubs. of Tex., N.Am. Butterfly Assn. Home: 1603 NW Keystone Dr Lawton OK 73505-2445 Office: In The Valley Of The Wichitas PO Box 6741 Lawton OK 73506-0741

ELLER, BRENDA ANN, elementary school educator, recreational director; b. Akron, Ohio, Apr. 25, 1959; d. Paul Ray and Wanda Ann (Ammons) Miller; m. Daniel Paul Eller, Aug. 31, 1985. BA, Bob Jones U., 1981; postgrad., U. Akron, 1985, The Citadel, 1990—. Cert. learning disabilities tchr., Ohio, S.C. Tchr. kindergarten Massillon (Ohio) Christian Sch., 1981-83, Henry Ctr. for Learning, Akron, 1984-85, Summit County Schs., Akron, 1985-86; tchr. high sch. Plain Local Schs., Canton, Ohio, 1986-90; spl. edn. resource tchr. Chicora Elem., Charleston (S.C.) County Schs., 1990-92; instr. evening classes Jackson Community Edn., Canton, 1986-88; exec. dir. Ohio Bapt. Acres, Massillon, 1988-89. Mem. AMA (aux. 1987—) Stark County Med. Aux., Aultman Hosp. Residents Spouses Orgn. (pres. 1987-88). Republican.

ELLETT, JOHN SPEARS, II, retired taxation educator, accountant, lawyer; b. Richmond, Va., Sept. 17, 1923; s. Henry Guerrant and Elizabeth Firmstone (Maxwell) E.; m. Mary Ball Ruffin, Apr. 15, 1950; children: John, Mary Ball, Elizabeth, Martha, Henry. BA, U. Va., 1948, JD, 1957, MA, 1961; PhD, U. N.C., 1969; CPA, Va., La.; bar: Va. 1957. Lab. instr. U. Va., Charlottesville, 1953-58; instr. Washington and Lee U., 1958-60; asst. prof. U. Fla., 1967-71; assoc. prof. U. New Orleans, 1971-76, prof. taxation, 1976-94; ret., 1994, pres. Maxwelton Farm and Timber Corp., 1994—; trainee Va. Carolina Hardware Co., Richmond, 1948-51; ac ct. Equitable Life Assurance Soc., Richmond, 1951-52; staff acct. Musselman & Drysdale, Charlottesville, 1952-54; staff acct. R.M. Musselman, Charlottesville, 1957-58; mem. U. New Orleans Oil and Gas Acctg. Conf., 1973-92; bd. dirs., publicity chmn. U. New Orleans Energy Acctg. and Tax Conf., 1993-94, bd. dirs. publicity com.; pres. Maxwelton Farm and Timber Corp., 1994—; treas. U. New Orleans Estate Planning Seminar, 1975-78, lectr. continuing edn.; CPCU instr. New Orleans Ins. Inst., 1975-78. Served with AUS, 1943-46. Mem. AICPA, Am. Acctg. Assn., Am. Assn. Atty.-CPAs (chmn. ptnrship. taxation continuing edn com. 1989, ptnrship. taxation com. 1990, organized La. chpt., v.p. 1991-93), Va. Soc. CPAs, La. Soc. CPAs, Va. Bar Assn. Democrat. Episcopalian. Author books; contbr. articles to profl. jours. Home: 177 Maxwelton Rd Charlottesville VA 22903-7801

ELLINGSEN, MARK, history of Christian thought educator; b. Bklyn., June 18, 1949; s. Emil and Edna (Nilssen) E.; m. Helen Betsey Shaw, Aug. 18, 1973; children: Patrick John, Elizabeth Ann, Peter Ellingsen. BA magna cum laude, Gettysburg Coll., 1971; MDiv magna cum laude, Yale Divinity Sch., 1974; MA, MPhil., Yale U., 1975, 76, PhD, 1980. Ordained to ministry Evang. Luth. Ch. Am. Vice pastor St. Luke's Luth. Ch., Hellertown, Pa., 1975-77, Cen. Pocono Luth. Parish, Scotrun, Pa., 1977-78; asst. prof. Luther-Northwestern Seminary, St. Paul, Minn., 1979-82; assoc. prof. Inst. for Ecumenical Rsch., Strasbourg, France, 1982-88; pastor Haven Luth. Ch., Salisbury, N.C., 1988-90, St. John's Luth. Ch., Asheboro, N.C., 1990-93; asst. prof. Interdenominational Theol. Ctr., Atlanta, 1993—; part-time instr. Randolph C.C., Asheboro, 1992-93; presenter in field. Author: Doctrine and Word, 1983, The Evangelical Movement, 1988, The Integrity of Bible Narrative, 1990, Preparation and Manifestation, 1992, The Cutting Edge: How Churches Speak on Social Issues, 1993, A Common Sense Theology, 1995; contbr. numerous articles to profl. jours. and newspapers. Mem. Christ Luth. Ch., Marietta, Ga., 1994—; cons. ecumenical affairs com. Southeastern synod Evang. Luth. Ch. Am., 1995—; recruiter and participant March of Dimes Walkathon, Asheboro, 1992-93; participant Crop Walk for Hunger, Salisbury, N.C., 1989-90; big bro. Big Bros./Bis Sister, Effort, Pa., 1978-79. Recipient Reader's Choice award Christianity Today, 1992. Mem. Am. Acad. Religion, Phi Beta Kappa. Democrat. Lutheran. Home: 4124 Gregory Manor Cir Smyrna GA 30082-4428 Office: Interdenominatl Theol Ctr 700 M L King Jr Dr SW Atlanta GA 30314-4112

ELLIOT, DOUGLAS GENE, chemical engineer, engineering company executive, consultant; b. Medford, Oreg., June 3, 1941; s. Don Joseph and Eleanor Joan (Sheets) E.; m. Noma Warnken, July 16, 1966 (div. 1979); 1 child, Jennifer M.; m. Patricia Jean Nichols, Mar. 15, 1980; children: Steven V. Bates, Michael A. Castillo. BSChemE, Oreg. State U., 1964; MS, U. Houston, 1968, PhD, 1971. Reservoir/prodn. engr. Humble Oil & Refining Co., Beaumont, Tex., 1964-66; co-founder, v.p. and bd. dirs. S.W. Wire Rope, Inc., 1967-70; cons. Gas Processors Assn., Houston, 1971; process/project engr. Hudson Enging. Co., Houston, 1971-78; mgr. process enging. Davy-McKee Corp., Houston, 1978-83, v.p. oil and gas, 1983-85; pres. D. G. Elliot & Assocs. Inc., Houston, 1985-86; pres., COO Internat. Process Svcs. Inc., Houston, 1986—, also bd. dirs.; adj. prof. Rice U., Houston, 1976-77; mem. indsl. adv. com. Okla. State U., Stillwater, 1979-83; mgmt. cons. Norsk Hydro Oil & Gas Div., Oslo, 1984—. Contbr. articles to profl. jours.; mem. editorial rev. bd. Energy Process mag., 1981—; patentee in field. Mem. Tex. Energy Adv. Com., Austin, 1978; founding mem., bd. dirs. Tex. Solar Energy Soc., Austin, 1978; mem. Ctr. of Excellence R&D rev. panel Okla Ctr. for Advancement of Sci. & Tech., Oklahoma City. Recipient Outstanding Achievement award Tex. Soc. Profl. Engrs., 1978, citation for merit Bechtel Corp., 1991, 92, 93. Fellow AIChE (sec.-treas. S. Tex. sect. 1979, chmn. elect 1980, chmn. 1981, bd. dirs. fuels and petrochem. divsn. 1982-85); mem. Soc. Petroleum Engrs., Gas Processors Assn. (sec.-treas. 1983), N.Y. Acad. Scis., Sigma Zi. Home: 506 Fairport Houston TX 77079

ELLIOT, J. H., museum director. Dir. Atlanta Mus. Office: Atlanta Museum 537-39 Peachtree St NE Atlanta GA 30308

ELLIOTT, ANNE NIXON, gifted and talented education educator; b. Hickory, N.C., Apr. 16, 1947; d. Robert William and Reba Blanton (Whisnant) Elliott; m. Allen Eugene Caldwell, June 9, 1968 (div. Aug. 1978); 1 child, Catherine Anne; m. George Thomas Pitner, Jan. 1, 1980 (div. Nov. 1996). BA, U. N.C., Greensboro, 1968; MA, Lenoir-Rhyne Coll., 1990. cert. tchr. elem. gifted and talented. Tchr. Raleigh (N.C.) Pub. Schs., 1968-69, Newton (N.C.)-Conover City Schs., 1970—; cons. N.C. Geog. Alliance, 1988—. Recipient Excellence in Geography Tchg. Regional award Rand McNally, 1990, Disting. Tchg. Achievement award Nat. Coun. for Geog. Edn., 1990, Outstanding Elem. Math. Tchr. award N.C. Coun. Tchrs. Math., 1991. Mem. ASCD, N.C. Assn. for Gifted and Talented, N.C. Coun. Social Studies, N.C. Assn. Educators (local sec. 1970—), N.C. Sci. Tchrs. Assn., Alpha Delta Kappa (Gamma Rho chpt. pres.-elect, 1986—). Baptist. Home: 215 11th Ave NW Hickory NC 28601-3658 Office: South Newton Elem Sch 306 W I St Newton NC 28658-3534

ELLIOTT, APRIL LEE, educational consultant; b. Richmond, Va., Nov. 23, 1972; d. Wallace Dean and Carol Lee (Burruss) E. BA in French, Va. Commonwealth U., 1995. Peer sexuality educator Student Health Ctr. Va. Commonwealth U., Richmond, 1992-95, tech. writer, 1994-95, rape crisis cons., 1993-95; pres. Outspoken Prodns., Richmond, 1996—. Author: (plays) Drawing the Shades, 1993, Chorus, 1995. Mem. exec. com. Nat. Student Coalition Against Sexual Assault, 1994—; vol. Juvenile Ct., Richmond, 1995. Recipient Leadership award State Coun. Higher Edn. in Va., 1994, Leadership award Va. Commonwealth U., 1995, Excellence in French award, 1995; Va. Commonwealth U. scholar, 1990-91. Office: Outspoken Productions 2314 Floyd Ave #2 Richmond VA 23220

ELLIOTT, BRADY GIFFORD, judge; b. Harlingen, Tex., Nov. 26, 1943; s. Clyde Andres Elliott and Mildred (Parker) Bounds; m. Rhea Elizabeth Ricks, May 15, 1967; children: Adrian Winthrope, Jason Lawrence. BBA, McMurray Coll., 1970; JD, South Tex. Coll. Law, 1973. Bar: Tex. 1973, U.S. Dist. Ct. (so. dist.) Tex. 1974, U.S. Tax Ct. 1974, U.S. Ct. Appeals (5th cir.) 1974, U.S. Supreme Ct. 1979, U.S. Ct. Appeals (11th cir.) 1981. Asst. sec., asst. treas., asst. gen. counsel Gordon Jewelry Corp., Houston, 1970-79; sec., gen. counsel Oshman's Sporting Goods, Inc., Houston, 1979-82; sole practice, Sugar Land, Tex., 1982-88; legal counsel Ft. Bend C. of C., Sugar Land, Tex., 1982-88; mcpl. judge Missouri City, Tex., 1983-88; judge 268th Dist. Ct., Fort Bend County, Tex., 1988—. Bd. dirs. Ft. Bend chpt. Texans' War on Drugs, Sugar Land, 1981-94; bd. dirs. Ft. Bend Boys Choir, 1984-94. Mem. ABA, Houston Bar Assn., Fort Bend County Bar Assn., Masons, Rotary (treas. 1983-85). Republican. Methodist. Office: County Ct House Richmond TX 77469

ELLIOTT, BRUCE MICHAEL, vascular surgeon; b. North Platte, Nebr., Nov. 7, 1951; m. Susan Elliott. BS, Nebr. Wesleyan U., 1974; MD, U. Nebr., 1977. Diplomate Nat. Bd. Med. Examiners, Am. Bd. Surgery; lic. physician Nebr., S.C. Intern Letterman Army Med. Ctr., 1977-78, resident in gen. surgery, 1978-82; fellow in peripheral vascular surgery Walter reed Army Med. Ctr., 1983-84; instr. dept. surgery Uniformed Svcs. of Health scis., 1983-84, clin. asst. prof. dept. surgery, 1984—; clin. asst. prof. gen. surgery U. Tex. Health Sci. Ctr., San Antonio, 1984-86; asst. prof. surgery Med. U. S.C., Charleston, 1986-91, assoc. prof. surgery, 1991—, co-dir. ann. postgrad. course in surgery, 1989—, head sect. vascular surgery, 1987—; staff gen. and peripheral vascular surgery svc. Letterman Army Med. Ctr., 1982-83; chief peripheral vascular surgery svc. Brooke Army Med. Ctr., 1984-86; lectr. in field. Editorial reviewer Jour. Am. Acad. Dermatology, 1990—; contbr. numerous articles to profl. jours., chpts. to books. With M.C., U.S. Army, 1977-86, USAR, 1986—. Decorated Army Commendation medal; recipient Chesapeake Vascular Soc. First Place award in ann. paper presentation, 1984. Fellow ACS; mem. Internat. Soc. Cardiovascular Surgery, Peripheral Vascular Surgery Soc. (program com. 1990—, exec. com. 1991—), S.C. Vascular Surg. Soc. (exec. com. 1991—, pres. 1993-94), So. Assn. Vascular Surgery, San Antonio Surg. Soc., Soc. for Mil. Surgeons, Southeastern Surg. Congress, Assn. Acad. Surgery, S.C. Med. Assn. (del. ho. of dels. 1993), Charleston County Med. Soc., Beta Beta Beta. Office: Medical Univ South Carolina Dept Vascular Surgery Charleston SC 29425

ELLIOTT, CHARLES MARK, Greek Orthodox priest; b. Richmond, Va., Mar. 3, 1960; s. Charles Raymond and Joyce Katherine (Crook) E.; m. Patti Gail Page, Aug., 1982; children: Matthew A., Andrew J. BA, Austin Coll., 1982, MA, Baylor U., 1984; MDiv, Holy Cross Orthodox Sch. of, Theology, Brookline, Mass., 1989; postgrad. studies, U. So. Miss., 1994—. Ordained to the diaconate 1989, to the priesthood 1990 for the Greek Orthodox Archdiocese of N. and S. Am. Asst. priest Sts. Peter & Paul Greek Orthodox Ch., Glenview, Ill., 1989-93; pastor Holy Trinity and St. John Greek Orthodox Ch., Jackson, Miss., 1993—; Contbr. to Dictionary of Christianity in America (book), Greek Orthodox Theol. Rev. (jour.), 1989, Touchstone (jour.), 1990. Recipient Exomologos and Oikonomos, Greek Orthodox Archdiocese, 1994. Mem. SCV. Home: 1110 Greenbriar St Jackson MS 39211 Office: Holy Trinity & St John Ch 1417 W Capitol St Jackson MS 39203-2122

ELLIOTT, DAVID PATRICK, pharmacist, educator; b. Edmonton, Canada, Mar. 16, 1956; came to the U.S., 1978; s. Clifford Albert and Lucia Catherine (Fuchs) E.; m. Anita Gertrude Lorenzo, Apr. 24, 1981; children: Matthew Paul, Sarah Anne, Mary Luisa. BS in Pharmacy, U. Manitoba, 1978; PharmD, U. Tex., 1981. RPh, W.Va., Tex. Resident in adult medicine U. Tex., Austin, 1980-81; asst. prof. pharmacy practice U. Ill., Chgo., 1981-84; asst. prof. clin. pharmacy W.Va. U., Charleston, 1984-90, assoc. prof., 1990—. Contbr. articles to profl. jours. Fellow Am. Soc. Cons. Pharmacists; mem. Am. Coll. Clin. Pharmacy. Roman Catholic. Office: W Va U Clin Pharmacy Dept 3110 Mac Corkle Ave SE Charleston WV 25304

ELLIOTT, EDWIN POWERS, JR., magazine editor, clergyman; b. Richmond, Va., June 18, 1947; s. Edwin Powers and Ellen Lee (Bridewell) E.; m. Anne Bindon Brisebois (dec. July 1968); children: Laura Bindon, Rebecca Tate, Elizabeth Catherine. AB in History, Coll. William and Mary, 1969; MDiv, Ref. Theol. Sem., Jackson, Miss., 1974; DLitt (hon.), Covenanter Coll., Ft. Worth, 1992. Ordained to ministry Presbyn. Ch. in Am., 1974. Tchr. Prince William County Schs., Manassas, 1969-71; pastor 1st Presbyn. Ch., Watervalley, Miss., 1972-78, Manassas Ref. Presbyn. Ch., 1978—; pres. Reformation Ednl. Found., Manassas, 1978—, Reformation Typesetting & Pub., Manassas, 1978—; mng. editor, writer Christian Observer, Manassas, 1986—; radio min. Way of Truth Broadcast, 1972-78; lectr. Covenant Bible Class, 1978—; rec. clk. gen. assembly Presbyn. Ch. in Am., 1975-82, rec. clk. Covenant Presbytery, 1974-78; moderator Hanover Presbytery, Ref. Presbyn. Ch.; cons. to over 50 religious, ednl., sci. and pub. interest periodicals, 1978—. Campaign cons. Manassas Rep. Com., 1986—. Mem. Royal Order Scotland, Masons (grand chaplain Miss. 1976-77, high priest Manasssas 1993-94), KT. Office: Christian Observer 9400 Fairview Ave Manassas VA 20110

ELLIOTT, HAROLD WAYNE, lawyer, retired army officer; b. Rock Hill, S.C., Jan. 18, 1946; s. Harold Livingston and Kathryne (Wright) E.; m. Marian Barton, Jan. 26, 1974; 1 child, Mary Kathryne. BA in Polit. Sci., The Citadel, 1968; JD, U. S.C., 1971; LLM, U. Va., 1982, postgrad. Bar: S.C. 1971. Commd. 1st lt. U.S. Army, 1971, advanced through grades to lt. col., 1991; chief internat. law U.S. Army JAG Sch., Charlottesville, Va., 1990-93; ret. U.S. Army, 1993. Contbr. articles and book revs. to profl. jours. Republican. Presbyterian. Home: 600 Carrsbrook Dr Charlottesville VA 22901

ELLIOTT, JAMES ROBERT, federal judge; b. Gainesville, Ga., Jan. 1, 1910; s. Thomas M. and Mamie Lucille (Glenn) E.; m. Brownie C. Buck, Aug. 3, 1949; children: Susan G., James Robert. Ph.B., Emory U., 1930, LL.B., 1934. Bar: Ga. 1934. Pvt. practice law Columbus, Ga., 1934-62; judge U.S. Dist. Ct. (mid. dist.) Ga., Columbus, 1962—; Mem. Ga. Ho. of Reps., 1937-43, 47-49; Democratic nat. committeeman, 1948-56. Served as lt. USNR, 1943-46, PTO. Mem. Ga. Bar Assn., Kiwanis, Lambda Chi Alpha, Phi Delta Phi, Omicron Delta Kappa. Home: 2612 Carson Dr Columbus GA 31906-1563 Office: US Dist Ct 120-12th St Rm 224 PO Box 2017 Columbus GA 31902

ELLIOTT, JAMES V., corporate lawyer; b. Washington, Feb. 8, 1944; s. James M. and Mary R. Elliott; m. Suzanne L. Elliott; children: Katherine, John. BA in Polit. Sci., Duke U., 1966; JD, U. Calif., Berkeley, 1969. Bar: Calif., Va., D.C. Dep. dist. atty. San Diego County, 1969-72; pvt. practice San Diego, 1972-74, Washington, 1981-89; sr. trial atty. Office Controller of Currency, Washington, 1974-78, dir. bank orgn. and structure divsn., 1978-81; sr. v.p., gen. counsel First Deposit Corp., San Francisco, 1989-95, Providian Corp., Louisville, 1995—. Office: Providian Corp 400 W Market St Louisville KY 40202-3346

ELLIOTT, JAMES WARD, lawyer; b. Norwich, N.Y., Mar. 4, 1954; m. Susan Talbot, Dec. 22, 1979; children: Shawn, Chris. BA, SUNY, Oneonta, 1976; JD, Union U., Albany, N.Y., 1979. Bar: N.Y. 1980, U.S. Dist. Ct. (no. dist.) N.Y. 1980, U.S. Ct. Mil. Appeals 1980, Va. 1991. Procurement counsel Grumman Aerospace Corp., Bethpage, N.Y., 1986-87, govt. contracts counsel, 1987-89; corp. counsel McDermott, Inc. (subs. The Babcock & Wilcox Co.), Lynchburg, Va., 1989—. Mem. Hazardous Waste Action Coalition, Nat. Security Indsl. Assn. (subcom. law), Am. Arbitration Assn. (panel of arbitrators). Republican. Office: The Babcock & Wilcox Co Law Dept 2220 Langhorne Rd Lynchburg VA 24501-1108

ELLIOTT, JENNIFER SUE, television producer; b. Chgo., Oct. 12, 1971; d. Terry John and Susan Marie (Smith) E. BS, Miami U., 1993. News producer Sta. WDTN-TV2, Dayton, Ohio, 1993-95, Sta. WNCN-NBC-17, Raleigh, N.C., 1995—. Mem. Soc. Profl. Journalists, Phi Beta Kappa. Roman Catholic. Home: 129 E Farrington Dr Raleigh NC 27615 Office: NBC-17 1205 Front St Raleigh NC 27609

ELLIOTT, JOHN FRANKLIN, clergyman; b. Neosho, Mo., June 11, 1915; s. William Marion and Charlotte Jeanette (Crump) E.; m. Winifred Margaret Key, July 6, 1939; children: Paul Timothy, Stephen Marion, Andrew Daniel. Student, Maryville Coll., 1933-35; A.B., Austin Coll., 1937; post-grad., Louisville Presbyn. Sem., 1937-38, U. Tenn., 1938, Dallas Theol. Sem., 1939-40; B.D., Columbia Theol. Sem., 1942, M.Div., 1971; D.Litt. (hon.), Internat. Acad., 1954. Ordained to ministry Presbyn. Ch., 1942. Founder Emory Presbyn. Ch., Atlanta, 1941, Wildwood Presbyn. Ch., Salem, Va., 1950; pastor Wylam Presbyn. Ch., Birmingham, Ala., 1942-47; asst. prof. Southeastern Bible Coll., 1942-43; pastor Salem Presbyn. Ch., 1947-51, Calvary Presbyn. Ch. Ind., Ft. Worth, 1952-86; founder, pastor, Grace Presbyn. Ch. Ind., Roanoke, Va., 1951-52; dean, dir. Fort Worth Bible Inst., 1952-55; founder, headmaster Colony Christian Sch., Ft. Worth, 1968-86; founder dir. Grace Ministries, Ft. Worth, 1986—; ministerial advisor bd. dirs. Reformed Theol. Sem., Jackson, Miss., 1973-83; chaplain Tex. Constl. Conv., 1974; bd. dirs. Graham Bible Coll., 1966-74, Scripture Memory Fellowship Internat., 1979-84, Messianic Ministry to Israel, Inc., Chattanooga, 1989-93; some-time chaplain Dallas Cowboys, Tex. Rangers, Kansas City Royals; founder, pres., assoc. prof. Bible, Covenanter Theol. Sem., Nagaland, Myanmar, 1993—. Bd. dirs., pres. Salem (Va.) Nursing Assn., 1949; charter mem. Fellowship Ind. Evang. Chs., 1951—, pres., 1967, nat. sec., 1971; founder, dir. Ft. Worth Home Bible Classes, 1954—; dir. Spanish Pubis., Inc., 1969-95, emeritus, 1995—; bd. dirs. Ind. Bd. for Presbyn. Home Missions, 1956-74; dist. committeeman Longhorn coun. Boy Scouts Am., Ft. Worth, 1960-66; bd. dirs. Union Gospel Mission, Ft. Worth, 1965-70, pres., 1968; mem. U.S. Coast Guard Aux., Ft. Worth, 1967-91; pilot, chaplain, col. CAP, Ft. Worth, 1970-92, chmn. nat. chaplain com., 1979-80, first chief of chaplains, 1980-82. Fellow Philos. Soc. Gt. Britain (Victoria Inst.), Royal Geog. Soc., Huguenot Soc. London,; mem. U.S. Holocaust Meml. Mus. (charter), Am. Yad Vashem Meml. Mus., Rotary (pres. 1988-89). Home: 3980 Edgehill Rd Fort Worth TX 76116-7303 Office: Ridglea Bank Bldg 6300 Ridglea Pl Ste 420 Fort Worth TX 76116-5706

ELLIOTT, MITCHELL LEE, financial analyst; b. Greenwood, Miss., Oct. 24, 1958; s. Charles Edward and Elizabeth Ann (Roberts) E.; m. Ann Bonham, June 7, 1986. BSBA, U. So. Miss., 1980. Mktg. analyst JFMA, Jackson, Miss., 1981-82; fin. analyst ERGON, Jackson, 1982—; v.p. bd. ERGON Cos. Credit Union, Jackson, 1987-90, pres., 1990—; v.p. ETE Devel., 1992—. Mem. Pine Ridge Homeowners Assn. (pres. 1994). Republican. Methodist. Home: 110 Meadowview Dr Brandon MS 39042-9224 Office: ERGON PO Box 23028 Jackson MS 39225-3028

ELLIOTT, MYRA TURNER, nursing educator; b. Martin, Ky., Aug. 19, 1958; d. Langley and Violet (Sparkman) Turner; m. Olin Andrew Elliott II, June 10, 1978; 1 child, Myranda Grance Elliott. ADN, Prestonsburg (Ky.) C.C., 1978; BSN, U. Ky., 1981; postgrad., U. Tenn., 1985; MSN, U. Ky., 1993. Clin. I/nursing care mgr. St. Joseph's Hosp., Lexington, 1978-83; clin. I/nursing care mgr., office nurse Dr. Andy Elliott, Martin, Ky., 1983-84; assoc. prof. Prestonburg C.C., 1984—, senator, 1995—; chairperson devel. and implementation of a clin. ladder program, Prestonburg, 1990—. Mem. Floyd County Cmty. Com. for Edn., 1992—; bd. dirs. Hospice of Big Sandy, 1987-95; Sunday sch. tchr., mem. choir First Bapt. Ch., Prestonburg. Recipient NISOD Excellence award, 1996. Mem. ANA, Ky. Dental Aux. (state historian), Ky. Nurses Assn., Coun. on Critical Care, Ky. Mountain Dental Aux. (pres.), Ky. Dental Alliance (pres.-elect). Home: 1391 Abbott Creek Rd Prestonsburg KY 41653-8930 Office: Prestonsburg Cmty Coll One Bert Combo Dr Prestonsburg KY 41653

ELLIOTT, RICHARD VERBRYCK, marine engineer; b. Yonkers, N.Y., Sept. 27, 1934; s. George Francis and Eileen Louise (Higgins) E.; m. Linda Lou Deinhardt, July 14, 1973; 1 child, June Louise. BS in Engring., Mcht. Marine Acad., 1958; postgrad. Georgetown U., 1959; MA in Psychology, New Sch. Social Research, 1973. Asst. to dir. info. Am. Mcht. Marine Inst., N.Y.C., 1962-63; asst. to pres. Marine Index Bur., N.Y.C., 1963-65; with Port Authority N.Y. and N.J., N.Y.C., 1965—, assoc. editor Via Port of N.Y., 1965-67, aviation pub. services rep., 1968-71, supr. personnel communications, 1971-80, energy task force editor, 1978-79, supr. employee communication systems, 1980-87, employee communication cons., 1988, editor Ann. Report, 1988, 89, coord. corp. projects, 1990-95, ret., 1995. Vice chmn. public relations marine sect. Nat. Safety Council, 1965; pres. Wilmington Steamboat Found., Inc., 1980-87; mem. com. Nat. Maritime Hall of Fame.; trustee Demarest Bd. Edn., 1989-92. Lt. USNR, 1958-61. Recipient Congressman Wainwright award for scholarship in Am. history, govt., 1958, award of Excellence, Internat. Assn. Bus. Communicators, 1975; Feature Editor award Mcht. Marine Acad., 1958, Bronze award Ann. Report, 1988, 89. Mem. S.S. Hist. Soc. Am. (High Seas editor Steamboat Bill Jour. 1962-68, v.p. Middle Atlantic states 1968-70), Internat. Assn. Bus. Communicators, U.S. Mcht. Marine Acad. Alumni Assn. Author: Last of the Steamboats-The Saga of the Wilson Line, 1970. Home: 124 Spring Cove Dr Cary NC 27511

ELLIOTT, RITTA FAYE, administrative assistant; b. Norfolk, Va., July 31, 1955; d. Walter Jr. and Wildred Helen (Harris) Turner; m. Eddie Elliott, Jr., Feb. 8, 1975; children: Elvin L'Mar and Kelvin Le'Quincy (twins). Student, Norfolk State U., 1973-79; diploma, Norfolk Bus. Coll., 1977. Clk.-typist, stenographer Norfolk State U., 1978-86, office svcs. specialist, 1986—. Author: My Name is..."Ritta" Poetry With a Story, 1996; contbr. poetry to various publs. Mem. Order Ea. Star (chpt. 197). Apostolic. Home: 805 Kramer Pl Chesapeake VA 23320-5930 Office: Norfolk State U 2401 Corprew Ave Norfolk VA 23504

ELLIOTT, RONALD LEE, agricultural engineer, educator; b. DeKalb, Ill., June 26, 1951; s. Lawrence Edgar and Mary Louise (Downey) E.; m. Judith Ann Steele, May 28, 1983; children: William, Michael, Sarah. BS in Agrl. Engring. with highest honors, U. Ill., 1973, MS in Agrl. Engring., 1974; PhD in Agrl. Engring., Colo. State U., 1981. Registered profl. engr., Ill., Colo. Grad. teaching asst. agrl. enging. dept. U. Ill., 1973-74; environ. protection engr. divsn. water pollution control Ill. EPA, 1974-77; grad. rsch. asst. agrl. and chem. enging. dept. Colo. State U., 1978-81; from asst. prof. to assoc.

prof. agrl. engring. dept. Okla. State U., Stillwater, 1981-90, prof., 1990—; summer asst. Ill. Coop. Extension Svc., Bureau County, 1971-73; rsch. specialist Denver office U.S. Bureau of Reclamation, 1989; cons. Randolph & Assocs., Peoria, 1980, Park, Nelson, Caywood & Park, Chickasha, Okla., 1986, Mitchell & DeClerck, Enid, Okla., 1992-93, Greenleaf Nursery Co., Park Hill, Okla., 1994—. Contbr. numerous articles to profl. jours. Usher First Christian Ch., 1985-86, pres. seekers class, 1985-86, pres. Christian Men's Fellowship, 1987-88, deacon, 1988, 90-93, mem. evangelism com., 1991—, chmn., 1991, mem. logos youth program, 1993—, elder, 1993—, chmn. ofcl. bd., 1996. Recipient James A. Whatley award Okla. State U., 1990; Grad. fellow NSF, 1973-74, Rockwell Internat., 1978-79; grantee Okla. State U. Water Rsch. Ctr., 1982-84, 84-85, Okla. Corp. Commn., 1984-86, U. Ctr. for Water Rsch., 1986-88, U.S. Bureau Reclamation, 1989, 91-93, U.S. Geol. Survey, 1989-91, 91-93, USDA-ARS Plant Sci. Rsch. Lab., 1988-92, USDA-ARS Specific Coop. Agreement, 1992—, 93—, USDA, 1988-93, 89-93, Okla. Dept. Commerce, 1988-90, 90-93, U.S. Dept. Agriculture, 1990—, 91—, 93—, Okla. Ctr. for Advancement Sci. and Tech., 1990-93, 91—, U. Ctr. for Energy Rsch., 1990-91, 91-92, Electric Power Rsch. Inst., 1991-92, 92—, USDA-CSRS, 1992—, Samuel Roberts Noble Found., 1994—. Mem. ASCE (irrigation water requirements com. 1991—, chmn. subcom. standards for automated weather stas. 1991—, chmn. tech. session nat. conf. irrigation and drainage engring. 1993), Am. Soc. Agrl. Engrs. (John G. Sutton award 1972, participant various coms. and confs., vice chmn. soil and water nomenclature com. 1992-93, chmn. 1993—, chmn. engring. practice subcom. surface irrigation com. 1982-87, vice chmn. 1983-86, chmn. 1986-89, chmn. local arrangements meeting s.w. region 1985, student paper award com. 1983-87, chmn. 1986-87, sec.-treas. Okla. sect. 1986-87, vice chmn. programs 1987-88, chmn.-elect 1988-89, chmn. 1989-90, vice chmn. awards 1990-91, vice chmn. career devel. 1993—), Am. Peanut Rsch. Edn. Soc. (tech. program com. 1988 meeting), U.S. Com. Irrigation, Drainage and Flood Control, Coun. Agrl. Sci. and Tech., Sigma Xi, Tau Beta Pi, Phi Kappa Phi, Alpha Epsilon (Disting. Svc. to Students award 1983, 84, 91), Gamma Sigma Delta, Phi Eta Sigma, Omicron Delta Kappa. Office: Okla State U Biosystems And Agrl De Stillwater OK 74078

ELLIOTT, SIGRID ISOLDE, clinical social worker; b. Hungerzell, Bavaria, Germany, Apr. 27, 1951; came to U.S., 1961; 1 child, Mark. BS in Germanics, Am. U., 1973. Tchr. fgn. lang. Canton Jr. High Sch., 1978-81; counselor Battered Women Hotline, 1988-89; vol. Homeless Shelter for Women Luther Pl., 1989; intern rehab. counselor St. Luke's House, Inc., 1989-90; extern psychotherapist The American U. Ctr. for Psychol. and Learning Svcs., 1990-91. Mem. Phi Kappa Phi. Home: PO Box 443 414 Fortress Way Occoquah VA 22125

ELLIS, ALFRED WRIGHT (AL ELLIS), lawyer; b. Cleve., Aug. 26, 1943; s. Donald Porter and Louise (Wright) E.; m. Kay Genseke, June 1965 (div. 1976); 1 child, Joshua Kyle; m. Sandra Lee Fahey, Feb. 11, 1989. BA with honors, U. Tex., Arlington, 1965; JD, So. Meth. U., 1971. Bar: Tex., U.S. Dist. Ct. (no., so., ea. and we. dists.) Tex., U.S. Ct. Appeals (5th cir.), U.S. Supreme Ct.; cert. personal injury and civil trial lawyer. Atty. Woodruff, Kendall & Smith, Dallas, 1972; ptnr. Woodruff & Ellis, Dallas; pvt. practice Dallas, 1983—; instr. So. Meth. U. Law Sch. Trial Advocacy; past pres. Law Focused Edn., Inc. Past mem. City of Dallas Urban Rehab. Standards Bd., Dallas Assembly, Salesmanship Club, Dallas; vol., fund raiser Habitat for Humanity; trustee Hist. Preservation League, 1992-94; tournament dir. Dallas Regional Golden Gloves Tournament, 1976-96; pres., bd. dirs. Dallas Coun. on Alcoholism, 1980. Capt. U.S. Army, 1965-69. Fellow Roscoe Pound Found.; named one of Outstanding Young Mem of Am., 1977, named Boss of Yr. Dallas Assn. Legal Secs., 1978; recipient Certs. of Recognition (8) D.I.S.D., 1971-83, Wall St. Jour. award So. Meth. U. Law Sch., 1972, Hayward McMurray award Dallas Jaycees, 1975-76, Spl. Recognition award All Sports Assn., 1977, Cert. of Appreciation for Exceptional and Disting. Vol. Svc. Gov. Mark White, 1983, Community Spirit award Dallas Bus. Jour., 1993, Disting. Svc. award Dallas All Sports Assn., 1993,award Nancy Garms Meml. for outstanding Contr. to Law Focus Edn., 1996-Leontaworsk award. Fellow Tex. Bar Found. (sustaining life), Dallas Bar Found. (trustee); mem. ATLA, ABA (chair youth edn. for citizenship com.), Am. Bd. Trial Advocates (diplomate), Am. Coll. Legal Medicine (assoc.), Legal Svcs. of North Tex. (bd. dirs., Outstanding Svc. award 1990), State Bar Tex. (lectr. seminars, bd. dirs. 1991-94, 95, Excellence in Diversity award 1994), Dallas Bar Assn. (bd. dirs. 1978, chmn. bd. dirs. 1986, v.p. 1987-88, pres. 1990), Dallas Lawyers Assn. (pres. 1977, Disting. Cmty. Svc. award 1990), Tex. Trial Lawyers Assn., Tex. Equal Access to Justice Found. (bd. dirs.), Dallas All Sports Assn. (pres.-1980). Office: 900 Jackson St Ste 560 Dallas TX 75202-4432

ELLIS, ANDREW JACKSON, JR., lawyer; b. Ashland, Va., June 23, 1930; m. Dorothy L. Lichliter, Apr. 24, 1954; children: Elizabeth E. Attkisson, Andrew C., William D. AB, Washington and Lee U., 1951, LLB, 1953. Bar: Va. 1952. Ptnr. Campbell, Ellis & Campbell, Ashland, 1955-70, Mays, Valentine, Davenport & Moore, Richmond, Va., 1970-88; ptnr. Mays & Valentine, Richmond, 1988-96, sr. counsel, 1996—; substitute judge County of Hanover (Va.) Ct., 1958-63, commonwealth atty., 1963-70, county atty., 1970-78l substitute judge 15th jud. dist., 1990-96; mem. Capital adv. bd. NationsBank of Va., 1960-93; judge 15th Dist. J&D Ct., 1996—. Mem. Ashland Town Coun., 1956-63, mayor, 1958-63; trustee J. Sargent Reynolds Community Coll., 1972-80. 1st lt. U.S. Army, 1953-55. Fellow Am. Coll. Trial Lawyers; mem. Am. Judicature Soc., Va. Bar Assn., Va. State Bar (coun. 1968-74), Va. Trial Lawyers Assn., S.R., Kiwanis. Episcopalian. Home: 15293 Old Ridge Rd Beaverdam VA 23015-1610 Office: Mays & Valentine PO Box 1122 Richmond VA 23208-1122

ELLIS, BERNICE ALLRED, personnel executive; b. Lincoln, Ala., Mar. 15, 1932; d. Bernard Bobo and Lucille (Hogue) Allred; m. Marvin Leonard Ellis; 1 child, Jeffrey Craig. Student, Ala. A&M U., 1990, U. Ala., Huntsville, 1990, Gadsden State C.C., Ala., 1993. Personnel staffing specialist Bd. of U.S. Civil Svc. Examiners, Anniston, Ala., 1957-66; personnel mgmt. specialist Dept. of Army, Anniston, 1966-73; tech. svcs. officer Dept. of Army, 1973-74; personnel mgmt. specialist Dept. of Army, Redstone Arsenal, Ala., 1974-79; supervisory personnel mgmt. specialist U.S. Army Europe, Mannheim, Fed. Republic of Germany, 1979-83; tech. svcs. officer U.S. Army Europe, Darmstadt, Fed. Republic of Germany, 1983-86; supervisory personnel mgmt. specialist Dept. of Army, Fort Ritchie, Md., 1986-87; ret., 1987; tax preparer H&R Block, Gadsden, Ala., 1994, 95; tax preparer H&R Block, Gadsden, 1994-95, Etowah Chem., Gadsden, 1995-96. Vol. Huntsville Bot. Gardens, 1989-92; mem. local group Master Gardeners, Huntsville, 1990, Huntsville Wildflower Assn, 1990-92, State and Local Master Gardeners Assn., 1990-93. Mem. Huntsville Bot. Soc. (vol.), Ala. Master Gardeners Assn. (local and state vol.), Huntsville Wildflower Assn. Home: 82 Ty Pl Ohatchee AL 36271-9231

ELLIS, BIANCA J., conservator; b. Corpus Christi, Tex.; d. Robert Beatty and Jacqueline Renne Marie (LeCompte) E.; m. Bill Denz (dec.). Student, U. Houston, 1971, U. St. Thomas, 1972. Owner Timber and Devel., Santa Cruz, Calif., 1981-92, Bianca Ellis Restoration, Austin and Nashville, 1991-96, B-Fish, Santa Cruz, Calif., 1992-93. Mem. Tex. Speological Assn. Democrat. Home: 604 Upson Austin TX 78701

ELLIS, DONALD LEE, lawyer; b. Dallas, Oct. 2, 1950; s. Truett T. and Rosemary (Tarrant) E.; children: Angela Nicole, Laura Elizabeth, Natalie Dawn, Donald Lee II. BS, U. Tulsa, 1973; JD, Oklahoma City U., 1976. Bar: Tex. 1979, Okla. 1977, U.S. Dist. Ct. (ea. dist.) Tex. 1978, U.S. Dist. Ct. (we. dist.) Okla. 1978, U.S. Ct. Appeals (5th cir.) 1984, U.S. Supreme Ct., 1984, U.S. Ct. Appeals (11th cir.) 1990. Spl. agt. FBI, Washington, 1976-78; asst. dist. atty. Smith County, Tyler, Tex., 1979-80; mem. firm Barron & Ellis, Tyler, 1980-84, Ellis & Woods law firm, 1984-85; sole practice, Tyler, 1985—. Bd. dirs. Mental Health Assn., Tyler, 1983-87. Mem. Assn. Trial Lawyers Am., Tex. Bar Assn., Okla. Bar Assn., Smith County Bar Assn., Soc. Former Spl. Agts. FBI, Tex. Trial Lawyers Assn., FBI Agents Assn., Lawyers-Pilot Bar Assn. Home: PO Box 131221 Tyler TX 75713-1221 Office: PO Box 131221 217 W Houston St Tyler TX 75702-8137

ELLIS, DONNELL, elementary school principal; b. Vicksburg, Miss., July 9, 1949; s. Jack and Edith (Ellis) Johnson. BS, Jackson State U., 1972, Miss. State U., Starkville, 1977; MEd, Miss. State U., Starkville, 1979. Tchr. Vicksburg Pub. Schs., 1976-85, asst. prin., 1985-87; prin. Vicksburg Warren Sch. Dist., 1987—. Recipient Outstanding Young Educator award Jaycees, 1980, Cmty. Svc. award Les Soeurs Charmantes, 1987. Mem. NAACP, Masons, Shriners. Democrat. Baptist. Home: 1336 East Ave Vicksburg MS 39180

ELLIS, GLEN EDWARD, JR., insurance agent, financial planner; b. Austin, Tex., Sept. 7, 1960; s. Glen Edward and Virginia Lee (Walter) E.; m. Sherry Kay Testolin, Aug. 8, 1992. BS, Stanford U., 1983. ChFC. Registered rep., sr. field underwriter Aetna Investment Svcs., Inc., Hartford, Conn., 1987—; fin. planner Aetna Fin. Svcs., Inc., Hartford, Conn., 1996—. Mem. Internat. Assn. for Fin. Planning, Million Dollar Round Table, Nat. Assn. Life Underwriters (Nat. Sales Achievement award 1988-89, 93-95, Nat. Quality award 1990-95). Office: Aetna Investment Svcs Inc 8911 N Capital of Tex Hwy Ste 2210 Austin TX 78759-7289

ELLIS, GRACE CAROL, real estate executive; b. Fairview, Mo., Dec. 4, 1935; d. Leo Leslie and Grace (Allinder) Eurit; m. Leonard Eugene Ellis, Dec. 17, 1955; children: Susan Diane, Linda Jeanne, Leonard Eugene. Grad. Draughon's Bus. Sch., 1954. Real estate broker, Stillwater, Okla., 1970—; ptnr., mgr. Crestview Estates, Stillwater, 1971-85, Crestview Quick Shop and Laundry, 1971—; ptnr., mgr. Classic Mini-Storage, 1996. Republican. Baptist. Avocations: reading; gardening; traveling. Office: Crestview Quick Shop 2319 E 6th Ave Stillwater OK 74074-6506

ELLIS, HERBERT WAYNE, lawyer; b. Jacksonville, Fla., Jan. 20, 1948; s. Herbert White and Sophie Cecilia (Myrna) E.; m. Diane Joyce Bookman, Apr. 2, 1977; children: Austin Wayne, Gordon Blake. BA, U. Fla., 1970, JD, 1975. Bar: Fla. 1978, U.S. Dist. Ct. (mid. dist.) Fla. 1979. Asst. pub. defender, div. chief 3d Jud. Cir. Fla., Lake City, 1978—. Deacon 1st Presbyn. Ch., Lake City, 1985-90, elder, 1991—; bd. dirs. Columbia Assn. for Retarded Citizens, Lake City, 1981-86. Mem. Columbia County Bar Assn. (pres., 1991), 3d Cir. Bar Assn. (pres. 1992), Mission Trail Shooting Club (pres. 1983-85). Democrat. Home: 17 Chapel Hill Blvd Lake City FL 32025-6565 Office: Office of Pub Defender PO Drawer 1209 200 N Marion St Lake City FL 32055

ELLIS, JAMES JOLLY, landscape resort official; b. Meadville, Pa., Mar. 3, 1937; s. Walter Harmon and Nerea Isabel (Farver) E.; A.A., Orlando Jr. Coll., 1959; B.S. in Bus. Adminstrn. and Econs., Rollins Coll., 1981. With Orlando (Fla.) Parks and Forestry Dept., 1961-70; supt. landscape dept. Walt Disney, coord. World, Fla., 1970-78, 81-82, Walt Disney Village Communities, 1979-90, landscape supr. Walt Disney MGM Studio, 1990-95, supr. Epcot Ctr., 1982—, Walt Disney Village Communities, Orlando, 1978-81, horticulture area mgr. over rd. maintenance and spl. projects, 1995—. Served with U.S. Army, 1959-60. Mem. Am. Mgmt. Assn., Fla. Turf Grass Assn. Republican. Lutheran. Home: 705 S Summerlin Ave Orlando FL 32801-4021 Office: PO Box 10000 Orlando FL 32830-1000

ELLIS, JEFFREY L., lawyer; b. Northampton, Pa., Sept. 23, 1949; s. Vernon P. and Doris (Barton) E. BS, Ea. Tex. State U., 1970, MS, 1971; JD, No. Ill. U., 1973. Dir. safety svcs. ARC, Rockford, Ill., 1971-73; staff Dist. Atty.'s Office, 6th Dist., Paris, Tex., 1973-79; pres. Wild Water Sports, New Braunfels, Tex., 1980-82; asst. dir. safety svcs. ARC, Houston, 1982-84; pres. Ellis & Assocs., Houston, 1983—; cons. World Water Park Assn., Prairie Village, Kans., 1985—, I.A.P.P.A., Alexandria, Va., 1985—; internat. safety adv. bd. Nat. Safety Coun., 1994-96. Author: National Pool and Waterpark Lifeguard Training Program Textbook, 1986, 2d edit., 1991, 5th edit., 1994, Nat. Safety Coun. Learn to Swim Program. Recipient Tex. Pub. Pool Coun. Aquatic Profl. of the Yr. award, 1991. Republican. Methodist. Home and Office: 3506 Spruce Park Cir Humble TX 77345-3033

ELLIS, JOHN CARROLL, JR., life insurance sales executive; b. Portsmouth, Va., Aug. 11, 1948; s. John Carroll and Sarah Edith (Pittman) E.; m. Janet Elizabeth Ackroyd, Nov. 17, 1973; 1 child, Mary Virginia. BA, Hampden-Sydney (Va.) Coll., 1970; postgrad., U. Richmond, 1971-72. CLU. Life ins. agt. Northwestern Mut. Life Ins. Co., Richmond, 1972-73, Conn. Mut. Life Ins. Co., Virginia Beach, Va., 1973-96, Mass. Mut. Life Ins. Co., Virginia Beach, Va., 1996—; bd. dirs. Jones Inst. devel. com. Med. Coll. Hampton Rds. Found. Bd. dirs. YMCA, Lynchburg, Va., 1981-89; elder First Presbyn. Ch., Virginia Beach, 1990—. Mem. CLU-ChFC (pres. Norfolk-Tidewater chpt. 1989-90), Norfolk C. of C. (bd. dirs. 1975-78), Million Dollar Round Table, Hampden-Sydney Coll. Alumni Assn. (pres.-elect 1989-91, pres. 1991-93, trustee 1995—), Cape Henry Racquet Club (pres. 1985-87), Exch. Club Virginia Beach (pres. 1980-81), Leaders Club. Home: 837 Greentree Arch Virginia Beach VA 23451-3787 Office: 3330 Pacific Ave Ste 401 Virginia Beach VA 23451-2983

ELLIS, JUNE B., human resource consultant; b. Portland, Ind., June 17; children: Kenneth G., Reyn K. BS, Mary Washington Coll., 1942; MSW, Tulane U., 1953; PhD, Internat. U., 1977. Asst. dir. social services East La. State Hosp., Jackson, 1960-62; instr. Tulane U. Sch. Social Work, New Orleans, 1962-63, asst. prof. dept. psyhiatry, Sch. Medicine, 1963-68; exec. dir. Family Service-Travelers Aid, Ft. Smith, Ark., 1967-71; pres. Child and Family Cons., Ft. Smith, 1971—; dir. Human Resource Devel. Ctr., Ft. Smith; mem. adv. bd. Suspect Child Abuse and Neglect; cons. Volvo Health Care, Goteborg, Sweden, 1974-92, Kontura Personal, 1974-92; mem. Tulane Alumni Bd., 1978-88; mem. continuing profl. edn. com. Tulane Univ. Sch. Social Work, 1996—. Author: TA Tally, 1974, TA Talk, terms and references in transaction, 1976, BEING, 1982. Mem. Ark. Gov.'s Commn. on Status of Women, 1970-73, Ark. Gov.'s Com. Drug Abuse Prevention; mem. adv. bd. Jr. League Am.; mem. scholarship selection com. Whirlpool Corp.; coord. Western Ark. Health Advocacy Svc., 1995—. Named Outstanding Alumni, Tulane U., 1984. Mem. ASTD, AAUW, Am. Acad. Psychotherapists, Am. Group Psychotherapy Assn., Am. Orthopsychiat. Assn., Acad. Cert. Social Workers, Western Ark. Mental Health Assn. (adv. bd.), Conf. for Advancement of Pvt. Practice in Social Work, Am. Assn. Ret. Persons. Episcopalian. Clubs: Town, Hardscrabble Country (Ft. Smith). Office: Child and Family Cons Inc PO Box 3816 Fort Smith AR 72913-3816 also: 3437 Westminster Dallas TX 75205

ELLIS, KARAN ANN, health care facility administrator. Student, East Tex. State U., Paris (Tex.) Jr. Coll. Bus. office employee Hunt Meml. Hosp. Dist., Greenville, 1960-64, bus. office mgr., 1964-67, asst. to adminstr., 1967-84, dir. support svcs., 1987-91, dir. materials mgmt., 1984—. Mem. Hunt-Rains County unit Am. Cancer Soc.; treas. Salem-Kinser United Meth. Ch. Named Exec. Woman of Greenville Bus. and Profl. Women's Assn., 1983. Mem. Am. Soc. Hosp. Materials Mgmt., Tex. Soc. Hosp. Purchasing and Materials Mgmt. (past pres.), Greenville C. of C. Home: 5008 Canton St Greenville TX 75402-6247

ELLIS, LONNIE CALVERT, educator; b. Oneida, Tenn., Sept. 18, 1945; s. Lewis Calvert and Alma Gean (Goad) E.; m. Karen Chambers, Dec. 16, 1967; children: Lonnie Christopher, James Gregory, Megan Lynn. BS, Cumberland Coll., 1968; MA, Tenn. Tech. U., 1974, EdS, 1985. Cert. Career Level II and III tchr. Coach Oneida Ind. Sch. Dist., Tenn., 1968-72, Scott County Sch. System, Huntsville, Tenn., 1972-78, 1979—, computer coord. Scott H.S., 1993—; mgr. pers. Tibbals Flooring Co., Oneida, 1978-79; instr. Roane State C.C., 1985-91, State Tech. Inst., Knoxville, 1985-86; bd. dirs. Scott Appalacian Industries, v.p., 1986. Chmn. Cissy Baker for Senate campaign, Huntsville, 1980; vice chmn. Scott County Recreation Com., 1984-90; active Huntsville Recreation Com., 1991—; pres. Scott County Youth Softball/Baseball League, 1992—. Recipient Dist. Coach of Yr. award Coca Cola Bottling Co., 1985, recognition award Tenn. Ho. of Reps., 1985, Citizens award E. Tenn. chpt. Nat. Football Found., 1978. Mem. Scott County Edn. Assn. (chmn. welfare com., state contact person, pres.-elect, chief negotiator 1987-88), East Tenn. Edn. Assn., Tenn. Edn. Assn., NEA. Baptist. Avocations: computers, athletics. Home: RR 1 Box 44 Helenwood TN 37755-9732 Office: Scott County High Sch Scott High Dr Huntsville TN 37756

ELLIS, MICHAEL DAVID, aerospace engineer; b. Sacramento, July 13, 1952; s. John David and Priscilla Agnes (Tupper) E.; m. Virginia Katherine Hanlon, Mar. 27, 1976; children: Gwendolyn Dawn, January Marie, Jennifer Noel. BS in Space Sci., Fla. Inst. Tech., 1975. With satellite ops., orbit analyst Western Union, Sussex, N.J., 1976-77; with satellite ops., 3 axis RCA Americom, Sussex, N.J., 1977-78; with satellite ops., Land Sat ATS-6 Goddard Space Flight Ctr., Greenbelt, Md., 1978-79; with Voyager System Lead Jet Propulsion Lab., Pasadena, Calif., 1979-82; STS ground ops. analyst Applied Rsch. Inc., El Segundo, Calif., 1982-83; mission ops. Aerospace Corp., El Segundo, Calif., 1983-88; space sta. mission ops. Johnson Spaceflight Ctr., Houston, 1988—. Mem. troop asst. San Jacinto Girl Scouts U.S., Houston, 1988-94; Confraternity Christian Doctrine tchr. St. Bernadette, Clear Lake, 1990; Clear Lake Drill Team support Starlettes, 1989-95, Clear Lake Flares, 1995-96. Mem. Soc. Automotive Engrs. (chmn. spacecraft com. 1986-87), Am. Inst. Aeronautics and Astronautics (chmn. 1972-75).

ELLIS, RAYMOND CLINTON, JR., association executive; b. Chgo., May 11, 1921; s. Raymond Clinton and Frances Geraldine (Hersma) E. PhB, U. Chgo., 1950, MBA, 1953. Cert. hospitality tech. profl., hospitality educator. Various positions Marshall Field & Co., Chgo., 1938-52, safety dir., 1953-55; staff rep., dir. small bus. program Nat. Safety Coun., Chgo., 1955-61; dir. mem. rels. Variety Stores Assocs., N.Y.C., 1961-64; fleet safety coord. Am. Ins. Assn., N.Y.C., 1964-67; group adminstr. Hotel Safety Group, N.Y.C., 1967-77; dir. risk mgmt. and ops. Am. Hotel and Motel Assn., N.Y.C., 1977-92; exec. v.p. Am. Hotel and Motel Assn. Gen. Agy., Inc., N.Y.C., 1977-92; sec., project dir. Am. Hotel and Motel Assn. Rsch. Found., N.Y.C., 1977-92; mem. bd. trustees Hotel Assn. Group Trust, 1977—; mem. occupational safety and health com. Bus. Rsch. Adv. Coun., Bur. Labor Stats., U.S. Dept. Labor, 1971—; mem. overseas security adv. coun. U.S. Dept. State; security cons. to lodging industry, 1993-94; ops. cons. Am. Hotel and Motel Assn., 1993-94; apptd. adj. prof. hotel and restaurant mgmt. Conrad N. Hilton Coll. of Hotel and Restaurant Mgmt., U. Houston, 1994—, dir. tech. rsch. and edn. ctr., 1994—, dir. loss prevention mgmt. inst., 1994—; mem. consumer adv. coun. Underwriters Labs. Author: Security and Loss Prevention Management for the Lodging Industry, 1985; editor: Student Manual-Security Course, 1978, Security and Loss Prevention Management Manual, 1996; contbr. articles to profl. jours; mem. tech. bd. Hotel & Motel Mgmt. Mag.; editl. advisor Hospitality Law; editl. adv. bd. Hotel/ Motel Secutiry and Safety Mgmt. Elder N.Y. Ave. Presbyn. Ch., D.C. With USAAF, 1943-46, ATO. Named to Hospitality Tech. Hall of Fame, Internat. Assn. Hospitality Accts., 1989. Mem. ASTM, Am. Soc. Safety Engrs., Vets. of Safety, Nat. Fire Protection Assn. (mem. exec. com. lodging sect.), Nat. Safety Coun. (Disting. Svc. to Safety award 1986, mem. exec. com. retail, trades and svcs. divsn.). Republican. Home: 4444 Cullen Blvd Apt 115 Houston TX 77004-2624 Office: Conrad Hilton Coll U Houston Rm 133 S 4800 Calhoun Blvd Houston TX 77204-3902

ELLIS, ROBERT SMITH, allergist, immunologist; b. Shawnee, Okla., July 13, 1926. MD, Northwestern U., 1950. Diplomate Am. Bd. Allergy and Immunology, Am. Bd. Internal Medicine. Intern Henry Ford Hosp., Detroit, 1950-51, resident in medicine, 1951-52, 54-55; resident in allergy U. Mich. Hosp., Ann Arbor, 1955-56; with Presbyn. Hosp., Oklahoma City; clin. prof. medicine U. Okal. Coll. Medicine. Mem. AMA, Am. Acad. Allergy and Immunology, Southern Med. Assn. Office: Okla Allergy & Asthma Clin PO Box 26827 Oklahoma City OK 73126-0827

ELLIS, SUSAN GOTTENBERG, psychologist; b. N.Y.C., Jan. 24, 1949; d. Sam and Sally (Hirschman) Gottenberg; B.S., Cornell U., 1970; M.A., Columbia U., 1971; M.A., Hofstra U., 1975, Ph.D., 1976; m. David Roy Ellis, July 23, 1972; children: Sharon Rachel, Dana Michelle. Instr. health edn. Nassau Community Coll., Garden City, N.Y., 1971-73; sch. psychologist public schs., Somerville, N.J., 1976-77; clin. psychologist Somerset County Community Mental Health Center, Somerville, 1976-77; sch. psychologist, Pinellas County, Fla., 1977-78; instr. St. Petersburg (Fla.) Jr. Coll., 1978; clin. psychologist, Largo, Fla., 1977—; cons. Fla. Dept. Health and Rehab. Services, Med. Center Hosp., Largo, Morton Plant Hosp., Clearwater, Fla., 1978-79, N.Y. State Regents scholar, 1966-71; adj. prof. Eckerd Coll. St. Petersburg, 1988. Author: Interpret Your Dreams, 1987, A Dream Primer, 1988, Make Sense of Your Dreams, 1988. Mem. Am. Psychol. Assn., Fla. Psychol. Assn., Pinellas Psychol. Assn. (treas. 1978, polit. action chmn. 1979), Kappa Delta Pi. Club: Cornell U. Suncoast (v.p. 1979-80). Office: 3233 E Bay Dr Ste 100 Largo FL 33771-1900

ELLIS, THOMAS SELBY, III, judge; b. Bogota, Columbia, May 15, 1940; came to U.S., 1951; s. Thomas Selby and Anne Leete (Sachs) E.; m. Rebecca Lynn Garron, Sept. 23, 1995; children: Alexander Reed, Parrish Selby. B.S.E., Princeton U., 1961; J.D. magna cum laude (Knox fellow), Harvard U., 1969; diploma in law Magdalen Coll. Oxford (Eng.) U., 1970. Bar: Va. 1970, D.C. 1970, U.S. Dist. Ct. (ea. and we. dists.) Va. 1970, U.S. Ct. Appeals (4th cir.) 1970, U.S. Ct. Appeals (5th cir.) 1976, U.S. Tax Ct. 1977, U.S. Ct. Appeals (D.C. cirs.), 1980, U.S. Ct. Appeals (10th cir.) 1980, U.S. Ct. Appeals (3d cir.) 1981. Assoc., Hunton & Williams, Richmond, Va., 1970-76, ptnr., 1976-87; judge U.S. Dist. Ct. (ea. dist.) Va., Alexandria, 1987—; temporary mem. sr. common rm. U. Coll., Oxford, 1984. lectr. law Coll. William & Mary, Williamsburg, Va., 1981-83; mem. adv. coun. dept. astrophysics Princeton U., 1984—; speaker in field. Bd. dirs. Va. Lung Assn., Richmond, Sci. Mus. of Va. Found. Served to lt. USN, 1961-66. Mem. ABA, Internat. Bar Assn., Va. Bar Assn., Bar Assn. City Richmond, Va. Trial Lawyers Assn., Va. State Bar Assn., Nat. Princeton Alumni Assn. Episcopalian. Office: US Dist Court 401 Courthouse Sq Alexandria VA 22314-5799

ELLIS, WALTER LEON, minister; b. McKinney, Tex., Oct. 22, 1941; s. Erwin Ballard and Mary Edra (Bray) E.; m. Susan Elizabeth Elder, Nov. 23, 1960; children: Bruce Walter, David Anthony, Patrick Durward. BA, U. North Tex., 1964, MA, 1966; MDiv, Va. Sem., 1977; DMin, Austin Presbyn. Theol. Sem., 1993. Ordained to ministry Episc. Ch., 1977. Vicar St. Michael & All Angels', Longview, Tex., 1977-79, St. Mark's, Gladewater, Tex., 1977-79; rector St. Michael & All Angel's, Longview, 1979-82, St. Christopher, League City, Tex., 1982—; dean Galveston Convocation, League City, 1989—; mem. Diocesan Standing Com., Houston, 1996—, Order of St. Luke Chaplain, 1996—; trustee St. James House, Baytown, Tex., 1983-84, 90-93, Camp Allen, Navasota, Tex., 1987-90, Bishop Quin Found., Houston, 1991—, St. Vincent's House, Galveston, 1996—; chmn. dept. environment Diocese of Tex., 1993-95; b.d dirs. Interfaith Caring Ministries, League City, 1993-94; stewardship cons. Episcopal Ch. Ctr., N.Y.C., 1990-95. Contbr. articles to profl. jours. Bd. dirs. pres. Parents Anonymous, Longview, 1980; mem. exec. bd. Bay Area coun. Boy Scouts Am., Tex., 1983-86; pres. Rotary Club, League City, 1989-90. Paul Harris fellow Space Ctr. Rotary Club, Houston, 1989. Mem. League City Ministers' Assn., Clear Lake Ministerial Alliance, Brotherhood of St. Andrew, Am. Acad. Ministry, Am. Assn. Christian Counselors, World Future Soc. Home: 18619 Prince William Ln Houston TX 77058-4224 Office: St Christopher Episc Ch 2100 St Christopher Ave League City TX 77574-0852

ELLISON, ALTON LYNN, JR., lawyer; b. Luling, Tex., Mar. 8, 1950; s. Alton Lynn and Patsy Jo (Agan) E.; m. Janet Rachel Fisher, Aug. 17, 1980; children: Rachel Lynn, Gretchen Lynn. BA cum laude, Tulane U., 1971; JD, U. Tex., 1974. Bar: Tex. 1974. Asst. city atty. City of Austin, Tex., 1975; asst. dist. atty. Travis County, Austin, 1975-77; counsel com. on pub. health Tex. Ho. of Reps., Austin, 1979, gen. counsel Office of the Speaker, 1983-84; staff counsel Tex. Dept. Mental Health and Mental Retardation, Austin, 1980-83, State Ethics Adv. Commn., Austin, 1984; spl. asst. State Property Tax Bd., Austin, 1984-85; asst. dist. atty. 81st Jud. Dist., Karnes City, Tex., 1985-91; dist. atty. 81st Jud. Dist., Jourdanton, Tex., 1991—. Treas. Atascosa Mental Health Adv. Bd., Jourdanton, Tex., 1988—; mem. Atascosa Child Care Bd., 1990—. Mem. Tex. Bar Assn. Atascosa County Bar Assnb. (treas., pres. 1990), Travis County Young Lawyers Assn. (com. on judiciary 1974-79), Tex. Dist. and County Attys. Assn., Atascosa County Law Enforcement Officers Assn., Phi Beta Kappa, Phi Eta Sigma, Sigma Nu (v.p. Tulane chpt. 1968-70). Democrat. Methodist. Home: 239 Liberty Ln Pleasanton TX 78064-4712 Office: Dist Attys Office Atascosa County Courthouse Jourdanton TX 78026

ELLISON, ROSEMARY, curator. Chief curator Indian Arts and Crafts bd. So. Plains Indian Mus. and Crafts Ctr., Anadarko, Okla. Office: So Plains Indian Mus PO Box 749 Anadarko OK 73005-0749

ELLISON, THORLEIF, consulting engineer; b. Lyngdal, Norway, May 13, 1902; s. Andreas Emanuel and Gemalie (Svensen) E.; CE, Christiania Coll. Tech., 1924; postgrad. George Washington U., U. Va.; m. Reidun Ingeborg

Skonhoft, Jan. 1, 1932; children: Earl Otto, Thorleif Glenn, Sonja Karen. Came to U.S., 1928, naturalized, 1933. Supervising engr. GSA, Washington, 1948-57; supervising airport and airways svc. engr. FAA, 1957-61; chief airways engring. AID, Iran, Pakistan, Turkey, 1961-67; cons. engr., Washington and Va., 1971-82; supervising structural engr. for reconstrn. of The White House, 1949-52; mission dir. Bethlehem, Israel, Holy Land Christian Mission, Kansas City, 1968-71. Recipient U.S. Navy commendation, 1945. Active Christian Bus. Men's Com., Washington, Boy Scouts Am. Registered profl. engr. Mem. Nat. Soc. Profl. Engrs. (dir.), Sons of Norway (pres. Washington chpt.), Norwegian Soc. (treas.). Presbyterian (ruling elder). Home: Svennevik Rosfjord, 4580 Lyngdal Norway Address: 6324 Telegraph Rd Alexandria VA 22310-2969

ELLOS, WILLIAM JOSEPH, priest, philosophy educator; b. Ironwood, Mich., May 15, 1937; s. Simon Francis and Leone Elizabeth (La Fave) E. A.B., St. Louis U., 1961, M.A. in Philosophy, 1962, Ph.L. in Philosophy, 1962, S.T.L. in Theology, 1969, M.A. in Theology, 1970; postgrad. U. Wash., 1966-70; Ph.D. in Philosophy, Pontifical Gregorian U., Rome, 1975. Ordained priest Roman Catholic Ch., 1968. Asst. prof., chmn. dept. philosophy Gonzaga U., Spokane, Wash., 1976-80; asst. prof. Loyola U., Chgo., 1980-83, assoc. prof., 1983-95, grad. dir., 1984-86; mem. Univ.-wide Com. Values and Ethics, Chgo.; mem. ethics com. VA Hines Hosp., Chgo., St. Mary Nazareth Hosp., Chgo; ethics cons. Motorola, 1994—. Author: Ethical Practice in Clinical Medicine, 1990. Contbr. articles to profl. jours. NEH grantee, 1980. Mem. Am. Philos. Assn., Am. Cath. Philos. Assn., Jesuit Philos. Assn., Soc. Health and Human Values, World Congress of Philosophy, Am. Soc. Law and Medicine, Hastings Ctr., Inst. Ultimate Reality and Meaning. Avocations: music, backpacking. Home: 7626 Callaghan # 2201 San Antonio TX 78229 Office: St Marys U 1 Camino Santa Maria San Antonio TX 78228

ELLSWORTH, BOB See WISE, ROBERT ELLSWORTH, JR.

ELLSWORTH, JOSEPH CORDON, real estate executive, lawyer; b. Washington, Aug. 13, 1955; s. Richard Grant and Betty (Midgley) E.; m. Rebecca Ann Moss, Nov. 2, 1979; children: Lindsey, Stephanie, Brian, Brittney. Grad., Brigham Young U., 1980; JD, Calif. Western U., 1983. Bar: Utah 1984, U.S. Dist. Ct. Utah 1984. Asst. legal counsel Meadow Fresh Farms, Inc., Salt Lake City, 1983; mgr. property and leasing Equitec Properties Co., Atlanta, 1984-85; sr. mgr. real estate and adminstrn. MCI Telecom. Corp., Atlanta, 1985—; with MCI Telecom. Corp., Englewood, Colo.; v.p. Rebecca's Sunnybrook Yogurt, Inc., Atlanta, 1985-90. Mem. Nat. Assn. Corp. Real Estate Execs. Internat., B.Y.U. Alumni Assn. (chmn. Atlanta region 1988-94), Phi Alpha Delta. Republican. Office: MCI Telecom Corp Ste 600E 6312 S Fiddlers Green Cir Englewood CO 80111-4949

ELLWANGER, JOHN P(AUL), minister; b. St. Louis, Nov. 7, 1931; s. Walter Henry and Jessie Lorraine (Hanger) E.; m. Jane Alice Taylor, Jan. 15, 1967; children: Jennifer Lynn, Jeremy Paul. BA, Concordia Sem., St. Louis, 1953; MDiv, Concordia Sem., 1956. Ordained to ministry Luth. Ch.-Mo. Synod, 1956. Pastor Luth. Ch. of Redeemer, Melbourne, Fla., 1956-62, Columbus, Ga., 1962-70; pastor Hope Luth. Ch., Austin, Tex., 1970—; sec. Fla.-Ga. Dist., Luth Ch.-Mo. Synod, Orlando, Fla., 1965-70, counselor Austin Cir., 1971-73, 89-94; bd. regents Concordia Coll., Austin, 1973-77; mem. Soc. Ministry Com., Tex. Dist. Luth. Ch.-Mo. Synod, 1978-88. Author: (children's devotions) My Devotions, 1964; editor: Fla.-Ga. edit. Lutheran Witness mag., 1960-65. Pres. Muscogee County Am. Cancer Soc., Columbus, 1965, vice chmn. Mayor's Com. on Fluoridation, Columbus, 1966-67, mem. Human Relations Bd., Columbus, 1968-70. Mem. Kiwanis (chpt. pres. 1985-86). Democrat. Home: 7406 Barcelona Dr Austin TX 78752-2005 Office: Hope Luth Ch 6414 N Hampton Dr Austin TX 78723-2043

ELLWOOD, BROOKS BERESFORD, geophysicist, educator; b. Chgo., July 18, 1942; s. John F.F. and Doris (Hammill) E.; m. Suzanne Higgins, Feb. 25, 1965; children: Amber B., Robin E., John Richard. BS, Fla. State U., 1970; PhD, U. R.I., 1976. Rsch. asst. U. R.I., Narragansett, 1970-76; rsch. assoc. Ohio State U., Columbus, 1976-77; asst. prof. U. Ga., Athens, 1977-81, assoc. prof., 1981-83; assoc. prof. U. Tex., Arlington, 1983-88, prof., 1988—, acting chair, 1989-92; dir. Ctr. for Geoarcheol. Studies, Arlington, 1987—. Author: Geology and America's National Park Areas, 1996; contbr. articles to Jour. Geophys. Rsch., Earth and Planetary Sci. Letters, Geology, Geoarcheology, Physics of Earath and Planetary Interiors, Geophys. Rsch. Letters, Science, Nature, and others; co-prodr.: (video) Applied Geoarcheology, 1988. With U.S. Army, 1964-66. Fellow Geol. Soc. Am., Geol. Soc. Can.; mem. Am. Geophys. Union, Soc. Exploration Geophysicists, Am. Assn. Petroleum Geologists, Sigma Xi. Office: U Tex Arlington Dept Geology PO Box 19049 Arlington TX 76019

EL-MALLAKH, RIF S., psychiatry educator, researcher; b. Alexandria, Egypt, Sept. 5, 1956; came to U.S., 1968; s. Shohdy Y. and Nadia Y. (Yousef) E.; m. Peggy L. Mickus; children: James, Thomas. BS, U. Ill., 1976, MS, 1979, MD, 1984. Adj. clin. asst. prof. George Washington U., Washington, 1989-92; asst. prof. U. Louisville, 1992—. Contbr. numberous articles to profl. jours. Office: Univ Louisville Psychiatry Dept Louisville KY 40292

ELMORE, PAULINE R., legal association administrator; b. Portland, Maine, June 8, 1943; d. Sidney William and Sabina Constance (Urban) Richard; m. James A. Mason, Sept.14, 1963 (div. Oct. 1983); children: Christine Mason Knego, Catherine Mason Lindsay, Cheryl J. Mason; m. William D. Elmore, June 6, 1987. Student, Mount Holyoke Coll., 1961-63, Old Dominion U., 1966-69; BA in English, Va. Commonwealth U., 1976, MBA, 1991. Staff writer Blue Cross of Va., Richmond, 1973-77; pub. affairs asst. United Va. Bankshares, Richmond, 1977; mgr. pub. rels. Metro Richmond C. of C., Va., 1977-80, v.p. comms., 1980-84, v.p. membership, 1984-86; dir. pub. rels. and tng. Security Fed. Savings and Loan, Richmond, Va., 1987-88; exec. dir. Advt. Club of Richmond, Va., 1989-90; grad. asst. Va. Commonwealth U., Richmond, 1991; exec. dir. Fairfax Bar Assn., Va., 1991—; mem. project mgmt. team Fairfax Cts. Expansion Study, 1993-96; Spanish translator project Fairfax Juvenile Ct., 1994—; mem. devel. team Ct. Internet Project, 1996. Author: History of Blue Cross and Blue Shield of Virginia, 1976 (Addy award 1977); editor: Guide to Health Resources in the Greater Richmond Area, 1974, 2d edit., 1975. Founder, 1st pres. Va. Heroes, Richmond, 1990-92. Recipient 7 awards of excellence Am. C. of C. Execs., 1979-86, scholarship Am. Bus. Women's Assn., 1988. Mem. Am. Soc. Assn. Execs., Nat. Assn. Bar Execs., Greater Washington Soc. Assn. Execs. (mentor program 1994-95), Leadership Fairfax, Humanities and Scis. Alumni Assn. Va. Commonwealth U. (founding mem., bd. dirs. 1983-84), Beta Sigma Gamma. Office: Fairfax Bar Assn 4110 Chain Bridge Rd Rm 303 Fairfax VA 22030

ELOFSON, GREGG STEVEN, computer information systems educator, consultant; b. L.A., May 4, 1956; s. Milo Horton and Beverly Jean (Fritz) E. BA in English, Econs., Occidental Coll., 1981; MS in MIS, U. Ariz., 1983, PhD in MIS, 1989. Rsch. asst. dept. MIS U. Ariz., 1983; systems cons. Arthur Andersen & Co., 1983-85; rsch. assoc. dept. MIS U. Ariz., 1985, 86; staff scientist Sci. Applications Internat. Corp., Tucson, 1986-88; rsch. assoc. dept. MIS U. Ariz., 1988, 89; asst. prof. computer info. systems U. Miami Sch. Bus., 1989-94; asst. prof. decision and info. analysis Emory U. Sch. Bus., Atlanta, 1994—. Contbr. articles to profl. jours. Rsch. grant U. Miami, 1992, Max Orovitz Found. award U. Miami, 1990, grant U. Ariz., 1986, grant Engring. Topographic Labs., 1987; Jordan fellowship, 1996; reciepient Outstanding scholar award, 1994, 95. Office: Emory U Sch Bus 1602 Mizell Dr Atlanta GA 30322

ELROD, JOHN WILLIAM, university president, philosophy and religion educator; b. Griffian, Ga., Jan. 21, 1940; s. John Charles and Carolyn (Barnette) E.; m. Mimi Cobb Milner, Aug. 3, 1963; children—Adam Milner, Joshua O'Beirne. BA, Presbyn. Coll., Clinton, S.C., 1962; MA, Columbia U., 1967, PhD, 1971. Asst. prof. philosophy Iowa State U., Ames, 1971-75, assoc. prof., 1975-81, prof., 1981-84, chmn. dept., 1979-84; prof. philosophy Washington and Lee U., Lexington, Va., 1984—, dean Coll., 1984-88, v.p. acad. affairs, 1987-95, acting pres., 1988, pres., 1995—; acad. cons. So. Assn. Colls. and Schs. Author: Being and Existence in Kierkegaard's Pseudonymous Works, 1975, Kierkegaard and Christendom, 1981; assoc. editor Jour. Philosophy of Religion, 1974; mem. adv. bd. Kierkegaard's Writings, 1977-85, Internat. Kierkegaard Commentary, 1981—; contbr. articles to profl. jours. NEH fellow, 1976; grantee Am. Philos. Soc., 1977, Iowa State U., 1977, 80, 82, Iowa Bd. for Pub. Programming in Humanities, 1980. Mem. Am. Philos. Assn., Am. Acad. Religion, Soc. Philosophy of Religion (v.p. 1985—), Metaphys. Soc. Am., Soc. for Christian Philosophy, Phi Beta Kappa, Omicron Delta Kappa. Democrat. Presbyterian. Office: Washington & Lee U Office of President Lexington VA 24450

ELROD, JOY CHEEK, nurse; b. Ft. Gordon, Ga., Dec. 16, 1955; d. Alton Waldo and Peggy Jim (Hewin) Cheek; children: Dana Maria, Zacharia Daniel. AA, Emmanuel Coll., 1984; BSN, Med. Coll. Ga., 1986. Coord. Wellness Systems Inc., Athens, Ga., 1986-87; staff nurse Athens Regional Med. Ctr., 1987-90; staff nurse Ty Cobb Health Care System, Royston, Ga., 1990—, healthy beginnings coord., 1991—; med. outreach tng. amb. Ty Cobb Health Care System, Ga. Hosp. Assn., Royston, 1991-92. Mem. No. Jud. Dist. Task Force for Family Violence, 1994—, Hart and Franklin Counties Families United, Franklin County Commn. for Children and Youth. Baptist. Home: PO Box 61 Bowersville GA 30516-0061

EL-SHISHINI, ALI SALEM, financial executive; came to U.S., 1963; children: Oliver William, Omar Salem. BS, Cairo U., 1960; MS, U. Tenn., 1968, PhD, 1971. CLU, chartered fin. cons. Teaching asst., physics dept. U. Tenn., Knoxville, 1968-71; postdoctoral rsch. assoc. U. Pa., Phila., 1971-74; fin. svcs. mktg. cons. Equitable Fin. Cos., N.Y.C. and Nashville, 1974—. Contbr. articles to profl. publs. Home: 737 Shadowood Dr Nashville TN 37205-4616 Office: 414 Union St Ste 1820 Nashville TN 37219-1758

ELSNER, JAMES BRIAN, meteorologist, educator; b. Milw., Oct. 16, 1959; s. Roger Allen and Diane Lucille (Richard) E.; m. Svetoslava Chtilianova Kavlakova, Jan. 7, 1989; children: Ian James, Diana Michelle. BSc, U. Wis., Milw., 1981, MSc, 1984, PhD, 1988. Rsch. scientist U. Wis., Milw., 1989, part-time lectr., 1989-90; asst. prof. meteorology Fla. State U., Tallahassee, 1990-95, assoc. prof., 1995—; cons. Risk Prediction Initiative, Bermuda, 1995. Contbr. articles to profl. jours. Grantee NOAA, 1992, NSF, 1993, 95. Mem. Am. Meteorol. Soc., European Geophys. Soc., Xi Epsilon Pi. Office: Fla State U Dept Meteorology Tallahassee FL 32306

ELSON, CHARLES MYER, law educator; b. Atlanta, Nov. 12, 1959; s. Edward Elliott and Suzanne Wolf (Goodman) E.; m. Aimee F. Kemker, Dec. 18, 1993. AB magna cum laude, Harvard U., 1981, postgrad., 1981-82; JD, U. Va., 1985. Bar: N.Y. 1987, D.C. 1988, U.S. Dist. Ct. (so. and ea. dists.) N.Y. 1987, U.S. Ct. Appeals (11th cir.) 1987. Law clk. to judge U.S. Ct. Appeals (11th cir.), Atlanta, 1985-86; assoc. Sullivan & Cromwell, N.Y.C., 1986-90; asst. prof. Stetson U. Coll. Law, St. Petersburg, Fla., 1990-93, assoc. prof., 1993-96, prof., 1996—; vis. prof. law U. Ill., Champaign-Urbana, 1995; vis. prof. Cornell Law Sch., Ithaca, N.Y., 1996; cons. Holland & Knight, 1995—. Bd. dirs. Big Apple Circus, Ltd., N.Y.C., 1987-93, Gulfcoast Legal Svcs. Corp., 1991—, Sunbeam Corp., 1996—, Tampa Mus. Art, 1993—; trustee Talladega Coll., 1994—. Salvatori fellow Heritage Found., 1993-94. Mem. ABA, Assn. Bar City N.Y., Chevaliers du Tastevin, Down Town Assn., Nat. Assn. Corp. Dirs. (commn. dir. compensation 1995, commn. dir. professionalism 1996), Harvard Club N.Y.C., Univ. Club N.Y.C. Home: 3315 W Mullen Ave Tampa FL 33609-4657 Office: Law Coll 1401 61st St S Saint Petersburg FL 33707-3246

ELSTER, ALLEN DEVANEY, radiologist, educator, scientific researcher; b. Houston, Jan. 26, 1954; s. Allen William and Martha Jo (Greene) E.; m. Jeanine Jones, June 6, 1980; children: Allen, Elizabeth, Martha, Patricia. BE, Vanderbilt U., 1976; MA, Oxford (Eng.) U., 1978; MD, Baylor Coll. Medicine, Houston, 1980. Diplomate Am. Bd. Radiology; lic. physician, Tex., N.C. Clin. fellow in surgery Harvard Med. Sch., Boston, 1980-83; resident in radiology U. Tex. Med. Sch., Houston, 1983-86; asst. prof. radiology Bowman Gray Sch. Medicine, Wake Forest U., Winston Salem, 1986-88, assoc. prof., 1988-91, prof., 1991—; dir. Ctr. for Magnetic Resonance Imaging, Winston Salem, 1987—. Author: Magnetic Resonance Imaging, 1988, Cranial Magnetic Resonance Imaging, 1989, Questions and Answers in MR Imaging, 1993; editor Jour. Computer Assisted Tomography, 1995—; mem. editl. bd. 8 sci. jours.; contbr. articles to profl. jours. Sci. advisor Triplet Connection, Stockton, Calif., 1989—. Rhodes scholar, 1976; recipient numerous sci. rsch. grants from govt. and industry, 1989—. Mem. Radiol. Soc. N.Am. (Scholar award 1990), Am. Coll. Radiology, Am. Soc. Neuroradiology, Am. Soc. Rhodes Scholars. Office: Bowman Gray Sch Medicine Medical Center Blvd Winston Salem NC 27157

ELWELL, HOWARD ANDREW, safety engineer; b. Wichita, Kans., July 21, 1940; s. Howard Andrew and Mary Helen (Uncapher) E.; m. Landis Elain Kerr, Sept. 10, 1965. BSME, Purdue U., 1963. Exptl. engr. Pratt and Whitney, West Palm Beach, Fla., 1968-75, performance analysis engr., 1975-78, system safety engr., 1978-81, asst. project engr., 1981-87, project engr., 1987-92; pres. Elwell & Assoc., Jupiter, 1992—; safety cons. Gary Robinson, Inc., Jupiter, Fla., 1988—; v.p. Profl. Safety, Inc., Royal Palm Beach, Fla., 1988—; sys. safety mgr. CCTT program Dynamics Rsch. Corp./IBM, 1992-93. Lt. USN, 1963-68. Mem. Sys. Safety Soc., World Safety Orgn. (affiliate), Am. Soc. Safety Engrs. (profl.), Soc. Risk Analysis, Soc. Automotive Engrs., Human Factors Ergonomics Soc. (assoc.), Vets. of Safety. Home and Office: 12454 184th Ct N Jupiter FL 33478-2035

ELWOOD, WILLIAM NORELLI, medical researcher; b. East Orange, N.J., Aug. 21, 1962; s. William Rogers and Frances Emma (Norelli) E. BS in Comm., U. Fla., 1985; MA in Human Comm., U. South Fla., 1989; PhD in Human Communication, Purdue U., 1992. Grad. teaching asst. U. South Fla., 1988-89; grad. teaching instr. Purdue U., 1989-91; asst. prof. Auburn (Ala.) U., 1992-94; rsch. assoc. Affiliated Systems Corp., Houston, 1994-96; adj. asst. prof. U. Tex. Sch. Pub. Health, Houston, Md., 1996—; co-prin. investigator Nat. Inst. on Drug Abuse, 1994-96; rsch. assoc. NOVA Rsch. Co., Bethesda, Md., 1995—; adj. asst. prof. Ctr. for Health Promotion Rsch. and Devel. U. Tex.-Houston Sch. of Pub. Health, 1996—. Author: Rhetoric in the War on Drugs, 1994, Public Relations Inquiry as Rhetorical Criticism, 1995; contbr. articles to profl. jours. Chmn. Grove St./Blossom Brook Neighborhood Improvement Project, Sarasota, Fla., 1990-92; poll sheriff Tippecanoe County, Ind. State Elections, 1990; precinct capt. Sarasota County, Fla., 1986-89. Recipient Alan H. Monroe Disting. Grad. scholar, and teaching award, 1990-91; Rsch. grantee, Auburn U., 1993. Mem. Houston Coun. on Substance Abuse Svcs., Tex. Drug Epidemiology Workgroup. Home: 402 Tuam Ave 1 Houston TX 77006

ELY, DUNCAN CAIRNES, human services executive, civic leader; b. Phila., Apr. 3, 1951; s. Donald and Barbara Dercum (Mifflin) E.; m. Elizabeth Caroline Wickenberg, June 14, 1984; 1 child, Penn Wickenberg. BA, U. Ariz., 1974; MDiv, Gen. Theol. Sem., N.Y.C., 1988; cert. mentor of edn. for ministry, U. of South, 1985. Cert. in clin. pastoral edn. Bapt. Med. Ctr., 1985; cert. human svcs. adminstrn. Human Svcs. Inst., 1991. Nat. exec. dir. Assn. for Independence of Disabled, Inc., Tucson, 1974-77; exec. dir. Frat. of Alpha Kappa Lambda, Inc., Indpls., 1977-79; asst. St. Stephen's Episcopal Ch., Phila., 1979-80; dir. The Youth Alternatives Camps, Inc., Tucson, 1980-83, Crisis Assistance Clothing Ministry, Charlotte, N.C., 1989-93; exec. dir. N.C. Harvest, Inc., Charlotte, 1993-96, Spartanburg (S.C.) Cmty. Events, Inc., 1996—; chmn. bd. advisors expanded foods and nutrition edn. program N.C. State U., Charlotte, 1989-96; mem. foster care rev. bd. child protective svcs. Dept. Social Svcs., Charlotte, 1991-96. Author, editor: The Truth and the Word, 1978; also numerous articles in books, jours., mag. and newspapers. Past pres. Ely Assn., Inc., N.Y.C.; trustee Wildlife Guard, Inc., 1973—, also past chmn. bd. advisors The Relatives, Inc., Charlotte, 1989-96, Ret. Sr. Vol. Program, Charlotte, 1990-96, Vol. Ctr. Charlotte, 1990—; bd. dirs. Charlotte Emergency Housing, Inc., 1989-96, Met. Music Ministries, Inc., 1993-96; mem. Vol. Leadership Devel. Program, Charlotte, 1991; mem. class XIII, LEadership Charlotte, 1991; mem. class III Carolinas Leadership Program, 1994; mem. class I Leadership N.C., 1995; commr. for nat. and cmty. svc. State of N.C.; mem. N.C. Gov.'s Commn. on Nat. and Cmty. Svc. Recipient gold pin Phila. State Hosp., 1973, One of Nine Who Care award Sta. WSOC-TV and United Way, Charlotte, 1991, 94. Mem. Am. Mgmt. Assn., Am. Soc. Assn. Execs., Nat. Christian Counselors Assn. (lic. pastoral counselor), Metrolina Assn. for Vol. Adminstrn. (past pres.), N.C. Assn. Vol. Adminstrs. (past v.p.), Penn Laurel Poets, Soc. Nonprofit Execs., Pen and Pencil Club, Alpha Kappa Lambda, Alpha Phi Omega, Theta Kappa Psi, Theta Omega, Psi Chi, Spartanburg Country Club, Fripp Island Club (S.C.), numerous others. Republican. Episcopalian. Home: Skidaway The Wood House 605 Crystal Dr Spartanburg SC 29302-2716 Office: Spartanburg Cmty Events Inc PO Box 1861 Spartanburg SC 29304-1861

ELY, ELIZABETH WICKENBERG, priest; b. Columbia, S.C., June 14, 1953; d. Charles Herbert Jr. and Margaret Smith (Gall) Wickenberg; m. Duncan Cairnes Ely, June 14, 1984; 1 child, Penn Wickenberg Ely. BA, Agnes Scott Coll., 1975; MS, Columbia U., 1976; MDiv cum laude, Gen. Theol. Sem., N.Y.C., 1989. Ordained to ministry Episcopal Ch. in U.S.A., 1990. Homes and real estate editor Providence Jour.-Bull., Providence, 1976-78; sports columnist Clarion-Ledger, Jackson, Miss., 1978-80; sports writer, copy editor Atlanta Jour., 1980; sports editor and columnist Natchez (Miss.) Dem., 1980-81; sports copy editor Dallas Times-Herald, 1982; sports copy editor/writer Ariz. Daily Star, Tucson, 1981-83; copy editor Phila. Inquirer, 1983-85; assoc. rector St. John's Episcopal Ch., Charlotte, N.C., 1989-93; vicar All Saints and St. Patrick Episcopal Chs., Charlotte, 1993-96; assoc. rector Episcopal Ch. of the Advent, Spartansburg, S.C., 1996—; mem. diocesan coun. Episcopal Diocese of N.C. Author: A Manual for Lay Eucharistic Ministers, 1991. Mem. instnl. rev. bd. Carolinas Med. Ctr., Charlotte, 1990-96. Home: Skidmore 605 Crystal Dr Spartanburg SC 29302-2716 Office: Episcopal Ch of the Advent 141 Advent St Spartanburg SC 29302-1904

ELY, RICHARD MCBRIER, video/film producer, writer; b. Erie, Pa., Oct. 20, 1948; s. Robert Thatcher and Jeanne Louise (Meiser) E.; m. Heidi Marie Brinig, June 28, 1980 (div. Dec. 1990); children: Cadence McBrier Ely-Mooney, Hannah Giles Ely-Mooney. Student, allegheny Coll., Meadville, Pa., 1967-71, Franklin Pierce Coll., Rindge, N.H., 1968-69, Schiller Coll., West Berlin, 1970-71. Songwriter/prodr. Erie, 1972-80; writer/prodr. TAL, Inc. Advt., Erie, 1980-85; prodr. Healey, Schutte Advt., Buffalo, 1986; pres., creative dir. The Big Picture, Charlotte, N.C., 1986—; judge awards competition New eng. Audio/Visual assn., Boston, 1989; judge art competition Erie Art Ctr., 1979. Featured artist Battered Women's Shelter, Erie, 1982.

ELZINGA, KENNETH GERALD, economics educator; b. Coopersville, Mich., Aug. 11, 1941; s. Clarence Albert and Lettie (Albrecht) E.; m. Barbara Ann Brunson, June 17, 1967 (dec. 1978); m. Terry M. Maguire, Aug. 9, 1981. BA, Kalamazoo Coll., 1963; MA, Mich. State U., 1966, PhD, 1967. Rsch. economist Sen. Antitrust & Monopoly Subcom., 1964; asst. instr. Mich. State U., 1965-66; asst. prof. U. Va., 1967-71; spl. econ. adv. to the asst. atty. gen., antitrust divsn. Dept. Justice, 1970-71; assoc. prof. U. Va., 1971-74; fellow in law and econs. U. Chgo., 1974; vis. prof. of econs. Trinity U., 1984; Thomas Jefferson fellow, prof. of econs. Cambridge U., 1990, Cavaliers Dist. Teaching Professorship, 1992—; bd. dirs. Hope Coll. Bd. Trustees, 1983-90, Inter-Varsity Christian fellowship, 1993—; mem. editl. bd. Antitrust Bulletin, 1977—. Author: (with others) The Antitrust Penalties, 1976, The Fatal Equilibrium, 1985, Murder at the Margin, 1993, A Deadly Indifference, 1995. Recipient Thomas Jefferson award U. Va., 1992, Commonwealth of Va. Outstanding Faculty award, 1992, Kenan Enterprise award for tchg. econs., William R. Kenan Jr. Charitable Trust, 1996; named Tchr. of the Yr. Phi Eta Sigma, 1992. Mem. ABA, Am. Econs. Assn., Mystery Writers of Am., So. Econ. Assn. (pres. 1991), Internat. J.A. Shumpeter Soc., Industrial Orgn. Soc. (pres. 1979). Presbyterian. Home: Pavilion IV East Lawn Charlottesville VA 22903 Office: U Va Dept Econs 114 Ross Hall Charlottesville VA 22903

EMANUELE, R.M., business executive. V.p. rsch. Cytrx Corp., Norcross, Ga. Office: Cytrx Corp Tech Park/Atlanta 154 Technology Pky Norcross GA 30092

EMBREE, JAMES RAY, construction company executive, director; b. Cheyenne Wells, Colo., Oct. 7, 1949; s. LeRoy Lloyd and Dorothy Jean (Herndon) E.; m. Yvonne C. Gieschen, June 10, 1972; children: Yvette, Adrienne, Ashley, Beau. AA in Archtl. Bldg. Constrn., Cen. Mo. State U., 1971. Estimator Neighbor's Constrn. Co., Inc., Kansas City, Mo., 1971-73; project engr. Western Auto Supply Co., Kansas City, 1973-75; v.p. Jay's Constrn. Co., Inc., Kansas City, 1976-79; constrn. coord. Winchell's Donut House, LaMirada, Calif., 1975-76; pres. Embree Constrn. Group (Corp.), Georgetown, Tex., 1979—. Office: 30226 Oakmont Dr Georgetown TX 78628-1109

EMBREE, LESTER EUGENE, philosophy educator; b. San Francisco, Jan. 9, 1938; s. Lester Bordon and Charlotte Ann (Hoffman) E.; m. Veronica Kennedy (div. 1988); children: Lester Kenneth, Michael William, Deirdre Gabrielle. BA, Tulane U., 1962; PhD, New Sch. for Social Rsch., 1972. Asst. prof. No. Ill. U., DeKalb, 1969-73; assoc. prof. philosophy Duquesne U., Pitts., 1974, prof., 1979-90; William F. Dietrich eminent scholar philosophy Fla. Atlantic U., Boca Raton, 1990—; pres. Ctr. for Advanced Rch. in Phenomenology, Inc., Dallas, 1981—. Author, editor, translator numerous books on philosophy and cultural sci., philosophy of archaeology, philosophy of tech. and environ. philosophy; contbr. numerous articles to profl. jours.; editor: Encyclopedia of Phenomenology, 1996. With USMC, 1957-59. Office: Philosophy Dept Fla Atlantic U Boca Raton FL 33431

EMBREY, CARL RICE, artist; b. Hamilton, Tex., Oct. 28, 1938; s. Carl Denby and Margaret Ellen (Rice) E.; m. Peggy Jo Teehee, Dec. 27, 1962; children: Dawn Marie, Rhys Mayo. BFA, U. Tex. Austin, 1962, MFA, 1964. Mus. asst. U. Tex. Austin, 1961-64, teaching asst., 1963-64; instr. Laguna Gloria, Austin, 1963-64; pres. and exhbn. chmn. Men of Art Guild, San Antonio, 1965-68; pres. Contemporary Art Group, San Antonio, 1969-70; prof. drawing and painting San Antonio Art Inst., 1964-92, mem. faculty, 1964-93; juror Jewish Community Ctr., Houston, 1968, Houston Met. Exhbn., 1968, Rio Grand Art Festival, Laredo, Tex., 1970. One-man shows include U. Tex. Austin, 1964, Gate House, San Antonio, 1965, Men of Art Guild's Galleries, San Antonio, 1965, 66, 68, N. Star Gallery, San Antonio, 1968, Courtney Gallery, Houston, 1969, 71, Fairmount Gallery, Dallas, 1969-72, Marion Koogler McNay Art Mus., San Antonio, 1974, Meredith Long and Co., Houston, 1976, 79, 81, 83, 85, Harari-Johns Galleries, Ltd., London, 1984, San Antonio Art Ins., 1988, numerous others; retrospective exhbn. at Marion Koogler McNay Art Mus., San Antonio, 1997; exhibited in group shows at Beaumont (Tex.) Mus. Fine Arts, 1964, TFAA Cir. Exhbn., 1964-66, Isaac Delgado Mus., New Orleans, 1967, Tex. Fine Arts Assn., Austin, 1964-65, 67, Inst. Texan Cultures, San Antonio, 1968, 10th Ann. Invitational Exhbn. 40 Tex. Artists, Longview, 1970, 72, Odyssey Gallery, San Antonio, 1970, 72, Witte Meml. Mus., San Antonio, 1977, San Antonio Art Inst., 1977-82, 84-85, Chgo. Internat. Art Dealers' Exhbn., 1984-86, McNay Art Mus., San Antonio, 1988, Martin-Rathburn Gallery, San Antonio, 1992, 94, Meredith Long and Co., 1992, Eva Cohon Gallery Ltd., Chgo., 1993, numerous others; represented in permanent collections Contemporary Art Mus., Sylvan and Mary Lang, Am. Nat. Life, San Antonio Art League, Emerson Gallery, Hamilton Coll., Clinton, N.Y., others; numerous pvt. collections. Mem. Tex. Fine Arts Assn. Mem. Christian Ch. Home and Studio: 9319 Nona Kay Dr San Antonio TX 78217-5020

EMBRY, KAREN THOMPSON, elementary education educator; b. Atlanta, Sept. 25, 1958; d. James Newton and Billie Reese (Cleveland) Thompson; m. Sterling Charters Embry, Aug. 14, 1982 (div. Jan. 1994); 1 child, Juliette Reese Embry; stepchildren: Hugh Cooper Embry III, Headen Davidson Embry. BA in Early Childhood Edn., LaGrange Coll., 1980; postgrad., North Ga. Coll., 1989-90, Lanier Tech. Inst., 1996—. Cert. EMT intermediate level, 1996. Kindergarten tchr. Hall County Bd. Edn., Gainesville, Ga., 1980-81; 1st grade tchr. Hall County Bd. Edn., 1981-90, ESOL tchr., 1990-95, 5th grade tchr., 1995—; mem. adv. com. on ESOL needs for Hall County, 1993—, curriculum devel. com. ESOL Tchrs. of Hall County, 1993—. Contbr. articles to newspapers. Vol. Gateway House for Battered Women, Gainesville, 1992, Meals on Wheels, Gainesville, 1993; vol. interpreter Good News at Noon Med. Clinic, Gainesville, 1994. Mem. Ga. Assn. Educators, Hall County Assn. Educators, Jr. League of Gainesville-Hall County. Democrat. Methodist. Home: 4588 Buckhorn Rd Gainesville GA 30506-3024 Office: Myers Elem Sch 2676 Candler Rd Gainesville GA 30507-8961

EMBRY, MICHAEL DALE, news correspondent; b. Louisville, Oct. 30, 1948; s. G.T. Dale and Dolores Lorraine (Colburn) E.; m. Mary Elizabeth Frederick, Aug. 7, 1971; children: Justin Michael, Sean Russell. AB in journalism, Ea. Ky. U., 1975. Sports editor Messenger, Madisonville, Ky., 1975-77; sports writer Lexington (Ky.) Herald, 1977-80; newsman AP, Louisville, 1980-82; sports writer AP, N.Y.C., 1982-83; state sports editor AP, Milw., 1983-85; corr. AP, Lexington, 1985—; mem. adv. bd. Ea. Ky. U. Dept. Comms., 1990-93, Ea. Ky. Progress, 1990-93. Author: Basketball in the Bluegrass State, 1983, March Madness, 1985; contbr. articles to profl. publs. With USAF, 1969-73. Recipient Writing award Ky. chpt. Am. Cancer Soc., 1986-87, 89-90, 93, Ea. Ky. U. Comms. Alumni of Yr. 1983, DeDe award Ky. Devel. Planning Coun., 1988. Mem. Nat. Sportscasters and Sportswriters Assn., Nat. Turf Writers Assn., Football Writers Assn. Am., Ky. Thoroughbred Media, Blue Grass Soc. Profl. Journalists (pres. 1985-86), U.S. Basketball Writers Assn., Milw. chpt. Basketball Writers Assn. (pres. 1983). Home: 1188 Mount Rushmore Way Lexington KY 40515-5467

EMBRY, RICHARD HENRY, real estate broker; b. Muskogee, Okla., May 27, 1934; s. Fred Embry and Ella Mae (Taylor) Barnett; m. Gloria J. Kinchen, July 3, 1959. AS, Altus Jr. Coll., 1970; BS, N.E. State U., 1979. Enlisted USAF, 1951, advanced through grades to T sgt., ret., 1971; postal clerk U.S. Post Office, Muskogee, 1971; dep. dir. Community Action Agy., Muskogee, 1972-74; owner, mgr. R&G Enterprises, Muskogee, 1973-80; recruiter, counselor Connors State Coll., Warner, Okla., 1976; employment interviewer Okla. State Employment Svc., Muskogee, 1979-89, employment mgr., 1989-96; retired Okla. State Employment Svcs., Muskogee, 1996; owner, broker, appraiser Embry Real Estate, Muskogee, 1980—. Vice chmn. precinct # 47 Dem. Party, Muskogee, 1975-79; mem., chmn. Met. Planning, Muskogee, 1989-93; v.p. Blacks in Govt., Muskogee, 1993-95; pres. Habitat for Humanity, Muskogee, 1993-95. Mem. Nat. Assn. Realtors, Nat. Assn. Real Estate Appraisers, Okla. Assn. Realtors, Okla. Cert. Pub. Mgrs. Acad., Muskogee Bd. Realtors (ethics com. 1983-84), Northeastern State U. Alumni, Masons (33 degree). Home and Office: 1905 S 24th St W Muskogee OK 74401-8029

EMELY, CHARLES HARRY, trade association executive; b. Phila., Oct. 30, 1943; s. Charles Walter and Jane Beatty (Stott) E.; m. Susan Elizabeth Lawton, June 18, 1966 (dec. Mar. 1977); 1 child, Charles Walter II; m. Mary Ann Horvath, Sept. 1, 1979; 1 stepchild, Wendy A. Vellrath. Student, Drexel Inst. Tech., 1961-62; BA, Temple U., 1967; MA, Fairfield U., 1974; postgrad., NYU, 1974-76; PhD, Calif. Western U., 1978; postgrad., Ohio U., 1981-82. Adminstrv. asst. City of Phila., 1966-68; nat. rep. ARC, Washington, 1968-70; exec. dir., chief exec. officer Bridgeport, Conn., 1970-77; pres., chief exec. officer Comprehensive Bus. Cons., Ft. Washington, Pa., 1977-86; exec. v.p., chief exec. officer Adhesive & Sealant Council, Washington, 1987-88; pres., CEO Comprehensive Bus. Cons., Inc., Fairfax, Va., 1988—; exec. dir., CEO Internat. Assn. Law Firms, 1988—; exec. dir., COO Am. Soc. Hort. Sci., Alexandria, Va., 1994—; chmn. Cmty. Cons. Corps, Ft. Washington, 1980—; sr. cons. Philippine Nutrition Ctr., Manila, 1980; adj. faculty Ohio U., Athens, 1982-83, bd. dirs. ICM Internat., Inc.; comunications officer, U.S.A. Nat. Disaster Med. Sys., 1992—. Mem. bd. mgrs. YMCA, Fairfield, Conn., 1971-75; bd. dirs. Hope Ctr., Inc., Bridgeport, 1972-76, Comprehensive Health Planning Agy., Bridgeport, 1973-74; mem. Mayor's Energy Adv. Com., Bridgeport, 1973-74, Fayetteville (N.Y.) United Meth. Ch., 1985; trustee, v.p. Mental Health Assn. Conn., 1973-77; mem. adminstrv. bd. Nichols United Meth. Ch., Trumbull, Conn., 1975-77; adv. com. campaign coun. Rep. Nat. Com.; mem. Patriots Soc. Germantown Acad., Ft. Washington, 1978-80; pres. Ambler (Pa.) Symphony Orchestra, 1979-80; mem. Pvt. Industry Council, Ambler, 1979-80, Zanesville, Ohio, 1981-83; mem. parents council Hartwick Coll., Oneonta, N.Y., 1987. Mem. Am. Mgmt. Assn., Adminstrv. Mgmt. Soc., Am. Soc. Assn. Execs. (cert. assn. exec. 1977), Nat. Assn. Corp. Dirs. (sec./treas. Washington chpt.), Found. for Internat. Meetings, Mensa, Officers Club, Am. Radio Relay League, Bethesda Nat. Naval Med. Ctr., Aircraft Owners and Pilots Assn., Armed Forces Comms. and Electronics Assn., Associated Pub. Safety Comm. Officers, Rep. Nat. Com. Campain Coun. Rep. Nat. Com. Pres.'s Club. Republican. Clubs: Phila. Aviation Country, Vesper, University, City of Washington, Nat. Assn. Execs. Lodges: Masons, Shriners, Rotary. Home: 9715 Oak Bridge Pl Fairfax VA 22039-3400 Office: Am Soc Hort Sci 600 Cameron St Alexandria VA 22314

EMELY, MARY ANN, association executive; b. Bridgeport, Conn., Aug. 10, 1947; d. John and Stefanie Maria (Hutta) Horvath; m. Timothy Vellrath, Sept. 7, 1968 (div. Mar. 1975); 1 child, Wendy Amethyst Vellrath Delbrook; m. Charles H. Emely, Sept. 1, 1979. BA, U. Conn., 1969; postgrad., U. Bridgeport, 1975-76, Ohio U., 1982-83. Adminstrv. asst. ARC, Bridgeport, 1973-78; dir. mem. svcs. Comprehensive Assn. Cons., Ft. Washington, Pa., 1978-81; exec. dir. Muskingum County Respiratory Disease, Zanesville, Ohio, 1981-83; assoc. exec. dir. The Vol. Ctr., Syracuse, N.Y., 1984-86; dir. mem. programs NEA, Rockville, Md., 1986-91; dir. mem., mktg. Am. Geophys. Union, Washington, 1991-93; sr. dir. membership Coun. for Exceptional Children, Reston, Va., 1993-94; dep. exec. dir. Spl. Librs. Assn., Washington, 1994-95; exec. dir. Fedn. Govt. Info. Processing Couns., Falls Church, Va., 1995—; cons. Comprehensive Assn. Cons., Fairfax, Va., 1991-96. Editor Husky P.A.W. Print, 1995-96, Fedn. Facts, 1995-96; columnist: Female Exec., 1994-95. Bd. dirs. Pub. Employees Roundtable, Washington, 1995-96; mem. Nat. Rep. Coalition for Choice, Washington, 1993-96, Jr. League of Washington, 1986-96. Mem. NAFE, Am. Soc. assn. Execs. (cert., mentor diversity programs 1994-95), Am. Radio Relay League, Greater Washington Soc. Assn. Execs., Found. for Internat. Meetings, Mercedes Benz Club of Am., U. Conn. Alumni Assn. (No. Va. chpt., pres. 1996—), Kappa Alpha Theta. Methodist. Home: 9715 Oak Bridge Pl Fairfax Station VA 22039-3400 Office: FGIPC 7777 Leesburg Pike #3LS Falls Church VA 22043

EMERSON, ANN PARKER, dietician, educator; b. Twin Lakes, Fla., Dec. 3, 1925; d. Charles Dendy and Gladys Agnes (Chalker) Parker; B.S., Fla. State U., 1947; M.S., U. Fla., 1968; m. Donald McGeachy Emerson, Sept. 22, 1950; children—Mary Ann, Donald McGeachy, Charles Parker, William John. Research dietitian U. Chgo., 1948-50; adminstrv. research dietitian U. Fla. Coll. Medicine, Gainesville, 1962-68, dir. dietetic edn., 1968-74, dir. dietetic internship program, 1968-75, dir. program in clin. and community dietetics, 1974-83; mem. Commn. on Dietetic Registration, 1974-77, Commn. on Accreditation, 1980-83. Pres., Gainesville chpt. Altrusa, Internat., 1977-78. VA Allied Health Manpower grantee, 1974-81; HEW Allied Health Manpower grantee, 1975-78, 78-81. Mem. Am., Fla. Dietetic Assns. Republican. Roman Catholic. Clubs: Jr. League, Altrusa.

EMERSON, DONALD MCGEACHY, JR., appraisal company executive; b. Clearwater, Fla., Oct. 21, 1952; s. Donald McGeachy and Ann (Parker) E. BS in Bus. Adminstrn. and Real Estate, U. Fla., 1975, MA in Real Estate, 1976. Appraiser Emerson Appraisal Co., Gainesville, Fla., 1973-75, v.p., 1975-87, pres., 1987—; treas. Emerson Realty, Inc., 1977-86, pres. Emerson Realty, 1986—; owner, appraiser Emerson Appraisal Co., 1973—, pres., 1986—. Registered real estate broker, Fla. Mem. Gainesville Bd. Realtors, Nat. Assn. Realtors, Southeastern Interfraternity Conf. (program dir. 1975-76), U. Fla. Interfrat. Council (pres. 1974-75), Fla. Blue Key (treas. 1976-77), Fraternity Purchasing Assn. (chmn. bd. 1979-87), Appraisal Inst. (vice chmn. gen. course devel. com. 1991, curriculum com. 1991, chmn. gen. seminar com. 1992-94, vice-chair edn. com. 1995—), Order of Omega (pres. U. Fla. chpt. 1975-76), Centurion Council (pres. 1981-82), Gainesville C. of C. (bd. dirs. 1985-87), Rotary (pres. Gainesville Sunrise chpt. 1994-95), Delta Tau Delta. Democrat. Roman Catholic. Home: PO Box 113 Gainesville FL 32602-0113 Office: PO Box PO Box 882 Gainesville FL 32602-0882

EMERSON, DOUGLAS THEODORE, lawyer; b. Sept. 25, 1952; s. Douglas Theodore and Dora Mae (Angle) E. BA, U. Nev., Las Vegas, 1985; JD, Calif. Western Sch. Law, 1987. Bar: Tex. 1988, U.S. Dist. Ct. (no. dist.) Tex. 1988, U.S. Ct. Appeals (5th cir.) 1994. Assoc. Parkhill, Parkhill, Cowden & Runge, Grand Prairie, Tex., 1987-89; pvt. practice, Ft. Worth, 1989-92; ptnr. Law Offices Nekhom, Behr, Barnett & Emerson, Ft. Worth, 1992-95; pvt. practice Ft. Worth, 1995—. With USMC, 1971-73. Mem. State Bar of Tex., Tarrant County Bar Assn., Tex. Criminal Def. Lawyers Assn., Tarrant County Criminal Def. Lawyers Assn., Phi Alpha Delta. Office: Ste 200 221 W Exchange Ave Fort Worth TX 76106

EMERSON, JOHN WILLIAMS, II, lawyer; b. Greeneville, Tenn., Nov. 9, 1929; s. John Williams and Dorothy Mae (Moore) E.; m. Carolyn Rose Buchanan, Dec. 21, 1956; children: John Williams III, Amy Elizabeth, Emily Alicia. JD, Vanderbilt U., 1960. Bar: Fla. 1960, Tenn. 1960, U.S. Dist. Ct. (so. dist.) Fla. 1961, U.S. Ct. Appeals (5th cir.) 1961, U.S. Supreme Ct. 1968, U.S. Dist. Ct. (ea. dist.) Tenn. 1982, U.S. Ct. Appeals (6th cir.) 1983, U.S. Dist. Ct. (mid. dist.) Tenn. 1988, U.S. Dist. Ct. (mid. dist.) Fla. 1990. Ins. agt. Emerson Ins. Agy., Greeneville, 1949-56; instr. Peabody Coll., Nashville, 1958-59; assoc. Henderson, Franklin, Starnes & Holt, Ft. Myers, Fla., 1960-63; ptnr. Parks & Emerson, Naples, Fla., 1963-72, Treadwell, Emerson & Elkins, Naples, 1972-79, Emerson & Emerson P.C., Johnson City, Tenn., 1979-83, Emerson & Emerson P.A., Naples, 1983—; judge Small Claims Ct., Collier County, Naples, Fla., 1963-64. Col. aide de camp gov.'s staff State of Tenn., 1963-66; lt. gov. dist. 11 Fla. Dist. of Kiwanis, 1970-71. Capt. U.S. Army, 1950-54, Korea. Fellow Fla. Kiwanis Found. (life); mem. ABA, The Fla. Bar (bd. govs. young lawyers sect. 1963-66), Fla. Acad. Trial Lawyers, Assn. Trial Lawyers Am., Araba Temple (Ft. Myers, Fla.), Masons (32 Degree). Democrat. Presbyterian. Home: 583 6th Ave N Naples FL 33940-5506 Office: Emerson & Emerson PA 385 13th Ave S Naples FL 34102

EMERSON, PETER MICHAEL, counselor; b. Portland, Oreg., Feb. 16, 1956; s. George and Rayola (Jones) E. BS in Psychology, Brigham Young U., 1980; M in Counseling, Idaho State U., 1982, EdD in Counselor Edn., 1987. Cert. Nat. Bd. Cert. Counselors; lic. profl. counselor. Counselor Cedar Valley Boys Home, Fairfield, Utah, 1978-79; dir. drug abuse prevention Blackfoot (Idaho) Sch. Dist. # 55, 1980; dir. Trio Programs Upward Bound and Spl. Svcs., So. Utah State Coll., Cedar City, 1980-85; doctoral tchg. asst. of counselor edn. Idaho State U., Pocatello, 1985-87; asst. prof. Southeastern La. U., 1987-88; asst. prof. U. New Orleans, 1988-90; assoc. prof. Southeastern La. U., 1990-93, head dept., 1996—. Editor La. Jour. of Coun., 1989—. Mem. ACA, La. Lic. Profl. Counselors (chmn. bd. examiners), Am. Assn. for Marriage and Family Therapy (clin.), Assn. Adult Devel. and Aging (pres. 1994-95), Am. Assn. of State Counselin Bds. (pres. 1995-96). Mormon. Office: Southeastern La U PO Box 863 Hammond LA 70404-0863

EMERSON, RUSSELL GEORGE, writer; b. Lowell, Mass., Sept. 24, 1929; s. George H. and Sadie E. (Bostwick) E.; m. Dorothy Betcher, Oct. 15, 1954 (div. 1963); children: George A., Brian K.; m. Linda Marie Burkes, May 28, 1983. Student, Kennesaw (Ga.) Jr. Coll., 1974-76, Kennestone Hosp. Radiol. Tech., 1976-78. Registered radiol. technologist. Enlisted USN, 1947; stationed at Naval Air Station Barber's Point, Calif.; served on USS Mindora; stationed at Naval Air Station Los Alamitos, Calif., Atlanta; ret., 1969; photo journalist Cartersville (Ga.) Tribune News, 1969-74; staff technician West Paces Hosp., Atlanta, 1980-86, Humana Hosp., Cartersville, 1986-92; writer Acworth, Ga., 1993—. Author: Sign of the Serpent, 1991, Forbidden Waters, 1992, Whispers in the Wind, 1993, Tears for the Clown, 1994. Mem. NRA, Fleet Res. Assn., Am. Legion, Am. Registry of Radiologic Technologists.

EMERSON, WILLIAM KARY, engineering company executive; b. Enid, Okla., July 15, 1941; s. Kary Cadmus and Mary Rebecca (Williams) E.; m. Marcie Louise Stogner, Mar. 13, 1965; children: Rebecca A., Phillip W. BS, Okla. State U., 1965, MS, 1974; diploma, Command and Gen. Staff Coll., 1979, Defense Systems Mgmt. Coll., 1980. Commd. 2d lt. U.S. Army, 1965; advanced through grades to lt. col., 1985; prin. program mgr. Honeywell, Inc., Minnetonka, Minn., 1985-90; sr. program mgr. Alliant Techsystems, Inc., Minnetonka, 1990-92; dep. dir. engring. Teledyne Brown Engring. Co., Huntsville, Ala., 1992-96, dir. advanced engring., 1996—. Author: Chevrons, 1983, Encyclopedia of Insignia, 1995; contbr. articles to profl. jours. and ency. Mem. adv. com. Dist. 281 Sch. Bd., Minn., 1986-88, mem. summer sch. concept com., 1988-89; mem. Huntsville Land Trust, 1994—; chmn. recycling com. N. Ala. Sierra Club, 1994—; citizen mem. City of Huntsville Ordinance Rewrite Com., 1995-96. Decorated Legion of Merit, Bronze Star with V and one oak leaf cluster, Purple Heart with two oak leaf clusters; inducted into Madison County (Ala.) Hall of Heros, 1996. Fellow Co. Mil. Historians (bd. dirs. 1983-86, editor 1986-92, Miller award 1977); mem. Am. Soc. Mil. Insignia Collectors (editor jour. 1993—, Best Nat. Display award 1984), Am. Def. Preparedness Assn., Assn. U.S. Army, Mil. Order Purple Heart, Heritage Club, Sierra Club (local chmn. recycling com.). Methodist. Office: Teledyne Brown Engring 300 Sparkman Dr NW Huntsville AL 35805-1912

EMERY, HERSCHELL GENE, lawyer; b. Hobart, Okla., Oct. 19, 1923; s. W. Herschell and L. Norean (Lewis) E.; m. Charlotte Chrisney, Oct. 29, 1948; children—Kathy Emery Miller, Steve . A.B., U. Ill., 1945; LL.B., Harvard U., 1948. Bar: Ind. 1949, Tex. 1955, U.S. Tax Ct. 1956, U.S. Ct. Appeals (5th cir.) 1980, U.S. Ct. Claims, 1980. Assoc., Ross McCord Ice & Miller, Indpls., 1948-55; assoc., ptnr. Thompson Knight Wright & Simmons, Dallas, 1955-65; ptnr. Rain Harrell Emery Young & Doke, Dallas, 1965-87, ptnr. Locke Purnell Rain Harrell, 1987—; lectr. various tax and legal insts. Former pres. Dallas Estate Council, North Tex. chpt. Arthritis Found. Served with U.S. Army, 1943. Fellow Am. Coll. Tax Counsel, Am. Coll. Trust and Estate Counsel; mem. ABA, Tex. Bar Assn., Dallas Bar Assn., Phi Beta Kappa. Presbyterian. Clubs: Dallas Country (pres. 1993), Dallas Petroleum, Old Baldy. Office: Locke Purnell 2200 Ross Ave Ste 2200 Dallas TX 75201-6766

EMICH, CHARLES HENRY, orthopedist, retired navy officer; b. N.Y.C., Jan. 14, 1930; s. Carl and Lillian (Huen) E.; m. Patricia Ann Hollis, Apr. 11, 1959; children: Charlisa Emich Becklund, Curtis. BA, Columbia U., 1951; MD, N.Y. Med. Coll., 1955. Diplomate Am. Bd. Orthopedic Surgery. Commd. lt. (j.g.) USN, 1955, advanced through grades to capt., 1971; intern U.S. Naval Hosp. St. Albans, N.Y., 1955-56; resident in orthopedics U.S. Naval Hosp, Portsmouth, Va., 1958-62; ret., 1980; pvt. practice, Alexandria, Va., 1980—. Fellow Am. Acad. Orthopaedic Surgeons. Home: 7707 Maid Marian Ct Alexandria VA 22306-2718 Office: 417 N Washington St Alexandria VA

EMICK, WILLIAM JOHN, real estate investor, retired federal executive; b. Atlantic City, Apr. 17, 1931; s. William and Mable Jeanette (Myers) E.; divorced; children: Richard, Cherie, James. AA, San Antonio Coll., 1975; BApplied Arts and Scis. Bus. Mgmt., S.W. Tex. State U., 1977. Dep. div. chief U.S. Air Force, 1956-86; real estate investor Emick Investments, San Antonio, 1986—; pres. Kelly Mgmt. Assn., San Antonio, 1978-79, Kelly Apprentice Club, San Antonio, 1957-59. Chmn. Sr. Olympics Racquetball Regional Competitions, 1990-91, Regional Sr. Olympics Champion Singles and Doubles, 1991, Regional Sr. Olympics Champion Singles, 1992; pres. Bent Oak Condo. Assn., 1982, 88; program chmn. San Antonio Youth Opportunities, 1979; mem. United San Antonio, 1981-82. With USAF, 1951-55. Mem. North San Antonio C. of C., Animal Defense League. Home and Office: 3426 Sunlit Grv San Antonio TX 78247-2953

EMMERT, EMERY MYERS, religious counselor; b. Lexington, Ky., May 28, 1938; s. Emery Myers and Hettie Elizabeth (Myers) E.; m. Eliazbeth Gay Disponette, Feb. 14, 1963; children: Ann, Amy, Emery, Kathryn. BA, U. Ky., 1961; MDiv, Lincoln (Ill.) Christian Sem., 1976; D of Ministry, Lexington Theol. Sem., 1978. Min. Ellery (Ill.) Christian Ch., 1963-69; prof. Ky. Christian Coll., Grayson, 1969-77, Gt. Lakes Bible Coll., Lansing, Mich., 1977-81; high sch. tchr. Lexington (Ky.) Christian Sch., 1981-83; pres., counselor Ky. Christian Counseling, Lexington, 1981—; bd. dirs. Christian Student Fellowship, Lexington, 1981—. Pres. Citizens Against Child Abuse, 1983; v.p. Pks. and Recreation Com., Grand Ledge, Mich.; dir., editor Grayson Rotary Club, 1973-77. Recipient Outstanding Young Men of Am. award Jaycees, Grayson, 1974, Outstanding Svc. award Christian Student Fellowship, Lexington, 1987. Fellow Am. Assn. of Pastoral Counselors; mem. Am. Assn. of Christian Counselors. Home: 387 Hill Ct Lexington KY 40503 Office: Ky Christian Counseling 118 Dennis Dr # B Lexington KY 40503-2917

EMMETT, MEREDITH, association administrator. Exec. dir. North Carolina Community Shares, Durham. Office: North Carolina Community Shares PO Box 783 Durham NC 27702-0783

EMMETT, WALTER CHARLES, business broker; b. Lawrence, Mass., July 6, 1925; s. Walter Thornton and Agnes Owens Emmett; m. Laurel Stinnett, Nov. 21, 1975; children Jeffrey, Nancy, Scott; stepchildren: Wayne S. Dammier, Victoria Blackburn. student Dartmouth Coll., 1942-43, 46-47; lic. real estate broker, Tex. Owner, pres. The Emmett Group, Inc., Amarillo, Tex., 1978-85, 87—; dealer, operator, pres. Emmett-Simm's Motor Co., Inc., Panhandle, Tex., 1985-86; bus. broker Boston and Chamblin Realtors, Inc. 1986-87; owner Your Graphics Are Showing, Amarillo, 1977-79; salesman Ada Realtors, Amarillo, 1976-78; salesman Stevenson Motor, 1969-74, Russell Buick, 1974-76; lectr. Amarillo Jr. Coll.; ptnr. S.W.O.R.D., small bus. seminar prodns.; pres. Bus. Appraisal Svcs. div. Emmet Bus. Brokers, cons. sales tng. and mgmt. Past bd. dirs. Maverick Boys Club; past mem. adv. com. on comml. art, fine arts adv. council Amarillo Coll., comml. arts adv. com. Amarillo Coll.; past bd. dirs. Tex. Aviation Hist. Soc.; lay reader St. Andrew's Episcopal Ch., Amarillo. With A.C., USN, 1943-46. Mem. Internat. Bus. Brokers Assn. (cert. broker), Tex. Assn. Bus. Brokers, Amarillo C. of C. (past chmn. small bus. council), Amarillo Club, Downtown Club, Kiwanis (bd. dirs. 1979-80, 1st v.p., pres.-elect 1987-88, pres. 1988-89), Masons, Shriners. Episcopalian. Home: 2 Woodstone St Amarillo TX 79106-4151 Office: 1st Bank Southwest 2201 Civic Cir Ste 503 Amarillo TX 79109-1843

EMMICK, PATRICIA ANNE, surgical nurse; b. Atlantic City, Nov. 5, 1952; d. Russell T. and Rose (Gabrysz) Smith; m. Roger Douglas Emmick Sr.; 1 child, Christa C. Schulte; stepchildren: Roger, Heather, Steven Emmick. RN, Atlantic Community Coll., Mayslanding, N.J., 1972; ME, Stockton State Coll., Pomona, N.J.; BS, St. Joseph's Coll., 1992; postgrad., Valdosta State U., 1994—. RN, Ga., N.J.; cert. inpatient obstetrics, 1995; completed legal nurse cons. program, 1995. Commd. USAF Nurses Corps, 1978, advanced through grades to maj., 1987; nurse pediatrics, staff nurse to charge nurse to evening supr. Childrens Seashore House, Atlantic City, N.J., 1972-77; evening charge nurse pediatrics Shore Meml. Hosp., 1977-78; staff nurse ob ward, charge nurse pediatrics George AFB, Calif., 1978-80; staff nurse ob, pediatrics, charge nurse ob-gyn clinic Elmendorf AFB, Alaska, 1980-83; asst. charge nurse ob, charge nurse ob-gyn clinic, multi svc. unit, ob unit, coord. hosp. quality assurance Moody AFB, Ga., 1983-87; charge nurse obstet. ward USAF Hosp., Bitburg Air Base, Germany, 1987-89, supr. outpatient nursing svcs., charge nurse ob-gyn clinic, 1989-90, hosp. quality assurance coord., 1990; dir. ambulatory svcs., supr. outpatient nursing svcs. USAF Hosp., Moody AFB, 1990-92, asst. chief nurse, 1990-92, mgr. primary care svcs., 1992-94, dir. maternal child care, 1994-95; ret., 1995; labor and deliver nurse South Ga. Med. Ctr, Valdosta, 1995—; PRN RN labor and delivery South Ga. Med. Ctr., Valdosta; case mgr. First Am. Home Care, Valdosta, 1995-96, clin. supr., 1996—. Decorated Air Force Commendation medal, 1983, Meritorious Svc. medal, 1990, 95. Mem. AWOHNN. Home: 804 E Northside Dr Valdosta GA 31602-1914

ENARSON, CAM EDWIN, medical educator; b. Edmonton, Alta., Can., Jan. 11, 1958; came to U.S., 1982; m. Carol Ann Spacht, Oct. 1, 1983; children: Edward, David. BA, Concordia Coll., 1978; MD, U. Alta., 1982; MBA, U. Pa., 1990. Diplomate Am. Bd. Anesthesiology. Asst. prof. pub. health scis. and anesthesiology Bowman Gray Sch. Medicine, Winston-Salem, N.C., 1990—. Mem. Am. Soc. Anesthesiologists. Republican. Lutheran.

ENDICOTT, JOHN EDGAR, international relations educator; b. Cin., Aug. 9, 1936; s. Charles Lafayette and Alice Willa (Campbell) E.; m. Mitsuyo Tiffani Kobayashi, Aug. 24, 1959; children: Charlene Nobel, John Edward. BA, Ohio State U., 1958; MA in History, Omaha U., 1968; MA in Internat. Rels., Tufts U., 1972, MALD, 1973, PhD, 1973. Commd. USAF, advanced through grades to col.; dep. head polit. sci. and philosophy dept. USAF Acad., 1969-71, 73-78; dep. Air Force rep. mil. staff com. UN Security Coun., 1979-81; dir. internat. affairs divsn. Air Force Plans, The Pentagon, 1978-81; assoc. dean Nat. War Coll., 1981-83; dir. rsch. directorate Nat. Def. U., 1983-86; dir. Inst. Nat. Strategic Studies, Dept. Def., 1986-89; prof. Sch. Internat. Affairs Ga. Inst. Tech., Atlanta, 1989—, founding dir. Ctr. Internat. Strategy Tech. and Policy, 1989—; apptd. Olympic attache Mongolian Olympic Com., Ulaan Bataar, 1995-96; co-chair Coun. U.S.-Japan Security Rels.; bd. dirs. Nat. Def. U. Found., UN Assn. Atlanta; cons. Dept. Def., Chmn. Joint Chiefs Staff, PAJE Process, NRC of NAS, Office Internat. Affairs, Def. Task Force, Inst. Def. Analysis, others. Mem. editl. bd. The Japan Digest, Small Wars and Insurgencies, New South Mag.; author: Japan's Nuclear Option, 1975; co-editor, contbr.; American Defense Policy, 1977, Regional Security Issues, 1991; co-author: Politics of East Asia, 1978; contbr. articles to profl. jours. Decorated Legion of Merit, Bronze Star, Meritorious Svc. medal, Air medal with oak leaf cluster, Air Force Commendation medal with oak leaf cluster; W. Alton Jones rsch. grantee Ploughshares Found.; Mike Mansfield award Japan-Am. Soc. Ga., 1996. Fellow Internat. Inst. Strategic Studies; mem. Internat. Studies Assn., Assn. Asian Studies, Army and Navy Club, Japan-Am. Soc. Ga. (recipient Mike Mansfield award 1996, exec. com., bd. dirs.), Georgian Club, Phi Beta Kappa. Office: Ga Inst Tech Ctr Internat Strategy Atlanta GA 30332

ENG, STEVE, freelance writer; b. San Diego, Oct. 31, 1940; s. Ransom Ludwig and Helen (Stephens) E.; m. Anne Jeanne Kangas, 1969; 4 children. BA in English Lit., George Washington U., 1963; MS in Edn. (Counseling), Portland State U., 1973. Positions with various corps. and govt. agys.; freelance writer Nashville. Author: A Satisfied Mind: The Country Music Life of Porter Wagoner, 1992, Jimmy Buffett: The Man From Margaritaville Revealed, 1996; editor: Elusive Butterfly and Other Lyrics (Bob Lind), 1971, Toreros (John Gawsworth), 1990, others; assoc. editor: The Romantist, 1979—; staff book reviewer The Tennessean, 1982-93, BookPage, 1988—, Nashville Banner, 1993—; contbr. numerous poems to mags., including The Lyric, Cumberland Poetry Rev., The Twilight Zone, The Romantist, Am. Collector, Fantasy Tales, Amazing, The Arkham Collector; also books, including Anthology of Mag. Verse, Yearbook of Am. Poetry, Monthly Terrors, Narcopolis and Other Poems, Hidden Places, Secret Words, SPWAO Showcase 8, The Spring Anthology; book revs. pub. in Tennessean, So. Reader, BookPage, The Romantist, Country Music People, Louisville Music News, Horror Fiction Newsletter, Tenn. Hist. Quarterly; contbr. essays, articles, chpts. to books and prefaces including Dictionary of Literary Biography; songs recorded by Lonnie Lynne La Cour. With USAFR, 1963-69. Mem. BMI, Small Press Writers and Artists Orgn. (poetry cons. 1980-90, chmn. poetry panel 1987, recipient Best Writer Poetry award 1979, 83, Spl. Achievement award 1985), Country Music Assn. Home: PO Box 111864 Nashville TN 37222

ENGEL, JONATHAN CLARK, educational association administrator; b. N.Y.C., Aug. 10, 1952; s. Louis Henry Jr. and Mary June (Montgomery) E.; m. Joanne Lorene Fromm, Apr. 7, 1983; 1 child, Louis Axel. BA, U. Tex., 1984, MA, 1987. Coord. adult edn. project San Marcos (Tex.) Pub. Libr., 1988-91; site dir., instr. adult and continuing edn. coop. Ten County Adult Edn., Georgetown, Tex., 1989-91; site coord. Job Tng. and Ptnrship Act/Tex. Literacy Coun., 1990-91; coord. Job Opportunities and Basic Skills Ten County Adult Edn. Co-op, Tex. Dept. Human Svcs., 1990-91; dir. Project Parents Learning US Ten County Adult Edn. Co-op, 1990-91; dir. Workforce Instrnl. Network, Ctr. Initiatives Edn. S.W. Tex. State U., 1991-92; dir. Workforce Instrnl. Network Family Svc. Ctr. Community Action Inc., 1992—; chair edn. sub-com. interagy. planning com. implementation Job Opportunities and Basic Skills Program Tex. Dept. Human Svcs., Austin, 1990-91; mem. quality workforce planning com. Capital Area Workforce Alliance, 1991—, chair edn. and tng. com., 1994—, chmn. bd., 1994—; mem. Tex. Literacy Resource Ctr. Collaborative Network, 1993—; presenter in field. Prin. writer Citizens' Task Force for a Better San Marcos, 1994. Mem. partnership action team San Marcos Consol. Ind. Sch. Dist., 1991-92; pres. San Marcos Literacy Action, 1991—; pub. rels. chair San Marcos 2000, 1991—; pub. rels. rep. family self sufficiency project Housing Authority of City of San Marcos, 1992—; mem. models working group United Way, 1993; charter mem. Austin C.C. San Marcos Liaison Team, 1994—. Mem. San Marcos C. of C. (mem. edn. coun. 1989—), Capital Area Workforce Alliance (exec. com., chair edn. and tng.). Lutheran. Home: 407 Pioneer Trl San Marcos TX 78666-2450 Office: Community Action Inc PO Box 748 101 Uhland Rd San Marcos TX 78666-6630

ENGELHARDT, HUGO TRISTRAM, JR., physician, educator; b. New Orleans, Apr. 27, 1941; s. Hugo Tristram and Beulah (Karbach) E.; m. Susan Gay Malloy, Nov. 25, 1965; children: Elisabeth, Christina, Dorothea. B.A., U. Tex., Austin, 1963, Ph.D., 1969; M.D. with honors, Tulane U., 1972. Asst. prof. U. Tex. Med. Br., 1972-75, assoc. prof., 1975-77; mem. Inst. Med. Humanities, 1973-77; Rosemary Kennedy prof. philosophy of medicine Georgetown U., 1977-82; sr. research scholar Kennedy Inst. Center for Bioethics, Washington, 1977-82; prof. depts. internal medicine, community medicine and ob-gyn. Baylor Coll. Medicine, Houston,

1983—; mem. Ctr. for Ethics, Med./and Health Policy, Houston, 1983—; prof. dept. philosophy Rice U., Houston, 1983—; chmn. adv. panel on infertility prevention and treatment for office of tech. assessment of the U.S. Congress, 1986-87. Author: Mind Body: A Categorial Relation, 1973, The Foundations of Bioethics, 1986, rev. edit., 1996, Bioethics and Secular Humanism, 1991; co-author: Bioethics: Readings and Cases, 1987; assoc. editor Ency. of Bioethics, 1973-78, Jour. Medicine and Philosophy, 1974-84; mem. editl. adv. bd. Lit. and Medicine, 1982—, Bioethics, 1987—, Ethik in der Medizin, 1988—, Bioetica, 1993—; editor Jour. Medicine and Philosophy, 1984—, (series) Philos. Studies in Contemporary Culture, 1992—; co-editor Philosophy and Medicine series, 1974—, Clin. Med. Ethics, 1991—, Christian Bioethics, 1995—; editor: (with others) Evaluation and Explanation in the Biomedical Sciences, 1975, Philosophical Medical Ethics, 1977, Mental Health, 1978, Clinical Judgment, 1979, Concepts of Health and Disease, 1981, New Knowledge in the Biomedical Sciences, 1982, Scientific Controversies, 1987, The Use of Human Beings in Research, 1988, Sicherheit und Freiheit, 1990. Mem. bioethics com. Nat. Found. March of Dimes, 1975—. Fulbright fellow, 1969-70, Woodrow Wilson vis. fellow, 1988; fellow Inst. for Advanced Studies, Berlin, 1988-89. Mem. Am. Philos. Assn., European Acad. Scis. and Arts. Home: 2802 Lafayette Houston TX 77005-3038 also: HC 3 Box 1 New Braunfels TX 78132-4101 Office: Baylor Coll Med Ctr Med Ethics Med Health Policy Houston TX 77030

ENGELHARDT, JOHN HUGO, lawyer, banker; b. Houston, Feb. 3, 1946; s. Hugo Tristram and Beulah Lillie (Karbach) E.; m. Jasmin Inge Nestler, Nov. 12, 1976; children: Angelique D, Sabrina N. BA, U. Tex., 1968; JD, St. Mary's U., San Antonio, 1973. Bar: Tex. 1973. Tchr. history Pearsall H.S., Tex., 1968-69; pvt. practice, New Braunfels, Tex., 1973-75; examining atty. Comml. Title Co., San Antonio, 1975-78, San Antonio Title Co., 1978-82; pvt. practice, New Braunfels, 1982—; adv. dir. M Bank Brenham, Tex., 1983-89. Fellow Coll. State Bar Tex.; mem. ABA, Pi Gamma Mu. Republican. Roman Catholic. Office: HC 3 Box 1 New Braunfels TX 78132-4101

ENGELMANN, RUDOLPH HERMAN, electronics consultant; b. Hewitt, Minn., Mar. 5, 1929; s. Herman Emil Robert and Minna Louise (Kniep) E.; children: Guy Robert, Heidi Louise. BA, U. Minn., 1953. Electronic designer Lawrence Livermore (Calif.) Lab., 1959-61; cons. Atlantic Rsch. Corp., Manchester, N.H., 1961-64, Gen. Radio Co., West Concord, Mass., 1963-69, Possis Engring., Mpls., 1970—, 3M Co., St. Paul, 1977-78, Pako Photo, Mpls., 1977-78, Litton Microwave, Mpls., 1977-79; Presenter papers at confs., 1988-89, 89-90. Contbr. articles to profl. jours. 1st lt. USAF, 1946-53. Office: PO Box 330117 Atlantic Beach FL 32233

ENGERRAND, DORIS DIESKOW, business educator; b. Chgo., Aug. 7, 1925; d. William Jacob and Alma Willhelmina (Cords) Dieskow; BS in Bus. Adminstrn., N. Ga. Coll., 1958, BS in Elementary Edn., 1959; M Bus. Edn., Ga. State U., 1966, PhD, 1970; m. Gabriel H. Engerrand, Oct. 26, 1946 (dec. June 1987); children: Steven, Kenneth, Jeannine. Tchr., dept. chmn. Lumpkin County H.S., Dahlonega, Ga., 1960-63, 65-68; tchr., Gainesville, Ga., 1965; asst. prof. Troy (Ala.) State U., 1969-71; asst. prof. bus. Ga. Coll., Milledgeville, 1971-74, assoc. prof., 1974-78, prof., 1978-90, chmn. dept. info. systems and comms., 1978-89, ret., 1990; cons. Named Outstanding Tchr. Lumpkin County Pub. Schs., 1963, 66; Outstanding Educator bus. faculty Ga. Coll., 1975, Exec. of Yr. award, 1983. Fellow Assn. for Bus. Communication (v.p. S.E. 1978-80, 81-84, 89-92, bd. dirs.), Nat. Bus. Edn. Assn., Ga. Bus. Edn. Assn. (Postsecondary Tchr. of Yr. award 10th dist. 1983, Postsecondary Tchr. of Yr. award 1984), Am. Vocat. Assn., Ga. Vocat. Assn. (Educator of Yr. award 1984, Parker Liles award 1989), Profl. Secs. Internat. (pres. Milledgeville chpt. 1996—), Ninety-nines Internat. (chmn. N. Ga. chpt. 1975-76, named Pilot of Year N. Ga. chpt. 1973). Methodist. Contbr. articles on bus. edn. to profl. publs. Home: 1674 Pine Valley Rd Milledgeville GA 31061-2465 Office: Ga Coll Milledgeville GA 31061

ENGLAND, ARTHUR JAY, JR., lawyer, former state justice; b. Dayton, Ohio, Dec. 23, 1932; s. Arthur Jay and Elsbeth (Weiskopf) E.; m. Morley Tenenbom, June 24, 1959 (div.); children: Andrea, Pamela, Ellen, Karen; m. Deborah J. Miller, Mar. 31, 1984; children: Rachel, Aaron. BS, U. Pa., 1955, LLB, 1961; LLM, U. Miami, 1971; LLD (hon.), John B. Stetson Coll. Law, 1979, Nova U., 1982. Bar: Fla. 1961, N.Y. 1962. Assoc. Dewey, Ballantine, Bushby, Palmer & Wood, N.Y.C., 1961-64; ptnr. Culverhouse, Tomlinson, Taylor & DeCarion, Miami, Fla., 1964-69, Scott, McCarthy, Steel, Hector & Davis, Miami, 1969-70; spl. tax counsel Fla. Ho. Reps., 1971-72; consumer adviser, spl. counsel to gov. Fla., 1972-73; ptnr. Paul & Thomson, Miami, 1973-74; justice Supreme Ct. Fla., 1975-81, chief justice, 1978-80; ptnr. Steel, Hector & Davis, Miami, 1981-84; ptnr. Fine Jacobson Schwartz Nash Block England, Miami, 1984-92, pres., chief exec. officer, 1988-89; ptnr. Greenberg Traurig Hoffman Lipoff Rosen & Quentel, Miami, 1992—; dep. chmn. Conf. of Chief Justices, 1978-80; chmn. Coun. of State Ct. Reps., Nat. Ctr. for State Cts., 1979-80; mem. Commn. on Interest on Lawyers' Trust Accounts, 1986-90, chmn., 1989-90; chmn. adv. bd. Nat. Interest on Lawyers' Trust Accounts Clearinghouse, 1983-86; adj. prof. Coll. Law, Fla. State U. Contbr. articles to legal jours. With AUS, 1955-57. Recipient Medal of Honor, Fla. Bar Found., 1983, Herbert Harley award Am. Judicature Soc., 1986, Jurisprudence award Anti-Defamation League, 1991. Mem. ABA (Pro Bono Pub. award 1988), Am. Acad. Appellate Lawyers (pres. 1990-92), Am. Law Inst., Fla. Bar Assn. (chmn. appellate practice cert. com. 1993-94, cert. appellate lawyers), N.Y. State Bar Assn., Order of Coif, Beta Gamma Sigma. Jewish. Home: 4897 SW 82nd St Miami FL 33143-8603 Office: Greenberg Traurig Hoffman Lipoff Rosen & Quentel 1221 Brickell Ave PO Box 012890 Miami FL 33131

ENGLAND, DAN BENJAMIN, accountant; b. Duncan, Okla., Aug. 23, 1955; s. Haskell Thomas and Lillian Lucille (Rouw) E.; m. Mary Elizabeth Metcalf, May 24, 1980; 1 child, Stuart Benjamin. BA, Southeastern Okla. State U., 1977, BS, 1982. CPA, Okla. Br. mgr. Curtis Distbg. Co., Durant, Okla., 1978-79; dist. agt. Prudential Ins. Co., Durant, 1980-82; acct. Reedrill Inc., Sherman, Tex., 1982; mgr. Williams and Co. CPAs Inc., Durant, 1983-85; v.p. England Enterprises Inc., Durant, 1985—; pvt. practice acctg., Durant, 1985—; adj. instr. Southeastern Okla. State U., Durant, 1985-86; investment advisor rep., 1993—. Bd. dirs. Red River Arts Coun., Durant, 1986-94. Mem. Nat. Assn. Tax Practitioners, Okla. Soc. CPAs, Durant Jaycees (bd. dirs. 1985), Durant C. of C. Republican. Mem. Ch. of Christ. Lodge: Kiwanis (treas. Durant, 1985, sec. 1986, v.p. 1988, pres. 1989). Office: 206 N 10th Ave Durant OK 74701-4328

ENGLAND, DAVID P., anesthesiologist, educator; b. Providence, Dec. 31, 1955; s. Norman A.W. and Edna C. (Vanasse) E.; m. Marty Jean Beck, May 29, 1987; children: Jozlyn, Addyson, Macy. Student, Providence Coll., summer 1976, U. Nebr., summer 1977; BS in Biology and Psychology, Creighton U., Omaha, 1978; MS in Physiology, Georgetown U., 1980; postgrad., No. Va. C.C., Alexandria, 1984; DO, U. Health Scis., Kansas City, Mo., 1989. Diplomate Nat. Bd. Osteopathic Med. Examiners. Intern Doctor's Hosp., Columbus, Ohio, 1989-90; resident Med. Coll. Va., Richmond, 1990-93, asst. prof. dept. anesthesiology, 1993-95; faculty No. Va. C.C., Annadale, 1983-84; emergency rm. physician Kenner Army Hosp., Ft. Lee, Va., 1991-95. Russell C. McCaughan scholar Nat. Osteopathic Found., E.F.N. Fed. scholar; Georgetown U. Nursing Sch. teaching fellow. Mem. Am. Soc. Anesthesiology, Ariz. Soc. Anesthesiology, Am. Osteo. Assn., Va. Osteo. Med. Assn., Psi Sigma Alpha, Sigma Sigma Phi, Ctrl. Va. Mustang Club. Office: Canyon State Anesthesiologists PC 4820 E Mcdowell Rd Ste 101 Phoenix AZ 85008-4226

ENGLAND, GARY ALAN, television meteorologist; b. Seiling, Okla., Oct. 3, 1939; s. Leslie Elwood and Hazel Wanda (Stong) E.; m. Mary Helen Carlisle, Aug. 27, 1961; 1 child, Molly Michelle. BS in Math. and Meteorology, U. Okla., 1965. Profl. meteorologist. V.p. mktg. Southwestern Weather Svc., Oklahoma City, 1965-67; cons. meteorologist A.H. Glenn & Assocs., New Orleans, 1967-71; v.p. mktg. England & May, Oklahoma City, 1971-74; v.p. meteorology U.S. Weather Corp., Oklahoma City, 1974-78; pres. The Gary Co., Oklahoma City, 1978-93, Weather Designs, Inc., Oklahoma City, 1994—; dir. meteorology Griffin TV, Oklahoma City, 1971—; cons. meteorologist Techrad, Okla., 1977-78; forensic meteorologist legal field, Okla., 1971—. Author: Oklahoma Weather, 1975, United States Weather, 1976, Those Terrible Twisters, 1987, Weathering the Storm, 1996. Fundraiser The Christmas Connection, Oklahoma City, 1982—, Harvest Fund Drive, Oklahoma City, 1982—; mem. adv. bd. Make-A-Wish Found., Oklahoma City, 1993. With USN, 1957-61. Named to Western Okla. Hall of Fame Western Okla. Hist. Soc., 1983, Dewey County Hall of Fame Dewey County Hist. Soc., 1989, Best Meteorologist Okla. Gazzette Newspaper, 1984—, Outstanding Young Men of Am., 1976; recipient Ptnrs. for Excellence award Okla. Sch. Pub. Rels. Assn., 1989, Emmy for Best Weather Anchor, Heartland divsn. NATAS, 1994. Mem. AAAS, Am. Meteorol. Soc., Am. Bus. Club, N.Y. Acad. Sci. Mem. Christian Ch. Office: Sta KWTV PO Box 14159 Oklahoma City OK 73113-0159

ENGLAND, JOHN DAVID, neurologist; b. Clarksburg, W.Va., Jan. 20, 1954; s. John Draper and Imogene Lucille (Alexander) E.; m. Cathy Ann Drummond, Nov. 22, 1975. BA in Chemistry, W.Va. U., 1976, MD, 1980. Diplomate Nat. Bd. Med. Examiners, Am. Bd. Psychiatry and Neurology, Am. Bd. Electrodiagnostic Medicine; lic. physician, S.C., Pa., Colo., La. Intern Med. U. S.C., Charleston, 1980-81, resident in neurology, 1981-84; clin. neuromuscular fellow dept. neurology Hosp. of U. Pa., Phila., 1984-85, postdoctoral rsch. fellow dept. neurology, 1985-87; asst. prof. neurology U. Colo., Denver, 1987-92; assoc. prof. neurology La. State U., New Orleans, 1992—; attending physician U. Colo. Health Scis. Ctr., Denver, 1987-92, dir. electromyography lab., 1987-92; attending physician Med. Ctr. La., New Orleans, 1992—; lectr. in field. Contbr. numerous articles to profl. jours.; editl. cons. Muscle and Nerve, 1987—, Ann. Neurol., 1990—, Brain, 1993—. Recipient Koehler award in chemistry, Handbook award Chem. Rubber Co., Whitehall award of dept. chemistry; W.Va. U. Bd. Regents scholar, Masonic scholar, others; grantee Muscular Dystrophy Assn., 1985-87, NIH, 1987-88, Nat. Inst. Neurol. Disorders and Stroke, 1988-93, Nat. Inst. Aging, 1991-94, La. State U. Neurosci. Ctr. for Excellence, 1993-94, Dept. Def., 1993—. Mem. AMA, W.Va. U. Alumni Assn., Am. Assn. Electrodiagnostic Medicine (profl. practice com. 1988-91, spl. interest group com. 1992-93, tng. program com. 1993—), liaison rep. 1991-92), Am. Acad. Neurology, N.Y. Acad. Scis., Am. Soc. Neurol. Investigation, Soc. for Neurosci., Alpha Omega Alpha, Phi Kappa Phi, Phi Lambda Upsilon, Phi Beta Kappa. Democrat. Methodist. Office: Louisiana State U Med Ctr Dept Neurology 1542 Tulane Ave New Orleans LA 70112-2825

ENGLAND, JOHN MELVIN, lawyer, clergyman; b. Atlanta, June 29, 1932; s. John Marcus and Frances Dorothy (Brown) E.; m. Jane Cantrell, Aug. 2, 1953; children: Kathryn Elizabeth, Janette Evelyn, John William, Kenneth Paul, James Andrew, Samuel Robert. Student Ga. State U., 1951-53; JD, U. Ga., 1956; BD magna cum laude with honors in Theology, Columbia Theol. Sem., Decatur, Ga., 1964. Bar: Ga. 1959, U.S. Dist. Ct. (no. dist.) Ga. 1967, U.S. Ct. Mil. Appeals 1976, U.S. Ct. Appeals (5th cir.) 1967, U.S. Ct. Appeals (11th cir.) 1981, U.S. Supreme Ct. 1977, U.S. Dist. Ct. (mid. dist.) Ga. 1986, U.S. Dist. Ct. (so. dist.) Ga. 1991, U.S. Dist. Ct. (no. dist.) Tex. 1991; ordained to ministry Presbyn. Ch., 1964. Spl. agt. FBI, Washington, 1956-57, Indpls., 1957-59, Charlotte, N.C., 1959, Greenville, S.C., 1959-60; student supply pastor Bethel and Buford Presbyn. Chs., Atlanta, 1960-63; pastor Mullins (S.C.) Presbyn. Ch., 1964-67; asst. dist. atty. Fulton County (Ga.), 1967-75; sr. ptnr. England and Weller, Atlanta, 1975-88, England, Wearer & Kytle, 1988-94, England & McKnight, 1994—; legal seminar lectr. and speaker throughout the country under auspices of Christian orgns.; spl. pros. for gov. Ga., 1976-79; spl. cons. on appellate reform Supreme Ct. Ga., 1979-80; state bar rep. to Superior Ct. Uniform Rules Com. Coun. Superior Ct. Judges, 1984, 93. Elder, tchr., evangelism coord. Presbyn. Ch. USA; chmn., Christian Bus. Men's Coms. of U.S.A., Atlanta, 1971-73, chmn. internat. conv., Atlanta, 1979, bd. dirs., 1971-81. Mem. ABA, ATLA, State Bar Ga., Atlanta Bar Assn., Lawyers Club Atlanta, Ga. Trial Lawyers Assn.; Nat. Assn. Criminal Def. Lawyers, Ga. Assn. Criminal Def. Lawyers, North Fulton Bar Assn. Office: 410 River Ridge 9040 Roswell Rd Atlanta GA 30350-1853

ENGLAND, LYNNE LIPTON, lawyer, speech pathologist, audiologist; b. Youngstown, Ohio, Apr. 11, 1949; d. Sanford Y. and Sally (Kentor) Lipton; m. Richard E. England, Mar. 5, 1977. BA, U. Mich., 1970; MA, Temple U., 1972; JD, Tulane U., 1981. Bar: Fla. 1982, U.S. Dist. Ct. (mid. dist.) Fla. 1982, U.S. Ct. Appeals (11th cir.) 1982; cert. clin. competence in speech pathology and audiology. Speech pathologist Rockland Children's Hosp., N.Y., 1972-74, Jefferson Parish Sch., Gretna, La., 1977-81; audiologist Rehab. Inst. Chgo., 1974-76; assoc. Trenam, Simmons, Kemker, Scharf, Barkin, Frye & O'Neill, Tampa, Fla., 1981-84; asst. U.S. atty. for Middle Dist. Fla. Tampa, 1984-87; asst. U.S. trustee, 1987-91; ptnr. Stearns, Weaver, Miller, Weissler, Alhadeff & Sitterson, P.A., 1991-94, Prevatt, England, Ambler, Snyder & Taylor, Tampa, Fla., 1994—. Editor Fla. Bankruptcy Casenotes, 1983. Recipient clin. assistantship Temple U., 1972-74. Mem. ATLA, Comml. Law League, Am. Speech and Hearing Assn., Tampa Bay Bankruptcy Bar Assn. (dir. 1990-95), Am. Bankruptcy Inst., Fla. Bar Assn., Hillsborough County Bar Assn., Order of Coif. Jewish. Office: PO Box 2920 1 Tampa City Ctr Ste 2505 Tampa FL 33601-2920

ENGLAND, ROBERT STOWE, writer; b. York, S.C., Jan. 14, 1944; s. Hershel Stowe and Myrtle Lorene (Deal) E. BA in English, Duke U., 1967. Reporter Hartford (Conn.) Times, 1967-68; editor, pub. Washington, A Tabloid Rev., 1973-76; editor Del. Valley Bus. Mag., Phila., 1976-77; sr. editor Ingersoll-Rand Co. Corp. Mag., Washington, N.J., 1977-79; editor Metro Newark Mag., 1982-84; writer Insight Mag., Washington, 1985-88; ind. writer bus., polit. mags., Arlington, Va., 1988—. Pres. Harsimus Cove Neighborhood Assn., Jersey City, 1982-84. Recipient Blue Smoke and Mirrors award Insight mag., Washington, 1986. Mem. Washington Ind. Writers. Episcopalian. Home: 3116 Military Rd Arlington VA 22207-4136

ENGLAND, RUDY ALAN, lawyer; b. Snyder, Tex., Sept. 29, 1959; s. Bud and Imo D. (Witcher) E.; m. Zenda Cherie Ball, Mar. 24, 1978 (div. June 1988); children: Aaron, Kyle; m. Susan Ann Steadman, Mar. 10, 1990. AA summa cum laude, Western Tex. Coll., 1979; BS summa cum laude, U. Houston, 1986, JD, 1989. Bar: Tex. 1990, U.S. Dist. Ct. (so. dist.) Tex. 1990, U.S. Dist. Ct. (no., ea. and we. dists.) Tex. 1994, U.S. Ct. Appeals (5th cir.) 1990. Adminstrv. asst. Tartan Oil & Gas, Houston, 1981-82; div. order analyst Moran Exploration, Inc., Houston, 1982-83; sr. lease analyst Integrated Energy Inc., Houston, 1983-84; landman Cambridge Royalty Co., Houston, 1984-85; supr. div. orders MCO Resources Inc., Houston, 1985-87; assoc. Hutcheson & Grundy, L.L.P., Houston, 1989—. Mem. Houston Law Rev., 1988-89, bd. dirs. Houston Law Rev. Alumni Assn., 1996—. Mem. taxi squad U. Houston, 1991; mgr. Little League Baseball, 1993-96; bd. dirs. Braeburn Little League, 1995-96. Mem. Coll. of State Bar, State Bar Tex. (professionalism com. 1996—), Houston Bar Assn. (lawyers for literacy com. 1991-92, lawyers in pub. schs. com. 1995—), Tex. Young Lawyers Assn. (bd. dirs. 1993-95, liaison to Lawyers Assn. (bd. dirs. 1993-95, liaison to Tex. lawyer's creed com. of State Bar 1994-95, co-chmn. profl. and grievance awareness com. 1994-95, chmn. profl. com. 1993-94, mem. legis. com. 1990-93, vice chmn. com. 1993-94, mem. local affiliates com. 1991-92, dropout prevention com. 1991-92, Tex. Young Lawyer Assn. sect. Tex. Bar Jour. com., 1991-93, profl. and ethics com. 1995-96, outstanding young lawyer com. 1995-96), Houston Young Lawyers Assn. (bd. dirs. 1991-93, sec. 1993-94, chmn. professionalism com. 1991-92, Law Day com. 1992-93, award achievement com. 1993-94, ops. com. 1993-94, outstanding young lawyers com. 1991-92, Liberty Bell award com. 1992-93), U. Houston Alumni Assn., Cougar Cager Club. Mem. Unity Ch. of Christianity. Office: Hutcheson & Grundy LLP 3300 Two Allen Ctr 1200 Smith St Houston TX 77002

ENGLE, JEANNETTE CRANFILL, medical technologist; b. Davie County, N.C., July 7, 1941; d. Gurney Nathaniel and Versie Emmaline (Reavis) Cranfill; m. William Sherman Engle (div. 1970); children: Phillip William, Lisa Kaye. Diploma, Dell Sch. Med. Tech., 1960; BA, U. N.C., Asheville, 1976; postgrad., Marshall U., 1991—. Instr. Dell Sch. Med. Tech., Asheville, 1960-67; rotating technologist Meml. Mission Hosp., Asheville, 1967-68, asst. supr. hematology, 1968-71; supr. Damon Subs. Pvt. Clinic Lab., Asheville, 1971-73; chemistry technologist VA Med. Ctr., Durham, N.C., 1973-74, 75-76, supr., 1974-75; asst. supr. microbiology VA Med. Ctr., Salem, Va., 1976-79; supr. rsch. Med. Svc. Lab., Salem, 1979-90; flow cytometrist VA Med. Ctr., Huntington, W.Va., 1990-92, cons. to clin. lab. flow cytometry dept., 1992—; reviewer Jour. Club, Roanoke-Salem, Va., 1980-90. Author: (poem) Reflections on a Comet, 1984; contbr. numerous articles and abstracts on med. tech. to profl. jours., 1982—. Mem. The Acting Co. Ensemble. Democrat. Episcopalian. Home: 4775 Green Valley Rd Huntington WV 25701-9793

ENGLE, JOHN DAVID, JR., poet; b. Yocum, Ky., Sept. 29, 1922; s. John David and Mary Angeline (Combs) E.; m. Anita Marie Jacobs, Aug. 20, 1948 (div. 1972); children: Mari, Brent. BA, U. Ky., 1950, MA, 1953. Tchr. English. Belfry (Ky.) High Sch., 1950, Jenkins (Ky.) High Sch., 1950-51, Athens (Ky.) High Sch., 1951-53; tchr. English and journalism Lafayette High Sch., Lexington, Ky., 1953-56; tchr. English and creative writing Princeton High Sch., Cin., 1956-78; editorial assoc. Writer's Digest, Cin., 1967—; writer-in-schs. Ohio Arts Coun., 1976-84. Author: (poetry) Modern Odyssey, 1971, Laugh Lightly, 1974, Sea Songs, 1977, Laugh Lightly II, 1989, Tree People, 1990. Recipient award for poetry Ind. U., 1970. Mem. Poetry Soc. Am., Ky. Poetry Soc. (bd. dirs. 1988-89, spl. recognition award 1985), Ohio Poetry Day (bd. dirs. 1978-82, svc. award 1980, various awards for poetry), Nat. Fedn. State Poetry Socs., Poets and Writers. Home: 6395 Old Highway 519 West Liberty KY 41472-8906

ENGLE, WILLIAM THOMAS, JR., lawyer; b. Galveston, Tex., Nov. 14, 1957; s. William Thomas Sr. and Dixie Faris (Moody) E.; m. Susan Byrnes Mann, Feb. 11, 1984; children: Erin Patricia, Julia Nicole, William Thomas III. BA, Tex. Christian U., 1980; JD, Baylor U., 1982. Bar: Tex. 1982, U.S. Dist. Ct. (no. dist.) 1983, U.S. Ct. Appeals (5th cir.) 1983. Assoc. Adams, Meier & Addison, Hurst, Tex., 1982-84; ptnr. Markey & Engle, Bedford, Tex., 1984, Markey, Ash & Engle, Bedford, 1984-86; sole practice Bedford, 1986-88; mgr., ptnr. Engle, Addison & Wright, P.C., Bedford, 1988-89; pvt. practice Grapevine, Tex., 1989-90; lawyer Chicago Title Ins. Co., Dallas, 1991-92; pvt. practice Bedford, 1992-95, Paris, 1995—. Mem. Bldg. Commn., Bedford, 1983, Planning and Zoning Commn., Euless, 1985-86; alt. mem. Parks and Recreation Bd., Euless, Tex., 1984-85. Mem. Tex. Bar Assn. Republican. Baptist.

ENGLEMAN, CHARLES EDWARD, newspaper editor and publisher; b. Greenfield, Mo., Jan. 25, 1911; s. Franklin Pierce and Mabel Claire (Wilson) E.; m. Lela Jean Garnett; children: Carol Ann Sander, Stephen Charles. BS in Journalism, U. Okla., 1933. Reporter Daily Times-Democrat, Altus, Okla., 1934-35; news editor Daily Democrat-Chief, Hobart, Okla., 1935-36; advt. mgr. Daily News, Elk City, Okla., 1936-37; editor and pub. The Walters (Okla.) Herald, 1937-40; editor, pub., owner The Clinton (Okla.) Daily News, 1940—. Pres. Clinton Regional Hosp. Bd. Trustees, 1979-80; pres. Foss Reservoir Master Conservancy Dist. Bd. Trustees, 1956—; mem. U. Okla. Bd. Regents, 1976-83, pres. 1982-83; bd. dirs. U. Okla. Found., 1975—. Recipient Disting. Alumni award, U. Okla. Sch. Journalism, 1984, Okla. Journalism Hall of Fame award, Cent. State U., 1985, Milt Phillips award for Excellence in Newspaper Journalism, Okla. Press. Assn., 1982, Stanley Draper Disting. Editorial award, Okla. Heritage Assn., 1983, Disting. Svc. award U. Okla., 1995; named Clinton Citizen of Yr., 1988. Mem. Okla. Press Assn. (pres. 1957-58), United Press Editors of Okla. (pres. 1961-62), Okla. Newspaper Found. (pres. 1985-86), Rotary (pres. Clinton chpt. 1947-48), Clinton C. of C. (pres. 1952-53), Univ. Okla. Alumni Assn. (pres. 1962-63). Democrat. Methodist. Home: 601 S 14th St Clinton OK 73601-4205 Office: The Clinton Daily News 522 Avant Ave Clinton OK 73601-3436

ENGLEMAN, DENNIS EUGENE, electrical engineer; b. Falls City, Nebr., July 24, 1948; s. Eugene Adolf and Mary Alice (Franklin) E.; m. Deborah Faye Paulson, May 4, 1985; children: John Nicholas, Lily Eugenia, Mary Victoria. Student, U. Nebr., 1966-70; B in Engring. Tech., Wichita State U., 1982. Ordained to ministry Holy Order of Mans, 1977; pres. Christian Community Atlanta, 1985-87; ordained acolyte/reader of Blessed John the Wonderworker, Eastern Orthodox Ch., 1988. Minister parishes various locations, 1977-81; elec. technician Kans. Gas & Elec. Co., Wichita, 1981-82; elec. engr. Boeing Mil. Airplane Co., Wichita, 1982; design engr. Nat. Data Corp., Atlanta, 1983, Raymond Carousel Corp., Atlanta, 1984; elec. designer Cons. & Designers, Inc., Atlanta, 1984; project engr. Nordson Corp., Norcross, Ga., 1984-85, sr. engr., 1985-90, engring. supr., 1990-92, sr. engring. supr., 1992-94; project engr. ACE group, 1994—; pres. Holy Mountain Imports, Atlanta, 1987-93, Engleman Photography Internat., Atlanta, 1989—, Liberty Imports, Atlanta; appeared on various radio broadcasts, Cin.; mem. dept. of ministry and evangelism Greek Orthodox Archdiocese of Vasiloupolis, 1992. Author: Ultimate Things, 1995, Beautiful America's Atlanta, 1996; co-editor: Tree of Life, 1992; prodr. programming People TV, Pub. Access TV, 1990-93; singer, songwriter, arranger, 1992, Pristine Records, 1993; prodr. various slide shows; writer, prodr. folk opera; contbr. some 85 articles to profl. publs. Dir. St. Cyril's Village Orch., 1987-91; mem. Atlanta Balalaika Soc. Orch., 1984-87; mem. Atlanta Mandolin Soc. Orch., 1994—. Republican. Orthodox Christian. Office: 2805 Peterson Pl Norcross GA 30071-1812

ENGLER, BRIAN DAVID, systems operations executive; b. Palmerton, Pa., Oct. 9, 1947; s. David James and Doreen Estelle (Sheldon) E.; m. Margaret Mary Hurlock, Dec. 31, 1969 (div. Apr. 1981); children: Donna, David; m. Maxine Sue Richard, May 24, 1981; children: Rachel, Stacey. BS with merit, U.S. Naval Acad., 1969; MS in Ops. Rsch., Naval Postgrad. Sch., Monterey, Calif., 1978; MBA in Fin., Acctg., Marymount U., 1986. Commd. ensign USN, 1969, advanced through grades to comdr., 1983, naval flight officer, mission comdr., ops. analyst, 1969-89, ret., 1989; ops. analyst, project leader Systems Planning and Analysis., Falls Church, Va., 1989-90, asst. program mgr., 1990-91, program mgr., 1991—. Assoc. editor (alumni newsletter) O.R. News, 1976-78. Mem. Big Bros./ Big Sisters of Balt., Annapolis, Md., 1968-69; sec.-treas. bd. dirs. Gov.'s Sq. Homeowners Assn., Williamsburg, Va., 1989—. Decorated Navy Commendation medals (2), Meritorious Svc. medal; recipient Juvenile Decency award Kiwanis Club, 1965, Cert. of Proficiency, Civil Air Patrol, 1963, Best Cadet award Temple U., 1965. Mem. Mil. Ops. Rsch. Soc. (bd. dirs. 1991—, sec.-treas. 1993-94, v.p. for adminstrn. 1994-95), Am. Legion, Delta Epsilon Sigma. Home: 5918 Clermont Landing Ct Burke VA 22015-2565 Office: Systems Planning and Analysis Inc Ste 400 2000 N Beauregard St Alexandria VA 22311

ENGLISH, BRUCE VAUGHAN, museum director and executive, environmental consultant; b. Richmond, Va., Aug. 6, 1921; s. Pollard and Lucy Kelly (Rice) E.; m. Virginia Tejas McCall Shaw, Feb. 6, 1949. BS in Physics and Math., Randolph-Macon Coll., 1942; MS in Physics and Math., Ind. U., 1943; PhD in Physics, U. Va., 1958. Grad. asst. instr. army specialized tng. program/rsch. asst. Manhattan Dist. Engrs. Project; physics instr. Ind. U., Bloomington; asst. prof. physics army specialized tng. program Randolph-Macon Coll., Ashland, Va., 1943-44, assoc. prof., acting chmn. dept. physics, 1948-58, prof., chmn. dept., 1958-64; physicist, head high pressure lab. U.S. Navy Underwater Sound Reference Lab., Orlando, Fla., 1946-48; physicist, cons. historic preservation, pollution control and environment Ashland, 1964—; dir. Poe Found., Inc., Richmond, 1969—, pres., 1973-92; pres., dir. Edgar Allan Poe Mus., Richmond, 1973-92; pres. Pollution Control Assocs., Richmond, 1967-70. Co-pub.: Poe's Richmond, 1978; columnist Herald-Progress, 1971—; contbr. numerous articles to Poe Messenger mag. Founding mem. Richmond Symphony, 1956; mem. Patrick Henry Scotchtown Com., Hanover County, Va., 1958—; pres. Hist. Richmond Found., 1967-70; bd. dirs. Church Hill Model Neighborhood Bd., Richmond, 1968-73; chmn. Bicentennial Com. for Hanover County, 1974-92, Drainage Com., Ashland, 1980s, Courthouse Com. for Hanover County, 1985—; lay reader, mem. vestry St. John's Ch., Church Hill, Richmond, Va., 1969-70. With USN, 1944-45. Named Hon. Citizen State of Md., 1990; Ford Faculty fellow, 1951-52, Danforth fellow, 1956-57, du Pont fellow, 1957-58. Mem. AAAS, Am. Phys. Soc., Va. Acad. Sci., Va. Hist. Soc., Soc. Archtl. Historians, Nat. Trust for Hist. Preservation, Irish Georgian Soc., Cousteau Soc. (founding), Air and Waste Mgmt. Assn., Nat. Soc. for Clean Air Gt. Britain, Soc. Descendants of Peter Francisco (founder, advisor), City Tavern Club, Commonwealth Club, Farmington Country Club, Downtown Club, Phi Beta Kappa, Sigma Xi, Omicron Delta Kappa, Chi Beta Phi, Pi Delta Epsilon. Episcopalian.

ENGLISH, JAMES WILLIAM, software engineer; b. Washington, July 4, 1951; s. Charles Corwin and Jane (Bottenfield) E.; m. Mary Jo Willis, Aug. 22, 1981; 1 child, Christine M. BS, Pa. State U., 1973, James Madison U., 1982; M in Computer Sci., U. Va., 1988. Assoc. engr. Sperry Marine Inc., Charlottesville, Va., 1982; engr Sperry Marine Inc., Charlottesville, 1983, sr. engr., 1986, prin. engr., 1990. Mem. Assn. Computing Machinery. Home: 2098 Tavernor Ln Charlottesville VA 22911-7200 Office: Sperry Marine Inc 1070 Seminole Trl Charlottesville VA 22901-2827

ENGLISH, JUJUAN BONDMAN, women's health nurse, educator; b. El Dorado, Ark., Dec. 16, 1947; d. Irvin Raymond and Ida Ruth (Payton) Bondman; m. Frederick J. English, Aug. 28, 1976; children: Michael, Christopher, Meagan. ADN, So. State Coll., Magnolia, Ark., 1970; BSN, U. Ark., 1988; MSN, U. Miss., 1992. Cert. childbirth educator. Charge nurse Union Med. Ctr., El Dorado; charge nurse Warner Brown Hosp., El Dorado, labor and delivery supr.; instr. nursing U. Ark., Monticello, asst. prof. nursing, 1993-95; dir. nursing edn. Area Health Edn. Ctr.-South Ark., 1995—; coord. Parenting Coalition of South Ark. Mem. ANA, Ark. State Nurses Assn. (mem. strategic planning com., sec. 1994-96, pres.-elect 1996-97, mem. exec. com., Outstanding Dist. Pres. 1994), Ark. Nursing Coalition (steering com., Salute to Nursing com. chair), So. Nursing Rsch. Soc. (rsch. reviewer for D. Jean Wood award 1993), Nat. League Nursing, Ark. League Nursing, So. Regional Heideggerian Hermeneutical Inst., So. Ark. Breast Feeding Coalition (chair edn. com.), Sigma Theta Tau.

ENGLISH, RUTH ANN COWDER, personnel consultant; b. Kearney, Nebr., June 3, 1948; d. John Leonard and Ethel Lou (Brower) Cowder; divorced; 1 child, Liesl Michele. BS, SW Tex. State U., 1970; MA, U. No. Colo., 1978. Tchr. Churchill High Sch., San Antonio, 1971-72; edn. dir. Houston Telephone Fed. C.U., 1972-73; property mgr. English Properties Mgmt., San Antonio, 1972—; instr. ESL U.S. Civil Service, San Antonio, 1975-79; instr. continuing edn. Alamo Community Coll. Dist., San Antonio, 1984—; pres., cons., instr. Profl. Growth Systems, San Antonio, 1986—; tchr. Keystone Sch., San Antonio, 1989—. Troop leader San Antonio Area Coun. Girl Scouts U.S., 1984-93. Presbyterian. Home and Office: 3734 Litchfield St San Antonio TX 78230-3966

ENIS, THOMAS JOSEPH, lawyer; b. Maryville, Mo., July 2, 1937; s. Herbert William and Loretta M. (Fitzmaurice) E.; m. Harolyn Gray Westhoff, July 24, 1971; children: Margaret Elizabeth, David Richard, John Anthony, Brian Edward. B.S., Rockhurst Coll., 1958; J.D., U. Mo.-Columbia, 1966. Bar: Mo. 1966, Okla. 1973. Law clk. U.S. Dist. Ct. (we. dist.) Mo., 1966-67; prof. coll. law U. Okla., Norman, 1967-74, assoc. dean, 1970-74; atty. Southwestern Bell Tel. Co., Oklahoma City, 1974-79; ptnr. Bulla and Enis, Oklahoma City, 1979-81; pvt. practice Law Offices of Thomas J. Enis, Oklahoma City, 1981-87; of counsel Fellers, Snider, Blankenship, Bailey & Tippens, Oklahoma City, 1988-89, ptnr., 1990—; lectr. Okla. Bar Rev., 1968—. Bd. dirs. Okla. Symphony Orch., 1978-88, legal counsel, 1981-88; spl. counsel Okla. Ethics Commn., 1986-88; trustee Okla. County Law Libr., 1989-91; Judge Temp. Ct. of Appeals Okla., 1991-92. Mem. ABA, Okla. Bar Assn., Mo. Bar Assn., Oklahoma County Bar Assn., Order of Coif, Phi Delta Phi. Republican. Roman Catholic. Editor-in-chief Mo. Law Rev., 1965-66. Home: 3016 Stoneybrook Rd Oklahoma City OK 73120-5716 Office: 120 N Robinson Ste 2400 Oklahoma City OK 73102

ENLOW, RICK LYNN, chiropractor; b. Fort Worth, June 9, 1956; s. John and Violet E.; m. Jana Lynch, Aug. 9, 1975; children: Shawna, Grace, Amy. BA in Theology, Bapt. Bible Coll., 1978; D of Chiropractic cum laude, Parker Coll., 1985. Chiropractor Enlow Chiropractic Ctr N.E., Ft. Worth; chief of staff North Hills Diagnostic and Rehab Ctr.; guest lectr. Parker Coll. of Chiropractic; examiner Tex. Bd. Chiropractic State Licensing Examination; mem. staff Tarrant Outpatient Ctr. Phys. edn. sponsor, guest lectr. Birdville Sch. Dist.; adult bible tchr. North Richland Hills Bapt. Ch. Mem. Am. Chiropractic Assn., Tex. Chiropractic Assn. (pres. dist. 4), Neuro-Musculoskeletal Diagnostic and Surg. Assn. (pres.), Gamma Beta Phi. Office: Enlow Chiropractic Ctr Northwood Plaza 6805 NE Loop 820 Fort Worth TX 76180-6687

ENNIS, RALPH COLWELL, religious organization administrator, educator; b. Wallace, N.C., Sept. 24, 1950; s. Elmore Bernard and Emory Jayne (Turner) E.; m. Jennifer Ann Heer, Oct. 7, 1973; children: David, Amy, Sarah, Nathan. BS in Edn. with honors, N.C. State U., 1972. Cert. math. tchr., N.C., Va. Math. tchr. Virginia Beach (Va.) Schs., 1972-74; layout draftsman Sheet Metal Specialty, Virginia Beach, 1974-75; campus ministry dir. The Navigators Princeton (N.J.) U., 1975-82; staff devel. coord. The Navigators, Richmond, Va., 1982-84; assoc. dir. Leadership Devel. Inst. The Navigators, Colorado Springs, Colo., 1984-87, rschr. U.S. Dir. Team, 1987-88; community rep. The Navigators, Raleigh, N.C., 1988-91; pastor adult edn. Crossroads Fellowship, Raleigh, N.C., 1991-92; dir. tng. curriculum and Russia leadership devel. rschr. The CoMission, Raleigh, N.C., 1992—; founding ptnr., cons. Lead Consulting, Raleigh, 1988—. Author: Breakthru: Discover Your Niche in the Body of Christ, 1992, Crosswalk: A Relational Discipleship Program, 1992, Successfit: Discover Your Niche in the Workplace, 1993; co-author: (with Jennifer Ennis) Biblical Foundations of Parenting, 1995, Introduction to the Russian Soul, 1995. Pers. cons. Building Together, Raleigh, 1993; math tutor vol. Dist. II Schs., Colorado Springs, 1984. Mem. Nat. Hon. Math. Frat. Office: Lead Consulting PO Box 32026 Raleigh NC 27622-2026

ENNS, JOHN BENJAMIN, polymer scientist; b. Chilliwack, B.C., Can., May 31, 1948; came to U.S., 1973; s. John and Louise (Toews) E.; m. Mary Louise Campbell, Apr. 27, 1975. BS in Chemistry, U. B.C., Vancouver, 1973; MS in Polymer Sci., Case Western Res. U., Cleve., 1975; MA in Chem. Engring., Princeton U., 1980, PhD in Chem. Engring., 1982. Rsch. assoc. Midland Macromolecular Inst., Midland, Mich., 1975-77; mem. tech. staff AT&T Bell Labs., Whippany, N.J., 1981-89; sr. scientist Vistakon, J&J Vision Products, Jacksonville, Fla., 1989—; cons. (N.J.) Princeton U., 1986-89, Plastics Analysis Instruments, Inc., Princeton, 1981—. Contbr. articles to profl. jours. including Jour. Applied Polymer Sci., Polymer Preprints, Jour. Macromolecular Sci.-Physics, chpts. to books; editor: N.Am. Thermal Analysis Soc. Conf. Proc., 1994. Mem. N.Am. Thermal Analysis Soc. (awards chmn. 1986-87, treas. 1989-93, pubs. chmn. 1994-95, conf. treas. 1990-96, exec. coun. 1986-87, 89-95), North Jersey Thermal Analysis Group (program chmn. 1988-89), Soc. Plastics Engrs. (tech. program com. 1994—), Am. Chem. Soc. (program chmn. 1987-89), Soc. Rheology, Soc. for Advancement of Material and Process Engring. Mennonite Brethren Ch. Home: 9251 Jaybird Cir E Jacksonville FL 32257-5276 Office: Vistakon J & J Vision Products Inc 5985 Richard St Jacksonville FL 32216-5926

ENOCH, CRAIG TRIVELY, state supreme court justice; b. Wichita, Kans., Apr. 3, 1950; s. Donald Kirk and Margery (Trively) E.; m. Kathryn Stafford Barker, Aug. 2, 1975. B.A., So. Meth. U., 1972, J.D., 1975; LLM, U. Va., 1992. Bar: Tex. 1975, U.S. Dist. Ct. (no. dist.) Tex. 1976, U.S. Ct. Appeals (5th cir.) 1979. Assoc., Burford, Ryburn & Ford, Dallas, 1975-77; ptnr. Moseley, Jones, Enoch & Martin, Dallas, 1977-81; judge 101st Dist. Ct., Dallas, 1981-87; Chief Justice Texas Court of Appeals Fifth Dist., 1987-92; justice Tex. Supreme Ct., Austin, 1993—. Chmn., Canterbury House Collegiate Chapel, Dallas, 1982-84; chmn. subcom. Scouting for Handicapped, Circle 10 Council, Dallas, 1982-84; exec. vice chmn. track and field events Area 10 Spl. Olympics, Dallas, 1984-85. Served to capt. USAFR, 1973-81. Fellow Am. State Bar Found., Tex. State Bar Found.; mem. ABA, Am. Law Inst., State Bar Tex., Dallas Bar Assn. (chmn. ct. dept. 1984), Tex. Young Lawyers Assn. Republican. Episcopalian. Club: Kiwanis (pres. Dallas 1982-83, lt. gov. Tex.-Okla. Dist. 1983-84). Home: 2614 Maria Anna Rd Austin TX 78703-1656

ENOCH, LESLIE BLYTHE, II, gas industry executive, lawyer; b. Ft. Jackson, S.C., Jan. 26, 1942; s. Leslie Blythe and Rose Nell (Clift) E.; m. Ann Ellis Parsley, July 17, 1965; children: Angela, David, Leslie III. BA, Vanderbilt U., 1964; JD, U. Tenn., 1967, cert. of attainment, 1978. Bar: Tenn. Atty. Lackey-Harwood and Alexander, Nashville, 1971-73; staff atty. State of Tenn., Nashville, 1973-74; corp. counsel Nashville Gas Co., 1974-77, gen. atty., sec., 1977-79, vp., gen. atty., 1979-82, v.p., customer svc., 1982-83, sr. v.p., gen. counsel, 1983-92; exec. v.p., CEO Mid. Tenn. Natural Gas Utility Dist., Smithville, 1992—; bd. dirs. Credit Bur. of Nashville, Gas Industry Standards Bd.; dir. energy adv. bd. State of Tenn., 1995—. Chmn. legis. and congrl. action com. C. of C., Nashville, 1985; bd. dirs. Watkins Inst., 1989-92; trustee Motlow Coll. Found., 1994—. Mem. ABA, Am. Pub. Gas Assn. (legis. com., bd. dirs. 1993—), S.E. Gas Assn. (bd. dirs. 1993-96, chmn. investment com. 1994), Fed. Energy Bar Assn., Nashville Bar Assn., Tenn. Gas Assn. (pres. 1985-86, legis. com. 1987-91, exec. com. 1992), Tenn. Assn. Utility Dists. (legis. com. 1992—), Rotary. Episcopalian. Office: Mid Tenn Natural Gas Utility District Smithville TN 37166

ENRIGHT, MICHAEL JOSEPH, radiologist; b. Richmond, Va., Mar. 27, 1955; s. Wlliam Joseph and Margaret (O'Connell) E.l (div.); children: Kelly Ann, Margeaux Elizabeth; m. Susan Ross Lemon, June 29, 1991; 1 child, Darby Michelle. BS in Pharmacy, Ohio State U., 1978; MD, Ea. Va. Med. Sch., 1981. Diplomate Nat. Bd. Med. Examiners, Am. Bd. Radiology, Va. Bd. Pharmacy. Resident in radiology Ea. Va. Grad. Sch. Medicine, Norfolk, 1981-85; radiologist U.S. Navy, Charleston, S.C., 1985-88; body imaging fellow U. Va. Med. Ctr., Charlottesville, 1988-89; radiologist Radiology Assocs. of Roanoke, Va., 1989—; treas. Low Country Imaging Soc., Charleston, 1986-87; sect. head Body and Musculoskeletal Magnetic Resonance Imaging, Radiology Assn. Roanoke, 1993—. Author (exhibit) Scrotal Ultrasonography at Am. Roentgen Ray Soc. Meeting, 1989. Lt. commdr. U.S. Navy, 1985-88. Mem. AMA, Am. Coll. Radiology, Radiol. Soc. N. Am., Roanoke Soc. Medicine. Republican. Home: 4400 Kings Chase Dr Roanoke VA 24014-6530 Office: Radiology Assocs of Roanoke Ste 435 2037 Crystal Spring Ave SW Roanoke VA 24014-2441

ENRIQUEZ, MANUEL HIPOLITO, physician; b. Angeles City, Philippines, Aug. 19, 1953; came to U.S., 1982; s. Antonio S. and Milagros D. (Hipolito) E.; m. Mary Diane Maloney, June 22, 1985; children: Steven. Katie. BS, U. of the East, 1974, MD, 1979. Diplomate internal medicine, pulmonary disease and critical care medicine. Intern Philippine Gen. Hosp., Manila, 1980; resident Mercy Hosp., Buffalo, 1982-85; fellow Wayne State U. Sch. Medicine, Detroit, 1985-87; dir. respiratory therapy Humana Hosp. Clinch Valley, Richlands, Va., 1987-88; staff pulmonologist VA Med. Ctr., Asheville, N.C., 1989—, also dir. med. ICU, 1990—; flight surgeon USAF Clinic, Charleston AFB, S.C., 1991—; cons. assoc. Duke U. Med. ctr., Durham, N.C., 1989—; cons. in field. Med. officer CAP, Asheville, 1990—, sr. programs officer, 1993—. Fellow ACP, Am. Coll. Chest Physicians; mem. Aerospace Med. Assn., Am. Thoracic Soc., Res. Officers Assn., Soc. USAF Flight Surgeons. Roman Catholic. Office: VA Med Ctr 1100 Tunnel Rd Asheville NC 28805-2043

ENSENAT, LOUIS ALBERT, surgeon; b. Merida, Mexico, Oct. 24, 1916; s. Frank and Guadalupe F. (Ensenat) E.; B.S., Tulane U., 1938, M.D., 1941; M.Sc. in Medicine, U. Pa., 1953; m. Ruth Ogden, July 9, 1943; children—Gloria Louise, Tinita Ruth, Louis Albert, Rita Joan, Barbara Jean, Michael Monroe. Intern, Charity Hosp., New Orleans, 1941-42; resident surgery Charity Hosp., Monroe, La., 1942, Lakeshore Hosp., New Orleans, VA hosp., New Orleans, Batavia, N.Y.; fellow in surg. pathology Tulane U. Sch. Med.; preceptorship in surgery Biloxi (Miss.) VA Hosp.; staff surg. VA Hosp., Montgomery, 1946-52; pvt. practice surgery, Pasadena, Tex., 1952-63, New Orleans, 1963—; adminstr. Mercy Hosp. Pasadena, 1954-63, chief surgery, 1954-63; founder, dir. Gulf Coast Home Builders, Inc.; trustee Angiology Research Found., 1986—. Trustee, Big State Factors Corp. Served from lt. (j.g.) to lt. comdr. USN, 1942-46. Decorated Purple Heart, Bronze Star. Diplomate Am. Bd. Surgery, Am. Bd. Abdominal Surgery. Fellow French Soc. Phlebology, Am. Coll. Angiology (pres.); mem. Hawthorne Surg. Soc., Am. Soc. Abdominal Surgeons, N.Y. Acad. Scis., Am. Med. Writers Assn. Author articles in field. Home and Office: 7630 Jeannette St New Orleans LA 70118-4064

ENSLEY, BILL, sports association executive. Commr. HPER Dept. Ga. Athletic Conf./North Ga. Coll., Dahlonega. Office: Ga Athletic Conf HPER Dept North Ga Coll Dahlonega GA 30597

ENTMAN, BARBARA SUE, broadcaster, writer, photographer; b. Glen Cove, N.Y., Sept. 24, 1954; d. Bernard Entman and Rose (Jacobson) Entman; m. Joseph P. Synnott, Oct. 16, 1993. BA, U. Conn., 1976. Freelance writer/photographer, 1975—; announcer, publicity dir. Sta. WHUS-FM, Storrs, Conn., 1974-76; announcer, copywriter Sta. WKAJ-AM-FM, Saratoga Springs, N.Y., 1976-77; traffic coord. Sta. WMHT-FM, Schenectady, 1977-79; ops. dir. Sta. WNIU-FM, Dekalb, Ill., 1980-82; ops. mgr. Sta. KUHF, Houston, 1982-86, announcer, 1987-88, membership dir., 1988-89; spl. projects dir. Sta. KPFT-FM, Houston, 1989-90, subscriptions dir., 1990-92; mgr. Quality Environments, 1992-94; mgr. of radio Taping For The Blind Inc., 1994-96; freelance writer, publicist, creativity coach, photographer, radioproducer, jeweler, 1992—; media cons. Ill. Heart Assn., DeKalb, 1982, Sojourner Women's Bookstore, DeKalb, 1980-81; exhibited photographs in galleries and univs., 1970—; contbr. articles and poetry to mags. and newspapers; newsletter editor Congregation Aytz Chayim, Houston, 1983-84. Founder DeKalb Area Women's Network, 1981; bd. dirs. newsletter editor Art Resources Open to Women, 1977-79; mem. Chgo. Artists Coalition, 1981-82; mem. adv. bd. Houston Women's Caucus for Art, 1985-88, 93-94, chairperson publicity nat. conf., 1988; del. Tex. Dem. Conv., 1984, 86, 90, 94; mem. performing arts screening com. Houston Internat. Festival, 1989-93; mem. Congregation Emanu El, 1993—. Mem. Nat. Coun. Jewish Women (co-v.p. pub. rels. career br. Houston sect. 1994-96), Houston Reconstructionist Havurah. Home: PO Box 980757 Houston TX 77098-0757

ENTMAN, ROBERT MATHEW, communications educator, consultant; b. Bklyn., Nov. 7, 1949; s. Bernard and Rose (Jacobson) E.; m. Francie Seymour, June 1, 1979; children: Max, Emily. AB, Duke U., 1971; PhD, Yale U., 1977; M Pub. Policy, U. Calif., Berkeley, 1980. Asst. prof. Dickinson Coll., Carlisle, Pa., 1975-77, Duke U., Durham, N.C., 1980-89; postdoctoral fellow U. Calif., 1978-80; assoc. prof. comm. Northwestern U., Evanston, Ill., 1989-94; prof. comm. N.C. State U., 1994—; adj. prof. U. N.C., Chapel Hill, 1995—; cons. subcom. on telecom. U.S. Ho. of Reps., Washington, 1982, Nat. Telecom. and Info. Adminstrn., Washington, 1984-85, Aspen Inst., Washington and Aspen, Colo., 1986—; mem. working group Commn. on TV Policy, 1990—; guest scholar Woodrow Wilson Ctr., Washington, 1989. Author: Democracy without Citizens, 1989, (monograph) Blacks in the News, 1991, Diversifying Broadcast Media, 1996; co-author: Media Power Politics, 1981; also articles. Recipient McGannon award for comm. policy rsch., 1993; rsch. grantee Markle Found., 1984, 86, 88, 95, Chgo. Cmty. Trust, 1989-92, 95; rsch. fellow Ameritech., 1989-90. Mem. Am. Polit. Sci. Assn. (coun. polit. comm. sec. 1990-91, treas, 1996— editl. bd. Polit. Comm. 1992—, sec.-treas., polit. comm. sec. 1996-97, editl. bd. Jour. Comm. 1994—, editl. bd. Comm. Law and Policy 1994—, treas. polit. comm. sect. 1996—), Social Sci. Rsch. Coun. (working group on media and fgn. policy 1990-93). Office: NC State U Dept Comm Box 8104 Raleigh NC 27695

EPLING, GERALD ARTHUR, consulting company executive; b. Hampton, Va., Apr. 6, 1955; s. Raymond and Marie Elsie (Larsen) E.; m. Valeria J. Epling, Feb. 14, 1985. AAS, Community Coll. of Air Force, 1979, Eastfield Community Coll., 1990; BS in Computer Sci., U. Tex., 1992; MS in Cognition and Neurosci., U. Tex., Dallas, 1995. With Texas Instruments, Dallas, 1978-90; CEO Arthur Epling Enterprises, Richardson, Tex., 1990-94, Arthur Epling Cons., Richardson, 1996—. Served to E-4, USAF, 1975-78. Home: PO Box 835956 Richardson TX 75083-5956

EPPERSON, JEAN WARNER, rancher; b. Waco, Tex., July 7, 1919; d. Asa W. and Annie Mae (Bell) Warner; m. Clinton W. Breeding, Feb. 20, 1942 (div. Nov. 1958); children: Bayard, Webb, Leanna; m. Robert Julius Epperson, June 5, 1965. B.A., Baylor U., 1941; cert. Gulf Park Coll., Miss., 1939; postgrad. So. Meth. U., 1970-71. Mng. dir. Baylor U. Sch. Drama, Waco, 1943; rancher, Satin, Tex., 1954—. Nat. Museum House chair Nat. Soc. Colonial Dames Am., Tex., 1982-88, pres. 1990-92; chmn. bd. Brazos Forum, 1982—, Greater Waco Beautification Assn., 1984; bd. dirs. Dallas Garden Ctr., 1967-69, Dallas Theatre Ctr., 1965-75. Editor: Guidelines for Museum Houses, 1984. Named Woman of Yr., Kappa Alpha Theta, 1985, Mortar Bd. Woman of the Yr., 1986; recipient Pathfinder award, 1986. Mem. Phi Theta Kappa, Kappa Alpha Theta. Clubs: Dallas Garden (v.p. 1979), Jr. League Garden (pres. 1970) (Dallas). Home: PO Box 170 Satin TX 76685-0170

EPPERSON, JOEL RODMAN, lawyer; b. Miami, Fla., Aug. 29, 1945; s. John Rodman and Ann Louise (Barrs) E.; m. Gretchen Jean Meyer, Apr. 16, 1968; children: Joel Rodman, David Michael, Sandra Elizabeth. BS, U. South Fla., 1967; JD, South Tex. Coll., 1976. Bar: Fla. 1976, U.S. Dist. Ct. (mid. dist.) Fla. 1976, U.S. Ct. Appeals (5th cir.) 1976, U.S. Supreme Ct. 1979, U.S. Ct. Appeals (11th cir.) 1991. Asst. states atty. State of Fla., Tampa, 1976-79; ptnr. Bryant & Epperson, 1979-86, Assocs. & Bruce L. Scheiner, Ft. Myers, Fla., 1987-88; ptnr. Epperson & Stahl, Ft. Myers, 1988-90, Epperson & DeMinico, Tampa/Ft. Myers, 1991-92, Epperson & Assocs., P.A., Tampa/Ft. Myers, 1993—. Served to capt. USMC, 1968-72. Mem. ABA, ATLA, Acad. Fla. Trial Lawyers Assn., Lee County Bar Assn., Hillsborough County Bar Assn. Democrat. Home: 1306 Anglers Ln Lutz FL 33549-5040 Office: Epperson & Assocs 11430 S Cleveland Ave Fort Myers FL 33907-2323 also: 4329 N Armenia Ave Tampa FL 33607-6427

EPPERSON, MARGARET FARRAR, civic worker; b. Hickman, Ky., Feb. 9, 1922; d. John Henry and Helen Margaret (Thompson) White; m. Liberty Weir Birmingham III, June 14, 1947 (dec. Feb. 1965); children: Margaret W., Elizabeth J., Richard L.; m. Ralph Cameron Epperson, Sept. 18, 1971. Student, Washington Sch. Art, 1940; BA magna cum laude, Judson Coll., Marion, Ala., 1945; postgrad., Lambuth Coll., Jackson, Tenn., 1964. Cert. secondary tchr., Ky. Tchr. biology and typing Robert L. Osborne High Sch., Marietta, Ga., 1945-46; tchr. typing Hickman High Sch., 1946-47; tchr. day care ctr. Southside Bapt. Ch., Jacksonville, Fla., 1972-73; sec. to min. of Edn. Jacksonville, Fla., 1973; file clk. Epperson Appraisers, Pensacola, Fla., 1986-87; formerly substitute tchr. various high schs. and jr. high schs., staff mem. Ridgecrest Bapt. Assembly, summer 1946, 1971. Exhibited in group shows, Jackson, Tenn., 1957, 58, West Tenn. Exec. Club, 1958-59. Pres. Alexander Sch. PTA, Jackson, 1959-60, devotional chmn., 1956-57, chmn. rm. mothers, 1957-58, 1st v.p., 1958-59; sec. Reelfoot Lake coun. Girl Scouts U.S.A., 1969-71, troop mother cookie chmn. 1958-65; PTA sec. Jackson, Tenn. H.S., 1967-68, 70-71; PTA 1st v.p. Jackson, Tenn. Ctrl. Coun., 1960-61; mem. aux. assn. Jackson-Madison County Bar, 1960-65; vol. ARC, Jackson, 1955, Meml. Med. Hosp. Aux., Jacksonville, 1978-86, Am. Heart Assn., 1987-90, Sacred Heart Hosp. Aux., Pensacola, 1986—; life mem. Jacksonville Children's Hosp. Aux., 1974—; hostess designer show house Pensacola Symphony Guild, 1979-80, show house com., 1996—; dir. Women's Missionary Union, Bapt. Ch., 1976-78, mission support chmn., 1992, 93, 94, sec., 1995; Newcomers Club Greater Pensacola Area, 1988-89, Bon Appetit Luncheon Group, 1986-87, sunshine chmn., 1987-88, sec., 1988-89, nom. com., 1993-94, scholarship com., 1993-94, newcomer's book club group program chmn., 1995-96; publicity chmn. MacDowell Music Club, Jackson, 1954-55, program chmn. 1957-58, social chmn. 1959-60, parliamentarian 1961; com. mem. Jackson Cmty. Concert Assn., 1958-64; mem. women's bd. Bapt. Health Care Found., 1993—, mem. invitations and tickets com. for Style Show, 1993-94, life mem., 1996—; active Friday Musicale of Jacksonville, Fla., 1979-86, Friends of Libr., 1993-94, Escambia Coun. on Aging, 1996. Mem. AAUW (sec. 1988-90, 2d v.p. 1990-92, tel. com. 1993—, br. area rep. cmty. problems Tenn. 1970-71, chmn. Tenn. divsn. cultural interests 1969-70, Fla. chmn. interest groups 1977-78), DAR (treas. 1981-82, chmn. Am. Heritage 1989-91, chmn. mag. 1991-93), UDC (sec. Jacksonville chpt. 1979-81, historian Jacksonville chpt. 1981-83, sec. Pensacola chpt. 1989-90, corr. sec. Pensacola chpt. 1992-94, mem. com. chmn. 1993-94, Christian Women's Club (prayer chmn. 1991—, book chmn. 1987, 88, 92-94, hostesses asst. chmn. 1994—), Pensacola Fedn. Garden Clubs (pres. Poinciana Circle 1989-91, pres. Bells of Ireland Circle 1978-80, civic chmn., 1991, sec. Alderman Park Cir., Jacksonville 1980-82), Judson Coll. Alumnae Assn. of Pensacola (pres. 1993—, exec. bd. 1993—), Tenn. Fedn. Garden Clubs (pres. Jackson Jr. 1958-60, 60-70, chmn. exec. bd. 1970-71, chmn. flower show 1968).

EPPES, WALTER W., JR., lawyer; b. Meridian, Miss., Oct. 9, 1929; s. Walter W. Sr. and Mary (Seymour) E.; m. Katherine Bailey, Oct. 17, 1952; children: Kathy Eppes Yarborough, Susan Eppes Whitehead. Student, U. Ala., Tuscaloosa, 1947-50; LLB, U. Miss., 1952. Bar: Miss. 1952, U.S. Dist. Ct. (so. dist.) Miss. 1952, U.S. Ct. Appeals (5th cir.) 1952. Adjuster U.S. Fidelity & Guaranty, Co., Meridian, 1952-54; ptnr. Shumate & Eppes, Meridian, 1954-63, Huff, Williams, Gunn, Eppes & Crenshaw, Meridian, 1963-73, Eppes, Watts & Shannon, Meridian, 1973-95, Eppes & Carter, Meridian, 1995—. Author: (with others) Mississippi Law Institute, 1975. Pres. Roundtable Investors, Meridian, 1992. Mem. Am. Bd. Trial Advs. (diplomate), Miss. Bar (pres. 1985-86), Internat. Soc. Barristers (gov. 1968—), Internat. Assn. Def. Counsel (comm. chmn. 1960—), Downtown Club Meridian (pres. 1972), Northwood Country Club (bd. dirs. 1972). Republican. Presbyterian. Home: 4833 15th Pl Meridian MS 39303 Office: Eppes & Carter Attys Broadmoor Mart Meridian MS 39303

EPPLEY, FRANCES FIELDEN, retired secondary education educator, author; b. Knoxville, Tenn., July 18, 1921; d. Chester Earl and Beulah Magnolia (Wells) Fielden; m. Gordon Talmage Cougle, July 25, 1942; children:Russell Gordon Eppley, Carolyn Eppley Horseman; m. Fred Coan Eppley, Mar. 8, 1953; 1 child, Charlene Eppley Sellers. BA in English, Carson Newman Coll., 1942; MA, Winthrop Coll., 1963. Tchr., East Corinth (Maine) Acad., 1942-43; tchr. pub. schs., Charlotte, N.C., 1950-53, 59-83, Greenville, S.C., 1954-56, Spartanburg, S.C., 1957-58; head start tchr., summers 1964-68. Mem. hist. com. N.C. Bapt. Conv., 1985-88. Alpha Delta Kappa grantee, 1970. Mem. NEA, N.C. Social Studies Conf., Writers Assn., Alpha Delta Kappa, Pi Kappa Delta, Alpha Psi Omega. Baptist. Author: First Baptist Church of Charlotte, North Carolina: Its Heritage, 1981, History of Flint Hill, 1983, The First Astrologer, 1983, Sammy's Song, 1984, No Show Dog, 1985, Sun Signs for Christians, 1985, Astrology and Prophecy, 1987, Our Heavenly Home, 1987, Men Like-, 1987, A Hammer in the Land, 1988, Aunt Lillian's Seafoam Candy, 1988, Women's Lib in the Bible, 1988, William Penn, 1988, Columbus Was a Christian, 1988, Horoscopes of the Presidents, 1988, Messiah, 1989, 93, The Signs of Your Life, 1994; (musical drama): The Place To Be, 1982, Praise in the West, 1987; (musical show): Songs of The People, 1983; (song): Katie, 1985, (cantata) How Come, Jesus?, Stubborn Stella and The Sitting Stone, 1990, Columbus: The Race Home, 1990, Religion and Astrology, 1991, Astrology and Prophecy, 1991, The Ghosts of Elmwood, 1992, Full Circle, 1992, Sonnet to Charlotte, 1992, How Children Learn, 1992, Your Child and Astrology, 1992, Use Astrology to Help Your Child, 1992, Christmas Magnus, 1993, Ah, Jericho!, 1993, The Parthenon, U.S.A., 1993, The Shepherds Fields, 1993, Another Spring and World War II, 1994, The Mystery of the Laura K. Barnes, 1994, Contamination, 1994, First Landings, 1994, The Signs of Your Life, 1994, Teach the Children to Read, 1994, Hiawatha, 1995, The Stalker, 1995, Search for an Ancestor, 1995; editor: Chester's Letters, 1994, An Immediate Family, 1996, The Return, 1996. Home: 6611 Rolling Ridge Dr Charlotte NC 28211-5428

EPPLEY, ROLAND RAYMOND, JR., retired financial services executive; b. Balt., Apr. 1, 1932; s. Roland and Verna (Garrettson) E.; m. LeVerne Pittman, June 20, 1953; children: Kimberly, Kent, Todd. B.A., Johns Hopkins U., 1952, M.A., 1953; D.C.S. (hon.), St. John's U., 1984. Pres., chief exec. officer Comm. Credit Computer, Balt., 1962-68; pres., chief exec. officer CIPC, Balt., 1968-71; vice chmn. Eastern States Monetary, Lake Success, N.Y., 1982-88; pres., chief exec. officer, dir. Affiliated Financial, Wilmington, Del., 1983-85, Eastern States Bankcard, Lake Success, N.Y., 1971-88; ret., 1988; chmn. bd. Eppley-Tongue Assocs., Inc.; adj. prof. St. John's U., 1973-88; bd. dirs. Ea. States Monetary, Veritas Inc., Hanover Investment Funds, Janel Hydraulics, Vista Funds; chmn. bd. Hanover Funds, 1989-96, Eppley-Tongue Assocs., Inc., 1992-95. Chmn. bd. trustees Calgary Bapt. Ch., Balt., 1969-71; chmn. investment com. Community Ch., Manhasset, N.Y., 1983-88; bd. advisors St. John's U., 1973-88; active Trinity Meth. Ch., Palm Beach Gardens, Fla.; mem. Johns Hopkins U. Alumni Coun., 1996—. Recipient Disting. Service award St. John's U., 1981, 84 Laucheimer grantee, 1952-53. Mem. Am. Bankers Assn., Data Processing Mgmt. Assn., Am. Mgmt. Assn. Pres.'s Assn., Electronic Funds Transfer Assn., Mensa, Madison Sq. Garden Club, Meadowbrook Club, Plandome Country Club (dir. 1977-86), Hillendale Country Club, PGA Country Club, City Club of the Palm Beaches, Ibis Country Club, Masons, Shriners, Phi Beta Kappa, Omicron Delta Epsilon, Beta Gamma Sigma, Sigma Phi Epsilon (citation). Republican. Home: 105 Coventry Pl West Palm Beach FL 33418-8001 also: 210 Belmont Forest Ct Lutherville MD 21093

EPPS, AUGUSTUS CHARLES, lawyer; b. Richmond, Va., Feb. 2, 1916; s. John Lindsey and Lily Madeline (Becker) E.; m. Rosalie Suzanne Garrett, Aug. 17, 1946; children: Augustus Charles, George Garrett, John Daniel. B.S., U. Va., 1936, LL.B., 1938. Bar: Va. 1937, U.S. Supreme Ct. 1950. Practice in Richmond, 1938-42, 46—; assoc. atty. Christian, Barton & Parker, 1938-42; ptnr. Christian, Barton, Epps, Brent & Chappell, 1946-91, of counsel, 1991—; bd. dirs., gen. counsel Richmond Life Ins. Co., 1952-69; bd. dirs. Wainwright Investment Co., Va. Legal Services Corp., Garrett Groves, Inc.; trustee emeritus U. Va. Law Sch. Found. Editorial bd., bd. mng. editors: Va. Law Rev, 1936-38; contbr. articles to profl. jours. Mem. Richmond Sch. Bd., 1963-70; past pres. Met. Richmond Legal Aid Project;

past pres., bd. dirs. Crippled Children's Hosp., Friends Richmond Pub. Library; past vice chmn., bd. dirs. Richmond YMCA; bd. dirs., exec. com. Legal Aid Soc. Met. Richmond, 1967-76, Richmond Symphony; Richmond Urban Forum; former bd. dirs. Carpenter Ctr. for Performing Arts, 1981-87; mem. Richmond Public Library Bd., 1978-84; past bd. dirs. Richmond Offender Aid and Restoration, 1969-75; trustee Va. Diocesan Ctr., Episcopal Diocese Va.; bd. dirs., sec. Va. Math. & Sci. Coalition; v.p., bd. dirs. V.O.I.C.E.; active U. Va. Coun. Arts and Scis. Served to maj. AUS, 1942-46. Fellow Am. Bar Found., Am. Coll. Trial Lawyers, Va. State Bar; mem. ABA (past mem. com. on specialization, past mem. grievance com., past chmn. state com. legal edn., admission to bar, commn. on law and the economy), Va. Bar Assn. (pres. 1966-67, chmn. com. on specialization, past chmn. joint com. legis., law reform, past mem. exec. com.), Richmond Bar Assn. (past chmn. legal aid com., past pres.), Am. Judicature Soc., Assn. Life Ins. Counsel, Fed. Jud. Conf. 4th cir., U. Va. Law Sch. Assn. (council, chmn. Law Day 1972, 73, past chmn. com. scholarships, pres. 1977-79, nat. chmn. ann. giving appeal, 1984-85, 85-86), Phi Beta Kappa (pres. Richmond assocs. 1987-88), Order of Coif, Phi Delta Phi, Alpha Tau Omega. Episcopalian. Home: 6323 Ridgeway Rd Richmond VA 23226-3201 Office: 1200 Mutual Bldg 9th and Main Sts Richmond VA 23219-3012

EPPS, EDWIN CARLYLE, English language educator; b. Columbia, S.C., Aug. 17, 1948; s. Edwin Carlyle and Alice (Fleetwood) E.; m. Helen Carol Edens, Dec. 20, 1975; children: Catherine Clair Edens, William Fleetwood Tennyson. BA, Emory U., 1970; MA, U. S.C., 1973, EdD, 1993. Tchr. Union Elem. Sch., Paulding County, Ga., 1970-71; teaching asst. U. S.C., Columbia, 1971-73; tchr., dir. debate Spring Valley High Sch., Columbia, 1973-79; gen. ptnr. Woodspurge Books, Staunton, Va., 1979-81; tchr. McCracken Jr. High Sch., Spartanburg, S.C., 1981-90; tchr.-in-residence Writing Improvement Network U. S.C., Columbia, 1990-94; tchr. McCracken Jr. H.S., Spartanburg, S.C., 1994—; co-dir. Spartanburg Writing Project, 1984—; coord. S.C. Writing Project, 1986—; presenter in field various assns. Editor newsletter S.C. Writing Tchr., 1990-94; asst. editor jour. Teaching Edn., 1988-93; mem. editorial staff Carolina English Tchr., 1984-89; contbr. articles to profl. jours.; contbr. poetry to magazines and anthologies. Tchr. incentive grantee S.C. Dept. Edn., 1984, dissemination grantee S.C. Dept. Edn., 1985, tchr. incentive grantee S.C. Dept. Edn., 1987, NEH summer grantee, 1986. Mem. NEA, Nat. Coun. Tchrs. English, S.C. Assn. for Supervision and Curriculum Devel., S.C. Coun. Tchrs. English (secondary dir., v.p., liaison, pres.-elect 1995—), S.C. Coun. of Tchrs. of English (pres. 1996—). Democrat. Methodist. Home: PO Box 18404 Spartanburg SC 29318-8404 Office: McCracken Jr HS 300 Webber Rd Spartanburg SC 29307-2615

EPPS, GREGORY DEAN, program director; b. St. Albans, W.Va., Dec. 23, 1958; s. Don McGhee and Lola Mae (Coleman) E. BS in Edn., W.Va. State Coll., 1981; MS in Pub. Adminstrn./Mgmt., W.Va. U., 1989, EdD, 1995. Playground asst. Kanawha County Parks and Recreation, St. Albans, 1976, playground dir., 1977-80; supr. CETA program Charleston Housing Authority, St. Albans, 1981; supr. Gov.'s Summer Youth Program, St. Albans, 1982-83; substitute tchr. Kanawha County Schs., Charleston, W.Va., 1983-85; tchr., dept. chair Hayes Jr. High Sch., St. Albans, 1985-89; dir. ROTC enhanced skills tng. program W.Va. State Coll., Institute, 1989—; coach track, football, and basketball Hayes Jr. High Sch., 1984-89; coord. PICK Program Pvt. Industry Coun. Kanawha County, St. Albans, 1985-89; track and field cons. W.Va. State Coll., 1989-96, legis. affairs com., 1996, adv. com., 1996. Active Black Male Coalition, Kanawha County, 1992—, NAACP, Charleston, W.Va., 1989—, Big Brother Role Model Program, Kanawha County, 1989—, Salvation Army, Kanawha County, 1985—. Mem. Assn. for Devel. Edn. (chair awards com. 1989—, polit. liaison W.Va. chpt. 1995-96), Assn. for Instnl. Rsch. (chair exhibit com. 1989—), Pan Hellenic Coun. (rep. 1990—, Svc. award 1994), Jaycees (dir. St. Albans chpt. 1978, Jaycee of Month 1984), Omega Psi Phi (Man of Yr. 1995, Superior Svc. award 1996). Democrat. Baptist. Home: 33 1/2 Miriam Ave Saint Albans WV 25177 Office: WVa State Coll PO Box 1000 Campus Box 64 Institute WV 25112

EPPS, JAMES HAWS, III, lawyer; b. Johnson City, Tenn., Sept. 15, 1936; s. James Haws and Anne Lafayette (Sessoms) E.; m. Jane Mahoney, Oct. 9, 1976; children from previous marriage—James Haws IV, Sara Stuart. B.A., U.N.C., 1955-59; J.D., Vanderbilt U., 1962. Bar: Tenn. 1962, U.S. Dist. Ct. Tenn. 1962, U.S. Ct. Appeals (6th cir.) 1971, Interstate Commerce Commn. Bar 1962, U.S. Supreme Ct. 1967. Prin. Epps & Epps, Johnson City, Tenn.; city atty. Johnson City, 1967—, Johnson City Bd. Edn., 1967-86; spl. counsel State of Tenn., 1966-70; former gen. counsel Appalachian Flying Svc. Inc., ET&WNC Transp. Co., Inc. Past bd. dirs. Washington County Mental Health Assn., East Tenn. and Western N.C. Transp. Co., East Tenn. and Western N.C. R.R., Tennolina Corp., Appalachian Air Lines, Inc., Appalachian Flying Svc., Inc., Farmers and Mchts. Bank, Limestone, Tenn., Tenn. Mental Health Assn., budget com. United Fund of Johnson City, 1964-68, Assault Crime Counsel Early Support Svcs. Inc., Safe Passage Inc., Johnson City Homeless Coalition, Home Base Adv. Coun.; former legal adviser Appalachian Council Girl Scouts U.S.A.; mem. Tenn. Law Revision Commn., 1970-71; legal counsel Salvation Army, mem. adv. bd. 1974—, exec. com. 1977—, 1st v.p. adv. bd. 1991, pres. adv. bd. 1993, 94, mem. property com.; chmn. Family Violence Coun.; mem. Civil Def., 1967—; chmn. Washington County for Tenn. Leukemia Soc., 1991; mem. exec. com. Washington County Dem. Party, Tenn. Bicentennial Commn., exec. and fin. coms. Fellow Tenn. Bar Found.; mem. ABA, Fed. Bar Assn., Nat. Orgn. Legal Problems Edn., Nat. Assn. R.R. Trial Counsel, Internat. Mcpl. Lawyers Assn., (chmn. Tenn. chpt. 1988-89, ethics and environ. coms. 1989—, regional v.p. 1989-92, chmn. resolutions com. 1989-90, dues and alternatives revenue com. 1996, lectr., trustee, 1992—), Nat. Legal Aid Defender Assn., Tenn. Bar Assn., Am. Judicature Soc., Washington County Bar Assn. (past pres.), Tenn. Trial Lawyers Assn., Tenn. Mcpl. Attys. Assn., Assn. ICC Practitioners (past com. profl. ethics and grievances), Transp. Lawyers Assn., Motor Carrier Lawyers Assn., Am. Counsel Assn., Johnson City C. of C. (Disting. Service award 1968), Internat. Platform Assn., Lawyers Com. for Civil Rights Under Law, World Peace Through Law Ctr., Tenn. Lung Assn., Tenn. Correctional Assn., Tenn. Taxpayers Assn. (past bd. dirs.), Tennesseans for Better Transp., U.S. Supreme Ct. Hist. Soc., Def. Research Inst., Tipton Haynes Hist. Assn. (past dir.), Phi Delta Phi, Phi Delta Theta. Episcopalian. Clubs: Hurstleigh, J.C. Country, Unaka Rd. and Gun, Highland Stable, North Johnson City Bus. (dir., past pres. 1966-67), Nat. Lawyers, East Tenn. State U. Century, Boys' Club (charter) (Johnson City/Washington County). Lodges: Masons, Elks (legal counsel 1963-67). First bd. govs. Transp. Law Jour. Office: 115 E Unaka Ave Johnson City TN 37601-4623 also: PO Box 2288 Johnson City TN 37605-2288

EPPS, WILLIAM DAVID, minister; b. Jan. 15, 1951; s. William E. Epps Jr.; m. Cynthia Scott Douglas; children: Jason, John, James. B in Social Work, East Tenn. State U., 1975; ThM, Internat. Sem., 1981; D Ministry, Berean Christian Coll., 1981; postgrad., Assemblies of God Theol. Sem. Lic. to ministry Assemblies of God, 1978, ordained, 1980. Youth worker State St. United Meth. Ch., Bristol, Va., 1971-72; minister youth Wesley Meml. United Meth. Ch., Johnson City, Tenn., 1973-74; pastor Taylor Meml. United Meth. Ch., Johnston City, 1974-75, Chuckey United Meth. Cir., Greene County, Tenn., 1975-77, Orebank Assembly of God, Kingsport, Tenn., 1978-79; minister edn. Trinity Assembly of God, Johnson City, 1979; minister outreach 1st Assembly of God, Grand Junction, Colo., 1979-83; sr. pastor Trinity Fellowship, Peachtree City, Ga., 1983—; presbyter South Atlanta sect. Ga. Dist. Assemblies of God; chaplain Peachtree City Police Dept., Fayette County Sheriff's Dept., Atlanta divsn. FBI, Fulton County Police Acad.; chmn. 1990 N. Ga. Intercessory Prayer Gathering, Atlanta; mem. Ga. Dist. Evangelism Com., area evangelism rep.; mem. Coll. of Fellows of The Acad. Parish Clergy. Contbg. editor, Strategies for the 90's: A Pastoral Evangelism Handbook; contbr. articles to profl. jours. With USMC; U.S. Army N.G. Recipient Ga. Press Assn. Editorial award 1986, Cert. of Appreciation, Ga. Dist. Women's Ministries, 1989, many others. Mem. Fellowship Christian Athletes, Evang. Tchr. Tng. Assn. (honor mem.), Internat. Conf. Police Chaplains (Ga. post cert. police officer, Ga. post cert. chaplain, cert. sr. chaplain), Fayette County Ministerial Assn. (past pres.). Office: Trinity Fellowship PO Box 2777 Peachtree City GA 30269-0777

EPRIGHT, CHARLES JOHN, engineer; b. Bklyn., Jan. 11, 1932; s. Charles and Margaret Mary (Tripoli) E.; m. Mary Lucy Bono, May 29, 1954; children: Daniel John, Michael James, Marisa R. Becker, Victoria Epright Carmona, Maria Carmela. BS in Math., U. Nev., 1965; MS in Engring. Mgmt., Northeastern U., 1971. Sr. engr. Raytheon, Andover, Mass., 1970-78, Delmo-Victor, Belmont, Calif., 1978-79; advanced systems engring. specialist Lockheed Missile & Space Co., Austin, Tex., Sunnyvale, Calif., 1979-87; engring. scientist Tracor Aerospace, Austin, Tex., 1987-89, staff engr. Lockheed Engring. and Sci. Co., Houston, 1989—; cons. Colo. Electronic Tng. Ctr., Colorado Springs., 1968-69. Civic adv. Salem-in-Action, N.H., 1977-79; dir. Reachout, Salem, 1976-79; community action com. mem. N.H. Com. for Adopted and Foster Children, Manchester, 1978-79, Runaway Hotline, Austin, 1984-88, Middle Earth Spectrum Shelter, 1987-89; mem. pub. responsibility com. Mental Health/Mental Retardation, Austin, 1988-89; bd. dirs., v.p. Assn. Retarded Citizens, 1989-93; mem. outreach Covenant House Tex., Houston, 1990—. With USAF, 1950-70. Decorated Legion of Merit, 1969; recipient Family of Yr. award Sons of Italy, 1968, 69. Mem. Internat. Assn. Elec. and Electronic Engrs., Air Force Assn. (life), Assn. Old Crows, Am. Inst. Am. Scientists, DAV. Roman Catholic. Lodge: KC (grand knight 1968-69). Avocations: stamp collecting; photography; collecting old books. Home: 2012 Fairfield Ct N League City TX 77573-3504 Office: Lockheed Engring and Sci Co Ste 100/S06 555 Forge River Rd Webster TX 77598

EPSTEIN, ANNE CAROL, physician; b. N.Y.C., Mar. 18, 1956; d. Jeremiah Fain and Ruth Louise (Sandberg) Epstein; m. Howard J. Curzer, May 31, 1981; 1 child, Mirah Epstein Curzer. BA with high honors and spl. honors, U. Tex., 1977; MD, Baylor U., 1981. Diplomate Am. Bd. Internal Medicine; lic. physician, Tex. Resident in internal medicine Baylor Affiliated Hosps., Houston, 1981-84; instr. dept. internal medicine Tex. Tech U. Health Scis. Ctr., Lubbock, 1985-87, asst. prof. dept. internal medicine, 1987-93, assoc. prof., 1993-94; pvt. practice internal medicine, Lubbock, 1995—; mem. clin. faculty Univ. Med. Ctr., Lubbock, 1985—; med. expert Social Security Adminstrn., Oklahoma City, 1990—; guest lectr. dept. philosopy Tex. Tech U., 1986-92; panelist, presenter in field. Author chpt. and articles. Tex. Tech U. grantee, 1987. Mem. ACP, Phi Beta Kappa. Democrat. Jewish. Office: 3502 9th St STe 360 Lubbock TX 79415

EPSTEIN, DAVID GUSTAV, lawyer; b. Alexandria, La., Dec. 7, 1943; s. Isaac and Alice (Fried) E.; m. Diane Floca, Feb. 16, 1969; children: Daniel Stewart, Charles Abraham. LL.B., U. Tex., 1966; LL.M., Harvard U., 1969. Bar: Tex. 1966, Ariz. 1967, Ark. 1979, Ga. 1989. Asst. prof. N.C. Sch. Law, 1970-74; prof. law U. Tex., 1974-79, Fulbright and Jaworski prof. law, 1982-85; dean Sch. Law, U. Ark., 1979-82; dean and prof. bankruptcy law Southeastern Bankruptcy Law Inst., Emory U., Atlanta, 1985-89; ptnr. King & Spalding, 1989—. Author: Basic Uniform Commerical Code Teachng Materials, 1977, 3d rev. edit., 1988, Cases and Materials on Debtors and Creditors, 1973, 4th edit., 1994, Debtor Creditor Law in a Nutshell, 1973, 5th rev. edit., 1995, Bankruptcy (3 vols.), 1992. Mem. ABA, Ga. Bar Assn., Tex. Bar Assn., Nat. Bankruptcy Conf., Am. Law Inst., Am. Coll. Bankruptcy, Order of Coif. Democrat. Jewish. Office: King & Spalding 191 Peachtree St NE Atlanta GA 30303-1740

EPSTEIN, JAYE MARK, city planner; b. Washington, Dec. 30, 1950; s. Samuel and Doris Lee (Peck) E.; m. Mona Remer, June 30, 1974; children: Brian, Elizabeth, Sara. BA in Sociology, U. Md., 1974; M City and Regional Planning, Cath. U. Am., 1976. Cert. urban planner. Transp. planner Md. Dept. Transp., Office of Sec., Balt., 1978-82; assoc. planner Broward County Office of Planning, Ft. Lauderdale, Fla., 1982-83, Broward County Planning Coun., Ft. Lauderdale, 1983-85; chief planner City of Coral Springs, Fla., 1985-89; dir. planning City of Coral Springs, 1989-92, dir. community and econ. devel., 1992-93, dir. devel. svcs., 1993—; vice chmn. Broward County Tech. Coordinating Com., 1989—; chmn. Coral Springs Devel. Rev. Com., 1989—. Mem. Am. Inst. Cert. Planners (cert.), Am. Planning Assn., Fla. Planning Assn., Broward County Planning Assn., Cath. U. Am. Alumni Assn., U. Md. Alumni Assn. (life). Office: City of Coral Springs 9530 W Sample Rd Pompano Beach FL 33065-4104

EPSTEIN, ROBERT MARVIN, anesthesiologist, educator; b. N.Y.C., Mar. 10, 1928; s. Nathan Batlan and Rebecca (Dickes) E.; m. Lillian Ray Cohen, Dec. 31, 1950; children: Judith Susan, Neal Myron, Charles Benjamin. B.S. with distinction, U. Mich., 1947, M.D. cum laude, 1951. Diplomate: Am. Bd. Anesthesiology (dir. 1972-84, pres. 1979-80). Intern U. Mich. Hosp., 1951-52; resident in anesthesiology Presbyterian Hosp., N.Y.C., 1952-53, 55-56; instr. in anesthesiology and fellow in medicine Columbia U., 1956-57, assoc., 1957-59, asst. prof., anesthesiology, 1959-65, assoc. prof., 1965-70, prof., 1970-72; prof. U. Va., Charlottesville, 1972-74, Alumni prof., 1974-87, Disting. prof., 1987-92, Harold Carron prof., 1992—, dept. chmn., 1972-96; mem. anesthesiology tng. com. Nat. Inst. Gen. Med. Scis., NIH, 1966-69; mem. com. on anesthesia NRC, 1970-71; mem. Nat. Bd. Med. Examiners, 1982-90. Editor Anesthesiology, 1974-79; contbr. numerous articles to profl. jours. Bd. dirs., sec. U.Va. Health Svcs. Found., 1980-90, pres., 1990-93; trustee Ednl. Commn. for Fgn. Med. Grads., 1991-95, vice chmn., 1993-95. With U.S. Army, 1953-55. Guggenheim fellow Oxford (Eng.) U., 1966-67; N.Y. Heart Assn. fellow, 1956-57; Scholar-in-Residence, Inst. Medicine NAS, 1997. Fellow Royal Coll. Anaesthetists (Eng.); mem. AAAS, Inst. Medicine NAS, Am. Physiol. Soc., Am. Soc. Anesthesiologists, Soc. Acad. Anesthesia Chmn. (mem. coun., rep. to Coun. Acad. Soc. Assn. Am. Med. Colls. 1984-91), Am. Soc. Pharmacy and Exptl. Therapeutics, Anaesthetic Rsch. Soc. (U.K.), Assn. Univ. Anesthesiologists (pres. 1973-74), Phi Beta Kappa, Sigma Xi, Alpha Omega Alpha. Office: U Va Hosp Jefferson Park Ave Charlottesville VA 22908

ERB, KARL ALBERT, physicist, government official; b. Chgo., June 30, 1942; s. Edgar Gillette and Dorothy (Carsten) E.; m. Betty G. Hesse, June 22, 1963 (div. 1995); children: Janet, Margaret. BA, NYU, 1965; MS, U. Mich., 1966, PhD, 1970. Instr. U. Pitts., 1970-72; instr., asst. prof., assoc. prof. Yale U., New Haven, 1972-80; staff scientist Oak Ridge (Tenn.) Nat. Lab., 1980-86; program dir. NSF, Washington, 1986-89, dep. dir. physics div., 1991; asst. dir. White House Office Sci. and Tech. Policy, Washington, 1989-91; acting assoc. dir. for phys. scis. & engring. White House Office of Sci. and Tech. Policy, Washington, 1991-92, assoc. dir. for phys. scis. engring., 1992-93; sr. sci. advisor NSF, 1993—; exec. sec. Pres.'s Com. for the Nat. Medal of Sci., 1993—; mem. U.S. Nuclear Sci. Adv. Com., Washington, 1983-86; vis. prof. J.W. Goethe U., Frankfurt, 1978. Contbr. articles to physics jours. and encys., chpts. to books. Fellow AAAS, Am. Phys. Soc. Office: NSF 4201 Wilson Blvd Arlington VA 22230-0001

ERDMAN, JOSEPH, lawyer; b. Havana, Cuba, Dec. 14, 1935; s. Jonas and Miriam (Rimsky) E.; children: Harley, Andrew; m. Rosemary Hill, Apr. 20, 1992. B.A., U. Va., 1956; postgrad. U. Mich. Law Sch., 1956-57; LL.B., Fordham U., 1960. Bar: N.Y. 1960, Fla. 1975. Assoc. Wormser Koch Kiely-Alessandroni, N.Y.C., 1960-62; ptnr. Greenbaum, Wolff & Ernst, N.Y.C., 1962-82; ptnr. Proskauer, Rose, Goetz & Mendelsohn, Fla. and N.Y.C., 1982—; chair, personal planning dept. 1991—; lectr. radio, panels, NYU Inst. Taxation, 1978. Author: Complete Guide to Marital Deduction in Estate Planning, 1978, Effective Drafting under the Revised Uniform Principal and Income Act, 1991; contbr. articles to publs. including Estate Planning Mag., J.K. Lasser Estate Tax Techniques, Miami Herald, U.S. News and World Report. Co-chmn. Westchester for Carter Campaign, 1976; pres. Scarsdale Synogogue, 1978-79; mem. planned giving coun. U. Va., 1992—. Served with U.S. Army, 1957-58. Fellow Am. Coll. Trust and Estate Coun.; mem. N.Y. State Bar Assn., Fla. Bar Assn., Phi Beta Kappa, Boca West Club, Atrium Club, Boca Raton Resort Club, Farmington Country Club (Va.). Home: 19539 Island Court Dr Boca Raton FL 33434-5153 also: 17 W 54th St New York NY 10019-5404 Office: Proskauer Rose Goetz & Mendelsohn 2255 Glades Rd Ste 340 Boca Raton FL 33431-7382 also: 1585 Broadway New York NY 10036-8200

ERDREICH, BEN LEADER, federal agency executive; b. Birmingham, Ala., Dec. 9, 1938; s. Stanley Marx and Corinne (Leader) E.; m. Ellen Cooper, May 30, 1965; children: Jeremy Cooper, Anna Bethia. BA, Yale U., 1960; JD with honors, U. Ala., 1963. Bar: Ala. 1963, D.C. 1984. Assoc. Kaye, Scholer, Fierman, Attys., N.Y.C., 1965-66; ptnr. Cooper, Mitch & Crawford, Birmingham, 1966-74; mem. 98th-102nd Congresses from 6th Dist. Ala., 1983-93. Mem. Ala. Ho. of Reps., Birmingham, 1970-74, Jefferson County Commn., 1974-82. 1st lt. U.S. Army, 1963-65. Mem. D.C. Bar Assn., Ala. Bar Assn., Birmingham Bar Assn. Democrat. Jewish. Home: 2900 Redmont Park Cir Apt 202 Birmingham AL 35205-2155 Office: US Merit Systems Protection Bd 1120 Vermont Ave NW Washington DC 20419-0001

ERENSTEIN, ALAN, emergency room nurse, medical education consultant, aeromedical specialist. Grad., Aliquippa Hosp Sch. Radiology, Pa., 1974; student, Aliquippa Hosp. Sch. Radiology, New Wilmington, Pa., 1974; AA in Gen. Studies, LPN, Beaver County C.C., Monaca, Pa., 1977, AS in Nursing, RN, 1979. RN, Fla.; registered radiologic technologist. LPN Hamot Med. Ctr., Erie, Pa., 1977-78; team leader Trauma-Neuro ICU and Stepdown Unit Allegheny Gen. Hosp., Pitts., 1979-81, staff nurse Emergency Room, 1981; flight nurse LifeWATCH HCA Wesley Med. Ctr., Wichita, Kans., 1981-91, contigency and float pool, 1991-92, hyperbaric nurse, 1991-92; ER nurse, relief charge nurse, clin. coord., team leader JFK Med. Ctr., Atlantis, Fla., 1992-95; aeromed. specialist Bizjet Air Ambulance, West Palm Beach, Fla., 1994-95; med. edn. cons. Med. Edn. Cons. Am., Tampa, 1994—; with disaster team Cutler Ridge (Fla.) Field Hosp., 1992; response team Kans. Tornado Wesley Med. Ctr., Wichita, 1991; emergency rm./trauma nurse DelRay Med. Ctr., 1995—; flight nurse Flight Nurse Air Ambulance Profl., Inc., Ft. Lauderdale, Fla., 1996—; paramedic clin. coord. Hutchinson (Kans.) C.C., 1989; skills lab coord. Advanced Trauma Life Support Course, HCA Wesley Med. Ctr., Wichita, 1989-92; lectr. various med. ctrs., univs. and confs. Author: Trauma in Pregnancy, 1990; co-author: LifeWATCH Transport Manual, 1988; author (Soc. Trauma Nursing course) Trauma Nursing: From Resuscitation through Rehabilitation, Module: The Pregnant Trauma Patient, 1996. Mem. Soc. Trauma Nurses, Nat. Flight Nurses Assn. Home: 308 Island Shores Dr West Palm Beach FL 33413-2105 Office: Delray Med Ctr 5352 Linton Blvd Delray Beach FL 33484

ERICKSON, JOY MARILYN, artist, graphic designer, inventor, photographer; b. Princeton, Ill., June 18, 1932; d. Albert Otto and Hirrel Viola (Young) E.; m. Gerald Eugene Miller, Aug. 13, 1950 (div. Oct. 1982); children: Patricia Blackburn, Pamela Miskawitz, Paula Eberspacher; m. George Leon Gannett, Nov. 25, 1989. Student, No. Ill. U., Kennedy Sch. Art; ind. study, Jung Inst., Kusnacht, Switzerland, Cuanahuac (Mex.) Inst. One-woman shows include Ch. of the Brethren Gen. Offices, Elgin, Ill., 1978, Manchester Coll., North Manchester, Ind., 1981, Cannon Office Bldg., Washington, 1982, Nat. 4-H Ctr., Washington, 1982, Humphrey Building, Washington, 1982, New Windsor Internat. Svc. Ctr., Md., 1983, Immanuel Congrl. Ch., Hartford, 1983, Ark. Coll., Little Rock, 1983, Weinberg Ctr. for Arts, Frederick, Md., 1984, Mt. Calvary Episcopal Ch., Camp Hill, Pa., 1986, Cedar Lane Unitarian Ch., Bethesda, Md., 1988, Tucker Anthony and R. L. Day Gallery, Princeton, N.J., 1989, Ctrl. Nat. Bank Sarasota, Fla., 1992, Unitarian Universalist Ch. Sarasota, 1993, 95, 96, Artwerx, Sarasota, 1994; exhibited in group shows at Chgo. and Vicinity Festival Religious Art, Barrington, Ill., 1973, Rockford (Ill.) Art Assn., 1975, Phidian Art Assn., Dixon, Ill., 1978-82, Nat. Assn. Women Artists, N.Y.C., 1985, 86, 87, Nat. Assn. Womens Artist, Fla., 1995, Tatem Art Ctr., Hood Coll., Frederick, Md., 1986, Rochester (N.Y.) Mus. and Sci. Ctr., 1990, Portland (Oreg.) Conv. Ctr., 1991, State of the Art '93, Boston, 1993, Artwerx Ctr., Sarasota, 1994; represented in numerous pub. and pvt. collections; author, illustrator: In Straw and Story, 1978, revised reprint, 1983; illustrator and book designer: A is for Angels, 1978; illustrator: Book of Worship, 1978; cover illustrator and book designer: jubilee, 1991; contbr. numerous articles to profl. mags. and newspapers; subject of numerous articles; TV interviews PBS Money Watch, 1988, ESPN Small Business Report, 1989. Co-founder, exec. officer Nat. Assn. Arts in the Ch. of the Brethren, 1971-82; cons. for visual arts and conf. environment Ch. of the Brethren Gen. Bd., Elgin, Ill., 1971-84; co-chair Cedar Lane Auction of Fine Art, Bethesda, Md., 1987; visual art cons., designer Families 2000 Conf., Nat. Coun. Chs. of Christ, Chgo., 1991; designer visual art and conf. environment Ctr. for Prevention of Sexual and Domestic Violence, Chgo., 1993; illustrator, designer Ch. Women United, N.Y.C., 1984-93. Recipient Best of Show award Phidian Art Assn., 1979, 80, hon. menion, 1981, Walgreen purchase award, 1982; DeRose Hinkhouse Award of Excellence, Nat. Religious Pub. Rels. Coun., Inc., 1984. Mem. Sarasota Art Assn., Nat. Assn. Women Artists, Nat. Assn. Casein and Acrylic Painters, N.Y. Assn. Women Artists, Fla. Assn. Women Artists (Award of Distinction 1995), John and Mable Ringling Mus. of Art Found. Unitarian Universalist. Home: 3652 Allenwood St Sarasota FL 34232-1202

ERICKSON, WAYNE KENNETH, English language educator; b. New Haven, Feb. 12, 1951; s. Donald Clifford and Valerie Anne (Morawski) E.; m. Martha Carolyn Alexander, Aug. 14, 1971 (div. Mar. 1987); children: Caitlin, Brett, Ruth. BA, So. Conn. State U., 1976, MA, 1977; PhD, U. N.Mex., 1982. Lectr. in English U. N.Mex., Albuquerque, 1982-84; from instr. English to asst. prof. English Ga. State U., Atlanta, 1984—. Author: Mapping the Faerie Queene, 1996; contbr. articles to profl. publs. NEH fellow, 1989. Mem. MLA, Spenser Soc., Southeastern Renaissance Conf. Home: 4027 Stoneview Cir Stone Mountain GA 30083 Office: Ga State U Univ Plz Atlanta GA 30303

ERICSON, PHYLLIS JANE, psychologist, psychotherapist, consultant; b. Ft. Worth, Aug. 16, 1947; d. John H. and Charlotte Marie (Turner) E.; divorced; children: Colleen Nichole Murphy Pass, Sean Matthew Murphy Pass. B. Gen. Studies in Bus. Mgmt. and Advt., U. Tex., Arlington, 1981; MA in Psychology and Psychotherapy, Antioch U., 1990; Grad. in Psychology, Union Inst., Cin., 1995. Registered and cert. hypnotist, Calif.; cert. chem. dependency counselor, Tex.; lic. profl. counselor, marriage and family therapist, chem. dependency counselor, Tex.; cert. nat. and neurolinguist programming master strategist. Clk.-typist Gen. Dynamics Corp., Ft. Worth, 1965-69; counselor Snelling & Snelling Pers., Ft. Worth, 1970-72; account exec. Ft. Worth Star Telegram, 1972-79; v.p., prin. Ericson Assocs., Inc., Hurst, Tex., 1979-83; account exec. L.A.Times, Times Mirror Corp., 1983; nat. advt. dir. Baker Comm., Beverly Hills, Calif., 1984; owner, prin., builder GE Rehabs, Ft. Worth, 1984-86; counselor Comprehensive Counseling (later Ctrl. Psychol. Svcs.), Hurst, 1988-91; dir., counselor, cons., awareness counseling of DFW Ctrl. Psychol. Svcs., St. Marteen, Ft. Lauderdale, Fla., 1988—; counselor J. Marszalek & Assoc., Dallas, 1984-87, Wynrose Outpatient Program, Arlington, Tex., 1988-89, HCA Richland Hosp., North Richland Hills, Tex., 1988-89; crisis intervention counselor Suicide and Crisis Ctr., Dallas, 1987-88; pvt. practice Ctr. for Counseling Devel. Svcs., Ft. Worth, 1987-88; group facilitator, clin. cons. Bedford Meadows Hosp., 1989-91; instr. psychology dept. Tex. Wesleyan U., 1989; mem. allied staff, group facilitator Charter Hosp.-Grapevine, Tex., 1991-92. Mem. ACA, Am. Assn. for Group Counseling, Nat. Assn. Alcohol and Drug Abuse Counselors, Tex. Assn. Alcohol and Drug Abuse Counselors, Internat. Soc. for Study Multiple Personality Disorders, North Tex. Assn. for Study Multiple Personality Disorders. Office: Ctrl Psychol Svcs PO Box 491938 Fort Lauderdale FL 33349

ERICSON, RUTH ANN, psychiatrist; b. Assaria, Kans., May 15; d. William Albert and Anna Mathilda (Almquist) E. Student, So. Meth. U., 1945-47; BS, Bethany Coll.; MD, U. Tex., 1951. Intern, Calif. Hosp., L.A., 1951-52; resident in psychiatry U. Tex. Med. Br., Galveston, 1952-55; psychiatrist Child Guidance Clinic, Dallas, 1955-63; clin. instr. Southwestern Med. Sch., Dallas, 1955-72; practice medicine specializing in psychiatry, Dallas, 1955—; cons. Dallas Intertribal Coun. Clinic, 1974-81, Dallas Ind. Sch. Dist., U.S. Army, Welfare Dept., Tribal Concerns, Alcoholism, Adv. Bd. Intertribal Coun. Fellow Am. Geriatrics Assn., Royal Soc. Medicine; mem. So. Med. Assn. (life), Tex. Med. Assn. (life), Dallas Med. Assns. (life), Am. Psychiat. Assn. (life), Tex. Psychiat. Assn., North Tex. Psychiat. Assn., Am. Med. Women's Assn., Dallas Area Women Psychiatrists, Alumni Assn. U. Tex. (Med. Br.), Navy League (life), Air Force Assn., Tex. Archaeol. Soc. (life mem.), Dallas Archaeol. Soc. (hon. life mem., pres. 1972-73, 82-84, 89-91, archival rschr.), South Tex. Archaeol. Soc., Tarrant County Archeol. Soc., El Paso Archeol. Soc., N.Mex. Archaeol. Soc., Paleopathology Soc., Internat. Psychogeriatric Assn. (Famous Women of the 20th Century), Alpha Omega Alpha, Delta Psi Omega, Alpha Psi Omega, Pi Gamma Mu, Lambda Sigma, Alpha Epsilon Iota, Mu Delta. Lutheran. Home: 4007 Shady Hill Dr Dallas TX 75229-2844 Office: 3026 Mockingbird Ln # 101 Dallas TX 75205-2323

ERINAKES, JANET LEVERNIE, health consulting company owner; b. East Greenwich, R.I., June 15, 1940; d. Norman Samuel and Doris Levernie (Essex) Kettelle; m. Dennis C. Erinakes, June 9, 1962; children: David, Michael. Diploma, Roger Williams Gen. Hosp., Providence, R.I., 1961; student, U. Maine, Pa. State U.; postgrad., Kennedy Western U. RN, Tex.,

R.I. Asst. head nurse med./surg. Roger Williams Gen. Hosp., Providence, 1961; head nurse pediatrics Kent County Meml. Hosp., Warwick, R.I., 1961-62; asst. head nurse pediatrics Eastern Maine Med. Ctr., Bangor, 1962-65; Lamaze instr. maternal and child health Bangor, 1965-68; Lamaze instr., tchr. maternal and child health State College, Pa., 1974-75; office nurse, surg. asst. Manuel Lagon, M.D., Fort Worth, Tex., 1982-83; from staff nurse to charge nurse dialysis unit Tarrant County Nephrology Ctr., Fort Worth; from asst. head nurse to interim head nurse dept. home dialysis dept. Tarrant County Nephrology Ctr., Ft. Worth, 1990; clin. supr. home health Total Home Health Svcs., Inc., Fort Worth, 1989-90; asst. adminstr. Total Home Health Svcs., Inc., Ft. Worth, 1990-95; owner, pres. Diversified Health Consultants, Inc., Burleson, Tex., 1995—; Lamaze instr., State College, Pa., 1974-75. Office: 228 NE Wilshire Blvd Ste H Burleson TX 76028

ERMER, JAMES, transportation company executive; b. Cleve., Sept. 26, 1942; s. John James and Dorthy (Lourison) E.; m. Deanna Jean Foltz, Jan. 6, 1968; children—Halle, Ashley. B.S., Ohio U., 1964; postgrad., Cleve. State U. Analyst Chessie System, Cleve., 1967-74; auditor Chessie System, Balt., 1974-76, sr. asst. treas., 1976-80; asst. v.p., treas. CSX, Richmond, Va., 1980-83, v.p., treas., 1983-85; sr. v.p. fin. CSX, Richmond, 1985—; lectr. in field; trustee Nations Fund Trust; bd. dirs. Lawyers Title Corp. Methodist. Clubs: Brandermill Country (Va.), Commonwealth (Richmond), The Foundry (Va.), Union League Club (N.Y.C.), The Foundary (Va.). Home: 13705 Hickory Nut Pt Midlothian VA 23112-4939 Office: CSX Corp 901 E Cary St Richmond VA 23219-4057

ERNSBERGER, FRED MARTIN, retired materials scientist; b. Ada, Ohio, Sept. 20, 1919; 4 children. AB, Ohio Northern U., 1941; PhD in Phys. Chemistry, Ohio State U., 1946. Rsch. chemist U.S. Naval Ordnance Test Sta., 1947-54, S.W. Rsch. Inst., 1954-56, Mellon Inst. of Indsl. Rsch., 1957; rsch. chemist Glass Rsch. Ctr. PPG Industries, Inc., 1958-82; ret., 1982; adj. prof. dept. material sci. and engring. U. Fla., Gainesville, 1982—; Teltech cons., 1982—. Recipient IR-100 award, 1981, Scholes award, 1989. Fellow Am. Ceramic Soc. (Frank Forrest award 1964, Toledo Glass and Ceramic award 1970, G.W. Morey award 1974, Albert Victor Bleininger award 1993); mem. Am. Chem. Soc., Am. Ceramic Soc. Home and Office: 1325 NW 10th Ave Gainesville FL 32605-5303

ERNST, CARL WILLIAM, religious studies educator, researcher; b. L.A., Sept. 8, 1950; s. William Rufus and Barbara Mae (Brown) E.; m. Judith Lynne Rouse, June 30, 1974; children: Sophia Lilian, Teresa Elinor. AB with honors, Stanford U., 1973; PhD, Harvard U., 1981. Asst. prof. religion Pomona Coll., Claremont, Calif., 1981-87, assoc. prof. religion, 1987-92, chair dept. religion, 1991-92; prof. religious studies U. N.C., Chapel Hill, 1992—, chair dept. religious studies, 1995—; mem. adv. bd. Pakistan Arts Coun., Pacific Asia Mus., Pasadena, Calif., 1990— grant proposal reviewer NEH, 1990—; mem. adv. bd. Ackland Art Mus., Chapel Hill, 1995—. Author: Words of Ecstasy in Sufism, 1984, Eternal Garden: Mysticism, History and Politics at a South Asian Sufi Center, 1992, Ruzbihan Baqli: Mysticism and the Rhetoric of Sainthood in Persian Sufism, 1996; assoc. editor: (with G.M. Smith) Manifestations of Sainthood in Islam, 1993. Recipient Fulbright Rsch. fellowship Coun. for Internat. Exch. of Schs., India, 1978-79, Pakistan, 1986, Translation grant NEH, 1989-90, Summer Rsch. grant NEH, 1993, Sr. Rsch. fellowship Am. Inst. Indian Studies, India, 1981. Mem. Am. Acad. Religion, Mid. East Studies Assn., Inst. for Ctrl. and W. Asian Studies, U. Karachi (life), Am. Inst. Pakistan Studies (exec. com. 1994—, trustee), Triangle S. Asia Consortium (exec. com. 1992—). Office: Univ NC Dept Religious Studies Chapel Hill NC 27599-3225

ERNST, DAVID JOHN, physicist, educator; b. St. Paul, May 29, 1943; s. Ben Edward and Grace Elizabeth (Peterson) E.; m. Vicki Lynn Monsees, Sept. 9, 1967; children: David Miguel, Carmen Linnea. SB, MIT, 1965, PhD, 1970. Asst. prof., prof. Centro de Investigacion y de Estudios Avanzados del I.P.N., Mexico City, 1970-71; rsch. assoc., instr. Case Western Res. U., Cleve., 1972-75; asst. prof. physics Tex. A&M U., College Station, 1975-80, assoc. prof., 1980-85, prof., 1985-93; assoc. dir. Ctr. for Theoretical Physics, College Station, 1988-93; interim dir. Internat. Inst. for Theoretical Physics Tex. A&M U., College Station, 1990-93; Deutsches Forschungsgemeinschaft prof. U. Frankfurt (Fed. Republic Germany), 1988-93; prof. Vanderbilt U., Nashville, 1992—, chair physics and astronomy, 1992-95, assoc. dean coll. arts & scis., 1995—; vis. rsch. scientist Los Alamos (N.Mex.) Nat. Lab., 1974-85, cons., 1985—; cons. Oak Ridge (Tenn.) Nat. Lab., 1983—; faculty affiliate Oak Ridge Assoc. US, 1983—; program adv. com. Los Alamos Meson Physics Facility, chmn. PION subcom., 1985-89; organizing com., Am. rep. Sino-Am. Spring Sch. on Medium and High-energy Nuclear Physics, Taipei, Republic of China, 1990, Internat. Conf. on Medium and High-Energy Nuclear Physics, Taipei, 1990, Mesons and Nuclei at Intermediate Energies and Workshop on Mesons in the Few-Body Systems, Dubna, Russia, 1994; bd. dirs. Southeast Univs. Rsch. Assn.; numerous other profl. activities. Editor: Progress in Particle Physics, 1991, Progress in Nuclear Physics, 1991; contbr. articles to Phys. Rev., others. Recipient Disting. Teaching award Assn. Former Students Tex. A&M U., 1983; William Barton Rogers scholar; NSF fellow. Fellow Am. Phys. Soc. (program com., nuclear divsn. 1983-85), Los Alamos Meson Physics Facility Users Group Inc. (program adv. com., chmn. bd. dirs. 1991); dir. Pan-Am. Assn. Physics, 1992—), Sigma Xi. Office: Dept Physics and Astronomy Vanderbilt Hospital Nashville TN 37232

ERNST, JAMES E., company executive; b. 1951. Degree in bus. adminstrn. and acctg., U. Minn., 1975. CPA. With Mc Gladry & Pullen CPA, Davenport, Iowa, 1976-82; gen. svc. ptnr. Mc Gladry & Pullen CPA, Davenport, 1982, sr. gen. svc. ptnr. Alter Cos. accounts, 1987, pres., CFO gaming related entities for Goldstein family, 1991, CFO Alter Cos. entities, 1991; pres. Riverboat Corp. Miss., Biloxi. Office: Riverboat Corp Miss 151 Beach Blvd Biloxi MS 39530-4708

ERNST BOGDAN, JANET LEE, interior designer; b. Winston-Salem, N.C., Apr. 16, 1955; d. William Lee Ernst and Marie Keith (Shouse) Snyder; m. Ivica Bodgan, Aug. 19, 1994; 1 child, Ivana Bogdan. BS in Home Econs., Interior Design, U. N.C., Greensboro, 1977. Instr. arts and crafts Craft Showcase, Winston-Salem, 1977-78; display design The Ltd., Inc., N.C. and S.C., 1978-79; designer ind. retail stores Winston-Salem, 1977-81; head design dept. Butler Enterprises, Inc., Winston-Salem, 1981-86; design prin. Carolina Contract Design, Winston-Salem, 1986—; pres. Triad Design Concepts, Inc., Winston-Salem and Greensboro, 1988-90; cons. design, catalog line drawings, photography contract furniture and lighting mfrs., N.C. and Ga.; mentor student interns U. N.C., Greensboro, 1983-84, 87-93; propr. Carolina Carpet Svcs., 1992. Vol. Humane Soc., Winston-Salem, 1977-78; bd. dirs. Jamestowne Homeowners Assn., 1991-94, treas., 1993, pres., 1994; invited participant citizen amb. program Comml. Interior Design Del. to People's Republic of China. Mem. Inst. Bus. Designers (affiliate, ednl. com. 1987), Nat. Trust Hist. Preservation., Internat. Interior Design Assn. (assoc.). Republican. Moravian. Office: Carolina Contract Design The Keystone 1386 Westgate Center Dr Ste F Winston Salem NC 27103-2948

ERO, MORGAN ZAN, political scientist, educator; b. Benin, Edo, Nigeria, Dec. 25, 1950; s. Paul and Osarenkhoe E.; children: Morgan Jr., Ivie, Isi. BS, Jackson State U., 1978, MA, 1980; PhD, Atlanta U., 1987. Reporter, sub editor Nigerian TV, Benin City, Nigeria, 1973-75; NYSP U. Benin, 1982-83; lectr. Ogun State U., Ago-Iwoye, Nigeria, 1983-85; assoc. prof., coord. pub. adminstrn. program Miss. Valley State U., Itta Bena, 1989—. Mentor Career Beginning, Miss. Valley State U., 1992—, adv. bd. mem., 1993—, speaker Option Program, 1992—, v.p. faculty senate, 1993; adv. bd. mem. Sta-Home Health, Grenwood, Miss., 1994—. Named Faculty of the Yr., State of Miss., 1993. Mem. Am. Polit. Sci. Assn. (adv. coun. 1993-96), Nat. Assn. Black Polit. Scientists, The Atlantic Coun. (faculty assn. 1991). Office: Miss Valley State U Dept Social Sci Itta Bena MS 38941

ERRICKSON, BARBARA BAUER, electronic equipment company executive; b. Pitts., Apr. 5, 1944; d. Edward Ewing Bauer and Margaret J. McConnell; m. James Jay Burcham, June 30, 1966 (div. May 1972); children: James Jay II, Linda Lee; m. William Newel Errickson, Apr. 9, 1976 (div. Feb. 1987). BA, U. Ill., 1966; MBA, So. Meth. U., 1981. Programming trainee Allstate Ins. Co., Northbrook, Ill., 1973; programmer, team leader Motorola, Inc., Chgo., 1974-78; supr. systems Tex. Instruments, Dallas, 1978-81, product line mgr. worldwide shipping systems, 1981-83, product line mgr. shipping, inventory systems, 1983-84, mgr. mktg. info. systems, 1985, mgr. benefit systems, 1986-89, mgr. S.W. case cons. and edn., 1990-92, western area advanced practices mgr., 1992—; dir., billing and software developer Spring Park Home Owners, Garland-Richardson, Tex., 1984—, pres. and chmn. fin., 1985, v.p. legal, 1986. Active Dallas Women's Ctr., 1984—; mem. bus. adv. council So. Meth U. Bus. Adv. Program; mem. bus. adv. coun. El Centro Coll. Rehab. for Physically Challenged Through Data Processing, 1987—; chmn. control and adminstrn./mktg. United Way, 1986-89. Recipient Women in Leadership cert. YWCA Met. Chgo., 1977. Mem. Am. Mgmt. Assn., Am. Women in Computing (bd. dirs. 1987—, pres. 1989), Community Assns. Inst., So. Meth. U. MBA Soc., Spring Park Racquet Club, Beta Gamma Sigma. Republican. Presbyterian. Home: 6702 Lake Shore Dr Garland TX 75044-2044 Office: Tex Instruments Inc PO Box 869305 6620 Chase Oaks Blvd Plano TX 75086

ERSEK, GREGORY JOSEPH MARK, lawyer, business administrator; b. Cleve., Aug. 30, 1956; s. Joseph Francis and Mary H. (Hurchanik) E. AB, Columbia U., 1977; MBA, U. Pa., 1979; JD, U. Fla., 1984. Bar: Fla. 1986, U.S. Dist. Ct. (so. dist.) Fla. 1987. Cons. fin. valuation Am. Appraisal Co., Princeton, N.J., 1979-80; mgr. import-export Marie L. Veslie Co., Coral Gables, Fla., 1980-85; assoc. Lunny, Tucker, Karns & Brescher, Ft. Lauderdale, Fla., 1986; dir. legal dept. Horizons Rsch. Labs. Inc., Ft. Lauderdale, 1986-89, sr. corp. planner, 1988-89; gen. counsel Unisco Corp., Ft. Lauderdale, 1989-93, TRICORD Corp., Ft. Lauderdale, 1990-93, Irish Times, Inc., Ft. Lauderdale, 1993—; dir. corp. fin. dept. & sr. corp. counsel Canton Fin. Svcs. Corp., subs. Cyber Am. Corp., Salt Lake City, 1995—; sec.-treas., dir. Sorkar Group, Inc., Ft. Lauderdale, 1987-89; CEO Am. CompuShopper, Inc., 1989—; with legal dept. Pfizer Inc., N.Y.C., 1983; co-founder, mgr. Poland/U.S. Trade and Mktg. Consortium, 1989—; mem. Philip C. Jessup Internat. Moot Ct. team, 1983. Editor Medscanner, med. industry newsletter, 1987-89. Mem. venture coun. forum. Mem. Fla. Bar Assn., Utah Bar (securities sect.), Nat. Assn. Securities Dealers (nat. arbitration com.), Coun. on Fgn. Rels. (local com.), Wharton Club South Fla. Republican. Episcopalian. Home: 17820 NW 18th Ave Miami FL 33056-4949 Office: 268 W 400 S Ste 300 Salt Lake City UT 84101-1855

ERVIN, SAMUEL JAMES, III, federal judge; b. Morganton, N.C., Mar. 2, 1926; s. Sam Ervin. B.S., Davidson Coll., 1948; LL.B., Harvard U., 1951. Bar: N.C. Pvt. practice law Morganton, 1952-57; solicitor Burke County (N.C.) Criminal Ct., 1954-56; mem. firm Patton, Ervin & Starnes and predecessors, Morganton, 1957-67; judge Superior Ct. 25th Jud. Dist. N.C., 1967-80; judge U.S. Ct. Appeals (4th cir.), Morganton, N.C., 1980-89, 96—, chief judge, 1989-96. Pres. Davidson Coll. Nat. Alumni Assn., 1973-74; trustee Davidson Coll., 1982-94, Grace Hosp., Inc., 1992—. Named Young Man of Yr. Morganton Jaycees, 1954. Office: US Ct Appeals PO Drawer 1488 Morganton NC 28680-1488

ERWIN, GOODLOE Y., physician, land company executive; b. Athens, Ga., June 14, 1919; s. Howell Cobb and Llucy Gratten (Yancey) E.; m. Patricia Graham, Sept. 27, 1947; children: Alexander Wales, Charles Graham, Leslie Erwin Moose, Catharine. BS in Chemistry, U. Ga., 1940; MD, Emory U., 1943. Diplomate Am. Bd. Internal Medicine. Intern Grady Meml. Hosp., Atlanta, 1944; resident in medicine VA Hosp., Salt Lake City, 1947-48; pvt. practice internal medicine St. Marys Hosp., Athens Ctrl. Hosp., 1948-87; pres. Erwin Land Co., Athens, 1987—; dir. respiratory therapy dept. Athens Gen. Hosp., 1963-75, dir. CCU, 1965-70. Pres. Athens Hist. Soc., 1992-94; bd. dirs. Athens Cmty. Chest, 1950-60. 1st lt. M.C., U.S. Army, 1944-46, ETO. Fellow Am. Coll. Chest Physicians, Am. Coll. Cardiology; mem. Ga. Heart Assn. (pres. 1957-58, Disting. Svc. award 1964), Ga. Lung Assn. (pres. 1973-74), Ga. Soc. Internal Medicine (pres.), Phi Beta Kappa, Alpha Omega Alpha. Baptist. Home: 354 Milledge Cir Athens GA 30606

ERWIN, JOHN SEYMOUR, writer, editor, composer; b. Vicksburg, Miss., Aug. 2, 1911; s. Victor Flournoy and Margaret Preston (McNeily) E.; m. Caterina Maria di St. Vigne, Dec. 31, 1929; 1 child, Giovanni di St. Vigne. Student Sch. Contemporary Arts and Crafts, 1929-31, Columbia U., 1939-40; student of Alexander Siloti, 1934, of Serge Rachmaninoff, 1938. Feature editor The Am. mag., N.Y.C., 1954-56; mus. editor World and Its Peoples, Greystone Press, N.Y.C., 1959-61; co-founding editor SHOW mag., N.Y.C., 1962-63; sr. editor Natural History mag., N.Y.C., 1964-66; ency. project editor The Reader's Digest, N.Y.C., 1966-67; med. editor Media Medica, N.Y.C., 1968-70; contbr. Ency. Americana. Served with RCAF, 1940-44. Decorated George VI medal, Vol. Service medal; Tiffany Found. fellow, 1934-35; Gloucester Sch. fellow, 1935. Mem. Authors Guild. Episcopalian. Author: Like Some Green Laurel: The Life and Letters of Margaret Johnson Erwin, 1821-1863, 1981; composer: The Trojan Women Suite, 1940; Sappho in Levkas, 1942; Bermuda Sketches, 1979; Six Nocturnes, 1991.

ERWIN, RICHARD CANNON, federal judge; b. McDowell County, N.C., Aug. 23, 1923; s. John Adam and Flora (Cannon) E.; m. Demerice Whitley, Aug. 25, 1946; children: Richard Cannon, Jr., Aurelia Whitley. BA, Johnson C. Smith U., 1947; LLB, Howard U., 1951; LLD, Pfeiffer Coll., 1980, Johnson C. Smith U., 1981. Bar: N.C. 1951, U.S. Supreme Ct. 1974. Practice law Winston-Salem, N.C., 1951-77; judge N.C. Ct. Appeals, 1978; judge U.S. Dist. Ct. (mid. dist.) N.C., 1980-88, chief judge, 1988-92, sr. judge, 1992—; rep. N.C. Gen. Assembly, chmn. hwy. safety com.; mem. law bd. vis. Wake Forest U., 1984—. Trustee Forsyth County Legal Aid Soc., Amos Cottage, Inc.; chmn. bd. trustees Bennett Coll.; bd. dirs. N.C. 4-H Devel. Fund, Inc.; bd. visitors Div. Sch., Duke U.; trustee Children's Home, Winston-Salem; mem. steering com. Winston-Salem Found.; bd. dirs. United Fund; bd. dirs., pres. Citizens Coalition Forsyth County and Anderson High Sch., PTA; mem. N.C. Bd. Edn., 1971-77, N.C. State Library Bd. Trustees, 1968-69; mem., chmn. personnel com. Winston-Salem/Forsyth County Sch. Bd.; chmn. bd. trustees St. Paul United Methodist Ch. Mem. N.C. Bar Assn. (v.p. 1983-84), N.C. Assn. Black Lawyers, Forsyth County Bar Assn. (pres.), N.C. State Bar. Office: US Dist Ct 223-A Federal Bldg 251 N Main St Winston Salem NC 27101-3984

ERWIN, SCOTT, sporting company executive. Pres. Comty. Golf. Address: 8787 Park Ln Dallas TX 75231

ERWIN, SHELIA KAYE, newspaper publisher; b. Knoxville, Tenn., Feb. 5, 1946; d. Melton James Jr. and Ortha Lee (Phillips) Robbins; m. James Ray Erwin, June 23, 1995. BS, Tenn. Tech. U., 1970. Social worker Scott County Hosp., Oneida, Tenn., 1970-73; pub. Scott County News, Oneida, 1973—. Mem. Oneida Bus. and Profl. Club, Oneida C. of C. (ladies divsn.). Baptist.

ERWIN, VAL L., business executive. Pres. Internat. Compliance Corp., Argyle, Tex. Office: Internat Compliance Corp 1911 E Jeter Rd Argyle TX 76226-9401

ESCARRAZ, ENRIQUE, III, lawyer; b. Evergreen Park, Ill., Aug. 30, 1944; s. Enrique Jr. and Mary Ellen (Bandy) E.; children from previous marriage; Erin Christine, Martina Mary; m. Patricia Jane Escarraz; children: Sarah Ellen, James Lee, Jason F. BA, U. Fla., 1966, JD, 1968. Bar: Fla. 1969, U.S. Dist. Ct. (so. and mid. dists.) Fla. 1969, U.S. Ct. Appeals (5th cir.) 1971, U.S. Ct. Appeals (11th cir.) 1981. VISTA atty. Community Legal Counsel, Chgo., 1968-69; mng. atty. Fla. Rural Legal Services, Ft. Myers, 1969-71; pvt. practice law St. Petersburg, Fla., 1971-82, 85-87, 88—; ptnr. Anderson & Escarraz, St. Petersburg, 1982-85; asst. gen. counsel U. South Fla., 1987-88; assoc. James L. Eskald Law Office, Largo, Fla., 1988; part-time atty. Pub. Defender's Office Fla. 6th Cir., St. Petersburg, 1973-74; bd. dirs. Gulf Coast Legal Svcs., Inc., 1989—, pres., 1994-96. Vol. Cmty. Law Prog., Inc.; coord. James B. Sanderlin for Judge, Pinellas County, Fla., 1972-76; mem. ACLU Legal Panel, St. Petersburg, 1972—; cooperating atty. NAACP Legal Panel, St. Petersburg, 1972—; cooperating atty. NAACP Legal Def. Edn. Funds, Inc., N.Y.C., 1973—; pres. Creative Care, Inc., Clearwater, Fla., 1974-80; mem. allocations com. United Way, Pinellas County, 1976, 1978-81; pres., treas. Cmty. Youth Svcs., Inc., St. Petersburg, 1977-82; co-chmn. Blue Ribbon Com. Pinellas County Dem. Exec. Com., 1977-82; mem. Fla. HRS Dist. V Adv. Coun., Pinellas County, 1982, St. Petersburg Human Rels. Rev. Bd., 1984, 90—, St. Petersburg Adult Cmty. Band, 1989—, Greater St. Petersburg Second Time Around Marching Band, 1990-92; mem. adv. bd. Jacquelyn Elvera Hodges Johnson Fund, 1990—. Mem. ABA, Assn. Trial Lawyers Am., Pinellas County Trial Lawyers Assn., St. Petersburg Bar Assn. (pro bono com. 1988, 95—), Bayshore Runners Club, Suncoast Runners Club, Greater Pinellas County Dem. Club (sec. or treas. 1989—), USA Track & Field. Office: 2121 5th Ave N Saint Petersburg FL 33713-8013 also: PO Box 847 Saint Petersburg FL 33731-0847

ESCHBACH, JESSE ERNEST, federal judge; b. Warsaw, Ind., Oct. 26, 1920; S. Jesse Ernest and Mary W. (Stout) E.; m. Sara Ann Walker, Mar. 15, 1947; children: Jesse Ernest III, Virginia. BS, Ind. U., 1943, JD with distinction, 1949, LLD (hon.), 1986. Bar: Ind. 1949. Ptnr. Graham, Rasor, Eschbach & Harris, Warsaw, 1949-62; city atty. Warsaw, 1952-53; dep. pros. atty. 54th Jud. Circuit Ct. Ind., 1952-1954; judge U.S. Dist. Ct. Ind., 1962-81; chief judge judge U.S. Dist. Ct. Ind., 1974-81; judge U.S. Ct. Appeals (7th cir.), W. Palm Beach, Fla., 1981-85, sr. judge, 1985—; Pres. Endicott Church Furniture, Inc., 1960-62; sec., gen. counsel Dalton Foundries, Inc., 1957-62. Editorial staff: Ind. Law Jour, 1947-49. Trustee Ind. U., 1965-70. Served with USNR, 1943-46. Hastings scholar, 1949; Recipient U.S. Law Week award, 1949. Mem. U.S. C. of C. (labor relations com. 1960-62), Warsaw C. of C. (pres. 1955-56), Nat. Assn. Furniture Mfrs. (dir. 1962), Ind. Mfrs. Assn. (dir. 1962), ABA, Ind. Bar Assn. (bd. mgrs. 1953-54, ho. dels. 1950-60), Fed. Bar Assn., Am. Judicature Soc., Order of Coif. Presbyn. Club: Rotarian (pres. Warsaw 1956-57). Home: 11709 N Lake Dr Boynton Beach FL 33436-5518 Office: US Ct Appeals 7th Cir 253 US Courthouse 701 Clematis St West Palm Beach FL 33401-5101

ESCHETE, MARY LOUISE, internist; b. Houma, La., Feb. 8, 1949; d. Marshall John and Louise Esther (Davis) E.; m. Lorphy Joseph Bourque, July 7, 1979. BS, La. State U., 1970; MD, La. State U. Med. Ctr., Shreveport, 1974. Diplomate, Am. Bd. Internal Medicine. Resident in internal medicine La. State U. Med. Ctr., Shreveport, 1974-77; staff instr. La. State U. Med. Ctr., 1979, fellow in infectious disease, 1979; pvt. practice Houma, 1980-83; staff, dept. internal medicine South La. Med. Assocs., Houma, 1983—; chmn. infection control, Terrebonne Gen. Hosp., 1981—, South La. Med. Ctr., 1983—. Contbr. articles to med. jours. Bd. dirs. Houma Battered Women's Shelter, 1983-87, Houma YWCA, 1987-94; mem. Roche Nat. AIDS Adv. Bd., 1993; Triparish vol. activist, 1994. Named Citizen of Yr. Regional and State Social Workers, 1992. Mem. ACP, AAAS, AMA, Infectious Disease Soc., Am. Soc. Microbiology, So. Med. Assn. (grantee 1978), N.Y. Acad. Sci., La. State Med. Soc., Terrebonne Parish Med. Soc. (sec. 1982-83, v.p. 1993-94, pres. 1994-95), Krewe of Hyachinthians (pres. 1989-90, 94-95, bd. dirs. 1990-96), Houma Jr. Women's Club (reporter 1988-89, rec. sec. 1989—, pres.-elect 1991-93, pres. 1993-95), Alpha Epsilon Delta. Democrat. Roman Catholic. Home: 3387 Little Bayou Black Dr Houma LA 70360-2840 Office: South La Med Ctr 1978 Industrial Blvd Houma LA 70363-7055

ESKEW, RUSSELL CLARK, programmer; b. Oklahoma City, Jan. 24, 1950; s. Patrick Fredrick and Helen (Brown) E. Student, U. Tex., 1968-83; tech., U.S. Army Electronics, 1973. Pvt. practice programmer Austin, 1983—. Author: (jour.) Undergrad Math, 1989, (computer program) SHARING, 1992. With U.S. Army, 1972-75. Recipient 2d place Dallas (Tex.) Art Show, 1965. Mem. Men's Coun. Austin, Toastmasters (cert. speaker, v.p. Tejax chpt.), Computer Supported Coop. Work. Democrat. Office: PO Box 8117 Austin TX 78713-8117

ESKIN, JIM, public affairs professional; b. Boston, July 3, 1953; s. David H. and Charlotte B. (Sheinkopf) E.; m. Leigh Hope Katz, May 23, 1987 (div. Sept. 1, 1989). BA in Urban Affairs, George Washington U., 1975. Dir. comms. Agr. Coun. Am., Washington, 1974-81, Assoc. Milk Prodrs., Inc., San Antonio, 1982-96; pvt. practice San Antonio, 1996—; bus. cons. Jr. Achievement, San Antonio, 1986-90; mem. bus. expansion task force Greater C. of C., San Antonio, 1996—. Contbr. articles to periodicals, jours. Exec. dir. San Antonio for a Major Sports Complex, 1983-89; pres. Louis D. Brandeis lodge B'nai B'rith, San Antonio, 1989-93, bd. dirs., 1993; bd. dirs. Jewish Cmty. Ctr., San Antonio, 1987—, Goodwill Industries, Southwest Cmty. Empowerment Ctr., treas., 1994—; bd. trustees Leukemia Soc., San Antonio, 1991—; mem. Bus. for Social Responsibility, 1995—. Democrat. Jewish. Home: 11851 Belair #204 San Antonio TX 78213-4858

ESPENANT, KAREN E. JEFFRIES, journalist; b. Bedford, Ind., Aug. 16, 1961; d. Willard Herschel and Kathleen (Adams) Jeffries; m. Richard Jean-Claude Espenant, June 30, 1994; children: Mary Kathleen, Patrick Michael. Editor in chief The Meter Tenn. State U., 1996-97. Pres. Ladies Aux. of the Met. Nashville Fire Dept., 1991-92; mem. Nashville Symphony Chorus, 1995. Recipient All-Am. scholar award U.S. Achievement Acad., 1995-96, Nat. Collegiate Minority Leadership award, 1995-96. Mem. Soc. of Profl. Journalist (Paul McMaster's First Amendment award 1995-96), Soc. of Broadcast Journalists, Phi Kappa Phi, Pi Delta Phi. Home: 2613 Joplin Dr Nashville TN 37210

ESPINOZA, LUIS ROLAN, rheumatologist; b. Pisco, Peru, July 3, 1943; came to U.S.A., 1969; s. Luis R. and Luz Lelia (Bernales) E.; m. Carmen G. Gonzalez, Dec. 20, 1969; children: Luis M., Gabriela M. MD, Cayetano Heredia, Lima, Peru, 1969. Intern Jersey City (N.J.) Med. Ctr., 1969-70; resident Washington U., St. Louis, 1970-72, rheumatology fellow, 1972-73; rheumatology fellow McGill U., Montreal, Can., 1973-74, asst. prof., 1976-78; immunology fellow The Rockefeller U., N.Y.C., 1974-76; assoc. prof. U. South Fla., Tampa, 1978-83, prof. medicine, 1983-90; prof. medicine La. State U. Sch. Medicine, New Orleans, 1991—, also chief rheumatology sect. Editor: Infection in the Rheumatic Diseases, 1988, Psoriatic Arthritis, 1985, Immun Complexes, 1983; guest editor Infectious Arthritis Rheumatic Disease Clin. N. Am., 1993. Chmn. Lupus Found. Am., Tampa, 1979-90. Recipient Rsch. award NIH, Tampa, 1981, Arthritis Found., Tampa, 1990. Fellow ACP, Am. Coll. Rheumatology; mem. Am. Assn. Immunologists, So. Soc. for Clin. Investigation, Soc. for Clin. Rsch., Can. Soc. Rheumatologists, Can. Soc. for Clin. Investigation. Home: 1212 Conery St New Orleans LA 70115-3340 Office: La State U Med Ctr 1542 Tulane Ave New Orleans LA 70112-2825

ESQUIBEL, EDWARD VALDEZ, psychiatrist, clinical medical program developer; b. Denver, May 28, 1928; s. Delfino C. and Beatrice (Solis) E.; m. Elaine F. Telk (div. 1961); children: Roxanne, Cyndi, Allen, James; m. Lillian D. Robb, 1961; children: Amanda, Ramona. MD, U. Colo., 1958. Diplomate Am. Bd. Psychiatry and Neurology. Assoc. chief svc. Ill. State Psychiat. Inst., Chgo., 1964-66; dir. undergrad. program psychiatry, asst. prof. psychiatry Chgo Med. Sch., 1966-68; cons. and supr. group therapy Lake County Mental Health Clinic, Gary, Ind., 1968-72; pvt. practice Daytona Beach, Jacksonville, Fla., 1972-82; chief forensic svcs., dir. div. maximum security and inst. rsch. Colo. State Hosp., Pueblo, 1981; assoc. clin. prof. psychiatry Quillen-Dishner Coll. Medicine, Johnson City, Tenn., 1982-84; clin. psychiatrist VA Outpatient Clinic, Riviera Beach, Fla., 1984-86; mental health coord., supr. VA, Pensacola, Fla., 1986-88; assoc. chief staff, ambulatory care VA Med. Ctr., Ft. Lyon, Colo., 1988-90, Carl Vinson VA Med. Ctr., Dublin, Ga., 1990-91; staff physician VA Med. Ctr., Sheridan, Wyo., 1993—; chief psychiat. svcs. VA Med. Ctr., Lake City, Fla., 1993-94; contract physician Annashae Corp., Cleve., 1995—. Contbr. articles to profl. jours. Sgt. U.S. Army, 1952-58. Recipient Plaque Recognition award Southeastern Psychiat. Inst., 1964, Internat. Pers. Creative award, 1972, Key to City Daytona Beach, 1975, Hosp. Dirs. commendation VA, 1991. Mem. Am. Soc. Psychoanalytic Physicians. Home and Office: 801 Gospel Island Rd Inverness FL 34450-3592

ESSIG, ALAN, legislative staff member; b. N.Y.C., Feb. 3, 1959; s. Solonan and Rosalind (Kassote) E.; m. Mary Finn, Sept. 23, 1988; children: Hillary, Corey. BA in history, SUNY, Buffalo, 1981; MPA, SUNY, Albany, 1985. Budget analyst N.Y. State Senate Finance Com., Albany, 1986-89; analyst Ga. Dept. of Labor, Atlanta, 1989-93, Ga. State Senate Rsch. Office, Atlanta, 1993-95; dir. Ga. State Senate Rsch. Office, 1996—.

ESSIN, EMMETT MOHAMMED, JR., obstetrician, gynecologist; b. Sherman, Tex., Jan. 2, 1920; s. Emmett Mohammed Sr. and Lela Priscilla (Tallent) E.; m. Margaret Cummings, Dec. 31, 1939; children: Emmett III, William Robert, Ellen Priscilla, Warren Namon. BA, Austin Coll., 1940; MD, U. Tex., Galveston, 1943. Intern U. Tex., John Sealy Hosps., Galveston, 1943-44, resident in ob./gyn., 1944-45; mem. med. staff Wilson

N. Jones Meml. Hosp., Sherman, Tex., 1946—; chief staff Wilson N. Jones Meml. Hosp., Sherman, 1976-77, chief ob-gyn., 1987-88; bd. dirs. Devel. Bd. Wilson N. Jones Meml. Hosp., Am. Bank, Sherman; ; founder, pres., ptnr. Essin Clinic, Sherman, 1946-89. Charter bd. dirs. Texoma Blood Bank, Sherman, 1975. Lt. USNR, 1945-46. Recipient disting. alumnus awards Austin Coll., 1987, Sherman H.S., 1993. Mem. Grayson County Med. Soc. (past pres.), Tex. Med. Assn., William R. Cooke Obstetrical & Gynecological Soc. (past pres.), Am. Coll. Ob-Gyn. (founding), So. Med. Soc., Am. Coll. Abdominal Surgery, Am. Soc. Fertility. Presbyterian. Home: 1430 Western Hills Dr Sherman TX 75092-5239 Office: Essin Med Bldg 600 N Highland Ave Sherman TX 75092-5646

ESSLINGER, ANNA MAE LINTHICUM, realtor; b. Clifton, Tenn., May 29, 1912; d. Wallace Prather and Minnie P. (Bates) Linthicum; student Miss. State Coll. Women, La. State U.; m. William Francis Esslinger, Sept. 29, 1932; children—Ann Lynn (Mrs. James C. Wilcox), Susan Angie (Mrs. Heinz J. Selig). Founder, Esslinger-Wooten-Maxwell Inc., real estate, Coral Gables, Fla., 1968-85 . Pres. Coral Gables Bd. Realtors, 1975. Mem. Fla. (dir.) Assn. Realtors, Nat. Assn. Realtors, DAR, Assistance League of Eugene, Am. Contract Bridge League, Eugene Country Club, Eugene Symphony Guild, Chi Omega. Christian Scientist. Home: 759 Fairoaks Dr Eugene OR 97401-2392 Office: 1360 S Dixie Hwy Miami FL 33146-2904

ESSMYER, MICHAEL MARTIN, lawyer; b. Abilene, Tex., Dec. 6, 1949; s. Lytle Martin Essmyer and Roberta N. Essmyer Nicholson; m. Cynthia Rose Piccolo, Dec. 27, 1970; children: Deanna, Mike, Brent Austin. BS in Geology, Tex. A&M U., 1972; postgrad., Tex. Christian U., 1976; JD summa cum laude, South Tex. Coll. Law, 1980. Bar: Tex. 1980, U.S. Dist. Ct. (no., so., ea. we. dists) Tex. 1982, U.S. Ct. Appeals (5th cir.) 1981, U.S. Ct. Appeals (9th cir.) 1990, U.S. Ct. Appeals (1st cir.) 1993, U.S. Ct. Appeals (7th cir.) 1995, U.S. Ct. Appeals (fed. cir.) 1995, U.S. Ct. Claims, 1981, U.S. Supreme Ct. 1991. Briefing atty. Supreme Ct. Tex., Austin, 1980-81, Haynes & Fullenweider, Houston, 1981-89; briefing atty. Essmyer & Hanby, Houston, 1989-92; pres. Essmyer & Assocs., Houston, 1992-94, Essmyer & Tritco, LLP, 1994—. Lead article editor South Tex. Law Jour., 1979. Dem. candidate for state rep., Bryan, Tex., 1972; del. Dem. Party, Houston, 1982, 84; precinct chmn. Harris County Dem. Exec. Com., Houston, 1983-86. Capt. USAF, 1972-78. Nat. Merit Scholar, 1968-72. Mem. ABA, Houston Bar Assn., Tex. Trial Lawyers Assn., Harris County Trial Lawyers Assn., Assn. Trial Lawyers Am., Tex. Criminal Def. Lawyers Assn., Tex. Bar Found., Harris County Criminal Lawyers Assn. (dir. 1986-87), Fed. Bar Assn., Houstonian Club. Roman Catholic. Home: 1122 Glourie Dr Houston TX 77055-7506 Office: Essmyer & Tritico LLP 4300 Scotland St Houston TX 77007-7328

ESTELL, DORA LUCILE, retired educational administrator; b. Ft. Worth, Mar. 3, 1930; d. Hugh and Hattie Lucile (Poole) E. BA, East Tex. Bapt. U., 1951; MA, U. North Tex., 1959; EdD, East Tex. State U., 1988. Tchr. Mission (Tex.) Ind. Sch. Dist., 1951-53; tchr., adminstr. Marshall (Tex.) Ind. Sch. Dist., 1953-68; dep. dir. Region VII Edn. Svc. Ctr., Kilgore, Tex., 1968-94, ret., 1994. Contbr. articles to profl. jours. Mem. Phi Delta Kappa. Baptist. Home: 611 W Bell Ave Rockdale TX 76567-2809

ESTEP, MYRNA LYNNE, systems analyst, philosophy educator; b. Whitesville, W.Va., Jan. 7, 1944; d. Modest Schaeffer and Mary Magdalene E.; m. Richard Keith Schoenig, June 5, 1971; 1 child, Debora Lynne. BA, Ind. U., 1970, MS, 1971, PhD, 1975; postgrad., U. Tex., 1993—. Assoc. instr. Ind. U., Bloomington, 1972-75; asst. prof. U. Tex., San Antonio, 1975-78; rsch. edn. specialist Acad. Health Scis., San Antonio, Tex., 1979-84; program systems analyst, field researcher USMC, U.S. Navy, Quantico, Va., 1984-87; grad. faculty, advisor U. Zimbabwe, 1987-89; rsch. systems analyst San Antonio, 1990—; adj. faculty in philosophy U. of Incarnate Word, San Antonio, 1996—; grad. faculty U. Zimbabwe, Harare; advisor to ministries of higher edn. and labour, manpower planning and social welfare, Zimbabwe; adj. faculty U. Tex., San Antonio, 1996—. Author: The Relation Between Theoretical and Procedural Knowing, 1975; co-author: (with E.S. Maccia) Women and Education, 1975; contbr. scientific papers and monographs to profl. publs. Recipient Best Paper award U. Vienna, Austria, 1992. Mem. AAAS, Internat. Soc. Gen. Systems Rsch., Austrian Soc. Cybernetics, N.Y. Acad. Sci., Phi Kappa Phi. Home: 16022 Oak Grove Dr San Antonio TX 78255-1128

ESTEP, WILLIAM ROSCOE, JR., church history educator, minister; b. Williamsburg, Ky., Feb. 12, 1920; s. William Roscoe and Rhoda Mae (Snyder) E.; m. Edna Alice McDowell, Dec. 23, 1942; children: William Merl, Rhoda Elaine, Mary McDowell, Lena Jane. BA, Berea (Ky.) Coll., 1942; ThM, So. Bapt. Theol. Sem., 1945; ThD, Southwestern Bapt. Theol. Sem., 1951. Ordained to ministry Baptist ch., 1941. Asst. prof. L.A. Bapt. Theol. Sem., 1946-47; adj. prof. Union Bapt. Sem., Houston, 1952-54; assoc. prof. Southwestern Bapt. Theol. Sem., Ft. Worth, 1954-62, prof. ch. history, 1963-83, disting. prof. ch. history, 1984-90, disting. prof. ch. history emeritus, 1990-96; Mem. commn. on doctrine and interchurch coop. Bapt. World Alliance, McLean, Va., 1970-85, mem. Bapt. heritage commn., 1985—; pres. Conf. Faith and History, Indiana, 1984-86; mem. hist. com. Bapt. Gen. Conv. Tex., Dallas, 1992-96, chairperson credentials com., Ft. Worth, 1996—; sr. lectr. S.W. Commn. on Religious Studies, Dallas, 1988-89. Author: The Anabaptist Story, 1st. edit., 1963, 2nd edit., 1975, 3rd edit., 1995, Baptists and Christian Unity, 1966, Colombia: Land of Conflict and Promise, 1968, La Fe de Los Apostoles, 1969, And God Gave the Increase, 1972, Renaissance and Reformation, 1986, 92, The Gaston Story, 1987, Religious Liberty: Heritage and Responsibility, 1988, Revolution within the Revolution: the First Amendment in Historical Context, 1612-1789, 1990, Whole Gospel--Whole World: The Foreign Mission Board of the Southern Baptist Convention, 1845-1995, 1994; editor: Anabaptist Beginnings, 1523-1533, 1976, The Lord's Free People in a Free Land, 1976, Belthasar Hubmaier, Anabaptist Theologian and Martyr, 1978, The Reformation: Luther and the Anabaptists, 1979, Fides et Historia, Ft. Worth, 1986-96; contbr. numerous articles to theol. jours. Pres. Tarrant County chpt. Nat. Cystic Fibrosis Found., Ft. Worth, 1965-67. Recipient Disting. Svc. awards, Hist. Commn. Southern Baptist Convention, 1994, Christian Life Commn. Baptist gen. convention Tex., 1995; fellow Eigth Inst. Reformation Rsch. Concordia Theol. Seminary, 1971. Mem. Am. Soc. Ch. History (chairperson membership com. 1988-91), Am. Soc. Reformation Rsch., So. Bapt. Hist. Soc., Wiliam H. Whitsitt Bapt. Heritage Soc., Tex. Bapt. Hist. Soc., Phi Kappa Phi. Home: 1 York Dr Fort Worth TX 76134 Office: Southwestern Bapt Theol Sem 2001 W Seminary Dr Fort Worth TX 76115

ESTES, CAROLYN ANN HULL, elementary school educator; b. Memphis, June 11, 1933; d. Elmer Franklin and Annie Vernon (Jeter) Hull; m. Robert Marion Estes, June 4, 1955; children: Robert Franklin, David Carlton. BS, Memphis State U., 1955; postgrad., U. Tenn., 1958, Nat. Coll. Edn., 1968, N. Tex. State U., 1970, Tex. Christian U., 1984, U. Tex., Arlington, 1985. Cert. elem. and secondary tchr., Tex. 4th grade tchr. Memphis City Schs., 1955-56, 63-66; 6th grade tchr. Knoxville (Tenn.) City Schs., 1957-58; 3d grade tchr. Elk Grove Village (Ill.) Schs., 1968-69; sci. tchr. Stripling Middle Sch., Ft. Worth Ind. Sch. Dist., 1970-76; 5th grade magnet tchr. Eastern Hills Sch., Ft. Worth Ind. Sch. Dist., 1976-78; 5th grade honors tchr. Westcreek Elem. Sch., Ft. Worth Ind. Sch. Dist., 1978-91, computer instr., technol. coord., 1991—. Author: Hull's Heritage, 1986; contbg. author: Hardeman County History, 1979, also curriculum materials. Life mem. Tex. Coun. PTA, program chairperson, 1984-86; mem., bd. dirs. Ft. Worth Geneal. Assn. Named Walt Disney Salutes the Am. Tchr. Alternate, 1994. Mem. Nat. Edn. Assn., DAR (Outstanding Am. History Tchr. award 1988), Tex. State Tchrs. Assn., Ft. Worth Classroom Tchrs. (faculty liaison 1983-86, chmn. Tchr. Ethics and Profl. Standards 1989, Tchr. of Yr. 1985), Sigma Kappa (alumnae chpt., Significant Sigma award 1990). Home: 6409 Poco Ct Fort Worth TX 76133-5217 Office: Westcreek Elem Sch 3401 Walton Ave Fort Worth TX 76133-2229

ESTES, EDWARD RICHARD, JR., engineering consultant, engineer, retired educator; b. Richmond, Va., Mar. 2, 1925; s. Edward Richard Sr. and Mamie Cleveland (Bugg) E.; m. Elizabeth Hood Lee, Oct. 28, 1950; children: Virginia Lee Zimmerman, Susan Page, Edward Richard III, Elizabeth Anne Hubben, William Thomas. B in Engring., Tulane U., 1945; MS, Va. Polytech. Inst., 1948. Structural engr. Baskerville & Son, Richmond, 1947-48; asst. prof. Sch. Engring. U. Va., Charlottesville, 1948-55; rsch. engr. Am. Inst. Steel Constrn., N.Y.C., 1955-60; dir. engring. Fla. Steel Corp., Tampa, 1960-66; dir. engring. dept. Montague-Betts Co., Lynchburg, Va., 1966-68; chief rsch. engr. Am. Iron & Steel Inst., N.Y.C., 1968-69; engring. mgr. Rep. Steel Corp., Youngstown, Ohio, 1969-72; cons. engr. Estes & Assocs., Youngstown, 1972-78, Norfolk, Va., 1978—; prof. Old Dominion U., Norfolk, 1978-94, prof. emeritus, 1994; chmn. civil engring. tech. dept. Old Dominion U., Norfolk, Va., 1978-84, assoc. dean coll. engring. and tech., 1984-88; tech. cons. Nat. Assn. Archt. Metal Mfrs., 1991—. Contbr. numerous articles to profl. jours. With USNR, 1943-46. Fellow Am. Soc. Civil Engrs. (pres. Norfolk, Va. chpt. 1983-84); mem. Am. Welding Soc. (disting., sect. chmn. 1986-87, A.F. Davis Silver medal 1964), Am. Rwy. Engrs. Assn. (sec. com. 15), Am. Soc. Testing and Materials, Am. Iron and Steel Inst. (specification com.), Rsch. Coun. on Structural Connections (chmn. 1974-79), Am. Arbitration Assn., Norfolk Yacht and Country Club, Cypress Point Country Club, Rotary. Republican. Methodist. Home and Office: 7611 Nancy Dr Norfolk VA 23518-4635

ESTES, JACK CHARLES, oil service company executive, scientist; b. Rogers, Ark., Apr. 7, 1935; s. Jack Russell and Merle Clara (White) E.; m. Sandra Jean Reeves, Nov. 10, 1961; children: Michael Lynn, David Russell, Cristi Yvonne. BS in Engring., U. Tulsa, 1965. Computer engr. Remington Rand Univac, Ilion, N.Y., 1960; rsch. tech. Pan Am. Petroleum Corp., Tulsa, 1960-65, rsch. engr., 1965-76; rsch. supr. Amoco Prodn. Co., Tulsa, 1976-89; pres. Environ. Drilling Tech., Inc., Tulsa, 1990—. Contbr. articles to profl. jours.; patentee in field. With USAF, 1955-59. Mem. ASME, N.E. Okla. Sq. Dance Assn. (bd. dirs. 1989-92), Am. Petroleum Inst. (chmn. internat. subcom. 13 1982-85, vice chmn. com. 13 1986-89, task group chmn. 1989—, Svc. award 1991), Internat. Drilling Contractors (chmn. drill bit standardization task group 1973-80), Am. Mgmt. Assn., Soc. Petroleum Engrs. (tech. editor Jour. Petroleum Tech. 1977-78, Svc. award 1985, program com. 1989-92), Am. Chem. Soc. (Svc. award 1984), Sci. Rsch. Soc. (internat. sci. fair judge), Sigma Xi.

ESTES, JEANNE MITTLER, psychiatrist; b. Chgo., May 5, 1946; d. Sidney and Leonore (Broder) Mittler; m. Glen Bruce Estes, June 4, 1972. BS in Zoology, No. Ill. U., 1967, MS in Genetics, 1968; MD, U. Ill., 1972. Diplomate Nat. Bd. Med. Examiners. Resident in psychiatry NYU, 1972-75; attending psychiatrist Monroe (Wis.) Clinic, 1975-78; pvt. practice Baton Rouge, 1979—. Mem. Am. Psychiat. Assn., La. Psychiat. Med. Assn., Baton Rouge Psychiat. Soc., La. State Med. Soc., East Baton Rouge Parish Med. Soc., Am. Med. Women's Assn. Office: 4521 Jamestown Ave Ste 3 Baton Rouge LA 70808-3234

ESTES, JOSIE ELIZABETH, counselor; b. Raleigh, N.C., May 13, 1952; d. Vernon Ashworth and Richia Elizabeth (Atkinson) King; m. Glenn R. Estes, Sept. 3, 1983; children: Rick, Christie. BA, Columbia (S.C.) Coll., 1982; MS, U. N.C., 1986; MA, U. North Tex., 1995. Lic. profl. counselor, Tex.; exercise specialist. Swimming instr. Columbia, 1977-83; cardiac rehab. coord. Rex Hosp., Raleigh, 1985-89, Harris Meth. Hosp., Ft. Worth, Tex., 1989-92; vol. coord., dir. region 8, recovery workshop coord. Adult Children Anonymous, Arlington, Tex., 1990—; counselor Center St. Counseling Svcs., Arlington, 1996—. Coord. Adults in Recovery Workshops, Arlington, 1990—, Marketplace 29AD, Arlington, 1992—; local minister Ch. of the Nazarene, 1994. Mem. ACA, Am. Coll. Sports Medicine. Home: PO Box 150331 Arlington TX 76015 Office: Center Street Counseling Svcs 101 E North St Arlington TX 76011

ESTES, MOREAU PINCKNEY, IV, real estate executive, lawyer; b. Nashville, Oct. 10, 1917; s. Moreau Pinckney III and Lillian (Cole) E.; m. Bertha Lewis, Jan. 14, 1941; children: Moreau Pinckney V, Robert Lewis, Victoria Susanne. Student, Vanderbilt U., 1935-36; LLB, Cumberland U., 1938. Bar: Tenn. 1938. Sole practice law Nashville, 1938-41, bldg. contractor, 1940-43, 46-53; dir. Davidson County Farm Bur., Nashville, 1950-56; v.p. Davidson Farmers Coop., 1955-56; gen. mgr. Harpeth Valley (Tenn.) Utilities Dist., 1963-67; founder, pres. Hillsboro-Harpeth Corp., 1964—; founder, sec.-treas. Alpha Publishing Co., Brentwood, Tenn., 1986—, also bd. dirs.; founder, owner Realty Investment Co., Nashville, 1964—. Mem. residents adv. bd. Tenn. Selective Svcs. System, 1941; atty. property div. State of Tenn., 1963-67, property adminstr., 1964-67; asst. commr. Tenn. Dept. Conservation, 1975; Dem. primary cand. U.S. Ho. of Reps., 1950; del. State Dem. Conv., 1951; sec. Williamson County Dem. Primary Commn., 1967-69; asst. dir. communications Tenn. Dem. Gubernatorial Campaign, 1974; Williamson County coord. Tenn. Dem. Primary Gubernatorial candidate, 1978; middle Tenn. coord. Dem. Primary and Gen. Election Gubernatorial candidate, 1982; bd. stewards, Sunday sch. tchr. Hobson Meth. Ch., 1940-42, 46-50; founder, chmn. bd., 1st pres. Rivermont Watershed Dist., Davidson County, Tenn., 1990-94; apptd. col., aide de camp Staff of Tenn. Gov. Frank Clement, 1963-67, Gov. Ray Blanton, 1975-79, Gov. Lamar Alexandar, 1979-87. Served to 1st lt. Signal Corps U.S. Army, 1942-46, with Res., 1946-51. Named Nashville Mcpl. Tennis Singles and Doubles champion, 1939, 40, Middle Tenn. Singles and Doubles Mcpl. Tennis champion, 1940. Mem. Nashville Home Builders Assn. (pres. 1950), Tenn. Horsemen's Assn. (dir. 1964), Tenn. Hist. Soc., Tenn. Bar Assn., Nashville Bar Assn., Bibl. Archaeology Soc., Nat. Audubon Soc., Smithsonian Assocs., Vanderbilt U. Alumni Assn., Nat. Geographic Soc., SAR, Internat. Bible Assn., Nature Conservancy, Sierra Club, Am. Legion, Wildwood Swimming and Tennis Club (founder, 1st chmn.), Delta Kappa Epsilon. Democrat. Methodist. Home: 6434 Panorama Dr Brentwood TN 37027-4823 Office: 4219 Hillsboro Pike Ste 228 Nashville TN 37215-3328

ESTES, STUART HARDISON, oil industry executive; b. Santa Ana, Calif., Dec. 6, 1954; s. Edison Best and Katherine (Lloyd) E.; m. Nancy Ruth Pierce, Apr. 24, 1993; 1 child, Kathrine Ann. Student in Bus. Adminstrn., Okla. State U., Stillwater, 1973-78; Cert. Oil and Gas paralegal, U. Okla., 1990; Energy and Environ. Resource Mgmt., Okla. State U., Okla. City, 1992—. Team leader quality control Firestone Tire Corp., Okla. City, 1978-79; landman J.M. Newman Co., Ardmore, Okla., 1979-80; land mgr. Quest Energy Corp., Williston, N.D., 1980-82, Resource Design Corp., Ardmore, 1982-85; field land mgr. Sun Exploration Co., Midland, Mich., 1985-86; contract in-house landman Marathon Oil Co., Okla. City, 1987-88, Conoco, Inc., Okla. City, 1991-92; land mgr. Producers and Refiners Corp., Okla. City, 1988—; pres. Oil and Gas Investment Group, Inc., 1989—; mgr. land legal dept. ABPS Energy, Inc., Chickasha, Okla., 1995—; mem. producer adv. group Petroleum Tech. Transfers Coun., 1994—; advisor Commn. on Marginally Producing Oil and Gas Wells, 1994— (chmn. fee com. 1993—). Mem. Am. Assn. Profl. Landmen (mem. cert. com. 1994—, chmn. Field Landman Task Force, 1996—, Ednl. Merit award 1991, Excellence award 1993, Local Assn. of Yr. award 1993), Oklahoma City Assn. Petroleum Landmen (mem. exec. com., chmn. edn. com. 1993-94, sec. 1994-95, chmn. Video Libr. Commn. 1994-95), So. Okla. Assn. Petroleum Landmen, Soc. Petroleum Engrs. (student). Home: 4425 N Barnes Ave Oklahoma City OK 73112-8863 Office: Oil & Gas Invest Group Inc 3535 NW 58th St 950 Landmark Towers E Oklahoma City OK 73112-4898

ESTRADA, ADAHLI, rheumatologist; b. Rio Pedras, P.R., Apr. 13, 1965. BS magna cum laude, U. P.R., 1987, MD, 1990; specialty in internal medicine, San Juan VA Med. Ctr., 1993. Diplomate Am. Bd. Internal Medicine. Med. clin. rsch. San Juan Va Med. Ctr., 1993; fellow in clin. rheumatology Duke U. Med. Ctr., Durham, N.C., 1994-96; chmn. paper chase system U. P.R. Sch. of Medicine, 1986-88. Vol. San Juan VA Med. Ctr., 1986. Mem. ACP, Am. Coll. Rheumatology. Office: 1015 SE 17th St Ste 100 Ocala FL 34471-3911

ESTRADA, DAVID ROBERT, quality engineering consultant; b. Caro, Mich., May 25, 1944; s. Pedro Luna and Juanita (Briones) E.; m. Dian Deal, Oct. 25, 1975 (div. Mar. 1981); m. Leonor Hernandez, Jan. 13, 1968 (div. 1975); children: Darlene, David R. Jr., Anthony C.; m. Toni Marie Rimovsky, Apr. 2, 1983; stepchild: Tammy Marie Redler. Mech. drafstman Acme Iron Works, San Antonio, 1965-67; mech. drafstman Tracor, Inc., Austin, Tex., 1967-69, electro-mech. designer, supr., 1976-81; mech. designer Swearingen Aircraft, San Antonio, 1969-70; mech. designer, contract adminstr. Hayes Internat., San Antonio, 1970-72; br. mgr. AAA Engring. and Drafting, Inc., San Antonio, 1972-74; contract adminstr., mech. designer. Woosley Engring., San Antonio, 1974-76; cons. San Antonio, 1976; mfg. engr. B. J. Hughes, Round Rock, Tex., 1981-83; supr. product design and documentation Wayne div. Dresser Industries, Austin, 1983-87; cons. D.E. Design & Svcs., Austin, 1987—; ind. sales rep. Process Integrity, Arlington, Tex., 1987—; founder Rimest Enterprises, 1995. Author: (manual) Statistical Process Control, 1988. Bd. dirs. Capital area Easter Seal Soc., 1996—. With U.S. Army, 1962-65. Mem. Am. Soc. Logistics Engrs., Am. Soc. Quality Control, Toastmasters Internat. (Able Toastmaster), Masons, Shriners (unit pres. Oriental band 1988-91). Republican. Office: DE Design & Svcs PO Box 9510 Austin TX 78766-9510

ESTRIN, MELVYN J., computer products company executive. Co-chmn., co-CEO Nat. Intergroup, Inc., Carrollton, Tex.; co-chmn, co-CEO FoxMeyer Health Corp., Carrollton, Tex.; also bd. dirs.; mng. ptnr. Centaur Ptnrs., L.P.; chmn., pres., CEO Am. Health Svcs.; v.p., dir. Spectro Industries; founder First Women's Bank of Md.; pres. FWB Bancorporation, Rockville, Md.; chmn. FWB Bancorporation.; chmn. Estrin Internat., Inc.; with Estrin Realty and Devel. Corp.; bd. dirs. Washington Gas Light Co. Trustee U. Pa.; active Endowment Bd. of the Kennedy Ctr., The Econ. Club of Washington, The Washington Opera; nat. vice chmn. State of Israel Bonds; apptd. by Pres. Bush commr.Nat. Capital Planning Commn.; apptd. Nat. Coun. for the Performing Arts, John F. Kennedy Ctr. Recipient Eleanor Roosevelt Humanities award for Community Svc., 1986. Office: Univ Rsch Corp 7200 Wisconsin Ave Ste 600 Bethesda MD 20814-4811 also: Foxmeyer Health 1220 Senlac Dr Carrollton TX 75006-7019

ESTROV, ZEEV, medical educator; b. Bialistok, Poland, May 1, 1947; arrived in Israel, 1950, arrived in Can., 1984; s. Shabtai and Masha (Portnoy) E.; m. Miriam Metzler, Nov. 19, 1970; children: Yuval, Shunit, Efrat. MD, Sakler Sch. Medicine, Tel-Aviv, 1975. Intern Kaplan Hosp., Rehovot, Israel, 1973-74; resident in internal medicine Kaplan Hosp., Rehovot, Israel, 1975-80, sr. physician, 1981-87; dep. head dept. medicine Kaplan Hosp., Rehovot, 1987-89; prin. investigator div. medicine hematopoiesis rsch. lab. MD Anderson Cancer Ctr., Houston, 1989—; dep. med. dir. Kaplan Hosp., Rehovot, 1988-89. Contbr. articles to profl. jours. Capt. Israel Def. Forces, 1965-67, 74-75. Recipient Dr. Rogijinsky Found. prize, Israel, 1981, Travel award Am. Soc. Clin. Oncology, 1986, Tisdall award U. Toronto, The Hosp. for Sick Children, Toronto, 1986; Terry Fox scholar U. Toronto, 1984-87. Mem. Am. Soc. Hematology, Internat. Soc. Hematology, Internat. Soc. Exptl. Hematology, Am. Assn. Cancer Rsch. Home: 5739 Birdwood Rd Houston TX 77096-2108 Office: MD Anderson Cancer Ctr PO Box 302 1515 Holcombe Blvd Houston TX 77030-4009

ETGEN, ANN, ballet educator, artistic director, choreographer; b. Dallas; d. Eddy R. and Myrtle (Applegate) Etgen; m. Bill Atkinson, Aug. 16, 1961. Dancer, Met. Opera Ballet N.Y.C., 1958-60, Broadway musicals Brigadoon, Carousel; guest dancer Omnibus History of Dance for Agnes De Mille, 1957; artistic dir. Etgen-Atkinson Sch. of Ballet, Dallas, 1962—, Dallas Met. Ballet, 1964—; host S.W. Regional Ballet Festival, 1973. Dance panel Tex. Fine Arts Com., 1978-79; active Arts Magnet Sch., 1980, 81, 82, 83. NEA choreography grantee, 1976, grantee Tex. Fine Arts Commn., 1973, 76-77, Mobile Oil, 1979, 500 Inc., 1978-79; recipient choreography plan award Nat. Assn. Regional Ballet, 1983. Mem. Nat. Assn. Regional Ballet, S.W. Regional Ballet Assn. (membership chmn. 1986-87). Presbyterian. Creator ballets for Dallas Met. Ballet. Office: Dallas Met Ballet 6815 Hillcrest Ave Dallas TX 75205-1308

ETHERIDGE, ELIZABETH WILLIAMS, history educator; b. McDonough, Ga., May 14, 1928; d. Roy Pierce and Robbie (Williams) E. AB in Journalism, U. Ga., 1949, PhD in Am. History, 1966; MA in Journalism, U. Iowa, 1962. Asst. dir. News Bur. U. Ga., Athens, 1949-61, 62-63; asst. prof., assoc. prof., prof. history Longwood Coll., Farmville, Va., 1966-92, prof. emeritus history, 1992—. Author: The Butterfly Caste: A Social History of the Pellagra in the South, 1972, Sentinel for Health: A History of the Centers for Disease Control, 1992; (with Sylvia Herd) The Neighborhood Mint: Dahlonega in the Age of Jackson, 1986. Mem. AAUP, Orgn. Am. Historians, So. Hist. Assn., Phi Beta Kappa, Phi Kappa Phi. Democrat. Presbyterian. Home: 706 High St Farmville VA 23901

ETHERIDGE, JACK PAUL, arbitrator, mediator, former judge; b. Atlanta, Mar. 16, 1927; s. Anton Lee and Jessie Shephard (Brown) E.; m. Ursula Schlatter, Feb. 2, 1952; children: Jack Paul, Margaret Ann, Mary Elizabeth. Grad., Darlington Sch., Rome, Ga., 1945; B.S., Davidson Coll., 1949; J.D., Emory U., 1955. Bar: Ga. 1955. Since practiced in Atlanta; mem. firm Huie, Etheridge & Harland, 1959-66; mem. Ga. Gen. Assembly from Fulton County, 1963-66; judge Fulton Superior Ct., 1966-76, sr. judge, 1977-91, litigation mgr., 1991; faculty Nat. Jud. Coll., Coll. Criminal Justice, Law Sch., U. S.C., 1977-80; assoc. dean Emory U. Law Sch., Atlanta, 1981-88; chief jud. officer Jud. Arbitration and Mediation Svcs., Inc., Atlanta, 1992—; mem. Ga. Crime Commn., 1971-73; bd. dirs. Atlanta Legal Aid Soc., 1960-70. Trustee Davidson Coll., 1966-75; trustee Arts Festival of Atlanta, 1971-74, Atlanta U., 1977-87; chmn. bd. dirs. Atlanta Neighborhood Justice, Inc., Wolfcreek Wilderness Schs., Inc.; Fellow Harvard Law Sch., 1980. Served with USNR, 1945-46; Served with with AUS, 1949-52. Named Young Man of Year in Professions Atlanta Jr. C. of C., 1962. Fellow ABA, Am. Bar Found., Ga. Bar Assn., Internat. Acad. Trial Judges, Ctr. for Pub. Resources; mem. Atlanta Bar Assn. (pres. 1962-63), Nat. Conf. State Trial Judges (chmn. 1978-79), Atlanta Hist. Soc. (trustee 1969-75), Nat. Acad. Pub. Adminstrn., Beta Theta Pi, Omicron Delta Kappa, Phi Alpha Theta. Presbyterian. Home: 4715 Harris Trl NW Atlanta GA 30327-4409

ETHIER, DONALD NOEL, professional association executive; b. Waterbury, Conn., Nov. 13, 1945; s. Donald N. and Margaret Elizabeth (Pickett) E.; m. Patricia Rene Carson, April 12, 1986; children: Philip D., Renee E., Thomas J. BA, Earlham Coll., 1967; MBA, U. Conn., 1974. Supr. agy. supplies Conn. Mut. Life Ins. Co., Hartford, 1968-70; dir. ednl. mktg. Channing L. Bete Co., South Deerfield, Mass., 1974-77; dir. mktg. services Nat. School Pub. Rels. Assn., Arlington, Va., 1977-79; mktg. mgr. Am. Assn. School Adminstrs., Arlington, 1979-83; dir. membership and mktg. Nat. Restaurant Assn., Washington, 1983-94; dir. mem. svcs. Am. Indsl. Hygiene Assn., Fairfax, Va., 1994—; Contbg. editor Assn. Mktg. Mag., Reston, Va., 1987-90. Author: (with others) Principles of Association Management, 1988; co-author: Basics of Association Membership: A Workbook for Membership Directors, 1996; contbr. articles to profl. jours. Mem. Am. Mktg. Assn. (exec.), Direct Mktg. Assn. Washington, Am. Soc. Assn. Execs. (cert. assn. exec.), Beta Gamma Sigma. Office: Am Indsl Hygiene Assn 2700 Prosperity Ave Ste 250 Fairfax VA 22031

ETHRIDGE, MAX MICHAEL, civil engineer; b. Aurora, Mo., Aug. 7, 1949; s. James and Muriel (Boswell) E.; m. Martha Inez Thomason, Jan. 2, 1970; children: Marcia Inez, Marguerite Muriel. BSCE, U. Mo., 1970; MSCE, Purdue U., 1975, PhD, 1977; MPA, Golden Gate U., 1983. Registered profl. engr., Ind.; cert. photogrammetrist. Chief photo party 65 Nat. Ocean Svc., Norfolk, Va., 1972-74; exec. officer NOAA Ship Whiting, Norfolk, Va., 1977-79; chief coastal mapping Nat. Ocean Svc., Norfolk, Va., 1981-82; policy analyst Nat. Ocean Svc., Washington, 1982-84, liaison officer to def. mapping agy., 1984-85; deputy chief nat. geodetic survey Nat. Ocean Svc., Rockville, Md., 1985-87, chief nat. geodetic survey, 1987-89; sr. sci. advisor U.S. Geol. Survey, Reston, Va., 1989-90, chief office of strategic analysis, 1990-93, staff asst. to the dir., 1993-94, acting asst. dir. for programs, 1994—; adj. assoc. prof. Old Dominion U., Norfolk, 1979-82. Contbr. articles to profl. jours. deacon Presbyn. Ch., West Lafayette, Ind., 1975-77; asst. U.S. Girl Scouts, Virginia Beach, Va., 1980-82. Recipient Unit Citation, Nat. Oceanic and Atmospheric Adminstrn., 1971, letters of commendation, 1972-85, dirs. ribbons, 1987, Commendation medal, 1990, U.S. Dept. Interior Superior Svc. award 1993. Fellow Am. Congress on Surveying and Mapping (tech. tour coord. 1990-91, fed. govt. rep. on presdl. task force 1991-92); mem. ASCE, Am. Geophysical Union, Am. Soc. Photogrammetry and Remote Sensing, Am. Cartographic Assn. (bd. dirs. 1993—), Nat. Assn. Hispanic Fed. Execs. Office: US Geol Survey 105 National Ctr Reston VA 22092

ETON, OMAR, oncologist; b. N.Y.C., Sept. 2, 1957. AB in Biochemistry cum laude, Harvard U., 1978; MD, NYU, 1983. Diplomate Am. Bd. Internal Medicine and Oncology. Intern Parkland Meml. Hosp., Dallas, 1983-84, resident in internal medicine, 1984-86; fellow in immunology/oncology Meml. Sloan-Kettering Cancer Ctr., N.Y.C., 1986-87, fellow in oncology/hematology, 1987-90; oncologist U. Tex. M.D. Anderson Cancer Ctr.,

Houston, 1990—; asst. prof. dept. med. oncology U. Tex., 1990—; attending physician adult emergency svcs. Bellevue Hosp., NYU Med. Ctr., 1986-90; internist, oncologist, hematologist Malcolm Grow USAF Med. Ctr., Andrews AFB, Washington, 1988—. Contbr. articles to profl. jours. Lt. col. USAFR, 1995—. Fellow ACP, Am. Cancer Soc.; mem. AMA, AAAS, Am. Assn. for Cancer Rsch., Am. Soc. Clin. Oncology, Tex. Med. Assn., Harris County Med. Soc. Home: 4204 Byron Houston TX 77005 Office: U Tex MD Anderson Cancer Ctr 1515 Holcombe Blvd Houston TX 77030-4009

ETSON, TIMOTHY DEMORRIS, social worker, management consultant; b. Jamaica, N.Y., July 27, 1965; s. Oland and Virginia Dell (Moore) E. BS in Econs., S.C. State U., 1988. Exec. asst. Edgefield County Concerned Parents and Adults Orgn., Johnston, S.C, 1991-92; basic skills counselor Telamon Corp., Aiken, S.C., 1992-94; middle sch. instr. Johnston Christian Acad., 1994-95; asst. program coord. Benedict Coll., Columbia, S.C., 1995-96; econ. support casemgr. Dekalb County Dept of Family and Children Svc., Decatur, Ga., 1996—; mem. Cmty. Svc. Network, Aiken, S.C., 1993-94, Ga. County Welfare Assn., 1996—. Author: (tng. manual) Life-Skills Training Program Manual, 1993. Mem. exec. com. S.C. Young Dems., Orangeburg, 1985-87; bd. dirs. Edgefield County Concerned Parents and Adults Orgn., Johnston, S.C., 1992-94, Leadership Aiken (S.C.) County, 1993-96; poll mgr. Aiken County Election Commn., 1994; vol. Joe Riley for Gov. Campaign, 1994; mem. Dems. Aiken County, 1994. Mem. championshp basketball team Aiken Parks and Recreation Dept. League, 1994-96. Mem. Masons (sublime prince C.C. Johnson Consistory 136 32d degree Scottish Rite), Omega Psi Phi (asst. sec. 1993, Man of Yr. 1995). Democrat. Baptist. Home: 1510 Reid St NW Aiken SC 29801 Office: Northampton Assocs Inc 1143 Chuck Dowley Blvd Mount Pleasant SC 29464

ETTE, EZEKIEL, minister, mental health counselor; b. Ikot Ekpene, Aks, Nigeria, Sept. 22, 1957; came to U.S., 1982; s. Umo Ette Amauke and Adiaha Essiet; m. Nse Udofa, Dec. 31, 1990. NCE, U. Uyo, Nigeria, 1981; BS in Edn., U. Tenn., 1984; cert. gerontology, Ga. State U., 1987; MDiv, Emory U., 1989. Master addiction counselor; cert. criminal justice specialist. Resident supr. Atlanta Christian Coun. Mental Health, 1989-92; case mgr. West Fulton Cmty. Mental Health, Atlanta, 1992—; asst. pastor George Meml. Bapt., Atlanta, 1995—; CPR instr. Am. Heart Assn., Atlanta, 1992—; presenter in field. City editor African News Weekly, Atlanta, 1993—, columnist, 1993; editor Emory Jour. Internat. Affairs, 1987-88; columnist Emory Wheel, 1987-89. Notary pub., Fulton County, Ga., 1995—; pres. NTO Annang Found., Atlanta, 1995—. Cameron Found. scholar, 1982-85, Sunshine Found. scholar, 1989. Mem. Nat. Assn. Case Mgmt., Nat. Assn. Forensic Counselors, African Studies Assn.

ETTERER, SEPP, industrial relations consultant; b. Munich, Aug. 31, 1944; came to U.S., 1955, naturalized, 1962; s. Josef and Ingeborg Anna (Fierlings) E.; m. Judith Annette Shell, Feb. 25, 1978; children, Johnathan Sepp, Julia Anne, Joseph William; children from previous marriage: Victoria Marie, Christina Diane, Kurt. BSEE, Mich. State U., 1966. Lic. comml. pilot. Assoc. ele. engr. Boeing Co., 1966-67; pulp mill supr., plant safety engr. Procter & Gamble Co., 1970-76; sr. safety rep. Bechtel Power Co., 1976-77; plant safety supt. Hooker Chems. & Plastics Corp., 1977-78; indsl. relations dir. Interstate Lead Co. Inc., Leeds, Ala., 1978-85; regional personnel and safety dir. Structl. Steel Fabrication div. Trinity Industries, Inc., Birmingham, Ala., 1985-89; safety mgr. freight car div. Trinity Industries, Bessemer, Ala., 1989-94; pres. Safety Maintenance Orgn., Inc., Birmingham, 1994—; inds. rels. cons.; v.p. Le Marche aud Fleurs, Inc., 1986—. Author: Take It--It's Yours, 1975, Sky Pig, 1976, Euiqty 5, 1980, (software) SMOSYS Indsl. Rels. Mgmt., 1995. Capt. USAF, 1967-70. Mem. Am. Soc. Safety Engrs. (past pres.), Am. Indsl. Hygiene Assn. Home: 2021 Tyson Dr Birmingham AL 35216-1953 Office: PO Box 661333 Birmingham AL 35266-1333

EUBANKS, GARY LEROY, SR., lawyer; b. North Little Rock, Ark., Nov. 22, 1933; s. Herman and Gertrude (Carmack) E.; m. Mary Joyce Gathright, 1955 (div. 1966); children: Gary Leroy Jr., Bobby Ray; m. Beverly Gayle Mauldin, Apr. 21, 1971 (div. 1983); 1 child, Shane Mauldin; m. Elizabeth Duncan, Dec. 18, 1987. JD, U. Ark., 1960. Bar: Ark. 1960, U.S. Dist. Ct. Ark. 1960, U.S. Supreme Ct. 1970. Ptnr. Bailey, Jones, and Eubanks, Little Rock, 1960-63, Eubanks and Deane, Little Rock, 1963-65, Eubanks, Hood, and Files, Little Rock, 1965-69, Eubanks, Files and Hurley, Little Rock, 1969-76, Haskins Eubanks and Wilson, Little Rock, 1976-79, Gary Eubanks and Assocs., Little Rock, 1979—. Mem. Ark. Ho. of Reps., 1963-66, Pulaski County (Ark.) Sch. Bd., 1967. Served with USN, 1952-54. Mem. ABA, Ark. State Bar Assn., Pulaski County Bar Assn., Ark. Trial Lawyers Assn., Assn. Trial Lawyers Am., Am. Bd. Trial Advocacy (civil trial advocate). Democrat. Methodist. Home: 211 Scenic Dr Diamondhead # 7281 Hot Springs National Park AR 71913-8764 Office: PO Box 3887 Little Rock AR 72203-3887

EUBANKS, MARIE HARRIS, medical librarian; b. Warren County, Tenn., May 28, 1941; d. Thomas Hollis and Thelma (Pryor) Harris; m. Glen Earl Eubanks, Dec. 17, 1961; children: Eric Dean, Robert Louis. BS, Mid. Tenn. State U., 1962; MSLS, Cath. U. Am., 1982. Med. libr. Alvin C. York VA Med. Ctr., Murfreesboro, Tenn., 1982—. Pres. Assn. for Preservation of Tenn. Antiquities, Murfreesboro, 1987; chmn., fundraiser Mid. Tenn. Symphony Guild, Murfreesboro, 1986, 87; active Oaklands Mus. Assn., Rutherford County Hist. Assn., Nashville Community Orch., Mid. Tenn. Choral Soc., Sam Davis Home Assn. Named Most Valuable Mem., Nashville Community Band, 1988. Mem. DAR, Bus. and Profl. Women, Bohannon Music Club, Order of Ea. Star (Worthy Matron 1986), Murfreesboro Woman's Club, United Daus. of Confederacy. Office: Alvin C York VA Med Ctr 3400 Lebanon Rd Murfreesboro TN 37129-1237

EUBANKS, OMER LAFAYETTE, data communications specialist; b. Atlanta, Nov. 28, 1956; s. Omer LaFayette and Frances (Dix) EuB.; m. Joy Kay Gantt, Nov. 15, 1979; children: Matthew Christopher, Timothy Mark. BS, Vanderbuilt U., 1979. Cert. computer profl., Ga. Systems programmer U. Tenn., Nashville, 1978-79, Equifax, Inc., Atlanta, 1979-85; sr. systems programmer Advanced Technologies, Inc., Norcross, Ga., 1985-86; sr. communications systems programmer Atlanta Jour. Constitution, 1987-89; systems programmer Suntrust Banks, Atlanta, 1989-90; sr. communications analyst Life Ins. Co. of Ga., Atlanta, 1990-91; cons. Systems Ctr., Inc., Reston, Va., 1991-93; cons. Corinthian Software, Marietta, Ga., 1987, North Fulton Healthcare Assn., Roswell, Ga., 1990—, ISSC-Windward Tech. Ctr., 1994—, AT&T Universal Card Svcs., 1994-96, Worldspan, 1994-96, Advantis, 1996—. Bd. dirs. Wills Park Youth Baseball Assn., 1995-96—; deacon Roswell First Bapt., 189—, vice chair deacon bd., 1994, vice chair pers. com., 1996-97, chmn. student minister search com., 1996, mem. future devel. com., 1991-94, chair, 1994; mem pers. com., 1995—. NSF grantee, 1974. Mem. NRA (life), N.Am. Hunting Club (life), Pi Kappa Alpha. Baptist. Home: 355 Hickory Flat Rd Alpharetta GA 30201-2612

EUBANKS, RONALD W., lawyer, broadcaster; b. Montgomery, Ala., Sept. 17, 1946; s. William Shell and Violet Lavern (Walker) E.; 1 child, Edward Todd. Student, Auburn U., 1964-65; BA, U. Ala., 1968; JD, U. Utah, 1974. Bar: Utah 1974, Nebr., 1979, Minn. 1983, Wash. 1985, U.S. Ct. Appeals (10th cir.), 1977, U.S. Ct. Appeals (8th cir.), 1979, U.S. Supreme Ct., 1977, U.S. Ct. Appeals (9th cir.) 1985. Gen. mgr. Sta. WVMI and Sta. WQID, Biloxi Gulfport, Miss., 1968-71; with FCC, Washington, 1974-75; assoc. Hansen & Hansen, Salt Lake City, 1975-77; with law dept. Union Pacific R.R., Omaha, 1977-83; asst. gen. counsel Burlington No. R.R. Co., St. Paul, 1983-84, gen. counsel Western region, 1984-87, v.p. law and corp. affairs, Glacier Park Co., 1987-88; exec. v.p. Ecos Corp., 1988; chief exec. officer Capital Communications, Montgomery, 1991—; pres. ET Communications, Montgomery, Ala., 1988—; dir. Camas Prairie R.R., Longview Switching Co. Bd. dirs., mem. exec. com., legal counsel Utah Boys Ranch, Salt Lake City, 1977-79; bd. dirs. Children and Youth Svcs., Salt Lake City, 1977-84, Nebr. affiliate Am. Diabetes Assn., 1982-83, Greater Montgomery Sickle Cell Found., 1990—; co-chmn. Montgomery Father and Son Banquet Com., 1993—; bd. dirs., mem. exec. com. Montgomery Mental Health Assn., 1995—, treas., 1996—. Recipient Friend of Youth award YMCA, 1993; named Role Model of Yr., Southlawn Sch., 1996-97. Mem. ABA (sect. on litigation, coms. on publs. and trial techniques, sect. on tort and ins. practice, com. on r.r. law), Washington State Bar Assn., Seattle-King County Bar Assn., Wash. R.R. Assn. (chmn. 1984-87), Def. Research Inst. (chmn. com. on r.r. law 1984-86, mem. com. on practice and procedure), Jason's Soc., Phi Alpha Delta, Alpha Tau Omega. Presbyterian. Co-author: Practical Law in Utah, 1978, Defense of Mary Carter, 1984; contbr. to profl. publs. Home: 119 Oak Ridge Ln Pike Road AL 36064-2730 Office: Capital Comm 648 Perry St Montgomery AL 36104

EURE, LINDA JORDAN, state agency administrator; b. Edenton, N.C., Mar. 19, 1955. BA in Anthropology with honors, U. Ariz., 1977, MA, 1979. Photog. rschr. Ariz. State Mus., Tucson, 1976-78, artifact analyst, rschr., 1977-79, dir. docent program, 1979-80; asst. site mgr. Town Creek Indian Mound N.C. Dept. Cultural Resources, Mt. Gilead, 1981-83, historic site mgr. Historic Edenton State Historic Site, 1983—; bd. dirs. Historic Albemarle Tour, Inc., Edenton, 1983—; bd. dirs. Chowan County Tourism Devel. Authority, Edenton, 1990—, vice chmn., 1993—; chmn. N.E. regional mgmt. team, historic sites sect. N.C. Dept. Cultural Resources, 1994. William Shirley Fulton scholar U. Ariz., 1977-79. Mem. Phi Beta Kappa, Phi Kappa Phi. Office: Historic Edenton PO Box 474 Edenton NC 27932-0474

EUSTIS, RICHMOND MINOR, lawyer; b. New Orleans, Nov. 24, 1945; s. David and Molly Cox (Minor) E.; m. Catherine Luise Baños, Apr. 15, 1971; children: Richmond Minor Jr., Julie Bransford, Joshua Leeds, Molly Minor. BA in Econs., U. Va., 1967; JD, Tulane U., 1970. Bar: La. 1970. Assoc. Phelps Dunbar, New Orleans, 1970-75; ptnr. Monroe and Lemann, New Orleans, 1975-96; founder, ptnr. Eustis & O'Keefe, LLC, New Orleans, 1996—. Bd. dirs. Children's Bur., 1976-88, treas., 1984. Mem. ABA, La. Bar Assn., New Orleans Bar Assn. (chmn. torts and ins. com. 1992-95), Maritime Law Assn., S.E. Admiralty Law Inst., Boston Club, La. Club. Republican. Episcopalian. Home: 289 Audubon St New Orleans LA 70118-4841 Office: Eustis & O'Keefe 228 Saint Charles Ave Ste 1010 New Orleans LA 70170-1000

EVANS, ARTHUR FORTE, real estate developer; b. Augusta, Ga., Dec. 23, 1957; s. Arthur Forte Jr. and Mary Lou (Nelson) E. Student, Mercer U., 1976-78. Broker Evans Butler Realty, Melbourne, Fla., 1978—; land developer Forte Macaulay Devel. Co. Inc., Melbourne, 1985—; securities broker Sand Dollar Securities, Melbourne, 1988—; founder Metro Devel. Co. Inc., 1993; pres. Harp Holding Co., Inc., TLDC, Inc., Willows II Devel. Co. Inc., Baymeadows Devel. Co. Inc.; mem. adv. bd. Prime Bank. Bd. dirs. Boy Scouts Am. Mem. Melbourne Area Bd. Realtors, Home Builders and Contractors Assn. (bd. dirs.), Melbourne C. of C., Melbourne Hunting and Fishing Club. Republican. Methodist. Office: Forte Maculay Devel Co Inc 1688 W Hibiscus Blvd Melbourne FL 32901-2631

EVANS, AUDREY ANNE, environmentalist; b. Baton Rouge, Mar. 23, 1962; d. Rex Willard and Katherine Azena (Nielsen) E. BA in Polit. Sci., La. State U., Baton Rouge, 1984; MA in Fgn. Affairs, U. Va., Charlottesville, 1987. La. State U. campus coord. Global Hunger Project Uniting Campus Ministry and Ctr. for Disarmament Edn., Baton Rouge, 1981-83; teaching asst. Woodrow Wilson dept. govt. and fgn. affairs U. Va., Charlottesville, 1986; internat. policy analyst Bread for the World, Washington, 1986-88; program assoc. OMB Watch, Washington, 1988-89; cmty. outreach coord. Tulane Environ. Law Clinic, New Orleans, 1989—; waterfront dir. S.E. La. Girl Scout Coun., Independence, summer 1983; work study intern Africa Regional Affairs Bur., U.S. Dept. State, Washington, fall 1985; acting economic officer U.S. Embassy U.S. Dept. State, Bangui, Central African Republic, summer 1986. mem. editl. bd. La. Forum, 1992—. Mem. 2 cmty. supported agr. projects, 1994—; mem. cmty. adv. bd. WYES Pub. TV, New Orleans, 1991-92; environ. advisor La. Preservation Alliance, 1993—; mem. environ. equity com. Region IV, U.S. EPA, 1993—; mem. adv. bd. La. Citizen Action, 1994—; mem. mayor's environ. adv. com. City of New Orleans, 1994—; judge campaign for cleaner corps. Coun. on Econ. Priorities, N.Y.C., 1994; waterfront dir. S.E. La. coun. Girl Scouts U.S., Independence, summer 1983. Inductee Grassroots Movement for Environ. Justice Honor Roll and Hall of Fame, Citizens Clearinghouse for Hazardous Waste, 1993; recipient Cmty. Svc. award So. Christian Leadership Conf., 1994. Mem. Sci. and Environ. Health Network, La. Environ. Action Network, Alliance for Affordable Energy, Coalition to Restore Coastal La., Ozark Organic Food Coop. Office: Tulane Environ Law Clinic 6329 Freret St New Orleans LA 70118

EVANS, BILLIE ARNELL, rehabilitation nurse, radiologic technologist; b. Oceanside, Calif., Jan. 20, 1952; d. William Amos and Peggy Joyce (Steele) Mann. Radiology Technologist, Norfolk Gen. Sch. Radiology, Va., 1975; ASN, Tidewater C.C., Portsmouth, Va., 1983; BS in Health Care Adminstrn., St. Joseph's Coll., 1989; MS in Health Care Adminstrn., Cen. Mich. U., 1990. Registered radiologic technologist; RN, Va., N.C.; cert. rehab. nurse; cert. renal lithotripisy specialist. Radiology technologist Norfolk Gen. Hosp., 1976-83; shift head nurse Brain Injury unit Med. Coll. of Va., Richmond, 1984-89; staff nurse Southeastern Regional Rehab., Fayetteville, N.C., 1989-90; staff primary nurse stroke acute care unit Duke Med. Ctr., Durham, N.C., 1990-91; clin. charge nurse II Cysto Ste. U. N.C., Chapel Hill, 1991-92, nurse edn. clinician divsn. neurosurgery, 1992-95; clin. evaluator for rehab. svcs. UNC Hosps., Chapel Hill, N.C., 1995—. Recipient Nursing Process award Med. Coll. Va., 1987, Excellence in Adminstrv. Practice award, 1988. Mem. Assn. for Rehab. Nursing, Am. Urol. Assn. (nursing mem.), Am. Registry of Radiologic Technologists, Am. Congress of Rehab. Medicine, Nat. Head Injury Found., N.C. Assn. Rehab. Nursing, N.C. Head Injury Found., Am. Lithotripsy Soc., Sigma Iota Epsilon. Roman Catholic. Home: 5122 Copper Ridge Dr Apt303 Durham NC 27707-6130 Office: Rehab Unit 3 Gravely Chapel Hill NC 27514

EVANS, BOB, research director. Office: Mudtech Labs Inc 5310 Milwee St Houston TX 77092

EVANS, BRUCE HASELTON, art museum director; b. Rome, N.Y., Nov. 13, 1939; s. E. Arnold and Joan Sawyer (Haselton) E.; m. Margo Elizabeth Frey, July 14, 1962; children: Barton Haselton, Christopher Andrew. B.A., Amherst Coll., 1961; M.A., NYU, 1964. Asst. curator Dayton (Ohio) Art Inst., 1965-66, curator, 1967-68, chief curator, 1969-72, asst. dir., 1973-74, dir., 1975-91; dir. Mint Mus. Art, Charlotte, N.C., 1991—; mem. adv. panels Nat. Endowment for Arts and Humanities, 1973—; v.p. Midwest Museums Conf. Council, 1981; active Dayton River Corridor Design Rev. Com., Historic Architecture Com., Charlotte-Mecklenburg Pub. Art Commn., 1994—. Author: Fifty Treasures of the Dayton Art Institute, 1969, The Paintings of Jean-Leon Gerome, 1972, The Paintings of Edward Edmondson, 1972. Trustee Arts Advs. N.C. Mem. Assn. Art Mus. Dirs. (pres. 1986), Ohio Mus. Assn. (past pres.), Intermus. Conservation Assn. (past pres.), Am. Assn. Museums, Internat. Council Museums. Home: 3735 Abingdon Rd Charlotte NC 28211-3746 Office: Mint Mus of Art 2730 Randolph Rd Charlotte NC 28207-2012

EVANS, CAROL ANN BUTLER, administrative assistant; b. Brenham, Tex., Mar. 4, 1938; d. Ben Thornton Butler and Evelyn Meyer Anderson; m. Jack Guy Courtney, June 30, 1956 (div. 1970); children: Elaine, J. Guy, David, Bruce Courtney; m. J. Warren Evans, Feb. 5, 1988. Student, McNeese State U., Lake Charles, La., 1956-57, Midland (Tex.) Coll., 1971, Am. Inst. Banking, 1970-84. Asst. to pres. San Felipe Bank N.A., Houston, 1977-79; reg. mgr. Gatoil (USA) Inc., Houston, 1979-81; office mgr. Rapada Corp., Houston, 1981-83; mktg. officer Park Tower Nat. Bank, Houston, 1984-85; mktg. dir. First City Bank Med. Ctr., Houston, 1985; asst. to pres. Med Ctr. Bank, Houston, 1985-86; dir. pub. affairs The Doctor's Club of Houston, 1986-87; mgr. The Faculty Club Tex. A&M U., College Station, 1987-90, spl. events coord. The Faculty Club, 1990-94, staff asst. Office of the Commandant, Corps of Cadets, 1994-95; asst. to pres. First Am. Bank, Bryan, Tex., 1995—; cons. in field; lectr. in field. Author handbook: Essentials of Business Etiquette. Mem. Am. Bus. Women's Assn., Internat. Assn. Bus. Communicators, Assistance League Houston, Bank Mktg. Assn. Houston, Assn. of Faculty Clubs. Republican. Methodist. Home: 3310 Belmont Cir College Station TX 77845-8210

EVANS, CAROL ROCKWELL, nursing administrator; b. New Orleans, Jan. 8, 1953; d. Daniel Raymond Sr. and Helen (Fischer) Rockwell; divorced; children: Nikki Elizabeth, Mimi Michelle. ADN, La. State Med. Ctr., 1990. RN, La.; cert. ACLS, BLS, cert. case mgr.; lic. life and health ins. agent. Life and health ins. agt. La. Ins. Agts. Assn., New Orleans, 1975-95; dir. case mgmt. and utilization rev. Associated Med. Rev. Svcs., Metairie, La., 1986-95; charge nurse med-surg. telemetry unit Elmwood Med. Ctr., Jefferson, La., 1990—; RN specialist III ICU St. Charles Gen. Hosp., New Orleans, 1993—; dir. med. mgmt. Nat. Health Resources, Inc., Metairie, La., 1995—. Lobby La. Health Care, Baton Rouge, 1991. Mem. ANA, Individual Case Mgmt. Assn., Assn. Rehab. Nurses Case Mgmt. Soc. Am., Assn. Respiratory Care, New Orleans Continuity Care, La. Managed Healthcare Assn., NAFE. Republican. Roman Catholic. Home: 6002 Mitchell Ave Metairie LA 70003-4254 Office: Nat Health Resources Inc Ste 800 3525 N Causeway Blvd Metairie LA 70002

EVANS, CATHERINE GULLEY, librarian; b. Orange, Tex., Oct. 9, 1950; d. Walter Raleigh Jr. and Elizabeth Whitfield (Walker) Gulley; m. Wayne Lea Randall, Jan. 18, 1969 (div. 1981); children: Mary Helen, Wayne Lea Jr.; m. John Edward Evans, June 25, 1983. BS, Miss. U. for Women, 1972; MS, Memphis State U., 1981; MLS, U. Tenn., 1994. Libr. Motley Sch., Columbus, Miss., 1972-75, Heritage Acad., Columbus, 1975-77, Northside Elem. Sch., Natchez, Miss., 1979-80, Magnolia Heights Acad., Senatobia, Miss., 1980-81; libr. Memphis U. Sch., 1981-90, head libr., 1990-95; libr. dir. St. Mary's Episcopal Sch., Memphis, 1995—; dir. Memphis Assn. Ind. Schs. Libr. Consortium, 1990—. Contbr. articles to profl. jours.; producer videos. Mem. altar guild, flower guild, clothes closet Holy Apostles Episcopal Ch., Memphis, 1983-88. Mem. ALA, Assn. for Ednl. Communication and Tech., Southeastern Libr. Assn., Tenn. Libr. Assn. (chair local arrangements 1989, chair honors and awards 1990, 91, 94, chair sch. libr. divsn. 1987, chair libr. instrn. roundtable 1994, Louise Meredith award 1990, James E. Ward Libr. Instrn. award 1993), TENN-SHARE (bd. dirs.), On-Line Audio-Visual Catalogers, Memphis Libr. Coun. (v.p. 1992, pres. 1993). Republican. Episcopalian. Office: St Marys Episcopal Sch Libr 60 Perkins Ext Memphis TN 38117-3125

EVANS, CHARLES WAYNE, II, biologist, researcher; b. Athens, Ohio, Aug. 9, 1929; s. Charles Wayne and Florence Louise (Sheets) Evans Claypool; m. Jo F. Burt, 1948 (div. 1959); children—Charles Wayne III, James Friedrich (dec.), John Burns, Elizabeth Burt; m. Patricia Anne Baker, 1971; children—Debbie Jo, Caralyn Michelle. Student, Tex. A&M U., 1947-51, B.A., 1957, postgrad., 1963-65; postgrad., U. Houston, 1969-70. Seismologist, Universal Seismic Expt., Beaumont, Tex., 1958-65; marine biologist CRI/VIERS, St. Thomas, U.S. Virgin Islands, 1965-71; geologist Dr. C. B. Claypool, Beaumont, 1971-76; research biologist Panthera-Marine-Internat., Ltd., Belize, C.A., Beaumont, 1976-79, pres., chief exec. officer, 1976—; research biologist Synectics, Inc., Las Vegas, 1979-82, bd. dirs., treas., 1979—; research biologist SAC Research Ctr., Beaumont, 1982-88; pres. Jordhammer, Inc., Las Vegas, 1980—; bd. dirs. Ant Fire, Inc., Beaumont, 1985-88, Caribbean World Enterprises, Ltd., New Orleans & Belize, 1987—; pres., dir. rsch. Invicta Corp., 1988—; cons. I.Q. Tech., Houston, 1994—; cons. Eradicator Corp., Houston, 1994—. Inventor Jordhammer, 1982, Earthfire Injection System, 1988. Sus. mem. Rep. Nat. Com., Washington, 1982—; charter mem. Ellis Island Found., N.Y.C., 1983—; founder, pres. Caribbean Inst. Natural Sci., St. Thomas, 1967-70. Served with N.G., 1945-47. SAC Research Ctr. grantee, 1983, Dr. C. B. Claypool grantee, 1963, 78. Mem. AAAS, Smithsonian Assocs., Am. Mus. Natural History (assoc.), N.Y. Acad. Sci., Internat. Oceanographic Found., World Wildlife Fund. Clubs: Aggie, Century (Tex. A&M U.). Lodge: Lions. Avocations: music; chess; big game fishing.

EVANS, CRAIG, foundation administrator, consultant, lobbyist; b. Klamath Falls, Oreg., Apr. 14, 1949; s. Joseph Fuller Evans and Toni Opel (Hooper) Johnson; m. Susan Jean Murphy, Dec. 27, 1980. BA in English, Calif. State U., San Jose, 1971. Reporter San Jose (Calif.) Mercury News, 1968-71; adventurer 1st person to walk end-to-end through the Alps North Face, Berkeley, Calif., 1972-73; freelance writer Los Gatos, Calif., 1973-75; editor Backpacker Mag., N.Y.C., 1975-77; author William Morrow & Co., N.Y.C., 1977-81; exec. dir. Am. Hiking Soc., Washington, 1979-81; owner, chief exec. officer Syntax, Mktg. Communications, Falls Church, Va., 1981-84; assoc. exec. dir. Population-Environment Balance, Washington, 1984-86; pres. The WalkWays Ctr., Washington, 1986-90; mktg. cons. Craig Evans, Inc., Washington, 1989-90; sr. assoc. Am. Farmland Trust, Washington, 1990-95; pres. Fla. Stewardship Found., Boca Raton, 1995—; pres., lobbyist Farming for the Future, Boca Raton, 1994—; mountain tour leader Better Camping Mag., French and Swiss Alps, 1972-73; trails cons. U.S. Dept. of Interior, Washington, 1979-81; U.S. rep. European Rambler's Assn., 1977-84. Author: (7 book series) On Foot Through Europe, 1982, (pub. law) Nat. Trails System Act Amendments of 1983, Purchase of Agrl. Conservation Easement Program (H.B. 483), Commonwealth of Ky., 1994, and Palm Beach County, Fla., 1995; (pub. law) Palm Beach County Agricultural Economic Development Program, 1994; project editor: (book) Backpacking Equipment Buyer's Guide, 1977, A Landowners' Strategy for Protecting Florida Panther Habitat on Private Lands in South Florida: A Project Report, 1995, Incentive-based Programs and Techniques to Protect Natural Resources and Florida Panther Habitat on Private Lands: A Field Manual, 1995; creator, author: (travel mag.) Tripping, 1973; contbr. articles to profl. jours. Treas. Am. Trails Network, Washington, 1988-89. Recipient One Show Merit award The Art Dirs. Club, Inc., N.Y.C., The Copy Club of N.Y., 1974. Democrat. Home: 1230 NW 8th St Boca Raton FL 33486-2102

EVANS, DEWITT HOWARD, foundation administrator; b. Bessemer, Ala., Aug. 5, 1929; s. William Marcus and Ura Lee (Jenkins) E.; m. Doris Costello Mays, May 25, 1956 (div. Jan. 1958); m. Jacqueline Carol Abel, June 23, 1990. Student, U. Md., 1960-61; BA, U. D.C., 1976, MAT, 1979; postgrad., Howard U., 1980, U. Mich., 1991-92, Auburn U., 1994. Pres. Inst. for Preservation of African Am. Lit., Inc., Washington, 1987—, Nat. Consortium for African Am. Affairs, Inc., Washington, 1994—; philanthropist Scholarship Fund Found., Inc., Washington, 1996. Contbg. writer Balt.-Washington, Afro-Am. Newspaper, 1983-89. With USN, 1946-68. Mem. Panhellenic Coun., Inc. (sec. 1985-89), Kiwanis Internat. (sec. 1985-89), Grand United Order Odd Fellows in Am. (sec. 1981-89), Omega Psi Phi (reporter 1983-89). Democrat. Home: Rte 1 Box 25A Fitzpatrick AL 36029 Office: Scholarship Fund Found Inc 6228 Georgia Ave NW Washington DC 20011

EVANS, DONALD FREDRICK, architect; b. South Bend, Ind., June 14, 1945; s. Donald J. and Beatrice (Bucher) E.; m. Janice Hess, Feb. 15, 1969; 1 child, Dawn Michele. BArch, U. Miami, Fla., 1969. Registered archiect, Fla., Ala., Ariz., Ga., Vt., N.J., S.C., N.C., N.Y., N.H. Architect Bill Cox Assocs., Miami, 1969-70, Rocco Pace Architects, Miami, 1970-71, Fair Jerome Llano Architects, Miami, 1971-72, Barry Berkus Architects, Miami, 1972-73, Fred Klein Architects, Miami, 1973-74, Schweizer Assocs., Orlando, Fla., 1974-75; founder The Evans Group, Orlando, Fla., 1975—; mem. spl. com. on design Nat. Assn. Home Builders, Washington, 1988—; chmn., founder New So. Home, Orlando, 1988-89. Monthly columnist S.E. Home Builder, 1985—, Home & Condo, 1987—. Chmn. fund raising U. Miami Architecture, 1988—; benefactor Annie Russell Home for Atypical children, Orlando, 1986—. Recipient Aurora awards S.E. Builders Conf., Tallahassee, 1982—, Profl. Achievement award Profl. Builder Mag., Chgo., 1988. Mem. Urban Land Inst., AIA (housing com. 1986—), Home Builders Assn. of Mid.-Fla., Fla. Coun. Housing Industry, Nat. Inst. Bldg. Scis. Republican. Roman Catholic. Office: The Evans Group 1030 N Orange Ave Ste 200 Orlando FL 32801-1030

EVANS, ELIZABETH ANN WEST, real estate agent; b. Xenia, Ohio, Mar. 28, 1933; d. Millard Stanley and Elizabeth Denver (Johns) West. BA, Ohio U., 1966, MA, 1968. Cert. GRI, 1993. Sec. various orgns., Ohio, 1952-61; tchr. Ohio U., Athens, 1966-67, Zanesville, 1968-72; tchr. Collier County Pub. Schs., Naples, Fla., 1972-77; sales Helen's Hang Ups, Naples, 1978-79; mgr. pvt. practice Wilmington, Ohio, 1979-87; adminstrv. asst. Powell Assocs., Cambridge, Mass., 1987-90; real estate agt. Bill Evans Realty, Inc., Naples, 1989-90, Howard Hanna Real Estate Svcs., Naples, 1991-93, Downing-Frye Realty, Inc., Naples, Fla., 1993—. Mem. The Women's Network of Collier County. Mem. AAUW, Nat. Assn. Realtors, Greater Naples Alumnae Panhellenic (prs. 1984-86), Nat. Soc. DAR (chaplain 1988-90, chmn. Motion Picture, Radio and TV 1992-94, asst. chaplain 1994-96), Naples Marco Kappa Alpha Theta Alumnae Club (treas. 1990-92), Women's Network of Collier County, Phi Beta Kappa, Phi Kappa Phi, Phi Sigma Iota. Republican. Presbyterian. Home: Apt A200 15117 Royal Fern Ct Naples FL 34110-8081 Office: Downing-Frye Realty Inc 3411 Tamiami Trl N Naples FL 34103-3700

EVANS, FRANK OWEN, JR., physician; b. Macon, Ga., Nov. 5, 1940; s. Frank Owen and Evelyn Anne (Bone) E.; m. Beverly Anne Lemon, Dec. 29, 1964; children: Katherine Evans Adams, Frank Owen III, Creed King. BS in Chemistry, Washington and Lee U., 1963; MD, Cornell U., 1967. Diplomate Am. Bd. Internal Medicine, Am. Bd. Infectious Diseases. Intern U. Ala., Birmingham, 1967-68, resident, 1968-69; fellow in infectious diseases U. Va., Charlottesville, 1972-73, fellow in internal medicine, 1973-74, resident rsch. in sinusitis, 1973-74; chief staff Baldwin County Hosp, Milledgeville, Ga., 1978-79. Mem. exec. bd. Boy Scouts Am., Macon, Ga., 1987-93, scoutmaster, Milledgeville, 1977-90. Maj. U.S. Army, 1969-71. Fellow ACP. Home: 177 O'Connor Dr NW Milledgeville GA 31061-8258 Office: PO Box 1600 Milledgeville GA 31061-1600

EVANS, GAIL HIRSCHORN, television news executive; b. N.Y.C., Dec. 17, 1941; d. David Louis and Violet Ideta (Burkart) Hirschorn; m. Robert Mayer Evans, Mar. 13, 1966; children: Jason, Jeffrey, Julianna. BA, Bennington Coll., 1963. Aide to rep. William Fitts Ryan U.S. Congress, Washington, 1960-63, aide to rep. James Roosevelt, 1963-64; exec. asst. senator Harrison Williams U.S. Senate, Washington, 1964-65; legis. asst. The White House, Washington, 1965-66; owner, ptnr. Global Rsch. Svcs., Atlanta, 1976-80; prodr. CNN, Atlanta, 1980-87, v.p., 1987-91, sr. v.p., 1991—; trustee Radio TV News Dirs. Found., Washington, 1993—; adj. faculty Emory U. Bus. Sch., Atlanta, 1994—; bd. advisors Ga. State U. Law Sch., Atlanta, 1995—. Bd. advisors Ga. State U. Law Sch., Atlanta, 1995—; mem. Citizens Rev. Panel of Juvenile Ct. Atlanta, 1995—; participant Leadership Atlanta, 1978-79; bd. dirs. Atlanta Clean City Commn., 1976-79, Ga. Endowment for Humanities, Atlanta, 1976-80, chairperson, 1980-81; bd. govs. Atlanta Press Club, 1994—. Selected Mem. of 1995, YWCA Acad. Women Achievers. Mem. Am. Women in Radio and TV. Democrat. Jewish. Home: 4700 Paran Vly NW Atlanta GA 30327-3507 Office: CNN PO Box 105366 1 CNN Ctr 100 International Blvd Atlanta GA 30348-5366

EVANS, GAREN LEE, laboratory director, regulatory compliance officer; b. Tucson, June 14, 1946; s. Roland Lee and Gertrude Helen (Prouty) E.; m. Theressa Ann Schaefer, Sept. 25, 1965; children: Lois Louise, Garen Lee II, Elaine Diane. Student, U. Wash., Seattle, 1965; BS, U. Ariz., 1973; MRE, SW Bap. Theol. Sem., Ft. Worth, 1973-80; post grad., North Tex. State, Denton, 1984-88. Sr. analytical chemist Skyline Lab., Tucson, 1966-73; sr. process engr. Bell Helicopter, Ft. Worth, 1974-81; chemist, metallurgist Amarillo Mining, Amarillo, Tex., 1982-83; process mgr. Chem. Dynamics, Weatherford, Tex., 1983-85; lab. dir., regulatory compliance officer Andritz Ruthner, Arlington, Tex., 1985—. Inventor, phosphate precipitation of cadmium, 1980, silicate solidification of hazardous waste, 1981. Served with USNR, 1964-71. Mem. TAPPI, Am. Filtration Soc., Am. Chem. Soc. Republican. Baptist. Home: 3333 Happy Meadows Dr Alvarado TX 76009-6425

EVANS, GARY WAYNE, computer engineer; b. Hackensack, N.J., Mar. 4, 1942; s. Daniel Walter Evans and Isabella (Remington) McLaughlin; m. Marie Dianė Ross, Mar. 30, 1963; 1 child, Scott Christopher (dec.). AA, Palomar Jr. Coll., 1971; BSBA, San Diego State U., 1975. Mgr. Integrated Microcomputer Sys., Rockville, Md., 1984-88; sr. engr. arch. Martin Marietta, Littleton, Colo., 1988-91; chief engr. security Loral Western Devel. Labs., King of Prussia, Pa., 1991-93; local area mgr. Area Sys., Inc., Vienna, Va., 1993-94; program mgmt. specialist Loral Western Devel. Labs., San Jose, Calif., 1994—. Mem. Data Processing Mgmt. Assn., Mustang Assn. Republican. Home: 2504 S Castlerock Ln Santa Maria CA 93455 Office: Loral Western Devel Labs Dept Program Mgmt Santa Maria CA 93455

EVANS, HARRY LAUNIUS, pathology educator; b. Mobile, Ala., June 11, 1948; s. Aurelius A. and Anne (Hathaway) E.; m. Cheryl J. Winfrey, June 6, 1970 (div. Dec. 1990); children: Thomas H., Sarah S. BS, Stetson U., 1970; MD, U. Fla., 1974. Diplomate Am. Bd. Pathology. Resident in pathology Vanderbilt U. Med. Ctr., Nashville, 1974-75; fellow in dermatopathology Mayo Clinic, Rochester, Minn., 1977-78; fellow in pathology U.Tex.-M.D. Anderson Cancer Ctr., Houston, 1975-77, asst. prof. pathology, 1978-82, assoc. prof., 1982-90, prof., 1990—. Contbr. articles to med. jours. Mem. U.S.-Can. Acad. Pathology, Arthur Purdy Stout Soc. Surg. Pathologists. Office: U Tex-MD Anderson Cancer Ctr Dept Pathology 1515 Holcombe Blvd Houston TX 77030-4009

EVANS, HELEN HORLACHER, state agency administrator, foundation adminstrator; b. Fortville, Ind., June 11, 1920; d. Levi Jackson and Vaneta (Thomas) H.; m. Joseph Carson Evans Sr., Aug. 14, 1948 (Dec. Apr. 1971); children: Joseph Carson Jr., Elizabeth Ellen Evans Cooke. BS, U. Ky., 1941. Cert. edn. tchr., Ky. Home econs. tchr. Versailles (Ky.) High Sch., 1941-42; sr. tng. officer VA, Louisville, 1946-51; vol. coord. Ky. Edn. TV, Lexington, 1972-74; dir. Lt. Gov. mansion Ky. State Govt., Frankfort, 1975, spl. projects adminstr., 1976-79, dir. state meeting house, 1979—; exec. officer Ky. Mansions Preservation and Mary Todd Lincoln House, Lexington, 1985—. Chmn. 175th anniversary Second Presbyn. Ch., 1990; com. Ky. Mil. History Mus., 1979-87, 95—. WAC Capt. U.S. Army, 1942-46, ETO. Recipient Svc. to Mankind award Sertoma Club, 1974. Fellow U. Ky., 1988— (dir. faculty club 1992—); mem. Gen. Fedn. Women's Clubs (nat. chmn. 1972-74), Erikson Soc., Scoville Soc., Ky. Fedn. Women's Clubs (pres. 1970-72, chmn. centennial 1994), Woman's Club Ctrl. Ky. (dir.), Lexington Woman's Club (pres. 1966-68), Kappa Delta. Home: 281 Taylor Dr Lexington KY 40511-2165 Office: Vest-Lindsey House 401 Wapping St Frankfort KY 40601-2607

EVANS, JAMES GILES, former chemistry and computer educator; b. Panama City, Fla., Apr. 30, 1930; s. John Perry Evans and Julia Aldrich Carter. BS, Fla. State U., 1953, MS, 1963. Tchr. Fla. high schools, 1953-91. Author: Charley of the Cherokees, 1993. Bd. dirs. Gilchrist County Edn. Found., 1991-96; vol. Boy Scouts Am., 1969—, Juvenile Rehab. Republican. Baptist. Home: 3869 NW 67th Terr Rd Bell FL 32619-9642

EVANS, JEANETTE MARIE, operating room nurse; b. Detroit, Dec. 1, 1964; d. Edward Francis and Virginia Mary (Schultz) Dolan; m. Peter Haywood Evans, Mar. 21, 1987. BSN, Ga. So. Coll., 1989; student, Auburn U. RN, CNOR, Ga. Med./surg. nurse Kennestone Hosp., Marietta, Ga., 1989-90, oper. room nurse, 1990-91; oper. room nurse Commanche County Meml. Hosp., Lawton, Okla., 1992—; nurse critical care unit St. Vincent's Hosp., Birmingham, Ala., 1992—, evening supr. operating room, 1993—. Mem. ANA, Assn. Operating Room Nurses.

EVANS, JO BURT, communications executive, rancher; b. Kimble County, Tex., Dec. 18, 1928; d. John Fred and Sadie (Oliver) Burt; m. Charles Wayne Evans II, Apr. 17, 1949; children: Charles Wayne III, John Burt, Elizabeth Wisart. BA, Mary Hardin-Baylor Coll., 1948; MA, Trinity U., 1967. Owner, mgr. Sta. KMBL, Junction, Tex., 1959-61; real estate broker, Junction, 1965-74; staff economist, adv. on 21st Congl. Dist., polit. campaign Nelson Wolff, 1974-75; asst. mgr., bookkeeper family owned ranches and rent property, Junction, 1948—; gen. mgr. TV Translator Corp., Junction, 1968—, sec.-treas., 1980—. Treas., asst. to coordinator Citizens for Tex., 1972; historian Kimble Hist. Soc.; mem. Com. of Conservation Soc. to Save the Edwards Aquifer, San Antonio, 1973; homecoming chmn. Sesquicentennial Year, Junction; treas., asst. coordinator New Constitution, San Antonio, 1974; legis. chair Hill Country Women, Kimble County, 1990—. AAUW scholarship named in honor, 1973; named an outstanding Texan, Tex. Senate, 1973. Mem. Nat. Translator Assn., AAUW, Daus. Republic Tex., Tex. Sheriffs Assn., Nat. Cattlewomens Assn., Internat. Platform Assn., Bus. and Profl. Women (pres. 1981-82). Republican. Mem. Unity Ch. Home: PO Box 283 Junction TX 76849-0283 Office: 618 Main St Junction TX 76849-4635

EVANS, LAWRENCE ERIC, military officer, systems analyst; b. Ruiclep, Eng., June 28, 1956; came to the U.S., 1960; s. Larry Earl Evans and Ada Mary (Georges) Corman; m. Michele Karen Evans, June 12, 1993; 1 child, Lawrence William. AAS, Mohegan Coll., 1987. Enlisted USN, 1975; technician USN, Norfolk, Va., 1975-81; engr. asst. Vitro Labs., USNR, Washington, 1981-83; technician USN, Norfolk, 1983-89; recruiter USN, Fredericksburg, Va., 1989-92; weapons chief USN, Norfolk, 1992—; systems cons. USN, Norfolk, 1984-89, trainer, educator, programmer, 1989—, local area network adminstr., 1992-93; freelance programmer, 1983—. Leader Boy Scouts Am., Culpeper, Va., 1990. Mem. Aircraft Owners Pilots Assn., Norfolk Flying Club, Navy Meml. Found.

EVANS, LINDA MARIE, secondary education educator; b. Mobile, Ala., Jan. 3, 1960; d. John Ronald and Joe Ann (Terrell) Evans; m. F. Joseph Risser, July 8, 1992. BS, S.W. Tex. State U., 1993. Unit clk. Meth. Hosp., San Antonio, 1980—; tchr. Providence H.S., San Antonio, 1993-94, Poth (Tex.) Ind. Sch. Dist., 1994—. Mem. Vocat. Home Econs. Tchrs. Assn. Tex. (bd. dirs.), Am. Assn. Family and Consumer Sci., Phi Upsilon Omicron (alumni). Home: 130 Sioux Cir Cibolo TX 78108-3607

EVANS, MARY ANN, county administrator; b. Marion, Va., Feb. 22, 1942; d. Joseph Emory and Ruth Hazel (Burnop) Cress; m. Robert C. Evans, Feb. 29, 1970; children: Michael, Steven, Jill. AS, Marion Coll., 1962. Cashier Roses, Marion, 1960-62; sec. Dr. Pepper Bottling Co., Marion, 1962-71; sec. then asst. county adminstr. County of Smyth, 1971—. Mem. Profl. Secs. Internat. Home: PO Box 126 Atkins VA 24311-0126

EVANS, MICHAEL DAVID, clergyman, author; b. Springfield, Mass., June 30, 1947; s. Robert and Jean (Levine) E.; m. Carolyn Sue Wedel, Nov. 25, 1970; children: Michelle, Shira, Rachel, Michael. AA, Southwestern Jr. Coll., Waxahachie, Tex., 1969. Cert. scuba diver. Pastor Church on the Move, Euless, Tex.; chmn. bd. Evang. Israel Friendship Coun., Metroplex Media, Bedford Books, Bradford Books, MEM Internat., Irving, Tex.; mem. exec. bd. Am. Coalition for Traditional Values, Washington for Jesus; trustee Internat. Charismatic Bible Ministries; advisor to world leaders, including leaders of Israel, Uganda, El Salvador, Philippines. Author, producer: (book and spl.) Let My People Go, (book and TV spls.) Jerusalem, D.C.; Israel, America's Key to Survival; The Return; Save Jerusalem. Cpl. U.S. Army, 1964-66, Korea. Home: PO Box 910 Euless TX 76039 Office: MEM Internat 1425 Greenway Ste 400 Irving TX 75038

EVANS, MICHAEL DEAN, financial planner; b. Carthage, Tex., Dec. 26, 1953; s. Charles Henry and Joy Jean (Jones) E.; m. Karen Ruth Hall, May 20, 1975; children: Shelly, David. BS in Econs. and Fin., La. Coll., 1976. Loan officer La. Savs. Assn., Alexandria, La., 1976-78; dist. mgr. Dixiecolor, Inc., Lafayette, La., 1978-80; fin. cons. A.G. Edwards & Sons, Inc., Holiday, Fla., 1980-88; account exec., cert. fin. planner Integrated Resources Equity Corp., Tarpon Springs, Fla., 1988-90; registered rep. Mutual Svc. Corp., New Port Richey, Fla., 1989-91; sr. investment officer Barnett Securities, Inc., St. Petersburg, Fla., 1991-94; v.p. Barnett Banks Trust Co. N.A., Clearwater, Fla., 1994—; instr. investments La. Coll. Continuing Edn. Program, Pineville, La., 1982-83; mem. First Provisional Support Bn. Chairborne Rangers, Clearwater, Fla., 1987—. U.S. Coast Guard aux. Mem. Internat. Assn. Cert. Fin. Planners, Internat. Assn. Registered Fin. Planners, Tampa Bay Soc., Inst. Cert. Fin. Planners. Republican. Baptist. Club: La. Coll. Bus. Adminstrn. Soc. (Pineville, pres. 1974-75). Office: Barnett Banks Trust Co NA 600 Cleveland St Fl 3 Clearwater FL 34615

EVANS, ORINDA D., federal judge; b. Savannah, Ga., Apr. 23, 1943; d. Thomas and Virginia Elizabeth (Grieco) E.; m. Roberts O. Bennett, Apr. 12, 1975; children: Wells Cooper, Elizabeth Thomas. B.A., Duke U., 1965; J.D. with distinction, Emory U., 1968. Bar: Ga. 1968. Assoc. Fisher & Phillips, Altanta, 1968-69; assoc. Alston, Miller & Gaines, Atlanta, 1969-74, ptnr., 1974-79; judge U.S. Dist Ct. (no. dist.) Ga., Atlanta, 1979—; adj. prof. Emory U. Law Sch., 1974-77; counsel Atlanta Crime Commn., 1970-71. Recipient Disting. award BBB, 1972. Mem. Atlanta Bar Assn. (dir. 1979). Democrat. Episcopalian. Office: US Dist Ct 1988 US Courthouse 75 Spring St SW Atlanta GA 30303-3309

EVANS, PHILIP RODNEY, educator; b. Sheffield, Yorkshire, U.K., Aug. 31, 1945; came to U.S., 1994; s. David and Betty (Fox) E.; m. Pamela Ridgway, Dec. 27, 1968 (div. Sept. 1995); children: Rebecca, Simon; m. Faith Ann McCarty, Nov. 29, 1996. BEd, U. Alta., Edmonton, 1977, MEd, 1979, PhD, 1989. Prin. Grande Cache (Alta.) Jr.-Sr. H.S., Grande Cache, Alta., 1979-81; asst. prof. U. Calgary, Alta., 1986-94; assoc. prof. dept. edn. U. Tenn., Chattanooga, 1994—. Contbr. articles to profl. jours. Recipient Isaac Walton Killam Found. award, 1983-85. Home: 1920 Gunbarrel Rd Apt 1116 Chattanooga TN 37421

EVANS, RICHARD TAYLOR, aerospace engineer, consultant; b. Denver, July 2, 1940; s. Lawrence T. and Geraldine E. (Shoemaker) Dorsey; m. Mary W. Kalmar, Apr. 10, 1965; children: Christine M., Richard G. AB Pre-Engring., Columbia U., N.Y.C., 1962; BS in Elec. Engring., Colo. U., Boulder, 1964; MS in Aerospace Engring., Air Force Inst. of Tech., Dayton, Ohio, 1969; PhD in Aerospace Engring., U. Tex., Austin, Tex., 1980. Launch crew commdr., instr. Minuteman Missile Wing, Malmstrom AFB, Mont., 1965-69; minuteman, guidance project officer Space and Missile Sys. Orgn., Norton AFB, Calif., 1969-74; tech. rep. Charles Stark Draper Lab, Cambridge, Mass., 1974-76; grad. student Aerospace & Engring. Mechanics, Austin, Tex., 1976-79; dep. dir. Aerospace-Mechs. Scis. F.J. Seiler Rsch. Lab. USAF Acad., USAF Acad., Colo., 1979-83; site activation commdr. Joint Cruise Missile Program Office Sicily, 1983-84; dir. Sys. Deployment Cruise Missile Program Office, Crystal City, Va., 1984-87; deputy dir. Advanced Strategic Missile Sys. USAF, Norton AFB, Calif., 1987-90, Minuteman program mgr., 1990-92; tech. cons. SDIO TASC, Arlington, Va., 1992-94; tech. cons. Iridium Satellite Comms. Iridium Satellite Comms. TASC, Inc., Chandler, Ariz., 1994-95; tech. cons. to Def. Mapping Agy., others TASC, Inc., Reston, Va., 1995—. Contbr. articles to profl. jours. Col. USAF, 1965-92. Mem. AIAA (sr., chpt. chair), Armed Forces Commn. & Electronics Assn., Air Force Assn. Republican. Home: 2181 Wolftrap Ct Vienna VA 22182 Office: TASC Inc 12100 Sunset Hills Rd Reston VA 22090

EVANS, ROBERT BYRON, software engineer, educator; b. Winchester, Va., July 8, 1942; s. Quentin Marcellus and Catherine Virginia (Ours) E.; m. Nancy Lee Irwin, Oct. 24, 1964 (div. Sept. 1983); children: Richard Todd, Christine Kay, Danielle René. AB in Math., Ind. U., 1963; M Engring. in Computer Sci., Vanderbilt U., 1991. Customer svc. rep. R.R. Donnelley & Sons, Warsaw, Ind., 1963-68, prodn. planner, 1968-74; prodn. planner R.R. Donnelley & Sons, Gallatin, Tenn., 1974-81, bindery mgr., 1981-85, sr. software engr., 1985—; adj. asst. prof. computer sci. Volunteer State C.C., Gallatin, 1991—; speaker Machine Learning Conf., U. Mass., 1993, Statis. Process Control Users Conf., Graphic Arts Tech. Found., New Orleans, 1995, Gravure Assn. Am., Mpls., 1996. Author numerous articles on applied machine learning. Sgt. Ind. Army N.G., 1963-69. Mem. IEEE, Am. Assn. Artificial Intelligence, Assn. for Computing Machinery, Mensa. Home: 820 Newton Ln Gallatin TN 37066

EVANS, ROBERT OWEN, English language educator, administrator; b. Chgo., Sept. 19, 1919; s. Franklin Bachelder and Arline Henrietta (Brown) E.; m. Margery Brooks, Aug. 2, 1941; children—Robert Jr., Michele Chosney, Douglas Brooks. A.B., U. Chgo., 1941; M.A., U. Fla., 1950, Ph.D., 1954; postgrad., Harvard U., 1950-51. Instr., U. Fla., Gainesville, 1948-54; instr. to prof. U. Ky., Lexington, 1954-80, dir. honors program, 1966-78, asst. to pres., 1966-67, prof. emeritus, 1980—; prof, English, dir. gen. honors U. N.Mex., Albuquerque, 1980-86, prof. emeritus, 1986—; vis. prof., U. Helsinki, Finland, 1958-59, U. des Saarlands, Saarbrucken, Germany, 1963-64, Lincoln Coll., Oxford U., England, 1963, U. Wis., Madison, 1967-68, Am. Coll., Paris, 1970-71, Miami (Fla.)-Dade C.C., 1991—, Ky. State U., Frankfort, 1993; dir. Nat. Collegiate Honors Coun., 1975—, pres. 1977-78. Author: Osier Cage, 1966; Metrical Elision, 1966. Editor: Style/Rhetoric/Rhythm, 1966; Graham Greene-Critical Considerations, 1964; Wm. Golding Critical Considerations, 1976. Contbr. articles to profl. jours. Bd. dirs. Macatawa Cottagers Assn., Mich., 1954-80, former pres.; pres. Macatawa Parking Corp, 1988. Mem. MLA (USA & Finland), Internat. Assn. Univ. Profs. English, Internat. Comparative Lit. Assn., Western Regional Honors Coun., Phi Beta Kappa, Phi Kappa Phi, Psi Upsilon. Democrat. Episcopalian. Home: PO Box 4 Macatawa MI 49434-0004

EVANS, RODNEY EARL, business educator; b. Pontiac, Mich., May 15, 1939; s. Hubert Elgene and Lillian Beatrice (Wilcox) E.; m. Judith Karen Garvin; children: Mark, Scott, Cynthia. BA, Mich. State U., 1961, MBA, 1963, PhD, 1966. Prof. dept. bus. adminstrn. U. Okla., Norman, 1970—, dir. office bus. and indsl. coop., 1986-90; chmn. bd. Southwestern Premier Foods, Inc., Anadarko, Okla. Contbr. articles to profl. jours.; co-author: Marketing Strategy and Management, 1976. Capt. USAF, 1967-69. Mem. Am. Mktg. Assn. Office: U Okla Coll Bus Adminstrn 307 W Brooks St Norman OK 73019-4000

EVANS, ROSEMARY KING (MRS. HOWELL DEXTER EVANS), librarian, educator; b. Forsyth, Ga., Nov. 16, 1924; d. Wiley Ginn and Mary (Goggans) King; B.S., Tift Coll., 1957; librarian's certificate Woman's Coll. of Ga., 1963; M. Library Edn., U. Ga., 1972, postgrad. in library edn., 1975; m. Howell Dexter Evans, June 29, 1945; children—Joseph William, Curtis McKenney. Tchr. elementary sch., Forsyth, Ga., 1946-48, 54-62; librarian Mary Persons High Sch., Forsyth, 1962-73; catalog librarian Tift Coll., Forsyth, 1973-74; head librarian Stratford Acad., Macon, Ga., 1974-77; head librarian, assoc. prof. Gordon Jr. Coll., Barnesville, Ga., 1977-87; chmn. regents' acad. com. libraries State Bd. Regents Univ. System of Ga.: Mem. Ga. State Bd. Certification of Librarians. Author: The Christmas Tree Farm, 1989. Spiritual edn. chmn. PTA, 1960-61; mem. Monroe County Hosp. Authority, 1988—, Monroe County Libr. Bd., 1990—. Named Star Tchr., 1966. Mem. Nat., Ga., Monroe County (sec. 1959-60, v.p. 1961-62, pres. 1962-63) edn. assns., Ga. (dis. pres. 1965), ALA, Southeastern library assns., Ga. Library Assn. Methodist (chmn. local edn. bd. 1964-65, chmn. commn. on Christian vocation 1965—, exec. com., tchr. adult Bible class). Author: Backhome Cuisine, 1984. Home: Evans Rd Smarr GA 31086

EVANS, ROXANNE ROMACK, retired military officer, hospital administrator; b. Idaho Falls, Idaho, Feb. 14, 1952; d. Richard Edward and Anne Elizabeth (Browning) R.; m. Paul Evans. BS, U. Idaho, 1974; postgrad., U. Md., 1979; MHA, Baylor U., 1982. Registered dietitian, Tex., S.C., Va., Okla. Commd. 2d lt. U.S. Army, 1974, advanced through grades to lt. col., 1990; dietetic intern Brooke Army Med. Ctr., Ft. Sam Houston, Tex., 1974-75; staff dietitian Walter Reed Army Med. Ctr., Washington, 1975-77; chief food service div. Kimbrough Army Hosp., Ft. George G. Meade, Md., 1977-80; adminstrv. resident Tripler Army Med. Ctr., Hawaii, 1981-82, chief clin. dietetics br., 1982-85; chief nutrition care div. Moncrief Army Community Hosp., Ft. Jackson, S.C., 1985-87; chief clin. dietetics div. Nutrition Care Directorate Walter Reed Army Med. Ctr., Washington, 1987-89; chief procurement activity Army Med. Specialist Corps, Dental Corps, Vet. Corp, 1989-92; chief nutrition care divsn. Reynolds Army Community Hosp., Ft. Still, Okla., 1992-93; hosp. adminstrn. Reynolds Army Cmty. Hosp., Fort Sills, Okla., 1993-94; retired U.S. Army, 1994, ret., 1994. Asst. leader cub scouts Boy Scouts Am., Columbia, S.C., 1985-86. Fellow Am. Dietetic Assn.; mem. Am. Coll. Healthcare Execs. (diplomate).

EVANS, THOMAS PASSMORE, business and product licensing consultant; b. West Grove, Pa., Aug. 19, 1921; s. John and Linda (Zeuner) E.; B.S. in E.E., Swarthmore Coll., 1942; M.Engring., Yale U., 1948; m. Lenore Jane Knuth, June 21, 1947; children—Paula S., Christina L., Bruce A., Carol L. Engr., Atomic Power div. Westinghouse Electric Corp., Pitts., 1948-51; dir. rsch. and devel. AMF, Inc., N.Y.C., 1951-60; dir. rsch. O.M. Scott & Sons Co., Marysville, Ohio, 1960-62; v.p. rsch. and devel. W.A. Sheaffer Pen Co., Ft. Madison, Iowa, 1962-67; dir. rsch. Mich. Tech. U., Houghton, 1967-80; dir. research, mem. faculty Berry Coll., Mt. Berry, Ga., 1980-88; prof. bus. adminstrn., 1980-86. Author, patentee in field. Served to lt. USN, 1943-46. Registered profl. engr., Pa. Mem. Am. Forestry Assn., Am. Def. Preparedness Assn., Am. Phys. Soc., IEEE, Soc. Plastics Engrs., Yale Sci. and Engring. Assn., Nat. Coun. Univ. Rsch. Adminstrs., Licensing Execs. Soc., Air Force Assn., Am. Legion, AAAS, High Mus. Art, Hunter Mus. Art, Nat. Trust Hist. Preservation, Yale Club of Ga., Rome Little Theatre, Rome Symphony, VFW, Rotary Club, Sigma Xi, Tau Beta Pi. Home: 25 Wellington Way SE Rome GA 30161-9417 Office: 97 Berry College Mount Berry GA 30149-0097

EVANS, TIMOTHY HARRIS, non-profit organization executive; b. Phoenix, Dec. 4, 1959; s. John Henry III and Elizabeth L. (Harris) E.; m. Karen Neola Murphy, May 21, 1983; children: Zachary Harris, Luke Samuel. BS in Psychology, Fla. State U., 1980; MDiv, Duke U., 1983; MA in Psychology, U. West Fla., 1989. Min. First United Meth. Ch., Jupiter, Fla., 1984-85, Melrose (Fla.) United Meth. Ch., 1985-87; supr. clin. Gulf Coast Youth and Family Svcs., Pensacola, Fla., 1989-91; exec. dir. 90 and 9 Boys' Ranch, Gonzalez, Fla., 1991-92, Manna Food Bank, Pensacola, 1993—; pres. adv. bd. Bay Area Food Bank, Mobile, Ala., 1995-96. Active First United Meth. Ch., Pensacola, 1987—. Mem. Am. Soc. Pub. Adminstrn. (pres. Gulf Coast chpt. 1996—), Nat. Soc. Fund Raising Execs. (v.p. West Fla. chpt. 1995-96). Democrat. Home: 1225 Langley Ave Pensacola FL 32504 Office: Manna Food Bank Inc 911 N Tarragona St Pensacola FL 32501-3178

EVANS, TRELLANY VICTORIA THOMAS, entrepreneur; b. Georgetown, S.C., Apr. 18, 1959; d. Abraham Lincoln and Jannie Ruth (Brown) Thomas; m. Leroy Michael Evans, Sr., June 18, 1983; children: Leroy, Jr., Thomas, Trellany Janiece. BS, S.C. State U., 1980; MHA, MBA, Pfeiffer Coll., 1995. Instr. Horry-Georgetown (S.C.) Tech. Coll., 1982-83, Big Bend C.C., Bad Kreuznach, Germany, 1986-87; statistician U.S. Govt.-Europe, Bad Kreuznach, Germany, 1987-89; budget analyst U.S. Govt.-Europe, Baumholder, Germany, 1989-91; acct. U.S. Govt.-DeCA, Fort Lee, Va., 1991; pres., CEO Abraham & Evans Assocs., Huntersville, N.C., 1990—, DocuPrep, Charlotte, N.C., Info. Rsch., Inc., Huntersville, N.C., 1996—; cons. Abraham and Evans Assocs., Huntersville, 1990—; part-time computer applications instr. Mitchell C.C., Mooresville, N.C., 1994—; grad. rsch. asst. Pfeiffer Coll., 1994. Project dir. Charlotte (N.C.) Ctr. for Cmty. Self-Help, 1994—. Mem. Am. Soc. for Quality Control, Order of Eastern Star. Baptist. Office: Abraham and Evans Assocs 15312 Curling Ct-1020 Huntersville NC 28078

EVANS, VALERIE ELAINE, elementary education educator; b. Winston-Salem, N.C., July 12, 1971; d. Lindsay McRay an Beverly Kaye (Moser) E. BS in Edn., U. Ctrl. Fla., 1993, postgrad., 1996—. Vol. Pershing Elem. Sch., Orlando, Fla., 1991-92; intern Waterford Elem. Sch., Orlando, Fla., 1993; tchr. kindergarten Orange Ctr. Elem. Sch., Orlando, Fla., 1993-94, tchr. 4th grade, 1994-96; tchr. 4th grade Little River Elem. Sch., Orlando, Fla., 1996—; mem. computer tech. team, 1994, 96-97, mem. childcare team, 1994, sci. amb., 1996-97. Democrat. Methodist.

EVANS, WALLACE ROCKWELL, JR., mechanical engineer; b. El Paso, Tex., Aug. 23, 1914; s. Wallace Rockwell and Margaret (Strickland) E.; m. Evelyn Lucille Osborne, Feb. 12, 1944; children: Lynda Lucille, Wallace Rockwell III. BS in Mech. Engring., Va. Poly. Inst. and State U., 1941. Registered profl. engr., N.C. Constrn. engr. Weigel Engring. Co., Chattanooga, 1941-42; air conditioning engr. Page Air Conditioning Co., Charlotte, N.C., 1946-48, Celanese Fibers Co., Rock Hill, S.C., 1948-54; utilities mgr. Celanese Fibers Co., Charlotte, 1954-79; pres. Evans Engring. Co., Rock Hill, 1979-95; ret., 1995. Contbr. articles on refrigeration, air conditioning and radiant heat to profl. jours. Pres. PTA, Rock Hill, 1952-53. Lt. USN, 1942-47. Mem. ASME (life, power generation div. 1942), ASHRA, Am. Soc. Profl. Engrs. (pres. Piedmont chpt. 1969, Engr. of Yr. 1976). Republican. Methodist. Home and Office: 411 Lakeside Dr Rock Hill SC 29730-6105

EVANS, WAYNE EDWARD, environmental microbiologist, researcher; b. Indpls., Nov. 17, 1962; s. Warren J. II and Susan Carol (Winans) E.; m. Kathleen Francis Herbst, Dec. 30, 1989; children: Matthew David, Elizabeth Paige. BS in Biology, BA in Chemistry, Purdue U., 1986; MS in Microbiology, Ball State U., 1992. Supr. lab. microbiology and chemistry Moseley Labs./Vivolac Cultures, Indpls., 1986-89; environ. chemist Ind. Dept. Environ. Mgmt., Indpls., 1989-90; chemist technician Hoosier Microbiol. Labs., Muncie, Ind., 1991-92; micro lab supr. Ball State U., Muncie, 1990-92; environ. microbiologists ASCI Corp. at Waterways Exptl. Sta., Vicksburg, Miss., 1992—. Fellow AAAS, Am. Soc. for Microbiology, Am. Chem. Soc., Soc. for Indsl. Microbiology. Home: 109 Ridgecrest Dr Ridgeland MS 39157-2538

EVANS, WILLIAM EARL, JR., lawyer; b. Phoenix, June 19, 1956; s. William Earl and Julie Catherine (Perry) E. BS, Fla. So. Coll., 1980; JD, Cumberland Sch. Law, 1983. Bar: Fla. 1983, U.S. Dist. Ct. (mid. dist.) Fla. 1984, U.S. Ct. Appeals (11th cir.) 1985, U.S. Ct. Vets. Appeals 1993. Assoc., then ptnr. Shannon, Naser & Corda, Lakeland and Ft. Meade, Fla., 1983-89; pvt. practice Bartow, Fla., 1990—. Named one of Outstanding Young Men of Am., 1985. Mem. ABA, Fla. Bar Assn., Lakeland Bar Assn., Jaycees (pres. Ft. Meade chpt. 1985-86), Rotary (pres. Ft. Meade club 1987-87), Lions (pres. Ft. Meade club 1989-90), Masons (Lakeland lodge 91).

Republican. Roman Catholic. Office: 341 W Davidson St Ste 301 Bartow FL 33830-3765

EVANS, WILLIAM ROBERT, III (BUTCH EVANS), anthropologist; b. Camden, N.J., May 13, 1940; s. William Robert Jr. and Bernice Kathleen (Randall) E.; widowed; 1 child, Sean William. Student, St. Petersburg Jr. Coll., 1965-67, Rollins Coll., Winter Park, Fla., 1979-81; BA in Anthropology, U. South Fla., Tampa, 1969; postgrad., U. South Fla., 1994—. Cert. food hygiene specialist, spl. fire safety insp., food mgmt. profl. Profl. touring musician writing and performing with various bands, 1963, 64-66; instr. Berklee Sch. Music, Boston, 1970; venereal disease investigator, pub. health sanitarian Pinellas County Health Dept., St. Petersburg, Fla., 1969-70; staff music arranger, musician Walt Disney World Prodns., Lake Buena Vista, Fla., 1972-84; environ. health specialist Orange County Health Dept., Orlando, Fla., 1984-85, Pinellas County Health Dept., 1985-91, Dept. Health and Rehab. Svcs., Pinellas Park, 1991-92; sanitation and safety specialist Fla. Dept. Bus. and Profl. Regulation, Tampa, 1992—; anthropology and music cons. St. Petersburg Hist. Mus., Flight One Mus., 1993—. Composer, arranger Disney jazz ensemble series Main Street Strut, 1977; arranger, composer jazz ensemble arrangement Moon Monkey, Tonight Show Band, 1978-79, Don Lamond and His Big Swing Band Extraordinary, 1982, Blues for Sean, 1984; arranger Make Tomorrows Memories Now, 1977. Served with U.S. Army, 1961-63. Downbeat Hall of Fame scholar, 1964. Mem. ASCAP, Am. Anthrop. Assn., Soc. for Med. Anthropology, Suncoast Orgn. Practicing Anthropologists, Fla. Anthrop. Soc., Am. Fedn. Musicians. Democrat. Unitarian-Universalist. Home: 2628 Kavalier Dr Palm Harbor FL 34684

EVANS, WILLIAM WILSON, journalism educator, retired newspaper editor; b. Okmulgee, Okla., Mar. 12, 1932; s. Robert Daniel and Hortense Bernice (Harris) E.; m. Peggy Gene Roberts, Sept. 29, 1962; children: Daniel Rhys, Rebecca Colleen. BA, U. Okla., 1953; postgrad., North Tex. State U., 1963. Reporter, editor The Daily Ardmoreite, Ardmore, Okla., 1955-56; copy editor The Dallas Morning News, 1956-69, news editor, 1969-78, sr. news editor, 1978-83, asst. mng. editor, 1980-83, mng. editor, 1983-90, exec. mng. editor, 1990-93; instr. journalism So. Meth. U., Dallas, 1973-74, 90-96. Served to 1st lt. U.S. Army, 1953-55, Korea. Recipient W.H. Seay award A.H. Belo Corp., 1994, Marryat award AMR, 1993; named Disting. Alumnus in Journalism, U. Okla., 1990; McMahon scholar U. Okla., 1951-52. Mem. Soc. Profl. Journalists, AP Mng. Editors Assn. (chmn. ethics com. 1987-88, 91-92, chmn. fgn. news com. 1988-90, chmn. readership com. 1992-93, bd. dirs. 1991-93), Am. Soc. Newspaper Editors, Sigma Chi (consul 1952-53), Dallas Press Club. Home: 8402 Richardson Branch Trl Dallas TX 75243-7436

EVANS-O'CONNOR, NORMA LEE, secondary school educator, consultant; b. Vanceburg, Ky., Sept. 4, 1952; d. Herbert Martin and Nellie Irene (Parker) E.; 1 child, Karen. AB, Morehead State U., 1975; MEd, Xavier U., 1982. Cert. tchr. Fla., Ky., Tenn., Ohio. Tchr. Forest Hills Sch. Dist., Cin., 1977-83, Osceola County Schs., Kissimmee, Fla., 1983—; chair sch. adv. coun. Osceola H.S. (named Tchr. of Yr. 1995-96, County Social Studies Tchr. of Yr. 1996), advisor Student Govt., Students Against Drunk Driving, Class of 2000, dept. head social studies; mem. student coun. bd. Nat. Assn. Secondary Sch. Prins., Va., 1990-91; cons. Walt Disney World, Lake Buena Vista, Fla., 1991—; security guard Walt Disney World Co., Lake Buena Vista, 1988—; movie checker Theatrical Entertainment Svcs., L.A., 1990—. Mem. NEA, Nat. Assn. Workshop Dirs., Osceola County Tchrs. Orgn. Democrat. Roman Catholic. Office: Osceola County Schs 420 S Thacker Ave Kissimmee FL 34741-5963

EVATT, PARKER, former state commissioner, former state legislator; b. Greenville, S.C., Aug. 27, 1935; s. H.D. and Ruby (Parker) E.; m. Jane Mangum, Sept. 2, 1960; children—Katherine, Alan. B.S., U. S.C., 1958, M.Criminal Justice, 1978; LL.D. (hon.), Presbyterian Coll., 1977. Exec. dir. Alston Wilkes Soc., Columbia, S.C., 1965-87; mem. S.C. Ho. of Reps., 1975-87; commr. S.C. Dept. Corrections, 1987-95. Mem. adminstrv. bd. Virginia Wingard Meml., United Methodist Ch., del. to gen. conf., 1972, del. to jurisdiction confs., 1972, 76, 80, 84; past lay leader Columbia Meth. Dist. Served with USN, 1958-60. Recipient numerous awards and citations from civic, religious and profl. orgns. Mem. S.C. Youth Workers Assn. (past pres.), Christian Action Council (bd. govs. 1968-71), St. Andrews Jaycees (life), Nat. Assn. Social Workers (named Citizen of Yr. S.C. chpt. 1978), Internat. Halfway Assn. (v.p. 1973-76), Res. Officers Assn. (v.p. Columbia chpt.), Naval Res. Assn. (past pres. Carolina chpt.), Pi Kappa Alpha. Lodge: Rotary.

EVEARITT, DANIEL JOSEPH, religion educator; b. Toledo, Ohio, Dec. 13, 1950; s. Cedric Conrad and Bernadine Patricia (Weirich) E.; m. Karen Louise Braidwood, June 11, 1971. BA, Nyack (N.Y.) Coll., 1974; MPS, Alliance Theol. Sem., Nyack, 1976; MA, Drew U., 1980, PhD, 1988. Adj. prof. philosophy St. Thomas Aquinas Coll., Sparkill, N.Y., 1987-88, Nyack Coll., 1988-89; asst. to assoc. prof. religion and theology Toccoa Falls (Ga.) Coll., 1989—. Author: Rush Limbaugh and the Bible, 1993, Body and Soul: Evangelism and the Social Concern of A.B. Simpson, 1994. Named Tchr. of the Yr., Toccoa Falls Coll., 1990-91, Faculty Scholar of the Yr., 1993. Mem. Am. Acad. Religion, Evang. Theol. Soc., Am. Soc. Ch. History, Soc. for Sci. Study of Religion, Religious Rsch. Assn., Assn. for Sociology of Religion. Democrat. Mem. Christian and Missionary Alliance Ch. Home: 120 Valley Rd Toccoa GA 30577 Office: Toccoa Falls College Box 800-838 Toccoa GA 30598

EVENSEN, ALF JOHN, engineer, researcher; b. Marquette, Mich., June 30, 1938; s. Alf and Alice (Edna) E.; m. Judith Lynne Dellinger, June 22, 1979. BS, U. Mich., 1959; MA, Wayne State U., 1966; BA, U. Ala., 1993. System engr. Computer Scis. Internat., Apledoorn, The Netherlands, 1969; project engr. System Devel. Corp., Huntsville, Ala., 1970-81; system engr. electronics div. AVCO Corp., Huntsville, 1981-82; project mgr. Sci. Applications Internat. Corp., Huntsville, 1982-85; staff engr. Teledyne Brown Engring. Corp., Huntsville, 1985-93; prin. rschr. Tech. Masters Inc., Huntsville, Ala., 1994-95; with Systems Devel. Corp., Huntsville, Ala., 1995—. Served to lt. USNR, 1961-68. Mem. IEEE, NRA, Masons, K.T., Royal Order of Scotland, Ancient Arabic Order Nobles Mystic Shrine, Alpha Chi Sigma, Phi Alpha Theta, Phi Iota Sigma. Home: 137 Eldorado Dr Madison AL 35758-7809 Office: Systems Devel Corp 6703 Odyssey Dr Huntsville AL 35806

EVENSON, MICHAEL DONALD, software engineer; b. Yokosuka, Japan, July 6, 1961; s. David Donald and Teresita (Perez) E.; m. Bernadette Larue, Aug. 13, 1994; children: Natalie, Maria. BS, Marquette U., 1984. Engr. Grumman Tech. Svcs., Kennedy Space Ctr., Fla., 1984-95, sr. engr., 1991-95; engr. software Lockheed Martin Space Ops., Kennedy Space Center, Fla., 1995-96, United Space Alliance, Kennedy Space Ctr., Fla., 1996—. Pres. St. Teresa Young Adult Club, Titusville, Fla., 1990-91, Cath. Young Adults, Brevard County, Fla., 1992—, diocese coord., 1993—; tutor Grumman Adopt-a-Sch. program. Recipient awards Grumman, NASA, 1987, 88, 91. Republican. Roman Catholic. Office: United Space Alliance USK-653 Kennedy Space Center FL 32899

EVERETT, CARL NICHOLAS, management consulting executive; b. Ardmore, Okla., June 4, 1926; s. Elmer Edwards and Cecile (Jones) E.; BS, Columbia U., 1948; MBA with distinction, Harvard U., 1951; m. Susan Blessing Lindstrom, Oct., 1975; children by previous marriages: Carl N., Karen Lee, E. Anthony. With Benton and Bowles, N.Y.C., 1951-54, asso. account exec. Gen. Foods Corp., asst. account exec. Hellmanns and Best Foods Mayonnaise; with Campbell Mithun, Mpls., 1954-56, sr. account exec. Pillsbury Mills, account exec. Pillsbury Refrigerated Products; with McCann Erickson, N.Y.C., 1956-62, bottle sales account exec. Coca Cola Co., sr. account exec. Esso. Standard Oil, accounts supr. Westinghouse Electric Corp., account dir. Liggett and Myers Tobacco, mem. marketing plans bd. and marketing and advt. cons. Coca Cola Co.; sr. v.p., dir. Western region operations Barrington & Co., N.Y.C., 1962-64; founder, pres. Everett Assos., Inc., marketing and mgmt. consultants, N.Y.C., 1964-74; founder, pres. Everett Corp., Scottsdale, Ariz., 1974—; cons. Chrysler Corp., Pepsico Inc., Michelin Tire Corp., GE Corp., Can. Dry Corp., Allied Van Lines, Continental Airlines; co-founder, dir. Precision Investment Co., Denver, 1977—; founder, mng. partner Wilmot Properties, Scottsdale, Ariz., 1979-90; prof. of Bus. Northwest Nazarene Coll. 1992-95; prof. Northeastern State U., Tulsa, 1995—, Oral Roberts U., Tulsa, 1995—. Chmn. bd. dirs. Phoenix Meml. Hosp. Primary Care; bd. dirs. Phoenix Meml. Health Resources, Inc.; chmn. bd. adjustment Town of Paradise Valley, Ariz.; chmn. Commn. on Salaries for Elective Officers; mem. Ariz. Cost Efficiency Commn. Served with USNR, 1944-46. Mem. Am. Mgmt. Assn., Sigma Alpha Epsilon. Unitarian. Clubs: Harvard Bus. Sch. (bd. dirs. Ariz.), Harvard (bd. dirs.), Harvard Club of ID. (pres.), Campfire. Patentee in field. Home: 12340 E 138th Broken Arrow OK 74011

EVERETT, DAVID DEAN, librarian; b. Barberton, Ohio, May 31, 1953; s. Horace H. and Elizabeth Jane (Steele) E.; m. Eileen Marie Burns, Aug. 27, 1977; children: Sheila, Molly. BA in History, Centre Coll., Danville, Ky., 1975; MA in History, Mont. State U., 1976; MLS, Syracuse U., 1982. Ref./interlibr. loan libr. and instr. Case Libr., Colgate U., Hamilton, N.Y., 1983-87; head ref. svcs. and asst. prof. duPont-Ball Libr., Stetson U., DeLand, Fla., 1987-88, assoc. dir. pub. svcs., 1988—, asst. prof., 1988-91, assoc. prof., 1991—. Contbr. articles to profl. jours. Mem. ALA, Assn. Coll. and Rsch. Librs. (nat. adv. coun. coll. librs. sect. 1989-92, exec. bd. Fla. chpt. 1990-96), Fla. Libr. Assn., Beta Phi Mu, Phi Alpha Theta. Office: Stetson Univ Libr N Woodland Blvd Deland FL 32720

EVERETT, ELBERT KYLE, marketing executive, consultant; b. Knoxville, Tenn., June 17, 1946; s. David Abraham and Lois (Hill) E.; student E. Tenn. U., 1965-67; m. Jane Harville, June 13, 1967; 1 child, Evelyn Anne. Sales rep. Met. Life Ins. Co., Knoxville, 1968-70, Creative Displays, Knoxville, 1970-73; market mgr. central and No. Calif., Nat. Advt. div. 3M Co., Stockton from 1973, dist. mgr. western dist., Fresno, 1984; owner Jane Everett's Country Wholesale Furniture Mfg.; sr. cons. Profl. Practice Systems, Inc., Eastern U.S., 1990—; ptnr. Everett Mgmt. Group, 1990—; advt. cons. athletic dept. U. Pacific, Fresno State U.; lectr. outdoor advt. and mktg. San Joaquin Delta Coll., Fresno City Coll., Fresno State U., W.Va. Optometric Conv., Ind. Optometric Conv.; mgmt. cons. in med. field; lectr. in field. Mayor City of Indian Hills, Ky.; mem. steering com. Jefferson County Governance; mem. subcom. on tourism State of Nev.; cons. Stockton Civic Theater. Served with AUS, 1964. Recipient cert. of recognition U.S. Treasury Dept., 1977-78, 82-83; recognition award for best design Advt. Age, 1974, 83, Ky. col., 1995; 2 recognition awards Outdoor Advt. Assn. Am., 1973; Cert. of Appreciation United Way, 1978, 81, 82, 83. Mem. U. Pacific Athletic Found., Fresno State Found., Stockton C. of C., Fresno C. of C., Advt. Club Sacramento, Advt. Club Fresno, Internat. Platform Assn., Fresno State Athletic Found., Phi Sigma Kappa. Baptist. Home and Office: 205 Shevvin Ave Louisville KY 40207-1726

EVERETT, JOHN HOWARD, diving business owner, paramedic; b. Beaumont, Tex., Feb. 10, 1948; s. Bennie Earl Everett and Margaret (Weston) Heartfield; m. Kathleen Loraine Savon, May 30, 1983 (div. Mar. 1985); m. Debra Edwinna Haymon, Oct. 31, 1990. Grad., Forest Park High Sch., Beaumont, Tex., 1966; paramedic, Beaumont Emergency Med. Svc., 1983. Svc. technician Bear's Bug Svc., Beaumont, 1966-70; gunsmith Tex. Gunman, Beaumont, 1970-72; owner, pres. Aquaventures Dive Shop, Inc., Beaumont, 1974-91; flight paramedic, Med-Link St. Elizabeth Hosp., Beaumont, 1988—; exam. coord. Nat. Registry of EMTs, Columbus, Ohio, 1984-91. Recipient Underwater Photography award Tex. Gulf Coast Coun. Dive Clubs, 1978. Mem. Profl. Assn. Diving Instrs. (master instr./master dive trainer). Methodist. Home: 3010 19th St Beaumont TX 77706-7925 also: 12 Coral Negro, Playa del Carmen Mexico Office: Med-Link Aeromedical Svcs 2830 Calder St Beaumont TX 77702-1809

EVERETT, OREL MICHAEL, family physician; b. Port Arthur, Tex., Oct. 31, 1963; s. Orel Ruiz and Guadalupe (Gonzalez) E.; m. Stacey Rose Cordes, Nov. 25, 1988. BS, U.S. Mil. Acad., 1986; MD, U. Tex. Med. Br., Galveston, 1995. 1st lt. U.S. Army, 1986-90. Decorated Army Commendation medal. Mem. AMA, Am. Acad. Family Physicians, Phi Delta Epsilon. Republican. Roman Catholic. Home: 4205 Valley Cir Corpus Christi TX 78414-2633

EVERETT, R. TERRY, congressman, farmer, newspaper executive, bank executive; b. Dothan, Ala., 1937; m. Barbara Gail Pitts. Farm, police reporter The Dothan (Ala.) Eagle, 1959-61, editor, sportswriter, 1966-68; leased oper. newspapers The News Herald, The Graceville (Fla.) News, Hartford, Ala., 1961-64; owner, publisher, editor, founder Daleville (Ala.) Today, The Enterpriser Enterprise, The Army Flier, Fort Rucker, Ala., 1968-79; founder, owner, publisher, editor DownHome Today, Dothan, Ala.; publisher, editor The Daily Ledger (now Enterprise (Ala.) Ledger), 1974-77; mgr. Walls-Smith (now Smith) Newspaper Group, 1977-82; owned, operated Everett Media, 1982-85, Gulf Coast Media Inc., 1984-88; owner Media Mktg. Rsch., 1984-88; owner, pres. Union Springs (Ala.) Herald, 1988—; pres. Premium Home Builders, Enterprise, 1988-94, Everett Land Devel. Co., Enterprise, 1988-94; farmer Counties of Houston, Geneva, Ala., 1988-92; mem. 103rd-104th Congress from 2nd Ala. dist., 1993—. Apppointee to Pres'. Environ. Protection Commn. for Southea. region of U.S.; former mem. Pres'. Adv. Coun. of Faulkner state Jr. Coll.; deacon, teacher coll. career Sunday Sch.; chmn. bd. Ala. Press Assn. (past pres.). With USAF 1955-59. Recipient Gov's. award for conservation reporting, over 100 Ala. Press Assn. and AP awards. Republican. Baptist. Office: US Ho of Reps 208 Cannon Washington DC 20515-0102

EVERETTE, MARLENE MILLER, nursing administrator, surgical nurse; b. Columbus, Ohio, Jan. 10, 1951; d. George Clem and Goldie Alberta (Linder) Miller; m. Edwin Lisk Everette Jr., May 21, 1978; 1 child, Kristy Leigh. ADN, Chowan Coll., 1973; BSN, Barton Coll., 1990. RN, N.C.; cert. nurse oper. rm., cert. autotransfusion specialist. Staff nurse surgery N.C. Meml. Hosp., Chapel Hill, 1973-74; open heart surg. nurse VA Hosp., Durham, N.C., 1974-78; staff nurse surgery Nash Gen. Hosp., Rocky Mount, N.C., 1978-80; dir. surg. svcs. Community Hosp. Rocky Mount, 1980-93; oper. rm. mgr. Nash Gen. Hosp., Rocky Mount, 1993—. Mem. Assn. Operating Rm. Nurses, Women's Coun. (pres.), Eastern N.C. Operating Rm. Nurses (pres.), Sigma Theta Tau.

EVERHART, KENNETH ALBERT, III, information services administrator; b. Winston-Salem, N.C., Jan. 7, 1952; s. Kenneth Albert and Iris Hayden (Simpson) E.; m. Sondra Johnston, Aug. 15, 1979 (div. Aug. 1993); children: Christopher Hayden, Michael Kenneth; m. Genie Talkington, Feb. 27, 1995. BS in Info. Svcs., High Point U., 1989. Cons. info. svcs. Mgmt. Info. Svcs. Group, Greensboro, N.C., 1986-94; info. svcs. mgr. QualChoice of N.C., Winston-Salem, 1994-95, Accordant Health Svcs., Inc., Greensboro, 1995—. Inventor body watch composition analyzer. Mem. AAAS, Nat. Computer Security Assn., Data Processing Mgmt. Assn., Mensa.

EVERITT, ALICE LUBIN, labor arbitrator; b. Washington, Dec. 13, 1936; d. Isador and Alice (Berliner) Lubin; BA, Columbia U., 1968, JD, 1971. Assoc. firm Amen, Weisman & Butler, N.Y.C., 1971-78; spl. asst. to dir. Fed. Mediation and Conciliation Svc., Washington, 1978-81; editor Dept. Labor publ., 1979, pvt. practice labor arbitration, Washington, N.Y.C. and Petersburg, Va., 1981—; dean admissions Hofstra U. Sch. Law 1985-89; mem. various nat. mediation and arbitration panels including Fed. Mediation and Conciliation Svc., U.S. Steel and United Steelworkers. Mem. Am. Arbitration Assn., Soc. Profls. Dispute Resolution, Indsl. Rels. Rsch. Assn., Civil War Roundtable of Washington, N.Y.C. and Richmond. Office: 541 High St Petersburg VA 23803-3859

EVERLY, JANE, gifted education educator; b. Corona, Calif., Nov. 13, 1964; d. John W. and Esther (Hubberstey) E. BS magna cum laude, Belhaven Coll., 1985; MS, MEd, Miss. Coll., Clinton, 1987, EdS, 1989. Cert. elem. edn., gifted edn., computer edn. and sch. adminstrn., Miss. Tchr. 6th grade Casey Elem., Jackson, Miss.; tchr. gifted Casey Elem., Jackson, Siwell Mid. Sch., Jackson; coord. Summer Challenge Camp. Author: Cavern's Quest, 1994. Coach 6 state champion teams Odessey of the Mind. Mem. Miss. Profl. Edn. Home: 4858 Maplewood Dr Jackson MS 39206-4817

EVERSOLE, SANDRA JOY, operating room nurse; b. Leesville, La., Nov. 15, 1955; d. Marvin Henry and Joy Marie (Caraway) Miller; m. Robert Dean Eversole, July 6, 1974; children: Brandi, Jennifer, Brian. ADN, Brazosport-Galveston Coll., 1977. cert. oper. rm. nurse, 1988. Staff nurse med.-surg. Sweeny (Tex.) Community Hosp., 1977-78; staff nurse oper. rm. Sweeny (Tex.) Cmty. Hosp., 1978-82; staff nurse oper. rm. Polly Ryon Hosp., Richmond, Tex., 1982-91, asst. mgr. oper. rm., 1991—; preceptor Polly Ryon Hosp., Richmond, 1992—, mem. safety and infection control com., Richmond, 1992—. Designer intraoperative record, 1990. Mem. PTA Needville Elem. Sch., Band Boosters Club; mem. United Ch. of Christ. Mem. Assn. Oper. Rm. Nurses (cert.), Brazos Bend Assn. Oper. Rm. Nurses (v.p. 1996), Live Oak Club. Home: 15426 John Miller Rd Guy TX 77444-9516 Office: Polly Ryon Hosp 1705 Jackson St Richmond TX 77469-3246

EWERS, JOHN CANFIELD, museum administrator; b. Cleve., July 21, 1909; s. John Ray and Mary Alice (Canfield) E.; m. Margaret Elizabeth Dumville, Sept. 6, 1934; children: Jane (Mrs. Robinson), Diane (Mrs. Peterson). AB, Dartmouth Coll., 1931, DSc, 1968; MA, Yale U., 1934; LLD, U. Mont., 1966; DLitt (hon.), Mont. State U., 1994. Field curator Nat. Park Service, Washington, Morristown, N.J., Berkeley, Calif., Macon, Ga., 1935-40; curator Mus. Plains Indian, Browning, Mont., 1941-44; assoc. curator ethnology U.S. Nat. Mus., Smithsonian Instn., Washington, 1946-56; planning officer U.S. Nat. Mus., Smithsonian Instn., 1956-59, asst. dir. Mus. History and Tech., 1959-64, dir., 1964-65; sr. scientist U.S. Nat. Mus., Smithsonian Instn. (Office Anthropology), 1965-79; now ethnologist emeritus U.S. Nat. Mus., Smithsonian Instn. (Dept. Anthropology); research assoc., hon. trustee Mus. Am. Indian Heye Found., N.Y.C., 1979-90; mus. planning cons. Bur. Indian Affairs, 1948-49, Mont. Hist. Soc., 1950-54; cons. Am. Heritage, 1959. Author: Plains Indian Painting, 1940, The Horse in Blackfoot Indian Culture, 1955 (reprinted in Classics of Smithsonian Anthropology Series, 1980), The Blackfeet: Raiders on the Northwestern Plains, 1958, Artists of the Old West, 1965, Indian Life on Upper Missouri, 1968, Murals in the Round: Painted Tipis of the Kiowa and Kiowa-Apache Indians, 1978, Plains Indian Sculpture, 1986; editor: Adventures of Zenas Leonard, Fur Trader, 1959, Crow Indian Medicine Bundles, 1960, Five Indian Tribes of the Upper Missouri, 1961, O-Kee-pa, A Religious Ceremony and Other Customs of the Mandans, (George Catlin), 1967, Jean Louis Berlandier's Indians of Texas in 1830, 1969, Jose Francisco Ruiz, Report on the Indian Tribes of Texas in 1828, 1972, Indian Art in Pipestone, George Catlin's Portfolio in the British Museum, 1979; editor Jour. Washington Acad. Scis, 1955-56; mem. editorial bd.: The American West, 1965-70; contbr. articles to profl. publs. Served with USNR, 1944-46. Recipient 1st Exceptional Svc. medal Smithsonian Instn., 1965, award for rsch. and publs. in Am. Indian art Native Am. Art Studies Assn., 1989, gold medal for contbn. to history of Am., West Buffalo Bill Hist. Ctr., 1991, award for disting. svc. Am. Assn. Mus., 1996. Fellow Am. Anthrop. Assn., Rochester Mus. Arts and Scis.; mem. Western History Assn. (hon. life, prize for disting. writing 1985), Am. Indian Ethnohist. Conf. (pres. 1960-61), Anthrop. Soc. Washington. Clubs: Cosmos (Washington); Explorers (N.Y.C.). Home and Office: 4432 26th Rd N Arlington VA 22207-4018

EWIN, DABNEY MINOR, surgeon; b. New Orleans, Dec. 7, 1925; s. James Perkins and Lucille Havard (Scott) E.; m. Ethelyn Alexander Sherrouse, June 6, 1951 (div. 1968); children: Dabney Jr., Constance, Walton, Christopher, Leila; m. Marilyn Allison Abernathy, June 29, 1968. MD, Tulane U., 1951. Intern Jefferson-Hillman Hosp. U. Ala., Birmingham, 1951, resident, 1951-54; resident Ochsner Found. Hosp., New Orleans, 1954-56; chief resident Huey P. Long Charity Hosp., Pineville, La., 1956-57; pvt. practice, 1957—; staff surgeon Touro Infirmary, New Orleans, East Jefferson Gen. Hosp. Metairie, La., Charity Hosp. La., St. Jude Med. Ctr. (now called Kenner (La.) Regional Hosp.); clin. prof. surgery and psychiatry Tulane Med. Sch; clin. prof. psychiatry La. State U. Contbr. articles to profl. jours. Bd. dirs. Christ Sch., 1979-85; sr. class Sunday sch. tchr. Trinity Episc. Ch., 1960-66. Fellow ACS; mem. AMA, Am. Trauma Soc. (dir. 1975-79), Am. Burn Assn., Am. Occupational Medicine Assn. (spkr. Ho. of Dels., 1973-75), Am. Bd. Med. Hypnosis (past pres.), Am. Soc. Clin. Hypnosis (past pres.), La. State Med. Soc., Orleans Parish Med. Soc., Surg. Assn. La., New Orleans Surg. Soc., Alton Ochsner Surg. Soc. (past sec.), So. Med. Assn. (chmn. sect. on indsl. medicine and surgery 1966-67), La. Indsl. Med. Assn., La. Occupational Med. Assn. (past pres.), Soc. for Clin. and Exptl. Hypnosis, La. Psychiat. Assn. Republican. Office: 318 Baronne St New Orleans LA 70112-1606

EWOH, ANDREW IKEH EMMANUEL, political science educator; b. Enugu, Nigeria, Nov. 20, 1959; came to U.S., 1981; s. Lazarus Ngene and Virginia Nnenna (Ani) E.; divorced; children: Tyrone, Emmanuel, Andy, Chelsey. BS in Bus. Adminstrn., U. Southwestern La., 1984; MPA in Pub. Adminstrn., So. U., Baton Rouge, 1986; MA in Polit. Economy, U. Tex., Dallas, 1991, PhD in Polit. Economy, 1993. Grad. intern Office Housing and Tech. Assistance La. Dept. Urban and Community Affairs, Baton Rouge, 1985-86; teaching asst. So. U., Baton Rouge, 1985-86; teaching asst. Sch. Social Scis., U. Tex.-Dallas, Richardson, 1990-92, rsch. asst., 1991, instr., 1993; instr. bus. divsn. Richland Coll., Dallas, 1993; adj. prof. dept. pub. affairs Tex. So. U., Houston, 1986-89, 93; adj. prof. Sch. Bus. and Pub. Adminstrn. U. Houston-Clear Lake, 1994; asst. prof. polit. sci. Prairie View (Tex.) A&M U., 1993—. Acting editor Issues in Polit. Economy, 1991-92. Grad. rsch. fellow Tex. Higher Edn. Coord. Bd., Rsch. Programs Divsn., Austin, Tex., 1990, grad. fellow Minnie K. Patton Scholarship Found., 1991-92, 92-93. Fellow Acad. Polit. Sci.; mem. Am. Soc. Pub. Adminstrn. (mem. Pub. Com.), Assn. for Budgeting and Fin. Mgmt., Am. Acad. Polit. and Social Sci., Am. Polit. Sci. Assn., Ctr. for Study of Presidency, Southwestern Social Sci. Assn. Home: PO Box 691824 Houston TX 77269-1824

EXUM, CYNTHIA PHILLIPS, headmaster; b. Phila., July 20, 1951; d. George William and Frankie (Michael) Phillips; m. Frank Emanuel Exum Jr., June 11, 1971 (div. Aug. 1991); children: Christine Karen, Frank Emanuel III. BA in Elem. Edn., Coker Coll., 1988; MEd in Edn. Adminstrn., Winthrop U., 1994. Tchr. 1st United Meth. Ch., Bennettsville, S.C., 1985-87, Marlboro County Schs. Dist., Bennettsville, S.C., 1988-91; headmaster Thomas Hart Acad., Hartsville, S.C., 1991-96; head sch. Patrick Henry Acad., Estell, S.C., 1996—. Co-chair Leadership Hartsville C. of C., 1993-94, chair edn. day, 1993-95; mem. Marlboro County adv. com. S.C. Govs. Early Childhood Devel. Coun., Bennettsville, 1985-86. Mem. ASCD, Nat. Coun. Tchrs. Math., Nat. Assn. Elem. Sch. Prins., Nat. Sci. Tchrs. Assn., S.C. State Headmaster's Assn. (v.p. 1994-95, pres. 1995-96), S.C. Ind. Sch. Assn. (bd. dirs., mem. exec. com. 1991-94), S.C. Assn. Sch. Adminstrs., Rotary, Phi Kappa Phi. Republican. Methodist. Home: 384 E Fifth St Estill SC 29918 Office: Patrick Henry Acad PO Box 788 Hwy 601 Estill SC 29918

EYERMAN, DAVID JOHN, computer company administrator; b. Oak Park, Ill., June 14, 1966; s. Thomas Jude and Mary Kathryn (Evans) E.; m. Regan Veasey, Aug. 5, 1995. BS in Computer Sci., Am. U., Washington, 1988, MS in Computer Sci., 1989. Microcomputer project mgr. U.S. Dept. Treasury, Washington, 1987-89; assoc. programmer IBM, Milford, Conn., 1989-90; adv. software engr. IBM, Dallas, 1990—; dir. Thomas J. and Mary Kay Eyerman Found., Chgo., 1992—. Mem. The 500, Inc., Dallas, 1991—, Voce Forte, The Dallas Opera, 1993—, Shakespeare Festival of Dallas, 1994—. Mem. IEEE, Assn. Computing Machinery. Roman Catholic. Home: 3570 Waldorf Dr Dallas TX 75229

EYNON, STEVEN SCOTT, minister; b. Jacksonville, Fla., July 4, 1961; s. John Jerry and Sally Ann (Stevens) E.; m. Lori Lee Hunter, June 25, 1983; children: Christopher, Steven. BA summa cum laude, Fla. Christian Coll., Kissimmee, 1984; MMin, Ky. Christian Coll., 1992. Ordained to ministry Christian Ch., 1984. Min. youth winter Haven (Fla.) Christian Ch., 1982-84, 1st Christian Ch., Clearwater, Fla., 1985-94; sr. minister Cmty. Christian Ch., Ft. Lauderdale, Fla., 1994—; adj. instr. Fla. Christian Coll., 1988, 90; v.p. Fla. Christian Youth Conv., Orl ando, 1986; bd. dirs. Christianville Mission, Haiti, 1991—, chmn. bd. dirs., 1993-94; sec. of trustee, Fla. Christian Coll., 1996—. Author: (with others) Ideas, vol. 42, 1987, Good Stuff, vol. 4, 1988. Mem. Nat. Right to Life, Washington, 1983—; vol. Spl. Olympics, Clearwater, 1985-94; scouting coord. Boy Scouts Am., Clearwater, 1986-94; pres. Fla. Christian Coll. Alumni Assn., Kissimmee, 1987-88, v.p., 1985-87; bd. trustees Fla. Christian Coll., 1995—. Named Outstanding Young Min., N.Am. Christian Conv., 1989. Mem. Christ in Youth Planning

Coun. (advisor 1986-88), Christian Edn. Conf. (dir. 1988), Nat. Eagle Scout Assn. Home: 9590 NW 31st Pl Sunrise FL 33351 Office: Community Christian Ch 155 N Hiatus Rd Fort Lauderdale FL 33325-2526

EYSMANS, DEBRA MORRISON, former university public relations executive; b. Huntington, W.Va., Oct. 2, 1955; d. Jimmy Donald and Barbara Ann (Penvose) Morrison; m. Julien Lycurgue E. IV, Aug. 27, 1977; children: Courtney Collamore, Seth Lycurgue, Cabell Elizabeth. Student, Averet Coll., 1973-75; BA in Journalism, Marshall U., 1977; MA in Journalism, Regent U., 1995. Asst. to adviser, chief typesetter Marshall U., Huntington, 1977-79; graphic artist Mobility, Inc., Richmond, Va., 1979-80; typesetter Nagel's Flexo, Inc., Ashland, Va., 1980-81; asst. dir. pub. rels. Randolph-Macon Coll., Ashland, 1981-84; designer Commonwealth Mag., Norfolk, Va., 1984, prodn. mgr., 1985; publs. editor Thomas Nelson C.C., Hampton, Va., 1985, coord. word processing, publs. and printing, 1985-87, dir. pub. rels., publs. and printing, 1987-92, dir. pub. rels., 1992-94, ret., 1994; free-lance graphic artist, 1984, 85. Mem. AAUW, Nat. Fedn. Press Women, Nat. Coun. Mktg. and Pub. Rels. (Best Catalog in U.S. award 1990), Internat. Assn. Bus. Communicators (local exec. bd. dirs., 3 Best in Va. awards 1989), Va. Press Women (3 Comm. awards 1991), Va. Assn. Pub. Rels. and Publs. Profls., Va. State Agy. Pub. Affairs Assn., Coun. Advancement and Support of Edn. (Dist. III award of Excellence 1991), Soc. Profl. Journalists, Peninsula Ad Club (exec. bd. dirs.). Republican. Episcopalian. Home: 202 Richard Run Yorktown VA 23693-4431

EZEAMII, HYACINTH CHINEDUM, public administration educator; b. Bukuru, Nigeria, Sept. 8, 1957; came to U.S., 1983, naturalized, 1993; s. Christopher Onuora and Regina Anyankwo (Ajagu) E.; m. Felicia Ngozi Nwambu, Dec. 30, 1991; children: Ikemefuna Hyacinth, Nkemakonam Michelle. BS in Acctg., Shaw U., 1984; MPA in Pub. Fin. Adminstrn., N.C. State U., 1987, EdD in Higher Edn. Adminstrn., Pub. Adminstrn. and Sociology, 1992. Tchr. primary sch. St. Paul's Ctrl. Sch., Achalla, Nigeria, 1974-75; tchr. math. Igwebuike Secondary Sch., Awka, Nigeria, 1976-78; tchr. math., dean studies Nimo (Nigeria) Girls Secondary Sch., 1978-79; adj. asst. prof. pub. adminstrn. program N.C. Ctrl. U., Durham, 1991-93; rsch. and mgmt. cons. Exami Rsch. & Mgmt. Cons. Svcs., Raleigh, N.C., 1993-95; asst. prof. pub. adminstrn. Albany (Ga.) State U., 1995—; vis. asst. prof. Ctr. for Alternative Programs in Edn., Shaw U., Raleigh, 1992-93; mem. S.-E. Regional Seminar on African Studies. Editor, pub. (newsletter) Ekwe Nimo; internat. editor Nimo in Perspective mag. With Biafran Army, 1969-70. Named Hon. Chieftaincy Nimo Cmty., Anambra State, Nigeria, 1996. Mem. Am. Assn. Higher Edn., Nat. Congress Black Faculty, Am. Soc. for Pub. Adminstrn., Assn. for Study of Higher Edn., Assn. for Instl. Rsch., Am. Nimo Unions (founder, 1st pres. 1987-96), Nigerian Assn. Rsch. Triangle Area (founder, 1st pres. 1987-88). Office: Albany State Univ Dept Hist & Polit Sci PO Box 72304 Albany GA 31708

EZEIKE, GABRIEL O.I., agricultural engineering educator; b. Nanka, Anambra, Nigeria, Mar. 3, 1944; came to U.S., 1995; s. Ezekiel Nwankwo and Adeline Nwama (Ezechigbo) E.; m. Sandra Kodilichukwu Ugokwe, Mar. 29, 1975; children: Richard, Brian, Darlene, Audrey, David. BS in Agrl. Engring., U. Nigeria, 1973; MS in Agrl. Engring., U. Guelph, Ont., Can., 1976; PhD in Agrl. Engring., U. Guelph, 1978. Profl. engr., Coun. for the Regulation of Engring. in Nigeria. Jr. rsch. fellow U. Nigeria, Nsukka, 1973-74; lectr. II U. Nigeria, 1978-80, lectr. I, 1980-82, sr. lectr., 1982-85, reader, 1985-88, prof., 1988—; tchg./rsch. asst. U. Guelph, 1976-78; rsch. scientist U. Ga., Athens, 1995—; mem. editl. bd. Internat. Agrophysics, Budapest, Hungary, 1988-92; editor Jour. Agrl. Engring. and Tech., NCAM, Ilorin, Nigeria, 1992—; assoc. dean engring. U. Nigeria, 1989-90; head agrl. engring. dept. U. Nigeria, 1990-93; chmn. consultancy mgmt. U. Nigeria, 1992-95; co-dir. CIDA-TUNS-UNN Linkage Project U. Nigeria, 1990-93; chmn. NUC accreditation Ahmadu Bello U., Zaria, Nigeria, 1992; internat. accreditation team Kaduna (Nigeria) Poly. U., 1982. Editor: (book) Book of Inventions and Creative Works, 1986; invented triple-pass solar collector, 1986. Mem. Nigerian Soc. Agrl. Engrs. (nat. sec. 1980-82), Am. Soc. Agrl. Engrs. (editl. reviewer 1996), Internat. Soc. Tropical Root Crops, Can. Soc. Agrl. Engrs., Nigerian Soc. Engrs., Sigma Xi. Mem. Anglican Ch. Office: U Ga Biol and Agrl Engring 1109 Experiment St Griffin GA 30223-1797

EZEKWE, MICHAEL OBI, reseach scientist; b. Abatete, Anambra, Nigeria, Nov. 16, 1944; came to U.S., 1972; s. Okudo Ebudike and Ogaobaka (Anyaralu) E.; m. Edith Ifeyinwa Uzodinma, May 18, 1974; children: Obi, Kenechi, Ifemefuna, Chijioke, Nneamaka. BS with honors, U. Nigeria, 1971; MS, Pa. State U., 1974, PhD, 1977. Rsch. scientist Va. State U., Petersburg, 1978—, coord. program, 1993—; cons. in field. Contbr. articles to Jour. Animal Sci., Growth, Devel. and Aging, Va. Jour. Sci., Nutrition Report Internat., Hormone and Metabolic Rsch., Jour. Am. Oil Chemists Soc., Ann. Reciprocal Meats Conf. Eucharistic min. St. Joseph's Ch., Petersburg, 1986—, chetechist, 1990—. USDA-CSRS grantee, 1986—. Mem. Am. Soc. Animal Sci., Am. Inst. Nutrition, KC, Sigma Xi, Gamma Sigma Delta. Roman Catholic. Office: Va State U Agrl Rsch Sta Box 9122 Petersburg VA 23806

EZELL, KENNETH C., design company executive. Sec.-treas. Clifton, Ezell & Clifton Design, Deltona, Fla. Office: Clifton Ezell & Clifton Design 505 Deltona Blvd Ste 201-a Deltona FL 32725-8069

EZELL, MARGARET PRATHER, information systems executive; b. New Orleans, Aug. 12, 1951; d. Bluford and Mildred Winston (Seab) E. BS, Brigham Young U., 1973; MS, Utah State U., 1975; PhD, Mich. State U., 1982. Asst. prof., extension specialist Coop. Extension Svc., Pa. State U., University Park, 1982-85; So. regional computer coord. Coop. Extension Svc./USDA, Athens, Ga., 1985-88; cons. info. tech. Coop. Extension Svc./USDA, Clemson, S.C., 1988-89; info. tech. cons., instructional designer Atlanta, 1989—; adminstr. info. svcs., ea. region Resolution Trust Corp./FDIC, Atlanta, 1990-93, mgr. database, 1994—. Scholar Mich. State U., 1981, Marie Dye scholar, 1981. Mem. Am. Assn. Family and Consumer Scis. (grantee 1983, family econ./home mgmt. sect., pre-conf. local arrangements chmn. 1984-85, mem. nat. electronic tech. com. 1986-89), Ga. Assn. Family and Consumer Scis. (dist. vice chmn. 1986-87), Cen. Pa. IBM-PC Assn. (charter, treas. 1983-84), Agrl. Communicators in Edn. (Excellence in Computers award 1989), Assn. Banyan Users Internat. (ATlanta chpt., pres. 1991), World Futures Soc., Epsilon Sigma Phi, Kappa Omicron Nu.

FABER, DAVID ALAN, federal judge; b. Charleston, W.Va., Oct. 21, 1942; s. John Smith and Wilda Elaine (Melton) F.; m. Deborah Ellayne Anderson, Aug. 24, 1968; 1 dau., Katherine Peyton. B.A., W.Va. U., 1964; J.D., Yale U., 1967. Bar: W.Va. 1967, U.S. Ct. Mil. Appeals 1970, U.S. Supreme Ct. 1974. Assoc. Dayton, Campbell & Love, Charleston, W.Va., 1967-68, Campbell, Love, Woodroe, 1972-74; ptnr. Campbell, Love, Woodroe & Kizer, Charleston, 1974-77, Love, Wise, Robinson & Woodroe, Charleston, 1977-81; U.S. atty. U.S. Dept. Justice, Charleston, 1982-86; ptnr. Spilman, Thomas, Battle & Klostermeyer, Charleston, 1987-91; judge U.S. Dist. Ct. (so. dist.) W.Va., Bluefield, 1991—; counsel to ethics commn. W.Va. State Bar, Charleston, 1974-76. Served to capt. USAF, 1968-72, to col. W.Va. Air N.G., 1978-92. Nat. law scholar Yale Law Sch. New Haven, 1964-65. Mem. W.Va. State Bar, W.Va. Bar Assn., Phi beta Kappa. Republican. Episcopalian. Office: US Dist Ct PO Box 4068 601 Federal St Rm 2303 Bluefield WV 24701

FABRE, FRED RUFFIN, small business owner; b. Baton Rouge, Sept. 22, 1939; s. Joseph Ruffin and Bessie S. (Solomon) F.; student La. State U. Engaged in automobile repair, 1961—; owner Carriage House Garage, Baton Rouge, 1978—; cons. Rolls-Royce restorations, 1971—. Bd. dirs., trainer, coord., counsellor Genesis House, crisis ctr., Baton Rouge, 1970-71. Recipient various svc. awards. Mem. Antique Automobile Club Am. (officer, award for article 1978), Rolls-Royce Owners Club (tech. cons., nat. dir., McFarlane award for best regional newsletter 1990), Rolls-Royce Enthusiasts Club, Rolls-Royce Heritage Trust, Bentley Drivers Club, Phanton III Tech. Soc., BMW Owners Assn., Vintage BMW Owners Club, Capital Area Health Planning Coun. Newsletter and tech. editor. Home: 4063 Mohican St Baton Rouge LA 70805-6024 Office: 3745 Prescott Rd # A Baton Rouge LA 70805-5081

FABRIZIO, LOUIS MICHAEL, computer educator, consultant; b. N.Y.C., Feb. 3, 1952; s. Fiore and Concetta (Del Bove) F.; m. Betsy Jo Jackson, Apr. 9, 1977 (div. Aug. 1984); 1 child, Erin; m. Katherine Kilburn, Nov. 21, 1987; children: Clair, Maria. BS in Physics, Georgetown U., 1974; MS in Edn. Adminstrn., N.C. State U., 1979. Tchr. math. and sci. Kalorama Children's Program, Washington, 1974; Head Start edn. dir. Wake County Opportunities, Inc., Raleigh, N.C., 1975; dir. head start Wake County Opportunities, Inc., Raleigh, 1975-77; edn. cons. N.C. Dept. of Pub. Instruction, Raleigh, 1978, evaluation cons., 1979-81; evaluation cons. CTB McGraw-Hill, Monterey, Calif., 1982-88, sr. evaluation cons., 1990-92; nat. evaluation cons., instr. software cons. CTB Macmillan/McGraw-Hill, Monterey, 1993; nat. assessment cons. CTB/McGraw-Hill, Monterey, Calif., 1994-96; dir. divsn. accountability svcs. N.C. Dept. Pub. Instrn., Raleigh, 1996—; fellow Edn. Policy Fellowship Program, Washington, 1979. Active Dem. Nat. Com., N.C., 1988—, N.C. Dem. Com., 1990—. Mem. ASCD, Coun. for Basic Edn., Am. Ednl. Rsch. Assn., N.C. Assn. for Rsch. Edn. (sec. 1984-87, pres. 1988), Georgetown U. Alumni Assn. (chmn. admissions com. ea. N.C. 1985-89), Phi Delta Kappa (bd. dirs. 1985-89, Svc. Key 1990). Home: 208 Hunters Xing Cary NC 27511-6825 Office: 301 N Wilmington St Raleigh NC 27601

FABRY, PAUL ANDREW, international association executive; b. Budapest, Hungary; came to U.S., 1949, naturalized, 1962; s. Andrew and Ilona (Gombos) F., m. Louise Hitchcock Fair, May 15, 1958 (div. 1968); children: Lydia Louise, Alexa Fair; m. Angela Andrews Rutledge, May 8, 1971 (div. 1979); m. Elizabeth Adams Garrett, 1988. BA, Godollo Jr. Coll., 1937; PhD, U. Budapest, 1942, JD, 1943. War corr. Central European Press Service, Warsaw, Poland, Berlin, Vienna, Austria, Zurich, Switzerland, Budapest, 1943-44; sec. Fgn. Office, Budapest, 1945; head Prime Minister's Cabinet, Budapest, 1945-46; charge d'affaires of Hungary, Ankara, Turkey, 1946-47; fgn. corr. Istanbul, Turkey, 1948-49; sect. chief Radio Free Europe, N.Y.C., 1950-53; freelance writer, lectr., N.Y.C., 1954; pub. relations adviser E.I. du Pont de Nemours & Co., Wilmington, Del., 1955-62; mng. dir. Internat. House, New Orleans, 1962-85; cons. World Trade Ctr. New Orleans, 1986—. Moderator: Fact and Opinion WYES-TV, 1965-74. Rep. Internat. Red Cross, Vienna-Budapest, 1945-46; adv. bd. Istanbul U., 1948-49, Internat. Econ. Cooperation Com., N.Y.C.; v.p. Cultural Services, Inc., N.Y.C., 1953-54; active United Fund, Wilmington, 1955-60; trustee, mem. exec. com. New Orleans Ednl. TV Found., 1970-75; founder Budapest chpt. Pulitzer Prize Found., 1989—. Served to capt. Royal Hungarian Arty., 1943. Mem. World Trade Ctrs. Assn. (founder, dir. emeritus).

FABRY, SUSAN KINGSLAND, pediatric nurse practitioner; b. N.Y.C., Apr. 14, 1953; d. J. Kenneth and G. Bonita (McCracken) Mart; m. David A. Fabry, Oct. 23, 1976. BSN, Cornell U., 1975; MS, Ohio State U., 1982; cert., U. Va., 1984. RN, W.Va. Staff nurse newborn nursery/postpartum unit Akron (Ohio) Gen. Med. Ctr.; staff nurse neonatal ICU Cabell Huntington (W.Va.) Hosp.; pediatric NP Pediatrics, Inc., Huntington; asst. prof. Sch. of Nursing Marshall U., Huntington, clin. asst. prof. Sch. of Medicine. Mem. ANA, W.Va. chpt. Am. Acad. Pediatrics, ANA, Phi Kappa Phi, Sigma Theta Tau. Home: 16 Sutherland Rd Huntington WV 25705-3638

FABRYCKY, WOLTER JOSEPH, engineering educator, author, industrial and systems engineer; b. Springfield, N.Y., Dec. 6, 1932; s. Louis Ludwig and Stephanie (Wadis) F.; m. Luba Swerbilow, 1954; children: David Jon, Kathryn Marie. BS, Wichita State U., 1957; MS, U. Ark., 1958; PhD, Okla. State U., 1962. Instr. indsl. engring. U. Ark., 1957-60; from asst. to assoc. prof. indsl. engring. and mgmt. Okla. State U., 1962-65; from assoc. prof. to prof. indsl. and sys. engring. Va. Poly. Inst. and State U., Blacksburg, 1965-88, John L. Lawrence prof., 1988-95, founding chmn. systems engring., 1969-75, assoc. dean engring., 1970-76, dean rsch. divsn., 1976-81; Lawrence prof. emeritus, sr. rsch. scientist, 1995—. Author: (with G.J. Thuesen) Economic Decision Analysis, 1974, 2d edit., 1980, (with B.S. Blanchard) Systems Engineering and Analysis, 1981, 2d edit., 1990, (with G.J. Thuesen) Engineering Economy, 1950, 8th edit., 1993, (with P.M. Ghare and P.E. Torgersen) Applied Operations Research and Management Science, 1984, (with J. Banks) Procurement and Inventory Systems Analysis, 1987, (with B.S. Blanchard) Life-Cycle Cost and Economic Analysis, 1991; editor: (with J.H. Mize) Prentice-Hall International Series in Industrial and Systems Engineering, 1972—. Recipient Lohmann medal Okla. State U., 1992; Ethyl Corp. doctoral fellow Okla. State U., 1960-62. Fellow AAAS, Inst. Indsl. Engrs. (exec. v.p. 1982-84, trustee, Book of Yr. award 1973, Outstanding Educator award 1990); mem. Am. Soc. Engring. Edn. (v.p. 1977-78, bd. dirs., Grant award 1995), Nat. Coun. on Sys. Engring. (charter, nat. bd. dirs. 1995—), Ops. Rsch. Soc. Am., Sigma Xi, Alpha Pi Mu, Sigma Tau. Home: 1200 Lakewood Dr Blacksburg VA 24060-2005 Office: Va Poly Inst and State U 302 Whittemore Hall Blacksburg VA 24061

FACKLER, NANCY GRAY, nursing administrator, military officer; b. Norfolk, Va., Jan. 24, 1941; d. Albert Edward and Rita Marie (Murray) Gray; m. Martin L. Fackler, Sept. 29, 1964. BSN, Fla. State U., 1962; postgrad., San Francisco State U., 1988, Golden Gate U., 1989-91; M of Adminstrn. and Health Svcs. Mgmt., Golden Gate U., 1991; postgrad., U. Fla., 1993-94. RN, Fla.; cert. gerontology; lic. pvt. and comml. pilot. Commd. ensign USNR, 1962, advanced through grades to rear adm. Nurses Corps, 1994; nurse Chelsea Naval Hosp., Boston, Yokosuka (Japan) Naval Hosp.; with N.W. Region, mem. navy med. command NW region policy bd. USNR, Oakland, Calif., 1986-89; readiness command nurse USNR, San Francisco, 1989-91; DON Univ. Nursing Care Ctr., Gainesville, Fla.; dep. dir. Navy Nurse Corps, 1995—; originator res. same day surgery program Naval Hosp. Jacksonville and Naval Hosp. Oakland. Mem. Sec. of Navy Nat. Navy Res. Policy Bd.; active Alachua County Health Coalition. Mem. ANA, Nat. Naval Res. (policy bd.), Nat. Gerontol. Nursing Assn., Naval Res. Assn., Am. Tennis Assn., Fla. Tennis Assn. Home: RR 4 Box 264 Hawthorne FL 32640-8043

FACKLER, NAOMI PAULA, librarian; b. N.Y.C., Sept. 30, 1935; d. Martin Theodore and Lucie Clara Louise (Cloeter) Steege; m. John Paul Fackler, Sept. 2, 1956; children: Katherine G., Cheryl R., Karla S., John M., Dorothy L. AA, Concordia Collegiate Inst., 1954; BA, Valparaiso U., 1956; MILS, U. Tex. Austin, 1986. Med. technician New Eng. Deaconess Hosp., Boston, 1956-60; libr. tech. svcs. Med. Scis. Libr. Tex. A&M U., College Station, 1986-94, mgr. collection devel. Med. Sci. Libr., 1995—. Editor: Collection Development Policy, 1993; editl. bd. mem. Biomed. Libr. Acquisitions Bulletin, 1993—, The Serials Libr., 1995—. Co-pres. LWV Brazos County, Tex., 1995-96, pres. 1993-94, South Euclid, Ohio chpt., 1975-77. Mem. ALA, Med. Libr. Assn. (chair Exch. Adv. com. 1995-96). Democrat. Lutheran.

FADEM, LLOYD ROBERT, oil production executive; b. Tulsa, Jan. 2, 1951; s. Albert and Theresa (Tublin) F.; m. Laura Lynn Grossich, Aug. 29, 1980 (div. 1993). BSBA, U. Okla., 1973; postgrad., U. Pa., 1976. Account exec. Eppler, Guerin, Turner, Houston, 1973-74; mng. ptnr. Fadem Rauch Supply Co., Houston, 1974-79; oil producer executive Great Southwestern Exploration, Inc., Tulsa, 1979—; bd. dirs. Fadem Pipe and Supply Corp., Tulsa, Buck Creek Oil and Gas; lectr. in field. Mem. B'nai Emanual Synagogue, Tulsa Jewish Cmty. Ctr. Mem. Soc. Petroleum Engrs., Okla. Well Log Libr., Okla. Ind. Oil Assn., Okla. Stripper Well Assn., Osage Oil Producers Assn., U.S. Golf Assn., PGA Tour Ptnrs. Assn., Meadowbrook Golf Club. Jewish. Home: 4931 S Mingo Rd Ste E Tulsa OK 74146-4917 Office: Great Southwestern Exploration Inc 4931 S Mingo Rd Ste E Tulsa OK 74146-4917

FADLEY, ANN MILLER, English language and literature educator, writer; b. Ft. Worden, Wash., Nov. 22, 1933; d. Albert Delmar and Helen Elizabeth (Bush) Miller; m. Mit Rowley White, June 19, 1953 (div. Apr. 1977); children: Don M., Sharon L. White Patterson, Barbara A. White Salzman, Brian A.; m. John Lewis Fadley, Oct. 13, 1979 (dec. Jan., 1996). Student, Denison U., 1951-53; BA cum laude, Ohio State U., 1974, MA, 1976, PhD, 1986. Lectr. Ohio State U., Columbus, 1981-84; instr. Ohio Dominican Coll., Columbus, 1984-87; asst. prof. English Marshall U., Huntington, W.Va., 1987-88, Fla. So. Coll., Lakeland, 1988—; adj. prof. Ohio U., Ironton, 1988; panelist pub. TV, Columbus, 1985; chmn. Nat. Poetry Day, 1991—; chmn. vis. creative writers Fla. So. Coll., Lakeland, 1994—. Author: (fiction and poetry) Onionhead, 1989, 95, (poetry) Birmingham Poetry Review, 1992, Heartbeat, 1994, also articles and lit. criticisms; asst. editor Ohio Jour., 1975-76; founder, editor Cantilever Jours., 1989-96. Organizer, pres. Tri-Village Jr. C. of C. Wives Club, Columbus, 1959-60; past awards chmn. Young Musician's competition; chair Ruth Flower Brown Scholarship, Huntington, 1988; contest supr., mem. com. SCORE, 1988; judge VFW Voice of Democracy contest, Lakeland, 1990, 91, Fla. state judge, 1992; trustee Christ United Meth. Ch., Lakeland, 1991—, sec. trustees, 1991-93, 95; mem. bldg. com., organ fund task force, 1993-94; judge short fiction contest Nat. League Am. Pen Women Fla. State Assn. 1995; judge creative writing Polk County Citrus Festival, 1993. Recipient Merit award Fla. Poets Competition, WORDART Soc., 1990, 96, Distinction award, 1991, hon mention for poems; recipient hon. mention Nat. League Am. Pen Women, Lakeland, 1993, 94; grantee Fla. Endowment for Humanities, 1991, award hanging poetry Arts in the Park, Lakeland, 1993, 94, hanging poetry display Lake Morton Libr., 1994. Mem. MLA, South Atlantic MLA, Southeastern Renaissance Conf., Renaissance Soc. Am., Nat. Coun. Tchrs. English (chair session 1990), Fla. State Poets Assn. (head Lakeland workshop 1991, 92), Popular Culture Assn. (chair session 1992), Delta Delta Delta. Republican. Office: Fla So Coll Dept English 111 Lake Hollingsworth Dr Lakeland FL 33801-5607

FAHERTY, JOHN KEVIN, insurance broker, consultant; b. San Benito, Tex., Nov. 1, 1952; s. Frank Patrick and Laura Lewis (Kelly) F.; m. Marion Cumming Kilpatrick, Nov. 29, 1980; children: Sean, Colin. BA with honors in behavioral scis., St. Edward's U., Austin, Tex., 1975; MS in counseling psychology, North Tex. State U., 1979; spl. edn. cert., U. Tex., Tyler, 1981. Lic. psychol. assoc., assoc. sch. psychologist, Tex. Tchg. fellow, rschr. North Tex. State U., Denton, 1977-80; sch. psychologist Windham Sch. Sys., Tennessee Colony, Tex., 1980-87; sch. psychologist Ft. Worth Ind. Schs., 1988-91, ednl. cons., 1991—; ins. broker Faherty Ins. Svcs., Ft. Worth, 1991—; mem. pub. rels. com. Palestine (Tex.) Ind. Schs., 1986-87; rep. area adv. coun. Tex. Youth Commn., 1989-91; ex-officio mem. Tex. Commn. on Alcohol and Drug Abuse, 1991-93; mem. broker adv. panel Harris Meth. Health Sys., Arlington, Tex., 1996—. Author: (coll. workbook) Statistical Measurement in Psychology, 1980; co-author 4 tech. reports; contbr. articles to profl. jours. Chpt. pres. Palestine Jr. Chamber, 1985-86, state program mgr., 1986-87, state v.p., 1987-88; den leader and treas. Cub Scout pack 499, Ft. Worth, 1991—. Named one of Outstanding Young Men Am., 1988, 91; recipient Seiji Horiuchi award U.S. Jaycees, 1987, Career Achievement award Gen. Agts. and Mgrs. Assn. Ft. Worth chpt., 1991; Jaycees Internat. senator, 1988. Mem. Ft. Worth Life Underwriters Assn. (exec. com., sec.-treas. 1995—), Tex. Jr. Chamber Senate (exec. com., pres. 1996—), Tex. Jaycees Found., Inc. (bd. dirs., rep. 1990-91), John Ben Shepperd Leadership Forum (governing bd., rep. 1990-91), Tex. Leaders Round Table (Lone Star leader 1994-96), Leading Producers Round Table (pres.'s coun. 1993-96). Republican. Roman Catholic. Home: 7200 Francisco Dr Fort Worth TX 76133 Office: Faherty Ins Svcs 3701 S University Dr Fort Worth TX 76109

FAHEY, SHARON ANNE, nurse administrator; b. Boston, Nov. 20, 1949; d. Thomas B. Jr. and Margaret Gannon (Hall) F.; m. Mark J. Safferstone, Nov. 22, 1986; children: Todd, Chad, Heather. A.D.N., Cape Cod Community Coll., 1979; BSN, U. Miami (Fla.), 1986; MSN in Critical Care, U. Va., 1989. CCRN; cert. ACLS. Nurse mgr. ICU Mercy Hosp., Miami, Fla., 1880-86; clinician B thoracic cardiovascular ICU U. Va., Charlottesville, 1987-89; nurse mgr. ICU and cardiac surgery ICU Richmond (Va.) Meml. Hosp., 1989-90; dir. critical care svcs. Maryview Med. Ctr., Portmouth, Va., 1990-91; dir. critical care/adult med. svcs. Mary Washington Hosp., Fredericksburg, Va., 1992-94, cardiac surgery case mgr., 1995—. Pub. in field. Mem AACN, Am. Heart Assn. Home: 6 Greenhaven Ct Stafford VA 22554-5139

FAHLGREN, H(ERBERT) SMOOT, advertising agency executive; b. Parkerburg, W.Va., Aug. 17, 1930; s. C. Herbert and Julia (Smoot) F.; m. Judith Anne Henniger, Dec. 7, 1952; children: Steven, Becky, John. Student, U. Va., 1949-52; BSBA, Marietta Coll., 1952. Chmn. bd. dirs. Fahlgren, Parkersburg, W.Va., 1962—; bd. dirs. United Nat. Bank. Elder 1st Presbyn. Ch., Parkersburg. Mem Am. Assn. Advt. Agys (treas. 1978-79, dir. 1981—), W.Va. Round Table. Home: RR 9 Box 218 Parkersburg WV 26101-9104 Office: PO Box 1628 Rosemar Rd & Seminary Dr Parkersburg WV 26102-1628

FAHRLANDER, HENRY WILLIAM, JR., management consultant; b. Hamilton, Ohio, June 24, 1934; s. Henry William and Frances L. (Mitchel) F.; m. Shirley Fontenot, July 16, 1955; children: Henry W. III, Pauline Ann. BSEE, McNeese State U., 1956; cert. indsl. mgmt., So. Meth. U., 1965. Registered profl. engr., Calif.; registered lead assessor, London; cert. profl. cons. Design engr. Gen. Electric Co., Evendale, Ohio, 1956-60; quality mgr. Gen. Electric Co., St. Petersburg, Fla., 1960-65; quality system evaluation mgr. Tex. Instruments Co., Dallas, 1965-68; quality assurance dir. Recognition Equipment Corp., Dallas, 1968-72; dir. engring. Gen. Computer Systems, Addison, Tex., 1972-75; prin. H.W. Fahrlander & Assocs., Richardson, Tex., 1976—; instr. Dallas County Community Coll., Mesquite, Tex., 1972-78. Contbr. articles to profl. jours. Dir. adv. com. Dallas County Community Coll. Dist. at Richland Coll., 1965-68. Served with USAF, 1952-56, including Korea. Sr. mem. Am. Soc. Quality Control (chmn. Dallas sect. 1971-72, chmn. adminstrv. applications div. Milw. 1976-77, cert. quality engr., reliability engr.). Republican. Roman Catholic. Office: HW Fahrlander & Assocs 640 Downing Dr Richardson TX 75080-6117

FAHY, MICHAEL P., civil and environmental engineer; b. St. Louis, Nov. 15, 1950; s. William P. and Constance V. (Stark) F.; m. Anna Louise Hyder, Feb. 23 1985; stepchildren: David Groseclose, Lisa Lingnau, Steven Groseclose, Michael Groseclose, Scott Groseclose. BS in Geol. Engring., U. Mo., Rolla, 1973; MS in Civil and Environ. Engring., U. Colo., 1977. Registered profl. engr., N.Mex., Kans., Tex.; registered profl. geologist, Mo. Geologist Willard Owens Assocs., Denver, 1973-75; rsch. specialist U.S. Geol. Survey, Denver, 1975; lab. rschr. U.S. Bur. of Mines, Boulder, Colo., 1975-77; staff engr. W.A. Wahler & Assocs., Palo Alto, Calif., 1977-78; water and fuel engr. Pub. Svc. of N.M., Albuquerque, 1978-88; asst. water engr. Topeka Water Divsn., 1989-94; water rights engr. El Paso (Tex.) Water Utilities, 1994—. Co-author reports, conf. procs., abstract in field. Tech. presenter Optimists Club, Topeka, 1992; developer water rights presentation for cmty. orgns. in El Paso, 1996. Recipient 1st Place presentation in groundwater sect. Ann. Conf. Assn. Engring. Geologists, 1995. Mem. NSPE (grader mathcounts 1994, 96), Am. Water Works Assn. (recipient rsch. proposal award 1994). Democrat. Roman Catholic. Home: PO Box 26883 El Paso TX 79926-6883 Office: El Paso Water Utilities PO Box 511 1154 Hawkins Blvd El Paso TX 79961-0001

FAHY, NANCY LEE, food products marketing executive; b. Schenectady, N.Y., Aug. 15, 1946; d. Christopher Mark and Frances (Lee) F.; m. Steven Neil Wohl, June 8, 1945 (div. Apr. 1978). BS cum laude, Miami (Ohio) U., 1968. Educator Palatine (Ill.) Pub. Schs., 1968-70, Glencoe (Ill.) Pub. Schs., 1970-78; sales rep. Keebler Co., Elmhurst, Ill., 1978-80, dist. mgr., 1980-82, account mgr., 1982-83, zone mgr., 1983-85, account mgr., 1985-89; regional mktg. mgr. Keebler Co., Morrow, Ga., 1989—. Vol. Lincoln Park Zool. Soc., Chgo., 1975-78. Mem. Food Products Club, Merchandising Execs. Club (bd. dirs. 1984-85), Grocery Mfgs. Sales Execs. Club (bd. dirs. 1984-85, asst. sec. 1987, treas. 1988, 1st v.p. 1989), Phi Beta Kappa. Office: Keebler Co 1135 Commerce Rd Morrow GA 30260-2913

FAIN, HOWARD DOUGLAS, mortician; b. Nicholasville, Ky., Nov. 18, 1962; s. Franklin D. Howard and Ruth Ann (Rhorer) F.; m. Amy Carol Pritchett, Apr. 22, 1995; 1 child, Haleigh Cecilia. Diploma, Mid-Am. Coll. Funeral Svc., 1991. Disc jockey WNVL Radio, Nicholasville, 1979-93; co-owner WNVL and WCKU Radio, Nicholasville, 1985-89; dep. clk. Jessamine County Clk.'s Office, Nicholasville, 1983-89; mortician Hager & Cundiff Funeral Home, Nicholasville, 1990—; mayor pro-tem, city commr. City of Nicholasville, 1994—. Active Jessamine County Cancer Soc., Jessamine County Fair Bd., Jessamine County Exceptional Citizens, Virginia Simpson Scholarship Fund, Jessamine County Sr. Citizens; master of ceremonies Miss Jessamine County Fair Beauty Pageant, 1980—, Miss Jessamine Jamboree Beauty Pageant, 1981—; announcer Jessamine County Football and Basketball, Jessamine County Fair Horse Shows. Recipient Chamber Civic award Jessamine C. of C., 1993, Outstanding Citizen of Jessamine County award Jessamine C. of C., 1995. Mem. Jessamine County Saddle Club (hon.), Lions (past pres., hon.), Phi Sigma Eta (pres. 1990-91, master artist). Democrat. Baptist. Home: 120 Cleveland Ct Nicholasville

KY 40356 Office: Hager & Cundiff Funeral Home PO Box 865 Nicholasville KY 40340

FAIN, JAY LINDSEY, brokerage house executive, consultant; b. Ft. Worth, July 16, 1950; s. James Joel Fain and Jeannine Yvonne (Routt) Ashner; m. Beth Jernigan, Oct. 18, 1968; children: Lisa, Jacob. BBA, U. Tex., 1974. Cert. fin. planner. Acct. exec. Dallas Coca-Cola Bottling Co., 1968-74; unit sales mgr. Procter & Gamble, Houston, 1974-80; assoc. v.p. Dean Witter Reynolds, Houston, 1981—; speaker in field; panelist hearing bd. N.Y. Stock Exchange, 1987—. Sr. warden St. Cuthbert Episc. Ch., Houston, 1983, 91; mem. fin. com. Episcopal Diocese of Tex. coun.; trustee Bishop Quin Found.; den leader Cub Scouts, troop com. Boy Scouts Am. Mem. Inst. Cert. Fin. Planners, CPA Club Houston, Bear Creek Assistance Ministries, Hearthstone Country Club. Episcopalian. Home: 14910 Beechmoor Dr Houston TX 77095-3306 Office: Dean Witter Reynolds 3200 Southwest Fwy Ste 2100 Houston TX 77027-7525

FAIR, STEVE EDWARD, pharmaceutical marketing executive; b. Elizabethon, Tenn., Oct. 4, 1957; s. Bill Moody and Georgia Edna (Hart) F. BS in Biology, East Tenn. State U., 1979, postgrad., 1981-82. Radiation monitor supr. Nuclear Fuels Inc., Erwin, Tenn., 1981-89; profl. sales rep. Adria Pharms., Columbus, Ohio, 1990-92; dir. specialty markets Adams Labs. (subs. of Medeva Inc.), Fort Worth, 1992—. Deacon, vice chmn. of bd. dirs. Brick Christian Ch., Watauga, Tenn.; bd. dirs. East Tenn. Christian Home for Children. Recipient Salesmaster's award Adria Labs., 1991. Mem. Free and Accepted Masons #622. Home: RR 1 Box 765 Watauga TN 37694-9735 Office: Adams Labs 393 Old Watauga Rd Watauga TN 37694-3149

FAIRALL, BONNIE JEAN MAY, pension services executive; b. El Paso, Tex., Dec. 10, 1937; d. Aaron Robert and Catherine Lucille (Wiggs) May; m. Jack Wesley Fairall, Dec. 22, 1956. BA, Tex. Western Coll., 1958; MEd, U. Tex., El Paso, 1967; EdD, Tex. Tech. U., 1976. Cert. profl. tchr., adminstr., supr., Tex.; lic. ins. agt., Tex. Tchr. El Paso Ind. Sch. Dist., 1958-63, asst. prin., 1963-72, cons., 1963-78, dir., 1978-91; dir. Region 19, ESC, El Paso, 1991-95; regional mgr. Regional Ptnrs., Inc., El Paso, 1995—; cons./mem. adv. bd. El Paso c.C., 1978-92; mem. coun. for pers. preparation for handicapped Tex. Edn. Agy., Austin, 1980-95. Mem. autism task force Gov.'s Office, State of Tex., 1984-85; v.p. Meml. Pk. Sch. Bd., El Paso, 1974-76; mem. Mayor's Citizen Adv. Com., El Paso. Named to Outstanding Young Women of Am.; Jones fellow Tex. Tech. U., 1976-77. Mem. Tex. Assn. for Supervision and Curriculum Devel. (pres. 1989-90), AAUW (El Paso br. pres. 1967-68), Rotary (Vista Hills El Paso chpt.), Phi Delta Kappa, Kappa Delta Pi. Office: Regional Partners Inc 6090 Surety Dr #100 El Paso TX 79905

FAIRBANKS, CLIFFORD ALAN, psychologist, consultant; b. Tampa, Fla., Oct. 30, 1946; s. Charles Wesley and Mary Ann (Heath) F.; m. Linda Barbara Lawrence, Aug, 15, 1970; children: Andrew David, Jeffrey Lawrence. BA, U. South Fla., 1969; MEd, Temple U., 1972; D of Psychology, Nova U., 1981. Lic. psychologist, Fla. Tchr. Vanguard Sch., Lake Wales, Fla., 1970-71, Paoli, Pa., 1971-73; sch. psychologist Vanguard Sch., Lake Wales, 1974-78; clin. psychologist Indian River Community Mental Health, Stuart, Fla., 1981-84; pvt. practice clin. psychologist Stuart, 1984—; cons. psychologist Martin County Schs., Stuart, 1985—; mem. Sch. Health Adv. Com., Stuart, 1988—. Mem. task force Martin County Safe Schs., 1994—, mem. sex. edn. curriculum com., 1994—. Mem. APA, Fla. Psychol. Assn., Nat. Register Health Svc. Providers in Psychology. Democrat. Home: 731 NE Bayberry Ct Jensen Beach FL 34957-6821 Office: 900 E Ocean Blvd # 253F Stuart FL 34994-2471

FAIRBANKS, JAMES DAVID, academic administrator; b. Youngstown, Ohio, Jan. 2, 1946; s. James Wilson and Ruth Niles F.; m. Ann Felica Kozuch, Dec. 27, 1970; 1 child, Kathryn Elisabeth. BA in Eng. and History, Greenville Coll., 1968; MA in Polit. Sci., Ohio State U., 1969, PhD in Polit. Sci., 1975. Instr. govt. Lamar U., 1969-71; rsch. asst. for senate rep. Ohio Legis., 1971-73; teaching assoc. Ohio State U., Mansfield and Columbus, 1973-75; from asst. prof. to prof. social sci. U. Houston, 1976—, prof. social sci., 1984—, asst. to chancellor for acad. affairs, 1984-85, asst. v.p. for acad. affairs, 1983-89, exec. dir. instl. rsch. and planning, 1989-91, assoc. v.p. for policy and planning, 1991—; vis. asst. prof. polit. sci. Wake Forest U., 1975-76; instr. polit. sci. Houston C.C., 1976-80; book rev. editor Tex. Jour. Polit. Studies, 1984-96. Contbr. articles to profl. jours. Mem. ASPA, Nat. Social Sci. Assn., Soc. for Coll. and U. Planners (comm. coord. 1994—), So. Assn. Instl. Rsch. (program com. mem. 1991—), Am. Polit. Sci. Assn., Southwestern Social Sci. Assn., Urban Affairs Assn., Conf. on Faith and History. Republican. Episcopalian. Home: 2432 Dryden Rd Houston TX 77030-1002 Office: Univ Houston 1 Main St Ste 621-s Houston TX 77002-1001

FAIRBANKS, ROBERT ALVIN, lawyer; b. Oklahoma City, July 9, 1944; s. Albert Edward and Lucille Imogene (Scherer) F.; m. Linda Gayle Geer, Aug. 26, 1967; children: Chele Lyn, Kimberly Jo, Robert Alvin II, Michael Albert, Richard Alan, Joseph Alexander. BS in Math., U. Okla., 1967, JD, 1973; MBA, Oklahoma City U., 1970, MCJA, 1975; LLM, Columbia U., 1976; MA, Stanford U., 1984; MEd, Harvard U., 1993. Bar: Okla. 1974, U.S. Dist. Ct. (we. dist.) Okla. 1974, U.S. Ct. Customs and Patent Appeals 1974, U.S. Ct. Mil. Appeals, 1974, U.S. Tax Ct. 1974, U.S. Claims Ct. 1975, U.S. Customs Ct. 1975, U.S. Ct. Appeals (10th cir.) 1975, U.S. Supreme Ct. 1977, U.S. Dist. Ct. (ea. dist.) Okla. 1984, Minn. 1993. Commd. 2d lt. USAF, 1967, advanced through grades to capt., 1970; col. USAFR, 1986; asst. staff judge adv., chief of claims div. Office of Staff Judge Adv., Tinker AFB, Okla., 1974-75; legal asst. to Justice William A. Berry, Okla. Supreme Ct., 1977; pvt. practice Norman, Okla., 1974—; instr. bus. adminstrn. U. Md. Far East div., Nha Trang, Viet Nam, 1970-71, Rose State Coll., Midwest City, Okla., 1974; rsch. assoc. in law U. Okla., Norman, 1974, spl. lectr., 1974-75, vis. asst. prof., 1976-77, adj. prof. law, 1984—; vis. asst. prof. law Oklahoma City U., 1977; asst. prof. law U. Ark., Fayetteville, Arks., 1977-81; assoc. prof. law La. State U., Baton Rouge, 1981; rsch. asst. dept. family, community and preventative medicine Stanford (Calif.) Med. Sch., 1981-82; adj. asst. prof. govt. contract law Air Force Inst. Tech., Wright-Patterson AFB, Ohio, 1985—; cons. Cheyenne Tribe, Clinton, Okla., 1977-81, 90, Citizens Band of Pottawatomie Tribe, Shawnee, Okla., 1977-79, Inst. for Devel. of Indian Law, Washington, 1976-81; dir. Native Am. Coll. Prep. Ctr. Bemidji State U., Minn., 1993—. Editor-in-chief Am. Indian Law Rev., 1973; editor Okla. Law Rev., 1971-73; producer, dir.: (with Barbara P. Ettinger) "Aa-Niin" film, 1994; author book revs.; contbr. articles to profl. jours. Mem. bd. control Fayetteville (Ark.) City Hosp., 1977-81; cubmaster Boy Scouts Am., Norman, 1982-83, asst. scoutmaster, Stanford, 1981, scoutmaster, Norman, 1990-91, com. mem., den leader, 1988; softball coach Jr. High Girls League, Fayetteville, 1977-81; mem. adv. bd. Native Am. Prep. Sch., Santa Fe; pres., chmn. bd. Native Am. Coll. Prep. Ctr., Bemidji, Minn.; mem. exec. adv. bd. Aerospace Sci. and Tech. Edn. Ctr. of Okla., Okla. City Univ. U.S. Dept. Edn. fellow Stanford U. Med. Sch.; Charles Evans Hughes fellow Columbia U. Law Sch., 1976; Sequoyah fellow Assn. Am. Indian Affairs, 1975-76; Mellon fellow Harvard U. Sch. Edn., 1993. Mem. ABA, Okla. Bar Assn., Fed. Bar Assn., Am. Trial Lawyers Assn., Okla. Trial Lawyers Assn., Okla. Indian Bar Assn., Oklahoma County Bar Assn., Assn. Am. Law Schs., N.G. Assn. U.S., Air Force Assn. (life), Res. Officers Assn. (life), Nat. Contract Mgmt. Assn., Soc. Logistics Engrs., Phi Alpha Delta, Phi Delta Epsilon, Phi Delta Kappa. Republican. Roman Catholic. Office: 2212 Westpark Dr Norman OK 73069-4012

FAIRCHILD, RAYMOND EUGENE, oil company executive; b. Bowling Green, Ohio, June 25, 1923; s. Ira Ethalbert and Bessie Louise (Gearhart) F.; m. Eleanor Faith Vaughan, Sept. 1, 1973. B.S., Ohio U., 1948; M.S., U. Mo., 1950. Dist. geologist Pan Am. Prodn. Co., Houston, 1950-56; gulf coast div. exploration mgr. Pan Handle Eastern subs., Houston, 1956-72; mayor City of Hunter Creek, Tex., 1967-71; exploration cons. Houston, 1972-73; exploration mgr. A.P. Moller, Copenhagen, 1973-80; v.p. Hunt Oil Co., Dallas, 1980, former sr. v.p. internat. exploration; ret., 1988; pres., dir. Mayfair Petroleum Inc., Mayfair Petroleum Corp., Mayfair Environ. Svcs., 1990—. Alderman, City of Hunter Creek, 1962-67; commr. Spring Br. Fire Dept., 1962. Fellow Geol. Soc. London, Am. Assn. Petroleum Geologists; mem. Petroleum Exploration Soc. Great Britain, Dansk Geologisk Forening, Gulf Coast Assn. Geol. Socs., Houston Geol. Soc., Dallas Geol. Soc., East Tex. Geol. Soc., Assn. Internat. Petroleum Negotiators. Club: Dallas Petroleum. Home and Office: DBA Fairchild Farms RR 6 Box 63866 Winnsboro TX 75494-9790

FAIRCLOTH, DUNCAN MCLAUCHLIN (LAUCH FAIRCLOTH), senator, businessman, farmer; b. Sampson County, N.C., Jan. 14, 1928; s. James Bascum McLaughlin and Mary (Holt) F.; m. Nancy Ann Bryan, May 26, 1967 (div.); 1 child, Anne. Various positions Faircloth Construction, car dealerships, land-clearing, milling, banking, concrete, comml. real estate; farmer Coharie and Faircloth farms; chmn. N.C. Hwy. Commn., 1969-73; sec. N.C. Commerce, 1977-83; U.S. senator from N.C. 103rd Congress, 1993—; mem. Banking Housing & Urban Affairs Com., chmn. subcom. HUD Oversight and Structure; chmn. Environ. & Pub. Works subcom. of Clean Air Wetlands Pvt. Property and Nuclear Safety;. Republican. Presbyterian. Office: US Senate 317 Hart Sen Office Bldg Washington DC 20510-3305

FAIRES, ROSS N., manufacturing company executive; b. Indpls., July 20, 1934; s. Herbert C. and Thelma (Wood) F.; m. Glady Ann Caley, Dec. 20, 1954; children: Kurt J., Eric S., Jay A. BA, Wabash Coll., 1958; MBA, Ind. U., 1959. Advt. mgr. Cummins Engine Co., Columbus, Ind., 1959-62; pres. Arvin Industries div. Housewares, Columbus, 1962-75, Tibbals Flooring Co., Oneida, Tenn., 1979-91; chmn. Faires Group, Chattanooga, 1991—; bd. dirs. First Am. Nat. Bank, Knoxville, Tenn. Bd. dirs., pres., Knoxville Zoo, Knoxville Mus. Art, Nat. Symphony Orch., Washington, Webb Sch., Knoxville, St. Mary's Hosp. Found., Am. Symphony Orch. League, East Tenn. Comm. Found., Helen Ross McNabb Found.; bd. regents State of Tenn., 1984-91; mem. bd. advisors McCallie Sch. for Boys, Chattanooga; trustee Wabash (Ind.) Coll., Maryville Coll. Mem. Tenn. Bus. Assn. (bd. dirs.), Leadership KNoxville, Cherokee Country Club, Club Le Conte. Republican. Presbyterian. Home and Office: 904 Cherokee Blvd Knoxville TN 37919-7847

FAIRLEIGH, MARLANE PAXSON, retired business consultant, educator; b. Three Rivers, Mich., Feb. 28, 1939; d. Ronald Edward and Evelyn May (Roth) Paxson; m. James Parkinson Fairleigh, June 25, 1960; children: William Paxson, Karen Evelyn. MusB, U. Mich., 1960; MBA, Jacksonville State U., 1986. Cert. econ. devel. fin. profl. Adj. faculty Providence Coll., 1976-80, R.I. Coll., Providence, 1978-80; grad. asst. news bur. and info. ctr. Jacksonville (Ala.) State U., 1983-84, grad. asst. Coll. Commerce, 1984-85; bus. cons. Jacksonville State U. Small Bus. Devel. Ctr., 1985-96; presenter in field. Contbr. articles to profl. jours.; performed as featured soprano soloist Coll. Music Soc. Internat. Conf., Berlin, 1995. Chair Jacksonville State U. campus United Way Calhoun County, 1986-87; bd. dirs. 2nd Chance, Inc.; mem. Anniston Mus. Natural History. Mem. Women's Exec. Network, Calhoun County C. of C., Coll. Music Soc., Sigma Beta Delta. Home: 512 Fairway Dr SW Jacksonville AL 36265-3301

FAIRMAN, JARRETT SYLVESTER, retail company executive; b. Anderson, Ind., Feb. 22, 1939; s. Charles Lawton and Ruth (Rich) F.; m. Delores Rae Anderson, Nov. 13, 1960; children: Adele Suzanne, Jarrett Scott, Angela Christine. BS, Purdue U., 1961. Exec. trainee, div. mgr. Sears, Marion, Ind., 1963-67, mdse. mgr., asst. store mgr., Bloomington, Ind., 1967-69, asst. retail sales mgr. sporting goods, Chgo., 1969-71, territorial mdse. mgr. sporting goods, toys and bus. equipment, Dallas, 1971-78; regional v.p. retail ops. White's Home and Auto Stores, 1978-81; pres. Banner, Hendrik & Grant Co., Inc., Dallas, 1981-86; pres. Rapid Distbg. Co. (subs. Otasco), Tulsa, 1986-88; v.p. devel. Coast-to-Coast Home and Auto, Denver, 1988-89; pres. Fairman and Assocs., Inc., 1989-94; pres., CEO Fairman Properties, Inc., 1994—. Served with U.S. Army, 1961-63. Republican. Lutheran. Home and Office: 2006 Hillcrest Ct Mc Kinney TX 75070-4010

FAISON, HOLLY, state agency administrator; b. Sherman, Tex., Aug. 11, 1953; d. Ronald Miller and Ann (LaRoe) F. BA, Tex. A&M U., 1976. Dispatcher College Station (Tex.) Police Dept., 1976-77; police communications operator Tex. Dept. Pub. Safety, Bryan, 1977-83; supr. police communications facility Tex. Dept. Pub. Safety, Austin, 1983-85, Victoria, 1985-87; supr. police communications facility Tex. Dept. Pub. Safety, Bryan, 1987-92, regional supr. police communications, 1993—; mem. Brazos County Emergency Mgmt./Civil Def. Coun., Bryan, 1987-92. Producer video tng. tapes. Mem. Associated Pub. Safety Comms. Officers, Exec. Women in Tex. Govt. (chair-elect Houston chpt. 1996). Methodist. Home: 5500 De Soto St Apt 903 Houston TX 77091-3646 Office: Tex Dept Pub Safety 10110 Northwest Fwy Houston TX 77092-8603

FAJARDO, VICTOR, state commissioner. Commr. P.R. Dept. Edn., San Juan. Office: PR Dept Edn Office of Gov PO Box 190759 San Juan PR 00901

FALK, LAWRENCE CLASTER, publisher, editor, public official; b. Birmingham, Ala., Oct. 6, 1942; s. August Lawrence and Mildred (Claster) F.; student U. Ala. Law Sch., 1963-64, BA, U. Ala., 1978, postgrad., 1978-79; m. Willo Ella Niebow, Mar. 16, 1974; children: Wendy Rebecca, Laura Davida. Reporter, Birmingham Post-Herald, 1964-65; newsman UPI, Raleigh, N.C., 1965-67, mgr., Charlotte, N.C., 1967-68, Birmingham, 1968-70, nat. editor, Chgo., 1970-74; news bur. editor AMA, Chgo., 1973-74; news mgr. Northwestern U., 1974-75; dir. info. services U. Ala., Tuscaloosa, 1975-78; asst. v.p. U. Louisville, 1978-82; pres., chief exec. officer Falsoft, Inc., 1981—; pub., editor Rainbow mag., 1981—, PCM mag., 1982—; pub. ScoreCARD mag., 1983—; pub. Soft Sector mag., 1984-87, Rainbow Books, 1983—; pub. VCR Mag., 1985—, Voice Newspaper, 1986-87, Louisville Skyline Newspaper, 1986-87, New Pilot mag., 1986-90; pub. Software Shopper, 1990—, Power User Newsletter, 1991—; pres., chief exec. officer FPSS, Ag., 1963—; chief exec. officer, chmn. Posh Travel Assistance, Inc., 1985—; pres. Falsoft Video Prodns., 1988—; instr. pub. rels., 1979—; cons. Gadsden Community Coll.; speaker, seminar leader Coun. for Advancement and Support Edn.; mem. City Coun., Prospect, Ky., 1992-93; mayor Prospect, 1994—; pres. Jefferson County League Cities, 1994—; mem. Jefferson County Governance Steering Com., 1994—, Ohio River Corridor Study Commn., 1994—. Recipient Louisville Creative Competition award, 1980, 81, Council for Advancement and Support of Edn. award, 1980, 81, citation Ala. Legislature, 1971. Mem. Pub. Rels. Soc. Am., U. Louisville Assocs. (v.p. 1989—), Sigma Delta Chi (Investigative Reporting award 1970). Jewish. Lodge: B'nai B'rith (Outstanding Adv. to Youth citation 1971) Club: Jewish Community Center, The Temple, Jefferson, Hunting Creek Country, Harrod's Landing Yacht Club, Churchill Downs Turf Club. Home: 5803 Timber Ridge Dr Prospect KY 40059-9317 Office: Falsoft Bldg 9509 Us Highway 42 Prospect KY 40059-9238

FALK, MARSHALL ALLEN, retired university dean, physician; b. Chgo., May 23, 1929; s. Ben and Frances (Kamins) F.; m. Marilyn Joyce Levoff, June 15, 1952; children: Gayle Debra, Ben Scott. B.S., Bradley U., 1950; M.S., U. Ill., 1952; M.D., Chgo. Med. Sch., 1956. Diplomate Am. Bd. Psychiatry. Intern Cook County Hosp., Chgo., 1956-57; resident Mt. Sinai Hosp., Chgo., 1964-67; gen. practice medicine Chgo., 1959-64; resident in psychiatry, faculty dept. psychiatry Chgo. Med. Sch., 1964-67, prof., acting chmn. dept. psychiatry, 1973-74, dean, 1974-92, v.p. med. affairs, 1981-82, exec. v.p., 1982-91, dean emeritus, emeritus prof. psychiatry, 1991—; med. dir. London Meml. Hosp., 1971-74; mem. cons. com. to commr. health City of Chgo., 1972-82; mem. Ill. Gov.'s Commn. to Revise Mental Health Code, 1973-77, Chgo. Northside Commn. on Health Planning, 1970-74, Ill. Hosp. Licensing Bd., 1981-91. Contbr. articles to profl. jours. Trustee John F. Kennedy Hosp., Atlanta, 1993-95, cons., 1991-92; trustee Quantum Found. for Health, Palm Beach, Fla., 1995—. Capt. AUS, 1957-59. Recipient Bd. Trustees award for rsch. Chgo. Med. Sch., 1963, Disting. Alumni award Chgo. Med. Sch., 1976, Alumnus of Yr. award Bradley U., 1990. Fellow Am. Psychiat. Assn., Am. Coll. Psychiatrists; mem. Ill. Coun. Deans (pres. 1981-83), Coun. Free Standing Med. Sch. Deans (bd. dirs. 1984-92, pres. 1989-91), Sigma Xi, Alpha Omega Alpha.

FALK, MYRON, fundraising consultant; b. New Orleans, May 8, 1906; s. Gustave Falk and Margurite Rodriguez; m. Roberta Gilkison, Sept. 2, 1934 (dec. 1980); 1 child, Elizabeth Falk Jones. BA, Tulane U., 1931, postgrad., 1932. Case worker New Orleans Dept. Pub. Welfare, 1932; exec. dir. Baton Rouge area Fed. Bur. Transients, 1933-36; field rep., sr. cons. La. State Dept. Pub. Welfare, 1936-41; dep. dir. La. Civilian Def. Office, 1941-42; exec. dir. Comty. Chest of Baton Rouge, 1944-52; organizer, exec. dir. United Givers Fund of Baton Rouge, 1952-64; dir. western region United Way of Am., N.Y., 1964-72; sr. fundraising cons. United Way of Am., Alexandria, Va., 1972-74; pvt. practice fundraising cons., 1974-78; organizer La. Coun. Migratory Labor and Transients, 1938-41, exec. sec., 1938-41; cons., dep. civilian def. coord. and evacuation officer State of La., 1952; vis. prof. Sch. Social Welfare, La. State U., 1952-64; organizer Comty. Fund for Arts, Baton Rouge exec. dir., 1988-89. Author several pamphlets; contbr. articles to profl. jours. Civilian def. coord. 5-state region 8th Svc. Command, Dallas, evacuation officer La., 1942-44; exec. dir. Baton Rouge Area Found., 1978-88, exec. dir. emeritus, 1990; dist. SCORE rep., La., 1982, 83; mem. adv. bd. Hospice Found. Baton Rouge, Found. Hist. La., Vols. Pub. Schs., Epilepsy Assn. Greater Baton Rouge, Cmty. Fund Arts, Arts Coun. Greater Baton Rouge, Cystic Fibrosis Stair Climb Com.; bd. dirs. ARC, Coun. Aging Baton Rouge Area, Consumer Edn. Found., YMCA. Recipient Cert. Disting. Svc. Pub. Edn., Phi Delta Kappa, 1989, Golden Rule award J.C. Penney Co., 1990, Spirit Giving award Nat. Soc. Fund Raising Execs., 1993, Humanitarian award Arthritis Found., 1994, Golden Apple award Vols. in Pub. Schs., 1994. Mem. Am. Assn. Social Workers (Baton Rouge chpt. pres 1938, nat. bd. dirs. 1946-48), United Way Retirees Assn. (nat. bd. dirs.), La. Conf. Social Welfare (pres. 1939), Rotary. Home: 1479 Pollard Pky Baton Rouge LA 70808-8851

FALK, RUSSELL LOUIS, forestry consultant; b. Hempstead, N.Y., Sept. 5, 1957; s. Ed and Phyllis (Dolin) F.; m. Marybeth Murphy; children: Katy, Carly, Ryan. BS in Forest Mgmt. cum laude, SUNY, Syracuse, 1979. Registered forester, Ga., S.C.; cert. appraiser. Forester Ga. Pacific Corp., Dublin, 1979-88; forestry cons. Timberland Resource Svcs., inc., Dublin, 1988—, now pres.; com. person dist. II Forest Stewardship Program, Ga. Forestry Commn., USFS, USDA, 1990—. Mem. Am. Soc. Rural Appraisers and Farm Mgrs., Soc. Am. Foresters, Forest Farmers Assn., Ga. Forestry Assn., Dublin C. of C., Dublin Lions Club (past pres.). Republican. Baptist. Home: 913 Mark Allen Ln Dublin GA 31021-1021

FALKINGHAM, DONALD HERBERT, oil company executive; b. Lexington, Ill., Dec. 13, 1918; s. William Bishop and Violet (Ashabran) F.; m. Mary Margaret Chalmers, Aug. 23, 1947 (dec. Nov. 1993); children: Deanna Beth Falkingham Worst, Janis Kay Falkingham Fenwick; m. Marjorie A. Cohenour, Aug. 12, 1994. BS, Mo. Sch. Mines, 1941; Profl. Engr., U. Mo., Rolla, 1973. Registered profl. engr., land surveyor, Wyo. Field engr. Amoco, Rangely, Colo., 1951-53; dist. engr. Amoco Producing Co., Cody, Wyo., 1953-59; div. engr. Amoco Producing Co., Casper, Wyo., 1959-61; dist. supt. Amoco Producing Co., New Orleans, 1961-68; pres. Amoco UK Exploration Co., London, 1968-70, Amoco Iran Oil Co., Tehran, 1970-71; co-chmn. bd. dirs. Pan Am. Iran Oil Co., Teheran, 1970-71; gen. mgr. producing dept. Amoco Internat. Oil Co., Chgo., 1972-77; pres. Amoco Drilling Svcs., Chgo., 1975-77, Oceanwide Constrn. Co., St. Helier, Isle of Jersey, 1977-78; chmn. bd. World Maritime, Bermuda, 1977-78; ptnr., co-owner Falcar Energy Co., Houston, 1978-83; mng. dir. hydrocarbon devel. McDermott Inc., Bucharest, Romania, 1994-95; mng. dir. EuroMAC, Sofia, Bulgaria, 1994-95; dist. chmn. Am. Petroleum Inst., 1961; com. mem. Am Bur. Shipping, Bldg. and Classing Offshore Drilling Units, N.Y.C., 1966-68; chmn. exploration and production forum, Oil Industry Internat., London, 1974-77. Pres. bd. trustees, Presbyterian Ch., Cody. Pilot U.S. Army, 1942-45, ETO, maj. ret. Decorated D.F.C., Air medal with oak leaf cluster. Mem. Soc. Petroleum Engrs. (dist. chmn. 1967), Petroleum Club (pres. Casper chpt.), Cody Country Club (pres.), Masons, Shriners. Republican. Home: 7201 S Atlanta Ave Tulsa OK 74136 Office: Falcar Energy Co PO Box 1323 Montgomery TX 77356-1323

FALKNER, WILLIAM CARROLL, lawyer; b. Baird, Tex., Mar. 26, 1954; s. Vernon Lee and Eunice Vera (Fore) F.; m. Linda May (Tilley), May 23, 1987; children: Heather Lynn, Holly Ann. BA in Govt., Tarleton State U., Stephenville, Tex., 1976; JD, Stetson U., Gulfport, Fla., 1984. Bar: Fla. 1984, U.S. Dist. Ct. (mid. dist.) Fla. 1985, U.S. Ct. Appeals (11th cir.) 1985. Asst. co. atty., sr. asst. co. atty. Pinellas County Atty.'s Office, Clearwater, Fla., 1985—. Editor Res Ipsa, Clearwater, Fla., 1992-93; contbr. articles to profl. jours. Lt. col. U.S. Army Res., 1976—. Mem. ABA, Fla. Bar Assoc., Clearwater Bar Assoc. Baptist. Office: Pinellas County Atty's Office 315 Court St Clearwater FL 34616-5165

FALKSTEIN, JASMINE DAUPHINE, writer; b. Ashland, Oreg., May 18, 1957; s. Barry Nosher and Sara (Hauser) F. BA in Journalism, U. South Tex.; MA, U. Tex., 1977, PhD in Edn., 1980. Writer, Austin, Tex., 1980—. Contbr. over 300 poems and short stories to various publs. Home: 6635 Valleyside Rd Austin TX 78731

FALLAW, CAROL FREEMAN, religious organization administrator; b. Aiken, S.C., Mar. 16, 1947; d. Homer Ronell Freeman and Olivia Peloree (Kirkland) Sullivan; m. Waynon D. Fallaw, June 20, 1965 (div. June 1983); 1 child, Adrienne Carol (dec.). Diploma, Christian Life Sch. Theology, Columbus, Ga., 1994. Founder, dir., conf. spkr. New Beginning Ministries, Warrenville, S.C., 1985—; legal sec. Leon E. Green, Aiken, S.C., 1995—; tchr. Christian Life Sch. Theology, 1995—; lectr. Ga. Addiction Counselors Assn., Atlanta, 1995—; condr. workshops, grief recovery and tng. seminars. Author: A New Beginning, A Final Destiny, 1983, The Balm of Gilead, A New Beginning, 1987, The Thing in My Life, 1988, Death Is Not a Killer, 1990, Restoration for the Grieving, A Support Group Leader's Guide, 1991, Restoration for the Grieving, A Student's Guide, 1991, Rivers in the Desert, 1991, Complete in Him, The Death of a Parent, 1993, Complete in Him, The Death of a Child, 1994, Don't Ask "What Can I Do?" 1995, Rivers in the Heavens, 1996, Ministering to the Grieving: A Positive Guide of Support, 1996, The Time of the Singing of Birds is Come, 1996. Assoc. Ask-A-Nurse program Univ. Hosp., Augusta, Ga., 1993—; dir. support group HCA-Aiken Regional Med. Ctr., 1990—, Whole Life Ministries, Augusta, 1992—, Pepperhill Nursing Home, Aiken, 1994, Cornerstone Bapt. Ch., Aiken, 1996—; mem. leadership program Daus. of Zion, Black Mountain, N.C., 1995. Recipient Time To Care award City of Augusta, 1995; featured in Aiken Std., 1995. Mem. Ga. Funeral Dirs. Assn. (affiliate). Home and Office: PO Box 426 Warrenville SC 29851

FALLIN, BARBARA MOORE, human resources director; b. Paducah, Ky., Nov. 12, 1939; d. James Perry Moore and Margaret Arminta (Winn) Kastner; m. Jon Ball, Jan. 21, 1961 (div. July 1963); m. Ralph Daniel Fallin, May 23, 1965; children: Wade, Cathi, Cindy Pergrim, Danielle. Student, Fla. Christian Coll., 1957-58. Cert. sr. profl. in human resource mgmt. Exec. asst. to contr. The Borden Co., Tampa, Fla., 1958-65; mktg. asst. Martin-Marietta Corp., Shalimar, Fla., 1965-71; asst. to pres. Browning-Marine, Ft. Walton Beach, Fla., 1973; pers. coord. Keltec Fla., Shalimar, 1974-78; pers. mgr. Metric Systems Corp., Ft. Walton Beach, 1979-87, pers. dir., 1987-92; dir. human resources Metric Sys. Corp., Ft. Walton Beach, 1992—; mem. Job Svc. Employer Com., Ft. Walton Beach, 1985—; adv. bd. Bay Area Vocat.-Tech. Ctr., Ft. Walton Beach, 1988-92, Okaloosa Applied Tech. Ctr. Sch. Adv. Coun., 1995—. First mistress Krewe of Bowlegs, Ft. Walton Beach, 1983-84, first lady to Cap'n Billy Bowlegs XXXII, 1986-87; mem. citizens adv. com. U. West Fla., Pensacola, 1991—; mem. funds distbn. com. Okaloosa County United Way, 1990-93; mem. BNA's Pers. Policies Forum, 1995-96; mem. Pacesetters fund raiser team Salvation Army Capital Campaign, 1996—. Mem. NAFE, Soc. Human Resource Mgmt., Emerald Coast Pers. Mgmt. Assn. (pres. 1986-88, bd. dirs. 1988-92), Nat. Mgmt. Assn., Ft. Walton Beach C. of C. (hosts com. 1991—), Sugar Beach Sertoma Club (bd. dirs. 1996-97), Beta Sigma Phi (exec. bd. dirs. 1996-97). Republican. Presbyterian. Office: Metric Sys Corp 645 Anchors St NW Fort Walton Beach FL 32548-3803

FALLIN, MARY COPELAND, state official; b. Warrensburg, Mo., Dec. 9, 1954; d. Jospeh Newton and Mary (Duggan) Copeland; m. Joseph Price Fallin, Jr., Nov. 3, 1984; children: Christina, Price. BS, Okla. State U., 1977. Bus. mgr. Okla. Dept. Securities, Oklahoma City, 1979-81; state travel coord. Okla. Dept. of Tourism, Oklahoma City, 1981-82; sales rep. Associated Petroleum, Oklahoma City, 1982-83; mktg. dir. Brian Head (Utah) Hotel & Ski Resort, 1983-84; dir. sales Residence Inn Hotel, Oklahoma City, 1984-87; dist. mgr. Lexington Hotel Suites, Oklahoma City, 1988-90; real estate assoc. Pippin Properties, Inc., Oklahoma City, 199ž-94; state rep. Okla. Ho. of Reps., Oklahoma City, 1990-94; lt. governor State of Okla.,

Oklahoma City, 1995—. Mem. Okla. Fedn. Rep. Women; mem. Am. Legis. Exch. Coun., Nat. Conf. State Legislatures. Mem., del. Okla. Fedn. Rep. Women; mem. Am. Legis. Exch. Coun., Nat. Conf. State Legislatures. Named Nat. Legislator of the Yr., Okla. Ladies in the News, Guardian of Small Bus. award. Presbyterian. Home: 2521 NW 59th St Oklahoma City OK 73112-7108 Office: State Capitol Rm 211 Office of Lt Governor Oklahoma City OK 73105

FALLON, PAUL DENNIS, linguistics educator; b. Winchester, Mass., Apr. 23, 1966; s. William J. and Catherine Anne F.; m. Christina Kakava, July 15, 1990. BS, Georgetown U., 1988, MS, 1989; MA, Ohio State U., 1991, postgrad., 1991—. Acad. program specialist Spoken English Program, Ohio State U., Columbus, 1992-93; lectr. Mary Washington Coll., Fredericksburg, Va., 1995—. Contbr. articles to profl. jours. Mem. MLA, TESOL, Linguistic Soc. Am., Internat. Phonetic Assn., Soc. for Study of Caucasia, Soc. for Study of Indigenous Langs. of the Ams., Phi Kappa Phi, Phi Beta Kappa. Home: 612 Greenbrier Ct Apt J Fredericksburg VA 22401 Office: Mary Washington Coll ELS Dept 1301 Ave Fredericksburg VA 22401

FALLOWS, NOEL, foreign language educator; b. Liverpool, Eng., Dec. 25, 1961; s. William Mitchel and Patricia (Currie) F.; m. Kristin Marie Pope, Aug. 7, 1993.; BA in French and Hispanic Studies, U. Liverpool, 1984; MA in Spanish, U. Ga., 1986; PhD in Spanish, U. Mich., 1991. Asst. prof. Spanish Southeastern La. U., Hammond, 1991-92; asst. prof. Spanish U. Ga., Athens, 1992-96, assoc. prof. Spanish, 1996—; senator U. Ga. Faculty Senate, Athens, 1994—, chair steering com., 1995-96. Author: The Chivalric Vision of Alfonso de Cartagena: Study and Edition of the "Doctrinal de los cavalleros," 1995, Un texto inédito sobre la caballería del Renacimiento español: "Doctrina del arte de la cauallería," de Juan Quijada de Reayo, 1996; contbr. chpts. to books and articles to profl. jours. Horace H. Rackham Grad. fellow U. Mich., 1987; Newberry-Folger Consortium Fund fellow Newberry Libr., Chgo., 1988; Sarah H. Moss fellow U. Ga., 1994, 96; Faculty Rsch. grantee U. Ga., 1992. Mem. MLA, South Atlantic MLA, Internat. Courtly Lit. Soc. (sec. N.Am. br. 1993-94, session chair N.Am. br. 1994-95), Renaissance Soc. Am., Medieval Acad. Am. (Van Courtlandt Elliott prize 1996), Brit. Soc. for Eighteenth-Century Studies, Sigma Delta Pi. Office: Univ Ga Dept Romance Langs 109 Moore Coll Athens GA 30602

FALSETTA, VINCENT MARIO, artist, educator; b. Phila., Nov. 5, 1949; s. Vincenzo and Diomira (Gagliardi) F.; m. Betsy Belcher, Dec. 27, 1975 (div. Aug. 1979); m. Martha Ann Wilhelm, Dec. 18, 1984; children: Trisa Evans, Mario, Alexander. BA, Temple U., 1972, postgrad., 1972-73; MFA, Temple U., Rome, 1974. Asst. prof. Ind. U., Bloomington, 1974-75; instr. U. Utah, Salt Lake City, 1975-77; lectr. U. North Tex., Denton, 1977-78, asst. prof., 1978-84, assoc. prof., 1984-92, painting and drawing coord., 1985-93, prof., 1992—; juror Temple U. Art Dept. Student Exhbn., Phila., 1972, Mex.-Am. Student Art Exhbn., Denton, 1980, Fort Worth Pub. Sch. System Exhbn., 1980, Bruce Hall Art Exhbn., Denton, 1986, Tex. A&M U. Student Art Exhbn., College Station, 1987, Arts Magnet H.S. Student Painting and Drawing Exhbn., Dallas, 1987, Richland Coll. Student Art Exhbn., Dallas, 1990, U. North Tex. at the Sheraton Student Art Exhbn., 1991; faculty cons., grader Coll. Bd. Advanced Placement Examinations in Studio Art, Trenton (N.J.) State Coll., 1996; lectr. in field; interviewed, exhbns. reviewed on various radio and TV programs. One-man shows include Paley Libr. Gallery, Phila., 1972, Tyler Sch. Art, Rome, 1974, Painted Bride Art Ctr., Phila., 1974, 76, Johnson-Whitty Gallery, New Orleans, 1975, 77, Ind. U. Art Mus., Bloomington, 1975, Weber State Coll. Art Dept. Gallery, Ogden, Utah, 1976, U. Utah Art Dept. Gallery, Salt Lake City, 1977, Rosenfeld Gallery, Phila., 1978, 80, 85, 90, Hansen Galleries, N.Y.C., 1978, Chautauqua (N.Y.) Art Assn. Galleries, 1979, Tex. Wesleyan Coll. Gallery 13, Ft. Worth, 1979, Austin Coll., Sherman Tex., 1980, 500 Exposition Gallery, Dallas, 1980, Mattingly Baker Gallery, Dallas, 1982, 83, 85, OK Harris, N.Y.C., 1986, 87, 90, 96, Amarillo (Tex.) Art Ctr., 1983, Soghor, Leonard & Assocs., N.Y.C., 1985, Longview (Tex.) Mus. and Arts Ctr., 1992, San Angelo (Tex.) Mus. Fine Arts, 1993, Sch. Visual Arts Gallery, U. N. Tex., Denton, 1993, Conduit Gallery, Dallas, 1995, El Paso (Tex.) Mus. Art, 1996, Galveston (Tex.) Arts Ctr., 1996, The Art Ctr., Waco, Tex., 1996, others; exhibited in group shows at Paula J. Yoe Gallery Fine Arts, Lehighton, Pa., 1972, Albore Centro d'Arte e Pensiero, Rome, Italy, 1974, Silvermine Guild Artists, New Canaan, Conn., 1974 (Gen. Telephone and Electronics Corp. award), 76, J. B. Speed Art Mus., Louisville, 1974, art dept. gallery U. Utah, Salt Lake City, 1976, Cheltenham Art Centre, Phila., 1976, Utah Mus. Fine Arts, U. Utah, 1976, Johnson-Witty Gallery, New Orleans, 1976, Mus. Phila. Civ. Ctr., 1978, Rosenfeld Gallery, 1978, Arlington (Tex.) Community Ctr., 1978, 500 Exposition Gallery, 1978, 79, 80, Dallas Theatre Ctr., 1980, E. Tex. State U., 1980, Soho Ctr. Visual Arts, N.Y.C., 1982, OK Harris, 1982, 84, 85, U. N. Tex., 1982, 1986, Dallas Mus. Art, 1984, Longview Mus., 1984, Brandywine Workshop, Phila., 1984, Laguna Gloria Art Mus., Austin, 1984, visual arts gallery U. Tex. Dallas, 1984, Mattingly Baker, 1983, 84, Rubiner Gallery, Detroit, 1986, Helander Gallery, Palm Beach, Fla., 1986, 500 X Gallery, Dallas, 1988, DW Gallery, Dallas, 1987, 88, Rosenfeld Gallery, 1988, Hahn Gallery, Phila., 1990, Art Mus. S.E. Tex., Beaumont, 1992, Museo Italo Americano, San Francisco, 1991, Conduit Gallery, Dallas, 1985, 90, 92, 94, Norman Parish Gallery, Washington, 1993, Firehouse Art Ctr., Phila., 1993, U.S. Info. Agy. Traveling Exhbn., No. Africa and The Middle East, 1994-96, Arlington (Tex.) Mus. Art, 1994, The Art Ctr., Waco, Tex., 1995, The Mac, Dallas, 1995, numerous others; represented in numerous permanent collections; subject numerous books, periodical and newspaper articles. Grantee State of Pa., 1968-72, U. North Tex., Denton, 1980-81, 82-83, 85-86, 87-88, 88, 95, Pollock-Krasner Found., 1992, Tex. Commn. Arts, 1993; Mid-Am. Arts Alliance grantee NEA, 1996; recipient Temple U. Abroad grad. assistantship, Rome, 1973-74, Brandywine Workshop vis. artist fellowship, Phila., 1983, 89. Home: 202 Forest St Denton TX 76201-2059 Office: Univ of North Texas Sch of Visual Arts Denton TX 76203

FALZARANO, JEFFREY MARK, naval architecture and offshore engineering educator, researcher; b. Passaic, N.J., Aug. 23, 1960; s. Anthony Vincent and Bertha (Myron) F. BS in Naval Architecture, Webb Inst., 1982; MS in Naval Architecture, U. Mich., 1985, MS in Applied Mechanics, 1987, MS in Aerospace Engring., 1989; PhD Naval Architecture, Marine Engring., 1990. Engr. Foster Wheeler Boiler Corp., Livingston, N.J., 1981; naval architect John J. McMullen & Assoc., N.Y.C., 1981-82, USCG Naval Engring., Washington, 1982-84; rsch. naval architect USCG Mcht. Marine Technical, Washington, 1985; computer specialist ship hydrodynamics lab. U. Mich., Ann Arbor, 1984-85; rsch. engr. R & D Am. Bur. Shipping, Paramus, N.J., 1986; teaching asst., instr., 1987, rsch. asst. naval architecture dept., 1986-90; asst. prof. naval architecture and marine engring. U. New Orleans, 1990-95, also assoc. mem. grad. rsch. and teaching faculty, assoc. prof., 1995—, mem. grad. rsch. and teaching faculty, 1995—; assoc. investigator USCG Vessel Stability Project, Ann Arbor, 1986-88, USCG Mich. Sea Grant Vessel Dynamics Project, Ann Arbor, 1989-90; vis. scholar Vienna Tech. U. Inst. for Mechanics, 1989. Mem. steering com. Grad. Employees Orgn., Ann Arbor, 1987; campaign vol. Dukakis for Pres., Ann Arbor, 1989; chair edn. com. student orgns. Webb Inst., Glen Cove, N.Y., 1981-82. Benton fellow U. Mich., 1985-86; grantee Rackham/Sigma Xi, 1989, Office of Naval Rsch., 1991-96, La. Sea, 1991-93, NSF, 1992—. Mem. ASME (applied mechanics divsn. OMAE divsn.), AAUP, Soc. Naval Archs. and Marine Engrs. (Wilbur Lander scholar 1984-85), Am. Acad. Mechanics, Internat. Soc. Offshore and Polar Engrs. Office: U New Orleans NA & ME 911 Engineering Bldg New Orleans LA 70148

FANCHER, RICK, lawyer; b. Tucson, July 27, 1953; s. James Richard and Margaret Mae (Gum) F.; m. Cecelia Francis Baney, July 12, 1975; children: Jeffery Reed, Ashley Kristin. BA, Trinity U., 1975; JD, U. Tex., 1978. Bar: Tex. 1979, U.S. Dist. Ct. (we. and so. dists.) Tex. 1981, U.S. Ct. Appeals (5th cir.) 1981. Law clk. U.S. Dist. Ct., Corpus Christi, Tex., 1978-80; asst. atty. City of Corpus Christi, 1980; assoc. Gibbins, Burrow & Bratton, Austin, Tex., 1981, John L. Johnson, Corpus Christi, 1982-85; ptnr. Thornton, Summers, Biachlin, Dunham & Brown, Corpus Christi, 1985—. Mem. Tex. Bar Assn., Tex. Bd. Legal Specialization (cert. personal injury trial law). Democrat. Home: 4502 Lake Bistineau Dr Corpus Christi TX 78413-5261 Office: Thornton Summers Biechlin Dunham & Brown Ste 600 Am Bank Pla Corpus Christi TX 78475

FANNING, JUDY G., mental health nurse; b. Baton Rouge, Sept. 21, 1942; d. James D. and Cleo L. (Fowler) Graham; m. Jerry W. Fanning, Nov. 18, 1977; children: Randy, Heather; stepchildren: Tom, Max, Bill. Diploma, Mercy Hosp. Sch. Nursing, Oklahoma City, 1965; student, Okla. U., 1960-62. Clinic dir. Altick-Clariday Surg. Clinics, Dallas; clin. dir. McBride Bone and Joint, Oklahoma City; dir. nursing Community Gen. Hosp., Oklahoma City; dir. nursing svc. Western State Hosp./Okla. Dept. Mental Health, Ft. Supply. Chmn. bd. dirs. Okla. Emergency Med. Svcs. Mem. Okla. Orgn. Nurse Execs.

FANT, GENE CLINTON, JR., English language educator; b. Laurel, Miss., June 30, 1963; s. Gene C. and Ramona Faith (Hankins) F.; m. Lisa Anne Williams, Mar. 25, 1989. BA, James Madison U., 1984; MA, Old Dominion U., 1987; MDiv, New Orleans Bapt. Theol. Sem., 1991; MEd, PhD, U. So. Miss., 1995. Instr. Hampton (Va.) City Schs., 1985-87; instr. of English Gloucester (Va.) County Schs., 1987-89, Phillips Coll., Metairie, La., 1989-90, William Carey Coll., Hattiesburg, Miss., 1991-92; teaching asst. in English U. So. Miss., Hattiesburg, 1992-94, asst. dir. dept. edn., 1994-95, aide to univ. pres., 1995; asst. prof. Miss. Coll., Clinton, 1995—; cons. Miss. River Ministry, Jackson, 1992. Author: Petrarchan Hagiography in Wroth, 1995; contbr. articles to profl. jours. Crisis counselor, New Orleans, 1990-92. Linwood Orange fellow U. So. Miss., 1993. Mem. MLA, Nat. Coun. Tchrs. English, Conf. on Christianity and Lit. (Daub-Maher prize 1994), Internat. Arthurian Soc., Philological Assn. La., Gamma Beta Phi. Office: Miss Coll Dept English Box 4227 Clinton MS 39058

FARACE, VIRGINIA KAPES, librarian; b. Hazleton, Pa., July 10, 1945; d. Elmer Bernard and Elizabeth E. (Kuntz) Kapes; m. Frank John Farace, May 9, 1970. BA, Rider U., 1967; MLS, Rutgers U., 1968. Reference and govt. documents librarian Hazleton Area Pub. Libr., 1968-70; libr. dir. Boynton Beach (Fla.) City Libr., 1970—; bldg. cons. Boynton Beach City Libr., 1973-74, 85-89, Palm Springs (Fla.) Pub. Libr., 1976, 86. Editor: (directory) Library Resources in Palm Beach County, 1979; Centennial Book Com. Boynton Beach: The First 100 Years. Chair legis. com. Edn. Alliance, Palm Beach County, 1987-94; mem. strategic planning task force Palm Beach County Sch. Bd., 1990-91; chair job opportunity task force Project Mosaic, Palm Beach County, 1990-93, transition team 1993; chair budget com. Book Fest! A Literary Festival, Palm Beach County, 1990-93, co-chair exhibitors com., 1994-95, chair steering com., 1995-96, chair bd. dirs., 1996—; edn. com. Govs. Initiative for Teens, 1992—, sec., 1993—; adv. coun. Santaluces H.S., 1991—, chair, 1994—; mem. Congress Mid. Sch. Adv. Coun., 1992—; mem. Palm Beach County Leadership Class of 1994, mem. pub. issues com., 1995—; mem. task force Boynton Beach Hist. Schs., Task Force, 1993; mem. cmty. network Palm Beach County Sch. Bd., 1993—, sch. bd. constrn. oversight and rev. com., 1996, chair pers. and tng. subcom., safe schs. task force; bd. dirs. Boynton Beach Hist. Soc., 1992—, chair by-laws com., 1993, chair nominating ocm., 1994-95, co-chair Hist. 1913 Schoolhouse Restoration Com., 1994—. Mem. ALA, AAUW (v.p. Boynton Beach br. 1989—, br. coord. 1995-96, br. pres. 1996—, state strategic planning com. 1990—, chair 1992, Woman of Change award 1991, state conv. planning com. 1992, chair credentials com. 1992, S.E. Fla. cluster rep. state bd. 1994-96, chair state nominating com. 1994-95, bylaws com. 1994-95, state parliamentarian 1996—), Southeastern Libr. Assn., Spl. Libr. Assn., Fla. Pub. Libr. Assn. (pres. 1989-90, chair libr. adminstrn. divsn. 1992-93, parliamentarian 1992-94, legis. com. 1993—, chair adult svcs. divsn. 1994-95, Pres. award for outstanding libr. leadership 1996), Palm Beach County Libr. Assn. (pres. 1979-80, citation for leadership and svc. 1980), Coop. Authority for Libr. Automation (treas. 1984-93, pres. 1993—), Boynton Beach C. of C. (chair edn. com. 1991—, bd. dirs. 1992—, vice chair 1994—, parliamentarian 1993—, chair nominating com. 1994, Outstanding Com. Chair award 1992, Dir. of Yr. 1993, 94, Ann Barrett award for outstanding svc. and leadership to cmty. 1996), Alpha Xi Delta (pres. 1980-84). Roman Catholic. Home: Lake Clarke Shores 1841 Caribbean Rd West Palm Beach FL 33406-8606 Office: Boynton Beach City Libr 208 S Seacrest Blvd Boynton Beach FL 33435-4452

FARAH, CYNTHIA WEBER, photographer, publisher; b. Long Island, N.Y., June 2, 1949; d. Andrew John and Aria Emma (Jelnikova) Weber; m. James Clifton Farah, Jan. 12, 1974 (div. 1992); children: Elise, Alexa. BA in Communications, Stanford U., 1971; MA, U. Tex., El Paso, 1992. Mem. prodn. staff Sta. KDBC-TV, El Paso, Tex., 1971-73; v.p. Sanders Co. Advt., El Paso, 1973-74, film critic El Paso Times, 1972-77; lectr. film studies U. Tex., El Paso, 1995—; freelance photographer, El Paso, 1974—; pres. CM Pub., El Paso, 1981-89. Photographer, co-author: Country Music: A Look at the Men Who've Made It, 1982; author: Literature and Landscape: Writers of the Southwest, 1988; film critic Sta. KTEP, 1993—. Bd. dirs. N. Mex. State U. Mus. Adv. Bd., Las Cruces, 1982-90; dir., vice-chmn. Shelter for Battered Women, El Paso, 1981-86; active Jr. League, 1977-90, sustaining mem. 1990—, C. of C. Leadership El Paso Program, 1983-84; mem. El Paso County Hist. Comm., 1984-89, vice chmn., 1986, 87, El Paso County Hist. Alliance (v. chmn. 1986-88); trustee El Paso Community Found., 1984—; adv. bd. El Paso Arts Resources dept., 1987-93, chmn., 1991-93; mem. adv. bd. Tex. Film Alliance, 1991—, Tex. Ctr. for the Book, 1987—; mem. literary adv. panel Tex. Commn. on Arts, 1991-93; mem. adv. coun. El Paso Bus. Com. for Arts, 1988-90; mem. adv. coun. Harry Ransom Humanities Rsch. Ctr. U. Tex., Austin; mem. Tex. Com. Humanities Bd., 1993—; mem. lit. panel Cultural Arts Coun. Houston, 1993; mem. adv. com. Tex. Book Fair, 1996. Recipient J.C. Penny Golden Rule award, 1989, Vol. Svc. award El Paso Bur. United Way, 1989, Clara Barton Medallion ARC, 1979, Conquistador award City of El Paso, 1991; named Outstanding Active Mem. Jr. League, 1987-88, Outstanding Sustaining Mem., 1993-94; named to El Paso Women's Hall of Fame, 1992. Mem. Western Lit. Assn., U. Tex. at El Paso Libr. Assn. (v.p. 1987-88, pres. 1989-91), Modern Lang. Assn., Stanford U. Alumni Assn. Episcopalian.

FARBER, ROSANN ALEXANDER, geneticist, educator; b. Charlotte, N.C., Nov. 21, 1944; d. J. Wilson Jr. and June Adell (Childs) Alexander; m. Gerald Lee Farber, July 28, 1966 (div. Jan. 1969); m. Thomas Douglas Petes, July 20, 1973; children: Laura Elizabeth, Diana Christine. AB in Biology, Oberlin Coll., 1966; postgrad., U. Pitts., 1967-68, Albert Einstein Coll. Medicine, 1969; PhD in Genetics, U. Wash., 1973. Diplomate in clin. cytogenetics and clin. molecular genetics Am. Bd. Med. Genetics. Postdoctoral fellow Nat. Inst. for Med. Rsch., London, 1973-75; rsch. assoc. Children's Hosp. Med. Ctr., Boston, 1975-77; from asst. prof. to assoc. prof. U. Chgo., 1977-88; assoc. prof. dept. pathology and lab. medicine, program molecular biology and biotechnology, curriculum genetics and molecular biology U. N.C., Chapel Hill, 1988—; mem. U. N.C. Lineberger Comprehensive Cancer Ctr., 1996—. Contbr. articles to profl. jours. NIH grantee, 1978—. Mem. AAAS, Am. Soc. Human Genetics. Home: 612 Morgan Creek Rd Chapel Hill NC 27514-4928 Office: U NC CB 7525 Brinkhous-Bullitt Bldg Chapel Hill NC 27599

FARCI, ANDRE, business executive. Mgr. documents and processing Electrocom Corp., Arlington, Tex. Office: Electrocom Corp 2910 Avenue F Arlington TX 76011

FARCUS, JOSEPH JAY, architect, interior designer; b. McKeesport, Pa., June 17, 1944; s. Howard E. and Fannie (Meyers) F.; m. Jeanne Cohen, Dec. 31, 1983. BArch, U. Fla., 1967. Registered architect, Fla.; cert. Nat. Coun. Archtl. Registration Bds. Designer Morris Lapidus Assocs., Miami Beach, Fla., 1967-77; prin. Joseph Farcus Architect, Miami, Fla., 1977—; featured speaker: Modern Ship Architecture, intl. conf., Natl. Maritime Museum, London, 1996. Published in newspapers and mags. including Hotel and Restaurant Design, Fabrics & Architecture, Travel Weekly, World Cruise Industry Rev., Internat. Cruise & Ferry, Seatrade Rev., Archtl. Record; mem. editl. adv. bd. Internat. Cruise and Ferry Rev., London, 1994; archtl. and interior designer for largest cruise ship ever built, 1996; patentee ship funnel design; spkr. in field. Bd. dirs. Am. Jewish Com., Miami, 1991—. Mem. Constrn. Specifications Inst. Home and Office: 5285 Pinetree Dr Miami FL 33140-2109

FARENTHOLD, FRANCES TARLTON, lawyer; b. Corpus Christi, Tex., Oct. 2, 1926; d. Benjamin Dudley and Catherine (Bluntzer) Tarlton; children: Dudley Tarlton, George Edward, Emilie, James Doughterty, Vincent Bluntzer (dec.). AB, Vassar Coll., 1946; JD, U. Tex., 1949; LLD, Hood Coll., 1973, Boston U., 1973, Regis Coll., 1976, Lake Erie Coll., 1979, Elmira Coll., 1981, Coll. of Santa Fe, 1985. Bar: Tex. 1949. Pvt. practice, 1949-65, 67-76, 80—; mem. Tex. Ho. of Reps., 1968-72; dir. legal aide Nueces County, 1965-67; asst. prof. law Tex. So. U., Houston; pres. Wells Coll., Aurora, N.Y., 1976-80; disting. vis. prof. Thurgood Marshall Tex. So. U., Houston, 1994-95. Mem. Human Relations Com., Corpus Christi, 1963-68, Corpus Christi Citizen's Com. Community Improvement, 1966-68; mem. Tex. adv. com. to U.S. Commn. on Civil Rights, 1968-76; mem. nat. adv. council ACLU; mem. Orgn. for Preservation Unblemished Shoreline, 1964—; Dem. candidate for Gov. of Tex., 1972; del. Dem. Nat. Conv., 1972, 1st woman nominated to be candidate v.p. U.S., 1972; nat. co-chmn. Citizens to Elect McGovern-Shriver, 1972; chmn. Nat. Women's Polit. Caucus, 1973-75; mem. Dem. platform com., 1988; trustee Vassar Coll., 1975-83; bd. dirs. Fund for Constl. Govt., Ctr. for Devel. Policy, 1983—, Mexican Am. Legal Def. and Ednl. Fund, 1980-83; chmn. Inst. for Policy Studies, 1986-91. Recipient Lyndon B. Johnson Woman of Year award, 1973. Mem. State Bar Tex. Office: 2929 Buffalo Speedway Apt 1813 Houston TX 77098-1710

FARHO, JAMES HENRY, JR., mechanical engineer, consultant; b. Omaha, June 28, 1924; s. James Henry and Mary (Mena) F.; m. Dummer Ree Mitchem, Nov. 12, 1946; children: Sandra, Joann, Wayne. BSME, U. Nebr., 1965. Enlisted USN, 1942, advanced through grades to sr. aviation chief machinist, 1942-62, ret., 1962; engr. Exxon Rsch. & Engring. Co., Florham Park, N.J., 1965-66, project engr., 1966-68, sr. project engr., 1968-70, engring. group head, 1970-71, engring. sect. head, 1971-78; sr. staff advisor Exxon Rsch. & Engring. Co., Clinton, N.J., 1978-85; cons. engr. Lighthouse Point, Fla., 1985—; cons. Exxon Prodn. Rsch., Houston, 1985, Swiki Anderson & Assocs., Bryan, Tex., 1986-87, Glaxo Pharms., Research Triangle, N.C., 1988-91. Mem. VFW, Fleet Res. Assn., Am. Legion, Elks, Sigma Xi. Republican. Roman Catholic. Home and Office: 2401 NE 33rd St Lighthouse Point FL 33064-8142

FARIELLO, MARY ANNA, museum director, art educator; b. Summit, N.J., Feb. 23, 1947; d. Leonard Angelo and Emily (Troianello) F.; m. William S. Rogers, Feb. 14, 1978; children: S. Clay Rogers, Lucas A.A. Rogers. BA, Rutgers U., 1970; MA, Va. Commonwealth, 1987; MFA, James Madison U., 1993. Art critic Style Weekly, Richmond, Va., 1987; adj. faculty U. Richmond, 1987; designer Sci. Mus., Richmond, 1987; event coord. Va. Mus., Richmond, 1987-88; dir. Radford (Va.) U. Galleries, 1988—; curators roundtable Va. Mus. Fine Arts, Richmond, 1992, 96; chair Nat. Coll. Art Assn., Boston, 1996; founder Regional Sculpture Competition, 1991-96. Author: (catalog) From Absurdity to Austerity, 1993 (Addy award 1994); co-author: Collaboration, Art and Technology, British Columbia, 1993; prodr.: (video series) Profiles of Women Artists, 1992; presenter/author: Appalachian Craft Revival, Washington, D.C., 1993. Mem. planning task force Arts Coun. Blue Ridge, Roanoke, Va., 1994-96; task force County Schs., Montgomery County, 1993; adv. panel Va. Commn. Arts, Richmond, 1989-92; task force Va. Craft, Richmond, 1989-91; steering com. Yr. of Am. Craft, Richmond, 1991-93; stds. com. Va. Artisans Assn., Richmond, 1991-93. Mus. Assessment grantee Inst. Mus. Svcs., Washington, 1993, Spl. Projects grantee, 1988, 89, 95, faculty devel. grantee Radford U., 1991, 92, 94, curator's travel grantee Mid-Atlantic Arts Assn., Balt., 1990, project grantee Va. Comm. Arts, Richmond, 1989. Mem. Am. Assn. Mus. Coll. Art Assn., Womens Caucus (v.p. 1986-89), Southeastern Coll. Art Assn. (nominating com. 1990). Democrat. Office: Radford U Galleries Powell 200 Box 6965 Radford VA 24142

FARIÑA DE WOODBURY, MARGARITA, psychotherapist; b. Santurce, P.R., Jan. 30, 1928; d. Feliciano and Mercedes (Lajara) Fariña; m. Michael A. Woodbury, Sept. 10, 1949; children: Michael A. Jr., Camille, Margarita, Peter. BA, Wheaton Coll., 1949; studies with Piaget, U. Geneva, 1964-66; studies with Claude Levis Strauss, U. Sorbonne, Paris, 1966-68; MSW, U. P.R., Rio Piedras, 1974; MD, San Juan Bautista Med. Sch., 1983. Psychiat. resident P.R. Inst. Psychiatry, Rio Pedras, 1986-89; dir. social svcs. Family Inst. of Mental Health, San Juan, P.R., 1974-79, dir. family and social svcs., 1989—. Author: (with Michael A. Woodbury) La Revolución Psiquiatrica - Del Manicomio a la Comunidad, 1987. Recipient 1st Year Residency award Upjohn Interamerica Confederation, 1986, 87, 3d Year Residency award DuPont Pharm. Pan-Am. Inc., 1989. Mem. AMA, NASW (sec. 1973-74), Asociacion de Trabajadores Sociales (vocal 1974-75), Am. Psychiat. Assn. (treas. Puerto Rico branch, 1995-96). Roman Catholic. Home and Office: 557A Calle Trigo San Juan PR 00907-2511

FARKAS, STEVEN, engineering executive; b. Gyor, Hungary, July 15, 1931; came to U.S., 1962; naturalized citizen, 1968; s. Imre and Margit (Egerhazy) FF.; m. Piri Kaposztas, Dec. 24, 1956; children: Steven E., Susan M. Farkas Breen, Thomas A. ME Metall. Engring., U. Miskolc, Hungary, 1953. Registered profl. engr. Asst. supt. melting Csepel Iron and Steel Works, Budapest, Hungary, 1953-56; sr. rsch. metallurgist Atlas Steels, Ltd., Welland, Ont., Can., 1957-62; supt. continuous casting Crucible Steel of Am., Midland, Pa., 1962-68; chief engr. Sanderson & Porter, Inc., N.Y.C., 1969-70; gen. supt. Phoenix Steel Corp., Claymont, Del., 1970-74; area mfg. mgr. Ford Motor Co., Flat Rock, Mich., 1974-80; works mgr. Griffin Pipe Products/AMSTED Inc., Florence, N.J., 1980-88; sr. rsch. engr. Griffin Pipe Products/Amsted Industries, Inc., Lynchburg, Va., 1988-91; dir. rsch. and devel. Griffin Pipe Products/AMSTED Inc., Lynchburg, Va., 1991—. Contbr. articles to profl. jours.; patents pending in field. Mem. Am. Inst. Metall. Engrs., Assn. Iron and Steel Engrs. (life), ASTM, Am. Soc. Metals, Am. Foundrymen Soc., Am. Water Works Assn., Nat. Assn. Corrosion Engrs., Assn. Profl. Engrs. of Ont., Am. Contract Bridge League (sect. master), U. S. Golf Assn., NRA. Home: 3539 Gregory Ln Lynchburg VA 24503-3207 Office: Griffin Pipe Products Co PO Box 740 Adams St Lynchburg VA 24505

FARLEY, BENJAMIN WIRT, religious studies educator, writer; b. Manila, The Philippines, Aug. 6, 1935; s. Wirt Pamplin and Bessie (Campbell) White F.; m. Alice Anne Gamble; children: John David, Bryan Kirk. AB, Davidson Coll., 1958; BD, Union Theol. Sem., Richmond, Va., 1963, ThM, 1964, PhD, 1976. Ordained to ministry Presbyn. Ch., 1963. Instr. Lees-MacRae Coll., Banner-Elk, N.C., 1973-74; asst. prof. bible, religion, philosophy Erskine Coll., Due West, S.C., 1974-78, assoc. prof., 1978-84, Younts prof., 1985—, chair bible, relgion, philosophy dept., 1978-91. Author: The Hero of St. Lo, 1986, Mercy Road, 1986, The Providence of God, 1988, Corbin's Rubi-Yacht, 1992, In Praise of Virtue, 1994; translator, editor: Calvins Sermons on the Ten Commandments, 1980, Calvin's Treatises Against the Anabaptists and Against the Libertines, 1982; co-translator: Calvin's Ecclesiastical Advice, 1991; contbr. articles to profl. jours. Chair Bi-Racial Com., Franklin, Va., 1967-68. Named Writer of the Season, Nostalgia mag., 1990; Fund for Theol. Edn. fellow, 1970; Thomas Carey Johnson scholar Union Theol. Sem., 1963. Mem. Am. Philos. Assn., Calvin Studies Soc., Coloquium on Calvin Studies, Internat. Calvin Congress, Omicron Delta Kappa. Republican. Office: Erskine Coll PO Box 595 Due West SC 29639-0595

FARLEY, GAIL CONLEY, retired librarian; b. Mead, Okla., July 9, 1936; s. William Conley and Marguerite Gaines (Austin) F.; B.S. in History, Sul Ross State U., Alpine, Tex., 1957; M.S. in L.S., East Tex. State U., Commerce, 1970. Served with U.S. Army, 1957-60; tchr. San Felipe Ind. Sch. Dist., Del Rio, Tex., 1963-64; tchr. Natalia (Tex.) Ind. Sch. Dist., 1964-65; librarian Medina Valley Ind. Sch. Dist., Castroville, Tex., 1965-77, La Pryor (Tex.) Ind. Sch. Dist., 1977-78, McCamey (Tex.) Ind. Sch. Dist., 1978-92. Reporter Medina County Sheriff's Res., 1973-75, pres., 1975-77. Mem. Tex. Library Assn., Tex. Assn. Sch. Librarians, Assn. Tex. Profl. Educators, Nat. Rifle Assn. (life), Tex. Rifle Assn. (life). Home: PO Box 965 Mc Camey TX 79752-0965

FARLEY, JOSEPH MCCONNELL, lawyer; b. Birmingham, Ala., Oct. 6, 1927; s. John G. and Lynne (McConnell) F.; m. Sheila Shirley, Oct. 1, 1958 (dec. July 1978); children: Joseph McConnell, Thomas Gager, Mary Lynne. Student, Birmingham-So. Coll., 1944-45; BSME, Princeton U., 1948; student, Grad. Sch. Commerce and Bus. Adminstrn., U. Ala., 1948-49; LLB, Harvard U., 1952; LHD, Judson Coll., 1974; LLD (hon.), U. Ala.-Birmingham, 1983. Bar: Ala. 1952. Assoc. Martin, Turner, Blakey & Bouldin, Birmingham, 1952-57; ptnr. successor firm Martin, Balch, Bingham & Hawthorne, 1957-65; exec. v.p., dir. Ala. Power Co., 1965-69, pres., dir., 1969-89; v.p. So. Electric Generating Co., 1970-74, pres., dir., 1974-89; exec. v.p. nuclear The So. Co., Birmingham, 1989-90; pres., CEO So. Nuclear Oper. Co., Birmingham, 1990-91, chmn., CEO, 1991-92, also bd. dirs.; exec. v.p., corp. counsel So. Co., 1991-92; of counsel Balch & Bingham,

Birmingham, 1993—; bd. dirs. N.A., Torchmark Corp., Stockham Valve & Fittings Co.; mem. exec. bd. Southeastern Electric Reliability Coun., chmn., 1974-76; bd. dirs. Edison Electric Inst.; bd. dirs. Southeastern Electric Exch., pres., 1984; adv. dir. So. Co.; dir. emeritus Am. South Bancorp, 1996—. Mem. Jefferson County Republican Exec. Com., 1953-65; counsel, mem. Ala. Rep. Com., 1962-65; permanent chmn. Ala. Rep. Conv., 1962; alternate del. Rep. Nat. Conv., 1956; bd. dirs. Ala. Bus. Hall of Fame, Birmingham Area YMCA (hon. dir.); chmn. bd. trustees So. Rsch. Inst.; trustee Tuskegee U.; trustee Children's Hosp. Birmingham, pres. bd. trustees 1983-85; mem. Pres.'s Cabinet U. Ala.-Tuscaloosa; bd. visitors U. Ala. Sch. Commerce, chmn., 1991-93. Served with USNR, 1948; now lt. ret. Mem. NAM (bd. dirs. 1987-92), Ala. Bar Assn., Birmingham Bar Assn., Inst. Nuclear Power Ops. (bd. dirs. 1982-89, chmn. 1987-89), U.S. Coun. for Energy Awareness (bd. dirs. 1985-92), Am. Nuclear Energy Coun. (chmn. bd. dirs. 1987-92), Newcomen Soc. N.Am., Birmingham Country Club, Shoal Creek Club, The Club, Mountain Brook Club, Princeton of N.Y. Club, Summit Club, Rotary, Phi Beta Kappa, Kappa Alpha, Tau Beta Pi, Beta Gamma Sigma (hon.). Episcopalian. Home: 3333 Dell Rd Birmingham AL 35223-1319 Office: Balch & Bingham PO Box 306 Birmingham AL 35201-0306

FARLOW, JOEL WRAY, school system administrator; b. High Point, N.C., Mar. 11, 1947; s. William Howard and Dorothy Elizabeth (Cook) F.; m. Judi Morris, Dec. 18, 1971; 1 child, Jodi. BA, High Point U., 1969; MS, N.C. A&T State U., 1979. Cert. prin. N.C.; cert. tchr. N.C. Tchrs. grade 7-9 High Point Pub. Schs., 1969-76; learning lab specialist Guilford C.C., High Point, 1975-78; chief adminstr. Wesleyan Edn. Ctr., Highpoint, 1976—; bd. dirs. Guilford C.C. Child Care Adv. Bd.; instr. internat. Sch. Project, 1993. Author: (with others) Handbook for Christian Living, 1991. Mem. Assn. of Christian Schs. Internat. (bd. dirs., seminar spkr.), Nat. Assn. of Elem. Sch. Prins., N.C. Assn. of Ind. Schs. Wesleyan. Home: PO Box 92 Trinity NC 27370-0092 Office: Wesleyan Edn Ctr 1917 N Centennial St High Point NC 27262-7602

FARMAN, ALLAN GEORGE, oral pathologist, radiologist; b. Birmingham, West Midlands, Eng., July 26, 1949; came to U.S., 1980; s. George and Lily (Hewitt) F.; m. Taeko Takenori, 1996. B Dental Surgery, U. Birmingham, Eng., 1971; PhD in Oral Pathology, U. Stellenbosch, Republic of South Africa, 1977; EdS in Adminstrn./Higher Edn., U. Louisville, 1983, MBA with distinction, 1987; C.Biol, M.I.Biol. (hon.), Inst. Biology, London, 1984; LDS, Royal Coll. Surgeons, 1992; DSc in Maxillofacial Radiology, U. Stellenbosch, South Africa, 1996. Diplomate Am. Bd. Oral and Maxillofacial Radiology. Gen. practice in dentistry Wolverhampton (Eng.) Dist. Schs., 1971-72; asst. prof. oral pathology, registrar U. Witwatersrand and South African Inst. Med. Research, Johannesburg, 1972-74; assoc. prof. oral pathology U. Stellenbosch, Tygerberg, Republic of South Africa, 1974-77; assoc. prof. oral medicine, sr. specialist radiology U. Western Cape, Cape Provincial Adminstrn., Tygerberg, Republic of South Africa, 1974-77; gen. practice in dentistry Doncaster, Eng., 1977-78; head oral biology and oral pathology U. Riyadh, Saudi Arabia, 1978-79; asst. prof. diagnostic sci. U. Louisville Dental Sch., 1979-82, assoc. prof. diagnostic sci., 1982-85, prof., dir. radiology, 1985—; external examiner oral pathology U. Pretoria, Republic of South Africa, 1974, U. Western Cape, Tygerberg, 1975-76; cons. nat. bd. Joint Commn. for Dental Exams, Chgo., 1986-95, Dental Assisting Nat. Bd. com., 1989-92; cons. NIH, 1993—; dir. radiology summer workshop course U. Ky., Lexington, 1984-93; Fulbright vis. prof. to India, 1987; clin. prof. diagnostic radiology U. Louisville Sch. Medicine, 1990—, adj. prof. anat. scis. and neurobiology, 1990—; mem. med. staff U. Louisville Hosp., Norton Hosp., Kosair Hosp., Vencor, Jewish Hosp., Louisville. Author: Oral and Maxillofacial Diagnostic Imaging, Handbook of Signs in Dental and Maxillofacial Radiology; editor oral and maxillofacial radiology sect. Oral Surgery, Oral Medicine and Oral Pathology, 1988-95; mem. editorial bd. Dento-Maxillo-Facial Radiology, 1986—, Acta Stomatologica Croatica, 1996—; editor: Intraoral Radiology, 2d edit., 1991; editor: Computer Assisted Radiology, 1996; editor and author: ADAA Dental Radiography Series ADAA, 1990; contbr. numerous articles to profl. jours. Instr. CPR Louisville area chpt. Am. Heart Assn., 1985—; advisor Ctr. for Devices and Radiol. Health, Washington, 1985-87. Recipient Leith-Neumann award, 1970, Philip Jennens award, 1971, Frank Stammers award, 1971, Grawemeyer award Metroversity, 1983, Harry Crossley awards Harry Crossley Found., 1975-76. Mem. N.Y. Acad. Sci., Royal Soc. South Africa, Am. Acad. Oral and Maxillofacial Radiology (councilor for communications 1986-87, ednl. affairs 1987-88, editor newsletter 1985-90, editor 1988-95), Am. Assn. Dental Schs. (sec. radiol. sect. 1986-87, vice chmn. 1987-88, chmn. 1988-89, del. coun. sects. 1987-89, legis. advocate 1988-95), Electron Microscopy Soc. (sec.-treas. Ohio River Valley area 1984-86, treas. local arrangements 1984-85), Radiol. Soc. N.Am., Internat. Assn. Oral Pathologists (charter), Internat. Assn. Dental-Maxillo-Facial Radiology (pres. 1994—, editor newsletter 1991—), Japanese Soc. Oral and Maxillofacial Radiology, Sands-Cox Soc., Soc. Computer Applications in Radiology, Internat. Congress and Exposition in Computer Assisted Radiology (mem. symposium com. 1994—), Internat. Congress and Exposition on Computed Maxillofacial Imaging (founder, program chair 1994—), Sigma Xi (pres. Louisville chpt. 1992-93), Phi Kappa Phi, Omicon Kappa Upsilon, Beta Gamma Sigma. Home: # 1604 800 S 4th St Louisville KY 40203 Office: U Louisville Sch Dentistry 501 S Preston St Louisville KY 40202-1701

FARMER, DEBORAH KIRILUK, marketing professional; b. Richmond, Va., June 6, 1956; d. Curtis Wayne Kiriluk and Lilan Baltz Starford; m. Roger Paul Schatzel, Oct. 1993. Student, J. Sargeant Reynolds Community Coll., 1974-78, Va. Commonwealth U., 1978-79, John Tyler Community Coll., 1986. Paralegal asst. Hunton Willams, Richmond, 1974; coord. office svcs. Va. Housing Devel. Authority, Richmond, 1975-78; dist. adminstr. Lanier Bus. Products, 1978-80; exec. asst. Old Dominion Emergency Med. Svcs. Alliance, Richmond; asst program dir. Sta. WRVA-AM, Richmond, 1981-83; coord. local sales Stas. WRNL-AM and WRXL-FM, Richmond, 1983-84; sr. account exec. Sta. WTVR-FM, Richmond, 1984-85; mgr. nat. sales Sta. WQSF-FM, Richmond, 1985-88; nat. account exec. HNW&H, Atlanta, 1988-89; mgr. local sales Sta. WTKN/WHVE, St. Petersburg, Fla., 1989-90; gen. sales mgr. WFNS-AM, Tampa, Fla., 1990-91; sr. bus. devel. mgr. Staff Leasing Group, Tampa, 1991—; cons. mem., gov. adv. bd. EMS Pub. Info. Edn., Richmond, 1986; bd. dirs. Travelers Aid Soc. Va., 1987-88, sec., mem. exec. commn. Contbr. articles to profl. jours. CPR instr. ARC, Richmond, 1979-87, mem. VOAD com., 1994; emergency med. tech. Manchester Vol. Rescue Squad, Richmond, 1979-86, sec. bd. dirs., 1979-81, pub. rels. officer, 1985-86; dir. disaster relief Tampa Bay Bapt. Assn., 1993—; chair pub. rels. com. FBC Brandon, 1990-94. Am. Bus. Women's Assn. scholar, 1975. Mem. Am. Women in Radio and TV (charter, v.p. 1987-91, pres.). Republican. Baptist.

FARMER, HARRY FRANK, JR., internist; b. Daytona Beach, Fla., Nov. 9, 1941; s. Harry Frank and Lottie (Ditson) F.; m. Peggy Hines, Oct. 26, 1973; children: Harry Frank III, Kevin. BA, Stetson U., 1964; MA in History, U. Ga., 1966, PhD in History, 1969; MD, Med. Coll. Ga., 1976. Asst. prof. history Ga. Southwestern Coll., Americus, 1968-69. 71-72; resident in family practice Halifax Hosp., Daytona Beach, Fla., 1976-77; resident in internal medicine Univ. Hosp., Jacksonville, Fla., 1977-80; pvt. practice, New Smyrna Beach, Fla., 1980-90; med. dir. for Medicare, Blue Cross/Blue Shield, Jacksonville, Fla., 1990-92; pvt. practice, Ormond Beach, Fla., 1992—. Pres. Endeavors-Physicians Ind. Physicians Assn., Volusia County, Fla., 1993—. Capt. U.S. Army, 1969-71, Vietnam. Decorated Bronze Star, Vietnamese Cross of Gallantry. Mem. AMA, Am. Soc. Internal Medicine, Fla. Soc. Internal Medicine (exec. bd. 1980—), Fla. Med. Assn. (bd. govs., exec. bd. 1990—, editor hist. issue of Jour. 1988-95). Republican. Home: 5 N Ravensfield Ln Ormond Beach FL 32174-3892 Office: 570 Memorial Cir Ormond Beach FL 32174-5070

FARMER, JAMES, civil rights leader, former trade union official; b. Marshall, Tex., Jan. 12, 1920; s. James Leonard and Pearl Marion (Houston) F.; m. Lula A. Peterson, May 21, 1949 (dec. May 1977); children: Tami, Abbey. BS, Wiley Coll., Marshall, 1938; BD, Howard U., 1941; also 22 hon. doctoral degrees. Founder Congress of Racial Equality (CORE), 1942, nat. chmn., 1942-44, 50, nat. dir., 1961-66; race relations sec. Fellowship of Reconciliation, 1941-45; organizer Upholsterer's Internat. Union N.Am., 1945-47; lectr. race and labor problems, 1948-50; student field sec. League Indsl. Democracy, 1950-54; internat. rep. State, County and Municipal Employees Union, 1954-59; program dir. NAACP, 1959-61; leader CORE Freedom Ride, 1961; pres. Center for Community Action Edn., from 1965; asst. sec. for adminstrn. HEW, 1969-70; pres. Council on Minority Planning and Strategy, 1973-76; exec. dir. Coalition of Am. Pub. Employees, 1977-82; adj. prof. NYU, 1968; prof. social welfare Lincoln (Pa.) U., 1966-67; chmn. bd. Fund for Open Soc., 1974-95; vis. prof. Antioch U., 1983-84; Disting. vis. prof. Mary Washington Coll., 1985-94, disting. coll. prof., 1994—; nat. exec. bd. Am. Com. on Africa, 1959-64; chmn. Coun. United Civil Rights Leadership, from 1963; sponsor Am. Negro Leadership Conf. on Africa, from 1962. Author: Freedom--When?, 1965, Lay Bare the Heart: An Autobiography, 1985; also author essay and numerous articles. Vice chmn. Liberal Party N.Y. County, 1954-61; Bd. dirs. League Indsl. Democracy, Friends of Earth, Nat. Citizens Com. Broadcasting, Black World Found., ACLU, Americans Dem. Action. Recipient Am. Vets. Com. award, 1962, John Dewey award League Indsl. Democracy, 1962, Disting. Postgrad. Achievement Alumni award Howard U., 1964, Omega Psi Phi award, 1961, 63. Office: Mary Washington Coll Monroe Hall 1301 College Ave Fredericksburg VA 22401

FARMER, JOE SAM, petroleum company executive; b. Hot Springs, Ark., Mar. 2, 1931; s. Walter L. and T. Naomi F.; m. Elizabeth Jean Keener, Dec. 27, 1952; children: J. Christopher, David E., Kathryn L. Student, Ohio State U., 1950-51; B.Sc., Tex. A & M U., 1955. Cert. petroleum geologist. Geologist Lion Oil Co., Shreveport, La., 1955; geologist, then asst. chief geologist Placid Oil Co., New Orleans, Shreveport and Dallas, 1958-68; exploration mgr. N.Am. div. Union Carbide Petroleum Corp., Houston, 1968-71; v.p. domestic exploration and prodn. Ashland Exploration Inc., Houston, 1971-73, exec. v.p., 1973-77; adminstrv. v.p. Ashland Oil Inc., Ashland, Ky., 1977-79; v.p. Mesa Petroleum Co., Houston, 1979-80; pres. chief operating officer Union Tex. Petroleum Corp., Houston, 1980-83; pres. JSF Interests, Inc., Houston, 1983—. Served with USAF, 1955-57. Mem. Am. Assn. Petroleum Geologists, Assn. Profl. Geol. Scientists, Am. Petroleum Inst., Ind. Petroleum Assn. Am. (bd. dirs.), Mid-Continent Oil and Gas Assn., Houston Geol. Soc. Clubs: April Sound Country (Conroe, Tex.); Petroleum. Office: JSF Interests Inc Ste 207 10100 Hwy 105 West Montgomery TX 77356

FARMER, JOSEPH CHRISTOPHER, physician; b. San Angelo, Tex., Apr. 6, 1956; s. Joe Sam and Elizabeth Jean (Keener) F.; m. Margaret Elizabeth Phelan, June 23, 1979; children: Christopher, Andrew, Mary Elizabeth, John Samuel, Abigail. BS, Tex. A&M U., 1978; MD, U. Tex., Houston, 1982. Diplomate Am. Bd. Internal Medicine. Resident internal medicine Wilford Hall Med. Ctr., San Antonio, 1982-85; fellow critical care St. Louis U., 1985-87; dir. spl. care units Scott Med. Ctr., Scott AFB, Ill., 1987-90; dep. dir. critical care Wilford Hall Med. Ctr., San Antonio, 1990-91, dir. critical care, 1991—; commd. 2d lt. USAF, 1978, advanced through grades to lt. col., 1994; med. dir. critical care aeromed. transport teams USAF, Washington, 1994-96; chief cons. critical care USAF Surgeon Gen., Washington, 1993-96; assoc. prof. Uniformed Svcs. U. Health Scis., 1990—. Author: Critical Care, 1st edit., 1988, 2nd edit., 1992, 3rd edit., 1996; editor: Fundamental Critical Care Support, 1995, Critical Care Review, 3 vols., 1989, 91, 93, Multidisciplinary Critical Care Review Course, 1991, 93. Asst. scoutmaster Boy Scouts Am., San Antonio, 1993—. Decorated Meritorious Svc. medals; recipient Paul W. Myers award Air Force Assn., 1996. Fellow ACP, Am. Coll. Chest Physicians; mem. Soc. Critical Care Medicine (editor-in-chief critical care knowledge assessment program 1991-94), Soc. Air Force Physicians (outstanding resident rsch. award 1984). Home: 29415 Seabiscuit Dr Fair Oaks Ranch TX 78015 Office: Wilford Hall Med Ctr 2200 Bergquist Ste 1 Lackland AFB TX 78236-5300

FARMER, LOLA KAY, middle school educator; b. Corpus Christi, Tex., Feb. 13, 1960; d. Billie Doyle and Ruth L. (Conklin) Grundy; m. Mark Wayne Huddleston, Mar. 19, 1981 (div.); children: Autumn Rene, Aaron Wayne; m. Raoul Gregorio Farmer, Nov. 8, 1987; 1 child, Deon Joseph. BS in Edn., Engring. and Biology, Wayland Bapt. U., Plainview, Tex., 1982; MS in Curriculum and Instrn., Tex. A&M U., 1990. Tchr./coach Kress (Tex.) Ind. Sch. Dist., 1982-83; tchr./coach h.s. volleyball Freer (Tex.) Ind. Sch. Dist., 1983-84; tchr./coach mid. sch. volleyball, basketball, track Aransas County Ind. Sch. Dist., Rockport, Tex., 1984-85; tchr./coach mid. sch. basketball, track Corpus Christi Ind. Sch. Dist., 1986-87, coach, phys. edn. tchr., 1987-92, tchr. math./sci., 1992-94, tchr. sci., 1994-95; tchr. life sci. Grant Mid. Sch., Corpus Christi, 1995—; master tchr. Math. Integration Lab., Tex. A&M U., 1994-96, Nat. Tchr. Tng. Inst., KEDT Pub. Broadcasting, Corpus Christi, 1995-96. Mem. ASCD, Tex. Marine Educators Assn., Sci. Tchrs. Assn. Tex. Home: 3762 Topeka Corpus Christi TX 78411 Office: Grant Middle School 4350 Aaron Dr Corpus Christi TX 78413

FARMER, MARY BAUDER, small business owner; b. San Diego, Nov. 30, 1953; d. Chester Robert and Dixie (Cook) Bauder; m. L. Michael Dowling, July 1990. BS, Auburn U., 1986; postgrad., Ga. State U., 1992—. Exec. dir. Birmingham Woman's Med. Clinic, Ala., 1975-80; pres. Beacon Clinic, Montgomery, Ala., 1980-83; ptnr. Hill, Rose and Farmer, Atlanta, 1988-90; owner, mgr. Mary Farmer Fine Art, Atlanta, 1990—; creative dir., pres. Twin Studios, Inc., Atlanta, 1995—; v.p. Global Interests Inc., 1990—. Author, pub.: The Landlord's Primer for Georgia: A Self-Help Guide for Inexperienced Landlords. Mem. pub. rels. com. Project Open Hand, Ga. Citizens for Arts; mem. Bus. Com. for Arts. Mem. LWV, Ga. Women's Agenda (founder), Omicron Delta Kappa. Democrat. Office: Twin Studios Inc 312 N Highland Ave Atlanta GA 30307

FARMER, PHILLIP W., company executive; b. 1939. BA, Duke U. Various mgmt. and tech. positions GE, 1962-82; v.p., gen. mgr. govt. support sys. divsn. Harris Corp., Melbourne, Fla., 1982-86, v.p. Palm Bay ops., govt. sys. sector, 1986-88, sr. v.p. sector exec., govt. sys. sector, 1988-89, pres. electronics sys. sector, 1989-91, exec. v.p., 1991, pres., CEO, 1995—; bd. dirs. Mfrs. Alliance, Aerospace Industries Assn. Bd. trustees Fla. Inst. Tech. Mem. Bus. Roundtable, Electronic Industries Assn. Office: Harris Corp 1025 W NASA Blvd Melbourne FL 32919-0001*

FARMER, REBECCA ANNE, counselor; b. Norton, Va., July 30, 1952; d. Frank Nelson and Mary Ella (Johnson) F.; m. Carleton Dennis Scully, July 13, 1985. BA in Social Work, U. Ky., 1974, MS in Spl. Edn., 1985. Tchr. Growing Together Presch., Lexington, 1981-84, staff devel. coord., 1984-85; tchr. Fayette County Schs., Lexington, 1985-88; assoc. project dir. early intervention team tng. project Human Devel. Inst., U. Ky., Lexington, 1988-89; family counselor United Cerebral Palsy and Handicapped Children's Assn., Elmira, N.Y., 1990—; adj. clin. assoc. dept. occupational therapy Coll. Allied Health and Nursing, Ea. Ky. U., Richmond, 1983-85; cons. Stephen August Early Intervention Ctr., Cheshire, Conn., 1990-91—, children with phys. disabilities Paceine Sch., Quito, Ecuador; exec. dir. Guilford (Conn.) Aftersch. Program, 1991-92; tech. assistance specialist Ky. systems change project U. Ky. Human Devel. Inst., 1993—. Mem. Assn. for Persons with Severe Handicaps, Ptnrs. of Am. Democrat. Home: 26 Mockingbird Valley Rd Winchester KY 40391-2352

FARNAM, JAFAR, allergist, immunologist, pediatrician; b. Tabriz, Iran, Dec. 18, 1945. MD, Faculty Medicine Tabriz, 1972. Diplomate Am. Bd. Allergy & Immunology, Am. Bd. Pediatrics. Intern U. Ill. Hosp., Chgo., 1977-78; resident in pediatrics Christ Hosp.- Rush U., Oaklawn, 1978-80; fellow in allergy & immunology U. Tex. Med. Br., Galveston, 1980-82; clin. assoc. prof. internal medicine U. Tex. Med. Br.; with Clear Lake Regional Hosp. Mem. Am. Acad. Pediat., Am. Acad. Allergy, Asthma, and Immunology, Am. Coll. Allergy, Asthma, and Immunology, Tex. Med. Assn., Tex. Allergy Soc. Office: Allergy Asthma Ctr 450 Medical Center Blvd #204 Webster TX 77598-4234

FARNSWORTH, CHERRILL KAY, corporate executive; b. Indpls., Oct. 11, 1948; d. John Walter and Winona (Revis) Bowers; children: Leslie Erin, T Brooke Jr. BS magna cum laude, Butler U., 1970. Pres., CEO Suburban Transp. Svcs., Inc., Houston, 1974-76, Dorill Enterprises, Inc., Houston, 1976-85, Maxworth Investments, Houston, 1979-85, F&L Ventures, Inc., Houston, 1982-85; chmn. bd., pres., CEO TME, Inc., Houston, 1984—, HealthHelp Networks Inc., 1995—. Named one of Women on the Move, Houston Post, 1986, High Tech. Entrepreneur of Yr. KPMG Peat Marwick, 1992. Mem. NAFE, Am. Mgmt. Assn., Am. Assn. Ambulatory Care Profls., Soc. Magnetic Resonance Imaging, Assn. for Corp. Growth, Nat. Venture Capital Assn. (exec. com.), Tex. Exec. Women. Office: TME Inc 333 N Sam Houston Pky E Ste 500 Houston TX 77060-2403

FARNSWORTH, T. BROOKE, lawyer; b. Grand Rapids, Mich., Mar. 16, 1945; s. George Llelwyn and Gladys Fern (Kennedy) F.; children: Leslie Erin, T. Brooke. BS in Bus., Ind. U., 1967; JD, Ind. U., Indpls., 1971. Bar: Tex. 1971, U.S. Dist. Ct. (so. dist.) Tex. 1972, U.S. Tax Ct. 1972, U.S. Ct. Appeals (5th cir.) 1977, U.S. Ct. Appeals D.C. Cir. 1977, U.S. Supreme Ct. 1978, U.S. Ct. Appeals (11th cir.) 1982, U.S. Dist. Ct. (we. dist.) Tex. 1988, U.S. Dist. Ct. (no. dist.) Tex. 1994. Adminstrv. asst. to treas. of State of Ind. Indpls., 1968-71; assoc. Butler, Binion, Rice, Cook & Knapp, Houston, 1971-74; counsel Damson Oil Corp., Houston, 1974-78; prin. Farnsworth & Assocs., Houston, 1978-90, Farnsworth & von Berg, Houston, 1990—; bd. dirs., corp. sec. Lomax Exploration, Inc. Contbr. articles on law to profl. jours. Mem. ABA, Fed. Bar Assn., State Bar Tex., Houston Bar Assn., Fed. Energy Bar Assn., Assn. Trial Lawyers Am., Tex. Trial Lawyers Assn., Comml. Law League Am., Petroleum Club (Houston), Champions Golf Club. Republican. Mem. Christian Ch. Home: 5903 Bermuda Dunes Dr Houston TX 77069-1303 Office: Farnsworth and von Berg 333 N Sam Houston Pky E Ste 30 Houston TX 77060-2403

FARQUHAR, KAREN LEE, commercial printing company executive, consultant; b. Warwick, N.Y., May 27, 1958; d. Wesley Thomas and Margaret Anne (Storms) Kervatt; m. David W. Farquhar, July 17, 1982 (div. Feb. 1990); 1 child, Lauren Nichole. Assoc. Sci., Roger Williams Coll., 1978, BS cum laude, 1980. Office mgr. Price-Rite Printing Co., Dover, N.J., summer 1975-76; cons. SBA, Bristol, R.I., 1978-80; account exec. P.M. Press Inc., Dallas, 1980-90, sales trainer, 1984-85; v.p. KDF Bus. Forms Inc., Dallas, Tex., 1984-90; account exec. Jarvis Press, Dallas, 1990—; pres. Print Trends, Dallas, 1990—. Printer, Tex. Aux. Charity Auction Orgn., Dallas, 1985, Crescent Gala, Dallas, 1986, Cystic Fibrosis, Dallas, 1989-93, L.E.A.P. Found., 1992—, Dallas Soc. of Visual Comm., 1992, AIDS Resources Com., Dallas chpt. Cerebral Palsy, 1994, Lloyd-Paxton AIDS Benefit, 1994, Lloyd-Paxton AIDS Charity, Cerebal Palsy Charity, Yellow Rose Gala for Multiple Sclerosis, 1996. Recipient various awards Clampitt Paper Co., Dallas, 1982, P.M. Press Inc., 1983-89, Mead Paper Co., 1985-89. Mem. Printing Industry in Am. (recipient Judges Favorite award 1992, Best of Show Hon. Mention award 1994, gold award Best of Tex. 1996), Internat. Assn. Bus. Communicators, Nat. Bus. Forms Assn. Republican. Baptist. Avocations: piano, aerobics. Home: 2600 Raintree Dr Southlake TX 76092

FARQUHAR, ROBERT MICHAEL, lawyer; b. Chelsea, Mass., Apr. 28, 1954; s. Robert Vociel and Helen Margaret (Stevens) F.; m. Carol Elizabeth Auch, Dec. 16, 1978; children: Stephanie Elizabeth, Andrew Michael. BS, So. Meth. U., 1977, JD, 1980. Bar: Tex. 1980, U.S. Dist. Ct. (no. and ea. dists.) Tex. 1980, U.S. Ct. Appeals (5th and 11th cirs.) 1980, U.S. Supreme Ct. 1990; cert. bus. bankruptcy law Tex. Bd. Legal Specialization, Am. Bankruptcy Inst. Assoc. Carter Jones MaGee Rudberg Moss & Mayes, Dallas, 1980-82; ptnr. Johnson & Cravens, Dallas, 1982-88; shareholder Winstead Sechrest & Minick, P.C., Dallas, 1988—. Mem. ABA, Dallas Bar Assn. Republican. Episcopalian. Office: Winstead Sechrest Minick PC 1201 Elm St Ste 5400 Dallas TX 75270-2144

FARR, CHARLES SIMS, lawyer; b. Hewlett, N.Y., June 29, 1920; s. John Farr and Hazel (Zealy) Sims; m. Mary Randolph Rue, Dec. 21, 1946 (dec. Dec. 1980); children: Charles Sims, Virginia Farr Ramsey, Randolph Rue, John II; m. Muriel Tobin Byrnes, Oct. 13, 1990. Student, Princeton U., 1938-40; LLB, Columbia U., 1948. Bar: N.Y. 1949, Fla. 1984. Assoc. White & Case, N.Y.C., 1948-58, ptnr., 1959-88, of counsel, 1989-92, ret.; mem. bd. visitors Columbia U. Sch. Law. Contbr. articles to profl. publs. Chmn. Commonwealth Fund, N.Y.C., 1976-93; trustee St. Luke's-Roosevelt Hosp. Ctr., 1968-92, Gen. Theol. Sem., 1968-77, N.Y. Zool. Soc., Kent Sch.; mem. bd. fgn. parishes Protestant Episcopal Ch., 1954-78, pres., 1977; chancellor to pres. bishop Protestant Episcopal Ch. in U.S.A., 1977-85; vestryman St. James' Ch., N.Y.C., 1966-76, sr. warden, 1973-76, jr. warden, 1984-86; mem. coun. Rockefeller U., 1980-92. Lt. Comdr. USN, 1941-45, ETO, MTO, PTO. Recipient medal Columbia U. Alumni Assn., 1977. Fellow Am. Coll. Probate Counsel (regent 1960-75), Am. Bar Found.; mem. Assn. of Bar of City of N.Y., Century Club (trustee 1992-95), Links Club, River Club, Pilgrims Club, Yeamen's Hall (S.C.). Republican. Home: 81 King St Charleston SC 29401-2509 also: Harbor House 7 Ocean Way Camden ME 04843-1755 also: 200 E 66th Apt E New York NY 10021

FARR, PATRICIA HUDAK, librarian; b. Youngstown, Ohio, Mar. 10, 1945; d. Frank Francis and Anna Frances (Tylka) Hudak; m. William Howard Farr, Aug. 28, 1971; children: Jennifer Anne, William Patrick. BA, Youngstown State U., 1970; MLS, U. Md., 1980. Children's libr. Pub. Libr. Youngstown and Mahoning (Ohio), 1970-71; asst. Fla. State U. Libr. Tallahassee, 1971-73; rsch. asst. John Hopkins U. Sch. Hygiene and Pub. Health, Balt., 1974-76; asst. Mary Washington Coll. Libr., Fredericksburg, Va., 1976-79; children's libr. Cen. Rappahannock Regional Libr., Fredericksburg, 1980-84, young adult svcs. coord., 1984-89, youth svcs. libr., 1989-91, young adult svcs. coord., 1991-94, children's libr., 1995—. Revision editor HEW pub. Thesaurus of Health Edn. Terminology, 1976; compiler Health Edn. Monographs, 1974-76. Youngstown State U. scholar, 1963-64; R.V. Lowery Meml. scholar, 1979-80. Mem. ALA, Va. Libr. Assn., Now and Then Doll Club. Democrat. Episcopalian. Club: Now and Then Doll. Home: 618 Kings Hwy Fredericksburg VA 22405-3156 Office: Cen Rappahannock Regional Library 1201 Caroline St Fredericksburg VA 22401-3701

FARR, WALTER EMIL, JR., insurance agent; b. Houston, Sept. 18, 1945; s. Walter Emil and Thelma Louise (Sanders) F.; m. Mary Katherine Childers, Nov. 17, 1967; children: Katherine Leigh, Sara Ruth. Student, Tex. A&M U., 1963-67, U. Houston, 1972-75. Agt. Prudential Ins. Co., Houston, 1972-96; prin. Farr & Assocs., Houston, 1996—. Bd. dirs. St. James Episcopal Ch., Conroe, Tex., 1985-87. Capt. U.S. Army, 1967-72, Res., 1972-92, Desert Storm/Desert Shield. Decorated DFC, Purple Heart, Air medals (6). Mem. Houston Assn. Life Underwriters, Houston Assn. Health Underwriters, Houston C. of C., Vietnam Helicopter Pilots Assn., Lions. Republican. Episcopalian. Home: 29007 Driftwood Ln Spring TX 77381-1020 Office: W E Farr & Co 1235 North Loop W Ste 815 Houston TX 77008-4710

FARRAR, MARTHA ANN, lay worker, retired gift shop owner; b. Victoria, Tex., July 13, 1943; d. Warrington Siebert and Byrd Lillian Bertha (Dreyer) F. Student, Victoria Coll., 1961-63; cert., Baldwin Bus. Coll., 1964; cert. in nursing, Renger Hosp. Sch. Nursing, 1966. Reporter Zion Luth Ch. Women, Mission Valley, Tex., 1970-76, sec., 1976-78, pres., 1980-82, mem. adult choir, 1957-61, 72-84, Sunday sch. tchr., 1982-93, mem. altar guild, 1990-94; ret., 1993; owner Martha' Gift Shoppe, Victoria, 1972-93; mem. choir Spirit of Zion Ch., Mission Valley, 1985-94; mem. Rebecca Cir. Bible Study Group, Mission Valley, 1981-93, pres., 1990-91. Co-organizer, sec. Golden Crescent Mayor's Com. for People With Disabilities, 1994-95, chmn. parade com., 1994—, treas., 1996—; owner/operator MicroServ Enterprises, 1996. Democrat.

FARRAR, PAULINE ELIZABETH, accountant, real estate broker; b. Madison, Wis., July 2, 1928; d. William Charles and Mary Anna (Killalley) Selmer; m. James Walter Byers, Aug. 15, 1950 (dec. June 1972); children: Marvin Lee, Marjorie Sue; m. Robert Bascom Farrar, Apr. 14, 1974; stepchildren: Katrinka Jo Farrar Sandahl, Jon Randle Farrar. Student, U. Wis., 1946-49, U. Houston, 1956-57. Acct. Sterling Hogan, Houston, 1951-54, Lester Prokop, Houston, 1959-64, Holland Mortgage Co., Houston, 1964-68, Jetero Bldg Corp., Houston, 1968-71; real estate assoc. Mills Paulea Realtors, Houston, 1976-80, ERA, Nelson & Assocs., Missouri City, Tex., 1980-81; owner, broker, owner Property-Wise Realty, Sugar Land, Tex., 1981-89; owner, broker Realty Execs.-Ft. Bent, Sugar Land, 1989—; tax assesor, collector Sequoia Utility Dist., Houston, 1969-71. Leader Girl Scouts U.S.A., Houston, 1962-72; organizer, coordinator ladies program Stafford (Tex.) Ch. of Christ, 1978-81. Mem. Nat. Assn. Realtors (dir. 1995—), Tex. Assn. Realtors (bd. dirs. 1986-87), Cert. Real Estate Brokers (v.p. Tex. chpt. 1986-87, sec.-treas. 1988-90, v.p. 1991, pres. 1992), Ft. Bend County Bd. Realtors (pres. 1987—), Women's Coun. Realtors (founding chmn. Ft. Bend-S.W. Houston chpt., pres. 1988, nat. bd. govs. 1991), Nat. Realtors Inst. (cert. residential specialist, real estate broker, grad. Realtors

Inst., leadership tng.). Office: Realty Execs 13333 Southwest Fwy Ste 1900 Sugar Land TX 77478-3545

FARRELL, JUNE ELEANOR, retired middle school educator; b. Ft. Atkinson, Wis., Dec. 31, 1916; d. Isaac Leslie and Thora Eleanor (Huppert) Winter; m. Martin Joseph Farrell, Sept. 21, 1946; children: Leslie June Kathryn, Robert Joseph. BA, DePauw U., Green Castle, Ind., 1939. Cert. secondary tchr. English, Latin, and drama, Fla. Tchr. English, Latin and drama Elmore (Ind.) Twp. High Sch., 1939-41; tchr. Latin and English Beach Grove High Sch., Indpls., 1941-46; v.p. Farrell Foods Inc., 1948-66; tchr. English Ft. Atkinson (Wis.) Jr. High Sch., 1966-67, Venice (Fla.) Jr. High Sch., 1967-82; tchr. sci. Venice Area Mid. Sch., 1982-89, ret., 1989. Contbr. articles to profl. jours. Bd. dirs. AARP, Venice, Fla., 1994—; pres. Friends of Venice Cmty. Ctr., 1984—. Mem. AAUW, Sarasota County Reading Coun. (pres. 1974-76), Sarasota County Tchrs. English (treas. 1975-79), Alpha Delta Kappa (pres. chpt. 1976-78, alturistic chmn. 1986-93), Delta Zeta. Republican. Methodist. Home: 640 W Venice Ave Venice FL 34285-2031 also: 603 Van Buren St Fort Atkinson WI 53538-1715

FARRELL, KAROLYN KAY MCMILLAN, adult education educator; b. Springfield, Mo., June 23, 1938; d. Octa H. and Ruth Marie (Funkhouser) McMillan; m. Donald Paul Farrell, June 19, 1960; children: Shawn McMillan, Beth Melanie. BS in Edn. cum laude, SW Mo. State U., 1960; M Adult Edn., U. Ark., 1983, EdS, 1991; postgrad., U. Mo., 1964. Cert. adult edn. adminstr. Instr. art, sci., vocat. home econs. Indian Head High Sch., Charles County, Md., 1960-62; instr., cons. Kansas City (Mo.) Bd. Edn., 1962-63, cons. enrichment, 1963-68; instr. art Fayetteville (Ark.) Arts Gallery, 1973-77; artist in residence Butterfield Sch., Fayetteville, 1973-77; creator, developer Curriculum Disseminating Ctr., U. Ark., Fayetteville, 1979-82; dir. community and adult edn. Fayetteville Community Schs., 1979—; dietary asst. Trinity Luth. Hosp., Kansas City, 1962-63;instr. health Fayetteville High Sch., 1976-79; freelance artist, Fayetteville, 1980—. Vol. visual arts com. Walton Arts Ctr., 1980—; vol. Nelson Atkins Mus., Friends of Art, Kansas City, 1988—; co-chmn. N.W. Ark. Project Literacy U.S., 1988—; cmty. trustee Ark. Arts Ctr., 1994—. Levi grantee, Fayetteville, 1983-85; recipient numerous art awards. Mem. Am. Assn. Adult and Continuing Edn., Ark. Assn. Adminstrs. Adult Edn. (pres. 1989-91, sec. 1992—), Nat. Cmty. Edn. Assn., Ark. Assn. Pub. Continuing and Adult Edn. (facilitator), Rotary (fellowship and cmty. devel. coms.), Phi Delta Kapa (found. com. 1988—). Baptist. Home: 1567 Anson Pl Fayetteville AR 72701-3705

FARRELL, ROBERT JOEL, II, counselor and therapist, educator, minister; b. Decatur, Ala., May 15, 1965; s. Robert Joel and Amanda Jane (Morrisson) F.; m. Robin Carrie Gosdin, Dec. 8, 1990; children: Revin Joel, Ryan Jordan. BS in Bldg. Sci., Auburn U., 1988; MS in Religion, Ala. Christian Sch., 1990; MEd in Counseling and Psychology, Auburn U., 1992, PhD in Counselor Edn. and Supervision, 1996. Landscape contractor Farrell Lawns, Oklahoma City, 1977-83; asst. student tchr. Auburn (Ala.) U., 1986-88; intern min. Cen. Ch. of Christ, Anniston, Ala., 1987, Auburn Ch. of Christ, 1989-91; mng. editor Spirit Mag., Auburn, 1988-89; rsch. asst. family and child devel. Auburn U., 1990, tutor, 1990-94; substitute tchr. Auburn City Schs., 1991-94; assoc. prof. counseling, dir. clin. tng. So. Christian U., 1995—, dir. Life Skills Ctr., 1996—; min. of family counseling Hoover Ch. of Christ, 1995—; adj. prof. Faulkner U., Montgomery, Ala., 1991—; grad. rsch. asst. Strategic Teams for Rural Intervention Through Drug Edn., 1992-93; doctoral tchg. asst. Auburn U., 1993-95; asst. prodn. mgr. Jour. Rsch. in Childhood Edn., 1993-95; counselor Auburn U., Montgomery, 1994-95. Asst. dir. BASIC, Auburn, 1985-90; bd. dirs. Southeastern Drama Workshop, Auburn, 1990; asst. coord. Lee County Ind. Living Ctr., 1991-92; agy. counselor Ala. Coun. Human Rels., Inc., 1992-93; bd. dirs., sec. of bd. Montgomery Mens Ctr., 1994-95; missionary Chs. of Christ; senator Grad. Student Orgn., 1991-92. Mem. ACA, Am. Coll. Pers. Assn., Assn. for Religious and Values in Counseling, Am. Assn. Christian Counselors, Ala. Counseling Assn. (grad. student rep. alternative chpt. VII exec. coun., jour. editor), Ala. Assn. Specialists in Group Work (bd. dirs., sec., chmn. membership com., pres., pres.-elect, newsletter editor), Auburn U. Counseling Assn. (bd. dirs. 1991-95), Am. Coll. Counseling Assn. Home and Office: 617 Shawnee St Auburn AL 36830-5121

FARRIGAN, JULIA ANN, small business owner, educator b. Albany, N.Y., July 19, 1943; d. Charles Gerald and Julia Tryon (Shepherd) F. BS in Elem. Edn., SUNY, Plattsburgh, 1965; MS in Curriculum Planning and Devel., SUNY, Albany, and U. Manchester, Eng., 1973; postgrad. in adminstrv. svcs. Calif. State U., Fresno, 1976-78. With Monroe-Woodbury Ctrl. Sch. Dist., Monroe, N.Y., 1965-90; dist. coord. gifted programs The Pine Tree Sch., 1979-90; ptnr. Baskets Plain and Fancy, Jackson, Ga., 1994—; adj. prof. Gifted Edn. Contbr. articles to profl. jours. Officer United Meth. Women, Jackson United Meth. Ch.; bd. dirs., Butts County Hist. Soc., docent, editor newsletter; coord. blood drive ARC Butts County. Mem. DAR (vice regent William McIntosh chpt., state chmn.), AFT, ASCD, NYUFT, Nat. Assn. for Gifted Children, Coun. Exceptional Children, Monroe-Woodbury Tchr's. Assn., Hawthorne Garden Club (officer), Kiwanis (officer), Delta Kappa Gamma (officer Upsilon chpt., state officer). Democrat. Methodist.

FARRINGTON, BERTHA LOUISE, nursing administrator; b. Poteet, Tex., Jan. 20, 1937; d. Leonard Gilbert and Janie (Hernandez) Lozano; m. James Charles Farrington, Jan. 30, 1965; children: Mark Hiram, Robert Lee. BSN, Tex. Women's U., 1960; NP, U. Tex., 1984. RN, Tex. Charge nurse emergency rm. Parkland Meml. Hosp., Dallas; head nurse emergency rm./day surgery Bapt. Meml. Hosp., Pensacola, Fla.; asst. dir. health svcs. U. Tex. Southwestern Med. Ctr., Dallas, dir. student health svcs.

FARRINGTON, JERRY S., utility holding company executive; b. Burkburnett, Tex., 1934. B.B.A., North Tex. State U., 1955, M.B.A., 1958. With Tex. Electric Service Co., 1957-60; v.p. Tex. Utilities Co. (parent co.), Dallas, 1970-76, pres., 1983-87, chmn., CEO, 1987-95; chmn., 1995—; pres. Dallas Power & Light Co., 1976-83; chmn., CEO Tex. Utilities Fuel Co., Tex. Utilities Mining Co., Dallas. Office: Tex Utilities Co Energy Plz 1601 Bryan St Dallas TX 75201-3411

FARRIOR, CHARLES WARRICK, adminstrative contracting officer; b. Vicksburg, Miss., May 20, 1960; s. Edward Vardaman and Sadie Pilkington F.; m. Candace Ann Daniels, July 12, 1986. BBA in Fin., Miss. State U., 1982; MBA, Miss. Coll., 1990. Purchasing agt. IRS, Jackson, 1983-84; procurement asst. Army Corp of Engrs., Vicksburg, 1984-86; mgmt. cons. Vicksburg, 1990-91; contract specialist Army Corp of Engrs. - WES, Vicksburg, 1986-91; contract adminstr. Navy Supervisory of Shipbuilding, New Orleans, 1991-94; supervisory contract specialist and corp. adminstrv. contracting officer Navy Supervisory of Shipbuilding, Pascagoula, Miss., 1994-95; mgmt. cons., Vicksburg, 1990-91; adj. instr. of econs. Hinds Comm. Coll., Vicksburg, 1991. Pres. Miss. State U. BSU Alumni Bd., Starkville, 1995—; vol. Cystic Fibrosis Found., New Orleans, 1990—; mem. ann. giving nat. com. Miss. State U., 1996, legis. nat. com., 1993—. Selected for Top 40 Under 40 in Miss., 1996. Mem. Nat. Contract Mgmt. Assn., Miss. Coast Assn. of Fed. Adminstrs., MBA Assn. of Miss., Lions Club. Republican. Baptist. Home: 8721 Boxwood Lane Gautier MS 39553

FARRIS, BRADLEY KENT, neuro-ophthalmologist; b. Oklahoma City, Nov. 27, 1952; s. Edward Merhige and Lucille (Baldwin) F.; m. Diane K. Dietrich, Nov. 25, 1983; children: Matthew Bradley, Adam Edward, Jacob Bailey. BA, U. Okla., 1976, MD, 1980. Diplomate Am. Bd. Ophthalmology. Intern U. Okla., Oklahoma City, 1980-81, resident in neurology, 1981-82, resident in ophthalmology, 1982-85, asst. prof. ophthalmology, 1986-91, assoc. prof. ophthalmology, 1991—, adj. asst. prof. neurology, neurosurgery, 1986-91, adj. assoc. prof. neurology, neurosurgery, 1991—, dir. neuro-ophthalmology svc. Sch. Medicine, 1986—; fellow in neuro-ophthalmology U. Miami, Fla., 1985-86; chief ophthalmology svc. O'Donahue Rehab. Inst., Oklahoma City, 1987—; mem. staff Mercy Hosp., Bapt. Hosp., Deaconess Hosp.; presenter, lectr. in field. Author, editor text: The Basics of Neuro-Ophthalmology, 1991; book rev. editor Jour. Clin. Neuro-Ophthalmology, 1986—, mem. bd. editors, 1986—; contbr. articles to profl. publs. Mem., advisor Okla. Heat Injury Found., Oklahoma City, 1990—; bd. dirs. Fellowship Christian Athletes, Oklahoma City, 1986—. Named one of Best Doctors in Am., Woodward & White, 1991-93. Fellow Am. Acad. Ophthalmology; mem. AMA (Physician Recognition award 1991-93), Am. Acad. Neurology, Okla. State Med. Assn., N.Am. Neuro-Ophthalmol. Soc., Internat. Neuro-Opthalmology Soc., Christian Ophthalmol. Soc. (pres. 1990—), Frank B. Walsh Soc., Okla. State Acad. Ophthalmology, Ctrl. Okla. Ophthalmology Jour. Club, Phi Alpha Theta. Republican. Office: Dean A McGee Eye Inst 608 Stanton L Young Blvd Oklahoma City OK 73104-5014

FARRIS, EDWARD THOMPSON, dentist, medical researcher, real estate developer and broker; b. Ft. Worth, Sept. 9, 1925; s. Chester Arthur and Bernice Boyd (Thompson) F.; m. Helen Dean Williams, Apr. 21, 1950 (div. 1976); children: Mark Alan, Glen Edward; m. Ethel Lynn Melnick, Dec. 10, 1984 (dec. Oct. 1993). AS, U. Tex., Arlington, 1944; BA in Biology, U. North Tex., 1948, MA in Biology, 1953; DDS, Baylor U., 1953. Lic. dentist, Tex., real estate broker. Dentist Dallas, 1953—; owner, pres., chmn. Celestial Ctr., Inc., Dallas, 1968—; pres. PEP II Ptnrs. Inc., Dallas, 1992-93, C.B.E., Inc., Sunshine Realty Co., Inc.; gen. ptnr. Edward T. Farris Co., Ltd. Producer: (ednl. film) Texas Our Texas, 1968; producer, pub.: Outdoor Plants of the Southwest, 1982; patentee in med./dental field, automotive safety systems. Active Circle Ten. coun. Boy Scouts Am., 1967-90; charter mem. Rep. Task Force, 1994—. Served as sgt. U.S. Army, 1944-46, ETO. Decorated Bronze Star. Recipient Award of Merit Boy Scouts Am., 1977, Silver Beaver award Boy Scouts Am., 1979. Mem. Beta Beta Beta (hon.), Omicron Kappa Upsilon (hon.). Baptist. Lodges: Shriners, Masons (32 degree). Home: 1928 Cobblestone Ln Garland TX 75042-4652 Office: Celestial Ctr Inc 4715 Greenville Ave Dallas TX 75206-4117

FARRIS, FRANK MITCHELL, JR., lawyer; b. Nashville, Sept. 29, 1915; s. Frank M. and Mary (Lellyett) F.; m. Genevieve Baird, June 7, 1941; 1 dau., Genevieve B. B.A., Vanderbilt U., 1937; postgrad. N.Y. Law Sch., 1938-39. Bar: Tenn., 1939, U.S. Tax Ct., 1948, U.S. Supreme Ct., 1968. Conciliation commr. in bankruptcy U.S. Dist. Ct. Middle Dist. Tenn., 1940-42; ptnr. Farris, Warfield & Kanaday, and predecessors, Nashville, 1946—; gen. counsel, trustee George Peabody Coll. for Tchrs., 1968-79; counsel 3d Nat. Corp., Nashville, Cherokee Equity Corp., Nashville. Commr. Watkins Inst., Nashville, 1953-95; trustee Vanderbilt U., 1979—; chmn. bd. Oak Hill Sch., Nashville, 1968-74, 80-81. Mem. ABA, Tenn. Bar Assn., Nashville Bar Assn. Home: 940 Overton Lea Rd Nashville TN 37220-1503 Office: Farris Warfield & Kanaday Third Nat Fin Ctr 19th Fl Nashville TN 37219

FARRIS, JAMES CLARENCE, internal medicine physician; b. New Tazewell, Tenn., May 23, 1939; s. Clarence Edward and Nannie Lou (Sharp) F.; m. Nancy Jean Penn, June 17, 1961; children: Scott Penn, Rena Kathryn, James Clarence. BS, U. Tenn., 1960; MD, U. Tenn., Memphis, 1963. Diplomate Am. Bd. Internal Medicine. Chief of staff LaFollette (Tenn.) Med. Ctr., 1992—; bd. dirs. First Nat. Bank, LaFollette. Bd. dirs. Campbell County Hist. Soc., LaFollette, 1992-93; deacon First Bapt. Ch., LaFollette, 1992—. Capt. USAF, 1968-70. Mem. ACP, AMA, Am. Soc. Internal Medicine, Tenn. Med. Assn. Republican. Baptist. Office: 110 East Ave La Follette TN 37766-2856

FARRIS, ROBERT GENE, transportation company executive; b. Bartlesville, Okla., June 21, 1930; s. Carlton Kittrell and Ruby Lee (Richeson) F.; m. Betty C. Raimond, Dec. 28, 1951; children: Robert Raimond, William Carlton, Jonathan Bradley. BBA, U. Tex., 1952. Safety dir. Valley Transit Co., Inc., Harlingen, Tex., 1955-56, pers. dir., 1956-57, v.p., 1957-62, pres., 1963—, also bd. dirs., 1963—; bd. dirs. Tex. State Bank, Harlingen, Tex. Regional Bancshares, McAllen, Tex., Phoenix Energy Group Inc., Houston. Pres. Harlingen Indsl. Found., 1968-69; v.p. Rio Grande Coun. Boy Scouts Am., 1971-72; trustee Marine Mil. Acad., Harlingen, 1977—; bd. dirs. Tex. Tourist Coun., Austin, 1980-84. lst lt. U.S. Army, 1952-54, Korea. Named Friend of Tex. Transit, Tex. Dept. Hwys. and Pub. Transp., 1978. Mem. Nat. Bus Traffic Assn. (bd. dirs. 1980-85), Tex. Motor Transp. Assn. (bd. dirs. 1976-80), Harlingen C. of C. (pres. 1967-68), Rio Grande Valley C. of C. (pres. 1975-76), Phi Gamma Delta. Methodist. Office: Valley Transit Co Inc 219 N A St Harlingen TX 78550-5413

FARRIS, SUSAN ANN, nursing home administrator, dietitian; b. Beaumont, Tex., May 16, 1958; d. LW and Marian (Hancock) Koch; m. John Michael Farris, July 11, 1992. BS in Natural Scis., U. Tex., 1987; student, Southwest Tex. State U., 1987. Lic. nursing home adminstr., Tex. Adminstr. Beverly Enterprises, Coleman, Tex., 1988-91, Ft. Worth, 1994-95; adminstr. Forum Group, Ft. Worth, 1991-92, HEA Mgmt., Lake Worth, Tex., 1992-94, Park Haven, Inc., Bridgeport, Tex., 1995—; mem. adv. bd. Osteo. Ctr. for Geriatric Excellence, 1992—. Mem. ombudsman adv. bd. Area Agy. on Aging, Tarrant County, Tex., 1993—. Mem. Tex. Health Care Assn. (bd. dirs. 1992—), Golden Key Nat. Soc. Office: Park Haven Healthcare Ctr 2108 15th St Bridgeport TX 76426

FARRUKH, USAMAH OMAR, electrical engineering educator, researcher; b. Beirut, Lebanon, Aug. 24, 1944; came to U.S., 1969; s. Omar Abdullah and Amenah (Helmi) F.; m. Samar M. Hussami, 1980; children: Muna, Omar, Marwa. BSEE, Am. U. Beirut, 1967; PhDEE, U. So. Calif., 1974. Lead analyst Wolf R & D Group, Riverdale, Md., 1975-76; sci. specialist Phoenix Corp., McLean, Va., 1976-77; sci. cons. Applied Sci. and Tech. Inc., Rosslyn, Va., 1978; staff scientist Inst. Atmosphenic Optics and Remote Sensing, Hampton, Va., 1978-85; assoc. prof. dept. elec. engring. Hampton U., 1985-93, prof., 1993—; cons. U.S. Army Rsch. Office, 1990-91; summer faculty Dept. Energy, 1995. Contbr. articles to profl. jours. Bd. dirs. Hypohidrotic Ectodermal Dysplasia and Related Disorders Found., Hampton, 1987—. Grantee NASA, 1986-95, U.S. Army Rsch. Lab., 1993-95, Dept. Energy Summer Faculty Subcontract, 1995. Mem. IEEE, Optical Soc. Am. Office: Hampton Univ Olin Engring Bldg Hampton VA 23601

FARST, DON DAVID, zoo director, veterinarian; b. Wadsworth, Ohio, Feb. 25, 1941; s. Walter K. and Ada (Stetler) F.; m. Jan Rae Harber, June 17, 1980; children: Julie K., Jenny Lynn, John David. D.V.M., Ohio State U., 1965. Veterinarian, mammals curator Columbus Zoo, Ohio, 1969-70; assoc. dir. Gladys Porter Zoo, Brownsville, Tex., 1970-74, dir., 1974—. Editor: Jour. Zoo Animal Medicine, 1973-77. Mem. Am. Assn. Zool. Parks and Aquariums (pres. 1979-80, chmn. ethics bd. 1990-91), Am. Assn. Zoo Veterinarians, Internat. Union Dirs. Zool. Home: 640 Edgewater Isle San Benito TX 78586-9209 Office: Gladys Porter Zoo 500 Ringgold St Brownsville TX 78520-7918

FARWELL, BYRON EDGAR, writer; b. Manchester, Iowa, June 20, 1921; m. Ruth Saxby; children: Joyce, Byron John, Lesley. Student, Ohio State U., 1939-40; A.M., U. Chgo., 1968. Dir. adminstrn. Chrysler Internat., Geneva, 1959-70; archeologist; delivered Anne S.K. Brown Meml. lectr. on mil. history, Brown U., Providence, R.I., 1996. Author: The Man Who Presumed, 1953, 4th edit., paperback, 1989, U.K. edit., 1958, Books on Tape, 1995, Burton: A Biography of Sir Richard Francis Burton, 1964, 75, U.K. edit., 63, 88, 95, Books on Tape, 1994, Prisoners of the Mahdi, 1967, paperback 1971, 89, UK edit., 1967, Books on Tape, 1994, Queen Victoria's Little Wars, 1972, U.S. paperback edit., 1985, 2d edit., 1989, U.K. edit., 1973, Books on Tape, 1994, The Great Anglo-Boer War, 1976, U.K. edit., 1977, paperback edit., 1990, Books on Tape, 1994, Mr. Kipling's Army, 1981, U.K. edit., 1987, Books on Tape, 1994, For Queen and Country, 1981, paperback edit., 1987, Books on Tape, 1994, The Gurkhas, 1984, U.K. paperback edit., 1985, U.S. paperback edit., 1990, Books on Tape, 1994, Eminent Victorian Soldiers, 1985, paperback edit., 1986, U.K. edit., 1988, Books on Tape, 1993, The Great War in Africa, 1914-1918, 1986, UK edit., 1987, U.S. paperback edit., 1989, Books on Tape, 1994, Armies of the Raj, 1989, U.K. edit., 1990, U.S. paperback edit., 1991,, Books on Tape, 1994, Ball's Bluff: A Small Battle and its Long Shadow, 1990, Books on Tape, 1994, Stonewall: A Biography of General Thomas Jackson, 1992, paperback edit., 1993, Books on Tape, 1993; contbg. editor: Military History, World War II; contbr. The Reader's Companion to Military History, Oxford Companion to American Military History, 1996; contbr. numerous articles to Colliers Ency., newspapers, revs., mags.; mem. edit. bd. Small Towns Inst.; lectr. in field. Former councilman and mayor, Hillsboro, Va.; hon. mem., bd. dirs. Oatlands of Nat. Trust; former trustee Am. Mil. Inst.; mem. adv. bd. Nat. History Soc. Capt. C.E., U.S. Army, 1940-45, ordnance corps, 1950-53. Fellow Royal Soc. Lit. (U.K.), Royal Geog. Soc. (U.K.). Address: PO Box 3200C Hillsboro VA 20134-1510

FASCELL, DANTE B., congressman, lawyer; b. Bridgehampton, NY, Mar. 9, 1917; s. Charles A. and Mary (Gullotti) F.; m. Jeanne-Marie Pelot, Sept. 19, 1941; children: Sandra J., Toni F. JD, U. Miami, Coral Gables, Fla., 1938; LLD (hon.), Fla. Internat. U., 1985, Middlebury Coll., 1985, The Am. U., 1987, U. Miami, 1988; PhD (hon.), Haifa U., 1990, Barry U., 1993; D Pub. Svc., George Washington U., 1993. Bar: Fla. 1938. Pvt. practice Miami, 1938-41, 46—; legal attaché state legis. del. Dade County, Fla., 1947-50; mem. Fla. Legislature, 1950-54, 84th-102d Congresses from 19th Fla. dist., 1954-92; chmn. House Fgn. Affairs com., 1984-92; U.S. rep. 24th Gen. Assembly UN, 1969; chmn. Commn. Security and Cooperation in Europe; chmn. house del. U.S. Can. Parliamentary Group, 1977-83, North Atlantic Assembly, 1984-92; mem. select com. Narcotics Abuse,, 1992-94; lawyer Holland & Knight, Miami, Fla., 1994—; vice chmn. U.S. delegation to CSCE Conf., Belgrade, Yugoslavia, 1977-78, Madrid, Spain, 1980-83; ofcl. observer Arms Control Talks, Geneva; chmn. subcom. on arms control Internat. Security & Sci. Affairs; sr. advisor Ctr. Strategic and Internat. Studies; bd. dirs. Ivax Corp.; mem. Forum for Internat. Policy, Washington Inst. Fgn. Affairs; chmn. bd. dirs. Kids Voting, Fla. Contbr. articles to profl. jours. Pres. Dade County Young Dem. Club, 1947-48; trustee U. Miami; bd. dirs. Miami Children's Hosp. Found.; founding chmn. Nat. Endowment for Democracy. Capt. AUS, 1946; with Fla. N.G., 1939-41. Named One of Ten Outstanding Legislators, Fla. Legislature, 1951, 53; One of Five Outstanding Men in Fla., Fla. Jr. C. of C., 1951; recipient Freedom award Christian Solidarity Internat., Young Dem. Am. Congl. award; Nat. Endowment Citizens Spl. award, Am. Fgn. Svc. award, Peace Corps 25th Anniversary award, Mothers Against Drunk Driving award, Nat. Endowment for Dem. award, Save Our Everglades award, Presdl. End of Hunger award, Jewish Nat. Fund Tree of Life award, Arms Control Leadership award, Spirit of the Carribean award, VOA Congl. award, IMDI World Leadership award. Mem. ABA, Miami Jr. C. of C. (pres. 1947-48), Fed. Bar Assn., Dade County Bar Assn., D.C. Bar Assn., Fla. Bar, Caribbean/L.Am. Action (bd. trustees), Close Up Found. (bd. advisor), Coun. Fgn. Rels., Am. Legion, Lions, Moose, AHEPA, Iron Arrow, Kappa Sigma, Omicron Delta Kappa, Phi Beta Delta, Phi Kappa Phi, Phi Mu Alpha, Order of Coif, Wig and Robe. Democrat. Club: Italian-American (pres. 1947-48). Office: Holland & Knight 701 Brickell Ave Ste 3000 Miami FL 33131-2847

FASHBAUGH, HOWARD DILTS, JR., lawyer, management educator; b. Monroe, Mich., Jan. 31, 1922; s. Howard Dilts and Ninetta Esther (Greening) F.; m. Joyce Dallas MacCurdy, Dec. 25, 1946; children: James Howard, Linda Carol, Patricia Lee. B.S.E., U. Mich., 1947, M.S.E. in Chem. Engring., 1948, M.B.A. with high distinction, 1960; J.D. cum laude, Wake Forest U., 1972; M.Law and Taxation, Coll. William and Mary, 1983. Bar: Va. 1973, Mich. 1975. Mgr. engring. and mfg. Dow Corning Corp., Midland, Mich., 1952-70; assoc. Williams, Worrell, Kelly & Greer, Norfolk, Va., 1972-76, ptnr., 1976-77; corp. counsel Va. Chems. Inc., Portsmouth, Va., 1977-83; ptnr. Williams, Worrell, Kelly & Greer, Norfolk, 1983-85, sole practice, Chesapeake, 1985—; gen. counsel CEP, Inc., 1985-87, pres., treas. and gen. counsel, 1987-89; sec., legal counsel UCB Chems. Corp., UCB Med. Industries, Inc., UCB Radcure, Inc., UCB-JSR Electronics, Inc., 1988—, UCB Pharma, Inc., 1988—; adj. prof. mgmt. Old Dominion U., Norfolk, Va., 1989—. Elder Presbyn. Ch., 1966—; chmn. adv. bd. Salvation Army, Midland, Mich., 1967-69, chmn. adv. bd., Portsmouth, 1996—, chmn. 1996—. Lt. USNR, 1943-46, 50-52; divsn. vice capt. USCG Aux. Decorated Bronze Star medal. Mem. ABA, Va. Bar Assn., Kiwanis (pres. Portsmouth chpt. 1977-78), Beta Gamma Sigma. Home and Office: 4121 Stephanie Boyd Dr Chesapeake VA 23321-4424

FATHERREE, LARAINE CAUDELL, hospital administrator; b. Toccoa, Ga., Aug. 14, 1948; d. Dwain and Nell Marie (Smith) C. BS in Home Econs., U. Ga., 1970; MBA, U. South Ala., 1979. Cert. health exec. Tng. instr. Davis Bros., Inc., Atlanta, 1970-72; asst. to food svc. dir. West Paces Ferry Hosp., Atlanta, 1972-74; dir. food svcs. Drs. Hosp., Mobile, Ala., 1974-79; adminstrv. asst. Indian Path Hosp., Kingsport, Tenn., 1979-80, asst. adminstr., 1980-82; adminstr. Johnson City (Tenn.) Specialty Hosp. (formerly Johnson City Eye & Ear Hosp.), 1982—; food svc. cons., 1974-79; faculty mem. Ctr. for Health Studies, Nashville, 1979-87; bd. dirs. Tenn. Hosp. Assn., exec. com., 1988-91. Pres. , bd. dirs., mem. exec. com. East Tenn. Regional Organ Procurement Agy.; Sunday sch. tchr. Colonial Heights Baptist Ch., 1980-82; adv. Experience Based Career Edn. Program, Murphy High Sch., 1977-79; bd. dirs. United Way Washington County, 1986-92, exec. com. 1988; bd. dirs. Washington County Am. Heart Assn.; pres. Upper East Tenn. Hosp. Dist., 1986-88; mem. fin. com. Munsey Meml. Meth. Ch., 1990-93, mem. mission com. Mem. AAUW (bd. dirs.), Am. Coll. Health Execs., Johnson City C. of C. (health svcs. coun., bd. dirs. 1987-92, v.p. 1988, 91), Johnson City Leadership 2000, U. Ga. Alumni Assn., U. South Ala. Alumni Assn., Christian Bus. and Profl. Women (bd. exec. com. 1987-88), Leadership Kingsport, 1995, Rotary (bd. dirs.). Home: 2228 Granite Ct Johnson City TN 37604-2170 Office: Johnson City Specialty Hosp 203 E Watauga Ave Johnson City TN 37601-4629

FAUBION, JAMES DANIEL, anthropologist, educator; b. Redmond, Oreg., Dec. 5, 1957; s. Aunald Jacob Faubion and Shirley Julia (Carter) Saunders. BA in Anthropology/Philosophy, Reed Coll., Portland, 1980; MA in Anthropology, U. Calif., Berkeley, 1984, PhD, 1990. Asst. prof. anthropology and humanities Reed Coll., Portland, 1990-93; asst. prof. anthropology Rice U., Houston, 1993—. Author: Modern Greek Lessons, 1993; editor: Rethinking the Subject, 1995. Mem. Am. Anthrop. Assn., Soc. for Anthropology of Europe, Am. Ethnological Soc. Office: Rice Univ Anthropology Dept 6100 S Main Houston TX 77005

FAUGHT, JOLLY KAY, English language educator; b. Corbin, Ky., Dec. 22, 1954; d. Joshua Pleas and Emma Olive (Patrick) Sharp; m. Kenneth Lyle Faught, June 8, 1974; children: Jessica Ruth, Joshua Paul. BA, Cumberland Coll., 1974; MA, Wright State U., 1988. English tchr. Cumberland (Ky.) H.S., 1982-83; English educator Cumberland Coll., Williamsburg, Ky., 1991—. Mem. Williamsburg PTA, 1991—, sec., 1993-94. Mem. MLA, South Atlantic MLA, Delta Kappa Gamma (Alpha Lambda chpt.). Republican. Baptist. Office: Cumberland Coll English Dept 7828 College Station Dr Williamsburg KY 40769

FAULK, MICHAEL ANTHONY, lawyer; b. Kingsport, Tenn., Sept. 10, 1953; s. Loy Glade and Rosella E. (Dykes) F.; m. Janet Lynn McLain, Aug. 31, 1974; children: Katherine Lea, Andrew McLain. BS, U. Tenn., 1975; M in Pub. Adminstrn., Memphis State U., 1978, JD, 1979. Bar: U.S. Dist. Ct. (we. dist.) Tenn. 1980, U.S. Dist. Ct. (ea. dist.) Tenn. 1985. Dep. clk. to presiding justice Shelby County Chancery Ct., Memphis, 1977-79; assoc. Weintraub & Dehart, Memphis, 1980-82; ptnr. Frazier & Faulk, Church Hill, Tenn., 1982-83; sole practice Church Hill, 1983-93; ptnr. Law Offices of Faulk, May & Coup, Church Hill, Tenn., 1993—; commr. Tenn. Human Rights Commn., Nashville, 1985—, vice chmn. 1988-92; referee Hawkins County Juvenile Ct., Rogersville, Tenn., 1985—; bd. dirs. Legal Services Inc., Johnson City, Tenn. Bd. dirs. Upper East Tenn. Div. Am. Heart Assn., Blountville, 1984—. Named one of Outstanding Young Men in Am. U.S. Jaycees, 1977. Mem. ABA, Hawkins County Bar Assn. (pres. 1987-88), Assn. Trial Lawyers Am., Ducks Unltd. (chmn. Holston River chpt. 1984-91). Republican. Baptist. Lodge: Moose. Office: 107 E Main Blvd Church Hill TN 37642-3729

FAUNCE, WILLIAM DALE, clinical psychologist, researcher; b. Lansing, Mich., Dec. 4, 1947; s. Lucius Dale and Wilhelmina (Hall) F. BA, Mich. State U., 1972; MA, Calif. State U., L.A., 1978; PhD in Clin. Psychology, U. So. Calif., 1983. Lic. psychologist, Alaska, N.C. Psychology intern Brentwood (Calif.) VA, 1981-82; clin. psychologist UCLA Neuropsychiat. Inst., Westwood, Calif., 1983, Coldwater Canyon Hosp., North Hollywood, Calif., 1983-84, So. Peninsula Community Mental Health Ctr., Homer, Alaska, 1984-86; pvt. practice Homer, Alaska, 1986-87; cons. Santa Cruz, Calif., 1987-90; clin. psychologist, program dir. Broughton State Hosp., Morganton, N.C., 1990—; mem. faculty Appalachian State U., Boone, N.C., 1992—. Co-author: (chpt.) Imagery, 1984; contbr. articles to profl. jours. Fellow NIMH; mem. APA, Union Concerned Scientists. Home: PO Box 241 Jonas Ridge NC 28641-0241 Office: Appalachian State U Dept Psychology Smith-Wright Hall Boone NC 28608

FAVARO, MARY KAYE ASPERHEIM (MRS. BIAGINO PHILIP FAVARO), pediatrician; b. Edgerton, Wis., Sept. 30, 1934; d. Harold Wilbur and Genevieve Catherine (Hyland) Asperheim; B.S., U. Wis., 1956; M.S., St. Louis Coll. Pharmacy, 1965; M.D., U. Wis., 1969; m. Biagino Philip Favaro, May 31, 1969; children—Justin Peter, Gina Sue. Instr. pharmacology St. Louis U. and St. Mary's Hosp. Sch. Practical Nurses, 1959-64; staff pharmacist U. Hosps., Madison, Wis., 1964-65; intern Albany (N.Y.) Med. Center, 1969-70, resident, 1970-71; resident in pediatrics U. S.C., Charleston, 1971-72, asst. prof. pediatrics, 1973-75; pvt. practice pediatrics, 1974—. Mem. A.M.A., Am. Med. Women's Assn. Roman Catholic. Author: Pharmacology, an Introductory Text, 1992; The Pharmacologic Basis of Patient Care, 1985. Home: 1866 Capri Dr Charleston SC 29407-7606 Office: 5390 Dorchester Rd Charleston SC 29418-5652

FAVROT, HENRI MORTIMER, JR., architect, real estate developer; b. New Orleans, Apr. 23, 1930; s. Henri Mortimer and Helen Rebecca (Parkhurst) F.; m. Kathleen Loker Gibbons, Sept. 16, 1956; children: James P., Kathleen Favrot VanHorn, T. Semmes, Caroline. BArch, Tulane U., 1953; MArch, Harvard U., 1957. Lic. architect, La., Miss., Fla. Architect Favrot, Reed, Mathes & Bergman, New Orleans, 1955-56, Curtis & Davis, New Orleans, 1957-58; ptnr. Favrot & Grimball, New Orleans, 1958-62; pvt. practice architecture New Orleans, 1962-64; ptnr. Mathes, Bergman, Favrot & Assocs., New Orleans, 1964-69, Favrot & Shane, Metairie, La., 1969—; chmn. La. Architects Selection Bd., Baton Rouge, 1976. Prin. works include: Parktowne Townhouses, 1971 (Design Honor award La. Architects Assn.), Favrot & Shane Office Bldg., 1982 (Design Honor award New Orleans chpt. AIA). Mem. City Planning Commn., New Orleans, 1970-84, chmn., 1976, 77; commr. La. Housing Commn., Baton Rouge, 1985-86; bd. dirs. Met. Area Com., New Orleans, 1985-96, New Orleans Mus. Art, 1985-91, v.p., 1986-87; bd. dirs. Preservation Resource Ctr. of New Orleans, 1988—, pres., 1994-96; mem. bd. adminstr. Tulane U., 1986—. Recipient Outstanding Alumnus award Tulane U. Sch. Architecture, 1985. Mem. AIA (pres. New Orleans chpt. 1982), La. Architects Assn. (pres. 1984), New Orleans Apt. Assn. (pres. 1980), So. Yacht Club, New Orleans Lawn Tennis Club, Boston Club, La. Club, Stratford Club. Republican. Roman Catholic. Home: 1400 State St New Orleans LA 70118-6047 Office: Favrot & Shane Cos Inc 3925 N Service Rd W Ste 105 Metairie LA 70002

FAWBUSH, ANDREW JACKSON, lawyer; b. Miami, Fla., Oct. 7, 1946; s. Andrew T. Fawbush; m. Melinda Wheeley, Dec. 18, 1982; children: Andrew J. Jr., Tyler S., Karin J., Michelle L. BSBA in Acctg., U. Fla., 1972, JD, 1974. Bar: Fla. 1975. Assoc. Smith & Hulsey, Jacksonville, Fla., 1975-80; ptnr. Smith & Hulsey, Jacksonville, 1980-88, LeBoeuf, Lamb, Greene & MacRae, Jacksonville, 1988—; chmn. employee benefits dept. LeBoeuf Lamb Greene & MacRae, Jacksonville, 1993—. Contbg. author The Tax Lawyer. Bd. dirs. YMCA, Jacksonville, 1981-83; bd. dirs., past pres. Employee Benefits Coun. N.E. Fla.; bd. dirs., exec. com. Gator Boosters, Inc.; trustee, tchr. Cert. Employee Benefits Specialists, U. North Fla., 1982-88; bd. dirs. U. Fla. Found., 1993. With U.S. Army, 1968-70. Mem. ABA, Fla. Bar Assn. (spkr. employee benefit sect. 1983-88), Jacksonville Bar Assn., D.C. Bar Assn., N.Y. Bar Assn., U. Fla. Alumni Assn. (bd. dirs. 1987-92, pres. 1994), Gator Club of Jacksonville (bd. dirs. 1981-90, past pres.). Office: LeBoeuf Lamb Greene MacRae 50 N Laura St Ste 2800 Jacksonville FL 32202-3656

FAWKS, DAVID ROBERT, psychiatric nurse; b. Moline, Ill., Sept. 13, 1962; s. David Edward and Lois Lovetta (Moore) F.; m. Kay Joanne Psaltis, Apr. 29, 1988; children: Gina Elizabeth, Johnathan David. BSN, Olivet Nazarene U., Kankakee, Ill., 1986. RN, Fla.; cert. HIV counselor, CPR Instr. Psychiat. nurse Sarasota (Fla.) Meml. Hosp., 1990—. Bd. dirs. Luth. Ministries Adv. Coun., Sarasota, 1990—; charter mem. Sarasota/DeSoto Community Tng. Project, 1991—. Mem. Fla. Assn. Partial Hospitalization (corp. mem.), Mental health Task Force of the Sarasota Health and Human Svcs. Planning Coun. Republican. Nazarene. Home: 5783 Vanderipe Rd Sarasota FL 34241 Office: Sarasota Meml Hosp 1650 S Osprey Ave Sarasota FL 34239-2928

FAY, ANITRA SHARANE, psychologist; b. Ft. Smith, Ark., Sept. 23, 1954; d. Clarence Russell and Katala Ann (Green) Williams; m. Edgar Dempsey Fay, Dec. 25, 1975; 1 child, Matthew Williams. BA, U. Ark., 1976, MA, 1978, PhD, 1981. Lic. psychologist. Intern pediatric psychology U. Okla., Oklahoma City, 1980-81; psychologist Holt Krock Clinic, Ft. Smith, 1981-83, 85—, Huisman/Fay Psychol. Cons. P.A., Ft. Smith, 1982-85; dir. psychol. svcs. Phillips Cancer Support House. Co-author: (book chapter) Handbook of Clinical Psychology, 1983. Mem. multi-disciplinary team child abuse cases Sebastian and Crawford Counties, Ark., 1990, profl. women's adv. bd. Westark Community Coll., Ft. Smith, 1988—; advisor Youth Fellowship 1st Presbyn. Ch., Ft. Smith, 1988-90, elder. Mem. APA (divsn. clin. child psychology and psychotherapy), Nat. Register Health Care Providers, Soc. Pediatric Psychology, Ft. Smith Arts Ctr., Ark. Psychol. Assn., Ft. Smith Symphony, Zonta (pres. local chpt. 1986-88). Office: Holt Krock Clinic 2901 S 74th St Fort Smith AR 72903-5156

FAY, PETER THORP, federal judge; b. Rochester, N.Y., Jan. 18, 1929; s. Lester Thorp and Jane (Baumler) F.; m. Claudia Pat Zimmerman, Oct. 1, 1958; children: Michael Thorp, William, Darcy. B.A., Rollins Coll., 1951, LL.D., 1971; J.D., U. Fla., 1956; LL.D., Biscayne Coll., 1975. Bar: Fla. 1956, U.S. Supreme Ct. 1961. Ptnr. firm Nichols, Gaither Green, Frates & Beckham, Miami, Fla., 1956-61, Frates, Fay, Floyd & Pearson (and predecessors), Miami, 1961-70; prof. Fla. Jr. Bar Practical Legal Inst., 1959-65; judge U.S. Dist. Ct. for So. Fla., Miami, 1970-76, U.S. Ct. Appeals (5th cir.), 1976-81; judge U.S. Ct. Appeals (11th cir.), 1981-94, sr. judge, 1994—; lectr. Fla. Bar Legal Inst., 1959—; faculty Fed. Jud. Center, Washington, 1974-94; mem. Jud. Conf. Com. for Implementation Criminal Justice Act, 1974-82, Adv. Com. on Codes of Conduct, 1980-87, Adv. Com. on Appellate Rules, 1987-90; co-chmn. Nat. Jud. Coun. for State and Fed. Cts., 1990—. Mem. Orange Bowl Com., 1974—; dist. collector United Fund, 1957-70; mem. adminstrv. bd. St. Thomas U., 1970—; trustee U. Miami, Fla., 1989—; mem., supr. Ind. Counsel, 1994—. With USAF, 1951-53. Mem. Law Sci. Acad., Fla. Acad. Trial Attys., Am., Fla., Dade County, John Marshall (past pres.) bar assns., Fla. Council of 100, U. Fla. Alumni Assn. (dir.), Miami C. of C., Medico Legal Inst., Order of Coif, Phi Delta Phi (past pres.), Omicron Delta Kappa (past pres.), Pi Gamma Mu (past pres.), Phi Kappa Phi, Phi Delta Theta (past sec.). Republican. Roman Catholic. Clubs: Wildcat Cliffs (N.C.); Snapper Creek Lakes (Miami), Coral Oaks (Miami), Miami. Office: US Ct Appeals 11th Cir 99 NE 4th St Rm 1255 Miami FL 33132-2140*

FAY, ROBERT WOODS, financial executive; b. Phila., Dec. 11, 1946; s. Wayne Xalpha and June Elizabeth (Balliet) F.; m. Holly Howell, May 11, 1974; children—Wayne H., Randall C. B.A., Duke U., 1968; B.S., Villanova U., 1974; M.B.A., Drexel U., 1977. Systems engr. IBM Corp., Phila., 1968-72; mgr. cash systems and ops. Certain-Teed Corp., Valley Forge, Pa., 1972-78; div. contr. Harris Corp., Melbourne, Fla., 1978-85, treas., 1985-87, v.p., treas., 1988—; mem. so. adv. coun. Arkwright Mut. Ins. Co., Atlanta, 1985—. Bd. dirs United Way Brevard County, Melbourne, 1985—; alumni recruiter Duke U. Served with U.S. Army, 1969-75. Mem. Machinery and Allied Products Inst., Fin. Execs. Inst. Office: Harris Corp 1025 W Nasa Blvd Melbourne FL 32919-0002

FAY, ROBERTA MARIE, nurse, educator; b. Boston; d. Nicholas and Catherine Shaughnessy; divorced; children: Mark, David, Karen. Diploma, Carney Hosp. Sch. Nursing, Boston; BS in Nursing Edn., Columbia U.; MS, St. John's U., N.Y.C.; postgrad., Tex. Women's U., 1984. From instr. to asst. prof. SUNY, Farmingdale, 1964-68; charge nurse med.-surg. unit Mercy Hosp., Rockville Centre, N.Y., 1964-68; mem. faculty Our Lady of Grace, Pitts., 1968-72; asst. prof. dept. nursing Bloomfield (N.J.) Coll., 1972-74, Morris County Coll., Randolph, N.J., 1974-76; asst. prof. Coll. Nursing Tex. Women's U., Denton, 1977-83; clin. care specialist Johnson & Johnson Home Health, Dallas, 1983-85; adminst., dir. nursing Collin County Home Health, Plano, Tex., 1985-86; acad. leader, internat. lectr. Nursing Inst.: Internat. Journeys, 1985—; med.-surg. cons. Martingale Rsch. Corp., 1986—; part-time psychiat. staff nurse Hosp. Corp. Am. Med. Ctr. (now Charter of Dallas), 1986—. Active Boy Scouts Am., Girl Scouts U.S., Safety Coun. and Recreational Adv. Council, Am. Field Svc., sr. citizen groups. Mem. AAUP, Am. Nurses Assn., Am. Rural Health Assn., Tex. Alcohol Rsch. Assn., Am. Heart Assn., Am. Cancer Soc., Oncology Nurses Soc., Assn. Clin. Care Specialists, Columbia U. Alumni Assn., St. John's of N.Y. Alumni Assn., Carney Hosp. Alumni Assn., Eta Sigma Gamma. Home: 1316 Auburn Pl Plano TX 75093-5046

FAYNE, GWENDOLYN DAVIS, air force officer, English educator; b. Toledo, Dec. 8, 1951; d. Robert Louis and Marietta Beatrice (Sautter) Davis; m. Barry Dennis Fayne, Jan. 6, 1979; children: Ashleigh Elizabeth, Zachary Alexandur-John. BFA, So. Meth. U., 1972; MEd, U. North Tex., 1978; MA, U. Denver, 1987. Cert. tchr., Tex., Ala. Substitute tchr. Toledo and Dallas, 1972-73; film dir. Channel 39 Christian Broadcasting Network, Dallas, 1973-75; engr., air operator Channel 40 Trinity Broadcasting Network, Tustin, Calif., 1978; commd. 2d lt. USAF, 1978, advanced through grades to maj., 1989, ret., 1995; mgr. western area Hdqrs. USAFR Officers Tng. Corp., Norton AFB, Calif., 1979-81; chief tng. systems support Hdqrs. Air Force Manpower Pers. Pentagon, Washington, 1981-84; pers. policies officer J1, Orgn. of Joint Chiefs of Staff Pentagon, Washington, 1984-85; asst. prof. English, dir. forensics USAF Acad., Colorado Springs, Colo., 1987-92; adj. faculty mem. dept. English Auburn U., Montgomery, Ala., 1994-95; adj. faculty mem. dept. arts and scis. Troy State U., Montgomery, 1994—; dir. Bullock County HS Learning Ctr., Union Springs, Ala., 1995—; assoc. editor The Airpower Jour., Maxwell AFB, Ala., 1992-94, mil. doctrine analyst, 1994-95; dir. Bullock County H.S. Learning Ctr., Union Springs, Ala., 1995—; chair mil. affairs Jr. Officer's Coun., Norton AFB, 1981; invited spkr. in field; chmn. program devel. com. for nat. orgn. Cross Exam. Debate Assn., 1990-91. Assoc. editor The Airpower Jour., Maxwell AFB, 1992-94; contbr. articles to profl. jours. Teacher, mem. choir, soloist various chs., 1973; chair publicity com. Birthright, Inc., Woodbridge, Va., 1983. Named Command Jr. Officer of Yr., Hdqrs. USAFR Officers Tng. Corps, 1979. Mem. Speech Comm. Assn., Am. Forensics Assn., Nat. Parliamentary Debate Assn. (co-founder, editor Parliamentary Debate jour. 1992-95), Phi Upsilon Omicron. Republican. Methodist. Home: 8200 Harrogate Hl Montgomery AL 36117-5118 Office: Bullock County H S Union Springs AL 36089

FAZIO, TOM, design firm executive, golf course designer; b. Norristown, Pa., 1945; married; 6 children. Landscape designer intern George Fazio, 1962-1945; prin. Fazio Golf Course Designers, Inc., Jupiter, Fla.; cons. architect major golf tournaments including U.S. Open, Duluth, Ga., 1974, Tulsa, Okla., 1977, Toledo, 1979, P.G.A. Championship, Rochester, N.Y., 1980, Duluth, 1991, Toledo, 1986, Palm Beach Gardens, Fla., 1987, U.s. Amateur Championship, Jupiter, Fla., 1987, U.S. Open Championship, Rochester, 1989. Prin. works include Edgewood Tahoe Country Club, Lake Tahoe, Nev., Jupiter Hills Club, Jupiter, Fla., Am. Great Gorge Resort, McAfee, N.Y., Cariari Internat. Club, San Jose, Costa Rica, Pinehurst (N.C.) # 6, Golf Club Okla., Tulsa, Windstar Country Club, Naples, Fla., The Vintage Club, Indian Wells, Calif., Shadow Creek, Las Vegas, Emerald Dunes, West Palm Beach, Fla., Karsten Creek-Okla. State U., Stillwater, The Quarry, La Quinta, Calif., The Champions Club at Summerfield, Stuart, Fla., Glen Oaks, Des Moines, Iowa, Wade Hampton Golf Club, Cashiers, N.C., Black Diamond Ranch, Lecanto, Fla., Caves Valley Golf Club, Balt., Pelican Hill, Newport Beach, Calif., numerous others. Active Boys and Girls Club. Named Favorite Present-Day Designer of Golf Courses, Golf Digest, 1991, 93. Office: Fazio Golf Course Designers Inc 17755 SE Federal Hwy Jupiter FL 33469-1749 also: 8675 W 96th St Ste 204 Overland Park KS 66212-3382 also: 109 S Main St Hendersonville NC 28792-5083

FEAGIN, CLARENCE ELMER, JR., microbiologist; b. Bay City, Tex., Mar. 25, 1953; s. Clarence E. and June Juanita (Mangum) F. AA, Coll. of Mainland, 1978; BA, U. Tex., 1982, MS, 1984; PhD, Tex. A&M U., 1995. Grad. tchg. asst. Tex. A&M U., College Station, 1987-89, rsch. assoc., 1988-95; technician diagnostic microbiology Tex. Vet. Med. Diagnostic Lab., College Station, 1993—. Contbr. articles to profl. jours. U. Tex. grantee, 1983. Mem. Coastal Soc., Am. Littoral Soc., Am. Planning Assn., Beta Beta Beta, Phi Theta Kappa. Home: 402 Ayrshire College Station TX 77840

FEAGIN, EUGENE LLOYD, pastor; b. Hendersonville, NC, July 19, 1950; s. Eugene Lloyd and Martha (Hodges) F.; m. Anna Johnson, July 3, 1972; children: James Eugene, Travis Lee, Melissa Ann. BA, U. S.C., 1972, MEd, 1976; MDiv, Candler Sch. Theology, 1981. Ordained to ministry Methodist Ch., 1984. Pastor Fingerville (S.C.) United Meth. Ch., 1974-79, Saxon United Meth. Ch., Spartanburg, S.C., 1979-85, Cherokee Springs United Meth. Ch., Spartanburg, 1982-85, Sharon (S.C.) United Meth. Ch., 1985-91, Aldersgate United Meth. Ch., Inman, S.C., 1991-95; Heath Springs (S.C.) United Meth. Ch., 1995—; dir. communications, Spartanburg United Meth. Dist., 1982-85; bd. dirs., Pastoral Counseling Svc., Spartanburg, 1982-85; cluster leader, York/Clover United Meth. Cluster, S.C., 1986-91. Firefighter Sharon Vol. Fire Dept., 1986-91; mem. Schs./Community Team, York, 1990-91. Mem. Western York Ministerial Assn. (pres. 1989-90), Rotary (pres. Inman chpt. 1994-95, pres. Kershaw chpt. 1996—). Home: PO Box 36 Heath Springs SC 29058 Office: 201 S Main St Heath Springs SC 29058

FEAGLES, ROBERT WEST, insurance company executive; b. Ft. Wayne, Ind., July 23, 1920; s. Ralph L. and Mary Anna (West) F.; m. Anita Marie MacRae, Sept. 15, 1951; children: Wendy Lee, Cuyler MacRae, Priscilla Jane, Patrick Emerson. B.S., Ga. Inst. Tech., 1943, Am. Grad. Sch. of Internat. Mgmt., 1951; cert. of banking, Rutgers U. Grad. Sch. Banking, 1958. Sr. v.p. Citibank, N.A., N.Y.C., 1951-76, Travelers Ins. Co., Hartford, Conn., 1976-86; chmn., chief exec. officer Travelers Asset Mgmt. Internat. Corp., N.Y.C., 1979-87; vice chmn., chief exec. offcier The Conn. Ins. Co., Farmington, 1988-90. Bd. fellows Am. Grad. Sch. Internat. Mgmt., Glendale, Ariz., 1973—; mem. adv. council Internat. Exec. Service Corps. Council, N.Y.C., 1970—; chmn. Hartford Area Manpower Planning Council, 1978-79, Hartford Area Pvt. Industry Council, 1979-83, State job Tng. Coordinating Council, Hartford, 1983-88; corporator The Inst. for Living, Hartford, 1989—. Served to capt. U.S. Army, 1943-47. Recipient Jonas Mayer award Am. Grad. Sch. Internat. Mgmt., 1978. Mem. Pers. Round Table (emeritus), Univ. Club (N.Y.C.), Royal Automobile Club (London), Fishers Island Club, Bent Pine Golf Club. Republican. Presbyterian. Home: 507 River Dr Vero Beach FL 32963-2127

FEARING, WILLIAM KELLY, art educator, artist; b. Fordyce, Ark., Oct. 18, 1918; s. George David and Frankie (Kelly) F. BA, La. Tech. U., 1941; MA, Columbia U., 1950. Classroom tchr. Windfield Pub. Schs., La., 1942-43; prodn. illustrator Consolidated Vultee Aircraft, Fort Worth, 1943-45; prof. art Tex. Wesleyan Coll., Fort Worth, 1945-47, U. Tex.-Austin, 1947-87, Ashbel Smith prof. emeritus, 1987—, Ashbel Smith prof., 1983—. Author: (with C.I. Martin and E. Beard) Our Expanding Vision, 1960, The Creative Eye, 1969, 2d edit., 1979; (with E. Beard, N. Krevitsky, C.I. Martin) Art and the Creative Teacher, 1971, (with E. L. Mayton, B. Francis, E. Beard) Helping Children See Art and Make Art, 1982; (with E.L. Mayton and R. Brooks) The Way of Art Inner Vision Outer Expression, 1986. One-man shows include El Paso Mus. Art, Esther Bear Gallery, Santa Barbara, 1964, Gallery Visual Arts, La. Tech. U., Ruston, 1966, U. Tex. Art Mus., Austin, 1967, Fort Worth Art Ctr., 1969, Witte Meml. Mus., San Antonio, 1969, U. Tex. Art Mus., Austin, 1974, Mary Moore Gallery, La Jolla, 1975, Mary Moffett Gallery, La. Tech. U., Ruston, 1976, DuBose Gallery, Houston, 1977, L and L Gallery, Longview, 1975, 78, Retrospective Spencer Gallery, Fine Arts Ctr., U. Ark.-Monticello, 1981, Mary Moffett Gallery, Sch. Art and Architecture, La. Tech. U., Ruston, 1981, Old Jail Art Ctr., Albany, Tex., 1985, Marion Koogler McNey Art Mus., San Antonio, 1986, Valley House Gallery, Dallas, 1992, 96, Robinson Galleries, Houston, 1995; exhibited in group shows at Carnegie Inst., Pitts., 1955, Pa. Acad. Art, Phila., 1954-56, Carnegie Inst., Pitts., 1956-57, Mus. Fine Arts, Houston, 1956-57, Dallas Mus. Fine Art, 1956-57, Munson-Williams-Proctor Inst., Utica, 1956-57, Edwin Hewitt Gallery, N.Y.C., 1957, Dallas Mus. Fine Art, 1958, Am. Fedn. Art, 1958, Mus. Fine Arts, Little Rock, 1961, Colorado Springs Art Ctr., 1961, 63 Philbrook Art Ctr., Tulsa, 1963, Fort Worth Art Ctr., 1963, U. Ill., Urbana, 1955, 59, 63, Denver Art Mus., 1963, U. Ariz. and Ark. Art Ctr., 1964-65, N.Y. World's Fair, Tex. Pavilion, 1964, Tex. Pavillion Hemistair, San Antonio, 1968, Tex. Tech. U. Mus. Art, Lubbock, 1978, U. Tex.-Austin, 1979, Art Gallery Sch. Art and Architecture, La. Tech. U., Ruston, 1984, Archer M. Huntington Art Gallery, U. Tex.-Austin, 1983-91, 92-96, Longview Mus. and Arts Ctr., Tex., 1962, 63, 75, 85, 90, 91, Amarillo Art Ctr., Tex., 1988, Dallas Mus. of Fine Arts, 1991, Robinson Galleries, Houston, 1993, Valley House Gallery, Dallas, 1994-96. Home: 914 Calithea Rd Austin TX 78746-2716

FEARN, ROBERT MORCOM, economics and business educator, consultant; b. Paterson, N.J., Oct. 10, 1928; s. William and Violet Emily (Bray) F.; m. Priscilla Anne Southard, Sept. 15, 1951; children: Diane C. Fearn Desrosiers, Deborah A. Sears, Priscilla L.Graham, Robert W. AA, Boston U., 1950; BS in Commerce, Ohio U., 1952; MA in Econs., Wash. State U., 1955; PhD in Econs., U. Chgo., 1968. Grad. asst. Wash. State U., Pullman, 1952-54; intelligence officer CIA, Washington, 1954-63; from asst. to prof. econs. and bus. N.C. State U., Raleigh, 1965—, dir. grad. programs econs., 1993—; vis. prof. Duke U., Durham, N.C., 1982, Sch. Econs. and Bus., Athens, 1986-87, Liaoning U., 1991; expert witness NLRB, Winston-Salem, N.C., 1981-83; cons. Research Triangle Inst., Research Triangle Park, N.C., 1968-75, Pres.'s Commn. Income Maintenance, Washington, 1970; mem. econ. study and ad hoc wage bd. City Raleigh, 1974, others. Author: Labor Economics: The Emerging Synthesis, 1981. Contbr. articles to profl. jours. Pres., v.p., bd. dirs. West Raleigh Civic Assn., 1968-72; vice chmn. Free Alliance for Improvement Raleigh, 1968-71; scoutmaster, asst. scoutmaster, committeeman Occoneechee council Boy Scouts Am., Raleigh, 1970-80. Served with U.S. Army, 1946-48. Noyes-Ford-Hillman fellow, 1963-65. Mem. Am. Econ. Assn., So. Econ. Assn. (mem. bd. editors 1975-77), Indsl. Relations Research Assn., Assn. Comparative Econ. Studies, N.C. Faculty Senate (chmn. 1984-85, vice chmn. 1983-84), U. Chgo. Club of N.C. (sec. 1982-83, 83-84, bd. dirs. 1981-84), Raleigh Area Masters Swimming, Phi Kappa Phi (pres. 1992-93), Beta Gamma Sigma, Acad. Outstanding Tchrs., Alpha Kappa Lambda. Democrat. Unitarian-Universalist. Avocations: swimming; long distance backpacking; camping; sailing. Home: 1202 Kent Rd Raleigh NC 27606-1915 Office: NC State U Dept Econs PO Box 8110 Raleigh NC 27695

FEARS, JESSE RUFUS, historian, educator, academic dean; b. Atlanta, Ga., Mar. 7, 1945; s. Emory Binford and Hazel Elizabeth (Davis) F.; m. Charlene Louise Bauer, July 6, 1966; children: Laura Elizabeth, Jesse Rufus IV. BA summa cum laude, Emory U., 1966; MA, Harvard U., 1967, PhD, 1971. Asst. prof. classical langs. Tulane U., New Orleans, 1971-72; asst. prof. history Indiana U., Bloomington, 1972-75, assoc. prof. history, 1975-80, prof. history, 1980-86; prof., chair classical studies Boston U., 1986-90, assoc. dean Coll. Liberal Arts, 1987-89, dir. humanities found., 1988-90; dean Coll. Arts and Scis. U. Okla., Norman, 1990-92, prof. Classics, 1990—, G.T. and Libby Blankenship prof. history of liberty, 1992—, dir. Ctr. for History of Liberty, 1992—. Author: Princeps A Diis Electus, 1977, (monographs) The Cult of Jupiter, 1981, The Theology of Victory, 1981, The Cult of Virtues, 1981; editor: (3 vols.) Selected Writings/Lord Acton, 1985-88; contbr. chpts. to books, numerous articles to profl. jours. Bd. dirs. Okla. Sch. Sci./Math., Oklahoma City, 1990—. Danforth fellow Danforth Found., 1966-71, fellow Am. Acad. in Rome, 1969-71, Guggenheim Found., 1976-77, Alexander Von Humboldt, 1977-78, 80-81, Ctr. for History of Freedom, Wash. U., 1989-90. Mem. AAUP, Am. Philol. Assn. Classical Assn. Middle West and South, Phi Beta Kappa. Office: U Okla Dept Classics Ctr History of Liberty Kaufman Hall Norman OK 73019

FEARS, LOUISE MATHIS, private school educator; b. Washington, Ga., Dec. 31, 1935; d. Ambrose Powell Jr. and Sarah Louise (Moon) Mathis; m. Henry Beane Fears, June 22, 1958; children: Scott Powell, Douglas Edward, Leslie Fears Carter. BA, Shorter Coll., 1958; MEd, Ga. State U., 1977. Cert. Profl. Tchr., Ga. Evaluator Ga. State Dept. Ed., Atlanta, 1958-60; asst. Pers. Dept. City of Atlanta, 1960-61; tchr. DeKalb County Ga. Bd. Edn., Decatur, 1977-90; ednl. dir. Learning Solutions Gwinnett Pl. Ctr., Duluth, Ga., 1990-91; tchr. Christ the King Sch., Atlanta, 1991-95, Providence Christian Acad., Lilburn, Ga., 1995—. Author: A Limousine is a Magazine About Lemons, 1987. Trustee Shorter Coll., 1987-92, 94—; U.S. del. joint U.S./Chinese Early Childhood Edn. Conf., Beijing, 1993. Mem. Ga. Assn. Young Children, So. Early Childhood Assn., Nat. Assn. Edn. Young Children. Democrat. Baptist.

FEASTER, CHARLOTTE JOSEPHINE S., school administrator; b. Asheboro, N.C., Aug. 5, 1951; d. Earlie Lenan Staley and McCoy (Cheek) Staley Gathings; m. Jasper Nathaniel Feaster, July 23, 1983. BS in Intermediate Edn., Winston-Salem State U., 1973; MS in Intermediate Edn., N.C. Agrl. & Tech. State U., 1981, MS in Ednl. Leadership, 1993; Asst. Prin.'s Exec. Program, U. N.C., 1995-96. Cert. tchr., N.C., La. Dormitory asst. Winston-Salem (N.C.) State U., 1969-73; emergency rm. receptionist Reynolds Meml. Hosp., Winston-Salem, 1969-73; office asst. Employment Security Commn., Asheboro, 1969-71; cottage home parent asst. Guilford County Dept. Social Svcs., High Point, N.C., 1971-73; intermediate grade tchr. Randolph County Bd. Edn., Asheboro, 1973-94, summer sch. instr., 1987-91, 4th and 5th grade tchr., 1983-94; 4th and 5th grade tchr. Ramseur (N.C.) Sch., 1973-94; asst. prin. Randleman (N.C.) Elem. Sch., 1994-95, Liberty (N.C.) Sch., 1995—; enrichment camp instr. N.C. Agrl. & Tech. State U., Greensboro, 1982-87; Can. studies group leader Duke U., Durham, N.C., 1991-93; 4-H summer camp leader N.C. Randolph County, Asheboro, 1973-82; co-leader N.C. Tchr. Acad., Meredith Coll., Raleigh, N.C., 1993-94; site mgr. N.C. Tchr. Acad., Fayetteville (N.C.) State U., 1995, E. Carolina U., Greenville, 1996; mem. Asst. Prins. Exec. Program U. N.C., Chapel Hill, 1996—. 4-H leader Randolph County Agrl. Ext., Ramseur, 1983-85; Christian edn. dir. Deep River Assn. Bapt. Chs., Lee, Chatham and Randolph Counties, 1980-93; youth edn. resource person Oakland Bapt. Ch., Ramseur, 1983-93. Recipient Lay Leadership award Deep River Assn. Chs., 1990, Gold Clover award Randolph County Home Ext., 1989, Excellence First Project award Greensboro Area Math & Science Edn. Ctr., U. N.C. at Greensboro, 1991-93; grantee First Am. Bank, 1990; named one of Outstanding Young Educators Jaycees, 1990. Mem. N.C. Conf. Tchrs. Math. (workshop presenter 1988-93, Outstanding Math. Tchr. award 1992), N.C. Assn. Educators (county pres. 1992-95), Order Eastern Star (fin. sec. 1987-93), Gamma Omicron (award Eta Phi Beta chpt. 1991). Home: 361 Thornbrook Rd Ramseur NC 27316-9309 Office: Liberty Sch Asst Prin Exec Program 206 Fayetteville St Liberty NC 27298

FEATHERLY, HENRY FREDERICK, lawyer; b. Stillwater, Okla., Aug. 10, 1930; s. Henry Ira and Lucy Anne (Borsch) F.; m. Dorcas Diane Rowley, July 19, 1952; children—Henry Frederick, Charles Alan. B.S., Okla. State U., Stillwater, 1952; LL.B., Okla. U., Norman, 1957. Bar: Okla. 1957, U.S. Dist. Ct. (we. and ea. dists.) Okla. 1957, U.S. Ct. Appeals (10th cir.) 1958. Assoc. Pierce, Mock & Duncan, Oklahoma City, 1957-63; ptnr. Chiles & Featherly, Oklahoma City, 1963-64; sole practice, Oklahoma City, 1964-66; ptnr. Lamun, Mock, Featherly, Baer & Timberlake, Oklahoma City, 1966-85; ptnr. Lamun, Mock, Featherly, Kuehling & Cunningham, Oklahoma City, 1986—. Mem. commrs. staff Dan Beard Dist. council Boy Scouts Am., 1966—, Last Frontier council; trustee Heritage Hall Sch., Oklahoma City, 1974-77. Mem. ABA, Okla. Bar Assn., Oklahoma County Bar Assn., Am. Trial Lawyers Assn., Okla. Trial Lawyers Assn., Okla. Assn. Def. Counsel, Am. Judicature Soc. Republican. Methodist. Lodge: Lions (pres. 1970-71, 83-84). Home: 2433 NW 46th St Oklahoma City OK 73112-8307

FEAZELL, THOMAS LEE, lawyer, oil company executive; b. Mount Hope, W.Va., Feb. 25, 1937; s. Thomas Lee and Drema Lyal (Walker) F.; m. Virginia Scott, Feb. 3, 1961; children—Ann Lindsay, Thomas Lee, Robert Kent. Student, W.Va. U., 1954-56; B.B.A., Marshall U., 1959; LL.B., Washington and Lee U., 1962. Bar: W.Va. 1962, Ky. 1965. Atty. Ashland Oil, Inc., Ky., 1965-74, sr. atty., 1975-76, gen. atty., 1976-78, asst. gen. counsel, 1978-79, assoc. gen. counsel, 1979-80, v.p., 1980, v.p., gen. counsel, 1981—; adminstrv. v.p. Ashland Oil, Inc., 1988-92, sr. v.p., gen. counsel, sec., 1992—; bd. dirs. Ashland Coal, Inc., Nat. City Bank of Ashland. Bd. dirs. Marshall U. Found., Inc., Huntington, W. Va., 1984—, The Conf. Bd.-Coun. Chief Legal Officers. Mem. ABA, W.Va. Bar Assn., Ky. Bar Assn., Maritime Bar assn., Assn. Trial Lawyers Am., Am. Corp. Counsel Assn. (API gen. com. on law), U.S. C. of C. (legal affairs coun.), Am. Soc. of Corp. Secs., Bellefonte Country Club. Democrat. Presbyterian. Office: Ashland Inc PO Box 391 Ashland KY 41105-0391

FEAZELL, VIC, lawyer; b. Monroe, La., June 8, 1951; 1 child, Gregory Victor. BA, Mary Hardin Baylor Coll., 1972; JD, Baylor U., 1979. Bar: Tex. 1979, U.S. Dist. Ct. (5th cir.) 1988, U.S. Dist. Ct. (no. dist) 1988, U.S. Dist. Ct. (so. dist) 1989. Dir. drug abuse treatment program Mental Health-Mental Retardation, Waco, Tex., 1975-79; pvt. practice Waco, 1979-82; dist. atty. McLennan County, Tex., 1983-88; pvt. practice Austin, Tex., 1989-94; of counsel Parker, Parks & Rosenthal, Austin, 1995—; pres.

McLennan County Peace Officers Assn., Waco, 1984-87; pro bono def. counsel Henry Lee Lucas, 1989-94; expert legal corr. O.J. Simpson Trial, KTBC T.V. Primary character: Careless Whispers, 1986 (Edgar award 1986); contbr. articles to profl. jours. Del. State Dem. Conv., Houston, 1988. Named Outstanding Young Alumni, U. Mary Hardin Baylor, Belton, Tex., 1985, Peace Officer of Yr., Waco JC's, 1986. Mem. Nat. Assn. Criminal Def. Lawyers (life), Tex. Trial Laywers Assn., Tex. Criminal Def. Lawyers Assn., State Bar Tex., Bar of U.S. Fifth Cir.

FECHEK, THERESA ANNE, professional society administrator; b. Bobtown, Pa., May 14. BS in Edn., Clarion State U., 1956; MA, Case Western Res. U., 1963; PhD, Ohio State U., 1970. Tchr. various elem. and secondary schs. Delta Kappa Gamma Soc. Internat., Cleve., Tex.; asst. prof. U. R.I., 1970-77; program svcs. adminstr. Soc. Acting Exec. Dirs., 1977-84, exec. dir., 1984-88, exec. coord., 1988—. Office: Delta Kappa Gamma Soc Internat PO Box 1589 Austin TX 78767-1589

FECHIK, LLOYD (BUCK FECHIK), medical products company executive; b. Steubenville, Ohio, July 6, 1955; s. Daniel and Helen Evangeline (Bristol) F.; m. Catherine Koebler, July 21, 1985. AA in Electronics, U.S. Navy Avionics Sch., 1974. Field svc. engr. Technicare Corp., Houston, 1980-83; sr. svc. engr. Medic Equipment Corp., Houston, 1983, svc. supr., 1983-84, svc. mgr., 1984-86, v.p., 1986; pres. Computed Imaging Svc., Inc., Houston, 1986—, also bd. dirs.; pres. Computer Imaging Systems, Inc., Houston, 1990—, bd. dirs. With USN, 1974-80. Home: 9827 Churchill Way Dr Houston TX 77065-4105 Office: Computed Imaging Svc 8700 Jameel Rd Ste 130 Houston TX 77040-5047

FECHTER, LAURENCE DAVID, toxicology educator, researcher; b. N.Y.C., Dec. 23, 1945. BA, Clark U., 1967; MA, Kent State U., 1969; PhD, U. Rochester, 1973. Asst. prof. Johns Hopkins U., Balt., 1976-84, assoc. prof., 1984-93, prof., 1993; Mosier prof. toxicology U. Okla. Health Scis. Ctr., Oklahoma City, 1993—; cons. World Health. Editor: Proc. 4th Internat. Conf. on Combined Exposures to Environ. Factors, 1990; assoc. editor Neurotoxicology and Teratology, 1996—, mem. editl. bd., 1989—. Fellow Acad. Toxicol. Scis.; mem. Soc. Toxicology (pres. neurotoxicology splty. sect. 1994), Soc. for Neuroscis. Office: U Okla Health Scis Ctr Coll Pharmacy PO Box 26901 Oklahoma City OK 73190-9999

FECHTNER, ROBERT DAVID, physician; b. Newark, Mar. 9, 1957; s. Jerome L. and Sondra (Reiss) F.; m. Nancy S. Fechtner, Dec. 16, 1989; 1 child, Benjamin D. BS in biomedical sci., Univ. Mich., 1979, MD, 1982. Diplomate Am. Bd. Ophthalmology. Instr. Univ. Calif., San Diego, 1989-91; dir. glaucoma svcs. Univ. Louisville, Louisville, Ky., 1993—, asst. prof., 1991-95, assoc. prof., 1995—. Medical review bd. Ky. Transportation Cabinet, Franfort, Ky., 1994; glaucoma adv. bd. Prevent Blindness of Am., Schaumburg, Ill., 1993—; adv. panel U.S. Pharmacopeial Conv. Ophthalmology, Rockville, Md., 1995—. Recipient Nat. Rsch. Svc. award Nat. Inst. Health, 1989-91, Young Investigator award Univ. Louisville, 1994. Fellow Am. Acad. Ophthalmology; mem. Am. Glaucoma Soc. (com. mem. 1995), Ky. Medical Assn. (del.-at-large 1991). Office: Univ Louisville 301 E Muhammad Ali Blvd Louisville KY 40202-1511

FEDER, ARLENE STERN, endocrinology educator; b. Pitts., Aug. 16, 1949; d. Gilbert and Florence (Rubin) Stern; m. Richard Rosling Feder, Jan. 28, 1973; children: Gail Debra, Mark Alan. BA, Columbia U., 1971; MD, Hahnemann U., 1975. Diplomate Am. Bd. Internal Medicine, Am. Bd. Endocrinology. Resident internal medicine N.Y Med. Coll. Affiliated Hosps., 1975-78; fellow Albert Einstein Med. Coll., 1978-80; asst. prof. medicine W.Va. U., Morgantown, 1981-86, assoc. prof., 1986—; div. head endocrine sect. Ohio Valley Med. Ctr., Wheeling, 1981—; cons. Wheeling Hosp., 1989—. Mem. Wheeling Symphony Aux. Rsch. grantee Pfizer Pharms., 1985-87, Merck Pharms., 1987-90. Mem. Am. Diabetes Assn. (W.Va. pres. 1986-88), Endocrine Soc. Office: Ohio Valley Med Ctr 2000 Eoff St Wheeling WV 26003-3871

FEDEWA, LAWRENCE JOHN, information technology company executive; b. Lansing, Mich., Oct. 31, 1937; s. Norman Anthony and Agnes G. (Murphy) F.; m. Theresa Kathryn Goeser, Aug. 18, 1962; children: Kirsten Ann, Eric Christian, Lawrence John Jr. BA, Sacred Heart Sem., Detroit, 1959; postgrad., Mich. State U., 1960-61; PhD, Marquette U., 1969. Cert. high sch. tchr., Colo. Mem. editorial staff Denver Cath. Register, 1962-63; columnist Hi-Time mag., 1963-64; assoc. prof. St. Norbert Coll., De Pere, Wis., 1966-71; prof. philosophy, v.p. Park Coll., Kansas City, Mo., 1971-76; dean of the coll. Park Coll., Kansas City, 1971-74; founder, provost Park Coll./Crown Ctr., Kansas City, Mo., 1974-76; dir. internat. projects Control Data Corp., Washington, 1976-79; pres. Fedewa and Assocs., Washington, 1979-81; co-founder Internat. Inst. for Advanced Tech., Manila, 1978; v.p., sec., bd. dirs. Cordatum Inc., McLean, Va., 1981-90, pres., CEO, bd. dirs., 1990; pres. CEO, chmn. bd. Washington Tech. Group, Inc., Springfield, Va., 1990—; pres. ex officio Washington Inst. Tech., 1990—; CFO, chmn. bd. dirs. Internat. Health Corp., 1991-94; mng. exec. K.W. Tunnell Co. Fed. Svcs., Washington, 1994—; chmn., CEO, bd. dirs. Plowshares Internat., Inc., 1992—; chmn. bd. dirs. Health Interventions, Inc., 1993-95, WTG Fin. Svcs. Corp., 1995—; pres. Rose Hall Arabians, 1994—; exec. dir. Edml. Computer Svc., NEA, Washington, 1983-87. Pub. Yellow Book of Computer Products for Edn., 1983-86; author, pub. Guide to the Software Assessment Procedure, 1983-87; author: The Ethics of Ecumenism, 1969, Social Ethics with a Big Beat, 1970, The Design and Development of Computer Interactive Videodisc (CIV) Lessons, 1985; Education in the Information Age, 1986, Safety Training For Railroad Operating Employees: Introduction of Interactive Video Disc Training to the Railroad Industry (A Case Study), 1987, Do Computers Help Teachers Teach?, 1987. Mem. rsch. and devel. com. Met. Washington YMCA, 1986-90; trustee The Dupuy Inst., Washington, 1992. Roman Catholic. Office: Washington Tech Group Inc #900 6564 Loisdale Ct Springfield VA 22150-1812

FEDRICK, JOHNNIE BEA, psychologist; b. San Francisco, Jan. 10, 1950; d. Darrell James and Sylvia (Hague) F. BS in Journalism, U. Okla., 1979, MA in Psychology, 1989, MBA. Lic. psychologist, Okla. Reception staspers. U.S. Army, Ft. Sill, Okla., 1980-83; logistics ctr. counselor USAF, Tinker AFB, 1984-89; mgr. dept. human svcs. State of Okla., Tulsa, 1989-91; state case work instr. Tulsa Jr. Coll., 1991—; counselor, dir. Domestic Violence Intervention Svc., Tulsa, 1990—. Contbr. essay and stories to profl. publs. Fundraiser, Dem. Party, Tulsa, 1990; treas. United We Stand, Tulsa. Mem. U. Okla. Alumni Assn. (Tulsa chpt. treas. 1992). Jewish. Home: PO Box 52472 Tulsa OK 74152-0472

FEENEY, FRANCIS X., cable company executive, accountant; b. 1939. BS, St. Joseph's U., 1961. CPA, Pa. Acct. Laventhol & Horwath, Phila., 1961-66, Touche Ross & Co., Phila., 1966-71; with Cadence Industries Corp., Pa., 1971-80, Sterling Extruder Corp., Pa., 1980-89; v.p. fin. CCX, Inc., Charlotte, N.C., 1989—. Office: CCX Inc 1901 Roxborough Rd Charlotte NC 28211

FEENEY, MICHAEL THOMAS, civil engineer; b. Greensboro, N.C., Sept. 14, 1956; s. William Thomas and Helen Rae (Davis) F.; m. Mary Ryan Phillips, Oct. 26, 1985; children: William Patrick, Michael Ryan, Mary Patricia. BCE, N.C. State U., 1978, MCE, 1981. Registered profl. engr., Ga., Ala., S.C., Kans., Ind., Tenn., N.C., Va. Engr. trainee U.S. Corps Engrs., Wilmington, N.C., 1977-78; civil engr. U.S. Corps Engrs., Wilmington, 5, 1979-80; engr. Golder Assocs. Inc., Atlanta, 1981-84, project engr., 1984-86, sr. engr., 1986-87, assoc., 1987-92; mgr. geotechnology Jordan, Jones & Goulding Inc., Atlanta, 1993—. Scoutmaster Boy Scouts Am., Atlanta, 1981-85; active pub. sch. system strategic planning team, Atlanta, 1990; com. mem. Homeowner's Assn., Atlanta, 1990—. Mem. ASCE, Nat. Groundwater Assn. Republican. Roman Catholic. Office: Jordan Jones & Goulding Inc 2000 Clearview Ave Atlanta GA 30340-2100

FEGELY, EUGENE LEROY, retired humanities educator; b. Allentown, Pa., Dec. 10, 1930; s. Leroy Tracy and Viola Eliza (Sterner) F.; m. Margaret Ann Maconaghy, Sept. 18, 1954; children: Barbara, Laura, Hugh. BS in Edn., Temple U., Phila., 1956, MS in Edn., 1960. Cert. prin., tchr., edn. specialist. Tchr. Bucks County C.C., Newtown, Pa., 1970-78; instr. Craven C. C., New Bern, N.C., 1988—; stage mgr., actor Bucks County Playhouse, New Hope, Pa., 1984-86, various dinner theaters, Pa., N.Y., N.J., N.C., 1984—; asst. to producer-dir. Worthy is the Lamb, Swansboro, N.C., 1988; pres. Imagers, Inc., Langhorne, Pa., 1984-90; cons., advisor various ednl. assns., schs., Pa., N.J., N.C., 1970—. Author: Best of the Least, 1973; editor: Temple PDK, 1960-70, Rebel Rouser, 1995—; N.C. editor SERA Jour., 1990—; contbr. articles to profl. jours. Recipient Citation, Pa. Ho. of Reps., Harrisburg, 1987. Mem. NEA (life), Actors Equity, Pa. State Edn. Assn. (life, pres. 1967-68, Plaque 1968), Phi Delta Kappa (life, area coord. 1970-78, plaque 1978). Republican. Methodist. Home: 115 Randomwood Ln New Bern NC 28562-9556 Office: PO Box 13311 New Bern NC 28561-3311

FEHLER, POLLY DIANE, neonatal nurse, educator; b. Harvard, Ill., Jan. 6, 1946; d. Arthur William and Charlotte (Stewart) Eggert; m. Gene L. Fehler, Dec. 26, 1964; children: Timothy, Andrew. AS, summa cum laude, Kishwaukee Coll., 1974; BSN, magna cum laude, No. Ill. U., DeKalb, 1977, MSN, summa cum laude, 1980. Cert. BLS, neonatal resuscitation instr. Obgyn. staff nurse Kishwaukee Hosp., 1977; community health nurse DeKalb County Health Dept., 1977-79; grad. teaching asst. No. Ill. Univ., 1978-80; adj. maternity instr. Auburn Univ., Montgomery, Ala., 1980-81; maternal/newborn nurse USAF Regional Hosp. Maxwell, Montgomery, Ala., 1980-81, nurse internship coord., 1981-83; edn. coord. USAF Hosp., Bergstrom, Austin, Tex., 1983-87; neonatal ICU & transport RN St. Mary's Hosp., Athens, Ga., 1988-90; nursing instr. Tri-County Tech. Coll., Pendleton, S.C., 1990—; EMT, course lectr. U. Tex., Austin, 1984-86; counselor, vol. Hospice, 1984-87; sec., v.p. Shared Resources for Nurses, Austin, 1984-87, high blood pressure instr.-trainer, 1986-87, home health staff nurse Interim Health Care, Anderson, S.C., 1991-94; expert witness St. Mary's Hosp., Athens, 1991-92; coord. NCLEX rev. course Health Edn. Systems, Inc., 1993—; lectr. on interculturalism in nursing, 1993—; mem. adv. bd. Tri-County Student Competencies, 1990—, mem. advising team, 1995—, mini grant sel. com., 1992-93, 95—, com. chmn., 1996-97. Nursing textbook reviewer Addison Wesley Pubs., 1993, Mosby Yearbook, 1995—. Nurse, med. evaluator Mass Casualty Exercises, Austin, 1984-87; tchr., sec. United Meth. Chs., Ill., Ala., Ga., S.C., 1970—; mem. alumni bd. No. Ill. Alumni, DeKalb, 1979-80; mem. Malta Dist. Bd. Edn., 1979-80; judge Austin Sch. Dist. Sci. and Math. Fair, Austin, 1983-84; S.C. Gov.'s Guardian ad Litem Vol., 1995—; vol. Oconee County Healthy Visions Task Force, 1996—, S.C. Good Health Appeal Coll. Campaign Mgr., 1996, Oconee County Humane Soc., 1996—. Capt. USAF, 1980-88. Decorated USAF Commendation medal with oak leaf cluster; recipient Sr. Nursing Class of Tri-County Tech. Coll. Instr. of the Yr. award, 1992, Nat. Inst. for Staff and Orgnl. Devel. Excellence award, 1995. Mem. AAUW, ANA, S.C. Nurses Assn., S.C. Assn. Perinatal Nurses, S.C. Tech. Edn. Assn., Nursing Faculty Orgn. (v.p. 1991-94), United Meth. Women, S.C. Internat. Edn. Consortium, Sigma Theta Tau, Lambda Chi Nu. Meth. Home: 106 Laurel Ln Seneca SC 29678-2705 Office: Tri-County Tech Coll PO Box 587 Pendleton SC 29670-0587

FEILD, CHARLES ROBERT, pediatrician, educator; b. Little Rock, May 16, 1953; s. Robert Mills and Irene (Edwards) F.; m. Christina Reid Docherty, Nov. 20, 1981; children: Daniel Robert, Hannah Christina. Student, Hendrix Coll., 1971-74; MD, U. Ark., 1978. Diplomate Am. Acad. Pediatrics; lic. physician, Ark.; cert. advanced trauma life support. Intern and resident in pediatrics U. Ark. for Med. Scis., Ark. Children's Hosp., 1978-81; pediatric registrar Guy's Hosp., London, 1981; fellow, hon. pediatric registrar Inst. Child Health-U. London-Hosp. for Sick Children, 1982; clin. asst. prof. pediatrics U. Ark. for Med. Scis., 1981-82, asst. prof. pediatrics, 1982-85, 88-92, assoc. prof. pediatrics, 1992—, chief community pediatrics and pub. policy dept. pediatrics, 1991—; attending physician Ark. Easter Seals Residential Facility, 1983-85, 88—; chief Exceptional Family Mem. Svc., 1985-88; attending pediatrician Ctrs. for Youth and Families, Little Rock, 1992—; assoc. dir. Tech. Adv. Bd. Ark. Reproductive Health Monitoring Svc., 1989—; mem.exec. com. Ark. Children's Hosp. Med. Staff, 1990-93, program chmn. 1992-93; mem. ACH outpatient care com., student promotions com. Coll. Medicine, U. Ark. for Med. Scis., 1991-96; adj. assoc. prof. Coll. Nursing, UAMS, 1995—; prin. investigator Comprehensive Child Devel. Project Dept. Health Human Svcs., 1995—. Contbr. articles to med. jours. Bd. dirs. Hillcrest Hist. Neighborhood Resident's Assn.; camp physician Quapaw coun. Boy Scouts Am.; mem. ops. coun. Remmel Child Devel. Ctr., Little Rock. Grantee Robert Wood Johnson Found., 1990, 92U.S. Dept. Housing and Urban Devel., 1991. Fellow Am. Acad. Pediatrics (regional dir. Community Access to Child Health program 1993—, mem., facilitator State Community Access to Child Health program 1989—); mem. So. Soc. Pediatric Rsch., Am. Sch. Health Assn., Ambulatory Pediatric Assn., Nat. Health Policy Coun. (mem. steering com. 1993—), Ctrl. Ark. Pediatric Soc. (v.p. 1992-93, pres. 1993-94), Ark. Perinatal Assn. Methodist. Office: Ark Children's Hosp South Campus Rm 610 800 Marshall St Little Rock AR 72202-3510

FEIN, MELVYN LEONARD, sociologist, educator; b. Bklyn., Aug. 22, 1941; s. Samuel J. and Florence D. (Tarriff) F. BA, Bklyn. Coll., 1963; PhD, CUNY, N.Y.C., 1983. Rehab. counselor Office of Vocational Rehab., Rochester, N.Y., 1978-90; assoc. prof. Kennesaw State U., Marietta, Ga., 1991-96; resocializer, counselor, Rochester, 1986-91; chair interdept. group for sociology Univ. Ctr. Ga., Atlanta, 1996—. Author: Role Change, 1990, Analyzing Psychotherapy, 1992, IAM: A Common Sense Guide to Coping With Anger, 1993. Mem. Sociol. Practice Assn. (bd. dirs. 1992—, editor 1994-96), Am. Sociol. Assn., Ga. Sociol. Assn. (bd. dirs. 1991-95), So. Sociol. Soc. Home: 4531 Blackwater Trace Marietta GA 30066 Office: Kennesaw State U Sociology Dept Kennesaw GA 20144-5591

FEINBERG, DAVID JAY, architect; b. Bklyn., Nov. 3, 1938; s. Theodore R. and Lillian A. (Robins) F.; m. Hannelore D. Krueger-Feinberg, June 19, 1963; children: Daniel Peter, Alexander Scott. BArch, U. Pa., 1961. Registered architect N.Y., Fla., Ga., Conn., Ohio. Draftsman Armand Bartos & Assoc., N.Y.C., 1962-68; project architect Gilbert Seltzer & Assoc., N.Y.C., 1968-72, Tripp & Skrip Archs., Miami, Fla., 1972-73; project arch. Arthur Frimet Archs., Hollywood, Fla., 1973-74; pvt. practice Feinberg & Assocs., AIA Archs., PA, Miami, Fla., 1974—. Prin. works include Miami Rehab. Inst., Coral Gables, Fla., 1988. Founder, pres. South Dade Community Coun., Cutler Ridge, Miami, Fla., 1984, 94. Capt. Infantry, 1961-63, Berlin. Recipient Good Neighbor award Riverdale (N.Y.) Comty. Coun., 1972; named Hon. Citizen, Spuyten Duyvil, N.Y., 1970. Mem. AIA (Miami chpt.), South Fla. Frequency Modulation Assn. Office: 4960 SW 72nd Ave Ste 306 Miami FL 33155-5550

FEINSTEIN, MARION FINKE, artistic director, dance instructor; b. Nov. 7, 1925; d. Charles and Anne (Krein) Finke; m. Seymour Feinstein, Apr. 2, 1944; children: Sandi, Sheree, Lori. Degree in sec. sci., U. S.C., 1944; student, Joffrey Ballet, N.Y.C., Am. Ballet Theatre, N.Y.C.; studied with Alvin Ailey, N.Y.C. Instr. dance Recreation Dept., Columbia, S.C., 1945; instr. ballet Furman Basketball Team, Greenville, S.C., 1950-55; instr. jazz U. S.C., Spartanburg, 1986-87; dance dir. Carolina Youth Dance Theatre, Spartanburg, 1980—; tchr. various pageant winners and profl. dancers, including Miss Black Am., Miss World, Miss Am. finalist, Jr. Miss Dance of S.C. Mem. USO troupe, Spartanburg, 1942-44; choreographer Spartanburg Little Theatre, 1955-62, Miss Spartanburg Pageant, 1963-72. Recipient Resolution award S.C. Ho. Reps. and Senate, 1988, Cert. Performance Appreciation, City New Orleans, Resolution of Appreciation award Spartanburg County Council, S.C., Cert. Performance Appreciation N.Y.C. com. for entertainment at the Statue of Liberty, Fund Raising award March of Dimes. Mem. Dance Educators Am. (regional dir.), Dance Masters Am., So. Coun. Dancemasters (v.p.), Cecchetti Coun. Am., Bus. and Profl. Women, Hadassah Club (Spartanburg), B'nai Israel Sisterhood Orgn. Democrat. Jewish. Address: 1206 Reidville Rd Spartanburg SC 29306-3930

FEIST-FITE, BERNADETTE, international education consultant; b. Linton, N.D., Sept. 28, 1945; d. John K. and Cecilia Feist; m. William H. Fite. BS in Dietetics, U. N.D., Grand Forks, 1967; MS in Edn., Troy (Ala.) State U., 1973; EdD U. So. Calif. Commd. officer USAF, 1965, advanced through grades to maj., 1983; prof. health and fitness Nat. Def. U., Ft. McNair, Washington, 1989—; pres. Feist Assocs., instr. internat.edn. programs, seminars and workshops. Mem. Alexandria Little Theatre. Decorated Air Force Commendation medal, Dept. Def. Meritorious Svc. medal. Mem. NAFE, VFW. Soc. Internat. Edn., Tng. and Rsch., Am. Dietetic Assn., Nat. Assn. Women Bus. Owners, Women in Defense, Japan-Am. Soc. Washington, Dieticians in Bus. and Industry, Sports and Cardiovascular Nutritionists, Nutritional Enterpreneurs, Andrews Officers Club. Home: 2442 Cerrillos Rd Ste 312 Santa Fe NM 87505-3262 Office: Feist Assocs PO Box 7105 Alexandria VA 22307-0105

FEITSMA, LAURINDA DAWN, business owner; b. Chipley, Fla., Sept. 4, 1968; d. David and Ethel LaMerle (Collins) F. BS, Troy (Ala.) State U., 1990; MBA cum laude, Orlando (Fla.) Coll., 1992. Sales assoc. J.c. Penney, Montgomery, Ala., 1989-90; sec. Olsen Staffing, Maitland, Fla., 1990-91; rental coord. Nat. Semi-Trailer Corp., Orlando, 1991-93; in sales Orlando Freightliner, Apopka, Fla., 1993-94; constrn. coord. Hallmark Builders, Longwood, Fla., 1994-95; owner D & J Mobile Repair Svc., Orlando, Fla., 1995—; mem. accreditation desk for Olympic Soccer, Orlando, 1996. Mem. Profl. Employment Network, Woodmen of the World (music coord. 1992—), Delta Sigma Pi (v.p. ops. 1988-90). Republican. Presbyterian. Office: D & J Mobile Repair Svc 1972 Lake Atriums Cir Apt 195 Orlando FL 32839-5327

FELÁN, GEORGE DANIEL, elementary school educator, education advocate; b. Ft. Worth, Nov. 12, 1963; s. George Jimenez and Valentina (Macias) F.; m. Leticia Castilleja, Dec. 31, 1986 (div. Oct. 30, 1987); m. Sylvia Yanes, Feb. 21, 1995. BS in Bus. Adminstrn., Tex. Christian U., 1985; postgrad., U. N. Tex., 1996—. Educator Ft. Worth Ind. Sch. Dist., 1995—. Mayor pro tem City of Sansom Park, Tex., 1988-90. Mem. Assn. Supervision and Curriculm Devel. Democrat. Roman Catholic. Home: 3507 N Main St Fort Worth TX 76106 Office: Ea Hills Elementary 5917 Shelton Fort Worth TX 76112

FELD, KENNETH J., entertainment executive; b. Washington, 1947. Degree in bus. adminstrn., Boston U., 1970. Pres., prodr. Ringling Bros. & Barnum & Bailey, Vienna, Va., 1971—; pres. Ice Follies & Holiday on Ice Combined Showsm Inc. Office: Irvin & Kenneth Feld Productions care Debbie Linde 8607 Westwood Center Dr Vienna VA 22182-7506

FELDCAMP, LARRY BERNARD, lawyer; b. Hannibal, Mo., Nov. 24, 1938; s. Bernard Ernest and Mildred Elizabeth (Lehenbauer) F.; m. Irma Elaine Dahse, Mar. 13, 1964; children: David Allen, Michael Neal. BS in Chem. Engring., U. Mo., 1961; JD, U. Tex., 1967. Bar: Tex. 1967, U.S. Dist. Ct. (so. dist.) Tex. 1968, U.S. Ct. Appeals (5th cir.) 1970, U.S. Supreme Ct. 1973. Chem. engr. Union Carbide Corp., Texas City, Tex., 1963-65; ptnr. Baker & Botts, Houston, 1967—; gen. counsel Tex. Chem. Coun., Austin, 1981-92; mem. U.S. EPA Clean Air Act Adv. Com., 1991—. Chmn. Houston Area Oxidant Study Steering Com., 1978-80, Greater Houston Partnership/Greater Houston C. of C., Clean Air Coordinating Coun., 1990-95; pres. Woodlands Med. Ctr. Inc., Tex., 1978-88; mem. Houston-Galveston Area Coun. Govts. Air Quality Planning Com., 1988—, Mayor's Environ. Com., Houston, 1992—; chmn. bd. dirs. Houston-Galveston Area Emission Reduction Credit Orgn., 1994—; co-chair pub. adv. com. State of Tex. Environ. Priorities Project, 1993—. Served to 1st lt. U.S. Army, 1961-63. Mem. ABA, Tex. Bar Assn. (chmn. environ. sect. 1989-90), Houston C. of C. (chmn. environ. com. 1976-78), Tex. Ozone Task Force (chmn. 1987-90), Order of Coif, Phi Delta Phi, Omicron Delta Kappa, Tau Beta Pi. Presbyterian. Office: Baker & Botts 3000 One Shell Plz 910 Louisiana St Houston TX 77002

FELDER, PAMELA THERESA, child care director; b. Natchez, Miss., Aug. 1, 1956; d. Albert and Yvonne (McMorris) Evans; m. Dennis Felder, Jan. 13, 1976; children: D'Antwanette, Demetric. BS, Alcorn State U., 1977, MS, 1980; PhD, Kans. State U., 1982. Resource rm. specialist Jefferson Elem. Sch., Fayette, Miss., 1977-79; GED instr. Alcorn State U., Lorman, Miss., 1980-81; dir. child devel. assn. Rust Coll., Holly Springs, Miss., 1982-84; dir. early childhood ctr. Winston Salem (N.C.) State U., 1984-90; owner Pam's Unique Technique, Winston Salem, 1990-93; coord. Uplift, Inc., Greensboro, N.C., 1993-94; dir. med. ctr. child care N.C. Bapt. Hosp., Winston-Salem, 1994—. Author: Dream....but Dream Big, 1992, I'm Black and I'm Beautiful, 1993, (poetry) Best Poems, 1996 (Merit 1996). Bd. visitors Tech. Assistance Ctr., Winston-Salem, 1996. Recipient Golden Poet award World of Poetry, 1995, Best Poem Nat. Libr. of Poetry, 1995. Mem. N.C. Day Care Assn., N.C. Assn. of Educators, So. Assn. for Edn. for Children, Fourth County Day Care.

FELDMAN, DAVID HALL, economics educator; b. Miami, Fla., July 17, 1956; s. David and Margaret Mary (Kearns) F.; m. Susan Marie Lontkowski, Apr. 23, 1988; children: Anthony David and Aidan Nathaniel. AB, Kenyon Coll., Gambier, Ohio, 1978; MA, Duke U., 1980, PhD, 1982. Asst. prof. Duke U., Durham, N.C., 1982-84; asst. prof., assoc. prof. Colgate U., Hamilton, N.Y., 1984-89; assoc. prof. econs. Coll. William and Mary, Williamsburg, Va., 1989—. Reviewer So. Econ. Jour., Econ. Inquiry, N.Am. Jour. Econs. and Fin., Rev. of Internat. Econs., Internat. Rev. Econs. and Bus., McGraw-Hill; contbr. articles to profl. jours. Fellow NIH, 1978-79, Earhart Found., 1980-81. Mem. Am. Econs. Assn., So. Econs. Assn., Western Econs. Assn., Internat. Econs. and Fin. Soc., Atlantic Coun. U.S. (acad. assoc.), Nature Conservancy. Home: 112 Wood Pond Cir Williamsburg VA 23185-3118 Office: Coll William and Mary Dept Econs Williamsburg VA 23187

FELDMAN, ISRAEL, dermatologist, educator; b. Phila., Sept. 1, 1904; s. Jacob Feldman and Anna-Rachel Kramer; m. Jean Mishler, June 25, 1933 (div. Mar. 1966); children: Roger P., Bruce D. PhG, Phila. Coll. Pharmacy & Sci., 1924, postgrad. cert. clin. chemistry, 1925; DO, Phila. Coll. Osteo. Medicine, 1940. Diplomate Am. Osteo. Bd. Dermatology. Head dept. dermatology Met. Hosp., Phila., 1944-73; clin. prof. dermatology Phila. Coll. Osteo. Medicine, 1963-73; chief dermatology Cherry Hill (N.J.) Hosp., 1961-73; clin. prof. dermatology Nova Southeastern U. Coll. Osteo. Medicine, 1981-96, prof. emeritus, 1994—; lectr. on dermatology to students, local, state and nat. med. groups, 1941-90; class chmn. 50th reunion Phila. Coll. Osteo. Medicine, 1990. Contbr. articles to med. jours. Active Jewish Nat. Fund, Simon Wiesenthal Ctr., Elderhostel; diplomat World Jewish Congress. Fellow Am. Osteo. Coll. Dermatology (program chmn. 1965, pres. 1966); mem. Osteo. Bd. Dermatology, Am. Osteo Assn. (life), Am. Physicians Fellowships for Israel Medicine (trustee 1971), Fla. State Osteo. Med. Assn. (life.) B'nai B'rith (bd. dirs. North Miami Beach Eastern Shores), B'nai B'rith Anti-Defamation League. Jewish. Home: 3600 NE 170th St Apt 203 Miami FL 33160

FELDMAN, LEONID ARIEL, rabbi; b. Kishinev, Moldavia, Russia, May 3, 1953; came to U.S. 1980; s. Moisey and Rebekkah (Aronova) F.; m. Melissa Kim Weinstein, Apr. 29, 1990; 1 child, Mikha Adam. MS in Physics, Kishinev Pedagogical Inst., Russia, 1975; MA in Edn., Hebrew U., 1979; LittB in Jewish Studies, U. Judaism, L.A., 1984; MA, Jewish Theol. Sem., N.Y.C., 1987; postgrad., U. Miami, 1991—. Ordained rabbi, 1987. Dir. Russian dept. Bur. of Jewish Edn., L.A., 1981-84; faculty Wexner Heritage Found., N.Y.C., 1986—, CLAL-Nat. Jewish Ctr. for Learning & Leadership, N.Y.C., 1986—; rabbi Temple Emanu-El, Palm Beach, Fla., 1988—; pres. Ami-Da Inst., Palm Beach, Fla.; vis. rabbi Jewish Cultural Assn., Kishinev, summer 1990; nat. bd. dirs. Union of Coun. for Soviet Jews, Washington, 1986—; scholar-in-residene Gen. Assn. of Coun. Jewish Fedns., San Francisco, 1990; keynote speaker Masorti Assn., London, 1987; lectr. in field; radio broadcaster to Russia, Voice of Am., 1985-86; mem. Rabbinic Cabinet of United Jewish Appeal, 1989—; pres. Palm Beach County Bd. Rabbis, 1992-94. Contbr. articles to profl. jours. Recipient Gates of Jerusalem medal State of Israel Bonds, 1990, Rabbinic Leadership award Coun. Jewish Fedns., 1990, Rabbi Simon Greenberg Rabbinic Leadership award Jewish Theol. Sem., 1994, Tree of Life award Jewish Nat. Fund, 1996, Jerusalem 3000 award State of Israel Bonds, 1996; fellow Shma Mag., 1984-85; hon. fellow Bar-Ilan U., Israel, 1991. Mem. Rabbinical Assembly, Assn. of Jewish Edn. (exec. com. 1990-94), Jewish Fedn. of Plam Beach County (bd. dirs.). Office: Temple Emanu-El 190 N County Rd Palm Beach FL 33480-3740

FELDMAN, ZEEV TUVIA, neurosurgeon; b. Tel-Aviv, Apr. 7, 1957; s. Shmuel Nachum and Erna-Esther F.; m. Netta Gilboa, June 5, 1983; children: Tal, Omer. MD, Tel-Aviv U., 1988. Cert. neurosurgeon, Israel. Resident in neurosurgery Baylor Coll. Medicine, Houston, 1990-91, faculty dept. neurosurgery, 1995—; resident in neurosurgery Soroka Med. Ctr./Ben-Gurion U., Beer-Sheva, Israel, 1991-93, faculty dept. neurosurgery, 1993-95. Mem. Am. Assn. Neurol. Surgeons, Israel Med. Assn., Israel Neurosurg.

Soc., European Assn. of Neurosurg. Socs., Harris County Med. Soc., Tex. Med. Assn., N.Y. Acad. Scis. Office: Baylor College Medicine Dept Neurosurgery 6560 Fannin #944 Houston TX 77030

FELDSTEIN, CLAIRE SZEP, psychotherapist; d. Edward and Margaret (Schiffer) Szep; children: Leslie Tory, Jamie Bisignano, Susan Feldstein. BA cum laude, Hunter Coll., 1975; MSW, Barry U., 1979. Lic. clin. social worker, Fla.; diplomate in clin. social work Am. Bd. Forensic Examiners. Preferred provider HMOs, EAPs and ins. cos., pvt.; pvt. practice North Miami, Fla. Mem. NASW, Fla. Soc. Clin. Social Work, Fla. Alcohol And Drug Abuse Assn., Psi Chi. Office: 2450 NE 135th St Apt 911 Miami FL 33181-3535

FELDSTEIN, STANLEY, dentist; b. Bklyn., Aug. 18, 1929; s. Israel and Anna (Waxman) F.; m. Selma Dorfman, Sept. 9, 1951; children: Adrianne, Michael. BS, CCNY, 1951; DMD, NYU Coll. Dentistry, 1955. Cert. dentist, N.Y. Bd. Regents, 1955. Pvt. practice Flushing, N.Y., 1958-95; ret. Contbr. articles to profl. jours. Capt. USAF, 1955-58. Recipient Disting. Svc. award, Queens County Dental Soc., 1993. Fellow Am. Coll. Dentistry; mem. ADA (del. 1982-91, coun. govt. affairs, Washington, 1991-95), N.Y. State Dental Soc. (chmn. polit. action com., 1989-94), Queens County Dental Soc. (pres. 1978-79), Greater L.I. Dental Meeting (past dir., gen. chmn. 1970-82), Woodfield Country Club, Willow Ridge Country Club. Democrat. Jewish. Home: 3896 NW 56th Rd Boca Raton FL 33496

FELDT, GLENDA DIANE, educational administrator; b. Mobile, Ala., Sept. 15, 1950; d. William and Thelma G. (Sullivan) Sanderson; m. Fitzhugh M. Nuckols, 1969 (div. 1979); children: Thomas F., William L.; m. Everett R. Feldt, Jr., July 26, 1980; 1 child, Everett R., III. Student, Radford Coll., 1967-69; BA, Averett Coll., 1974; M of Pub. Admnistrn., Old Dominion U., 1981; EdD in Ednl. Leadership, Nova U., Ft. Lauderdale, Fla., 1993. Cert. tchr. voct. edn., adminstr., sociology, evaluator, work adjustment specialist, sch. supt., Va. Clk. typist Naval Air Sta., Norfolk, Va., 1968; clk., typist B Danville (Va.) Social Svc. Bur., 1970-71, welfare eligibility technician, 1971-73, social worker I, 1973-74; counselor, evaluator Fred T. Hatcher Ctr., Danville, 1974-75; vocat. evaluator Va. Dept. Vocat. Rehab., Danville, 1975-78; vocat. evaluator Va. Beach City Pub. Schs., 1978-80, work adjustment specialist, 1980-87; program leader vocat. spl. needs Norfolk (Va.) Pub. Schs., 1987-93; asst. prin. Bayside High Sch., Virginia Beach, Va., 1993-94; prin. New Horizons Regional Edn. Ctr., Newport News, Va., 1994—; project dir. Tidewater (Va.) Regional Nursing Articulation Project, 1988-90; cons. Johnson & Wales U., Norfolk, 1992-93; project dir. High Schs. that Work So. Regional Edn. Bd., 1993-94; presenter numerous confs. Presenter Coun for Exceptional Children, Boston, 1985, Nashville, 1987, Albuquerque, 1993; keynote speaker W. Va. Tech. prep. health occupations, Charleston, 1991. Bd. dirs Danville Jaycees Wives Assn., 1976-78, Goodwill Industries, Danville, 1977-78; pres. PTA, Danville, 1977-78; score keeper Great Bridge Little League, Chesapeake, Va., 1982-84. Named Woman of Day, WBTM Radio, Danville, 1974. Mem. NEA, ASCD, Nat. Assn. Secondary Sch. Prins., Va. Edn. Assn., Am. Vocat. Edn. Assn. (bd. dirs. Va. 1987-93, 96), Nat. Assn. Vocat. Edn. Spl. Needs Pers., Va. Assn. Vocat. Spl. Needs Pers. (pres. 1983-85, Va. Tchr. of Yr. 1986, Va. Adminstr. Yr. 1993), Jr. League Hampton Rds., Va. Women's Network, Exch. Club of York. Baptist. Home: 405 Marlbank Dr Yorktown VA 23692-4306 Office: New Horizons Regional Edn Ctr 13400 Woodside Ln Newport News VA 23602-1364

FELIX, JUDITH JOAN, elementary educator; b. Chilliwack, B.C., Canada, May 2, 1941; came to the U.S., 1963; d. Peter Augustus and Doris Victoria (Thiemer) Grossman; m. Robert Louis Felix, Sept. 25, 1962; children: Danielle Williams, Bridget Kneece, R. Nicholas, Conan P. BA, U. B.C., 1962; postgrad., Duquesne U., U. S.C., Furman U. Tchr. St. Joseph Sch., Columbia, S.C., 1984-91; tchr. Cardinal Newman Middle Sch., Columbia, 1991—, adminstrv. asst., 1992—; mem. adv. bd. Cardinal Newman Middle Sch., 1983-85; mem. inspection team Diocese of Charleston, S.C., 1993, 95. Bd. dirs. YWCA, Columbia, 1974-76; vol. VA. Hosp., Columbia, 1972-74; pres. sch. bd. St. Joseph Sch., 1980. Named Tchr. of Month Greater Columbia C. of C., 1992. Mem. Univ. Womens Club, Investment Club (pres. 1993-95), Book Club (pres. 1991-92), Univ. Club, Alpha Delta Pi. Home: 6233 Macon Rd Columbia SC 29209

FELKER, OUIDA JEANETTE WEISSINGER, special education educator; b. Vicksburg, Miss., Oct. 31, 1931; d. Eugene Liddell and Alice Byron (Cato) Weissinger; m. George Hugh Boyd Jr., Feb. 5, 1958 (div. 1968); children: James Eugene, Ouida Ann Boyd Baldwin, Alice Emelyn Boyd Dewey, Rosalie Jeanette, George Hugh III; m. Paul Henry Felker Jr., Mar. 4, 1983. BS, U. Tenn., 1952; MA, U. South Fla., 1974, EdS, 1985; EdD, U. Sarasota, 1987; grad. gemologist, Gemological Inst. Am., 1993. Cert. ins. appraiser. Tchr. health, phys. edn. South High Sch., Knoxville, Tenn., 1953; founder, exec. dir. Happyland Kindergarten, Clayton, Ga., 1955-56; tchr. spl. edn. Laurel (Fla.) Student Ctr., 1968-72; tchr. spl. edn., vocat. coord. Sarasota (Fla.) County Student Ctr., 1972-78; founder, exec. dir. Exceptional Industries, Venice, Fla., 1979-82; tchr. Sarasota (Fla.) County Student Ctr., 1985-88; staffing specialist Nokomis (Fla.) Elem. Sch., 1988-90, Englewood (Fla.) Elem. Sch., 1990—, Taylor Ranch Elem. Sch., Venice, Fla., 1990—; tchr. of handicapped Venice (Fla.) Area Rotary Clubs, Rio de Janeiro, 1982; liaison for exception student edn. Ideal Alternative High Sch. and Life Program, 1990—; owner Jewelry by Appointment. Bd. dirs. St. Mark's Day Sch., Venice, 1986-89; mem. St. Mark's Choir; past pres. Episcopal Ch. Women, Venice Area Coll. Club. Mem. Fla. Rehab. Assn. (past chpt. treas. and pres.), Suncoast Gesneriad Soc. (v.p. 1987-91), Accredited Gemologist Assn. (cert. 1992—), Phi Mu Alumnae Assn. (treas. 1992-93, v.p. 1994-95, pres. 1995—), Nat. Jewelry Appraisal Registry. Republican. Episcopalian. Home: 729 Apalachicola Rd Venice FL 34285-1605 Office: Ideal H S & ESE Spl Programs 3550 Wilkinson Rd Sarasota FL 34231-7547

FELLER, THOMAS ROBERT, director of special projects; b. Monroe, Wis., Sept. 28, 1954; s. Robert Charles and Wanda (Gaarder) F. BA, Ripon Coll., 1976. Cert. hotel adminstr. Desk clk. Holiday Inn-East, Baton Rouge, 1978-79, night auditor, 1979-80, front office supr., 1980-81; internal auditor Miss. Mgmt., Jackson, 1981-86; sr. auditor MMI Hotel Group, Jackson, 1986-96; dir. special projects MMI Hotel Group, Jackson, Miss., 1996—. Editor newsletter Smart-Ash, 1987-93, editor newsletter Southern Fandom Confedn. Bull., 1995—. Mem. Internat. Assn. Hospitality Accts., Nat. Restaurannt Assn. (internal audit exec. study group 1982—), Chimneyville Fantasy and Sci. Fiction Soc. (corr. sec. 1987—), Fantasy Amateur Press Assn., So. Fandom Confedn. (pres. 1995—). Office: MMI Hotel Group PO Box 16807 Jackson MS 39236-6807

FELLMAN, BARRY L., computer systems company executive; b. Miami, Fla., Jan. 25, 1954; s. Morton R. and Marilyn (Newman) F.; Sc.B. in Applied Math. magna cum laude, Brown U., 1975. Pres. Telemetry Controls, Inc., Miami, Fla., 1975-82, Morlin Group, Inc., Miami, 1982—; bd. dirs. Ctr. for Visual Communication, 1985—. Local admissions interviewer Brown U., 1976—; founding mem., hon. adviser Photogroup Miami, 1982-86; bd. dirs. Ctr. VIsual Communication. Mem. Assn. Computing Machinery, IEEE, Assn. Energy Engrs., AAAS, Builders Assn. South Fla., Greater Miami C. of C., Nature Conservancy, Tigertail Assn., Siggraph.

FELSKI, RITA, language educator; b. Birmingham, Eng., Apr. 15, 1956. BA, Cambridge U., Eng., 1979; MA, Monash U., 1982, PhD, 1987. Asst. prof. Murdoch U., Perth, Australia, 1987-93; prof. U. Va., Charlottesville, 1994—. Author: Beyond Feminist Aesthetics, 1989, The Gender of Modernity, 1995. Fellow Soc. for Humanities, 1988-89, Commonwealth Ctr., 1991; grantee Australian Rsch. Coun., 1993. Office: U Va Dept English Bryan Hall Charlottesville VA 22903

FELSTED, CARLA MARTINDELL, librarian, travel writer; b. Barksdale Field, La., June 21, 1947; d. David Aldenderfer Martindell and Dorthe (Hetland) Horton; m. Robert Earl Luna, Aug. 24, 1968, (div. 1972); m. Hugh Herbert Felsted, Nov. 2, 1974. BA in English, So. Meth. U., 1968, MA in History, 1974; MLS, Tex. Woman's U., 1978. Cert. secondary tchr., Tex.; cert. learning resources specialist, Tex. Tchr. Bishop Lynch High Sch., Dallas, 1968-72, Lake Highlands Jr. High Sch., Richardson, Tex., 1973-75; instr. Richland Coll., Richardson, Tex., 1973-76; library asst. So. Meth. U., Dallas, 1977-78; librarian Tracy-Locke Advt., Dallas, 1978-79; corp. librarian Am. Airlines, Inc., Ft. Worth, 1979-84; research librarian McKinsey & Co., Dallas, 1984-85; reference librarian St. Edward's U., Austin, Tex., 1985—, assoc. prof., 1994—; ptnr. Southwind Info. Svcs. and Southwind Bed-Breakfast, Wimberley, Tex., 1985-92; bd. dirs. Women's S.W. Fed. Credit Union, 1978-81. Editor, compiler: Youth and Alcohol Abuse, 1986; co-editor Mexican Meanderings, 1991—; contbr. to Frommer's travel guides, 1991—. Mem. adv. bd. Sch. Libr. and Info. Scis., Tex. Women's U., Denton, 1982-84; mem. curriculum com. Wimberley Ind. Sch. Dist., 1986; bd. dirs. Hays-Caldwell Coun. on Alcohol and Drug Abuse, San Marcos, Tex., 1986-88, Inst. Cultures for Wimberley Valley, 1989-91, Tex. Alliance Human Needs, 1992—. Grantee St. Edward's U., 1986-89, 96. Mem. ALA, Tex. Libr. Assn. (dist. program com., membership com. 1986-88, Tex.-Mex. rels. com. 1992—), Wimberley C. of C. (bd. dirs. 1987-88). Unitarian. Home: PO Box 33057 Austin TX 78764-0057

FELTON, NORMAN LEE, JR., alcohol and drug abuse services specialistt; b. Rochester, N.Y., Apr. 27, 1957; s. Norman Lee and Ina Dean (Quinn) F.; m. Gretel Belvador Massey, Sept. 6, 1979; children: Norman Lee III,David, Justin, Jonathan, Armand. BS in Biology, Fisk U., 1979; degree in pharmacy, Mercer U., 1983. Pharmacy mgr. night shift Ga. Bapt. Med. ctr., Atlanta, 1979-87; dir. pharmacy svcs. West End Med. Ctr., Atlanta, 1984-86; chmn. dept. pharmacy tech., instr., counselor Atlanta Coll. Med. and Dental Careers, 1989-93; edn. and prevention specialist Coun. on Substance and Alcohol Abuse, Montgomery, Ala., 1994—; lectr., condr. workshops in field. Autthor: Street Smart Drug Dictionary Guide for Parents and Children, 1996. Recipient student recognition award Atlanta Coll. Med. and Dental Careers, 1992, leadership and svc. award Mercer U. So. Sch. Pharmacy chpt. Student Nat. Pharm. Assn., 1988, award for presentation Head Elem. Sch., Montgomery, 1995. Mem. Assn. Pharmacy Technicians, Am. Soc. Hosp. Pharmacists, Alpha Phi Alpha. Home: 4824 Parktowne Way Apt 149 Montgomery AL 36116 Office: Coun on Substance Abuse 207 Montgomery St Ste 400 Montgomery AL 36104-3534

FELTON, WARREN LOCKER, II, surgeon; b. Bartlesville, Okla., Oct. 25, 1925; s. Warren Locker and Elizabeth (Keller) F.; m. Judith Ann Mead, July 25, 1969; children: Warren Locker, III, Susan Elizabeth Felton Skove, Richard John Conrad, Alecia Ann Felton George, Christina Jane. B.S., Washington U., St. Louis, 1949, M.D., 1949. Diplomate: Am. Bd. Surgery, Am. Bd. Thoracic Surgery. Intern, then resident in surgery and instr. Yale-New Haven Med. Center, 1949-56; practice medicine specializing in thoracic and vascular surgery Oklahoma City, 1958-86; med. dir. Okla. Found. for Peer Rev. Inc., Oklahoma City, 1986-91; mem. staff Mercy Health Center, St. Anthony Hosp., Baptist Med. Center; clin. prof. U. Okla. Med. Sch. Contbr. articles to med. jours. Bd. dirs. Travelers Aid Soc., Oklahoma City, 1961-64; mem. U. Okla. Assocs., 1980; bd. dirs. City Health Dept., Oklahoma City, 1987-96; mayor Nichols Hills, Okla., 1993-94, 96—. Served with USN, 1943-45, with M.C., U.S. Army, 1956-58. Mem. AMA, A.C.S., Am. Thoracic Soc., Am. Assn. Thoracic Surgery, Soc. Thoracic Surgeons, Southwestern Surg. Congress, Sigma Xi, Alpha Omega Alpha. Episcopalian. Club: Oklahoma City Golf and Country. Home: 1612 Dorchester Dr Oklahoma City OK 73120-1205

FELTS, JOAN APRIL, elementary school educator; b. Tulsa, Apr. 8, 1940; d. John Hickland and Dorris Retha (Finley) Matlock; m. Wayne Keith Felts, Aug. 19, 1962; children: David Wayne, Michael Scott, Steven Doyle. BS in Edn., Northeastern State U., Tahlequah, Okla., 1962. Cert. tchr., Okla. Tchr. Ruby Ray Swift Elem. Sch., Arlington, Tex., 1962-64; co-owner Felts Family Shoe Store, Muskogee, Okla., 1966-79; tchr. Hilldale Elem. Sch., Muskogee, 1979—. Leader Neosho dist. Boy Scouts Am., 1969-78, trainer, 1978-88. Recipient Dist. award of merit Boy Scouts Am., 1982, Wood Badge tng. award Nat. coun., 1983, Silver Beaver award Tulsa coun., 1985; Tchr. of Yr. award Hilldale Ind. Schs., 1988. Mem. Hill Assn. Classroom Tchrs. (chmn. staff devel. 1985-89, newsletter editor 1988-90), Northeastern State U. Alumni Assn (bd. dirs. 1976—, pres.-elect 1990-91, pres. 1991—), Beta Sigma Phi (pres. Xi Zeta Zeta chpt. 1993-95, Woman of Yr. award Muskogee chpt. 1987), Kappa Kappa Iota. Republican. Methodist. Home: 109 Grandview Blvd Muskogee OK 74403-8608 Office: Hilldale Elem Sch 315 E Peak Blvd Muskogee OK 74403-8515

FENDER, FREDDY (BALDEMAR HUERTA), singer; b. San Benito, Tex., June 4, 1937; s. Serapio and Margarita (Garza) Huerta; m. Evangalina Muniz, Aug. 10, 1957; children: Baldemar, Tammy, Daniel. Student, Del Mar Jr. Coll., Corpus Christi, Tex., 1973-74. Country music performer and rec. artist: records include Tex Mex, Enter My Heart, Swamp Gold, Before the Next Teardrop Falls, 1985, Are You Ready for Freddy, If You're Ever in Texas, Rock 'n' Country, The Texas Balladeer, Best of Freddy Fender, Christmas Time in the Valley, (with Delbert McClinton) Sometimes Country, Sometimes Blue, Conciones De Mi Barrio, The Freddy Fender Collection. Served with USMC, 1954-56, Korea. Recipient Grammy, Billboard awards, Outstanding Mexican-Am. award 1977. Mem. Country Music Assn., AFTRA, Am. Fedn. Musicians U.S. and Can., Broadcast Music Inc. Office: care The Jim Halsey Co Inc 3225 S Norwood Ave Tulsa OK 74135

FENDLER, OSCAR, lawyer; b. Blytheville, Ark., Mar. 22, 1909; s. Alfred and Rae (Sattler) F.; m. Patricia Shane, Oct. 26, 1946; children: Tilden P. Wright III (stepson), Frances Shane. B.A., U. Ark., 1930; LL.B., Harvard, 1933. Bar: Ark. bar 1933. Practice in Blytheville, 1933-41, 46—; spl. justice Ark. Supreme Ct., 1965; Mem. Ark. Jud. Council, 1959- 60; pres. Conf. Local Bar Assn., 1958-60; pres. bd. dirs. Ark. Law Rev., 1961-67; mem. Ark. Bd. Pardons and Paroles, 1970-71. Mem. Miss. County Democratic Central Com., 1948—. Served with USNR, 1941-45. Fellow Am. Coll. Trust and Estate Counsel, Am. Bar Found.; mem. ABA (chmn. gen. practice sect. 1966-67, mem. council sect. gen. practice 1964—, ho. dels. 1968-80, mem. com. edn. about Communism 1966-70, chmn. com. legal aid and indigent defendants 1970-73, chmn. com. law lists 1973-76, Founders award 1992), Ark. Bar Assn. (chmn. exec. com. 1956-57, pres. 1962-63), Am. Judicature Soc. (dir. 1964-68), Scribes, Nat. Conf. Bar Presidents (exec. council 1963-65), Blytheville C. of C. (past v.p., dir.), Navy League, Am. Legion. Club: Blytheville Rotary (past pres.). Home: 1062 Hearn St Blytheville AR 72315-2659 Office: 104 N 6th St Blytheville AR 72315-3326

FENDLEY, WILLIAM RAY, JR., university administrator, educator; b. Tuscaloosa, June 24, 1941; s. William Ray Sr. and Minnie Lee (Moore) F.; m. Carolyn Kay DeLon, June 12, 1965; 1 child, Howell DeLon. BA, U. Tenn., 1963, MS, 1968; PhD, Fla. State U., 1977. Asst. to dean U. Tenn., Knoxville, 1963-68, dir. student info., 1968-73; rsch. asst. Bd. Regents State Univ. System, Tallahassee, 1973-74; rsch. assoc. U. Tenn., 1974-79; asst. dir. Instnl. Rsch. U. Va., Charlottesville, 1979-81, assoc. dir. Instnl. Rsch., 1981-94; dir. Instnl. Rsch. U. Ala., Tuscaloosa, 1994—; adj. faculty Piedmont Va. C.C., Charlottesville, 1987-94; working group Nat. Ctr. for Edn. Stat., Washington, 1993-95, nat. postsecondary edn. consortium, 1995—. Editor: Reference Sources: An Annotated Bibliography, 1993. Mem. adv. bd. Charlottesville Tennis Patrons Assn., Charlottesville, 1985-90, Soccer Orgn. Albemarle County, Charlottesville, 1980-85; cert. referee U.S. Tennis Assn. Umpires Coun., N.Y., 1987-89. Recipient Pres.'s award Va. Assn. for Mgmt., Analysis and Planning, 1983. Mem. Assn. Instnl. Rsch. (advancement and devel. taskforce 1991-93, taskforce for student right to know 1993-95, forum chair 1994-95, Forum Chair award 1995), So. Assn. Instnl. Rsch. (treas., program chair, pres. 1989-94, Pres.'s award 1994, Svc. award 1996), Ala. Assn. Instnl. Rsch., Soc. Coll. and Univ. Planning, Rotary. Episcopalian. Home: 214 Tanglewood Circle Tuscaloosa AL 35406-2389 Office: Univ Ala University Blvd Office of Instnl Rsch Tuscaloosa AL 35487-0166

FENDRICK, ALAN BURTON, retired advertising executive; b. Bronx, N.Y., Mar. 22, 1933; s. Louis and Esther (Silberberg) F.; m. Beverly R. Schoenfeld, June 12, 1960; children: Sara Fendrick Shifrin, Lisa Rubinstein. A.B. with honors in Econs, Columbia U., 1954; M.B.A., Harvard U., 1958. Asst. sales mgr. splty. div. Hankins Container Co., 1958-60; mgr. bus. adminstrn., ops. and engring. NBC, 1960-67; exec. v.p., sec., treas. Grey Advt. Inc., N.Y.C., 1967-89, exec. v.p., chmn. fin. com., 1990-93. Trustee Woodlands H.S. Scholarship Fund, Greenburgh, N.Y., pres., 1977-78; trustee Jewish Child Care Assn. N.Y., 1985—, SAG Producers Pension and Health Plans, 1993—; mem. sch. bd. Mt. Plesant Cottage Sch., 1985—; bd. dirs. Columbia Coll. Alumni Assn., 1989-96. With AUS, 1954-56. Mem. Am. Assn. Advt. Agys. (chmn. com. on fiscal control 1979-81), Advt. Agy. Fin. Mgmt. Group (chmn. exec. com. 1980-82, pres. 1982-84), Exec. Svc. Corps of Manasota, Harvard Bus. Sch. Club N.Y., Fin. Execs. Inst., Otis Woodlands Club Inc. (bd. dirs. 1985-89, treas. 1984-88). Jewish (trustee temple). Home: 5880 Midnight Pass Rd Sarasota FL 34242-2184

FENG, JINAN, plant and soil science researcher; b. Xiaogan, Hubei, China, May 20, 1954; came to U.S., 1986; m. Pinfang Xu, May 1, 1982; children: Shuguang, Lisa Y. BS in Soil and Agrochemistry, Huazhong Agri. U., Wuhan, China, 1981; MS in Plant and Soil Scis., U. Mass., 1988, PhD in Plant and Soil Scis., 1992. Instr., rschr. dept. soil and agrochemistry Huazhong Agri. U., 1982-86; rsch. asst. dept. plant and soil scis. U. Mass., Amherst, 1986-92; post-doctoral rsch. assoc. dept. soil sci. N.C. State U., Raleigh, 1992-93; rsch. assoc. Fla. A&M U., Tallahassee, 1993—. contbr. papers, abstracts to profl. jours. Home: 1857 Hopkins Dr Tallahassee FL 32303 Office: Fla A&M U Wetland Ecology Program Tallahassee FL 32307

FENN, JIMMY O'NEIL, physicist; b. Brunswick, Ga., Nov. 18, 1937; s. Raymond Hume and Mae Elizabeth (Maxwell) F.; m. Nancy Sue Smith, Nov. 18, 1958 (div. 1974); children: Daniel Stewert, Nancy Anne, Margaret Elizabeth; m. Deborah Broadway, Sept. 2, 1989. BS, Lincoln Meml. U., 1963; MS, Emory U., 1967; PhD, Ga. Inst. Tech., 1980. Instr. dept. radiology Emory U., Atlanta, 1967, asst. prof., 1973-74; asst. prof. Med. U. S.C., Charleston, 1968-73, 74-82; assoc. prof. radiol. oncology Med. U. S.C., Charleston, ;, 1978-93; prof. radio oncology Med. U. S.C., Charleston, 1993—; med. bd. advisors radiation oncology Gen. Electric, 1992. Contbr. articles to So. Med. Jour., Cancer, Internat. Jour. Hyperthermia, Jour. Cell Biology, Jour. S.C. Med. Assn. Fellow Am. Coll. Med. Physics (chair, sec. 1984-91), Am. Coll. Radiology, Am. Assn. Med. Physicists (bd. dirs. 1984-88). Presbyterian. Office: Med U SC 171 Ashley Ave Charleston SC 29425-0001

FENN, SANDRA ANN, programmer, analyst; b. Sugar Land, Tex., Oct. 31, 1953; d. William Charles and Helen Maxine (Kyle) F.; m. Jimmie Dan Watts, May 21, 1973 (div. June 1988); children: Gabriel Nathaniel Watts, Lindsay Nichelle Garza. AA in Gen. Studies summa cum laude, Alvin (Tex.) C.C., 1994; student, U. Houston, 1994—. Shampoo asst. LaVonne's Salon of Beauty, Houston, 1972-73; coding clk. Prudential Ins. Co., Houston, 1974-75; word processing operator MacGregor Med. Assn., Houston, 1983-85; computer applications analyst Computer Scis. Corp., Houston, 1987-92; program support adminstr. Sci. Applications Internat. Corp., Houston, 1992-95, programmer/analyst, 1995—. Vol. tutor, Adopt-A-Sch. Program. Mem. Am. Bus. Women's Assn. (newsletter chair), Phi Theta Kappa. Home: 107 Clearview Ave Apt 1206 Friendswood TX 77546-4058 Office: Sci Applications Internat Corp 16511 Space Center Blvd Houston TX 77058-2017

FENNER, CATHERINE MUNRO, medical association administrator; b. Bronxville, N.Y., Oct. 31, 1959; d. James Hardie and Carol Munro (Stanley) F.; m. W. Todd Bender, Oct. 3, 1981 (div. Sept. 24, 1987); children: Sara Munro Bender, William Hardie Bender. BS in Natural Resources, U. of the South, Sewanee, Tenn., 1981. Exec. dir. Tenn. Keeping Abortion Legal and Safe, Nashville, 1987-93; Tenn. Chpt. Am. Acad. Pediatrics, 1994—; chair, pres. Tenn. Alliance for Choice, Nashville, 1990-93; trainer Nat. Abortion Rights Action League, Washington, 1992; steering com. Nashville Immunization Coalition, Nashville, 1996—; exec. dir. planning com. Am. Acad. Pediatrics, 1994—. Mem. Women's Task Force, Tenn. Dem. Party, Nashville, 1996; mem., vol. Jr. League of Nashville, 1985-88. Recipient Mayor's Acts of Excellence Award of Merit Metro. Bd. Edn., Nashville, 1994. Mem. Am. Soc. Assn. Execs., Tenn. Soc. Assn. Execs. Office: Tenn Chpt Am Acad Pediatrics PO Box 159201 Nashville TN 37215

FENSCH, THOMAS CHARLES, journalism educator, writer; b. Ashland, Ohio, Nov. 29, 1943; s. Edwin August and Heloise (Moore) F.; m. Jean Robinson, Dec. 27, 1977 (dec. July 1991); children: William Robinson, Susan Robinson Schwartz, Lynn Robinson Marrable; m. Sharon Wanslee, June 14, 1994; 1 child, Morris Johnson. AB in Psychology, History, Ashland Coll., 1965; MA in Journalism, U. Iowa, 1967; PhD in Comm., Syracuse U., 1977. Faculty mem. Shippensburg (Pa.) State U., 1970-71; asst. prof. journalism Ohio State U., Mansfield, 1971-73; assoc. prof. journalism U. Tex., Austin, 1977-91; Warner prof. journalism Sam Houston State U., Huntsville, Tex., 1991—; lectr. in field. Author: The Lions and the Lambs, 1970, Alice in Acidland, 1970, Films on the Campus, 1970, Smokeys, Truckers, CB Radios & You, 1976, Steinbeck and Covici: The Story of a Friendship, 1979 (Biographical Book of Yr., Ohioana Libr. Assn. 1980), paperback edit., 1984, Skydiving, 1980, The Hardest Parts: Techniques for Effective Non-Fiction, 1984, Conversations with John Steinbeck, 1988, The Sports Writing Handbook, 1988, 2d edit. 1995, Writing Solutions: Beginnings, Middles & Endings, 1988, Conversations with James Thurber, 1989, Best Magazine Articles: 1988, 1989, Associated Press Coverage of a Major Disaster: The Crash of Delta Flight 1141, 1990, Nonfiction for the 1990s, 1991, Television News Anchors, 1993, Oskar Schindler and His List, 1995; photographs have appeared in 6 books; contbr. over 115 articles to profl. jours. and mags. Mem. AAUP, Am. Soc. Journalists and Authors, Assn. Edn. in Journalism and Mass Comm. Home: 692 Elkins Lk Huntsville TX 77340-7317 Office: Sam Houston State Univ Dept Journalism Huntsville TX 77341

FENSKE, NEIL A., dermatologist; b. Blue Earth, Minn., Apr. 14, 1947. MD, St. Louis U., 1973. Diplomate Nat. Bd. Med. Examiners, Am. Bd. Dermatology, Am. Bd. Pathology. Resident U. Wis. Ctr. for Health Scis., Madison, 1974-77; prof. medicine and dir. divsn. dermatology/ cutaneous surgery U. South Fla., Tampa, prof. pathology, co-dir. interdepartmental dermatopathology svc.; chief dermatology sect. James A. Haley VA Hosp., Tampa, H. Lee Moffitt Cancer and Rsch. Inst., Tampa. Contbr. numerous articles to profl. jours., chpts. to books. Recipient AMA Physician's Recognition award, 1977, 80, 83, 86, 89, 92, Am. Acad. Dermatology CME award, 1978, 80, 83, 86, 89, 92, Male Decade achievement award, Gustavus Adolphus Coll., 1979, Disting. Alumni Citation in field of medicine, 1989. Fellow Am. Acad. Dermatology (regional coord. nat. melanoma/skin cancer screening program 1984—), Am. Soc. Dermatopathology; mem. AMA, Am. Cancer Soc. (bd. dirs. Hillsborough County Met. Unit 1991—, elected med. advisor 1992), Am. Dermatol. Assn., Inc., Am. Soc. Dermatology, Am. Soc. Dermatologic Surgery, Am. Fedn. Clin. Rsch., Pan Am. Med. Assn. (mem. coun. 1981—), Dermatology Found. (state vice chmn. Fla. 1991), Fla. Med. Assn., Fla. Soc. Dermatology (pres. 1994—), Fla. West Coast Soc. Dermatology (meeting program dir. 1989—, adv. coun. rep. 1980—, pres. 1992-93), Ctrl. Fla. Soc. Dermatology, Fla. Soc. Dermatol. Surgeons, Hillsborough County Med. Assn. (editorial bd. The Bull. 1988-91), South Ctrl. Dermatologic Congress (arrangements chmn. 1991-94), Southeastern Dermatol. Assn. (pres. 1988), So. Med. Assn. (co-coord. 79th Ann. Sci. Assembly 1985, vice chmn. 88th Ann. Sci. Assembly 1994), Skin Phototrauma Found. (chmn. adv. bd. 1992-93), Soc. Investigative Dermatology, Soc. Internat. Dermatol. Tropical, Dermatologic Therapeutic Assn., Assn. Profs. of Dermatology, Inc., Skin Cancer Found., Assn. Acad. Dermatologic Surgeons, Noah Worcester Soc. Office: U South Fla Coll Med Divsn Dermatology 12901 Bruce B Downs Blvd Tampa FL 33612-4742

FEOLA, RALPH LEONARD, insurance agent; b. Cohasset, Mass., Aug. 24, 1946; s. Randolph Archibald and Marie (Dyson) F.; m. Jeraldine Chapman, Aug. 28, 1970; 1 child, Lisa R. Vines. BS in Bus. Mgmt., Fla. So. Coll., 1969. Mgr. retail sales J.M. Fields Dept. Stores, Winter Haven, Fla., 1970-78; ins. agt. Feola Ins. Agy., Lakeland, Fla., 1978-85, Allstate Ins. Co., Plant City, Fla., 1986-94, Feola Ins. Agy., Plant City, 1994—. Fellow Life Underwriting Tng. Coun. (sgt. 1989); mem. Am. Soc. CLU and ChFC (v.p. 1991-92, pres. 1992-93, 93-96), Profl. Ins. Agts. Fla., Nat. Assn. Life Underwriters, Nat. Assn. Health Underwriters, Plant City C. of C., Estate Planning Coun. of Polk County, Elks, Moose. Democrat. Roman Catholic. Home: 5314 Woodhaven Ln Lakeland FL 33813-2656 Office: Feola Ins Agy 1003 S Collins St Plant City FL 33566-6507

FERAN, RUSSELL G., sales executive; b. New Orleans, Oct. 1, 1948; s. Fred and Jean (Zyslina) F.; m. Phyllis Sobel, 1973; 1 child, Leslie. BS in Indsl. Engring., La. State U., 1973. Cert. audio cons.; cert. technician Nat. Assn. Bus. and Ednl. Radio. Engr. South Cen. Bell. Telephone Co., New Orleans, 1973-75; SMIA mgr. Tandy Corp., Fort Worth, 1975-87; regional sales mg. Internat. Union Police Assns., Alexandria, Va., 1987-93; regional mgr. S.W. Pub., Phoenix, 1993—; bd. dirs. Book Rack Metairie, La., Crohn's & Colitis Found. Am.; cons. Vietnam Vets. Am., Washington, 1987—; arbitrator Better Bus. Bur. New Orleans, 1984-90. With USMC, 1967-70. Mem. Am. Philatelic Soc., Vietnam Vets. Am., Patrolman's Assn. New Orleans (hon. life 1988), Westside Amateur Radio Club (pres. 1983-85), JWV-USA (post # 580), Am. Radio Relay League (DCXX award 1971), B'nai B'rith (pres. lodge # 182 1986-88, 93-95, v.p. New Orelans coun. 1990-92). Home: 101 Fairway Dr New Orleans LA 70124 Office: RGF Enterprises Inc 333 Saint Charles Ave New Orleans LA 70130-3111

FERGUS, PATRICIA MARGUERITA, English language educator emeritus, writer, editor; b. Mpls., Oct. 26, 1918; d. Golden Maughan and Mary Adella (Smith) F. BS., U. Minn., 1939, M.A., 1941, Ph.D., 1960. Various pers. and editing positions U.S. Govt., 1943-59; mem. faculty U. Minn., Mpls., 1964-79, asst. prof. English, 1972-79, coord. writing program conf. on writing, 1975, dir. writing centre, 1975-77; prof. English and writing, dir. writing ctr., assoc. dean Coll. Mt. St. Mary's Coll., Emmitsburg, Md., 1979-81; dir. writing seminars Mack Truck, Inc., Hagerstown, Md., 1979-81; writer, 1964—; editorial asst. to pres. Met. State U., St. Paul, 1984-85; coord. creative writing, writer program notes for Coffee Concerts, The Kenwood, 1992-94; dir. Kenwood Scribes Presentation, 1994; speaker and cons. in field; dir. 510 Groveland Assocs.; bus. mgr. Eitel Hosp. Gift Shop. Author: Spelling Improvement, 5th edit., 1991; contbr. to Midwest Chaparral, Downtown Cath. Voice, Mpls., Mountaineer Briefing, ABI Digest; contbr. poems to Minn. English Jour., Mpls. Muse, The Moccasin, Heartsong and Northstar Gold, The Pen Woman, Midwest Chaparral, Rhyme Time; contbr. short stories to anthologies. Mem. spl. vocal octet St. Olaf Ch. Choir, St. Olaf Parish Adv. Bd., Windmore Found. for the Arts. Recipient Outstanding Contbn. award U. Minn. Twin Cities Student Assembly, 1975; Horace T. Morse-Amoco Found. award, 1976, Golden Poet award, World of Poetry, 1992; Ednl. Devel. grantee U. Minn., 1975-76; Mt. St. Mary's Coll. grantee, 1980; 3d prize vocal-choral category Nat. Music Composition Contest, Nat. League Am. Pen Women, speaker and Bronze Medalist, 13th Internat. Biographical Congress, 1986. Mem. AAUW, Am. Biog. Inst. (dep. gov.), Internat. Biog. Ctr. (hon. mem. adv. coun.), Nat. Coun. Tchrs. English (regional judge 1974, 76-77, state coord. 1977-79), Minn. Coun. Tchrs. English (chmn. career and job opportunities com., spl. com. tchr. licensure, sec. legis. com.), Nat. League Am. Pen Women (1st pl. Haiku nat. poetry contest 1992), World Lit. Acad., Mpls. Poetry Soc. (numerous poetry prizes), League Minn. Poets, Midwest Fedn. Chaparral Poets (numerous poetry prizes, 1st prize 1993), Poetry Soc. Va., Windmore Found. for the Arts, Va. Writers, Windmore Writers Group, Woman's Club of Culpepper, No. Dist. Woman's Club (2nd prize poetry 1996). Roman Catholic. Home and Office: 651B Southview Ct Culpeper VA 22701-3794

FERGUSON, BRUCE KIRKMAN, landscape architect, educator; b. Boston, Apr. 10, 1949; s. Albert Barnett Jr. and Louise (Enequist) F.; m. Rosemarie Emanuele, Sept. 15, 1979; children: Benjamin, Derek, John. BA, Dartmouth Coll., 1971; M in Landscape Architecture, U. Pa., 1975. Lic. landscape architect, Pa., Ga. Landscape architect Rahenkamp, Sachs, Wells and Assocs., Phila., 1973-75, Washington (Pa.) Ctr. for Design, 1975-80; instr. Pa. State U., State College, 1980-82; asst. prof. U. Ga., Athens, 1982-88, assoc. prof., 1988-93, prof., 1993—, MLA coord., 1992—; faculty advisor U.S. Bur. Mines, Pitts., 1980-83; cons. Beall, Gonnsen & Co., Athens, 1984—. Author: Stormwater Infiltration, 1994; co-author: On-Site Stormwater Management, 1990; contbr. articles to profl. jours. Active Squaw Run Area Watershed Assn., Pitts., 1977-80; dir. Pa. Environ. Coun., Phila., 1979-82, Clear Water Conservancy, State College, 1980-82. Fellow Am. Soc. Landscape Architects (founder water conservation com., chmn. 1991-93, Bradford Williams medal 1992); mem. Coun. Educators in Landscape Architecture (pres. 1991-92), Am. Water Resources Assn. Office: U Ga Sch Environ Design Caldwell Hall Athens GA 30602

FERGUSON, DAVID ROBERT, energy research manager; b. Atlanta, Dec. 26, 1949; s. Robert H. and Elizabeth (Whatley) F.; m. Marilyn Shuptrine, Dec. 13, 1970; children: Mary Elizabeth, Michelle Lynn. BBA in Mktg., Ga. State U., 1973. Mgr. market research Standard Fed. Savs., Atlanta, 1973-77; mgr. new constrn. First Union Nat. Bank, Charlotte, N.C., 1977-82; mgr. constrn. div. Cen. Carolina Bank, Durham, N.C., 1982-86; mgr. residential and comml. program Alternative Energy Corp., Research Triangle Park, N.C., 1986-93, dir. comml. market rsch., 1994—. Mem. AIA, Am. Mktg. Assn., Illuminating Engring. Soc., Bldg. Owners and Mgrs. Assn. Carolinas (pres. N.C.-S.C.-W.Va. chpt. 1990, bd. dirs. So. region 1990-92), Kiwanis, Charles M. Setzer Lodge. Democrat. Methodist. Home: 4102 Talcott Dr Durham NC 27705-2851 Office: Alternative Energy Corp PO Box 12699 Durham NC 27709-2699

FERGUSON, EMMET FEWELL, JR., surgeon; b. DeSoto, Ga., Mar. 28, 1921; s. Emmet Fewell Sr. and Emma Ruth (Smith) F.; Edith Geraldine Strozier, Nov. 26, 1954; children: Berrylin, Joann, Virginia, Fran, Emmet III. Student, U. Ga., 1938-40; MS in Zoology with honors, US Naval Acad., 1943; MD, Med. Coll. Ga., 1950. Diplomate Am. Bd. Surgery, Am. Bd. Colon-Rectal Surgery. Rsch. assoc. U.S. Naval Hosp., St. Albans, N.Y., 1950-51; surg. resident U. Fla., Jacksonville, 1951-53, 54-55, U. Ala., Brimingham, 1953-54; pvt. practice Jacksonville, 1955-93; pres. staff Meth. Hosp., Jacksonville, 1958-60, U. Hosp., Jacksonville, 1972-73; chief colon rectal surgery Bapt., Meth., and St. Vincents Hosps.; clin. prof. surgery coll. medicine U. Fla., 1960-93; mem. med. missions to Honduras, Costa Rica, Nicaragua, Ecuador; del., speaker Pan Am. Med. Meeting, Buenos Aires, 1967; mem. adv. com. coll. medicine U. Fla., Gainesville, 1976-82; chmn. bd. dirs. N.E. Fla. Health Svc. Agy., 1980-83; mem. Statewide Health Coun., 1980-89, chair, 1980-82. Contbr. articles to profl. jours. Del., speaker from Jax C. of C. to Internat. Exhbn., Moscow, 1959; tchr. Sunday sch. Riverside Bapt. Ch., 1955—, deacon, 1960, 90; del. from Am. Cancer Soc. to Internat. Cancer Soc., Tokyo, 1966; mem. United Way Bd., Jacksonville, 1970-80, chmn. profl. divsn., 1980; chmn. Fla. host com. Pres. Carter's Inauguration, Washington, 1977; life mem. Jacksonville Hist. Soc., pres., 1986-88; mem. Jacksonville Indigent Care Com.; bd. regents Nat. Libr. Medicine, Washington, 1977-81; founder bd. dirs. Bapt. Towers, 1970—; trustee, pres. bd. trustees Riverside Bapt. Day Sch., 1971-75; trustee health sci. ctr. libr. U. Fla., 1972-93; trustee Bartram Sch., 1974-84, pres., 1976-77; mem. exec. com., mem. office state commn. rsch., profl. svc. Am. Cancer Soc. With USN, 1940-46, 50-51, capt. M.C. res. Decorated Am. Def. medal, Naval Res. medal; recipient Disting. Svc. award Fla. divsn. Am. Cancer Soc., Tampa, 1972, 75, Silver Beaver award Boy Scouts Am., 1986, Emmet Ferguson award U. Fla. Health Sci. Ctr. Fellow ACS (pres. Fla. chpt. 1968), Am. Soc. Surgery Alimentary Tract, Am. Soc. Colon Rectal Surgeons, Piedmont Soc. Colon Rectal Surgeons (pres. 1996-97), Fla. Soc. Colon Rectal Surgeons (pres. 1972-74, 76-78); mem. AMA, Fla. Med. Assn. (life), So. Med. Assn., Southeastern Surg. Congress (Best Motion Picture award 1975), Duval County Med. Soc. (life, editor bull. 1970-73, pres. 1975-76), Navy League (life, pres. Jacksonville coun. 1983-84, Commendation award 1984), Sons Confederate Vets., Rotary (bd. dirs. 1978-80, chmn. com. polio plus 1987-88, Commendation award 1989), St. John's Dinner Club (pres. 1975-78, Commendation award 1978), Fla. Yacht Club (life), River Club. Democrat.

FERGUSON, ERIK TILLMAN, transportation consultant; b. Seattle, Apr. 3, 1957; s. Charles Harvey and Alice Eloise (Storaasli) F.; m. Elaine Ana Samayoa, May 17, 1985; children: Britnay Alexandra, Erik Tillman II. BA in History, U. So. Calif., L.A., 1979; PhD., U. So. Calif., 1988; M.C.R.P., Harvard U., 1982. Engring. aide Burmah Oil Co., Huntington Beach, Calif., 1975-77; roustabout Union Oil, Carpinteria, Calif., 1977-79; fabricator Lockheed Aircraft, Burbank, Calif., 1979-82; community planner Transp. Systems Ctr., Cambridge, Mass., 1982-84; projects specialist Commuter Transp. Svcs., L.A., 1984-86; assoc. planner Orange County Transit Dist., Garden Grove, Calif., 1986-88; asst. prof. Ga. Inst. Tech., Atlanta, 1988-95; sr. assoc. Ekistic Mobility Cons., Gardena, 1986-94; prin. ETF Assocs., 1990—. Editor newsletter/jour. Transp. Planning, 1990-94; mem. editl. bd. Jour. Planning Edn. and Rsch., 1991-94; contbr. articles to profl. jours. Mem. Task force on Regionally Important Resources, State of Ga., 1990. German Marshall Fund scholar, 1982-83, Nat. Merit scholar, 1974; Fed. Transit Adminstrn. grantee, 1991, 92, 94, 95; Lilly Found. Tchg. fellow, 1990-91; recipient Rsch. Practitioner award Western Govtl. Rsch. Assn., 1988. Mem. Am. Planning Assn. (chair transp. planning divsn. 1993-94, chair divsn. coun. 1994-96), Transp. Rsch. Bd., Assn. for Commuter Transp. (bd. dirs. 1990-94). Home: 2419 Leisure Lake Dr Atlanta GA 30338-5318 Office: PO Box 888729 Dunwoody GA 30356

FERGUSON, JAMES EDWARD, II, obstetrician, gynecologist, maternal-fetal medicine specialist; b. Glendale, Calif., Oct. 25, 1951; m. Lynn Corpening, June 21, 1975; children: James Edward III, David Gregory, Joshua Scott. Student, USCG Acad., 1969-71; AB in History, Marquette U., 1973; MD, Wake Forest U., 1977. Diplomate Nat. Bd. Med. Examiners, Am. Bd. Ob/Gyn with a subspecialty in maternal-fetal medicine. Intern USPHS Hosp., San Francisco, 1977-78; resident ob/gyn Stanford (Calif.) U. Sch. Medicine, 1978-80, postdoctoral fellow ob/gyn, 1982-84, asst. prof. ob/gyn, 1984-87, chief divsn. maternal-fetal medicine dept. ob/gyn., 1985-87, dir. prenatal diagnosis program dept. ob/gyn., 1986-87; chief resident Bowman Gray Sch. of Medicine, Winston-Salem, N.C., 1980-81, mem. clin. faculty, 1981-82; pvt. practice Pollak, Zammit, Ferguson, MD, P.C., Winston-Salem, N.C., 1981-82; asst. prof. ob/gyn. U. Va. Sch. Medicine, 1987-90, assoc. prof. depts. ob/gyn. and radiology, 1990-91, assoc. prof. dept. ob/gyn., assoc. prof. dept. radiology, 1991-96, dir. prenatal diagnosis and treatment unit dept. ob/gyn., 1989—, dir. divsn. maternal-fetal medicine dept. ob/gyn., 1990—, John Nokes prof. ob/gyn., 1996—, prof. dept. radiology, 1996—; med. dir. perinatal svcs. U. Va. Hosp., 1990—; attending staff mem. U. Va. Hosp., 1987—, Va. Bapt. Hosp., 1996—, Stanford U. Hosp., 1982-87, Forsyth Meml. Hosp., Winston-Salem, 1981-82, Med. Park Hosp., Winston-Salem, 1981-82; assoc. staff mem. Va. Bapt. Hosp., Lynchburg, 1992-96, Santa Clara Valley Med. Ctr., San Jose, Calif., 1982-87; cons. Mid-Coastal Calif. Perinatal Outreach Program, Stanford U., 1982-87, San Joaquin Gen. Hosp., Stockton, Calif., 1985-87, Va. Bapt. Hosp., Lynchburg, 1992—; fellow Project Hope, maternal-fetal medicine program, Krakow, Poland, 1987, 89, others; mem. numerous coms. in field. Editl. referee Am. Jour. Ob-Gyn., Ob-Gyn. Jour., Clin. Chemistry Jour., Am. Jour. Human Genetics, Am. Jour. Perinatology, Jour. Reproduction, Fertility and Devel., Jour. Maternal-Fetal Medicine; obstet. editl. cons. Perinatal Continuing Edn. Program, 1991—; contbr. articles to profl. jours., chpts. to books in field. Hon. chmn. March of Dimes Walkathon, U. Va. Health Scis. Ctr., 1990; active task force on smoking and pregnancy, Am. Lung Assn. of Santa Clara-San Benito Counties, 1983; active First Presbyn. Ch., Charlottesville; coach Soccer Orgn. Charlottesville-Albemarle; bd. dirs. Ednam Forest Owners Assn., Inc.; vol. physician Camp Va., Goshen. Recipient numerous grants in field, including Dept. Mental Health, Retardation and Substance Abuse, Commonwealth of Va., 1992-93, Perinatal Nurse Liaison Contract, 1991-92, others. Fellow ACOG (examiner for specialty oral bds. 1995—, mem. health care partnerships adv. com. to DMAS Va. sect. 1995); mem. AAAS, Am. Gynecol. and Obstetrics Soc., Am. Physiol. Soc., Am. Inst. Ultrasound in Medicine, Internat. Cytokine Soc., South Atlantic Assn. Obstetricians and Gynecol., Calif. Perinatal Assn., Peninsula Ob-Gyn. Assn., Peninsula Gynecol. Soc., Shufelt Soc., Soc. Perinatal Obstetricians (bd. dirs. 1996—), Frank Lock Soc., Assn. Profs. Ob-Gyn., So. Ob-Gyn. Seminar, Va. Obstet.-Gynecol. Soc., U. Va. Residents' Soc. (hon.), N.C. Obstet.-Gynecol. Soc. (hon.), Phi Beta Kappa, Phi Alpha Theta. Office: U Va Sch Medicine Div Maternal and Fetal Medicine PO Box 387 Charlottesville VA 22908

FERGUSON, MADELYN KRISTINA, education educator; b. Miami Beach, Fla., July 14, 1948; d. Francis Robb and Shirley Anne (Walsh) F.; m. Eugene Francis Zenobi, June 25, 1988. AA, Miami Dade Jr. Coll., 1968; BA in Edn., Fla. Atlantic U., 1975; MEd in Reading, U. LaVerne, Calif., 1981. Tchr. elem. edn. Sumner County Pub. Schs., Gallatin, Tenn., 1975-77; tchr. elem. edn. Dade County Pub. Schs., Miami, 1977-78, tchr. compensatory edn., 1979-81, tchr. elem. edn., 1981-83, tchr. acad. excellence, 1983—; leader Dade County 4-H, Miami, 1984— mem. coun. adv. com., 1989—; mem. overall adv. com. Fla. Coop. Extension, Miami, 1989—. Co-author, editor: Hands on Science Activities, 1988; editor: Miami Celebrity Cookbook, 1987. Member Urban League, Miami, 1984-95, ACLU, Miami, 1989-95. U. Fla. grantee, 1986, 87; Dade Pub. Edn. Fund grantee, 1989; Chevron/U. Fla. grantee, 1990, Nat. Gardening Assn. youth garden grantee, 1994; 4-H Cmty. Pride grantee, 1994; named Leader of Yr. Dade County 4-H, 1987, Tchr. of Yr. Lorah Park Elem. Sch., 1987; recipient Commendation, U.S. Congl. Record, 1991, Outstanding Vol. award Metro Dade County Coop. Ext., 1994. Mem. ASCD, Nat. Sci. Tchrs. Assn., League Environ. Educators of Fla., Fla. Assn. for the Gifted, Nature Conservancy, Friends of Va. Key (bd. dirs. 1991—). Democrat. Home: 3942 SW 5th St Miami FL 33134-2035

FERGUSON, R. NEIL, computer systems consultant; b. Dallas, June 22, 1952; s. Roy and Hellon Ferguson; m. L. Jean Ferguson, Aug. 12, 1977; 1 child, Rheachel Claire. BA in Psychology, U. Tex., 1976. Systems engr. EDS, Dallas, 1976-77; systems programmer Collins Radio/Rockwell Internat., Richardson, Tex., 1977-78; systems programmer/analyst Moore Bus. Systems, Denton, Tex., 1978-79; supr., computer graphics Atlantic Richfield Co., Dallas, 1979-85; software engring. specialist E-Systems, Inc., Garland, Tex., 1986-90; dir. product mgmt., graphics and database systems MPSI, Inc., Irving, Tex., 1990-92; pvt. practice computer cons. Lewisville, Tex., 1990—; tech. program dir. Internat. Microcomputer Exposition, Dallas, 1978. Recipient Golden Eagle award Am. Acad. Achievement, Tymshare award Tymshare Corp., Panasonic Sci. Achievement award Matsushita Electric Corp. of Am. and Jr. Engring. Tech. Soc., NASA award, 1st Place award in math. and computers 21st Internat. Sci. Fair; named Regional Class Champion, Sports Car Club of Am. Mem. Assn. for Computing Machinery (spl. interest group on computer graphics), Am. Congress Surveying and Mapping, Am. Soc. Photogrammetry and Remote Sensing. Home and Office: 1097 Holly Ln Lewisville TX 75067-5711

FERGUSON, WENDELL, private school educator; b. Sandersville, Ga., May 6, 1954; d. Isadore and Willie Mae (Roberts) Jordan; m. Larry Brown Sr., May 28, 1971 (div. Dec. 1985); children: Larry Brown Jr., Dwyne Lamont Brown, Anthony Patrick Brown; m. Jerry Lang Ferguson, Sept. 28, 1992. Diploma, Alphena C.C., 1972; student, Ga. State U., 1983-87. Sales clk. U.S. NAS, Albany, Ga., 1972-74, 76-77; substitute tchr. Ga. Dept. Edn., Houston County, 1976-77; nutritionist (nursery) Howard AFB, Panama Canal, 1980; joined Sweet Adelines, Inc., Tulsa, 1981; data entry operator dept. budget mgmt. Atlanta City Hall, 1982; mgr., operator Atlanta Connections, 1982-83; asst. supr. micro-film Ga. Dept. Revenue, Atlanta, 1986-88; promotional sales rep. RG Clothier/L.B. Holyfield, Atlanta, 1992-95; substitute tchr. Old Nat. Christian Acad., College Park, Ga., 1995—; ptnr. Internat. Carpet Creations, Inc., Atlanta, 1989-96; co-prodr., writer, owner Jeri-Del Prodns., Atlanta. Actress, singer, dancer various prodns. (Irving Berlin award 1982); author: Times In Life, 1996. Vol. persona bus. broker Asst. Sec. of State, Atlanta, 1994; coord. nominees judgeship position Fayette, Pike, Upson & Spaulding Counties, Ga., 1992; surveyor for st. lights, Atlanta, 1982; vol. Fulton County Dept. Parks and Recreation, Burdett Gym; active We Are Today, Tomorrow. Democrat. Home: 2853 The Meadows Way College Park GA 30349 Office: Jeri-Del Prodns PO Box 490221 College Park GA 30349-0221

FERILLO, CHARLES TRAYNOR, JR., public relations executive; b. Charleston, S.C., Nov. 2, 1945; s. Charles Traynor and Mae Girard (Mathewes) F.; children: Joseph Todd, Margaret Amelia; m. Julia Blanding Holman Ferillo, Dec. 11, 1993. BA, Coll. of Charleston, 1972. Accredited in pub. rels. Legis. asst. S.C. House of Reps., Columbia, 1973-74, exec. dir. Office of Rsch. and Personnel, 1974-82; deputy lt. gov. State of S.C., Columbia, 1982-86; pres. pvt. practice, Columbia, S.C., 1987—. mem., bd. dirs. Habitat for Humanity of Ctrl. S.C., Columbia, 1992-95, City Yr. of Columbia, S.C., 1993-95, Planned Parenthood of Ctrl. S.C., 1991-95; vice chmn. United Way of the Midlands, Columbia, S.C., 1994. Sgt. U.S. Army, 1967-69, Vietnam. Mem. Pub. Rels. Soc. Am. Democrat. Home: 1938 College St Columbia SC 29201-3922 Office: Ferillo & Assocs Inc 1711 Pickens St Columbia SC 29201-2646

FERLAUTO, JERRY JOSEPH, neonatologist; b. Bronx, Sept. 7, 1944; s. Julius and Rose F.; m. Natalina, June 1969; children: Marina, Michael, Robert, Kimberly. BA, Seton Hall U., 1966; MD, U. Bologna, 1971. Diplomate Am. Bd. Pediatrics. Intern. in pediatrics Muhlenberg Hosp., Plainsfield, N.J., 1972-73; resident in pediatrics Muhlenberg Hosp., 1973-74; fellow in neonatology Rockford (Ill.) Sch. Medicine, 1975-76; pvt. practice neonatology and gen. pediatrics Middletown, N.Y., 1975-76; assoc. dir. nurseries Greenville (S.C.) Hosp. System, 1976-80; dir. neonatal programs Children's Hosp., Greenville, 1980—; med. dir. neonatal devel. follow-up clinic Children's Hosp., 1980—, med. dir. apnea program, mem. needs assessment com., 1991—, chmn., 1994, maternal child health adv. bd., newborn nursery com., chmn. com. on admitting privileges pediatrics, dir. neonatal transport team, steering com. for devel. women/children/infants svc.; assoc. prof. Med. U. S.C., 1976—; mem. Maternal and Infant Health Com. S.C.; chmn. Piedmont Perinatal Governance Bd. Recipient S.C. Maternal Child Health award, 1991. Fellow Am. Acad. Pediatrics (perinatal sect., S.C. chpt.); mem. Nat. Perinatal Assn., S.C. Perinatal Assn., S.C. Med. Soc., So. Soc. Pediatric Rsch., So. Perinatal Assn., Nat. Assn. Apnea Profls. Office: Greeneville Neonatology PA 701 Grove Rd Greenville SC 29605-5601

FERLITA, THERESA ANN, clinical social worker; b. Pinar del Rio, Cuba, Sept. 8, 1944; came to U.S., 1945; d. Sam Marion and Maria (Garcia-Collia) F. AB in Sociology, Spalding Coll., Louisville, 1966; MS in Social Work, U. Louisville, 1972. Lic. clin. social worker, Fla. Various positions, 1966-70; sr. resource program developer Children's Bd. Hillsborough County, Tampa, Fla., 1990-92; supr. homefinding unit Ky. Dept. Child Welfare, Louisville, 1972-73; foster care worker Fla. Dept. Health and Rehabilitative Svcs., Tampa, 1974; homemaker supr. Family Counseling Ctr., Clearwater, Fla., 1974; sr. social worker, mem. intake team London Borough of Newham Social Svcs., 1976; clin. social worker Alcoholism Svcs. Hillsborough Community Mental Health Ctr., Tampa, 1977-78; clin. social worker The Children's Home, Inc., Tampa, 1978-80; case coord., coord. tng. and edn., supr. teen mother program The Child Abuse Coun., Inc., Tampa, 1980-90, clin. supr. Rainbow Family Learning Ctrs., 1989-90; pvt. practice family therapy, adults abused as children, 1991; social worker med.-surg. and trauma Tampa (Fla.) Gen. Hosp., 1992-95; mgr. family svcs. Hillsborough County Headstart Dept., Tampa, 1995-96; clin. social worker St Joseph's Home Health Svc., 1996—; adj. instr. Hillsborough C.C., Tampa, 1988; cons. The Spring Battered Spouse Shelter, Tampa, 1984; coord. Parents Anonymous Children's Group, Tampa, 1980-85; mem. state health adv. com. Redlands Christian Migrant Assn., Immokalee, Fla., 1982—; mem. policy coun. Hillsborough County Headstart, Tampa, 1986-89; mem. Cmty. Action Bd., Hillsborough County. Editor, compiler manuals for child abuse and neglect investigations, 1986, 87. Pres. Fair Oaks Condominium Assn., Tampa, 1990-91; past pres. Child Abuse Com., Fla., Inc.; bd. dirs., v.p. Centro Tampa, 1989-90. Mem. NASW (sec. Tampa Bay unit 1981-83, vice-chmn. 1990-91, Social Worker of Yr. award 1988, sec. Fla. chpt. 1986-88, del. assembly 1986-91), Acad. Cert. Social Workers, Nat. Network Social Work Mgrs. Democrat. Roman Catholic. Home: 3810 N Oak Dr Apt N-31 Tampa FL 33611-2574 Office: St Joseph's Healthcare Svc 2727 W Dr Martin Luther King Blvd Tampa FL 33607

FERN, EMMA E., state agency administrator; b. Columbus, Ohio, July 22, 1927; d. Frederick and Wilhelmina (Boxheimer) Brauler; m. Joseph S. Fern, Mar. 31, 1956. AA in Criminal Justice, Miami-Dade C.C., 1975. Adminstrv. asst. Lucayan Beach Hotel, Bahamas, 1956-68, Loew's Hotels, Miami Beach, Fla., 1968-70; intelligence analyst Metro-Dade Police Dept., Miami, 1970-78; crime intelligence analyst supr. Fla. Dept. Law Enforcement, Miami, 1978—. Recipient award Fla. Dept. Law Enforcement for disting. contbn. to criminal justice, 1984, U.S. Dept. Justice award for pub. svc. Mem. Internat. Assn. Law Enforcement Intelligence Analysts (charter, pres. 1990-96). Home: 1365 NW 192nd Ter Miami FL 33169-3442

FERNÁNDEZ, ALBERTO ANTONIO, security professional; b. Santiago de Cuba, Oriente, Cuba, May 21, 1945; came to the U.S., 1962; s. Carlos and Lydia (Sotera) F.; m. Alexis Quesada, July 19, 1968 (div. July 1984); children: Gyselle, Alexander; m. Rebeca Perez, Sept. 7, 1984; 1 child, Yanelle. Computer programmer, Fla. Computer Coll., 1968; police officer, Metro Dade Police Acad., 1970; AA, Miami (Fla.) Dade C.C., 1973; BS in Criminology, Fla. Internat. U., 1994; drug enforcement spl. agt., DEA Spl. Tng. Sch., 1977. Lic. pvt. investigator, Fla. Police officer Metro Dade Police, Miami, 1969-75; spl. agt. Drug Enforcement Adminstrn., 1976-88; ret., 1988; chief security advisor A.P.A. Internat. Airline, Miami, 1995-96, Faucett Internat. Airline, Miami, 1995-96, Servivensa Internat. Airline, Miami, 1996—. Recipient Recognition award for fighting against drugs Dominican Govt., 1987; named Police Officer of Yr., Kiwanis Club, Miami, 1971. Mem. Assn. Former Fed. Narcotic Agts., Fla. Internat. U. Alumni.

FERNANDEZ, GUILLERMO J., ophthalmologist, medical-paralegal consultant; b. San Juan, P.R., Dec. 25, 1928; s. Guillermo and Margarita (Marti) F.; m. Casilda Sanchez Toro. MD, U. Madrid, 1958; postgrad. in ophthalmology, NYU, 1959-60. Diplomate P.R. Bd. Med. Examiners. Intern Presbyn. Hosp., San Juan, P.R., 1958-59; preceptor in ophthalmology Eye Inst. P.R., San Juan, 1960-63; pvt. practice ophthalmologist San Juan, 1963—; chief of surgery Eye Inst. P.R., 1972-76, 83-90, bd. dirs., 1963-90. Chmn. Orlando (Fla.) Civil Svc. Bd., 1994—. Fellow ACS, Am. Acad. Ophthalmology; mem. AMA, Fla. Med. Assn., Fla. Soc. Ophthalmology, P.R. Med. Soc. Home: 3924 Orange Lake Dr Orlando FL 32817

FERNANDEZ, HENRY A., professional association administrator, lawyer; b. Bklyn., Dec. 5, 1949; s. Henry and Pura (Perez) F. BA Sociology, St. John's U., 1971; student, Empire State Military Acad. Army Reserve Nat. Guard, Peekskill, N.Y., 1972-73; JD, Bklyn. Law Sch., 1977. Bar: N.Y. 1978, U.S. Dist. Ct. (so. and ea. dists.) N.Y. 1978, U.S. Dist. Ct. (no. dist.) N.Y. 1981. Supr. Hornblower & Weeks Hemphill-Noyes, 1967-72; ednl. counselor, devel. exec. Aspira of N.Y. and Am., Inc., 1972-74; field placement counselor Bur. Coop. Edn. N.Y.C. Bd. Edn., 1974-75; dir. Coll. Adapter Program Higher Edn. Devel. Fund, 1975-77; vis. atty., grad. honors fellow Puerto Rican Legal Defense and Edn. Fund Inc., 1977-79; staff atty. Williamsburg Legal Svcs., 1979-81; asst. counsel N.Y. State Office Mental Health, 1981-86; dir. adminstrn. Capital Dist. Psych. Ctr., 1986-88; dir. Bur. Investigation and Audit N.Y. State Office Mental Health, 1988; state rev. officer N.Y. State Edn. Dept., 1990-93; dep. commr. U. State N.Y., 1988-93; pres., CEO Assn. of Univ. Programs in Health Adminstrn., Arlington, Va., 1993—; bd. dirs., pres. Coun. Licensure Enforcement & Regulation, program com., fin. com. 1989, vice chair fin. com. 1989-90, pres.-elect 1991-92, treas. 1991-92, pres. 1992-93; bd. dirs. Am. Occptl. Therapy Certification Bd. Mem. N.Y. State Coun. Grad. Med. Edn., 1990-93; bd. dirs. N.Y. State Divsn. Youth Independent rev. bd., 1977-88, Legal Aid Soc. Northeastern N.Y., chair labor rels. com., exec., policy, nomination com. Recipient Disting. Svc. Citation N.Y. State Chiropractic Assn., 1991, Presdl. Citation Assn. Architects, AIA, 1991; Hispanic Health Leadership fellow Nat. Coalition Hispanic Health and Human Svc. Orgns., Kellogg Found., 1990-91; DeGray Meml. scholar St. John's U., 1967-71; Bklyn. Law Sch. scholar, 1973-77. Fellow N.Y. Acad. Medicine, N.Y. State Bar Found.; mem. N.Y. State Bar Assn. (chair com. Minorities in Profession 1990-94, Labor and Employment law sect. 1982-92, com. Mental and Phys. Disabilities 1986-88, com. atty. professionalis 1989-92, Action Unit 4 1993-94), Puerto Rican Bar Assn. (Capital dist. chpt. pres. 1986-88), N.Y. Health Careers (adv. coun.), Coun. State Govs. (exec. com. 1992-93, VA bd. nursing home adminstrn. 1993—, Coalition Hispanic Health Human Svc. Orgn. (treas., bd. dirs. 1994—). Home: 9607 Crosspointe Dr Fairfax Station VA 22039 Office: Assn Univ Prog Hlth Admin 1911 Fort Myer Dr Ste 503 Arlington VA 22209-1603

FERNANDEZ, ISABEL LIDIA, human resources specialist; b. Miami, Fla., Jan. 23, 1964; d. Rafael Juvencio and Lidia Rafaela (Morin) Fernandez. BBA, Fla. Internat. U., Miami, 1984, MS in Hospitality Mgmt., 1990. Personnel cons. Miami, 1984—; asst. dir. human resources Turnberry Isle Yacht & Country Club, Miami, 1985-87; dir. personnel Sheraton River House, Miami, 1987-88; program dir. hospitality mgmt. programs Miami-Dade Community Coll., 1988-89; dir. human resources Doubletree Hotel, Miami, 1989-91, Sky Chefs, Miami, 1991-93; tng. cons. Barnett Banks Inc., Miami, 1993—. Editor newspaper The Sunblazer, 1983-84; contbr. articles to profl. jours. Founder South Fla. Diversity Coun. Named Employee of the Month, Coconut Grove Hotel, Miami, 1985. Mem. NAFE, Am. Hotel and Motel Assn. (pres. Greater Miami chpt.), Young Reps. Club (pub. rels. coun.). Republican. Lutheran. Home: 8510 NW 3rd Ln # 501 Miami FL 33126-3857

FERNANDEZ, JOSEPH ANTHONY, educational administrator; b. 1935. BA in Edn., U. Miami, 1963; MEd, Fla. Atlantic U., 1970; EdD, Nova U., 1985; HHD (hon.), Marymount Manhattan Coll., N.Y.C., 1990, Bank St. Coll. Edn., N.Y.C., 1990, CUNY, 1990; LHD, CUNY, 1990, Bank Street Coll. Edn., 1990. Former tchr. math., former supt. Dade County Pub. Schs., Miami; chancellor N.Y.C. Pub. Schs., 1990-93; pres., CEO Sch. Improvement Svcs., Inc., Winter Park, Fla., 1993—. Pres. Coun. of the Great City Schs., Washington. Office: Sch Improvement Svcs Inc 1240 Wellington Ter Maitland FL 32751

FERNÁNDEZ, YOLANDA GARZA, librarian; b. Weslaco, Tex., Mar. 8, 1954; d. Faustino and Teresa (Palacios) Garza; m. James Michael Fernández, June 9, 1979; children: Javier René, Ana Yadira. BA, Pan Am. U., Edinburg, Tex., 1975; MLS, Sam Houston State U., 1989. Cert. secondary tchr., Tex. Reading tchr. Mercedes (Tex.) Jr. High, 1975-76; tchr. English Mary Hoge Jr. High., Weslaco, Tex., 1976-84; libr. Santa Maria (Tex.) Ind. Sch. Dist., 1985-89; head libr. high sch. South Tex. Ind. Sch. Dist., Mercedes, 1989—; libr. h.s. Progreso (Tex.) Ind. Sch. Dist., 1994—. Pres. Parish Pastoral Coun., Progreso, Tex., 1989—. Mem. Assn. Tex. Profl. Educators (pres. Weslaco chpt. 1980-81), Tex. Assn. Sch. Librs., Tex. Libr. Assn., Valley Interfaith. Democrat. Roman Catholic. Home: PO Box 146 Toluca Ranch Progreso TX 78579 Office: Progreso Ind Sch Dist Farm Rd 1015 Progreso TX 78579

FERNANDEZ-MARTINEZ, JOSE, physician; b. San Juan, P.R., Apr. 2, 1930; s. Telesforo and Luisa (Martinez) Fernandez; m. Carmen Dolores Noya, Dec. 26, 1954. BS, Villanova U., 1951; MD, U. Pa., 1955. Diplomate Am. Bd. Internal Medicine, Sub-Bd. Cardiovascular Diseases. Intern U. Pa. Hosps., Phila., 1955-56, resident in internal medicine, 1956-59, fellow in hypertension and cardiovascular diseases, 1956-57; practice medicine specializing in cardiovascular diseases Santurce, P.R., 1961—; attending physician in internal medicine San Juan City Hosp., 1961—; assoc. prof. medicine U. P.R., 1978-88, prof. Sch. of Medicine, 1988—. Served to capt. U.S. Army, 1959-61. Fellow ACP, Am. Coll. Cardiology; mem. P.R. Med. Assn. (pres. sci. coun. 1968), Alpha Omega Alpha. Office: Ashford Med Ctr Ashford & Washington Sts Ste 208 Santurce PR 00907

FERO, LESTER K., aerospace engineer, consultant; b. Beaver Dams, N.Y., Feb. 28, 1919; s. Ray L. and Bertha (Kniffin) F.; m. Margery G. Wilde, Sept. 11, 1944; children: Gregory G. (dec.), Leslie Kay. BS in Aerospace Engring., U. Mich., 1940. Structures engr. Curtiss-Wright, Buffalo, 1940-46; v.p. Dansaire Corp., Dansville, N.Y., 1946-47; chief structural engr. Bell Aircraft, Niagara Falls, N.Y., 1947-56; program mgr. Martin Co., Balt., 1956-63, NASA Hdqrs., Washington, 1963-70; staff asst. NASC/Exec. Office of Pres., Washington, 1970-72; dir. space transp. plans NASA Hdqrs., Washington, 1972-82; pres., chief engr. Fero Enterprises, Inc., Bowie, Md., 1984-87, Loudon, Tenn., 1987—; guest lectr. U. Mich., Ann Arbor, 1953. Pres. Community Assn., Lutherville, Md., 1960. Recipient Achievement awards NASA, 1969, 75, 82. Assoc. fellow AIAA (chmn. Balt. sect. 1961).

FERRANTI, JENNIFER, journalist; b. Perth Amboy, N.J., Jan. 19, 1954; d. Joan D. (Vorhauer) McCarthy; m. Daniel V. Ferranti, Nov. 10, 1990. BA in Journalism, Marquette U., 1975. Dir. planning and devel. N. Def. Trust, Washington, 1988-89; press sec. Fred Koory for Ariz. Gov. Campaign, Phoenix, 1990; freelance journalist, Dunn Loring, Va., 1991—. Mng. editor Ideas Mag., 1991-94; publ., editor: Footprints Publs., Phoenix, 1984-88; contbr. articles to mags. and periodicals including McCall's, Saturday Evening Post, Charisma, Christianity Today, World, Christian Legal Soc.'s quar. jour., Focus on the Family's Citizen, numerous others. Named Writer of the Yr. Am. Christian Writers, Washington, 1995, Greater Phila. Christian Writers Fellowship, 1995. Mem. Soc. Profl. Journalists, Evang. Press Assn., No. Va. Christian Writers Fellowship, Washington Ind. Writers. Republican. Office: PO Box 629 Dunn Loring VA 22027

FERRARI, THOMAS J., physician; b. Rockville Ctr., N.Y., Dec. 12, 1955; s. Reynold Louis and Veronica Ethel Ferrari. BS in Pharmacology, Fla. A&M U., 1978, PharmD, 1984; MD, Am U. of the Caribbean, Montserrat, 1988, MS, 1986. Residency in internal medicine Mt. Sinai Med. Ctr., Milw., 1991; chief of staff Appling Gen. Hosp., Baxley, Ga., 1993—. Home: RR 7 Box 650-c Baxley GA 31513-8703

FERRAZ, FRANCISCO MARCONI, neurological surgeon; b. Floresta, Pernambuco, Brazil, Aug. 14, 1951; came to U.S., 1976. Student, Colegio Nobrega, Recife-Brazil, 1967-69; MD, Faculdade de Medicine da Universidade Federal de Pernambuco-Brazil, 1975. Diplomate Am. Bd. Neurol. Surgery. Intern, Jamaica Hosp., N.Y.C., 1976-77; resident Georgetown U. Med. Ctr. and Affiliated Hosps., Washington, 1977-82; pvt. practice medicine specializing in neurol. surgery, Washington, 1982—; staff Georgetown U. Hosp., 1982—, Arlington Hosp., 1982—; chief div. neurosurgery, faculty clin. instr. Georgetown U. Sch. Medicine, 1988—; faculty clin. assoc. prof. George Washington Sch. Medicine; cons. in field. Contbr. articles to profl. jours. Mem. AMA, Am. Assn. Neurol. Surgeons, Pan Am. Med. Soc., D.C. Med. Soc., Arlington Med. Soc., Neurosurg. Soc. of D.C., Washington Medico Surg. Soc., Washington Acad. Neurosurgery, Congress of Neurol. Surgery.

FERRE, ANTONIO LUIS, newspaper publisher; b. Ponce, P.R., Feb. 6, 1934; s. Luis A. and Lorenza (Ramirez de Arellano) F.; m. Luisa Rangel, Feb. 23, 1963; children: Maria Luisa, Antonio Luis, Luis Alberto, Maria Eugenia, Maria Lorenza. AB magna cum laude, Amherst Coll., 1955, PhD in Humanities (hon.), 1995; MBA, Harvard U., 1957; student, Inst. for Sr. Mgmt. and Govt. Execs., Dartmouth Coll.; PhD in Comm. Sci. (hon.), U. Turabo, 1992. Chmn Puerto Rican Cement Co.; vice chmn. Banco Popular; pres., editor El Nuevo Dia, 1968—; mem. adv. coun. Met. Life; chmn. P.R. Conservation Trust. Author: (essays) Un Alto en el Camino; Pan, Paz y Palabra; also numerous newspaper editorials. Pres. P.R. Coun. on Higher Edn., 1966-68, Gov.'s Adv. Coun., 1968-72; mem. Gov.'s Labor Adv. Coun., 1975; pres. Com. for Econ Devel. P.R.; vice chmn. Ponce Mus. Art. With U.S. Army, 1958. Recipient Presdl. citation, 1976. Mem. P.R. Mfrs. Assn. (pres. 1965-66), Am. Mgmt. Assn. (President's Assn. 1963—), Coun. of Fgn. Rels., Inter-Am. Dialogue, P.R. C. of C., Dorado Beach and Golf Club, Bankers Club P.R., Club Deportivo de Ponce, Phi Beta Kappa. Roman Catholic.

FERRÉ, FREDERICK POND, philosophy, religion, technology and ethics educator; b. Boston, Mar. 23, 1933; s. Nels F.S. and Katharine Louise (Pond) F.; m. Marie Booth, June 8, 1954 (div. July 18, 1980); 1 child, Katharine Marie.; m. Barbara Meister, June 12, 1982. Student, Oberlin Coll., 1950-51; A.B. summa cum laude (Prof. Augustus Howe Buck fellow), Boston U., 1954; M.A., Vanderbilt U., 1955; Ph.D. (Fulbright fellow, Kent fellow), U. St. Andrews, Scotland, 1959. Comml. pilot certified flight instr. Vis. asst. prof. philosophy Vanderbilt U., 1958-59; asst. prof. religion Mt. Holyoke Coll., 1959-62; asso. prof. philosophy Dickinson Coll., Carlisle, Pa., 1962-67, prof. philosophy, 1967-80, Charles A. Dana prof., 1970-80; prof. philosophy, head dept. philosophy and religion U. Ga., Athens, 1980-84, head dept. philosophy, 1984-88, chmn. faculty of environ. ethics, 1984-91; research prof. of philosophy U. Ga., 1988—; vis. prof. So. Meth. U., 1964-65, Bucknell U., 1965-66, Pitts. Theol. Sem., 1968-69, Princeton Theol. Sem., 1970-71, Vancouver Sch. Theology, 1978, Iliff Sch. Theology, 1983, U. Erlangen-Nürnberg, Fed. Republic Germany, 1986; Eli Lilly vis. prof. sci., theology and human values Purdue U., 1974-75; vis. prof. philosophy and tech. and pub. policy Vanderbilt U., 1977-78. Author: Language, Logic and God, 1961, Exploring the Logic of Faith, 1962, Paley's Natural Theology, 1963, Basic Modern Philosophy of Religion, 1967, Comte's Introduction to Positive Philosophy, 1970, Shaping the Future, 1976, The Challenge of Religion, 1982, God and Global Justice, 1985, Philosophy of Technology, 1988, Concepts of Nature and God, 1989, Hellfire and Lightning Rods, 1993, Ethics and Environmental Policy, 1994, Being and Value, 1996; gen. editor Research in Philosophy and Tech., 1986-94; chief cons. New World View film series, 1985-92; editorial bd. Am. Jour. Theology and Philosophy, Jour. of Religion, Personalist Forum, Am. Philos. Quar., Environ. Ethics, Philos. Forum, Proteus, Faith and Philosophy; editorial bd. U. Ga. Press. dir. Concepts of Nature and God, NEH, Athens, 1987. NEH fellow, 1969-70; NEH fellow Nat. Humanities Inst., U. Chgo., 1978-79. Mem. Am. Assn. U. Profs. (nat. council 1973-76), Am. Philos. Assn. (program com. 1973-74, nominating com. 1980-82), Philosophy Sci. Assn., Metaphys. Soc. Am. (program chmn. 1971-72, councillor 1975-79), Am. Theol. Soc. (exec. com. 1970-73, treas. 1972-73, v.p. 1975-76, pres. 1976-77), Nat. Humanities Faculty, Am. Council Learned Socs. (del. 1982-85), Soc. Philosophy of Religion (pres. 1985-86), Phi Beta Kappa (pres. chpt. 1971-74). Home: 275 Davis Estate Rd Athens GA 30606-5009

FERRÉ, SUSAN INGRID, musician; b. Boston, Sept. 5, 1945; d. Gustave Adolf and Dorothy Elizabeth (Fredericks) F.; m. K. Charles Lang, June 18, 1980; 1 child, Carl Christophe Ferré-Lang. BA, BMus, Tex. Christian U., 1968; diploma, Schola Cantorum, Paris, 1969; MMus, Eastman Sch. Music, 1971; DMA, North Tex. State U., 1979. Instr. U. Paris, Vincennes, France, 1969-70; mem. adj. faculty U. North Tex., Denton, 1974-79, Perkins Sch. Theology, Dallas, 1982-92, So. Meth. U., Dallas, 1987-93; concert artist worldwide, 1980—; organ cons. chs. Tex., 1980—, dir. music, organist, 1962—; guest conductor Am. southwest, 1975—. Dir. Tex. Baroque Ensemble, 1981—, Early Music at Round Top, Tex., 1986—. Fulbright Found. grantee, 1968-69. Mem. Am. Guild Organists (dean 1991-93), Am. Organ Academy (bd. dirs.), Am. Bach Soc., Westfield Ctr. for Early Keyboard Studies, Organ Hist. Soc., Early Music Am. Home: 2221 Royal Crest Dr Garland TX 75043

FERREE, PATRICIA ANN, corporate managed care analyst, nurse; b. Middletown, N.Y., Oct. 5, 1947; d. William Harry and Florence Arlene (Sarr) Krenrich; m. Daniel Milton Ferree, Feb. 13, 1972; children: Patricia Ann, Daniel Milton Jr. AS, Cen. Fla. Community Coll., Ocala, 1969; BS in Nursing, Va. Commonwealth U., 1985. Cert. cardiac nurse therapist. Critical care nurse Fla. Hosp., Orlando, 1969-76, cardiac nurse therapist, 1976-80, head nurse cardiac rehab., 1980-82; nurse adminstrn., rsch. nurse Va. Heart Inst., Richmond, 1982-86; coord. health care cost containment Cir. City Stores, Inc., Richmond, 1986, mgr. health and safety, 1986-89, corp. mgr. workers' compensation and safety, 1989-93, corp. mgr. workers compensation, 1993-94, corp. sr. analyst for managed care unit in risk mgmt. dept., 1994—. Choir dir. Courthouse Rd. Seventh-Day Adventist Ch., Richmond, 1983-89, min. music, 1989-94; mem. curriculum com. Richmond Acad. Home and Sch. Leader; chmn. cardiovascular task force Am. Heart Assn., 1984-85. Recipient svc. plaque cardiology dept. Fla. Hosp., 1982; Peggy Gibson Meml. nursing scholar, 1967, Fla. Bd. Edn. nursing scholar, 1967-69. Mem. Am. Assn. Occupational Health Nurses, Am. Soc. Safety Engrs., Soc. Nursing Profls., Am. Assn. for Cardiovascular and Pulmonary Rehab. (founding), Richmond Met. Soc. for Cardiac Rehab. (founding), Phi Kappa Phi, Sigma Zeta. Republican. Office: Cir City Stores Inc 9950 Mayland Dr Richmond VA 23233-1463

FERRELL, J(AMES) GLENN, minister; b. Majestic, Ky., May 6, 1949; s. Carl Hanson and Lillian (Blankenship)uF.; m. Barbara Jean Humphreys, Nov. 2, 1979; children: Blake Anthony, Micah Judah, Hannah Maryah, Noah Baruch. BA, Warren Wilson Coll., 1971; postgrad., Princeton Theol. Sem., 1971-72, Louisville Theol. Sem., 1972-73, U. Dayton, 1976-78; MDiv, Fuller Theol. Sem., 1986. Ordained to ministry Evang. Presbyn. ch., 1988. Tng. mgr. Communicam, Inc., Culver City, Calif., 1981-84; sr. analyst data comms. World Vision U.S., Monrovia, Calif., 1984-86; community devel. cons. World Vision U.S., Ea. Ky., 1986—; evangelist, ch. planter Evang. Presbyn. Ch., Ea. Ky., 1988—; exec. sec. Appalachin Evang. Mission, Denniston, Ky., 1991—. Contbr. articles Christian Observer. Del. Nat. Conv. U.S. Taxpayers Party Conv., New Orleans, 1992. With U.S. Army, 1973-76. Home: PO Box 98 Denniston KY 40316-0098 Office: Appalachin Evang Mission PO Box 98 Denniston KY 40316-0098

FERRELL, MICHAEL TIMOTHY, academic administration; b. Oakland, Calif., Sept. 26, 1949; s. William Tiffany and Mamie Sue (Kent) F.; m. Elizabeth Suzanne Nessmith, Apr. 2, 1977; children: Richard Leonard, Michael Timothy II. BS, La. State U. in Shreveport, 1975. Office mgr. H&H Oil Co., Shreveport, 1975-77; from asst. dir. acctg. svcs. to vice chancellor bus. affairs La. State U., Shreveport, 1977—. Fin. com. Fellowship United Meth. Ch., Bossier City, La., 1995; coach Bellaire Baptist Ch., Bossier City, 1985-89, YMCA, Bossier City, 1975-84. Served in U.S. Navy, 1968-74. Office: LA State U in Shreveport One University Pl Shreveport LA 71115

FERRELL, MILTON MORGAN, JR., lawyer; b. Coral Gables, Fla., Nov. 6, 1951; s. Milton M. and Annie (Blanche) Bradley; m. Lori R. Sanders, May 22, 1982; children: Milton Morgan III, Whitney Connolly. BA, Mercer U., 1973, JD, 1975. Bar: Fla. 1975. Asst. state's atty. State's Atty.'s Office, Miami, 1975-77; ptnr. Ferrell & Ferrell, Miami, 1977-84; sole practice Miami, 1985-87; ptnr. Ferrell & Williams, P.A., Miami, 1987-90, Ferrell & Fertel, P.A., Miami, 1990—. Trustee Mus. Sci. and Space Transit Planetarium, 1977-82; mem. Ambs. of Mercy, Mercy Hosp. Found., Inc., 1985-94; trustee, mem. legal com., chair com. U. Miami Project to Cure Paralysis, 1985-94. Fellow Nat. Assn. Criminal Def. Lawyers, Am. Bd. Criminal Lawyers (bd. govs. 1981-82, sec. 1983-84, v.p. 1984-86, pres. 1987-88); mem. ABA (grantee 1975), Fla. Bar Assn. (jury instrns. com. 1987-88, chmn. grievance com. 11-L 1989-91), Dade County Bar Assn. (bd. dirs. 1977-80), Bath Club (bd. govs. 1992-95), Miami Club, Banker's Club, Cat Cay Yacht Club, Ltd. Home: Bay Point 4511 Lake Rd Miami FL 33137-3372 Office: Ferrell & Fertel PA 201 S Biscayne Blvd Ste 1920 Miami FL 33131-4329

FERRIS, JAMES LEONARD, academic administrator; b. Bellingham, Wash., Jan. 15, 1944; s. Gerald Durward and Esther Evelyn (Larson) F.; m. Virginia Marie Dowde, June 23, 1972; children: Eric, Heidi. BSChemE, U. Wash., 1966; MS in Pulp and Paper Sci., Lawrence U., Appleton, Wis., 1969, PhD in Pulp and Paper Sci., 1974; Advanced Mgmt. Program, Harvard Bus. Sch., 1992. Mill engr. Weyerhaeuser Paper Co., Everett, Wash., 1966-67, scientist R & D dept., 1974-75; mgr. tech. svcs. pulp div. Weyerhaeuser Paper Co., Tacoma, 1975-80, dir. R & D, 1980-85, mgr. mfg. pulp div., 1985-88, v.p. rsch., 1988-96; pres. Inst. Paper Sci. and Tech., Atlanta, 1996—; trustee Pulp and Paper Found., Miami U., Oxford, Ohio, 1989—, Ga. Tech. Rsch. Corp., 1996—. Lt. (j.g.) USN, 1970-72, Vietnam. Mem. TAPPI (chmn. rsch. com.). Office: Inst Paper Sci and Tech 500 Tenth St Atlanta GA 30318

FERRIS, KATHLEEN RICHARD, English language educator and professional; b. Baldwin, La., Sept. 30, 1941; d. Arthur Edward and Loretta Anne (Bienvenu) Richard; m. Norman Bernard Ferris, Feb. 24, 1961; children: Kennedy Adams, Julie Elizabeth; stepchildren: Allison Ferris Pierce, Cheryl, Adrienne Ferris Johnson. BA in English and French, Mid. Tenn. State U., 1974, MA in English, 1980; PhD in English, Emory U., 1989. Assoc. prof. English Lincoln Meml. U., Harrogate, Tenn., 1988—. Author: James Joyce and the Burden of Disease, 1995. Mem. Rutherford County Dem. Women, Murfreesboro, 1971—, pres., 1972. Recipient Houston award for excellence in teaching, 1993, Lincoln award for profl. achievement, 1995; Mellon Appalachian fellow Faculty Scholars Program, U. Ky., 1994-95. Mem. MLA, AAUW, AAUP, South Atlantic MLA, Am. Conf. for Irish Studies, James Joyce Internat. Found. Home: 3210 E Compton Rd Murfreesboro TN 37130-6868 Office: Lincoln Meml U PO Box 1685 Harrogate TN 37752-1000

FERRIS, NORMAN BERNARD, history educator; b. Richmond, Va., Nov. 29, 1931; s. Paul Whyte and Elizabeth (Gillette) F.; m. Kathleen Anne Richard, Feb. 21, 1961; children: Allison Paige Ferris Pierce, Cheryl Adair, Adrienne Leigh Ferris Johnson, Kennedy Adams, Julie Elizabeth. AA, Lamar Coll., 1951; BA, George Washington U., 1953; LLB, Blackstone Law Sch., Chgo., 1956; MA, Emory U., 1957, PhD, 1962. Instr. Emory U., Atlanta, 1959-60; asst. prof. U. Southwestern La., Lafayette, 1960-61; asst. prof. Mid. Tenn. State U., Murfreesboro, 1962-65, assoc. prof., 1965-69, prof., 1969—; mem. Tenn. Humanities Coun., Nashville, 1979-85, chair, 1983-84; chair Tenn. Bd. of Regents Faculty Subcoun., Nashville, 1987-88. Author: Desperate Diplomacy, 1976, The Trent Affair, 1977 (Pulitzer nominee 1977); contbr. numerous articles to profl. jours. Secretary Rutherford County Dems., Murfreesboro, 1972-78; mem. Rutherford County U.S. Constn. Bicentennial Commn., Murfreesboro, 1987-91. Lt. (j.g.) USN, 1953-57. NEH grantee, 1979-80. Mem. AAUP (pres. Tenn. Conf. 1978-80, 84, coun. 1980-83, 85-89, chair nat. assembly state confs. 1985-87, Claxton award 1991, Sumberg award 1996), Am. Hist. Assn., Orgn. Am. Historians, Southern Hist. Assn., Soc. for Historians of Am. Fgn. Rels. Home: 3210 E Compton Rd Murfreesboro TN 37130-6868 Office: Mid Tenn State U Dept Of History Murfreesboro TN 37132

FERRISS, ABBOTT LAMOYNE, sociology educator emeritus; b. Jonestown, Miss., Jan. 31, 1915; s. Alfred William Overby and Grace Chiles (Mitchell) F.; m. Ruth Elizabeth Sparks, Dec. 21, 1940; children—John Abbott, William Thomas. B.J., U. Mo., 1937; M.A., U. N.C., 1943, Ph.D., 1950. Asst. prof. sociology Vanderbilt U., 1949-51; research social scientist Human Resources Research Inst., Air U., 1951-54; chief unit effectiveness br. Air Force Personnel and Tng. Res. Ctr., 1954-57; chief health survey br. Bur. of Census, 1957-59; supervisory survey statistician Outdoor Recreation Resources Rev. Commn., 1959-62; asst. study dir. NSF, 1962-67; research sociologist Russell Sage Found., 1967-70; prof. sociology Emory U., 1970-82, chmn. dept., 1970-76; lectr. George Washington U., 1958-59, U. Md., 1959-61, No. Va. Ctr. of U. Va., 1960-70; guest prof. ZUMA, Mannheim, Fed. Republic Germany, 1989. Served with USAAF, 1943-46; CBI. NSF grantee, 1976-78. Mem. Internat. Soc. Quality of Life studies, Am. Sociol. Soc., Sociol. Research Assn., So. Sociol. Soc. (pres. 1986-87, editor The So. Sociologist 1981-84), Population Assn. Am. (sec.-treas. 1968-71), Ga. Sociol. Assn. (cert. of merit 1989), D.C. Sociol. Soc. (sec.-treas. 1965-68, pres. 1969-70, Stuart Rice award 1984), Midsouth Sociol. Assn., Internat. Sociol. Assn. Democrat. Episcopalian. Club: Cosmos (Washington). Author: National Recreation Survey, 1962; Indicators of Trends in the Status of American Women, 1971; Indicators of Change in the American Family, 1970; Indicators of Trends in American Education, 1969; Attitudes of Far Eastern Air Force Personnel Toward Natives, 1953; editor: Research and the 1970 Census, 1971; (with J.C. Glidwell) Reducing Traffic Accidents by Use of Group Discussions-Decision: An a priori Evaluation, 1957; editor, pub. SINET (Social Indicators Network News), 1984-95; editor So. Sociologist, 1981-84; assoc. editor Social Forces, 1976-79; editor PAA Affairs, 1968-71, SINET Selections, 1990—; mem. editorial bd. Social Indicators Research, 1980—. Home: 1273 Oxford Rd NE Atlanta GA 30306-2426

FERRITOR, DANIEL E., university official; b. Kansas City, Mo., Nov. 8, 1939; m. Patricia Jean Ferritor; children: Kimberly Ann, Kristin Marie, Sean Patrick. BA, Rockhurst Coll., 1962; MA, Washington U., St. Louis, 1967, PhD, 1969. Tchr. grade sch. Raytown, Mo., 1962-64; program assoc., asst. dir. Nat. Program on Early Childhood Edn., 1970-71; asst. program dir. CEMREL Inc., St. Ann, Mo., 1969-70, assoc. dir. instrnl. systems program, 1970-71; asst. prof. sociology U. Ark., Fayetteville, 1967-68, assoc. prof., 1973-79, prof., 1979-85, chmn. dept., 1973-85, vice chancellor for acad. affairs, provost, 1985-86, chancellor, 1986—. Author: (with Robert L. Hamblin, D. Buckholdt, M. Kozloff and L. Blackwell) The Humanization Processes, 1971; contbr. articles to profl. jours. Office: U Ark Office of Chancellor Fayetteville AR 72701*

FERRY, JAMES P., physical education educator; b. Mineola, N.Y., Feb. 7, 1970; s. Richard E. and Barbara D. (Birley) Jedrey. BS in Edn., Troy State U., 1993. Cert. tchr., Ga. Tchr., coach Metter (Ga.) H.S., Candler County Bd. Edn., 1994—. Mem. AAHPERD, Nat. Coun. Tchrs. Math., Kappa Delta Pi, Gamma Beta Phi, Phi Eta Sigma. Home: 200 Candler St Metter GA 30439

FERSTEL, VICKI HUTT, reporter; b. N.Y.C., Feb. 24, 1954; d. Abraham and Shirley Irene (Kizelstein) Hutt; m. John William Ferstel, May 11, 1974 (div. 1984); 1 child, Sarah Dorothy Ferstel. AB in Journalism, Polit. Sci., Syracuse U., 1976. Reporter The Daily News, Jennings, La., 1977-78; reporter The Daily Iberian, New Iberia, La., 1978-80; VISTA coord. So. Mut. Help Assn., Jeanerette, La., 1980-81; news dir. Sta. KANE-AM, New Iberia, 1981-87, Sta. WYNK-FM, Baton Rouge, La., 1987-88; bur. chief The Advocate, Baton Rouge, 1988—. Author: (article, speech) Future of Black-Jewish Relations, Nat. Conf. of Blacks-Jews, Dillard U., 1993. Mem. Press Club of Baton Rouge, 1988-90, La. Press Women, 1988—. Recipient La.-Miss. AP Managing Editors award, 1995, Environ. Reporting award Nat. Fedn. Press Women, 1992, 94, 95, Broadcast award Mental Health Assn. in La., 1987-88, Broadcast Editorial award Radio-TV News Dirs. Assn. La./Miss., 1985, Broadcast Reporting award La. Assn. Educators, 1983. Jewish. Home: 15135 Woodlore Dr Baton Rouge LA 70816-1557 Office: The Advocate River Parishes Bur PO Box 1295 Gonzales LA 70707-1295

FERTEL, RUTH U., restaurant owner; b. 1927. Pres. Ruth's Chris Steak House, New Orleans, 1965—. Office: Ruth's Chris Steak House 711 N Broad St New Orleans LA 70119

FERTITTA, ROBERT S., dean; b. Balt., Oct. 26, 1940. BA, U. Md., 1962; LLB, U. Md., Balt., 1964. Bar: Md. 1964, Tex. 1974. Clk. Ct. of Appeals of Md., 1964-65; asst. state's atty. Md., 1966-71; assoc. dean Nat. Coll. of Dist. Attys., Houston, 1971-94; dean, 1994—. Mem. ABA, Houston Bar Assn., Tex. Bar Assn., Tex. Dist. and County Attys. Assn., Nat. Dist. Attys. Assn. Office: Nat Coll Dist Attys Univ Houston Law Ctr 4800 Calhoun Rd Houston TX 77204-6382

FESTA, EDWARD J., company executive. Pres. Seabrook Enterprises, Atlanta. Office: Seabrook Enterprises 100 Galleria Pky Ste 580 Atlanta GA 30339

FETCHERO, JOHN ANTHONY, JR., otorhinolaryngologist; b. Jeannette, Pa., June 4, 1951; s. John Anthony Sr. and Cleda (Byerly) F.; m. Wynona Ann Kestler, Feb. 26, 1982; children: John Anthony III, Christopher Jason, Dominic Vincent, Victor Thomas. BS in Biology, St. Vincent Coll., 1973; DO, Coll. Osteo. Medicine, Des Moines, 1976. Intern Des Moines Gen. Hosp., 1976-77; Flight surgeon Naval Aero. Med. Inst., Pensacola, Fla., 1977-78; resident Nat. Naval Med. Ctr., Bethesda, Md., 1980-84; otorhinolaryngologist, oro-facial plastic surgeon Am. Co. Osteo. Opthalmology and Otorhinolaryngology, 1987; otolaryngologist Am. Coll. Otolaryngology, Chgo., 1988; pvt. practice Orange Park, Fla., 1988—. Mem. Julington Creek (Fla.) Civic Assn., 1988—. With USNR, 1973—. Med. Sch. scholar USN, 1973-76. Mem. Fla. Osteo. Assn., Osteo. Acad. Otorhinolaryngology, Am. Acad. Otolaryngology, Am. Osteo. Assn., Fla. Med. Assn., Clay County Med. Soc. Republican. Roman Catholic. Home: 1474 Fruit Cove Forest Rd Jacksonville FL 32259-2811

FETTERMAN, ANNABELLE, packing company executive. Ceo. Lundy Packing Co., Clinton, N.C. Office: Lundy Packing Co PO Box 49 Clinton NC 28328-0049*

FETTERMAN, JAMES C., lawyer; b. Charleston, W.Va., Apr. 13, 1947; s. Kenneth Lee and Sara Jane (Shaffer) F.; m. Patricia Alice Shewmake, June 8, 1968; children: Janet, Paula, Kenneth, David. BA, Miss. State U., 1969, MA, 1970; JD, U. Miss., Oxford, 1972; MBA, St. Louis U., 1985. Bar: Miss. 1972, Sarasota County, U.S. Dist. Ct. (no. dist.) Miss. 1972, U.S. Ct. Mil. Appeals 1972, U.S. Dist. Ct. (mid. dist.) Fla. 1986, U.S. Tax Ct. 1986, U.S. Ct. Appeals (11th cir.) 1986. Staff atty. First Miss. Corp., Jackson, 1976-77; cert. of need adminstr. Office of Gov. State of Miss., Jackson, 1977-78; adminstrator, prin. investigator Miss. Bd. Nursing, Jackson, 1978-79; asst. prof., head dept. fin. Jackson State U., 1979-82; asst. prof. dept. mgmt sci. St. Louis U., Mo., 1982-86; ptnr. Borza Fetterman, Sardelis, Chartered, Sarasota, 1986-89, James C. Fetterman, P.A., Sarasota, Fla., 1989—; sr. res. adviser to gen. counsel and assoc. gen. counsel Def. Lobistics Agy., 199--94; assoc. prof. U. Sarasota, 1987—; judge advocate I.M.A. USAF, 1987; spl. master for zoning and code enforcement Sarasota County, 1991—; vol. counsel Am. Radio Relay League, 1995—. Editor Midwest Law Review U. Kans., 1984-86, also textbooks. Bd. dirs., v.p., chaperone Sarasota Boy's Choir, 1992-93; asst. scoutmaster Boy Scouts Am., 1991-95, scoutmaster, 1995—. Capt. USAF, 1972-76, ETO; col. res. 1972—. Named one of Outstanding Young Men of Am., Jaycees, 1982. Mem. Am. Bus. Law Assn., Res. Officer Assn. (Sarasota chpt. pres. 1989-91, v.p. 1991-92), Fla. Bar (vice chmn. mil. law com. 1991-94, chmn. 1994-95), Ret. Officer's Assn. (bd. dirs. Sarasota chpt. 1991-93), Am. Legion, Nat. Eagle Scout Assn. Republican. Roman Catholic. Office: 2375 S Tamiami Trl Sarasota FL 34239-3808

FEUER, A.B. BUD, retired journalist, historian, writer; b. Freeport, Ill., Nov. 5, 1925; s. Samuel R. and Betty R. Feuer; m. Gloria Stuart, Mar. 19, 1950 (div. Sept. 1972); children: Robert, James, Ellen Feuer Greenberg; m. Millie Marietta Martin Cox, Apr. 20, 1985. Student, U. Notre Dame. Journalist City News Agy., South Bend, Ind., 1946-80; book reviewer Mil Rev. mag., Mil. History mag., WWII mag.; lectr., seminar leader Va. Western C.C., Blue Ridge Writers Conf. Author: Combat Diary, 1991, Coast Watching in Solomon Islands, 1992, General Chennault's Secret Weapon, 1992, Santiago Campaign of 1898, 1993, The Spanish-American War At Sea, 1995, Commando!, 1996; editor: Bilibid Diary, 1987; co-author: (with James T. Murphy) Skip Bombing, 1993; contbr. articles to profl. publs. With USN, 1942-46. Mem. Am. Soc. Journalists and Authors, Soc. Profl. Journalists, U.S. Naval Inst. (life), Navy League U.S. (life), Am. Mil. Inst. Home: 2318 Avenham Ave SW Roanoke VA 24014-1606

FEUVREL, SIDNEY LEO, JR., lawyer, educator; b. Birmingham, Ala., June 7, 1948; s. Sidney Leo and Tommie Eula (Nolan) F.; m. Glenda Kay Erwin, May 8, 1970 (div. 1979); 1 child, William Michael; m. Lillian Torrence, Apr. 22, 1989. BA, Mercer U., 1978, JD, 1981; student comparative criminal law, Moscow U., Russia, 1979; student East-West trade law, Warsaw U., Poland, 1979; student U.S. govt. law studies, U. Utah, 1980. Bar: Fla. 1981, Ga. 1981, U.S. Dist. Ct. (no. dist.) Ga. 1981, U.S. Dist. Ct. (mid. dist.) Fla. 1983, U.S. Ct. Appeals (11th cir.) 1983, U.S. Supreme Ct. 1989; cert. mediator and arbitrator, Federal Dist. Ct., U.S. Bankruptcy Ct. (mid. dist.), Fla. Air traffic controller FAA, Memphis, 1970-74, Atlanta, 1974-76; pvt. practice law Atlanta, 1981, Orlando, Fla., 1981—; adj. prof. Fla. Inst. Tech., Melbourne, 1983-91, Velenica C.C., Orlando, 1990—, Webster U., Orlando, 1990—; cert. family mediator, ins. mediator, county ct. mediator Fla. Supreme Ct. Bd. dirs. Griffin Prep. Sch., Ga., 1977. With USN, 1966-69, Vietnam 1967-68. Mem. ATLA, Rotary (treas. 1985), 3d Degree Mason, 32 Degree Scottish Rite Mason, Noble of Shrine (Atlanta), Orange County Bar Assn. (pro bono panel), Am. Arbitration Assn. (apptd. panel of arbitrators), Am. Trial Lawyers Assn., Acad. of Fla. Trial Lawyers. Office: 1520 E Livingston St Orlando FL 32803-5436

FEWEL, HARRIETT, lawyer; b. Chickasha, Okla., Nov. 28, 1943; d. Orson Harry Jr. and Dorothy (Jones) Maricle; m. John Gerrard Fewel, Sept. 10, 1966. BA, Okla. Coll. Liberal Arts, 1966; MA, U. Ky., 1969; JD, St. Mary's U., San Antonio, 1979. Bar: Tex. 1980, Mass. 1985, U.S. Dist. Ct. (no. dist.) Tex. Pvt. practice, San Antonio, 1980-83; paralegal Office U.S. Atty. for Dist. Mass., Boston, 1983-84; mng. atty. Hyatt Legal Svcs., Arlington, Tex., 1985-87; pvt. practice Lancaster, Tex., 1987—. Mem. Million Dollar Advocates Cir. Democrat. Roman Catholic. Office: 519 Martindale Dr Lancaster TX 75146-3140

FICHENBERG, ROBERT GORDON, newspaper editor, consultant; b. Phila., Jan. 1, 1920; s. Samuel Harrison and Katherine (Gordon) F.; m. Ruth Pollard, Sept. 14, 1947; children: Ruth Ann, Kathryn Leigh. B.S., Syracuse U., 1940. City editor Adirondack Daily Enterprise, Saranac Lake, N.Y., 1940-42; reporter, copy editor, asst. city editor Binghamton (N.Y.) Press, 1942-57; mng. editor Knickerbocker News, Albany, N.Y., 1957-66; exec. editor Knickerbocker News, 1966-78; chief Washington bur. Newhouse Newspapers, editor Newhouse News Svc., 1979-91; writer, cons. Nat. Assn. Dist. Attys., Washington, 1991—; bd. dirs. Nat. Press Found. Served to 1st lt. Signal Corps AUS, 1942-46; to capt. U.S. Army, 1951-52. Mem. Am. Soc. Newspaper Editors, N.Y. State Soc. Newspaper Editors (pres.), AP Mng. Editors Assn., White House Corrs. Assn., N.Y. State AP Assn. (past pres.), Soc. Profl. Journalists, Nat. Press Club, Army and Navy Club, Fed. City Club, Univ. Club Washington, Gridiron Club (Washington). Home: 1605 Mason Hill Dr Alexandria VA 22307-1930 Office: Nat Dist Attys Assn 99 Canal Center Plz Ste 510 Alexandria VA 22314-1588

FICHTER, ROBERT WHITTEN, artist; b. Ft. Myers, Fla., Dec. 30, 1939. BFA, U. Fla., 1963; MFA, Ind. U., 1966. Asst. curator exhbns. George Eastman House Mus., Rochester, N.Y., 1966-68; asst. prof. UCLA, 1968-71; prof. Fla. State U., Tallahassee, 1971—; vis. assoc. prof. art UCLA, 1976. One-man shows include The Univ. Gallery, Memphis State U., 1989, U. South Fla., Tampa, 1984, Southeastern Ctr. Comtemporary Art, Winston-Salem, N.C., 1986, Internat. Mus. Photography, Rochester, 1982-85; represented in group shows Kunsthaus, Zurich, 1977, Whitney Mus., N.Y., 1981, San Francisco Mus. Modern Art, 1985, L.A. County Mus., 1987, Munchner Kunstverein, Munchen, Germany, 1989, Nat. Gallery Can., Ottawa, 1989, Harnett Gallery, U. Rochester, 1990. Fla. Fine Arts fellow, NEA fellow. Home and office: 612 W 8th Ave Tallahassee FL 32303-5302

FICKEN, CARL FREDERICK WILHELM, theology educator; b. Augusta, Ga., Sept. 16, 1935; s. Carl F.W. Sr. and Alice Eugenia (Mobley) F.; m. Terrell Anne Holderfield, June 16, 1962; children: Catherine Anne, Mark Jonathan. AB, Lenoir-Rhyne Coll., 1957, DD (hon.), 1995; BDiv, Luth. Theol. Sem., Phila., 1960; STM, Luth. Theol. So. Sem., Columbia, S.C., 1968; PhD, U. S.C., 1972. Pastor St. Mark's Luth. Ch., Sullivan's Island, S.C., 1960-62; campus rector Luth. Ctr. U. S.C., Columbia, 1962-68, instr., rsch. asst., 1969-72; instr. Luth. Theol. So. Sem., Columbia, 1966-70; asst. prof. English Elon Coll., Burlington, N.C., 1972-75; prof. Theology & Culture Luth. Theol. So. Sem., Columbia, 1976—; dir. Luth. Theol. Ctr., Atlanta, 1988—; mem. Interfaith Coalition Atlanta, Atlanta, 1990—, Interfaith Taskforce for 1996 Olympic Games, Atlanta, 1992—. Author: God's Story and Modern Literature, 1985; editor: (jour.) Taproot, 1986-88. Treas. CROP com., Columbia, 1979-83; coord. Bread for the World, Columbia, 1981-88; bd. dirs. Community Care Inc., Columbia, 1987-88. John S. Reynolds fellow U. S.C., Columbia, 1971-72, Franklin Clark Fry fellow Luth. Ch. Am., 1982. Office: Luth Theol Ctr 1703 Clifton Rd NE # 1 Atlanta GA 30329-4044

FICKLING, WILLIAM ARTHUR, JR., health care manager; b. Macon, Ga., July 23, 1932; s. William Arthur and Claudia Darden (Foster) F.; m. Neva Jane Langley, Dec. 30, 1954; children: William Arthur III, Jane Dru, Julia Claudia, Roy Hampton. BS cum laude, Auburn U., 1954. Exec. v.p. Fickling & Walker, Inc., Macon, 1954-74; chmn. bd. dirs., chief exec. officer Charter Med. Corp., Macon, 1969-85, pres., chmn. bd. dirs., 1985-93; chmn. bd. Beech St. Corp., Macon, 1986—; bd. dirs. Ga. Power Co., Riverside Ford. Trustee Wesleyan Coll., Macon, Auburn Univ. Found.; mem. adv. bd. Med. Coll. Ga. Mem. Macon Bd. Realtors, Kappa Alpha, Delta Sigma Phi, Phi Kappa Phi. Methodist. Home: 4918 Wesleyan Woods Dr Macon GA 31210-4119 Office: Beech St Corp PO Box 307 577 Mulberry St Ste 1100 Macon GA 31202

FIDDICK, PAUL WILLIAM, broadcasting company executive; b. St. Joseph, Mo., Nov. 20, 1949; s. Lowell Duane and Betty Jean (Manring) F.; m. Julie Hanna Lorms, July 31, 1983; children: Lea Elizabeth, Hanna Manring. BJ, U. Mo., 1971. Account exec. Sta. KCMO-KFMU, Kansas City, Mo., 1971-72; account exec. Sta. WEZW, Milw., 1972-74, dir. sales mktg., 1974-76, v.p., gen. mgr., 1976-81; sr. v.p. Multimedia Broadcasting Co., Milw., 1981; pres. Multimedia Radio, Cin., 1982-86, Radio Group, Heritage Communications, Inc., Des Moines, 1986-87, Radio Group, Heritage Media Corp., Dallas, 1987—; bd. dirs. Nat. Assn. Broadcasters, Washington, 1994—, Radio Advt. Bur., N.Y.C., 1983—, chmn. 1993-94, mem. acad. staff U. Wis., Milw., 1978-81. Elder Westminster Presbyn. Ch., Dallas. Named one of 40 Most Powerful People in Radio, Radio Ink Mag., 1996, Fifth Estater, Broadcasting Mag., 1990, Up and Coming Radio Exec. of Yr., Radio Only Mag., 1983. Mem. Phi Eta Sigma, Kappa Tau. Office: Heritage Media Corp One Galleria Tower 13355 Noel Rd Ste 1500 Dallas TX 75240-6650

FIEDLER, HANS KARL, communications analyst, consultant; b. Milw., Dec. 26, 1955; s. Leon Dale and Wilma Pauline (Mercer) F.; m. Teresa Cox. AAS, U. Louisville, 1980, BS, 1983. Dir. Bus. Sch. Microcomputer Lab. U. Louisville, 1983-85, programmer, analyst, 1985-88, systems programmer, 1988-94; comm. analyst, 1994—; owner HF Cons., Louisville, 1983—. Mem. ACM, NRA, IEEE, Digital Equipment Computer Users Soe., Order Ky. Cols., Sports Car Club of Am., Ohio Falls Sports Car Assn. Republican. Methodist. Home: 10201 Cambrie Ct Louisville KY 40241-1187 Office: Univ Louisville Systems Program Dept Louisville KY 40292

FIEGLE, FRANCIS EDWIN, II, civil engineering manager; b. Berwyn, Ill., Sept. 8, 1948; s. Francis Edwin and Mary Sue (McCrory) F.; m. Shera Lynn Hudson, June 17, 1972 (div. Apr. 1986); m. Evelyn Louise Brock, May 11, 1986; 1 stepchild, Joel Ashley Reeves. BS in Civil Enging., Ga. Inst. Tech., 1973. Registered profl. engr., Ga. Project mgr. John A. Todd Co., Atlanta, 1972-73; chief of constrn. inspection DeKalb County Rds. and Drainage, Decatur, Ga., 1974-77; county engr. Rockdale County, Conyers, Ga., 1977-79; environ. engr. Ga. Safe Dams Program, Atlanta, 1979-84, classification mgr., 1984-85, program mgr., 1985—. Dir. Rockdale County Humane Soc., Conyers, 1977-80. Recipient Outstanding Individual Contbn. of Yr. award Ga. Tech. Students Ctr., 1971; recipient Disting. Svc. Key award Alpha Phi Omega, 1971. Mem. NSPE/Ga. Soc. Profl. Engrs. (v.p. 1988, chpt. pres. 1989, chmn. math. cts. 1990-91, chmn. continuing edn. 1993, Engr. of Yr. in Govt. 1992-93), Assn. State Dam Safety Ofcls. (Ga. state rep. 1992—, bd. dirs. 1994—, sec.-treas. 1996—). Republican. Roman Catholic. Home: 2967 Antioch Rd Franklin GA 30217-3621 Office: Ga Safe Dams Program 4244 International Pky Ste 110 Atlanta GA 30354-3906

FIEHN, GEORGE ROGER, home building company executive, consultant; b. Norfolk, Nebr., July 10, 1943; s. George William and Wilhelmina Adeline (Gee) F.; m. Marlene Mae Frink, July 15, 1962; children: Alan, Brenda, Christine, Tiffany. Gen. mgr. F.W. Woolworth Co., N.Y.C., 1961-71; cons. Am. Housing Guild, San Diego, 1971-73, US Home Corp., Houston, 1973-78, Genstar Ltd., Toronto, Ont., Can., 1978-80; div. pres. David Weekley Homes, Houston, 1980-88; pres. Roger Fiehn & Assocs., Houston, 1988—, Am. Classic Homes, Houston, 1992—. Co-author: Certified Site Professional, 1992. Named Nat. Sales Person of Yr., Nat. Assn. Home Builders, 1983, Nat. Sales Mgr. of Yr., 1985, Nat. Mktg. Dir. of Yr., 1986. Mem. Inst. Residential Mktg. (mem. faculty 1983—, nat. pres. 1991-92), Builder-Realty Coun. Internat. (bd. dirs. 1993—), Nat. Sales and Mktg. Coun. (trustee 1988-92), Nat. Assn. Home Builders, Tex. Assn. Builders.

FIELD, ELLEN, association executive; b. Marlinton, W.Va., Dec. 26, 1952; d. George S. and Vivienne W. Sharp; m. John A. Field, May 7, 1977; children: MArgaret Elaine, George William Butler. BS, W.Va. U., 1974; MA, Coll. Grad. Studies, 1976. Rsch. assoc. Nat. Gov.'s Assn., Washington, 1978-80; mem. presdl. pers. Reagan-Bush Transition Team, Washington, 1980; vice chmn. McLean (Va.) Cmty. Ctr., 1987-90; spl. asst. Office Drug Control Policy, Washington, 1990-93; vol. coord., dir. spl. events Tom Davis Campaign, Springfield, Va., 1994-95; field dir. Bobbie Kilberg for Lt. Gov., McLean, 1993, George Allen for Gov., McLean, 1993; legis. dir. Congressman Tom Davis, Washington, 1995. Author: Governing the American States, 1978; editor: Governor's Policy Initiatives, 1980, Reflections on Being Governor, 1981. Treas. Dranesville Rep. Party, McLean, 1994—, mem. Fairfax County Rep. Commn., 1994—; pres. Greater McLean Republican Women's Club, 1987. Mem. Nat. Fedn. Rep. Women, Va. Fedn. Rep. Women. Presbyn.

FIELD, FRANCIS EDWARD, electrical engineer, educator; b. Casper, Wyo., Nov. 20, 1923; s. Jesse Harold and Persis Belle (St. John) F.; m. Margaret Jane O'Bryan, Oct. 13, 1945; children: Gregory A., Christopher B., Sheridan Diane. BSEE, U.S. Naval Acad., 1945; MA in Internat. Affairs, George Washington U., 1965; AMP, Harvard Bus. Sch., 1970. Master cert. graphoanalyst; comml. pilot. Owner Field Lumber Co., Lander, Wyo., 1948-50; commd. ensign, U.S. Navy, 1945, advanced through grades to capt. 1966, ret., 1975; rsch. engr., George Washington U., 1975-90, adj. faculty, 1977-90; program dir. NSF, Washington, 1982-90; pres. EXTANT, cons. firm, McLean, Va., 1981—. Author: Chronicle of a Workshop, 1977. Mem. Internat. Graphoanalysis Soc. (award of merit 1984), Masons, Sigma Xi. Republican. Home: 8122 Dunsinane Ct Mc Lean VA 22102-2719 also: 280 S 3rd St Lander WY 82520

FIELD, THOMAS HAROLD, software engineer; b. Flint, Mich., May 13, 1951; s. Harold Franklin and Evelyn Agnus (DeHate) F.; m. Sharon Deborah Patronis, Dec. 11, 1982; 1 child, Gabriel. BSEE, U. Mich., Dearborn, 1973; MS in Computer Sci., Fla. Inst. Tech., 1986. Sr. field engr. Martin Marietta Def. Systems, Pittsfield, Mass., 1974—. Mem. IEEE, Assn. for Computing Machinery. Roman Catholic. Home: 305 Grant Ave Indian Harbour Beach FL 32937 Office: Lockheed Martin Def Sys PO Box 246 Cape Canaveral FL 32920-0246

FIELDER, BARBARA LEE, management, leadership and communications trainer; b. Long Beach, Calif., Dec. 6, 1942; d. Thomas G. Coultrup and Elizabeth L. (Doran) Cox; m. Alford W. Fielder, Apr. 14, 1970; children: Kris, Kimberly, Brian. BSBA, Redlands U., 1979. Cert. tchr., Calif. Sr. compensation analyst Irvine Co., Newport Beach, Calif., 1973-76; pers. adminstr. Shiley divsn. Pfizer Co., Irvine, Calif., 1976-78; asst. dir. human resources BASF-Video Corp., Fountain Valley, Calif., 1978-79; pres. Barbara L. Fielder & Assoc., Roseville, Calif., 1979-89, Fielder Group, Ky., 1989—; instr. U. Calif., Irvine and Riverside, 1981-85, Davis, 1985-88; instr. Orange Coast Coll., Long Beach C.C., Coastline C.C.; workshop leader Inst. Applied Mgmt. and Law, 1981—, Nat. Seminars Group, 1989-94, SkillPath, 1994—. Contbr. articles to profl. publs., articles on mgmt. and bus. to Tribune Courier Newspaper; author: I'm Communicating, But...Am I Being Heard?, Motivation in the Workplace. Pres. Calif. Employers Coun., 1983-86; mem. Pvt. Industry Coun., Orange County, Calif., 1983-84; past mem. Foothill Adv. Bd., 1987-89; bd. dirs. Industry Edn. Coun. Calif., 1987-89. Recipient Outstanding Svc. award Interstate Conf. Employment Security Agys., Indpls., 1984. Mem. Nat. Speakers Assn., Tenn. Speakers Assn., Internat. Platform Assn., Lions Club. Presbyterian.

FIELDING, INEZ VICTORIA BROWN, community health nurse; b. Lewisburg, St. Mary, Jamaica, July 12, 1933; came to the U.S., 1968; d. Stanley J. and Nora (Facey) Thomas; m. Wynford Brown, Mar. 14, 1958 (dec. 1968); children: Laurel, Seymour; m. Clay Burton, Aug. 15, 1981. Diploma in nursing, Wolverhampton Sch. Nursing, England, 1960; BS in Spl. Studies, St. Francis Coll., Bklyn., 1978. RN, N.Y., Fla. Nursing supr. Wilson Hosp., Mitcham Surrey, England, 1966-68, Far Rockaway (N.Y.) Nursing Home, 1968-69; staff nurse Down State Med. Ctr., Bklyn., 1968-70; asst. head nurse Kingsbrook Jewish Med. Ctr., Bklyn., 1970-82, St. Albans (N.Y.) Vets. Hosp., 1982-83; paramedic examiner Insurex Corp., 1983-85; visiting nurse Trico Home Visit Svc., 1984-86; area nurse Visiting Nurse Assn. Indian River County, Vero Beach, Fla., 1985-87; sr. community health nurse, specialist, coord. Indian River County Health Unit, Vero Beach, 1987—. supr. Fellsmere Outreach clinic; bd. dirs. Mental Health Assn., Vero Beach, 1988, Am. Cancer Soc., Vero Beach, 1990; active Sebastian Property Owners Assn. Mem. ANA (coun. cultural diversity 1991, Nurse Excellence award 1991), AAUW, Fla. Nurses Assn. (treas., conv. del. 1988-94, healthy start coalition rep. Nurse of Yr. Dist. #17 1989, Mary Cash award 1994), Fellsmere Health Care Coalition, Fla. Pub. Health Assn. Democrat. Methodist. Home: 1197 Gardenia St Sebastian FL 32958-8215 Office: Indian River County Pub Health Dept 1900 27th St Vero Beach FL 32960-3383

FIELDS, ANITA, dean; b. Amarillo, Tex., Oct. 29, 1940; d. Dera and Mamie Maureen (Craig) Bates; 1 child, William Kyle. Grad. nursing, Jefferson Davis Hosp., 1962; BSN, Tex. Christian U., 1966; MSN, Northwestern State U. La., 1974; PhD, Tex. Women's U., 1980. C.E. coord., asst. prof. Northwestern State U., Shreveport; prof., dean McNeese State U., Lake Charles, La.; gov.'s appointee Southwest La. Hosp. Dist. Commn., 1989-91, chmn., 1989-91. Mem. allocations com. and loaned exec. United Way, 1991-92, Am. Heart Assn., Am. Cancer Soc., ARC. Recipient Ben Taub award, 1962, Ann Magnussen award ARC, 1977. Mem. ANA (del.), La. Nurses Assn. (past pres. and 1st v.p., spl. recognition award 1993), Lake Charles Dist. Nurses Assn. (bd. dirs., Nurse of Yr. award 1972, 80), Nat. League Nursing (agy. mem.), Sigma Theta Tau (Image of Nursing award 1993), Delta Kappa Gamma, Phi Kappa Phi. Home: 1723 Fox Run Dr Lake Charles LA 70605-6404

FIELDS, BILLY WAYNE, executive assistant; b. Madison, Tenn., May 13, 1957; s. William Carter and Polly Fields; m. Donna Linton. AS, Volunteer State C.C., Gallatin, Tenn., 1977; BS, Austin Peay State U., Clarksville, Tenn., 1979; MA, Western Ky. U., 1988. Coord. student pubs. Austin Peay State U., Clarksville, 1979-80; editor/reporter Middle Tenn. Newspaper, Clarksville, 1980-82; dir. news and info. Ky. Wesleyan Coll., Owensboro, 1982-86; press sec. U.S. Congressman Bill Boner, Nashville and Washington, 1986-88; press sec./spl. asst. Mayor of Nashville, 1988-90; exec. asst. to judge Davidson County Juvenile Ct., Nashville, 1990—. Mem. Victim Awareness Coun., Nashville, 1988—; pres. Lockeland Springs Neighborhood Assn., Nashville, 1992-95, v.p. Nashville Neighborhood Alliance, 1995—; bd. dirs. ARC, Owensboro, Ky., 1984-86, Hist. Edgefield, East Nashville Caucus; mem. Child Death Rev. Team, Nashville, 1993—; tchr. Sunday sch. Connell Meml. United Meth. Ch., Goodlettsville, Tenn., 1988—; nat. bd. dirs. Coll. Media Advisors, Inc., 1983-86; owner rep. Juvenile Justice Ctr.; chmn./facilitator Mayor's Anti-Crime Summit; chmn. for coun. Airport Transition Adv. Group. Recipient ARC Svc. award. Mem. Soc. Profl. Journalists, Tenn. Juvenile Ct. Svcs. Assn., Nashville Neighborhood Alliance, Gamma Beta Phi, Omicron Delta Kappa. Democrat. Home: 902 Boscobel St Nashville TN 37206-3730 Office: Davidson County Juvenile Ct 100 Woodland St Nashville TN 37213-1215

FIELDS, HALL RATCLIFF, finance educator; b. Gilbert, La., Nov. 24, 1937; s. Frederick Deacue and Mary Elodie (Moore) F.; 1 child, Demetria Charise Gable Fields Hunt; m. Ruby Jean James, Feb. 23, 1980; 1 child, Brandon Hall. BS, So. U., Baton Rouge, 1965; MEd, McNeese State U., 1975; Coop. Edn. cert., La. Tech. U., 1968; postgrad., Grambling State U., 1990; postgrad. in higher edn., Nova Southeastern U., 1991—. Lic. ins. agt. Bus. tchr., head dept. bus. edn. Armstrong High Sch., Rayne, La., 1965-70; bus. edn. tchr., advisor Future Bus. Leaders Am. Rayne High Sch., 1970-80, gen. coop. edn. coord., 1978-80; acct., bookkeeper Housing & Urban Devel. Community Block, Grambling, La., 1980-81; bus. edn. tchr. Ft. Necessity (La.) High Sch., 1981-82, Ruston (La.) High Sch., 1982-83; acct. Grambling State U., 1983-87, acad. counselor, asst. prof., 1987—; bus. edn. and career counselor vact. edn. Acadia Parish Sch. Bd., Crowley, La., 1965-78; adv. sec. Minority Affairs, La. Commr./Ins., Baton Rouge, 1989—, com. 1994; mem. Gov.'s Adv. Com. Equal Opportunity, Baton Rouge, 1991, sec., 1994; lectr. continuing edn. spkrs. bur. Grambling State U.; bus. counselor career, pres., CEO Fields Career and Fin. Svcs., 1990. Chmn. Accreditation Sub-Com. III, Grambling State U., 1989, Accreditation, Adminstrn., Rayne H.S., So. Assn. Colls. and Schs., 1979. Photographer, lectr., organizer Ivy Camera Club, Ft. Lewis, Wash., 1961-62; treas. Acadia Parish Edn. Assn., Crowley, 1967-71; pres. Acadia Assn. Edn., Crowley, 1980; deacon Starlight Bapt. Ch., Rayne, La., 1966; deacon, Mt. Olive Bapt. Ch., Grambling, 1980, chmn. deacon bd., 1993—; chmn. sustaining membership enrollment Boy Scouts Am., Grambling, 1993, scoutmaster, mem. bd. Ouachita Valley Coun., 1994. With U.S. Army Signal Corps, 1960-63, Vietnam. Recipient Thunderbird Dist. award Boy Scouts Am., 1994; named Outstanding Tchr. Yr., 1991. Mem. AACD, Am. Assn. Christian Counselors (charter), Nat. Career Devel. Assn., Am. Coll. Personnel Assn., Am. Assn. Multi-Cultural Counseling & Devel., Am. Counseling Assn., Internat. Platform Assn., La. Assn. Multi-Cultural Counseling & Devel., Am. Assn. Religious & Values Issues in Counseling, La. Assn. Religious & Values Issues in Counseling, Nat. Acad. Advising Assn., La. Acad. Advising Assn., Southern U. Alumni Fedn. (life), Omega Psi Phi (Pi Tau chpt. editor, historian). Democrat. Home: 703 College Ave Grambling LA 71245-2413 Office: Grambling State U Coll Bas Study PO Box 567 C Grambling LA 71245-0567

FIELDS, HARRIET GARDIN, counselor, educator, consultant; b. Pasco, Wash., Feb. 25, 1944; d. Harry C. and Ethel Jenell (Rochelle) Gardin; m. Avery C. Fields; 1 child, Avery C. BS in Edn., S.C. State U., Orangeburg, 1966; MEd, U. S.C., 1974. Lic. profl. counselor and supr.; nat. bd. cert. counselor and career counselor. Tchr. Richaldn Sch. Dist., Columbia, S.C., 1966-67 73-76; counselor supr. S.C. Dept. Corrections, Columbia, 1971-73; counselor Techinal Edn. System, West Columbia, S.C., 1967-70; exec. dir. Bethlehem Community Ctr., Columbia, 1976-79; human rels. cons. Calhoun County Schs., St. Matthews, S.C., 1979-82; admission counselor Allen U., Columbia, 1982-83; pres., cons. H.G. Fields Assn., Columbia, 1973—; exec. dir. Big Bros./Big Sisters, Columbia, 1984-87. Mem. Richland County Coun., Columbia, 1989-92, chair, 1993, 94, 95, 96; 2d vice chair Richland County Dem. Party, Columbia, 1984-88; sec. Statewide Reapportionment Com., 1990—. Recipient inaugural Woodrow Wilson award Greater Columbus C. of C., 1994, Pres.'s Disting. Svc. award Nat. Orgn. Black County Ofcls., 1996, numerous human rels. and outstanding svc. awards. Mem. ACA (resolutions chair So. br. 1993-94), S.C. Assn. Counselors (chair govt. rels. 1985—, pres. 1982-83), Assn. Multicultural Counseling Devel., S.C. Coalition Pub. Health, Nat. Assn. Counties (bd. dirs., employment steering com., chair youth sub-com., legis. com., revenue, fin. and econ. devel. steering com.), S.C. Assn. Counties (employment and tng. steering com., taxation and fin. com. 1994), Am. Bus. Women's Assn. Democrat. Methodist. Office: Richland County Coun PO Box 192 2020 Hampton St Columbia SC 29202

FIELDS, JAMES PERRY, dermatologist, dermatopathologist, allergist; b. Sherman, Tex., July 30, 1932; s. John Galloway and Alma (Goff) F.; m. Linda Hensley, May 30, 1958; children: Timothy Austin, Amy Elizabeth. BS, U. Tex., 1953, MS, 1957; MD, U. Tex., Galveston, 1958. Diplomate Am. Bd. Dermatology, Am. Bd. Allergy and Immunology, spl. competence cert. in dermatoapathology. Dir. dept. dermatology USPHS, S.I., N.Y., 1964-78; assoc. prof. medicine and pathology Vanderbilt U. Sch. of Medicine, Nashville, 1978-88; pvt. practice, Nashville, 1988—; dir. dermatopathology Lab. of the Mid-South, Nashville, 1988—; from instr. to assoc. clin. prof. dermatology and pathology Columbia-Presbyn. Hosp. and Coll. of Physicians and Surgeons, N.Y.C., 1968-88; assoc. clin. prof. medicine Vanderbilt U. Sch. Medicine, Nashville, 1988—. Author (with others): Mycobacterial Diseases, 1991; contbr. articles to profl. jours. Bd. dirs. Am. Leprosy Missions Internat., Greenville, S.C., 1974—; vol. med. missionary, United Meth. Vols. in Mission, 1984—. Capt. USPHS, 1958-79. Recipient citation for meritorious svcs. President's Com. on Employment of Handicapped, 1970, Meritorious Svc. medal USPHS, 1978. Fellow ACP, Am. Acad. Allergy and Immunology, Am. Acad. Dermatology, Am. Coll. Allergy and Immunology, Am. Soc. Dermatopathology, Am. Soc. for Dermatologic Surgery, N.Y. Acad. Medicine (sec. 1976-77, chmn. sect. on dermatology 1977-78). Home: 411 Lynwood Blvd Nashville TN 37205-3434 Office: 4301 Hillsboro Rd # 200 Nashville TN 37215-3314

FIELDS, KAREN KEYSE, physician; b. Berea, Ohio, Apr. 24, 1956; d. Dale Russell and Barbara Mae (Offenberg) Keyse; m. Paul Henry Fields III, Sept. 4, 1982; 1 child, Michael Fisher. BA, Ohio No. U., 1978; MD, Ohio State U., 1981. Diplomate Am. Bd. Internal Medicine, Am. Bd. Med. Oncology, Am. Bd. Hematology, Nat. Bd. Medicine. Intern and resident Jewish Hosp. Cin., 1981-84; fellow in hematology and oncology Coll. Medicine U. Cin., 1986-88; fellow in hematology and oncology Health Sci. Ctr. U. Fla., Jacksonville, 1988-89; asst. prof. internal medicine U. South Fla., Tampa, 1989-94, assoc. prof., 1994—; asst. chief Bone Marrow Transplant Svc. H. Lee Moffitt Cancer Ctr. and Rsch. Inst., Tampa, 1992—, assoc. dir. div. bone marrow transplantation, dept. medicine, 1996—, interim program leader bone marrow transplant program, 1996—; lectr., presenter in field. Contbr. 100 articles and abstracts to profl. jours. Mem. Keel Club, United Way, Tampa, Fla., 1992—. Named one of Outstanding Young Women of Am., 1985; grantee U. South Fla., 1990, H. Lee Moffitt Cancer Ctr. and Rsch. Inst., 1991, Lederle Labs., 1992, Bristol Myers, 1993. Mem. Am. Soc. Clin. Oncology, Am. Soc. Hematology, Am. Soc. Bone Marrow Transplantation, Internat. Soc. for Exptl. Hematology, N.Am. Assn. Bone Marrow Transplantation (breast cancer subcom.), Phi Alpha Kappa, Phi Kappa Phi, Beta Beta Beta, Tau Beta Sigma. Office: H Lee Moffitt Cancer Ctr Bone Marrow Transplant Svc 12902 Magnolia Dr Tampa FL 33612-9416

FIELDS, W(ADE) THOMAS, dental educator; b. McKenzie, Tenn., Oct. 15, 1942; s. Thomas N. and Rachel (Reynolds) F.; m. Sherry J. Jolly, Aug. 12, 1966; children: Jeffrey Thomas, Susan Michele. DDS, U. Tenn., 1965; MPH, U. N.C., 1970. Clin. dentist N.C. State Bd. of Health, Raleigh, 1966-69; asst. prof. U. Louisville, 1972-75, assoc. prof., dept. chmn., 1975-79; assoc. prof., dept. chmn. U. Tenn., Memphis, 1979-83, assoc. prof., div. dir., 1983-90, prof., div. dir., 1990—; faculty cons. Memphis VA Hosp., 1981—; cons. Asst. Surgeon Gen. and Chief Dental Officer, USPHS, Washington, 1985; project cons. Am. Bd. Dental Pub. Health, Gainesville, Fla., 1984. Reviewer Jour. of Acad. of Gen. Dentistry, 1984—; content cons. monographs (Am. Dental Assn., 1983, 86), abstract reviewer (Am. Assn. Pub. Health Dentistry, 1985); contbr. over 30 articles to profl. jours. Head coach Little League, Elizabeth City, N.C., 1968-69, Peewee Baseball, Louisville, 1976-78; asst. den leader Boy Scouts Am., Louisville, 1978-79; pres. Germantown (Tenn.) H.S. Band Boosters, 1985-86, 89-90. Recipient Traineeship, USPHS, 1969-71. Mem. Am. Dental Assn., Tenn. Dental Assn. (cons. Coun. on Dental Edn. 1984-87), Memphis Dental Soc., Am. Assn. Dental Schs., Am. Assn. Pub. Health Dentistry (sec.-treas. 1979-82, pres.-elect, pres. 1982-84), Deans' Odontological Soc. (elected mem.), Omicron Kappa Upsilon. Home: 1536 Carr Ave Memphis TN 38104-4901 Office: Univ Tenn Coll Dentistry 875 Union Ave Memphis TN 38103-3513

FIELDS, WANDA LEE, special education educator; b. Manchester, Ky., Jan. 23, 1955; d. Henry and Kathleen (Hensley) Bishop; m. William Henry Fields, Sept. 16, 1968; children: Vonda, Willetta, Karen, William. BS in Edn., Cumberland Coll., 1984, MA in Edn., 1993. Cert. std. elem. tchr., provisional cert. tchr. exceptional children. Tchr. asst. Clay County Pub. Schs., Manchester, Ky., 1984-85; tchr. exceptional children Jackson County Pub. Schs., McKee, Ky., 1985—; presenter in field. Mem. NEA, Ky. Edn. Assn. Republican. Baptist. Home: Rte 2 Box 574B Manchester KY 40962 Office: Tyner Elem Sch Hwy 30 PO Box 190 Tyner KY 40486

FIELDS, WILLIAM COFFIELD, III, artist; b. Fayetteville, N.C., Sept. 27, 1917; s. William Coffield Jr. and Elizabeth Mitchell (Gibson) F. BFA, U. N.C., 1938; postgrad., Sch. of Mus. of Fine Arts, Boston, 1942-44; DHL (hon.), Dowling Coll., Oakdale, N.Y., 1975; Dr. Humanities (hon.), Meth. Coll., Fayetteville, 1984. Dir. Fed. Art Project Ctr., Sanford, N.C., 1938-39, Fed. Art Project Ctr. and N.C. State Art Soc. Gallery, Raleigh, 1939-40; asst. state dir. N.C. Fed. Art Project, 1940-42; Editor: (books) Cumberland County, N.C. Court Minutes, 1755-1791, Vol. I, 1978 Vol. II, 1981, A Guide to Historic Sites in Fayetteville and Cumberland County, N.C., 1993, Cumberland County, N.C., Deeds, 1754-70, Vol. I, 1994. Artist painting portraits including the late Pope Pius XII, Prince Enrico Barberini, Prince Urbano Barberini, Princess Maria Barberini, Prince Ludovico Chigi-della Rovere-Albani, Grand Master of Sovereign Mil. Order of Malta, Prince Raimondo Orsini, Princess Maria Silvia Boncompagni-Ludovisi, Princess Maria Elena Pignatelli, Vittorio Orlando, Prime Minister of Italy during World War I, others; numerous one-man shows in Rome, N.Y., N.C. and numerous group shows in eastern galleries. Vice pres. N.C. Symphony Soc., also exec. and fin. coms.; mem. Carolina Charter Tercentenary Commn., 1962, mem. com. on arts and chmn. dance-drama com.; adv. com. N.C. Recreation Commn., 1964; mem. N.C. Arts Coun.; bd. dirs. Carolina Charter Corp., Raleigh, 1963—, Friends of Archives, Raleigh, 1990—; pres. N.C. Ballet Co., 1967-69. Recipient N.C. Award in Fine Arts, 1974. Fellow Royal Soc. Arts (London, life); mem. Assoc. Artists of N.C. (pres. 1961-64). Democrat. Home and Office: RR 23 Box 143 Fayetteville NC 28301-9123

FIELDS, WILLIAM JAY, investment banker; b. Pasadena, Calif., Nov. 8, 1936; s. Jason and Mary Elizabeth (Bell) F.; m. Marilyn Catherine Lamberton, June 11, 1960; children—Kathryn P., Gregory M. B.B.A. in Fin., Calif. Western U., 1960. Ops. mgr. Dempsey Tegeler & Co., San Diego, 1960-65; v.p., nat. credit mgr. Bache & Co., Inc., N.Y.C., 1965-72; mng. dir., chief adminstrv. officer Wheat First Butcher Singer Inc., Richmond, Va., 1972—; regulatory policy com. N.Y. Stock Exchange, 1983—. Chmn. bd. YMCA, Richmond, 1983-92; bd. dirs. Va. Opera, Carpenter Ctr. Performing Arts, HandWorkshop-Va. Ctr. Craft Arts, Ctrl. Richmond Assn., YMCA Greater Richmond. Served with U.S. Army, 1957-59. Republican. Methodist. Club: Downtown. Home: 8912 Norwick Rd Richmond VA 23229-7716 Office: PO Box 1357 Richmond VA 23211-1357

FIERKE, THOMAS GARNER, lawyer; b. Boone, Iowa, Nov. 12, 1948; s. Norman Garner and Mary Margaret (Mullen) F.; m. Susan Marie Butler, July 17, 1976 (div. Mar. 1983); m. Debra Lynn Clayton, Sept. 17, 1988; children: Veronica Helen, Caroline Margaret. BS in Metall. Engring., Iowa State U., 1971; JD, U. Minn., 1974; LLM, Boston U., 1978. Bar: Ill. 1974, U.S. Dist. Ct. Mass. 1976, U.S. Dist. Ct. (no. dist.) Ill. 1976, U.S. Ct. Appeals (1st cir.) 1976, U.S. Tax Ct. 1978, U.S. Supreme Ct. 1978, Mass. 1980, N.Y. 1981, U.S. Ct. Appeals (fed. cir.) 1989. Commd. 2d lt. U.S. Army, 1974, advanced through grades to capt., 1980; trial ct. prosecutor Ft. Devens, Mass., 1974-77; group judge adv. 10th Spl. Forces Group, 1975-78; chief adminstrv. law sect. Ft. Devens, 1977-78; chief legal counsel, contracting officer U.S. Def. Rep., Am. Embassy, Tehran, Iran, 1979; chief adminstrv. law Ft. Devens, 1979-80; judge adv. gen. corps, 1974-80; various to col./comdr. 2d Judge Advocate Gen.'s Det. U.S. Army Res., 1980—; atty., advisor Army Materiel Command, 1980-82; mgr. contracts policy and review Martin Marietta Michoud Aerospace, Martin Marietta Corp., New Orleans, 1982; gen. counsel Lockheed Martin Manned Space Sys., Lockheed Martin Corp., New Orleans, 1984—; apptd. to La. Gov.'s Mil. Adv. Commn., 1991—; bd. dirs. La. Orgn. for Jud. Excellence; mem. La. state com. Employer Support of Guard and Res., 1988—, regional ombudsman, 1989-92, dep. state ombudsman, 1992-94, state ombudsman, 1994—, chmn. New Orleans sect., 1992-94. Col. USAR, 1980—. Recipient Most Valuable Employer Support for the Guard and Res. award, NASA Pub. Svc. medal, 1992, La. Cross of Merit award State of La., 1994, Outstanding Vol. Svc. medal Dept. Def., 1994, 95, 96. Mem. Am. Corp. Counsel Assn. (bd. dirs. New Orleans chpt. 1987—, v.p. 1989-90), Internat. Assn. Def. Counsel. Republican. Episcopalian. Office: Lockheed Martin Manned Space Sys PO Box 29304 New Orleans LA 70189-0304

FIERRO-CARRION, GUSTAVO ADOLFO, internist; b. Quito, Ecuador, Dec. 11, 1961; came to U.S., 1990; s. Gustavo A. and Fany (Carrion) Fierro. MD, Central U., Quito, 1986. Diplomate Am. Bd. Internal Medicine. Resident St. Paul Med. Ctr., Dallas, 1990-93; hypertension rsch. fellow U. Tex. S.W. Med. Ctr., Dallas, 1994—. Mem. AMA, ACP, Wilderness Med. Soc., Am. Alpine Club. Office: Univ of Texas SW Med Ctr 5323 Harry Hines Blvd Dallas TX 75235

FIERROS, RUTH VICTORIA, retired secondary school educator; b. McRoberts, Ky., Mar. 29, 1920; d. Willie A. and Harriet (Wright) Cornett; m. Jose Fernando Fierros, Nov. 22, 1945 (dec.); children: Cedric Joseph, Philip Alonso, Stephen Michael. BA in English, Berea Coll., 1942; MA in English and Edn., Tex. A&I U., 1954. Cert. tchr., Tex. Tchr. Jenkins Ind. Schs., McRoberts, 1942-43, Laredo (Tex.) Ind. Schs., 1951-87; ret., 1987. Editor: Class '42 Yearbook, 1982, 87, 92; author: Upon the Easel of My Heart, 1982, Love's Collage of Rose Petals, 1996; contbr. poems to anthologies. Chairperson 50th and 55th anniversary reunions Berea Coll. Class of 1942; pres. Tuesday Music & Literature, 1986-88. With USN, 1943-46. Recipient Tchr. Excellence award U. Tex., 1987, Golden Apple award Alpha Delta Kappa, 1987, Golden Poet award, 1988, Cert. of Citation State of Tex. Ho. of Reps., 1987, Armed Forces award, 1988, Leadership award, 1988. Mem. AAUW (1st v.p. 1966-68), NEA, Gifted and Talented Assn., Nat. Coun. Tchrs. English, Tex. State Tchrs. Assn., So. Poetry Assn. (Critics Choice award), Nat. Libr. of Poetry, Webb County Unit Ret. Tchrs. Assn. (2d v.p. 1994-95), Charles T. Morgan Soc., Delta Kappa Gamma (pres.), Internat. Poetry Assn. Democrat. Roman Catholic. Home: 1801 Fremont St Laredo TX 78043-2606

FIFE, WILLIAM FRANKLIN, retired drug company executive; b. Buffalo, W.Va., Nov. 6, 1921; s. Alfred Charles and Grace (Pitchford) F.; children: Scott Franklin, Susan Elizabeth, Cindy Francine. AB, Berea Coll., 1949; MS, U. Wis., 1950. Operating mgr. McKesson & Robbins, Chgo. and Kansas City, Mo., 1950-56, Cleve. Wholesale Drug Co., 1956-58; with Owens, Minor & Bodeker, Inc., 1958-91; pres., exec. v.p., sr. v.p. Owens & Minor, Inc., Richmond, Va., 1981-87, chief oper. officer, 1987-91, exec. v.p., 1989-91, ret., 1991—, now cons., bd. dirs., mem. exec. and audit coms. Capt. C.E. U.S. Army, 1942-46. Home: 507 Gaskins Rd S Richmond VA 23233-5709 Office: Owens & Minor Inc 4800 Cox Rd Glen Allen VA 23060-6292

FIGARI, ERNEST EMIL, JR., lawyer, educator; b. Navasota, Tex., Feb. 18, 1939; s. Ernest Emil and Louise (Campbell) F.; children: Alexandra Caroline, Audrey Elizabeth. BS, Tex. A&M U., 1961; LLB, U. Tex.-Austin, 1964; LLM, So. Meth. U., 1970. Bar: Tex. 1964, U.S. Ct. Appeals (5th cir.) 1965, U.S. Dist. Ct. (no. dist.) Tex. 1964, U.S. Supreme Ct. 1967. Law clerk to judge U.S. Dist. Ct. (no. dist.) Tex., Dallas, 1964-65; assoc. Coke & Coke, Dallas, 1965-70, ptnr., 1970-75; ptnr. Johnson & Swanson, Dallas, 1975-86, Figari & Davenport, Dallas, 1986—; adj. prof. law So. Meth. U., Dallas, 1974-79, 81-82, U. Tex., 1980 . Contbr. articles to legal jours. Fellow ABA, Tex. Bar Found., Dallas Bar Found.; mem. State Bar Tex., ABA. Roman Catholic. Office: Figari & Davenport 4800 Nations Bank Pla 901 Main St Dallas TX 75202-3714

FIGGE, FREDRIC J., II, bank executive. Chmn. credit policy NationsBank Corp., Charlotte, N.C. Office: NationsBank Corp NationsBank Corp Ctr 100 N Tryon St Charlotte NC 28202-4000*

FIGUEIRA, ROBERT CHARLES, history educator; b. N.Y.C., Jan. 30, 1951; s. Charles Manoel and Marion (Gentile) F. BA in History and German, Wesleyan U., Middletown, Conn., 1973; MA in Medieval Studies, Cornell U., 1976, PhD in History, 1980. Asst. dean Emory Coll. Emory U., Atlanta, 1983-85; vis. asst. prof. history So. Meth. U., Dallas, 1986-87, Wright State U., Dayton, 1987-88; assoc. prof. history St. Mary's Coll. Minn., Winona, 1988-91; assoc. prof. and prof. history, chair history & polit. sci. Lander U., Greenwood, S.C., 1991—; book reviewer; presenter papers at confs., 1983-96; faculty peer reviewer Bush Found. Grants St. Mary's Coll., Minn., 1988; manuscript referee Ch. History, 1988, U. Pa. Press, 1987, 94, Yale U. Press, 1996; grant applications referee NEH, 1993; state examiner Bavarian Ministry fro Edn. and Culture, 1986; vis. scholar U. Calif., Berkeley, Inst. Medieval Canon Law/Robbins Collection, 1982, 84, 88, 90, 91. Contbr. articles to profl. jours. Bd. dirs. S.C. Humanities Coun. Recipient scholarships Wesleyan U., 1969-73, N.Y. State Regents, 1969; grantee NEH, 1988, 91, 92, 93, Lander Found., 1991, 93, 94, 95, Bush Found., 1988-89, 89-90; rsch. fellow Deutscher Akademischer Austauschdienst, 1993; Cornell U. fellow, 1977-78, Fulbright, 1973-74. Mem. Am. Cath. Hist. Assn., Am. Hist. Assn., Medieval Acad. Am., Am. Soc. Ch. History, Soc. for Medieval Canon Law, Am. Polit. Sci. Assn., So. Hist. Assn. (European sect.), Selden Soc., Phi Beta Kappa, Phi Alpha Theta. Roman Catholic. Office: Lander U Willson St Greenwood SC 29649

FILBERT, ELEANOR JANE, special education educator; b. McCall Creek, Miss., July 26, 1949; d. Ervin Erastus and Hellon Ruth (Palmer) Fleming; m. Robert Morris Filbert Jr., Sept. 27, 1969; children: Robert III, Eleanor, Hellon, Michael, Paul, Paula. Student, S.W. C.C., Summit, Miss., 1991-92, Copiah-Lincoln C.C., 1992; BS in Elem. Edn., U. So. Miss., 1994; postgrad., Alcorn U., 1995-96. Cert. tchr., Miss. Justowriter Enterprise Jour., McComb, Miss., 1967-69; tchr. asst. Valpraiso (Fla.) Elem. Sch., 1975-76; computer operator Enterprise Jour., McComb, 1983-86; tchr. spl. edn. Amite County H.S., Liberty, Miss., 1994—. Mem. CEC (sponsor 1994-95), Miss. Assn. Educators. Republican. Baptist. Home: Rt 1 Box 22-B Smithdale MS 39664 Office: Amite County H S Liberty MS 39645

FILBIN, CHARLES EVERETT, loss control representative; b. Clarksburg, W.Va., Sept. 12, 1955; s. Robert Lloyd and Margaret Mary (Hoyt) F.; children: Charles Everett Jr., Collin Eugene. BSBA, Ohio State U., 1978. Cert. safety profl. Pers. analyst City of Dallas, 1979-81, safety officer, 1981-87, safety specialist, 1987-89; risk mgr. City of Mesquite, Tex., 1989-92; sr. loss control rep. Berkley Adminstrs., Dallas, 1992—. Author newsletter Dallas Water Utilities, 1981-87; author, editor Dallas Risk Mgmt. Newsletter, 1987-89. Cubmaster Boy Scouts Am., Dallas, 1988-94; coord. Bike-A-Thon, Mesquite chpt. Am. Heart Assn., 1991. Recipient Commitment to Excellence award Dallas Water Utilities, 1987. Mem. Am. Soc. Safety Engrs. (mem. govtl. affairs com. 1993—), Tex. Pub. Risk and Ins. Mgmt. Assn., Tex. Safety Assn., Am. Assn. Agts. and Adjusters. Republican. Office: Berkley Adminstrs 16775 Addison Rd Ste 325 Dallas TX 75248-1867

FILER, EMILY SYMINGTON HARKINS, social services administrator; b. Balt., May 12, 1936; d. Frank Fife and Grace (Cover) Symington; m. George Archer Harkins, June 21, 1958 (div. 1982); children: Montgomery Fox, Emily Harrison (dec. Apr. 1978); m. Robert Hoagland Filer, June 24, 1989. Degree, Villa Julie Med. Sec. Sch., Balt., 1955. Cert. vol. adminstr. Registrar Johns Hopkins Hosp., Balt., 1955-57, sec. hearing and speech ctr., 1957-58; pres. Distaff Wives, San Francisco, Boston, 1958-63; v.p., bd. dirs. The Planning Council, Tidewater, Va., 1969-78; pres. Jr. League of Norfolk (Va.)-Virginia Beach, 1972-74; founder, coord. Lee's Friends, Norfolk, 1978-86, exec. dir., 1986—; chmn. Tidewater dist. Va. Council Soc. Welfare, 1985-87, Va. Council Social Welfare, 1988; bd. dirs. Va. Wesleyan Coll., Norfolk, 1979—, Olde Huntersville Devel., Norfolk, 1985-87. Lic. pastoral caregiver The Ch. of Good Shepherd, 1992—; bd. dirs. Westminster Canterbury of Virginia Beach, 1992—, exec. com. sec., 1993—; mem. Mayor's Com. on Paine. Recipient (Lee's Friends awards) Vol. Action Ctrs., 1981, Cmty. Svc. award Jewish Cmty. of Tidewater, 1982, Pres. Vol. Action award, 1982, Spl. Vol. Action award South Hampton Roads, 1988, 1989 Gov.'s Gold medal for Vol. Excellence, 1990 J.C. Penney Golden Rule award Hampton Roads, Merit citation NCCJ, 1992, award First Nat. Congress on Cancer Survivorship, 1995; recipient Women-In-Transition award YWCA, 1989, Spl. award as Outstanding Bus. Woman of Hampton Roads, 1989, Disting. Merit citation NCCJ, 1992, Va. Vol. Adminstr. of Yr. award, 1992, Outstanding Outstanding Orgn. award Tidewater Dist., 1992, Vol. of Distinction award Jr. Leagues Internat., 1994; named Great Citizen of Hampton Roads, 1987. Mem. Internat. Assn. for Vol. Adminstrs. (cert. liaison, region IV 1986, profl. devel. liaison assn. 1987-88, region IV 1987-88, 93-94, recertification chair 1990-92, exec. com. Internat. Conf. on Vol. Adminstrn. 1997), Colonial Va. Assn. for Vol. Adminstrs. (dep. sec. 1986-87, pres. 1987-89), Tidewater Cancer Network (assoc. 1986), Nat. Hospice Orgn. (profl.), Va. Assn. for Hospice Orgn. (assoc.), Jr. League of Norfolk-Va. Beach (sustainer, past pres., First Sustainer award). Episcopalian. Office: Lee's Friends 618 Stockley Gdns Norfolk VA 23507-2017

FILES, MARK WILLARD, business and financial consultant; b. Bartlesville, Okla., Dec. 5, 1941; s. Francis Marion and Alice Wade (Webb) F.; m. Elizabeth Kay Maltby; children: Patrick, Jennifer Leigh. BBA, U. Okla., 1963, MA, 1964, postgrad. Stanford U. CPA, Okla., La. From asst. acct. to ptnr. Peat, Marwick, Mitchell & Co., Tulsa, 1964-80; vice chmn., dir. Braeloch Holdings, Inc., Covington, La., 1980-93; ptnr. Graham Ptnrs. Fin. Cons. and Investments, Covington, 1993—. Exxon Corp. fellow U. Okla., 1964. Trustee Christ Episc. Sch., Covington, 1993—. Mem. AICPA, Okla. Soc. CPAs (chmn. ethics com. 1975-76), La. Soc. CPAs, Am. Petroleum Inst., Beau Chene Golf and Racquet Club (Mandeville, La.), Phi Eta Sigma, Beta Gamma Sigma, Pi Kappa Alpha. Republican. Episcopalian. Home: 712 N Beau Chene Dr Mandeville LA 70471-1616 Office: Graham Ptnrs 5000 Highway 190 Ste A-1 Covington LA 70433-4950

FILIPP, CAROLYN FRANCINE, music educator, insurance agent; b. Houston, Oct. 11, 1950; d. Emil Frank and Augustina Joyce (Klozik) Filipp. B.Music, U. Houston, 1973; M.Ed., Stephen F. Austin State U., 1977; postgrad. Houston Baptist U., 1979-80. Band dir. Ft. Bend Ind. Sch. Dist., Stafford, Tex., 1973-74, choral dir., 1974-76; choral dir., Missouri City, Tex., 1976-77, Houston Ind. Sch. Dist., 1977—, band dir., 1985-86, 1994-95; choral dir. Aldine Ind. Sch. Dist., 1995-96; pianist Houston Brethren Ch., 1964-73, choral dir., 1968-70; pianist Cy-Fair Community Ch.; clarinetist, saxophonist, vocalist Space-City Dutchmen Orch., 1965-75; clarinetist Kovanda Orch., 1987-95; pvt. tchr. clarinet, saxophone and piano, Houston; ins. agt. Western Frat. Life Assn., Cedar Rapids, Iowa, 1977-86, Farmers' Mut. Protective Assn. Tex., Temple, 1978—, Slavonic Benevolent Order of the State of Tex., 1987—; treas. Houston Brethren Ch. Christian Sisters Soc., 1991-94; trustee Hus Sch., sec., 1991-94, treas., 1991-94. Mem. Congress Houston Tchrs. (rec. sec. 1980-82, exec. v.p. 1982-84), Tex. Classroom Tchrs. Assn., Tex. Music Educators Assn., Conf., Tex. Bandmasters Assn., Am. Choral Dirs. Assn. (life), Alpha Delta Kappa, Tau Beta Sigma, Gamma Sigma Sigma (chpt. sec.-treas. 1971-73, life). Clubs: Coll. Women's, Houston Liederkranz. Lodges: Western Fraternal Life Assn. (local sec. 1977-81, Tex. liaison officer 1985-86), Slavonic Benevolent Order Tex., Farmers Mut. Protective Assn. Tex., Sons of Hermann, Sokol Houston. Home: 2515 Lazybrook Dr Houston TX 77008-1003

FILIPS, NICHOLAS JOSEPH, management consultant; b. Garrett, Ind., June 10, 1925; s. John and Elizabeth (Grigore) F.; children by previous marriage: Steven, Mary Beth, Fred John; m. Kathryn V. McDowell, Apr. 6, 1982. Student, U. Detroit, 1942-45, Ind. U., 1945-47; BS in Biology, Am. U., 1948; postgrad., Ind. U., 1979. V.p., mgr. Wayne Pharmacal Supply Co., Ft. Wayne, Ind., 1949-67, pres., chmn. div. Bendway, Inc., South Bend, Ind., 1955-67; v.p., gen. mgr. Karel First-Aid Supply Co., Chgo., 1967-71; pres., gen. mgr. Amedic Surg. Supply Co., Miami, 1971-78; pres., chief exec. officer Med. Supply Co., Inc., Jacksonville, Fla., 1978-81; pres., chmn. bd. KNF Med. Enterprises, Inc., Jacksonville, 1985—; cons. Wholesale Distbrs. Contbr. articles to profl. jours. Benefactor numerous non-profit hosps. and clinics, Colombia, S.Am. Recipient Am. Legion Leadership award, 1939; named Cons. and Mktg. Dir. of Yr. Retiree Skills, Inc., Tucson, 1990. Mem. Am. Surg. Trade Assn. (Distinctive Svc. award 1960), Lions, Fla. Sheriffs Assn. Democrat. Roman Catholic. Office: Health Distbrs Mgmt and Cons Co Ltd 150 Belvedere St Atlantic Beach FL 32233-4107

FILLEY, WARREN VERNON, allergist, immunologist; b. Topeka, Kans., Oct. 27, 1950. MD, U. Kans. Sch. Medicine, 1976. Diplomate Am. Bd. Allergy & Immunology, Am. Bd. Internal Medicine. Intern U. Okla., 1976-77, resident in internal medicine, 1977-79; fellow allergy & immunology Mayo Clin., Rochester, 1979-81; with Presby. Hosp., Okla. City; clin. asst. prof. medicine U. Okla. Mem. AAAI, ACP, ASIM. Office: Okla Allergy and Asthma Clinic 750 NE 13th St Oklahoma City OK 73104-5051

FILLMAN, STEPHEN DOUGLAS, physician; b. Donaldsville, La., July 6, 1950; s. Jack M. and Alice H. (Hollub) F.; m. Lee Ann Lane, June 2, 1973; children: Matthew T., Alice Lane. BA in Chemistry, So. Meth. U., 1972; MD, U. Tex. Med. Br., 1976. Intern U. Tex. Med. Br., Galveston, 1976-77, resident, 1977-79; assoc. N.W. Diagnostic Clinic, P.A., Houston, 1982—. Maj. USAF, 1979-82. Mem. ACP, AMA, Tex. Med. Assn.

FINAZZO, KATHY JO, primary school educator; b. Leonardtown, Md., Dec. 18, 1971; d. Curtis Brent and Charlotte Rosalie (Withrow) Noel. BA in Elem. Edn. and Eng. Lit., Rider Coll., 1993. Cert. tchr., Va., N.J. Presch. tchr. Bldg. Blocks Sch., King George, Va., 1993; sutstitute tchr. King George and Colonial Beach (Va.) sch. dists., 1993-94; 3d-5th grade tchr. King George Summer Sch., 1994; 1st grade tchr. Colonial Beach Elem. Sch., 1994—; cheerleading coach Colonial Beach. H.S., 1994—. Fundraiser Martin House Child Learning Ctr., Trenton, N.J., 1993. Mem. Va. Edn. Assn., Colonial Beach Edn. Assn., Kappa Phi Kappa (co-founder, v.p. 1991-93), Sigma Tau Delta. Home: PO Box 780 Dahlgren VA 22448

FINCH, DIANE SHIELDS, retail sales administrator; b. Detroit, Aug. 25, 1947; d. Earl Arthur and Carrie (Steele) Shields; m. Glenn A. Finch III, Oct. 5, 1968; 1 child, Jennifer Lynn. AA, U. Houston, 1969; student, U. St. Thomas, 1970-73, Rice U., 1980. Apt. mgr. Moonmist Manor, Houston, 1972-75; sales merchandiser Mattel Toys, Houston, 1975-77; sales merchandiser Plough Sales, Houston, 1977-79, ter. mgr., 1979-80, area mdse. mgr., 1980-84, dist. sales mgr., 1984-86; dist. mdse. mgr. Schering-Plough Healthcare Product, Houston, 1986-92; dist. retail merchandising mgr. McNeil Consumer Products, Houston, 1992-95; dist. sales mgr. Walt Disney Home Video, Houston, 1995—. Area chmn. Assn. Cmty. TV, Houston, 1985-87; mem. Friends of Ronald McDonald House; mem. Citizens Animal Protection. Mem. Nat. Assn. Female Execs., Am. Mgmt. Assn., Tex. Exec. Women (bd. dirs.), Houston Fedn. Profl. Women. Office: Walt Disney Home Video 5020 Longmont Dr Houston TX 77056-2420

FINCH, EVELYN VORISE, financial planner; b. Marietta, Ohio, Jan. 20, 1930; d. Richard Raymon Juantzee and Oreatha Fay (Carnes) Metcalf; m. Herman Frederick Ahrens, May 13, 1948 (div. Nov. 1957); children: Erick K.F., Hilda Kate (dec.), Nicole Schwartz; m. James Derwood Finch, June 29, 1973 (dec. Oct. 1993). BS in Music Edn., Concord Coll., 1961. Registered health underwriter, 1990. Music tchr. Prince George's County (Md.) pub. schs., 1961-72; pvt. piano tchr. Washington, 1961-73; china and crystal sales rep. Quality Products Co., Washington, 1973-80; ins. agt. Mut. of Omaha Cos., Washington, 1980-92, Memphis, 1992-94; pvt. practice fin. planner Alamo, Tenn., 1994—; registered mem. Internat. Fin. Exch., Inc., Memphis, 1996—; mem. internat. mktg. and investments divsn. TriOcean Internat., LLC, Emeryville, Calif., 1995—. Pianist for Sunday sch. class; supporting mem. Nat. Mus. Women in the Arts, Washington, 1990—, Women's Philharm., San Francisco, 1993—. Mem. NAFE, AAUW (br. pres. 1994-96, Tenn. chair endl. found. 1996—), Nat. Assn. Health Underwriters (v.p. pub. rels. Memphis chpt.), Internat. Assn. for Fin. Planning, Jackson (Tenn.) Assn. Life Underwriters (publicity dir.), Nat. Boating Fedn. (pres. 1985-87), Internat. Order of Blue Gavel, Chesapeake Commodores Club, Potomac River Yacht Clubs Assn. (legis. chair 1978-87), Chesapeake Bay Yacht Clubs Assn. (commodore 1982), Corinthian Yacht Club, Prince George's Yacht Club (commodore 1978), Pi Mu, Kappa Delta Pi. Home: Finch Rd Box 226A Alamo TN 38001-9734 Office: Finch Fin Svcs Finch Rd Box 226A Alamo TN 38001

FINCH, MICHAEL PAUL, lawyer; b. Galveston, Tex., Jan. 4, 1946; s. Albert Lynn and Ila Belle (Robertson) F.; m. Rebecca Jean Minnear, Dec. 27, 1969; children: Michael Paul, Rachelle Jean. BEE cum laude, Rice U., 1969, MEE, 1969; JD magna cum laude, U. Houston, 1972. Bar: Tex. 1973. Petroleum engr. Exxon Corp., Houston, 1969-72; assoc. Vinson & Elkins, Houston, 1972-79, ptnr., 1980—. Dir. Houston Pops Orch., 1988-89. Mem. ABA, Tex. Bar Assn., Houston Bar Assn., Am. Contact Bridge League (life master 1964—). Republican. Methodist. Clubs: Houston Ctr., Rice U. (founder). Home: 12531 Overcup Dr Houston TX 77024-4915 Office: Vinson & Elkins 3300 First City Tower 1001 Fannin St Houston TX 77002

FINCH, RAYMOND LAWRENCE, judge; b. Christiansted, St. Croix, V.I., Oct. 4, 1940; s. Wilfred Christopher and Beryl Elaine (Bough) F.; m. Lenore Luana Hendricks, June 8, 1963; children—Allison, Mark, Jennifer. A.B., Howard U., 1962, J.D., 1965. Bar: V.I. 1971, Third Circuit Ct. of Appeals 1976. Law clk. Judge's Municipal Ct. of V.I., 1965-66; partner firm Hodge, Sheen, Finch & Ross, Christiansted, 1970-75; judge Territorial Ct. of V.I., Charlotte Amalie, 1975-86, Ct. of Appeals, V.I., Charlotte Amalie, 1986-94, U.S. Dist. Ct. of V.I., 1994—; instr. Grad. div., Coll. of V.I., Am. Inst. Banking, 1976—. Bd. dirs. Boy Scouts Am., Boys Club Am. Served to capt. U.S. Army, 1966-69. Decorated Army Commendation medal, Bronze Star medal. Mem. Am. Judges Assn., Am., Nat. bar assns., Internat. Assn. Chiefs of Police. Democrat. Lutheran. Office: PO Box 24051 Christiansted VI 00824-0051

FINCH, ROGER DEAN, labor activist, legislative administrator; b. Greenville, S.C., Jan. 29, 1952; s. John Simpson and Kathryn Tabitha (Dean) F.; m. Memory Lynn Lynch, Apr. 16, 1982; children: Erin Joel, Megan Tabitha. Student, George Meany Ctr., Silver Spring, Md., 1984, 94. Agt. Norfolk So. R.R., Greenville, 1972—; dist. chmn. Transp. Comm. Internat., Greenville, 1984-91, state legis. dir., 1990—. Instr. ARC, Greenville, 1990-94; coord. United Way, Greenville County, 1990-95; adminstr., dir. Greenville U.U. Fellowship, 1993-95; exec. committeeman Greenville County Dem. Party, 1996—; mem. Dem. Leadership Coun., 1994-96, AFL-CIO. Mem. Carolina Alliance for Fair Employment, Keowee Sailing Club, Sierra Club (spl. events coord., exec. com. 1990-93). Unitarian Universalist. Office: Transportation Communications Internat PO Box 2151 Greenville SC 29602

FINCH, SUSAN MCGUIRE, urban planner; b. Sarasota, Fla., Sept. 9, 1965; d. Carroll Philip and Doris Jeannette (Montgomery) McG.; m. Steven Preston Finch, Nov. 30, 1991. BA, U. South Fla., 1988. Cmty. planner Hillsborough County, Tampa, Fla., 1990-93; sr. planner Hillsborough County, Tampa, 1993-94; planner Engelhardt, Hammer and Assocs., Tampa, 1994—. Mem. Am. Planning Assn., Delta Gamma (options chmn. 1986—). Republican. Home: 919 S Rome Ave Unit #14 Tampa FL 33606-3079

FINCHER, HUGH MCCOMMON, III, foreign language educator; b. Gaffney, S.C., Nov. 29, 1945; s. Hugh McCommon Jr. and Flora Neva (Bonner) F. AB with honors in classics, U. N.C., 1967, MA in Classics, 1969; PhD in Humanities, Fla. State U., 1979. Lic. tchr., S.C., N.C. Asst. prof. classics Birmingham (Ala.)-So. Coll., 1969-70; instr. English U. Ala., Huntsville, 1973-75; tchr., headmaster Gaffney (S.C.) Day Sch., 1975-82; tchr. Trinity Sch., Rutherfordton, N.C., 1982-84, Cherokee County (S.C.) Schs., Gaffney, 1984—; adj. prof. French Limestone Coll., Gaffney, 1985-87; adj. prof. Latin Converse Coll., Spartanburg, S.C., 1988-92; mem. state coms. Dept. Edn., S.C., 1988-95; developer, tchr. French FLES Program, Cherokee County Schs., Gaffney, 1990-93, ESL program, 1993-96. Editor: Caesar's Bellum Helveticum, 1994. Mem. NEA, Carolina TESOL, Classical Assn. Midwest and South, South Atlantic MLA, Am. Assn. Tchrs. French, Am. Assn. Tchrs. German. Presbyterian. Home: 509 E Frederick St Gaffney SC 29340

FINDLEY, JOHN SIDNEY, dentist; b. Bryan, Tex., Oct. 3, 1942; s. Sidney Albert and Leila Mae (Reading) F.; m. Patricia Ann Reep, June 10, 1967 (div. 1977); children: John Brett, Sidney Alan; m. 2nd Judith Ann Smith, May 22, 1981. Student USAF Acad., 1961-62, N. Tex. State U., 1963-65; DDS, Baylor U. Coll. Dentistry, 1970, Disting. Grad., 1996. Pvt. practice dentistry, Plano, Tex., 1970—; bd. dirs. Fin. Svcs. Inc. Contbr. articles to profl. jours. Formerly bd. dirs. Plano YMCA, United Way of Plano, Park Bd. City of Plano, Charter Rev. Commn. City of Plano; pres. Colleagues of the Plano Police, City of Plano; chmn. advancement com. North Trail Dist. Boy Scouts Am.; campaign chmn. Plano YMCA Fund Dr., 1978; councilman City of Cross Rds., Tex., 1988-89, mayor, 1992-94; chmn. bd. trustees Oak Grove United Meth. Ch.; gen. chmn. Dallas Midwinter Dental Clinic. Recipient Cert. of Recognition Am. Acad. Dental Radiology, 1970; Paul Harris fellow Rotary Internat., 1979. Fellow Am. Coll. of Dentists, Internat. Coll. Dentists; mem. ADA, Tex. Dental Assn., pres. elect, 1996; (chmn. coun. govt. affairs, Pres. award 1994, 95, pres.-elect 1996—), Dallas County Dental Soc. (bd. dirs., editor DDS News, gen. chmn. Dallas Midwinter Dental Clinic 1992, pres.-elect 1992-93, pres. 1994, dentist of yr. 1995), Acad. Gen. Dentistry, Rotary (Plano, bd. dirs., pres. 1977-78). Methodist. Home: RR 3 Box 498 Aubrey TX 76227-9528 Office: 1410 14th St Plano TX 75074-6359

FINE, A(RTHUR) KENNETH, lawyer; b. N.Y.C., June 29, 1937; s. Aaron Harry and Rose (Levin) F.; m. Ellen Marie Jensen, July 11, 1964; children: Craig Jensen, Ricki-Barie, Desiree-Ellen. AB, Hunter coll., 1959; JD, Columbia U., 1963; C.L.U. cert. Coll. Ins., 1973; diploma Command and Gen. Staff Coll., 1978. Bar: N.Y. 1974; registered rep. and limited prin., Nat. Assn. Securities Dealers, Inc. Joined U.S. Army N.G., 1955, advanced through grades to maj., 1973, ret., 1980; cons. U.S. Life Ins. Co., N.Y.C., 1970-74, atty., 1975-78, asst. gen. counsel, 1978; asst. counsel USLIFE Corp., N.Y.C., 1978-79, assoc. counsel, 1979-93; asst. v.p., counsel Western Res. Life Assurance Co. of Ohio, Largo, Fla. Mem. ABA, Am. Soc. CLU and ChFC (Suncoast chpt.), N.Y. State Bar Assn., Nat. Guard Assn. U.S., Militia Assn. N.Y. (chmn. vet. officers com. 1981-90), Am. Legion (7th regt. post), Ret. Officers Club St. Petersburg, Fla. Republican. Lutheran. Home: 5953 36th Ave N Saint Petersburg FL 33710-1835 Office: Western Res Life Assurance Co of Ohio 201 Highland Ave NE Largo FL 33770-2512

FINE, J(AMES) ALLEN, insurance company executive; b. Albemarle, N.C., May 2, 1934; s. Samuel Lee and Ocie (Loflin) F.; m. Marie Nan Morris, Sept. 1, 1957 (dec. Apr. 1989); children: James A(llen), William Morris. Student Pfeiffer Coll., 1957-58; BS, U. N.C., 1961, MBA, 1965. Sr. accountant Haskins & Sells, CPAs Charlotte, N.C., 1961-62, Watson, Penry, & Morgan, Asheboro, N.C., 1962-64; instr. U. N.C., Chapel Hill, 1964-65; asst. prof. Pfeiffer Coll., Misenheimer, N.C., 1965-66; treas., v.p. adminstrn. Nat. Lab. for Higher Edn. (formerly Regional Edn. Lab. Carolinas and Va.), Durham, N.C., 1966-72; organizer, CEO, treas., dir. Investors Title Ins. Co., Inc., Chapel Hill, 1972—; CEO, treas., dir. Investors Title Ins. Co., Inc., Columbia, S.C., 1973—; pres., dir. Investors Title Co., Inc., Chapel Hill, 1976—; developer Carolina Forest Subdiv., Chapel Hill, 1970-78, Springhill Forest subdiv., Chapel Hill, 1977-80, Stoneycreek subdiv., 1978—; lectr. accounting U. N.C., Chapel Hill, 1967-70. Area officer ann. alumni giving U. N.C., Chapel Hill, 1968-69, 71-73, 75—. With USN, 1953-57. Recipient Haskins & Sells Found. award for excellence in accounting, 1961; N.C. Assn. CPAs award for most outstanding accounting student U. N.C., 1961. Mem. Am. Inst. CPA's, N.C. Assn. CPAs, Am. Accounting Assn., Am. Land Title Assn. (research com. 1983—, membership com. 1984-85, exec. com. underwriters sect. 1986, recruitment, retention subcom., 1985), Nat. Assn. Ins. Commrs. (liaison com. 1987-88, 1994—), U. N.C. Nat. Devel. Com. 1994—, CEDAR Bus. Mgrs. (chmn. nat. exec. com. 1971), Phi Beta Kappa, Beta Gamma Sigma (treas. 1961). Home: 112 Carolina Frst Chapel Hill NC 27516-9033 Office: 121 N Columbia St Chapel Hill NC 27514

FINE, JO-DAVID, dermatologist; b. Louisville, Apr. 9, 1950; s. Lewis and Bernice Rhea (Friedman) F.; m. Catherine Miles Evans, June 3, 1972; children: David, Jeffrey, Kenneth. BS in Chemistry, Yale Coll., 1972; MD with distinction, U. Ky., 1976; MPH in Epidemiology, U. N.C., 1992. Diplomate Am. Bd. Internal Medicine, Am. Bd. Dermatology (gen. and immunologic dermatology). Intern and jr. asst. resident Duke U. Med. Ctr., Durham, N.C., 1976-78; resident dermatology Harvard Med. Sch. and Mass. Gen. Hosp., Boston, 1978-80; sr. resident dermatology Harvard Med. Sch. and Lahey Clin. Found., Boston, 1980-81; med. staff fellow dermatology br. Nat. Cancer Inst./NIH, Bethesda, Md., 1981-83; asst. prof. dermatology U. Ala. Sch. of Medicine, Birmingham, 1983-85, assoc. prof. dermatology, 1985-90; assoc. prof. dermatology U. N.C. Sch. Medicine, Chapel Hill, 1990-92, prof. dermatology, 1992—; clin. prof. epidemiology U. N.C. Sch. of Pub. Health, Chapel Hill, 1993—; prin. investigator Nat. Epidermolysis Bullosa Registry, Chapel Hill, 1986—; trustee Dystrophic Epidermolysis Bullosa Rsch. Assn. of Am., Inc., N.Y.C., 1989—; mem. med. sch. admission com. U. N.C. Sch. of Medicine, Chapel Hill, 1990-96; ad hoc reviewer grants NIH, 1986—. Editl. bd.: Clinical and Experimental Dermatology, London, 1994—; dep. editor: Jour. of Investigative Dermatology, 1992-93; editor/author: (book) Bullous Diseases, 1993; contbr. approximately 125 articles to profl. jours. Vice-pres. Yale Club of Ala., Birmingham, 1989; dir. cen. N.C. alumni schs. com., Yale U., New Haven, Conn., 1994—. Recipient Disting. Svc. award Dystrophic Epidermolysis Bullosa Rsch. Assn. of Am., N.Y.C., 1984, New Investigator Rsch. award, NIH, Bethesda, 1985, rsch. grants, 1985—, rsch. grants Vet. Adminstrn., Washington, 1984-88. Fellow Am. Acad. Dermatology, Am. Coll. Physicians, Royal Soc. of Medicine (London); mem. Soc. for Investigative Dermatology, Am. Fedn. for Clin. Rsch., Am. Pub. Health Assn., Am. Dermatol. Assn. Jewish. Office: Univ NC Dept Dermatology 3100 Thurston CB #7287 Chapel Hill NC 27599

FINE, JOEL TED, marketing and management consultant; b. Balt.; s. Albert and Ida (Sapperstein) F. BS in Econs., Johns Hopkins U., 1956. Exec. v.p. Pallette Prodns., Miami, Fla., 1966-80; founder, pres. Fin. Synergetix Corp., Miami, 1970—; pres. Profl. Mktg. Services, Miami, 1975—; founder, chmn., sec., treas. The Knowledge Coll., Miami, 1986—. Producer TV series Paint Along with Conni Gordon, 1973-78; exec. producer TV ballets and other cultural arts prodns., 1975—. Telethon talent coordinator United Cerebral Palsey, Miami, 1971-77; co-founder, chmn. bd. dirs., Cultural Arts Soc. S. Fla., 1972—; bd. dirs., v.p. Miami chpt. Leukemia Soc. Am., 1977-79; bd. dirs. Retinitis Pigmentosa Found., 1979-85, Miami Local Bus. and Homeowners Assn., 1986-87; bd. advisors Greater Miami Internat. Film Festival, 1979-80, Bakehouse Art Complex, Miami, 1986—; pres. Nat. Voluntary Health Agys., Miami, 1984-85. Mem. Greater Biscayne Blvd. C. of C. (exec. bd. dirs.), N. Miami Soc. of Arts, Phi Epsilon Pi. Lodge: Masons (32d degree). Office: Profl Mktg Services PO Box 1 Miami FL 33153

FINE, JOYCE CAPLAN, education educator; b. Balt., July 4, 1945; d. Daniel and Ruth (Block) Caplan; m. Roger Alan Fine, Dec. 22, 1965; children: Laura Fine Freedman, Andrew David. BA in Edn., Goucher Coll., 1967; MS in Reading Edn., Fla. Internat. U., 1983, EdD in Curriculum and Instrn., 1991. Adult ESOL tchr. L.A. Pub. Schs., 1968-69; elem. tchr. Dade County Pub. Schs., Miami, Fla., 1973-79, grant dir., 1986-87; pvt. practice as tutor Miami, 1979-91; instr. Fla. Internat. U., Miami, 1991—; adj. prof. Fla. Internat. U., 1983-89, vis. prof., 1990-91, asst. prof., 1992—; ednl. cons. Macmillan Pub., Miami, 1984-89, Harcourt Brace Jovanovich, Miami, 1990. Contbr. articles to profl. jours. and chpts. to books. Dir. STAR: Students Teaching Adults Reading, Miami, 1992-94, REAL: Reading Experiences in Adult Literacy, Miami, 1995. Recipient Youth Corps award for svc. to Greater Miami Svc. Corps Nat. Assn. for Svc. and Conservation Corps, 1992. Mem. Fla. Orgn. Tchr. Educators (pres. 1993—), Fla. Reading Assn. (bd. dirs. 1993—). Office: Fla Internat U 220 SE 2nd Ave Fort Lauderdale FL 33301-1905

FINE, NORMAN DAVID, investment management executive; b. Boston, Nov. 28, 1935; s. Jack and Frances (Abrams) F.; m. Joan Jablow, June 23, 1956; children: Bonnie E. Fine Harding, Michael J. BS in Mgmt., Boston U., 1957, JD, 1959. Bar: Mass. 1959. Account exec. various N.Y.Stock Exchange firms, 1959-72; mgr. floor ops. L.M. Rosenthal & Co., Boston, 1972-75; specialist Boston Stock Exchange, 1975-76; sr. v.p. Fla. Coast Banks, Inc., Pompano Beach, Fla., 1976-83; sr. v.p., sr. inv. officer Midlantic Nat. Bank and Trust Co., Ft. Lauderdale, Fla., 1983-88; pres. Fine Capital Mgmt. Group, Inc., Boca Raton, Fla., 1988—; bd. dirs., Banyan Bank, Boca Raton, 1991-96. Bd. dirs., Pompano Beach sect. Am. Cancer Soc., 1985-87, Am. Suicide Found. Fla. Div., 1996—; chmn., Pompano Beach Indsl. Devel. Commn., 1983-85. Fellow Fin. Analysts Soc. South Fla.; mem. Greater Pompano Beach C. of C. (bd. dirs. 1985-87), Tower Club, Rotary Club of Boca Raton. Republican. Office: Fine Capital Mgmt Group Inc 2000 Glades Rd Ste 204 Boca Raton FL 33431-8504

FINE, ROBERT M., allergist, immunologist, dermatologist; b. Little Rock, Ark., Jan. 9, 1930. MD, Tulane U., 1955. Diplomate Am. Bd. Allergy & Immunology, Am. Bd. Dermatology. Intern Charity Hosp., New Orleans, 1955-56, resident, 1956-57, 59-61; with Dekalb Med. Ctr., Decatur, Ga., Vets Affairs Med. Ctr., Decatur, Ga.; prof. Emory U., 1986—. Mem. FAS-MOHSMicroS, Am. Acad. Allergy & Immunology, Am. Acad. Dermatology, Am. Coll. Allergy & Immunology, Am. Coll. Physicians, Am. Dermatological Assn. Office: Fine Derm Assoc 2675 N Decatur Rd Ste 601 Decatur GA 30033-6134

FINEGOLD, RONALD, computer services executive; b. Bklyn., Nov. 17, 1942; s. Herman Hearsch and Ethel (Kanner) F.; BS, CCNY, 1963; m. Ellen Carole Sehr, Mar. 22, 1964; children: Sherry Dawn, Edward Jon. Supr. programming Celanese Chem. Co., N.Y.C., 1962-66; v.p. marketing Automation Scis., Inc., N.Y.C., 1966-69; pres. Computer Horizons Corp., N.Y.C., 1969-82, chmn. bd., 1977-82, dir., 1969-82; chmn. bd. Stamford Assos., Inc., N.Y.C., 1969-75; pres., dir. Rizons Brokerage, Inc., 1970-71, chmn. bd., dir., 1972-75; chmn. bd. Custom Terminals Corp., 1976-82; pres. Skylane Corp., 1977—; chmn. bd., dir. Starlex Systems & Services, Inc., 1983-89; bd. dirs. Atlantic Sports & Entertainment, Ltd., Exec. Sports Network, Inc. Mem. Data Processing Mgmt. Assn., Am. Mgmt. Assn., Young Pres.'s Orgn., Aircraft Owners and Pilots Assn., Tau Epsilon Phi. Home: 5686 NW 38th Ter Boca Raton FL 33496-2719

FINELLI, PATRICK MICHAEL, theater educator; b. Boston, May 14, 1949; s. Patrick Louis and Catherine Theresa (Di Palma) F. BA, U. Calif., Berkeley, 1972, MA, 1975; MBA, U. South Fla., 1982; PhD, U. Calif., Berkeley, 1991. Prof. U. South Fla., Tampa, 1976—; theatre cons. Robbins, Bell & Kuehlem, Architects, Tampa, 1992—, Criswell, Blizzard & Blouin, Architects, St. Petersburg, Fla., 1993—, Howard & Assocs., Tampa, 1994; bd. cons. SMW Comm., Sacramento, 1994. Author: Directory of Software, 1988, Sound for the Stage, 1989; editor Theatre Design and Technology, 1989-94, Stage Directions, 1994. Mem. Greenpeace, Washington, 1980—, Smithsonian Assocs., Washington, 1983—, The Nature Conservancy, Arlington, Va., 1988—. Recipient Eisner prize U. Calif. at Berkeley, 1972; named Outstanding Tchr., U. South Fla., 1994; Regents fellow, 1973, Holloway grantee U. South Fla., 1990. Mem. Am. Soc. for Theatre Rsch., Assn. Theatres in Higher Edn., U.S. Inst. for Theatre Tech., Nat. Computer Graphics Assn., Univ. and Coll. Theatre Assn. Home: 608 E River Dr Tampa FL 33617-7836 Office: U South Fla 4202 E Fowler Ave Tampa FL 33620-9900

FINEMAN, STANLEY MARK, allergist, immunologist, pediatrician; b. Phila., 1948. MD, Emory U. Sch. Medicine, 1973. Diplomate Am. Bd. Allergy & Immunology, Am. Bd. Pediatrics. Intern Children's Hosp. Med. Ctr., Cin., 1973-74, resident pediatrics, 1974-76; fellow allergy & immunology Children's Hosp. Med. Ctr., Boston, 1976-78; clin. asst. prof. pediatrics Emory U. Sch. Medicine. Mem. Am. Acad. Allergy & Immunology, Am. Acad. Pediatrics, Am. Thoracic Soc. Office: 790 Church St Ste 410 Marietta GA 30060-7290

FINGER, BERNARD L., financial services consultant; b. N.Y.C., Aug. 21, 1927; s. Morris and Anna (Weinberg) F.; m. Naomi Wesler, Feb. 1, 1948; children: Stephanie, Eric. BA, CCNY, 1949; MA, Columbia U., 1950. Securities investigator Securities and Exch. Commn., N.Y.C., 1957-61; dir. fl. procedures and allocations Am. Stock Exch., N.Y.C., 1961-67; compliance dir. Purcell Graham & Co., N.Y.C., 1967-69, Bruns, Nordeman, Rea & Co., N.Y.C., 1969-81, Securities Settlement Corp., N.Y.C., 1981-91; pvt. practice West Palm Beach, Fla., 1992—; arbitrator N.Y. Stock Exch., N.Y.C., 1987—, Nat. Assn. Securities Dealers, N.Y.C., 1987—. With U.S. Army, 1944-46. Mem. Securities Industry Assn. (compliance and legal divsn.), Phi Beta Kappa (Gamma chpt. of N.Y.).

FINK, CHARLES AUGUSTIN, behavioral systems scientist; b. McAllen, Tex., Jan. 1, 1929; s. Charles Adolph and Mary Nellie (Bonneau) F.; m. Ann Heslen, June 1, 1955 (dec. June 1981); children: Patricia A., Marianne E., Richard G., Gerard A. AA, Pan-Am. U., 1948; BS, Marquette U., 1950; postgrad., George Washington Med. Ctr., Walter Reed Army Med. Ctr., 1969-70, No. Va. C.C., 1973, George Mason U., 1974; MA, Cath. U. Am., 1979. Journalist UP and Ft. Worth Star-Telegram, 1950-52; commd. 2d lt. U.S. Army, 1952, advanced through grades to lt. col., 1966, various positions telecommunications, 1952-56, instr., 1956-58, exec. project mgmt., 1958-62, def. analysis and rsch., 1962-65, fgn. mil. rels., 1965-67, def. telecommunications exec., 1967-69, chief planning, budget and program control office Def. Satellite Communications Program, Def. Communications Agy., 1969-72, ret., 1972; pvt. practice cons. managerial behavior Falls Church, Va., 1972-77; pres. Behavioral Systems Sci. Orgn. (and predecessor firms), Falls Church, 1978—; leader family group dynamics, 1958-67; home hemodialysis technician, 1969-81; pub (jour.) Circle, 1985—; computer program cons. Hubble Space Telescope Servicing Mission, NASA, 1993. Developer hierarchial theory of human behavior, 1967—, uses in behavioral, social and biol. sci. and their applications, 1972—, behavioral causal modeling research methodology, 1974—, computer-aided behavior systems coaching for persons and orgns., 1982—, telecoaching, 1989; microbiol. chromatographic profiling, 1989—; public domain Portable Personal Health Record, 1994; adv. for copyrighting computer graphics displays and multi-media communications in scis. Adv. bd. Holy Redeemer Roman Cath. Ch., Bangkok, Thailand, St. Philip's Ch., Falls Church, Va., 1971-73. Decorated Army Commendation medals, Joint Services Commendation medal; named to Fink Hall of Fame, 1982; recipient Behavior Modeling award Internat. Congress Applied Systems Rsch. and Cybernetics, 1980, Mission Pin award NASA, 1993. Mem. AAAS, Nat. Genealogical Soc., Internat. Soc. Systems Scis., Am. Soc. Cybernetics, Internat. Assn. Cybernetics, Internat. Network Social Network Analysis, Assn. U.S. Army, Ret. Officers Assn., Finks Internat. (v.p. 1981—), KC. Home: 3305 Brandy Ct Falls Church VA 22042-3705 Office: PO Box 2051 Falls Church VA 22042-0051

FINK, HAROLD KENNETH, retired psychotherapist, technical writer; b. East Orange, N.J., Oct. 15, 1916; s. Colin Garfield and Lottie (Muller) F.; m. Sue Evans Carrico Fox, July 2, 1977; 1 stepchild, Burke Fox. A.B., Princeton U., 1938; M.S., Calif. Inst. Tech., 1941; Ph.D., Cornell U., 1943; postgrad. William White Inst. Psychiatry, N.Y.C., 1946-47, Postgrad. Ctr. for Mental Health, N.Y.C., 1948-50. Lic. clin. psychologist. Pvt. practice, N.Y.C., 1946-50, 53-57, La Jolla, Calif., 1951-53, Ft. Lauderdale, Fla., 1957-62; prof., chmn. dept. psychology, guidance dir. Ft. Lauderdale Coll., 1967-71, dean, 1971-73; asst. dir. Phoenix Club Half-way House, Ft. Lauderdale, 1972-73; clin. psychologist forensic service So. Fla. State Hosp. Hollywood, Fla., 1974-75; pvt. practice Plantation, Fla., 1977-82; intake clin. psychologist Hawaii State Hosp., Kaneohe, 1982-84; pvt. practice Honolulu, 1983-84, Kihei, Maui, 1984-89, ret., 1989; intake clin. psychologist Maui Community Mental Health Ctr., Kahului, 1985; instr. psychology adult edn. div. Broward County Sch. Bd., Ft. Lauderdale, Fla., 1960-82; instr. sr. citizens outreach program Broward Community Coll., Ft. Lauderdale, 1979-81; test examiner and evaluator sheltered workshop Mental Health Rehab. Found., Ft. Lauderdale, 1982. Author: Long Journey, 1954, Mind and Performance, 1954. Contbr. over 150 articles to prof. jours. Served to lt. j.g. USNR, 1943-45. Mem. Am. Psychol. Assn. (life), Hawaii Psychol. Assn. (life), N.Y. Acad. Scis. (life mem. psychol. div.), Insts. Religion and Health (charter life mem.), Ft. Lauderdale Acad. of Scis. (charter life mem. and founding mem.), Hawaii Psychol. Assn. (life, sec. pvt. practice com. 1983-84). Democrat. Home and Office: 6025 NW 100th Way Parkland FL 33076-2579

FINK, NORMAN STILES, lawyer, educational administrator, fundraising consultant; b. Easton, Pa., Aug. 13, 1926; s. Herman and Yetta (Hyman) F.; m. Helen Mullen, Sept. 1, 1956; children: Hayden Michael, Patricia Carol. AB, Dartmouth Coll., 1947; JD, Harvard U., 1950. Bar: N.Y. 1951, U.S. Dist. Ct. (ea. and so. dists.) N.Y. 1954, U.S. Supreme Ct. 1964. Mem. legal staff Remington Rand, Inc., N.Y.C., Washington, 1949-54; ptnr. Lans & Fink, N.Y.C., 1954-68; counsel devel. program U. Pa., Phila., 1969-80; v.p. devel. and univ. rels. Brandeis U., Waltham, Mass., 1980-81; dep. v.p. devel. and alumni rels., assoc. gen. counsel devel. Columbia U., N.Y.C., 1981-89, sr. counsel John Grenzebach & Assocs., Inc., Chgo., 1989-91; v.p. Am. Australian Studies Found., cons. v.p. Engle Consulting Group, Inc., Chgo.; mem. bd. vis. Brevard Coll., 1995—. With U.S. Army, 1945-46. Recipient Alice Beeman award for excellence in devel. writing Coun. Advancement and Support of Edn., 1984; Lilly Endowment grantee, 1979-80. Mem. ABA (mem. com. on exempt orgns. sect. taxation and com. estate planning and drafting, charitable giving), Coun. Advancement and Support of Edn. (various coms.), Am. Arbitration Assn. (panelist), Assn. of Bar of City of N.Y.C. (com. on tax-exempt orgns. 1987-90), Dartmouth Lawyers Assn., Harvard Law Sch. Assn., Nat. Soc. Fund Raising Execs (Contbn. to Knowledge award 1985), Harvard Club N.Y., Democrat. Jewish. Editor: Deferred Giving Handbook, 1977; author: (with Howard C. Metzler) The Costs and Benefits of Deferred Giving, 1982.

FINKELDAY, JOHN PAUL, retail sales executive; b. Pleasantville, N.J., Nov. 20, 1943; s. Charles John Henry and Viola Sybilla (Eastlack) F.; m. Karen Lynn Mattoon, Nov. 16, 1963; 1 son, John Paul. Student, Glassboro State Coll., 1961-63, Rider Coll., 1965. With McGraw Hill Publ. Co., Hightstown, N.J., 1963-65; asst. controller Exel Wood Products Co., Inc., Lakewood, N.J., 1965-66, office mgr., 1966-82, mgr. data processing, 1970-78, v.p., dir. data processing, 1978-83, v.p. MIS, 1983-86, v.p. adminstrn., 1983-84; v.p. Amici Systems, Inc., Brick, N.J., 1986-88; data processing mgr. Hamilton Beach, Inc., Washington, N.C., 1988-90, Hamilton Beach/Proctor-Silex, Inc., Washington, N.C., 1990-91; owner J&L Enterprises d/b/a Karen's Gifts, Greenville, N.C., 1991—; pres. ESP plus Inc., Greenville, N.C., 1993—; mem. Del. Valley Computer Users Group. Third v.p. exec. com. Adm. Farragut Acad. Parents Assn., 1980-81. Mem. Am. Mgmt. Assn., U.S. Golf Assn. (assoc.), N.C. Aquarium Soc., Greenville Country Club. Home: 3044 Dartmouth Dr Greenville NC 27858-6745 Office: ESP plus Inc 803A Red Banks Rd Greenville NC 27858-5834

FINKELDAY, KAREN LYNN, manufacturing executive; b. Orange, N.J., July 21, 1944; d. Gordon Dayton and Dorothy Laura (Chesseman) Mattoon; m. John Paul Finkelday, Nov. 16, 1963; 1 child, John Paul. Student, Glassboro State Coll., 1962-63, Ocean County Coll., 1978-83. Multiple listing svc. mgr. Ocean County Bd. of Realtors, Toms River, N.J., 1976-79; acct. supr. Paco Packaging Inc., Lakewood, N.J., 1980-83; office mgr. Warne Surgical Products Inc., Eatontown, N.J., 1983-84; sales mgr. TFX Medical Inc., Eatontown, N.J., 1984-86; coord. mktg. and sales Standard-Keil Mfg. Co., Allenwood, N.J., 1986-87; exec. asst. to pres. Standard-Keil Mfg. Co., Allenwood, N.J., 1987-89; mgr. United Refrigerated Svcs., Inc., Tarboro, N.C., 1989—. Creator: (advertisement) Signatures Series, 1987, Nat. Restaurant Assn., 1987, Ptnrs. for Progress, 1988; contbr. articles to profl. jours. Mem. Greenville Mus. Art. Mem. NAFE, Am. Mgmt. Assn., N.J. Bd. Realtors, U.S. Golf Assn., Greenville Country Club. Home: 3044 Dartmouth Dr Greenville NC 27858-6745 Office: United Refrigerated Svcs Inc PO Box 7006 Tarboro NC 27886-7006

FINKENBERG, MEL EDWARD, physical education administrator; b. Bklyn., Aug. 25, 1948; s. Harry and Charlotte (Putterman) F.; m. Juanita Maria Miles, June 17, 1984; 1 child, Amber Lynn. BS, So. Conn. State U., 1970; MEd, Stephen F. Austin State U., 1971; EdD, U. Houston, 1975. presenter, textbook reviewer in field. Phys. edn. instr. West Haven (Conn.) Pub. Schs., 1970-71, Whitcomb Elem. Sch., Clear Creek, Tex., 1972-74; exercise physiologist NASA/Johnson Space Ctr., Houston, 1974-76; various to asst. prof. phys. edn. and athletics Calif. State U., L.A., 1978-80, chmn., prof. dept. phys. edn., recreation, 1980-89; chmn., prof. dept. kinesiology and health scis. Stephen F. Austin State U., Nacogdoches, Tex., 1989—. Co-author: Three Domains of Physical Education, 1973; contbr. articles to profl. jours. Recipient univ. rsch. grant Stephen F. Austin U., 1990, Teaching Excellence award, 1990; rsch. grantee Tex. Assn. Intercollegiate Athletics for Women, 1990, Calif. State U., L.A./lottery grant awards, others; nominated Outstanding Univ. Prof., Calif. State U., 1979-86; named to Outstanding Young Men of Am., 1980. Mem. AAHPERD, Tex. Assn. Health, Phys. Edn., Recreation and Dance, Rotary, Am. Coll. Sports Medicine, Am. Acad. Underwater Scientists, Phi Delta Kappa, Phi Epsilon Omega, others. Home: 2529 Carole St Nacogdoches TX 75961-2247 Office: Stephen F Austin State U Po Box 13015 SFA Sta Nacogdoches TX 75962-3015

FINLAY, STEVEN CLYDE, art director, electronic designer; b. Crossville, Tenn., Mar. 13, 1963; s. Clyde Eric and Linda Dail (Singleton) F.; m. Clarivel Gonzalez, Apr. 13, 1991; 1 child, Ethan Clarke. BFA in Comml. Art, Western Ky. U., 1985. Asst. art dir. Stockwell and Friends, Nashville, 1985; computer graphics artist Marshall Prodns., Inc., Nashville, 1985-87; computer animator, designer Video Ventures Prodns., Inc., Miami, Fla., 1987-91; art dir. Fla. Power and Light Co., Juno Beach, Fla., 1991—; owner Gravics, 1994—. Recipient Bronze Addy award in sales, promotion, computer animation Greater Miami Advt. Fedn., 1989, Gold Addy award for poster Palm Beach Advt. Fedn., 1995, Silver Quill award 1st pl. for newsletter design Internat. Assn. Bus. Communicators, 1995; NATAS nominee in animation, 1989. Mem. Electronic Design Assn. Methodist. Home: 1059 Fairfax Cir W Lantana FL 33462-7402 Office: Fla Power and Light Co PO Box 14000-cce Juno Beach FL 33408

FINLEY, GEORGE ALVIN, III, wholesale executive; b. Aurora, Ill., Apr. 25, 1938; s. George Alvin, II, and Sally Ann (Lord) F.; m. Sue Sellors, June 20, 1962 (dec. 1995); children: Valerie, George Alvin IV. BBA, So. Meth. U., 1962; postgrad. Coll. Grad. Program, Ford Motor Co., 1963. Rep. for Europe, Finco Internat., 1959-61; trainee Ford Motor Co., Dearborn, Mich., 1962-63; v.p. mktg. Internat. Motor Cars, Oakland, Calif., 1963-64, Sequoia Lincoln lease mgr., 1965; regional mgr. Behlen Mfg. Co., Dallas, 1965-67; pres. C C Disbtrs., Corpus Christi, Tex., 1967—; guest instr. Sch. Bus., So. Meth. U., pres., 1986-91, Nueces River Authority, 1975—; bd. dirs. MD Anderson Hosp. U. Tex., Coastal Bend Alcoholic Rehab. Ctr. Inc., Tex., 1973-93, McDonald Obs., U. Tex., exec. com.; treas. Intergovtl. Commn. on Drug and Alcohol Abuse, 1989—, bd. dir.; mem. Del Mar Coll. Pres.' Coun. Mem. Tex. Wholesale Hardware Assn. (pres. 1991-92), Nat. Assn. Wholesalers, Am. Supply Assn., Wholesale Distbrs. Assn. (bd. dirs. 1994—), Impact Industries Inc. (chmn. bd. Sandwich, Ill. 1986-93) , Nat. Retail Hardware Assn., So. Hardware Assn., Rotary Internat., Phi Delta Theta. Democrat. Methodist. Asst. in design, engring., production, mktg. Apollo Automobile, 1963-64. Home: 3360 Ocean Dr Corpus Christi TX 78411-1457 Office: PO Box 9153 210 Mcbride Ln Corpus Christi TX 78408-2338

FINLEY, JACK DWIGHT, investments and consultation executive; b. Lawrence County, Ind., Aug. 7, 1927; s. Paul and Esther Irene (Keithley) F.; m. Beverly Janice Burpee, June 11, 1949; children: Janice Blair, Jennifer Brooke Finley Nichols, Jena Blake. BS, U.S. Mil. Acad., 1949; MS in Elec. Engring., U. Ill., 1953; DLitt (hon.), Westbrook Coll., 1996. Commd. 2d lt. U.S. Air Force, 1949, advanced through grades to capt., 1955, resigned, 1956; mem. tech. staff Ramo-Wooldridge Corp., L.A., 1956-60; v.p. R&D Data Corp., Dayton, Ohio, 1960-68; v.p., tech. dir., chmn. bd. dirs., founder EIKONIX Corp., Bedford, Mass., 1968-86, cons. investments, dir. svcs., 1986—; cons. R-W, L.A., 1960-61; vis. lectr. Rochester Inst. Tech. (N.Y.), 1966-68; bd. dirs. Quipp, Inc., Miami, Fla., 1989—, chmn., 1995—. Contbr. articles to profl. jours; patentee in field. Trustee Westbrook Coll., Portland, Maine, 1987-96, vice chmn. bd., 1988-90, chmn. bd., 1990-95; trustee U. New Eng., 1996—. Fellow Soc. Photo Optical Instrumentation Engrs.; mem. Missile Range and Space Pioneers (life charter mem.), IEEE (life sr. mem.), AIAA, Am. Soc. Photogrammetry, Am. Soc. Photogrammetry and Remote Sensing (emeritus), Soc. Photog. Scientists and Engrs., U. Ill. Alumni Assn., Assn. Grads. U.S. Mil. Acad., Eta Kappa Nu, Nashawtuc Country Club, Wyndemere Country Club. Home and Office: 338 Edgemere Way N Naples FL 34105-7105 also: 30 Washington Dr Acton MA 01720-3122

FINLEY, MARY LOU GUINN, artist, craft designer; b. Knoxville, Tenn., Mar. 24, 1941; d. Marvin Carl and Louise (Underwood) Guinn; m. Michael Douglas Finley, Apr. 3, 1959; children: Kelly Melora, Kevin Michael, Scott Douglas, Sean David. AS, Cleve. State C.C., 1982. Sec. George C. Heap Jewelry, Knoxville, 1959; substitute tchr. Bradley County Sch. System, Cleve., 1971-77; bank teller Cleve. Nat. Bank, 1977-82; adminstrv. asst. First Am. Nat. Bank, Cleve., 1982-86; artist, craft designer Cleve., 1989—; helping artist Decoart Products, Stanford, Ky., 1994—. Author instructional art and craft books. Recipient art awards and craft design awards. Mem. Ocoee Artists Assn. (bd. dirs. 1995—). Home: 3020 Lilac Dr NW Cleveland TN 37312-1446

FINLEY, ROBERT VAN EATON, minister; b. Charlottesville, Va., May 2, 1922; s. William Walter and Melissa (Hoover) F.; BA, U. Va., 1944; postgrad. U. Chgo. Div. Sch., 1946-47; LittD, Houghton Coll., 1952; m. Ethel Drummond, Dec. 23, 1949; children: Deborah Ann, Ruth Ellen. Ordained to ministry Bapt. Ch., 1957. Evangelist, Youth for Christ Internat., Chgo. and Inter-Varsity Christian Fellowship, Chgo., 1945-46, overseas, 1948-51; pastor Evang. Free Ch., Richmond, Calif., 1951-52; minister to fgn. students 10th Presbyn. Ch., Phila., 1952-55; pastor Temple Bapt. Ch., Washington, 1965-66; founder, gen. dir. Christian Aid Mission, Charlottesville, Va., 1953-70, chmn., pres., 1970—; founder, gen. dir. Overseas Students Mission, Ft. Erie, Ont., Can., 1954-68, pres., 1969-85; founder, pres. Christian Aid Mission Can., 1985-88, chmn. bd. dirs., 1989—; pres. Bharat Evang. Fellowship, Washington, 1973-87; chmn., bd. dirs., Internat. Fellowship Indigenous Missions, Harrisburg, Pa., 1988—; editor Conquest for Christ, 1954-74, Christian Mission mag., 1974—; founder, pres. Internat. Students, Inc., Colorado Springs, Colo. 1952-67, chmn., 1968-70. Mem. Omicron Delta Kappa. Republican. Office: Christian Aid Mission 3045 Ivy Rd Charlottesville VA 22903-9302 also: Christian Aid Mission, 201 Stanton St, Fort Erie, ON Canada L2A 3N8

FINLEY, SARA CREWS, medical geneticist, educator; b. Lineville, Ala., Feb. 26, 1930; m. Wayne H. Finley; children: Randall Wayne, Sara Jane. B.S. in Biology, U. Ala., 1951, M.D., 1955. Diplomate Am. Bd. Med. Genetics; cert. clin. geneticist; cert. clin. cytogeneticist. Intern Lloyd Noland Hosp., Fairfield, Ala., 1955-56; NIH fellow in pediatrics U. Ala. Med. Sch., Birmingham, 1956-60; NIH trainee in med. genetics Inst. Med. Genetics, U. Uppsala, Sweden, 1961-62; mem. faculty U. Ala. Med. Sch., 1960—, co-dir. lab. med. genetics, 1966—, prof. pediatrics, 1975—, occupant Wayne H. and Sara Crews Finley chair med. genetics, 1986—; Disting. Faculty lectr. Med. Ctr., U. Ala. at Birmingham, 1983; mem. staff Univ., Children's hosps.; mem. ad hoc com. genetic counseling Children's Bur., HEW, 1966; mem. ad hoc rev. panel for genetic disease and sickle cell testing and counseling programs, 1980; mem. genetic diseases program objective rev. panel Bur. Maternal and Child Health and Resources Div., HHS, 1989, mem. adv. group on lab. quality assurance, 1989; Birmingham bd. dirs. Compass Bank. Author papers on clin. cytogenetics, human congenital malformations, human growth and devel. Mem. White House Conf. Health, 1965; mem. rsch. manpower rev. com. Nat. Cancer Inst., 1977-81; mem. Sickle Cell Disease Adv. Com., NIH, 1983-87; chairperson physician's campaign bd. dirs. United Way, 1993-95. Recipient Disting. Alumna award U. Ala. Sch. Medicine Alumni Assn., 1989, Med. award Ala. Assn. for Retarded Children, 1969, Turlington award Planned Parenthood of Ala., 1982, Nat. Outstanding Alumnae award Zeta Tau Alpha, 1992, Disting. Alumna award U. Ala. Nat. Alumni Assn., 1994; named Top Ten Women in Birmingham, 1989, Top 31 Most Outstanding Alumnae U. Ala., Tuscaloosa, 1993. Fellow AMA (founding), Am. Coll. Med. Genetics; mem. Am. Soc. Human Genetics, Am. Fedn. Clin. Rsch., Soc. Exptl. Biology and Medicine, N.Y. Acad. Scis., So. Soc. Pediatric Rsch., Med. Assn. Ala., Ala. Assn. Retarded Children (Ann. Med. award 1969), Ala. Acad. Sci., Jefferson County Med. Soc. (pres. 1990), Jefferson County Pediatric Soc., The Harrison Soc., Rotary Club of Birmingham, Phi Beta Kappa, Sigma Xi, Alpha Omega Alpha, Alpha Epsilon Delta, Omicron Delta Kappa, Phi Kappa Phi, Zeta Tau Alpha. Home: 3412 Brookwood Rd Birmingham AL 35223-2023 Office: U Ala UAB Station Birmingham AL 35294

FINLEY, SARAH MAUDE MERRITT, social worker; b. Atlanta, Nov. 19, 1946; d. Genius and Willie Maude (Wright) Merritt; m. Craig Wayne Finley, Aug. 10, 1968; children: Craig Wayne Jr., Jarret Lee. BA, Spelman Coll., 1968; postgrad., Atlanta U., 1968-69. Job placement advisor Marsh Draughton Bus. Coll., Atlanta, 1971-72; child attendant Fulton County Juvenile Ct., Atlanta, 1972; social worker Fulton County Dept. Family and Children Svcs., Atlanta, 1972—, casework suprs., 1976—, Title VI customer svc. coord. Ctrl. City/North Area office, 1990—. Mem. Am. Pub. Welfare Assn., Ga. County Welfare Assn., Ga. Conf. on Social Welfare, Atlanta Pub. Schs. Parents, Tchrs. and Students Assn., Nat. Assn. Counties, Nat. Alumnae Assn. Spelman Coll., Womens Aux. Ga. VFW, Atlanta Urban League. Baptist. Office: Fulton County Dept Family and Children Svcs 84 Walton St NW Atlanta GA 30303-2125

FINLEY, T.J., evangelist, songwriter, poet, writer; b. Mountain Home, Ark., Mar. 14, 1924; s. Thomas Jackson and Vada Lee (King) F.; m. Gwendolyne Williams, Nov. 18, 1944; children: Jerial Lynn, Donna Gwen, Deborah Ann. BA, Abilene Christian U., 1948. Evangelist Ch. of Christ, Tex., 1948-68; v.p. Camp Red Oak, Orange, Tex., 1958-62; established siinging sch. Ch. of Christ, Haskell, Tex., 1965—. Author: (short course) How to Win Soul and Influence Christians. Cpl. USAF, 1943-46. Republican. Home: 129 E Florence Cordell OK 73632

FINLEY, WAYNE HOUSE, medical educator; b. Goodwater, Ala., Apr. 7, 1927; s. Byron Bruce and Lucille (House) F.; m. Sara Will Crews, July 6, 1952; children: Randall Wayne, Sara Jane. BS, Jacksonville State U., 1948; MA, U. Ala., 1950, MS, 1955, PhD, 1958, MD, 1960; postgrad., U. Uppsala, Sweden, 1961-62. Cert. clin. cytogenetics Am. Bd. Med. Genetics, 1983. Sci. tchr. High Sch., Tuscaloosa, Ala., 1949-51; intern U. Ala. Hosps. and Clinics, 1960-61; from asst. prof. to assoc. prof. pediat. U. Ala. Sch. Medicine, 1962-70, from asst. prof. to assoc. prof. biochemistry, 1965-77, asst. prof. physiology and biophysics, 1968-75; prof., 1970-96; chmn. med. student rsch. day U. Ala. Sch. Medicine, 1965-75, from asst. prof. to assoc. prof. biochemistry, 1965-77, chmn. faculty coun. Sch. Medicine, 1977-78, 84-87, assoc. prof., 1975-96, prof., 1977-96, asst. prof. physiology and biophysics, 1968-75, dir. Lab. Med. Genetics, 1966-96, assoc. prof., 1975-96, prof. epidemiology, pub. health and preventive medicine, 1975-96, prof. emeritus, 1996—, adj. prof. biology, 1980-96, dir. Lab. Med. Genetics, 1966-96, chmn. med. student rsch. day, 1965-75, chmn. faculty coun. Sch. Medicine, 1977-78, 84-87; dir. med. genetics grad. program U. Ala. Sch. Medicine, 1983-96, dir. med. genetics program, 1978—; chmn. Carey Phillips Travel Fellowship, 1972—; nat. adv. rsch. resources coun. NIH-HEW, 1977-80; sr. scientist Comprehensive Cancer Ctr., Cystic Fibrosis Rsch. Ctr.; bd. dirs. Southeastern Regional Genetics Group; chmn. steering com. Reynolds Hist. Libr. Assocs., 1981—, Carmichael Fund for Grad. Students, 1989—; faculty rep. U. Ala. Sys. Bd. Trustees, 1995-96; senator U. Ala. Faculty Senate, 1995-96. Contbr. articles on human malformations and clin. cytogenetics to tech. jours. With AUS, 1945-46, 51-53; lt. col. Res.; ret. Recipient Med. award Ala. Assn. Retarded Children, 1969, Turlington award, 1982, Disting. Faculty Lectr. award U. Ala. Med. Ctr., 1983, Wayne H. and Sara C. Finley chair in med. genetics U. Ala., Birmingham, 1986, Alumnus of Yr. award Jacksonville State U., 1989, Portrait Reynolds Libr., 1991. Fellow Am. Coll. Med. Genetics (founder, edn. com. 1993—, program dir. 1996); mem. AMA (Physicians Recognition award 1971, 75, 81, 84, 87, 90, 93), AAAS, N.Y. Acad. Scis., Soc. Exptl. Biology and Medicine, Am. Inst. Chemists, Am. Fedn. Clin. Rsch., Am. Soc. Human Genetics, So. Med. Assn., So. Soc. Pediat. Rsch., Med. Assn. Ala. (counsellor 1990—), Jefferson County Med. Soc. (maternal and child health com. 1975-79, chmn. 1976-77, pres. 1983), Jefferson County Pediat. Soc., Caduceus Club (pres. 1984-86), U. Ala. Sch. Medicine Alumni Assn. (pres. 1974-75, Disting. Alumni award 1978), Greater Birmingham Area C. of C. (bd. dirs. 1983-86), Newcomen Soc., Kiwanis (pres. Shades Valley 1973-74), Rotary, Sigma Xi, Kappa Delta Pi, Phi Delta Kappa, Alpha Omega Alpha, Phi Beta Pi, Omicron Delta Kappa. Baptist. Home: 3412 Brookwood Rd Birmingham AL 35223-2023 Office: U Ala Lab Med Genetics Univ Station Birmingham AL 35294-0017

FINN, GLORIA INEZ, geriatrics nurse; b. Frederick, Md., Nov. 12, 1932; d. Carl Ray and Inez Rebecca (Watkins) Holland; m. James Ronald Finn, May 5, 1956 (div. Sept. 1985); children: Lisa Gaye Harris, Tara Lane Finn. Degree in nursing, Ch. Home Hosp., Balt., 1953. RN, Md., Va.; cert. geriat. Asst. head nurse, supr. Church Home Hosp., Balt., 1953-55; IV therapist Union Meml. Hosp., Balt., 1955-58; supr. U. Okla., Oklahoma City, 1958-59; RN newborn nursery Alexandria (Va.) Hosp., 1959-62; RN gen. duty Annaburg Manor Nursing Home, Manassas, Va., 1974-79; RN charge nurse Loudoun Longterm Care, Leesburg, Va., 1979-90; RNC supr. Loudoun Longterm Care Ctr., Leesburg, Va., 1990—; owner Home Owner Orgn., Va., 1960—. Mem. Va. State Nurses Assn., Am. Legion (assoc.). Methodist. Home: 45473 Lakeside Dr Sterling VA 20165-2523

FINNELL, DALLAS GRANT, fundraising executive; b. Scott, Sask., Can., Jan. 10, 1931; s. Grant and Della (Loadman) F.; m. Shirley Mae Sproule, Nov. 25, 1954 (div. 1977); children: Kenneth Wayne, Karlyn Sue, Darryl Dallas; m. Patricia Frances Irving Lewis, Mar. 20, 1982; stepchildren: Stephen Joseph Lewis, Janine Lewis Strozzieri. BSBA, Lewis and Clark Coll., 1954. Trust adminstr. U.S. Bank Oreg., Portland, 1955-60; alumni dir. Lewis and Clark Coll., Portland, 1960-62; dir. annual fund Austin Coll., Sherman, Tex., 1962-65; corp. relations officer Duke U., Durham, N.C., 1965-69; exec. dir. U. Oreg. Med. Sch. Found., Portland, 1969-73; asst. to pres., dir. devel. Salk Inst., San Diego, 1973-74; western area dir. Cystic Fibrosis Found., San Diego, 1974-78; pres. Gen. Hosp. Found., Everett, Wash., 1978-89; prin. Dallas Finnell & Co., 1989-91; pres. Dallas Finnell & Co., Inc., Alexandria, Va., 1991—; cons. Finnell Assocs., Portland and San Diego, 1971-78. Bd. dirs. Bishop Sch. of Everett, 1980-84, pres., 1983. Mem. Assn. for Healthcare Philanthropy (bd. dirs. 1985-86), Northwest Devel. Officers Assn. (pres. 1982), Nat. Soc. Fund Raising Execs. (greater Washington chpt., cert. 1991—, bd. dirs. Wash. state chpt. 1988-89), Rotary. Republican. Home and Office: 8721 Waterford Rd Alexandria VA 22308-2356

FINNEY, CARL RICHARD, emergency medical technician; b. Texarkana, Tex., Dec. 16, 1964; s. Lloyd Edward and Elsie Jo (George) F.; m. Rita Lea Cardenas, July 21, 1990. Grad. H.S., Natalia, Tex. Cert. EMT and basic trauma life support, Tex. Lifeguard Northside Sch. Dist., San Antonio, 1985-88, lifeguard supr., 1988-89, 4th grade swimming instr., 1989; EMT Superior Ambulance Co., San Antonio, 1988-89; med. tech./safety tech. Ohbayashi Corp., San Antonio, 1988—. Contbr.: A Sea of Treasures, 1995 (Editor Choice award 1995), Best Poems of the 90's, 1996. Vol. ARC, San Antonio, 1986-90, first aid instr., 1987-90, minor events coord., 1987; trustee Temple Bapt. Ch., San Antonio, 1989; youth worker New Covenant Ch., San Antonio, 1990. Named Outstanding Vol., ARC, 1989, Outstanding Tchrs. Aid, Key Club Internat., 1989. Mem. Internat. Soc. Poets. Baptist.

FINNEY, ERNEST ADOLPHUS, JR., state supreme court chief justice; b. Smithfield, Va., Mar. 23, 1931; s. Ernest A. Sr. and Collen (Godwin) F.; m. Frances Davenport, Aug. 20, 1955; children: Ernest A. III, Lynn Carol (Nikky) Finney, Jerry Leo. BA, Claflin Coll., 1952; JD, S.C. State U., 1954, LHD (hon.), 1996; HHD (hon.), Claflin Coll., 1977; LLD, U. S.C., 1991, The Citadel, 1995, Johnson C. Smith U., 1995, Morris Coll., 1996; LHD (hon.), Coll. of Charleston, 1995; LLD, Morris Coll., 1996. Bar: S.C. 1954, U.S. Dist. Ct. S.C. 1957, U.S. Ct. Appeals (4th cir.) 1964. Pvt. practice law Conway, S.C., 1954-60, Sumter, S.C., 1960-66; assoc. Finney and Gray, Attys.-at-Law, Sumter, 1966-76; mem. S.C. Ho. of Reps., Columbia, 1973-76; judge S.C. Cir. Ct., Columbia, 1976-85; assoc. justice S.C. Supreme Ct., Columbia, 1985-94, chief justice, 1994—. Chmn. S.C. Legis. Black Caucus, Columbia, 1973-75; chmn. bd. dirs. Buena Vista Devel. Corp., Sumter, 1967—; mem. S.C. State Elections Commn., Columbia, 1968-72; trustee Claflin Coll., Orangeburg, S.C., 1986—, chmn. bd. trustees, 1987-95; sch. law minority adv. com. U. S.C., 1988—. Recipient Disting. Alumni of Yr. award Nat. Assn. Equal Opportunity Edn., 1986, Achievement award C. of C., Sumter, 1986, Presdl. Citation Morris Coll., Sumter, 1986; named 1987 Citizen of Yr. Charleston (S.C.) Med. Soc., 1987; inductee Nat. Black Coll. Alumni Hall of Fame, 1988. Mem. ABA, Am. Judges Assn., Am. Law Inst., Conf. Chief Justices, Sumter County Bar, S.C. Bar, Assn. Trial Lawyers Am., Nat. Bar Assn. (appellate com.), S.C. Trial Lawyers Assn. (hon.), Masons, Shriners. Methodist. Home: 24 Runnymede Blvd Sumter SC 29153-8742 Office: SC Supreme Ct Rm 100 PO Drawer 1309 Sumter County Courthouse Sumter SC 29151-1309

FINNEY, JAMES OWEN, JR., cardiologist; b. Gadsden, Ala., Feb. 3, 1938; s. James Owen and Margaret (Pride) F.; m. Pattie Perry Robinson, June 8, 1960; children: Margaret Carlisle, Pattie Perry, James Owen III, Mabel Pride. BA, Vanderbilt U., 1960, MD, 1965. Diplomate Am. Bd. Internal Medicine and Cardiovascular Diseases. Intern Univ. Ala., Birmingham, 1965-66, resident, 1966-68; fellow cardiology Univ. Chgo., 1968-69; fellow Univ. Ala., Birmingham, 1969-70, chief resident, 1970-71; pvt. practice Southview Med. Group, Birmingham, Ala., 1973—. Major USAF, 1971-73. Fellow ACP, Am. Coll. Cardiology, Coun. on Clin. Cardiology, Am. Heart Assn. (dir. Ala. alliance 1975—); mem. Vanderbilt Med. Alumni Assn. (v.p. 1992-94, pres. 1994-96). Office: Southview Med Group 833 Saint Vincents Dr Ste 300 Birmingham AL 35205-1613

FINNEY, MARCIA DAY, medical educator, academic administrator; b. Grand Rapids, Mich., June 25, 1948; d. Robert Sheldon and Jean Louise (Thompson) D.; m. Charles M. Finney, May 12, 1979 (div. 1988); 1 child, Brendan. BA in English with high honors, Mich. State U., 1970; MA, U. Va., 1976, PhD, 1996. Instr. English Northwestern U., Evanston, Ill., 1974-75; editor medicine U. Va., Charlottesville, 1975-78, info. officer medicine, 1978-88, instr. medicine, 1988-91, spl. asst. to v.p. and provost for health scis., 1989-95, asst. prof. med. edn. (med. humanities), 1991—; co-dir. humanities in medicine U. Va. Sch. Medicine, 1996—; assoc. scholar Va. Health Policy Ctr., U. Va., 1991—; ethics com. U. Va. Med. Ctr., 1984—, ethics consultation svc., 1988-89; dir. lit. and medicine U. Va. Sch. Medicine, 1991—. Author: (with others) Introduction to Clinical Ethics, 1991, Essentials of General Surgery, 1992, Managing in Academics: An Academic Medicine Model, 1993; adv. editor: International Dictionary of Medicine and Biology, 1986, Churchills Medical Dictionary, 1989; contbr. articles to profl. jours. Bd. dirs. Oratorio Soc. Charlottesville-Albemarle, 1988-91, Zephyrus, 1994—; lector, chalice bearer Christ Episcopal Ch., Charlottesville, 1991—, vestry registrar, 1993-95. Fellow Woodrow Wilson, 1970-71, Danforth, 1972-74. Mem. Soc. for Health and Human Values, The Narrative Circle, Phi Beta Kappa. Democrat. Episcopalian. Home: 116 Oak Forest Cir Charlottesville VA 22901-1610 Office: U Va Sch Medicine HSC Box 389 Charlottesville VA 22908-0389

FINNEY, PATRICIA ANN, elementary education educator; b. Ft. Worth, Aug. 7, 1936; d. Thomas Lee and Mary Myrtle (Austin) Carleton; m. Roy Jack Finney, Nov. 9, 1957; children: Roy Jack Finney III, Thomas Lee Finney. BS in Edn., North Tex. State U., 1957. Cert. tchr., Tex. Tchr. art Ft. Worth Ind. Sch. Dist., Ft. Worth, 1957-67; tchr. Ft. Bend Ind. Sch. Dist., Sugar Land, Tex., 1979-85, tchr. elem. art, 1985—. One-woman gallery shows, 1972—; illustrator children's books, 1991, 92, 93. Vol. artist Audubon Soc. newsletter, Houston, 1991—; vol. Houston Mus. Natural Sci., 1994—. Mem. Tex. Art Edn. Assn., Nat. Art Edn. Assn., Soc. Children's Book Writers, PTA. Methodist. Home: 10019 Towne Brook Ln Sugar Land TX 77478-1642

FINNEY, ROY PELHAM, JR., urologist, surgeon, inventor; b. Gaffney, S.C., Dec. 7, 1924; s. Roy P. Finney Sr. and Mary Frances (Cannon) Woodard; m. Kay Harkness, Apr. 5, 1962; children: Wright C., James L., Joella R., Gray, Kevin. MD, Med. U. S.C., 1952. Diplomate: Am. Bd. Urology. Resident in urology Johns Hopkins U., Balt., 1952-57; prof. surg. urology U. South Fla., Tampa, 1972-84, dir. div. urology, 1972-84; ret. Designer and inventor implantable prostheses incontinence device inflatable penile prostheses treatment impotence, Double J ureteral stent, developer new surg. procedures treatment impotence; patentee in field. Fellow ACS; mem. Am. Urology Assn., Soc. Internationale D'Urologie, Internat. Continence Soc., Urodynamic Soc. Republican. Home: 4382 Cortez Blvd Spring Hill FL 34607-1201

FINSTAD, GUY W., educational association executive; b. Cranfills Gap, Tex., Sept. 12, 1933; m. Geneva Allen, Aug. 9, 1952; children: Sherry G. Roberts, Garry, Terry, Barry. BS in Agrl. Edn., Tex. Tech., 1959. Tchr. Maypear (Tex.) Ind. Sch. Dist., 1959-61; tchr./farmer/ranch mgr. Cal Farley's Boys Ranch, Boys Ranch, Tex., 1961-80; com. staff Tex. Senate, Austin, 1981-88; adminstrv. asst. U.S. Congressman Sarpolius, Washington, 1988-90; exec. dir. Vocat. Agr. Tchrs. Assn. tex., Austin, 1990—. Exec. bd. Future Farmers Am. Found., Austin, 1985—; bd. dirs. Future Farmers Am. (Tex. chpt.), Austin, 1990—; bd. dirs. Vocat. Agrl. Tchrs. Assn. Tex. Credit Union, Austin, 1981-88. Named Disting. Alumnus, Sch. Edn., tex. tech., 1994. Lutheran. Home: PO Box 148 Cranfills Gap TX 76637 Office: Vocat Agrl Tchrs Assn Texas 614 E 12th St Austin TX 78701-1908

FINTOR, LOUIS JOHN, epidemiologist, researcher, writer; b. Detroit, Oct. 12, 1958; s. Louis and Thelma (Estepp) F. BA, U. Mich., 1984; MA, Am. U., 1986; MPH, U. Calif., Berkeley, 1990; postgrad., Johns Hopkins U., George Washington U. Reporter L.A. Times, 1987-88, The Detroit News, 1988-89, The Hartford Courant, 1989-90; analyst NIH, Bethesda, Md., 1990-95; epidemiologist CDC, Atlanta, 1995-96; health comm. specialist NIOSH Appalachian Regional Lab., Morgantown, W.Va., 1996; commr. Mayor's Commn. on Food, Nutrition and Health, Washington, D.C. HIV Prevention Planning Commn., Washington. Contbrn. author: Science and Practice of Cancer Prevention and Control, 1995, Encyclopedia of AIDS, 1996. Mem. APHA, Am. Soc. Health Svcs. Rsch., White House Corr. Assn., Nat. Press Club (employment com. chair). Office: NIOSH Appalachian Regional Lab MS-B167 1095 Willowdale Rd Morgantown WV 26505

FIORENTINO, CARMINE, lawyer; b. Bklyn., Sept. 11, 1932; s. Pasquale and Lucy (Coppola) F. LL.B., Blackstone Sch. Law, Chgo., 1954, John Marshall Law Sch., Atlanta, 1957. Bar: Ga., D.C., U.S. Supreme Ct., U.S. Dist. Ct. D.C., U.S. Ct. Appeals (2d cir.), U.S. Dist. Ct. (no. dist.) Ga., U.S. Ct. Appeals (5th cir.), U.S. Ct. Claims. Mem. N.Y. State Workmen's Compensation Bd., N.Y. State Dept. Labor, 1950-53; ct. reporter, hearing stenographer N.Y. State Com. State Counsel and Attys., 1953; public relations sec. Indsl. Home for Blind, Bklyn., 1953-55; legal stenographer, researcher, law clk., Atlanta, 1955, 57-59; sec. import-export firm, Atlanta, 1956; sole practice, Atlanta, 1959-63, 73—; atty., advisor, trial atty. HUD, Atlanta and Washington, also legal counsel Peachtree Fed. Credit Union, 1963-74; acting dir. Elmira (N.Y.) Disaster Field Office, HUD, 1973; former candidate U.S. Adminstrv. Law Judge. Recipient State of Victory World Culture prize. Mem. Smithsonian Instn., pres., dir., gen. counsel The Hexagon Corp., Republican Nat. Com., Rep. Presdl. Task Force, Nat. Hist. Soc.; Inducted into Rep. Presdl. Legion Merit, 1993; Life Dynamics fellow; mem. Atlanta Hist. Soc., Atlanta Bot. Gardens, Am. Mus. Natural History, Mus. Heritage Soc. Mem. ABA, Fed. Bar Assn., Atlanta Bar Assn., Decatur-DeKalb Bar Assn., Am. Judicature Soc., Old War Horse Lawyers Club, Assn. Trial Lawyers Am., AAAS, Internat. Platform Soc., Nat. Audubon Soc. Presbyterian. Clubs: Toastmasters, Gaslight, Sierra. Writer non-fiction and poetry; composer songs and hymns. Home and Office: 4717 Roswell Rd NE Apt R4 Atlanta GA 30342-2915

FIORENTINO, THOMAS MARTIN, transportation executive, lawyer; b. Washington, Aug. 4, 1959; s. Thomas Martin Sr. and Julia (Bray) F.; m. Mary Ann Hammer, June 12, 1983; children: Sara Elizabeth, Caroline McKay, Thomas Martin III. BA, U. Fla., 1980; JD, Mercer U., 1983. Bar: Fla. 1984. Claims rep. Seaboard System R.R., Evansville, Ind., 1983-84; claims atty. Seaboard System R.R., Jacksonville, Fla., 1984-86; dir. risk mgmt. CSX Corp., Jacksonville, 1986-87; asst. to pres. CSX Tech., Jacksonville, 1987-89; chief of staff Fed. R.R. Adminstrn., 1989-90; counselor to dep. sec. of transp. Office of the Sec., Dept. Transp., Washington, 1990-91; asst. v.p. pub. affairs CSX Transp., Jacksonville, 1991-94, v.p. govt. affairs, 1994-95, v.p. corp. comms. and pub. affairs, 1995—. Mem. bd. visitors The Bolles Sch., 1990-96; bd. dirs. St. Mark's Episcopal Day Sch., 1992-94, Theatreworks, 1992-95, Boys and Girls Clubs of N.E. Fla., 1992-95, Mus. Sci. and History, 1993-96, Jacksonville Urban League, 1993-95, Bapt. Health Systems Found., 1992—, I.M. Sultzbacher Ctr. for the Homeless, 1994-95, Gov. Coun. Sustainable Devel., 1996, Children's Home Soc. of Jacksonville, 1996—. Mem. Fla. Bar Assn., Fla. C. of C., Jacksonville C. of C., First Coast Mfrs. Assn., River Club, Marsh Landing Country Club, The Lodge and Bath Club (Ponte Vedra Beach), Kappa Alpha Alumni Assn. (bd. dirs. Jacksonville chpt. 1987-88), Phi Delta Phi. Republican. Presbyterian. Home: 140 Indian Hammock Ln Ponte Vedra Beach FL 32082-2155

FIORIO, GIANFRANCO R., financial consultant; b. Washington, Jan. 14, 1951; s. Franco Emilio and Maria (Lanzillotto) F. AA, Broward C.C., 1971; BA, Fla. Atlantic U., 1973. Exec. v.p. Global Intermktg., Washington, 1977-87; pres. Pilott Inc., Arlington, Va., 1987-91; fin. cons. Arlington, Va., 1991—; real estate agt. GRA 5 Star Properties, Va., 1987-93; real estate cons., 1987-93; real estate mgmt. cons., 1987—. Author screenplay: Noble Element, 1985. Athletic scholar Fla. Atlantic U., 1971.

FIRESTONE, JUANITA MARLIES, sociology educator; b. Wurzburg, Germany, Jan. 30, 1947; d. Harrison and Marlies (Breit) Gillette; m. Kenneth Todd Firestone, Aug. 31, 1968 (div. Oct. 1993); children: Jason Dean, Krystillin Elisabeth. BS in Sociology cum laude, Black Hills State U., 1979; MA in Sociology, U. Tex., 1982, PhD in Sociology, 1984. Office mgr. Silver Wings Aviation, Rapid City, S.D., 1975-76; pub. rels. mgr. Pacer Mining Co., Custer, S.D., 1976-79; lectr. sociology U. Tex., Austin, 1980-87; asst. prof. sociology U. Tex., San Antonio, 1987-94, assoc. prof., 1994—; cons. in field; attendee Nat. Security Forum, 1994; mem. Chancellor's Faculty Adv. Coun., U. Tex. Sys., 1994-96; testimony U.S. Congress Black Polit. Caucus, 1996. Contbr. articles to profl. jours. Mem. spkrs. bur. Rape Crisis Ctr., Austin and San Antonio, 1984-94; bd. dirs. AIDS Found., San Antonio, 1992; coord. workshop Expanding Your Horizons, San Antonio, 1992-96; mem. Task Force on Crime and Violence, San Antonio, 1990. Recipient Rsch. award U. Tex. Sys., Austin, 1991, 95; Congrl. fellow, Washington, 1983. Mem. Internat. Sociol. Assn., Am. Sociol. Assn., S.W. Soc. Social Sci. (pres. women's caucus 1994-95), Golden Key (faculty advisor 1990-96), Alpha Kappa Delta. Office: U Tex at San Antonio Divsn Social and Policy Sci San Antonio TX 78249

FIRESTONE, SHEILA MEYEROWITZ, gifted and talented education educator; b. Bronx, N.Y., Dec. 20, 1941; d. Boris and Bella Meyerowitz; m. Bruce Firestone, Oct. 1, 1961; children: Wayne, Evan. AA, Miami-Dade Community Coll., North Miami, Fla., 1969; BA in Edn., Fla. Atlantic U., 1972; MS in Spl. Edn., Fla. Internat. U., 1973. Cert. learning disabilities, elem., gifted, early childhood, emotionally disturbed, Fla. Tchr. to gifted Highland Oaks Elem. Sch., North Miami Beach, Fla., 1973—; chairperson Dade County Very Spl. Arts Festival, 1989-93. Composer: Premiere - Psalm 117, Because I Love, South Florida Youth Symphony, 1994. Mem. choir Temple Sinai, North Miami Beach, 1979-92; pub. speaking coach Optimist Oratorial Contests, North Miami Beach, 1988-89, Theodore Gibson Oratorical Contest, Miami, 1989-90; state evaluator Future Problem Solving, 1989-96; creative writing supt. Dade County Youth Fair, 1982-87; founder "Songs for a New Day; pub. teaching curriculum and leadership/citizenship tng. thematic music and interdisciplinary whole lang. learning units, 1990; mem. choir Aventura Turnberry Jewish Ctr., 1993. Named Master Tchr., State of Fla., 1985; recipient Very Spl. Arts Honor award Dade County Bd. Pub. Instns., 1990, 1st pl. Jim Harbin Fame award Fla. Media Educators, 1994, Tchr. of Note, Young Patronesses of the Opera, 1996; Freedom Found. grantee, summers, 1983, 84, 87, 90, Nancy Givens Instrnl. grantee, Fla. Coun. Exceptional Children, 1995, Javitts grant Nat. Evaluator F.P.S., 1992-93, grantee Dade Pub. Edn. Fund Impact II Adapter, 1994. 1Mem. ASCAP, Coun. for Exceptional Children (various offices 1963—, chpt. pres. 1988, Fla. Exceptional Tchr. of Yr. finalist 1989, Chpt. 121 Dade County Exceptional Student Tchr. of Yr. award 1989, Highland Oaks Elem. Sch. Tchr. of Yr. 1990), Fla. Assn. Gifted Children, Dade County Reading Coun., Sigma alpha Iota (patroness 1996). Democrat. Home: 19520 NE 18th Pl Miami FL 33179-3642 Office: Highland Oaks Elem Sch 20500 NE 24th Ave Miami FL 33180-1307

FISCH, BRUCE JEFFREY, physician; b. Indpls., May 9, 1952; s. Charles and June Louise (Spiegal) F.; m. Susan Elizabeth Resneck, July 31, 1977; children: Ian Lawrence, Paul Jeffrey. BA, Ind. U., 1974, MD, 1978. Diplomate Am. Bd. Psychiatry and Neurology, Am. Bd. Clin. Neurophysiology, Am. Bd. Sleep Medicine. Intern in internal medicine Mich. State U., Lansing, 1978-79; resident in neurology Ind. U. Sch. Medicine, 1979-81, chief resident in neurology, 1981-82, postdoctoral fellow in electromyography, 1982; postdoctoral fellow in electroencephalography Mayo Clin. Grad. Sch. of Medicine, 1982-83; asst. prof. neurology Columbia U. Coll. Physicians and Surgeons, N.Y.C., 1984-90; dir. Epilepsy Monitoring Unit Columbia-Presbyn. Med. Ctr., N.Y.C., 1985-90; assoc. prof. neurology La. State U. Sch. Medicine, New Orleans, 1990—; dir. Clin. Neurophysiology Program and Labs. U. Hosp. and Charity Hosp./La. State U. Sch. Medicine, 1990—; dir. Sleep Disorders Ctr Univ. Hosp., New Orleans, 1991—; dir. Clin. Neurophysiology Lab., Harlem Hosp., N.Y.C., 1985-90; dir. Quantitative EEG Analysis Lab., Neurol. Inst. N.Y., Columbia-Presbyn. Med. Ctr., 1986-90; clin. asst. in neurology St. Vincent's Hosp., N.Y.C., 1986-90; mem. curriculum com. La. State U., 1992—; reviewer books and jours. in field. Author: Spehlmann's EEG Primer, 1992; contbr. articles to profl. jours. Grantee Charles S. Robertson Meml. Gift for Alzheimer's Disease, The Banbuy Fund, 1987-88, NIH-BRSG, 1991-92, The Upjohn Co., 1994-95. Fellow Am. Electroencephalographic Soc. (sec. 1992-95, presenter confs., various coms.), Am. Sleep Disorders Assn.; mem. Am. Acad. Neurology (conf. presenter, rev. abstracts), Am. Epilepsy Soc. (mem. and program coms. 1992-93, bd. dirs. S.E. La. coun. 1992—, platform session chmn. 1992), AMA, Am. Acad. Clin. Neurophysiology. Home: 5 Dunleith Ct New Orleans LA 70118-5142 Office: La State U Sch Medicine 1542 Tulane Ave New Orleans LA 70112-2825

FISCHELL, TIM ALEXANDER, cardiologist; b. Washington, Feb. 10, 1956; s. Robert Ellentuch and Marian (Standard) F.; m. Anne Elizabeth Arbetter, Sept. 23, 1984; children: Evan Daniel, Jonathan Morris. AB, Cornell U., 1977, MD, 1981. Diplomate Am. Bd. Internal Medicine, subspecialty cardiovascular disease. Intern internal medicine Harvard/Mass. Gen. Hosp., Boston, 1981-82, resident, 1982-84; fellow cardiology Stanford (Calif.) U., 1984-87, asst. prof. medicine, 1987-92; assoc. prof. medicine Vanderbilt U., Nashville, 1992—; mem. med. adv. bd. Scimed, Mpls., 1992—, Cordina, Inc., Fremont, Calif., 1993—, Isostent, Inc., San Carlos, Calif., 1995—. Patentee in field; contbr. articles to profl. jours., chpts. to books. Recipient Fischbach Residency Scholarship, 1986, Nat.Rsch. Svc. award grant NIH, 1986-87, clin. investigator award NIH, 1987-92, biomed. rsch. support grant NIH/Stanford U., 1988-90; finalist Inventor of Yr. prize First Thoraxcenter Course on Intracoronary Stenting, Rotterdam, The

Netherlands, 1994. Fellow Am. Coll. Cardiology, Soc. Cardiac Angiography and Interventions, Andreas Gruntzig Soc., Am. Heart Assn. (coun. on circulation, advanced fellowship award Calif. affiliate 1987, grant in aid award 1988-90), Phi Beta Kappa, Phi Kappa Phi, Alpha Omega Alpha. Home: 1018 Chancery Ln Nashville TN 37215 Office: Vanderbilt U Hosp Rm 1201 21st & Garland St Nashville TN 37232

FISCHER, ALVIN EUGENE, JR., marketing executive; b. Glendale, Calif., July 31, 1942; s. Alvin Eugene Sr. and Roberta Maxine (Barker) F.; m. Michel Jane Gorham, Dec. 20, 1960 (div. Oct. 1982); children: Theresa Michele, Todd Alan, Alvin Eugene III; m. Laurie Ann Simpson, Aug. 22, 1986. Student, Orange Coast Coll., 1960-70, UCLA, 1967, U. Calif., Irvine, 1970. Lic. bldg. contractor, Calif. Supt. constrn. K.W. Koll Builders, Costa Mesa, Calif., 1960-65; gen. sales mgr. Mills Inc., Santa Ana, Calif., 1965-70; gen. mgr. Royal Interiors Inc., Santa Ana, 1970-72; v.p. nat. ops. Larwin Home Ctr., Beverly Hills, Calif., 1972-74; broker Village Real Estate, Huntington Beach, Calif., 1975-78; v.p. sales Phillips Floor Covering, Santa Ana, 1978-81; gen. sales mgr. G.A.F./Tarkett/Star Distbn., Commerce, Calif., 1981-83; v.p. sales and mktg. LaSalle-Deitch Co., Tustin, Calif., 1983-84; gen. sales mgr. LD Brinkman, Ontario, Calif., 1984-85; sales mgr. western region Nat. Floor Products Inc., Florence, Ala., 1986—; panelist Western Floor Covering Assn., 1979. Mgr. pubs. Newport Theatrical Arts, Newport Beach, Calif., 1983; mem. South Coast Community Ch., Irvine, Calif. Mem. Am. Mgmt. Assn., So. Calif. Floor Covering Club, Newport Sail Club. Office: Nat Floor Products Inc PO Box 354 Florence AL 35631-0354

FISCHER, ASHTON JOHN, JR., investor; b. New Orleans, Nov. 24, 1952; s. Ashton John and Elizabeth Lee (Nicholson) F.; m. Roxanne Wright Stoehr, Dec. 28, 1978 (div. Mar. 1983). BA, Tulane U., 1978. Investor, 1978—. Contbr. poetry to Nat. Libr. Poetry (Editor's Choice award 1993). Mem. Internat. Soc. Poets (charter, life). Home and Office: 5420 S Liberty St New Orleans LA 70115-5007

FISCHER, CARL ROBERT, health care facility administrator; b. Rahway, N.J., Nov. 15, 1939; s. Robert Carlton and Elsie Marie (Wolfarth) F.; m. Lynn Elaine Ekstrand, Mar. 12, 1966; children: Kristen, Leslie, Meredith, Kelly. B.S. in Nursing, Wagner Coll., 1964; M.S., SUNY-Buffalo, 1966; M.P.H., Yale U., 1968. With Yale-New Haven Hosp., 1968-77, assoc. dir., 1975-77; exec. assoc. adminstr. U. Cin. Med. Ctr., 1977-80; exec. dir. clin. programs U. Ark. for Med. Scis., Little Rock, 1980-86; assoc. v.p. health scis. and exec. dir. Med. Coll. of Va. Hosps., Richmond, 1986—; active Univ. Hosps., Richmond, 1986—; active Univ. Hosp. Consorium Svcs. Corp., 1987, chmn. bd. dirs. 1988-89, chmn. supply and svcs. divsn., 1988-89, 95—. Mem. Am. Assn. Med. Colls., Am. Hosp. Assn., Va. Hosp. Assn. (bd. dirs. 1986-91, chmn. coun. on adminstrn. and health planning 1988, coun. on assn. devel. 1987-88, physician liaison com. 1989-90), Univ. Health Systems Consortium (bd. dirs. 1981—, exec. com. 1983-96), Ctrl. Va. Health Planning Agy. (pres. 1991-93). Lutheran. Office: Med Coll Va Hosps Va Commonwealth U PO Box 980510 Richmond VA 23298

FISCHER, DANIEL EDWARD, psychiatrist; b. New Haven, Apr. 22, 1945; s. Alexander and Miriam (Kramer) F.; m. Linda Lee Bradford, June 12, 1969; children: Meredith Tara, Alexis Anne. B.A., Boston U., 1969, M.D., 1969; J.D., Coll. William and Mary, 1986. Bar: Va. 1986, U.S. Dist. Ct. (ea. dist.) Va. 1986, U.S. Ct. Appeals (4th cir.) 1986. Intern in medicine Baylor Affiliated Hosps., Houston, 1969-70; resident in psychiatry Washington U. Sch. Medicine, St. Louis, 1970-73; practice medicine specializing in psychiatry Virginia Beach, Va., 1975—; chmn. dept. psychiatry DePaul Hosp., Norfolk, Va., 1978-79, Bayside Hosp., Virginia Beach, 1980-81, 88-89, 1990-91; assoc. med. dir. adult in-patient svcs. rapid stabilization unit Tidewater Psychiat. Inst., Norfolk, 1989-94; med. dir. Norfolk (Va.) Psychiat. Ctr., 1995-96. Contbr. articles to profl. jours.; patentee in field. Bd. dirs. Tidewater Pastoral Counseling Svc., Norfolk, 1976—, Kempsville Conservative Synagogue, Virginia Beach, 1982-86, Beth Chavarim, 1987-90; pres. Am. Investment Mgmt. Svcs., Inc., Virginia Beach, 1987—. Served as maj. U.S. Army, 1973-75. Decorated Army Commendation medal. Fellow Acad. Psychosomatic Medicine, Am. Psychiat. Assn.; mem. AMA, Va. Med. Soc., Va. Psychiat. Assn., Virginia Beach Med. Soc., Tidewater Acad. Psychiatry. Democrat. Jewish. Office: 621 Lynnhaven Pky Ste 366 Virginia Beach VA 23452-7300

FISCHER, DAVID JON, lawyer; b. Danville, Ill., July 27, 1952; s. Oscar Ralph and Sarah Pauline (Pomerantz) F. BA, U. Miami, 1974, JD, 1977. Bar: Fla. 1977, Iowa 1978, U.S. Dist. Ct. (so. dist.) Iowa 1978, (mid. dist.) Fla. 1993, U.S. Ct. Appeals (8th cir.) 1978, D.C. 1979, U.S. Ct. Appeals (D.C. cir.) 1979, U.S. Dist. Ct. D.C. 1980, U.S. Ct. Appeals (llth cir.) 1984, U.S. Tax Ct. 1987, Ga. 1989, U.S. Dist. Ct. (no. dist.) Ga. 1990, U.S. Supreme Ct. 1990, U.S. Dist. Ct. (mid. dist.) Fla., 1993. Atty. Iowa Dept. Social Svcs., Des Moines, 1978; assoc. Parrish & Del Gallo P.C., Des Moines, 1978-79, Donald M. Murtha & Assocs., Washington, 1979-80; assoc. editor Lawyers Coop. Pub. Co., Washington, 1980-82; pvt. practice law Washington, 1982-83, Des Moines, 1983-84, Atlanta, 1984-93; pvt. practice Tampa, Fla., 1993; asst. dist. legal counsel Fla. Dept. Health and Rehab. Svcs., Largo, 1993-95; pvt. practice law Atlanta, 1995—; part-time atty. Fla. Dept. of Children and Families, 1996-97; prof. John Marshall Law Sch., Atlanta, 1986-88; instr. legal studies program dept. ins. and risk mgmt. Ga. State U., 1988-93, instr. aviation adminstrn. program Coll. Pub. and Urban Affairs, 1989-93; apptd. gen. counsel Techwerks, Inc., Mo., 1990-92; instr. Bridge the Gap seminar, Inst. CLE in Ga., 1993; presenter State of Fla. Dept. Health and Rehabilitative Svcs. Dist. Legal Counsel Workshop, 1994, 96; spkr. Clearwater Bar Assn., 1993, 94, 95. Author: The Aeronaut's Law Handbook, 1986, (with others) Georgia Corporate Practice Forms for the Small Business Attorney, 1992; contbg. editor Balloon Life mag., 1986—; editor: (suppl.) Georgia Corporate Forms, 1993—, Florida Criminal Sentencing, 1997—. Vol. liaison Atlanta Com. for the Olympic Games, 1991-92. Mem. ABA (sect. com. 1980-82), Fed. Bar Assn., Iowa Bar Assn., State Bar Ga., Atlanta Bar Assn., Fla. Bar Assn., D.C. Bar Assn., Polk County Bar Assn., Pros. Attys. Coun. Ga. (tech. editor Computer Crime Jour.), Gwinnett County Bar Assn., U. of Miami Alumni Assn., Balloon Fedn. Am. (chmn. com. 1986-91), Carolinas Balloon Assn., Ga. Balloon Assn. (chmn. com. 1985-90), Chesapeake Balloon Assn., Great Ea. Balloon Assn., Alpha Epsilon Pi (hon., faculty advisor). Jewish.

FISCHER, JOHN ARTHUR, financial analyst; b. Mpls., Oct. 23, 1929; s. Carl Frederick and Kathryn Dorothy (Gehrenbeck) F.; m. Betty Louise Christopher, May 23, 1953; children: Mark Alan, Cris Lynn. B in Gen. Studies, U. Nebr., 1969. Customer engr. IBM, Jacksonville, Fla., 1956, Poughkeepsie, N.Y., 1956-57, systems engr., Kingston, N.Y., 1957-58, Kansas City, Mo., 1958-60, programmer, project mgr., Omaha, 1960-69, site mgr. Lowry AFB, Denver, 1969-71, Leesburg, Va., 1971-72, project mgr., Manassas, Va., 1972-76, staff programmer, 1976-79, staff bus. controls analyst fed. systems div., 1979-87, chmn. supervisory com. Employees Credit Union, 1979-88, dir. 1983-91, chmn. bd. dirs., 1988-91; pres. Foxleith Assocs., 1987—, John Fischer & Assocs., 1988—. Mem. county and state com. Va. Rep. Com. With USN, 1947-56; ETO. Mem. NRA (life), Assn. Computing Machinery, Prince William County Beekeepers Assn. (treas. 1977-89), Prince William County Community Svcs. Bd. (dir. 1990-92). Home: 4407 Sanders Ln Catharpin VA 20143-1016 Office: Foxleith Assocs 4407 Sanders Ln Catharpin VA 20143-1016

FISCHER, LEROY HENRY, historian, educator; b. Hoffman, Ill., May 19, 1917; s. Andrew LeRoy and Effie (Risby) F.; m. Martha Gwendolyn Anderson, June 20, 1948; children: Barbara Ann, James LeRoy, John Andrew. B.A., U. Ill., 1939, M.A., 1940, Ph.D., 1943; postgrad., Columbia U., 1941. Grad. asst. history U. Ill., 1940-43; asst. prof. history Ithaca (N.Y.) Coll., 1946; asst. prof. history Okla. State U. at Stillwater, 1946-49, assoc. prof. history, 1949-60, prof. history, 1960-73, Oppenheim Regents prof. history, 1973-78, Oppenheim prof. history, 1978-84, Oppenheim prof. emeritus, 1984—; exec. sec. honors program, 1959-61; chmn. Old Ctrl. Com., 1971—. Author: Lincoln's Gadfly, Adam Gurowski, 1964; (with Muriel H. Wright) Civil War Sites in Oklahoma, 1967, The Civil War Era in Indian Territory, 1974, The Western States in the Civil War, 1975, Territorial Governors of Oklahoma, 1975, The Western Territories in the Civil War, 1977, Civil War Battles in the West, 1981, Oklahoma's Governors 1907-1979, 3 vols., 1981-85, Oklahoma State University Historic Old Central, 1988; co-author: A History of Governance at Oklahoma State University, 1992; editor: The History of the Oklahoma State University Centennial Histories Project, 1993; contbr articles to profl. jours. Vice chmn. Honey Springs Battlefield Park Commn., 1968-92, Okla. Civil War Centennial Commn., 1958-65; mem. adv. com. Okla. Hist. Preservation Rev. Commn., 1978—, chmn. adv. com., 1969-78, vice chmn., 1978-81, chmn., 1981-83; bd. dirs. Nat. Indian Hall of Fame, 1969—, YMCA, 1951-54, 83-85; bd. dirs. Assocs. Western History Collections, U. Okla., 1981—, pres., 1989-90; bd. dirs. Stillwater Mus. Assn., 1987-93, pres., 1990-91; mem. Okla. Chisholm Trail Centennial Commn., 1967-68; bd. dirs. Friends of Honey Springs Battlefield Park, 1991—, pres., 1994—. With Signal Corps, AUS, 1943-45. Recipient Lit. award Loyal Legion U.S., 1963; named tchr. of Yr., Okla. State U.-Okla. Edn. Assn., 1969; inducted in Okla. Historians Hall of Fame, 1995. Mem. Am. Hist. Assn., Southern Hist. Assn., Western History Assn., Am. Assn. State and Local History, AAUP, Okla. Heritage Assn. (Disting. Svc. award 1989), Okla. Hist. Soc. (bd. dirs. 1966—, treas. 1984-87), Ill. Hist. Soc., Orgn. Am. Historians, Omicron Delta Kappa, Pi Gamma Mu, Phi Alpha Theta, Alpha Kappa Lambda. Methodist (chmn. various coms. 1946—, adminstrv. bd. 1950-77, chmn. 1976-77, lay leader 1970-71). Home: 1010 W Cantwell Ave Stillwater OK 74075-4603

FISCHER, MARSHA LEIGH, civil engineer; b. San Antonio, May 9, 1955; d. Joe Henry and Ellen Joyce (Flake) F. BSCE, Tex. A&M U., 1977. Engring. asst. Tex. Dept. Hwys. and Transp., Dallas, 1977-79; outside plant engr. Southwestern Bell Telephone Co., Dallas, 1979-82, staff mgr. for budgets, 1982-84; area mgr. engring. design Southwestern Bell Telephone Co., Wichita Falls, Tex., 1984-86; area mgr. Southwestern Bell Telephone Co., Ft. Worth, 1986-88; dist. mgr., local provisioning application Bell Communications Rsch., Piscataway, N.J., 1988-91; dist. mgr. engring. Southwestern Bell Telephone, Ft. Worth, Tex., 1992-94, dir. customer svcs., 1994-95, dir. network engring., 1996—. Named one of Outstanding Women of Am., 1987. Mem. NSPE, Tex. Soc. Profl. Engrs., Tex. Soc. Civil Engrs., Profl. Engrs. in Industry, Tex. A&M Assn. Former Students. Republican. Home: 6724 Johns Ct Arlington TX 76016-3622 Office: Southwestern Bell Telephone 1 Bell Plz Rm 1870 Dallas TX 75218-4053

FISCHER, NORMAN, JR., media broker, appraiser, broadcast consultant; b. Washington, Mar. 14, 1924; s. Norman and Agnes Columbia (May) F.; m. Ela Cecile Ragland, Mar. 28, 1959; 1 child, Norman Terrill. BS, Washington and Lee U., 1949. Lic. real estate broker, Tex. Owner, operator radio stas. Sta. KUKA-AM, San Antonio, 1961-67, Sta. WEBB-AM, Balt., 1967-70, Sta. KBER-AM, Abilene, Tex., 1976-82; account exec. radio stas. Sta. KTSA-AM, San Antonio, 1957-60, Sta. KONO-AM, San Antonio, 1960-61; ptnr. Holt-Fischer, Austin, Tex., 1970-72; v.p. R. Miller Hicks Co., Austin, 1972-75; pres. Advance Inc., owners Sta. KRMH, Austin, 1972-75; pres. Norman Fischer & Assocs., Inc., Austin, 1974—; guest instr. U. Tex. Sch. Comm., 1979. Mem. Bexar County Dem. Com., 1966; active Austin chpt. March of Dimes, 1973-77, chpt. chmn., 1976; mem. adv. coun. Humanities Rsch. Ctr., U. Tex. Served with Signal Corps, AUS, 1943-46. Mem. Nat. Assn. Broadcasters, Tex. Assn. Broadcasters, La. Assn. Broadcasters, Nat. Radio Broadcasters Assn., Nat. Media Brokers Assn., Austin C. of C., Tarry House Club, Austin Club, Headliners Club, Rotary. Episcopalian. Office: Norman Fischer & Assocs Inc 2201 N Lamar Blvd # 5308 Austin TX 78705-4920

FISCHER, ROBERT LEE, engineering executive, educator; b. Huntington, W.Va., Feb. 4, 1947; s. Charles Lee and Frances Louise (Pennington) F.; m. Mona Lynn Reeser, Oct. 27, 1966; children: Robert Lee Jr., Amy Lynn, Cory Brandon. Cert. in electronics tech., Huntington East Vocat. Tech., 1965; BA in Physics and Gen. Sci., Marshall U., 1970, MS in Vocat. Tech. Edn., 1976; PhD in Elec. Engring., Kennedy-Western U., 1993. Registered profl. electrical engr.; lic master electrician; cert. plant engr. Electrical engr. J.F. & M. Co., Huntington, 1970-71; electronics prodn. supr. polan ind. div. Wollensak, Inc., Huntington, 1971-72; electrical maintenance supr. ACF Industries, Inc., Huntington, 1972-76, electrical maintenance supt., 1976-78, sr. maintenance engr., 1978-80, plant engr., 1980-84, mgr. plant, prodn. and tooling engring., 1984-85; engr., prin. cons. Fischer Tech. Svcs., Huntington, 1979—; electrical, instrumentation and utilities mgr. Calgon Carbon Corp., Catlettsburg, Ky., 1985-93, maintenance mgr., 1993-94, maintenance svcs. mgr., 1994—; robotics instr. Marshall U. Community and Tech. Coll., Huntington, 1986—; instrumentation and control engring. curriculum adv. com. Shawnee State U., Portsmouth, Ohio, 1985—. patentee electronic height control device, robot safety mechanism. Elected to West Jr. High Sch. Hall of Fame, Huntington, 1988; recipient Sr.-Under Black Belt-Open 3d Place award United Fighting Arts Fedn. Nat. Karate Tournament, 1984; named W.Va. ambassador of sci. and engring. among all people, 1982. Mem. NSPE, W.Va. Soc. Profl. Engrs., W.Va., Acad. Sci., Ohio Valley Astron. Soc., Am. Radio Relay League, Six Meter Internat. Radio Club. Democrat. Home: 3606 Route 75 Huntington WV 25704 Office: Calgon Carbon Corp PO Box 664 Catlettsburg KY 41129-0664

FISCHLER, ABRAHAM SAUL, academic administrator; b. Bklyn., Jan. 21, 1928; s. Morris and Esther P. Fischler; m. Shirley Balter, Apr. 9, 1949; children: Bruce Evan, Michael Alan, Lori Faye. BS in Soc. Sci., CUNY, 1951; MA in Sci. Edn., NYU, 1952; EdD, Columbia U., 1959; DSc (hon.), N.Y. Inst. Tech., 1981; LLD (hon.), Nova U., 1992. Sci. tchr., supr. Ossining (N.Y.) Pub. Schs., 1952-58; instr. Columbia U., N.Y.C., 1958-59; asst. prof. edn. Harvard U. Grad. Sch., Cambridge, Mass., 1959-62; assoc. prof. then prof. edn. U. Calif., Berkeley, 1962-66; dean grad. studies Nova U., Ft. Lauderdale, Fla., 1966-70, James Donn prof., 1966—, exec. v.p., 1969-70, pres., 1970-92; pres. emeritus, univ. prof., 1992—; mem. Broward County Sch. Bd., 1994—; visiting prof. nat. and internat. univs., 1963-65; cons. numerous sch. dists., Calif., 1962-67; advisor ednl. pubs.; mem. bus.-edn. adv. com. Alameda-Contra Costa Counties, Calif.; mem. Calif. Elem. Sci. Adv. Com., Sacramento; mem. Overseas Tchrs. Examining Team, Berkeley; bd. dirs. Cardio-Metrics, Inc., Inst. Learning Techs., Inc., Hollywood (Fla.) Fed. Savs. & Loan Assn., Hollywood Med. Ctr. Author: Modern Science, Grades 7,8,9, 1963; (with others) Science: A Modern Approach, 1966, Modern Science, 1967, Modern Elementary Science: Grades 1 through 8, 1971, Nova U.'s Three National Doctoral Degree Programs: An Analysis and Formative Evaluation, 1977; contbr. numerous articles to profl. jours., author monograp and research reports. Pres. United Way Broward County (Fla.), 1984-85, bd. dirs., 1973—, chmn. budget com., 1976-81; chmn. Broward County Overall Econ. Devel. Com., 1980—, Broward Edn. and Tng. Coun., 1989-90; pres. S.E. Fla. Holocaust Meml. Ctr., 1985-87, Temple Beth El, Hollywood, 1988-90; adv. bd. Leadership Broward; mem. 17th Jud. Nominating Commn., Broward County, 1982-86, Ft. Lauderdale Mus. Art, Ft. Lauderdale Symphony Orch. Assn., Broward County Crime Commn., Broward Workshop Edn. Task Force, Town of Davie, Fla. Econ. and Indsl. Devel. Bd.; bd. dirs. Hollywood (Fla.) Med. Ctr., 1982—, chmn. bd. dirs., 1985—; pres. Health Care Rsch. and Edn. Found., 1988-89, United Ways Fla., 1990-91; bd. govs. Fla. Bar, 1991—. Served with USN. Recipient Outstanding Mgmt. and Leadership award Sales and Mktg. Execs., Ft. Lauderdale, 1978, Leader of Yr. award Leadership Broward, 1991, Humanitarian of Yr. award E.A.S.E. Found., 1991, Disting. Educator award Assn. Ind. Schs. Fla., 1992, Tree of Life award Jewish Nat. Fund, 1993, Spirit of Broward award, 1994, Lifetime Achievement award Urban League, 1994; DuPont fellow UCLA, 1958, Sci. Manpower fellow Columbia U., 1958-59. Fellow AAAS, Phi Delta Kappa; mem. Assn. for Edn. Tchrs. Sci. (past pres.), Assn. Supervision and Curriculum Devel., Nat. Assn. Research in Sci. Teaching, Nat. Science Tchrs. Assn., Soc. Advancement Edn., Soc. Research Adminstrs., Am. Assn. Higher Edn., Nat. Council Univ. Research Adminstrs., Com. of 100, Hollywood; Hundred Club Broward County (pres. 1985-86), Kappa Delta Pi. Clubs: Cosmos (Washington), 110 Tower (Ft. Lauderdale), Tower Club. Office: Nova U Office of Pres Emeritus College Ave Fort Lauderdale FL 33314-7796

FISCHLER, SHIRLEY BALTER, lawyer; b. Bklyn., Oct. 9, 1926; d. David and Rose (Shapiro) Balter; m. Abraham Saul Fischler, Apr. 9, 1949; children: Bruce Evan, Michael Alan, Lori Faye. BA, Bklyn. Coll., 1947, MA, 1951; JD, Nova U., Ft. Lauderdale, Fla., 1977. Bar: Fla. 1977, D.C. 1980, U.S. Ct. Appeals (D.C. cir.) 1980. Tchr., N.Y.C. Bd. Edn., 1948-50, Richmond (Calif.) Pub. Schs., 1965-66; assoc. Panza, Maurer, Maynard, Platow & Neel, Ft. Lauderdale, 1977-85; pro bono atty. Broward Lawyers Care, 1982-86. V.p. Gold Circle Nova Southeastern U., 1995—; bd. govs. Nova. U. Law Ctr., 1982—; mem. Commn. on Status of Women, Broward County, Fla., 1982-87, vice chair, 1983-84, PACERS Broward County Ctr. for Performing Arts. Mem. Fla. Bar Assn., D.C. Bar Assn., Broward County Bar Assn. Home: 5000 Taylor St Hollywood FL 33021-5839

FISCUS, DONNA RAU, chemical company executive; b. La Porte, Ind., May 5, 1948; d. Harry Noble and Mary Harness; m. Thomas James Fiscus, Sept. 24, 1929. BS in Chemistry and Biology, Valparaiso U., 1969. Tech. trainee Bethlehem Steel, Chesterton, Ind., 1969-71, engr., 1971-73, chief spectrographer, 1975, tin plate engr., 1975-76, asst. chem. supr., 1976-82, metall. svc. engr., 1982-86; mktg. specialist Calgon, St. Louis, 1986-89; lab. supr. Occidental Chem., Caslte Hayne, N.C., 1989-94; mgr. silicate safety/hygiene Occidental Chem., Dallas, 1994-96, plant mgr., 1996—. Co-patentee in field. Roman Catholic. Home: 114 Soundview Dr Hampstead NC 28443-2510 Office: Occidental Chem 4201 W 69th St Chicago IL 60629

FISH, HOWARD MATH, aerospace industry executive; b. Melrose, Minn., Aug. 1, 1923; s. Nathaniel and Louise Magaret (Gaetz) F.; m. Jamie Katherine Tom, May 15, 1948; 1 child, Howard Math Jr. Student, Air Command and Staff Coll., 1954; MBA, U. Chgo., 1957; postgrad., Armed Forces Staff Coll., 1960, Air War Coll., Montgomery, Ala., 1964; MAIA, George Washington U., 1964. Enlisted USAF, 1942, commd. 2d lt., 1944, capt., 1950, col., 1965, advance through grades to lt. gen., 1974, retired, 1979; deputy asst. sec. defense internat. security affairs Dept. Defense, Washington; asst. vice chief of staff USAF, Washington; chmn. U.S. Mil. Delegation to UN; v.p. internat. LTV Aerospace and Defense Co., 1980-82, Loral Corp., 1992-96; sr. advisor Internat. Lockheed-Martin Vought Sys., Dallas, La., 1996—; mem. Def. Policy Adv. Com. on Trade, Washington, 1987-94; chmn. Am. League for Exports and Security Assistance, Washington, 1986-94. Decorated Def. DSM, Air Force DSM, Legion of Merit, DFC, Air medal, Purple Heart, POW medal. Mem. Am. Def. Preparedness Assn. (chmn. internat. div. 1984-94), Army Navy Club, Air Force Assn., Beta Gamma Sigma. Roman Catholic. Home: 1223 Capiland Dr Shreveport LA 71106

FISH, THOMAS EDWARD, English language educator; b. Redbud, Ill., Aug. 1, 1952; s. Edward Charles and H. Grace (Thomas) F.; m. Kathryn Jane Griffith, Nov. 17, 1979; children: Dana Rose, Sally Kathryn. BA, Iowa State U., Ames, 1974; MA, U. Kans., 1976, MPhil, 1979, PhD, 1981. Asst. instr. in English U. Kans., Lawrence, 1974-81, staff mem. communications resource ctr., 1978, 80; adj. asst. prof. English Iowa State U., 1981-84; asst. prof. English Cumberland Coll., Williamsburg, Ky., 1984-86, assoc. prof. English, 1986-96, prof. English, 1996—. Self-study editor SACS, 1992-95. Elder Corbin (Ky.) Presbyn. Ch., 1986, 90-92. Lilly grantee Cumberland Coll., 1990, named Prof. for Excellence in Teaching, 1990. Mem. Modern Lang. Assn., Nat. Coun. Tchrs. of English, Popular Culture Assn., Browning Inst., South Atlantic Modern Lang. Assn., Phi Beta Kappa, Phi Kappa Phi. Democrat. Home: 260 Brush Arbor Rd Williamsburg KY 40769-1717 Office: 7193 College Station Dr Williamsburg KY 40769-1382

FISHBAUGH, CAROLE SUE, secondary school educator; b. Newark, Ohio, Mar. 11, 1938; d. Lawrence William Baird and Thelma Irene (Kennon) Baird-Thogmartin; m. Emerson LaVerna Fishbaugh, Sept. 11, 1961. BS in Edn., Ohio U., 1962; postgrad., Ohio State U., 1963-65, U. North Fla., 1985—, Jacksonville U., 1994. Cert. elem., K-12 reading tchr., K-12 tchr. mentally retarded, Fla. Elem. tchr. Greenfield (Ohio) Exempted Village Schs., 1958-60; elem. tchr. Newark Pub. Schs., 1960-61, tchr. mentally retarded, 1961-62. 63-65; tchr. mentally retarded Alexandria (Va.) Pub. Schs., 1962-63; vice prin. Lincoln Jr. High Sch., Newark, 1964-65; tchr. reading Nassau County Pub. Schs., Fernandina Beach, Fla., 1986-93; contact person reading dept. Fernandina Beach Mid. Sch., 1990-93, mem. sch. adv. coun., 1991—, contact person for alternative edn., chair dept. alternative edn., 1993-94, chair sch. improvement adv. coun., 1994-96, tchr. varied exceptionalities, 1994—, ESE dept. chair, 1996-97, mem. dist. team, 1994-96; mem. grant com. Fernandina Beach Mid. Sch., 1992—, mem. tech. com. Mem. ch. and soc. com., organizer drug abuse fight Meml. United Meth. Ch., Fernandina Beach, 1987, mem. steering com. Habitat for Humanity; mem. adminstrv. coun. Meth. Children's Home Soc. for United Meth. Ch., 1987—; mem. Fernandina Beach Task Force to Fight Crime, 1992-06; dist. rep. Sch. Adv. Coun., 1994-96. Mem. ASCD, Nat. Mid. Sch. Assn., Fla. League Mid. Schs., Nassau Tchrs. Assn. (sch. rep. 1987-90, treas. 1988-90, rep. on sch. improvement 1992, sec. 1994, treas. 1995—), Order Eastern Star. Democrat. Office: Fernandina Beach Mid Sch 315 Citrona Dr Fernandina Beach FL 32034-2739

FISHE, GERALD RAYMOND AYLMER, engineering executive; b. Farnham Royal, Eng., Feb. 22, 1926; s. Daniel Hamilton and Dorothy Vida (Norton) F.; m. Patricia Ann Roach, Aug. 18, 1949; children: Martha Vida Bindshedler, Raymond Patrick Hamilton, G. Keith Hamilton. BS in Mech. Engring., Duke U., 1949. Registered profl. engr. Fla., Ga., Ill., Iowa; Ala., Mo., Tenn., W.Va. (inactive). Project engr. E.I. DuPont de Nemours & Co., Martinsville, Va., 1952-58; architect's staff engr. So. Ill. U., Carbondale, 1958-63; sec. Adair Brady & Fishe, Inc., Lake Worth, Fla., 1965-66; chief engr. Gamble Pownall & Gilroy, Ft. Lauderdale, Fla., 1963-65; cons. forensic engr. Ft. Lauderdale, 1966—; Pres. Fishe and Kleeman, Inc., Ft. Lauderdale, 1974-85, Fidelity Inspection & Svc. Co., Ft. Lauderdale, 1983-91, Farletot Found., Inc., Ft. Lauderdale, 1985-91. Patentee in field. With U.S. Army, 1944-45. Fellow Nat. Acad. Forensic Engrs., Am. Acad. Forensic Scis. (chmn. engring. sect. 1988-89, bd. dirs. 1990-93); mem. ASHRAE, Constrn. Specification Inst., Nat. Fire Protection Assn. Republican. Episcopalian. Home: 2031 SW 36th Ave Fort Lauderdale FL 33312-4208 Office: GRA Fishe Cons Engr 601 S Andrews Ave Fort Lauderdale FL 33301-2833

FISHER, ANITA JEANNE, English language educator; b. Atlanta, Oct. 22, 1937; d. Paul Benjamin and Cora Ozella (Wadsworth) Chappelear; m. Kirby Lynn Fisher, Aug. 6, 1983; 1 child by previous marriage, Tracy Ann. BA, Bob Jones U., 1959; postgrad., Stetson U., 1961, 87, U. Fla., 1963; MAT, Rollins Coll., 1969; PhD in Am. Lit., Fla. State U., 1975; postgrad., Writing Inst., U. Ctrl. Fla., 1978, NEH Inst., 1979, U. Ctrl. Fla., 1987, Stetson U., 1987, U. Fla., 1987, 90, Disney U./U. Ctrl. Fla., 1996. Cert. English, gifted and adminstn. supr.; cert. in ESOL. Chairperson basic learning improvement program, secondary sch. Orange County, Orlando, Fla., 1964-65; chmn. composition Winter Park H.S., Fla., 1978-80; chmn. English depts. Orange County Pub. Schs., Fla., 1962, 71; reading tchr. Woodland Hall Acad., Reading Rsch. Inst., Tallahassee, 1976; instr. edn., journalism, reading, Spanish, thesis writing Bapt. Bible Coll., Springfield, Mo., 1976-77; prof. English, S.W. Mo. State U., Springfield, 1980-84, instr. continuing edn., courses in music and creative writing, 1981-82, editor LAD Leaf; tchr. Volusia County Schs., Fla., 1984-88, 95—, gifted students, 1986-88; tchr. Lee County Schs., 1988-95; adj. prof. Edison C.C., 1989-95, U. So. Fla., 1990-95, Barry U., 1993; mem. steering com. So. Assn. Colls. and Schs., 1989-90; speaker in field. Contbr. writings to publs. in field, papers to nat. profl. confs. Vol. Greene County Action Com., 1977, Heart Fund, 1982; book reviewer Voice of Youth Advs. Writing Program fellow U. Cen. Fla., 1978. Named Lee County Tchr. of Distinction 1994-95. Mem. Volusia County Coun. Tchrs. English/Fla. Coun. Tchrs. English, Kappa Delta Pi, Phi Delta Kappa. Republican. Presbyterian.

FISHER, BARBARA TURK, school psychologist; b. Bklyn., Feb. 21, 1940; d. Jack and Reva (Miller) Turk; m. Ronnie Herbert Fisher, Aug. 15, 1961; children: Sylvia Kay, Mark Lee. BA, Fla. State U., 1961; MS, Barry U., 1966, EdS, 1977; EdD, Nova U., 1989. Coord. of counseling Immaculate La Salle High Sch., Miami, Fla., 1966-69; rehab. counselor Miami Adult Tng. Ctr., 1969-70; sch. psychologist Dade County Sch. Sys., Miami, 1970—; instr. Miami Dade C.C., 1991; presenter at profl. assn. meetings and social sci. seminars, 1993, 94, 95. Fellow AAUW; mem. Dade County Assns. Sch. Psychologists. Republican. Jewish. Home: 234 Antiquera Ave Apt 3 Miami FL 33134-2914 Office: Dade County BPI Region I Office 733 E 57th St Hialeah FL 33013-1357

FISHER, CHARLES WILLIAM, biochemist; b. Augsburg, Germany, Dec. 15, 1953; s. Charles Kay and Ruth Elnora (Hamilton) F.; m. Anna Patricia Piro, Dec. 15, 1974; 1 child, Christy Ann; m. Carolyn Roberta Bartay, June 15, 1984; children: Charles Edward, Camille Frances. BS, U. Ga., 1975, MS in Entomology, 1979; PhD in Biochemistry, Tex. A&M U., 1983. Rsch. assoc. Northeastern Ohio U. Coll. of Medicine, Rootstown, 1983-86, Case Western Res. U., Cleve., 1986-89; instr. biochemistry U. Tex. Southwestern Med. Ctr., Dallas, 1989—. Home: 438 Summit Dr Richardson TX 75081-5118 Office: U Tex Southwestern Med Ctr 5323 Harry Hines Blvd Dallas TX 75235-9038

FISHER, DENISE BUTTERFIELD, marketing executive; b. San Diego; d. Wyartt Grant and Therese Marie (Hoffman) Butterfield; m. Paul Elliott Fisher, June 15, 1985. BS, Old Dominion U., 1978; MA, U. Va., 1984. Environ. planner Rappahannock Area Devel. Commn., Fredericksburg, Va., 1978-80; grants coord. Va. State Water Control Bd., Richmond, 1980-81, project mgr., 1981-83; mgmt. analyst City of Newport News, Va., 1984-88; intergovtl. rels. mgr. City of Newport News, 1988-91; mktg. mgr. Malcolm Pirnie, Inc., Newport News, 1991—; cons. Va. State Water Control Bd., Virginia Beach, 1984. Contbr. articles to profl. jours. Chmn. United Way Campaign, Newport News, 1985, 86, 87; v.p. North Suffolk Cir. Children's Hosp. of King's Daus., Suffolk, Va., 1989, 90. Recipient Betty Crocker Homemaker of Am. award Gen. Mills, 1972; tuition scholar Old Dominion U., 1973, Wallerstein scholar Va. Mcpl. League, U. Va., 1983. Mem. Internat. City Mgmt. Assn., Soc. Mktg. Profl. Svcs., Am. Soc. Pub. Adminstrn. (pres. Hampton Rds. chpt. 1992). Office: Malcolm Pirnie Inc 11832 Rock Landing Rd Ste 400 Newport News VA 23606-4278

FISHER, GLENN EDWARD, computing specialist, researcher, retired; b. Birdville, Tex., Sept. 17, 1936; s. Leeman Smith and Maggie Mae (Phipps) F.; m. Maryanna Catharine Cluggish, Aug. 11, 1961; children: Marjorie Gail, Robert Leeman. BS in Math., Arlington State Coll., 1962. Sci. computer engr. Gen. Dynamics Corp., Ft. Worth, 1962-67; computing specialist U. Houston, 1967-82, mgr. operating systems, 1982-95, retired, 1995. Contbr. articles to profl. jours. Mem. IEEE (hon.), Assn. for Computing Machinery (hon.), Math. Assn. Am., Univac Share Exch., Honeywell Large Scale Users Assn. Methodist. Home: 22402 Diane Dr Spring TX 77373-7504 Office: Univ Houston 4800 Calhoun Rd Houston TX 77004-2610

FISHER, JACOB ALEXANDER SHULTZ, clergyman; b. Wichita Falls, Tex., Apr. 22, 1925; s. Hiram Herbert Fisher and Mary Elizabeth Shultz; m. Nell Davidson , Aug. 13, 1949; children: Michael D., Kelly Paige Fisher Matthews. BA, Centenary Coll., 1950; MDiv, S.W. Bapt. Theol. Sem., 1953. Ordained to ministry Bapt. Ch., 1951. Commd. ensign USN, 1953, advanced through grades to lt. comdr., 1959, chaplain, 1953-72, ret.,, 1972; dir. pastoral care La. State U. Med. Ctr. (formerly Confederate Meml. Med. Ctr), Shreveport, 1972-95; ret., 1995. Founding pres. Ret. Srs. Vol. Program, Shreveport, 1976-78. With USNR, 1943-46, 47-55. Decorated Navy Letter of Commendation with combat star. Mem. Coll. of Chaplains, La. Chaplains Assn. (pres. 1982, 83), Greater Shreveport Ministerial Assn. (pres. 1980), Masons. Democrat. Home: 305 Baycliff Ln Shreveport LA 71105-4815 Office: La State U Med Ctr 1541 Kingshighway Shreveport LA 71105

FISHER, JANET WARNER, secondary school educator; b. San Angelo, Tex., July 7, 1929; d. Robert Montell and Louise (Buckley) Warner; m. Jarek Prochazka Fisher, Oct. 17, 1956 (div. May 1974); children: Barbara Zlata Harper, Lev Prochazka, Monte Prochazka. BA, So. Meth. U., 1950, M of Liberal Arts, 1982; student various including, Columbia U., U. Dallas,, U. Colo., U. London and others. Cert. English, German and ESL tchr., K-12, Tex., N.Y. Bd. dirs., sec. Masaryk Inst., N.Y.C., 1968-71; with orphan sect. Displaced Persons Commn., Washington, 1950; fgn. editor Current Digest of the Soviet Press, N.Y.C., 1953-55; cable desk clk. Time, Inc., N.Y.C., 1955-56; tchr. of English and reading, langs. Houston Ind. Sch. Dist., 1975-80; tchr. Carmine Ind. Sch. Dist., Round Top, Tex., 1980-82; instr. English Houston Community Coll., 1983-88; adj. prof. English U. Houston, 1983-87; tchr. Royal Ind. Sch. Dist., Brookshire, Tex., 1989-92, Hempstead Ind. Sch. Dist., Waller County, Tex., 1992-94; adj. prof. English, U. Houston, Houston C.C., 1983-87; tchr. Amnesty Program, Houston, 1988-90; adj. prof. English Blinn Coll., Brenham, Tex., 1995—. Candidate sch. bd., South Orangetown, N.Y., 1962, state rep., Houston, 1980; del. Dem. State Conv., 1996, Houston Tchrs. Assn., 1975-80; officer LWV, Nyack, N.Y., 1960-62; trustee Shepherd Drive United Meth. Ch., Houston; del. Tex. ann. conf. United Meth. Ch., 1996; del. Tex. State Dem. Conv., 1996. Recipient award for Svc. to Missions, United Meth. Ch., Houston, 1985. Mem. AAUW, NOW, WILPF, Harris County Women's Polit. Caucus. Home: PO Box 66067 Houston TX 77266-6067

FISHER, (MARY) JEWEL TANNER, retired construction company executive; b. Port Lavaca, Tex., Oct. 31, 1918; d. Thomas M. and Minnie Frances (Dunks) Tanner; grad. Tex. Luth. Coll., 1937; m. King Fisher, Aug. 13, 1937; children: Ann Fisher Boyd, Linda Fisher LaQuay. Sec. treas. King Fisher Marine Svc., Inc., Port Lavaca, 1959-82; dir., cons. King Fisher Marine Svc.; artist, poet. Trustee Meml. Med. Ctr., 1976-81, 90-94, pres. bd. trustees, 1992-93; trustee Golden Crescent Coun. Govts., 1980-81, Crisis Hotline Calhoun County, 1985-93. Lic. pvt. pilot. Mem. DAR (regent Guadalupe Victoria chpt. 1986-88), Daus. Republic Tex., 99's, Internat. Orgn. Women Pilots, Calhoun County Hist. Commn. Home: PO Box 166 Port Lavaca TX 77979-0166 Office: PO Box 108 Port Lavaca TX 77979-0108

FISHER, JIMMIE LOU, state official; b. Delight, Ark., Dec. 31, 1941. Student, Ark. State U.; grad. John F. Kennedy Sch. Govt., Harvard U., 1985. Treas. Greene County, Ark., 1971-78; auditor State of Ark., Little Rock, 1979, treas., 1981—; sec. Ark. State Bd. Fin. Trustee, ex-offico mem. Ark. Pub. Employees Retirement System, Ark. Tchr. Retirement System; trustee Ark. State Hwy. Retirement System; former vice chair Dem. State Com.; former mem. Dem. Nat. Com.; del. Dem. Nat. Conv., 1988; past pres. Ark. Dem. Women's Club; mem. Ark. Devel. Fin. Authority. Mem. State Bd. Fin. (sec.), State Bd. Election Commrs., Nat. Assn. State Treas. (pres.). Office: Treasury Dept 220 State Capitol Bldg Little Rock AR 72201-1059

FISHER, JOSEPH JEFFERSON, federal judge; b. San Augustine County, Tex., 1910; s. Guy B. and Lula (Bl) F.; m. Kathleen Clark; children—Leila (Mrs. Leila F. Thomas), Joseph Jefferson, John Clark, Guy Cade, Anne Fisher Winslow. Student, Stephen F. Austin Coll., 1929; LL.B., U. Tex., 1936. Bar: Tex. 1936. Served as county atty. San Augustine County, 1936-39; dist. atty. 1st Jud. Dist. Tex., 1939-46, dist. judge, 1956-59; partner firm Fisher, Tonahill & Reavley, Jasper, Tex., 1947-56; U.S. dist. judge Eastern Dist. Tex., 1959—, chief judge, 1967—. Mem. ABA (chmn. jud. sect. 1957), 1st Jud. Bar Assn. (pres. 1956), Tex. Bar Assn., State Bar Tex. (legis. and exec. coms. 1957-59), Am. Judicature Soc., Tex. Hist. Assn., Sons of the Republic of Tex., Ex-Student Assn. U. Tex. (life), Stephen F. Austin State U. Ex-Students Assn. (life), Delta Kappa Epsilon. Methodist. Clubs: Mason, Lion (dist. gov., internat. dir., mem. exec. com. 1952-54), Order San Jacinto. Home: 130 Central Caldwood Dr Beaumont TX 77707-1916 Office: PO Box 88 Beaumont TX 77704-0088

FISHER, KING, marine contracting company executive; b. Port Lavaca, Tex., Jan. 14, 1916; s. Charles Everett and Kittie (Moss) F.; student pub. schs., Port Lavaca; m. Jewel Tanner, Aug. 13, 1937; children: Ann Fisher Boyd, Linda Fisher LaQuay. Pres. King Fisher Marine Svc., Inc., Port Lavaca, 1941-96, chmn. of bd., 1959—; corp. sec. Fisher Channel & Dock Co., Port Lavaca, 1954—; bd. dirs. First Nat. Bank of Port Lavaca, Seaport Bank, Seadrift, Tex. Mem. Tex. Mid-Coast Water Devel. Assn., Gulf Coast Intracoastal Canal Assn., Port Lavaca C. of C. Home: Fisher Rd Chocolate Ba Port Lavaca TX 77979 Office: PO Box 166 Port Lavaca TX 77979-0166

FISHER, MARGARET ELLA, medical/surgical nurse; b. Toronto, Ont., Can., Mar. 26, 1929; d. Andor and Emma (Bukovan) Jakab; m. Floyd F. Fisher, Nov. 12, 1994; children: Emmalee Crosson, Keith E. Taylor. Diploma, St. John's Sch. Nursing, Springfield, Mo., 1972. Cert. nursing home adminstr. House supr. Golden Valley Meml. Hosp., Clinton, Mo., 1978-81; inservice dir. Golden Valley Meml. Hosp., Clinton, 1978-81; dir. nurses Windsor (Mo.) Hosp., 1981-82; expert witness pvt. practice, Hemet, Calif., 1984-90. Pub. author poetry (Non-Fiction Poetry awards 1988-96). Mem. Hemet Caregivers (founder 1988).

FISHER, PAUL DOUGLAS, psychologist, program director; b. Nashville, Aug. 6, 1956; s. John Clark and Iris (Pierce) F.; m. Donna Nichols, May 28, 1988. BS magna cum laude, Vanderbilt U., 1978; PhD, U. Ala., 1983. Psychologist, mental health dir. USAF, worldwide, 1982-85; resident Wilford Hall Med. Ctr., San Antonio, 1983; v.p. Profl. Performance Devel. Group, San Antonio, 1983-86; pvt. practice psychology Houston, various other locations, 1986-88; clin. dir., psychologist Addiction Recovery Corp., Harrison, Tenn., 1988-90; cons. dir. Tenn. Dept. Corrections-S.E. Region, 1988—; owner, dir. Tenn. Transitional Living Ctrs., Harrison, 1989—; examiner Tenn. Bd. Psychol. Examiners, 1988—; cons. Centurion Police Stress Program, 1990—; pres. Tenn. Transitional Living Ctrs., 1988-90. Author: Issues in Human Adjustment, 1980; contbr. articles to profl. publs. Rsch. edn. dir. Gov's. Alliance for a Drug-Free Tenn., 1988—; mem. Rep. Senatorial Com., Washington, 1982—, Tenn. Pub. Broadcasting, 1987—, Tenn. Friends of Folk Music, 1988—. Capt. USAF, 1982-86. Recipient Presdl. Order of Merit from Pres. George Bush, 1991; Smithsonian Instn. fellow, 1978-81, NIMH fellow, 1978-80. Mem. APA, Psychologists for Advancement of Conservative Thought (v.p. 1981—), Am. Police Assn. (life), Tenn. Sheriffs Assn., Tenn. Assn. for Child Care, Mensa. Office: Tenn Transitional Living Ctrs PO Box 1006 Harrison TN 37341-1006

FISHER, RICHARD WELTON, venture capitalist; b. L.A., Mar. 18, 1949; s. Leslie Welton and Magnhild (Andersen) F.; m. Nancy Collins, Sept. 8, 1973; children: Andersen, Alison, James Leslie, Texana. BA cum laude, Harvard U., 1971; student, Oxford (Eng.) U., 1972-74; MBA, Stanford U., 1975. Asst. to Robert Roosa Brown Bros. Harriman & Co., N.Y.C., 1975-77, sr. mgr., 1983-87; exec. asst. to sec. of treas. Head of Policy Planning U.S. Treasury Dept., Washington, 1977-79; mng. ptnr. Fisher Capital Mgmt., Dallas, 1987—, Fisher Ewing Ptnrs., Dallas, 1989—; chmn. Stanford U. Sch. Bus. Trust, Palo Alto, Calif., 1982-84; adj. prof. L.B.J. Sch., U. Tex., 1996; dir. Utimco, Inc., 1996—. Bd. dirs., mem. exec. com. Dallas Mus. Art, 1985-89; bd. dirs. Goodwill Industries Dallas, 1989—, treas., 1991—, chmn., 1993—; bd. dirs. Boys Club Dallas, 1984-84, Dallas Assembly, 1983—, Progressive Policy Inst., Washington, 1989—, Russian Am. Enterprise Fund, 1993—; mem. Dallas Citizens Coun., 1986—; active Dallas Com. Fgn. Rels., chmn., 1987—; dir. fgn. policy issues Perot Presdl. Campaign, 1992; mem. visitors com. Kennedy Sch. Govt. and Ctr. for Internat. Affairs, Harvard U., 1992—; Dem. candidate U.S. Senate, 1994. Decorated gran oficial Order of Bernardo O'Higgins (Chile); U.S.-Japan leadership fellow Japan Soc., 1989; recipient Outstanding Achievement award Stanford U. Assocs., 1986; named one of 10 Rising Stars of Tex., Tex. Bus. Mag., 1988; named Admiral of Tex. Navy, 1987. Mem. Inst. Ams. (chmn. 1987-93), Inter-Am. Dialogue (exec. com. 1992—), Am. Coun. on Germany (bd. dirs. 1985-94), Philos. Soc. Tex., Harvard Club, Petroleum Club. Presbyterian. Office: Fisher Capital Mgmt 4600 Texas Commerce Towers Dallas TX 75201

FISHER, ROBERT BRUCE, priest; b. Paragould, Ark., Feb. 6, 1937; s. Lawrence Bruce Fisher and Georgia M. (Paris) Kasper. BA, Divine Word Seminary, Techny, Ill., 1961, MA, 1965; STB, STL, Gregorian Univ., Rome, 1966; STD, Pont. Ateneo di Sant' Anselmo, Rome, 1969. Ordained priest Roman Cath. Ch., 1965. Adminstrv. attache Nunciature of Holy See, Accra, Ghana, 1982-83; pastor Good Shepherd Ch., Tema, Ghana, 1984-86; asst. pastor St. Matthias Ch., New Orleans, 1990-94; asst. prof. Xavier U., New Orleans, 1988-95; dir. studies A. Tolton House of Studies, New Olreans, 1991-96; dist. superior Divine Word Soc. New Orleans, 1990-96; promoter New African Cinema film series. Editor: (liturgical ordo) Ordo for the Phillipines, 1972. Co-chmn. Cath. Returnee Crisis Com., Accra, 1982-83; mem. Mayor Morial's Coun. of Religious Advisors, 1994. Mem. Coll. Theology Soc., Semiotic Soc. Am., Am. Acad. Religion, KC (chaplain Met. chpt. 1993-96); African Assn. for Study of Religions. Democrat.

FISHER, ROSALIND ANITA, personnel executive; b. Jackson, Tenn., Feb. 5, 1956; d. Hartwell E. Fisher and Gwendolyn C. Miller. BS in Psychology, Cen. Mo. State U., 1978; MS in Community Devel., So. Ill. U., 1986. Specialist Human Relations dept. City of Kansas City, 1982-85, vol. mediator, 1985-87; employee relations and tng. mgr. Personnel and Risk Mgmt. dept. U. Nebr., Lincoln, 1985-87; asst. dir. personnel services dept. Kans. State U., Manhattan, 1988-89; dir. personnel svcs. Kansas State U., Manhattan, 1989-90; dir. human resources U. West Fla., Pensacola, 1990—, asst. v.p. EEO/AA and Diversity, 1995—; cons. Chancellor's Commn. on Sexual Harassment, Lincoln, 1987—; speaker women's issues. Cons., trainer Stop Violence Coalition, Kansas City, 1984-85; arbitrator Cornhusker Better Bus. Bur., Lincoln, 1985-87; bd. dirs. YMCA, Lincoln, 1986-87; active Leadership Pensacola Class of 1992. Recipient Appreciation award Stop Violence Coalition, 1984. Fellow Coll. and Univ. Personnel Assn.; mem. AAUW, Univ. Assn. for Adminstrv. Devel. (exec. com., chair profl. devel. 1986-87), 100 Black Women, Nat. Assn. Negro Bus. and Profl. Women (outstanding vol. of yr. 1985), Women of Color Task Force (chair 1986-87), Soc. Human Resource Mgrs. (profl. devel. com. 1990—), Am. Assn. Affirmative Action. Democrat. Home: 6102 Alicia Dr Pensacola FL 32504 Office: U West Fla Office Human Resources 11000 University Pky Pensacola FL 32514-5732

FISHER, WILLIAM PAUL, JR., medical educator, medical outcomes researcher; b. Moline, Ill., Aug. 16, 1955; s. William Paul and Grace Elizabeth (Castelein) F.; m. Rebecca Ann Lee, May 1974 (div. Oct. 1976); m. Adeline Marie Masquelier, June 28, 1986; children: Margaux Victoria, Zella Eleonore, Julia Alexandra. AA in Liberal Arts, Black Hawk Coll., Moline, 1976; BA in Anthropology, So. Ill. U., Carbondale, 1981; MA in Social Sci., U. Chgo., 1984, PhD in Edn., 1988. Rsch. asst. in rehab. R & D, Hines (Ill.) VA Hosp., 1984-87; rsch. assoc. Marianjoy Rehab., Wheaton, Ill., 1988-92, sr. rsch. scientist, 1992-94; assoc. prof. pub. health and preventive medicine La. State U. Med. Ctr., New Orleans, 1994—; rsch. assoc. MESA Labs., U. Chgo., 1984—. Editor issue Internat. Jour. Ednl. Rsch., 1995; assoc. editor Jour. Outcome Measurement, 1996—; contbr. articles to profl. jours. Spencer Found. dissertation fellow U. Chgo., 1987-88. Mem. ASTM (head measurement working group electronic med. record com.), APHA, Am. Med. Informatics Assn., Am. Ednl. Rsch. Assn. (reviewer), Am. Congress Rehab. Medicine (reviewer), Assn. for Health Svcs. Rsch., Rasch Measurement Spl. Interest Group (reviewer). Office: La State U Med Ctr 1600 Canal St Rm 809 New Orleans LA 70112

FISHMAN, BARRY STUART, lawyer; b. Chgo., June 14, 1943; s. Jacob M. and Anita (Epstein) F.; B.A., U. Wis., 1965; J.D., DePaul U., 1968; m. Meredith Porte, Mar. 27, 1976; 1 child, Janna. Admitted to Ill. bar, 1968, Fla., Calif. bars, 1969; partner firm Fishman & Fishman, Chgo., 1968-72; counsel real estate fin. dept. Baird & Warner, Inc., Chgo., 1972-75; gen. counsel Biscayne Fed. Savs. & Loan Assn., Miami, Fla., 1976-79; mem. firm, Ea. regional council Logs Nationwide Representation of Lenders; mem. firm Pallot, Poppell, Goodman & Slotnick, Miami, 1977-80; sr. ptnr. Shapiro & Fishman, North Miami Beach, Tampa, Jacksonville, Orlando and Boca Raton, Fla., 1984—; dir. investment div. Cushman and Wakefield of Fla., 1978—. Mem. big gifts com. Greater Miami Jewish Fedn., 1977—; dir. Neighborhood Housing Services, Dade County, Fla., 1977—. Mem. Fla., Calif., Ill., Chgo., Dade County bar assns., Nat. Assn. Realtors, Real Estate Securities and Syndication Inst., Mortgage Bankers Assn., Fla. Mortgage Bankers Assn., Comml. Law League. Jewish. Clubs: Turnberry Isle Yacht & Racquet, Turnberry C.C. Home: 1025 NE 203rd Ln Miami FL 33179-2529 Office: 20803 Biscayne Blvd Ste 300 Miami FL 33180-1429

FISHMAN, LEWIS WARREN, lawyer, educator; b. Bklyn., Dec. 19, 1951; BA in Polit. Sci., Syracuse U., 1972; MPA, Maxwell-Syracuse U., 1973; JD, U. Miami, 1976. Bar: Fla. Supreme Ct. 1976, U.S. Dist. Ct. (so. dist.) Fla. 1977, D.C., 1978, U.S. Ct. Appeals (5th and 11th cirs.) 1981. Assoc. Simons & Fishman P.A. (and predecessor firm), Miami, 1976-80, ptnr., 1980-81; assoc. law firm Wood, Lucksinger & Epstein, Miami, 1981-82; pres. Lewis W. Fishman P.A., Miami, 1982—; adj. prof. law Fla. Internat. U., 1981, 83, 84, 91. Mem. Fla. Acad. Healthcare Attys. (bd. dirs., sec. 1986-88, pres. 1990-92), Nat. Health Lawyers Assn. (lectr. 1983, 88-89), Fla. Hosp. Assn. (lectr., sec. 1986-88, v.p. 1988), Fla. Med. Records Assn. (lectr. 1982, 83, 84), Am. Acad. Hosp. Attys. (lectr. 1989, 90, 91), Nat. Health Lawyers Assn., Cath. Health Assn., Fla. Bar Assn. (mem. exec. coun. health law sect., chmn. health law sect. 1995-96, cert. health law atty., mem. health law cert. com., 1994—, vice-chmn. 1995-96, chmn. 1996—). Jewish. Home: 14140 SW 104th Ave Miami FL 33176-7064 Office: 9130 S Dadeland Blvd Miami FL 33156-7818

FISHMAN, MARK BRIAN, computer scientist, educator; b. Phila., May 17, 1951; s. Morton Louis and Hilda (Kaplan) F.; m. Alice Faber, Feb. 20, 1977 (div. 1986); m. E. Alexandra Baehr, Apr. 13, 1992. AB summa cum laude, Temple U., 1974; postgrad. Northwestern U., 1974-76; MA, U. Tex., 1980. Bilingual tchr. Wilmette Pub. Schs., 1974; rsch. assoc., programmer, asst. instr. U. Tex., Austin, 1976-80; instr. computer and info. scis. U. Fla., Gainesville, 1980-85; asst. prof. computer sci. Eckerd Coll., St. Petersburg, Fla., 1985-90, dept. coord., 1988-90, 91—, assoc. prof. computer sci., 1991—; instrnl. cons. to IBM, 1980—; cons. artificial intelligence, Battelle Corp., 1987-89, USN Naval Tng. Systems Ctr., 1987—, Advanced Techs., Inc., 1988—, LBS Capital Mgmt., 1990—. Series editor: Advances in Artificial Intelligence Rsch., Vol. I, 1989; editor: Proc. of the First Florida Artificial Intelligence Rsch. Symposium, 1988, Proc. of the Second Florida Artificial Intelligence Rsch. Symposium, 1989, Advances in Artificial Intelligence Research, vol. I, 1989, vol. II, 1992, Proc. of the Third Florida Artificial Intelligence Rsch. Symposium, 1990, Proc. of the Fourth Florida Artificial Intelligence Rsch. Symposium, 1991, Proc. of the Fifth Artificial Intelligence Rsch. Symposium, 1992; guest editor: International Journal of Expert Systems, Vol. 5, no. 2; steering com. First Internat. Conf. Human and Machine Cognition; contbr. articles to profl. jours; presenter in field. U. Tex. fellow, 1978-80; F.C. Austin scholar, 1975; Nat. Def. Fgn. Lang. fellow, 1974. Mem. Assn. Computing Machinery (Tchr. of Yr. award U. Fla. 1984), IEEE Computer Soc., Am. Assn. Artificial Intelligence, Assn. Computational Linguistics, Fla. Artificial Intelligence Research Soc. (proc. chair 1988—, sec. 1988-89, v.p. 1989-91, pres. 1991—), Am. Soc. Engring. Edn. (faculty research fellow summer 1986, 91), Internat. Soc. Philosophical Enquiry, Sigma Xi, Phi Beta Kappa, Phi Kappa Phi, Upsilon Pi Epsilon. Home: 20505 US Highway 19 N # 12175 Clearwater FL 34624-6001 Office: Eckerd Coll Dept Computer Sci Saint Petersburg FL 33733

FISHMAN, ROBERT JACK, publisher; b. Memphis, Nov. 1, 1934; s. Saul Jack and Katherine (Little) F.; m. Nancy Lee Allen, Nov. 25, 1955; children: Jeffrey Daniel, Robert Michael. BS, U. Memphis, 1955; grad. Southeastern Inst. Orgnl. Mgmt., U. N.C., 1958, grad. Acad. Orgn. and Mgmt., 1961; grad. Indsl. Devel. Inst., U. Okla., 1964. Dir. Camden (Tenn.) H.S. Band, 1955; mgr. Jesup (Ga.) C. of C., 1956-59, Morristown (Tenn.) C. of C., 1959-65; exec. dir. Mid. Tenn. Indsl. Devel. Assn., Nashville, 1965-66; pub., editor Citizen Tribune, Morristown, 1966—; pres., CEO Lakeway Pubs., Inc., Morristown, 1966—; dir. Suntrust Bank, Morristown; pres. Tenn. Press Svc., Knoxville, Tenn., 1981-86. Vice chair Gov.'s Econ. Study Com., Nashville, 1971-72; chmn. Tenn. Indsl. and Agrl. Devel. Commn., Nashville, 1970-71; chmn. fin. com. Tenn. Indsl. and Agrl. Devel. Com., Nashville, 1974-75; chmn. Gov.'s Citizen's Com. on Compensation, Nashville, 1973; mem. Gov.'s Travel and Tourist Coun., Nashville, 1963-66; mem. Tenn. Bd. Regents, Nashville, 1991—, chmn. fin. com., 1995—; newspaper rep. Nat. Info. Infrastructure Adv. Coun., Washington, 1994-96; chmn. Pvt. Industry Coun. Dist. II, 1983-84; mem. Hamblen County Juvenile Ct. Adv. Bd., Morristown, Tenn., 1985-86; chmn. Area Wide Devel. Corp., Knoxville, 1994-95. 1st lt. USNG, 1955-66. Recipient Nursing award Walters State C.C., 1978, Vol. of Yr. award Tenn. Indsl. Devel. Coun., 1982, Presdl. Citation Pvt. Industry Coun., 1986, Vol. of Yr. award So. Indsl. Coun. Econ. Devel., 1982, Super Booster award West High Booster Club, 1983, Paul Harris fellow award Rotary Club, 1991, Journalism Alumni Citation, Memphis State U., 1985, Silver Beaver award Boy Scouts Am.; named Morristown Outstanding Young Man of Yr., 1964, Tenn. Outstanding Young Man of Yr., 1964. Mem. Nat. Newspaper Assn. (chmn. 1995-96), Tenn. Press Assn. (pres. 1986-87, Pres. award 1980), Tenn. C. of C. Exec. Assn. (pres. 1963), Kiwanis Internat. (life, pres. 1974-75, lt. gov. 1975-76), Tenn. Assn. AP (pres. 1980), East Tenn. Indsl. Coun. (pres. 1971-75), Knoxville Area Newspaper Network (v.p. 1994-95). Episcopalian. Office: Citizen Tribune 1609 W 1st North St Morristown TN 37814-3724

FISHMAN, SEYMOUR, fundraising executive; b. Newark, Feb. 10, 1915; s. Samuel G. and Ethel (Raffman) F.; m. Sylvia Shemel, Feb. 14, 1937; children: Steven Joel., Judith Lynn Fishman Singer. MA, CCNY, 1937. Lic. psychologist, N.Y. Pvt. practice psychology Bellevue Hosp., N.Y.C., 1935-41; vocat. counselor Nat. Refugee Svc., 1941-43; dir. Pacific Ocean area USO, 1943-47; nat. dir. orgn. Am. Jewish Congress, 1947-51; fundraiser Israel Bonds, 1951-55; with Greater Chgo. office V.P. Divine and Fishman, Inc.(N.Y.S.E.), 1955-63; exec. v.p. Am. Friends of Hebrew U., 1963-80; pres. Sy Fishman Assocs., Inc., 1980—; fin. cons., nat., 1980—; cons. Am. Friends of Hebrew U. With USO, 1943-47, PTO. Decorated Merit award Dept. Def. Mem. Am. Psychol. Assn., Mason, B'nai B'rith. Home: 3625 N Country Club Dr Apt 240 Miami FL 33180-1711

FISK, ARTHUR DANIEL, psychology educator; b. Grand Rapids, Mich., Mar. 24, 1954; s. Arthur Daniel Fisk and Jacqualin (Rector) Johnson. BS in Psychology, Ohio State U., 1978; AM in Psychology, U. Ill., 1980, PhD in Psychology, 1982. Supr. human factors engring. AT&T Communications, 1982-84, mgr. human factors engring., 1984-85; asst. prof. U. S.C., 1985-87; asst. prof. psychology Ga. Inst. Tech., Atlanta, 1987-90, assoc. prof., 1990-94, prof., 1994—; vis. scientist in human factors, vis. assoc. prof. psychology Ind. U., 1991; mem. schooling, tng. and measurement program USAF; mem. HUD2 study sect. NIH, 1991—. Editorial bd.: Human Factors jour., 1987-89, editor, 1989—; editorial bd. Applied Ergonomics, 1988—; contbr. articles to profl. jours., chpts. to books in field. Dallenbach fellow psychology dept. U. of Ill., 1981-82; recipient fellowship, 1980-81, undergrad. rsch. scholarship Ohio State U., 1977-78; grantee NIH, 1987-90, 91—, Nat. Inst. Health Biomed. Rsch., 1985-86, Nat. Inst. on Aging, 1986, S.C. Venture Fund, others. Fellow APA (pres.-elect div. applied exptl. and engring. psychologists), Human Factors Soc. (mng. editor publs. 1986-89, gen. chmn. ann. conf. 1992, exec. coun 1991—); mem. Gerontol. Soc. Am., Psychonomic Soc., So. Soc. Philosophy and Psychology, Sci. Rsch. Soc., Sigma Xi. Office: Ga Inst Technology Sch of Psychology Atlanta GA 30332-0170

FISK, FRANCINE JOAN, librarian; b. Tulsa, Okla., Mar. 3, 1953; d. Francis Charls and Alberta Joan (Fink) F.; m. Scott Franklin McClung, Nov. 30, 1991; 1 child, Miranda Fisk McClung. BS, U. Tulsa, 1974; MLS, U. Okla., 1976. Media specialist Moore (Okla.) Pub. Schs., 1976-85; coord. media svcs. U. Tulsa, 1985-87, head reference libr., 1987-89, coord. libr. info. svcs., 1989-92, coord. libr. info. svcs. and collections, 1992-93, coord. gen. svcs., 1993—. Mem. ALA, Okla. Libr. Assn. (chair Adminstrn. Roundtable 1995-96), Tulsa Area Libr. Coop. (bd. dirs., vice chmn. 1991-92), Beta Phi Mu. Office: McFarlin Libr U Tulsa 2933 E 6th St Tulsa OK 74104

FISK, RAYMOND PAUL, marketing educator; b. Yuma, Ariz., Sept. 27, 1953; s. Elwin Lee and Verleen Thelma (Rafferty) F.; m. Jamie Tucker, Aug. 8, 1980. BS, Ariz. State U., 1976, MBA, 1977, PhD, 1980. Faculty assoc. Ariz. State U., Tempe, 1977-80; instr. Am. Grad. Sch. Internat. Mgmt., Glendale, Ariz., 1978; asst. prof. mktg. Okla. State U., Stillwater, 1980-84, assoc. prof. mktg., 1984-89; mktg. analyst Nat. U. Teleconf. Network, 1983; dir mktg. Teleconf. Consortium, 1984-85; faculty assoc. Ctr. for Internat. Trade Devel., 1986-89; assoc. prof. mktg. U. Ctrl. Fla., Orlando, 1989-96; prof., chair dept. mktg. U. New Orleans, 1996—. Fulbright scholar Klagenfurt U. of Edn. Scis., 1987; dissertation research grantee dept. mktg. Ariz. State U., 1980; Dean's excellence fund summer grantee Okla. State U., 1981-82; rsch. grantee Okla. State U./Asian Inst. Mgmt. Coop. Rsch. Program, 1983; summer bus. extension grantee Okla. State U., 1983, 86; rsch. grantee Mktg. Sci. Inst., 1985-86, Ariz. State U., 1986-88. Mem. AAAS, Am. Mktg. Assn. (doctoral consortium fellow 1979, editor mktg. newsletter 1984-86, dir. Svcs. Mktg. Spl. Interest Group, 1993-95; sr. v.p. for Teaching/Info. Dissemination, Acad. Coun., 1994-96; pres. Ctrl. Fla. chpt. 1994-95), Assn. Consumer Rsch., So. Mktg. Assn., Southwestern Mktg. Assn., Beta Gamma Sigma. Author: (with Jamie T. Fisk) Airways: A Marketing Simulation, 1986; editor: (with Stephen W. Brown) Marketing Theory: Distinguished Contributions, 1984; (with Patriya S. Tansuhaj) Services Marketing: An Annotated Bibliography, 1985; (with Patriya S. Tansuhaj and Lawrence A. Crosby) Servmark: The Electronic Bibliography of Services Marketing Literature, 1987; cons. editor Mktg. News, 1981-82; editorial rev. bd. Jour. Health Care Mktg., 1983-89; contbr. articles to profl. jours. Office: U New Orleans Coll Bus Admin Dept Mktg New Orleans LA 70148

FISMER, ROBERTA D., nursing administrator; b. Nanticoke, Pa., Dec. 30, 1947; d. Robert D. and Violet Myrtle (Garey) Benscoter; m. Carl Edward Fismer, Nov. 8, 1974; children: Lee Alan, Diana Lynn. AA, Manatee Jr. Coll., 1967. RN, Fla.; CCRN; cert. BLS, ACLS, PALS. Staff nurse telemetry Sarasota (Fla.) Meml. Hosp., 1967-68, staff nurse ICU, 1968-80; paramedic instr. Sarasota County Vocat. Sch., 1973-78; nurse mgr., co-founder cardiac rehab. Sarasota County YMCA, 1977-80; staff nurse SICU South Miami Hosp., Miami, Fla., 1981-86; staff nurse ICU Mariners Hosp., Tavernier, Fla., 1986-88, supr. ICU, 1988-94, nursing quality assurance mgr., 1990—, nurse mgr. ICU and emergency dept., 1994—. Pres. Am. Heart Assn., Sarasota County, 1975-76; mem. Pride, Tavernier, 1989-91. Mem. AACN, Fla. Assn. Quality Assurance Profls. Republican. Home: 179

Azalea St Tavernier FL 33070-2201 Office: Mariners Hosp 50 High Point Rd Tavernier FL 33070-2006

FITCH, MARK KEITH, lawyer; b. Ardmore, Okla., Nov. 8, 1957; s. Charles Aubrey and Helen Wanda (Lively) F. B in Accountancy, U. Okla., 1980, JD, 1983. Bar: Okla. 1983, U.S. Dist. Ct. (we. dist.) Okla. 1983, U.S. Tax Ct. 1983. Assoc. Speck, Philbin, Fleig, Trudgeon & Lutz, P.C., Oklahoma City, 1983-85; prin., ptnr. Nash & Fitch P.C., Oklahoma City, 1985-95; prin., owner Mark K. Fitch, Atty., Oklahoma City, 1995—. Treas. Ctrl. Okla. Young Reps., 1986-87; dir. Gatewood Neighborhood Assn. Recipient Presdl. Achievement award Nat. Rep. Congl. Com., 1987; named to Outstanding Young Men of Am., 1987. Mem. ABA, Okla. Bar Assn. (com.), Oklahoma City Estate Planning Coun., Gatewood Neighborhood Assn. (bd. dirs.), Okla. Mus. Art Assn., Allied Arts Found., Phaythopen Charity Soc., U. Okla. Coll. Law Assn., Bachelor's Club. Office: 50 Penn Pl Ste 1300 Oklahoma City OK 73118

FITCH, TONI LYNN, public relations coordinator association; b. Richmond, Va., June 20, 1970; d. James Harold and Gaynell (Gibson) F. BA in English, History, Queens Coll., 1992. Tchg. asst. Dance Arts Ctr., Jacksonville, N.C., 1984-88; news intern WJNC Radio News, Jacksonville, summer 1989; student intern Office Comm., Queens Coll., Charlotte, N.C., 1990; resident asst. Residence Life Queens Coll., Cbarlotte, 1989-91; adminstrv. asst. Comm. Health Svcs., Cbarlotte, 1992-93, comm. coord., 1993-94; pub. rels. coord. Safety and Health Coun. of N.C., Charlotte, 1994-96; mem. adv. bd. career ctr. Queens Coll., Charlotte, N.C., 1994—; bd. dirs. Charlotte Mecklenberg Safe Kids Coalition, Charlotte, 1996—. Performing mem. N.C. 4H Performing Arts Troupe, 1983-90; editor, designer (quartetrly publs.) Community Health Focus, 1993-94. Sr. Health News, 1993-94, (bimontly publ.) Safety Net, 1994—. Honor coun. rep. Queens Coll, Charlotte, 1989-92; publicity dir. Coll. Union Activities Coun., Queens Coll., Charlotte, 1991-92; vol. leader Mecklenburg County 4H, Charlotte, 1992-94. Named Outstanding Mem. 4H, Jacksonville and N.C. State, 1979-91; recipient Devel. Fund scholarship N.C. 4H, 1988; State Winner for Achievement, Nat. Congress 4H, 1990. Mem. Nat. Safety Coun. (youth divsn.), Nat. Assn. Desktop Pubs., Am. Soc. Assn. Execs. Office: Safety and Health Coun of NC 500 E Morehead St Ste 103 Charlotte NC 28207

FITCHETT, JUNE WISEMAN, health care facility administrator; b. Marion, N.C., May 29, 1942; d. Coy and Lena (Ellis) Wiseman; m. Bruce Harvey Fitchett, Jan. 19, 1963 (div. Aug. 1977); chlidren: Alisa Michelle Fitchett Ashe, William Shawn. BA, Western Carolina U., 1968. Cert. activity dir., N.C. Tchr. English and remedial edn. Jackson County Pub. Schs., Sylva, N.C., 1966; tchr., counselor Asheville (N.C.) Buncombe Tech. Inst., County of Buncombe Neighborhood Youth Corp., 1971-75; coord. Buncombe County Title II County of Buncombe and City of Asheville, 1975—; job placement coord. of handicapped, orgn. devel. coord. Thoms Rehab. Hosp., Asheville, 1976-81; personnel dir., rehab. coord. Lions Industries for Blind, 1982-83; social worker food stamp office County of Buncombe Social Svcs., Asheville, 1984-85; res. svcs. assoc. Givens Estate Retirement Ctr., Asheville, 1985—; dir. resident activity therapy and volunteers Victoria Health Care Ctr., Asheville, 1986—; pres. Social Svcs. Coun., County of Buncombe, 1982-83; corr. Asheville Citizen Times. Recipient Outstanding Young Woman of Am. award, 1971, Outstanding Svc. to Handicapped award Asheville Area Mayor's Com., 1980. Mem. N.C. Activity Profls. (state bd. 1991-92, pres. western dist. 1991-92, writer state newsletter 1991-92, membership chair state bd.), Asheville Toastmistress Club (v.p. 1973), Beta Sigma Phi. Baptist. Home: 226 Forest Hill Dr Asheville NC 28803-2406 Office: Victoria Health Care Ctr 455 Victoria Rd Asheville NC 28801-4827

FITCHETT, W(ILLIAM) CALVIN, insurance executive; b. Nassawadox, Va., Nov. 28, 1948; s. William and Gloria Jane (Kellam) F.; m. Dorothy Sharon Johnson, July 6, 1950; 1 child, Katherine Anne. BS, U. Richmond, 1971. Tchr. Accomack (Va.) County Sch. Bd., 1971-73; examiner Am. Internat. Group, Atlanta, 1974-75; regional supr. Life of Va., Atlanta, 1973-74, 75-80; dir. of claims Ga. Internat. Life, Atlanta, 1980-82; asst. v.p. Capital Holding Corp., Louisville, 1982-84; v.p. Citizens and So. Life Ins. Co., Tucker, Ga., 1984-87; pres. Citizens and So./Sovran Ins. Group, Tucker, Ga., 1987-91, C&S/Sovran Ins. Group, Atlanta, 1991-92, Nations Banc Ins. Svcs. Inc., Atlanta, 1992—. Pres. Georgetown Homeowners Assn., Lilburn, Ga., 1985-86; councilman City of Lilburn, 1986-89, mayor pro tem, 1989-90, mayor, 1990-94; bd. dirs. Gwinnett County Coalition Human Resouce Devel., 1989-90, Gwinnett County Water and Sewer Authority, 1990. Fellow Life Office Mgmt. Assn. (soc. rep. 1989-90); mem. Ga. Assn. Life. Cos. (bd. dirs. 1988-89, v.p. 1990-91), Gwinnett C. of C. (bd. dirs. 1988-89). Republican. Baptist. Home: 73 Lancaster Ct SW Lilburn GA 30247-5144 Office: Nations Banc Ins Svcs Inc 2059 Northlake Pky Tucker GA 30084-5321

FITE, KATHLEEN ELIZABETH, education educator; b. Houston, June 26, 1948; d. Daniel Patrick and Edith Elizabeth (Burnett) F. BS in Edn., S.W. Tex. State U., 1969, MEd, 1970; EdD, N. Tex. State U., 1972. Cert. tchr. Prof. S.W. Tex. State U., San Marcos, 1973—, dir. Ctr. for Study of Basic Skills, 1980, dir. Race Integration Tng. Inst., 1982-83, dir. elem. edn. dept., 1983-84, assoc. dir. sponsored projects, 1984-86, dir. sponsored projects, 1986-87; cons. U.S. Dept. Edn., numerous pub. cos.; mem. adv. bd. Dushing Pub. Group, Inc. Co-author: A few Favorites of the Total Teacher, The Super Ideas Book, Creative Art Ideas; asst editor SW Tex. U. Faculty Bull., 1977-78, editor, 1978-81; contbr. numerous articles, reports and book revs. to profl. jours. and manuals. Mem. sr. citizens adv. com. San Marcos City Coun., Commn. for Women; facilitator, dir. numerous community workshops; pres. Jr. Svc. League; activity chmn. Tex. Spl. Olympics; numerous other civic activities. Named Ky. Col., 1975; elected to Hall of Fame, San Marcos Commn. for Women, 1991; grantee U.S. Dept. Edn., L.B. Johnson Inst., 1988, 89, also others. Mem. ASCD, Nat. Assn. Edn. Young Children, Tex. Assn. Tchr. Educators, Kindergarten Tchrs. Tex., Tex. Computer Edn. Assn. (bd. dirs. 1984-87, publs. editor, state conf. asst. 1984-88), San Marcos Assn. for Edn. Young Children (treas.), S.W. Tex. State U. Alumni Assn. (Teaching award of honor, Key of Excellence award, Strutter Hall of Fame), Golden Key, Phi Delta Kappa (pres. 1981, v.p., faculty advisor, mem. ritual team 1986-89), Kappa Delta Pi (hon.). Methodist. Home: 602 Larue Dr San Marcos TX 78666-2410 Office: SW Tex State U Dept Curriculum & Instrn San Marcos TX 78666

FITILIS, THEODORE NICHOLAS, portfolio manager; b. N.Y.C., July 6, 1937; s. Theris and Katherine (Barbara) F.; married, Sept. 1991; children from previous marriage: Jennifer, Hillary. BA in Econs., NYU, 1959, MBA, 1965. Cert. fin. analyst, 1969. Fin. analyst Moody's Investment Service, N.Y.C., 1960-70; fin. analyst Alliance Capital Mgmt., L.P., N.Y.C., 1970-93, sr. v.p., 1986-93; pres., investment portfolio mgr. Fitilis Capital Mgmt. Co., N.Y.C., 1993—; v.p. Printing and Pub. Analyst Group, N.Y.C., 1973-74. Served with U.S. Army, 1960-61. Mem. N.Y. Soc. Security Analysts, Media and Entertainment Analysts Assn. N.Y. Greek Orthodox. Office: Fitilis Capital Mgmt Co Ste 102N 2600 S Ocean Blvd Apt 102N Palm Beach FL 33480-5418

FITKIN, BARBARA WELDON, oil company executive; b. Comanche, Okla., July 1, 1938; d. Harold and Virginia Flora (Anderson) Weldon; m. Kelsie Cron Beauchamp, May. 24, 1958 (dec. Feb. 1962); 1 child, Weldon Harold; m. A. Edward Fitkin II, Dec. 22, 1971 (dec. Mar. 1992). Student, Cen. State Coll., 1956,57,58. V.p., sec. Fitkin Petroleum, Oklahoma City, 1974-80, CEO, 1980-92, pres., 1992—. Named Bus. Women of Yr. Okla. City Women's Forum, 1982. Mem. Beacon Club, English Speaking Union, Soc. of St. Andrews, Okla. City Geological Soc., Edgemere Park Preservation Assn. (sec.). Republican. Episcopalian. Office: Fitkin Petroleum Corp 2809 NW Expressway Ste 200 Oklahoma City OK 73112

FITTON, HARVEY NELSON, JR., former government official, publishing consultant; b. Washington; s. Harvey Nelson and Ada Hortense (Marshall) F.; m. Bernice Jeanette Sutton, Jan. 8, 1946. Student, Nat. Acad. Theater, 1940; degree in Am. Studies, George Washington U., 1949, degree in Am. Lit. and Cultural History, 1956; postgrad., Am. U., 1963. Editor, rsch. asst. Nat. Acad. Scis., Nat. Rsch. Coun., Washington, 1949-56; med. writer and editor NIH, Bethesda, Md., 1956-58; info. specialist farmer cooperative svc. USDA, Washington, 1958-61, publs. editor office of info., 1961-63, chief editorial br. office of info., 1963-66, head pub. div. office govtl. and pub. affairs, 1966-84, dep. dir. of info., office govt. and pub. affairs, 1984; cons. in writing, editing, publishing and continuing edn. Washington, 1985—; instr. USDA Grad. Sch., Washington, 1962-92; elected Internat. Poetry Hall of Fame, 1996. Editor, rsch. asst.: Atlas of Tumor Pathology, 1949-56; editor: NIH Record, 1956-58; contbr. articles to profl. jours. Pres. Clermont Woods Community Assn., Fairfax County, Va., 1968, No. Va. Family Svc., Falls Church, 1972-73; elder local Presbyn. Ch. With USN, 1942-45. Recipient Hart award Edn. Coun. of Graphic Arts Industry, 1980. Fellow Soc. for Tech. Comm. (pres. Washington chpt. 1972-73, asst. to pres. for recognition programs 1976-77); mem. Acad. Am. Poets, Internat. Soc. Poets, Haiku Soc. Am., Agrl. Communicators in Edn. (pres. Washington chpt. 1968, Spl. Achievement award 1986), Am. Assn. Engring. Schs. (pubs. com.), Nat. Assn. Govt. Communicators (pres. Washington chpt. 1979, nat. pres. 1980, mem. editl. bd. Govt. Comm., Communicator of Yr. 1984), St. Andrews Soc., Nat. Assn. Scholars, Assn. Lit. Scholars and Critics, Toastmasters (pres. Alexandria chpt. 1959-60), SAR. Home and Office: 5624 Glenwood Dr Alexandria VA 22310-1323

FITTS, R. LEWIS, minister, business administrator; b. Pontotoc, Miss., Aug. 26, 1930; s. Raymond B. and Bertha P. (Ladd) F.; m. Mary Frances Crain, Apr. 21, 1951; children: Debra D. Schaffner, Steven L., Myra F. Pullin. BS in Secondary Edn., Memphis State U., 1958; M in Religious Edn., Southwestern Bapt. Theol. Sem., 1959, MA in Religious Edn., 1983. Cert. in church adminstrn. So. Bapt. Conv. Min. edn. Carlisle Ave. Bapt. Ch., Louisville, 1966-70; min. edn. and adminstrn. First Bapt. Ch., Baton Rouge, 1970-79; ch. adminstr. Tallowood Bapt. Ch., Houston, 1979-85, Prestonwood Bapt. Ch., Dallas, 1985-89; min. bus. adminstrn. First Bapt. Ch., Wichita Falls, Tex., 1989-96. Contbr. material to profl. mag. V.p. Downtown Kiwanis Club, Baton Rouge, 1978-79; pres. Spring Br. Kiwanis Club, Houston, 1983-84. Master sgt. USAF, 1950-58. Mem. Nat. Assn. Ch. Bus. Adminstrn. (v.p. 1983-85, pres. Houston chpt. 1983-84, pres. Texoma chpt. 1989-91, Outstanding Ch. Adminstr. award 1995), WAC Bapt. Assn. (fin. com. 1989-91), So. Bapt. Ch. Bus. Adminstrn. Assn. Home: 14 Westchester Dr Conroe TX 77304

FITZGERALD, CAROL, administrative assistant; b. Pitts., Aug. 18, 1942; d. Edward Anton and Catherine Elizabeth (Mc Kay) Bloch; m. John Michael Mc Kee, July 10, 1965 (div. Sept. 1977); children: John Michael Jr., James Scott; m. Jean Fitzgerald, Dec. 19, 1984. BA, U. Miss., 1964. Adminstrv. aide to county commr. Broward County Commn., Ft. Lauderdale, Fla., 1978—. Trustee Cleve. Clinic Hosp., Ft. Lauderdale, 1987—, Humane Soc. Broward County, 1984-87; bd. dirs. The Opera Guild, Ft. Lauderdale, 1990-91, Light of the World Clinic, 1996—; founder Broward Libr. Found., Ft. Lauderdale, 1986—. Mem. U. Miss. Alumni Assn., Grolier Club (N.Y.C.). Democrat. Home: 2100 S Ocean Dr Apt 10-CD Fort Lauderdale FL 33316-3806

FITZGERALD, ERNEST ABNER, retired bishop; b. Crouse, N.C., July 24, 1925; s. James Boyd and Hattie Pearl (Chaffin) F.; m. Sara Frances Perry; children: James Boyd, Patricia Anne Poole. AB, We. Carolina U., 1947; BD, Duke U., 1951; DD, High Point Coll., 1969, Pfeiffer Coll., 1986, Union Coll., 1994; LLD, Greensboro Coll., 1993; DD, Union Coll., 1994. Ordained to ministry United Meth. Ch. as deacon, 1949, as elder, 1950. Pastor Webster Circuit, N.C., 1944-47, Liberty Circuit, 1947-50, Calvary United Meth. Ch., Asheboro, N.C., 1950-55, Abernathy United Meth. Ch., Asheville, N.C., 1955-59, Purcell United Meth Ch., Charlotte, N.C., 1959-64, Grace United Meth. Ch., Greensboro, N.C., 1964-66, Centenary United Meth. Ch., Winston-Salem, N.C., 1966-82, West Market St. United Meth. Ch., Greensboro, 1982-84; bishop United Meth. Ch., Atlanta Area, 1984-92; mem. United Meth. Devel. Fund, Adminstrv. Coun., Southeastern Jurisdiction, Nat. United Meth. Found. for Christian Higher Edn.; bd. trustees Emory U.; bd. visitors Duke U. Author: A Time to Cross the River, 1977, How to be a Successful Failure, 1978, God Writes Straight with Crooked Lines, Diamonds Everywhere, 1983, Keeping Pace: Inspirations in the Air, 1988, others; contbr. AMTRAK mag. Home: 2536 Huntington Woods Dr Winston Salem NC 27103-6634

FITZGERALD, JOHN THOMAS, JR., religious studies educator; b. Birmingham, Ala., Oct. 2, 1948; s. John Thomas and Annie Myrtle (Walters) F.; m. Karol Bonneaux, May 23, 1970; children: Kirstin Leigh, Kimberly Anne. BA, Abilene Christian U., 1970, MA, 1972; MDiv, Yale U., 1975, PhD, 1984. Instr. Yale Coll., New Haven, Conn., 1979, Yale Divinity Sch., New Haven, Conn., 1980-81; instr. U. Miami, Coral Gables, Fla., 1981-84, asst. prof., 1984-88, assoc. prof., 1988—; vis. assoc. prof. Brown U., Providence, 1992; dir. honors. program U. Miami, 1987-91, master Hecht Residential Coll., 1987-91, chmn. Rhodes Scholarship com., 1987-91. Author: Tabula of Cebes, 1983, Cracks in an Earthen Vessel, 1988; editor New Testament and Christian Origins sect. Religious Studies Rev., 1994—; editor: Friendship, Flattery and Frankness of Speech, 1996; contbr. articles to profl. jours. Judge for Silver Knight awards The Miami (Fla.) Herald, 1988, 90. Recipient Max Orovitz Summer Rsch. award U. Miami, 1985, 87, 94, 95; Rotary Internat. fellow, Tuebingen, Fed. Republic Germany, 1974-76, Two Bros. fellow Yale Div. Sch., 1974-75. Mem. Soc. Bibl. Lit. (chmn. com. 1989—, editor Texts and Translations Series: Greco-Roman Religion 1993—), Iron Arrow Honor Soc., Omicron Delta Kappa, Golden Key Nat. Honor Soc. (chmn. scholarship com. 1990-91), Phi Kappa Phi (chpt. pres. 1988-89). Home: 15215 SW 78th Ct Miami FL 33157 Office: U Miami PO Box 248264 Miami FL 33124-4672

FITZGERALD, JOSEPH MICHAEL, JR., lawyer; b. Norfolk, Va., Oct. 9, 1943; s. Joseph Michael and Grace Elizabeth (Finegan) F.; m. Lynne Marie Leslie, May 3, 1973; children: Joseph Glenn, Leslie Marie. BS, Mt. St. Mary's Coll., 1965; JD, Cath. U. Am., 1970; LLM, U. Miami, 1973; JCL, St. Thomas Aquinas, 1986; MA, St. Thomas U., 1988; D of Ministry, Grad. Theological Found., 1993. Bar: Fla. 1970, D.C. 1991, Va. 1993, U.S. Dist. Ct. (so. dist.) Fla. 1971, U.S. Ct. Appeals (11th cir.) 1973, U.S. Supreme Ct. 1980; cert. mediator. Investigator, Retail Credit Co., Miami, Fla., 1965-66; intelligence analyst Def. Intelligence Agy., Washington, 1966-70; ptnr. Fitzgerald & Fitzgerald, Miami, 1970-79, McDermott, Will & Emery, Miami, 1979-84, Wood, Lucksinger & Epstein, Miami, 1984-88, Fitzgerald, Portela & Portuondo, Miami, 1989-92, Fitzgerald, Charlip, Delgado, Befeler & Portuondo, P.A., Miami, 1992-94, Fitzgerald & Portuondo, 1994—; adj. facility Sch. of Law and Isnt. of Pastoral Ministry, St. Thomas U., 1989—; bd. dirs. Security Bank, Ft. Lauderdale, Fla.; lectr. environ. law and health law at various symposiums and univs.; advisor to Office Environ. Affairs, Fla. Dept. State, 1971; spl. counsel Broward County Environ. Quality Control Bd., 1975-82; spl. asst. state's atty. for environ. crimes Broward County, Fla., 1974-76; appeals judge Met. Tribunal of Archdiocese of Miami, 1986—. Contbr. articles to profl. jours. Trustee Fla. Ind. Coll. and Univs. Found., 1977-79, Inst. on Man and the Oceans, 1976-81, Boystown of Fla., 1978-83, Kiwanis Youth Found., 1980-81, Seton Shrine Ctr., 1980-81, St. Francis Hosp. Found., 1981-85, Legal Svcs. Miami, 1985-87, 89—; chmn. Mediation Ministries, 1990—, Ctr. for Law and Ministry, 1990—, Charlottesville Housing Found., 1995—. Mem. ABA, Fla. Bar Assn., Va. State Bar, D.C. Bar, Dade County Bar Assn. (award of merit 1975, 76), Cath. Lawyers Guild (pres. 1984), Serra Internat. (trustee 1979-80, pres. 1984-85), Kiwanis, Knights of Malta, Knights of St. Gregory. Avocations: golf, tennis, bicycling, reading, sailing. Home: 5710 S Le Jeune Rd Coral Gables FL 33146-2816 also: 888 Tanglewood Rd Charlottesville VA 22901-7817 Office: 2665 S Bayshore Dr Ste M-103 Miami FL 33133-5448

FITZGERALD, LYNNE MARIE LESLIE, family therapist; b. Berea, Ohio, Aug. 21, 1946; d. Glenn Willis and Blanche Marie (Monkosky) Leslie; m. J. Michael Fitzgerald, May 3, 1974; children: Joseph Glenn, Leslie Marie. BA, U. Miami, 1968; MS, St. Thomas U., 1983; PhD, Nova Univ., 1994. Lic. marriage and family therapist, Fla. Sml. group facilitator U. Miami Med. Sch., 1988; family therapist Family Life Ctr. of Fla., Inc., Coral Gables, 1985—; facilitator stress, depression and suicide prevention program Mental Health Assn., Charlottesville, Va., 1995—; facilitator Dade County Pub. Schs./Depression and Suicide Prevention, Miami, 1985-92, Mental Health Assn. Charlottesville/Albemarle/Depression and Suicide Prevention Program for Schs., 1996—; cons. Mediation Ministries, Miami, 1990—, Counseling Ctr., St. Louis Cath. Ch., Miami, 1990-92. Mem. Jr. League, Va., St. Anne's-Belfield Sch. parents aux. bd.; bd. dirs. The Vizcayans, Miami, 1979-83, Party Parade, Charlottesville, 1995, gen. chmn. 1995-96, pres. 1996—; active Marian Ctr. Aux., Miami. Named Woman of Yr., Kappa Kappa Gamma Alumnae Assn., Miami, 1973. Mem. Am. Assn. Marriage and Family Therapists (approved supr.), Am. Orthopsychiat. Assn., Am. Assn. Christian Counselors, Mental Health Assn Charlottesville (profl. bd. dirs. 1995—), Kappa Kappa Gamma (U. Va. house bd., 1995—, alumnae exec. bd. 1994—, Woman of Yr. 1973). Roman Catholic. Home: 888 Tanglewood Rd Charlottesville VA 22901-7817 Office: Family Life Ctr of Fla Inc 1550 Madruga Ave Miami FL 33146-3039

FITZ GERALD-BUSH, FRANK SHEPARD, historian, poet; b. Hialeah, Fla., Oct. 11, 1925; s. Frank Shepard and Lady Irene (Coburg-FitzGerald) Bush; A.B., U. Miami (Fla.), 1953, M.A., 1964. Instr. Ransom Sch., Coconut Grove, Fla., 1957-58, St. Johns Country Day Sch., Orange Park, Fla., 1959-61; instr. in history Homestead AFB Extension, Fla. State U., 1961-64; reference librarian, curator Floridiana, John F. Kennedy Meml. Library, Hialeah, 1966-71; historian City of Opa-locka (Fla.), 1975—; dir. South Fla. Archaeol. Museum, 1975; instr. Vivian Laramore Rader Poetry Group, 1973—, Inst. Continuing Studies U. Miami, 1990; author: (poetry) Native Treasure, 1943, Sonnets In Search of Sequence, 1968, Remembered Spring, 1974; Memories of a Golden Land, 1985; (history) A Dream of Araby: Glenn H. Curtiss and the Founding of Opa-locka, 1976, MacGyver-The Dramatic Art of Richard Dean Anderson, 1995; contbr. numerous articles, revs. and poems to profl. jours. in Gt. Britain, France, U.S., 1942—; trustee Friends of Opa-locka Library, 1976—; mem. bd. advisers South Fla. Poetry Inst., 1975. Served with RCAF, 1943-44, USMCR, 1948-51 Am. Field Service, 1944-45, USAF, 1951-55. Recipient Recognition award Laramore Rader Poetry Group, 1975, 76; named knight comdr. Order Holy Sepulcher, knight Orders Holy Cross Jerusalem, St. Stephen the Martyr, St. Gregory the Illuminator, St. Basil the Gt. Mem. Fla. Hist. Soc., Hist. Assn. So. Fla., Dade Heritage Trust, Irish Georgian Soc., County Kildare Archaeol. Soc. (life), Fla. Anthropol. Soc., RAF Assn. (life), Opa-locka C. of C. (asso.), S.R., SAR, Magna Charta Barons, English-Speaking Union, Viscayans, DAV (life), Am. Legion. Author: Young Alfred: The Forgotten Prince, 1979. Home: 3030 NW 171st St Opa Locka FL 33056-4332

FITZPATRICK, JAMES WARD, JR., engineering technology educator; b. Birmingham, Ala., June 17, 1921; s. James Ward and Ellen Barbara (Vogtle) F.; m. Ruth Bertha Horn, June 19, 1948; 1 child, James Ralph. BS in Indsl. Engring., Auburn (Ala.) U., 1942, BS in Mech. Engring., 1947, postgrad., 1950-53; postgrad., MIT, 1949-50. Registered profl. engr., Ala. Indsl. engr. O'Neal Steel, Birmingham, 1947-48; plant engr. Stockham Valves & Fittings, Birmingham, 1948-49; instr. mech. engring. Auburn U., 1950-53; structural engr. Decatur (Ala.) Iron & Steel Co., 1953-56, chief engr. jail and prison equipment, 1956-64; engring. and project mgr. Monsanto Co., St. Louis, 1964-72, engring. supt., 1972-82; v.p. personnel and ops. Continental Commodities, Inc., Charlotte, N.C., 1982-83; instr. York Tech. Coll., Rock Hill, S.C., 1985—; cons. Assn. Systems, Inc., Charlotte, 1985-95; cons. textbook revs. various pubs., 1987—. Author software: Workplan, 1984. Capt. U.S. Army, 1942-46, ETO. Decorated Bronze Star. Mem. ASCE, Am. Soc. for Engring. Edn., Charlotte Philatelic Soc. (pres. 1985-89). Republican. Presbyterian. Office: York Tech Coll 452 S Anderson Rd Rock Hill SC 29730-7318

FITZPATRICK, JOE ALLEN, music minister; b. Cushing, Okla., Aug. 8, 1959; s. Bill J. and G. Marilyn (Dawes) F.; m. Gwenn Marie Robertson, June 27, 1987. B. Music Edn., Okla. State U., 1982; M. Ch. Music, Southwestern Bapt. Theol. Sem., 1984. Minister of music 1st Bapt. Ch., Yale, Okla., 1976-82, Mandarin Bapt. Ch., Jacksonville, Fla., 1985-89, Park Hill Bapt. Ch., North Little Rock, Ark., 1989—; music intern Travis Ave. Bapt. Ch., Ft. Worth, 1983-84; dir. music Jacksonville Bapt. Assn., 1987-89, cons. youth music, ch. music coun., 1986-87; state and associational festival adjudicator State Convs. of Ark., Ga. and Fla., 1986—; tenor The Centurymen, 1988—. Mem., soloist Ark. Symphony Chorus. Recipient Outstanding Young Men of Am. award U.S. Jaycees, 1984. Mem. So. Bapt. Ch. Music Conf., Ark. Bapt. Singing Men "MasterSingers", Am. Choral Dirs. Assn., Choristers Guild. Office: Park Hill Bapt Ch 201 E C St North Little Rock AR 72116-8807

FITZPATRICK, JOHN J., bishop; b. Trenton, Ont., Can., Oct. 12, 1918; s. James John and Lorena (Pelkey) F. Ed., Propaganda Fide Coll., Italy, Our Lady of Angels Sem.; B.A., Niagara U., 1941. Ordained priest Roman Catholic Ch., 1942. Titular bishop of Cenae and Aux. of Miami Fla., 1968-71; bishop of Brownsville Tex., 1971-91; bishop emeritus, 1991—. Office: 1904 Barnard Rd Brownsville TX 78520-8247

FITZPATRICK, J(OSEPH) F(ERRIS), JR., biology educator, consultant; b. New Orleans, Mar. 8, 1932; s. Joseph Ferris and Ethel Beatrice (Sanders) F.; m. Sarah Lynn Ebersole (div.); children: Joseph Ferris, Kathleen Anne, Eileen Elizabeth, Daniel Thomas; m. Barbara Ann Laning; 1 child, Stephen Ferris. B.S., Tulane U., 1959, M.S., 1961; Ph.D., U. Va., 1964. Instr. zoology U. Ky., Lexington, 1964; asst. prof. zoology Miss. State U., State College, 1964-69; assoc. prof. biology Randolph-Macon Woman's Coll., Lynchburg, Va., 1969-73; assoc. prof. biology U. South Ala., Mobile, 1973-78, prof., 1978—. adj. curator of crustacea Tulane U. Mus. Natural History, New Orleans, 1991—; adj. prof. ecology, evolution and organismic biology Tulane U., 1994—. Served with U.S. Army, 1952-54. NSF grantee; Philip Francis DuPont fellow, Henry Clay Marchant fellow, 1961-64. Fellow AAAS, Internat. Assn. Astacology (founder), Crustacean Soc. (founder), Phi Sigma, Sigma Xi. Author: How to Know the Freshwater Crustacea, 1983; contbr. articles to sci. jours. Office: U South Ala Dept Biol Scis Mobile AL 36688

FITZPATRICK, PAUL FREDERICK, biochemist; b. Chgo., Aug. 16, 1953; s. Frederick William and Joan Catherine (Kilsdonk) F.; m. Susan Colette Daubner, Aug. 23, 1980; children—Andrew Liam, Eileen Susan. B.A., Harvard Coll., 1975; Ph.D., U. Mich., 1981. Research assoc. U. Mich., Ann Arbor, 1981-82, Pa. State U., University Park, 1982-86; asst. to assoc. prof. biochemistry and biophysics, Tex. A&M U., College Station, 1986-96, prof. 1996—; investigator Am. Heart Assn., 1991-96. Rackham predoctoral fellow, U. Mich., 1979-80; recipient Ind. Research Service award NIH, 1982-84. Mem. Am. Chem. Soc., AAAS, Am. Soc. Biol. Chemistry. Office: Tex A&M U Dept Biochem and Biophysics College Station TX 77843

FITZSIMONS, CORINNE MARIE, medical/surgical nurse; b. Fairfield, Ala., Dec. 7, 1925; d. William Dixon and Marie Rose (Moss) DeBardeleben; m. L. E. FitzSimons, Mar. 18, 1948 (div.); children: Annette, John, Robert. RN, Emory U. Hosp., 1947; BSN, McNeese State U., 1972; MSN, U. Tex. Med. Br., Galveston, 1976. RN, La., Tex. Staff/sch. nurse various hosps./schs., various locations, 1947-77; asst. prof. nursing Tex. Woman's U., Houston, 1977-79, U. S.W. La., Lafayette, 1979-81; coordiantor nursing edn. St. Patrick Hosp., Lake Charles, La., 1981-82; dir. nursing staff/svc. DeQuincy Nursing Home, Kinder (La.) Nursing Home, 1982-84; charge nurse med./surg. West Calcasieu-Cameron Hosp., Sulphur, La., 1984-86; ind. nurse practitioner Analytical Nurse Mgmt., Lake Charles, La., 1986-88; nurse clinician surgery floor Lake Charles Meml. Hosp., 1988-92, clin. nurse specialist edn. dept. & relief nursing supr., 1992—; clin. nurse specialist Sawela Tech. Inst. Mem. ANA, La. Nurses Assn., Cath. Daus. Am., Oncology Nursing Soc., Am. Cancer Soc., Am. Diabetic Assn., Am. Bus. Women's Assn., Sigma Theta Tau.

FIX, DOUGLAS MARTIN, electrical engineer; b. Lincoln, Nebr., Oct. 20, 1953; s. Raymond Harold and Juliana Marie (Spatz) F. BSEE, BSCS, U. Colo., 1979; MSEE, Southern Meth. U., 1983. Registered profl. engr. Tex. Computer ops. Seismograph Svc. Corp., Denver, 1974-78, seismic analyst, 1978-80; design engr. Tex. Instruments, Dallas, 1980-85, sr. engr., 1985-88, lead engr., 1988—; adj. prof., Eastfield Coll., Mesquite, Tex., 1983—; cons. Computers U2, Allen,Tex., 1990—. Contbr. article to profl. jours.; patent pending for digital video monitor interface arch. Elder, tchr. Zion Luth. Ch., Dallas, 1992—; crime watch coord. Neighborhood Homeowners, Dallas, 1988. Recipient Sundstrand scholarship Sundstrand Corp., 1978. Mem. IEEE, Eta Kappa Nu (sec. 1978), Soc. Info. Display, Mensa, Tau Beta Pi. Republican. Lutheran. Home: 761 Livingston Dr Allen TX 75002 Office: Texas Instruments 13510 N Central Expressway Dallas TX 75243

FLACY, FRANK LANDOM, family therapist; b. San Antonio, Sept. 11, 1943; m. Martha; one child, three stepchildren. AA in Psychology, San Antonio Coll., 1975; BA in Psychology, Sociology, U. Tex., San Antonio,

1980, MA in Counseling, 1981; MA in Biblical and Religious Studies, Abilene Christian U., 1987, MDiv in Bible, Counseling, Ministry, 1988; PhD in Psychology and Theology, Calif. Grad. Sch. Theology, 1993. Ordained minister, Ch. of Christ, 1978; lic. profl. counselor, marriage and family therapist, chemical dependency counselor, Tex. From carrier to supr. San Antonio Light Newspaper, 1956-89; minister Helotes Christian Ch., San Antonio, 1978-90; substance abuse counselor Ctr. for Health Care Svcs., San Antonio, 1990—; counselor drug edn. and prevention Wackenhut Corrections, San Antonio, 1992-94; family therapist Kyle (Tex.) NewVision, 1994—; dep. sheriff San Antonio (reserve) 1964-85, Denver, 1967-68; counselor, conductor of seminars and workshops. Author: (book) Who is This One Called Christ?, 1991, (book) Lady Cop/Lady Killer, 1996; contbr. numerous articles to various publs. Mem. Am. Assn. Marriage and Family Therapists. Home: 6167 Deer Valley Dr San Antonio TX 78242-1517 Office: Kyle NewVision 701 S IH 35 Kyle TX 78640-9999

FLADING, JOHN JOSEPH, brokerage house executive; b. Pitts., Sept. 1, 1960; s. William F. and Mary E. (McGowan) F.; m. Laura Mansfield, Feb. 20, 1993; children: Evan, Elizabeth, John Joseph. BSBA, Fordham U., 1982. Regional sales mgr. U.S. Lines, Atlanta, 1982-86; v.p. Drexel Burnham Lambert, Atlanta, 1986-88; v.p. investments Lehman Bros. div. Shearson Lehman Bros., Atlanta, 1988-92; v.p. Alex. Brown and Sons, Atlanta, 1992—. Mem. Rep. Senatorial Inner Cir., Senatorial Comm., Rep. Nat. Com. Republican. Roman Catholic. Office: Alex Brown and Sons One Piedmont Ctr Ste 400 Atlanta GA 30305

FLADUNG, RICHARD DENIS, lawyer; b. Kansas City, Mo., Aug. 1, 1953; s. Jerome Francis and Rosemary (Voeste) F.; m. Leslie Lynn Cox, June 1, 1985; children: Daniel Edwin, Erica Anne, Derek Richard. BSCE, U. Kans., 1976, postgrad., 1977; JD, Washburn U., 1980. Bar: Kans. 1980, U.S. Dist. Ct. Kans. 1980, Ind. 1981, U.S. Dist. Ct. (so. dist.) Ind. 1981, U.S. Patent and Trademark Office 1982, Mo. 1983, Tex. 1984, U.S. Dist. Ct. (we. dist.) Mo. 1983, U.S. Dist. Ct. (so. dist.) Tex. 1984, U.S. Ct. Appeals (fed. cir.) 1984, U.S. Ct. Appeals (5th cir.) 1987, U.S. Supreme Ct. 1987, U.S. Dist. Ct. (we. dist.) Tex. 1988. Engr. Black and Veatch Cons. Engrs., Kansas City, 1975-80; corp. counsel CTB Inc., Milford, Ind., 1980-82; patent atty. Chase & Yakimo and predecessor firm, Kansas City, 1982-83, Bush, Moseley, Riddle and Jackson and predecessor firm, Houston, 1983-87, Pravel, Hewitt, Kimball & Krieger, Houston, 1987—. Contbr. articles on patent applications and ins. coverage for intellectual property matters to profl. edn. programs. Legal aide to spkr. of Kans. Ho. of Reps., Topeka, 1980. Named One of Outstanding Young Men of Am., 1985. Mem. ABA (vice chmn. patent, trademark sect. young lawyer div. 1988-89), ASCE, Houston Bar Assn. (ex officio bd. dirs. 1987-88, vice chmn. profl. responsibility com. 1991—), Am. Intellectual Property Law Assn., Tex. Young Lawyers Assn. (bd. dirs. 1988), Mo. Bar Assn., Ind. Bar Assn., Houston Young Lawyers Assn. (pres. 1987-88, exec. mem. bd. dirs. 1987-88, Outstanding Com. Chmn. award 1984-86), Kansas City Bar Assn., Houston Intellectual Property Law Assn., Pi Alpha Kappa (treas. 1974-75). Roman Catholic. Office: Pravel Hewitt Kimball & Krieger 1177 West Loop S Fl 10 Houston TX 77027

FLAGE, DANIEL ERVIN, philosophy educator; b. Postville, Iowa, May 18, 1951; s. Irvin Elmer and Delois Louise (Fiet) F.; m. Dana Rae Olmstead, Aug. 7, 1976; children: Tristan Phillip, Angela Irene. BA, Luther Coll., 1973; MA, U. Iowa, 1976, PhD, 1977. Asst. prof. Ill. State U., Normal, 1979; lectr. in philosophy U. Wis., La Crosse, 1979-83; asst. prof. U. Tex., Austin, 1983-90, James Madison U., Harrisonburg, Va., 1990-93; assoc. prof. James Madison U., Harrisonburg, 1993—. Author: Berkeley's Doctrine of Notions, 1987, David Hume's Theory of Mind, 1990, Understanding Logic, 1995. University Tchrs. fellow NEH, 1988-89, Summer Seminar Coll. Tchrs., 1995; recipient Edna P. Shaeffer Humanist award James Madison U., Harrisonburg, 1994. Mem. Am. Philosophical Assn., Am. Assn. Univ. Profs., Internat. Berkeley Soc., Hume Soc. Republican. Methodist. Home: 523 Viewmont Ct Harrisonburg VA 22801 Office: James Madison Univ Harrisonburg VA 22807

FLAGG, RAYMOND OSBOURN, biology executive; b. Martinsburg, W.Va., Jan. 31, 1933; s. Dorsey Slemons and Dorothy (Hobbs) F.; m. Ann Quinlan Birmingham, May 19, 1956; children: Richard Matthew, Elizabeth Ann, Catherine Garnett. BA with honors, Shepherd Coll., 1957; PhD in Biology, U. Va., 1961; diploma in advanced mgmt. program, U. N.C., Chapel Hill, 1994. Math tchr. Boonsboro (Md.) High Sch., 1957; rsch. asst. Blandy Exptl. Farm, Boyce, Va., 1957-61; rsch. assoc. U. Va., Charlottesville, 1961-62; dir. Botany Carolina Biol. Supply Co., Burlington, N.C., 1962-80, v.p., 1980—; v.p. Wolfe Sales Corp., Burlington, 1985—; head Cabisco Biotech., Burlington, 1988-91; v.p. Found. for Ednl. Devel., Research Triangle Park, N.C., 1983-85; vice chmn. N.C. Plant Conservation Bd., Raleigh, 1984-88. Contbr. articles to profl. jours. Chmn. Beautification Commn., Burlington, 1976-80, Hist. Dist. Commn., 1981-82; bd. dirs. United Way of Alamance County, Burlington, 1984-88; vice chmn. Tree Adv. Com., Burlington, 1993—. Rsch. grant Am. Cancer Soc., 1960, rsch. equipment grant Va. Acad. Sci., 1961; recipient Community Leadership award No. Piedmont Devel. Assn., 1977. Mem. AAAS, Assn. Southeastern Biologists (pres. 1978-79), N.C. Acad. Sci. (pres. 1983-84), Va. Acad. Sci., Rotary (pres. Alamance A.M. 1988-89). Democrat. Presbyterian. Office: Carolina Biol Supply 2700 York Rd Burlington NC 27215-3387

FLAGG DAVIS, VIVIAN ANNETTE, librarian, researcher, public policy consultant; b. Milledgeville, Ga., July 18, 1960; d. Rufus and Sandra Ann (Seals) F.; m. Joe H. Davis Jr., Jan. 16, 1993. BA, Ga. State U., 1982, MPA, 1988. Purchasing and sales clk. Reed Drugs, Atlanta, 1980-81; libr. assoc. Atlanta Jour. & Constn., 1981-84, libr. asst., 1984-89, assoc. libr., rsch. supr., 1989-91, systems libr., 1991—. Tutor Lit. Action, Atlanta, 1981-83; bd. dirs. Odyssey Family Counseling Ctr., Hapeville, Ga., 1983-85; mem. adv. coun. Vol. Atlanta, 1984-87, pres., 1983-85; mem. svc. coun. Youth Devel. Allocations and Evaluation Com., Atlanta, 1987—, planning and allocations com. United Way, Atlanta, 1987—, co-chair Task Force for Homeless and Hungry, 1992—; chmn. social action com. social svcs. and human resources dir. Greater Piney Grove Bapt. Ch.; mem. Atlanta Ballet Assocs.; bd. dirs. Higher Plain Ministries, 1994—. Recipient Outstanding Leader award Vol. Ga., 1984. Mem. ASPA, Nat. Young Profls. Forum, NAACP, Am. Soc. Info. Sci., Spl. Librs. Assn. Democrat. Home: 3735 Landgraf Cv Decatur GA 30034-4775 Office: Atlanta Jour Constn 72 Marietta St NW Atlanta GA 30303-2804

FLAH, RICHARD, life insurance executive; s. Richard Davis and Margaret (Minton) F.; m. Patricia Rose McLean; children: Elliot, Nathan, Hannah Rose. Grad., U. Colo., 1978, Am. Coll., 1983. CLU. Assoc. Hurwitz Assocs., Miami, Fla., 1979-82; v.p. Flah & Stoller, P.A., West Palm Beach, Fla., 1982-88; pres. Flah & Co., West Palm Beach, 1988—; bd. dirs. The Ptnrs. Group. Co-founder Planned Giving Coun. Mem. Nat. Assn. Life Underwriters (bd. dirs., chair regional ethics), Million Dollar Roundtable (top of table, legis. liaison, chair regional membership comm. com.); mem. Assn. for Advanced Life Underwriting; mem. numerous civic boards of trustees. Office: Flah & Co 222 Lakeview Ave West Palm Beach FL 33401-6145

FLAHERTY, CAROLE L., medical, surgical and mental health nurse; b. Des Moines, Feb. 27, 1938; d. Albert L. and Edythe Evelyn (Kuehl) Hildreth; m. Gary Alan Flaherty, June 2, 1956; children: Brian Keith, Kelly Blaine. BS in Sociology-Psychology, Iowa State U., 1970; BSN, U. Iowa, 1972. Lic. counselor drugs and chem.; cert. alcohol and drug abuse counselor. Charge nurse., ortho. H.E.B. Harris Hosp., Bedford, Tex., 1984-87; relief charge nurse-psychiat., clin. nurse specialist Med. Plaza Hosp., Ft. Worth, 1987-88; charge nurse children's unit Psych. Inst., Ft. Worth, Tex., 1988-90; head nurse psychiat. and behavioral medicine unit N.E. Community Hosp., Bedford, Tex., 1990-91; counselor alcohol and drug abuse and coord. supr. Schick-Shaddel Hosp., Ft. Worth, 1991-94; asst. dir. nursing, med. unit mgr. Park View Ctr., Ft. Worth, 1994-95; supr. weekends Baylor Med. Ctr., Grapevine, Tex., 1995—; instr. Queens Med. Ctr., Honolulu, 1982. Spl. support group for minorities-Univ., Iowa, 1970. Recipient Delta Airline award and pin, 1984; Health and Profl. grant Univ. Iowa, 1970-72; Am. Legion award Univ. Iowa. Mem. ANA-IA, Mensa. Home: River Forest Estates 2508 Peach Blossom Ct Bedford TX 76021-7235

FLAHERTY, DAVID THOMAS, JR., lawyer; b. Boston, June 17, 1953; S. David Thomas Sr. and Nancy Ann (Hamill) F.; m. Margaret Lynn Hoyle, Oct. 2, 1986; children: Alexandra Lynn, David Thomas III. BS in Math., German, U. N.C., 1974, JD, 1978. Bar: Mass. 1979, N.C. 1979, U.S. Dist. Ct. (we. dist.) N.C. 1979, U.S. Dist. Ct. (mid. dist.) N.C. 1981, U.S. Ct. Appeals (4th cir.) 1981, U.S. Tax Ct. 1982, U.S. Supreme Ct., 1987, U.S. Ct. Fed. Claims, 1992. Assoc. Wilson & Palmer, Lenoir, N.C., 1979-80, Ted West P.A., Lenoir, 1980-82; ptnr. Robbins, Flaherty & Lackey, Lenoir, 1982-85, Robbins & Flaherty, Lenoir, 1985-88, Delk, Flaherty, Swanson & Hartshorn, P.A., Lenoir, 1988-89, Delk, Flaherty, Robbins, Swanson & Hartshorn, P.A., Lenoir, 1989-90, Flaherty, Robbins, Swanson & Hartshorn, P.A., 1990-95; dist. atty. 25th Prosecuratorial Dist., Lenoir, 1995—; mem. N.C. Ho. of Reps., 46th dist., 1988-94, N.C. Cts. Commn., 1989—. Mem. exec. com. Caldwell County Reps., Lenoir, 1985-86, 88—. Mem. N.C. Bar Assn., Assn. Trial Lawyers Am., N.C. Acad. Trial Lawyers, N.C. Conf. Dist. Attys., 25th Judicial Dist. Bar Assn. (mem. exec. com. 1987-88), Reps. Men's Club, Blue Key. Methodist. Home: 228 Pennton Ave SW Lenoir NC 28645-4316 Office: Office of Dist Atty Caldwell County Courthouse PO Box 718 Lenoir NC 28645

FLAHERTY, SERGINA MARIA, ophthalmic medical technologist; b. Düsseldorf, Germany, Nov. 22, 1958; came to U.S., 1962; d. Austin W. and Evelyn (Kähl) F. Cert. ophthalmic med. technologist. Ophthalmic asst. U.S. Army, Ft. Rucker, Ala., 1978-82; ophthalmic technician Wiregrass Total Eye Care Clinic, Enterprise, Ala., 1983-86, Straub Hosp. and Clinic, Honolulu, 1986-90; ophthalmic technologist Eye Cons. of San Antonio, San Antonio, 1993-96, Stone Oak Ophthalmology, San Antonio, 1996—. Mem. Assn. Tech. Pers. in Ophthalmology, Ophthalmic Photographer Soc., Hawaii Ophthalmic Assts. Soc. (founding mem., sec. 1987-89, pres. 1989-90), Ophthalmic Pers. Soc. San Antonio (program dir. 1994-95, pres. 1996—). Home: 5650 Grissom Rd Apt 807 San Antonio TX 78238-2251 Office: Stone Oak Ophthalmology Ste 450 540 Madison Oak San Antonio TX 78258

FLAMING, WADE A., software engineer; b. Goessel, Kans., Aug. 7, 1965; s. Abe Jacob and Velma Bernice (Heibert) F. AA, Hutchinson (Kans.) Community Jr. Coll., 1985; BS, Biola U., 1987. Math, physics tutor Hutchinson (Kans.) Community Jr. Coll., 1984-85; co-op. student engr. divsn. tng. and control systems Honeywell, West Covina, Calif., 1986-87; software engr. Hughes Tng. Inc., West Covina, Calif., 1988—, Hughes Tng., Inc., Arlington, Tex., 1993—. Republican. Home: 2455 Jefferson Court Ln Arlington TX 76006-4243 Office: Hughes Tng Inc PO Box 6171 Arlington TX 76005-6171

FLAMMER, CAROL MORGAN, public relations specialist; b. Knoxville, Tenn., Oct. 9, 1967; d. Hugh Whitford and Margaret (Houze) Morgan; m. William Flammer, June 8, 1991. BA in Bus. and Behavioral Sci., Oglethorpe U., 1989. Assto dir. Art Gallery, Otlethorpe U., Atlanta, 1987-89; mgr. mus. shop, tchg. asst. High Mus. at Ga.-Pacific Ctr., Atlanta, 1989-90; pub. rels. asst. Atlanta Bot. Garden, 1990-91, interim pub. rels. mgr., 1991-92, pub. rels. specialist, 1992-94; Editor (newsletter) Clippings, 1994-96. Editor newsletter Clippings, 1992—. Pub. rels. mgr. Zoo Atlanta; vol. N.W. Ga. Coun. Girls Scouts U.S.; alumni bd. Oglethorpe U. Mem. Pub. Rels. Soc. Am. (younger profls. planning com. Ga. chpt. 1992—, profl. devel. com. 1994—, founding mem. environ. sect. 1996, host/orientation chair), South Magnolia Garden Club, Ga. Hunter Jumper Assn., Psi Chi, Chi Omega. Office: Zoo Atlanta 800 Cherokee Ave SE Atlanta GA 30315

FLAMMIA, MADELYN JANE, communication educator; b. Neptune, N.J., June 17, 1956; d. Francis and Ann (Burbank) F. BA, U. Bridgeport, 1979; MAT, Monmouth U., Long Branch, N.J., 1983; PhD, Rutgers U., 1988. Grad. tchg. asst. Rutgers U., New Brunswick, 1983-88; asst. prof. Murray (Ky.) State U., 1988-90; assoc. prof. tech. comm. U. Ctrl. Fla., Orlando, 1990—. Editor: Perspectives on the Profession of Technical Communication, 1995; contbr. articles to profl. jours. Mem. MLA, Assn. Tchrs. Tech. Writing (treas. 1995-96, mem. exec. coun. 1995-96), Soc. for Tech. Comm., Nat. Coun. Tchrs. English. Methodist. Home: 533 Lexingdale Dr Orlando FL 32828 Office: University of Central Florida Dept English Alafaya Trail Orlando FL 32816

FLANAGAN, CLYDE HARVEY, JR., psychiatist, psychoanalyst, educator; b. Louellen, Ky., Aug. 21, 1939; s. Clyde H. Sr. and Ruby Marie (Caldwell) F.; m. Gloria Kay Glymph, June 1,1961 (div. Feb. 1974); children: Clyde H. III, Christpher Shane; m. Carol Anne Ross, Apr. 13, 1974; children: Patrick Ross, Colleen Helen. BS, Maryville Coll., 1962; MD, U. Tenn. Med. Unit, Memphis, 1966. Diplomate Am. Bd. Psychiatry and Neurology, Am. Bd. Child and Adolescent Psychiatry and Neurology, Nat. Bd. Med. Examiners. Commd. 2d lt. U.S. Army, 1965, advanced through grades to col., 1980; rotating med. intern U.S. Army Tripler Gen. Hosp., Honolulu, 1966-67; gen. psychiatry resident U.S. Army Walter Reed Gen. Hosp, Washington, 1967-69, child psychiatry resident, 1969-71; asst. chief child guidance svc. Walter Reed Army Med. Ctr., Washington, 1971-80; chief cmty. mental health activity Ft. Belvoir, Va., 1980-86; asst. head tri-svc. alcohol rehab. dept. Nat. Navy Hosp., Bethesda, Md., 1986-88, ret., 1988; dir. gen. psychiat. residency program W.S. Hall Psychiat. Inst., Columbia, S.C., 1988-92; prof. dept. of psychiatry/behavioral sci. Sch. Medicine U. S.C., Columbia, 1988—, dir. divsn. psychoanalysis dept. psychiat./behavioral sci., 1992—; candidate in psychoanalysis Washington Psychoanalytic Inst., 1978-88; tng. and supervising analyst U. N.C./Duke PSA Ednl. Program, Chapel Hill, 1991—. Contbr. chpt. to books in field. Fellow Am. Psychiat. Assn., Am. Acad. Child and Adolescent Psychiatry (Franklin Robinson award 1975); mem. Am. Psychoanalytic Assn. (councilor 1989—, cert. in adult, adolescent, and child psychoanalysis Bd. Profl. Stds.), Am. Coll. Psychiatrists, Washington Psychoanalytic Soc., N.C. Psychoanalytic Soc. (councilor 1989—), S.C. Psychiat. Soc. (membership chmn. 1991—), Am. Coll. Forensic Examiners (cert. forensic examiner), Am. Group Psychotherapy Assn. (cert. group psychotherapist). Office: U SC Sch Medicine Dept Neuropsychiatry 3555 Harden St Ext #104A Columbia SC 29203

FLANAGAN, JUDITH ANN, marketing and entertainment specialist; b. Lubbock, Tex., Apr. 28, 1950; d. James Joseph II and Jean (Breckenridge) F. BS in Edn., Memphis State U., 1972; postgrad., Valencia C.C., Rollins Coll.; postgrad. in theme park mgmt., Disney Univ. Area/parade supr. Entertainment div. Walt Disney World, Orlando, Fla., 1972-81; parade dir. Gatlinburg (Tenn.) C. of C., 1981-85; entertainment prodn. mgr. The 1982 World's Fair, Knoxville, 1982; cons. Judy Flanagan Prodns./Spl. Events, Gatlinburg, 1982—, Miss U.S.A. Pageant, Knoxville, 1983; prodn. coord. Nashville Network, 1983; dir. sales River Terr. Resort, Gatlinburg, 1985-86; account exec. Park Vista Hotel, Gatlinburg, 1986-88; project coord. Universal Studios, Fla., 1988-90; dir. spl. events in univ. rels. U. Tenn., Knoxville, 1990—; prodn. mgr. 1984 World's Fair Parades and Spl. Events, New Orleans, Neil Sedaka rock video, Days of Our Lives daytime soap opera. Named One of Outstanding Young Women Am., 1981; recipient Gatlinburg Homecoming award, 1986, World Lifetime Achievement award, 1993. Mem. ASPCA, Human Soc. U.S., Internat. Spl. Events Soc., Defenders of Wildlife, U. Tenn. Pres. Club, Doris Day Animal League. Roman Catholic. Home: 350 Bruce Rd Gatlinburg TN 37738-5612

FLANIGAN, ROBERT DANIEL, JR., educational finance official; b. Lithonia, Ga., Apr. 14, 1949; s. Robert Daniel and Maggie (Mabry) F.; BA, Clark Coll., 1970; MBA, Emory U., 1982; m. Anne Butler, Dec. 12, 1970. Auditor, Arthur Andersen & Co., Atlanta, 1969-70; comptroller Spelman Coll., Atlanta, 1970-75, bus. mgr., 1975-81, exec. dir. bus. and fin. affairs, 1981-82, v.p. bus. and fin. affairs, 1982-94; v.p., treas., 1994—; fin. cons. NIH, U.S. Dept. Edn.; fin. com., bd. dirs. The Coll. Bd., Inc.; mem. Atlanta Bus. League, Inc.; bd. dirs. Managed Comp Ins. Co., The Common Fund. Bd. dirs. Leadership Atlanta, Paideia Sch.; mem. Leadership Atlanta, Inc. Mem. Nat. Assn. Accts., Nat. Assn. Coll. Aux. Svcs., Nat. Assn. Coll. and Univ. Bus. Officers, So. Assn. Coll. and Univ. Bus. Officers (fin. cons.), Am. Mgmt. Assn., 100 Black Men of Atlanta, Inc., Kiwanis (Atlanta chpt.), Alpha Phi Omega. Democrat. Methodist. Office: 350 Spelman Ln Atlanta GA 30314

FLANNAGAN, BENJAMIN COLLINS, IV, lawyer; b. Richmond, Va., Sept. 7, 1927; s. Benjamin Collins and Virginia Carolyn (Gay) F.; B.A., U. Va., 1947, M.A. in Econs., 1948, J.D., 1951; LL.M., Georgetown U., 1956. Admitted to Va. bar, 1951; trial atty. Justice Dept., Washington, 1955—, chief civil litigation unit, appellate and civil litigation sect., internal security div., 1971-73, spl. asst. internal security sect. criminal div., 1973-74, sr. trial atty. spl. litigation sect., 1974-79, sr. legal adv. gen. litigation and legal advice sect., 1979-93; retired 1993. Mem. editorial bd. Va. Law Rev., 1949-50, book rev. editor, 1950-51. Served to 1st lt. U.S. Army, 1952-55. Recipient Sustained Superior Service award Justice Dept., 1964, 74, 82, Spl. Commendation for Outstanding Service award criminal div., 1976, 84. Mem. Va. Bar Assn., Beta Gamma Sigma. Episcopalian. Clubs: Country of Va. (Richmond), Deep Run Hunt (Manakin-Sabot). Home: 210 Nottingham Rd Richmond VA 23221-3115

FLANNERY, EDWARD E., municipal official; b. Irvine, Ky., Nov. 7, 1945; s. Garth E. and Thelma B. (Blevins) F. BSBA, Bowling Green State U., 1967; MBA, U. Dayton, 1976. Acctg. dir. Lee County Clk. of Cts., Ft. Myers, Fla., 1976-85, dir. cts., 1986—. Sgt. U.S. Army, 1967-69, Vietnam. Recipient Outstanding Citizenship award Dayton Bar Assn., 1962. Home: 4803 SW 5th Pl Cape Coral FL 33914-6501 Office: Lee County Clk Cir Ct 1700 Monroe St PO Box 2396 Fort Myers FL 33901-3071

FLANNERY, JOHN PHILIP, II, lawyer; b. N.Y.C., May 15, 1946; s. John Philip and Agnes Geraldine (Applegate) F.; m. Bettina Gregory, Nov. 14, 1981. BS in Physics, Fordham Coll., 1967; BS in Engring., Columbia U., 1969, JD, 1972; student Art Students League, 1972-73. 1 child, Diana Elizabeth. Bar: N.Y. 1973, U.S. Dist. Ct. (so. dist.) N.Y. 1973, U.S. Ct. Appeals (2d cir.) 1973. Mem. staff Ford Found. Project to Restructure Columbia U., 1968; news rep. nat. press relations IBM, 1970; law clk. Adminstrv. Conf. U.S., 1971; law clk. U.S. Ct. Appeals 2d cir., 1972-74; asst. U.S. atty. Narcotics and Ofcl. Corruption units So. Dist. N.Y., 1974-79; sr. assoc. Poletti Freidin Prashker Feldman & Gartner, N.Y.C., 1979-82; spl. counsel U.S. Senate Judiciary Com., 1982; spl. counsel U.S. Senate Labor Com., 1982-83; Dem. candidate for U.S. Congress from Va. 10th Dist., 1983-84; sole practice in civil and criminal litigation, 1984—; spl. counsel Sen. Howard Metzenbaum, 1985-87; asst. dist. atty., Bronx, N.Y., 1986-87; counsel, bd. dirs. Washington Internat. Horse Show Assn., 1989-91; legal expert "Crime in D.C.", Fox-TV, 1993, "Crime Bill", Wis. Pub. Radio, 1994, "People vs O.J. Simpson", ABC Network Radio, 1994-95, "Va.'s No Parole" Larry King Live CNN, 1994, "Imprisonment" CBS Morning Show, 1994; spl. counsel U.S. House Judiciary Com., 1996—; lectr. in field. Committeeman Dem. Party N.Y. County, 1979-80; mem. legis. commn. Citizen's Union, 1971-72; mem. Arlington Transp. Commn., 1983-85; chmn. bus. coun. Va. Gov.'s War on Drugs Task Force, 1983-84; committeeman Dem. Party Arlington County, 1983-84; coord. N.Y. State Lawyers Com. for Senator Edward M. Kennedy, 1979-80; dir. Citizens for Senator M. Kennedy, 1980; pres. Franklin Soc., 1979-80; del. Dem. Nat. Conv., 1988, Va. Assembly U. W.Va., 1990; committeeman Loudoun County Dem. Com., 1995—, sec. 1995—, chmn., 1996—. Recipient U.S. Justice Dept. award for Outstanding Contbns. in the Field of Drug Law Enforcement 1977; U.S. Atty. Gen.'s Spl. Commendation for Outstanding Svc., 1979. Mem. ABA, Bar Assn. of City of N.Y., N.Y. County Lawyers Assn., Arlington County Bar Assn., Loudon County Bar Assn., Nat. Assn. Criminal Def. Lawyers (chair briefbank com. 1990-91, legis. co-chair 1991—, dir. 1993—, President's commendation 1991, 92, 95), Acad. Polit. Sci., Va. Coll. Criminal Def. Attys. (bd. dirs. 1993—). Democrat. Author: Commercial Information Brokers, 1973; Habeas Corpus Bores Hole in Prisoners' Civil Rights Action, 1975; Pro Se Litigation, 1975; Prison Corruption: A Mockery of Justice, 1980; Conspiracy: A Primer, 1988, Is Innocence Relevant to Execution? If Not, Isn't that Murder?, 1994, Equal Justice For All, 1995. Home and Office: Shamrock Farm 38138 Forest Mills Rd Leesburg VA 22075

FLATO, WILLIAM ROEDER, JR., software development company executive; b. Corpus Christi, Tex., Apr. 20, 1945; s. William Roeder and Juanita Flato; m. Beatrice Pesl, Aug. 22, 1974; children: Amanda Leigh, William Roeder III. BBA, U. Houston, 1967. CPA, Tex. Acct. Hughes Tool Co., Houston, 1966-67; acct. Milchem, Inc., Houston, 1967-72, accounting mgr., 1972-73, asst. contr., 1973, corp. contr., 1973-78; v.p. fin., sec., treas. Baker Performance Chems. Inc. (formerly Magna Corp.), Houston, 1978-82, exec. v.p. fin. and planning, sec.-treas., 1982-93; CFO, v.p. fin. CoToCo Techs., Inc., 1993-96, Connective Techs., Inc., 1996—; founder, CFO, v.p. fin. Connective Techs., Inc., 1996—. Active Country Village Civic Assn.; state chmn. Young Ams. for Freedom, 1964; precinct chmn. Harris County Rep. Exec. Com., 1966-67. With U.S. Army, 1968-69. Decorated Army Commendation medal. Mem. Am. Inst. CPA's, Tex. Soc. CPA's, Mensa. Presbyterian. Home: 11931 Drexel Hill Dr Houston TX 77077-3009 Office: 7676 Hillmont St Ste 120 Houston TX 77040-6423

FLAX, FLORENCE ROSELIN P., photographer; b. Brockton, Mass., June 23, 1936; d. Samuel and Aida (Liebowitz) Polinsky; m. Barry Melvin Flax, Mar. 23, 1963; children: Amy Rhonda, Matthew David. Student, Chandler Sch. for Women, Boston, 1955. Sec. Northeastern U., Boston, 1956-63; ind. artist, art dealer Vienna, Va., 1974-82; ind. photographer specializing in infrared and macro-photography Vienna, 1982—. Featured in group exhbns. A.S.M.P., 1991-95, Tartt Gallery, Washington, 1991, Internat. Platform Assn., Washington, 1991, 92 (Judges Choice award, 2d prize 1993, 1st prize 1994, 3d prize 1994, 1st prize 1995), Ellipse Art Ctr., Arlington, Va., 1991, Capital Hill Art League, 1994-96, 96— (recipient Best in Show award), Springfield Art Guild, 1995; solo exhibits (spon. by Capital Hill Art League) include Capital Hill Art League, 1995-96, At "Provisions", Washington, 1996, Home of Stewart Mott, Washington, 1996; photo editor, photography columnist Old Dominion Sierran, 1993, 94, 95; contbr. photographs to 1995 Town of Vienna Calendar. Vol. Rep. Presdl. Campaign hdqrs., 1976, 80, 84; vol. Va. Chpt. Sierra Club, 1993—; mem. Women's Cabinet, Northeastern U., Boston, 1978; co-coord. photography teaching sessions Beauty I See Around Me, 1995. Mem. Am. Soc. Media Photographers (Mid Atlantic bd. mem. 1995-96), Washington Figure Skating Club (charter), Sierra Club, World Wildlife Fund, World Found. Successful Women (charter), Internat. Platform Assn., Capital Hill Art League. Home and Office: 104 Saratoga Waye NE Vienna VA 22180-3663

FLECKENSTEIN, JAMES LAWRENCE, radiologist; b. Omaha, Mar. 18, 1957. BS in Biology, U. Washington, 1979, MD, 1984. Diplomate Nat. Bd. Med. Examiners, Am. Bd. Radiology. Intern U. Tex. Southwestern Affiliated Hosps., Dallas, 1984-85; resident in radiology U. Tex. Southwestern Med. Ctr., Dallas, 1985-89, fellow in musculoskeletal MRI and spectroscopy, 1987-88, fellow in neuroradiology, 1989-91, dir. neuroradiology magnetic resonance, 1991-94; med. dir. Algur H. Meadows Diagnostic Imaging Ctr., U. Tex. Southwestern Med. Ctr., Dallas, 1991-94, acting med. dir. Aston Radiology, 1991, assoc. prof. radiology, 1994—. Fellow Am. Coll. Sports Medicine; mem. AMA, Am. Roentgen Ray Soc., Am. Soc. Neuroradiology, Tex. Med. Assn., Tex. Radiol. Soc., Internat. Soc. Magnetic Resonance in Medicine, Dallas County Med. Assn. Home: 4223 Lomo Alto Ct Dallas TX 75219-1540 Office: U Tex SW Med Ctr Algur H Meadows Diagnostic Imaging Ctr 5171 Harry Hines Blvd Dallas TX 75235-7707

FLEER, MARILYN JUNE, editor; b. Laredo, Tex., July 17, 1931; d. Cecil Howard and Bernice Elizabeth Fleer. BA, U. Okla., 1954, MA, 1971. Pvt. practice editor Norman, Okla., 1969—. Author: Medieval Sweets, 1990, Feudal Food, 1990, (play) Saladin and the Knight, 1992; author of poetry. Active Okla. U. Theater Guild, Norman, 1994, Cleveland County Okla. U. Alumni, Norman, 1994, Friends of the Libr., Norman, 1994; block capt. Hardie Rucker Neighborhood Assn., Norman, 1994; founder Medieval Days Soc., 1994. Mem. Okla. U. Journalism Alumni Assn., Okla. Writers Fedn., Norman Galaxy of Writers (past pres.), Medieval Fair Bd. (historian 1976-93), Mut. Unidentified Flying Objects Networks (rsch. asst. 1990), Okla. U. Arts and Scis. Alumni (charter), McFarlin Singles Plus, Lionheart Reenactment Soc., Gt. Books Discussion Group, Norman Arts and Humanities Coun. Republican. Methodist. Home and Office: Near Campus Wordprocessing 1406 George Ave Norman OK 73072-6209

FLEETWOOD, MARY ANNIS, education association executive; b. Winfield, Ala., July 31, 1931; d. George A. and Martha Ann (Perry) Sullivan; m. Lewis N. Fleetwood, Aug. 19, 1950; children: Juanita, Dexter Lewis, Melanie Louise. Student, HCC Community Coll., 1973-80. Gen. office staff Able Rose Mercentile Co., Birmingham, Ala., 1949-51; with auditing dept. Bank for Savs. & Trusts, Birmingham, Ala., 1951; account receivables clk. I.W. Phillips, Tampa, Fla., 1972-77; account clk. Sch. Bd. Hill County, Tampa, Fla., 1980, office mgr., 1981-90. V.p. PTA, 1961-62;

pres. Woman's Missionary Union, Birmingham, 1963-64. Mem. DAR, Nat. Inst. Govt. Purchasing (cert. profl. buyer). Baptist. Home: 601 W Sylvan Dr Brandon FL 33510-3542

FLEGLE, JIM L., lawyer; b. Paducah, Ky., Dec. 3, 1951; s. J.L. and Alice M. (Goodman) F.; m. Ophelia Flegle Camina; children: Lauren Tyler, Brittanie Len, James Brendan. BA, U. Ky., 1974; JD, U. Va., 1977. Bar: Tex. 1977, U.S. Dist. Ct. (so. dist.) Tex. 1977, U.S. Dist. Ct. (no. dist.) Tex. 1984, U.S. Dist. Ct. (we. dist.) Tex. 1988, U.S. Dist. Ct. (ea. dist.) Tex. 1989, U.S. Ct. Appeals (5th and 11th cirs.) 1981, U.S. Ct. Appeals (9th cir.) 1991, U.S. Ct. Appeals (fed. cir.) 1994, U.S. Supreme Ct. 1993. Assoc. Bracewell & Patterson, Houston, 1977-83, ptnr., 1983-92; head of office Bracewell & Patterson, Dallas, 1992—, mem. adv. com., 1996—; mem. Criminal Justice Act Vol. Atty. Panel for the U.S. Dist. Ct. (no. dist.) Tex. Vol. Houston Pro Bono Program; active Tex. Lawyers and Accts. for Arts, Houston, 1982-85, St. Paul's Chamber Music Soc.; mem. corp. campaign com. Dallas Mus. Art, 1994-95, Dallas Hist. Soc., 1991-92. Mem. ABA, Tex. Bar Assn., Houston Bar Assn., Dallas Bar Assn., Houston Bar Found., Tex. Bar Found., Dallas Bar Found., Am. Bd. Trial Advocates, Raven Soc., Phi Beta Kappa, Omicron Delta Kappa, Sigma Nu. Methodist. Office: Bracewell & Patterson 4000 Lincoln Plz Dallas TX 75201-3320

FLEISCHER, ALAN BERNARD, JR., dermatologist, educator; b. St. Louis, June 6, 1961; s. Alan Bernard and Eileen Barbara (Meyer) F.; m. Anne Bridget Fitzsimmons, Aug. 12, 1989; 1 child, Gerrit James. AB, U. Mo., 1982, MD, 1987. Diplomate Am. Bd. Dermatology, Nat. Bd. Med. Examiners. Internal medicine intern U. N.C., Chapel Hill, 1988, resident in dermatology, 1988-91; asst. prof. dermatology Bowman Gray Sch. Medicine, Winston-Salem, N.C., 1991-96, assoc. prof. dermatology, 1996—. Contbr. 2 chpts. to books, numerous articles to profl. jours. Med. Found. Teaching scholar, 1993. Mem. Am. Acad. Dermatology, So. Med. Assn., European Acad. Dermatology, Soc. for Investigative Dermatology, Internat. Dermatoepidemiology Assn. (bd. dirs. 1996—), Phi Beta Kappa, Sigma Xi, Alpha Omega Alpha. Office: Bowman Gray Sch Medicine Dept Dermatology Medical Center Blvd Winston Salem NC 27157

FLEISCHMANN, ROY MITCHELL, rheumatologist, educator, researcher; b. N.Y.C., Apr. 2, 1944; s. Isaac and Bessie Fleischmann; m. Laura Stockman, Aug. 27, 1967; children: Amy, Allison, Erica. AB in Zoology, Columbia U., 1964; MD, SUNY, Bklyn., 1969. Diplomate Am. Bd. Internal Medicine, Am. Bd. Rheumatology, Nat. Bd. Med. Examiners. Intern and asst. resident in medicine Maimonides Med. Ctr., N.Y.C., 1969-71; resident Mt. Sinai Hosp., N.Y.C., 1971-72; fellow in arthritis Columbia U. Coll. Physicians and Surgeons, N.Y.C., 1972-74, asst. in clin. medicine, 1974-75; pvt. practice, Dallas, 1975—; assoc. attending in internal medicine div. rheumatology Baylor U. Med. Ctr., Dallas, 1975-78; attending in internal medicine, chief div. rheumatology St. Paul Med. Ctr., Dallas, 1978—, dir. Arthritis Ctr., 1984—; jr. active attending in internal medicine Dallas County Hosp. Dist., Dallas, 1975—; instr. medicine Mt. Sinai Hosp., N.Y.C., 1971-72; asst. physician Presbyn. Hosp., N.Y.C., 1974-75; clin. instr. medicine U. Tex. Health Sci. Ctr., Dallas, 1975-84, clin. asst. prof., 1984-85, clin. assoc. prof., 1986—; mem. med. and sci. com. North Tex. chpt. Arthritis Found., 1975—, mem. med. adv. com., 1978—, bd. dirs. North Ctrl. chpt., 1985-92, chmn. pub. edn. com., 1985-89, mem. exec. com., 1986, mem. long range planning com., 1986-89; presenter in field. Contbr. articles and abstracts to med. jours. Fellow Am. Coll. Rheumatology; mem. Tex. Rheumatism Assn. (governing bd. 1980-83), Tex. Rheumatism Soc. (pres. 1983-84), Tex. Med. Assn., Dallas County Med. Soc., N.Y. State Soc. Internal Medicine, N.Y. Acad. Internal Medicine, Dallas-Ft. Worth Rheumatology Club (pres. 1980—), Rheumatology Rsch. Internat. (pres., CEO). Office: Rheumatol Assocs Ste 400 5939 Harry Hines Blvd Bldg 400 Dallas TX 75235-6243

FLEIT, MARTIN, lawyer; b. Bklyn., Apr. 5, 1926; s. Samuel and Nellie (Greenfield) F.; m. Lois Lenefsky, Dec. 29, 1979; children—Julie, Pam, Douglas, Lauren, David. Student Tufts U., 1944-45; B.S. in Ch.E., U. N.H., 1948, J.D., Georgetown U., 1952. Bar: D.C., 1952, Fla., 1974, N.Y., 1980. Ptnr., Stevens, Davis, Miller & Mosher, Washington, 1948-69, Keck, Mahin & Cate, Washington, 1992—; sr. ptnr. Fleit, Jacobson, Cohn & Price, Washington, 1969-92. Mem. adv. bd. Patent, Trademark and Copyright Jour., Bur. Nat. Affairs Inc. Served with USNR, 1943-46. Mem. ABA, Am. Intellectual Property Law Assn., Pat. and Trdmk. Inst. Can., Internat. Assn. Protection Indsl. Property, Inter-Am. Assn. Indsl. Property, Fedn. Internat. Des Conseils en Propriete Industrielle, Internat. PAT-GOT Assn. (founder) Home: 520 Brickell Key Dr Miami FL 33131-2620 Office: Penthouse 1201 New York Ave NW Washington DC 20005-3917

FLEMING, CHRISTINA SAMUSSON, special education educator; b. Ft. Belvoir, Va., Dec. 20, 1950; d. Lewis Frew and Gayle Virginia (Pribnow) Samusson; m. Hal Alex Fleming, July 16, 1977; children: Hilary Anne, Alex Andrew. BS, Tex. Woman's U., 1972, MEd, 1974. Cert. tchr., Tex. Spl. edn. tchr. Richardson (Tex.) Ind. Sch. Dist., 1972-81; ednl. diagnostician Mental Health Mental Retardation, Plano, Tex., 1985-90; pre-kindegarten tchr. U. Gymnastics, Plano, 1987-90; spl. edn. tchr. Plano Ind. Sch. Dist., 1990—; mem. spl. edn. task force Plano Ind. Sch. Dist., 1994—; ednl. diagnostician Collin County Mental Health Mental Retardation, Plano, 1985-90; mem. Blue Ribbon Sch. Writing Team, 1996. Author: (manual) Self Concept in the Primary Years, 1974, (booklet) Heart to Heart: A Parent's Guide to Congenital Heart Disease, 1981. Mem. exec. bd. Child Guidance Clinic, Plano, 1984-91; mem. exec. bd. Shepard Elem. Sch. PTA, Plano, 1985-89, pres., 1987; mem. exec. bd., founding mem. Heart to Heart, Dallas, 1980-86; leader Girl Scouts U.S.A., Tex., 1985-94. Mem. Tex. Assn. Gifted and Talented, Richardson Learning Disabilities Assn. (exec. bd. 1974-87), Assn. Tex. Profl. Educators, Parent Tchr. Student Assn. Republican. Methodist. Home: 1217 Monterey Cir Plano TX 75075-7315 Office: Plano ISD Weatherford Elem 2941 Mollimar Dr Plano TX 75075-6306

FLEMING, CHRISTOPHER GEORGE, physical education educator; b. Hartford, Conn., Aug. 7, 1965; s. William Hayden and Jane (Randel) F.; m. Cynthia Lynn White, July 30, 1988; 1 child, Christina Elizabeth. BA in Health and Phys. Edn., Furman U., 1988; MEd in Health and Phys. Edn., The Citadel, 1990; diploma in profl. edn., U. Conn., 1992. Dana tchg. fellow, Dana rsch. fellow Furman U., Greenville, S.C., 1987-88; grad. asst. The Citadel, Charleston, S.C., 1988-90, U. Conn., Storrs, 1990-92; fitness dir. The Fitness Club, St. Charles, Md., 1992-93; exercise physiologist Anderson (S.C.) Phys. Therapy, 1993-94; project health coord., instr. Prestonburg (Ky.) C.C., 1994—. Columnist Md. Ind. newspaper, 1993, Index-Jour., 1993-94, Floyd County Times, 1994—. Mem. AAHPERD, Am. Coll. Sports Medicine (cert. health fitness instr.). Home: PO Box 204 Allen KY 41601 Office: Prestonburg CC 1 Bert T Combs Dr Prestonsburg KY 41653

FLEMING, DORIS AVEN, mental health nurse; b. Pinehurst, N.C., Sept. 12, 1958; d. Robert Leslie and Margaret Louise (Hunt) F. AS in Nursing, Sandhills C.C., Pinehurst, 1985; BSN, U. N.C., 1995. Cert. biofeedback Biofeedback Cert. Inst. Am.; cert. chem. dependency nurse Consolidated Assn. Nurses in Substance Abuse Internat. Cert. Bd. Nurse, biofeedback therapist Moore Regional Hosp., Pinehurst, 1985—. Mem. ANA (cert. psychiat. and mental health nurse), N.C. Biofeedback Assn. Office: Moore Regional Hosp PO Box 3000 Pinehurst NC 28374-3000

FLEMING, HORACE WELDON, JR., higher education administrator, educator; b. Elberton, Ga., Jan. 14, 1944; s. Horace Weldon Sr. and Alma G. (Dove) F.; m. Orene Stephens Greene, Feb. 8, 1970; children: Susan Renee, Patrick Weldon. BA, U. Ga., 1965, MA, 1966; PhD, Vanderbilt U., 1973. Mem. faculty Clemson (S.C.) U., 1971-87; chief economist U.S. Senate Judiciary Com., 1981; staff dir. Office of Pres. Pro Tem U.S. Senate, 1981-82; founding dir. Strom Thurmond Inst. Govt. and Pub. Affairs, Clemson, 1982-90; exec. v.p. U. of the Pacific, Stockton, Calif., 1990-92; exec. v.p., provost Mercer U., Macon, Ga., 1992-96; pres. U. So. Miss., Hattiesburg, 1997—; cons. to fed., state and local govt. agys. on fin., orgn. and mgmt., energy and water policy; frequent media columnist and speaker. Charter trustee Dropout Prevention Fund, 1986-90, The Palmetto Project, 1987-90; v.p. Hill Found., 1982—; mem. Pres.'s Nat. Vol. Adv. Coun., 1986-89; mem. Assembly on the Future of S.C., 1988; mem. Gov.'s Transition Task Force on Govt. Reform, 1986-87; mem. S.C. Reorgn. Commn., 1987-90; mem. Stockton-San Joaquin (Calif.) Conv. and Visitors Bur., 1990-92; mem. Vision 2000 task force Stockton Bus. Coun., 1990-92. Capt. U.S. Army, 1969-71, Vietnam. Recipient Order of Palmetto, S.C., 1990, award of merit S.C. Water Resources Commn., 1990, Palmetto Pride award The Palmetto Project, 1990, others; Faculty fellow Leadership Hilton Head Island, 1989. Mem. Scabbard and Blade, Blue Key, Tiger Brotherhood, Phi Mu Alpha, Pi Sigma Alpha, Sigma Phi Epsilon, Omicron Delta Kappa, Phi Kappa Phi, numerous orgns. in higher edn. Office: U So Miss 1400 Coleman Ave Hattiesburg MS 39406

FLEMING, JON HUGH, psychology educator, business executive, educational consultant; b. Dallas, Oct. 8, 1941; s. Durwood and Lurlyn (January) F.; m. Cheryl Lindberg; children: Marcus, Phillip, Jon Mark, Mallory, Elaine, Jonathan Robinson. B.A., So. Meth. U., 1963, Th.M., 1966; Rel.D., Sch. Theology at Claremont, 1968; postgrad., U. Tex., Austin, 1970-71. Exec. asst. to dean, dir. devel. U. Tex. Med. Sch., Houston, 1970-73; dir. devel., exec. dir. health sci. ctr. rels. U. Tex. Health Sci. Ctr., Houston, 1973-76, lectr. dept. psychiatry, 1971-76, adj. prof. psychiatry, 1976-78; exec. v.p., prof. psychology and human devel. Tex. Woman's U., Denton, 1976-78; pres., prof. psychology Tex. Wesleyan U., Ft. Worth, 1978-84; pres., CEO EData, Inc., Dallas, 1984-87, Asset Cons. Inc., Dallas; exec. v.p. The Unimark Cos., Dallas, 1984—; chmn. bd. dirs. The Fleming Group and the January Cos.; grad. tchg. asst. Sch. Theology at Claremont, Calif., 1966-68; cons. Sadler Clinic and Doctor's Hosp., Conroe, Tex. Telemetrics Internat., 1974-75; chmn. The Fleming Group and The January Cos. State chmn. Educators for Reagan-Bush, 1980; mem. chancellor's coun. U. Tex. System; mem. Tex. Gov.'s Select Com. on Pub. Edn., chmn. educating the child, vice chmn. teaching profession; mem. exec. com. Gov.'s Criminal Justice Task Force; mem. bd. visitors McDonald Obs., U. Tex. Mem. Council Advancement and Support Edn., Philos. Soc. Tex., Assn. Higher Edn. North Tex. (mem. bd.), Ft. Worth Club, Ramada Club, Doctor's Club (Houston), Headliners Club (Austin, Tex.), Kappa Alpha. Republican. Methodist. Office: The Fleming Group The January Cos 3878 Oak Lawn Ave Dallas TX 75219-4460

FLEMING, JOSEPH Z., lawyer; b. Miami, Fla., Jan. 30, 1941; s. Richard Marion and Lenore C. F.; m. Betty Corcoran, Feb. 12, 1947; 1 child, Katherine Anne. BA in Engish, U. Fla., 1958; non-credit courses U. Chgo., 1959, Hague Acad. of Internat. Law, 1966; JD, U. Va., 1965; LLM in Labor Law, NYU, 1966. Bar: Fla. 1965, D.C. 1981. Assoc. Paul & Thomson, Miami, 1966-72, ptnr., 1972-74; ptnr. Fleming & Neuman, 1974-81, Fleming & Huck, Miami, 1981-86; sole practice, Miami, 1986-87; Fleming and Klink, 1987-88; pvt. practice, 1988-96, 1996—; Alley & Alley-Ford & Harrison; lectr. profl. programs, seminars. Author: Airline and Railroad Labor Law, 1981-1996, 8th edit., 1996; editor, contbg. author Environmental Regulation and Litigation in Florida, 1980, 82, 84, 85, 87, 88, 90, 91, 93, 94, 95; contbg. author: Environmental Pollution and Individual Rights, 1978, Reporter's Handbook, 1979—, Historic Preservation Law, 1984, 85, 86, 87, Entertainment Arts and Sports Law, 1989, 90, 91. Trustee Met. Dade County Ctr. for Fine Arts, 1982-86; mem. Biscayne Bay Environ. Task Force Subcom., 1982-83, well field protection adv. com. Dade County Task Force, 1984-87; mem. Noguchi-Bayfront Park Trust, Miami, 1983-89; pres., bd. dirs. Fla. Rural Legal Svcs., 1967-78, Pres.'s Water Policy Implementation Workshops, Dept. of Interior Water Task Force, 1979; bd. dirs. Miami chpt. Am. Jewish Com. Recipient conservation award Fla. Audubon Soc., 1981, 89, Tropical Audubon Soc., 1979, award Dade County Mental Health Assn., 1974, award Miami Design Preservation League, 1982, 83, award Progressive Architecture, 1982, Am. Jewish Com. award. Mem. Am. Law Inst.-ABA (continuing profl. edn. com. 1985—), Fla. Bar Assn. (past chmn. environ. and land use law sect., labor law and employment discrimination law sect., entertainment, arts and sports law sect.), City Club. Home: 34 Lagorce Cir Miami Beach FL 33141-4520 Office: 620 Ingraham Bldg 25 SE 2nd Ave Miami FL 33131-1506

FLEMING, MICHAEL PAUL, lawyer; b. Orlando, Fla., June 25, 1963; s. Joseph Patrick and Therese (Eccles); m. Natalie Jackson, Oct. 15, 1988; children: Shannon Isabel, Nicholas Patrick, Patrick Edward, Michael Paul. BA, U. St. Thomas, 1984; JD, U. Houston, 1987. Bar: Tex. 1987; U.S. Dist. Ct. (so. dist.) Tex. 1988; U.S. Ct. Appeals (5th cir.) 1988, U.S. Supreme Ct. 1991; cert. personal injury. Ptnr. Fleming & Fleming, Houston, 1987-91; asst. county atty. Harris County, Houston, 1991-96; elected Harris county atty., 1996—. Mem. Houston Young Profl. Reps., 1984—. Mem. State Bar of Tex., Ancient Order of Hibernians, KC, Phi Delta Phi. Roman Catholic. Home: 6046 Lymbar Dr Houston TX 77096-4713 Office: Harris County Atty 1001 Preston St Ste 634 Houston TX 77002-1816

FLEMING, RANDOLPH INGERSOLL, food products executive; b. Macon, Ga., July 15, 1944; s. Robert Ingersoll and Margaret Brockett (Slayton) F.; m. Vivianna Chopitea Burlingame, June 28, 1970; children: David, Baird, Aurora, Rebeccah, Nancy, Rafael. BA in Econs., Yale U., 1966; MBA, Harvard U., 1972. Staff economist Louis Berger, Inc., East Orange, N.J., 1972-74; dept. mgr. Green Thumb Corp., Apopka, Fla., 1974-76; mgr. diversification Std. Fruit Co.-Honduras, La Ceiba, 1976-78, divsn. contr., 1980-83, divsn. gen. mgr., 1983-90; corp. budget dir. Castle & Cooke, Inc., San Francisco, 1978-79; prodn. adminstr. Dole Fresh Fruit, San Francisco, 1980; pres., gen. mgr. Dole Dominicana, Miami, Fla., 1990-95; mgr. Dole Terminal, Gulfport, Miss., 1995-96; mem. fgn. rels. com. Consejo Nacional Hombres de Empresa. Santo Domingo, 1992-94. Sec., bd. dirs. Carol Morgan Sch., Dominican Republic, 1994-95. Lt. USN, 1966-69. Mem. Am. C. of C., Dominican Republic (pres. 1992-94), Assn. Am. C. of C. Latin Am. (v.p. Caribbean 193—), Agribus. Coun. (bd. dirs. 1990-93), Wianno Club (Osterville, Mass.), Wianno Yacht Club, Santo Domingo Country Club, Body Health Club. Republican. Episcopalian. Office: Dole PO Box 1689 Gulfport MS 39502

FLEMING, RONALD A., clinical pharmacologist; b. Urbana, Ill., Aug. 19, 1961; s. Henry Pridgen and Irene (Murray) F.; m. Colleen Elizabeth Fitzgerald, Sept. 10, 1988; 1 child, Alicia Nicole. BS, N.C. State U., 1983; DPharm, U. N.C., 1988. Cert. pharmacy Tenn., N.C. Postdoctoral fellow U. Tenn., Memphis, 1988-90, Centre Antoine Lacassagne, Nice, France, 1990-91; asst. prof. Bowman Gray Sch. Medicine, Winston-Salem, N.C., 1991—. Office: Bowman Gray Sch Medicine Medical Ctr Blvd Winston Salem NC 27157

FLEMING, TIMOTHY WOODBRIDGE, fine arts and communications educator; b. Lincoln, Nebr., May 23, 1944; s. George Monroe and Ruth Nadine (Compton) F.; m. Nancy Carol Old, Aug. 16, 1977 (div. Mar. 1989); children: Allison Paige, Lauren Elizabeth; m. Marilynn Back Liddell, June 20, 1991. MusB, Baylor U., 1966, MusM, 1974; EdD, U. Houston, 1984. Cert. all-level music tchr., Tex. Choral music instr. Waco (Tex.) Independent Sch. Dist., 1972-76; chair music dept. San Jacinto Coll. North, Houston, 1976-81, chair fine arts/comm. divsn., 1981—. Contbr. articles to profl. jours. Pres. North Channel Crimestoppers, Houston, 1986; ch. music dir. Holy Trinity United Meth. Ch., Houston, 1977-81; mem., asst. conductor Houston Symphony Chorale, 1976-77; ch. music dir. 1st Presbyn. Ch., 1972-76. With U.S. Army, 1969-72. Mem. ASCD, Tex. Assn. Music Schs. (pres. 1990, bd. dirs. 1978-91), Tex. Music Educators Assn. (instnl. rep.), Galena Park Rotary (bd. dirs. 1992-94, sec. 1995-96). Office: San Jacinto Coll N 5800 Uvalde Rd Houston TX 77049-4513

FLEMM, EUGENE WILLIAM, concert pianist, educator, conductor, chamber musician; b. Rahway, N.J., Jan. 16, 1944; s. Julius Eugene and Helen Frances (May) F. MusB, Coll.-Conservatory of Music, U. Cin., 1965, MusM, 1972, D in Mus. Arts, 1990. Music dir., condr. Cin. Civic Orch., 1979-83; assoc. prof., chmn. music dept. Mid. Ga. Coll., Cochran, 1983-90; concert pianist, studio tchr. Dunedin, Fla., 1990—; founder, condr. Mid. Ga. Choral Union, 1983-90; chamber musician, founder, dir. The Omega soloists, Dunedin, 1987, Nuveau Ensemble piano quartet, It Takes Three; music dir., condr. Suncoast Symphony Orch., 1996—; ch. musician; bandmaster St. Petersburg Jr. Coll. Symphony Band; guest condr. Clearwater Cmty. Symphony Band. European concert tours include Amsterdam, Baden, Barcelona, Berlin, Brussels, Edinburgh, Geneva, Glasgow, The Hague, Innsbruck, London, Lüneburg, Lucerne, Milan, Monza, Munich, Oslo, Paris, Prague, Püttlingen, Rotterdam, Saarbrücken, Salzburg, Trier, Vienna; solo recitals include Carnegie Recital Hall, Lincoln Ctr., Atlanta-High Mus. Art, Dayton Art Inst., Tampa Bay Performing Arts Ctr., Anderson House, Washington. Mem. Fla. Hist. Soc., Pi Kappa Lambda. Republican. Lutheran. Home and Office: 1615 Santa Anna Dr Dunedin FL 34698-3722

FLEMMONS, MARI ROBERTSON, secondary school educator, writer; b. Flint, Mich., Jan. 10, 1959; d. Thomas Eugene Robertson and Arlene Mae (Kramer) Behmer; m. Kenneth Alan Flemmons, Aug. 20, 1982; 1 child, Geoffrey Thomas. BS in Journalism, Ark. State U., 1981; teaching cert., U. Ctrl. Ark., 1985. Cert. tchr., Ark. Layout artist, typist comms. dept. Ark. State U., Jonesboro, 1977-80; reporter Helena (Ark.) World, 1981-83; instr. photographer Phillips County C.C., Helena, 1983; feature writer Ark. Dem., Little Rock, 1983-85; instr. journalism, yearbook, newspaper and photography Parkview Arts/Sci. Magnet H.S., Little Rock, 1986—; curriculum writer for photography Little Rock Sch. Dist.; mem. Parkview pub. com. Parkview Arts/Sci. Magnet H.S., 1986—, sponsor Quill and Scroll, 1986—, sr. sponsor, program chmn., 1986—, advisor photography staff, 1986—, advisor sch. yearbook, 1986—, advisor sch. newspaper, 1986—; founding sponsor Challenger Ctr. Editor, writer: (newsletter) Student Rev., 1986-89, Progress Report, 1986, Newcomers Guide to North Little Rock, 1986, 88, Easy Mag., 1986-87. Vol. Pulaski County Humane Soc., Ark. Old State House Gift Shop; mem. Atty. Gen.'s Youth Gang Task Force, Parent/Tchr./Student Assn. Mem. NEA, Nat. Scholastic Press Assn., Soc. Profl. Journalists (edn./scholarship com.), Journalism Edn. Assn., Ark. H.S. Press Assn., Ark. Edn. Assn., Little Rock Classroom Tchrs. Assn., Ark. Journalism Advisers Assn. Lutheran. Home: 719 Mellon St Little Rock AR 72205-2744 Office: Parkview Arts/Sci Magnet HS 2501 Barrow Rd Little Rock AR 72204-3332

FLESHMAN, LINDA EILENE SCALF, private investigator, writer, columnist, consultant, communications and marketing executive; b. Oklahoma City, Sept. 17, 1950; d. James Truman and Dortcha Virginia (Stiles) Scalf; children: Leatha Michele, Misty Dawn. AA, Tarrant County Jr. Coll., 1977; BA, North Tex. State U., 1979. Copywriter, Advt., Graphics & Mktg., Ft. Worth, 1978-80; editor Ft. Worth mag. Ft. Worth C. of C., 1980-81; mktg. prodn. coord. City of Fort Worth, 1981-83; dir. pub. rels. Circle T coun. Girl Scouts U.S., Ft. Worth, 1983-85; mgr. corp. tng. Am. Airlines Direct Mktg., 1984-87; dir. corp. communications LeasPak Internat., 1987-89; mgr. background svcs. AMR Svcs. (div. Am. Airlines), 1989-94; owner The Private Investigators, Ft. Worth, Tex. Mem. Internat. Bus. Communicators, Am. Women in Radio and TV, Women in Communication. Democrat. Roman Catholic. Office: The Private Investigators PO Box 14807 Fort Worth TX 76117-0807

FLETCHER, JOHN GREENWOOD II, state judge; b. Phila., July 27, 1937; s. John Greenwood and Verna Mildred (DeVoe) F.; m. Donna Lynn Gould, Oct. 30, 1965; children: John Greenwood III, Rebecca Lynn. BA, U. Miami, 1959; JD, U. Fla., 1962. Bar: Fla. Asst. county atty. Pinellas County Fla., Clearwater, Fla., 1963-67, Dade County Fla., Miami, 1967-73; city atty. Sweetwater, Fla., 1975-77, Naples, Fla., 1977-78; gen. counsel Sanibel (Fla.)-Captiva Water Assn., 1978-85; spl. counsel Broward County Expressway Authority, Ft. Lauderdale, Fla., 1985-88, Dade County Sch. Bd., Miami, 1991-96; pvt. practice, South Miami, Fla., 1973-96; dist. judge 3d Dist. Ct. Appeal Fla., Miami, 1996—; asst. adj. prof. U. Miami, Coral Gables, Fla., 1971-73; cons. Dade County Sch. Bd., 1991-96. Contbr. articles to profl. jours., chpt. to book. 1st lt. JAGC, U.S. Army, 1963-68. Mem. Fla. Bar Assn. (grievance com. 1986-88, ethics com. 1989-91), Dade County Bar Assn., Phi Eta Sigma. Home: 11511 Nogales St Miami FL 33156-4231 Office: 3d Dist Ct Appeal Fla Bldg 2001 SW 117th Ave Miami FL 33175-1716

FLETCHER, KATHERINE ANN PATRICK, pediatrics, emergency nurse; b. Rotan, Tex., Sept. 9, 1950; d. John Andrew and Elsie Louise (Moore) Patrick; m. James Lawson Fletcher, Dec. 23, 1971; children: James Jr., Janice, Carol. ADN, Nicholls State U., 1988. CEN, La.; cert. ACLS, pediatric advanced life support, trauma nursing. Staff nurse med. surg. South La. Med. Ctr., Houma, 1988-89, staff nurse pediat. emergency rm., 1990-92, charge nurse emergency rm., 1992-94; head nurse pediat. Chabert Med. Ctr., Houma, 1994—. Fellow Emergency Nursing Assn. Democrat. Baptist. Home: PO Box 42 Raceland LA 70394-0042

FLETCHER, NORMAN S., state supreme court justice; b. July 10, 1934; s. Frank Pickett and Hattie Sears Fletcher; m. Dorothy Johnson, 1957; children: Mary Kiker, Elizabeth Coan. BA, U. Ga., 1956, LLB, 1958; LLM, U. Va., 1995. Assoc. Matthews, Maddox, Walton and Smith, Rome, Ga., 1958-63; pvt. practice LaFayette, Ga., 1963-90; city atty. City of LaFayette, 1965-89; county atty. County of Walker, 1973-88; spl. asst. atty. gen. State of Ga., Atlanta, 1979-89; justice Supreme Ct. of Ga., Atlanta, 1990—; mem. State Disciplinary Bd., 1984-87, chair investigative panel, 1986-87. Ruling elder Peachtree Presbyn. Ch., Atlanta; former officer First Presbyn. Ch. of Rome, Ga., LaFayette Presbyn. Ch., Cherokee Presbytery; former commr. Presbyn. Ch. USA Gen. Assembly, 1984, 85; bd. visitors U. Ga. Sch. Law, 1992-95, chmn., 1994-95. Master Joseph Henry Lumpkin Inn of Ct.; fellow Am. Bar Found., Ga. Bar Found.; mem. State Bar Ga. (chair local govt. sect. 1977-78), U. Ga. Law Sch. Alumni Assn. (pres. 1977), Rotary. Office: Supreme Ct Ga 527 State Judicial Bldg Atlanta GA 30334

FLETCHER, PATRICE TOMASKY, special education educator; b. Euclid, Ohio, Aug. 19, 1958; d. George William and Margaret Louise (Zapotosky) Tomasky; m. Richard Jan Fletcher, Dec. 30, 1988. BA, W.Va. U., 1982; BS, California U. Pa., 1987; MS, Nova U., 1990. Cert. tchr., spl. edn. tchr., Pa., Mass., Fla., edn. leadership, Fla. Residential program worker Greene County Assn. Retarded Citizens, Waynesburg, Pa., 1985-87, Twin Trees, Inc., Connellsville, Pa., 1985-87; spl. edn. tchr. May Inst. Autistic Children, Chatham, Mass., 1987-88, Eckerd Youth Devel. Ctr., Okeechobee, Fla., 1988-90, Cypress Hammock Sch., Canal Point, Fla., 1990-92, Crestwood Mid., Royal Palm Beach, Fla., 1992-95, H.L. Johnson Elem. Sch., Royal Palm Beach, Fla., 1993—; presenter workshops in field. Mem. Fla. Edn. Assn., Coun. Exceptional Children.

FLETCHER, RILEY EUGENE, lawyer; b. Eddy, Tex., Nov. 29, 1912; s. Riley Jordan and Lelih Etta (Gill) F.; m. Hattie Inez Blackwell, June 11, 1954. BA, Baylor U., 1950, LLB, 1950. Bar: Tex. 1950, U.S. Dist. Ct. (no. dist.) Tex. 1958, U.S. Ct. Appeals (5th cir.) 1959, U.S. Ct. Mil. Appeals 1965, U.S. Ct. Appeals (11th cir.) 1981, U.S. Supreme Ct. 1965. Asst. county atty. Navarro County, Corsicana, Tex., 1951-52, county atty., 1952-54, sole practice, 1955-56; asst. atty gen. Atty. Gen. dept., Austin, Tex., 1956-62, chief Law Enforcement div., 1958-61, chief Tax div., 1961-62; asst. gen. counsel Tex. Mcpl. League, Austin, Tex., 1962-63, gen. counsel, 1963-78, spl. counsel, 1978-88, ret., 1988. Capt. AUS, 1942-46, PTO, lt. col. ret. Recipient Disting. Svc. award Tex. Mcpl. Courts Assn. 1980, Appreciation award Tex. City Atty.'s Assn. 1982, Assn. Mayors, Councilmen & Commrs. Tex. 1984, City Bowie, Tex. 1984, Appreciation Resolution City Round Rock, Tex., 1988. Mem. ABA, State Bar Tex., Travis County Bar Assn., Judge Advocates Assn., Texas City Attys. Assn. (hon. life mem). Baptist. Home: 1525 E 2nd St Apt 509 Granbury TX 76048-2641

FLETCHER, SARAH CAROLYN, retired elementary education educator; b. Webb, Ala., May 7, 1925; d. James Harvey and Emma Freddie (Scarborough) Lee; m. Gaston Maurice Fletcher, June 24, 1948; children: S. Daphne, Lee Maurice, Timothy J. Student, Bob Jones Coll., 1943-44, 46-47, Calhoun Coll., 1968-70, Troy State U., 1970-72; BA, Bethany Theol. Seminary, 1995, MA, 1996. With Atlanta and Andrews Rwy. Co., 1944-46; sec. to pub. The Dothan Eagle, 1944-46; tchr. Morgan County Schs., Decatur, Ala., 1967-69, Newton (Ala.) Pub. Schs., 1969-72, Trinity Christian Schs., Oxford, Ala., 1972-73, Berachah Christian Academy, Huntsville, Ala., 1973-75; sec. Dominion Textile, Yarmouth, Nova Scotia, 1975-76; tchr. Mueller Christian Sch., Miami, 1976-79, Berean Christian Sch., Dothan, Ala., 1979-86, Grace Bible Acad., Dothan, 1987-90, Clinton Christian Acad., Upper Marlboro, Md., 1990-91; cons. Mary Kay Cosmetics, 1982—. Author: To Love Again, 1996; contbr. articles to profl. jours. Active in ch. Mem. Troy State U. Creative Writing Club, Dothan Creative Writing Group. Baptist.

FLETCHER, THELMA, musician, performing company executive. MusB, Northwestern U. Appearances with Suzanne Summers, Johnny Desmond, June Valli, Victor Borge, Diahann Carroll, Phyllis Diller, Henny Youngman, Robin Leach, Kay Stevens, Rip Taylor, Patti Page, Roberta Peters, John Denver, Smothers Bros., others; show pianist 1776, Shubert Theatre, Chgo.,

Hello Dolly, Jupiter (Fla.) Theater; pianist Acad. Award Ceremony, 1989; appears nationally leading hotels, country clubs, jazz festivals; society orch. leader, pianist, 1984—; recordings include (with Cantor Jerome Frazes) High Holiday Memories and (with Cantor Howard Tushman) Chanukah Songs. Address: 9345 Kolmar Ave Skokie IL 60076-1614 also: 485 Lake Dora Dr West Palm Beach FL 33411-2309

FLICKINGER, JOE ARDEN, telecommunications educator; b. Cadillac, Mich., Feb. 4, 1949; s. Arden Henry and Stella Frances (Hurst) F.; m. Judith Marie Gardner, Sept. 18, 1971; children: Jan Elsa, Jill Kimberly. BA, Kalamazoo Coll., Mich., 1971; MA, U. So. Calif., 1975; AS, Clatsop Community Coll., 1985; PhD, U. Oreg., 1993. Asst. chief engr. Sta. KUSC-FM, L.A., 1972-74; sta. engr. Sta. KAST-AM-FM, Astoria, Oreg., 1974-75; studio operator, instr. Clatsop Community Coll., Astoria, 1975-88; grad. teaching fellow in telecommunications U. Oreg., Eugene, 1988-90; sr. mktg. cons. RKM Corp., Vancouver, Wash., 1990-93; vis. asst. prof. communications Lewis and Clark Coll., Portland, Oreg., 1991-92; asst. prof. communications Radford (Va.) U., Va., 1992—; dir. grad. program, corp. and profl. comm. Radford (Va.) U., 1996—; session organizer on high definition TV, Northcon, 1989, IEEE and ERA Tech. Conf., 1989. Dir. TV muscular dystrophy telethon Astoria Jaycees, 1980, 81; canvasser Friends of Coll., Astoria, 1982; pres. bd. dirs. Sta. KMUN-FM Tillicum Found., Astoria, 1983-84. Mem. IEEE, IEEE Computer Soc., IEEE Comm. Soc., Am. Radio Relay League (life), Pacific Telecomm. Coun., Northcom Inner Circle, N.Y. Acad. Scis., Nat. Model R.R. Assn., Sunset Empire Amateur Radio Club (sec. 1978-81), Radford Host Lions Club (v.p.). Democrat. Presbyterian. Avocations: amateur radio, golf, fishing, astronomy, cooking.

FLIEGEL, ROBERT AALBU, park administrator; b. Mpls., Feb. 6, 1940; s. Ernie and Evelyn Aileen (Aalbu) F.; m. Elizabeth Margaret Kelly, July 22, 1972 (div. Apr. 1983); 1 child, Troy Robert; m. Nena Louise Thames Whittemore, Apr. 2, 1983 (dec. Jan. 1993); m. Ellen Hand, July 8, 1995. BA, Carleton, 1961; MPA, Harvard U., 1989. Politico-mil. asst. U.S. Consulate Gen., Nassau, Bahamas, 1971-73; polit. adviser Iceland Def. Force, Keflavik, Iceland, 1976-78; legis. affairs officer, lt. comdr. Office of Chief of Naval Ops., Washington, 1981-82; rep. Scott & Stringfellow, Inc., Roanoke, Va., 1985-86; coord. Columbus Quincentenary Castillo de San Marcos Nat. Park Svc., St. Augustine, Fla., 1991-92, head of adminstrn., 1992—; fgn. mil. sales cons. Control Data Corp., Mpls., 1983-84. Contbr. articles to profl. jours. Recipient Def. Meritorious Svc. medal Sec. of Def., 1978. Mem. Nat. Genealogical Soc., U.S. Naval Inst., Mil. Order of World Wars, Ret. Officers Assn. Office: Nat Park Svc 1 Castillo Dr South Saint Augustine FL 32084-3252

FLINN, DAVID LYNNFIELD, financial consultant; b. Atlanta, Aug. 6, 1943; s. William Adams and Caroline Elizabeth (Blackshear) F.; divorced; children: Raymur Elizabeth, Marion Orme. BA, Ga. State U., 1967. With Citizens & So. Nat. Bank, Atlanta and Miami, Fla., 1967-70; asst. to pres. Panelfab Internat. Corp., Miami, 1970-72; v.p. Citibank, Miami, 1972-76; ind. fin. cons. Miami, 1976—; CFO, Aljoma Lumber, Inc., Miami, 1990—; cons. various fgn. corps., 1981—; bd. dirs. Aljoma Lumber, Inc., Medley, Fla., Continental Trust Mortgage Corp., Miami, Shoma Devel. Corp. Bd. dirs., former pres. La Gorce Island Assn., 1974-89; bd. dirs. Children's Home Soc., Miami, 1980-83. Mem. La Gorce Country Club (Miami Beach, Fla.), Fisher Island Club (Miami), Com. of 100 (Miami). Republican. Episcopalian. Home: 1717 N Bayshore Dr Apt 1231 Miami FL 33132-1150 Office: 10300 NW 121st Way Miami FL 33178-1003

FLOHR, DANIEL P., company executive. Pres. Target Techs., Wilmington, N.C. Office: 6714 Netherlands Dr Wilmington NC 28405

FLOM, EDWARD LEONARD, retired steel company executive; b. Tampa, Fla., Dec. 10, 1929; s. Samuel Louis and Julia (Mittle) F.; m. Beverly Boyett, Mar. 31, 1956; children—Edward Louis, Mark Robert, Julia Ruth. B.C.E., Cornell U., 1952. With Fla. Steel Corp., Tampa, 1954—; v.p. sales Fla. Steel Corp., 1957-64, pres., dir., 1964—; bd. dirs. Teco Energy Inc., Outback Steakhouse Inc. Bd. dirs., mem. exec. com. Com. of 100, Tampa, United Fund Tampa; mem. adv. com. St. Joseph's Hosp., Tampa; bd. dirs. Family Svc. Assn. Tampa, Jewish Welfare Fedn. Tampa; bd. dirs. temple. With C.E., U.S. Army, 1952-54. Mem. Am. Iron and Steel Inst. (bd. dirs.), Fla. Engrng. Soc., Young Pres. Orgn., Univ. Club, Palma Ceia Golf and Country Club, Tampa Yacht Club, Gasparilla Krewe, Rotary (bd. dirs. Tampa). Home: 4936 St Croix Dr Tampa FL 33629-4831 Office: PO Box 31328 1715 W Cleveland St Tampa FL 33606-1810

FLOOD, JOAN MOORE, paralegal; b. Hampton, Va., Oct. 10, 1941; d. Harold W. and Estalena (Fancher) M.; 1 child by former marriage, Angelique. B.Mus., North Tex. State U., 1963, postgrad., 1977; postgrad. So. Meth. U., 1967-68, Tex. Women's U., 1978-79, U. Dallas, 1985-86. Clk. Criminal Dist. Ct. Number 2, Dallas County, Tex., 1972-75; reins. libr. Scor Reins. Co., Dallas, 1975-80; corp. ins. paralegal Assocs. Ins. Group, 1980-83; corp. securities paralegal Akin, Gump, Strauss, Hauer & Feld, 1983-89; asst. sec. Knoll Internat. Holdings Inc., Saddle Brook, N.J., 1989-90, 21 Internat. Holdings, Inc., N.Y.C., 1990-92; dir. compliance Am. Svc. Life Ins. Co., Ft. Worth., 1992-93; v.p., sec. Express Comm., Inc., Dallas, 1993-94; fin. transactions paralegal Thompson & Knight, Dallas, 1994-96; corp. transactions paralegal Jones, Day, Reavis & Pogue, Dallas, 1996—. Mem. ABA, Tex. Bar Assn. Home: PO Box 190165 Dallas TX 75219-0165

FLORA, PHILIP CRAIG, magazine publisher; b. Roanoke, Va., June 2, 1950; s. Kenneth Van and Betty Louellen (Crum) F. Student, Va. Poly. Inst., 1968-72. Pub. Robotics Age mag., La Canada, Calif., 1979-81, A-I mag. (of the Am. Assn. for Artificial Intelligence), Menlo Park, Calif., 1980-81; editor and pub. Computerized Mfg., Orlando, Fla., 1983-90, Robot Systems and Products; owner, prin. TecSpec Publs., Orlando; editor, pub. Fla. Prodn. Guide, 1988-93; editor Location Prodn. Guide, 1988—. Editor International Computer Vision Directory, 1985; assoc. producer film The Aurora Encounter, 1985; creator TV series Nuts and Bolts, 1980; writer, dir. (motion picture) Generation War, 1996; author (web series) Generation War; pub. www.webmovie.com, 1996. Mem. devel. com. The Reason Found., Santa Monica, Calif., 1984. Mem. Internat. TV Assn., Union Internat. de la Marionnette, Puppeteers of Am. Office: Location Prodn Guide 5849 Lost Mountain Rd Roanoke VA 24018

FLORELL, KENNETH MICHAEL, medical dosimetrist; b. Topeka, June 29, 1957; s. Loren Thurlow and Ruth Arlene Florell; m. Sandra Lee Tuttle, Dec. 17, 1983. BS in Biology, Averett Coll., Danville, Va., 1984. Cert. in radiologic tech., radiation therapy, med. dosimetry. Radiation therapist R.I. Hosp., Providence, 1985-87; rsch. dosimetrist Quality Assurance Rev. Ctr., Providence, 1987-90; med. dosimetrist Roger Williams Med. Ctr., Providence, 1990-92, Moore Regional Hosp., Pinehurst, N.C., 1992—. Mem. Am. Assn. Med. Dosimetrists (com. on protocol and ethics 1994), Am. Soc. Radiologic Technologists, Beta Beta Beta. Office: Moore Regional Hosp Dept Radiation Oncology PO Box 3000 Pinehurst NC 28374-3000

FLORES, MARION THOMAS, advertising executive; b. Bradford, Pa., Mar. 8, 1946; d. Charles Gordon and Marion Eleanor (Hoffman) Thomas; m. I.D. Flores III, Aug. 31, 1968; 1 child, Whidden. BA magna cum laude, Wellesley Coll., 1968; MBA, Columbia U., 1971. Trainee Citibank, N.Y.C., 1971-72; officer First Nat. Bank, Dallas, 1972-74; cons. Booz, Allen & Hamilton, Dallas, 1974-77, assoc., 1977-80, prin., 1980-82; sr. v.p., chief fin. officer The Bloom Cos., Inc., Dallas, 1983-85; exec. v.p., CFO, dir. Publicis/Bloom Inc., Dallas, 1985-94; exec. v.p. Brierley and Ptnrs., Dallas, 1995-96; bd. dirs., exec. com. North Tex. Corp. for Pub. Broadcasting, 1988—. Trustee, pres. Non-Profit Loan Fund, Dallas, 1987-90; bd. dirs. YWCA, Dallas, 1984-89, Ctr. Non-Profit Mgmt., 1988-92; trustee Alliance for Higher Edn. Mem. Tex. Coun. Advt. (treas., bd. dirs. 1984-94), Wellesley Coll. Alumnae Assn. (treas., bd. dirs. 1989-91), Charter 100, Dallas Forum, Fin. Execs. Inst. Home: 4218 Fairfax Ave Dallas TX 75205-3025 Office: Brierley and Ptnrs 1201 Main St Ste 2500 Dallas TX 75202-3936

FLORES, PATRICK F., archbishop; b. Ganado, TX, July 26, 1929. Grad., St. Mary's Sem., Houston. Ordained priest Roman Catholic Ch., 1956; ordained titular bishop of Italica and aux. bishop San Antonio, 1970; apptd. bishop of El Paso, 1978; archbishop of San Antonio, 1979. Office: Chancery Office PO Box 28410 2718 W Woodlawn Ave San Antonio TX 78228-0410 also: 2600 W Woodlawn Ave San Antonio TX 78228-5196

FLORES-MANGES, IRMA, library administrator; b. Laredo, Tex., June 14, 1953; d. Miguel Jr. and Andrea (Rodriguez) Flores; children: Kristina Isabel Manges, Aisha Shelonda Manges, Joshua Miguel Manges. BA in Anthropology, U. Tex., 1974, MLS, 1983. Libr. clk. info. svcs. Tex. State Libr., 1983; reference libr. Ctrl. Libr., Austin, 1983-85; refernce libr. Austin Pub. Libr., 1983-84, br. libr., 1984-93, youth svcs. mgr., 1993—. Vol. archives clerk Tex. State Libr., 1983. GLISSA scholar U. Tex., 1982; Title IIB fellow U. Tex., 1982, U. Tex. fellow, 1983. Mem. Am. Libr. Assn., Tex. Libr. Assn., Hispanic Network Internat. City Mgmt. Assn. Democrat. Roman Catholic. Office: Austin Pub Libr Dept Youth Svcs 800 Guadalupe St Austin TX 78701-2314

FLORES-NAZARIO, MARGARITA, human resources director; b. Naguabo, P.R., Oct. 17, 1951; d. Juan and Victoria (Nazario) Flores; m. Antonio Rodriguez; children: Antonio IV, Diana Margarita. BA in Psychology, U. P.R., Rio Piedras, 1973, MPA, 1981. Cert. sr. human resources profl. Dir. fed. programs Municpality of Naguabo, 1973-77; pers. rep. BD Catheters Co., Canovanas, P.R., 1977-79; mgr. pers. Products Control Clorox Inc., Ceiba, P.R., 1979-81, Bard Cardiosurgery, Las Piedras, P.R., 1981-88; dir. human resources Whitehall Robins Labs., Guayama, 1988—. Mem. P.R. Mfrs. Assn. (bd. dirs. 1993, Mgr. of Yr. award 1986), Labor Practitioners P.R., Pharm. Industries Assn., Soc. Human Resources Mgmt. (pres. 1986). Home: Box 10162 CUH Sta Humacao PR 00792 Office: Whitehall Robins Labs PO Box 208 Guayama PR 00785-0208

FLORI, ANNA MARIE DIBLASI, nurse anesthetist, educational administrator; b. Amsterdam, N.Y., Oct. 29, 1940; d. Tony and Maria (Macario) DiBlasi; children: Tammy, Tina, Toni; m. Gilberto Flori, May 24, 1986. Grad., Albany Med. Ctr. Sch. Nursing, 1962, Fairfax Hosp. Sch. Nurse Anesthetists, Va., 1972; BS in Anesthesia, George Washington U., 1979; M. in Bus. and Pub. Adminstrn., Southeastern U., Washington, 1982; PhD, Columbia Pacific U., 1983. Cert. registered nurse anesthetist. Staff nurse West Seattle Gen. Hosp., 1962-64; office nurse Filmore Buckner, M.D., Seattle, 1964-66; staff nurse anesthetist Fairfax Hosp., 1972-73; staff nurse anesthetist Potomac Hosp., Woodbridge, Va., 1973, chief nurse anesthetist, 1973—; dir. Potomac Hosp. Sch. for Nurse Anesthetists and Sch. for Nurse Anesthesia; faculty mem. Columbia Pacific U., 1973-90; chief nurse anesthetist No. Va. Anesthesia Assn., 1988—; guest lectr. No. Va. Community Coll., Inservice Potomac Hosp., George Washington U.; coord. Free Clinic Prince William County, Woodbridge, Va. Contbr. books on anesthesia. Mem. Am. Assn. Nurse Anesthetists, Va. Nurse Anesthesia Assn., Nat. Italian Am. Found. Home: 12954 Pintail Rd Woodbridge VA 22192-3831

FLORY, ROBERT MIKESELL, computer systems analyst, personnel management specialist; b. Bridgewater, Va., Feb. 21, 1912; s. John Samuel and Vinnie (Mikesell) F.; m. Thelma Thomas, Sept. 14, 1942; 1 child, Pamela. B.A., Bridgewater Coll., 1932; M.A., U. Va., 1938; postgrad. U. Chgo., 1946-51. Job/methods analyst United Air Lines, Chgo., 1945-47; job analyst Julian Baer, Chgo., 1948; asst. to v.p. Fairbanks, Morse, Chgo., 1949-60; mgmt. cons. Yarger & Assocs., Falls Church, Va., 1961; computer systems analyst, various fed. agys., Washington, 1962-82; tchr. Roosevelt U., Chgo., 1956-61; seminar leader U. Chgo., 1960-61; cons. Va. Gov.'s Commn. for Reorgn. State Govt., 1961. Served to lt. comdr. USN, 1942-45, PTO. Home: 5501 Seminary Rd Apt 1204S Falls Church VA 22041-3907

FLOSS, MARK THADDEUS, civil engineer, computer scientist; b. Alexandria, Va., June 5, 1958; s. Charles Robert Jr. and Shirley Lee Ann (Bliss) F.; m. Alice LeeAnn Scholl, Aug. 10, 1985; children, Jennifer Ann, Johnathon Alexander. BSCE, The Citadel, 1980. Registered profl. engr., S.C. City engr. City North Charleston, S.C., 1985-92; constrn. insp. City of Savannah, Ga., 1993-94, facilities project coord., 1994; field engr. Town of Mt. Pleasant, S.C., 1994-96; asst. pub. works dir., city engr., chief bldg. ofcl. City of Goose Creek, 1995—. Author road codes, computer macros. With USAFR, 1985. Home: 18 Briarcliff Dr Charleston SC 29407-6612 Office: City of Goose Creek Dept Pub Works PO Drawer 1768 Goose Creek SC 29445

FLOURNOY, JACOB WESLEY, internal audit director; b. Odessa, Tex., June 18, 1956; s. Dan Dunn and Vonnie Rea (Morrow) F.; m. Tina Charlene Hargis, Jan. 5, 1980; children: Daniel Edward, Samuel Wesley. BBA, U. North Tex., 1978; MBA, U. Okla., 1984. CPA, cert. internal auditor; cert. info. sys. auditor; cert. fraud examiner. Asst. bank examiner Fed. Deposit Ins. Corp., Oklahoma City, Okla., 1978-80; internal auditor City of Oklahoma City, 1980-82; sr. internal auditor U. Okla., Norman, 1982-86; internal audit dir. U. Tex. Health Sci. Ctr., San Antonio, 1986-91, U. Ark. Sys., Little Rock, 1991—. mem. AICPA, Inst. Internal Auditors (pres., v.p., sec., treas.), Info. Sys. Audit and Control Assn., Assn. Coll. and Univ. Auditors (chair acctg. principles com. 1991-92). Office: U Ark 1123 S University Ave Ste 915 Little Rock AR 72204-1616

FLOWER, WALTER CHEW, III, investment counselor; b. New Orleans, Mar. 3, 1939; s. Walter Chew II and Anne Elisa (Lusk) F.; m. Ella Smith Montgomery, Dec. 21, 1966; children: Anne Stuart, Lindsey Montgomery. BA in Econs., Tulane U., 1960; MBA in Fin., Harvard U., 1964. Cons. AID, State Dept., 1964-65; fin. analyst Delta Capital Corp., New Orleans, 1965-66; v.p., mng. partner Loomis Sayles & Co. Inc., New Orleans, 1967-78; pres. Walter C. Flower & Co., Investment Counsel, New Orleans, 1978—; dir. Starmount Cos., Tulane Med. Ctr.; bd. dirs. Longue Vue Found., 1983—; dir GPOA Found., 1985—; vestryman, mem. parish council Trinity Ch., 1978—; dir., fin. adv. Jr. League New Orleans, 1978-82; fin. adv. Hermann Grima House, 1978—, Beauregard House, 1979—, Metairie Park Country Day Sch., 1991—. Lt. USNR, 1960-62. Mem. Boston Club, La. Club., Pickwick Club, New Orleans Lawn Tennis Club, So. Yacht Club (New Orleans), Fishers Island Yacht Club, Stratford Club, Lakeshore Club, Wyvern Club, Confrerie Des Chevaliers Du Tastevin, Phi Beta Kappa. Office: 408 Magazine St New Orleans LA 70130-2427

FLOWERS, JUDITH ANN, marketing and public relations director; b. Oxford, Miss., Feb. 21, 1944; d. Woodrow Coleman and Ola Marie (Harding) Haynes; m. Sayles L. Brown Jr., Apr. 20, 1963 (div. Apr. 1974); children: Sayles L. III, Gregory A., Matthew C., Stephen W.; m. Taylor Graydon Flowers Jr., Apr. 27, 1979. Grad. high sch., Clarksdale, Miss. Office mgr. The KBH Corp., Clarksdale, 1964-69; office mgr., estimator Willis & Ellis Constrn., Clarksdale, 1969-75; with advt. prodn. Farm Press Pub., Clarksdale, 1975-79, advt. mgr., 1979-86, dir. advt. svcs., 1986-93; dir. mktg. and pub. rels. Cotton Club Casino, Greenville, Miss., 1992-95; dir. spl. projects C. of C., Clarksdale, Miss., 1996—. Counselor County Youth Ct., Clarksdale, 1985—; sec. Keep Clarksdale Beautiful, 1990-92; bd. dirs. Delta Arts Coun., 1994-95, Miss. Tourism Promotion Assn., 1996—, Miss. Delta Arts Coun., 1996—; co-chair Tennessee Williams Festival, 1996. Mem. NAFE, Bus. and Profl. Women (corr. sec. 1987-88, 1st v.p. 1989-90, pres. 1992-93), Agri-Women Am., Nat. Agri-Mktg. Assn. (v.p. mid-south chpt. 1989-90, pres. 1990-91, nat. dir. 1991-93), Clarksdale C. of C. (chmn. agribus. commn. 1989-92, bd. dirs. 1989-92), So. Garden History Soc. (bd. dirs. 1992-95), The Garden Conservancy (city beautification 1996—), Miss. Tourism Promotion Assn. (bd. dirs. 1996—), Miss. Delta Arts Coun. (bd. dirs. 1996—). Republican. Baptist. Home: PO Box 3126 Dublin MS 38739-0126 Office: C of C PO Box 160 Clarksdale MS 38614

FLOWERS, KATHY RENÉ, elementary school educator; b. Memphis, Feb. 15, 1959; d. Charles Edward and Thelma Ophelia (Watson) F. BS in Elem. Edn., Le Moyne-Owen Coll., 1980; MS in Elem. Edn., LeMoyne-Owen Coll., 1994. Recreation dir. Memphis Park Commn., 1978; tchr.'s asst. Lamplighter Montessori Sch., Memphis, 1979; elem. sch. tchr. Memphis City Schs., Hanley Elem. Sch., 1980—; facilitator Parent-to-Parent Tng. Workshops, Me and My Shadow Workshops; participant Newspaper in the Classroom-Newspaper Fair. Storyteller in shopping malls and children's birthday parties. Chairperson Memphis in May Children's Poster Contest, 1993-96; mem. com. dr. Martin Luther King's Jr. 4th Annual Solidarity Day Banquet, 1993. Recipient Outstanding Social Studie tchr. award State of Tenn., 1993. Fellow Memphis Edn. Assn., Tenn. Edn. Assn., NEA, Nat. Sci. Tchrs. Assn., Women in Edn.; mem. West Tenn. Reading Assn. (sch. liaison rep.), Tenn. Coun. for Social Studies, Zeta Phi Beta (grammateus 1978-80, Miss Blue Revue chairperson 1995, 3rd Anti-Basileus 1995, Membership cert. 1978). Democrat. Baptist. Home: 1500 Ball Rd Memphis TN 38106-8203

FLOWERS, WILLIAM HOWARD, JR., food company executive; b. Thomasville, Ga., Nov. 14, 1913; s. William Howard and Flewellyn Evans (Strong) F.; m. Fontaine Maury Tice, June 22, 1936; children: Fontaine (Mrs. Fontaine Flowers McFadden), Maury (Mrs. Joseph V. Shields Jr.), Daphne (Mrs. C. Martin Wood III), Taliaferro (Mrs. Robert P. Crozer). B.A. in Bus. Adminstrn, Washington and Lee U., 1933. With Flowers Baking Co. div. Flowers Industries, Inc., Thomasville, Ga., 1933-68, pres., chief operating officer, 1937-65, chmn., chief operating officer, 1966-68; chmn., chief exec. officer Flowers Industries, Inc., Thomasville, 1974-76, chmn., 1976-81, chmn. exec. com., 1981—, chmn. emeritus, 1984-96, retired chmn. bd., 1996—. Chmn. Southeastern Legal Found., Atlanta, 1983-87, emeritus, 1987—; dir. The Prayer Book Soc., 1984-87, Thomas County Bi-Centennial/Sesqui-Centennial Commn.; mem. spl. adv. com. on pub. opinion U.S. Dept. State, 1970-72; mem. Thomas County Sch. Bd., 1953-58, Madeira Sch. Corp., Greenway, Va., 1960-68, Ga. Senate, 1964-68; city commr., Thomasville, 1941; pres. Thomasville YMCA, 1949-52; trustee John D. Archbold Meml. Hosp., 1953-71, Thomasville; pres. William Howard Flowers Jr. Found. Recipient Ga. Freedom award, 1994, Pinnacle award Thomasville-Thomas County, 1994; named Man of Yr., Thomas County C. of C., 1964. Mem. NAM (dir. 1962-66), Young Pres.'s Orgn., Chief Execs. Orgn., Ducks Unltd. (nat. trustee 1967—), University Club (N.Y.C.), Rotary, Lyford Cay (Nassau), Wildcat Cliffs Country (Highlands, N.C.), Ga-Fla Field Trial, Glen Arven Country (Thomasville), Farmington Country (Charlottesville, Va.), Omicron Delta Kappa. Episcopalian. Office: Flowers Industries Inc PO Box 1338 US Highway 19 S Thomasville GA 31799-1338

FLOYD, CINTHIA ANN, secondary school educator, coach; b. Mobile, Ala., July 26, 1961; d. Joe Merle and V. Marolyn (Whiddon) Crump; children: Cory James, Courtney Marie; m. Martin A. Floyd, Aug. 12, 1994. BS in Phys. Edn., U. South Ala., 1983, MEd, 1984. Cert. phys. edn. tchr., Ala. Grad. teaching asst. U. South Ala., Mobile, 1984-85; tchr. phys. edn., volleyball coach Palmer Pillans Mid. Sch., Mobile, 1985—; softball coach B.C. Rain High Sch., Mobile, 1989—; mem. health curriculum adv. bd. Mobile County Pub. Sch. System, 1990-91; program dir. Racquetball Club Mobile, 1980-87. Named Pillans Mid. Schs. Ala. Tchr. of Yr., Mobile County Pub. Sch. System, 1991, Outstanding Tchr. of Yr., Mobile C. of C., 1991, One of Top Three in Nation, Disney's Am. Tchr. awards, 1993. Mem. AAHPERD, NEA, Nat. Assn. Girls and Women in Sports, Ala. Assn. Health Phys. Edn. Recreation and Dance (State Coach of Yr. 1991), Ala. Edn. Assn., Ala. High Sch. Athletic Assn., Coaches and Phys. Educators Mobile (v.p. 1989-91), Kappa Kappa Iota (pres. 1991). Baptist. Home: 607 Montclaire Way Mobile AL 36609 Office: Pillans Mid Sch 2051 Military Rd Mobile AL 36605-3132

FLOYD, FRANK ALBERT, JR., management executive; b. Florence, S.C., Dec. 23, 1929; s. Frank Albert Sr. and Alline Heard (Campbell) F.; m. Ruby Joye VanKeurin, Mar. 15, 1951; children: Frank Albert III, Joye Lynn, Frances Alline. BS in Chemistry and Psychology, U. S.C., 1950; postgrad., U. N.C., 1950-51, U. Denver, 1952, Trinity Coll., San Antonio, 1953. Lic. real estate broker, S.C. Indsl. engr. Excelsior Mills, Union, S.C., 1955-58; chief chemist Milliken & Co., Union, 1958-59; prodn. mgr. Kingstree (S.C.) Mfg. Corp., 1959-62; pres., CEO Computer Acctg. Corp., Columbia, S.C., 1962-69, Frank A. Floyd Co., Columbia, 1969-86; chmn., CEO Comml. and Investment Realty, Inc., Columbia, 1969—; chmn. bd. dirs. InterMark Mgmt. Corp., Columbia, 1986—; mem. adv. bd. First Citizens Bank, Columbia, 1991—; v.p., treas. Bear Investments, Inc., Palmetto Guaranty Investment Corp.; agt. Aetna Ins. Co., Am. Gen. Life Ins. Co.; pres. First Guaranty Investment Corp. Bd. deacons, First Presbyn. Ch.; supt. Sunday sch., tchr., mem. long range planning com., mem. christian edn. com., bldg. com., fin. and budget com. N.E. Presbyn. Ch. Mem. U. S.C. Alumni Assn., Kiwanis (past pres. Union club), Union County Club, Exec. Club of Columbia, Skyhawk Club, Palmetto Club. Republican. Presbyterian. Home: 6317 Olde Knight Pky Columbia SC 29209-1523 Office: InterMark Mgmt Corp InterMark Bldg 3830 Forest Dr Ste 202 Columbia SC 29204-4145

FLOYD, JAMES BURRIS, electrical engineer; b. Olanta, S.C., Nov. 27, 1939; s. William Claude Jr. and Cherrie Selema (Ward) F.; m. Barbara Elizabeth Hart, Oct. 23, 1965; children: Kimblery Anne, James B. Jr. BSEE, Clemson U., 1962; MSEE, Cath. U., 1975. Elec. sys. designer Newport News (Va.) Shipbuilding, 1962; elec. sys. designer Naval Sea Sys. Command, Arlington, Va., 1969-87, program mgr. elec./magnetic sys., 1987-94; prin. engr. Gibbs & Cox, Inc., Arlington, Va., 1994—; cons. Program Exec. Office Mine Warfare, Arlington, 1992—. Author: (tech. book) Magnetic Ranging, Testing and Calibration of Non-Magnetic Mine Countermeasure Ships, 1996; editor: (tech. book) Magnetic Treatment Procedures, 1985, (workbooks) Magnetic Silencing, 1989. Tchr., com. chmn. So. Bapt. chs., S.C., Md. and Va., 1966—, deacon, 1967—; leader Cub and Boy Scout troops, Springfield, Va., 1978-85; soccer coach Springfield Youth Club, 1978-83. Capt. U.S. Army, 1963-64, 65-69. Recipient Disting. Svc. award Charleston Heights Bapt. Ch., 1967, Meritorious Civilian Svc. award, 1994. Mem. Assn. Sr. Engrs. (symposium pub. com. 1972, 77). Home: 7200 Ming Tree Ct Springfield VA 22152-3613 Office: Gibbs & Cox Inc Naval Architects Marine Eng 1235 Jefferson Davis Hwy Arlington VA 22202-3283

FLOYD, JOHN MALCOM, lawyer; b. Decatur, Ala., Aug. 16, 1963; s. Kenneth Ray and Linda Sue (Hughes) F.; m. Marsha Debra Moon, July 20, 1985. BS, Samford U., 1985; JD, Cumberland Sch. Law, 1988. Bar: Ala. 1989. Supr. claims and litigation Corp. Risk Dept. Vulcan Materials Co., Birmingham, Ala., 1988—, pres., 1995-96; v.p. Nat. Alumni Found., Am. Jour. Trial Advocacy, Birmingham, 1991-92; mem. Vulcan Materials Co. Nat. Mgmt. Assn., v.p., 1990-91, pres., 1991-92, chmn., 1992-93; bd. dirs. Product Liability Adv. Coun. Mng. editor Am. Jour. Trial Advocacy, 1984-85. Mem. Ala. State Bar Assn., Def. Rsch. Inst., Assn. Trial Attys. Am., Ill. Self Insurers Assn. (bd. dirs.). Republican. Baptist. Home: 5141 Meadow Brook Rd Birmingham AL 35242 Office: Vulcan Materials Co One Metroplex Dr Birmingham AL 35209

FLOYD, JULIE A., management analyst; b. Washington, Feb. 11, 1952; d. Lawrence Eugene and Marion Rose (King) Floyd; m. E. Scott Royce, June 9, 1984. AA, Immaculata Coll., Washington, 1971; BA, Dunbarton Coll., Washington, 1973; MA, Marymount U., 1994. Traffic mgmt. specialist Mil. traffic Mgmt. Command, Falls Church, Va., 1975-80; mgmt. asst. U.S. Army Concepts and Analysis Agy., Bethesda, Md., 1981-84; orgnl. analyst Chief of Naval Ops., Arlington, Va., 1984-91; mgmt. analyst Bur. Naval Pers., Arlington, 1991-93, dir., 1993—, mem. workforce transition team, 1995—; co-chair Naval Dist. of Washington Tng. Coun., 1988. Editor Arlington NOW News, 1978-79. Regional legis. chair Federally Employed Women, Washington, 1988-89, membership chair Pentagon I chpt., Arlington, 1988; intern Women's Equity Action League, Washington, 1981; dist. chair 10th Congl. Dist. Va. Libertarian Party, 1980-81; vols. coord. Arlington, VA Clark (Libertarian) For Pres. campaign, 1980; pub. edn. chair Arlington County Task Force on Domestic Violence, 1979; vol. Muskie for Pres. campaign, 1972; pres. Arlington chpt. NOW, 1978-79, membership chair, 1977-78. Named to Outstanding Young Women of Am., 1981. Mem. Am. Soc. Tng. and Devel., Soc. for Human Resources Mgmt. Home: PO Box 10607 Arlington VA 22210

FLOYD, KAY CIRKSENA, medical technologist, educational association administrator; b. Hastings, Nebr., Mar. 30, 1943; d. Frank H. and Mary Gertrude (Martini) Cirksena; m. Richard Clark Floyd, Jr., May 20, 1967; children: Scott, Matthew. BA, Hastings Coll., 1965. Registered med. technologist. Electrocardiogram technician Bishop Clarkson Meml. Hosp., Omaha, 1964-65, med. technologist, 1965-66; teaching med. technologist Rochester (N.Y.) Gen. Hosp., 1966-70; teaching technologist Presbyn. Hosp. Ctr., Albuquerque, 1970-71; asst. lab. supr. Anna Kaseman Hosp., Albuquerque, 1971-72; dir. govt. rels. Oklahoma State Sch. Bds. Assn., 1995—. Traffic commr. Oklahoma City, 1980-85; PTA pres. Stonegate Elem. Sch., 1979-80, Hoover Mid. Sch., Oklohoma City, 1984-85; v.p., pres. Oklahoma City Bd. Edn., 1985-92 (v.p. 1987-88, pres. 1988-89); bd. dirs. Oklahoma City Pub. Sch. Found., 1990-91; active The Referral Ctr. for Alcohol and Drug Svcs., 1990—, v.p., 1994—; active Met. Area Projects Oversight,

1994—; grad. Leadership Oklahoma City, 1993. Mem. Am. Soc. Clin. Pathologists (assoc.), Okla. State Sch. Bds. Assn. (bd. dirs. 1985-92), Nat. Sch. Bds. Assn., Orch. League (bd. dirs. 1994), Okla. City Rep. Women's Club (2d v.p. 1994). Republican. Presbyterian. Home: 2401 NW 119th St Oklahoma City OK 73120-7407 Office: Okla State Sch Bds Assn 2801 N Lincoln Blvd Oklahoma City OK 73105

FLUHARTY, JERRY KENNETH, JR., mathematics educator; b. Wheeling, W.Va., Mar. 2, 1956; s. Jerry Kenneth and Dorothy Irene (White) F.; m. Mary Regina Sinon, May 31, 1986; 1 child, Carrie Lynn. BS in Math., W. Liberty (W.Va.) State Coll., 1978; MS in Maths., W.Va. U., 1984. Assoc. prof. Ea. Shore C.C., Melfa, Va., 1984—, coord. summer youth employment and tng. program, 1987-93, mgr. Local Area Network, 1992—; tchr. physics Nandue High Sch., Onley, Va., 1985-87; computer cons. Northampton-Accomack Meml. Hosp., Nassawadox, Va., 1993. Sec.-treas. Eastern Shore Country Fair, Melfa, 1987—; bd. dirs. Ea. Schore Coalition Against Domestic Violence, 1990; asst. cubmaster pack 313 Boy Scouts Am., 1992-93. Mem. Math. Assn. Am., Va. Math. Assn. Two Yr. Colls. Home: PO Box 342 Onancock VA 23417-0342 Office: Ea Shore C C 29300 Lankford Hwy Melfa VA 23410-3001

FLUNO, JOHN ARTHUR, entomologist, consultant; b. Appleton, Wis., July 21, 1914; s. Arthur Swetland and Elsie (Younger) F.; m. Ruth Margaret Johnson, Aug. 15, 1942; children: Ruth Adaire, Jo Anne. BS, Rollins Coll., 1937; MS, Ohio State U., 1939. Field aide U.S. Dept. Agr., Orlando, Fla., 1937-38; entomologist Orlando, Fla., 1946-56, Beltsville, Md., 1956-72; asst. Ohio Biol. Survey, Columbus, 1938-40; instr. Rollins Coll., Winter Park, Fla., 1941; jr. entomologist USPHS, 1941-46; now cons. Served with AUS, 1943-46. Mem. Entomol. Soc. Washington, Rollins Coll. Alumni Assn. (past pres.), The Lepidopterists Soc., Am. Mosquito Control Assn. Home and Office: 1234 Lakeview Dr Winter Park FL 32789-5038

FLY, JAMES LAWRENCE, JR., construction executive; b. N.Y.C., Aug. 15, 1928; s. James Lawrence and Mildred Marvin (Jones) F.; m. Annette Mary Williams, Dec. 12, 1959 (div. June 1966); 1 child, James Lawrence III; m. Rosa Zidelis, Sept. 15, 1979 (div. 1993). BA, Yale U., 1950; postgrad., Columbia U., 1955-56. Cert. AA gen. contractor, Fla. Adminstrv. asst. film dept. CBS TV, N.Y.C., 1953-55; with sales svc. CBS Radio Network, N.Y.C., 1955-56; salesman Katz Agy., N.Y.C., 1956-58, Sta. WNTA TV, N.Y.C., 1958-59; pres., chief exec. officer Gibraltar Constructors, Inc., Daytona Beach, Fla., 1959—; known and recognized dedicated environmentalist; pres. Daytona Beach (Fla.) chpt. Nat. Assn. Home Builders, 1965-66; mem. South Daytona Bd. of Zoning Appeals, 1981-83. 1st lt. USMC, 1951-53, Korea. Mem. Yale Club N.Y.C., Halifax River Yacht Club. Democrat. Presbyterian. Home: 915 Pine Tree Ter Deland FL 32724-2967 Office: Gibraltar Constructors Inc PO Box 4006 S Daytona Sta Daytona Beach FL 32121

FLYNN, DANIEL CLARKE, human resources executive, educator; b. San Francisco, May 10, 1939; U.S. and Ireland citizen; s. John Lawrence and Elizabeth Kathryne (Stumpf) F.; m. Kathleen Ann McNally, Feb. 3, 1990; children: Theresa, Daniel Joseph. BA, U. Santa Clara, 1961; JD, Georgetown U., 1975. Bar: Va, 1975. Sr. pers. rep. COMSAT, Washington, 1967-72; assoc. dir. Am. Bankers Assn., Washington, 1975-79; sr. mgr. MCI Communications, Washington, 1982-87; v.p. pers. svcs. Lafarge Corp., Reston, Va., 1987—, Lafarge Can. Inc., Montreal, 1987—; adj. prof. Am. U., Washington, 1987—; mem. conf. bd. Can. Compensation Ctr. 1st lt. U.S. Army, 1961-63. Mem. Am. Compensation Assn. (cert. compensation profl., mem. faculty 1985-93), Internat. Inst. Soc. Human Resources Mgmt., Belgian-Am. Assn. Home: 4619 4th Rd N Arlington VA 22203-2347 Office: Lafarge Corp 11130 Sunrise Valley Dr Reston VA 20191-4393 also: Lafarge Can Inc, 606 Cathcart, Montreal, PQ Canada H3B 1L7

FLYNN, DAVID WAYNE, secondary school educator; b. Lafayette, Tenn., May 25, 1969; s. Wayne Morris and Linda Gail (Doss) F.; m. Leigh Anne Rich, July 30, 1993. BS in Edn., Tenn. Technol. U., 1991, MEd in Adminstrn. and Supervision, 1995, postgrad., 1995—. Cert. elem. sch. tchr., cert. tchr. psychology and secondary biology, cert. ednl. adminstr. and supervisor, Tenn. Educator-coord. JOBS program Macon County Sch. Sys., Lafayette, 1991-92; tchr. English grades 7-8 Macon County Jr. H.S., Lafayette, 1992-93; tchr. 5th grade Ctrl. Mid. Sch., Lafayette, 1993-94; tchr. sci. Macon County H.S., Lafayette, 1994—; cons. Tenn. Sci. Tchrs. Insvc., Fossil Record, 1995. Bd. dirs. Macon County Edn. Found., 1995—. Mem. NEA, Nat. Planetary Soc., Nat. Sci. Tchrs. Assn., Tenn. Edn. Assn., Tenn. Sci. Tchrs. Assn., Macon County Edn. Assn. (pres. 1995—), Kappa Delta Pi. Home: 141 Dixon Rd Lafayette TN 37083 Office: Macon County HS Hwy 52 Bypass E Lafayette TN 37083

FLYNN, DONALD F., entertainment company executive. Grad., Marquette U., 1961. Employee David Himmelblau & Co., 1961-65; acct. Arthur Andersen & Co., 1965-72; comptroller Waste Mgmt. Inc.; dir., stockholder Blockbuster Entertainement Corp., 1987—; chmn. bd., CEO Discovery Zone, Inc., Fort Lauderdale, Fla., 1992—. Office: Discovery Zone Inc 110 E Broward Blvd Fl 23 Fort Lauderdale FL 33301

FLYNN, KIRTLAND, JR., accountant; b. Orange, N.J., Aug. 27, 1922; s. Kirtland and Jane Elizabeth (Miller) F.; m. Lucy Jane Andrews, June 11, 1948; children: Patricia Carson Flynn Moore, Gail Miller, James Kirtland. BA, Colgate U., 1943. Acctg. staff Celanese Corp., Newark, Houston and Charlotte, N.C., 1947-65; sec.-treas. Little Constrn. Co., Inc., Charlotte, 1965-66; mem. controller's staff J.P. Stevens & Co., Inc., Charlotte, 1966-81, mgr. info. services div., Charlotte and Greer, S.C., 1981-85; pvt. practice acctg., 1985-92; mem. staff Larry R. Swartz, CPA, 1993—. Bd. dirs., treas. Charlotte Exchange Student Program, 1979-83; chmn. Tryon Fire Protection Dist. Bd. Commrs., 1986—; bd. dirs. Tryon Fine Arts Ctr., 1987-89; bd. dirs., treas. Polk County Sheltered Workshop, 1987-91, exec. v.p. 1991-93, pres., 1993-96. 1st lt. USMCR, 1943-46. Decorated D.F.C., Air medals. Mem. Inst. of Mgmt. Accts. (chpt. pres. 1966-67, nat. dir. 1971-73, pres. Carolinas Council 1973-74, nat. v.p. 1978-79), Stuart Cameron McLeod Soc. (bd. govs. 1979-81, treas. 1981-82, sec. 1982-83, v.p. 1983-85, pres. 1985-86), Tryon C. of C. (bd. dirs. 1985-93, treas. 1985-90, v.p. 1990-92). Lodges: Masons, Shriners, K.T. Home: Sourwood Ridge PO Box 1138 Tryon NC 28782-1138 Office: One Tryon Pl Tryon NC 28782-3709

FLYNN, PATRICK, designer, programmer; b. Washington, Aug. 11, 1953; s. Walter L. and Virginia B. Flynn. BS in English, East Carolina U., 1977; AAS in Bus. Computer Programming, Coll. of the Albemarle, 1996. Disc jockey Sta. WBXB-FM, Edenton, N.C., 1976; copy coord. BDM Corp., McLean, Va., 1977-80; editor HBH Co., Arlington, Va., 1980-81; audio/visual technician Projection, Inc., Arlington, 1982; carpenter Sandalwood Construction Co., Kitty Hawk, N.C., 1983-86; ind. contractor Patrick Painting, Kitty Hawk, 1986-92; game designer TurnKey Design Group, Kitty Hawk, 1993—; media cons., 1973—; pub. SandTraveler, Kitty Hawk, 1992-93. Contbr. articles and editls. to mags. and newspapers; designer Cutthroat Chess, 1993; appeared as extra Matlock series NBC-TV, 1989, (film) Toy Soldiers, 1990. Vol. Transp. Fishnet Ministries, Inc., Front Royal, Va., 1993, Rock Ch. Kitty Hawk, 1983-96. Mem. Alpha Phi Gamma, Phi Theta Kappa. Republican. Office: Airline Tariff Publ Co PO Box 17415 Washington DC 20041-0415 also: 5869-C Post Corner Trl Centreville VA 20120

FLYNN, PAUL ARTHUR, marketing professional; b. Portland, Maine, Sept. 29, 1946; s. Hugh Francis Flynn and Carolyn Mae (Pettingill) Barber; m. Terri Ann Smith, May 22, 1970; children: Heather Naomi, Ryan Paul. BS, U. Maine, 1968, MS, 1971. Tchr. U. Maine, Gorham, 1970-71, MSAD #6, Buxton, Maine, 1971-73; specialist merchandise Panama Canal Co., Canal Zone, 1973-79; buyer H.J. Wilson Co., Baton Rouge, La., 1980-82; buyer/designer Western Auto Supply Co., Kansas City, Mo., 1983-86; mgr. mktg. Roadmaster Corp., Olney, Ill., 1986-90; with Firestone, Duluth, Ga., 1990—; cons. Thailand Govt., Bankok, 1985-86, Chinese Govt. Light Industry, Shanghai, 1985. Contbr. articles to profl. jours. Served with U.S. Army, 1968-70. Named Father Taiwan Bicycle Asahi Enterprises, 1985. Mem. U. So. Maine Alumni Assn., Phi Sigma Pi. Republican. Roman Catholic. Home: 1373 Sunrise Way Lawrenceville GA 30245-7619 Office: Wells Fargo/Kraft Gen Foods The Myrick Co 6205 Best Friend Rd Norcross GA 30071

FLYNN, SHARON ANN, marketing executive, educator; b. Kings Park, N.Y., Apr. 14, 1955; d. John Joseph and Mary Rose (Dwyer) F.; 1 child, Carl J. Roell III. Degree in Nursing Sci., Suffolk County Community Coll., 1976; R.N., NY State Psychiat. Sch. Nursing, 1977; student Barry Univ., 1987—. Psychiat. therapist Kings Park Psychiat. Ctr., N.Y., 1971-77, psychiat. registered nurse, 1977-79; acute hemodialysis nurse Boca Raton Community Hosp., Fla., 1981-83; home infusion therapy educator Am. Hosp. Supply Corp., S.E. Fla., 1983-84, mktg. territory mgr., 1984-85; mktg. devel. specialist home infusion therapy Hosp. Corp. Am., Ft. Lauderdale, Fla., 1985—, designer and mgr. Apnea Monitoring Service, 1986-88; adminstrv. dir. Diabetes Mgmt. Ctr. Health Trust, Inc., Plantation, Fla., 1988-90; dir. dialysis program Home Intensive Care, Inc., Ft. Lauderdale, Fla., 1990-91; gen. mgr. ops. Home Intensive Care, 1991-92; v.p., dir. clin. ops. Blue Chip Healthcare Inc., 1992-95, residence sch. nurse, St. Andrews, Boca Raton, Fla., 1995—; cons. in field 1984-91; instr. continuous ambulatory peritoneal dialysis Boca Raton Community Hosp., 1982, instr. diabetic edn., 1981. Mem. Aspartame Consumer Safety Network, chmn. med. com. on aspartame consumer safety, 1987. Mem. NAFE, Discharge Planners Assn., Assn. Profl. Saleswomen, Internat. Platform Assn., Am. Legion Aux. Republican. Roman Catholic. Office: Saint Andrews Sch 3900 Jog Rd Boca Raton FL 33434-4455

FOCHT, WILLIAM JARRELL, geology educator; b. Dayton, Ohio, Dec. 21, 1950; s. Estill Leroy F. and June Francis (Collins) Baker; m. Thaisa Gail Mauk, Aug. 19, 1978 (div. Apr. 1986); 1 child, Kendrea Layne; m. Toni Sue Shaklee, May 12, 1990. BS in Zoology magna cum laude, Ohio U., 1973, postgrad., 1973-75; BCE magna cum laude, Vanderbilt U., 1979; MA in Polit. Sci. summa cum laude, Okla. State U., 1992, PhD in Environ. Sci., 1995. Crew leader, equipment operator Underground TV Inspection, Inc., Durham, N.C., 1975-76, St. Petersburg, Fla., 1975; computer dept. mgr., project mgr. McCullough Assocs., Inc., Murfreesboro, Tenn., 1976-78; environ. engr. region IV U.S. EPA, Atlanta, 1980-81; environ. engr. region VI U.S. EPA, Dallas, 1981-87; sr. environ. engr. hdqrs. U.S. EPA, Washington, 1987-88; instr. Okla. State U., Stillwater, 1988-94, asst. prof. Sch. Geology, 1994—; sr. regulatory scientist Sci. Applications Internat. Corp., Columbus, Ohio, 1990-95; expert witness, regulatory expert, 1989-94; instr. various courses and seminars throughout U.S. Contbr. articles to profl. jours. Recipient Spl. Recognition award U.S. EPA, 1983, 87, Superior Achievement award, 1985, Bronze medal, 1986, Spl. Recognition award Soc. Environ. Scientists, 1990, various grants, 1991-96; Okla. State U. Centennial scholar, 1990, Dean Norman Cohn scholar Ohio U., 1972-73, Hiram Roy Wilson grad. fellow Ohio U., 1973-75, McAlester Scottish Rite grad. fellow Okla. State U., 1991-92, disting. grad. fellow Okla. State U. Found., 1989-93; presdl. fellow Univ. Ctr. Water Rsch., Okla. State U., 1988-92. Mem. Nat. Assn. Environ. Communicators (bd. dirs., co-chair ethics task force 1993), Soc. Risk Analysis, Nat. Ground Water Assn., Risk Assessment and Policy Assn. (charter), Internat. Soc. Sci. Study Subjectivity, Okla. Acad. Sci. (vice-chair social scis. sect. 1990-91), Okla. Coun. on Grad. Edn. and Rsch. (Okla. State U. rep. 1993-94), Okla. State U. Soc. Environ. Scientists (pres. 1989, historian 1992), Phi Kappa Phi, Alpha Epsilon Lambda, Tau Beta Pi, Chi Epsilon, Pi Sigma Alpha. Democrat. Office: Okla State U 105 Noble Rsch Ctr Stillwater OK 74078

FODIMAN, AARON ROSEN, publishing executive; b. Stamford Conn., Oct. 10, 1937; s. Yale J. and Thelma F.; BS, Tulane U., 1958; LLB, N.Y. U., 1960, MBA, 1961; grad. L'Academie de Cuisine Canardier, Washington, 1977. Bar: N.Y. 1960, D.C. 1961, Va. 1965; White House counsel, Washington, 1961-78; FTC, Washington, 1961-65; practiced in Arlington, Va., 1965-78; pres. Fast Food Operators, Inc., N.Y.C., 1978-84; pres. Hampton Healthcare, 1984-91, Tampa Bay Publs., 1986—; pub., editor Tampa Bay Mag.; bd. dirs. Tampa Players Inc., Washington Ballet, Manhattan Punch Line Theatre; pres. Dunedin Art Ctr.; chmn. Pinellas County Arts Council, Golda Meir Ctr., Bay Ballet Theatre; bd. dirs. Kent Jewish Community Ctr.; community advisor Clearwater Dunedin Jr. League.; mem. adv. bd. Am. Film Inst.; chmn. Ford Presdl. Campaign, 1976; cons. spl. services U.S. Dept. State spl. envoy to Iran, Poland, Russia, Senegal, 1964-78; TV host local sports show, Dine Line, Tampa Bay Mag.; advisor Fed. Res. Bank Atlanta. Participant, Leadership Pinellas; participant, founder Leadership Tampa Bay, Nat. Conf. Christians and Jews; chmn. A Taste of Pinellas; pres. Bay Ballet Theatre; Pinellas County amb. to Ringling Mus. Art. Recipient Hyam Soloman Freedom award, 1974, Miniature Palette award Miniature Art Soc. of Fla., 1987, Order of Salvador medal Dali Mus., 1989; honoree, award winner Friends of Arts Pinellas County, Congressional medal of honor, Silver Star, Nat. Legion of Merit, Meritorious Svc. U.N. Svc. Mem. Pinellas County Restaurant Assn. (pres.), Tampa Bay Restaurant Assn. (pres.), Fla. Restaurant Assn. (bd. dirs.), Chaine des Rotisseurs (chpt. officer), Internat. Legal Frat., Phi Delta Phi. Club: Barrister Inn (pres.) (Washington). Lodge: B'nai Brith (pres. Washington).

FOERSTER, DAVID WENDEL, JR., counselor, consultant, human resources specialist; b. Jacksonville, Fla., Jan. 7, 1953; s. David Wendel Foerster and Estelle Jones Williams. BA cum laude, U. Fla., 1977. Cert. and registered gen. mediator, Ga. Founding dir. Addictive Disease Resouce Ctr., Atlanta, 1979-84; founding exec. dir., crisis mediator Resource Ctr., Atlanta, 1984—; cons. Hansel Post (name changed to Jones, Day, Reavis & Pogue), Peterson, Dillard, Young, Asselin & Powell, Parker, Johnson, Cook & Dunlevie, Garland Samuel & Loeb, King & Spalding, State Bar Ga., Atlanta Falcons Football Club, SAFE Recovery Ctrs., Coca-Cola, Wachovia Bank Ga., Sun Trust Bank, Hayes Microcomputer Products, Inc.; lectr. Ga. State U., Atlanta, 1984—, Atlanta Pub. Schs. Contbr. articles to profl. jours.; interviewee, expert CBS, PBS, ABC, CNN, Bus. Week, Atlanta Jour. Cosntn., 1978—. Bd. dirs. Resource Ctr., Atlanta, 1984—; instr. All Saints Episcopal Ch., Atlanta, 1985—. Recipient merit award Mended Hearts, Inc., 1985; grantee HBO, 1987; Will Watt Fellow, 1995. Mem. ACA, Ga. Addiction Counselors Assn., Ga. Employee Assistance Forum, Nat. Assn. Addiction Counselors, Employee Assistance Profl. Assn., Rotary (Paul Harris fellow 1994). Home: 300 Brentwood Dr NE Atlanta GA 30305 Office: Resource Ctr 2921 Piedmont Rd NE Ste D Atlanta GA 30305-2785

FOGARTY, NANCY CLARK, librarian; b. Greensboro, N.C., June 13, 1944; d. Boatman Eugene and Willie Carey (Glosson) Clark; m. Stephen Henry Fogarty, Apr. 7, 1973; children: Michael Patrick Fogarty, Stephanie Clark Fogarty. BA in English, U. N.C., Greensboro, 1966, MA in Communication Studies, 1980; MSLS, U. N.C., 1969. Eng. tchr. Walter Hines Page H.S., Greensboro, 1966-68; reference libr. Wilson Library, U. N.C., 1969-70; reference libr. Jackson Library, U N.C., Greensboro, 1970-76, head reference libr., 1976-94, head bibliographic instruction, 1995—. Mem. Nat. Fedn. of Music Clubs Euterpe Club (treas. 1995—), Southeastern Libr. Assn. (mem. exec. bd., N.C. rep. 1994—), N.C. Libr. Assn. (mem. exec. bd., treas., N.C. rep. 1994—). Democrat. Presbyterian. Office: Jackson Library Reference Dept Greensboro NC 27412

FOGEL, DANIEL MARK, English language educator, author; b. Columbus, Ohio, Jan. 21, 1948; s. Ephim and Charlotte Edith (Finkelstein) F.; m. Rachel Kahn, June 24, 1973; children: Nicholas Alden Kahn-Fogel, Rosemary Kimlat Kahn-Fogel. BA in English magna cum laude, Cornell U., 1969, MFA in Creative Writing, 1974, PhD in English, 1976. Tchr. English East Lyme (Conn.) High Sch., 1969-71; asst. prof. English La. State U., Baton Rouge, 1976-80, assoc. prof. English, 1980-84, prof. English, 1984—, assoc. dean grad. sch., 1990-92, assoc. vice chancellor acad. affairs, dean grad. sch., 1992—; tchr. poetry writing workshops, Baton Rouge, 1980-87; instr. creative writing and lit. Instituto Allende, San Miguel de Allende, Guanajuato, Mex., 1972; mem. adv. com. Publs. MLA, 1986-90. Author: Henry James and the Structure of the Romantic Imagination, 1981 (Pulitzer prize nomination), Daisy Miller: A Dark Comedy of Manners, 1990, Covert Relations: James Joyce, Virginia Woolf, and Henry James, 1990, A Companion to Henry James Studies, 1993; author: (with others) The Aspern Papers Souvenir Book, 1988, The World Book Encyclopedia, 1991; author foreword: The Henry James Encyclopedia, 1989; editor/co-editor, author introduction: American Letters and the Historical Consciousness, 1987, New Essays on the Portrait of a Lady, 1987; editor: The Princess Casamassima, The Tragic Muse, The Reverberator, 1989; editor, founder Henry James Rev., 1979-95; gen. editor Henry James Soc. Monographs, 1991—; mem. editorial staff Epoch, 1974-76; poetry editor Epoch, 1974, Nat. Forum 1981-86; editorial cons. Nat. Forum, 1980-84; consulting editor UMI Rsch. Press, 1983-89; author articles in field; contbr. poems to anthologies and periodicals. NEH summer stipend, 1977, 87; grantee La. Endowment for Humanities, 1990, Manship rsch. grantee, 1991-92. Mem. MLA, Henry James Soc. (exec. dir.). Democrat. Jewish. Office: Office Acad Affairs 146 Thomas Boyd Hall Baton Rouge LA 70803

FOGG, ERNEST LESLIE, minister, retired; b. Butte, Mont., June 4, 1920; s. Ernest L. Fogg Sr. and Gertrude G. (Waller) Fogg-Parker; m. Margaret E. Fogg, June 17, 1943 (dec. Oct. 1962); children: Judith E., Dennis M. (dec.), Stephen William; m. Carolee Little, Sept. 1, 1965; 1 stepchild, Stephen Babcock. BA, Trinity U., San Antonio, 1943; MDiv, McCormick Theol. Seminary, Chgo., 1946; DD (hon.), Mary Holmes Coll., 1981. Ordained to ministry Presbyn. Ch., 1946. Missionary Bd. of Fgn. Missions/Presbyn. U.S.A., Thailand, 1946-59; field exec. Nat. Coun. of Chs., Indonesia, 1959-65; exec. Commn. on Ecumenical Mission and Rels./Presbyn. U.S.A., N.Y.C., 1965-70, Bd. Nat. Missions/Presbyn. U.S.A., N.Y.C., 1970-72; dir., Fund for Indochina World Coun. Chs., Geneva, 1973-76; sr. minister Cen. Presbyn. Ch., Montclair, N.J., 1977-87; chmn. Am. Leprosy Mission, 1979-86. Contbr. articles to profl. jours. Mem. World Affairs Coun., San Antonio. Mem. Rotary (pres. 1986-87). Democrat. Home: 10782 Oakland Rd San Antonio TX 78240-2025

FOGLE, PATRICIA MAHOOD, physical education educator; b. Snyder, Tex., Sept. 10, 1956; d. Robert H. and Wanda Sue (Busby) Mahood; m. Ronald A. Fogle, June 16, 1979 (div. Sept. 1995); children: Whitney Lee Ann, Nicholas Arthur. BS, Hardin-Simmons U., 1979; MA, Tex. Women's U., 1986. Tchr., coach Smithfield Mid. Sch., North Richland Hills, Tex., 1979-81, Odessa (Tex.) H.S., 1981-83, Abilene (Tex.) H.S., 1983-86; instr. Hardin-Simmons U., Abilene, 1989-96; instr. lang. arts Coppell Ind. Sch. Dist. Chmn. project rsch., computer, pub. affairs, ticket sales carousel Jr. League of Abilene, teen outreach com., membership devel. com., 1987-96; membership chmn. PTO, Abilene, 1991-96; new mem. com. First Bapt. Ch., Abilene, 1989-96. Mem. AAHPHERD, Tex. Assn. Phys. Edn., Recreation & Dance, Golden Key. Republican. Home: 4300 Rosemeade Pkwy # 1313 Dallas TX 75287

FOLDESY, LYNN, mental health nurse; b. Newark, Apr. 6, 1953; d. George and Elizabeth (Hango) F. BA, Chadron State Coll., 1975; AAS, Bergen Community Coll., 1979. RN, N.C., N.J.; cert. psychiat. and mental health nurse, N.C., N.J. Staff nurse St. Josephs Hosp., Paterson, N.J., 1979-81, Duke U. Med. Ctr., Durham, N.C., 1981—. Mem. Am. Psychiat. Nurses Assn.

FOLEA, RICHARD VICTOR, SR., educational business management administrator; b. Lorain, Ohio, Feb. 3, 1931; s. Victor John Folea; m. Martha Ina Ingham (div. Oct. 1994); children: Richard Victor Jr., Carol Ann, Ruth Virginia, Victor John. BA in Biology, Miami U., Oxford, Ohio, 1956; MA in Pub. Pers. Adminstrn., Am. U., 1960; PhD in Info. System Mgmt., Edn. Policy, Plan, and Adminstrn., U. Md., 1991. Pers. officer, specialist various fed. govt. agys., Washington, 1950-60; computer bus. mgr. Goddard Space Flight Ctr./NASA, Greenbelt, Md., 1960-66; tech. Payroll-Pers. Sys. advisor Office Sec. HEW, Washington, 1970-73; dir. Office Mgmt. Policy USPHS, Washington, 1981-83, dir. Mgmt. Initiatives and Studies Rsch., 1983-94; pres. AELOF Assocs., Lusby, Md., 1987—. Founder, producer, editor newspaper City of New Carrollton Echo, 1959-63; contbr. articles to various computer and info. system mgmt. profl. jours. Troop chmn. Boy Scouts Am., 1979-84. With U.S. Army Med. Corps, 1951-54. Mem. Office Automation Soc. Internat. (contbg., cert.).

FOLEY, HELEN CLAIBORNE, university administrator; b. Columbia, S.C., June 8, 1945; d. David Bartholemew and Helen Irving (DuBose) F. BS magna cum laude, U. S.C., 1984; MEd, Vanderbilt U., 1986. Staff asst. U. S.C., Columbia, 1971-77; assoc. dir. U. S.C. Alumni Assn., Columbia, 1977-80; dir. devel. coll. pharmacy U. S.C., Columbia, 1980-85; dir. devel. Va. Poly. Inst., Blacksburg, 1987-90; v.p. devel. Tenn. Performing Arts Ctr., Nashville, 1991-92, fundraising cons., 1992; dir. spl. gifts La. State U. Found., Baton Rouge, 1992—. Vol. Richland Meml. Hosp., Columbia, 1970-75, Spl. Olympics, Columbia, 1976-78; tchr. Literacy Coun., Columbia, 1987. Named one of Disting. Alumni U. S.C., 1988. Mem. Rotary (chmn. mentor com. Blacksburg-Christiansburg chpt. 1989), Blacksburg C. of C. (chmn. legis. com. 1989). Epsicopalian. Home: 9024 Fox Run Ave Baton Rouge LA 70808-8103

FOLEY, MARK ADAM, congressman; b. Newton, Mass., Sept. 8, 1954. Student, Palm Beach C.C. Owner, mgr. The Lettuce Patch Restaurant, 1975-81; real estate broker, pres. Foley-Smith & Assocs., Inc., 1975-94; commr. City of Lake Worth, 1977-79, commr., vice mayor, 1982-84; state rep. dist. 85 Fla., 1990-92; state senator dist. 35 Fla., 1992-94; mem. 104th Congress from 16th Fla. dist., 1995—. Republican. Address: 506 Cannon Washington DC 20515

FOLEY, PETER MICHAEL, lawyer; b. Detroit, Feb. 10, 1947; s. Paul Emmet and Sophye (Balicki) F.; m. Jane Thurlow Foley, Apr. 25, 1987. BA, Johns Hopkins U., 1969; JD, Georgetown U., 1973. Bar: N.C. 1974, U.S. Supreme Ct., U.S. Ct. Appeals (4th, 5th, & 11th cirs.), U.S. Dist. Ct. (ea., mid. & we. dists.) N.C. Law clk. to Hon. Cornelia Kennedy U.S. Dist. Ct. for Ea. Dist. Mich., Detroit, 1973-75; assoc., ptnr. Moore Ragsdale Liggett Ray & Foley, P.A., Raleigh, N.C., 1975-87; ptnr. LeBoeuf Lamb Leiby & MacRae, Raleigh, 1987-93, Ragsdale, Liggett & Foley, Raleigh, 1994—; adj. prof. Campbell U. Law Sch., Buies Creek, N.C., 1984-87. Mem. Def. Rsch. Inst., N.C. Assn. Def. Lawyers. Office: 2840 Plaza Pl PO Box 31507 Raleigh NC 27622

FOLINSBEE, LAWRENCE JOHN, physiologist, researcher; b. Vancouver, B.C., Can., Nov. 28, 1945; came to U.S., 1963; s. John Allan and Agnes Emily (Colpitts) F.; m. Jane Elizabeth Furchner, Aug. 24, 1969; children: John Alan, Emily Jane. BS, U. Oreg., 1967, MS, 1969; PhD, U. Calif., Davis, 1972. Rsch. assoc. U. Calif., Davis, 1969-72; postdoctoral fellow U. Toronto, Ont., Can., 1972-74, asst. prof., 1973-74; assoc. rsch. physiologist U. Calif., Santa Barbara, 1974-84; sr. scientist ABB Environ. Svcs., Chapel Hill, N.C., 1984-90; rsch. physiologist EPA, Research Triangle Park, N.C., 1990-95; chief environ. media assessment br. Nat. Ctr. Environ. Assessment, EPA, Research Triangle Park, N.C., 1995—; cons. Am. Petroleum Inst., Washington, 1983-84; mem. adv. bd. Electric Power Rsch. Inst., Palo Alto, Calif., 1987-93. Mem. editorial bd. Toxicology and Indsl. Health Jour., 1983-93; editor: Environmental Stress: Individual Human Adaptations, 1978; assoc. editor: Medicine and Science in Sports and Exercise; author chpts. in books; contbr. over 70 articles to profl. jours. Rsch. grantee NIH, EPA, Electric Power Rsch. Inst. Fellow Am. Coll. Sports Medicine; mem. Am. Physiol. Soc., Am. Thoracic Soc. Democrat. Episcopalian. Home: 227 Old Forest Creek Dr Chapel Hill NC 27514-5424 Office: EPA Nat Ctr Environ Assessment Mail Drop #52 Research Triangle Park NC 27711

FOLK, KATHERINE PINKSTON, English language educator, writer, journalist; b. Corsicana, Tex., Feb. 8, 1925; d. Lucian Albert and Katherine (Shell) Pinkston; m. Elmer Ellsworth Folk, Apr. 21, 1946; children: Russell Harter, David Shell, Barbara Kay Folk Nowotny. BA in Journalism, Tex. Tech. U., 1946; postgrad., U. Houston, 1960-71. Reporter Scurry County Times, Snyder, Tex., 1946; dir. advt. Dunlaps Dept. Store, Lubbock, Tex., 1946; instr. English Odessa (Tex.) Coll., 1948-53; dir. communication, editor Viva Mag. Houston Met. Ministries, 1979-80; dir. communication for continuing edn. Houston Community Coll. System, 1989-90, instr. English, 1980—; auditor creative writing Rice U., Houston, 1966; tutor English Spring Br. Ind. Sch. Dist., Houston, 1970-75. Contbr. articles to popular mags. Ann. sponsor Odessa Coll., 1950-53; mem. Harris County Heritage Soc., Houston, 1985-91, Nat. Fedn. Rep. Women, Houston, 1987-95, Country Playhouse Little Theatre, 1987-96; bd. dirs. Spring Br. YWCA, Houston, 1990-91. Mem. AAUW, Jr. League Houston (patron tea rm.), Nat. Fedn. Press Women, Soc. Children's Book Writers, Romance Writers Am., Delta Delta Delta (chmn. scholarship com. 1972). Episcopalian. Office: Houston C C Sys 22 Waugh Dr Houston TX 77007-5813

FOLLIN, RODNEY HUGH, municipal official; b. Arlington, Va., Aug. 16, 1955; s. John Walker and Anne Dibrell (Fulcher) F. BA with distinction, U. Va., 1977, MA in Pub. Adminstrn., 1980; grad. Regional Exec. Devel. Inst., George Mason U., 1995. Clk. II Pub. Works Dept.-Solid Waste Divsn., Fairfax County, Va., 1977-78; adminstrv. intern Office of County Adminstr.,

Loudoun County, Va., 1979-80; adminstr. Office of Youth Svcs., Loudoun County, Va., 1980-86; mgmt. and budget analyst Office of Exec. Mgmt., Prince William County, Va., 1986—. Named to Dean's list, 1973-77; Baumes fellowship Va. Mcpl. League, 1978-79. Mem. ASPA (No. Va. chpt. coun. 1985-87), Govt. Fin. Officers Assn., Am. Mgmt. Assn., Va. Delinquency Prevention and Youth Devel. Assn. (founding mem., treas. 1985-86). Office: Prince William County 1 County Complex Ct Woodbridge VA 22192-9201

FOLSOM, HYTA PRINE, educational grant writer, consultant; b. Day, Fla., Jan. 6, 1948; d. John Wesley and Estelle Melissa (Weaver) Prine; m. Terrence Franklin Folsom, Aug. 25, 1968 (div. 1995); children: Heather V., Laura E., Teresa A., Tyson F. AA, North Fla. Jr. Coll., Madison, 1967; BS in Elem. Edn., Fla. State U., 1969, cert. in early childhood edn., 1981; MS in Ednl. Leadership, Nova U., 1991. Cert. Fund Raising Executive (CFRE) Nat. Soc. of Fund Raising Execs. (INSFRE), 1996. Tchr. Gladys Morse Elem. Sch., Perry, Fla., 1969-72, 73-74; owner, operator Hyta's Presch. and Nursery, Mayo, Fla., 1979; tchr. Lafayette Elem. Sch., Mayo, 1975-77, 81-93; grants writer Lafayette County Sch. Dist., Mayo, 1990-93; cons. Grant Writers Directory, Jostens Learning Corp., 1991—; dir. alt. resources Coun. of Govts., Odessa, Tex., 1993—; owner, CEO Devel. Strategies, Inc.; mem. tchr. edn. coun. Layafette County Sch. Dist., 1983-85, coord. pre-kindergarten program, 1989-93; rep. Nat. Child Devel. Assocs., 1992; mem. Lafayette Dist. Adv. Coun., 1990-93, Schoolyear 2000 Pub. Schs. Coun., 1991-93; chairperson Lafayette County Early Childhood Coun., 1989-92. Co-author: Rainbows of Readiness, 1990. Leader Brownie troop Girl Scouts U.S., 1984-85; mem.-at-large Suwannee River Resource Conservation Devel., 1991, sec., 1992-93; nursery coord., tchr. Sunday sch., leader children's ch. Brewer Lake Bapt. Ch., 1984-85. Named Master Tchr., State of Fla., 1986. Mem. Nat. Soc. Fund Raising Execs., Lafayette Edn. Assn. (v.p. 1976-77, 87-89, pres. 1990), Kiwanis (sec. Mayo chpt. 1992), Alpha Delta Kappa. Democrat. Home: 1513 Custer Ave Odessa TX 79761 Office: Coun of Govts City Municipal Plz 119 W 4th Odessa TX 79761-4502

FOLSOM, ROGER LEE, healthcare administrator; b. Hahira, Ga., May 17, 1952; s. Jesse Lee and Virginia (LeGette) F. BS in Biology, Valdosta (Ga.) State U., 1975; postgrad., U. Ga., 1975. From radiol. technologist to adminstrv. asst. Smith Hosp., Inc., Hahira, 1971-78; pharm. rep. The Upjohn Corp., Dublin, Ga., 1979-85; cmty. rels. rep. Am. Med. Internat., Dublin, Ga., 1985-86; dir. mktg., pub. rels. Parkside Med. Svcs. Corp., Dublin, 1986-88, corp. mktg. dir. and pub. rels. S.E., 1988-94; owner, CEO Medlst Healthcare, Dublin, 1995—; adv. bd. Ga. Coop. Health Edn. Program, Dublin, 1987, pres., bd. dirs., 1992-95. Mem. Friends of Libr., Dublin, 1983—; coach, mem. adv. bd. Dublin Recreation Dept., 1986—; bd. dirs. Am. Heart Assn., Dublin, pres., 1989-90, chmn. bus. industry com.; adminstrv. bd., fin. com. Pine Forest United Meth. Ch., Dublin; chmn. planning and devel. com. Laurens 2000. Mem. Acad. Hosp. Mktg., Pub. Rels. and Planning/Am. Mktg. Assn., Dublin-Laurens C. of C. (charter leadership class 1989, mem. alumni com. 1990, bd. dirs. 1990, v.p. 1992, v.p. cmty. devel. 1992-93, pres. 1996—), Rotary (fund-raising chmn. Dublin 1986, bd. dirs. 1990-94, pres. Dublin club 1993-94, found. com. dist. 6920gov.'s group rep., 1996—), Dublin Country Club (bd. dirs., v.p. 1995—). Republican. Home: 506 Brookwood Dr PO Box 972 Dublin GA 31040 Office: Medlst Healthcare 1016 Claxton Dairy Rd Ste 2-c Dublin GA 31021-7941

FOLSOM, WYNELLE STOUGH, retired wood products manufacturing executive; b. Bankston, Ala., July 19, 1924; d. Richard Carey and Ora Beatrice (Fowler) Stough; m. Eugene Bragg Folsom, Sept. 3, 1944; children: Don Wayne, Dana L. Student U. Ala., Livingston U., 1962-63, Draughan Bus. Coll., Montgomery, Ala., 1941-42, Alexander State Coll., Alexander City, Ala., 1967-68, Chilton Vocat. & Tech. Sch., Clanton, Ala., 1969-70. Sec., Ala. Power Co., Birmingham, 1942-44; med. librarian Santa Rosa Hosp., San Antonio, 1944-46; payroll clk. Dow Chem. Co., Freeport, Tex., 1946-48; with audit dept. Sears, Roebuck & Co., Selma, Ala., 1956-66; sec.-treas. Oakline Chair Co., Inc., Selma, 1967-83, pres., 1983-86. Chmn. publicity Cahaba Regional Libr. (Friends of the Libr.), Clanton, Ala., 1979; mem. Selma-Dallas County Historic Preservation Soc., 1982-87. Mem. Selma C. of C., Hemorcallis Garden Club (pres. 1979), Woman's Study Club (chmn. publicity 1967-69). Republican. Mem. Ch. of Christ. Avocations: needlework, fishing, reading, painting, gardening. Home: 803 Lay Dam Rd Clanton AL 35045-2923 Office: Oakline Chair Co Inc Hwy 31 N PO Box 1698 Clanton AL 35045-1698

FOLTS, WILLIAM EDWARD, academic administrator, educator; b. Tuscaloosa, Ala., May 10, 1950; s. Howard Allen and Kathryn Fletcher (Harris) F.; m. Sandra Sue Wright, Feb. 2, 1950; 1 child, Steven Edward. BS, U. Ala., 1977, MS, 1979; PhD, U. Fla., 1987. Chief engr., radio announcer Sta. WJRD Radio, Tuscaloosa, 1967-70, Sta. WNPT Radio, Tuscaloosa, 1970-79; asst. in social gerontology/grants rsch. coord. U. Fla., Gainesville, 1979-83; rsch. assoc. Juvenile Justice Audit Project, Gainesville, 1987; asst. prof. U. North Tex., Denton, 1987-91; dir. gerontology program Appalachian State U., Boone, N.C., 1991—, assoc. prof., 1991—. Author: Old Homes New Families: Shared Living for the Elderly, 1984, Housing and the Aging Population: Options for the New Century, 1994, Aging Well, 1995; contbr. articles to profl. jours. Mem. So. Gerontol. Soc. (bd. dirs. 1991—), S.W. Soc. on Aging (bd. dirs.), Sigma Phi Omega, Sigma Xi, Alpha Kappa Delta, Phi Alpha. Office: Appalachian State U 219 Chapell Wilson Hall Boone NC 28608

FONTAINE, JOHN C., newspaper company executive, corporate lawyer. BA, U. Mich., 1953; LLB, Harvard U., 1956. Bar: N.Y. 1957. Pres. Knight-Ridder, Inc., Miami, Fla. Office: Knight-Ridder Newspapers Inc One Herald Plz Miami FL 33132-1693*

FONTANA, AL, director of Miami Metropolitan Zoo. Office: Miami Met Zoo 12400 SW 152nd St Miami FL 33177-1402

FONTANA, MARIO H., nuclear engineer; b. West Springfield, Mass., Mar. 30, 1933; s. Remo and Sabina (De Angelis) F.; m. Sue Janeway, Apr. 12, 1958; children: Richard, Edward. BS, U. Mass., 1955; MS, MIT, 1957; PhD, Purdue U., 1968. Registered engr., Tenn. Instr. Purdue U., Oak Ridge, Tenn., 1964-65; dir. industry degraded core program Tech for Energy, Inc., Knoxville, Tenn., 1981-84; v.p. engring. Energex Oak Ridge, 1984-85; dir. nuclear safety tech. IT Corp. and Tenera, L.P., Knoxville, 1985-90; sr. scientist Avco Rsch. and Advanced Devel., Wilmington, Mass., 1963-64; instr. Purdue U., 1964-65; mem. rsch. staff Oak Ridge Nat. Lab., 1957-63, 65-81, 1990-94, asst. dir. nuclear safety rsch., 1968-72, head advanced concepts devel. engring. tech. div., 1972-81, asst. dir. engring. tech. div., 1990-93; group leader Advanced Concepts, 1993-94; ret., 1994; cons. U.S. AEC, Washington, 1972-73, U.S. NRC, Washington, 1979-81, 91—, U.S. Dept. Energy, Washington, 1986-89; adj. prof. U. Tenn., 1995—; mem. Adv. Com. on Reactor Safeguards, 1995—. Author more than 100 reports and articles. Fellow Am. Nuclear Soc. (chmn. nuclear reactor safety divsn. 1972-73, 94-95); mem. AAAS, ASME, Am. Mgmt. Assn., Soc. Risk Analysis, Rotary Internat., Sigma Xi, Tau Beta Pi. Office: Oak Ridge Nat Lab PO Box 2009 Oak Ridge TN 37831-2009

FONTENELLE, LARRY JULES, cardiothoracic surgeon; b. New Orleans, Jan. 2, 1938; s. Ernest Jules and Violet (Hingle) F.; m. Brenda Porter, June 11, 1960; children: Michele, Leslie, Renee, Rhett, Paulette, Chad, Laurence, Jarrod, Jason. MD, La. State U., New Orleans, 1962. Diplomate Am. Bd. Surgery, Am. Bd. Thoracic Surgery; lic. physician, La., Miss. Intern Wilford Hall USAF Med. Ctr., Lackland AFB, Tex., 1962-63, resident in gen. surgery, 1963-67; fellow in thoracic surgery Wilford Hall Med. Ctr., Lackland AFB, Tex., 1968-70; resident in surgery U. Tex. Med. Sch./Bexar County Hosp., San Antonio, 1970; chief surg. svc. VA Med. Ctr., Biloxi, Miss., 1981—, acting chief staff, 1992-93; program chmn. gen. thoracic surgery fellowship Keesler Med. Ctr. and VA Med. Ctr., Biloxi, 1984—. Contbr. numerous articles to profl. jours. Pres., Mercy Cross High Sch. Bd., Biloxi, 1983-87, pres. PTA, 1983. Served to col. M.C., USAF, to 1981. Decorated Legion of Merit; recipient Surgeon Gen.'s award, 1969, Excalibur award Soc. of Air Force Clin. Surgeons, 1994. Fellow ACS; mem. So. Thoracic Surg. Assn., Assn. Mil. Surgeons, Assn. Acad. Surgeons, Nat. Assn. VA Physicians, Assn. VA Surgeons, Phi Kappa Theta (pres. 1957). Republican. Roman Catholic. Home: 701 Holly Hills Dr Biloxi MS 39532-4362 Office: Dept Vets Affairs Chief Surg Svc (112) 400 Veterans Ave Biloxi MS 39531-2420

FONTENOT, JACKIE DARREL, safety and health consultant; b. Leesville, La., Sept. 22, 1946; s. Oliver Huel and Ida Cora (Abshier) F.; m. Carolyn Luetta Brown, Jan. 2, 1968 (div. Dec., 1968); 1 child, Duane Alan; m. Hilda Marie Lopez, June 7, 1969; 1 child, Kayla Marie. Student, San Houston State U., 1964-66, Lee Coll., 1989-91. Cert. safety profl. (bd. cert. safety profls.); hazard control mgr. (bd. hazard control mgmt.); authorized crane inspector; cert. instr.; approved profl. source Tex. Workers Comp. and Field Safety Rep. Commn. Safety engr. Brown & Root, Monroe City, Tex., 1968-70; field safety rep. Tex. Gulf Sulphur Co., Fannett, Tex., 1970-72; plant safety supr. NL Baroid, Channelview, Tex., 1972-73; prodn. dept. safety coord. NL Baroid, Houston, 1973-76, regional safety mgr., 1976-81; mgr. safety and health NL Baroid Petroleum Svcs., Houston, 1981-86, NL Petroleum Svcs., Houston, 1986-88, Baroid Corp., Houston, 1988-91; safety and health cons. pvt. practice, Anahuac, Tex., 1991—; mem. indsl. com. NFPA, Boston, 1976—; instr. driver safety-fire suppression Tex. Safety Assn., Tex. A&M Extension Svc., 1976—; project dir. Tex. A&M Indsl. Fire Sch., master instr., 1993—; cert. instr. MSHA; speaker in field. Contbr. articles to Safety Coun. Newsletter, 1982-93. Sch. bd. trustee, Anahuac Ind. Sch. Dist., 1981-93; umpire Anahuac Youth Athletic Assn., 1980-82; Anahuac vol. fireman, 1976-86. Recipient Instr. Achievement award Tex. Safety Assn., Austin, 1977. Mem. Am. Soc. Safety Engrs. (nominated for Safety Profl. of Yr. Gulf Coast chpt. Houston 1986), Nat. Safety Coun. (chmn. petroleum sect. 1981—, Masons (past master lodge #995). Home and Office: PO Box 1207 104 Bayview Anahuac TX 77514-1207

FONTENOT, JAMES NOLAN, JR., orthopedist; b. Aug. 28, 1949. BS in zoology, La. State U., 1971; MD, Tulane U., 1975. Diplomate Am. Bd. Orthopaedic Surgeons. Rsch. asst. Walter Reed Army Medical Ctr., Washington, summer 1972, 73; internship Tulane U. Charity Hosp., New Orleans, 1975-76; residency dept. orthopedics Tulane U., New Orleans, 1978-82; resident Veterans Adminstrn. Hosp., New Orleans, 1978, chief adminstrn. resident, 1981; resident Touro Infirmary, New Orleans, 1979, Tulane Med Ctr., New Orleans, 1979-81, Childrens Hosp., New Orleans, 1980; third yr. resident, chief adminstrv. Veterans Adminstrn. Hosp., Alexandria, La., 1981, U.S. Pub. Health Svc. Hosp., New Orleans, 1981; instr. Tulane U. Sch. Medicine Dept. Orthopedics, Northeastern La. State U., 1981; staff privileges Clay County Hosp., Henrietta, Tex., Bowie meml. Hosp., Bethania Regional Health Care Ctr., 1984—, Wichita Gen. Hosp., 1984—; chief of staff Bethania Regional Health Care cCtr., 1992. With U.S. Army, 1976-78. Fellow Am. Acad. Orthopaedic Surgeons, Internat. Coll. Surgeons; mem. Tex. Orthopaedic Soc., N.Am. Spine Soc., So. Med. Orthopaedic Assn.; mem. Southern Med. Assn., Tulane Caldwell Soc., Wichita County Med. Soc., Tex. Med. Soc., So. Orthopedic Assn., Tex. Med. Foun. Home: 2002 Ardath St Wichita Falls TX 76301-6006 Office: Wichita Falls Clinic 501 Midwestern Pky E Wichita Falls TX 76302-2302

FONTES, J. MARIO F., JR., lawyer; b. São Paulo, Brazil, Jan. 17, 1964; m. Gladys Fontes, Jan. 7, 1995. BA cum laude in Econs. and Internat. Studies, Am. U., Washington, 1987; JD, Cath. U., Washington, 1992. Bar: Pa. 1993, Fla. 1995, U.S. Ct. Claims 1993, U.S. Ct. Internat. Trade 1993. Exec. v.p. Interbanque, 1989-92; assoc. Porter, Wright, Morris & Arthur, Washington, 1992-93, Hughes Hubbard & Reed, Miami, Fla., 1993—. Mem. ABA, Inter-Am. Bar Assn., Pa. Bar Assn., Brazilian-Am. Chamber (mem. program com. 1994—), Phi Kappa Phi. Office: Hughes Hubbard & Reed 201 S Biscayne Blvd Fl 25 Miami FL 33131-4325

FONVIELLE, CHARLES DAVID, lawyer; b. Melbourne, Fla., Dec. 28, 1944; s. Charles David Fonvielle Jr. and Margaret Jordan Palmer; m. Deborah Konas, July 25, 1970; children: C. Caulley, D. Jordan. BA, U. Fla., 1968; JD, Fla. State U., 1972. Bar: Fla. 1972, U.S. Dist. Ct. (no., mid. and so. dists.) Fla. Asst. pub. defender Fla. Pub. Defender Assn., Tallahassee, 1972-74; pvt. practice Tallahassee, 1974-77; ptnr. Thompson, Wadsworth, Messer, Turner & Rhodes, Tallahassee, 1977-80, Green & Fonvielle, Tallahassee, 1980-84, Green, Fonvielle & Hinkle, Tallahassee, 1984-85, Fonvielle & Hinkle, Tallahassee, 1985—. Bd. dirs. Fla. State U. Coll. of Law, endowed prof. litigation. Mem. ALTA (sustaining), Tallahassee Bar Assn. (bd. dirs. 1978-79), Acad. Fla. Trial Lawyers (Eagle sponsor 1990—), Nat. Bd. Trial Advocacy (cert.), Fla. Bar Assn. (bd. legal specialization and edn. 1991—), Fla. State U. Pres.'s Club (bd. visitors). Office: Fonvielle & Hinkle 3375A Capital Cir NE Tallahassee FL 32308-3736

FOOTE, AVON EDWARD, webmaster, communications educator; b. Burnsville, Miss., Sept. 24, 1937; s. Avon Ruble and Lila Frances (Broughton) F.; BS, Florence State U., 1963; MS, U. So. Miss., 1968; PhD, Ohio State U., 1970; m. Dorothy Veronica Gargis, Mar. 15, 1960; children: Anthony E., Kevin A., Michele. Announcer, Sta. WJOI, Florence, Ala., 1958-60; prodn. mgr. Sta. WOWL-TV, Florence, 1960-64; advt. coordinator Plough Inc., Memphis, 1964-66; faculty adviser Sta. WMSU, U. So. Miss., Hattiesburg, 1966-67; producer-dir. telecomm. Ohio State U., Columbus, 1967-69; assoc. prof. broadcasting U. Miss., Oxford, 1971-72; project dir. Ohio Valley TV System, Columbus, 1972-74; mem. faculty, coordinator grad. studies Sch. Journalism and Mass Communication, U. Ga., Athens, 1974-80; prof. broadcasting U. North Ala., Florence, 1980—; prof., London, 1990, 91; awards judge Ohio State Awards, 1968-73; chmn. faculty screening com. Peabody Radio-TV Awards, 1976-79. Bd. dirs. Florence YMCA, 1982-86; founder Worldwide Web Pages including Worldserver, 1995. NDEA fellow, 1967, Nat. Acad. TV Arts and Scis. Meml. fellow, 1970; recipient Cmty. Svc. award Florence Civitan Club, 1990, 1st pl. award Corp. Video Profl. Competition Nat. Broadcasting Soc., 1991; regional 1st pl. award, Nat. 3d pl. award Coll. Emmy award Hollywood Acad. TV Arts and Scis., 1984, Honorable Mention Comedy awards Nat. Broadcasting Soc., 1987, Industry Faculty Seminar fellow Internat. Radio-TV Soc., 1987. Mem. Broadcast Edn. Assn., Alpha Epsilon Rho, Alpha Lamba Delta. Republican. Anglican. Editor: The Challenges of Educational Communications, 1970; CBS and Congress: "The Selling of the Pentagon" Papers, 1972. Author: (with Koenig and others) Broadcasting and Bargaining, 1970; Chotankers, 1982. Editor Nat. Assn. Ednl. Broadcasters Broadcasting Rev., 1969-73. Producer ednl. TV programs. Home: 222 Shirley Dr Florence AL 35633-1434 Office: Comm Bldg Box 5158 Florence AL 35632

FOOTE, EDWARD THADDEUS, II, university president, lawyer; b. Milw., Dec. 15, 1937; s. William Hamilton and Julia Stevenson (Hardin) F.; m. Roberta Waugh Fulbright, Apr. 18, 1964; children: Julia, William, Thaddeus. BA, Yale U., 1959; LLB, Georgetown U., 1966; LLD (hon.), Washington U., St. Louis, 1981, Barry U., 1991; hon. degree, Tokai U., Tokyo, 1984; LLD (hon.), Barry U., 1991. Bar: Mo. 1966. Reporter Washington Star, 1963-64, Washington Daily News, 1964-65; exec. asst. to chmn. Pa. Ave. Commn., Washington, 1965-66; assoc. Bryan, Cave, McPheeters & McRoberts, St. Louis, 1966-70; vice chancellor, gen. counsel, sec. to bd. trustees Washington U., St. Louis, 1970-73, dean Sch. Law, 1973-80, spl. adv. to chancellor and bd. trustees, 1980-81; pres. U. Miami, Coral Gables, Fla., 1981—; mem. exec. com., bd. dirs. Am. Coun. Edn., 1986-88; chmn. citizens com. for sch. desegregation, St. Louis, 1980; chmn. desegregation monitoring and adv. com., St. Louis, 1980-81. Author: An Educational Plan for Voluntary Cooperation Desegregation of School in the St. Louis Met. area, 1981. Mem. Coun. on Fgn. Rels.; founding pres. bd. New City Sch., St. Louis, 1967-73; mem. gov.'s task force on reorganization State of Mo., 1973-74, steering com., chmn. governance com. Mo. Gov.'s Conf. on Edn., UN Assn. Greater St. Louis chpt., 1977-79, adv. com. Naval War Coll., 1979-82, Fla. Coun. of 100, Southern Fla. Metro-Miami Action Plan, exec. com. Miami Citizens Against Crime; founding chmn. Miami Coalition for a Drug Free Community, 1988—. Recipient Order of Sun (Peru). Democrat. Office: U Miami PO Box 248006 Miami FL 33124

FOOTE, FRANCES CATHERINE, association executive, living trust consultant; b. Chgo., Apr. 3, 1935; d. Peter and Ellen Gertrude (Quinn) F. BS in Edn., Cardinal Stritch Coll., 1957; MS in Edn., Ill. State U., 1966. Cert. tchr., Ill. Tchr. Sch. Dist. 123, Oak Lawn, Ill., 1959-84; asst. prin. Sch. Dist. 123, Oak Lawn, 1971-80; pres. Am. Now, St. Petersburg, Fla., 1985—; instr. geography workshops for tchrs., 1967-70, use of newspaper in classroom workshops, 1973-75; co-chair social Studies Curriculum Revision; living trust cons. Accurate Bus. Assocs., Inc., St. Petersburg; ind. rep. Watkins Products. Officer PTA, Oak Lawn, 1973-76; mem. Rep. Nat. Com., Washington, vol. State of Fla. Guardian ad litem, St. Vincent de Paul Soc. Mem. Am. Fedn. Tchrs. Roman Catholic. Home: 280 126th Ave E Apt 203 Treasure Island FL 33706-4442

FOOTE, NATHAN MAXTED, retired physical science educator; b. Woodlawn, Pa., Oct. 8, 1913; s. Myron Tinkham and Ada May (Maxted) F.; m. Laura Belle Gruey, Sept. 5, 1936; children: Jonathan W., L. Nadine, Frances C., Willard G. AB, DePauw U., 1935; MS, Purdue U., 1939. Rsch. engr. RCA, Camden, N.J., 1940-49; rsch. scientist Colgate Palmolive, Jersey City, N.J., 1950-52; rheologist B.F. Goodrich Chem. Co., Avon Lake, Ohio, 1953-58; acting head, Dept. Physics Baldwin Wallace Coll., Berea, Ohio, 1958-60; vis. asst. prof. Physics Pa. State U., University Park, 1960-61; asst. prof. Physics, Behrend Coll. Pa. State U., Erie, 1964-78, ret., 1979; assoc. prof. Phys. Sci. SUNY, Geneseo, 1961-64. Author: Industrial and Engineering Chemistry, 1944, Industrial and Engineering Chemistry, 1947. Del. Ohio Coun. Am. Bapt. Men, 1955-58. Mem. AAAS, Am. Chem. Soc. (50 Yr. award 1993), Sigma Xi. Home: 14 E Main St Lot B Mount Dora FL 32757-3470

FOOTE, SHELBY, author; b. Greenville, Miss., Nov. 17, 1916; s. Shelby Dade and Lillian (Rosenstock) F.; m. Gwyn Rainer, Sept. 5, 1956; children: Margaret Shelby, Huger Lee. Student, U. N.C., 1935-37; D.Litt. (hon.), U. of the South, 1981, Southwestern U., 1982, U. S.C., 1991, U. N.C., 1992; D.Litt (hon.), Millsaps U., 1993, Notre Dame U., 1994. Novelist lectr., U. Va., 1963, playwright in residence, Arena Stage, Washington, 1963-64, writer in residence, Hollins Coll., Va., 1968; Author: novels Tournament, 1949, Follow Me Down, 1950, Love in a Dry Season, 1951, Shiloh, 1952, Jordan County, 1954, September September, 1978; history The Civil War, A Narrative: Vol. I, Fort Sumter to Perryville, 1958, Vol. II, Fredericksburg to Meridian, 1963, Vol. III, Red River to Appomattox, 1974; play Jordon County: A Landscape in the Round, 1964; editor: Chickamauga and Other Civil War Stories, 1993. Mem. acad. adv. bd. U.S. Naval Acad., 1988-89. Recipient Disting. Alumnus award U. N.C., 1975, Dos Passos prize for Lit., 1988, Charles Frankel award 1992, St. Louis Literary award 1992, Nevins-Freeman award 1992; Guggenheim fellow, 1955-57, Ford Found. fellow, 1963-64. Mem. Am. Acad. Arts and Letters, Fellowship of So. Writers, soc. Am. Historians. Office: 542 E Parkway S Memphis TN 38104-4362

FORBES, ARTHUR LEE, III, lawyer; b. Houston, Sept. 3, 1928; s. Arthur Lee Jr. and Corinne (Mayfield) F.; m. Nita R. Harrison, Mar. 25, 1957; children—Tricia, Kim, Arthur Lee. B.S.C.E., U. Tex.-Austin, 1952; J.D., S. Tex. Coll. Law, 1959. Bar: Tex. 1959, U.S. Ct. Appeals (5th cir.) 1960, U.S. Supreme Ct. 1967. Ptnr. firm Lee & Forbes, Houston, 1960-73, Shapiro, Forbes & Cox, Houston, 1974-88; gen. counsel Bay Houston Towing Co., 1989—. Served to lt. USMC, 1952-54. Mem. ABA, Tex. Bar Assn., Houston Bar Assn., Assn. Trial Lawyers Am., Houston Trial Lawyers Assn., Sigma Chi, Phi Delta Phi, Unitarian. Club: Houston Racquet. Home: 5 Leisure Ln Houston TX 77024-5123 Office: Three Riverway Ste 450 Houston TX 77056

FORBES, MORTON GERALD, lawyer; b. Atlanta, July 12, 1938; s. Arthur Mark and Mary Dean (Power) F.; m. Eunice Lee Haynsworth, Jan. 25, 1963; children: John, Ashley, Sarah. AB, Wofford Coll., 1962; JD, U. Ga., 1965. Bar: Ga. 1965, U.S. Dist. Ct. (mid. dist.) Ga. 1965, U.S. Dist. Ct. (so. dist.) Ga. 1968, U.S. Dist. Ct. (no. dist.) Ga. 1993, U.S. Ct. Appeals (5th cir.) 1974, U.S. Ct. Appeals (4th cir.) 1972, U.S. Ct. Appeals (11th cir.) 1981. Assoc. Pierce, Ranitz, Lee, Berry & Mahoney, 1967-70; ptnr. Pierce, Ranitz, Berry, Mahoney & Forbes, 1970-76, Pierce, Ranitz, Mahoney, Forbes & Coolidge, 1976-81; ptnr., sec. Ranitz, Mahoney, Forbes & Coolidge, P.C., 1981-91, Forbes & Bowman, 1991—; gen. counsel Ga. Fen. Young Rep. Clubs, 1971-72; guest lectr. dept. dental hygiene Armstrong State Coll., 1970-72. Mem. Savannah Port Authority, 1973—, chmn., 1979-81; mem. Chatham County Devel. Authority, 1973-80; mem. nat. com. Nat. Fedn. Young Reps., 1973; mem. econ. adv. coun. Coastal Area Planning and Devel. Authority, 1980—; bd. dirs. Savannah Symphony Soc., 1971-75; Ga. del. to Japan/Southeast Trade Mission, Kyoto, Japan, 1983, S.E. U.S.A./Japan Assn. meeting, Birmingham, Ala., 1984. Served with USN, 1965-67. Recipient Outstanding Service award Savannah Port Authority, 1981. Mem. ABA, State Bar Ga., Am. Judicature Soc., Nat. Assn. Bond Counsel, Ga. Def. Lawyers Assn. (v.p. 1987—, mem. exec. com. 1988, bd. dirs., exec. v.p. 1990-91, pres. 1991-92), Savannah Bar Assn. (exec. com. 1989—, pres. 1992-93), Libel Def. Resource Ctr., Def. Rsch. Inst. (state chmn. 1992—), Savannah Econ. Devel. Action Council (founding), Savannah Area Wofford Coll. Alumni Club (past pres.), Soc. of the Cincinnati (Va.), St. Andrews Soc., Soc. Colonial Wars, Sons of Revolution (sec. 1988-92). Republican. Presbyterian. Clubs: Chatham, Savannah Yacht, 1st City, The Landings Club. Office: Forbes & Bowman PO Box 13929 Savannah GA 31416-0929

FORBES, SARAH ELIZABETH, gynecologist, real estate corporation officer; b. Currituck, N.C., May 4, 1928; d. Dexter and Mary (Brock) Forbes. BA, U. Rochester, 1949; MD, Med. Coll. of Va., 1954. Diplomate Am. Bd. Ob-Gyn. Intern Norfolk (Va.) Gen. Hosp., 1954-55; resident obgyn Johnston-Willis Hosp., 1955-56; resident ob-gyn Norfolk Gen. Hosp., 1956-57, chief resident, 1957-58; pvt. practice gynecologist Newport News, Va., 1958—; pres., real estate investor Mary B. Forbes Land Corp., Newport News, 1972—; pres. Sebrof Corp., Newport News, 1978—, Haras, Inc., Newport News, 1984—, S.S. U.S., Inc., Newport News, 1984—; bd. dirs. Family Planning Coun.; mem. teaching staff ob-gyn dept. Riverside Hosp. Pres. Peninsula Soc. for Prevention Cruelty to Animals, 1966—; mem. adv. bd. Peninisula chpt. Parents without Ptnrs.; bd. dirs. Newport News chpt. Am. Cancer Soc., pres., 2d v.p., 1971-72, 1st v.p., 1972-73, pres., 1973-74, chmn. rsch., 1961-69; candidate for Newport News City Coun., 1986; bd. dirs. Va. Peninsula Boys and Girls Club, 1991—. Recipient AMA Physicians Recognition award for Continuing Edn., 1973-76, Twin award Va. Peninsula YWCA, 1987, Medallion award Peninsula Boys and Girls Club, 1993; named Woman of Yr. for Peninsula Area, 1975. Mem. Va. Peninsula Acad. Medicine (pres. 1973-74, v.p. 1972-73, sec., treas. 1971-72); fellow AMA, Va. Med. Soc., Newport News Med. Soc. Am. Coll. Ob-Gyn, Tidewater Ob-Gyn Soc. Office: 12420 Warwick Blvd Newport News VA 23606-3001

FORBIS, MELVIN RICHARD, construction executive; b. Joliet, Ill., Mar. 2, 1934; s. Arthur J. and Mary Louise (Cassineri) F.; m. Jean Myrna Berry, Nov. 17, 1956; children: Richard, Robert, Ronald, Craig, David. Project mgr. Berry, Chgo., 1960-82; pres. Forbis Systems, Inc., Naples, Fla., 1982—; pres. Prestige Lighting & Design, Chgo.-Leasing, Custom Store Lighting, Premier Electricity of S.W. Fla.; adv. bd. Am. Subcontractors, Naples, 1990—, Collier County Govt. homeless com., Naples, 1993—. Adv. bd. Salvation Army, Naples 1986—; state dir. U.S. Jaycees, Joliet, 1963-70; dir. Diabetes Found., Naples, 1995; adv. bd. Econ, Naples, 1995.With U.S. Army, 1952-54, Korea. Home: 2770 Coach House Lane Naples FL 33942 Office: Forbis Systems Inc 1876 Trade Center Way Naples FL 33942

FORCE, CRYSTAL ANN, school counselor; b. Atlanta, Jan. 4, 1947; d. Raymond Ralph and Mary Ellen (Sticher) Bennett; m. Edward James Force, June 26, 1971; children: Lane Bennett, Patrick Brendan. BA, Carson-Newman Coll., 1969; MEd, Fla. Atlantic U., 1971. Cert. sch. counselor, Ga. Tchr. English Clewiston (Fla.) High Sch., 1969-71, sch. counselor, 1971-72; sch. counselor Greenport (N.Y.) Sch., 1972-75; dir. after sch. program LaBelle Elem. Sch., Marietta, Ga., 1985-89; sch. counselor LaBelle and Fair Oaks Elem. Schs., Marietta, 1989-90, LaBelle and King Springs Elem. Schs., Marietta, Smyrna, Ga., 1990-91; sch. counselor King Springs Elem. Sch., Smyrna, 1991—, creator Peacewalk and Peacegardens; co-dir. Smart Kids Orgn., Smyrna, 1992—. Chair parent edn. com. Griffin Mid. Sch. Parent Teacher Student Assn., Smyrna, 1993-94, exec. bd. sec. 1988; chmn. celebrating differences multicultural com. King Springs Elem., chmn. parent edn. com. PTA; mem. Citizens Adv. Coun., Smyrna, 1984-85, 93-94; mentor Campbell High Sch., Smyrna, 1992-93; mem. nat. adv. coun. Inst. Human Resource Devel., Building Esteem in Students Today Program. Recipient Am. Hero in Edn. award Reader's Digest Assn., 1993, Today's Kids award Brawner Hosp., 1993, Elem. Sch. Counselor of Yr. for Cobb County, Ga., 1994. Mem. AAUW, Am. Counseling Assn., Am. Sch. Counselor Assn., Ga. Sch. Counselor Assn., Nat. Sch. Age Child Care Alliance, Ga. Sch. Age Child Care Assn., Cobb County Sch. Counselor Assn. (program chmn. 1995-96, profl. recognition com. 1994-95), Campbell High Sch. Booster Club. Republican. Baptist. Home: 4227 Deerwood Pky Smyrna GA 30082-3929 Office: King Springs Elem Sch 1041 Reed Rd Smyrna GA 30082-4230

FORCE, ELIZABETH ELMA, retired pharmaceutical executive, consultant; b. Phila., Sept. 6, 1930; d. Harry Elgin and Loretta G. (Werner) F. BA, Temple U., 1952; postgrad., U. Pa., 1965-67; MPh, George Washington U., 1972, PhD, 1973. Cons. sr. scientist Booz-Allen Hamilton, Bethesda, Md., 1967-68; rsch. cons. scientist GEOMET, Inc., Rockville, Md., 1968-70; profl. assoc. div. med. scis. NAS-NRC, Washington, 1970-74; mgr. clin. adminstrn. dept. clin. rsch. and devel. Wyeth Labs., Radnor, Pa., 1974-77; exec. dir. regulatory affairs Merck Sharp and Dohme Rsch. Labs., West Point, Pa., 1977-88; cons. Clin. Regulatory Systems, Sarasota, Fla., 1988-91; asst. professorial lectr. epidemiology and environ. health Sch. Medicine George Washington U., Washington, 1972-74; vis. assoc. prof. cmty. health and preventive medicine Med. Coll. Jefferson U., Phila., 1981-83. Editor Clin. Rsch. Practice and Drug Regulatory Affairs, 1983-85, Drug Info. Jour., 1984-88; contbr. 60 articles to profl. jours. Ruhland Pub. Health fellow George Washington U. Sch. Medicine, 1971-73. Mem. Drug Info. Assn. (pres. 1986-87, Outstanding Dir. award 1985). Office: 7555 Northport Dr Boynton Beach FL 33437-5066

FORD, ANN SUTER, family nurse practitioner, health planner; b. Mineola, N.Y., Oct. 31, 1943; d. Robert M. and Jennette (Van Derzee) Suter; m. W. Scott Ford, 1964; children: Tracey, Karin, Stuart. RN, White Plains Hosp. Sch. Nursing (N.Y.), 1964; BS in Nursing with high distinction, U. Ky., 1967; MS in Health Planning, Fla. State U., 1971, PhD, 1975; MSN, Fla. State U., 1992. Nurse, U. Ky. Med. Ctr., 1964-65, Tallahassee Meml. Hosp., 1968-69; guest lectr. health planning dept. urban and regional planning Fla. State U., Tallahassee, 1973-76, health planner and research assoc., 1974-76, vis. asst. prof., 1976-77, asst. prof. and dir. health planning splty., 1977-83, assoc. prof., 1982-83; health care analyst and policy cons., 1983-86; med., health program analyst Aging and Adult Svcs. for State of Fla., 1986-90; coordinator Fla. Alzheimer's Disease Initiative, 1986-90; family nurse practitioner Capital Area Physicians' Svcs., 1993-94; assoc. prof. nursing Fla. A&M U., 1994—; bd. dirs. Regional Fla. Lung Assn., 1986-91; mem. exec. com. human services and social planning tech. dept. Am. Inst. Planners, 1977-83. Author: The Physician's Assistant: A National and Local Analysis, 1975; contbr. numerous articles on health edn. and health planning to profl. jours.; contbr. chpts. to books; author rsch. reports. USPHS grantee, 1965-67; HEW grantee, 1978; Univ. fellow Fla. State U., 1971-72; recipient Am. Inst. Planners' Student award, 1975. Mem. Am. Planning Assn. (charter mem. human services and social planning tech. dept. 1976-83, chmn. health planning session Oct. 1978, 79, health policy liaison 1979-83, author assn. health policy statement), Am. Health Planning Assn., Fla. Nurses Assn., Phi Kappa Phi, Sigma Theta Tau. Address: 2602 Cline St Tallahassee FL 32312-3110

FORD, DEBORAH LYNNE, dean; b. Owensboro, Ky., Dec. 1, 1965; d. Philip Olin and Nancy J. (Shively) Akers; m. John David Ford, June 10, 1989; 1 child, Abigail Lynne. BS in Edn., U. Louisville, 1987, EdD, 1996; MS in Coll. Student Pers., Ind. U., 1989. Coord. student devel. Spalding U., Louisville, 1989-91, dean of students, 1991—. Chair Child Watch Greater Louisville, 1994—. Fellow Scottish Rite Found., 1991—; named one of Outstanding Young Women Am., 1989. Mem. Nat. Assn. Student Pers. Adminstrs., Am. Coll. Pers. Assn., Nat. Orgn. on Legal Problems of Edn. Office: Spalding U 851 S 4th St Louisville KY 40203-2115

FORD, FRANCES ANNETTE, secondary educator; b. Tulsa, Okla., Feb. 11, 1947; d. William Warren and Esther Ernestine (Spivey) F. BS, East Carolina U., 1969; MEd, U. Ga., 1973, EdS, 1983, EdD, 1993. Cert. tchr. Ga. Tchr. Jones County Bd. Edn., Trenton, N.C., 1969-70, Charlotte-Mecklenburg Bd. Edn., Charlotte, N.C., 1970-72, Dougherty County Bd. Edn., Albany, Ga., 1973-75; tchr., coord. Fayette County Bd. Edn., Fayetteville, Ga., 1976—; English instr. Gordan Jr. Coll., 1995; mem. Career Planning Bd., Atlanta, 1982-83, Vocat. Evaluation Team, Atlanta, 1984-85; mem. Leadership Team, Fayette County H.S., 1990—, chairperson, 1994-96. Elder Brooks (Ga.) Christian Ch. Disciples of Christ, 1992-95. Mem. NEA, Ga. Assn. Educators, Am. Vocat. Assn., Ga. Vocat. Assn., Delta Kappa Gamma (1st v.p. 1996—), Phi Delta Kappa. Office: Fayette County High Sch 205 Lafayette Dr Fayetteville GA 30214

FORD, GORDON BUELL, JR., English language, linguistics, and medieval studies educator, author, retired hospital industry financial management executive; b. Louisville, Sept. 22, 1937; s. Gordon Buell Sr. and Rubye (Allen) F. AB summa cum laude in Classics, Medieval Latin, and Sanskrit, Princeton U., 1959; AM in Classical Philology and Linguistics, Harvard U., 1962, PhD in Linguistics, 1965; postgrad., U. Oslo, 1962-64, U. Sofia, Bulgaria, 1963, U. Uppsala, Sweden, 1963-64, U. Stockholm, 1963-64, U. Madrid, 1963. Yeager, Ford, and Warren Found. Disting. prof. Indo-European, Classical, Slavic, and Baltic linguistics, Sanskrit, and Medieval Latin Northwestern U., Evanston, Ill., 1965—; Lybrand, Ross Bros., and Montgomery Found. Disting. prof. English and linguistics U. No. Iowa, Cedar Falls, 1972—; sr. exec. v.p. for real estate fin. mgmt. Gorgay, Inc., Louisville, 1976-77; sr. exec. v.p. for reimbursement and rates acctg. fin. mgmt. Humana, Inc., The Hosp. Co., Louisville, 1978-93; dir. Southeastern Investment Trust, Inc., Louisville, 1978-93; ret., 1993; rsch. prof. The Southeastern Investment Trust, Inc. Rsch. Found., Louisville, 1976—; vis. prof. Medieval Latin, U. Chgo., 1966—; vis. prof. linguistics U. Chgo., Downtown Ctr., 1966—; prof. English evening divs. Northwestern U., Chgo., 1968-69, prof. anthropology, 1971-72. Author: The Ruodlieb: The First Medieval Epic of Chivalry from Eleventh-Century Germany, 1965, The Ruodlieb: Linguistic Introduction, Latin Text with a Critical Apparatus, and Glossary, 1966, The Ruodlieb: Facsimile Edition, 1965, 3d edit. 1968, Old Lithuanian Texts of the Sixteenth and Seventeenth Centuries with a Glossary, 1969, The Old Lithuanian Catechism of Baltramiejus Vilentas (1579): A Phonological, Morphological, and Syntactical Investigation, 1969, Isidore of Seville's History of the Goths, Vandals, and Suevi, 1966, 2d edit. 1970, The Letters of Saint Isidore of Seville, 1966, 2d edit. 1970, The Old Lithuanian Catechism of Martynas Mazvydas (1547), 1971, others; translator: A Concise Elementary Grammar of the Sanskrit Language with Exercises, Reading Selections, and a Glossary (Jan Gonda), 1966, The Comparative Method in Historical Linguistics (Antoine Meillet), 1967, A Sanskrit Grammar (Manfred Mayrhofer), 1972; contbr. numerous articles to many scholarly jours. Appointed to Hon. Order Ky. Cols. (life). Mem. Linguistic Soc. Am. (life, Sapir life patron), Internat. Linguistic Assn., Societas Linguistica Europaea (charter, life), Am. Philol. Assn. (life), Classical Assn. Middle West and South (life), Medieval Acad. Am. (life), MLA (life), Am. Assn. Tchrs. Slavic and East European Langs., Am. Assn. Advancement Slavic Studies (life), Assn. for Advancement Baltic Studies (life), Inst. Lithuanian Studies (life), Tchrs. of English to Speakers of Other Langs. (charter, life), SAR (life), Princeton Club (N.Y.C., Chgo.), Princeton Alumni Assn. (Louisville), Harvard Club (N.Y.C., Chgo., Louisville, Lexington, Ky.), Pres.'s Soc. Bellarmine Coll. (life), Louisville Country Club, KC (life), Phi Beta Kappa (life). Baptist. Home: 3619 Brownsboro Rd Louisville KY 40207-1863 also: PO Box 2693 Clarksville Br Jeffersonville IN 47131-2693

FORD, JAMES HENRY, JR., hospital executive; b. Brownfield, Miss., May 25, 1931; s. James H. and Katie Sue F.; m. Peggy Simpson, Mar. 1959; children: Renee, James, Randy, Penny. B.S. in Acctg., Memphis State U., 1953; M.H.A., St. Louis U., 1969. Auditor Sears, Roebuck & Co., Memphis, 1955-60; adminstrv. asst. Meth. Hosp., Memphis, 1964-67; asst. adminstr. Druid City Hosp., Tuscaloosa, Ala., 1969-76, adminstr., from 1976, now pres.; pres. DCH Healthcare Authority, Tuscaloosa; past pres., now bd. dirs. West Ala. Emergency Med. Svcs.; past pres. West Ala. Hosp. Coun., 1974; treas. Ala. Vol. Hosps. Am., 1986-87. past pres. Phoenix House of Tuscaloosa, 1974; loaned exec. United Fund in Tuscaloosa County, 1974, 75; past chmn. adminstrv. bd. First Meth. Ch. of Tuscaloosa, 1973; bd. dirs. Blue Cross-Blue Shield Ala., 1986-92, 94—; mem. Black Warrior Coun. Boy Scouts Am., 1978—. Recipient William G. Follmar award, Robert H. Reeves award Hosp. Fin Mgmt. Assn., 1975. Mem. Ala. Hosp. Hosp. Execs. (pres. 1981-82), Am. Coll. Adminstrs., Ala. Hosp. Assn. (trustee 1978-84, 88-94, chmn. 1993-94, gold medal 1991). Office: DCH Regional Med Ctr 809 University Blvd E Tuscaloosa AL 35401-2029

FORD, JOE THOMAS, telephone company executive, former state senator; b. Conway, Ark., June 24, 1937; s. Arch W. and Ruby (Watson) F.; m. Jo Ellen Wilbourn, Aug. 9, 1959; children: Alison, Scott. BS, U. Ark., 1959. With Allied Telephone Co., Little Rock, 1959-83, v.p.-treas., 1963-77, pres., 1977-83; pres. ALLTEL Corp., 1983-87, pres., chief exec. officer, 1987-91, chmn., pres., chief exec. officer, 1991-93, chmn., CEO, 1993—; now chmn. Alltel Corp., Little Rock, A.R.; mem. Ark. Senate, 1967-82; dir. Comml. Nat. Bank, 1970-85, Little Rock, Security Bank, Conway. Recipient Disting. Alumni cert. U. Ark., 1987. Baptist. Home: 2100 Country Club Ln Little Rock AR 72207-2040 Office: Alltel Corp PO Box 2177 1 Allied Dr Little Rock AR 72202-2013

FORD, KATHLEEN MARIE, home health nurse, trainer; b. N.Y., May 3, 1937; d. Gregory Henry and Mary Rose (Spinella) Kanellos; m. William Henry Ford, Jan. 8, 1958; children: William Henry Jr., Theresa Marie. AAS, Nassau C.C. RN N.Y., N.Mex., Tex. Staff nurse ICU, CCU North Shore U. Hosp., Manhassett, N.Y., 1973; LIJ Hillside Med. Ctr., New Hyde Park, N.Y., 1974-75; utilization rev. coord., med. auditing asst. Terrace Heights Hosp., Jamaica, N.Y., 1975-76; utilization review coord., supr. Belen area, freelance discharge planning coord., key nurse for quality assurance program in N.Mex. Hosp. Home Health Care, 1976-78; utilization review coord. Huguley Meml. Hosp., Fort Worth, Tex., 1981-82; admissions nurse, acting supr., field RN Upjohn Healthcare Svcs., 1983-84; field nurse Med. Plz. Home Health Care, Fort Worth, 1984-86, PMI, Fort Worth, 1986-88, Fort Worth Osteopathic Med. Ctr., 1989; supr. Home Health of Tarrant County, 1989-91; patient care coord. Family Svc. Inc., Fort Worth, 1991-94; home health field trainer Total Home Health Svcs., Fort Worth, 1994-95; field supr. Vis. Nurse Assn., Ft. Worth, 1995—. Host parent fgn. exch. student Aspect Found., San Francisco, 1989-90, 94-95. Roman Catholic. Home: 7525 Nutwood Pl Fort Worth TX 76133-7512 Office: Vis Nurse Assn 1300 S University Fort Worth TX 76107

FORD, KELLY CURTIS, educational consultant; b. Duncan, Okla., Sept. 22, 1945; s. Orlando and Lucille (Chesnut) F. BAA, Cameron U., 1971; postgrad., U. Okla., 1979, Okla. State U., 1973-74. Cert. in grammar and composition, Am. and English lit., speech and drama, yearbook, newspaper, social studies, bus. English, chemistry, Okla. Tchr. English Walters (Okla.) Pub. Schs., 1971-75; tchr. English Oologah (Okla.)-Talala Pub. Schs., 1975-94, coach acad. team, 1985-93; ednl. cons. pvt. practice, Claremore, Okla., 1994—; co-dir. writing project Okla. State U., Stillwater, 1992—, dir. summer youth writing project, 1993; mem. com. to develop objective for lang. arts competency test for tchr. cert. Okla. Dept. Edn., also mem. com. to develop lang. arts competency test, editorial coord. Okla. Centennial Anthology, other coms.; workshop presenter in field; guest lectr. Cameron U., 1971; supr. student tchrs. Northeastern State U., 1988, 93, Tulsa U., 1990; instr. Headlands Indian health careers program U. Okla., 1991. Mem. grant selection com. for Chautauqua Inst., Okla. Found. for Humanities, 1993. Recipient cert. of recognition Oologah-Talala Bd. Edn., 1986-87, 90-91, citation State of Okla. and Gov.'s Com. To Hire Handicapped, 1981, letter of commendation Carleton Coll., 1987, achievement merit award Claremore Optimist Club, 1991, Tchr. of Yr. award Oologah-Talala Pub. Schs., 1991, citation of congratulations Okla. Senate, 1991, citation of recognition Okla. Ho. of Reps., 1991, outstanding writing tchr. award Writing Conf., 1993, also others. Mem. NEA, Okla. Edn. Assn. (sec.-treas. English, speech and journalism tchrs. so. dist. 1972-73, chmn. 1973-74), Nat. Coun. Tchrs. English (judge 1987—), Okla. Coun. Tchrs. English (bd. dirs. 1971—, 1st v.p. 1978-79, pres.-elect 1979-80, pres. 1980-81, editorial bd. Okla. English Jour. 1987—, Lifetime Achievement award 1993), Oologah-Talala Classroom Tchrs. Assn. (sec. local staff devel. com. 1986-87, chmn. 1987-88, editor newsletter 1987-88, 90-91, 93-94). Home: 29B Riverhill New Hope PA 18938-1262

FORD, MARCYANNE ROSE, computer consultant; b. New Britain, Conn., July 17, 1941; m. John E. Ford, Jr., Aug. 3, 1991; children: William, Todd, Christopher, Kerilee, Alyssa, Derrick. BA in Math., St. Joseph Coll., West Hartford, Conn., 1963; MS in Computer Sci., Rensselaer Poly. Inst. Tchr. math. St. Paul High Sch., Bristol, Conn., 1980-81; analyst telecommunications Hartford (Conn.) Ins. Group, 1981-95; cons. Computer Profls. Inc., Cary, N.C., 1995—. mem. mentoring program St. Joseph Coll., 1992. Republican. Roman Catholic. Home: 6925-16 Spring Creek Cove Raleigh NC 27513 Office: Computer Profls Inc 2000 Regency Pkwy Cary NC 27511

FORD, ROBERT DAVID, lawyer; b. New Orleans, Oct. 30, 1956; s. Thomas Paul and Inez Mary (Rodriguez) F.; m. Jean Ann Burg, May 5, 1979; children: Robert David Jr., Charlene Elizabeth, Timothy Michael. BA, U. New Orleans, 1978; JD, Loyola U., 1983. Bar: La. 1983, U.S. Dist. Ct. (ea. dist.) La. 1983, U.S. Ct. Appeals (5th cir.) 1985. Claims rep. State Farm Mut. Auto Ins. Co., Metairie, La., 1978-80; assoc. Hammett, Leake & Hammett, New Orleans, 1983-86; ptnr. Thomas, Hayes, Beahm & Buckley, New Orleans, 1986-95; mem. Chehardy, Sherman, Ellis, Breslin & Murray, Metairie, La., 1995-96; with Hailey, McNamar, Hall, Larmann & Papale, Metairie, 1996—. Mem. ABA (coms. on health law, profl. liability and products liability litigation 1992, subcoms. on hosp. and clinic med. devices and med. malpractice liability 1992), Fed. Bar Assn., La. Bar Assn., New Orleans Bar Assn., La. Assn. Def. Counsel, Am. Soc. Law and Medicine, La. Soc. Hosp. Attys. of La. Hosp. Assn., Def. Rsch. Inst., Phi Kappa Theta, Pi Alpha Delta. Republican. Roman Catholic. Home: 8 Caney Ct Kenner LA 70065-3944 Office: Hailey McNamara Hall Larmann & Papale 1 Galleria Blvd Ste 1400 Metairie LA 70001

FORD, WENDELL HAMPTON, senator; b. Owensboro, Ky., Sept. 8, 1924; s. Ernest M. and Irene (Schenk) F.; m. Jean Neel, Sept. 18, 1943; children: Shirley Jean (Mrs. Dexter), Steven. Student, U. Ky., 1942-43. Past ptnr. Gen. Ins. Agy., Owensboro; chief asst. to gov. Ky., 1959-61; mem. Ky. Senate, 1966-67; lt. gov. Ky., 1967-71, gov. Ky., 1971-74, U.S. senator from Ky., 1974—, Dem. whip, 1991—, asst. minority leader 104th Congress; past chmn. Dem. Senatorial Campaign Com., Nat. Dem. Gov.'s Caucus; chmn. Dem. Nat. Campaign Com., 1976; ranking minority mem. Commerce, Sci. and Transp. Subcom. of Aviation, Rules and Adminstrn. Com.; mem. Energy and Natural Resources Com., Joint Com. on Printing, Senate Dem. Policy Com., Senate Dem. Steering and Coordination Com., Senate Dem. Tech. and Comm. Com. Served with AUS, 1944-46, Ky. N.G., 1949-62. Baptist. Club: Elk, Jaycees.

FORDE, JOHN ELLIS, communication educator; b. Laurel, Miss., Mar. 20, 1961; s. Jerry and Anne (Mayfield) F.; m. Connie J. McMullan, Dec. 19, 1985; children: John David, Daniel. AA in Liberal Arts, Jones County Jr. Coll., Ellisville, Miss., 1981; BA in Comms., Miss. State U., 1983; MS in Pub. rels., U. So. Miss., 1984, PhD in Comm., 1988. Teaching asst. in Spanish U. So. Miss., Hattiesburg, 1983, comm. grad. teaching asst., 1983-84, pub. rels. intern, 1984, coord. divsn. lifelong learning, 1985; dir. pub. rels. William Carey Coll., Hattiesburg, 1985-87; instr. Miss. State U., Starkville, 1987-89, asst. prof. comms., 1989—. Contbr. articles to profl. jours. Mem. fin. com. First United Meth. Ch., Starkville, 1994, adminstrv. bd., 1993, co-pres. Koinonia Sunday sch. class 1993; mem. Starkville Men's Ch. Softball League, 1988—; coach T-ball Starkville Baseball Assn., 1993—, Starkville Youth Soccer Orgn., 1992-94, bd. dirs., 1992-93; co-sec. Starkville Pub. Schs. PTA, 1993-94; media com. chair Parents for Pub. Schs., 1994, others. Mem. Pub. Rels. assn. Miss. (chpt. pres. 1992, 93, bd. dirs. 1990—, State Practitioner of the Yr. 1992, charter pres. Starkville/MSU chpt. 1992, bd. dirs. 1991—), So. Pub. Rels. Fedn. (bd. dirs. 1990—), Coll. Pub. Rels. Assn., Soc. Advancement Mgmt. (nat. bd. dirs., v.p. pub. rels. 1993-94), Miss. Speech Comm. Assn. (pres. 1991-92), Pub. Rels. Soc. Am. (educators sect.), Assn. Edn. Journalism and Mass. Comm., Speech Comm. Assn., So. States Comm. Assn., Miss. Press Assn., Phi Kappa Phi. Office: Miss State Univ Dept Comm PO Drawer PF Mississippi State MS 39762

FORDER, REG ARTHUR, publishing executive; b. Edmonton, Alta., Can., Jan. 4, 1943; s. William A. and Janet A. (Williams) F.; m. Eleonore J. Bergan, July 30, 1984; children: Jerry, Donna, Sharon, Mark, Dale. Grad. high sch., Canada. Mgr. Nat. Real Estate Svc., Vancouver, Can., 1965-77; prin. Century Vending, Phoenix, 1981—; pub. Christian Communicator Mag., Phoenix, 1994—; dir. confs. Am. Christian Writers, 1981—. Author: Soulwinning: An Action Handbook for Christians, 1985. Office: Am Christian Writers PO Box 110390 Nashville TN 37222

FORDHAM, CHRISTOPHER COLUMBUS, III, university dean and chancellor, medical educator; b. Greensboro, N.C., Nov. 28, 1926; s. Christopher Columbus and Frances Long (Clendenin) F.; m. Barbara Byrd, Aug. 16, 1947; children: Pamela Fordham Richey, Susan Fordham Crowell, Betsy Fordham Templeton. Cert. in medicine, U. N.C., 1949; MD, Harvard U., 1951. Diplomate Am. Bd. Internal Medicine. Intern Georgetown U. Hosp., 1951-52; asst. resident Boston City Hosp., 1952-53; prof. medicine emeritus U. N.C. Sch. Medicine, 1993—; sr. asst. resident N.C. Meml. Hosp., Chapel Hill, 1953-54; fellow in medicine U. N.C. Sch. Medicine, 1954-55, instr. medicine, 1958-60, asst. prof., 1960-64, assoc. prof., asst. dean, Sch. Medicine, 1964-68, prof., assoc. dean, 1968-69; acting asst. sec. for health Dept. HEW, Washington, 1977; dean Sch. Medicine U. N.C., 1971-79; prof. medicine U. N.C. Sch. Medicine, 1971—, vice chancellor for health affairs, 1977-80, chancellor, 1980-88, chancellor emeritus and prof. medicine, 1988-93, chancellor emeritus, dean emeritus, prof. medicine emeritus, 1993—; prof. medicine, v.p. for medicine, dean Sch. Medicine, Med. Coll. Ga., Augusta, 1969-71; practice medicine, specializing in internal medicine Greensboro, N.C., 1957-58; chair Gov.'s Com. on N.C. Awards, 1993—. Bd. dirs. Royal Soc. Med. Found., N.Y.C., 1990-95; chmn. N.C. Awards Com., 1993—. Officer USAF, 1955-57. Fellow ACP, AAAS; mem. AAUP, AMA (spl. award 1990), Nat. Assn. State Univs. & Land Grant Colls. (chair coun. univ. governance 1990-91), N.C. Med. Soc., So. Soc. Clin. Investigation, Am. Soc. Nephrology, Am. Fedn. Clin. Rsch., Soc. Health and Human Values, Am. Assn. Med. Colls. (exec. coun. 1975-78, rep. liaison com. med. edn. 1977-79), Am. Assn. Med. Coll. So. Regional Deans (chmn. 1972-73, 75-76, chmn. nat. coun. deans 1977), N.Y. Acad. Scis., Inst. Medicine of Nat. Acad. Sci. (council 1985-90), Elisha Mitchell Sci. Soc., Order Golden Fleece, Sigma Xi, Alpha Omega Alpha. Office: Univ NC Sch Medicine Campus Box 7000 Rm 5023 Clin Wing Chapel Hill NC 27514

FORDHAM, SHARON ANN, food company executive; b. Somerset, N.J., Jan. 30, 1952; d. Thomas Anthony and Gladys Maryann (Hagaman) F. BA in History with honors, Rutgers U., 1975; MBA in Mktg., U. Pa., 1977. Asst. product mgr. Bristol-Myers (Drackett Co.), Cin., 1977-78, product mgr., 1979; product mgr. Borden, Inc., Columbus, Ohio, 1979-8l, Nabisco Brands Inc., East Hanover, N.J., 198l-82; group product mgr. Nabisco Brands, Inc., East Hanover, N.J., 1982-84, dir. mktg., 1984-86; sr. dir. new bus. Nabisco, Brands Inc., East Hanover, N.J., 1986-91, v.p. new bus., 1991-94; v.p., gen. mgr. Life Savers Co., 1994—. Originator, dir. Almost Home (Cookie Wars), 1983, Low Salt Nabisco Crackers, 1987, Teddy Grahams, 1988, Mr. Phipps, 1991, Snack Wells, 1992, Nabisco Breakfast Snack Line, 1994. Mem. Woodbridge (N.J.) Wind Ensemble, 1982-83, Hillsborough Wind Ensemble, Somerset, N.J., 1984-87. Recipient award Point of Purchase Advt. Inst., 1983, 89, Gold Effie award Assn. Nat. Advertisers, 1986, 89, 92, New Product of Yr. award Bus. Week, 1988, Food and Beverage Mktg., 1988, 91, 93, New Snack Product of Yr. award Consumer Network, 1988, Gorman Pub., 1988, 91, Am. Mktg. Assn., 1989, 91, 92, 94. Mem. Mensa, Wharton Club N.Y. (bd. dirs.). Republican. Roman Catholic. Office: The Life Savers Co 1100 Reynolds Blvd Winston Salem NC 27105

FORDICE, KIRK, JR. (DANIEL KIRKWOOD FORDICE), governor, construction company executive, engineer; b. Memphis, TN, Feb. 10, 1934; s. Daniel Kirkwood and Clara Aileen (Augustine) F.; m. Patricia Louise Owens, Aug. 13, 1955; children: Angela Leigh Fordice Roselle, Daniel K. III, Hunter L., James Owens. BSCE, Purdue U., 1956, MS in Indsl. Mgmt., 1957. Registered profl. engr., Miss., La. Engr. Exxon, Baton Rouge, 1956-62; ptnr. Fordice Constrn. Co., Vicksburg, Miss., 1962-76, pres., chief exec. officer, from 1976; gov. State of Miss., 1992—; bd. dirs. Mchts. Nat. Bank, Vicksburg, Miss.; vice-chmn. So. Gov.'s Assn., 1992—, chmn., 1994—. Sec. Miss. Rep. Party, Jackson, 1981-88; vice-chmn. Vicksburg-Tallulah Dist. Airport Bd.; chmn. Econ. Devel. Found., Vicksburg, 1984. Served to col. C.E., USAR. Recipient Teddy Roosevelt award Cons. Engrs. Coun. Miss., 1992, Captain of Industry award Miss. Cystic Fibrosis Found., 1992; named one of Outstanding Young Men of Am., U.S. Jaycees, 1969, Vol. Laureate in Indsl. Devel., Gov. of Miss., 1985; achievement recognition Engineering News Record mag., 1982, 91, A Grade for Fiscal Policy award Cato Inst., 1994. Fellow ASCE (pres. Vicksburg br. 1982, Outstanding Civil Engr. of Yr. Miss. sect. 1992); mem. NSPE, NRA, Associated Gen. Contractors of Miss., (Outstanding Mem. of Yr. award 1992), Am. Inst. Constructors, Cons. Constructors Coun. Am., Soc. Am. Mil. Engrs., Assoc. Gen. Contractors Am. (nat. pres. 1990, nat. life dir., pres. Miss. Valley flood control br. 1970, Man of Yr. award 1992), Am. Constrn. Industry Forum (pres. 1991), Confederation Internat. Contractor's Assns. (v.p. 1990—), So. Govs. Assn. (chmn.), Aircraft Owners and Pilots Assn., Nat. Aero. Assn., Reserve Officers Assn., Quiet Birdmen, Am. Quarter Horse Assn., Safari Club Internat., Game Conservation Internat., Rivertown Club (Vicksburg), The Moles, Nature Conservancy, Sigma Chi (Significant Sig award 1993), Tau Beta Pi, Chi Epsilon. Republican. Methodist. Office: Office of the Governor PO Box 139 Jackson MS 39215 also: Fordice Constrn Co 4111 Warrenton Rd Vicksburg MS 39180-5517

FORE, CAROLYN LOUISE B., pediatrics nurse; b. Pitts., June 7, 1937; d. Paul Wade and Lilan Ettibell (Doughty) Baltz Binning; m. Robert L. Fore, Sept. 27, 1958; children: Paul William, Mark Lee. Diploma, Grace Hosp. Sch. Nursing, Richmond, Va., 1958; student, Hillsborough Community Coll., Polk Community Coll., U. Fla., 1984-85; BS in Health Care Adminstrn., St. Joseph Coll., 1991. Head nurse pediatric surgery unit Med. Coll. Va., Richmond, 1958-65; supr., open heart pump operator Dr. Louis Bosher, Richmond, 1964-68; indsl. nurse Holly Farms Poultry Ind., West Glen Allen, Va., 1969-70; case mgr. Henrico County Health Dept., Richmond, 1971-77; nursing supr. Porta Medic, Tampa, Fla., 1977-78; ins. agt. Life of Ga., Tampa, 1978; sr. community health nurse Childrens Med. Svc., Tampa, 1978-82; sr. community health nurse Childrens Med. Svc., Lakeland, Fla., 1982-84, RN specialist, 1984-88, supr. sr. community health nursing, 1988-89, DON, 1989—. Recipient Essay award. Mem. Va. Nurses Assn., Fla. Nurses Assn. Home: 3010 King John Pl Seffner FL 33584-6167

FOREHAND, ROBERT JACKSON, education administrator; b. Goldsboro, N.C., Nov. 16, 1951; s. Loyd Jackson and Almeta Rae (Batten) F.; m. Celia Ann Marshburn, July 10, 1976; children: Samuel Aaron, Benjamin Joel. BRE, Heritage Bible Coll., 1976; BA in Religion, N.C. Wesleyan Coll., 1978. Ordained to ministry Pentecostal Holiness Ch., Falcon, N.C., 1974. Mem. Christian edn. bd. N.C. Conf. Pentecostal Holiness Ch., Falcon, 1976-82, sec.-treas. Christian edn., 1982-86, asst. dir. Christian edn., 1986-87, conf. dir. Christian edn., mem. Gen. Christian Edn. Bd., 1987—; bd. dirs. Ch. Edn. Ministries IPHC, 1993—. Nat. comdr. Royal Rangers, IPHC, 1993; coord. re-election com. Senator Jesse Helms, 1984. Recipient Instrumental Solo award Pentecostal Holiness Ch., 1971. Republican. Home and Office: PO Box 60 Falcon NC 28342-0060

FOREHAND STILLMAN, MARGARET P., library director; b. Nov. 12, 1951; m. Peter R. Stllman, Feb. 11, 1995; children: Lindsay Howell, Walker Harrison. BA in Edn., U. Richmond, 1973; MA in Edn., Va. Commonwealth U., 1974; MLS, U. Md., 1977. Libr. hdqrs. Chesapeake Libr. Systems, 1979-85, dir. librs. and rsch. svcs., 1985—. Bd. dirs. Tidewater ARC, 1980-83, Western Tidewater Area Health Edn. Ctr., 1980—, exec. coun. 1982—; v.p. Va. Stage Co., 1981-82, bd. dirs., 1979-85; bd. dirs. the Planning Coun. Cultural Alliance of Greater Hampton Roads, 1985—, exec. coun. 1986-88; bd. dirs. Am. Cancer Soc. Portsmouth-Chesapeake Bds., 1987—, pres., 1991—; mem. Mayor's Com. on Protocol, 1987, Mayor's Commn. on Bicentennial Constitution, 1987; co-chmn. Mayor's Task Force on Libr., 1989—, Gov.'s Rural Econ. Devel. Task Force, 1990-91. Named Outstanding Young Career Woman Va. Fedn. Bus. and Profl. Women's Clubs, 1978, Outstanding Bus. and Profl. Woman, 1993. Mem. ALA (Va. chair nat. libr. week 1985-86), Va. Libr. Assn. (coun.mem. 1978-86, chair Va. Pub. Libr. sect. 1978-79), Va. State Libr. Bd. (vice chmn. 9186-87, chmn. 1987-88, chmn. bldg. com. 1988—), State Adult Literacy Com. (chmn. 1989—), Chesapeake C. of C. (chmn. pub. rels. com. 1989—, planning coun., bd. dirs., UVA adv. bd., Hampton Roads Bd.), DAR (bd. dirs. Chesapeake chpt. 1983—). Office: Chesapeake Pub Libr 298 Cedar Rd Chesapeake VA 23320-5512

FOREMAN, EDWARD RAWSON, lawyer; b. Atlanta, May 15, 1939; s. Robert Langdon and Mary (Shedden) F.; m. Margaret Reeves, Oct. 19, 1968; children: Margaret Langdon, Mary Rawson. BA, Washington & Lee U., 1962; JD, Emory U., 1965. Bar: Ga. 1965. Assoc. Jones, Bird & Howell, Atlanta, 1965-70, ptnr., 1970-82; ptnr. Alston & Bird, Atlanta, 1982—; chmn. McAliley Endowment Trust, 1978—; lectr. Inst. for Continuing Legal Edn. in Ga., 1989; panelist, moderator Bus. Atlanta's Office Leasing and Tenant Opportunities in 1990s. Bd. dirs. Ansley Park Beautification Found., Atlanta, 1984—; bd. dirs. Midtown Bus. Assn., Atlanta,

1988—, sec., chmn. fundraising com., 1989-91, v.p., 1991, pres., 1992; trustee Paidela Sch. Endowment Fund, Atlanta, 1980—, Woodruff Arts Ctr., Atlanta, 1985-90; chmn. Emory U. Law Fund, Atlanta, 1981; chmn. legal divsn. United Way Met. Atlanta, 1984; chmn. strategic planning com. High Mus. Art, 1986-95, v.p., bd. dirs. 1986-95, chmn. nominating com., 1993-95; vestryman, sr. warden St. Luke's Episc. Ch., 1975-94, mem. com., 1975—; pres. Atlanta Legal Aid Soc., 1975-76, Atlanta Preservation Ctr., 1986-91; trustee Miss Hall's Sch., Pittsfield, Mass., 1990—. Recipient Cmty. Svc. award Martin Luther King Jr. Ctr. Nonviolent Social Change, 1980, Outstanding Svc. award Atlanta Preservation Ctr., Inc., 1983. Mem. ABA (mem. comml. leasing com. 1987—), State Bar Ga. (chmn., panelist, moderator comml. leasing seminars 1979-86), Atlanta Bar Assn. (chmn., panelist, moderator leasing seminars 1979-86, chmn. hdqrs. search com. 1988—), Lawyers Club Atlanta (chmn. long-range planning com. 1989-90), Atlanta Bar Found. (bd. dirs.), Old War Horse Lawyers Club, Nine O'Clocks Club (mem. centennial com. 1983), Highlands Country Club N.C. Democrat. Episcopalian. Home: 238 15th St NE # 16 Atlanta GA 30309 Office: Alston & Bird 4200 One Atlantic Ctr 1201 W Peachtree St Atlanta GA 30309

FOREMAN, EDWIN FRANCIS, economist, real estate broker; b. Syracuse, N.Y., July 24, 1931; s. Herve Joseph and Ruth Margaret F.; m. Colleen Frances Tapp, July 7, 1962; children: Lisa C., Eric E. BAE in Econs. and Fgn. Trade, U. Fla., 1957; postgrad. in real estate Fla. Internat. U., 1974-75. Owner, prin. Edwin F. Foreman, Mortgage Broker, Hollywood, Fla., 1974—; with Consol. Energy Corp., Hollywood, 1977—, pres., chmn. bd., 1977—; v.p. Ea. State Securities, Inc., 1977—; owner, prin. Edwin F. Foreman, Real Estate Broker, 1978—; pres., chmn. One-Fore-Devel., Inc., 1985, Three-Fore-Devel., Inc., 1985, L&E Comm. Inc., 1985; chmn., CEO Universal Traction, Hollywood, 1988—; gen. ptnr. Four-Fore Devel. Ltd., Five-Fore-Devel. Ltd., Six-Fore Devel., Ltd., 1987—, CCS Ventures, 1990—. Econ. cons. Michael I. Warde de Colombia Ltd.; guest lectr. econs. Xavier U., Bogota, Colombia. Served with USAF, 1950-53. R.J. Reynolds fellow U. N.C., 1961. Mem. Hollywood C. of C. (econ. devel. com.), Ft. Lauderdale World Trade Council. Democrat. Unitarian. Clubs: Jockey, Grove Isle (Miami), Fisher Island. Avocations: camping, fishing, music, photography, travel. Office: PO Box 7570 Hollywood FL 33081

FOREST, PHILIP EARLE, finance consultant; b. San Mateo, Calif., Dec. 4, 1931; s. Percy Egbert and Charlotte Elizabeth (Copeland) F.; m. Sally Annette Cauble, Apr. 30, 1988. BS, U. Md., 1972. Enlisted U.S. Army, 1950, advanced through grades to maj., 1964; various pos. FHA, HUD, Washington, 1966-77; spl. asst. to asst. sec. for housing HUD, Washington, 1977-78, spl. asst. to dep. asst. sec. for single family housing, 1978-83, spl. asst. to undersec., 1979, acting dep. asst. sec. for single family housing, 1980-81; housing and housing finance cons. Arlington, Va., 1983—. Author: Building the Single Family Loan Package, 1988, Collection Department Responsibilities and Operations, 1986, Processing the Loan, 1986, FHA/VA Servicing Handbook, 1990, Mortgage Loan Servicing, 1994. Pres. Columbia (Md.) Commuter Bus Corp., 1975-83. Mem. Mortgage Bankers Assn. Am. (assoc. signle family and loan adminstrn. coms. 1983—), Nat. Assn. Rev. Appraisers and Mortgage Underwriters (sr., registered mortgage underwriter 1983-93), Suburban Md. Bldg. Industry Assn. (fin., program coms., edn. inst. 1984—), Nat. Assn. Home Builders (standing com. housing fin. 1989-91, 93-96, single family govtl. subcom., vice-chmn. 1990, chmn. 1991, single family subcom., vice-chmn. 1995, chmn. 1996, task force on crisis in fin. housing prodn., chmn. HUD subcom. 1990, task force on internat. bus. devel. 1991), Am. Alliance for Loan Mgmt. (incorporator, dir., exec. v.p. 1989—).

FORESTER, KARL S., federal judge; b. 1940. BA, U. Ky., 1962, JD, 1966. With Eugene Goss Esp., 1966-68; mem. firm Goss & Forester, 1968-75, Forester, Forester, Buttermore & Turner, P.S.C., 1975-88; judge U.S. Dist. Ct. (ea. dist.) Ky., Lexington, 1988—. Mem. Ky. Bar Assn., Harlan County Bar Assn., The Champions. Office: US Dist Ct PO Box 2165 Lexington KY 40595-2165

FORÊT, RANDY BLAISE, insurance executive; b. New Orleans, June 29, 1954; s. John Morris and Della Antoinnette Forêt; m. Tanya Lynn Mason, May 28, 1977; children: Tabitha, Blaise, Marshall, Joshua. BS, Liberty Coll., 1977; A in Claims, Ins. Inst. Am., 1991. English instr., football coach Liberty High Sch., Pensacola, Fla., 1979-84; editor Wise Publs., Denton, Tex., 1984-85; field claims rep. State Farm Ins. Co., Dallas, 1985-89; claims supt. State Farm Ins. Co., Abilene, Tex., 1989—; lic./ordained cons. Liberty Fellowship, Pensacola, 1977-85. Pres. Denton TTA, 1984; precinct chmn. Rep. Party, Ft. Worth, 1984, mem. exec. com., 1994-96, chmn. permanent orgn. com., 1996; instr. Jr. Achievement. Mem. Abilene Claims Assn. Office: State Farm Ins 3025 SW Dr PO Box 7137 Abilene TX 79608

FORINA, MARIA ELENA, gifted education educator; b. Santiago, Cuba, Apr. 10, 1942; came to U.S., 1972; d. Jorge Fernando and Maria Elena (De Gongora) Chaves; m. Antonio Forina, May 28, 1961; children: Maria Elena, Amalia, Jose, Jorge Antonio. AA, Somerset County Coll., 1975; BS magna cum laude, U. Tex. Pan Am., Edinburg, 1982, M in Gifted Edn., 1995. Cert. elem. tchr., bilingual tchr., gifted edn. tchr., Tex.; SOI cert. trainer. 1st grade tchr. Pharr-San Juan-Alamo (Tex.) Ind. Sch. Dist., 1981-83, gifted edn. resource tchr., 1983-88, 6th grade gifted edn. tchr., 1988—, AMS writing trainer, 1991—. Eucharistic minister Resurrection Cath. Ch., Alamo, 1982—, CCD tchr., 1986—, mem. blue ribbon com., 1988—, mem. pastoral coun., 1993—. Mem. ASCD, Nat. Coun. Tchrs. Math., Nat. Coun. Tchrs. English, Tex. Assn. for Gifted and Talented, Phi Kappa Phi, Delta Kappa Gamma. Republican. Home: 842 Fannin Box 3901 Alamo TX 78516 Office: Alamo Mid Sch 1819 W US Highway 83 Alamo TX 78516-2102

FORKS, THOMAS PAUL, osteopathic physician; b. Great Lakes Naval Station, Ill., Apr. 15, 1952; s. Louis John and Rhoda Joan (Miles) F.; m. Sharron Elizabeth Wells, Dec. 15, 1979; 1 child, Joseph Miles. BA, St. Mary's U., 1975; MS, U. Tex., San Antonio, 1977; PhD, U. So. Miss., 1981; DO, U. Health Scis., Kansas City, Mo., 1988. Teaching asst., instr., then asst. prof. biology U. So. Miss., Hattiesburg, 1977-82; asst. prof. biology Wilkes Coll., Wilkes-Barre, Pa., 1982-83; intern Corpus Christi (Tex.) Osteo. Hosp., 1988-89; resident, then chief resident in family practice U. Miss., Jackson, 1989-91; emergency rm. physician Rush Hosp., Newton, Miss., 1989-91, Lackey Meml. Hosp., Forest, Miss., 1991—; physician N.E. Family Practice, San Antonio, 1992-93; family physician Morton, Miss., 1993—; lectr. in emergency med. mgmt. of snakebites. Contbr. articles to profl. publs. Charity physician Stewpot Free Clinic, Jackson, 1990-91; adv. bd. Cath. Charities, Jackson, 1990-91. Mem. AMA, AAFP, Am. Osteo. Assn., Miss. Acad. Sci., So. Med. Assn., Soc. for Study Amphibians and Reptiles, Chgo. Herpetological Soc. Republican. Roman Catholic. Home: 1809 Sarah Ln Jefferson City MO 65101

FORLINES, FRANKLIN LEROY, minister, educator; b. Winterville, N.C., Nov. 14, 1926; s. John Leroy and Leta Nanny (Manning) F.; m. Carolyn Le Fay Gilbert, Aug. 4, 1956; children: Jonathan Gilbert, James Franklin. BA, Freewill Bapt. Bible Coll., Nashville, 1952; MA, Winona Lake Sch. of Theology, Ind., 1959; BD, No. Bapt. Theol. Sem., Chgo., 1962; ThM, Chgo. Grad. Sch. of Theology, 1970. Ordained to ministry Free Will Bapt. Ch., 1951. Pastor 1st Free Will Bapt. Ch., Newport News, Va., 1952-53; mem. faculty Free Will Bapt. Bible Coll., 1953-59, 1962—, chmn. Bible dept., 1965—, dean of men, 1953-59, 65-71, dean of students, 1971-74. Author: Biblical Ethics, 1973, Systematics, 1975, Romans, The Randall House Bible Commentary, 1987. Mem. Evang. Theol. Soc., Bible Sci. Assn. Nashville (v.p. 1988—). Home: 3801 Rolland Rd Nashville TN 37205-2537 Office: Free Will Bapt Bible Coll 3606 W End Ave Nashville TN 37205-2403

FORMAN, HARRIET, nursing publication executive; b. Bklyn., Dec. 13, 1936; d. Herman Schulman. Diploma, The Mount Sinai Hosp. Sch. of Nursing; BS in Nursing cum laude, Adelphi U.; M of Health Care Adminstrn., L.I. U.; EdD, Tchr.'s Coll. Columbia U. RN, N.Y., Fla. Adminstrv. nursing supr. to asst. dir. nursing The Jewish Inst. for Geriatric Care, 1971-73, assoc. dir. nursing, 1973-76; dir. nursing svcs. Kingsbrook Jewish Med. Ctr., 1976-78, asst. adminstr., 1977-78; dir. of nursing to exec. dir. nursing Hempstead Gen. Hosp. Med. Ctr., 1978-81, assoc. adminstr., 1981-88; adminstr. Met. Jewish Geriatric Ctr., 1988-89; exec. dir. Greater N.Y./N.J. met. edit. The Nursing Spectrum, 1989-92, corp. editorial dir., 1992-93; exec. editor, start-up mng. editor HT-The Mag. for Health Travel Profls., 1993-94; exec. dir. Fla. divsn. Nursing Spectrum, Ft. Lauderdale, 1994—; cons. in mgmt. and edn.; adj. faculty Adelphi U. Sch. Nursing, Tchrs. Coll. Columbia U.; adv. com. nursing edn., nursing edn. and nursing adminstrn. com. Contbr. articles to profl. jours. Mem. ANA, Fla. State Nurses Assn., Am. Med. Writers Assn., Am. Orgn. Nurse Execs., Fla. Orgn. Nurse Execs., Sigma Theta Tau. Home: 520 N Ocean Blvd Apt 20 Pompano Beach FL 33062-4621

FORMAN, PETER GERALD, marketing professional; b. N.Y.C., June 26, 1946; s. Charles Richard and Gertrude (Flushing) Formaniak; m. Jane Ann Clark, Sept. 13, 1969 (div. 1980); children: Clark, Ellen; m. Pamela Blackbourn, Jan. 27, 1990. BSEE, U. Rochester, 1968, MSEE, 1972; MBA, U. Dallas, 1984. Programmer Gen. Dynamics, Rochester, N.Y., 1969-70, Stromberg-Carlson, Rochester, 1970-73; sr. programmer Xerox Corp., Dallas, 1973-76; tech. program mgr. Mostek, Carrollton, Tex., 1976-83; v.p. Am. Micro Products, Dallas, 1983-84; software mgr. ElectroCom Automation, Arlington, Tex., 1984-89, mgr. mktg., 1989-95; tech. mgr. GE, 1995—. Author 2 poems. Mem. Am. Mgmt. Assn., Toastmasters (pres. local club 1986-87), Sigma Iota Epsilon. Home: 302 Pecos Trl Irving TX 75063-4541

FORMO, BRENDA TERRELL, travel company executive; b. Greensboro, N.C., May 18, 1946; d. Walter C. Terrell and Eunice W. Kirkman; m. Robert A. Formo, Oct. 14, 1978; 1 child, Eric Victor. BSBA, East Carolina U., 1968; MA in Bus. Adminstrn., Webster U., 1977; postgrad., 1970, 72, 77, 84, 87; grad., Army War Coll., 1990. Commd. 2d lt. U.S. Army, 1969, advanced through grades to col., 1991, ret., 1993; acctg. instr. U.S. Army Fin. Sch., Ft. Harrison, Ind., 1969-71; women's officer recruiter U.S. Army Kansas City Recruiting Main Sta., 1971-73; recruiting ops. officer U.S. Army SW Recruiting Command, San Antonio, 1973-75; area comdr. U.S. Army San Antonio Dist. Recruiting Command, 1975-77; chief pay and examination divsn. U.S. Army Fin. and Acctg. Office, Yongsan, Korea, 1977-78; asst. chief acctg. U.S. Army Mil. Dist. Washington Fin. and Acctg. Office, 1978-80; banking officer U.S. Army Europe Office of the Dep. Chief of Staff for Resource Mgmt., 1980-84; fin. and acctg. officer Def. Nuclear Agy., 1984-87; investigator Office of Dept. of the Army Inspector Gen., 1987-91; chief programs and analysis divsn. Dept. Army Office of Dep. Chief of Staff for Logistics, 1991-93; fin. mgmt. cons., 1993-96; co-founder, pres. BRE Inc., 1996—. Pres. Browne Acad. PTA, Alexandria, Va., 1987; active Washington Farm United Methodist Ch., Alexandria. Decorated Legion of Merit with oak leaf cluster (2 awards), Meritorious Svc. medal with 3 oak leaf clusters (4 awards), Army Commendation medal with 4 oak leaf clusters (5 awards). Mem. Am. Soc. Travel Agts., Assn. of the U.S. Army, Terrell Soc. Am., Mt. Vernon Yacht Club (Alexandria). Address: 9416 Forest Haven Dr Alexandria VA 22309

FORMWALT, LEE WILLIAM, history educator; b. Springfield, Mass., Dec. 19, 1949; s. William E. and Claire E. (Letendre) F.; m. Dorothea M. Mumm, Dec. 30, 1972; children: Jennifer, Zachary, Meghan. BA in History, Cath. U., 1971, PhD in History, 1977; MA in History, U. Mass., 1972. Asst. prof. Albany (Ga.) State U., 1977-82, assoc. prof., 1982-88, prof., 1988—; rsch., editorial asst. Md. Hist. Soc., Balt., 1974-77, asst. editor, 1977-80; vis. assoc. editor Am. Philosophical Soc., Phila.,1980-81; adj. prof. Brewton-Parker Coll.-Lee Correctional Inst., Leesburg, Ga., 1983-85. Editor: (5 vols.) Papers of Benjamin Henry Latrobe, 1977-86; editor Jour. of Southwest Georgia History, 1983-87, 89—; monthly columnist Albany Ind., 1982; contbr. articles to profl. jours. Bd. dirs. Thronateeska Heritage Found., Albany, 1982-88, 89-92, 94—; treas. Mt. Zion Albany Civil Rights Movement Mus., Inc., 1994-96, v.p., 1996—; v.p. St. Teresa Sch. Bd., Albany, 1984-86. Grantee Am. Philos. Soc., 1981, Am. Assn. for State and Local History, 1988-89, Ga. Humanities Coun., 1993-94; NEH fellow, 1985-86. Mem. AAUP, Am. Hist. Assn. (grantee 1986-87), Orgn. Am. Historians, Soc. for Historians of the Early Republic, So. Hist. Assn., Ga. Assn. Historians (editl. bd. 1989-92), Ga. Hist. Soc. (editl. bd. 1991—). Democrat. Roman Catholic. Home: 939 Barbragale Ave Albany GA 31705-9576 Office: Albany State Coll Dept History And Sci Albany GA 31705

FORNELL, MARTHA STEINMETZ, art educator, artist; b. Galveston, Tex., Dec. 19, 1920; d. Joseph Duncan and Martha Lillian (McRee) Steinmetz; m. Earl Wesley Fornell, Sept. 20, 1947 (dec. Mar. 1969). B.Mus. cum laude, U. Tex., 1943; postgrad. U. Houston, 1953-56, Lamar U., 1957-60. Music cons., fgn. program editor Voice of America, USIA, N.Y.C., 1944-46; advt. cons. fed. agys., San Antonio, 1946-47; tchr. music secondary schs., Houston, 1953-56; tchr. art Beaumont (Tex.) Ind. Sch. Dist., 1956-79; collages exhibited Galerie Paula Insel, N.Y.C., 1974-84, Ponce, P.R., 1976-79, 82, 84, 87; group show participant Ann. Am. Nat. Miniature Show, Laramie, Wyo., Beaumont Art Mus. Annual, 1960, Houston Art League Easter Annual, 1960, Austin Women's Club, 1961. Recipient Circuit awards Tex. Fine Arts Assn., 1962-64, Invitational awards, 1964-65. Mem. Tex. Fine Arts Assn., Mu Phi Epsilon. Contbr. articles to Am.-German Rev. Address: 2303 Evalon St Beaumont TX 77702-1309

FORNEY, VIRGINIA SUE, educational counselor; b. Little Rock, Sept. 15, 1925; d. Robert Millard and Susan Amanda (Ward) Tate; m. J.D. Mullen, Jr., Oct. 13, 1945 (div. 1966); children: Michael Dunn, Patricia Sue; m. Bill E. Forney, Apr. 29, 1967. Student Tex. State Coll. for Women, 1943-46; BFA, U. Okla., 1948; postgrad. Benedictine Heights Coll., Tulsa, 1957-58; M.Teaching Arts, Tulsa U., 1969; postgrad. Okla. State U., intermittently, 1969—. Cert. secondary tchr., sch. counselor, vis. sch. counselor, Okla. With Sta. WNAD, U. Okla., 1947-49; tchr. lang. arts Tulsa Bd. Edn., 1959-73; women's counselor Tulsa YWCA, 1980; vis. sch. counselor Tulsa County Supt. of Schs. Office, 1980-86; dir. spl. project Tulsa County Supt. Schs. Office, 1986-91; owner, dir. Svc. to Families in Bus. and Industry, 1991—. Mem. budget com. United Way Greater Tulsa, 1980-86, edn. com. Planned Parenthood Greater Tulsa, 1980-86; mem. Tulsa County adv. coun. Okla. State U., 1983-85; chairperson Tulsa Coalition for Parenting Edn., 1983-84; chairperson problems of youth study Tulsa Met. C. of C., 1984-85; mem. gen. bd. March of Dimes Greater Tulsa, 1985; pres. evening alliance All Souls Unitarian Ch., 1993-94. Mem. Am. Assn. for Counseling and Devel., Internat. Assn. Pupil Personnel Workers (state bd. dirs. 1982-86), Okla. Assn. Family Resource Programs (regional v.p. 1982-86, state pres. 1986-87), Program Internat. Ednl. Exchange (community coordinator for Tulsa 1986-90), LWV Okla. (chairperson juvenile justice study 1976-77), LWV Met. Tulsa (mem. exec. bd. 1993-95), Tulsa Parents As Tchrs. Inc. (founding pres. 1991-92, exec. bd. 1992—). Democrat. Unitarian. Avocation: piano.

FORRAY, GABE, information systems executive; b. Apr. 1, 1946. BS, Concordia U., Montreal, Que., Can., 1970; MBA, U. Toronto, 1973. Cert. project mgmt. profl. Rsch. asst. RCA Ltd., Montreal, Que., Can., 1967-71; from planning analyst to project leader No. Telecom, Montreal, 1973-76; from sr. fin. analyst to mgr. corp. systems devel. Teleglobe, Montreal, 1976-90; systems devel. mgr. Cen. and Southwest, Dallas, 1991-94; sr. cons. Dallas, 1995; mng. prin. Oracle Corp., Irving, Tex., 1996—. Mem. Assn. Sys. Mgmt., Data Processing Mgmt. Assn., Project Mgmt. Inst. Home: PO Box 261119 Plano TX 75026-1119

FORREST, ALLEN WRIGHT, accounting firm executive, accountant; b. Quincy, Mass., Nov. 8, 1941; s. Edwin Wright and Sylvia (Locke) F.; m. Helen Frances Kolb, Nov. 10, 1962; children: Deborah, Teresa, Sandra, William. BBA, U. N. Fla., 1980, MS in Acctg., 1981. Enrolled agt., IRS. Enlisted USN, 1958, advanced through grades to sr. chief petty officer, 1972, resigned, 1977; treas., contr. Fla. Bonded Pools, Inc., Jacksonville, 1977-89; pvt. practice Jacksonville Beach, Fla., 1982-89; pres. Profl. Computer Support Inc., Jacksonville Beach, 1988-90, Forrest & Co., Inc., Jacksonville, Fla., 1989—. Treas. Beaches United Citizens, Jacksonville Beach, 1982. Recipient Carl Burger Meml. Manuscript Nat. Assn. Accts., 1982-83. Mem. Fla. Assn. Ind. Accts., Fleet Res. Assn., Beaches Bus. Assn., Phi Kappa Phi, Beta Gamma Sigma. Home: 259 Coral Way Jaxville Bch FL 32250-2911 Office: Forrest & Co Inc 1500 Roberts Dr Jacksonville Beach FL 32250-3222

FORRESTER, EUGENE PRIEST, former army officer, management marketing consultant; b. Watertown, Tenn., Apr. 17, 1926; s. Robert L. and Christine Elizabeth (Phillips) F.; B.S., U.S. Mil. Acad., 1948; M.A. in Internat. Relations, George Washington U., 1967; LL.D., Chung Ang U. (Republic of Korea), 1981; grad. Command and Gen. Staff Coll., Armed Forces Staff Coll., Brit. Staff Coll., Nat. War Coll.; m. Mary Louise Wagner, Dec. 28, 1953 (dec. 1971); children—Eugene Priest, II, Pamela Louise, Elizabeth Wagner. Commd. 2d lt. U.S. Army, 1948, advanced through grades to lt. gen., 1978; with Command and Gen. Staff Coll., Ft. Leavenworth, Kans., 1958-59; staff officer Supreme Hdqrs. Allied Powers Europe, 1961-63; dep. battle group comdr. 504th Inf., 82d Airborne Div., later asst. chief of staff for ops. 82d Airborne Div., Ft. Bragg, N.C., 1963-65; mil. asst. to Sec. Army, Washington, 1966; chief forces devel. U.S. Army, Vietnam, 1967-68, comdr. 3d Brigade, 4th Inf. Div., 1968; exec. officer to vice chief of staff Dept. Army, Washington, 1968-70; asst. div. comdr. 1st Cav. Div., Vietnam, 1970; dep. asst. chief of staff Civil Ops. and Rural Devel. Support, Hdqrs. Mil. Assistance Command, Vietnam, 1970-71; dir. officer personnel, later dir. procurement, tng. and distbn., then dir. plans, program and budget, Hdqrs. Dept. Army, 1971-73; comdr. U.S. Army Adminstrn. Center, Ft. Ben Harrison, Ind., 1973-75; comdr. U.S. Army Recruiting Command, Ft. Sheridan, Ill., 1975-78; comdr. 6th U.S. Army, Presidio, San Francisco, 1978-79; comdr. Combined Field Army, Korea, 1979-81; comdr. U.S. Army Western Command, Ft. Shafter, Hawaii, 1981-83; ret., 1983; mgmt. mktg. cons., corp. dir., 1983—. Trustee Nat. Def. U. Found., 1986—. Decorated D.S.M. with oak leaf cluster, Silver Star, Legion of Merit with 3 oak leaf clusters, D.F.C., Bronze Star with 2 oak leaf clusters, Air medal with 18 oak leaf clusters, Joint Service Commendation medal, Combat Inf. badge (2), Nat. Order Vietnam 4th-5th class, Gallantry Cross with 2 palms and gold star (Vietnam), Armed Forces Honor medal 1st class (Vietnam), Order of Nat. Sec. Merit Tong-Il medal (Korea), numerous others. Clubs: Army-Navy, Bohemian. Address: 1101 S Arlington Ridge Rd # 902 Arlington VA 22202-1951

FORRESTER, KEN, retired military officer; b. Hamilton, Ont., Can., Apr. 21, 1941; came to U.S., 1955; s. William H. and Lucille (Hayes) F.; m. Pamela Campbell, Mar. 19, 1976; children: Allyson, Christi, Stephen, Pamela. AS, Miami-Dade Jr. Coll., 1966; BS, U. of N.Y., 1987; MS, Troy State U., 1990. Lic. funeral dir., Fla. Commd. 2d lt. Fla. Nat. Guard, St. Augustine, 1967, advanced through grades to lt. col., 1986; tng. officer 146h signal batt. Fla. Nat. Guard, Jacksonville; fiscal acctg. supr. Fla. Nat. Guard, budget analyst, supervisory auditor, pub. affairs officer, 1986-94, ret., 1994; fin. and acctg. dir. Dept. Mil. Affairs, 1994—; mem. St. Augustine Airport Authority, 1982-94. Mem. St. Johns County Water and Sewer Authority; lay reader, mem. Trinity Episcopal Ch. Named Outstanding Young Man St. Augustine Jaycees, 1976. Mem. St. Johns C. of C., Assn. of the U.S. Army, Fla. Nat. Guard Officer's Assn., Kiwanis, Elks 129, Elks Club, ARC, Am. Cancer Soc., Am. Legion. Home: 604 Teeside Ct Saint Augustine FL 32085-1008

FORSTNER, JAMES ROBERT, family practice physician; b. L.A., Jan. 9, 1947; s. James Lee Jr. and Emily Erin (Lipford) F.; m. Elizabeth Burks, Oct. 20, 1973 (div. 1987); children: James Dean, William Robert. AB, Princeton U., 1969; MD, U. N.C., 1973. Diplomate Nat. Bd. Med. Examiners, Am. Bd. Family Practice. Intern U. So. Calif. Med. Ctr., 1973-74. Chmn. bd. edn., Brunswick County, N.C., 1982-86. Office: 250 E 11th St Southport NC 28461

FORSYTH, GEORGE LIONEL, psychotherapist, author; b. Bridgetown, N.S., Can., July 14, 1934; came to U.S., 1969, naturalized, 1978, dual citizen Can./U.S.; s. Frederick Chesley and Mildred Estella (MacNeill) F.; m. Carolyn Gail Rood, Aug. 20, 1955 (div. June 1982); children: George Eric, Gail Lori Forsyth Smith, Helen-Ray Norton, Oct. 2, 1983; step-children: Pamela Darie Norton White, Helen Jeanne Norton Berry. BS, Thomas A. Edison Coll., Palm Beach, Fla., 1969, MS in Psychology, 1970, PhD in Psychotherapy, 1972, DD, 1975; BD, Universal Brotherhood, Atlanta, 1993. Lic. psychotherapist, hypnotherapy, psychology, biofeedback, instr.-tchr.; ordained priest Order of St. John of Jerusalem, 1975; ordained min. Universal Brotherhood Movement, Inc., 1994. With Maritime Telegraph & Telephone Co. Ltd., 1952-56, 58-68; with spl. projects dept. Bell Can., 1956-58; master electrician Glen Dorman Electric; part owner Evangeline Enterprises; with spl. projects dept. Bell Telephone Co. Can., Montreal, Que., Can., 1956-58; with So. Bell Telephone Co., Ft. Lauderdale, 1970-84; owner Marvo Talent Agys.; pvt. practice hypnotherapy Ft. Lauderdale, Fla., 1972-76; tchr. hypnosis Broward County Schs., 1972-84; mem. Lauderdale Psychiat. Group, Ft. Lauderdale, 1975-85; rsch. assoc. World Rsch. Ctr. for Hypnosis Studies, Inc., Miami, Fla., 1975-76; adminstrv. v.p. Internat. Coll. Hypnosis Studies, Inc., Miami Beach, 1975-78; prof. Broward C.C., Ft. Lauderdale, 1972-80, Miami-Dade C.C., North Miami Campus, 1972-80; adult edn. instr. Broward County Cmty. Schs., 1972-85; owner Video Memories; charter mem., co-founder, treas., stand in preacher, instr., psychic healer Inner Light Metaphys. Ctr., Ft. Lauderdale, 1977-80; instr., prof. Nova-Davie Cmty. Sch., Piper Cmty. Sch., Pembroke Pines Cmty. Sch., Broward C.C., Miami Dade C.C., Applied Hypnosis Inst.; cons. Ocean Med. Hypnotherapy and Biofeedback Ctr. Inc., 1974-84. Author: How to Enjoy Eating the North Atlantic Lobster, 1994, All About Lobsters and Dulse, 1995; stage mgr., actor, singer, hypnotist, magician's asst., lighting and sound engr. various stage shows over the years; inventor in field including spl. hypnosis induction light, 1975. TV antenna inspector Town of Wolfville, N.S., 1954-56; dir. civil defence Town of Kentville, N.S., 1960-65; choir mem., soloist, mem. bd. stewards United Ch. of Can., Berwick, N.S., 1950—; chmn. N.S. Folk Arts Coun., 1967. Recipient various awards and plaques for pub. orgns. for hypnosis, N.S. and Ft. Lauderdale, Fla., 1969-80's. Mem. Hypnosis Soc. N.S. (hon. life), Clan Forsyth Soc. (life), Telephone Pioneers Am. (life), Fla. State Assn. Spiritualist Ministers Inc., Internat. Brotherhood Elec. Workers (hon. life), Comm. Workers Am. (hon. life), Comm. Workers Am. Retiree's Club, Can. Inst. Hypnotism, Nat. Guild Hypnotherapists, N.S. Hypnotists Soc. (hon.), Masons (32 degree). Home: Sunshine Ranches 14420 Stirling Rd Fort Lauderdale FL 33330

FORT, ARTHUR TOMLINSON, III, physician, educator; b. Lumpkin, Ga., Sept. 24, 1931; s. Thomas Morton and Gladys (Davis) F.; m. Jane Wilmer McClelland, June 15, 1957; children: Abby Lucinda, Arthur Tomlinson, Jr., Juliana Melody, Ernest Arlington, II. B.B.A., U. Ga., 1952; M.D., U. Tenn., 1962. Diplomate: Am. Bd. Ob-Gyn, Am. Bd. Family Practice. Intern, then resident in ob-gyn U. Tenn.-City of Memphis Hosp., 1962-66; asst. prof. U. Tenn. Med. Sch., 1966-70; prof. ob-gyn, head dept. Sch. Medicine La. State U., Shreveport, 1970-73; prof. maternal-child health and family planning, head program family health Sch. Pub. Health Tulane U., 1973-74; practice medicine specializing in rural family medicine Vacharie, La., 1974-79; prof. ob-gyn and family medicine, head dept. family medicine and comprehensive care Sch. Medicine La. State U., Shreveport, 1980—. Author articles in field. Adv. bd. mem. State of La. Dept. Health and Human Resources, 1986-88. With USAF, 1952-57. Recipient Golden Apple Teaching award Student AMA, 1969, Golden Apple Teaching award Western Interstate Commn. on Higher Edn., 1973. Fellow Am. Coll. Ob-Gyn, Am. Acad. Family Practice; mem. AMA. Office: PO Box 33932 Shreveport LA 71130-3932

FORT, BRENDA LOUISE, critical care nurse; b. Detroit, Aug. 19, 1955; d. William Talmadge and Hattie Belle (Walton) Walker; m. John Allen Fort, Jan. 29, 1983; children: Christopher Jeremy, Daniel Nicholas, Bethany Lynne. BA, U. Mich., 1977; BSN, Ga. State U., 1987. RN. Staff nurse VA Med. Ctr., Decatur, Ga., 1987-95, critical care nurse, 1995—. Disaster health nurse ARC, Atlanta, 1994—, health fair coord., 1994, CPR instr., 1993—. Mem. ANA, AACN (cert.), Sigma Theta Tau, Phi Kappa Phi. Home: 3453 Wren Rd Decatur GA 30032 Office: VA Med Ctr 1670 Clairmont Rd Decatur GA 30033

FORT, CLAIRE CAUDILL, business development executive; b. Birmingham, Ala., Aug. 19, 1943; d. Joe Sanford and Elizabeth Hendon (Martin) Caudill; m. Lewis Heyward Fort (div. May 1981); 1 child, Michelle Fort Willm. Student, Fla. State U., 1964-67, U. S.C., 1983-84; grad., U. of South. Mgr. divsn. security dept. Pan Am. World Airways, Patrick AFB, Fla., 1961-64; adminstrv. asst. II Ednl. TV Commn., State of Fla., Tallahassee, 1964-67; employment counselor Snelling & Snelling Pers., Sumter, S.C., 1967-68; legal sec. McNair Law Firm, P.A., Columbia, S.C., 1971-73, office mgr., 1973-84, exec. asst. client rels., 1984-93, mgr. client devel., 1994-95, dir. bus. devel., 1995—; coordinating dir. Columbia Econs. Club, 1995—. Mem. agy. rels./rev. panel United Way of Midlands, Columbia, S.C.; mem. steering com. Corp. Vol. Coun. of United Way; bd. dirs., mem. exec. com. Cultural Coun. of Richland and Lexington Counties, 1996—; chair Cultural Devel. Fund, 1997; vice chair bd., dir. funding/resources divsn. of bd. dirs.

S.C. chpt. Nat. Ctr. Missing & Exploited Children, Columbia; mem. S.C. affiliate Am. Diabetes Assn., bd. dirs., 1994—; chaplain crisis intervention Lexington County (S.C.) Sheriff's Dept.; charter mem./organizer New Life Ctr., Lexington; mem. diocesan Christian edn. task force Episcopal Diocese of Upper S.C., 1978-81, lay rector, pres. Cursillos in Christianity, 1982-86, mem. diocesan evangelism program task force, 1988—; youth dir./Sunday sch. coord. St. Alban's Episcopal Ch., Lexington, S.C., 1976-82, lay rector Discovery Weekend, 1982, originator/co-leader Cathechumanate Process, 1983-85, mem. vestry, 1975-78, 80-83, 85-88, 90-93, clk., 1975-78, 80-81, sr. warden, 1982-83, leader adult Sunday sch. 3 yrs., leader adult Bible study/prayer group 3 yrs. Mem. Nat. Law Firm Mktg. Assn., Greater Columbia C. of C. (bd. dirs. Com. of 100, 1993-96, unified mktg. task force, ann. meeting task force, Vol. of Month for May 1993). Democrat. Office: McNair Law Firm PA 1301 Gervais St Columbia SC 29201-3326

FORTE, STEPHEN FORREST, interior designer; b. Shreveport, La., Oct. 18, 1947; s. Forrest Lee and Alva (Clary) F. BA, Centenary Coll., Shreveport, 1971; postgrad., La. Tech U., 1971, Parsons Sch. Design, Paris, 1981. Lic. interior designer, La., Fla. Interior designer Interiors, Inc., Shreveport, 1974-75, Yarbrough Interior Designers, Shreveport, 1975-85; pres. Stephen Forte Interior Design, Shreveport, 1985—. Prin. works include: Strand Theatre Restoration, Shreveport, 1981-85, One Tex. Ctr., Shreveport, 1986, Southdown Retirement Ctr., Baton Rouge, 1988, Goodrich Oil Co., 1990, Caddo Parish Commn. Offices, 1993, Champion Lake Complex, Shreveport, La., 1995-96; featured in The Designer, Designers West and So. Living mag. articles. Mem. Internat. Interior Design Assn. Democrat. Roman Catholic. Office: 6505 Line Ave # 48 Shreveport LA 71106

FORTENBERRY, CAROL LOMAX, real estate appraiser; b. Charlotte, N.C., Apr. 23, 1959; d. Henry Clyde and Anne Tristram (Holt) Lomax; m. Mark Kevin Fortenberry, July 14, 1984; children: Liza Holt, Joseph Tristram. BA in radio, TV, motion pictures, U. N.C., Chapel Hill, 1981; MBA, Queens Coll., Charlotte, 1988. Lic. real estate salesman, N.C.; cert. gen. real estate appraiser, N.C.; MAI. Various positions Jefferson Pilot Communications Co., Charlotte, 1981-85; asst. show mgr. So. Shows, Inc., Charlotte, 1985-87; bus. mgr. Mark Fortenberry Photography, Charlotte, 1987-88; comml. real estate appraiser Stout-Beck & Assocs., Charlotte, 1988-94, Fitzhugh L. Stout & Assoc., Charlotte, 1994—. Mem. outreach com. St. John's Episc. Ch., Charlotte, 1990. Mem. Appraisal Inst., Comml. Real Estate Women, U. N.C. Alumni Assn., Nat. Bone Marrow Registry, Cool Hand Investing and Conversing Soc. Home: 128 Wonderwood Dr Charlotte NC 28211-4010 Office: Fitzhugh L Stout & Assoc 505 East Blvd Charlotte NC 28203-5109

FORTENBERRY, ELIZABETH WALLER, private school educator; b. Chattanooga, Tenn., Jan. 2, 1947; d. Henry Albert and Alice Rushing Waller; m. John Kent Fortenberry, Aug. 18, 1973; 1 child, Kevin Douglas. BS, U. Tenn., Chattanooga, 1969; M in Bus. Edn., Mid. Tenn. State U., 1985. Cert. tchr. secondary edn., Tenn.; cert. profl. sec. Head edn.-bus. dept. Lookout Valley H.S., Chattanooga, 1971-74; adminstrv. asst. Associated Water and Air Resource Engrs., Nashville, 1974-78; dir. placement Branell Tech. Ctr., Nashville, 1984-85; exec. dir. Elizabeth Fortenberry Sch. of Bus., Nashville, 1986-90; bus. cons. Tng. for Tomorrow, Inc., Brentwood, Tenn., 1989-92; coord. summer youth program S.E. Tenn. Pvt. Industry Coun., Chattanooga, 1995; coord. edn. Challenge Acad., Chattanooga, 1995—; mem. adv. bd. secretarial sci. Nashville State Tech. Inst., 1983-85; workshop leader Tenn. Divsn. AAUW, Clarksville, 1990, Tenn. Vocat. Edn. Conf., Murfreesboro, 1991. Author: (training manuals) Shifting Gears and Changing Lanes, Part I: Reframing Today's Classroom, Part 2: Career Management and Job Transition Skills, 1994. Mem. edn. com. Chattanooga Mfrs. Assn., 1996. Mem. Delta Pi Epsilon. Home: 7106 Saratoga Ln Chattanooga TN 37421

FORTENBERRY, JACK CLIFTON (CLIFF FORTENBERRY), mass communications educator; b. Laurel, Miss., Jan. 6, 1955; s. Claude Henry and Margaret Ann (Jordan) F.; m. Melanie Caroline Leigh, Oct. 29, 1983; children: Elizabeth, Ryan. Student, Jones County Jr. Coll., Ellisville, Miss., 1973-74; BS, Miss. Coll., Clinton, 1975, MS, 1976; PhD, U. So. Miss., Hattiesburg, 1991. Salesman Surplus City, Jackson, Miss., 1977; instr. U. So. Miss., Hattiesburg, 1977-78; minister music Pattison (Miss.) Bapt. Ch., 1978-79; dir. media svcs. St. Dominic/Jackson Meml. Hosp., 1979-82; instr. gen. studies Southeastern La. U., Hammond, 1982-83; minister music Westside Bapt. Ch., Ponchatoula, La., 1983-85, Bowie St. Bapt. Ch., Hattiesburg, 1979-83; instr. communications Southeastern La. U., Hammond, 1983-85, media cons., 1983-85; asst. prof. mass communications Miss. Coll., Clinton, 1985—; pres. faculty coun. Miss. Coll., 1994—. Contbr. articles to profl. jours. Minister music Twin Lakes Bapt. Ch., 1991. Mem. Speech Communication Assn., Miss. Speech Communication Assn. (v.p. elect 1991-92, pres. 1992-93). Baptist. Home: 555 Linda Dr Clinton MS 39056 Office: Miss Coll PO Box 4207 Clinton MS 39058

FORTIER, ROBERT ELVE, healthcare company executive; b. Milford, Mass., June 23, 1948; s. Robert and Edith (Letourneau) F.; m. Barbara Y. Szlerjko, June 5, 1960 (div. May 1975); m. Frances Anne Byron, Sept. 4, 1984; children: Jenipher Michelle, Robert Francis. BA in Polit. Sci. and Econs., Coll. of Holy Cross, 1970; MBA, St. Louis U., 1972. CLU. Police officer St. Louis County Police Dept., 1970-73; sales rep. Travelers Ins. Co., Worcester, Mass., 1973-75, State Mutual Life Assurance Co., St. Louis, 1975-77; group mgr. Greatwest Life Assurance Co., Milw., 1977-80; regional mgr. Crown Life Ins. Co., Hartford, Conn., 1980-84; v.p. Am. Internat. Group, Wilmington, Del., 1984-88; v.p., chief mktg. officer Transport Ins. Co., Ft. Worth, 1988-89; pres., chief exec. officer Provider Networks Am., Ft. Worth, 1989-91; chmn., CEO Health Corp. Internat., Inc., 1991—; bd. dirs. Benefits Mgmt. Internat., Dubai, United Arab Emirates, Euro Health and Diagnostic Clinic, Dubai; cons. Ministry of Health, State of Oman, 1987, United Arab Emirates, 1987. Contbr. articles to profl. publs. Chmn. Victims of Violent Crimes, St. Louis, 1976; mem. Milw. Healthcare Coalition, 1980; bd. dirs. Milw. Employee Benefits Coun., 19779-80, Am. Bus. Coun., Dubai, 1987. Mem. Self Ins. Inst. Am., Am. Assn. Preferred Provider Orgns., Am. Soc. Assn. Execs., Profl. Ins. Mktg. Assn., Am. Soc. CLUs, Life Ins. Mktg. Inst., Group Health Assn. Republican. Roman Catholic. Home: 3304 Langley Hill Ln Colleyville TX 76034-4942 Office: Health Corp Internat Inc 701 Highlander Blvd Ste 450 Arlington TX 76015-4325

FORTMUELLER, HEINZ WILLIAM ERICH, quality assurance professional; b. N.Y.C., Aug. 26, 1933; s. Gustav August and Ida Marie (Jahns) F.; m. Monika Mareile Nissner, June 5, 1956 (div. Feb. 1989); children: Barbara Ann, Linda May, Aren Chris. AS, Jones Coll., 1977, BBA, 1982. Mgr. inspection and test NCR Corp. (formerly Scott Electronics Co.), Orlando, Fla., 1965-77; quality control engr. NCR Corp. (formerly Scott Electronics Co.), Lake Mary, Fla., 1977-84; sr. quality control engr. quality assurance Orlando divsn. Martin Marietta Esc., 1984-90; quality assurance mgr. RAF Technologies, Inc., Deland, Fla., 1990—; Chief Indian Guides, Orlando, 1968-72; leader Boy Scouts Am., Orlando, 1972-76. Cpl. U.S. Army, 1953-55, Europe. Republican. Lutheran. Home: 267 E Constance Rd Debary FL 32713-3505

FORTNER, BILLIE JEAN, small business owner; b. Tarrytown, Ga.; d. Willard and Sara (Beckworth) Burch; m. Randall Carroll; m. David Jones (div.); m. Robert F. Fortner, Jr., Sept. 20, 1981; children: Gina Sumner, Simone Dixon, Natalie Garner. AA summa cum laude, Brewton Parker Coll., 1970; BS, Ga. So. Coll., 1972, MEd, 1975, EdS, 1977. Math & sci. tchr. Toombs County Schs., Lyons, Ga., 1971-76, gifted tchr., 1976-81; gifted tchr. Montgomery County Schs., Mt. Vernon, Ga., 1985-88; ptnr. Rabbit's Quik Stop, Vidalia, Ga., 1985—, Rabbit's Cargo Inc., Vidalia, 1987—, Fortner Rentals, Vidalia, 1988—, Rabbit On the Strip, Vidalia, 1988—, Fortner Farms, Vidalia, 1989—; artist-in-residence, ptnr. F.C.F. Investments, Vidalia, 1992—; ptnr. Kipling B. Collins; artist-in-residence, Vidaliak, Ga. Troup leader Girl Scouts, Vidalia, 1972-76; block coord. Ga. Heart Assn., Vidalia, 1976. Mem. Phi Beta Kappa. Baptist. Home: 404 Slayton St Vidalia GA 30474-2546 Office: Rabbit's Quik Stop Hwy 292 W Vidalia GA 30474

FORWARD, RICHARD BLAIR, JR., marine biology educator; b. Washington, Jan. 13, 1943; s. Richard Blair and Ruth (Angwin) F.; m. Margaret Heumann, Aug. 8, 1969; children: Zoe A., Quincy V. BS, Stanford U., 1965; PhD, U. Calif., Santa Barbara, 1969. Rsch. asst. U. Calif., Santa Barbara, 1966-68, teaching asst., 1968-69; rsch. assoc. Yale U., New Haven, 1969-71; asst. prof. Duke U., Durham, N.C., 1971-77, assoc. prof., 1977-88, prof., 1988—, asst. dir. Marine Lab., 1991—. Contbr. articles to profl. jours. Mem. Am. Soc. Limnology and Oceanography, Am. Soc. Zoologists, Cruustacean Soc. Office: 135 Duke Marine Lab Rd Beaufort NC 28516

FOSBERG, BARRY L., research consultant; b. New Orleans, Mar. 18, 1953; s. Irving A. and Betty (Perlman) F.; m. Gloria Lynn Connelly, Jan. 5, 1986. BS in Internat. Security Affairs, U.S. Naval Acad., 1975; MPA, U. New Orleans, 1990. Cert. tng. cons. Adminstrv. asst. Downtown Devel. Dist., New Orleans, 1985-87; econ. devel. coord. planning and zoning St. Charles Parish, Hahnville, La., 1987-89; mgr. Met. Coll. Pub. Svc. Tng. Project U. New Orleans, 1989-92; salesman Remington Shavers and Knives, New Orleans, 1993-94; art sales Street Scene, New Orleans, 1994—; polit. policy cons. New Orleans, 1993—; tng. cons. Met. Coll. U. New Orleans; instr. computer skills Delgado U. La. Job Link Program, New Orleans, 1992-93; pub. policy cons. mayoral and concilman campaigns, New Orleans, 1994. Bd. mem. Touro Synagogue Brotherhood, New Orleans, 1986—, 1st v.p., 1992-94. Lt. USN, 1975-84. Grantee La. Randolph-Sheppard Programs, State La.Divsn. Rehab. Svcs., U. New Orleans, 1990-93. Mem. U.S. Naval Inst., Am. Soc. Pub. Adminstrn. Democrat. Jewish. Home: 1632 4th St Apt 3 New Orleans LA 70130-5949

FOSNAUGHT, PATRICIA S., art educator; b. Jersey City, Mar. 20, 1943; m. Robert A. Fosnaught, Nov. 26, 1964; 1 child, Nancy. BFA, U. Dayton, 1969; M. Art Edn., Wright State U., 1973. Art tchr. Dayton (Ohio) Pub. Schs., 1972-73; art tchr. Trotwood-Madison Schs., Trotwood, Ohio, 1973-78; instr. art Tenn. Tech. U., Cookeville, 1979-91; artist in residence Tenn. Tech. U./Tenn. Arts Commn., 1989-90; asst. curator edn. Tampa Mus. Art, 1992—. Photographs of art included in Soft Jewelry, 1977, (Nancy Howell-Koehler, author) Photo Art Processes, 1980; exhibited in many shows. Recipient Purchase award Tenn. Arts Com., Cookeville, 1981, Gov.'s award/arts State of Tenn., 1982; named Profl. Woman of Yr. Cookeville Bus. and Profl. Women, 1991. Mem. Nat. Art Edn. Assn., Fla. Art Edn. Assn., Fla. Assn. Mus., Arts Complete Edn. Coalition. Home: 1185 Shipwatch Cir Tampa FL 33602-5728

FOSS, JOHN HOUSTON, writer, consultant, educator; b. Cleveland, June 20, 1925; s. Clifford Paul and Isabella Har (Bull) F.; m. Jean Willard, Oct. 26, 1985. BS in Agriculture, Wash. State U., 1951; MA in Am. Lit., Duke U., 1953. Tech. writer Douglas Aircraft Co., El Segundo, Calif., 1954-56; cons., writer Palos Verdes Estates, Calif., 1956-79, Seattle, 1979-84; mgr. tng. programs Am. Radio Relay League, Newington, Conn., 1984-87; pvt. practice pubs. cons. N.Y.C., 1987—; adj. vis. instr. U. S.C., Beaufort, 1992-93; asst. prof. English Calif. Lut. Coll., Thousand Oaks, 1953-54; cons. Green River C. C., Auburn, Wash., 1981-83. Author: (coll. textbook) Horseshoeing Theory and Hoof Care, 1977; editor (coll. textbook) Anatomy and Physiology of Farm Animals, 1965; contbr. articles to profl. jours. Pres. Southland Juvenile Found., Inc. With U.S. Army, 1943-46. Mem. Am. Radio Relay League, Am. Horse Shows Assn., Am. Horse Protection Assn. (dir. 1991—), Authors Guild, Authors League Am., Phi Gamma Delta. Republican. Home and Office: 15 Pier Pointe New Bern NC 28562

FOSTER, ARTHUR KEY, JR., lawyer; b. Birmingham, Ala., Nov. 22, 1933; s. Arthur Key and Vonceil (Oden) F.; m. Jean Lyles Foster, Jan. 7, 1967; children: Arthur Key III, Brooke Oden. B.S.E., Princeton U., 1955; JD, U. Va., 1960. Bar: Ala. 1960. Ptnr. Balch & Bingham, Birmingham, 1965—. Trustee Episcopal Found. Jefferson County; bd. dirs. Met. YMCA, Downtown Club, Highlands Day Sch., Altamont Sch. Served to lt., USN, 1955-60. Mem. ABA, Ala. Bar Assn., B'ham Bar Assn., Estate Planning Council of Birmingham, Nat. Assn. Bond Lawyers, Newcomen Soc. of U.S. Republican. Episcopalian. Club: Kiwanis (bd. dirs.). Office: Balch & Bingham PO Box 306 Birmingham AL 35201-0306

FOSTER, BETTY JO, academic administrator; b. Danville, Va., Mar. 30, 1947; d. Archer Gardner and Frances (Brown) Whitlow; m. David W. Foster, Sept. 14, 1968; children: Brian, Tracey. BS, Radford U., 1969; MS, Va. Polytech U. & State U., 1979; EdD, Nova U., 1993. Prof. office sys. tech. Danville (Va.) C.C., 1971-90, dir. Ctr. for Bus., Industry, Govt., 1990-93, dean instrn., student devel., 1993—. Bd. Dirs. Danville Regional Med. Ctr. Mem. Va. Cmty. Coll. Assn., Pitt County and Danville City C. of C. (com. chair, Pittsylvania County Citizen of Yr. 1994), Riverview Rotary (bd. dirs.). Baptist. Office: Danville Cmty Coll 1008 S Main St Danville VA 24541

FOSTER, BILL See FOSTER, WILLIAM EDWIN

FOSTER, BILL C., newspaper publisher; b. Waco, Tex., Nov. 20, 1931; s. Willie Stephen and Vera (Chadwick) F.; m. Camelia Rentz, Oct. 3, 1953 (dec. May 1990); children: Cheryl, Jennifer Foster Martin; m. Ellen Campbell, May 14, 1993. Student, Baylor Coll., 1950s. Owner, pub. Waco Citizen, 1946-50, pub., 1950—; pub. Citizen Newspapers, Inc., Waco, 1960—, pres., 1994—; pub. The Moody (Tex.) Courier, 1988—; pres. Bill Foster & Assocs., Waco, 1995—; pres. Bill Foster & Assocs., Waco, 1970—. Author Brazos Trails column in Waco Citizen. Active Salvation Army; history com. chmn. 1st United Meth. Ch.; former dir. McLennan County Miss Tex. U.S.A. Pageant, Waco Calendar Girl Pageant; former dir. Tex. Press Assn. Recipient 50 Yr pin award Tex. Press Assn., 1993. Mem. Hotel/Motel Assn., Waco Bd. Realtors, Waco C. of C., Bellmead C. of C., Nat. Newspapers Assn., Tex. Cmty. Newspaper Pubs., Lions (dist. pub. rels. chmn.). Home: 3833 Huaco Ln Waco TX 76710-5073

FOSTER, BRAD WAYNE, publishing executive; b. San Antonio, Apr. 26, 1955; s. Byron and Yvonne (Kirst) F.; m. Cindy R. Guyton, Sep. 14, 1991. B in Environ. Design, Tex. A&M Univ., 1977. Owner Jabberwocky Graphix, Irving, Tex., 1981—. Author, artist (mag. series) Mechthings, 1987-88; artist (mag. series) Amazing Stories, 1982-91, (book) Monica the Computer Mouse, 1984; photographer: Cat in a Box, 1992. Recipient Hugo award SF Worldcon Inc., 1987-89, 92, 94, Chesley award Assn. Sci. Fiction Artists, 1989.

FOSTER, CHARLES CRAWFORD, lawyer, educator; b. Galveston, Tex., Aug. 1, 1941; s. Louie Brown and Helen (Hall) F.; m. Marta Brito, Sept. 7, 1967 (div. Apr. 1986); children: John, Ruth; m. Lily Chen, Jan. 7, 1989; children: Zachary, Anthony. AA, Del Mar Jr. Coll., 1961; BA, U. Tex., 1963, JD, 1967. Bar: Tex. 1967, N.Y. 1969. Assoc. Reid & Priest, N.Y.C., 1967-69, Butler & Binion, Houston, 1969-73; ptnr. Tindall & Foster, Houston, 1973—; hon. consul gen. Kingdom of Thailand, 1996—; adj. prof. immigration law U. Houston, 1985-89; vice chmn. World Trade Divsn. Greater Houston Partnership, 1996—; sec. Houston World Affairs Coun., 1990—; bd. dirs. Houston Forum, Inst. Internat. Edn., Houston Protocol Alliance, Brit. Am. Bus. Assn., DARE. Contbr. articles to profl. jours. Chmn. Immigration Reform Gov.'s Task Force on Tex., 1984-87; mem. exec. coun. Houston chpt. CARE Found., 1996—. Rotary Internat. fellow U. Concepción, Chile, 1964; recipient Houston Internat. Svc. award Houston Jaycees, 1996. Mem. ABA (chmn. immigration com. internat. law and practice sect. 1982-90, chmn. coordinating com. on immigration and law 1987-89), Am. Immigration Lawyers Assn. (pres. 1981-82, Outstanding Svc. award 1985), Tex. Bar Assn. (chmn. com. law on immigration and nationality 1984-86), Tex. Bd. Legal Specialization (chmn. immigration adv. commn. 1979—), Houston Bar Assn., Asia Soc. (trustee 1992—, chmn. Houston Ctr. 1992—), Rotary. Methodist. Home: 17 Courtlandt Pl Houston TX 77006-4013 Office: Tindall & Foster 2800 Tex Commerce Tower 600 Travis St Houston TX 77002

FOSTER, DALE WARREN, political scientist, educator, management consultant, real estate broker, accountant; b. Bryan, Tex., Mar. 7, 1950; s. William Henry and Maysie Blanche (Hembree) F. BBA, Tex. A&M U., 1972, MA, 1979, Cert. in Profl. Teaching, 1987; BS, U. Houston, 1981, MEd, 1983; AAS, Houston C.C. Sys., 1982. Cert. in property mgmt. Dept. mgr. J.C. Penney Co., Bryan, 1973-74; shopper advt. mgr. Harte-Hanks Newspapers/Daily Eagle, Bryan, 1975-76; bus. mgr., contr. S.M. Hardee Enterprises, College Station, Tex., 1976-78; ops. mgr. Western Food Svcs., Inc., Pasadena, Tex., 1978-80; internal auditor Hermann Hosp., Houston, 1980-82; high sch. tchr. Cypress-Fairbanks Independent Sch. Dist., Houston, 1983-84; alternative sch. tchr. Alief Independent Sch. Dist., Houston, 1984-88; gov. prof. Houston C.C. System, 1980—, chmn. govt. dept. co-op program, 1992—, lead instr., 1993—; supr. student tchr. U. Houston, 1989-90; adj. instr. North Harris County Coll., Houston, 1983-96; fin. cons. Pro-Trac Econ. Planning Adv. Bd., Denver, 1985-86; Presdl. Scholars lectr. Minority Students Honors Program, Houston, 1986-89; coord. legis. practicum Harris County Congl. Internship Program, 1988—; exch. tchr., The Netherlands, 1992. Co-editor textbook supplement, curriculum guide, departmental political reader; author classroom instructional project. Mem. adv. com. Hermann Affiliated Fed. Credit Union, Houston, 1980-82; mem. fin. coun. Harris County Dem. Com., 1991-93; mem. dean's coun. U. Houston, 1992-96; trustee, treas. Wilmington-Barnard Found., 1992-97. Named Tchr. of Yr., Cy.-Fair H.S., 1984, Individualized Study Ctr., 1987, Master Tchr. Nat. Leadership Inst. U. Tex., Austin, 1991, host tchr. Washington Week Intern Program, 1995; recipient Adj. Teaching and Comty. Svc. award North Harris County Coll. Dist., 1990, Teaching Excellence medal Nat. Inst. Staff and Orgn. Devel., 1991; Fulbright scholar, 1992; Acad. Polit. Sci. inductee, 1994; Robert A. Taft fellow L.B.J. Sch. Pub. Affairs, 1995. Fellow Am. Bd. Master Educators; mem. ASCD, Tex. Jr. Coll. Tchrs. Assn., Tex. Coun. Social Studies, Inst. Mgmt. Accts., Internaat. Platform Assn., Am. Fin. Assn., Fulbright Assn., Houston C.C. Sys. Faculty Assn. (Outstanding Tchr. award 1991), Phi Theta Kappa, Alpha Phi Omega, Kappa Delta Pi. Democrat. Baptist. Office: Houston C C NW 5514 Clara Rd Houston TX 77041-7204

FOSTER, DANIEL GEORGE, minister of music, organist, choirmaster; b. South Bend, Ind., Feb. 28, 1958; s. E. D. and Barbara Warlick (Yount) F. AA, Western Piedmont Coll., 1978; BS, U. N.C., 1980. Substitue organist Luth. Ch.-Mo. Synod, Newton and Conover, N.C., 1971-74; organist, choirmaster 1st Bapt. Ch., Claremont, N.C., 1974-78, Holy Cross Luth. Ch., Newton, 1979-85, 88—; dir. music. organist, choirmaster Concordia Evang. Luth. Ch-Mo. Synod, 1985-88. Mem. Luth. Laymen's League (asst. league svcs. chmn. N.C. and S.C. dist. 1982-84, sec. local chpt. 1985—). Republican. Home: 210 3rd St NE Conover NC 28613-2047 Office: Holy Cross Luth Ch-Mo Synod 612 S College Ave Newton NC 28658-3416

FOSTER, EUGENE LEWIS, engineering executive; b. Clinton, Mass., Oct. 9, 1922; s. George Frank and Georgie Nina (Lewis) F.; m. Mavis Estelle Howard, July 30, 1944; children—Kaye Louise, Eugene Howard, Mark Edward, Carol Anne. B.S.M.E., U. N.H., 1944, M.S., 1951; Mech. E., M.I.T., 1953, Sc.D., 1954. Research engr. Procter and Gamble, Cin., 1946-47; instr. U. N.H., 1947-49; asst. prof. mech. engring. M.I.T., Cambridge, 1950-56; pres., chmn. Foster-Miller Assocs., Inc., Waltham, Mass., 1956-72; cons. Office of Sec. of Transp., Washington, 1972-73; chmn. Foster-Miller Assocs., 1974—; pres. UTD, Inc., Alexandria, Va., 1976-93; pres. emeritus UTD, Inc., Alexandria, 1993—; mem. U.S. nat. com. for tunneling tech. Nat. Acad. Sci., 1975-79. Author: (with W.A. Wilson) Experimental Heat Power Engineering, 1956; also articles. Mem. Recreational and Environ. Com. Fairfax County, Va., 1976-78. Served with C.E. U.S. Army, 1943-46. Mem. ASME, ASCE, N.Y. Acad. Scis., AAAS, Nat. Soc. Profl. Engrs. Home: PO Box 267 Alton Bay NH 03810-0267 Office: UTD Inc 8560 Cinder Bed Rd Ste 1300 Newington VA 22122

FOSTER, GAYLA CATHERINE, musician; b. Oklahoma City, June 3, 1946; d. Jon B. and Betty Louise (Swidensky) Wagner; m. Bart Lewis Foster III, Mar. 9, 1974; children: Jason Scott (dec.), Jacob Bart, Joseph Matthew. MusB in Piano Performance, U. Okla., 1969, MusM in Piano Performance, 1971; postgrad., U. So. Calif., 1971-73; D of Musical Arts in Piano/Pedagogy, U. Okla., 1995. Cert. tchr. K-12, Okla. Grad. asst. in piano U. Okla., 1969-71, spl. instr. in piano, 1990, Okla. artist-in-residence, 1993—; instr. music theory and chorus C.E. Donart High Sch., Stillwater, 1974-78; pvt. practice Stillwater, 1974—; instr. music theory Okla. State U., 1979, adj. keyboard faculty, 1993-95; team instr. keyboard skills, U. Okla., 1991; workshop leader, Okla. and Tex., 1991-97; pianist Stillwater Chamber Singers, 1986-91, Okla. All-State Band, Oklahoma City, 1976, Thanksgiving Choral Festival Okla. State U., 1985, chorus mem. Pres. Masterworks Chorus, 1984, accompanist, 1985-89, accompanist for summer choir, 1982; adjudicator Okla. Fedn. Music Clubs, Okla. State U., Am. Coll. Musicians Piano Guild. Solo recitals include U. Okla., Norman, 1966-69, 71, 86, 89, 91, Okla. State U., Stillwater, 1971, 77, 84-85, 89, 91, 96, Cameron U., Lawton, 1988, Tulsa Performing Arts Ctr., 1988, 90, Graz, Austria, 1992, So. Meth. U., Dallas, 1993, U. Nebr., 1995; ensemble recitals include Okla. State U., 1988-96, Composers Symposium U. Okla., 1991, St. Cecilia Music Club, Stillwater, 1975, 80-85, 88, Okla. Fedn. Music Club State Conv., Ponca City, 1977, Arts & Scis. Grad. Banquet Program Okla. State U., 1979. Dir. music Highland Park United Meth. Ch., Stillwater, 1976—; pianist St. Cecilia Christmas Choir, Stillwater, 1981-88, Town & Gown Community Theatre Prodns., Stillwater; performance pianist Cushing-Chandler Community Chorus, 1985. Recipient Outstanding Svc. award United Meth. Women, Stillwater, 1990, 3rd prize Mid-Am. Chopin Festival, 1990; named one of Outstanding Young Women of Am., 1981, 97. Mem. Music Tchrs. Nat. Assn. (cert., Nat. Arts Advocacy com. 1996—), Okla. Music Tchrs. Assn. (cert. bd. 1990—, adjudicator), Stillwater Area Music Tchrs. Assn. (by-laws com. mem. 1984, exec. adv. bd. dirs. 1985-86, sec.-treas. 1986-89, v.p. 1993—), Friends Music for Okla. State U. (exec. bd. dirs. 1983, sec.-treas. 1984-88), St. Cecilia Music Club (Stillwater coord. for N.W. dist. jr. festival 1985—, exec. bd. dirs. 1986-89, pres. 1982-84, 1st v.p. 1980-82, Outstanding Achievement Svc. award 1986), Okla. Fedn. Music Clubs (state exec. bd. 1982-87, state chmn. Nell Keaton Cook scholarship 1984-87), Chamber Music Soc. Palos Verdes, Pi Kappa Lambda, Sigma Alpha Iota (treas. 1969-70, Sword of Honor 1969). Home: 3619 S Washington St Stillwater OK 74074-5909

FOSTER, JOHN DAVID, surfing instructor; b. Atikoken, Ontario, Can., May 1, 1935; came to U.S., 1981; s. Malcolm Burton and Carol Bertha (Royce) F. MD, McGill U., Montreal, Can., 1978. Emergency physician Wierton (W. Va.) Med. Ctr., 1981-83; surfing instr. John D. Foster P.A., Atlantic Beach, Fla., 1983—. Author: (books) Ras Tafari Makkonen in Medical Ethics: An Overview, 1982, Debt is Slavery, 1994. Libertrian. Office: John D Foster PA 36801 Atlantic Blvd Atlantic Beach FL 32233

FOSTER, JOHN ROBERT, communications educator, minister; b. Sapulpa, Okla., Apr. 30, 1948; s. John McDonald and Jane Ann (Barris) F.; m. Teresa Maye Morrow, Sept. 3, 1967; children: John A., Mary B., Emily A., James P. BA, Northwestern State Coll. La., 1970; M of Religious Edn., Tex. Christian U., 1972; postgrad., La. State U., 1993—. Ordained to ministry Christian Ch. (Disciples of Christ, 1972. Commd. 2d lt. U.S. Army, 1972, advanced through grades to lt. col., 1992; min. Marthaville (La.)/Bèlah United Meth., 1993—; instr. speech comm. Northwestern State U. La., Natchitoches, 1992—; club soccer coach Northwestern State U. La., 1993—; women's commr. Gulf S. Soccer Conf., Baton Rouge, 1994, 96, commr., 1996—. Parade chairperson Natchitoches Christmas Festival, 1993, 94. Mem. Speech Comm. Assn., So. States Comm. Assn., Religious Speech Comm. Assn., Am. Legion. Home: 514 Royal St Natchitoches LA 71457 Office: Northwestern State Univ La Dept Lang and Comm Natchitoches LA 71497

FOSTER, JOSEPH JAMES, III, creative writer; b. St. Louis, Oct. 26, 1942; s. Joseph H. and Theresa M. (Welch) F.; m. Karen M. Spies, Dec. 5, 1970 (div. July 1980); children: Michael J., Vickie A., DeAnna, Joseph W., Donna M.; m. Trudi L. Kitchner, Aug. 8, 1992. Student, beauty sch., St. Louis, 1968. Former draftsman, cook, carpenter. Co-author: How To Change Your Life for the Better, 1989, (manuscript) The Gamblers Blue Book, 1986, Back to the Future Again, Stories for Children of All Ages, 1987. With U.S. Army, 1959-61. Home: 8227 Riverboat Dr Tampa FL 33637-6579

FOSTER, KATHRYN WARNER, newspaper editor; b. Charleston, S.C., Sept. 16, 1950; d. Jack Huntington Warner and Theodora (Heinsohn) Miller; m. William Chapman Foster, Sept. 11, 1971; children: William Huntington, Jonathan Chapman. BA in English, Newberry Coll., 1972. Obituary writer, TV editor Greenville (S.C.) News-Piedmont, 1971-72, asst. lifestyle editor, 1972-73, feature editor, 1973-78; Living Today copy editor Miami (Fla.) Herald, 1978-83, asst. weekend editor, 1984-86, asst. travel editor, 1986-91,

96—, editor in home and design dept., 1992-93, editor Getaways midweek travel page, 1993-94, assoc. editor Health Beat, 1995-96; editor Miami Herald Dining Guide, 1988-91, asst. editor Destinations mag., 1990-91; speaker S.W. Fla. Writer's Conf., Ft. Myers, 1992. Contbr. articles to newspapers. Sec. Palmetto Elem. PTA, Miami, 1990-91. Recipient Penney-Mo. 1st pl. award for feature sects. U. Mo. Sch. Journalism, Columbia, 1978. Lutheran. Office: Miami Herald Travel Dept 1 Herald Plz Miami FL 33132-1609

FOSTER, MARTHA TYAHLA, educational administrator; b. Coaldale, Pa., Apr. 22, 1955; d. Stephen and Frances (Solomon) Tyahla; m. David Marion Foster, Jan. 3, 1981. BA with distinction, U. Va., 1977, MEd, 1981, EdS, 1981. Legis. asst. U.S. Ho. of Reps., Washington, 1977-79; asst. dean summer session U. Va., Charlottesville, 1981; program cons. campus activities U. Houston, 1981; coordinator student affairs Capitol Inst. Tech., Kensington, Md., 1982-83, asst. dean students, Laurel, Md., 1983-84, assoc. dean students, 1984-86, dean students, 1986-87; bd. dirs. Curry Sch. Edn. Found. U. Va., 1987-90. Mem. Arlington County Commn. on Status of Women, 1985-88; chmn. Christian edn. Christ Meth. Ch., 1994—; coun. mem.- at-large Arlington United Way, 1995—. Named Woman of Yr. Bus. and Profl. Women's Club, Vienna, Va., 1986. Methodist. Lodge: Order of Eastern Star (worthy matron 1988-89, trustee 1993-96).

FOSTER, MICHAEL PAUL, sales and marketing representative; b. Lubbock, Tex., Dec. 21, 1947; s. William Paul and Helen Warren (Chapman) F.; m. Sheryl Leigh Steffens, Feb. 16, 1974. BA, Baylor U., 1970; MBA, U. South Fla., 1986. Tech. specialist Sci. Product div. Am. Hosp. Supply Corp., Dallas, 1974-79; instrument salesman diagnostics div. Boehringer Mannheim Gmbh, Tampa, Fla., 1979-84; area sales mgr. Cooper/Technicon, Tampa, 1985-89; sales mgr. southeastern region Chemistry div. Coulter Electronics, Inc., Tampa, 1989—; nat. sales mgr. Serono Diagnostics, 1993—; med. mktg. cons. Ferraz and Foster, Tampa, 1986—. Mem. Radiology Soc. Am., Am. Assn. Clin. Chemistry. Republican. Methodist. Home: 2103 Isle Of Palms Dr Valrico FL 33594-7256

FOSTER, MIKE, food products executive; b. 1948. BS, U. Ill., MS. With Morman Mfg. Co., Inc., Quincy, Ill., 1971—; pres. Quincy Soybean Co. Ark., Helena, 1989—. Office: Quincy Soybean Co Ark Hwy 20 S Helena AR 72342

FOSTER, MURPHY J., JR. (MIKE FOSTER), governor; b. Shreveport, La.; married. BSCE, La. State U. Sugar cane farmer La.; founder Bayou Sale, La.; pres. Sterling Sugars, Inc.; senator St. Mary/Assumption Parish Dist. La. State Senate, 1987, chmn. commerce com., 1991; gov. State of La. Jr. warden St. Mary's Episcopal Ch.; pres. St. Mary Parish Farm Bur. With USAF, Korea. Mem. Am. Legion. Office: Office of the Governor PO Box 94004 Baton Rouge LA 70804

FOSTER, R. PAM, interior designer; b. Fleet, Hants, Eng., June 17, 1946; came to U.S., 1991; d. William Henry and Mabel (Selby) Melville; m. Ernest William Bracken, Feb. 4, 1991; children from a previous marriage: Paul Melville, Nina Kathleen. Student in Bus., Clark's Coll., Guildford, Surrey, Eng., 1964. From sec. to dir. sales Brit. Caledonian Airways, Gatwick, Eng., 1969-71, sr. mktg. exec., 1985-89; v.p. Transcontinental Svcs., London, 1973-81; owner, pres. Claremont Travel Ltd., Hurstpierpoint, Eng., 1981-85; mgr. interior design Brit. Airways, London, 1989-91; pres., owner House of Melville, Inc., Leesburg, Va., 1993—. designer interior for Airbus A320 Launch Aircraft for Brit. Airways. Local organizer Cystic Fibrosis Rsch. Trust, Sussex, Eng., 1974-84. Office: House of Melville RR 1 Box 361 Leesburg VA 22175-8811

FOSTER, RICHARD DONITHAN, journalist, freelance writr; b. Richmond, Va., Jan. 11, 1971; s. Roger Lee Foster and Sandra Kay (Sheffield) Boclair; m. Lisa Kayne Bricker, May 28, 1994. AA in Liberal Arts, J. Sargeant Reynolds C.C., Richmond, 1992; BS in Mass Comm., Va. Commonwealth U., 1994. Contbr. editor and writer Pure Immagination Pub., N.Y.C., 1992-93; staff writer, intern Richmond Times-Dispatch, 1992-94; news editor Commonwealth Times, Richmond, 1993; staff writer Reflections in Ink, Richmond, 1993, Roanoke (Va.) Times, 1994—. Acad. scholar FBI Nat. Acad. Alumni Assn., 1992, 93, journalism scholar Scripps-Howard Found., 1993. Mem. Soc. Profl. Journalists (Regional Mark of Excellence award 1994). Home: 3382-G Rasmont Rd SW Roanoke VA 24018 Office: The Roanoke Times PO Box 2491 Roanoke VA 24010

FOSTER, ROBERT LAWSON, retired judge, deacon; b. Putnam, Okla., Nov. 17, 1925; s. Mark M. and Jessie Marie (Gregory) F.; m. Mary Jo Hull, July 1, 1949 (dec.); children: Candace Ann (Mrs. Dan Sebert), Martha Denise (Mrs. Gerald Speed), Karen Sue Greenfield, Robert L., John Michael (dec.), Cynthia Kay. B.A., U. Okla., 1949, LL.B., 1950, J.D., 1970. Bar: Okla. 1950; ordained deacon Roman Cath. Ch., 1979. Pvt. practice Chandler, 1950-51; county judge Lincoln County, Okla., 1951-69; assoc. dist. judge 23d Jud. Dist., Chandler, Okla., 1969-87. Chmn. dist. council Boy Scouts Am., 1968-69; chmn., an organizer Chandler Combined Appeal, 1954—; sec., pres. Lincoln County Jr. League Baseball, 1960-68; county dir. Civil Def., 1953-70; mem. bd. Permanent Deacon Candidates for Okla., mem. deacon perceiver team, 1985—; adv. to registrants Selective Svc., 1953—. Served with USAF, 1944-45. Mem. Lincoln County Bar Assn. (pres. 1965, sec. 1960-64, 67-69, 70-73), C. of C. (sec. 1964-68), Okla. Assn. County Judges (sec.-treas. 1964-67), Okla. Jud. Conf. Club: Chandler Parents. Lodge: Lion (dir. 1964-65, pres. 1967, treas. 1968-70, zone chmn. 1973-74, dep. dist. gov. 1974—).

FOSTER, VIRGINIA, retired botany educator; b. Joseph, Oreg., Feb. 4, 1914; d. Perry Alexander and Genevieve (Shain) F. BS, U. Wash., 1949, MS, 1950; PhD, Ohio State U., 1954. Prof. Judson Coll., Marion, Ala., 1956-58; prof. Miss. State Coll. for Women, Columbus, 1958-59, LaVerne (Calif.) Coll., 1959-60, Calif. Western U., San Diego, 1960-61, Pensacola (Fla.) Jr. Coll., 1962-84. Author: (lab. manual) The Botany Laboratory, 1976, rev. edit., 1985, 3d edit., 1991. Home: 9270 Scenic Hwy Pensacola FL 32514-8054

FOSTER, WILLIAM EDWIN (BILL FOSTER), nonprofessional basketball coach; b. Ridley Park, Pa., Aug. 19, 1930; s. Howard M. and Viola Jane (Beaston) F.; m. Shirley Ann Junkin, June 17, 1957; children: Vicki R., Debra Jo, Julia Ann, Mary K. BS, Elizabethtown Coll., 1954; MEd, Temple U., 1957. Coach, tchr. Chichester (Pa.) High Sch., 1954-57, Abington (Pa.) High Sch., 1957-60; coach, instr. Bloomsburg (Pa.) State Coll., 1960-63; head basketball coach Rutgers U., New Brunswick, N.J., 1963-71, U. Utah, Salt Lake City, 1971-74; head basketball coach, asst. athletic dir. Duke U., Durham, N.C., 1974-80, U. S.C., Columbia, 1980-86; head basketball coach, interim athletic dir. Northwestern U., Evanston, Ill., 1986-93, athletic dir., 1993; assoc. commr. S.W. Conf., Dallas, 1993-96; pres. BF Sports Ltd., Carrollton, Tex., 1996—; chmn. of the bd. Naismith Meml. Basketball Hall of Fame; pres. Nat. Sports Video Seminars; cons. to commr. of Big 12 for Basketball. Served with USAF, 1951-52. Named Nat. Coach of Yr., Sporting News Playboy Mag., 1978, S.C. Coach of Yr., 1981; named to Elizabethtown Coll. Sports Hall of Fame, Pa., Pa. Sports Hall of Fame, Rutgers Basketball Hall of Fame, Delaware County (Pa.) Hall of Fame. Mem. Nat. Assn. Basketball Coaches (past pres., co-coach of yr. 1978), Nat. Speakers Assn. Office: BF Sports Ltd 1039 Stemmons Fwy Ste 307 Carrollton TX 75006

FOSTER, WINFRED ASHLEY, JR., aerospace engineering educator; b. Greensboro, N.C., Jan. 30, 1945; s. Winfred Ashley and Pauline Crouse Foster; m. Doris Thelma Murphree, Aug. 28, 1966; children: Kimberly Ann, Elizabeth Carol. B of Aerospace Engring., Auburn U., 1967, MS of Aerospace Engring., 1969, PhD of Aerospace Engring., 1974. Registered profl. engr., Fla., Ala. Student trainee NASA George C. Marshall Space Flight Ctr., Huntsville, Ala., 1963, NASA/ASEE faculty rsch. fellow, summer 1977; grad. rsch. and teaching asst. dept. aerospace engring. Auburn (Ala.) U., 1967-69, instr. dept. aerospace engring., 1969-70, grad. teaching and rsch. asst. dept. aerospace engring., 1970-74, asst. prof. dept. aerospace engring., 1974-78, 79-83, assoc. prof. dept. aerospace engring., 1983-96; prof. dept. aerospace engring., 1996—; sr. design engr. Pratt & Whitney Aircraft Co., West Palm Beach, Fla., 1978-79; cons. Sci. Analysis, Inc., Montgomery, Ala., Eaglemark, Inc., Auburn, Ala., Hardin, Taber and Tucker, Attys. at Law, Birmingham, Ala., Mitternight Boiler Works, Inc., Satsuma, Ala., Ala. Cast Iron and Pipe Co., Birmingham, Hayes Internat. Corp., Dothan, Ala., Pratt & Whitney Aircraft Co., West Palm Beach, Fla., REMTECH, Inc., Huntsville, Ala.; presenter in field. Patentee aerial seeder and method; contbr. articles to profl. jours. Recipient Award for aircraft row-seeder Indsl. Rsch. Mag., 1973. Mem. AIAA, Sigma Xi, Sigma Gamma Tau, Phi Kappa Phi. Republican. United Methodist. Home: 903 Cherokee Rd Auburn AL 36830-2724 Office: Auburn U Dept Aerospace Engring 211 Aerospace Engring Bldg Auburn AL 36849

FOTHERGILL, JOHN WESLEY, JR., systems engineer, design company executive; b. San Francisco, June 24, 1928; s. John Wesley and Madeline Mary (Frates) F.; m. Nancy F. Bacon, 1990; children from previous marriage: Nancy Gay, Wesley Daykin, Michael James, Karen Renee. BS, Calif. State U., Sacramento, 1955, postgrad., 1956-59; postgrad., Utah State U., 1960-63, SUNY, 1964-67; D of Environ. Engring. (hon.), World U., 1985. Mem. staff theoretical div. U. Calif. Radiation Lab., Livermore, 1955-56; mem. staff computer div. Aerojet Gen. Corp., Sacramento, Calif., 1957-59; computer div. Thiokol Chem. Corp., Brigham City, Utah, 1959-64; staff engr. Link group Gen. Precision Systems, Inc., Binghamton, N.Y., 1964-67; mgr. sci. dept., link Info. Sci. div. Gen. Precision Systems, Inc., Silver Spring, Md., 1967-69; gen. mgr. Washington div. Singer Info. Services Corp., Bethesda, Md., 1969-72; pres., chief scientist, chmn. bd. Integrated Systems, Inc., Brunswick, Md., 1972-86, Analytic Adv. Group, Inc., McLean, Va., 1980-86; project engr. firefighting tng. system Link Sim System div. CAE Corp., Silver Spring, Md., 1986-90, Contraves USA-SSI, Tampa, Fla., 1990-91; cons. engr. smoke control tech, firefighting tng. systems, facilities tech. and equipment, 1992—. Contbr. articles to profl. jours. Served with U.S. Army, 1945-46, with USAF Res., 1947-53, USNR, 1955-73. Mem. Smoke Control Assn., Nat. Fire Protection Assn., AAAS, N.Y. Acad. Scis., Naval Inst., ASHRAE. Home and Office: 203 W Laurel Ave Sterling VA 20164-3734

FOULKE, EDWIN GERHART, JR., lawyer; b. Perkasie, Pa., Oct. 30, 1952; s. Edwin G. and Mary Claire (Keller) F. BA, N.C. State U., 1974; JD, Loyola U., New Orleans, 1978; LLM, Georgetown U., 1993. Bar: S.C. 1979, U.S. Dist. Ct. S.C. 1979, U.S. Ct. Appeals (4th cir.) 1979, Ga. 1986, U.S. Ct. Appeals (11th cir.) 1986, D.C. 1989, U.S. Ct. Appeals (D.C. cir.) 1989, U.S. Supreme Ct. 1990. Assoc. Thompson, Mann & Hutson, Greenville, S.C., 1978-83, Rainey, Britton, Gibbes & Clarkson, Greenville, 1983-85; ptnr. Constangy, Brooks & Smith, Columbia, S.C., 1985-90; chmn. Occupational Safety and Health Rev. Commn., Washington, 1990-95; of counsel Jackson Lewis, Greenville, S.C., 1995—; instr. St. Mary's Dominican Coll., New Orleans, 1977-78. Field rep. Reagan/Bush Campaign, Columbia, 1980, S.C. state coord., 1984; sec., treas. Employment Labor Law Sect., Columbia, 1981-82. Mem. ABA, S.C. Bar Assn., Ga. Bar Assn., Greenville County Bar Assn. (chmn. pub. rels. com. 1984-85), Am. Inst. Parliamentarians, SAR, Rotary. Roman Catholic. Office: Jackson Lewis & Krupman 301 N Main St Ste 2100 Greenville SC 29601

FOUNTAIN, ANDRE FERCHAUD, academic program director; b. Oklahoma City, Nov. 12, 1951; s. J. E. and Neaumatta Abilene (Edwards) F.; m. Linda K. Young. BS in Nursing, U. Okla., 1978. RN, Okla; cert. master hyrdotherapist, Kniepp Inst., Germany, massage therapist. Exec. dir. New Life Programs, Oklahoma City, 1981-87; dir. Praxis Coll. Health, Arts and Scis., Oklahoma City, 1988—; speaker in field. Author: A Psychoprophylactic Workbook, 1981; co-author: Psychological Reports, 1977. Found. Caucus for Men in Nursing, Norman, 1976. Recipient 1st Pl. award Internat. Sci. Fair Balt., 1970. Mem. Internat. Childbirth Edn. Assn. (state coord. 1982-84), Am. Soc. Psychoprophylaxis in Obstetrics, Body Workers and Wellness Therapies Assn., Okla. Sports Massage Assn., Masons.

FOUNTAIN, ANNE OWEN, Spanish language educator; b. Buenos Aires, Aug. 30, 1946; d. George Earle and Margaret Frances (Richards) Owen; m. Alvin Marcus Fountain II, June 20, 1970; children: Catherine Anne, Elizabeth Moore. BA with honors in Spanish, Ind. U., 1966, MA, 1968; PhD, Columbia U., 1973, cert. in Latin Am. studies, 1973. Publs. asst. The Hispanic Soc. Am., N.Y.C., 1970-71; Spanish instr. Peace Coll., Raleigh, N.C., 1972-75, spl. studies coord., 1975-85, ind. study/honors coord., 1985-87, Alumnae Disting. prof. Spanish, 1988—; cons. Acad. Alliances, N.C. World Ctr., N.C. Global Lang. Camps Inc. Contbr.: Essays on Comedy and the Gracioso in Plays by Agustin Moreto, 1986; contbr. articles to profl. jours. Co-chair cultural exhibits Internat. Festival of Raleigh, 1990-91; vol. Meals on Wheels, Raleigh, 1985—; active Hillyer Meml. Christian Ch. Nat. def. fgn. lang. fellow Ind. U., Bloomington, 1966-67; faculty fellow Columbia U., N.Y.C., 1967-70. Mem. MLA, Am. Assn. Tchrs. Spanish and Portuguese (pres. N.C. chpt. 1984-86, Tchg. award 1994), Assn. Depts. Fgn. Langs., S.E. Coun. L.Am. Studies (exec. coun. 1990—, pres.-elect 1992-93, pres. 1993-94, chmn. 1995-96), So. Conf. on Lang. Tchg. (adv. bd., bd. dirs., vice chmn. 1993-95, chmn. 1995-96), Fgn. Lang. Assn. N.C. (hon. life, pres. 1987-89), Delta Kappa Gamma, Sigma Delta Mu (v.p. 1988-92, pres. 1992—). Home: 2620 Mayview Rd Raleigh NC 27607-6917 Office: Peace Coll 15 E Peace St Raleigh NC 27604-1194

FOUNTAIN, EDWIN BYRD, minister, educator, librarian, poet; b. Manassas, Ga., Mar. 11, 1930; s. David Theodore and Laura Bertha (Phillips) F. BFA, U. Ga., 1951; BRE, BTh, Lexington Bapt. Coll., 1980, MRE, 1981, DD (hon.), 1990; MLS, U. Ky., 1984, ABD in Edn., 1993; postgrad., U. Bibl. Studies, 1993—. Ordained to ministry Bapt. Ch., 1982. Pastor Riverview Bapt. Ch., Lexington, Ky., 1982-87; libr. asst. Lexington Bapt. Coll., 1980-81, tchr., libr., 1981-90; divisional chmn. libr. svcs. Tenn. Temple U., Chattanooga, 1990-91; librarian Statesboro (Ga.) Regional Libr., 1991-93. Compiler indexes for religious books: (by B.H. Carroll) An Interpretation of the English Bible, (by T.P. Simmons) A Systematick Study of Bible Doctrine, (with Jim Jeffries) A Student's Writers Guide; contbr. articles to profl. publs., poetry to anthologies. Mem. alumni bd. Armstrong State Coll., Savannah, Ga. U. Ky. fellow, 1990. Mem. ALA, SAG, SAR (local sec.), S.R., SCV, Christians Librs. Assn., Actors Equity Assn., Bulloch Co. Hist. Soc., Lexington Bapt. Coll. Alumni Assn. (pres. 1982-87, 89-90), Armstrong State Coll. Alumni Assn. (bd. dirs.) Beta Phi Mu. Home: 2365 Womack East Garfield GA 30425-9521

FOUNTAIN, JOANNA F., library consultant, business owner; b. Huauchinango, Puebla, Mexico, May 2, 1945; d. Thomas E. and Iona F.; m. Raymond L. Schroeder, 1985; 1 child, Stacey H. Chambers. BA, Syracuse U., 1966; MLS, U. Tex., 1970; PhD, Tex. Woman's U., 1982. Libr. Emerson Elem. Sch., Miami, Fla., 1967-69; libr., dir. Oak Springs Br. Oak Springs br. Austin (Tex.) Pub. Libr., 1970-72; bilingual rsch. libr., Edn. Svc. Ctr., Region 13, Austin, 1972-76, tng. specialist, 1976-78; editorial dir. Voluntad Pubs., Austin, 1978-79; assoc. dir. for collection devel. Tex. So. U. Libr., Houston, 1981-83; dir. libr. tech. svcs. Southwestern U., Georgetown, Tex., 1983-90; adj. faculty U. Tex., Austin, 1990—; owner, sole propr. Bibliotechnics, Georgetown, 1990—; tech. svcs. libr. Austin Ind. Sch. Dsit., 1995—. Author: Headings for Children's Materials, 1993, Hey, Miss! You Got A Book For Me?, 1978, 81, Subject Headings for School and Public Libraries, 1996; editor, compiler bibliography CARTEL, 1973-76, Guide to Title VII Bilingual Bicultural Education Programs, 1973-75. Mem., officer La Sertoma, Georgetown, 1983-88. Recipient Grad. fellowship Tex. Woman's U., 1979-81, Higher Edn. Act grant U. Tex. at Austin, 1969-70. Mem. ALA. Presbyterian. Home and Office: 603 Serenada Dr Georgetown TX 78628-1633

FOUNTAIN, LINDA KATHLEEN, health science association executive; b. Fowler, Kans., Apr. 30, 1954; d. Ralph Edward and Ruth Evelyn (Cornelson) Young; m. Andre Fountain. BS in Nursing, Cen. State U., Edmond, Okla., 1976. RN, Okla. Staff nurse med./surg. and coronary care unit Presbyn. Hosp., Oklahoma City, 1976-79; mgr. nursing Hillcrest Osteo. Hosp., Oklahoma City, 1979-80; staff nurse, mgr. Oklahoma U. Teaching Hosp., Oklahoma City, 1981-82; pres. New Life Programs, Oklahoma City, 1981-88, Nursing Entrepreneurs, Ltd., Oklahoma City, 1988—; mgr. Internat. Health Supply, Oklahoma City, 1988—; coord. lactation cons. program State of Okla., 1981—, new life car seat rental program at various hosps., 1983-92, also speaker Success Co., Oklahoma City, 1984—; owner Rainbows Overhead Graphic Media, Oklahoma City, 1984-91; speaker in field. Founder Praxis Coll., Oklahoma City, 1988. Named Mentor of Yr., Okla. Metroplex Childbirth Network, Oklahoma City, 1984. Mem. Am. Nurses Assn., Internat. Lactation Cons. Assn., Internat. Platform Assn., Bodyworkers and Wellness Therapies Assn. Office: Nursing Entrepreneurs Ltd PO Box 75393 Oklahoma City OK 73147-0393

FOURNIER, DONALD CHARLES, allergist, immunologist; b. Lewiston, Maine, Apr. 16, 1949; s. Charles A. and Doris L. (Lessard) F.; m. Linda Faye Dix, Feb. 10, 1977; children: Dana, Alyson, Ashley. AA, Blinn Coll., Brenham, Tex., 1966-68; BA, Trinity U., 1970; MD, U. Tex. Med. Br., Galveston, 1974. Diplomate Am. Bd. Allergy and Immunology, Am. Bd. Internal Medicine. Commd. med. officer USAF, 1970, advanced through grades to chief allergy immunology, 1983; intern Wilford Hall USAF Med. Ctr., 1974-75, resident, 1975-77, fellow, 1977-79; mem. staff Wilford Hall USAF Med. Ctr., Lackland AFB, 1979-80; chief internal medicine svc. USAF Med. Ctr., Scot AFB, Ill., 1981-83, chief allergy immunology, 1980-83; lt. col. USAFR, 1983—; allergist, immunologist Collom and Carney Clinic, Texarkann, Tex., 1983-85; pvt. practice Texarkana, Tex., 1985—; courtesy faculty St. Louis U., 1980-83; clin. asst. prof. allergy immunology La. State U., Shreveport, 1986—, assoc. dir. allergy tng. program; asst. clin. prof. Area Health Edn. Ctr., S.W., U. Ark. Med. Sci., 1987—; cons. in field. Contbr. articles to profl. jours. State bd. dirs. Am. Lung Assn., Little Rock, 1986-92; mem. AIDS adv. com. Tri State chpt. ARC, Texarkana, Tex., 1988—. Recipient Baylor award Assn. Mil. Allergists; decorated Air Force Commendation medal. Fellow ACP, Am. Acad. Allergy Asthma Immunology, Am. Coll. Chest Physicians, Am. Assn. Cert. Allergists, Am. Coll. Allergy Asthma Immunology; mem. AMA, Tex. Allergy & Immunology Soc. (bd. dirs. 1994-97, chair practice standards com. 1994-97). Home: RR 1 Box 111 B Hooks TX 75561-9801 Office: 2435 College Dr Ste 5 Texarkana TX 75501-2784

FOURNIER, JOSEPH ANDRE ALPHONSE, nurse, social worker, psychotherapist; b. Norwich, Conn., Jan. 11, 1942; s. Alphonse J. and Eva Marie (Duhaime) F.; children from previous marriage: Elizabeth A., Michael J., Michelle D.; m. Lorinda Bonnette, Dec. 29, 1990; 1 child, Eva M. AA, U. Md., 1977; BSN, Med. Coll. Ga., 1981; MSW, U. Ga., 1987. RN; cert. employee assistance profl.; cert. in marriage and family therapy; bd. cert. diplomate in clin. social work. Sr. staff nurse, psychiatry Med. Coll. Ga., Augusta, 1982-94; psychotherapist employee, faculty assistance program Med. Coll. Ga., 1988—; mgr. homeless vets. program VA Med. Ctr., Augusta, 1987-88; psychotherapist Family Counseling Ctr. of CSRA, 1992—. Founder Comfort House, Inc. Recipient 79th Point of Light award Pres. George Bush, 1990, Vol. Svc. award Augusta chpt. ARC, 1995. Fellow Am. Orthopsychiat. Assn.; mem. NASW (Social Worker of Yr. award Augusta unit 1993, Ga. chpt. 1994), Employee Assistance Profl. Assn., Sigma Theta Tau. Home: 214 Taft Dr Evans GA 30809-9650

FOURNIER, SERGE RAYMOND-JEAN, orchestra conductor; b. Mayet, France, Sept. 28, 1931; came to U.S., 1961, naturalized, 1969; s. Raymond and Genevieve (Brisset) F.; 1 child, Genevieve Elizabeth. Grad., Conservatoire Nat. Superieur de Musique, Paris, 1956; student, Berkshire Music Center, 1961-62, Friedelind Wagner's Master Class, Bayreuth, 1963; D.F.A. (hon.), U. Toledo, 1974. Lic. comml. pilot, flight instr. Flutist, Lamoureux Orch., France, 1958-60, condr., Compagnie Madeleine Renaud and Jean Louis Barrault, Theatre de France, 1960, asst. to Leonard Bernstein, condr., N.Y. Philharmonic Orch., 1962, 63, music dir., condr., Toledo Symphony Orch., 1964-79, guest appearances, Radio Diffusion and Television Francaise, Paris, 1963, Orch. Grand Casino de Vichy, 1957, 58, Berkshire Music Festival, 1961; guest condr. in, Europe, U.S., Mexico City, Japan and, Can., (Recipient Premiere Medaille de Solfege 1948, Premier Prix de Flute 1949, Premier Prix d'Histoire de la Musique 1951, Premier Prix d'Ensemble Instrumental 1952, Premier Prix de Direction d'Orchestre 1956, Deuxieme accessit de Contrepoint 1956, Koussevitzky Meml. Conducting prize 1961, decorated chevalier Ordre des Arts et Lettres (France)). Served in French Army, 1952-54. Named One of Ten Outstanding Young Men Toledo C. of C., 1965. Home: PO Box 3995 Largo FL 34645-0995

FOUSE, ANNA BETH, education educator; b. Austin, Tex., Jan. 11, 1947; d. Wilfred Davis and Doris Faye (Thomas) Chrisner; m. William Douglas Fouse; children: Douglas Lee, Alan Dale, Michael Wade, Robert Lynn. BS, U. Tex., Austin, 1967; MEd, Tex. Woman's U., 1973, PhD, 1976; various postgrad., Tex., 1980-81, 85-89. Cert. elem. tchr., spl. edn. tchr., Tex. 1st grade tchr. Austin Ind. Sch. Dist., 1967-68, Pasadena Ind. Sch. Dist., 1968-69; 3rd grade tchr. Harlingen (Tex.) Ind. Sch. Dist., 1969-70; homebound tchr. Irving (Tex.) Ind. Sch. Dist., 1970-71, tchr. emotionally disturbed, 1971-73; spl. edn. dir. Paris (Tex.) Ind. Sch. Dist., 1975-85, Region VII ESC, Kilgore, Tex., 1985-91; instr. U. Tex., Tyler, 1990-91, asst. prof., 1991—; consulting editor bd. Acad. Therapy Jour., Austin, 1988-89. Co-author: (tech. asst. manual) Assessment Manual for Appraisal Personnel, 1987, Guidelines for Speech Pathologists, 1987, Accreditation for Special Educators, 1988, A Primer About Attention Deficit Disorder, 1993. Chairperson Paris Regional Habilitation Ctr. Adv. Bd., 1980-85, High Priority Infant Transitional Svcs. Adv. Bd., Longview, Tex., 1989-90; profl. adv. bd. so. region Attention Deficit Disorders Assn., 1990—; mem. adv. bd. Lamar County Alcohol and Drug Ctr., Paris, 1984-86. Mem. Tex. Coun. for Exceptional Children (v.p., pres., pres.-elect, bd. dirs.), Tex. Coun. of Adminstrs. in Spl. Edn., Assn. for Children with Learning Disabilities, Tex. Ednl. Diagnosticians Assn., Internat. Coun. for Exceptional Children, Phi Delta Kappa (pres. chpt. 1324 1991-93). Home: 517 E Fairmont St Longview TX 75601-3804 Office: U Tex 3900 University Blvd Tyler TX 75799-0001

FOUTCH, MICHAEL JAMES, actor, dancer, period dance researcher, producer; b. Dallas, Dec. 18, 1951; s. G.E. and Mary Muriel (Stanphill) F. BFA in Theatre, So. Meth. U., 1973. Cert. tchr. theatre and speech. Tech. dir. Eastfield Theatre, Dallas, 1973-77; dancer San Antonio Ballet, 1982, Dallas Concert Ballet, 1982-83; gen. ptnr. Stanphill Energy Partnership, Dallas, 1990-91; exec. dir. The Dallas Gilbert and Sullivan Soc., 1991-92; lighting designer Dallas Repertory Theatre, 1975; dancer TV Project, Shreveport, La., 1981; tchr. various ballet cos., Tex., La., 1983—; hist. dance study Early Dance Inst., Balt., 1988. Appeared in play The Mousetrap, 1976, ballets Giselle, 1980, Les Sylphides, 1982, The Nutcracker, 1983, 84, 92, 93, 94, Cinderella, 1983, Swan Lake, 1983, Romeo and Juliet, 1984, dancer in operas Orfeo, 1986, Andrea Chenier, 1987, Iolanthe, 1989. Mem. S.W. Theatre Assn., Am. Assn. Comty. Theatre, Am. Indian Arts Coun., Am. Indian C. of C., Mensa, Intertel. Office: PO Box 17711 Dallas TX 75217-0711

FOUTS, JAMES FREMONT, mining company executive; b. Port Arthur, Tex., June 3, 1918; s. Horace Arthur and Willie E. (Edwards) F.; m. Elizabeth Hanna Browne, June 19, 1948; children: Elizabeth, Donovan, Alan, James. BChemE, Tex. A&M U., 1940. Div. supt. Baroid div. N.L. Industries, U.S. Rocky Mountain area and Can., 1948-60; pres. Riley-Utah Co., Salt Lake City, 1960-67, Fremont Corp., Monroe, La., 1967—, Auric Metals Corp., Salt Lake City, 1972—; bd. dirs. La Fonda Hotel, Santa Fe, N.Mex., High Plains Natural Gas Co., Canadian, Tex. Hon. asst. sec. of State of La. Served to lt. col. arty U.S. Army, 1942-46. Mem. Wyo. Geol. Assn. (v.p. 1958), Rocky Mountain Oil & Gas Assn. (bd. dirs. 1959), Res. Officers Assn. Wyo. (pres. 1948), Am. Assn. Petroleum Geologists, Internat. Geol. Assn., Mont. Geol. Assn., Ind. Petroleum Producers Assn. Republican. Episcopalian. Club: Univ. Lodge: Elks. Home: 4002 Bon Aire Dr Monroe LA 71203-3015 Office: Fremont Corp PO Box 7070 Monroe LA 71211-7070 also: Auric Metals Corp 2464 Wilson Ave Salt Lake City UT 74108

FOUTZ, TIMOTHY LEE, engineering educator; b. Ahoskie, N.C., Dec. 4, 1957; s. Billy L. and Zelma V. (Plaster) F.; m. Karen N. Thompson, Sept. 8, 1990; 1 child, James Copley. BS, N.C. State U., 1980, MS, 1983, PhD, 1988. Rsch. engr. USDA-Agrl. Rsch. Svc., Raleigh, N.C., 1982-85; asst. prof. U. Ga., Athens, 1988-94, assoc. prof., 1994—. Contbr. articles to profl. jours. Grantee Southeastern Poulty and Egg Assn., 1990. Mem. ASME, Am. Soc. Agrl. Engrs. (com. vice chair 1992), Am. Soc. Engring. Educators. Office: U Ga Driftmier Engring Ctr Athens GA 30602

FOWLER, ARDEN STEPHANIE, music educator; b. N.Y.C., May 24, 1930; d. Arthur Simon and Lenore Irene (Strouse) Bender; m. Milton

Fowler, Aug. 6, 1951; children: Stacey Alison, Crispin Laird. Student, Traphagen Sch., 1947-49; BA, Marymount Coll., Tarrytown, N.Y., 1976; MusM, U. So. Fla., 1978. Designer Rubeson's Sportswear, N.Y.C., 1949-51; free-lance designer Dobb's Ferry, N.Y., 1952-72; organist/choir dir. Children's Village, Dobb's Ferry, N.Y., 1972-74; music specialist Highland Nursery Sch., Chappaqua, N.Y., 1972-76; pvt. voice tchr., vocal coach, 1972—; music therapist Cedar Manor Nursing Home, Ossining, N.Y., 1974-76; founder, pres. Gloria Musicae Chamber Chorus, Sarasota, Fla., 1979-85, mng. dir., 1985-89; soloist various chs. and choruses, N.Y., Fla., 1953—; mem. faculty vocal music dept. St. Boniface Conservatory, Sarasota, 1979-81; music critic Sarasota Herald Tribune, 1986-91; lectr. music history Edn. Ctr., Longboat Key, Fla.; vol. music for early childhood Head Start. Freelance travel writer, 1985—. Mem. Dem. Exec. Com of Manatee County, Fla. Mem. Chorus Am., Assn. Profl. Vocal Ensembles, Friends of the Arts (hon.), Sigma Alpha Iota, Phi Kappa Phi. Episcopal. Home: 4244 Marina Ct Cortez FL 34215-2518

FOWLER, CHARLOTTE ANN, occupational health nurse; b. Shreveport, La., June 10, 1954; d. William James Jr. and Erin Kathleen (Taylor) F. Student, N.E. La. U., 1973-74, La. State U., Shreveport, 1977-78; ADN, Northwestern State U., Shreveport, 1982. RN, La. RN in oper. rm. Schumpert Med. Ctr., Shreveport, 1982-85; RN in oper. rm. La. State U. Med. Ctr., Shreveport, 1985-86, RN in recovery rm. and surg. ICU, 1986-87, RN in psychiatry, 1987-88, RN in recovery rm., 1988-89, RN in surg. ICU, 1989-90, RN clin. coord. dept. of surgery divsn. oral maxifacial surgery, 1990-93, nursing adminstrn. RN, house mgr., 1993—. Author: (with others) American Poetry Anthology, 1989. Dist. coord. La. Nurses' Network for Impaired Profls., 1987-90; bd. dirs., lay rep. Met. Cmty. Ch., Shreveport. Mem. ANA, Am. Assn. Occupl. Health Nurses, Critical Care Soc., La. State Nurses Assn., Shreveport Dist. Nurses Assn. Home: 625 Wilkinson Shreveport LA 71104 Office: La State U Med Ctr Occupl Health Clinic 1501 Kings Hwy PO Box 33932 Shreveport LA 71130-3932

FOWLER, DELBERT MARCOM, design and construction engineer; b. Ladonia, Tex., Sept. 14, 1924; s. Robert Delbert and Floy Ethel (Marcom) F.; B.S., U.S. Mil. Acad., 1945; M.S. in Civil Engring., Tex. A. and M. U., 1954; M.S. in Internat. Affairs, George Washington U., 1965; grad. Indsl. Coll. Armed Forces, 1965; m. Betty Alouise Reichey, Dec. 11, 1948; children: Kathryn Lewis (Mrs. David Irwin), John D. Marcom, Francine Floy. Commd. 2d lt. C.E., U.S. Army, 1945, advanced through grades to col., 1966; assigned Austria, 1945-48, Korea, 1950-52, W. Ger., 1958-61, policy and planning positions, Washington, 1961-67, 70-72, Vietnam, 1968-69, ret., 1972; project mgr. Urban Systems Devel. Corp., Arlington, Va., 1973; regional adminstr. Fed. Energy Adminstrn., Dallas, 1973-77; sr. assoc. Planergy Inc., Austin, 1978-79; pres. Blum Building Automation, Security, and Comm., Dallas, 1979-85; dir. design and constr., Dallas Ind. Sch. Dist., 1985-92; pres. FS Cons., 1985—. Mem. energy task force Goals for Dallas, 1976-77; mem. Austin Energy Conservation Commn., 1979. Decorated Legion of Merit, Bronze Star, Air medal. Fed. Exec. fellow Brookings Instn., 1971-72. Registered profl. engr., Tex.; cert. energy mgr. Mem. Nat., Tex., Dallas socs. profl. engrs., Am. Soc. Mil. Engrs., Soc. Energy Engrs., SAR, Internat. Platform Assn. Presbyterian. Author articles, papers. Home: 5708 Willow Ln Dallas TX 75230-2150 Office: FS Cons 5708 Willow Ln Dallas TX 75230-2150

FOWLER, HARRIET WHITTEMORE, art museum director; b. Geneva, N.Y., Apr. 6, 1946. B.A., Cornell U., 1977, Ph.D., 1981; student Smith Coll., 1964-67. Interim dir. U. Ky. Art Mus., Lexington, 1982, curator, 1981-90. Author (exhbn. catalogue) New Deal Art, WPA Works at the Univ. of Ky., 1985, Handbook of the Collection, 1991; (introduction) A Spectacular Vision-The George and Susan Proskauer Collection. Mem. Hist. Properties Adv. Commn. of Ky., 1985-88; state dir. Southeast Mus. Conf., 1992-95. Recipient Frances Sampson Fine Arts prize Cornell U., 1977. Mem. Ky. Assn. Mus. (pres. 1992-94), Phi Kappa Phi. Home: 1175 Bakers Ln Nicholasville KY 40356-8716 Office: U of Ky Art Mus Rose & Euclid Lexington KY 40506

FOWLER, LINDA MCKEEVER, hospital administrator, management educator; b. Greensburg, Pa., Aug. 7, 1948; d. Clay and Florence Elizabeth (Smith) McK.; m. Timothy L. Fowler, Sept. 13, 1969 (div. July 1985). Nursing diploma, Presbyn. U. Hosp., Pitts., 1969; BSN, U. Pitts., 1976, M in Nursing Adminstrn., 1980; D in Pub Adminstrn., Nova U., 1985. Supr., head nurse Presbyn. Univ. Hosp., Pitts., 1969-76; mem. faculty Western Pa. Hosp. Sch. Nursing, Pitts., 1976-79; acute care coord. Mercy Hosp., Miami, 1980-81; asst. adminstr. nursing North Shore Med. Ctr., Miami, 1981-84, v.p. patient care, 1984-88, Golden Glades Regional Med. Ctr., Miami, 1988-89, Humana Hosp.-South Broward, Hollywood, Fla., 1989-91, assoc. exec. dir. nursing; v.p./CNO Columbia Regional Med. Ctr. at Bayonet Point, 1991-96; COO/CNO Greenbrier Valley Med. Ctr., 1996—; mem. adj. faculty Barry U., Miami, 1984—, Broward C.C., Ft. Lauderdale, 1984—, Nova U., 1986—; cons. Strategic Health Devel. Inc., Miami Shores, Fla., 1986—, So. Coll., Cleveland, Tenn., 1995-96. Bd. dirs. Pasco County Am. Cancer Soc., 1992-95. Dept. HEW trainee, 1976, 79-80. Recipient Pres.'s award Columbia Healthcare Corp., 1995. Mem. Am. Orgn. Nurse Execs. (legis. com. 1988-90), Fla. Orgn. Nurse Execs. (bd. dirs. 1986-88), South Fla. Nurse Adminstrs. Assn. (sec. 1983-84, bd. dirs. 1984-86), U. Pitts. Alumni Assn., Presbyn. U. Alumni Assn., Portuguese Water Dog Club Am. (bd. dirs. 1988-89), Ft. Lauderdale Dog Club (bd. dirs. 1981-82, 83-85, v.p. 1982-83), Am. Kennel Club (dog judge), Sigma Theta Tau. Lutheran. Home: 27 Potomac Crossway Lewisburg WV 24901-8917 Office: Columbia Greenbrier Valley Med Ctr PO Box 497 202 Maplewood Ave Ronceverte WV 24970

FOWLER, PAUL RAYMOND, physician, lawyer, educator; b. Washington, Apr. 30, 1958; s. Charles Raymond and Dora E. (Burger) F.; m. Mary Jane Weber, Oct. 4, 1986; children: Christina D., Laura M. BS, U. Md., 1980, postgrad., 1980-81; DO, U. Osteopathic Medicine, Des Moines, Iowa, 1985; JD with honors, Drake U., 1994. Diplomate Am. Bd. Family Practice. Intern Des Moines Gen. Hosp., 1985-86; resident Ea. Va. Grad. Sch. Medicine, Norfolk, 1986-88; pvt. practice Sentara Norfolk Gen. Hosp., Norfolk, 1988-90; staff Iowa Meth. Med. Ctr., Des Moines, 1990-96, Mercy Med. Ctr., Des Moines, 1992-94; med. dir. Occupational Health Svcs., Des Moines, 1990-94; dean for clin. affairs Fla. Coll. Medicine, Tarpon Springs, 1994-96; chief physician Ford Motor Co., Hapeville, Ga., 1996—; assoc. clin. prof. U. Osteo. Medicine, 1990—; judge Nat. Mock Trial Coll. Comp., 1992; mem. mock trial team Drake U. Law Sch., 1992, Med. Malpractice Rev. Bd., Commonwealth of Va., 1988-90. Contbr. articles to profl. jours. Active Silver Spring Vol. Fire Dept., 1978-81; mem. bioethics com. Iowa Meth. Med. Ctr., Des Moines, 1992—; elder Gloria Dei Ch., Des Moines, 1992-94. Maj. USAR, 1988—. Recipient Good Citizen award Clifton Park Citizens Assn. Fellow Am. Acad. Family Physicians, Am. Coll. Legal Medicine; mem. Fla. Bar Assn., Ill. Bar Assn., D.C. Bar Assn., Am. Bd. Med. Specialties, Fla. Acad. Family Physicians, Phi Sigma (pres. 1984-85). Home: Ste 6A 1220 Evergreen Way Stockbridge GA 30281 Office: 340 Henry Ford II Ave Hapeville GA 30354

FOWLER, RAY HARLAND, engineering consultant; b. Ishpeming, Mich., Jan. 28, 1929; s. James and Minnie Katherine (Karbum) F.; m. Judith Sue Shirkey, Aug. 30, 1952; children: Karen Elise Fowler-Sneed, Douglas Ray. BSCE, Mich. Tech. U., 1957; MS in Transp. Engring., U. Calif., Berkeley, 1969. Lic. profl. engr., Tex. Resident engr. FAA, Ft. Worth, Tex., 1957-60; design engr. FAA, Ft. Worth, 1960-65; chief airport planning FAA, Houston, 1966-69, asst. dist. chief, 1969-73; project mgr. airports FAA, Washington, 1973-75, program mgr. R & D, 1975-85; v.p. R & D Resource Internat. Inc., Columbus, Ohio, 1985-87; dept. head Mitech. Inc., Washington, 1987-92; cons. R.H. Fowler & Assoc., Springfield, Va., 1992—; mem. transp. rsch. bd. NAS, Washington, 1976-95. Fellow ASCE; mem. ASTM, AIAA, Soc. Automotive Engrs., Inst. of Transp. Engrs., Air Traffic Control Assn. Home: 6403 Wyngate Dr Springfield VA 22152 Office: RH Fowler & Assocs 6403 Wyngate Dr Springfield VA 22152

FOWLER, SHARMILA MATHUR, marketing and planning executive; b. New Delhi, India, Nov. 3, 1963; came to U.S. 1965; d. Vishnu S. and Kusum Mathur; m. John William Fowler Jr., May 19, 1990; 1 child, John Nikhil. BA in Computer Sci./Math., U. Rochester, 1985; MBA, U. Pa., 1990. Rsch. asst. NW Systems, Rochester, N.Y., 1984; mktg. rep. nat. distbn. div. IBM Corp., Columbia, S.C., 1985-86, systems engr. S.W. mktg. div., 1986-88; mktg. intern Myoflex/Perdiem Brand Group Rorer Pharm. Corp., Ft. Washington, Pa., summer 1989; bus. devel. assoc. DNA Plant Tech. Corp., Cinnaminson, N.J., 1990-92; strategic info. mgr. Sonoco Products Co., Hartsville, S.C., 1992-94; mktg. projects mgr. internat. bus. devel. Consumer Products Group, Sonoco Products Co., 1994—; cons. in field. Contbr. articles to profl. jours. Mem. Am. Mktg. Assn., Soc. for Competitive Intelligence Profls. Home: 1516 Fair St Camden SC 29020-2923

FOWLER, THOMAS HOWARD, social services administrator; b. Houston, Aug. 31, 1943; s. John Howard and Lovie O'Danial (Westbrook) F.; m. Cheryl Lynn Pampe, Aug. 27, 1966; children: Joseph Westbrook, Amy Catherine. BA, U. Houston, 1966, MA, 1970, MSW, 1975. Social svcs. adminstr. Tex. Dept. Human Resources, Houston, 1971-81; dir. planning United Way Brazoria County, Angleton, Tex., 1982-85; exec. dir. United Way Brazoria County, Angleton, 1985—; founding mem. Cmty. Found. Brazoria County, 1993—; bd. dirs. United Way Tex.; mem. state adv. com. State Employee Charitable Campaign, 1996. Del. Dem. State Conv., Houston, 1992. With U.S. Army, 1968-70. Mem. Tex. Assn. United Ways (v.p. 1994-95, pres. 1996), Pvt. Industry Coun. (Gulf Coast). Methodist. Home: 107 Tamarisk Trl Lake Jackson TX 77566-4101 Office: United Way Brazoria County 1212 N Velasco St Angleton TX 77515-3064

FOWLER, TILLIE KIDD, congresswoman; b. Milledgeville, Ga., Dec. 23, 1942; d. Culver and Katherine Kidd; m. L. Buck Fowler, 1968; children: Tillie, Elizabeth. BA in Polit. Sci., Emory U., 1964, JD, 1967. Legis. asst. Rep. Robert G. Stephens, 1967-70; counsel White House Office of Consumer Affairs, 1970-71; mem. 103d-104th Congresses from 4th Fla. dist., 1993—. Pres. Jr. League Jacksonville, Fla., 1982-83; chmn. Fla. Humanities Coun., 1989-91; pres. Jacksonville City Coun., 1989-90, mem., 1985-91; mem. bd. visitors U.S. Naval Acad., 1995-96. Republican. Office: US Ho of Reps 413 Cannon House Office Bldg Washington DC 20515

FOWLER, VIVIAN DELORES, insurance company executive; b. Knoxville, Tenn., Sept. 26, 1946; d. Rance James Pierce and Margaret Willadene (Crowe) Compton; m. James Hubert Fowler, May 12, 1979. Student, U. Tenn., Knoxville. CPCU. Clk. The Travelers Ins. Co., Knoxville, 1967-84, adminstv. staff, 1984, comml. mktg. asst., 1984-86; comml. account analyst The Travelers Ins. Co., Nashville, 1986-89, sr. account analyst, 1989-90, account mgr., 1990-93; regional asst. mgr. small bus. unit coml. lines The Travelers Ins. Co., Atlanta, 1993—; regional underwriting mgr. select accounts mktg. Travelers/Aetna Ins. Co., Atlanta, 1996. Lay witness speaker, United Meth. Ch., Knoxville 1979-82; charter mem. St. Thomas Hosp. Found. Soc., 1990; mem. Arthritis Found., 1991. Mem. NAFE, Soc. CPCU, Soc. Cert. Ins. Counselors (cert. 1987), Nat. Assn. of Ins. Women (cert. Profl. Ins. Woman 1975), Internat. Platform Assn. Republican. United Methodist. Home: 604 Ashley Forest Dr Alpharetta GA 30202-6133 Office: Travelers Aetna Ins Co 3500 Piedmont Rd NE Ste 400 Atlanta GA 30305

FOWLER, WILLIAM DIX, construction company executive; b. Glendale, Calif., Jan. 29, 1940; s. H. Dix and Bertha Grace (Graveling) F.; m. Shela Antonia Sandstrom, Feb. 8, 1964; children: Kurtis Walter Dix, Kara Antonia Grace, Kevin William Victor, Keir Andrew Bexar. B.B.A., Tex. Christian U., 1964, M.P.A., 1967. C.P.A., Alaska, Tex. Sr. v.p., mgr. J.L. Cox & Son, Inc., Kansas City, Mo., 1973-74; project adminstrn. mgr. Perini Arctic Assn., Delta Junction, Alaska, 1974-77; Alaska div. mgr. Majestic Wiley Contractor, Fairbanks, Alaska, 1974-77; v.p., treas. Frank Moolin & Assocs., Anchorage, 1977-78; sr. v.p., gen. mgr. Alaska Internat. Constrn. Inc., Fairbanks, 1978-80; pres., COO Alaska Internat. Constrn. Inc., 1980-85; pres. FANCO Engring. & Constrn.Inc., 1986—, Southeast Pipeline Contractors, Inc., Ariz. and Alaska, 1986-88; pres., COO Cherrington Corp., Calif., Tex., Alaska, and Can., 1989-90; chmn., CEO Underwater Construction, Inc., Alaska, 1990-92, Sound Environ. Svcs. Inc., Alaska, Calif., Tex., 1992—. U. Alaska Found. fellow. Mem. Am. Inst. CPA's, Alaska Soc. CPA's, Tex. Soc. CPA's, Associated Gen. Contractors (bd. dirs. Fairbanks 1984-86), Beta Alpha Psi. Republican. Episcopalian. Lodge: Rotary. Office: Sound Environ Svcs Inc 600 E Sandy Lake Rd Ste 124 Coppell TX 75019

FOX, ANTHONY N., lawyer; b. Lynhurst, N.J., Apr. 26, 1958; s. Vincent James and Mary Anne (Garafolo) F.; m. Sandra Leigh Son, Oct. 15, 1983; children: Brittany Amber, Stephanie Nicole. BA in Polit. Sci., Maryville (Tenn.) Coll., 1980; JD cum laude, Cumberland Sch. Law, Birmingham, Ala., 1983. Assoc. Gonce, Young, Howard & Westbrook, Florence, Ala., 1983-86, Clark & Scott P.C., Birmingham, Ala., 1986-91; ptnr. Clark & Scott P.C., Birmingham, 5, 1991-94, mng. ptnr., 1994—; statewide corp. counsel CBS Inc., Cin., 1994—. Sec. Hickory Ridge Homeowners, Birmingham, 1989. Mem. Ala. State Bar Assn., Ala. Claims Assn., Workmen's Compensation Assn. Ala., Phi Alpha Delta (pres. 1982-83). Methodist. Home: 5008 Longleaf Ln Birmingham AL 35242-3452 Office: Clark & Scott PC PO Box 380548 Birmingham AL 35238-0548

FOX, BETH WHEELER, library director; b. Oklahoma City, May 4, 1945; d. Robert R. and Marjorie (Woodberry) Wheeler; m. Dennis Dean Fox, July 15, 1963; children: Rebecca, Julia, Bryce. BS in Libr. Sci./History cum laude, U. North Tex., 1967. Cataloger George Williams Coll., Downers Grove, Ill., 1967-68; br. libr. Libr., Ft. Benning, Ga., 1968-69; ref. libr. Palos Verdes (Calif.) Pub. Libr., 1969-72; libr. vol. Am. Luth. Sch. Libr., Burbank, Calif., 1979-81, Stevenson Elem. Sch. Libr., Burbank, 1981-82; libr. dir. Westbank Community Libr., Austin, Tex., 1983—; presenter in field. Author: The Dynamic Community Library: Practical, Creative and Inexpensive Ideas of the Library Director, 1988, Behind the Scenes at the Dynamic Library: Simplifying Essential Operations, 1990. Bd. dirs. Westbank Community Bds. Recipient Hon. Svc. award Burbank Coun. PTA, 1981, Vol. of Yr. award, 1982. Mem. ALA (John Cotton Dana award 1986, 90), Tex. Libr. Assn. (co-founder small cmty. libr. round table 1986, program chmn. dist. III 1986, rep. state fin. rev. 1991, structure/orgn. coun. 1994, rsch. grant recipient 1987, pub. rels. com. 1995-98, scholarship com. 1995-98, Access Tex. com. 1996—Cmty. Libr. of Yr. 1988), Ctrl. Tex. Libr. Sys. (automatiion com. 1986), Network for Smaller Librs. (founder 1985), Tex. Mcpl. Libr. Dirs. Assn., Vol. League of Austin, Rotary (scholarship com. 1996), Rotary (tchr. excellence com. 1997). Home: 1606 Bay Hill Dr Austin TX 78746-6248

FOX, CAROLYN ELAINE, psychiatric nurse; b. Swannanoa, N.C., Aug. 28, 1933; d. William Marion and Sereptha (West) F. Diploma in Nursing, Rutherford Hosp., 1955; BS in Nursing, Western Carolina U., 1978, MA in Edn., 1981. RN, N.C. Staff nurse Highland Hosp., Asheville, N.C., 1955-64, head nurse, 1964-71, supr., 1972-73, acting dir. of nursing service, 1974-75, 84-85, asst. dir. of nursing service, 1975-79, clin. coord., 1979-84, assoc. dir. nursing service, 1985-91, asst. coord. utilization rev., patient advocate, 1991-92, utilization rev. coord., 1992-93; cons. First Mental Health Inc., Nashville, Tenn., 1993—. Contbr. articles to profl. publs. Mem. ANA, N.C. Nurses Assn., Dist. 1 Nurses Assn. (bd. dirs., v.p.), Sigma Theta Tau. Baptist. Avocations: crafts, spectator sports, bowling, music, art. Home: 219 Richmond Ave Swannanoa NC 28778-3112

FOX, GERALD G., county manager; m. Dolores Fox; 3 children. BA in Polit. Sci., Beloit (Wis.) Coll., 1954; MPA, Kans. U., 1958. Adminstrv. asst. to city mgr. City of San Antonio, 1957-59; city mgr. City of Ennis, Tex., 1959-63, City of Camden, Ark., 1963-66, City of Fayetteville, Ark., 1966-69, City of Wichita Falls, Tex., 1969-80; county mgr. Mecklenburg County, Charlotte, N.C., 1980—; mem. N.C. Gov.'s Crime Commn., 1983-95; vice chmn. Carolinas Innovation Group, chmn., 1991-92, exec. bd. innovation groups, 1993-96; bd. dirs. Cable TV Info. Ctr.; county mgrs. adv. com. State of N.C. Dept. Human Resources, 1982-85, income maintenance simplification adv. com., 1983; bd. dirs., exec. com., treas. Coun. on Health Costs, Inc., 1984-90; state and local govt. rev. U. Ga., 1992-94. Editl. bd. Am. City and County Mag., 1992; contbr. articles to profl. jours. Co-chmn. YMCA Cmty. Svcs. Project; adv. bd. Boy Scouts Am.; divsnl. campaign chmn., bd. dirs. Arts and Sci. Coun., 1990—, Ben Craig Ctr., 1990—, United Fund, Vis. and Conv. Bur., 1983—, Carolinas Partnership Econ. Devel. Corp., 1986—, exec. com., 1991—; chmn. St. Patrick's Cathedral, Parish Coun., 1984-86; mem. Charlotte/Mecklenburg Citizen's Forum; dir. Univ. Rsch. Park, 1990—; exec. com. Charlotte Organizing com. NCAA Tournament Basketball, 1990-94, mem. Final Four, 1994-96. Recipient Ann. award for Outstanding Fin. Adminstrn. Tex. Mcpl. Adv. Coun., 1961; named One of ten mems. invited ICMA European Task Force to visit and study European cities in Eng., Holland, West Germany, 1977. Mem. ASPA, Tex. City Mgmt. Assn. (bd. dirs. 1971-73, scholarship com. chmn. 1970-73, others), Tex. Innovation Group (chmn. exec. com. 1978-79), Internat. City Mgmt. Assn. (futureVisions 1989-91, pub. policy com. 1986-88, strategic planning com. 1984, chmn. conf. planning com. 1983, others, L.P. Cookingham award for career devel. 1979, Ann. Program Excellence award for environ. mgmt. 1990), Urban and Regional Info. Sys. Assn. (pres. 1973-74, bd. dirs. 1972-75), Nat. League of Cities (labor rels. policy com. 1979-80), N.C. City-County Mgmt. Assn. (conf. planning chmn. 1986-87, bd. dirs. 1984-86), Nat. Assn. County Adminstrs. (exec. bd. 1984-86), Nat. Assn. Counties (fin. and taxation steering com. 1987—, AIDS Task Force 1988, vice chmn. bonds subcom.), govt. Fin. Officers Assn. (state and local govt. budget practices com. 1995—), Omicron Delta Kappa. Home: 428 Robmont Rd Charlotte NC 28270-5331 Office: PO Box 31781 Charlotte NC 28231-1781

FOX, JAMES CARROLL, federal judge; b. Atchison, Kans., Nov. 6, 1928; s. Jared Copeland and Ethel (Carroll) F.; m. Katharine deRosset Rhett, Dec. 30, 1950; children: James Carroll, Jr., Jane Fox Brown, Ruth Fox Jordan. BSBA, U. N.C., 1950, JD with honors, 1957. Bar: N.C. 1957. Law clk. U.S. Dist. Ct. (ea. dist.) N.C., Wilmington, 1957-58; assoc. Carter & Murchison, Wilmington, N.C., 1958-59; ptnr. Murchison, Fox & Newton, Wilmington, N.C., 1960-82; judge U.S. Dist. Ct. (ea. dist.) N.C., Wilmington, 1982—; lectr. in field. Contbr. articles to profl. jours. Vestryman, St. James Episcopal Ch., 1973-75, 79-82. Mem. Hew Hanover County Bar Assn. (pres. 1967-68), Fifth Jud. Dist. Bar Assn. (sec. 1960-62), N.C. Bar Assn. Office: US Dist Ct Alton Lennon Fed Bldg PO Box 2143 Wilmington NC 28402-2143

FOX, JAY WILLIAM, microbiology educator; b. Springfield, Ill., Sept. 18, 1952; s. William Jay Jr. and Phylis Colleen (Anderson) F.; m. Nena S. Fox, Nov. 20, 1989. BA, Monmouth Coll., 1974; PhD, Colo. State U., 1978. Asst. prof. microbiology U. Va. Med. Sch., Charlottesville, 1981-86, assoc. prof. microbiology, 1986-93, prof. microbiology, 1993—. Recipient Humboldt Rsch. fellowship Av Humboldt Stiftung, Munchen, Fed. Republic of Germany, 1990-91. Mem. Am. Chem. Soc., Am. Peptide Soc., Internat. Soc. Toxicology, Am. Soc. Biochem. Molecular Biologists, Biophysics Soc. Office: Univ Va Health Sci Ctr PO Box 441 Charlottesville VA 22908

FOX, KENNETH IAN, company manager; b. Chgo., Mar. 27, 1943; s. Edward and Rochelle (Drexler) F.; m. Eileen Hayes, Jan. 11, 1975. BS, U. Ill., 1965; MS, Mich. State U., 1967, PhD, 1971. Dir. rsch. J. R. Short Milling Co., Kankakee, Ill., 1971-76; supr. regulatory compliance Kraft Inc., Chgo., 1976-77; dir. rsch. FMC Corp., Lakeland, Fla., 1977-87; dir. new bus. devel. FMC Corp., Lakeland, 1988—; dir. tech. svcs. Chiquita Brands Inc., Cin., 1987-88. Home: 4736 Highlands Place Dr Lakeland FL 33813-2161 Office: FMC Corp PO Box 1708 Lakeland FL 33802-1708

FOX, LLOYD ALLAN, insurance company executive; b. Bklyn., Sept. 20, 1945; s. Samuel Morris and Adele (Sheingold) F.; m. Lenore Judith Weinstock, Aug. 10, 1968; children: Jennifer Lynn, Elizabeth Susan. BS in Pharmacy, Long Island U., 1968; JD, U. Mich., 1974. Bar: Ga. 1974, D.C. 1979; lic. ins. agent, Ga. Mng. ptnr. Stokes, Shapiro, Fussell, Fox & Wedge, Atlanta, 1974-87; exec. v.p., gen. counsel Splty. Systems, Inc., Indpls., 1987-90; chmn., CEO Environ. Mgmt. Group Inc., Atlanta, 1987-90; pres. Environ. Mgmt. Ins. Svcs. Inc., Atlanta, 1990—, Am. Safety Casualty Ins. Co., 1993—; bd. dirs. Performance Contracting Group, Inc., Charlotte, N.C., Am. Safety Casualty Ins. Co., 1993—, Am. Safety Ins. Group, Ltd., 1995—. Author: Employer's Guide to Employee Retirement Income Security Act, 1974, Businessman's Guide to Mergers and Acquisitions, 1977, Business Planning for the Closely-Held Company, 1980, Asbestos Management and Removal-Legal Considerations and Planning, 1985, Legal Considerations of Asbestos Management Plans, 1987. Pres. Chastain Park Civic Assn., Atlanta, 1976; bd. dirs., v.p. Nat. Kidney Found., Atlanta, 1977-88, bd. dirs. emeritus, 1988—; bd. dirs. Asbestos Abatement Coun. Assn. Wall and Ceiling Industries Internat., Washington, 1987-90, pres., 1989-90; bd. dirs., pres. Asbestos Info. and Rsch. Coalition, 1990—. Lt. USPHS, 1968-71. Recipient Pres.'s award Nat. Kidney Found. Ga., 1984. Mem. State Bar Ga., D.C. Bar, Environ. Info. Assn., Alpha Zeta Omega. Jewish. Office: Ste 200 1845 The Exchange NW Atlanta GA 30339-2022

FOX, MARIAN CAVENDER, mathematics educator; b. Paris, Tenn., Dec. 12, 1947; d. G.W.F. and Marilee (Boden) Cavender; m. James H. Fox, Jan. 24, 1973; children: Brendon Dutch, Michael Garrett. BS in Math., Miss. U. for Women, 1969; MA in Edn., George Washington U., 1973; PhD in Math. Edn., Ga. State U., 1989. Secondary tchr. math., Mo., Va., 1970-77; instr. math. North Cen. Tech. Coll., Mansfield, Ohio, 1979-81; prof. Manatee C.C., Bradenton, Fla., 1981-86; grad. tchr., rsch. asst. Ga. State U., Atlanta, 1986-89; asst. prof. Math. Kenesaw State Coll., Marietta, Ga., 1989-95; rsch. assoc. U. Tex., Austin, 1995—; cons. Manatee County Schs., Bradenton, 1983-85, State of Ga. Dept. of Edn., Atlanta, 1987-90, Fulton County Schs., Atlanta, 1987-90. Mem. Assn. Tchr. Educators, Nat. Coun. Tchrs. Math., Math. Assn. Am., Ga. Coun. Tchrs. Math., Phi Delta Kappa. Office: Univ of Texas-Austin 5ZB 462 Dept C & I Austin TX 78705

FOX, MARY FRANK, sociology educator and researcher. BA, U. Mich., 1967, MA, 1969, PhD, 1978. Prof. sociology Sch. of History, Tech. and Soc., Ga. Inst. Tech., Atlanta; rsch. study panel Nat. Rsch. Coun., Washington, 1995—; adv. bd. on women in sci. and engring. Alfred Sloan Found., 1993-95; mem. editl. bd. Social Studies of Sci., 1996—. Assoc. editor Sex Roles, 1992—, Gender and Society, 1986-90. Rsch. grants NSF, 1985-88, 91-95. Mem. Sociologists for Women in Soc. (pres. 1995), Am. Sociol. Assn. (chair sex and gender sect. 1986-87, coun. sex and gender sect. 1993-96, publs. com. 1989-92), Soc. for Social Studies of Sci. (chair ednl. bd., handbook of sci. and tech. studies 1990-95). Office: Ga Inst Tech 214 DM Smith Bldg Atlanta GA 30332-0345

FOX, RAYMOND GRAHAM, educational technologist; b. Portland, Oreg., May 31, 1923; s. George Raymond and Georgia Dorothy (Beckman) F.; B.S., Rensselaer Poly. Inst., 1943; m. Harriet Carolyn Minchin, Apr. 17, 1948; children—Susan, Christine, Ellen, Laura, John. Salesman IBM Corp., N.Y.C., 1946-48, br. mgr., 1949-56, systems mgr., 1957-65, edn. systems devel. mgr., 1965-76; chmn. bd. Learning Tech. Inst., Warrenton, 1975—. Mem. Va. Council for Deaf, 1978-84; chmn., 1980-83; mem. Sec. of Navy Adv. Bd. on Edn. and Tng., 1972-77; cons. for tech. Va. Legis. Adv. Com. on Handicapped, 1970; mem. Nat. Def. Exec. Reserve, 1970-83; mem. emeritus, 1983—. Served with USNR, 1943-46. Mem. Soc. Applied Learning Tech. (pres. 1972—), Nat. Security Indsl. Assn. (chmn. tng. group 1974-76). Anglican. Clubs: Army & Navy (Washington); Fauquier (Warrenton, pres. 1993-94); Columbia Country (Chevy Chase, Md.); Moorings (Vero Beach, Fla.). Patentee interactive multimedia instruction delivery sys. Home: PO Box 376 Warrenton VA 22088-0376 Office: 50 Culpeper St Warrenton VA 22086-3238

FOX, ROGER WILLIAMS, allergist and immunologist, educator; b. Belleville, Ill., Jan. 13, 1949; s. Frank Xavier and Eleanor Betty (Williams) F.; m. Cynthia Jayne Swetland, June 3, 1972; children: Russchelle Lynn, Rawley Williams, Travis Paul. MD, St. Louis U., 1975. Diplomate Am. Bd. Internal Medicine, Am. Bd. Allergy & Immunology. Asst. prof. medicine divsn. allergy & immunology U. South Fla., Tampa, 1980-86, assoc. prof., 1986—, assoc. prof. pub. health dept. occupl. & environ. health Coll. Pub. Health, 1988—; investigator various pharm. cos., 1980—. Co-author: Circulating Immune Complexes in Clinical Medicine, 1982, Proceedings of the Symposium on Biological Response Modifiers in Human Oncology and Immunology, 1983, Annual Review of Chronopharmacology, 1984, Bronchial Asthma, 1986, Current Treatment of Ambulatory Asthma, 1986, Immunology and Allergy Medical Clinica of North America, 1991, Medical Clinics of North America, 1992, Anaphylaxis, 1993, Bronchias Asthma: Principles of Diagnosis and Treatment, 1994, Environmental Medicine, 1994; contbr. articles to profl. jours. Fellow ACP, Am. Acad. Allergy & Immunology; mem. AMA (Physicians Recognition award 1987), Fla. Med. Assn., Fla. Allergy Soc. (pres. 1980-83). Office: Tampa Bay Allergy Asthma & Immunology Assocs 13801 Bruce B Downs Blvd Tampa FL 33613-3946

FOX, RUTH ELLEN, personal care industry executive; b. Indpls., Oct. 7, 1947; d. Willard Lycurgus and Ruth Ellen (Egan) Cameron; m. Cameron Fox, Mar. 2, 1975; 1 child, Cameron Michael. BS, Ind. U., 1969. Owner

Creative Reflections Cards and Gifts, Grand Island, Nebr., 1980-85; sales rep. Am. Greetings, Cleve., 1985-88; registered rep. Red River Fed. Savs. and Loan, Lawton, Okla., 1988-89, sales mgr., 1989-91; sales mgr. fin. svcs. div. Pacific S.W. Bank, Corpus Christi, Tex., 1991-93; owner, mgr. Physicians Weight Loss Ctr., Corpus Christi, Tex., 1993—; cons. Marketing One, Inc., Portland, Oreg., 1989-91. Advisor Salvation Army, Lawton, 1990-91, Marie Detty Youth & Family Ctr., Lawton, 1990-91, Keywanette-MacArthur High Sch., Lawton, 1991, Builder's Club - MacArthur Jr. High, Lawton, 1991, United Way, 1991. Mem. Nat. Assn. Life Underwriters, Demolay Mother Club (sec. 1991), Eastern Star, Boy Scouts Am., Kiwanis (pres. Lawton br. 1991). Republican. Presbyterian. Home: 5949 Crooked Creek Dr Corpus Christi TX 78414-2507 Office: Physicians Weight Loss Ctr Windchase Shopping Ctr 2033 Airline Rd Ste H1 Corpus Christi TX 78412-4694

FOX, SUSAN E., legal assistant; b. Uniontown, Pa., June 17, 1955; d. James Ira Sr. and Elizabeth Ann (Kirk) F. BS in Journ., W.Va. U., 1977; Cert. Completion, Nat. Ctr. for Paralegal Tng., Atlanta, 1977. Legal asst. Jackson, Kelly, Holt & O'Farrell, Charleston, W.Va., 1978-79, Dennis, Corry, Webb & Carlock, Atlanta, 1979-84, Dennis, Corry, Porter & Thornton, Atlanta, 1984-89, Ga.-Pacific Corp., Atlanta, 1989—. Bd. dirs. Met. Atlanta Coun. on Alcohol and Drugs, 1991-92, treas., 1992-93, pres., 1993-94; bd. dirs. DeKalb Rape Crisis Ctr., 1994-96; bd. dirs. Ga.-Pacific Svc. Force, 1995-96; chmn., mem. devel. Jr. League of DeKalb County, Decatur, Ga., 1989-90, cmty. rsch. chmn., 1990-91, corr. sec., 1991-92, pres.-elect, 1994-95, pres., 1995-96; mem. Leadership DeKalb, 1995; Olympic vol., Equestrian Venue Comm. Ctr., 1996. Mem. Ga. Assn. Legal Assts. (newsletter asst. 1980-81, mem. chmn. 1981-82), Embroiderers Guild of Am., Atlanta Needlepoint Guild (sec. 1992-93, chmn. cmty. projects), High Mus. of Art. Republican. Presbyterian. Home: 2207 Harbor Pointe Pkwy Dunwoody GA 30350-3158 Office: Georgia-Pacific Corp 133 Peachtree St Atlanta GA 30303

FOX, THOMAS CHARLES, foreign language educator; b. Norwalk, Conn., July 19, 1953; s. Charles Ralph and Margaret Teresa (Grigonis) F.; m. Karin Barbara Fischer, June 10, 1995; 1 child, Katharina Charlotte Barbara. BA, Wesleyan U., 1975; PhD, Yale U., 1983. English tchr. Maedchen Gymnasium, Lingen, Germany, 1975-76; asst. dir. Wesleyan Program in Germany, Bonn, 1976-77; instr. in German Yale U., New Haven, 1978-83; dir. German programs Coun. on Internat. Ednl. Exch., N.Y.C. and Bonn, 1983-84; asst. prof. German Washington U., St. Louis, 1984-92; assoc. prof. German, dir. Concordia Coll., Inst. German Studies, Bemidji, Minn., 1992-95; assoc. prof. German, chair dept. German and Russian U. Ala., Tuscaloosa, 1995—. Author: Louise von François: A Feminist Reading, 1988, Border Crossings, 1993; editor: Disenchantment of the World, 1989; editor GDR Bulletin, St. Louis, 1984-92. Fellow German Acad. Exch. Svc., Germany, 1981-82, 86, 95, Am. Coun. Learned Socs., 1988-89; grantee Goethe Inst., Germany, 1991, 95. Mem. MLA, Am. Assn. Tchrs. German, German Studies Assn. Office: Univ Ala Box 870262 Tuscaloosa AL 35487

FRACKER, ROBERT GRANGER, retired librarian, consultant; b. Spout Spring, Va., Sept. 29, 1928; s. Dudley Granger and Ruby Walker (Page) F.; m. Sandra Elizabeth Snyder, June 5, 1965; 1 child, Mary Susan F. McCann. Student, Va. Poly. Inst. and State U., 1946-49, Roanoke Coll., 1948; BS, East Tenn. State U., 1954; MA, Appalachian State U., 1957; postgrad., U. Ill., 1957-59, Duke U., 1962-65, U. N.C., 1977, N.C. Central U., 1978. Coach, tchr. English and social studies Beaver Creek High Sch., West Jefferson, N.C., 1954-56; counselor univ. coun. on tchr. edn. U. Ill., Urbana, 1957-59; mem. faculty Meredith Coll., Raleigh, N.C., 1962-93, reference libr., media coord. Carlyle Campbell Libr., 1977-93, ret., 1993. Campus chmn. United Way Wake County, 1976. With U.S. Army, 1951-53. Mem. N.C. Assn. Tchr. Educators (pres. 1975-76), Internat. Phenomenological Soc., Assn. Tchr. Edn., Philosophy of Edn. Soc., Am. Soc. Mil. Insignia Collectors, Kami Kaze, Kappa Komma Kappa, Kappa Delta Pi, Phi Delta Kappa, Order Silver Sunset. Democrat. Presbyterian. Home: 307 Oakridge Rd Cary NC 27511-4515

FRAGALE, MARY LYNCH, emergency nurse; b. Clarksburg, W.Va., July 1, 1950; d. A. Carl and Angela (Wanstreet) Lynch; m. Ernest S. Fragale, Feb. 19, 1982; 1 child, Stephen. ADN Sci., Salem (W.Va.) Coll., 1973; student, Allegheny Gen. Hosp., Pitts., 1978. RN, W.Va.; CEN; cert. nurse practitioner, Pa. Staff nurse W.Va. U. Med. Ctr., Morgantown; staff nurse emergency room United Hosp. Ctr., Clarksburg, W.Va., emergency nurse practitioner, instr. in-hosp. edn. svcs., 1988. Mem. Am. Acad. Nurse Practitioners.

FRAILEY, DAVID CODORI, communications consultant; b. Emmitsburg, Md., Jan. 4, 1921; s. Clarence George and Estelle Marie (Codori) F.; m. Lea Alexander, Dec. 27, 1950; children: Joan Murphy Rosenzweig, Stephen Alexander Frailey. BA, Mt. St. Mary's Coll., 1942. Editor, reporter AP, Balt., Annapolis, 1942, 46; pub. rels. exec. Am. Airlines, Washington, various, 1946-82, asst. v.p., 1972-73, corp. v.p., 1973-82; adj. prof. So. Meth. U., Dallas, 1984-90; editorial, communications cons. Dallas, 1983—. Editor: Eagle by Robert Serling, 1986, (textbook) Notes on Editing, 1985, How Long? by Earl Ditmars, 1994. Master Sgt. U.S. Army, 1943-46. Mem. Nat. Press Club, Delta Epsilon Sigma. Roman Catholic. Home and Office: 3635 Asbury St Dallas TX 75205-1848

FRALEY, DEBRA LEE, critical care nurse; b. San Antonio, June 19, 1961; d. Billy C. and Martha Sue (Schooler) F. BSN, U. Tex., San Antonio, 1983. CCRN; cert. ACLS, ACLS instr. Nursing care coord. Univ. Hosp.; asst. head nurse Med. Ctr. Hosp., San Antonio; surg. ICU insvc. coord. Med. Ctr. Hosp., chmn. ICU flow sheet com., SICU rep. for transplant liaison com., product evaluation com., expert rater for patient acuity. Recipient George W. Brackenridge Nursing scholarship. Mem. AACN, Sigma Theta Tau. Address: 227 Twilight Terrace St San Antonio TX 78233-6557

FRANCE, BELINDA TAKACH, lawyer, business owner; b. Jacksonville, Fla., June 10, 1964; d. Bruce Albert and Bertha Loretta (Hawkins) Takach; m. Alden Whitney France, July 27, 1985. BS, U. Tampa, Fla., 1985; JD, Stetson U., 1987; LLM in Taxation, U. Fla., 1989. Bar: Fla. 1989, U.S. Dist. Ct. (mid. dist.) Fla. 1989, U.S. Ct. Claims 1989, U.S. Tax Ct. 1989, U.S. Ct. Appeals (11th cir.) 1989, U.S. Ct. Appeals (Fed. cir.) 1990. Tax preparer H&R Block, Tampa, 1983-84; acct. Robert Osborne & Assocs., Tampa, 1984-85; assoc. Thomas C. Little, P.A., Clearwater, Fla., 1987-88; co-counsel Bruce R. Young, P.A., Clearwater, 1988; prin. Belinda Takach France, P.A., Tallahassee, Fla., 1988—; prof. Ft. Lauderdale Coll., Tallahassee, 1989; adj. instr. Tallahassee C.C., 1991—; vice chmn. bd. dirs. Someplace Else, Tallahassee; owner Catalyst Seminars; expert witness in taxation and pension matters. Mem. Tallahassee Rep. Women, 1989-90. Mem. ABA (com. domestic rels. tax problems, com. attys. in small law firms), Fla. Bar Assn., Tallahassee Bar Assn., Tallahassee Women Lawyers Assn., Tallahassee C. of C. Office: 703 E Tennessee St Tallahassee FL 32308-4984

FRANCE, RICHARD WILLIAM, finance executive; b. Evanston, Ill., Oct. 24, 1947; s. Norman Marshall and Carolyn (Andersen) F.; m. Dianne M. Vlasak, May 5, 1979; children: Jennifer Sara, Hilary Ann, Justine Elizabeth. AA, Kendall Coll., 1968; BS in Bus. Adminstrn., Am. U., 1970. Auditor Pick Hotels Corp., Chgo., 1970-72; comptroller K St. Hotel Corp., Washington, 1972-74; controller Registry Hotel Corp., Dallas, 1974-83, Fairmont Hotel Co., Dallas, 1983-86; corp. controller Signet Hotel Corp., Dallas, 1986-87, v.p. fin., 1987-92, chief fin. officer, 1992—. Mem. Internat. Assn. Hospitality Accts. (v.p., pres., and chmn. Minn. Chpt. 1975-82). Republican. Roman Catholic. Office: Signet Hotel Corp 15851 Dallas Pky Ste 925 Dallas TX 75248-3362

FRANCE-DEAL, JUDITH JEAN, parochial school educator; b. Falls City, Nebr., June 27, 1941; d. Paris and Georgia Elizabeth (Reiger) France; m. Gary Arthur Deal, Dec. 30, 1960; children: Kevin, Timothy. Student, Bapt. Inst. Christian Workers, Bryn Mawr, Pa., 1959; grad., Liberty Bible Inst., 1994. Vol. worker with many orgns., 1957—; receptionist Central Ins. Co., Omaha, Nebr., 1960-62; vol. PTA, Cub Scouts, etc., Wis., 1966-76; tchr. spl. edn. First Bapt. Ch., Dallas, 1985-88, vol. tutor ESL, 1985—; inspirational spkr.; tchr. English and Bible studies 1st Bapt. Ch., Richardson, Tex., 1989—; pres., founder God's Internat. ABCs, Inc.; model for numerous advts. and commls. Author: Center of Our Lives, 1994. Chaplain-min. to cancer patients Tulsa Cancer Treatment Ctr. Recipient numerous writing awards. Mem. Internat. Platform Assn. Republican. Office: Gods Internat ABC Inc 1000 14th St Ste 122 Plano TX 75074-6249

FRANCESCHETTI, DONALD R., physicist, educator; b. Oceanside, N.Y., Nov. 21, 1947; s. Nicholas and Lucile frances (Powell) F.; m. Alice Frizzell, Oct. 2, 1982. BS, Bklyn. Coll., 1969; MA, Princeton U., 1971, PhD, 1974. Rsch. assoc. U. N.C., Chapel Hill, 1975-77, rsch. asst. prof., 1977-79; asst. prof. U. Memphis, 1979-83, assoc. prof., chmn. dept. physics, 1983-86, prof. physics, 1986-91, interim assoc. v.p. for rsch., 1990-93, interim vice provost for rsch., 1993-96, Disting. Svc. prof., 1996—; vis. lectr. State U., Utrecht, Netherlands, 1982. Contbr. over 55 articles to profl. jours. Woodrow Wilson Grad. fellow, 1969-70, NSF Grad. fellow, 1969-72, Postdoctoral Energy-related fellow, 1975-76. Mem. AAAS, Am. Chem. Soc., History of Sci. Soc., N.Y. Acad. Sci., Sigma Xi, Phi beta Kappa. Office: University of Memphis Dept of Physics Memphis TN 38152

FRANCIS, CLIFFORD LARRY, retired career officer, management analyst; b. Chesapeake, Ohio, Apr. 29, 1940; s. Clifford Dale and Ruth Elizabeth (Queen) F.; m. Sarah Helen Clark, Feb. 28, 1961; children: Elaine, Todd, Wyatt. AA in Data Processing, No. Va. C.C., Annandale, 1975, AA in Acctg., 1976; BBA, Columbia Coll. Mo., 1985; M in Mgmt., Webster U., 1986. Commd. 2nd lt. USAR, 1964, advanced through grades to lt. col., 1983; adminstrv. asst. U.S. Army Engring. Ctr., Ft. Belvoir, Va., 1972-74, gen. supply supr. splst., 1974-76, chief, dir. res. component direct, 1976-83; mgmt. analyst Force Integration Agy. U.S. Army, Ft. Belvoir, Va., 1992—; chief transp. bur. U.S. Army Res., St. Louis, 1983-84, chief personnel mgmt. supr. divsn. Personnel Ctr., 1984-86, chief combat svcs. supr. divsn. Personnel Ctr., 1986-88, plans officer, dep. chief program analysis and evaluation officerl Personnel Ctr., 1988-92; adv. Chem. and MP Ctrs. U.S. Army Res., Ft. McClellan, Va., 1988-92; ret., 1992. Leader Boy Scouts Am., Va., Mo., Ala., 1980-93, Eagle Scout, 1955. Mem. Assn. U.S. Army, NRA, Retired Officers Assn., Profl. Mil. Comptroller Assn., Res. Officer's Assn. (pres. DC chpt. 1964). Home: 5340 Pond Mountain Rd Broad Run VA 20137 Office: US Army Integration Agy 9900 Belvoir Rd Fort Belvoir VA 22060

FRANCIS, KAREN See RUGALA, KAREN FRANCIS

FRANCIS, LA FRANCIS DIANA, nursing administrator, career officer; b. Brewton, Ala., Nov. 30, 1955; d. Lucian Webster Jr. and Mary (McMillan) Johnson; m. Denis Hinds Francis, Oct. 25, 1980; children: Amanda Rachel, Vanessa Nicole. BSN, U. No. Colo., 1978. Med.-surg. staff nurse Penrose Community Hosp., Colorado Springs, 1978; gen. surg. staff nurse Meml. Hosp., Colorado Springs, 1978-81; PRN reg. staff nurse Alpha Nurse Registry PRN, El Paso, Tex., 1981; head nurse North Park Community Hosp., El Paso, Tex., 1982; lt. jr. grade, post-part. staff nurse Naval Hosp., San Diego, 1982-83; lt., 1984—; post-part. asst. charge nurse Naval Hosp., San Diego, 1983, ortho. staff nurse, 1984, maj. jnt. ortho. staff nurse, 1984-85, EENT asst. charge nurse, 1985; ortho.-neurol. charge nurse Meml. Hosp., Colorado Springs, 1985-86; staff nurse ICU Naval Hosp. Beaufort, S.C., 1986-87, staff nurse gen. med.-surg., 1987, asst. charge nurse gen. med.-surg., 1988-89, div. officer acute care, 1989-90, charge nurse sickcall, 1990-91, sr. nurse quality assurance/coord., 1991; div. officer sickcall Br. Med. Clinic Naval Sta. Va., Norfolk, Va., 1992; dept. head sickcall Br. Med. Clinic NAVSTA, Norfolk, Va., 1992-95; total quality leadership facilitator/leader, BLS instr., 1990—; divsn. officer Family Practice Clinic USNH, Yokosaka, Japan, 1995-96, dept. head Family Care, 1996—; BLS instr., 1990—, instr., trainer, 1995—. Contbr. articles of rsch. to profl. jours. Budget chair Religious Ministries, Parris Island, S.C., 1990-91; vol. Help of Beaufort, S.C. Recipient Help of Beaufort Vol. of Yr. award, 1991. Mem. ANA, Am. Acad. Ambulatory Care Nursing. Baptist. Home: PSC475 Box 1671 FPO AP 96350-1671

FRANCIS, LEE, III, trade association administrator; b. Albuquerque, May 21, 1945; m. Mary Elaine Allen, Aug. 12, 1972; 1 child, E. Lee Francis IV. BA, San Francisco State Univ., 1983, MA, 1984; PhD, Western Inst. Social Rsch., 1991. Tchr. San Francisco State U., 1984, U. Calif., Santa Barbara, 1989, Calif. State Univ., Long Beach, 1990; dir. Wordcraft Circle of Native Writers, Fairfax, Va., 1992—; spl. asst. to Lt. Gov. N.Mex., Santa Fe, 1967-71, U.S. Senator Pete V. Domenici, 1977; cons., 1971-76; leg. asst. U.S. Senator Hugh Scott, 1976-77; staff assoc. Jt. Com. Congl. Ops., Washington, 1978; sr. ptnr. Associated Bus., Inc., Albuquerque, 1978-81; adminstrv. coord. student affirmative action program, San Francisco State Univ., 1981-83, asst. dir. ednl. opportunity program, 1983-84; sr. faculty Meta-Life Adult Profl. Tng. Inst., Washington, 1984-88; student affairs officer U. Calif., Santa Barbara, 1989; dir. student rels. and activities Calif. State Univ., Long Beach, 1990, dir. pre-engring. intensive learning acad., 1991; core faculty Western Inst. Social Rsch., Berkeley, Calif., 1989-93; indian youth specialist U.S. Dept. Interior Bur. Indian Affairs, Office Alcohol and Substance Abuse Prevention, 1994; v.p. First Am. Rsch., 1993-95, Washington Internships for Native Students, Am. Univ., Washington, 1994-96; tchr. George Mason U., Fairfax, 1994, 95, Am. Univ., Washington, 1995; bd. dirs. Greenfield Rev. Lit. Ctr.; chmn. Am. Univ. native Adv. Coun., 1994—; trustee-at-large Laguna (N.Mex.) Pueblo Ednl. Found., 1996—; lectr., presenter in field. Author: (books) BEST Course: A Cultural Communications Handbook, 1986, Native Time: A Historical Time Line of Native America, 1996, Reclaiming The Vision--Past, Present and Future: Native Voices for the Eighth Generation, 1996 (short stories) Callaloo: A Journal of African-American and African Arts and Letters-Native American Literatures: A Special Issue, 1994, Blue Dawn, Red Earth: New native American Storytellers, 1996; issue editor Prevention Quar., Jan. 1995, Moccasin Telegraph, Jan. 1995; contbr. introductions to books, articles and essays to profl. publs.; lit. adv. Native Playwrights' Newsletter, 1993—; manuscript reviewer, grant application reviewer various organizations. Mem. diversity com. United Way Am. Nat. Offices, Alexandria, Va., 1994—. Honor's scholar N.Mex. State Univ., 1967; recipient Emminent Svc. citation Office of Lt. Gov. N.Mex., 1967, Cert. Appreciation, Student Affirmative Action Program, San Francisco State Univ., 1981-82, Spl. Commendation cert. Asst. Sec. Edn., Office Ednl. Rsch. and Improvement, U.S. Dept. Edn., 1992, Medallion of Honor, Inds. of the Ams. (IOTA) Soc., 1994, Tech. Rev. award Office Indian Edn., Indian Fellowship Program, U.S. Dept. Edn., 1995. Mem. Nat. Coalition Indian Edn., Nat. Indian Edn. Assn., Nat. Psychiatric Assn., Nat. Congress Am. Indians, Native Writers' Circle Ams. (bd. dirs.), Wordcraft Circle Native Writers and Storytellers (bd. dirs.). Office: Wordcraft Circle of Native Writers & Storytellers 9 E Burnam Rd Columbia MO 65203-3511

FRANCIS, MARK LOUIS, composer, educator, musician; b. Dunkirk, N.Y., Sept. 24, 1958; s. Richard S. Francis and Marie A. Messina-Francis. BA in Music Theory, SUNY, Fredonia, 1981; MusM in Composition, U. Conn., 1984; DMA in Composition, U. Ky., 1989. Grad. asst. U. Conn., 1982-84; tutor Minority Learning Ctr. U. Ky., 1987-88; mem. Hoffman-Francis Duo, 1988-90; with flute and guitar duo McDermott-Francis Duo, 1992—; dir. musicianship and theory Ashland Sch. of Music, Lexington, Ky., 1989-90; instr. La. Sch. for Math., Sci. and the Arts, Lexington, 1990—, Northwestern State U., 1991-96; instr. Regional Acad. Enrichment Conf., 1990; presenter in field; state advisor south ctrl. jour. of music scores N.W. State U., 1994. Composer numerous works including Fireworks, 1984, Intermezzo, 1985, Four Poems, 1986, Waltz-Reverie, 1987, Concerto 1987-89, Duettino, 1988, Two Pieces, 1989, Two Etudes, 1989, Divertimento, 1990, A Dream Suite, 1990, Fractures, 1991-92, 2 Bagatelles, 1992-93, Nelsongs, 1992-93, Dear Linda, 1992-94, The African Vesper, 1993, 3 Machado Songs, 1994, 3 Pieces, 1994, Malice, 1994, Land of the Vampires, 1994, 7 Dickinson Songs, 1992-95, Found Objects, 1994, Landscapes, 1995-96, Sonatina, 1995, Trio 1996; book reviewer: The New Shostakovich for The New Jour. of Music, 1992; CD reviewer: Stephen Paulus Songs for The New Jour. of Music, 1992, Frates for 20th Century Music, 1996, Meet the Composer: A Conversation with James Guthrie, 1994, Meet the Composer: A Conversation with Michael Kallstrom, 1994. Recipient Gordon Kinney prize Chamber Music Soc. of Ctrl. Ky., Std. award ASCAP, 1995, 96; N.Y. State Regents scholar. Mem. Soc. of Composers, Inc., Southeastern Composers League (treas. 1995), Coll. Music Soc., South Ctrl. Soc. for Music Theory, Guitar Found. Am., Pi Kappa Lambda. Home: 179 Twin Lakes Rd Natchitoches LA 71457-6535 Office: La Sch Math Sci and Arts 715 College Ave Natchitoches LA 71457-3915

FRANCIS-FELSEN, LORETTA (LOREE FRANCIS-FELSEN), nursing educator; b. Youngstown, Ohio, May 26, 1947; d. Frank Anthony and Ann (Beraduce) Capuzello; 1 child, Julie Frances Felsen. AAS, Youngstown State U., 1972, BS, 1976; MSN, Cath. U. Am., 1981; PhD, Columbia Pacific U., San Rafael, Calif., 1991. Lic. nurse, Fla., D.C., Md., Ohio. Employee health nurse lamp plant GE, Youngstown, 1972-76; charge nurse intermediate and med./surg. clients St. Elizabeth Med. Ctr., Youngstown, 1976-78; head nurse SICU/CCU Sibley Meml. Hosp., Washington, 1978-79; instr. dept. nursing Anne Arundel C.C., Annapolis, Md., 1979-81; instr. Marymount Coll., Arlington, Va., 1981; dir. ICU/CCU So. Md. Hosp. Ctr., Clinton, Md., 1981-82; clin. nurse specialist Office of Dr. Edwin Westura, Camp Springs, Md., 1982-84; instr. ADN program Charles County C.C., LaPlata, Md., 1984-85; asst. prof., coord. undergrad. program dept. nursing Bowie (Md.) State U., 1987-91; on-call asst. DON Greater Laurel-Beltsville Hosp., Laurel, Md., 1989-91; asst. prof. Coll. Nursing U. Fla., Gainesville, 1991—; mem. minority mentor program, mem. adminstrv. coun. U. Fla., 1994—; mem. nursing adv. coun. Bowie State U., 1989-91; mem. profl. practice com. Alachua Gen. Hosp., Gainesville, 1992—; vice chair, chair dist. HHS Bd., 1994; presenter in field. Mem. editl. adv. bd. Nursing Health S.C.O.P.E., Jacksonville, Fla., 1991-93; contbr. or co-contbr. articles to profl. publs. Vol. nurse Westwood Mid. Sch., Gainesville, 1993-94; vol. Kids Am. Day, Glen Springs Elem. Sch., Gainesville, 1992, treas. safety patrols, 1991-92; vol. Career Day, Fairland Elem. Sch., Silver Spring, 1991. Recipient nurse traineeship Cath. U. Am., 1988. Mem. ANA (cert. in gerontol. nursing), NLN, Nat. Rural Health Assn., Fla. Rural Health Assn., Sigma Theta Tau (pres.-elect Alpha Theta chpt. 1994-95, chpt. vice-chairperson, chpt. program chairperson 1993-94, pres. 1995—, faculty advisor, co-chairperson induction 1992-93, chpt. eligibility chairperson 1992-93). Home: 4127 NW 34th Pl Gainesville FL 32606-6151

FRANCO, ALEXANDER, construction company executive; b. Havana, Cuba, Sept. 5, 1963; came to the U.S., 1963; s. Sotero and Maria Franco. BA, Columbia U., 1983; MBA, Pace U., 1987. CPA. Sr. auditor Price Waterhouse, N.Y.C., 1987-92; legis. asst. Fla. Ho. of Reps., Tallahassee, 1993-94; exec. dir. Interamerican Businessmen's Assn., Miami, Fla., 1995—; mgr. Coastal Constrn. Products, Miami, 1996—; v.p. Cuba Consulting Group, Miami, 1995—. Author: Business Opportunities in a Free Cuba, 1995, The Cuban Business and Legal Environment in the 1950s, 1996. Founder, pres. Ronald Reagan Rep. Alliance, Miami, 1989&; active Hispanic leadership tng. program Cuban Am. Nat. Coun., Miami, 1992; active Leadership Miami, Greater Miami C. of C., 1993. Named Outstanding Young Man of Am., 1989; recipient Outstanding Achievement award Cuba Bus. Roundtable, Miami, 1995. Republican.

FRANCO, ANNEMARIE WOLETZ, editor; b. Somerville, N.J., Sept. 18, 1933; d. Frederick Franz and Bertha (Laugginger) Woletz; m. Frederick Nicholas Franco, June 11, 1977. Student, Wood Coll. of Bus. Editorial asst. Internat. Musician, then assoc. editor, 1965-88, ret., 1988. Republican. Presbyterian. Home: 166 Wellstone Dr Palm Coast FL 32164-4111

FRANEY, ERIC D., advertising agency executive; b. Little Rock, Oct. 5, 1970. BBA in Mktg., U. Ark., Little Rock, 1993. Computer support asst. The Computer Shoppe, Little Rock, 1988; cash mgmt. asst. 1st Comml. Bank, Little Rock, 1989-90; mktg. asst. Babcock & Wilcox-ST Co., Little Rock, 1991-92; account exec. Cranford Johnson Robinson Woods, Little Rock, 1992-94; pres., owner Franey Inc., Little Rock, 1994—. Author: (screenplay) The American Dream, 1992, (book) Black America: An Economic Powerhouse in the Dark, 1996. Mem. Leadership Roundtable, 1996—. Mem. Greater Little Rock C. of C., Alpha Kappa Psi.

FRANK, HARVEY, foodservice distributing company executive; b. Jacksonville, Fla., Oct. 22, 1944; s. Perry and Mildred (Lieberman) F.; m. Linda Howard, Nov. 15, 1978; 1 child, Jonathan Perry. Student, Daytona Beach Community Coll., 1962-64; BS in Bus., U. South Fla., 1966; postgrad. in law, Stetson U., 1967. Vice pres. City Provisioners, Daytona Beach, Fla., 1973-78, pres., 1978-88, chmn., chief exec. officer, 1988—; bd. dirs., mem. fin. com. ComSource, Inc., Atlanta. Recipient ind. appreciation award Volusia County Bus. Devel. Ambs., 1987, Industry of Yr. award City of Ormond Beach, 1992. Mem. Nat.-Am. Wholesale Grocers' Assn. (edn. com. 1981—, bd. dirs. 1992), Nat. Assn. Credit Mgrs. (1st v.p. Fla. 1988—), U.S. C. of C., Am. Culinary Fedn. (hon.), Daytona Beach C. of C. (bd. govs. 1981-84, svc. award 1984), Internat. Food Distbrs. Assn. (bd. dirs. 1988—, Disting. Svc. award 1990, Internat. Distbr. award 1991). Jewish. Home: PO Box 2063 Daytona Beach FL 32115-2063 Office: CP Foodsvc PO Box 2246 Daytona Beach FL 32115-2246

FRANK, MARK BARTON, immunogeneticist, molecular biologist; b. Denver, June 24, 1953. BA in Zoology, UCLA, 1975; MS in Biomed. Scis.-Genetics, U. Hawaii, 1977, PhD in Biomed. Scis.-Genetics, 1980. Postdoctoral rschr. dept. microbiology & molecular genetics U. Calif., Irvine, 1980-81, postgrad. rschr. dept. microbiology and molecular genetics, 1981-86; asst. mem. Arthritis & Immunology Program, Okla. Med. Rsch. Found., Oklahoma City, 1986—; adj. asst. prof. U. Okla. Health Scis. Ctr., Oklahoma City, 1986—, lectr. grad. sch.; mem. Okla. Ctr. for Molecular Medicine, Oklahoma City, 1991—. Contbr. articles and revs. to profl. jours. Grantee NIH, Arthritis Found., Lupus Found. Am., others. Mem. Am. Assn. Immunologists, Am. Soc. Human Genetics, Am. Coll. Rheumatology, Sigma Xi (Faculty Rsch. award 1990). Home: 2118 Brookhaven Dr Edmond OK 73034-4824 Office: Okla Med Rsch Found Arthritis & Immunology 825 NE 13th St Oklahoma City OK 73104-5005

FRANK, MARY LOU BRYANT, psychologist, educator; b. Denver, Nov. 27, 1952; d. W.D. and Blanche (Dean) Bryant; m. Kenneth Kerry Frank, Sept. 9, 1973; children: Kari Lou, Kendra Leah. BA, Colo. State U., 1974, MEd, 1983, MS, 1986, PhD, 1989. Tchr. Cherry Creek Schs., Littleton, Colo., 1974-80; from grad. asst. to dir. career devel. Colo. State U., Ft. Collins, 1980-86; intern U. Del., Newark, 1987-88; psychologist Ariz. State U., Tempe, 1988-93; assoc., lead prof. psychology Clinch Valley Coll. U. Va., Wise, 1992-96, asst. acad. dean, 1993-95; head psychology dept., prof. North Ga. Coll., Dahlonega, 1996—; instr. Colo. State U., Ft. Collins, 1981-82, counselor, 1984-85, 86-87; psychologist Ariz. State U., Tempe, 1989-92; assoc. prof. psychology Clinch Valley Coll. U. Va., 1992-96. Author: (program manual) Career Development, 1986; contbr. book chpts. on eating disorders and existential psychotherapy. Mem. APA, AACD, Phi Kappa Phi, Phi Beta Kappa, Pi Kappa Delta, Psi Chi. Office: North Ga Coll Psychology Dept 207 Dunlap Hall Dahlonega GA 30533

FRANK, MICHAEL M., physician; b. Bklyn., Feb. 28, 1937; s. Robert and Helen (Prakin) F.; m. Ruth Sybil Pudolsky, Nov. 5, 1961; children: Robert E., Abigail B., Brice S.H. AB, U. Wis., 1956; MD, Harvard U., 1960. Intern Boston City Hosp., 1960-61; resident in pediatrics Johns Hopkins Hosp., 1961-62, 64-65; vis. scientist Nat. Inst. Med. Research, London, 1965-66; with NIH, 1967-90; chief lab. of clin. investigation, clin. dir. Nat. Inst. Allergy and Infectious Diseases, Bethesda, Md., 1977-90; prof., chmn. dept. pediatrics Duke U. Med. Ctr., Durham, N.C., 1990—. Mem. ACP, Assn. Am. Physicians, Am. Soc. Clin. Investigation, Soc. Pediatric Rsch., Am. Pediatric Soc., Infectious Diseases Soc., Am. Acad. Allergy, Am. Acad. Pediatrics.

FRANK, MYRA LINDEN, consultant; b. Richmond, Va., Oct. 26, 1950; d. J. C. and Myra Teresa (Lanzarone) Frank; m. Timothy Franklin Long (div. Jan. 1981); m. Robert Andrew Hudson (div. 1994). BA, Erskine Coll., 1972; student, Inst. Fin. Edn., 1982-88. Chief activities therapist S.C. Dept. Corrections, Columbia, 1973-75, acting prin., 1975-77, coll. coord., 1977-78; owner, operator Carolina Coast Seafood, Aiken and Beaufort, S.C., 1978-80; from teller to savs. counselor Security Fed. Savs. & Loan, Aiken, 1981-83; customer svc. rep. Bankers 1st Savs. & Loans, Augusta, Ga., 1983-84, mgr. br. adminstrn., 1984-85; coord. automated teller machines, banking officer 1st Fed. Savs. Bank, Brunswick, Ga., 1985-88; ptnr., cons. electronic banking/software devel. RAH Systems, Brunswick, 1988-93; ptnr. specific application computer programming, software tng. Details & More, Greenville, S.C., 1989-90, ptnr. event planning, various mfg. positions and mktg./sales, 1989-91; cons. office and computer svcs. Mauldin, S.C., 1992-93; lectr. S.C. Edn. Tchrs. Assn., Columbia, 1974, S.C. Assn. Social Workers, Columbia, 1975, Bus. and Profl. Women's Club, Columbia, 1978; small bus. owner, distbr. Nuskin product line, 1987-90; ind. mktg. rep. Network 2000/

U.S. Spring, 1988-92; computer specialist Top Food Svcs. Carolina, Inc., Duncan, S.C., 1989-9o; adminstrv./sales mgr. Custom Catering, Duncan, 1990; cons. Contract Office/Computer Svcs., Greenville, 1992—. Book rev. writer A Class Act, Greenville, 1996—; appeared with Aiken Cmty. Theatre, 1981. Bd. dirs. Quest Soc., Greenville, 1992-95; mem. hospice com. Am. Cancer Soc., Augusta, 1981; lectr. St. John's United Meth. Ch., 1981-82; registrar, treas. Sugar Creek Soccer Club, Greenville, 1996—. Mem. A Creative Gathering Writers Group. Democrat. Home and Office: PO Box 333 Mauldin SC 29662-0333

FRANK, RONALD EDWARD, marketing educator; b. Chgo., Sept. 15, 1933; s. Raymond and Ethel (Lundquist) F.; m. Iris Donner, June 18, 1958; children: Linda, Lauren, Kimberly. BSBA, Northwestern U., 1955, MBA, 1957; PhD, U. Chgo., 1960. Instr. bus. statistics Northwestern U., Evanston, Ill., 1956-57; asst. prof. bus. adminstrn. Harvard U., Boston, 1960-63, Stanford U., 1963-65; assoc. prof. mktg. Wharton Sch., U. Pa., 1965-68, prof., 1968-84, chmn. dept. mktg., 1971-74, vice dean, dir. rsch. and PhD programs, 1974-76, assoc. dean, 1981-83; dean, prof. mktg. Krannert Grad. Sch. Mgmt., Purdue U., 1984-89; dean, Asa Griggs Candler prof. mktg. Goizueta Bus. Sch. Emory U., Atlanta, 1989—; bd. dirs. Lafayette (Ind.) Life Ins. Co., The MAC Group, Home Hosp., Lafayette; cornerstone rsch. cons. to industry; mem. strategic issues com. Am. Assembly Collegiate Schs. of Bus., 1988-92, bd. dirs., 1992-96, chmn. audit com., 1993-94, mem. strategic planning and ops. com,. 1994-95; chmn. Orgn. for the Future Task Force, 1996—. Author: (with Massy and Kuehn) Quantitative Techniques in Marketing Analysis, 1962, (with Matthews, Buzzell and Levitt) Marketing: an Introductory Analysis, 1964, (with William Massy) Computer Programs for the Analysis of Consumer Panel Data, 1964, An Econometric Approach to a Marketing Decision Model, 1971, (with Paul Green) Manager's Guide to Marketing Research, 1967, Quantative Methods in Marketing, 1967, (with Massy and Lodahl) Purchasing Behavior and Personal Attributes, 1968, (with Massy and Wind) Market Segmentation, 1972, (with Marshall Greenberg) Audience Segmentation Analysis for Public Television Program Development, Evaluation and Promotion, 1976, The Public's Use of Television, 1980, Audiences for Public Television, 1982. Bd. dirs., fin. com. Home Hosp. of Lafayette, 1985-89; bd. dirs. The Washington Campus, 1984-89, 95—. Recipient pub. TV rsch. grants John and Mary R. Markle Found., 1975-82. Mem. Am. Mktg. Assn. (dir. 1968-70, v.p. mktg. edn. 1972-73), Inst. Mgmt. Sci., Assn. Consumer Rsch. Home: Westfield Sq 6 Downing Ln Decatur GA 30033-1403 Office: Emory U Goizueta Bus Sch Atlanta GA 30322

FRANK, WILLIAM EDWARD, JR., executive recruitment company executive; b. Pitts., Aug. 28, 1943; s. William Edward and Grace (Hankey) F.; m. Lesley Ann Austin, July 22, 1992; children: William John, Jorell. BS in English, Slippery Rock U., 1965. Corp. employment mgr. Wometco Enterprises, Inc., Miami, Fla., 1967-71; v.p. human resources ITT Community Devel. Corp., Miami, 1971-79; ptnr. TASA, Inc., Coral Gables, Fla., 1979-80; pres. The Curtiss Group, Inc., Boca Raton, Fla., 1980—. Bd. dirs. IIC Ptnrs. Mem. Boca Grove County Club. Home: 7859 Mandarin Dr Boca Raton FL 33433-7427 Office: The Curtiss Group No Trust Plz 301 Yamato Rd Ste 2112 Boca Raton FL 33431-4929

FRANK, WILLIAM FIELDING, computer systems design executive, consultant; b. N.Y.C., Oct. 27, 1944; s. Karl Frederick and Margaret Ruth (Denisson) F.; m. Linda Carol Hainfield, Dec. 20, 1965 (div. 1972); children: Aaron, Tobin. BA, Middlebury Coll., 1966; MA, U. Chgo., 1969; PhD, U. Pa., 1976. Assoc. prof. Oreg. State U., Corvallis, 1969-79; mem. tech. staff Bell Labs., Whippany, N.J., 1979-81; pres. Enterprise Engring. Inc., Warren, Vt., 1982—; vis. scholar MIT, Cambridge, 1981-85; cons. Citibank, 1982—, AT&T, 1984, N.Y. Times, 1985, Bank of Am., 1985, State of Calif., 1986—, Digital Equipment Corp., 1987-89, Soviet Ministry of Trade, 1990, Bankers Trust, 1991, Fidelity Investments, 1993—, Reuters, 1996—. Contbr. articles to profl. jours. Rsch. grantee NSF, 1971, 77, NEH, 1976, 81. Mem. Assn. for Computing Machinery, Computer Soc. IEEE. Republican. Congregationalist. Home: 1230 Broadwater Dr Fort Myers FL 33919 Office: EEI 18 Foxcroft Dr Marlboro NJ 07746

FRANKEL, ANDREW JOEL, manufacturing company executive; b. N.Y.C., Oct. 7, 1945; s. Lazar Hirsch and Estelle Rose (Fuchs) F.; m. Marilyn Judith Marcus, Dec. 24, 1967; children: Jennifer Lauren, Jonathan Matthew. BSChemE, N.J. Inst. Tech., 1968; M in Nuclear Engring., NYU, 1970; postgrad., U. Hartford, 1971-72. Cert. paralegal mediator Am. Arbitration Assn. Physicist ABB Combustion Engring., Windsor, Conn., 1970-76, lead engr., 1976-77; dir. non-proliferation programs Oak Ridge (Tenn.) Nat. Lab., 1977-78; mgr. mkt. intelligence dept. NAC Internat., Inc., Atlanta, 1978-80; gen. mgr., dir. fuel-trac divsn. NAC Internat., Inc., 1980-86; mgr. mktg. info. systems Martin Marietta Energy Systems, Inc., Oak Ridge, 1986-89, mgr. info. resources, 1989-91, mgr. bus. analysis and decision support, 1991-92; cons. bus. devel. Martin Marietta Corp., Bethesda, Md., 1992-93; mgr. fin. analysis Martin Marietta Utility Svcs., Inc., Oak Ridge, 1993-94; mgr. cost reduction programs Lockheed Martin Utility Svcs., Inc., Bethesda, Piketon, Ohio, Paducah, Ky., 1994—. Contbr. articles to profl. jours. U.S. del. Internat. Nuclear Fuel Cycle Evaluation, Washington, 1977-78; nuclear safety advisor Conn. Gov.'s Office, Hartford, 1975-77. NSF fellow, 1968-70. Mem. Am. Nuclear Soc. (sec. Conn. chpt. 1976-77), Tau Beta Pi (v.p. N.Y.C. Met. chpt. 1969, pres. 1970). Republican. Methodist. Home: 200 Jalusian Trail Paducah KY 42001-8856 Office: Lockheed Martin Utility Svcs Inc 5600 Hobbs Rd Paducah KY 42002-1410

FRANK-FITZNER, FONTAINE LYNNE, geriatrics, medical and surgical nurse; b. Detroit; m. George H. Fitzner. AA with honors, Jackson Community Coll., Mich., 1984; BSN with honors, Ea. Mich. U., 1988; Assoc. in Geriatric Nursing Care, Ea. Mich. U.-Mich. State U., 1990. RN, Mich., Fla. Staff nurse Suncoast Hosp., Largo, Fla., 1988-89; charge nurse VA Hosp., Ann Arbor, Mich., 1989; infection control practitioner Med. Ctr. Hosp., Punta Gorda, Fla., 1992-93; health svcs. coord. Cigna Health Plan of Fla. Inc., Tampa, 1993-96; clin. rev. specialist Liberty Mut. Ins. Co., Tampa, 1996—. Mem. ANA, Fla. Nurses Assn., Nat. League of Nursing, Sigma Theta Tau.

FRANKLAND, ERICH GENE, political science educator, researcher; b. Iowa City, Mar. 13, 1968; s. E. Gene and Diane L. (Malone) F.; m. Tammy N. Noble, Sept. 3, 1994; 1 child, Amber Shay. Student, Westminster Coll., Oxford, Eng., 1988; BA with honors, Earlham Coll., 1990; MA, U. Okla., 1994, PhD, 1997. Centennial rsch. fellow dept. polit. sci. U. Okla., Norman, 1990-94, instr., 1991—, editl. and rsch. asst., 1993—. Contbr. articles to profl. jours. Mem. Am. Polit. Sci. Assn., Acad. Polit. Sci., Internat. Studies Assn., Nat. Wildlife Fedn., Phi Beta Kappa. Democrat. Unitarian. Office: U Okla Dept Polit Sci 455 W Lindsay St Rm 205 Norman OK 73019

FRANKLIN, BILLY JOE, international higher education specialist; b. Honey Grove, Tex., Jan. 30, 1940; s. John Asia and Annie Mae (Castle) F.; m. Sonya Kay Erwin, June 1, 1958; children: Terry Daylon, Shari Dea. BA, U. Tex., 1965, MA, 1967, PhD, 1969. Asst. prof. sociology U. Iowa, Iowa City, 1969-71; chmn. Western Carolina U., Cullowhee, N.C., 1971-72, Wright State U., Dayton, Ohio, 1973-75; dean S.W. Tex. State U., San Marcos, 1975-77; v.p. acad. affairs Stephen F. Austin State U., Nacogdoches, Tex., 1977-81; pres. Tex. A&I U., Kingsville, 1981-85, Lamar U., Beaumont, Tex., 1985-91; exec. v.p. Tex. Internat. Edn. Consortium, Austin, 1991-96, pres., 1996—; mem. nat. agrl. rsch. com. USDA, 1982-85; policies and purposes com. Am. Assn. State Colls. and Univs., 1985-91, nominating com., 1986-88, mem. exec. com. bd. dirs., 1990-91; pres. Assn. Tex. Colls. and Univs., 1985-86, Tex. Acad. Sci., 1986-87; commr. commn. on colls. So. Assn. Colls. and Schs., 1985-90, chmn., 1987-90, pres.-elect, 1990-91; chmn. Coun. Pub. Univ. Pres. and Chancellors, 1988-91; bd. dirs. Tex. Ptnrs. of Am. Co-editor: Research Methods: Issues and Insights, 1971, Social Psychology and Everyday Life, 1973; contbr. articles to profl. jours. Mem. sr. adv. bd. Tex. Lyceum, Inc., 1982-88; bd. dirs. United Way of Coastal Bend, 1981-84, United Way of Beaumont, Tex., Tex. Ptnrs. of the Ams., 1994—; chmn. Austin-Oita (Japan) Sister Citis, 1995-96; ; bd. dirs. Energy Mus., 1987, pres., 1987-90; mem. exec. com. Muscular Dystrophy Assn., 1985-91. Presbyterian. Fellow Tex. Acad. Sci.; mem. Am. Sociol. Assn., Kingsville C. of C. (bd. dirs. 1981-83, pres. 1984), Beaumont C. of C. (bd. dirs. 1986-91, chmn. 1988-89), East Tex. C. of C. (bd. dirs. 1985-87), East Tex. Venture Capital Group (bd. dirs. 1985-87), Sigma Xi. Presbyterian. Office: PO Box 7667 Austin TX 78713-7667

FRANKLIN, BOBBY JO, state education agency administrator; b. Canton, Miss., Nov. 14, 1951; s. Robert Lee and Gladys Julia (Thompson) F.; m. Nelda Ann Allbritton, Apr. 5, 1986; children: Elizabeth Leann, Caleb Lee, John Winston. AS, East Cen. Jr. Coll., Decatur, Miss., 1971; BS, U. So. Miss., 1973; MEd, Auburn U., 1987; PhD, La. State U., 1992. Cert. tchr., Miss., La. Tchr. Warren County Schs., Vicksburg, Miss., 1973-84; environ. technician U.S. Corps Engrs., Vicksburg, 1981-84; grad. asst. dept. chemistry La. State U., Baton Rouge, 1984-85, grad. asst. dept. curriculum and instrn., 1986-89; lab. technician Baddley Chem. Co., Baton Rouge, 1985-87; adminstr. edn. sect. office of R&D La. Dept. Edn., Baton Rouge, 1989—; cons. La. Acad. Rally, U. So. La., 1987; mem. Parkview Bapt. Sch. Bd., Baton Rouge, 1992-94; chair AERA Sig: Sch. Indicators and Report Cards, 1994-96. Contbr. articles to profl. jours. Mem. Warren County Rep. party, 1983-84. Named Star Tchr. Miss. Econ. Coun., 1983; recipient tchr. commendation Internat. Sci. and Engring. Fair, 1983. Mem. NSTA, Nat. Assn. Rsch. in Sci. Teaching, Am. Edn. Rsch. Assn., Mid-South Edn. Rsch. Assn., La. Edn. Rsch. Assn., Phi Delta Kappa. Baptist. Home: 2131 Firewood Dr Baton Rouge LA 70816-2814 Office: La Dept Edn 626 N 4th St Baton Rouge LA 70802-5363

FRANKLIN, DONALD BENJAMIN, JR., nephrologist; b. Statesboro, Ga., Oct. 7, 1955; m. Julie Duff, Oct. 8, 1983; children: Donald III, James D., Leslie A. BBA, Ga. So. U., 1977; BS, Shorter Coll., 1980; MD, Med. Coll. Ga., 1985. Diplomate Am. Bd. Internal Medicine in Internal Medicine and Nephrology. Intern U. Tenn. Coll. Medicine/Erlanger Med. Ctr., Chattanooga, 1985-86, resident, 1986-88; fellow nephrolgy Vanderbilt Univ. Med. Ct., Nashville, 1988-90; assoc. clin. prof. U. Tenn. Coll. Medicine, Chattanooga, 1990—. Mem. AMA, Am. Soc. Nephrology, Renal Physicians Assn., Nat. Kidney Found. Presbyterian. Office: Nephrology Assocs 979 E 3rd St Ste 1111 Chattanooga TN 37403-2143

FRANKLIN, JOHN HOPE, historian, educator, author; b. Rentiesville, Okla., Jan. 2, 1915; s. Buck Colbert and Mollie (Parker) F.; m. Aurelia E. Whittington, June 11, 1940; 1 son, John Whittington. AB, Fisk U., 1935; AM, Harvard, 1936, PhD, 1941; hon. degrees, Morgan State Coll., Va. State Coll., Lincoln (Pa.) U., Cambridge (Eng.) U., Drake U., Mich. State U., U. Ill. at Chgo., Carnegie-Mellon U., Columbia U., Columbia Coll., Chgo., Loyola U., Chgo., Bklyn. Coll., Bard Coll., Boston Coll., Brown U., Tuskegee Inst., Grand Valley Coll., Marquette U., Lincoln Coll., Ill., Princeton, Hamline U., Fisk U., R.I. Coll., Dickinson Coll., Howard U., U. Md., U. Notre Dame, Tulsa U., Morehouse Coll., Miami U., Johnson C. Smith U., Lake Forest Coll., Tougaloo Coll., Union Coll., Northwestern U., Whittier Coll., U. Mass., U. Mich., Seattle U., U. Toledo, Yale U., L.I. U., Catholic U. Am., Tulane U., Temple U., Kalamazoo Coll., Washington U., St. Louis, Trinity Coll. (Conn.), Ariz. State U., SUNY, Albany, No. Mich. U., U. Utah, Coll. New Rochelle, George Washington U., Governors State U., Harvard U., U. Pa., Ripon Coll., Atlanta U., Wayne State U., U. N.C.-Chapel Hill, Dillard U., Manhattan Coll., Roosevelt U., N.C. Central U., Ind. State U., St. Olaf Coll., Emory U., U. Miami, U. Conn., U. N.C.-Charlotte, Brandeis U., Wake Forest U., Wilkes Coll., Queen's Coll., N.Y., Wilmington Coll., Hope Coll., Bryant Coll., SUNY-Binghamton, Indiana U., N.C. Weslyan U., N.C. State U., So. Meth. U., Berea Coll., Grad Ctr. CUNY, Suffolk U., Washington Coll., Eckerd Coll., Rutgers U., U. N.C., Greensboro, St. Augustine Coll., U. Okla., Oreg. State U., Winston-Salem State U., Queens Coll., Charlotte, N.C., Ill. State U., Bates Coll., Williams Coll., U. of the South, U. N.C.-Wilmington, Am. U.; hon. degree, Furman U., Georgetown U., Tufts U., Elizabeth City State U., Shaw U., San Francisco U., Washington and Lee U., Columbia U., Chgo. Instr. history Fisk U., 1936-37; prof. history St. Augustine's Coll., 1939-43, N.C. Coll. at Durham, 1943-47, Howard U., 1947-56; chmn. dept. history Bklyn. Coll., 1956-64; prof. Am. history U. Chgo., 1964-82, chmn. dept. history, 1967-70, John Matthews Manly Distinguished Service prof., 1969-82; James B. Duke prof. history Duke U., 1982-85; prof. legal history Duke U. Law Sch., 1985-92; Elizabeth City State U., Shaw U., U. San Francisco, Washington and Lee U.; Pitt prof. Am. history and instns. Cambridge U., 1962-63; vis. prof. Harvard U., U. Wis., Cornell U., Salzburg Seminar, U. Hawaii, U. Calif., Cambridge U.; chmn. Bd. Fgn. Scholarships, 1966-69, Nat. Coun. on Humanities, 1976-79; trustee Nat. Humanities Ctr., 1980-91; Fulbright prof., Australia, 1960; Jefferson lectr. in humanities, 1976; Fulbright disting. lectr., Zimbabwe, 1986. Author: Free Negro in North Carolina, 1943, From Slavery to Freedom: A History of African Americans, 7th edit, 1994, Militant South, 1956, Reconstruction After the Civil War, 1961, The Emancipation Proclamation, 1963, A Southern Odyssey, 1976, Racial Equality in America, 1976, George Washington Williams, A Biography, 1985, Race and HIstory, 1990; (with others) Land of the Free, 1966, Illustrated History of Black Americans, 1970, The Color Line: Legacy for the 21st Century, 1993; editor: Civil War Diary of James T. Ayers, 1947, A Fool's Errand by Albion Tourgee, 1961, Army Life in a Black Regiment by Thomas Higginson, 1962, Color and Race, 1968, Reminiscences of an Active Life by John R. Lynch, 1970; editor: (with August Meier) Black Leaders in the Twentieth Century, 1982 (with Abraham Eisenstadt) Harlan Davidson's American History Series; mem. editorial bd.: Am. Scholar, 1972-76, 94—. Bd. dirs. Salzburg Seminar, Mus. Sci. and Industry, 1968-80, DuSable Mus., 1970—; trustee Chgo. Symphony, 1976-80, Fisk U., 1947-80. Recipient Cleanth Brooks medal Fellowship So. Writers, 1989, Gold medal Ency. Brit., 1990, Caldwell medal N.C. Coun. on Humanities, N.C. medal, 1992, 93, Charles Frankel medal, 1993, NAACP Spingarn medal, 1995; Bruce Catton award Soc. Am. Historians, 1994, Cosmos Club award, 1994, Sidney Hook award Phi Beta Kappa Soc., 1994, Pres. Medal of Freedom, 1995; named to Okla. Hall. of Fame, 1978; Edward Austin fellow, 1937-39, Guggenheim fellow, 1950-51, 73-74, Pres.'s fellow Brown U., 1952-53, Ctr. for Advanced Study in Behavioral Scis. fellow, 1973-74, sr. Mellon fellow. Fellow Am. Acad. Arts and Scis.; mem. Am. Hist. Assn. (pres. 1978-79), So. Hist. Assn. (pres. 1970-71), Orgn. Am. Historians (pres. 1974-75), Assn. for Study Negro Life and History, Am. Studies Assn. (past pres.), Am. Philos. Soc. (Jefferson medal 1993), AAUP, Phi Beta Kappa (senate 1966-82, pres. 1973-76), Phi Alpha Theta.

FRANKLIN, LARRY BROCK, publishing executive; b. Greenville, S.C., June 28, 1951; s. Billy Center and Elizabeth (Brock) F.; m. Janice Ann Roberts, Jan. 8, 1972; children: Stacie Lyn, Kevin Brock. BA in Journalism, U. S.C., 1974. Mgr. advt. Clinton (S.C.) Chronicle, 1974-78, mng. editor, 1978-86, gen. mgr., 1986-89, pub., 1989—. Recipient News Photograph award S.C. Press Assn., 1979-81, Best Column award, 1985, 87, 90, 93, Best Editorial award, 1987, Reporting In Depth award, 1990, Best Investigative Series award Nat. Newspaper Assn., 1991. Baptist. Office: Clinton Chronicle PO Box 180 Clinton SC 29325-0180

FRANKLIN, MARK NEWMAN, political science educator; b. Grahamstown, South Africa, Jan. 29, 1942; came to U.S., 1989; s. Norton Norris and Ethel Maureen (Leonard) F.; m. Margery Helen Mason, 1967 (div. 1980); children: David, Caroline. BA, Oxford U., 1964, MA, 1968; PhD, Cornell U., 1970. Teachng asst. Cornell U., Ithaca, N.Y., 1964-67; lectr. U. Strathclyde, Scotland, 1969-89; prof. polit. sci. U. Houston, 1989—; John and Rebecca Rooves prof., 1996; vis. prof., Fulbright fellow U. Iowa, 1984-85. Author: Decline of Class Voting in Britain, 1985, Community of Science in Europe, 1988, Electoral Change, 1992, Parliamentary Questions, 1993, Choosing Europe?, 1996. Newton Farr fellow Cornell U., 1967-69. Office: U Houston Dept Polit Sci Houston TX 77204

FRANKLIN, MARY ANN WHEELER, retired administrator, educator, higher education and management consultant; b. Boston; d. Arthur Edward Wheeler and Madeline Ophelia (Hall) Wheeler-Brooks; m. Carl Matthew Franklin; 1 child, Evangeline Rachel Hall Franklin-Nash. BS, U. N.H., 1942; MEd, U. Buffalo, 1948; EdD, U. Md., 1982. Cert. tchr., N.Y., Ga. Instr. edn. W.Va. State Coll., Institute, 1947; tchr. gen. sci. John Marshall Jr. High Sch., Bklyn., 1952; assoc. prof. sci. Elizabeth City (N.C.) State Coll., 1960; asst. dean coll. Morgan State U., Balt., 1967-77, asst. dean Coll. Arts and Scis., 1977-78, asst. v.p. acad. affairs, 1978-82; asst. prof. bus. Catonsville (Md.) Community Coll., 1982; asst. to dean evening and weekend coll. So. U. New Orleans, 1983-92; cons. numerous locations Herford County Tchrs., Murfreesboro, N.C., 1961, St. Catherine's Sch., Elizabeth City, 1962-64, Archbishop Keough H.S., Balt., 1970-80, Hampton Inst. Va. St. Paul Coll., 1972; bd. dirs. Archbishop Keough H.S.; presenter confs., seminars and workshops; spkr. in field. Editor Academic Affairs Newsletter, 1980-82, Morgan State Coll. Catalog, 1969-82; author: The How and Why of Testing at Elizabeth City State College, 1962, Report on Princeton University Program for Physics Teachers in HBCU's, 1964, Learning Summer Camp Code, National Library of Poetry, 1992, 93, 94, 95, Interrogations of a Metropolis, 1993, Who Are We/Who We ARe, 1994. Mem. com. higher edn. Citizens League, Balt., 1979-81; assoc. dir. youth camp NCCJ, 1974-75, bd. dirs., 1969-80; dir., originator Vestibule Program and Parents Workshop for New Citizens and Residents, SUNO Summer Learning Camp, 1984-95; pres. Lake Willow Homeowners Assn., 1994-96. Fellow NSF, Harvard U., 1958-59, Carnegie-Ford-NSF, Princeton U., 1964; recipient Education award Am. Assn. of Coll. Tchrs. Edn., 1966. Mem. AAUW, Am. Mgmt. Assn., Nat. Coun. Negro Women (bd. dirs. 1984), Am. Assn. Higher Edn., Am. Assn. Continuing Higher Edn., Nat. Assn. Trainers and Educators for Alcohol and Substance Abuse Counselors (pres. accreditation coun.'s alcohol and drug counseling program in higher edn.), La. Assn. Continuing Higher Edn., Md. Assn. Higher Edn., Urban League, Delta Sigma Theta, Phi Sigma, Pi Lambda Theta.

FRANKLIN, PAUL DEANE, financial consultant, financial planner; b. Shreveport, La., Oct. 17, 1942; s. Paul Amerideth and Marjorie (Hyde) F,; m. Carol Fillmore Talley, Aug. 30, 1966 (div. July 1982); children: Kyle D., Sean R.; m. Barbara Joyce, Oct. 12, 1985. BS in Bus., La. Tech. U., 1964; MBA in Fin., La. State U., 1965. CFP; cert. sr. profl. human resources. Pers. rep. Monsanto Co., El Dorado, Ark., 1966-68; supr. pers. Monsanto Co., Muscatine, Iowa, 1968-70; supt. pers. Monsanto Co., Stonington, Conn., 1970-71, Comml. Solvents Corp., Terre Haute, Ind., 1971-74; mgr. human resources Mobay Chem. Corp., Baytown, Tex., 1974-85; pres. Micro Energy Sys., Inc., Pitts., 1985-88; mgr. human resources Miles Inc. (name now Bayer Corp.), Charleston, S.C., 1988—; dir. human resources Bayer Corp., Charleston, S.C., 1995—; bd. dirs. Goodwill Industries Lower S.C., Inc. Co-chmn. United Way, Baytown, Tex., 1983-84; coach Boys Club Am., Terre Haute, 1972-74; scoutmaster Boy Scouts Am., Baytown, 1975-76; bd. dirs. Pvt. Industry Coun., Charleston County, 1994-95, Goodwill Industries of Lower S.C., Inc., 1996—, Pvt. Industry Coun. Berkeley County, 1996—; bd. govs. Trident Area Consortium for Tech., 1994—. Mem. Inst. CFPs, Trident Indsl. Rels. Com., Charleston Metro C. of C., Rotary (sgt.-at-arms), Beta Gamma Sigma (scholastic achievement award 1964), Delta Sigma Pi (internat. mem.). Republican. Home: 648 Harbor Creek Pl Charleston SC 29412-3203 Office: Ste 105 147 Wappoo Creek Dr Charleston SC 29412

FRANKLIN, RITA SIMS, retail executive; b. Selma, Ala., May 18, 1943; d. Emmett McClain and Mary Frances (O'Brien) Sims; children: Susan Lenore Sims Franklin, Sarah Louise Sims Franklin. Student, Judson Coll., 1961-62, Huntingdon Coll., Montgomery, Ala., 1962-65. Retail salesperson, acct. Sims Furniture & Interiors, Selma, Ala., 1965—. Councilwoman Selma City Council, 1980-84, 88—; mem. Old Depot Mus. Soc., Selma, 1976—; bd. dirs. Med. Family Practice Bd., Selma, 1980—, Easter Seal Rehab. Bd., 1980—; exec. bd. Community Action Agy., Selma, 1980—. Mem. Selma Dallas County Hist. Soc., Friends of the Selma Library, Selma Beautification Coun., Women in Mcpl. Govt. (nat. bd. dirs.), Class VII Leadership Ala., Third Conf. on Ala. State Cts. Democrat. Baptist. Home: 1904 Tippett Dr Selma AL 36701-6641 Office: Sims Furniture PO Box 1058 Selma AL 36702-1058

FRANKLIN, ROBERT DRURY, oil company executive; b. Mead, Okla., June 6, 1935; s. Sam Wesley and Frankie Marjorie (Gooding) F.; m. Barbara Jean Bellis, May 30, 1958 (div. 1973); children: Philip Foster, Elizabeth Jean. BS in Petroleum Engring., U. Okla., 1957; JD, So. Methodist U., 1964. Registered profl. engr., Tex. Petroleum engr. Mobil Oil Corp., Denver City, Tex., 1957-59; prodn. mgr. Bayview Oil Corp., Dallas, 1959-65; sec., dir. Siboney Corp., Dallas, 1965-70; pres., dir. Northland Oils Ltd., Dallas, 1970-89, Costa Resources, Inc., Dallas, 1972—; v.p., dir. Internat. Oil & Gas Corp., Dallas, 1979-84. Mem. Rep. Eagles, Washington. Mem. State Bar Tex., Ind. Petroleum Assn. Am., Soc. Petroleum Engrs., Am. Petroleum Inst., Energy Club of Dallas, Mensa. Presbyterian. Clubs: Willow Bend Polo, Midland Country, Beverly Hills. Home: 4138 Crossing Ln Dallas TX 75220-5036 Office: Costa Resources Inc 3103 W Golf Course Rd Midland TX 79701-2914

FRANKLIN, ROOSEVELT, minister; b. Chattanooga, Aug. 30, 1933; s. James R. and Cora Ann (Ponds) F.; m. Darnell Pinkston, Sept. 30, 1972; children: Sophia, Dellazar. BS, Northeastern U., 1958; MA (hon.), Savannah State Coll., 1962; M. of Cybernetics, Grad. Sch. Wicca, St. Charles, Mo. Lic. metaphysician. Pastor Free For All Bapt. Ch., Greenwood, S.C., 1959-61; radio min. Spiritual Ch., Aiken, S.C., 1961-63; nat. lectr. United Coun. Spiritual Ch., Raleigh, N.C., 1963-66; min. Holy Trinity House of God, Macon, Ga., 1966—; youth dir. Holy Trinity Ch., Macon, 1966-72, talent coord., 1966-73; dir. Spiritual Singers, 1966—; lectr. in field; world renown authority on witchcraft and transcendental meditation; expert in clairvoyance, spiritual meditation. Organizer voters registration, Macon, 1977; pub. relations vol. Nat. Dem. Party, Atlanta, 1984; bd. dirs. Retired Persons Assn., 1980—. Capt. U.S. Army, 1951-54, Korea. Named extrovert promoter Music Workshop, 1979; recipient Hunt Bond Troop award Ft. Valley State Alumni, 1980, Afro Am. Heritage award Afro Am. Heritage Mus., 1987, Golden Eagle award Macon Courier, 1988. Mem. NAACP (life), SCLC (life), Inner Circle Congl. Aids, C. of C., Minister's Alliance (v.p. 1966—, Citizens award 1979), Ga. Black Am. Pageant (coord. 1980—, Leadership award 1982), Direct Sellers League, Smooth Ashler (dist. dep. 1970—), Rolls-Royce Club, Woodsmen of Am., Pioneer Club, Shriners (nat. amb.), Masons (33 deg., sovereign grand gen. inspector), Optimist, Kiwanis, Civitan, Elks, Nat. Lodge (treas. 1987—), Potentate of the Rosicruscins, Sertoma, Lions. Democrat. Office: Holy Trinity House of God 280 Straight St Macon GA 31204-6100

FRANKLIN, RUDOLPH MICHAEL, ophthalmologist, medical association administrator; b. Elizabeth, N.J., May 16, 1943. AB, Johns Hopkins U., 1965, MD, 1969, MA, 1979. Diplomate Am. Bd. Ophthalmology, Nat. Bd. Med. Examiners. Intern in medicine associated hosps. SUNY, Buffalo, 1969-70; resident in ophthalmology Wilmer Inst. Johns Hopkins U. Sch. Medicine, Balt., 1970-71; fellow in ophthalmology Johns Hopkins U. Sch. Medicine, Balt., 1975-76, instr. in ophthalmology, 1977-78, asst. physician retinal vascular clinic, 1978; staff assoc. allergenic products sect. lab. bacterial products divsn. biologics stds. NIH, 1971-73; asst. prof. ophthalmology sch. medicine La. State U. Med. Ctr., New Orleans, 1978-82, assoc. prof., 1982-86, prof., 1986-91, dir. med. retina and uveitis svc., 1978-91; pvt. practice ophthalmologist New Orleans, 1991—; dir. Bob Hope Eye Rsch. Ctr., Houston, 1991—; mem. corneal diseases panel Nat. Eye Adv. Coun., 1980-81; mem. sect. on microbiology and immunology com. ARVO, 1981-83, chmn. sect. microbiology and immunology, 1983; mem. exec. com. NIH Med. Student Tng. Grant, 1981; examining physician prospective evaluation radial keratotomy study NEI-NIH Multicenter Clin. Study, 1981-82; mem. grant rev. com. Fight for Sight, 1982; ad hoc mem. neuroscience study sect. NEI, Bethesda, Md., 1983; mem. spl. study sect. visual scis. NIH, Washington, 1985, spl. study sect. small bus. innovation rsch. program, Bethesda, 1985, AIDS and Related Rsch. Group, 1990-92; mem. corneal diseases panel midcourse evaluation Nat. Eye Adv. Coun./NIH, 1985; mem. steering com. Studies Ocular Complications AIDS, 1990. Contbr. over 116 articles, papers and abstracts to med. and profl. jours. Officer USPHS, 1971-73. Recipient Alfred P. Sloan award, 1967, Seeing Eye, Inc. award, 1968, Rsch. award Fight for Sight, 1977; grantee NIH, 1978-93, 82-89, 89-91, NIH/Pfizer, 1983-88, Fidia Pharm. Corp., 1987-89, Alcon Labs., 1991-93. Mem. Am. Acad. Ophthalmology (basic and clin. sci. course faculty 1990-95), Am. Assn. Immunologists, Am. Uveitis Soc. (sec.-treas.), Assn. for Rsch. in Vision and Ophthalmology, La. State Med. Soc., La.-Miss. Ophthal. and Otolaryn. Soc., Orleans Parish Med. Soc., New Orleans Acad. Ophthalmology (exec. com. 1986-92, v.p. 1988-90, pres.-elect. 1990-92, pres. 1992-94). Address: 3535 Bienville St Ste W380 New Orleans LA 70119-5253

FRANKS, ALLEN, research institute executive, educator; b. Cleve., Nov. 12, 1936; s. Stanley Arthur and Helen Dorothy (Kulwicki) F.; m. Cary Bajko, Feb. 2, 1963; children: Mathew, Sara. BS, U. Miami, 1959; LLB, Case Western Res. U., 1963, JD, 1968; Cert. chem. engr. Patent atty. B.F. Goodrich Co., Akron, Ohio, 1963-65; chemist, mgr. paint testing lab. P.P.G. Industries, Barberton, Ohio, 1965-66; tech. dir., lab. mgr. Reichhold Chems., Ind., Cuyahoga Falls, Ohio, 1966-76; instr. Inst. Astral Studies, Inc., Akron,

1974-80, pres., 1977-80; mgr. tech. sales Sovereign Chem. Co., Cuyahoga Falls, 1980-86; pres. I.A.S. Inc., 1986-94; sec.-treas. rsch. divsn. IAA, 1990-95, pres., 1995—; CEO Cary Franks Inc., 1995—; lectr. astrology, biorhythms, tennis Akron U., 1974-79, Kent (Ohio) State U., 1973-77. Contbr. articles to profl. jours. Bd. dirs. Persephone Found., Bath, Ohio, 1974-80, chmn., 1981-86; instr. tennis YWCA, Goodyear Racquet Club. Served with USCGR, 1954-62. Fellow Am. Inst. Chemists; mem. N.Y. Acad. Scis., AAAS, Ohio Inst. Chemists (treas. 1976-84, pres. 1984-90). Am. Chem. Soc., Akron Rubber Group, Northeast Ohio Rubber Group, Mensa, Intertel, Crystal Lake Country Club, Phi Delta Phi, Univ. Club, Goodyear Racquet Club, Towpath Racquet Club. Office: 4211 NE 12th Ave Pompano Beach FL 33064-5939

FRANKS, HERSCHEL PICKENS, judge; b. Savannah, Tenn., May 28, 1930; s. Herschel R. and Vada (Pickens) F.; m. Judy Black; 1 child, Ramona. Student U. Tenn.-Martin, U. Md.; JD, U. Tenn.-Knoxville; grad. Nat. Jud. Coll. of U. Nev. Bar: Tenn. 1959, U.S. Supreme Ct. 1968. Claims atty. U.S. Fidelity & Guaranty Co., Knoxville, 1958; ptnr. Harris, Moon, Meacham & Franks, Chattanooga, 1959-70; chancellor 3d Chancery div. of Hamilton County, 1970-78; judge Tenn. Ct. Appeals, Chattanooga, 1978—; spl. justice Tenn. Supreme Ct., 1979, 86, 87; presiding judge Hamilton County Trial Cts., 1977-78; spl. judge Tenn. Ct. of Criminal Appeals, 1990-92; mem. commn. to study appellate cts., 1990-92. Served with USNG, 1949-50, USAF, 1950-54. Mem. ABA (award of merit), Tenn. Bar Assn. (award of merit 1968-69), Tenn. Bar Found., Chattanooga Bar Found., Chattanooga Bar Assn. (pres. 1968-69, Founds. of Freedom award 1986), Am. Judicature Soc., Inst. Jud. Adminstrn., Optimists (pres. 1965-66), Community Service award 1971), Mountain City Club, LeConte Club, City Farmers Club, Phi Alpha Delta. Mem. United Ch. of Christ. Address: 540 Mccallie Ave Ste 562 Chattanooga TN 37402-2089

FRANKS, HOLLIS BERRY, retired investment executive; b. Sugar Tree, Tenn., Jan. 18, 1916; s. Louis Berry and Mary Maggie (Oxford) F.; m. Anne Moody, June 22, 1940 (dec. Jan 1993); children: Robert Berry, June Anne Franks Johnson. BS in Agr., U. Tenn., 1937; MEd, U. Mo., 1940. Cert. tchr. Tchr. Tenn. Dept. Edn., various locations, 1922-39; tchr. vocat. agriculture Sardis, Tenn., 1937-38; tchr. vocat. agr. and vocat. edn. U. Mo., Columbia and Richland, 1939-42; mgr. The Large Mo. Turkey Show, Richland, 1940-41; regional mgr. Ralston Purina Co., 1942-60; stock and commodity broker Bache & Co., Greensboro, N.C., 1960-70; 2d v.p. investments Shearson Lehman & Hutton, Memphis, 1970-81; fin. advisor to sr. citizens, 1982—; gen. sales mgr. adv. bd. Ralston Purina Co., 1947-57. Mem. Henderson County Ret. Tchrs. (v.p. 1986—), Lexington Rotary Club (bd. dirs. 1989-90), Phi Kappa Phi, Phi Delta Kappa. Republican. Baptist. Home: 336 N Broad St Lexington TN 38351-1677

FRANKS, ROBERT YATES, college administrator; b. Dallas, Apr. 10, 1948; s. B. Jack and Betty Jean (Bankston) F.; m. Jane Ellen Franks, May 16, 1977 (div. Feb. 1991); children: Ellen, Robert, Joseph, Carolyn. BS in Edn., Tex. A&M U., 1969, MEd in Curriculum and Instrn., 1970; postgrad., U. North Tex., 1991—. Cert. tchr. Tex. Sci. tchr. Birdville Ind. Sch. Dist., Fort Worth, 1972-75, Brazosport Ind. Sch. Dist., Freeport, Tex., 1975-78; ops. mgr. Am. Cyanamid Co., Carrolton, Tex., 1978-83; petroleum engr. Profile Control Svcs., Lewisville, Tex., 1983-84; prodn. mgr., human resource mgr. Ecolab, Inc., Garland, Tex., 1984-86; sci. tchr. Ford Bend Ind. Sch. Dist., Sugarland, Tex., 1986-87; petroleum engr. CPE Assocs., Denton, Tex., 1987-89; sci. tchr. Krum (Tex.) Ind. Sch. Dist., 1989-91; tech prep coord. Navarro Coll., Corsicana, Tex., 1991—; adv. mem. Tex. SPECAP, Tex. Tech U., Lubbock, 1995—; mktg. adv. com. Tex. Tech. Prep Dirs., Austin, 1991—; adv. mem. N.C. Tex. Sch.-to-Work Com., Arlington, 1995—; presenter in field. Author: Lizard Labs, 1995. Explorer advisor Boy Scouts Am., Freeport, Tex., 1974-77, Haltom City, Tex., 1972-74, asst. scoutmaster, 1971-72. Mem. ASCD, Am. Vocat. Assn., Nat. Tech Prep Network, Tex. Tech Dirs. Assn., Phi Delta Kappa (pres. 1996—, v.p. programs 1995-96). Episcopalian. Home: 301 Miracle Dr Apt 207 Corsicana TX 75110 Office: Navarro Coll 3200 West 7th Corsicana TX 75110

FRANSE, JEAN LUCILLE, secondary school educator; b. Comanche, Okla., Jan. 24, 1932; d. Robert Sydney and Mary Lee (Hooper) McDonald; children: Steven E. Franse, John K. Franse, James M. Franse. BS, Eastern N.Mex. U., 1969, MA, 1976; postgrad., Tex. Tech. U. Cert. ESL, mid-mgmt. Telephone operator Mountain States Telephone, Clovis, N.Mex., 1950-51; mktg. rschr. Opinions Unltd., Amarillo, Tex., 1985-88; sch. tchr. Farwell (Tex.) Ind. Schs., 1969—; bookkeeper, pres. Franse Irrigation, Inc., Farwell, 1985—. Author: (poetry) World of Poetry Anthology, 1991 (Golden Poet award 1991), Our World's Favorite Poems (Outstanding award 1993), Outstanding Poets of 1994, 1994 (Merit award 1994). Mem. Christian Coalition, Dallas, 1994, Ctr. for Am. Values, Washington, 1993-94, Liberty Alliance, Forest, Va., 1994. Mem. ASCD. Home: PO Box 580 Farwell TX 79325-0580 Office: Farwell Ind Sch Dist Box F Farwell TX 79325

FRANTZ, CECILIA ARANDA, psychologist; b. Nogales, Ariz., Aug. 6, 1941; d. Tomas Navarro and Maria Guadalupe (Covarrubias) A.; m. Roger Allen Frantz, May 27, 1972; 1 child, Kimberly Marie Whelan. BA, U. Ariz., 1966; MA, Ariz. State U., 1972, PhD, 1975. Lic. clin. psychologist, Ariz., sch. psychologist, Va. Tchr. Wilson Sch. Dist., Phoenix, 1966-70; psychologist Child Evaluation Ctr., Phoenix, 1973-75; sch. psychologist Wilson Sch. Dist., Phoenix, 1975-78, spl. edn. dir., 1977-78, schs. supt., 1978-81; acting dir. Nat. Inst. Handicap Rsch. U.S. Dept. Edn., Washington, 1981-82, dep. asst. sec. dept. elm. and secondary edn., 1982-87; asst. dir. Bush's Nat. Steering Com. Campaign Hdqrs., Washington, 1987-88; pvt. practice Washington, 1988—; sch. psychologist Cath. Diocese of Arlington, Va., 1990-92; Arlington County Schs., Arlington, Va., 1992—; cons. U.S. Dept. Edn., Washington, 1987—. Mem. APA, Am. Assn Sch. Adminstrs., Ariz. State Psychol. Assn., Ariz. State Sch. Psychologists Assn., Maricopa Soc. Clin. Psychologists (sec. 1976-77). Republican. Roman Catholic. Home: 4501 Arlington Blvd Apt 609 Arlington VA 22203-2740

FRANZ, FRANK ANDREW, university president, physics educator; b. Phila., Sept. 16, 1937; s. Russell Ernest and Edna (Keller) F.; m. Judy Rosenbaum, July 11, 1959; 1 child, Eric Douglas. BS in Physics, Lafayette Coll., 1959; MS in Physics, U. Ill., 1961, PhD in Physics, 1964. Research assoc. U. Ill., Urbana, 1964-65; asst. prof. physics Ind. U., Bloomington, 1967-70, assoc. prof., 1970-74, prof., 1974-85, assoc. dean Coll. Arts and Scis., 1974-77, dean faculties, 1977-82; prof. physics, provost, v.p. academic affairs and research W.Va. U., Morgantown, 1985-91; prof. physics, pres. U. Ala., Huntsville, 1991—; guest scientist Swiss Fed. Inst. Tech., Zurich, 1965-67, U. Munich, 1978. Contbr. articles to profl. jours. NSF fellow, 1965-67, Alfred P. Sloan fellow, 1968-70. Fellow Am. Phys. Soc.; mem. AAAS, AAUP (pres. Bloomington, Ind. chpt. 1972-73), Am. Assn. Physics Tchrs., Sigma Xi. Office: Office of President Univ Alabama Huntsville AL 35899

FRANZ, RAYMOND VICTOR, editor, publisher; b. Dayton, Ky., May 8, 1922; s. Herman Frederick and Hazel Lucille (Atkins) F.; m. Cynthia Marie Badame, Feb. 28, 1959. Diploma, Bible Sch. Gilead, 1944, Bible Sch. Gilead, 1964. With Watch Tower Bible and Tract Soc., Jehovah's Witnesses, 1940-80; supt., traveling supr. P.R. and V.I., 1946-51; supt. Dominican Republic, 1961-65; mem. editorial staff Bklyn., 1965-71; mem. internat. governing body, 1971-80; clerical worker Gregerson's Supermarkets, Gadsden, Ala., 1980-85; founder, editor, pub. Commentary Press, Atlanta, 1983—. Author: Crisis of Conscience, 1983 (8 printings, 9 langs.), In Search of Christian Freedom, 1991, (3 langs.); co-author: Aid to Bible Understanding, 1971. Office: Commentary Press PO Box 43532 Atlanta GA 30336-0532

FRARY, MICHAEL, artist, educator; b. Santa Monica, Calif., May 28, 1918; s. Ira Earl Frary and Henrietta Chittenden; m. Gloria Marvin (div. 1951); 1 child, Michael Jr. (dec.); m. Lola Marguerite Finch, July 21, 1951; children: Mark, David. BArch, U. So. Calif., 1940, MFA in Painting, 1941; diploma, Acad. de la Grande Chaumiere, Paris, 1950. Instr. aviation subjects USN, Jacksonville, Fla., 1941-45; asst. art dir. Goldargus Paramount Universal Studios, Hollywood, 1946-48; art instr. UCLA, 1948-50; art instr., faculty chmn. San Antonio Art Inst., 1950-52; prof. art U. Tex., Austin, 1952-86, ret., 1986. Author: Impressions of the Texas Panhandle, 1977, Watercolors of the Rio Grande, 1984; one man shows include Witte Mus., San Antonio, McNay Mus. Art, San Antonio, Art Mus. South Tex., Corpus Christi, Springfield Mus. Art, Mo., Colorado Springs Fine Arts Mus., Peabody Mus., Salem, Mass., Inst. Texan Cultures, San Antonio, Amarillo Art Ctr., Tex., Huntington Art Gallery U. Tex., Austin, Rudder Ctr. Tex. A&M, College Station, Performing Arts Ctr. U. Tex., Austin, IC2 Inst. U. Tex., Austin, U. Tex. Med. Sch., San Antonio, Dalzell Hatfield Gallery, L.A., Janet Nessler, N.Y., Sante Fe East, Gallery, Scottsdale, Ariz., Meredith Long, Houston, Valley House, Dallas, The Gallery, Palm Springs, Calif., and numerous others; executed murals at Inner Space Caverns, Georgetown, Tex., Brackenridge Hosp., Austin, Tex., Forest Oil Co., Nat. Bank of Commerce, San Antonio, Headliners Club, Austin, KTBC Bldg., Austin; represented in permanent collections at Nat. Mus. Am. Art, Smithsonian Instn., Washington, Interior Bldg., Washington, Butler Inst. Am. Art, Youngtown, Ohio, L.A. County Mus., Santa Barbara Mus. Art, Dallas Mus. Fine Arts, Phillips Petroleum Bldg., Bartlesville, Okla., Springfield Art Mus., Mo., Va. Mus. Fine Arts, Richmond, Virginia Scott Mus., Pasadena, Amarillo Art Ctr., Tex., McNay Mus., San Antonio, Tex. Instruments, Dallas. Mem. Athletics Coun., Utah, 1977-81. Recipient medal of honor AIA Austin Chpt., 1974, citation of honor Tex. Soc. Architects, 1974, and numerous others. Mem. Nat. Watercolor Soc. (bd. dirs.), Watercolor USA Honor Soc., Southwestern Watercolor Soc. (hon. life), Tex. Watercolor Soc. (purple sage status), Waterloo Watercolor Group (hon. life), Miss. Watercolor Soc. (signature mem.). Home and Studio: 3409 Spanish Oak Dr Austin TX 78731

FRASE, LARRY LYNN, internist, medical association administrator; b. Austin, Tex., June 18, 1957; s. Leland Leo and Mary Dawn (Courtney) F.; m. Debra Lynn Kimble, May 26, 1979; children: Scott, Laura, Kevin. BS summa cum laude, Baylor U., 1979; MD, U. Tex. Southwestern, 1983. Diplomate Am. Bd. Internal Medicine. Chief med. resident, asst. instr. internal medicine U. Tex. Southwestern Med. Sch., Dallas, 1986-87; internist, v.p. Internal Medicine Assn. Longview, Tex., 1988—; chief of medicine Good Shepherd Med. Ctr., Longview, 1990-92, pres. med. staff, 1993-94, med. dir. transitional care unit, 1994—. Contbr. articles to med. jours. Pres. Am. Heart Assn., Longview, 1992-93. Student rsch. fellow Am. Gastroenterol. Assn., 1981. Mem. ACP, Tex. Soc. Internal Medicine (bd. dirs. 1991-93), Tex. Med. Assn., Oak Forest Country Club, Phi Beta Kappa, Alpha Omega Alpha. Republican. Methodist. Home: 1108 Stillmeadow Ln Longview TX 75604-2822 Office: Internal Medicine Assn 703 E Marshall Ave Ste 101 Longview TX 75601-5563

FRASER, CLEVELAND ROBERT, political science educator; b. Portland, Oreg., June 23, 1953; s. Cleveland and Camilla Rosalie (Rosefield) F.; m. Sandra Louise Tapia, July 29, 1978. BA, U. Ariz., 1976; MA in Internat. Rels., Can. Politics, U. Toronto, 1977; PhD in Internat. Rels., Northwestern U., 1987. Teaching fellow Northwestern U., Evanston, Ill., 1978-82, teaching asst., 1981-82, rsch. asst., 1982-83; instr. Furman U., Greenville, S.C., 1983-86, asst. prof. polit. sci., 1986-91, assoc. prof. polit. sci., 1991—; co-dir. Eng./European Communities Program, 1987, 89, Baltic Study Program, 1989, 93; dir. Washington Term Program, 1989, 94, Latin Am. Program. Co-author: (with H. Paul Friesema and Janice A. Beecher) Blowing in the Wind: The Prospects for Utility Adoption of Wind Energy Systems, 1981; contbr. articles to profl. jours. Mem. house selection com. Greenville Habitat for Humanity, 1986; mem. internat. studies adv. com. Southside High Sch., Greenville, 1992. H.B. Earhart fellow, 1979-81, fellow Northwestern U., 1978; grantee NCR Corp., 1985, faculty devel. grantee Furman U., 1983, 91, 92, rsch. and profl. growth grantee, 1987, 88, Can. studies faculty enrichment grantee, 1989, 93, Que. studies faculty enrichment grantee, 1991. Mem. Am. Polit. Sci. Assn., Internat. Studies Assn., Internat. Studies Assn./South, Assn. for Can. Studies in U.S., S.E. Coun. for Can. Studies, Latin Am. Studies Assn., Southeastern Coun. of Latin Am. Studies. Home: 10 Old Mill Rd Greenville SC 29607-5312 Office: Furman Univ Dept Polit Sci 3300 Poinsett Hwy Greenville SC 29613-0002

FRASER, DAVID BEN, psychiatrist; b. Houston, Oct. 20, 1926; s. Malcolm Joseph and Edith Frieda (Faber) F.; m. Joan Beckley Isley, Mar. 12, 1951 (div. Feb. 1979); m. Nell Ann Brumley, June 30, 1979; children: Susan Lynn, David Ben Jr., John Randall, Vicki Ann. BA, U. Tex., 1948; MD, U. Tex., Galveston, 1952. Diplomate Am. Bd. Psychiatry and Neurology. Intern Meml. Hosp, Corpus Christi, 1952-53; resident in psychiatry VA Hosp., North Little Rock, 1965-68; chief psychiat. outpatient sect. VA Hosp., North Little Rock, Ark., 1974-76; chief psychiatry So. Ark. Hosp. Med. Ctr., El Dorado, 1979—; asst. prof. psychiatry La. State U., Shreveport, 1986—, U. Ark. for Med. Scis., Little Rock, 1969—; med. dir. So. Ark. Regional Health Ctr., El Dorado, 1979—. Recipient Disting. Svc. award Ark. Coun. Cmty. Mental Health Ctrs., 1984, Physician's Recognition award AMA, Washington, 1995—. Fellow Am. Psychiat. Assn. (life); mem. Ark. Psychiat. Soc. (pres. 1973), Gulf Coast Acad. Gen. Practice (pres. 1969). Methodist. Office: So Ark Regional Health Ctr 715 N College Ave El Dorado AR 71730-4403

FRASER, HOWARD MICHAEL, foreign language educator, editor; b. N.Y.C., Nov. 11, 1943; s. Irving Jacob and Melvina (Epstein) F.; m. Ruth Carole Rea, June 17, 1967; children: Megan, Benjamin. BA, Columbia U., 1964; MA, N.Mex. U., 1966; AM, Harvard U., 1967; PhD, N.Mex. U., 1970. Grad. asst. instr. Spanish U. N.Mex., Albuquerque, 1964-66, instr. English, 1967; lab. asst. Southwestern Coop.-Edn. Lab., Albuquerque, 1968; assoc. Portuguese U. N.Mex., 1969-70, instr. Spanish, 1970; asst. prof. U. Wis., Madison, 1970-74; from asst. to assoc. prof. William and Mary Coll., Williamsburg, Va., 1974-82, prof., 1982—; prof. NEH, 1993—; review editor Latin Am. Literary Review, Pitts., 1975-85; assoc. editor Chasqui, Tempe, Ariz., 1972—, Hispania, L.A., 1986-95. Author: (books) Magazines and Masks, 1987, In the Presence of Mystery: Modernist Fiction and the Occult, 1992. Mem. Am. Assn. Tchrs. Spanish and Portuguese (editl. bd., pres. 1986-95), MLA. Office: Coll William & Mary Dept Modern Langs Williamsburg VA 23187

FRASER, JOHN WAYNE, insurance executive, consultant, underwriter; b. Ashland, Ala., Jan. 19, 1944; s. Elliott Nathaniel and Maurice Jennette (Glenn) F.; m. Diana Louise Renn, Jan. 20, 1963; children: Christine Celeste, Sean Elliott. AA in Bus. Adminstrn., St. Petersburg Jr. Coll., 1969; BA with honors, U. South Fla., 1974. Dir. mfg. svcs. Milton Roy Co., St. Petersburg, Fla., 1965-74; sales rep. Fla. Forms Co., Tampa, 1975-76, Graphic Bus. Systems, St. Petersburg, 1976-79; dist. mgr. Blue Cross/Blue Shield Fla., St. Petersburg, 1979-86; sr. v.p. Wittner Cos., 1986—. Mem. Internat. Found. Employee Benefit Welfare Plans. With U.S. Army, 1962. Mem. Bay Area Benefits Assn. (pres. 1989-90), Fla. West Coast Employee Benefit Coun. (bd. dirs. 1994—), Nat. Assn. Health Underwriters (trustee West Coast chpt. 1988—, pres. 1992-93), Fla. Assn. Health Underwriters (bd. dirs. 1992-93, 1st v.p. 1993-94, pres. 1994-95), Cen. Pinellas Jaycees (treas. 1975, v.p. 1976), U. South Fla. Alumni Assn. Democrat. Unitarian-Universalist. Office: 5999 Central Ave Ste 400 Saint Petersburg FL 33710-8535

FRASURE, CARL MAYNARD, political science educator; b. Morgantown, W.Va., Aug. 21, 1938; s. Carl Maynard and Louise (Durham) F.; m. Beverly Brown, Sept. 1, 1962 (div. Aug. 1980); 1 child, Stephanie Frasure Goff. BS, W.Va. U., 1962, MA, 1965, MS, 1966, PhD, 1980; postgrad., Ohio U., 1985. Cert. secondary tchr., W.Va. Extension prof. W.Va. U., Morgantown, 1966-82; dir. student svcs. Bluefield (W.Va.) State U., 1982-83; prof. Salem (W.Va.)-Teikyo U., 1983—, chmn. polit. sci. dept., 1983—, asst. to acad. dean, 1984-86; cons. W.Va. Dept. Edn., Charleston, 1990; chairperson social scis. divsn., 1994—. Author, editor: W.Va. U. Non-credit Programs Catalog, 1980. Treas. Polit. Action Com. for Better Edn., Clarksburg, 1990; mem. Bridgeport (W.Va.) Police Civil Svc. Commn., 1993—; mem. Clarksburg Police Civil Svc. Commn, 1994—. Sgt. U.S. Army, 1957-63. U.S. Dept. Edn. grantee, 1966-70, 82-87, Options grantee Brown U., 1991. Mem. Am. Polit. Sci. Assn., W.Va. Polit. Sci. Assn., Phi Delta Kappa (treas. W.Va. U. chpt. 1984), Lions (treas. Bridgeport chpt. 1987-93, pres. 1993—), Elks (essay judge Clarksburg chpt. 1983—). Democrat. Episcopalian. Home: 1088 Taylor St Clarksburg WV 26301-4227 Office: Salem-Teikyo U Penn Ave Political Sci Dept Salem WV 26426

FRATES, RALPH CORYELL, JR., pediatrician, educator; b. San Francisco, Dec. 8, 1943; s. Ralph Coryell and Elizabeth (Bedford) F.; m. Sarah Ann Burnett, Dec. 20, 1969. BA in Biol. Scis., Stanford U., 1965; MD, Tulane U., 1969. Diplomate Am. Bd. Pediatrics. Intern L.A. County/U. So. Calif. Med. Ctr., L.A., 1969-70; resident in Pediatrics Baylor Coll. Medicine, Houston, 1972-74, pulmonary fellow, 1974-76; asst. prof. Pediatrics U. Calif., Davis, 1976-82, Baylor Coll. Medicine, Houston, 1982-84; rsch. med. officer NIH, Bethesda, Md., 1984-86; assoc. prof. Pediatrics med. br. U. Tex., Galveston, 1986-92; assoc. prof. Health Scis. Ctr. U. Tex., Houston, 1992—. Capt. U.S. Army, 1970-72, Vietnam; Lt. Col. U.S. Army, 1990-91, Desert Storm. Office: U Tex Health Sci Ctr Dept Pediat 6431 Fannin St Houston TX 77030-1501

FRAZER, DAVID HUGH, JR., allergist; b. Montgomery, Ala., Mar. 31, 1937; s. David H. and Sue Ray (Durrett) F.; m. Johnnie Bowie Swetenburg, July 5, 1941; children: David Hugh III, Bowie Swetenburg, Wills Findley. BS, Tulane U., 1958, MD, 1961. Private practice Atlanta, 1966-67, Montgomery, 1967—. Bd. dirs. S. Ala. State Fair, Montgomery, Brantwood Children's Home. With USAF, 1962-64. Fellow Am. Coll. Allergy and Immunology; mem. Am. Acad. Allergy and Immunology. Republican. Presbyterian. Office: 1420 Narrow Lane Pky Montgomery AL 36111-2654

FRAZER, JAMES NISBET, JR., artist, photographer; b. Atlanta, Oct. 6, 1949; s. James Nisbet and Rebecca (Young) F.; m. Kathryn Lenore Johnson, May 31, 1980; children: Jamieson, John Nisbet, Katie. BA, Amherst Coll., 1971; MVA, Ga. State U., 1973. instr. Atlanta Coll. Art, Ga. State U. and Mercer U. Atlanta, 1972-82; founding pres. Nexus, Inc. (now Nexus Contemporary Art Ctr.), Atlanta, 1973-74, bd. dirs., 1973-81. One-man shows include Heath Gallery, Atlanta, 1977, 80, 83, 87, 93, Photography Gallery, Va. Intermont Coll., Bristol, 1992, Gallery A, Savannah (Ga.) Coll. Art and Design, 1984, Southeastern Ctr. Contemporary Art, Winston-Salem, N.C., 1982, High Mus. Art, Atlanta, 1981, Nexus Gallery, 1973, 75, others; exhibited in group shows at Bird-in-Hand Photography Gallery, Arlington, Va., 1972, Ctrl. Wash. State Gallery, Ellensburg, 1973, Nexus Gallery, 1975, Ohio Silver Gallery, L.A., 1975, U.S. Info. Agy. (travelled to Ctrl. and S. Am.), 1976, The High Mus. Art, Atlanta, 1979, travelling shows: Mus. Art, Ft. Lauderdale, El Paso Mus. Art, Holzman Art Gallery, Towson (Md.) State U., Mus. of the Rockies, Mont. State U., Bozeman, The Nickle Arts Mus., U. Calgary, Can., Wichita Falls Mus. and Art Ctr., Midland (Mich.) Ctr. for Arts, numerous others, group shows at Marcuse Pfeifer Gallery, N.Y.C., 1984, Chapelle de La Sorbonne, Paris, Centre d'Action Culturelle, Angoulême, Refectoire des Jacobins, Toulouse, 1985, Detroit Inst. Arts, 1985, Atlanta Botanical Garden, 1990, Nexus Contemporary Art Ctr., 1993, numerous others; represented in permanent collections and commissions Hurt, Richardson, Garner, Todd & Cadenhead, Atlanta, McDonald's Corp., HBO & Co., Atlanta, Robinson-Humphrey, Atlanta, Prudential Life Ins., Jacksonville, Fla., Omni Internat. Hotel, Atlanta, VA Med. Ctr., Atlanta, Michael C. Carlos Mus., Emory U., Atlanta, Montgomery (Ala.) Mus. Fine Arts, Vassar Coll. Art Gallery, Poughkeepsie, N.Y., The High Mus. Art, Addison Gallery Am. Art, Andover, Mass.; works published in books: The Southern Ethic, 1975, The Creative Camera (Nancy Howell-Koehler), 1989; contbr. articles to profl. jours.

FRAZER, RUSSELL THEODORE, general engineer; b. Chattanooga, Mar. 10, 1956; s. Chalmers Fletcher and Dorothy Ruth (Gonzalez) F. BA, Columbia U., 1978; BSChemE, La. State U., 1981; postgrad., U. Calif., Berkeley, Calif. State U., Pomona and Northridge; BSEE, George Mason U., 1996. Teaching asst. dept. chemistry and physics Dept. Chemistry and Physics, La. State U., Baton Rouge, 1978; quality control technician Airco Indsl. Gases, Port Allen, La., 1979-80; nuclear sci. lab. technician dept. natural resources Nuclear Sci. and Environ. Monitoring Lab., Baton Rouge, 1980-81; gen. engr. Dept. of the Navy, Calif., 1981-84; gen. engr. and electronics engr. Dept. of Army, Warrenton, Va., 1984—. Mem. IEEE. Office: Signals Warfare Directorate US Dept Army Warrenton VA 20187

FRAZER, STUART HARRISON, III, cotton merchant; b. Montgomery, Ala., Feb. 13, 1948; s. Stuart Harrison Jr. and Myrta Frances (Garrett) F.; m. Linda Gail Patterson, Nov. 21, 1971 (div. 1983); 1 child, Heather Allison; m. Mary Prue Coleman, Oct. 28, 1983; 1 child, Meredith Jane. Student, Huntingdon Coll., Montgomery, 1966-68, Auburn (Ala.) U., 1970-73. V.p. Weil Bros. Cotton Inc., Montgomery, 1970-88; sr. v.p. Rollins Cotton Co., Montgomery, 1988-92; pres. Rollins Cotton Co., Montomery, 1992—; mem. USDA adv. com. con Cotton Clasing, Washington, 1988—; bd. dirs. N.Y. Cotton Exch., Cotton Coun. Internat., Nat. Cotton Coun.; mem. agrl. adv. com. to Commodity Futures Trading Commn., Washington. Mem. YMCA Boys Work Com., pres. 1986-87. With U.S. Army, 1968-69. Mem. Am. Cotton Shippers Assn. (dir., 1st v.p. 1992, 2nd v.p. 1991, pres. 1993), Nat. Cotton Coun., Atlantic Cotton Assn. (pres. 1981-82), Montgomery Cotton Exch. (pres. 1976—), Montgomery Country Club. Episcopalian. Home: 2517 Darrington Rd Montgomery AL 36111-1527 Office: Rollins Cotton Co 301 Church St Montgomery AL 36104-3427

FRAZER, VICTOR OLANZO, lawyer. BA in History, Fisk U., 1964; JD, Howard U., 1971. Pvt. practice Washington, N.Y., Md., V.I.; del. at large, V.I. U.S. Ho. Reps., Washington, 1995—; mem. com. on internat. rels. U.S. Ho. Reps., mem. subcom. on Africa, mem. congl. black caucus, arts caucus, boating caucus, tourism and travel caucus, edn. caucus, ho. renewable energy caucus, congl. caucus on India and Indian-Ams., African trade and investment caucus, congl. coastal caucus, congl. caucus on Hong Kong, mem. task force against anti-semitism. Office: US Ho Reps 1711 Longworth Washington DC 20515-5501

FRAZIER, ALTON EUGENE, interior designer; b. Minden, La., Sept. 11, 1922; s. Carlton Randolph and Gertrude (Sexton) F.; m. Irene Sipple; children: Joan Marie, Dan Jay, Carol Ann, Robert Eugene, Carlton Todd; m. Jacquelyn Heller. Student, La. Tech. U., 1940-42; LLB, La. State U., 1949, JD, 1968. Bar: La. 1949; cert. interior designer, N.Y.; registered interior designer, Tex. Pvt. practice in law Minden, 1949-60; profl. instr. Dale Carnegie Leadership, Ark., La., Tex., 1960-69; interior designer Sangers Design Studio Inc., Dallas, 1960-63, Eugene Frazier Studio, Dallas, 1963—; dir. distbr. Alpine Air Purifiers, Dallas, 1995; independent distbr. Nikken, Inc., Dallas, 1994; instr. So. Meth. U., Dallas, 1956=59; bd. dirs. Cosmopolitan Life Ins. Co.; writer Park Cities People Newspaper, Dallas. Author: Good Taste Begins With You, 1969, Kitchens, The Miracle Room, 1979, New Fashions in Floors, 1979, Glamourize With Lighting, 1979. Patron 500 Inc., Dallas; active Dallas Mus. Fine Arts. Mem. Am. Soc. Interior Designers (profl. mem.), Allied Design Profls., Nat. Writers Assn., Smithsonian Inst., Airliner Gourmet Study Club, Primetimers Internat. Methodist. Home: 4400 Lakeside Dr Dallas TX 75205-3820 also: 624 Elm St Minden LA 71055 Office: 3922 Lemmon Ave Dallas TX 75219-3734

FRAZIER, ANN LYNETTE, medical/surgical nurse; b. Oxford, N.C., Jan. 18, 1960; d. James Edward and Gerald Rene (Hite) F. BSN, Atlantic Christian Coll., Wilson, N.C., 1982. RN, N.C.; cert. med.-surg. nurse ANCC. Staff nurse med.-surg. unit, asst. head nurse Duke U. Med. Ctr., Durham, N.C., 1988-92, advanced staff nurse, 1992—. Recipient Spl. Achievement-Excellence in Nursing Practice award Duke U. Med. Ctr. Friends of Nursing, 1989. Mem. ANA. Home: 3476 Sandy Creek Dr Durham NC 27705-6033 Office: Duke U Med Ctr PO Box 3714 Durham NC 27710

FRAZIER, CLAUDE CLINTON, III, dermatologist, chemistry consultant; b. Hattiesburg, Miss., Aug. 27, 1948; s. Claude Clinton Frazier Jr. and June Elizabeth (Gibson) Geissler; m. Nancy L. Peters, 1977 (div. 1985); 1 child, Clinton Evan; m. Angela D. Haas, 1996. BS, Memphis State U., 1970; MS, Oreg. Grad. Inst., 1972; PhD, Calif. Inst. Tech., Pasadena, 1976; DO, Kirksville Coll. Osteo. Med., 1992. Rsch. fellow Institut for Stralenchemie Max Planck Inst. for Kohlenforschung, Mulheim, Fed. Republic of Germany, 1975-76; rsch. assoc. U. Ga., Athens, 1976-78; asst. prof. U. Minn., Duluth, 1978-82; sr. scientist Martin Marietta Labs., Balt., 1982-88; pvt. practice sci. cons., 1988—; intern Franklin Sq. Hosp. Ctr., Balt., 1992-93; resident in dermatology Gulf South Med. and Surg. Inst., Kenner, La., 1993-96; pvt. practice Bay St. Louis, Miss., 1996—, Slidell, La., 1996—, Picayune, Miss., 1996—; chemistry cons. Martin Marietta Labs., Balt., 1988-91. Contbr. articles to profl. jours.; patentee in field. Mem. Am. Chem. Soc., The Cranial Acad., Am. Osteo. Assn., So. Med. Assn., Sigma Xi. Home: 139 Woodcrest Dr Covington LA 70433-6501 Office: Gulf Coast Dermatology and Dermatologic Surgery Ctr 641 Dunbar Ave Bay Saint Louis MS 39520

FRAZIER, EUGENE RICHARD, designer; b. Columbus, Ohio, Feb. 12, 1947; s. Richard Claire and Catherine Otillia (Abel) F.; m. Nancy Ellen Willeman, Aug. 16, 1969 (div. June 1974); 1 child, Melissa Rachelle; m. Virginia Louise Abel, Aug. 26, 1995. Student, Chippewa Falls Vocat. High, Wis., Wis. U., Calif. Coll. Arts and Crafts, 1965-66; grad. in Interior Design, Rudolph Schaeffer Sch. Design, 1968-70. Lic. designer, Fla., Tex. Archtl. draftsman Pacific Telephone Co., San Francisco, 1966-71; interior designer Western Contract Furnishers, San Jose, Calif., 1971; archtl. designer Irving Caster, Inc., San Mateo, Calif., 1971-74, Eugene R. Frazier & Assocs., San Francisco, 1974-75; comml. photographer Gene Frazier Photography, Mill Valley, Calif., 1975-77; designer to mng. dir. design devel. S&A Restaurant Corp. (The Pillsbury Co.), Dallas, 1977-87; cons. Trump Plaza, West Palm Beach, Fla., 1988-92; design mgr. Furr's/Bishop's Incorporated, Lubbock, Tex., 1992—; participant, advisor Personnel Decisions, Inc., Mpls., 1986. Concept designer and developer Bennigan's Tavern Restaurants, 1977-84; mng. dir. S&A Restaurant Corp. concepts; also Plaza Grills and Lynx Nightclubs for Embassy Suites Hotels, 1985-87. Trustee Am. Indian Relief Coun., 1994—; mem. Rep. Nat. Com., Washington, 1985—, Nat. Rep. Senatorial Com., Austin, 1984—. Recipient Award of Excellence Chgo. Lighting Inst., 1985, Award of Achievement Bennigan's Mgmt. Team, 1983, Nat. Graphics Award of Excellence for Art Direction of S&A's Plaza Grill. Mem. AIA, Am. Soc. Interior Designers, Foodsvc. Cons. Soc. Internat., Internat. Assn. Lighting Designers, Acad. Model Aeros., Planetary Soc., DAV (gold leader Comdrs. Club), Nat. Parks and Conservation Assn., Sedona Mag. Soc., Constrn. Specifications Inst., Am. Archtl. Found., Humane Soc. U.S., Statue of Liberty Found., Nat. Trust for Hist. Preservation. Roman Catholic. Office: Furr's/Bishop's Inc 6901 Quaker Ave Lubbock TX 79413-5943

FRAZIER, TERRY FRANCIS, engineering manager; b. St. Louis, Nov. 23, 1953; s. Francis William and Marilyn Mae (Miller) F.; m. Alma A. Barrera, Mar. 24, 1984; 1 child, Micheal Franklin. BSChemE, Washington U., 1978. Devel. engr. Proctor & Gamble-Latin Am., Cin., 1978-79; sr. rsch. engr. Dow Chem. Energy Rsch., Freeport, Tex., 1979-80, Baton Rouge, 1980-81; project leader Dow Chem. Hydrocarbons Rsch., Freeport, Tex., 1982-85, Dow Chem. Specialty Chems., Freeport, 1985; rsch. leader Dow Chem. R&D Computing, Freeport, 1986-87; group leader R&D computing expert systems and modeling group Dow Chem. Co., Freeport, 1988-91, group leader engring. sci., 1991-93, group leader engr. sci./applied info. sci., 1993; global R&D portfolio mgr., 1993-95; bd. dirs. CyberSoft Inc., Sugarland, Tex.; customer adv. bd. Bolt, Berenek & Newman, Boston, 1991-92. Author: (software) Lifestyles USA. Mem. IEEE, Assn. Computing Machinery. Home: 3035 Golden Hills Ln Missouri City TX 77459-5737 Office: Dow Chemical Bldg B1216 Freeport TX 77541

FRAZIER, WALTER RONALD, real estate investment company executive; b. Dallas, Mar. 3, 1939; s. Walter and Gracie Neydene (Bowers) F.; m. Bertina Jan Simpson, May 10, 1963; children: Ronald Blake, Stephen Bertram. BS in Civil Engring., Tex. A&M U., 1962, BS in Archtl. Constrn., 1962. Tech. dir. Marble Inst., Washington, 1965-68; dir. mktg. Yeonas Co., Vienna, Va., 1969-72; pres. McCarthy Co., Anaheim, Calif., 1972-76, The Frazier Group, Annandale, Va., 1977-79; chmn. Equity Programs Investment Corp., Falls Church, Va., 1980-85; pres., dir. Community Constrn. Co., Falls Church, 1982-85; pres. Palestrina Corp., Falls Church, 1986—; pres. bd. dirs. Annandale Jaycees, 1967-69, Annandale Nat. Little League, 1983-85. Served to 1st lt. U.S. Army, 1963-65. Named to Outstanding Young Men Am., U.S. Jaycees, 1973. Mem. Nat. Assn. Home Builders (bd. dirs. 1991-95), No. Va. Bldg. Industry Assn., (1st v.p., bd. dirs. 1991-95, pres. 1994), Prince William County C. of C. (pres. bd. dirs. 1989-92). Republican. Methodist. Avocations: golf, boating. Home: 4203 Elizabeth Ln Annandale VA 22003-3668 Office: Palestrina Corp 5119A Leesburg Pike Ste 249 Falls Church VA 22041

FRAZIER, WILMA RUTH, emergency nurse, clinical educator; b. Dimmitt, Tex., Dec. 16, 1949; d. Charles William and Agnes May (Behrends) Pennington; m. Robert Lee Frazier, Aug. 25, 1967; children: Troy Linn, Matthew A., Robbie G., Brandy R., Nathan L. AAS, No. Okla. Coll., 1992; postgrad., Okla. U. Health Sci., 1994—. RN. Tchr. Perry Head Start, 1988-90; purchasing clk. Perry (Okla.) Meml. Hosp., 1984-88, nursing asst., 1990-92, med./surg. nurse, 1992-94, inpatient supr., 1994, emergency rm. nurse, 1992—, preceptor nurse externs, 1993—, dietary quality assurance team, 1994, clin. educator, 1996—; Sunday sch. tchr. First Christian Ch., Perry, 1988—, mem. Christian Women's Fellowship, 1968—; mem. Perry Band Boosters Perry Sch. Bands, 1987—; active PTA, Perry Pub. Schs., 1975—. Mem. Student Nurse Assn., Phi Theta Kappa. Republican. Home: RR 2 Box 59 Perry OK 73077-9802 Office: Perry Meml Hosp 501 N 14th St Perry OK 73077-5021

FRAZIER-PETTY, ESTHER IRENE, nursing educator, registered nurse; b. Jones Springs, W.Va., Dec. 9, 1938; d. Daniel Abraham and Rachel Gertrude (Rinaca) Frazier; m. Lewis Phillip Close, Feb. 6, 1959 (div. July 5, 1988); children: Stephen F. (dec.), Karen L. (dec.), Judy L. (dec.); m. Gary Wallace Petty, July 10, 1993; 1 step son, Nathan Wallace Petty. Diploma Nursing, City Hosp. Sch. Nursing, Martinsburg, W.Va., 1959; BSN, George Mason U., Fairfax, Va., 1982. Registered nurse, Va. State Bd. Nursing. Staff nurse War Meml. Hosp., Berkeley Springs, W.Va., 1959-62, 63-64; obstetrical supv. Culpeper (Va.) Meml. Hosp. Inc., 1965-70; asst. dir. nursing, acting dir. nursing, dir. nursing, 1970-73; dir. nursing Orange (Va.) County Nursing Home, 1974-75; clin. nursing instr. Piedmont Tech. Edn. Ctr., Culpeper, Va., 1977-79; pre-clinical nursing instr., dir. nursing, 1982—; dir. nursing program, 1982—, HOSA adv., 1987—, Piedmont Tech. Edn. Ctr.; Culpeper County Health adv. bd. 1993—; tech. prep health care steering com. Germanna C.C., Locust Grove, Va., 1995—; adv. VA Health Occupations Students of Am., state advisor exec. coun. 1993-95; adv. Va. Health Occupational Students of Am., 1993-95. Named Outstanding Health Occupations Students of Am. Adv. Health Occupations Students Am., 1992, Culpeper County Tchr. of Yr. Women's Club of Culpeper, 1996, Va. REgion IV Health Occupations Edn. Tchr. of Yr., 1996. Mem. Am. Vocat. Assn., Va. Vocat. Assn., Va. Health Occupations Edn. Assn., Health Occupations Students Am., Sigma Theta Tau. United Methodist. Home: Rt 1 Box 118 Orange VA 22960 Office: GW Carver-Piedmont Tech Edn Ctr PO Box 999 Culpeper VA 22701

FRAZLER, ROD, agricultural products executive; b. 1948. Asst. terminal mgr. Continental Grain Co., Chgo., 1969-75, mgr., 1984—; v.p. Quincy Soybean Co. of Ark., Helena. Office: Quincy Soybean Co of Ark Hwy 20 S Helena AR 72342

FREAS, GEORGE WILSON, II, computer consultant; b. Franklin, Ky., Oct. 27, 1955; s. George Wilson and Audrey Carolyn Freas; m. Cynthia Anne Fleming, Feb. 19, 1984 (div. Oct. 1990); 1 child, Alexander Morange. BS in Computer Sci., Western Ky. U., 1979; MS in Computer Sci., U. Ala., Huntsville, 1994. Software cons. Bell South Telecom., Birmingham, Ala., 1995—; pres. Synergistic Cons., Inc., Huntsville, 1991—. Author: Canny Canon, 1990; author: (software) GEN7 Desktop, 1993, LALL-LL(1), 1992. Home: PO Box 2885 Huntsville AL 35804-2885 Office: Synergistic Consultants Inc Box 18888 Huntsville AL 35804-8888

FRECH, KENNETH RALSTON, JR., hospital administrator; b. Somerville, N.J., May 22, 1947; s. Kenneth Ralston Sr. and Ann Delores (Vones) F.; m. Sheila Theresa Foley (div.); 1 child, Kenneth Ralston III; m. Pia Helen Kabin; 1 child, Harold William. B of Profl. Studies, Barry U., 1983; M of Health Mgmt., St. Thomas U., 1990; DPA, Nova U., 1996. Cert. solo aviation pilot. Owner, mgr. Ken's Carpets, Hawaiian Gardens, Calif., 1968-70; transp. team leader Fisher Sci., Somerville, 1970-74; constrn. crew chief Best Air-Conditioning Co., Pompano Beach, Fla., 1978-80; patient adv. Jackson Meml. Hosp., Miami, 1980-93, adminstr. on duty, 1993—; pers./adminstrv. officer 324th Combat Support Hosp., Perrine, Fla., 1992-94. Spkr. Southeastern Conf. for Pub. Adminstrn., Cocoa, Fla., 1993. With USNR, 1964-68, sgt. U.S. Army, 1974-78. Decorated Nat. Def. Svc. medal with one star Dept. of the Army, 1974, Good Conduct medal, 1978, Army Achievement medal with one oak leaf cluster, 1987, Army Commendation medal, 1992, Meritorious Svc. medal, 1994. Mem. Acad. Polit. Sci., Res. Officers Assn., Am. Soc. for Pub. Adminstrn., Adjutant Gen. Corps, Am. Legion, Disabled Am Vets. Comdrs. Club. Home: 1595 NE 129th St Miami FL 33161

FREDERIC, CHERYL ANN, theatre educator; b. Pascagoula, Miss., Oct. 11, 1952; d. Louis Augustus and Clara Elizabeth (Rust) F.; m. Ronald A.J. Nuzzo, May 28, 1980 (div. Jan. 1986); 1 child, Aaron John Nuzzo. BFA in Theatre, U. So. Miss., 1973; MS in Gifted Edn., Coll. New Rochelle, 1981; PhD in Theatre, Fla. State U., 1993. Cert. tchr. theatre, speech, English, gifted edn., reading, Miss., Fla., Ala., N.Y. Actress N.Y.C., 1974-78; tchr. Gautier (Miss.) Jr. High Sch., 1984-86, Pascagoula High Sch., 1986-90; teaching asst. Sch. Theatre, Fla. State U., Tallahassee, 1991-93; asst. prof. dept. comm. and theatre Southeastern La. U., Hammond, 1993—. Dir. various plays, 1984—; appeared on TV including All My Children, ABC, One Life to Live, ABC (comml.) Am. Express; in films including Short Eyes, Bermuda, Accepting for Winkelmeyer, Coney Island; in theatre including An Evening of Futurism, A Streetcar Named Desire, Aria Da Capo, After the Rain, He Ain't Done Right by Nell, The Bremen Town Musicians, Summer and Smoke, The Lion in Winter. Co-dir. playABILITIES theatre troupe. Fellow Fla. State U., 1990-91; grantee Southea. La. U., 1995-96. Mem. Assn. Theatre in Higher Edn., Southea. Theatre Conf., Assn. Theatre Accessibility, Mid Am. Theatre Conf., Am. Theatre and Drama Soc., Pi Beta Phi (continuing edn. scholar 1991), Phi Kappa Phi, Alpha Psi Omega. Roman Catholic. Office: Southeastern La Univ Dept Comm and Theatre SLU 451 Hammond LA 70402

FREDERICK, MYRNA SUE LABRY, sales executive, beauty consultant; b. Abbeville, La., Nov. 22, 1950; d. Noah and Jeanne (Vincent) LaBry; m. Conley J. Frederick, Jan. 22, 1972; children: Dawn M. Frederick Vincent, Shauri Frederick Richard, Ryan C., Brett J. Student, U. Southwestern La., Lafayette, 1968-69. Ins. office mgr. and cashier Kaplan, La., 1969-73; owner Baton Studio, Kaplan, 1973-79; mgr., fashion buyer, bookkeeper, cashier Kaplan, 1973-91, landscape artist, 1973—; ind. profl. sales dir. Mary Kay Cosmetics, 1992—; ind. profl. beauty cons., 1989—. Mem. Vermilion Arts Coun. Mem. Am. Bus. Women (sec., treas., v.p., pres. 1985-90, Outstanding Woman of Yr. 1990), Krew Chic Alapie (v.p., sec., treas., reporter), Kaplan Jaycee Jaynes (sec., treas., pres. 1974-79, Oustanding Woman of Yr. 1977, Dist. Woman of Yr. 1977-78), Kaplan Chamber of Commerce. Democrat. Roman Catholic. Home: 115 Pelican St Kaplan LA 70548-5652

FREDERIKSEN, RAND TERRELL, cardiologist; b. Lubbock, Tex., Nov. 21, 1941; s. R.T. Frederiksen and Ruth Simpson (Stanford) F.; m. Patricia Kelly Woolwine, May 23, 1989; children; Ruth Reed Frederiksen DeRosa, David Ellis. Student, Tex. Tech. U., Lubbock, 1960-63; MD, Washington U., 1967. Diplomate Am. Bd. Internal Medicine. Cardiologist St. Thomas Hosp., Nashville, 1974—, pres. med. staff, 1990-92; mng. ptnr. Page Campbell Cardiology Group, P.C., Nashville, 1996—; assoc. prof. clin. medicine Vanderbilt U., Nashville, 1988—. Maj. U.S. Army, 1970-73. Fellow Am. Coll. Cardiology, Am. Coll. Chest Physicians, Soc. Cardiac Angiography and Intervention; mem. Am. Heart Assn. (coun. clin. cardiology), Soc. Echo Cardiography, Soc. Critical Care Medicine. Home: 589 Harpeth Trace Dr Nashville TN 37221-3132

FREDERIKSEN, RICHARD ALLAN, plant pathology educator; b. Renville, Minn., Aug. 9, 1933; s. Oscar Price and Sylvia (Anderson) F.; m. Phyllis Krinke, July 19, 1958; children: Johnathan K., Kristin J. BS, U. Minn., St. Paul, 1955, MS, 1957, PhD, 1961. Plant pathologist USDA, St. Paul, 1958-63; asst. prof. plant pathology Tex. A&M U., College Station, 1963-70, assoc. prof., 1970-73, prof., 1973—. With U.S. Army, 1956-58. Fellow Am. Phytopath. Soc. Office: Tex A&M U Dept Plant Pathology College Station TX 77843

FREDRICKSON, MARK ALLAN, health facility administrator, physician; b. Denver, June 12, 1956; s. Lloyd Allan and Dolly Maxine (Waters) F. BS in Chem. Engring., U. Colo., 1978; MS in Chem. Technology, Iowa State U., 1981; MD, UT Southwestern Med. Ctr., Dallas, 1988. Diplomate Am. Acad. Physical Medicine and Rehab., Am. Acad. Pain Mgmt., Tex. State Bd. Medical Examiners. Chem. engr., process chem. support, chem. rsch. and devel. Rockwell Internat., Golden, Colo., 1978-79; rsch. asst. Iowa State U. of Sci. and Tech., Ames, Iowa, 1979-81; teaching asst. Iowa State U. of Sci. Tech., Ames, Iowa, 1980-81; rsch. engr., advanced products in nephrology COBE Labs., 1981-82; lab. mgr., dept. surgery UT Southwestern Med. Ctr., Dallas, 1983-84; intern in internal medicine Presbyn. Hosp., Dallas, 1988-89; resident in physical medicine and rehab. Parkland Hosp., Dallas, 1989-92; resident physical medicine and rehab. UT Southwestern Med. Ctr., Dallas, 1992; med. dir., physician The Health South Rehab. Hosp. of Midland Odessa, Midland, 1992—; corporate physician adv. bd. Nat. Med. Enterprises, 1992-93. Contbr. to profl. jours. NIH Summer Rsch. fellow, 1985, Exxon Rsch., 1980, Monsanto Teaching fellow, 1980; Sabin scholar, 1975. Fellow Am. Acad. Physical Medicine and Rehab.; mem. AMA, Dallas Ft. Worth Metroplex Physical Medicine and Rehab., Texas. Med. Assn., Am. Acad. Pain Mgmt., Am. Coll. Physician Execs. Mem. Protestant Ch. Office: 4904 Island Dr Midland TX 79707-1411

FREE, FLOYD MONROE, social services administrator; m. Lisa Presley; children: Katlyn, Kolton. BA in Religion/Psychology, Mobile (Ala.) Coll.; MDiv, Southeastern Bapt. Theol. Sem.; postgrad., Troy State U. Ordained So. Bapt. Min., Bapt. Ch. Pastor Pleasant Grove Bapt. Ch., Atmore, Ala., 1979-80; chaplain Bapt. Hosp., Pensacola, Fla., 1982-83; program dir. adminstrv. asst. Waterfront Rescue Mission, Inc., Pensacola, 1983-85; pres. Knox Area Rescue Ministries, 1985—; Fla. gov.'s task force on homeless and hungary; mem. mayor's coalition on homeless. Chmn. Knox County Homeless Coalition; mem. Inner City Challenge com. Recipient Book of Golden Deeds award Exch. Club, 1991. Mem. Knoxville C. of C., Christian Ministries Mgmt. Assn., Internat. Union of Gospel Missions (v.p. Southeastern dist.). Office: Knox Area Rescue Ministries PO Box 3352 Knoxville TN 37927-3352

FREE, KENNETH A., athletic conference commissioner; b. June 8, 1937; s. Lee W. and Margaret (McMurray) F.; children: Delana (dec.) Kenneth Jr., Benjamin. BS, N.C. A&T State U., 1970. Profl. baseball player KC/Detroit Stars Negro Baseball League, 1959, Hickory Negro Baseball League, 1960, N.Y. Mets., 1960-64, Ctrl. Motor Lines, Greensbor, N.C., 1964-67; adminstr. recreation ctr. Greensboro Parks and Recreation, 1968-69; cons. parks and recreation N.C. Dept. Resources, Fayetteville, 1970-78; commr. Mid Eastern Athletic Conf., Greensboro, N.C., 1978—; mem. NCAA Men's Basketball Com., Overland Park Kans., 1987-92; bd. dirs. NCAA Honda award, Overland Park, NCAA Exec. Com., Overland Park, 1992, NCAA Pro Sports Liason, 1993, NCAA Postgrad. Scholarship Com., NASC. Bd. dirs. N.C. Parks and Recreation Found., Guilgord County AIDS Task Force; mem. citizens' adv. com. Greensboro Bats, Greensboro Sports Commn., Greensboro Sports Coun., Greensboro Coliseum Planning Com.; trustee and mem. Chancellor Choir-United Meth. Ch. With U.S. Army, 1955-58. Named to Nat. All-Star Team, Negro Baseball League, 1959, CIAA Basketball and Football Officials Hall of Fame, N.C. A&T Sports Hall of Fame. Fellow N.C. Recreation and Parks Assn.; mem. Collegiate Commrs.' Assn., Nat. Basketball and Football Coaches Assn., Nat. Assn. Coll. Dirs. of Athletics (exec. com.), Univ. Commrs. Assn., Masons, Kappa Alpha Psi. Home: 4 Bent Oak Ct Greensboro NC 27455

FREE, MARY MOORE, anthropologist; b. Paris, Tex., Mar. 6, 1933; d. Dudley Crawford and Margie Lou (Moore) Hubbard; m. Dwight Allen Free Jr., June 26, 1954 (dec.); children: Hardy (dec.), Dudley (dec.), Margery, Caroline. BS, So. Meth. U., 1954, MLA, 1981, MA, 1987, PhD, 1989. Instr. So. Meth. U., Dallas, 1982-89, prof. continuing edn., 1989-90, prof. Dedman Coll., 1990—, adj. asst. prof. dept. anthropology, 1990—; prof. Richland C.C., Dallas, 1986; house anthropologist Baylor U. Med. Ctr., Dallas, 1990—; adv. bd. geriatrics Vis. Nurse Assn., Dallas, 1984-91; presenter in field anthropology, medicine; bd. Dedman Coll. SMU Excellence in Sci. Lecture Series. Author: The Private World of the Hermitage: Lifestyles of the Rich and Old in an Elite Retirement Home, 1995; contbr. chpts. in sci. books, ednl. TV, and articles to Anthropology Newsletter, Am. Anthropologist, Am. Jour. Cardiology, Cahiers de Sociologie Economique et Culturelle-Ethnopsycholie, Jour. Heart Failure, Jour. Internat. Soc. Dermatology, other profl. jours.; mem. editl. bd. Baylor U. Med. Ctr. Procs. Bd. dirs. New Hearts & Lungs, Baylor Med. Ctr., 1994; active various svc. and social orgns. Named one of Notable Women of Tex., 1984. Fellow Am. Anthrop. Assn., Inst. for Study of Earth and Man; mem. AAAS, Internat. Soc. Heart Failure (sci. adv. bd.), Dallas Women's Club, Dallas Petroleum Club, Brook Hollow Golf Club, Pi Beta Phi. Methodist. Home: 4356 Edmondson Ave Dallas TX 75205-2602 Office: Baylor U Med Ctr 3500 Gaston Ave Dallas TX 75246-2045

FREEDLAND, JACOB BERKE, dentist, endodontist; b. Wilmington, N.C., Mar. 19, 1913; s. Morris and Molly (Burke) F.; m. Charlotte Soble, Sept. 7, 1939; children: Martin B., Leslie Ann Freedland Locke. Student, U. N.C.; DDS, Emory U., 1936; D of Pub. Svc. (hon.), U. N.C., Charlotte, 1990. Diplomate Am. Bd. Endodontists. Pvt. practice dentistry Charlotte, N.C., 1938—; adj. prof. U. N.C., Chapel Hill, 1963—; vis. lectr. Columbia, Pa., N.Y., 1970—; cons. lectr. U.S. Army Dental Corps, Walter Reed, 1964-86, USN Dental Corps, Nat. Naval Ctr., 1964-78, Area Health Edn. Ctrs., Charlotte; dir. dental programs Charlotte Area Health Edn. Ctr., Carolinas Med. Ctr., Charlotte; dir. program devel. AHEC, 1990. Contbr. articles to profl. jours. Bd. dirs. Charlotte Symphony, Mecklenburg Red Cross, Mecklenburg County Blood Bank; bd. visitors U. N.C., 1985-89. Maj. Dental Corps U.S. Army, 1941-45, ETO. Recipient Charlotte Dental Soc. award, 1965, Disting. Alumnus award U. N.C., 1979, Edgar D. Collidge award, L.A., 1980, Disting. Practitioner award Nat. Acad. Dentistry, 1987, Thomas P. Hinman Disting. Svc. award, 1988, Louis Grossman Internat. award Soc. Francaise d'Endodontie, New Orleans, 1989, Achievement award Am. Fund Dental Health, Chgo., 1990, Disting. Svc. scroll N.C. Dental Soc., 1990, Distg. Philanthropist award Am. Rsch. and Endowment Found., Chgo., 1993; Jacob B. Freedland D.D.S. Conf. Rm. Spl. Care Dental Ctr., Huntersville Oaks Nursing Home named in his honor, 1990; Jacob B. Freedland Chair endowed in his honor U. N.C. Sch. Dentistry; Freedland Scholarship in endodontics established U. N.C. Sch. Dentistry, 1993. Fellow Am. Coll. Dentists, Internat. Coll. of Dentists, Am. Assn. Endodontists (1st Disting. Philathropist award Rsch. Edn. Found. 1993), Acad. Dentistry Internat. (named Internat. Dentist of Yr., 1994); mem. ADA (cons., commn. on accreditation, coun. on dental edn. 1964-86, del. to internat. profl. orgns. 1982, 86, 87, Presdl. citiation 1988), Am. Assn. Endodontists (pres. 1964-65), N.C. Dental Soc. (pres. 2nd dist. 1964-65), Am. Inst. Oral Scis. (pres. 1965-67), Am. Assn. Hosp. Dentists, Am. Fund Dental Health (trustee, adviser), Dental Found. N.C. (pres. 1975, bd. dirs.). Jewish. Home: 2633 Richardson Dr Charlotte NC 28211-3355 Office: 721 Doctors Bldg Charlotte NC 28283

FREEDLENDER, SUSAN See HOMESTEAD, SUSAN E.

FREEDMAN, JONATHAN ANDREW, clinical sociologist; b. Bklyn., Feb. 13, 1936; s. Meyer Joel and Florence Esther (Bernstein) F.; m. Jo Ann Sanders, June 28, 1959; children: Lorin John, Michael James, Noah David. BA, Wesleyan U., Middletown, Conn., 1957; MA, Brandeis U., 1964, PhD, 1973. Cert. clin. sociologist. Research coord. Community Action Tng. Ctr., Syracuse, N.Y., 1965-66; lectr. sch. social work Syracuse U., 1966-71; dir. edn. & tng. Hutchings Psychiat. Ctr., Syracuse, 1971-93; spl. asst. to exec. dir. for orgnl. change, 1990-93; asst. prof. Health Scis. Ctr., Syracuse, 1973-93; adj. prof. Syracuse U., 1977-93; adj. faculty New Sch. for Social Research, N.Y.C., 1980-93; pres. FreedMuse, Atlanta, 1988—; pres. The Syracuse Ctr., 1988-93; exec. dir. Inst. for Human Evolution, Salem, Mass., 1986-87, bd. dirs.; cons., trainer, bd. dirs. several orgns. in Syracuse. Author: Clinical Sociology, 1979, Choicepoint, 1989, Choose Health, 1991; contbr. articles to profl. jours. Past pres. Max Gilbert Hebrew Acad., Syracuse. Recipient Disting. Career in Sociol. Practice award, 1989. Mem. Am. Soc. Tng. and Devel. (Profl. Practice Area Achievement award Greater Atlanta Chpt. 1995), Sociol. Practice Assn. (pres. 1983-85). Democrat. Jewish. Office: FreedMuse 1175 Kingsley Cir NE Atlanta GA 30324-3221

FREEDMAN, LOUIS MARTIN, dentist; b. Newark, Mar. 19, 1947; s. Morris and Sylvia (Swimmer) F.; m. Elizabeth Norine Palmer, June 17, 1978; children: Steven, Julie, Brian. Student, Emory U., 1963-66, DDS, 1970. Gen. dentist Freedman, Freedman & Weitman DDS, P.C., Atlanta, 1970—; clin. instr. Emory U. Dental Sch., Atlanta, 1970-77; team dentist Atlanta Hawks Basketball Team, 1971—, Atlanta Flames Hockey Team, 1979-80, Atlanta Knights Hockey Team, 1992, Atlanta Fire Ants Roller Hockey Team, 1994—. Mem. Exch. Club, Atlanta, 1970-73; mgr. Sandy Springs Youth Sports Little League Baseball, 1979—; head coach Sandy Springs United Meth. Ch. basketball program, 1991—. Mem. Alpha Epsilon Delta, Omicron Kappa Upsilon. Jewish. Office: Freedman Freedman & Weitman 3111 Piedmont Rd NE Atlanta GA 30305-2507

FREEDMAN, PAUL HARRIS, history educator; b. N.Y.C., Sept. 15, 1949; s. Alfred M. and Marcia (Kohl) F.; m. Bonnie Jean Roe, Aug. 15, 1982. BA, U. Calif., Santa Cruz, 1971; PhD, U. Calif., Berkeley, 1978. Prof. history Dept. of History Dept. of History, Vanderbilt U., Nashville, 1979—. Author: The Diocese of Vic, 1983, The Origins of Peasant Servitude in Medieval Catalonia, 1991 (Premio del Rey prize 1993). Fellowship Guggenheim Fund, 1994-95. Mem. Medieval Acad. of Am. (councillor 1995—), Am. Hist. Assn. Office: Dept History Vanderbilt Hospital Nashville TN 37232

FREEDMAN, SANDRA WARSHAW, former mayor; b. Newark, Sept. 21, 1943; m. Michael J. Freedman; 3 children. BA in Govt., U. Miami, 1965. Mem. Tampa (Fla.) City Coun., 1974—, chmn., 1983-86; mayor City of Tampa, 1986-95. Bd. dirs. Jewish Community Ctr., 1974-75, Boys and Girls Clubs Greater Tampa, Hillsborough Coalition for Health, Tampa Community Concert Assn.; mem. sports adv. bd. Hillsborough Community Coll., 1975-76; sec. Downtown Devel. Authority, 1977-78; bd. dirs., v.p. Fla. Gulf Coast Symphony, 1979-80; vice chmn. Met. Planning Orgn., 1981-82; corp. mem. Neighborhood Housing Service; bd. fellows U. Tampa; mem. steering com. Hillsborough County Council of Govt.'s Constituency for Children; mem. exec. bd. Tampa/Hillsborough Young Adult Forum; chmn. bd. trustees Berkeley Prep. Sch.; trustee Tampa Bay Performing Arts Ctr., Inc., Tampa Mus.; mem. ethics com. Meml. Hosp.; mem. Tampa Preservation, Inc., Tampa/Hillsborough County Youth Council, Davis Islands Civic Assn., Tampa Hist. Soc., Met. Ministries Adv. Bd., Rodeph Sholom Synagogue, Sword of Hope Guild of Am. Cancer Soc., Friends of the Arts. Recipient Spessar L. Holland Meml. award Tampa Bay Com. for Good Govt., 1975-76, Human Rights award City of Tampa, 1980, award Soroptimist Internat. Tampa, 1981, Status of Women award Zonta of Tampa II, 1986, Woman of Achievement award Bus. & Profl. Women, Jewish Nat. Fund Tree of Life award, Disting. Citizen award U. South Fla., 1995, Nat. Conf. of Christian and Jews Humanitarian award, 1995; named to Fla. Home Builders Hall of Fame. Mem. Hillsborough County Bar Aux., Greater Tampa C. of C., C. of C. Com. of 100 (exec. com.), Fla. League of Cities (bd. dirs.), Tampa Urban League, Nat. Council Jewish Women, U. Miami Alumni Assn., Athena Soc., Hadassah. Office: 3435 Bayshore Blvd Apt 700 Tampa FL 33629-8800

FREELAND, ALAN EDWARD, orthopedic surgery educator, physician; b. Youngstown, Ohio, July 30, 1939; s. Harold Edward and Esther Amelia (Hanley) F.; m. Janis Ann Foerschl, Oct. 11, 1969; children: Matthew, Jennifer, Rebecca, Michael. BA, Johns Hopkins U., 1961; MD, George Washington U., 1965. Cert. hand surgery Am. Bd. Orthopaedic Surgery. Intern Church Home and Hosp., Balt., 1965-66; resident Johns Hopkins Hosp., Balt., 1967-70, Letterman Army Med. Ctr., San Francisco, 1973-75; prof. dept. orthopaedic surgery U. Miss. Med. Ctr., Jackson, 1978—; chief staff U. Med. Ctr., Jackson, 1986-87; chief surgery Miss. Meth. Rehab. Ctr., Jackson, 1991-93, pres. elect med. staff, 1994, pres. med. staff, bd. dirs., 1995—. Author: Stable Internal Fixation of the Hand and Wrist, 1986, The First Twenty-Five Years: History of the American Association for Hand Surgery, 1996; mem. editl. bd. Orthopedics, Slack, Inc., 1986—, Jour. Orthopaedic Trauma, Raven Press, 1993—. Mem. Fire Protection Dist., Brandon, Miss., 1990-93. Lt. col. U.S. Army, 1971-78. Fellow Am. Acad. Orthopaedic Surgeons, Am. Orthopaedic Assn.; mem. Am. Soc. Surgery of Hand (governing coun. 1989-92), Am. Assn. Hand Surgeons (parliamentarian 1994, historian 1995, mem. exec. com., bd. dirs. 1994—, treas. 1996), Internat. Fedn. Socs. for Surgery of Hand (chmn. bone and joint com. 1992—), Miss. State Orthopaedic Assn. (pres. 1986, pres. Jackson chpt. 1985). Home: 303 Swallow Dr Brandon MS 39042-6454 Office: 2500 N State St Jackson MS 39216-4500

FREELAND, JAMES M. JACKSON, lawyer, educator; b. Miami, Fla., Feb. 17, 1927; s. Byron Brazil and Mary Helen (Jackson) F.; m. Valerie; children: Carole Leigh, Thomas Byron, James Jackson Jr. A.B., Duke U., 1950; J.D., U. Fla., Gainesville, 1954; postgrad. fellow, Yale U. Law Sch., 1960-61. Bar: Fla. 1954. Assoc. firm Dowling & Culverhouse, Jacksonville,

1954-57; mem. faculty U. Fla. Law Sch., 1957-60, 61-62, 65—, prof. law, 1970-95, dir. grad. tax law program, 1977-82, disting. svc. prof. law, emeritus, 1995—; of counsel August, Comiter, Kulunas & Schepps, P.A., West Palm Beach, Fla., 1995—; prof. law N.Y. U. Law Sch., 1963-65; vis. prof. U. Ariz. Law Sch., Tucson, 1969-70; mem. tax faculty Practicing Law Inst., 1969-76; vis. tax prof. Leiden U., The Netherlands, 1983. Co-author: Federal Income Taxation of Estates, Trusts and Beneficiaries, 1970, 2d edit., 1993, The Florida Will and Trust Manual, 1983, The Tennessee Will and Trust Manual, 1984, Fundamentals of Federal Income Taxation, 1972, 9th edit., 1996; adv. editor Jour. Corp. Taxation, 1977—, S Corp. Tax Jour., 1989—. Served with USNR, 1944-46. Named Outstanding prof. U. Fla., 1968, Outstanding Law Prof., 1970-73, 75; Designated Disting. Service Prof. Law, 1982. Mem. ABA, Am. Law Inst., Am. Coll. Tax Counsel, The Fla. Bar (exec. com. tax sect. 1971—, Outstanding Tax Lawyer State of Fla. 1982), Order of Coif, Blue Key, Phi Kappa Phi. Republican. Methodist. Home: 7700 NW 41st Ave Gainesville FL 32606-4114

FREEMAN, ANNE HOBSON, writer, English language educator; b. Richmond, Va., Mar. 19, 1934; d. Joseph Reid Anderson and Mary Douthat (Marshall) Hobson; m. George Clemon Freeman, Jr., Dec. 6, 1958; children: Anne Colston McEvoy, George Clemon, Joseph Reid Anderson. AB, Bryn Mawr Coll., 1956; postgrad. London U., 1956-57; MA, U. Va., 1973. Fiction writer, 1956—; reporter Internat. News Svc., Eastern Europe, 1957; editor Va. Mus. Fine Arts, Richmond, 1959-63; lectr. English, U. Va., Charlottesville, 1973-88; chmn. adv. com. Bryn Mawr Bull., Pa., 1978-81. Author: The Style of a Law Firm: Eight Gentlemen From Virginia, 1989, A Hand Well Played, the Life of Jim Wheat Jr., 1994; contbr. stories to various mags., anthologies, lit. jours. Bd. dirs. Va. Hist. Soc., 1984-90, Va. Commn. for Humanities and Pub. Policy, 1985-89, Nat. Coun. Friends of Kennedy Ctr., Washington, 1983-85, Mus. of Confederacy, Richmond., 1994—. Fulbright scholar, 1956-57; Va. Ctr. for Creative Arts fellow; MacDowell Colony fellow. Mem. Va. Writers Club, Country of Va. Club, Woman's (Richmond) Club. Episcopalian. Home: Oyster Shell Point Farm Callao VA 22435-0680

FREEMAN, ARTHUR MERRIMON, III, psychiatry educator, dean; b. Birmingham, Ala., Oct. 10, 1942; s. Arthur Merrimon Freeman II; m. Linda Poynter; children: Arthur M. IV, Katherin Leigh, Edward Todd. AB in Philosophy, Harvard U., 1963; MD, Vanderbilt U., 1967. Diplomate Am. Bd. Psychiatry and Neurology; lic. psychiatrist, Ala., N.C., La. Asst. prof. dept. psychiatry and behavioral scis. Stanford (Calif.) U., 1974-77; prof., vice chmn. dept. psychiatry U. Ala., Birmingham, 1977-90; med. dir. Appalachian Hall Hosp., Asheville, N.C., 1990-91; prof., chmn. dept. psychiatry La. State U. Med. Ctr., Shreveport, 1991—, dean, 1993-96; regional med. dir. divsn. mental health La. Dept. Health and Hosps., 1992-94. Author: Psychiatry for the Primary Care Physician, 1979. Bd. dirs. Vols. of Am., Shreveport, 1993—, Shreveport Symphony, C. of C., 1993-96. Lt. comdr. M.C., USN, 1972-74. Nat. Merit scholar Harvard U., 1959-63; Biochemistry fellow Karolinska Inst., Stockholm, 1965, fellow in hepatic disease Royal Free Hosp., London, 1966. Fellow APA, Am. Coll. Psychiatrists (Laughlin fellow 1971), Acad. Psychosomatic Medicine, So. Psychiat. Assn.; mem. Am. Assn. Chmn. of Depts. of Psychiatry, Biomed. Rsch. Found. N.W. La. (bd. dirs. 1993-96). Home: 5929 E Ridge Dr Shreveport LA 71106-2423 Office: La State U Med Ctr Dept of Psychiatry 1501 Kings Hwy Shreveport LA 71103-4228

FREEMAN, BRUCE L., JR., physicist, researcher; b. Wharton, Tex., Apr. 2, 1949; s. Bruce L. Sr. and Audrey May (Wear) F.; m. Susan Hope Balog, Jan. 9, 1982; 1 child, Laura Hope. BS, Tex. A&M U., 1970; MS, U. Calif.-Davis, Livermore, 1971, PhD, 1974. Staff physicist Los Alamos (N.Mex.) Nat. Lab., 1974-95; pres. Centrus Plasma Techs., Inc., Denton, 1995—. Contbr. articles to profl. jours. Mem. IEEE, Am. Phys. Soc. Republican. Office: Centrus Plasma Techs Inc PO Box 5073 Denton TX 76203-0073

FREEMAN, CLIFFORD ECHOLS, JR., investment banker; b. Dallas, Jan. 15, 1959; s. Clifford Echols Sr. and Dorris (Sowder) F. BSBA, U. Tex., 1987; BSEE, Rice U., 1987, MBA, 1989. Lic. real estate broker, Tex. Gen. mgr. R.K.J. Enterprises, Houston, 1981-83; cons. Clifford E. Freeman & Assocs., Dallas, 1983-86; rep. Kidder, Peabody & Co., Inc., Houston, 1989-93; assoc. First Nat. Bank So. Africa, Johannesburg, Republic of South Africa, 1988—; pres. Clifford E.Freeman & Assocs. Inc., Houston, 1991—; mng. dir. Tex. Capital Securities, Inc., Houston, 1993—; chmn., CEO Island Internat. Restaurant Group, Inc., Houston, 1995—. Mem., class chmn. ann. fund. Rice Fund Coun. Office: Island Internat Restaurant Group Inc 4311 Willowview Ct Sugar Land TX 77479

FREEMAN, DAVID FRANKLIN, psychoanalyst, psychiatrist; b. Raleigh, N.C., Apr. 13, 1925; s. Lemuel Elmer MacMillan and Katharine (Parker) F.; m. Constance Covell, Mar. 28, 1953; children: Julia Freeman-Woolpert, Martha Somers, David F. Jr. BS, Wake Forest Coll., 1948; MD, Bowman Gray Sch. Medicine, 1951. Diplomate Am. Bd. Psychiatry and Neurology Psychiatry, Am. Bd. Psychiatry and Neurology Child Psychiatry, Nat. Bd. Med. Examiners; lic. psychiatrist, N.C. Intern Phila. Gen. Hosp., 1951-52; resident in psychiatry Boston Psychopathic Hosp., 1952-55, fellow child psychiatry, 1954-55; fellow child psychiatry Worcester Youth Guidance Ctr., 1955-56; pvt. practice Lincoln, Mass., 1956-61, Chapel Hill, N.C., 1963—; dir. North Ctrl. Mental Health Consultation Svc., Fitchburg, Mass., 1956-57; from staff psychiatrist to chief psychiatrist Douglas A. Thom Clinic for Children, Boston, 1957-61; staff psychiatrist Walden Clinic, Concord, Mass., 1958-59; dir. child psychiatry outpatient clinic N.C. Meml. Hosp., Chapel Hill, 1961-63; asst. prof. psychiatry U. N.C. Sch. Medicine, 1961-63, clin. asst. prof., 1963-66, clin. assoc. prof., 1966-84, clin. prof., 1984-94, adj. prof., 1994—; asst. dir. psychoanalytic edn. program U. N.C. and Duke U., Chapel Hill, 1984-92, dir., 1992-95, edn. com., 1973—, chmn. candidate progression com., 1992; chair bd. dirs. N.C. Psychoanalytic Found., 1995—; cons. U.S. Army Hosp., Ft. Devans, Mass., 1957-58, Waltham Family Svc. League, 1957-58, Va. Treatment Ctr. for Children, Richmond, Va., 1964-66, U. N.C. Sch. Medicine, Chapel Hill, 1966-88; N.E. Home for Little Wanderers, Boston, 1959-61; lectr. and presenter in field. Contbr. articles to profl. jours. Study commn. N.C. Emotionally Disturbed Children, chmn. com. pvt. practice, 1970-71; active Gov.'s Adv. Com. on Youth Devel., 1972-73. Sgt. U.S. Army, 1943-46, France. Fellow Am. Psychiatric Assn. (life, peer reviewer 1983-87), N.C. Psychiatric Assn. (life, com. mem. 1963—); mem. Am. Acad. Child & Adolescent Psychiatry (life), Am. Psychoanalytic Assn. (life, cert., del. to exec. coun. 1977-82, 84-88, alt. del. to exec. coun. 1982-84, 88—), Assn. for Child Psychoanalysis, Internat. Psychoanalytic Assn., N.C. Med. Soc., N.C. Coun. Child Psychiatry (founding mem., pres. 1971-72, exec. com. 1973-80), N.C. Psychoanalytic Soc. (founding mem., pres. 1982-84, exec. com. 1977—), N.C. Psychoanalytic Found. (chair bd. dirs. 1995—), Orange County Med. Soc., Alpha Omega Alpha, Gamma Sigma Epsilon. Home: 101 Ashe Pl Chapel Hill NC 27514-4943

FREEMAN, DAVID LEE, artist, educator; b. Columbia, Mo., Nov. 10, 1937; s. Melvin C. and Helen Marie F.; m. Mildred P. Kern, Apr. 12, 1960; children: Lori, Kevin. BA, U. Mo., 1960, MA, 1961; MFA, U. Iowa, 1963. From instr. to asst. prof. U. Wis., Madison, 1963-70; prof. Winthrop U., Rock Hill, S.C., 1970—. One man shows include Carlson Lobrano Gallery, Atlanta, 1990, Fridholm Fine Arts Galleries, N.C., 1993. Home: 630 University Dr Rock Hill SC 29730-3708 Office: Winthrop Univ Dept Art & Design Rock Hill SC 29733

FREEMAN, DONALD WILFORD, real estate developer, horse breeder; b. Brooksville, Fla., Sept. 25, 1929; s. Fred Maxwell and Dovie (Keef) F.; m. Ruby Jane Lewis, Feb. 25, 1956; children: Clifton Lewis, Susan Anne. BS, U. Ala., 1953, JD, 1953; LLM, NYU, 1957. CPA, Ga. Acct., Ernst & Ernst, Atlanta, 1953-55; tax atty. Office Chief Counsel, U.S. Treasury Dept., N.Y.C., 1955-57, West Point Mfg. Co. (Ga.), 1957-58; treas. Ryder System, Inc., Miami, Fla., 1958-61; v.p., dir. Henderson's Portion Pak, Inc., 1961-63; pres. Biscayne Capital Corp., Miami, Fla., 1964-66; sr. asso. Lazard Freres & Co., N.Y.C., 1967-69; pres. James A. Ryder Corp., Miami, 1969-78; owner Kiyara Arabians, 1978—. With AUS, 1946-48, PTO. Mem. Fla. Inst. CPAs, Phi Kappa Sigma, Beta Gamma Sigma. Episcopalian. Home: 13965 Caloosa Blvd Palm Beach Gardens FL 33418

FREEMAN, GILL SHERRYL, lawyer; b. N.Y.C., June 24, 1949; d. Norman and Arlene (Vigdor) Jacovitz. BS in Edn. cum laude, Temple U., 1970; student, U. Wis., 1966-68; MEd, U. Miami, Miami, Fla., 1973; JD cum laude, U. Miami, 1977. Bar: Fla. 1977, U.S. Dist. Ct. (so. dist.) 1977, U.S. Dist. Ct. (mid. dist.) Fla. 1984, U.S. Ct. Appeals (5th cir.) 1977. Tchr. Dade County Pub. Schs., Miami, 1970-76; assoc. Walton, Lantaff, Schroeder & Carson, Miami, 1977-82; assoc. Ruden, McClosky, Smith, Schuster & Russell, Miami, 1982—, ptnr., 1983—; vice chair Fla. Supreme Ct. Gender Bias Commn., 1987-90; chair Fla. Supreme Ct. Gender Bias Study Implementation Commn. Elected Fellow of the ABA, 1993; Master, Family Law Inns. of Ct., 1992. Mem. Fla. Bar Assn. (pres. 1984-85), Fla. Assn. Women Lawyers. Office: Ruden McClosky Smith Schuster & Russell 701 Brickell Ave Ste 1900 Miami FL 33131-2860

FREEMAN, JAMES ATTICUS, III, lawyer, insurance and business consultant; b. Gadsden, Ala., Jan. 27, 1947; s. James Atticus and Dorothy Mae (Watson) F.; m. Judith Gail Davis, June 19, 1970; children: Gwendolyn Gail, James Atticus IV, Laura Marie. BS, Vanderbilt U., 1969, JD, 1972. Bar: Tenn. 1972. Broadcaster, newsman GE Broadcasting, Nashville, 1965-72; atty. The Murray Ohio Mfg. Co., Nashville, 1972-73, legal officer, 1973-81; asst. v.p., legal officer, asst. sec. The Murray Ohio Mfg. Co., Brentwood, Tenn., 1981-86, asst. v.p., legal officer, dir. risk mgmt., 1986-90, sec., 1988-90; of counsel Blackburn, Little, Smith & Slobey, Nashville, 1990-92; atty. Blackburn & Slobey, 1992-94; shareholder Blackburn Slobey Freeman & Happell PC, 1995—; pres. Litigation Mgmt. Specialists, Inc., 1989—; founder Nat. Alternative Dispute Resolution Svcs. Tenn., Inc.; bd. dirs. Puhl Leasing, Inc., Some Assembly Required, Inc., Phoenix Property Mgmt. Svcs., Inc., Williamsom Investments, Inc.; asst. sec. Product Assembly, Inc., 1991—; sec. B & D Transp. Inc., 1993—; lectr. corp. law, mem. bd. advisers Southeastern Inst. Paralegal Edn., Nashville, 1982—; guest lectr. U. Wis. Sch. Engring., Madison, 1983—; resource cons. Med Marc Ins., 1992—. Mem. ABA, Tenn. Bar Assn., Nashville Bar Assn. (chmn. membership com. 1984, program chmn. corp. sect. 1985-86), Def. Rsch. Inst., Tenn. Def. Lawyers Assn., Am. Soc. Metals (mem. adj. faculty Cleve. chpt. 1984-88), Outdoor Power Equipment Inst. (chmn. corp. counsel com. 1976-84), Bicycle Mfrs. Assn. (chmn. legal affairs com. 1978-81), Vanderbilt Alumni Assn., Risk and Ins. Mgmt. Soc. (v.p. Cumberland chpt. 1988, 89, Def. Rsch. Inst. (corp.), Phi Alpha Delta. Episcopalian. Office: Litigation Mgmt Specialists One Nat Bank Plaza 414 Union St Ste 2051 Nashville TN 37219-1758 also: Blackburn Slobey Freeman& Happell One Nat Bank Plaza 414 Union St Ste 2050 Nashville TN 37219

FREEMAN, JAMES I., executive. Office: Dillard Dept Stores Inc PO Box 486 900 W Capitol Ave Little Rock AR 72201-3108

FREEMAN, MARY ANNA, librarian; b. Sentinal, Okla., July 24, 1943; d. Wylie Lee and Thelma Anna (Elam) Johnson; m. Charles Edward Freeman, Jr., Aug. 26, 1963; children: Charles Edward III, Juliana Elizabeth, Mark Adrian, Lee Agustin. BS, Abilene Christian U., 1963; M.L.S., Tex. Woman's U., 1981. Tchr. 4th grade Las Cruces Pub. Sch. (N.Mex.), 1963-64; tchr. 2d grade, 1964-67; head audiovisual dept. El Paso (Tex.) Pub. Library, 1972; head librarian Guillen Jr. H.S., El Paso, 1974-95; asst. librarian Andress H.S., El Paso, 1995-96, head libr., 1996—. Treas., Guillen PTA, El Paso, 1983-85, 86-89; mem. partnership in edn. liaison, 1986-90. Mem. ALA, Tex. Library Assn. Office: Andress HS 5400 Sun Valley El Paso TX 79924

FREEMAN, NATASHA MATRINA LEONIDOW, nursing administrator; b. Nyack, N.Y., June 12, 1958; d. Paul and Matrina (Butich) L.; m. Douglas Edward Freeman, Oct. 20, 1990; children: Alexandra, Mary. AAS, Rockland C.C., 1979; BS in Nursing cum laude, SUNY Coll. Technology, Utica, 1982; MS in Nursing magna cum laude, Syracuse U., 1985. RN, N.Y.; cert. nurse adminstr. Staff nurse Englewood Hosp., N.J., 1979-80; charge nurse Mary Imogene Bassett Hosp., Cooperstown, N.Y., 1980-82, nursing svc. coord., 1983-86, asst. dir. sys. devel., 1986-87; assoc. nursing practice coord. Strong Meml. Hosp.-U. Rochester, N.Y., 1987-88, asst. dir. nursing Bayfront Med. Ctr., St. Petersburg, Fla., 1988—. Translator: Excellence in Russian Language, 1976 (Otrada award). Served as 1st lt. USAFR, 1990-91, Persian Gulf War, Saudi Arabia. Mem. Fla. Orgn. Nurse Execs., Tampa Bay Orgn. Nurse Execs., Sigma Theta Tau. Office: Bayfront Med Ctr 701 6th St S Saint Petersburg FL 33701-4814

FREEMAN, SIDNEY LEE, minister, educator; b. Madison, Wis., Jan. 23, 1927; s. Jack and Gertrude (Kaifetz) F.; m. Evelyn Marie Gronberg, Feb. 3, 1950 (div. 1965); children: Lynn Claire, David Eugene, Michael John; m. Gaynell Bradley, Apr. 28, 1967. BS, U. Wis., 1947; MA, Bowling Green State U., 1949; PhD, Cornell U., 1951. Ordained to ministry Unitarian Universalist Assn., 1957. Min. Unitarian Ch. Charlotte, N.C., 1957-89, min. emeritus, 1989—; instr. communication arts Cen. Piedmont Community Coll, Charlotte, part-time 1987—; chaplain Cedar Spring Hosp., Pineville, N.C., part-time 1989—; pres. So. Unitarian Coun., Atlanta, 1953, Thomas Jefferson Unitarian Dist., Charlotte, 1963-64; lectr. Albert Schweitzer Coll., Churwalden, Switzerland, summer 1959, Starr King Sch. for Ministry, Berkeley, Calif., summer 1965. Pres. Charlotte Mental Health Assn., 1978-80; chair consulting bd. Cedar Spring Hosp., Pineville, N.C., 1993—. Recipient Disting. Svc. award Charlotte Mental Health Assn., 1983. Mem. Unitarian Universalist Mins. Assn. (past sec.), Charlotte Area Clergy Assn. (past com.). Home: 4500 Rockford Ct Charlotte NC 28209-2924

FREEMAN, WALDEN SHANKLIN, retired history educator, college administrator; b. Indpls., Aug. 31, 1930; s. Harry Z. and Ellen (Shanklin) F.; m. Carolyn Louise Robertsdahl, Aug. 19, 1978. BA, Butler U., 1952, MA, 1959; PhD, Ind. U., 1967. Instr. in history Gettysburg (Pa.) Coll., 1963-68; assoc. prof. history William Woods Coll., Fulton, Mo., 1968-72, assoc. dean acad. affairs, registrar, prof. history, 1973-83, chair humanities divsn., prof., 1983-85; v.p. acad. affairs, prof. history Schreiner Coll., Kerrville, Tex., 1986-94; ret., 1994; vis. assoc. prof. history Ind. U., Bloomington, 1972-73. Chpt. treas. ARC, Kerrville, 1995—, bd. dirs., 1993—; mem. steering com. Leadership Kerr County, Kerrville, 1988-93; chair campaign subcom. United Way, Fulton, 1982, 83. Comdr. USNR, 1954-76. Mem. Orgn. Am. Historians, Am. Hist. Assn., Ind. Hist. Soc., Kiwanis (pres. Fulton 1981-82, Kerrville 1995-96), Alpha Chi (nat. sec. 1991-95). Home: 411 Coronado Dr Kerrville TX 78028

FREEMAN-LANDGRAF, DOLORES J., administrative assistant; b. Ft. Worth, Tex., Sept. 1, 1946; d. Tommy Drexel McCulley and Dorothy Jean (O'Bryant) Mathis; m. Jerry Bob Freeman (div.); 1 child, Lori Jean Freeman-Smith; m. David Lorin Landgraf, July 22, 1995. BSPA magna cum laude, U. Tex., 1989; MPA, U. N. Tex., 1993. Adminstrv. asst., City Mgr.'s Office City of Garland, Tex., purchasing dir., asst. dir. fleet mgmt., engr. asst.; mem. purchasing coun. C. of C., Garland, 1993-94. Mem. Kiwanis (newsletter editor 1995-96), Pi Alpha Alpha, Pi Sigma Alpha, Phi Theta Alpha. Office: City of Garland PO 469002 Garland TX 75046-9002

FREIBERT, LUCY MARIE, humanities educator; b. Louisville, Oct. 19, 1922; d. Joseph Anthony and Amelia Josephine (Stich) F. BA in English, Nazareth Coll., 1957; MA in English, St. Louis U., 1962; PhD in English, U. Wis., 1970. Joined Sisters of Charity of Nazareth. Elem. tchr. St. Cecilia Sch., Louisville, 1947-51, Holy Name Sch., Louisville, 1951-57; secondary tchr. Presentation Acad., Louisville, 1957-60; prof. English Spalding Coll., Louisville, 1960-71; prof. English U. Louisville, 1971-93, prof. emerita of English, 1993—. Co-editor: Hidden Hands, An Anthology of American Women Writers, 1790-1870, 1985; contbr. articles to profl. jours. Named Woman of Distinction, Ctr. for Women and Families, 1993. Mem. MLA (life), NOW, Nat. Women's Studies Assn., Melville soc. Roman Catholic. Home: 1507 Hepburn # 2 Louisville KY 40204 Office: U Louisville Dept English Louisville KY 40292

FREIMARK, JEFFREY PHILIP, retail supermarket executive; b. Bklyn., Mar. 11, 1955; s. Benjamin and Fay (Lefton) F.; m. Hollis Joan Hauser, Aug. 27, 1978; children: Samara, Brandon. BS, U. So. Fla., 1976; MBA, NYU, 1980; JD, N.Y. Law Sch., 1984. Bar: N.J. 1985; CPA, N.J., Fla. Sr. staff acct. Abraham and Straus, Bklyn., 1976-78; internal audit dir. Stern's Dept. Store, Paramus, N.J., 1978-79; dir. acctg. Kings Super Markets, West Caldwell, N.J., 1979-82, controller, 1982-83, controller, sec., 1983-84, v.p. fin., 1985-86; sr. v.p. fin. and adminstrn., chief fin. officer, treas., dir. PXC & M Holdings Inc./Pueblo Xtra Internat. (formerly Pueblo Internat. Inc.), Pompano Beach, Fla., 1986-91, exec. v.p., chief fin. officer, sec., 1992—; exec. v.p., CFO, sec., dir. Pueblo Xtra Internat., Inc., Pompano Beach, Fla., 1993—, PXC&M, Inc., Pompano Beach, 1993—. Vol. dir. NYU Grad. Sch. Bus. Mgmt. Decision Lab., 1980-81. Mem. ABA, N.J. Bar Assn., Am. Inst. CPA's, Fla. Soc. CPA's, N.J. Soc. CPA's, Assn. MBA Execs., Fin. Execs. Inst. Republican. Jewish. Home: 21180 Oakley Ct Boca Raton FL 33433-7435 Office: PXC&M Holdings Inc and Pueblo Xtra Internat 1300 NW 22nd St Pompano Beach FL 33069-1426

FREITAG, ROBERT FREDERICK, retired government official; b. Jackson, Mich., Jan. 20, 1920; s. Fred J. and Beatrice (Paradise) F.; m. Maxine Pryer, Apr. 13, 1941 (dec. Mar. 1995); children: Nancy Marie Freitag Sprague, Janet Louise Freitag Wasserstrom, Fred John II, Paul Robert. B.S.E. in Aero. Engring., U. Mich., 1941; postgrad., MIT, 1941-42. Commd. ensign USNR, 1941; lt. comdr. U.S. Navy, 1946, advanced through grades to capt., 1960; various guided missile programs, 1941-55; project officer Jupiter and Polaris intermediate range ballistic missiles (Chief Naval Operations), 1955-57; range planning officer, also spl. asst. to comdr. (Pacific Missile Range), Point Mugu, Calif., 1957-59; astronautics officer (Bur. Naval Weapons), 1959-63; ret., 1963; dir. launch vehicles and propulsion NASA, 1963; dir. Manned Space Flight Field Center Devel., 1963-72, dir. manned space flight advanced programs, 1973-82; dep. dir. NASA Space Sta. Task Force, 1982-85, dir. Space Sta. Office of Policy, 1985, dep. assoc. adminstr. for Space Sta., 1985—; Mem. NACA Com. Propellers, 1944-46, Sec. Def. Spl. Com. Adequacy Range Facilities, 1956-58, Joint Army-Navy Ballistic Missile Com., 1955-57, NACA Spl. Com. Space Tech., 1958-59; re-adv. com. missile and spacecraft aerodynamics NASA, 1960-63; joint Def. Dept.-NASA-Astronautics Coordinating Bd. (on launch vehicles panel), 1960-64. Author tech. papers. Decorated Legion of Merit, 1959; recipient Spl. Commendation from Comdr.-in-Chief U.S. Pacific Fleet, 1953, Spl. Commendation from Sec. Def., 1958, Sec. Navy Commendation medal, 1959, Disting. Alumnus award U. Mich., 1957, Sesquicentennial medal and cert., 1967, NASA Exceptional Service medal, 1969, 81, Outstanding Leadership medal, 1985, Bronze medal Brit. Interplanetary Soc., 1979; named Meritorious Exec., 1987; elected to Mich. Aviation Hall Fame, 1991. Fellow AIAA (pres. Cen. Calif. sect. 1958-59, dir. Washington sect. 1964-65, 69, Internat. Cooperation award 1990), Am. Astronautical Soc., Royal Aero. Soc.; mem. Internat. Acad. Astronautics (Allen D. Emil award 1986), Deutsche Gesellschaft für Luft-und Raumfahrt (hon.). Home: 4110 Mason Ridge Dr Annandale VA 22003-2034

FREMONT-SMITH, RICHARD, retired federal health care executive; b. Boston, Mar. 11, 1935; s. Maurice and Mary Dixon (Thayer) F.-S. Student, Harvard U., 1954-56; MBA, Columbia U., 1969; grad. cert., George Washington U., 1971; cert., Yale U., 1986. Enlisted USCG, 1956, advanced through grades to lt., 1966, served in Vietnam, 1965-66, resigned from active duty, 1966; advanced from lt. comdr. to capt USCGR, 1966-82; recalled to active duty USCG, 1982, dir. special projects Washington hdqrs., 1982-84, released from active duty, 1984, asst. chief med. adminstrn. Washington hdqrs., 1985-87, liaison officer to Asst. Sec. Defense, 1987-94; fed. account rep. Xerox Corp., Boston, 1970-71; stockbroker Paine, Webber, Jackson & Curtis, Boston, 1969-70; asst. dir. Peter Bent Brigham Hosp., Boston, 1972-75; assoc. dir. Bay State Profl. Stds. Rev. Orgn., Boston, 1975-78; v.p. Qualicare Inc., Boston, 1978-80, R.A. Wiegand and Co. Inc., Boston, 1980-81; dir. internal mgmt. controls directorate Office of Asst. Sec. Def., Washington, 1993-94; dir. spl. projects USCG Hdqtrs., Washington, 1994; ret., 1994. Contbr. articles to profl. jours. Bd. dirs. ARC, Boston, L.A., disaster relief officer nat. ARC staff, 1952—; chmn. ops. Boston chpt., 1980, vice chmn. disaster svcs., 1978-82, mem. exec. com., 1978-82, bd. dirs., 1972-82, chief asst. med. disaster officer Boston, chmn. emergency med. svcs. transp. com. Boston, 1973-78. Decorated Bronze Star medal, and many others; fellow Kings Fund Coll., London, 1972. Mem. ARC Disaster Svc. Human Resource Sys., Mil. Order Loyal Legion (hon.). Home: 2401 E Las Olas Blvd Fort Lauderdale FL 33301-1572

FRENCH, BERTHA DORIS, medical, surgical and geriatrics nurse; b. Augusta Center, N.Y., Jan. 18, 1911; d. Charles Madison and Tillie (Hallenbeck) F. Diploma, Faxton Hosp. Sch. Nursing, Utica, N.Y., 1933. RN, N.Y., Tex. Pvt. duty nurse Brownsville, Tex.; dir. nurses Retama Manor Nursing Home, Brownsville, 1972, Valley Grande Manor Nursing Facility, Brownsville, 1973-76, PRN Home Health Agy., Brownsville; staff nurse Brownsville Med. Ctr.; relief dir. nursing svc. Village at Valley Inn, Brownsville, Brownsville Good Samaritan Ctr.; DON Ebony Lake Convalescent Ctr., 1990; nursing cons. Casa del Sol Adult Day Care Ctr., Brownsville, Harlingen, and San Benito, Tex., 1992-94; charge nurse, dir. Casa del Sol Adult Day Care Ctr. # 2, Brownsville, 1991—; adv. dir. J & J Home Health Agency; asst. Mary Lou Watkins, MD, PhD, 1994-95, 96—; charge nurse Casa del Sol Day Care Ctr. # 3, Brownsville, 1993—; cons. San Benito (Tex.) Adult Day Care Ctr., 1996—, Happy Hearts Adult Day Care Ctr., Brownsville; guest spkr. LVN program Tex. Southmost Coll., 1990; pvt. duty for Gladys Porter; founder Gladys Porter Zoo, 1980. Recipient Recognition award Mayor of Brownsville, 1992. Home: 6070 Emilia Ln Brownsville TX 78521-9701

FRENCH, EARL ALLAN, principal; b. Popular Bluff, Mo., July 1, 1955; s. Earl Aston and Mary Ethel (Gisi) F. BS in Social Sci., U. Okla., 1978; AA in History/Lang. Arts, South Okla. City Jr. Coll., 1981; MEd in Social Sci., Ctrl. State U., Edmond, Okla., 1984, MEd in Edn. Adminstrn., 1987; supt. cert., Tex. A&M U., Corpus Christi, 1993. Cert. tchr., Tex., Okla., Mo., Colo., Kans., Va. Student tchr. Moore (Okla.) High Sch., 1978; social studies instr., English instr., asst. athletic dir. West Elk Ind. Sch. Dist., Howard, Kans., 1979-81; social studies instr., gifted students instr. Perkins-Tryon (Okla.) High Sch., 1981-85; social studies instr., English instr. Air Force Acad., Colo. Springs, Colo., 1985-86; exec. traveling sec. to William C. McIntosh II Washington, 1986-87; social studies instr., jr. high athletic adminstr. Caddo Mills (Tex.) Jr. High Sch., 1987-88; social studies instr., phys. edn. instr. Chico (Tex.) Ind. Sch. Dist., 1988-89; vice prin. Alice (Tex.) High Sch., 1989-95; prin. James Monroe H.S., Fredericksburg, Va., 1995—; Mem. numerous school coms.; workshop adminstr. in field. Active Am. Diabetes Assn., Am. Cancer Assn., Boys/Girls Club of Am. Named Southeast Kans. Track Coach of Yr., 1980, Member of Ctrl. Okla. Football Coaching Staff of Yr., 1983, 84, Okla. Baseball Coach of Yr., 1984, Ft. Worth Area Coach of Yr., 1989, Outstanding Young Adminstr. for South Tex., U.S. Marine Corps, 1991. Mem. ASCD, NASSP, Am. Baseball Coaches Assn. (Southwest Coach of Yr. 1984), Am. Football Coaches Assn., Nat. Baseball Assn., Nat. H.S. Coaches Assn., Nat. Strength Coaches Assn., Nat. Interscholastic Athletic Adminstrs., Assn. Tex. Secondary Sch. Prins., Tex. H.S. Baseball Coaches Assn., Tex. H.S. Coaches Assn., Affective Educators Assn., Va. Assn. Secondary Sch. Prins., U. Okla. Alumni Assn., Kappa Delta Pi, Delta Upsilon. Democrat. Baptist.

FRENCH, ELIZABETH IRENE, biology educator, violinist; b. Knoxville, Tenn., Sept. 20, 1938; d. Junius Butler and Irene Rankin (Johnston) F. MusB, U. Tenn., 1959, MS, 1962; PhD, U. Miss., 1973. Tchr. music Kingsport (Tenn.) Sympony Assn., 1962-64, Birmingham (Ala.) Schs., 1964-66; NASA trainee in biology U. Miss., Oxford, 1969-73; asst. prof. Mobile (Ala.) Coll. (name now U. Mobile), 1973-83, assoc. prof., 1983-94, prof., 1994—; orch. contractor Am. Fedn. Musicians, 1983—; 1st violin Kingsport Symphony Orch., 1962-64, Birmingham Symphony Orch., 1964-66, Knoxville Symphony Orch., 1965-68, Memphis Symphony Orch., 1970-73, Mobile Opera-Port City Symphony, 1974—. Violin recitalist Ala. Artists Series, 1978-81. Named Career Woman of Yr., Gayfer's, Inc., 1985. Mem. Assn. Southeastern Biologists, Human Anatomy and Physiology Soc. (nat. com. to construct standardized test on anatomy and physiology), Wilderness Soc., Ala. Acad. Scis. (presenter 1996), Ala. Ornithol. Soc., Mobile Bay Audubon Soc., Am. Fedn. Musicians, Ala. Fedn. Music Clubs (chmn. composition contest 1986—, historian 1991-95), Schumann Music Club (pres. 1977-79, 85-87, 94—). Republican. Episcopalian. Home: 36 Ridgeview Dr Chickasaw AL 36611-1317 Office: U Mobile PO Box 13220 Mobile AL 36663-0220

FRENCH, JAMES HAROLD, JR., plastic surgeon; b. Oxford, Miss., Mar. 25, 1946; s. James Harold and Arlene (Howard) F.; m. Kathleen Brelsford, Dec. 23, 1987; children: James Harold III, Katheryn Chandler. BA, U. Ark., 1968; MD, La. State U., 1975. Diplomate Am. Bd. Plastic Surgery. Intern, resident La. State U. Sch. Medicine, New Orleans, 1975-79; resident plastic surgery Vanderbilt U., Nashville, 1979-81; asst. prof. plastic surgery Johns Hopkins U., Balt., 1981-85; co-dir. Ctr. for Facial Rehab. Fairfax Hosp., Falls Church, Va., 1986—; ptnr. Ctr. for Plastic Surgery, Annandale,

Va., 1985—. Fellow NYU, 1982-83. Fellow ACS. Office: Ctr for Plastic Surgery 3299 Woodburn Rd Annandale VA 22003

FRENCH, JAMES THOMAS, historian, educator; b. Monroe, La., July 21, 1947; s. Harvey Thomas and Hazel Laura (Roberts) F.; m. Cathy Dianne Newsom, Aug. 10, 1974; children: Rebecca, Michael, Elizabeth, Patrick, Sarah. BA in Psychology, La. Tech. U., 1974, MA in History, 1983; MA in Edn., Chapman Coll., 1980. Chief Military Studies Branch Curriculum Divsn. Headquarters Air Force Reserve OfficerTng. Corps, 1984-87; chief Air Base Operability 26th Combat Support Group, Zweibrucken, Germany, 1988-89; chief Command and Control Divsn. 26th Tactical Reconnaissance Wing, 1989-91; commd. USAF, 1975-92, advanced through grades to maj., ret., 1992; marine NCO Vietnam, 1968-69, 70-71; asst. prof. history (adj. faculty) Tidewater C.C., Chesapeake, Va., 1995—. Home: 4 Woodhaven Dr Poquoson VA 23662

FRENCH, KARI LYN, sales representative; b. Rochester, N.Y., Sept. 21, 1967; d. Ronald Lewis and Karla K. (Pfeifer) F. BS in Edn., Lubbock Christian U., 1990. Cert. tchr., Tex. Tchr. Frenship Ind. Sch. Dist., Wolfforth, Tex., 1990-96; sales rep. Mary Kay Cosmetics, Inc., 1996—. Singer, dancer, actress Texas!, Canyon, Tex., 1988, Viva Santa Fe!, Hobbs, N.Mex., 1990, 92, Streetcar Named Desire, 1993, Blithe Spirit, 1994. Named to Outstanding Young Women of Am., 1988. Mem. Assn. Tex. Profl. Educators, West Tex. Speech Tchrs. Assn., Tex. Forensics Assn., Univ. Interscholastic League (acad. coord. 1992-96), Nat. Forensics League. Mem. Ch. of Christ. Home: 5211 C 73rd St Lubbock TX 79424-4448

FRENCH, KENNETH WAYNE, radio station executive, consultant; b. Damascus, Va., May 18, 1952; s. Kenneth Park and Adelphia (Sluder) F.; m. Patsy Baker, Sept. 1, 1979. BA in Broadcast Journalism, U. S.C., 1974. Cert. radio mktg. cons. Sports announcer Sta. WSSC, Sumter, S.C., 1974-76; gen. sales mgr. Sta. WWDM-FM, WFIG, Sumter, S.C., 1976-80; gen. mgr. Sta. KIXY-FM, KQSA, San Angelo, Tex., 1981-83; v.p., gen. mgr. Sta. KELS-FM, Ardmore, Okla., 1983-84; gen. sales mgr. Sta. KKCS-FM KKHT, Colorado Springs, Colo., 1984-85; local sales mgr. KEYN-FM/KQAM, Wichita, Kans.; gen. mgr. Sta. KBUY-FM, KDJW, Amarillo, Tex., 1986-87; operating ptnr., gen. mgr. Sta. KMVR-FM KOBE, Las Cruces, N.Mex., 1987-88; gen. mgr. Sta. WYBB-FM/WNST-FM, Charleston, S.C., 1989—; exec. v.p. The French Group, Charleston, S.C., 1990—. Actor in films Rich In Love, 1993, Die Hard III, 1995, Stranger Than Fiction, 1996, TV movies Queen, 1993, Class of '61, 1993, Scarlet, 1994, Bionic Everafter, 1994, The Romeo and Juliet Murders, 1996, TV series Sweet Justice, 1995. Bd. dirs. YMCA, San Angelo, 1981-82, Conv. and Visitors Bur., Las Cruces, 1987-88, Aggie Sports Assn., Las Cruces, 1987-88; dir.-elect Las Cruces C. of C., 1988-89, Dona Ana Arts Coun., 1988-90; bd. dirs. Happy Days, Spl. Times, Charleston, 1993—, v.p., pres.-elect, 1994—. Recipient Key Man award Jaycees, 1980, N.Mex. Gov. award of appreciation, 1989, S.C. Gov.'s Vol. award, 1996. Mem. Charleston Area Broadcasters (pres. 1993-94). Baptist. Office: Sta WYBB-FM/WNST-FM 59 Windermere Blvd Charleston SC 29407-7411

FRENCH, LOUIS BERTRAND, engineering educator; b. Louisville, May 23, 1939; s. William Louis and Mary Elizabeth (Heuser) F. BSEE, Christian Bros. Coll., 1966; MS in Tech. Edn., Memphis State U., 1988. Design engr. Eaton Yale and Towne, Forrest City, Ark., 1966-68; instr. to assoc. prof. State Tech. Inst. at Memphis, 1968—. With USMC Res., 1956-61. Mem. IEEE, Assn. for the Advancement of Med. Instrumentation, Soc. of Biomed. Equipment Technicians (bd. dirs. 1984-87). Home: 530 Greenbriar Eads TN 38028 Office: State Tech Inst at Memphis 5983 Macon Cv Memphis TN 38134-7642

FRENCH, MICHAEL BRUCE, beverage company executive; b. Arlington, Va., Sept. 18, 1954; s. Orville Sidney and Doris (Goldberg) F.; m. Robin Ann Abenstein, Oct. 15, 1978; children: Brian Michael, Matthew Jeffrey, Sean Thornton. BA, Princeton (N.J.) U., 1976; M in Mgmt., Northwestern U., Evanston, Ill., 1978. Brand asst., asst. brand mgr. Procter & Gamble Co., Cin., 1978-80, brand mgr., 1981-84; mktg. dir. Coca-Cola Bottling Mideast Inc. subs. P&G, Lexington, Ky., 1984-85; v.p. mktg. Coca-Cola Botting Mideast, Inc., Lexington, 1985-87; brand mgr. Coca-Cola USA, Atlanta, 1987-89; mktg. mgr. chain accounts Coca-Cola Fountain, Atlanta, 1989, dir. channel mktg., 1989-93, dir. product definition and devel., 1993, asst. v.p. mktg. ops., 1993-94, v.p. mktg., 1994-95; dir. edn. mktg. Coca-Cola Co., Atlanta, 1995—. Mem. Rep. Party of Ga., Atlanta, 1988—; mem. baseball steering com. U. Ky., Lexington, 1986-87; fundraising chmn. Jr. Achievement of the Bluegrass, Lexington, 1986-87; chmn. pub. awareness subcom. Gov.'s Anti-Substance Abuse Commn., Frankfort, Ky., 1986-87; divsn. coord. Coca-Cola United Way Campaign, 1996. Named to Hon. Order of Ky. Cols., 1986. Mem. Princeton Club of Ga. Home: 4352 Highborne Dr Marietta GA 30066-2429 Office: Coca-Cola USA Coca-Cola Plz Atlanta GA 30313

FRENDAHL, DENNIS MICHAEL, beverage company executive; b. Beloit, Wis., Aug. 16, 1959; s. Arnold Edward and Cecilia Eugenia (Ballesteros) F.; m. Lisa M. Qui, Aug. 14, 1983; children: Christopher, Bryan. B in Indsl. Engring., Ga. Tech., 1983; MBA, U. Chgo., 1988. Cert. practitioner in inventory mgmt. Shipping supr. Frito-Lay, Inc., San Jose, Calif., 1983-84, material svcs. mgr., 1984-85; facilities ops. mgr. Frito-Lay, Inc., Chgo., 1985-86, zone indsl. engr., 1986-88; prin. Paragon Cons. Group, Dallas, 1988-91; mgmt. cons. Cleveland Cons. Assn. (purchased Paragon in Jan. 1991), Dallas, 1991-94; mgr. ops. engring. Coca-Cola Co., Atlanta, 1994-96; procurement account mgr. Coca-Cola Trading Co., 1996—. Author (computer program) Linear Programs for Commodities, 1989-90. Pres., treas. Ga. Tech. Alumni Club, Dallas, 1991; pres., treas. edn. com. Atonement Luth. Ch., Plano, Tex., 1990-91. Mem. Inst. Indsl. Engrs. (sr., treas. 1982-83, scholarship 1982), Am. Prodn. and Inventory Control Soc. (sr., cert. practitioner inventory mgmt.), Beta Gamma Sigma. Home: 5355 Wild Sonnet Path Norcross GA 30092 Office: Coca-Cola Co One Coca-Cola Plz Atlanta GA 30301

FRENETTE, LUC, anesthesiologist, educator; b. LaTuque, Que., Can., June 14, 1958; came to U.S., 1990; s. Liguori and Colette (Charland) F.; m. Marie Claude, Feb. 11, 1991. BS, Coll. Three Rivers, Trois-Riviere, Que., Can., 1978; MD, U. Montreal, Que., Can., 1984; BA, U. Pitts., 1991. Chief dept. anesthesiology Hotel Dieu Hosp., Amos, Que., Can., 1988-90; asst. prof. anesthesiology U. Ala., Birmingham, 1991—; cons. R.I.S., Boantree, 1991—, Tonorstric, Hoskinton, 1992—. Author numerous abstracts; contbr. articles to profl. jours. Mem. AMA, Internat. Soc. Perioperative Care in Liver Transplantation, Internat. Anesthesia Rsch. Soc., Am. Soc. Anesthesiology, Am. Soc. Regional Anesthesiologists, Can. Med. Assn., Can. Soc. Anesthesiologists, Quebec Med. Assn., Quebec Soc. Anesthesiologists. Office: Univ Ala Dept Anesthesiology 619 19th St S # 845 Birmingham AL 35233-1924

FRENGER, PAUL FRED, medical computer consultant, physician; b. Houston, May 9, 1946; s. Fred Paul and Frances Mae (Mitchell) F.; m. Sandra Lee Van Schreeven, Aug. 17, 1979; 1 child, Kirk Austin. BA in Biology, Rice U., 1968; MD, U. Tex.-San Antonio, 1974. Lic. physician, Tex., Colo. Pediatric intern Keesler USAF Med. Ctr., Biloxi, Miss., 1974-75; course dir. U.S. Air Force Physician Assistant Sch., Sheppard AFB, Tex., 1976-78; spl. projects cons. Med. Networks, Inc., Houston, 1979-81; dir. med. products Microprocessor Labs., Inc., Houston, 1983; chief med. officer, dir. Mediclinic, Inc., Houston, 1984-85; pres., cons. Working Hypothesis, Inc., Houston, 1981-83, 85-87; project leader Telescan, Inc., Houston, 1987-89; med. dir. McCarty Clinic, 1989-90, Ft. Bend Family Health Ctr., 1990-91, Doctors at the Galleria, 1991-92; chief med. officer Health Testing, Inc., 1991; med. dir. Houston Pro Med., 1992-93, Heights Occupational Med. Clinic, 1994, Suburban Physician's Ctr., 1995-96. Contbr. over 80 articles to profl. jours.; patentee life raft test device, 3 patents. Mem. Rocky Mountain Bioengring. Symposium. Served to lt. col. USAF, 1969-78. Decorated Air Force Commendation medal. Mem. IEEE, Am. Assn. Med. Dirs., Am. Assn. Med. Systems and Informatics, Assn. for Computing Machinery (editor SIG Forth Newsletter 1990-94, ACM News Houston chpt. 1990-91, assoc. editor ACM Sigplan Notices 1995-96), Internat. Neural Network Soc., Mensa. Episcopalian. Avocations: model engineering, railroading. Home: 814 Silvergate Dr Houston TX 77079-5001

FRENQUELLE, PETER MICHAEL, legislative analyst, organization official; b. Cambridge, Mass., Aug. 28, 1969. BA in Polit. Sci., U. South Fla., 1991. Sales clk. The Edge in Electronics, Fairfax County, Va., 1991-92; office asst. Hogan & Hartson, L.L.P., Tyson's Corner, Va., 1992-94; legis. analyst Motorcycle Industry Coun., Inc., Arlington, Va., 1994—. Vol. reporter Broadside newspaper George Mason U., Fairfax, Va., 1993, Dole/Kemp Campaign, Washington, 1996. Mem. U. South Fla. Alumni Assn. Home: 1500 Lincoln Cir Apt 141 McLean VA 22102 Office: Motorcycle Industry Coun Inc Ste 600 1235 Jefferson Davis Hwy Arlington VA 22202

FRENZE, KARIN M.E. ALEXIS, art historian; b. Bethesda, Md., Mar. 26, 1956; d. Carl O. and Maj-Britt (Lennerup) Alexis; m. Christopher John Frenze, July 25, 1987; children: Maj-Britt Kristina, Peter Christopher-Erik. BS, Am. U., 1976, MA in art history, 1978; PhD in art history, U. Va., 1986. Rsch. asst. The Frederick Law Olmsted Papers, Washington, 1986-87; arch. historian, surveyor Montgomery County (Md.) Preservation Commn., 1988; coord., moderator, lectr. Smithsonian Inst., Washington, 1984—; coord. Smithsonian Assocs. Art History Series Cert. Program, 1989—; art and architecture historian, rsch. asst. to Kress Prof. Nat. Gallery of Art, Washington, 1990-93; instr. No. Va. C.C., Alexandria, 1979-81, Southeastern U., 1980-81, The Am. U., 1983, Montgomery Coll., Rockville, Md., 1984-86, Germantown, Md., 1979, Mt. Vernon Coll., Washington, 1984-86, Georgetown U., 1987, Gallaudet U., Washington, 1989; tchg. asst. U. Va., 1983; bd. adv. Smithsonian Art History Series, 1989-91, 93; guest lectr. Fgn. Svc. Inst., U.S. Dept. State, 1992—; lectr. in field. Co-author: National Museum, 1992; contbr. articles to profl. jours. and pubs. Parents' steering com. Daytime Devel. Ctr., Fairfax, Va., 1993-94; bd. dirs. Parents of Children with Down Syndrome; mem. Nat. Down Syndrome Congress; bd. dirs. Inter-faith Coalition Family Friend, Easter Seal Soc., Northern Va. Recipient Rsch. Trip, Nat. Gallery Art, 1991, 92, 93, award of merit Records of Columbia Hist. Soc., 1989; Thord-Gray Meml. Fund grantee Am.-Scandinavian Found., 1992; named Scandinavian-Am. Citizen of Yr. award Scandia Touch, Occoguan, Va., 1996. Mem. Ctr. Advanced Study in Visual Arts, The Soc. Archtl. Historians, The Coll. Art Assn., Am.-Scandinavian Assn., Soc. Advancement of Scandinavian Studies, Smithsonian Assocs. Lutheran. Home: 2449 Villanova Dr Vienna VA 22180-6956

FRERET, RENÉ JOSEPH, minister; b. Pass Christian, Miss., Jan. 3, 1944; s. James Carroll and Pearl (Gordy) F.; m. Freda Rester; children: Katherine, Grace, Stephen, Rachel. AA, Perkinston Jr. Coll., 1964; BA, Bapt. Christian Coll., 1973; MA, Bapt. Christian U., 1978, PhD, 1984. Ordained to ministry Ind. Bapt. Ch., 1967. Pastor New Hope Bapt. Ch., McNeil, Miss., 1966-68, Cen. Bapt. Ch., Gulfport, Miss., 1968-70, Forest Hills Bapt. Ch., Benton, Ark., 1970-72; assoc. pastor Bapt. Tabernacle, Shreveport, La., 1972-73; pastor Temple Bapt. Ch., Gulfport, Miss., 1973—; adminstr. Temple Christian Acad., Gulfport, Miss., 1974—; pres. Temple Bapt. Inst., 1981—; instr. Maranatha Inst. Missions, Natchez, Miss., 1983—; dir. Maranatha Mens Retreat, Natchez, 1990—; bd. dirs. Meml. Hosp., Gulfport. Author: Patriotism, 1990. Chmn. Harrison County (Miss.) Fire Commn., 1990; chmn., mayor Gulfport City Councilmen Task Force, 1994—; chaplain Orange Grove Vol. Fire Dept., Gulfport, 1989, Harrison County Bd. Suprs., 1992-95; bd. trustees Meml. Hosp. Gulfport, 1996—. Mem. Miss. State Assn. Christian Schs. (exec. dir. student state competition 1984-93, v.p. 1988-93, pres. 1993-95, exec. dir. 1996—), Am. Assn. Christian Schs. (bd. dirs. 1996—). Home: 13092 Quail Ridge Rd Gulfport MS 39503-4835 Office: Temple Bapt Ch 14190 Dedeaux Rd Gulfport MS 39503-3358

FRERICHS, EDWIN NATHAN, retail planning consultant; b. Buffalo Center, Iowa, Feb. 3, 1926; s. Onno H. and Elmina Ann (Davis) F.; m. Elizabeth A. Ryals, Dec. 23, 1948; children: Lori, Derek. BA in Art & Indsl. Design, U. Iowa, Iowa City, 1950. Registered Interior Designer, Realtor. Interior designer Adleta Showcase Co., Dallas, 195-63; retail planning cons. Rya Retail Design, Dallas, 1963-69, Frerichs Assn., Dallas, 1965-71; dir. store planning constrn. McRaes Dept. Stores, Jackson, Miss., 1971-72; v.p. prodn. dir. RYA Retail Design, Dallas, 1972-79; retail planning cons. RE Assocs., Dallas, 1979-83, ENF Design Group, Dallas, 1983-88; store design project mgr. J.C. Penney Co., Dallas, 1988-92; retail planning cons. ENF Design Group, Dallas, 1992—. Sgt. U.S. Army, 1944-46, 50-51, Korea. Mem. Am. Inst. Interior, Inst. Store Planners. Mem. Christian Ch. Office: ENF Design Group 982 Sylvania Dr Dallas TX 75218-2941

FRESH, EDITH MCCULLOUGH, behavioral medicine educator, psychologist; b. Quincy, Fla., Sept. 23, 1942; d. Harry Moses and Edith (Anderson) McCullough; m. Frederick Anthony Fresh, July 2, 1940; children: Kevin, Bradford, Carla, Eric. AB in Sociology, Ind. U., 1970; MSW, U. Mich., 1972; MA in Clin. Psychology, Ga. State U., 1988, PhD in Clin. Child and Family Psychology, 1993. Cert. Acad. Cert. Social Workers; lic. psychologist, Ga.; lic. marriage and family therapist, Ga. Human resources specialist Pub. Tech., Inc., Washington, 1973-77; outpatient program dir. Project Headline, Detroit, 1972-73; asst. prof. Fla. A&M U., Tallahassee, 1977-83; clin. social worker Morehouse Sch. Medicine, Atlanta, 1983-88; clin. social worker, adminstr. Spelman Coll., Atlanta, 1988-90; marriage and family therapist, psychologist in pvt. practice Atlanta, 1990—; instr. DeKalb Coll., North Campus, Dunwoody, Ga., 1991-94; divsn. chief, asst. prof. Morehouse Sch. Medicine, Atlanta, 1994—; vis. staff Gestalt Inst. Cleve., 1981-88; site visitor commn. for accreditation for marriage and family edn., Am. Assn. Marriage and Family Therapists, Washington, 1983—. Bd. dirs. Reston (Va.) Black Focus, 1976; charter bd. mem. The Capitol Outlook newspaper, Tallahassee, 1980-84; regional coord., Nat. Hook-Up of Black Women, South Atlantic region, 1980-83; chair SPRC Hoosier Meml. United Meth. Ch., Atlanta, 1995—. Recipient Rep. Gwen Cherry Meml. award, So. Regional Journalists Assn., 1980; named Woman of the Yr., Zeta Phi Beta, 1982. Mem. NASW, APA, Nat. Assn. Black Psychologists, Am. Assn. Marriage and Family Therapists (clin. mem.; mem. ethics com., 1992-95), Soc. Tchrs. of Family Medicine, Ga. Assn. Marriage and Family Therapists (chair ethnic and minority tas force, 1991-92). Office: Morehouse Sch Medicine Dept Family Medicine 505 Fairburn Rd SW Atlanta GA 30331

FRETWELL, LINCOLN DARWIN, career officer, dentist, consultant; b. Moulton, Ala., Sept. 20, 1944; s. Lincoln Coolege and Katherine Alice (Gargis) F.; m. Connie Ruth Comer, Aug. 17, 1974; children: Darbi, Christina, Benjamin. AA, Daytona Beach Jr. Coll., 1969; BA, Fla. State U., 1971; DDS, Med. Coll. Va., 1975. Diplomate Fed. Svcs. Bd. of Gen. Dentistry, Certifying Bd. Gen. Dentistry. Resident in dentistry U. Va., Charlottesville, 1975-77; asst. prof. Sch. Dentistry Med. Coll. Va., Richmond, 1977-81; dental officer, officer in charge Lyster Army Hosp. Dental Clinic, Richmond, Va., 1984-87; instr. Acad. Health Scis., 1987-91; comdr. Ft. Irwin DENTAC, 1991-93; dental cons. U.S. Army, Ft. Sam Houston, Tex., 1993-95; comdr. DENTAC, Ft. Hood, Tex., 1995—. Author: Handbook of Preventive Dentistry, 1978; contbr. articles to profl. jours. Coach U.S. Army Youth Activities, 1986—; leader Boy Scouts Am., Tex. and Calif., 1989—. Recipient Family of Yr. award U.S. Army, 1990-91. Fellow Internat. Coll. Dentists; mem. ADA, Soc. U.S. Army Flight Surgeons, Acad. Gen. Dentistry (pres. 1996—), Pierre Fauchard Acad. (chmn. mil. affairs 1990-93), Omicron Kappa Upsilon. Home: 6762 Marshall St Fort Hood TX 76544 Office: US Army DENTAC Fort Hood TX 76544

FREUND, ADRIAN PAUL, county official; b. Tunbridge Wells, Kent, Eng., July 15, 1950; came to U.S., 1956; s. Eric Conrad and Beryl Lillian (Elphick) F.; m. Marlene Alicia Porter, June 1972 (div.); m. Karin Lee Krueger Fox, Oct. 11, 1986; 1 child, Justin Kent. B in Urban Planning, U. Ill., 1972. Transp. coord. City of Springfield, Ill., 1972-73; program mgr. water quality mgmt. Rock Valley Met. Coun. Govts., Rockford, Ill., 1973-75; asst. water program dir., program adminstr. Dane County 208 Water Quality Program Dane County Regional Planning Commn., Madison, Wis., 1975-85; chief environ. officer Office Environ. Resource Mgmt., Austin, Tex., 1985-86; dep. dir. Dept. Environ. Protection, Austin, 1986-88; asst. dir. Environ. and Conservation Svcs. Dept., acting dir. Resource Mgmt. Dept., Austin, 1988-89; chief Bur. Water Mgmt. Conn. Dept. Environ. Protection, 1989-92; dir. dept. planning and environ. mgmt. Jefferson County, Louisville, Ky., 1992—; organizer, instr. U. Wis.-Extension Planning and Zoning Insts., Wis. and Colo., 1983-85; presenter Am. Planning Assn. Nat. Conf., 1995-96. Mem. Am. Planning Assn. (dir.-at-large 1986-94, nat. bd. dirs. 1986-94, pres. Wis. chpt. 1980-82, chmn. environ. quality task force), Am. Inst. Cert. Planners (charter). Democrat. Home: 10304 Long Home Rd Louisville KY 40291-4020 Office: Jefferson County Dept Planning and Environ Mgmt 527 W Jefferson St Ste 600 Louisville KY 40202-2854

FREUND, ALAN EUGENE, petrochemical company executive; b. Emporia, Kans., Dec. 5, 1953; s. Eugene Francis and Doris Emily (Bennett) F.; m. Denelle Kay Allen, Sept. 15, 1984; children: Courtney A., Hillary A., Meredith A. BS, Emporia State U., 1975; MBA, U. Kans., 1978. CPA, Ohio. Planning assoc. Standard Oil Co., Cleve., 1978-79, mgr. products control, 1979-81, mgr. crude oil acctg., 1981-82, controller petroleum products and refining, 1982-84, controller crude trading and transp., 1984-85; mgr. adminstrn. and control BP Am., Cleve., 1985-92; dir. adminstrn. and control, corp. sec. Global Octanes Corp. (Mitsui USA), Houston, 1992-96; dir. supply and distribition Global Octanes Corp., Houston, 1996—. Mem. Tex. Soc. CPAs, Fin. Execs. Inst., Ohio Soc. CPAs, Risk and Ins. Mgmt. Soc., Kans. Alumni Assn. Office: Global Octanes Corp 1000 Louisiana St Ste 5680 Houston TX 77002-5013

FREUND, EMMA FRANCES, medical technologist; b. Washington; d. Walter R. and Mabel W. (Loveland) Ervin; m. Frederic Reinert Freund, Mar. 4, 1953; children: Frances, Daphne, Fern, Frederic. BS, Wilson Tchrs. Coll., Washington, 1944; MS in Biology, Catholic U., Washington, 1953; MEd in Adult Edn., Va. Commonwealth U., 1988; cert. in mgmt. devel. Va. Commonwealth U., 1975, supr. devel.; student SUNY, New Paltz, 1977, J. Sargeant Reynolds C.C., 1978. Cert. Nat. Cert. Agy. for Clin. Lab. Pers, supervisory devel., Va. Tchr. math. and sci. D.C. Sch. System, Washington, 1944-45; technician in parasitology lab., zool. div., U.S. Dept. Agr., Beltsville, Md., 1945-48; histologic technician dept. pathology Georgetown U. Med. Sch., Washington, 1948-49; clin. lab. technician Kent and Queen Anne's County Gen. Hosp., Chestertown, Md., 1949-51; histotechnologist surg. pathology dept. Med. Coll. Va. Hosp., Richmond, 1951—, supr. histology lab., 1970-88, mgr., supr. 1988—; cons. profl. meetings and workshops histotechnology, head infosvcs. Histo-Help; mem. exam. coun. Nat. Cert. Agy. Med. Lab. Pers. Asst. cub scout den leader Robert E. Lee coun. Boy Scouts Am., 1967-68, den leader, 1968-70. Co-author: (mini-course) Instrumentation in Cytology and Histology, 1985; editor Histo-Scope Newsletter. Mem. AAAS, NAFE, AAUW, Am. Soc. CLin. Lab. Sci. (rep. to sci. assembly histology sect. 1977-78, chmn. histology sect. 1983-85, 89-96), Va. Soc. Med. Technology, Richmond Soc. Med. Technologists (corr. sec. 1977-78, dir. 1981-82, pres. 1984-85), Va. State Soc. Histotechnology (pres. 1994—), Nat. Certification Agy. (clin. lab. specialist in histotech., clin. lab. supr., clin. lab. dir.), N.Y. Acad. Scis., Am. Assn. Clin. Chemistry (assoc.), Am. Soc. Clin. Pathologists (cert. histology technician), Nat. Geog. Soc., Va. Govtl. Employees Assn., Nat. Soc. Histotech. (by-laws com. 1981—; C.E.U. com. 1981—, program com. regional meeting 1984, 85, chmn. regional meeting 1987, program chmn. regional mtg. 1992), Am. Mus. Natural History, Smithsonian Instn., Am. Mgmt. Assn., Clin. Lab. Mgmt. Assn., Nat. Soc. Historic Preservation, Sigma Xi, Phi Beta Rho, Kappa Delta Pi, Phi Lambda Theta, Omicron Sigma. Home: 1315 Asbury Rd Richmond VA 23229-5305

FREVERT, JAMES WILMOT, financial planner, investment advisor; b. Richland Twp., Iowa, Dec. 19, 1922; s. Wesley Clarence and Grace Lotta (Maw) F.; m. Jean Emily Sunderlin, Feb. 12, 1949; children: Douglas James, Thomas Jeffrey, Kimberly Ann. BS in Gen. Engrg., MIT, 1948. Prodn. mgr. Air Reduction Chem. Co., Calvert City, Ky., 1955-61; plant mgr. Air Products & Chems., West Palm Beach, Fla., 1961-62; pres. Young World HWD, Ft. Lauderdale, Fla., 1962-66; v.p. Shareholders Mgmt. Co., L.A. 1966-73. Founder, past pres. MIT Club Palm Beach County, dir., 1976—, edn1. council mem., 1977-81. Served to 1st lt. USAF, 1943-46. Mem. Palm Beach Pundits, City Club of the Palm Beaches. Republican. Presbyterian. Home: 883 Country Club Dr North Palm Beach FL 33408-3742

FREY, BOB HENRY, psychotherapist, sociologist, educator, poet; b. Porterdale, Ga., Mar. 7, 1953; s. George Loyd Sr. and Betty Montine (Canup) F.; m. Deborah Ann Dunn Mar. 8, 1980. BA, Immanuel Coll., Peachtree City, Ga., 1976; MA, Immanuel Sem., Peachtree, 1977, DRE, 1980; EdD in Counseling and Adminstrn., Immanuel Sem., Atlanta, 1988; PhD in Sociology, Columbia Pacific U., 1985; MA in Counseling, Luther Rice Sem., 1992; postgrad., U. Bibl. Studies, 1992-95, South Fla. Bible Coll. & Sem., 1996—; LLD (hon.), Christian Bible Coll., 1996. Cert. med. psychotherapist, Am. Bd. Med. Psychotherapists and Psychodiagnosticians. Dean Calvary Bapt. Bible Coll., Jonesboro, Ga., 1977-78; chief of police City of Hagan, Ga., 1986-87; caseworker prin. Toombs County Dept. Family and Children Svcs., Lyons, Ga., 1987; adj. faculty mentor Columbia Pacific U., San Rafael, Calif., 1987-89; adj. prof. Newport U., Newport Beach, Calif., 1989—; coord., mgr. Tidelands Community Mental Health, Mental Retardation and Substance Abuse Ctr., Savannah, Ga., 1990-91; psychotherapist, clin. dir. social and clin. svcs. Mel Blount Youth Home Ga., Vidalia, 1992-94; psychotherapist, clin. supr. Clayton Ctr. for Mental Health, Substance Abuse and Devel. Svcs., Riverdale, Ga., 1994—; mentor adj. faculty Christian U. Kuaui, Hawaii, 1993—; adj. faculty St. Martin's Coll. and Sem., Milw., 1995—; poet, Nat. Libr. Poetry, Owings Mills, Md. Author: A Biblical Perspective-The Writing of Divorcement, 1993, A Biblical Study Guide, 1993, The Frey Initiative on Accreditation-Discriminatory Practices Regional vs National, 1994, (pamphlets) The Bible, The Christian, Non-Christian and Nudism, 1982, The Frey Manifesto On Accreditation Issues, 1995, Christians Out-Of-Step With God, 1985. Lobbyist MADD, Atlanta, 1983; rsch. bd. advisors nat. divsn. Am. Biographical Inst., Raleigh, N.C., 1994—. Sgt. U.S. Army, 1970-77. Partial scholar Columbia Pacific U., 1982. Mem. APA (student affiliate). Democrat. Home: 8478 Shiloh Ct Jonesboro GA 30236

FREY, HERMAN S., publishing company executive; b. Murfreesboro, Tenn., Apr. 19, 1920; s. Saleem McCool and Minnie May (Felts) F.; m. Daisy Rook Corlew, Apr. 3, 1946; 1 child, Pamela Anne. Student electronic Navigation MIT, 1943; cert. in Commerce, U. Va., 1958; cert. internat. law, internat. ct. justice, The Netherlands, 1959; Course in naval intelligence U.S. Naval War Coll., 1948; BA, Am. U., 1964; MBA, George Washington U., 1965; student Oxford U., 1974; cert. constl. history, Oxford U., 1974, cert. fgn. and imperial policy, 1975. Commd. ensign USN, 1942; advanced through grades to lt. comdr., 1955; with navigation dept. USS Quincy, 1937-41, navigator USS Sagamore, 1941-42, asst. navigator USS Iowa, 1942-44, with Naval Schs., Norfolk, Va., N.Y.C., Miami, 1944-45, navigation and gunnery officer USS Zuni, 1945-46, exec. officer USS Chickasaw, 1946-47, comdg. officer, 1947-48; instr. Naval Sch., Boston, 1948-51; comdg. officer USS Sisken, 1951-52; conducted Cts. Inquiry for comdr. Mine Force Atlantic Fleet, 1953; comdr. mine divsn., task unit, 1952-54; exec. officer USS McClellan, 1954-55; officer detailer Bur. Naval Pers., Washington, 1955-58; advisor, liaison Am. Embassy, The Netherlands, 1958-61; stock broker Auchincloss, Parker & Redpath, Arlington, Va., 1966-67; asst. prof. Georgetown U., Washington, 1967, U. Va., Charlottesville, 1967-69; freelance journalist Europe, U.S., 1972-76; pres. Frey Enterprises, 1976—; faculty U. Md., College Park, 1978; condr. cts. inquiry Comdr. Mine Force Atlantic Fleet, 1953-54; mem. bd. govs. Am. Sch. of Hague, Netherlands, 1959-61; cons. State of Tenn., 1969-70; mem. World Affairs Coun., Washington, 1994—. Author: Jefferson Davis, 1977. Ran for U.S. Senate, Tenn., 1970, 72; mem. adv. com. Nat. Naval Meml. Found., Washington, nat. adv. coun. A Tribute to the United States Navy, 1941-45; bd. govs. Meth. Ch., Arlington, 1962-64; mem. U.S. Hist. Soc., Nat. Trust for Hist. Preservation, Battle of Normandy Found., 50th ann. Coun. Battle of Normandy; honorary citizen Colonial Williamsburg, Va. Mem. AAUP, VFW (life), Am. Bus. Men's Assn., The Hague, 1958-61, Naval Order of U.S. (life), World Inst. Achievement, Soc. Advancement Mgmt. (pres. 1964), Internat. Platform Assn., U.S. Naval Inst. (life), U.S. Capitol Hist. Soc., Tenn. Hist. Soc., Tenn. Sheriff's Assn., Ret. Officers Assn. (life), Nat. Assn. Uniformed Services (life), World Affairs Coun. (Washington), Am. Legion (life), Navy League of U.S., Vets. Assn. of USS Iowa, Mil. Dist. Officer's Club (Washington), Phi Alpha Theta. Democrat. Avocations: history, literature, collecting rare books, travel, amateur cooking. Participant in the atom bomb tests at Bikini Atoll, 1946. Office: Frey Enterprises Ste 115-12 1007 Murfreesboro Pike Nashville TN 37217-1509

FREYER, VICTORIA C., fashion and interior design executive; b. Asbury Park, N.J.; d. Spiros Steven and Hope (Pappas) Pappaylion; m. Cyril Steven Arvanitis, Dec. 26, 1950 (div. 1975); children: Samuel James, Hope Alexandra. BA, Georgian Court Coll., 1950; student, N.Y. Sch. Interior Design, 1971-72. Mgr. Homestead Restaurant, Ocean Grove, N.J., 1946-58; art supr. Lakewood (N.J.) Pub. Schs., 1950-51; interior designer London, 1975-76, F. Korasic Assocs., Oakhurst, N.J., 1977-78; owner, operator Virginia Interiors, McLean, Va., 1974-90; interior designer Anita Perlut Interiors, McLean, 1986; owner, operator Victoria Freyer Interiors, McLean, 1986—; fashion cons. Nordstrom Splty. Store, McLean, 1988-92; fashion seminar coord. Nordstrom Splty. Store, Tysons Corner, Va., 1992—; lectr. Girl Scouts U.S., Rep. Women of Capitol Hill, Washington Hosp. Ctr., Women's Am. ORT, Nat. Assn. Cath. Women, Bethesda Naval Hosp., NIH, others. Pres. Monmouth County Med. Aux., 1964; originator 1st lecture series Monmouth Coll., Long Branch, N.J., 1965; guest moderator Alexandria (Va.) Hosp. Series, 1988; mem. Women's Symphony Com., Washington, 1988—; guest speaker Girl Scouts U.S. Coun. Nation's Capitol, 1988-90, Nuclear Energy Coun., 1989, pers. dept. CIA, 1989-90, Internat. Women's Group Washington, 1989-90. Recipient Recognition awards Girl Scout Coun. Nation's Capitol, 1991, No. Region Beta Pi, 1991, Beta Sigma Pi, 1991. Mem. AAUW (program chmn. 1968, guest speaker many orgns.). Greek Orthodox. Home and Office: 7630 Provincial Dr Mc Lean VA 22102-7631

FREYTAG, ADDIE LOU, nurse; b. Crestview, Fla., May 16, 1941; d. William Harold and Nellie (Davis) McCullough; m. Charles Lee Freytag, Oct. 14, 1961 (dec. 1992); children: Cassandra Duncan, Camilla Gay, C. Preston. RN, Orange Meml. Hosp., 1961; grad., Tex. Woman's U., 1973; BS in Edn., U. Tenn., 1988, MSN, 1991. RN, Tenn., Fla.; cert. pediat. nurse practitioner, family nurse practitioner. Staff nurse Hariman (Tenn.) Hosp., 1961-66, Oak Ridge (Tenn.) Hosp., 1966-70; office nurse Dr. Lewis Preston, Oak Ridge, 1970-74; family nurse practitioner Mountain Peoples Health Coun., 1974-76; with Child Health & Devel., Wartburg, Tenn., 1977-80, Community Health Ctr., Deer Lodge, Tenn., Highland Health Ctr., Elgin, Tenn.; staff nurse Parkwest Hosp. Knoxville Superior Home Health, Wartburg, 1989; family nurse practitioner Oak Grove Primary Care Clinic, Oneida, Tenn., 1992—; mem. med. staff Scott County Hosp., Oneida, 1992. Past county commr. Morgan County. Recipient honorable mention Felder Photo Contest, 1988, 95; George B. Boland Nurse's scholar. Mem. ANA (cert. family nurse practitioner 1982), Tenn. Nurses Assn., Nat. Assn. Pediat. Nurse Assocs. and Practitioners (cert. pediat. nurse practitioner 1977), Nurse Practitioners Assn. for Continuing Edn., Tenn. Pac, Nurses in Advanced Practice. Home: 226 Letorey Rd Wartburg TN 37887-3135

FREYTAG, SHARON NELSON, lawyer; b. Larned, Kans., May 11, 1943; d. John Seldon and Ruth Marie (Herbel) Nelson; children: Kurt David, Hillary Lee. BS with highest distinction, U. Kans., Lawrence, 1965; MA, U. Mich., 1966; JD cum laude, So. Meth. U., 1981. Bar: Tex. 1981, U.S. Dist. Ct. (no. dist.) Tex. 1981, U.S. Ct. Appeals (5th cir.) 1982, U.S. Supreme Ct. 1993; cert. civil appellate law. Tchr. English, Gaithersburg (Md.) H.S., 1966-70; instr. English, Eastfield Coll., 1974-78; law clk. U.S. Dist. Ct. for No. Dist. Tex., 1981-82, U.S. Ct. Appeals 5th Cir., 1982; ptnr. litigation and appellate sect. Haynes and Boone, Dallas, 1983—, vis. prof. law Southern Meth. U., 1985-86; faculty Appellate Adv. program NITA. Editor-in-chief Southwestern Law Jour., 1980-81; contbr. articles to law jours. Woodrow Wilson fellow. Recipient John Marshall Constl. Law award, Baird Cmty. Spirit award, 1995. Mem. ABA (mem. litigation sect., chair subcom. on local rules), Fed. Bar Assn. (co-chmn. appellate practice and advocacy sect. 1990-91), Tex. Bar Assn. (mem. appellate coun.), Dallas Bar Assn. (mem. appellate coun.), Higginbotham Inn of Ct., Barristers, Order of Coif, Phi Delta Phi, Phi Beta Kappa. Lutheran. Office: Haynes & Boone 3100 NationsBank Plz Dallas TX 75202

FRIAR, GEORGE EDWARD, lawyer, state official; b. Coxton, Ky., Aug. 18, 1916; s. George Allen and Ida Mae (Crutchfield) F.; m. Margaret Ellen Riggin; children: George Edward Jr., Cynthia L. Smith, Elizabeth Ralston. Ed., Maryville Coll., Princeton U., Vanderbilt U., U. Tenn. Sch. Law. Chmn. bd., pres. Corporate Concepts, Inc.; sec. of state State of Tenn.; gen. counsel So. Govs. Conf. With USN, World War II. Mem. ABA (ho. of dels.), Nat. Assn. Bar Execs. (pres.). Home: 6548 Draw Ln Sarasota FL 34238-5147

FRIBERG, EMIL EDWARDS, mechanical engineer, consultant; b. Wichita Falls, Tex., Apr. 11, 1935; s. John Walter and Anne (Edwards) F.; m. Jo Ann Rutta, Jan. 26, 1957; children: Emil Edwards Jr., Vicki Lynn, Joe Alan. BSME, U. Tex., 1958. Registered profl. engr., Tex. Engr. Steam Electric Sta., TU Electric, Wichita Falls, 1958-60, engr. power sales, 1960-64; engring. cons. mktg. dept. TU Electric, Ft. Worth, 1964-69; prin. Cowan, Love & Jackson Inc., Ft. Worth, 1969-73; pres. Friberg Assocs. Inc., Ft. Worth, 1973—. Contbr. articles to ASHRAE Trans. Sec. mech. engring. class of 1958, U. Tex., Austin, 1965—; chmn. Ft. Worth Energy Conservation Adv. Com., 1981. 1st lt. U.S. Army, 1959-60. Recipient award of excellence Cons. Engrs. Coun. Tex., 1977. Fellow ASHRAE (regional chmn. 1975-78, bd. dirs. 1979-82, award of merit 1975, Disting. Svc. award 1979, Regional award of merit 1981, Crosby Field award 1991), ASME, Tex. Soc. Profl. Engrs. (pres. 1972-73, Young Engr. award 1968, Engr. of Yr. award 1992), Ft. Worth Club, Rotary, Delta Upsilon (pres. Tex. Found. 1970). Baptist. Office: Friberg Assocs PO Box 2080 Fort Worth TX 76113-2080

FRICKS, WILLIAM PEAVY, shipbuilding company executive; b. Byron, Ga., Aug. 14, 1944; s. Walker Nathaniel and Mary (Peavy) F.; m. Deanie Dudley, Aug. 27, 1966; children: Holly Anne, William Peavy, Austin Nathaniel. B.S. in Indsl. Mgmt, Auburn (Ala.) U., 1966; M.B.A. in Fin, Coll. William and Mary, Williamsburg, Va., 1970; A.M.P., Harvard U., 1983. With Newport News Shipbldg. and Dry Dock Co., Va., 1966—; adminstrv. asst. to pres., then contr. and treas. Newport News Shipbldg. and Dry Dock Co., 1979-80, v.p. fin., 1980-83, v.p. tech., 1983-84, v.p. mktg., 1984-85, v.p. human resources, 1985-88, sr. v.p., 1988-92, exec. v.p., 1992-94, pres., COO, 1994-95, pres., CEO, 1995—. Office: Newport News Shipbldg 4101 Washington Ave Newport News VA 23607-2734

FRIDAY, WILLIAM CLYDE, university president emeritus; b. Raphine, Va., July 13, 1920; s. David L. and Mary E. (Rowan) F.; m. Ida Howell, May 13, 1942; children: Frances H., Mary H., Ida E. Student, Wake Forest Coll., 1937, LLD (hon.), 1957; BS, N.C. State Coll., 1941; LLB, U. N.C., 1948; DCL (hon.), U. N.C., Chapel Hill and Greensboro, 1988; LLD (hon.), Belmont Abbey Coll., 1957, Duke U., 1958, Princeton U., 1958, Elon Coll., 1959, Davidson Coll., 1961, U. Ky., 1970, Mercer U., 1977, U. N.C., Wilmington, 1992, U. N.C., Wilmington, 1992; DCL (hon.), St. Augustine's Coll., 1986, U. of South, 1976; DPS (hon.), U. N.C., Charlotte, 1986, N.C. State Coll., 1991; DFA (hon.), N.C. Sch. Arts, 1987. Bar: N.C. 1948. Asst. dean student U. N.C., 1948-51, asst. to pres., 1951-55, sec. of univ., 1955-56, acting pres., 1956, pres., 1956-86; Mem. Carnegie Commn. on Higher Edn., Commn. to Study SUNY, So. Regional Edn. Bd.; chmn. President's Task Force on Edn., 1966-67; mem. Commn. White House Fellows, 1965-68. Mem. Nat. Com. for Bicentennial Era, Am. Coun. Edn., Commn. Nat. Changes in Higher Edn.; chmn. Ctr. Creative Leadership, 1981-96, Gov.'s Commn. on Literacy,1987, Regional Literacy Ctr. Commn., 1989-90, So. Growth Policies Bd., 1989—, Knight Found. Nat. Commn. on Intercollegiate Athletics, 1989-93. Mem. Assn. Am. Univs. (pres. 1971). Democrat. Baptist. Office: Univ NC The William R Kenan Jr Fund PO Box 3858 Bowles Dr Chapel Hill NC 27515-3808

FRIED, LAWRENCE PHILIP, insurance company executive; b. N.Y.C., Mar. 20, 1938; s. Louis Israel and Gertrude May (Carlin) F.; m. Elaine Lois Raskin, Nov. 28, 1959 (div. 1986); children: Diane, Howard, Elliott; m. Diane Lynn Williford, Nov. 10, 1994. BBA in Mktg., Adelphi U., 1960. Lic. life health ins. and variable annuities agt.; registered rep. Nat. Assn. Securities Dealers; cert. ins. inspector. Prodn. mgr. Verdi Handbags, N.Y.C., 1960-73, Express Handbags, North Bergen, N.J., 1973-74; gen. mgr. Victoria Needlework, Inc., N.Y.C., 1974-79; v.p. sales J&L Hardwood Lumber Sales, Bellmore, N.Y., 1979-81; plant mgr. Jade Handbags and Belts, N.Y.C., 1981-83; mgr. Glamour Glove, Inc., N.Y.C., 1983-87; dir. prodn. Campaign, Inc., Portsmouth, Va., 1987-89; pres. Larry Fried & Assocs., Boca Raton, Fla., 1989-94; sr. v.p. The Philips Group, Inc., Lake Worth, Fla., 1989-93; v.p., ptnr. The Securance Agy., Inc., Roswell, Ga., 1994—; pres. Servpro of Chamblee-Dunwoody, Roswell, Ga., 1994—; area mgr. Broward County Atlantic Plan; cons. Elf Ceations, Inc., Bellmore, 1970-83; regional dir. Eagle Internat. Mktg., Inc., Oklahoma City, 1981-87; lectr. Help Overweight, Inc., Bklyn., 1974-75; bd. dirs. Nassau County Epilepsy Found., 1979-86; active local polit. campaigns, 1979-85; pres. Winning Edge Network, Ft. lauderdale, Fla.; bd. mem. South Broward Jewish Family Svcs.; bd. com. mem. Jewish Family Svcs. of Atlanta; mem. Alumni Recruiters Coun. Adelphi U.. Bd. dirs. Nassau County Epilepsy Found., 1979-86; active local polit. campaigns, 1979, Adelphi U. Alumni adv. coun.; pres. Winning Edge Network, Ft. Lauderdale, Fla.; bd. mem. South Broward Jewish Family Svcs., 1993-94; mem. pers. practice com. Jewish Family Svc. Atlanta; mem. Alumni Recruiters Coun. Adelphi U. Life Underwriters Tng. Coun. fellow. Mem. Jewish Geneal. Soc. Ga., Bellmore C. of C. (bd. dirs., v.p. 1979-83), Hampton Roads C. of C., Great Neck Power Squadron, U. Mich. Alumni Club Atlanta, Masons, Rotary, Pi Sigma Epsilon (life). Jewish. Home: 620 Brickleberry Ct Roswell GA 30075-3077 Office: Servpro Chamblee-Dunwoody Adminstrn Office 10930 Crabapple Rd #20 Roswell GA 30075

FRIEDEN, JANE HELLER, art educator; b. Norfolk, Va., Aug. 25, 1926; d. Samuel Ries and Saida (Seligman) Heller; m. Joseph Lee Frieden, Dec. 23, 1950 (dec. 1990); children: Nancy Frieden Crowe, Robert M., Andrew M. AA, Coll. of William and Mary, Norfolk, Va., 1945; BA, Coll. of William and Mary, Williamsburg, Va., 1947; MA, Columbia U., 1950. Lic. pvt. pilot. Tchr. art City of Norfolk Pub. Schs., 1947-48, Hudson Day Sch., New Rochelle, N.Y., 1948-49, Mt. Vernon (N.Y.) Pub. Schs., 1949-50, City of Norfolk Pub. Schs., 1950-51; prof. art Coll. William and Mary Extension, Williamsburg, 1957-72, U. Va. Extension, Norfolk, 1972-78, Community Colls. State of Va., Chesapeake and Hampton, 1978-82, St. Leo Coll., Norfolk, 1982-95; travel agt., 1977-89. Author: (dictionary) A is For Art, 1978-82; artist water color paintings and ink drawings at several shows. Asst. Gen. Douglas MacArthur Meml. Archives, Norfolk, 1945-95; vol. Chrysler Mus. Art, Norfolk, 1991—, Va. Symphony Aux., 1992—, Norfolk Little Theatre Box Office, 1991—, Meals on Wheels, 1962-66, Make-A-Wish Found., 1996, ARC, 1953-95, greylady project, 1956-62, bloodmobile project, 1966-80; tchr. drawing Ghent Venture, 1993; reader for the visually handicapped Intouch Network WHRO-TV, 1991—; mem. archives com. Ohef Sholom Temple; bd. dirs. Norfolk Little Theatre, 1996. Mem. Internat. Orgn. Women Pilots (treas. 1978-85), Tidewater Artists Assn. (bd. dirs. 1975-80, 91—, treas. membership coun.), Tidewater Orchid Soc., Am. Orchid Soc., Norfolk Soc. Arts, United Daus. Confederacy, Hermitage Soc., Norfolk Ex Libris Soc. Coll. William & Mary (mem. steering com. 1993—), Va. Belles (reunion com. 1993—). Republican. Jewish. Home: 221 Oxford St Norfolk VA 23505-4354

FRIEDLAND, BILLIE LOUISE, former human services administrator; b. Los Alamos, New Mex., Jan. 6, 1944; d. William Jerald and Harriet Virginia (Short) Van Buskirk; m. David Friedland. BS in Edn., Calif. U. of Pa., 1972, MS in Psychology, 1986; postgrad., W.Va. U., 1992—. Sales mgr., buyer Friedland's Ladies Ready-To-Wear, Monessen, Pa., 1969-72; tchr. Belle Vernon (Pa.) Area Schs., 1973-74; head social scis. dept. Yeshiva Achei Tmimim, Pitts., 1974-75; caseworker, outreach to children and their families project Fayette County Mental Health and Mental Retardation Clinic, Uniontown, Pa., 1975, ctr. supr. outreach to children and their families project, 1976; case mgr., family support svcs. coord. Diversified Human Svcs. Inc., Monessen, 1978-89, supr. cmty. living arrangements, 1989-92; grad. asst. Affiliated Ctr. for Deve. Disabilities W.Va. U., Morgantown, 1992-93, grad. asst. dept. spl. edn., 1993—; founder 1st Infant/Toddler Day Care Project, Fayette County, 1976-78. Mem. NAACP, Am. Assn. Mental Retardation, Coun. for Exceptional Children, W.Va. Fedn. Coun. for Exceptional Children (chairperson divsn. mental retardation/developmental disabilities), Nat. Assn. Dual Diagnoses, Conf. on Black Basic Edn. Office: WVa U Sch Human Resources Dept Spl Edn 507 E Allen Hall Morgantown WV 26506-6122

FRIEDLANDER, EDWARD JAY, journalism educator; b. Portland, Maine, Apr. 24, 1945; s. Otto and Marguerite Evelyn (Smith) F.; m. Roberta Kay Burford, July 12, 1975; 1 child, Erika Anne. BS, U. Wyo., 1967; MA, U. Denver, 1970; EdD, U. No. Colo., Greeley, 1973. Reporter The Denver Post, 1967-68, U.S. Info. Agy., Washington, 1968-69; publicist Universal Pictures, N.Y.C., 1969-70; mag. editor Daily Times-Call, Longmont, Colo., 1970-71; media coord. Centaurus High Sch., Lafayette, Colo., 1972-73; asst. prof. mass communication Cen. Mo. State U., Warrensburg, 1973-75; asst. prof. dept. journalism U. Ark., Little Rock, 1975-77, assoc. prof. dept. journalism, 1977-81, prof. dept. journalism, 1981-95, chairperson dept. journalism, 1988-95; dir., prof. U. South Fla. Sch. Mass Comms., Tampa, 1995—; cons. Bur. Indian Affairs, Washington, 1972, The White House, Washington, 1979, Ark. Press Assn., Little Rock, 1980-95; cons., editor FCC, Washington, 1979-81. Author: Excellence in Reporting, 1987, Feature Writing for Newspapers and Magazines, 1988, 2nd rev. edit., 1993, 3d rev. edit., 1996, Modern Mass Media, 1990, 2nd rev. edit., 1994, Medios de Comunicación Social, 1992. William Robertson Coe fellow U. Wyo., 1973, German Acad. Exch. Svc. fellow, Bonn, 1982, European Acad. fellow, Berlin, 1984. Mem. Assn. Edn. in Journalism and Mass Comm., Soc. Profl. Journalists (officer exec. bd. Ark. profl. chpt. 1986-89, 92-94, v.p. 1989-91, pres. 1991-92), Kappa Tau Alpha. Office: U South Fla Sch Mass Comms 4202 E Fowler Ave # 1040 Tampa FL 33620-9900

FRIEDLINE, JOHN ALLEN, pathologist; b. Somerset, Pa., Aug. 3, 1954; s. Clarence William and Elizabeth Jean (Peebles) F. BS, U. Pitts., 1976; MD, Jefferson Med. Coll., 1980. Diplomate Nat. Bd. Med. Examiners. Attending physician Shadyside Hosp., Pitts., 1983-86, Jenkins (Ky.) Cmty. Hosp., 1986-92; resident pathologist Fisher Inst. of Pathology, Pitts., 1992-95. Vol. in mission United Meth. Ch., Ky., 1987—. Mem. AAAS, N.Y. Acad. Scis., Am. Soc. Tropical Medicine and Hygiene, Am. Chem. Soc., Am. Soc. Clin. Pathology, Coll. Am. Pathologists, Phi Beta Kappa. Home: 18 Highland St Morgantown WV 26505 Office: WVa U Med Ctr Dept Pathology Morgantown WV 26505

FRIEDMAN, BARRY, financial marketing consultant; b. Bklyn., Apr. 8, 1938; s. Samuel I. and Marion (Meltzer) F.; m. Ellen Barbara Rotkin, Aug. 30, 1958 (div. Nov. 1986); children: Scott Evan, Bradley Howard, Andrea Iris; m. Shirli Redlich Laufer, Nov. 19, 1993; children: Jamie Candance, Taylor Gene, Cameron Lee. BSBA, Lafayette Coll., 1959; cert. in fin. planning, Coll. for Fin. Planning, 1982. Cert. fin. planner. Owner Garden State Promotional, South Orange, N.J., 1959-68; v.p. Pa. Securities Co., East Orange, N.J., 1968-73; sr. v.p. McMillen Fin. Svcs., Jacksonville, Fla., 1973-75; pres. Enerdyne Corp., Richardson, Tex., 1975-80; sr. v.p. Murray Fin. Corp., Dallas, 1980-84; owner Barry Friedman Assocs., Southlake, Tex., 1984—; pres. Conifer Investment Group, Southlake, 1990—; bd. dirs. Bancon Corp.; dir. mktg. Foresters Equity Svcs., San Dieto, 1995—; pres. North Tex. Fin. Planners, Dallas, 1982-84, chmn., 1984-85; speaker; seminar leader. Contbr. articles to profl. jours. Mem. Internat. Assn. for Fin. Planning (chmn. 1969-72, pres. 1980-85), Mensa. Home and Office: Barry Friedman Assocs 102 Killdeer Ct Southlake TX 76092

FRIEDMAN, DEBORAH LESLIE WHITE, educational administrator; b. Grand Rapids, Mich., July 5, 1950; d. Edward Charles and Luella Jane (Carr) White; children: Karen Elizabeth, David Edward. BS, Cen. Mich. U., 1972; MBA, U. Toledo, 1980; D in Higher Ednl. Adminstrn., N.C. State U., 1995. Traffic mgr. WTOL-TV, Toledo, Ohio, 1972-74; catering cons. Gladieux Food Svcs., Toledo, 1974-75; mktg. rsch. analyst Owens-Ill., Toledo, 1978; instr. Sampson C.C., Clinton, N.C., 1980-81, instr. in bus. adminstrn., 1980-81, chmn. acctg., bus. adminstrn., real estate, 1981—, pres. faculty senate, 1983-84; faculty advisor Phi Beta Lambda, 1981-88; adj. trainer N.C. Dept. Community Colls., Raleigh, 1989—; mem. bd. dirs. Sampson County United Way, Inc., 1996—. Bd. dirs. Clinton (N.C.) Found. for Edn., 1984-89, appropriations chmn., 1984-88, sec., 1988-89; com. mem. Clinton City Schs. Com. on Stds. of Excellence, 1986-87; vol. Girl Scouts Am., Clinton, 1983, 85; mem. N.C. C.C. Leadership Program, 1990. Named Outstanding Young Educator, Clinton Jaycees, 1985; recipient Outstanding Svc. award Clinton Student Govt. Assn., 1982, Excellence in Tchg. award N.C. State Bd. C.C., 1989, Cert. of Appreciation, State of N.C. for Vol. Svcs., 1987, EXCEL finalist, 1991, 93-94. Mem. Am. Assn. Women in Cmty. Colls. (membership dir. 1988-89), N.C. Assn. Bus. Chair and Dept. Heads (pres.-elect), Bus.-Industry Assocs., Am. Bus. Women Assn. (pres. 1983-84, Sampson County Woman of Yr. 1984), Beta Gamma Sigma, Phi Kappa Phi. Home: 411 W Elizabeth St #D Clinton NC 28328-3052 Office: Sampson C C PO Box 318 Clinton NC 28329-0318

FRIEDMAN, DONALD FLANELL, foreign language educator; b. Savanah, Ga., May 28, 1953; s. Jacob and Elaine (Flanell) F. BA in English summa cum laude, Armstrong State Coll., 1974; MA in Comparative Lit., U. Ga., 1976; PhD in Comparative Lit., NYU, 1985. Instr. English Bundesgymnasium Bruck-Mur, Styra, Austria, 1976-78; rsch. libr. Internat. Atomic Energy Agy., Vienna, Austria, 1978; instr. St. Leo's Coll., Savannah, Ga., 1979-80; translator, freelance writer Doubleday, Crown and Quarto Publs., 1971-86; instr. Pace U., N.Y.C., 1985-86; asst. prof. French, German Wofford Coll., Spartanburg, S.C., 1986-88; asst. prof. French, German Winthrop U., Rock Hill, S.C., 1988-91, assoc. prof., 1991—. Co-author: Viennese Cuisine, The New Approach, 1987, author: The Symbolist Dead City: A Landscape of Poesis, 1990, Anthology of Belgian Sumbolist Poets, 1992; translator Elle disait dormir pour mourir, 1992, Un pays noyé; editor series Francophone Belgian lit., Belgian cultural studies; contbr., translator numerous articles and papers to profl. publs. Mem. Am. Comparative Lit. Assn., So. Comparative Lit. Assn., South Atlantic Modern Lang. Assn., Internat. Comparative Lit. Assn., Conseil Internat. d'Etudes Francophones. Office: Winthrop U Dept Fgn Lang Rock Hill SC 29732

FRIEDMAN, GEORGE, business intelligence executive; b. Budapest, Hungary, Feb. 1, 1949; came to U.S., 1951; s. Emil and Friderika (Deckner) F.; m. Meredith Ruth Smith; stepchildren: Meredith Michelle LeBard, Waverly Edward LeBard; children: David Aaron, Jonathan Robin. BA, CUNY, 1970; MA, Cornell U., 1973, PhD, 1976. Prof. polit. sci. Dickinson Coll., Carlisle, Pa., 1974-92; adj. prof. in residence The Am. U., Washington, 1992-94; dir. Ctr. Geopolit. Studies La. State U., Baton Rouge, 1994-96; chmn., dir. GPA Strategic Forecasting Group, Baton Rouge, 1996—; bd. dirs. Inst. Geopolit. Studies, Baton Rouge; adj. prof. Tulane U., New Orleans, 1996—; cons. Shape Tech. Ctr., The Hague, The Netherlands, 1980-81, McDermott, 1996, Albemarle, 1996, Fin. Times TV, 1996. Author: The Political Philosophy of the Frankfurt School, 1981, The Coming War with Japan, 1991, The Future of War, 1996, (screenplay) TV Asahi, 1991; contbr. articles to Baltimore Sun, L.A. Times, Psychology Today, Detroit Free Press, CEO International Strategies, Sociological Theorym Jour. Social Philosophy and Policy. Seminar dir. Nat. Endowment for the Humanities, Washington, 1984, 85, 87, mem. grant review panel, 1984-87. Rsch. grantee Esri Corp., Sun Microsyss. Corp., 1994, Pew Charitable Trust, 1994, Earhart Found., 1996. Mem. Am. Polit. Sci. Assn., Soc. Competitive Intelligence Profls., Naval Surface Warfare Assn., Author's Guild. Jewish. Office: GPA Strategic Forecasting C 7600 GSRI Rd Baton Rouge LA 70820 Address: PO Box 84180 Baton Rouge LA 70884-4180

FRIEDMAN, HAROLD BERTRAND, retired chemical company executive; b. Montgomery, ala., Oct. 13, 1904; s. William B. and Esther (Lipson) F.; m. Maxine Cohen, Mar. 1, 1953; children: Martin D., Carol and Cathy (twins). BA, U. Ala., 1923; PhD in Chemistry, U. Va., 1927. Math. tchr. Sidney Lanier H.S., Montgomery, 1923-24; tchg. fellow chemistry U. Va., 1925-27; instr. chemistry U. Maine, Orono, 1927-28; rsch. asst., instr. Columbia U., N.Y.C., 1925-29; asst. prof., then assoc. prof. chemistry Ga. Inst. Tech., Atlanta, 1929-42; chief R & D ZEP Mfg. Co., Atlanta, 1944-66; v.p. R&D Zep Mfg. Co., 1966—. Contbr. articles to profl. jours. Lt. col. U.S. Army, 1942-47. Mem. Phi Beta Kappa, Sigma Xi, Phi Kappa Phi. Home: Apt 10F 2575 Peachtree Rd NE Atlanta GA 30305

FRIEDMAN, HERBERT, physicist; b. N.Y.C., N.Y., June 21, 1916; s. Samuel and Rebecca (Seligson) F.; m. Gertrude Miller, 1940; children—Paul, Jon. BA, Bklyn. Coll., 1936; PhD in Physics, Johns Hopkins U., 1940; DSc (hon.), U. Tübingen, Fed. Republic Germany, 1977, U. Mich., 1979. With U.S. Naval Rsch. Lab., Washington, 1940—, supt. atmosphere and astrophysics div., 1958-63, supt. space sci. div., 1963-80; chief scientist E. O. Hulburt Ctr. Space Rsch. U.S. Naval Rsch. Lab., 1963-80, Emeritus, 1980—; adj. prof. physics U. Md., 1960-80, U. Pa., 1974—; vis. prof. Yale U., 1966-68; Martin-Marietta fellow in Space Sci., NASM, 1986-87; mem. space sci. bd. Nat. Acad. Scis.-NRC, 1962-75, 86—, chmn. com. on solar-terrestrial rsch., 1968-71; mem. com. sci. and pub. policy Nat. Acad. Scis., 1967-71, mem. geophysics rsch. bd., 1969-71, chmn., 1976-79, mem. adv. com. internat. orgns. and programs, 1969-77; pres. Interunion Com. on Solar-Terrestrial Physics, 1967-74; pres. spl. com. on solar-terrestrial physics ICSU, 1975-80; chmn. COSPAR working group II, Internat. Quiet Sun Yr.; v.p. COSPAR, 1970-75, 86—; mem. Gen. Adv. Com. on Atomic Energy, 1968-73; mem. Pres.'s Sci. Adv. Com., 1970-73, Advisory Bd. Fermi Lab., 1986-88; chmn. commn. on phys. scis., math and resources NRC, 1984-86. Recipient Disting. Svc. award Dept. Navy, 1945, 80; medal Soc. Applied Spectroscopy, 1957; Disting. Civilian Svc. award Dept. Def., 1959; Disting. Achievement in Sci. award, 1962; Janssen medal French Photog. Soc., 1962; Presdl. medal for disting. fed. svc., 1964; Eddington medal Royal Astron. Soc., 1964; R.D. Conrad medal Dept. Navy, 1964; Rockefeller Pub. Svc. award, 1967; Nat. Medal Sci., 1969; medal for exceptional sci. achievement NASA, 1970, 78; Michelson medal Franklin Inst., 1972; Dryden Rsch. award, 1973; Wolf Found. prize in physics, 1987; Russell award Am. Astron. Soc., 1980; Sci. award Nat. Space Club, 1990; Janssen medal French Astron. Soc., 1990; Massey medal, Royal Soc. London, 1992. Fellow AIAA (hon., Space Sci. award 1963, Internat. Cooperation in Space Sci. medal 1991), Am. Phys. Soc., Am. Optical Soc., Am. Geophys. Union (pres. sect. on solar-planetrary relationships 1967-70, Bowie medal 1981), Am. Astronautical Soc. (Lovelace award 1973), AAAS (v.p. 1972); mem. NAS (council 1979-82, chmn. assembly of math. and phys. scis. 1980-83), Am. Acad. Arts and Scis., Internat. Acad. Astronautics, Am. Philos. Soc. (coun. 1992—); hon. mem. Spl. Com. on Solar-Terrestrial Physics, 1984. Club: Cosmos. Home: 2643 N Upshur St Arlington VA 22207-4025 Office: Naval Rsch Lab Code # 7690 Washington DC 20011

FRIEDMAN, JOEL WILLIAM, law educator; b. N.Y.C., Mar. 16, 1951; s. Max Aaron and Muriel (Yudien) F.; m. Vivian Stoleru, Apr. 5, 1987; 1 child, Alexa Erica. BS, Cornell U., 1972; JD, Yale U., 1975. Bar: Calif. 1975, U.S. Dist. Ct. (cen. dist.) Calif. 1975. Asst. prof. Tulane U., New Orleans, 1976-79, assoc. prof., 1979-82, prof. law, 1982—, C.J. Morrow prof. law, 1985-86; vis. prof. law U. Tel Aviv, Israel, 1983, U. Tex. Law Sch., 1985-86, Chuo Law Sch., Tokyo, 1988, Hebrew U. of Jerusalem Law Sch., 1990; lectr. Fed. Jud. Ctr., Washington, 1987—; cons. La. Ho. of Reps., Baton Rouge, 1982-85; bd. dirs. Legal Aid Bur., New Orleans, 1982-90; spl. master Pasadena Ind. Sch. Dist., Houston, 1987-93. Editor: Cases and Materials on Law of Employment Discrimination, 1983, 3d edit., 1993; contbr. articles to law revs. Pres., bd. dirs. Woldenberg Village, Inc., 1995—; v.p., bd. dirs. Jewish Fedn. Greater New Orleans, 1995—. Recipient Felix Frankfurter faculty award for disting. tchg. Tulane Law Sch., 1989; Fulbright scholar Israel, 1990. Co-chmn. New Orleans Cmty. Rels. Com., 1984. Mem. Am. Assn. Law Schs. (chair sect. on employment discrimination law 1987-88), Am. Law Inst., B'nai B'rith Hillel Found. (pres. New Orleans 1987-91), Internat. Assn. of Jewish Lawyers and Jurists La. Br. (pres. 1994-95). Democrat. Avocations: running, squash, scuba diving, skiing. Home: 1230 State St New Orleans LA 70118-6027 Office: Tulane Law Sch 6329 Freret St New Orleans LA 70118-6231

FRIEDMAN, LINDA ANNE, lawyer; b. Cleve., Oct. 6, 1952; d. Thomas John and Elaine (Urban) Bunsey; m. Doug Friedman, Aug. 6, 1978; children: Jessica, Rachel. Student, Sorbonne U., Paris, 1971-72; AB, Kenyon Coll., 1973; JD, Vanderbilt U., 1976. Bar: Ala. 1976. Law clk. U.S. Dist. Ct. (no. dist.) Ala., Birmingham, 1976-77; ptnr. Bradley, Arant, Rose & White, Birmingham, 1977—; legal editor Channel 6 TV, Birmingham, 1993-94. Co-author: Protecting Intellectual Property, 1988, Unfair Competition in Alabama, 1989; editor: (chpts. in books) State Trademark and Unfair Competition, 1986—, State Antitrust Practice and Statutes, 1991. Fundraiser March of Dimes, Birmingham, 1990; co-chmn. bus. leaders divsn. Birmingham Jewish Fedn., Birmingham, 1992, 93; VIP Starathon, United Cerebral Palsy, Birmingham, 1993—. Named one of Top 40 under 40, Birmingham Bus. Jour., 1992. Mem. Ala. Bar Assn. (chmn. antitrust 1986-90, bd. bar examiners 1988-89, other offices, Continuing Legal Edn. award 1990), Am. Law Inst., Bus. and Profl. Women (steering com. 1992-93), Kiwanis. Office: Bradley Arant Rose & White 1400 Park Place Tower 2001 Park Pl Birmingham AL 35203-2735

FRIEDMAN, LINDA JOY, senior litigation paralegal, journalist; b. N.Y.C., Sept. 24, 1965; d. Stanley and Jo-Anne (Elliot) Zipper; m. David A. Friedman, Nov. 25, 1989. Student, Georgetown U., 1986, U. Balt. Sch. of Law, 1987; BS, U. Miami, 1987. Freelance journalist The Daily Record,

Balt., 1989; paralegal Whiteford, Taylor, Preston, Balt., 1990-92; sr. litigation paralegal Cooney & Mattson, Ft. Lauderdale, Fla., 1992—. Writer, producer: (cable TV show) The College Experience, 1985-86; editor The Miami Hurricane, 1986-87. V.p. NOW, U. Miami, Fla., 1986-87; pres. Pi Chi Sorority, 1987; young profl.'s bd. mem. Miami (Fla.) Skyline Theatre, 1993. Recipient P.A.B. Widener scholarship Georgetown U. Inst. on Polit. Journalism, 1986. Mem. Soc. Profl. Journalists (v.p. 1985—), Nat. Press Club. Republican. Home: 10487 N W 10 Ct Coral Springs FL 33071 Office: Cooney & Mattson PO Box 14546 301 E Las Olas Blvd Fort Lauderdale FL 33302

FRIEDMAN, RICHARD JOEL, orthopaedic surgeon; b. Toronto, Ont., Can., Mar. 25, 1956; s. Morris and B. Beverley (Kalles) F.; m. Vivian Sara Lichtman, Sept. 19, 1981; children: Arielle, Leah. MD with honors, U. Toronto, 1980. Diplomate Nat. Bd. Med. Examiners, Royal Coll. Physicians and Surgeons Can., Am. Bd. Orthopaedic Surgery. Intern in surgery Johns Hopkins Hosp., Balt., 1980-81; resident in surgery Mass. Gen. Hosp., Boston, 1981-82, resident in orthopaedic surgery, 1982-85; asst. in orthopaedic surgery Brigham and Women's Hosp., Boston, 1985; asst. prof. orthopaedic surgery Med. U. S.C., Charleston, 1986-90, faculty Coll. Grad. Studies, 1987—, assoc. prof. orthopaedic surgery, 1990-95, prof. orthopaedic surgery, 1995—; chief orthopaedic sect. Vets. Adminstrn. Med. Ctr., Charleston, 1986-91; attending staff dept. orthopaedic surgery Charleston Meml. Hosp. and Vets. Adminstrn. Hosp., 1986—; cons. St. Francis Xavier Hosp., Charleston, 1988—; mem. ARC Southeastern Transplantation com., 1988-90; mem. instnl. rev. bd. for human rsch. Med. U. S.C., 1986—, ethics com., 1990—, continuing edn. com., 1991-95; mem. pharmacy and therapeutics com. Med. U. Hosp., 1986-90, utilization rev. com., 1987—, chmn. post surgery recovery task force com., 1988, search com. for dir. of procurement, 1989; presenter in field. Reviewer clin. orthopaedics and related rsch., 1988—, Jour. Shoulder and Elbow Surgery, 1991—, Jour. Bone Joint Surgery, 1992—, Jour. Orthop. Rsch., 1995—; contbr. over 150 articles to profl. jours. V.p. Charleston Jewish Fedn., Charleston, 1993—, bd. dirs. Charleston Symphony Orch., 1993—. Recipient Ann Sheppard Meml. scholarship, 1976, P.S.I. Found. summer scholarship, 1977, Walter F. Watkins scholarship, 1978, George Ruderfer Meml. grant, 1978, R.I. Harris Undergrad. award, 1979, Crocker Found. grant, 1980, Edwin French Cave Traveling fellowship, 1985, John A. Seigling Teaching award, 1990; named Vol. of Yr., Am. Red Cross Southeastern Transplantation Svcs., 1989. Fellow ACS, Mass. Med. Soc., Royal Coll. Physicians and Surgeons Can., S.C. Orthop. Assn., Am. Acad. Orthop. Surgeons (sec. biomed. engring. 1992—, CPT coding com. 1992—, evaluations com. 1993—); mem. Am. Coll. Rheumatology, S.C. Med. Assn., Am. Orthop. Assn. (N.Am. Traveling fellowship 1987), Soc. for Biomaterials (local arrangements com. 1990), Bioengring. Alliance S.C. (rsch. coord. 1990—), Am. Shoulder and Elbow Surgeons (fin. com. 1992-93, rsch. com. 1993—), European Rheumatoid Arthritis Surg. Soc., Can. Orthop. Assn., Ea. Orthop. Assn., So. Orthop. Assn., So. Med. Assn., Charleston County Med. Soc., Assn. VA Orthop. Surgeons, Orthop. Rsch. Soc., Assn. Bone and Joint Surgeons. Office: Med Univ SC 171 Ashley Ave Charleston SC 29425-0001

FRIEDMAN, ROBERT MICHAEL, lawyer; b. Memphis, June 19, 1950; s. Harold Samuel and Margaret (Siegel) F.; m. Elaine Freda Burson, Dec. 21, 1975; children: Daniel Justin, Jonathan Aaron. B.S., U. Tenn., 1973, J.D., 1975; postgrad., Exeter U., Eng., 1974, Nat. Coll. Trial Advocacy, 1985. Bar: Tenn. 1976, U.S. Dist. Ct. (we. dist.) Tenn. 1977, U.S. Dist Ct. (no. dist.) Miss. 1979, U.S. Ct. Appeals (5th cir.) 1979, U.S. Supreme Ct. 1983, U.S. Dist. Ct. (so. dist.) Tex. 1986, U.S. Ct. Appeals (6th cir.) 1986. Assoc. Cassell & Fink, Memphis, 1976-78; pres., sr. ptnr. Friedman & Sissman, P.C., Memphis, 1978-91, Friedman, Sissman & Heaton, P.C., Memphis, 1991—; commr. State of Tenn. Jud. Selection Commn., 1994-96; corp. legal/litigation counsel, dir. Tenn. Interpreting Svc. for Deaf, Memphis, 1981-89, Mid-South Hospitality Mgmt. Ctr., Inc., Memphis, 1984-88; legal counsel Moss Hotel Co., Inc., 1986-89, Helena Hotel Co., 1986-89, Charlestown Hotel Co., 1986-89, Jackson Hotel Co., 1986-89, Murfreesboro Hotel Co., 1986-89, Santee Hotel Co., 1986-89, Kingsport Hotel Co., 1986-89, Raleigh Hotel Assocs., Ltd., 1986-89, Ozark Regional Eye Ctr., 1986—, Brookfield Mortgage Co., Inc., 1987—, Mt. Pleasant Hotel Co., 1987-89, Hattiesburg Hotel Assocs. Ltd., 1987-89, Wright and Assocs. Constrn. Co. Inc., 1987—, Pro Billiards Tour Assn. Inc., 1996—; legal counsel, pres. Biloxi Hotel Co., Inc., 1986-89; litigation counsel Independence Fed. Bank Batesville, Ark., 1987-88; legal counsel Autorama, Inc., 1988—; bd. dirs./legal counsel Evan R. Harwood Day Tng. Ctr., 1989—; legal/litigation counsel Super D Drugs, Inc., 1989—, So. Comm. Vols., Inc., WEVL FM Cmty. Radio, 1990—; mem. staff, contbr. Tenn. Law Rev., 1974-75, recipient cert., 1975; corp. gen., litigation counsel U.S. for Inversiones Tesmo, Sociedad Anonima, Republic of Costa Rica, 1990—; rep. of Tenn. Bar Assn. and State of Tenn. to Nat. Summit Crime and Violence, 1994; legal counsel Pro Billiards Tour Assn., Inc., 1996—. Bd. dirs. Project 1st Offenders, Shelby County, Tenn., 1976-78; bd. dirs., legal counsel Memphis Community Ctr. for Deaf and Hearing Impaired, 1980-81; bd. dirs. Eagle Scout Day, Chickasaw coun. Boy Scouts Am., 1978—, Ea. Dist. committeeman, 1991—, mem. adv. bd., 1993—, chmn. Eagle Scout recognition day, 1993-94; scoutmaster Boy Scouts Am., Memphis, 1991—; mem. U. Tenn. Coll. Law Alumni Adv. Coun., Dean's Cir., 1992—; rep. of Tenn. Bar Assn. and State of Tenn. Nat. Summit Crime and Violence, 1994. With USCG, 1971-77. James E. West fellow, 1996; A.S. Graves Meml. scholar, 1974-75; recipient Outstanding Svc. award and Key, Alpha Phi Omega, 1972, Am. Jurisprudence award Lawyers Co-op. Pub. Co. and Bancroft-Whitney Co., 1973-74, Chancellor's Honor award George C. Taylor Sch. Law, U. Tenn., 1975, Robert W. Richie Outstanding Svc. award Tenn. Assn. Criminal Def. Lawyers, 1993, Order of Arrow, Vigil of Honor, 1994, Nat. award Boy Scouts Am., 1996. Mem. ABA, Assn. Trial Lawyers Am., Tenn. Bar Assn. (ho. dels. 1991-94, chmn. criminal justice sect. 1991-94, atty./solicitor Tenn Supreme Ct. 1994), Tenn. Jud. Selection Commn. (Tenn. state commr. 1994—), Tenn. Trial Lawyers Assn., Tenn. Assn. Criminal Defense Lawyers (bd. dirs. 1994), Nat. Assn. Criminal Def. Lawyers (vice chmn. law practice mgmt. com. 1990-93, co-chmn. forfeiture abuse task force 1991-93), Memphis and Shelby County Bar Assn., Fed. Bar Assn., Nat. Criminal Justice Assn. (charter 1984—), Alpha Phi Omega, Delta Theta Phi. Democrat. Jewish. Home: 3303 Spencer Dr Memphis TN 38115-3000 Office: Friedman Sissman & Heaton PC 100 N Main St Ste 3400 Memphis TN 38103-0534

FRIEDMAN, SOL, inventor, writer; b. N.Y.C., June 10, 1922; s. Marcus and Ida (Wolf) F.; m. Rose Schenkerman, July 19, 1945 (dec. 1981); children: Miles, Alan; m. Paula Jacobson, Sept. 17, 1982. Student, Cooper Union U., N.Y.C., 1945-47. Profl. inventor Sol Friedman and Assocs., N.Y.C., 1950—. Inventor toys and games, including Operation Orbit, 1960 (donated to Smithsonian Inst. Air and Space Mus.), Johnny Astro, 1967 (Boys Toys of Yr., Nat. Assn. Toy Retailers U.K. 1967), Baby Party, Walt Disney World. Sgt. U.S. Air Corps Army, 1942-45. Recipient Presdl. citation Pres. Harry S Truman, 1994, cert. of merit Eleanor Roosevelt Dem. Club, Monsey, N.Y. Home and Office: Sol Friedman & Assocs Apt 106 310 Racquet Club Rd Bldg 118 Fort Lauderdale FL 33326-1155

FRIEDMAN, SUSAN LYNN BELL, job training and community relations specialist; b. Lafayette, Ind., May 23, 1953; d. Virgil Atwood and Jean Loree (Wiggins) B.; m. Frank H. Friedman, July 31, 1976; 1 child, Alex Charles. B.A., Purdue U., 1975; M.S., Ind. State U., 1981. Asst. dir. pub. relations Vincennes U. Jr. Coll., Ind., 1977-83; dir. Knox County C. of C., Vincennes, 1983-84; asst. to pres. Am. Assn. Community and Jr. Colls., Washington, 1985-87; owner/pres. SBF Promotions, 1987—; mgr., program developer Family Resources, Inc., 1988-89; partnership coord. Beaufort (S.C.) County Sch. Dist., 1989-90; job tng. coord. Heart of Ga. Tech. Inst., 1990-92, econ. devel. v.p., 1992-96; exec. dir. Tex. Assn. Ptnrs. in Edn., 1996—. Bd. dirs. Women in Need of God's Shelter, Inc., 1991-96, Ga. Common Cause, 1992-96, pres., 1993-95; mem. Dublin-Laurens Leadership Class, 1994-95; Hoosier scholar, 1971, 72; pres. Annandale BPW, Vincennes, Ind. and Beaufort, S.C., 1995-96; pres. BPW Dublin. Mem. NAFE, Am. Assn. Women in Community and Jr. Colls. (nat. liaison 1985-87), LWV (chpt. v.p. 1982-84), ACLU, BPW Austin, TSAE, TSPRA, NAPE, TAPE, NOW, Austin Kiwanis. Home: 8612 Bobcat Dr Round Rock TX 78681-3700 Office: 400 W 15th St Ste 910 Austin TX 78701-1647

FRIEDMAN, SYLVIA, librarian; b. Cape Town, Republic of South Africa, Jan. 17, 1940; came to U.S., 1977; d. Benjamin and Minna (Kahn) Daniels; m. Basil Asher Friedman, Jan. 19, 1964; children: Michelle, Alan. Assoc. Trinity Coll., London; student, Maas Drama Sch., 1958-62. Libr. Hebrew Youth Acad. Sch., West Caldwell, N.J., 1977-81, Adath Yeshurun Temple, North Miami Beach, Fla., 1983-91, Temple Sinai, Hollywood, Fla., 1987-89, Toras Emes Acad. Elem. Sch., 1993-94, Congregation Beth David Library, Miami, 1994. Mem. adv. coun. Judaic studies Barry U., 1986-91. Mem. Assn. Jewish Libraries (v.p. 1983-86, pres. South Fla. chpt. 1985-88), ALA. Democrat. Jewish. Home: 17201 NE 11th Ct Miami FL 33162-2623

FRIEDRICH, GUSTAV WILLIAM, communication educator; b. Hastings, Nebr., Mar. 2, 1941; s. Edwin August and Ellen Marie (Meyer) F.; m. Erena Rae, Aug. 4, 1962; 1 child, Bruce Gregory. AA, Concordia Coll., St. Paul, 1961; BA summa cum laude, U. Minn., 1964; MA, U. Kans., 1967, PhD with honors, 1968. 7th grade tchr. St. John's Sch., Young America, Minn., 1961-62; asst. instr. U. Kans., Lawrence, 1964-68; asst. prof., then assoc. prof. Purdue U., West Lafayette, Ind., 1968-77; prof., chair communication dept. U. Nebr., Lincoln, 1977-82, U. Okla., Norman, 1982—; cons. in field. Author: Classroom Communication, 1976, Public Communication, 1983; editor: Education in the 80's, 1981; author, editor: Teaching Communication, 1990. Recipient Outstanding Young Tchr. award CSCA, 1970, Svc. award CSCA, 1978. Mem. Speech Communication Assn. (pres. 1988-89, Golden Anniversary award 1974), Internat. Communication Assn. (bd. dirs. 1983-85), Cen. State Communication Assn. (exec. sec. 1975-77, pres. 1980). Democrat. Home: 1007 Thistlewood Dr Norman OK 73072-3941 Office: U Okla Burton Hall # 226 Norman OK 73019

FRIEDRICH, KATHERINE ROSE, educational researcher; b. Ft. Benning, Ga., Mar. 16, 1964; d. Robert Louis and Judith Ann (Dupont) F. BS in Math. and Psychology, S.W. Tex. State U., 1987; MS in Edn1. Psychology, Tex. A&M U., 1990, postgrad. Grad. rsch. asst. dept. sociology Tex. A&M U., College Station, 1989, grad. rsch. asst. dept. ednl. psychology, 1989-91, grad. teaching asst., 1991-92; program evaluator Ctr. for Alternative Programs Bryan (Tex.) Ind. Sch. Dist., 1991; rsch. specialist dept. rsch. and evaluation Houston Ind. Sch. Dist., 1993—; rsch. cons. U. Oreg., Eugene, 1987-88, Tex. A&M U., 1991-92. Vol. Doing Something, Washington, 1992-93. Am. Ednl. Rsch. Assn. rsch. fellow with NSF, 1992-93; scholar for acad. excellence Tex. A&M U., 1990-91. Mem. Advanced Studies of Nat. Databases (sec. 1994-95), Am. Ednl. Rsch. Assn., So. Ednl. Rsch. Assn. Roman Catholic. Office: Houston Ind Sch Dist Dept Rsch Evaluation 3830 Richmond Ave Houston TX 77027

FRIEDRICHS, ARTHUR MARTIN, manufacturing company executive, retired; b. N.Y.C., May 8, 1911; s. Arthur C. and Olga A. (Knoepke) F.; m. Juanita Elizabeth Barrett, Nov. 2, 1968. Student, Union Coll., 1930-31; BS, NYU, 1935. Bookkeeper Corn Exchange Bank, N.Y.C., 1935-37; with E.H. & A.C. Friedrichs Co., 1937-71, pres., 1958-71; bd. dirs. Fredrix Artists Canvas, Inc., Lawrenceville, Ga. Bd. dirs. Wartburg Home, Mt. Vernon, N.Y., 1974-96; pres. Artists Material Mfrs. Assn., 1965-68; life mem. Imperial Point Hosp. Aux., Ft. Lauderdale; mem. Norwalk Hosp. Vols. Mem. Fraternal Order Police (assoc.), Artists Fellowship, Weston Hist. Soc., Met. Opera Guild, Art Material Mfrs. Assn. N.Y. (past pres.), Salamagundi Club (N.Y.C., life), Lighthouse Point Yacht and Racquet Club, Corinthians, Quiet Birdmen. Clubs: Salmagundi (life) (N.Y.C.); Lighthouse Point Yacht and Racquet (Fla.); Quiet Birdmen; Corinthians. Home: 2510 NE 35th St Lighthouse Point FL 33064-8157

FRIEND, HAROLD CHARLES, neurologist; b. Chgo., Nov. 28, 1946; s. Leonard Nathan and Sharlee (Friedman) F.; m. Joyce Friend; children: Reed, Chad. BA, U. Tex., 1968, MD, 1972. Diplomate Am. Bd. Neurology. Resident Upstate Med. Ctr., Syracuse, N.Y., 1972-73, Albert Einstein Coll. Medicine, Bronx, N.Y., 1973-75; mem. staff Boca Raton (Fla.) Community Hosp., 1975—; pres. Neurosci. Ctr., Boca Raton, 1984—; spl. expert witness Fla. Agy. for Health Care Adminstrn.; expert med. advisor divsn. workers compensation Fla. Dept. Labor and Employment Security; bd. dirs. So. Security Bankcorp.; pres. Puget Sound Yellow Taxi, Inc., 1994-95. Author: Territorial Marking, 1968, Bell's Palsy, 1975, Transient Global Amnesia, 1987. Bd. dirs. Boca Raton Children's Mus., 1989-92; dist. chmn., assoc. lodge advisor Boy Scouts Am., 1980-89, mem. exec. bd., v.p. Gulfstream coun., 1988-90, pres. coun., 1993-95, area I v.p., 1990-92, area IV v.p., 1993-95, area IV pres., 1995—, mem. so. region exec. bd., 1993—; exec. bd. United Way, Palm Beach County Agy. Rels. Com., 1992-95, mem. allocation com., 1990-92. Recipient Vigil Honor award Boy Scouts Am., 1983, Dist. Merit award, 1987, Silver Beaver award, 1990, Wood Badge, 1990, Disting. Commr. award, 1991, Disting. Eagle Scout, 1996; James West fellow, 1993. Fellow Am. Acad. Disability Evaluating Physicians, Am. Acad. Neurology, Am. Bd. Quality Assurance and Utilization Rev. Physicians; mem. Am. Soc. Neuroimaging (cert.), So. Clin. Neurol. Soc., Fla. Soc. Neurology, Am. Epilepsy Soc., Am. Med. EEG Assn., Am. Assn. Study Headache, N.Y. Acad. Scis. (life), Sierra Club (life), Palm Beach Med. Svc. (vice chmn. med./legal com.), Rotary (bd. dirs., pres. Boca Raton chpt., dist. world fellowship chmn. 1992-94, 96-97, dist. found. chmn. 1994, chmn. dist. conf. 1995, gov.'s rep. 1994-95, 96—, Paul Harris fellow, Dist. Svc. award 1992, 95, Pres. Salute Commendation 1993), Internat. Fellowship Running and Fitness Rotarians (internat. chmn. 1992-97), Internat. Fellowship Scouting Rotarians (N.Am. sect. chmn. 1995-96, internat. sec. 1996—), Boca Raton Road Runners Club (pres. 1992-93), Phi Beta Kappa, Phi Kappa Phi, Theta Xi, Alpha Phi Omega. Office: 1500 NW 10th Ave Ste 105 Boca Raton FL 33486-1344

FRIEND, WILLIAM BENEDICT, bishop; b. Miami, Fla., Oct. 22, 1931; s. William Eugene and Elizabeth (Paulus) F. Student, U. Miami, 1949-52; cert. in philosophy, St. Mary's Coll., St. Mary, Ky., 1955; cert. of ordination, Mt. St. Mary's Sem., Emmittsburg, Md., 1959; M.A. in Edn., Cath. U. Am., 1965; L.L.D., St. Leo Coll., 1986. Ordained priest Roman Cath. Ch., 1959. Parish priest, educator, counselor, adminstr., 1959-68; acting dir. ednl. research U. Notre Dame, Ind., 1968-71; vicar for edn., supt. schs. Diocese of Mobile, Ala., 1971-76, chancellor adminstrn., vicar for edn., 1976-79; aux. bishop Diocese of Alexandria-Shreveport, La., 1979-83, diocesan bishop, 1983-86; first bishop of Shreveport La., 1986—; chmn. campaign for human devel. Nat. Conf. Cath. Bishops, 1982-85; mem. sci. and human values com. Commn. of Bishops and Scholars, 1983-86, chmn., 1986-92, cons., 1993—; bd. dirs. La. Cath. Conf., 1986-92; mem. Pontifical Coun. for Culture. Editor handbooks and study guides for Cath. edn., 1971-77; editor: (with Ford and Daues) Evangelizing the Cultures in A.D. 2000, 1990, co-editor (with J. Anderson) The Culture of Bible Belt Catholics, 1995; contbr. articles on Cath. edn., Cath. ch. leadership and mgmt., theol. relections to profl. publs. Bd. dirs. S.E. Regional Hispanic Ctr., 1986—, Miami (Fla.) Interchurch Conf.; trustee Notre Dame Sem., 1976, St. Joseph Coll. Sem., New Orleans, 1976—. Decorated Order of Fleur de Lis K.C., 1980, knight comdr. with star Knights of Holy Sepulchre of Jerusalem, 1983; recipient Presdl. award Nat. Cath. Ednl. Assn., 1978, O'Neil D'Amour award Nat. Assn. Bds. Edn., 1982, NCCJ Brotherhood and Humanitarian award, 1987. Mem. AAAS, KC, Am. Acad. Religion, Cath. Acad. Sci., U.S.A., N.Y. Acad. Sci., Soc. for Biblical Lit., World Futures Soc., Univ. Club (Shreveport). Office: Diocese of Shreveport Catholic Ctr 2500 Line Ave Shreveport LA 71104-3022

FRIES, HELEN SERGEANT HAYNES, civic leader; b. Atlanta; d. Harwood Syme and Alice (Hobson) Haynes; student Coll. William and Mary, 1935-38; m. Stuart G. Fries, May 5, 1938. Bd. mem. Community Ballet Assn., Huntsville, Ala., 1968—; mem. nat. nurses aid com. ARC, 1958-59; dir. ARC Aero Club, Eng., 1943-44; supr. ARC Clubmobile, Europe, 1944-46; mem. women's com. Nat. Symphony Orch., Washington, 1959—, chmn. residential fund drive for apts., 1959; bd. dirs. Madison County Republican Club, 1969-70; mem. nat. council Women's Nat. Rep. Club N.Y., 1963—, chmn. hospitality com., 1963-65; bd. dirs. League Rep. Women, 1952-61; patron mem., vol. docent Huntsville Mus. Art, Huntsville Lit. Assn.; vol. docent Weeden House, Twickenham Hist. Preservation Dist. Assn., Inc., Huntsville; mem. The Garden Guild, Huntsville, The Collectors Guild Constn. Hall Village, Huntsville, Historic Huntsville Found., Hunstville Mus Art. Recipient cert. of merit 84th Div., U.S. Army, 1945. Mem. Nat. Soc. Colonial Dames Am., Daus. Am. Colonists, DAR, Nat. Trust Hist. Preservation, Va., Nat., Valley Forge (Pa.), Eastern Shore Va., Huntsville-Madison County hist. socs., Assn. Preservation Va. Antiquities, Greensboro Soc. Preservation, Tenn. Valley Geneal. Soc., Friends of Ala. Archives, Nat. Soc. Lit. and Arts, Va. Hist. Soc., English Speaking Union, Turkish-Am. Assn., Army-Navy Club, Washington Club, Capitol Hill Club, Army-Navy Country Club, Garden Club, Redstone Yacht Club, Huntsville Country Club, Heritage Club, Botanical Garden Club. Home: 409 Zandale Dr SW Huntsville AL 35801-3462

FRIGO, JAMES PETER PAUL, industrial hardware company executive; b. Iron Mountain, Mich., Jan. 11, 1942; s. Louis and Giustina (Carollo) F.; m. Patricia Mary Nellen, June 21, 1969; children: Christine, Catherine, P.J., Pamela, Steven, Sandy. BBA, U. Miami, 1966. Sales rep. Great Dane Trailers, Miami, 1966-67, Foster Inc., Miami, 1968, Lawson Products Inc., Miami, 1968—; pres. Jim Frigo Inc., Miami, 1972—. Mem. Nat. Speakers Assn., Fla. Speakers Assn., Internat. Platform Assn., Knights of Columbus. Republican. Roman Catholic. Office: Jim Frigo Inc 7420 SW 175th St Miami FL 33157-6313

FRINK, WILLIAM DAVID, JR., senior systems engineer; b. Birmingham, Ala., Dec. 9, 1955; s. William David and Bettye Jean (Haynes) F.; m. Chanthaphen Mongkolcharti Winkler; children: Kesvadee. AS in Math., Marion Mil. Inst., 1975; BS in Physics, Auburn (Ala.) U., 1977, MBA, 1978; MSES, Naval Postgrad. Sch., Monterey, Calif., 1990. Commd. 2d lt. U.S. Army, 1977, advanced through grades to maj., 1990, air def. officer, 1979-82; physicist sci. and tech. info. team U.S. Army, Frankfurt, Germany, 1982-85; rsch. and devel. officer U.S. Army Matl. Command, 1985-90; missile engr. U.S. Army Missile Command, Redstone Arsenal, Ala., 1991-92; systems engr. CAS, Inc., Huntsville, Ala., 1992—. Decorated Army Commendation medal; recipient Meritorious Svc. Medal, 1985, nat. Def. Svc. Medal, Dept. of Def., 1991, Aircraft Survivability award, Naval Postgrad. Sch., 1990. Mem. AIAA, Air Def. Assn., Army Acquisition Corps, Sigma Pi Sigma. Home: 4712 Whitehall Dr NW Huntsville AL 35816-1232 Office: CAS Inc PO Box 1284 Huntsville AL 35807-0284

FRISBIE, SAYER LOYAL, newspaper publisher, copyeditor; b. Biloxi, Miss., Mar. 6, 1915; s. Sayer Lloyd and Marguerite Elizabeth (Bernard) F.; m. Louise Kelley, June 30, 1937 (dec. 1989); 1 child, S.L. IV. BA, Fla. So. Coll., 1937, LittD (hon.), 1985. Reporter Polk County Dem., Bartow, Fla., 1935-37, mng. editor, 1937-46, editor, columnist, 1946-64, pub., columnist, 1964-82, copyeditor, columnist, 1982—; adj. instr. editl. and column writing Fla. So. Coll., 1976-86; pres. Fla. Press Assn., 1948-49, Frisbie Pub. Co., Inc., Bartow, 1964—. Chmn. Polk County Mental Health Coun., Bartow, Polk County Juvenile Ct. Coun., Bartow; treas. Bartow Rotary Found., 1987-90. With Infantry, 1944-46. Named to Fla. Newspaper Hall of Fame, Fla. Press Assn., 1989. Mem. Bartow Rotary Club (bd. dirs. 1939-40, pres. 1940-41, Paul Harris fellow), Sigma Delta Chi (chpt. chmn. 1947-49). United Methodist. Office: Frisbie Pub Co Inc 190 S Florida Ave Bartow FL 33830

FRISCHENMEYER, MICHAEL LEO, sales executive; b. Ottawa, Kans., Feb. 8, 1951; s. Edwin Francis and Patricia Louise (Scheibmeir) F.; m. Helen N. Bright, May 19, 1974; children: Lindsay Patrice, David Edward. BA in Chemistry, U. Mo., 1973, MBA in Mtkg., 1975. Mktg. asst. Mallinckrodt Inc., St. Louis, 1975, asst. product mgr., 1975-77; mgr. tech. services Standard Havens, Inc., Kansas City, Mo., 1977-79, nat. sales mgr., 1979-83; sales engr. Nat. Filter Media Corp., St. Louis, 1983; div. sales mgr. Nat. Filter Media Corp., Memphis, 1983-85, Hamden, Conn., 1986-88; nat. sales mgr. Nat. Filter Media Corp., Memphis, 1985-86, Salt Lake City, 1988-90; v.p., div. mgr. Nat. Filter Media Corp., Memphis, 1991—. Recipient 5 Star Major Advancement award Pollution Engring. mag. 1978, 79. Mem. Air Pollution Control Assn. Home: 2107 Glenalden Dr Germantown TN 38139 Office: 8895 Deerfield Dr Olive Branch MS 38654-3815

FRISCHKORN, DAVID EPHRAIM KEASBEY, JR., investment banker; b. Huntington, W.Va., Apr. 11, 1951; s. David Ephraim Keasbey Frischkorn and Permele Elliott (Francis) Booth; m. Anne Cochran, May 9, 1981. BA magna cum laude, Tufts U., 1973; MBA, Columbia U., 1976. Corp. fin. assoc. Rotan Mosle, Houston, 1976-77, asst. v.p., 1977-79, v.p., 1979-82, sr. v.p., 1982-85; v.p. Kidder, Peabody & Co., Houston, 1985-87, Frischkorn & Co. Investment Bankers, Houston, 1988-92; sr. v.p., mng. dir. Rauscher Pierce Refsnes, Inc., Houston, 1993-96; mng. dir. Jefferies & Co. Bd. dirs. Houston Child Guidance Ctr., 1981-88, pres. bd. dirs. 1984-86; trustee The Hill Sch., Pottstown, Pa., 1978-80, Presbyn. Sch., Houston, 1990-94. Mem. N.Y. Athletic Club, Houston Country Club, Coronado Club (Houston), Argyle Club (San Antonio), Mill Reef Club (Antiqua, W.I.). Republican. Presbyterian. Office: 909 Fannin Ste 3100 Houston TX 77010

FRISHMAN, LAURA JEAN, visual physiologist; b. Washington, Dec. 21, 1947; d. Daniel and Ruth Lenore (Bolker) F.; m. Dan Schweitzer-Tong, June 4, 1972 (div. Feb. 1980). BA in Sociology and Biology, Vassar Coll., 1969; MS in Psychobiology, U. Pitts., 1975, PhD in Psychobiology, 1979; postgrad., Northwestern U., 1979-83. Rsch. asst. Harvard, Princeton U., 1969-72; asst. rsch. physiologist UCSF, 1983-90; assoc. prof. optometry U. Houston, 1990—; vis. scientist U. Mich., 1990, U. Zurich, 1990; adj. asst. prof. ophthalmology, UCSF, 1987-90; editl. bd. Visual Neuroscience, 1993-95, assoc. editor, 1997—. Author chpts. to books; contbr. articles to profl. jours. Active animal care com. U. Houston 1991—, faculty senate, 1992—, faculty life com., 1992, edn. policies com., 1993, faculty affairs com., 1994—, rsch. initiation grant and peer rev. com., 1991, 96; grant reviewer NIH, 1995—, NSF, 1991—. Recipient NIMH fellow, 1975-77, 79-83; rsch. grants in field. Mem. Assn. Rsch. in Vision and Ophthalmology, Soc. Neuroscience, Internat. Soc. Clinical Electrophysiology Vision, Am. Soc. Advancement Scis., Sigma Xi. Home: 3403 Stanford St Houston TX 77006-4316 Office: U Houston Coll Optometry 4901 Calhoun Rd Houston TX 77204-6052

FRIST, THOMAS FEARN, JR., hospital management company executive; b. Nashville, Aug. 12, 1938; s. Thomas Fearn and Dorothy (Cate) F.; m. Patricia Champion, Dec. 22, 1961; children: Trisha, Thomas III, Bill. BS, Vanderbilt U., 1961; MD, Washington U., 1966. Chmn., chief exec. officer Hospital Corp. of Am., Nashville; exec. v.p. Hosp. Corp. Am., Nashville, 1969-77, pres., chief oper. officer, 1977-82, pres., chief exec. officer, 1982-85, chmn., 1985-95; vice chmn. Columbia/ Hosp. Corp. of Am. Healthcare Corp., Nashville, 1995—; bd. dirs. Columbia Healthcare. Trustee Vanderbilt U., Nashville, 1987, United Way of Am., Alexandria, Va., 1987. Fellow Am. Coll. Healthcare Execs. (hon.); mem. Bus. Roundtable, Bus. Coun., Belle Meade Country Club. Presbyterian. Office: Hosp Corp Am PO Box 550 Nashville TN 37202-0550

FRIST, WILLIAM H., senator, surgeon; b. Nashville, Feb. 22, 1952; m. Karyn Frist; children: Harrison, Jonathan, Bryan. AB, Princeton U., 1974; MD, Harvard U., 1978. Resident Mass. Gen. Hosp., 1979-84; chief resident Stanford U. Med. Ctr., 1985; founder, surgeon Vanderbilt Transplant Med. Ctr., 1986—; U.S. senator from Tenn., 1995—; mem. banking, housing & urban affairs com., budget com., labor & human resources com., small bus. com. U.S. Senate, 1995. Republican. Office: US Senate 565 Dirksen Senate Office Bldg Washington DC 20510*

FRITSCH, ALBERT JOSEPH, director environmental demonstration center; b. Maysville, Ky., Sept. 30, 1933; s. Albert Anthony and Mary Elizabeth (Schumacher) F. BS in Chemistry, Xavier U., 1955, MS in Chemistry, 1956; PhD in Chemistry, Fordham U., 1964; S.T.L. in Theology, Loyola U., Chgo., 1968. Ordained priest Roman Cath. Ch., 1967. Postdoctorate rsch. assoc. U. Tex., Austin, 1969-70; sci. cons. Ctr. for Study of Responsive Law, Washington, 1970-71; co-dir. Ctr. for Sci. in the Pub. Interest, Washington, 1971-77; dir. Appalachia--Sci. in the Pub. Interest, Lexington, Ky., 1977—; mem. A.S.P.I.; adv. coun. Ky. Appalachian Regional Commn.; Ky Outlook 2000, Sci. cons. Ctr. for Study of Commericalism, U.S. C.C. Environmental Justice Program, D.C.; bd. dirs. Tenn. Valley Energy Reform Coalition, 1993—, Nat. Cath. Rural Life Conf., 1994, U.S. Cath. Conf. Environ. Taskforce, Washington, 1994—. Author: A Theology of Earth, 1972, The Contrasumers: A Citizens Guide to Resource Conservation, 1974, 99 Ways to a Simple Lifestyle, 1976, Special Topics in Hetereocyclic Chemistry Vol. 30, Interscience, 1977, Household Pollutants Guide, 1978, Environmental Ethics, 1980, Green Space, 1982, Appalachia: A Meditation, 1987, Communities at Risk, Renew America, 1989, Eco-Church, 1991, Down to Earth Spirituality, 1992, Waste Minimization: Widening the Perspectives, 1993, Earth Healing, 1994; chpts. in Embracing the Earth, 1994, Ecological Prospects, 1994, The Greening of Faith, 1996. Named Gamaliel Chair Lectr. Lutheran Ministry, U. Wis.. Milw., 1991, Bannon Chair lectr. U. Santa Clara, Calif., 1994; recipient St. Francis Xavier medal,

Xavier U., Cin., 1993. Mem. Soc. of Jesus, Sigma Xi, Phi Lambda. Roman Catholic. Home: 50 Lair St Mount Vernon KY 40456

FRITSCH, BILLY DALE, JR., construction company executive; b. Pensacola, Fla., May 10, 1956; s. Billy Dale Fritsch Sr. and Cleta Thiel; children: Mackenzie, Billy Dale III, Jessica. BS, No. Mich. U., 1978. CPA, Ill. Staff acct. Jonet, Fontain, Vande Loo, et al, Green Bay, Wis., 1979; asst. contr. Carpenter Contractors of Am., Pompano Beach, Fla., 1979-81, contr., 1981-84, v.p. fin., 1984-90, exec. v.p., 1990—; cons. Jade Industries, Coral Springs, Fla., 1983-86; mem. team of taxation and acctg. specialists Citizen Ambassador Program, 1988. Mem. AICPA, Fla. Inst. CPAs, Ill. CPA Soc., Constrn. Fin. Mgmt. Assn., Greater Ft. Lauderdale C. of C. (founding trustee 1990), Internat. Platform Assn. Republican. Office: Carpenter Contractors Am 941 SW 12th Ave Pompano Beach FL 33069-4610

FRITSCH, DEREK ADRIAN, nurse anesthetist; b. Cuero, Tex., Sept. 12, 1957; s. Adrian Henry and Virginia Emma (Bernshausen) F.; m. Jacqueline Ann Joyce, June 8, 1985; children: Alexander Derek, Adrienne Joyce. AA, Wharton County Jr. Coll., Wharton, Tex., 1978; BSN, U. Tex. Health Sci. Ctr., 1980; CRNA, Harris County Hosp. Dist., Houston, 1983. Cert. registered nurse anesthetist. Anesthesia tng. Ben Taub Gen. Hosp., The Meth. Hosp., VA Hosp., others, Houston, 1979-88; staff anesthetist Anesthesia Specialists of Houston/The Woman's Hosp. Tex., Houston, 1988-94, 95—; freelance staff anesthetist Schick Shadel Hosp., Houston, 1990, Gulf Coast Regional Med. Ctr., Wharton, 1994-95; staff anesthetist, anesthesia specialists of Houston/The Woman's Hosp., Houston, 1995—. Colo. County emergency vol. Ambulance Corps, 1976-78; provider anesthesia internat. eye surgery team, Benovolent Missions Internat., Belize, Boliva, El Salvador, 1993-94, 93-95, gen. surgery team, Guatemala, 1996. Recipient Luth. Brotherhood scholarship, 1979, Rotarian scholarship, Houston, 1979, others. Mem. AANA, Tex. Assn. Nurse Anesthetists, Internat. Anesthesia Rsch. Soc., Gulf Coast Assn. Nurse Anesthetists (bd. dirs. 1987-89, pres. 1988-89), Greater New Eng. Acad. Hypnosis, Phi Theta Kappa (State Recognition award, chpt. pres. 1977-78), Sigma Theta Tau. Lutheran. Home: 410 Lake Bend Dr Sugar Land TX 77479-5804 Office: Anesthesia Specialists Houston 7800 Fannin Ste 101 Houston TX 77054

FRITTS, LILLIAN ELIZABETH, retired nurse; b. N.Y.C., July 19, 1923; d. William Franklin and Elzora Jane (Hodge) Bowen; A.D.N., R.N., Central Peidmont Community Coll., 1969; m. Thurman Luther Fritts, Aug. 5, 1944; children—William Luther, Franklin Lee, George Allen. Emergency room nurse Lexington (N.C.) Meml. Hosp., 1953-58; office nurse James T. Welborn, M.D., Lexington, 1958-60; staff nurse Haven Nursing Ctr., Lexington, 1960-61; pvt. duty nurse, 1961-63; owner, ptnr. Buena Vista Nursing Ctr., Lexington, 1964-91, ret., 1991; adult extension tchr. Davidson County Community Coll., 1978, adv. bd. nursing program, 1969-79; pres. Piedmont dist. Long Term Nursing Dirs., 1986-88, Long Term Care Piedmont Nurses Assn., 1987-89. Mem. Am. Nurses Assn., N.C. Nurses Assn., Lic. Practical Nurse Orgn. (state sec. 1958-60), N.C. Lic. Practical Nurse Assn., Dist. 9 Nurse Assn. N.C., N.C. Health Care Facilities Services Assn., Gideons Internat. Baptist. Home: 797 Hill Everhart Rd Lexington NC 27295-7102

FRITZ, CAROL SCHWEINFORTH, nurse administrator, consultant; b. Hudson Falls, N.Y., May 13, 1944; d. Leon B. and Dorothy (Keech) Schweinforth; m. John E. Fritz, Aug. 1, 1969. Diploma, Presbyn. Hosp. Sch. of Nursing, Phila., 1965. RN, N.Y., N.C.; cert. case mgr. Team leader, asst. head nurse Sunnyview Rehab. Ctr., Schenectady, N.Y., 1966-71; dir. nursing Sandhills Nursing Ctr., Pinehurst, N.C., 1973-74; occupational health nurse mgr. Good Mark Foods, Inc., Raleigh, N.C., 1975-82; rehab. mgr. Intracorp, Raleigh, 1982-88; dist. mgr. Resource Opportunities, Inc., Raleigh, 1988—; audiologic cons. N.C. State U., Raleigh, 1982-84. Vol. N.C. Food Bank. Mem. N.C. Assn. Rehab. Profls. (officer at large 1989—). Democrat. Home: 3900 Meadow Field Ln Raleigh NC 27606-4470

FRITZ, EDWARD WILLIAM, mechanical engineer; b. Kenosha, Wis., Nov. 30, 1953; s. Edward Wilgar and Marilyn Jean (Pflug) F.; m. Cindy Susan Smith, Nov. 25, 1977; children: Edward W. Jr., Michael V. BS, U.S. Merchant Marine Acad., 1975. Registered profl. engr., N.C., S.C. Test engr. Ingalls Shipbuilding, Pascagoula, Miss., 1975-77, shift test engr., 1977-78; assoc. engr. Duke Power Co., Charlotte, N.C., 1978-80, design engr., 1980-87, sr. engr., 1987-91; engring. supr., 1991—; York, S.C. Mem. ASME, Am. Nuclear Soc. Presbyterian. Office: Duke Power Co Catawba Nuclear Sta 4800 Concord Rd York SC 29745-9635

FRITZ, JOANNE LEE (JONI FRITZ), association executive; b. Bklyn., May 5, 1936; d. Theodore Roosevelt and Josephine (Chandler) L.; m. John D. Allen Jr., June 16, 1956 (div. Jan. 1970); children: John D. III, Cynthia Allen de Ramos, Victoria Lee Burnett; m. Nicholas Fritz Jr., July 4, 1970. Student, Cornell U., 1954-56; BA in Sociology with distinction, George Washington U., 1971. Tchr. Enon Elem. Sch., Chester, Va., 1958-59; med. records analyst Fairax (Va.) Hosp., 1962-66; med. asst. Drs. Apter and Morrissey Ltd., 1966-72; assoc. dir. Am. Network Community Options and Resources (formerly Nat. Assn. Pvt. Residential Resources), Falls Church, Va., 1972-76; exec. dir. Am. Network Community Options and Resources, Falls Church, Va., 1976—; panelist Office Human Devel., HHS, 1980-83, Health Care Financing Adminstrn., 1991; speaker pvt. residential svcs. nat. and state confs.; sec. Consortium for Citizens with Disabilities, 1974-82, chmn. housing task force, 1983-85, chmn. staff wage and hour task force, 1986-88; mem. steering com. Forum on Long Term Care, Washington, 1979-84; bd. dirs. Accreditation Coun. on Svcs. to People with Disabilities, 1979-80; mem. adv. panels various orgns. Author, editor, Links, 1976—. Trustee Commn. on Accreditation Rehab. Facilities, 1984-89, chmn. standards com., 1985-87. Recipient Ark. Traveler award; Ky. col. Mem. Am. Assn. Mental Retardation, Assn. Retarded Citizens, Nat. Brain Injury Found., Nat. Fire Protection Assn. (subcom. bd. & care). Office: Am Network Community Options and Resources 4200 Evergreen Ln Ste 315 Annandale VA 22003-3255

FRITZ, KATHLYN ANN, sociology educator; b. Whitmire, S.C., Aug. 9, 1946; d. William Richard and Evelyn Rogers (Ackerman) F.; m. Bruce Hager Mayhew, June 3, 1977 (dec. Mar. 1988); m. Bruce Wilton Nell-Smith, Dec. 29, 1992. AB, Lenoir Rhyne Coll., 1968; PhD, Yale U., 1975. Asst. prof. U. S.C., Columbia, 1974-78; dir. Fairfield County Mus., Winnsboro, S.C., 1983-88; assoc. prof. Newberry (S.C.) Coll., 1990—; chair dept. sociology and psychology, 1995—; vis. asst. prof. U. S.C., Columbia, 1986-87, 88-89; cons. So. States Energy Bd., 1979, S.C. Energy Rsch. Inst., 1978. Bd. dirs. Fairfield Arts Coun., Winnsboro, 1982; mem. Cen. Midlands Hist. Preservation, Columbia, 1983-85, Pine Tree Players, pres., 1982-84, 89, 90; pres. Fairfield Friends of the Libr., 1983-84. Nat. merit scholar, 1964. Mem. So. Sociol. Soc., S.C. Sociol. Assn., Inquirendo Club (pres. 1990-91), Winnsboro Women's Club (bd. dirs. 1982-83), Popular Culture Assn in the South. Home: 233 S Vanderhorst St Winnsboro SC 29180-1447 Office: Newberry Coll Dept Sociology and Psychology 2100 College St Newberry SC 29108-2126

FRITZ, TERRENCE LEE, investment banker, strategic consultant; b. Ft. Dodge, Iowa, Mar. 10, 1943; s. George and Julia Evelyn (Katnik) F.; m. Pam Fritz; children: Erich, Kevin, Tanya. BS in Indsl. Engring., Iowa State U., 1967. Registered profl. engr., Colo. Mfg. system analyst Martin-Marietta, Denver, 1967-68; system fin. analyst N.Am. Philips, Denver, 1968-69; mgmt. cons. Denver, 1970-74; exec. dir. Met. Transit Authority-Iowa Dept. Transp., Des Moines, 1974-78; sr. v.p. mktg., strategic planning Holiday Inns, Trailways, Dallas, 1978-80; pres. Strategic Actions, Dallas, 1984-88; regional dir. capital markets group Grant Thornton, Dallas, 1988-90; pres. Capital Mkts. Group, Inc., Dallas, 1990—; mem. adv. bd. So. Meth. U., 1981-84, local adv. bd. Dallas Fed. Res., 1982-84; advisor transp. rsch. bd. NAS, 1980. Bd. dirs. Dallas-Ft. Worth Adv. bd., 1980-84; cons. Dallas-Ft. Worth Transp. Authority, 1980; mem. Gov.'s Com. on Tech., Austin, 1982-83; Dallas rep. U.S. President's Carribean Initiatives Program to Jamaica, Costa Rica, 1981-83; exec. dir. Japan-Tex. Conf., 1981-84; mem. adv. bd. So. Meth. U. Cox Sch. Bus., 1981-84. Mem. Dallas C. of C. (pres., chief exec. officer 1980-84). Home: 9347 Briarhurst Dr Dallas TX 75243-6139 Office: Ste 300 2911 Turtle Creek Blvd Dallas TX 75219-6243

FRITZE, JULIUS ARNOLD, marriage counselor; b. Albuquerque, Dec. 30, 1918; s. Martin Herman and Mary (Staerkel) F.; m. Marion Caroline Becker, June 4, 1944; children: Christine, Timothy; m. 2d, Anita Carol Dozier, May 18, 1973. Student St. Paul's Jr. Coll., 1937-39; diploma Concordia Sem., 1944; B.A., in Edn., U. N.Mex., 1943; M.S., Central Mo. State Coll., 1969. Nat. cert. counselor; lec. marriage and family therapist, Tex. Ordained to ministry Lutheran Ch., 1944; pastor in Corpus Christi, Tex., 1944-48, Higginsville, Mo., 1948-57; exec. dir. Marriage and Parenthood Center, Dallas, 1957-59; pvt. practice marriage counseling, Dallas, 1959—; indsl. psychologist N. Am. Mktg., 1975-76; mgmt. cons. Concord Systems, Inc., 1978—; therapist Proctor & Gamble, Dallas, 1991—. Cons. Mo. Snyod, Luth. Ch., St. Louis, 1961, Tex. dist., 1976—; lectr. to profl. and laymen's insts., 1956—; lectr. Dallas County Jr. Coll. Bd. dirs. Dallas area Am. Lung Assn., 1976—. Lic. profl. counselor, Tex. Mem. Am. Assn. Marriage Counselors, Am. Personnel and Guidance Assn., Nat. Vocat. Guidance Assn., Nat. Council Family Relations, Am. Psychol. Assn., Southwestern Psychol. Assn., Tex. Psychol. Assn., Am. Orthopsychiat. Assn., Internat. Platform Assn. Author: The Essence of Marriage, 1969; Mini Manual for Ministers, 1978, The Essence of Life, 1990; contbr. series of articles to nat. mags. Home: 10531 Castlegate Dr Dallas TX 75229-5102 Office: 3198 Royal Ln Ste 100 Dallas TX 75229-3777

FRITZE, RONALD HAROLD, historian, educator; b. Ft. Wayne, Ind., Dec. 8, 1951; s. Harold Albert and Mary Eleanor (Cordray) F. BA in History, Concordia Coll., 1974; MA in History, La. State U., 1976, MLS, 1982; PhD, U. Cambridge, Eng., 1982. Rsch. assoc. dept. history La. State U., Baton Rouge, 1979-80, rsch. asst. catalog project, 1980, instr. western civilization, dept. history, 1981-82; instr. Am. history Houston C.C., 1983-84; librarian reference/collection devel. history, polit. sci. Rice U., Houston, 1982-84; asst. prof. history Lamar U., Beaumont, Tex., 1984-89, assoc. prof., 1989-95, prof., 1995—, Univ. prof., 1996—. Co-author: (with Randy Roberts, James Olson) Reflections on Western Civilization: A Reader, 1990, (with Brian Coutts, Louis Vyhnakek) Reference Sources in History: An Introductory Guide, 1990, (with Randy Roberts, James Olson) Reflections on World Civilization: A Reader, 1993; author: Legends and Lore of the Americas before 1492; An Encyclopedia of Visitors, Explorers and Immigrants, 1993, Historical Dictionary of Stuart Britain, 1996; editor-in-chief Historical Dictionary of Tudor Britain, 1991; contbr. articles to acad. and profl. jours. Mem. Am. Hist. Assn., Cambridge Hist. Soc., Hist. Assn., Past and Present Soc., ALA, Library History Round Table, Sixteenth Century Studies Conf., Conf. on British Studies, Phi Alpha Theta, Phi Kappa Phi, Phi Beta Mu. Lutheran. Office: Lamar U Dept History Beaumont TX 77710

FRIZZELL, GREGORY KENT, lawyer; b. Wichita, Kans., Dec. 13, 1956; s. D. Kent and Shirley Elaine (Piatt) F.; m. Kelly Susan Nash, Mar. 9, 1991; children: Benjamin Newcomb, Hannah Kirsten, Robert Nash, David Gregory. BA, U. Tulsa, 1981; JD, U. Mich., 1984. Bar: Okla. 1985, U.S. Dist. Ct. (no., ea. and we. dists.) Okla. 1985, U.S. Ct. Appeals (10th cir.) 1985, U.S. Supreme Ct. 1990. Jud. clk. to judge U.S. Dist. Ct. for No. Dist. Okla., Tulsa, 1984-86; pvt. practice Tulsa, 1986-95; gen. counsel Okla. Tax Commn., 1995—; vol. atty. Legal Aid to Elderly, Legal Svcs. of Ea. Okla., Tulsa, 1988—. Mem. Tulsa County Rep. Exec. Com., 1986-92; Tulsa County chmn. Dole for Pres. Com., 1987-88; counsel bd. dirs. Tulsa Speech and Hearing Assn., 1987-95, pres., 1994-95. Mem. Okla. Bar Assn. (young lawyers rep. to client security fund com. 1990-92), Am. Inns of Ct. (barrister). Home: 2947 S Quaker Ave Tulsa OK 74114-5309 Office: Okla Tax Commn Gen. Counsel's Office 2501 N Lincoln Blvd Oklahoma City OK 73194 also: Rm 501 440 S Houston Tulsa OK 74127

FRIZZELL, LUCILLE BRIDGERS, retired librarian; b. Yazoo City, Miss., Dec. 17, 1925; d. Thomas Alfred Bridgers and Maie Hollingsworth; m. Byron Waters Frizzell, July 24, 1952; children: Peter Graham, David Edward, Mark Dillard. BS, East Tenn. State U., 1977, MS, 1980. Sec. U.S. Steel Corp., 1946-53; libr. Steed Coll., Johnson City, Tenn., 1980-82, Bristol Coll., Johnson City, 1982-84, Draughons Jr. Coll., Johnson City, 1984-90. Lic. lay eucharistic min. St. John's Episcopal Ch. Mem. AAUW, DAR (treas. Johnson City chpt. 1959-60), Nat. Soc. So. Dames (v.p. East Tenn. chpt. 1986-88, v.p. Tenn. state chpt. 1990-92), Watauga Assn. Genealogists (charter), Washington County Hist. Soc. (charter), Monday Club, Delta Kappa Gamma. Republican. Home: 3320 Bondwood Cir Johnson City TN 37604-8907

FRNKA, JEROME VICTOR, chemistry educator; b. Elcampo, Tex., July 20, 1941; s. Frank William and Laura Emily (Kosler) F.; m. Vickie Johnette Halbert, May 29, 1966; children: Scott Anthony, Laura Allison. BS, Sam Houston State U., 1963; PhD, Tex. A&M U., 1973. Cert. secondary tchr. Rsch. fellow U. Minn., Mpls., 1974-76, rsch. assoc., 1976-77, asst. prof., 1977-78; asst. prof. Elmira (N.Y.) Coll., 1978-84, assoc. prof., 1984-86; tchr. honors chemistry J.L. McCullough High Sch., The Woodlands, Tex., 1986-87; asst. prof. Baylor U. Coll. of Medicine, Houston, 1987-90; tchr. honors chemistry Klein (Tex.) Sr. High Sch., 1990—. Contbr. articles to profl. jours. Regional asst. dir. Univ. Interscholastic League Baylor U., 1995-96. Mem. Am. Chem. Soc., AAAS. Episcopalian. Office: Klein Sr High Sch 16715 Stuebner Airline Klein TX 77379

FROCK, TERRI LYN, nursing educator and consultant; b. Uniontown, Pa., Sept. 18, 1953; d. Samuel Edward and Louise Harriet (Hooper) F. BSN, U. Miami, 1975, MS in Nursing, 1980; EdS, Fla. Atlantic U., 1987, EdD, 1994. Asst. head nurse North Broward Med. Ctr., Pompano Beach, Fla., 1976-79; instr. nursing Broward C.C., Ft. Lauderdale, Fla., 1980-85, Fla. Internat. U., Miami, 1994—; asst. prof. nursing Fla. Internat. U., North Miami, 1994—; nursing edn. cons. Fla. Bd. Nursing, 1988-92; camp nurse Kanuga Camp and Conf. Ctr., Hendersonville, N.C., summers 1980-81. Editor newsletter Fla. League for Nursing, 1996-97. Bd. dirs. Am. Heart Assn., Boca Raton; mem. St. Martins-in-the-Fields Episc. Ch., Pompano Beach. Mem. Nat. League for Nursing, Fla. Nurses Assn., Fla. Atlantic U. Alumni Assn. (bd. dirs.), Sigma Theta Tau, Phi Kappa Phi, Kappa Delta Pi, Phi Delta Kappa. Home: 2210 NE 40th Ct Lighthouse Point FL 33064-7328

FROEHNER, STANLEY C., neurobiology educator; b. Gonzales, Tex., Feb. 17, 1946; s. Elmar Paul and Estelle Florence (Kattner) F.; m. Sandra Evans, Feb. 2, 1968.; BS, U. Tex., 1968; PhD, Calif. Inst. Tech., 1972. Guest researcher Svenska Traforskings Inst., Stockholm, 1972-74; rsch. fellow neurobiology Harvard U., Boston, 1974-76, rsch. fellow neuropathology, 1976-78; asst. prof. biochemistry Dartmouth U., Hanover, N.H., 1978-84, assoc. prof. biochemistry, 1984-89, prof. biochemistry, 1989-91; prof., chair physiology U. N.C., Chapell Hill, 1992—; mem. rev. bd. Howard Hughes Med. Inst., Chevy Chase, Md., 1995—; mem. study sect. NIH, Bethesda, Md., 1985-87, molecule and cell neurosci. com. Internat. Union Physiol. Scis., 1995—; mem. sci. adv. bd. Cambridge (Mass.) Symposia, 1995—; Javitz neurosci. investigator NIH, 1995—. Rsch. grantee NIH, 1979—, Muscular Dystrophy Assn., 1979—. Office: U NC Sch Medicine Dept Physiology 266 Medical Sci Rsch Bldg Chapel Hill NC 27599-7545

FROELICHER, FRANZ, chemist, geologist, environmental consultant; b. Ridgewood, N.J., Jan. 11, 1936; s. Victor and Helen (Stehli) F.; m. Margarete (Grundmann), Jan. 23, 1976; children: Britta, Niels. BA in Biology, Alaska Meth. U., 1971, BA in Geology, 1972; PhD in Geology, Sedimentology, Paleoecology, Edinburgh U., Scotland, 1977. Researcher, instr. U. Tübingen, Fed. Republic Germany, 1977-79; asst. prof. geology U. So. Miss., Hattiesburg, Miss., 1979-88; dir. European geology field camp U. So. Miss., Hattiesburg, 1980-88; dir. ctr. for coal and coal products rsch. U. So. Miss., Gulfport, 1986-88; chemist nat. monitoring and residue analysis lab. USDA, Gulfport, Miss., 1988-90; v.p. environ. issues DeWitt & Co., Gulfport, Miss., 1990-92; chemist hazardous waste sect. U.S. Army Corps Engrs., Savannah, Ga., 1992—. Author monthly newsletter EcoIssues; contbr. articles to profl. jours., presented papers at profl. meetings. Grantee Miss. Mineral Resources Inst., 1979-86, GCAGS, 1986, TSI, Inc., 1986-87, Army Corps Engrs., 1987, Leaf River Forest Products, Inc., 1987. Mem. Geol. Soc. Am. (coal div.), Miss. Acad. Scis., N.Am. Coal Petrographers, Soc. Organic Petrology, Palaeontologische Gesellschaft, Paleontol. Assn., Sonderforschungsbereich 53, Soc. Organic Petrology Publs. (rev. bd.). Home: 6 Coquena Dr Savannah GA 31410-1331 Office: US Army Corps Engrs Savannah Dist EN-GH Savannah GA 31402

FROIS, THEODORE MICHAEL, lawyer; b. New Orleans, Dec. 14, 1944; s. Theodore Charles and Lois Rita (Bordes) F.; m. Louana Hime; 1 child, Monica. BA in Bus. Adminstrn., Southeastern La. U., 1962-66; JD, Loyola U., 1966-69. Bar: La. 1969, Tex. 1985. Trial atty. Kierr and Gainsburgh, New Orleans, 1969-70; atty. Exxon Co., U.S.A., New Orleans, 1970-74, Houston, 1976-78; refinery atty. Exxon Co., U.S.A., Baton Rouge, 1978-81; divsn. atty. Exxon Co., U.S.A., New Orleans, 1981-84; chief atty. Exxon Co., U.S.A., Houston, 1984-85, gen. counsel, 1995—; supervisory atty. Creole Petroleum Corp., Caracus, Venezuela, 1974-75; gen. counsel EssoInter-Am., Inc., Coral Gables, Fla., 1986; asst. gen. counsel Exxon Co., Internat., Florham Park, N.J., 1986-90; sr. counselor coord. Exxon Corp., N.Y.C., 1990, Dallas, 1990-94; adv. bd. Southwestern Legal Found., Dallas, 1995—; dean's adv. com. Loyola U. Law Sch., New Orleans, 1988—. Author: (jour.) Loyola Law Reviewer, Vol. XIV, No. 1 and No. 2, 1967-68, (manual) Louisiana Mineral Law Institute, 1983; assoc. editor (jour.) Loyola Law Review, 1968-69. Mem. ABA, State Bar of Tex., La. State Bar, Houston Bar Assn., Houston Bar Found. (bd. dirs. 1995—, dir.). Office: Exxon Co USA 800 Bell Houston TX 77252-2180

FROMKIN, AVA LYNDA, management consultant, healthcare risk management services; b. Toronto, Ont., Can., May 3, 1946; d. Joseph and Sara Ann (Hurovitz) F.; came to U.S., 1948, naturalized, 1953; BSN, U. Miami, 1969, cert. adminstrv. scis., 1975, MBA, cert. health adminstrn., 1983. Diplomate Am. Bd. Risk Mgmt. of Healthcare; lic. risk mgr. Nurse, Mt. Sinai Med. Ctr., Miami Beach, Fla., 1970-71, 73-76; dir. surg. svcs. Cedars of Lebanon Health Care Ctr., Miami, 1976-82; adj. prof. intraoperative nursing program Miami (Fla.)-Dade C.C., 1982-83; prin. A. Lynda Fromkin, Inc., Miami, Fla., 1982-94. Mem. ANA, Fla. Nurses Assn., Am. Soc. Post Anesthesia Nurses, Assn. Oper. Rm. Nurses (dir. Miami chpt. 1979-80), F.H.A. Soc. Healthcare Risk Mgmt., Alzheimer's Care Com. Notables, U. Miami Pres. Circle. Home: 555 NE 34th St Apt 2306 Miami FL 33137-4059

FROMM, ERWIN FREDERICK, insurance company executive; b. Kalamazoo, Oct. 24, 1933; s. Erwin Carl and Charlotte Elizabeth (Wilson) F.; student U. Mich., 1951-52, Flint Jr. Coll., 1952-53; BA, Kalamazoo Coll., 1959; postgrad. Ill. State U., 1970-72; CPCU, CLU; cert. nursing home adminstr. Underwriter, State Farm Ins., 1959-72; cons. Met. Property & Liability Ins. Co., Warwick, R.I., 1972-73, dir. underwriting and policyholders svcs., 1973, asst. v.p., 1973-74, v.p., 1974—; sr. v.p. Royal Ins. Co., Charlotte, N.C., 1979-90; ret., 1990; nursing home exec. Royal Crest Health Care Ctr., Inc., 1990-92; pres. Royal Monarch Cons., Inc., 1990—; past chmn. All Industry Ins. Com. for Arson Control; chmn. Nat. Coun. on Compensation Ins.; past chmn. Comml. Lines Com. Ins. Svc. Office; past mem. adv. com. underwriting program Ins. Inst. Am. Mem. adv. coun. Bus. Sch., U. R.I.; past bd. dirs. Charlotte Symphony; bd. dirs. N.C. Ins. Edn. Served to 1st lt. U.S. Army, 1953-56. Mem. CPCU Assn. (N.C. chpt.), CLU Assn. (N.C. chpt.), Am. Coll. Health Care Adminstrs. English Speaking Union, Masons, Shriners. Home and Office: 2740 Montgomery St Durham NC 27705-5718

FROSCH, PATRICIA ANN, non-profit organization executive; b. Deming, N.Mex., Mar. 22, 1954; d. Malcolm Lee and Dorothy Jane (Card) F. BA, McMurry Coll., 1976. Caseworker Child Protective Svcs., Abilene, Tex., 1976-77; med. social worker, dir. admissions, pub. rels. coord. West Tex. Rehab. Ctr., Abilene, 1977-82; sales and mktg. support rep. Abilene Bus. Equipment, Abilene, 1982-84; dist. field rep. Tex. divsn. Am. Cancer Soc., 1984-86; exec. dir. Mend-a-Child, 1986—. Bd. dirs. Abilene Zool. Soc., 1994—, Taylor County Hist. Commn., Abilene, 1993; past pres., bd. dirs., sec. Friends of Abilene Pub. Libr., 1988-94; grad. steering com. Leadership Abilene, 1988-91; chair steering com., mem. adv. com. Young Leadership Abilene, 1989-93; sustaining mem. Jr. League of Abilene, chair pub. affairs, 1991-92; mem. adv. com. Abilene Mental Health/Mental Retardation Child and Adolescent Svcs., 1992. Named Friend of Yr., Friends of Abilene Pub. Libr., 1993. Republican. United Methodist. Office: Mend-a-Child 1246 N 6th St Abilene TX 79601-5807

FROST, JOHN ELLIOTT, minerals company executive; b. Winchester, Mass., May 20, 1924; s. Elliott Putnam and Hazel Lavera (Carley) F.; m. Carolyn Catlin, July 12, 1945 (div. 1969); children: John Crocker, Jeffrey Putnam, Teresa Baird, Virginia Nicholl; m. Martha Hicks, June 6, 1969 (div. 1984); m. Catherine Kearns, July 27, 1985; 1 stepchild, Colleen Depew. BS, Stanford U., 1949, MS, 1950, PhD, 1965. Geologist Asarco, Salt Lake City, 1951-54; chief geologist, surface mines supt. Philippine Iron Mines Inc., Larap, Camarines Norte, 1954-60; chief geologist Duval Corp. (Pennzoil Corp.), Tucson, 1961-67; minerals exploration mgr. Exxon Corp., Houston, 1967-71; minerals mgr. Esso Eastern Inc. div., 1971-80; sr. v.p. Exxon Minerals Co. div., Houston, 1980-86; pres., Exxon Minerals Internat., Houston, 1980-86; v.p. Kalahari Resources, 1996—, Frost Minerals Internat., 1986—; bd. dirs., United Engring. Trustees, N.Y.C., 1981-94, chmn. real estate com., 1986-89, v.p., 1989-91, pres., 1991-93. Mem. adv. bd. Sch. Earth Scis., Stanford (Calif.) U., 1983-85; pres. SEG Found., 1984, bd. dirs. 1981-84, 1994—. Served to 1st lt. USAAF, 1943-45, PTO. Fellow Geol. Soc. Am., Soc. Econ. Geologists (pres. 1989-90, councilor 1982-84, program com., nominating com. chmn. 1982); mem. AIME (chmn. edn. com. Soc. Mining Engrs. 1971; Charles F. Rand medal 1984, Disting. Mem. award 1984, Dist. Svc. award 1991), Australian Inst. Mining and Metallurgy; mem. Am. Inst. Profl. Geologists, The Houston Club, Sigma Xi. Republican. Methodist. Home and Office: 602 Sandy Port St Houston TX 77079-2419

FROST, JONAS MARTIN, III, congressman; b. Glendale, Calif., Jan. 1, 1942; s. Jack and Doris (Marwil) F.; m. Valerie Hall, May 9, 1976; children: Alanna Shaw, Mariel Jeanne, Camille Faye. BA, U. Mo., 1964, BJ, 1964; J.D., Georgetown U., 1970. Bar: Tex. 1970. Law clk. U.S. Dist. Ct. Judge Sarah T. Hughes, Dallas, 1970-71; legal commentator Sta. KERA-TV, Dallas, 1971-72; pvt. practice law Dallas, 1972-79; mem. 96th-104th Congresses from 24th Tex. dist., Washington, D.C., 1979—; mem. rules com.; chmn. Dem. Congl. Campaign Com. Del. Dem. Nat. Conv., 1976, 84, 88, 92, 96; coord. North Tex. Carter-Mondale Campaign, 1976. Office: US Ho of Reps 2459 Rayburn Office Bldg Washington DC 20515

FROST, JUANITA CORBITT, hospital foundation coordinator; b. Rockford, Ill., Aug. 4, 1926; d. Mervin Charles and Eva Marie (Moberg) Corbitt; m. Thomas Tapenden Frost, Jan. 3, 1954; children: Annamarie, Thomas Tapenden. Student, Little Rock U., Ark., 1959-61. Med. sec. asst. clinical pathology lab. VA, Whipple, Ariz., 1951-54; exec. dir. Camp Fire Girls, Temple, Tex., 1967-73; exec. sec. Scott & White Meml. Hosp. Found., Temple, Tex., 1973-82; hosp. found. coordinator, exec. asst. to bd. Scott & White Meml. Hosp., Scott Sherwood and Brindley Found, Temple, Tex., 1982—. Vestry mem. Episcopal Ch., Temple, Tex., 1985—, sr. warden, 1987, worship com., 1995—; active Com. on Bishops Address NW Region Diocese Episcopal Ch., Houston, 1988, Bell County Choral Group, Belton, Tex., 1988-92, Tchr. Literacy Coun., Temple, 1988-93. Mem. Am. Hosp. Assn. Exec. Assts. Home: 3001 Las Moras Dr Temple TX 76502-1643 Office: Scott & White Meml Hosp Found 2401 S 31st St Temple TX 76508-0001

FROST, PHILIP, company executive. Pres. Ivax Corp., Miami, Fla. Office: Ivax Corp 4400 Biscayne Blvd Miami FL 33137-3212

FROST, SUSAN HENSON, academic administrator; b. Atlanta, Aug. 17, 1948; d. Charles Walton and Sue (Hutchens) Henson; m. John Randall Frost, June 27, 1970; children: Susannah, Charles. BA, Agnes Scott Coll., 1970; MEd, North Ga. Coll., 1984; EdD, U. Ga., 1989. Prof. Brenau Coll., Gainesville, Ga., 1983-91; dir. instl. planning and rsch. Emory U., Atlanta, 1991-95, vice provost instnl. planning and rsch., and adjunct prof., 1995—; cons. in field. Author: Academic Advising for Student Success: A System of Shared Responsibility, 1991, (with Ronald D. Simpson) Inside College: Undergraduate Education for the Future, 1993; contbr. articles to profl. jours. Bd. dirs. Gateway Shelter Women, Gainesville, 1980-81; treas. Northeast Ga. Speech Ctr., Gainesville, 1988-91, Gainesville Jr. Svc. League, 1978-80; charter chmn. Parents Coun. Edn., Gainesville, 1987-90. Recipient Student Rsch. award, 1988. Mem. Am. Assn. Higher Edn., Nat. Acad. Advising Assn., So. Assn. Instl. Rsch., Assn. Study Higher Edn., Assn. Instl. Rsch., Soc. Coll. and Univ. Planning, Kappa Delta Pi, Phi Delta Kappa, Phi Kappa Phi. Office: Emory U 108 Administration Bldg Atlanta GA 30322

FROST, WAYNE N., lawyer; b. Winters, Tex., Nov. 24, 1953; s. J.F. and Dorothy (Martin) F.; m. Susan Amini, Aug. 15, 1981; children: Daniel Morgan, Charlotte Nicole. BA in Criminal Justice, U. Tex., Odessa, 1976; M Criminal Justice Adminstrn., Oklahoma City U., 1978; JD, Detroit Coll. Law, 1984; postgrad., U. Houston, 1987. Bar: Tex. 1986, U.S. Dist. Ct. (we. dist.) Tex. 1990. Law clk. U.S. Atty.'s Office, Detroit, 1984; tchg. fellow, dir. moot ct. program Detroit Coll. Law, 1984; asst. dist. atty. Midland County Dist. Atty.'s Office, Midland, Tex., 1984—, chief narcotics prosecutor, 1992—; pvt. practice, Midland, 1986—; guest lectr. Tex. Crime-Stoppers, West Tex. Area Peace Officers Assn. Contbr. articles to legal mag. Hon. dep. Ector County Sheriff's Dept., Odessa, Tex., 1974—; bd. dirs. MADD, Midland, 1993—. Mem. Nat. Dist. Attys. Assn., Tex. Dist. and County Attys. Assn., Tex. Narcotics Officers Assn. (guest lectr., counsel gen.), Sheriffs Assn. Tex., Masons (32d degree), DeMolay (Legion of Honor). Republican. Baptist. Home: 4503 Teakwood Trace Midland TX 79707-1626 Office: Midland County Dist Atty's Office 200 W Wall St Ste 201 Midland TX 79701-4507 also: PO Box 2233 119 N Colorado St Ste 306 Midland TX 79701

FRUMKIN, HOWARD, medical educator, epidemiologist; b. Poughkeepsie, N.Y., Oct. 14, 1955; s. Barnett A. and Eileen (Brooks) F.; m. Beryl Ann Cowan, June 8, 1986; children: Gabriel, Amara. AB, Brown U., 1977; MD, U. Pa., 1982; MPH, Harvard U., 1982, DrPH, 1993. Diplomate Am. Bd. Internal Medicine, Am. Bd. Preventive Medicine. Asst. prof. medicine U. Pa., Phila., 1988-90; chmn. environ. and occupational health Emory Sch. Pub. Health, Atlanta, 1990—; mem. Ga. Hazardous Waste Mgmt. Authority, 1991-93. Editl. bd. Am. Jour. Indsl. Medicine, 1990—, Internat. Jour. Occupational and Environ. Health, 1994—, Jour. Agromedicine, 1993—. Mem. Atlanta Regional Commn. Vision 2020 Environ. Task Force, 1994-96. Fellow ACP, Am. Coll. Occupl. and Environ. Medicine; mem. APHA (governing coun. 1993—), Assn. Occupation and Environ. Clinics (exec. bd. 1991—, pres. 1995-96), Soc. Occupl. and Environ. Health (exec. bd. 1992—), Physicians for Social Responsability (exec. bd. 1995—). Home: 1770 E Clifton Rd NE Atlanta GA 30307-1252 Office: Rollins Sch Pub Health Emory Univ 1518 Clifton Rd NE Atlanta GA 30322

FRUSH, JAMES CARROLL, JR., real estate development company executive; b. San Francisco, Oct. 18, 1930; s. James Carroll and Edna Mae (Perry) F.; m. Patricia Anne Blake, Oct. 29, 1960 (div. 1977); children: Michael, Gloria; m. Carolyn Fetter Bell, Aug. 23, 1978; 1 child, Stephen. BA, Stanford, 1953; postgrad., U. Calif., San Francisco, 1957-58; MA, Saybrook Inst., 1981, PhD, 1985. Ptnr. James C. Frush Co., San Francisco, 1960-70; v.p., bd. dir. Retirement Residence, Inc., San Francisco, 1964-70, pres., 1970—; pres. Nat. Retirement Residence, San Francisco, 1971-89, Casa Dorinda Corp., 1971-89; chairperson Retirement Residence Inc. Ala., Daphne, 1995—; pres. Marin Shakespeare Festival, 1971-73, James C. Frush Found., 1972-78; adj. prof. gerontology, psychology and theology Spring Hill Coll., Mobile, Ala., 1988—; adj. prof. counseling edn. U. South Ala., Mobile; bd. dirs. Gwynned Inc., Blue Bell, Pa.; dir. Heritage Retirement Housing, Inc., 1996—. Author (with Benson Eschenbach): The Retirement Residence: An Analysis of the Architecture and Management of Life Care Housing, 1968, Self-Esteem in Older Persons Following a Heart Attack: An Exploration of Contributing Factors, 1985; contbr. articles to profl. jours.; producer ednl. films. Bd. dirs. San Francisco Sr. Ctr., 1973-78, Found. to Assist Calif. Tchrs. Devel. Inc., 1987-89; mem. adv. bd. Christus Theol. Inst., Mobile, Ala., 1992-95; mem. ethics com. adv. bd. Westminster Village, Spanish Ft., 1994—. Mem. Gerontol. Soc., Southeastern Psychol. Assn., Assn. for Anthropology and Gerontology, Stanford Alumni Assn., RSVP (adv. bd. Mobile chpt. 1988-94), C.G. Jung Soc. of Gulf Coast (pres.), Ala. Humanities Found. Speakers Bur. (presenter 1993-94, 94-95). Office: care T Pimsleur 2155 Union St San Francisco CA 94123-4003

FRY, RUSSELL JACKSON, plastics company executive; b. Winamac, Ind., Feb. 19, 1928; s. Russell Frederick and Mary (Jackson) F.; m. Peggy York, Sept. 1, 1956; children: Margaret, Charles. BA, DePauw Univ., 1952. Sales mgr. Ekco Products, Chgo., 1952-66; v.p. mktg. and sales Fesco, Pitts., 1966-77, Beacon Plastics, Detroit, 1977-87; pres., chief exec. officer, owner Emruss Corp., Ponte Vedra Beach, Fla., 1987—. Sgt. U.S. Army, 1946-48, Korea. Mem. Sawgrass Country Club, Lodge at Ponte Vedra. Republican. Presbyterian. Home: 3120 Timberlake Pt Ponte Vedra Beach FL 32082-3720 Office: Emruss Corp at Park Place Sawgrass Village PO Box 682 Ponte Vedra Beach FL 32004-0682

FRYBURGER, LAWRENCE BRUCE, lawyer, mediator, writer; b. Cin., Apr. 7, 1933. BA, U. Cin., 1956; LLB with honors, U. Tex., 1958. Bar: Tex. 1959, U.S. Dist. Ct. (we. dist.) Tex. 1961, U.S. Ct. Appeals (5th cir.) 1962, U.S. Supreme Ct. 1963, U.S. Dist. Ct. (so. dist.) Tex. 1972, U.S. Dist. Ct. (no. dist.) Tex. 1981, U.S. Ct. Appeals (11th cir.) 1981; bd. cert. labor and employment law Tex. Bd. Legal Specialization. Pvt. practice San Antonio, 1959—; spl. prof. labor relations law San Antonio Coll., 1968—. Author: Policies, Procedures and People: A Blueprint for Human Resources, 1996; contbr. articles to law jours.; mem. editorial bd. Tex. Lawyers Practice Guide, 1964. Mem. San Antonio Bd. Adjustment, 1969-72; chmn. lawyer's div. United Fund, San Antonio and Bexar County, 1967-68. Sutphin scholar U. Cin., 1956. Mem. ABA, Tex. Bar Assn. (program chmn. current devels. in labor law inst. 1978, mem. coun. labor law sect. 1978-80), Tex. young Lawyer's Inst. (originator), San Antonio Bar Assn. (chmn. lawyer reference plan 1970-73), Tex. Young Lawyers Assn. (bd. dirs. 1964-66), San Antonio Young Lawyers Assn. (pres. 1963-64, Outstanding Young Lawyer award 1967), Tex. Assn. of Residential Care Communities (spl. labor law counsel 1996—), Phi Delta Phi, Sigma Chi.

FRYD, VIVIEN GREEN, fine arts educator; b. Bklyn., May 14, 1952; d. Herbert and Stefanie (Ries) Green; m. Martin Fryd, Aug. 17, 1983; 1 child, Emma Renee. BA, Ohio State U., 1974, MA, 1977; PhD, U. Wis., 1984. Asst. to assoc. dean Coll. Letters and Sci. Student Acad. Affairs U. Wis., 1981-84; vis. asst. prof. Ariz. State U., 1984-85; asst. prof. Vanderbilt U., Nashville, 1985-92, assoc. prof. dept. fine arts, 1992—; instr. Pitts. State U., summer 1978; participant, lectr. various symposiums and confs.; co-dir. Transatlantic Voyages: Discovery of the New World and the Old, Robert Penn Warren Ctr. for Humanities, Vanderbilt U., 1991-92. Author: Art and Empire: The Politics of Ethnicity in the United States Capitol, 1815-1860, 1992; reader book manuscripts Cambridge U. Press,Cambridge Monographs in American Art, Penn State Press; contbr. articles and revs. to profl. jours., chpts. to books. Vanderbilt U. Rsch. Coun. grantee, 1986, Smithsonian Short Term Visitor grantee, 1987; Capitol Hist. Soc. fellow, 1987, Am. Coun. Learned Soc. fellow alt., 1988-89, Vanderbilt U. Rsch. Coun. fellow, 1988-89, Robert Penn Warren Ctr. Humanities fellow, 1993-94; Am. Coun. Learned Soc. grantee-in-aid, 1989, Keenan-Venture Fund grantee Vanderbilt U., 1990. Mem. Am. Studies Assn. (Rourke prize com. 1992, program com. 1994, John Hope Franklin publ. prize com. 1994). Democrat. Jewish. Home: 1715 Beechwood Ave Nashville TN 37212-5501 Office: Vanderbilt U Dept Fine Arts Nashville TN 37235

FRYE, HENRY E., state supreme court justice; b. Ellerbe, N.C., Aug. 1, 1932; s. Walter A. and Pearl Alma (Motley) F.; m. Edith Shirley Taylor, Aug. 25, 1956; children: Henry Eric, Harlan Elbert. BS in Biol. Scis., A & T U., N.C., 1953; JD with honors, U. N.C., 1959. Bar: N.C. 1959. Asst. U.S. atty. (middle dist.), N.C., 1963-65; prof. law N.C. Central U., Durham, 1965-67; practice law Greensboro, N.C., 1967-83; rep. N.C. Gen. Assembly, 1969-80, N.C. Senate, 1980-82; assoc. justice N.C. Supreme Ct., Raleigh, 1983—; organizer, pres. Greensboro Nat. Bank, 1971-80. Deacon Providence Baptist Ch. Capt. USAF, 1953-55. Mem. ABA, N.C. Bar Assn., Greensboro Bar Assn., Nat. Bar Assn., Am. Judicature Soc. (chair bd. dirs. 1995—), Kappa Alpha Psi. Office: NC Supreme Ct PO Box 1841 Raleigh NC 27602-1841

FRYEFIELD, PETER JAY, judge; b. Brookline, Mass., Feb. 27, 1949; s. Warren Baer and Ann (Steinhouse) F.; m. Diane Michelle Buerger, June 4, 1978; children: Arden Whitney, Warren Buerger, Branham Laine. BS, U. Fla., 1971, JD, 1974. Bar: Fla. 1975, U.S. Dist. Ct. (mid. dist.) Fla. 1975, U.S. Ct. Appeals (5th cir.) 1978, U.S. Supreme Ct. 1980, U.S. Ct. Appeals (11th and fed. cirs.) 1983; cert. in civil trial law 1995. Pub. defender 4th Jud. Cir., State of Fla., Jacksonville, 1974-77; ptnr. Allen, Margol & Fryefield, Jacksonville, 1977-85, Margol, Fryefield & Pennington, Jacksonville, 1985-87; pvt. practice Jacksonville, 1987-91; ptnr. Fryefield & Whitman, Jacksonville, 1992-95; cir. ct. judge 4th Jud. Cir. of Fla., Jacksonville, 1995—. Pres. Blackhawk Bluff Civic Assn., Jacksonville, 1983, Kids in Concert, 1990; treas. Aslam House Inc.; bd. dirs. N.W. Mental Health Svcs. Inc. Mem. Jacksonville Bar Assn. (mem. ethics com.), Assn. Trial Lawyers Am., Acad. Fla. Trial Lawyers, DPT Litigation Group, Aquatic Injury Safety Group. Jewish. Office: Duval County Courthouse 330 E Bay St Jacksonville FL 32202-2921

FU, LIMIN, biomedical and computer science educator; b. Taipei, Taiwan, Dec. 8, 1953; came to U.S., 1987; s. Tsai-Yi and Jen-Yui (Huang) F.; m. Lienfen Yueh, May 22, 1989; children: Katherine, Edward. MD, Nat. Taiwan U., 1978; MS, Stanford U., 1983, PhD, 1985. MD, Fla. Assoc. prof. Nat. Taiwan U., Taipei, 1985-87; rsch. scientist Allied Signal Inc., Washington, 1987-88; asst. prof. U. Wis., Milw., 1988-90; asst. prof. then assoc. prof. U. Fla., Gainesville, 1990—; cons. Info. Industry Inst., Taipei, 1985-87. Author: Neural Networks in Computer Intelligence, 1994; patentee neural network invention, 1995. Recipient Dr. T.M. Du's award Med. Soc. Taiwan, 1978, Overseas Outstanding Young Man medal Fedn. Overseas Chinese Assn., 1994. Mem. IEEE, Am. Assn. Artificial Intelligence, Computer and Medicine Assn. (v.p. 1993—, Disting. Svc. award 1993), N.Y. Acad. Sci., Sigma Xi. Office: U Fla Dept Computer and Info Scis 301 CSE Gainesville FL 32611

FUCHS, OLIVIA ANNE MORRIS, lawyer; b. Louisville, May 2, 1949; d. H.H. Morris Jr. and Betty Jean Wills Saltkill; m. Robert Edward Fuchs, Dec. 27, 1969. BA, U. Louisville, 1977, JD cum laude, 1980. Bar: Ky. 1980, U.S. Dist. Ct. (we. dist.) Ky. 1985, Ind. 1986, U.S. Dist. Ct. (so. dist.) Ind. 1987, U.S. Tax Ct. 1987. Assoc. Brown, Todd & Heyburn, Louisville, 1981-87; mem. Conliffe, Sandmann & Sullivan PLLC, Louisville, 1987—. Notes editor Jour. Family Law, 1979-80. Vol. advocate R.A.P.E. Relief Ctr., Louisville YWCA, 1981-87. Mem. ABA, Ind. Bar Assn., Ky. Bar Assn., Louisville Bar Assn. (probate sect. chmn. 1990, profl. responsibility com. chmn. 1988), U. Louisville Law Alumni Coun. (bd. dirs., 1st v.p. 1996—), Exec. Club Louisville (pres. 1996—), Jefferson Club, Phi Alpha Delta. Democrat. Presbyterian. Office: Conliffe Sandmann & Sullivan PLLC 621 W Main St Louisville KY 40202-2967 also: 141 E Spring St New Albany IN 47150-3434

FUCHS, OWEN GEORGE, chemist; b. Austin, Tex., June 22, 1951; s. Emil George and Hazel June (Johnson) F.; children from previous marriage: Ginny Lynn, William Oberholz, Owen George; m. Caroline S. Crook, Dec. 15, 1990; 1 child, Evan Ashbey. AA, Lee Jr. Coll., 1970, AS, 1973; BS, U. Houston, 1972. Chemist, Merichem Co., Houston, 1972-73; lab. mgr. Superintendence Co., Inc., Houston, 1973-78; dir. labs. and hydrocarbon research Chas. Martin Internat., Pasadena, Tex., 1978-79; pres., chief exec. officer Alpha-Omega Labs., Inc., Houston, Tex., 1979-88; bd. dirs. A.O.L. Inc., Houston, 1988—; pres., chief exec. officer Owen G. Fuchs & Assocs., Houston, 1988—, Texas City Testing Inc., 1989—, Environ. Testing Enterprises, Inc., 1991—, La. Testing Labs., Inc., 1992—. Mem. ASTM, Am. Chem. Soc. Home: PO Box 613 Highlands TX 77562 Office: PO Box 3921 Texas City TX 77592-3921

FUENTE, D. I., office supply manufacturing executive; b. 1946. Prof. Case Western Reserve U., 1970-75; with Gould Inc., Cleve., 1975-79; pres. paint stores group Sherwin-Williams Co., 1979-87; CEO, chmn. bd., dir. Office Depot Inc., Boca Raton, Fla., 1987—, OD Internat., Inc., Delray Beach, Fla. Office: Office Depot Inc 2200 Old Germantown Rd Delray Beach FL 33445-8223

FUGAZZI, PAUL ANTHONY, sales executive; b. Lexington, Ky., Jan. 8, 1959; s. Paul Edward and Joyce Allen (Hall) F. Student, U. Ky., 1978—. Sales rep. Nat. Tchrs. Assocs., Ky., 1979-80; product merchandiser A&P Tea Co., Inc., Lexington, Ky., 1975-81; with McCormick and Co., Inc., Eastern, Ky., 1981—; regional sales trainer eastern U.S. McCormick and Co., 1984-85; dist. sales mgr. McCormick and Co., Inc., various states, 1985-87, zone sales mgr., 1987—; chief exec. officer Fugazzi Real Estate Ventures, Lexington, Ky., 1987—. Organizer, adminstr. Addison County Neighborhood Soc., Lexington, 1987. Mem. Nat. Sales Bd. of McCormick. Republican. Roman Catholic. Home and Office: 631 Elsmere Park Lexington KY 40508-1405

FUHRMANN, CHARLES JOHN, II, strategic and finance consultant; b. Seattle, Feb. 21, 1945; s. Carl I. and Darlene (Reynolds) F.; m. Eugenie A. Livanos, June 24, 1967 (div. 1982); children: Katharine Reynolds, Alexandra Livanos; m. Martha M. Harris, Oct. 17, 1987; children: Arianna Taylor, Charles J. III. AB summa cum laude, Harvard Coll., 1967, MBA with honors, 1969. Sr. v.p. White Weld & Co., Inc., N.Y.C., 1969-78; mng. dir. Merrill Lynch Capital Markets, N.Y.C., 1978-91; pres., CEO 50-Off Stores, Inc., 1996—; bd. dirs. 50-Off Stores, Inc., The Sunshine Cottage, Children's Rehab. Ctr., 1996—. Vestry, St. James' Episcopal Ch., N.Y.C., 1979-84, treas. 1981-84; bd. trustees San Antonio Mus. Art, 1994—, San Antonio Mus. Assn., 1993—, The Witte Mus., 1994—, San Antonio Pub. Libr. Found., 1995—. Mem. River Club (N.Y.C.), Delphic Club (Cambridge, Mass.), Country Club (Prout's Neck, Maine), San Antonio Country Club, Argyle Club, Majestic Club (chmn. 1994-96). Home and Office: 550 Ivy Ln San Antonio TX 78209-2825

FUJIMOTO, ICHIRO, mathematics educator, researcher; b. Hyogo, Japan, Oct. 1, 1951; came to U.S., 1985; s. Shigeichi and Shizuko Fujimoto. BS in Physics, U. Tokyo, 1975; MS in Maths., Hiroshima (Japan) U., 1982; postgrad., U. Rochester, N.Y., 1985-86; PhD in Math., U. Fla., 1990. Vis. asst. prof. U. Fla., Gainesville. Mem. Math. Soc. Japan, Am. Math. Soc. Office: U Fla Dept Math Gainesville FL 32611

FUKUDA, AISAKU ISAAC, reproductive endocrinologist; b. Kyoto, Japan; s. Kenji and Akiko (Nishimura) F.; m. Kiyomi Hayata, Feb. 11, 1979; children: Ayumi, Aya. MD, Kansai Med. U., 1978; PhD, D of Med. Sci., Kyoto U., 1989. cert. Am. bd., of Bioanalysis, 1996. Resident in ob/gyn Kyoto U., 1978-80; dir. dept. ob/gyn Maizuru City Hosp., Kyoto, 1980-84, NTT Kyoto Hosp., 1988-89; dir. In Vitro Fertilization program Ishida Hosp., Osaka, Japan, 1989-90; from rsch. assoc. to dir. lab. assisted reproductive tech. East Tenn. State U., Johnson City, 1990—; asst. prof. ob/gyn East Tenn. State U., 1991—. Mem. Am. Soc. Reproductive Medicine, Soc. Study of Reproduction, mem. Am. Assn. of Bioanalysis, Japan Soc. Obstetrics and Gynecology. Home: 2104 Hickory Springs Rd Johnson City TN 37604 Office: East Tenn State U Dept Ob/Gyn Box 70569 Johnson City TN 37614

FUKUI, GEORGE MASAAKI, microbiology consultant; b. San Francisco, May 25, 1921; s. Tsunejiro and Kimiko (Wada) F.; m. Yuri Lillyn Kenmotsu, Sept. 23, 1944; children: Lisa Jo, Tenley Kay. BS, U. Conn., 1945, MS, 1948; PhD, Cornell U., 1952. Instr. bacteriology U. Conn., Storrs, 1948-49; lab. instr. Cornell U., Ithaca, N.Y., 1949-52, mem. adv. bd. microbiology dept., 1985-88; asst. br. chief U.S. Army, Frederick, Md., 1952-60; dir. microbiology and immunology Wallace Labs., Cranbury, N.J., 1960-77, Hazelton Labs., Vienna, Va., 1977-78; dir. microbiology Abbott Labs., North Chicago, Ill., 1978-79; rsch. microbiologist Abbott Labs., Irving, Tex., 1979-86; pres. Internat. Cons. in Microbiology, Irving, 1986—. Contbr. articles to sci. jours. Asst. scoutmaster troop 712, Boy Scouts Am., Topaz, Utah, 1943; recruiter Cornell U., Princeton, N.J., 1964-69. With U.S. Army, 1945-46. Recipient commendation Rsch. Soc. Am., 1959, medal for sci. achievement Hiroshima (Japan) U., 1973, Gran Amigo de Mex. commendation Nat. U. Mex., 1982, commendation Tohoku U., Sendai, Japan, 1983. Fellow Am. Acad. Microbiology (charter, diplomate); mem. Am. Soc. for Microbiology, Rutgers Soc. Japan (hon.), Phi Beta Kappa, Sigma Xi. Republican. Episcopalian. Home and Office: 3813 E Greenhills Ct Irving TX 75038-4819

FULCHER, HUGH DRUMMOND, author; b. Lynchburg, Va., Feb. 4, 1945; s. Lewis Page and Frances Louise (Drummond) F.; m. Cheryl Brenn Phelps, July 29, 1972 (div. July 1990); children: Keston Hugh, Kara Brenn. BS in Physics, Math., Va. Poly. Inst. and State U., 1967, MS in Nuclear Engring., 1970. Lic. nuclear reactor operator, Md. Physics instr. Va. Poly. Inst. and State U., Danville, 1968-69, Danville C.C., 1969-71; nuclear engr. Babcock & Wilcox Inc., Lynchburg, 1971-82, Energy Inc., Richmond, Va., 1982-85; computer engr. Ariz. Pub. Svcs., Phoenix, 1985-90; nuclear engr. Scientech, Inc., Rockville, Md., 1990-91; writer H.D. Fulcher Pubs., Inc., Lynchburg, 1992—; cons. engr. Fla. Power and Light, Miami, 1985, Westinghouse Svannah River, Aiken, S.C., 1991-92. Author: Emotional Mind Modeling, 1995. Argonne Nat. Lab. Grad. Engring. scholar, 1969. Methodist. Home: Rt 7 Box 62MB Lynchburg VA 24503 Office: H D Fulcher Publishers Inc Rt 7 Box 62MB Lynchburg VA 24503

FULDA, MICHAEL, political science educator, space policy researcher; b. Liverpool, Eng., Apr. 21, 1939; came to U.S., 1962, naturalized, 1966; s. Boris and Catherine (Von Dehn) F.; m. Rosa Bongiorno, July 19, 1970; children: Robert, George. Student Polytechnique, Grenoble, France, 1956-57, Tech. U., West Berlin, Germany, 1957-58, Karl Eberhardt U., Tubingen, Germany, 1963-66; MA, Am. U., 1968, PhD in Internat. Studies, 1970. Prof. polit. sci. Fairmont State Coll., W.Va., 1971—; internat. rls. specialist NASA, Washington, 1979; fellow NASA Marshall Ctr., Huntsville, Ala., summer 1977, Langley Ctr., Hampton, Va., 1976. Author: Oil and International Relations, 1979; (with others) United States Space Policy, 1985. Contbr. articles to profl. jours. Bd. dirs. Fairmont Chamber Music Soc., 1983—; W.Va. state com. chmn., dir. space policy Nat. Unity Campaign for John Anderson, 1980; mem. nat. adv. com. John Glenn Presdl. Com., 1984, space policy group Dukakis/Bentsen Com., 1988. With U.S. Army, 1962-66. Woodrow Wilson Found. fellow, 1969-70; Humanities Found. W.Va. grantee, 1978-80, NASA W.Va. Space Grant Consortium grantee, 1991—; named Del. to Aerospace States Assn. by the Gov. of W.Va.; Fellow AIAA (assoc.); mem. Am. Astronautical Soc., Nat. Space Soc. (dir. 1991-93), British Interplanetary Soc., Deutsche Gesellschaft fur Luft und Raumfamrt, Nat. Space Club, Inst. for the Social Sci. Study of Space (pres. 1988—), Assn. Argentina Tech. Space. Home: 1 Timothy Ln Fairmont WV 26554-1331

FULGHUM, ROBERT SCHMIDT, microbiologist, educator; b. Washington, Mar. 3, 1929; s. James Hooks and Frances (Witcraft) F.; m. Esther Marie Slagle, June 17, 1953; children: Robert Slagle, David James, Joseph Christopher. BS in Biology, Roanoke Coll., 1954; MS in Bacteriology, Va. Poly. Inst. and State U., 1959, PhD in Bacteriology, 1965. Approved cons. bacteriologist, Pa. Grad. asst. Va. Poly. Inst. and State U., Blacksburg, 1956-60; instr. Susquehanna U., Selinsgrove, Pa., 1960-63; asst. prof. Susquehanna U., Selinsgrove, 1963-64, N.D. State U., Fargo, 1964-68; asst. prof. Coll. Dentistry U. Ky., Lexington, 1968-71; dir. anaerobic products Robbin Lab. div. Scott Labs., Carrboro, N.C., 1971-72; assoc. prof. East Carolina U., Greenville, 1972-90, prof., 1990-96, asst. chair dept., 1989-96, prof. emeritus, 1996—; cons. Scott Labs., Fiskeville, R.I., 1972-73; cons., spkr. Norwich Eaton Pharm, Inc., 1987, Abbott Labs., Chgo., 1988, Otitis Media Rsch. Ctr. Children's Hosp., Pitts., 1988; program co-chmn. 3d ednl. strategies workshop tchg. microbiology and immunology Med. Students Assn., Med. Sch. Microbiology and Immunology Chairs, 1990, 4th ednl. stratgies workshop, 1992, 5th ednl. strategies workshop, 1994, 6th ednl. strategies workshop, 1996; mem. organizing com. Ednl. Strategies for Basic Scis. Workshop, Charleston, S.C., 1993. Regional editor newsletter The Anaerobist, 1973-75; contbr. articles to profl. jours. Troop committeeman, treas. Boy Scouts Am., Lexington, Ky., 1968-71, Greenville, 1981-83; bd. dirs. Wesley Found., Greenville, 1979-82; bd. dirs., fin. com. Greenville Community Shelter, 1989-91. With USAF, 1952-56. Rsch. grantee Nat. Inst. Dental Rsch., Washington, 1969, N.C. United Way, 1974, Deafness Rsch. Found., N.Y.C., 1979-88, Block Drug Co., N.J., 1991. Mem. Am. Soc. Microbiology (alternate councilor N.C. br. 1972, 83, ednl. rep. 1973-77, sec.-treas. 1978-81, 89-94, treas. 1994-96, v.p. 1983-84, pres. 1984-85, editor 1988—), Sigma Xi (Helms award 1982). Methodist. Home: PO Box 512 Greenville NC 27835-0512 Office: East Carolina U Dept Microbiology Greenville NC 27858

FULLARD, DANIEL, business education educator, retired, financial secretary; b. Tuberville, S.C., July 19, 1929; s. Henry Joseph and Estelle (Butler) F.; m. Merlene Singletary, June 6, 1961; children: Nathaniel, Samuel, Gwendolyn. BS, Benedict Coll., 1960; MEd, Clemson U., 1981. Farmer S.C., 1942-51; tchr. H.S. Sch. Dist. # 50, Greenwood, S.C., 1960-85, ret., 1985; ins. agt. N.C. Mut., Durham, 1985-88; sales and rental employee Good Cents Sales and Rental, Greenwood, 1989; assoc. credit dept. Rhodes Furniture Co., Greenwood, 1990; pres. S.C. Bus. Edn. Assn., Columbia, 1972-73. Author poems and songs. Cpl. U.S. Army, 1951-54. Mem. Am. Legion. (fin. com. 1991-96). Democrat. Baptist. Home: 116 Russell St Greenwood SC 29646

FULLER, IRA CALVIN, town manager; b. Wendell, N.C., Aug. 2, 1942; s. Herman Edward and Algie (Medlin) F. A in Criminal Justice, Nash C.C., Rocky Mount, N.C., 1982. Police officer Town of Wendell, N.C., 1966-69; asst. chief of police Town of Wendell, 1969-74, chief police, 1974-83, town mgr., 1983—. Mem. Internat. City Mgrs. Assn., Internat. Assn. Chiefs Police (assoc.). Democrat. Baptist. Home: PO Box 295 412 Old Zebulon Rd Wendell NC 27591-9335 Office: Town Wendell PO Box 828 Wendell NC 27591-0828

FULLER, LILLIAN MARY, radiation oncologist, educator; b. Stratford, Ont., Sept. 11, 1923; came to U.S., 1950; d. David Stanley and Grace Annie (Ellerby) F.; m. Rudolph Joseph Royer, Oct. 29, 1956 (dec. June 1974). MD, U. Western Ont. Med. Sch., 1947. Diplomate Am. Bd. Radiology. Intern Victoria Hosp., London, Ont., Can., 1947-48; sr. intern in pathology Gen. Hosp., Hamilton, Ont., Can., 1948-49; resident in radiology Strong Meml. Hosp., Rochester, N.Y., 1950-53; asst. radiologist Strong Meml. Hosp., Rochester, 1953-54; fellow in radiotherapy Sloan Kettering Inst., 1954-55; Am. Cancer Soc. fellow Radium Inst., Liverpool, England, 1956; asst. prof. M.D. Anderson Cancer Ctr., Houston, 1956-61, assoc. prof., 1961-80, prof., 1981—, dep. chmn. dept. clin. radiotherapy, 1986-90; vis. prof. Hematology Inst. Rio de Janeiro, 1987, Dept. Radiation Oncology U. Istanbul, 1990, King Faisal Specialist Hosp. and Rsch. Ctr., Riyadh, Saudi Arabia, 1991, Osler Inst., Hem. Inst. Rad. Oncol., Louisville, 1991. Editor, prin. author: Hodgkin's Disease and Non Hodgkin's Lymphomas in Adults and Children, 1988; contbr. articles to profl. jours. Recipient Svc. to Mankind award Leukemia Soc., Tex. Gulf Coast chpt., 1987, Past State Pres.' award Tex. Fedn. Bus. and Profl. Women, 1987. Fellow Am. Coll. Radiology; mem. Am. Radiol. Soc., Am. Soc. Clin. Oncology, Am. Soc. Therapeutic Radiology, Radiol. Soc. N.Am., Soc. Surg. Oncology. Home: 5111 Paisley St Houston TX 77096-4123 Office: MD Anderson Cancer Ctr 1515 Holcombe Blvd Houston TX 77030-4009

FULLER, MAXINE COMPTON, retired secondary school educator; b. Tiny, Va., Aug. 23, 1921; d. Perry and Lillie (Sutherland) Compton; m. David Thompson Fuller Jr., 1946 (dec. Mar. 1975); children: Davine Miller, Patricia Machen, Shirley Brodeur, Dorothy Brunson, David Thompson III. BS, Longwood Coll., 1943; MA, U. Ala., 1966; AA in Edn., U. Ala., Birmingham, 1980. Receptionist Goodyear Tire and Rubber Co., Richmond, Va., 1943; office mgr. trainee Goodyear Tire and Rubber Co., Selma, Ala., 1943-44; office mgr. Goodyear Service, Bessemer, Ala., 1944-46; sec., ops. mgr. Birmingham So. Coll., 1966; tchr. Manpower-Bessemer State Tech. Coll., 1966-68, McAdory High Sch., 1968-71; bus. edn. coord. Hueytown High Sch., 1971-88, ret., 1988; vis. com. mem. So. Assn. Secondary Schs. and Colls., 1980, 84. Sunday sch. tchr. Pleasant Ridge Bapt. Ch., Hueytown, Ala., 1962-88, pers. com., 1980-83; mem. Hueytown High PTA, 1986-87; liaison officer Adopt-A-Sch. program Hueytown High/Lloyd Noland Hosp., 1987-88; chmn. bus. edn. dept. Hueytown High Sch., 1971-88. Mem. NEA, Am. Vocat. Assn., Nat. Ret. Tchrs. Assn., Ala. Ret. Tchrs. Assn., Longwood Coll. Alumni Assn., Alpha Delta Kappa (corr. sec. XI chpt. 1982-84), Delta Kappa Gamma (treas. Gamma Lambda chpt. 1976-80), Echo Book Club (Bessember, pres. 1986-88, sec. 1994-96), Hueytown Culture Club (pres. 1994-96). Baptist.

FULLER, ORA, nursing administrator; b. Brenham, Tex., Nov. 5, 1944; d. Ella Mae Davis; m. Lonnie E. Fuller, Feb. 18, 1989. ADN, Coll. of the Mainland, 1974; BSN, U. Tex., Galveston, 1980, MS in Nursing, 1983. Lic. voc. nurse U. Tex. Med. Branch, Galveston, 1964-68; clinical supvr., charge nurse Meml. Hosp. Galveston County, Texas City, 1968-82; emergency room charge nurse Danforth Meml. Hosp., Texas City, 1982-83; instr. Coll. of the Mainland, Texas City, 1976-83; asst. dir. nursing U. Tex. Med. Branch Hosps., Galveston, 1983-85, dir. nursing, 1986-88; head nurse Emory U. Hosp., Atlanta, 1988-91; dir. patient svcs.-case mgmt. South Fulton Med.

Ctr., East Point, Ga., 1991—. Adv. com. Grad. Sch. Nursing Mgmt. Tract, 1985-88; bd. dirs. LaMarque Tigers Youth Football Assn., 1980; mem. Galveston Hist. Soc., 1986-88; coord. voter regirstration drives, 1980-92. Nursing scholar Ladies Aux. Mainland Ctr. Hosp., 1973, Pub. Svc. award NAACP, 1982. Mem. ANA, Am. Bus. Womens Assn., Am. Orgn. Nurse Execs., Ga. Orgn. Nurse Execs., Women Health Care Execs., Nat. Assn. Healthcare Quality, Ga. Assn. Healthcare Quality. Home: 190 Morning Springs Walk Fairburn GA 30213-3460 Office: 1170 Cleveland Ave East Point GA 30344-3600

FULLER, STEVEN EDWARD, accountant; b. Atmore, Ala., May 21, 1950; s. Joe Ivy and Lilly Grace (Griffith) F.; m. Linda Diane Simpson, Dec. 30, 1974; children: Crystal Ann, Brett Alan. AA, Albany (Ga.) Community Coll., 1973; BBA, Valdosta (Ga.) State Coll., 1975; MS in Mgmt., Fla. Internat. U., 1980. CPA, Fla. Revenue agt. IRS, Ft. Lauderdale, Fla., 1975-79; sr. mgr. Ernst and Young, CPA's, Ft. Lauderdale, 1979-90; ptnr. Adair, Fuller, Witcher & Malcom, P.A., CPAs, Ft. Lauderdale, Fla., 1990—. Bd. dirs., treas. Twig House Inc., Ft. Lauderdale, 1982-89; chmn. bd. dirs. Samaritan Ctr. South Fla., Ft. Lauderdale, 1989-91, bd. dirs., 1986-92; advisor planned giving adv. coun. Boys Club, Ft. Lauderdale, 1987; dep. treas. Nick Navarro for Sheriff, Ft. Lauderdale, 1987. Recipient Pres.'s Merit award Twig House, Inc., 1986. Mem. AICPA's, Fla. Inst. CPA's, Estate Planning Coun. of Broward County, Commerce Club of Ft. Lauderdale (bd. dirs. 1986—, pres. 1989). Republican. Episcopalian. Office: Adair Fuller Witcher & Malcom PA 100 W Cypress Creek Rd Fort Lauderdale FL 33309-2181

FULLER, SUSAN JOAN, broadcast executive; b. Rockwood, Tenn., Aug. 25, 1964; d. Richard David and Sylvia Joan (Sellars) F.; m. G. Christopher Elder, May 29, 1993. BS in Journalism, U. Tenn., 1986; postgrad., So. Sem., 1988-90. ESL tchr. Fgn. Mission Bd., Nagasaki, Japan, 1987; campus minister Roane State C.C., Harriman, Tenn., 1987-88, N.W. Bapt. Convention, Portland, Oreg., 1989-90; childcare worker Home of the Innocents, Louisville, 1988-89; news dir., sta. mgr. Radio Covington (Ga.), Inc., 1990—; news affiliate Ga. Network, Atlanta, 1990—, Channel 2 WSB-TV, Atlanta, 1990—. Recipient Comms. award Am. Cancer Soc., 1993. Mem. Ga. Assn. Broadcasters (Sta. of Yr. award 1991). Democrat. Office: WGSF-AM 1430 1151 Hendricks St SW Covington GA 30209-3733

FULLER, THEODORE, JR., elementary education educator; b. Hempstead, Tex., Nov. 4, 1937; s. Theodore and Bernice V. (Rutledge) F.; B.S., Prairie View (Tex.) A&M U., 1959, M.Ed., 1980. Tchr. vocat. agr., Richards, Tex., 1960; elem. tchr. Houston Ind. Sch. Dist., 1963—. Served with USAR, 1961-63. Mem. NEA, Nat. Council Tchrs. English, Assn. Childhood Edn., Assn. Supervision and Curriculum Devel., Internat. Reading Assn., Soc. Children's Book Writers, Tex. Tchrs. Assn., Houston Tchrs. Assn., Audubon Soc., Sierra Club, Nature Conservancy. Author feature stories, articles in field. Home: 7709 Claiborne St Houston TX 77016-3909 Office: 10130 Aldine-Westfield St Houston TX 77093

FULLER, WILLIAM HARRISON, technology company executive; b. Peru, Ind., Dec. 10, 1957; s. Gordon Lee and Betty Marie (Campbell) F.; m. Donna Marie Karrick, July 10, 1981. BS in Engring. Physics, U. Ariz., 1982. Project engr. Vega Biotechnologies, Tucson, 1981-83; systems engr. VISA Anasazi, Phoenix, 1983-86; v.p. Vidnetics Ltd., VISA, Phoenix, 1986-88; chief engr. Executone, Scottsdale, Ariz., 1988-89; v.p. Spectradyne Inc., Richardson, Tex., 1989—. Patentee in field. Mem. AAAS. Home: 728 Moddle Cave Plano TX 75023

FULLERTON, JYMIE LUIE, pharmaceutical company executive, consultant; b. Ft. Worth, Oct. 25, 1943; s. Vernon Luie and Ruth (Boyer) F.; m. Martha Jane Smothers; children: Laurie, Patrick, Tammie, Janie, Emily. BBA, Cen. State U., 1971, MBA, 1973. Tchr.-coordinator distributive edn. Stigler (Okla.) High Sch., 1971-72; regional sales rep. Johnson Wax, Racine, Wis., 1973-75; div. sales mgr. Fox-Vliet Retail Computer Service, Oklahoma City, 1975-77; corp. dir. computer services Fox-Vliet Drug Co., Oklahoma City, 1977-78; corp. sales mgr. Foxvliet Drug Co., Oklahoma City, 1978-79; v.p. merchandising Foxmeyer Drug Co., Oklahoma City, 1979-81, v.p. retail ops., 1981-83; v.p. healthmart Foxmeyer Drug Co., Dallas, 1983-84; div. pres. Okla. div. Foxmeyer Drug Co., Oklahoma City, 1985-86, sr. v.p. so. region, 1986-90, sr. v.p. of mktg. and bus. devel., 1990-93; pres. Foxmeyer Internat. Trading Co., 1990-93, A.T.I. Internat. Trading Corp., 1993—. Served with U.S. Army, 1966-69. Mem. Am. Mgmt. Assn., Nat. Drug Wholesalers Assn., Dallas. C. of C. Republican.

FULLERTON, THOMAS MANKIN, JR., economist; b. Ft. Worth, Aug. 31, 1959; s. Thomas Mankin and Katherine Jane (Copeland) F.; 1 child, Kristina Marie. BBA, U. Tex., El Paso, 1981; MS, Iowa Stata U., 1984; MA, U. Penn., 1988; PhD, U. Fla., 1996. Jr. economist El Paso (Tex.) Electric Co., El Paso, 1981-83; economist Exec. Office of the Gov., Boise, Idaho, 1984-87; internat. economist Wharton Econometrics, The WEFA Group, Bala Cynwyd, Pa., 1988-91; sr. economist U. Fla., Gainesville, 1991-96; rsch. assoc. U. Fla. Ctr. for Latin Am. Studies, Gainesville, 1991-96; asst. prof. U. Tex. El Paso, 1996—; regional economist Tex. Ctr. for Border Econ. Devel., 1996—; alternate, Nat. Gov.'s Assn. Energy Com., Boise, 1985-86; Idaho state expert, Wharton Econometrics Regional Network, Boise, 1986-87; Idaho coord., Fed. Program Population Estimates, Boise, 1985-87; broadcaster, Radio YSKL, San Salvador, El Salvador, 1976-77. Sponsor Save the children, Bogota, Colombia, 1985—; Dem. precinct mgr., Boise, 1986; commr, U. Tex. Student Election Bd., El Paso, 1978-79, mortar bd. U. Tex., El Paso, 1981. Dean's fellow, Wharton Sch., 1987-88. Mem. Nat. Assn. Bus. Economists (policy panel 1989—, forecast panel 1984-88), Phila. Coun. Bus. Economists, Wharton Alumni Assn., Phi Kappa Phi, Alpha Chi. Presbyterian. Office: Dept Econs and Fin UTEP El Paso TX 79968-0543

FULLINGIM, JOHN POWERS, consulting firm executive; b. Amarillo, Tex., Dec. 10, 1951; s. Jim F. and Wanda (Powers) F.; m. Kristin Kepner, Apr. 27, 1979. BA, Baylor U., 1975; MBA, U. Tex., Dallas, 1979. Broadcaster Sta. KVIL Radio, Dallas, 1976-79; regional sales mgr. Control Data Corp., Dallas, 1979-83; dir. mktg. TOCOM Div. Gen. Instrument, Dallas, 1983-87; pres. Addison Mktg. Group, Dallas, 1987—. Author: Professional Services Marketing, 1988, Strategic Value Selling Using Financial Modeling, 1989, Whole Brain Marketing, 1994; contbr. articles to profl. jours.; patentee in field. Bd. dirs., officer 500 Inc., Dallas, 1984-87; v.p. mktg. dir. Allegro Dallas, 1987-90; advisor So. Meth. U. Bus., Dallas, 1988—; bd. dirs. Theatre Three, Dallas, 1991—; grad. Leadership Dallas, 1988. Mem. Am. Mktg. Assn. (exec.), Junto II Dallas (founder, sec. 1988—), Univ. Club of Dallas (chmn. mem. com. 1994—). Office: Addison Mktg Group 15851 Dallas Pky Ste 725 Dallas TX 75248-3360

FULMER, ROBERT IRWIN, gynecologist; b. Phila., Feb. 14, 1936; s. Wilmer Paul and Roberts Crawford (Irwin) F.; m. Grace Earlene Anderson, Sept. 2, 1961 (dec. Apr. 1995); children: Robert Paul, Thomas Scott; m. Patricia Ann, Seidenberg, Nov. 24, 1995. BA in Philosophy, Rice U., 1959; MS with honors, Baylor U., 1963; MD, Baylor Coll. Medicine, 1966. Diplomate Am. Bd. Ob-Gyn.; lic. physician, Tex. Rotating intern Baylor Affiliated Ben Traub and Jeff Davis Hosps., Houston, 1966-67; resident Baylor Affiliated Hosps., Houston, 1967-70; obstetrician-gynecologist Gynics Assocs., Austin, Tex., 1972-76; pvt. practice specializing in ob-gyn. Austin, 1976-87, pvt. practice specializing in gynecology and infertility, 1987—; rsch. asst. Bio-Med. Rsch., Austin, 1992-94; active staff St. David's Cmty. Hosp., 1972—, Seton Med. Ctr., 1988—, Seton N.W. Hosp., 1991—, Austin Diagnostic Med. Ctr. Hosp., 1996—; mem. courtesy staff Breckenridge Hosp., Austin, 1993—. Maj. USAF, 1970-72. Fellow ACOG, Am. Fertility Soc., Tex. Assn. Ob-Gyn.; mem. AMA, Tex. Med. Assn. (alt. rep. 1970-72), South Ctrl. Ob-Gyn. Soc. (state rep. 1980-84, pres. 1995-96), Travis County Med. Soc. Republican. Episcopalian. Home: 7601 Ridgestone Dr Austin TX 78731-1453 Office: 805 E 32nd St Ste 203 Austin TX 78705-2529

FULP, ESTELLE MARIE, retired nursing administrator; b. Braddock, Pa.; children: Linda M. Creedon, Carole A. Rhodes, Janice C. Rowe. Diploma, Braddock Gen. Hosp. Sch. Nursing, 1944; BSN, Duquesne U., 1962; MPH, U. N.C., 1966. Pub. health nurse supr. State of Pa., Greensburg; nursing cons. N.C. Div. Health Svcs., Raleigh; chief nurse N.C. Dept. Environ. Health & Natural Resources, Raleigh. Recipient Margaret B. Dolan award, Fiquett-Holley award. Mem. ANA, APHA, N.C. Nurses Assn. (bd. dirs., chmn. multiple constituency assn. 13, past pres., pres.-elect, past chmn. mgmt. com., 1st v.p., Outstanding Svc. Bd. Dirs. award), Nat. League for Nursing, N.C. Pub. Health Assn., N.C. Woman's Forum, Sigma Theta Tau, Delta Omega.

FULP, JAMES ALAN, securities firm executive; b. Kernersville, N.C., July 11, 1951; s. Charles Lee and Doris (Allen) F.; m. Patricia Jane Withers, May 19, 1973 (div. Apr. 1984); children: Jonathan Charles, Brian Emory; m. Sally Jo Case, Dec. 4, 1984; 1 child, Casey Vance. BA, N.C. State U., 1973; MBA, Wake Forest U., 1975. Comml. loan officer First Union Nat. Bank, Charlotte, N.C., 1975-78; v.p. Citizens Fidelity Bank and Trust, Louisville, 1978-81; pres. Hilliard-Lyons Equipment Mgmt., Inc., Louisville, 1981-84, Walnut St. Securities, Inc., St. Louis, 1984-90; sr. v.p. Robert Thomas Securities, Inc., St. Peterburg, 1990—. Mem. Internat. Assn. for Fin. Planning. Republican. Presbyterian. Office: Robert Thomas Securities Inc 880 Carillon Pky Saint Petersburg FL 33716-1102

FULP, SAM RUSSELL, gastroenterologist; b. Lexington, N.C., Feb. 24, 1957; s. Bill Russell and Charlotte Josephine (Leonard) F.; m. Robin Renee Waitman, Aug. 4, 1979; children: Julie Michelle, Andrew Michael. BS in Biol. Scis. magna cum laude, N.C. State U., 1979; MD, Wake Forest U., 1983. Intern Grady Meml. Hosp., Atlanta, 1983-84; resident Emory U. Affiliated Hosps., Atlanta, 1984-86; fellow in gastroenterology N.C. Bapt. Hosp., Winston-Salem, 1988-90; internist, med. dir. Athens (Ga.) Neighborhood Med. Ctr., 1986-88; internist, gastroenterologist Mecklenburg Med. Group, Charlotte, N.C., 1990—; lectr. in field. Contbr. articles to profl. jours. Mem. ACP, Am. Coll. Gastroenterology, Am. Gastroenterol. Assn., Am. Soc. Gastrointestinal Endoscopy, AMA, Crohn's and Colitis Found. of Am., Mecklenburg County Med. Soc., N.C. Med. Soc. Office: Mecklenburg Med Group 3535 Randolph Rd Charlotte NC 28211-5004

FULTON, JANE SLEETH, family and consumer science educator; b. Morgantown, W.Va., Sept. 21, 1949; d. Clark Kendall and Nellie J. (Strouss) Sleeth; m. David Michael Fulton, Nov. 8, 1969 (div.); children: Jeffrey Michael, Joseph David. BA, W.Va. U., 1971; MEd, The Citadel, 1996. Diversified coop. tng. coord. Monogalia County Schs., Morgantown, 1975-77; family and consumer scis. tchr. Charleston County Schs., Mt. Pleasant, S.C., 1978—; sponsor Students Against Drunk Driving, Mt. Pleasant, 1986-88, Future Homemakers of Am., Mt. Pleasant, 1978-96, Miss Wando Pageant, Mt. Pleasant, 1979-92, Teen Inst. of S.C., Florence, 1987-88. Den leader, asst. cubmaster Boy Scouts Am., Mt. Pleasant, 1978-82, 85-92. Mem. NEA. Methodist. Office: Wando High Sch 1560 Mathis Ferry Rd Mount Pleasant SC 29464

FULTON, JOE KIRK, JR., banker, investor; b. Lubbock, Tex., Sept. 12, 1957; s. Joe Kirk Sr. and Mary Alice (Braselton) F. Student, Tex. Tech U., 1976-79. Profl. motorcycle racer, 1970-76; diesel mechanic R.H. Fulton, Inc., Lubbock, Tex., 1970-76; specialist Pantera Specialist Inc., Calif., 1976-78; sec.-treas. Quien Sabe Investments, Lubbock, 1979—;, 1982-87; pilot Profl. Airshows, 1979—; with Kirk Fulton Gen. Contractor, Inc., Lubbock, 1988—, Paige & Fulton Constrn., Lubbock, 1988-89; field rep. Robbe Model Sport, 1988—; ptnr. Sierra Home Builders, Lubbock, 1991—. Recipient numerious aerobatic flying awards. Mem. Internat. Coun. Airshows, Nat. Aerobatics Assn., Internat. Aerobatic Club (v.p. 1986-89), Aircraft Owners and Pilots Assn., Exptl. Aircraft Assn., Fedn. Aero. Internat., Am. Model Aeros., Profl. Banker's Assn. Republican. Office: Quien Sabe Investments 1601 W Loop 289 Lubbock TX 79416-5124

FULTON-ADAMS, DEBRA ANN, nurse practitioner; b. Anne Arundel, Md., Dec. 16, 1961; d. William D. and Patricia A. (Rensel) Fulton; m. Howard T. Adams, June 3, 1995. BSN, U. Tex., Galveston, 1983, MSN, 1986. Advanced RN practitioner, Fla.; cert. profl. nurse practitioner. Clin. nurse specialist Arnold Palmer Hosp. for Childen and Women, Orlando, Fla., 1988; pediatric and internal medicine nurse practitioner Office of Dr. Shirley Nagel, Mt. Dora, Fla., 1991-92; project leader in med. policy-med. rev.-fraud and abuse Medicare Fraud Br., Jacksonville, Fla., 1993-96, med. cons., outreadh educator, project mgr., 1996—; med. cons., 1996—; advanced RN practitioner part time Dr. Perry G. Carlos, 1996—. Home: 1210 Signal Point Dr Jacksonville FL 32225-4560 Office: Medicare Fraud Br 532 Riverside Ave Ste 11 T Jacksonville FL 32202-4914

FULTS, KENNETH WYATT, civil engineer, surveyor; b. Center, Tex., Feb. 20, 1949; s. Raymond Weldon and Dovie Marie (Tindal) F.; m. Carolyn Kay Barnett, Feb. 27, 1971 (div. Aug., 1985); 1 child, Wendy Carol. BS in Civil Engring., Tex. A&M U., 1971. Engring. asst. Tex. Dept. Transp., Crockett, Tex., 1971-73; design engr. Tex. Dept. Transp., Lufkin, Tex., 1973-76; dist. lab. engr. Tex. Dept. Transp., Lufkin, 1976-85, dist. planning engr., 1985-89; bituminous engr. Tex. Dept. Transp., Austin, 1989-90, soils and aggregate engr., 1990-93, dir. pavements, 1993—; chmn. Coll. Curriculum Com., Lufkin, Tex., 1988-89; instr. pavement design, Tex. Dept. Transp., Austin, 1990, asphalt mix design, 1990-91; co-chmn. Joint Spl. Devel. Com., Austin, 1993—. Contbr. reports to Tex. Dept. Transp. Publs. Regional pres. Tex. Pub. Employee Assn., Region II, Tex., 1976; chmn. bd. dirs. Dist. II Credit Union, Lufkin, Tex., 1978-82. Mem. ASCE (v.p. 1989), ASTM, Transp. Rsch. Bd., Assn. State Hwy. and Transp. Officials (jt. task force 1993—), NCHRP. Mem. Ch. of Christ. Home: 111 Powder Horn Trail San Marcos TX 78666 Office: Tex Dept Transp 125 E 11th St Austin TX 78701

FUNDERBURK, AMY ELIZABETH, artist, art educator, exhibition coordinator; b. Charlotte, N.C., Feb. 16, 1966; d. Carl Lee and Dorothy Jean (Hooks) F.; m. James Carl Williams, Oct. 26, 1991. BS in Graphic Design summa cum laude, Appalachian State U., 1988. Art instr. Sawtooth Ctr. Visual Art, Winston-Salem, N.C., 1989—, graphics coord. asst., 1990-91, acting graphics coord., 1991, 92; art instr. Forsyth Tech. C.C., Winston-Salem, N.C., 1989—; exhbns. coord. Winston-Salem Forsyth County Arts Coun., 1992-96, Babcock Sch., Worrell Profl. Ctr. Bus. Mgmt., Wake Forest U., Winston-Salem, 1996—, Greater Winston-Salem C. of C., 1993—. Illustrator: (book) Candle Lovefeast, 1990; one person shows include Louise Gilbert Meml. Art Gallery, Mitchell Cmty. Coll., Statesville, N.C., 1994, Davidson County Mus. Art, Lexington, N.C., 1994, Parsons Gallery, Spartanburg (S.C.) Mus. Art, 1996; exhibited in group shows at Catherine Smith Gallery, Appalachian State U., Boone, N.C., 1987, 88, 93, 95, Milton Rhodes Gallery, Winston-Salem, 1993, 95, Delaplaine Visual Arts Ctr., Frederick, Md., 1994, Woman Made Gallery, Chgo., 1995, Davidson County Mus. Art, Lexington, 1995; represented in permanent collections including Forsyth Tech. C.C. Emerging artist fellowship grantee Winston-Salem County Arts Coun., 1990-91; recipient hon. mention Ctr. Gallery, 1991. Mem. Assoc. Artists of Winston-Salem (bd. dirs. 1991-95, v.p. 1994-95, pres. 1996—), Davidson County Mus. Art (hon. mention Spotlight '95 juried art exhbn. 1995, annual members open exhbn. 1995). Home and Office: 416 Corona St Winston Salem NC 27103-2817

FUNDERBURK, DAVID B., congressman, history educator, former ambassador; b. Langley Field, Va., Apr. 28, 1944; married; 2 children. B.A., Wake Forest Coll., 1966; M.A., Wake Forest U., 1967; Ph.D., U. S.C., 1974. Instr. Wingate (N.C.) Coll., 1967-69, U. S.C., Columbia, 1969-70; assoc. prof. history Hardin-Simmons U., Abilene, Tex., 1972-78; prof. history Campbell U., Buies Creek, N.C., 1978-81, 85-86; U.S. ambassador to Romania Bucharest, 1981-85; cons. U.S. Dept. Edn., 1987-88; mem. Nat. Edn. Com. on Internat. Ednl. Programs, 1987-90, 104th Congress from 2nd N.C. dist., Washington, DC, 1995—. Candidate for U.S. Senate from N.C., 1986; exec. dir. Conservatives for Freedom Polit. Action Com., 1988-94; chmn. Internat. Romanian Relief Fund, 1990-94; chmn. U.S. Coalition to Recognize Croatia, 192; elected to U.S. Congress, 1994. Office: US Congressman 427 Cannon HOB Washington DC 20515

FUNDERBURK, H(ENRY) HANLY, JR., college president; b. Carrollton, Ala., June 19, 1931; s. Henry Hanly and Mary (Ferguson) F.; m. Helen Hanson, July 26, 1953; children: Debra Funderburk Dahl, Kenneth. BS in Agrl. Sci., Auburn U., 1953, MS in Botany, 1958; PhD, La. State U., 1961. Asst. dean grad. sch. Auburn U., 1967-68, pres., 1980-83, Alumni prof., 1966; v.p., chief adminstrv. officer Auburn U., Montgomery, 1968-78, chancellor, 1978-80; dir. govt. and community affairs Auburn U., Montgomery, Montgomery, 1983-84; pres. Ea. Ky. U., Richmond, 1985—. 1st lt. U.S. Army, 1953-55. Mem. Kiwanis (hon. life Montgomery), Rotary, Sigma Xi, Phi Kappa Phi, Alpha Zeta, Gamma Sigma Delta, Omicron Delta Kappa. Methodist. Home: 507 Lancaster Ave Richmond KY 40475-2150 Office: Ea Ky U Office of President Richmond KY 40475

FUNDORA, THOMAS, artist, journalist, composer; b. Havana, Cuba, Mar. 7, 1935; came to U.S., 1960; s. Evangelio and Juana Evangelina (Rodriguez) F.; m. Marlene Delgado, Feb. 10, 1954 (div. June 1957). Degree in art journalism, Candler Coll., 1953; degree in modern art and restoration, Escola Arte Bologna, Italy, 1961; student, Escuela San Alejandro, Havana, 1950. Dir. gen., dir. exhbns. Fundora Gallery, Miami, Fla.; pres., bd. dirs. Song Festival, N.Y.C., Internat. Song Festival, Trujillo, Internat. Song Festival, Chiclayo, Festival of Song, Buenos Aires, Internat. Song Festival, Viña del Mar, Miami, others; former sr. v.p. Record World, Internat. Music Rev. mag.; pub., editor USA 23 Millones, Miami. Author: Union Panamericana, Washington, 1959, Galeria Duneen Graham, N.Y.C., 1959, Condon Relley Gallery, N.Y., 1959, Muestra Arquitectonica Neocolonial Colegio de Arquitectos, Havana, 1959, Emociones, 1963 (award 1964), Lo Mejor de Mi Vida, 1984, Inquietudes, 1988 (award 1990), Tu y Ellos, 1989; exhbns. include Lyceum de La Havana, 1949, Asociacion de Reporters, Havana, 1954, Galeria Gratacielo, Milan, 1961, Galeria del Canale, Venice, Los Grandes de Am., Hotel Woodstock, N.Y., 1964, Mamma Leones Art Show, N.Y., 1965, Glovier Club, N.Y., 1965, Exposition of Contemporary Art, Hotel Turistas, Trujillo, Peru, 1965, IRT Art Exhibit, Bklyn., 1966 (medalla de plata), Internat. Exhibition Friends of P.R., N.Y.C., 1967, Bienal de Sao Paulo, 1967, Roland de Aenlle Gallery, N.Y., 1967, Cayre Art Exhibit, 1968, Strokes and Motion of Light and Matter, Miami, 1989-90, Martin's Art Gallery, Coral Gables, Fla., 1990. Mem. Assn. Painters N.Y. (pres. 1969-73). Republican. Home: 205 Camelot Dr Tavernier FL 33070-2805 Office: Fundora Art Gallery 103400 Overseas Hwy Key Largo FL 33037

FUNK, CHARLOTTE MARIE, art educator, artist; b. Milw., Sept. 27, 1934; d. Ernest Louis and Stacy Cecile (Radomski) Mueller; m. Verne James Funk, June 8, 1956; children: Tracy B., Kory V., Christopher J. BS, U. Wis., 1972; MS, Ill. State U., 1975, MFA, 1976. Instr. art dept. Tex. Tech. U., 1978—; instr. Arrowmont Sch. Arts & Crafts Summer program, 1981, spring 1988. One-person shows include McMurray U., Alilene, Tex., 1993, Hueser Art Ctr., Bradley U., 1990; exhibited in group shows at UT-PB, Odessa, Tex., 1993, Nat. Juried Exhbn., Iowa City, 1992, 93, Arrowmont Collection Eastern Shore Art Ctr., Fairhope, Ala, 1993, Nat. Women's Art Exhbn., Eastern New Mex. U., 1992, Textile Arts Ctr., Chgo., 1990, Waco Art Ctr., 1988, Downey Mus., Calif., 1987, Milw. Art Mus.,1987, Tenn. Fine Arts Ctr., Nashville, 1985, West Tex. Mus., 1985, and others. Mem. Am. Craft Coun. Home: 2312 58th St Lubbock TX 79412-2534

FUNK, ELLA FRANCES, genealogist, author; b. Domino, Ky., Apr. 7, 1921; d. Roy William and Edna Rene (Cummins) Roach; m. Eugene Boyd Funk, June 20, 1942; children: Susan Teresa, Eugene Boyd. B of Liberal Studies, Mary Washington Coll., 1982. Exec. sec. Lang. Labs., Inc., Bethesda, Md., 1969-70; office mgr. legal firm Donovan Leisure Newton & Irvine, Washington, 1970-76; genealogist, hist. researcher, writer, 1976—; class lectr., bd. dirs. Mary Washington ElderStudy Program; vol. Assn. Preservation Va. Antiquities; mem. Presbyn. Ch., Fredericksburg, Va. Named Exec. of Week, Sta. WGMS, Washington, June 1975; recipient Blue Ribbon winner for poem Va. Fedn. Women's Clubs, 1994. Life mem. Nat. Geneal. Soc.; mem. Hist. Fredericksburg Found., DAR, Alpha Phi Sigma, Sigma Phi Gamma. Club: Woman's (Fredericksburg, Va.). Lodge: Order Eastern Star. Author: Cummins Ancient, Cummins New, vol. 1, 1978, vol. 2, 1980, Joseph Funk, a biography, 1984, Benjamin's Way, 1988, (short stories) Christmas In The Abbey, 1988 (ribbon winner 1989), Dangerous Mission (Va. Fedn. Women's Clubs ribbon 1991), The Phobia (Va. Fedn. Women's Clubs ribbon 1994), My Son and the Westwind (Women's Club blue ribbon 1996). Recipient ribbon for poem "The Good Ship", 1990. Home: 4405 Turnberry Dr Fredericksburg VA 22408-9548

FUNK, GARY LLOYD, control engineer; b. Fairfax, Okla., Oct. 12, 1944; s. George N. and Maymie Lou (Harrell) F.; BS, Rose Hulman Inst. Tech., 1966; MS, Purdue U., 1969; PhD, U. Pitts., 1974. Registered profl. engr., Okla., Tex. Rsch. engr. systems control div. Gulf Rsch. & Devel. Co., Harmarville, Pa., 1969-72, engr. exploration div. on systems and instrumentation, 1972-75; systems and control engr. Applied Automation subs. Phillips Petroleum Co., Bartlesville, Okla., 1975, mem. process tech. div., 1975-77, sr. process control engr. computer systems, 1977-83, prin. engr., 1983-87; mgr. process control application and simulation tech. combustion engring. Simcon, Houston, 1987-88; dir. advanced control tech., Brown & Root, USA, Inc., Houston, 1988-91; dir. computer intergrated mfg. processor Cooper and Lybrand Mgmt. Consulting Svcs., 1991-92. V.P. Computer Integrated Mfg. Process Industry, Systemhouse Inc., 1992—; chief scientist, 1993-95, prin. cons., 1995—. Precinct chmn. Democratic Com., 1981. Mem. Okla. Soc. Profl. Engrs. (v.p. 1980-81, 82-83), IEEE, AIChE (treas. mgmt. divsn. 1995, 96, pres. chpt. 1983-84), Nat. Soc. Profl. Engrs., Tex. Soc. Profl. Engrs., ISA (nat. dir. automatic control divsn. 1996), Jaycees, Masons, Moose, Elks, Kiwanis. Presbyterian. Contbr. 69 articles to profl. jours.; 31 patents in field. Home: 600 S 6th St Fairfax OK 74637-5002

FUNK, SMITH ADAM, construction executive; b. Washington, Oct. 12, 1925; s. Raymond Adam and Vera May (Smith) F.; m. Irene Tolis, Nov. 28, 1946; children: Susan Karen Funk Nute. BArch, U. Notre Dame, 1950, BCE, 1952; postgrad., Fairleigh Dickinson U., 1966-67. Registered architect, profl. engr.; cert. roof cons. Architect, engr. Chas. W. Cole & Son, South Bend, Ind., 1950-56; architect design and sales dept. Reynolds Metals Co., Chgo., 1956-62; architect Whirlpool Corp., St. Joseph, Mich., 1962-63; archtl. rsch. mgr. Barrett div. Allied Chem., Morristown, N.J., 1963-67; mgr. product devel. Jim Walter Rsch. Corp., St. Petersburg, Fla., 1967-76; gen. mgr. tech. adminstrn. Celotex Corp., Tampa, Fla., 1976—; faculty mem. Roofing Industry Edn. Inst., Denver, 1985—; adv. panel Oak Ridge (Tenn.) Nat. Lab., 1986—; chmn. Hillsborough County Roof Adv. Com., Tampa, 1989—. Patentee plastic roofing system. Active Conservative Caucus, Washington, Children's Home, Tampa, Salvation Army, Tampa. With USNR, 1944-46. Mem. AIA, Structural Engring. Assn. Ill., Naval Inst., Am. Concrete Inst., Roof Cons. Inst. Presbyterian. Home: 5016 W Dickens Ave Tampa FL 33629-7515 Office: Celotex Corp 4010 W Boy Scout Blvd Tampa FL 33607-5727

FUNK, VICKI JANE, librarian; b. Frankfurt am Main, Hesse, Fed. Republic of Germany, Apr. 7, 1951; d. George N. and Maymie Lou (Harrell) F.; m. David Robert Koble, July 11, 1986. BS, Ind. State U., 1971; MLS, Okla. U., 1975; cert. in comparative libraries, Oxford U., Eng., Summer 1978; cert. in Scottish lit., St. Andrews U., Scotland, Summer 1985. Elem. open concept team tchr. Plainfield (Ind.) Pub. Schs., 1971-72; media specialist, tchr. elem. schs. Enid (Okla.) Pub. Schs., 1972-73, librarian, 1973-74; libr. media specialist Bartlesville (Okla.) Sr. H.S., 1975—; chmn. library evaluation teams North Cen. Assn., Okla., 1982-86; pres. V.I.E.W. adv. bd. Okla. State Dept. Vocat. Edn., 1980-81; tchr. pub. library continuing adult edn. program, Bartlesville, 1986. Storyteller Ednl. TV Bartlesville Cable, 1975-77, Oral Children's Program Pub. Library, 1985-86; book reviewer Okla. State Dept. Libraries "Gushers and Dusters", 1986-87; mem. book rev. selection com. Bartlesville Pub. Library. V.P. Friends of the Pub. Library, Bartlesville, 1986. Recipient Outstanding Svc. award Okla. Dept. Vocat. Edn., 1981; Emiline Libr. scholar Ind. State U., 1970; Innovative Edn. grantee Bartlesville Pub. Edn. Found., 1990, 91. Mem. NEA, AAUW (edn. officer 1980-81), Okla. Edn. Assn., Bartlesville Edn. Assn., Bartlesville Art Assn., Okla. Libr. Assn., Kappa Kappa Iota (v.p. 1990-91). Democrat. Presbyterian. Office: Bartlesville Sr High Sch 1700 Hillcrest Dr Bartlesville OK 74003-5825

FUNK ORSINI, PAULA ANN, health economist; b. Marietta, Ohio, May 16, 1956; d. James Corwin and Inez Aline (Smith) Funk; m. Michael Joseph Orsini, May 4, 1991. BS, Ohio State U., 1979, MS, 1986, PhD, 1992. Pharmacy resident Hosp. of U. Pa., Phila., 1979-80; staff pharmacist Nursing Ctr. Svcs., Hilliard, Ohio, 1984-85; mktg. rsch. assoc. Strategic Mktg. Corp., Bala Cynwyd, Pa., 1986; staff pharmacist Hahnemann U. Hosp., Phila., 1986-87, Mt. Carmel East Drugstore, Columbus, Ohio, 1987-91, Ohio State U. Hosps., Columbus, 1980-86, 87-91; asst. prof. U. Md., Balt., 1991-95; sr. dir. health econs. Parexel State and Fed. Assocs., Alexandria, Va., 1995—; presenter in field. Author: (with others) Modern Medicine Dermatology Pocket Guide, 1982; reviewer Am. Jour. Hosp. Pharmacy, 1987; contbr. articles tp profl. publs., including Jour. Pharm. Mktg. and Mgmt., Am. Jour.

Hosp. Pharmacy, Hosp. Pharmacy, Hosp. Formulary. Scholar in pharm. scis. IAPS-Am. Found. Pharm. Edn., 1988; Nat. Assn. Bds. Pharmacy-Am. Found. Pharm. Edn. fellow in pharmacy adminstrn., 1990, Albert B. Fisher Jr. PhD Citation fellow Am. Found. Pharm. Edn., 1989. Mem. Coun. Grad. Students in Pharm. Scis. (pres. 1990-91), Am. Assn. Pharm. Scientists, Am. Soc. Hosp. Pharmacists, Am. Pharm. Assn., Assn. for Consumer Rsch., Am. Mktg. Assn., Assn. for Health Svcs. Rsch., Rho Chi. Office: State & Fed Assocs 1101 King St Ste 600 Alexandria VA 22314-9999

FUQUA, JAMES FRANKLIN, pharmaceutical executive; b. Shelbyville, Tenn., Feb. 12, 1954; s. James F. and Mary Ruth (Simpkins) F.; m. Sena Kay Steenbergen, Dec. 19, 1981; children: Sena Meredith, Bradley Elizabeth. BA in Biology, Vanderbilt U., 1976. Dir. influenza vaccination program Met. Health Dept., Nashville, 1976-78; head coach women's track Vanderbilt U., Nashville, 1977-79; hosp. rep. Merck & Co., Inc., Nashville, 1979-81; corrd. health edn. Merck & Co., Inc., West Point, Pa., 1981-82; assoc. dir. field devel. Merck & Co., Inc., West Point, 1987-92; dist. mgr. Merck & Co., Inc., Houston, 1982-87; region exec. Merck & Co., Inc., Birmingham, Ala., 1992-96; cons. orgnl. devel. and corp. change Performance Impact, Inc., San Diego, 1989-92. Bd. dirs. Mountain Brook (Ala.) Athletics, 1996—; pres., bd. dirs. 4215 Harding Rd. Homeowners, Nashville, 1977-80. Named Best Trained Sales Force, Fin. World Mag., 1991. Mem. Mid. Tenn. Soc. Healthcare Execs., Mountain Brook Swim/Tennis Clubb. Republican. Methodist. Home: 4527 Pine Mountain Rd Mountain Brook AL 35213 Office: Merck & Co Inc 5 Concourse Pkwy Ste 2430 Atlanta GA 30328

FUQUA, JOHN BROOKS, retired consumer products and services company executive; b. Prince Edward County, Va., June 26, 1918; s. J.B. Elam and Ruth F.; m. Dorothy Chapman, Feb. 10, 1945; 1 son, John Rex. Grad. high sch., Prospect, Va.; LLD (hon.), Hampden-Sydney Coll., 1972, Duke U., 1973, Fla. Meml. Coll., 1982, Oglethorpe U., 1986; LHD (hon.), Queens Coll., 1987, Longwood Coll., 1990; LLD (hon.), U. Tulsa, 1991, Mercer U., 1991; DHL (hon.), Queens Coll., Charlotte, 1995; D in Adminstrn. (hon.), Cumberland Coll., 1995. Chmn. Fuqua Industries, Inc., Atlanta, 1965-89; mem. adv. bd. Norfolk So. Corp.; established Ctr. for USSR Mgr. Devel., tng. program for top Soviet mgrs. at Fuqua Sch. Bus. Duke U., 1990. Mem. Augusta Aviation Commn., 1945-67; past mem., fin. chmn. Augusta Hosp. Authority; past mem. Ga. Sci. and Tech. Commn.; mem. Ga. Ho. of Reps., 1957-62, chmn. House Banking Com., 1959-63; mem. Ga. Senate, 1963-65, chmn. Senate Banking and Fin. Com., Dem. Party and Exec. Com. Ga., 1962-66; bd. visitors Emory U., 1970-76; former mem. adv. council Ga. State U.; former trustee Ga. State U. Found.; trustee Duke U., 1974-87; trustee Hampden-Sydney Coll., 1976-91; bd. dirs. Horatio Alger Assn. Disting. Americans; bd. dirs. Lyndon B. Johnson Found; bd. visitors Fuqua Sch. Bus., Duke U.; past dir. Atlanta C. of C.; donor $10 million to found Fuqua Sch. Bus., Duke U., 1980, $5.5 million to build the Dorothy Chapman Fuqua Conservatory, Atlanta Bot. Gardens, 1989, $10 million to establish Fuqua Sch., Va., 1993; founder Internat. Sch. Christian Comm., 1991, $3 million to establish the Faqua Heart Ctr. of Atlanta at Piedmont Hosp., 1995, $1.5 million to Atlanta Com. for Spl. Games, 1996. Recipient Horatio Alger award, 1984, award U. Pa. Wharton Grad. Sch. Bus., 1985, Disting. Entrepreneurship award, 1985, Free Enterprise medal Entrepreneur of Yr. Shenandoah Coll., 1991; named Boss of Yr. Augusta Jaycees, 1960, Broadcaster-Citizen of Yr. Ga. Assn. Broadcasters, 1963, Broadcast Pioneer of Yr., 1979, Outstanding Bus. Leader Northwood Inst., 1986, Mktg. Statesman Sales and Mktg. Execs. Internat., 1986, Bus. Statesman Harvard Bus. Sch. Club Met. Atlanta, 1987, Georgian of Yr., 1989, Philanthropist of Yr. Ga. chpt. Nat. Soc. Fund Raising Execs., 1989, Philanthropist of Yr. Nat. Assn. Fund Raising Execs., 1993, Entrepreneur of Yr. Stanford Bus. Sch. Alumni Assn., 1992, Pinnacle award Sales and Mktg Execs. Internat. Acad. Achievement, 1993, Fellow of the Coll. award Capitol Coll., 1994; The Fuqua Heart Ctr. of Atlanta at Piedmont Hosp. named in his honor. Mem. Chief Exec. Orgn. Home: 3574 Tuxedo Rd NW Atlanta GA 30305-1049 Office: The Fuqua Cos 1201 W Peachtree St NW Ste 5000 Atlanta GA 30309-3400

FURBAY, WALTER M., economist; b. Cardington, Ohio, May 27, 1920; s. Walter R. and Leta (Young) F.; BS, Ohio State U., 1941; MS, 1956, PhD, 1960; m. Margie V. Beckwith, June 18, 1941 (dec.); children: Rebecca Lee, Virginia Dale; m. Camelia G. Tuthill Apr. 3, 1980. Vocat. agr. tchr. Ohio schs., 1941-44, h.s. tchr., 1946-52; sales Bankers Life Ins. Co., Des Moines, 1952-54; vocat. agr. tchr. Ohio h.s., 1954-56; econ. rschr. Ohio Agrl. Expt. Sta., 1957-60; agrl. economist Campbell Soup Co., 1960-63, U.S. Dept. Agr., Farmer Coop. Svc., 1964-68; head bus. and econs. dept. King's Coll., 1968-81, Shelton Coll., Cape May, N.J., 1981-87; mem. Madagascar Survey Team, 1966. Served to lt. USNR, 1944-46. Mem. Am. Mktg. Assn., Am. Econ. Conv., Gamma Sigma Delta. Mem. Soc. of Friends. Lodges: Lions, Kiwanis. Address: 224 Southwinds Dr Sarasota FL 34231-4062

FURCHTGOTT, ERNEST, psychology educator; b. Zlate Moravce, Czechoslovakia, Nov. 2, 1922; came to U.S., 1938; s. Bela and Sara (Schor) F.; m. Mary Wilkes, July 23, 1953; children: David G., Harold W., Margaret N. Frazier. BA, U. Calif., L.A., 1946, MA, 1948, PhD, 1950. Asst. prof. to prof. psychology U. Tenn., Knoxville, 1949-69; prof. psychology U. S.C., Columbia, 1969-92, head dept. psychology, 1969-78, disting. prof. emeritus, 1992—; cons. VA, 1955—; NIH grant rev. com., Bethesda, 1963-78. Contbr. articles to profl. jours. Named Phi Kappa Phi Lectr., U. Tenn., 1969; recipient Rosamond Boyd award, S.C. Gerontol. Soc., NIH Career Devel. award, U. Tenn., 1963-68. Fellow APA, Gerontology Soc. Am.; mem. S.E. Psych. Assn. (mem. coun. 1968-71). Home: 4600 Perry Ct Columbia SC 29206

FURCI, JOAN GELORMINO, early childhood education educator; b. Torrington, Conn., Jan. 3, 1939; BS, Western Conn. State Coll., Danbury, 1960; MS, U. Hartford, 1966; Ed.D., Nova U., Ft. Lauderdale, Fla., 1975. Tchr., Conn., 1960-68, dir. Early Childhood Program Univ. Sch., Nova U., 1971-90; asst. prof. Nova Coll., 1990-94, early childhood tchr., N.C. Tng. and Tech. Assistance Ctr., Morganton, 1995—; cons. Early Childhood Program, N.Y., N.C., 1968—; bd. dirs. United Way Child Care Centers, Broward County. Pres. Kids in Distress, 1987-88. Mem. Nat. Assn. for Edn. Young Children, Assn. for Childhood Edn. Internat. Home: 281 Cold Creek Rd Canton NC 28716-9612

FURGIUELE, MARGERY WOOD, vocational educator; b. Munden, Va., Sept. 28, 1919; d. Thomas Jarvis and Helen Godfrey (Ward) Wood; BS, Mary Washington Coll., 1941; postgrad. U. Ala., 1967-68, Catholic U. Am., 1974-76, 80; m. Albert William Furgiuele, June 19, 1943; children—Martha Jane Furgiuele MacDonald, Harriet Randolph. Advt. and reservations sec. Hilton's Vacation Hide-A Way, Moodus, Conn., 1940; sec. TVA, Knoxville, 1941-43; adminstrv. asst., ct. reporter Moody AFB, Valdosta, Ga., 1943-44; tchr. bus. Edenton (N.C.) H.S., 1944-45; tchr. bus., coord. Culpeper (Va.) County High Sch., 1958-82; ret., 1982; tchr. Piedment Tech. Edn. Ctr., 1970—. Co-leader Future Bus. Leaders Am., Culpeper, mem. state bd., 1979-82; state advisor 1978-79, Va. Bus. Edn. Assn. Com. chmn., 1978-79. Certified geneal. record Searcher; author of two books, contbr. articles to profl. jours. Mem. Am. Orchid Soc., African Violet Soc., Country Club (Culpeper). Home: 1630 Stoneybrook Ln Culpeper VA 22701-3336

FURLOW, EDWARD PENNINGTON, consulting forester; b. Lakewood, Ohio, June 4, 1924; s. Calvin Edward and Emmie Nancy (Pennington) F.; m. Marjorie Graves, Sept. 8, 1946 (dec. May 1970); children: Edward Jr., Harold, Calvin; m. Margaret Diehl, Nov. 27, 1971 (div. June 11, 1980); m. Anne Stewart, Aug. 22, 1981 (dec. May 13, 1984); m. Birgit Andersen, June 14, 1986. BS in Forestry, Purdue U., 1949, MS in Forestry, 1950; postgrad., George Wash. U., 1964-65. Registered forester, Md., W.Va. Trust officer Washington Loan and Trust, 1951-52; West African rep. Fordom Forest Products Corp., N.Y.C., 1950-52; svc. forester Va. Forest Svc., Charlottesville, 1952-55; acting dir. ops., dir. investigation, chmn. staff Tariff Commn. and Internat. Trade Commn., Washington, 1955-83; owner, cons. forester Edward P. Furlow Forest Products, Arlington, Va., 1983—. Contbr. articles to profl. publs. Asst. Office of V.P. Spiro Agnew, Washington, 1969; staff aide Congressman George Bush, Washington, 1969. With U.S. Army, 1942-46, ETO, lt. col. USAR, 1948-76. Decorated Bronze Star with oak leaf cluster, Meritorious Svc. medal and Combat Medics badge, U.S. Army; Congl. fellow Am. Polit. Sci. Assn., 1968-69. Mem. Assn. Cons. Foresters, Soc. Am. Foresters, Va. Forestry Assn., Xi Sigma Pi. Home: 4876 Old Dominion Dr Arlington VA 22207-2743 Office: E P Furlow Forest Products 4876 Old Dominion Dr Arlington VA 22207-2743

FURMAN, HOWARD, mediator, lawyer; b. Newark, Nov. 30, 1938; s. Emanuel and Lilyan (Feldman) F.; m. Elaine Sheitleman, June 12, 1960 (div. 1982); children: Deborah Toby, Naomi N'chama, David Seth; m. 2d Janice Wheeler, Jan. 14, 1984. BA in Econs., Rutgers U., 1966; JD cum laude, Birmingham Sch. Law, 1985. Bar: Ala. 1985, U.S. Dist. Ct. (no. dist.) Ala. 1986, U.S. Dist. Ct. (so. dist.) Ala. 1996. Designer/draftsman ITT, Nutley, N.J., 1957-61; pers. mgr. Computer Products Inc., Belmar, N.J., 1962-64, Arde Engrng. Co., Newark, 1964-66; econs. instr. Rutgers U., New Brunswick, N.J., 1966-74; dir. indsl. rels. Harvard Ind. Frequency Engrng. Labs. Divsn., Farmingdale, N.J., 1966-74; commr. Fed. Mediation and Conciliation Service, Birmingham, Ala., 1974-96; pvt. practice specializing in mediation and arbitration, Birmingham, 1985—; instr. bus. law Jefferson State C.C., 1989-95; instr. human resources mgmt. Nova U., 1993; prof. personal property, adminstrv. law, sales and alternative dispute resolution Birmingham Sch. Law, 1993—. Pres. Ocean Twp. Police Res. (N.J.), 1968. Recipient ofcl. commendation Fed. Mediation and Conciliation Svc., 1979, 81, 82, 88. Mem. ABA, Ala. Bar Assn., Birmingham Bar Assn., Ala. Trial Lawyers Assn., Soc. Profls. in Dispute Resolution, Fed. Soc. Labor Rels. Profls., Indsl. Rels. Rsch. Assn., Sigma Delta Kappa. Jewish. Home: 900 Kathryne Cir Birmingham AL 35235-1722 Office: Fed Mediation and Conciliation Svc 900 Kathryne Cir Birmingham AL 35235-1722

FURNISH, SHEARLE LEE, English and modern languages educator; b. Denver, Mar. 30, 1953; s. C. Wilbur and Ruth S. Furnish; m. Karen F. Merris, July 29, 1984 (div. Feb. 1990); m. Patricia Lee Huneycutt, May 18, 1990. AB in English Lit., Transylvania U., 1975; MA in English Lit., U. Ky., Lexington, 1978, PhD in English Lit., 1984. Teaching asst. dept. English U. Ky., 1975-81, instr., 1981-84; vis. asst. prof. dept. lit., lang. and comm. U. N.C., Asheville, 1984-86; asst. prof. dept. English Meredith Coll., Raleigh, N.C., 1986-89; asst. prof. dept. English and modern langs. West Tex. State U. (now West Tex. A&M U.), Canyon, 1989-93, assoc. prof., 1993—; presented papers various confs. Publs. com. Panhandle-Plains Hist. Rev., 1991—; editorial bd. KPA Bull., 1985; contbr. articles to profl. jours. Bd. dirs. Friends of the Cornette Libr., West Tex. A&M U., 1993—. Grantee West Tex. State U., 1990, West Tex. A&M U., 1990, 94. Mem. Modern Lang. Assn., Southeastern Medieval Assn., Panhandle-Plains Hist. Soc., Assn. for Study Lit. and Environ., New Chaucer Soc., Medieval and Renaissance Drama Soc., Tex. Medieval Assn., Coll. Lang. Assn. Democrat. Home: 2606 14th Ave Canyon TX 79015-5518 Office: West Tex A&M U PO Box 908 Canyon TX 79015-0908

FURRER, JOHN RUDOLF, retired manufacturing business executive; b. Milw., Dec. 2, 1927; s. Rudolph and Leona (Peters) F.; m. Annie Louise Waldo, Apr. 24, 1954; children: Blake Waldo, Kimberly Louise. B.A., Harvard U., 1949. Spl. rep. ACF Industries, Madrid, 1949-51; asst. supr. thermonuclear devel. and test Los Alamos, Eniwetok Atoll, 1952-53; dir. product devel. ACF Industries, N.Y.C., 1954-59; dir. machinery, systems group, central engrng. labs. FMC Corp., San Jose, Calif., 1959-68, gen. mgr. engineered systems div., 1968-70; v.p. in charge planning dept., cen. engrng. labs. and engineered systems div. FMC Corp., Chgo., 1970-71; v.p. material handling group FMC Corp., Chgo., 1971-77, v.p. corp. devel., 1977-88, sr. v.p., 1988-90. Patentee in field. Trustee Ravinia Festival, 1986-90. Served with USN, 1945-46. Mem. ASME, Coun. Planning Execs. (chmn. conf. bd. 1986-87), Harvard Club N.Y.C., Riomar Bay Yacht Club, Mid-Am. Club, Chgo. Yacht Club, Vero Beach Yacht Club, Ocean Reef Club. Home: 203 Spinnaker Dr Vero Beach FL 32963-2953

FURST, ALEX JULIAN, thoracic and cardiovascular surgeon; b. Augusta, Ga., Aug. 21, 1938; m. George Alex and Ann (Segall) F.; m. Elayne Kobrin, Aug. 11, 1962; children: James Andrew, Jeffrey Michael, Joseph Robert. Student, U. Fla., 1963; M.D., U. Miami, 1967. Intern U. Miami Hosp., 1967-68, resident, 1968-72, clin. instr. dept. surgery, 1974-91; chief resident in thoracic and cardiovascular surgery Emory U. Hosp., Atlanta, 1972-73, sr. surg. registrar of thoracic unit, 1972-73; sr. surg. registrar of thoracic unit Hosp. for Sick Children, London, 1973-74; practice medicine specializing in thoracic and cardiovascular surgery Miami, Fla.; assoc. prof. surgery and cardiology, chief surg. svc. Miami VA Med. Ctr., 1991—, prof., surgery and medicine; chief thoracic surgery, pres. med. staff Mercy Hosp.; mem. staff Bapt. Hosp., South Miami Hosp., Doctor's Hosp. (all Miami), North Ridge Gen. Hosp., Ft. Lauderdale. Served with U.S. Army, 1958-60. Fellow Am. Coll. Cardiology, Am. Coll. Chest Physicians, A.C.S.; mem. Dade County Med. Assn., Fla. Med. Assn., Heart Assn. Greater Miami, Soc. Thoracic Surgeons, So. Thoracic Surg. Assn. Home: 8802 Arvida Dr Miami FL 33156-2302

FURSTMAN, SHIRLEY ELSIE DADDOW, advertising executive; b. Butler, N.J., Jan. 26, 1930; d. Richard and Eva M. (Kitchell) Daddow; grad. high sch.; m. Russell A. Bailey, Oct. 1, 1950 (div. Oct. 1967); m. William B. Furstman, Dec. 24, 1977. Asst. corporate sec. Hydrospace Tech., West Caldwell, N.J., 1960-62; sec. to pres. R.J. Dick Co., Totowa, N.J., 1962-63, Microlab, Livingston, N.J., 1963; asst. corporate sec. Astrosystems Internat., West Caldwell, N.J., 1963-65; corporate sec. Internat. Controls Corp., Fairfield, N.J., 1965-73; sec. to pres. Global Financial Co., Nassau, Bahamas, 1974-75; office mgr. Internat. Barter, Nassau, 1975-76; sec. to pres., corp. sec. Haas Chem. Co., Taylor, Pa., 1976-77; asst. to pres., pub. Am. Home mag., N.Y.C., 1977-78; v.p., office mgr. Gilbert, Whitney & Johns, Inc., Whippany, N.J., 1979-95; ret., 1996. Home: 4 Oceans West Blvd # 606D Daytona Beach FL 32118

FUSELIER, LOUIS ALFRED, lawyer; b. New Orleans, Mar. 26, 1932; s. Robert Howe and Monica (Hanemann) F.; m. Eveline Gasquet Fenner, Dec. 27, 1956; children: Louis Alfred, Henri de la Claire, Elizabeth Fenner. B.S., La. State U., 1953; LL.B., Tulane U., 1959. Bar: La. 1959, Miss. 1964, U.S. Supreme Ct. 1965. Trial atty. NLRB, New Orleans, 1959-62; v.p., ptnr. Young, Williams, Henderson & Fuselier, P.A., Jackson, Miss., 1994—. Capt. USAF, 1953-56. Fellow Am. Acad. Hosp. Attys.; mem. ABA (practice and procedure com. of labor law sect.), La. Bar Assn. (past chmn. labor law sect.), Am. Law Inst., Miss. Bar Assn., Hinds County Bar Assn., Miss. Bar Found., Miss. Def. Lawyers, Miss. Wildlife Fedn. (pres. 1975-77), Newcomen Soc., Soc. Human Resource Mgmt. (accredited pers. diplomate), Miss. Econ. Coun. (dir. 1996—), Miss. Mfrs. Assn., Boston Club (New Orleans), Country Club, Univ. Club (Jackson), Rotary. Home: 3804 Old Canton Rd Jackson MS 39216-3521

FUSSELL, RONALD MOI, aerospace engineer; b. Lakeland, Fla., Jan. 12, 1956; s. Moi Monroe and Ima Jean (Thomas) F.; children: Scott Monroe, Dayna Michelle. B in Profl. Studies, Barry U., 1993; grad., Fla. Inst. Tech., 1995. Diesel mechanic Refrigerated Transport, Inc., Dundee, Fla., 1975-76; pvt. investigation Rsch. Reports, Inc., Tampa, Fla., 1977-79; chief operator Mil. Affiliate Radio System, Taegue, Republic of Korea, 1979-80; avionics technician McDonnell Douglas Svcs., Inc., Dhahran, Saudi Arabia, 1982-83; quality control analyst avionics div. McDonnell Douglas Svcs., Inc., Taif, Saudi Arabia, 1983-84; program support tng. specialist avionics McDonnell Douglas Space Systems Co., Kennedy Space Center, Fla., 1986-89; ops. engr. Spacelab Life Scis. Mission1 McDonnell Douglas Space Systems Co., 1989-91; spacecraft avionic systems educator McDonnell Douglas Space Systems Co., Kennedy Space Center, Fla., 1986-91; pres. Advanced Human Techs., Inc., Titusville, Fla., 1988-90; ops. engr. McDonnell Douglas Space Systems Co., Kennedy Space Center, Fla., 1989-94; sr. program integration engr. McDonnell Douglas Space and Def. Sys., Kennedy Space Center, Fla., 1994-95, sr. mission engr., 1995—. Mem. Fla. Farm Bur. Served with USAF, 1976-82. NASA Launch honoree, 1988. Mem. Nat. Mgmt. Assn., McDonnell Douglas Mgmt. Assn. Democrat. Baptist. Home: 5120 Patricia St Cocoa FL 32927-3240 Office: McDonnell Douglas Space & Def Systems PO Box 21233 Kennedy Space Center FL 32815-0233

FUSTÉ, JOSÉ ANTONIO, federal judge; b. 1943. BBA, U. P.R., San Juan, 1965, LLB, 1968. Ptnr. Jimenez & Fuste, Hato Rey, P.R., 1968-85; judge U.S. Dist. Ct. P.R., San Juan, 1985—; prof. U. P.R., 1972-85. Office: US Courthouse CH-133 150 Carlos Chardon Ave Hato Rey San Juan PR 00918-1758

FUTRELL, ROBERT FRANK, military historian, consultant; b. Waterford, Miss., Dec. 15, 1917; s. James Chester and Sarah Olivia (Brooks) F.; m. Marie Elizabeth Grimes, Oct. 8, 1944 (dec. 1978); m. Jo Ann McGowan Ellis, Dec. 15, 1980. BA with distinction, U. Miss., 1938, MA, 1939; PhD in History, Vanderbilt U., 1950. Spl. cons. U.S. War Dept., Washington, 1946; historian USAF Hist. Office, Washington, 1946-49; assoc. prof. mil. history Air U., Maxwell AFB, Ala., 1950-51, prof., 1951-71, sr. historian, 1971-74, prof. emeritus mil. history, 1974—; professorial lectr. George Washington U., 1963-68; guest lectr. Air U. Squadron Officer Sch., Air Command and Staff Coll., Air War Coll., Air Force Acad., Army War Coll., Militärgeschichtliches Forschungsamt, German Fed. Republic, 1951—, Sch. Advanced Airpower Studies; participant Air Force Acad. Mil. History Symposia, 1968—, Militärgeschictliches Forschungsamt, Freiburg, German Fed. Republic, 1988; vis. prof. mil. history Airpower Rsch. Inst., Ctr. for Aerospace Doctrine Rsch. and Edn., Air U., 1982-85, hist. advisor to USAF project Corona Harvest, 1969-74; cons. East Avionics Svcs. & Tech., Inc., Chantilly, Va.; hist. advisor Lafayette Mus. Found., Air Force Acad., 1990. Author: Ideas, Concepts, Doctrine: A History of Basic Thinking in the United States Air Force, 1907-1964, 1971, rev. edit., 1907-84, 2 vols., 1989, The United States Air Force in Korea, 1950-1953, 1961, rev. edit., 1983, The United States Air Force in Southeast Asia: The Advisory Years to 1965, 1981, (with Wesley Frank Craven, James L. Cate) The Army Air Force in World War II, 1948-1958; contbr. chpts. to hist. books, articles to scholarly publs. Served to capt. USAAF, 1941-45, lt. col. USAF Res., ret. Recipient Meritorious Civilian Svc. award USAF, 1970, Exceptional Civilian Svc. decoration Sec. of USAF, 1973. Mem. Ala. Hist. Assn., The Ret. Officers Assn., SAR (pres. Montgomery County chpt. 1971-74), So. Hist. Assn., Air Force Hist. Found. (mem. editorial advisors 1969-81, trustee 1985—), Inst. Mil. Affairs, Montgomery Capital City Club, Kiwanis Club of Montgomery, Phi Eta Sigma, Pi Kappa Pi. Methodist. Address: 908 Lynwood Dr Montgomery AL 36111-2514

FUZEK, BETTYE LYNN, secondary education educator; b. Knoxville, Tenn., Oct. 24, 1924; d. Wallace Paul and Bess (Wallace) Bean; m. John F. Fuzek, May 31, 1943; children: Mary Ann, Mark Lynn, Martha Elizabeth. Student, U. Tenn., 1944-45, East Tenn. State U., 1959-64; BS, Milligan Coll., 1966; postgrad. summers, various schs., 1966—. Sci. tchr. Dobyns-Bennett High Sch., Kingsport, Tenn., 1969-72; subs. tchr. Sullivan County High Schs., Kingsport, 1973-86; violin tchr. Symphony Assn. of Kingsport Talent Edn. Prog., 1973-80, Kingsport Suzuki Assn., 1980-90; pvt. tchr. violin, 1990—; violinist Kingsport Symphony Orch., 1980-85. Tchr. Literacy Coun. Kingsport, Inc., 1990—. Mem DAR. Presbyterian. Home: 4603 Mitchell Rd Kingsport TN 37664-2125

FUZEK, JOHN FRANK, chemical consultant; b. Knoxville, Tenn., Dec. 21, 1921; s. John and Maria (Pucher) F.; m. Bettye Lynn Bean, May 31, 1943; children: Mary Ann, Mark Lynn, Martha Elizabeth. BS in Chem. Engring., U. Tenn., 1943, MS in Phys. Chemistry, 1945, PhD in Phys. Chemistry, 1947; post PhD fellow, Office Naval Rsch., 1947-48. Chemist Hercules Powder Co., Wilmington, Del., 1943-44; research chemist N. Am. Rayon Corp., Elizabethton, Tenn., 1948-55; head research physics dept. Beaunit Fibers, Elizabethton, 1955-66; sr. research chemist Tenn. Eastman Co., Kingsport, 1966-70; research assoc. chemicals div. Eastman Kodak Co., Kingsport, 1970-86; cons. Kingsport, 1986—. Author: (with others) (chpt.) Clothing Comfort, 1977, Water in Polymers, 1980; contbr. articles in Jour. Am. Chem. Soc., I&EC Product R&D, ASTM Standard News; patents dyeable polypropylene fibers, process for spinning viscose, silk-like polyester fiber, silk-like textile fiber; contbr. articles to profl. jours. Recipient Sci. Research award Oak Ridge (Tenn.) Inst. of Nuclear Studies, 1950. Fellow AAAS, ASTM (vice chmn. com. D-13 on textiles 1984-90, Cert. of Appreciation 1983, Merit award 1990), Am. Inst. Chemists (pres. Tenn. chpt. 1971-72); mem. Am. Chem. Soc. (nat. councilor 1964-66, chmn. N.E. Tenn. chpt. 1957-58, nat. alt. councilor 1978-80, Speaker of Yr. 1979), Fiber Soc. (Lectr. of Yr. 1980-81), Coblentz Soc., Am. Crystallographic Assn., Am. Assn. Textile Chemists and Colorists, Sigma Xi. Republican. Presbyterian. Home: 4603 Mitchell Rd Kingsport TN 37664-2125

GAA, PETER CHARLES, organic chemist, researcher; b. Springfield, Ill., Mar. 30, 1955; s. Peter Carl and Patricia (Stewart) G.; m. Sheila Bourque, Aug. 2, 1980; children: Lily, Charlie. BS in Chemistry, U. Notre Dame, 1977; PhD in Organic Chemistry, Ga. Tech. Inst., 1982. Rsch. chemist PPG Industries, Pitts., 1982-84, sr. rsch. chemist, 1984-87, rsch. project chemist, 1987-91, group leader, 1987-91, rsch. assoc., 1989-91; dir. R&D Wilsonart Internat., Temple, Tex., 1991—. Contbr. articles to profl. jours. Mem. TAPPI (vice chmn. div. indsl. nonwoven materials 1989—, chmn. tech. program div. nonwovens 1991-92), Am. Chem. Soc. (PPG Indsl. sponsor and rep. div. polymers 1987—), Product Devel. Mgmt. Assn., Adhesion Soc. Republican. Roman Catholic. Home: 600 S General Bruce Dr Temple TX 76504-5149 Office: Ralph Wilson Plastics 600 S General Bruce Dr Temple TX 76504-5149

GABBARD, (JAMES) DOUGLAS, II, judge; b. Lindsay, Okla., Mar. 27, 1952; s. James Douglas and Mona Dean (Dodd) G.; m. Connie Sue Mace, Dec. 30, 1977 (div. Feb. 1979); m. Robyn Marie Kohlhaas, June 18, 1981; children: Resa Marie, David Ryan, James Douglas III, Michael Drew. BS, Okla. U., 1974, JD, 1977; grad., Nat. Jud. Coll., 1987. Bar: Okla. 1978. Ptnr. Stubblefeild & Gabbard, Atoka, Okla., 1978; sole practice Atoka, 1979; asst. dist. atty. State of Okla., Atoka, 1979-82; 1st asst. dist. atty. State of Okla., Atoka, Durant and Coalgate, 1982-85; dist. judge 25th Jud. Dist. State of Okla., Atoka and Coalgate, 1985—; presiding judge South East Adminstrn. Dist., Okla., 1992—, State Ct. Tax Review, Okla., 1992—; presiding judge of emergency panel of State Ct. Criminal Appeals; dir. Okla. Trial Judges Assn.; mcpl. judge City of Atoka, 1978-79; atty. Town of Wapanucka, Okla., 1979-80; legal advisor Counties of Atoka, Coal and Bryan, 1982-85. Mem. Bryan County/Durant Arbitration Com., 1984; negotiator Bryan Meml. Hosp. Bd., Durant, 1984-85. Mem. Okla. Bar Assn. (legal ethics com. 1988-90, jud. adminstrv. com. 1988-90), YLD state law and edn. com. 1988-90), Nat. Dist. Attys. Assn., Okla. Jud. Conf., Nat. Jud. Coll. (regional planning com. 1988), Jaycees, Masons. Democrat. Methodist. Home: 1401 S Walker Dr Atoka OK 74525-3611 Office: County Ct House Atoka OK 74525

GABBARD, GREGORY NORMAN, poet; b. Ft. Smith, Ark., Oct. 4, 1941; s. Norman Walter and Weema Pauline (Littlejohn) G. BS, MIT, 1962; MA, U. Tex., 1964, PhD, 1968. Instr. English Old Dominion COll., Norfolk, Va., 1967-68; asst. prof. English N.Mex. Highlands U., Las Vegas, 1968-69, U. Nev., Reno, 1969-74; clk.-typist Red River Army Depot, Texarkana, Tex., 1983-91. Author: Tiger Webs, 1982, Dragon Raid, 1985, A Mask for Beowulf, 1990, Knights Errand, 1992. Recipient Boit Essay prize, MIT Humanities Dept., 1961, Boit Creative prize, 2d pl., 1961, 1st pl., 1962, John Masefield award Poetry Soc. Am., 1978. Home: 602 Cannon St New Boston TX 75570-2206

GABBERT, J(OSEPHINE) ANN, nurse, administrator; b. Ft. Worth, Feb. 19, 1956; d. Weldon Saye Darnell and Mary E. (Richards) Darnell Strasheim; children: Amanda, Maryann; m. Adam Gabbert. BS in Nursing, Mary Hardin Baylor Oll., Belton, Tex., 1978; postgrad., U Tex., Arlington, Dallas Bapt. U. Clinician II Surg. ICU/Recovery Rm. M.D. Anderson Hosp. and Tumor Inst., Houston, 1977-84; staff nurse emergency rm. DFW Med. Ctr., Grand Prairie, Tex., 1984-87; agcy. nurse Spl. Care Nurses, Dallas, 1988-89; nurse mgr. emergency rm. Charlton Meth. Hosp., Dallas, 1988-89; claims rep. AMNA Corp., Dallas, 1990; staff nurse emergency svcs. dept. Parkland Meml. Hosp., Dallas, 1990-92; PRN, staff nurse emergency rm., relief supr. Midway Park Med. Ctr., Lancaster, Tex., 1989-91, dir. home health, 1993-94; CEO, owner Elite Care II Home Health Agy., Midlothian, Tex. Mem. ANA, Tex. Nurses Assn. Home: 1033 Glen Oak Dr Burleson TX 76028-6267

GABEL, GEORGE DESAUSSURE, JR., lawyer; b. Jacksonville, Fla., Feb. 14, 1940; s. George DeSaussure and Juanita (Brittain) G.; m. Judith Kay Adams, July 21, 1962; children: Laura Gabel Hartman, Meredith Gabel Harris. AB, Davidson Coll., 1961; JD, U. Fla., 1964. Bar: Fla. 1964, D.C. 1972. With Toole, Taylor, Moseley, Gabel & Milton (and predecessor firms), Jacksonville, 1966-74, Gabel & Hair (formerly Wahl & Gabel), Jacksonville, 1974—; mem. Fla. Jud. Nominating Commn., 4th Circuit, 1982-86. Pres. Willing Hands, Inc., 1971-72; chmn. N.E. Fla. March of Dimes, 1974-

75; mem. budget com. United Way, 1972-74, chmn. rev. com., 1976; bd. dirs. Central and South brs. YMCA, 1973-79, Camp Immokalee, 1982-86; elder Riverside Presbyterian Ch., 1970-77, 80-86, 90-92, clk. session, 1975-76, 85-86, trustee, 1988-91; pres. Riverside Presbyn. Day Sch., 1977-79; chmn. Nat. Eagle Scout Assn., 1974-75; pres. Boy Scouts Am., North Fla. Coun. 1993-96, Silver Beaver award, 1978; trustee Davidson Coll., 1984-95; Norwegian Consul, 1989—; pres. Jacksonville Consular Corps., 1992-93, 96—. Capt. U.S. Army, 1964-66. Fellow Am. Coll. Trial Lawyers, Am. Bar Found.; mem. ABA (chmn. admiralty and maritime law com. 1980-81, chmn. media law and defamation torts com. 1988-89, tort and ins. practice sect.), World Assn. Lawyers (founding mem.), Am. Counsel Assn. (bd. dirs. 1980-82, pres. 1992-93), Assn. Trial Lawyers Am., Am. Judicature Soc., Maritime Law Assn. U.S. (bd. dirs. 1994—), Assn. Average Adjusters (overseas subsriber), Fla. Bar (chmn. grievance com. 1973-75, chmn. admiralty law com. 1978-79, chmn. media and communications law com. 1990-91), Acad. Fla. Trial Lawyers, Southeastern Admiralty Law Inst. (bd. govs. 1973-75), Duval County Legal Aid Assn. (bd. dirs. 1971-74, 81-84), Am. Inn of Ct. (master of bench, sec.-treas. 1990-95), Rotary of Jacksonville (bd. mem. 1982-84, 1988-89, pres. 1987-88). Democrat. Home: 1850 Shadowlawn St Jacksonville FL 32205-9430 Office: Gabel & Hair 76 S Laura St Ste 1600 Jacksonville FL 32202-5443

GABELER-BROOKS, JO, artist; b. Baton Rouge, Feb. 14, 1931; d. Gustav Adolph Jr. and Ruth Adelaide Stein; m. Charles Pierce Gabeler Jr., Feb. 17, 1951 (div. Feb. 1973); children: Ann Speed, Charles Pierce III, T. Dolph, Caroline Hart; m. Ralph Brooks, Aug. 8, 1990. BA, Stephens Coll., 1950; studied with Edward Betts, Judi Betts, Al Brouillette, Jeanne Dobie, Ray Ellis, Dong Kingman, Fred Messersmith, John Pike, Tony Van Hasselt, Millard W, ells. illustrator: (with others) The Golf Courses at the Landings on Skidaway Island, 1993. Currently showing at John Tucker Fine Arts, Savannah, Ga.; one-woman shows include Elliott Mus., Stuart, Fla., 1986, Scarborough House, Savannah, 1988; exhbns. include Fla. Watercolor Soc., Mus. Arts and Scis., Daytona, Fla., 1978, Brevard Art Ctr. and Mus., Melbourne, 1981, State Capitol, Tallahassee, 1982, Boca Raton Mus. Art, 1984, 86, Houston Pub. Libr., 1981, Galveston (Tex.) Art League, 1983; represented in permanent collections The Moody Found., Elliott Mus., The Rosenberg Libr., Transco Energy Co. Houston, Allied Bank of Seabrook, Tex. Mem. Fla. Watercolor Soc. (Pres.'s award 1981, 82, Purchase award 1986, signature life mem.), Salmagundi Club, Galveston Art League (pres. 1981-82, Purchase award 1982), Profl. Artist Guild, Landings Art Assn. (pres. 1990). Home: 11 Mainsail Crossing Savannah GA 31411-2723

GABERMAN, HARRY, lawyer, economic analyst; b. Springfield, Mass., May 6, 1913; s. Nathan and Elizabeth (Binder) G.; m. Ingeborg Luise Gruda, Sept. 24, 1953; children—Claudia Natalie Gaberman Razzook, Victor Lucius. JD George Washington U., 1941; LLM, Catholic U. Am., 1954. Bar: D.C. 1942. Atty.-investigator, atty.-advisor U.S. Mil. Govt. and U.S. High Commn. for Germany, Berlin, Frankfurt, Bonn, 1945-53, also indsl. specialist, bus. economist, legal and intercorp. relations analyst, asst. chief industry control sect.; asst. legal advisor and attache Am. embassy, Rome, 1953; dep. U.S. agent before Italian-U.S. Conciliation Commn.; sole practice, Washington, 1953-55; intelligence analyst Army Transp. Intelligence Agy., Gravelly Point, Va., 1955-56; supervisory atty.-advisor, atty.-advisor Air Force Systems Command, Andrews AFB, Md., 1956-75; asst. to U.S. mem. Four-power liquidation of German War Potential Com., Berlin, 1946; chief deconcentration br. U.S. High Commn., Frankfurt, 1949; acting dep. U.S. mem. law com. Allied Kommandatura, Berlin, 1951; U.S. mem. 3-power Film Reorgn. Com., Bonn, 1949-50; dep. U.S. agt. Italian-U.S. Conciliation Commn. Contbr. articles to profl. jours. Recipient Profl. Achievement award George Washington U. Law Alumni, 1983. Mem. Fed. Bar Assn. (chmn. govt. contracts council 1970-75, 78-79, dep. chmn. sect. internat. law, editor internat. law sect. newsletter, numerous Disting. Service awards, others), D.C. Bar Assn. (chmn. govt. contracts com. 1964-66), charter mem.. Diplomatic and Consular Officers Ret., Am. Fgn. Svcs. Assn., Air Force Assn. Avocations: walking, reading, listening to classic and semi-classic music. Address: 5117 Overlook Park Annandale VA 22003-4361

GABERT, HARVEY A., obstetrician, gynecologist, educator; b. Yorkton, Sask., Can., July 16, 1927; came to U.S., 1967; s. Robert and Emma (Wiedman) G.; m. Ave Maria Terre; children: Kathryn, Stephen (dec.), Susan. MD, U. Alta., 1962. Diplomate Am. Bd. Ob-Gyn., sub-bd. Maternal-Fetal Medicine. Asst. prof. U. Utah, Salt Lake City, 1967-73, assoc. prof., 1973-78; prof., dir. maternal-fetal medicine Tulane U., New Orleans, 1978-80, U. Tex., Galveston, 1980-82; prof., head ob-gyn. La. State Med. Sch., New Orleans, 1982—. Contbr. chpt. to book, numerous articles to profl. jours. Fellow Royal Coll. Surgeons (Can.), Am. Coll. Ob-Gyn. Republican. Methodist. Office: La State Med Sch Dept Ob-Gyn 1542 Tulane Ave New Orleans LA 70112-2825

GABLE, KAREN LYNN, social worker; b. Washington, Apr. 19, 1964; d. Edward Brennan and Dorothy Ann (Sear) G. BA, Mt. St. Marys Coll., 1986; MSW, Catholic U., 1994. Psychiat. tech. Chestnut Lodge Hosp., Rockville, Md., 1987-88, Psychiat. Inst. Washington, 1988-89; ropes therapist Baywood Hosp., Webster, Tex., 1989-90; aftercare counselor Psychiat. Inst. Wash., 1990-92; intern George Washington Univ. Med. Ctr., 1993-94; foster care and family preservation social worker No. Va. Family Svcs., Falls Church, 1995—; addictions cons. No. Va. Family Svc., Falls Church, 1994—. Mem. NASW, Nat. Assn. Alcoholism and Drug Abuse Counselors, Phi Beta Kappa. Roman Catholic. Home: 10809 Keller St Silver Spring MD 20902 Office: No Va Family Svc 100 N Washington St Falls Church VA 22046

GABOR, JEFFREY ALAN, insurance and financial services executive; b. Cambridge, Mass., July 7, 1942; s. Frank and Selma (Cluck) G.; m. Ann Steinholtz, June 15, 1963; children: Elissa, Andrea, William. Student, U. Miami, 1960-64. Cert. fin. planner. Pres. The Gabor Agy., Inc., Tallahassee, Fla., 1964—, Gabor Settlements Inc., Tallahassee, 1994—. Mem. Nat. Assn. Life Underwriters, Tallahassee Life Underwriters Assn. (bd. dirs. 1985—), Inst. CFP, Nat. Structured Settlements Trade Assn., Gen. Agts. and Mgrs. Assn. (pres. 1983-84), Million Dollar Round Table (life). Home: 3050 Fermanagh Dr Tallahassee FL 32308-3333 Office: Gabor Cos 3534 Thomasville Rd Ste 601 Tallahassee FL 32308-3413

GABRIEL, RICHARD WEISNER, lawyer; b. Greensboro, N.C., Nov. 2, 1949; s. George Deeb and Lillian (Weisner) G.; m. Elizabeth Diane Burton, June 23, 1979; children: Margaret Elizabeth, Richard Weisner Jr. AB, Duke U., 1971; MBA, U. N.C., Greensboro, 1977; JD, Wake Forest U., 1975. Bar: N.C. 1975, U.S. Supreme Ct. 1978, U.S. Tax Ct. 1981, U.S. Dist. Ct. (mid. dist.) N.C. 1975. Pvt. practice law Greensboro, 1975-77; mng. ptnr. Gabriel, Berry & Weston, Greensboro, 1978—; vis. lectr. Guilford Coll., Greensboro, 1977-81; counsel Internat. Home Furnishings Reps. Assn., High Point, N.C., 1988—. Co-author: (manuals) Proving Damages in North Carolina, 1989, Trial Advocacy in North Carolina, 1990, Trying the Automobile Injury Case in North Carolina, 1992-93, 95, Counseling the Small Business Client in North Carolina, 1996; contbg. articles to popular mags., 1988—; editor-in-chief Wake Forest Jurist, 1975. With N.C. Army N.G., 1971-77. Recipient award for exemplary svc. Upjohn Health Care Svcs., 1988, Presdl. Citation, IHFRA, 1991. Office: Gabriel Berry & Weston 214 Commerce Pl Greensboro NC 27401-2427

GADSON, RONALD CEDRIC, middle school educator; b. Hartford, Conn., Aug. 7, 1964; s. Rushiel Frederick and Mildred Anquinette (Thomas) G.; m. Dorethea Hall, Mar. 25, 1989; children: Alexis, Kiara. MAT in Social Scis., Grambling (La.) State U., 1988, BA in History, 1986; Cert. in Adminstrn. and Supervision, West Ga. Coll., 1995. Cert. tchr., Ga. Mid. sch. tchr. Randolph County Bd. Edn., Cuthbert, Ga., 1988-90, Cobb County Sch. Dist., Marietta, Ga., 1990-91, Stewart County Bd. Edn., Lumpkin, Ga., 1991-92; tchr. social scis. Atlanta Pub. Schs., 1992—; adj. prof. history Andrew Coll., Cuthbert, summer 1990; pvt. tchr. Motown/Biv10 Records, L.A., 1991; feature panelist Nat. Report on Edn., Jet Mag., 1995. African-Am. teenage male group developer. Named to Outstanding Young Men of Am., 1989. Mem. Ga. Coun. for Social Studies, Ga. Assn. Educators, Met. Atlanta Assn. for Classroom Edn., Alpha Phi Alpha. Democrat. Methodist.

GAEDE, JANE TAYLOR, pathologist; b. Washington, July 8, 1941; d. Raleigh Colston and Margaret (Lamb) Taylor; m. William Hanks Gaede, Feb. 12, 1966; children: Geoffrey Terence, Bruce Lucas. BA, U. Miss., 1962; MD, Duke U., 1966. Diplomate Am. Bd. Pathology. Intern in surgery N.C. Bapt. Hosp., Winston-Salem, N.C., 1966-67; resident in pathology Duke Med. Ctr., Durham, N.C., 1967-71, asst. prof. pathology, 1974—; asst. prof. pathology Med. Univ. S.C., Charleston, 1971-74; staff pathologist VA Med Ctr., Durham, 1974—. Author: Clinical Pathology for the House Officer, 1982. Fellow Am. Soc. Clin. Pathologists; mem. DAR (1st vice regent local chpt. 1992-94, regent 1996—), N.C. Soc. Pathologists. Presbyterian. Office: Duke Univ Med Ctr Dept Pathology PO Box 3712 Durham NC 27710

GAGE, DAVID FLOYD, business owner, entrepreneur; b. Rochester, N.Y., June 11, 1945; s. Ward Edward and Virginia Mary (Thibault) G. Grad., Art Inst. Pitts., 1966. Illustrator U.S. Dept. Navy, Alexandria, Va., 1971-75; visual info. specialist, art dir. Surface Warfare mag., Arlington, Va., 1975-88; arts and info. specialist Naval Sea Systems Command, Arlington, 1988-92; chmn. bd. dirs. The Graphic Edge Ltd., Reston, Va., 1989-91; pres., CEO The Advantage Group, Reka Micro-Fiber Non-Toxic Cleaning Products, Elcombe Systems, Ltd., The Mainstreet Messenger, Manassas, Va., 1990—, Lodestone Techs., Manassas, 1991—; cons. freelance comml. artist, computer graphics desktop pub. and design specialist, Manassas, Va., 1980—; artist Paintings by David F. Gage, Manassas, 1984—. Prin. works include legal and letterhead designs Com. To Re-elect Pres., 1984, emblem Surface Navy, 1985, flag Washington chpt. Naval Engrs., 1986; commd. paintings of Thoroughbred horses include Shadow, 1984, Alabama, 1986, Thoroughbred Horses, 1987, mag. covers, 1979, 82. With USN, 1966-71. Mem. Graphic Artist's Guild. Home: 8592 Liberia Ave Manassas VA 22110-4640 Office: The Advantage Group PO Box 2165 Manassas VA 22110-0824

GAGE, E. DEAN, university administrator; b. San Saba, Tex., Oct. 24, 1942; s. Jim M. and Mary Kathryn (Golden) G.; m. Kathy Hugo, Dec. 25, 1965; children: Michelle Renee, Andrea Nicole. BS, Tex. A&M U., 1965, DVM, 1966; MS, Auburn U., 1969. Diplomate Am. Coll. Vet. Surgeons. Rsch. assoc. Auburn (Ala.) U., 1966-68, asst. prof., 1969; asst. prof. Tex. A&M U., College Station, 1969-72, assoc. dean, 1982-88, exec. asst. pres., 1989, sr. v.p., provost, 1990-93, pres., 1993-94, exec. dir. ctr. exec. devel., 1995—; bd. dirs. Victorial Bank and Trust, Bryan, Tex. Mem. exec. bd. Tamu-BC Coun., College Station, 1990. Mem. AVMA, Am. Assn. for Accreditation Lab Animal Care (trustee, bd. dirs. 1990), Nat. Assn. State Univs. and Land Grant Colls., Am. Animal Hosp. Assn. (Veterinarian of Yr. 1983), Tex. Acad. Vet. Practice (Pres's. Achievement award 1989), Assn. Am. Vet. Med. Colls. (pres. 1986-87, chmn. coun. educators 1984-85), Am. Coll. Vet. Surgeons (bd. regents 1983-86). Baptist. Office: Tex A&M Univ M/S 4114 Office of Exec Devel College Station TX 77843

GAGE, GASTON HEMPHILL, lawyer; b. Charlotte, N.C., June 16, 1930; s. Lucius Gaston and Margaret (White) G.; m. Jane Basinger, July 11, 1959; children: Gaston Hemphill Jr., John Robert, Stephen Matheson. BA, Duke U., 1953; LLB, U. N.C., 1958. Bar: N.C. 1958, U.S. Ct. Appeals (4th cir.) 1964, U.S. Ct. Appeals (7th and fed. cirs.) 1983, U.S. Supreme Ct. 1965, U.S. Ct. Fed. Claims. Ptnr. Grier, Parker, Poe, Thompson, Bernstein, Gage & Preston, Charlotte, 1964-84, Parker, Poe, Thompson, Bernstein, Gage & Preston, Charlotte, 1984-90, Parker, Poe, Adams & Bernstein, Charlotte, 1990—. Dir. Elon Homes for Children, Elon Coll., N.C., 1986—, vice chair, 1995—; pres. Boys Town of N.C., Charlotte, 1974-78, A.G. Jr. High PTA, Charlotte, 1974-75, Mecklenburg Kiwanis, Charlotte, 1968; sec., ofcl. bd. Myers Park United Meth. Ch., Charlotte, 1970-72. Mem. ABA, N.C. Bar Assn., N.C. State Bar Assn., Mecklenburg County Bar Assn., Kiwanis (lt. gov. Carolinas dist. 1995-96). Methodist. Home: 324 Lockley Dr Charlotte NC 28207-2330 Office: Parker Poe Adams & Bernstein 201 S College St Charlotte NC 28244-0002

GAGE, JOHN, opera company executive; b. Grand Rapids, Mich., Nov. 25, 1937; s. John McKay and Frances Charlotte (Hulswit) Criner. BA, Wayne State U., 1965, MA, 1969. Instr. speech and theatre Heidelberg Coll., 1966-70; mem. faculty speech and theatre Hamline U., 1971-73; gen. mgr. Friar's Theatre, Mpls., 1971-72; artistic dir. Chimera Theatre Co., St. Paul, 1971-73; stage mgr. St. Paul Opera, 1972-74; gen. mgr. Theatrical Rigging Systems, Mpls., 1974-77; prodn. stage mgr. Dallas Civic Opera, also Miami Opera, 1977-80; gen. mgr. Florentine Opera Co., Milw., 1980-89, Opera Am.; gen. dir. Opera/Columbus, Ohio, 1989-91; dir. prodn. Dallas Opera, 1991—. Served with USAF, 1956-60.

GAGE, ROBERT CLIFFORD, minister; b. Beverly, Mass., Nov. 20, 1941; s. George V. and Elizabeth B. (May) G.; m. Mary Neefe, June 17, 1961; children: Joanna, Jonathan, Judith, Joshua, Joy. Student, Tenn. Temple U., 1961-62; BA, Phila. Coll. of Bible, 1964; postgrad., Ea. Bapt. Theol. Sem., 1966-67, New Sch. Soc. Rsch., 1975-76; D of Religion, Newport U., 1983. Ordained to ministry Gen. Assn. Regular Bapt. Chs., 1964. Pastor Whitehall Bapt. Ch., Phila., 1964-65, Glencroft Bapt. Ch., Glenolden, Pa., 1966-68; pastor 1st Bapt. Ch., Newfield, N.J., 1969-70, Hackensack, N.J., 1971-79; pastor Wealthy St. Bapt. Ch., Grand Rapids, Mich., 1979-88; evangelist, 1988-91; pastor Haven Bapt. Ch., Winter Haven, Fla., 1991—; radio min., 1965—. Author: The Birthmarks of the Christian Life, 1976, Our Life in Christ, 1978, The Pastor's Counseling Workbook, 1983, The Pre-Marriage Counseling Workbook, 1984, Discipleship Evangelism, 1985, Cultivating Spiritual Fruit, 1986, basic Discipleship, 1987, Why Me, Lord, 1988, The Unveiling, 1990; editor sword and Shield, 1969—; contbr. sermons to ch. publs.; weekly columnist Pers. Pub. Clinics, Winter Haven News Chief. Home: 1388 Avenue H SW Winter Haven FL 33880-2608 Office: 2105 King Rd SW Winter Haven FL 33880

GAHAGAN, THOMAS GAIL, obstetrician, gynecologist; b. Brush Valley, Pa., Apr. 14, 1938; s. Ben D. and Zula C. (Brown) G.; m. Mary A. Miller, Dec. 23, 1960; children: David, Diane, Kevin, Keith. BA, Washington and Jefferson Coll., 1960; MD, U. Pa., Phila., 1964. Diplomate Am. Bd. Ob/Gyn. Intern U. Ky., Lexington, 1964-65, resident in ob/gyn., 1965-68; group practice Dr. Jones and Kelch P.A., Newark, Ohio, 1970-71, Naples (Fla.) Ob/Gyn., 1971-85; pvt. practice Naples, 1985—. Capt. USAF, 1968-70. Fellow ACOG, Fla. Ob-Gyn. Soc.; mem. AMA, Am. Cancer Soc. (life, bd. dirs. Collier unit 1973-93, bd. dirs. Fla. div. 1976-91, pres. 1986-87, St. George medal 1990), Fla. Med. Assn., Collier County Med. Soc. (exec. com. 1989-94, pres.-elect 1991-92, pres. 1992-93). Republican. Presbyterian. Office: 700 2nd Ave N Ste 305 Naples FL 34102-5702

GAILLARD, GEORGE SIDAY, III, architect; b. Miami, Fla., Apr. 24, 1941; s. George Siday and Sarah Margaret (Crawford) G.; m. Charlalee Bailey, 1965 (div. 1969); m. Sylvia Gayle Bridgewater, July 18, 1977; 1 child, Barron Matthew. B.S., Ga. Inst. Tech., 1965; postgrad., Ga. State U. Registered architect Ga. Sole propr. Fox Magnanimus, Atlanta, Ga., 1971-78, Gaillard & Assocs., Atlanta, 1978-81, 1983—; mgr. design dept. Deca Inc., Miami, 1982. Sculpture exhibited in group shows at Piedmont Arts Festival, 1971, 73. Cubmaster Cub Scouts Am., Stone Mountain, Ga., 1988-89. With USMCR, 1962-68. Mem. AIA (chmn. liason com. So. Coll. Tech. for Atlanta chpt. 1989-90), Huguenot Soc. S.C., Clan Lindsay Assn. U.S.A. Inc. (Ga. rep. 1989-95), St. Andrew's Soc. Atlanta (bd. dirs.). Avocations: reading, camping, constructing and competing with blackpowder rifles.

GAINER, LEILA JOSEPHINE, media relations strategist, consultant; b. Balt., Dec. 4, 1948; d. Theodore and Leila Lee Dworkowski (dec.); stepmother: Madeline Dworkowski; m. Robert M. Gainer, Aug. 21, 1971. BA, Frostburg (Md.) State Coll., 1970. Reporter, editor Labor Law Guide, Coll. and Univ. Report, Commerce Clearing House, Inc., Washington; dir. Ctr. for Regional Action Nat. Assn. Regional Coun. Local Govts., Washington; dir. nat. affairs Am. Soc. for Tng. and Devel., Alexandria, Va.; dir. pub. rels. Lesnik, Himmelsbach, Wilson & Hearl, Advt. and Pub. Rels., Myrtle Beach, S.C.; freelance editor, writer. Co-author: Training in America: The Organization and Strategic Role of Training, Workplace Basics: The Essential Skills Employers Want, Workplace Basics: Training Manual, Training the Technical Workforce; author tng. monographs, articles on women's golf, golf course revs., and equipment. Honored by Pres. Carter for Leadership on 1980 Rural Devel. Act.

GAINES, PAUL B., airport executive. Dir. Dept. Aviation City of Houston; also dir. aviation Ellington Field, Houston Intercontinental Airport, William P. Hobby Airport. Office: Houston Tex Dept of Aviation PO Box 60106 Houston TX 77205-0106

GAINES, SARAH FORE, retired foreign language educator; b. Roxobel, N.C., Aug. 21, 1920; d. Stonewall Jackson Fore and Ethel Gattis; m. Clyde Ritchie Bell (div. 1974); m. John Coffman Gaines. AB, U. N.C., 1941, MA, 1944, PhD, 1968, MLS, 1982. Instr. U. N.C., Greensboro, 1967-69, asst. prof., 1970-75, assoc. prof., 1976-85, assoc. prof. emeritus, 1985—. Author: Charles Nodier, 1971; also articles, book revs. Home: 3017 Robin Hood Dr Greensboro NC 27408-2618

GAL, RICHARD JOHN, industrial engineer; b. Youngstown, Ohio, Oct. 30, 1957; s. John and Maria (Hesch) G.; m. Connie Marie Norton, 1996; children: Stephanie, Kristin. B in Engring., Youngstown State U., 1979; MBA, Ea. Mich. U., 1981. Indsl. engr. trainee Nat. Steel, Ecorse, Mich., 1979-81; indsl. engr. Republic Steel, Massillon, Ohio, 1981-84; div. indsl. engr. Avery, Painesville, Ohio, 1984-87; assoc. prin. engr. Sverdrup Tech., Niceville, Fla., 1987-94; quality dir. Sverdrup Tech., Elgin AFB, Fla., 1995—; examiner F.L. Sterling Award, 1995, 96, 97; IRCA auditor. Contbr. articles to profl. jours. Advisor Jr. Achievement, Canton, Ohio, 1981-82. Mem. Inst. Indsl. Engrs. (sr.), Am. Soc. Quality Engrs. Home: 125 Baywind Dr Niceville FL 32578-4801 Office: PO Box 1935 Eglin AFB FL 32542

GALANDIUK, SUSAN, colon and rectal surgeon, educator; b. N.Y.C., Mar. 6, 1957; d. Joseph and Dora (Neu) G.; m. Hiram C. Polk Jr., Dec. 22, 1991. BS cum laude, SUNY, Albany, 1976; MD summa cum laude, Julius Maximilians U., Wuerzburg, Germany, 1982. Diplomate Am. Bd. Surgery, Am. Bd. Colon and Rectal Surgery. Surg. intern Chirurgische Univ. Klinik, Julius Maximilians U., Wuerzburg, Germany, 1982-83; surg. intern Cleve. Clinic Found., 1983-84, surg. resident, 1984-88; Price fellow in surg. rsch., dept. surgery U. Louisville, 1988-89, instr. dept. surgery, 1990-91, asst. prof. dept. surgery, 1991—, assoc. prof., 1996—; colon and rectal surgery fellow Mayo Clinic, Rochester, Minn., 1989-90; presenter in field. Author chpts. to books; contbr. articles to profl. jours. Chmn. fund raising com. ARC, Louisville, 1993; chair med. adv. com. Ky. chpt. Crohn's and Colitis Found. Am., Louisville, 1993—. William E. Lower Fellow Thesis prize Cleve. Clinic Found., 1986. Fellow ACS, Am. Soc. Colon and Rectal Surgeons (mem. rsch. found. young rschrs. com., mem. program com. 1994—); mem. AMA, Am. Med. Women's Assn., Am. Soc. Microbiology, Am. Soc. Univ. Profs., Assn. Acad. Surgery, Assn. Surg. Edn., Assn. Women Surgeons, Collegium Internat. Chirurgiae Digestivae, Jefferson County Med. Soc., Ky. Med. Assn. (mem. cancer com.), Louisville Surg. Soc., Hiram C. Polk Jr. Surg. Soc., Ohio Valley Soc. Colon and Rectal Surgeons, Priestly Soc., Soc. Surg. Alimentary Tract, Soc. Am. Gastrointestinal Endoscopic Surgeons, Soc. Surg. Oncology, Southeastern Surg. Congress, Surg. Infection Soc., Soc. of Univ. Surgeons, Am. Soc. Gastrointestinal Endoscopists, Ctrl. Surg. Assn. Greek Catholic. Office: U Louisville Dept Surgery 550 S Jackson St Louisville KY 40202-1622

GALARD, MAURICE JAOQUIM, family practice physician; b. Cosenza, Italy, Aug. 16, 1948; parents U.S. citizens; s. Gaetano and Nerina (Cassano) G.; m. Sharon Evalee Young, Oct. 23, 1981. MD, U. Siena, 1972. Intern in surgery Regional Hosp., Cosenza, 1972-73; intern in family practice Bay Front Med., St. Petersburg, Fla., 1973-74; asst. dir. Blood Bank, Cosenza, 1974-76; resident in internal medicine Nassau Hosp., Mineola, N.Y., 1976-77; family practice attending physician Tampa (Fla.) Gen. Hosp., 1977-80; family practice physician Harborside Hosp., St. Petersburg, 1980-86; emergency svcs. dir. Jackson-Campbellton-Sneeds, Fla., 1980-86; CEO Emergency Med. Assocs., Plantation, Fla., 1988-91, Bay Walk In Clinic, Marianna, Fla., 1991—; ptnr. Torretta Med. Inc., Tampa, 1977-80; owner, dir. Gateway Clinic, Gen. Clinic, St. Petersburg, 1980-86; vis. assoc. prof. dept. biostatistics U. Ala., Birmingham, 1993. Mem. Fla. patient advocacy com. Office of the Gov., Tallahassee, 1993-94. Fellow Am. Acad. Family Practice, Am. Coll. Clin. Pharmacology; mem. MENSA, Toastmasters Internat. Republican. Jewish. Home: RR 2 Box 203-na-1 Bonifay FL 32425-9802 Office: Bay Walk In Clinic 4325 Lafayette St Marianna FL 32446-2915

GALATAS, LAUREEN, psychiatric nurse; b. New Orleans, Nov. 21, 1958; d. Floyd G. and Carol E. (Jacobs) G. M. Nursing; BSN, La. State U., New Orleans, 1980, MSN, 1989. RN, Tex., La.; cert. clin. nurse specialist in adult psychiat.-mental health nursing. Staff nurse St. Charles Gen. Hosp., New Orleans, 1980-90, DePaul Hosp., New Orleans, 1985-86, Tulane U. Hosp., New Orleans, 1987-90, The Cedars Hosp., DeSoto, Tex., 1990; clin. nurse specialist Ctr. for Adolescent and Family Care, Duncanville, Tex., 1990—; cons. geropsychiat. program Physician's Regional Hosp., Wylie, Tex., 1992-93; insvc. coord. Geropsychiat. Svc. Opportunities, Inc., Duncanville, Tex., 1994—. Mem. Am. Psychiat. Nurses Assn., Sigma Theta Tau.

GALATI, JOSEPH STEPHEN, hepatologist; b. Rockville Centre, N.Y., Apr. 19, 1959; s. Joseph S. and Agnes G. (Petrucci) G.; m. Geraldine Theresa Ward, Sept. 28, 1991; 1 child, Joseph Stephen. BS, Syracuse U., 1981; MD, St. George's U., 1987. Diplomate Am. Bd. Internal Medicine, sub-bd. Gastroenterology. Intern, resident in medicine SUNY Health Sci. Ctr., Bklyn., 1987-90, chief resident in medicine, 1991; fellow in gastroenterology & hepatology U. Nebr. Med. Ctr., Omaha, 1991-94; asst. prof. medicine U. Tex. Med. Sch., Houston, 1994—, med. dir. transplant hepatology, 1996—. Mem. Am. Coll. Physicians, Am. Assn. Study of Liver Disease, Am. Gastroenterol. Assn., Tex. Liver Coalition (sec. 1995). Office: U Tex Health Sci Ctr-Houston 6431 Fannin, MSB4-234 Houston TX 77030

GALEAZZO, CONSTANCE JANE, neonatal nurse; b. Daytona Beach, Fla., Dec. 3, 1946; d. O.D. and Ruth (Centers) Bales; m. James Guy Galeazzo, Oct. 8, 1966; children: James Bryan, Amy Caroline, Rebecca Jane. BA, Wesleyan Coll., Macon, Ga., 1987; BSN, Ga. Coll., Milledgeville, 1990; MSN, U. South Ala., 1996. RN; cert. nurse practitioner. Program coord. Rape Crisis Line Macon-Bibb County, Ga.; mental health technician Med. Ctr. Ctrl. Ga., Macon, nurse extern; neonatal nurse practitioner, 1991—. R.A. Bowen scholar, Whitehead Found. scholar. Mem. Sigma Theta Tau, Psi Chi, Gamma Beta Phi. Home: 1702 River Forest Dr Macon GA 31211-9783

GALES, ROBERT ROBINSON, judge; b. N.Y.C., Feb. 15, 1941; s. Arthur S. and Gertrude L. (Robinson) G.; m. Karen A. Terry, Nov. 25, 1986; children: Laurie Ann, Thomas Michael, Robert Robinson II, Brian Timothy, Victoria Marie. BA in History and Geography, Ohio Wesleyan U., 1962; JD, Syracuse U., 1965; LLM, George Washington U., 1966; postgrad. U. Philippines, 1969, Indsl. Coll. Armed Forces, 1971. Bar: N.Y. 1966, U.S. Dist. Ct. (so. and ea. dists.) N.Y. 1967, U.S. Dist. Ct. (we. dist.) Wash. 1967, U.S. Ct. Appeals Armed Forces 1967, U.S. Ct. Claims 1967, U.S. Ct. Appeals (9th cir.) 1968, D.C. 1973, U.S. Dist. Ct. (ea. dist.) Va. 1973, U.S. Ct. Appeals (4th cir.) 1973, U.S. Ct. Appeals (2d cir.) 1975, U.S. Customs Ct. 1977, U.S. Ct. Customs and Patent Appeals 1978, Ill. 1978, U.S. Ct. Internat. Trade, 1980, U.S. Ct. Appeals (Fed. cir.) 1982, U.S. Ct. Appeals (7th cir.) 1983, U.S. Dist. Ct. (no. dist.) Ill. 1983, U.S. Dist. Ct. (so. dist.) Ill. 1984. Travel cons. ESSO Touring Svc., N.Y.C., 1960; dep. dir. internat. law 13th Air Force, Philippines, 1969-71; asst. legal advisor U.S. del. Renegotiation of Philippines-U.S. Status of Forces Agreement, 1969-71; chief civil law Tactical Air Command, USAF, Hampton, Va., 1971-72, chief adminstrv. law, 1972-73; assoc. Herzfeld & Rubin, P.C., N.Y.C., 1973-77; task force coord. Volkswagen of Am., Inc., Englewood Cliffs, N.J., 1977; sr. atty. Velsicol Chem. Corp., sec. fgn. subsidiaries, 1977-80; asst. atty. gen. Consumer Protection div. Office of Ill. Atty. Gen., Bensenville and Joliet, 1981-83; chief Utility and Acquisition Law, 375th Air Base Group, Scott AFB, Dept. Air Force, Belleville, Ill., 1984-87; dept. counsel Def. Legal Services Agy., Directorate for Indsl. Security Clearance Rev., Arlington, Va., 1987-88, mem. appeal bd., 1988-90, chief adminstrv. judge, 1990-94; chief adminstrv. judge Def. Legal Svcs. Agy., Def. Office Hearings and Appeals, 1994—; mobilization asst. to dir. Judiciary USAF, 1987-89; dir. Civil Law Office of Judge Adv. Gen., 1989-91; sr. res. advisor to staff judge adv. Air Force Dist. of Wash., 1991-92; vis. adj. lectr. Manhattan Coll., 1973-77, N.J. Inst. Tech., 1975-77, Ill. Inst. Tech., 1978-84, So. Ill. Univ., Carbondale, 1984-86. Contbg. editor, writer to newspapers. Mem. Wash. State Soccer Commn., 1967-68; chmn. exploring com. Far East council Philippine dist. Boy Scouts Am., 1969-71; dist. judge adv. Va. VFW, 1972-73; pres., chmn. exec. com. Briarcliff Citizens for Responsive Govt., 1973-74; bd. dirs. Ossining (N.Y.) Area Jaycees, 1973-74, sec., 1974-75; pres. Ossining Hist. Soc., 1974-76; Rep. dist. leader Town of Ossining, 1974-78; dir. Soc. Prevention of Cruelty to Animals of Westchester, 1974-77; bd. dir. Briarcliff-Ossining-Scarborough br. ARC, 1975-76; mem. Westchester County Rep. Com., 1975-

78; commr. Wayne Twp. (Ill.) Soccer, 1979-83; Rep. precinct committeeman Wayne Twp., 1979-82; adv. bd. Elgin (Ill.) High Sch., 1979-83; trustee Wayne Twp., 1979-85; pres. Melstone neighborhood bd. Little Rocky Run Homeowners Assn., 1987-92. Ret. col. USAFR, Vietnam. Decorated Legion of Merit, Bronze Star, Meritorious Service medal with 3 oak leaf clusters, Air Force Commendation medal with 3 oak leaf clusters, Air Force Achievement medal (U.S.) Air Force Recognition Ribbon; various medals Republic of Vietnam, Outstanding Contribution to Contracting award USAF, 1986, Master of the Bench and mem. Prettyman-Leuenthal Am. Inn of Court, 1996—. Mem. Am. Judges Assn., Nat. Assn. Adminstrv. Law Judges, mem. bd. advs. to the Journal of The Nat. Assn. of Adminstn. Law Judges, 1995—. Vietnam Vets. Bar Assn. (air force judge adv.), Arnold Air Soc., Delta Phi Epsilon, Phi Alpha Delta. Republican. Contbr. articles to profl. jours. Avocations: sports, travel, collecting model soldiers, dining, writing. Home: 6638 Rockland Dr Clifton VA 20124-2501

GALIN, JERRY DEAN, college dean; b. Cullman, Ala., May 22, 1945; s. Herman William and Evelyn B. (McManus) G. BA, St. Bernard (Ala.) Coll., 1967; MA, U. Ala., Tuscaloosa, 1970; EdD, Nova U., 1981. Tchr. math. Morgan County Sch. Sys., Eva, Ala., 1967-74; chmn. mgmt. dept. Wallace State Coll., Hanceville, Ala., 1974-90, dean faculty devel., 1990-93, acad. dean, 1993—; pres. Cullman Tchrs. Credit Union, 1982-85; mem. survey team So. Assn. Colls. and Schs., 1984—; ptnr. G & G Properties, Cullman, 1989—; participant radio and TV shows. Bd. dirs., mem. fin. com. Hospice of Cullman County, Cullman, 1989-91; bd. dirs. Helen Keller Eye and Temporal Bone Bank, Florence, Ala., 1990-91, Ala. Sight Conservation Assn., Birmingham, 1990-91, Cullman County Family Recreational Complex, 1990—; pres. Cullman County Electric Coop. Operation Round-Up Commn., 1995—; chmn. Cullman County Quality Cmty. Coun., 1991-93; mem. Cullman Rural Devel. Com., 1989—; lectr. to social, civic and cmty. groups; master of ceremonies for local events. Recipient Knights of Blind award Eye and Temporal Bone Bank, 1990, 100 percent Dist. Govs. award Internat. Lions Club, 1991, Henry and Lucille Sweet award Ala. Lions Club, 1992. Mem. Ala. Econ. Devel. Orgn., Cullman Area C. of C. (pres. bd. dirs. 1993-94), Wallace State Athletic Assn. (treas. 1989—), Cullman Investment Club (pres. 1989—), Lions (numerous offices 1972—, Lion of Yr. award 1988, Melvin Jones fellow 1991). Democrat. Methodist. Home: 294 County Road 591 Hanceville AL 35077-6048 Office: Wallace State Coll 801 Main St Hanceville AL 35077

GALINDO-CIOCON, DAISY JABRICA, critical care nurse, educator; b. Cotabato, The Philippines, Nov. 10, 1954; d. Deogracias Dano and Salud (Jabrica) Galindo; m. Jerry Ochoa Ciocon, May 14, 1988; children: Jay, Jessica, Jeremy. BSN, U. Santo Thomas, Manila, 1977; MSN, Russell Sage Coll., 1981; PhD, U. Miami, 1990. RN, The Philippines, N.Y., Nebr., Fla. Nurse Greene County Meml. Hosp., Catskill, N.Y., 1977-79, Albany (N.Y.) Med. Ctr., 1979-82; staff nurse critical care unit Cedars Med. Ctr. Hosp., Miami, Fla., 1982-85, U. Nebr. Med. Ctr., Omaha, 1987-88; asst. prof. U. Miami (Fla.) Sch. Nursing, 1982—; adj. nurse rschr. VA Med. Ctr., Miami, 1990-92, nurse rschr. Geriatric Rsch., Edn. and Clin. Ctr., 1992—. Home: 7360 SW 121st St Miami FL 33156-5307 Office: PO Box 248153 Coral Gables FL 33124-8153

GALITELLO-WOLFE, JANE MARYANN, artist, writer; b. Torrington, Conn., Aug. 27, 1942; d. Morris D. and Rose A. (Abate) Galitello; children: Henry Berg III, Jason Sterling, Marissa Tracy. Student, Ward Sch. Elec., 1961, Porter-Chester Coll., 1982. Nurse aide Palm Bay, Fla., 1989; decorator, designer Waterbury, Conn.; electronic engr. Torrington, Conn.; sales rep. Thomaston, Conn.; dance tchr. San Jose, Calif.; freelance artist, writer Torrington. Author: Your Gift of Life, 1991 (award 1993), Snow Bird Melt, 1991, Tody, Heart Desire; published 3 songs including Shadow of Love. Faith healer; active Govt. for Abuse Through Nation and Unity of Nation; advocate for the homeless; active Untied We Stand in Love; min. Your Gift of Life, WBCC-CoCo Radio. Home: PO Box 61851 Palm Bay FL 32906-1851

GALLAGHER, ANNE PORTER, business executive; b. Coral Gables, Fla., Mar. 16, 1950; d. William Moring and Anne (Jewett) Porter; m. Matthew Philip Gallagher, Jr., July 31, 1976; children: Jacqueline Anne, Kevin Sharkey. BA in Edn., Stetson U., 1972. Tchr. elem. schs., Atlanta, 1972-74; sales rep. Xerox Corp., Atlanta, 1974-76, Fed. Systems, Rosslyn, Va., 1976-81; sales rep. No. Telecom Inc. Fed. Systems, Vienna, Va., 1981-84, account exec., 1984-85, sales dir., 1985-94, mktg. dir., 1995-96; v.p. Fed. Pub. Sector Timeplex Fed. Systems, Inc., Fairfax, Va.; bus. devel. dir. Informix Software, Vienna, Va., 1996—. Mem. exec. com. N. Va. United Way; bd. dirs. Make A Wish Friends. Mem. NAFE, Info. Tech. Assn. of Am. (exec. com.), Armed Forces Comm. and Electronics Assn., Pi Beta Phi. Episcopalian. Avocations: skiing, jogging, aerobics. Home: 4052 Seminary Rd Alexandria VA 22304-1646 Office: Informix Software Inc 8605 Leesburg Pike Ste 700 Vienna VA 22182

GALLAGHER, MATTHEW PHILIP, JR., advertising agency executive; b. Providence, June 17, 1944; s. Matthew Philip and Roberta Marie (Tierney) G.; m. Anne Weathers Porter, July 31, 1976; children: Jacqueline Anne, Kevin Sharkey. BA, St. Bonaventure U., 1966. Systems engr. IBM Corp., Arlington, Va., 1967-71; sales rep. Xerox Corp., Silver Spring, Md., 1971-75; dir. mktg. Taft Corp., Washington, 1976-78; dir. devel. World Wildlife Fund, Washington, 1978-79; pres. advt. agy. Gallagher & Assocs., Inc., Alexandria, Va., 1979—; songwriter, entertainer, Atlanta, 1975-76. Author: Hans and the Gold Nugget, 1993; cons. editor: Corporate Foundation Directory. Bd. dirs. Alexandria Sheltered Enterprises, 1980-89, ARC Found. of No. Va., 1991-95. 1st lt. USAFR, 1966-71. Mem. Direct Mktg. Assn. Washington (Internat. Dir. Mktg. Leader award 1983). Home: 4052 Seminary Rd Alexandria VA 22304-1646 Office: Gallagher & Assocs Inc 115 S Union St Ste 308 Alexandria VA 22314-3361

GALLAGHER, VICKI SMITH, real estate agent; b. Norfolk, Va., Dec. 6, 1950; d. James Colan and Margaret Helen (Brewer) Smith; m. Steven Robert Gallagher, Nov. 19, 1977. BS in Music Performance, Old Dominion U., 1973. Agt. GSH Residential, Chesapeake, Va., 1979-84, Realty Cons., Virginia Beach, Va., 1984-90, Leading Edge Realty, Virginia Beach, 1990—. Recipient Nat. Assn. Home Builders Million Dollar Sales award, 1993, Internat. Cat Assn. Mid-Atlantic Region Humanitarian of Yr., 1996; named Leading Edge Realty Resale Agt. of Yr., 1995. Mem. Tidewater Bd. Realtors (Million Dollar Sales Club Gold award 1993, Silver award 1994, others), Tidewater Builders Assn. (Million Dollar Sales Club 1993, Silver Hammer award Million Dollar Sales Circle 1994, Million Dollar Circle 1995, others), Va. Assn. Realtors, Tidewater Assn. Realtors (Million Dollar Club 1995), Leading Edge Realty Achievers Club (Listing Agt. of Yr. 1995), Tidewater Bd. Realtors Million Dollar Circle, Tidewater Assn. Realtors Million Dollar Club. Home: 2236 Crossroad Trl Virginia Beach VA 23456-3538 Office: Leading Edge Realty Expressway Ctr 4772 Euclid Rd Ste B Virginia Beach VA 23462-3800

GALLARDO, HENRIETTA CASTELLANOS, writer; b. San Antonio, July 16, 1934; d. Francisco Garcia and Elisa Duarte (Moreno) Castellanos; m. Albert Joseph Gallardo, Aug. 19, 1965; children: Frank Cantu, Roger Cantu, Gloria Michelle. Cert., Draughn's Bus. Coll., San Antonio, 1952. Sec. Kelly Air Force Base, San Antonio, 1952-53; exec. sec. U. Tex., Dallas, 1974-82; interior decorator Plano, Tex., 1983-85, writer. Author: Tangled Web of Destiny, 1992, Marsh & Co., 1993. Mem. Internat. Platform Assn. Democrat. Catholic. Home: 2212 Parkhaven Dr Plano TX 75075-2013

GALLIAN, VIRGINIA ANNE, music educator; b. St. Louis, Dec. 29, 1933; d. Martin Charles and Flora Olinda (Rocklage) Schake; children: John Charles, Paige Renee. BS, U. Mo., 1955, MS, 1966; student, U. San Jose, Calif., 1961, U. North Tex., Denton, 1971. Tchr. Hazelwood (Mo.) Pub. Schs., 1955, Ft. Dix Post Sch., Trenton, N.J., 1956, Ft. Bragg Post Sch., Fayetteville, N.C., 1956-58, Ferguson-Florrisant (Mo.) Pub. Schs., 1958-59; music supr. Jefferson City (Mo.) Pub. Schs., 1959-60; tchr. Union Sch. Dist., San Jose, 1960-63, 67, 68, Bridgeport (Calif.) Pub. Schs., 1963-65, Columbia (Mo.) Pub. Schs., 1965-67; music tchr. Denton Ind. Sch. Dist., 1970-95; adj. Tex. Woman's U., 1996—; instr. U. North Tex., 1995. Mem. AAUW, Tex. State Tchrs. Assn. (lobbyist 1985—, bd. dirs. 1988-93), Denton Edn. Assn. (chmn. 1985-95), Sigma Alpha Iota (chaplain 1972-74), Phi Delta Kappa. Republican. Methodist.

GALLIMORE, MARGARET MARTIN, real estate executive; b. Winston Salem, Mar. 20, 1947; d. Holland Henry and Dallas Cornell (Robbins) Martin; m. Elmer Harold Holden Jr., Feb. 14, 1965; children: Andrew Harold, Amy Darlene, John Alan; m. Timothy Milton Gallimore, May 9, 1986. Student, High Point (N.C.) Coll., 1989. Lic. real estate broker, N.C. With AT&T Network Sys., Winston-Salem, 1965-69, 73-75, prodn. operator, 1979-89; real estate salesperson Lambe-Young Real Estate Co., Kernersville, N.C., 1975-79; leasing cons. Vinyard Gardens Apts./S.E. Atlantic Properties, Winston-Salem, 1994-95; comm. assoc. AT&T Phone Ctr., Winston-Salem, 1995-96; real estate salesperson Triad Piedmont Properties, Kernersville, 1996; real estate broker Winston-Salem, 1996—. Author poetry. Recipient Editors Choice awards (2) Nat. Libr. of Poetry, 1995; named to Internat. Poetry Hall of Fame, Nat. Libr. Poetry, 1996. Mem. Nat. Assn. Realtors, N.C. Assn. Realtors, Western Piedmont Assn. Realtors, Internat. Soc. Poets (Disting. mem.). Home: 2534 Union Cross Rd Winston Salem NC 27107-4420

GALLO, VINCENT JOHN, financial planner; b. N.Y.C., Aug. 13, 1943; s. Nicholas and Catherine (Vitiello) G.; m. Blanche Marie Poplin, Apr. 15, 1972; children: Steven, Mark. BA, U. Dayton, 1965. Registered fin. planner; CLU; Chartered Fin. Cons. Mgr. methods engrng. Daniel Internat. Corp., Greenville, S.C., 1971-75; exec. v.p. Am. Ind. Elec. Contractors Assn., Arlington, Tex., 1975-77; pres. Vincent J. Gallo & Assocs., Inc., Winston-Salem, N.C., 1977—; adj. instr. Am. Coll., Bryn Mawr, Pa., 1984-86. Capt. USAF, 1966-71. Served to capt. USAF, 1966-71. Mem. Am. Soc. CLUs and Chartered Fin. Cons. (continuing edn. chmn. 1984, pres. 1988-89), Internat. Assn. Fin. Planners, Nat. Assn. Securities Dealers, Nat. Soc. Pub. Accts., Winston-Salem Estate Planning Coun. (v.p.), N.C. Soc. Accts., Mensa, Million Dollar Round Table. Home: 8800 Harwick Ct Clemmons NC 27012-9737 Office: 3775 Vest Mill Rd Ste C Winston Salem NC 27103-2990

GALLUPS, VIVIAN LYLAY BESS, federal contracting officer; b. Vicksburg, Miss., Jan. 14, 1954; d. Vann Foster and Lylay Vivian (Stanley) Bess; m. Ordice Alton Gallups, Jr., July 12, 1975. BA, Birmingham So. Coll., 1975, MA in Mgmt., 1985; MA in Edn., U. Ala., Birmingham, 1975. Cert. purchasing mgr. Nat. Assn. Purchasing Mgmt. Counselor Columbia (S.C.) Coll., 1975-76; case mgr. S.C. Dept. Social Services, Lexington, 1976; benefit authorizer, payment determination specialist then recovery reviewer Social Security Adminstrn., Birmingham, 1977-85; adminstrv. contracting officer U.S. Dept. Def., Birmingham, Ala., 1992-94; supr. contract adminstr. Def. Logistics Agy. U.S. Dept. Def., Ft. Belvoir, Va., 1994-95; contract adminstr., now supervisory contract adminstr. Def. Logistics Agy., Ft. Belvoir, Va., 1995—. Hospice vol. Bapt. Med. Ctr.-Montclair, Birmingham, 1982; trustee, treas. Resurrection House, Birmingham, 1984-85; vol. counselor Cathedral Ch. of Advent, Birmingham, 1987. Mem. Nat. Contract Mgmt. Assn. (cert. profl. contracts mgr., chpt. sec. 1987, pres. 1990-93, nat. dir. 1993-94), Assn. of Luth. Ch. Musicians. Lutheran. Home: 14144 Reverend Rainsford Ct Upper Marlboro MD 20772 Office: US Def Dept Def Logistics Agy 2875 John J Kingman Rd Rm 4422 Fort Belvoir VA 22060

GALT, JOHN WILLIAM, actor, writer; b. Jackson, Miss., Apr. 4, 1940; s. William Neal and Lyndel Janes (Fortenberry) G.; m. Anna Marie Kolenovsky, Dec. 14, 1965 (div. 1973); children: Joseph William, Edward Wayne; m. 2d, Diane Renee Wallace, June 6, 1981; children: Christopher Wallace, Geoffrey Warren. Student U. Md. at Munich (W.Ger.), 1960-61, Mountain View Coll., 1970-72; BA, Univ. Scis. Am., L.A., 1992. Toured as folksinger U.S.A. and Europe, 1960-62; voice talent on numerous radio and TV comls., Dallas, 1965-78, 80—, L.A., 1978-80; 31 film appearances as actor; looped characters in 4 movies; voice of Lyndon B. Johnson in Oliver Stone's JFK, 1992, Forrest Gump, 1994; writer film script Iceman, 1976; contbg. writer For The Love of Benji, 1977; writer screenplay Step Back From Anger, 1986, The Guardians, 1987; contbg. writer The Internal Affair, 1988; v.p. Tex. Ind. Feature Prodns., Inc., 1981—, Jackson Galt Creative Enterprise Inc, 1991—. Co-author (with Philip Jackson): Into Invisible Light, 1991, Crossover, 1992, also numerous short fiction. Served with USAF, 1957-62. Recipient Dallas Citizen's Cert. Merit, 1973, Clios (26), Tellys (25), N.Y. Film Festival Silver, Addys (43), CHA Gold Spirit award; several Tops in advertising awards. Mem. NATAS (Heartland chpt.), Actor's Equity Assn., Screen Actor's Guild, AFTRA, Writers Guild of Am., Acad. for Preservation of Talking Pictures. Avocation: Martial Arts (2nd degree black belt Tae Guek Kwan Kung Fu 1993, advanced oriental broad sword combat forms, brown belt Hapkido OHTC 1989). Office: Kim Dawson Agy 2710 N Stemmons Fwy Ste 700 Dallas TX 75207-2208

GALUCKI, FRANCES JANE, nursing educator, medical/surgical nurse; b. Waverly, N.Y., May 5, 1925; d. Clarence Watson and Edith Agnes (LaFever) McCray; m. Edward W. Galucki, Feb. 17, 1947; children: Clarence W., Linda S. Galucki Schmidt, Edward F., Alan J., Donna J. Galucki Plewes. RN, Buffalo (N.Y.) Gen. Hosp., 1947. Staff nurse Buffalo Gen. Hosp., 1949-52, 58-63, 73-76, acting head nurse, 1963-64, insvc. instr., 1964-69, supr. blood team, ward clks., 1965-69; staff nurse Kimberly Quality Care, St. Petersburg, Fla., 1986-93; ret., 1994. Mem. N.Y. State Nurses Assn. (dist. 1), ANA, Nurses Official Registry of Buffalo (nomination com., past chmn. grievance com.). Office: 10901 Roosevelt Blvd N Ste 100 Saint Petersburg FL 33716-2305

GALYA, THOMAS ANDREW, geologist; b. New Brunswick, N.J., July 11, 1947; s. Andrew Peter and Geraldine Rose G.; m. Lanora Lucille Bucklew, Jan. 8, 1970. BS, W.Va. U., 1971; MS, N.E. La. U., 1975; PhD, Miami U., Oxford, Ohio, 1983. Geologist, Sewell Coal Co.-Pittston Co., Nettie, W.Va., 1972; chief geologist, Clinchfield Coal Co.-Pittston Co., Dante, Va., 1978-82; sr. coal geologist, head coal quality group Exxon Coal Resources USA, Inc., Houston, 1982-86; staff geologist, Exxon Coal and Minerals Co., Houston, 1986-89; owner, pres. Galya & Assocs., Katy, Tex., 1989; sr. geologist Occidental Petroleum-Island Creek Coal Corp., 1989-91; geologist III, W.Va. Divsn. Environ. Protection, Logan, 1991-96, lead geologist so. ops., 1996—; tchg. asst. Northeast La. U., Monroe, 1973-75; teaching fellow Miami U., Oxford, Ohio, 1975-77, fellow, 1977-78. Mem. Am. Inst. Profl. Geologists, Am. Assn. Petroleum Geologists, Soc. Sedimentary Geology, Geol. Soc. Am., Sigma Xi, Sigma Gamma Epsilon. Democrat. Roman Catholic. Home: 65 Dogwood Ln Madison WV 25130-1268 Office: WWV Divsn Environ Protection 525 Tiller St Logan WV 25601-3438

GAMBLE, MARY G(RACE), marketing and quality professional; b. Evanston, Ill., Feb. 23, 1950; d. John D. and Bertha E. (Flynn) G. BA with honors, U. Fla., 1971, MBA, 1993. Mgr. maj. market Gillette Co., Chgo., 1977-83; asst. regional sales mgr. Atlanta, 1983-85; v.p. sales and mktg. Hemochek Corp., Gainesville, Fla., 1985-89; div. mgr. Environ. Sci. & Engring., Gainesville, Fla., 1989-93; v.p., chief quality officer Hellmuth, Obata & Kassabaum, St. Louis, 1993—; judge Fla. Quality Sterling Award. Bd. mem. Gov.'s Sterling Coun., 1989—, United Way of Alachua County, 1990-93; bd. examiners Malcolm Baldridge Nat. Quality Award. Mem. Am. Soc. Quality Control, Assn. Jr. Leagues, Univ. Club, Rotary. Republican. Office: 1 Tampa City Ctr Ste 3000 Tampa FL 33602-5817

GAMBLE, RAYMOND WESLEY, marriage and family therapist, clergyman; b. East Orange, N.J., Feb. 11, 1933; s. Kenneth Nelson and Lillian Clare (Appgar) G.; m. Margaret Gamble, Sept. 11, 1954 (div. 1964); children: Karen F., Roy B.; m. Penelope Louise Hansen, Nov. 19, 1979; 1 child, Wesley B. BA, Houghton (N.Y.) Coll., 1956; MDiv, Union Theol. Sem., Richmond, Va., 1960; postgrad., Yale U., 1967; D Ministry, Columbia Theol. Sem., Decatur, Ga., 1990. Ordained to ministry Presbyn. Ch., 1960. Student chaplain Va. State Penitentiary, 1958-60; asst. pastor Immanuel Presbyn. Ch., Lake Park, Fla., 1960-62; founder, pastor Westminster Presbyn. Ch., Palm Beach Gardens, Fla., 1962-67; exec. dir. Mental Health Assn. Palm Beach County, West Palm Beach, 1967-73; pvt. practice marriage and family therapy, West Palm Beach, Stuart, Fla., 1973—; founder, sr. pastor Palm City (Fla.) Presbyn. Ch., 1984—; guest instr. Indian River Community Coll., 1978; cons., chaplain Lake Hosp., Lake Worth, Fla., 1973-75; chaplain Savannas Hosp., Port St. Lucie, Fla., 1986—; program dir., aftercare counselor narcotic addict rehab. program NIMH, West Palm Beach, 1969-73. Active numerous drug abuse rehab. programs, Palm Beach County; past mem. Com. for Mental Health Edn.; active Presbytery Tropical Fla., 1960—; mem. ch.-coll. coun. Montreat Coll., 1988—; past mem. bd. dirs. Alcohol and Drug Abuse Coun. Palm Beach County, North County Drug Abuse Bd., Boca Raton (Fla.) Drug Abuse Found.; past pres. Drug Abuse Rehab. Team, Inc. Mem. Am. Assn. for Marriage and Family Therapy (clin.), Am. Assn. Christian Counselors. Home and Office: 288 NE Alice St # 101S Jensen Beach FL 34957-6006

GAMBLE, STEVEN G., academic administrator. Pres. Southern Ark. U., Magnolia. Office: Southern Arkansas U Office of President Magnolia AR 71753

GAMBLE, WESLEY, information technology consultant; b. Buffalo, May 4, 1970; s. Wayne Wesley Gamble and Ella Elizabeth (Hooker) Cawein. BSEE, Cornell U., 1992. Software programmer IBM, East Fishkill, N.Y., 1990-91; cons. Andersen Cons., N.Y.C., 1992-95, Informix Software Inc., Houston, 1995—. Mem. Ctr. for Healing of Racism. Home: 4207 Drake St Apt 5 Houston TX 77005 Office: Informix Software Inc 1330 Post Oak Blvd Ste 2350 Houston TX 77056

GAMBLIN, JAMES E., quality assurance specialist; b. St. Louis, Nov. 10, 1954; s. Donald Burton and Bette Sue (Welch) G. AA, Johnson County Community Coll., 1978; BA in Math. cum laude, Avila Coll., 1979; MS in Ops. Mgmt. summa cum laude, U. Ark., 1991; postgrad., Kennesaw State Coll., 1996—. Lic. pilot, FAA. Instr. U. Ark., Fayetteville, Ark., 1979-80; quality assurance specialist Def. Logistics Agy., Wichita, 1980-86, St. Louis, 1986-89; chief quality assurance specialist Def. Logistics Agy., Camden, Ark., 1989-91, Warner Robins, Ga., 1991-94; indsl. property/plant clearance officer Def. Logistics Agy., Marietta, Ga., 1994—; instr. quality Def. Logistics Agy., St. Louis, 1984-89; site adminstr. Def. Contract Mgmt. Command Atlanta World Wide Web, 1996—. Frequent contbr. articles to Def. Contract Mgmt. Command, Atlanta Total Quality Eagle, Def. Contract Mgmt. Dist. South Southern Exposure, and other publs. Editor Singles' newsletter First Bapt. Ch., Canton, Ga., 1994-96. Mem. Am. Soc. Quality Control (sr.; mid. Ga. sect. treas. 1993-94, vice chmn. 1994-95), U. Ark. Alumni Assn. (life), Aircraft Owners and Pilots Assn., NRA (life), Good Sam Club (life), Shriners, York Rite, Scottish Rite, Masons (32d degree). Baptist. Office: US Govt Def Logistics Agy 805 Walker St Ste 1 Marietta GA 30060-2789

GAMBONE, VICTOR EMMANUEL, JR., physician; b. Phila., Aug. 28, 1949; s. Victor Emmanuel and Eleanor Joyce (Porambo) G.; BS, Pa. State U., 1971, MD, 1975. Cert. Med. Dir. in Long Term Care; diploma Am. Bd. Quality Assurance and Utilization Rev. Physicians. Intern and resident in internal medicine U. South Fla., Tampa, 1975-78; practice medicine specializing in internal medicine and geriatrics, Dunedin, Fla., 1978—; coord. geriat. medicine curriculum Morton Plant Mease/U. South Fla. Family Practice Residency Program, 1996—; med. dir. Stratford Ct. Marriott Health Ctr., Palm Harbor, Fla., 1991—, St. Mark Village, Palm Harbor, 1993—, Mease Continuing Care, Dunedin, Fla., 1993—, Manor Care Nursing Ctr., Dunedin, 1994—, Spanish Gardens Nursing Ctr., Dunedin, 1994—, Gulfcoast Nursing Ctr., Clearwater, Fla., 1995—, Hospice Care, Inc., Pinellas County, 1982-86, Regency Oaks Nursing Ctr., Clearwater, 1996—, Bayside Nursing Pavillion, Clearwater, 1996—, Mariner Health of Clearwater, 1996—; chmn. dept internal medicine Mease Health Care, Dunedin, Fla., 1989. Diplomate Am. Bd. Internal and Geriatric Medicine. Mem. AMA, ACP, Am. Med. Dirs. Assn., Am. Geriatrics Soc., Am. Soc. Internal Medicine. Author: Post Operative Recall of Intra-Operative Events, 1975 (research award U. Miami Med. Sch.). Office: 601 Main St Dunedin FL 34698-5848

GAMBRELL, LUCK FLANDERS, corporate executive; b. Augusta, Ga., Jan. 17, 1930; d. William Henry and Mattie Moring (Mitchell) Flanders; m. David Henry Gambrell, Oct. 16, 1953; children: Luck G. Davidson, David Henry, Alice Kathleen, Mary G. Rolinson. AB, Duke U., 1950; diplome d'etudes françaises, L'Institut de Touraine, Tours, France, 1951. Chmn. bd. LFG Co., 1960—. Mem. State Bd. Pub. Safety, 1981-90; bd. dirs. Atlanta Symphony Orch., 1982-85; mem. Chpt. Nat. Cathedral, Washington, 1981-85; mem. World Service Council YWCA, 1965—, council Presbytery Greater Atlanta, 1988; elder First Presbyn. Ch., Atlanta; chmn. bd. dirs. Student Aid Found., Atlanta, 1992—; mem. Bd. Councilors The Carter Ctr., Emory U. Mem. Atlanta Jr. League, Alpha Delta Pi.

GAMBRILL, CHRISTOPER WAYNE, physical education educator; b. Cullman, Ala., Sept. 11, 1965; s. Terry Warren and Nancy Wynona (Roden) G. BS, U. Ala., Birmingham, 1992. Cert. tchr., Ala. Phys. edn. tchr. Birmingham City Schs., 1992—; fitness instr. Steve's Gym, Cullman, 1988-93. Mem. AAHPERD. Democrat. Baptist. Home: 431 County Rd 639 Cullman AL 35055

GAMMAGE, ROBERT ALTON (BOB GAMMAGE), lawyer; b. Houston, Mar. 13, 1938; s. Paul and Sara Ella (Marshall) G.; m. Judy Ann Adcock, Aug. 3, 1962 (div. 1979); children: Terry Lynne, Sara Noel, Robert Alton Jr.; m. Lynda Ray Hallmark, July 4, 1980; 1 child, Samuel Paul. AA, Del Mar Coll., Corpus Christi, Tex., 1958; BS, U. Corpus Christi, (now Tex. A&M U.), 1963; MA, Sam Houston State U., 1965; JD, U. Tex., 1969; LLM, U. Va., 1986. Bar: Tex. 1969, U.S. Dist. Ct. (so. dist.) Tex. 1970, U.S. Ct. Appeals (5th cir.) 1970, U.S. Supreme Ct. 1973, U.S. Ct. Appeals (11th cir.) 1981, U.S. Dist. Ct. (we. dist.) Tex. 1983, U.S. Ct. Mil. Appeals 1986, U.S. Ct. Appeals (D.C. cir. 1993). Tchg. fellow, dir. fraternities Sam Houston State U., Huntsville, Tex., 1963-65; dean of men, dir. student activities U. Corpus Christi, 1965-66; property mgr. Harrison-Wilson-Pearson, Austin, Tex., 1966-69; pvt. practice law Houston, 1969-79; mem. Tex. House of Reps., Austin, 1971-73, Tex. Senate, Austin, 1973-76; del. Tex. Constl. Conv., Austin, 1974; mem. U.S. House of Reps., Washington, 1977-79; asst. atty. gen. State of Tex., Austin, 1979-80; pvt. practice Austin, 1980-82; spl. cons. U.S. Dept. of Energy, 1980; justice Tex. Ct. Appeals, Austin, 1982-91, TX State Supreme Ct, Austin, TX, 1991-95; pvt. practice Austin, 1995—; mem. Tex. Jud. Budget Bd., Austin, 1983-88, Supreme Ct. Jud. Edn. Exec. Com., 1985-93, Tex. Jud. Coun., Austin, 1986-93, Jud. Com. on Ct. Funding, Austin, 1988-91; instr. govt. San Jacinto Coll., Pasadena, Tex., 1969-70; adj. prof. South Tex. Coll. Law, Houston, 1971-73. With U.S. Army, 1959-60, USAR, 1960-64, USNR, 1965-95. Named Outstanding Sen. Tex. Intercollegiate Students Assn., 1973; recipient Disting. Svc. award Alcoholism Coun. Tex., 1976. Mem. ABA, State Bar Tex. (Disting. Svc. award 1975, vice chmn. funding judiciary com. 1988-91), Am. Judicature Soc., Inst. Jud. Adminstrn., Coll. State Bar Tex. Democrat. Baptist. Office: PO Box 13226 Austin TX 78711

GAMMON, JACK ALBERT, computer scientist; b. Baytown, Tex., June 9, 1950; s. Jack Albert and Thalia (Montgomery) G. BS in Computer Sci. summa cum laude, U. Tex., Richardson, 1988, MS in Computer Sci., 1990. Engr., electronics Anaconda Aluminum Rolling Mill Products, Terre Haute, Ind., 1979-81; project engr., developer KAVCO Inc., Terre Haute, Ind., 1981-83; tng. instr. Hane Indsl. Tng. Inc., Terre Haute, Ind., 1983-85, tech. svcs. mgr., 1985-87; instr. U. Tex., Richardson, 1988-93; with Cyrix Corp., Richardson, 1993-95; engr. Access Tech. Sys., Addison, Tex., 1995-96; project engr. New Micros Inc., Dallas, 1996; progamming cons. Cybertek, Dallas, 1996—. Author: Understanding Induction Heating, 1984, Understanding Serial Communications, 1986, Understanding D.C. Drives, 1986, Understanding A.C. Drives, 1986. Mem. student union activities adv. bd., U. Tex., 1988-89, student life com., 1988-90, acad. expansion task force student life and activities, 1989-90; mem. Hillcrest Ch. Mem. IEEE, NorTex QRP, Pi Mu Epsilon.

GAMMON, JAMES EDWIN, SR., clergyman; b. San Diego, Jan. 23, 1944; s. Jack Albert and Thalia Gammon; BA, Tex. Christian U., 1970, postgrad., 1970-72; m. Sharon Elaine Head, June 27, 1965; children: John Paul, James Edwin, Jeffrey David. Ordained to ministry Ch. of Christ, 1966; minister Carter Park Ch., Ft. Worth, 1966-69, Scotland Hills Ch., Ft. Worth, 1969-70, Northside Ch., Dallas, 1970-73, Central Ave Ch., Valdosta, Ga., 1973-78; debate coach Christian Coll. S.W., Dallas, 1971-73; pres. So. Bible Inst., Valdosta, 1977-78; minister Trinity Oaks Ch. of Christ, Dallas, 1978-80, Parkview Ch. of Christ, Sherman, Tex., 1980-85; pres. Texoma Bible Inst., 1980-85; minister Eisenhower Ch. of Christ, Odessa, Tex., 1985-86; minister, Cen. Ch. of Christ, McMinnville, Tenn., 1986—; pres. Eagle Trust, 1994; chmn. Warren County Hist. Commn., 1995—. Author: Notes on the Acts, 1983, Notes on I, II Corinthians, 1984, Thessalonians, 1985, Notes on James, 1985, Notes on Romans, 1988, Notes on the Beatitudes, 1989, Notes on II Peter, 1994. With U.S. Army, 1963-66. Republican. Home: 203 S Arrowhead Dr Mc Minnville TN 37110-2930 Office: Court Sq PO Box 536 Mc Minnville TN 37110-0536

GAMMON, MALCOLM ERNEST, SR., surveying and engineering executive; b. Chattanooga, Tenn., Sept. 7, 1947; s. George A. and Frances Helen (Conway) G.; m. Glenna Dee Shirk, June 5, 1971; children: Malcolm Ernest Jr., Christopher Brian. BS, Miss. State U., 1970. Ops. mgr. Pyburn & Odom, Inc., Baton Rouge, 1970-84; chief exec. officer, prin. owner Hydro Cons., Inc., Baton Rouge, 1984—. Tech. contbr. (textbook) 4567 Review Questions for Surveyors, 11th edit., 1985, Elementary Surveying, 8th edit., 1989. State chmn. La. Trig Star Program, Baton Rouge, 1988-89; mem. adv. bd. La. Math. Coalition. Mem. La. Soc. Profl. Surveyors (registered, pres. 1990), Miss. Assn. Land Surveyors (registered), Nat. Soc. Profl. Surveyors (profl. mem., bd. govs.), Am. Congress on Surveying and Mapping (profl. mem., cert. hydrographer), Ark. Soc. Profl. Surveyors (registered), Ala. Profl. Land Surveyors (registered). Home: 440 Rue De Laplace Baton Rouge LA 70810-4557 Office: Hydro Cons Inc 10275 Siegen Ln Baton Rouge LA 70810-4926

GANAWAY, GEORGE KENNETH, psychiatrist; b. Davenport, Iowa, Mar. 22, 1946; s. Kenneth Joseph and Elizabeth Earl (Baker) G.; m. Elzada Lawson, Dec. 27, 1969; children: Heather, Erin. BS in Clin. Psychology, Duke U., 1968; MD, Emory U., 1973. Diplomate Am. Bd. Psychiatry and Neurology; lic. physician, Ga. Resident in psychiatry Emory Affiliated Hosps., Atlanta, 1973-76; candidate Emory Psychoanalytic Inst., 1993—; pvt. practice in gen. adult and adolescent psychiatry Atlanta, 1976—; founder, program dir. Ridgeview Ctr. for Dissociative Disorders, Smyrna, Ga., 1987-96; med. cons. dissociative disorder Ridgeview Inst., 1996—; asst. prof. psychiatry Emory U. Sch. Medicine, Atlanta, 1976-80, clin. asst. prof. psychiatry, 1981—; clin. asst. prof. psychiatry Morehouse Sch. Medicine, Atlanta, 1990—; psychiat. cons. Disability Adjudication br. Social Security Adminstrn., Atlanta, part-time, 1980-87, Douglas County Mental Health Clinic, Douglasville, 1977-81, South Cobb Mental Health Ctr., Austell, Ga., 1978-80, Atlanta Depression Clinic of Ctr. Metabolic Studies, 1976-77, others; ann. chmn. S.E. Regional Conf. Dissociative Disorders, 1987—; active staff Ridgeview Inst.; cons. staff Kennestone Hosp., Marietta. Asst. editor Dissociation: Progress in Dissociative Disorders, 1988—, Internat. Jour. Clin. and Exptl. Hypnosis, 1995—; mem. editl. adv. bd. Insight mag.; editl. reviewer Am. Jour. Psychiatry, Child Abuse and Neglect: The Internat. Jour., Jour. Psychology and Theology, Jour. Nervous and Mental Disease, Dissociation: Progress in the Dissociative Disorders; contbr. articles to profl. jours. Adv. bd. False Memory Syndrome Found., 1992—. Fellow Internat. Soc. for Study of Dissociation (task force on stds. of practice 1991—); mem. Am. Psychiat. Assn., Ga. Psychiat. Physicians Assn., So. Med. Assn., Am. Soc. Clin. Hypnosis, Atlanta Hypnosis Soc. Office: D-201 5064 Roswell Rd NE Atlanta GA 30342-2252

GANDY, BONNIE SERGIACOMI, oncological and intravenous therapy nurse; b. Bridgeton, N.J., July 12, 1952; d. Albert A. and Jean (Goodwin) Sergiacomi; m.Robert H. Gandy, Aug. 15, 1981 (dec.); 1 child, Anthony Robert. BA, Glassboro (N.J.) State Coll., 1974; ADN, Cumberland County Coll., Vineland, N.J., 1985. RN, N.J., N.C.; cert. tchr., N.J.; cert. oncology nurse, intravenous nurse. Staff nurse, charge nurse William B. Kessler Meml. Hosp., Hammonton, N.J., 1985-86; supr. med. outpatient unit South Jersey Hosp. System-Millville (N.J.) Div., 1986-93; dir. home care nursing Med IV Home Health Svcs., Hickory, N.C., 1994-95; IV nurse cons., IV therapist Am. Pharm. Svcs., Hickory, N.C., 1995—. Mem. Nat. Intravenous Therapy Assn., Oncology Nursing Soc., Phi Theta Kappa.

GANDY, JAMES THOMAS, meteorologist; b. Memphis, Tenn., Nov. 25, 1952; s. Thomas Marion and Sible Christaline (McBride) G.; m. Ann Cuppia, Apr. 12, 1986. BS, Fla. State U., 1974; postgrad., U. S.C. Meteorologist Sta. WREG-TV (CBS affiliate), Memphis, 1975-77; staff meteorologist Sta. KTVY-TV (NBC affiliate), Oklahoma City, 1977-82; dir. ops. Weather Data, Inc., Wichita, Kans., 1982-84; meteorologist Kans. State Network (NBC affiliate), Wichita, 1982-84; chief meteorologist Sta. WIS-TV (NBC affiliate), Columbia, S.C., 1984—; guest lectr. U. S.C., Columbia, 1991, 95. Named Best TV Weather Forecaster, The State Newspaper, Columbia, S.C., 1993, Best TV Weather Personality, Columbia Met. Mag., 1994, 95, 96. Mem. AAAS, Am. Meteorol. Soc. (TV Seal of Approval 1985, Memphis chpt. sec. 1976-77, chmn. 1977, Ctrl. Okla. chpt. sec.-treas. 1979, 82, pres. 1980, Palmetto chpt. v.p. 1988-89, pres. 1989-90), Nat. Weather Assn., Planetry Soc. (charter mem.), N.Y. Acad. Scis., Order Internat. Fellowship (charter). Home: 101 W Ashford Way Irmo SC 29063-8325 Office: WIS Television 1111 Bull St Columbia SC 29201-3722

GANGAROSA, RAYMOND EUGENE, epidemiologist, engineer; b. Rochester, N.Y., July 1, 1951; s. Eugene John and Rose Christine (Salamone) G. BA, Emory U., 1972; MSEE, Ga. Inst. Tech., 1976; MD, Med. Coll. Ga., 1980; M in Pub. Health, Emory U., 1991. Diplomate Am. Bd. Internal Medicine. Rsch. technician Electromagnetic Scis., Inc., Altanta, 1973-74; med. resident U. Md., Balt., 1980-81; clin. scientist Picker Internat., Cleve., 1981-88; vis. scientist Ctrs. for Disease Control, Atlanta, 1990—; doctoral candidate Emory U., Atlanta, 1990—; rsch. fellow Emory U. Ethics Ctr., 1994—; med. epidemiologist Ga. Divsn. Pub. Health, 1995—; coord. Instl. Rev. Bd., Cleve., 1982-84, 86-87; cons. Novel Imager Design Team, Cleve., 1987-88. Editor Picker Internat. Newsletter, 1985-87; coord. audiovisual tng. courses for magnetic resonance imaging, 1982-84; contbr. articles to profl. and law jours. Campaign dir. David Drexel for State Senate, Chapel Hill, N.C., 1972; sculptor Toys on Request, 1982—; coord. Control Alcohol, Tobacco and Drug Use, Atlanta, 1989—. Mem. AAAS, Am. Pub. Health Assn., N.Y. Acad. Scis., Soc. for Epidemiologic Rsch.

GANGEMI, J(OSEPH) DAVID, microbiology educator, biomedical researcher, research administrator, hospital administrator; b. Wilmington, Del., July 3, 1947; s. Joseph C. and Lavern (Wagener) G.; m. Nancy Elizabeth Thompson, Aug. 22, 1970; children: Stephanie Elizabeth, Alyssa Lavern, Jennifer Anne. BS, Clemson U., 1969; PhD, U. N.C., 1973. Commd. 2nd lt. U.S. Army, 1969; rsch. virologist U.S. Army, Frederick, Md., 1973-78; ret. U.S. Army, 1978; asst. prof. microbiology, immunology Sch. Medicine U. S.C., Columbia, 1978-82, assoc. prof. Sch. Medicine, 1982-90, assoc. dir. tech. transfer, 1989-92, dir. tech. transfer, 1991-92, prof. microbiology, immunology Sch. Medicine, 1991-92; sabbatical Ciba-Geigy, Basel, Switzerland, 1987-88; prof. microbiology Clemson (S.C.) U., 1991—, dir. Greenville Hosp. System/Clemson U. Biomed. Coop., 1992—; rsch. cons. Charles Pfizer Labs., Groton, Conn., 1980-83, Ciba-Geigy, Basel, 1986—, Drug Innovation and Design, Inc., Newton, Mass., 1990—; mem. tech. adv. bd. S.C. Rsch. Authority, 1996—. Contbr. articles to profl. jours.; editl. bd. Letters in Applied Microbiology, 1988—. Lt. col. USAR, 1989. Mem. AAAS, Internat. Soc. Antiviral Rsch., Am. Soc. Tropical Medicine and Hygiene, Am. Thoracic Soc., S.C. Acad. Sci., S.C. br. Am. Soc. Microbiology (pres. 1983-85, Outstanding Microbiologist 1993). Roman Catholic. Office: Clemson Univ 445 Brackett Hall Clemson SC 29634

GANGI, ANTHONY FRANK, geophysics educator; s. Frank Paul and Sarah Lucille (Cosenza) Gangi; m. Enrichetta De Gange, Jan. 26, 1961 (dec. Oct. 1987); m. Beverly Ann Goebel, Aug. 19, 1992. BS in Applied Physics, UCLA, 1953, MS in Applied Physics, 1954, PhD in Physics, 1960. Mem. tech. staff Space-Electronics Corp., Glendale, Calif., 1959-61; mgr. Space-Electronics Corp.(now Space Gen. Corp.), Glendale, Calif., 1961-64; assoc. prof. geophysics MIT, Cambridge, 1964-67; assoc. prof. geophysics Tex. A&M U., College Station, 1967-70, prof. geophysics, 1970—; vis. prof. U. Federal de Bahia, Salvador, Brazil, 1982-83, 84; mem. working group on mass transport in lithosphere and upper mantle U.S. Geodynamics Project, 1972-82; mem. tech. adv. bd. Consortium on Continental Reflection Profiling, 1975-85; cons. and lectr. in field. Contbr. articles to profl. jours. With U.S. Army, 1946-48, Korea. Shell fellow, 1957, NATO fellow, 1975-76. Mem. IEEE (adminstrv. com. 1975-78, membership chmn. 1975-78), Am. Geophys. Union, Seismological Soc. Am., Soc. Expln. Geophysicsts (rsch. com. 1972—), Geosci. Electronics Soc., Sigma Pi sigma, Sigma Xi. Home: 3804 Sunnybrook Ln Bryan TX 77802-3925 Office: Tex A&M U Dept Geology and Geophysics College Station TX 77843-3115

GANGOPADHYAY, NIRMAL KANTI, mining company executive; b. Dacca, Bengal, India, Apr. 23, 1943; came to U.S. 1970; s. Madhusudan and Sudha Rani (Chakravarty) G.; children: Molly, Dolly. B.Engring., U. Calcutta, India, 1965; M.Tech., Indian Inst. Tech., Kharagpur, India, 1968; MS, U. Idaho, 1971. Registered profl. engr., Ky., Pa., Va., W.Va. Office engr. Mt. State Constrn., Charleston, W.Va., 1971-73; project engr. The Pioneer Constrn. Co., Charleston, 1973-75; chief engr. Perry & Hylton, Inc., Beckley, W.Va., 1975-87; v.p. engring. WRM, Inc., Perry & Hylton, Inc., Beckley, 1987—. Contbr. articles to profl. jours. Fund raiser Raleigh County Bus. Coalition com., Beckley, 1986. Dept. Civil Engring., U. Idaho research fellow, 1970. Mem. W.Va. Mining and Reclamation Assn. (tech. com.). Republican. Hinduism. Home: PO Box 93 Mabscott WV 25871-0093

GANN, JEAN POPE, insurance agency executive, fine arts appraiser; b. Winfield, Ala., Dec. 5, 1917; d. Garvin and Clara (Couch) Pope; m. John Henry Gann, Apr. 6, 1935 (dec.); children: John Garvin, W. Gerald, Jean Gann Nelson. Student, U. Howard Coll., 1949-52, U. Ala., 1964-68, Montevallo, Ala., 1983-84, Samford U., 1983-85. Lic. ins. agt.; cert. appraiser fine arts and antiques. Owner, mgr. Sylacauga (Ala.) Ins. Agy., 1952—; instr., trainer Sylacauga High Sch., 1960—; co-chmn. Citywide Sales Clinic, Sylacauga C. of C., 1972. Contbr. articles to profl. jours. Mem. Birmingham (Ala.) Mus. Art, 1979—; exec. bd. dirs. United Givers Fund, Sylacauga, 1978-81; charter mem. Sylacauga Mus. and Arts Ctr., 1982—; v.p. Sylacauga High Sch. PTA, 1961-62; chmn. edn. Am. Cancer Soc., South Talladega County, Ala., 1953-61; bd. dirs. Sylacauga Boys Club, 1988—; charter bd. dirs., parliamentarian B.B. Comer Meml. Libr. Found., 1991—; mem. Ala. Women's Polit. Caucus, 1978—, Nat. Dem. Com., Ala. Dem. Com., Ala. Citizens for ERA; tchr. adult Bible class 1st Bapt. Ch., 1945—, mem. long range planning com., 1950-58, 89—; chmn. com. that established Ave. of Flags in Sylacauga, 1972; pres. Bapt. Women's Orgn., 1964-65, 76-80; chmn. prayer breakfast Nat. Bus. Women's Week, 1979-85. Named Sylacauga Woman of Yr., Sylacauga Exch. Club, 1961; recipient cert. in Christian tng. Howard Coll., Samford U., 1983; cert. of recognition 1st Bapt. Ch., 1985 (stewardship chmn.1996—). Mem. Soc. Fine Arts U. Ala., Ala. Ind. Ins. Agts. (legis. com. 1978-79, 84-85), Nat. Assn. Ind. Ins. Agts., Ala. Fedn. Bus. and Profl. Women (dist. chmn. for young careerists 1972-73, regional legis. chmn. Sylacauga chpt. 1983—, pres. 1962, 62, 73, dist. VI chmn. 75th Hist. Celebration), Sylacauga Bus. & Profl. Women's Club (legis. chmn. 1980—, chmn. internat. com. 1987—, named Woman of Achievement 1976, Sylacauga Woman of Yr. 1994), U.S.A. Young Careers (chmn. 1987-88, internat. chmn. 1988), Nat. Trust for Hist. Preservation, Sylacauga C. of C. (mem. com. 1952—, chmn. ann. membership 1974-75), Sylacauga Antique Group, LWV, Nat. Mus. Women in the Arts (charter 1987—), Bus. and Profl. Women's Found., Coosa Valley Country Club (charter mem.), Matrons Study Club, Alpha Lambda Delta. Avocations: collecting antiques, study of historical sites and buildings. Home: 300 Bay St Sylacauga AL 35150-3410 Office: Sylacauga Ins Agy PO Box 598 Sylacauga AL 35150-0598

GANN, PAMELA BROOKS, law educator; b. 1948. BA, U. N.C., 1970; JD, Duke U., 1973. Bar: Ga. 1973, N.C. 1974. Assoc. King & Spalding, Atlanta, 1973; assoc. Robinson, Bradshaw & Hinson, P.A., Charlotte, N.C., 1974-75; asst. prof. Duke U. Sch. Law, Durham, N.C., 1975-78, assoc. prof., 1978-80, prof., 1980—, dean, 1988—; vis. asst. prof. U. Mich. Law Sch., 1977; vis. assoc. prof. U. Va., 1980. Author: (with D. Kahn) Corporate Taxation and Taxation of Partnerships and Partners, 1979, 83, 89; article editor Duke Law Jour. Mem. Am. Law Inst., Coun. Fgn. Rels., Order of Coif, Phi Beta Kappa. Office: Duke Univ Sch Sci Dr and Towerview Rd Box 90362 Durham NC 27708-0362 Home: 3712 Darwin Rd Durham NC 27707

GANNON, JOHN SEXTON, lawyer, management consultant; b. East Orange, N.J., Apr. 7, 1927; s. John Joseph and Agnes (Sexton) G.; m. Diane Ditchy, Aug. 11, 1951; children: Mary Catherine, John, Lanie Elizabeth, James. BA, U. Mich., 1951; JD, Wayne State U., Detroit, 1961. Bar: Mich. 1962, Tenn. 1971, U.S. Ct. Appeals (6th cir.) 1977, U.S. Dist. Ct. (mid. dist.) 1989. Labor negotiator, mgr. employee rels. Chrysler Corp., Highland Park, Mich., 1951-61; labor counsel, mgr. employee rels. Ex-Cell-O Corp., Highland Park, 1961-65; assoc. Constangy & Powell, Atlanta, 1966; v.p. employee rels., labor counsel Werthan Industries, Nashville, 1967-80; ptnr. Dearborn & Ewing, Nashville, 1980-90; pvt. practice Nashville, 1991—; mem. adj. faculty Owens Sch., Vanderbilt U., Nashville, 1975-85; instr. SHRM cert. program Mid. Tenn. State U., 1993—; pres. Employee Rels. Svcs., Inc., Nashville, 1987—. Contbr. articles to profl. jours. Mem. Birmingham (Mich.) Bd. Zoning Appeals, 1963-66; mem. Human Rels. Commn., Nashville, 1979-89; chmn. Tenn. Citizens for Ct. Modernization, Nashville, 1979-80; mem. Pvt. Industry Coun., Nashville, 1986-95. With USN, 1945-47. Mem. ABA, FBA, Tenn. Bar Assn., Mich. Bar Assn., Nashville Bar Assn., Soc. Human Resource Mgmt., Am. Arbitration Assn. (mem. panel of employment mediators and arbitrators), Univ. Club, Hillwood Country Club, Kiwanis. Home: 216 Jackson Blvd Nashville TN 37205-3300

GANSKOPP, WILLIAM FREDRICK, oil company executive; b. Nanticoke, Pa., July 24, 1915; s. Herman and Ida Helene (Hecht) G.; m. Neale Irene Crosby, July 9, 1942; children: Jennifer Winell, Daryl Stephen. AB in Physics, Lafayette Coll., 1938; diploma in advanced mgmt., Northwestern U., Caracas, Venezuela, 1960. Engr. Standard Oil Co. of N.J., Elizabeth, 1938-42; capt. 703d engrs., Africa, Italy, 1942-45; gas engr. Creole Petroleum Corp., Caracas, Venezuela, 1946-51, mgr. gas sect., 1954-62; drilling engr. Creole Petroleum Corp., Jusepin, Venezuela, 1952-54; natural gas dept. head Esso Nederland, Hague, The Netherlands, 1962-65; natural gas exec. Esso Ea., Sydney, Australia, 1965-68; pres. Gan-Ed, Inc., Columbus, N.C., 1970-78, chief exec. officer, 1978-81; dir., cons. Owosso Gan, Inc., Gainesville, Fla., 1981—. Patentee self-propelled golf cart; patentee in Can., Japan and Mex. Recipient Barge Math. award Lafayette Coll., Easton, Pa., 1936, citation MTO, Livorno, Italy. Mem. Ret. Officers Assn. (life, program chmn. 1981-82), Gainesville Golf and Country Club, Masons. Republican. Lutheran. Home and Office: 5511 SW 35th Way Gainesville FL 32608-5232

GANT, HORACE ZED, lawyer; b. Van Buren, Ark., Apr. 1, 1914; s. George Washington and Ida Elizabeth (Stephenson) G.; m. Edith Imogene Farabough, Oct. 10, 1937; children: Alice Margaret, Linda Beth, Zed George, Paul David. LLB, U. Ark., 1936, JD, 1969. Bar: Ark. 1936, U.S. Dist. Ct. (we. dist.) Ark. 1937, U.S. Supreme Ct. 1943. Asst. pros. atty., Van Buren, 1936-41; sole practice, Van Buren, 1941-43; atty. War Relocation Authority, Washington, 1943, U.S. Dept. Interior, Washington, 1947; field atty. VA, Little Rock, 1947-73; chancery judge Ark. 15th Jud. Dist., Van Buren, 1973-75; ptnr. Gant & Gant, Van Buren, 1975—; chmn. bd. dirs. Western Ark. Legal Svcs., Ft. Smith, 1991, pres. bd. dirs., 1991-92; chancery ct. master Ark. 12th Jud. Dist., Ft. Smith, 1976-91. Bd. dirs. Harbor House and Gateway House, Ft. Smith, Ark., 1974-84; chmn. Western Ark. Adv. Council, Ft. Smith, 1976-81; pres. Mental Health Assn., Ft. Smith, 1978; trustee Boggan Edn. Scholarship Trust Fund, chmn., 1979—; deacon 1st Baptist Ch., Van Buren. Lt. comdr. USN, 1943-46. Mem. Ark. Bar Assn., Masons (master 1942-43). Democrat. Home: 403 S 7th St Van Buren AR 72956-5813 Office: Gant & Gant Attys at Law 200 S 7th St PO Box 416 Van Buren AR 72956

GANT, LINDA ANN, dietitian, consultant; b. Independence, La., July 21, 1951; d. James and Dorothy Mae (Cryer) Ryan; m. Eymel Gant, June 5, 1971; children: Shajuandra Reche, Eymel III, Enre Alfan. BS in Instn. Mgmt., Grambling State U., 1972. Licensed, registered dietitian. Intern U. Mich. Hosp., Ann Arbor, 1973; pub. health nutritionist Jefferson Health Unit, Metairie, La., 1975-85; clin. dietitian VA Med. Ctr., New Orleans, 1985-89; home care dietitian VA Hosp., New Orleans, 1989—; cons. RD United Med. Ctr., New Orleans, 1991—, New Orleans Gen. Hosp., 1991—, Stuart Home Health, New Orleans, 1991—; speaker in field. Participant Health Fairs including Irish Channel Cmty. Ch., 1993, Am. Cyanamid, 1993, Lakeside Mall, 1992, Earth Fest, others; vol. serve meals to homeless Ozanam Inn, 1992-93; mem. program planning com. nutrition month Am. Cancer Soc., 1993. Mem. Am. Soc. Parenteral and Enteral Nutrition, Nat. Kidney Found. La., Am. Dietetic Assn., La. Dietetic Assn. (planning program com. 1990, nominating com. 1994-95), New Orleans Dietetic Assn. (chair year book 1988-89, chair long range planning 1987-88, sec. 1990-91, pres. 1992-93, nominating com. 1989-90, edn. program planning com. ann. seminar 1991), Kappa Omicron Phi. Democrat. Baptist. Home: 353 Bertolino Dr Kenner LA 70065-2532 Office: VA Med Ctr 1601 Perdido St New Orleans LA 70112-1207

GANTT, PHYLLIS CROWLEY, secondary education educator; b. Augusta, Ga., May 12, 1961; d. Robert Lee Olin Crowley and Mildred Louise (Garvin) Traynham; m. William Ray Gantt, Sept. 8, 1978; children: Aaron, Adam, Abby, Andrew, Addison. BA in Secondary Edn., U. S.C., 1990. Cert. tchr. S.C. Social studies and history tchr. Wagener (S.C.)-Salley High, 1990—. Poll mgr. S.C. Election Com., Columbia, S.C., 1989—; exch. student host World Heritage, Washington, 1993-95. Named Summer Inst. attendee Nat. Endowment for Humanities, Chapel Hill, N.C., 1996; Gender Equity grantee Dr. Trudy Henson, U. S.C., Aiken, 1994; Filling the Void grantee Aiken (S.C.) Electric Co., 1996-97. Mem. ASCD, So. Poverty Law Ctr., U. S.C. Aiken Alumni, Gamma Beta Phi, Sigma Tau Delta. Democrat. Deist. Home: 20 Rodeo Loop Wagener SC 29164 Office: Wagener Salley High 272 S Main St Wagener SC 29164

GANTZ, ANN CUSHING, artist, educator; b. Dallas, Aug. 27, 1936; d. Maurice Kendrick and Margaret (Hughes) Cushing; m. Everett Ellis Gantz, Sept. 20, 1958; children: Elaine Gantz Wright, Melissa Cushing. BFA, Newcomb Coll., 1955. Tchr. Dallas Mus. of Art, 1956-65; pres. Cushing Galleries, Inc., Dallas, 1962-79; tchr. Cushing Studio Inc., Dallas, 1979—; dir. Cushing Atelier, 1962—; chair Six Operas in Six Artists Exhibition/Dallas Opera, 1996. One-woman shows and group shows including Mary nye Gallery, Dallas, Black Tulip Gallery, Dallas, Lawrence Gallery, Dallas, The Elms Gallery, Midland, Tex., Landmark, Tennison, Stewart, Cushing, Park Cities galleries, Dallas, Shrednk Gallery, Denver, Hockaday Gallery, Dallas, Dallas Visual Art Ctr., 1996; pvt. collections Dallas Mus., Norfolk Mus., Boston Mus., Denver Mus., New Orleans Mus., Brook Meml., Memphis. Bd. dirs. Dallas Opera, Dallas Theatre Ctr. Recipient Durrell award Dallas Mus., 1979. Mem. Tex. Fine Arts Assn. (hon.), Dallas Print and Drawing Soc. (pres. 1972-80), Tex. Printmakers (pres. 1956-70), Phi Delta Kappa, Alpha Omicron Pi. Episcopalian. Office: Cushing Studio 11333 N Central Expy Dallas TX 75243-6708

GANZ, CHARLES, laboratory executive. Pres. En Cas Analytical Lab., Winston-Salem, N.C. Office: 2359 Farrington Point Dr Winston Salem NC 27107

GANZARAIN, RAMON CAJIAO, psychoanalyst; b. Iquique, Chile, Apr. 18, 1923; s. Eusebio Gastanaga and Maria Cajiao; m. Matilde Vidal Soto, Oct. 10, 1953; children: Ramon, Mirentxu, Alejandro. BS, St. Ignacio Coll., Santiago, Chile, 1939; MD, U. Chile, Santiago, 1947; postgrad., Chilean Psychoanalytic Inst., 1947-50, cert. tng. analyst, 1953. Assoc. prof. psychiatry U. Chile, Santiago, 1955-68, dir. dept. med. edn., 1962-68; prof. depth psychology, sch. psychology Cath. U., Santiago, 1962-68; dir. Chilean Psychoanalytic Inst., Santiago, 1967-68; tng. analyst Topeka Inst. Psychoanalysis, 1968-87; dir. group psychotherapy services The Menninger Found., Topeka, 1978-87; geog. tng. analyst Columbia U. Ctr. for Psychoanalytic Tng. and Research, Atlanta, 1987; assoc. prof. psychiatry Emory U., Atlanta, 1988—; tng. analyst Emory U. Psychoanalytic Inst., 1988—. Author: Fugitives of Incest, 1988, Objects Relations Group Psychotherapy, 1989; contbr. articles to profl. jours., chpts. to books. Fellow Am. Group Psychotherapy Assn.; mem. AMA, Internat. Assn. Group Psychotherapy (bd. dirs., exec. counselor 1986), Am. Group Psychotherapy Assn. (bd. dirs. 1984-87, 93-96), Internat. Psychoanalytic Assn., Am. Psychoanalytic Assn., Kans. Med. Soc., Topeka Psychoanalytic Soc. (pres. 1985-87). Roman Catholic. Office: Emory U Psychoanalytic Inst Dept Psychiatry PO Box AF Atlanta GA 30337-0503

GARBER, ERIC A.E., chemistry educator, researcher; b. N.Y.C., Mar. 31, 1958; s. George A. and Miriam (Kasimer) G. BS magna cum laude, CCNY, 1978; PhD, Brandeis U., 1983. Rsch. assoc. U. Ill., Chgo., 1990-92; asst. dir. Ctr. for Biotechnology Northwestern U., 1992; adj. asst. prof. Roosevelt U., 1993; asst. prof. dept. chem. W.Va. State Coll., 1993—; vis. rsch. specialist U. Ill. Chgo. Coll. Medicine, 1993. Contbr. articles to profl. jours. Recipient Am. Cancer Soc. fellow, 1984-85, NRSA fellow, 1983, Jesse Smith Noyes fellow, 1981. Mem. AAAS, Am. Chem. Soc., Am. So. Biochemistry and Molecular Biology, Am. Soc. Engring. Edn., Am. Soc. Microbiology, The Protein Soc., Phi Beta Kappa, Sigma Xi. Democrat. Jewish. Home: 5427 Hillbrook Dr Charleston WV 25313 Office: W Va State Coll Dept Chemistry Institute WV 25112

GARBER, HAROLD MICHAEL, lawyer; b. St. Louis, July 22, 1954; s. Allen Lee and Beverly (Schnurman) G. BS, Syracuse U., 1976; JD, Nova U., 1990. Bar: Mo. 1990, Fla. 1991, D.C. 1991, U.S. Dist. Ct. (so. dist.) Fla. 1991. Pres. Garber Graphic Svcs., Inc., St. Louis, 1977-87; shareholder Garber & Campbell, P.A., Miami, Fla., 1991—. Mem. ABA, St. Louis Bar Assn., Dade County Bar Assn. (Pro Bono award Fla. 11th Jud. Cir. 1995), Comml. Law League, Phi Delta Phi. Office: Garber & Campbell PA 12000 Biscayne Blvd Ste 216 Miami FL 33181-2720

GARBER, MARY ELLEN, retired sports reporter; b. N.Y.C., Apr. 19, 1916. AB in Philosophy, Hollins Coll., 1938. Society editor Twin City Sentinel, Winston-Salem, N.C., 1940-41, mem. news staff, 1941-44, 45-46, sports editor, 1944-45; mem. sports staff Jour., Winston-Salem, 1946-86, part-time mem. sports staff, 1986—. Recipient over 40 awards for sports writing, including 1st prize Coll. Baseball Coaches, U.S. Basketball Writers, N.C. Press Assn.; prizes N.C. Press Women, Grady Elmore award N.C. Tennis Assn., Tennis Writer of Yr. award, Disting. Svc. award N.C. H.S. Athletic Assn., Lifetime Achievement award YWCA, adult award for N.C. Tennis, Skeeter Francis award for svc. to Atlantic Coast Conf., Atlantic Coast Sportswriters Assn., 1995; named Baseball Writer of Yr., Raleigh Hot Stove League; named to Winston-Salem/Forsyth County H.S. Sports Hall of Fame, N.C. Journalism Hall of Fame, Hollins Coll. Sports Hall of Fame, N.C. Sports Hall of Fame, 1996; PACIS award for best all-around sports program, N.W. N.C. H.S. woman basketball player of yr., reater Winston-Salem Kiwanis Club tennis tournament,Atlantic Coast Conf. woman athlete of yr., Assn. for Women in Sports Media scholarship program all named in her honor. Mem. Atlantic Coast Conf. Sportswriters (past mem. bd. dirs. and pres.), Football Writers Assn. (past mem. bd. dirr.). Home: 419 N Stratford Rd Winston Salem NC 27104-3135

GARCIA, ANTONIO DE JESUS, manufacturing executive; b. Havana, Cuba, Oct. 10, 1943; came to U.S., 1983; s. Constantino and Hildelisa E. (Fernández) G.; m. Anna H. Swiech, Mar. 22, 1967 (div. Dec. 1980); 1 child, Marcin; m. Mireya Melgar Hubert, Oct. 22, 1985; children: Jean-Philippe, Jean-Charles, Alexandra Hubert. BS, Candler Coll., Havana, 1960; M.Mech. Engring., Poly. Inst., Warsaw, Poland, 1969. Project mgr. Machinery Constrn. Enterprises, Havana, 1969-74; tech. assessor Steel Foundry, Havana, 1974-79; program mgr. Direction for Raw Material, Havana, 1979-80; gen. mgr. Tin Mine, Madrid, 1981; pvt. tutor Paris, 1982-83; machine operator A.P.T., Inc., Miami, Fla., 1983-84, ops. mgr., 1984-92, v.p. mfg., 1992-96. Mem. Soc. Mfg. Engrs. Republican. Roman Catholic. Home: 4601 SW 58th Ave Miami FL 33155

GARCIA, HENRY FRANK, finance and administration executive; b. San Antonio, Aug. 29, 1943; s. Henry V. and Lucia (Dominguez) G.; m. Rose Lozano, Feb. 28, 1970; children: John Henry, Rebecca. BA in Psychology, St. Mary's U., San Antonio, 1969, MA in Econs., 1974. Cert. purchasing mgr., Tex. Buyer purchasing Southwest Research Inst., San Antonio, 1967-70, asst. mgr. purchasing, 1970-74, mgr. purchasing, 1974-78, asst. dir. materials mgmt., 1978-80, dir. corp. travel, 1980-87, dir. materials mgmt., 1980-87; dir. fin. and adminstrn. Ctr. for Nuclear Waste Regulatory Analyses, San Antonio, Tex., 1987—; instr. U. Tex., San Antonio, 1976-77; instr. materials mgmt. and econs., San Antonio Coll., 1975-83; instr. econs. St. Marys U., San Antonio, 1976-81; adj. prof. econs. Webster U., San Antonio, 1980—. Contbr. articles to profl. jours. Chmn. San Antonio Regional Minority Purchasing Council, 1983. Mem. Nat. Purchasing Inst. (pres. 1979-80, Outstanding Svc. award 1986), Nat. Assn. Purchasing Mgmt. (cert., v.p. dist. II 1987-89, Pro-D Man of Yr. award 1985, Congrove Outstanding Mem. award 1991, President's award 1994), Purchasing Mgmt. Assn. San Antonio (pres. 1981-82, Conway L. Holmes award 1984), Nat. Bus. Travel Assn. (v.p. 1985-86), Nat. Assn. Bus. Economists (pres. local chpt. 1978), Project Mgmt. Inst. Democrat. Roman Catholic. Office: Ctr Nuclear Waste Regulatory Analyses 6220 Culebra Rd San Antonio TX 78238-5166

GARCIA, IRIS ESCOBEDO, public health nurse; b. McAllen, Tex., July 9, 1962; d. Genaro and Gloria (Estrada) Escobedo; m. Julian Garcia, Jr., Aug. 7, 1987. AS, Pan Am. U., 1986; cert., Tex. Women's U., 1991. Staff nurse Knapp Meml. Meth. Hosp., Weslaco, Tex., 1984-86, Edinburg (Tex.) Gen. Hosp., 1986-87; supr., pediatric nurse practitioner Hidalgo County Health Dept., Elsa Clinic, Edinburg, 1987-91; self-employed Iris' Well Child Physicals, 1991—. Home: PO Box 1882 Elsa TX 78543-1882

GARCIA, RAYMOND LLOYD, dermatologist; b. Paterson, N.J., Jan. 24, 1942; s. Raymond and Ruth Elaine (De Graff) G.; m. Cynthia Ruth Towne (div.); m. Toy Ping Woo, Dec. 22, 1984; 1 child, Christopher Drew. BA cum laude, Drew U., 1963; MD, Temple U., 1967. Diplomate Am. Bd. Dermatology, Am. Bd. Dermatology-Pathology. Commd. Col. USAF, 1966; intern Wilford Hall USAF Med. Ctr., San Antonio, 1967-68; dermatology resident, 1969-72; vice-chmn. residency tng. program Wilford Hall USAF Med. Ctr., San Antonio, 1972-82; asst. chief aerospace medicine USAF Acad., Colorado Springs, Colo., 1968-69; chief dermatology Carswell USAF Hosp., Ft. Worth, 1982-86; pvt. practice Irving, Tex., 1986—; asst. prof. U. Tex. Med. Sch., San Antonio, 1972-82; assoc. prof. Tex. Coll. Osteo. Medicine, Ft. Worth, 1982-92; cons. to surgeon gen. USAF, 1979-86. Editor: Jour. the Assn. Mil. Dermatologists, 1978-86, Handbook of Dermatology, 1980; contbr. over 50 articles to profl. jours. Decorated Nat. Defense medal USAF, 1972, Meritorious Svc. medal 1982. Fellow Am. Acad. Dermatology (legis. liaison com. 1972-78); mem. Assn. Mil. Dermatologists (sec., treas. 1973-75, v.p. 1977-78, pres. 1980), Tex. Med. Assn., Tarrant County Med. Soc., Babcock Surg. Soc. of Temple U. Med. Sch., Tex. Dermatol. Soc., Biol. Honor Soc. of Drew U., Alpha Kappa Kappa, Beta Beta Beta. Republican. Baptist. Home: 1110 San Juan Ct Arlington TX 76012-2750 Office: Dermatology Center 2015 W Park Dr Irving TX 75061-2113

GARCIA, YOLANDA VASQUEZ, educational services manager, educator; b. San Antonio, Nov. 27, 1948; d. Eleodoro and Antonia (Hernandez) Vasquez; (div. 1985); children: Yvette Flores, Marisa Flores, Julie Garcia. BA, Our Lady of the Lake, 1971; MA, U. Tex., San Antonio, 1977. Cert. counseling and guidance. Elem. sch. tchr. San Antonio (Tex.) Ind. Sch. Dist., 1972-76; elem. sch. tchr. Northside Ind. Sch. Dist., San Antonio, 1977-81, itenerant ESL tchr., 1981-87, sch. counselor, 1988-93, adminstr.; student tchr. supr. U. Tex., Austin, 1993—. Scholar Our Lady of the Lake, San Antonio, 1968, U. Tex., San Antonio, 1976, Inst. de Cooperacion, Madrid, Spain, 1985; fellow U. Tex., Austin, 1993. Mem. TESPA, Am. Edn. Rsch., Coun. for Exceptional Children, Tex. Assn. Bilingual Edn., Kappa Delta Pi. Democrat. Roman Catholic. Home: 6834 Brookvale San Antonio TX 78238 Office: Northside Pre-K Ctr 11937 I H 10 W San Antonio TX 78230

GARCÍA-CASTAÑÓN, SANTIAGO, Spanish educator, researcher, translator, poet; b. Avilé, Asturias, Spain, Sept. 23, 1959; came to U.S., 1985; s. Rufino García Miranda and Piedad Castañon Fierro. Lic. in Anglo-Germanic philology, U. Oviedo, Spain, 1983; MA in Spanish Lit., U. Ill., 1987, PhD in Spanish Golden Age Lit., 1990. Rsch. asst. U. Oviedo, 1979-80; tchr. English, chmn. dept. Colegio Santo Angel, Avilés, 1983-84; grad. tchg. asst. U. Ill., Urbana-Champaign, 1985-89, rsch. asst., 1986-89, grad. asst., 1987-89; instr. Spanish, Ill. Wesleyan U., Bloomington, 1989-90, asst. prof., 1990-92; asst. prof. U. Ga., Athens, 1992—; lectr., presenter in field. Author: (play) El "tenure es sueño, 1991; Tiempo imperfectos (Poetry) 1994. Entre las sombras (poetry) 1996, contbr. articles and book revs. to profl. jours., poetry to various publs. Grantee Spanish Ministry Edn., 1976-79, U. Ill., 1988; Univ. fellow U. Ill., 1987. MLA, Am. Assn. Tchrs. Spanish and Portuguese, Assn. Cervantistas, Assn. for Hispanic Classical Theater, Assn. Licenciados y Doctores Españoles en los Estados Unidos, Soc for Renaissance Barogue Hispanic Poetry, Sociedad Numismatia Avilesina Phi, Sigma Delta Pi (hon.). Roman Catholic. Office: U Ga Dept Romance Langs Athens GA 30602

GARCÍA-GODOY, CRISTIÁN, historian, educator; b. Mendoza City, Argentina, June 3, 1924; came to the U.S., 1963; s. Cristián García Pontis and Renee Godoy Ponce; children: María Celina Heeter, María Inés García Robles, María Susana García Robles. Degree in law, U. Buenos Aires, 1950; diploma, U. Nacional de Cuyo, 1952; postgrad., Washington U., 1969, Cath. U., 1971. Official various banks, Argentina, 1941-62; sec. gen. Secretaria de Comercio de la Nación, Argentina, 1958-59; cabinet mem. Ministro de Economía, Río Negro, Argentina, 1959-60; pres.-organizer Banco de la Provincia de Río Negro, Argentina, 1960; internat. civil servant GS/OAS, 1962-89; prof. history Argentine Sch., Washington, 1981—. Author: San Martin en el Reino Unido, 1996, Jefes Espanoles en la Formacion Militar de San Martin, 1995, Correspondencia Inedita de Tomas Godoy Cruz con su Padre Clemente Godoy y Videla, 1993, The Essential San Martin, 1993-94, Tomas Godoy Cruz: Su tiempo, su vida, su drama, 1991, Tomas Godoy Cruz, Dictamen Federalista, Introduccion y estudio, 1991, Los XII Presidentes 1850-1910, 1989, The San Martin Papers, 1988, Selected U.S. Supreme Court Decisions Related to Constitutional Law, 1986, San Martin y Unanue en la Liberacion del Peru, 1983, Evolucion Historica y Constitucional de la Argentina, 1982, San Martin, Selected Bibliography, 1978, Ampliaciory Actualizacion 1978/96, Tribute to the Liberator General San Martin, 1978; contbr. articles to profl. jours. Lt. Argentine Army, 1946. Mem. Academia Nacional de la Historia, Premio Republica Argentina, Soc. Argentina de Historiadores Buenos Aires, Nat. Geneal. Soc. USA, Inst. Argentino de Ciencias Genealogicas, Inst. Bonaerense de Numismatica y Antiguedades, Acad. Nacional Sanmartiniana Buenos Aires, Junta de Estudios Historicos Mendoza, Inst. de Estudios Ibericos Buenos Aires, Internat. Inst. Pub. Adminstrn. (U.K.), Acad. Polit. Sci. USA, Am. Soc. Internat. Law, Washington Fgn. Law Soc. USA, San Martin Soc. (pres., Hermandad Ysabel la Catolica (chancellor). Home: 1128 Balls Hill Rd Mc Lean VA 22101-2653 Office: San Martin Soc PO Box 33 Mc Lean VA 22101-0033

GARCIA-MELY, RAFAEL, retired education educator; b. N.Y.C., Dec. 28, 1921; s. Rafael and Vivian (Mely) G.; m. Lucy ortiz, Mar. 2, 1951 (div. Dec. 1968); children: Martin, Christine. B.S. in Social Sci., CCNY, 1946; BD, Yale U., 1949, MDiv, 1972; MA, NYU, 1951, PhD, 1959; LHD (hon.), World U. (P.R.), 1975. Ordained to ministry United Ch. of Christ U.S.A., 1949. Dir., cmty. coord. Brownsville Houses Cmty. Ctr., N.Y.C. Housing Authority, 1949-51; assoc. pastor, assoc. dir. Ch. of the Good Neighbor and Cmty. Ctr., N.Y.C., 1951-53; dir. New Neighbors Project, Hudson Guild, N.Y.C., 1953-54; youth min. First Reformed Ch., Schenectady, 1954-56; prof. edn. Inter-Am. U., San German, P.R., 1957-65, dean co-campus programs, 1962-63, dean adminstrn., 1963-65, prof. grad. edn. program metro campus, 1984-94; ret., 1994; dep. gen. sec. World Council Christian Edn., Geneva, 1966-68; dean of acad. affairs World U., San Juan, P.R., 1969-78; dean grad. program Internat. Inst. World U. Am. San Juan, 1978-83; adj. prof. Caribbean Residence Ctr. Dowling Coll., San Juan; dean U. of the Air, 1985-86. Editor Jour. World Christian Edn., 1966-68. Sec., bd. gov. World Univs., San Juan, 1968-83; v.p., treas. Latin Am. Evang. Council Christian Edn., Lima, Peru, 1968-81; bd. dirs., co-founder World Univs., Inc., San Juan, 1965-83; bd. dirs. govs. World Council Edn., Geneva, 1968-71; regional sec. Scholarship Commn. World Council of Chs., Geneva, 1971-80; co-founder Fomento de la Opera, San Juan, 1977. Mem. ASCD, Am. Assn. Higher Edn., Am. Sociol. Assn., Religious Edn. Assn., Adult Edn. Assn., Phi Epsilon Chi, Phi Delta Kappa. Avocations: music, educational activities, sports.

GARCIA-RILL, EDGAR ENRIQUE, neuroscientist; b. Caracas, Venezuela, Oct. 31, 1948; came to U.S., 1973; s. Juan Garcia and Aracelis (Rill) Ramirez; m. Sherrie Hunt, Oct. 2, 1978 (div.); children: Sarah Thais; m. Susan Gene Ebel, May 13, 1984. BA, Loyola of Montreal, 1968; PhD, McGill U., 1973. Rsch. asst. dept. psychiatry McGill U., Montreal, 1972-73; postdoctoral fellow UCLA, 1973-78; asst. prof. anatomy U. Ark. for Med. Scis., Little Rock, 1978-82, assoc. prof., 1982-87, prof., 1987—, prof. psychiatry, 1990—; dir. NSF Exptl. Program to Stimulate Competitive Rsch., Ark. Neurobiology Rsch. Ctr., 1989—; mem. biomed. rsch. study sect. NIAAA, Washington, 1983-87, biopsychology study sect. NIH, Washington, 1988-93; chmn. biopsychology rev. com. NIH, 1991-93; reviewer several neurosci. jours., 1979—, small bus. innovative rsch. study sect. NIH, 1988-92; exec. office of pres. Office of Sci. and Tech. Policy Forum, 1994. Editor: (videotape) The Basal Ganglia and the Locomotor Regions, 1986; patentee in field. V.p., bd. dirs. Morris Found., Little Rock, 1985—. Postdoctoral fellow Que. Med. Rsch. Coun., 1973; grantee NSF, 1980-85, 88—, NIH, 1983—. Mem. Soc. for Neurosci. (chpt. com. 1991-93), Am. Assn. Anatomists. Office: U Ark for Med Scis 4301 W Markham St Little Rock AR 72205-7101

GARDE, DANIEL FREDERICK, safety engineer; b. Bklyn., June 17, 1940; s. Daniel Frederick and Mary A. G.; children—Kim Marie, Daniel, Michael. B.S., Fordham, U., 1962; M.A. in Safety and Health, NYU, 1977. Commd. 2d lt. U.S. Army, 1962, advanced through grades to capt., 1965; served as comdr. 426th Supply and Service Co., 101st Airborne Div., Vietnam, 1969, comdr. 577th Q.M. Co., Aerial Delivery, Germany, 1971-73, ret., 1973; safety dir. Metro Containers, Carteret, N.J., 1973-75; safety and tng. dir. LCP Chems., Linden, N.J., 1975-79; sr. safety engr. Lederle Labs., Pearl River, N.Y., 1979-81; dir. safety and security Exxon Bayway Refinery, Linden, 1981-92; mgr. safety, health, fire protection Hess Oil Virgin Islands Corp., St. Croix, 1992—; faculty Middlesex Coll., 1978, 79, Mercy Coll., 1980-81, NYU, 1983—; chmn. petroleum sect. exec. com. Nat. Safety Coun.; chmn. local emergency planning com., St. Croix. Contbr. articles to profl. publs. Decorated Bronze Star, Air Medal, Vietnamese medal of honor. Mem. Am. Soc. Safety Engrs., Am. Indsl. Hygiene Assn., Nat. Fire Protection Assn. Roman Catholic. Home: 43 Wilson Ave Iselin NJ 08830-1414 Office: HOVIC Dept 31 PO Box 127 # 31 Kingshill VI 00851-0127

GARDE, SUSAN REUTERSHAN, accountant; b. Southampton, N.Y., Sept. 5, 1953; d. Robert Gordon and Ann Patricia (Cronin) Reutershan; m. John Franklin Garde III, May 20, 1989; children: John Franklin IV, Sean Robert. BS, Skidmore Coll., 1975; MBA, Fla. Inst. Tech., 1983, MS in Mgmt., 1991. Budget analyst Grumman Aerospace Corp., Bethpage, N.Y., 1975-76, program planner, 1976-79; sr. budget planner Grumman Aerospace Corp., Stuart, Fla., 1979-81, program planner, 1981-82; adminstr. rsch. ctr. United Technologies, West Palm Beach, Fla., 1982-86; sr. adminstr. United Technologies Inc., West Palm Beach, 1986-87, United Technologies Optical Systems Inc., West Palm Beach, 1988-94; cost acct. Harbor Br. Oceanog. Inst., Inc., Fr. Pierce, Fla., 1994-96, sr. cost acct., 1996—. Mem. Am. Bus. Women's Assn. (pres. Orchid chpt. 1986-87, Sailfish chpt. 1985), Skidmore Alumni Assn., Skidmore Club S.E. Fla. Republican. Roman Catholic. Home: 5100 9th St Vero Beach FL 32966-2841 Office: Harbor Br Oceanog Inst 5600 N Us Highway 1 Fort Pierce FL 34946-7320

GARDIOL, RITA MAZZETTI, foreign language educator; b. Pitts.; d. Joseph and Grace (Ivey) Mazzetti; m. Rene Gardiol. BA, Mt. Mercy Coll., Pitts., 1959; MA, Middlebury Coll., 1963; PhD, Ind. U., 1968. Asst. prof. fgn. lang. Ball State U., Muncie, Ind., 1969-72, assoc. prof., 1972-76, prof., 1976-93, interim provost, 1980-81, chairperson dept. fgn. langs., 1978-91, dir. Asian studies, 1990-94; chair dept. Spanish, Italian and Portugues U. S.C., Columbia, 1994—; mem. exec. coun. fgn. langs. Ind. Dept. Edn., 1986-92. Fulbright scholar Spain, 1963-64; grantee Ind. Dept. Edn., 1988-93, NEH, 1990; recipient Coll. Tchr. of Yr. award Ind. Fgn. Lang. Tchrs. of Spanish and Portuguese. Mem. Tchrs. of Spanish and Portuguese. Office: Univ SC Dept Spanish Italian & Portuguese Columbia SC 29208

GARDNER, DALE RAY, lawyer; b. Broken Arrow, Okla., May 8, 1946; s. Edward Dale and Dahlia Faye (McKeen) G.; m. Phyllis Ann Weinschrott, Dec. 27, 1969. BA in History, So. Ill. U., 1968; MA in History, St. Mary's U., San Antonio, 1975; JD, Tulsa U., 1979. Bar: Okla. 1979, Colo. 1986, Tex. 1991, U.S. Ct. Mil. Appeals 1988, U.S. Ct. Claims 1989, U.S. Dist. Ct. (no. dist.) Okla. 1981, U.S. Dist. Ct. Colo. 1986, U.S. Dist. Ct. (so. dist.) Tex. 1992, U.S. Ct. Appeals (10th cir.) 1986. Pvt. practice, Sapulpa, Okla., 1979-80; asst. dist. atty. child support enforcement unit 24th Dist. Oklahoma, Sapulpa, 1980-86, 94-95; pvt. practice Aurora, Colo., 1986-91, Houston, 1991-94, Sapulpa, Okla., 1994—; mng. atty. Hyatt Legal Services, Aurora, 1988-89. Author: Immigration Act of 1965: The Preliminary Results, 1974, Teapot Dome: Civil Legal Cases that Closed the Scandal, 1989. Mem. Child Support Enforcement, Sapulpa, 1980-86, 94-96; trustee United Way, Sapulpa, 1985, 95; Domestic Violence Counsel, Sapulpa, 1985; chmn. bd. trustees 1st Presbyn. Ch., Sapulpa, 1985. Capt. U.S. Army, 1969-75, Vietnam., lt. col Res., judge adv. Mem. ABA, Okla. Bar Assn., Tex. Bar Assn., Creek County Bar, Gold Coat Club (pres.), Sertoma (pres. Sapulpa 1985, pres. Columbine 1988, 90, Sertoman of Yr. 1985). Democrat. Home: 1533 Terrill Circle Sapulpa OK 74066 Office: 5433 Westheimer Rd Ste 825 Houston TX 77056-5305 also: 7 South Park St Sapulpa OK 74066

GARDNER, DAN NOBLES, deacon, church official; b. Austin, Tex., July 30, 1942; s. Dan B. and Virginia (Nobles) G.; m. Mary K. Gardner, Apr. 15, 1965; children: Ginger L., Dan B. BBA, U. Tex., 1966. Deacon Hyde Park Bapt. Ch., Austin, 1965—, bus. coord., 1975—; instr. ch. mgmt. Austin C.C., 1988-90; tchr. Hyde Park Bapt. Sch., Austin, 1990-91; high sch. baseball coach, 1990-93. Contbg. author: Church Administration, 1985. Lt. col. U.S. Army, Vietnam, 1966-67, mem. Res. Recipient Faith in God award Austin Jaycees, 1969, Good Shepherd award Boy Scouts Am., 1990. Mem. Nat. Assn. Ch. Bus. Adminstrs., Am. Assn. Baseball Coaches, Tex. High Sch. Coaches Assn. Home and Office: Hyde Park Bapt Ch 3901 Speedway Austin TX 78751-4625

GARDNER, EDWARD CLINTON, JR., gastroenterologist; b. Raleigh, N.C., Aug. 25, 1951; s. Edward Clinton Sr. and Ruth Woodward (Cohen) G.; m. Karen Louise Holmes, June 24, 1978; children: Jessica Jean, Rebecca Ruth, Edward Clinton III. BA in Chemistry, Emory U., 1973, MD, 1977. Diplomate Am. Bd. Internal Medicine, Am. Bd. Gastroenterology. Intern Emory U., Atlanta, 1978, resident in internal medicine, 1980, fellow in digestive diseases, 1982; Onwer, pres. Athens (Ga.) Gastroenterology Assocs., P.C., 1982—; med. staff St. Mary's Hosp., Athens, 1982—, Athens Regional Med. Ctr., 1982—. Fellow Am. Coll. Gastroenterology; mem. ACP, Am. Gastroenterol. Assn., Am. Soc. Gastrointestinal Endoscopy, Ga. Gastroenterol. Soc., Crawford W. Long Med. Soc., Med. Assn. Ga., Phi Beta Kappa. Methodist. Office: Athens Gastroent Assocs PC Bldg 1 Office C 740 Prince Ave Athens GA 30606-5909

GARDNER, GWENDOLYN SMITH, retail executive; b. Bristol, Va., Mar. 2, 1948; d. Julian B. and Margaret Smith; m. Clyde Eugene Gardner Jr., July 20, 1968; children: Jennifer Ellen, Julie Anne. Student, U. N.C., Charlotte, 1966-67, King's Bus. Coll., Charlotte, 1967-68, Cen. Piedmont Community Coll., 1969. Cert. store profl. Asst. bookstore mgr., textbook mgr. Cen. Piedmont Community Coll., Charlotte, 1969-90; bookstore mgr. Davidson (N.C.) Coll., 1990—. Mem. Nat. Assn. Coll. Stores (tchr., facilitator, Stanford, Calif., 1990-91, nominating and cert. coms., 1991, chair cert. com. 1993, 94, store evaluator 1993, bd. trustees 1996—, Pres.' award 1994), Coll. Stores Assn. N.C. (pres. 1990, southeast regional com. 1994-95, course materials com. 1995-96). Office: Davidson Coll Bookstore Main St Davidson NC 28036-9086

GARDNER, HAROLD STEPHEN, economics educator, researcher; b. Dallas, May 17, 1951; s. Clarence Eugene and Nora Evelyn (Stephenson) G.; m. Kathy Susan Stokes, July 2, 1971; children: Daniel Eugene, Jessica Emily. BA, U. Tex., 1973; PhD, U. Calif.-Berkeley, 1978. Instr., Grinnell Coll, Iowa, 1977-78; Herman Brown prof. econ. and dir. Ctr. for Internat. Bus., Baylor U., Waco, Tex., 1978—. Author: Soviet Foreign Trade, 1983, Comparative Economic Systems, 1988. Rsch. fellow Am. Council of Learned Socs., 1980, Presdl. fellow Salzburg Seminar, 1995. Mem. Am. Econ. Assn., Assn. Slavic Studies, Assn. Comparative Econs. Baptist. Avocation: piano. Office: Baylor U Dept Econs Waco TX 76798-8003

GARDNER, J. STEPHEN, lawyer; b. Dayton, Ohio, May 10, 1944; s. David L. and Mary (Webb) Gardner; m. Sandra Ellen Ott, Dec. 23, 1967; children: Stephen, Truett, P.J. BS, U. Fla., 1966, JD, 1969. Bar: Fla. 1969, U.S. Dist Ct. (mid. dist.) Fla. 1971. Atty. Ott & Gardner, Tampa, Fla., 1971-72, Bucklew, Ramsey, Ott & Gardner, Tampa, 1972-75, Trinkle & Redman, Brandon, 1976-81, Bush Ross Gardner Warren & Rudy, Tampa, 1981—. Bd. dirs. Tampa Downtown Partnership, 1989—, also past pres. Capt. U.S. Army, 1970-71. Mem. Tampa Yacht and Country Club (past pres.), Davis Islands Civic Assn. (past pres.), Exch. Club of Tampa (past pres.), Univ. Club of Tampa (bd. dirs., pres.). Methodist. Office: Bush Ross Gardner Warren & Rudy PA 220 S Franklin St Tampa FL 33602-5330

GARDNER, JAMES, recreational management executive, personal care industry executive; b. Ridgeland, S.C., May 27, 1953; s. Shirley Mae Gardner; m. Cathy Brantley, Dec. 27, 1986; 1 child, Jasmine Charese. BA, St. Augustine's Coll., 1975. Med. lab. technician Beaufort-Jasper Comprehensive Health Svcs., Ridgeland, S.C., 1975-76; asst. mgr. Liberty Loans Inc., Hampton, S.C., 1976-77; sr. asst. mgr. Household Fin. Corp., Beaufort, S.C., 1977-79; nigh auditor Hyatt Hotels Corp., Hilton Head, S.C., 1979-80; machinist Gen. Carbide Corp., Jasper, 1979-80; chem. unloader/machinist apprentice St. Regis Paper Co., Jacksonville, Fla., 1981-82; night auditor/mgr., front desk clk. Holiday Inn, Jacksonville, Fla., 1982; owner, operator Gardner's Barber Styling Salon, Ridgeland, S.C., 1984—; parks and recreation dir. Jasper County Coun., Ridgeland, 1992—. Mem. Ridgeland Mid. Sch. Improvement Coun. 1992; bd. dirs. Jasper County Dept. Social Svcs., 1991, Beaufort-Jasper Comprehensive Health Svcs.; mem. recreation task force Jasper County Coun., 1991; pres., dir. Low Country Amateur Athethics, Inc. 1993; active Ridgeland Mid. Sch. Youth Basketball Program; youth program coord. Rep. Juanita White's Campaign Com., Ridgeland, 1980. Mem. NAACP, Citizen's Organized for Pub. Svc. Home: PO Box 399 Ridgeland SC 29936-0399

GARDNER, JOAN, medical, surgical nurse; b. Ft. Worth, Oct. 5, 1950; d. Bert and Pearl (Sandgarten) G. BS in Edn., U. Tex., 1972, BS in Communication, 1976; diploma, Brackenridge Hosp., 1982. RN, Tex. Trust asst. Austin (Tex.) Nat. Bank; tchr. English and reading Columbus (Tex.) Ind. Schs.; staff orthopedics nurse Seton Med. Ctr., Austin, 1982-83, staff nurse gyn. surgery and post partum, 1983-84, staff nurse post partum, 1984-85, staff nurse gyn. surgery and ear, nose, throat, and eye, 1986, charge nurse gen. surgery, 1988-92, staff nurse short-term surgery, 1992—. Home: 1602 Leigh St # A Austin TX 78703-2452 Office: 1201 W 38th St Austin TX 78705-1006

GARDNER, JOEL SYLVANUS, tempest products company executive; b. New Bern, N.C., Aug. 12, 1942; s. John and Josephine R. (Tilghman) m. Jessie Hall Gardner, Aug. 18, 1963; children: John H., Jeremy L. BS in Textiles, N.C. State U., 1970; Diploma in Law, LaSalle Ext. U., Chgo., 1979; MBA, Va. Poly. Inst., 1976; D in Mgmt., Calif. U., Petaluma, 1990. Mgr. contracts Foster Assocs., Washington, 1973-75, Hazleton Labs., Vienna, Va., 1975-77; mgr. contracts and bus. devel. Dynamac Corp., Rockville, Md., 1977-79; procurement mgr. Sperry Corp., Reston, Va., 1977-81; asst. to pres. PE Systems, Alecandria, Va., 1981-84; pvt. cons. Alecandria, Va., 1984-85; pres. Quality Tempest Products, Fairfax, Va., 1985-88; owner TEPs, McLean, Va., 1988—; bd. advisors Westco Inc., Silver Spring, Md., 1986, 87. Mem. Nat. Contract Mgmt. Assn. (cert.). Adventist. Home: 635 Frederick St SW Vienna VA 22180-6360

GARDNER, KATHRYN JOHANNA, nursing educator, community health nurse; b. Cleora, Okla., Nov. 2, 1933; d. Raymond John and Nora Jane (Paul) Yost; m. James F. Gardner, Sept. 29, 1956; children: Julie, Kevin, Kari, Michelle, Gregory. Diploma, St. Johns Sch. of Nursing, Tulsa, 1955; BA, U. Corpus Christi, Tex., 1972; MPH, U. Tex. Sch. of Pub. Health, 1981, DPH, 1988; cert. in Gerontology, 1993, cert. in Infection Control, 1994. Dir. student health svcs. U. Corpus Christi; health ctr. charge nurse City of Houston Dept. HHS, coord. nursing staff devel., supr. clin. health edn.; coord. staff devel. Seven Acres Jewish Geriatric Ctr.; continuous Quality Improvement Coord. Past mem. adv. com. March of Dimes. Recipient Svc. award ARC, Cert. of Appreciation, March of Dimes. Mem. ANA, APHA, Nat. Assn. Health Care Quality, Tex. Nurse's Assn., Tex. Gulf Coast Assn. Healthcare Quality, Assn. Profl. in Infection Control and Epidemiology.

GARDNER, KERRY ANN, librarian; b. Honolulu, May 19, 1955; d. Byron Patton and Claire (Teig) G. BA in Polit. Sci. magna cum laude, Temple U., 1976; MA in Latin Am. Studies, U. Ariz., 1983, MLS, 1990. Vol. libr. Doylestown Pub. Libr., Richlandtown, Pa., 1972-73; documents libr. FMC Corp., Chgo., 1977-78; grad. rsch. asst. U. Ariz., Tucson, 1983-86; libr. asst. I Phoenix Pub. Libr., 1988-89; freelance libr. and rsch. cons. Tucson, 1984-88, 89-92; project mgr. U. Ariz., 1990-91, 91-92; mgr. faculty resource libr. U. Ariz. Ctr. English as 2d Lang., 1989-90, 91-92; pub. svcs. libr. Bryan Wildenthal Meml. Libr., Sul Ross State U., Alpine, Tex., 1992—. Contbr. articles to profl. publs. Tchr. English Literacy Vols. Am., Pima County, Ariz., 1991-92. Grad. scholar U. Ariz., 1976-77, 81-82. Mem. ALA, Assn. Coll. and Rsch. Librs., Tex. Libr. Assn. (legis. com. coll. and univ. librs. divsn. 1993—), Assn. Borderlands Scholars, Big Bend User's Group, Rocky Mountain Coun. Latin Am. Studies, Beta Phi Mu. Office: Sul Ross State U Bryan Wildenthal Meml Alpine TX 79832

GARDNER, RICHARD CALVIN, elementary school educator, librarian; b. Indpls., Sept. 21, 1931; s. Selby A. and Mary E. (Armstrong) G.; B.S., Butler U., 1951; M.A., East Tenn. U., 1955; postgrad. U. Del., 1959, U. Tenn., 1960, 72, U. Wis., 1965; m. Dorothy Faye Fleenor, Aug. 25, 1951; children—Sylvia Jeannine, Kirby Hunter, Trevor Christian. Tchr. elem. sch. Kingsport Pub. Schs., Tenn., 1951-55; asst. prof. edn. SUNY, Oneonta, 1955-57; elem. sch. supr. Kingsport City Schs., 1957-61, asst. supt. schs., 1961-65, 69-71; supr. curriculum devel. Tenn. Dept. Edn., Nashville, 1966-67, coordinator div. instrn., 1972; supt. schs. Norton (Va.) City Schs., 1972-79; supr. elem. edn. Wise County Pub. Schs., Va., 1979-80; tchr.-librarian Hamilton Elem. Sch., Mendota, Va., 1980-83, tchr., 1983-85, prin., 1985-91; tchr. Greendale Elem. Sch., Abingdon, Va., 1991-96, sub, tchr. and vol., wash., Co. (Va.) Public Sch., 1996—; extension instr. E. Tenn. State U., Johnson City, 1959-65, U. Va., Charlottesville, 1967—, U. Tenn., Knoxville, 1967-72, Va. Poly. Inst. and State U., Blacksburg, 1973-80; vis. prof. St. Mary of the Plains Coll., Dodge City, Kans., summer 1971; mem. tchr. edn. adv. council Clinch Valley Coll., U. Va., 1974-76; mem. adv. council Wise Speech and Hearing Clinic, 1975; cons. to Day Care Services, Tenn. Dept. Public Welfare, 1959-71; bldg. coord. Mendota Community Ctr., 1993-94. Bd. dirs. Regional Child Devel. Ctr., 1974-79, chmn. bd. dirs., Mendota Cmty. Health Ctrs, 1996—, Wash. Co. Planning Commn., 1992—, Appalachian Regional Lab., 1971-72, Kingsport Community Chest; bd. dirs. Dilenowisco Ednl. Co-op, chmn., 1972-73. Recipient Good Citizenship award Jaycees, 1962. Mem. NEA, Va., Washington County edn. assns., Local State Nat. PTA' s,1951—, PTA Life mem., Tenn. Va., Kentucky Colonel, 1985. Kappa Delta Pi, Phi Kappa Phi. Mem. Universalist Ch. (trustee 1955-57, ch. sch. dir. 1955-57). Club: Kiwanis (dir. 1972-75, v.p. local chpt. 1974-75). Home: Hunter's Oak 10353 Mendota Rd Abingdon VA 24210-4057

GARDNER, ROBERT CHARLES, systems analyst, administrator; b. Charlotte, N.C., June 11, 1961; s. Gary Kent and Betty Joyce (Sells) G.; m. Ginger Adair Lawing, Feb. 23, 1985; children: Robert Cameron, Sarah Ashley. Student, Western Carolina U., 1979-83. Systems support analyst Miller Svcs., Charlotte, N.C., 1983-85; program mgr. Computer Task Group, Charlotte, 1986-87; installation support analyst Systems Assocs., Inc., Charlotte, 1985-86, programmer, analyst, 1987; systems analyst Day Data Systems subs. E.I. DuPont, Charlotte, 1987-90, systems specialist, 1990-91; project leader Tultex Corp., Martinsville, Va., 1991-92; cons. Am. Systems Profls., Charlotte, 1992-93; systems adminstr. 3 HBO & Co. (formerly First Data Corp.), Charlotte, 1993-96; systems engr. First Union Nat. Bank, Charlotte, 1996—. Mem. Optimists (little league baseball coach 1986), Pi Lambda Phi. Democrat. Methodist. Home: 3508 Kelly Rd Charlotte NC 28216-5731

GARDNER, STANLEY DWAIN, communications company executive; b. Waco, Tex., Nov. 9, 1956; s. Luther Winford Jr. and Frances Leona (Guest) G.; m. Sara Lee Denman, Nov. 23, 1985; children: John Madison, Helen Frances, Luther Winford III. BBA in Fin., U. Tex., Austin, 1979; postgrad. on bus. adminstrn., U. Tex., Arlington, 1982. V.p., chief fin. officer Farmers Propane Gas Co., Inc., Hamilton, Tex., 1979-81, Syntek Investment Properties, Inc., Dallas, 1981-84; mng. ptnr. Gardner & Co., Inc., Dallas, 1984—; CEO, pres. Personalized Comm., Dallas, 1987—. Bd. dirs. Washington St. Presbyn. Mission, Dallas, 1986—, Am. Heart Assn., 1980-81, Dallas Heart Ball, 1986—. Named one of Outstanding Young Men in Am., 1980, 88. Mem. Dallas Mus. of Art, Tex. Ex-Students Assn. (life), Dallas C. of C. Republican. Home: 4311 Potomac Ave Dallas TX 75205 Office: Personalized Comm 8609 NW Plaza Dr Ste 300 Dallas TX 75225-4214

GARDNER, WILLIAM WAYNE, academic administrator; b. LaFayette, Ga., Oct. 13, 1946; s. James Hobson and Minnie Ruth (LeCroy) G.; m. Verlene Sue Stoddard, June 29, 1968; children: Julie Anne, Suzanne Angelique, Michelle Elaine. BS in Missions, Toccoa Falls Coll., 1969; MDiv,

Luther Rice Sem., 1985; M of Profl. Studies, Alliance Theol. Sem., 1986. Cert. Fund Raising Exec. Pastor Deere Creek Chapel, Winterset, Iowa, 1970-71; asst. pastor Ft. Payne (Ala.) Alliance Ch., 1971-73, Grace United Meth. Ch., Wyckoff, N.J., 1973-75; assoc. regional dir. World Vision Internat., Ridgewood, N.J., 1975-76; regional dir. World Vision Internat., Atlanta, 1976-83; v.p. for advancement Toccoa Falls (Ga.) Coll., 1983—; gen. mgr. TFC Network, 1995—; sec. dist. exec. com. Christian & Missionary Alliance, Charlote, N.C., 1986—, interim dist. supt., 1989; chmn. Comm. Commn. Accrediting Assn. of Bible Colls. Pub., founder Toccoa Falls Mag.; prodr.: (film) Changing Lives, (video) Building Servants for Service, (audiotapes) In His Name, Make His Praise, Sounds of Praise, Exalt His Name. Pres. Toccoa Falls Alumni Assn., 1977-80. Mem. Am. Assn. Bible Colls. (com.), Coun. for Advancement for Secondary Edn., Christian Stewardship Assn., Christian Mgmt. Assn., Assn. of Instl. Devel. Officers of Christian Edn., Rotary. Republican. Home: 1007 Oak Cliff Dr Toccoa GA 30577-8982 Office: Toccoa Falls Coll Office of Advancement Rt 17 Toccoa GA 30598

GARFIELD, ROBERT EDWARD, medical educator; b. Douglas, Wyo., Jan. 27, 1939; s. Robert Edward and Caryl (Brush) G.; m. Josett Garfield, Mar. 7, 1964; children: John, Patricia. BSc in Biology, U. Wyo., 1968, MSc in Physiology, 1969; PhD in Pharmacology, U. Alta., Edmonton, Can., 1973. Assoc. prof. McMaster U., Hamilton, Ont., Can., 1979-83, acting chmn., 1984-85, prof., 1983-91; prof. and dir. U. Tex. Med. Br., Galveston, 1991—, dir. reproductive scis., 1991—; external grant reviewer USDA, Washington, 1995, The Wellcome Trust Corp., London, 1995, NIH, Washington, 1994. Author: Uterine Contractility, 1990, Control of Uterine Contractility, 1994, Basic Mechanisms Controlling Term and Preterm Birth, 1994. Mem. basic rsch. adv. com. March of Dimes, White Plains, N.Y., 1993—. Mem. Soc. Gynecol. Investigation, Romanian Acad. Med. Scis., Soc. for Study of Reproduction, Sigma Xi. Office: Univ of Texas Medical Br 301 University Blvd Galveston TX 77555-1062

GARISON, LYNN LASSITER, real estate executive; b. El Dorado, Ark., Dec. 19, 1954; d. Robert Weaver and Iris Amy (Horton) Lassiter. Student, Randolph-Macon Woman's Coll., 1973-76; BS, Tex. A&M U., 1978. Lic. real estate broker, Tex. From broker assoc. to regional mgr. J. B. Goodwin, Realtors, Residential, Inc., Austin, Tex., 1979-82; comml. broker assoc. Christon Co., Realtors, Inc., Dallas, 1983-87; v.p. Dallas Mkt. Ctr., Dallas, 1987-89; regional v.p. Tenenbaum and Assocs., Inc., Dallas, 1989-92; pres. Artemis Co., Dallas, 1992—; bd. dirs. Consumer Credit Counseling Svc. Bd. dirs. Dallas Coun. World Affairs; mem. Mayor's Task Force on Child Abuse, Highland Pk. Presbyn. Ch. Mem. DAR, Daus. of the Republic of Tex., Nat. Assn. Corp. Real Estate, Cert. Comml. Investment Mem., Urban Land Inst., Rotary Internat. (bd. dirs. Park Cities club, v.p.). Home: PO Box 12681 Dallas TX 75225

GARLAND, LARETTA MATTHEWS, educational psychologist, nursing educator; b. Jacksonville, Fla.; d. Wilburn L. and Clyde-Marian (Chamberlin) Matthews; diploma Fla. State Sch. Nursing, 1942; BSN, Emory U., 1950, MEd, 1953; BA in Edn., U. Fla., 1951; cert. cardiovascular nurse specialty Tex. Med. Center, 1965; EdD, U. Ga., 1975; postgrad. in counseling and guidance Ga. State U., 1969, grad. cert. in gerontology, 1981; Cert. nat. counselor, 1986; m. John B. Garland, Mar. 2, 1946; children: John Barnard, Brien Freeling, Amy-Gwin. Office and staff nurse, Lakeland, Fla., 1942, 45; nurse ARC, Buffalo, 1956; asst. prof. nursing Med. Coll. Ga., 1965-67; instr. Emory U., 1952-54, assoc. prof., 1967-71, prof., 1972-86; prof. emeritus, 1987—; ednl. psychologist, dir. gerontol. nurse practitioner program, 1978-80, asst. to dean, 1983-86. Author: (with Carol Bush) Coping Behavior and Nursing, 1982; contbr. articles to profl. jours. Served with Nurse Corps, U.S. Army, 1942-45. Decorated Bronze Star; recipient Outstanding Teaching award Emory U. Sch. Nursing Grad. Srs., 1977, appreciation award So. Region Constituent Leagues, Nat. League for Nursing award, 1987, Mabel Korsell award of appreciation Ga. League for Nursing, 1987, Spl. Recognition award Ga. Nurses Assn., 1988, 90, Nurse of Yr. award, 1992, appreciation Ga. Assn. Nursing Students, 1990, Van de Vrede award Ga. League Nursing, 1993; HEW fellow, 1967-68. Mem. APA, AACD, Am. Nurses Assn., Ga. Assn. Nursing Students (hon.), Nat. League Nursing, Bus. and Profl. Women, China Burma India VA Assn., Hump Pilots Assn., Fla. Fed. Garden Clubs, Fla. Fed. Womens Clubs, Nat. Assn. Women Vet. (steering com.), Women in Mil. Svc. Meml. Found. (charter), Alpha Chi Omega, Sigma Theta Tau, Kappa Delta Pi, Alpha Kappa Delta, Omicron Delta Kappa. Methodist. Office: Emory U Nell Hodgson Woodruff Sch Nursing Atlanta GA 30322

GARLAND, RAY LUCIAN, investment company executive, columnist; b. Roanoke, Va.; s. Walter Buhrman and Minnie (Allen) G.; m. Jane Morriss, Dec. 30, 1982. BA, Roanoke Coll., 1958; MA, U. Va., 1966. Ptnr. Garland's Drug Stores, Roanoke, 1949-60; instr. Roanoke Coll., Salem, Va., 1960-66; mem. Va. Ho. of Dels. Commonwealth of Va., Richmond, 1968-80, mem. Va. Senate, 1980-84; mng. ptnr. W.B. Garland and Son, Investment, Roanoke, 1974—. Columnist Roanoke Times, and others, 1985—. Recipient Disting. Alumni award Roanoke Coll., 1992. Republican. Methodist. Home and Office: RR 1 Box 103 Goode VA 24556-9712

GARLAND, RICHARD ROGER, lawyer; b. Princeton, Ill., Aug. 20, 1958; s. Louis Roger and Irene Marie (Tonozzi) G. BA in Polit. Sci. summa cum laude, U. S. Fla., 1979; JD with honors, U. Fla., 1982. Bar: Fla. 1982, U.S. Dist. Ct. (mid. dist.) Fla. 1983, U.S. Ct. Appeals (11th cir.) 1987, U.S. Supreme Ct. 1988, U.S. Ct. Appeals (fed. cir.) 1995; Fla. Bar cert. in appellate practice, 1995. Instr., supr. appellate advocacy U. Fla., Gainesville, 1981-82; assoc. Dickinson, O'Riorden, Gibbons, Quale, Shields & Carlton, Venice, Fla., 1983-85, Sarasota, Fla., 1986-90; ptnr., sr. atty. Dickinson & Gibbons, Sarasota, Fla., 1991—. Pres. parish coun. San Pedro Cath. Ch., North Port, Fla., 1986-92; barrister, program chair John M. Scheb Inn of Ct. Mem. ABA, FBA, Sarasota County Bar Assn. (editor newsletter 1991-93, bd. dirs. 1994-96, treas. 1996-97), U. South Fla. Alumni Assn., Phi Kappa Phi, Pi Sigma Alpha. Democrat. Roman Catholic. Office: Dickinson & Gibbons PA 1750 Ringling Blvd Sarasota FL 34236-6836

GARLING, CAROL ELIZABETH, real estate executive and developer; b. Detroit, Sept. 23, 1939; d. Elmer Daniel and Elizabeth Aldene (Kish) Champagne; m. Fred C. Garling, Mar. 7, 1963 (dec. Nov. 1972). BA, U. Detroit, 1960, degree in criminology, 1972. Lic. real estate broker. Asst. dir. prodn. programming and control Ford Motor Co., Dearborn, Mich., 1960-62; land developer, builder Garling Bldg. Co., Dearborn, 1962-73; specialist indsl. security Cen. Security, Inc. and Garling Security Services, Dearborn, 1973-79; owner, realtor, broker Carol Garling Realty, Inc., Dearborn, 1976-80; broker, realtor Embassy Realty, Inc., Ft. Lauderdale, Fla., 1981—; land developer Garling Bldg. and Devel., Raleigh, N.C., 1986—. Mem. Ft. Lauderdale Bd. Realtors, Plum Hollow Golf Club (Southfield Mich., life mem.). Home: 7750 N Via De La Sombre Scottsdale AZ 85258-3210

GARMER, WILLIAM ROBERT, lawyer; b. Balt., May 8, 1946; s. William M. and Grace (DeLane) G.; divorced; 1 child, Lindsey DeLane. B.A., U. Ky., 1968, J.D., 1975. Bar: Ky. 1975, U.S. Dist. Ct. (ea. dist.) Ky. 1977, U.S. Ct. Appeals (6th cir.) 1980, U.S. Supreme Ct. 1979. Law clk. to chief judge U.S. Dist. Ct. (ea. dist.) Ky., Lexington, 1975-76; assoc. prof. law litigation skills U. Ky. Law Sch., Lexington, 1981—; ptnr. Savage, Garmer & Elliott, P.S.C., Lexington, 1984—. Casenote editor St. Mary's Law Jour., 1975; contbr. articles to profl. jours. Deacon Presbyn. Ch. With USAF, 1969-73. Fellow Am. Coll. Trial Lawyers; mem. ABA, ATLA (chair coun. state pres.), Ky. Bar Assn. (com. on specialization and cert. 1982—, litigation com. 1989—), Fayette County Bar Assn., Ky. Acad. Trial Attys. (bd. govs. 1984-89, treas. 1990, sec. 1991, v.p. 1992, pres. 1994), Phi Delta Phi (named one of Best Lawyers in Am. 1989-96). Democrat. Office: Savage Garmer & Elliot PSC 141 N Broadway St Lexington KY 40507-1230

GARNER, CINDY ANNE, account executive; b. Fayetteville, N.C., Aug. 2, 1957; d. William Marvin and Virginia Ruth (Wheeler) G. MAT, BA, Rollins Coll., 1979. Collector Creditors Mercantile, Inc., Orlando, Fla., 1980-82; supr. collection Credinrs Mercantile Inc., Orlando, Fla., 1982-83, mgr. collection, 1983-84, regional mktg. dir., 1984-86; mgr. collection AMI Tampa (Fla.) Cen. Bus. Office, 1986-87, dir., 1987-89; pres. Marc Inc., Charlotte, N.C., 1989—. Mem. Am. Guild Patient Account Mgmt. (publs. com. 1990-91, 2d v.p. Carolina chpt.), Am. Collectors Assn., Nat. Fin. Mgmt. Assn., Nat. Health Collectors Assn. Office: 1012 S Kings Dr Charlotte NC 28283-0001

GARNER, DAVID PAUL, defense analyst; b. Painesville, Ohio, July 3, 1942; s. Cecil Larue and Kamilla Margaret (Kardos) G.; m. Teresia Elaine Espinosa, June 14, 1969; children: Deborah, Margaret, Kathryn, Jennifer. BBA, U. Notre Dame, 1964; MBA, Harvard U., 1970; Disting. Grad., U.S. Naval War Coll., Newport, R.I., 1983. Commd. 2d lt. USMC, 1964, advanced through grades to col., 1985; served two tours USMC, Vietnam; chief of mblzn. plans Orgn. Joint Chiefs Staff USMC, 1985-88, ret., 1988; rsch. fellow Logistics Mgmt. Inst., McLean, Va., 1989—. Fin. chmn. St. Elizabeth Seton Parish, Lake Ridge, Va., 1985-90, mem. liturgy com., 1991—, mem. parish coun., 1987-94. Decorated Bronze Star for valor, 1966; recipient Pres.'s award Logistics Mgmt. Inst., 1995, Def. Superior Svc. medal Sec. of Def., Washington, 1988. Mem. Assn. of Nat. Def. Execs., Marine Exec. Assn., Notre Dame Club of Washington, Harvard Bus. Sch. Club of Washington. Roman Catholic. Home: 3506 Caledonia Cir Woodbridge VA 22192 Office: Logistics Mgmt Inst 2000 Corporate Ridge Mc Lean VA 22102

GARNER, DIANNE GRAHAM, special education consultant, early childhood consultant; b. Ft. Worth, Jan. 8, 1943; d. Raymond Duke and Iris Alberta (Pierce) Reed; widowed; 1 child, Kirk Thomas Garner. BS, Tex. Tech. U., 1964, MEd, 1976. Ednl. diagnostician Tex. Tech. U., supervision U. N. Tex. Elem. sch. tchr. Colorado Springs (Colo.) Ind. Sch. Dist., 1964-69; spl. edn. tchr. Lubbock (Tex.) Pub. Schs., 1971-75, ednl. diagnostician, 1975-77, spl. edn. specialist, 1977-87; coord. IDEA part H. Colo. Dept. Edn., Denver, 1987-92; ednl. specialist Region XI Edn. Svc. Ctr., Fort Worth, 1992-95; spl. edn. supr. Denton (Tex.) Ind. Sch. Dist., 1995—; mem. Head Start advisory, Lubbock, Tex., 1985-87; pres., treas. Tchg. Tex. Tots, Stateville, Tex., 1980-85; cons. Children Resources Internat., Washinton, 1994-96, Childcare Assn., Ft. Worth, 1994-96. Mem. Trophy Club Women's Club, Assn. Edn. Young Children (Ft. Worth area). Republican. Mem. Ch. of Christ. Office: Denton Ind Sch Dist 1117 Riney Rd Denton TX 76107

GARNER, DOUGLAS MICHAEL, gymnastics fitness center executive, team coach; b. Camden, Ark., Sept. 10, 1959; s. Thomas Clark and Naomi (Colvert) G.; m. Becky Lynn Cathcart, Dec. 26, 1982; children: Tyler, Michael. BA in Psychology and Sociology, Centenary Coll., Shreveport, La., 1980; MS in Behavioral Sci., Kennedy Western U. Instr. Am. Coaching Effectiveness Program; meet dir. USGF; dir. U.S. Gymnastics Fedn. Men's Program; co-owner, head team coach Hot Springs Gymnastics Fitness Ctr., 1980—; adj. prof. Garland County C.C.; instr. elem. phys. edn. pvt. sch.; dir. Ark. Springers Gymnastics Camp; guest presenter Youth Clinics, Head Start Conf. for Movement Edn. Mem. adv. bd. Collegiate Press. Youth coach Wheelchair Sports, H.S. Boys Club; dir., head coach Ark. Jr. Rollin' Razorbacks Wheelchair Sports Team; vol. youth coach, Hot Springs, Shreveport; rated ofcl. Ark. Activities Assn. Mem. AAPHERD, ASCD, APA, Nat. Assn. Girls and Women Sports (citizen amb. program del. to Russia 1993), U.S. Assn. Ind. Gym Clubs, U.S. Gymnastics Fedn. (safety cert.), Ark. Ofcls. Assn., Wheelchair Sports USA, Nat. Handicapped Sports, Nat. Wheelchair Basketball Coaches Assn. Home: 122 Mesa Trl Hot Springs National Park AR 71913-9088 Office: Hot Springs Gymnastics and Fitness 1860 Higdon Ferry Rd Hot Springs National Park AR 71913-7218

GARNER, DOUGLAS RUSSELL, science writer; b. Orange, Tex., Aug. 7, 1953; s. Jim Buck and Ruthie Delores (Seastrunk) G. BA in Biology, U. Tex., 1975; postgrad. in medicine, Creighton U., 1976-77. Pub. health investigator Houston Health Dept., 1979-84; freelance tech. writer, translator Houston, 1984-86; tech. translations editor McElroy Translation Co., Austin, Tex., 1986-96; freelance sci. writer and editor, Austin, 1989—; sci. researcher Calif. Afro-Am. Mus., L.A., 1991—. Author: The Adventures of Teddy Wallace, 1991. Recipient award Charles Palmer Davis Found., 1970. Mem. AAAS. Home and Office: PO Box 8428 Austin TX 78713-8428

GARNER, JO ANN STARKEY, elementary school educator; b. Ft. Hamilton, N.Y., Dec. 25, 1934; d. Joseph Wheeler and Irene Dorothy (Vogt) Starkey; m. James Gayle Garner, Mar. 2, 1957; children: Mary Vivian Pine, Margaret Susan Gillis, Kathryn Lynn. BA in History, Govt., Law, U. Tex., Austin, 1956; postgrad., Trinity U., 1973. Cert. deaf edn. and elem. tchr., Tex. Kindergarten tchr. Platenstrasse Internat. Sch., Frankfurt, Fed. Republic Germany, 1964-66; tchr. of deaf Sunshine Cottage Sch. for Deaf, San Antonio, 1966—; speech cons. Trinity U., 1978, cooperating tchr., 1978-87. Mem. San Antonio Fiesta Commn. Mem. Tex. Alexander Graham Bell Assn. (charter), Tex. State Geneal. and Hist. Soc., San Antonio Geneal. and Hist. Soc., The Bright Shawl, Rep. Nat. Com., German-Texan Heritage Soc., Ind. Hist. Soc., Pioneers of Ind., Mecklenburg (N.C.) Geneal. Soc., Pioneers of Ill., Ill. Geneal. Soc., Tex. Pioneers, Alpha Delta Pi. Republican. Mem. Catholic Episcopal Ch. Home: 2027 Edgehill Dr San Antonio TX 78209-2023 Office: Sunshine Cottage Sch for Deaf 103 Tuleta Dr San Antonio TX 78212-3176

GARNER, JOHN KENNETH, lithography company executive; b. Washington, June 16, 1953; s. John Daniel and Dorothy Aldridge (Hicks) G.; m. Mary Anne Walton, Aug. 7, 1976; 1 child, Emily Aldridge. BA, Randolph-Macon Coll., 1975. Account mgr. United Litho, Falls Church, Va., 1981-87, dir. mktg., 1987-89, v.p. mfg., 1989, v.p. sales and mktg., 1989-90, exec. v.p., chief operating officer, 1990-93, pres., CEO, 1993—; cons., speaker Graphic Arts Coun. N.Am., Alexandria, Va., 1989—, Graphic Comm. Assn., Alexandria, 1989—, Fla. Mag. Assns., Tallahassee, 1989—; mem. adv. com. exec. devel. program. Printing Industry of Am., Alexandria, 1989—; bd. dirs. Printing Industries Va., 1992—. Internal v.p. Merrifield (Va.) Jaycees, 1977-78. Recipient Key Man award Merrifield Jaycees, 1978, Wallace Stettinius Educator of Yr. award, 1993. Mem. Nat. Assn. Printers and Lithographers (bd. dirs. 1993—), Va. Printing Found. (bd. dirs. 1993—), Graphic Arts Edn. and Rsch. Found. (peer review com. 1994—)., Walter E. Soderstrom Soc. Office: United Litho 2818 Fairfax Dr Falls Church VA 22042

GARNER, JULIE LOWREY, occupational therapist; b. Paris, Tex., Aug. 6, 1953; d. John Robert and Rachel (Garner) Lowrey; m. Kenneth Wayne Garner, Jan. 29, 1983. BS, U. Tex., Galveston, 1975; MS, Tex. Woman's U., 1982. Cert. occupational therapist, Tex.; cert. to administer and interpret So. Calif. Sensory Integration Tests Sensory Integration Internat., neurodevel. treatment approach to cerebral palsy. Occupational therapist Presbyn. Hosp. Dallas, 1976-77; occupational therapist region X Ednl. Svc. Ctr., Richardson, Tex., 1977; occupational therapist Duncanville (Tex.) Ind. Sch. Dist., 1977-81, 89-90, Grand Prairie (Tex.) Ind. Sch. Dist., 1978-81, U. Tex., Dallas, 1981-83, Lewisville (Tex.) Ind. Sch. Dist., 1983-85, Collin County Coop. Spl. Svcs., Wylie, Tex., 1983-89, Commerce (Tex.) Ind. Sch. Dist., 1990—. Bd. dirs. United Cerebral Palsy Assn. Dallas, 1980-84. Recipient Hurdle Cert. of Honor Soroptimist Internat., Dallas, 1976. Mem. Am. Occupational Therapy Assn., Sensory Integration Internat. Methodist. Home: 1313 Flameleaf Dr Allen TX 75002-4424

GARNER, PAUL TRANTHAM, auditor; b. Cameron, Tex., May 25, 1951; s. W.H. and Dorothy L. (Gohmert) G.; children: Paul Christopher, Gregory Trantham. BBA, U. Tex., 1973; MS in Bus. Adminstrn., U. No. Colo., 1980. Cert. systems profl. Engr. Tex. Instruments, Inc., Austin, 1980; mgr. performance audit divsn. State of Tex. Auditor's Office, Austin, 1980-95; dir. data svcs. Tex. Workers Compensation Commn., Austin, 1995—; mem. faculty Austin C.C., 1982; seminar lectr. in field. Mem. Bergstrom-Austin Community Coun. Capt. U.S. Army, 1973-80. U.S. Army ednl. scholar, 1969. Mem. Assn. for Systems Mgmt. (pres.), Am. Evaluation Assn., Legis. Prog. Evaluation Soc., Austin Endowment Soc. (bd. dirs.), Austin Bus. Club., Rotary. Home: 7804 Wykeham Dr Austin TX 78749 Office: Tex Workers' Compensation Commn 4000 S IH35 Austin TX 78704

GARNES, DELBERT FRANKLIN, clinical and consulting psychologist, educator; b. Lorain, Ohio, Jan. 13, 1943; s. Delbert Chauncey and Virginia (Scott) G.; m. Bertha J. Smith (div.); m. Joyce M. Roberts; children: Franklin Chauncey, Charles Deltre. BA, Ohio State U., 1969; MA, Xavier U., 1974; PhD, St. Louis U., 1980. Lic. clin. psychologist. Counselor Fairfield Sch. for Boys, Lancaster, Ohio, 1970-71; instr. Met. Coll., St. Louis, 1974-75; psychologist Narcotics Svc. Coun., St. Louis, 1974-75, Roxbury Ct. Clinic, Boston, 1975-77, Fuller Mental Health Ctr., Boston, 1976-77; asst. prof. psychology Tex. So. U., Houston, 1980-86, assoc. prof., 1986—; chmn. dept. counseling and psychology, 1990—; cons. Mass. Bar Assn., Boston, 1976-77, Mass. Parole Bd., Boston, 1977, Harris County Juvenile Probation, Houston, 1981—, Harris County Dept. Edn., Houston, 1988—. Judge, Internat. Sci. and Engring. Fair, 1982, Houston Sci. and Engring. Fair, 1983-85. Cpl. USMC, 1961-65. Recipient Disting. Svc. award Nat. Tech. Assn., 1985, Svc. award Student Nat. Pharm. Assn., 1987, Sam Houston Area coun. Boy Scouts Am., 1987; NIMH fellow, 1977; Boston U. Sch. Medicine teaching fellow, 1975. Mem. Houston Assn. Black Psychologists (pres. 1981-82), Am. Psychol. Assn., Nat. Assn. Black Psychologists, Am. Fedn. Tchr., Tex. State Tchrs. Assn. Office: Tex So U 3100 Cleburne St Houston TX 77004-4501

GARNES, RONALD VINCENT, marketing executive, finance broker, consultant; b. Washington, Mar. 7, 1947; s. Ernest W. Love and Vauda Hall Love G.; student U. Dayton, 1965-68; BS, U. Md., 1975. Adminstrv. mgr. Western Union Electronic Mail, Inc., McLean, Va., 1976; dir. mktg. Communications Cons., Inc., Silver Spring, Md., 1977; ptnr. CAC, Washington, 1977; account mgr. PRC Computer Ctr., Inc., McLean, Va., 1978-79, sr. account mgr., 1979—; mktg. exec. Dun and Bradstreet Corp.; prin., chief exec. officer RVG Assocs., Ltd., 1990—. Cons. Mem. Fairfax County Republican Com. Mem. Nat. Coun. Tech. Svc. Industries, Nat. Assn. Market Developers, Am. Entrepreneurs Assn., Internat. Assn. Bus. and Fin. Cons., Mortgage Bankers Assn. Am., Internat. Assn. Entrepreneurs Am., Greater Washington Bd. Trade, Fairfax County C. of C., Lincoln Club, U.S. Senatorial Club. Roman Catholic. Office: 7918 Jones Branch Dr Ste 600 Mc Lean VA 22102

GARNETT, LINDA KOPEC, nurse, researcher; b. Springfield, Mass.; d. Frank J. and Anna (Paul) Kopec; m. Thomas R. Garnett, Oct. 6, 1990. BS in Nursing cum laude, Fitchburg (Mass.) State Coll., 1983; MS in Health Svcs. Adminstrn., Ctrl. Mich. U., 1996. RN. Nurse intern Med. Coll. Va. Hosps., Richmond, nurse clinician in neurosci. ICU; terr. mgr., patient care specialist Kinetic Concepts Therapeutic Svcs., Richmond; rsch. coord. dept. neurology Med. Coll. Va./Va. Commonwealth U., Richmond. Mem. Sigma Theta Tau.

GARREANS, LEONARD LANSFORD, protective services official, criminal justice professional; b. Glenwood, Iowa, Mar. 25, 1942; s. Ernest Lyle and Kathryn Hermine (Seeger) G.; m. Wanda Marian Ackley, Aug. 24, 1963; children: Kirk Anthony, Debra Renee, David Lance, Diana Jasmine. BSE summa cum laude, John Brown U., 1973; MSE, State Coll. Ark., 1974; postgrad., U. Ark., 1978-79; PhD, Internat. U., Independence, Mo., 1984. Cert. secondary tchr., guidance counselor. Draftsman Pacific Pumping Co., Oakland, Calif., 1963; chem. operator Allied Chem. Corp., El Segundo, Calif., 1963-69; asst. swimming coach John Brown U., Siloam Springs, Ark., 1972-73; grad. asst. State Coll. Ark., Conway, 1973-74; tchr./coach, dir. athletics The Alliance Acad., Quito, Ecuador, 1974-78; teaching asst. U. Okla. Summer Inst. Linguistics, Norman, 1979-81; dir. guidance and counseling Lomalinda High Sch. Summer Inst. Linguistics, Colombia, 1981-87; internat. trainer, cons. Summer Inst. Linguistics, Dallas, 1987-89, pers. devel. officer, 1989-93; cmty. supervision officer Dallas County, State of Tex., Dallas, 1993-95; community supr. officer Dallas County Community Supervision and Corrections Dept., 1993-95; detention officer Richardson (Tex.) Police Dept., 1995—; internat. dir. of intercultural comm. course Summer Inst. Linguistics, Dallas, 1988-89. Vol. probation officer Benton County (Ark.) Juvenile Youth Authority, 1970-72; mem. Jaycees, 1970. With USMC, 1960-63. Mem. Am. Assn. Ret. Persons. Republican. Evangelical. Home: 7346 Cave Dr Dallas TX 75249-1303 Office: Richardson Police Dept 140 N Greenville Richardson TX 75081

GARREN, SAMUEL BAITY, English language educator; b. Greensboro, N.C., Jan. 20, 1943; s. Martin Thompson and Birdie Mary (Rowland) G.; m. Christine Elizabeth Branham, May 24, 1980. BA, Davidson Coll., 1965; MA, La. State U., 1967, PhD, 1976. Instr. English La. State U., Baton Rouge, 1971-74; asst. prof. Grambling (La.) State U., 1976-77; vis. lectr. U. N.C., Wilmington, 1979-80; vis. asst. prof. English N.C. A&T State U., Greensboro, 1977-79, asst. prof., 1980-86, assoc. prof., 1986-95, prof., 1995—, sec. faculty senate, 1988-90, del. faculty assembly, 1993-96, mem. black studies task force, 1992-94; short story contest judge O. Henry Festival, Greensboro, 1994. Mem. editl. bd. Growing Up mag., 1988-89; contbr. articles to profl. jours. and Dictionary of Literary Biography. Faculty devel. grantee N.C. A&T State U., 1993. Mem. MLA, Coll. Lang. Assn., Samuel Beckett Soc., Nat. Coun. Tchrs. English, South Atlantic MLA. Democrat. Mem. Soc. of Friends. Office: NC A&T State U English Dept 1601 E Market St Greensboro NC 27411

GARRETT, FRANKLIN MILLER, historian; b. Milw., Sept. 25, 1906; s. Clarence Robert and Ada (Kirkwood) G.; LLB, Woodrow Wilson Coll. Law, 1941; PhD, Oglethorpe U., 1970; m. Frances S. Finney, 1978; children by previous marriage: Patricia Abbott, Franklin Miller. Br. mgr. Western Union Telegraph Co., Atlanta, 1934-38; salesman Ward Wight & Co., Atlanta, 1939-40; mem. exec. staff pub. relations, historian Coca-Cola Co., Atlanta, 1940-68. Chmn., Fulton County (Ga.) Civil Service Bd., 1955-72; ofcl. historian City of Atlanta, 1973—, Fulton County, 1975—. Bd. dirs. Children's Center Met. Atlanta, 1958-70. Served with AUS, 1942-45. Named a City Shaper, Atlanta mag., 1976; recipient Meritorious Pub. Service medal Nat. Assn. Secs. of State, 1985, Shining Light award for Svc. as Atlanta's Historian, 1993; mainline diesel locomotive Ga. R.R. named in his honor, 1980. Mem. Nat. Ry., Va., Ga., Atlanta (chmn. bd. trustees 1967-68, dir. 1968-74, historian 1974—, trustee 1932—), DeKalb County hist. socs., Newcomen Soc. N.Am., Atlanta Art Assn., Atlanta Civil War Round Table, Grand Jurors Assn. Fulton County, Ga. Geneal. Soc. Presbyterian. Clubs: Rotary, Commerce, Piedmont Driving. Author: Atlanta and Environs I-III, 1954, rev. edit., 1969; Yesterday's Atlanta, a picture history, 1974. Home: 3650 Randall Mill Rd NW Atlanta GA 30327-2712 Office: 130 W Paces Ferry Rd NW Atlanta GA 30305-1366

GARRETT, GEORGE PALMER, JR., creative writing and English language educator, writer; b. Orlando, Fla., June 11, 1929; s. George Palmer and Rosalie (Toomer) G.; m. Susan Parrish Jackson, June 14, 1952; children: William, George, Rosalie. Grad., Hill Sch., 1947; A.B., Princeton U., 1952, M.A., 1956, Ph.D., 1985; DLitt (hon.), U. South, 1995. Asst. prof. English Wesleyan U.; writer-in-residence, resident fellow in creative writing Princeton U., 1964-65; former assoc. prof. U. Va.; prof. English Hollins Coll. Va., 1967-71; prof. U. S.C., Columbia, 1971-73, Princeton U., 1974-78, U. Mich., 1979-80, 83-84; Hoyns prof. creative writing U. Va., Charlottesville, 1984—; prof. Bennington Coll., 1980; Coal Royalty chair U. Ala., 1994. Author The Reverend Ghost: Poems (Poets of Today IV), 1957, King of the Mountain, 1958, The Sleeping Gypsy and Other Poems, 1958, The Finished Man, 1959, Which Ones Are the Enemy, 1961; (poems) Abraham's Knife, 1961, In the Briar Patch, 1961; (plays) Sir Slob and the Princess, 1962, Cold Ground Was My Bed Last Night, 1964; (screenplays) The Young Lovers, 1964, The Playground, 1965, Do, Lord, Remember Me, 1965, For a Bitter Season, 1967, A Wreath for Garibaldi, 1969, Death of the Fox, 1971, The Magic Striptease, 1973, Welcome to the Medicine Show, Postcards/Flashcards/Snapshots, 1978, To Recollect a Cloud of Ghosts: Christmas in England 1602-03, 1979, Luck's Shining Child: Poems, 1981, The Succession: A Novel of Elizabeth and James, 1983, The Collected Poems of George Garrett, 1984, James Jones, 1984, An Evening Performance: New and Selected Short Stories, 1985, Poison Pen, 1986, Understanding Mary Lee Settle, 1988, Entered from the Sun, 1990, The Sorrows of Fat City, 1992, Whistling in the Dark, 1992, My Silk Purse and Yours, 1992, The Old Army Game, 1994, The King of Babylon Shall Not Come Against You, 1996; editor The Girl in the Black Raincoat, 1966, The Sounder Few, 1971, Film Scripts I-IV, 1971, Craft So Hard to Learn, 1973, The Writer's Voice, 1973, Intro V, 1974, Intro 6: Life As We Know It, 1974, Intro 7: All of Us and None of You, 1975, Botteghe Obscure Reader, 1975, Intro 8: The Liar's Craft, 1977, Intro 9: Close to Home, 1978, Eric Clapton's Lover, 1990, The Wedding Cake in the Middle of the Road, 1992, Elvis in Oz, 1992, That's What I Like (About the South), 1993. Served in occupation of Trieste, Austria and Germany. Recipient Rome prize Am. Acad. Arts and Letters, 1948-59, Sewanee Rev. fellow poetry, 1958-59, Am. Acad. and Inst. of Letters award, 1985, T.S. Eliot award Ingersoll Found., 1990, Bernard Malamud PEN/Faulkner award, 1990, Hollins Coll. medal, 1992, U. Va. Pres.'s Report award, 1992; named Cultural Laureate of Va., 1986; Ford Found. grantee in drama, 1960, Nat. Found Arts grantee, 1966, Guggenheim fellow, 1974. Fellow Am. Acad. in

Rome; mem. MLA, Author's League, Writers Guild Am. East, Poetry Soc. Am., PEN, Fellowship So. Writers (vice chancellor 1988, chancellor 1993—). Democrat. Episcopalian. Home: 1845 Wayside Pl Charlottesville VA 22903-1630 Office: Univ Va Dept English Charlottesville VA 22903

GARRETT, GLORIA SUSAN, social services professional; b. Tampa, Fla., Nov. 30, 1951; d. Howard Leon and Marie Leonora (Garcia) G.; m. Michael Thomas McClain, May 16, 1973; children: Molly Kathleen Garrett McClain, Andrew Michael Garrett McClain. Student, Agnes Scott Coll., 1969-71, U. South Fla., 1971-72; BA, Ga. State U., 1977, MEd, 1979. Sr. caseworker DeKalb County Dept. Family and Children Services, Decatur, Ga., 1979-80, 82-84, prin. caseworker, 1980-82, 84-85, casework supr., 1985-86, sr. casework supr., 1986-91; disability adjudicator Ga. Disability Adjudication Sect., Decatur, 1991-93, sr. disability adjudicator, 1993-94, case cons., 1994-96, disability adjudication casework supr., 1996—. Mem. Nat. Assn. Disability Examiners, Ga. Assn. Disability Examiners. Office: Disability Adjudication PO Box 1187 Decatur GA 30031-1187

GARRETT, JAMES LEO, JR., theology educator; b. Waco, Tex., Nov. 25, 1925; s. James Leo and Grace Hasseltine (Jenkins) G.; m. Myrta Ann Latimer, Aug. 31, 1948; children: James Leo III, Robert Thomas, Paul Latimer. BA, Baylor U., 1945; BD, Southwestern Bapt. Theol. Sem., 1948, ThD, 1954; ThM, Princeton Theol. Sem., 1949; Ph.D., Harvard U., 1966; postgrad. Oxford U., 1968-69, St. John's U., 1977, Trinity Evang. Divinity Sch., 1989. Ordained to ministry Baptist Ch., 1945. Pastor, Bapt. chs. in Tex., 1946-48, 50-51; successively instr., asst. prof., assoc. prof., prof. theology, disting. prof. Southwestern Bapt. Theol. Sem., Fort Worth, 1949-59, 79—, assoc. dean for PhD degree, 1981-84; prof. Christian theology So. Bapt. Theol. Sem., Louisville, 1959-73; dir. J. M. Dawson Studies in Ch.-State, prof. religion Baylor U., Waco, Tex., 1973-79, Simon M. and Ethel Bunn prof. Ch.-State Studies, 1975-79; interim pastor Bapt. chs. in Tex., D.C., Ind. and Ky.; guest prof. Hong Kong Bapt. Theol. Sem., 1988; coord. 1st Conf. on Concept of Believers' Ch., 1967; chmn. Study Commn. on Coop. Christianity, Bapt. World Alliance, 1968-75; sec. Study Commn. on Human Rights, 1980-85; theol. lectr. Wake Forest, N.C., Torreon, Mex., Cali, Colombia, Recife, Brazil, Montevideo, Uruguay, Oradea, Romania, Dallas. Mem. Am. Soc. Ch. History, Am. Acad. Religion, So. Bapt. Hist. Soc., Conf. on Faith and History. Author: The Nature of the Church According to the Radical Continental Reformation, 1957, Baptist Church Discipline, 1962, Evangelism for Discipleship, 1964, Baptists and Roman Catholicism, 1965, Reinhold Niebuhr on Roman Catholicism, 1972, Living Stones: The Centennial History of Broadway Baptist Church, Fort Worth, Texas, 1882-1982, 2 vols., 1984-85, Systematic Theology Vol. 1, 1990, Vol. 2, 1995; co-author: Are Southern Baptists "Evangelicals"?, 1983; co-editor: The Teacher's Yoke: Studies in Memory of Henry Trantham, 1964; editor: The Concept of the Believers' Church, 1970, Baptist Relations with Other Christians, 1974, Calvin and the Reformed Tradition, 1980; editor Southwestern Jour. Theology, 1958-59, Jour. of Ch. and State, 1973-79. Home: 5525 Full Moon Dr Fort Worth TX 76132-2309 Office: PO Box 22117 Fort Worth TX 76122

GARRETT, JAMES LOWELL, contractor; b. Stillwater, Okla., Dec. 29, 1946; s. Calvin L. Garrett and Jetta L. (Hubbel) Newberry; m. Deborah F. Files, Sept. 3, 1987; 1 child, Kristina D. BS in Indsl. Engring. and Mgmt., Okla. State U., 1969. Pres. Garrett Devel., Oklahoma City, 1970-80, T.A.O. Inc. Gen. Contractor (merged with Garrett Devel.), Tulsa, 1981—. Mem. Investments and Constrn. Mgmt., Tulsa C. of C. Office: T A O Inc Gen Contractor 8218 E 121st St Bixby OK 74008-2700

GARRETT, JOHN C., electrical engineer, manufacturing executive; b. 1943. BEE, U. Conn., 1964. Engr. GE Co., 1964-87; from engring. supr. to exec. v.p. Square D Co., 1987-93; pres. Harris Corp., Melbourne, Fla., 1993—. Office: Harris Corp 1025 W NASA Blvd Melbourne FL 32919

GARRETT, JOHN CHARLES, economist; b. Englewood, N.J., Feb. 17, 1957; s. John Battaille Jr. and Charlotte Anna (Milstrey) G. BA in Econs., Tex. Christian U., 1978; PhD in Econs., U. Tex., 1982. Teaching asst. U. Tex., Austin, 1979, asst. instr., 1980, 81-82; assoc. economist Chase Econometrics, Bala Cynwyd, Pa., 1982-83; economist BellSouth Telecomms., Birmingham, Ala., 1983-91, 93—; econ tech. staff Bell. Comms. Rsch., Livingston, N.J., 1991-93. Chancellor scholar, 1975-78, Nat. Merit scholar, 1975-78. Mem. Am. Econ. Assn. Republican. Presbyterian. Home: 3925 Cannock Dr Birmingham AL 35242-5835 Office: BellSouth Bus Systems Ste 500 3000 Galleria Pkwy Birmingham AL 35244

GARRETT, JOSEPH EDWARD, aerospace engineer; b. Hendersonville, N.C., Mar. 4, 1943; s. Kenneth Pace and Anna Lou (Lytle) G.; m. Aurelia Jane Pryor, Aug. 7, 1971. BS in Aerospace Engring., N.C. State U., 1966; MS in Aerospace Engring., Ga. Inst. Tech., 1978. Registered profl. engr., Ga. Basic and fatigue loads assoc. aircraft engr. LASC-Ga. (formerly Lockheed-Ga.), Marietta, 1966-67, basic and fatigue loads structures engr., 1967-75, fatigue and fracture mechanics sr. structures engr., 1975-80, company planning, 1980-82, fracture mechanics structures engr., 1982-91, advanced structures sr. engr., 1991-96; fatigue and fracture mechanics sr. structures engr., 1996—. Loaned exec. United Way, Atlanta, 1984, Cobb County chmn. for Individual Gifts, Marietta, 1985, chmn. Cobb County Adv. Com., Marietta, 1987-88, bd. dirs., Atlanta, 1987-88. Assoc. fellow AIAA (dir. Regional II 1990-96), Mem. of Yr. Atlanta sect. 1986, Booster of Yr. 1988, 92, 94, 95); mem. Inst. Cert. Mgrs. Lockheed Ga. Mgmt. Assn. (v.p. mem. achievement 1988-89, v.p. adminstrn. 1989-90, Booster of Month 1980, 1st Cert. Mgr. of Yr. 1989). Republican. Baptist. Home: 2291 Goodrum Ln Marietta GA 30066-5200 Office: LASC-Ga Dept 73-25 Zone 0160 86 S Cobb Dr Marietta GA 30063-0160

GARRETT, KATHRYN ANN (KITTY GARRETT), legislative clerk; b. Antlers, Okla., July 10, 1930; d. Stansell Harper and Vena Clifford (Crawford) Byers; m. William Donald Garrett, Jan. 13, 1955 (dec. June 1992); children: William Mark, Amy Kathryn, Ann Elizabeth Garrett Jenni. Student, Okla. A&M U., 1948-50. Sec. Garform Industries, Wagoner, Okla., 1951-52; sec. to exec. sec. Okla. Edn. Assn., Oklahoma City, 1952-55; sec. revenue and taxation com. Ho. Reps., State of Okla., Oklahoma City, 1969-76, bill clk./ins. clk., 1976-84, asst. chief clk./jour. clk., 1985-93; ret., 1994. Mem. Am. Soc. Legis. Clks. and Secs. (assoc.), Okla. Heritage Assn., Sooner Book Club. Democrat. Home: 1429 Wilburn Dr Oklahoma City OK 73127-3253

GARRETT, LARRY CARLTON, sales executive; b. Elizabeth City, N.C., Oct. 17, 1950; s. Carlton Bray and Norma (Smithson) G.; m. Cheryl Dawn Fishel, Nov. 19, 1972; children: Christopher M., Stephen E. BA, Atlantic Christian Coll., 1972. Sales trainee Graybar Electric, Norfolk, Va., 1972-75; sales specialist Broudy Kantor Co. Inc., Norfolk, 1975-77, divisional mgr., 1977-84; sales specialist Boehringer Mannheim Diagnostics, Virginia Beach, Va., 1984-88, sr. sales specialist, 1988; regional sales mgr. Boehringer Mannheim Corp., Chesapeake, Va., 1988—. Vol. Kempsville Rescue Squad, Virginia Beach, 1981-84. Mem. ADA (bd. dirs. Hampton chpt. 1987-88), Seven Springs Golf Club, Sigma Phi Epsilon. Home: 544 Warrick Rd Chesapeake VA 23320-7230

GARRETT, LEE (HOMER SIMMONS HOLCOMB), retired broadcaster; b. Roanoke, Va., Sept. 29, 1925; s. Homer Simmons and Dorothy (Pollard) H.; m. Charlotte Wade Holcomb, Feb. 28, 1953; childre: David Lee Holcomb, Sharon Kay Holcomb Thompson. Student, Shenandoah Coll., Dayton, Va., 1946-47. Announcer Sta. WSVA, Harrisonburg, Va., 1946-47; program dir. Sta. WROV, Roanoke, 1948-53; announcer, reporter, news anchor, mgr. community svcs., commentator Sta. WSLS-TV, Roanoke, 1953-87. Mem. Roanoke County Bd. Suprs., 1986-89, vice chmn., 1987, chmn., 1988-89; vice chmn. Roanoke County Social Svcs. Bd., 1986-87, mem., 1987-89; mem. Va. Aviation Bd., 1990-94; vice chmn. Roanoke Regional Airport Commn., 1988-89; mem. Roanoke County Ext. Leadership Coun., Va. Poly. Inst. and State U., 1992—. with USAAF, 1943-45; 2d lt. USAF, 1952-53, Korea; lt. col. USAFR ret. Recipient Coll. medallion Va. Western C.C., 1966, Pres.'s award Ferrum (Va.) Coll., 1970. Mem. Ret. Officers Assn. (pres. 1993-94, 97), Mil. Order World Wars (comdr. 1992-94), Am. Legion (chmn. nat. D-Day Meml. Found. 1992-94), Nat. D-Day Meml. Found. (chmn. 1992-94), Quiet Birdmen, AARP, League Older Ams., Silver Falcons Assn., Torch Club (v.p.), Hunting Hills Country Club, Rotary, Optimists (pres.). Democrat. Baptist. Home: 4501 Tanglewood Ln Roanoke VA 24018-2455

GARRETT, LINDA OAKS, theology educator; b. Oklahoma City, Sept. 4, 1957; d. Monzell F. and Doris H. (Lovett) O.; m. John Charles Garrett, July 20, 1996. MDiv, Southwestern Bapt. Theol. Sem., 1986, PhD, 1993. Tchg. asst., fellow Southwestern Bapt. Theol. Sem., Ft. Worth, 1986-93; tchg. fellow U. No. Tex., Denton, 1994-95; asst. prof. religion Judson Coll., Marion, Ala., 1995-96; instr. Jefferson State C.C., Birmingham, Ala., 1996—; music dir. 1st Presbyn. Ch., Grand Prairie, Tex., 1993-95, Trinity Bapt. Ch., Bonham, Tex., 1986-87. Author: Biblical Illustrator, 1994-95. Mem. Am. Acad. Religion and Soc. Bibl. Lit. Home: 3925 Cannock Dr Birmingham AL 35242

GARRETT, LOUISE LIN, secondary school educator; b. Atlanta, May 19, 1956; d. Linton Monroe and Mamie Louise (Drewry) G.; m. Thomas H. Rochester, Dec. 10, 1979 (div. 1983); 1 child, Linda Louise Carmella; m. James Larry Kent, Feb. 20, 1993. BS in Zoology, U. Ga., 1971. Cert. mid. sch. sci. tchr., secondary sch. sci. tchr., gifted edn. tchr., Fla. Sci. tchr. Atlanta Area Vocat. Tech. Sch., 1970-72, So. Jr. H.S., Columbus, Ga., 1972-74, Hardaway H.S., Columbus, 1974-75, Grady H.S., Atlanta, 1975-78, Steward Mid. Sch., Douglasville, Ga., 1979-80, Paulding County H.S., Dallas, Ga., 1982-83, Jinks Mid. Sch., Panama City, Fla., 1986-89, Brown Mid. Sch., Panama City, 1989-93, Everitt Mid. Sch., Panama City, 1993—; head Transcoastal Trucking Co., Atlanta, 1980-86; notary pub. State of Fla., 1989—; amb. first Internat. Physics Edn. Del. to Vietnam, Eisenhower Found., 1993; rep. Peace Corp World-Wide Sch., 1992-93; presenter in field. Author: Toys in the Science Classroom, 1992; co-author pamphlet, Energy Experiments for Enthusiastic Experimentors; contbr. articles to profl. jours. Vol. forester Fla. Dept. Forestry, 1986-93; vis. tchr. Withlachoochee Environ. Ctr., 1987; Daisy leader Girl Scouts U.S., 1988-89, asst. Brownie troop leader, 1989-91, troop leader, bus driver, 1991-92, 93; vol. Kaleidoscope Theater, 1989-94; bd. suprs. Bay County Soil and Water Conservation Dist. Group V, State of Fla., 1990—, chairperson spkr. contest, 1987-91; lector, Sunday sch. tchr., vacation bible sch. tchr. St. Andrew's Episcopal Ch., 1983—, mem. Altar Guild, wedding ministry; active local schs. Recipient 1st Pl. award Ga. Instrnl. Fair for Tchrs., 1980, cert. of merit Withlachoochee Environ. Ctr., 1987, Outstanding Sci. Tchr. cert., 1988, Conservation Tchr. of Yr. award, 1989, Outstanding Conservation of Yr. award, 1990. Mem. NSTA, FTA/NEA (rep. del. 1990-96), Assn. Bey County Educators (chair grievance com. 1991), Fla. Assn. Sci. Tchrs., N.W. Fla. Physics Allegiance, Bay District Sci. Coun., Assn. Bay County Educators, Notary Assn. Fla. Episcopalian. Home: 2213 W 27th St Panama City FL 32405 Office: Everitt Mid Sch 608 School Ave Panama City FL 32401-5256

GARRETT, MARILYN, tax consultant; b. San Francisco, Feb. 19, 1955; d. Jerry B. and Mary Alice (Mitchell) Williams; m. Michael Anthony Garrett, Sept. 10, 1982 (div. Oct. 1991); children: Michael Amin Jamiel, Mario Antonio Ray, Mitchell Andrae Jerry. Student, Tex. So. U., Houston, 1992—. Notary pub., Tex. Children's protective svcs. worker, eligibility specialist I Tex. Dept. Human Svcs., Houston, 1986-93; tax cons., Missouri City, Tex., 1993—; receptionist Tex. So U. Coll. Pharmacy, Houston, 1993—. Contbr. poetry to anthologies (Silver Poet award). Troop leader Boy Scouts Am., Houston, 1991-93; v.p. James H. Law Elem. Sch. PTA, Houston, 1992-94; vol. parent Project Headstart, Houston, 1993. Democrat. Mem. Ch. of Christ. Home: 1214 Cowden Ct Missouri City TX 77489-3130 Office: Tex So U Coll Pharmacy Gray Hall 240 3200 Cleburne St Houston TX 77004

GARRETT, PAUL R., JR., physician; b. Salem, Ohio, Nov. 22, 1947; s. Paul Robert and Lois Elizabeth (Schooley) G.; m. Roberta Karen Kampshulte, Nov. 26, 1977; children: Samantha, Kelly. BA, Case Western Res. U., 1969; MD, Med. Coll. Ohio, Toledo, 1972. Diplomate Nat. Bd. Med. Examiners, Am. Bd. Internal Medicine, Am. Bd. Med. Oncology. Intern Emory U. Affiliated Hosps., 1972-73, resident, 1973-75; fellowship in oncology and hematology Emory U., 1975-77; pvt. practice Orlando, Fla., 1977-94; chief med. officer Fla. Hosp. Healthcare Sys., 1995—; asst. cons. prof. medicine Duke U. Sch. Medicine, 1990—; pres. med. staff Fla. Hosp., Orlando, 1994; med. dir. Hosp. Ctrl. Fla., Orlando, 1992—. Contbr. articles to profl. jours. Med. dir. Leukemia Soc. Ctrl. Fla., 1978-82, 84-88; mem. med. adv. bd. Hospice Ctrl. Fla., 1990—; mem. physician adv. com. Sun Health Plans Fla., 1992—. Emory U. Affiliated Hosps. Hematology and Oncology fellow, 1975-77; recipient Glidden L. Brooks award for Scholastic Excellence, 1972, Mead-Johnson Rsch. award, 1972, Mosley Book award, 1972. Mem. Am. Soc. Clin. Oncology, Am. Soc. Hematology, Am. Soc. Internal Medicine, Fla. Soc. Clin. Oncology, Fla. Med. Assn., Orange County Med. Soc., Acad. Hospice Physicians, Am. Coll. of Physician Execs., Alpha Omega Alpha. Office: 601 E Rollins St Orlando FL 32803

GARRETT, RANDY JACK, commercial real estate broker; b. Plainview, Tex., Jan. 17, 1952; s. Jack Charles and Veda Faye (Ramsower) G.;m. Marialice Williams; children: Alissa Marie, Clayton Chase. BBA, Tex. Christian U., Ft. Worth, 1974. Advt. salesman Dallas Morning News, 1974-77; advt. dir. John Watson Landscape Illumination, Dallas, 1977-80; catalogue prodn. mgr. Inovision-An EDS Co., Dallas, 1980-82; advt. mgr. Casa Bonita Inc., Dallas, 1982-85; broker Coldwell Banker Comml., Dallas, 1985-90; broker, salesman Joe Foster Comml. Real Estate, Dallas, 1990-92; broker Barclay Comml., Dallas, 1992-94, Fults-Oncor, Dallas, 1994—. Vice chmn. Park Cities YMCA, 1996, major gifts chmn., 1995; bd. mem. Chem. Awareness Coun./Com., 1995—. Named Vol of Yr.. Park Cities YMCA, Dallas, 1995. Mem. North Tex. Comml. Assn. Realtors (editl. bd. chmn. 1994). Republican. Christian Scientist. Office: Fults Oncor Internat 9400 N Central Expy 5th Fl Dallas TX 75231

GARRETT, REGINALD HOOKER, biology educator, researcher; b. Roanoke, Va., Sept. 24, 1939; s. William Walker and Lelia Elizabeth (Blankenship) G.; m. Linda Joan Harrison, Mar. 15, 1958 (div.); children: Jeffrey David, Randal Harrison, Robert Martin; m. Catherine Leigh Touchton, June 12, 1989. BS, Johns Hopkins U., 1964, PhD, 1968. Asst. prof. biology U. Va., 1968-73, assoc. prof., 1973-82, prof., 1982—; sci. cons. Contbr. articles to profl. jours.; author textbook. NIH fellow, 1964-68; Fulbright Hays fellow, 1975-76; Thomas Jefferson vis. fellow, 1983; grantee NIH, NSF. Mem. Am. Soc. Biochemistry and Molecular Biology, Am. Soc. Microbiology, Am. Soc. Plant Physiology, Soc. Gen. Physiology, Sigma Xi, Phi Lambda Upsilon, Phi Sigma. Office: U Va Dept Biology Gilmer Hall Charlottesville VA 22903

GARRETT, RICKI RAYNER, educational administrator; b. Tupelo, Miss., Jan. 28, 1951; d. Charles Evans and Lucille (Moore) Rayner; m. Jesse Ivy Garrett III, Dec. 21, 1974; children: Charles Walker, Jesse Oliver. BA in English, Miss. U. for Women, 1973; MA in English, U. Miss., 1974. Tchg. asst. English U. Miss., Oxford, 1974-75; tchr. English Jackson (Miss.) Preparatory Sch., 1975-78; owner, mgr. Hinughi Trading Post, Jackson, 1978-85; bd. dirs. State Instns. of Higher Learning, 1992-2004; bd. dirs. Miss. Ednet Bd., Miss. Commn. on Vol. Svc. Charter mem., pres. Clinton (Miss.) Jr. Aux., 1990-91; pres. Clinton Newcomers, 1989-90, Miss. U. for Women Alumni Assn., Columbus, 1991-92; co-pres. Clinton H.S. Band Boosters, 1996-97; bd. dirs., treas. Arts Coun. Clinton, 1995—; bd. dirs. Clinton PTA, 1986—; mem. coun. ministries 1st United Meth. Ch., 1995—. Republican. Methodist. Home: 114 Cedar Crest Dr Clinton MS 39056

GARRETT, ROBERTA KAMPSCHULTE, nurse; b. Amityville, N.Y., Aug. 15, 1947; d. Robert Henry and Gertrude Ann (Schweitzer) Kampschulte; m. Paul R. Garrett Jr., Nov. 26, 1977; children: Samantha Kristine, Kelly Nicole. BS, U. Fla., 1969. RN, Fla.; cert. in oncology nursing. Staff nurse Valley Hosp., Ridgewood, N.J., 1969-70; asst. head nurse Broward Gen. Hosp., Ft. Lauderdale, Fla., 1970-71; CCU nurse Grady Meml. Hosp., Atlanta, 1972-77; nurse to pvt. physician Orlando, Fla., 1977-94; case mgmt. Fla. Healthcare Sys., Orlando, 1996—. Republican. Lutheran.

GARRETT, RONALD DOYLE, electronics company executive; b. Atlanta, Feb. 14, 1955; s. Doyle Clayton and Ernestine Marge (Anderson) G.; m. Deborah Loran Steinman, Apr. 29, 1955 (div. Jan. 1992); children: Richard, Ronda, Patrick; m. Sandra Jean Horn, 1994. Enlisted USN, 1973, resigned, 1981; sr. design engr Loral Electronics, Atlanta, 1981-84; dir. rsch. and devel. Tangent Techs., Norcross, Ga., 1984-88; dir. engring. DayStar Digital, Flowery Branch, Ga., 1988-90; pres. IIR, Inc., Cumming, Ga., 1990-93; v.p. mktg. Spectra Systems Corp., Alpharetta, Ga., 1993—. Inventor computer network card, computer keyboard. Recipient Beneficial Invention award U.S. Govt., 1980. Mem. IEEE, North Fulton Amateur Radio Soc., Atlanta MacIntosh Users Group. Libertarian. Unitarian. Home: PO Box 29 Cumming GA 30130-0029 Office: Internet Works LLC 6295 Barrett Rd 2nd Fl Cumming GA 30128

GARRETT, SANDRA, elementary education educator; b. Salina, Kans., Feb. 7, 1955; d. Ralph Thurston and Sybil (Cook) Renfro; m. Richard Hugh Garrett, may 15, 1977; children: Bobbie Jean, Alex Hugh. BSE, Henderson State U., 1976; MSE, U. Cen. Ark., 1977; EdD, U. N. Tex., 1996. Reading specialist in elem. edn., English; currirulum and instrn. specialist. Tchr. fourth grade Pub. Sch., Springdale, Ark., 1977; tchr. second grade and spl. edn. Pub. Sch., Nashville, Ark., 1977-80; tchr. grades four, five and six Pub. Sch., Dallas, 1990-93; tchr. grade seven and eight Pub. Sch., Mesquite, Tex., 1993-95; asst. prof. Southeastern Okla. State U., Durant, Okla., 1995-96. Founder and pub. (children's mag.): Young Writers' Craft, 1992-95; columnist, co-editor: The Lantern, 1995—. Mem. Southeast Regional Reading Consortia, Okla., 1995-96; pres. Friends of the Pub. Libr., Mesquite, 1989. Recipient Meadows Excellence in Tchg. fellowship, U. North Tex., 1978, Comm. Svc. award The Exch. Club, Mesquite, 1994. Mem. AAUW, ASCD, Assn. Childhood Educators Internat., Internat. Reading Assn., Nat. Coun. Tchrs. of English, Alpha Upsilon Alpha (asst. counselor 1996), Kappa Delta Pi (asst. counselor 1996), Phi Delta Kappa. Home: 5317 Arroyo Trail Sherman TX 75090

GARRETT, WILLIAM E., general surgeon; b. Chgo., Jan. 27, 1945; s. William and Virginia (Martin) G. BS, DePaul U.; MD, U. Chgo. Plastic surgeon Harlem Hosp., N.Y.C., 1985-86; asst. prof. U. Tenn., Memphis, 1986-93; asst. prof. surgery Meharry Med. Coll., Nashville, 1993-96, assoc. prof. surgery, 1996—, faculty coun. chair, 1994-96; asst. chief surgery Met. Gen. Hosp., 1996—.

GARRIS BOWMAN, MARY LOUISE, poet, singer, songwriter; b. Wadesboro, N.C., Oct. 9, 1946; d. Roscoe and Tinnie Bell (Taylor) Garris; m. Willie James Bowman, Dec. 18, 1983; children: James T. Robinson, Maurice Robinson. Grad., Anson C.C., Polkton, N.C., 1994. Author: (poems) Masterpiece, Don't Let A Dream Die, Why Did Men Reject Jesus Christ, The Angel Rolled the Stone Away, From Poverty to a Throne, Heaven, I Imagined, God Can Lift Heavy Burdens, The Earth Was Once Like a Paradise, I Just Took Time to Pray; contbr. articles tp profl. jours. Named to World of Poetry Hall of Fame, 1991. Mem. World of Poetry. Home: PO Box 835 Wadesboro NC 28170-0835

GARRISON, CLIFFORD DAVIS, JR., physical education educator; b. Memphis, May 15, 1940; s. Clifford Davis and Mabel (Parker) G.; m. Maribeth Woodfin, Mar. 26, 1965; children: Gregory Davis, Lee Woodfin. BS in Edn., U. Ctrl. Ark., 1962, MEd, 1965. Jr. high coach, tchr. Wynne (Ark.) Pub. Schs., 1962-63, asst. sr. high sch. coach, tchr., 1963-64; head basketball coach, asst. football coach, tchr. Stuttgart (Ark.) High Sch., 1964-70, dean of students, coach, 1970-71; asst. basketball coach, phys. edn. instr. Henderson State U., Arkadelphia, Ark., 1971-72; head basketball coach, phys. edn. instr. Hendrix Coll., Conway, Ark., 1972-88, head basketball coach, prof. phys. edn., 1989-93; also athletic dir. Hendrix Coll., Conway, 1992—. Named Outstanding Young Educator Stuttgart Jaycees, 1968; life mem. Naismith Meml. Basketball Hall of Fame. Mem. AAHPERD, Ark. H.S. Coaches Assn., Ark. Intercollegiate Conf. (Coach of Yr. 1979-80, 80-81, 90-91, So. Collegiate Athletic Conf. Coach of Yr. 1994-95, Winningest Basketball Coach in Hendrix History), Nat. Assn. Basketball Coaches Assn., Nat. Assn. Collegiate Dirs. Athletics. Methodist. Office: Hendrix Coll 1600 Washington Ave Conway AR 72032-3001

GARRISON, GEORGE HARTRANFT HALEY, curator; b. Norfolk, Va., Aug. 6, 1938; s. George Hartranft Haley and Ione (Taylor) G.; m. Hannelore Emmy Lydia Buckel, June 6, 1968; 1 child, Ione Gerhild. BA in History, Va. Mil. Inst., 1961; translators cert., U. Heidelberg. Commd. 2d lt. U.S. Army, 1961, advanced through grades to capt., 1967; trust mgr. pvt. estate Nags Head, N.C., 1976-79; curator of scrip, dir. rsch. and sales Antique Stocks & Bonds Co., Williamsburg, Va., 1979—. Author: (workbook) Insider's Guide to Antique Securities, 1987; contbr. articles to internat. newspapers and jours. Pres., sr. curator, trustee Soc. for Preservation Am. Bus. History; trustee Am. Mus. Fin. History. Recipient Disting. Svc. award as ofcl. Scripophilist, State of Va., 1981; named Entrepreneur on the Go, Entrepreneur Mag., 1991. Mem. Bond and Share Soc. (pres. Am. br.). Home and Office: Antique Stocks & Bonds Drawer JH Williamsburg VA 23187-3632

GARRISON, GEORGE WALKER, JR., mechanical and industrial engineering educator; b. Statesville, N.C., May 21, 1939; s. George Walker and Gladys Mary (Bell) G.; BSME, N.C. State U., 1961, MS, 1963; PhD, 1966; MBA, Vanderbilt U., 1980; m. Nancy Carole Mayfield, June 10, 1961; children: Jennifer Renee, George W. Rsch. and tchg. asst. N.C. State U., 1964-66; rsch. engr. Sverdrup/ARO, Inc., Arnold Air Force Sta., Tenn., 1966-70, sr. lead engr., 1970-75, sect. supr., 1975-78, br. mgr., 1978-80, dir. energy systems Sverdrup Tech. Inc., Tullahoma, Tenn., 1980-81; prof. mech. engring. U. Tenn., Tullahoma, 1981—, chmn. engring. mgmt. program, 1994—; tech. dir. Ctr. for Advanced Space Propulsion, 1987-89, dir., 1989—; exec. dir. Ctr. Space Transp. and Applied Rsch. John W. Harrelson Scholarship award, 1957; NDEA fellow, 1961; named Outstanding Profl. of Yr., 1987. Fellow ASME; mem. AIAA, Nat. Mgmt. Assn. (pres. 1991-92, Silver Knight Mgmt. award 1992), Sigma Xi. Mem. Christian Ch. (Disciples of Christ) (elder, chmn. bd. 1984-87). Contbr. articles to sci., tech. jours. Home: 567 Waters Edge Dr Estill Springs TN 37330-3668 Office: U Tenn Space Inst Tullahoma TN 37388

GARRISON, MARK DAVID, psychology educator, writer; b. Edmund, Okla., Jan. 15, 1955; s. William Floyd and Marjorie Jo (Barton) G.; m. Diane Louise Nelson, Jan. 2, 1981; children: Erik Peter, Astrid Linnea, Nels Stephen. BA, Shimer Coll., 1976; MA in Psychology, U. Dallas, 1978; PhD in Interdisciplinary Psychology, Emory U., 1983. Instr. Bethel Coll., McKenzie, Tex., 1982-84; prof. Ky. State U., Frankfort, Ky., 1984—; assessor Toyota Assessment Ctrs., Frankfort, Ky., 1986-90. Author: Introduction to Psychology, 1992, Human Relations: Porductive Approaches for the Workplace, 1997; contbr. article to Jour. Mind and Behavior; editor: (bookseries) Integrative Studies Series, 1991—. Grantee U.S. Dept. Edn., Ky., 1986-89, 95—, NEH, 1989-90. Mem. APA, So. Soc. Philosophy and Psychology. Home: 107 E Third Frankfort KY 40601 Office: Dept Psychology Ky State U Frankfort KY 40601

GARRISON, PATRICIA A., mathematics educator; b. New Orleans, Apr. 2, 1942; d. Wilmer and Leatha (Roussell) Garrison; m. Klem Wendell Jones, Aug. 13, 1966 (div. Apr. 1981); 1 child, Katrice Wynnett Jones Morgan. BS in Secondary Edn., Southern U., Baton Rouge, 1965; MEd in Curriculum and Instrn., Boston Coll., 1996. Tchr. math. Jefferson Parish Sch. Dist., Harvey, La., 1965-67, 82—, Knoxville City Sch. Sys., 1968-81; instr. math. Boston Coll., Chestnut Hill, 1990-91, Goellen Smith Psychiat. Hosp., New Orleans, 1987. Vol. math. tutor LaFamille Nouvelle Civic Orgn., Harvey, 1983-85, Jefferson Parish Sch. Sys., 1989-90; vol. Jefferson Parish Juvenile Dept.; active voter registration NAACP, Harvey, 1987—. Named Outstanding Mother of the Yr., Civic and Social Club, New Orleans, 1996, Woman of the Yr. Westside Missionary Bapt. Assn., 1996. Mem. ASCD, Nat. Coun. Tchrs. Math., Order Eastern Star (Queen Esther chpt. program chair 1996—, Walk-A-Thon chair 1996), Alpha Kappa Alpha (v.p. 1996—, vol. math. tutor 1995-96, tutorial program chair 1995-96, Outstanding Svc. award 1996). Democrat. Baptist. Home: 2152 Caddy Dr Marrero LA 70072-4722 Office: West Jefferson High School 8th St Harvey LA 70058

GARRISON, PAUL F., retail executive; b. Black Mountain, N.C., Aug. 12, 1929; s. AWilliam Garfield and Ellen Mitchell (Burgin) G.; m. Joyce C. Silver, Mar. 21, 1952; children: Phillip B., James G. Student, Berea (Ky.) Coll., 1950-52; BS in Agr., U. Tenn., 1954; postgrad., Mich. State U., 1956-57. Mgmt. trainee Kroger Co., Atlanta, 1954-55, store mgr., 1955-56, produce buyer, 1957-60, field merchandiser, 1960-62, zone mgr., 1962-69; dir. ops. Bruno's Inc., Birmingham, Ala., 1969-70; v.p., dir. Bruno's Inc.,

Birmingham, 1970-88, pres. Birmingham div., 1990-91, sr. exec. v.p., 1991—; pres. Piggly Wiggly So., Vidalia, Ga., 1988-90. Bd. dirs. Southwestern Acad., Vidalia, 1988-90. Sgt. USMC, 1946-49. Mem. Kiwanis, Masons. Republican. Baptist. Home: 1730 Cornwall Rd Birmingham AL 35226-2610 Office: Bruno's Inc PO Box 2486 800 Lakeshore Pkwy Birmingham AL 35211

GARRISON, PITSER HARDEMAN, lawyer, mayor emeritus; b. Lufkin, Tex., Mar. 7, 1912; s. Homer and Mattie (Milam) G.; m. Berneice Jones, Dec. 3, 1936 (dec. Apr. 1992); m. Reba Brent, Sept. 29, 1993. Student Lon Morris Jr. Coll., 1929-30, student Stephen F. Austin State U., 1930-32; LL.B., U. Tex., 1935. Bar: Tex. 1935; U.S. Dist. Ct. (ea. dist.) Tex. 1936, U.S. Dist. Ct. (so. dist.) Tex. 1938, U.S. Ct. Appeals (5th cir.) 1939. Ptnr. Garrison, Renfrow, Zeleskey, Cornelius & Rogers, Lufkin, 1935-52, sr. ptnr., 1952-68; chmn., gen. counsel Lufkin Nat. Bank, 1968-81; sole practice, Lufkin, 1981—. Mayor City of Lufkin, 1970-88, mayor emeritus, 1988—; past bd. dirs., past pres. Angelina and Neches River Authority, Lufkin; past pres. Deep East Tex. Council of Govts., Jasper; past bd. dirs., past chmn. Angelina County Tax Appraisal Dist., Lufkin; bd. dirs. Meml. Hosp., Lufkin, 1975-91 . Served to maj. U.S. Army, 1942-46. Recipient Disting. Alumnus award Lon Morris Jr. Coll., 1974; Disting. Alumnus award Stephen F. Austin State U., 1976; named East Texan of the Month, East Tex. C. of C., 1966, East Texan of the Yr., East Tex. C. of C., 1981, East Texan of Yr., Deep East Tex. Council of Govts., 1980. Fellow Am. Coll. Trial Lawyers, Tex. Bar Found. (charter); mem. Angelina County Bar Assn. (past pres.), Tex. Bar Assn., ABA, Phi Delta Phi. Democrat. Methodist. Lodges: Rotary (past pres.), Masons, Shriners. Home: 1302 Tom Temple Dr Apt 302 Lufkin TX 75904-5552 Office: PO Box 150537 515 S First St Lufkin TX 75915-0537

GARRISON, WANDA BROWN, environmental consultant; b. Madison County, N.C., Sept. 16, 1936; d. Roy Lee Brown and Zella Arizona (Miller) Brown Hannah; m. Charles Mitchell Garrison, July 9, 1955; children—Roy Lee, Marsha Joan; 1 step-son, Charles Mitchell, Jr. Student air-line hostess Weaver Airlines, St. Louis, 1954-55; student Haywood Tech. Coll., Clyde, N.C., 1967-68; student IBM, Asheville, N.C., 1977; student in data processing Agy. Record Control, Atlanta, 1978. Operator Day Co., Waynesville, N.C., 1954-57; driver Haywood County Schs., Waynesville, 1970-71; operator Am. Enka, N.C., 1972-75; bookkeeper L. N. Davis Ins. Co., Waynesville, 1975-80; stock preparation Champion Internat., Canton, N.C., 1980-89; cons. Garrison and Assocs. Environ. Solutions, Pensacola, Fla. Sec./treas. James Chapel Baptist Ch., Haywood County, N.C., 1965-77; pres. Fire Dept. Aux., Crabtree, N.C., 1973—; pres. Women Mission Union, Crabtree Bapt. Ch., Haywood County, 1977-80; v.p. Gideon Aux., Haywood County, 1982-84, pres., 1984-87; state aux. follow-up rep., 1984-87, state zone leader, 1987-88. Recipient Life Saving plaque Lion's Club, Waynesville, 1972. Mem. AFL-CIO. Republican. Home: 513 S 2nd St Pensacola FL 32507-3313

GARRITY, RAYMOND JOSEPH, community college administrator, consultant; b. New Orleans, Sept. 15, 1939; s. Frank Patrick and Troy Elizabeth (Welborn) G.; m. Madelyn Rita Smith, Oct. 28, 1977. BS, Loyola U., New Orleans, 1961, MS, 1966; EdD, Ind. U., 1972. Instr. sci. and chemistry New Orleans Pub. Schs., 1961-70; evaluation/edn. specialist La. State U. Med. Ctr., New Orleans, 1970-73; assoc. dir. edn. office Meharry Med. Coll., Nashville, 1973-75; dir. curriculum Delgado C.C., New Orleans, 1975-88, dean City Park campus, 1988-90, provost, v.p. for acad. affairs, 1990—; trustee Coun. for Adult and Experiential Learning, Chgo., 1993—; state coord. Nat. Coun. Instrnl. Adminstrs., 1986—; bd. dirs. Nat. Assn. Pvt. Non Traditional Schs. and Colls., Grand Junction, Colo., 1990—. Author jour. articles, book revs., curriculum materials. Chmn. Mayor's Adv. Commn. on Hazardous Materials, New Orleans, 1980-86; mem. exec. bd. New Orleans Ednl. TV Consortium, 1993—, treas., 1996; bd. dirs. Family Devel. Found., New Orleans, 1994—. Decorated knight Equestrian Order of the Holy Sepulchre of Jerusalem (Vatican City); Fulbright scholar, 1994. Fellow Georgian-Am. Acad. Medicine and Surgery; mem. KC, Order of Alhambra, Deutsches Haus (pres. 1971, 78), Schlaraffia Nova Orleans (v.p. 1985—). Roman Catholic. Home: 4533 Transcontinental Dr Metairie LA 70006 Office: Delgado CC 501 City Park Ave New Orleans LA 70119

GARROTT, FRANCES CAROLYN, architectural technician; b. Bowling Green, Ky., Mar. 10, 1932; d. Irby Reid and Carrie Mae (Stahl) Cameron; m. Leslie Othello Garrott, Oct. 12, 1951 (dec. Feb. 1978); children: Dennis Leslie, Alan Reid; adopted children: Carolyn Maria, Karen Roxana; m. Raymond William Scerbo, May 31, 1978 (div. Oct. 1990). Student Fla. State U., 1951, St. Petersburg Jr. Coll., 1962-74; grad. Pinellas Vocat. Tech. Inst., 1975. With Sears, Roebuck and Co., Rapid City, S.D., 1951-52, St. Petersburg, Fla., 1961-62; bookkeeper Ohio Nat. Bank, Columbus, 1953-54, Sunbeam Bakery, Lakeland, Fla., 1955-56; with Christies Toy Sales, Pennsauken, N.J., 1958-60; exec. sec. Gulf Coast Automotive Warehouse, Inc., Tampa, Fla., 1970-73, office mgr., 1975-78; sec., treas., chief pilot, co-owner Tech. Devel. Corp., St. Petersburg, Fla., 1970-78; freelance archtl. draftsman and designer, archtl. cons., constrn. materials estimator, 1975—, Fla. state judge Vocat. Indsl. Clubs of Am. Skills Olympics, 1986. Nat. Assn. Women in Constrn. scholar, 1974. Mem. Nat. Assn. Women in Constrn., Alpha Chi Omega. Democrat. Home and Office: 8156 Timberidge Loop W Lakeland FL 33809

GARSIDE, MARLENE ELIZABETH, advertising executive; b. Newark, Dec. 1, 1933; d. Abraham and Shirley (Janow) Carnow; BS in Commerce and Fin., Bucknell U., 1955; m. Stanley Kramer, Aug. 7, 1955 (dec. 1967); children: Deborah Frances, Elizabeth Anne; m. Martin Lutman, Aug. 27, 1969 (dec. 1981); m. Michael J. Weinstein, Apr. 9, 1983 (dec. 1984); m. Normand Garside, Apr. 5, 1986. Asst. rsch. dir. Modern Materials Handling Co., Boston, 1955-57; econ. analyst, project adminstr. United Rsch. Co., Cambridge, Mass., 1957-58; free lance tech. writer, econ. analyst, 1958-66; asst. mgr. survey planning and mkt. rsch. IBM, White Plains, N.Y., 1967-69; mgr. rsch. svcs. McKinsey & Co., Cleve., 1969-72; former v.p., dir. Am. Custom Homes, former dir. Liberty Builders, Inc., Cleve.; owner, v.p., dir. Am. Custom Builders Inc., Cape Coral, Fla., 1978—; ptnr., dir. Star Realty Inc., Cape Coral, 1980—; account exec. Media Graphics, Inc., Naples, Fla., 1984; advt. mgr. Fox Electronics, Ft. Myers, Fla., 1984-86; v.p. Langdon Advt., Ft. Myers, 1987-88; asst. mgr. facility svcs. State of Fla. Dept. Health and Rehabilitative Svcs., Ft. Myers, 1988-90, facility svcs. mgr., 1990-92, gen. svcs. mgr., 1992—. Mem. Econ. and Indsl. Devel. Task Force, City of Cape Coral, 1979. Mem. Nat. Assn. Homebuilders, Bldg. Industry Assn., Constrn. Industry Assn., Nat. Bd. Realtors. Home: 1482 Sautern Dr Fort Myers FL 33919-2744 Office: State of Fla Dept Health Rehab Svcs 2295 Victoria Ave Fort Myers FL 33901-3884

GARSON, HELEN SYLVIA, English language educator, writer; b. N.Y.C.; d. Louis and Faye (Saks) Perlman; m. H. Neil Garson; children: Wendy, Eliot, Lisa. BA, George Washington U.; MA, U. Ga.; PhD, U. Md.; cert., Worcester Coll., Oxford, Eng. Instr. George Washington U., Washington, U. Md., College Pk.; asst. prof. George Mason U., Fairfax, Va.; assoc. prof. George Mason U., assoc. dean Coll. Arts and Scis., prof., prof. emeritus; freelance lectr. Smithsonian Instn., others; freelance writer; cons. TV documentary; peer reviewer. Author: Truman Capote, 1981, Short Fiction of Truman Capote, 1992, Tom Clancy, 1996; contbr. numerous articles to profl. jours. and reference books. Mem. MLA, Popular Culture Assn., Am. Studies Assn., European Assn. Am. Studies, Phi Kappa Phi, Pi Lambda Theta. Office: George Mason U Dept English 4400 University Dr Fairfax VA 22030

GARSTANG, MICHAEL, atmospheric sciences educator, consultant; b. Utrecht, Natal, South Africa, Apr. 4, 1930; s. Tom and Ethel May Garstang; m. Elizabeth Jacoba Mostert, Jan. 10, 1953; children: Stephen Raymond, Elizabeth Michele Garstang Jarman. BA, U. Natal, 1952, MA, 1958; MS, Fla. State U., Tallahassee, 1961, PhD, 1964. Cert. cons. meteorologist. Teaching assoc. U. Natal, 1951; rsch. assoc. African Explosives/Chem. Industries, Natal, 1952; meteorologist Brit. Colonial Svc., Trinidad, 1953-56; rsch. assoc. Woods Hole (Mass.) Oceanographic Inst., 1957-64; from asst. prof. to prof. Fla. State U., Tallahassee, 1962-71; prof. atmospheric scis. U. Va., Charlottesville, 1971—; v.p. Simpson Weather Assocs., Charlottesville, 1976-80, exec. v.p., 1980-85, pres., 1985—. Editor Bull. Am. Meteorol.Soc., 1968, Jour. Applied Meteorology, 1995—; assoc. editor Mon. Weather Rev., 1984-86; co-editor monographs. Recipient Philip Frandsen award NUCEA, 1992; Erskine fellow U. Canterbury, New Zealand, 1990. Fellow Am. Meteorol. Soc.; mem. Am. Geophys. Union. Office: U Va Dept Environ Sci Mccormick Rd Charlottesville VA 22903

GART, ALAN, finance educator, consultant; b. Phila., June 7, 1940 s. Herman J. and Zelda M. (Goldstein) G.; m. Davida B. Winderman, June 5, 1966; children: Steven, Lisa. BA, U. Pa., 1961, MA, 1963, PhD, 1967. V.p. Mfrs. Hanover Trust, N.Y.C., 1969-74; sr. v.p. Girard Bank, Phila., 1974-77; chief economist INA, Phila., 1977-80; sr. v.p. Parkway Mgmt., Phila., 1980-84; prof. Lehman Coll., CUNY, N.Y.C., 1984-88, U. Mass., Dartmouth, 1988-91, Nova U., Ft. Lauderdale, Fla., 1991—; vis. prof. Columbia U., N.Y.C., 1987-91; bd. dirs. Market St. Fund, Phila.; cons. numerous cos. Author: Insiders Guide to the Financial Services Revolution, 1934, Handbook of the Money and Capital Markets, 1988, Analysis of the New Financial Institutions, 1989, Regulation, Deregulation: The Future of the Banking, Insurance and Securities Industries, 1994; Banking Redefined: How Super Regional Powerhouses are Reshaping Financial Services, 1996; contbr. articles to profl. jours. Mem. Am. Statis. Assn., Am. Econ. Assn., Nat. Assn. Bus. Economists, Western Fin. Assn., Acad. Fin. Svcs. Home: 978 Warfield Ln Huntingdon Valley PA 19006-3338 Office: Nova U 3301 College Ave Fort Lauderdale FL 33314-7721

GARTMAN, MAX DILLON, language educator; b. Mobile, Ala., May 3, 1938; s. Noah Christopher and Edna Olga (Schwartzauer) G.; m. Marcia Ann Hubbard, Aug. 31, 1962; children: Noel Don, Polly Antoinette, Paul Dillon. AB in French and History, Samford U., Birmingham, Ala., 1960; MA in French, U. Ala., Tuscaloosa, 1962, PhD in Romance Langs., 1974; cert., U. Nice, France, 1985. NDEA fellow U. Ala., Tuscaloosa, 1960-65; prof. Romance langs. Samford U., 1965-82, head dept. fgn. langs., 1975-82; chair dept. fgn. langs., prof. Romance langs. U. North Ala., Florence, 1982—; pres. Internat. Edn. Travel, Florence, 1982—. Editor SU Faculty Forum Ann., 1967-72; performer rec. The Holy City, 1976. Chair Ala. Assn. Fgn. Lang. Tchrs., 1973, 74, So. Conf. Lang. Tchg., 1976. Mem. Ala. Assn. Tchrs. of French (chairperson 1995-97), Ala. Consortium for Fgn. Langs. (chairperson 1995-97), Rotary (sec. Oxmoor club 1981-82, music dir. 1982—). Baptist. Home: 122 Lambeth St Florence AL 35633 Office: U North Ala Box 5074 Florence AL 35632-0001

GARVER, JAMES AMOS, municipal official; b. Tylertown, Miss., Dec. 4, 1937; s. Harold Ray and Alyce Delores (Walters) G.; m. Nancy Jo Crowl May 3, 1959; children: Dale Lee, Delores Elizabeth, Brian Keith. Student Kans. State Coll., 1955-56, U. Md., 1957-58, Kings Coll., Cambridge, Eng. 1958, U. Ark., 1959-60, Drury Coll., 1961-62, Kans. U., 1962-63. Certified econ. developer Am. Econ. Devel. Council. Various positions Dun & Bradstreet, Inc., Kansas City, Mo., 1960-66, Mid-Am., Inc., Parsons, Kans., 1966-70; v.p. Com. of 100, Charleston, W.Va., 1970-72; exec. v. p. Bus. & Indsl. Devel. Corp., Charleston, W. Va., 1972-77; prin. Jamon Realty, Charleston, 1977-78; dep. dir. Gov.'s Office Econ. Devel., Charleston, 1977-79; sales and mktg. dir. Md. Economic Growth Assn., Balt., 1979-82; pres., CEO Broward Econ. Devel. Bd., Ft. Lauderdale, Fla., 1982-91; pres. Browards Com. of 100 Inc., Ft. Lauderdale, 1986-91, Broward Econ. Devel. Coun., Inc., Ft. Lauderdale, 1991—; assoc. cons. Vismor, McGill & Bell, Columbia, S.C., 1969-79; assoc. Walter W. Harper & Assocs., Greensboro, N.C., 1969-79; prin. Assoc. Cons., Charleston, 1969-79. Chmn. legis. com. Fla. Econ. Devel. Coun., 1984-85, bd. dirs., 1986-89, pres., 1987, mem. exec. com., 1987-89; mem. svc. resolution Broward Sch. Bd., 1988; mem. bd. advisors Cleve. Clinic Fla., 1989—; bd. dirs. Jr. Achievement South Fla., 1982-93, Ronald McDonald Children Charities/South Fla., 1990-93. With USAF, 1956-60. Named Econ. Devel. Profl. of Yr. State of Fla., 1986. Fellow Am. Econ. Devel. Coun. (bd. dirs. 1973-77, 89—, vice chair so. region 1991-93, exec. com. 1992—, vice chair sects. 1993-95, 2d vice chair 1995-96, 1st vice chair 1996-97, Pres.' award 1977, Dist. Svc. award 1992); mem. So. Indsl. Devel. Coun. (pres. 1988-89, hon. life), Am. C. of C. Execs., Nat. Assn. Indsl. and Office Parks, Profl. Assocs., Indsl. Devel. Rsch. Coun., Internat. Assn. Corp. Real Estate (treas. assoc. com. 1990-94), Ft. Lauderdale Bd. Realtors (Outstandinf Svc. award 1987), Tower Club (bd. govs. 1988), Rotary. Presbyterian. Home: 5540 Bayview Dr Fort Lauderdale FL 33308-3442 Office: Broward Econ Devel Coun Inc 200 E Las Olas Blvd Ste 1850 Fort Lauderdale FL 33301-2248

GARVEY, SHEILA, office administrator; b. Takoma Pk., Md., Aug. 5, 1954; d. Donn Edward and Regina Barbara (Zysk) G. BA in English, Randolph-Macon Coll., 1976; cert. paralegal, George Washington U., 1977. Dep. clk. Fairfax County (Va.) Cir. Ct., 1977-78, Alexandria (Va.) Cir. Ct., 1978-88, Fed. Dist. Ct. Ea. Dist. Va., Alexandria, 1988-90; paralegal Donn Edward Garvey, Esq., Alexandria, 1980-94; adminstrv. asst. Fortran Corp., Newington, Va., 1996—. Contbg. author: (poem anthologies) Between The Raindrops, 1995 (Editor's Choice award 1995), Best Poems of 1996 (Editor's Choice award 1996), Spirit of the Age, 1996 (Editor's Choice award 1996). Mem. props dept. Little Theatre of Alexandria, 1984. Recipient Hon. Mention Washington Lit. Soc., 1976, J.C. Penney Golden Rule award United Way of Am., Alexandria, 1994. Mem. Smithsonian Instn., Internat. Soc. Poets (assoc.). Home: 9213 Craig Ave Alexandria VA 22309

GARVIN, PATRICK PATILLO, internet systems architect, computer security; b. Macon, Ga., Jan. 14, 1963; s. Patrick Pattillo and Margaret Mary (McCrary) G.; m. Karen Elizabeth Quigg, Apr. 6, 1991; 1 child, Elizabeth Agnes (previous marriage). BS in Computer Sci., U Md., 1988. Systems engr. BTG Internet Svcs., Vienna, Va., 1986-91; sr. systems engr. BTG Internet Svcs., Vienna, 1991-94, tech. dir., 1994—. mem. tech. com. No. Va. Hospice, Falls Ch., Va., 1993-94. mem. Internet Soc., USENIX, SAGE, Phi Kappa Tau (pres.). Avocation: homebrewing. Office: BTG Inc 1944 Old Gallows Rd Vienna VA 22182

GARWOOD, WILLIAM LOCKHART, federal judge; b. Houston, Tex., Oct. 29, 1931; s. Wilmer St. John and Ellen Burdine (Clayton) G.; m. Merle Castlyn Haffler, Aug. 12, 1955; children: William Lockhart, Mary Elliott. BA, Princeton U., 1952; LLB with honors, U. Tex., 1955. Bar: Tex. 1955, U.S. Supreme Ct. 1959. Law clk. to judge U.S. Ct. Appeals (5th cir.), 1955-56; mem. Graves, Dougherty, Hearon, Moody & Garwood (and predecessor firms), Austin, Tex., 1959-79, 81; assoc. justice Supreme Ct. Tex., Austin, 1979-80; judge U.S. Ct. Appeals (5th cir.), 1981—; dir. Anderson, Clayton & Co., 1976-79, 81, exec. com., 1977-79, 81. Pres. Child and Family Service of Austin, 1970-71, St. Andrew's Episcopal Sch., Austin, 1972; bd. dirs. Community Council Austin and Travis County, 1968-72, Human Opportunities Corp. Austin and Travis County, 1966-70, Mental Health and Mental Retardation Ctr. Austin and Travis County, 1966-69, United Fund Austin and Travis County, 1971-73; mem. adv. bd. Salvation Army, Austin, 1972—. Served with U.S. Army, 1956-59. Fellow Tex. Bar Found. (life); mem. Tex. Law Rev. Assn. (pres. 1990-91, dir. 1986-96), Am. Law Inst., Am. Judicature Soc., Order of Coif, Chancellors, Phi Delta Phi. Episcopalian. Office: US Ct Appeals Homer Thornberry Jud Bldg 903 San Jacinto Blvd Austin TX 78701-2450

GARY, ETHEL, minister; b. Tuscaloosa, Ala., May 11, 1953; d. Joe Nathan and Ethel (Williams) G.; children: Farrand, D'Tra LaDawn. Cosmetology Diploma, Dekalb Coll., Nurses Aide Diploma; Modeling and Design Diploma, Massey Jr. Coll., Atlanta. Office mgr., receptionist Action Digital Color, Marietta, Ga., Fratelli Studios, Marietta; nanny Smith and Stone Family, Atlanta; hair salon owner, operator Decatur, Ga.; talent scout and agt. Kiddin Around Talents, Atlanta; emergency tech. Dekalb Med. Ctr., Decatur. Author: (brochure) God's Women of Excellence, (study sheet) The Pattern of God. Home: 2422 Shamrock Dr Decatur GA 30032

GARY, JULIA THOMAS, minister; b. Henderson, N.C., May 31, 1929; d. Richard Collins and Julia Branch (Thomas) G. BA, Randolph-Macon Woman's Coll., 1951; MA, Mt. Holyoke Coll., 1953; PhD in Chemistry, Emory U., 1958; MDiv cum laude, Candler Sch. Theology, 1986. Ordained to Meth. Ch. as deacon, 1986, as elder 1989. Instr. Mt. Holyoke Coll., South Hadley, Mass., 1953-54, Randolph-Macon Woman's Coll., Lynchburg, Va., 1954-55; from asst. prof. to prof. chemistry Agnes Scott Coll., Decatur, Ga., 1957-84, dean, 1969-84; pastor-in-charge St. Matthew United Meth. Ch., East Point, Ga., 1987-92; bd. dirs. Global Health Action, Inc., Atlanta, treas., 1991—; chair coord. coun. Decatur Area Emergency Assistance Ministry, 1995—. Contbr. articles to profl. jours. Recipient Alumnae Achievement award Randolph-Macon Woman's Coll., 1990. Mem. Zonta of Atlanta (pres. 1979-81, Zonta of the Yr. 1988), Phi Beta Kappa, Sigma Xi. Home: 117 Bruton St Decatur GA 30030-3767

GARY, RICHARD DAVID, lawyer; b. Richmond, Va., Apr. 25, 1949; s. Morton Nathan and Blanche (Rudy) G.; m. Linda Levene, Aug. 6, 1972; children: Brent Ryan, Lauren Renee. AB in Econs., U. N.C., 1971; JD, U. Va., 1974. Bar: Va. 1974. From assoc. to ptnr. Hunton & Williams, Richmond, 1974—; guest lectr. law Coll. William and Mary, Williamsburg, 1983-90. Pres. Beth Sholom Home Cen. Va., Richmond, 1989-91; chmn. Beth Sholom Home Va., 1991-92. Recipient Disting. Svc. award Beth Sholom Home Cen. Va., 1984. Mem. ABA (pub. utilities sect. council mem.), Va. State Bar (chmn. adminstrn. law sect. 1982-83), Va. Bar Assn., Richmond Bar Assn., Fed. Energy Bar Assn. Home: 1518 Helmsdale Dr Richmond VA 23233-4722 Office: Hunton & Williams Riverfront Plz East Twr 951 E Byrd St Richmond VA 23219-4040

GARY, ROGER VANSTROM, marketing executive; b. Kingsville, Tex., Nov. 28, 1946; s. Enos Edward and Rosadel Josephine (Vanstrom) G.; m. Janice Ruth Krueger, Apr. 5, 1974; 1 child, Vanessa Lorine. BBA, U. Tex., 1971. Tax examiner IRS, Austin, Tex., 1967-71; locomotive engr. So. Pacific Transp. Co., San Antonio, 1971-79; roadforeman engines So. Pacific Transp. Co., Victoria, Tex., 1979-80; controller RailTex, Inc., San Antonio, 1980-86; gen. mgr. shortline devel. RailTex, Inc., 1986-88; gen. mgr., bd. dirs., corp. sec. Tex. So. RR, San Antonio, 1989-90; chief exec. officer Gary Mktg. Group, 1990—; chmn. bd. dirs. Tex. Western Enterprises, Inc., 1996—; bd. dirs., chmn. Tex. and Pacific Numis. Corp., 1984-87; bd. dirs., treas. Tex. Independence Express, 1984-86; bd. dirs. San Antonio River Authority, 1993—. State chmn. Libertarian Party Tex., San Antonio, 1984-88, vice chmn. fin., 1991-92; mem., vice chmn. local bd. Selective Svc. Sys., San Antonio, 1982—; mem. citizens adv. bd. South Tex. Regional Blood Bank, San Antonio, 1986—; bd. dirs. Beacon Hill Neighborhood Assn., San Antonio, 1982-86; bd. dirs. Unity Ch., 1989-92, v.p., sec., pres., 1990-92; life mem. dist. 2-A-2 Lions Sight and Tissue Found.; v.p. Provisional Govt. of the Republic of Tex., 1995-96. With U.S. N.G., 1968-74, Tex. State Guard, 1991-96. Recipient spl. recognition S. Tex. Regional Blood Bank, 1986-88. Mem. Mensa, Sons Republic of Tex., 21st Century Congress, U. Tex. Ex-Students Assn. (life), Lions (bd. dirs. San Antonio 1986-87, 90-91, v.p. 1993-96, pres. 1996-97). Home: 723 Aganier Ave San Antonio TX 78212-3317

GARZA, EMILIO M(ILLER), federal judge; b. San Antonio, Tex., Aug. 1, 1947; s. Antonio Peña and Dionisia (Miller) G. BA, U. Notre Dame, 1969, MA, 1970; JD, U. Tex., 1976. Assoc. Clemens, Spencer, Welmaker & Finck, San Antonio, 1976-82; ptnr. Clemens, Spencer, Welmaker & Finck, San Antonio, Tex., 1982-87; dist. judge 225th Dist. Ct., Bexar County, San Antonio, 1987-88; U.S. dist. judge U.S. Dist. Ct. (we. dist.) Tex., San Antonio, 1988-91; U.S. cir. judge U.S. Ct. Appeals (5th cir.), San Antonio, 1991—. Bd. dirs. Symphony Soc. San Antonio, 1987-89; mem. Century Club San Antonio, 1987-88; adv. coun. U. Tex. San Antonio Coll. Fine Arts and Humanities, 1992—; adv. bd. Pan Am. Inst. for Polit. Studies (now the Phoenix Inst.) 1992—; bd. advisors Hispanic Law Jour. U. Tex. at Austin Sch. Law, 1992—. Mem. State Bar Tex., San Antonio Bar Assn. Office: 8200 IH-10 W Ste 501 San Antonio TX 78230

GASIOROWSKI, MARK JOSEPH, political scientist, educator; b. N.Y.C., Oct. 9, 1954; s. John P. and Abby F. (Geroski) G. BA, U. Chgo., 1976; MA, U. N.C., 1980, PhD, 1984. Prof. La. State U., Baton Rouge, 1984—. Author: U.S. Foreign Policy and the Shah, 1991; co-author: Neither East Nor West, 1990. Office: La State U Dept Political Sci Baton Rouge LA 70803

GASKINS-CLARK, PATRICIA RENAE, dietitian; b. Ft. Sill, Okla., July 24, 1959; d. Jay Frank and Iwana (Robinson) Gaskins; m. Gene Martin Clark, June 6, 1986; children: Taylor Renae, Kyle Gene. BS, Cameron U., 1982; MS, Cen. State U., 1986. Cert. home econ.; registered dietitian. Nutrition specialist William E. Davis & Sons, Inc., Oklahoma City, 1985-87; dietitian intern Okla. Teaching Hosps., Oklahoma City, 1987; clin. dietitian Grady Meml. Hosp., Chickasha, Okla., 1987-89; chief clin. dietitian Presbyn. Hosp., Oklahoma City, 1989-90; mgr. nutrition svcs. Norman (Okla.) Regional Hosp., 1990—. Mem. Am. Dietetic Assn., Cameron U. Alumni Assn., Oklahoma City Dist. Dietetic Assn., Okla. Dietetic Assn., Cen. State U. Alumni Assn., Phi Upsilon Omicron. Republican. Baptist. Office: Norman Regional Hosp 901 N Porter Ave Norman OK 73071-6404

GASPERONI, ELLEN JEAN LIAS, interior designer; b. Rural Valley, Pa.; d. Dale S. and Ruth (Harris) Lias; student Youngstown U., 1952-54, John Carrol U., 1953-54, Westminster Coll., 1951-52; grad. Am. Inst. Banking; m. Emil Gasperoni, May 28, 1955; children: Sam, Emil, Jean Ellen. Mem. Coeurde Coeur Heart Assn., Orlando Opera Guild, Orlando Symphony Guild. Mem. Jr. Bus. Women's Club (dir. 1962-64), Sweetwater Country Club (Longwood, Fla.); Lake Toxaway Golf and Country Club (N.C.). Presbyterian. Home: 1126 Brownshire Ct Longwood FL 32779-2209

GASPERONI, EMIL, SR., realtor, developer; b. Hillsville, Pa., Nov. 13, 1926; s. Attico and Rose Mary (Sarnicola) G.; m. Ellen Jean Lias, May 28, 1955; children: Samuel Dale, Emil Attico, Jean Ellen. Diploma real estate U. Pitts., 1957. Owner, pres. Gasperoni Real Estate, New Castle, Pa., 1956-63, Ft. Lauderdale, Fla., 1965-86, Gasperoni Internat. Group, Longwood, Fla., 1986—; founder, chmn. bd. Fill-R-Up Auto Wash Systems Inc., Ft. Lauderdale, 1967-72. Served with U.S. Army, 1945-46, ETO. Mem. Nat. Inst. Real Estate Brokers, Fla. Assn. Mortgage Brokers, Sweetwater Country Club (Longwood, Fla.), Lake Toxaway (N.C.) Country Club. Home: 1126 Brownshire Ct Longwood FL 32779-2209 Office: 505 Wekiva Springs Rd Ste 800 Longwood FL 32779-6050

GASQUE, DIANE PHILLIPS, funding specialist; b. Madison, Wis., Mar. 31, 1954; d. Codie Odel and Ruth Elaine (Oimoen) Phillips.; m. Wyndham Henry Burriss, Feb. 5, 1977 (div. 1989); m. Allard Harrison Gasque, Nov. 14, 1992; 1 child, Folline Elaine Gasque. BA, Midlands Tech., Columbia, S.C. Cert. Notary S.C. With inventory control Oxford Industries, Columbia, S.C.; processing agent NCR, Columbia, S.C.; comml. loan officer S.C. Nat., Columbia, S.C.; personnel dir. Witten Sales, Columbia, S.C.; funding agt. Resource Bankshares Mortgage Group, 1995—. Mem. The Order of the Confederate Rose. Republican. Presbyterian. Home: 3728 Linbrook Dr Columbia SC 29204

GASQUE, (ALLARD) HARRISON, radio air personality, entertainer; b. Richmond, Va., Oct. 10, 1958; s. Thomas Nelson and Susan (Folline) G.; m. Diane Cynthia Phillips, Nov. 14, 1992; 1 child, Folline Elaine. Grad., Columbia Sch. Broadcasting, Washington, 1982. Announcer, disc jockey Sta. WKDK-AM, Newberry, S.C., 1981-82, Sta. WEEL-AM, Washington, 1983-85; announcer Sta. WWGO-FM, Columbia, 1986-87, Sta. WNOK-AM, 1987-88, Sta. WODE-AM, 1989-90, Sta. WYYS-FM, 1991, Sta. WSCQ-FM, Columbia, 1991-94, Sta. WCOS-FM, Columbia, 1994—; v.p. transp. Palmetto Optical Supply, 1986—. Extra in movie Chattahoochie. Trustee Presdl. Task Force, 1991; mem. S.C. Hist. Soc.; mem. Rep. Presdl. Task Force; mem. Nat. Right to Work Com., mem. Nat. Assn. Alcholism Drug-Abuse Counselors, 1996—. Recipient Presdl. Order of Merit award, 1991. Mem. S.C. Assn. Alcoholism and Drug Abuse Counselors, Sons Confederate Vets., Sons Am. Revolution, Phi Kappa Psi, Alpha Epsilon Rho. Avocations: singing, coin, stamp and record collecting, tennis, basketball, football. Home: 3728 Linbrook Dr Columbia SC 29204

GASSMAN, ALAN SCOTT, lawyer; b. Ft. Worth, July 29, 1959; s. Marvin P. and Sara F. Gassman; m. Marcia Rabinovich, June 14, 1981; children: Nicole Rose, Brent Daniel. BA with distinction in Bus. Adminstrn., Rollins Coll., 1980; JD with honors, U. Fla., 1982, LLM in Taxation, 1983. Bar: Fla. 1983, U.S. Tax Ct. 1984; cert. in estate planning and probate law. Assoc. Larson, Conklin, Stanley & Probst, Belleair Bluffs, Fla., 1984-85; ptnr. Larson, Conklin, Stanley, Probst & Gassman, Clearwater, Fla., 1985-87; pvt. practice, Clearwater, 1987—; assoc. prof. Tampa Coll., Clearwater, 1985; lectr. Am. Law Inst., ABA, Practical Lawyer, Practical Tax Lawyer. Contbr. articles to legal publs.; contbg. author Jour. Asset Protection. Bd. dirs., v.p. Pinellas Ctr. for Visually Impaired, Inc., Dunedin, Fla., 1987—, v.p., 1988. Mem. Fla. Bar Assn. (chmn. unauthorized practice of law com. tax sect. 1987, mem. exec. om. tax sect. 1987), Clearwater Bar Assn. (chmn.

tax sect. 1987, chmn. bus., banking and tax law sect. 1996), Pinellas County Estate Planning Counsel (bd. dirs. 1987—, pres. 1993). Jewish. Office: 1245 Court St Ste 102 Clearwater FL 34616-5856

GASTON, EDWIN WILLMER, JR., retired English language educator; b. Nacogdoches, Tex., Feb. 22, 1925; s. Edwin Willmer and Fannie (Meisenheimer) G.; m. Martha Middlebrook, Feb. 16, 1946; children: John E. F., Thomas M., Weldon K. BS, Stephen F. Austin State U., 1947, MA, 1951; PhD, Tex. Tech U., 1959. Editor various mags. and newspapers, 1947-50; radio broadcaster, 1947-50; dir. publs., asst. prof. English and journalism Stephen F. Austin State U., Nacogdoches, 1950-53, assoc. prof., 1955-64, prof., 1965-86, chmn. dept. English, 1965-69, dean Grad. Sch., 1976-81, v.p. for acad. affairs, 1981-86, prof. emeritus, 1986—; instr. Tex. Tech U., 1953-55. Author: The Early Novel of the Southwest, 1961, A Manual of Style, 1961, Conrad Richter, 1963, (updated ed. 1989), Eugene Manlove Rhodes, 1967; editor: (with others) Southwestern American Literature: A Bibliography, 1980; contbr. articles to anthologies, encys., profl. jours. Served as cpl. USMC, 1942-46, PTO. Recipient Disting. Prof. award Stephen F. Austin State U.; Fulbright scholar U. Helsinki, Finland, 1964-65. Mem. MLA (south cen. region), Nat. Coun. Tchrs. English, Southwestern Am. Lit. Assn., Western Am. Lit. Assn., Tex. Folklore Soc. (treas. 1970-96, past pres.), Alpha Chi (pres. 1967-79, pres. emeritus 1979—). Home: 709 Bostwick St Nacogdoches TX 75961-2416

GATES, BETTY RUSSELL, artist; b. Davenport, Okla., Aug. 10, 1927; d. Robert R. Russell and Lela May (Brannon) Creekmore; m. David W. Gates, July 1, 1945; children: Jerry (dec.), David E., Ann Fiser, Julie Lenderman, Alexander. Student, Ark. A&M, Monticello; grad., Art Instruction Inc., Mpls. One-woman shows include Sheraton Gallery, Dallas, 1988, Top of the Linfe Gallery, Ft. Worth, 1990, 91, White Oak Gallery, Edina, Minn., 1990, 91, 92, Woodbridge Gallery, Gualala, Calif., 1993, Irving (Tex.) Art Assn., 1994, Bismarck State Coll., 1996; group shows include Channel 13 Gallery, Dallas, 1982, U. Tex., Arlington, 1983, Art About Town, Dallas, 1986, Fed. Bldg. Lobby Gallery, N.Y.C., 1987, Wartburg Coll., Waverly, Iowa, 1988, Living History Farms, Des Moines, 1988-91, Am. Artists Profl. League Grand Nat., N.Y.C., 1988, Mus. Prairie Pioneer, Grand Island, Nebr., 1989, Rough Rider Internat., Williston, N.D., 1989, 90, 91, 92, 93, Salmugundi 12th Ann. Exhbn., N.Y.C., 1989, White Oak Gallery, Edina, 1990, 91, 92, Gov. Western and Wildlife Show, Nebr., 1991, 93, B. Swartz Meml. Libr., L.I., N.Y., 1991, Cannon Ho. Rotunda Room, Washington, 1992, Nat. League Am. PEN Women, Washington, 1992, Chang Kai-Chek Meml. Hall, Taipei, Taiwan, 1993, Bismarck State Coll. Mus., 1993, Perry House Galleries, Washington, 1993, Dr. Sun-Yat-Sen Mus., Taipei, 1993, Gene Autrey Mus., L.A., 1994, 95, Knickerbocker Grand Nat. Mus., Washington, 1994, Catherine Lorrilard Wolfe Art Club, 1995, numerous others; permanent collections include Wise County Art Mus., Decatur, Tex., Dr. Sun-Yat-Sen Mus., Taiwan, Bismarck State Coll., The Baird Family. Ofcl. artist USCG. Recipient Merit cert. Harrisburg (Pa.) Art Ctr., 1985, Grand prize Rough Rider Internat., 1989, Buckskin award, 1993, ACA award Artists & Craftsman Associated, 1992, Winsor Newton and MJ Design award, 1993, Traditional Oil award Cork Gallery, 1993, Holbein and Winsor-Newton awards Dallas Artists and Craftsmen, 1994, Best of Show in Traditional Oil award Visual Individualists United, N.Y., 1995, Henrietta Sabetsky Meml. award Visual Individualist United, 1995. Mem. Dallas Artists and Craftsman Associated (Grumbacher Gold medallion 1990, Watson Guptil award 1991), Nat. League Am. PEN Women (Spl. award 1981), Catherine Lorillard Wolfe Art Club (Katherine T. Lovell Meml. award 1982, Anna Hyatt Huntington Bronze medal 1986, Still Life award 1989), Am. Artists of Rockies, Women Artists of West, Visual Individualists United (assoc.), Western Acad. Women Artists. Home: 4900 Wondol Ct Hurst TX 76053-3819

GATES, CAROLYN HELM, municipal official; b. Scooba, Miss., July 23, 1935; d. Benjamin LaBaum Helm and Frances Kimbrough Gilbert; m. James Pickens Gates, Aug. 21, 1955; children: James Stephen, Carolyn Kimbrough, Charles Christian. Student, U. Ala., 1954; BA, Memphis State U., 1975, postgrad., 1975—. Pres. C.H. Gate Constrn., Memphis, 1976; chair Shelby County Bd. Commrs., Memphis, 1977—; chair budget com. Shelby County Bd. of Commerce, Memphis, 1983-84, chair edn. com., 1983-86, chair, 1988-89; mem. Tenn. County Svcs., Nashville, 1984-86; steering com. Nat. Assn. Co. Gov., Washington, 1986-90; bd. mem. Govs. Com. on Excellence, Memphis, 1984-86. Editor: Pizza Lovers Cookbook, 1976; author: Keeping The Fire, Keeping the Faith, 1990; columnist In Touch, 1980-89. Del. Rep. Nat. Conv., 1976-92; chmn. Salvation Army Adv. Bd., Memphis, 1987-89; mem. presdl. search com. Memphis State U. Named Outstanding Female Grad. Memphis State Alumni, 1983. Mem. Mission for Memphis (team capt.), Memphis State U. Nat. Alumni Assn. (pres. 1989-92), Shelby County Rep. Career Women (pres. 1986-88). Republican. Methodist. Home: 7430 Mimosa Dr Memphis TN 38138-5804 Office: Office Bd Commrs 160 Mid-America Mall N Ste 619 Memphis TN 38103

GATES, DARYL LAMAR, special education educator, musician; b. Shreveport, La., Sept. 23, 1956; s. Leonard and Hattie (Franklin) G. BA in Elem. Edn., La. Tech. U., 1984, MA in Spl. Edn., 1987. Cert. ednl. admintrn. Educator Caddo Parish Sch. Bd., Shreveport, La., 1977—; radio announcer KBCL Radio Station, Shreveport, 1988—; sales rep. Gospel Today Mag., 1992—; adv. Greater Shreveport Human Rels. Com., 1995—, Winward Hosp., Shreveport, La., 1995—. Composer (religious music): Gates Collection Vols. I, IV, 1973. Mem. African-Am. Culture Coalition, Shreveport, 1994; bd. dirs. La. Mass Choir, 1988. Recipient music awards La. Mass Choir, 1988-94; named Living Legend Lakeside Bapt. Ch., 1996. Mem. NAACP, ASCD, Nat. Edn. Assn., Caddo Assn. Educators (Emerging Leader 1994), La. Assn. Educators. Home: PO Box 8279 Shreveport LA 71148

GATES, ROBERTA PECORARO, nursing educator; b. Elmira, N.Y., May 22, 1948; d. Patrick George and Verle Elizabeth (Warriner) Pecoraro; m. William Franklin Gates III, May 20, 1972; 1 child, William Franklin IV. BSN, U. Ariz., 1970; MSN in Family Nursing, U. Ala., Huntsville, 1981. Cert. clin. specialist in med.-surg. nursing. Charge nurse St. Mary's Hosp. and Mental Health Ctr., Tucson, 1970-72; asst. head nurse Torrance (Calif.) Meml. Hosp., 1973-74; dist. nurse Sierra Sands Sch. Dist., Ridgecrest, Calif., 1974-76; instr. Albany (Ga.) Jr. Coll., 1978-80, John C. Calhoun Coll., Decatur, Ala., 1981-83; learning resources coord. Albany State Coll., 1984-85; asst. prof. Sinclair C.C., Dayton, Ohio, 1990-91, Darton Coll., Albany, 1986-89, 92—; cons. Cmty. Health Inst., Albany, 1993, Early County Bd. Edn., Blakely, Ga., 1994. Author: A Model for Adolescent Health Promotion in the Dougherty County Community, 1993. Mem. Ga. Coun. Prevention of Child Abuse, Albany, 1988, 93; mem. Albany Mus. Art, 1993—; mem. Cmty. Ptnrs. Health Care Initiative, Dayton, 1990-91; bd. dirs. March of Dimes, Albany, 1986-89; mem. Albany-Dougherty 2000, DOCO Alternative Adv.Bd., State Consortium Early Intervention, Babies Can't Wait, 1995. Named to Outstanding Young Women of Am., 1983. Mem. Sigma Theta Tau, Phi Kappa Phi. Office: Darton Coll 2400 Gillionville Rd Albany GA 31707-3023

GATES, SHEREE HUNT, elementary education educator, writer; b. Buford, Ga., Oct. 3, 1958; d. Erwin Albion and Betty Joyce (Herndon) Hunt; m. Roger Lee Gates Jr., Jan. 29, 1960; children: Roger L. III, Christopher A. BS, U. Md., 1984; MEd, Boston U., 1985; EdD, U. Ga., 1992. Cert. tchr., sch. counselor. Placement dir., dir. student svcs. Phillips Jr. Coll., Augusta, Ga., 1985-86; client svcs. coord., battered women counselor Safe Homes, Augusta, 1986-87; tchr. Richmond County Bd. Edn., Augusta, 1987-89; sch. counselor Redcliffe Elem. Sch., Aiken, S.C., 1989-91; tchr. Barton Chapel Elem. Sch., Augusta, Ga., 1991-93; instr. English, U. Izmir, Turkey, 1993-95; tchr. E. Vaughan Elem. Sch., Woodbridge, Va., 1995—. With U.S. Army, 1979-83. Mem. Am. Assn. Counseling and Devel., Ednl. Leadership Assn., Adult Edn. Quar., Alpha Sigma Lambda. Democrat. Office: E Vaughan Elem Sch PSC 88 2200 York Dr Woodbridge VA 22026

GATES, SHERRIE MOTT, chemotherapy nurse; b. Selma, Ala., Aug. 3, 1943; d. Walter Glover and Elvin (McKinney) Mott; m. Frederick Kilbourne Gates Jr., May 29, 1964; children: Dannial Kilbourne, William Shawn. Diploma, Carraway Meth. Sch. Nursing, Birmingham, Ala., 1964. Cert. med.-surg. nurse, ANCC. Staff med.-surg. nurse Good Samaritan Hosp., West Palm Beach, Fla., 1964-67; relief evening supr., emergency nurse, staff nurse Belle Glade (Fla.) Gen. Hosp., 1970-74; emergency rm. nurse Prattville (Ala.) Gen. Hosp., 1976-92; head nurse emergency rm. Autauga Med. Ctr., Prattville, 1986-90, 3-11 shift supr., 1990-92; ambulatory care staff/relief supr. VA Hosp., Montgomery, Ala., 1992-93; chemotherapy nurse VA Med. Ctr., Montgomery, Ala., 1993—. Office: VA Medical Center 215 Perry Hill Rd Montgomery AL 36109-3725

GATES, STEVEN LEON, physician; b. Newton, Kans., Aug. 13, 1954; s. Leon Martin and Mary Lorine (Adams) G.; m. Paula Ellen Banwart, Jan. 1, 1977; children: Stephanie, Scott, Jeffrey. BS in Pharmacy summa cum laude, S.W. Okla. State U., 1976; DO, Okla. State U., 1986. Diplomate Am. Bd. Internal Medicine; lic. pharmacist, Okla. Intern Osteopathic Med. Ctr. Tex., Ft. Worth, 1986-87; resident in internal medicine Dallas/Ft. Worth Med. Ctr., Grand Prairie, Tex., 1987-90; pharmacist M & D Star Drug Store, Okmulgee, Okla., 1976-80; pharmacist, mgr. Wal-Mart Pharmacy Div., Okmulgee, Okla., 1980-82; chief med. resident Ready Care Minor Emergency Ctr., Bedford, Tex., 1987-90; jail physician Tarrant County Sheriff's Dept., Ft. Worth, 1989-90; pvt. practice internal medicine Grand Prairie, 1990—; internal medicine physician and minor emergency physician Ready Care Med. Clinic, Bedford, Tex., 1990—; dir. med. edn. Dallas/Ft. Worth Med. Ctr.-Grand Prairie, 1990—; clin. asst. prof. dept. medicine Tex. Coll. Osteopathic Medicine, Ft. Worth, 1990—. Mem. AMA, Am. Coll. Osteopathic Internists (bd. cert.), Am. Osteopathic Assn., Tex. Osteopathic Med. Assn., Tex. Med. Assn., Tarrant County Med. Soc., Sigma Sigma Phi. Republican. Home: 3110 Sunny Meadows Ct Arlington TX 76016-5948

GATEWOOD, ROBERT PAYNE, financial planning executive; b. Nebr., Mar. 4, 1923; s. Robert Harvey and Bess (Payne) G.; m. Marilyn Wengert, June 6, 1946; children: Robert, Lottie, Traber, Cy, Marilyn, Bess, John, Anthony, Judemarie, Anne, Tressa, Joseph, Ruth. BS, U.S. Naval Acad., 1946; postgrad. La. State U., 1974. CLU. Estate planner J.D. Marsh & Assocs., 1950-56; pres. estate planning Fin. Corp. Am., 1956-61; pres. Robert P. Gatewood & Co., specialists in tax and estate planning, 1961—; internat. lectr.; mem. sales execs. adv. bd. Inst. Ins. Mktg., La. State U., 1970-79. Contbr. articles to profl. jours. Bd. dirs. Planned Giving Coun. Palm Beach. Served with USN, 1946-50. Recipient Bernard L. Wilner Meml. award. Mem. D.C. Assn. Life Underwriters (pres. 1965-66), Assn. Advanced Life Underwriting, Million Dollar Round Table, Am. Soc. CLUs & Chartered Fin. Cons. (pres. 1975-76), Washington D.C. Estate Planning Coun., East Coast Estate Planning Coun., Fla. Assn. CLUs and ChFCs, Palm Beach Assn. Life Underwriters, 25 Million Dollar Internat. Forum (founder), Knights of Malta. Republican. Roman Catholic. Home: 1171 N Ocean Blvd Delray Beach FL 33483

GATEWOOD, TELA LYNNE, lawyer; b. Cedar Rapids, Iowa, Mar. 23; d. Chester Russell and Cecilia Mae (McFarland) Weber. BA with distinction, Cornell Coll., Mt. Vernon, Iowa, 1970; JD with distinction, U. Iowa, 1972. Bar: Iowa 1973, Calif. 1974, U.S. Supreme Ct. 1984. Instr. LaVerne Coll., Pt. Mugu, Calif., 1973; asst. city atty. City of Des Moines, 1973-78; sr. trial atty. and supervisory atty. EEOC, Dallas, Phila., 1978-91, acting regional atty. Dallas Dist., 1987-89; adminstrv. judge EEOC, Dallas, 1991-94; adminstrv. law judge Social Security Adminstrn., Oklahoma City, 1994—. Bd. dirs. Day Care Inc., Des Moines, 1975-78, sec., 1977, pres., 1978. Mem. ABA (labor law, litigation, govt. svc., judiciary sects.), AAUW, NAFE, Nat. Assn. Female Judges, Fed. Bar Assn., U.S. Supreme Ct. Bar Assn., Calif. Bar Assn. Office: Social Security Adminstrn Office of Hearings and Appeals 420 W Main St Ste 400 Oklahoma City OK 73102

GATEWOOD, WILLARD BADGETT, JR., historian; b. Pelham, N.C., Feb. 23, 1931; s. Willard Badgett and Bessie Lee (Pryor) G.; m. Mary Lu Brown, Aug. 9, 1958; children: Willard Badgett III, Elizabeth Ellis. BA, Duke U., 1953, MA, 1954, PhD, 1957. Asst. prof. history East Tenn. State U., 1957-58, East Carolina U., 1958-60; assoc. prof. N.C. Wesleyan Coll., 1960-64; prof. U. Ga., 1964-70; Alumni Disting. prof. history U. Ark., 1970—, provost and chancellor, 1984-85. Author: Theodore Roosevelt and the Art of Controversy, 1970, Smoked Yankees, 1971, Black Americans and the White Man's Burden, 1975, Slave and Freeman, 1979, Free Men of Color, 1982, Aristocrats of Color, 1990, Arkansas Delta, 1993; mem. bd. editors Ga. Rev., 1968-70, Jour. Negro History, 1972-74, Ark. Hist. Quar., 1992—. Bd. dirs. Winthrop Rockefeller Found., 1990—. Recipient Parks Excellence in Teaching award Phi Alpha Theta, 1970, Michael Rsch. award, 1967; Outstanding Teaching award Omicron Delta Kappa, 1979, rsch. award U. Ark. Alumni Assn., 1980, Gingles award Ark. Hist. Assn., 1982, Chancellor's medal, 1994, Ledbetter prize, 1994; Truman Libr. fellow, 1963; Acad. Arts and Scis. grantee, 1962. Mem. Am. Hist. Assn., So. Hist. Assn. (pres. 1986-87), Ark. Hist. Assn., Orgn. Am. Historians, Assn. Study Afro-Am. Life and History, Phi Beta Kappa. Presbyterian. Office: U Ark Old Main # 416 Fayetteville AR 72701

GATHRIGHT, JOHN BYRON, JR., colon and rectal surgeon, educator; b. Oxford, Miss., Sept. 29, 1933; s. J. Byron Sr. and Connie (Love) G.; m. Barbara Cooper, Sept. 19, 1959; children: John Byron III, Lin, John Miles, Peter C. BS, U. Miss., 1955; MD, Northwestern U., 1957. Diplomate Am. Bd. Colon and Rectal Surgery (pres. 1989-90). Intern Charity Hosp., New Orleans, 1957-58, resident in gen. surgery, 1958-62; fellow in colon & rectal surgery Alton Ochsner Med. Found., New Orleans, 1962-63; mem. staff So. Bapt. Hosp., New Orleans, 1963-69; mem. staff Ochsner Found. Hosp., New Orleans, 1969—, chmn. colon and rectal surgery dept.; clin. prof. surgery Tulane U., New Orleans, 1991—; vis. surgeon So. La. Med. Ctr., Houma, 1977—; trustee, exec. com., bd. dirs. Alton Ochsner Med. Found., 1980—. Assoc. editor Diseases of the Colon and Rectum, 1977-93, Perspectives in Colon and Rectal Surgery, 1987—, Colon and Rectal Surgery Outlook, 1987—; mem. bd. editors Current Concepts in Gastroenterology, 1980-89. Fellow ACS (grad. edn. com. 1981-89, Am. Soc. Colon and Rectal Surgeons (pres. 1989-90), Soc. Coloproctology of Eng. and Ireland (hon.), Internat. Soc. Univ. Colon and Rectal Surgeons (sec. 1990—). Republican. Presbyterian. Office: Ochsner Clinic & Hosp 1514 Jefferson Hwy New Orleans LA 70121-2483

GATIPON, BETTY BECKER, medical educator, consultant; b. New Orleans, Sept. 8, 1931; d. Elmore Paul and Theresa Caroline (Sendker) Becker; m. William B. Gatipon, Nov. 22, 1952 (dec. 1986); children: Suzanne, Ann Gatipon Sved, Lynn Gatipon Pashley. BS magna cum laude, Ursuline Coll., New Orleans, 1952; MEd, La. State U., 1975, PhD, 1983. Tchr. Diocese of Baton Rouge, 1960-74, edn. cons. to sch. bd., 1974-78; dir. Right to Read program Capital Area Consortium/Washington Parish Sch. Bd., Franklington, La., 1978-80; dir. basic skills edn. Capital Area Consortium/Ascension Parish Sch. Bd., Donaldsonville, La., 1980-82; instr. Coll. Edn. La. State U., Baton Rouge, 1982-84; evaluation cons. La. Dept. Edn., Baton Rouge, 1984-85; dir. basic skills edn. Capital Area Basic Skills/East Feliciana Parish Sch. Bd., Clinton, La., 1985-86; program coord. La. Bd. Elem. and Secondary Edn., New Orleans, 1987-89; dir. divsn. of med. edn., dept. family medicine Sch. Medicine La. State U. Med. Ctr., New Orleans, 1989—; evaluator East Feliciana Parish Schs., 1982-86; presenter math. methods workshops Ascension Parish Schs., 1980-84. Author curriculum materials, conf. papers; contbr. articles to edn. jours. Curatorial asst. La. State Mus., New Orleans, 1987—; soprano St. Louis Cathedral Concert Choir, New Orleans, 1988—; chmn. Symphony Store, New Orleans Symphony, 1990—; lector St. Angela Merici Ch. Mem. Am. Ednl. Rsch. Assn., Assn. Am. Med. Colls., Midsouth Ednl. Rsch. Assn., La. Ednl. Rsch. Assn., Soc. Tchrs. Family Medicine, New Orleans Film and Video Buffs, Phi Kappa Phi, Phi Delta Kappa. Roman Catholic. Home: 105 10th St New Orleans LA 70124-1258 Office: LA State U Med Ctr Sch Medicine 1542 Tulane Ave New Orleans LA 70112-2825

GATLIN, EUGENE S., JR., retired English language educator, consultant; b. Columbia, S.C., Aug. 30, 1935; s. Eugene S. Sr. and Alma (Lee) G.; m. Carolyn Maier, Feb. 14, 1976; children: David Ryan, Elizabeth Lee. AB, Furman U., 1957; MEd, U. S.C., 1967, MA, 1970, PhD, 1973. Tchr. dept. head Columbia Pub. Schs., 1961-69; instr. U. S.C., Columbia, 1967-81; prof. English, speech Midlands Tech. Coll., Columbia, 1969-91, head dept., 1973-78, chmn. Faculty Senate, 1979, 82, disting. prof. emeritus, 1991; speech and bus. comm. cons., 1971—; guest prof. U. Wyo., Laramie, summer 1974, Coker Coll., Fort Jackson, S.C., 1983—; pvt. cons. 1995—. mem. standing rev. com. and editorial coms. various pubs.; tchr., developer syllabus on bus. corr. and indsl. managerial comm.; monitor new coll. instrs., 1974-78; mem. editorial bd. numerous pub. cos. Author: Language of Community College Freshmen, Oral and Written Maturity in Writing, An Alternate Form of Composition, 1974; mem. editorial bd. bus. writing - concepts and applications, 1984-85, 86-90, pub. speaking and bus. communications texts; contbr. articles to profl. jours. Mem. Midlands Tech. Edn. Found., Columbia, 1979-82; mem. adv. bd. Midlands Tech. Aux. Svcs., 1981-82. Named Faculty Mem. of Yr., A.C. Flora High Sch., 1969, Midlands Tech. Coll., 1972, 81, 82; U.S. Com. on Humanities grantee, 1965, 79. Mem. NEA, Coll. English Assn., Ga.-S.C. Conf. on English, Southeastern Conf. on English in Two-Yr. Colls., S.C. Speech Communication Assn. (evaluator 1979, 81, 83), S.C. Tech. Edn. Assn. Republican. Baptist. Club: Toastmasters (cons. 1981-82) (Columbia). Avocations: theatre, boating, reading, singing, chess. Home and Office: 4533 Ivy Hall Dr Columbia SC 29206-1228

GATLIN, LINDA SUE, secondary educator; b. Gallopolese, Ohio, July 25, 1950; d. Earl Brewer and Martha Elizabeth (Crane) Pickering; m. Bruce E. Gatlin, May 29, 1972; children: Timothy Earl, Melinda Elizabeth. AA, Copiah Lincoln Coll., 1970; BS, Delta State U., Cleveland, 1972; M.Ed., U. So. Miss., 1976; postgrad., U. New Orleans, 1993—. Tchr. St. Tammany Parish Schs., Slidell, La., 1985—, Jackson County Schs., Pascagoula, Miss., 1972-85; camp co-director KidKam Camps, Mandeville, La., 1993-95; mentor tchr. St. Tammany Schs., Covington, La., 1984—; chair dept. North-shore H.S., Slidell, 1991-95; TV guest La. Pub. Broadcasting, 1995; presenter in field. Author: (state approved secondary science course) Science Research and Discovery, 1995, The Science Teacher, 1996; (grants) Biotechnology NAET, 1994, Creative Teaching, 1996; coach: Science Olympied Team. Mem. SACS, Baton Rouge, La. 1992—. Howard Hughes fellow, 1990, 96; named Tchr. Rschr. of Yr., Sigma Xi., 1995. Fellow Am. Assn. Immunologists; mem. ASCD, Am. Ednl. Rsch. Assn., Nat. Assn. Biology Tchrs., La. State Tchrs. Assn., La. Assn. Biology Tchrs., St. Tammany Sci. Tchrs.,. Baptist. Home: 704 Caesar Rd Picayune MS 39466 Office: Northshore HS 100 Panther Dr Slidell LA 70461

GATTI, ELLEN GRANDY, educational administrator, real estate broker; b. S.I., N.Y., Aug. 13, 1931; d. Joseph Grandy and Ann (Coppola) Galasso; m. Arthur J. Gatti, Oct. 13, 1950 (ddec. 1971); children: Glenn, Gary, Robin, Greg, Gene, Randy (dec.). BSBA, Monmouth U., 1966; MEd, U. Miami, 1970; edn. specialist, U. Fla., 1982. Tchr. Dade County Schs., Miami, 1967-95; owner, prin., broker A.J. Gatti & Assocs., Miami and Holiday, Fla., 1971—; owner, dir. Prodigy Sch., Holiday, 1995—; real estate instr. Fla. Real Estate Commn., 1987—. Author: (column) Miami Times, 1972-76, Propwash-Personality Profiles, 1986-88, (bi-monthly newsletter Holmes Currents, 1972-76. Vol. Rep. Party, San Diego, Miami, 1980—, Miami Jackson Hosp., 1988. Mem. Civil Air Patrol (instr. 1987—, capt. 1987—), Toastmasters Internat. (Best Humorous Speech 1990, Evaluation Speech 1991), Literary Coun. Am., Alpha Delta Pi. Republican. Office: Prodigy Sch PO Box 3378 Holiday FL 34690-0378

GAUBERT, LLOYD FRANCIS, shipboard and industrial cable distribution executive; b. Thibodaux, La., Jan. 6, 1921; s. Camille J. and Leonise (Henry) G.; children: Lloyd Francis, Leonise, Bruce, Blane, Gwen, Greg. Student Southwestern La. Inst., 1939-41, U.So. Calif., 1941-42, Tex. Christian U., 1946-47. Tool engr. Consol.-Vultee Aircraft Corp., San Diego, 1941-45; tool project engr. Fort Worth plant Convair, 1946-47; founder, owner, pres. L.F. Gaubert & Co., Inc., New Orleans, 1947—; pres. Michoud Indsl. Complex, Inc., Marine Indsl. Cable Corp., Carmel Devel. Corp.; dir. First Nat. Bank Commerce, New Orleans; pres. Holiday Inn Thibodaux. Chmn. regional planning commn. New Orleans Mayor's Coordinating Com. for NASA, 1961-63, chmn. mfrs. com., 1961-63; bd. dirs. Better Bus. Bur., New Orleans, Met. New Orleans Safety Coun., New Orleans Pub. Belt R.R., New Orleans Port Com., New Orleans Traffic and Transp. Bur., USCG Acad., New Orleans Opera House Assn., Christian Bros., New Orleans; trustee Sta. WYES-TV, New Orleans; exec. com. Sugar Bowl Football; founder, chmn. Greatest Bands in Dixie; pres. Holiday Inn of Thibodaux; dir., USCG Acad.; state pres. navy league adv. coun. Loyola U., New Orleans. Served with USAAF, 1942-45. Recipient St. Louis medallion Archdiocese of New Orleans, 1990; named Man of the Yr., Christian Bros.' Sch., 1989. Mem. Am. Soc. Tooling and Mfg. Engrs. (pres. 1948-49), Soc. Naval Architects and Marine Engrs., Am. Soc. Naval Engrs., La. Engring. Soc., Navy League (past pres. New Orleans coun., nat. dir., state pres. La.), New Orleans Petroleum Club, Sugar Bowl (exec. com.), Am. Legion, Plimsoll Club, Bd. of Trade Club, Internat. House, Optimists (pres. 1957-58, lt. gov. 1959-60), K.C., Ancient Order Hibernians in Am. Republican. Roman Catholic. Home: 5668 Bancroft Dr New Orleans LA 70122-1306 Office: LF Gaubert & Co Inc 700 S Broad St New Orleans LA 70119-7417

GAUDET, JEAN ANN, librarian, educator; b. Oakland, Calif., Dec. 28, 1949; d. Edwin Joseph and Teresa Maureen (McDonnell) G. BS, Madison Coll., Harrisonburg, Va., 1971; MLS, George Peabody Coll. for Tchrs, Nashville, 1973. Libr., gifted edn. tchr. Prince William County Schs., Manassas, Va., 1971—. Chmn. Site-Based Mgmt. Com., Dumfries, Va., 1989-92; chmn. Cmty. Choir, Woodbridge, Va., 1983-85; citizen ambassador People to People, Russia and Poland, 1992, China, 1993, Australia, 1994. Mem. ALA, Va. Edn. Media Assn., Va. Assn. for Edn. of Gifted, Delta Kappa Gamma (sec. 1994—), Beta Phi Mu, Alpha Beta Alpha. Home: 16820 Francis West Ln Dumfries VA 22026-2110 Office: Potomac Sr High Sch 16706 Jefferson Davis Hwy Dumfries VA 22026-2130

GAULDEN, MARY ESTHER, medical/science educator; b. Rock Hill, S.C., Apr. 30, 1921; d. Daniel Harley and Jessye Virginia (Carson) G.; m. John Jagger, Oct. 19, 1956; children: Thomas Alexander Jagger, Yvonne Jagger Mellinger. BS, Winthrop Coll., 1942; MA, U. Va., 1944, PhD, 1948. Rsch. assoc. U. Ala., 1945-46, NIH, 1946-47; instr. U. Tenn., 1947-49, lectr., 1956-65; sr. biologist Oak Ridge (Tenn.) Nat. Lab., 1949-60; mem. staff Cmty. Cancer Ctr., U. Tex. Southwestern Med. Ctr., Dallas, 1975-92; adj. assoc. prof. environ. scis. U. Tex., Dallas, 1982-87; asst. prof., chief radiation biology sect. dept. radiology Southwestern Med. Sch. U. Tex., Dallas, 1965-68, assoc. prof., 1968-92, adj. prof., 1992—; med. staff affiliate Baylor U. Med. Ctr., Dallas, 1974—; vis. prof. U. N.C., 1954; cons. Oak Ridge Nat. Lab., 1960-70, Rsch. and Evaluation Assocs., Inc., Chapel Hill, N.C., 1988-93; mem. radiation bio-effects and epidemiology adv. com. FDA, 1972-75; advisor to U.S. Army NAS-NRC, 1973-76, mem. com. on toxicology, 1987-93; mem. risk assessment guidelines adv. com. U.S. EPA, 1985. Co-editor: Medical Radiation Biology, 1973; contbr. chpt. to: Mitogenesis, 1959, The Cell Nucleus, 1960, Aneuploidy: Mechanisms of Origin, 1989; co-contbr. chpt. to 8 books, most recently: Chemical Mutagens, 1984; contbr. articles to profl. jours. and conf. procs.; mem. editl. bd. Environ. Mutagenesis, 1981-90; mem. panel of reviewers Jour. Nuclear Medicine, 1985-91. Fellow AAAS (past mem. coun.); mem. Am. Soc. for Cell Biology (founding), Am. Soc. Photobiology (founding), Assn. Southeastern Biologists (past sec., past pres.), Radiation Rsch. Soc. (founding), Radiol. Soc. N.Am., Environ. Mutagen Soc. (founding, councilor 1976-79), Am. Soc. Preventive Oncology (founding), Sigma Xi. Democratic. Unitarian. Office: Univ Tex Southwe Med Ctr Dept Radiology 5323 Harry Hines Blvd Dallas TX 75235-7200

GAULTNEY, JOHN ORTON, life insurance agent, consultant; b. Pulaski, Tenn., Nov. 7, 1915; s. Bert Hood and Grace (Orton) G.; m. Elizabethine Mullette, Mar. 30, 1941; children: Elizabethine G. McClure, John Mullette, Walker Orton, Harlow Denny. Student, Am. Inst. Banking, 1936; diploma, Life Ins. Agy. Mgmt. Assn., 1948, Little Rock Jr. Coll., 1950; Mgmt. C.L.U. diploma, 1952; grad. sales mgmt. and mktg., Rutgers U., 1957. CLU. With N.Y. Life Ins. Co., 1935—; regional v.p. N.Y. Life Ins. Co., Atlanta, 1956-64; v.p. N.Y. Life Ins. Co., N.Y.C., 1964-67; v.p. in charge group sales N.Y. Life Ins. Co., 1967-68, v.p. mktg., 1969-80, agt., 1980—; life ins. cons., 1981—; v.p. N.Y. Life Variable Contracts Corp., 1969-80; hon. dir. Bank of Frankewing (Tenn.), 1984—. Elder Presbyn. Ch., 1952; chmn. Downtown YMCA, Atlanta, 1963-65; mem. Bd. Zoning Appeals, Bronxville, N.Y., 1970-80; mem. Nashville YMCA, 1981—; mem. pub. rels. com. Nat. Coun. YMCAs, 1965-80; mem. internat. world svc. com. YMCA, 1968-80; chmn. Vanderbilt YMCA, N.Y.C., 1974-76, bd. dirs., 1966-76; bd. dirs. Memphis YMCA, 1939-40, Little Rock YMCA, 1941-55, Atlanta YMCA, 1959-65, Greater N.Y. YMCA, 1975-80; dir. Internat. Assn. Y's Men's Club, 1936-42. Capt. inf. AUS, 1942-45, MTO. Decorated Silver Star, Bronze Star with 3 clusters, Purple Heart with 2 clusters.; recipient Devereux C. Josephs award N.Y. Life Ins. Co., 1954, Cross of Mil. Svc. UDC, 1973; named Ark. traveler, 1955; hon. citizen Tenn., 1956; Tenn. ambassador, 1981-87; Ky. col., 1963. Mem. Am. Soc. CLUs, Tenn. Soc. CLUs, Nat. Assn. Life

Underwriters, Tenn. Assn. Life Underwriters, Heritage Found., Carnton Assn. (bd. dirs. 1981-90, pres. 1987-88), N.Y. So. Soc. (trustee 1965-80), Williamson County Hist. Soc. (pres. 1983-85), Brentwood Hist. Trust, Giles County Hist. Soc., 361st Inf. Assn. World War II (pres. 1967-70), Mass. Soc. of the Cin., SAR (N.Y. state dir. 1970-80), Soc. Colonial Wars, Descendants of ColonialClergy, Tenn. Sons of Revolution, Assn. Preservation Tenn. Antiquities (trustee 1984-93), Tenn. Soc. in N.Y. (pres. 1971-74, trustee 1980-85), Newcomen Soc. in Am., English Speaking Union, Capital City Club (Atlanta), Athletic Club Md. Farms (Brentwood, Tenn.), Nashville City Club, Victory Svcs. Club (London), Sojourners, Heroes of '76 (commdr. 1993-94), Sovereign Mil. Order of the Temple of Jerusalem, Rotary, Masons, York Rite, Scottish Rite, Shriners. Home: 6109 Johnson Chapel Rd Brentwood TN 37027-5720 Office: NY Life Ins Co Nations Bank Plz 17th Fl Nashville TN 37219

GAUMOND, GEORGE RAYMOND, librarian; b. Watertown, N.Y., May 4, 1946; s. Francis George and Hazel Mae (Ellis) G.; m. Arlene Mae Lynch, June 7, 1969; 1 son, Gregory Wade. B.A., U. S.C., 1969; M.S., U. Ill., 1975; PhD, U. N.C., Chapel Hill, 1988. Librarian, U. N.C.-Wilmington, 1975-78; dir. library Shepherd Coll., Shepherdstown, W.Va., 1981-88; dir. libr., Valdosta (Ga.) State U., 1989—. Mem. employee adv. council W.Va. Bd. Regents, Charleston, 1983-86; mem., chmn. library resources adv. com. W.Va. Bd. Regents, 1985-88; mem. grant rev. panel for library edn., research and resources br. U.S. Dept. Edn.; mem. acad. com. librs. Bd. Regents U. Sys. Ga. Served to lt. USN, 1969-74. Mem. ALA, Ga. Libr. Assn., Southeastern Library Assn., W.Va. Library Assn., So. Ga. Associated Lirs. (chmn. 1991-92), Beta Phi Mu. Democrat. Methodist. Lodges: Masons, Kiwanis (dir. 1983-84). Home: 2603 Lakewood Dr Valdosta GA 31602-2148 Office: Valdosta State U Odum Libr Valdosta GA 31698

GAUTHIER, DOREEN ANN, librarian; b. Davenport, Iowa, July 18, 1941; d. Clifford H. and Dorothy H. Wildman; m. William E. Gauthier, July 18, 1989. BA, Midland Coll., Fremont. Nebr., 1972; grad. cert., U. Omaha, 1972; MA, U. South Fla., 1996. Children's libr. Keene Meml. Libr., Fremont, Nebr., 1967-77; circulation libr. Pompano Beach (Fla.) Libr., 1978-79; libr. dir. Lighthouse Point (Fla.) Libr., 1979—; dir. Fla. Pub. Libr. Assn., Lakeland, Fla., 1992—. Mem. ALA, Fla. Libr. Assn., Broward County Libr. Assn. Episcopalian. Home: 1990 NE 32nd Ct # 44 Lighthouse Point FL 33064-7684 Office: Lighthouse Point Library 2200 NE 38th St Lighthouse Point FL 33064-3913

GAVALER, JUDITH ANN STOHR VAN THIEL, bio-epidemiologist; b. Pitts., Aug. 5; d. Frank Howell and Nancy Helen (Hoovler) Stohr; m. John Raymond Gavaler, Nov. 17, 1962 (div. Apr. 1974); children: Joan Susan, Christopher Paul; m. David Hoffman Van Thiel, May 13, 1978 (separated March, 1995). BS, Hood Coll., 1961; PhD, U. Pitts., 1986. Jr. engr. Westinghouse Rsch., Pitts., 1961-63; rsch. asst. U. Pitts. Sch. Medicine, 1974-78, rsch. assoc., 1978-86, asst. prof., 1986-88, assoc. prof., 1988-92, prof., 1993; asst. prof. dept. epidemiology U. Pitts. Grad. Sch. Pub. Health, 1988-93; mem., head women's health rsch. program rsch. program Okla. Med. Rsch. Found., Okla. City, 1993—; sr. scientist women's rsch. Okla. Transplantation Inst., Bapt. Med. Ctr. Okla., chief women's rsch., 1994—, chief statis. and database svcs., 1994—; head Inst. Medicine Conf. Com., 1991; adj. prof. biostats. and epidemiology U. Okla. Health Sci. Ctr.; mem. rsch. rev. com. biochem. physiol. medicine NIAAA, 1993—; mem. rsch. rev. com. NIH, 1996—. Mem. editl. bd. Alcoholism, Clinical and Experimental Research jour., 1989-94 (assoc. editor 1994—), Digestive Diseases and Scis. jour., 1990-94; contbr. articles to profl. jours. Active LWV, Pitts., 1965-93, Oklahoma City, 1993—; mem. Oklahoma City Art Mus. Assocs., 1995—. Grantee Nat. Inst. Alcohol Abuse and Alcoholism, 1985—; recipient Young Investigator award Rsch. Soc. Alcoholism, 1990. Fellow Am. Coll. Nutrition; mem. Internat. Assn. Study of the Liver, Rsch. Soc. on Alcoholism (Young Investigator award 1990), Internat. Soc. Biomed. Rsch. on Alcoholism, Am. Assn. for Study of Liver Diseases, Am. Gastroenterol. Assn. Democrat. Home: 1816 Huntington Ave Oklahoma City OK 73116-4317 Office: Okla Med Rsch. Found 825 NE 13th St Oklahoma City OK 73104-5005

GAVANDE, SAMPAT ANAND, agricultural engineer, soil scientist; b. Nasik, India, Mar. 1, 1936; came to U.S., 1960; s. Ananda Bala and Saraja G. Gavande; m. Shaila Sawant, Feb. 25, 1968; children: Neil, Vikram. MS in Agrl. Engring., Kans. State U., 1962; PhD in Soils, Irrigation and Drainage, Utah State U., 1966. Registered profl. engr., Tex.; cert. profl. soil scientist; cert. profl. agronomist. Tech. officer FAO, UN, Turrialba, Costa Rica, 1966-69, Chapingo, Mex., 1969-72, Saltillo, Mex., 1973-77; chief tech. advisor FAO, UN, Rome and Asuncion, Paraguay, 1987-89; sr. scientist/engr. Radian Corp., Austin, Tex., 1977-82; hydrologist/sr. engr. Tex. Water Commn., Austin, 1983-87; chief tech. support br. Tex. Dept. Health, Austin, 1989-92; team leader Tex. Natural Resources Commn., Austin, 1992—; cons. soil/water FAO, UN, Kenya, 1985, watershed cons., Chile, 1987, India, 1989, watershed mgmt. cons., Iran, 1989, Indonesia, 1990. Author: (textbook in Spanish lang.) Soil Physics and Its Applications, 1972; contbr. over 60 articles to tech. publs., 1968-77. Mem. Rep. Presdl. Task Force, Austin and Washington, 1989-91; bd. dirs. India Community Ctr., Inc., Austin, 1991—. Mem. ASTM, Am. Soc. Agrl. Engrs., Am. Soc. Soil Sci., Am. Soc. Agronomy. Home: 4501 Upvalley Ct Austin TX 78731-3666 Office: Tex Natural Resources Conservation PO Box 13087 Austin TX 78711-3087

GAVANT, MORRIS LEONARD, radiologist; b. Atlanta, July 25, 1955; m. Ann Ellen Blockman; children: Joshua, Aaron, Jonathan, Judah. BS in Health Systems Engring., Ga. Inst. Tech., 1976; MD, Emory U., 1980. Diplomate Nat. Bd. Med. Examiners. Resident in diagnostic radiology U. Tenn. Ctr. for Health Scis., Memphis, 1980-83, chief resident, 1983-84, fellow in interventional and cardiovascular radiology, 1983-84, instr., 1984-85, asst. prof., 1985-89, assoc. prof., 1989-90, assoc. prof. with tenure, 1990—, internat. radiology fellowship dir., 1992—; mem. faculty senate U. Tenn., Memphis, 1993—; sec. dir. vascular/interventonal radiology William F. Bowld Hosp/U. Tenn. Memphis, 1991—; sect. co-dir. Regional Med. Ctr. Memphis/Elvis Presley Meml. Trauma Ctr., 1991—; asst. chief radiology svc. Memphis VA Med. Ctr., 1987-91, sect. chief uroradiology, 1984—, vacular/interventional radiology, 1984—; cons. Le Bonheur Children's Med. Ctr., 1984—. Contbr. articles to profl. jours. Grantee Squibb Labs., 1984-85, Squibb Med. Diagnostics, 1986-87, 87-88, Winthrop Pharms., 1988-89, Merck, Sharp & Dohme Rsch. Labs., 1989—. Mem. Am. Coll. Radiology, Radiol. Soc. N.Am., Am. Roentgen Ray Soc., Assn. Program Dirs. in Radiology, Soc. Cardiovascular and Interventional Radiology, Soc. Uroradiology, Assn. Univ. Radiologists, Tenn. Radiol. Soc., Memphis Roentgen Soc., AMA, So. Med. Assn., Tenn. Med. Assn., Memphis and Shelby County Med. Soc., Am. Soc. of Emergency Radiology. Office: U Tenn Memphis Dept Radiology 800 Madison Ave Memphis TN 38103-3400

GAVEY, JAMES EDWARD, investment and real estate brokerage company executive; b. Buffalo, June 6, 1942; s. George W. and Clara E. (Hanley) G.; m. Joan M. Moran, June 6, 1964; children: Philip W., Peter J., John P. BS, LeMoyne Coll., 1964; MBA, Columbia U., 1965. Acct. Peat, Marwick, Mitchell & Co., Buffalo, 1960-64; bus. cons. Arthur Andersen & Co., N.Y.C., 1965-73; pres. Gavey & Company, Inc., N.Y.C., 1973-87; founder, 1988—; pres. Island Investment Realty, Marco Island, Fla., 1990—. Contbr. articles to profl. jours. Chmn. com. United Fund, Bronxville, N.Y., 1970—; commr. Tuckahoe (N.Y.) Housing Authority, 1974-76, chmn., 1976-81; capt. N.Y. ann. fund Fordham Prep. Sch., 1980-83. Recipient various achievement awards. Mem. AICPA, N.Y. State Soc. CPAs, Fla. Soc. CPAs, Nat. Assn. Rev. Appraisers, Internat. Inst. Valuers, Nat. Apt. Assn., Nat. Assn. Home Builders, Internat. Platform Assn., Newcomen Soc. N.Am., Rotary, Union League, Cooperstown Country Club. Republican. Roman Catholic. Home and Office: PO Box 2158 Marco Island FL 33969-2158

GAVIAN, PETER WOOD, investment banker; b. Brewster, Mass., Dec. 8, 1932; s. Sarkis Peter and Ruth Millicent (Wood) G.; m. Natalie Greenough, Sept. 10, 1955 (div. 1966); children: Sarah, Deborah Gavian Costolloe; m. Kathleen Byrne Covert, Aug. 30, 1975; 1 child, Margaret Elizabeth. BA, Yale U., 1954; MBA, Harvard U., 1959. Chartered fin. analyst; USCG master's lic. Assoc. McKinsey & Co., N.Y.C., 1959-61; sec./treas. Greater Washington Investors, 1961-64, 70-71; v.p. fin. NUS Corp., Washington, 1965-66; asst. to group v.p. internat. Carborundum Co., Niagara Falls, N.Y., 1966-68; pvt. investment banking, Washington, 1968-70, 71-76; pres. Corp. Finance of Washington, Inc., 1976—; expert witness in bus. valuation, 1980—; lectr. Am. U., Washington, 1978-80; trustee Calvert Group Funds, Bethesda, Md., 1980—; dir. Am. Civil Liberties Union Va., 1993-95. Contbr. articles to profl. jours. Lt. USN, 1954-57. Dir. Washington Soc. Investment Analysts (pres. 1978-79); mem. Am. Soc. Appraisers (dir. Washington chpt. 1993—), Assn. Investment Mgmt. and Rsch. Club: Naval Acad. Sailing Squadron. Avocation: sailboat racing. Home: 3005 N Franklin Rd Arlington VA 22201-3917

GAWARECKI, CAROLYN GROSSÉ, watercolor artist and educator; b. Rahway, N.J., Oct. 30, 1931; d. Charles Grossé; m. Stephen Jerome Gawarecki, Apr. 3, 1954; children: Susan Lynn, Cathy Ann. BA, Douglass Coll., 1953. High sch. art tchr. Highland Park (N.J.) High Sch., 1953-55; exhibits artist Smithsonian Mus. Natural History, Washington, 1956-57; ind. watercolor workshop organizer and tchr. Gawarecki Assocs., Falls Church, Va., 1980-91; watercolor instr. Falls Church City Recreation Dept., 1963—; tchr. workshops in Md., W.Va., Grand Tetons, Acapulco, Mex., Ireland, Eng., Greece and France. Represented in permanent collections Dunnegan Art Gallery, Bolivar, Mo., Texaco Corp., Georgetown U., James River Corp., Cygnus Corp., Olivar Carr Corp., Indsl. Coll. Armed Forces, 1st Va. Bank, Md. Casualty, Comsat; contbr. articles to profl. jours.; paintings appeared in Best of Watercolor, 1995, Best of Watercolor Places, 1996. Judge nat. watercolor show Panama City Art Assn., 1983, Ctrl. Va. Watercolor Soc., 1994. Recipient Monetary award for art Va. Watercolor Soc., 1987, 88, 89, 92, 93, 95, Mid-Atlantic Regional, 1981, 84, Nat. Watercolor Soc., 1989, Md. Fedn. Art, 1990, 2d Place award La. 22d Internat., 1992, W.Va. Watercolor Soc., 1994, 96, 1st place award Wash. Watercolor Soc., 1994, So. Watercolor Soc., 1994, Best in Show award Springfield Art Guild Washington and No. Va., 1996. Mem. Nat. Watercolor Soc. (signature mem.), Potomac Valley Watercolorists (founder, 1st pres. 1974-77), Art League, Washington Watercolor Soc., Knickerbocker Artists (signature mem.), So. Watercolor Soc., Va. Watercolor Soc. Home: 7018 Vagabond Dr Falls Church VA 22042-3944

GAWEHN-FRISBY, DOROTHY JEANNE, freelance technical writer; b. Omaha, Jan. 20, 1931; d. Robert Floyd and Margaret Marie (Sitzman) Sealock; m. Kenneth Emil Gawehn, Apr. 17, 1951 (div. Jan. 1985); children: Marilyn Gawehn Jeffries, Kenneth M., Eric M., Celeste Gawehn-Yates; m. Charles Frisby, Mar. 17, 1990. Grad. high sch., Omaha. Systems technician Nat. Welding Co., Richmond, Calif., 1962-63; lead data entry operator United Grocers Co., Fresno, Calif., 1964-68, data processing mgr., 1968-72, computer operator shift supr., Oakland, Calif., 1972-76, documentation specialist, 1976-82; mgr. adminstrv. systems Baddour, Inc., Memphis, 1983-89; with Fed. Express Corp., 1989-91; sr. tech. writer Autozone, Memphis, 1991-95; freelance writer; contract tech. writer with Ctrl. Technical Svcs. Reader for the blind Sta. WTTL, Memphis, 1983-89; vol. worker Crisis and Suicide Intervention, Memphis, 1985-89, Docent for Ramesses exhibit, 1987. Recipient Key to Memphis. Mem. Internat. Tng. Communication (club pres. 1989-90, 96—, Communicator of Yr. award, Dixie region 1988-89, coun. 4 exec. bd. 1992-93), Data Processing Mgmt. Assn (Performance award 1973, Yosemite chpt.), Mensa (chmn. 1989-90, 96). Republican. Roman Catholic. Avocations: backpacking, reading, writing, travel, hiking. Home and Office: 6644 Elkgate Memphis TN 38141-1205

GAWRONSKI, PEGGY, healthcare worker; b. Buffalo; m. Dennis Gawronski, 1973; 1 child, Shawn Hasan. BS in Sociology, BS in Psychology, Ariz. State U., 1981; MA in Sociology, Morehead (Ky.)) State U., 1994. Case worker Mountain Comprehensive Care, Prestonsburg, Ky., 1991—. Treas. Ariz. Youth Soccer Assn., 1982-84, pres., 1984-90; officer subregion 2B U.S. Youth Soccer, 1993—. Named to Ariz. Youth Soccer Assn. Hall of Fame, 1990. Mem. Aux. to Am. Pharm. Assn. (life, v.p. 1992-94, pres. 1994-96). Home: 305 W Old Middle Creek Rd Prestonsburg KY 41653

GAY, FRANCES MARION WELBORN, private school educator; b. Charleston, S.C., Feb. 18, 1956; d. Melvin Floyd and Frances Helen (Looper) G. BA in English, Hollins Coll., 1979; MAT in English, The Citadel, Charleston, 1989. Cert. tchr. grades 5-12, S.C. Tchr. English, grades 7-8 Charleston Day Sch., 1986-87; tchr. grades 3-4 St. Paul's Acad., Ravenel, S.C., 1987-88; dir. devel. Charleston Day Sch., 1988-89, dir. devel. and admissions, 1989-92; tchr. science, grade 5 Ashley Hall, Charleston, 1992—, tchr. Lang. Arts, grade 6, 1992—. Editor: School Year Book, 1986-87; author/editor (bi-ann. newsletter) The CDS Gateway. Named one of Outstanding Young Women of Am., 1991. Mem. DAR, Hollins Alumnae Club of Charleston (pres. 1983-93), Garden Club of Charleston, Jr. League of Charleston (chmn. violence on view 1989, corrs. sec. 1992), Huguenot Soc. of S.C. (ch. docent 1985-86), English Speaking Union, Friends of the Confederate Home and Coll., Nat. Soc. Colonial Dames of the 17th Century, The Scottish Soc. of Charleston. Episcopal. Home: 8 King St Charleston SC 29401-2714 Office: Ashley Hall 172 Rutledge Ave Charleston SC 29403-5821

GAY, JOHN MARION, federal agency administrator, organization-personnel analyst; b. Houston, Sept. 23, 1936; s. John Henry and LolaBell (Collins) G.; m. Rebecca Jane Gay; children—John Marion II, Dierdre, Michael, Michelle (dec.), Steven, Christina. B.A., Tex. So. U., 1956; MSW, U. Richmond, 1968, B.S., Fla. Meml. Coll., 1976, MBA, Nova U., 1977. Cert. tchr., Fla. Compensation analyst SE Banks, N.A., Miami, Fla., 1976-78; personnel job analyst Kaiser Transit Group, Miami, 1978-80; tribal adminstr. Miccosukee Indians, Everglades Nat. Park, Fla., 1980-81; tchr. Broward County Schs., Fort Lauderdale, Fla., 1981-83, Dade County Schs., Miami, 1983-84; postal employee U.S. Postal Service, North Miami Beach, Fla., 1984—, consumer affairs officer, 1985-87, supt. Sta. Br. OONS, 1987—, supr. Mails/Delivery, 1988—, coord. for on-line computerized mail forwarding system, 1989, div. rte. insp., 1992—; inspection team leader S. Fla. Postal Ops., 1993—. Corp. coord. United Negro Coll. Fund, Dade County, 1977. Served with USAF, 1956-59. Max Fleischmann scholar United Negro Coll. Fund, 1975; recipient mems. award of honor Alpha Kappa Mu, 1974; award Fla. Meml. Coll. Alumni Assn., 1978. Fellow NEA; mem. Nat. Assn. Postal Suprs. Democrat. Avocations: tennis, bowling, writing. Home: 2780 NW 34th Ter Lauderdale Lakes FL 33311-1888

GAY, SPENCER BRADLEY, radiologist, educator; b. Washington, June 12, 1948; s. Lendall Croxton and Claudine (Moss) G.; m. Debie Farris (div. Sept. 1982); 1 child, Colin Bradley; m. Marit Corinne Anderson; children: Chelsea Britt, Kristen Corinne. BS, U. Miami, Fla., 1973; MD, U. Va., 1983. Dir. Full Circle Farm, Somerset, Va., 1974-78; pres. Cen. Va. Title Agy., Orange, 1977-79; resident in radiology U. Va. Health Scis. Ctr., Charlottesville, 1983-87, fellow in radiology, 1987-88, asst. prof., 1988-94, assoc. prof., 1994—. Mem. Med. Soc. Va., Am. Roentgen Ray Soc., Radiol. Soc. N.Am. Episcopalian. Office: U Va Health Sci Ctr PO Box 170 Charlottesville VA 22902-0170

GAY, SYLVIA FRANCE, critical care and pediatrics nurse; b. Macon, Ga., June 10, 1941; d. Sydney Taylor and Katharine Bernice (Gostin) France; m. Carl C. Gay, June 14, 1958; children: Mike, Katharine, Greg. AA, AS in Nursing, Brevard Community Coll., Cocoa, Fla., 1979; BA, U. Cen. Fla., 1985. RN, Fla.; lic. prescribed pediatric extended care. Staff nurse III, Wuesthoff Meml. Hosp., Rockledge, Fla.; staff nurse III neonatal ICU, neonatal transport nurse Holmes Regional Med. Ctr., Melbourne, Fla.; founder, dir. Kids Individual Devel. Svcs., alt. health care facility for medically fragile children. Mem. ANA (cert. high risk perinatal nurse), NAACOG (cert. low risk neonatal nurse), Nat. Assn. Neonatal Nurses, Nat. Perinatal Assn. Home: 407 Berwick Way Melbourne FL 32940-2112

GAY, WILLIAM KARL, systems integration program manager; b. N.Y.C., Mar. 14, 1945; s. William Michael and Emmi Katherine (LaFranz) G.; m. Diane Marr Pugh, Aug. 29, 1970; children: Jennifer M., Sarah H. BCE, CCNY, 1967; M of Engring., U. Fla., 1976. Registered profl. engr., D.C.; cert U.S. Army material acquisition mgr. Commd. 2d lt. U.S. Army, 1970, advanced through grades to lt. col., 1984; project dir. U.S. Army Engring. Studies Ctr., Washington, 1976-78; spl. asst. for R&D Dept. of the Army, Washington, 1978-80; area facilities engr. Dept. of the Army, Taegu, Korea, 1980-82; chief engr. plans and ops. U.S. Forces Korea, Seoul, 1982-83; divsn. chief systems integration and configuration mgmt. Dept. of Def., Washington, 1983-87; ret., 1987; prin. spl. systems Sverdrup, Arlington, Va., 1987-93; asst. v.p. comml. and internat. programs SAIC, McLean, Va., 1993—; chmn. task force Future/Build 2000 Conf. procs., 1990; mem. expert panel Intellibat procs., Paris, 1993, Designing to Avoid Obsolescence, Nat. Rsch. Coun., 1993. With USMC, 1967-69, U.S. Army, 1970-87. Decorated Legion of Merit, 1980, Def. Superior Svc. medal, 1987. Mem. NSPE, Intelligent Bldg. Inst. (chmn. tech. com. 1988-93), Bldg. Futures Coun. (innovation com. 1992-93), Electronics Industry Assn. (standards com. 1992), Chi Epsilon, Tau Beta Pi, Phi Kappa Phi. Episcopalian. Home: 612 Walker Hill Ln Great Falls VA 22066-3901 Office: SAIC 1710 Goodridge Dr Mc Lean VA 22102-3701

GAYLIS, NORMAN BRIAN, internist, rheumatologist, educator; b. Johannesburg, South Africa, May 31, 1950; came to U.S., 1976; s. Bernard Gaylis and Jesse Gaylis Berelowitz; m. Natalie Dagnin, June 6, 1976; children, Brett-Ari, Jarrod Michael. M.B.Ch.B. U. Witwatersrand, Johannesburg, South Africa, 1973. Diplomate Am. Bd. Internal Medicine. Intern Mt. Sinai Med. Ctr., Miami, 1976, resident, 1977-78, chief resident in medicine, 1978-79; clin. research fellow U. Miami, 1979-81; practice medicine specializing in rheumatology and internal medicine, North Miami, Fla. 1981—; mem. staff Parkway Med. Ctr., North Miami Gen. Hosp., North Shore Hosp., Biscayne Med. Ctr.; clin. assoc. prof. U. Miami, 1982—; host health talk show sta. WINZ, Miami. Editor: Problems in Rheumatology, 1981, 82 (award Arthritis and Rheumatology Assn. Bd. dirs., adviser Lupus Found. South Fla., 1981-83; bd. dirs., mem. council edn. Arthritis Found. South Fla., 1982-83. Mem. ACP, Am. Rheumatism Assn. (S.E. 1st prize for case presentation 1981), South African Med. Assn., Brit. Med. Assn., AMA. Jewish. Home: 520 N Parkway Miami FL 33160-2253 Office: 160 NW 170th St Miami FL 33169-5521

GAYLORD, EDWARD LEWIS, publishing company executive; b. Denver, May 28, 1919; s. Edward King and Inez (Kinney) G.; m. Thelma Feragen, Aug. 30, 1950; children: Christine Elizabeth, Mary Inez, Edward King II, Thelma Louise. A.B., Stanford U., 1941; LL.D., Oklahoma City U., Okla. Christian Coll., Pepperdine U., 1984. Chmn. Okla. Pub. Co., Oklahoma City; also bd. dirs. Okla. Pub. Co.; editor, pub. Daily Oklahoman, Sunday Oklahoman; pres. Sun Resources, Inc., Greenland (Colo.) Ranch, OPUBCO Resources, Inc., OPUBCO Devel. Co.; chmn. Gaylord Entertainment, Nashville; chmn. Opryland U.S.A., Inc., Nashville, chmn. bd. Gayno, Inc., Colo. Springs; ptnr. Cimarron Coal Co., Denver, Lazy E Ranch, St. Jo, Tex.; chmn., CEO, bd. dirs. Broadmoor Hotel, Colo. Springs. Chmn., trustee Okla. Industries Authority; hon. chmn. bd. govs. Okla. Christian Coll.; bd. dirs. Okla. State Fair, pres., 1961-71; chmn. bd. dirs. Nat. Cowboy Hall of Fame and Western Heritage Ctr.; vice chmn. bd. govs. Am. Citizenship Ctr.; chmn. Okla. Med. Research Found., 1983—; past trustee Casady Sch., Oklahoma City U. Served with AUS, 1942-46. Recipient Brotherhood award NCCJ named to Okla. Hall of Fame, 1974; first recipient Spirit of Am. award U.S. Olympic Com., 1984; Disting. Service award U. Okla., 1981; Golden Plate award Am. Acad. Achievement, 1985. Mem. Oklahoma City C. of C. (dir., past pres.), So. Newspaper Pubs. Assn. (past pres.). Congregationalist. Home: 1506 Dorchester Dr Oklahoma City OK 73120-1203 Office: The Daily Oklahoman PO Box 25125 9000 Broadway Ext Oklahoma City OK 73114-3708

GAYNOR, LEAH, radio personality, commentator, broadcaster; b. Irvington, N.J.; d. Jack and Sophia Kamish; AA, Miami Dade C.C., 1970; BA, Fla. Internat. U., 1975, postgrad., 1975—; m. Robert Merrill, Mar. 27, 1954 (dec.); children: Michael David (dec.), Lisa Heidi (dec.), Tracy Lynn (dec.). Owner, operator Lee Gaynor Assos., pub. relations, Miami, Fla., 1970-72; exec. dir. Ft. Lauderdale (Fla.) Jaycees, 1970-71; host interview program Sta. WGMA, Hollywood, Fla., 1971-73, stas. WWOK and WIGL-FM, Fla., 1973-79; occupational specialist Lindsey Hopkins Edn. Ctr. Dade County Pub. Schs., publicity-pub. rels., Miami, 1971-91; ednl. specialist Office Vocat., Adult, Career and Community Edn. Dade County Pub. Schs. 1991-94; broadcaster talk show sta. WEDR-FM, 1983-93; host, producer weekly half-hour pub. service talk program, The Leah Gaynor Show, 1985-94. Mem. Citizens Adv. Com. Career and Vocat. Edn., 1973; mem. adv. com. North Miami Beach High Sch., 1977-79; mem. publicity Com. Ctr. Fine Arts, Mus. Sci.; mem. Coalition Community Edn.; bd. dirs. Alternative Programs, Inc. Mem. Women in Comm., Am. Women in Radio and TV (dir. publicity Goldcoast chpt. 1974-76), Alliance Career Edn. (publicity chmn.). Democrat. Home: 1255 NE 171st Ter Miami FL 33162-2755

GEARHART, JOHN WESLEY, III, musician, educator; b. Hampton, Va., Apr. 3, 1950; s. John Wesley Jr. and Carolyn (Scott) G.; m. Laurie Brasfield, June 10, 1972; children: Jennifer B., Courtney S. Student, Guilford Coll., 1968-69; BA, Coll. William & Mary, 1972; MusM, Temple U., 1975; postgrad., Westminster Choir Coll. Organist First Presbyn. Ch., Hampton, Va., 1965-68, First Bapt. Ch., Greensboro, N.C., 1968-69; asst. organist/choirmaster Bruton Parish Ch., Williamsburg, Va., 1969-73; asst. organist John Wanamaker Store, Phila., 1973-78; organist/choirmaster Grace Presbyn. Ch., Jenkintown, Pa., 1973-78; recording artist, harpsichordist Independence Hall, Phila., 1974-78; organist/choirmaster St. Paul's Episc. Ch., Mobile, Ala., 1978-93; harpist Biloxi Symphony, 1990-93, Port City Symphony, 1990-93; dir. music St. John the Divine Episcopal Ch., 1993—; lectr., recitalist Colonial Williamsburg Found., 1971-73; lectr. Coll. William & Mary, 1972-73; faculty mem. Spring Hill Coll., 1980-93; cons. 1973-93. Contbr. articles to profl. jours.; composer 48 Hymn Descants, 1980; performed for 12 segments The Protestant Hour (nat. radio broadcasts) 1987-88. Treas., chmn. fin. Mobile Theatre Guild, Inc., 1980-85; mem. bd. Mobile Student Symphony, 1991-93; treas. Mobile chpt. Am. Guild Eng. Handbell Ringers, 1987-93; dir. 70-voice St. Paul's Comty. Choral Soc., Mobile, 1985-93; founder/dir. 20-voice Mobile Vocal Arts Ensemble, 1979-93; del. 4th Internat. Congress Organists, Cambridge, Eng., 1988. Ala. State Arts Coun. Individual fellow, 1990. Mem. Am. Guild Organists (dean 1980-82, treas. Mobile chpt. 1983-88, 92-93, chmn. region VI conv. Mobile 1991), Am. Harp Soc. (pres. Gulf Coast chpt. 1992-94), Assn. Anglican Musicians, Organ Hist. Soc., Phi Mu Alpha. Republican. Episcopalian. Home: 12511 Woodthorpe Ln Houston TX 77024-4110 Office: St John The Divine Episcopal Ch 2450 River Oaks Blvd Houston TX 77019-5826

GEARY, DAVID LESLIE, communications executive, educator, consultant; b. Connellsville, Pa., Sept. 30, 1947; s. Harry and Edith Marie (Halterman) G. BA, Otterbein Coll., 1969; MSJ, W.Va. U., 1971; postgrad., U. Denver, 1974-75; diploma, Def. Info. Sch., 1971, exec. communications curriculum, U. Okla., 1978, Def. Dept. Sr. Pub. Affairs Officers Course, 1984, Fgn. Svc. Inst., U.S. Dept. State, 1984, Nat. Def. U., 1986; postgrad., U. Sarasota, 1992—. Admissions counselor Otterbein Coll., 1968-69; instr. English, staff counselor Office of Student Ednl. Svcs. W.Va. U., Morgantown, 1969-71; dir. info. Luke AFB, Ariz., 1971-72; course dir. English and comm. U.S. Air Force Acad., Colo., 1972-76; dir. pub. affairs Loring AFB, Maine, 1976-79; spl. asst. pub. affairs Seymour Johnson AFB, N.C., 1980; dir. pub. affairs USAF Engring. and Svcs., Tyndall AFB, Fla., 1980-84, UN and US Air Forces, Korea, 1984-85; asst. prof., asst. dept. chmn., mem. coun. of assoc. and asst. deans U. Ala., 1985-88; acting dir. pub. affairs USAFR, 1988-92; prin. Leadership Comm. Counsel, 1992-95; comm. program mgr., dir. pub. affairs U.S. Dept. Energy, Albuquerque, 1995—; adj. prof. pub. rels. Ga. State U., Atlanta, 1993-95, mem bd., profl., pub. rels. reviiew; guest lectr. U. Maine, 1976-79, USAF Inst. Tech., 1981-82, Fla. State U., 1982-83, U. Md., 1984-85, U.So. Calif., 1984-85, Seoul (Korea) Nat. U., 1985, U. Ala., 1988, Ga. State U., 1991, U. Ga., 1991. Contbr. articles to profl. jours.; mem. bd. prcfls. Pub. Rels. Rev.: A Jour. of Rsch. and Comment, 1996—; editl. bd. Jour. of Employee Communication Mgmt., 1996—. Decorated 4 U.S. Meritorious Svc. medals, 2 Air Force Commendation medals, Air Force Achievement medal, Armed Forces Res. medal, Humanitarian Svc. medal, 2 Nat. Def. Svc. medals, Pres.'s Extradinary Svc. award Otterbein Coll., 1969, Hon. Citizen of Ariz. award, 1971, Mayor's Community Svc. medallion, Songtan, Korea, 1985, Nat. Disting. Svc. medal Arnold Air Soc., 1986, Nat. citation Angel Flight, 1986, George Washington Honor medal from Freedom's Found., 1988, Outstanding Faculty Advisor award U. Ala. Student Govt. Assn., 1988, Exemplary Svc. award Nat. Com. for Employer Support of Guard and Res., 1991, U.S. Dept. Energy Quality award, 1995, U.S. Dept. Energy Spl. Orgnl. Achievement Recognition, 1995, 96; Readers Digest Found. grantee, 1970. Mem. NATAS, Assn. for Edn. in Journalism and Mass Commn., Internat. Comm. Assn., Pub. Rels. Soc. Am., Internat. Assn. Bus. Communicators, SAR, Am. Legion, N.Mex. Pub. Affairs Roundtable (founding). Republican. Episcopalian. Office: Office Pub Affairs US Dept Energy PO Box 5400 Albuquerque NM 87185-5400

GEARY, DAVID PATRICK, criminal justice educator, consultant, author; b. Milw., May 20, 1928; s. Cornelius John and Madeline (Cushway) G.; m. Mary Ann Delavan, June 19, 1954; children: Patrick, John, Daniel, Peter. BS, LaVerne U., L.A., 1971; MPA, U. So. Calif., 1972; PhD, Marquette U., 1979; postgrad., U. Mich., 1980. Cert. life teaching credential, Calif. Police officer City of Greendale, Wis., 1950-55; chief police City of Hales Corners, Wis., 1955-61, City of Salem, Oreg., 1961-65, City of Ventura, Calif., 1965-72; assoc. prof. criminal justice U. Wis., Milw., 1972-76, U. South Fla., Tampa, 1976-79, U. Nev., Reno, 1979-82; assoc. prof. criminal justice Va. Commonwealth U., Richmond, 1982—, pres. faculty senate, 1989; mem. vis. faculty Ventura Coll., 1966-72, Carthage Coll., Kenosha, Wis., 1974; cons. Commn. on Accreditation for Law Enforcement Agys., Fairfax, Va., 1990; cons. to city Va. State Police, 1994, Richmond Va. Police, 1996—; cons. to city atty. and police dept. City of Dallas, 1990; cons. to atty. gen. City of Birmingham, 1991; cons. to postal insp. U.S. Postal Svc., Washington, 1992. Author: How To Deliver Death News, 1981; editor: Community Relations, 1976; also articles. Gen. chmn. Arts in Justice, Anderson Gallery, Richmond, 1989. With U.S. Maritime Svc., 1944-46. Named Outstanding Young Man, U.S. Jaycees, Hales Corners, 1965; rsch. fellow U.S. Govt. Law Enforcement Assistance Adminstrn., 1976. Mem. AAUP (pres. Va. Commonwealth U. chpt. 1987, 94), Va. Assn. Criminal Justice Educators (pres. 1985-87). Home: 7678 Yarmouth Dr Richmond VA 23225 Office: Va Commonwealth U Box 2017 816 W Franklin St Richmond VA 23284

GEARY, PAMELA BLALACK, community health and medical/surgical nurse; b. Shelby County, Tenn., Oct. 27, 1961; d. Walker Ernest Jr. and Pauline Eliose (Holbrook) Blalack; m. Carl Dewayne Geary, Oct. 17, 1981; children: Michelle Dawn, Micheal Dewayne. Diploma, Meth. Hosp. Sch. Nursing, Memphis, 1984. RN, Tenn. Supplemental nurse Meth. Home Care, Memphis, staff home health nurse; staff nurse Meth. Hosp.-North, Memphis, Bapt. Meml. Hosp.-Tipton, Covington, Tenn. Named one of Celebrate Nursing Top 100, 1996.

GEARY, PATRICK JOSEPH, naval security administrator; b. Milw., Mar. 6, 1957; s. David Patrick and Mary Ann (Delavan) G. BS, Va. Commonwealth U., 1984; MA, U. Richmond, 1987. Tech. publs. writer Dept. Def. Security Inst., Richmond, Va., 1987-88; ops. security officer David Taylor Naval Rsch. Ctr., Bethesda, Md., 1988-91, Space and Naval Warfare Sys. Command, Arlington, Va., 1991-92; divsn. head office of security Naval Sea Sys. Command, Arlington, 1992—. Pres. Ybor City Jaycees, Tampa, Fla., 1979, Reno Jaycees, 1980-81; regional/dist. dir. Nev. Jaycees, Reno, 1981-83; co-campaign mgr. state assembly Rep. Party of Nev., Reno, 1982; senator Jaycees Internat., Coral Gables, Fla., 1983, life mem.; active West End Jaycees Richmond, 1983—. Decorated superior civilian svc. medal Dept. Navy, 1995; recipient Charles Kulp meml. award U.S. Jaycees, 1981; Albright grad. fellow U. Richmond, 1985. Mem. NRA, KC, Am. Def. Preparedness Assn. (life), Ops. Security Profls. Soc. (charter, nat. bd. dirs. 1995—), Nat. Assn. Parliamentarians, Am. Inst. Parliamentarians, Nat. Mil. Intelligence Assn. (life), Pi Sigma Alpha, Alpha Phi Sigma. Roman Catholic. Home: 816 Cresthill Rd Fredericksburg VA 22405-1614

GEDDIE, THOMAS EDWIN, retired small business owner; b. Athens, Tex., Oct. 7, 1930; s. Nolen Dawson and Fannie (Troublefield) G.; BS in Agr., Okla. State U., 1951; postgrad. Tex. A&M U., 1951; m. Minnie Maxine Smith, Feb. 18, 1968; children: Susan, Tommy, Sherry. Owner, operator Thomas E. Geddie Assocs., Athens, 1955-96, ret. 1996; active as pvt. investor. Served with U.S. Army, 1952-54. Republican. Presbyterian. Mem. Masons (32 deg.). Home: 901 Clifford St Athens TX 75751-2959 Office: 314 N Faulk St Athens TX 75751-2030

GEDDINGS, CHARLES MCIJOR, III, librarian; b. Sumter, S.C., Mar. 6, 1953; s. Charles McIjor Jr. and Ruby (Christmas) G.; m. Terry Diana Ludwig, Dec. 28, 1985. BA, Wofford Coll., 1975; postgrad., Duke U., 1977; MLS, U. S.C., 1980. Cert. libr. media specialist, libr.; cert. instr. oil painting. Tchr. English Hillcrest H.S., Dalzell, S.C., 1975-80; libr. media specialist Ebenezer Jr. H.S., Sumter, 1980-82, High Hills Mid. Sch., Shaw AFB, S.C., 1982-96, Hillcrest Mid. Sch., Dalzell, 1996—; reference libr. Cen. Carolina Tech. Coll., Sumter, 1986—. Artist oil paintings. Precinct v.p. local Rep. party, Sumter, 1990; deacon Pine Grove Bapt. Ch., chmn., 1994—, Sunday sch. tchr., 1985—. Mem. S.C. Assn. Sch. Librs. (dist. network contact 1993-95, regional network contact 1995-96, Bol award nominee com. 1984-86). Home: 2430 Tindal Rd Sumter SC 29150 Office: Cen Carolina Tech Coll 506 N Guignaid Sumter SC 29110

GEDDY, VERNON MEREDITH, JR., lawyer; b. Norfolk, Va., Apr. 12, 1926; s. Vernon Meredith and Carrie Cole (Lane) G.; m. Marie Lewis Sibley, Dec. 22, 1949; children: Anne Lewis Geddy Cross, Vernon M. Geddy III. A.B. cum laude, Princeton U., 1949; LL.B., U. Va., 1952. Bar: Va. Ptnr. Geddy & Harris (and predecessor firms), Williamsburg, Va., 1952-80; ptnr. McGuire, Woods, Battle & Boothe (and predecessor firms), Williamsburg, Va., 1980-91; Geddy, Harris & Geddy, 1991—; former dir. United Va. Bankshares, Nat. Ctr. for State Cts. Mem. Williamsburg City Coun., Va., 1968-80; trustee Colonial Williamsburg Found., 1981-95, Va. Hist. Soc., Richmond, 1981-88, 94—, Va. Mus. Fine Arts, 1982-91; bd. dirs. Williamsburg Cmty. Hosp., 1969-85, WHRO, Jamestown-Yorktown Found. Sgt. USAAF, 1944-46, PTO. Named to Raven Soc. Fellow Am. Bar Found. (award 1976); mem. ABA, Va. Bar Assn. (pres. 1972-73), Va. State Bar, Williamsburg Bar Assn. (pres. 1975-93), Omicron Delta Kappa, Commonwealth Club. Episcopalian. Home: PO Box 379 Williamsburg VA 23187-0379 Office: Geddy Harris & Geddy 516A S Henry St PO Box 379 Williamsburg VA 23187

GEE, KENT LEONG, management consultant; b. Houston, Oct. 27, 1949; s. Wallace ChowDung and Lucille (Louie) G. BA, Houston Bapt. U., 1972, M Liberal Arts, 1989, MS in Mgmt., Computing & Systems., 1991; BS in Accountancy, U. Houston-Ctrl., 1978. Missionary appointee Home Mission Bd., So. Bapt. Convention, Atlanta, 1972-74; account exec. Search Cons., Inc., Houston, 1974-76; acct., supr. Elder Leasing Co., Houston, 1978-79, Mitchell Energy & Devel. Corp., The Woodlands, Tex., 1979-85; sr. cons. Deloitte Haskins & Sells, Houston, 1985-86; sr. EDP auditor Transco Energy Co., Houston, 1986-90; mgmt. cons. in cultural diversity/systems integration, owner DiversiTech Cons., Houston, 1990—; adj. lectr. U. Houston-Downtown, 1992—. Bd. mgrs. Greater Harris County 9-1-1 Emergency Network, Houston, 1992—; past chmn./bd. dirs. Asian Am. Coalition, Houston, 1991-92; mem. attendance boundary com. Houston Ind. Sch. Dist., 1992-93; bd. dirs. Electronic Data Processing Auditors Assn., Houston, 1986-90. Mem. IEEE, Nat. Emergency Number Assn., Tex. Emergency Number Assn., Assn. Pub. Safety Comms. Ofcls. Internat. Inc., Assn. Cert. Fraud Examiners.

GEEKER, NICHOLAS PETER, lawyer, judge; b. Pensacola, Fla., Dec. 15, 1944. B.A. in English, La. Poly. Inst., 1966; J.D., Fla. State U., 1969. Bar: Fla. 1969, U.S. Dist. Ct. 1970, US. Supreme Ct., 1980. Assoc. firm Merritt & Jackson, Pensacola, 1969; law clk. U.S. Dist. Judge D.L. Middlebrooks, Tallahassee, 1970-73; asst. state atty. Fla. 1st Jud. Circuit, 1973; asst. U.S. atty. No. Dist. Fla., 1973-76, U.S. atty., 1976-82; sole practice Pensacola, Fla., 1982-85; circuit judge Fla. 1st Jud. Circuit, 1985—; mem. Fed.-State Joint Com. on Law Enforcement. Mem. Fla. Bar Assn., Fla. Trial Lawyers Assn. (editor Newsletter 1975), Phi Delta Phi. Office: 190 Governmental Ctr Pensacola FL 32501

GEEN, TIM DOW, restaurant executive; b. Beaumont, Tex., Nov. 27, 1944; s. James M. and Thelma N. (Vannostran) G.; divorced; 1 child, Kevin. BA in Criminal Justice, La. State U., 1975. Supervising sgt. Beaumont Police Dept., 1973-88; owner, mgr. Party Music, 1978-88, Peppermel Club, Tulsa; owner Embers Club, Tulsa, 1991—. Security chief ops. Ducks Unltd., Beaumont, 1978-86. Sgt. USMC, 1963-69, Vietnam. Recipient Deptl. Medal of Valor, Beaumont Police Dept., 1979. Home and Office: PO Box 702643 Tulsa OK 74170-2643

GEENTIENS, GASTON PETRUS, JR., former construction management consultant company executive; b. Garfield, N.J., Apr. 6, 1935; s. Gaston Petrus and Margaret (Piros) G.; m. Barbara Ann Chamberlin, Oct. 14, 1960; children: Mercedes Frith, Faith Piros. BSCE, The Citadel, 1956. Registered profl. engr., 15 states. Plant engr. Western Elec. Co., Inc., Kearny, N.J., 1956-58, owner's rep., N.Y.C., 1960-64; v.p. Gentyne Motors, Inc., Passaic, N.J., 1958-60; project engr. Ethyl Corp., Baton Rouge, La., 1964-65; mgr. Timothy McCarthy Constrn. Co., Atlanta, 1965; asst. to v.p. A.R. Abrams, Inc. and Columbia Engring., Inc., Atlanta, 1965-66; supr. engring. and constrn. Litton Industries, N.Y.C., 1966-71; pres. G.P. Geentiens Jr., Inc., Charleston, S.C., 1971-82; gen. ptnr. Engineered Enterprises Co., Charleston, 1973-76; dir. Cayman Broadcasting Assos., Cayman Islands, B.W.I., 1977-82. Mem. Ramapo (N.Y.) Republican Com., 1961-64. Served to 1st lt. C.E., AUS, 1956-58. Mem. ASCE, Tau Beta Pi. Home: 1219 Pembrooke Dr Charleston SC 29407-7748

GEESLIN, GARY LLOYD, lawyer; b. Grenada, Miss., Oct. 31, 1940. BA, Miss. State U., 1962; JD, U. Miss., 1968. Bar: Miss. 1968, U.S. Dist. Ct. (no. dist.) Miss. 1968, U.S. Dist. Ct. (so. dist.) Miss. 1972, U.S. Ct. Appeals (5th cir.) 1974, U.S. Ct. Appeals (fed. cir.) 1987. Assoc. Threadgill & Smith, Columbus, Miss., 1968-79; ptnr. Lipscomb, Geeslin & McClanahan, Columbus, 1991-94; pvt. practice, Columbus, 1979-91, 94—. Mem. Old Waverly Golf Club, Rotary (pres. Columbus 1976). Office: 107 Merle Dr Columbus MS 39702-7205

GEGGUS, DAVID PATRICK, history educator; b. Romford, Essex, Eng., Nov. 19, 1949; came to U.S., 1983; s. David and Alice Winifred (Thorne) G.; m. Josiane Bassal, 1994; 1 child, Sarah Valentine. BA, Oxford (Eng.) U., 1971, MA, 1976; MA with distinction, London U., 1972; DPhil, York (Eng.) U., 1979. Jr. rsch. fellow Wolfson Coll., Oxford U., 1976-80; rsch. fellow Southampton (Eng.) U., 1980-82; from asst. prof. to assoc. prof. history U. Fla., Gainesville, 1983-93, prof., 1993—. Author: Slavery, War and Revolution, 1982; editor (with D.B. Gaspar) A Turbulent Time, 1997; also over 50 articles. Guggenheim fellow, 1984, Woodrow Wilson fellow, 1986, fellow Nat. Humanities Ctr., Research Triangle Park, N.C., 1989, Social Scis. Rsch. Coun., 1992. Office: U Fla Dept History Gainesville FL 32611

GEHLE, JANICE MARIE, news research manager; b. Chgo., Apr. 21, 1949; d. William Edward and Genevieve Victoria (Pocius) Jaeger; m. Robert Wayne Gehle, June 18, 1972. BA, No. Ill. U., 1971; MA, U. So. Fla., 1984. Cert. English tchr., Fla. Lang. arts tchr. Oak Lawn-Hometown Sch. Dist., Ill., 1971-73; English tchr. Manatee County Sch. Bd., Bradenton, Fla., 1973-79; coord. newspaper in edn. Bradenton Herald, 1979-81, news librn., 1981-84; news librn. Sarasota (Fla.) Herald-Tribune, 1984-93, news rsch. mgr., 1994—. Author tchg. guides: Newspaper in Edn., Lang. Arts, Sci.-Health, Math., Social Studies, 1980. Mem. Spl. Librs. Assn. news divn., Fla. Newspaper Librns. Office: Sarasota Herald-Tribune 801 S Tamiami Trl Sarasota FL 34236-7824

GEHRKE, TIMOTHY ROBERT, social worker; b. St. Joseph, Mich., Apr. 14, 1960; s. Robert Henry and Elaine Mae (Ulrich) G.; m. Mary Ann Brazil, Feb. 22, 1986. BS, Eastern Mich. U., 1983, MA, 1989. Lic. social worker; lic. profl. counselor. Youth attendant Washtenaw County Juvenile Ct., Ann Arbor, Mich., 1983, youth counselor, 1983-86, 87-90, intensive probation officer, 1986-87, program coord., 1990; case mgr. Dept. Justice Fed. Prison System, Milan, Mich., 1987; career devel. asst. Eastern Mich. U., Ypsilanti, 1989-90; probation agt. II Washtenaw Count 14A Dist. Ct., Ypsilanti, Mich., 1992-93; program dir. Serious Habitual Offender Program Agency for Cmty. Devel., Tampa, Fla., 1993—. Mem. Am. Assn. Counseling and Devel., Eastern Mich. U. Alumni Orgn. (alumni program trustee, Huron Valley chpt. v.p. 1991-92), Kiwanis (bd. dirs. 1991-93). Republican. Lutheran. Home: 2214 Arbor Oaks Dr Valrico FL 33594-5103 Office: Juvenile Ct 6612 Stark Rd Seffner FL 33584-2704

GEHRON, MICHAEL MCDERMOTT, information technology company executive; b. N.Y.C., Aug. 18, 1954; s. William Jules and Patricia (Coleman) G.; m. Nancy Wirth, Mar. 26, 1988; children: Katherine Charleswirth, Luke Coleman. BA, Denison U., 1977; MS, Am. U., 1985. Systems analyst J.A. Reyes, Washington, 1984-87; asst. v.p. Network Mgmt. Inc., Fairfax, Va., 1987-90; v.p. Marasco Newton Group, Arlington, Va., 1990—; adj. faculty Bowie (Md.) State U., 1988-89. Vol. U.S. Peace Corps, Togo, West Africa, 1978-80. Jenny Moore fellow George Washington U., 1982. Office: Marasco Newton Group 1600 Wilson Blvd Arlington VA 22209-2505

GEIGER, JAMES NORMAN, lawyer; b. Mansfield, Ohio, Apr. 5, 1932; s. Ernest R. and Margaret L. (Bauman) G.; m. Paula Hunt, May 11, 1957; children: Nancy G., John W. Student Wabash Coll., Crawfordsville, Ind., 1950-51; BA, Ohio Wesleyan U., 1954; JD, Emory U., 1962, LLD, 1970. Bar: Ga. 1961, U.S. Dist. Ct. (mid. dist.) Ga. 1966, U.S. Ct. Appeals (5th and 11th cirs.) 1980, U.S. Dist. Ct. (so. dist.) Ga. 1983. Ptnr. Henderson, Kaley, Geiger and Thurmond, Marietta, Ga., 1962-64, Geiger and Pierce and predecessors, Perry, Ga., 1964-88, Geiger & Pierce, P.C., 1986—. Trustee Westfield (Ga.) Schs., 1970-74; mem. civilian adv. bd. Warner Robins AFB, 1976; chmn. coun. ministries Perry United Meth. Ch., 1970-71, mem. adminstrv. bd., 1968—. Capt. USAF, 1954-57. Mem. ABA, Ga. Bar Assn., Houston County Bar Assn., South Ga. C. of C. (bd. dirs.) Perry C. of C. (pres. 1976, 90), Perry Kiwanis (pres. 1968, Man of Yr. 1968), Perry Club Coun. (pres. 1967), Phi Delta Phi, Pi Sigma Alpha. Methodist. Home: 821 Forest Hill Rd Perry GA 31069-3645 Office: Geiger & Pierce 1007 Jernigan St Perry GA 31069-3325

GEIGER, RALPH BRUCE, physician; b. Wyandotte, Mich., Feb. 10, 1947; s. Robert Bruce and Gwen (Shone) G.; m. Stephanie Frances Gentile, Oct. 30, 1983 (div. Nov. 1992, remarried Feb. 1996); children: Jeremy Sean, Lauren Nicole. BA cum laude, Kenyon Coll., 1969; candidat en medicine, U. Liege, Belgium, 1973; MD, U. Miami, 1977. Diplomate Am. Bd. Internal Medicine. Intern, resident in internal medicine U. Miami, 1980; ptnr. Cummings, Geiger, Van Haasteren, Miami, 1980-88; ptnr. Gold, Vann, White, Vero Beach, Fla., 1988—, also bd. dirs.; chief of medicine Coral Reef Hosp., Miami, 1987. Office: Gold Vann White 2300 5th Ave Vero Beach FL 32960-5169

GEIGER, RICHARD BERNARD, engineer, retired federal agency administrator; b. Huron County, Mich., May 4, 1936; s. Clement T. and Elizabeth A. (Volmering) G.; m. Norma J. Edwards, Sept. 6, 1958; children: Brenda, Jeffrey, Lisa, Paula, Pamela. AAS, St. Clair C.C., Port Huron, Mich., 1961; BS in Civil Engring., George Washington U., 1972; M in Urban Affairs, Va. Poly. Inst. & State U., 1980. Registered profl. engr., Mich., D.C. Engring. technician Bur. Pub. Rds., Gatlinburg, Tenn., 1958-63; hwy. engr. Bur. Pub. Rds., Arlington, Va., 1964-67; planning engr. Fed. Hwy. Adminstrn., Arlington, 1967-73, environ. engr., 1973-77; environ. engr. Fed. Hwy. Adminstrn., Washington, 1977-80, hwy. engr., 1980-89; asst. chief, divsn. transp. Bur. Indian Affairs, Washington, 1989-91, chief, divsn. transp., 1991-94, ret., 1994; mem. Nat. Rsch. Coun. (Transp. Rsch. Bd.), Washington, 1989—. V.p. Ch. Share Com., Annandale, Va., 1990-91. With U.S. Army, 1954-56. Recipient Svc. award Am. Assn. State Hwy. and Transp. Ofcls., 1983, Superior Achievement award Fed. Hwy. Adminstrn., 1986. Mem. ASCE (Outstanding Student award 1971), NSPE, Nat. Assn. County Engrs., Order of the Engr., Am. Legion, Disabled Am. Vets. (life). Home: 6903 Fern Ln Annandale VA 22003-1909

GEIGERMAN, CLARICE FURCHGOTT, writer, actress, consultant; b. Charleston, S.C., Sept. 24, 1916; d. Melvin and Doreta (Brown) Furchgott; m. Henry D. Geigerman, Jr., July 4, 1941 (dec. Nov. 1967); children: Henry D. III, Robert M.; m. Bruce Franklin Woodruff, Jr., Dec. 11, 1982. A in Bus., Draughon Sch. Commerce, 1935; student, U. Ga., 1935-36, Am. Inst. Banking, 1936-41, Ga. Inst. Real Estate, 1972. Dir. payroll and pers. Atlanta Ordnance Dept., 1935-41, 45-46; freelance writer Atlanta Press Club, 1964—; pvt. practice as pub. rels. cons. Atlanta, 1970—; ins. agent Am. Family Life, Atlanta, 1970—; real estate agent Ackerman & Co., Atlanta, 1972—; freelance actress Women-In-Film, Atlanta, 1974—. Writer TV Digest, 1961-62; writer, contbg. editor Arts Mag., 1962-63; author, editor newsletter, mag. Atlanta Music Club, 1973; columnist Jewish Georgian, 1989—, Buckhead Weekly, 1995—; appeared in motion picture Driving Miss Daisy, 1991. Pres. Atlanta Civic Ballet, 1962-64, So. Regional Opera, Atlanta, 1968-75; mem. Atlanta Funds Rev. Bd., 1973-75; v.p. Atlanta Playhouse Theatre, pres., bd. dirs.; 1st v.p. Met. Atlanta Better Films, 1992-96, pres., 1996—; active Salvation Army, Atlanta History Ctr., Atlanta Bot. Garden, High Mus., Art English Speaking Union; bd. dirs. Active Voters, 1965-75; bd. dirs., v.p. Atlanta Symphony, 1966-68; bd. dirs. Alliance Theatre Guild. Named Hon. Lt. Col. on Gov.'s Staff, Gov. Zell Miller, 1994-95. Mem. NAFE, NATAS, Atlanta Ballet Assn., World Assn. Women Journalists, Pub. Rels. Soc. Am., Nat. Trust for Hist. Preservations. Democrat. Jewish. Home and Office: 620 Peachtree St NE Atlanta GA 30308-2313

GEIMAN, STEPHEN ROYER, secondary school educator, coach; b. Waynesboro, Va., Aug. 10, 1947; s. David Samuel and Frances Elizabeth (Davis) G.; m. Donna Lisa Hanger, Aug. 9, 1974; children: Stephen Colburn, Charles Dolan, Brecken Elisabeth. BS in Phys. Edn., Appalachian State U., 1969. Cert. tchr., Va. Phys. edn. instr. Orange (Va.) County H.S., 1969-70; driver edn. instr. Wilson Meml. H.S., Fishersville, Va., 1970-72, phys. edn. instr., coach, 1974—; phys. edn. instr., English tchr. Fishburne Mil. Sch., Waynesboro, Va., 1972-74. Mem. Waynesboro/Augusta County Drug Advocacy Com., 1972-74; mem. adv. com. State Dept. Edn. Spl. Edn. Phys. Edn. Va., 1982; mem. quality com. State Dept. Edn. Phys. Edn. Stds., 1983; mem. sch. evaluation team State Dept. Edn., 1983. Mem. ASCD, AAHPERD, Nat. H.S. Coaches Assn., Va. H.S. Coaches Assn. (legis. coun. 1982-85, 92—), Va. Assn. Health, Phys. Edn., Recreation and Dance, Am. Running and Fitness Assn., Assn. for the Advancement of Health Edn., Nat. Assn. Sport and Phys. Edn., Nat. H.S. Track Coaches Assn. Home: RR 2 Box 310 Waynesboro VA 22980 Office: Wilson Meml HS RR 1 Box 260 Fishersville VA 22939-9620

GEIS, TARJA PELTO, educational coordinator, consultant, counselor, teacher, professor; b. Pietarsaari, Finland, Mar. 31, 1945; m. John J. Geis, June 18, 1966; children: Jeffrey, Steven. BS in Edn. and Art, Towson State U., Balt., 1967, MEd in Elem. Edn., 1970; EdD in Edn., Nova U., Ft. Lauderdale, 1986. Tchr. Balt. County, Balt., Md., 1967-70, Prince George's County, Bowie, Md., 1970-73; tchr. Dade County, Miami, Fla., 1979-84, ednl. specialist fed. programs, 1984-85, tchr., chairperson, 1985-89; co-originator, saturn coord. Gilbert L. Porter Elem., Miami, Fla., 1990-96; counselor Kendale Lakes, Miami, 1995—; adj. prof. Barry U., 1996—. Editor: Chapter I Connection newsletter, 1984, Leo-T Times newsletter, 1987, Phi Delta Kappa newsletter, 1987. Validator NAEYC, Dade Reading Coun.; chair Restructuring Pub. Edn. Internat. Conf., Miami, 1990; mem. Lindgren Lakeowner Assn., Miami, 1991—; svc. Feeding the Needy, Miami, 1990—. Named Tchr. of Yr. South Area Dade County Pub. Schs., 1987, Fla. Master Tchr. Dept. Edn. Fla., 1988; grantee Found. for Excellence, 1986, 88, 89, 91. Mem. U. Miami Sporty Gals, Phi Delta Kappa (pres. U. Miami chpt. 1991-92, Svc. Key award 1994). Home: 12764 SW 112th Ter Miami FL 33186-4721

GEISENDORFF, TYSON BAINE, marine corps officer; b. Kountze, Tex., May 15, 1968; s. Donald Baine Geisendorff and Jessie Marie (Strozier) Graves; m. Kim Yvonne Sabo, June 1, 1990. BS in Criminal Justice, Lamar U., Beaumont, Tex., 1990. Commd. 2d lt. U.S. Marine Corps, 1990, advanced through grades to capt., 1995; various assignments Korea and Japan, 1991-94; Marine Corps ground safety program mgr. Naval Safety Ctr., Norfolk, Va., 1994—. Decorated Navy Achievement medal. Home: Po Box 2833 Virginia Beach VA 23450 Office: NAV SAFECEN 375 A St Norfolk VA 23511

GEISERT, WAYNE FREDERICK, educational consultant, retired administrator; b. Elmo, Kans., Dec. 20, 1921; s. Frederick Jacob and Martha E. (Lauer) G.; m. Ellen Maurine Gish, July 2, 1944; children: Gregory Wayne, Bradley Kent, Todd Wilfred. AB, McPherson Coll., Kans., 1944; PhD in Econs, Northwestern U., 1951; LLD (hon.), Manchester Coll., 1987; HHD (hon.), James Madison U., 1992; LHD (hon.), Bridgewater Coll., 1994, McPherson Coll., 1994. Instr. Hamilton (Kans.) High Sch., 1946-48; part-time instr. Kendall Coll., Evanston, Ill., 1948-50; grad. asst. Northwestern U., 1950-51; from assoc. prof. to prof. and head dept. econs. and bus. Manchester Coll., North Manchester, Ind., 1951-57; dean coll. McPherson Coll., 1957-64; pres. Bridgewater (Va.) Coll., 1964-94, pres. emeritus, 1994—; chmn. bd. First Va. Bank of the Shenandoah Valley, 1994-95; cons. in ednl. field; pres. Assn. Va. Colls., 1970-71; exec. com. Church-related Colls. and Univs. in the South, 1973-74. Bd. dirs. Univ. Center in Va., 1964-78; pres. Council Ind. Colls. in Va., 1984-85; bd. dirs. Shenandoah Valley Ednl. TV, chmn. bd., 1979-84; bd. dirs. Va. Found. Ind. Colls., v.p., 1974-76, pres., 1976-78; moderator Ch. of Brethren, 1973-74, chmn. rev. and evaluation com., 1975-77, mem. gen. bd., 1977-82, vice chmn., 1977-78, chmn. gen. services commn., 1979-82, chmn. pension bd., 1979-82; chmn. United Way campaign, 1979-80; ednl. del. Dalian U. Fgn. Langs., Peoples Republic China, 1985, 90, 94. Served with USNR, 1944-46, PTO. Recipient Alumni Citation of Merit, McPherson Coll., 1974, Profl. Educator of Yr. award James Madison U., 1983; Geisert Hall named in his honor by Bridgewater Coll., 1990; named Meritorious Alumnus, Chapman (Kans.) H.S., 1994. Mem. Am. Econ. Assn., Harrisonburg-Rockingham County C. of C. (bd. dirs. 1977-82, pres. 1980-81), Rotary, Omicron Delta Kappa, Pi Kappa Delta, Alpha Psi Omega, Lambda Soc. Home: 1492 Cumberland Dr Harrisonburg VA 22801-8608 Office: Bridgewater Coll Office of the Pres Emeritus Bridgewater VA 22812

GEISINGER, JANICE ALLAIN, accountant; b. Iroquois County, Ill., June 21, 1927; d. Carl Oliver and Constance Kathryn (Risser) Irps Allain; m. Robert Bond Geisinger, Oct. 17, 1947 (div. 1976); children: Jacque K., Holly D., Terry Joe. AA, Blackburn U., Carlinville, Ill., 1947. Lab. technician Mich. Health Lab., East Lansing, 1947-48; with Southwestern Bell Telephone, Tulsa, 1948-49; bookkeeper Geisinger Ent., Dallas, 1951-69; salesman Earl Page Real Estate, Irving, Tex., 1969-71; food purchaser Town & Country vending, Dallas, 1971-75; bookkeeper/sec. Belco C & I Wiring Inc., Irving, 1976-85; leasing bookkeeper Copiers Etc., Inc., Dallas, 1985-89; bookkeeper Kennedy Elec. Inc., Mesquite, Tex., 1989; ret., 1990; cons. Ross Mech., Irving, 1989-95; asst. bookkeeper Metroplex Dental Group, 1990—. Crew leader Census Bur., Dallas, 1990. Mem. Am. Contract Bridge Assn. Home: 1216 E Grauwyler Rd Irving TX 75061-5031

GEISSLER, WILLIAM BENNETT, orthopaedic surgeon; b. Omaha, Apr. 8, 1959; s. Wilfred Waldo and Cathryn (Bennett) G.; m. Susan Morgan. BS in Chemistry/Biology summa cum laude, Washburn U., 1981; MD, Tulane U., 1985. Lic. physician, Miss. Orthopaedic surgery intern U. Miss. Med. Ctr., Jackson, 1985-86, resident in orthopaedic surgery, 1986-90; fellow in orthopaedic trauma surgery Aarau, Switzerland, 1988; fellow in arthroscopic surgery and sports medicine Orthopaedic Rsch. of Va., Richmons, 1990-91; fellow in hand and upper extremity surgery U. Miss. Med. Ctr., 1991-92, asst. prof. orthopaedic surgery, 1992—; mem. staff VA Med. Ctr., Jackson, Miss. Meth. Rehab. Ctr., Jackson. Contbr. numerous articles to profl. jours. Sports Medicine fellow, 1992. Mem. AMA, Miss. State Med. Assn., Miss. Orthopaedic Soc. (treas. Jackson chpt. 1992-93), Ctrl. Med. Soc., Arthroscopy Assn. N.Am., So. Orthopaedic Assn. (editorial bd. 1992-93). Republican. Methodist. Home: 67 Terrapin Dr Brandon MS 39042-2513 Office: Univ Med Ctr 2500 N State St Jackson MS 39216-4500

GEITHNER, PAUL HERMAN, JR., banker; b. Phila., June 7, 1930; s. Paul Herman and Henriette Antonine (Schuck) G.; m. Irmgard Hagedorn, Sept. 6, 1956; children: Christina, Amy, Paul. B.A. cum laude, Amherst Coll., 1952; M.B.A. with distinction, U. Pa., 1957. Sec.-treas. Ellicott Machine Co., Balt., 1964-68; successivley v.p., sr. v.p., exec. asst to the chmn., First Va. Banks, Inc., Falls Church, 1968-85, pres., chief adminstrv. officer, 1985-95, also bd. dirs., vice chmn., 1986-95; pres. First Va. Life Ins. Co., 1974—. Bd. dirs. Fairfax (Va.) Symphony Orch., 1988—, pres., 1991-92; bd. dirs. Va. Coll. Fund, 1987-91; trustee Va. Banker Sch. Bank Mgmt., 1988-92, Bridgewater Coll., 1989—; dir. Ellicott Machine Corp., 1996—. Lt. USNR, 1952-55. Mem. Va. Bankers Assn. (pres. 1992-93). Home: 5406 Colchester Meadow Ln Fairfax VA 22030-5444 Office: 1st Va Banks Inc 6400 Arlington Blvd Falls Church VA 22042-2336

GELBAND, CRAIG HARRIS, physiologist; b. San Clemente, Calif., Aug. 30, 1963; s. Henry and Ellen Brooke (Charin) G.; m. Susan Judith Cataldo, June 2, 1991; 1 child, Jessica Ellen. BS, Duke U., 1985; PhD, U. Miami, Fla., 1990. Predoctoral fellow U. Miami, 1985-90; postdoctoral fellow U. Nev., Reno, 1990-93, rsch. asst. prof., 1993-94; asst. prof. physiology and pharmacology U. Fla., Gainesville, 1994—, asst. prof. pharmacology, 1995—. Mem. editl. bd. Circulation Rsch., 1995—. Recipient First Prize award Eastern Student Rsch. Forum, 1989, Young Investigator Rsch. award Summer Conf. Smooth Muscle, 1991; Nat. Kidney Found. grantee, 1994-95, NIH F.I.R.S.T. Award grantee, 1996—; NIH Presdoctoral fellow, 1985-90,

Lucille P. Markey Found. fellow, 1988-90; Tobacco Rsch. Coun. scholar, 1996—. Mem. Am. Physiol. Soc. (Rsch. Career Enchancement award), Am. Heart Assn. (Initial Investigatorship 1995—), Biophys. Soc. Democrat. Jewish. Office: U Fla Dept Physiology PO Box 110274 Gainesville FL 32610

GELFAND, FRANCINE LOSEN, psychiatrist, educator; b. N.Y.C., Mar. 27, 1939; d. David and Celia (Burman) Losen; m. Philip N. Gelfand, June 22, 1963; children: Corinne Lipnick, Shoshana, Miriam Oberstein, Deborah. BA, Barnard Coll., 1961; MD, N.J. Coll. Medicine, 1965, post-grad., 1966-72. Diplomate Am. Bd. Psychiatry and Neurology; cert. in child and adolescent psychiatry and geriatric psychiatry. Pvt. practice N.Y.C., 1972, Leesburg, Fla., 1973—; instr. child psychiatry N.Y. Med. Coll., N.Y.C., 1972; clin. asst. prof. psychiatry U. Fla. Med. Coll., Gainesville, 1973—. Pres. Beth Shalom Synagogue, Leesburg, 1984-85. Fellow Am. Psychiat. Assn., Am. Acad. Child and Adolescent Psychiatry, Fla. Psychiat. Soc. (chair com. on childhood and adolescence 1990-92, pres. 1993-94); mem. Lake County Med. Soc. (bd. dirs. 1975-85, pres. 1983-84), Altrusa (chair nominating com. 1988-90). Office: 1208 W Dixie Ave Leesburg FL 34748-6314

GELHAUSEN, MARVIN DUANE, newspaper editor; b. Grafton, W.Va., May 15, 1957; s. William W. and Catherine Marie (Fortney) G. AA, Ohio Valley Coll., 1977; BA in Mass Comms., Pub. Rels., Abilene Christian U., 1979. Circulation asst. Mountain Statesman, Grafton, 1980-81; graphic design Epler & Sons Printers, Grafton, 1981-82; from staff writer to editor Mountain Statesman, 1982—. Mem. Grafton Cmty. Chest, 1992—, Econ. Devel. Authority, 1992—; former Grafton Vol. Fire Dept. Mem. Rotary (pres. Grafton club 1993-94), Taylor County Geneal. Soc., Taylor County Hist. Soc., Alpha Phi Omega. Democrat. Mem. Ch. of Christ. Home: RR 3 Box 206 Grafton WV 26354-9536 Office: Mountain Statesman 914 W Main St Grafton WV 26354-1028

GELLER, JANICE GRACE, nurse; b. Auburn, Ga., Feb. 25, 1938; d. Erby Ralph and Jewell Grace (Maughon) Clack; m. Joseph Jerome Geller, Dec. 23, 1973; 1 child, Elizabeth Joanne. Student, LaGrange Coll., 1955-57; BS in Nursing, Emory U., 1960; MS, Rutgers U., 1962. Nat. cert. group psychotherapist; cert. clin. nurse specialist. Psychiat. staff nurse dept. psychiatry Emory U., Atlanta, 1960; nurse educator Ill. State Psychiat. Inst., Chgo., 1961; clin. specialist in mental retardation nursing Northville, Mich., 1962; faculty Coll. Nursing Rutgers U., Newark, 1962-63, faculty Advanced Program in Psychiat. Nursing, 1964-66; faculty Coll. Nursing U. Mich., Ann Arbor, 1963-64; faculty, Teheran (Iran) Coll. for Women, 1967-69; clin. specialist psychiat. nursing Roosevelt Hosp., N.Y.C., 1969-70; faculty, guest lectr. Columbia U., N.Y.C., 1969-70; supr. Dept. Psychiat. Nursing Mt. Sinai Hosp., N.Y.C., 1970-72; pvt. practice psychotherapy N.Y.C., 1972-77, Ridgewood, N.J., 1977-96; faculty, curriculum coord. in psychiat. nursing William Alanson White Inst. Psychiatry, Psychoanalysis and Psychology, N.Y.C., 1974-84; mem. U.S. del. of Community and Mental Health Nurses to People's Republic of China, 1983. Contbr. articles to profl. jours.; editorial bd. Perspectives in Psychiat. Care, 1971-74, 78-84; author: (with Anita Marie Werner) Instruments for Study of Nurse-Patient Interaction, 1964. Mem. Bergen County Rep. Com., 1989. Recipient 10th Anniversary award Outstanding Clin. Specialist in psychiat.-mental health nursing in N.J., Soc. Cert. Clin. Specialists, 1982; Fed. Govt. grantee as career tchr. in psychiat. nursing, Rutgers U., 1962-63; cert. psychiat. nurse and clin. specialist, N.J., N.Y. Mem. AAAS, ANA (various certs.), N.C. Nurses Assn., Soc. Cert. Clin. Specialists in Psychiat. Nursing (chmn.), Coun. Specialists in Psychiat./Mental Health Nursing, Am. Group Psychotherapy Assn. (cert. group psychotherapist), Am. Assn. Mental Deficiency, World Fedn. Mental Health, Sigma Theta Tau. Address: 307 Chatterson Dr Raleigh NC 27615-3137

GELLER, ROBERT BURNS, medical educator, researcher; b. Cin., July 31, 1953; s. Abe and Lil (Smolin) G. BS, MS in Physics, MIT, 1976; MD, Harvard Med. Sch., 1983. Intern Hosp. of U. of Pa., Phila., 1983-84, resident, 1984-86; med. oncologist Johns Hopkins Oncology Ctr., Balt., 1986-89; dir. allogeneic bone marrow transplantation, asst. prof. U. Chgo., 1989-92; dir. leukemia svc., assoc. prof. medicine Emory U., Atlanta, 1992-96; dir. blood and marrow transplant program St. Luke's Hosp. of Kansas City, Mo., 1996—; mem. Oncology Hematology Assocs. of Kansas City, 1996—; med. dir. Hospice Atlanta, 1993-96, Nat. Marrow Donor Program Emory U., 1993—. Home: 306 W 7th St Kansas City MO 64105 Office: Saint Luke's Hosp Kansas City 4400 Wornall Rd Kansas City MO 64111

GELLER, ROBERT JEROME, pediatric toxicologist; b. Bronx, N.Y., July 11, 1955; m. Janice Lee Mettler, May 16, 1981; 1 child, Kenneth Bryan Geller. BA, Boston U., 1979, MD, 1979. Resident in pediatrics Med. Coll. Va., Richmond, 1979-82, instr., chief resident Dept. Pediatrics, 1982-83; fellow in clin. Pharmacology and Toxicology U. Va. Med. Ctr., Charlottesville, 1983-84; asst. prof. pediatrics Coll. Community Health Scis. U Ala., Tuscaloosa, 1984-88; asst. prof. pediatrics Emory U., Atlanta, 1988-92, assoc. prof. pediatrics, 1992—; co-med. dir. Ala. Poison Ctr., Tuscaloosa, 1984-86; med. dir. Ala. Poison Ctr., Tuscaloosa, 1986-88, Ga. Poison Ctr., Atlanta, 1988—. Fellow Am. Acad. Pediatrics, Am. Acad. Clin. Toxicology. Office: Emory U Dept Pediatrics 69 Butler St SE Atlanta GA 30303-3033

GELSTHORPE, JOANNE CARINI, nursing supervisor, military officer; b. Porticello, Sicily, Italy, Jan. 1, 1945; came to U.S., 1948; d. Giuseppi and Benedetta (Sanfilippo) Carini; m. Joseph Dean Gelsthorpe, Oct. 5, 1968; children: David, Anne, Catherine, John. BSN, Alverno Coll., 1966; MSN, Troy State U., 1993. RN, Wis.; cert. nurse adminstr. Commd. 2d lt. U.S. Army, 1964, advanced through grades to col., 1994; head nurse Kimbrough Army Hosp., Ft. Meade, Md., 1971-73; evening supr. 121st Evacuation Hosp., Seoul, Republic of Korea, 1975-76; staff nurse Leavenworth, Kans., 1979; head nurse emergency rm. McDonald Army Community Hosp., Ft. Eustis, Va., 1979-82; head nurse, supr. 2d Gen. Hosp., Landstuhl, Fed. Republic of Germany, 1982-85; nursing supr. Darnall Army Community Hosp., Ft. Hood, Tex., 1985-91; asst. chief nurse Lyster Army Community Hosp., Ft. Rucker, Ala., 1991-93, Darnall Army Cmty. Hosp., Ft. Hood, 1994-96; chief nurse Reynolds Army Hosp., Ft. Sill, Okla., 1996—. Mem. ANA, Tex. Nurses Assn., Ret. Army Nurses Assn. (assoc.), Sigma Theta Tau. Roman Catholic. Home: 702 White Oak Ln Harker Hts TX 76543-1712 Office: Reynolds Army Hosp Fort Sill OK 73503

GELTNER SCHWARTZ, SHARON, communications executive; b. Lakeland, Fla., Dec. 10, 1958; d. Bernard Benjamin and Gail (Bergad) G.; m. Eric Michael Schwartz, Dec. 30, 1995. AA, Wm. Rainey Harper Coll., 1978; BJ, U. Ill., 1980. Editor White House Weekly Feistritzer Publs., Washington, 1980, Instl. Investor, Washington, 1981-83; freelance writer Alexandria, Va., 1984-90; feature writer, investigative reporter, fgn. corr. Knight Ridder Newspapers, Boca Raton, Fla., 1990-92; book editor Weiss Rsch., Palm Beach Gardens, Fla., 1993-95; comm. mgr. Achievers Unltd., West Palm Beach, Fla., 1995—; writer, rschr. The Naisbitt Group, Washington, 1985-86; legal rschr. David James Ltd., Bethesda, Md., 1986-87; invited panelist The Poynter Inst. Media Studies, 1992. Author: (with others) Weekends Away from Washington, D.C., 1989, Fodor's Wall Street Journal Guide to Business Travel, 1991; contbr. articles to Quill, Washington Journalism Rev., Media Bus. Quar., Am. Writer. Participant Women's March on Washington, 1986; fundraiser United Jewish Appeal, Washington, 1986-88.; rep. D.C. writers in Bangkok Royal Thai Embassy, Washington, 1986, Palm Beach County, Fla., Yellow Feathers gridiron, 1990-91. Recipient Nat. Headliner award for outstanding news reporting Press Club of Atlantic City, 1993. Mem. NOW, Washington Ind. Writers (Michael Halberstam award 1983), House and Senate Periodical Corrs., Amnesty Internat., Fla. Press Assn., Nat. Writers Union (del. nat. conv. 1994), Regional Reporters Assn., Nat. Women's Art Mus. (charter), U. Ill. Alumni Assn. Investigative Reporters and Editors, Women in Comms. (Ace award 1996). Home: 9982-B Watermill Cir Bounton Beach FL 33437

GEMMA, PETER BENEDICT, JR., political, public relations and fund raising consultant; b. Providence, Sept. 13, 1950; s. Peter B. and Jane M. (St. Amand) G.; m. Fran Griffin, Oct. 3, 1981 (div. Oct. 1986); children: Peter B. Gemma III; m. Jodi Moody, Oct. 13, 1989; 1 child, Adrienne Grace. Student, Roger Williams Coll., 1968-70, Providence Coll., 1975-76. Employment cons. Bus. Careers, Inc., Providence, R.I., 1970-71; sales mgr. C.E. Ryder Corp., Bristol, R.I., 1972-74; mayoral campaign mgr. Vincent A. Cianci, Providence, R.I., 1974; mayoral aide City of Providence, Providence, R.I., 1975-77; campaign cons. various clients, N.J./Maine, 1978; exec dir. Nat. Pro-Life P.A.C., Falls Church, Va., 1979-88; pres. Associated Direct Mktg. Svcs., Inc., Arlington, Va., 1979-88; devel. counsel The Funding Ctr., Alexandria, Va., 1991—; writer editorials USA Today, 1985—. Contbr. articles and commentaries to profl. jours. Mem. Providence Rep. City Com., 1974-77; chmn. R.I. 10th Senatorial Com., 1975-77; mem. exec. com. R.I. Young Reps., 1974-76; treas. Friends Roger Williams Park, 1974-76; del. Va. Rep. Conv., 1981, 83, 85, 86, 91, 93, 94; mem. Fairfax County Rep. Com., 1983-85, Arlington (Va.) Rep. Com., 1990—, mem. exec. com., 1992-93; mem. cmty. health svcs. bd. Arlington County Bd. Suprs., 1991-93; bd. dirs., chmn. Arlington County chpt. ARC, 1994-95; bd. dirs. Falls Church (Va.) Players, 1982-83. Recipient commendation for leadership Commonwealth of Ky., 1985, hon. Ky. col., 1991; George Washington honors medal Freedoms Found. at Valley Forge, 1989. Mem. Nat. Soc. Fund Raising Execs. (pub. rels. com. Greater Washington chpt. 1989-90, bd. dirs. 1992—, newsletter editor 1992-94, Abel Hanson award 1993). Home and Office: 5810 25th Rd Arlington VA 22207

GENDZWILL, JOYCE ANNETTE, retired health officer; b. Milw., Aug. 8, 1927; d. Felix Vincent and Antoinette Marie (Borske) G.; m. Lauren E. Trombley, June 13, 1952 (div. Jan. 1960); children: Regan Eve Trombley Kovacich, Eugene Vincent, Paul Quentin. BS, U. Mich., 1949, MD, 1952, MPH, 1961. Cert. pub. mgr., Ala. Internship USPHS, Detroit, Cleve., 1952-53; dir. extern edn. Beyer Meml. Hosp., Ypsilanti, Mich., 1953-54; resident in radiology St. Luke's Hosp., Denver, 1954-55; health officer Dickinson-Iron Dist. Health Dept., Stambaugh, Mich., 1959-76; dir. bur. local health svc. Ala. Dept. Pub. Health, Montgomery, Ala., 1976-81; asst. state health officer Ala. Dept. Pub. Health, Montgomery, 1981-91; ret., 1991. Mem. AMA, So. Med. Assn., Mensa, Phi Beta Kappa, Delta Omega, Phi Kappa Phi. Home: 6580 Thorman Rd Port Charlotte FL 33981-5579

GENNIN, GEORGE STRATFORD, defense company executive, aviation consultant; b. Tylertown, Miss., May 15, 1944; s. ned Andrew and Linda (Fortenberry) G.; m. Laureen Ann Martin, May 16, 1981; children: Ashley, Chris. BA in Biology, U. Miss., 1966; MS in Personnel Mgmt., Troy State U., 1985; Graduate, USAF Air War Coll., USAF Fighter Weapons Sch. Commd. 2nd lt. USAF, 1966; advanced through ranks to col.; fighter weapons instr., fighter pilot USAF, 1966-73; mgr. F-16 program, advanced avionics Nellis AFB, Nev., 1973-77; opers. staff officer Ramstein Air Base, Germany, 1977-78; opers. officer, comdr., project pilot F-16 MOT&E Hill AFB, Utah, 1978-81; squadron comdr., F-16 OT&E test dir., pilot Nellis AFB, Nev., 1981-84; chief Asia divsn., directorate internat. programs Pentagon USAF, 1985-88; vice wing comdr. tactical air command Bergstrom AFB, Tex., 1988-90; ret. USAF, 1990; dir. internat. opers. SRS Internat., 1990-91; pres., CEO SDS Internat., Arlington, Va., 1991—; also bd. dirs.; cons. US Govt., Dept. Def., Internat. Air Force. Decorated Air medal with twenty oak leaf clusters, D.F.C. with five oak leaf clusters, Legion of Merit with one oak leaf cluster, Air Force Commendation medal, Combat Readiness medal, Overseas Short Tour Medal with one oak leaf cluster, Overseas Long Tour medal, Air Force Longevity medal with four oak leaf clusters, Expert Marksmanship medal, Republic of Vietnam Cross with palm, Republic of Vietnam Campaign medal; recipient Air Force Organizational Excellence award with fourteen oak leaf clusters and valor device. Mem. Am. Legion, Order of Daedalians, Air Force Assn., Veterans of Fgn. Wars. Office: SDS Internat 2011 Crystal Dr Arlington VA 22202-3709

GENSHEIMER, ELIZABETH LUCILLE, software specialist; b. Louisville, Jan. 25, 1955; d. Theodore Rudolph and Florence Virginia (Nieder) G. BS in Computer Sci., U. Louisville, 1976, postgrad., 1977-78; postgrad., U. Tex., Dallas, 1993—. Weapons analyst CIA, Washington, 1975-76; engr. software Tex. Instruments, Dallas, 1978-81, No. Telecom, Inc., Richardson, Tex., 1981-83; mem. sci. staff Bell No. Rsch., Richardson, 1983-88, magnet mgr. univ. interrels. program U. Southwestern La., 1986-88, mgr. product test Meridian Data Network Sys., 1988-89; mgr. devel. software test Convex Computer Corp., Richardson, Tex., 1989-93; software cons. Ft. Worth Techs. Cons., 1993-95; in software devel. Tandem Telecom., 1995—. Mem. APA, Soc. Computers in Psychology, Nature Conservancy, Nat. Geog. Soc., North Tex. Water Garden Soc., Whale Watch Soc., Soc. Rsch. in Child Devel. Home: PO Box 796005 Dallas TX 75379-6005

GENTER, JOHN ROBERT, winery executive; b. Huntsville, Ala., Oct. 16, 1957; s. John C. and Madge (McDaniel) G.; m. Margaret F. MacNaughton, Sept. 5, 1981; children: John Thomas, Lois Katharine. BS in Mktg. and Bus., U. Ala., 1980. Sales rep. food div. Procter & Gamble, Cin. and Jacksonville (Fla.), 1980-81, dist. field rep., 1981; unit mgr. Procter & Gamble, Cin., Tampa (Fla.), 1982-84; div. trade devel. mgr., regional mgr. Frito-Lay, Inc., Dallas, Tampa, 1984-85; field mktg. mgr. vintage div. E&J Gallo Winery, Modesto (Calif.), Tampa, 1985, state mgr., 1986, div. mgr., 1986-91, region mgr. chain div., 1992-95; dir. mktg. Purity Wholesale Grocers, Boca Raton, Fla., 1995-96; exec. Acosta Sales Co., Tampa, 1996—; trainer Sales Mgmt. Tng. Sch. Procter & Gamble, Cin., 1982-83, Sales Devel. Program Frito-Lay, Dallas, 1984-85. Author: (with others) E&J Gallo Field Marketing Manual, 1986. Mem. St. John's Ch., Tampa, 1985—, active Father's Ministry; youth soccer, baseball and basketball coach YMCA; trustee Patrons of St. John's Sch. Mem. U. Ala. Alumni Assn. (chmn. Every Mem. Canvass), Soc. de Vinum Honoratus, Beta Gamma Sigma. Republican. Episcopalian. Home: 559 Ladrone Ave Tampa FL 33606-4036 Office: Acosta Sales Co Ste 301 5650 Breckenridge Park Dr Tampa FL 33610

GENTNER, PAUL LEFOE, architect, consultant; b. Seattle, Feb. 24, 1944; s. Edward George and Opal Eloise (Davis) G.; m. Glenda Frank Hoy, May 25, 1975; 1 stepchild, Robert Michael Hurd. AA in Architecture, Anne Arundel C.C., Arnold, Md., 1970; BS in Engring., Century U., 1984. Registered arch., Md. Project rep. RTKL Assocs., Inc., Balt., 1970-73; staff architect James R. Grieves Assocs., Balt., 1973-77; sr. engr. Morrison-Knudsen (MKSAC), Columbia, Md., 1977-79; staff engr. Morrison-Knudsen (MKSAC), Saudi Arabia, 1979-81; planning mgr. Morrison-Knudsen Internat. Inc., Barranquilla, Colombia, S.Am., 1981-86; staff architect RTKL Assocs., Inc., Balt., 1986-92; specifications writer Sverdrup Cpr., Arlington, Va., 1992-93; mgr. specifications Daniel, Mann, Johnson, & Mendenhall, Balt., 1993-95, Arlington, Va., 1995-96. With USNR, 1965-68, Vietnam; Persian Gulf, 1990-91. Mem. AIA, Constrn. Specifications Inst. (cert. constrn. specifier, bd. dirs. Balt. chpt. 1991-92, 1st v.p. 1993-94, pres. 1994-95), Soc. Am. Mil. Engrs., Bricklayers (local # 1), Naval Res. Mobile Constrn. Bn. Home: 2028 Park Ave Baltimore MD 21217-4816

GENTRY, CYNTHIA SUE, childhood education executive; b. Hattiesburg, Miss., Oct. 6, 1930; d. Hiram Edward and Amanda Norfleet (Cox) Liles; m. Timothy Peters Gentry, Nov. 28, 1953 (dec. Dec. 1985); children: Sandra Carol Case, Timothy Edward, Stephen Bradford, Karen Ruth. BS, U. Houston, 1952; MS, Corpus Christi State U., 1983. Cert. tchr., reading tchr., diagnostician, Tex. Tchr. Houston (Tex.) Ind. Schs., 1952-54, 56-57, Corpus Christi (Tex.) Ind. Sch. Dist., 1968-78; libr. First Bapt. Ch., Corpus Christi, 1988-89, dir. childhood edn., 1989-91; dir. First Bapt. Sch., Corpus Christi, 1991—. Mem. AAUW, Tex. Assn. Bapt. Schs., Corpus Christi State U. Alumni Assn. Baptist. Office: First Baptist Sch 3115 Ocean Dr Corpus Christi TX 78404-1614

GENTRY, DAPHNE SUE, historian; b. Danville, Va., Oct. 7, 1941; d. Arthur Merritt Jr. and Lucy Marguerite (Humphreys) G. BA, U. N.C., Greensboro, 1963, MA, 1964. Archivist Libr. Va., Richmond, 1964-79, historian, 1979—. Author: Dog Art: A Selection from the Dog Museum, 1996; asst. editor: Key to Survey Reports, 1990; editor Westie Imprint, 1991—, Mag. Va. Genealogy, 1993-96. Mem. West Highland White Terrier Club Am. (bd. dirs., v.p., pres. 1989-91, Pres.' award 1986, 94, 96), West Highland White Terrier Club Greater Wash. (sec.), West Highland White Terrier Club Ind., Va. Kennel Club (sec., pres., bd. dirs.). Home: 604 Arlie St Richmond VA 23226 Office: Libr Va 8th and Broad Sts Richmond VA 23219

GENTRY, DAVID RAYMOND, engineer; b. Easley, S.C., Sept. 26, 1933; s. Thomas Herbert and Rosalie (Howard) G.; m. Mary Lynn White, June 5, 1955; children: David R. Jr., Mary Diane Gentry Farley. BS, Clemson Coll., 1955; MS, Inst. Textile Tech., Charlottesville, Va., 1957; PhD, Clemson U., 1972. Rsch. engr. WestPoint (Ga.) Mfg. Co., 1957-60; asst. prof. Clemson (S.C.) U., 1960-67; mgr. testing and evaluation Phillips Fibers Corp., Greenville, S.C., 1967-73; assoc. prof. Ga. Inst. Tech., Atlanta, 1973-78; sr. devel. engr. Amoco Fabrics & Fibers Co., Atlanta, 1978-80, mgr. fibers devel., 1980-84, dir. fibers devel., 1985-90, rsch. assoc., 1990-92, sr. rsch. assoc., 1992—. fellow NSF, 1966, Sirrine Found., 1965-67, Inst. Textile Tech., 1955-57. Mem. ASTM (sec. com. D-13 textiles 1974-80), Am. Assn. Textile Technologists (sec. Piedmont chpt. 1963-65), The Fiber Soc., The Textile Inst. (assoc.), Phi Psi (sec., pres. Iota chpt. 1953-55, faculty adviser 1961-65), Phi Kappa Phi. Home: 3456 Embry Cir Atlanta GA 30341-5612 Office: Amoco Fabrics and Fibers Co 260 The Bluffs Atlanta GA 30336-1143

GENTRY, GAVIN MILLER, lawyer; b. N.Y.C., Oct. 5, 1930; s. Curtis Gavin and Grace (Wattenbarger) G.; m. Mary Jane Coleman, Sept. 28, 1963; children—Janie Coleman, Grace Eleanor. B.S., U. Tenn., 1954, J.D., 1954. Bar: Tenn. 1954, U.S. Dist. Ct. (we. dist.) Tenn. 1956, U.S. Supreme Ct. 1978. Trial counsel U.S. Army, 1954-56; with Armstrong, Allen, Prewitt, Gentry, Johnston & Holmes, Memphis, 1956—, sr. ptnr., 1976—; mem. redrafting com. Tenn. Corp. Law; guest lectr. Memphis State U., U. Tenn. Ctr. Health Scis.; dir. corps. Author: Great Destinations in the Smokies, 1995. Mem. Pres.'s coun. Rhodes Coll., 1970—; bd. dirs. Girl Scouts U.S.A., 1973-75; pres. Memphis Tennis Assn., 1960-66, Tenn. Tennis Assn., 1960-61; treas. Tenn. br. Maureen Connelly Brinker Tennis Found., 1972-79; pres. Les Passees Rehab. Ctr., 1977, Lausanne Sch., 1975-78; elder Idlewild Presbyn. Ch. 1st lt. AUS, 1954-56. Recipient Faculty prize U. Tenn., 1953, 1st prize will writing U. Tenn., 1954; numerous awards and prizes for tennis, 1947—. Mem. ABA, Memphis and Shelby County Bar Assn. (bd. dirs. 1989-90), Tenn. Bar Assn., Am. Soc. Hosp. Attys., Tenn. Hosp. Assn., Nat. Health Lawyers Assn., Am. Soc. Law and Medicine. Club: Univ. (Memphis). Office: Armstrong Allen Prewitt Gentry Johnston & Holmes Brinkley Plz 80 Monroe Ave Ste 700 Memphis TN 38103-2467

GENTRY, JUDITH ANNE FENNER, history educator; b. Balt., May 28, 1942; d. Charles Albert and Mildred (Atkinson) Fenner; m. Robert Joseph Gentry, May 25, 1969; 1 child, James Andrew Sayle. BA, U. Md., 1964; PhD, Rice U., 1969. Prof. history U. Southwestern La., Lafayette, 1969—; adv. editor Jefferson Davis Papers. Contbr. articles to profl. jours. Mem. dist. com. Boy Scouts Am., Lafayette, 1987-95. Fellow NEH, 1980; rsch. grantee NEH, 1978-81. Fellow La. Hist. Assn. (pres. 1991-92); mem. AAUP (state pres. 1977-79), Am. Hist. Assn., Orgn. Am. Historians, So. Hist. Assn., So. Assn. Women Historians (pres. 1978-79). Office: Univ Southwestern La Dept History Lafayette LA 70504

GENZMAN, ROBERT WAYNE, lawyer; b. Fairbanks, Alaska, Sept. 13, 1951; s. Glendon Carl and Catherine Eileen (Brugger) G.; m. Martha Pauline Ingle, Jul. 6, 1991; children: Robert Glendon, Jacqueline Eileen. BA magna cum laude, Univ. Pa., 1973; postgrad., Univ. Manchester, Manchester, Eng., 1971-72; MS, Univ. London, 1974; JD, Cornell Univ., 1977. Bar: Fla., Ohio, D.C. Staff counsel House Select Com. on Assassinations, Washington, 1977-78; leg. asst. U.S. Rep. Robert L. Livingston, Washington, 1979-80; asst. U.S. Atty. U.S. Dept. Justice, Orlando, Fla., 1980-83; assoc. Rumberger, Kirk, Caldwell, Cabaniss, Burke, Orlando, Fla., 1983-85, Baker & Hostetler, Orlando, Fla., 1985-88; assoc. minority counsel. House Iran-Contra Com., Washington, 1987; U.S. Atty. U.S. Dept. Justice, Orlando, 1988-93; shareholder Akerman, Senterfitt & Eidson, Orlando, 1993—; mem. practioners adv. group U.S. Sentencing Commn., Washington, 1993—. Mem. Citrus Club, Orange County Bar Assn., Federal Bar Assn. (pres. Orlando chpt. 1984-86). Republican. Lutheran. Office: Akerman Senterfitt & Eidson 255 S Orange Ave Orlando FL 32801-3445

GEOGHEGAN, JOSEPH EDWARD, retired electrical engineer; b. N.Y.C., Aug. 2, 1932; s. Roderick and Florence (Post) G.; m. Kathleen Bourké, Dec. 3, 1966. BEE, SUNY, Stony Brook, 1976; MBA, U. Phoenix, 1986. Engr. Otis Elevator Co., N.Y.C., 1956-66; sr. design engr. The Peelle Co., Bayshore, N.Y., 1966-78; sr. project engr. Westinghouse Electric Corp., Pitts., 1978-80; tech. rep., logistics mgr. Raytheon Co., Sudbury, Mass., 1980-94; instr. Worcester (Mass.) Pub. Schs., 1991, Camden County (Ga.) High Sch., 1994; radio broadcaster Sta. WKBX, Ga., 1993-94; profl. speaker and seminar leader. Producer/host tv show Careers, 1983. Chmn. Northborough (Mass.) Coun. on Aging, 1988-92; bd. dirs. Audio Jour., Worcester, 1989-92; mem. Rep. Com., Northborough, 1989-92; judge Mass. Acad. Decathlon, 1986-92; vol. Vol. Income Tax Assistance, Sr. Health Ins. Info. Program, Ret. Sr. Vol. Program. Sgt. U.S. Army, 1952-54. Mem. Toastmasters Internat. (area gov. 1988-89, Disting. Toastmaster award), Am. Legion, K.C.

GEORGE, ANTHONY DALE, lawyer; b. West Palm Beach, Fla., Apr. 21, 1962; s. Anthony Dale and Satyra McMurrian (Askeland) G.; m. Kim Norheim, Aug. 11, 1984; children: Satyra June, Chandler Saul. BA, U. Fla., 1983, JD, 1989; postgrad., U. of the South, 1986. Bar: Fla., U.S. Dist. Ct. (so. dist.) Fla. Pharmacy technician North Fla. Regional Hosp., Gainesville, 1983-85, Shands' Teaching Hosp., Gainesville, 1985-86; staff rsch. atty. Search, Denney, Scarola, Barnhart & Shipley, P.A., West Palm Beach, Fla., 1989-90; pvt. practice Stuart, Fla., 1990—. Mem. Dist. 2 Martin County Sch. Bd., 1992—, chmn., 1995-96; mem. Rep. Exec. Com., 1991—, mem. Coun. of 100, 1991—; mem. Martin County Estate Planning Coun., 1991—; mem. Leadership Martin County, 1991-92, mem. alumni bd. planning com., 1992—; mem. Martin County Children's Svcs. Coun., 1992-95, chmn., 1994, 95. Mem. Martin County Bar Assn. (probate and guardianship subcom. 1991—, mentor Edn. for Ministry, 1993—). Episcopalian. Home: 3121 SE Bedford Dr Stuart FL 34997-5449 Office: 759 SE Federal Hwy Ste 219 Stuart FL 34994-2972

GEORGE, CAROLE SCHROEDER, computer company executive; b. Bloomington, Ind., Mar. 20, 1943; d. Melburne Evert and Neva Mae (Bechtel) Gibson; m. Richard D. White, Aug. 31, 1962 (div. 1972); 1 child, Kenneth Donald; m. Charles R. Schroeder, Apr. 7, 1973 (div. 1983); m. Thomas H. George III, May 4, 1991. BS in Pharmacy, Wayne State U., 1972 postgrad., Va. Commonwealth U., 1980-83. Registered pharmacist, Mich. Va. Staff pharmacist St. Joseph Hosp., Pontiac, Mich., 1972-73; dir. pharmacy St. Mary Hosp., Livonia, Mich., 1974-76; resident Detroit Receiving Hosp., 1977-78; clin. faculty pharmacy Med. Coll. of Va., Richmond, 1978-83; dir. pharmacy ops. Med. Coll. Va. Hosps., Richmond, 1978-33; mktg. mgr. TDS Healthcare Systems Corp., Atlanta, 1983-86; sr. cons. Gerber Alley, Norcross, Ga., 1986; dir. product mgmt. Baxter Healthcare Systems, Reston, Va., 1986-89; sr. v.p. Integrated Systems Tech. Inc., Reston, 1989-96; prin. Intelligent Bus. Consulting, Reston, 1996—; v.p. Horizon Data Corp., Reston, 1996—. Mem. Am. Soc. of Hosp. Pharmacists, Am. Pharm. Assn., Nat. Assn. for Healthcare Quality, Rho Chi.

GEORGE, EDWARD VINCENT, classical languages educator; b. Buffalo, Dec. 10, 1937; s. Vincent Edward and Anna Marie (Santora) G.; m. Cecilia Fisher, Aug. 28, 1968; children: Mary Margaret, Paula Catherine, Andrew Vincent. BA in Classical Langs., Niagara U., 1959; MS in Edn., Canisius Coll., 1962; MA in Classics, U. Wis., 1962, PhD in Classics, 1966. Cert. secondary tchr. Latin, N.Y. Instr. classics U. Tex., Austin, 1966-67, asst. prof., 1967-71; assoc. prof. Tex. Tech U., Lubbock, 1971-77, prof., 1977—; chair Tex. Com. for the Humanities, 1990-91. Editor,translator J.L. Vives, Commentary on the Dream of Scipio, 1989, Sullan Declamations, 1988; author: Aeneid 8 and the Aitia of Callimachus; contbr. articles to profl. jours. Trustee Vergilian Soc. Am., 1974-79. NEH grantee, 1981-83. Mem. AAUP, Classical Assn. Mid. West and South, Am. Philol. Assn., Renaissance Soc., Am. World History Assn., South Cen. Renaissance Conf., Internat. Assn. Neo-Latin Studies, Am. Classical League (v.p. 1981-82, coord. diversity task force), Tex. Classical Assn. (pres. 1986-87). Office: Tex Tech U Classical and Modern Langs and Lits MS 2071 Lubbock TX 79409-2071

GEORGE, ERNEST THORNTON, III, financial consultant; b. Charleston, S.C., Dec 29, 1950; s. Ernest Thornton and Betty (Long) T.; m. Frances Thomson, Sept. 30, 1977; children: Ernest Thornton IV, Andrew Neal, Katherine Frances. Student, U. Miss., 1970-71; BS in Mktg., Miss. State U., 1973. CFP; CLU; registered investment advisor. Field underwriter Mut. of N.Y., 1974—, Mfrs. Life Ins. Co., 1981—; prin. N.Y. Stock Exch., 1977—; rep. Investment Mgmt. & Rsch., Starkville, Miss., 1989—; owner, prin. Investment and Mgmt. Group Inc., Starkville, 1982—, Wealth Mgmt.

Group, Inc.; founding mem. bd. dirs. First Bank of Starkville; guest lectr. Miss. State U. Mem. editorial bd. Life and Health Ins. Sales; contbr. articles to profl. jours. Bd. dirs. exec. bd. Pushmataha area coun. Boy Scouts Am., Republican party; past pres. Men of Ch., Presbyn. Ch., chmn. bd. deacons, elder, men's Sunday Sch. tchr.; bd. dirs. Oktibbeha County Libr., Oktibbeha Devel. Coun., Starkville Acad. Mem. Nat. Assn. Life Underwriters (nat. committeeman nat. mtg.), Nat. Assn. Securities Dealers, East Miss. Life Underwriters Assn. (past pres.), CLU (bd. dirs. Miss. chpt.), Internat. Assn. for Fin. Planning (bd. dirs. Miss. chpt.), Million Dollar Round Table (life, qualifying), Ct. Round Table (honor roll chpt.), Quarterback Club, Oktibbeha County C. of C. (exec. bd.), Rotary (bd. dirs. Starkville), Sigma Chi, Pi Sigma Epsilon. Home: 1672 Valley Hills Cir Starkville MS 39759-9806 Office: Investment Mgmt and Rsch 102 S Jackson St PO Box 963 Starkville MS 39759

GEORGE, FRANK WADE, small business owner, antiquarian book dealer; b. Austin, Tex., Aug. 22, 1918; s. Frank Wade and Rosa Scott (Slaughter) W.; m. Marjorie Ann Miller, Dec. 27, 1948 (div. Jan. 1955); children: Frank Wade III, Gregory Scott, Barbara Lee; m. Martha Jeanne Wagner, Feb. 8, 1964 (dec. 1996); m. Wenona Thoma, 1996. Student, Tex. Sch. Fine Arts, 1936-41, Mexico City Coll., 1947; BJ, U. Tex., 1948. Office mgr. Tex. Sch. Fine Arts, 1936-41; mgr. Austin Symphony Orch., 1946-48, Erie (Pa.) Philharmonic Orch., 1948-49, Birmingham (Ala.) Symphony Orch., 1949-50; asst. cashier First Nat. Bank Birmingham, 1950-80; mgr. Ala. Pops Orch., Birmingham, 1955-62, Town and Gown Theatre, Birmingham, 1962-65; pres. Birmingham Opera Co., 1973-75; owner Books! By George, Birmingham, 1981—. Treas. Greater Birmingham Arts Alliance, 1971-75, Birmingham Opera Guild, 1971-74, So. Regional Opera, 1981-84; trustee Birmingham Symphony Assn., 1973-75; chmn. artist hospitality Arts Hall of Fame, Birmingham, 1974; judge nat. coun. auditions Met. Opera Assn., 1981; docent Birmingham Mus. Art, 1980-82. Mem. Gideons Internat. (pres. 1980-83), Allegro Mus. Club (v.p. 1993-94), Ala. Symphonic Assn. (dir. speakers bur. 1995). Home: 2120 5th Pl NW Birmingham AL 35215-3314 Office: Books! By George 2424 7th Ave S Birmingham AL 35233-3318

GEORGE, JAMES EDWARD, accountant; b. Mt. George, Ark., May 22, 1943; s. Opal W. Sr. and Mildred M. (Dacus) G.; m. Corliss Ann Johnson, Sept. 3, 1965; children: J. Mark, Ty C., Ryan E. BA in Acctg., U. Ark., Little Rock, 1967; MS in Logistics, Air Force Inst. Tech., 1979; grad., Air Command and Staff Coll. of USAF, 1987, USAF Air War Coll., 1992. CPA, Ark. Commd. 2d lt. USAF, 1967, advanced through grades to capt.; commdr. Field Tng. Detachment, Mt. Clemens, Mich., Kadena AFB, Japan and Kunsan AFB, Korea, 1967-73; supr. maintenance Field Maintenance Squadron, Craig AFB, Ala., 1973-75; flightline br. chief Royal AFB, Bentwater, Eng., 1976-77; officer in charge quality control Tactical Fighter Wing, Royal AFB, Bentwater, 1977-78; left active duty USAFR, 1978, advanced through grades to lt. col., 1988, ret., 1994; pub. utility auditor Ark. Pub. Svc. Commn., Little Rock, 1979—; lectr. pub. utility income taxes and depreciation 12th and 13th ann. ea. utility rate seminar Nat. Assn. Regulatory Utility Commrs., 1984, 85. Bd. dirs. North Little Rock 1st Ch. of Nazarene, 1989-94. Mem. AICPA (mem. info. retrieval com. 1987-90), Ark. Soc. CPA's (pres. Ctrl. Ark. chpt. 1992-93, 95-96, chmn. membership com. 1991-93, bd. dirs. 1994-97, mem. exec. com. 1996-97, Outstanding Ark. CPA in Industry and Bus. award 1995), Toastmasters (pres. Uptown chpt. 1985, Able Toastmaster award 1988), Officers Club (bd. dirs. Kadena AFB 1971-72). Home: 906 Karla Circle Sherwood AR 72120-6032

GEORGE, JAMES NOEL, hematologist-oncologist, educator; b. Columbus, Ohio, Sept. 23, 1938. BA, MD, Ohio State U., 1962. Diplomate Am. Bd. Internal Medicine, subspecialty in hematology; lic. Okla. Bd. Med. Licensure and Supervision, Tex. State Bd. Med. Examiners, Ohio State Med. Bd. Intern, resident dept. medicine Vanderbilt U. Sch. Medicine, Nashville, 1962-63, 66-67; resident in medicine, hematology fellow, chief resident med. Strong Meml. Hosp., U. Rochester (N.Y.) Sch. Medicine, 1967-70; rsch. hematologist Walter Reed Army Inst. Rsch., Washington, 1963-66; from asst. prof. to assoc. prof. dept. med. divsn. hematol. U. Tex. Health Sci. Ctr., San Antonio, 1970-81, prof. dept. medicine divsn. hematology, 1981-89; rsch. assoc. Theodor Kocher Inst., Berne, Switzerland, 1975-76; prof. dept. medicine, chief hematology-oncology sect. U. Okla. Health Sci. Ctr., Oklahoma City, 1990—; staff physician Okla. Blood Inst., Oklahoma City, 1994—; vis. prof. dept. physiol. chemistry U. Wis., Madison, 1987-88; prof. associe U. Paris VII, Hopital Lariboisiere, Paris, 1988-89; mem. transfusion com. Bexar County Hosp., 1970-87; chmn. hematology peer rev. panel NASA Life Scis. Space Flight Experiment Program, 1978; mem. NIH Hematology Study Sect. I, 1986-94; mem. adv. bd. Gladstone Found. Labs. for Cardiovasc. Rsch., U. Calif., San Francisco, 1991; bd. trustees Gorgas Sci. Found., Inc., Brownsville, Tex., 1992—. Mem. editl. bd. Blood, 1985-90. Mem. oncology task force Midwest City Regional Hosp., 1995—. Capt. M.C., U.S. Army, 1963-66. Recipient 1st Ann. Lyndon B. Johnson award Tex. affiliate Am. Heart Assn., 1976. Fellow ACP; mem. Am. Fedn. for Clin. Rsch., Am. Heart Assn. (thrombosis coun.), Am. Soc. Clin. Investigation, Am. Soc. Hematology (com. on ednl. affairs and tng. 1986-89, sci. subcom. on platelets 1986-89, chmn. subcom. on platelets 1995, com. on publs. 1991—, chmn. edn. program on platelets 1993, 94, 96, ad hoc com. on practice guidelines 1994—, nominating com. 1995), Cen. Soc. Clin. Rsch., So. Soc. for Clin. Investigation, Alpha Omega Alpha (councilor Tex. Epsilon chpt. 1978-81). Office: U of Okla Health Scis Ctr Dept Medicine Hemat-Onc Sec PO Box 26901 Oklahoma City OK 73190

GEORGE, JOHN DAVID, JR., management educator; b. Salem, Oreg., Apr. 10, 1936; s. John David Sr. and Lillian (Dahl) G.; m. Judith Elaine Early, June 4, 1958; children: Jeffrey Michael, Jennifer Lee. BS, U.S. Mil. Acad., 1958; MBA, U. Ala., 1971, PhD, 1975; MA, Liberty U., 1990. Commd. 2d lt. U.S. Army, West Point, N.Y., 1958; retired U.S. Army, Washington, 1980; officer U.S. Army, Vietnam., 1967-68, 71-72, Rsch. Inst. for Behavioral and Social Scis. U.S. Army, Washington, Va., 1978-79; prof., chmn. mgmt. dept. Liberty U., Lynchburg, Va., 1990—. Decorated Legion of Merit, U.S. Army, Bronze star with oak leaf cluster. Mem. So. Mgmt. Assn. Republican. Presbyn. Office: Liberty U Box 20000 Lynchburg VA 25406

GEORGE, JULIE BERNY, epidemiologist; b. Nigeria, Feb. 12, 1953; came to U.S., 1976; d. George Akabogu and Marie-Therese Nzeribe; m. Joshua, Feb. 14, 1976 (div. Dec. 1978); 1 child, Michael Ifeanyi. MD, Med. Coll. Va., 1984; MPH, UCLA, 1987; MOH, Harvard Sch. Pub. Health, 1994. Diplomate Am. Bd. Family Practice. Med. practitioner Advantage Care/Prairie Med. Group, L.A., 1988-90; med. epidemiologist Ctrs. for Disease Control, Atlanta, 1990-92; HIV/AIDS surveillance WHO, Brazzaville, Congo, 1992-93. Lt. comdr. USPHS, 1990-92. Roman Catholic. Office: Exxon Chem Co Rm W1-166 13501 Katy Frwy Bldg KFY Houston TX 77079

GEORGE, LESTER LEE, golf course architectural firm executive; b. July 6, 1955. BA in Health and Phys. Edn., U. Richmond, 1977. Assoc. designer Golf Svcs. Internat., 1987-91; pres., prin. golf course arch. Colonial Golf Design, Inc., Richmond, Va., 1991—. Prin. works include Colonial Williamsburg, Va., Golf Parks, New Brunfels, Tex., Pinnacle Valley Ranch, Little Rock, Ark. Office: Colonial Golf Design Inc 619A Twinridge Ln Richmond VA 23235-5268

GEORGE, STEPHEN CARL, insurance company executive, educator, consultant; b. Miami, Fla., July 11, 1959; s. Joseph P. and Beatrice P. George; 3 children. BS in MIS, Fla. State U., 1983; MBA in Health Adminstrn., U. Miami, 1986. Provider rels. spec. Travelers Health Network, Phila., 1987-89; prin. Tyler & Co., Atlanta, 1989-93; risk mgmt. cons. John Alden - Provider Group, Miami, 1994; pres. Provider Risk, Inc., Miami, 1995—; instructor U. Miami, 1995—; article rev. coun. Med. Econs. Mag., 1991—; adj. prof. Nova Southeastern U., 1996—; spkr. in field. Contbr. articles to profl. jours. Worker Habitat for Humanity, Miami, Fla., 1995—. A.A. Green scholar. Mem. Am. Assn. of Physician Hosp. Orgns. (regional dir. 1995—), Soc. for Healthcare Planning and Mktg., Am. Coll. of Health Care Execs. (mem. regents adv. coun. 1995—), Toastmasters Internat. (CTM), South Fla. Exec. Forum, Alpha Kappa Psi. Office: Provider Risk Inc 9761 SW 123rd St Ste 1000 Miami FL 33176-4929

GEORGE, SUSAN E. GOULD, health facility administrator; b. Bedford, Pa., Sept. 21, 1952; d. Robert Neil and Joan Louise (Robertson) Gould; m. Scott O. George, Aug. 17, 1974; children: Seth, Seleste. BSN cum laude, U. Pitts., 1974. RN, Fla. Staff nurse med./surg. unit Bedford (Pa.) County Meml. Hosp., 1974; staff nurse surg. unit Gainesville (Fla.) Hosp., 1974-75; staff nurse neurol.-med. unit James A. Haley Vets. Hosp., Tampa, Fla., 1975-76, staff nurse surg. ICU, 1976-78, staff nurse post anesthesia care unit, 1978-82, head nurse operating room, 1982-83, coord. operative svcs., 1983-92, asst. chief nursing svc., ICU/operative svcs., 1992—; cons. Health Care Auditors; nat. cons. for implementation of automated med. record for surg. svcs.; lectr. in field. Developer surg. computer package. Mem. Assn. Operating Room Nurses (exec. bd. Tampa Bay chpt. 1988-91, bd. dirs. 1991-93), U. Pitts. Alumni Assn., Sigma Theta Tau.

GEORGE-LEPKOWSKI, SUE ANN, echocardiographic technologist; b. Altoona, Pa., Sept. 17, 1948; d. Charles Frederick and E. Anita (Haller) G.; m. Walter Lepkowski. AS, BS in Agronomy, Pa. State U., 1968, 70, MEd in Agronomy, Biol. Scis., Edn., 1972; PhD, Columbia & Columbia Pacific U., 1980; DS, Columbia Pacific U., 1981. Internship echocardiology West Pa. Hosp., Pitts., 1979-80; echocardiography tech. Bronson Meth. Hosp., Kalamazoo, 1981-82; echocardiographic technologist Nalle Clinic, Charlotte, 1983-85; tech. dir. Carolina Cardiology, Asheville, N.C., 1985-86; chief echocardiolographic technologist Candler Gen. Hosp., Savannah, Ga., 1986-88; echocardiolography, clin. specialist, technical spl. edn. specialist, chief technologist Self Meml. Hosp., Greenwood, S.C., 1988—; cons., rschr., lectr. in field. Contbr. articles to profl. jours.; co-author: Clinical 2-D Echocardiography. Mem. choir, Carolina Mountain Brass, Gospell Quartet; percussionist Images; edn. chmn. Greenwood Lupus Group, pres.; edn. chmn. S.C. Lupus Found.; team leader Fibromyalgia Syndrome. Recipient ACP award, Berkeley-Whittinger award for rsch. and acad. excellence. Mem. Am. Soc. Ultrasonic Tech. Specialists, Am. Inst. Ultrasonic Medicine, Soc. Diagnostic Med. Sonographers, Am. Registry Diagnostic Med. Sonographers (registered diagnostic med. sonographer, registered diagnostic cardiac sonographer), Altoona/Pa. State U. Alumni Assn., Columbia Pacific U. Alumni Assn., Altoona High Alumni Assn., IPTAY, S.C. Ultrasound Soc., N.C. Ultrasound Soc., Am. Soc. Echocardiography, Pa. State Carolina Club, USGA, PGA, LPGA, Rolling "S" Platform Assn., Phi Epsilon Phi. Mem. Dutch Reformed Ch. Home: 531 Willson St Apt 3 Greenwood SC 29649-1560 Office: Self Meml Hosp 1325 Spring St Greenwood SC 29646-3860

GEORGIOU, RUTH SCHWAB, retired social worker; b. Milford, Del., June 9, 1922; d. Lafayette and Ola (Moody) Burlingame; m. Matheos Georgiou, July 16, 1960 (dec. Sept. 1984); children: Eleni Georgiou Strawn, Diana Maria, Theodora Evtychia. BA in Liberal Arts with honors, U. Mich., 1943; MS in Social Adminstrn., U. Pitts., 1945. Lic. social worker, N.Y. Child welfare officer Unitarian Svc. Com., Germany, 1947-48; dir. Camp Bluebird Jewish Bd. of Guardians, N.Y.C., 1949; asst. dir. Girls Club of Bklyn. Bklyn. Hebrew Orphan Asylum, 1949-52; asst. dir. Suburban Agy., Hempstead, N.Y., 1954-57; co-dir. Suburban Homemakers & Maternity Agy., Hempstead, 1957-61; med. social worker Glen Oaks (N.Y.) Nursing Home, 1967-68; sr. care worker N.Y. Dept. Health-Social Svcs. Dept., Mineola, 1968-69; social work supr. Tampa (Fla.) Lighthouse for the Blind, 1976-78; med. social worker Global Home Health Svcs., Pinellas and Pasco, Fla., 1979-89; ret., 1989; social work cons. Spanish Gardens Nursing Home, Dunedin, Fla., 1980-82, St. Mark's Village, Palm Harbor, Fla., 1982-83; mem. adv. bd. Med. Pers. Pool, New Port Richey, 1986—. Author: (manual) Homemaker's Manual, 1956. Co-chmn. sr. care of Planned Approach to Community Health, New Port Richey, 1988-89; pres. Community Svc. Coun. West Pasco, New Port Richey, 1985-86, bd. dirs., 1985-91. Recipient cert. of appreciation Cmty. Svc. Coun. West Pasco, 1986, 91. Mem. NASW (membership chmn. Pasco subunit Fla. chpt. 1991—, chmn. membership Tampa Bay unit 1992—), Acad. Cert. Social Workers. Home: 300 S Walton Ave Apt 53 Tarpon Springs FL 34689-6011

GEORGITIS, JOHN, allergist, educator; b. Columbus, Ohio, June 19, 1950; s. William James and Mary Helen (Wyman) G.; m. Marilyn Howard; children: Nancy Lynn, Kathryn Mary, Matthew Walter. BA, Bowdoin Coll., Brunswick, Maine, 1972; MD, U. Vt., 1976. Diplomate Am. Bd. Pediatrics, Am. Bd. Allergy and Immunology. Resident in pediatrics James Whitcomb Riley Hosp., Indpls., 1976-78, pulmonology fellow, 1978-79; allergy fellow SUNY, Buffalo, 1979-81, rsch. asst. prof., 1981-84; assoc. prof. Bowman Gray Sch. Medicine, Winston-Salem, N.C., 1984-94, prof., 1994—; dir. allergy and immunology tng. program Bowman Gray Sch. of Medicine, Winston-Salem, 1987—. Office: Bowman Gray Sch of Medicine Med Ctr Blvd Winston Salem NC 27157

GEORGIUS, JOHN R., bank executive; b. 1944. BBA, Ga. State U., 1967. With 1st Union Nat. Bank N.C., Charlotte, 1975—, chmn., CEO, 1988-93; pres. 1st Union Corp., Charlotte, 1993—, mem. corp. mgmt. com., also bd. dirs. Office: 1st Union Corp 1 First Union Ctr Charlotte NC 28288

GERARD, ALMA ELIZABETH, financial planner; b. Johnson City, Tenn., Aug. 1, 1955; d. Charles E. and Alma L. Flaherty; 1 child, Daniel H. Gerard III. Student, East Tenn. State U., 1973-77, Am. Coll., Cambridge, Mass., 1991-94. Data processing supr., asst. mgr. Cox and Rich Wholesale Co., Inc., H.T. Hackney Co., Inc., Johnson City, 1973-86; internal mgr. Smith Wholesale, Inc., Johnson City, 1986-88; prin. PCA Planning Group, Morristown, Tenn., 1988-95; sr. ptnr. Jireh Svcs., Morristown, 1995—; speaker in field; condr. time mgmt. workshops. Author: I Miss My Time With You, Christian Time Management Principles, 1996. Active Lakeway AG; area coord. Christian Music Connection; head Spkr.'s Bur. Mem. NALU, Internat. Assn. Fin. Planners, Nat. Assn. Exec. Women, C. of C. Home: 4836 W AJ Hwy Morristown TN 37814 Office: Jireh Services PO Box 1776 Morristown TN 37816-1776

GERBER, BRIAN LYNN, science educator, consultant; b. Orrville, Ohio, July 11, 1960; s. Russell Johnson and Gwendolyn Jeanette (Graber) G.; m. Mary Elizabeth Raczkowski, Nov. 4, 1995. AAS, Hocking Tech. Coll., Nelsonville, Ohio, 1980; BS in Biology, Kent State U., 1983, BS in Edn., 1986, MA, 1987; PhD, U. Okla., 1996. Sci. tchr. Escuela Bella Vista, Maracaibo, Venezuela, 1988-92, sci. curriculum coord., 1990-92; rsch. asst. Project EARTHSTORM, Norman, 1992-93, instr., 1992-93; instr. U. Okla., 1995; asst. dir. Ctr. for Energy Edn., Norman, 1996; asst. prof. sci. edn., dept. secondary edn. Valdosta State U., Ga., 1996—. Editor: (sci. text) Investigations in Natural Sciences: Biology, 1995; contbr. articles to profl. jours. including Jour. of Rsch. in Sci. Tchg., Sci. and Children, others; presenter in field. Founder Project Hope, Maracaibo, 1992. Recipient Tchr. Sponsor award NASA, 1991, 92; City of Dolton C. of C. scholar, 1978, U. Okla. Sci. Edn. scholar, 1994, U. Okla. Coll. of Edn. scholar, 1995. Mem. Am. Ednl. Rsch. Assn., Assoc. Edn. Tchrs. in Sci., Nat. Sci. Tchrs. Assn., Nat. Assn. of Biology Tchrs., Nat. Assn. for Rsch. in Sci. Tchg., Visitor Studies Assn. Home: 4400 Willow Wood Gate Valdosta GA 31602-6708 Office: Valdosta State U Dept Secondary Edn Valdosta GA 31698-0101

GERBERDING COWART, GRETA ELAINE, lawyer; b. Ft. Wayne, Ind., Aug. 17, 1960; d. Miles Carston G. and Ruth (Hostrup) G., stepmother Joanie Wyatt Gerberding; m. T. David Cowart, Aug. 12, 1995. BS with high distinction, Ind. U., 1982; JD cum laude, 1985. Bar: Ind. 1985, U.S. Dist. Ct. (so. dist.) Ind., CPA, Ind., CEBS. Sr. tax cons. Ernst & Whinney, Indpls., 1985-87; assoc. Klineman, Rose, Wolf and Wallack P.C., Indpls., 1987-89, Hall Render Killian Heath & Lyman P.C., Indpls., 1989-95; of counsel Haynes and Boone, L.L.P., Dallas, 1996—; presenter at seminars. Author: (with G.P. Gooch) Trust and Estate Income Tax Reporting and Planning, 1985; contbr. chpts. to books, articles to profl. jours. Chmn. hospitality area Virginia Slims Tennis Tournament, Indpls., 1987-89; vol. Jello Tennis Classic Tennis Tournament, Indpls., 1990-91; coord. Hospitality and Ball Kids, 1990, Jr. Jamboree GTE Tennis Tournament, Indpls., 1990; vol. Ctr. for Exploration The Children's Mus., Indpls., 1991-94; mem. com. on funding Vision 2002 Luth. Camp Assn., Inc., 1993-94. Glen Peters fellow Ind. U., 1984. Fellow Ind. Bar Found.; mem. ABA (com. marital deduction legis. real property and probate sect. 1986-87, tax section, gen. income tax com. 1987-89, employee benefits com. 1988—, subcom. health plan design and state regulation 1993—, health care task force 1994—), Ind. Bar Assn. (acct.-lawyers com. 1986-89, co-chmn. com. on legis. 1988-92, coun. tax sect. 1988—, sec.-treas. 1991-92, v. chmn. tax sect. 1992-93, chair elect 1993-94, chair 1994-95), Indpls. Bar Assn., Indpls. Jaycees (treas. 4th Festival 1987 monthly dinner meetings 1988), West Indy Racquet Club (USTA Volvo Tennis Team 1986-87, RCA Tounament Credentials Com. 1993-94), Indpls. Racquet Club (USTA Volvo Tennis Team 1988-91). Office: Haynes and Boone LLP 901 Main St Ste 3100 Dallas TX 75202-3789

GEREAU, MARY CONDON, corporate executive; b. Winterset, Iowa, Oct. 10, 1916; d. David Joseph and Sarah Rose (Stack) Condon. Student, Mt. Mercy Jr. Coll., 1935-37; BA, U. Iowa, 1939, MA, 1941; m. Gerald Robert Gereau, Jan. 14, 1961. Program dir. ARC, India, 1943-45; dean of students Eastern Mont. Coll., 1946-48; supt. pub. instrn. state of Mont., 1948-56; sr. legis. cons. NEA, 1957-73; dir. legis. Nat. Treasury Employees Union, 1973-76; legis. asst. to Senator Melcher, Mont., 1976-86; pres. Woman's Party Corp., 1991—. Contbr. articles on state govt. and edn. to profl. jours. Co-chmn. Truman Commerative Com., 1994—. Mem. Coun. Chief State Sch. Officers (bd. dir. 1953-56, pres. 1956), Rural Edn. Assn. (exec. bd. 1953-56), Nat. Women's Party (v.p. 1984-91), Equal Rights Ratification Coun. (nat. chmn.), NEA. Named Conservationist of Yr. Mont. Conservation Coun., 1952, Roll Call Cong. Staffer of Yr., 1985; recipient Disting. Svc. award VFW, 1951, Disting. Svc. award, Chief State Sch. Officers, 1956. Mem. U.S. Congress Burro Club (pres. 1983-84).

GEREIGHTY, ANDREA SAUNDERS, polling company executive, poet; b. New Orleans, July 20, 1938; d. Andrew Jackson and Jeanne Teresa (Martin) Saunders; m. Dennis Anthony Gereighty Jr., May 19, 1959 (wid.); children: Deni Ann, David Dennis, Peggy T. Cert., Exeter Coll., Oxford, Eng., 1972; BA, U. New Orleans, 1974, MA in English with distinction, 1978. Cotton analyst Anderson-Clayton, Metairie, La., 1956; records retrieval profl. Shell Oil Co., New Orleans, 1956-60; census coord. St. Vincent De Paul Ch., New Orleans, 1960-65; bldg. funds dir. St. Francis Xavier Ch., Metairie, 1965-70; tchr. spl. edn. Deckbar Elem. Sch., Jefferson, La., 1966-70; tchr. secondary edn. Chalmette (La.) H.S., 1971-72; assoc. prof. English dept. U. New Orleans, 1972-73; tchr. secondary edn. Berlin-Am. H.S., 1980-81; owner, founder, CEO New Orleans Field Svcs. Assocs., 1974—; guest speaker Delgado Coll., New Orleans, 1989; guest presenter Rabouin Vo-Tech., New Orleans, 1980; lectr., guest presenter poetry at New Sarpy Sch., 1994, 95; guest presenter St. Mark's Episcopal Ch., Latter Libr., N.O. Pub. Libr., others. Author: Asking Questions, 1980, (poetry books) Illusions and Other Realities, 1974, Restless for Cool Weather, 1990, Season of the Crane, 1994; contbr. to poetry mags. Recipient Coda award Poets and Writers, 1983, Poetry award of honor Nat. League Am. Pen Women, 1973, Deep South Writers, 1984, 88, 90, 92, 94, 2d place award Nuyarikin Poet's Cafe, N.Y.C. Mem. Am. Mktg. Assn., Mktg. Rsch. Assn., Nat. Geneal. Soc., Jefferson Geneal. Soc., New Orleans Poetry Forum (dir. 1990—), New Orleans Track Club. Democrat. Roman Catholic. Home: 257 Bonnabel Blvd Metairie LA 70005-3738 Office: New Orleans Field Svcs Rear Office Ste 257 Bonnabel Blvd Metairie LA 70005-3738

GEREN, BRENDA L., business educator; b. Cleveland, Tenn., Sept. 9, 1950; d. Benny L. and Betty R. (Still) Elmore; m. Gilbert L. Geren; children: Melissa, Kristi. BBA, U. Tenn., Chattanooga, 1987; MBA, U. Tenn., 1989; postgrad., U. Manchester (Eng.) Bus. Sch., 1987; EdD, U. Tenn. Owner Waterville Grocery, Cleveland, 1973—; asst. prof. Cleveland State C.C., 1989, U. Tenn., Chattanooga, 1989. Mem. Creative Arts Guild, Cleveland; vol. Spl. Olympics, Cleveland; docent Hunter Art Museum, Chattanooga; advisor Jr. Achievement. Recipient rsch. honorarium U. Tenn., 1987, letter of merit U. Manchester Bus. Sch., 1987; bus. and econ. rsch. fellow U. Pitts., Ea. Europe, summer 1992. Mem. Soc. Advancement of Mgmt., Am. Soc. Quality Control, Assn. Pvt. Enterprise Edn., Tenn. Edn. Assn., Cleveland C. of C. (Quality Coun.), Omicron Delta Epsilon, Beta Sigma Phi. Home: 3731 Trewhitt Rd Cleveland TN 37323

GERHARDT, GLENN RODNEY, sales executive; b. Chgo., Aug. 3, 1923; s. Louis Arther and Myrtle (Wallander) G.; m. Ruth Jean Lorch, Oct. 18, 1923; children: Robert L., Thomas F., Kim. Student, Iowa State Coll., 1941-43; BBA, U. Wis., 1949. Salesman Eppler, Guerin and Turner Investments, Dallas, 1952, Holeproof Hosiery-Kayser-Roth, Dallas, 1952-56, Lillan Russell Originals, Mobile, Ala., 1956-58; sales mgr. Evenflo Products, Ravenna, Ohio, 1958-88, J. Myers Sales Co., Dallas, 1988—; pres. H.A. Investors, Dallas, 1952; pres. Rumhil Arabians, Inc., McKinney, Tex., 1963-85. Pres. Culleoka (Tex.) Water Supply Corp., 1980. Served with USAF, 1943-45, PTO, India. Mem. USCG Auxillary, U.S. Power Squadron, N.Tex. Arabian Horse Club (pres. 1965), Arabian Horse of Tex. (treas. 1964). Republican. Episcopalian. Home: 2308 San Gabriel Dr Plano TX 75074-3463

GERHARDT, ROSARIO ALEJANDRINA, materials scientist; b. Lima, Peru, May 20, 1953; d. Jacob K. and Tarcila (La Cruz) G.; m. Michael Paul Anderson, Sept. 27, 1980; children: Heidi Margaret, Kathleen Elizabeth. BA, Carroll Coll., 1976; MS, Columbia U., 1979, D Engring. Sci., 1983. Teaching asst. Columbia U., N.Y.C., 1978-79, grad. asst., 1979-83, research assoc., 1983-84; postdoctoral fellow Rutgers U., Piscataway, N.J., 1984-86, asst. rsch. prof., 1986-90; assoc. prof. Ga. Inst. Tech., 1990—; cons. in field. Contbr. articles to profl. jours. Mem. Am. Ceramic Soc., Am. Phys. Soc., N.Y. Acad. Sci., Electron Microscopy Soc. Am., Materials Rsch. Soc., Sigma Xi, Materials Sci. Club N.Y. (sec. 1988-90). Roman Catholic. Home: 124 Infantry Way Marietta GA 30064-5000

GERHARDT, WILLIAM PAUL, army officer, university administrator; b. Lake Forest, Ill., Oct. 26, 1955; s. William James and Virginia Gail (Mecham) G.; m. Sandra Ann Montez, Dec. 31, 1991; 1 child, Zack. B.Bus., Western Ill. U., 1977; MS in Human Resources Mgmt., Troy State U., Dothan, Ala., 1994. Commd. 2d lt. U.S. Army, 1977—, advanced through grades to lt. comdr., 1994; instr., tng. officer Dir. Combined Army Tng., Ft. Rucker, Ala., 1985-86; comdr. 260th FA detachment 1st Brigade, Ft. Rucker, 1986-87; divsn. chief Directorate of EVAL & STDZN, Ft. Rucker, 1987-88; HHC comdr. 3-3 ATK HEL Bn., 3d Infantry Divsn., Wurzburg, Germany, 1988-89, battalion ops. officer, 1989-90, battalion exec officer, 1990-91; chief aviation planning group Army Aviation Ctr. and Sch., Ft. Rucker, 1992-94; course dir./instr. Armed Forces Staff Coll., Norfolk, Va., 1994—. Lay minister, mem. parish coun. Geibelstadt Cmty. Parish, St. Ignatius Ch., Leavenworth, Kans., AFSC Cmty. Parish. Recipient St. Barbara award Field Artillery Assn., 1989. Mem. Soc. for Human Resource Mgmt., Army Aviation Assn. Am. (St. Michael award 1989), Tidewater Soccer Referee Assn. (mentorship com./EVAL com. 1995—), Delta Mu Delta. Home: 1210 Porter Rd Norfolk VA 23511 Office: Armed Forces Staff College 7800 Hampton Blvd Norfolk VA 23511

GERHART, GLENNA LEE, pharmacist; b. Houston, June 11, 1954; d. Henry Edwin and Gloria Mae (Mrnustik) G. BS in Pharmacy, U. Houston, 1977. Registered pharmacist, Tex. Staff pharmacist Meml. City Med. Ctr., Houston, 1977-84, asst. dir. pharmacy, 1984—. Mem. Am. Pharm. Assn., Am. Soc. Hosp. Pharmacists, Tex. Pharm. Assn., Tex. Soc. Health-System Pharmacists, Harris County Pharm. Assn., Plumeria Soc. Am., U. Houston Alumni Orgn. (life), Houston Cat Club, Nat. Cougar Club, Slavonic Benevolent Order of Tex., Greentrails Ladies Club, Kappa Epsilon. Republican. Methodist. Home: 19811 Cardiff Park Ln Houston TX 77094-3031 Office: Meml City Med Ctr 920 Frostwood Dr Houston TX 77024-2312

GERLACH, GARY G., botanical garden director, columnist; b. Louisville, Apr. 28, 1945; s. Henry Elmer and Lorraine (Curry) G.; m. Kathryn Lynn Arnold, Feb. 8, 1969; children—Lynnette, Christopher. B.S. in Hort., U. Ky., 1967; M.S. in Hort., U. Del., 1969. Dir. Birmingham Bot. Gardens, Ala. Columnist garden adv. Birmingham, also radio shows. Home: 3607 E Lakeside Dr Birmingham AL 35243-1943 Office: Birmingham Bot Garden 2612 Lane Park Rd Birmingham AL 35223-1802*

GERLACH, JEANNE ELAINE, English language educator; b. Charleston, W.Va., Oct. 20, 1946; d. Lafayette and Edith Lorraine (Robinson) Marcum; m. Roger Thomas Gerlach Sr., Dec. 30, 1966; children: Roger Thomas Jr., Kristen Elaine. BS, W.Va. State Coll., Institute, 1974; MA, W.Va. State Coll., 1979; EdD, W.Va. U., 1985, U. North Tex., 1992. Lang. arts tchr. Ohio County Schs., Wheeling, W.Va., 1974-79; English instr. West Liberty (W.Va.) State Coll., 1979-82; continuing edn. instr. Seattle Pacific U., 1982-85; asst. prof. English W.Va. U., Morgantown, 1985-86, Tarrant County Jr. Coll., Ft. Worth, 1986-88; dir. Communications Unlimited, Dallas, Pitts., 1986—; assoc. prof. English edn. W.Va. U., Morgantown, 1989—, spl. asst. to the provost, 1994—, dir. ctr. women's studies, 1993-94; cons. to bus. and corps., 1986—; co-dir. advanced writing project W.Va. U., Morgantown, 1989, lang. arts camps, 1988, 89, 90, young writers inst. Editor: English Internat.; contbr. articles to profl. jours. Mem. LWV, W.Va., DAR, Young Republicans, W.Va. Faculty Devel. grantee W.Va. U., 1989; recipient 1st. place Creative Writing award W.Va. Women's Clubs, 1976. Mem. AAUW, AAUP, Nat. Coun. Tchrs. English (chair women's com. 1986—, chair nominating com. 1988-89, Outstanding Tchr. in Coll. of Human Resources and Edn. award W.Va. U. 1992, Rewey Belle Inglis award 1992), Am. Ednl. Rsch. Assn., W.Va. U. Alumni Assn. (sec. 1990, pres.), Nat. Women's Studies Assn., Nat. Soc. Daus. Am. Revolution. Republican. Methodist.

GERLIN, ANDREA L., journalist; b. El Paso, Tex., July 24, 1962; d. Ronald E. and Valerie J. G. BA, Harvard Coll., 1984; MA, Cambridge U., 1987; MS with honors, Columbia U., 1992. Stringer The N.Y. Times, Boston, 1983-84; researcher The N.Y. Times Mag., N.Y.C., 1987-88; reporter The Register Citizen, Torrington, Conn., 1989-91; staff reporter Wall Street Jour., Dallas, 1992—. Contbg. author: Collectanea Augustiniana, 1991. Cissy Patterson fellow Am. Press Inst., Reston, Va., 1991; recipient Christopher Light Editing award Columbia U., 1992, Tex. Gavel award State Bar Tex., 1995. Mem. Soc. Profl. Journalists (Stephen A Collins Pub. Svc. award 1990), Harvard Club N.Y., Harvard Club Dallas (v.p. 1993—). Episcopalian. Office: Wall Street Jour 1233 Regal Row Dallas TX 75247-3613

GERLOVICH, KAREN J., historian, musicologist; b. Duluth, Minn., Apr. 28, 1944; m. Edward Gerlovich, Apr. 27, 1974. Grad. high sch., Duluth. Freelance accordian historian. Composer polkas; author: Happy Gals USA & Their Wonderful Music USA. Home: 3277 Beneva Rd Unit 104 Sarasota FL 34232

GERMAN, RONALD STEPHEN, health care facility administrator; b. Jersey City, May 26, 1946; s. Steve and Eleanor (Gruttke) G.; m. Diana Lynn Jones, Dec. 3, 1972 (div. 1983); m. Cheryl Dunbar Gardner, Apr. 26, 1985; children: Scott James Gardner, Brian Dunbar Gardner. BSBA cum laude, U. Tenn., 1974; MBA summa cum laude, Bristol U., 1991. With Bankers Trust Co., N.Y.C., 1969-70; dir. employee tng. and devel. personnel dept. U. Tenn., Knoxville, 1975-78; mgr. East Tenn. Orthopaedic Ctr., Knoxville, 1978—; bd. dirs. Knoxville Acad. Medicine Med-Staff Placement Inc. Mem. First United Meth. Ch., Knoxville, 1987—. Served with USAF, 1965-69. Mem. Med. Group Assn. (pres. 1982), Nat. Orthopaedic Mgrs. Assn., Profl. Assn. Health Care Office Mgrs., Am. Mgmt. Assn., Am. Coll. Med. Group Adminstrs., Am. Coll. Med. Practice Execs. (cert.), Knoxville Med. Group Mgrs. Assn. (pres. 1992), Tenn. Valley Pers. Assn. (treas. 1987-88, sec. 1989), Knoxville Rotary (Paul Harris fellow). Republican. Home: 420 Dixieview Rd Knoxville TN 37922-2609 Office: East Tenn Orthopedic Ctr 2701 Kingston Pike Knoxville TN 37919-4619

GERMINARIO, LOUIS THOMAS, materials scientist; b. Molfetta, Apuglia, Italy, Sept. 27, 1947; came to U.S., 1956; s. Diego and Angela Germinario; m. Violet Joan Maas, May 19, 1984; children: Stephanie, Victoria. BA, Gettysburg (Pa.) Coll., 1970; MS, Cath. U. Am., 1972, PhD, 1973. Staff scientist, cons. EMV Assocs. Microanalysis Lab., Rockville, Md., 1972-73; postdoctoral rsch. assoc. Ariz. State U., Tempe, 1973-75; NIH fellow Johns Hopkins U., Balt., 1975-78; sr. rsch. assoc. Case Western Res. U., Cleve., 1978-81; rsch. chemist Eastman Chem. Co., Kingsport, Tenn., 1981-86, sr. rsch. chemist, 1986-91, prin. rsch. chemist, 1991-95; rsch. assoc., 1995—; session chmn. IUPAC Internat. Symposium on Macromolecules, Akron, 1995. Contbr. articles to profl. jours. Grantee Sigma Xi, 1972, Biophys. Soc., 1978. Mem. Am. Chem. Soc., Electron Microscopy Soc. Am. (session chmn. 1975), N.Y. Acad. Sci., Microscopy Soc. Am. (session chmn. 1995), Sigma Xi, Beta Beta Beta. Office: Eastman Chemical Co Eastman Rd Kingsport TN 37662-1972

GERMROTH, DAVID SCOTT, trade association executive; b. Phila., May 6, 1961; s. Richard and Jeanette (Barrette) G.; m. Rebecca Jean Hudson, May 7, 1990. A.German/Dutch, Linguor Sprach Schule, Trier, Germany, 1982; BA in Polit. Sci., Temple U., 1987, MA in Pub. Adminstrn./Pub. Policy, 1991. Support mgr. Wilhelm Knod & Co., Traben, Germany, 1982-85; legis. asst. to Congressman Bob Edgar, U.S. Ho. of Reps., Washington, 1985-86; asst. to chair dept. polit. sci. Temple U., Phila., 1987-89; asst. dir. govt./program outreach Fulbright Tchr. Exch. Program, USIA, Washington, 1989-91; asst. dir. govt./pub. affairs Eisenhower World Affairs Inst., Washington, 1991-93; vis. fellow The Brookings Inst., Washington, 1993-94; dir. govt./corp. affairs Nat. Vets. Legal Svcs. Program, Washington, 1994-96; govt. affairs exec. Art Freight and Forwarders Assn., Alexandria, Va., 1996—; adj. faculty Exec. MBA Program, Temple U., 1987-90, dept. polit. sci., 1989-91; adj. faculty dept. polit. sci. LaSalle U., Phila., 1989-91, evening/weekend divsn. Widener U., Wilmington, Del., 1990—, Sch. Law, Legal Edn. Inst., 1992—; mem. Eisenhower Leadership Program Bd., U.S. Dept. Edn., 1993-94. Contbr. articles to profl. jours. Sgt. USAF, 1979-82. Temple U. Grad. scholar, 1989-90. Mem. Internat. Studies Assn., German Soc. of Pa., European Cmty. Studies Assn., Ctr. for Study of the Presidency, Am. Fgn. Svc. Assn., Am. Soc. Assn. Execs., Am. Soc. Internat. Law, Assn. of Govt. Affairs Execs. Home: PO Box 20652 Alexandria VA 22320

GERNERT, IRWIN WILLIAM (BILL GERNERT), real estate developer, industrial designer, entrepreneur; b. Nashville, May 18, 1929; s. Irwin William and Mary Alice (Comingore) G. Student, Parsons Sch. Design, Manhattan, 1949-50, Peabody Coll., Nashville, 1950, U. Louisville, 1951. Art dir. CBS Channel 5, Nashville, 1955-57, Bill Gernert Industries, Nashville, 1970-80; tchr. Montgomery Bell Acad., 1961-67; art dir. Hee Haw, 1969-79; devel. Jupiter of Nashville, 1987-93; devel. Gernert Retirement Community, Nashville, 1990—. Bd. dirs., mem. adv. bd. Nashville Tech. Sch., 1990-93; Empire Studios, 1996, active Nashville Jr. C. of C., 1958. With U.S. Army, 1952-53. Mem. Nashville Artist Guild (sec. 1948-51). Lutheran. Home: 936 Caldwell Ln Nashville TN 37204-4016

GERNON, CLARKE JOSEPH, SR., mechanical and forensic engineering consultant; b. New Orleans, Dec. 27, 1944; s. Edward James and Mary Emma (Harvey) G.; m. Mila Du Bois Chutz, Dec. 28, 1963; 1 child, Clarke Joseph Jr. BSME, La. State U., 1969, MS in Engring. Mechanics, 1971. Registered profl. engr., La., Tenn., S.C. Mech. engr. Barnard and Burk, Inc., Baton Rouge, 1969-72; project engr. Lurgi-Knost, Inc., Baton Rouge, 1972-73; project mgr. The Rust Engring. Co., Baton Rouge, 1973-78, Imes and Assocs., Inc., Baton Rouge, 1978-86; mech. engr. and owner Futuretech Design, Baton Rouge, 1986—. Patentee in field. Vice chmn. Dixie Elec. Adv. Bd.; founding chmn. Capital Resource Conservation and Devel. Coun., Inc.; major supporter A Child's Wish; mem. Aero-space Task Force of MetroVision Partnership of New Orleans; incorporator and bd. dirs. Plantation Estates Civic Assn., Inc.; past pres. and bd. dirs. La. Miss. Christmas Tree Assn.; bd. dirs. Nat. Christmas Tree Assn.; mem. quarantine adv. com. La. Dept. Agr. for Christmas Trees. Mem. ASME, Am. Welding Soc., So. Bldg. Code Congress Internat., Nat. Fire Protection Assn., Am. Acad. Forensic Scis. Roman Catholic. Office: Futuretech Design PO Box 40672 Baton Rouge LA 70835-0672

GERNON, GEORGE OWEN, JR., civil engineer; b. New Orleans, Dec. 15, 1950; s. George Owen and Loretta Cecile (Conners) G.; m. Vilma Velozo de Souza, June 11, 1974; children: Marco Antonio, Adrianna Elizabeth. BS, U. Southwestern La., 1972. Registered profl. engr., La. Field engr. Oceanic Contractors SE Asia, Brazil and Trinidad, 1972-74; structural engr. J. Ray McDermott, New Orleans, 1974-75; sr. design engr. Santa Fe Engring. Svcs., Orange, Calif., 1975-77; sr. project engr. Santa Fe Engring. and Constrn. Co., Houma, La., 1978-79, project mgr., 1979-87; asst. ops. mgr. Pipelines Unltd. Svcs., Houma, La., 1987-88, ops. mgr., 1989-90; sr. ops. engr. McDermott Inc., Morgan City, La., 1990-93, sr. project mgr., 1993—. Mem. NSPE, Project Mgmt. Inst., Am. Welding Soc., La. Engring. Soc., Mensa. Republican. Roman Catholic. Home: 2810 Mission Hills Ct Katy TX 77450 Office: McDermott Inc 5718 Westheimer Ste 500 Houston TX 77057

GERONEMUS, DIANN FOX, social work consultant; b. Chgo., July 4, 1947; d. Herbert J. and Edith (Robbins) Fox; BA with high honors, Mich. State U., 1969; MSW, U. Ill., 1971; 1 dau., Heather Eileen. Diplomate Am. Bd. Clin. Social Work; lic. clin. social worker, marriage and family therapist, Fla.; cert. case mgr.; bd. cert. diplomate clin. social work. Social worker neurology, neurosurgery and medicine Hosp. of Albert Einstein Coll. Medicine, 1971-74; prin. social worker ob-gyn and newborn infant service Rush-Presbyn.-St. Luke's Med. Center, Chgo., 1974-75; social worker neurology, adminstr. Multiple Sclerosis Treatment Center, St. Barnabas Hosp., Bronx, N.Y., 1975-77, socio-med. researcher (Nat. Multiple Sclerosis Soc. grantee), dept. neurology and psychiatry, 1977-79, dir. social service, 1979-80; field work instr. Fordham U. Grad. Sch. Social Service, 1979-80; preceptor, social work program Fla. Atlantic U., Fla. Internat. U.; mem. edn. com., med. adv. bd., program cons. Nat. Multiple Sclerosis Soc., 1980-83, area service cons., 1983-86 ; pvt. practice psychotherapy; social work cons.; cons. in gerontology, rehab. and supervision, 1980—. Mem. Ombudsman Coun., 1992-94, vice chmn. 1993-94. Mem. NASW, Acad. Cert. Social Workers, Registry Clin. Social Workers, Am. Orthopsychiat. Assn. Jewish. Contbr. articles to profl. jours. Home: 833 NW 81st Way Fort Lauderdale FL 33324-1216

GERRETSEN, GILBERT WYNAND (GIL GERRETSEN), marketing and management consultant; b. Rotterdam, The Netherlands, May 8, 1955; arrived in Can., 1957, Can. citizen, 1960; arrived in U.S., 1980, naturalized, 1983; s. Everhardus Hubertus and Johanna (Boers) G.; m. Susan Boggs, June 27, 1980. B in Commerce, U. Calgary, Alberta, Canada, 1976. Group ins. adminstr., asst. supr. group acctg. Great-West Life Assurance, Winnipeg, Canada, 1978-80; supr. policyholder svc. Founders Life Ins., Tampa, Fla., 1980-81; cons. specialist group ins. William M. Mercer, Inc., Tampa, Fla., 1981-82; exec. dir. Junior Achievement, Greenville, S.C., 1982-85; pres. Jr. Achievement So. Ariz., Tucson, 1985-88; sr. dir. devel. Junior Achievement, Seattle, 1988-90; sr. dir. mktg. Washington Special Olympics, Seattle, 1990-92; chief mktg. officer ALM Internat., Greenville, 1992-94; pres. ListenUp Mktg., Inc., Greenville, 1994—; developer Flashpoint Mktg.; founder Biz-Trek Mktg. Inst. Pub. (newsletter) Bizfax. Bd. dirs. Jr. Achievement, 1996—, Greenville Humane Soc., 1996—, S.C. Soc. for Prevention of Cruelty to Animals, 1996—, Child Evangelism Fellowship, 1996, C. of C. Small Bus. Coun., 1996, Clemson U. Small Bus. Devel. Coun., 1996, Greenville Chamber Edn. Com. and CEO Roundtable, Greenville Rehab. Ctr., chmn.-elect, 1996—. Fellow Life Mgmt. Inst.; mem. Nat. Soc. Fund Raising Execs., Christian Businessmen's Com., Leadership Greenville. Office: ListenUp 2718D Wade Hampton Blvd Greenville SC 29615

GERSHENSON, DAVIS MARC, oncology educator, university administrator; b. Mt. Vernon, Ill., Feb. 10, 1946; s. David Abraham and Lucille Clara (Cunningham) G.; m. Jo Anne Vaughan, Aug. 2, 1969 (div. May 1977); m. Michelle Renacci; children: Rebecca, Rachel, Hannah, David Marc. BA, U. Penn., 1967; MD, Vanderbilt U., 1971. Diplomate Am. Bd. Ob-Gyn, Am. Bd. Gynecologic Oncology, Nat. Bd. of Med. Examiners. Assoc. prof. gynecology, assoc. surgeon U. Tex. M.D. Anderson Hosp. and Tumor Inst., Houston, 1984-87; assoc. prof. U. Tex. M.D. Anderson Hosp., Houston, 1987-88, clin. assoc. prof. gynecologic oncology, 1987-88, assoc. v.p. for patient care, 1989-92, prof., dep. chmn. dept. gynecology, 1988—. Editor Clin. Consultations in Ob-Gyn, Gynecologic Oncology, 1990—, Operative Techniques in Gynecologic Surgery; editor textbook: Operative Gynecology; assoc. editor Ob-Gyn Clin. Alert, 1989—. Maj. USAF, 1975-77. Recipient Favorite Son award So. Ill. Med. Assn., 1995. Mem. Soc. Gynecol. Oncologists (pres. 1996—, President's award), Felix Rutledge Soc., Houston Gynecologic and Obstet. Soc., Alpha Omega Alpha. Office: U Tex MD Anderson Cancer Ct 1515 Holcombe Ave Houston TX 77030

GERSHON, ELAINE A., medical/surgical nurse; b. Ft. Worth, Sept. 23, 1963; d. Jim Joseph and Rose Margaret (Anello) Bezdek; m. J. Robert Gershon Jr., Sept. 9, 1989. AAS in Nursing, Cooke County Coll., Gainesville, Tex., 1985. RN, Tex.; cert. CPR, intravenous therapy. Nurse med.-surg. outpatient unit Denton Regional Med. Ctr., 1989-91; nurse Denton (Tex.) Home Health Care, 1991-92; DON, DON Kern Manor, Pilot Point, Tex., 1992—. Office: 2501 Scripture Ste 100 Denton TX 76207

GERSON, MARTIN LYONS, secondary school educator; b. Morristown, Tenn., Sept. 12, 1961; s. Allan Jerome and Bernice (Misner) G. BS, Purdue U., 1984; MA for Tchrs., Ga. State U., 1986, cert. ednl. specialist, 1994. Cert. secondary math. tchr., Ga. Tchr. math. Cross Keys High Sch., Atlanta, 1984—; instr. math. Ga. State U., Atlanta, 1988-90, Dekalb Coll., Atlanta, 1990—. Named Tchr. of Month math. students Cross Keys High Sch., 1989, HERO Club, Cross Keys High Sch., 1990, Tchr. of Yr. faculty Cross Keys High Sch., 1990, West Dekalb Rotary Club, Atlanta, 1991. Mem. Nat. Coun. Tchrs. Math., Ga. Coun. Tchrs. Math., B'nai B'rith. Jewish. Home: 1000 Liberty View Ct Norcross GA 30093-4800 Office: Cross Keys High Sch 1626 N Druid Hills Rd NE Atlanta GA 30319-4156

GERST, STEVEN RICHARD, healthcare director, physician; b. N.Y.C., Oct. 20, 1958; s. Paul Howard and Elizabeth (Carlsen) G.; m. Isabelle Sylvie Meier, Apr. 21, 1987 (div.); 1 child, Chantal Elizabeth. BA, Columbia U., 1981, MD, 1986, MPH, 1987; MBA, Emory U., 1996. Lic. ins. broker, N.C. Med. affairs coord. Sun Health Care Plans, Charlotte, N.C., 1987-88, cons., 1988-90; asst. v.p., dir. Preferred Provider Orgns. Crawford & Co., Atlanta, 1994, Preferred Provider Arrangements Crawford & Co., Atlanta, 1990-94; v.p. Imaginative Devices Inc., Atlanta, 1993-94, Columbia/HCA Healthcare Corp., Nashville, Tenn., 1994-95; pres., CEO Health Advantage Network, Orlando and Atlanta, Fla., 1994—, Woodland Hills, Calif., 1994-95; sr. cons. Coopers & Lybrand, Atlanta, 1995—; interim pres. PCA Health Plans Ga. (HMO), Atlanta, 1996—; interviewer Columbia Coll., N.C., 1987; adj. prof. Emory U., 1997. Editor-in-chief: Handbook Coll. Physicians and Surgeons (Alumni award), 1983, Columbian (Robert Shellow Gerdy award), 1981. Vol. Presbyn. Hosp., N.Y.C., 1979-81, St. Lukes Hosp., N.Y.C., 1978-79. Mem. AMA, Am. Acad. Med. Dirs., Am. Coll. Med. Staff Affairs, Am. Coll. Physician Execs., Am. Coll. Health Care Execs., Am. Assn. Physician-Hosp. Orgns., Am. Assn. Preferred Provider Orgns., Andover Alumni Soc. N.Y. (dir. 1986-87), Alliance Francaise (v.p. Charlotte, N.C. chpt. 1987-88). Home: 5450 Glenridge Dr NE Apt 372 Atlanta GA 30342-4921 Office: 1155 Peachtree Rd Atlanta GA 30309

GERSTEIN, ESTHER, sculptor; b. N.Y.C., May 20, 1924; d. Leon and Lillian (Peretz) Grizer; m. Leonard B. Gerstein, Mar. 31, 1946; children: Lee Steven, Laurie Susan. Student, Pratt Inst., 1941-42, NYU, 1942-43; pvt. study, various sculptors; student, Cooper Union, 1946-48. Asst. tchr. Art Students League, N.Y.C., 1944-46; painting tchr. pvt. sch. Great Neck, N.Y., 1961-63; founder, instr. sculpture and painting Studio 33, Westbury, N.Y., 1964-72; sculptor and painter pvt. studios, Boca Raton, Fla.; lectr. Norton Mus., Palm Beach, Fla., 1985. Exhibited in group shows at Hecksher Mus., Huntington, N.Y., Norton Mus., Palm Beach, Fla., Kellenberg Gallery, C.W. Post Coll., L.I., Firehouse Gallery, Nassau Cmty. Coll., L.I., Lever House, N.Y.C., Grace Bldg., N.Y.C., Hofstra U., Lighthouse Gallery, Tequesta, Fla., Montoya Art Gallery, Palm Beach, Del-Aire Country Club, Boca Raton, Fla., Bocaire Country Club, Boca Raton, Polo Country Club, Boca Raton, Nathan Rosen Gallery, Boca Raton, Lynn U., Boca Raton, Naza Gallery, Boca Raton; one man show includes TV spl.; represented in numerous pvt. and corp. collections throughout U.S. Art Students League scholar, 1944, Cooper Union scholar, 1946. Mem. Artists Guild Norton Mus., Nat. League Am. Pen Women.

GERTSCH, WILLIAM DARRELL, university research administrator, consultant; b. Montpelier, Idaho, Mar. 27, 1940; s. Ezra Eugene and Lucile (Brimhall) G.; m. Christine Carter, June 7, 1962; children: Larry, Dawn, Debbie, Amy. BS in Engring. Sci., U.S. Mil. Acad., 1962; MA in History, U. Wash., Seattle, 1969, PhD in Econ. History, 1974. Instr. in econs. and history Utah State U., Logan, 1972-74; mem. staff Los Alamos (N.Mex.) Nat. Lab., 1974-77; gr. mgr. Idaho Nat. Engring. Lab., Idaho Falls, 1977-79; pres. Gertsch, Juncal & Assocs., Ltd., Idaho Falls, 1979-87; assoc. dir. Advanced Tech. Devel. Ctr. Ga. Inst. Tech., Atlanta, 1987-91; assoc. v.p. for rsch., dir. Energy Ctr. U. Okla., Norman, 1992—; pres. U. Okla. Rsch. Corp., 1992—; adj. prof. U. N.Mex., Albuquerque, 1974-77; cons. in field. Contbr. articles to profl. jours. Scoutmaster Boy Scouts Am., Albuquerque, 1963-67; leader ch. youth groups, Los Alamos, 1974-86. Capt. USAF, 1962-70. NDEA fellow, 1972. Mem. AAAS, Geothermal Resources Coun. (chpt. pres. 1982-83). Office: Univ Okla Dept of Rsch Norman OK 73069

GERVAIS, KEVIN MICHAEL, computer network engineer; b. Troy, N.Y., Sept. 11, 1956; s. Jeremiah Arthur and Thelma Marion (Gokey) G.; m. Linda Ann Henneberry, 1984; children: David, Nicholas, Aubrey. BS in engring. tech., U. Nebr., 1982. Prod. engr. Telemed Cardio Pulmonary Systems, Omaha, 1978-81; field engr. Harris Corp., Omaha, 1981-83; communications anaylst ConAgra Corp., Omaha, 1983-86; data communications anaylst Mutual of Omaha, Omaha, 1986-87; sr. engr. Sci. Applications Internat. Corp., 1987-93; network engr. New Technology, Inc., Huntsville, Ala., 1993-95, ERC, Inc., 1995-96; engr., scientist TRW, Inc., Huntsville, 1996—. Mem. IEEE (assoc.), Armed Forces Communications and Elec. Assn. Home: 2926 Old 431 Hwy S Owens Cross Roads AL 35763 Office: TRW Inc 213 Wynn Dr Huntsville AL 35805

GERWIN, LESLIE ELLEN, public affairs and community relations executive, lawyer; b. L.A., May 18, 1950; d. Nathan and Beverly Adele (Wilson) G.; m. Bruce Robert Leslie, July 3, 1978; 1 child, Jonathan Gerwin Leslie. BA, Prescott Coll., 1972; JD, Antioch Sch. Law, 1975; MPH, Tulane U., 1988. Bar: D.C. 1975, N.Y. 1981, U.S. Dist. Ct. D.C. 1977, U.S. Dist. Ct. (so. dist.) N.Y. 1980. Staff asst. U.S. Congress, Washington, 1970-72; cons. Congl. Subcom., Washington, 1972-73; instr. U. Miami Law Sch., Coral Gables, Fla., 1975-76; assoc. prof. law Yeshiva U., N.Y.C., 1976-86; vis. assoc. prof. law Tulane Law Sch., New Orleans, 1983-84; pub. policy cons. New Orleans, 1987—; pres. Ariadne Cons., New Orleans, 1994—; dir. devel. and community rels. Planned Parenthood La., Inc., New Orleans, 1989-90; legal advisor La. Coalition for Reproductive Freedom, 1990-92; exec. v.p. Met. Area Com., New Orleans, 1992-94; exec. dir. Met. Area Com. Edn. Fund, New Orleans, 1992-94; bd. dirs. Inst. for Phys. Fitness Rsch., N.Y.C., 1982-86, Challenge/Discovery, Crested Butte, Colo., 1977-80; cons. FDA, Washington, 1977-78, U. Judaism, L.A., 1974-75; mem. Met. Area Com. Leadership Forum, New Orleans, 1988. Contbr. articles to profl. jours. Mem. Ind. Dem. Jud. Screening Panel, N.Y.C., 1980; bd. dirs. New Orleans Food Bank for Emergencies, 1987-89; profl. adv. com. MAZON-A Jewish Response to Hunger, L.A., 1986-89; bd. dirs. Second Harvesters Food Bank Greater New Orleans, 1989-94, La. State LWV, 1990-91, Anti-Defamation League, New Orleans, 1989-95, Jewish Endowment Found., 1987-93; trustee Jewish Fedn. Greater New Orleans, 1989-95, Fed. Emergency Mgmt. Agy. Bd., Emergency Food and Shelter Program, S.E. La., 1988—; v.p. Tulane U. B'nai B'rith Hillel Found., 1987-90; steering com. Citizens for Pers. Freedom, 1989-91; steering com. Metro 2000, 1989-90; sec. New Orleans sect. Nat. Coun. Jewish Women, 1990-91, state pub. affairs chmn., 1992-96; bd. Contemporary Arts Ctr., 1993—; chair, bd. advocates Planned Parenthood La., 1995—; v.p. Edn. Tikvat Shalom Conservative Congregation, 1995—, chair New Orleans Israel Bonds, 1996—; me. Cmty. Rels. Com., 1986—, vice chair, 1995—. Fellow Inst. of Politics, 1990-91; scholar Xerox Found., 1972-75; Decorated Order of Barristers; named One of Ten Outstanding Young Women of Am., 1987; recipient Herbert J. Garon Young Leadership award Jewish Fedn. Greater New Orleans, 1990; named YWCA Role Model, 1992. Mem. ABA, N.Y. Bar Assn., N.Y. Acad. Scis., Am. Pub. Health Assn., D.C. Bar Assn., Nat. Moot Ct. Honor Soc., Pub. Health Honor Soc., Calif. State Dem. Club (Key Svc. award 1988), Delta Omega.

GERY, JOHN ROY OCTAVIUS, secondary education educator; b. Reading, Pa., June 2, 1953; s. Malcolm Dougherty and Eugenie Gunesh (Guran) Gery. BA in English with honors, Princeton U., 1975; MA in English, U. Chgo., 1976; MA in Creative Writing, Stanford U., 1978. Lectr. English San Jose (Calif.) State U., 1977-79, Stanford (Calif.) U., 1977-79; instr. English U. New Orleans, 1979-84, asst. prof. English, 1984-88, assoc. prof. English, 1988-95, prof. English, creative writing, 1995—; vis. assoc. prof. U. Iowa, Iowa City, 1991, 93; dir. creative writing U. New Orleans, 1986-90, 96; dir. Philological Assn. of La., Lafayette, New Orleans, 1986-88; bd. dirs. New Orleans Poetry Jour. Press, 1987—; second v.p. Gulf Coast Creative Writing Tchrs. Assn., Mobile, Ala., 1996—; Yeats Chair in Poetry Ezra Pound Ctr. for Literature, Brunnenburg Castle, Italy, 1990, 92; resident poet Cummington (Mass.) Cmty. of the Arts, 1993. Author: Charlemagne: A Song of Gestures, 1983, The Enemies of Leisure, 1995, Nuclear Annihilation and Contemporary American Poetry, 1996; author various poems. Treas. Educators for Social Responsibility, New Orleans, 1982-90; co-chair political action New Orleans Progressive Alliance, 1986-90. Recipient Deep South Poetry awards Deep South Writers Conf., Lafayette, 1984, 87, Critics' Choice award for Poetry, 1995-96; poetry fellow Wesleyan U. Writers Conf., Middletown, Conn., 1989; creative writing fellow Nat. Endowment for the Arts, 1992-93. Mem. Assoc. Writing Programs, Poets & Writers, Modern Language Assn., La. State Poetry Soc. Democrat. Office: U New Orleans Dept English Lakefront New Orleans LA 70148-0001

GETMAN, ROBERTA See PEARL, ROBERTA LOUISE

GETTING, VLADO ANDREW, medical and public health educator, consultant; b. Pitts., July 20, 1910; s. Milan Alexander and Harriet (Almasy) G.; m. Rose Madeline Klaus, Dec. 2, 1937 (dec. June 1992). AB wih honors, Johns Hopkins U., 1931; MD, Harvard U., 1935, MPH magna cum laude, 1939, DrPH cum laude, 1940. Diplomate Am. Bd. Preventive Medicine and Pub. Health. Asst. epidemiologist Mass. Dept. Pub. Health, Boston, 1937-39, epidemiologist, 1939-40; commr. pub. health City of Worcester, Mass., 1941-42; commr. Mass. Dept. Pub. Health, Boston, 1943-53; prof. pub. health practice U. Mich. Sch. Pub. Health, Ann Arbor, 1953-61, prof., chmn. dept. community health, 1961-73; prof., chmn. dept. allied health svcs. U. Ctrl. Fla., Orlando, 1973-75; asst. dir. community medicine, dept. med. edn. Fla. Hosp., Orlando, 1975—; clin. prof. U. South Fla., Tampa, 1976—; mem. adv. com. resident program in preventive medicine Palm Beach County Health Dept., 1978—; cons. Mayflower Retirement Ctr. Health Ctr., Winter Park, Fla., 1991—; cons. in preventive medicine USAF, 1965-66; cons. in pub. health to many states, Can. provinces and cities and counties. Author more than 125 pub. health publs.; numerous talks, articles and radio and TV programs. Bd. dirs., chmn. bd. dirs. Mayflower Retirement Ctr., 1975-91; U.S. rep. to 3d World Health Assembly, Geneva. Recipient numerous cers. for svc. from various State of Fla. agys., 1975—. Mem. AMA, Fla. Med. Assn., Orange County Med. Assn., Am. Pub. Health Assn. (various offices), Mass. Med. Assn. (non-resident mem.). Congregationalist. Home: 1630 Mayflower Ct Apt B109 Winter Park FL 32792-2568 Office: Fla Hosp Dept Med Edn 2501 N Orange Ave Ste 235 Orlando FL 32804-4641

GETZ, LOWELL VERNON, financial advisor; b Schenectady, Feb. 28, 1932; s Leon and Harriet Esther (Friedman) G.; BS in Econs., U. Pa., 1953; MBA, Harvard U., 1955; m. Judith Ruth Schwartz, Oct. 14, 1956; children: Marshall, Andrew. Treas., R. Dixon Speas Assos., Inc., Manhasset, N.Y., 1969-72, Coverdale & Colpitts, Inc., N.Y.C., 1972-74; fin. mgr. Bovay Engrs., Inc., Houston, 1974-79; sec., treas. Rice Center, Houston, 1979-82; guest lectr. U. Houston, 1980-81, Harvard Grad. Sch. Design, 1985—; overseas instr. Hong Kong Mgmt. Assn., 1986—, Advanced Mgmt. Inst. for Architecture & Engring., 1993-95; cons. in fin. mgmt. to architects, engring. firms., 1980—; overseas instr. Tongji U., Shanghai, People's Republic of China, 1990, Shanghai Mcpl. Constrn. Commn., 1992, Assn. Consulting Engrs., London, 1995; condr. seminars in field. Served as lt. USNR, 1955-58. Mem. Profl. Svcs. Mgmt. Assn. (pres. 1988, treas. 1981-82, bd. dirs. 1979-88, 86-88), Tex. Soc. CPAs (chmn. mgmt. adv. svcs. com. Houston chpt. 1982-83), Am. Inst. CPAs (mem. various mgmt. adv. svcs. subcoms. 1981-87), Am. Soc. Appraisers (sr.), Inst. Mgmt. Cons. (cert.). Author: Financial Management and Project Control for Consulting Engineers, 1983; Financial Management for the Design Professional, 1984, Business Management in the Smaller Design Firm, 1986, Managing Ownership Transition in Design Firms, 1987, Mergers, Acquisitions, and Sales, 1987; co-author: Ownership Transition, Options and Strategies, 1996; contbg. editor: Valuation Survey of Design Firms, 1991-95, Insider's Guide to Cashing in on your Equity in an A/E/P or Environmental Consulting Firm, 1993, Architect's Handbook of Professional Practice, 1993, Financial Management for Design Firms, 1994; contbr. articles to profl. publs. Home: 11701 Spriggs Way Houston TX 77024-2615 Office: 820 Gessner Rd Ste 265 Houston TX 77024-4258

GETZ, MORTON ERNEST, medical facility director, gastroenterologist; b. Bklyn., May 22, 1930; s. Jacob Michael and Regina (Kohn) G.; m. Carol Washer, Aug. 12, 1956; children: Jacob Michael, Deborah Etta. AB, Emory U., 1950; MS, Purdue U., 1952; MD, Wake Forest U., 1956. Intern Jackson Meml. Hosp., Miami, Fla., 1956-57; resident in medicine Jackson Meml. Hosp., 1957-58; sr. surgeon NIH, Atlanta and Bethesda, Md., 1958-60; chief resident in medicine Jackson Meml. Hosp., 1960; NIH fellow in gastroenterology U. Miami, 1960-61; pvt. practice internal medicine and gastroenterology Coral Gables, Fla.; mem. courtesy staff South Miami Hosp.; attending physician Cedars Med. Ctr. Contbr. articles to profl. jours. With

USPHS, 1958-60. Mem. Miami Fla. Gastroenterologic Soc., Dade County Soc. Internal Medicine, Am. Soc. Internal Medicine, So. Med. Assn., Fla. Med. Assn., Dade County Med. Assn., AMA, Ind. Acad. Scis., N.C. Acad. Sci., Phi Rho Sigma. Democrat. Jewish. Office: # 370 14100 Palmetto Frontage Rd Miami Lakes FL 33016

GEWIRTZMAN, GARRY BRUCE, dermatologist; b. Albany, N.Y., Mar. 26, 1947; s. Benjamin Joseph and Mary (Leibowitz) G.; m. Sheila Ellen Cuba, July 4, 1971; children: Beth Lauren, Aron Jeffrey. BA, Rutgers U., 1969; MD, Albany Med. Coll., 1973. Diplomate Am. Bd. Dermatology. Intern U. Miami (Fla.), 1973-74; resident in dermatology SUNY-Buffalo, 1974-77; practice medicine specializing in dermatology; attending staff Humana Hosp., Plantation (Fla.) Gen. Hosp.; pres. Arbet Enterprises Inc. Author: Smooth as a Baby's Bottom, Skin Care Tips and Skin Sense; contbr. articles to profl. jours. Fellow Am. Acad. Dermatology; mem. AMA, Fla. Med. Assn., Broward County Med. Assn., Fla. Soc. Dermatology, Soc. Dermatol. Genetics, Broward Bus. and Profl. Assn. (pres.), Broward County Dermatol. Soc. Office: Bennett Med Park 201 NW 82nd Ave Plantation FL 33324-7808

GEX, WALTER JOSEPH, III, federal judge; b. Bay St. Louis, Miss., Mar. 20, 1939. BA, U. Miss., LLB, 1963. Bar: Miss. 1963. With Satterfield, Shell, Williams & Buford, Jackson, Miss., 1963-72, ptnr., 1966-72; ptnr. Gex, Gex & Phillips, Bay St. Louis, Miss., 1972-86; judge U.S. Dist. Ct. (so. dist.) Miss., Biloxi, 1986—. Fellow Miss. State Bar Found.; mem. Fed. Bar Assn., Miss. State Bar Assn.. Republican. Roman Catholic. Office: US Dist Ct 725 Washington Loop Rm 238 Biloxi MS 39530-2267

GEYER, BILL R., lawyer; b. Hodgenville, Ky., Dec. 6, 1948; s. Walter Richard and Frances D. (Jaggers) G. BA, U. Okla., 1970; JD, U. Tulsa, 1975. Bar: Okla. 1975. Staff atty. Okla. Dept. of Human Svcs., Oklahoma City, 1975-84; pvt. practice Norman, Okla., 1984—; assoc. Grethen, Blythe and Tracy, Purcell, Okla., 1988-89. Editor: Directory of Legal Resources for Older Americans, 1982. Recipient Cert. of Recognition Legal Svcs. Corp., 1983; named mem. Hon. Order Ky. Cols. Mem. ABA (young lawyers div. com. on delivery of legal svcs. to elderly 1978-83, co-chmn. 1981-82, exec. coun. 1983-84, young lawyers div. Nat. Community Law Week com. 1981-84, exec. coun. 1983-84, mem. sect. family law 1991—), Okla. Bar Assn. (lawyer referral com. 1983-84, Law Day com. 1982-84, law related edn. com. 1986—, young lawyer div. Community Law Week com. 1982-84, chmn. 1982-83, young lawyers div. legal svcs. to the elderly 1978-83, mem. sect. family law 1992—, Dean Earl Sneed award 1982, Cert. of Appreciation 1984), Cleveland County Bar Assn. Baptist. Home: 2612 Lynnwood Cir Norman OK 73072 Office: PO Box 721632 Norman OK 73070

GEYER, FREDERICK FRANCIS, chemical company executive; b. Hopkins, Min., Dec. 3, 1949; s. Lester E. and Viol Marie (Moran) G.; m. Karen Ann Lowe, July 3, 1971; children—Brian, Stephanie. B.S., St. Mary's Coll., Minn., 1971; M.S., Purdue U., 1974, Ph.D., 1979. Research scientist Kodak Research Labs., Rochester, 1979-82, sr. research scientist, 1982-83; dep. head U.S. Apparatus div., 1983-85, mgr. systems devel. Mass Memory Bus. unit, 1985; gen. mgr. magneto-optic drive and media Verbatim, Sunnyvale, Calif., 1985-88; dir. optical recording divsn. Kodak Rsch. Labs., dir. R&D mass memory divsn., 1988-89, dir. electronic Imaging Rsch. Labs., 1989-91; assoc. dir. Imaging Rsch. Labs., 1991-93, gen. mgr., v.p. CD Imaging, 1993-94; v.p. mktg. and sales Digital & Applied Imaging, 1994-95; v.p. Equipment and Software Design Ctr., 1995-96; sr. v.p. digital video Tex. Instruments, Dallas, 1996—. Patentee in optical disks. Mem. Sigma Xi, Sigma Pi Sigma. Office: Tex Instruments 13510 N Central Expy Dallas TX 75243

GEYER, G. NICHOLAS, investment banker; b. Cape May, N.J., June 24, 1951; s. George B. and Rosalind C. (Myers) G.; m. Theresa F. Arbach Geyer, Feb. 14, 1984; children: Nicole Christine, Sean Alexander. Pres. pvt. practice, Cape May Court House, N.J., 1976-79; dir. Fine Art Internat. Investment, Cape May Court House, N.J., 1980-84; dir. Trade and Fine Art Internat. Investment & Trade, Ocala, Fla., 1984—. Mem. Internat. Soc. Financiers, Irish Wolfhound Club Am. Office: Internat Investment & Trade 3341 SE 45th St Ocala FL 34480-8485

GHALY, EVONE SHEHATA, pharmaceutics and industrial pharmacy educator; b. Cairo; d. Shehata Ghaly Shenouda and Amalia Elias Tadros; m. Nagdy Roshdy Mehany; children: Maichel Nagdy Roshdy, Mary Nagdy Roshdy. B in Pharm. Scis., Assiut U., Egypt, 1970; M in Pharm. Sci., Cairo U., 1979, PhD of Pharmaceutics, 1984; postdoctoral fellow, Phila. Coll. Pharm., 1986-88. Specialist and pharmacist in R&D Arab Drug Co., Cairo, 1970-75, sr. pharmacist in R&D, mgr. rsch. devel., 1975-86; assoc. rschr. Phila. Coll. Pharm., 1988-89; vis. prof., asst. prof. Sch. Pharmacy U. P.R., San Juan, 1989-92, assoc. prof., 1992—; cons. Smith Kline & Beecham, Inc., P.R., 1990—, Eli Lilly found., P.R., 1993—, Merck Sharp and Dohme Inc., P.R., 1994; instr., lectr. FDA, 1991, Warmer Lambert Inc., P.R., 1993-94, Ciba Geigy Inc., P.R., 1995. Contbr. articles to profl. jours. Grantee Colorcon Pharm. Inc., 1993-94, Baker Norton Pharm. Inc., 1993, INDUNIV Rsch. Ctr., 1990-92, 92-93, IBM, NIH-BRSG, 1991-92, Knoll AG Co., 1983, others. Mem. AAAS, Fed. Internat. Pharmaceutics, Am. Assn. Pharm. Scientists, Am. Pharm. Assn., Am. Assn. Coll. Pharmacy, Controlled Release and Bioactive Material, Sigma Xi, Rho Chi. Home: Condominio Puerta Sol 2000 San Juan PR 00926 Office: Univ PR Sch Pharmacy GPO Box 5067 San Juan PR 00936

GHOLSON, HUNTER MAURICE, lawyer; b. Columbus, Miss., Feb. 19, 1933; s. Leonidas Carter and Hunter Marie (McDonell) G.; m. Hortense Jones, June 3, 1961; children: Emily Gholson Bailey, William Webster. BA, U. Miss., 1954, LLB, 1955, JD, 1955. Bar: Miss. 1955, U.S. Ct. Appeals (5th and 11th cirs.) 1955, D.C. 1975, U.S. Supreme Ct. 1975. Ptnr. Gholson, Hicks & Nichols, Columbus, Miss., 1959—; sec., dir. Columbus Marble Works, Inc., 1970—, NBC Capital Corp., Starkville, Miss., 1984—; dir. Gulf States Mfr., Starkville, 1968-94. Sr. warden St. Paul's Ch., Columbus, 1990-93. Lt. USNR, 1955-59. Mem. Old Waverly Golf Club. Episcopalian. Home: 1100 N 6th St Columbus MS 39701 Office: Gholson Hicks & Nichols 605 2nd Ave N Columbus MS 39701-4567

GIALLANZA, CHARLES PHILIP, lawyer; b. Hornell, N.Y., Nov. 18, 1950; s. Charles Joseph Jr. and Rena Eugena (Foster) G.; 1 child: Charles Edward. AS in Aerospace Sci., U. Albuquerque, 1977; BA in Polit. Sci. and English, U. South Fla., 1979; JD, John Marshall Law Sch., 1982. Bar: Ga. 1983, U.S. Dist. Ct. (no. dist.) Ga. 1983; cert. air traffic contr. FAA. With USAF, 1971-79; air traffic contr. USAF Res., Tampa, 1977-79, Dobbins AFB, 1980-81; air traffic contr. USN Res., Dobbins AFB; assoc. James B. Pilcher, Atlanta, 1982-83; pvt. practice Snellville, Ga., 1983—. Advocate assisting Cubans detained in Atlanta prison, 1985, 86; capt. Ga. Def. Force, 1985-86. Recipient photography awards USAF, 1975. Mem. Ga. Bar Assn., Atlanta Bar Assn., Gwinnet Bar Assn. (law day com. 1987-88). Office: 3881 Stone Mountain Fwy Ste 5 Snellville GA 30278

GIANCOLA, JOYCE A., psychotherapist; b. Youngstown, Ohio, Nov. 12, 1948; d. Benedict Paul Giancola and Annis Mary (Fieldhouse) Mahan; 1 child, Mary Stephanie Bolton. BS in Psychology and Sociology, Kennesaw (Ga.) State Coll., 1989; MS in Cmty. Counseling, Ga. State U., 1991, EdS in Cmty. Counseling, 1992; postgrad., U. Ga., 1995. Lic. profl. counselor; nat. cert. counselor; cert. Nat. Bd. Cert. Clin. Hypnotherapists. Counselor Atlanta Women's Ctr., 1988-89; vice chmn. jud. citizens rev. panel Cobb County Juvenile Ct., Marietta, Ga., 1992-96; pvt. practice psychotherapy, Atlanta, 1996—; coord. rsch. project maternal substance abuse study dept. psychiatry Emory U. Sch. Mediciine, Atlanta, 1990—; presenter in field to profl. confs., schs. and organs; group facilitator for incest survivors, nurturing parent facilitator Ga. Coun. on Child Abuse, Atlanta. Co-author: The Children's Program, Preventing Domestic Violence: Therapeutic Intervention with Young Children, 1993. Vol. counselor Cobb County Rape Crisis Ctr., Marietta, 1987-89; project coord. VISTA Ret. Sr. Vols., Marietta. Recipient Golden Rule award J.C. Penney, 1992. Mem. ACA, Southeastern Region Assn. for Women in Psychology, Ga. Coun. on Child Abuse, Atlanta Play Therapy Assn., Atlanta Hypnosis Soc. Home: 120 Bramble Oak Dr Woodstock GA 30188 Office: Emory Sch Medicine 1256 Briarcliff Rd Rm 323W Atlanta GA 30306

GIANELLI, VICTOR F., mathematics and physics educator; b. Valparaiso, Chile, June 27, 1939; came to the U.S., 1966; s. Santiago and Elena Teresa (Gil) G.; m. Margaret Kay Carter, Feb. 3, 1967; children: Paul, James. BS, U. So. Colo., 1970; MA, U. No. Colo., 1973. Cert. secondary edn. in math. and physics. Physics and chemistry tchr. Re-3 Platte Valley Sch. Dist., Sedgwick, Colo., 1970-75; head physics divsn. Chilean Ministry of Edn., Santiago, 1975-78; math. and physics tchr. Ysleta Ind. Sch. Dist., El Paso, Tex., 1978—; math, physics and electronics instr. El Paso (Tex.) C.C., 1979—; state textbook selection com. mem. Tex. Edn. Agy., Austin, 1982; prin.'s adv. com. pres. Riverside H.S., El Paso, 1986-87; math curriculum alignment mem. Ysleta Ind. Sch. Dist., El Paso, 1992-95. Co-author: Projecto de Mejoramiento de la Ensenanza de la Fisica, 1977, Curriculum Para la Ensenanza de la Fisica, 1977. Recipient Student Body award Revere Student Coun., Sedgewick, 1975; named Tchr. of Most Influence by Ex-Students, MIT, Cambridge, 1980. Mem. NEA, Nat. Coun. Math. Tchr., Tex. State Tchrs. Assn., Greater El Paso Coun. Tchrs. Math. Home: 1948 Preview Pl El Paso TX 79936

GIANGROSSO, PATRICIA ANN, editorial consultant; b. New Orleans, Mar. 14, 1948; d. James Louis and Nola Patricia (Hebert) G. BA cum laude, Loyola U. of the South, 1969; MA, U. N.C., 1972, PhD, 1978. English tchr. part time St. Ursula Schule, Geisenheim, Germany, 1973-75; lab. instr. U. N.C., Chapel Hill, 1969-70, teaching asst., 1970-73, 76-78; asst. prof. German N.E. La. U., Monroe, 1978-87; data control specialist Tulane Med. Sch., New Orleans, 1991-94; editorial cons. La. State U. Med. Ctr., New Orleans, 1994—; adj. prof. German, Univ. Coll. of Tulane U., New Orleans, 1989-90, Delgado C.C., New Orleans, 1991—. Contbr. articles to profl. jours. Recipient stipend Norwegian Fgn. Ministry to attend U. Bergen, 1977, NEH Summer stipend, 1979, NEH Summer Rsch. stipend, 1980, NEH stipend, 1982. Mem. La. Classical Assn. (sec./treas. 1994-96), Southeastern Medieval Assn., South Atlantic MLA, Am. Assn. Tchrs. German (sec./treas., newsletter editor La. chpt. 1985-89), The Medieval Acad. Office: La State U Med Ctr Dept Pediatrics 1542 Tulane Ave Rm 827 New Orleans LA 70112-2822

GIARDINA, SUSAN PETRINI, association executive; b. Alexandria, Va., Mar. 3, 1967; d. Bart and Rosemary (DiRicci) Petrini; m. Christopher Evan Giardina, Oct. 26, 1991; 1 child, Nicholas Francis. BS in Hotel & Restaurant Mgmt., U. Nev., 1989. Student mgr. Marriott Food Svc. and Mgmt., Las. Vegas, Nev., 1986-89; sr. housekeeping mgr. Santa Clara (Calif.) Marriott, 1989-92; meeting and event coord. Innovative Mgmt., Charleston, W.Va., 1992-95; dir. membership svcs. and meeting planning Fur Info. Coun. Am., Herndon, Va., 1995—. Event coord. Deepwood Homeowner Assn., Reston, Va., 1996. Mem. Am. Soc. Assn. Execs. Roman Catholic. Office: Fur Info Coun Am 655 15th St # 320 Washington DC 20005

GIARRANO, THOMAS, marketing executive; b. Cleve., June 26, 1953; s. James Bartholamew and Joanna Maria (Sclimenti) G.; m. Mandy Panfil, May 12, 1979; children: Luciano, Gabriella, Nicolo. Grad. high sch., Twinsburg, Ohio. Acct. C.W. Kollman, P.A., Twinsburg, 1972-73, R.M. Beatty, CPA, Mayfield Village, Ohio, 1973; acct., owner Thomas Giarrano Acctg. Svcs., Princeton, Ind., 1973-79; dir. fin. svcs. Scott Carpet Mills, Inc., Beachwood, Ohio, 1979-81; dir. ops. The Scott Group, Inc., Beachwood, 1981-83, S.W. mktg. dir., 1983-84; mfg. and operational cons. (textile) T. Giarrano & Assoc., Atlanta, 1984-87; v.p. EPI Internat., Inc., Atlanta, 1987-92, C and N Systems Corp., Marietta, Ga., 1992—; mem. exec. com. PEI Internat., Inc.; mktg. cons. for tech. industry start-ups, 1992—; registered rep. The Equitable, Atlanta, 1993—. Elder, min. East Cobb Congregation Jehovah's Witness, Marietta, Ga., 1986—. Office: The Equitable 3414 Peachtree Rd NE Ste 1000 Atlanta GA 30326-1113

GIBBES, WILLIAM HOLMAN, lawyer; b. Hartsville, S.C., Feb. 25, 1930; s. Ernest Lawrence and Nancy (Watson) G.; m. Frances Hagood, May 1, 1954; children: Richard H., William H. Jr., Lynn. BS, U. S.C., 1952, LLB, 1953. Bar: S.C. 1953, U.S. Ct. Mil. Appeals 1954, U.S. Dist. Ct. S.C. 1956, U.S. Supreme Ct. 1959, U.S. Ct. Appeals (4th cir.) 1965. Asst. atty. gen. Columbia, S.C., 1957-62; ptnr. Berry & Gibbes, Columbia, 1962-68, Berry, Lightsey, Gibbes, Columbia, 1968-72; mem. Gibbes Law Firm, P.A., Columbia, 1985—; house of dels. S.C. Bar, 1994-96; chief judge U.S. Army Legal Svcs. Agy., 1980-83. Author: Control of Highway Access - Its Prospects and Problems, Legal Dimensions of Community Health Planning, 1969; mem. Law Rev. Digest, 1960. Chmn. bd. dirs. U. S.C. YMCA. Brig. gen. JAGC, USAR 1980-83. Recipient Legion of Merit, U.S. Army, 1983. Mem. ABA (mil. laws com. 1984-90, meml. com.), S.C. Bar Assn. (exec. com. 1961-62), Am. Bd. Trial Advocates (sec.-treas. 1994-95, pres-elect 1995-96, pres. 1996-97), Judge Advs. Assn. (pres. 1982-83), Richmond County Bar Assn., S.C. Credit Ins. Assn. (gen. counsel 1963-94), Tarantella Club, Caprician Club, Summit Club, Forest Lake Country Club, Kiawah Island Club, Kappa Sigma Kappa, Omicron Delta Kappa. Episcopalian. Home: 287 Windward Point Rd Columbia SC 29212-8417 Office: 1518 Washington St Columbia SC 29201-3469

GIBBINS, BOB, lawyer; b. Seminole, Okla., Feb. 27, 1936; s. Robert Lee and La-Ceile Rene (Shackelford) G.; m. Suzanne K. Gibbins (div. Oct. 1975); children: Bob Jr., Steven, Jenny Durbin Kyndall Krebs; m. Pam Reed, Feb. 26, 1982. BBA, U. Tex., 1958, LLB, 1961. Bar: Tex. 1961, U.S. Dist. Ct. (no. dist.) Tex. 1961, U.S. Ct. Appeals (5th cir.) 1971, U.S. Supreme Ct. 1974, Colo. 1991; diplomate Am. Bd. Trial Advs., Am. Bd. Profl. Liability Attys. Assoc. Morehead, Sharpe, Tisdale & Gibbins, Plainview, Tex., 1961-71; ptnr. Gibbins & Spivey, Austin, Tex., 1971-76; pvt. practice, Austin, 1976-78; sr. ptnr. Gibbins, Wash and Bratton, Austin, 1978-79, Gibbins, Burrow, Wash & Bratton, Austin, 1979-81, Gibbins, Burrow & Bratton, Austin, 1981-86, Gibbins & Bratton, Austin, 1986-89, Gibbins, Winckler & Bayer, Austin, 1989-91, Gibbins, Winckler & Harvey, Austin, 1991—. Co-author: Texas Practical Guide: Personal Injury, 1988, Products Liability Litigation: Trial Strategy, 1988. Recipient War Horse award So. Trial Lawyers Assn., 1991, Faculty Svc. award, Univ. Tex. Sch. of Law, 1992; Bob Gibbins endowed presdl. scholarship named in his honor U. Tex. Sch. of Law, Austin, 1991. Fellow Internat. Acad. Trial Lawyers, Internat. Soc. Barristers, State Bar Tex., Coll. of the State Bar Tex.; mem. Assn. Trial Lawyers Am. (pres. 1991-92), Nat. Bd. Trial Advocacy (civil trial adv.), Trial Lawyers for Pub. Justice (bd. dir.s 1993), Tex. Trial Lawyers Assn. (dir. emeritus). Office: 500 W 13th St Austin TX 78701-1827

GIBBONS, CELIA VICTORIA TOWNSEND (MRS. JOHN SHELDON), editor, publisher; b. Fargo, N.D.; d. Harry Alton and Helen (Haag) Townsend; student U. Minn., 1930-33; m. John Sheldon Gibbons, May 1, 1935; children: Mary Vee, John Townsend. Advt. mgr. Hotel Nicollet, Mpls., 1933-37; contbg. editor children's mags., 1935—; partner Youth Assos. Co., Mpls., 1942-65; pub. art dir. Mines and Escholier mags., 1954-65; founder Bull. Bd. Pictures, Inc., Mpls., 1954, pres., 1954—; founder Periodical Litho Art Co., Mpls., 1962, pres., 1962-65; artist Cath. Boy mag., 1938; artist, designer book Palaces That Went To Sea, 1990; chief photographer Cath. Miss mag., 1955. Mem. Women's aux. Mpls. Symphony Orch.; mem. Fort Lauderdale (Fla.) Art. Mus. Republican chairwoman Golden Valley, Minn., 1950; alternate del. Hennepin County Rep. Conv., 1962. Mem. Mpls. Inst. Arts, Internat. Inst., St. Paul Arts and Sci., Art Guild Boca Raton. Clubs: Woman's, Minikahda; Deerfield Beach Women's. Home: 1416 Alpine Pass Tyrol Hills Minneapolis MN 55416 Office: 1057 Hillsboro Mile Hillsboro Beach FL 33062

GIBBONS, JULIA SMITH, federal judge; b. Pulaski, Tenn., Dec. 23, 1950; d. John Floyd and Julia Jackson (Abernathy) Smith; m. William Lockhart Gibbons, Aug. 11, 1973; children: Rebecca Carey, William Lockhart Jr. B.A., Vanderbilt U., 1972; J.D., U. Va., 1975. Bar: Tenn. 1975. Law clk. to judge U.S. Ct. Appeals, 1975-76; assoc. Farris, Hancock, Gilman, Branan, Lanier & Hellen, Memphis, 1976-79; legal advisor Gov. Lamar Alexander, Nashville, 1979-81; judge 15th Jud. Cir., Memphis, 1981-83, U.S. Dist. Ct. (we. dist.) Tenn., Memphis, 1983—. Fellow Am. Bar Found., Tenn. Bar Found.; mem. ABA, Tenn. Bar Assn., Memphis Bar Assn., Order of Coif, Phi Beta Kappa. Presbyterian. Office: US Dist Ct 1157 Federal Bldg 167 N Main St Memphis TN 38103-1816

GIBBONS, MICHAEL LAWRENCE, software engineer; b. New Haven, Conn., May 15, 1969; s. Robert Joseph and Kathryn Antoinette (Sheldon) G.; m. Mary Juanita Dewhirst, Apr. 15, 1992. Student, Villanova U., 1986-88; AS, Ohlone Coll., Fremont, Calif., 1990-92; BS in Computer Sci. Engring., U. Tex., Arlington, 1994. Systems engr. Tandy Corp., Phila., 1986-87; systems engring. mgr. Tandy Corp., Orange, Conn., 1988; systems engr. Grid Systems, Stamford, Conn., 1989; mktg. mgr. Grid Systems, Fremont, Calif., 1990-92, Fort Worth, 1992-93; instr. U. Tex., Arlington, 1994; software engr. Digital Print, Inc., Ft. Worth, 1995-96; systems engr. Telxon Corp., Dallas, 1996—. Mem. Aircraft Owners and Pilots Assn., Alpha Gamma Sigma. Home: 1814 Hunters Ridge Dr Grapevine TX 76051-7923

GIBBS, JAMES ALANSON, geologist; b. Wichita Falls, Tex., June 18, 1935; s. James Ford and Clovis (Robinson) G.; m. Judith Walker, June 18, 1966; children: Ford W., John A. BS, U. Okla., 1957, MS, 1962. Cert. profl. geologist. Geologist Calif. Co., New Orleans, 1961-63, Lafayette, La., 1963-64; cons. geologist, oil producer, Dallas, 1964—; pres., CEO Five States Energy Co., 1984—. Author: Finding work as a Petroleum Geologist: Hints to the Jobseeker, 1984. Trustee Inst. for Study Earth and Man, So. Meth. U. Lt. USNR, 1957-59. Recipient William B. Heroy Disting. Svc. award Am. Geol. Inst., 1994. Mem. AAAS, Am. Geological Inst. (trustee), Geol. Soc. Am., Dallas Geol. Soc. (pres. 1975-76, hon. mem. 1986), Am. Assn. Petroleum Geologists (sec. 1983-85, pres. 1990-91, Disting. Svc. award 1987, hon. mem. 1995), Am. Inst. Profl. Geol., Ind. Petroleum Assn. Am., Nat. Petroleum Coun., Tex. Ind. Producers and Royalty Owners Assn., Houston Geol. Soc., Lafayette, La. Geol. Soc., Soc. Ind. Profl. Earth Scientists (past chmn. Dallas chpt.), Petroleum Engrs. Club, Dallas Country Club, Dallas Petroleum, Explorers Club, Sigma Xi, Sigma Gamma Epsilon, Phi Delta Theta. Republican. Methodist. Home: 3514 Caruth Blvd Dallas TX 75225-5001 Office: 4925 Greenville Ave Ste 1220 Dallas TX 75206

GIBBS, JAMES CALVIN, editor, publisher, composer, educator; b. Asheville, N.C., Mar. 28, 1924; s. Jeter Prichard and Inez Louise (Hilton) G.; m. Clara Camps, June 20, 1947 (dec. June 1973); m. Carmen Castell, Jan. 4, 1976; children: Paula Delores Hickman, Javier Octavio Hickman. BA in Human Rels., U. Miami, 1954; graduate, Inst. of Psychorientology, Laredo, Tex., 1973. Chief clk. U.S. Govt., Cherry Point, N.C., 1942; mgr. Pan Am Airways, Miami, 1946-79; tchr. Assoc. Schs., North Miami Beach, Fla., 1980-85; pub., editor Gibbs Pub. Co., North Miami Beach, 1956—. Contbr. articles on parapsychology to various mags. and primary publs. Sgt. USMC, 1943-46. Mem. Am. Parapsychol. Rsch. Found. (charter), Life Dynamics Fellowship (assoc.), Inst. of Cosmic Sci. (charter, Parapsychology award 1977), MENSA. Office: Gibbs Pub Co PO Box 600927 Miami FL 33160-0927

GIBBS, JOHN PATRICK, physician, educator; b. Tecumseh, Nebr., Mar. 17, 1948; s. Leonard Keith and Mary Myrtle (Murphy) G.; m. Elise Marie Buras, Aug. 30, 1973; 1 child, Caroline Michelle. BS in Chem. Engring. with high distinction, U. Nebr., 1970; MD, U. Tex., Galveston, 1976. Diplomate Am. Bd. Preventive Medicine, Nat. Bd. Med. Examiners. Rsch. engr. Shell Oil Co. div. Shell Devel. Co., Houston, 1970-73; resident in internal medicine U. Okla. Health Ctr., Oklahoma City, 1976-77; contract emergency physician Houston, 1980-90, Pasadena, Tex., 1981-91; plant med. dir. Ethyl Corp., Pasadena, 1981-88, asst. corp. med. dir., 1988-91; corp. med. dir. Kerr-McGee Corp., Oklahoma City, 1990-95; v.p. health mgmt. Kee-McGee Corp., Oklahoma City, 1995—. Mem. planning com. community awareness and emergency response Chem. Mfrs. Assn., Harris County, Tex., 1987-89, health programs task group, 1991—; mem. occupational health com. Am. Mining Congress, 1991—. Lt., flight surgeon USMC, USNR, 1977-80. Fellow Am. Coll. Occupational Medicine (sec., treas. Tex. chpt. 1987); mem. AMA (Physicians Recognition award 1981, 85), Okla. State Med. Assn., Tex. Med. Assn. Home: 2201 Augusta Ave Edmond OK 73034-3016 Office: Kerr-McGee Corp PO Box 25861 Oklahoma City OK 73125-0861

GIBBS, ROSE L., interior designer; b. Waynesboro, Ga., July 15, 1940; d. James C. Sr. and Julie Mae (Ward) Lovett; m. Edward Mason Gibbs, Nov. 1967; children: Anthony Wayne, Robert Wesley. BS, U. Ga., 1962. Receptionist FBI, Atlanta; asst. store mgr. Franklin Simon, Atlanta; buyer, mgr. J.C. Penney Co., Atlanta; co-owner, interior designer E. & R. Interiors, Riverdale, Ga., 1971—. Mem. NAFE. Address: 7426 Highway 85 Riverdale GA 30274-3429

GIBERSON, THOMAS PAUL, emergency medicine physician; b. Cedar Rapids, Iowa, Feb. 17, 1949; s. Walker Eugene and Helen Z. (Crenshaw) G.; m. Ram Sorat, Jan. 1, 1973; 1 child, Nahlunat Sorat. BS in Microbiology, Calif. Poly., Pomona, 1977; DO, Coll. Osteo. Medicine & Surg., 1983. Bd. cert. emergency medicine. Chief emergency medicine William Beaumont Army Med. Ctr., El Paso, Tex., 1988-90; asst. dir. emergency dept. Athens (Ga.) Regional Med. Ctr., 1990-91; staff physician Gwinnett Med. Ctr., Laurenceville, Ga., 1991—, chief dept. emergency medicine, 1995—. Mem. Coverdell Bus. Task Force, Atlanta, 1993—. Maj. U.S. Army, 1986—. Fellow Am. Coll. Emergency Physicians; mem. So. Med. Assn., Ga. Coll. Emergency Physicians. Republican. Home: 510 River Bottom Rd Athens GA 30606-1986

GIBILISCO, STANLEY PHILIP, science writer, graphic artist; b. Birmingham, Ala., Sept. 26, 1953; s. Joseph Anthony and Josephine Sterling (Welch) G. BS in Math., U. Minn., 1976; postgrad., Conn. Sch. Broadcasting, 1978, U. Miami, 1985-86, U. Iowa, 1989. Freelance sci. writer and editor Miami, Fla., 1982—; freelance exptl. and abstract artist Miami, 1993—; v.p. Internat. Electronic Sys., Inc., Miami, 1979-81; tech. writer ITT North Electric Co., Cape Canaveral, Fla., 1980; asst. tech. editor QST Mag. Am. Radio Relay League, Newington, Conn., 1978-79, radio station technician, 1977-78. Author: Understanding Einstein's Theories of Relativity, 1983, 91, Japanese edit., 1989, Black Holes, Quasars and Other Mysteries of the Universe, 1984, Violent Weather: Hurricanes, Tornadoes and Storms, 1984, Comets, Meteors and Asteroids: How They Affect Earth, 1985, Mex. edit., 1993, Spanish edit., 1993, Basic Transistor Course, 2d edit., 1985, Encyclopedia of Electronics, 1985, Puzzles, Paradoxes and Brain Teasers, 1990, International Encyclopedia of Integrated Circuits, 1989, Understanding Lasers, 1989, Japanese edit., 1991, More Puzzles, Paradoxes and Brain Teasers, 1990, Reaching for Infinity, 1990, Mex. edit., 1993, Spanish edit., 1993, Optical Illusions, 1990, Mex. edit., 1993, Spanish edit., 1993, International Encyclopedia of Integrated Circuits, 2d edit., 1992, Hot ICs for the Electronics Hobbyist, 1993, Concise Illustrated Dictionary of Science and Technology, 1993, Amateur Radio Encyclopedia, 1993, Teach Yourself Electricity and Electronics, 1993, The Illustrated Dictionary of Electronics, 6th edit., 1994, McGraw-Hill Encyclopedia of Personal Computing, 1995; co-author: The ARRL Technician/General Q&A Book, 1979, The Illustrated Dictionary of Electronics, 3d edit., 1985, Fundamentals of Transducers, 1985, Italian edit., 1987, Principles and Practice of Impedance, 3d edit., 1987, Electronic Conversions, Symbols and Formulas, 2d edit., 1988, The Illustrated Dictionary of Electronics, 4th edit., 1988, Encyclopedia of Electronics, 2d edit., 1990, Italian edit., 1994, The Illustrated Dictionary of Electronics, 5th edit., 1991; contbr. articles to profl. publs.

GIBNEY, PAMELA, physician. BA in Art History, Drew U., 1973; premed, U. Va., 1981-83, U. Tulsa, 1983-85; DO, Okla. State U., 1989. Intern Tulsa Regional Med. Ctr., 1989-90; emergency rm. physician 56th FW Hosp., MacDill AFB, Tampa, Fla., 1990-93; family practice resident Pinellas Cmty. Hosp., Pinellas Park, Fla., 1993-95; pvt. practice emergency room physician St. Petersburg, 1995—. Capt. USAF, 1990-93. Recipient Regeants award, 1989, recognition award Am. Med. Women's Assn.; decorated achievement medal USAF, 1993. Mem. Am. Osteo. Assn., Assn. Mil. Osteo. Physicians and Surgeons, Sigma Sigma Phi, Delta Omega (v.p. 1987-88).

GIBRAN, DANIEL KAHLIL, international relations educator, researcher; b. Hague, Guyana, Nov. 21, 1945; came to U.S., 1991; m. Joan MArie Harrison, Nov. 12, 1976; children: Kerstin Marianne, Nicole Kamala. BA in History and Secondary Edn., Mid. East Coll., Lebanon, 1976; diploma in social scis., U. Stockholm, 1984; MA in Internat. Rels., U. Kent, Canterbury, Eng., 1982; PhD in Internat. Rels., U. Aberdeen, Scotland, 1990; postgrad in Bus. Adminstn., Heriot-Watt U., Scotland; mil. history student, West Point, 1993; nat. security law student, U. Va., 1994. Lic. aircraft dispatcher, FAA. Tutor in politics and internat. rels. U. Aberdeen, 1989-90; sr. economist, researcher Planning Inst. Jamaica, 1987-90; asst. prof. internat. rels. Shaw U., Raleigh, 1991-96; assoc. prof., chmn. dept. history, geography, polit. sci. Tenn. State U., Nashville, 1996—; cons. World

Bank, Washington, 1990, DOD tech. asst. program to HBCUS and minority instns., 1994-95; prin. investigator DOD, Army Pentagon, Washington, 1993-94; lectr. govt. U. W.I., Barbados, 1990-91, Chs. Tchrs. Coll., Mandeville, Jamaica, 1986, Jamaican Inst. Mgmt., Kingston, 1987-89; vis. lectr. internat. rels. and polit. sci. N.C. State U., Raleigh; adminstrv. mgr. Island Life Ins. Co., Ltd., Kingston, 1986-87; participated in numerous profl. confs. Author: Tug of War: Strategy Versus Economics in British Defence Policy, 1994, The Exclusion of Black Soliders from the Medal of Honor: The Study Commissioned by the U.S. Army to Investigate Racial Bias in the Award of the Nation's Highest Military Decoration, 1996, The Falklands War: History, Legality and British Defence Policy, 1997, (with Joe Galloway) Debt of Honor, 1997. Religious liberty dir. Raleigh (N.C.) Seventh-Day Adventist Ch., 1992-94. Mem. Royal United Svcs. Inst. for Def. Studies (U.K.), Coun. for Arms Control (U.K.), U.S. Naval Inst., Def. Intelligence Coll. Found. Home: 428 Raleighview Rd Raleigh NC 27610-4624

GIBSON, BARBARA ARLENE, nurse, writer; b. Port Jefferson, N.Y., July 6, 1942; d. David M. and Marion G. (Nyman) Ramos; m. Robert R. Gibson, Feb. 10, 1979; children: Joan M. Gunther, Karen L. Mullins. AAS, Suffolk County C.C., 1976. RN, Fla. Team leader Tarpon Springs (Fla.) Gen. Hosp., 1977-80; office mgr. Bob's Concrete Pumping Svc., Clearwater, Fla., 1980-89; nurse team leader St. Anthony's Hosp., St. Petersburg, Fla., 1981-89; founder Fibromyalgia Network Greater Tampa Bay, Fla., 1989-90; lectr. on fibromyalgia syndrome, 1989—; freelance writer. Author, pub.: The Fibromyalgia Handbook, 1990, 2d edit., 1995, Fibromyalgia: Exploring the Possibilities, Vol. I, Sumatriptan, 1994; freelance writer; former med. columnist Suncoast CFIOS Support Group Newsletter. Home: 1443 Mission Dr W Clearwater FL 34619-2744 Office: Gemini Press PO Box 4546 Clearwater FL 34618-4546

GIBSON, CHARLES WALTER, minister; b. Jersey City, N.J., Feb. 16, 1930; m. Reva Jean Taylor, June 16, 1951; children: Charles Michael, Stephen Taylor, Dwayne Watkins. Student, U. Richmond, 1948-52. Pastor Graceland Bapt. Ch., Clayville, Va., 1951-53, Cosby Meml. Bapt. Ch., Richmond, Va., 1953-61, Emmanuel Bapt. Ch., Manassas, Va., 1961-66, 67-71, Bethlehem Bapt. Chapel now Lyndale Bapt. Ch., Richmond, 1966-67, Oak Grove Bapt. Ch., Richmond, 1971-78, Wilroy Bapt. Ch., Suffolk, Va., 1978-81, Amelia Bapt. Ch., Amelia Court House, Va., 1981-87, Woodbine Bapt. Ch., Manassas, 1987-92; intentional interim pastor Cornerstone Bapt. Ch., Falmouth, Va., 1992-94, Kentwood Heights Bapt. Ch., Quinton, Va., 1994-96, Hillcrest Bapt. Ch., Mechanicsville, Va., 1996—; participant numerous missions; chaplain Prince William County Hosp., Manassas, 1969-71, Chippenham Hosp., Richmond, 1973-78, Louise Obici Meml. Hosp., 1979-81, assoc. chaplain Chippenham Hosp., 1992-96; Sunday sch. supt. Potomac Assn., 1971, vice moderator, 1971; mem. teaching staff Eagle Eyrie Sunday Sch. and Ch. Tng. Trustee Children's Home of Va. Bapt., Inc., 1996—; pres. Woodstock Civic Assn.; officer local PTA; mem. edn. com. Richmond chpt. Nat. Found. Ileitis and Colitis; mem. police chaplaincy program Suffolk Police Dept., 1980; mem. exec. com. and com. on pub. edn. Alcohol-Narcotics Edn. Coun., Inc. of Va. Chs.; moderator Amelia Interfaith Coun., 1982-84, 86-87; coord. chaplaincy program Prince William Hosp., 1988-92; commr. Prince William Commn. on the Future, 1989-90; bd. dirs. Coalition of Human Svcs., 1990-92, Prince William Interfaith Vol. Caregivers Program, 1990-92. Home: 19510 Oakwood Ln Jetersville VA 23083

GIBSON, ERNEST L., III, healthcare consultant; b. Baton Rouge, Oct. 29, 1945; s. Ernest L. Jr. and Ethel (Dunning) G.; m. Susan R. Wilson, Aug. 29, 1970; children: E. Lee, Elizabeth K. BS in Pharmacy, U. of the Pacific, 1968, PharmD, 1969. Resident hosp. pharmacy U. Tex. Med. Br., Galveston, 1972; assoc. dir. pharmacy U. Calif. Med. Ctr., Sacramento, 1970-78; dir. pharmacy mgmt. Svc. Master Industries, Downers Grove, Ill., 1978-82; exec. v.p. DOSE Sys., 1982-93; pres. HealthCare Solutions Group, Plano, 1992—; lectr. Sacramento Jr. Coll., 1975-78. Stephens min. Custer Rd. United Meth. Ch., Plano, Tex., adminstrv. bd. dirs., 1984-87; bd. dirs. Lupus Found. North Tex. Mem. Health Info. Mgrs. Soc., Am. Soc. Hosp. Pharmacists, Tex. Soc. Hosp. Pharmacists (bd. dirs. 1976-77, chmn. legal affairs com.), Sacramento Valley Soc. Hosp. Pharmacists (prs. 1975), Jaycees (state chmn. drug abuse campaign 1976). Republican. Home: 4549 Miami Dr Plano TX 75093-5511 Office: Healthcare Solutions Group 4549 Miami Plano TX 75093

GIBSON, (RAMONA) FERNE G(RIMMETT), assistant principal, music coordinator; b. Lawlon, W.Va., June 9, 1939; d. Oakley Oren and Wilsie Graden (Massie) Grimmett; m. Robert G. Gibson, Aug. 18, 1962; children: Thomas Loring, Anne Paige Gibson Wilson. BS in Music Edn., U. Richmond; MEd in Adminstrn. and Supervision, West Ga. Coll. Music tchr. Newport News (Va.) Pub. Schs., 1961-62, Charlotte (N.C.) Pub. Schs., 1963-67; music cons. Raleigh (N.C.) Pub. Schs., 1967-73; music specialist Pepperell Elem. Sch., Lindale, Ga., 1973-79, Pepperell Mid. Sch., Lindale, Ga., 1979-81; asst. prin. Pepperell H.S., Lindale, Ga., 1986—; music coord. Floyd County Schs., Rome, Ga., 1979—; evaluation coms. So. Assn. Colls. and Schs., 1978, 84, 87, 89, 92, 93, 94; cons. Whitfield County Schs., 1988; rewrite com. Tchr. Cert. Test in Music, State of Ga., 1987-90, 93-94; interview/audition com. Gov.'s Honors Program, annually; curriculum guide developer and editor; workshop leader. Bd. dirs. Regal Day Care Ctr., Rome Area Coun. for Arts, Rome Boys Choir/Children's Choir, Christmas in Rome, Coosa River Christmas, Heritage Holidays, Mayfest On the Rivers, Rome Sesquecentennial; program chair, v.p. Cedartown Federated Music Club; vol. Cedartown Civic Auditorium; com. mem. Olympic Arts and Cultural Events; active Friends of Dance Arts, Cedartown Cmty. Chorus, Bus. and Profl. Women's Club. Named Music Educator of Yr., Pub. Sch. Divsn., Am. Music Conf., 1981. Mem. Floyd County Assn. Educators (pub. rels. chair), Ga. Assn. Educators (conv. del 1978, State Pub. Rels. award), NEA, Ga. Music Educators Assn. (chair dist. VII elem. divsn.), Music Educators Nat. Conf. (conv. del.), ASCD, Ga. ASCD, Ga. Assn. Ednl. Leaders, Alpha Delta Kappa (pres.), Sigma Alpha Iota, Phi Delta Kappa. Home: 10 Mitchell Cir Rome GA 30161-5938

GIBSON, MARK ANTHONY, secondary school educator; b. Glasgow, Ky., June 26, 1967; s. Thomas Eugene and Louise Elizabeth (Garmon) G. AS, Draughons Jr. Coll., Bowling Green, Ky., 1990; BS, Wester Ky. U., 1994. Cert. bus. edn. tchr., Ky. Clk., product mgr. Cavenah's IGA Foodliner, Edmonton, Ky., 1985-92; substitute tchr. Metcalfe County Bd. Edn., Edmonton, 1992-94, bus. edn. tchr., 1994—; clk. Edmonton Livestock Market, Inc., 1993—. Mem. NEA, Nat. Bus. Edn. Assn., Ky. Edn. Assn., Golden Key Honor Soc., Phi Eta Sigma, Kappa Delta Pi. Office: Metcalfe County HS PO Box 379 Edmonton KY 42129

GIBSON, WILLIAM WILLARD, JR., law educator; b. Amarillo, Tex., Mar. 5, 1932; s. William Willard and Genelle (Works) G.; m. Beth Smyth, July 31, 1953; children—William Willard, Michael Murray, Timothy Thomas, Elizabeth Mills. B.A., U. Tex., Austin, 1954, LL.B., 1956. Assoc. Gibson, Ochsner, Harlin, Kinney & Morris, Amarillo, Tex., 1956-60, ptnr., 1960-65; assoc. prof. U. Tex.-Austin Sch. Law, 1965-69, prof., 1969-76, Albert Sydney Burleson prof. law, 1976-83, Sylvan Lang prof. law, 1983—, dir. continuing legal edn., 1981-85, assoc. dean, 1979-86; Austin; provost jud. edn. Supreme Ct. Tex., 1992-93. Author: Teaching Materials on Wills and Estates, 1967; Selected Provisions from Texas Statutes Pertaining to Wills and Estates, 1973; also articles. Vice chancellor Diocese of Tex., Protestant Episcopal Ch. Recipient Leon Green award Tex. Law Rev. Assn. of Ex-Editors, Austin, 1983. Fellow Am. Coll. Trust and Estate Counsel (academician); mem. Am. Coll. Real Estate Lawyers. Democrat. Office: U Tex Sch Law 727 E 26th St Austin TX 78705-3224

GIDDENS, LYNN NEAL, adoption educator; b. Gastonia, N.C., Apr. 29, 1952; d. James Ernest and Evelyn (Lineberger) Neal; m. David Stan Giddens, Aug. 22, 1980. BA in Sociology, U. N.C., 1977. Adoption educator N.C. Post Adoption Ctr., Chapel Hill, N.C., 1994—. Author: Eternal Inspirations, 1983, Faces of Adoption, 1984, When Love Is Not Enough, 1995. Mem. N.C. Adoption Connections (coord. 1991-95). Democrat. Baptist. Office: NC Post Adoption Ctr PO Box 2823 Chapel Hill NC 27515

GIDEL, ROBERT HUGH, real estate investor; b. Ft. Dodge, Iowa, Sept. 19, 1951; s. Wayne D. and Mary A. (Ziegler) G.; m. Linda Carol Lombardo, Oct. 23, 1976; children: Jill, Allison, Robert. BSBA, U. Fla., 1973. Comml. loan officer Century Bank, St. Petersburg, Fla., 1975-77; asst. v.p. N.Y. Life, Washington, 1977-81; exec. v.p. Heller Real Estate Fin. Co., Chgo., 1981-86; pres., mng. dir., bd dirs. Alex Brown Realty Advisors, Balt., 1986-90; mng. dir., bd. dirs. Alex Brown Kleinwort Benson Realty Advisors, Balt., 1990-93; pres., bd. dirs. Brazos Ptnrs. L.P., Dallas, 1993—; bd. dirs. Brazos Asset Mgmt., Brazos Fund, L.P.; pres., COO, bd. dirs. ParagonGroup Inc., 1996—. Contbr. articles to profl. publs. Mem. Nat. Coun. Real Estate Investment Fiduciaries, Nat. Assn. Real Estate Investment Trusts, Pension Real Estate Assn., Urban Land Inst., Assn. Fgn. Investors in Real Estate, L'Hirondelle Club (Balt.), Bent Tree Country Club (Dallas). Republican Roman Catholic. Home: 5427 Edgehollow Pl Dallas TX 75287-7506 Office: Paragon Group Inc 7557 Rambler Rd Ste 1200 Dallas TX 75231

GIDUZ, ROLAND, journalist; b. Fall River, Mass., July 24, 1925; s. Hugo and Edith May (Baker) G.; children: William Roland, Robert Baker, Thomas Tracy. AB in Journalism, U. N.C., 1948; MS in Journalism, Columbia U., 1949; postgra., Harvard U., 1959; postgrad., Ga. Inst. Tech., 1979. Editor Chapel Hill (N.C.) News Leader, 1954-59, News of Orange County, Chapel Hill, 1960-66, Gen. Alumni Assn., U. N.C., Chapel Hill, 1966-81; news dir. Sta. WCHL, Chapel Hill, 1981-82; dir. pub. affairs Village Cos., Chapel Hill, 1982-96; columnist Chapel Hill newspaper, 1952-82; owner, pub. The Triangle Pointer Mag., Chapel Hill, 1960-77; cable TV show host/producer Chapel Hill Almanac, 1982—. Author: Who's Gonna Cover 'Em Up?, 1985. Alderman, mayor pro-tem Town of chapel Hill, 1957-69; pres. Friends of chapel Hill Libr., 1975; chmn. cmty. bd. Hillhaven Convalescent Home, 1984; sec. Arts Ctr., 1988-89; trustee Preservation Soc., 1986—, Pub. Sch. Found., 1988-92. Served with U.S. Army, 1943-45, ETO. Named Young Man of Yr. Chapel Hill Jaycees, 1960, Citizen of Yr. Sons Am. Revolution, 1969, Sertoma, 1976; recipient Silver Beaver award Boy Scouts Am., 1977. Mem. Harvard U. Alumni Assn. (regional dir. 1995—), N.C. Train Host Assn. (editor 1995—). Democrat. Presbyterian. Club: Toastmasters, Rotary (pres. local club 1971). Lodge: Masons. Home: 325 Tenney Cir Chapel Hill NC 27514-7804

GIELISSE, VICTOR A.L., food company executive. Student, Tech. Coll. Hotel Sch., The Hague, Netherlands, 1966-69; Grad. Diploma Cert. Food/Beverage Exec., Ednl. Inst. of AH&MA, 1989; Cert. Master Chef magna cum laude, Culinary Inst. Am., 1989; BS, MBA, Calif. Coast U., 1991, 93; D (hon.), Johnson and Wales U., Norfolk, 1995. Commis de cuisine Park Hotel, Monchengladbach, Germany, 1970-71, Eurotel, St. Moritz, Switzerland, 1971-72; garde-mgr. Rhein Hotel Dreesen, Bonn-Bad Godesberg, Germany, 1972-73; from garde mgr. to sous chef Carlton Hotel, Johannesburg, South Africa, 1973-79; exec. sous chef The Westin Oaks Hotel, Houston, 1979-80, exec. chef, 1980-82; exec. chef The Westin Hotel, Dallas, 1982-84, The Adolphus Hotel, Dallas, 1984-85; chef/co-owner Actuelle Restaurant, Dallas, 1985-93; prin. ptnr. Culinary Fast-Trac & Assocs., Inc., Dallas, 1992—. Contbg. editor Chef Mag., Chgo., 1993—; contbr. articles to profl. jours. Recipient numerous awards including Tyson award for culinary excellence grand prize, 1985, Restaurateur of Yr. award Tex. Restaurant Assn., 1991, Chef of Yr. award Culinary Inst. Am., 1991, Professionalism award Am. Culinary Fedn., Ctrl. Region, 1992, Jefferson award for pub. svc., Tex. Bluebonnet award Tex. Dietetic Assn., 1992, Grand prize Nat. Recipe Contest, Cervena Co., 1993; inducted into Am. Acad. Chefs, 1991. Mem. Am. Acad. Chefs, Am. Culinary Fedn., Tex. Chef's Assn., Chaine des Rotisseurs. Office: Culinary Fast Trac & Assocs Inc 6642 Garlinghouse Ln Dallas TX 75252

GIERON-KORTHALS, MARIA ANTONINA, pediatrician, neurologist, medical educator; b. Poland, Feb. 2, 1947. Grad., Med. Sch., Warsaw, Poland, 1971. Diplomate Am. Bd. Psychiatry and Neurology; lic. physician, N.Y., Fla. Rotating intern in internal medicine, pediatrics, surgery, ob-gyn. Mcpl. Hosp., Sandomierz, Poland, 1971-72; fellow in clin. pathology, bacteriology and clin. chemistry, rschr. in immunology dept. lab. medicine Med. Inst. for Post Grad. Edn., Warsaw, 1972-73; rsch. asst. in exptl. neuropathology, peripheral nerve ischemia Albert Einstein Coll. Medicine, Bronx, N.Y., 1974-75; resident in pediatrics Bronx Lebanon Hosp./Downstate Med. Ctr., Bklyn., N.Y., 1975-77; resident in pediatric neurology Downstate Med. Ctr., 1977-80, chief resident, 1980-81; prof. pediats. U. South Fla., 1987-90, co-dir. Muscular Distrophy Assn. Clinic, 1981-90, program dir. Children's Ctr., Coll. Edn., 1981-91, cons. Children's Ctr., 1991-93; mem. active staff Tampa Gen. Hosp., 1981—; Electroencephalography fellow Mayo Clinic, Richarster, Minn., 1987, vis. scientist Peripheral Nerve Ctr., 1987; Epilepsy minifellow Bowman Gray Sch. Medicine, Wake Forest U., Winston-Salem, N.C., 1988; cons. TGH-Psychiatry Ctr., Tampa, 1982—, H. Lee Moffitt Cancer Ctr., Tampa, 1985—, Shriner's Hosp., Tampa, 1985—; lectr. and presenter papers in field. Contbr. 44 articles to med. and sci. jours. Grantee VA Med. Rsch., 1981-85, 86-89, Phizer Drug Co., 1984-85; Recipient Excellence in Pub. Edn. award Hillsborough County Pub. Schs., 1988. Mem. AMA (Physician's Recognition award 1985), Am. Acad. Neurology, Am. Electroencephalographic Soc., Child Neirology Soc., Hillsborough County Med. Assn. Office: U South Fla 1 Davis Blvd Ste 200 Tampa FL 33606-3422

GIESECKE, ADOLPH HARTUNG, anesthesiologist, educator; b. Oklahoma City, Apr. 19, 1932; s. Adolph H. and Goldia (Lynn) G.; m. Veronica Morel, June 11, 1954; children: Carl E., Suzanne G., Noel M., Hans E. MD, U. Tex. Med. Br., Galveston, 1957. Diplomate Am. Bd. Anesthesiology. Intern William Beaumont Army Hosp., El Paso, Tex., 1957-58; resident U. Tex., Dallas, 1960-63, from asst. prof. to prof. anesthesiology, 1963-81, chmn. anesthesiology, 1981-92; Fulbright lectr. Johannes Gutenberg U., Mainz, Germany, 1970-71. Lay reader Episcopal Ch., Irving, Tex., 1968—. Capt. USAR, 1957-60. McLaughlin Scholar, 1955. Mem. Am. Soc. Anesthesiology, So. Soc. Anesthesiology (pres. 1972), Internat. Trauma Anesthesiology and Critical Care Soc. (pres. 1992—), Japan Soc. Anesthesiologist (hon.), Tex. Med. Assn. (del. 1992-94), Wood Libr. Mus. (bd. dirs. 1990-94), U. Tex. Med. Br. Alumni Assn. (Disting. Ashebell Smith Alumnus award 1989), Alpha Omega Alpha. Republican. Episcopalian. Office: U Tex Southwestern Med Sch 5322 Harry Hines Blvd Dallas TX 75235-7209

GIESEN, HERMAN MILLS, engineering executive, consultant, mechanical forensic engineer; b. San Antonio, Sept. 22, 1928; s. Herman Iglehart and Emeline Barbara (Frey) G.; m. Linda B. Williams, Aug. 9, 1979; 1 child, Jonathan; children by previous marriage: John Herman, David Douglas, Amy Lynn. Student Tex. A&M U., 1946-47; BS in Engring., U.S. Naval Acad., 1951; MSEE, USAF Inst. Tech., 1960; MS in Ops. Mgmt., U. So. Calif., 1966. Commd. 2d lt. USAF, 1951, advanced through grades to maj., 1966; served as aircraft maintenance mgr., 1954-56, flight instr., 1957-59, rsch. and devel. program officer, 1960-63, aircraft, flight commdr., 1963-64, elec. engr.-analyst, 1964-66, resigned, 1966, now col. Res., ret.; exec. adviser in program control McDonnell-Douglas Corp., Huntington Beach, Calif., 1966-68; sr. bus. planner E-Systems, Inc., Greenville, Tex., 1968-71; pres. Giesen & Assos., Inc., indsl. mgmt. engring. cons., Dallas, 1971-72, 78—; plant engr. Dixie Metals of Tex., Dallas, 1972-73; plant engr. Murph Metals Div., R.S.R. Corp., Dallas, 1973-74, ops. maintenance/engring. mgr., 1974-76; mfg. mgr. Ferguson Industries, Dallas, 1976-78; self-employed cons. design engr., 1978-84; mech. forensic engr. AID Cons. Engrs., Inc., Dallas, 1985-90; pres., mech. forensic engr. Environ. Issues Support, Inc., 1990—. Decorated Air medal, USAF Commendation medal, Air Force Meritorious Service medal; registered profl. engr., Tex., environ. assessor; cert. flight instr., advanced instrument ground aircraft instr. FAA. Mem. NSPE, Tex. Soc. Profl. Engrs. Contbr. articles to profl. jours. Home: 3636 Shenandoah St Dallas TX 75205-2119

GIESSELMANN, MICHAEL GUENTER, electrical engineer, educator, researcher; b. Basel, Switzerland, Oct. 15, 1956; came to U.S., 1986; s. Guenter Fritz and Hedwig (Schenck) G. MSEE, Tech. U. Darmstadt, Fed. Republic Germany, 1981, PhDEE, 1986. Rsch. assoc. Tech. U. Darmstadt, 1981-86; asst. prof. Tex. Tech U., Lubbock, 1986-92, assoc. prof., 1992—, grad. advisor, chair grad. com., 1994—; cons. West Pub., San Francisco, 1988, OCR Diasonics, Salt Lake City, 1990-92, ESP Inc., 1995—; researcher Lawrence Livermore (Calif.) Nat. Lab., 1988-90, Tex. Advanced Tech. program, 1992-94, Ballistic Missile Def. Orgn., 1995—. Contbr. tech. papers and reports to confs., symposia and profl. jours. Recipient Halliburton award Halliburton Edn. Found., 1988, New Faculty award Tex. Tech. U. Ex-Students Assn., 1990, Outstanding Faculty award, 1991, Charles L. Burford Faculty award, 1994, Pres.'s Excellence in Teaching award, 1995. Mem. IEEE (sr., sec. 1990-91, treas. 1992-95), Aircraft Owners and Pilots Assn. Office: Tex Tech U Elec Engring Ms # 3102 Lubbock TX 79409

GIFFORD, DONALD ARTHUR, lawyer; b. Derry, N.H., Nov. 21, 1945; s. George Donald and Bertha Margaret (Gibbs) G.; m. Sandra Louise Robaldo, July 25, 1964; children: Adriana, Roy, Stacy. BA, U. S. Fla., 1967; JD with high honors, Fla. State U., 1970. Bar: Fla. 1970, U.S. Dist. Ct. (mid. dist.) Fla. 1970, U.S. Dist. Ct. (no. dist.) Fla. 1981, U.S. Dist. Ct. (so. dist.) Fla. 1982, U.S. Ct. Appeals (5th cir.) 1975, U.S. Ct. Appeals (11th cir.) 1981, U.S. Supreme Ct. 1980. Assoc. Raymond, Wilson, Karl, Conway & Barr, Daytona Beach, Fla., 1972; law clk. U.S. dist. ct. (mid. dist.) Fla., Tampa, 1972-73; with Shackleford, Farrior, Stallings & Evans, P.A., Tampa, 1973—. Chair. divsn. allocations United Way Greater Tampa, 1987-94, treas., 1991-93, pres., 1994-96; mem., trustee U.S. Fla. Found., 1986—, New Coll. Found., 1990-93. Fellow ABA (ho. of dels. 1991-92), Am. Judicature Soc.; mem. Fed. Bar Assn., Fla. Bar (bd. govs. 1989-95, mem. exec. com. 1993-94, chair legis. com. 1993-94, legis. com. 1995—), Fla. Bar Found. (bd. dirs. 1996—), Hillsborough County Bar Assn. (bd. dir. 1981-90, pres. 1988-89), U. S. Fla. Nat. Alumni Assn. (pres. 1976, bd. dir. 1970-92, Outstanding Alumnus 1976, Outstanding Sci. award 1996), Fla. State U. Coll. Law Alumni Assn. (bd. dir. 1982—, pres. 1987-88), Fla. State U. Alumni Assn. (bd. dirs. 1987—, chmn. 1992-94), Fla. Bar Found. (bd. dirs. 1996—), F.L.A. Inc. (bd. dirs. 1995—), Outback Bowl (mem team rels. com. 1986-95), Tiger Bay Club (bd. dirs. 1988-92). Office: Shackleford Farrior Stallings & Evans PA PO Box 3324 Tampa FL 33601-3324

GIGLIO, DAVID THOMAS, small business owner; b. Stamford, Conn., Feb. 24, 1958; s. John Joseph and Gertrude Marie (Healy) G. Student, Loyola U., New Orleans, 1975-76. Mgr. customer svc. Oreck Corp., New Orleans, 1975-80; customer rep. Baldwin-Gegenheimer, Stamford, Conn., 1980-81; contract adminstr. Smith & Smith Aircraft, New Orleans, 1981-85; owner Frames, Inc., New Orleans, 1986—. Adv. bd. mem. Mayor's Algiers Adv. Bd., New Orleans, 1994—; v.p. Artina, New Orleans, 1996; sec. Algiers Econ. Devel. Found., New Orleans, 1993—. Mem. Profl. Picture Framing Assn. (Gulf Coast chpt.), Algiers Point Assn. (adv. bd. mem., dir. Point Clean Team), Old Algiers Main St. Program (adv. bd.), Crescent City Peace Alliance (steering com.), Delcazal Pals (founding). Office: Frames Inc 3439 Kabel Dr New Orleans LA 70131

GIGLIO, STEVEN RENE, lawyer; b. Denver, Feb. 13, 1952; s. Dominic Mark and Ruth (Strain) G.; m. Susan Dale Carver, Feb. 12, 1987. BA in Russian Studies, La. State U., 1973, JD, 1976. Bar: La. 1976, U.S. Dist. Ct. (ea., mid. and we. dists.) La. 1979, U.S. Ct. Claims 1990, U.S. Ct. Appeals (5th cir.) 1979, U.S. Supreme Ct. 1981. Sole practice Baton Rouge, 1976-79; asst. gen. counsel La. Dept. Health, Baton Rouge, 1979-87; ptnr. Olds & Giglio, Baton Rouge, 1987-88, Kleinpeter, Schwatzberg & Stevens, Baton Rouge, 1988-93; pvt. practice Baton Rouge, 1993—. Patentee in field. Mem. La. Bar Assn. Roman Catholic. Office: 2900 Westfolk Dr Ste 200 Baton Rouge LA 70827

GIKAS, CAROL SOMMERFELDT, museum director; b. St. Louis; m. Ken Gikas. Student, U. Mo., 1968-70; BA in Studio Art, U. Ark., Little Rock, 1975; MA, U. Tex., 1977; postgrad. Mus. Mgmt. Inst., U. Calif., summer 1981. Asst. mus. registrar Ark. Arts Ctr., Little Rock, 1972-74; assoc. curator Leeds Gallery, U. Tex., Austin, 1977-80; exec. dir. La. Arts and Sci. Ctr., Baton Rouge, 1980—; mem. grants adv. panel So. Arts Fedn., 1981, Arts & Humanities Council Greater Baton Rouge, 1982, 83, div. arts La. State Arts Council, 1981, 85; mem. adv. bd. U.S.S. Kidd/La. Naval Mus., Baton Rouge, 1981, 84, La. Dept. Edn., 1981; state rep. to council S.E. Mus. Conf., 1984, 85. Sec. Gov.'s commn. for Anniversary of La. State Capitol, 1981, 82; active Baton Rouge C. of C. Goals Conf., 1984, 85, Leadership Greater Baton Rouge, C. of C., 1985, 86; trustee ARC, 1986—; mem. Mayor's Commn. for Bicentennial of U.S. Constn. Mem. Am. Assn. Mus., Art Mus. Assn. (regional rep. 1983—). Office: Lousianna Arts & Science Ctr Inc PO Box 3373 Baton Rouge LA 70821-3373

GILBERT, ARTHUR CHARLES, aerospace engineer, consulting engineer; b. N.Y.C., Sept. 23, 1926; s. Phillip Saul and Annie (Taishoff) G.; children: Pamela Stephanie Gilbert Remis, Randi Ilene Gilbert Cutler. B Aero. Engring., NYU, 1946, M Aero. Engring., 1947, ScD in Engring., 1956. Registered profl. engr., N.Y., Mich., D.C. Rsch. engr., sr. exec. aerospace manufacturer various orgns., 1947-67; v.p., mng. ptnr. Systems Technology Lab., Inc., 1968-70; founder Auto-Train Corp., 1968-79; chief scientist Chief Naval Ops. Exec. Panel, 1970-75; v.p., dir. engring. R & D Data Solutions Corp., 1975-77; v.p. Unified Industries, 1977-78; with OAO Corp., 1978-81; pres. Arthur C. Gilbert, SCD, PE, Arlington, Va., 1981—; consulting engr. in field; special asst. to USN-sec. Nav R&D, Washington, 1987—; vis. prof. Navy War Coll., Newport, R.I., 1979. Mem. Spitfire Soc. U.K., Cosmos Club Washington. Home and Office: Arthur C Gilbert SCD PE 1201 S Eads St Apt 910 Arlington VA 22202-2840

GILBERT, DAVID WALLACE, aerospace engineer; b. Berkeley, Calif., June 20, 1923; s. Wallace William and Elizabeth Wilson (Findlay) G.; m. Jeanne Wilson Gillette, June 27, 1948; children: Laurence R., LeeAnn, Dean A., Barbara L., John L., Mary H. BSME, U. Calif., Berkeley, 1948. Flight test analyst Convair, San Diego, 1948-51, dynamics engr., 1951-55, design specialist, 1955-59, chief GN&C systems, 1959-62; mgr. GN&C JSC Apollo Project Office NASA, Houston, 1962-64, br. chief GN&C Systems div., 1964-89. With U.S. Army, 1942-45, ETO. Mem. AIAA (assoc. fellow). Home: 10019 Cedarhurst Dr Houston TX 77096-5102

GILBERT, JAMES RILEY, II, career officer; b. Plainview, Tex., Sept. 15, 1946; s. William Frederick and Ada Louise (Pate) G.; m. Christine Ann Barta, Sept. 1969 (div. Aug. 1981); children: Priscilla Gail, James Riley III, Jamie Reyna, Paula Gaye, Crystan Anthony; m. Julia Bryan Futrell Gilbert, Aug. 14, 1982 (div. Aug. 1994); 1 chld, Rachael Ann Gilbert; m. Julie Ceria, Nov. 25, 1994. BBA in Mgmt. Sci., U. North Tex., Denton, 1975; naval officer commn., Officer Candidate Sch., Newport, R.I., 1977; MS in Fin., Naval Postgraduate Sch., Monterey, Calif., 1989, MA in Middle East History, 1989. Cert. naval surface line officer, command-at-sea, joint svc. officer. Div. officer USS Charles F. Adams, Mayport, Fla., 1969-77; instr. Anti-Submarine Warfare Sch., Norfolk, Va., 1977-80; dept. head USS McCloy, USS Biddle, Norfolk, Va., 1980-83; student Naval Postgraduate Sch., Monterey, Calif., 1987-88; exec. officer USS Stump, Norfolk, Va., 1989-90; student Marine Command and Staff Coll., Quantico, Va., 1990-91; naval ops. branch chief U.S. Ctrl. Command, MacDill AFB, Fla., 1991-94; ops. directorate So. Command, Panama City, 1994—. Contbr. articles to profl. jours. Comdr. USN, 1969—. Mem. Naval Inst.

GILBERT, JERRY LON, petroleum geologist; b. Fort Worth, Feb. 14, 1947; s. Joe Pershing and Josephine Elizabeth (Bunch) G.; m. Katherine Anne Snyder, Aug 30, 1969; children: Jennifer Christine, Julie Anna, John Bryan. BS, West Tex. State U., 1970, MS, 1975. Geologist, Sohio Petroleum, Oklahoma City, 1975-76; geologist, Petroleum Inc., Oklahoma City, 1976-79; geologist Search Drilling Co., Amarillo, Tex., 1979-81; v.p. geol. Spur Petroleum, Amarillo, 1981-83; sr. geologist Santa Fe Minerals, Tulsa, 1983-84; consulting petroleum geologist Strat Land Exploration, Tulsa, 1984-85; cons. Tulsa, 1985-87; mgr. exploration Bridwell Oil Co., Wichita Falls, Tex., 1987—. Served to 1st lt. CE U.S. Army, 1971-73, capt. Okla. NG. Mem. Panhandle Geol. Soc. (sec. 1980-81, v.p. 1981-82, pres. 1982—), Am. Assn. Petroleum Geologist (cert. 1983), North Tex. Geol. Soc., Tulsa Geol. Soc., Simga Gamma Epsilon. Republican. Methodist. Avocations: golf, rock collecting. Home: 2414 Barbados St Wichita Falls TX 76308-4732 Office: Bridwell Oil Co PO Box 1830 Wichita Falls TX 76307-1830

GILBERT, JOHN CARL, chemistry educator; b. Laramie, Wyo., Jan. 30, 1939; m. Lucia Albino, Dec. 18, 1965; 1 child, Melissa. BS with honors, U. Wyo., 1961; MS, Yale U., 1962, PhD, 1965. Asst. prof. dept. chemistry/biochemistry U. Tex., Austin, 1965-71, assoc. prof., 1971-84, prof., 1984—, chmn. dept. chemistry/biochemistry, 1987-91; vis. assoc. prof. chemistry Iowa State U., 1974-75; cons. Alcon Labs., Inc. Referee Jour. Am. Chem. Soc., Jour. Organic Chemistry, Tetrahedron, Tetrahedron Letters, Can. Jour. Chemistry; contbr. numerous articles to profl. jours. Grantee Robert A. Welch Found., 1994—, Alcon Labs., 1990-96, THECB, 1994-96. Office: Univ of Texas Dept of Chemistry/Biochem Austin TX 78712

GILBERT, VIRGINIA LEE, English language educator, poet, photographer; b. Elgin, Ill., Dec. 19, 1946; d. Blair Edward and Florence Amelia (Swailes) G. BA in English, Iowa Wesleyan Coll., 1969; MFA in Creative Writing-Poetry, U. Iowa, 1971; postgrad., U. Utah, 1974-75; PhD in English and Creative Writing-Poetry, U. Nebr., 1991. English instr. Peace Corps, South Korea, 1971-73; tchg. fellow U. Utah, Salt Lake City, 1974-75; instr. ESL, test writer Dept. of Def. Sub-Contracts, Iran, 1976-79; asst. prof. English Ala. A&M U., Normal, 1980-92, assoc. prof. English, 1992—; adminstr. Acad. Am. Poets and the Writers' Community, N.Y.C., 1976; instr. ESL Coll. of Lake County, Grayslake, Ill., 1979; teaching asst. U. Nebr., Lincoln, 1984-87, sec. English Grad. Student Assn., 1986-87; dir. Program in Creative Writing and Visiting Reading Series, Ala. A&M U., mem. Gwendolyn Brooks Com., 1980—, Honors Day Com., 1980-84; poetry reader. Author: (poems) To Keep at Bay the Hounds, 1985, The Earth Above, 1993, The Other Brightness, 1995; contbr. poems and articles to jours. and anthologies. Recipient spl. merit award Kodak Internat. Photography Competition, 1986, Photography Best of Show award B&W N.E. Ala. State Fair, 1988, 2d place Hackney lit. award, 1990, 1st place award Sakura Festival Haiku Contest, 1992, 1st place travel photography award Huntsville Times, 1994; creative writing fellow Nat. Endowment for Arts, 1976-77; Title III faculty devel. grantee Ala. A&M U., 1990-91, Fulbright-Hays travel grantee, China, 1993. Mem. MLA, Assoc. Writing Programs, Poets and Writers, Poetry Soc. Am. (past mem. internat. com.), Pen Women (pres. Huntsville br. 1990-94), Huntsville Arts Coun. (rep. 1994), Ala. Poetry Soc. (newsletter editor 1992-94), Huntsvile Lit. Assn., Huntsville Photog. Soc. (ann. award for best photographs 1980-82, v.p. 1996—). Democrat. Methodist. Office: Ala A&M U Dept of English PO Box 453 Normal AL 35762-0453

GILBREATH, ROBERT DEAN, management consultant, author; b. Panama Canal Zone, Dec. 29, 1949; s. William O. and Frances S. Gilbreath; m. Linda Susan Wurst, June 27, 1970; children: Robert Dean, Alice Beth. Student, U.S. Mil. Acad., 1967-70; BS in Civil Engring., U. Ky., 1973; MS in Engring. Mgmt., U. Tenn., 1976. Registered profl. engr. Engr. TVA, Knoxville, 1973-76; dept. mgr. Gilbert/Commonwealth, Jackson, Mich., 1976-79; worldwide practice dir. Andersen Cons., Chgo., 1979-89; pres., CEO Change Mgmt. Assocs., Atlanta, 1989-93; CEO Proudfoot Change Mgmt., Atlanta, 1993-94; v.p. IBM Consulting Group, 1995-96, Pritchett & Assoc., 1996—; lectr. Ministry Internat. Trade and Industry, 1981-83, Harvard U. Grad. Sch. Bus., Boston, 1987, MIT, Cambridge, 1987. Author: Winning at Project Management, 1986, Forward Thinking, 1987, Save Yourself, 1991, Managing Construction Contracts, 1992, Escape from Management Hell, 1993, Mergers: Growth in the Fast Lane, 1996. Served with U.S. Army, 1970-72. Decorated Army Commendation medal.

GILCHRIST, WILLIAM RISQUE, JR., economist; b. Lexington, Ky., July 16, 1944; s. William Risque and Susan (McLemore) G.; B.B.A., U. Miami, 1966, M.B.A., 1970; postgrad. Northwestern U., 1973—; m. Peggy Linder Gardner, Mar. 20, 1968; children: William Risque, Shannon Linder, Heather Susan. Assoc. dir. conf. services div. continuing edn. U. Miami, Coral Gables, Fla., 1966-71; asst. dir. edn. and tng. Mortgage Bankers Assn. Am., Washington, 1971-73; pres. Ventura Fin. Corp., Fort Lauderdale, Fla., 1973-76; pres. Gilchrist and Assocs., Pompano Beach., Fla., London, and Santiago, Chile, 1976—; pres. Intervault, Inc., Ft. Lauderdale and Basel, Switzerland; cons. in field. Recipient Cert. of Achievement, Savs. and Loan Execs. Seminar, 1971. Mem. Broward County (Fla.) C. of C., NAB, Econ. Soc. South Fla., Mortgage Bankers Assn., Nat. Assn. Pvt. Security Vaults (pres. 1986-92)., Senatorial Inner Circle. Republican. Episcopalian. Clubs: Kiwanis. Marina Bay, Mutiny. Author: International Monetary System-s—Alternatives, 1969; Eurodollar Outlook-OPEC and the LDC's, 1978. Home: 1341 SE 9th Ave Pompano Beach FL 33060-9558

GILDAN, PHILLIP CLARKE, lawyer; b. West Palm Beach, Fla., July 17, 1959; s. Herbert Leonard and Kathleen (Yeager) G.; m. Laurie Beth Leinwand, Aug. 25,1985; children: Tyler Ross, Jacob Lee. AB magna cum laude, Dartmouth Coll., 1981; JD cum laude, Harvard U., 1984. Bar: Fla. 1984, U.S. Ct. Appeals (11th cir.) 1986, U.S. Supreme Ct. 1989. Assoc. Nason, Gildan, Yeager, Gerson & White, P.A., West Palm Beach, 1984-89, shareholder, 1989—; lectr. Reinventing Govt. Symposium, Hollywood, Fla., 1994, Risk Mgmt. State Conf., Deerfield Beach, Fla., 1995. Contbr. articles to profl. jours. Dir. Com. for Good Govt., Palm Beach, Fla., 1990-94. Mem. Fla. Bar Assn. (appellate rules com. 1990-92, 95—), Palm Beach County Bar Assn. (appellate practice chmn. 1993—), Am. Inns of Ct. LIV (exec. com. 1991-94), Phi Beta Kappa. Office: Nason Gildan Yeager Gerson & White Ste 1200 1645 Palm Beach Lakes Blvd West Palm Beach FL 33401-2217

GILES, AUDREY ELIZABETH, reference librarian; b. Menomonie, Wis., Oct. 31, 1931; d. Walter Fredrick and Gladys Merle (Drake) Stewart; m. Joe B. Giles, Nov. 18, 1950 (div. July 1979); children: Joe C., Fred A., Mark J., Laura E., John A. AS, North Ark. Cmty. Coll., 1977; BS in Edn., U. Ark., 1979; MLS, Tex. Womans U., 1987. Kindergarten tchr. Berryville (Ark.) Schs., 1979-84, KISD, Killeen, Tex., 1984-86; libr. Ark. Tech. U., Russellville, 1989-90; reference libr. U. of Mary Hardin Baylor, Belton, Tex., 1991—; cons. libr. Fray Bartolme Libr., San Cristobal de las Casas, Chiapas, Mex., 1988; info. specialist Midwives Info. Libr. and Resource Ctr., London, 1987. Mem. ALA, AAUW, Tex. Libr. Assn., Am. Soc. Indexers, Assn. of Christian Librs., Kappa Delta Pi. Baptist. Office: Univ Mary Hardin Baylor Libr UMHB Campus Box 8016 Belton TX 76513

GILES, KATHARINE EMILY (J. K. PIPER), administrative assistant, writer; b. Jackson Hole, Wyo., Jan. 9, 1938; d. William Lamar and Grace Hawley (Domrose) G.; children: Piper Lee Shanks, John Richard Hamlin. Diamond cert., Gemological Inst. Am., 1971. Adminstrv. asst. Matthiesen Equipment Co., San Antonio, 1993—. Author: The Marvelous Bean, 1989, The Lost Trident, 1991, The Missing Crystal, 1992, Jewel of Avalon, 1992, The Lost Kingdom, 1991, The Desert Sun, 1992, The Fire Sled, 1991, Knights of Glass, 1992, Black Pagoda, 1992, Memories from the Kitchen of Grace & Rich Williams, 1992. Home: PO Box 201025 San Antonio TX 78220-8025

GILES, MICHAEL COMER, physical education educator, aquatics consultant; b. Huntsville, Ala., Sept. 14, 1946; s. Comer E. and Temple (Harton) G.; m. Bobby Jean Morris, July 27, 1984; children: Mary Temple Giles Stewart, Michel Comer Jr. BS, U. Ala., 1968; MS, U. So. Miss., 1972. Cert. in aquatics, lifeguard instr. trainer, water safety instr., lifeguard, CPR instr., first aid instr. trainer ARC. 0dir. aquatics, swimming coach Tuscaloosa (Ala.) YMCA, 1968-69; dir. aquatics, instr. phys. edn. John C. Calhoun Community Coll., Decatur, Ala., 1969-71, 72-75, varsity tennis coach, 1972-75; grad. asst. dept. athletic adminstrn. and coaching U. So. Miss., Hattiesburg, 1971-72, dir. aquatics, instr., 1975—, varsity swimming coach, 1979-87; tennis coord. Decatur Recreation Dept., 1972-75; mem. nat. aquatics faculty ARC, Washington, 1988—; presenter in field, 1975—; condr. clins. for Spl. Olympic athletes and lifeguard instr. trainers; supr., trainer lifeguards M.C. Johnson Natatatorium and Lake Sehoy; cons. on safety and lifeguard personnel to numerous pub. and pvt. pools, Miss.; tech. advisor for films Home Pool Safety and Preventing Water Emergencies, ARC, 1990. Prin. author: Safety Training for Swimming Coaches, 1988; contbg. author: Basic Water Safety Testbook, 1988; editor: Instructor Trainer Manual on Lifeguarding, 1991. Mem. Hattiesburg Arts Coun., 1990—. Mem. AAHPER and Dance, Am. Swim Coaches Assn., Coll. Swim Coaches Assn., Nat. Assn. Underwater Instrs. (cert. asst. scuba diving instr.), Nat. Intramural and Recreational Sports Assn., Miss. Assn. Health, Phys. Edn. and Recreation, U.S. Swimming. Episcopalian. Home: 3012 Magnolia Pl Hattiesburg MS 39402-2430 Office: U So Miss Ss Box # 5124 Usm Hattiesburg MS 39406

GILES, SCOTT ANDREW, public affairs consultant; b. Ithaca, N.Y., Aug. 6, 1960; s. Peter Giles and Marilyn Kay Redman; m. Catherine Elizabeth Lalley, Oct. 10, 1987; children: Abagael Brennan, Eliza Roe, William Samuel. BA, St. Lawrence U., 1982; MA, U. Va., 1995, postgrad., 1995—. Spl. asst. to Hon. Frank Horton, Washington, 1982-84, legis. asst., 1984-86; assoc. Cassidy & Assocs., Washington, 1986-90, interim dir. rsch., 1991-92; pub. affairs cons. Charlottesville, Va., 1990—; editl. asst. Biolaw, 1993—; presenter Am. Assn. Cmty. Colls., Nat. Leadership Acad.; keynote spkr. Calif. C.C., 1996. Adv. to bd. dirs. Tougaloo Coll., 1987-90; adv. to bd. Alexander Graham Bell Assn. for Deaf, 1986—, panelist, seminar leader internat. conv., 1988, moderator, seminar leader centennial conv., 1990, panelist biennial conv., 1992. Mem. Am. Assn. Higher Edn., Assn. Study Higher Edn., Assn. Instl. Rsch., Kennedy Inst., Hastings Ctr., Raven Soc., Am. Assn. Cmty. Colls. Home: 317 Parkway St Charlottesville VA 22902-4630

GILES, SUSAN MICHELE, medical/surgical nurse; b. Inglewood, Calif., Mar. 28, 1965; d. Michael Paul and JoAnn Patricia (Margan) Stash.; m. Sept. 7, 1991. BSN, Westminster Coll., Salt Lake City, 1987. RN, Calif.; cert. med.-surg. Staff nurse gen. surg. unit St. Joseph Hosp., Orange, Calif., 1987-91; staff nurse gen. med. surg. unit Castle Med. Ctr., Kailua, Hawaii, 1992-94; staff nurse renal/pulmonary/telemetry unit Mary Washington Hosp., Fredericksburg, Va., 1994-95; intermediate med. care unit staff nurse Onslow Meml. Hosp., Jacksonville, N.C., 1995—. Mem. ANA, Sigma Theta Tau.

GILES, WILLIAM ELMER, journalism educator, former newspaper editor; b. Somerville, N.J., July 5, 1927; s. Elmer and Mary Jane (Reed) G.; m. Gloria Mastrangelo, June 4, 1949; children: William J., Michael E., Richard H. and Paul L. (twins), Joseph R. A.B. in Government, Columbia U., 1950, M.S. in Journalism, 1951. Reporter Plainfield Courier-News, N.J., 1946-47; copyreader, reporter Wall Street Jour., 1951- 58; mng. editor S.W. edit. Wall Street Jour., Dallas, 1958-61, news editor Washington bur., 1961; an organizer nat. weekly newspaper Nat. Observer, 1961, editor, 1962-71; asst. gen. mgr. Dow Jones & Co., Inc.; pub. Dow Jones & Co., Inc. (Wall Street Jour. and Nat. Observer), 1971-76; dir. mgmt. programs, mem. Dow Jones mgmt. com., 1972-76; disting. editor in residence Baylor U., 1976; exec. editor Detroit News, 1976-77, editor, v.p., 1977-83; editor-in-residence, lectr. Mich. State U., East Lansing, 1983—; Sunday editor Singapore Monitor, 1984-85; v.p. Sandy Corp., Troy, Mich., 1985-87; prof. journalism La. State U., Baton Rouge, 1987-91, dir. Manship Sch. Journalism, 1988-91; prof. So. U., Baton Rouge, 1992—. Mem. Assn. Educators in Journalism and Mass Comm., Soc. Profl. Journalists. Home: 667 College Hill Dr Baton Rouge LA 70808-4950

GILGER, MARK ALAN, pediatrician, educator; b. Kansas City, Mo., May 19, 1954; s. Virgil Lee and Odillia Anne (Erker) G.; m. Donna Lee Short, Sept. 5, 1982; children: Michael Alan, Katherine Anne, Caroline Leigh. BA in Sociology, Creighton U., 1976, MD, 1980. Diplomate Am. Bd. Pediatrics, sub.-bd. Pediatric Gastroenterology and Nutrition. Resident in pediatrics U. Rochester, 1981-83; clin. dir. USPHS Indian Health Svc., Yuma, Ariz., 1984-86; fellow in pediatric gastroenterology Baylor Coll. Medicine, Houston, 1986-89, asst. prof. pediatrics, 1989—. Contbr. chpts. to books, articles to profl. jours. Served as comdr. USPHS, 1983-86. Recipient Health Emphasis Campaign Role Model award Indian Health Svc., 1985, Nat. Rsch. Svc. award NIH, 1987, 88, 95; Baylor Pediatric award for excellence in teaching. Fellow Am. Acad. Pediatrics; mem. N.Am. Soc. Pediatric Gastroenterology and Nutrition. Office: Baylor Coll Medicine 1 Baylor Plz Houston TX 77030-3411

GILHAM, ELIZABETH LYNNE, journalist; b. Bellaire, Ohio, Aug. 15, 1944; d. William Donald and Wilma (Kopyar) G.; m. Ali Akbar Tabatabai (div. June 1967); 1 child, Tiffany. BA in Internat. Rels., Am. U., 1970; cert., U. Paris (Sorbonne), 1973; MA in Journalism, Regent U., 1992. Segment prodr. Newsight (TV show), Virginia Beach, Va., 1987-92; founding editor, editor-in-chief Focus mag., Virginia Beach, 1989-90; media negotiator Victor King Advt., Virginia Beach, 1989-91; asst. prodr. The 700 Club, Virginia Beach, 1993-94; media rschr. CBN spl. programming, Virginia Beach, 1993-94; journalist Thomson Newspapers, The Register-Herald, Beckley, W.Va., 1995—. Mem. Soc. Profl. Journalists, Mensa. Democrat. Office: The Register-Herald 801 N Kanawka St Beckley WV 25801

GILHAM, JAMES RICHARD, mechanical engineer; b. Athens, Ohio, Sept. 8, 1953; s. James H. and Wanda N. (Andrews) G.; m. Laura Elisabeth Brookins, Mar. 19, 1976; 1 child, Kaitlin Lauryn Ashley. BSME, Ohio U., 1979. From ops. mgr. to plant mgr. CYRO Industries, Osceola, Ark., 1990—; mech. engr. Rockwell-Collins, Cedar Rapids, Iowa, 1979-80; mech. design engr. Borg-Warner Chemicals Control Engring., Parkersburg, W.Va., 1980-83; from process engr. to process mgr. Borg-Warner Chemicals, Waveland, Miss., 1983-88; process mgr. Borg-Warner Chemicals/GE Plastics, Oxnard, Calif., 1988-90. Home: 104 W Alicia St Osceola AR 72370

GILKEY, HERBERT TALBOT, engineering consultant; b. Boulder, Colo., Nov. 27, 1924; s. Herbert James and Mildred Virginia (Talbot) G.; B.S. in Mech. Engring., Iowa State U., 1947, M.S., 1949; postgrad. U. Ill., 1950-53; m. Romona Marie Olsen, June 28, 1946 (dec. 1970); children: Virginia Anne, Herbert David, Edele Christine, Arthur Talbot, Martha Olive; m. 2d, Mary Louise Tucker Brown, Apr. 26, 1974. Research asso. in mech. engring. U. Ill., Urbana, 1949-55; dir. tech. services Nat. Warm Air Heating and Air Conditioning Assn., Cleve., 1955-67; research dir. Waterloo Register div. Dynamics Corp. of Am., Cedar Falls, Iowa, 1967-70; dir. of govt. and consumer affairs Air Conditioning and Refrigeration Inst., Arlington, Va., 1971-77, exec. dir. pub. affairs, 1977-80; dir. codes and govt. liaison Sheet Metal and Air Conditioning Contractors Nat. Assn., Vienna, Va., 1980-85; engring. cons., Vienna, 1985—; cons. on chlorofluorocarbons to The World Bank, 1990—. Scoutmaster, Greater Cleve. council Boy Scouts Am., 1964-67, commr. Wapsipinicon and Nat. Capital Area councils, 1967-70; mem. Bd. Zoning Appeals, Cedar Falls, 1969-70; mem. Energy Conservation Task Force, Fairfax County, Va., 1977-78; chmn. task group Halocarbon Emission, 1988-91, guideline project com. Reducing CFC Refrigerant Emission, 1988-91; elder Presbyn. Ch., Cleveland Heights, Ohio, 1960-62, Cedar Falls, 1968-70. Served with C.E., U.S. Army, 1943-45. Recipient Award of Merit, Boy Scouts Am., 1974; registered profl. engr., Va., Md., D.C., Ohio, Iowa. Fellow ASHRAE (Disting. Service award 1970, chmn. research and tech. com. 1971-72, chmn. govt. affairs com. 1975-76, chmn. energy conservation com. 1976-77); mem. ASME (life), Nat. Fire Protection Assn. (air conditioning com. 1960-67), Uniform Boiler and Pressure Vessel Laws Soc. (council 1973-79). Contbr. articles on heating and air conditioning engring. to profl. jours.; editor various air conditioning design and installation manuals, 1955-67. Home and Office: 2606 E Meredith Dr Vienna VA 22181-4039

GILL, EVALYN PIERPOINT, editor, publisher; b. Boulder, Colo.; d. Walter Lawrence and Lou Octavia Pierpoint; student Lindenwood Coll., BA, U. Colo.; postgrad. U. Nebr., U. Alaska, MA, Cen. Mich. U., 1968; m. John Glanville Gill; children: Susan Pierpoint, Mary Louise Glanville. Lectr. humanities Saginaw Valley State Coll., University Center, Mich., 1968-72; mem. English faculty U. N.C., Greensboro, 1973-74; editor Internat. Poetry Rev., Greensboro, 1975-92; pres. TransVerse Press, Greensboro, 1981—. Bd. dirs. Eastern Music Festival, Greensboro, 1981—, Greensboro Symphony, 1982—, Greensboro Opera Co., 1982—, Weatherspoon Assn.; chmn. O. Henry Festival, 1985, 95. Mem. Am. Lit. Translators Assn., MLA, N.C. Poetry Soc., Phi Beta Kappa. Author: Poetry By French Women 1930-1980, 1980, Dialogue, 1985, Southeast of Here: Northwest of Now, 1986, Entrances, 1996; editor: O. Henry Festival Stories, 1985, 87, Women of the Piedmont Triad: Poetry and Prose, 1989, Edge of Our World, 1990; contbr. poetry to numerous mags. Home: 2900 Turner Grove Dr N Greensboro NC 27455-1977

GILL, GEORGE NORMAN, newspaper publishing company executive; b. Indpls., Aug. 11, 1934; s. George E. and Urith (Dailey) G.; m. Kay Baldwin, Dec. 28, 1957; children—Norman A., George B. A.B., Ind. U., 1957. Reporter Richmond (Va.) News Leader, 1957-60; copy editor, reporter, acting Sunday editor, city editor, mng. editor Courier-Jour., Louisville, 1960-74; v.p., gen. mgr. Courier-Jour. and Louisville Times Co., 1974-79, sr. v.p. corp. affairs, 1979-80, pres., chief exec. officer, 1981-86; chief exec. officer affiliates Standard Gravure Corp., WHAS, Inc., 1981-86; pres., pub. Courier-Jour. and Louisville Times Co., 1986-93. Served with USNR, 1954-56. Recipient Picture Editors award Nat. Press Photographers Assn., 1965. Mem. Am. Soc. Newspaper Editors, Asso. Press Mng. Editors, Louisville Com. on Fgn. Relations, Alpha Tau Omega, Sigma Delta Chi. Club: Mason. Home: PO Box 108 Pewee Valley KY 40056-0108

GILL, GERALD LAWSON, librarian; b. Montgomery, Ala., Nov. 13, 1947; s. George Ernest and Marjorie (Hackett) G.; m. Nancy Argroves, Mar. 5, 1977 (div. 1982). AB, U. Ga., 1971; MA, U. Wis., 1973. Cert. profl. libr., Va. Cataloger James Madison U., Harrisonburg, Va., 1974-76, reference libr., 1976-87, bus. reference libr., 1987—, instr., 1974-80, asst. prof., 1980-90, assoc. prof., 1990—; lectr., speaker nat., regional groups; cons. new product devel. Gale Rsch., 1990—; speakers Bureau James Madison Univ., faculty senate, 1975-79, 1996—, cirriculum and instruction com., sec., 1976-78, chair 1978-79, univ. coun. 1996—. Mem. editorial bd. James Madison Jour., 1977-80; contbr. articles to profl. jours. Mem. libr. adv. com. State Coun. for Higher Edn. in Va., 1986-87; virtual Va. Coord. Mgmt. Bus. com. Mem. ALA (chmn. bus. reference svcs. com. 1984-86, sec. law and polit. sci. sect. 1982-85, chmn. bus. reference svcs. discussion group 1986-87, chmn. bus. reference in acad. librs. com. 1988-91, Gale Rsch. award 1991), AAAS, Am. Mgmt. Assn., Am. Soc. for Info. Sci., Va. Libr. Assn. (coun. 1986-87, parliamentarian 1979, 81), Spl. Librs. Assn. (treas. Va. chpt. 1983-85, pres. 1986-87), Internat. Platform Assn., World Future Soc., Harrisonburg C. of C. Democrat. Roman Catholic. Home: 1379 Devon Ln Harrisonburg VA 22801-5201 Office: James Madison U Library Harrisonburg VA 22807

GILL, MILTON RANDALL, minister; b. Cheverly, Md., Dec. 8, 1950; s. Milton Thomas and Patricia Georgiana (King) G.; m. Carroll Ann Bennett, Nov. 10, 1979; 1 child, Laura Grace. BS, U. Md., 1973; MDiv, Princeton Sem., 1977; DMin, South Fla. Ctr. Theol. Studies, Miami, 1995. Ordained to ministry Presbyn. Ch., 1979. Pastor First Presbyn. Ch., Theresa, N.Y., 1979-84, Weirsdale (Fla.) Presbyn. Ch., 1984-89, First Presbyn. Ch., Boynton Beach, Fla., 1989—; sem. del. Gen. Assembly Presbyn. Ch. (U.S.A.), Balt., 1976; pres. Thousand Island Clergy Assn., Alexandria Bay, N.Y., 1982-83, Boynton Beach Ministerial Assn., 1994-96. Mem. bd. visitors Presbyn. Coll., Clinton, S.C., 1993-96. Mem Rotary, Kiwanis (pres. Lake Weir, Fla. club 1986-87). Republican. Office: First Presbyn Ch 235 SW 6th Ave Boynton Beach FL 33435-5517

GILLAN, ALLAN WAYNE, airline captain, consultant; b. Norfolk, Va., Oct. 6, 1946; s. Luke Allan Gillan and Esther (Santmyer) Hayes; m. Kerry Bradford, Jan. 23, 1980. BA, Pa. State U., 1968. Demonstration test pilot Rockwell Internat., St. Louis, 1973-76; airline capt. Am. Airlines, Dallas, 1976—; check airman Am. Airlines, Dallas, 1978-80; flight and simulator instr. Flight Safety Internat., 1976-77. Lt. USN, 1968-73. Fellow Allied Pilots Assn. Republican. Office: DFW Internat Airport Am Airlines Dallas TX 75261

GILLANI, NOOR VELSHI, atmospheric scientist, researcher, educator; b. Arusha, Tanzania, Mar. 8, 1944; came to U.S., 1963, naturalized, 1976; s. Noormohamed Velshi and Sherbanu (Kassam) G.; m. Mira Teresa Pershe, Aug. 13, 1971; children: Michael, Michelle, Nicole. GCE (Ordinary Level Div. I), U. Cambridge, 1960, (Advanced Level), U. London, 1963; AB cum laude, Harvard U., 1967; MS in Mech. Engring., Washington U., St. Louis, 1969, DSc, 1974. Vis. sci. Stockholm U., 1977; rsch. assoc. Washington U., 1975-76, rsch. sci., 1976-77, asst. prof., 1977-80, assoc. prof. 1981-84, prof. mech. engring., 1985-91, faculty assoc. CAPITA, 1979-91, dir. air quality spl. studies data ctr., 1981-88, mech. engring rsch. computing facility, 1988-90; pres. N.V. Gillani & Assocs., Inc., 1991—; prof. atmospheric sci. N.C. State U., 1993-95; prin. sci. NASA-UAH Global Hydrology & Climate Ctr., U. Ala., Huntsville, 1995—; vis. sci. Brookhaven Nat. Lab., 1990-91, EPA/RTP, 1992, TVA Environ. Rsch. Ctr., 1994-95; organizer NATO CCMS 15th internat. tech. meeting on air pollution modeling and its applications, St. Louis, Apr. 1985; mem. Sci. Bd. NATO/CCMS Air Pollution Pilot Study, 1986-94; mem. tech. adv. bds. U.S. EPA, DOE and others, 1980—; hon. mem. Aga Khan Bd. Edn. for the U.S.A., 1987-90. Author 2 chpts. in EPA Critical Assessment Document on Acid Deposition, 1984; author: (with others) EPA Criteria Document for Particulate Matter, 1994-95; editor: Air Pollution Modeling and Its Applications V, vol. 10, 1986; contbr. articles on superconductivity, bioengring., atmospheric scis. and air pollution to nat. and internat. profl. jours. Dir., founder Nat. Aga Khan Bd. Edn. Program for Parental Involvement in Children's Edn., USA; Aga Khan scholar and travel grantee, 1961-63; Harvard Coll. scholar, 1963-67; Washington U. Grad. Engring. fellow, 1967-69; research assistantships NIH, EPA, 1971-74; Rsch. grantee, EPA, DOE, EPRI, TVA, 1978—. Mem. N.Y. Acad. Scis., Am. Meteorol. Soc., Am. Chem. Soc., ASME, Nat. Assn. for Edn. Young Children. Avocations: religious studies, music, tennis, early childhood education, computers. Office: NASA-UAH Global Hydrology & Climate Ctr U Ala 977 Explorer Blvd Huntsville AL 35806

GILLARD, BAIBA KURINS, medical educator, research scientist; b. Dickholzen, Germany, May 14, 1946; came to U.S., 1950; d. Martins Rudolfs and Velta (Mizis) K.; m. Charles Francis Gillard, Sept. 9, 1967; 1 child, Laine Kristine. BS, Purdue U., 1967; MA, Washington U., St. Louis, 1969, PhD, 1972. Fellow Baylor Coll. Medicine, Houston, 1972-73, asst. prof., then assoc. prof., 1983—; fellow, then asst. prof. UCLA, 1973-83. Contbr. articles to profl. publs. Rsch. grantee Am. Cancer Soc., 1991-95. Mem. AAAS, Am. Chem. Soc., Am. Soc. for Biochemistry and Molecular Biology, Am. Latvian Assn., Houston Latvian Women's Orgn., Glycoconjugate Soc. Office: Baylor Coll Medicine Dept Medicine 1 Baylor Plz Houston TX 77030

GILLARD, JAMES HENRY, naval officer, ocean engineer; b. Charleston, W.Va., Sept. 11, 1944; s. Joseph Harold and Elizabeth Grace (Edwards) G.; m. Carole Marie Thomas, June 11, 1966; 1 child, Thomas. BS, U.S. Naval Acad., 1966; MS, OE, MIT, 1982. Cert. ocean engr. Commd. ensign USN, 1966, advanced through grades to capt., 1987; engring. officer USS Nathan Hale, Pearl Harbor, Hawaii, 1971-75; mem. nuclear propulsion exam. bd. Comdr. in Chief, U.S. Atlantic Fleet, Norfolk, Va., 1975-76; dept. head Navy Nuclear Power Sch., Orlando, Fla., 1977-79; nuclear repair officer Portsmouth (N.H.) Naval Shipyard, 1982-84; asst. program mgr. Naval Sea Sys. Command, Arlington, 1985-86; program mgr. submarine launched Tomahawk cruise missiles Naval Air Sys. Command, Arlington, 1987-92, dir. submarine design and sys. engring. group, 1992-93; sr. project engr. Hughes Missiles Sys. Co., Arlington, 1994-95; dir. submarine programs Gray Hawk Sys., Inc., 1996—. Pres. Woodlawn Little League, Alexandria, Val., 1988-89, mgr., coach, 1985-92; coach Am. Legion Baseball, Alexandria, 1992-93, Mt. Vernon Youth Athletic Assn., Alexandria, 1985-90. Decorated Legion of Merit (2 awards). Mem. Soc. Naval Architects and Marine Engrs., Am. Soc. Naval Engrs., U.S. Naval Inst. Home: 9110 Volunteer Dr Alexandria VA 22309-2923 Office: Gray Hawk Sys Inc 6225 Edgewater Dr Falls Church VA 22041

GILLASPIE, LYNN CLARA, education educator, director clinical experience; b. Winchester, Ky., Oct. 23, 1953; d. Bramblette Francis and Annette (Faulconer) G. BS in Elem. Edn., U. Tenn., 1976, MS in Elem. Edn./Reading, 1979; EdD in Curriculum and Supervision, Vanderbilt U., 1993. Cert. elem. educator, reading, gifted educator, Ky., Tenn. Tchr. lang. arts Morristown (Tenn.) City Schs., 1976-78; tutor, grad. asst. U. Tenn., Knoxville, 1978-79; reading tchr., migrant math. tchr., adult basic educator Clark County Schs., Winchester, Ky., 1979-90; vis. instr., supr. student interns Eastern Ky. U., Richmond, 1990-91; teaching asst. Vanderbilt U., Nashville, 1991-93; assoc. prof., dir. clin. experiences U. North Ala., Florence, 1993—, mem. grad. faculty, 1996—; cost ctr. head U. North Ala., Florence, 1993—, tchr. edn. coun. mem., 1993—, mem. first yr. tchr. survey task force, 1993—, internat. program steering com., 1996—, graphics standards com., 1996—. Co-author: University of North Alabama Teacher Education Handbook, 1994, Facilitating Reform: One Laboratory School's Collaborative Enterprise, 1994; author: University of North Alabama Student Internship Handbook, 1994; contbr. articles to profl. jours. Recipient Eliza Claybrooke Meml. scholarship Vanderbilt U., 1993. Mem. ASCD, Internat. Reading Assn., Am. Edn!. Rsch. Assn., Assn. Tchr. Educators, Am. Assn. Colls. for Tchr. Edn., Ala. Assn. Tchr. Educators (sec.-treas. 1995-96), Kiwanis, Phi Delta Kappa (v.p. U. North Ala. chpt. 1994-95), Alpha Upsilon Alpha, Kappa Delta Pi, Alpha Delta Kappa. Disciples of Christ. Office: U North Ala Box 5125 U North Alabama Florence AL 35632-0001

GILLEAN, WILLIAM OTHO, JR., physician, psychiatrist; b. Stamford, Tex., Jan. 24, 1935; s. William Otho and Esther (Parish) G.; m. Doris Milan Gillean, Nov. 4, 1964; children: William O. Gillean III, Julie R., Martha A., Anne E. BA, U. Tex., Austin, 1957; MD, U. Tex. Med. Branch, Galveston, 1961. Cert. in psychiatry. Intern, resident in psychiatry and neurology U. Tex. Med. Br. Hosp., Galveston, 1961-65; chief psychiatry svc. Brooke Army Hosp., 1967-68; pvt. practice, 1968—; clin. asst. prof. psychiatry U. Tex.

Health Sci Ctr., San Antonio, 1968—; staff psychiatrist VA, San Antonio, 1969-74, 90—; chief psychiatry dept. Baptist Meml. Hosp., 1969; chmn. psychiatric policy com. Villa Rosa Hosp., 1973; chief psychiatrist Ctr. for Health Care Svcs., San Antonio, 1973-89, med. specialist, 1990—; cons. Bexar County, San Antonio, 1968—; bd. dirs. Half Way House Inc., San Antonio, 1969-71. Capt. US Army, 1966-68. Named Cmty. Mental Health Worker of Yr. Mental Health Assn. Greater San Antonio, 1983. Mem. AMA, Titus Harris Soc., Bexar County Med. Soc., Tex. Med. Assn., Tex. Soc. Psychiat. Physicians, Am. Psychiat. Assn., Bexar County Psychiat. Soc., So. Med. Assn., Longhorn Found., Phi Beta Pi, Kappa Kappa Psi. Home and Office: PO Box 40308 San Antonio TX 78229

GILLELAND, DIANE SUITT, state official. BS in Edn., U. Ark., 1968, MEd, 1970; PhD in Higher Edn., So. Ill. U., 1992; postgrad., Bryn Mar Coll., 1978. Dir. Higher Edn. Dept., Little Rock. Toll. fellow, 1992. Office: Higher Edn Dept 114 E Capitol Ave Little Rock AR 72201-3820

GILLEN, HOWARD WILLIAM, neurologist, medical historian; b. Chgo., Nov. 25, 1923; s. John Howard and Emily Elizabeth (Bayley) G.; m. Corinne V. Neese, July 24, 1948. BS, U. Ill., 1947; MD, U. Ill., Chgo., 1949. Hon. active neurologist New Hanover Regional Med. Ctr., Wilmington, N.C., 1973-93, emeritus neurologist, 1993—; cons. neurologist Cape Fear Meml. Hosp., Wilmington, 1973-93; clin. prof. neurology U. N.C., Chapel Hill, 1973-93, clin. prof. emeritus, 1993—; adj. prof. biol. sci. U. N.C., Wilmington, 1986—; rsch. assoc. I.R.I.S.C., Wilmington, 1989-93, sr. investigator, 1993—. Capt. USNR, ret. Home: 2038 Trinity Ave Wilmington NC 28405-7880

GILLEN, WILLIAM ALBERT, lawyer; b. Sanford, Fla., May 26, 1914; s. William D. and Marie Carolyn (Holt) G.; m. Lillian Stevens Thornton, Aug. 19, 1939 (dec. May 1981); children: William Albert, Susan Marie Gillen Casper; m. Anita Thomas Hapner, Mar. 19, 1988. Student, U. Fla., 1931-32, 33-36, JD, 1936; student, U. Tampa, Fla., 1932-33; LLD (hon.), U. Tampa, 1983. Bar: Fla. 1936, U.S. Dist. Ct. (mid. and so. dists.) Fla. 1937, U.S. Supreme Ct. 1950, U.S. Ct. Appeals (5th and 11th cirs.) 1981. Practice law Tampa, Fla., 1936—; mem. Fowler, White, Gillen, Boggs, Villareal and Banker, P.A., 1946-89, of counsel, 1989—, chmn. bd., pres., 1970-86; mem. Hillsborough County Home Rule Charter Com., 1969-70, 13th Circuit Jud. Nominating Com., 1972-76, Fla. Supreme Ct. Jud. Nominating Commn., 1979-83; bd. dirs. Freedom Savs. and Loan Assn., Tampa, 1972-84, chmn., 1978-84. Assoc. editor: Am. Maritime Cases, 1948-89. Bd. dirs. Exec. Svc. Corps. Tampa, Inc., 1989-95, United Fund Tampa, 1956-64, Greater Tampa Citizens Safety Coun., 1966-69, U. South Fla. Found., 1965-68, pres., 1967-68; pres. Gulf Ridge coun. Boy Scouts Am., 1959. Maj. inf. AUS, 1942-46. Fellow Am. Coll. Trial Lawyers, Am. Bar Found., Fla. Bar Found.; mem. Hillsborough County Bar Assn. (pres. 1953), Fla. Bar Assn. (gov. 1951-57), Fedn. Ins. Counsel (pres. 1960-61, chmn. bd. dirs. 1961-62), Internat. Assn. Def. Counsel, Def. Research Inst. (v.p. 1961-62), Maritime Law Assn. U.S., ABA (co-chmn. conf. lawyers, ins. cos. and adjusters 1975-78), Com. of 100, Tampa C. of C. (pres. 1968-69), Am. Legion, Gasparilla Krewe (capt. 1968-70, King LVII 1970-71), Rotary Internat. Found., Phi Delta Phi, Sigma Alpha Epsilon, Sigma Alpha Epsilon Found. Democrat. Episcopalian. Clubs: Tampa Yacht and Country (bd. dirs. 1962-64), Univ. (bd. dirs. 1976-79, pres. 1978-79), Merrymakers, Palma Ceia Golf and Country (Tampa). Lodges: Rotary (pres. Tampa chpt. 1959-60), Masons. Home: 3109 W Sunset Dr Tampa FL 33629-5207 Office: Fowler White Gillen Boggs Villareal & Banker PA 501 E Kennedy Blvd Ste 1700 Tampa FL 33602-5200

GILLENWATER, JAY YOUNG, urologist, educator; b. Kingsport, Tenn., July 27, 1933; s. Jay King and Ann Marion (Young) G.; m. Shirley Joyce Brockman; children: Linda, Ann, Jay. BS, U. Tenn., 1954, MD, 1957. Diplomate Am. Bd. Urology (pres. 1988). Intern U. Pa. Grad. Hosp., 1958-59, resident, 1959-60, 62-65; asst. prof. U. Va. Med. Sch., Charlottesville, 1965-67, prof., chmn. urology dept., 1967-95; prof., 1995—; mem. coun. Nat. Inst. Diabetes and Digestive and Kidney Diseases, NIH, 1987-93; pres. AUA, 1991-92. Editor: Adult and Pediatric Urology, 1987, 91, 95; editor Urology Yearbook, 1978-94; assoc. editor Jour.Urology, 1985-93, editor, 1994—. Capt. U.S. Army, 1960-62. Mem. Am. Urol. Assn. (exec. com. 1987—, Hugh Young award, 1989, Mary Scott Hughes edn. award 1985, pres. 1991-92), Health Svc. Found. (pres. 1980-91), Am. Bd. Urology (pres. 1988), Am. Found. Urol. Diseases (pres. 1992—). Republican. Methodist. Home: 648 Dry Bridge Rd Charlottesville VA 22903-7630 Office: U Va Hosps Dept Urology Box 422 Charlottesville VA 22908

GILLER, NORMAN MYER, banker, architect, author; b. Jacksonville, Fla., Feb. 14, 1918; s. Morris and Esther (Seltzer) G.; m. Frances Schwartz, June 30, 1946; children: Ira D., Anita Giller Grossman, Brian. Student, Ga. Inst. Tech., 1943-44; BArch, U. Fla., 1945; postgrad. in banking, Bankers Adminstrn. Inst., 1965-66. Chmn. bd. Norman M. Giller and Assocs., Architects, Miami Beach, Fla., 1945—; chmn. bd., pres. Interam. Nat. Bank, Miami Beach, 1964-68; vice chmn. Jefferson Bancorp, Miami Beach, 1968—; pres., vice chmn. Jefferson Nat. Bank, Sunny Isles, Fla., 1968—; bd. dirs. Jefferson Nat. Bank, Miami Beach, Jefferson Nat. Bank of Palm Beach, Boca Raton, Fla., Jefferson Bank of Broward, Hollywood, Fla.; cons. U.S. Dept. State, Washington, 1961-70, Govts. Panama, Nicaragua, Brazil, Colombia, El Salvador, 1961-70. Author: An Adventure in Architecture, 1977, A Century in America, 1986; contbr. articles on architecture to profl. jours. Chmn. Miami Beach Housing Authority, 1970, Fla. State Bd. Architecture, Tallahassee, 1979, Design Rev. Bd. City of Miami Beach, 1985; pres. So. Fla. coun. Boy Scouts Am., 1961-63, Concerned Citizens of N.E. Dade County, Miami Beach, 1970; sec. Nat. Coun. Archtl. Registration Bd., S.E. Atlanta, 1981; mem. Sunny Isles Task Force, Fla., 1982; pres. Mosaic-Jewish Mus. Fla., 1992—. Lt. (j.g.) USNR, 1942-46. Named Man of Yr., Gold Coast C. of C., 1973; bridge named in his honor Fla. Legis., Miami Beach, 1983; recipient Man of the Decade award, 1989; named to Hall of Fame, Gold Coast C. of C., 1994. Fellow AIA (pres. South Fla. chpt. 1945—, Silver medal 1979); mem. Fla. Assn. Architecture (bd. dirs. 1945—, Cmty. Svc. award 1982), Am. Bankers Assn., Fla. Bankers Assn. (mem. com. 1965—), Fla. Bankers Holding Co. Assn., Miami Beach C. of C. (Citizen of the Yr. 1995, pres. 1970—). Democrat. Jewish. Lodges: Masons, Shriners. Office: Jefferson Bancorp Inc 975 Arthur Godfrey Rd Miami FL 33140-3329

GILLESPIE, BETTY GLOVER, critical care nurse; b. Abbeville, La., Aug. 7, 1939; d. Thomas F. and Idas (Baumgardner) Glover; m. Alfred H. Gillespie, Dec. 9, 1960; children: Kim Hammonds, Rick T. Hammonds, Mark W. BSN cum laude, Nicholls State U., 1987; postgrad., La. State U. RN, La.; cert. pediatric advanced life support; CCRN, ACLS. Staff nurse, rehab. unit Terrebonne Gen. Med. Ctr., Houma, La., staff nurse, telemetry; staff nurse, ICU Chabert Med. Ctr., Houma, 1989—; adj. facutly, precepetor BSN nursing program Nicholls State U. Mem. AACN (CCRN), Soc. Critical Care Medicine, Sigma Theta Tau. Home: 16 Parkway Cir Houma LA 70364-2812

GILLESPIE, JAMES DAVIS, lawyer; b. Elkin, N.C., Apr. 30, 1955; s. John Banner and Jerry Sue (Swaim) G.; m. Tommie Lee Johnson, Aug. 13, 1977; 1 child, John Foster. BA, U. N.C., 1977; JD, Samford U., 1980. Bar: N.C. 1980, U.S. Dist. Ct. (mid. dist.) 1982, U.S. Dist. Ct. (we. dist.) N.C. 1983, U.S. Ct. Appeals (4th cir.) 1984. Ptnr. Neaves & Gillespie, Elkin, 1980-91; mem. Surry-Yadkin Mental Health Authority, Mt. Aiy, N.C., 1981-91, vice chmn., 1987-89, chmn. 1990-91. Bd. editors: Cumberland Law Rev., 1978-80. Commr. Town of Jonesville, N.C., 1983-85, mayor, 1985-93; mem. exec. com. N.W. Piedmont Coun. Govts., 1987, sec., 1988-89, chmn., 1990-91; active Surry-Yadkin Mental Health, Mental Retardation and Substance Abuse Authority, 1981-91, vice chmn., 1987-89, chmn., 1990-91; bd. dirs. Foothills Art Coun., 1987-90. Mem. ABA, Assn. Trial Lawyers Am., N.C. Bar Assn., N.C. Trial Lawyers Assn., Surry and Yadkin Counties Bar Assn., Elkin Jaycees (bd. dirs. 1981-83, v.p. 1983-84), N.C. Acad. Trial Lawyers, Greater Elkin-Jonesville C. of C. (charter, bd. dirs. 1987-90), Phi Alpha Delta, Soc. Curia Honoris. Democrat. Baptist. Home: 371 Wagoner St Jonesville NC 28642-2658 Office: Neaves & Gillespie 124 W Main St Ste A Elkin NC 28621-3433

GILLETT, VICTOR WILLIAM, JR., title insurance company executive; b. El Paso, Tex., Feb. 4, 1932; s. Victor William and Alice Cecelia (Kemper) G.; BBA, Tex. A&M U., 1953; m. Anita Johanne Dexter, Mar. 1, 1975; children: Victor William, III, Blake Andrew. V.p., dist. mgr. Stewart Title Guaranty Co., Corpus Christi, Tex., 1955-61; pres., chief exec. officer Stewart Title & Trust Co., Phoenix, 1961-77, dir., 1965-77; sr. v.p., nat. mktg. dir. Stewart Title Guaranty Co., Houston, 1977-91, dir., 1981-91; sr. v.p. Stewart Title Guaranty Co., Irvine, Calif., 1988-91; pres. Old Republic Title Co. Bell County, Temple, Tex., 1992—; dir. Stewart Info. Svcs. Corp., 1983-91. Bd. dirs. Ariz. Heart Assn., 1970-73; bd. dirs., sec. Phoenix Civic Improvement Corp., 1974-76. With AUS, 1953-54. Mem. Am. Land Title Assn. (gov. 1969-71), Temple-Belton Bd. Realtors, Temple C. of C., Temple Rotary Club, Wildflower Country Club, Temple Area Homebuilders Assn., Assn. U.S. Army (pres., dir. 1968), Navy League, Former Students Assn. Tex. A&M U., 12th Man Found. (Tex. A&M U.). Episcopalian. Home: 5007 Sterling Dr Temple TX 76502-7108 Office: 2704 Exchange Plz Temple TX 76504-7059

GILLETTE, FRANK C., JR., mechanical engineer; m. Jane Gillette; 3 children. BS in Mech. Engring., U. Fla. Mech. designer Pratt & Whitney, 1962-77, chief of structures, 1977-80, engring. mgr. YF119 program, dir. engring. programs F119 engine projects for Govt. Engines and Space Propulsion, 1980-95, dir. advanced mil. programs, 1995—; presenter numerous papers to profl. socs. Recipient Disting. Svc. award U. Fla. Coll. Engring., Laurels award Aviation Week, 1991. Mem. AIAA (Nat. Engr. of Yr. award 1991), ASME, Soc. Automotive Engrs. (Cliff Garrett Turbomachinery Engring. award 1994). Home: 8325 Nashua Dr Palm Beach Gardens FL 33418-6047 Office: Pratt & Whitney Aircraft Govt Prop Division PO Box 109600 West Palm Beach FL 33410-9600

GILLETTE, HALBERT GEORGE, mathematics educator; b. Kansas City, Mo., Sept. 18, 1926; s. Halbert Reginald and Vinada Pearl (Varnado) G.; m. Dorothy Helene Youmans, Apr. 20, 1947; children: Richard Wayne, Susan Helene, Kenneth George, Eric Glen. BA, U. Nebr., 1964; MEd, Tulane U., 1974; EdS, Stetson U., 1983. Math., sci. and sci. research tchr. L.B. Johnson Jr. High Sch., Melbourne, Fla., 1974-76; math tchr. J. Madison Middle Sch., Titusville, Fla., 1976-77; math./sci. tchr. Titusville High Sch., 1977-78; tchr. math. Cocoa H.S., Fla., 1978-94; chmn. dept. math. Cocoa H.S., 1987-94; adj. math. instr. Brevard C.C., Cocoa, 1983—; assoc. math. instr. Keiser Coll., Melborne, Fla., 1996; question writer/judge Fla. H.S. Acad. Tournament, 1985—, Nat. Tournament for Acad. Excellence, 1987—. Del. leader People-to-People Friendship Caravan to USSR, 1990, to Australia, 1991; mem. del. 1st Joint U.S./Russia Conf. on Math. Edn., 1993. Lt. comdr. USN, 1944-74, ret. Named Tchr. of the Yr., Cocoa High Sch., 1983-84. Mem. NEA, Nat. Coun. Tchrs. Math., Fla. Coun. Tchrs. Math., Brevard Coun. Tchrs. Math. (treas. 1983—), Fla. Teaching Profession, Assn. Former Intelligence Officers (Nat. and Satellite chpts., v.p. Satellite chpt. 1994—), The Ret. Officers Assn. (Nat. and Cape Canaveral chpts.), Naval Investigative Svc. Retirees Fla. (sec. 1994—), Assn. Ret. Naval Investigative Svc. Spl. Agts., Astronaut Trail Shell Club, Fla. Ret. Educators Assn., Ctrl. Brevard Ret. Educators Assn. Home: 3740 Ocean Beach Blvd # 404 Cocoa Beach FL 32931-3425

GILLEY, JAMES WADE, university president; m. Nanna Beverly, 1961; children: Cheryl Rice, Wade Jr. Doctorate, Va. Tech.; postgrad., U. Fla., Harvard U. Past sec. edn. State of Va.; past. sr. v.p. George Mason U.; pres. Marshall Univ., Huntington, W. Va., 1991—. Author 3 books; contbr. articles to profl. jours. Active Huntington Mus. Art, W. Va. Jobs Investment Trust, Huntington Area Devel. Coun., 5th Ave. Bapt. Ch., other orgns. Mem. W. Va. Roundtable, Huntington Rotary Club, Huntington C. of C., Guyan Country Club. Office: Marshall Univ Office of Pres 400 Halgreer Blvd Huntington WV 25755*

GILLEY, W. KAY, small business owner, consultant, writer; b. Ft. Wayne, Ind., May 1, 1949; d. Howard R. and Evelyn M. (Alcorn) G.; m. James R. Hargreaves, Aug. 31, 1986 (div. Jan. 1995). BS, U. Oreg., 1989, MS, 1991. Author, editor: Hargreaves on HR and Focused Intent, 1991—, Leading From the Heart Choosing Courage Over Fear in the Workplace, 1996; co-author: (book) The New Bottomline-Blending Commerce With Consciousness, 1996; columnist The Human Factor, 1991-95.

GILLIAM, BRUCE LAWRENCE, internist; b. Harbor City, Calif., Sept. 2, 1962; s. Lawrence Noah and Julianne (Free) G. AB in Chemistry, Occidental Coll., 1984; MS in Pharm. Sci., U. Ariz., 1986; MD, Jefferson Med. Coll., 1990. Diplomate Am. Bd. Internal Medicine, Nat. Bd. Med. Examiners. Resident in internal medicine U. Calif. David Med. Ctr., Sacramento, 1990-93; fellow in infectious diseases U. N.C., Chapel Hill, 1993-96; rsch. physician Henry M. Jackson Found., Rockville, Md., 1996—. Named to Rho Chi Pharm. Soc., U. Ariz., 1985, Hobart Amory Hare Med. Honor Soc., Jefferson Med. Coll., 1988. Mem. AMA, ACP, IDSA. Home: 418 Little Quarry Rd Gaithersburg MD 20878 Office: Henry M Jackson Foundation 13 Taft Ct Ste 200 Rockville MD 20878

GILLIAM, GEORGIE ANN, primary education educator; b. Houston, Jan. 11, 1973; d. George W. and Nancy K. (Adams) G. BS in Interdisciplinary Studies, Stephen F. Austin State U., 1996. Desk clk. Castle Motel, Beaumont, Tex., 1990-93; mgr. Yo Ski Inc., Beaumont, 1993—; pres. reading coun. Stephen F. Austin State U., Nacogdoches, 1995-96. Mem. AAUW, Tex. State Reading Assn., Kappa Delta Pi. Republican. Office: Yo Ski Inc 1125 N 11th St Beaumont TX 77702

GILLIAM, NANCY D., operating room nurse; b. Nurenberg, Fed. Republic of Germany, Nov. 22, 1965; d. Leroy E. and Anne Marie (Döertler) G. ADN, Marymount U., Arlington, Va., 1987, BSN, 1989. RN, VA. Clinician II Fairfax Hosp., Falls Church, Va., 1987-92; oper. rm. nurse. Arlington (Va.) Hosp., 1992—. Capt. Nurse Corps, USAR, 1990—.

GILLICE, SONDRA JUPIN (MRS. GARDNER RUSSELL BROWN), sales and marketing executive; b. Urbana, Ill.; d. Earl Cranston and Laura Lorraine (Rose) Jupin; m. Gardner Russell Brown, Jan. 12, 1980; 1 child, Thomas Alan Gillice. BS, Lindenwood Coll.; MBA, Loyola Coll. Pers. officer N.Y. Citibank, 1968-70, 1st Nat. Bank of Chgo., 1970-72; mgr. human resources Potomac Electric Power Co., Washington, 1973-81; dir. pers. U.S. Synthetic Fuels Corp., Washington, 1981-86, v.p. human resources, Guest Svcs., Inc., 1987-90; v.p. sales and mktg., 1990-93; pres. Rus Son, Inc., 1994—; sr. v.p. govt. rels. Drake Beam Morin, Inc., 1994—. Mem. bd. govs. Loyola Coll., Nat. Coal Coun., mem. exec. com.; mem. nat. bd. Med. Coll. Pa.; bd. dirs. KHG Dance Theatre, Nat. Women's Econ. Alliance. Mem. AAUW (pres. Falls Church br. 1976-78), Edison Electric Inst. (chmn. tng. and mgmt. devel. com.), Am. Soc. Pers. Adminstrs., Greater Met. Washington Bd. Trade, Soroptimists (pres. Washington chpt. 1979-80), DAR, Army Navy Country Club, Soc. Magna Charta Dames, Edgartown Yacht Club, Georgetown Club. Republican.

GILLILAN, WILLIAM J, III, construction company executive; b. Pitts., June 20, 1946; s. William J, II and Sara Parker (Wynn) G.; BS in Indsl. Engring. with honors, Purdue U., 1968; MBA, Harvard U., 1970; m. Susan Woodyard, June 20, 1970; children: William J, Mary, John C., Mark. With Centex Corp., 1974—, exec. v.p. ops. Centex Homes Midwest, Inc. subs. Centex Corp., Palatine, Ill., 1978, pres., 1978-83; v.p. Centex Homes, 1980-83, exec. v.p., 1983-86, pres., COO, 1986-89, pres., CEO, 1989-90, chmn., CEO, 1990-91, chmn., 1991—; chmn., pres., CEO Centex Constrn. Group, 1990—; exec. v.p. Centex Corp., 1989-90, exec. v.p., COO, 1990-91, pres., COO, 1991—. Served to lt. USNR, 1970-74. Mem. Northwood Country Club, Delta Tau Delta. Republican. Presbyterian. Home: 6115 Shadycliff Dr Dallas TX 75240-5337 Office: Centex Corp 3333 Lee Pky Dallas TX 75219-5111*

GILLILAND, IRENE LYDIA, nursing educator; b. Phila., Nov. 30, 1950; d. Michael and Tatiana (Koziol) Chodan; m. Charles Donald Gilliland, Mar. 23, 1974 (div. Dec. 1990); children: Ami, Charles, Robert. BSN, Villanova U., 1972; MSN, U. Va., 1986. Lectr. nursing Radford (Va.) U., 1986-87; nursing instr. Va. Western C.C., Roanoke, Va., 1984-90, U. of the Incarnate Word, San Antonio, 1991—; hospice case mgr. Santa Rosa Hospice, San Antonio, 1994—; cost containment cons. ins. cos. in field, 1988—. Mem. ANA, AAUP, Women in Bus., Am. Holistic Nurses Assn., Am. Assn. Holistic Aromatherapy, Sigma Theta Tau. Home: 21527 Longwood San Antonio TX 78259 Office: Univ of the Incarnate Word San Antonio TX 78209

GILLILAND, MARION CHARLOTTE S., volunteer; b. Duluth, Minn., Dec. 29, 1918; d. John Oscar and Jenny Olympia (Wangberg) Spjut; m. Charles Herbert Gilliland, Mar. 6, 1942; children: Charles Herbert Jr., Marion Charlotte Jr., Patricia Ann, Norman Paul, Cynthia Eileen. BA in Anthropology with honors, U. Fla., 1963, MA in Anthropology, 1965. Author: The Material Culture of Key Marco, Florida, 1976, Key Marco's Buried Treasure, 1989, Dearest Daught and Popsy Wells; Two Artists named Sawyer, 1995, The Calusa Indians of Florida, 1995; contbr. articles to newspapers and profl. jours. Pres. Alachua County (Fla.) Childrens Com., 1959-61, Alachua County Scholarship and Loan Fund, 1960-62, Gainesville (Fla.) Womens Forum 1993-94; v.p. govtl. rels. div. Gainesville C. of C., 1977-79; health com. Human Svcs. Planning Coun., Gainesville, 1980-84; bd. dirs. Fla. Arts Celebration, Gainesville, 1984-91; sec. Friends of Music U. Fla., 1994—, pres., 1990-92; pres. Gainesville Women's Forum, 1993-94. Recipient Peggy Wilcox Svc. award State of Fla., 1985, Woman of Distinction award Santa Fe C.C., 1993, Women Who Make a Difference award Girl Scouts U.S., 1996. Mem. Fla. Med. Assn. Aux. (pres. 1969-70, bd. dirs. 1970-73), AMA Aux. (sec. 1975-76, v.p. so. regional 1976-78, historian 1978-79), Alachua County Med. Aux. (pres. 1960-61), So. Anthropol. Soc., Fla. Anthropol. Soc., Archael. Inst. Am., Nat. Assn. Underwater Investigators, Fla. Mus. Assocs., Fla. Women's Alliance (charter mem.), Mortar Bd. (hon.), Phi Kappa Phi. Home: 3031 SW 70th Ln Gainesville FL 32608-5216

GILLILAND, MARY MARGARETT, healthcare consultant; b. Leland, Miss., Dec. 23, 1942; d. Lindon Edward and Allie Earlene (Saulters) Palmore; m. Carl Ralph Gilliland, Jan. 12, 1963; children: Carl Ralph, Gini Lynn. Diploma in Nursing, Greenwood Leflore, 1963; B of Healthcare Adminstrn., East Tex. State U., 1976; M of Human Rels. and Mgmt., Abilene Christian U., 1978; BS, Tex. Woman's U., 1991, MS, 1993. RN, Tex. Staff nurse Sunflower County Health Dept., Indianola, Miss., 1965-66; asst. dir. nursing Presbyn. Hosp. Dallas, 1966-80, assoc. dir. nursing, 1980-87, assoc. exec. dir., 1987-91; healthcare cons. G&S Healthcare Cons., Allen, Tex., 1991—; adj. faculty Tex. Woman's U., Denton. Contbr. articles to profl. jours. Mem. ANA, Am. Orgn. Nurse Execs., Tex. Orgn. Nurse Execs., Tex. Nurses Assn. (continuing edn. com, Great 100 Nurses 1991), Nurses Alumni Assn. (sec.) Sigma Theta Tau, Phi Kappa Phi. Home: 2101 Rigsbee Dr Plano TX 75074-4913 Office: G&S Healthcare Cons Raceway Profl Bldg I 200 Boyd Pl Allen TX 75002-2560

GILLILAND, TERRI KIRBY, accountant; b. Tuscaloosa, Ala., Oct. 4, 1954; d. William Park and Bobbie (Fitts) Kirby; m. Glenn Scott Gilliland, Aug. 31, 1991; 1 child, Joshua Scott. BS in Commerce and Bus. Adminstrn., U. Ala., Tuscaloosa, 1977. CPA, Ala. Staff acct. Yeager & Christian CPAs, Tuscaloosa, 1979-84; chief acct. HealthSouth Rehab. Corporation, Birmingham, Ala., 1984-86; sr. acct. DeWitt & DeWitt CPAs, Tuscaloosa, 1986-93; acct. II-tax Hunt Refining Co., Tuscaloosa, 1993—; mem. regional adv. com. U.S. Small Bus. Adminstrn., Birmingham, 1991-93. Participant Leadership Tuscaloosa, 1988-89. Mem. AICPA, Am. Soc. Women Accts. (treas. West Ala. chpt. 1991-92, sec. 1992-93), Ala. Soc. CPAs, Inst. Mgmt. Accts. (acquisition dir.). Baptist. Home: 3015 1st Ct Tuscaloosa AL 35405-2201 Office: Hunt Refining Co PO Box 038995 Tuscaloosa AL 35403-8995

GILLILLAND, THOMAS, art gallery director; b. Bladen, Nebr., Feb. 14, 1932; s. Whitney and Virginia (Wegmann) G.; m. Cora Lee Critchfield, Aug. 23, 1956; children: Shaun, Ruth, Virginia. Grad., Wentworth Mil. Acad., 1952; BA, Am. U., 1963, MA, 1967. Dep. dir. congl. liaison AID, Washington, 1969-75; congl. liaison officer USDA, Washington, 1975-76, dir. legis. affairs Animal and Plant Health Inspection Svc., 1976-83; dir. external affairs Fin. Mgmt. Svc. U.S. Dept. Treasury, Washington, 1983-93; owner Art in the Hand Gallery, St. Augustine, Fla., 1994—. Contbr. mag. articles. Mem. Nat. Assn. Govt. Communicators (Blue Pencil award 1986), Soc. for Preservation and Encouragement of Barbershop Quartet Singing in Am., Nat. Press Club. Republican. Presbyterian. Home: 65 Fullerwood Dr Saint Augustine FL 32095-2167

GILLIS, RICHARD PAUL, management consultant; b. El Paso, Tex., Dec. 16, 1953; s. Richard Paul Gillis and Gloria (Quinonez) Pena; children: Aric Adam, Tory Evan. BS in Mgmt., Park Coll., 1986. Studio rec. engr. various orgns., El Paso and Denver, 1978—; sales rep. Wilmot Printing, El Paso, 1983-84; fleet/leasing mgr. Casa Ford/Nissan, El Paso, 1984-86; leasing mgr. Koger Properties, El Paso, Jacksonville, Fla., 1986-90; gen. mgr. Koger Mgmt., El Paso, Jacksonville, 1990—; v.p. Tara Designs & Mktg., El Paso; ptnr. Steele/Gillis Prodns., El Paso and Nashville. Mem. Reach for a Star, El Paso, 1988; arbitrator Better Bus. Bur. of El Paso, 1989; bd. dirs. Ronald McDonald House of El Paso. With USAF, 1975-76. Mem. Rotary Club El Paso. Office: Koger Properties Ste 120 444 Executive Center Blvd El Paso TX 79902-1014

GILLISPIE, RONNIE STEPHEN, health science facility administrator; b. Eden, N.C., Feb. 28, 1948; s. Earl Warren and Katherine (Stowe) G.; m. Verona Lynette Gusler, Nov. 6, 1971; children: Ronald Kevin, Byron Lee, Stephen Glenn. Grad., Watts Hosp. Sch. Radiologic Technologists, 1969; various coll. courses, 1969—. Emergency room charge technologist Watts Hosp., 1969-72, instr., 1972-73, asst. chief technologist, dir. edn., 1973-75, acting chief technologist, 1975, adminstrv. asst., 1975-76; adminstrv. asst. Durham Regional Hosp., 1976-79, dir. radiology services, 1979-92, dir. cardiac catheterization svcs., 1987-92; asst. v.p. facility svcs., co-coord. high tech. assessment com., co-chair corp. capital expenditur com. Durham County Hosp. Corp., 1992—. Mem. adv. com. on radiol. sci. Vance-Granville C.C. Mem. Am. Soc. Radiologic Technologists (counselor 1973-75, membership com. 1974), Am. Mgmt. Assn., N.C. Soc. Radiologic Technologists (life with honor; bd. dirs. 1974-75, 1st v.p. 1975-76, pres. 1978-79, jr. bd. dirs. 1979-80, chmn. bd. dirs. 1980-81, also numerous coms.), Triangle Soc. Radiologic Technologists (bd. dirs. 1971-72, 73-76, chmn. bd. dirs. 1975-77, co-chmn. 1974-76, chmn. program com. 1973-75, chmn. nominating com. 1974-76, chmn. seminar com. 1976, chmn. fin. com. 1976-77), Am. Hosp. Radiology Adminstrs., Assn. Univ. Radiologic Technologists, Am. Radiol. Nurses Assn. Methodist. Home: 5804 Koback Dr Durham NC 27712-3612 Office: Durham County Hosp Corp 3643 N Roxboro Rd Durham NC 27704-2702

GILLMAN, BARBARA SEITLIN, artist, gallery owner; b. Miami, Fla.. Student, Tulane U., 1955-57; BA, U. Miami, 1958. pvt. art dealer/cons., 1968-79; head JCC Cultural Arts afterschool program Pinecrest Elem. Sch., 1970s; juror Gasparilla Art Festival, Tampa, Fla., 1988; Silver Knight awards art juror, spons. Miami Herald, 1988, 90, 91; lectr. S. Fla. Art Ctr., 1990, Boca Mus. Art, Fla., 1991; curator City of Orlando Aqui! Hispano Arte en Orlando, 1992; panelist in field. Brought works of Andy Warhol to Miami with Toby Ansin, Beth David Fine Arts and the Lowe Mus., 1980; brought Internat. Water Sculpture Competition exhibit from New Orleans World Fair to Miami, 1984 (One of Top Ten exhibits of Yr. Miami Herald); opened Barbara Gillman Gallery, Miami, 1979 (Best Art Gallery, Miami S. Fla. Mag. 1985, New Times Newspaper 1991), Miami Beach, 1992; subject numerous media articles. Trustee Dade County (Fla.) Performing Arts Trust, 1991; mem. First Cultural Colloquium, spons. Dade County Arts and Sci. Coun. Office: Barbara Gillman Gallery The Sterling Bldg 939 Lincoln Rd Miami Beach FL 33139-2601

GILMAN, ALFRED GOODMAN, pharmacologist, educator; b. New Haven, July 1, 1941; s. Alfred and Mabel (Schmidt) G.; m. Kathryn Hedlund, Sept. 21, 1963; children: Amy, Anne, Edward. BS, Yale U., 1962; MD, PhD, Case Western Res. U., 1969; DSc (hon.), U. Chgo., 1991, Case Western Res. U., 1995. Pharmacology research assoc. NIH, Bethesda, Md., 1969-71; from asst. prof. to assoc. prof. pharmacology U. Va., Charlottesville, 1971-77, prof., 1977-81, dir. med. sci. tng. program, 1979-81; prof. pharmacology, chmn. dept. U. Tex. Southwestern Med. Ctr., Dallas, 1981—, Raymond Willie prof. molecular neuropharmacology, 1987—; mem. pharmacology study sect. NIH, 1977-81, mem. nat. adv. gen. med. scis. coun., 1992-95; bd. sci. counselors Nat. Heart, Lung & Blood Inst. NIH, 1982-86; sci. adv. com. Am. Cancer Soc., N.Y.C., 1982-86; adv. com. Lucille P. Markey Charitable Trust, Miami, Fla., 1984-96; sci. rev. bd. Howard Hughes Med. Inst., Bethesda, 1986-93; dir. Regeneron Pharmaceutics, 1989—, Eli Lilly and Co., Inc., 1995—. Editor: The Pharmacological Basis of Therapeutics, 1975, 80, 85, 90; contbr. over 200 articles to profl. jours. Recipient Poul Edvard Poulsson award Norwegian Pharmacology Soc., 1982, GairdnerFound. Internat. award, Can., 1984, Albert Lasker Basic Med.

Rsch. award, 1989, Passano Sr. award Passano Found., 1990, Waterford Biomedical Sci. award Scripps Clinic and Rsch. Found. 1990, Basic Sci. Rsch. prize Am. Heart Assn., 1990, Steven C. Beering award Ind. U., 1990, City of Medicine award, Durham, N.C., 1991, CIBA-GEIGY Drew award, 1991, Nobel Prize in Physiology or Medicine, 1994. Mem. Am. Soc. Pharmacology & Exptl. Therapeutics (John J. Abel award in pharmacology 1975, Louis S. Goodman and Alfred Gilman award 1990), Am. Soc. Biol. Chemistry, Nat. Acad. Scis. (Richard Lounsbery award 1987), Am. Acad. Arts and Scis., Inst. Medicine of NAS. Office: U Tex Southwestern Med Ctr Dept Pharmacology 5323 Harry Hines Blvd Dallas TX 75235-9041*

GILMAN, JOSEPH MICHAEL, telecommunications executive; b. Sullivan, Ind., Nov. 12, 1952; s., Bruce Arnold and Joy Maxine (Sharpe) G.; m. Susan Ann Wine, Aug. 28, 1951; children: Emily Marie, Natalie Elizabeth, Hannah Irene. BS in Math., Morehead State U., 1974; MS in Mgmt. of Tech., MIT, 1990. Mgr. South Ctrl. Bell, Louisville, 1974-85, dist. mgr., 1985-87; ops. mgr. South Ctrl. Bell, Birmingham, Ala., 1987-90; dir. BellSouth Svcs., Atlanta, 1990-92; v.p. BellSouth Internat., Atlanta, 1992-94, BellSouth Europe, Brussels, 1994—; bd. dirs. Bell South Asia/Pacific Enterprises, Atlanta, 1992—. Mem. corp. gifts com. Woodruff Arts Ctr., Atlanta, 1993, 94. Mem. Australian C. of C., Am. C. of C. Office: BellSouth Internat 1100 Peachtree St NE Ste 400 Atlanta GA 30309-4529

GILMAN, RONALD LEE, lawyer; b. Memphis, Oct. 16, 1942; s. Seymour and Rosalind (Kuzin) G.; m. Betsy Dunn, June 11, 1966; children—Laura M., Sherry I. B.S., MIT, 1964; J.D. cum laude, Harvard U., 1967. Bar: Tenn. 1967, U.S. Supreme Ct. 1971. Mem. Farris, Mathews, Gilman, Branan & Hellen, Memphis, 1967—; judge Tenn. Ct. of Judiciary, 1979-87; lectr. trial advocacy U. Memphis Law Sch., 1980—. Contbr. articles to profl. jours. Regional chmn. ednl. coun. MIT, 1968-88; bd. dirs. Memphis Jewish Home, 1984-87, Chickasaw coun. Boy Scouts Am., 1993—; mem. Leadership Memphis. Recipient Sam A. Myar Jr. Meml. award for outstanding service to legal profession and community, 1981. Mem. ABA (ho. of dels. 1990—), Am. Law Inst., Am. Judicature Soc., Am. Coll. Trust and Estate Counsel, Memphis Bar Assn. (pres. 1987), Tenn. Bar Assn. (spkr. ho. of dels. 1985-87, pres. 1990-91), 6th Cir. Jud. Conf. (life), Am. Arbitration Assn. (mem. large, complex case panel 1993—), Econ. Club, Kiwanis. Democrat. Jewish. Address: Farris Mathews Gilman One Commerce Sq Ste 2000 Memphis TN 38103

GILMAN, SHELDON GLENN, lawyer; b. Cleve., July 20, 1943. BBA, Ohio U., 1965; JD, Case Western Res. U., 1967. Bar: Ohio 1967, Ky. 1971, Ind. 1982, Fla. 1984, D.C. 1985, Tenn. 1985, U.S. Supreme Ct., 1987. Mem. staff accts. tax dept. Arthur Andersen & Co., Cleve., 1966-68; assoc. Handmaker, Weber & Meyer, Louisville, 1971-74, ptnr., 1974-83; ptnr. Barnett & Alagia, Louisville, 1984-87; ptnr. Lynch, Cox, Gilman & Mahan, P.S.C., 1987—; gen. counsel Louisville Assn. Life Underwriters, 1977, 78, 90; adj. prof. law U. of Louisville Sch. of Law. Bd. dirs., chmn. Louisville Minority Bus. Resource Ctr., 1975-80; pres. Congregation Adath Jeshurun, 1986-88; bd. dirs., v.p., sec. Louisville Orch., 1982-85; bd. dirs. City of Devondale (Ky.), 1976, United Synagogue of Cons. Judaism, N.Y., 1989—, also pres. Ohio Valley region. With JAGC, AUS, 1968-71. Mem. Ky. Bar Assn. (ethics com. 1982-86), Louisville Employee Benefit Council (pres. 1980). Office: Lynch Cox Gilman & Mahan 500 Meidinger Towers Louisville KY 40202

GILMORE, DAVID SCHNEITER, administrator; b. St. Louis, Nov. 27, 1951. BS in Psychology, S.E. Mo. U., 1974, MA in Psychology, 1981. Bd. cert. pyschotherapist; cert. hypnotherapist. Chief psychologist State of Mo., Farmington, 1975-80; pvt. practice Farmington, 1978-80; prof. State of Mo., Flat River, 1978-80; rehab. cons. Ft. Myers, 1980-85; adminstr., dir. Ctr. for Pain Control, Ft. Myers, 1985-91; adminstr. Bayshore Workplaces, Ft. Myers, 1990-91, Vocat. and Rehab. Svcs., Ft. Myers, 1980—; prin. The Gilmore Clinic, Ft. Myers, Sarasota, St. Petersburg, Orlando, St. Louis, Miami, Fla., 1986—. Mem. Am. Psychol. Assn., Fla. Rehab. Assn. (pres. S.E. chpt.).

GILMORE, JAMES STUART, III, state attorney general; b. Richmond, Va., Oct. 6, 1949; s. James Stuart, Jr. and Margaret Kandle G. BA, U. Va., 1971, JD, 1977. Atty. Harris, Tuck, Freasier & Johnson, 1977-80, Benedetti, Gilmore, Warthen & Dalton, 1984-87; formerly commonwealth's atty. Henrico County, Va.; now atty. gen. State of Va.; alt. del. Rep. Nat. Conv., 1976; chmn. Henrico County Rep. Com., 1982-85, now vice chmn.;. With U.S. Army, 1971-74. Mem. Nat. Dist. Atty. Assn., Va. Bar Assn., Va. Trial Lawyers Assn., Va. Commonwealt Attys. Assn,, Phi Delta Phi. Methodist. Office: Office Atty Gen 900 E Main St Richmond VA 23219*

GILMORE, KENNY B., career officer; b. Carthage, Miss., Mar. 18, 1961; s. Kendal and Joan (Ware) G.; m. Carleen J. Jones, May 26, 1984; children: Lacey Anne, Tyler Jennings. BS, Agrl. Extension Edn., 1983; MEd, Miss. State U., 1986. Cert. tchr. Miss. Tchr. Sturgis (Miss.) H.S., 1983-86; ops. officer Newton (Miss.) Nat. Guard, 1986-95, adminstrv. officer, 1995—; cons. Double G Farms, Union, Miss., 1992—. Served to maj. N.G. Decorated Meritorious Svc. medal, Army Commendation medal, others. Mem. Nat. FFA Alumni (life), Air Def. Arty. Assn., Field Arty. Assn., Miss. Nat. Guard Assn. Home: 1049 Hwy 21 S Union MS 39365 Office: Miss Army Nat Guard 412 Northside Dr Newton MS 39345-2381

GILMORE, LINDA LOUISE TRAYWICK, nursing educator; b. Alexander City, Ala., Dec. 4, 1962; d. James Winston and Vena Louise (Curlee) Traywick; m. Gerald Bates Gilmore, Aug. 24, 1985; 1 child, Ethan Bates Gilmore. AS, Alexander City State Jr. Coll., 1984; RN, Sylacauga Hosp. Sch. Nursing, 1985; BSN, U. Ala., Birmingham, 1988; MSN, Troy State U., 1992. RN, Ala.; cert. med.-surg. nurse, chemotherapy, and oncology clin. nurse, BLS instr., oncology nurse. Staff nurse U. Ala. Hosps., Birmingham, 1985-89, S.E. Ala. Med. Ctr., Dothan, 1989-94; ADN instr. Wallace Coll., Dothan, 1991-95; asst. prof. BSN program Troy (Ala.) State U., 1996—; quality assurance rep. perinatal divsn. Univ. Hosp., Birmingham, 1986-88; discharge planning rep. S.E. Ala. Med. Ctr., Dothan, 1989-91; faculty advisor Wallace Assn. Nursing Students, Dothan, 1993-95; mem. courtesy com. Wallace Coll., 1994-95; mem. drug computation com. Wallace ADN, 1994-95. Choir mem., soloist Bay Springs Bapt. Ch., Dothan, 1990—, guest speaker Hospice care Sr. Citizen Group, 1992, guest speaker nursing Bible Sch. Class, 1993, discipleship tng. tchr., 1993—, dir. children's choir grades 1-3, 1995—; vol. firefighter Bay Springs Vol. Fire Dept., Dothan, 1993—. Mem. ANA, Oncology Nursing Soc., Ala. State Nurses Assn. (v.p. dist. 7 1993-95). Baptist. Office: Troy State U Collegeview Bldg Troy AL 36082

GILMORE, LORETTA TUTTLE, social worker; b. Newark, June 12, 1949; d. Lester Banks and Doris Elizabeth (Carey) Rodgers; married, Jan. 16, 1971 (div. 1978); children: Nicole, Mark. Student, Langston (Okla.) U., 1967-71; BA, Rutgers U., 1975, postgrad. Grad. Sch. Social Work, 1977-78. Social caseworker Dept. Pub. Welfare, Newark, 1968-69, Essex County Welfare Bd., Newark, 1972-73; adminstrv. asst. to prin. tchr. St. Rocco Sch., Newark, 1975-77; social worker juvenile rehab., juvenile justice system Essex County Div. Youth Svc., Newark, 1985-94; counselor Children and Family Svcs. Foster Care, West Palm Beach, Fla., 1994-95; dir. social svcs. Sutton Pl. Rehab. and Health Care Ctr., Lakeworth, Fla., 1995—; counselor Essex County Div. Youth Svc., Newark 1973-85, Girls Ctr. of Essex County, 1974-76. Mem. Delta Sigma Theta. Roman Catholic. Home: 1401 Village Blvd Apt 2116 West Palm Beach FL 33409-2794

GILMORE, LOUISA RUTH, retired nurse, retired firefighter; b. Pitts., Oct. 31, 1930; d. Albert Leonard and Bertha Christina (Birch) Huber; m. William Norman Kemp, May 27, 1950 (div. 1975); children: Janyce Louise Kemp Lipson, Barbra Lea Kemp Bilharz, Robert William, Paul Lee, Charles Albert; m. Robert James Gilmore, Sept. 1, 1989. Diploma in nursing, San Bernardino C.C., Needles, Calif., 1983. Office nurse Santa Fe Clinic, Needles, 1953-57; spl. duty nurse Needles Cmtys. Hosp., 1957-62; nurse supr. Santa Fe Clinic, 1962-79; staff nurse in surgery Needles Desert Cmtys. Hosp., 1979-90; Cell Tech ind. distbr. Reliv Products, Temple, Tex., 1991—; instr. CPR Needles Desert Cmtys. Hosp., 1987-90; med. officer San Bernardino County Fire Dept., Needles, 1980-83, pub. info. officer, 1983-85, vol. fire fighter, 1983-90; ind. distbr. Reliv Products, 1991-95, Cell Tech., 1996—. Mem. Calif. State Fireman Assn., Needles Firefighters Assn. (treas. 1987, 88), Beta Sigma Phi-Zeta Gamma (treas. 1966, sec. 1967, v.p. 1968, pres. 1969, named Sweetheart Queen 1969), Order of Rose (life).

GILMORE, MARJORIE HAVENS, civic worker, lawyer; b. N.Y.C., Aug. 16, 1918; d. William Westerfield and Elsie (Medl) Havens; AB, Hunter Coll., 1938; JD, Columbia, 1941; m. Hugh Redland Gilmore, May 8, 1942; children: Douglas Hugh, Anne Charlotte Gilmore Decker, Joan Louise. Admitted to N.Y. State bar, 1941, Va. bar, 1968; rsch. asst. N.Y. Law Revision Commn., 1941-42; assoc. firm Spence, Windels, Walser, Hotchkiss & Angell, N.Y.C., 1942, Chadbourne, Wallace, Parke & Whiteside, N.Y.C., 1942-43; atty. U.S. Army, Washington, 1948-53. Sec., Thomas Jefferson Jr. High Sch. PTA, 1956-58; chmn. by-laws rev. com., Long Point Corp., Ferrisburg, Vt., 1981-93; parliamentarian Wakefield High Sch. PTA, 1959-60, chmn. citizenship com., 1960-61; publicity chmn. Patrick Henry Sch. PTA, sec., 1964-65; parliamentarian Nottingham PTA, 1966-69; mem. extra-curricular activities com. Arlington County Sch. Bd.; area chmn. fund drive Cancer Soc., 1955-56; active Girl Scouts U.S.A., 1963-70; mem. '41 com. Columbia Law Sch. Fund. Recipient Constl. Law award Hunter Coll., 1938. Mem. Arlington Fedn. Women's Clubs (rec. sec. 1979-80), No. Dist. Va. Fedn. Women's Clubs (chmn. legis. com. 1986-88, chmn. pub. affairs No. dist. 1988-90), Columbia Law Sch. Alumni Assn., Alpha Sigma Rho. Presbyn. Club: Williamsburg Woman's of Arlington (corr. sec. 1970-72, 1st v.p. 1972-74, pres. 1974-76, chmn. communications 1981-82, chmn. legis. com. 1982-86, 90—). Home: 3020 N Nottingham St Arlington VA 22207-1268

GILMORE, ROBIN HARRIS, emergency department nurse; b. Wilmington, N.C., Apr. 23, 1964; d. John Sidney and Emily (Newton) Harris; m. Christopher Alan Gilmore, Feb. 20, 1993. AAN, Southeastern C.C., 1987. RN, ACLS, BTLS, MICN. From staff nurse to asst. nurse mgr. ER Columbus County Hosp., Whiteville, N.C., 1993-95; critical care nurse mgr., current CCU, ICU, ED Columbus County Hosp., Whiteville, 1995—. Mem. Emergency Nurses Assn. Republican. Baptist. Home: PO Box 1835 Rd#1546 Whiteville NC 28472 Office: Columbus County Hosp 500 Jefferson St Whiteville NC 28472

GILMORE, STEPHEN VINCENT, actuary; b. Fremont, Ohio, June 23, 1952; s. Harold S. and Florence K. (Ramseyer) G.; m. Sharon Ann Conkle, June 21, 1986. BS, Miami U., Oxford, Ohio, 1974, MS in Stats., 1975. Lic. actuary, U.S. Treas. With Cowan Actuarial Co., Cin., 1975-82; assoc. actuary Maccabees Mut. Life Ins. Co., Southfield, Mich., 1982-86; sr. cons. Peat Marwick Mitchell & Co., Cleve., 1986-87; sr. actuarial cons. Compensation Systems, Inc. of Am., Flint, Mich., 1987-89; enrolled actuary J.T. Comer & Assocs., Charlotte, N.C., 1989-90; actuary Miami Valley Pension Svc., Dayton, 1991-92; enrolled actuary Advanced Pension Systems, Inc., Charlotte, 1992—. Mem. Soc. Actuaries (assoc., cert.), Am. Acad. Actuaries, Am. Soc. Pension Actuaries, Pi Mu Epsilon. Home: 10305 Shelter Rock Ct Charlotte NC 28214-8674 Office: Advanced Pension Systems 2432 N Sharon Amity Rd Charlotte NC 29205

GILMORE, THOMAS MEYER, trade association administrator, secretary; b. Millheim, Pa., Mar. 10, 1942; s. Harold Grant and Phyllis (Meyer) G.; m. Linda Steiglitz, June 23, 1972; children: Joshua Paul, Megan Elizabeth. BS, Lock Haven (Pa.) U., 1965; MS in Organic Chemistry, U. Del., 1970; PhD in Food Sci., Pa. State U., 1976. Instr. U. Del., Georgetown, 1967-72; prof. Del. Tech. and C.C., Georgetown, 1975-78; asst. prof. S.D. State U., Brookings, 1978-82; sr. food technologist Hershey (Pa.) Foods Corp., 1982-85; tech. dir. Dairy and Food Industry Supply Assn., McLean, Va., 1985—; tech. rep. to ANSI/ISO TC-199 (safety and hygiene requirements for machinery). Contbr. articles to profl. jours. Pres. Brookings Lions, 1981. Mem. NEA (life), ASTM, Am. Soc. Agrl. Engrs., Internat. Assn. Milk, Food, Environ. Sanitations, Am. Dairy Sci. Assn. (profl.) sec. dairy food div. 1987-90, Inst. Food Tech. (counselor Washington chpt. 1987-93, treas. Keystone chpt. 1985, exec. coun. dairy tech. div. 1987-88), N.E. Dairy Practice Coun., Internat. Dairy Fedn. (com. mem. experts on hygenic design dairy processing equip., chem. rep. to Frederick Co. sludge task force). Independent. Episcopalian. Home: 4645 Lynn Burke Rd Monrovia MD 21770-9428 Office: Dairy & Food Industries 1651 Dolley Madison Blvd Mc Lean VA 22101-3418

GILMOUR, JOHN BRAYTON, political science educator; b. Richmond, Va., Feb. 22, 1955; s. Neil and Martha Doris (Myers) G.; m. Ann Reid Kendrick, May 28, 1988; 1 child, Elizabeth Ann. AB, Oberlin Coll., 1977; MA, U. Va., 1980; PhD, U. Calif., 1985. Asst. prof. polit. sci. Washington U., St. Louis, 1987-95; asst. prof. govt. Coll. William and Mary, Williamsburg, Va., 1995—. Author: Reconcilable Differences?, 1990, Strategic Disagreement, 1995; contbr. articles to profl. jours. Office: Coll William and Mary Dept Govt Williamsburg VA 23187

GILPIN, PETER RANDALL, retired state government insurance regulator; b. Danville, Ill., Oct. 3, 1927; s. Ralph Theodore Gilpin and Harriet Ellen (Randall) Medford; m. Wilma Poovey, Nov. 10, 1979; children: Lisa Kent Tan, Jeffrey Randall, Scarlett Hartzoge. BA in Journalism, U. Houston, 1950. Reporter, asst. mag. editor Houston Chronicle, 1950-58; reporter, city editor Asheville (N.C.) Citizen-Times, 1958-65; dir. pub. rels. U. N.C., Asheville, 1966-78; Congl. press asst. U.S. Rep. Lamar Gudger, Washington, 1978-81; office mgr. Washington Area Intergroup, 1982; spl. asst., asst. supr., dept. western/regional affairs N.C. Dept. Insurance, Raleigh and Asheville, 1982—; spl. cons. N.C. Dept. Inst., Asheville, 1995—. Co-author: Lunsford/Minstrel of Appalachians, 1966. Mem. Mayor's Com. on Employment of Handicapped, Asheville, 1975-78; mem. Mayor's Com. on Alcohol and Drug Abuse, Washington, 1982; trustee emeritus Crossnore (N.C.) Sch., 1966-86; mem. alumni coun. Christ Sch., Arden, N.C., 1990-93. Recipient Med. Press award N.C. Med. Soc., 1962, Order of Long Leaf Pine, Gov. of N.C., 1994. Democrat. Episcopalian. Home: 468 Old Haw Creek Rd Asheville NC 28805

GILSTRAP, LEAH ANN, media specialist; b. Seneca, S.C., Sept. 12, 1950; d. Raymond Chester and Eunice Hazel (Long) G. BA in History, Furman U., 1976, MEd, 1982; MLS, U. S.C., 1991. Cert. tchr., media specialist, S.C. Tchr., spl. edn. Greenville (S.C.) County Sch. Dist., 1978-79, tchr., 1978-92, media specialist, 1992—. Mem. NEA (del. 1991-95), ALA, S.C. Assn. Sch. Librs., S.C. Edn. Assn. (bd. dirs. 1994—), Greenville County Edn. Assn. (bd. dirs. 1988—, governance chair 1988—, v.p. 1996—), Greenville County Coun. Media Specialists (bd. dirs. 1993-94). Democrat. Baptist. Home: 150 Howell Cir Apt 184 Greenville SC 29615-4915 Office: Bryson Mid Sch 3657 S Industrial Dr Simpsonville SC 29681-3238

GIMENEZ, CARLOS ANTONIO, fire chief; b. Havana, Cuba, Jan. 17, 1954; came to U.S., 1960; s. Carlos Antonio and Mitzi Ann (de Llano) G.; m. Lourdes Maria Portela, June 20, 1975; children: Carlos Julio, Julio Francisco, Lourdes Marie. AA in Gen. Studies, Miami Dade C.C., 1984. Firefighter Miami Fire Rescue, 1975-79, fire lit., 1979-84, fire capt., 1984-87, exec. asst., 1987-88, div. chief, 1988-91, fire chief, 1991—. Bd. dirs. Coral Gables Youth Ctr., 1989—. Mem. Dade County Chief Fire Officers Assn. (bd. dirs. 1991—). Republican. Roman Catholic. Home: 4061 S Le Jeune Rd Miami FL 33146-2843 Office: Fire Rescue and Inspection Svcs 44 SW 2nd Ave10th Fl Miami FL 33130*

GIMENEZ, RAPHAEL ANTOINE, French and Spanish languages educator, writer; b. Montauban, France, Dec. 31, 1948; came to the U.S., 1968; BA in French, Calif. State U., San Diego, 1974; MA in French, Calif. State U., Fullerton, 1976; postgrad., Université de Neuchâtel, Switzerland, 1974-75; cert. in syntax, Université de la Sorbonne, 1982; PhD in French, U. So. Calif., 1983. Lectr. U. So. Calif., 1982-84, Chapman U., 1986-87; asst. prof. dept. French Scripps Coll. Claremont Colls., 1984-85; lectr. faculté des lettres Université de l'Institut Catholique, Paris, 1985-86; asst. prof. So. Oreg. State U., 1987-89, U. New Orleans, 1990-93; lectr. Spanish So. U. New Orleans, 1993—; translator Soc. Advancement Racial and Religious Unity; cons. So. Oreg. State U., 1988; presenter in field. Author: L'Espace de la douleur chez Loaisel de Tréogate (1752-1812), 1992; editor (weekly radio broadcast) Les Quatre Saisons, Sta. KTYM, 1982-84; contbr. articles to profl. jours. Scholar U. So. Calif., 1977-83. Mem. Pi Delta Pi. Home: 6409 Saint Roch Ave New Orleans LA 70122-5627 Office: So U New Orleans Dept Fgn Langs 6400 Press Dr New Orleans LA 70126-1009

GINDY, BENJAMIN LEE, insurance company executive; b. Detroit, July 23, 1929; s. Roy E. and Anne M. Gindy; B.S., U. Fla., 1951; m. Judith Youngerman, Dec. 20, 1953; children—Deborah, Daniel, David. Field rep. Penn Mut. Ins. Co., 1957-59; brokerage mgr. Mass. Indemnity Co., Miami, Fla., 1959-68; gen. agt. Guardian Life Ins. Co. Am., Miami, 1968—; pres. Internat. Risk Cons., Inc.; mktg. dir., Party Magic, Inc.; instr. Life Underwriter Tng. Council, C.L.U. diploma course U. Miami; past columnist Miami Rev.; guest speaker in field. Recipient Nat. Health Ins. award Guardian Life Ins. Co. Am., 1977, 83. C.L.U. Mem. Am. Soc. C.L.U.'s (past pres. Miami chpt., named Man of the Yr., 1987), S. Fla. Inter-Profl. Council (past pres.), Gen. Agts. and Mgrs. Assn. (past pres.), Miami Assn. Life Underwriters (past pres., Man of Yr. 1972). Home: 1018 Aduana Ave Coral Gables FL 33146-3326 Office: Gindy Agy/Guardian Life 7615 SW 62nd Ave Miami FL 33143-4906

GINGRICH, NEWT(ON LEROY), congressman; b. Harrisburg, Pa., June 17, 1943; s. Robert Bruce and Kathleen (Daugherty) G.; children: Linda Kathleen, Jacqueline Sue.; m. Marianne Ginther, Aug. 1981. B.A., Emory U., 1965; M.A., Tulane U., 1968, Ph.D. in European History, 1971. Faculty W. Ga. Coll., Carrollton, 1970-78; asst. prof. history W. Ga. Coll., until 1978; mem. 96th-105th Congresses from 6th Ga. dist. U.S. Ho. of Reps., Washington, 1979—; speaker U.S. Ho. Reps., 104th Congress, 1995—, 105th Congress, 1997—; speaker, chmn. emeritus GOPAC; co-founder Conservative Opportunity Soc., congl. mil. caucus, space caucus; mem. joint com. on printing, house adminstrn. com.; co-chmn. Leader's Task Force on Health; adj. prof. Reinhardt Coll., Waleska, Ga., 1994-95. Author: (with Marianne Gingrich) Window of Opportunity, 1984, Renewing American Civilization, 1995, (with William Forschen) 1945, 95, To Renew America, 1995. Named Man of Yr., 1995/. Mem. AAAS, Ga. Conservancy. Republican. Baptist. Lodges: Kiwanis, Moose. Office: US Ho of Reps 2428 Rayburn Bldg Washington DC 20515-0005*

GINN, B(ARBARA) MERRIELYN, history educator; b. Tylertown, Miss., Feb. 13, 1947; d. Bobby Merriel Ginn and Carrolene (Brock) Hope. BS, Miss. State Coll. for Women, Columbus, 1969; MA, Southeastern La. U., Hammond, 1980. History tchr. Slidell (La.) Jr. H.S., 1969-87; history instr., leadership devel. (Phi Theta Kappa) S.W. Miss. Comml. Coll., Summit, 1988—; co-sponsor Scholars Bowl, Summit, 1990—. Mem. Friends of the Library, Tylertown, 1996, Human Soc. of the U.S., 1994—, Miss. Farm Bur., 1988—, Miss. Humanities Coun., 1995— (Humanities Tchr. of Yr. 1995-96). Named one of Outstanding Elem. Tchrs. of Am., 1973, Outstanding Young Educator Slidell Jaycees, 1974, Outstanding La. Educator, 1981. Mem. Miss. Hist. Assn., So. Hist. Assn., Orgn. Am. Historians. Home: 407 Enochs St Tylertown MS 39667 Office: SW Miss Cmty College 2000 College Dr Summit MS 39666

GINN, CONNIE MARDEAN, nurse; b. Nevada, Mo., July 22, 1951; d. Walter Jess and Marjorie Dean (Bowman) Andrews; 1 child, Justin Andrew Hutchinson; m. Robert Bob Ginn, Feb. 18, 1978; 1 child, Heather Diane. LPN, Okla., Pa.; cert. gastrointestinal nurse clinician. Med./surgical nurse Jane Phillips Mem. Med. Ctr., Bartlesville, Okla., 1971-72, Baptist Med. Ctr., Oklahoma City, 1972-73; emergency rm. nurse Baptist Med. Ctr., 1973-75, with, 1975-77; with South Community Hosp., Oklahoma City, 1977-79; digestive disease nurse James L. Stammer, M.D. and area hosps., Oklahoma City, 1979-86; clin. coord. Regional Gastroenterology Assocs., Ben G. Lazarus, D.O., Lancaster, Pa., 1986-88; nurse Springer Clinic, Paul W. Hathaway, M.D., Tulsa, 1988-90; gastrointestinal clinician Hillcrest Med. Ctr., 1990-94; nurse coord. Family Med. Care of Tulsa, 1994—; dir. Okla. Ednl. Seminars, 1983-85, course coord., 1983-85. Presented articles on diseases and patient care to various confs. Pro rescuer and vol. ARC, vol. health and safety, vol. first aid and safety, first responder, instr. Mem. Soc. Gastroenterology Nurses and Assocs. (regional del. to nat. seminars 1982-85, dir. at large 1984-86, co-divsn. chmn. regional socs. 1984, mem. program com. 1985, mem. scholarship com. 1987-88), Regional Soc. Gastrointestinal Assts. (pres.-elect Okla. and Ark. 1981-82, pres. Okla. 1980-85, founder and first pres. Okla. 1982), Northeastern Okla. Soc. Gastrointestinal Nurses and Assocs. (founder, bd. advisors 1991—), Pa. Soc. Gastrointestinal Assts., Nat. Soc. Gastrointestinal Nurses and Assocs., Nat. Assn. LPNs, LPN Assn. Pa., Nat. Soc. Physicians Nurses, Nat. Coun. Nurses, Am. Assn. Christian Counselors. Republican. Home: 11386 S Date St Jenks OK 74037-3240 Office: Family Med Care of Tulsa 7600 S Lewis Ave Tulsa OK 74136-6836

GINN, JOHN ARTHUR, JR., insurance agent; b. Palatka, Fla., June 2, 1918; s. John Arthur and Violet Maude (Merwin) g.; m. Lou Eliska Cone, Feb. 4, 1945; children: Judith Ann, John Arthur III. BS, Fla. So. Coll., 1940. CLU; chartered fin. cons. Agt. N.Y. Life, Palatka, Fla., 1938—; chmn. N.Y. Life Chmn. Coun., 1981, bd. dir. N.Y. Life Adv. Bd. Dirs., 1981-95. Pres. Jaycees, Palatka, 1952—. Mem. Fla. Assn. Life Underwriters (pres. 1969), Nat. Assn.Life Underwriters. Republican. Methodist. Office: Ginn & Assocs 417 St Johns Ave Palatka FL 32177-4724

GINN, VERA WALKER, educational administrator; b. Jacksonville, Fla., Dec. 22, 1949; d. Grady (dec.) and Pearl Walker; m. Perry L. Ginn, Mar. 16, 1969; children: Perry Jr., Spencer. BA in Edn., Fla. Atlantic U., 1972; MS, Nova U., 1985; specialist in edn., Barry U., 1991. Cert. ednl. leadership, reading, elem. edn., ESOL. Tchr. grades 3 and 4 Plantation (Fla.) Park Elem., 1973-82, Griffin Elem., Cooper City, Fla., 1982-85; tchr. grades 6-8 Seminole Middle, Plantation, 1985-90; lead tchr. Chpt. 1 Adminstrv. Office, Ft. Lauderdale, 1990-92, tchr. on spl. assignment, 1992-93, specialist chpt. 1 secondary, 1993—; adj. prof. Fla. Atlantic U., Ft. Lauderdale, 1995; advisor Fla. Future Educators Am., Plantation, 1990-91. Mem. ASCD, Internat. Reading Assn., Fla. Reading Assn., Fla. Assn. Sch. Adminstr., Secondary Reading Coun. Fla., Broward County Reading Coun., Phi Delta Kappa. Democrat. Baptist. Home: 6700 SW 20th St Plantation FL 33317-5107 Office: Chpt 1 Adminstrv Office 701 NW 31st Ave Fort Lauderdale FL 33311-6627

GINSBERG, ALAN HARVEY, social sciences educator; b. San Antonio, Sept. 29, 1942; s. Sam and Lillian (Gindler) G.; m. Emily Lewis Van Duyvendijk, Apr. 9, 1966; children: Stephanie Rebekah, Leah Susannah. BA, Trinity U., 1963; MA, La. State U., 1968, PhD, 1973. Math. tchr. Edgewood Independent Sch. Dist., San Antonio, 1963-64; Spanish tchr. Southwest Independent Sch. Dist., San Antonio, 1964-66; prof. social scis. Coll. of Mainland, Texas City, Tex., 1969-70, 77—, chmn. social scis. div., 1970-77; election analyst Tex. radio stas.; cons. in field. Translator hosp. booklet; contbr. articles, book revs. to newspapers. Precinct chmn. Galveston County Rep. Com., 1986-90; del. Rep. State Conv., Dallas, 1986; speaker to various civic orgns. NDEA fellow, 1966-69. Mem. Tex. Jr. Coll. Tchrs. Assn. Jewish. Home: 1711 Winnie St Galveston TX 77550 Office: Coll of Mainland Texas City TX 77591

GIORDANO, DAVID ALFRED, internist, gastroenterologist; b. South Bend, Ind., Feb. 3, 1930; s. Alfred S. and Alice (Gracy) G.; m. Sally Kay Buchanan, Jan. 30, 1960; children: Steven David, Michael Bruce. BS, Northwestern U., 1951; MD, Ind. U., Indpls., 1955. Diplomate Am. Bd. Internal Medicine. Intern Univ. Hosp., Cleve., 1955-56; resident in internal medicine Ind. U. Med. Ctr., Indpls., 1958-60; instr. medicine Duke U. Med. Ctr., Durham, N.C., 1960-61, Ind. U. Med. Ctr., Indpls., 1961-63; cons. gastroenterology Vets. Hosp., Univ. Hosp., Indpls., 1961-63; pvt. practice Sarasota, Fla., 1963—; active staff Sarasota Meml. Hosp., chief of staff, 1970-71, assoc. staff Drs. Hosp., Sarasota; mem. West Cen. Fla. Profl. Standards Review Orgn., 1976, Sarasota County Local Govt. Study Commn., 1967-69; sec. Sarasota County Comprehensive Health Planning Coun., 1969-70, exec. com., 1969-72; bd. dirs. Blue Shield, 1973-80, chmn. Governmental Affairs Com., 1978-80; rep. of state ins. commr. to Russia, Denmark, Sweden, Eng. and France, 1979. Contbr. articles to profl. jours. Med. advisor Planned Parenthood Assn., 1965-70. Lt. comdr. USN, 1956-58. Fellow Am. Coll. Physicians (rep. Fla. coun. med. specialists 1973—, health and pub. policy com. 1987—, governing bd. 1987—), Am. Coll. Gastroent.; mem. AMA, Fla. Soc. Internal Medicine (med. adv. coun. 1971-90), Fla. Gastroent. Soc. (pres. 1972), West Coast Acad. Internal Medicine (pres. 1977-78), Sarasota County Med. Soc. (co-chmn. peer review com. 1970-71), Fla. Med. Assn., Am. Soc. Internal Medicine, Fla. Med. Assn., Am. Soc. Gastrointestinal Endoscopy, Am. Gastroent. Assn. Home: 6 Lands End Ln Sarasota FL 34242-1148 Office: David A Giordano MD PA 1950 Arlington St Ste 119 Sarasota FL 34239-3508

GIORDANO, JAMES JOSEPH, neuroscientist, educator; b. Staten Island, N.Y., Sept. 22, 1959; s. James and Gloria (Timpone) G.; m. Ginger Heathman. BS, St. Peter's Coll., Jersey City, 1981; MA, Norwich U., 1982; MPhil, CUNY, 1985, MS, PhD cum laude, 1986. Diplomate Am. Acad. Pain Mgmt. Rsch. asst. Einstein Med. Coll., Bronx, N.Y., 1983-86; rsch. fellow Johns Hopkins U., Balt., 1986-88; asst. prof. neurosci. Drake U., Des Moines, Iowa, 1988-92; dir. pain rsch. Iowa Meth. Hosp., Des Moines, 1990-92; commd. lt. USN, 1992; divsn. officer USN, Pensacola, Fla., 1992-93; dept. head aerospace physiology USN, Cherry Point, N.C., 1993-95; neurology prof. Lamar U., Tex., 1996—; coord. pain mgmt. S.E. Tex. Med. Ctr., 1996—; vis. prof. dept. neurology U. Tex. Med. Br., Galveston, 1996—. Textbook author; contbr. numerous articles to profl. jours. Recipient Presdl. Point of Light award Pres. George Bush, 1991. Fellow Am. Coll. Sports Medicine; mem. Acad. Sports Medicine, Soc. Neurosci., Soc. USN Flight Surgeons.

GIORDANO, JOHN READ, conductor; b. Dunkirk, N.Y., Dec. 31, 1937; s. John C. and Mildred G.; m. Sept. 3, 1960; children: Anne, Ellen, John. MusB, Tex. Christian U., 1960, MusM, 1962. Mem. music faculty North Tex. State U., 1965-72; mem. faculty, condr. univ. symphony Tex. Christian U., 1972—; chmn. jury Van Cliburn Internat. Piano Competition, 1973; permanent chmn. jury Van Cliburn Internat. Piano Competition, Ft. Worth, 1974—; founder, music dir. Ft. Worth Symphony Orch., Ft. Worth Chamber Orch. (formerly Tex. Little Symphony), 1976—, also condr. Appeared as saxophone soloist and with orchs. throughout Europe and U.S., 1965-72; music dir. youth orch. Greater Ft. Worth, 1969—; guest condr. Ft. Worth Symphony, 1971, music dir. and condr., 1972—; guest condr. with various orchs. including Nat. Symphony of Belgium, Nat. Symphony of El Salvador, Amsterdam Philharm., Brazilian Nat. Symphony, Belgian Nat. Radio Orch., Nat. Symphony of Portugal, English Chamber Orch.; composer: Composition for Jazz Ensemble and Symphony Orchestra, 1974; subject of feature film Symphony, 1978. Served with USAR, 1960-68. Recipient Premiere Prix with distinction Royal Conservatory Brussels, 1965; Fulbright scholar Royal Conservatory, Brussels, 1965. Mem. Phi Mu Alpha Sinfonia, Phi Kappa Lambda, Kappa Kappa Psi. Office: Ft Worth Symphony Orch 4401 Trail Lake Dr Fort Worth TX 76109-5201*

GIOVANNONI, JOHN MICHAEL SAFFOLD, financial services firm executive; b. Washington, Feb. 20, 1952; s. Daniel Henry and Virginia Reach (Saffold) G.; m. Catherine Marie Biggs, Mar. 7, 1979 (div. 1987); 1 stepchild, Jason Matthew Allen Twining. Student in bus. acctg., Montgomery Coll., 1973-76; student in acctg., USDA Grad. Sch., 1976-78; student tax insts., U. Md., 1977-80; student, Eckerd Coll., 1988. Lic. pub. acct., Washington. Controller ID Sys./Lamco Inc, Washington, 1971-73; sole practitioner John M. S. Giovanonni PA, Washington, 1973-77; mng. ptnr. Giovannoni & Assocs., Washington, 1977-81; controller, CFO Gardner Group-Jacobs Gardner, Washington, 1981-83; tax mgr. Rogers, Wood, Hill, Starman & Gustason, Naples, Fla., 1983-86; exec. tax mgr. Berthelot, Taylor & Meacham, Ft. Myers, Fla., 1987; prin., CEO The Washingtonian Group, Tallahassee, Fla., 1987—; bd. dirs. Fed. News Svc. Group, Washington, Fla. Physicians Found., Cape Coral, Fla.; v.p., bd. dirs. Poling & Assocs., Inc., Edgewater, Fla., 1995—, Euro-Pan Am. Trade Orgn., Miami, Fla., 1992—; spkr. in field. Conv. del. Fla. GOP 1995 Presdl. Conv., Orlando, 1995; precinct chmn. Rep. Party, Leon County, Fla., 1996—, Montgomery County, Md., 1971-74; candidate Register of Wills Rep. Party, Montgomery County, 1974; chmn. 20th Dist. Club, Silver Spring, Md., 1975; bd. dirs. Salvation Army Comty. Named Mem. of Yr., Nat. Assn. Accts., 1978, Dir. of Yr., Nat. Assn. Accts., 1980. Mem. Nat. Soc. Pub. Accts. (mem. scholar found. com.), Fla. Soc. Enrolled Agts. (chpt. v.p. 1991-92), Inst. Mgmt. Accts. (chpt. pres. 1987-88). Office: The Washingtonian Group # B 5039 Louvinia Dr Tallahassee FL 32311-8719

GIPE, JOAN PATRICIA, education educator; b. Louisville, Oct. 15, 1948; m. Charles A. Duffy, Oct. 22, 1983. BA with honors, U. Ky., 1970, MA, 1971; PhD, Purdue U., 1977. Cert. reading specialist, Ky., Ind. Substitute tchr. Fayette County Schs., Lexington, Ky., 1970-71; tchr. remedial reading Scott County Schs., Sadieville, Stamping Ground, 1971-72; elem. tchr. Tippecanoe Sch. Corp., Lafayette, Ind., 1972-75; grad. instr., supr. reading clinic, supr. student tchrs. Purdue U., West Lafayette, Ind., 1974-77; asst. prof. dept. curriculum and instrn. U. New Orleans, 1977-80, assoc. prof., 1980-85, chmn. dept., 1985-88, prof., 1987—, coord. teaching enhancement, 1992-93, rsch. prof., 1994—; dir. exemplary collaborative program Minority Student Achievement, 1991. Author: Corrective Reading Techniques, 1987, 3d edit., 1995; contbr. articles to profl. jours. Recipient Tchg. award U. New Orleans Alumni Assn., 1981, Amoco Found., 1985, Purdue Disting. Edn. Alumni, 1996; grantee Network Performing and Visual Arts Schs., 1988, 89, 90, La. Edn. Quality Support Fund, 1991—. Mem. Am. Edn. Rsch. Assn., Internat. Reading Assn. (editorial adv. bd. 1989, 90, 91, 92), Orgn. Tchr. Educators Reading. Office: U New Orleans Dept Curriculum & Instrn New Orleans LA 70148

GIRARDIN, DAVID WALTER, chaplain, military officer; b. Detroit, July 9, 1951; s. David Louis and Anna Marie (Didyk) G.; m. Barbara Kimberly White, June 27, 1976; children: David John, Emily Grace. BA in Theology, Andrews U., Berrien Springs, Mich., 1982, MDiv, 1985; postgrad., U. San Diego, 1994-95. RN, Calif. RN Harper Grace Hosp., Detroit, 1973-74, Detroit Indsl. Clinic, 1974-76; physician's asst. thoracic surgery Harper Grace Hosp., Detroit Med. Ctr., 1976-80; commd. ensign USN, 1983, advanced through grades to lt. comdr., 1994, chaplain, 1983-87; chaplain naval mobile constrn. bn. THREE USN, Port Hueneme, Calif., 1986-89; chaplain Marine Corps Recruit Depot USN, San Diego, 1989-91, chaplain USS COWPENS (CG-63), 1991-94; chaplain marriage family therapy program U. San Diego, 1994-95; chaplain U.S. Naval Sta., P.R., 1995-96; chaplain/dir. family svc. ctr. U.S. Naval Sta., P.R., 1996—; trainer, Leadership, Edn. and Devel. Cons., Reynoldsburg, Ohio, 1985—; pastoro Minn. Conf. Seventh-day Adventists, Three River Falls, 1984-86; trainer, prevention & relationship enhancement program, 1994—; facilitator, Critical Incident Debriefing Team, 1996—; trainer, Sexual Assault Advocate Team, 1993. Contbr. articles to newspapers and jours. Decorated Navy-Marine Corps Commendation medal, Meritorious Svc. medal, Navy Achievement medal, Southwest Asian War medal, Kuwait Liberation medal. Mem. Naval Res. Assn. (life), NRA (life), Adventist Chaplaincy Ministry, Adventist Mil. and Vets. Orgn. Office: Office Of Chaplains Psc 1008 Box 3031 FPO AA 34051-3031

GIRARDIN, LINDA JANE BECKER, editor; b. Glen Cove, N.Y., June 5, 1949; d. George Walter and Helen Elisabeth (Lynch) Becker; m. David Louis Girardin, Jan. 8, 1977. BA, Hartwick Coll., 1971; MPA, U. N. Fla., 1993. Rsch. asst. Smithsonian Instn., Ft. Pierce, Fla., 1973-76; coord. adult and continuing edn. St. Johns River C. C., Palatka, Fla., 1978-90; sr. tech. report editor St. Johns River Water Mgmt. Dist., Palatka, 1991—; local officer Fla. Assn. Com. Colls., Palatka, 1980-90. Contbr. articles to profl. jours. Bd. dirs. local unit Am. Cancer Soc., Palatka, 1996. Mem. Soc. for Tech. Comm., Am. Soc. Pub. Adminstrn. Home: PO Box 392 East Palatka FL 32131 Office: St Johns River Water Mgmt Dist PO Box 1429 Palatka FL 32178

GIRARDS, JAMES EDWARD, lawyer; b. Manhasset, N.Y., Aug. 16, 1963; s. H.V. and Barbara (Davis) G.; m. Julie Ann Calame, June 27, 1987; children: Jessica Lauren, James Edward. BS, Baylor U., 1986; JD, St. Mary's Law Sch., 1989. Bar: Tex. 1989, U.S. Dist. Ct. (no., so. and ea. dists.) Tex. 1991. Assoc. Law Offices Windle Turley, P.C., Dallas, 1989-94; prin. Tracy & Girards, Dallas, 1994—. Contbr. articles to profl. jours. Recipient Am. Jurisprudence Contracts award AmJur Pub. Co., 1986. Mem. ABA, ATLA, Tex. Trial Lawyers Assn., Dallas Trial Lawyers Assn., Dallas Bar Assn., Dallas Assn. Young Lawyers, State Bar Tex., Coll. of State Bar of Tex., Am. Mensa, Ltd. Office: Tracy & Girards Two Forest Plz 12201 Merit Dr Ste 220 Dallas TX 75251

GIRGIS, MAURICE A., economist, consultant; b. Cairo, June 29, 1940; came to U.S., 1963; s. Awad and Helena (Qudsi) G.; m. Barbara B. Wilkes, Aug. 29, 1967; children: Helana A., Christina M., Charles P. BA, Cairo U., 1961, MA, 1965; PhD, Ind. U., 1970. Prof. econs. Ball State U., Muncie, Ind., 1967-81, dept. chmn., 1974-77; rsch. fellow Inst. of Econs., Kiel, Germany, 1972-74; sr. scientist, divsn. dir. Inst. for Sci. Rsch., Kuwait, 1981-90; sr. v.p. Gulf Investment corp., Kuwait, 1990-92; sr. econ. advisor Ministry of Fin., Bahrain, 1992-94; pres. LTC Techno-Econs., Inc., Raleigh, N.C., 1994—. Author: Industrialization in Egypt, 1977; editor: Oil Economies, 1984. Deacon, Coptic Ch., Raleigh, 1992-94. Named Outstanding Educator, Ball State U., 1970; recipient A.F. Edelman award Ops. Rsch. and Mgmt. Sci., 1996. Office: LTC Techno-Economics Inc 204 Dalton Dr Raleigh NC 27615

GIRONE, JOAN CHRISTINE CRUSE, commercial real estate agent, former county official; b. Kingston, Ont., Can., Aug. 30, 1927; naturalized U.S. citizen; d. Arthur William and Helen Wilson Cruse; m. Joseph Michael Girone, June 26, 1954; children: Susan, Richard, William. Buyer, Franklin Simon, Inc., N.Y.C., 1946-54; supr. Midlothian dist. Chesterfield County (Va.) Bd. Suprs., 1976-88, vice chmn., 1976-82. Founding mem. Capitol Area Agy. on Aging, 1973-89, Med. Coll. Va. Women's Health Adv. Coun., 1990—, Chesterfield County Citizens for Responsible Govt., 1991—; bd. dirs. Cen. Va. Ednl. TV Corp., 1989-94; commr., chmn. Richmond (Va.) Regional Planning Dist. Commn., 1976-88; Va. Power Consumer adv. bd.; chmn. community edn. adv. com. Va. Bd. of Edn., 1972-79; mem. Va. Gov.'s Adv. Bd. on Aging, 1980-82; chmn. Richmond Met. Transp. Planning Orgn., 1981-88; bd. visitors Va. State U., 1980-84; chmn. Chesterfield County Com. to elect John Warner and Paul Trible to U.S. Senate, 1979, 82, 84; Chesterfield chmn. Marshall Coleman for Gov., 1981—; chmn. Women for Reagan-Bush, 1984, vice chair Rt 288 Freeway Comm., 1996, Va. Fedn. Rep. Women, mem. candidate recruitment com., 1985; mem. Central Va. River Basin com., 1985; mem. evaluation task force United Way of Greater Richmond, 1985; bd. dirs. Maymont Found., 1982-89, YMCA Greater Richmond Metro, ARC Va. Capital chpt., Family and Children's Services, 1988, Chesapeake Bay Local Assistance Bd. Adv. Com., Midlothian Village Vol. Coalition Adv. Bd., Midlothian YMCA, 1994—, Caucus for Future Ctrl. Va., 1994—; chmn. steering com. Bon Air Village Preservation, 1995—. Recipient Good Govt. award Richmond First Club, 1985; Joan C. Girone Libr. named in her honor, 1995. Mem. Va. Assn. Counties (exec. bd. 1982-87), Richmond Metro C. of C. (bd. dirs. Chesterfield Bus. Coun. 1989—), Huguenot Rep. Woman's Club (Rep. Woman of Yr. 1983). Home: 2609 Dovershire Rd Richmond VA 23235-2815

GIROUARD, PEGGY JO FULCHER, ballet educator; b. Corpus Christi, Tex., Oct. 25, 1933; d. J.B. and Zora Alice (Jackson) Fulcher; m. Richard Ernest Girouard, Apr. 16, 1954 (div. Mar. 1963); children: Jo Linne, Richard Ernest; m. James C. Boles, May 4, 1996. BS in Elem. Edn., U. Houston, 1970. Ballet Instr. Emmamae Horn Studio, Houston, 1951-81; owner, dir. Allegro Acad. Dance, Houston, 1981—; artistic dir. Allegro Ballet Houston, 1976—; asst. mgr. Sugar Creek Homes Assn., Sugar Land, Tex., 1979-90. Choreographer (with Glenda W. Brown) Masquerade Suite, 1983, Sebelius Suite, 1983, Shannan, 1984, Papa Shamus, 1986, Silhouettes, 1987, Aspirations, 1989, Here Come the Clowns, 1990. Mem. Cultural Arts Coun. Houston. Mem. Dance Masters Am. (dir. 1977-80), S.W. Regional Ballet Assn. (chmn. craft of choreography 1983-85, coord. to nat. assn. 1983—, Stream award 1986), Regional Dance Am. (bd. dirs. 1986—). Democrat. Home: 9945 Warwana Rd Houston TX 77080-7609

GISSEL, L. HENRY, JR., lawyer; b. Houston, Oct. 20, 1936. BA, Rice U., 1958; LLB, So. Meth. U., 1961; postgrad., Georgetown U. Bar: Tex. 1961. Sr. ptnr. Fulbright & Jaworski, Houston, v.p., 1991-93. Fellow Am. Coll. Trust and Estate Counsel (pres. 1995-96, regent 1981-87, 91—), Am. Bar Found. (bd. cert. estate planning and probate lab. Tex. bd. legal specialization); mem. ABA (sect. real property probate and trust law, chair 1988-89, coun. 1981-90, 94—), Houston Bar Assn. (sect. del. 1994—). Office: Fulbright & Jaworski 1301 Mckinney St Ste 5100 Houston TX 77010

GIST, GINGER LEE, environmental scientist; b. Detroit, Aug. 28, 1954; d. Donald Wesley and Wanda Maxine (Lovelace) Dycus; m. Richard Franklin Collins, Dec. 21, 1989. BS in Edn., Ark. State U., 1976, MS in Edn., 1979; PhD, U. Tenn., 1983. Asst. mgr. Mangel's Dress Shop, Jonesboro, Ark., 1972-75; sci. tchr. Bay-Brown Secondary Schs., Bay, Ark., 1976-78; grad. asst. biology dept. Ark. State U., Jonesboro, 1978; biology tchr. Manila (Ark.) H.S., 1978-79; grad. tchg. asst. dept. microbiology U. Tenn., Knoxville, 1979-81, grad. rsch. asst. dept. entomology and plant pathology, 1981-83; actress Cinetel Prodns., Knoxville, 1984; asst. prof. dept. environ. health E. Tenn. State U., Johnson City, 1985-89, asst. dean Sch. Pub. and Allied Health, 1988-90, assoc. prof. dept. environ. health, 1989-90, mem. adv. coun., 1992—; sr. environ. health scientist exposure and disease registry divsn. health studies Agy. Toxic Substances and Disease Registry, Atlanta, 1990—, acting branch chief health investigations branch divsn. health studies, 1996; mem. adv. coun. U. Ga. Environ. Health Program, Atlanta, 1993—; mem. planning com., facilitator environ. and pub. health surveillance workshop Nat. Ctr. Environ. Health, Coun. State and Territorial Epidemiologists, Nat. Environ. Health Assn., Atlanta, 1995—; mem. Environ. and Pub. Health Coun. Underwriters Labs., Northbrook, Ill., 1996—. Contbr. numerous articles to profl. jours., chpts. to books. Multimedia first aid instr. ARC, Knoxville, Tenn., 1980-83, CPR instr., 1981-84; mem. Johnson City (Tenn.) Clean Team Sch. Task Force Keep Am. Beautiful Found., 1987-90; judge Upper E. Tenn. Sci. Fair, bd. dirs., Johnson City, 1989-90, bd. dirs., 1989-90. Fellow Summer Geriatric Inst. Ohio Valley Appalachia Regional Geriatric Edn. Ctr., Lexinton, 1987-88; grantee ETSU Rsch. Devel. Com., Johnson City, Tenn., 1985, USEPA, 1988, 89; recipient Environ. Health Scientist of Yr. Agy. Toxic Substances and Disease Registry, Atlanta, Ga., 1992, Outstanding Poster Presentation Fifth Internat. Conf. Internat. Soc. Evinon. Epidemiology, 1993. Mem. Am. Acad. Sanitarians (diplomante, bd. dirs. 1993—), AAAS, Am. Pub. Health Assn., Ga. Environ. Health Assn., Ga. Pub. Health Assn., Internat. Soc. Exposure Analysis (nomenclature com. 1994-96), Nat. Environ. Health Assn. (mem. pub. com. 1990-94, ad hoc com. on student affairs 1992-94, chair ad hoc com. on sect. realignment 1993-94, reviewer Jour. Environ. Health 1989—, bd. dirs. coun. dels. 1987-88, 95—, proxy 1989, ex officio 1990-95, tech. sect. chair, air, land, water sect. 1990-95, second v.p. 1995-96, first v.p. 1996—, mem. numerous other coms.), Nat. Coun. Environ. Health and Protection Accreditation (treas. 1990-93), Soc. Occupl. and Environ. Health, Soc. Toxicology (Southeastern regional chpt. 1989—), Alpha Lambda Delta, Gamma Beta Phi, Phi Kappa Phi, Gamma Sigma Delta, Epsilon Nu Eta, Omicron Delta Kappa, Sigma Xi. Office: Agy Toxic Substances and Di 1600 Clifton Rd E-31 Atlanta GA 30333

GITELMAN, MORTON, law educator, dean, publisher; b. Chgo., Feb. 7, 1933; s. Jack and Molly (Sponke) G.; m. Norma C. Linkow, Dec. 23, 1956 (dec. Feb. 1976); children: Neil, Eliot, Ronald; m. Marcia L. McIvor, May 15, 1977. Cert. in personnel adminstrn., Roosevelt U., 1954; JD, DePaul U., 1959; LLM, U. Ill., 1965. Bar: Ill. 1959, U.S. Ct. Appeals (10th cir.) 1963, Ark. 1972, U.S. Dist. Ct. (ea. and we. dists.) Ark. 1972, U.S. Ct. Appeals (8th cir.) 1972, U.S. Supreme Ct. 1974. Teaching fellow U. Ill., Urbana, 1959-60; research assoc. Duke U., Durham, N.C., 1960-61; assoc. prof. law U. Denver, 1961-65; prof. law U. Ark., Fayetteville, 1965—, assoc. dean, 1991—; chief exec. officer M&M Press; chmn. Ark. Adv. Com. U.S. Commn. Civil Rights, 1972-82, mem., 1966—. Author: Unionization Attempts in Small Enterprises, 1963; (with others) Arkansas Rules of Evidence, 1988; co-editor Land Use, 1976, 4th rev. edit., 1990. Chmn. Fayetteville Planning Commn., 1972-76, mem., 1967-76; nat. bd. dirs. ACLU, 1969-72, pres. Ark. chpt., 1969-70. Served with U.S. Army, 1954-56. Recipient Disting. Teaching award U. Ark. Alumni Assn., 1978; named Civil Libertarian of Yr. ACLU Ark., 1983, Disting. Prof. of Law, 1989. Mem. Ill. Bar Assn., Ark. Bar Assn. Jewish. Home: 1229 W Lakeridge Dr Fayetteville AR 72703-2031 Office: U Ark Sch Law Fayetteville AR 72701

GITTELSON, GEORGE, physician; b. N.Y.C., Sept. 11, 1920; s. Harry and Frances (Spiro) G.; m. Mildred Greenberg, 1942 (div. 1974); children: Howard, Alan, Gary; m. Shari Saslaw, July 24, 1983. BA, Pa. State Coll., 1941; MD, U. Pa., 1951. Diplomate Am. Bd. Allergy and Immunology. Intern Jackson Meml. Hosp., 1951-52; resident Cook County Grad. Sch. Medicine, 1954; pvt. practice Miami, Fla., 1952—; clin. assoc. prof. Sch. Medicine, U. Miami, 1954-79. Capt. USAF, 1942-46, ETO. Fellow Am. Acad. Allergy and Immunology, Am. Coll. Allergy and Immunology. Office: 10691 N Kendall Dr Miami FL 33176-1551

GITTENS, ANGELA, airport executive. Dep. dir. San Francisco Internat. Airport, 1994; gen. mgr. William B. Hartsfield Internat. Airport, Atlanta. Office: Atlanta Ga City Dept of Aviation General Mgrs Office Hartsfield Atlant Intnat Airport Atlanta GA 30320

GITTLIN, ARTHUR SAM, industrialist, banker; b. Newark, Nov. 21, 1914; s. Benjamin and Ethel (Bernstein) G.; m. Fay Lerner, Sept. 18, 1938; children: Carol Franklin, Regina (Mrs. Peter Gross), Bruce David, Steven Robert. BCS, Newark U., 1938. Ptnr. Gittlin Bag Co. (name now changed to Gittlin Cos. Inc.), Livingston, N.J., No. Miami, Fla., N.Y.C., 1935-40; v.p., dir. Gittlin Bag Co., 1954—, chmn. bd., 1963—; v.p., dir. Abbey Record Mfg. Co., Newark, 1958-60; chmn., treas. Packaging Products & Design Co. (now PPD Corp.), Newark and Glendale, Calif., 1959-71, chmn. exec. com., treas., 1972—; chmn. Pines Shirt & Pajama Co., N.Y.C., 1960-85, Pottsville Shirt & Pajama Co. (Pa.), 1960—, Barrington Industries, N.Y.C., 1963-72, First Peninsula Calif. Corp., N.Y.C., 1964-68, Peninsula Savs. and Loan, San Francisco and San Mateo, Calif., 1964-68, Wall-co Imperial, Miami, Fla., 1965-87, Levin & Hecht, Inc., N.Y.C., 1966-72, Wallco of San Juan (P.R.), Brunswick Shirt Co., N.Y.C., 1966-72, Fleetline Industries, Garland, N.C., 1966-72, All State Auto Leasing & Rental Corp., Beverly Hills, Calif., 1968-72, Packaging Ltd., Newark, 1970-76, Kans. Plastics, Inc., Garden City, 1970-76, Bob Cushman Distbrs., Inc. (now Wallpapers Inc.), Phoenix, 1972-87, Wallpaper Supermarkets, Phoenix, 1976-80, Wallco Internat. Inc., Miami, 1976, Overwrap Equipment Corp., Fairfield, 1978-86, GCI Ala. Inc., Birmingham, 1981—; chmn. Wallpapers Inc., Oakland, Calif., 1982-86, Portland, Oreg., Honolulu, Denver, L.A. and Phoenix, 1982-86; pres. Covington Funding Co., N.Y.C., 1963—; vice chmn. bd. Peninsula Savs. and Loan Assn., San Mateo and San Francisco, 1964-67, chmn., 1967-68; chmn. bd., treas. Bob Cushman Painting & Decorating Co. (now Wallco West), Phoenix, 1972-86; treas., dir. Flex Pak Industries, Inc., Atlanta, 1973-76, Ploy Plax Films, Inc., Santa Ana, Calif., 1973-76; sec., chmn. exec. com. Zins Wallcoverings, Newark; v.p., bd. dirs. JKG Printing & Graphics, Boca Raton, Fla., 1994—; ptnr. Benjamin Co., Livingston, N.J., Laurel Assocs. (Md.), Seaboard Realty Assocs., Miami, 1980—, GHG Realty Assocs., N.Y.C., 1980, Parkway Assocs., Miami, 1987—; ptnr., investors cons. Mission Pack, Inc., L.A.; vice chmn., dir., chmn. exec. com. Falmouth Supply, Ltd., Montreal, Que., Can., Ascher Trading Corp., Newark, Aptex, Inc., Newark; v.p., dir. JKG Printing and Graphics, Boca Raton, Fla., 1994—; bd. dirs., fin. cons. Ramada Inns, Phoenix; bd. dirs., fin. cons. Aztar Corp., Phoenix; bd. dirs. Harris Paint & Wall Covering Super Marts, Miami, Morgan Hill Mfg. Co., Reading, Pa., Douglas Gardens Home for the Aged, Miami. Chmn. N.C. com. B'nai B'rith, 1940; treas. N.C. Fedn. B'nai B'rith Lodges, 1941-43, v.p., 1943-44, pres., 1944-47; mem. com. to rev. dept. banking and ins. N.J. Commn. on Efficiency and Economy in State Govt., 1967-69; trustee Benjamin Gittlin Charity Found., Newark, BAMA Master Retirement Program, Hillel Found. at Rutgers U., Temple Emanuel, Miami, hon. v.p., bd. dir.; founders bd. Miami Gardens Home Aged. Mem. Greenbrook Country Club (Caldwell, N.J.), B'nai B'rith. Jewish (trustee Temple Emanuel, Miami, 1987—). Home: 59 Glenview Rd South Orange NJ 07079-1060 also: 9801 Collins Ave Bal Harbour FL 33154 Office: 2875 NE 191st St Miami FL 33180-2801 also: 21 Penn Plz New York NY 10001-2727 also: 70 S Orange Ave Livingston NJ 07039-4903

GIVHAN, EDGAR GILMORE, physician; b. Montevallo, Ala., Aug. 6, 1935; 7. AB in German Lit., Washington & Lee U., 1956; MD, Washington U., St. Louis, 1960. Diplomate Am. Bd. Internal Medicine. Intern Vanderbilt U., 1960, resident in internal medicine, 1965, instr. in hematology, 1965-66; instr. in hematology Auburn U. Sch. Lab. Tech., 1967-85; co-owner Commercial Garden Design, Montgomery, Ala., 1982—; pres. med. staff Montgomery Bapt. Hosp., 1974-75; cons. physician Ala. Medicaid Program, 1982-86; bd. dirs., cons. Humana Hosp. East Montgomery; med. dir. Humana Ins. Co. Ala.; horticulture lectr. Author: (guide and video) How to Grow Great Southern Gardens, 1992, Flowers for South Alabama Gardens, 1980, (with others) Heritage Gardens, 1992; contbr. articles to profl. jours. Chmn. bd. South Montgomery YMCA, 1973; bd. dirs. ARC, Montgomery, 1970-73, med. dir. blood processing ctr., Montgomery, 1973-80; bd. dirs. Montgomery Symphony Orch., Blue Cross and Blue Shield Ala., 1979-85, Montgomery C. of C., 1980-84; bd. vis. for the humanities Auburn U. Capt. USAF, 1962-64. Vanderbilt U. fellow, 1965-66. Fellow ACP; mem. AMA, Ala. Soc. Internal Medicine, Montgomery Soc. Internal Medicine (pres. 1970), Montgomery County Med. Soc. (pres. 1976), Ala. Soc. Clin. Oncology (v.p. 1982), Am. Soc. Hematology, So. Garden History Soc. (pres., bd. dirs.), Phi Beta Kappa. Office: 6912 Winton Blount Blvd Montgomery AL 36117

GIVHAN, ROBERT MARCUS, lawyer; b. Mineral Wells, Tex., May 10, 1959; s. Walter Houston Givhan and Marion Blackwell Callen Stothart; m. Janet Lee Dothard, May 6, 1989; children: Vivian Lee, Charlotte Ann. BA, U. Ala., Tuscaloosa, 1981; JD, Cumberland Sch. Law, Birmingham, Ala., 1986. Bar: Ala. 1987, D.C. 1989, U.S. Supreme Ct. 1989, U.S. Ct. Appeals (D.C. and 11th cirs.). Assoc. Perry and Russell, Montgomery, Ala., 1987-88; dep. dist. atty. 15th Jud. Cir. of Ala., Montgomery, 1988-91; dep. atty. gen. Office of Atty. Gen. of Ala., Montgomery, 1991-95; counsel Johnston, Barton, Proctor & Powell, Birmingham, 1995—. Fellow Am. Coll. Pros. Attys.; mem. ABA (vice chmn. antitrust competition and trade regulation com. of adminstrv. law sect. 1994), Ala. State Bar Assn. Episcopalian. Home: 427 Cliff Pl Birmingham AL 35209 Office: 2900 AmSouth/Harbert Plz 1901 6th Ave N Birmingham AL 35203-2618

GLACEL, BARBARA PATE, management consultant; b. Balt., Sept. 15, 1948; d. Jason Thomas Pate and Sarah Virginia (Forwood) Wetter; m. Robert Allan Glacel, Dec. 21, 1969; children: Jennifer Warren, Sarah Allane, Ashley Virginia. AB, Coll. William and Mary, 1970; MA, U. Okla., 1973, PhD, 1978. Tchr. Harford County (Md.) Schs., 1970-71; tchr. Dept. Def. Schs., W.Ger., 1971-73; ednl. counselor U.S. Army, Germany, 1973-74; mgmt. cons. Barbara Glacel & Assocs., Anchorage, 1980-86, Washington, 1986-88; ptnr. Pracel Prints, Williamsburg, Va., 1981-85; sr. mgmt. tng. specialist Arco Alaska, Inc., 1984-85; gen. mgr. mgmt. programs Hay Systems, Inc., Washington, 1986-88; CEO VIMA Internat., Burke, Va., 1988—; 2d v.p., bd. dirs. Chesapeake Broadcasting Corp. Md.; adj. prof. U. Md., 1973-74, Suffolk U., Boston, 1974-77, C.W. Post Ctr., L.I. U., John Jay Coll. Criminal Justice, N.Y.C., 1979-80, St. Thomas Aquinas Coll., N.Y.C., 1981, St. Mary's Coll., Leavenworth, Kans., 1981, Anchorage C.C., 1982; acad. adviser Ctrl. Mich. U., 1981-82; asst. prof. U. Alaska, Anchorage, 1983-85; mem. adj. faculty Ctr. for Creative Leadership, 1986—; guest lectr. U.S. Mil. Acad.; mem. U.S. Army Sci. Bd., 1986-90; mem. U.S. Dept. Def. Sci. Bd. Quality of Life Panel, 1994-95. Author: Regional Transit Authorities, 1983; (with others) 1000 Army Families, 1983, The Army Community and Their Families, 1989, Light Bulbs for Leaders, 1994. Chmn. 172d Inf. Brigade Family Coun. Recipient Comdr.'s award for pub. svc. U.S. Dept. Army, 1984, U.S. Army Patriotic Civilian Svc. award 1991, U.S. Army Forscom Svc. award 1993; AAUW grantee, 1977-78. Mem. ASTD (bd. dirs. Anchorage chpt.), Am. Psychol. Assn., Soc. for Indsl. and Organizational Psychology, Instrnl. Systems Assn. (v.p. 1993-96), Soc. of Alumni Coll. of William and Mary (bd. dirs. 1992—). Home: 5290 Lyngate Ct Burke VA 22015-1688 Office: VIMA Internat 5290 Lyngate Ct Burke VA 22015-1688

GLADDEN, JOSEPH RHEA, JR., lawyer; b. Atlanta, Oct. 5, 1942; s. Joseph Rhea Sr. and Frances (Baker) G.; m. Sarah Elizabeth Bynum, Aug. 21, 1965; children: Joseph III, Elizabeth. AB, Emory U., 1964; LLB, U. Va., 1967. Bar: Ga. 1968, U.S. Dist. Ct. (no. dist.) Ga. 1968, U.S. Ct. Appeals (5th cir.) 1968, U.S. Ct. Appeals (11th cir.) 1985. Assoc. King & Spalding, Atlanta, 1967-73, ptnr., 1973-85; v.p., sr. staff counsel Coca-Cola Co., Atlanta, 1985-87, v.p. dep. gen. counsel, 1987-90, v.p., gen. counsel, 1990-91, sr. v.p., gen. counsel, 1991—; chmn. bd. dirs. Coca-Cola Beverages, Toronto, Ont.; bd. dirs. Wesley Homes, Inc. Chmn., bd. trustees Agnes Scott Coll.; trustee The Food and Drug Law Inst., The Atlanta Ballet, The Lovett Sch. Mem. ABA (com. on corp. law depts.), Am Corp. Counsel Assn., Ga. Bar Assn., State Bar Ga., Assn. Gen. Counsel, Atlanta Bar Assn., Commerce Club, Piedmont Driving Club. Office: The Coca-Cola Co PO Drawer 1734 Atlanta GA 30301-1734

GLADECK, SUSAN ODELL, social worker; b. Honesdale, Pa., Apr. 28; d. Lester Albert and Esther Grace (Fleming) Odell; children: Amy Frances, Esther Lena. BA with honors, Cedar Crest Coll., 1960; M. Social Svc., Bryn Mawr Coll., 1962. Lic. clin. social worker, Va.; cert. piano tchr. Social worker Family Svc. of Phila. and Family Svc. of Del. County, Media, Pa., 1962-63, Lehigh U. Child Devel. Ctr., Bethlehem, Pa., 1966, South Terr. Area Neighborhood Ctr., Bethlehem, Pa., 1969-71, Lehigh County Children's Bur., Allentown, Pa., 1971-73; social worker II Farifax (Va.) County Dept. Human Devel., 1987-90; sr. social worker adult svcs. Loudoun County Dept. Social Svcs., Leesburg, Va., 1990-94; pvt. practice McLean, 1994—. Organist, choir dir. Chesterbrook Presbyn. Ch., Falls Church, Va., 1995—. Mem. NASW, Acad. Cert. Social Workers, Am. Coll. Musicians, Am. Guild Organists, Music Tchrs. Nat. Assn., Nat. Fedn. Music Tchrs., Va. Fedn. Music Tchrs., No. Va. Music Tchrs. Assn. Home and Office: 6516 Fairlawn Dr Mc Lean VA 22101-5235

GLADFELTER, WILBERT EUGENE, physiology educator; b. York, Pa., Apr. 29, 1928; s. Paul John and Marea Bernadette (Miller) G.; m. Ruth Isabelle Ballantyne, Jan. 26, 1952; children: James W., Charles D., Mary A. AB magna cum laude, Gettysburg (Pa.) Coll., 1952; PhD, U. Pa., 1960. NSF fellow U. Pa., Phila., 1956-58, NIH fellow, 1958-59, asst. instr., 1954-56; instr. physiology W.Va. U., Morgantown, 1959-61, asst. prof., 1961-69, assoc. prof., 1969-96, prof. emeritus, 1996—. Contbr. articles to profl. jours. Treas., Monongalia County chpt. W. Va. Heart Assn., 1976-95. With USN, 1946-48. NSF fellow, 1956-58. Mem. Am. Physiol. Soc., Soc. Neurosci., Soc. for Integrative and Comparative Biology, Sigma Xi, Phi Beta Kappa, Beta Beta Beta. Lutheran. Home: 70 Pine Tree Ln Morgantown WV 26505-9118 Office: WVa U Health Sci Ctr Dept Physiology Morgantown WV 26506

GLASER, ROBERT HARVEY, SR., pastor; b. Phila., May 4, 1935; s. Harvey A. and Janet (McKechnie) G.; m. Joan Williams, Nov. 16, 1957 (div. July 1979); children: Linda Hartwell, Diane Lim Myra Ward, Linda Carrano, Robert Sr., Teresa Garcia, David Glaser; m. Virginia Sue Fischer, May 27, 1990. AB, Grove City (Pa.) Coll., 1957; MDiv, Princeton (N.J.) Theol. Sem., 1960. Pastor Smithfield Presbyn. Ch., Amenia, N.Y., 1960-64; organizing pastor Westminster Presbyn. Ch., Warner Robins, Ga., 1964-69; pastor First Presbyn. Ch., Forest Hills, N.Y., 1967-81; mem. ch. redevelopment Prospect Heights Presbyn. Ch., Bklyn., 1981-86; pastor Colcord (W.Va.) and Clear Creek Presbyn. Chs., 1987-89; interim pastor First Presbyn. Ch., Nitro, W.Va., 1989; pastor First Presbyn. Ch., Hinton, W.Va., 1989—; moderator Presbytery of N.Y.C., 1976-77; cmn. Maj. Mission Fund, N.Y.C., 1979-81; bd. sec. Edwin Gould Svcs. for Children, N.Y.C., 1987-89. Mem. Second Chance panel D.A.'s Office, Queens, 1977-81. Named Eagle Scout Boy Scouts Am., 1950. Mem. Lions (treas. 1991—), Omicron Delta Kappa, Pi Gamma Mu. Home: 1519 Fayette St Hinton WV 25951-2018 Office: First Presbyn Ch Third Ave Hinton WV 25951

GLASER, WOLFRAM, psychiatrist; b. Breslau, Germany, Feb. 27, 1944; came to U.S., 1957; s. Rudolf Friedrich and Hilde Erna (Mordt) G.; m. Emily Ann Pitts, May 5, 1979; children: Richard, Alan, Michael, Maria. Student, U. Ala., Tuscaloosa, 1963-64; BA, Birmingham-So. Coll., 1967; MD, U. Ala., Birmingham, 1971. Diplomate Am. Bd. Psychiatry and Neurology, Am. Bd. Forensic Medicine; lic. physician, Ala. Pediatric intern Children's Hosp., Birmingham, 1971-72; psychiatry resident Univ. Hosp., Birmingham, 1972-75; chmn. dept. psychiatry Lloyd Noland Hosp. and Health Ctr., Fairfield, Ala., 1976-88, staff psychiatrist, 1988-89; staff psychiatrist Taylor Hardin Secure Med. Facility, Tuscaloosa, 1989-90, dir. acute care and evaluation program, 1990-92; assoc. psychiatrist Cmty. Psychiat. Svcs., Birmingham, 1992-93; med. dir. Eastside Mental Health Ctr., Birmingham, 1992-93, Western Mental Health Ctr., Birmingham, 1994—; cons. U. Ala.-Birmingham Regional Drug Abuse Program, 1976, Birmingham Health Care for the Homeless Coalition, 1988-89; physician advisor Ala. quality Assurance Found., 1989—; profl. staff Bryce Hosp., Tuscaloosa, 1979-86; courtesy staff Hill Crest Hosp., 1978—, Birmingham VA Med. Ctr., 1989-92; clin. instr. psychiatry U. Ala., Birmingham, 1976-91, clin. asst. prof., 1994—; active staff Bapt. Med. Ctr., Montclair, 1992-96, U. Hosp. and Kirklin Clinic, 1996—; courtesy staff Brookwood Med. Ctr., 1992—, St. Vincent's Hosp., 1992—, Med. Ctr. East, 1995—, Bapt. Med. Ctr., Montclair, 1996—. Maj. USAR, 1975-80. Mem. AMA, Am. Psychiat. Assn., Am. Coll. Forensic Examiners, Ala. Psychiat. Soc., Med. Assn. State of Ala., Jefferson County Med. Soc., Nat. Alumni Soc. of U. Ala. in Birmingham (dir. 1980-81, Scroll of Appreciation), Alpha Omega Alpha. Office: Western Mental Health Ctr 1701 Avenue D Birmingham AL 35218-1532

GLASGOW, AGNES JACKIE, social welfare administrator, therapist; b. El Paso, Tex., July 23, 1941; d. Carl Lecota Pace and Henrietta Ford (Cozart) Robertson; m. Morgan Walton, Sept. 20, 1958 (div. 1979); children: Scotty Gene, Carley Earlene Walton DeVore; m. Phillip Sidney Glasgow, Aug. 9, 1986. Lic., Trinidad State Jr. Coll., Colo., 1968; AAS, Met. State Coll., Denver, 1979, BS, 1980; MPA, U. Colo., Denver, 1987. Cert. substance abuse counselor, Colo., Tenn. Pvt. practice Life Counseling Ctr., Denver, Memphis, 1980—; coord. masters program for substance abuse Met. State Coll., Denver, 1980-81; exec. dir. Concord Commons Counseling Ctr., Decatur, Ill., 1981-82; child care specialist Adams Community Mental Health Ctr., Commerce City, Colo., 1982-84; adolescent family counselor Parkside Lodge Colo., Thorhton, Colo., 1984-86; family therapist Charter Lakeside Hosp., Memphis, 1986-87; counselor, coord. Shelby State Community Coll., Memphis, 1987-88; supr. adolescent and young adult program Meth. Outreach, Memphis, 1988-90; sr. mental health specialist dual diagnosis unit Meth. Hosp. Cen., 1990—, relapse prevention specialist, 1994—; cons., part-time instr. Shelby State C.C., Memphis. Contbr. articles to profl. jours. Com. mem. Youth Suicide Task Force, Memphis, 1988—. Recipient Vol. of Yr. award United Way, Decatur, Ill., 1982, Cmty. Svc. award scholarship Mental Health Soc., 1983, Outstanding Svc. award, 1989, Disting. Svc. award Sheriff Dept., Memphis, 1988; nominated Diamond award Memphis Mental Health Assn., 1994. Mem. Nat. Orgn. Human Svc. Workers, Nat. Orgn. Substance Abuse Counselors, Am. Assn. Counseling & Devel., Psi Chi (treas. 1979-80). Republican. Methodist. Office: 10 Thomas 1265 Union Ave Memphis TN 38104-3415 also: 1835 Union Ave Ste 203 Memphis TN 38104-3900

GLASGOW, HAROLD GLYN, military academy administrator; b. Heflin, Ala., Feb. 4, 1929; s. Ralph Stephens and Vera Floretta (Johnson) G.; m. Jean Carol Cunningham, Sept. 4, 1954; children: John Stephen, Jeffrey Glyn, Jennifer Leigh. BS in Phys. Edn., U. Ala., Tuscaloosa, 1951; MS in Internat. Affairs, George Washington U., 1972. Commd. USMC, 1951, advanced through grades to maj. gen., 1980; active duty USMC, Korea, 1951-53; staff sec. Marine Corps Recruit Depot USMC, Paris Island, S.C., 1953-56; exec. officer co. B 1st battalion 4th Marines 1st Marine Brigade USMC, Kanoehe, Hawaii, 1956-58; coach USMC, Camp Lejeune, N.C., 1958-60; commdr. co. A 3rd reconnaissance battalion 3rd Mainre divsn. USMC, Okinawa, 1960-62; insp., instr. 40th rifle co. USMCR, Lubbock, Tex., 1962-65; exec. officer 2nd battalion 2nd Marines, staff sec., asst. chief staff USMC, Camp Lejeune, 1966-68; commdg. officer 2nd battalion 1st Marines 1st Marine Divsn. USMC, Vietnam, 1968-69; head, gen. officer/col./adminstrv. assignment sect. Hdqrs. Marine Corps USMC, 1969-71, exec. asst. to asst. commandant, 1972-75, commdg. officer 6th Marines, 1975-76, commdg. officer 36th Marine amphibious unit, 1975-76, commdg. gen. Marine Corps. AIr Ground Combat Ctr., 1978-80, commdr. Combined Arms Command, 7th Marine Amphibious Brigade, 1980-81; dep. for devel., dir. devel. ctr. Marine Corps Devel. and Edn. Command USMC, Quantico, Va., 1981-82; dir. ops. divsn. plans policies and orgns. dept. Hdqrs. Marine Corps USMC, 1982-84; commdg. gen., III Marine Amphibious Force, 3rd Marine divsn. FMF USMC, Okinawa, 1984-86; commdr. ea. recruiting region Marine Corps. Recruit Depot. USMC, Paris Island, 1986-87; ret. USMC, 1987; gen. Marine Mil. Acad., Harlingen, Tex., 1987—. Decorated D.S.M., Legion of Merit with Combat "V," Bronze Star with Combat "V," M.S.M. with one bronze star, Korean Svc. medal with three bronze stars, Vietnam Svc. medal with four bronze stars, Korean Order Mil. Merit, Republic of Vietnam Cross of Gallantry with palm, UN Svc. medal, Vietnam Campaign medal. Mem. Harlingen Rotary. Office: Marine Military Acad 320 Iwo Jima Blvd Harlingen TX 78550-3627

GLASGOW, VAUGHN LESLIE, museum curator and administrator; b. Portland, Ind., Apr. 23, 1944; s. Leslie Lloyd and Garnet Lucile (Confer) G. BA, La. State U., 1967; MA, Pa. State U., 1970, postgrad. Rsch. asst., asst. to curator Anglo-Am. Art Mus., La. State U., 1965-67; instr. art history, adminstrv. asst. dept. art history Pa. State U., 1970-71; asst. prof. art history Middle Tenn. State U., 1972-73; arts mgr. La. Council for Music and Performing Arts, 1973-75; chief curator La. State Mus., New Orleans, 1975-83, assoc. dir. for spl. projects, 1983-87; dir. for spl. projects La. State Mus., 1987—; lectr. dept. art Newcomb Coll., Tulane U., New Orleans, 1975-79; Am. commr. Sun King: Louis XIV and the New World, 1982-85; mem. adv. panel youth and student programs NEH, 1970-73; cons. Madewood Arts Festival; bd. dirs. La. Alliance for Arts Edn., 1978-79; bd. dirs., treas. Photography Council La.; cons. Hermann-Grima Historic House Mus., New Orleans; art adv. bd. St. Mary's-Dominican Coll. Author: L'Amour de Maman: La Tradition acadienne du tissage en Louisiane, 1983, A Social History of the American Alligator: The Earth Trembles with His Thunder, 1991 (AASLH award 1992); contbr. articles to profl. jours. Mem. La. State Folklife Commn., 1982. Named Internat. Hon. Citizen, City of New Orleans, 1982, La Rochelle, France, 1982, Poitiers, France, 1982, Chevalier des Palmes Academiques, 1984, Chevalier des Arts et des Lettres, 1986, La. Mus. Employee of Yr., 1990. Mem. Inst. La. Music and Folklore (bd. dirs. 1976-78), Am. Assn. for State and Local History (nat. awards com. 1989-92), Am. Assn. Museums (curators com.), Internat. Coun. Museums (internat. exhbn. exch. com.), Southeastern Mus. Conf., La. Assn. Museums. Office: La State Mus 751 Chartres PO Box 2448 New Orleans LA 70176-2448

GLASKOWSKY, ELIZABETH POPE, nutritionist, dietitian; b. Surginer, Ala., Jan. 13, 1924; d. Hubert Collins and Amanda Elizabeth (Alston) Pope; m. Nicholas Alexander Glaskowsky Jr., June 13, 1953; children: Peter Nicholas, Alexandra Elizabeth. BS with honors, U. Montevallo, 1945. Lic. dietitian, nutritionist, Fla.; registered dietitian. Dietetic internship Brooke Army Med. Ctr., San Antonio, 1945-46; 2d lt., 1st lt., hosp. dietitian Oliver Gen. Hosp., Augusta, Ga., 1946-49; asst. prof. home econs. U. Montevallo, Ala., 1949-51; 1st lt., capt. U.S. Army, 1951-54; chief dietitian Camp Breckenridge, Ky., 1951-52; instr. dept. adminstrn. Med. Field Svc. Sch., Fort Sam Houston, Tex., 1952; chief ward food svc., nutrition instr. Letterman Army Hosp., San Francisco, 1952-54; asst. dir. Stern Dining Hall, dir. Encina Hall Stanford (Calif.) U., 1954-55, 55-57; head dietitian Masonic Hosp.-U. Minn., Mpls., 1958-59; consulting nutritionist, dietitian Dade County (Fla.) Pub. Health Dept., 1978-87, 87—. Mem., 2d officer Old Cutler Women's Rep. Club, Dade County, 1980—; del. Rep. Sate Conv., 1990-91, 95; mus. guide Vizcaya Mus., Date County, 1981—. Mem. Am. Dietetic Assn., Fla. Dietetic Assn., Miami Dietetic Assn. Republican. Episcopalian. Home: 13421 SW 69th Ct Miami FL 33156-6943

GLASPEY, BEN LEE, family practice physician; b. Phila., Feb. 19, 1964; s. Ben Lee and Audrey (Bauer) G. BA in Biology, Franklin & Marshall Coll., Lancaster, Pa., 1986; MS in Anatomy, Hahnemann U., Phila., 1988; DO, U. Osteo. Med. & Health Scis., Des Moines, 1992. Med. intern Youngstown (Ohio) Osteo. Hosp./Cafaro, 1992-93; family practice resident U. Fla./Shands Hosp./Alachua Gen. Hosp., Gainesville, Fla., 1993-96; ACLS instr. U. Osteo. Medicine and Health Scis., Des Moines, 1989-90, teaching asst. gross and neuroanatomy, 1989-90. Author: Saunders Manual of Medical Practice. Mem.Sigma Sigma Phi. Baptist. Home: 837 SE Sweetbay Ave Port Saint Lucie FL 34983 Office: Family Care Assocs PA 1432 Tiffany Ave Fort Pierce FL 34982

GLASS, DAVID D., department store company executive, professional baseball team executive; b. Liberty, Mo., 1935; married. Gen. mgr. Crank Drug Co., 1957-67; v.p. Consumers Markets Inc., 1967-76; exec. v.p. fin. Wal-Mart Stores Inc., Bentonville, Ark., to 1976, vice chmn., CFO, 1976-84, pres., 1984—, COO, 1984-88, CEO, 1988—, also bd. dirs.; CEO, chmn. bd. dirs. Kansas City Royals, 1993—. Office: Wal-Mart Stores Inc 702 SW 8th St Bentonville AR 72712-6209 also: Kansas City Royals PO Box 419969 Kansas City MO 64141*

GLASS, DOROTHEA DANIELS, physiatrist, educator; b. N.Y.C.; d. Maurice B. and Anna S. (Kleegman) Daniels; m. Robert E. Glass, June 23, 1940; children: Anne Glass Roth, Deborah, Catherine Glass Barrett, Eugene. BA, Cornell U., 1940; MD, Woman's Med. Coll. Pa., 1954; post-grad., U. Pa., 1960-61; DMS (hon.), Med. Coll. Pa., 1987. Diplomate: Am. Bd. Phys. Medicine and Rehab. (guest bd. examiner 1978, 89). Intern Albert Einstein Med. Center, Phila., 1954-55, clin. asst. dept. medicine, 1956-59, attending phys. medicine and rehab., 1968-70, chmn. dept. phys. medicine and rehab., sr. attending, 1971-85; chief rehab. medicine VA Med. Ctr., Miami, Fla., 1985-95; clin. prof. dept. orthopaedics and rehab. U. Miami Sch. Medicine, 1985—; Lois Mattox Miller fellow preventive medicine Woman's Med. Coll. Pa., 1955-56, instr. preventive medicine, 1956-59, instr. medicine, 1960-62; resident phys. medicine and rehab. VA Hosp., Phila., 1959-62, chief phys. medicine and rehab., 1966-68, cons., 1968-82; asst. clin. dir. Jefferson Med. Coll. Hosp., Phila., 1963-66, Camden County Stroke Program, Cooper Hosp., Camden, N.J., 1963-66; gen. practice medicine, Phila., 1956-59; asst. med. dir., chief rehab. medicine and rehab. Moss Rehab. Hosp., Phila., 1968-70, med. dir., 1971-82, sr. cons., 1982—; mem. active staff Temple U., Phila., 1968—, asso. prof. rehab. medicine, 1968-73, prof., 1973—, dir. residency tng. rehab. medicine, 1968-82; program dir. Rehab. Research and Tng. Center, 1977-80, chmn. dept. rehab. medicine, 1977-82; staff physician Hosp. Med. Coll. Pa., Phila., 1955-59, vis. asso. prof. neurology, 1973-79, clin. prof., 1977-82, vis. prof., 1982-96; mem. cons. staff Frankford Hosp., Phila., 1968-82, Phila. Geriatric Center, 1975-82; mem. active staff Willowcrest-Bamberger Hosp., Phila., 1980-82; asso. phys. medicine and rehab. U. Pa. Sch. Medicine, Phila., 1962-66; asst. prof. clin. phys. medicine and rehab., 1966-68; asst. clin. dir. dept. phys. medicine and rehab. Jefferson Med. Coll., Phila., 1963-66. Contbr. articles to profl. jours. Mem. profl. adv. com. Easter Seal Soc. Crippled Children and Adults Pa., 1975-82; active Goodwill Industries Phila., 1973-82, Cmty. Home Health Svcs. Phila., 1974-82, Ea. Pa. chpt. Arthritis Found., 1968-82. Recipient humanitarian svc. cert. Gov.'s Com. on Employment Handicapped, 1974, Outstanding Alumnae award Commonwealth of Pa. Bd., Hosp. Med. Coll. Pa., 1975, humanitarian award Pa. Easter Seal Soc., 1981, John Eiselie Davis award Am. Kinesiotherapy Assn., 1988, Carl Haven Young svc. award, 1994. Mem. AMA, Am. Acad. Med. Dirs., Am. Acad. Phys. Medicine and Rehab. (disting. clinician award 1995), Am. Assn. Electromyography and Electrodiagnosis (assoc.), Am. Assn. Sex Educators, Counselors and Therapists, Am. Burn Assn., Am. Coll. Antiology, Am. Coll. Utilization Rev., Am. Congress Rehab. Medicine (bd. govs., pres. 1986-87, gold Key award 1989), Am. Heart Assn. (coun. on cerebrovascular disease), Am. Lung Assn. Phila. and Montgomery County (bd. dirs. 1977-79), Am. Med. Women's Assn., Assn. Acad. Physicatrists, Assn. Med. Rehab. Dirs. and Coordinators, Coll. Physicians Phila., Emergency Care Rsch. Inst., Gerongol. Soc., Internat. Assn. Rehab. Facilities, Internat. Rehab. Medicine Assn., Pan Am. Med. Assn., Fla. Med. Assn., Fla. Soc. Phys. Medicine and Rehab. (pres. 1975-77), Pa. Med. Soc. (phys. medicine and rehab. adv. com. 1975-82), Pa. Thoracic Soc., Martin County Med. Soc., Delaware Valley Hosp. Coun. Forum, Phila. Med. Soc., Phila. PSRO (bd. dirs. 1975-82), Phila. Soc. Phys. Medicine and Rehab. (pres. 1968-69), Laennec Soc. Phila., Martin County Med. Assn., Royal Soc. Health, Alpha Omega Alpha.

GLASS, FRED STEPHEN, lawyer; b. Asheboro, N.C., Oct. 17, 1940; s. Emmett Frederick and Colene F. (Foust) G.; m. Gloria A. Grant, June 12, 1964; 1 child, Elizabeth Foust; m. Martha G. Daughtry, June 9, 1982. BA, Wake Forest U., 1963, JD, 1966. Bar: N.C. 1966, U.S. Dist Ct. (ea. dist.) N.C. 1966, (mid. dist.) N.C., (we. dist.) N.C.; U.S. Ct. Appeals (4th cir.), U.S. Supreme Ct. Research asst. presiding justice N.C. Supreme Ct., 1966-67; ptnr. Miller, Beck, O'Briant and Glass, Asheboro, N.C., 1971-77; exec. dir. and legal counsel N.C. Democratic Party, 1977-78; dep. commr. N.C. Indsl. Commn., 1978; spl. Congl. asst. 4th Congl. Dist. N.C., 1979; ptnr. Harris, Cheshire, Leager and Southern, Raleigh, N.C., 1979-86; ptnr. Poyner and Spruill, Raleigh, 1987-94; Brooks, Stevens & Pope, P.A., Cary, 1994—; prof. law and govt. Asheboro Jr. Coll. Bus., 1973-76. Author: Legal Guide for Reserve Commanding Officers; contbg. editor: N.C. Will Drafting and Probate Practice Handbook, 1983; contbr. articles to profl. jours. Basketball coach and fitness instr. Randolph County YMCA; pub. chmn., United Appeal; bd. dirs., Randolph County Emergency Med. Technician Bd.; mem. adv. bd. Naval War Coll. operations law; active Dem. campaigns, Boy Scouts Am., council commr. for Roundtables, 1980-89, asst. dist. commr. 1979-84, asst. scoutmaster; mem. nat. com. Boy Scouts of Am., council ex. bd., council commr., chancellor, council commrs. coll., 1980-83, Boy Scouts Am. Nat. Com., 1987-90, coun. pres. 1995-96; force judge adv. COMRNCF, 1985-89. Rear adm. JAGC, USNR. Disting. Svc. Medal award, 1996. Meritorious Svc. medal with gold star, Meritorious Unit Commendation, Nat. Meritorious Svc. award USNR, 1995, Navy Commendation medal with Gold Star, Nat. Defense Svc. medal with Bronze Star, Seabee Combat Warfare Specialist Cert.; recipient numerous Scouters Tng. award Boy Scouts Am., Disting. Eagle Scout award, 1991, Young Man of Yr. award City Asheboro. Mem. ABA (studying com. on armed forces law), Randolph County Bar Assn. (pres. 1971-74), 19th Jud. Dist. Bar Assn. (pres. 1974-75), N.C. Bar Assn. (chmn. young lawyer sect. Randolph County), Dist. Criminal Law Symposium (chmn. 1976), N.C. Def. Lawyers Assn. (computer in litigation support 1989), N.C. Bar Assn. (computers in law office 1995), Sovereign Mil. Order Temple Jerusalem, Naval Order U.S. Democrat. Episcopal. Home: 113 Whispering Pines Ct Cary NC 27511-4059 Office: 2000 Regency Pky Ste 150 Cary NC 27511-8506

GLASS, GARY, psychiatrist; b. San Antonio, June 30, 1947; m. Carol Faget, Sept. 22, 1979; children: Matthew, Sarah. BS, Tulane U., 1969; MD, U. Rochester, 1973. Intern Bexar County Hosp., San Antonio, 1973-74; resident Sepulveda (Calif.) VA Hosp., 1974-77, chief resident, 1977-78; pvt. practice L.A., 1978-79, Austin, Tex., 1981—; med. head mental health/mental retardation clinic Rosewood Human Devel. Ctr., Austin, 1979-84. Mem. Am. Psychiat. Assn., Tex. Med. Assn., Travis County Med. Soc. Office: 5806 Mesa Dr Ste 220 Austin TX 78731-1616

GLASS, J. KENNETH, bank executive; b. 1946. Grad., Harding U., 1969. With Arthur Andersen & Co., Memphis, 1970-74; with First Tenn. Nat. Corp., Memphis, 1974—, pres. Tenn. banking group. Office: First Tenn Nat Corp 165 Madison Ave Memphis TN 38103-2723*

GLASS, LAWRENCE, business executive. Sr. v.p., dir. devel. SRA Technologies, Inc., Falls Church, Va. Office: SRA Technologies Inc Ste 600 West Tower 8110 Gatehouse Rd Falls Church VA 22042

GLASS, ROBERT DODDS, foundation administrator; b. Bristol, Va., Dec. 1, 1950; s. Frank Walter and Sarah Eugene (Dodds) G.; m. Karen Leigh Rhodes, Feb. 28, 1977; children: Alta Gail, Sarah Marie, Robert Noah, Asa Frank. BS in Psychology, Duke U., 1973; MEd in Spl. Edn., U. Louisville, 1980, EdD in Spl. Edn., Ednl. Rsch. and Adminstrn., 1992. Acct. exec., spl. events coord. Stas. WKQQ/WBLG Radios, Lexington, Ky., 1974-76; acct. exec. broadcast and print media mktg. Mktg. Cons., Lexington, 1976-77; rsch. assoc., ednl. rsch. and materials devel. Am. Printing House for Blind, Louisville, 1977-88; dir. Enabling Technologists of Ky. and Ind., Louisville, 1988-89; program developer Found. and Alliance for Tech. Access, San Rafael, Calif., 1989—; instr. Leadership Inst. in Spl. Tech. Harvard U., Cambridge, Mass., 1988; cons. Apple Computer, Cupertino, Calif., Nat. Spl. Edn. Alliance. Author: (with others) Elementary Problem Solving, 1979, (with others) Elementary Computation, 1979, (with F.L. Franks) Metric Measurement for Blind Students, 1980, (with F.L. Franks) Biological Models Development, 1980, (with others) Blindness, Visual Impairment and Deaf-Blindness: Annual Listing of Current Literature, 1982-87, (with others) Guide to Computer Resources for People with Disabilities, 1994; author numerous reports and tng. materials; contbr. articles to profl. jours. Broecker Found. scholar, 1980, 87-90. Mem. Ky. Assistive Tech. Svc. Network (charter, mem. adv. bd., chair subcom. on pub. policy reform, co-chair long range planning com.). Home: 1531 Dawn Dr Louisville KY 40216-1617 Office: Alliance for Tech Access 1531 Dawn Dr Louisville KY 40216-1617

GLASS, VICKY LYNN RHAME, office manager; b. LeCompte, La., June 9, 1954; d. Tommy E. and Vera T. (Barton) Rhame; m. Tommy G. Glass, June 7, 1975 (div. 1982); 1 child, Jacob E. BA, Northwestern State U. of La., 1975. Cert. dep. assessor, La. Assessors Assn. Dep. assessor Rapides Parish Assessor Office, Alexandria, La., 1980-95, office mgr., bookkeeper, 1995—. Mem. Rapides Parish Sr. Citizen Day com., Alexandria, 1993, 94, 95, 96. Democrat. Baptist. Office: Rapides Parish Assessor PO Box 2002 Alexandria LA 71309

GLASSMAN, ARMAND BARRY, physician, pathologist, scientist, educator, administrator; b. Paterson, N.J., Sept. 9, 1938; s. Paul and Rosa (Ackerman) G.; m. Alberta C. Macri, Aug. 30, 1958; children: Armand P., Steven B., Brian A. BA, Rutgers U., N.J., 1960; MD magna cum laude, Georgetown U., Washington, 1964. Diplomate Am. Bd. Pathology, Am. Bd. Nuclear Medicine. Intern Georgetown U. Hosp., Washington, 1964-65; resident Yale-New Haven Hosp., West Haven VA Hosp., 1965-69; asst. prof. pathology, Coll. Medicine U. Fla.; chief radioimmunoassary lab. Gainesville VA Hosp.; practice lab. and nuc. medicine, 1969-71; dir. clin. labs., assoc. prof., prof. pathology, cellular, molecular biology Med. Coll. Ga., Augusta, 1971-76; cons. physician in pathology VA Hosp., Augusta, 1973-76; cons. physician in nuclear medicine Univ. Hosp., Augusta, 1973-76; med. dir. clin. labs. Med. U. S.C. Hosp., Charleston, 1976-87; attending physician in lab. and nuclear medicine Med. U. S.C., Charleston, 1976-87, assoc. med. dir. Med. U. Hosp. and Clinics, 1982-86; med. dir. clin. labs. Charleston Meml. Hosp., S.C., 1976-87; cons. VA Hosp., Charleston, 1976-87; prof., chmn. dept. lab. medicine Med. U. S.C., 1976-87, med. dir. MT and MLT programs, 1976-87, clin. prof. pathology, lab. medicine, and radiology, 1987—, acting chmn. dept. immunology and microbiology, 1985-87, assoc. dean Coll. Medicine, 1979-85, asst. and assoc. dean Coll. Allied Health Sci., 1984-87, chmn. hosp. exec. com., 1985-86, acting med. dir. Univ. Hosp. and Clinics, 1985-86; sr. v.p. med. affairs, prof. lab. medicine and nuclear medicine Montefiore Med. Ctr. and Albert Einstein Coll. Medicine, Bronx, N.Y., 1987-89; v.p., lab. dir. Nat. Reference Lab., Nashville, 1989-92; cons., 1992-95; clin. prof. dept. pathology Vanderbilt U., Nashville, 1990-92, prof. pathology, 1992-94; dir. Vanderbilt Pathology Lab. Svcs., 1992-94; dir. clinical labs. Vanderbilt U. Med. Ctr., 1993-94, O. Stribling chair, prof., 1994—; head and chair divsn./dept. lab. medicine U. Tex., M.D. Anderson Cancer Ctr., Houston, 1994-96; also med. dir. Med. Tech. & Cytogenic Tech. programs, 1994—, also dir. sect. of cytogenetics, 1994—; mem. adv. coun. Trident Tech. Coll., 1976-87; bd. dirs. Fetter Family Health Ctr.; founding dir., bd. dirs. Sealite, Inc., 1987—, chmn. bd. dirs., 1995—; mem. med. adv. com. Nashville Red Cross Blood Ctr., 1991-94, acting med. dir., 1991-92; mem. bd. sci. advisors Nat. Health Labs./Nat. Reference Lab., 1992-94, cons., 1992-95; bd. dirs. Gulf Coast Cmty. Blood Ctr.; founding bd. dirs. Sealife, Inc., 1991—. Editor, co-editor 4 books; contbr. over 120 refereed articles to profl. jours., 30 chpts. to books. Trustee Coll. Prep. Sch., 1979-84, chmn. bd., 1983-84; trustee, bd. dirs., v.p. Mason Prep. Sch., 1984-87; bd. dirs. United Way, 1983-87, Am. Cancer Soc., 1984-87. Served with USMCR, 1956-64. Johnson and Avalon Found. scholar Georgetown U., 1961-64; State scholar Rutgers U., 1956-60. Fellow Coll. Am. Pathologists (numerous coms.), ACP, Assn. Clin. Scientists (Diploma of Honor 1987, pres. 1990-91, exec. com. 1990-95, Clin. Scientist of Yr. 1993, C.P. Brown lectr. 1995), Am. Soc. Clin. Pathology (coun. immunohematology and blood banking 1983-89, Commr.'s award for CCE 1989), Am. Bd. Pathology (transfusion medicine/blood bank test com. 1984-88), Am. Coll. Nuc. Medicine, N.Y. Acad. Medicine; mem. Internat. Acad. Pathology, Am. Assn. Pathologists, Soc. Nuc. Medicine (chmn. edn. com. 1973-77, acad. coun. 1979-92), AMA (Physician's Recognition award, instnl. rep. to sect. on med. schs.), So. Med. Assn., Am. Geriatric Soc. (founding fellow So. divsn.), Am. Soc. Microbiology, Am. Assn. Blood Banks (chmn. cryobiology com. 1974-83, edn. com. 1978-85, sci. program com. 1981-84, autologous transfusion com. 1979-83, bd. dirs. 1984-87, transfusion practices com. 1992-96), Assn. Schs. Allied Health Professions (bd. editors jour. 1979-83), Soc. Cryobiology (treas., bd. dirs. 1978-80), AAAS, N.Y. Acad. Scis., Acad. Clin. Lab. Physicians and Scientists (exec. coun. 1978-85, pres. 1982-83), S.E. Area Blood Bankers (pres. 1979-81, exec. coun. 1980-85), Tenn. Assn. Blood Banks (treas. 1993-94), Am. Coll. Physician Execs., Sigma Xi, Alpha Eta, Alpha Omega Alpha. Office: MD Anderson Cancer Ctr Lab Medicine Box 73 1515 Holcombe Blvd Houston TX 77030-4095

GLASSMAN, STEVE, humanities educator; b. Hays, Kans., Sept. 4, 1946; s. Eugene and Marguerite G. BA, Kans. U., 1971; MA, U. Southwest Louisiana, 1981; MFA, Vermont Coll., 1983. Assoc. prof. Embry-Riddle U., Daytona Beach, Fla., 1984—. Author: Blood on the Moon, 1990; editor: Zora in Florida, 1991. Bd. dirs. Sister Cities of Volusia County, Fla., 1993—. Fulbright scholar, Belize, 1992. Mem. Fla. Assn. Depts. English (pres. 1994-96), Fla. Coll. English Assn. (pres. 1991-92). Democrat. Office: Embry-Riddle Aeron U Regional Airport Daytona Beach FL 32114

GLASSON, LINDA, hospital security and safety official, healthcare consultant; b. Nassawadox, Va., July 2, 1947; d. William Robert and Doris (Savage) G.; m. Charles William Lemon, Jr., Mar. 21, 1969 (div. 1973). Student Eastern Shore Br. U. Va., 1965-67, J. Sargent Reynolds C.C., 1976-80, Old Dominion U., 1981, Va. Wesleyan Coll., 1985. Cert. ambulance emergency med. technician. Clk.-typist G.L. Webster Co., Inc., Cheriton, Va., 1962-70; tchrs. aide Cape Charles High Sch., Va., 1970-72; dir. recreation and infirmary asst. United Meth. Children's Home, Richmond, Va.,

1972-73; stockroom mgr. Flair Clothing Store, Richmond, 1973-74; with med. record dept. Richmond Meml. Hosp., 1974-75, asst. utilization rev. coord., 1975-80, hosp. police sgt., 1977-80; dir. safety and security Maryview Hosp., Portsmouth, Va., 1980—, chmn. hosp. safety com., 1980—, mem. disaster com., 1980—, chmn., 1986—. Contbg. author tng. manuals; contbr. articles to profl. publs. Instr. first aid and personal safety ARC, 1970-85, multimedia first aid instr., 1983-88, first aid chmn. bd. dirs. Henrico chpt., 1979-80, vol. emergency med. technician ambulance state fair annually 1974—. Mem. Internat. Assn. Hosp. Security (sr., chmn. Region III 1985, v.p., sec. 1985-88, spl. appointee to bd. 1988-89), Am. Soc. Indsl. Security (mem. nat. standing com. healthcare security 1979-84, v.p. 1983-84), Internat. Assn. Healthcare Security & Safety (pres.-elect 1990, pres. 1991-92, past pres. 93—), Internat. Healthcare Security and Safety Found. (pres. 1994-95). Baptist. Avocations: golf, softball, swimming, reading, classical music. Office: Maryview Hosp 3636 High St Portsmouth VA 23707-3236

GLAVINE, TOM (THOMAS MICHAEL GLAVINE), professional baseball player; b. Concord, Mass., May 25, 1966; m. Carri Dobbins, Nov. 7, 1992. Grad. high sch., Mass. Pitcher Atlanta Braves, 1984—. Recipient Cy Young award Baseball Writers' Assn. Am., 1991, Silver Slugger award, 1991, 95; named Nat. League Pitcher Yr., Sporting News, 1991, named to Nat. League All-Star Team, 1991-93, 96. Office: Atlanta Braves PO Box 4064 Atlanta GA 30302-4064*

GLAZE, THOMAS A., state supreme court justice; b. Jan. 14, 1938; s. Phyllis Laser; children: Steve, Mike, Julie, Amy, Ashley. BSBA, U. Ark., 1960, JD, 1964. Exec. dir. Election Research Council Inc., 1964-65; legal advisor, 1965-66; staff atty. Pulaski County Legal Aid, 1966-67, asst. then dep. atty. gen., 1967-70; pvt. practice law, 1970-79; chancellor Ark. Chancery Ct., 6th Jud. Cir., 1979-80; judge Ark. Ct. Appeals, 1981-86; assoc. justice Ark. Supreme Ct., 1987—; co-author Ark. Election Act, 1969, Ark. Consumer Act; lectr. U. Ark. Bd. dirs. Vis. Nurses Corp., Youth Home Inc. Office: Ark Supreme Ct 625 Marshall St Little Rock AR 72201-1020*

GLAZER, FREDERIC JAY, librarian; b. Portsmouth, Va., Feb. 20, 1937; s. Moses Herman and Charlotte Esther (Blachman) G.; B.A., Columbia U., 1958, M.S., 1964; m. Sylvia Katherine Lerner, Aug. 18, 1963; children: Hoyt Eric, Hilary Alison. Librarian, Kirn Meml. Library, Norfolk, Va., 1964-67; dir. Chesapeake (Va.) Pub. Library, 1967-72; exec. sec.-dir. W.Va. Library Commn., Charleston, 1972—; cons. in field. Vice pres. Tidwater Lit. Council, 1970-71; exec. dir. Va. Nat. Library Week, 1970, 71. Served with AUS, 1960-62. Recipient Presdl. certificate appreciation, 1968; spl. recognition Grolier Nat. Library Week, 1970; Gold award 15th Internat. TV and Film Festival, 1972; Region III Outstanding Citizen's award HEW, 1977; Dora R. Parks award W.Va. Library Assn., 1979; Libr. fellow Libr. Fgn. Lit., Moscow, 1994. Mem. ALA (gen. chmn. membership com. 1974-77, councilor 1975-80). Creator Library Six-Pack, Library Book Bucks, Instant Carousel Library, Outpost Library; contbr. articles to profl. jours., commd. by ALA to write, produce and direct media presentation commemorating 25th anniversary of fed. library services and constrn. act legislation. Avocations: reading, brewing beer. Home: RR 1 Box 330 Charleston WV 25312-9727 Office: Libr Commn Sci & Cultural Ctr 1900 Kanawha Blvd E Bldg E Charleston WV 25305-0002

GLEATON, HARRIET E., retired anesthesiologist; b. Altoona, Pa., Aug. 25, 1937; d. Munsey Sinclair and Anna Morgan (Scofield) G. BA, Franklin & Marshall Coll., 1959; MD, Temple U., 1962. Diplomate Am. Bd. Anesthesiology. Intern Mt. Sinai Hosp., N.Y.C., 1962-63; resident in anesthesiology Hosp. U. Pa., 1963-65; fellow Hosp. U. Pa., Phila., 1965-66, instr. anesthesiology, 1966-69; clin. anesthesiologist Michael Reese Hosp., Chgo., 1969-71; assoc. prof. U. Okla., Oklahoma City, 1971-81; clin. anesthesiologist Jane Phillips Episcopal Meml. Med. Ctr., Bartlesville, Okla., 1981-92; pvt. practice, 1992. Mem. AMA, Am. Soc. Anesthesiologists, Nature Conservancy, World Wildlife Fedn., Environ Def. Fund, Sierra Club.

GLEATON, MARTHA MCCALMAN, English language educator; b. Troy, Ala., Oct. 29, 1943; d. Isaiah Williams and Martha Frances (McCalman) G.; m. Ansley Giddens Brown, Jr., Feb. 11, 1967 (div. 1986); children: Anne Martha, Ansley Giddens III. BS, Troy State U., 1967; MA, U. N.C., Greensboro, 1975; PhD, U. N.C., 1980. Asst. prof. Bennett Coll., Greensboro, N.C., 1985-89; asst. prof. High Point (N.C.) U., 1989-94, assoc. prof., 1994—; chr. English dept., 1996—; faculty advisor Alpha Gamma Delta, High Point, 1990—, Jr. Yr. Abroad Westminster Coll., Oxford, England, 1991—. United Negro Fund grantee, 1986, 88. Mem. Nat. Coun. Tchrs. of English, Coll. Composition Comm., Southea. Am. Soc. 18th Century Studies.

GLEAVES, EDWIN SHEFFIELD, librarian; b. Nashville, Feb. 28, 1936; s. Edwin Sheffield and Hazel Boyd (Hunter) G.; m. Jane Ann Thompson, May 20, 1978; children: Susan Kay, David Hunter. BA, David Lipscomb Coll., 1958; MA, Emory U., 1960, PhD, 1964. Head libr., assoc. prof. english David Lipscomb Coll., Nashville, 1964-65; dir., chmn. dept. libr. and info. sci. Peabody Coll. Vanderbilt U., Nashville, 1967-87; state libr., archivist Tenn. State Libr. and Archives, Nashville, 1987—; Fulbright lectr., San Jose, Costa Rica, 1971; Univ. lectr., cons. Colombia, 1971, 84, 92, Mex., 1971, 74, 79-81, 85-86, 94, Paraguay, 1977-79; mem. Tenn. Humanities Coun. Bd. Author (with others): Reference Services and Library Education: Essays in Honor of Frances Neel Cheney, 1982; contbr. over 150 articles to profl. jours. Mem. Bread for World, Washington, 1984—; chmn. Tenn. Hist. Records Adv. Bd., 1988—; bd. dirs. Tenn. Hist. Soc., 1994—, Tenn. Hist. Commn., 1987—, Disciples of Christ Hist. Soc., 1995—, Tenn. Ctr. for the Book, 1996—. With USAFR, 1954-63. Mem. ALA (translator World Ency. 1986), Assn. Specialized and Coop. Libr. Agys. (chair state libr. agy. 1996-97), Tenn. Libr. Assn. (Frances Neel Cheney award 1986, Honor award 1990), Soc. Am. Archivists, Tenn. Hist. Soc. (bd. dirs.), Assn. Records Mgmt. Adminstrs., Chief Officers State Libr. Agys. Democrat. Home: 1004 Norfleet Dr Nashville TN 37243-0312 Office: Tenn State Libr & Archives 403 7th Ave N Nashville TN 37219-1409

GLEMANN, RICHARD PAUL, accounting executive; b. Bklyn., May 7, 1949; s. Walter and Norma (Adler) G.; m. Lorraine Glemann (div. Dec. 1972); 1 child, Nicole. BBA, Fla. Internat. U., 1980, MS in Taxation, 1985. CPA, Fla. Sr. v.p. staff Citicorp, N.Y.C., 1969-71; asst. treas. Crawford Door Co., Hialeah, Fla., 1971-74; controller Air Carrier Supply Inc., Miami, Fla., 1974-75; supr. Fiske & Co., Miami, 1979-81; mgr. Mallah, Furman & Co., Miami, 1981-83, Morrison, Brown, Argiz & Co., Miami, 1983-85; pres., prin. Richard P. Glemann CPA PA, Miami, 1985-88; U. North Fla., 1988-89; nat. tax lectr. Gear Up Tax Seminars, 1994. Chmn. Hugh O'Brian Youth Found., Miami, 1984-85. Mem. Am. Inst. CPA's, Fla. Inst. CPA's (vice chmn. small bus. adv. com. Dade County chpt. 1987, chmn. practice mgmt. com. 1988), Coconut Grove Jaycees (bd. dirs. 1981, 83-84). Office: 806 3rd St Ste A Neptune Beach FL 32266-5063

GLENN, DAVID WRIGHT, mortgage company executive; b. Brigham City, Utah, Nov. 22, 1943; s. Alma Wray and Lois (Wright) G.; m. Cherie Jean Tilleman, June 9, 1967; children: David Wray, Shannon, Chelece, Daniel William, Kellie. BS, Weber State Coll., 1968; MBA, Stanford U., 1971, PhD, 1974. Asst. prof. U. N.C., Chapel Hill, 1973-74; vis. asst. prof. Stanford U., (Calif.), 1974-75; asst. prof. U. Utah, Salt Lake City, 1975-78; vis. asst. prof. Harvard U., 1977; assoc. prof. U. Utah, 1978-83; dir. Fed. Savs. & Loan Ins. Corp., Washington, 1983-84; sr. v.p. planning and acquisitions Calfed, Inc., 1984-87; pres., COO Fed. Home Loan Mortgage Corp., Mc Lean, Va., 1987—. Author numerous articles in bus. and fin. Office: Fed Home Loan Mortgage Corp 8200 Jones Branch Dr Mc Lean VA 22102-3107*

GLENN, JEANNETTE CHARLES, health facility administrator; b. Florence, S.C., Dec. 3, 1944; d. Harry S. and Ather (Jackson) Charles; m. Rodney Steven Glenn, Jan. 28, 1967; children: Michelle Y., Felicia J. Diploma of Nursing, Kate Bitting Reynolds Sch., Winston Salem, N.C., 1966; BSN, U. S.C., 1985; MSN, Med. U. S.C., 1988. Asst. dir. practice devel., dir. staff devel., McLeod Meml. Hosp., Florence, S.C.; surgical clin. coord. head RN med. unit McLeod meml. Hosp., Florence, S.C.; dir. ednl. systems; v.p. human resources and edn., assoc. v.p. practice devel. McLeod Regional Med. Ctr., Florence, S.C. Mem. allocations com., bd. dirs. Florence United Way. Mem. ANA, S.C. Nurses Assn. (coun. on practice), Pee Dee Nurses Assn. (sec., past del. to S.C. Nurses Assn., past bd. dirs.), S.C. Hosp. Soc. Educators (bd. dirs., patient edn. liaison, pres.), S.C. Soc. for Health Edn. and Tng., Am. Soc. Health Educators and Trainers, Am. Hosp. Assn., Sigma Theta Tau. Home: PO Box 694 2515 Whirlaway Ave Florence SC 29505

GLENN, JOE DAVIS, JR., retired civil engineer, consultant; b. Fair Play, S.C., Aug. 12, 1921; s. Joe Davis and Elise Glenn; m. Margaret Glenn, Feb. 21, 1946 (dec. Mar. 1986); children: Joe Davis III, William Harry, Diane Elizabeth, Mary Kathryn; m. Ruth Robinson, Mar. 21, 1987. BSCE, Clemson U., 1942; MSCE, U. Tenn., 1955. Asst. prof. civil engring. Clemson (S.C.) U., 1946-56; structural engr. Tidewater Constrn. Corp., Norfolk, Va., 1956-60; owner, pres. Joe D. Glenn Jr. & Assocs., Norfolk, 1960-76; pres. Glenn-Rollins & Assoc., Inc., Norfolk, 1976-82; pres. Joe D. Glenn & Assoc., Inc., Norfolk, 1982-89, chmn., 1989-91; chmn. Glenn and Sadler Assoc. Inc., Norfolk, 1991-93; retired, 1993. Past elder Coleman Place Presbyn. Ch., Norfolk. Served with C.E. U.S. Army, 1942-46. Decorated Bronze Star. Mem. ASCE (life, Hardy Cross Hall of Fame 1991), NSPE (bd. dirs. 1976-80), Va. Soc. Profl. Engrs. (pres. 1975-76, Engr. of the Yr. 1976), Cons. Engrs. Coun. of Va., Hampton Rds. Engrs. Club (pres. 1974), Soc. Am. Mil. Engrs., Norfolk-Princess Anne Club, Kiwanis (pres. 1963). Home: 4516 Mcgregor Dr Virginia Beach VA 23462-4531

GLENN, ROBERT LEE, internist; b. Rainelle, W.Va., May 6, 1931; m. Nancy Lee Brinkley, Mar. 8, 1958; children: David Robert, Susan Diane. BA in Biology, Berea (Ky.) Coll., 1953; Md, U. Va., 1953. Intern in medicine N.Y. Hosp., N.Y.C., 1957-58, asst. resident in medicine, 1958-59, fellowship in gastroenterology, 1959-60; chief resident in medicine U. Va. Hosp., Charlottesville, 1960-61; pvt. practice Lynchburg, Va., 1963-96; chief of staff Meml. Hosp., Lynchburg, Va., 1967; active staff Va. Bapt. Hosp. Divsn. Centra Health, Inc., Lynchburg, 1963—, exec. staff, 1971-73, mem. med. record and audit com., chmn., chmn. joint intensive care com., 1979-80, mem. cardiac monitoring com., 1981, mem. of skilled care adv. com., 1981, con. for utilization rev. com., 1978-82, mem. utilization rev. com., 1983, 86, mem. institutional rev. com., 1981-96, mem. profl. ethics com., 1983-93, joint intensive care unit com., 1984-85; active staff Lynchburg Gen. Hosp. Divsn. of Centra Health, 1963—, mem. patient care com., various joint coms.; fin. com. Centra Health Inc., Lynchburg, 1987, exec. com. 1988-90; bd. dirs. Integrated Health Care. Mem. Lynchburg Symphony Orch.; bd. deacons First Presbyn. Ch., elder, 1978-80, 82-86, 91-94, sr. high youth fellowship adult advisor, 1980-83, officer nominating com., vice chmn. 1992-93, chmn. 1993-94); bd. trustees Va. Bapt. Hosp., Lynchburg, 1984-86. Fellow ACP; mem. AMA, Lynchburg Acad. of Medicine (bd. dirs. 1969-75, sec.-treas. 1971, v.p. 1972, pres.-elect 1973, pres. 1974, rep. Acad. to Lynchburg Health Care Coalition 1984-85), Med. Soc. of Va. (Va. pharmacy com. 1973-81), Va. Soc. of Internal Medicine, Am. Soc. of Internal Medicine, Va. Gastroenterology Soc., Lynchburg C. of C., Piedmont Heart Soc. (adv. com.), Omicron Delta Kappa, Alpha Omega Alpha. Home: 1436 Club Dr Lynchburg VA 24503 Office: Med Assocs of Ctrl Va Inc PO Box 2719 2215 Landover Pl Lynchburg VA 24501

GLENN, STEVEN CLAUDE, financial executive; b. N.Y.C., Jan. 26, 1947; s. Jack and Lillian (Dankner) Goloshin; m. Penelope Wertz, Aug. 9, 1969 (div. 1982); m. Kathy Mathews, May 23, 1985; children: Darren, Ryan, Chad Mathews, Tara Mathews, Roscoe Goloshin. BA, U. Miami, Fla., 1970; postgrad., Am. Coll., 1976, 82, 87, 88; MS in Fin. Svcs., The Am. Coll., MS in Mgmt. CLU; Chartered Fin. Cons. Agt. Occidental Life Ins. Co., Miami, 1970-75; assoc. gen. agt. Conn. Mut. Life Ins. Co., Miami, 1975-78; agy. mgr. Bankers Life Ins. Co., Jacksonville, Fla., 1978-84; v.p. Lincoln Planning Group, Inc., Jacksonville, 1985-88; pres. The Glenn Planning Group, Inc., Orange Park, Fla., 1989—. Contbr. to books: Your Money and Your Life, 1979, ABC's of Investing Your Retirement Funds, 1980; contbr. articles to profl. jours. Bd. dirs. Jacksonville Gen. Agts. and Mgrs. Assn., 1981-84. Mem. Internat. Assn. Fin. Planning, Jacksonville Soc. CLUs and Chartered Fin. Cons. Home: 319 Scenic Point Dr Orange Park FL 32073-7110 Office: PO Box 755 Orange Park FL 32067-0755

GLICKMAN, RANDOLPH DAVID, ophthalmology educator, researcher; b. N.Y.C., Aug. 24, 1949; s. Stanley Irwin and Ruth Marion (Kaiser) G.; m. Pauline Po-Ling Leung, July 12, 1985. AB, Columbia U., 1971; PhD, U. Toronto, Ont., Can., 1978. Postdoctoral fellow Harvard U., Cambridge, Mass., 1978-79; rsch. fellow Schepens Eye Rsch. Inst., Boston, 1979-81; assoc. rsch. scientist Technology, Inc., San Antonio, 1981-86; rsch. scientist KRUG Life Scis., San Antonio, 1986-92; assoc. prof. U. Tex. Health Sci. Ctr., San Antonio, 1992—; assoc. dir. Ctr. for Environ. Radiation Toxicology. Guest editor: Neurosci. and Biobehavioral Revs., 1993; reviewer Lasers in Surg. Med.; contbr. chpt. to book, articles to profl. jours. Bd. dirs. Terra-Genesis, San Antonio, 1993—, pres., 1994—; adv. bd. Lions Sight and Tissue Found., San Antonio, 1985-89. Recipient U. Toronto open fellowship, 1972, U. Toronto Mary H. Beatty fellowship, 1972-73, Nat. Rsch. Coun. Can. postgrad. fellowship, 1973-76, Nat. Eye Inst., postdoctoral fellowship, 1978-81. Mem. AAAS, Soc. Neuroscience (Alamo chpt. v.p. 1992-93, pres. 1993-94), Assn. Rsch. in Vision and Ophthalmology, Internat. Brain Rsch. Orgn., Oxygen Soc., Sigma Xi. Office: U Tex Health Sci Ctr Dept Ophthalmology 7703 Floyd Curl Dr San Antonio TX 78284-6200

GLINES, CARROLL VANE, JR., magazine editor; b. Balt., Dec. 2, 1920; s. Carroll Vane and Elizabeth Marion (Cross) G.; m. Mary Ellen Edwards, Oct. 1, 1943; children: Karen Ann, David Edwards, Valerie Jean. Student, Drexel Inst. Tech., 1938-40, Canal Zone Jr. Coll., 1946-48, U. Munich, 1948; BBA, U. Okla., 1952, MBA, 1954; MA, Am. U., 1969. Commd. 2d lt. USAF, 1942, advanced through grades to col., 1965; military service, 1941-68; mgr. publs. Nat. Bus. Aircraft Assn., Washington, 1968; assoc. editor Armed Forces Mgmt. mag., Washington, 1969-70; editor Air Cargo mag., Washington, 1970-71; editor Air Line Pilot mag., Washington, 1971-85, cons. editor, 1985-86, contbg. editor, 1989—; sr. editor Aviation Space mag., 1982-85; editor Profl. Pilot Mag., Alexandria, Va., 1986-88, sr. contbg. editor, 1988-95; sr. contbg. editor Aviation History mag. (formerly Aviation Heritage mag.), Leesburg, Va., 1990—; mgr. publs. Air Line Pilots Assn., 1971-85, dir. comms., 1983-85; lectr. U. Dayton, U. Alaska, Am. U. Author 30 books; contbr. articles to mags.; gen. editor MacMillan, Air Force Acad. series, 1970-74; editl. cons. Van Nostrand Reinhold, 1980-85; contbg. editor Nation's Bus., 1981-86; mem. adv. bd. Hist. of Aviation Collection, U. Tex., Dallas, 1981-90, 94—, Alaska Aviation Heritage Mus., Anchorage, 1993—; curator Doolittle Libr., U. Tex., Dallas, 1995—. Asst. to v.p. for spl. projects Evergreen Internat. Aviation, 1988-93; active Frontiers of Flight Mus., Dallas. Recipient numerous awards from press assns. Freedoms Found. Mem. Aviation-Space Writers Assn. (Lauren D. Lyman award), Air Force Assn., Air Force Hist. Found., Quiet Birdmen, Soc. Profl. Journalists, Order of Daedalians, Army-Navy Club. Home: 1531 San Rafael Dr Dallas TX 75218-4444

GLINSKI, HELEN ELIZABETH, operating room nurse; b. Gouverneur, N.Y., Apr. 9, 1944; d. Arthur Andrew and Lillian May (MacKenzie) Turnbull; m. David Lee Joseph Glinski, May 13, 1967; children: David Lee Joseph II, Christopher John. Diploma of Nursing, House of Good Samaritan, Watertown, N.Y., 1965; registered nurse 1st asst., Del. County C.C., 1992. RN, N.Y., Cert. Nurse Operating Room. Staff nurse operating rm. House of Good Samaritan, Watertown, N.Y., 1965-66; staff nurse operating rm. Cmty. Gen. Hosp., Syracuse, N.Y., 1966-68, acting headnurse operating rm., 1968-69, 70, acting asst. head nurse, inservice instr., 1969-70, 70-71; staff nurse operating rm. E.J. Noble Hosp., Gouverneur, N.Y., 1971-72; head nurse, supr. operating rm. Edward John Noble Hosp., Gouverneur, N.Y., 1972-77; sr. staff nurse operating rm. Mercy Hosp., Watertown, N.Y., 1978-79; staff nurse operating rm. Roswell Pk. Meml. Inst., Buffalo, 1979-85, Buffalo VA Med. Ctr., 1985-95; nurse 1st asst. oper. rm. VA Med. Ctr., West Palm Beach, Fla., 1995—; mem. RN First Asst. Spl. Assembly, 1992—. Collector Am. Cancer Assn., Buffalo, 1991, 92, 93. Recipient Performance award Dept. Vet. Affairs, Buffalo, 1988, 91, 93. Mem. Assn. Oper. Rm. Nurses (bd. dirs. 1992-93, 96—, corr. sec. 1986-91, pres.-elect 1993-94, pres. 1994-95, officer western N.Y. chpt.). Episcopalian. Home: 737 Mill Valley Pl West Palm Beach FL 33409-7613

GLISSON, MELISSA ANN, dietitian; b. Arlington, Tex., May 19, 1962; d. Benjamin Louis and Mary Francis Doskocil; m. Fredric Brown Glisson Jr., May 11, 1985; children: Zachary David, Ashley Marie. BS in Food, Nutrition and Dietetics, Tex. Christian U., 1985. Dietitian Woodridge Convalescent Ctr., Grapevine, Tex., 1985; clin. dietitian Thunderbird Samaritan Hosp., Glendale, Ariz., 1988-89; dietitian III Abilene (Tex.) State Sch., 1992-94; mgr. health and wellness program Doskocil Mfg. Co., Arlington, Tex., 1994—. Treas., chmn. fin. com., membership coord. Am. European Dietetic Assn., 1989-92. Mem. Am. Dietetic Assn. (Young Dietitian of Yr. 1992). Home: 5102 Chad Dr Arlington TX 76017-6475 Office: Doskocil Mfg Co 4209 Barnett Blvd Arlington TX 76017-5801

GLOBER, GEORGE EDWARD, JR., lawyer; b. Edwards AFB, Calif., Aug. 10, 1944; s. George Edward and Catharine (Crain) G.; m. Deirdre Denman, May 22, 1971; children—Denman, Nancy King. A.B., Cornell U., 1966; J.D., Harvard U., 1969. Bar: Tex. 1969, U.S. Sup. Ct. 1976. Assoc., Vinson & Elkins, Houston, 1969-77; dir. Houston Dept. Pub. Service, 1977-78; mem. law dept. Exxon Corp. and Affiliates, 1978—, counsel Exxon Corp., 1995—, asst. gen. counsel Exxon Chem. Co., 1991-94; chief atty. refining, environ. and health Exxon Co. USA, 1988-91; gen. counsel Exxon Prodn. Rsch. Co., 1982-88.

GLOVER, EVERETT WILLIAM, JR., environmental engineer; b. Fairmont, W.Va., Apr. 4, 1948; s. Everett William and Pearl Irene (Bollman) G.; m. Joyce Ann Linville, May 24, 1969 (div.); 1 child, Alison Renee. BSCE with high honors, W.Va. U., 1970, MSCE, 1975. Registered profl. engr. Md., Va., N.C., S.C., Ga., Fla., Ala. Project engr. Law Engring. Testing Co., Atlanta, 1972-78; project mgr. Soil & Material Engrs. Inc. (S&ME), Atlanta and Raleigh, N.C., 1978-87; br. mgr. Westinghouse Environ. & Geotech. Svcs. (formerly S&ME), Atlanta, 1987-90, project dir., 1990-92; project dir. Rust Environment & Infrastructure (formerly SEC Donohue, Inc.), 1992—. Mem. ASCE, Project Mgmt. Inst., Chi Epsilon, Tau Beta Pi.

GLOVER, KYLE STEPHEN, English language educator; b. Bentonville, Ark., Feb. 14, 1950; s. John Logan and Bonnie Janelle (Ford) G.; m. Deborah Ann Plummer, Aug. 19, 1972; 1 child, Mark Brandon. BA in English, Okla. Bapt. U., 1972; MA in English, Baylor U., 1977; PhD in English, U. Mo., 1985. Mgr. product devel. MPSI Sys. Inc., Tulsa, 1982-93; asst. prof. English Okla. State U., Stillwater, 1993—. With U.S. Army, 1972-75, Germany. Mem. MLA, Assn. Tchrs. of Tech. Writing, Soc. for Tech. Comm., Soc. for Lit. and Sci. Office: Okla State Univ Dept English Stillwater OK 74078

GLOVER, NANCY ELLIOTT, elementary school administrator; b. Nashville, Dec. 10, 1950; d. Walter Leroy and Mary Ruth (Draughon) Elliott; m. Donald R. Hamlett, Aug. 1971 (dec. Nov. 1981); children: Joshua Hamlett, Kyle Hamlett; m. Charles H. Glover, Feb. 14, 1986; stepchildren: Chris, Troy. BS, David Lipscomb Coll., 1971; MA, Austin Peay State U., 1975; Edn. Degree Specialist, Tenn. Tech. U., 1982; EdD, Tenn. State U., 1994. Asst. ext. agt. U. Tenn. Ext. Svc., Dover, 1971-73; kindergarten/resource tchr. Lakeside Elem. Sch., New Johnsonville, Tenn., 1974-76; 3d grade tchr. Union Elem. Sch., Gallatin, Tenn., 1976-78; 1st grade tchr. Vena Stuart Elem. Sch., Gallatin, Tenn., 1978-81; 7th grade sci. tchr. Gallatin Mid. Sch., 1984-85; 5th and 6th grade math./sci. tchr. Friendship Christian Sch., Lebanon, Tenn., 1985-87; Home Bound/resource tchr. Gallatin H.S., 1988-89; 4th and 5th grade tchr. Clyde Riggs Elem. Sch., Portland, Tenn., 1989-93; asst. prin. Howard Elem. Sch., Gallatin, 1993—; vis. evaluation com. So. Assn. Colls. and Schs., 1994. Vol. coll. coord. United Way, Howard Elem. Sch., Gallatin, 1993—; Bible sch. tchr. Ch. of Christ, Castalian Springs, Tenn., 1976—; campaign vol. various polit. candidates, Sumner County, 1968—. Recipient Gras. assistantship Tenn. State U., 1982-83, scholarship David Lipscomb U., 1968-71. Mem. ASCD, NEA, Tenn. Edn. Assn., Sumner County Edn. Assn., Gallatin Edn. Assn., Phi Delta Kappa. Democrat. Home: 115 Computer Ln Gallatin TN 37066-0821 Office: Howard Elem Sch 805 Long Hollow Pike Gallatin TN 37066-2605

GLUECK, SYLVIA BLUMENFELD, writer; b. Tulsa, Dec. 23, 1925; d. Maurice and Sina (Turk) Blumenfeld; m. Norton Shushan Glueck, June 15, 1947; children: Nancy Eisen, Milton Glueck. BJ, U. Mo., Columbia, 1949. Publicity dir. Sta. WDSU, New Orleans, 1946-47; advt. copywriter Swiftway Direct Mail, New Orleans, 1961; freelance writer and author New Orleans and San Antonio, 1965—. Author book, 1990; contbr. fiction articles to mags. and newspaper features, 1984-85, 90 (Golden Pro award 1986). Mem. AAUW, Women in Communication, Alamo Writers, San Antonio Profl. Writers Group, Mensa. Home and Office: 309 W Magnolia Ave Apt 1 San Antonio TX 78212-3216

GLUSHKO, GAIL M., military officer, physician; b. Griffiss AFB, N.Y., Apr. 22, 1960; d. Wasil and Mary Patricia (Hanchowsky) G.. BA, Miami U., Oxford, Ohio, 1982; MD, Wright State U., 1993. From cashier to asst. mgr. Scarff's Garden Ctr., New Carlisle, Ohio, 1983-85; intelligence rsch. specialist Fgn. Tech. Divsn., Wright Patterson AFB, Ohio, 1985-89; commd. U.S. Army, 1989, advanced through grades to capt., 1993; resident in internal medicine William Beaumont Army Med. Ctr., Ft. Bliss, Tex., 1993-96, army physician; army physician U.S. Army Aeromed. Ctr., Ft. Rucker, Ala., 1996—. Mem. AMA, Phi Sigma (treas 1981-82), Phi Rho Sigma. Russian Orthodox. Office: US Army Aeromed Ctr Dept Internal Medicine Fort Rucker AL 36362

GLYNN, ERNEST B., civil engineer, environmental engineer; b. Cambridge, Mass., Dec. 19, 1911; s. Frederick Stanley G. and Maude Lillian Landers; m. Beatrice Beverly Bakerink, Jan 27, 1951; children: Nancy Belva, Priscilla Beverly. Diploma Structural Design, MIT, 1939; BS, U. Md., 1956. Registered profl. engr., Washington. Archtl. engr. Office Chief of Engrs. U.S. Army, Washington, 1942, 45-47; archtl. engr. Hq. 2nd Army U.S. Army, Balt., 1947-48; ports engr. bd. engr. river and harbors U.S. Army, Washington, 1948-51, engr., intelligence specialist, asst. chief of staff G-2, 1951-63; sr. engr. rsch. specialist Def. Intelligence Agy., Washington, 1963-73; pvt. practice Washington, 1973-85, Alexandria, Va., 1985—; prof. engring. George Washington U., Washington, 1982-85; Presenter, lectr. in field. Contbr. over 30 articles to profl. jours. Mem. Mt. Vernon dist. Fairfax (Va.) Falls Ch., 1959-65; mem. citizen adv. com. Met Wash COG, Washington, 1965-96. Served in U.S. Army, 1942-45. Decorated Croix de Guerre with palm, France; recipient two presdl. citations. Fellow Am. Soc. Civil Engrs. (chair solid waste com. 1950, 51); mem. Am. Acad. Environ. Engr. (diplomate), Va. Soc. Profl. Engrs., Nat. Soc. Profl. Engr. (pres. George Washington chpt. 1976, outstanding engr. 1976, engr. of yr. award 1984), Solid Waste and Environ. Protection, Masons (master lodge 4 Washington). Home and Office: 4306 Ferry Landing Rd Alexandria VA 22309-3025

GNIECH, THOMAS ANTHONY, public relations executive, consultant; b. Chgo., Nov. 11, 1948; s. Robert John and Jacqueline (Heintz) G.; m. Mary Frances Hoffmann, Dec. 22, 1973 (div. Aug. 1992); 1 child, James Philip; m. Nancy Irene Mills, Feb. 14, 1994. BS, Chgo. Tech. Coll., 1970; BA, Northeastern Ill. U., 1974, MA, 1975; postgrad., Loyola U., 1975-76. Cert. pub. rels. cons., Fla. Indsl. engr. Rodman Lab., Rock Island, Ill., 1970-71; project mgr. U.S. Army Armament Command, Rock Island, 1975-77; pub. affairs officer U.S. Army Corps of Engrs., Washington, 1977-81, USN Sea Systems Command, Washington, 1981-83, Comptr. of the Currency, Washington, 1983-85; exec. comm. mgr. Blue Cross/Blue Shield, Jacksonville, Fla., 1985-93; re-engring. cons. Blue Cross/Blue Shield, Jacksonville, 1993—; judge, med. comm. Fla. Med. Assn., Jacksonville, 1990-92; adv. bd. U. North Fla., Jacksonville, 1993—. Sgt. U.S. Army, 1971-72, Vietnam. Sgt. U.S. Army, 1971-72, Vietnam. Recipient Mercury award Nat. Media Conf., N.Y.C., ARC award Nat. Annual Report Conf., N.Y.C., Bronze award Fin. World Mag., N.Y.C., 1986, 89. Mem. Pub. Rels. Soc. Am. (accredited practitioner, dir. 1988-93, nat. del. 1989-93, jud. rev. panel 1992—, chpt. pres. 1992), Fla. Pub. Rels. Assn. (Golden Image award 1986, 88, 89, 90, 91, 92). Republican. Roman Catholic. Home: 2261 The Woods Dr Jacksonville FL 32246 Office: Blue Cross & Blue Shield Fla PO Box 1798 Jacksonville FL 32202

GOANS, JUDY WINEGAR, lawyer; b. Knoxville, Tenn., Sept. 27, 1949; d. Robert Henry and Lula Mae (Myers) Winegar; m. Ronald Earl Goans, June 18, 1971; children: Robert Henson, Ronald Earl Jr. Student, Sam Houston State U., 1967-68; BS in Engring. Physics, U. Tenn., 1971, postgrad., 1971-74, JD, 1978. Bar: Tenn. 1978, U.S. Dist. Ct. (ea. dist.) Tenn. 1979, U.S. Patent Office 1980, U.S. Ct. Appeals (Fed. cir.) 1980, U.S. Supreme Ct. 1983. Instr. legal rights Knoxville Women's Ctr., 1977-78; patent analyst nuclear div. Union Carbide Corp., Oak Ridge, Tenn., 1978-79; patent atty. U.S. Dept. Energy, Washington, 1979-82; legis. and internat. intellectual property specialist Patent and Trademark Office, Washington, 1982-89; pvt. practice law Clinton, Tenn., 1990-96; cons. internat. intellectual property law Clinton and Washington, 1993—; judge Rich Moot Ct. competition, Washington, 1984, Knoxville, 1991; head U.S. Del. 13th session World Intellectual Property Orgn. Permanent Com. for Devel. Cooperation Related to Intellectual Property, 1989; mem. hearing com. Bd. Responsibility of the Supreme Ct. Tenn., 1992—; dir. and chief of party SIPRE Project, Cairo. Del. Nat. Women's Conf., Houston, 1977; bd. dirs. Nat. Orgn. for Women, Washington, 1977-79, Good Shepherd Kingergarten, 1987, Knoxville Women Ctr. 1992-93; legal adv. bd. Knoxville Rape Crisis Ctr., 1979. Mem. ABA, Tenn. Bar Assn., Am. Intellectual Property Law Assn., Govt. Patent Lawyers Assn. (sec. 1981-83), Patent and Trademark Office Soc. (bd. dir. 1986-88), East Tenn. Laywers Assn. for Women (pres. elect 1990-91, pres. 1992, bd. dirs.), Knoxville Assn. Women Execs. (bd. dirs.), Greater Knoxville Lions Club, Tau Beta Pi (bd. dirs. Greater Smoky Mountain Alumni Chpt. 1991—), Sigma Pi Sigma, (sec. U. Tenn. chpt. 1970-71). Episcopalian. Home: 1422 Eagle Bend Rd Clinton TN 37716-4009 Office: SIPRE Project-Cairo care Janice Dance 2021 Wilson Blvd Ste 1200 Arlington VA 22201

GOBLE, ROBERT THOMAS, planning consultant; b. Newton, N.J., Feb. 6, 1947; s. Harold Kenneth and Elizabeth (Snook) G.; m. Camilla Jane Cordray, June 6, 1968; children: Erin Lee, Carrie Elizabeth. BFA, Ohio U., 1969; M Urban Planning, U. Ill., 1971. Research asst. Bur. Urban and Regional Research, Urbana, Ill., 1970-71; sr. planner Dallas Planning Dept., 1971-72; asst. dir. planning Wilbur Smith & Assocs., Columbia, S.C., 1973-75; prin. Carter Goble Assocs. Inc., Columbia, 1975—, also bd. dirs.; bd. dirs. Columbia Leasing, Inc., CGA Facilities, Inc., St. Johns Devel. Corp., Palmetto Trails; planner projects in 48 states and 4 countries, 1975—. Chmn. adv. com. S.C. Outdoor Recreation Planning Council, Columbia, 1977-78, Leadership Columbia Com, 1982-83, chmn. Gov.'s Com. on Jobs and Econ. Devel., Columbia, 1982; chmn. bd. Children's Bur. S.C., Columbia, 1985-86. Mem. Am. Planning Assn., Am. Inst. Cert. Planners, Nat. Acad. Scis. (chmn. rural transp. com. 1983-88, sect. G com. 1988-89, group 1 coun. 1989-93, com. on transit mgmt. and performance 1993—), Nat. Sheriff's Assn., Am. Jail Assn., Am. Correctional Assn., Palmetto Conservation Found. (founding mem., chmn. bd. dirs.). Palmetto Trails (bd. dirs.). Presbyterian. Office: Garter Goble Assocs 1619 Sumter St Columbia SC 29201

GOBLIRSCH, KURT GUSTAV, foreign language educator; b. Rochester, N.Y., Jan. 31, 1962; s. Richard Paul Goblirsch and Marilyn Paulson La Bounta. AB, Washington U., St. Louis, 1984; MA, U. Minn., 1987, PhD, 1990. Asst. prof. La. State U., Baton Rouge, 1991-96; asst. prof. dept. Germanic langs. U. S.C., Columbia, 1996—. Contbr. articles to profl. jours. Am. Swedish Inst. summer study scholar, 1987; German Acad. Exch. Svc. rsch. fellow, Bonn, 1990-91; Swedish Inst. rsch. fellow, Stockholm, 1992; La. State U. grantee, 1993. Mem. MLA, Am. Assn. Tchrs. German, Soc. for Germanic Philology, Soc. for Advancement of Scandinavian Study. Office: U SC Dept Germanic Langs Columbia SC 29208

GOCKLEY, (RICHARD) DAVID, opera director; b. Phila., July 13, 1943; s. Warren and Elizabeth S. Gockley; m. Adair Lewis; children: Meredith, Lauren, Adam. BA, Brown U., 1965; MBA, Columbia U., 1970. Dir. music Newark Acad., 1965-67; dir. drama Buckley Sch., N.Y.C., 1967-69; mgr. box office Santa Fe Opera, 1969-70; bus. mgr. Houston Grand Opera, 1970-71, assoc. dir., 1971-72, gen. dir., 1972—. Bd. dirs. Tex. Inst. Arts in Edn. Recipient Tony award League of N.Y Theaters and Producers, 1977, Dean's award Columbia Bus. Sch., 1982, Music Theater award Nat. Inst. Music Theater, 1985; named one of Outstanding Men Am., Nat. Jr. C. of C., 1976. Mem. Opera Am. (pres. 1985—). •

GODBEY, LUTHER DAVID, architectural and engineering executive; b. Friend, Nebr., May 28, 1938; s. Luther Dobbs and Ruth (Thomas) G.; m. Priscilla White, Oct. 6, 1963 (div. May 1985); children: Emily, Patrick David. BArch, U. Nebr., 1961. Registered architect, Tex. Archtl. designer Selmer A. Solheim & Assoc., Lincoln, Nebr., 1961-63; architect, prin. Golemon & Rolfe Assoc. Inc., Houston, 1963-88; v.p. CRSS, Houston, 1988-90; dir. Corp. program Henningson Durham & Richardson, Dallas, 1990-92; asst. dir. phys. plant Tex. A&M, College Station, 1992—. Author: 52 Ways to Overcome Tennis Elbow, 1980; prin. works include 5000 Montrose Condos., Houston, 1979, Richmond Commerce Bank Office Bldg., Houston, 1980, One Capitol Sq. Office Bldg., Austin, 1985, Marriott Riverwalk Hotel, San Antonio, 1980, Westin O'Hare Hotel, Chgo., 1985, Wyndham Hotel, San Antonio, 1986, L'Hotel Sofitel, Miami, Fla., 1987, Bell Northern Rsch. Ctr., Ottawa, Can., 1988, Yukon Ltd. R & D Complex, Taejon, Korea, 1990, Godbey Residence, Bryan, Tex., 1995; watercolor exhibits include Jefferson Nat. Exhibition, New Orleans, 1963, Houston Art League Show, 1968, Southwestern Watercolor Soc. Regional Exhibition, Dallas, 1969, Houston Arts Festival, 1969, 72, Watercolor U.S.A., Springfield, Mo., 1970, circuit exhibition, 1970-71, 48th Ann. Regional Jury Exhibition Shreveport (La.) Art Guild, 1970, Southwestern Watercolor Soc. 2d Ann. Jury Exhibition, Houston, 1972. Mem. AIA (Brazos chpt. 1992—), Tex. Soc. Architects (honor award 1972), Tex. Assn. Phys. Plant Adminstrs., Briarcrest Country Club, Tex. A&M Faculty Club. Office: Tex A&M Phys Plant MS 1371 College Station TX 77843-1371

GODBOLD, FRANCIS STANLEY, investment banker, real estate executive; b. Charleston, S.C., Mar. 4, 1943; s. Francis Stanley and Ula Leigh (Waddey) G.; m. Lelia Elizabeth Harman, Sept. 24, 1966; children: John A., Laura H. BS in Indsl. Engring. with honors, Ga. Inst. Tech., 1965; MBA, Harvard U., 1969. V.p. Raymond, James & Assocs., Inc., St. Petersburg, Fla., 1969-74, sr. v.p., 1974-78, exec. v.p., 1978—; pres., bd. dirs. Raymond James Fin., Inc. 1987—; mem. regional firms adv. com. N.Y. Stock Exch., 1990-93. Pres. Baypoint Middle Sch. parent Action Com., 1982-83, Bay Vista Parent Action Com., 1979-80; Leadership St. Petersburg, 1974—; mem. Lakewood High Sch. Parent Action com., 1984-90, pres. 1987-88; dir. Ga. Tech. Indsl. and Systems Engring. Alumni Adv. Bd., 1995-96 mem. Tampa Bay area regional devel. coun. Capt. AUS, 1965-67. Mem. Securities Industry Assn. (vice chmn. So. dist. 1980, chmn. 1987, treas. 1986, exec. com. 1988—, nat. dir. 1995, regional firms com. 1995, tax policy com.), Tau Beta Pi, Phi Kappa Phi, Alpha Pi Mu, Phi Delta Theta. Republican. Presbyterian. Clubs: Harvard of West Coast Fla. (sec.-treas. 1971-72, v.p. 1972-73, pres. 1973-74), Harvard Bus. Sch. (treas. 1984), Squires, Quarterback, Lakewood Country, Elk River. Office: Raymond James Fin Inc 880 Carillon Pkwy Saint Petersburg FL 33716-1102*

GODBOLD, JOHN COOPER, federal judge; b. Coy, Ala., Mar. 24, 1920; s. Edwin Condie and Elsie (Williamson) G.; m. Elizabeth Showalter, July 18, 1942; children: Susan, Richard, John C., Cornelia, Sally. BS, Auburn U., 1940; JD, Harvard U., 1948; LLD (hon.), Samford U., 1981, Auburn U., 1988, Stetson U., 1994. Bar: Ala. 1948. With firm Richard T. Rives, Montgomery, 1948-49; ptnr. Godbold & Hobbs and successor firms, 1949-66; cir. judge U.S. Ct. Appeals (5th cir.), 1966-81, chief judge, 1981; chief judge U.S. Ct. Appeals (11th cir.), 1981-86, sr. judge, 1987—; dir. Fed. Jud. Ctr., Washington, 1987-90. Mem. Fed. Jud. Ctr. Bd., 1976-81. With field arty. AUS, 1941-46. Mem. ABA, Fed. Bar Assn., Ala. Bar Assn., Montgomery County Bar Assn., Alpha Tau Omega, Omicron Delta Kappa, Phi Kappa Phi. Episcopalian. Office: US Ct Appeals 11th Circuit PO Box 1589 Montgomery AL 36102-1589*

GODCHAUX, FRANK AREA, III, food company executive; b. Nashville, Feb. 5, 1927; s. Frank Area, Jr. and Mary Lawrence (Ragland) G.; m. Agnes Kirkpatrick, May 23, 1953; children: Katherine Area, Mary Lawrence, Leslie Kirkpatrick, Frank Kirkpatrick. BBA, Vanderbilt U., 1949. Pres. Lastarmco Inc., Abbeville, La., 1964-78; chmn. bd. Lastarmco Inc., 1978—, Riviana Foods Inc., Houston, 1965—; chief exec. officer Riviana Foods Inc., 1980-84; v.p. Colgate-Palmolive Co., N.Y.C., 1976—; dir. New Orleans br. Fed. Res. Bank Atlanta, 1958-63, Acadian TV Corp., Lafayette., La., 1957-83, Chart House, Inc., Lafayette, First Nat. Bank Lafayette, Coastal Chem. Co. Inc., Abbeville, Diversifoods, Inc., Itasca, Ill., 1984-85; bd. dirs. First Commerce Corp., New Orleans, Pacific Ocean Enterprises, Inc., Solana Beach, Calif.,Sysco Corp.; mem. nat. rice adv. com. Dept. Agr., 1964-66, 71-73, 76. Mem. Evangeline area coun. Boy Scouts Am., dist. chmn., 1954-55; trustee Vanderbilt U., 1967—; mem. U. Southwestern La. Found., 1955—. With USNR, 1945-46. Mem. Vanderbilt Alumni Assn. (bd. dirs. 1959-63), Atlantic Salmon Fedn. (bd. dirs. 1987), Phi Delta Theta. Episcopalian. Clubs: Augusta Nat. Golf, Augusta Country, Abbeville Country (La.), City (Lafayette, La.), Mark's (London), The River (N.Y.C.), River Oaks Country (Houston), Belle Meade Country (Nashville). Home: 501 S Main St Abbeville LA 70510-6508 Office: Riviana Foods Inc 2777 Allen Pky Houston TX 77019-2141*

GODDARD, ROBERT DEFOREST, III, management administrator, consultant; b. Bridgeport, Conn., Jan. 28, 1940; s. Robert DeForest Jr. and June Ruth (Bruce) G.; m. Jean Rae Donaldson, Sept. 18, 1986; children: Donald, Gerald, Michael; m. Bonnie Guy, July 19, 1986; 1 child, Benjamin. AA, Palm Beach Jr. Coll., 1967; BS, Fla. Atlantic U., 1969; MBA, U. North Fla., 1974; PhD, U. S.C., 1981. Draftsman Missile Test Project RCA, Cape Canaveral, Fla., 1959-61; computing aide R&D Pratt & Whitney Aircraft, West Palm Beach, Fla., 1965-67; sr. systems analyst Sperry-UNIVAC/RCA CSD, Orlando, Jacksonville, Fla., 1969-73; grad. teaching asst. U. S.C., Columbia, 1974-78; prof. mgmt. Appalachian State U., Boone, N.C., 1978—; pres. Orgnl. Devel. Assn., Boone, 1976—; presenter in field. Co-author: Behavior in Organizations, 1990, Instructor's Manual-Organizational Behavior, 1993, 96; editor Rsch. News, 1982-84; text reviewer; mem. editorial bd. Jour. Global Bus., 1990—; contbr. more than 30 articles to profl. jours. Mayor Town of Seven Devils, N.C., 1981-84; bd. dirs. Region D Coun. Govt., Boone, 1981-83, Sorrento Skies Property Owner's Assn., Boone, 1993—; pres. Somerset Homeowner's Assn., Casselberry, Fla., 1971; steering com. Watauga United Way Campaign, 1986; mem. bd. of adjustment City of Casselberry, Fla., 1971, zoning bd., 1971, planning bd., 1970. With USAF, 1961-65. Recipient Coach of Yr. award So. Women's Soccer Assn., 1991, 93, Outstanding Svc. award Region D Coun. Govt., 1981-84, Gov.'s Community of Excellence award Town of Seven Devils, 1981, 82, 83, Acad. fellowship U. North Fla., 1973-74. Mem. Assn. Global Bus., Acad. Internat. Bus., So. Mgmt. Assn., Pacific Asian Mgmt. Inst., Charlotte Sales and Mktg. Execs., Epsilon Chi Omicron (bd. dirs. 1987—), Pi Sigma Epsilon (v.p. educator programs 1986-87, 87-88, nat. sec. 1985-86), Mu Kappa Tau, Beta Gamma Sigma. Home: 128 Bella Vista Dr Boone NC 28607-8410 Office: Appalachian State Univ 4086 Raley Hall Boone NC 28608

GODDARD, THELMA TAYLOR, critical care nurse, nursing educator; d. James Oscar and Goldie Pearl (Hawkins) Taylor; m. Kenneth L. Goddard; children: Catherine, Sharon, K. John. ADN, W.Va. No. Community Coll., Weirton, 1980; BSN, West Liberty State Coll., 1986; MSN, W.Va. U. Staff critical care nurse Weirton (W.Va.) Med. Ctr., Pitts., West Pa., Pitts.; instr. nursing W.Va. No. C.C., W.Va. U., Morgantown; staff critical care nurse Cen. Med. Ctr., Pitts.; nursing instr. Waynesburg (Pa.) Coll., 1991-92, Carlow Coll., Pitts., 1992-94; instr. nursing Allegheny County C.C., Pitts., 1993-94; asst. prof. Wheeling (W.Va.) Jesuit Coll., 1994—; critical care nurse Ctrl. Med. Ctr., Pitts., 1990-94. Mem. ANA, AACCN, Sigma Theta Tau, Phi Theta Kappa. Office: Wheeling Jesuit Coll 342 Donahue Hall Wheeling WV 26003

GODFREY, ALINE LUCILLE, music specialist, church organist; b. Providence, R.I., Dec. 4, 1943; d. Bernard Almasse and Rita Linda (Laramee) Brindamour; m. George Ruben Godfrey, Aug. 22, 1981; 1 child, Murray Aaron. BA, Rivier Coll., 1970; cert. of attendance, Am. Conservatory of Music, Fontainebleau, France, 1972; M of Music, U. Notre Dame, 1975. Cert. tchr. profl. all level music, provisional elem.-gen., Tex. Choir dir. Scituate (R.I.) High Sch., 1970-74; tchr. grade 4 McDowell Intermediate Sch., Hondo, Tex., 1974-75; tchr. grade 5 Wilson Elem. Sch., Harlingen, Tex., 1975-76; organist St. Albans Episcopal Ch., Harlingen, 1977-80; music specialist St. Mary's Sch. and Immaculate Conception Sch., Brownsville, Tex., 1977-79; choral accompanist Harlingen H.S., 1979-80; tchr. grade 6 Sam Houston Sch., Harlingen, 1980-81; music dir. St. Alban's Episcopal Sch., Harlingen, 1987-90; choral accompanist Marine Military Acad., Harlingen, 1988-90; tchr. Stuart Place Elem. Sch., Harlingen, 1990-91; msic specialist Harlingen Ind. Sch. Dist., 1991—; organist St. James Ch., Manville, R.I., 1972-74, First United Meth. Ch., Mercedes, Tex., 1987-93; pianist, accompanist Cardinal Chorale, Harlingen, 1980-81. Composer: Songs for Tots, 1983; playwright: (musical) Why the Bells Rang, 1988, American Tribute, 1995; arranger, dir. (musicals) Across the U.S.A., 1988, Around the World at Wilson School, 1992; dir. Under the Big Top, 1989, United We Stand, 1991; music dir.: Together, 1995, Christmas in the West, 1995, Every Day is Earth Day, 1996. Vol. Hosts Program, Harlingen, 1981, Riofest, 1983, Dishman Spring Festival, Combes, Tex., 1993, 94, Wilson Spring Fest, 1996; dir. Crockett Sch. dedication, 1993. Mem. Tex. State Tchrs. Assn., Tex. Music Educators Assn., Smithsonian Instn., PEO Sisterhood (historian), Am. Assn. Ret. Persons. Home: PO Box 875 Combes TX 78535-0875 Office: Wilson Elem Sch Primera Rd Harlingen TX 78552

GODFREY, GARLAND ALONZO, retired academic administrator; b. Booneville, Ark., Nov. 5, 1909; s. William Wylie and Lelia (Clay Coatney) G.; m. Merriam Jocille Morris, Nov. 4, 1933; children: Merriam Rose Godfrey Paul, Anna Lee Godfrey Reynolds, Joseph William, Jon Thomas. AA, Ark. Tech. U., 1931; BS, Okla. State U., 1933, MA, 1936, EdD, 1957. From tchr. to supt. schs. pubs. schs., Okla., 1933-60; pres. U. Ctrl. Okla., Edmond, 1960-75. Democrat. Home: 11 Carter Cir Bella Vista AR 72714-3229

GODFREY, HERB, air transportation executive. BS in Air Transp. and Econs., U. Tenn. Dir. aviation Hillsborough County Aviation Authority, Tampa, Fla., 1958-66; mgr. Lindbergh Field, San Diego; v.p. Eastern Divsn. United Airlines, 1966-81; exec. v.p. Dolphin Airways, 1981-82; regional v.p. fin. svcs. and securities firm, 1982-87; dir. aviation Broward County Fla., 1987-90; exec. dir. Greater Orlando (Fla.) Aviation Authority, 1990-92; dir. aviation Jacksonville (Fla.) Port Authority, 1993—. With USN. Mem. Am. Assn. Airport Execs. (accredited), Airports Coun. Internat. N.Am. (past chmn.), Fla. Airport Mgrs. Assn. (past bd. dirs.). Office: Jacksonville Port Authority PO Box 3005 Jacksonville FL 32206

GODFREY, PAUL, publisher. Chmn. bd. dirs. Fla. Sun Pubs., Bradenton. Office: Fl Sun Publ Inc 717 1st St Bradenton FL 34208-1947*

GODING, JUDITH GERMAINE, residential facility administrator, musician; b. Lynchburg, Va., Mar. 8, 1947; d. John Lewellyn and Louise Irene (McCormick) G. BA in Music, Lynchburg Coll., 1969, MEd in Spl. Edn., 1975; EdD in Sch. Adminstrn., Vanderbilt U., 1984. Cert. tchr., Va. Tchr. Cen. Va. Tng. Ctr., Lynchburg, 1969-79, program coord., 1979-82, ctr. dir., 1982—; tchr. Cen. Va. Cmty. Coll., Lynchburg, 1978, 86; organist, choirmaster Peakland United Meth. Ch., Lynchburg, 1970-79, 84-87; interim organist, choir dir. Madison Hts. (Va.) Bapt. Ch., 1990-91; interim organist First Christian Ch., Lynchburg, 1989-90, Euclid Christian Ch., Lynchburg, 1991—; pianist Piedmont Club, Lynchburg, 1975-93; presenter workshops. Contbr. articles to profl. jours. Mem. Cmty. Concerts Assn.; bd. dirs. Lynchburg Symphony. Recipient Edith Carrington award Lynchburg Fine Arts Ctr., 1988, Outstanding Achievement of Accomplishment in Human Svcs. Mgmt., Devel. Disabilities Svcs. Mgrs., Inc., 1989, Disting. Alumni award Lynchburg Coll., 1993, T. Gibson Hobbs award, 1995 and others. Mem. Ctrl. Va. Alumni Club (pres. 1990-94), Lynchburg Coll. Alumni Assn. (pres. 1994—). Home: 1911 Mimosa Dr Lynchburg VA 24503-2329 Office: Cen Va Tng Ctr PO Box 1098 Lynchburg VA 24505-1098

GODSEY, R(ALEIGH) KIRBY, university president; b. Birmingham, Ala., Apr. 2, 1936; m. Joan Stockstill; children—Raleigh, Hunter, Erica, Stephanie. BA, Samford U., 1957; BD, New Orleans Baptist Theol. Sem., 1960, ThD, 1962; MA, U. Ala., 1967; PhD, Tulane U., 1969; LHD, U. S.C., 1984. Asst. prof. philosophy and religion Judson Coll., Marion, Ala., 1962-67; Danforth assoc. Danforth Found., 1964-67; v.p., dean Averett Coll., Danville, Va., 1969-77; dean Coll. Liberal Arts Mercer U., Macon, Ga., 1977-78, exec. v.p., 1978-79, pres., 1979—; trustee So. Assn. Colls. and Schs.; pres. Ga. Fund Ind. Colls.; chief cons. Comprehensive Instl. Devel. Project; cons. Mgmt. Higher Edn. and Organizational Devel. Problems, Planning and Data Systems for Pvt. Colls., Carnegie Found., Task Force on Acad. Affairs for Council of Ind. Colls.; mem. exec. com. Nat. Workshop on Faculty Devel., Lilly and Kellogg Founds.; lectr. Confs. on Personnel Relations, New Orleans, Chgo., Detroit, Seminars on Philos. Ethics for Med. Students, Tulane U., regional confs. and workshops, Chgo., St. Louis, Atlanta, Kansas City. Contbr. articles to profl. jours. Speaker at civic clubs and organs. and bus. and profl. groups including Rotary, Kiwanis, Exchange, Civitan, Sertoma. Recipient Citizenship award, Danville, Va., 1971. Mem. Am. Assn. Higher Edn. (chmn. conf. on institutional planning), Am. Philosophical Assn., So. Soc. for Philosophy and Psychology, Macon C. of C. (bd. dirs.), Phi Alpha Theta, Phi Kappa Phi. Baptist. Lodge: Rotary. Office: Mercer Univ Cen Office 1400 Coleman Ave Macon GA 31207-1000*

GODSEY, WILLIAM COLE, physician; b. Memphis, Dec. 11, 1933; s. Monroe Dowe and Margaret Pauline (Cole) G.; m. Norma Jean Wilkinson, June 18, 1958; children: William Cole, John Edward, Robert Dowe. B.S., Rhodes Coll., 1955; M.D., U. Tenn., 1958. Diplomate Am. Bd. Psychiatry and Neurology. Intern John Gaston Hosp., Memphis, 1958-59; resident in psychiatry Gailor Meml. Hosp., Memphis, 1960-63; practice medicine specializing in psychiatry and neurology; asst. supt. Memphis Mental Health Inst., 1965-74; supt. Cen. State Hosp., Nashville, 1974-75; med. dir. Whitehaven Mental Health Ctr., Memphis, 1975-84, St. Joseph Hosp. Life Ctr., 1984-88; pres. Civilian Material Assistance, Memphis, 1988—; mem. staff St. Joseph Hosp., Eastwood Hosp.; asst. prof. U. Tenn. Coll. Medicine, 1965-74, Coll. Pharmacy, 1972-75; chief of staff Lakeside Hosp., Memphis, 1976-77; songwriter, pub.; pres. Memphis Country Music, Inc. Fellow Am. Psychiat. Assn. (life; past pres. West Tenn. chpt.); mem. Tenn. Psychiat. Assn. (exec. coun., past pres.), So. Med. Assn., NRA, Moose. Methodist. Office: 5118 Park Ave Ste 323 Memphis TN 38117-5711

GODWIN, NANCY ELIZABETH, home economics supervisor; b. Ft. Bragg, N.C., Sept. 17, 1951; d. Nathan Harold and Opal Elizabeth (Hickox) G. AS, South Ga. Coll., 1971; BS, North Ga. Coll., 1973; MEd, Ga. So. Coll., 1978, edn. specialist, 1982. Tchr. Nicholls (Ga.) Pub. Sch., 1974-78; instr. Swainsboro (Ga.) Vocat. Sch., 1978-82; supr. Ga. Dept. Edn., Swainsboro, 1982-91; tchr. Camden County (Ga.) High Sch., 1992—. Mem. Arts Coun., 1987-91, Clean Community Commn., Emanuel County, Ga., 1988-89. Mem. Am. Vocat. Assn., Am. Home Econs. Assn., Future Homemakers Am. Alumni Assn., Ga. Assn. Future Homemakers Am. (hon.), Ga. Home Econs. Assn. (chmn. area scholarship and legis. com. 1985-89, chmn.-elect 1991-92), Ga. Vocat. Assn., Nat. Assn. Suprs. Home Econs., Home Econs. Edn. Assn., Swainsboro C. of C., Pilot Club (pres.-elect 1986-87, pres. 1987-88, bd. dirs. 1988-89, pub. rels. area leader 1990-91, state outreach coord. 1990-91, and others). Democrat. Baptist.

GODWIN, PAUL MILTON, musician, educator; b. Hot Springs, Ark., June 18, 1942; s. Walter Franklin and Mamie Viola (Meek) G.; BA, Ark. Tech. U., 1964; MA, Ohio State U., 1969, PhD, 1972; m. Mary Mae Wolfe, July 22, 1967; children: Katherine Elizabeth, Kimberly Ann, Jeremy Wolfe. Band dir. Lewisville (Ark.) Sch., 1966-67, Lee Sr. H.S., Marianna, Ark., 1972-73; tchg. assoc. Ohio State U., 1970-71; mem. faculty Belmont U., Nashville, 1973—, assoc. prof. music, 1975-80, prof., 1980—, coord. music theory, 1973-89, band dir., 1973-79, chmn. dept. acad. studies, 1983-93, univ. coord. acad. advising, 1993—; choir dir. Crievewood United Meth. Ch., Nashville, 1973-74; dir. Middle Tenn. Jr. High Clinic Honors Band, 1979. With USAR, 1964-66. Mem. Soc. Music Theory, Coll. Music Soc., Mid. Tenn. Sch. Band and Orch. Assn., Music Educators Nat. Conf., Tenn. Music Educators Assn., Assn. Tech. Music Instrn., Nat. Acad. Advising Assn., Phi Mu Alpha Sinfonia. Methodist. Home: 5709 Shetland Ct Nashville TN 37211-6215 Office: Belmont U Sch Music 1900 Belmont Blvd Nashville TN 37212-3758

GOEHL, THOMAS JOSEPH, chemist; b. Phila., Apr. 29, 1942; s. John F. and Catherine M. (McDevitt) G.; m. Judith M. Fortier (dec. Apr. 1993); children: Eric T., Alexandra M. BS in Chemistry, U. Notre Dame, 1964; PhD in Biochemistry, Wayne State U., 1969. Analytical chemist Nalco Chem. Co., Chgo., 1964; rsch. asst. Wayne State U., Detroit, 1965-69; rsch. biochemist, group leader Sterling Winthrop Rsch. Inst., Rensselaer, N.Y., 1969-75; asst. prof. medicinal chemistry dept., assoc. dir. Lab. U. Pitts., 1975-78; rsch. chemist, project officer divsn. biopharmaceutics FDA, Washington, 1978-82; chemistry, inhalation, tech. & toxicokinetics leader Nat. Inst. Environ. Health Scis., Research Triangle Park, N.C., 1982-94; sci. editor Environmental Health Perspectives, Durham, N.C., 1994—; expert witness FDA, 1979; lectr. U.S. FDA, 1979, U. Mex.-Mexican Chem. Soc., ;1981, Nat. Inst. Environ. Health Scis., 1984, Spectroscopy Soc. Pitts., 1992, Czechoslovak-U.S. Sci. and Tech. Program, 1993, Taiwan NIOSH, 1995. Reviewer Jour. Pharm. Scis., Environ. Toxicology and Chemistry, Pharm. Rsch., Environ. Health Perspectives; contbr. articles to profl. jours. Wolf Meml. Found. scholar, 1960-64; NASA fellow, 1967-69; recipient award of merit FDA, 1981, Quality Work Performance award NIH, 1984, 88, 91, 92. Mem. Am. Chem. Soc. (scholarship com. 1983-87). Democrat. Roman Catholic. Home: 112 Holly Creek Rd Morrisville NC 27560-9508

GOEHRING, MAUDE COPE, retired business educator; b. Persia, Tenn., Jan. 5, 1915; d. James Lawrence and Bobbie C. (Ross) Cope; m. Harvey John Goehring Jr., Aug. 12, 1950 (dec. Mar. 1992). BS in Edn., Ind. U. of Pa., 1948; MEd, U. Pitts., 1950; student, Lebanon Valley Coll., 1944-45. Tchr. Penn Hills Sr. High Sch., Pitts., 1948-68; tchr. U. Pitts., 1959-60, ret., 1968; vol. chmn. ICU, operating rm. info. desk Margaret R. Pardee Meml. Hosp., Hendersonville, N.C., 1989-95; vol. Carolina Village Health Ctr., 1994—; coord. Henderson County Ct. House Vols., Hendersonville, 1983-89; cons., counselor tax aid program Am. Assn. Ret. Persons, Hendersonville, 1981-96. Neighborhood chmn. Girl Scouts U.S., Butler County Pa., 1976-79; bd. dirs. ARC, Hendersonville, 1986-91; sec.-treas., bd. dirs. Crime Stoppers of Henderson County, 1991-96; nat. bd. dirs. Second Wind Hall of Fame, 1991-95. Mem. AAUW (officer 1975-76), Gideon Internat. Aux. (pres., sec. 1969-70), Delta Pi Epsilon (life, Gamma chpt., pres., sec. 1956-59, nat. del. 1957). Republican. Lutheran. Home: 21 Kestrel Ct Hendersonville NC 28792-2838

GOELZER, RONALD ERIC, surgeon; b. Chilton, Tex., Oct. 12, 1933; s. Robert August and Genevieve Pamelia (Suttle) G.; m. Carolyn Beth Williams, Aug. 31, 1956; children: Karen G. Garrett, Linda G. Morton, Julianne G. Dayton, Ronald Eric Jr. Pre-med. cert., Baylor U., 1953, MD, 1957. Surg. intern Yale-New Haven Med. Ctr., Conn., 1957-58, surg. rsch. fellow, 1958-59, surg. residency, 1959-61; cardiovascular, thoracic & gen. surgery resident Yale-New Haven Med. Ctr., 1961-63; chief res. gen. cardio-vascular, thoracic surg., 1961-63; gen. and thoracic surgeon Rugeley & Blasingame Clinic, Wharton, Tex., 1966-74, Diagnostic & Surg. Clinic, El Campo, Tex., 1974—; bd. trustees El Campo Meml. Hosp.; team physician H.S. football team, El Campo, 1983—. Bd. dirs. Pub. Sch. Bd. Trustees, Wharton, Tex., 1972-75; chmn. bldg. com. First Bapt. Ch., El Campo, 1982-84; v.p. El Campo Meml. Hosp., 1977-85, bd. trustees, 1992—; Lt. comdr. USN, 1963-65. Mem. Am. Coll. Surgery (cert.), Am. Coll. Thoracic Surgeons (cert.), Tex. Med. Assn. (com. mem.), Elks, Rotary. Baptist. Home: PO Box 391 1701 Saint Lukes Dr El Campo TX 77437-9368 Office: Diagnostic & Surg Clinic 303 Merchant St El Campo TX 77437-4519

GOERKE, GLENN ALLEN, university administrator; b. Lincoln Park, Mich., May 15, 1931; s. Albert W. Goerke and Cecile P. (Crowl) G.; m. Joyce Leslie Walker, Mar. 3, 1973; children: Lynn, Jill, Kurt. A.B., Eastern Mich. U., 1952, M.A., 1955; Ph.D., Mich. State U., 1964. Dean univ. svcs. Fla. Internat. U., Miami, 1970-71, assoc. dean faculty, 1971-72, assoc. v.p. acad. affairs, provost North campus, 1972-73; v.p. community affairs Fla. Internat U., Miami, 1973-78; dean coll. continuing edn. U. R.I., 1978-81; chancellor Ind. U. East, Richmond, 1981-86; pres. U. Houston, Victoria, 1986-89; interim chancellor U. Houston Sys., 1989; pres. U. Houston, Clear Lake, 1991-95, 1995—; adminstr. first VISTA tng. program and Operation Head Start, 1964; cons. adult higher edn., Bahamas, 1975-79, Jamaica, Bahamas, El Salvador, Colombia, Bahamas. Bd. dirs. Reid Meml. Hosp. Found.; bd. dirs. Richmond Symphony Orch.; chmn. edn. adv. panel Ind. Arts Commn. Recipient Outstanding Service award Adult Educators Assn. U.S., 1975; recipient Eastern Mich. U. Disting. Alumni award, 1982. Mem. Nat. Univ. Continuing Edn. Assn. (pres. 1973-74), Nat. Assn. State Univs. and Land Grant Colls. (dell. 1980-81), Am. Assn. State Colls. and Univs., Phi Delta Kappa. Democrat. Methodist. Office: U Houston Office of Pres 4800 Calhoun Houston TX 77204-2162*

GOETZ, STEPHAN JUERGEN, agricultural economics educator; b. Nairobi, Kenya, Feb. 25, 1960; came to U.S., 1983; m. Kathleen J. Weiss, Apr. 30, 1983; children: Alexandra K., Lukas R. BSc in Agrl. Econs. with distinction, U. Guelph, Can., 1984; MSc in Agrl. Econs., Mich. State U., 1986, PhD in Agrl. Econs., 1990. Grad. rsch. asst. dept. agrl. econs. Mich. State U., 1984-86; project mgr., prin. researcher Food Security in Africa

Coop Agreement, Mich. State U./USAID, 1986-87; vis. specialist, grad. rsch. asst. dept. agrl. econs. Mich. State U., 1988-90; asst. prof. agrl. econs. U. Ky., Lexington, 1990-94, assoc. prof. agrl. econs., 1994—; speaker profl. meetings, 1988—. Contbr. articles to profl. jours., chpts. to books; mem. editl. coun. Rev. Agrl. Econs., 1993-96, Jour. Agrl. and Applied Econs., 1996—; manuscript reviewer Econ. Jour. Eng., Am. Jour. Agrl. Econs., Econ. Devel. and Cultural Change, So. Jour. Agrl. Econs./Jour. Agrl. and Applied Econs., Rev. Agrl. Econs., Agrl. and Resource Econs. Rev., Econ. Devel. Quar., Jour. Productivity Analysis, Jour. on Agricultural and Resource Econs. Growth and Change. Bd. dirs. Ky. Econ. Assn., 1996—. Mem. Am. Agrl. Econs. Assn., Internat. Assn. Agrl. Economists, Am. Econ. Assn. Econometric Soc., Internat. Regional Sci. Assn., So. Agrl. Econs. Assn., Western Agrl. Econs. Assn., N.Am. Regional Sci. Assn., So. Regional Sci. Assn., So. Regional Info. Exch. Group (assoc.), Cmty. Econs. Network. Office: U Ky Dept Agrl Econs 317 Agrl Engring Bldg Lexington KY 40546-0276

GOFF, JAMES RUDOLPH, JR., history educator; b. Goldsboro, N.C., Jan. 9, 1957; s. James R. and Kathryn (Forehand) G.; m. Connie Wynn Crawford, Dec. 22, 1978; children: Gideon, Kacy. AA, Emmanuel Coll., 1976; BA, Wake Forest U., 1978; MDiv, Duke U., 1981; PhD, U. Ark., 1987. Instr. Watauga High Sch., Boone, N.C., 1987-88; lectr. Appalachian State U., Boone, 1986-89, asst. prof., 1989-94, assoc. prof., 1994—; presenter numerous workshops in field; asst. minister Creedmore (N.C.) United Meth. Ch., 1979-80, Evangelistic Temple Pentecostal Holiness Ch., Cary, N.C., 1980-81. Author: Fields White Unto Harvest: Charles F. Parham and the Missionary Origins of Pentecostalism, 1988; contbr. articles to religious publs. Pres. Boone Jaycees, 1990-91, chmn. 1991-92; sport dir. Camp Adventure Day Camp, Raleigh, 1980; mem. Duke Divinity Sch. Choir, 1980-81, Emmanuel Coll. Choir, 1974; pres. Emmanuel Ministerial Fellowship, Emmanuel Coll., 1975-76, v.p. 1974-75; pres. PTSA, Parkway Elem. Sch., 1992-93; sponsor numerous camps. Mary Hudgins scholar, 1984, 85; grantee Ctr. for Ark. and Regional Studies, 1984, Hubbard Ctr. Funds, Xerox, also others, 1990-93, So. Gospel Music Assn. and Singing News mag., 1996-97; Charles Oxford scholar U. Ark., 1983-84. Mem. Orgn. Am. Ch. Historians, Orgn. Am. Historians, Soc. Pentecostal Studies, So. Hist. Assn., Phi Theta Kappa. Republican. Pentecostal Holiness. Home: 117 Stirrup Ln Boone NC 28607-9805 Office: Appalachian State U Dept History Boone NC 28607

GOFFIGAN, CHRISTOPHER WAYNE, research associate; b. Norfolk, Va., June 10, 1960; s. James Edward and Lillie Pearl (Jones) G. AAS in Mgmt., Tidewater C.C., 1982, AAS in Merchandising, 1982. Cert. in profl. communication. Libr. aide Tidewater C.C., Virginia Beach, Va., 1980-82; inventory taxer Miller Rhodes, Virginia Beach, Va., 1984, 88; telephone sales rep. Energy Savs. Exterior Inc., Virginia Beach, Va., 1985, Sears Svc. Ctr., Virginia Beach, Va., 1985-86; credit clerical Sears Credit Ctrl., Virginia Beach, Va., 1986-87; telephone interviewer Issues Answers, Norfolk, Va., 1988; rsch. assoc. Leading Nat. Advertisers/Competitive Media Reporting, Virginia Beach, 1990—; new mem. adv. panel Am. Mktg. Assn., Chgo., 1992-93. Vol. City of Virginia Beach, 1989. Recipient Cert. of Appreciation, Mil. Mail Call, 1984, Editors Choice award Nat. Libr. Poetry, 1996; named Knight Chevalier Venerable Order of the Knights of Michael the Archangel, 1992, Hon. Sgt. At Arms, Nat. Assn. Chiefs of Police, 1993. Mem. Am. Fedn. Police, Am. Police Hall of Fame & Mus., U.S. Marshals and Peace Officers Assn. Am., Nat. Assn. Chiefs of Police (hon. chief 1995, Good Samaritan award 1995, Gold Seal award 1995), Internat. Soc. Poets (Internat. Poet of Merit award 1996). Home: 740 Cason Ln Virginia Beach VA 23462

GOFORTH, DANIEL REID, computer scientist, consultant; b. L.A., Mar. 19, 1960; s. Buddy Gene and Judy LaRae (Law) G.; m. Rebecca Clarice Holt, Dec. 19, 1981; children: Emily Clarice, Grason Holt. BA, U. Ala., Huntsville, 1984. Sr. engring. programming Sperry/Unisys Corp., Huntsville, 1983-91; computer scientist Boeing Computer Support Svcs., Huntsville, 1991-93; sr. computer cons. Computer Horizons Corp., Atlanta, 1993—. Recipient Achievement Excellence award Unisys Corp., 1989, Editor's Choice award Nat. Libr. Poetry, 1994, 95, Pres.'s award for lit. excellence Nat. Authors Registry, 1996. Mem. Nat. Mgmt. Assn., Gideons Internat. Office: Computer Horizons Corp Ste 160 3340 Peachtree Rd NE Atlanta GA 30326

GOGGANS, ROBERTA DAILY, retired school system administrator; b. Colbert Co., Ala., Jan. 11, 1926; d. Henry Delofton and Lou Ella (Taylor) Daily; m. Maurice Dow Goggans, Nov. 16, 1946; (wid. 1960); children: Martha Jane, Sheri Susan, Edsel Dow, Maurice Daily. BS, Florence State Tchr., Florence, 1957; AA,MA, U. Ala., Tuscaloosa, 1964-81. Tchr. Colbert Co. Bd. Edn., Tuscumbia, Ala., 1949-52, Marion Co. Bd. Edn., Hamilton, Ala., 1954-66; prin. Byrd Jr. High Sch., Detroit, 1966-69; tchr. Marion County Bd. Edn., Hamilton, supt., 1985-89, ret., 1989; clk. typist Office Scientific Research Wash., 1944-45; farmer Pvt. Practice Marion county, 1982-89. Mem. Gov. Council JTPA Alabama, 1982-86, TVA Commission Alabama, 1986-89, Shottsville United Methodist Ch. Alabama, 1958—. Named Outstanding Woman Leader of Yr., Bevil State C.C., 1995. Mem. AASA ,AEA, NEA, MCEA, Farm Bur., Forestry, Cattlemen's Assn., Co. Devel. Com. Co., Health Com., V.P. Alpha Delta Kappa, Phi Delta Kappa, BPW Hamilton, Fine Arts Hamilton. Democrat. Methodist. Home: 11946 County Hwy 11 Hamilton AL 35570-9805

GOHIL, MAHENDRA NANDLAL, radiologist, educator; b. Bhavnagar, India, Nov. 7, 1928; came to U.S., 1967; BS, U. Bombay, India, 1951; MS in Chemistry, U. Gujarat, India, 1953; MD, Free U. Berlin, 1963. Diplomate Am. Bd. Radiology, Am. Bd. Nuclear Medicine; lic. physician Tex., Calif., Kans., Ky., Tenn. Postdoctoral fellow, rsch. fellow Free U. Berlin, 1963-66; sr. postdoctoral fellow Dept. Radiology, Div. Nuclear Medicine, U. Wash., Seattle, 1967-68; intern St. Francis Hosp., Wichita, Kans., 1968-69; urology intern VA Hosp., Wichita, 1969-70; rotating intern Christ Hosp., Cin., 1970-71; diagnostic radiology resident U. Louisville, 1971-74; pvt. practice radiology and ultrasonography, 1974-84; asst. prof. radiology U. Tex. Med. Br., Galveston, 1990—; cons. in diagnotstic radiology, nuclear medicine and ultrasonography VA Ctr., Wichita, 1979-84, Sedgwick County Cmty. Health Ctr., Wichita, 1979-84; chief tng. and cons. in diagnostic radiology Winfield (Kans.) State Hosp. and Tng. Ctr., 1979-84; chief dept. radiology William Newton Meml. Hosp., Winfield, 1979-84, Security Forces Hosp., Riyadh, Saudi Arabia, 1984-87; cons. radiologist Hamad Gen. Hosp., Doha, Qatar, Arabian Gulf, 1987-89, King Fahad Armed Forces Hsop., 1989-90; dir. radiology sect. Tex. Dept. Criminal Justice Hosp., 1994—. Contbr. articles to profl. jours. State Govt. Saurashtra, India acad. merit fellow, 1951-53, West German Acad. Merit fellow, 1960-64. Mem. Am. Coll. Radiology, Am. Roentgen Ray Soc., Assn. Univ. Radiologists, Tex. Radiol. Soc., Galveston County Radiol. Soc., Soc. of Breast Imaging. Office: Univ Tex Med Branch Dept Radiology Galveston TX 77555-0709

GOHLKE, LILLIAN MARIE, retired secondary school educator; b. Nada, Tex., Feb. 2, 1937; d. Fred Joe and Frieda (Meismer) Kubesch; m. William Carlton Gohlke, Aug. 1, 1964; children: David, Kristi Gohlke Price. AA, Wharton County Jr. Coll., 1957; BA, Sam Houston State U., 1959, MA, 1963. Tchr. English/Spanish Sheridan (Tex.) High Sch., 1959-70; tchr. English Rice High Sch., Altair, Tex., 1970-81, high sch. libr., 1981-92; pub. libr. vol. Sheridan Meml. Libr., 1992-94; univ. interscholastic league coord. Rice High Sch., Altair, 1970-92, future tchr. adviser, 1971-92. Author: Tex. Outlook Mag., 1964. Summer swimming instr. Sheridan Swimming Pool, 1960-80; bd. dirs. San Bernard Electric Coop, Bellville, Tex., 1980-96; instrumental in initiation of STEP for Libr. Sr. Texan Employment Program, Waco, 1993-94. Named Outstanding Secondary Educators of Am., Rich H.S., 1974; recipient John H. Lovelady Lifetime for Youth award Future Tchrs. Am., 1992; NDEA fellow in Spanish U. Tex., 1960, NDEA fellow in English U. Tex., 1962; Sheridan Meml. Libr. grantee, 1993, 94, 95. Mem. Tex. State Tchrs. Assn., Tex. Libr. Assn., Tex. Assn. Family and Cmty. Edn., Sheridan Meml. Libr. Bd., Cath. Das. of Am., Delta Zeta. Democrat. Roman Catholic. Home: PO Box 181 Sheridan TX 77475-0181 Office: Sheridan Meml Libr PO Box 274 Sheridan TX 77475-0274

GOINS, RICHARD ANTHONY, lawyer, educator; b. New Orleans, Mar. 1, 1950; s. James Milton and Vivian (Wiltz) G.; m. Jane Parker, Aug. 18, 1973 (div. Sept. 1987); m. Nannette Smith, Mar. 3, 1990. BA in History cum laude, Yale U., 1972; JD, Stanford U., 1975. Bar: La. 1975, Calif. 1977. Dep. dir. New Orleans Legal Asst. Corp., 1977-78, exec. dir., 1978-81; law clk. to Hon. A. Duplantier U.S. Fed. Dist. Ct., New Orleans, 1982; asst. prof. Loyola U. Law Sch., New Orleans, 1981-84; ptnr. Adams and Reese, New Orleans, 1987—; asst. bar examiner torts La. Bar Exam., 1991-96, bar examiner civil procedure, 1996—; mem. merit selection panel for selection and appt. of U.S. Magistrate for Ea. Dist. La., 1992—; mem. host com. jud. conf. Fed. 5th Cir. Ct. Appeals, 1995. Mem. Mayor of New Orleans Overall Econ. Devel. Plan Com., 1991, Orleans Intercmty. Coun., 1992; mem. spl. gifts. com. Yale Alumni Fund, 1991-92; bd. dirs. New Orleans Home Mortgage Authority, 1991-94, City Trust, New Orleans, 1983-94, State Mental Health Advocacy Sys., New Orleans, 1983-84, New Orleans Legal Assistance Corp., 1982-83, Milne Asylum for Destitute Orphan Boys, Inc., 1994—. Reginald Heber Smith fellow, 1975; Nat. Achievement scholar Yale U., 1968-72, Leadership La. scholar, 1992. Mem. ABA (Conf. of Minority Ptnrs. 1990—), La. State Bar Assn. (legal aid com. 1978-81, uniform fed. rules com. 1991-92, fed. ct. bench-bar liaison com. 1993—), Nat. Bar Assn. (comml. law sect. 1989—), Fed. Bar Assn. (bd. dirs. New Orleans chpt. 1992—), 5th Cir. Bar Assn., Calif. State Bar Assn., Thomas More Inn of Ct. (barrister). Democrat. Roman Catholic. Home: 4412 Mandeville St New Orleans LA 70122-4928

GOIZUETA, ROBERTO CRISPULO, food and beverage company executive; b. Havana, Cuba, Nov. 18, 1931; came to U.S., 1964; s. Crispulo D. and Aida (Cantera) G.; m. Olga T. Casteleiro, June 14, 1953; children: Roberto S., Olga M., Javier C. BS, BChemE, Yale U., 1953; degree (hon.), U. Notre Dame, 1995. Process engr. Indsl. Corp. Tropics, Havana, 1953-54; tech. dir. Coca-Cola Co., Havana, 1954-60; asst. to sr. v.p. Coca-Cola Co., Nassau, Bahamas, 1960-64; asst. to v.p. R & D Coca-Cola Co., Atlanta, 1964-66, v.p. engring., 1966-74, sr. v.p., 1974-75, exec. v.p., 1975-79, vice chmn., 1979-80, pres., COO, 1980-81, chmn. bd., CEO, 1981—; bd. dirs. SunTrust Banks, Inc., Ford Motor Co., SONAT, Inc., Eastman Kodak; trustee Emory U., 1980—, The Am. Assembly, 1979—, Boys and Girls Clubs Am., Robert W. Woodruff Arts Ctr., 1990—. Recipient Svc. to Democracy award Am. Assembly, 1990, Equal Justice award NAACP Legal Def. Fund, 1991, Disting. Pub. Svcs. award Advt. Coun., 1994. Mem. Bus. Coun., Bus. Roundtable Policy Com., Points of Light Initiative Found. Office: Coca-Cola Co PO Drawer 1734 Atlanta GA 30301-1734

GOKEL, GEORGE WILLIAM, organic chemist, educator; b. N.Y.C., June 27, 1946; s. George William and Ruth Mildred G.; BS in Chemistry, Tulane U., 1968; PhD in Organic Chemistry, U. So. Calif., 1971; m. Kathryn Smiegocki, June 2, 1978; children: Michael Robert, Matthew George, Mark Arlington. Postdoctoral fellow UCLA, 1972-74; chemist cen. rsch. dept. E.I. Du Pont de Nemours & Co., Wilmington, Del., summer 1974; asst. prof. chemistry Pa. State U., University Park, 1974-78; assoc. prof. chemistry U. Md., College Park, 1978-82, prof. chemistry, 1982-85, U. Miami, Coral Gables, Fla., 1985-93; prof. dept. molecular biology & pharmacology Sch. Medicine, dir. bioorganic chemistry program Washington U., 1993—; cons. W.R. Grace Co., 1977-86; cons. Lion Detergent Co., Tokyo, 1985—, Seal Sands Chem. Co., Stockton-on-Tees, Eng., 1983-88, Monsanto Co., St. Louis, 1989-91, A.H. Marks, Eng., 1990—; lectr. in field. Recipient Allan C. Davis medal Md. Acad. Sci., 1979; Leo Schubert award Washington Acad. Scis., 1980, Macrocycle Chemistry award Izatt-Christensen, 1996; Petroleum Research Fund grantee, 1976-78; NIH grantee, 1979—. Mem. AAAS, Am. Chem. Soc., Chem. Soc. (London), Am. Assn. Adv. Sci., Sigma Xi, Alpha Chi Sigma. Republican. Methodist. Author: Phase Transfer Catalysis in Organic Synthesis, 1977; Experimental Organic Chemistry, 1980; Macrocyclic Polyether Syntheses, 1982; editor Cation Binding by Macrocycles, 1996; editor Advances in Supramolecular Chemistry, vols. 1-3, 1990-93, Comprehensive Supramolecular Chemistry, vol. 1, 1996; contbr. numerous articles to profl. jours. Home: 1817 Stenton Path Chesterfield MO 63005-4733 Office: Washington U Sch Medicine Dept Molecular Biology & Pharmacology Saint Louis MO 63110

GOKHALE, ARUN MAHADEO, materials science and engineering educator; b. Vadodara, Gujarat, India, Apr. 28, 1948; came to U.S., 1987; s. Govnd Mahadeo and Shanta Gokhale; m. Sulabha Joshi, Dec. 27, 1975; children: Sonali, Amit. B Tech. in Metall. Engring., Indian Inst. Tech., Kanpur, India, 1970, M Tech. in Metall. Engring., 1972; PhD in Materials Sci. and Engring., U. Fla., 1977. Lectr. dept. metall. engring. Indian Inst. Tech., Kanpur, 1977-80, asst. prof. metall. engring., 1985-87; sr. asst. mgr. R & D Ctr. Hindustan Brown Boveri Vadodara, India, 1980-85; asst. prof. metallurgy Ind. Inst. Sci., Bangalore, 1985; vis. assoc. prof. Sch. Materials Engring. Ga. Inst. Tech., Atlanta, 1987-89, assoc. prof., 1989-92, prof., 1992—; lectr., rschr. in field; presenter at confs. and symposia in field; reviewer rsch. proposals NSF; mem. internat. adv. bd. 8th Internat. Congress for Stereology, Irvine, Calif., 1991, keynote lectr. 6th European Congress for Stereology, Czech Republic, 1993. Contbr. articles to sci. publs.; mem. editl. bd. Jour. Microscopy. Recipient Kamani Gold medal Indian Inst. Metals, 1985. Mem. Internat. Soc. for Stereology (v.p. 1992—), Soc. for Quantitative Morphology (exec. bd. 1992—), Sigma Xi (chmn. inst. com. for best PhD thesis award 1992-93). Home: 660 Yorkshire Dr Marietta GA 30068-5210 Office: Ga Inst Tech 778 Atlantic Dr Atlanta GA 30332

GOLAN, LAWRENCE PETER, mechanical engineering educator, energy researcher; b. Newark, June 20, 1938; s. Joseph and Francis (Duda) G.; m. Helen Imelda Hemko, June 30, 1962; children: Lisa Marie, Wanda Marie, Lawrence P. II. BSME, W.Va. U., 1961, MSME, 1964; PhD, Lehigh U., 1968. Mech. engr. Picatinny Arsenal, Dover, N.J., 1961-62; instr. W.Va. U., Morgantown, 1962-64, Lehigh U., Bethlehem, Pa., 1964-68; engring. assoc. Exxon Rsch. and Engring., Florham Park, N.J., 1968-86; founder/mgr. Doe advanced gas turbine sys. rsch. prog., dir. S.C. Energy Rsch. and Devel. Ctr., Clemson, 1986—; prof. mech. engring. Clemson U., 1986—; chmn. 2d World Congress Chem. Engring. on Coal Utilization; cons. State of Ill. Ctr. for Coal Rsch., 1987-90; mem. S.C. Energy Products Evaluation Com.; chair Nat. HEat Transfer Conf., 1996. Contbr. articles to profl. jours. Mem. adv. com. W.Va. U., 1985-94. Mem. AIChE (East Coast membership chmn., vice chair nat. meeting 1991, chair elect heat transfer divsn. 1990, chair 1991, co-chair 1992, nat. heat transfer conf. best paper, chair AIChE Kern award 1994, chair ASME-AIChE Jakob award 1994), Am. Petroleum Inst. (chmn. sampling project 1985-89), S.C. Energy Mgrs. Roman Catholic. Home: 333 Lowkirk Aly Seneca SC 29672-2273 Office: SC Energy Rsch and Devel 386-2 College Ave Clemson SC 29634

GOLAND, MARTIN, research institute executive; b. N.Y.C., July 12, 1919; s. Herman and Josephine (Bloch) G.; m. Charlotte Nelson, Oct. 16, 1948; children—Claudia, Lawrence, Nelson. M.E., Cornell U., 1940; LL.D. (hon.), St. Mary's U., San Antonio. Instr. mech. engring. Cornell U., 1940-42; sect. head structures dept. research lab., airplane div. Curtiss-Wright Corp., Buffalo, 1942-46; chmn. div. engring. Midwest Research Inst., Kansas City, Mo., 1946-50; dir. for engring. scis. Midwest Research Inst., 1950-55; v.p. Southwest Research Inst., San Antonio, 1955-57; dir. Southwest Research Inst., 1957-59, pres., 1959—; pres. S.W. Found. Biomed. Rsch. (formerly S.W. Found. Rsch. & Edn), San Antonio, 1972-82; dir. Nat. Bancshares Corp. Tex., 1972-87; chmn. subcom. vibration and flutter NACA, 1952-60; chmn. research adv. com. on aircraft structures NASA, 1960-68, chmn. materials and structures group, aeros. adv. com., 1979-82; sci. adv. com. Harry Diamond Labs., U.S. Army Materiel Command, 1955-75; adv. panel com. sci. and astronautics Ho. of Reps., 1960-73; mem. adv. bd. on undersea warfare Dept. Navy, 1968-70, chmn., 1970-73; mem. spl. aviation fire reduction com. FAA, 1979-80; sci. adv. panel Dept. Army, 1966-77; chmn. U.S. Army Weapons Command Adv. Group, 1966-72; mem. materials adv. bd. NRC, 1969-74; vice-chmn. Naval Research Adv. Com., 1974-77, chmn., 1977; dir. Nat. Bank Commerce, San Antonio, 1969-90; dir. Engrs. Joint Council, 1966-69; mem. adv. group U.S. Armament Command, 1972-76; mem. sci. adv. com. Gen. Motors, 1971-81; mem. Nat. Commn. on Libraries and Info. Scis., 1971-78; chmn. NRC Bd. Army Sci. and Tech., 1982-89; chmn. Commn. Engring. and Tech. Systems, NRC, 1980-86. Editor: Applied Mechanics Review, 1952-59; editorial adviser, 1959-84. Bd. govs. St. Mary's U., San Antonio, 1970-76, 85-94; pres. San Antonio Symphony, 1968-70, chmn. bd., 1970-71; bd. dirs. So. Meth. U. Found. Sci. and Engring., Dallas, 1979-90; trustee Univs. Rsch. Assocs., Inc., 1979-84; mem. Tex. Nat. Rsch. Lab. Commn., 1986-91. Recipient Spirit of St. Louis Jr. award ASME, 1945, Jr. award, 1946, Alfred E. Noble prize ASCE, 1947, Outstanding Civilian Svc. award U.S. Army, 1972, 88, Nat. Engring. award, 1985, W.W. McAllister Patriotism award, 1986, Herbert Hoover medal, 1987; named Employer of Yr. Nat. Employee Svcs. and Recreation Assn., 1993. Fellow AAAS, Am. Inst. Aeros. and Astronautics (pres. 1971); hon. mem. ASME (dir., mem. bd. tech., mem. tech. devel. com., v.p. communications); mem. NAE, Soc. Automotive Engrs., C. of C. (bd. dirs.), Sigma Xi, Tau Beta Pi. Home: 306 Country Ln San Antonio TX 78209-2319 Office: Southwest Rsch Inst PO Box 28510 San Antonio TX 78228 also: 6220 Culebra Rd San Antonio TX 78238-5166

GOLANT, STEPHEN MYLES, geographer, gerontologist, educator; b. Toronto, Can., Dec. 14, 1945; married; 1 child. BA in Geography with honors, U. Toronto, Can., 1968, MA in Geography, 1969; PhD in Geography, Social Gerontology, U. Wash., 1972. Asst. prof. Behavioral Scis. U. Chgo., 1972-79, assoc. prof. Geography, 1979-80; assoc. prof. Geography U. Fla., Gainesville, 1980-84, chair dept. Geography, 1982-88, prof. Geography, adj. prof. Urban and Regional Planning, 1984—. Various radio and TV appearances including ABC's 20/20, 1988; author: The Residential Location and Spatial Behavior of the Elderly, 1972, Location and Environment of Elderly Population, 1979, A Place to Grow Old: The Meaning of Environment in Old Age, 1984, Housing America's Elderly: Many Possibilities, Few Choices, 1992, Smart Housing, 1994; assoc. editor (book) The Columbia Retirement Handbook, 1994; contbr. articles, book revs. to profl. jours. Can. coun. scholar, 1969-70, 70-71. Mem. Gerontol. Soc. Am. (sec.-treas. behavioral and social scis. sect. 1993—), Nat. Coun. on the Aging, Am. Assn. on Aging, Am. Sociol. Assn., Am. Assn. of Homes for the Aging, Fla. Assn. of Homes for the Aging, Am. Psychol. Assn. (divsn. 34), Environ. Design Rsch. Assn., Assn. Am. Geographers (Southeastern divsn.), So. Gerontol. Soc. Office: U Fla Dept Geography 3142 Turlington Hall Gainesville FL 32611

GOLD, ALAN STEPHEN, judge, lawyer, educator; b. N.Y.C., Jan. 8, 1944; s. Frank and Geraldine (Guenzberg) G.; m. Susan Fine, May 28, 1965; children: Carol, Natalie. BA with high honors, U. Fla., 1966; JD, Duke U., 1969; M in Taxation, U. Miami, Fla., 1974. Bar: Fla., 1969, Dade County, Fla. (11th judicial cir.), 1992. Law clk. to Hon. Charles Carrol Fla. 3d Dist Ct. Appeal, Miami, 1969-71; asst. atty. Met. Dade County Atty's Office, Miami, 1971-75; ptnr. Greenberg, Traurig, Hoffman, Lipoff, Rosen & Quentel, P.A., Miami, 1975-92; apptd. judge 11th Circuit Ct., Dade County, Fla., 1992—. Contbr. articles to legal jours. Co-gen. counsel Fla. High Speed Rail Transp. Commn., 1985—; city atty. Village of Bal Harbour, Fla., 1976-82; spl. counsel Broward County, Fla., 1984-88; trustee Palmer Sch., Miami, 1987-88; bd. dirs. Actor's Playhouse, Miami, 1989—, South Dade Jewish Community Ctr., Miami, 1985-85; apptd. Fla. Environ. Land Mgmt. Com., 1987. Disting. scholar Fla. State U., 1990; recipient award for outstanding contbn. in field of legis. affairs South Fla. Bldrs. Assn., 1989. Mem. ABA, Fla. Bar. Assn. (com. on environment and land use law 1983-84, Disting. Svc. award 1984), Urban Land Inst. (nat. policy coun. 1988—), Greater Miami C. of C. (chmn. land use com. 1989-90), Am. Coll. Real Estate Attys. Democrat. Jewish. Office: Dade County Ct House 73 W Flagler St Fl 7 Miami FL 33130-1731

GOLD, CATHERINE ANNE DOWER, music history educator; b. South Hadley, Mass., May 19, 1924; d. Lawrence Frederick Dower and Marie (Barbieri) Barber; m. Arthur Gold, Mar. 24, 1994; children: Carolyn D. Gold, Judith G. Enteen. AB, Hamline U., 1945; MA, Smith Coll., 1948; PhD, The Cath. U. Am., 1968. New Eng. rep. Gregorian Inst. Am., Toledo, 1948-49; tchr. music, organist St. Rose Sch., Meriden, Conn., 1949-53; supr. music Holyoke (Mass.) Pub. Schs., 1953-55; instr. music U. Mass., Amherst, 1955-56; prof. music Westfield (Mass.) State Coll., 1956-90; columnist and freelance writer Holyoke Transcript Telegram, 1991-93; organist St. Theresa's Ch., South Hadley, 1937-41, St. Michael's Ch., N.Y., 1945-46; concert series presenter Westfield State Coll., 1987-91, rschr. tchr.; vis. scholar U. So. Calif., 1969; vis. assoc. prof. music Herbert Lehman Coll. CUNY, 1970-71. Author: Puerto Rican Music Following the Spanish American War, 1898-1910, 1983; (monograph) Yella Pessl, 1986, Alfred Einstein on Music, 1991, Yella Pessl: First Lady of the Harpsichord, 1993; presenter Irish Concert Springfield Symphony Orch., 1981 (plaque 1982). Pres. Coun. for Human Understanding Holyoke, 1981-83, Friends of Holyoke Pub. Libr., 1990-91; bd. dirs., chmn. nominating com. Holyoke Pub. Libr., 1987-89; bd. dirs. Holyoke Pub. Libr. Corp., 1991-94, Women's Symphony League, The Symphony Orch., 1992-94; bd. dirs., sec. Life Long Learning Soc. of Fla. Atlantic U., 1994—; presiding officer inauguration Dr. Irving Buchman pres. of Westfield State Coll.; mem. ethics com. Holyoke Hosp., 1988-94; sec. Haiti Mission, 1982-94; bd. overseers Mullen U., 1993; hon. mem. bd. Coun. Human Understanding, 1994; hon. mem. WSC Found., 1994; co-chair United Jewish Appeal/Jewish Fedn. Boca Lago Women's Divsn., 1996-97. Recipient citation Academia InterAmericana de P.R., 1978, Holyoke Pub. Libr., 1983, plaque Mass. Tchrs. Assn., Boston, 1984, medal Equestrian Order Holy Sepulchre of Jerusalem, Papal Knighthood Soc., Boston, 1984, Performance award Gov. Dukakis, Mass., 1988, award for Puerto Rican Jour. Al. Margens, 1992, Human Rels. award Coun. for Human Understanding, Holyoke, 1994, award Trustee's Cir. Westfield State U., 1994; named Lady Comdr., 1987, with star, 1990, Career Woman of Yr., 1988; fellow Internat. Biographical Assn., 1991; Westfield State U. concert series named Catherine A. Dower Performing Arts Series in her honor, 1991; recipient 1st prize in Raddock Eminent Scholar Chair Essay Contest of Fla. Atlantic U., 1996. Mem. Am. Musicol. Soc., The Coll. Mus. Soc., Ch. Music Assn. Am. (journalist), Acad. Arts and Scis. of P.R. (medal 1977), Internat. Platform Assn., Friends of the Holyoke Pub. Libr. (pres. 1990-91), Irish Am. Cultural Inst. (chmn. bd. 1981-89), Holyoke Quota (v.p. 1976-79, pres. 1979-81, 90-92, chmn. speech and hearing com. 1987-94), B'nai B'rith of Boca Lago (sec. bd. dirs. 1994—), Lifelong Learning Soc. Fla. Atlantic U. (sec. 1994—). Democrat. Home: 8559 Casa Del Lago Boca Raton FL 33433-2107

GOLD, DANIEL HOWARD, ophthalmologist, educator; b. N.Y.C., Sept. 21, 1942; s. Isadore and Leona (Cotton) G.; m. Joann Aaron, Oct. 22, 1966 (div. Sept. 1985); m. Barbara Wood, June 19, 1988; children: David, Abigail, Michael. Student, U. Mich., 1959-66. Diplomate Am. Bd. Ophthalmology. Asst. chief dept. ophthalmology Walter Reed Army Med. Ctr., Washington, 1972-74; asst. prof. dept. ophthalmology Montefiore Hosp. Med. Ctr., Bronx, N.Y., 1974-76; asst. clin. prof. med. br. U. Tex., Galveston, 1977-85, assoc. clin. prof. med. br., 1986-91; physician, ophthalmologist Eye Clinic of Tex., Galveston, 1977—; clin. prof. ophthalmology med. br. U. Tex., Galveston, 1991—; mem. med. staff exec. com. St. Mary's Hosp., Galveston, 1989-90, 95-96, chmn. dept. surgery, 1995-96. Editor: (textbook) The Eye in Systemic Disease, 1990; sec. editor Duanes Clinical Ophthalmology, 1974—, Current Opinion in Ophthalmology, 1991—; contbr. articles to profl. jours. Maj. U.S. Army, 1972-74. Fellow Am. Acad. Ophthalmology (mem. self-assessment com. 1989-92, Honor award 1985), Royal Coll. Ophthalmologists Gt. Britain, N.Y. Acad. Medicine; mem. Macula Soc., Assn. for Rsch. in Vision and Ophthalmology, Pan Am. Assn. Ophthalmology, Galveston Physicians Svc. Assn. (bd. dirs. 1985—, pres. 1993—), Tex. Med. Assn. (coun. on pub. health 1995—). Jewish. Office: Eye Clinic Tex 2302 Avenue P Galveston TX 77550-7992

GOLD, DEBORAH T., gerontology and sociology educator; b. Chgo., Apr. 1, 1951; d. James Samuel and Flora Jane (Schwartz) G. BA, U. Ill., 1973; MEd, Nat. Coll., 1979; PhD, Northwestern U., 1986. Reading specialist High Sch. Dist. 113, Highland Pk, Ill., 1973-83; dir., secondary tchr. preparation program Northwestern U., 1983-86; sr. fellow Aging Ctr. Duke U., Durham, N.C., 1988—, assoc. prof. dept. psychiatry and dept. sociology, 1988—; cons. family support program long-term care project Duke U., 1988—, spl. care units project U. N.C., Chapel Hill, 1988—; cons. Office Tech. Assessment, Washington, 1990-93; mem. nat. osteoporosis data group Nat. Inst. for Arthritis Musculoskeletal and Skin Diseases; mem. sci. adv. bd. Nat. Osteoporosis Found. Contbr. numerous articles to profl. jours., chpts. to books. Northwestern U. fellow, 1982-84, Retirement Rsch. Found. fellow, 1985. Mem. APA, Am. Soc. on Aging, Am. Sociol. Assn. (chmn. dissertation com. 1992-93), Gerontol. Soc. Am. (chair membership com. 1993-95), So. Gerontol. Soc., Sigma Xi. Office: Duke U Med Ctr PO Box 3003 Durham NC 27715-3003

GOLD, HAZEL, Spanish language educator; b. Bklyn., May 5, 1953; d. Robert Murray and Thelma (Steinberg) Gold. BA, Mt. Holyoke Coll., 1973; MA, U. Pa., 1974, PhD, 1980. Asst. prof. Columbia U., N.Y.C., 1980-85, Northwestern U., Evanston, Ill., 1985-92; assoc. prof. Emory U., Atlanta, 1992—; cons. and reader Spanish advanced placement exams Ednl.

Testing Svc., Princeton, N.J., 1989—; rev. panelist NEH, Washington, 1990. Author: The Reframing of Realism: Galdo's and the Discourses of the 19th Century Spanish Novel; mem. editorial bd. Jour. for Interdisciplinary Lit. Studies, Anales Galdosianos; contbr. articles to profl. jours. Grantee U.S.-Spain Joint Com. Cultural and Ednl. Cooperation, 1986, Am. Coun. Learned Socs., 1990, fellow 1988. Mem. AAUP, MLA (divsn. exec. com. Spanish lit. 1991-95, Katherine Singer Kovacs prize selection com. 1996—), Soc. Study Narrative Lit., Asociacion Internacional de Galdosistas (v.p. 1993-95, pres. 1996—), Asociacion Internacional de Hispanistas, Midwest MLA. Office: Emory Univ Dept Spanish Atlanta GA 30322

GOLD, I. RANDALL, lawyer; b. Chgo., Nov. 2, 1951; Albert Samuel and Lois (Rodrick) G.; m. Marcey Dale Miller, Nov. 18, 1978; children: Eric Matthew, Brian David. BS with high honors, U. Ill., 1973, JD, 1976. Bar: Ill. 1976, U.S. Dist. Ct. (no. dist.) Ill. 1976, Fla. 1979, U.S. Dist. Ct. (so. dist.) Fla. 1979, U.S. Ct. Appeals (5th and 7th cirs.) 1979, U.S. Tax Ct. 1979, U.S. Ct. Appeals (11th cir.) 1981, U.S. Supreme Ct. 1982, U.S. Dist. Ct. (mid. dist.) Fla. 1987; CPA, Ill., Fla. Tax staff Ernst & Ernst, Chgo., 1976-77; asst. state atty. Cook County, Ill., 1977-78, Dade County, Miami, Fla., 1978-82; spl. atty. Miami Strike Force U.S. Dept. Justice, Fla., 1982-87; pvt. practice Miami, 1987-92; asst. U.S. atty. U.S. Dist. Ct. (mid. dist.) Fla., 1992—; lectr. Roosevelt U., Chgo., 1976-77; vice chmn. fed. practice com. on criminal sect. Fla. Bar, 1986-88, profl. ethics com., 1992—; instr. Rollins Coll. paralegal program, 1992—; adj. prof. criminal justice program U. Ctrl. Fla., 1994—. Co-chmn. Greater Oviedo Cmty. Devel. Program, 1992-93; adviser Jr. Achievement, Chgo., 1976-78, Miami, 1982-84; coach, judge Nat. Trial Competition, U. Miami Law Sch., 1983-86, 88, 90; mentor Seminole County Sch., 1994—; coach mock trial program legal project Dade County Pub. Schs., 1985-89, 91-92, ptnr. program, 1989-92. Mem. ABA (govt. litigation counsel com., complex crimes com. litigation sect.), FBA, AICPA, Fla. Bar, Ill. Bar Assn., Ill. Soc. CPAs, Fla. Inst. CPAs (com. on rels. with Fla. Bar 1985-86, bd. dirs. South Dade chpt. 1987-92), Orange County Bar Assn. (professionalism com.), Seminole County Bar Assn., Am. Assn. Atty. CPAs, Am. Inns of Ct., U. Ill. Alumni Club (v.p.), Delta Sigma Pi. Jewish. Office: 80 N Hughey Ave Ste 201 Orlando FL 32801-2224

GOLDBERG, ALAN JOEL, lawyer; b. Bklyn, Jan. 22, 1943; s. Ralph and Dorothy (Rolnick) G.; 1 child, Cary Adam. BA, U. Miami, 1965, JD, 1968. Bar: Fla. 1968, U.S. Supreme Ct., U.S. Ct. Appeals (4th cir.). Ptnr. Goldberg, Young, Goldberg & Borkson, P.A., Ft. Lauderdale, Fla., 1968-82; atty. City of Margate (Fla.), 1969-70, City of Tamarac (Fla.), 1970-71; pvt. practice, Ft. Lauderdale, 1982—; pres. Diversified Oil Co., 1996—, Diversified Realty Holdings Co., 1996—; pres. PSI. Mem. Citizen's Task Force on Transp., State of Fla.; mem. Broward County Planning Coun., 1984-92, chmn., 1988, 91. Mem. ABA, Fla. Bar Assn. Republican. Office: 6227 N Federal Hwy Fort Lauderdale FL 33308

GOLDBERG, BERNARD R., news correspondent; b. N.Y.C., May 31, 1945; s. Sam and Sylvia (Abovitz) G.; m. Nancy Solomon, Jan 18, 1986; children: Brian Erik, Catherine Michelle. BA, Rutgers U., 1967. Writer, reporter AP, N.Y.C, 1967-69; writer, prodr. Sta. WTVJ-TV, Miami, Fla., 1969-70; prodr., reporter Sta. WPLG-TV, Miami, 1970-72; corr. CBS News, Atlanta, San Francisco, N.Y.C., Miami, 1972—; staff corr. 48 Hours, 1988-89, spl. corr., 1988-93; corr. Eye to Eye, 1993-95; spl. corr. CBS Evening News, 1995—. Recipient 6 Emmy awards NATAS, 1988, 89, 92, George Foster Peabody award Sch. Comm. U. Ga., 1988, Ohio State U. award, 1994, Edward R. Murrow Brotherhood award Cinema/Radio/TV unit B'nai B'rith, 1989, Cert. of Merit ABA, 1979, Silver Gavel award 1990, Cert. of Merit, 1994, Award Sigma Delta Chi, 1994. Office: CBS News # 1170 4770 Biscayne Blvd Ste 1170 Miami FL 33137-3251

GOLDBERG, EDWARD JAY, general contractor; b. Atlanta, Apr. 30, 1950; s. J. Elliott and Sarah (Spiegelman) G.; m. Susan Ellen Jacobson, Dec. 19, 1976; children: Marc Samuel, Robin Beth, Allison Gayle. BS in Fin., U. Ga., 1972. Acctg. coordinator Panasonic, Atlanta, 1972-76; account supr. Oscar Mayer Co., Birmingham, Ala., 1976-81; pres. Alscan, Inc., Birmingham, 1981—. Mem. Birminahm Mus. Art, 1987, Birmingham Symphony Orch., 1987; bd. dirs. Temple Beth-El, Young Leadership Cabinet; v.p. Birmingham Jewish Fedn., gen. campaign chmn., 1993-95; bd. dirs., treas. Birmingham Jewish Day Sch.; chmn. ways and means Birmingham Jewish Cmty. Ctr. Mem. Am. Soc. Indsl. Security, Associated Gen. Contractors, Ala. Alarm Assn., Birmingham C. of C., Pine Tree Country Club, B'nai B'rith (v.p. 1981-83). Jewish. Home: 3504 Branch Mill Rd Birmingham AL 35223-1608 Office: Alscan Inc 237 Oxmoor Cir Birmingham AL 35209-6425

GOLDBERG, HAROLD JOEL, history educator; b. N.Y.C., Apr. 23, 1945; s. Abraham Goldberg and Frances (Spector) Rosen; m. Nancy Sloan Goldberg, June 15, 1969; children: Alexander, Zachary. BA, SUNY, Buffalo, 1967; MA, U. Wis., 1970, PhD, 1973. Asst. prof. U. of the South, Sewanee, Tenn., 1974-81, assoc. prof., 1982-89, prof., 1990—; sec., treas. So. Conf. on Slavic Studies, 1993—. Editor: Documents of Soviet-American Relations, vol. 1, 1993, vol. 2, 1995. Mem. Am. Assn. for the Advancement of Slavic Studies (bd. dirs. 1996—). Home: 111 Oak Hill Circle Sewanee TN 37375 Office: Univ of the South 735 University Ave Sewanee TN 37383

GOLDBERG, IVAN BAER, real estate executive; b. Newport News, Va., Apr. 20, 1939; s. David and Sara (Levy) G.; m. Mary Linda Caffee, Oct. 27, 1968 (div. 1978); children: Stephen Morris, Michael Scott. Student, U. Va., 1957-58, Coll. of William and Mary, 1958-60. Exec. v.p. Bedding Supply Co., Inc., Newport News, 1961-72; sec.-treas. Mut. Realty Corp., Newport News, 1972—; pres. Goldkress Corp., Newport News, 1972—; gen. ptnr. Goldkress Investment Co., Newport News, 1972—; bd. dirs. Goldkress Corp., Mut. Realty Corp. With USCGR, 1962. Mem. Newport News-Hampton Bd. Realtors, Nat. Assn. Realtors. Jewish. Home: 15 Ferguson Cv Newport News VA 23606-2016 Office: Mut Realty Corp 11116 Jefferson Ave Newport News VA 23601-2551

GOLDBERG, PAUL BERNARD, gastroenterologist, clinical researcher; b. Bklyn., Apr. 11, 1950; s. Samuel and Eva (Turkenitz) G.; m. Harriet Ruth Ferrer, July 8, 1973 (div. 1987); children: Deborah Lynn, Susan Michelle; m. Mary Alice Denaro, June 23, 1990; 1 child, Laura Alicia. BA in Chemistry summa cum laude, Cornell U., 1967-71, MD, 1971-75. Diplomate Am. Bd. Internal Medicine, Am. Bd. Gastroenterology. Intern in medicine Hosp. of U. of Pa., Phila., 1975-76, resident in medicine, 1976-78, fellow in gastroenterology, 1978-80, fellow in nutritional support svc., 1979-80; med. coord. and founder nutritional support svc. Lakeland (Fla.) Gen. Hosp., 1980-81; attending physician Halifax Med. Ctr., 1980—, Ormond Meml. Hosp., 1980—, Humana Hosp., 1980—, Fish Meml. Hosp., New Smyrna Beach, Fla., 1989—, Peninsula Med. Ctr., 1989-94; pres. Sunshine Health Care Plan, Inc., 1983-86, v.p., 1986-87; chief staff Humana Hosp., Daytona Beach, 1986-88, trustee, 1986-89, mem. exec. comj., 1984-91; mem. rev. bd. Coastal Instnl. Rev., 1990-93, chmn. rev. bd., 1993—; expert reviewer Fla. Dept. Profl. Regulation, 1990—; pres. med. staff Halifax Hosp., 1996-97; clin. asst. prof. medicine dept. family medicine U. South Fla. Rschr. and author in field. Physician adv. Daytona chpt. Crohn's and Colitis Found., 1991-95. Recipient Nat. award Ford Future Scientists of Am., 1967, Westinghouse Sci. Talent Search finalist, 1967. Fellow ACP, Am. Coll. Gastroenterology; mem. Am. Gastroent. Soc., Am. Soc. Gastrointestinal Endoscopy, Am. Soc. for Parenteral and Enteral Nutrition (pres. Fla. chpt. 1991-92), Volusia County Med. Soc. (exec. com. 1991-94, co-chmn. mini internship program 1992-94), Fla. Gastrointestinal Soc., Fla. med. Assn. (alt. del. to ho. of dels. 1990-95), Fla. Assn. Nutritional Support (1st pres.), Rotary, Phi Beta Kappa, Alpha Omega Alpha. Office: Gastrointestinal Assocs 201 N Clyde Morris Blvd Ste 100 Daytona Beach FL 32114-2765

GOLDBERG, STANLEY IRWIN, real estate executive; b. Newport News, Va., May 13, 1934; s. David and Sara (Levy) G.; m. Marilyn Levin, Nov. 22, 1963 (dec. Oct. 1970); 1 child, Andrew Garfield. Student, Coll. William and Mary, 1952-54, U. Va., 1954-55. Lic. real estate broker, Va. V.p. Bedding Supply Co., Inc., Newport News, 1956-59, exec. v.p., 1960-61, pres., 1962-70; gen. ptnr. Goldkress Investment Co., Newport News, 1970—, also bd. dirs.; pres. Mutual Realty Corp., Newport News, 1973—. Trustee Temple Sinai, Newport News. Served with USAF, 1957-58. Mem. Nat. Assn. Realtors, Va. Assn. Realtors, Newport News-Hampton Bd. Realtors. Lodge: Elks. Home: 19 Hopemont Dr Newport News VA 23606-2146 Office: 11116 Jefferson Ave Newport News VA 23601-2551

GOLDBERG, STEPHEN LESLIE, research psychologist; b. N.Y.C., June 7, 1947; s. Jacob William and Mae (Siegelheim) G.; m. Elaine Sharon Singer, Feb. 2, 1974; children: Jordan Marc, Benjamin Scott. BA, SUNY, Buffalo, 1969, PhD, 1974. Rsch. psychologist U.S. Army Rsch. Inst., Alexandria, Va., 1974-80; rsch. psychologist/team leader U.S. Army Rsch. Inst., Ft. Knox, Ky., 1980-84; chief sci. coordination office U.S. Army Rsch. Inst., Ft. Monroe, Va., 1984-89; chief rsch. unit U.S. Army Rsch. Inst., Orlando, Fla., 1989—; vis. assoc. prof. U. Ctrl. Fla., Orlando, 1994—. Editl. bd. Jour. Mil. Psychology, 1995—. Bd. dirs. Spring Lake Assn., Altamonte Springs, Fla., 1991—. Mem. APA (pres. divsn. mil. psychology), Human Factors and Ergonomics Assn. Home: 225 Spring Lake Hills Dr Altamonte Springs FL 32714 Office: US Army Research Inst 12350 Research Pkwy Orlando FL 32826-3261

GOLDBERG, WILLIAM JEFFREY, accountant; b. Chgo., Jan. 18, 1950; s. Harry and Bernice Dorothy (Benson) G. m. Brenda Liebling; children: Leslie Claire, Melissa Liebling. BA, Knox Coll., 1971; JD, Cornell U., 1974; postgrad. U. Chgo., 1976-78. Bar: Ill. 1974, U.S. Dist. Ct. (no. dist.) Ill. 1974; CPA. Fin. counseling officer Continental Ill. Nat. Bank, Chgo., 1974-79; supr. KPMG Peat Marwick, Houston, 1979-80, mgr., 1980-82, ptnr., 1982—; nat. dir. Personal Fin. Planning Svcs., 1984-93, southwest ptnr.-in-charge, 1993—; instr. law Ill. Inst. Tech. Chgo. Kent Coll. Law, 1977-78. Dir. Acad. Fin. Svcs., 1988-89; trustee Jewish Fedn. of Greater Houston, 1985—; trustee Endowment Fund of Jewish Community of Houston, 1987—. Mem. AICPA (personal fin. planning div., exec. com. 1986-89, 94—, chmn. legis. and regulation subcom. 1989-91), Tex. Soc. CPAs, Houston Estate & Fin. Forum, Houston Bus. and Estate Planning Coun., Knox Coll. Club Houston (pres. 1981-82), Westwood Country Club (bd. dirs. 1996—). Office: KPMG Peat Marwick PO Box 4545 Houston TX 77210-4545

GOLDEN, BETH, community college administrator; 1 child, Molly E. Student, Eureka Coll., 1970; BA, U. N.C., Asheville, 1985; postgrad., Western Carolina U., 1993. Instr. adult basic edn. Blue Ridge C.C., Flat Rock, N.C., 1988, 90-91; tng. rep. Blue Ridge C.C., Flat Rock, 1989-90, compensatory edn. and spl. populations specialist, 1990-91, coord. spl. populations office, 1991—; cognitive retraining therapist Thomas Rehab. Hosp., Asheville, 1988-89, cons. in field. Chair Henderson County Mayor's Com. for Persons with Disabilities, 1992-95; chair respite care com. Parents' Assistance League, 1994-95. Grantee State of N.C., 1985, Ednl. Found., 1991, 92, 93, Melvin Lane Charitable Trust, 1992, 93. Mem. N.C. Head Injury Found. (profl. coun.), Henderson County Coun. on Women (pres. 1991-93), Job Devel. Coun. Henderson County, Inter-Agy. Coun.

GOLDEN, EDDIE LEE, optometrist; b. Forest, Miss., Jan. 3, 1955; s. James Madison and Hazel E. (Tucker) G.; m. Kathy Patricia Davis, Nov. 27, 1982; children: Jonathan, Heather, Jeremy, Matthew. AA, East Cen. Jr. Coll., Decatur, Miss., 1975; MS, U. Miss., 1977; OD, So. Coll. Optometry, 1982. Pvt. practice Golden Eye Clinic, Hattiesburg, Miss., 1983—. Deacon, mem. Temple Bapt. Ch., Hattiesburg; discipleship tng. dir.; missionary Bapt. Student Union, 1974, mem. state coun., 1974-75; vol. optometric missions in Cen. Am. Mem. Am. Optometric Assn. (contact lens sect., sports vision sect.), Nat. Eye Rsch. Found., Internet. CKR Soc., So. Coun. Optometry, Miss. Optometric Assn., Miss. Club (pres. 1981-82, Optometric Recognition award 1985-92), U. So. Miss. Eagle Club, Rotary. Office: Golden Eye Clinic 10336 Shrewsbury Run W Collierville TN 38017-8860

GOLDEN, E(DWARD) SCOTT, lawyer; b. Miami, Fla., Sept. 25, 1955; s. Alvan Leonard and Fay Betty (Gray) G.; m. Jane Eileen DeKlavon, June 9, 1979; children: Daniel Bryan, Kimberly Michelle. Student, So. Fla. Christian Coll., 1975-76; BS, MIT, 1978; JD, Harvard U., 1981. Bar: Fla. 1981, U.S. Dist. Ct. (so. dist.) Fla. 1982, U.S. Tax Ct. 1982, U.S. Supreme Ct. 1991, U.S. Dist. Ct. (mid. dist.) Fla. 1993. Assoc. Roberts and Holland, Miami, 1981-82, Valdes-Fauli, Richardson, Cobb & Petrey, P.A., Miami, 1982-83; v.p. Buck and Golden, P.A., Ft. Lauderdale, Fla., 1983-88; sole practice, 1988—. Editor-in-chief Harvard Jour. of Law and Pub. Policy, 1980-81; contbr. articles to profl. jours. Active West Lauderdale Bapt. Ch., Broward County, Fla., 1994—, chmn. deacons, 1984-86, 87-88, elder, 1994—; mem. MIT Ednl. Coun., 1995; del. Fla. Rep. Conv., 1987, 90; mem. Rep. Exec. Com., Broward County, 1984-94. Named one of Outstanding Young Men of Am., 1986; nominee Order of Silver Knight; Western Electric grantee, 1972-74. Mem. Christian Legal Soc., Zeta Beta Tau. Lodge: Optimists (treas. Dade County Carol City High Sch., 1971-72). Home: 5410 Buchanan St Hollywood FL 33021-5708 Office: 644 SE 4th Ave Fort Lauderdale FL 33301-3102

GOLDEN, JEFFREY A., banker, holding company executive; b. 1940. With Sun Fin. Corp., Nashville, City Bank and Trust Co., Inc., Mc Minnville, Tenn., 1966—; pres. City Bank and Trust Inc., Mc Minnville, Tenn., 1981—. Office: City Bank & Trust Co House Office Bldg 101 E Main St Mc Minnville TN 37110-2505*

GOLDEN, KIMBERLY KAY, critical care, flight nurse; b. Munich, July 31, 1961; came to U.S., 1961; d. Henry Davis and Mary Walker G. AA, Hinds Jr. Coll., Raymond, Miss., 1980, ASN, 1984; BSN, U. Miss., Jackson, 1987, AS in EMT-Paramedic, 1990. Cert. ACLS instr., PALS provider and instr.; emergency nurse, crit. care RN; cert. paramedic, Miss., Tenn. Staff nurse neuro ICU U. Miss. Med. Ctr., 1984-85, staff nurse surg. ICU, 1985-87; staff nurse emergency rm. Rankin Gen. Hosp., Brandon, Miss., 1987-88; flight nurse Lifestar Helicopter Flight Svc., 1988-91; staff nurse emergency rm., ICU Nightingale Nursing, Jackson, 1988-91, Riveroaks Hosp., Jackson, 1990-91; staff RN emergency rm., Aerovesta flight Midland Meml. Hosp., Tex., 1991-93; flight nurse Hosp. Wing BTLS, Memphis, Tenn., 1993—; examiner Nat. Registry EMT-P; advanced trauma life support station instr.; affiliate faculty paramedic program U. Miss. Faculty scholar Hinds Jr. Coll., 1983. Mem. AACN, Nat. Flight Assn., Emergency Nurses Assn. Baptist. Office: PO Box 140466 Austin TX 78714-0466

GOLDEN, LEAH WALLER, elementary education educator; b. Richmond, Va., Mar. 6, 1950; d. Raymond Taylor and Leah Rubinette (Fleet) Waller; m. Timothy Paul Golden, June 29, 1974; children: Catherine Fleet, John Rudolph. BA in History, Mary Baldwin Coll., 1972; MA in Edn., James Madison U., 1994. Cert. profl. tchg., reading specialist, Va. Tchr. Hampton (Va.) City Schs., 1972-73, Chesapeake (Va.) City Schs., 1973-74, Buena Vista (Va.) Pub. Schs., 1974-78, Rockbridge County Schs., Lexington, Va., 1987—. Mem. adv. bd. Literacy Vol. of Rockbridge area, Lexington, 1995—. Named Tchr. of Week Roanoke Times, 1996. Mem. NEA, ASCD (participant consortium 1993-96), Va. Edn. Assn., Rockbridge Edn. Assn., Shenandoah Valley Reading Coun., Delta Kappa Gamma (parliamentarian 1996-98). Episcopalian. Home: 301 S Jefferson St Lexington VA 24450 Office: Box 280 Natural Bridge VA 24579

GOLDEN, LESLIE BLACK, real estate agent; b. Dallas, Aug. 21, 1955; d. Aubrey C. Jr. and Martha (Cartwright) Black; m. G. Hawkins Golden II, Sept. 21, 1985; children: G. Hawkins III, John Houston. BBA, U. Tex., 1977. Advt. prodn. asst. Neiman Marcus, Dallas, 1977-78; group account exec. Registry Hotel, Dallas, 1978-80, sales mgr., 1982-83; sales mgr. Doubletree Inn., Dallas, 1980-82, Sheraton Park Cen., Dallas, 1983-85; real estate agt. Golden-King Properties, Dallas, 1985-94, Golden Homes, Dallas, 1994—. Mem. Jr. League Dallas, 1988—; bd. dirs. Innovators of Dallas Symphony Orch., 1986-89, chmn. arrangements 1988, chmn. coloring book fundraiser, 1989, hon. trustee Dallas Symphony Orch., 1988-89; chair phone com., auditor chmn. jr. group Dallas Garden Club, 1983—, bd. dirs. 1987-89; bd. dirs. Yellow Rose Gala com. Multiple Schlerosis, Dallas, 1985-89; chmn. Easter Egg Hunt Dallas So. Meml. 1987-96. bd. dirs. 1987-89; docent Dallas Zoo, 1989-93; vol. Freedom Ride Found., 1987; Highland Park Presbyn. Day Sch. Parents Coun., 1990-96, auction solicitations com.; Dallas Children's Theatre Guild, 1992—; vol. Equest., 1993—; co-chair Ridefest, 1994, 95, chair ann. awards banquet, 1996—, Equest. aux., 1991—, bd. dirs. 1995-96, Showcase com. 1980, 96; chmn. Equest 96 Boot Scootn' Ball Auction. Mem. The Science Pl., Dallas Mus. Art, Dallas Zoo, Channel 13, Dallas Childrens Theater Guild, Dallas Country Club, Park Cities Club, Kappa Alpha Theta Alumni. Office: Golden King Properties 8533 Ferndale Rd Ste 202 Dallas TX 75238-4401

GOLDEN, PATRICIA FARIS, social worker; b. Nashville, Sept. 13, 1948; d. Robert Mark Finks and Josephine Elizabeth (King) Finks; m. William Richard Golden, Sept. 6, 1969; children: James Christian, Thomas Courtenay. BS in Edn., U. Tenn., 1970; MSW, U. Ga., 1992. Lic. clin. social worker, grief counselor. Elem. sch. tchr. Knox County Sch. Bd., Knoxville, Tenn., 1970-71; counselor Dept. Human Svcs., Nashville, 1971-76, field supr. I, 1976-80, field supr. II, 1980-81, regional field supr., 1981-82; social worker II Wesley Woods Geriatric Hosp. Emory U., Atlanta, 1992—; group leader Bereavement Group Wesley Woods Ctr., Atlanta, 1993—. Mem. NASW, Assn. Death Edn. and Counseling. Republican. Methodist. Home: 3226 Classic Dr Snellville GA 30278-3530 Office: Emory Univ Wesley Woods Geriatric Hosp 1821 Clifton Rd NE Atlanta GA 30329-4021

GOLDEN, ROBERT NEAL, psychiatrist, researcher; b. Phila., Aug. 27, 1953; s. Maxwell Solomon and Rosalie (Shragowitz) G.; m. Shannon Celeste Kenney, May 27, 1979; children: Troy, Blair, Sean. BA, Yale U., 1975; MD, Boston U., 1979. Diplomate Am. Bd. Psychiatry and Neurology. Resident in psychiatry U. N.C., Chapel Hill, 1979-83, chief resident, 1982-83, asst. prof. psychiatry, 1985-89, assoc. prof. psychiatry, 1989-94, prof., chair, 1994—; assoc. dir. Gen. Clin. Rsch. Ctr. U. N.C., 1990-95, Mental Health Clin. Rsch. Ctr. U. N.C., 1989-94. Contbr. articles to profl. jours. Ginsburg fellow Group Advancement Psychiatry, 1981-82, Laughlin fellow Am. Coll. Psychiatry, 1983. Mem. AAAS, Am. Psychiat. Assn., Soc. Biol. Psychiatry, Internat. Soc. Psychoneuroendocrinology. Office: U NC Sch Medicine Dept Psychiatry Chapel Hill NC 27599

GOLDEN, SANDRA JEAN, nurse; b. Portsmouth, Va., Nov. 18, 1954; d. Richard Elmer and Catherine Mae (Zenisek) Haungs; m. Gerald Thomas Golden, Jan. 18, 1980 (div. 1989); 1 child, Sarah Catherine. AAS, No. Va. Community Coll., 1974; postgrad., Shepherd Coll., 1980-81. Staff nurse, charge nurse surg. ICU/CCU Good Samaritan Hosp., Lebanon, Pa., 1974-77; staff nurse, charge nurse ICU/CCU Jefferson Meml. Hosp., Alexandria, Va., 1977-78; staff/charge nurse ICU/CCU City Hosp., Inc., Martinsburg, W.Va., 1978-79; office nurse Shenandoah Surg. Group, Inc., Martinsburg, 1980-87; case mgr., preceptor, home health Shenandoah Meml. Hosp., Woodstock, Va., 1988—. Mem. AACN. Republican. Roman Catholic. Office: Home Care of Shenandoah Meml Hosp Drs Office Bldg PO Box 3 Woodstock VA 22664

GOLDFARB, NANCY DENA, English literature educator; b. Cin., July 22, 1964; d. Lee I. and Theresa (Eckman) G. BA, Brandeis U., 1985; MA, U. Mich., 1989, PhD, 1994. Vis. lectr. Gutenberg U., Mainz, Germany, 1993-94; asst. prof. English Western Ky. U., Bowling Green, 1995—; faculty advisor Women in Transition, Bowling Green, 1996—. Jr. Faculty Rsch. grantee Western Ky. U., 1996. Mem. MLA, Am. Comparative Lit. Assn. Office: Western Ky U One Big Red Way Bowling Green KY 42101

GOLDKRAND, JOHN WOLF, obstetrician/gynecologist; b. Boston, Sept. 16, 1940; m. Ann Steinberg; children: Judith, Howard. AB, Bowdoin Coll., 1962; MD, Tufts U., 1966. Diplomate Am. Bd. Ob-Gyn., Am. Bd. Maternal/Fetal Medicine. Intern surg. svc. Bureau City Hosp., 1966-67, resident in surg. svcs., 1967-68; resident in ob-gyn. Yale-New Haven Hosp., 1970-73; dir. resident edn. in ob/gyn, assoc. dir. perinatology Meml. Med. Ctr., Savannah, Ga., 1989—, dir. med. edn. ob-gyn., 1989—. Maj. M.C. U.S. Army, 1968-70. Mem. Phi Beta Kappa. Office: Meml Med Ctr 4750 Waters Ave Savannah GA 31404-6200

GOLDMAN, ALAN H., philosophy educator; b. N.Y.C., Aug. 7, 1945; s. Lawrence I. and Florence (Goodman) G.; m. Joan Roslyn Berkowitz, May 29, 1968; children: Michael, David. BA, Yale U., 1967; PhD, Columbia U., 1972. Instr. Columbia U., N.Y.C., 1970-72; asst. prof. Ohio U., Athens, 1972-74, U. Idaho, Moscow, 1974-76; assoc. prof. U. Miami, Coral Gables, Fla., 1977-81; prof. U. Miami, 1981—; vis. prof. U. Mich., Ann Arbor, 1980; vis. fellow U. Colo., Boulder, 1983, Princeton (N.J.) U., 1976; chmn. philosophy dept. U. Miami, 1988—; editor series in applied ethics Garland Publ., N.Y.C., 1993—. Author: Aesthetic Value, 1995, Moral Knowledge, 1988, Empirical Knowledge, 1988, Moral Foundations of Professional Ethics, 1980, Justice & Reverse Discrimination, 1979. NEH grantee, 1991; NEH fellow, 1976-77. Mem. Am. Philos. Assn. (program com. 1990-92). Office: U Miami Dept Philosophy Coral Gables FL 33124

GOLDMAN, JOHN ABNER, rheumatologist, immunologist, educator; b. Cin., June 9, 1940; s. Leon and Belle (Hurwitz) G.; children from previous marriage: Joey, Beth; m. Deborah J. Staples, Aug. 1, 1993; children: Shelley, Michael. BS, U. Wis., 1962; MD, U. Cin., 1966. Diplomate Am. Bd. Internal Medicine, subspecialty in rheumatology, allergy-immunology. Intern, U. Oreg. Med. Sch., Portland, 1966-67; resident U. Cin. Med. Center, 1967-69, postdoctoral fellow in rheumatology and immunology, 1969-71 clin. prof. medicine Emory U. Sch. Medicine, Atlanta, 1973—. Contbr. numerous articles to sci. jours. Bd. dirs. Atlanta Arthritis Found.; med. div. council Lupus Erythematosus Found, Inc. Maj. U.S. Army, 1971-73. Fellow ACP, Am. Soc. Lasers in Medicine and Surgery (bd. dirs.), Am. Coll. Rheumatology; mem. Ga. Soc. Rheumatology (pres. 1974-75), Med. Assn. Atlanta, Med. Assn. Ga. (council of splty. socs.), Met. Atlanta Rheumatology Soc. (pres.). Office: Med Quarters Ste 293 5555 Peachtree Dunwoody Rd NE Atlanta GA 30342-1711

GOLDMAN, LISA EACHUS, health facility administrator; b. Waltham, Mass., June 24, 1955; d. George Bloomfield and Genivive (Foti) Gallub; m. Edward Elliot Goldman, July 1, 1984; children: Melissa Ann, Audrey Carol. BS, Barry U., 1983, MBA, MPA, 1994. Tchr. Dade County and Miami (Fla.) Tech. Inst., 1982-84; v.p. Point Adult Communities, North Miami Beach, Fla., 1984-92; CEO, owner Fla. Behavioral Network, Miami, 1993—; pres. Statewide Mgmt. & Fin. Svcs. Corp., Miami, 1993—; exec. v.p. Assocs. in Geriatric Psychology, Inc., Pembroke Pines, 1992—; ptnr. Goldsel Inc., Fort Lauderdale, Fla., 1990-92; real estate investor, Miami, 1976-88; instr. acctg. Barry U., 1993. Co-author: Bi-Lingual Resource Jour., 1990, 91. Active Miami Shores Performing Theater; mem. bd. overseers U. Miami. Mem. Alzheimer's Assn. (v.p. 1993), Fla. State Coun. on Alzheimer's Disease, Nat. Long Term Care Com. (bd. dirs. Dade County chpt. 1991), Nat. Coun. Jewish Women (v.p. 1989-91), S.O.A.R.I.N.G. (chpt. pres.), Infants in Need Inc. Home: 7120 W Cypresshead Dr Parkland FL 33067 Office: Fla Behavioral Network 1001 Ives Dairy Rd Ste 206 Miami FL 33179-2501

GOLDMAN, NATHAN CARLINER, lawyer, educator; b. Charleston, S.C., Mar. 19, 1950; s. Reuben and Hilda Alta (Carliner) G.; m. Judith Tova Feigon, Oct. 28, 1984; children: Michael Reuben, Miriam Esther. BA, U. S.C., 1972; JD, Duke U., 1975; MA, Johns Hopkins U., 1978, PhD, 1980. Bar: N.C. 1975, Tex. 1985, U.S. Dist. Ct. (mid. dist.) N.C. 1975. Paralegal City Atty.'s Office, Durham, N.C., 1975-76; asst. prof. govt. dept. U. Tex., Austin, Tex., 1980-85; pvt. practice Houston, 1985-86; assoc. Liddell, Sapp, Zivley, Hill & LaBoon, Houston, 1986-88; pvt. practice Houston, 1988—; adj. prof. space law U. Houston, 1985-88; rsch. assoc. Rice U. Inst. Policy Analysis, 1986—; lectr. bus. law, 1988-95; mem. coordinating bd. Space Architecture, U. Houston, 1985—; v.p. Internat. Design in Extreme Environments Assn., U. Houston, 1991—; vis. asst. prof. U. Houston-Clear Lake, 1989-91; adj. prof. South Tex. Coll. Law, 1994-95; gen. counsel Internat. Space Enterprises, 1993—, Globus Ltd. Co., 1994—; info. officer Israel Consulate, 1996—. Author: Space Commerce, 1985, American Space Law, 1988, 2d edit., 1995, Space Policy: A Primer, 1992; editor: Space and Society, 1984; assoc. editor Jour. Space Commerce, 1990-91; exec. editor Space Governance, 1996—; also articles. Mem. com. on governance of space U.S. Bicentennial Commn., 1986-88, Clear Lake (Tex.) Area Econ. Devel. Found., 1987, Space Collegium, Houston Area Rsch. Ctr., 1987; pres. Windermere Civic Assn., 1990-92; bd. dirs. Hebrew Acad., 1994-96, Men's Club United Orthodox Synagogues, 1994—. U.S. Dept. Justice grantee, 1979-80, U. Tex. Inst. for Constructive Capitalism U. grantee, 1983; E.D. Walker Centennial fellow, 1984; NASA Summer fellow U. Calif., 1984. Fellow Internat. Inst. Space Law; mem. ABA, Tex. Bar Assn., Nat. Space Soc. (v.p. 1989-91), Inst. for Social Sci. Study Space (mem. adv. bd. 1990, editor Space Humanization Jour. 1993—), Am. Astrronautical Soc., Inst. for Design in Extreme Environment Assn. (v.p. 1991—), Space Bus. Roundtable. Home: 2328 Dryden Rd Houston TX 77030-1104 Office: Rice U PO Box 1892 Houston TX 77252

GOLDSMITH, H. RANDALL, management consultant; b. Abilene, Tex., Dec. 28, 1946; s. Ardouth Carrell and Harriann (Rice) G.; m. Mary Lue Keele, Jan. 8, 1981; children: Randa, Gregory. BA, Hardin Simmons U., 1970; M in Urban Planning, Tex. A&M, 1990, PhD in Econ. Devel., 1994. Pres. R. Goldsmith, Inc., College Station, Tex., 1971-88; assoc. dir. technology bus. devel. Tex. A&M, College Station, 1988-92; dir. Clear Lake Technology Transfer Ctr. U. Houston, 1992-96; pres. Okla. Alliance for Mfg. Excellence, Inc., Tulsa, 1996—; strategic planning Fed. Labs., 1992-96; technology transfer U.S. Corps., 1992-96; econ. devel. cons., 1988-96, product commercialization cons., NASA, 1992-96. Advisor U.S. 6th Congl. Dist., College Station, 1986. 2d lt. U.S. Army, 1970-71. Named to Outstanding Young Men of Am., 1974. Mem. Tex. Technology Transfer Soc. (bd. dirs. 1994-95), Internat. Comm. Devel. Soc. Office: The Alliance Ste 500 525 S Main Tulsa OK 74103

GOLDSMITH, J(OSEPH) PATRICK, psychologist; b. Lancaster, S.C., July 18, 1944; s. Brooks Pope and Margaret (Ussery) G.; m. Jean Horton; 1 child, Brook. BA in Psychology, Presbyn. U., 1966; MEd, U. Ga., 1967; EdD, Auburn U., 1976. Lic. psychologist, S.C.. Vocat. rehab. counselor State Ga., Athens, 1970-71; grad. teaching asst. Auburn (Ala.) U., 1971-74; sales rep. Xerox Corp., Cola, S.C., 1974-76, Pfizer Corp., Springfield, Va., 1976-77; psychologist Catawba Ctr. for Growth and Devel., Lancaster, S.C., 1976-78; program dir. Community Living Svc. Western Carolina Ctr. and Broughton Hosp., Morganton, N.C., 1977-78; psychologist Psychol. Assocs., Lancaster, 1978—; cons. alcohol and drug abuse Elliott White Springs Meml. Hosp., Lancaster, 1978—; cons. staff psychologist Rebound, Lancaster, Piedmont Med. Ctr., Rock Hill, S.C.; psychologist Dept. Juvenile Placement and Aftercare, Dept. Social Svcs.; sec. Lancaster County Child Abuse Com.; mem. Multidisciplinary Steering Com. for Child Abuse; bd. dirs., treas. Catawba Ctr. for Growth and Devel.; bd. dirs. Lancaster County Commn. on Alcohol and Drug Abuse; chmn. Lancaster and Rock Hill Vocat. Rehab. Workshops. Author: (pamphlet) Loving Yourself: The Psychology of Self-Esteem. Capt. U.S. Army, 1968-70. Mem. Am. Assn. Marriage and Family Therapists (clin.). Baptist. Home: 703 W Barr St Lancaster SC 29720-1953 Office: Psychol Assocs PO Box 669 Lancaster SC 29721-0669

GOLDSMITH, KAREN LEE, lawyer; b. Bridgeport, Conn., Jan. 10, 1946; d. James Joseph and Marjorie (Crowley) Minto; m. Michael Goldsmith, Oct. 12, 1968 (dec. May 1979); children: Susan Chapman, Pamela S., Neil J.; m. Jeffery S. Hooie, June 13, 1980. AA summa cum laude, Seminole Jr. Coll., 1969; BA summa cum laude, U. Cen. Fla., 1975; JD cum laude, U. Fla., 1978. Bar: Fla. 1979, U.S. Dist. Ct. (mid. dist.) Fla. 1979, U.S. Dist. Ct. (so. and no. dists.) Fla. 1981, U.S. Ct. Appeals (11th cir.) 1981. Assoc. Pitts, Eubanks & Ross P.A., Orlando, Fla., 1978-80; assoc. Dempsey & Slaughter P.A., Orlando, 1980-83, ptnr., 1983; ptnr. Dempsey & Goldsmith P.A., Orlando, 1984-90, Goldsmith & Grout, P.A., Winter Park, Fla., 1990—; lectr. Interhome '86, Ft. Lauderdale, Fla., 1986—, health care related legal issues various orgns., 1978—; speaker profl. meetings, 1982—; speaker Harborside Healthcare Annual Convention, 1992, 94. Author: Advance Directives in Florida, 1993; sr. editor U. Fla. Law Rev., 1978; contbr. articles to profl. jours. Mem. ABA, Am. Health Care Assn. (legal subcom. 1991-95, lectr. ann. symposium), Fla. Bar Assn. (chmn. state law week 1985, 86), Orange County Bar Assn. (Outstanding Chmn. 1982), Nat. Health Lawyers Assn. (speaker), Nat. Conv. Med. Dirs. Assn. (speaker 1992), Fla. Assn. Dirs. Nursing (speaker 1992, 96), Fla. Health Care Assn. (various seminars), U. Ctrl. Fla. Alumni Assn. (bd. dirs., exec. com., sec. 1988), Am. Soc. Assn. Execs., Order of Coif, Phi Kappa Phi. Roman Catholic. Office: Goldsmith & Grout PA 385 W Fairbanks Ave Ste 300 Winter Park FL 32789-5018

GOLDSTEIN, BARRY DAVID, pharmacology educator, university administrator; b. Bklyn., Jan. 7, 1953; m. Gail Goldstein, June 26, 1976; children: Melissa, Beth, Lori. BA in Biology, Adelphi U., 1975; PhD in Pharmacology, U. Medicine and Dentistry N.J., 1979. Rsch. assoc. dept. pharmacology U. Ill., Chgo., 1979-81; asst. prof. dept. pharmacology and toxicology Med. Coll. Ga., Augusta, 1981-86, assoc. prof., 1986-91, interim v.p. for acad. affairs, assoc. prof., 1991-92, prof. dept. pharmacology and toxicology, 1991—, v.p. for acad. affairs, 1992—; chairperson State Healthcare Pers. Planning Com., 1996—; mem. top mgmt. adv. com. Internat. Mgmt. Coun., 1994-96; chairperson Gov.'s Health Care Study Com., 1992-93. Contbr. articles to profl. jours. Bd. dirs. Walton Way Temple, 1985-88, 92—; bd. dirs. Augusta Jewish Cmty. Ctr., 1984-93, treas., 1989-90, pres., 1987-89; bd. dirs. Congregation of Children of Israel, 1992—, treas., 1996—; bd. dirs., treas. Augusta Open Door Kindergarten; mem. budget allocation com. United Way, 1992, chair budget panel, 1993, bd. dirs., 1994—; mem. Ga. Environ. Techs. Consortium, 1992—, Augusta Players Bus. and Profl. Alliance, 1993-94, Coll. Bd.-Acad. Assembly, 1992; chmn. Gov.'s Health Care Pers. Study Commn., 1992-93; mem. Ga. Ladders in Nursing Careers planning com. Ga. Hosp. Assn., 1993; judge area sci. fair, 1984. Named to Hicksville Pub. Sch. Hall of Fame, 1987; NRSA postdoctoral fellow in neurotoxicology, 1979; recipient numerous rsch. grants. Mem. AAAS, Am. Assn. Higher Edn., Am. Soc. Pharmacology and Exptl. Therapeutics, Soc. for Neurosci. (CSRA chpt.), Am. Pain Soc., Internat. Assn. for Study Pain, Soc. Toxicology, Rotary. Home: 308 Gloucester Rd Martinez GA 30907-9069 Office: Med Coll Ga 1120 15th St Augusta GA 30901-7605

GOLDSTEIN, BERNARD, transportation and casino gaming company executive; b. Rock Island, Ill., Feb. 5, 1929; s. Morris and Fannie (Borenstein) G.; m. Irene Alter, Dec. 18, 1949; children: Jeffrey, Robert, Kathy, Richard. BA, U. Ill., 1949, LLB, 1951. Bar: Iowa 1951. With Alter Co., Bettendorf, Iowa, 1951—, chmn. bd., 1979—; chmn. bd. Valley Corp., Bettendorf, 1984—, Casino Am. Inc., Biloxi, Miss., 1992—. Pres. Quad City Jewish Fedn., 1975. Jewish.

GOLDSTEIN, BURTON BENJAMIN, JR., communications executive; b. Atlanta, Mar. 11, 1948; s. Burton B. and Grace Goldstein; m. Kathleen N. Gurley, Aug. 22, 1970; children: Katherine Claire, Alexander Max. AB, U. N.C., 1970; MEd, U. Mass., 1973; JD with honors, U. N.C., 1976. Bar: Ga. 1976. Assoc. dir. urban internat. Yale U., New Haven, 1970-72; assoc. Long, Aldridge & Norman, Atlanta, 1976-80; gen. counsel Solinet, Atlanta, 1980-81; CEO Info. America, Atlanta, 1981—; ex-officio dir. Info. Industry Assn., Washington, 1992-93. Exec. com. SciTrek, Atlanta, 1988—; chmn. adv. bd. Inst. for Arts & Humanities, Chapel Hill, N.C., 1991—; chmn. Info. Industry Assn. Investment Conf., N.Y.C., 1992-93; bd. dirs. Atlanta chpt. Am. Jewish Com. Named Fast Tech 50, Arthur Andersen, Atlanta, 1988—, Runner-up Entrepreneur of Yr., Ernst & Young & INC Mag., 1991, Entrepreneur of the Yr., Info. Industry, 1991. Mem. ABA, Ga. Bar Assn., Am. Jewish Com., The Temple, Chancellor's Club U. N.C., Phi Beta Kappa. Democrat. Jewish. Office: Information America 600 W Peachtree St NW Atlanta GA 30308

GOLDSTEIN, CARL, art educator; b. N.Y.C., June 24, 1938; s. Aaron and Rose (Tannenbaum) G.; m. Alicia Creus, Mar. 6, 1990; children: Antonia Bess, Alexander Solomon. BA, Bklyn. Coll., 1960; MA, Columbia U., 1962, PhD, 1966. Asst. prof. Brown U., 1966-71; assoc. prof. U. N.C., Greensboro, 1971-80, prof., 1980—; vis. instr. Wheaton Coll., spring 1966; vis. assoc. prof. U. N.H., Durham, summer 1973, 75; vis. prof. U. N.C.-Chapel Hill, spring 1990; acting dir. Wheaton Coll. Art Gallery, spring 1966; vis. curator Mus. Art, R.I. Sch. Design, spring 1968 and 1970; v.p. Unicorn Found. for Advancement of Modern Poetry, Greensboro, 1974-79; co-chair Friends of Unicorn Press, 1974-79; chair panel meeting Coll. Art Assn., Toronto, 1984; mem. task force of acad. planning of vice-chancellor U. N.C., Greensboro, 1985-87, acting head art dept., 1990-91; grant reviewer, judge NEH, 1992, 93; presenter numerous confs., seminars. Author: Visual Fact over Verbal Fiction, A Study of the Carracci and the Criticism, Theory, and Practice of Painting in Renaissance and Baroque Italy, 1988, Teaching Art: Academies and Schools form Vasari to Albers, 1996; contbr. chpts. to books, articles to scholarly publs. William Bayard Cutting traveling fellow Columbia U., 1964-65, S.H. Kress Found. fellow, 1965, Howard Found. fellow, 1970-71; Am. Philos. Soc. grantee, 1977, 82.

GOLDSTEIN, DEBRA HOLLY, judge; b. Newark, Mar. 11, 1953; d. Aaron and Erica (Schreier) Green; m. Joel Ray Goldstein, Aug. 14, 1983; children: Stephen Michael, Jennifer Ann. BA, U. Mich., 1973; JD, Emory U., 1977. Bar: Ga. 1977, Mich. 1978, D.C. 1978, Ala. 1984. Tax analyst atty. Gen. Motors Corp., Detroit, 1977-78; trial atty. U.S. Dept. Labor, Birmingham, Ala., 1978-90; U.S. adminstrv. law judge office hearing and appeals Social Security Adminstrn., Birmingham, 1990—; new judge faculty U.S. adminstrv. law judges Social Security Adminstrn., 1991, 93—. Mem. editorial bd. The Ala. Lawyer, 1994—, The Addendum, 1995—. Chairperson Women's Coordinating Bur., Birmingham, 1983-85; active United Way, Birmingham, 1983, 87, 90, active adult edn. Temple Beth-El, bd. dirs., 1993-94, co-chair workshop initiative group, 1993-94; program chmn. Sisterhood, 1987-88, adminstrv. v.p., 1989-90, 90-92; scholarship chairperson Nat. Coun. Jewish Women, 1986; mem. steering com. Birmingham Bus. and Profl. Women Fedn., 1987-88, 95—; leader Brownie Troop, 1992—, bd. dirs. Cahaba Girl Scout Coun., 1996—; mem. enrichment com. Cherokee Bend Sch., 1992-93, 94-95, chmn. enrichment com., 1995-96; mem. edn. com. Temple Emanu-El, 1995—; active Leadership for Diversity Initiative, 1995-96. Mem. ABA, Ga. Bar Assn., D.C. Bar Assn., Mich. Bar Assn., Birmingham Bar Assn. (mem. law day com., scholarship com. 1994—), Ala. Bar Assn., Zonta (v.p. 1983-84, bd. dirs. 1988-89, 90-92, intercity chmn. 1995, co-pres. 1996—), B'nai B'rith Women (chair S.E. region 1984-86, counselor 1986-88, Women's Humanitarian award 1981), Hadassah (local bd. dirs. 1979-83, adminstrv. v.p. 1989-90, 90-92). Jewish. Office: Social Security Adminstrn Office of Hearings and Appeals 117 Gemini Cir Birmingham AL 35209-5840

GOLDSTEIN, JOSEPH LEONARD, physician, medical educator, molecular genetics scientist; b. Sumter, SC, Apr. 18, 1940; s. Isadore E. and Fannie A. Goldstein. BS, Washington and Lee U., Lexington, Va., 1962; MD, U. Tex., Dallas, 1966; DSc (hon.), U. Chgo., 1982, Rensselaer Poly. Inst., 1982, Washington and Lee U., 1986, U. Paris, 1988, U. Buenos Aires, 1990, So. Meth. U., 1993, U. Miami, 1996, U. Miami, 1006. Intern, then resident in medicine Mass. Gen. Hosp., Boston, 1966-68; clin. assoc. NIH, 1968-70; postdoctoral fellow U. Wash., Seattle, 1970-72; mem. faculty U. Tex. Southwestern Med. Ctr., Dallas, 1972—, Paul J. Thomas prof. medicine, chmn. dept. molecular genetics, 1977—, regental prof., 1985—; Harvey Soc. lectr., 1977; mem. sci. rev. bd. Howard Hughes Med. Inst., 1978-84, mem. med. adv. bd., 1985-90, chmn. med. adv. bd., 1995—; non-resident fellow Salk Inst., 1983-94; chmn. Albert Lasker Med. Rsch award jury, 1996—; mem. sci. adv. bd. Scripps Rsch. Inst., 1996—. Co-author: The Metabolic Basis of Inherited Disease, 5th edit., 1983; editorial bd. Jour. Biol. Chemistry, 1981-85, Cell, 1983—, Jour. Clin. Investigation, 1977-82, Ann. Rev. Genetics, 1980-85, Arteriosclerosis, 1981-87, Sci. 1985—. Mem. bd. trustees Rockefeller U., 1994—; mem. sci. adv. bd. Welch Found., 1986—; bd. dirs. Passano Found., 1985—. Recipient Heinrich-Wieland prize, 1974, Pfizer award in enzyme chemistry Am. Chem. Soc., 1976; Passano award Johns Hopkins U., 1978; Gairdner Found. award, 1981; award in biol. and med. scis. N.Y. Acad. Scis., 1981, Lita Annenberg Hazen award, 1982; Rsch. Achievement reward Am. Heart Assn., 1984; Louisa Gross Horwitz award, 1984; 3M Life Scis. award, 1984, Albert Lasker award in Basic Med. Rsch., 1985; Nobel Prize in Physiology or Medicine, 1985, Trustees' medal Mass. Gen. Hosp., 1986, U.S. Nat. medal of Sci., 1988. Mem. NAS (Lounsbery award 1979, coun. 1991—), ACP (award 1986), Assn. Am. Physicians, Am. Soc. Clin. Investigation (pres. 1985-86), Am. Soc. Human Genetics (William Allan award 1985), Amer. Acad. Arts and Scis., Am. Soc. Biol. Chemists, Am. Fedn. Clin. Research, Am. Philos. Soc., Inst. Medicine, Royal Soc. London (fgn. mem.), Phi Beta Kappa, Alpha Omega Alpha. Home: 3831 Turtle Creek Blvd Apt 22B Dallas TX 75219-4415 Office: U Tex Southwestern Med Ctr 5323 Harry Hines Blvd Dallas TX 75235-9046

GOLDSTEIN, LARRY BRUCE, neurologist, educator; b. N.Y.C., May 27, 1955; s. Daniel and Sharon (Kantrowitz) G.; children: Sarah, Daniel. AB magna cum laude, Brandeis U., 1977; MD, Mt. Sinai Med. Sch., 1981. Intern Mt. Sinai Hosp., N.Y.C., 1981-82, resident in neurology, 1982-85, chief resident, 1985; fellow Duke U., Durham, N.C., 1985-86, assoc., 1986-88, asst. prof. medicine, 1989-95, assoc. prof., 1995—, asst. rsch. prof. Ctr. for Health Policy, 1989—. Fellow Am. Acad. Neurology (G. Milton Shy award 1979); mem. Nat. Stroke Assn., Internat. Behavioral Neurosci. Soc., Soc. for Neurosci., Am. Heart Assn. (fellow stroke coun.). Office: Duke Med Ctr Box 3651 Durham NC 27710

GOLDSTEIN, ROBERT MICHAEL, transplant surgeon; b. Elizabethton, Tenn., Mar. 21, 1953; s. Buford Jack and Mary Jane Goldstein; m. Amanda Elizabeth Goldstein, May 16, 1992. BA, U. Tenn., 1975; MD, U. Tenn., Memphis, 1981. Diplomate Am. Bd. Gen. Surgery., Am. Bd. Surg. Care. Pediatric intern Ohio State U., Columbus, 1981-82; surgery resident W.Va. U., Morgantown, 1982-84, 85-87; rsch. fellow Johns Hopkins, Balt., 1984-85; transplant fellow U. Pitts., Pa., 1987-88; transplant fellow Baylor U. Med. Ctr., Dallas, 1987-88, asst. dir. transplant svcs., 1988—, dir. transplant intensive care, 1990—. Fellow ACS; mem. Am. Bd. Surg. Critical Care. Office: Baylor Univ Dept Transplantation Dallas TX 75246

GOLDSTEIN, THOMAS, lawyer; b. Pitts., Jan. 27, 1944; s. Louis and Ethel (Joseph) G.; m. Azhaniah Borhan, July 23, 1977; 1 child, Azlina. BA, Wabash Coll., Crawfordsville, Ind., 1965; MA, Washington U., St. Louis, 1968; JD, Howard U., Washington, 1973. Bar: D.C. 1973, Fla. 1974, U.S. Dist. Ct. (so. dist.) Fla. 1975, U.S. Mil. Ct. Appeals (11th cir.) 1976, U.S. Supreme Ct. 1978; cert. civil trial lawyer Fla. Bar. 1983. Asst. atty. gen. U.S. Dept. Justice, Washington, 1973-75; asst. county atty. Met. Dade County, Miami, Fla., 1975—; lectr. CLE Eminent Domain, 1990, 94, 95, Am. Law Inst.-ABA Condemnation Seminar, 1996; statutory rev. com., Fla., 1993-94; Gov.'s pvt. property rights legis. ad hoc working group, 1995. Mng. editor Howard U. Law Jour., 1972-73; contbr. to books: Florida Eminent Domain Practice and Procedure, 1988, Nichols on Eminent Domain, 1993, Florida Eminent Domain Practice and Procedure Update, 1993. Mem. auto ins. reform com. Met. Dade County, 1977—; legis. lobbyist, Tallahassee, Fla., 1983, 93, 94, 95, 96. Fulbright scholar, 1968-69; Ford Found./Indian Govt. Parliamentary fellow Inst. Constl. and Parliamentary Studies, New Delhi, 1969-70; recipient Outstanding Svc. award Police Benevolent Soc., Miami, 1982, Golden Poet awards World of Poetry, 1985-92. Mem. Internat. Law Soc. (v.p. 1972-73), Fulbright Alumni Club (life). Democrat. Office: Dade County Atty Office 111 NW 1st St Ste 28 Miami FL 33128-1902

GOLEMBIEWSKI, ROBERT THOMAS, public and business administration educator, consultant; b. Lawrenceville, N.J., July 2, 1932; s. John and Pauline (Pelka) G.; m. Margaret M. Hughes, Sept. 1, 1956; children—Alice, Hope, Geoffrey. A.B., Princeton U., 1954; M.A., Yale U., 1956, Ph.D., 1958; DSc (hon.), U. Lethbridge, 1996. Instr. politics Princeton U., 1958-60; asst. prof. mgmt. U. Ill., 1960-63; lectr. indsl. adminstrn. Yale U., 1963-64; research prof. pub. mgmt. U. Ga., Athens, 1964—; cons. UNIDO, AT&T Co., Smith Kline Corp., others; Killam vis. scholar, 1980; disting. vis. scholar U. Calgary (Alta., Can.), 1981-86, 89. Author: The Small Group, 1962, Behavior and Organization, 1962, Men, Management and Morality, 1965, Public Administration, 1967, Renewing Organizations, 1972, Learning and Change in Groups, 1976, Public Administration As A Developing Discipline, Parts 1 and 2, 1977, Approaches To Planned Change, Vols. 1 and 2, 1979, Toward the Responsive Organization, 1979, Approaches to Organizing, 1981, Public Budgeting and Finance, 1983, The Costs of Federalism, 1984, Humanizing Public Organizations, 1985, Stress in Organizations, 1986, Phases of Burnout, 1988, High Performance and Human Costs, 1988, Ironies in Organization Development, 1990, Handbook of Organizational Consultation 1993, Practical Public Management, 1994, Managing Diversity in Organizations, 1995; 30 other books; contbr. over 500 articles to profl. publs. Recipient Douglas McGregor Meml. awards for excellence in application behavioral scis., 1975, 87, Chester I. Barnard Meml. award, 1980, Hosp. Adminstr.'s Book of Yr. award, 1966, award Am. Soc. Tng. Dirs., 1969, Creative Rsch. medal U. Ga., 1984, Third Century award in social and behavioral scis., 1988; Ford fellow, 1961; Lilly Found. grantee, 1962-64; NIMH grantee; named to hon. Order Ky. Cols., 1984; named Cons. of Yr., 1989. Fellow Acad. Mgmt. (Mgmt. Laureate 1991); mem. Internat. Assn. Applied Social Scientists, Am. Soc. Pub. Adminstrn., Am. Soc. for Tng. and Devel., Am. Polit. Sci. Assn., So. Polit. Sci. Assn. (v.p. 1979, pres. 1980), Org. Devel. Inst. (bd. dirs.). Roman Catholic. Club: Princeton (N.Y.C.). Home: 145 Highland Dr Athens GA 30606-3211

GOLIAN, LINDA MARIE, librarian; b. Woodbridge, N.J., Mar. 27, 1962; d. Joseph John Golian and Mary Grace (Juba) Rodriguez; m. Gary S. Lui, Oct. 6, 1988. BA, U. Miami, 1986; MLIS, Fla. State, 1988; EdS, Fla. Atlantic U., 1995, postgrad., 1996—. Libr. tech. asst. U. Miami, 1981-86; serials control libr. U. Miami Law Sch., 1986-89; serials dept. head Fla. Atlantic U., Boca Raton, 1990—; adj. instr. Fla. Atlantic U. Coll. Continuing & Distance Edn., 1993—, U. So. Fla. Coll. Libr. Sci., 1995—; program specialist Marriott Statford Ctr. Sr. Living Comty., Boca Raton, 1994-96. Vol. storyteller Aid to Victims of Domestic Assault, Delray Beach, Fla., 1994-96. Mem. NOW, AAUW, NAFE, NLA, Spl. Libr. Assn., N.Am. Serials Interest Group, ASCD, Southeastern Libr. Assn., Assn. Libr. and Info. Sci. Educators, ALA (mem. ACRL, ALCTS, LAMA and RASD divsns., mem. CLENE, IFRT, LIRT, NMRT and SORT Round Tables, women's studies sect. comm. com. 1994—, serials com. nomination com., Miami local arrangements com. 1994, chair libr. sch. outreach 1994—, 3M profl. devel. grantee 1995), Laubach Literary Vols. of Am., Am. Assn. Adult and Continuing Edn., Fla. Libr. Assn. (serials libr. or yr. 1994, grantee 1987). Republican. Roman Catholic. Office: Fla Atlantic U Wimberly Libr PO Box 3092 Boca Raton FL 33431

GOLIS, PAUL ROBERT, lawyer; b. San Francisco, Sept. 25, 1954. BA with high distinction, Calif. State U., Long Beach, 1977; JD, Syracuse U., 1981. Bar: Fla. 1984, U.S. Dist. Ct. (so. dist.) Fla. 1985. Assoc. Russell L. Forkey, P.A., Ft. Lauderdale, Fla., 1984-85, Josias & Goren, P.A., Ft. Lauderdale, 1985-88; sr. trial atty. State of Fla. Dept. Transp., Ft. Lauderdale, 1988-90; asst. county atty. Palm Beach County, West Palm Beach, Fla., 1990-91; assoc. Scott, Royce, Harris, Bryan & Hyland, Palm Beach Gardens, Fla., 1991-93, Watterson, Hyland, Baird & Klett, Palm Beach Gardens, 1993—. Bd. dirs. Aid to Victims of Domestic Assault, Inc., 1990—, v.p., 1993—. Mem. ABA, Fla. Bar Assn. (eminent domain com. 1989—), Palm Beach County Bar Assn. (vice chmn. environ., land use and eminent domain CLE com. 1993-95, chmn. 1995—). Office: Ste 112 4100 RCA Blvd Ste 100 Palm Beach Gardens FL 33410

GOLLER, EDWIN JOHN, chemistry educator; b. Lawrence, Mass., Jan. 28, 1940; s. Edwin Charles and Mary Helen (Dubovy) G.; m. Ana Amelia Smith, Dec. 22, 1984; 1 child, Maria Teresa. BS in Chemistry, Marrimack Coll., 1961; MS in Organic Chemistry, Northeastern U., 1964; PhD in Organic Chemistry, U. N.H., 1969. Instr. chemistry Merrimack Coll., North Andover, Mass., 1963-66; asst. prof. organic chemistry Va. Mil. Inst., Lexington, 1969-73, assoc. prof., 1973-79, prof., 1979—, chem. dept. head, 1989—, sci. div. dir., 1992-96; cons. Wiley & Wilson, Lynchburg, Va., 1990, Clean Air for Rockbridge County, Lexington, 1991-93. Contbr. articles to profl. jours. Active Va. Jaycees, Lexington, 1973-74. Mem. Am. Chem. Soc. (alt. nat. counselor 1982-83). Office: Va Mil Inst Chemistry Dept Lexington VA 24450-0304

GOLLIVER, CHERYL RENA, nurse; b. St. Louis, Feb. 5, 1955; d. Howard James and Nolia Lavelle (Shaw) G. BSN, U. N. Ala., 1978. Staff nurse, charge nurse NICU Regional Med. Ctr., Memphis; staff nurse, newborn Kapiolani Med. Ctr., Honolulu; staff RN med./surg. Hinds Gen. Hosp., Jackson, Miss.; transport nurse newborn ICU Regional Med. Ctr., Memphis. Home: 7074 Windsor Dr Horn Lake MS 38637-1225

GOLOBY, GEORGE WILLIAM, JR., environmental scientist, ornithologist, aviculturist; b. Franklin, Ky., Mar. 21, 1949; s. George William Sr. and Katherine Jacqueline (Panchot) G.; m. Diane Grayson, Dec. 29, 1974; children: Amy Vanessa, George William III. BS in Wildlife Sci., Tex. A&M U., 1971. Zookeeper of birds Houston Zool. Gardens, 1971-72; warehouseman, driver Houston Ind. Sch. Dist., 1972-76; lab. mgr. Empak Inc., Houston, 1976-80; asst. sect. chief City of Houston Dept. Pub. Works, 1980-90; environ. quality specialist III City of Houston Dept. Pub. Works & Engring., 1990—; owner Penfeathers Tours, Houston. Editor (newsletters) Water Environment Assn. Tex. (WEAT) Pipeline, 1984—, Tex. Ornithol. Soc. Newsletter, 1989—, Penfeathers Newsletter, 1986—, Panchot Paper, 1989-93, Houston Audubon Soc., 1977-80, The Naturalist, 1986-89; asst. editor (books) Houston, 1978, Encyclopedia of American Cities, 1979. Mem. Houston Proud, 1986, Cy-Fair Houston C. of C., 1986, Greater Houston Conv. and Vis. Bur., 1986-88. Mem. Water Environ. Assn. Tex. (com. chmn. 1984—), Tex. Water Utilites Assn., Houston Audubon Soc. (v.p. adminstrv. affairs 1986-89), Am. Birding Assn., Outdoor Nature Club, Parrot People Club (v.p. Houston chpt. 1985-86), Purple Martin Conservation Assn., Whooping Crane Conservation Assn., Tex. Nature Conservancy. Office: City Houston 3100 Old Galveston Rd Houston TX 77017

GOLSON, SISTER AFTON ALMEDA, health facility administrator, nun; b. Prattville, Ala., July 12, 1932; d. Grady Everett and Sarah Virginia (Roy) G. Diploma in Nursing, St. Margaret's Hosp., Montgomery, Ala., 1958; BSN, Marillac Coll., 1969; MS in Hosp. and Health Svcs. Adminstrn., U. Ala., 1977. Joined Daus. of Charity, 1965; RN, Ala. Asst. dir. nursing Hotel Dieu, New Orleans, 1961-64; dir. nursing Sr. Margaret's Hosp., Montgomery, 1969-71, asst. adminstr., 1971-75, pres., 1985-87, 1980-85; asst. adminstr. St. Vincent's Hosp., Birmingham, 1977-78, 1985-87; pres., chief exec. officer St. Thomas Hosp., Nashville, 1989—, also bd. dirs.; chmn. bd. dirs. Providence Hosp., Mobile, Ala., St. Margaret's Svcs., Montgomery, Providence Hosp. Bd., Southfield, Mich.; bd. dirs. Seton Health Corp., Nashville; mem. chief exec. officer adv. com. east cen. region Daus. of Charity, 1989—, numerous others. Active Cath. Charities Tenn., Inc., Nashville, St. Mary Orphanage, Inc., Nashville, Villa Child Care, Inc., Nashville, Villa Maria Manor, Inc., Social Svc. Commn. of Met. Govt., Nashville, HEALTHCO Bd., Murfreesboro, Tenn., Community Health Consortium, also pres. 1991—; mem. adv. com. Tenn. Donor Svcs., 1989—, mem. ethics and legis. com., 1989—. Mem. Am. Coll. Healthcare Execs., Tenn. Hosp. Assn. (Blue Cross liaison 1989—, govt. rels. and rep. legal affairs com. 1989—), Nashville C. of C. (bd. dirs.), Leadership Nashville. Office: Saint Thomas Hosp PO Box 380 Nashville TN 37202-0380*

GOMES, NORMAN VINCENT, retired industrial engineer; b. New Bedford, Mass., Nov. 7, 1914; s. John Vincent and Georgianna (Sylvia) G.; grad. U.S. Army Command and Gen. Staff Coll., 1944; BS in Indsl. Engring. and Mgmt., Okla. State U., 1950; MBA in Mgmt., Xavier U., 1955; m. Carolyn Moore, June 6, 1942 (dec. Apr. 1983); m. Helen Groesbeck Kurzawa, April 22, 1995. Asst. chief engr. Leschen divsn. H.K. Porter Co., St. Louis, 1950-52; staff mfg. cons. Gen. Electric Co., Cin., 1952-57: lectr. indsl. mgmt. U. Cin., 1955-56; vis. lectr. indsl. mgmt. Xavier U. Grad. Sch. Bus. Adminstrn., 1956-57; staff indsl. engr. Gen. Dynamics, Ft. Worth, 1957-60; chief ops. analysis Ryan Electronics, San Diego, 1960-64; sr. engr., jet propulsion lab. Calif. Inst. Tech., Pasadena, 1964-67, mem. tech. staff, 1967, mgr. mgmt. sys., 1967-71; industry rep. and cons. U.S. Commn. on Govt. Procurement, Washington, 1970-72; adminstrv. officer GSA, Washington, 1973-78, program dir., 1979; vis. lectr. mgmt. San Antonio Coll., 1982-85. Active Serra, Internat.; mem. Drug and Alcohol Adv. Coun. N.E. Ind. Sch. Dist., San Antonio, 1989-95. 2d lt. to maj. C.E., AUS, 1941-46; engring. adviser to War Manpower Bd., 1945. Decorated Army Commendation medal, Armed Svcs. Res. medal; recipient Apollo Achievement award, 1969; Outstanding Performance award GSA, 1974- 75, 76, 77, 79. Mem. Am. Inst. Indsl. Engrs. (nat. chmn. prodn. control research com., 1951-57; bd. dirs. Cin., Fort Worth, San Diego, Los Angeles, San Antonio chpts. 1954-84, pres. Cin. chpt. 1956-57, pres. Los Angeles 1970-71, nat. dir. community services 1969-73), Ret. Officers Assn. U.S. (chpt. pres. 1968-69, recipient Nat. Pres. certificate Merit 1969), Nat. Security Indsl. Assn. (mgmt. systems subcom. 1967-69), Vis. Nurse Assn. of San Antonio (mem. adv. coun. 1988-95), Freedoms Found. at Valley Forge (v.p. edn. and youth leadership programs San Antonio chpt. 1987-89), Pillars San Fernando Cathedral, Old Dartmouth Hist. Soc., Equestrian Order of the Holy Sepulchre of Jerusalem (knight comdr.). Republican. Roman Catholic. Club: K.C. (4th deg.). Home: RR 1 Box 45A Burnet TX 78611-9714

GOMEZ, LUCAS, assistant treasurer, credit manager; b. Socorro, Colombia, Oct. 18, 1940; came to U.S., 1963; s. Carlos Julio and Maria Luisa (Reyes) G.; m. Alicia Barney, July 31, 1964; children: Fabian, Eric. BA in Econs., Queens Coll., 1972; MBA in Internat. Fin., St. Johns U., 1975. Billing clk. Laury Rich, N.Y.C., 1963-67; sr. sales rep. Scott Jrs., N.Y.C., 1967-72; fin. ops. mgr. Exxon Internat. Co., N.Y.C./Houston, 1973-81; fin. ops. supr. Exxon Chem. Americas, Houston, 1981—. Contbr. articles to profl. jours. Mem. Nat. Chem. Credit Assn. (internat. div. chmn. 1986-87, exec. bd. chmn. 1988-90, Outstanding Svc. award, 1987, '90), Nat. Assn. Credit Mgmt. (conf. speaker, panel mem., bd. dirs.), Fin. Credit and Internat. Bus.-Nat. Assn. Credit Mgmt. (bd. dirs.). Roman Catholic.

Home: 702 Saint Ives Ct Houston TX 77079-2412 Office: Exxon Chem Americas 13501 Katy Fwy Houston TX 77079-1305

GOMEZ, LUIS CARLOS, manufacturing executive; b. San Jose, Costa Rica, June 17, 1943; came to U.S., 1961; s. Luis and Julietta (De Blanco) G.; children: Robert, Marie; m. Donna J. Lewis; children: Terri Munoz, Mikell Simmons. Grad., San Jose High Sch., 1959. Pres. Vitalizer, Hialeah, Fla. Patentee for retro fit device to lower emissions and save fuel The Vitalizer III. Roman Catholic. Office: 2344 W 77th St Hialeah FL 33016-1868

GOMEZ-SOUTO, JOSEPH, hospital administrator; b. Santiago de Compostela, Galicia, Spain, Aug. 18, 1958; came to U.S., 1969; s. Jose and Maria (Varella) Gomez. BA in Chemistry, Fla. Atlantic U., 1982; MD, U. Juarez, Mex., 1987; PhD, Biomed. Inst., Chihuahua, Mex., 1989; MBA in Health Care, U. Calif., Irvine, 1996. Med. technologist U. Miami (Fla.)-Jackson Hosp., 1982-84; med. clk. in internal medicine Albert Einstein Sch. Medicine, N.Y.C., 1987-88; clerkship in anat. pathology U. Miami-Mt. Sinai Med. Ctr., 1993; clin. lab. supr. Hialeah Hosp., Miami; prof. hematology U. Miami-Mt. Sinai Hosp.; adminstr. profl. clin. svcs. U. Miami-South Shore Hosp. Med. Ctr., Miami Beach, 1995—; tech. dir. Internat. Red Cross, Juarez, 1986-87. Bd. dirs. South Fla. Audubon Soc., Miami, 1977. Recipient Key to City, City of Miami, 1977, 78. Mem. South Fla. Orchid Soc. Republican.

GONG, ALICE KIM, neonatologist, educator, researcher; b. Canton, People's Republic China, Sept. 28, 1954; came to U.S., 1963; d. Kwing Sheung and Grace (Tong) G.; m. Richard John Gong, 1982; children: Karis Anne, Kathleen Rose, Paul Michael. BS, Miss. Coll., 1976; MD, U. Miss., 1980. Diplomate, bd. cert. in pediatrics; sub-bd. cert. in neonatal-perinatal medicine. Resident U. Tex., Galveston, 1980-82; resident SUNY, Buffalo, 1982-83, fellow neonatology, 1983-85; asst. clin. prof. U. Tex. Health Sci. Ctr., San Antonio, 1985-86, asst. prof., 1986-94; assoc. prof., 1994—; dir. nurseries Bapt. Meml. Hosp. System, San Antonio, 1988—; cons. Bur. Chronically Ill and Disabled Children, Austin, 1989—; regional instr. Neonatal Resuscitation Course, San Antonio, 1989—. Contbr. articles to profl. jours. Physician cons. and instr. Safe Sitter, San Antonio, 1989—. Grantee March of Dimes, San Antonio, 1987. Mem. Am. Acad. Pediatrics, Southern Soc. Pediatric Rsch., Tex. Perinatal Assn., Women's Faculty Assn., Tex. Pediat. Soc., San Antonio Pediat. Soc. Baptist. Office: U Tex Health Sci Ctr Dept Pediatrics 7703 Floyd Curl Dr San Antonio TX 78284-6200

GONG, JEH-TWEEN, physicist, philosopher; b. Taipei, Taiwan, Republic of China, Feb. 24, 1950; came to U.S., 1975; s. Lo-Cheen and Sing-in (Hu) G.; m. Gwendolyn J. Glenn, Dec. 15, 1975; children: Andrew, Gloria, Jason, Henry. BS, Chung-Yuan U., Chung-Li, Taiwan, 1972; MS, Taiwan Nat. U., 1974, PhD, 1978. Assoc. prof. Taiwan Nat. U., 1978-82, prof., 1982-85; pres. Soc. World Philosophy, 1985—; editor in chief Adams Press, 1985—; invited speaker XIX World Congress of Philosophy, Moscow, 1993, 6th Internat. Conf. on Thinking, MIT, 1994. Author: Super Unified Theory, 1984, Truth, Faith, and Life, 1990, Divine Constitution, 1992. Advisor gifted program Washington County Sch. Bd., Va. Mem. AAAS (invited speaker 1994 conf.), Am. Philos. Assn., Nat. Ctr. Teaching Thinking, Chinese Acad. Scis., N.Y. Acad. Scis. Office: PO Box 1857 West Covina CA 91793-1857

GONONG, ZOILA OBMANA, medical/surgical nurse; b. Labo Cam Norte, The Philippines, June 29, 1938; d. Felix V. and Eugenia (Villaluz) Obmana; m. Oscar J. Gonong, Oct. 3, 1970; children: Annagene, John Felix (dec.). Nursing diploma, U. Nueva Caceres, Naga City, The Philippines, 1963. RN. Gen. duty nurse Orlando (Fla.) Regional Med. Ctr., 1976-82, Naval Hosp., Orlando, 1985-86; RN vis. nurse Humana Hosp. Lucerne, Orlando, 1986-88; nurse Walt Disney World, Orlando, 1989-90, Orlando Meml. Convalescent Ctr., Lucerne Terrace, Fla., 1990-91, Associated Health Care and Orlando Health Care Home Visits and IV Therapy, 1992-92; Paragon Nursing, 1992—; nurse Trans-World Nurses, Orlando; with XL-CARE Agy., Winter Park, Fla., 1990—, FIRSTAT, Winter Park, Fla., 1990—; staff builder agy. Nations Helath Care, Orlando, 1995—; with Nurse Finders, 1985—, Staff Builders, Nations Health Care, 1995. Vol. Ministry for the Sick; active Social Justice Com., AIDS Ministry; active Respect Life Ministry and Pro-Life Movement. Fellow Internat. Biographical Assn.; mem. Nat. Assn. Physicians' Nurses, Bayanihan Internat. Ladies Assn., Philippine-Am. Club, Bally Health Club, Fava Club. Home: 701 Nana Ave Orlando FL 32809-6442

GONSHAK, ISABELLE LEE, nurse; b. Newark, Apr. 4, 1932; d. Robert John and Clara Kate (Cooperman) McClelland; m. David M. Gonshak, Aug. 8, 1953; children: Evan J., Brett A., Kathryn Susan. RN, N.J. Nurse Newark City Hosp., 1953. Tchr. Ideal Sch. for Nurse's Aides, Miami, Fla., 1972-74; vocal soloist numerous TV and social affairs. Bd. dirs. Miami Beach Symphony, 1971—, pres. 1978-79; bd. dirs. South Fla. Symphony; mem. Opera Guild Soc. Ft. Lauderdale (life); active Statue of Liberty Refinishing Com. Mem. Greater Miami Opera Assn., Hadassah (life). Jewish. Home: 1700 SW 72nd Ave Plantation FL 33317-5037

GONWA, THOMAS ARTHUR, nephrologist, transplant physician; b. Chgo., Sept. 2, 1949; s. George Joseph and Darline (Sears) G.; m. Mary Alice Westrick, Sept. 28, 1974; children: Claire, Charlotte. BS, St. Joseph's Coll., 1971; MD, U. Ill., 1975. Diplomate Am. Bd. Internal Medicine, Nephrology, Critical Care Medicine. Resident Bowman Gray, Winston-Salem, N.C., 1975-78, renal fellow, 1978-80; postdoctoral rsch. fellow U. Calif., San Francisco, 1980-82, instr., 1982-83; asst. prof. U. Iowa, Iowa City, 1983-86; staff physician Dallas Nephrology, 1986—; assoc. dir. transplant Baylor U. Med. Ctr., Dallas, 1987—; clin. assoc. prof. medicine Southwestern Med. Sch., 1993—. Assoc. editor Jour. Immunology, 1985-86; contbr. more than 100 articles to profl. jours. Recipient rsch. award VA, 1984. Fellow ACP; mem. Am. Soc. Transplant Physicians (sec., treas. 1990-93, pres.-elect 1993-94, pres. 1994-95, Upjohn award 1983), Am. Soc. Nephrology, Am. Assn. Immunologists, Transplantation Soc. Office: Dallas Nephrology 3601 Swiss Ave Dallas TX 75204

GONYNOR, FRANCIS JAMES, lawyer; b. Cambridge, Mass., Nov. 6, 1959; s. James Francis and Beverly Joan (Lintz) G.; m. Deborah Lynn Snyder, July 25, 1981; children: Brian Christopher, Caroline Jane. AA, U. Fla., 1978, BA, 1980; JD, U. Houston, 1983. Bar: Tex. 1983, U.S. Dist. Ct. (so. dist.) Tex. 1983, U.S. Ct. Appeals (5th cir.) 1983. Assoc. Eastham Watson Dale & Forney, Houston, 1983-88, ptnr., 1988—; mediator Am. Arbitration Assn., 1992. Contbr. articles to profl. jours. Mem. Maritime Law Assn., Houston Bar Assn., Houston Young Lawyers Assn., Galveston Bay Found. Home: 3327 Spring Trail Dr Sugar Land TX 77479-3050 Office: Eastham Watson Dale Forney 808 Travis St Fl 20 Houston TX 77002-5706

GONZALES, DIANA ESPAÑA, journalist; b. San Antonio, Nov. 12, 1947; d. Gregorio Quintero Gonzales and Virginia (España) Nuncio; m. Rudy A. Peña, Apr. 23, 1992. Student, San Antonio Coll., 1968-71; BA, S.W. Tex. State U., 1973; postgrad., Sul Ross State U., 1994—. Reporter Yakima (Wash.) Herald Republic, 1974-78, San Antonio Express, 1978-81; news editor News-Herald, Del Rio, Tex., 1982-83, mng. editor, 1983-94; mng. editor Del Rio Sun Newspaper, 1995—; editl. cons. Spirit Val Verde, Del Rio, 1983-84; writing cons. Dow Jones Newspaper Workshop, San Antonio, 1991; adj. prof. English S.W. Tex. Jr. Coll., Del Rio. Sec., vice chmn. Val Verde Hist. Commn., Del Rio, 1987-89; mem. Child Welfare Bd., Del Rio, 1989; pres. Del Rio Adult Literacy Coun., 1990—; mem. com. Recycle Del Rio, 1991. Am. Newspaper Pubs. fellow, 1985; recipient Outstanding Communicator award Toastmasters Internat., 1974, 1st Pl. Feature Writing award Washington Press Women, 1975, 2d Pl. Pub. Affairs Reporting award Sigma Delta Chi, 1976, Outstanding Former Student award San Antonio Coll., 1991. Home: 306 Mclymont St Del Rio TX 78840-6547 Office: Del Rio Sun 306 McLymont Del Rio TX 78840-6547

GONZALES, EDMOND TASSIN, pediatric urologist; b. New Orleans, Oct. 1, 1940; s. Edmond Tassin and Leona (Bolhalter) G.; m. Lynn Smith, June 19, 1965; children: Michelle, Cheryl, Lisa, Edmond III. BS, Loyola U., 1962; MD, Tulane U., 1965. Diplomate Am. Bd. Urology, La. State Bd. Med. Examiners, N.C. State Bd. Med. Examiners, Tex. State Bd. Med. Examiners. Intern Charity Hosp. La., New Orleans, 1965-66; asst. resident in urology Duke U. Med. Ctr., Durham, N.C., 1969, jr. asst. resident in surgery, 1969-70, asst. resident in urology, 1970-71, sr. resident in urology, 1971, chief resident in urology, 1972, fellow in investigative urology, 1968, instr. in urology, 1972; asst. prof. urology Sch. Medicine Wayne State U., Detroit, 1973-74; assoc. prof. urology Baylor Coll. Medicine, Houston, 1974-82, prof., 1982—; mem. med. staff, chief pediatric urology svc., head dept. surgery Tex. Children's Hosp., Houston, pres. med. staff, 1988; active med. staff Meth. Hosp., Ben Taubman Gen. Hosp., St. Joseph Hosp., Houston; courtesy med. staff St. Luke's Episcopal Hosp., Hermann Hosp., Tex. Woman's Hosp., Houston; past mem. med. staff Children's Hosp. Mich., VA Hosp., Hutzel Hosp., Detroit Gen. Hosp., Detroit; mem. urology resident rev. com. Baylor Coll. Medicine, 1974—, mem. acquistions com. learning resources ctr., 1974—; mem. dept. ambulatory svc. Tex. Children's Hosp., 1974—; mem. various coms.; mem. joint oper. rm. com. Tex. Children's Hosp., St. Luke's Episcopal Hosp., Tex. Heart Inst., Houston, 1976—; presenter in field. Author: (with others) Urological Surgery, 1975, 3d edit., 1980, Pediatric Therapy, 1975, 6th edit., 1980, Handbook of Pediatric Surgery, 1974, Current Pediatric Therapy, 1975, Comparative Operative Urology, 2d edit., 1981, Genitourinary Cancer Surgery, 1982, Major Topics in Pediatric and Adolescent Oncology, 1982, International Perspectives in Urology, 1983, Clinical Pediatric Urology, 2d edit., 1985, others; co-editor: Common Problems in Pediatric Urology, 1990; asst. editor: Urologic Surgery, 4th edit., 1991; author various audiocassettes; contbr. articles to profl. jours. With USPHS, 1966-68. Mem. Duke Urol. Alumni Soc., Harris County Med. Soc., Houston Pediatric Soc., Tex. Med. Assn., Soc. Univ. Urologists, Tex. Pediatric Soc., Am. Acad. Pediatrics (mem. exec. com. sect. on urology 1982-84, chmn. 1992, sec. 1987-90), Am. Urol. Assn. (South Ctrl. sect. 1976—, exam. com. of Am. Bd. Urology 1975-79, program chmn. sect. urology 1979, 1st prize Montague L. Boyd Essay Contest 1972), Soc. for Pediatric Urology (exec. com. 1984—, program chmn. 1984), Tex. Urol. Soc., Genitourinary Soc., Alpha Sigma Nu, Alpha Omega Alpha. Office: Tex Childrens Hosp Clin Care Ctr 6621 Fannin St # 270 Houston TX 77030-2303

GONZALES, SAM C., police chief; b. Aug. 24, 1941; married; 2 children. BS in Criminal Justice, Abilene Christian Coll., 1975; grad., FBI Nat. Acad., 1979; grad. Sr. Mgmt. Inst. for Police, Harvard U., 1989; grad., U.S. Secret Svc. Dignitary Protection Sch., 1990; grad. Nat. Exec. Inst., FBI Sch. Mgmt., 1991. Spl. investigator organized crime unit La. State Police, 1969-70; patrol officer Dallas Police Dept., 1963-67, investigator narcotics, vice, and organized crime unit Intelligence Unit, 1967-69, investigator vice divsn., 1970-71, police sgt. detention svcs. divsn., supervisory sgt. Internal Affairs and Patrol, 1971-75, police lt. cmty. svcs. divsn. and auto theft sect., 1975-79, police capt., exec. officer S.E. and S.W. patrol divsns., identification divsn., and detention svcs. divsn., 1979-87, dep. chief divsn. commdr. N.W. patrol divsn., 1987-88, asst. chief of police patrol east, 1988-90, exec. asst. chief of police office of spl. svcs., 1990, acting chief of police, 1990, 1st exec. asst. chief of police, 1990-91; chief of police Oklahoma City Police Dept., 1991—; presenter drug initiatives and cmty. policing S.W. Law Enforcement Inst., 1989, Cmty. Policing and Drugs Conf., Mich. State, 1990, Ala. Mayor's Conf., 1990. Bd. dirs. New Horizons Ranch for Disadvantaged Youth; mem. Criminal Justice Task Force; mem. steering com. Edna McConnell Clark Found.; mem. adv. commn. Truth in Sentencing. Recipient Spl. Recognition award City Coun., 1990, Excellence in Svc. award City Mgr., 1990, Presdl. commendation, 1990, Neighborhood Initiative Program award City Mgr., 1992. Mem. Internat. Assn. Chiefs of Police, Police Exec. Rsch. Forum (presenter drug initiatives and cmty. policing 1989), Major Cities Chiefs Assn. Office: Police Department 701 Couch Dr Oklahoma City OK 73102-2211

GONZALEZ, ALAN FRANCIS, lawyer; b. Tampa, Fla., Nov. 28, 1951; s. Frank R. and Marina (Font) G.; m. Hilda Martinez, July 28, 1973 (div. May 1982); 1 child, Adria; m. Yolanda Alvarez, Mar. 28, 1986; 1 child, Carly. BA in Mktg., U. South Fla., 1973; MBA, Samford U., Birmingham, Ala., 1977; JD, Samford U., 1977; LLM, U. Fla., 1978. Bar: Fla. 1977, U.S. Tax Ct. 1977, U.S. Ct. Claims 1978, U.S. Dist. Ct. (mid. dist.) 1977, U.S. Ct. Appeals (5th cir.) 1977, U.S. Ct. Appeals (11th cir.) 1995. Assoc. Salem, Salem, Musial & Morse P.A., Tampa, Fla., 1978-79; ptnr. Gonzalez & Scaglione, Attys. at Law, Tampa, 1979-90; pvt. practice Tampa, 1990-92; ptnr. Sierra, Gustafson & Gonzalez, Tampa, 1992-95; pvt. practice Tampa, 1995—; instr. Royalton Coll., South Royalton, Vt., 1973-74, Rollin Coll., 1993; adj. prof. Ala. Christian Coll., Birmingham, 1975-76, Hillsborough C.C., Tampa, 1978-81; asst. prof. U. Ctrl. fla., 1990-92. Author: (Fla. student pocket accompaniment text) Civil Litigation for the Paralegal, 1992. Mem. ABA, Fla. Acad. Trial Lawyers, Hillsborough County Bar Assn. Home: 4719 Foxshire Cir Tampa FL 33624-4307

GONZALEZ, ANTONIO, academic administrator, mortgage company executive; b. Edinburg, Tex., Mar. 14, 1943; s. Manuel Gonzales and Natalia Torres; m. Elma De Luna, Oct. 10, 1975; 1 child, Julissa Priscilla. BA, U. Md., Balt., 1971; MA, U. Tenn., 1973; JD, Miles Coll., 1979. Law clk. Crain Caton James & Oberwetter, Houston, 1979-81; instr. U. Houston, 1981-83, asst. dir., 1983-86; instr. Houston C.C., 1982-85, 95; assoc. dir. No. Ill. U., Dekalb, 1986-88; adminstr. Prairie View (Tex.) A&M U., 1988-95; instr. Houston Internat. U., 1988-89, pres., CEO, 1989-90; pres., CEO Am. Fidelity Mortgage & Title Co., Houston, 1992-95; instr. North Harris Coll., Houston, 1994-95; mem. adv. com. Houston C.C., 1994-95. Editor: Mexican-American Musicians, 1987; mem. editl. bd. Jour. Minority Issues, 1993-94. Chair tng. and devel. LULAC Dist. 18, Houston, 1994-96; dir. Inst. Chicano Culture, Houston, 1995; mem. SER Jobs for Progress, Houston, 1994-96; Dem. candidate Tex. Ho. Reps. Dist. 130, 1994. With USAF, 1966-70, Vietnam. Named Man of Yr. LULAC, Ill., 1987. Mem. AAUP, ABA,VFP, Am. Hist. Assn., Tex. Assn. Chicanos in Higher Edn., Tex. Assn. Coll. Admissions Counselors, Tex. Assn. Coll. Univ. Student Pers. Adminstrs., Phi Delta Kappa, Delta Theta Phi. Roman Catholic. Home: 16614 Dounreay Dr Houston TX 77084 Office: Prairie View A&M U PO Box 532 Prairie View TX 77446

GONZÁLEZ, CARLOS A., lawyer; b. Havana, Cuba, July 24, 1960; s. Jorge A. and Ondina (Santos) G.; m. Marilyn Marvin, Aug. 22, 1988; children: Matthew M., Jordan R. BS, Fla. State U., 1983; MA in Religion, Yale U., 1986; JD, Vanderbilt U., 1989. Bar: Ga. 1989, U.S. Dist. Ct. (no. dist.) Ga. 1991, U.S. Ct. Appeals (11th cir.) 1992, U.S. Dist. Ct. (mid. dist.) Ga. 1993. Law clk. to Judge Harold C. Murphy U.S. Dist. Ct. (no. dist.) Ga., Rome, 1989-91; fed. ct. monitor, spl. master U.S. Dist. Ct. (no. dist.) Ga., Atlanta, 1993—; assoc. Rogers & Hardin, Atlanta, 1992-93; pvt. practice Atlanta, 1993—; cons. in higher edn., 1994—. Fellow Inst. for Ministry, Law and Ethics, Salt Lake City. Mem. ABA, Am. Judicature Soc., Atlanta Bar Assn., Fed. Bar Assn., Phi Delta Phi. Methodist. Home: 3087 Belingham Dr Atlanta GA 30345 Office: PO Box 450888 Atlanta GA 31145-0888

GONZALEZ, EFREN, airport executive. Asst. aviation dir. City of San Antonio Aviation Dept. San Antonio Internat. Airport. Office: San Antonio Internat Airport Dept of Aviation 9800 Airport Blvd San Antonio TX 78216-4837

GONZALEZ, EMILIO BUSTAMANTE, rheumatologist, educator; b. Asuncion, Paraguay, Jan. 9, 1949; came to U.S., 1974; s. Emilio Gonzalez-Jovellanos and Clara (Bustamante) Gonzalez; m. Elizabeth Ferreira, Jan. 4, 1973; 1 child, Daniel. BS in Scis. and Humanities, C.A.L. Coll., Asuncion, 1972; MD summa cum laude, Nat. U., Asuncion, 1972. Diplomate Am. Bd. Internal Medicine, Am. Bd. Rheumatology, Am. Bd. Allergy and Immunology. Intern Univ. Hosp., Asuncion, 1973-74; resident Danbury (Conn.) Hosp., 1975-78; teaching fellow allergy/clin. immunology U. Pitts. Sch. Medicine/VA Med. Ctr., 1978-79; mem. staff allergy/clin. immunology Nat. Jewish Hosp. and U. Colo. Affiliated Hosps., Denver, 1979-80; mem. staff clin. immunology/rheumatology U. Tex. Med. Br., Galveston, 1980-81, clin. instr. dept. medicine, 1981-82, asst. prof. medicine, 1982-89, assoc. prof. medicine, 1989—; chief rheumatology svc. Grady Meml. Hosp./Emory U. Sch. Medicine, Atlanta, 1989—; attending physician rheumatology sect. med. svc. VA Med. Svc., Emory U., Decatur, Ga., 1989—; attending physician divsn. rheumatology Emory U. Hosp., Atlanta, 1989—; cons., part-time mem. divsn. rheumatology The Emory Clinic/Emory U., Atlanta, 1989—; bd. dirs. Arthritis Found., Ga., sci. com., 1993—; presenter in field. Contbr. numerous articles to profl. jours.; nat. manuscript reviewer jours. in field. Fellow ACP, Am. Coll. Rheumatology; mem. AMA, Am. Acad. Allergy and Immunology, Ga. Rheumatism Soc. (program chmn. 1993-94), Ga. Soc. Rheumatology (pres. 1995-96), Sigma Xi. Home: 2019 Starfire Dr NE Atlanta GA 30345-3961 Office: Emory U Dept Rheumatology 69 Butler St SE Atlanta GA 30303-3033

GONZALEZ, GERARDO MERCED, university dean; b. Placetas, Las Villas, Cuba, Sept. 24, 1950; came to U.S., 1962; s. Elio A. and Armantina (Torres) G.; m. Marjorie A. Reilly, Apr. 10, 1976; children: Justin, Jarrett, Ian, Julie. BA in Psychology, U. Fla., 1973, PhD in Counselor Edn., 1978. Nat. cert. counselor. Asst. dean, dir. U. Fla., Gainesville, 1977-86, assoc. prof., 1987-89, prof. and chmn., 1989-92, assoc. dean edn., 1992—; mem. nat. planning group Higher Edn. Prevention Ctr., Washington, 1990-96. Author: Preventing Substance Abuse in Higher Education, 1994; editor: Challenges of Cultural Diversity to Counseling, 1992; contbr. articles to profl. jours. Chmn. bd. Vista Pavilion Rehab. Hosp., Gainesville, 1990-96; mem. nat. adv. coun. Alcohol, Drug Abuse and Mental Health Adminstrn., Rockville, Md., 1987-90; mem. prevention com. Gov.'s Commn. on Drug Abuse, Tallahassee, 1984-86. Recipient Presdl. Letter of Recognition, Pres. Reagan, 1986, Cert. of Appreciation, Sec. of Health and Human Svcs., 1989, Pres.'s award Am. Coll. Pers. Assn., 1986. Mem. ACA, Assn. for Multicultural Counseling, Am. Assn. Colls. for Tchr. Edn. Home: PO Box 12126 Gainesville FL 32604 Office: Univ of Florida 140 Norman Hall Gainesville FL 32611-2053

GONZALEZ, HENRY BARBOSA, congressman; b. San Antonio, Tex., May 3, 1916; s. Leonides and Genevieve (Barbosa) G.; m. Bertha Cuellar, 1940; children: Henry B., Rosemary, Charles, Bertha, Stephen, Genevieve, Francis, Anna Marie. LLB, St. Mary's U., 1943, LLD (hon.), 1943, JD, 1967; HHD, Our Lady of Lake U., 1984; LLD (hon.), U. D.C., 1984. Formerly with father's translating co., dep. dir. San Antonio Housing Authority; chief probation officer Bexar County, 1946; exec. sec. Jr. Deps. of Am. (predecessor Pan Am. Progressive Assn.); mem. San Antonio City Coun., 1953-56, mayor pro-tem, 1955-56; state senator, 1956-61; mem. 87th-104th Congresses from 20th Tex. Dist., Washington, D.C., 1961—; chmn. bank, fin. and urban affairs com. 1989-95. Civilian cable and radio censor Army and Naval Intelligence, World War II. Recipient Philip Hart Pub. Svc. award Consumer Fedn. Am., 1993, Outstanding Govt. Svc. award Am. Fedn. Trial Lawyers, 1993, Outstanding Govt. Svc. award Am. Numismatic Assn., 1993, Amicus award ATLA, 1993, John F. Kennedy Profile in Courage award John F. Kennedy Libr. Found., 1994, Wayne Morse Integrity in Politics award Wayne Morse Hist. Park Corp., 1994. Mem. Order Mil. Med. Merit (hon.). Democrat. Office: US Ho of Reps 2413 Rayburn Bldg Washington DC 20515-0005 Home: 238 W Kings Highway San Antonio TX 78212

GONZALEZ, JOE MANUEL, lawyer; b. N.Y.C., Aug. 18, 1950; s. Reinaldo Fabregas and Mary Louise (Cermeno) G.; m. Ruia Jane Whiteside, Dec. 30, 1977; children: Matthew Ray, Jane Marie, Jeffrey Joseph, Joseph Manuel. BA, U. South Fla., 1972; JD, Gonzaga U., 1980; LLM in Taxation, Georgetown U., 1981. Bar: Fla. 1981, U.S. Tax Ct. 1983, U.S. Dist. Ct. (mid. dist.) Fla. 1984, U.S. Ct. Appeals (11th cir.) 1984, U.S. Supreme Ct. 1985. Atty. Gonzaga U. Legal Services, Spokane, Wash., 1980; mng. ptnr. Cotterill, Gonzalez, Hayes & Grantham, Fla., 1981-88, Cotterill & Grantham, Pa., 1982-92, Cotterill, Gonzalez & Grantham, Pa., Pa., 1992-93; prin. Joe M. Gonzalez, P.A., 1993—; atty. Hispanic Def. League, Tampa, Fla., 1982-90. Assoc. editor Gonzaga Law Rev. Spl. Report: Pub. Sector Labor Law, 1980. Mem. Sheriff's Hispanic Adv. Coun., Hillsborough County, Fla., 1982-93, City of Tampa Hispanic Adv. Coun., 1983-93, chmn. 1993—; chmn. citizens adv. com. Hillsborough County Planning Commn., 1988-90; pres. Tampa Hispanic Heritage, Inc., 1985-93; founder Carnavale En Tampa, Inc., 1986-90; master of ceremonies Gasparilla Sidewalk Art Festival, 1988; mem. police chief's adv. com., 1988-93; sec. Hispanic Bus. Inst. Fla., Inc., 1988-93. Mem. ABA, Fla. Bar Assn. (jud. nominating prodedures com. 1988-89), Hillsborough County Bar Assn., Assn. Trial Lawyers Am., Nat. Inst. for Trial Advocacy, Complete Census Count Com., Rotary, Phi Delta Phi. Democrat. Presbyterian. Home: 1708 W Richardson Pl Tampa FL 33606-3227 Office: 620 E Twiggs St Ste 100 Tampa FL 33602-3929

GONZALEZ, JORGE JOSE, medical educator; b. Valdivia, Chile, Aug. 13, 1945; came to U.S., 1973; s. Manuel and Emma (Clasing) G.; m. Barbara Hayworth, May 22, 1971; children: Carla Andrea, Maria Cristina. MD, U. Chile, 1971. Resident in internal medicine New Hanover Meml. Hosp., Wilmington, N.C., 1973-76; fellow in endocrinology Med. U. S.C., Charleston, 1976-78; from asst. prof. to assoc. prof. medicine U. N.C. Sch. Medicine, Chapel Hill, 1978-92, prof. medicine, 1992—; program dir. Internal Medicine Tng. Program, Wilmington, 1991. Recipient N.C. Pub. Health Assn. Adult Health Promotion Sect. Spl. commendation, 1989. Fellow Am. Coll. Clin. Endocrinology; mem. Am. Diabetes Assn., Endocrine Soc., Am. Assn. Clin. Endocrinology. Episcopalian. Home: 113 Chelsea Ln Wilmington NC 28409-8103 Office: Coastal AHEC 2131 S 17th St Wilmington NC 28401-7407

GONZALEZ, JOSE ALEJANDRO, JR., federal judge; b. Tampa, Fla., Nov. 26, 1931; s. Jose A. and Luisa Secundina (Collia) G.; m. Frances Frierson, Aug. 22, 1956 (dec. Aug. 1981); children—Margaret Ann, Mary Frances; m. Mary Sue Copeland, Sept. 24, 1983. B.A., U. Fla., 1952, J.D., 1957. Bar: Fla. 1958, U.S. Dist. Ct. (so. dist.) Fla. 1959, U.S. Ct. Appeals 1959, U.S. Supreme Ct. 1963. Practice in Ft. Lauderdale, 1958-64; claim rep. State Farm Mut., Lakeland, Fla., 1957-58; assoc. firm Watson, Hubert and Sousley, 1958-61, ptnr., 1961-64; asst. state atty. 15th Cir. Fla., 1961-64; cir. judge 17th Cir. Ft. Lauderdale, 1964-78, chief judge, 1969-70; assoc. judge 4th Dist. Ct. Appeals, West Palm Beach; U.S. dist. judge So. Dist. Fla., 1978—. Bd. dirs. Arthritis Found., 1962-72; bd. dirs. Henderson Clinic Broward County, 1964-68, v.p., 1967-68. Served to 1st lt. AUS, 1952-54. Recipient Kupferman award Laymen's Nat. Bible Assn., 1991; named Broward County Outstanding Young Man, 1967, one of Fla.'s Five Outstanding Young Men, Fla. Jaycees, 1967, Broward Legal Exec. of Yr., 1978. Mem. ABA, Am. Judicature Soc., Fed. Bar Assn., Fla. Bar Assn., Broward County Bar, Ft. Lauderdale Jaycees (dir. 1960-61), Fla. Blue Key, Sigma Chi (Significant Sig), Phi Alpha Delta. Democrat. Club: Kiwanian (pres. 1971-72). Home: 631 Intracoastal Dr Fort Lauderdale FL 33304-3618 Office: US Dist Ct 205 US Courthouse 299 E Broward Blvd Fort Lauderdale FL 33301-1944

GONZALEZ, JOSE L., pediatrician, educator; b. Havana, Cuba, July 11, 1951; s. Eugenio and Maria Angela (Rodriguez) G.; m. Caryl A. Sherman, Nov. 26, 1994. BS, U. Miami, 1972, MD, 1976. Bd. cert. Am. Bd. Pediatrics, Pediatric Endocrinology & Diabetes. Intern in pediatrics Children's Med. Ctr., Dallas, 1976-77, resident in pediatrics, 1977-79, co-chief resident in pediatrics, 1979-80; clin. and rsch. fellow in pediatric endocrinology U. Iowa Hosps. & Clinics, Iowa City, 1980-82; clin. asst. prof. pediatric endocrinology U. Tex. Health Sci. Ctr.-JPSH, Ft. Worth, 1982-87, Southwestern Med. Sch., Dallas, 1987; pvt. practice Dallas-Ft. Worth, 1982-94; asst. prof. pediatric endocrinology and diabetes U. Tex. Health Sci. Ctr.-Southwestern Med. Sch., Dallas, 1994—; chmn. instnl. rev. bd. Ft. Worth/Cooks Children's Hosp., 1984-86; cons. mem. newborn screening program Tex. Bd., 1982—; mem. Ft. Worth Genetics Adv. Com., 1983-87; mem. admissions com. U. Tex. Health Sci. Ctr. S.W., 1993—. Mem. Tarrant County Community Adv. Com., Tex. Youth Coun., 1984-87; bd. dirs. Juvenile Diabetes Found., 1990-93; mem. adv. bd, 1993—; bd. dirs. Am. Diabetes Assn., 1990-91, So. Diabetes Found., 1994—; chmn. Med. Adv. Com. to Camp Sweeney, 1990—. Fellow Am. Acad. Pediatrics, Lawson Wilkins Pediatric Endocrine Soc.; mem. Greater Dallas Pediatric Soc. (pres. 1992-93).

GONZALEZ, JOSE RAMÓN, academic administrator; b. Barranquitas, P.R., June 11, 1930; m. Rosaura Figueroa. BAEd, U. P.R., 1955, MPHE, 1957; PhD in Pub. Health and Edn., U. N.C., 1967. Tchr. Dept. Edn., P.R., 1950-57, zone health supr., 1958-59, supr. student teaching, 1960-61; coord. U. P.R., Rio Piedras, 1961-63, asst. dean sch. edn., 1963-65; assoc. v.p., v.p. acad. affairs Inter Am. U. P.R., San Juan, 1980-90; acad. adminstr., pres. Inter Am. U. P.R. Ctr. Office, San Juan, 1990—; cons. various pub. and pvt. schs., P.R., U. P.R.; organizer 1st Congress Higher Edn. P.R. Editor, contbg. author: Options for the Development of Higher Education; contbr. articles to profl. jours. Pres. Com. Ann. Conf. Gen. Edn. Mem. ASCD,

Assn. Student Teaching, Pub. Health Assn., Am. Assn. Higher Edn., Am. Assn. Colls., Phi Delta Kappa. Office: Inter Am U PR Ctr Office Office of the Pres PO Box 363255 San Juan PR 00936-3255*

GONZALEZ, JUAN (ALBERTO VAZQUEZ), professional baseball player; b. Vega Baja, Puerto Rico, Oct. 16, 1969. Outfielder Tex. Rangers, 1986—. Named Am. Assn. MVP, 1990; named to Am. League Silver Slugger Team, 1992-93, Sporting News Am. League All-Star team, 1993. Office: Tex Rangers 1000 Ballpark Way Arlington TX 76011-5168*

GONZALEZ, MARIA ELENA, SR., religious organization executive. Pres. Instituto de Liturgia Hispana.

GONZALEZ, MICHAEL JOHN, nutrition educator, nutriologist; b. N.Y.C., July 5, 1962; s. R. Miguel and Daisy (Guzman) G.; m. Enid J. Bauza, Mar. 28, 1987; children: Michael John Jr., Michael Joseph. BS in Biology, Cath. U., 1983; MS in Cell Biology, Nova Coll., 1985; MNS in Nutrition and Biochemistry, U. P.R., 1986; NMD in Nutrition, John F Kennedy, 1988; DSc in Health Sci, Lafayette U., 1989; PhD in Tumor Biology, Mich. State U., 1993; postgrad. in geriatrics, U. P.R., 1993-95. Rsch. asst. dept. chemistry Cath. U., Ponce, P.R., 1982-83; lab. instr. dept. biology U. P.R., Mayaguez, 1983-85; rsch. asst. dept. biochemistry U. P.R., Rio Piedras, 1985-86; mem. dept. biology faculty Cath. U., Ponce, 1986-87; rsch. asst. dept. human nutrition Mich. State U., East Lansing, 1987-90; sci. instr. dept. Upward Bound, 1990-91, lab. instr., rsch. asst. dept. food sci. and pharmacology, 1991-93; asst. prof. U. P.R. Med. Sci., San Juan, 1993-96, assoc. prof., 1996—; mem. faculty Sch. Pub. Health U. P.R. Med. Scis., 1989-93. Reviewer, contbr. articles to profl. jours. Fellow Am. Nutritional Med. Assn. (v.p. 1991—); mem. Am. Inst. Nutrition, Am. Assn. Cancer Rsch., Soc. for Exptl. Biology, N.Y. Acad. Sci., Am. Assn. Police, United Farmers. Democrat. Roman Catholic. Office: Univ PR Med Sci Sch of Pub Health B-456 GPO Box 365067 San Juan PR 00936

GONZALEZ, PATRICIA, television news reporter; b. Miami, Fla., Sept. 17, 1972; d. Pedro and Silvia (Noa) Hurtado de Mendoza; m. Joaquin Fernando Gonzalez, Dec. 17, 1994. BS in Telecomm., U. Fla., 1992. Reporter, anchor, prodr. Sta. WRUF-AM & FM, Gainesville, Fla., 1991-92; reporter, anchor Sta. WUFT-TV, Gainesville, Fla., 1991-92; reporter Sta. WLTV-TV, Miami, 1993-94; reporter, fill-in anchor Sta. WSCV-TV, Miami, 1994—. Mem. NATAS, Soc. Profl. Journalists, Investigative Reporters and Editors, Nat. Assn. of Hispanic Journalists, Radio-Television News Dir. Assn. Roman Catholic. Office: WSCV 2340 W 8 Ave Miami FL 33012

GONZALEZ, RAQUEL MARIA, pharmacist; b. Veguitas, Oriente, Cuba, June 1, 1952; d. Ernesto Esteban and Evora Cristina (Ramirez) G. BS in Biology, Ga. Coll., 1974; BS in Pharmacy, Mercer U., 1977. Registered pharmacist, Ga., Fla., Tenn.; registered pharmacist cons., Fla. Staff pharmacist Cobb Gen. Hosp., Austell, Ga., 1978; staff pharmacist VA Hosp., Nashville, 1978-79, Decatur, Ga., 1979-81; staff pharmacist Lewisburg (Tenn.) Community Hosp., 1981-89; pharmacist Pharmacy Staffing Svcs. Inc., Brentwood, Tenn., 1989—; chief pharmacist Super D Drug Store # 50, Fayetteville, Tenn., 1989-93; chief of pharmacy Fred's Discount Pharmacy, Lewisburg, Tenn., 1993—; relief pharmacist Farmer's Market Pharmacy (Kroger), Nashville, 1989—. Mem. Ducks Unltd. Republican. Roman Catholic. Club: Atlanta Ski. Home: RR 1 Box 35 Belfast TN 37019-9801 Office: Pharmacy Staffing Svcs Inc 1413 Bowman Ln Brentwood TN 37027-6922 Office: Fred's Discount Pharmacy 1800 Mooresville Hwy Lewisburg TN 37091-2010

GONZALEZ, RAUL A., state supreme court justice; b. Weslaco, Tex., Mar. 22, 1940; s. Raul G. and Paula (Hernandez) G.; m. Dora Blanca Champion, Dec. 22, 1963; children—Celeste, Jaime, Marco, Sonia. BA in Govt., U. Tex., Austin, 1963; JD, U. Houston, 1966; LLM, U. Va., 1986. Bar: Tex. 1966. Asst. U.S. atty. U.S. Dist. Ct. (so. dist.) Tex., Brownsville, 1969-73; atty. Gonzalez & Hamilton, Brownsville, 1973-78; judge 103d Dist. Ct. Tex., Brownsville, 1978-81, U.S. Dist. Ct. Appeals (13th cir.), Corpus Christi, Tex., 1981-84; justice Tex. Supreme Ct., Austin, 1984—. Bd. dirs. Brownsville Boy's Club, Brownsville Community Devel. Corp., So. Tex. Rehab. Ind. Sch. Dist.; U.S. Recipient Outstanding Performance Rating award Dept. Justice, 1972, Toll fellow, 1987. Mem. Christian Legal Soc., Christian Conciliation Service, ABA, Tex. Bar Found. Lodge: Rotary. Home: 2300 Pebble Beach Dr Austin TX 78747-1615 Office: Tex Supreme Ct Capitol Sta PO Box 12248 201 W 14th St Austin TX 78711-2248*

GONZALEZ, RICHARD THEODORE, photographer; b. Trona, Calif., Nov. 9, 1939; s. Alfonso Contreras and Mary (Duarte) G.; m. Gerry Price, Oct. 30, 1958 (div. 1972); children: Richard K., Debra G., Maria E., Felicia F.; m. Yolanda Quijano, Apr. 18, 1991; 1 child, Andrea. Degree in profl. still photography, N.Y. Inst. Photography, 1962. Photographer Kerr McGee Chem. Corp., Trona, 1962-86, San Bernadino, Calif., 1987-89; founder Gonzalez's Modeling Agy., Midwest City, Okla., 1996—; newspaper photographer Trona Argonaut, 1962-86; freelance photographer, Trona, 1962-86. Democrat. Roman Catholic. Home: 769 NW 1st St Moore OK 73160 Office: Ste D-366 700 S Air Depot Blvd Midwest City OK 73110-4833

GONZALEZ, ROLANDO NOEL, secondary school educator, religion educator, photographer; b. Rio Grande City, Tex., Sept. 10, 1947; s. Ubaldo and Beulah (Gutierrez) G. BA, U. Tex., 1968; MA, Tex. A & I U., 1972. Cert. tchr. all scis., guidance and counseling. Tchr., head sci. dept. Roma (Tex.) Jr. High Sch., 1968-71; migrant/Title I counselor Roma Elem. and Roma Jr. High Sch., 1972-76; head sci. dept. Rio Grande High Sch., Rio Grande City, Tex., 1976-78; tchr., head sci. dept. Ringgold Jr. High Sch., Rio Grande City, 1982-83, Pharr-San Juan-Alamo High Sch., Pharr, Tex., 1986—; seminarian Diocese of Brownsville, San Antonio, 1979-82; pastoral asst. Our Lady, Queen of Angels Ch., La Joya, Tex., 1982-83; coord., lay ministries Brownsville Diocese, McAllen, Tex., 1983-85; lectr., tchr. on scripture Perpetual Help Ch., McAllen, 1986-88, Holy Spirit Ch., McAllen, 1989—; scripture tchr., lectr. St. Mary Margaret Ch., Pharr, 1988; instr. history of chemistry U. Tex.-Pan Am., Edinburg, 1990; wedding and portrait photographer, 1973—. Contbr. articles to profl. jours. tchr. scripture, lectr. Sts. Mary and Margaret Ch., Pharr, 1988, Sacred Heart Ch., Mercedes, Tex., 1990. Recipient Appreciation award Sacred Heart Ch., 1990. Home: 2800 W Iris Ave Mcallen TX 78501-6200

GONZALEZ, ROSEMARY MASSEY, library media specialist; b. Orrville, Ala., Sept. 16, 1937; s. Edgar Pearson and Lillian Pearl (Stone) M.; m. Rene David Gonzalez, Aug. 23, 1958 (div. Aug. 16, 11988); children: Marina Hardin, Anna Rose, Michael, Gregory. BS in Libr. Sci., U. So. Miss., 1972, MLS, 1977. English tchr. Bristol Va. Sch., 1958-59, Cedartown (Ga.) Georgis Schs., 1959-60; libr. media specialist Miss. Dept. Human Svcs. Div. Youth Svcs., Columbia, 1969—. Reporter Columbia Jaycees, 2d v.p., 1963, 1st v.p., 1964-65, pres., 1966; v.p. Picayune Jaycees, 1967; pres. Hist. Culture Club, 1966; reporter, v.p. Fine Arts Club, 1970-79; active Girl Scouts Am., Boy Scouts Am., 1968-81, Columbia Sch. Sys. Parents groups, 1967-81, Holy Trinity Cath. Ch., 1993-94, mem. parish group, 1993-94, sec. parish coun., 1994—. Mem. Miss Libr. Assn., U. So. Miss. Libr. Sci. Alumni, State Employees Miss. Orgn. (sec.), Miss. Bus. and Profl. Women (dist. I dir., state nominations chair 1992-93, nat. conv. chair 1993-94, 95-96, 96-97, expansion chair 1994—), Columbia Bus. and Profl. Women (pres. 1990-91, pres. elect 1988-90, 94—, rec. sec. 1989-90, 96-97), U. So. Miss. Alumni Assn., Miss. Bus. and Profl. Women, U. So. Miss. Spirit Alumni Assn., Phi Mu Alumni Assn. (Hattiesburg area chpt.), Beta Sigma Phi. Home: 1704 Ridgewood Dr Columbia MS 39429-2640 Office: Miss Dept Human Svcs Columbia Campus 1730 Highway 44 Columbia MS 39429-9709

GONZALEZ-MOLINA, GABRIEL, research center executive; b. Teziutlan, Puebla, Mex., May 12, 1958; came to U.S., 1990; s. Ignacio and Josefina (Molina) G.; m. Belinda Acosta; children: Gabriel, Jose-Ignacio. BA, Iberoamericana U., Mexico City, 1982; MA in Comm. Rsch., Leicester (U.K.) U., 1983, PhD, 1990. Rsch. dir. U. of the Americas, Mex., 1985-90; dir. Hispanic studies The Gallup Orgn., Lincoln, Nebr., 1990-92; dir. World Hispanic Rsch. Ctr., The Gallup Orgn., Lincoln, 1992-93; pres. Latin Am. divsn. The Gallup Orgn., Lincoln, 1993. Corr. editor Media, Culture and Society, 1983-89; contbr. articles to jours. in Spain, Mex., Peru, Colombia, Ecuador, U.S. and U.K. Recipient Overseas Rsch. award Com. Vice Chancellors and Prins. Univs. and Colls. United Kingdom, 1983, 84. Mem. U.S. Hispanic C. of C. Office: Gallup Orgn 7205 NW 19th St Ste 302 Miami FL 33126-1229

GONZALEZ-PITA, J. ALBERTO, lawyer; b. Havana, Cuba, Aug. 20, 1954; came to U.S., 1960; s. Benigno Jesus and Maria Modesta (Diaz) G.P.; m. Suzanne J. Martin, Apr. 7, 1984; children: Roberto Martin, Antonio Martin. AA, Miami-Dade Community Coll., 1973; BA, U. Miami, 1974; JD, Boston U., 1977. Bar: Fla. 1977, U.S. Dist. Ct. (so. dist.) Fla. 1977, U.S. Ct. Appeals (5th cir.) 1977, U.S. Ct. Appeals (11th cir.) 1981. Assoc. Walton, Lantaff, Schroeder & Carson, Miami, Fla., 1977-80; assoc. Patton & Kanner, Miami, 1980-82, ptnr., 1982-86, mng. ptnr., 1986-89; ptnr. McDermott, Will & Emery, Miami, 1989-91, White & Case, Miami, 1991—; chair Worldwide Privatization Practice Group; co-chair Latin Am. Practice Group. Mem. Acad. for Community Edn., Miami, 1980-90; bd. dirs. Inst. Innovative Intervention, Miami, 1980-90; trustee St. Thomas U., Miami, 1991-96. Mem. ABA, Internat. Bar Assn., Inter-Am. Bar Assn., Internationale des Avocats, Cuban-Am. Bar Assn., Maritime Law Assn. U.S. Roman Catholic. Club: Miami. Office: White & Case 200 S Biscayne Blvd Ste 4900 Miami FL 33131-2310

GONZALEZ-VALES, LUIS ERNESTO, historian, educational administrator; b. Rio Piedras, P.R., May 11, 1930; s. Ernesto and Carmen (Vales) G.; B.A. with honors, U. P.R., 1952; M.A., Columbia U., 1957; doctorate (hon.) Pontifical Catholic U. P.R., 1995; m. Hilda González, July 16, 1952; children—Carmen L., Luis E., Antonio S., Maria G., Rosa Maria, Gerardo, Rosario, Hildita. Instr. humanities U. P.R., Rió Piedras, 1955-58, asst. prof. humanities, 1958-64, asso. prof. humanities, 1964-67, asso. prof. history, 1967, prof. history, 1983, asst. dean faculty gen. studies, 1960-65, asso. dean faculty gen. studies, 1965-67. Author: Gabriel Gutierrez de Riva: Albores del Sigle XVIII en Puerto Rico, 1990. Dir. P.R. Acad. History, 1992—; exec. sec. Council on Higher Edn., 1967-83; exec. sec. Commonwealth Post Secondary Commn., 1973-83; chancellor P.R. Jr. Coll., 1985-87; bd. dirs Inst. Puerto Rican Culture; mem. Collegiate Ednl. adv. panel Cadet Command, U.S. Army, 1986—. Served to 2d. lt. inf. U.S. Army, 1952-55, adj. gen. P.R. N.G., 1983-85, ret. maj. gen. U.S. Army, 1990. Mem. Am. Hist. Assn., Acad. Polit. Scis., P.R. Acad. History, Am. Acad. Polit. and Social Scis., Latin Am. Studies Assn., Assn. U.S. Army, N.G. Assn., Mil. Order World Wars, Res. Officers Assn., P.R. Acad. of Arts and Scis. Phi Alpha Theta (pres. 1962-63). Roman Catholic. Author: Alejandro Ramirez: La Vida de un Intendente Liberal, 1972; contbg. author: Puerto Rico: A Political and Cultural History, 1983; contbr. articles on Puerto Rican history (in Spanish) to hist. jours.; editorial bd. Revista Historia, 1960-67.

GOOCH, CAROL ANN, psychotherapist consultant; b. Meridian, Miss., Apr. 17, 1950; d. James Tackett and Chris M. Page; (div.); 1 child, Aaron Patrick Gooch. BS, Fla. State U., 1972, DS, 1975; MS, Troy State U., 1974. Lic. profl. counselor, Tex.; lic. chem. dependency counselor, Tex.; lic. marriage and family therapist, Tex.; cert. chem. dependency specialist, Tex.; cert. compulsive gambling counselor, Tex. Tchr. Okaloosa Sch. Dist., Fort Walton, Fla., 1972-77; counselor USAF, Osan AFB, Korea, 1977-79; sch. counselor Tomball (Tex.) Sch. Dist., 1983-90; cons. Montgomery (Tex.) Sch. Dist., 1992—; psychotherapist pvt. practice, Houston, 1990—; cons. school systems, Houston, 1990—; coord. sr. program Forest Springs Hosp., Houston, 1993—, Cypress Creek Hosp., 1994—. Vol. cons. PTO, Woodlands, Tex., 1990. Recipient fellowship Fla. State U., Tallahassee, 1973, Nat. Disting. Svc. award Ex Coun. U.S. Pubs., N.J., 1989; named Outstanding High Sch. Counselor, Tomball Ind. Sch. Dist., 1989. Mem. AAUW, ACA, ASCD, Tex. Sch. Counselors Assn., Am. Mental Health Counselors Assn., Tex. Mental Health Counselors Assn., Am. Bus. Women's Assn., Fla. State U. Alumni Assn., Kappa Delta Pi. Home and Office: Carol A Gooch MS LPC PO Box 1308 Montgomery TX 77356

GOOD, GREGORY ALAN, science history educator; b. Latrobe, Pa., May 18, 1952; s. Albert Harry and Hildegard Rosemary (Stauffer) G.; m. Lynn Beverly Sobolov, Sept. 9, 1956; children: Colleen, Anna. BS in Physics, St. Vincent Coll., 1974; MA in History of Sci., U. Toronto, 1976, PhD in History of Sci., 1982. Lectr. U. Winnipeg, Man., Can., 1979-80; asst. prof. W.Va. U., Morgantown, 1983-89, assoc. prof., 1989—. Editor: The Earth, the Heavens and the Carnegie Institution of Washington, 1994, History of the Geosciences: An Encyclopedia, 1996. Mem. exec. com. W.Va. Sierra Club, 1985-88, tng. cons., 1985-88, outings chair, 1988-90. Post-doctoral fellow Smithsonian Inst., Washington, 1982, Fgn. Rsch. fellow Humboldt Stiftung, Hamburg, Germany, 1990-91; Rsch. grantee NSF, 1987-88. Mem. Can. Sci. and Tech. Hist. Assn., History of Sci. Soc., History of Earth Scis. Soc., Am. Soc. for Environ. History, Arbeitskreis Geschichte Geophysik, Forest History Soc., Monongalela Group (chair S.C. 1995-96), Sigma Xi (treas. W.Va. U. 1995-96, v.p. 1996-97). Democrat. Office: WVa U PO Box 6303 Morgantown WV 26506-6303

GOOD, RAPHAEL S., psychiatrist, obstetrician, gynecologist; b. Phila., July 5, 1921; s. Herman and Esther (Wergeles) G.; m. Eleanor Ackerman, Oct. 31, 1943 (dec. Jan. 1975); children: Heidi Hancock, Bonnie; m. Sharon Ann Killeen, Mar. 1, 1981. MD, SUNY, Buffalo, 1948. Diplomate Am. Bd. Psychiatry and Neurology, Am. Bd. Ob-Gyn., Nat. Bd. Med. Examiners. Intern Millard Fillmore Hosp., Buffalo, N.Y., 1948-49; resident in ob-gyn. Millard Fillmore Hosp., Buffalo, 1949-50; resident in ob-gyn. Fordham Hosp., N.Y.C., 1952-53, chief resident in ob-gyn., 1953-54; pvt. practice Hialeah, Fla., 1957-71, So. Miami, 1989-92; Boca Raton, Fla., 1992-95; pvt. practice Coconut Grove, Fla., 1995—; resident in psychiatry U. Miami/Jackson Meml. Med. Ctr., 1971-74; clin. instr. ob-gyn U. Miami Sch. Medicine, 1957-62, clin. asst. prof. ob-gyn., 1962-69, clin. assoc. prof. ob-gyn., 1970-74, asst. prof. psychiatry and ob-gyn., 1974-78, assoc. prof. psychiatry and ob-gyn., 1979-81, prof. clin. psychiatry and ob-gyn., 1987-89, clin. prof. psychiatry and ob-gyn., 1989—, dir. continuing profl. edn. dept. psychiatry, 1987-89; assoc. prof. psychiatry and ob-gyn. med. br. U. Tex., Galveston, 1981-84, prof. clin. psychiatry and ob-gyn., 1984-86, vice chmn. dept. psychiatry and behavioral scis., 1981-86; chief ob-gyn. Hialeah Hosp., 1959-61; editl. reviewer Am. Jour. Psychiatry, Jour. Nervour and Mental Diseases, Ob-Gyn., Psychosomatics, Contemporary Ob-Gyn., Jour. Psychosomatics Ob-Gyn.; dir. psychiat. consultation-liaison svc. U. Miami, Jackson Meml. Med. Ctr., 1974-81, acting dir., 1989, rsch. scientist Comprehensive Cancer Ctr., 1975-81; ad hoc site visit com. chmn. Nat. Cancer Inst., 1980, ad hoc rev. com. for grant proposals, 1980, 88; mem., chmn. various coms. med. br. U. Tex., 1981-86, mem. task force group practice med. sch., mem. patient care mgmt. team dept. psychiatry and behavioral scis.; mem. various coms. sch. medicine U. Miami, mem. task force departmental goals and objectives dept. psychiatry; presenter in field. Author: (with others) Frontiers of Radiation Therapy and Oncology, 1980, Controversy in Obstetrics and Gynecology III, 3d edit., 1983, Psychosomatic Obstetrics and Gynecology, Gynecology and Obstetrics, 1987; mem. editl. bd. Jour. Reproductive and Infant Psychology; contbr. articles to profl. jours. Mem. Dade-Monroe Profl. Stds. Rev. Orgn., 1979-81, trustee, 1981, quality assurance com., 1981, confidentiality com., 1981, nominating com., 1980; mem. med. adv. com. South Fla. chpt. National Found., March of Dimes, 1975-81; mem. psychiatry com. Cancer and Acute Leukemia Group B, 1976-80; cons. for reproductive issues ACLU. Maj. USAF, 1950-52, 54-57. Grantee NIMH, 1983-86, 81-86, 76-81, Nat. Cancer Inst., 1973-76. Fellow Am. Psychiat. Assn. (mem. task force family planning and population 1973-75, chmn. sub-com. fgn. guests and invited speakers ann. meeting 1976, mem. host com. ann. meeting 1976, mem. planning com. inst. hosp. and community psychiatry 1986, 87, mem. adv. panel panic disorders 1989), Am. Coll. Ob-Gyn. (mem. com. psychosomatics 1972-77), Miami Obstet. and Gynecol. Soc. (life, mem. exec. com. 1968-70, 72-75, treas. 1968-70, v.p. 1972-73, pres. 1973-74, mem. nominating com. 1974-81, 86—); mem. AMA, Am. Soc. for Psychosomatic Ob-Gyn. (mem. exec. com. 1974-81, mem. program com. ann. meeting 1974-78, chmn. 1979, pres. elect 1979, pres. 1980, chmn. exec. com. 1980, mem. nominating com. 1981), Am. Assn. Sex Educators, Counselors and Therapists (mem. exec. com. 1974-80, nat. v.p. 1978-80, exec. com. 1975-80, chmn. S.E. dist. 1976-77, mem. long-range planning com. 1980, mem. nominating com. 1983), Fla. Obstet. and Gynecol. Soc. (life), South Fla. Psychiat. Soc. (mem., chmn. various coms., v.p. 1988, dep. rep. area V coun. and assembly dist. brs. 1989, pres.-elect 1990-91, pres. 1991-92), Internat. Soc. Psychosomatic Ob-Gyn. (exec. bd. dirs. 1985-88), Soc. for Reproductive and Infant Psychology (mem. adv. bd. 1985—), Tex. Psychiat. Soc. (mem. continuing med. edn. com. 1982-86, mem. program com. 1982-86, ann. symposium chmn. 1986), Titus Harris Psychiat. Soc. (program com. chmn. 1986), William A. Little Obstet. and Gynecol. Soc. (mem. program com. 1981, mem. exec. com. 1987—, bd. dirs. 1986—, pres.-elect 1993, pres. 1994—), Mental Health Assn. Dade County Fla. (mem. new mom's com. 1974-81, mem. prevention com. 1976-81). Office: 2980 Mcfarland Rd Ste 203 Coconut Grove FL 33133-6030

GOOD, STEWART EARL, accountant; b. Kitchner, Ont., Aug. 27, 1943; came to the U.S., 1968; s. Mevin and Carrie (Reist) G.; m. Linda Jane Good, Apr. 19, 1991. BS in Acctg., Bob Jones Coll., 1972; MBA, Furman U., 1976. CPA. Tchr. Rutledge Coll., Greenville, S.C., 1972-79; auditor Liberty Life, Greenville, 1979-84; asst. prof. Liberty U., Lynchburg, Va., 1984-89; stockholder Good & Mather, Greenville, 1989-94; loan originator Norwest Mortgage Inc., Greenville, 1994—. Office: Norwest Mortgage Inc 530 Howell Rd Ste 207B Greenville SC 29615-2044

GOODBRED, RAY EDWARD, artist, educator; b. Bklyn., Dec. 7, 1929; s. Edward Stone and Rose Raymond (White) G.; m. Barbara Jean Zorn, Oct. 29, 1977. Student, Am. Art Sch.; ASL, NYU; student, Nat. Acad. Sch. Fine Arts. Freelance artist Charleston, S.C., 1961—; instr. art Hastle Sch. Art, Charleston, S.C., 1961-63, Art Students League N.Y., N.Y.C., 1975-81. Illustrator Omni Mag. (collectors edit.), 1979; painter of portraits, figures and still lifes. With USNR, 1951-53. Recipient medal of merit Knickerbocker ARtists, N.Y.C., 1979. Mem. Pastel Soc. Am. (Trump award 1st prize 1978, McCowan Tuttle 1st prize 1979), Charleston Artists Guild, Salmagundi Club N.Y.C. (1st prize 1978). Republican. Episcopalian. Home and office: 85 Montagu St # D-2 Charleston SC 29401-1236

GOODE, CONSTANCE LOPER, elementary school assistant principal; b. Camden, N.J., Dec. 8, 1950; d. Joseph R. and Cora F. (Loper) Stallings; m. Thomas L. Goode, Mar. 24, 1973; children: Bryan Thomas, James Robert. BS, Duquesne U., 1973; MEd, Coll. William and Mary, 1989; EdS in Adminstrn. and Supervision, George Washington U., 1996. Cert. elem. tchr., Va. Tchr. spl. edn. Las Cruces (N.Mex.) Pub. schs., 1973-74; elem. tchr. Va., 1974-89; elem. counselor Newport News (Va.) Pub. Schs., 1989-91, staff devel. coord., 1991-95; asst. prin. Carver Elem. Sch., Newport News, 1995—. Recipient outstanding svc. award; scholar Mennon Co. Mem. NEA, Va. Edn. Assn., Newport News Edn. Assn. (past pres.), Newport News Reading Coun., Sigma Lambda Delta, Delta Kappa Gamma. Home: 112 Hilda Cir Hampton VA 23666-4723 Office: Carver Elem Sch 6160 Jefferson Ave Newport News VA 23605

GOODE, DAVID RONALD, transportation company executive; b. Vinton, Va., Jan. 13, 1941; s. Otto and Hessie M. (Maxey) G.; m. Susan Skiles, June 22, 1963; children: Christina, Martha. AB, Duke U., 1962; JD, Harvard U., 1965. Bar: Va. 1965. Tax atty. Norfolk & Western Ry., Roanoke, Va., 1965-66, asst. gen. tax atty., 1967, gen. tax atty., 1968-70, dir. taxation, 1971-81; asst. v.p. taxation Norfolk So. Corp., Roanoke, 1982-85, v.p. taxation, 1985-91, exec. v.p. adminstrn., 1991, pres., 1991-92, chmn., pres., CEO, dir., 1992—; bd. dirs. Assn. Am. R.R., Bus. Com. for Arts Caterpillar, Inc., C. of C. of U.S.A., Ga.-Pacific Corp., Tex. Instruments, Inc., TRINOVA Corp., Va. Econ. Devel. Partnership. Bd. trustees Gen. Douglas MacArthur Meml. Found., Hollins Coll., Va. Faound. Ind. Colls.; bd. visitors Fuqua Sch. Bus., Duke U.; mem. Am. Soc. Corp. Execs., Bus. Roundtable, Nat. Freight Transp. Assn., Nat. Grain Car Coun., Norfolk Mil./Civilian Liaison Group, Transp. Rsch. Bd. Exec. Com., Va. Bus. Coun., Va. Bus. Higher Edn. Coun.; bus. adv. coun. Northwestern U.; Coal Industry Adv. Bd., Gov.'s adv. coun. on Revenue Estimates; vice chmn. Kennedy Ctr. Corp. Fund. Bd. Mem. ABA, Va. Bar Assn., Roanoke Bar Assn., Norfolk Bar Assn., Bayville Golf Club, Harbor Club, Hunting Hills Country Club, Laurel Valley Golf Club, The Links, Met. Club, Norfolk Yacht and Country Club, Shenandoah Club, Town Point Club, Virginian Golf Club. Democrat. Presbyterian. Home: 7301 Woodway Ln Norfolk VA 23505-3149 Office: Norfolk So Corp 3 Commercial Pl Norfolk VA 23510-2191*

GOODE, JEAN-VENABLE R. (KELLY), pharmacy educator; b. Roanoke, Va., July 4, 1964; d. Robert Hundley and Jean (Glasgow) Robertson; m. William Bagwell Goode IV, May 8, 1993. BS in Agrl. Econs., Va. Poly. Inst. and State U., 1986; BS in Pharmacy, Med. Coll. Va./Va. Commonwealth U., 1989; PharmD, MCV/VCU, 1994. Lic. pharmacist, Va.; cert. pharmacotherapy specialist, Bd. Pharm. Specialties. Staff pharmacist Peoples Drug Stores, Richmond, Va., 1989; staff pharmacist MCV Hosps., Richmond, 1989-92, 93-94, supr. ambulatory care, 1994-96; clin. instr. pharmacy Sch. Pharmacy, MCV/VCU, Richmond, 1994-96, asst. prof., 1996—; cons. pharmacist Manor Care Imperial, Richmond, 1995—; cons. Heritage Info. Sys., Inc., Richmond, 1994—. Vol. Am. Heart Assn., 1994, 96; mem. Va. Hist. Soc., 1996, Va. Mus. Fine Arts, 1990—. Breast cancer screening fellow Am. Cancer Soc., 1993. Mem. Am. Coll. Clin. Pharmacy, Am. Soc. Cons. Pharmacists, Am. Soc. Health Sys. Pharmacists, Am. Pharm. Assn., Va. Pharmacists Assn., Va. Soc. Hosp. Pharmacists (sec. treas. region IV 1995—), Rho Chi. Republican. Home: 5118 Caledonia Rd Richmond VA 23225 Office: MCV/VCU Sch Pharmacy PO Box 980533 Richmond VA 23298

GOODE-HADDOCK, CELIA ROSS, title company executive; b. Bryan, Tex., May 22, 1950; d. Phillip Barron and Sara June (Council) Goode; m. Wallace Leonard Williams, Jan. 13, 1968 (div. 1969); 1 child, Quinn Williams; m. Robert Sherman Stallings, Aug. 19, 1972 (div. 1986); children: Ashley, Leigh; m. Billy Dan Haddock, Dec. 11, 1994. BS, Tex. A&M U., 1972. Sec. Univ. Title Co., College Station, Tex., 1972-77; mgr. Univ. Title Co., 1977-83; pres., 1983—; adv. com. Ticor Title Ins., Dallas, 1988-90; mem. adv. com. for continuing edn. State Bd. Ins., Austin, 1989-91; bd. dirs. Pvt. Enterprise Rsch. Ctr., Tex. A&M U. Election judge Brazos County, Tex., 1983—; mem. loan com. Community Devel. Loan Com., College Station, 1988-91; commr. Brazos County Ctrl. Appraisal Dist., 1985-95; mem. adv. com. Congressman Joe Barton, 1987-92; bd. dirs. Humana Hosp. of Brazos Valley, 1988-91, Tex. A&M U. Pvt. Enterprise Rsch. Ctr., 1996—; bd. dirs. Columbia Hosp. Brazos Valley, 1994-96, vice chmn. bd., 1996; pres. Brazos Valley Devel. Coun. Revolving Loan Fund; bd. dirs., publicity chmn. Family Outreach, 1988-90; pres. bd. trustees Christ Meth. Ch., 1996—; vol. Sta. KAMU-TV, 1979—, active in past numerous civic and polit. orgns.; mem. Operation Child Save Task Force, 1990-92; divsn. leader Brazos County United Way, others. Winner 1994-95 of Bryan Rotary Club Newman 10 award. Mem. Tex. Land Title Assn. (legis. chmn. 1990—, Outstanding Young title Person 1982), Bryan/College Station Bd. Realtors (Affiliate of Yr. 1985), Bryan College Station Homebuilders Assn., Bryan/College Station C. of C. (v.p. for leadership 1994—), Tex. A&M/Bryan College Station Coun Bd., Opera and Performing Arts Guild (chmn.), Leadership Brazos Alumni Assn. (Outstanding Alumni award for Leadership 1996). Methodist. Office: Univ Title Co 1021 University Dr E College Station TX 77840-2120

GOODEN, BENNY L., school system administrator. Supt. Ft. Smith (Ark.) Pub. Schs. State finalist Nat. Supt. Yr. award, 1993. Office: Ft Smith Pub Schs 3205 Jenny Lind Rd Fort Smith AR 72901-7101

GOODEN, PAMELA JOYCE, lawyer; b. Tuscaloosa, Ala., Nov. 21, 1954; d. Robert Joseph and Betty Jo (Bullock) G.; m. Johnnie Wade Hope, Apr. 26, 1980 (div. Feb. 1984); m. James Douglas Cook, Aug. 3, 1985; children: Cullen, Connor. BA, Judson Coll., 1975; JD, U. Ala., 1978. Bar: Ala. 1978, U.S. Dist. Ct. (mid. dist.) Ala. 1980, U.S. Ct. Appeals (11th cir.) 1993. Staff atty. Legal Svcs. of Ala., Montgomery, 1978-80; assoc. Segrest & Pilgrim, Montgomery, 1980-82; ptnr. Pilgrim & Gooden, Montgomery, 1983-92; pvt. practice Montgomery, 1992—. Mem. ABA, Ala. Bar Assn., Ala. Young Lawyers Assn. (exec. com. 1984-85), Montgomery Young Lawyers Assn. (pres. 1984), Am. Legion (judge state oratorial contest Montgomery chpt. 1986-90), Soroptimist Internat. (2d v.p. 1981-82, 1st v.p. 1984-85, pres. 1985-86, corr. sec. 1989-90). Baptist. Home: 2443 Belcher Dr Montgomery AL 36111-2147 Office: Pamela J Gooden Atty at Law 1138 S Mcdonough St Montgomery AL 36104-5044

GOODGAME, GORDON CLIFTON, minister; b. Jones County, Miss., Oct. 8, 1934; s. J. Clyde and Eloise Hertha (Smith) G.; m. Dianne Fraser, July 29, 1961; children: Gordon Clifton Jr., Gregory Carson, Cathey. BS in Law and Bus., U. Tenn., 1955; MDiv, Emory U., 1958; STM, San Francisco Theol. Sem., 1970, STD, 1974. Sr. min. 1st United Meth. Ch., Pulaski, Va., 1973-74; leader devel. cons. Holston Conf. Coun. Ministries, Johnson City,

Tenn., 1974-77; sr. min. 1st United Meth. Ch., Oak Ridge, Tenn., 1977-81, 1st-Centenary United Meth. Ch., Chattanooga, 1981-90; dir. Holston Conf. Coun. Ministries, Johnson City, 1990-93; exec. dir. Southeastern Jurisdictional Adminstrv. Coun., Lake Junaluska, N.C., 1994—; del. United Meth. Gen. Conf., 1976, 80, 84, 88, 92, 96, Southeastern Jurisdictional Conf., United Meth. Ch., 1972, 76, 80, 84, 88, 92, 96; dir. United Meth. Bd. Global Ministries, N.Y.C., 1980-88; mem. World Meth. Coun., 1986—; mem. United Meth. Gen. Coun. Ministries, 1992—. Bd. dirs. Chattanooga United Way, 1983-89, Hospice Chattanooga, 1982-90; trustee Hiwassee Coll., Madisonville, Tenn., 1979—, pres. bd. trustees; trustee Meth. Med. Ctr. Oak Ridge, 1977-81; mem. United Meth. Gen. Coun. on Ministries, 1992—. Mem. Emory U. Alumni Assn. (bd. govs.), Candler Sch. Theology Alumni Assn. (pres., Svc. award 1992), Rotary (sgt. at arms 1989-90). Democrat. Home: 11-4 Tri Vista Villas Lake Junaluska NC 38740 Office: SEJ Adminstrv Coun PO Box 67 Lake Junaluska NC 28745-0067

GOODING, LELA MOORE, language educator, department chairman; b. St. Patrick's, Grenada, May 24, 1944; s. Raymond Clarence P. Moore and Rolda A. Coomasingh; m. Earl N.M. Gooding, Aug. 22, 1965; children: Earl Gooding Jr., Ndala Gooding Booker. PhD in English, Vanderbilt U. Instr. English Oakwood Coll., Huntsville, Ala., 1972-76, asst. prof. English, 1976-89, assoc. prof. English, 1989-93, chair dept. English and comms., 1992—, prof. English, 1993—. Author: (drama) No More a Stranger, 1993. Mem. Assn. Supervision and Curriculum Devel., Assn. Depts. of English, Nat. Coun. Tchrs. English. Mem. SDA Ch. Home: 3528 Nathalee Ave Huntsville AL 35810 Office: Oakwood Coll Dept English and Comms Huntsville AL 35810

GOODLATTE, ROBERT WILLIAM, congressman, lawyer; b. Holyoke, Mass., Sept. 22, 1952; s. Robert Swan and Doris (Mentzendorff) G.; m. Maryellen Flaherty, Oct. 6, 1974; children: Jennifer, Robert. BA, Bates Coll., 1974; JD, Washington & Lee U., 1977. Bar: Mass. 1977, Va. 1978, U.S. Ct. Appeals (4th cir.) 1981. Adminstrv. aid congressman M. Caldwell Butler U.S. Ho. of Reps., Washington, 1977-79; pvt. practice Roanoke, Va., 1979-81; ptnr. Bird, Kinder & Huffman, Roanoke, 1981-93; mem. 104th Congress from 6th Va. dist. 103rd Congress from 6th Va. dist., Washington, D.C., 1993—, asst majority whip; chmn. dept. ops. subcom. nutrition and fgn. agrl. 103rd Congress from 6th Va. dist., Washington. Mem. bldg. better bds. adv. com. United Way of Roanoke Valley, Roanoke, 1988-92; chmn. Roanoke City Rep. Com., 1980-83, 6th Cong. Dist. Rep. Com., Va., 1983-88. Mem. Civitan (pres. Roanoke chpt. 1989-90). Office: US Ho of Reps 123 Cannon House Office Bld Washington DC 20515

GOODMAN, DARLENE EARNHARDT, nursing educator; b. Concord, N.C., Dec. 22, 1953; d. Hugh J. and Juanita J. (Paxton) Earnhardt; div.; 1 child, Aaron Locke. BSN, U. N.C., Charlotte, 1977, postgrad., 1991—. Staff nurse Cabarrus Meml. Hosp., Concord, N.C., 1977-81; nursing instr. sch. of nursing Cabarrus Meml. Hosp., Concord, 1981-84, cert. neonatal resuscitation instr., 1991—; nurse mgr. birthing ste. Lake Norman Regional Hosp., Moorsville, N.C., 1990-91; nursing instr. maternity Louise Harkey Sch. of Nursing, Concord, N.C., 1991—; patient edn. nurse childbirth Lake Norman Regional Hosp., Mooresville, 1990-91; diabetes educator Cabarrus Meml. Hosp., Concord, 1994; advisor Assn. Nursing Students, Cabarrus Meml. Hosp., 1990—. Chmn. United Way Lake Norman Regional Hosp., Mooresville, N.C., 1990, Cabarrus Meml. Hosp., Concord, N.C., 1994. Mem. ANA, N.C. Nurses Assn., Assn. Women's Health, Obstet. and Neonatal Nurses, Sigma Theta Tau (charter Gamma Iota chpt.). Democrat. Presbyterian. Office: Louise Harkey Sch Nursing 431 Copperfield Blvd Concord NC 28025

GOODMAN, DAVID WAYNE, research chemist; b. Glen Allen, Miss., Dec. 14, 1945; s. Henry G. and Anniebelle G.; m. Sandra Faye Hewitt, June 9, 1967; 1 child, Jac Hewitt. BS, Miss. Coll., 1968; PhD, U. Tex., 1974. NATO postdoctoral fellow Tech. Hochschule, Darmstadt, Fed. Republic of Germany, 1974-75; NRC postdoctoral fellow NBS, Washington, 1975-76, mem. research staff, 1976-80; mem. research staff Sandia Labs., Albuquerque, 1980-85, head surface sci. div., 1985-88; prof. chemistry, Tex. A&M U., College Station, 1988-94, head phys. and nuc. divsn., 1991-94, Welch prof., 1994—. Recipient Humboldt Rsch. award, 1995. Mem. Am. Chem. Soc. (treas. div. colloid and surface sci. 1980-83, vice chair 1983, chmn. 1984, Colloid or Surface Chemistry award 1993), Am. Vacuum Soc. (mem. exec. council 1981, 85-87). Office: Tex A&M University Dept of Chemistry College Station TX 77843

GOODMAN, ERNEST MONROE, air force officer; b. Casper, Wyo., May 14, 1955; s. Gordon Lee and Georgia Lee (Lent) G.; m. Songkran Sana, Sept. 30, 1976 (div. Feb. 1995). BSEE, U. Okla., 1982; MBA in Mgmt., Cen. State U., Edmond, Okla., 1986. Registered profl. engr., Okla. Avionics technician USAF, N.D., Okla., and S.E. Asia, 1973-78, USAFR, Tinker AFB, Okla., 1978-83; project engr., mgr. engring. Okla. City Air Logistics Ctr., Tinker AFB, 1982-90, 90—; commd. 2d lt. USAF, 1983, advanced through grades to maj.; engring. officer USAFR, Tinker AFB, 1983—. Mem. NSPE, Okla. Soc. Profl. Engrs., Air Force Assn., Res. Officers Assn., Tinker Mgmt. Assn., Toastmasters Internat. Democrat. Lutheran. Home: 4221 SE 53rd St Apt 13 A Oklahoma City OK 73135-2413 Office: USAF OC-ALC/LASKRF Bldg 3220 Tinker AFB OK 73145

GOODMAN, GERTRUDE AMELIA, civic worker; b. El Paso, Tex., Oct. 24, 1924; d. Karl Perry and Helen Sylvia (Pinkiert) G. BA, Mills Coll., 1945. Pres. El Paso chpt. Tex. Social Welfare Assn., 1963-65, bd. dirs. 1965-70, state bd. dirs., 1965-70; state bd. dirs. Pan-Am. Round Table, El Paso, 1966—, bd. dirs. 1970-71, sec., 1973-74, life mem.; founder, 1st chmn. El Paso Mus. Art Mem. Guild, 1962-68; bd. dirs. Mus. Art Assn., 1962-69, also v.p.; chmn. dir. El Paso C. of C. women's Dept., 1976-77; bd. dirs. Rio Grande Food Bank, 1988-94; bd. dirs. El Paso Pub. Libr., 1972-80, pres. bd. dirs., 1978-80; pres. El Paso County Hist. Soc., 1981-82, bd. dirs., 1986-92; mem. planning com. El Paso United Way, 1953—; mem. El Paso Mus. Art Bd. Coun. Recipient Hall of Honor award El Paso County Hist. Soc., Nat. Human Rels. award NCCJ, 1981, numerous awards for civic vol. work. Home: 905 Cincinnati Ave El Paso TX 79902-2435

GOODMAN, KAREN LACERTE, financial services executive; b. Mesa, Ariz., Nov. 9, 1946; d. Howard Lee and Margaret (Duncan) G.; m. Grant A. Lacerte, Feb. 1, 1964; children: Arthur Grant Jr., Arcel Leon Rene. Student, George Washington U., 1974-76. Prodn. mgr. Data Corp. of Am., Reston, Va., 1967-73; pres. Transco Leasing Co., Washington, 1974-78; sec., treas. to v.p. Certa Data Corp., Orlando, Fla., 1989—; pres. Fin. Rsch. Assocs., Inc., Orlando, 1979—; cons. in field, 1979—; dir. statis. seminars in field. Editor, pub.: Financial Studies of the Small Business (annual publ.), 1976—. Mem. Am. Heart Assn., Winter Haven, Fla., MADD, 1985—. Mem. Greater Orlando C. of C. Republican. Home: 6759 Winterset Gardens Rd Winter Haven FL 33884-3154 Office: Financial Rsch Assocs 510 Avenue J SE Winter Haven FL 33880-3781

GOODMAN, KATHERYNE LOCKRIDGE (KAY GOODMAN), church administrator, elder; b. Raphine, Va., Dec. 11, 1941; d. Lancelot Charles and Katheryne Marie (Wade) Lockridge; m. Charles Robert Goodman, July 6, 1963 (dec. Jan. 1983); children: Ktaheryne Gibbs Goodman, Elizabeth Claire Goodman Michael. BS in Edn., Longwood Coll., 1963. Ordained elder Presbyn. Ch. U.S.A., 1975; cert. prof. tchr., Va. Tchr. Pub. Sch. of Rockbridge County, Va., 1963-66; nutrition specialist Valley Program for Aging Svcs., 1978-80; field rep. for devel., cons. Va. and Pitts. regions Ch. World Svc./Nat. Coun. Chs., Elkhart, Ind., 1987-89; hunger action enabler Shenandoah Presbytery, Harrisonburg, Va., 1983-89, interum assoc. exec. presbyter for program/hunger action enabler, 1989-90, assoc. exec. presbyter, 1990—; workshop and small group leader Women's Global Mission, Hunger Action Enabler and Peacemaking Confs., Montreat and Ghost Ranch, 1984—; moderator Shenandoah Presbytery, 1985; Presbyn. hunger program rep. World Food Day Nat. Com., 1987-91; rep. Synod of Mid-Atlantic Presbyn. Ch., Australia-U.S. Exch., World Coun. Chs. Decade of Ch. in Solidarity with Women, 1990-91; mem. South Africa work/study trip, evaluator Operation Hunger, 1992; mem. N.Am. bd. South African Orgn. Operation Hunger, Inc., 1992—, vice chmn., 1993, 94; participant UN 4th World Conf. on Women, Beijing, China, 1995. Organizer and chair Ecumenicals for Polit. Action, Harrisonburg, 1987-89; participant Volga Peace Cruise, 1987; dir. Blue Ridge Area Food Bank, 1984-89, mem. exec. com., 1987, 88, 89; founding dir. Friendship House, 1988-90; voting mem. Va. Interfaith Ctr. Pub. Policy, 1986—; founding mem., co-convener Va. Hunger Congress, 1986—; voting mem. Shenandoah Presbytery; mem. Trinity Presbyn. Ch., Harrisonburg. Named Woman of Yr., Harrisonburg, 1992, Woman of Distinction, Girl Scouts Am., 1995. Democrat. Home: 708 Rhododendron Ct Mc Gaheysville VA 22840-9202 Office: Presbytery of Shenandoah PO Box 1214 1111 N Main St Harrisonburg VA 22801-1214

GOODMAN, LENN EVAN, philosopher; b. Detroit, Mar. 21, 1944; s. Calvin Jerome and Florence Jeanne (Cohen) G.; m. Madeleine Joyce Goodman, Aug. 29, 1965 (dec. Oct. 2, 1996); children: Allegra Sarah Karger, Paula Goodman Fraenkel. BA summa cum laude, Harvard U., 1965; PhD, Oxford (Eng.) U., 1968. Vis. asst. prof. philosophy and Near Eastern studies UCLA, 1968-69; from asst. to assoc. prof. philosophy U. Hawaii, Honolulu, 1969-80, prof. philosophy, 1981-94; prof. philosophy Vanderbilt U., Nashville, 1994—; v.p. Inst. for Islamic/Judaic Studies, Denver, 1984-85. Author: Monotheism, 1981, Saadiah's Book of Theodicy, 1988, On Justice, 1991, Avicenna, 1992, God of Abraham, 1996; editor: Brown Judaic Studies: Studies in Medieval Judaism; editor Jewish philosophy subject, Routledge Encyclopedia of Philosophy. Mem. Am. Philos. Assn., Acad. for Jewish Philosophy, Am. Oriental Soc. Office: Vanderbilt U Furman Hall 111 Nashville TN 37240

GOODMAN, LEWIS ELTON, JR., lawyer; b. Lynchburg, Va., Jan. 27, 1936; s. Lewis Elton and Mary (Oliver) G.; m. Elizabeth Shumaker, July 10, 1960; children: William L., Lee E. JD, U. Richmond, 1973. Bar: Va. 1973, U.S. Dist. Ct. (we. dist.) Va. 1973, U.S. Ct. Appeals (4th cir.) 1979, U.S. Supreme Ct. 1986. Pvt. practice Danville, Va., 1973—. Office: 222 Masonic Bldg Danville VA 24541

GOODMAN, LOUIS JOEL, medical society executive; b. Paterson, N.J., Sept. 29, 1948; m. Joann R. Goodman, Feb. 28, 1971; children: Melissa H., Wendy E. BS, NYU, 1970, MPA, 1972, PHD, 1975. Cert. assn. exec. Intern Health Ins. Plan, N.Y.C., 1973-74; systems analyst Health and Hosp. Corp., N.Y.C., 1972-74; dept. dir. AMA, Chgo., 1974-85; v.p. Michael Reese Hosp., Chgo., 1985-87; exec. v.p., CEO Tex. Med. Assn., Austin, 1987—. Bd. dirs. Am. Assn. Med. Soc. Execs., Pinnacle of Success award, 1992-94. Mem. Am. Soc. Assn. Execs. (coms. 1988—), Tex. Soc. Assn. Execs. (coms. 1987—). Office: Tex Med Assn 401 W 15th St Austin TX 78701-1665

GOODMAN, MICHAEL FREDERICK, advertising executive; b. Ringgold, Ga., Dec. 15, 1951; s. Frederick Doherty and Hilda Naomi (Benton) G.; m. Renee Elizabeth Penny, Mar. 24, 1980. BS in Mktg., Ventura (Calif.) Coll., 1973; postgrad., Chattanooga State U., 1976, U. Tenn., Knoxville, 1996. V.p., gen. mgr. Comml. Advt. Corp., Chattanooga, 1971-73; pres. Michael Goodman & Assocs., Inc., Chattanooga, 1973-78; nat. sales mgr. Pennco Internat., Inc., Mansfield, Ohio, 1978-84; pres., CEO M. Goodman & Co., Inc., Chattanooga, 1984—; bd. dirs. Leisure Life Care, Inc., CCS Internat., Inc.; pres. MG&A, Inc.; speaker in field. Mem. Tenn. Govt. Affairs Com., 1986—, Fed. Govt. Affairs Com., Chattanooga, 1987; publicity chmn. Chattanooga Bus.-to-Bus. Expo, 1987; chmn. Chattanooga Bus. Week, 1988; coord. Key Mkt. Partnership for a Day, Free Am., 1989—. Mem. Am. Assn. Advt. Agys., Chattanooga Small Bus. Council. Republican. Presbyterian. Club: Optimist. Office: M Goodman & Co Inc 4206 South Ter Chattanooga TN 37412-2620

GOODMAN, THOMAS ALLEN, psychiatrist, educator; b. Henryetta, Okla., Dec. 28, 1931; s. John Howard and Pauline Nadine (Murphy) G.; m. Barbara Ann Straw, Dec. 14, 1957; children: Kelli, Katherine, Jennifer. Student, Loyola U., 1950-53; MD, U. Okla., 1957; postgrad., Seattle Psychoanalytic Inst., 1966-72; JD, U. Tulsa, 1986. Diplomate Am. Bd. Psychiatry and Neurology. Intern, resident George Washington U., Washington, 1957-59; resident psychiatry U. Calif., San Francisco, 1959-62; chief mental hygiene clinic Seattle VA Hosp., 1966-68; pvt. practice Psychoanalytic Inst., Seattle, 1968-78; cons. U. Tex., Austin, 1978-82; prof. psychiatry U. Okla., Tulsa, 1983-88; pvt. practice Tulsa, 1988—; dir. forensic psychiatry Dept. Mental Health, Tulsa, 1986-88. Contbr. articles to profl. jours. Maj. USAF, 1959-66. Mem. AMA, Internat. Psychoanalytic Assn., Am. Psychiat. Assn., Am. Psychoanalytic Assn. Home: 312 E 20th St Tulsa OK 74120-7421 Office: 1980 Utica Sq Ste 204A Tulsa OK 74114-1611

GOODRICH, ALAN OWENS, lawyer; b. Dallas, Sept. 15, 1958; s. David Earle and Elizabeth (Owens) G. BA, U. Va., 1981; JD, So. Meth. U., 1984. Bar: Tex. 1984. Assoc. Jones, Day, Reavis & Pogue, Dallas, 1984-87; assoc. Gardere & Wynne, Dallas, 1988-89; atty. Sunbelt Savs., Irving, Tex., 1989-92; ptnr. Goodrich & Mays, 1992-94; lawyer Basic Capital Mgmt., Inc., Dallas, 1994—; bd. dirs. The Soliloquy Project, Inc., 1992—. Bd. dirs. Vol. Ctr., Dallas, 1988—. Mem. ABA, Tex. Bar Assn., Dallas Bar Assn. Republican. Presbyterian. Home: 4723 W Amherst Ave Dallas TX 75209-3127 Office: Basic Capital Mgmt Inc Ste 600 10670 N Central Expy Dallas TX 75231

GOODRICH, JAMES ALAN, veterinarian, researcher; b. June 20, 1961; s. Neil E. and Barbara F. (Weeks) G. BS in Pathobiology, U. Conn., 1983; DVM, Tufts U., 1988. Intern New Haven (Conn.) Ctrl. Hosp. for Veterinary Medicine, 1988-89; pvt. practice Conn., 1989-91; fellow Med. U. S.C., Charleston, 1991-94, Bowman Gray Sch. Medicine, Winston-Salem, N.C., 1994-95; asst. prof. Med. U. S.C., 1995—. Eagle Scout Boy Scouts Am., Cheshire, Conn., 1978. Mem. Am. Veterinary Med. Assn., Assn. Primate Veterinarians, S.C. Assn. Veterinarians, Assn. Lab. Animal Practitioners. Office: The Med U of South Carolina 171 Ashley Ave Charleston SC 29425

GOODRICH, SAMUEL MELVIN, obstetrician, gynecologist; b. Milledgeville, Ga., May 4, 1936; s. Ellis and Frieda (Bergman) G.; m. Ellen Schneider, Mar. 31, 1971; children: Jason Alexander, Harriet Schneider, Ashley Ann, Rachel Leigh. BS, U. Ga., 1957; MD, Med. Coll. of Ga., Augusta, 1961. Diplomate of Am. Bd. Ob-Gyn. Asst. prof. ob-gyn Med. Coll. of Ga., 1968-69; pvt. practice ob-gyn Milledgeville Ob-Gyn, 1969—; asst. clin. prof. Med. Coll. of Ga., 1969—; bd. dirs. First Nat. Bank Baldwin County, Milledgeville. Maj. U.S. Army Med. Corps, 1966-68. Mem. Ga. State Ob-Gyn Soc. (pres. 1978-79, chmn. sect. 1985-88), South Atlantic Assn. Ob-Gyn (v.p. 1992-94, pres. 1994-95), So. Med. Assn. (sec. gynecol. sect. 1989—, sect. chmn. 1996), Med. Coll. Ga. Medicine Alumni (pres.-elect 1990-91, pres. 1991-92). Home and Office: Milledgeville Ob-Gyn Assocs 750 N Cobb St Milledgeville GA 31061-2390

GOODRICH, THOMAS MICHAEL, engineering and construction executive, lawyer; b. Milan, Tenn., Apr. 28, 1945; s. Henry Calvin and Billie Grace (Walker) G.; m. Gillian Comer White, Dec. 28, 1968; children: Michael, Braxton, Charles, Grace. BSCE, Tulane U., 1968; JD, U. Ala., 1971. Bar: Ala. 1971. Adminstrv. asst. Supreme Ct. Ala., Montgomery, 1971-72; various mgmt. positions BE & K, Inc., Birmingham, Ala., 1995, pres., CEO, 1995—, also bd. dirs.; bd. dirs. First Comml. Bank, Birmingham. Bd. dirs. Birmingham Civil Rights Inst., Constrn. Industry Inst., Birmingham Area coun. Boy Scouts Am., U. Ala. Health Scis. Found., So. Rsch. Inst. Capt. U.S. Army, 1968-72. Mem. TAPPI, ABA, Ala. State Bar Assn., Assn. Builders and Contractors (pres. 1990), Constrn. Pres.'s Industry Forum. Presbyterian. Office: B E & K Inc PO Box 2332 2000 Internat Park Dr Birmingham AL 35243

GOODRUM, LINDA ANN, physician; b. Lima, Ohio, Mar. 5, 1963; d. James Ellis and Judith Ann (Hansen) G. BS, La. State U., Baton Rouge, 1985; MD, La. State U., Shreveport, 1989. Resident La. State U., Shreveport, 1989-93; fellow in maternal-fetal medicine Baylor U. Coll. Med., Houston, 1993-95; asst. prof. maternal fetal medicine divsn. U. Tex. Med. Br., Galveston, 1995—. Contbr. articles to profl. jours. Mem. AMA, Am. Coll. Ob-Gyn., Am. Med. Womens Assn., Phi Kappa Phi. POL Republican. Baptist. Office: Div Maternal Fetal Medicine 301 University Blvd Galveston TX 77555-0587

GOODSON, CAROL FAYE, librarian; b. Detroit, Mar. 28, 1947; d. Norman Elwood and Wilma Mary (Harmon) G.; m. Lawrence J. Price, May 10, 1974 (div. 1977). BA, SUNY, Buffalo, 1970, MLS, 1972; MA, West Ga. Coll., 1996. Libr. SUNY, Buffalo, 1970-72, St. Louis Pub. Libr., 1973-77; community sch. dir. St. Louis Bd. Edn., 1977-80; reference libr. Ga. Dept. Edn., Atlanta, 1981-84; head pub. svcs. Atlanta campus Mercer U., Chamblee, Ga., 1985; mem. Dominican Sisters of Nashville, 1985-90; asst. dir. Clayton County Libr. System, Jonesboro, Ga., 1990-91; coord. off-campus libr. svcs. West Ga. Coll., Carrollton, 1991—; state coord. Ga. Summer Reading Club, 1991; owner and moderator, ALA-PLAN listserv., FISC-L listserv and WOODY-L listserv. Editor GA Conf., AAUP Summary. Pres. Tower/Literacy Vols. Am., Clayton County, 1991; active Leadership, 1990-91. Mem. AAUP (exec. com. 1994—, editor Ga. newsletter 1996—), ALA, Ga. Libr. Assn., Southeastern Libr. Assn., Libr. Info. Tech. Assn., (program planning com. 1992—, sec. 1993—), Assn. Coll. Rsch. Librs. (clip notes com. 1992—, extended campus libr. svcs. sect., comm. com. 1994—), Beta Phi Mu, Phi Kappa Phi, Omicron Delta Kappa, Sigma Tau Delta. Home: 210 Oak Ave Carrollton GA 30117-3726 Office: West Ga Coll Ingram Libr Carrollton GA 30118

GOODSON, CAROLE EDITH MCKISSOCK, mathematics and technology educator; b. Des Moines, Dec. 31, 1946; d. William Thompson and Edith (Johnson) McKissock; m. Robert Wayne Peterson, July 1978; 1 son, David Shelby Peterson. B.S., U. Houston, 1968, M.Ed., 1971, Ed.D., 1975. Tchr., Spring Branch Ind. Sch. Dist., Houston, 1968-69; mem. faculty Coll. Tech., U. Houston, 1972—, instr., 1972-75, asst. prof., coll. counselor, 1975-78, assoc. prof., coll. counselor, 1978-81, assoc. prof., chmn. related courses tech., 1981-89, assoc. dean, assoc. prof. tech. math., 1982-89; prof., 1988—, chmn. civil, mech. and related techs., 1989-94, chmn. indsl. tech., 1994—. Author: (with S.L. Miertschin) Technical Mathematics With Applications, 1983, 2d edit., 1986; Technical Mathematics with Calculus, 1985; Technical Algebra with Applications, 1985, Technical Trigonometry with Applications, 1985; prodn. editor Jour. Engring. Tech., 1991-93, editor in chief, 1993-95; contbr. articles to publs. Recipient Dow Outstanding Young Faculty award Am. Soc. Engring. Edn., 1982. Mem. Am. Soc. Engring. Edn. (dir. 1992-94, ERM divsn. vice chmn. 1985-86, chmn. 1987-89, sec.-treas., bd. dirs. 1989-90, Gulf S.W. regional chair 1982-83), Nat. Coun. Tchrs. Math., Math. Assn. Am., Am. Statis. Assn., Tau Alpha Pi, Phi Kappa Phi (chpt. pres. 1985), Tex. Assn. of Sch. Engring. Tech. (sec./treas. 1986—). Presbyterian. Office: U Houston Coll Tech 312 # T2 Houston TX 77204-4083

GOODSON, SHANNON LORAYN, behavioral scientist, author; b. Beaumont, Tex., May 26, 1952; d. James Ernest and Lorayn (Miller) G. BS in Psychology, Lamar U., 1974, MS in Organizational Psychology, 1977. Co-founder, pres., CEO Behavioral Scis. Rsch. Press, Inc., Dallas, 1979-92, pres., 1992—; presenter in field; guest on various radio talk shows. Co-author: (with G.W. Dudley) Earning What You're Worth?, 1992, Psychology of Call Reluctance, 1986; contbr. articles to profl. jours. and periodicals. Mem. SE Psychol. Assn. Office: Behavioral Scis Rsch Press 12803 Demetra Dr Ste 100 Dallas TX 75234-6101

GOODWIN, BILLY WAYNE, chemical engineer; b. Memphis, Nov. 12, 1954; s. Jess W. and Florence (Adams) G.; m. Carole McCutcheon, July 25, 1992; 1 child, Hayley M. BSChemE, La. State U., 1992. Fin. cons. Goodwin & Assocs., Inc., Baton Rouge, 1976-86, with, 1986-87; mgr. Cadgis Rsch. Lab., La. State U., Baton Rouge, 1987-89; student engr. Ethyl Corp. R & D, Baton Rouge, 1989-92; engr. Walk, Haydel & Assocs., Inc., New Orleans, 1992-95; prodn. mgr. vinyl chloride monomer Ga. Gulf Corp., Plaquemine, La., 1995—. Grantee Air & Waste Mgmt. Assn., Baton Rouge chpt., 1991. Mem. AIChE, Am. Inst. Chemists (hon.), Air and Waste Mgmt. Assn. (hon.), Golden Key, Omega Chi Epsilon, Tau Beta Pi, Phi Eta Sigma. Republican. Episcopalian. Home: 37149 Shadow Ct Prairieville LA 70769 Office: Ga Gulf Corp PO Box 629 Hwy 405 Plaquemine LA 70765-0639

GOODWIN, CRAUFURD DAVID, economics educator; b. Montreal, Que., Can., May 23, 1934; came to U.S., 1962; s. George G. and Roma (Stewart) G.; m. Nancy Virginia Sanders, June 7, 1958. B.A., McGill U., 1955; Ph.D., Duke U., 1958. Econ. research asst. Courtauld's Can., Ltd., 1955; lectr. econs. U. Windsor, Ont., 1958-59; exec. sec. Commonwealth Studies Center, Duke U., also; vis. asst. prof., 1959-60; hon. research fellow Australian Nat. U., 1960-61; asst. prof. econs. York U., Toronto, 1961-62; asst. prof. econs., asst. to provost Duke U., Durham, N.C., 1962-63; assoc. prof. econs., sec. to Univ., asst. to provost Duke U., 1963-64, asso. prof. econs., sec. Univ., asst. provost, 1964- 66, assoc. prof. econs., asst. provost, dir. internat. studies, 1966-68, prof. econs., vice provost for internat. studies, 1968-69, prof. econs., vice provost, dir. internat., 1969-71, prof. econs., 1971-74, James B. Duke prof. econs., 1974—, dean Grad. Sch., vice provost for research, 1980-86; Smuts vis. prof. Cambridge U., 1967-68; officer in charge European and internat. affairs Ford Found., 1971-77. Author: Canadian Economic Thought: The Political Economy of a Developing Nation 1814-1914, 1961, Economic Enquiry in Australia, 1966, The Image of Australia, 1974, (with M. Nacht) Absence of Decision, 1983, Fondness and Frustration, 1984, Decline and Renewal, 1986, Abroad and Beyond, 1988, Missing the Boat, 1991; editor: (with W.B. Hamilton and Kenneth Robinson) A Decade of the Commonwealth 1955-64, 1966, (with I.B. Holley) The Transfer of Ideas, 1968, (with R.D.C. Black and A.W. Coats) The Marginal Revolution in Economics, 1973, Exhortation and Controls, 1975, Energy Policy in Perspective, 1981, Economics and National Security, 1991, International Investment in Human Capital, 1993, (with Alan Smith, Ulrich Teichler, and Peggy Blumenthal) Academic Mobility in a Changing World: Regional and Global Trends, 1996, (with M. Nacht) Beyond Government, 1995, Talking to Themselves, 1995; editor: (jour.) History of Political Economy, 1969—, (series) Historical Perspectives on Modern Economics, 1981—. Guggenheim fellow, 1967-68. Home: PO Box 957 Hillsborough NC 27278-0957

GOODWIN, ELIZABETH CAROL, special education educator; b. Jacksonville, Fla., Aug. 14, 1946; d. Arthur Lee and Florence Mabery (Ivey) Dunnam; m. James Stanley Goodwin, May 29, 1970; 1 child, Carolyn Sue. AA, Fla. Jr. Coll., 1967; BA, U. W. Fla., 1969; MEd, U. N. Fla., 1987; postgrad., Jacksonville U., 1991—. Cert. spl. edn. tchr., Fla. Substitute tchr. Duval County Schs., Jacksonville, 1970-71, 79-87, 1988—, spl. edn. tchr., 1987-88; spl. edn. tchr. Twin City Bapt. Temple, Lunenberg, Mass., 1976-77, Univ. Christian Sch., Jacksonville, 1977-78; tchr. Am. and western history Victory Christian Sch., Jacksonville, 1978-79. Author: (poems) Sunshine and Daisies, 1981. Leader Awanas, Tampa, Fla., 1972-74; Sunday sch. tchr., choir tchr. local ch.; foster parent. 2d lt. U.S. Army, 1970. Scottish Rite scholar, 1976-77; named Outstanding Tchr. of Yr., Twin City Christian, 1976-77. Mem. Coun. for Exceptional Children, Duval Tchrs. United, Kappa Delta Pi. Democrat. Baptist. Home: 2140 Westcott St Jacksonville FL 32206-4271

GOODWIN, JOEL FRANKLIN, SR., dentist; b. Shawnee, Okla., Sept. 9, 1924; s. Abb L. and Ethel Elizabeth (Broyles) G.; m. Betty Mashburn; children: Mary Carolyn, Joel Franklin Jr., John and Gene (twins). BS, Baylor U., 1951, DDS, 1952. Gen. practice dentistry Dallas, 1952—; instr. oral surgery Coll. Dentistry Baylor U., Dallas, 1952. Vice chmn. Dallas Mid-Winter Dental Clinic, 1961, gen. chmn., 1962; dental dir. United Fund, Dallas, 1966-67; sec. bd. trustees Baylor Coll. Dentistry, 1976-79, chmn. building com., 1971-77, trustee 1971-82; bd. dirs. War on Poverty, City of Dallas, 1966-67. Mem. Dallas County Dental Soc. (v.p. 1963-64, pres. 1966-67), Am. Coll. Dentists (Hon. degree 1968), Baylor U. Coll. Dentistry Alumni Assn. (v.p. 1985-86, sec., treas. 1954-85, pres. elect 1986-87, pres. 1987-88, trustee 1988-90, Disting. Svc. award 1969, Disting. Alumni award 1976), Dallas C. of C. (med. and dental coms. 1966-67). Baptist. Home: 6110 Sul Ross Ln Dallas TX 75214 Office: Baylor Doctors Bldg 3707 Gaston Ave Ste 716 Dallas TX 75246-1540

GOODWIN, JOHN ROBERT, law educator, author; b. Morgantown, W.Va., Nov. 3, 1929; s. John Emory and Ruby Iona G.; m. Betty Lou Wilson, June 2, 1952; children: John R., Elizabeth Ann Paugh, Mark Edward, Luke Jackson, Matthew Emory. B.S., W.Va. U., 1952, LLB, 1964, J.D., 1970. Bar: W.Va., U.S. Supreme Ct. Formerly city atty., county commr., spl. pros. atty., then mayor City of Morgantown; prof. bus. law W.Va. U.; prof. hotel and casino law U. Nev., Las Vegas; Author: Legal Primer for Artists, Craftspersons, 1987, Hotel Law, Principles and Cases, 1987. Served with U.S. Army, Korea. Recipient Bancroft-Whitney award in Constl. Law'; named Outstanding West Virginian, State of West Virginia. Democrat. Author: Twenty Feet From Glory; Business Law, 3d edit.; High Points of Legal History; Travel and Lodging Law; Desert Adventure;

Gaming Control Law; editor Hotel and Casino Letter; past editor Bus. Law Rev., Bus. Law Letter. Home: Casa Linda 48 5250 E Lake Mead Blvd Las Vegas NV 89115-6751

GOODWIN, PAUL RICHARD, transportation company executive; b. N.Y.C., Feb. 6, 1943; s. Paul Richard Fetyko and Ellen Mary Goodwin; m. Nina Presant, Oct. 10, 1965; children: Elizabeth, Ross. B.C.E., Cornell U., 1965; M.B.A., George Washington U., 1970. Mgmt. trainee Chessie System, Balt., 1965-66, in various mgmt. positions fin. dept., 1966-76; asst. to v.p. fin. Chessie System, Cleve., 1977-78, asst. v.p. fin., 1978-80, v.p. fin., 1980-81, sr. v.p. fin., 1982-85; sr. v.p. fin. and planning Chessie System, CSX Transp., Jacksonville, 1985-88; exec. v.p. CSX Transp., Jacksonville, 1989—; bd. dirs. Cen. Fla. Pipeline Corp.; mem. adv. bd. First Union Bank. Trustee U. North Fla. Office: CSX Transp 500 Water St Jacksonville FL 32202-4422

GOODWIN, PHILLIP HUGH, hospital administrator; b. Paragould, Ark., Sept. 10, 1940; s. Ray H. and Helen L. (Griffin) G.; m. Pamela J. Davis, June 24, 1962; children: Philip Grey, Julie Ann. BA in Bus. and Econs., Hendrix Coll., 1962; M in Hosp. Adminstrn., Washington U., St. Louis, 1968; LLD (hon.), U. Charleston, 1995. Bus. mgr. Stuttgart (Ark.) Meml. Hosp., 1962-64; asst. adminstr. Union Meml. Hosp., El Dorado, Ark., 1964-67; adminstrv. asst. to assoc. adminstr. Hillcrest Med. Ctr., Tulsa, 1968-77, v.p., adminstr., chief operating officer, 1977-82; exec. v.p. Charleston (W.Va.) Area Med. Ctr., 1982-87, pres., chief exec. officer, 1987—; adj. faculty Wash. U., St. Louis, W.Va. U., Med. Coll. Va., W.Va. Coll. Grad. Studies; bd. dirs. Auther B. Hodges Nursing Home, Charleston, One Valley Bank N.A., Charleston, One Valley BanCorp of W.Va.; frequent speaker ednl., profl. and bus. assns. Co-author: Time Management for Hospital Administrators; contbr. articles to profl. publs. Bd. dirs. Kanawha Hospice Inc., Charleston, 1987-89, W.Va. Bus. Roundtable, Wellness Coun. Am., Nat. Com. for Quality Health Care; vol. Mgmt. Assistance Program, Charleston, 1987-89, Nat. Inst. Chem. Studies, Charleston, 1988-91, Charleston Renisance Corp., Bus. and Industry Coun. of W.Va., Pvt. Industry Coun. of W.Va.; pres. Civitan Club, Tulsa, 1970. Fellow Am. Coll. healthcare Execs.; mem. W.Va. Hosp. Assn. (pres. 1987, 88), Am. Hosp. Assn. (ho. of dels. 1988—), Vol. Hosps. Am. (bd. dirs. 1978-82, bd. Wellness Coun. of Am. 1994), Charleston Ranaisance Soc., W.Va. C. of C., Charleston C. of C., Ducks Unltd., Berry Hill Country Club. Republican. Methodist. Office: Charleston Area Med Ctr PO Box 1547 Charleston WV 25326-1547

GOODWIN, ROBERT, human resources specialist; b. Paterson, N.J., July 1, 1937; s. Herbert and Lodia (Czajkowski) Jackson; m. Paula Flo Wininger, Dec. 15, 1959 (div. Dec. 1980); children: Robert, Roger, Richard; m. Bertha Ann Walker, Apr. 14, 1984; stepchildren: Susan, Kerry. BS, U. of the State of N.Y., 1986. Tng. system analyst U.S. Navy, NATOPS coord.; air program mgr., surface program mgr., dir. tng. divsn. Naval Tng. Systems Ctr. Regional Office, 1983-87; tech. tng. equipment officer U.S. Atlantic Fleet, 1987-88, tng. systems advisor, 1988-94; tech. advisor, mem. steering com. IEEE Stds. for DIS, 1994-95; human resources exec. Goodwin Assocs., Virginia Beach, Va., 1995—. With U.S. Navy, 1955-73. Mem. Fleet Res. Assn., Soc. Computer Simulation, ASTD, Navy League (life mem.), Assn. Naval Aviation (life mem.), Surface Navy Assn. (charter mem.), Nat. Tng. Systems Assn. Home and Office: Goodwin Assocs 909 Pillow Dr Virginia Beach VA 23454-2624

GOODWIN, SHARON ANN, academic administrator; b. Little Rock, May 19, 1949; d. Jimmy Lee and Eddie DeLois (Cluck) G.; m. Mitchell Shayne Mick, May 4, 1968 (div. Mar. 1973); 1 child, Heather Michelle; m. Raymond Eugene Vaclavik, June 24, 1974 (div. Aug. 1982); 1 child, Tasha Rae Vaclavik. BA in Psychology, U. Houston-Clear Lake, 1980; MEd in Higher Edn. Adminstrn., U. Houston, 1990. Various clerical positions Gen. Telephone Co., Dickinson, Tex., 1969-80; state dir. Challenge, Inc., Oklahoma City, 1980-82; gen. mgr. Mr. Fix It, Houston, 1982-85; assoc. dir. admissions U. Houston, Tex., 1985-92; adminstr. Inst. for the Med. Humanities U. Tex. Med. Br., Galveston, 1992—. Mem. legis. com. Comm. Workers, Dickinson and Austin, 1975; mem. centennial choir U. Tex. Med. Br., Galveston, 1992-95; vol. Dickens on the Strand, Galveston, 1993—. Recipient Honorable Mention, World of Poetry, 1986, Golden Poet award World of Poetry, 1987, Silver Poet award 1990, Golden Poet award 1991. Mem. AAUW, Assn. of Am. Med. Colls.-Group on Institutional Planning. Home: PO Box 517 League City TX 77574-0517 Office: Univ Tex Med Br Inst for the Med Humanities 301 University Blvd Galveston TX 77555-1311

GOODWIN, S(HEILA) DIANE, drug information scientist; b. Durham, N.C., Jan. 19, 1958; d. Leon Jackson and Mattie (Wilson) G. BS in Pharmacy, U. N.C., 1981; PharmD, Med. Coll. Va., 1986. Registered pharmacist, N.C., Va., Colo. Staff pharmacist Durham (N.C.) County Gen. Hosp., 1981-84; asst. prof. U. Fla. Coll. Pharmacy, Gainesville, 1988-89; clin. rsch. pharmacist Duke U. Med. Ctr., Ctr. AIDS Rsch., Durham, 1990-91; asst. prof. U. Colo., Sch. Pharmacy, Denver, 1991-94; drug info. sci. Burroughs Wellcome Co., Research Triangle Park, N.C., 1994-95; mgr. HIV program devel. Care Mgmt. divsn. Glaxo Wellcome, Inc., Research Triangle Park, 1995—; cons., reviewer, researcher, lectr. in field. Contbr. articles to profl. and sci. jours. Clin. pharmacy fellow Duke U. Med. Ctr., 1986-87, Millard Fillmore Hosp., 1987-88. Mem. Am. Coll. Clin. Pharmacy (chmn. pub. and profl. rels. com. 1991-92, Schering rsch. grantee 1990, chmn. pubs. com. 1996), Am. Soc. Health Sys. Pharmacists, Am. Soc. Microbiology, Soc. Infectious Diseases Pharmacists, Am. Soc. Clin. Pharmacology and Therapeutics, Kappa Epsilon, Rho Chi. Democrat. Baptist. Office: Glaxo Wellcome Inc 5 Moore Dr Research Triangle Park NC 27709

GOODWIN, WILLIAM DEAN, oil and gas company executive; b. Independence, Kans., Aug. 3, 1937; s. William Brice and Rozella Delia (Lillibridge) G.; m. Jane Louise Varnum, Oct. 23, 1960 (div. 1973); children: Deborah Diane, Laura Louise; m. Linda Ann Booth, July 26, 1980; 1 child, William D. II. BS in Advt. and Bus., U. Kans., 1961. Editor Marshall County News, Marysville, Kans., 1961-63; dir. pub. relations U.S. Jaycees, Tulsa, 1963-67; account exec. Carl Byoir & Assocs., Chgo., 1967-68, Holder, Kennedy & Co., Nashville, 1968-70; press sec. U.S. Senator Bill Brock, Washington, 1970-74; exec. v.p. Nat. Energy Corp., Nashville, 1974-78, Tenn. Land & Exploration, Nashville, 1979-80; pres. Commerce Oil Co., Nashville, 1980-83; pvt. practice oil producer Crossville, Tenn., 1984-91; v.p. Tom Jackson & Assocs., Nashville, 1991-96; prin. Akins & Tombras, Nashville, 1996—; treas. Tenn. Oil Producers Polit. Action Com., Nashville, 1983-88. Editor-in-chief Future mag., 1966-67; editor Nat. Young Reps. mag., 1971-72, The Oilpatch newsletter, PLS News mag. Chmn. Davidson County Reps., Nashville, 1979; nominee Candidate for U.S. Congress 5th Dist. Tenn., 1978; cons. Nat. Rep. Senatorial Com., Washington, 1973; dir. publicity Com. to Reelect the Pres., 1972; vice chmn. Tenn. Commn. on Status of Women, 1979-80. Served with USN, 1956-57. Mem. Nat. Assn. Royalty Owners Assn. (life, bd. govs. 1986—), Tenn. Oil and Gas Assn. (exec. v.p. 1975-82, named Tenn. Oil Man of Yr. 1981), VFW, Nashville City Club, Downtown Kiwanis. Methodist. Club: Lake Tansi (Crossville). Home: 900 Hawthorne Ct Franklin TN 37069 Office: 222 Second Ave N Ste 370M Nashville TN 37201

GOODWIN, WILLIAM LEGREE, JR., health care food service administrator, retired army officer; b. Aiken, S.C., Oct. 31, 1946; s. Wiliam Legree and Susie Lurine (Young) G.; m. Brenda Kay Windham, Oct. 5, 1968; children: Melissa, Bradford, Madeline. BS, Berry Coll., 1968; MS, U. Tenn., 1976. Dietetic intern Brooke Army Med. Ctr., Ft. Sam Houston, Tex., 1969; advanded through grades to col. U.S. Army, 1972; staff dietitian Fitzsimons Army Med. Ctr., Aurora, Colo., 1969-72; chief prodn. and food svc. U.S. Army Hosp., Ft. Campbell, Ky., 1972-76; chief prodn. and svc., staff officer Walter Reed Army Med. Ctr., Washington, 1976-79; chief nutrition care divsn. Moncrief Army Hosp., Ft. Jackson, S.C., 1979-83, Frankfurt (Germany) Army Regional Med. Ctr., 1983-87; col. nutrition care divsn. Eisenhower Army Med. Ctr., Ft. Gordon, Ga., 1987-90; chief Army Med. Specialist Corps br., officer pers. mgmt., dir. U.S. Army Pers. Command, Alexandria, Va., 1990-94; ret. U.S. Army, 1994; health care dist. mgr. Valley Mgmt. Svcs., Jackson, Miss., 1994—; cons. Army Surgeon Gen., Washington, 1976-79; mem. program com. Nat. Rsch. Coun., Washington, 1980-82; chmn. com. on mgmt. practice Ga. Dietetic Assoc., 1988-89. Mayor U.S. Army Mil. Housing Area, Heilsburg, Germany, 1985-87. Recipient "A" Prefix award Army Surgeon Gen., 1988, Order of Mil. Med. Merit award Army Surgeon Gen., 1989; decorated Legion of Merit. Mem. Am. Dietetic Assn. (registered), Miss. Dietetic Assn., Interagy. Inst. for Fed. Healthcare Execs. Methodist. Home: 445 Annandale Pky Madison MS 39110-7862 Office: Valley Mgmt Svcs 4400 Mangum Dr Jackson MS 39208-2113

GOODWIN-DAVEY, ALICE ANNE, English language educator; b. Springdale, Ark., Aug. 22, 1959; m. Colyn Roy Davey, Dec. 4, 1993; 1 child, Christopher Davey. BA in English and Sociology magna cum laude, William Jewell Coll., 1981; grad. lang./tchr. tng. program, U.S. Peace Corps, 1981; grad. cert. tchg. English as fgn. lang., U. S.C., 1986, MA in Linguistics, 1989, postgrad., 1992-94. Head proctor writing ctr. William Jewell Coll., Liberty, Mo., 1979-81; tchr. English lang. U. S.C., Columbia, 1985-88, tchr. English for fgn. students, 1986—, tchr. grammar writing English Programs for Internats., 1986—, grammar/writing coord. English Programs for Internats., 1989—; tchr. English Linchwe II Sch., Mochudi, Botswana, 1984, Internat. Sch. Panama, Panama City, 1990, Am. Tng. Inst., Panama City, 1990; instr. English to vis. Korean bus. profls. Sch. Bus., U. S.C., 1992; assoc. dir. summer inst. for English educators from South Africa and Namibia, USIA, 1992, 93, acad. specialisty in writing skills devel., 1993; instr., presenter many Eng. lang., writing, composition workshops, confs.; trainer tchg. profls. in field; contbg. grantwriter various internat. agys.; programmer writing ctr. student svcs. bur. U. S. Africa, Pretoria, 1994-95, writing and acad. lang. ESL cons. Bur. for univ. tchg., 1995—. Contbr. articles to profl. publs. Vol. tchr. English lang. and lit. U.S. Peace Corps, Botswana, 1981-83. Mem. TESOL (Broward County, Fla., Carolina, Brazilian and Panamanian affiliates), Nat. Coun. Tchrs. of English, South Atlantic MLA, Conf. on Coll. Composition and Comm., Conf. on Computers and Writing, So. African Applied Linguistics Assn. Office: U SC English Programs Internats Columbia SC 29208

GOODWYN ROSEBORO, WANDA, medical/surgical nurse; b. Newark, Jan. 1, 1964; d. David Manuel and Velma (Jay) Goodwyn; m. Thomas Douglas Roseboro, Apr. 7, 1989. BSN, Seton Hall U., South Orange, N.J., 1987. Psychiat. asst. Clara Maas Med. Ctr., Belleville, N.J.; staff nurse Community Health Care of North Jersey, Orange; clin. nurse Walter Reed Army Med. Ctr., Washington; clin. nurse labor and delivery Johns Hopkins Hosp., Balt., Andrews AFB, U. N.C., Chapel Hill. 1st lt. U.S. Army, 1987-91. Mem. ANA.

GOODYKOONTZ, CHARLES ALFRED, newspaper editor, retired; b. Radford, Va., Dec. 29, 1928; s. Charles A. and Claudine (Noell) G.; m. Jean Shirley Beasley, Sept. 17, 1955; 1 child, Charles Alfred. Student, Emory and Henry Coll., 1946-48. Sports editor Radford News Jour., 1948-50; mem. staff Richmond (Va.) Times-Dispatch, 1952-81, mng. editor, 1969-81; v.p., exec. editor Richmond (Va.) Times-Dispatch and The Richmond News Leader, 1982-93, ret., 1993; former chmn. Va. AP, UPI. Bd. trustees Emory and Henry Coll., 1985-92; chmn. Trinity United Methodist Ch., Richmond, 1995, bd. trustees; bd. govs. Va. Home for Boys, 1995. With AUS, 1950-52. Recipient George Mason award for service to Va. journalism, 1973; inducted into Va. Comm. Hall of Fame, 1992. Mem. AP Mng. Editors Assn. (treas. 1988-90), Va. Press Assn. (bd. dirs. 1986-89, life), Soc. Profl. Journalists, Sigma Delta Chi (regional dir. 1971-74, nat. officer 1975-79, pres. 1978, Wells Key award 1982, pres. Found. 1985-87), Va. Inst. of Pastoral Care (bd. dirs. 1995). Home: 8207 Shannon Hill Rd Richmond VA 23229-4911

GOOLRICK, ROBERT MASON, lawyer, consultant; b. Fredericksburg, Va., Mar. 25, 1934; s. John T. and Olive E. (Jones) G.; m. Audrey J. Dippo (div.); children—Stephanie M., Meade A. B.A. with distinction, U. Va., 1956; J.D., 1959. Bar: Va. 1959, D.C., 1959, U.S. Dist. Ct. D.C. 1961, U.S. Ct. Appeals (D.C. cir.) 1961. Assoc. Steptoe & Johnson, Washington, 1959-65, ptnr., 1965-79; sole practice, Alexandria, Va., 1979-83; cons. bus., oil and gas fin.; instr. U. Va. Law Sch. Mem. ABA (corps. sect.), Jefferson Soc., Raven Soc., Order of Coif, Phi Beta Kappa. Author: Public Policy Toward Corporate Growth, 1978; Corporate Mergers and Acquisitions under Federal Securities Laws, 1978. Home: Apt 22 3320 Woodburn Village Dr Annandale VA 22003-6860 Office: 6720 Curran St Mc Lean VA 22101-3803

GOORLEY, JOHN THEODORE, consulting chemist; b. Galion, Ohio, Mar. 12, 1907; s. William H. and Emma (Ness) G.; BS, Ohio State U., 1930; MS, Purdue U., 1932, PhD, 1934; m. Ethel L. Coleman, Nov. 27, 1935; children: John, Alice (Mrs. Harold A. Breard, Jr.), Robert, Richard. Chief control chemist Burroughs Wellcome & Co., Tuckahoe, N.Y., 1933-38; research dir. Labs. Lex, Havana, Cuba, 1939-42, Ben Venue Labs., Bedford, Ohio, 1946-48, Johnson & Johnson de Argentina, Buenos Aires, 1948-50; owner, dir. Labs. Goorley, Buenos Aires, 1950-55; prof. pharm. chemistry Ohio No. U., Ada, 1956-57; v.p., gen. mgr. Inland Alkaloid Co., Tipton, Ind., 1957-58; prof. pharm. chemistry N.E. La. U., Monroe, 1958-68, prof. pharmacognosy, 1968-72; chemist Laboratorios Finlay, S.A., San Pedro Sula, Honduras, 1974-76; prof. chemistry and pharmacy U. Nacional Autonoma de Honduras, Tegucigalpa, 1976; Fulbright prof. U. Honduras, 1966-67, cons. chemist, 1967—; exec. v.p. Enviro-Med Labs., Ruston, La., 1978-82; vis. prof. U. El Salvador, 1968; cons. pharm. industries. Active Little Theater, Monroe. Served to capt. AUS, 1942-46; lt. col. AUS, 1956-63. Col. staff govs. Ky., La. Mem. AAAS, Am. Pharm. Assn., Am. Chem. Soc., N.Y. Acad. Scis., Sigma Xi, Rho Chi, Phi Delta Chi, Tau Kappa Epsilon. Research in pharm. chemistry and biochemistry. Contbr. articles to profl. jours. Patentee in field. Home: 776 Thora Blvd Shreveport LA 71106

GORANSON, STEPHEN CRAFT, history of religions educator, researcher; b. Surrey, Eng., Nov. 5, 1950; arrived in U.S., 1952; s. Harold Theodore and Brinkley (Craft) G.; 1 child, Anna Marie P. BA, Brandeis U., 1972; MA, Duke U., 1986, PhD, 1990. Instr. Judaic civilization Duke U., Durham, N.C., 1988, 90, U. N.C., Chapel Hill, 1988-89; asst. prof. O.T., N.T. and religions of world N.C. State U., Raleigh, 1990-93; asst. prof. history of religions Wake Forest U., Winston-Salem, N.C., 1994; mem. Sepphoris Archaeol. Excavation; presenter in field. Contbr. articles to profl. jours. and Anchor Bible Dictionary. Mem. Soc. Bib. Lit. Home: 706 Louise Cir Apt 30J Durham NC 27705

GORAY, GERALD ALLEN, real estate executive, lawyer; b. Detroit, Aug. 22, 1939; s. James A. and Lucille (Rankin) G.; m. Donna Marie Belian, Apr. 26, 1958; children: Brian M., Gregory D. BBA magna cum laude, U. Detroit, 1963; JD, U. Mich., 1965. Bar: Mich. Atty. Parsons, Tennant et al, Birmingham, Mich., 1966-70, U.S. Dept. of Housing, Detroit, 1970-71, Rodgers & Goray, Southfield, Mich., 1971-75; pres. Goray Devel. Co., Boca Raton, Fla., 1975—; bd. dirs. Monroe (Mich.) Bank & Trust, 1968-70; ptnr. Nat. Self-Storage Equities Fla., Tucson, 1984—; pres. Stonemark Devel. Co., Boca Raton, 1988—. Vice-chmn. Lathrup Village (Mich.) Zoning Bd. Appeals, 1981. Mem. Village Athletic Club (pres. 1975-76). Office: Goray Devel Co 621 NW 53rd St Ste 255 Boca Raton FL 33487-8236

GORDIN, BARBARA, foundation administrator; b. Washington, Sept. 18, 1947; d. Julius and T. Rose (Adler) G.; children: Joseph Barr, Sarah Barr. BA, Am. Univ., 1969. Cert. rsch. adminstr. Grants/contracts mgmt. specialist NIH, Bethesda, Md., 1969-72; adminstrv. asst. to adminstrv. assoc. Baylor Coll. Medicine, Houston, 1973-75, 76—; exec. dir. Internat. Atherosclerosis Soc., Houston, 1990—; adminstr. Rice U., Houston, 1975-76; cons. in field; mem. credit com. Baylor Coll. Med., supervisory com., nominating com. Mem. Nat. Coun. Univ. Rsch. Adminstrs., Soc. Rsch. Adminstrs., Adminstrs. Internal Medicine. Office: Baylor Coll Medicine Dept Medicine 6550 Fannin St Ste 1423 Houston TX 77030-2720

GORDON, BARBARA ELAINE, school counselor; b. Villa Rica, Ga., Aug. 11, 1947; d. Joseph Carl and Ludie (Busby) G. BA, West Ga. Coll., 1971, MEd, 1986, EdS, 1987. Cert. mid. sch. tchr., specialist in counseling, Ga. Counselor Herschel Jones Mid. Sch., Dallas, Ga. Named Paulding County Counselor of Yr., 1994. Mem. NEA, Ga. Assn. Sch. Counselors, Ga. Assn. Educators, Paulding Assn. Educators, Phi Kappa Phi, Alpha Lambda Delta. Home: 638 Old Tanyard Rd Villa Rica GA 30180-2407

GORDON, BARON JACK, stockbroker; s. George M. and Rose (Salsbury) G.; midshipman U.S. Naval Acad., 1946; BS, Lynchburg Coll., 1953; m. Ellin Bachrach, Aug. 20, 1954; children: Jonathan Ross, Rose Patricia, Alison. V.p. Consol. Ins. Agy., Norfolk, 1948-55; asst. treas. Henry Montor Assos., Inc., N.Y.C., 1956; v.p., sec. Propp & Co., Inc., N.Y.C., 1957-58; ptr. Koerner, Gordon & Co., N.Y.C., 1959-62; sr. ptnr. Gordon, Kulman Perry, and predecessor firm, N.Y.C., 1962-71, pres., chmn. bd., 1971-74; pres., chmn. bd. Palison, Inc., mem. N.Y. Stock Exch., White Plains, N.Y., 1974—; chmn. bd. Rojon, Inc., real estate and investments, Williamsburg, Va., 1979—. Mem. Harrison (N.Y.) Archtl. Rev. Bd., 1970-72, Harrison Planning Bd., 1975-77; bd. dirs. Montefiore Hosp. Assn., YM-YWHA, Lafayette Ednl. Fund., Inc., 1986-92; internat. adv. coun. Mus. of Am. Folk Art, 1990—; naval aide-de-camp to gov. State of Va., 1989—. Lt. USNR, 1953-55, capt., 1989. Mem. Folk Art Soc. (bd. dirs. 1987-95, mem. nat. adv. bd. 1996—), U.S. Naval Acad. Alumni Assn. (life). Clubs: Stock Exch. Luncheon (N.Y.C.), Kingsmill Sports (Williamsburg, Va.), Buttonwood, N.Y. Stock Exch. Home: 113 Elizabeth Meriwether Williamsburg VA 23185-5107 Office: Drawer JG Williamsburg VA 23187

GORDON, BARTON JENNINGS (BART GORDON), congressman, lawyer; b. Murfreesboro, Tenn., Jan. 24, 1949; s. Robert Jennings and Margaret Louise (Barton) G. B.S., Middle Tenn. State U., 1971; J.D., U. Tenn., 1973. Bar: Tenn. 1974. Congressman 99th-105th Congresses from 6th Tenn. dist., Washington, D.C., 1985—. Mem. Tenn. Democratic Exec. Com., 1974-83, exec. dir., 1979-81, chmn., 1981-83; bd. dirs. Middle Tenn. State U. Found.; chmn. Rutherford County United Givers Fund, Rutherford County Cancer Crusade. Mem. Rutherford County C. of C. (bd. dirs.). Methodist. Office: US Ho of Reps 2201 Rayburn HOB Washington DC 20515

GORDON, DAVID STOTT, lawyer; b. Atlanta, Mar. 10, 1951; s. Alexander Stott and Kathleen Marie (Maxwell) G.; m. Melodye Anne Vanoy, Oct. 25, 1991. AB in Psychology with honors, U. Ga., 1972; MA, Trinity Evang. Div. Sch., 1995; JD, U. Ga., 1977; postgrad., Judge Adv. Gen. Sch., 1982-83, Georgetown U., 1984-86, U. N.C., 1991; MA in History, Trinity Evang. Div. Sch., 1995. Bar: Ga. 1977, U.S. Supreme Ct. 1983, U.S. Ct. Internat. Trade 1985, Md. 1986, N.C. 1989. Legal assistance officer 1 Armored Divsn., U.S. Army, Grafenwoehr, Germany, 1978; officer in charge Grafenwoehr Law Ctr., U.S. Army, 1979; chief legal instr. Combined Arms Tng. Ctr., U.S. Army, Vilseck, Germany, 1979-80; atty. internat. law Hqrs. U.S. Army Europe, Heidelberg, 1980-82; legal advisor 1st U.S. Army Recruiting Brigade, Ft. Meade, Md., 1983-86; corp. counsel Caldwell Aircraft Trading Co., Charlotte, N.C., 1987-90; sr. v.p., gen. counsel Caldwell Aircraft Trading Co., Charlotte, 1990—, bd. dirs.; ops. officer HQ XVIII Airborne Corps., U.S. Army, Rafha, Saudi Arabia, 1991; internat. law officer 360th Civil Afffairs Brigade, USAR, Columbia, S.C., 1987—. Contbr. articles to profl. jours. Active mem. Christ Ch. (Episcopal), Charlotte, 1991—. Major U.S. Army, 1977-86, 91; lt. col. Res. Decorated Army Commendation medal with two oak leaf clusters, Army Achievement medal. Mem. ABA, N.C. State Bar Assn. (sect. internat. law), Civil Affairs Assn., Robert Burns Soc. Charlotte, S.E. Renaissance Conf., Renaissance Soc. Am., Phi Beta Kappa. Republican. Home: 2916 Forest Park Dr Charlotte NC 28209-1402 Office: Caldwell Aircraft Trading Ste 1011 4801 E Independence Blvd Charlotte NC 28212-5403

GORDON, ELLA DEAN, women's health nurse; b. Chgo., Jan. 19, 1947; d. Ed and Mozelle (Jordan) Hall; m. Starling Alexander Gordon, Aug. 2, 1969; children: Gerald Alexander, Dana Rolean. Diploma, Grady Meml. Hosp., 1968; student, Ga. State U., 1969-75; BSN, Med. Coll. Ga., 1976; M in Health Sci., Armstrong State Coll., 1983. RN, Ga., Tex. Charge nurse pediatrics evenings Grady Meml. Hosp., Atlanta, 1968-71; staff nurse pediatrics Dr.'s Meml. Hosp., Atlanta, 1971; charge nurse Pediatricians Office, Decatur, Ga., 1971-72; staff nurse VA Hosp., Atlanta, 1972-76; nurse primary care med. ICU VA Hosp., San Antonio, 1983; charge nurse, army nurse corps Eisenhower Army Med. Ctr., Ft. Gordon, Ga., 1976-79; staff nurse obstet. Noble Army Hosp., Ft. McClellan, Ala., 1984; instr. clin. nursing Jacksonville (Ala.) State Coll. Nursing, 1984-85; clin. nurse obstet. Gorgas Army Hosp., Republic of Panama, 1987-89; charge nurse oncology days Eisenhower Army Med. Ctr., Ft. Gordon, Ga., 1989-90; charge nurse obstet. Brooke Army Med. Ctr., Ft. Sam Houston, Tex., 1990-96; mem. labor & delivery Wilford Hall Air Force Med. Ctr., Lackland AFB, Tex., 1996—; cons. health edn. ETOWAH County Clinics, Gadsden, Ala, 1985; health educator Cardiovascular Coun. of Savannah, Ga., 1983, Parent/Child Devel. Svcs., Savannah, 1982. Contbr. articles to profl. jours. Instr. ARC, Ft. McClellan, 1985-86, chmn., vols., 1986-87. Capt. U.S. Army, 1976-79; col. USAR, 1991. Named One of Outstanding Young Women in Am., 1979, 83. Mem. Assn. Mil. Surgeons, Assn. of Women's Health, Obstets. and Neonatal Nurses, Res. Officer Assn., Officers Wives Club (publicity chmn. 1982-83), Sigma Theta Tau. Democrat. Home: 12810 El Marro St San Antonio TX 78233-5832 Office: Wilford Hall AF Med Ctr Lackland AFB TX 78236

GORDON, EUGENE ANDREW, judge; b. Guilford County, N.C., July 10, 1917; s. Charles Robert and Carrie (Scott) G.; m. Virginia Stoner, Jan. 1, 1943; children: Eugene Andrew, Rosemary Anne. AB, Elon Coll., 1938, LLD (hon.), 1982; LLB, Duke U., 1941. Bar: N.C. 1941. Practiced law, 1946-64; mem. firm Young, Young & Gordon, Burlington, 1947-64; solicitor Alamance Gen. County Ct., 1947-54; county atty. Alamance County, 1954-64; U.S. judge Middle Dist. N.C., 1964-82, sr. judge, 1982—; instr. U.S. Atty. Gen.'s Sch. Former chmn. adv. bd. Salvation Army.; Former nat. committeeman N.C. Young Democrats; former pres. Alamance County Young Democrats; chmn. Alamance County Dem. Exec. Com., 1954-64; mem. U.S. Jud. Conf. Adv. Com. on Criminal Rules, 1976-84. Capt. AUS, 1942-46, N.C. Army N.G., 1946-47. Mem. Greensboro Bar Assn., Assn. U.S. Dist. Judges (past pres.). Office: Middle Dist Ct 324 W Market St, Ste 303 Greensboro NC 27401-2544*

GORDON, FELTON HAYS, public relations executive; b. Eastville, Ga., Oct. 1, 1915; s. Emory Emanuel and Claudia (Bush) G.; m. Margaret McKinnon Brooke, May 4, 1944 (div.); child: Chiera Margaret; m. Eisie Pauline Cochran, Nov. 23, 1949 (dec.); children: Richard Alan, Terry Emory; m. Vivian Wilma Pritchard, Sept. 5, 1981. BJ, U. Ga., 1938; postgrad., Auburn U., 1939-41, U. Hawaii, 1942-44; LLB, Atlanta Law Sch., 1952-55. Sports editor Ledger-Enquirer Newspaper, Columbus, Ga., 1938-42; dir. news bur. Automobile Club of So. Calif., Los Angeles, 1945; news dept. staff Times-Dispatch, Richmond, Va., 1946-47; account exec. So. Pub. Rels. Inst., Atlanta, 1948-49; pres. Felton Gordon Pub. Rels., Inc., Atlanta, 1949—; instr. indsl. rels. U. Ga., Atlanta, 1957; mem. adv. com. U.S. Treasury Dept., Washington, 1969-72; supr. seminar presentations on eyecare in 40 countries, 1978-89. Mem. pub. rels. adv. com. World Congress Ctr., Atlanta, 1973. Lt. sr. grade USNR, 1941-45, PTO. Inducted into Ga. Pub. Relations Hall of Fame, U. Ga., 1988. Mem. Pub. Rels. Soc. Am. (pres. Atlanta chpt. 1966, Dyar Massey award 1967, Dist. Chmn. award 1970), Pub. Rels. Rsch. and Edn. Found., Internat. Assn. of Ops. Execs. (pres. 1957), Associazione Professionale Italiana Ottica, Internat. Assn. Med. Assistance to Travelers, Phoenix Soc., Kiwanis (chmn. pub. rels. com. Atlanta chpt. 1967). Republican. Lutheran.

GORDON, HELEN TATE, nurse assistant; b. Washington, Ga., Dec. 17, 1948; d. Geraldine Tate; m. Marvin Gordon (div. 1968); children: Stedric, Itanza. Grad. high sch., Atlanta; cert. acad. excellence, Atlanta Met. Coll., 1990. Cert. nurse asst. Data transcriber IRS, Chamblee, Ga., 1966-67; sec.-steno IRS, Atlanta, 1967-70, U.S. Dept. Labor, Atlanta, 1970-77; sec.-steno U.S. Dept. Transp., Atlanta, 1977-80, equal opportunity specialist, 1980-83, adminstrv. officer, safety officer, 1984-85; adminstrv. sec. Atlanta Job Corps/MTC, Atlanta, 1986-90; adminstrv. asst. Spelman Coll., Atlanta, 1990-93; nurse asst. Imperial Health Care Ctr., Atlanta, 1993—. Recipient Adminstr. Safety award Fed. Hwy. Adminstrn., 1985. Baptist. Office: Imperial Health Care Ctr 2645 Whiting St NW Atlanta GA 30318

GORDON, IAN ROBERT, geophysicist, geologist; b. Portland, Oreg., Oct. 30, 1966; s. James Robert Gordon and Sheila Kay (Lorain) Brown; 1 child, Deveron. BS in Geology with honors, Oreg. State U., 1988; MS in Geology, U. Wyo., 1990. Geology instr. Oreg. Mus. Sci. and Industry, Portland, 1984-85; field mapping asst. U.S. Geol. Survey, Lakewood, Colo., 1988; geologist British Petroleum Am., Houston, 1989; geophysicist Conoco, Inc., Casper, Wyo., 1990-94; sr. geophysicist Conoco, Inc., Corpus Christi, Tex., 1994—; chair supervisory com. Conoco Fed. Credit Union, Casper, Wyo., 1991-92. Recipient Westinghouse Sci. Talent Search, Sci. Svc., 1987, W.A. Tarr award Sigma Gamma Epsilon. Mem. Geol. Soc. Am., Mensa. Office: Conoco Inc 4444 Corona St Corpus Christi TX 78411-4321

GORDON, JEFF, race car driver; b. Aug. 4, 1971; m. Brooke Sealy. Stock race car driver DuPont Chevrolet, 1993—; Season highlights: winner NASCAR Winston Cup, 1994, winner Busch Clash, 1994, finished fourth Daytona 500, 1994, winner Winston Select Open, won the pole for Coca-Cola 600, 1994, winner Brickyard 400, 1994, winner Goodwrench 500, 1995, winner Purolator 500, 1995, winner Food City 500, 1995, winner Pepsi 400, 1995, winner Slick 50 300, 1995, winner Mountain Dew Southern 500, 1995, winner MBNA 500, 1995, others. Named to McDonald's All-star team, 1994, 95; 1993 Maxx Race Cards Rookie of the Yr., 2d youngest Winston Cup Champion NASCAR ever at age 24. Office: NASCAR PO Box 2875 Daytona Beach FL 32120-2875

GORDON, MARCIA LAURA, psychiatrist; b. Lynn, Mass., Oct. 13, 1925; d. Jacob and Rebecca (Portnoy) G.; children: Mark D., Julie D., Susan R. AB, Radcliffe Coll., 1946; MD, Harvard Med. Sch., 1949. Diplomate Am. Bd. Psychiatry and Neurology. Intern U. Ill. Rsch. and Ednl. Hosps., Chgo., 1949-50; resident in pscyhiatry Boston State Hosp., 1950-51; fellow in psychiatry Beth Israel Hosp., Boston, 1951-52, Judge Baker Child Guidance Clinic & Children's Med. Ctr., Boston, 1952-53; staff Mass. Dept. Pub. Health, Quincy, Mass., 1953-54, Community Clinic Mass. Mental Health Ctr., Boston, 1955-56; instr. dept. psychiatry U. Miami Sch. Medicine, 1956-57, asst. prof., 1957-58; chief psychiat. outpatient svcs. Jackson Meml. Hosp. Psychiat. Inst., Miami, 1957-58; clin. asst. prof. U. Miami Sch. Medicine, 1958-79; staff, acting dir. Dade County Child Guidance Clinic, Miami, 1957-60; psychiat. cons. Sunland Ctr., Miami, 1975-78; sr. fellow U. Miami, 1976-77; dir. child psychiatric consultation-liaison svcs. U. Miami Sch. Medicine, 1977-79; psychiatrist pvt. practice Pinellas County, Fla., 1980—. Regional bd. mem. Anti-Defamation League of West Fla., Tampa, 1989-93; com. Tampa Bay Region Campaign for the Third Century of Harvard Medicine, 1990. Fellow Am. Orthopsychiat. Assn.; mem. Am. Psychiat. Assn., Fla. Psychiat. Assn., Am. Arbitration Assn., Pinellas County Psychiat. Assn. (pres. 1982-83, exec. bd. 1983-85), Fla. Med. Assn., Am. Med. Women's Assn. (pres. Suncoast br. 1982-83), B'nai B'rith (unit # 2603), Phi Beta Kappa. Jewish. Home and Office: 1949 Cove Ln Clearwater FL 34624-6426

GORDON, MICHAEL D., electronics engineer and nurse, air force officer; b. St. Louis, Dec. 30, 1946; s. Hardin G. and Lola D. (Wadlow) G.; m. Karen Lynn Minor, May 17, 1967 (dec. Oct. 1967); m. Debra Horton, Nov. 5, 1995; adopted children: Li Nin, Maria, Tina Johnathan. Diploma in respiratory therapy, U. Calif., San Diego, 1970; BSN, UCLA, LA, 1973; BA in Theology, NCA Coll. & Sem., Gatlinburg, Tenn., 1981; BS, MS in Electronic Engring., UCLA, 1989. RN, Calif.; cert. electronics engr., respiratory therapy tech., physician's asst. Respiratory therapist USAF, 1970—; RN, pediatrics, gen. nursing USAF, UNICEF, 1973—; commd. officer USAF, 1973, advanced through grades to brig. gen., 1993; chaplain, counselor USAF, UNICEF, 1981—; elec. engr. USAF, 1989—; flight nurse; emergency nurse; helicopter pilot; cons. Muscular Dystrophy Assn., N.Y.C., 1982—, Children's Hosp., L.A., 1982—; chief bd. dirs., founder Children of an LOC Found., 1970. Goodwill amb. Muscular Dystrophy Telethon, 1974—, Holt Internat. Children's Svcs., 1974—, children's hosps., 1982—, UN, UNICEF, 1982—; vol. nurse, chaplain ARC; vol. Oklahoma City Bombing Disaster Team, 1995. Recipient UNICEF Hall of Fame award, 1980, Disting. Svc. award, 1981. Mem. VFW, ANA, Nat. Chaplain's Assn. (life, Legion of Honor, Chaplain's medal of honor 1981, named to Chaplains Hall of Fame 1983), Am. Assn. Respiratory Care, Am. Legion, Phi Beta Kappa. Baptist.

GORDON, RICHARD E., publishing executive; b. N.Y.C., June 22, 1958; s. Donald Edward and Anne Elizabeth (Waterson) G.; m. Marie C. Dillon, Mar. 11, 1989. BA in History, U. Pa., 1980. Bur. chief Richmond (Va.) Times-Dispatch, Fredericksburg, Va., 1981-82, Petersburg, Va., 1982-85; reporter, editor Richmond (Va.) Times-Dispatch, Richmond, 1985-87; asst. city editor, projects editor The Palm Beach Post, W. Palm Beach, Fla., 1988-90; weekend editor Broward edition The Miami Herald, Hollywood, Fla., 1990-94; newsroom technology coord. The Miami Herald, Miami, 1995, online svcs. mgr., 1996—.

GORDON, ROBERT DANA, transplant surgeon; b. N.Y.C., Jan. 25, 1945; s. Gerson George and Muriel Ruth (Danish) G.; m. Linda Susan Svirsky, July 9, 1970; children: David Charles, Daniel Lawrence. BA, Amherst Coll., 1966; MD, Cornell U., 1971. Diplomate Am. Bd. Surgery. Intern in surgery Mass. Gen. Hosp., Boston, 1971-72, resident in surgery, 1972-74, 77-78; vis. scientist transplantation biology unit Clin. Rsch. Ctr., Harrow, U.K., 1974-76; rsch. fellow Mass. Gen. Hosp./Harvard Med. Sch., Boston, 1974-76; clin. fellow Harvard Med. Sch., Boston, 1977-78; asst. prof. surgery U. Colo., Denver, 1979-83; asst. prof. surgery U. Pitts., 1983-88, assoc. prof. surgery, 1988-92; prof. surgery, chief liver transplant svc. Emory Univ., Sch. Medicine, Atlanta, 1992—; attending surgeon Egleston Children's Hosp., Atlanta, 1992—; attending surgeon, co-dir. organ transplant svcs., Emory U. Hosp., Atlanta, 1992—; chmn. fgn. rels. com. United Network Organ Sharing, Richmond, Va., 1987-90. Bd. dirs. Pitts. chpt. ARC; corp. trustee The Jackson Lab., Bar Harbor, Maine, 1994—. Fellow ACS; mem. Internat. Soc. Cardiovascular Surgery, Ctrl. Surg. Assn., Soc. Univ. Surgeons, Am. Soc. Transplant Surgeons, Transplantation Soc., Internat. Liver Transplantation Soc., Am. Assn. for Study Liver Diseases, Pan Am. Med. Assn. (pres. sect. organ transplantation 1992-94), Ga. Surg. Soc., Pa. Soc. Biomed. Rsch. (bd. dirs. 1991-92). Office: Emory U Hosp 1364 Clifton Rd NE Atlanta GA 30322-1059

GORDON, T. DUANE, reporter; b. Jackson, Miss., Dec. 30, 1974; s. Tommy Miles and Sharon Kaye (Hudson) G. BA in Comms., Miss. State U., 1996. Staff writer The Reflector, Miss., 1992-95, features editor, 1995-96; editor UHP Chronicle, Miss., 1993-94; asst. bookkeeper Rehab., Rsch. and Tng. Ctr. on Blindness, Miss., 1995-96; reporter Madison County Jour., Ridgeland, Miss., 1996—; Adv. pub. rels to author Raymond Houston, Water Valley, Miss., 1996. Contbr. articles to jour. and mag. Vol. counselor, pub. rels. officer Summer Scholars Theatre Camp, Miss. State U., 1994, 95; mem. ACLU Miss., Jackson, 1992-96; pres. Gays, Lesbians, Bisexuals and Friends Miss. State U., 1993-94; mem. Nat. Dem. Party. Recipient 5 awards Miss. Press Assn., 1995, 96. Mem. Soc. Profl. Journalists (v.p. local chpt. 1993-96), Phi Kappa Phi. Democrat. Presbyterian. Home: 345 Fulton Canton MS 39046 Office: Madison County Jour PO Box 219 Ridgeland MS 39158

GORDY, CHARLIE LEON, real estate broker, insurance broker, consultant; b. La Marque, Tex., Aug. 11, 1938; s. Charlie Melville and Mattie Agnes (Williams) G.; children from previous marriage: Chad Leon, Casey Leanne. BBA, U. Houston, 1961. Lic. real estate broker, mgr., Tex.; registered property tax cons., Tex. Pres. Gordy & Gordy, Inc., La Marque, 1964—; adj. faculty Coll. of he Mainland, Texas City, Tex., 1975—, San Jacinto Coll., Pasadena, Tex., 1986. Mem. League City Planning Commn., 1975-78, La Marque Zoning Commn., 1986-88, Texas City Econ. Devel. Commn., 1986-89, 96; chmn. real estate adv. com. Coll. of Mainland, Texas City, 1975-96; mem. La. Marque Bus. Coun. Lt. col. USAR, 1961-89. Mem. Nat. Assn. Realtors, Tex. Real Estate Tchrs. Assn., Tex. Assn. Realtors (bd. dirs. 1982-83), Realtors Nat. Mktg. Inst., Houston Assn. Realtors, Texas City-La Marque Bd. Realtors (pres. 1972-73), Texas City-La Marque C. of C. (bd. dirs. 1987-90), La Marque C. of C. Office: Gordy & Gordy Inc PO Box 608 714 Bayou Rd La Marque TX 77568-0608

GORE, DAVID CURTISS, software company executive, consultant; b. Conway, S.C., Dec. 4, 1964. BS in Fin., U. S.C., 1986. Co-owner, v.p. Gem-Clarke Co., Inc., Columbia, S.C., 1985-89; pvt. practice Columbia, S.C., 1989—. Mem. Lambda Chi Alpha (treas. 1984-85). Republican. Baptist. Office: PO Box 7304 Columbia SC 29202-7304

GORELICK, RISA PAIGE, secondary education educator; b. N.Y.C., Aug. 30, 1969; d. Martin and Valerie G. BA, Goucher Coll., 1991; MA, Miami U., 1994. Editl. cons. Discover Card Svcs., Inc., Riverwoods, Ill., 1991-92; pvt. practive tchg. cons., tutor Oxford, Ohio, 1992-94, Lafayette, La., 1994—; instr., tchg. asst. Miami U./English Dept., Oxford, 1992-94, U. S.W. La./English Dept., Lafayette, 1994—; bd. dirs. freshman English com. U. S.W. La., 1995—; v.p. programming Acadiana Coun. of the Tchrs. of English, Lafayette, 1995—; tchg. cons. Nat. Writing Project, 1995—. Editor: (newsletters) Active Voice, Scribe, 1995—; editl. asst. Readerly/Writerly Texts, 1995—. Cookbook editor (fundraiser) St. Joseph's Diner (soup kitchen), Lafayette, 1994-95. Tchg. fellow Nat. Writing Project of Acadiana, Lafayette, 1995. Mem. Nat. Couns. of the Tchrs. of English, Rsch. Network Forum (assoc. chair 1996—), Modern Language Assn., La. Assn. of Coll. Composition (newsletter editor 1995—), Sigma Tau Delta. Democrat. Jewish. Home: 215 Buena Vista Blvd # 2 Lafayette LA 70503 Office: USL Dept of English PO Box 44691 Lafayette LA 70504-4691

GORES, CHRISTOPHER MERREL, lawyer; b. N.Y.C., Aug. 27, 1943; s. Guido James and Mary (Callaway) G.; children: Ellen, Eugenia, James. AB, Princeton U., 1965; LLB, Columbia U., 1968. Bar: N.Y. 1968, Tex. 1973, U.S. Dist. Ct (no. dist.) Tex. 1977. Assoc. Akin, Gump, Strauss, Hauer & Feld, L.L.P., Dallas, 1973-79, ptnr., 1979—. Bd. dirs. Shakespeare Festival of Dallas, 1982-88. Lt. USNR, 1969-72. Office: Akin Gump Strauss Hauer & Feld LLP Ste 4100 1700 Pacific Ave Dallas TX 75201-7322

GORGES, HEINZ AUGUST, research engineer; b. Stettin, Germany, July 22, 1913; came to U.S., 1959; s. Gustav and Marga (Benda) G.; m. Sapienza Teresa Coco, Sept. 2, 1957. ME, Tech. U. Dresden (Germany), 1938; PhD, Tech. U. Hannover (Germany), 1946. Registered profl. engr., D.C. Group leader LFA Aero Research Establishment, Braunschweig, Germany, 1940-45; with Royal Aircraft Establishment, Farnborough, Eng. 1946-49; prin. sci. officer Weapons Research Establishment, Adelaide, South Australia, 1949-59; sci. asst. George C. Marshall Space Flight Center, NASA, Huntsville, Ala., 1959-61; dir. advanced projects Cook Technol. Center, Morton Grove, Ill., 1961-62; sci. adviser Ill. Inst. Tech. Research Inst., Chgo., 1962-66; asst. v.p. environ. and phys. scis. Tracor, Inc., Austin, Tex., 1966—; v.p. Tracor-Jitco Inc. Rockville, Md., 1972-75; pres. Vineta Inc., Falls Church, Va., 1975—; prof. Redstone extension U. Ala., 1960. Fellow AIAA (assoc.); mem. ASME, Acoustical Soc. Am., cosmos Club. Research super and hypersonics, resources mgmt., environ. scis., system engring. and analysis. Address: 3705 Sleepy Hollow Rd Falls Church VA 22041-1021

GORMAN, CHARLES MATTHEWS, JR., landscape architect; b. Florence, S.C., July 8, 1924; s. Charles Matthews and Martha Catherine (Gresham) G.; m. Edith Nelle Burnette, Oct. 6, 1956; children: Julia C. Gorman Price, Charles M. III, John B., Susan C. Gorman Moore. BS in Indsl. Mgmt., Ga. Tech. U., 1949; B in Landscape Arch., U. Ga., 1963. Hwy. commr. staff Tenn. Hwy. Dept. and Tenn. State Parks, 1963-67; architect U.S. Navy, Charleston, S.C., 1967-70, Combustion Engring. and L.B.C. & W. Architects, Columbia, S.C., 1970-76; freelance site planner Charleston, 1976-80; sr. project mgr. Fluor-Saudi Arabia, 1981, 82 & 88; planner Lockwood-Greene Engrs., Atlanta, 1983-84, 87-88, Sci. Applications Internat. Corp., Oak Ridge, Tenn., 1989-93. V.p. Mid. Tenn. Conservancy Coun., Nashville, 1967; mem. Tenn. Hist. Commn., 1965-68. Served with U.S. Army, 1943-45, ETO. Decorated Purple Heart. Presbyterian. Home: 49 Carriage Sq Clinton TN 37716

GORMAN, CHRIS, state attorney general; b. Frankfort, Ky., Jan. 22, 1943; m. Vicki Lynn Beekman; two sons. Grad., U. Ky. Bar: Ky., 1967. Former ptnr. Conliffe, Sandman, Gorman, and Sullivan, Louisville; former dir. civil div. Jefferson County Attys. Office; atty. gen. Ky., 1992—. Office: Office of Atty Gen Capitol Bldg Frankfort KY 40601

GORMAN, LAWRENCE JAMES, banker; b. Albany, N.Y., Mar. 22, 1948; s. Lawrence Edward and Olive Gertrude (MacDowell) G.; grad. Nat. Grad. Trust Sch., 1980; BS, Syracuse U., 1970; JD, Albany Law Sch. Union U., 1973; m. Barbara J. Pisarek, Aug. 4, 1973; children: Ryan Patrick, Michael Patrick. Admitted to N.Y. bar, 1976; assoc. Grasso, Rivizzigno & Woronov, Syracuse, 1973-76; asst. v.p. Trust and Investment div. Lincoln 1st Bank N.A., Syracuse, 1976-79; v.p. Trust and Investment div. Bank of N.Y., Syracuse, 1979-83; v.p. 1st Va. Banks, Inc., 1983-88; pres. Retirement Plan Svcs. Inc., 1988—; adj. prof. Onondaga County Community Coll.; faculty N.Y. State Bar, 1980-81. Dir. Our Town Fredericksburg, 1985-89, pres., 1986-87; mem. investment com. Am. Cancer Soc. N.Y. State chpt., 1981-83; trustee N.Y.C. chpt. Leukemia Soc. Am., 1982-83. Mem. N.Y. State Bar Assn., Onondaga County Bar Assn. (chmn. bank liaison com. 1980-82), Fredericksburg Bar Assn., Estate Planning Council Fredericksburg (pres.). Clubs: Fredericksburg Country, Commonwealth. Home: 3 Russell Rd Fredericksburg VA 22405-2301 Office: PO Box 763 Fredericksburg VA 22404-0763

GORMAN, ROBERT W., food products executive; b. 1942. Various positions Dart Industries, Deerfield, Ill., 1970-80; exec. TreeSweet Products, Houston, 1980-86, Sunkist, Orange, Calif., 1986-88, J.G. Boswell Co., L.A., 1988-92; pres., CEO Winter Garden (Fla.) Citrus PDTS Coop., 1993—. Office: Winter Garden Citrus PDTS Coop 355 9th St Winter Garden FL 34787-3651

GORMAN-GORDLEY, MARCIE SOTHERN, personal care industry franchise executive; b. N.Y.C., Feb. 25, 1949; d. Jerry R. and Carole Edith (Frendel) Sothern; m. N. Scott Gorman, June 14, 1969 (div.); children: Michael Stephen, Mark Jason; m. Mark A. Gordley, June 26, 1994. AA, U. Fla., 1968; BS, Memphis State U., 1970. Tchr., Memphis City Sch. System, 1970-73; tng. dir. Weight Watchers of Palm Beach County and Weight Watchers So. Ala., Inc., West Palm Beach, Fla., 1973—, area dir., then pres., 1977—; pres. Markel Ads, Inc. Cubmaster Troop 130. Hon. lt. col. a.d.c. Ala. Militia. Mem. Women' Am. ORT (program chmn. 1975), Optometric Soc. (sec. 1973), Weight Watchers Franchise Assn. (chair mktg. com., mem. advt./mktg. coun., chairperson region IV bd. dirs., treas., 2d v.p. 1991, 1st v.p.), Nat. Orgn. Women, Exec. Women of the Palm Beaches, Am. Bus. Women's Assn., Nat. Assn. Female Execs., Zonta. Home: 429 N Country Club Dr Lake Worth FL 33462-1003 Office: 2459 S Congress Ave West Palm Beach FL 33406-7613

GORMLEY, DENNIS MICHAEL, consulting company executive; b. Meriden, Conn., Feb. 1, 1943; s. Lawrence Edward and Anna (Seitz) G.; m. Elizabeth Carol Festa, Aug. 12, 1967 (div. Sept. 1984); children: Douglas Lawrence, Jennifer Marie; m. Janet Lee Johnson, Mar. 23, 1985. BA, U. Conn., 1965, MA, 1966. Advanced through grades to 1st lt. U.S. Army; rsch. specialist fed. civil svc. Army Materiel Command, Washington, 1969-72; chief fgn. intelligence U.S. Army Harry Diamond Labs, Washington, 1972-79; sr. v.p. Pacific-Sierra Rsch. Corp., Arlington, Va., 1979—; cons. Sandia Nat. Labs., Albuquerque, 1992—, Rand Corp., Santa Monica, Calif., 1987-90, The Brookings Instn., Washington, 1973-75; govt. adv. com. mem. Dept. Def., Washington, 1983—; vis. scholar Geneva Ctr. for Security Policy, 1996—. Author: Double Zero and Soviet Military Strategy, 1988, rev. paperback, 1990; co-author: Swords and Shields, 1987, Doctrine, The Alliance and Arms Control, 1987, ATBMs and Western Security, 1988, Controlling the Spread of Land-Attack Cruise Missiles, 1995; contbr. articles to profl. jours. and newspapers. 1st lt. U.S. Army, 1966-69. Rsch. fellow Internat. Inst. for Strategic Studies, London, 1984. Mem. AAAS, Internat. Inst. for Strategic Studies, Arms Control Assn., Security Affairs Support Assn., Nat. Liberal Club, London, Phi Alpha Theta. Home: 4864 33rd Rd N Arlington VA 22207-2802 Office: Pacific Sierra Rsch Corp 1400 Key Blvd Arlington VA 22209-1518

GORR, LOUIS FREDERICK, investment consultant; b. North Platte, Nebr., Aug. 1, 1941; s. Ernest Frederick and Eileen Bethel (Green) G.; m. Madeleine Zangla, Dec. 12, 1967; 1 dau., Michaela. B.A., U. Nebr., 1963, M.A., 1967; postgrad., U. Md., 1972; M.B.A., U. Dallas, 1981; mgmt. and real estate courses, So. Meth. U. Spl. asst. to dir. Nat. Mus. Am. History and Tech., Smithsonian Instn., Washington, 1969-73; dir. div. museums and historic preservation Fairfax (Va.) County Govt., 1973-77; dir. Dallas County (Tex.) Heritage Soc., 1977-79, Dallas Mus. Natural History, 1979-86, Dallas Aquarium, 1979-86; dep. dir. fin and adminstrn., treas. Winterthur (Del.) Mus. and Gardens, 1986-89; owner East End Devel. Corp., 1984-86; pres. Janus Mgmt. Advisors, 1985-86; exec. dir. Mus. of the Confederacy, Richmond, Va., 1989-92; investment cons. Branch Cabell & Co., Richmond, Va., 1993-96; fin. cons. Lincoln fin. group Profl. Fin. Planning Corp., Richmond, 1996—; pres. Harbor Fin. Advisors, LLC, Richmond, 1996—; real estate broker, Tex.; cons., lectr. mus. and mgmt. fields, 1970—; adj. prof. mus. studies U. Okla., 1982-93; mem. bd. commerce Dallas Nat. Bank, 1980-84; dir., mem. exam. and shareholder rels. coms. Fidelity Nat. Bank, 1985-86, advisory dir., 1986-88—; chmn. bd. commerce Republic Bank Dallas East, 1983-84. Author numerous articles, revs. in field. Pres. Fairfax Symphony Orch., 1976-77; bd. dirs. No. Va. Youth Symphony, 1975-77, Met. Washington Cultural Alliance, 1976, Prince George's County (Md.) Arts Council, 1973, Fairfax County Assn. Civic Orgns., 1976-77, Cen. Va. Pub. Broadcasting, 1990—; mem. arts and culture adv. com. Dallas Ind. Sch. Dist., Leadership Dallas, 1983; leadership devel. trainer United Way, 1980-83; mem. adv. bd. March of Dimes Found.; mem. community adv. bd. Med. Coll. Va., 1991-93. Served with USAF, 1963-64. Research fellow Smithsonian Instn., 1971; Research fellow Naval Inst. Mem. Am. Assn. Mus. (bd. dirs. 1982-83), Va. Assn. Mus. (bd. dirs. 1989-93), Tex. Assn. Mus. (pres. 1981-83, dir.), Am. Mgmt. Assn., Turn-Around Mgmt. Assn., Assn. Sci. Mus. Dirs. (v.p. 1983), Dallas Bus. League, Dallas 40, Dallas C. of C., East Dallas C. of C., Leadership Dallas Alumni Assn., Bus. Workout Coun. (bd. dirs. Richmond), Internat. Assn. Fin. Planning, Inst. CFPs, Masons (32 degree), Shriners, Sigma Iota Epsilon, Lambda Chi Alpha. Republican. Home: 2310 E Marshall St Richmond VA 23223-7147 Office: 9011 Arboretum Pky Ste 320 Richmond VA 23236

GORYN, SARA, textiles executive, real estate developer, psychologist; b. Lima, Peru, Dec. 28, 1944; came to U.S., 1988; d. Ricardo and Lola (Braiman) Grunfeld; m. Jorge Goryn, June 18, 1966 (dec. Sept. 1985); children: Karen, Monica, Lea. B in Psychology, Cath. U., Lima, 1978, M in Psychology, 1985; BA in Bus., Queens Coll., 1989-91. Sec. Inst. Internat. Edn., Lima, 1963-66; head dept. clin. psychology Coll. Leon Pinelo, Lima, 1978-85; pvt. practice Lima, 1978-85; founder Nido Picaflores, Lima, 1980; gen. mgr. Fabritex Peruana, Lima, 1985-88, Michelle Textiles, Charlotte, N.C., 1989—; v.p. Monica Investment, Charlotte, 1990-93, pres., 1993—; bd. dirs. Fabritex Peruana, Lima, MLK Internat., Charlotte, SOFAS y MAS, Lima. Author learning disabilities curriculum, 1980. Mem. Soc. Israelita Peru, Lima, 1966—, Hebraica, Lima, 1966—. Mem. Peru Psychol. Soc. Democrat. Home: 3600 Castellaine Dr Charlotte NC 28226-6386

GOSE, WILLIAM CHRISTOPHER, chemist; b. Dante, Va., Oct. 8, 1940; s. Willie Gibson and Lillian Beatrice (Addington) G.; m. Mary Hildreth Gross, Dec. 31, 1974. BS in Chem. and Math., East Tenn. State U., 1976; MBA in Bus. Mgmt., U. Tenn., 1983. Chief lab. analyst Holston Def. Corp., Kingsport, Tenn., 1961-74; sr. technician Holston Def. Corp./Tenn. Eastman Co., Kingsport, 1974-78; rsch. chemist Tenn. Eastman Co., Kingsport, 1978-85; tech. rep. Eastman Chem. Products, Inc., Kingsport, 1985-94; prin. tech. rep. Eastman Chem. Co., Kingsport, 1994—. Contbr. papers to profl confs. including Schotland Conf., Houston, 1990, Polymer Conf., Lucerne, Switzerland, 1991. With USN, 1958-61. Mem. Soc. Plastics Engrs. (sr., author papers plastics recycle conf. Atlanta 1992, additives conf. Orlando, Fla. 1993), Am. Chem. Soc., Elks (exalted ruler 1991-93, state officer 1991—, Merit award 1991-93), Optimist Internat. (pres. local chpt. 1993-94). Republican. Methodist. Office: Eastman Chem Co PO Box 1974 Kingsport TN 37662-5230

GOSLAWSKI, VIOLET ANN, nurse, substance abuse counselor; b. Bangor, Mich., Aug. 31, 1929; d. George and Ethel Pikal; m. Stephen T. Goslawski, Jan. 18, 1975; children: John F. Cappetto, Steve Goslawski, Carol Smurawski. AAS in Nursing, Morton Coll., 1986; AAS in Mental Health, Loop Coll., 1987. RN, Fla., Ill.; clin. nurse specialist; cert. substance abuse counselor; nat. cert. addictions counselor, internat. cert. addictions counselor. Psychiat. nurse and addictions counselor HCA Riveredge Hosp., Forest Park, Ill., 1987-90; psychiat. nurse, counselor Choices of Pinellas Cmty. Hosp., Choices of Pinellas Park, Fla., 1990—, Medfield/Charter Psychiat. Hosp., Largo, Fla., 1990-96, Rader Inst., Seminole, 1990.

GOSLEN, FRANK ODELL, insurance adjustment company executive, lawyer; b. Forsyth County, N.C., Nov. 19, 1927; s. Henry Benjamin and Josephine L. (Boner) G.; m. Mary Anne Raines; children: Benjamin Neely, Clifton William, Theodore Henry, Katherine Josephine. AA, Mars Hill Jr. Coll., 1948; LLB, Wake Forest U., 1951, JD, 1970. Bar: N.C. 1953. From trainee to pres. Southeastern Adjustment Co., Greensboro, N.C., 1953—; former bd. dirs. and mem. faculty Inst. Piedmont; past bd. dirs. N.C. Ins. Edn. Found.; condr. state-wide ednl. seminar N.C. Ins. Women, 1975; guest lectr. Southeastern Inst. for Ins. Agts., 1975, 76; condr. interruption workshop Greensboro Ins. Women, 1981; speaker on ins. to Civitans, Fire and Casualty Underwriting Forum, Greensboro Ins. Women, also others; instr. courses Ind. Ins. Agts., 1962, 63, 73, CPCU, 1974, 77, 78. Assoc. editor Adjuster's Report, former editor. Mem. tennis com. Lawndale Pool, Inc.; bd. dirs. Piedmont Bapt. Recreation Assn.; deacon, trustee, Sunday sch. tchr. and supt., chmn. fin. com., pulpit com. Lawndale Bapt. Ch., chmn. ins. com., 1973—; mem. program for advanced tech. crime and prevention N.C. Justice Acad., 1976; former softball and basketball coach. Recipient Outstanding Counselor award Piedmont Bapt. Assn., 1968, Boss of Yr., Ins. Women Greater Greensboro, 1972, Greensboro Ins. Women, 1974. Mem. Nat. Assn. Ind. Ins. Adjusters (past com. mem.), N.C. Bar Assn., Greensboro Bar Assn., N.C. Adjusters Assn. (charter, past pres., cert. of merit 1966, Adjuster of Yr. award 1971), Greensboro Claims Assn. (charter, past pres., Adjuster of Yr. award 1967, 70), Soc. CPCU's (charter Piedmnt chpt., past pres.), VFW, Greensboro Mystery Club, Lions. Home: 303 Pineburr Rd Greensboro NC 27455-2713 Office: Southeastern Adjustment Co PO Box 9395 Greensboro NC 27429-0395

GOSNELL, CANDACE SHEALY, industrial sociologist, educator; b. Alexandria, La., July 26, 1948; d. James Monroe and Joyce (Graves) Shealy; m. Reginald L. Gosnell (div. 1988); children: Juliette Elizabeth, Kimberly Joyce. BA in Humanities, U. Houston, 1983, MS in Future Studies, 1985; EdD, Clemson U., 1994. Coord. residency tng. U. Houston, 1982-85; dir. adminstrn. Marshall & Stevens, Inc., L.A., 1985-88; adj. instr. Tri-County Tech. Coll., Pendleton, S.C., 1989-90, dir. curriculum, 1990—; charter mem., cons. S.C. Internat. Edn. Consortium, Greenville, 1991; mem. task force, cons. S.C. Assn. for Devel. Edn., Greenwood, 1991. Recipient Outstanding Leadrship award Am. Bus. Inst., 1991; named one of 2000 Notable Am. Women Am. Bus. Inst., 1991. Mem. NAFE, S.C. Tech. Edn. Assn., Am. Vocat. Soc., World Future Soc., Women in Higher Edn., Phi Delta Kappa. Presbyterian. Home: 135 Grandview Ct Vance SC 29163-9552 Office: Tri County Tech Coll PO Box 587 Pendleton SC 29670-0587

GOSS, DONALD DAVIS, consultant, author, lecturer; b. Marblehead, Mass., May 18, 1923; s. Donald Chapin and Ruth Alden (Johnson) Goss; m. Marilyn Elizabeth Riddle, Jan. 1, 1948; children: Daniel Griffith, Cynthia Davis, Charles Chapin. Student, Chauncy Hall Sch., Boston; grad., Sch. Practical Art Boston. Freelance comml. artist; art dir. various advt. agys. and comml. printers; advt. mgr., dir. mktg. Vogue Dolls Inc., until 1958; founder consulting firm Ideation, 1958—; founder Goss Galleries, Inc., Dallas, until 1990. Author: Problem Solving Through Innovation, Imaginative Skills Development, Take Time to Think, Turning Problems Into Profits. With U.S. Army, WW II. Home and Office: Ideation 1404 Carrollton Ave Metairie LA 70005-1811

GOSS, PORTER J., congressman; b. Waterbury, Conn., Nov. 26, 1938; m. Mariel Robinson; children: Leslie, Chauncey, Mason, Gerrit. BA, Yale U., 1960. Clandestine svcs. officer CIA, 1962-71; co-founder newspaper Island Reporter, Sanibel, Fla., 1973; mayor City of Sanibel, coun. mem., 1974-82; commr. County of Lee, Fla., 1982-88, chmn. commn., 1985; mem. 100th-104th Congresses from 14th Fla. Dist., 1988—; chmn. rules subcom. on legis. process, mem. stds. of ofcl. conduct com., mem. select com. on intelligence; port commr. S.W. Fla. Regional Airport. Dir. Lee County Mental Health Ctr., J.N. "Ding" Darling Found.; dir. chmn. Sanibel-Captiva Conservation Found.; chmn. bd. Canterbury Sch.; mem. S.W. Fla. Mental Health Dist. Bd. Intelligence officer U.S. Army, 1960-62. Republican. Presbyterian. *

GOSSEN, EMMETT JOSEPH, JR., motel chain executive, lawyer; b. Kenosha, Wis., Aug. 23, 1942; s. Emmett J. and Julia (Tribur) G.; m. Patricia E. Zele, June 14, 1968; children: André, Nicole. BA, Case Western Res. U., 1965; PhD, Yale U., 1970; JD, Harvard U., 1974. Bar: Mass. 1974, D.C. 1975. Assoc. Hale and Dorr, Boston, 1974-77; counsel The Sheraton Corp., Boston, 1977-83, sr. v.p., dir. devel., 1983-86; exec. v.p. corp. devel. Inter-Continental Hotels, Montvale, N.J., 1988-90; sr. v.p., dir. devel. Motel 6, L.P., Santa Barbara, Calif., 1986-88; exec. v.p. corp. affairs and devel. Motel 6, L.P., Dallas, 1990—. Office: Motel 6 LP 14651 Dallas Pky Ste 500 Dallas TX 75240-7480

GOSSETT, DANETTE ESTELLE, marketing professional; b. Richmond, Va., Oct. 31, 1958; d. Robert Alton and Charlesanna (Logan) G. BS in Mktg. Mgmt., Old Dominion U., 1980. Market rsch. analyst Southeastern

Inst. Rsch., 1979-81; with Dentsu Corp., N.Y., 1981-83; sr. media planner, account exec. Compton Advt., 1983-85; advt. and mktg. mgr. Metromedia Long Distance; nat. advt. mgr. Avis Rent A Car Systems, Inc., 1988-90; dir. mktg. svcs. Royal Caribbean Cruise Line, 1990-92; founder Mktg. Firm, 1992—; instr. Women's Bus. Devel. Ctr., Fla. Internat. U., 1994—. Mem. Women in Bus., Coral Gables (Fla.) C. of C., 1992-94, chmn. women's bus. network, 1995-97, bd. dirs., 1996—; mem. Greater Miami (Fla.) Conv. Bur., 1994; chmn. mktg. subcom. Coral Gables (Fla.) Retail Coun., 1993-94. Mem. Nat. Assn. Women Bus. Owners.

GOSSETT, MARK VALTON, minister; b. Dallas, Oct. 28, 1956; s. James Valton and Jo (Shelton) G.; m. Lynda Kay Genevay, Jan. 3, 1981; children: Jonathan Daniel, Andrew Mark, Sarah Jo. BA, Baylor U., 1979; MDiv, Southwestern Bapt. Theol. Sem., 1982. Pastor Mt. Olive Bapt. Ch., Talco, Tex., 1980-82, Lone Oak (Tex.) Bapt. Ch., 1982-85, Ctrl. Baptist Ch., Baytown, Tex., 1985—. Vol. St. James House, Baytown, 1990—, Baytown N. Little League, 1991-95; United Way spkr. for Bay Area Rehab. Ctr., 1993-95. Mem. San Jacinto Bapt. Assn. (adminstrv. coun. 1986—, chmn. camp com. 1986-88, chmn. long range planning com. 1988-91, chmn. credentials and petitionery com. 1991-94, vice-moderator, treas. 1994-96), Sulphur Springs Masonic Lodge, Dallas Scottish Rite Bodies. Office: Ctrl Bapt Ch 1800 King St Baytown TX 77520-7537

GOSSMAN, FRANCIS JOSEPH, bishop; b. Balt., Apr. 1, 1930; s. Frank M. and Mary Genevieve (Steadman) G. BA, St. Mary Sem., Balt., 1952; S.T.L., N. Am. Coll., Rome, 1955; J.C.D., Cath. U. of Am., 1959. Ordained priest Roman Cath. Ch., 1955; asst. pastor Basilica of the Assumption, Balt., 1959-68; asst. chancellor Archdiocese of Balt., 1959-65, vice chancellor, 1965-68; pro-synodal judge Balt. Tribunal, 1961; vice officialis Tribunal of Archdiocese of Balt., 1962-65, officialis, 1965-68; made papal chamberlain with title Very Rev. Monsignor, 1965; elected to Senate of Priests of Archdiocese, 1967-68; adminstr. Cathedral of Mary Our Queen, 1968-70; named aux. bishop of Balt. and titular bishop of Aguntum, 1968-75, apptd. vicar gen., 1968; apptd. to Bd. Consultors, 1969; urban vicar Archdiocese of Balt., 1970-75; bishop of Raleigh N.C., 1975—; Mem. Balt. Community Relations Commn., 1969-75; mem. exec. com. Md. Food Com., Inc., 1969-75. Bd. dirs. United Fund Central Md., 1974-75. Mem. Canon Law Soc. Am., Nat. Conf. Cath. Bishops, U.S. Cath. Conf. Home: 1601 Westbridge Ct Raleigh NC 27606-2656 Office: 300 Cardinal Gibbons Dr Raleigh NC 27606-2108*

GOTSOPOULOS, BARBARA LYNN, computer consultant; b. Paterson, N.J., Mar. 16, 1948; d. Albert Raymond and Vivian Betty (Polkoph) Parker; m. Nicholas Solon Gotsopoulos, Mar. 15, 1970. BS, Rensselaer Poly. Inst., 1969; postgrad., Sheridan Vocat. Tech. Ctr., 1991. Prin. in wholesale distbg. co. Hollywood, Fla., 1981-84; pvt. practice commodities trading cons. Hollywood, 1984-87; pres. Blue Springs Capital Corp., Hollywood, 1985-86, 1st Fla. Commodities, Inc., North Lauderdale, 1987; ptnr. Multinat. Svcs., Hollywood, 1986-87; br. office mgr. Ind. Brokers Group, Inc., North Lauderdale, 1987; asst. to sr. v.p. E.F. Hutton and Co., Inc., North Miami Beach, Fla., 1987-88, Prudential-Bache Securities, North Miami Beach, 1988; comm. cons. Telus Communications, North Miami, 1988-89, Metagram Am., Inc., Hollywood, Fla., 1989-90; computer cons. pvt. practice, Hollywood, 1992; v.p. ops. Bankcard Ctr. Miami, Miami Lakes, Fla., 1992-94; adminstrv. asst. Fla. ops. and devel. Consumer Health Svcs., Pembroke Pines, Fla., 1994-95; adminstrv. asst. planning and zoning City of Hallandale, Fla., 1995—. Mem. NAFE (charter), United Greeks Am. (co-founder), Alpha Psi Omega, Phi Beta Lambda.

GOTT, MARJORIE EDA CROSBY, conservationist, former educator; b. Louisville; d. Alva Baird and Nellie (Jones) Crosby; m. John Richard Gott, Jr., Mar. 12, 1946 (dec. Sept. 1993); 1 child, J. Richard III. AB in Math., U. Louisville, 1934; postgrad., U. Ky., 1938-42. Nationally accredited flower show judge, landscape design critic and judge. Underwriter Commonwealth Life Ins. Co., Louisville, 1934-37; tchr. English Hikes Sch., Buechel, Ky., 1937-43; civilian chief statis. control unit Materiel Command, Army Air Force, Dayton, Ohio, 1943-46; tchr. psychology Bapt. Hosp. and Gen. Hosp., Louisville, 1950-52; dedicated Ky.'s Floral Clock to All Kentuckians Who Take Pride in the Beauty of Their State Commonwealth of Ky.,1961. Author: (booklet) How a Garden Club Beautifies a City, 1967. Pres. Young Women's Rep. Club of Louisville and Jefferson County, 1938-40; pres. Beautification League Louisville and Jefferson County, 1963-64; co-chair Keep Ky. Cleaner-Greener, 1963-68; bd. dirs. Scenic Ky., Inc., 1989—, Nat. Coun. State Garden Clubs, 1961-83. Recipient Conservation award of merit Commonwealth of Ky., 1963, Landscape Design Critics award Nat. Coun. State Garden Clubs, 1979. Mem. Woman's Club of Louisville (pres. 1973-75, hon. 1991—), Garden Club of Ky. (pres. 1961-63), Nat. Assn. Parliamentarians (founder, pres. Louisville unit 1961-63), Louisville Astron. Soc. (hon.). Presbyterian. Home: 136 Indian Hills Trl Louisville KY 40207-1541

GOTTESMAN, IRVING ISADORE, psychology educator; b. Cleve., Dec. 29, 1930; s. Bernard and Virginia (Weitzner) G.; m. Carol Applen, Dec. 23, 1970; children—Adam M., David B. B.S., Ill. Inst. Tech., 1953; Ph.D., U. Minn., 1960. Diplomate in clin. psychology and psychol. assessment; lic. psychologist Minn., Calif., Va. Intern clin. psychology VA Hosp., Mpls., 1959-60; lectr. dept. social relations Harvard U., 1960-63; USPHS fellow in psychiat. genetics Inst. Psychiatry, London, 1963-64; assoc. prof. psychiat. & genetics, dept. psychiatry U. N.C., 1964-66; prof. dept. psychology, psychiatry and genetics U. Minn., 1966-80; prof. dept. psychiatry and genetics Washington U., St. Louis, 1980-85; Commonwealth prof. psychology U. Va., Charlottesville, 1985-94, Sherrell J. Aston prof. psychology, 1994—; cons. NIMH, Washington, 1975-79, 92-96, NIMH Nat. Plan for Schizophrenia, 1988-89; mem. Pres.'s Commn. on Huntington Disease, 1977; tng. cons. VA, Washington, 1968-85; fellow Ctr. for Advanced Studies in the Behavioral Scis., Stanford, Calif., 1987-88; Inst. of Medicine Com. cons. Vietnam War Experience Study, 1987-88; NRC cons. Workshop on Schizophrenia, 1995-96. Author: Schizophrenia and Genetics, 1972 (Hofheimer prize), Schizophrenia The Epigenetic Puzzle, 1982, Schizophrenia Genesis: The Origins of Madness, 1991 (transl. into Japanese and German, William James Book award, Phi Beta Kappa U. Va. Book award 1992), Schizophrenia and Genetic Risks, 1992, Schizophrenia and Manic Depressive Disorder: Biological Roots of Mental Illness Revealed by Study of Identical Twins, 1994, transl. into Japanese, 1997, Seminars in Psychiatric Genetics, 1994; editor: Man, Mind and Heredity, 1971, Vital Statistics, Demography and Schizophrenia, 1989. Served with USNR, 1956-61. Guggenheim fellow U. Copenhagen, 1972; recipient R. Thornton Wilson prize Ea. Psychiat. Rsch. Assn., 1965, Stanley Dean award Am. Coll. Psychiatrists, 1988, Eric Stromgren medal Danish Psychiat. Soc., 1991, Kurt Schneider prize, Bonn, 1992, Alexander Gralnick prize Am. Assn. Suicidology, 1992, Jonathan Logan award Nat. Alliance for Mentally Ill, 1995; David C. Wilson lectr. U. Va. Sch. Medicine, 1967; Parker lectr. Ohio State U. Sch. Medicine, 1983, 93. Fellow APA (Disting. Scientist award divsn. 12, sect. 3 1994), AAAS, Am. Psychopathol. Assn., Royal Coll. Psychiatrists (hon.), Am. Psychol. Soc. (human capital initiative task force for psychopathology rsch. agenda 1993-96); mem. Minn. Human Genetics League (v.p. 1969-71), Soc. Study Social Biology (v.p. 1976-80), Behavior Genetics Assn. (pres. 1976-77, T. Dobzhansky award 1990), Am. Soc. Human Genetics (editl. bd. 1967-72), Soc. Rsch. in Psychopathology (pres. 1993). Home: 260 Terrell Rd W Charlottesville VA 22901-2167 Office: Univ Va Gilmer Hall Charlottesville VA 22903

GOTTFRIED, BEVERLY JANE SICKLER, dental hygienist; b. Takoma Park, Md., Aug. 19, 1947; d. Orion Harding and Doris Helen (Herrmann) Sickler; m. Myron Leon Gottfried, Dec. 28, 1969; children: Heather Sherene, Haley Marie. BS in Dental Hygiene, Loma Linda U., 1969. Registered dental hygienist, N.C. Pvt. practice, 1969—; instr. preventive and community dentistry Loma Linda (Calif.) U. Sch. Dentistry, 1970-76, instr. clin. dental hygiene, 1972-76; instr. clin. dental hygiene Asheville (N.C.) Buncombe Tech. Sch., 1977-78; pres. Jr. Dental Aux., Loma Linda, 1975-76. Editor: Taste of Home, 1993; author: School Health Magazine, 1974-77; author: (cartoon) Sparkles, Your Friend, 1975; patentee bouquet in a can; contbr. articles to mags. Dental health educator with puppets, Loma Linda, N.C. and Dublin, Ireland, 1969—; pres. Dental Hygiene Alumni Assn., Loma Linda, 1974-75; exec. com. mem. Seventh-day Adventists, N.C. and S.C., 1987—, com. mem. Assn. Bd. for Carolina Conf., 1987—. Home and Office: 1415 Patton Ave Asheville NC 28806-1721

GOTTLIEB, MARISE SUSS, epidemiologist; b. N.Y.C., July 16, 1938; d. Lester J. and Fannie (Freeman) Suss; m. A. Arthur Gottlieb, June 8, 1958; children: Mindy Cheryl, Joanne Meredith. AB, Barnard Coll., 1958; MD, NYU, 1962; MPH, Harvard U., 1966. Intern, Mass. Meml. Hosp., 1962-63; resident preventative medicine dept. epidemiology Harvard U. Med. Sch., 1965-68, instr. dept. medicine, H.M., Boston, 1969-70, also fellow, asst. in Medicine Peter Bent Brigham Hosp.; dir. chronic disease control N.J. Dept. Health, Trenton, 1970-75; asst. prof. dept. community medicine Rutgers Med. Sch., Piscataway N.J., 1972-75; assoc. prof. dept. medicine Tulane U. Sch. Medicine, New Orleans, 1975-91; assoc. prof. dept. epidemiology Sch. Pub. Health, 1975-80; chief chronic disease control, La. Dept. Health and Human Resources, New Orleans, 1975-85; dir. clin. and regulatory affairs, v.p. med. affairs Imreg Inc., New Orleans, 1985—; mem. epidemiology and disease control study sect. NIH, Bethesda, Md., 1982-85. NIH traineeship, 1965-66, spl research fellow Nat. Inst. Arthritis, Metabolism and Digestive Diseases, 1966-68. Diplomate Am. Bd. Preventive Medicine. Fellow Am. Coll. Preventive Medicine, Am. Coll. Epidemiology; mem. Am. Diabetes Assn., Soc. Epidemiol. Rsch., Am. Fedn. Clin. Rsch., Am. Pub. Health Assn. Contbr. articles to profl jours. Office: Imreg Inc 144 Elk Pl Ste 1400 New Orleans LA 70112

GOTTLIEB, SIDNEY ALAN, optometrist; b. Pitts.; s. Walter Coleman and Jennie (Moskovitz) G.; m. Kathie Sue Block, Apr. 30, 1989; 1 child, Jamie Lauren. BSA, U. Ga., 1981; BS, Pa. Coll. of Optometry, 1982, OD, 1985. Lic. optometrist. Optometrist Gottlieb Vision Group, Stone Mountain, Ga., 1985-88, Opticare Assocs., Marietta, Ga., 1988, Stephen E. Schock and Assocs., Norcross, Ga., 1988-94; pvt. practice Woodstock, Ga., 1994—; vision cons. Ga. Ctr. for Multi-handicapped, Atlanta, 1986-88, Peachtree Reentry Program for the Head Injured, Lawrenceville, Ga., 1986-88, Shephard Spinal Ctr., Atlanta, 1988-94, DeKalb Med. Ctr., Decatur, Ga., 1991—. Mem. Am. Optometric Assn., Ga. Optometric Assn., So. Coun. of Optometry, Brain Injury Assn., Ga. Assn. for Children with Learning Disabilities, Young Couples Club (v.p. 1989-90). Democrat. Jewish. Office: Lenscrafters 210 Gatsby Pl Alpharetta GA 30202-6160

GOTTWALD, BRUCE COBB, chemical company executive; b. Richmond, Va., Sept. 28, 1933; s. Floyd Dewey and Anne Ruth (Cobb) G.; m. Nancy Hays, Dec. 22, 1956; children: Bruce Cobb Jr., Mark Hays, Thomas Edward. BS, Va. Mil. Inst., 1954; postgrad., U. Va., Inst. Paper Chemistry, Appleton, Wis., U. Richmond; LLD (hon.), Va. Union U., 1990. Chemist Albemarle Paper Mfg. Co., Richmond, Va., from 1956, asst. sec., 1960; v.p. Ethyl Corp., Richmond, Va., 1962-64, sec., 1962-69, exec. v.p., 1964-69, pres., COO, 1969-92, pres., CEO, 1992-94, chmn., CEO, 1994—; bd. dirs. James River Corp., CSX Corp., Tredegar Industries, First Colony Corp. Former pres. Va. Mus. Fine Arts; bd. visitors Va. Mil. Inst.; bd. govs. Va. Coun. Econ. Edn. Named Outstanding Industrialist, Sci. Mus. Va., 1990. Office: Ethyl Corp PO Box 2189 Richmond VA 23218-2189

GOTTWALD, FLOYD DEWEY, JR., chemical company executive; b. Richmond, Va., July 29, 1922; s. Floyd Dewey and Anne (Cobb) G.; m. Elisabeth Morris Shelton, Mar. 22, 1947; children: William M., James T., John D. BS, Va. Mil. Inst., 1943; MS, U. Richmond, 1951. With Albemarle Paper Co., Richmond, 1943-62, sec., 1956-57, v.p., sec., 1957-62, pres., 1962; exec. v.p. Ethyl Corp., Richmond, 1962-64, vice chmn., 1964-68, chmn., 1968-94, CEO, 1970-92, chmn. exec. com., 1970-94, vice chmn., 1994-96; bd. dirs. Tredegar Industries, Inc.; chmn., CEO Albemarle Corp. Past bd. dirs. Nat. Petroleum Coun.; trustee U. Richmond; mem. River Rd. Bapt. Ch.; past trustee V.M.I. Found., Inc.; bd. visitors The Coll. of William & Mary, 1993—; pres. bd. trustees Va. Mus. Fine Arts, 1994-96. Decorated Bronze Star, Purple Heart. Mem. NAM (former bd. dirs.), Am. Petroleum Inst. (bd. dirs.) Chem. Mfrs. Assn. (former bd. dirs.), Internat. Game Fish Assn. (trustee 1992—), Alfalfa Club, Country Club Va., Commonwealth Club. Office: Albemarle Corp PO Box 1335 Richmond VA 23218

GOUGE, BETTY MERLE, family therapist; b. Colbert, Okla., Nov. 8, 1937; d. Clifford Carlton and Cleo (Sims) Gage; m. W. Frank Wolfenbarger, July 26, 1980; children: Carol Gouge-Blanchard, Jeff Gouge, Gretchen Wolfenbarger-Doll. BS, Tex. Womans U., 1968, MS, 1971, PhD, 1975. workshop leader shcs. and profl. orgns. Co-author: Choices! Choices! Choices!, 1985, Wonderful You, 1985, My Feelings and Me, 1985, Let's Share, 1985, Land of Listening, 1985, The Feeling Fun House, 1985, A Lasting Friend, 1985, Rules at my House, 1986, An Island Adventure, 1986. Mem. APA, AACD, DGPA, AGPA, DAMFT, Am. Assn. Marriage and Family Therapy. Office: Family Counseling Ctr Ste 280 2925 Lyndon B Johnson Fwy Dallas TX 75234-7614

GOUGELMAN, PAUL REINA, lawyer; b. Chgo., Mar. 16, 1951; s. Paul Reina Gougelman and Jayne Bohus; m. Maureen S. Sikora, 1984. BA, Fla. Internat. U., Miami, 1975; JD, Nova Law Sch., Ft. Lauderdale, 1980. Bar: Fla. 1981, U.S. Ct. Appeals (11th cir.) 1981, US. Dist. Ct. (mid. dist.) Fla. 1983. Atty. 1st Dist. Ct. Appeals, Tallahassee, 1980-83; of counsel Maguire, Voorhis, & Wells, P.A., Melbourne, Fla., 1996—; city atty. Indialantic, Fla., 1989—, Melbourne Beach, Fla., 1990—, Melbourne, Fla., 1996—; spl. counsel for land use and growth mgmt. City of Maitland, 1984-88; spl. counsel for code enforcement bd. City of Longwood, Fla., 1985-87; cons. growth mgmt. City of Lake Mary, Fla., 1985-87; gov.'s appointee East Ctrl. Fla. Regional Planning Coun., 1986—; mem. Seminole County Charter Adv. Com., 1987-88; gen. counsel City of Cocoa Redevel. Agy., 1990—, Brevard Met. Planning Orgn., 1993—, Space Coast League of Cities, 1991—; adv. coun. Fla. Met. Planning Orgn., 1994—. Mem. Orange County Bar Task Force, 1985, Brevard County Planning and Zoning Bd., 1989-92, chmn., 1991-92, Brevard County Charter Com. (chmn. 1993—); chmn. bd. dirs. Harbor City Vol. Ambulance Squad, 1994—. Mem. ABA, Fla. Bar (local govt. law sect., elected exec. coun. environ. and land use law sect.). Republican. Presbyterian. Office: Maguire Voorhis & Wells PA 1499 S Harbor City Blvd Melbourne FL 32901

GOUGH, CAROLYN HARLEY, library director; b. Paterson, N.J., Sept. 23, 1922; d. Frank Ellsworth and Mabel (Harrison) Harley; m. George Harrison Gough, Sept. 21, 1944; children: Deborah Ann Gough Bornholdt, Douglas Alan. B.A., Coll. William and Mary, 1943; M.L.S., Drexel U., 1966. Research asst. Young and Rubicam, Inc., N.Y.C., 1943-44; library dir., asst. prof. Cabrini Coll., Radnor, Pa., 1966-81; chmn. Palm Beach County Library Bd., 1984-86. Mem. resources study com. Tredyffrin Twp. Library, 1964-65; docent Henry Morrison Flagler Mus., 1982—. Mem. Tri-State Coll. Library Coop. (v.p. 1973-74, pres. 1974-75), Assn. Coll. and Research Libraries (dir. 1978-81), AAUP, DAR (Palm Beach chpt.), Beta Phi Mu, Kappa Delta. Republican. Episcopalian. Clubs: Questers, Inc. (1st nat. v.p. 1964-66), Atlantis Golf, Atlantis Women's (co-pres. 1982-83), Sir Robert Boyle Soc. Home: 458 S Country Club Dr Atlantis FL 33462-1238

GOUGH, GEORGIA BELLE, art educator; b. Oklahoma City, Dec. 21, 1920; d. George John and Lillie Belle (Massongill) Leach; m. Clarence Ray Gough, Feb. 7, 1975. BS, Ctrl. State Coll., 1941; MS, North Tex. State U., 1946; PhD, U. Okla., 1962. Tchr. elementary Dist. 16/Noble County Okla., Lucien, 1941-42; tchr. elementary, art Denison (Tex.) Sch. Dist., 1942-43; tchr. elementary art Oklahoma City Sch. Dist., 1943-47; instr., asst. prof., assoc. prof., prof., prof. emerita U. North Tex., Denton, 1947—; sec. Nat. Coun. on Edn. Ceramic Arts, 1970-73; craftsman/trustee Am. Crafts Coun., 1976-80; U.S. Del. World Crafts Coun., 1978, 80; sec., pres., hon. mem. Tex. Designer/Craftsmen. Contbr. articles to profl. jours.; designer of wall hanging Greater Denton Arts Coun., 1985. Bd. dirs. Greater Denton Arts Coun. Recipient Cmty. Arts Recognition award Denton Arts Coun., 1995. Democrat. Home: 1813 Willowwood Denton TX 76205-6992

GOUGH, JESSIE POST (MRS. HERBERT FREDERICK GOUGH), retired education educator; b. Nakon Sri Tamaraj, Thailand, Jan. 26, 1907 (parents Am. citizens); d. Richard Walter and Mame (Stebbins) Post; B.A., Maryville Coll., 1927; M.A. in English, U. Chgo., 1928; Ed.D., U. Ga., 1965; m. Herbert Frederick Gough, June 30, 1934; children: Joan Acland (Mrs. Alexander Reed), Herbert Frederick. Tchr. English, Linden Hall, Lititz, Pa., 1930-32; tchr. Fairyland Sch., Lookout Mountain, Tenn., 1955-64; rsch. asst. English curriculum studies ctr. U. Ga., 1964-65; asso. prof. elem. edn. LaGrange (Ga.) Coll., 1965-73, prof., 1973-75; prof. N.W. Ga. area tchr. edn. svcs., 1969-71. Mem. Walker County (Ga.) Curriculum Coun., 1959-61, Walker County Ednl. Planning Bd., 1958-60. Mem. Am. Ednl. Rsch. Assn., Internat. Reading Assn., Nat., Ga. edn. assns., Delta Kappa Gamma. Home: 1005 Mountain Creek Rd Chattanooga TN 37405-1638

GOULART, PAUL A., computers educator, electronics educator; b. Ayer, Mass., July 5, 1940; s. Bravel and Marie Anne (Boucher) G.; m. Theresia Schreiber Fields, Dec. 12, 1961 (div. Nov. 11, 1977); children: Michael T., Stephen B., Angela S., Deborah S., Alex S.; m. Glenda Mae Spencer, Oct. 13, 1979. AAS, C.C. Air Force, Randolph AFB, Tex., 1978; BSEd, Athens (Ala.) State Coll., 1992. Commd. USAF, 1959, MSGT, ret., 1979; area supr. Datagraphix, Inc., Birmingham, Ala., 1979-88; tchr., tech. dir. RETS Electronic Inst., Birmingham, Ala., 1988-92; tchr. Baldwin County Bd. Edn., Robertsdale, Ala., 1992—. Home: 23386 Hwy 98 Foley AL 36535 Office: S Baldwin Ctr Tech PO Box 549 Robertsdale AL 33333

GOULD, ALAN BRANT, academic administrator; b. Aug. 2, 1938; m. Mary Nell; children: Adam, Charles, Christopher. BA in History cum laude, Marshall U., 1961, MA in History, 1962; PhD in Am. History, W.Va. U., 1969. Grad. instr., dept. history W.Va. U., Morgantown, 1962-65; instr., dept. history D.C. Tchrs. Coll., 1965-66; asst. prof. history No. Va. Community Coll., 1966-69; prof., dept. history Marshall U., Huntington, W.Va., 1969—, sr. v.p., 1988-89, provost, 1989-92, interim pres., 1990-91, v.p. for acad. affairs, 1991-94, dean Coll. Liberal Arts, 1980-88, acting v.p. acad. affairs, 1984-86, asst. to pres. for spl. projects, 1986, chmn. dept. history, 1977-80, asst. to v.p. acad. affairs, 1976-77, coord. Regents BA degree program, 1976-80, 86-94; exec. dir. John Deavin Drinko Acad. John Deaver Drinko Acad., 1994—; adj. prof. history W.Va. Coll. Grad. Studies, 1976—; lectr. Ohio U., Ironton, 1970-74; vis. lectr. for Project Newgate, Fed. Youth Correction Inst., Summit, Ky., fall 1970. Contbr. articles to hist. jours, also conf. papers. Chmn. Cabell County Hist. Landmark Commn., 1983-92; trustee Huntington Mus. Art, 1983-93, chmn. edn. com., mem. exec. com.; pres. River Cities Cultural Coun., 1985-91; bd. dirs. W.Va. Humanities Coun., 1986—, v.p., 1989-91, pres., 1991-94, W.Va. Coalways, Inc., 1987—, Mayor of Huntington's Main St. Project, 1987-92, Marshall U. Rsch. Corp., 1988, mem., 1982-86; mem. W.Va. Antiquities Commn., 1975-77, Cabell County Commn. on Crime, Delinquency and Corrections, 1982-86, statewide steering com. Ideas That Built Am., 19856, Carter G. Woodson Meml. Commn., 1986—; mem. steering com. Ethics W.Va. Program, 1983-84, chmn. Great Books Program; mem. affirmative action bd. City of Huntington, 1989-91, mem. hist. landmark commn., 1989-91, 94—; bd. trustees W. Va. Ednl. Found., Inc., 1993—. Inducted into Huntington East High Sch. Hall of Fame, Class of 1986. Mem. Am. Hist. Assn. (com. on status of history in schs. 1974-76), Orgn. Am. Historians (state rep.), W.Va. Hist. Assn. (sec. 1974, v.p. 1975, pres. 1976), W.Va. Assn. Acad. Deans (mem. exec. bd. 1982-86). W.Va. Bd. Regents (univ. rep., acad. affairs adv. com. 1984-86), Soc. Yeager Scholars (steering com. 1986-87), W.Va. Humanities Ctr. (exec. com. 1987—), Gamma Theta Upsilon, Omicron Delta Kappa, phi Alpha Theta, Phi Eta Sigma, Pi Sigma Alpha. Office: Marshall U John Deaver Drinko Acad 400 Hal Greer Blvd Huntington WV 25755-0001

GOULD, CHRISTOPHER, English language educator; b. Pearl River, N.Y., Oct. 7, 1947; s. Harry Simeon, Jr. and Jeanne Priscilla (Petersen) G.; m. Kathleen Joann Hallmark, July 16, 1946; 1 child, Emily Jeanne. BA with hons., U. Va., 1969; MA, U. S.C., 1975, PhD, 1977. Assoc. prof. English U. N.C., Wilmington, 1986-92, prof. English, 1992—, chmn. dept. English, 1995-96; editor N.C. English Tchr., 1992—; bd. dirs. North Car. English Tchrs. Assn.; dir. Cape Fear Writing Project, Wilmington, 1987-90. Co-author: (book) Writing, Reading and Research, 1990, 4th edit. 1997; prin. author: Critical Issues in Contemporary Culture, 1997. Mem. Nat. Coun. Tchrs. English, Conf. on Coll. Composition and Commn., Rhetoric Soc. Am. Democrat. Episcopalian. Office: Univ N C at Wilmington 601 South College Rd Wilmington NC 28403

GOULD, GLENN HUNTING, marketing professional, consultant; b. Martinsburg, W.Va., June 15, 1949; s. Glenn Hunting Sr. and Margaret Alice (Otto) G.; m. Marilyn Kay Jones, July 12, 1953; 2 children: Courtney Lynn, Angela Pace. BA in Sociology, W.Va. U., 1973, MS in Indsl. Relations, 1974. Mgr. human resources Hillenbrand Ind., Batesville, Ind., 1979-81; mgr. human resources, MIAD div. Bausch & Lomb, Balt., 1981-82; dir. human resources Universal Security Inst., Balt., 1982-83; chief exec. officer M.K. Jones & Assocs., Largo, Fla., 1983—; bd. dirs. Pitts. Inst. Mortuary Soc.; cons. Colombian Fin. Group, 1995-96, Wilbert Inc. Contbg. author: Successful Funeral Service Practice, 1987. Served as sgt. USAF, 1967-71, Vietnam. Named one of Outstanding Young Men Am., 1980. Mem. Soc. Human Resource Mgmt. (cert. sr. profl.), Alpha Kappa Delta. Democrat. Presbyterian. Office: 1501B Belcher Rd S Largo FL 34641-4505

GOULDER, GERALD POLSTER, retail executive; b. Columbus, Ohio, Apr. 30, 1953; s. Norman Ernest and Betty (Polster) G. BA, Ohio State U., 1975; JD, Washington U., 1978. Bar: Ohio 1978, N.C. 1985. Asst. atty. gen. Ohio Atty. Gen.'s Office, Columbus, 1979-83; atty. James M. Schottenstein & Assocs., Columbus, 1983-84; chmn., chief oper. officer Carolina Drug Distbrs., Inc. and Emporium Stores, Ltd., Greensboro, N.C., 1984—. Assoc. editor Washington U. Urban Law Ann., 1977-78; contbr. articles to profl. jours. Trustee Wexner Heritage Village, Columbus, 1983-84, bd. dirs. Eastern Music Festival, Greensboro, 1991-94, U. N.C.-Greensboro Spartan Club, 1991-95; v.p. Beth David Synagogue, Greensboro, 1992-94, pres., 1996; participant Leadership Greensboro, 1985, Triad Leadership, 1991; mem. Crime Study Commn., Greensboro, 1992, Greensboro Devel. Corp., 1993. Mem. N.C. Bar Assn., Greensboro Bar Assn., Leadership Greensboro Alumni Assn., Bexley (Ohio) Dem. Club (founder, pres.). Republican. Jewish.

GOULDING, JUDITH LYNN, surgical technologist; b. Worcester, Mass., Aug. 13, 1957; d. Robert Daniel and Marion Eva (Whittaaker) G. Cert. operating room technologist, David Hale Fanning Sch. Health, Worcester, 1976; student, Community Coll. R.I., 1978-79; BA in Interior Design, Ringling Sch. Art and Design, Sarasota, Fla., 1988, student, 1988—; student, St. Petersburg Jr. Coll., Clearwater, Fla., 1992-95. Surg. technologist peripheral vascular team Sarasota Meml. Hosp., 1988-89; contract surg. technologist UCLA Med. Ctr., 1989-90, Alachua Gen. Hosp., Gainesville, Fla., 1990, El Camino Hosp., Mountain View, Calif., 1990, Hoag Meml. Hosp., Newport Beach, Calif., 1990-91, Aurora (Colo.) Presbyn. Hosp., 1991, Yale-New Haven Med. Ctr., 1991-92; surg. technologist Del Rey Community Hosp., Del Rey Beach, Fla., 1992; pvt. surg. asst. HCA Largo (Fla.) Med. Ctr., 1992—. Mem. Am. Soc. Interior Designers, Assn. Surg. Technologists. Democrat. Home: 10600 4th St N Apt 818 Saint Petersburg FL 33716-3206

GOURLEY, JAMES LELAND, editor, publishing executive; b. Mounds, Okla., Jan. 29, 1919; s. Samuel O. and Lodema (Scott) G.; m. Vicki Graham Clark, Nov. 24, 1976; children: James Leland II, Janna Lynn Gourley, Kelly Clark, Brandon Clark. B in Liberal Studies, U. Okla., 1963. Editor, pub., pres. Daily Free-Lance, Henryetta, Okla., 1946-73; editor Oklahoma City Friday, 1974—; chmn. Nichols Hills Pub. Co., 1974—; pres. Suburban Graphics, Inc., 1991-93; pres. Central Okla. Newspaper Group, 1987, 90, 93, 96; pres. Sta. KHEN, KHEN-FM, Henryetta, 1955-63; pres. Hugo (Okla.) Daily News, 1953-63; chief of staff gov. Okla., 1959-63; chmn., pres. State Capitol Bank, 1962-69; v.p. sta. KXOJ Sapulpa, 1972-75; treas. Sta. KJEM-FM, Oklahoma City, 1962-67. Mem. Pres. Nat. Pub. Advisory Com. to Sec. Commerce, 1963-66; exec. dir. Gov's Comm. Higher Edn., 1960-61; Dem. candidate for gov. Okla., 1966. Dist. chmn. Boy Scouts Am., 1963-65; bd. dirs. So. Regional Edn. Bd., 1959-67, Okla. Symphony Soc., 1976-88, Oklahoma City Crimestoppers, 1982—, Salvation Army, Oklahoma City, 1985-87, Okla. Goodwill Industries, 1989-91; mem. Gov.'s Reform Com., 1984. Maj. AUS, 1942-46, ETO. Recipient Best Okla. Small Daily newspaper awards, 1949-58, 69-72, Best Large City Weekly newspaper awards, 1977-80, 83-85, 87-91; inducted into Okla. Journalism Hall of Fame, 1980. Bd. trustees Okla. City Univ., 1993—; bd. dirs. Okla. City Edn. Round Table, 1992—. Mem. UP Internat. Editors Okla. (pres. 1958-59), Okla. Disciples of Christ Laymen (pres. 1964-65), Suburban Newspapers Am. (dir. 1980-89), Nat. Newspaper Assn., Okla. Press Assn. (pres. 1988-89, treas. 1991-93), Oklahoma City C. of C. (dir. 1975—), Henryetta C. of C. (pres. 1955), Oklahoma City Golf and Country Club (bd. dirs. 1991-95), Econ. Club Okla., Oklahoma City Com. of 100, Rotary (pres. Oklahoma City club 1992-93), Pi Kappa Alpha. Republican. Home: 6449 Grandmark Dr

Oklahoma City OK 73116-5006 Office: 10801 Quail Plaza Dr Oklahoma City OK 73120-3123

GOURLEY, PAULA MARIE, art educator, artist, designer bookbinder; b. Carmel, Calif., Apr. 29, 1948; d. Raymond Serge Voronkoff and Frances Eliseyvna (Kovtynovich) G.; m. David Clark Willard, Feb. 10, 1972 (div. Oct. 1973). AA, Monterey (Calif.) Peninsula Coll., 1971; BA, Goddard Coll., 1978; MFA, U. Ala., 1987; pvt. bookbinding study with, Donald Glaister, Roger Arnoult, Paule Ameline, Michelene de Bellefroid, Francoise Bausart, Sun Evrard, James Brockman. Radiologic technologist Cen. Med. Clinic, Pacific Grove, Calif., 1970-71, Community Hosp. of Monterey, 1972-75, Duke U. Med. Ctr., Durham, N.C., 1975-77; dept. head, ultrasound technologist Middlesex Meml. Hosp., Middletown, Conn., 1977-79; asst. prof. U. Ala., Tuscaloosa, 1985-93, assoc. prof., 1993—; asst. dir. Inst. for the Book Arts, U. Ala., 1985-88, coord., 1988-94, co-dir. M.F.A. program in the book arts, 1994—; U.S. rep. Les Amis de la Reliure d'Art, Toulouse, France, 1989—; founding dir. Southeastern chpt. Guild of BookWorkers, 1995—; coord. journalist for U.S. to Art et Metiers du Livre, Revue Internat., Paris; established Pelegaya Press and Paperworks, 1978. Editor First Impressions (newsletter), 1988—; contbr. articles to profl. jours.; numerous nat. and internat. bookbinding exhbns., 1978-95. Vol. PLUS Literacy Program, Tuscaloosa, 1991—. U. Ala. grantee, 1988, 89, 90, 92; recipient Diplome of honneur Atelier d'Arts Appliques, France, 1986, Craft fellowship Ala. State Coun. on Arts, 1993-94. Mem. Am. Registry Radiologic Technologists, Am. Registry Diagnostic Med. Sonographers, Guild of Bookworkers (founder and bd. dirs. Southeastern regional chpt., editor, pub. newsletter True Grits), Hand Bookbinders Calif., Bookbinders Internat. (v.p. U.S. 1989—), Pacific Ctr. for the Book Arts, Am. Craft Coun., Ala. Craft Coun., Can. Bookbinders and Book Artists Guild, Nat. Mus. Women in Arts, Am. Craft Coun. Nat. Trust for Historic Preservation, Phi Beta Kappa Internat. Scholars. Home: 2811 6th St Tuscaloosa AL 35401-1759 Office: U Ala Main Libr # 517 Tuscaloosa AL 35487

GOUTI, SAMMY YASIN, psychology educator, psychotherapist; b. Gaza, Jordan, June 19, 1963; came to the U.S., 1981, naturalized, 1994; s. Yasin Ahmed and Helala Yossef (Abomarie) G.; 1 child, Chelsey Ann. AS, San Jacinto Coll., Pasadena, Tex., 1984; BS with honors, U. Houston-Ctrl., 1987; MA, U. Houston-Clear Lake, 1989, postgrad., 1993-95; Cert. Massage Therapy, Phoenix Sch. Massage, Houston, 1992; student, TVI Actors Studios, Hollywood, Calif., 1995; cert. in acting, The Mayo Hill Sch., 1994; postgrad., Sam Houston State U., 1995. Lic. profl. counselor-intern. Asst. tchr. presch. U. Houston Human Lab. Sch., 1986-87; social sci. instr. George I. Sanchez High Sch., Houston, 1989-90; psychotherapist Life Resource-A Mental Health Ctr., Beaumont, Tex., 1990-91; psychology instr. Lamar U., Orange, Tex., 1991; assoc. clin. psychologist Tex. Dept. Mental Health and Mental Retardation, Beaumont, 1991-92; counseling program Sam Houston State U., 1995; massage therapist The Houstonian Health Club, 1993-95; prof. psychology U. Houston-Downtown, 1992—; founder The Ctr. for stress Release, Houston, 1992, The SHUMS World Magic Ctr., Houston, 1992; adj. prof. psychology Kingwood Coll., 1996—, San Jacinto Coll., 1996—; DNC rep. State of Tex., 1995—. Trade Mark (TM) Super Human Universal Monkeys, 1993; appeared music videos Clay Walker's, Clinton Gregory's, 1995; appeared on John Bradshow TV Talk Show, 1996; guest appearance The Bradshaw Difference, 1996; featured in 5 Hollywood motion pictures including The Evening Star, Apollo II, Cable TV, Rough Riders; TV host Arab-Am. TV and TV Houston, 1996—; author (poems) The Shums, 1993, The Encounter, 1994, Princess, 1995; contbr. articles to profl. jours. Rep. Dem. Nat. Com., 1995—. Recipient Editor's Choice award Nat. Libr. Poetry, 1993, 94, 95; U. Houston scholar, 1986-87, 88-89. Mem. ACA, Am. Film Inst., Internat. Soc. Poets (life), Assn. for Humanistic Psychology, Inst. Noetic Scis., Nat. Guild Hypnotists, Assn. for Body and Massage Profls., Golden Key, Psi Chi, Alpha Epsilon Delta. Office: U Houston Downtown Dept Social Scis 1 Main St Houston TX 77002-1001

GOVER, ALAN SHORE, lawyer; b. Lyons, N.Y., Sept. 5, 1948; s. Norman Marvin and Beatrice L. (Shore) G.; m. Ellen Rae Ross, Dec. 4, 1976; children: Maxwell Ross, Mary Trace. AB, Tufts U., 1970; JD, Georgetown U., 1973. Bar: Tex. 1973, D.C. 1980, U.S. Dist. Ct. (so. dist.) Tex. 1974, U.S. Dist. Ct. (we. dist.) Tex. 1976, U.S Dist. Ct. (no. dist.) Tex. 1988, U.S. Dist. Ct. (ea. dist.) Tex. 1990, U.S. Ct. Appeals (5th cir.) 1974, U.S. Ct. Appeals (D.C. cir.) 1977, U.S. Dist. Ct. (we. dist.) 1979, U.S. Ct. Appeals (2d cir.) 1979, D.C. 1980, U.S. Ct. Appeals (9th and 11th cirs.) 1981, U.S. Ct. Appeals (8th cir.) 1981, U.S. Supreme Ct. 1976. Assoc. Baker & Botts, Houston, 1973-80, ptnr., 1981-85; ptnr. Weil, Gotshal & Manges, Houston, 1985—. Co-author: The Texas Nonjudicial Foreclosure Process, 1990; editor, chmn. editorial bd. P.L.I. Oil and Gas and Bankruptcy Laws, 1985. Trustee Congregation Beth Israel, Houston, 1980-86, v.p., 1996—; trustee Houston Ballet, 1986—, v.p., 1993-96; chmn. ann. fund St. John's Sch., Houston, 1993-95; trustee Retina Rsch. Found., Houston. Fellow Tex. Bar Found.; mem. ABA, Coronado Club, N.Y. Athletic Club. Jewish. Office: Weil Gotshal & Manges 700 Louisiana St Ste 1600 Houston TX 77002-2722

GOVETT, BRETT CHRISTOPHER, lawyer; b. Corpus Christi, Tex., May 17, 1965; s. Raymond Weston and Martha Lenora (Barton) G.; m. Cynthia Lynn Rowell, June 5, 1993. BA in Chemistry cum laude, The Citadel, 1987; JD cum laude, Tex. Tech U., 1990. Bar: Tex. 1990, U.S. Ct. Appeals (5th cir.) 1990, U.S. Dist. Ct. (so. dist.) Tex. 1990, U.S. Dist. Ct. (no. dist.) Tex. 1991. Jud. clk. for judge Reynaldo G. Garza U.S. Ct. Appeals (5th cir.), Brownsville, Tex., 1990-91; participating assoc. Fulbright & Jaworski L.L.P., Dallas, 1991—. Note editor Tex. Tech. Law Rev., 1989-90, contbr. articles. Mem. Southwestern Legal Found. Mem. Order of Coif. Office: Fulbright & Jaworski LLP 2200 Ross Ave Ste 2800 Dallas TX 75201

GOWDA, NARASIMHAN RAMAIAH, financial consultant; b. Mallasandra, Karnataka, India, Nov. 21, 1949; came to U.S., 1982; s. Ramaiah and Kamalamma Gowda; m. Padma Gowda, Oct. 11, 1981; children: Shyla, Shilpa. BS, Bangalore U., India, 1971, MS, 1975; MBA, Armstrong U., 1985, U. Cin., 1986, Clayton U., 1989. Sales exec. Elys Chem. Lab., Bangalore, 1975-80; mgr. Health Clinic, Cin., 1982-87; account exec. Stuart James Co., Cin., 1987-88; fin. cons. Quest Capital Strategies, Inc., Cin., 1988-90; pres. Gowda Fin. Svcs., 1988—, Investors Funding Group, 1989—; sr. v.p. Gowda Glass & Assocs., 1990—; fin. cons. Merrill Lynch, Pierce, Fenner & Smith, Inc., 1991-92, Montano Securities Corp., Orange, Calif., 1993—; prof. fin. Shepherd's Coll., 1992-93. Adminstr. Rural Devel. Program, Bangalore, 1985—; pres. Indian Developers Bangalore, 1995—. Mem. Real Estate Investors Assn., Internat. Assn. Registered Fin. Planners, Inc., Assn. MBA Execs., U.S. Golf Assn., Cmty. Assns. Inst., Internat. Policy Inst., Potomac C. of C., Scandinavian Health Club. Republican. Home: 12261 Greenleaf Ave Potomac MD 20854

GOWDY, ROBERT HENRY, physics educator, researcher; b. Putnam, Conn., Apr. 7, 1941; s. Henry Willard and Helen Mary (McCarthy) G.; m. Cellissa Norcross, Apr. 16, 1966; children: Jay Willard, Cellissa Brown, William Henry. BS, Worcester Poly. Inst., 1963; MS, Yale U., 1964, PhD, 1968. AEC fellow in physics Yale U., New Haven, 1968-70; postdoctoral fellow in physics U. Md., College Park, 1970-72, asst. prof., 1972-78; asst. prof. Va. Commonwealth U., Richmond, 1978-82, assoc. prof., 1981—, chmn. physics dept., 1982-89, 91-92. Contbr. articles to profl. jours. Grad. fellow NSF, 1963-68, rsch. fellow Sloan Found., 1974-76. Roman Catholic. Home: 3 Clarke Rd Richmond VA 23226-1621 Office: Va Commonwealth U Dept Physics Box 842000 Richmond VA 23284-2000

GOWER, BOB G., gas and oil industry executive; b. 1937. With Atlantic Richfield Co., L.A., 1963-88; pres., CEO, bd. dirs. Lyondell Petrochem. Co., Houston, 1988—. Office: Lyondell Petrochem 1221 McKinney St Houston TX 77010*

GOWLER, DAVID BRIAN, dean; b. Mt. Vernon, Ill., Sept. 24, 1958; s. Cedric Maynard and Betty Lou (Runnels) G.; m. Rita Kay Stookey, July 16, 1983; children: Camden Douglas, Jacob David. BA, U. Ill., 1980; PhD, MDiv, So. Bapt. Theol. Sem., Louisville, 1982-89; postgrad., Cambridge (Eng.) U., 1987. Instr. So. Bapt. Theol. Sem., Louisville, 1988-89; asst. prof. Berry Coll., Rome, Ga., 1989-90; asst./assoc. prof. Chowan Coll., Murfreesboro, N.C., 1990—, asst. dean acad. affairs, 1996—; assoc. editor Emory Studies in Early Christianity, Scholars Press/Emory U., Atlanta, 1992—. Author: Host, Guest, Emmy, and Friend, 1991; editor 5 books; contbr. numerous articles to profl. jours. NEH grantee, 1995. Mem. Westar Inst., Cath. Bibl. Assn., Soc. Bibl. Lit. (rhetoric and N.T. sect. steering com. 1990—). Presbyterian. Office: Chowan College 1848 Jones Dr Murfreesboro NC 27855

GOYAL, AMITA, information systems educator, consultant; b. New Delhi, June 21, 1968; came to U.S., 1975; d. Shiv Narain and Swarn Lata (Aggarwal) G. BS, U. Md., 1987, MS, 1991, PhD, 1994. Tech. cons. U. Md., College Park, 1985-87, dir. deans, 1987-88, workstation tech. cons., 1988-89, acad. computing coord., 1989-93; asst. prof. Va. Commonwealth U., Richmond, 1993—; program chair Worldwide Conf. on IS Edn., Colo., 1995. Editor procs. of WISE, 1995; mem. editl. bd. Jour. IS Edn., 1993—, Jour. Mgmt. Sys., 1996; contbr. articles to profl. jours. Mem. Internat. Assn. for Math. Modelling, Assn. Next Step Developers, Inc. Office: Va Commonwealth U PO Box 844000 1015 Floyd Ave Richmond VA 23284

GOYNE, RODERICK A., lawyer; b. Denver, Aug. 13, 1949. BA with highest honors, U. Tex., Arlington, 1971; JD with honors, Harvard U., 1974. Bar: Tex. 1974. Ptnr. Baker & Botts LLP, Dallas. Mem. ABA, State Bar Tex. (chmn. legal opinions com. bus. law sect. 1992—), Am. Coll. Investment Counsel (trustee 1993—), Tex. Assn. Bank Counsel, Dallas Bar Assn. Office: Baker & Botts LLP 2001 Ross Ave Dallas TX 75201-8001*

GRABEEL, DENNIS CRAIG, federal quality specialist; b. Pennington Gap, Va., Dec. 4, 1946; s. Charles Lavoy and Reba Virginia (Smith) G.; m. Deborah Kathryn Jodlowski, Sept. 27, 1980; children: Nathan Charles, Justin Adam. BS in Edn., U. Va., 1970; MPA, Fla.-Atlantic U., 1981. Cert. strategic planning facilitator. Educator Va. Pub. Schs., 1970-71; mcpl. adminstr. City of Boynton Beach, Fla., 1978-92, asst. planner; asst. to city mgr., dir. mgmt. svcs., 1986-92; cons., instr. Dept. of Navy, Sr. Leader Seminar-TQL, 1992—. Coord. Boynton Beach handicapped adv. com., 1985; chmn. City Emergency preparedness com., Boynton Beach, 1986, adult scouting vol., 1988—; lay spkr. Salem United Meth. Ch., 1993—. Lt. USN, 1971-77, comdr. USNR, ret., 1992. Mem. ASTD, Am. Soc. Pub. Adminstrs., Nat. Eagle Scout Assn. (life), Fla.-Atlantic U. Alumni Assn. (life), U. Va. Alumni Assn. (life), Assn. United Meth. Scouters (life), Pi Alpha Alpha Nat. Hon. Soc., Palm Beach Rugby Football Club (co-founder, past pres.). Home: 1212 Eagle Way Virginia Beach VA 23456-5869 Office: Naval Leader Tng Unit Little Creek 1575 Gator Blvd Ste 338 Norfolk VA 23521-2740

GRABER, HARRIS DAVID, sales executive; b. Bronx, N.Y., Mar. 31, 1939; s. Charles and Ella (Shapiro) G.; m. Esther Estelle Feldman, Dec. 28, 1957; children: Donald Irwin, Gregory Stuart, Monique Cheryl, Roy Scott. AS, Queensborough Community Coll., 1973; BS cum laude, CUNY, 1975; MBA, St. Johns U., 1979. Draftsman Paramount Designs Co., N.Y.C., 1956-58; design draftsman Milgo Electronic Co., Miami, Fla., 1961-62; design engr. Cons. and Designers Co., N.Y.C., 1958-61, 62-64; with engrng. and engrng. mgmt. depts. Grumman Aerospace Co., Bethpage, N.Y., 1964-74, mktg. and sales engr., 1974-75, group head customer engrng. tech. requirements, 1975-78, internat. bus. analyst, 1978; govt. sales mgr. Systems-East div. Conrac Corp., West Caldwell, N.J., 1978-80; dir. govt. mktg. Telephonics Corp., Huntington, N.Y., 1980-82; regional sales mgr. Measurement Systems div. Gould Inc., Oxnard, Calif., 1982-83; sales mgr. govt. bus. Servonic div. Gulton Industries Inc., Costa Mesa, Calif., 1983-84; dir. mktg. systems ILC Data Device Corp., 1984-88; mgr. bus. and systems devel. Paramax Systems Corp., Great Neck, N.Y., 1988-92; dir. mktg., contracts and sales Ferranti Venus, Inc., Holtsville, N.Y., 1992-94; OEM account mgr. Lambda Electronics Inc., Melville, N.Y., 1994—. Mem. Navy League, Armed Forces Communications and Electronics Assn. Home: # 2050 15935 Bent Tree Forest Cir Dallas TX 75248

GRABER, JOHN PAUL, elementary education educator; b. Stillwater, Okla., July 7, 1941; s. Paul James and Lucy Ilene (Raxter) G.; m. Jane Zhi-Rong Zhao, June 27, 1987; one child, Julia Lantian. BS in mathematics, U. Okla., 1963; BS in elementary edn., U. Tulsa, 1971; MS in edn., U. of So. Calif., 1976; EdD, U. Tulsa, 1993. Cert. tchr., Okla., Calif. Tchr. math Sapulpa (Okla.) Jr. H.S., 1972-73; tchr. North Girls' MS, Chungju, Korea, 1973-74, 1976-79; assoc. dir. St. Louis H.S./Adult Divsn., Seoul, Korea, 1974-75; assoc. prof. Hong Ik U., Seoul, 1980-82; tchr. math Tulsa (Okla.) Pub. Schs., 1984—; adj. instr. Tulsa Jr. Coll., 1992-94; bldg. rep. Tulsa Classroom Tchrs. Assn., 1994-96; mem. Shared Decision Coun., Tulsa Pub. Schs., 1995-96. Contbr. articles to profl. jours. Captain U.S. Army, 1963-70, Lt. Col. Army Reserve, 1970-91. Recipient Bronze Star. Mem. Nat. Coun. of Tchrs. of Math, Nat. Edn. Assn. (bldg. rep.), Am. Defense Preparedness Assn., U.S. Army Armor Assn., Nat. Rifle Assn. (cert. rifle instr.), Phi Delta Kappa. Republican. Baptist. Home: 11417 E 5th St Tulsa OK 74128

GRABOFF, PAUL, chemist, consultant; b. Bklyn., Sept. 23, 1929; s. Joe and Esther (Tobokowitz) G.; m. Helene Friedman, July 4, 1957; children: Ellen Shemesh, Marcy LeSieur. AAS in Chemistry, N.Y.C. C.C., 1949; BA in Chemistry, NYU, 1956; MS in Chemistry, Stevens Inst. Tech., Hoboken, N.J., 1965. Lab. technician Drew Chem., Boonton, N.J., 1949-51, IFF, Elizabeth, N.J., 1953-54; analytical chemist SUNY, Bklyn., 1956; rsch. chemist Columbia U., N.Y.C., 1957; ops. mgr. Epoxy Products, Irvington, N.J., 1957-66; instr. N.J. Inst. Tech., Newark, 1975-85; tech. mgr. Dart Industries, Paramus, N.J., Augusta, Ga., 1966-88; cons. Augusta, 1988—; lectr. ISO 9000; assessor for lab. accreditation AZLA; mem. U.S. Tech. Adv. Group to Internat. Orgn. for Standardization Tech. Com. 61 on Plastics, 1970—; mem. total quality adv. coun. Augusta Tech.Coll., 1992-94; spkr. ASTD, 1993, Am. Soc. for Quality Control, 1996. Contbr. articles to profl. jours.; reviewer tech. papers. Corp. USMC, 1951-53. Fellow ASTM (chmn. D-20 com. on plastics 1992—, mem. D-20 adv. bd. 1980—, mem. D-20 exec. bd. 1974—, mem. Merit award selection com. 1992-94, bd. dirs. appointee com. on stds. 1997—, mem. bd. dirs. nominating com. 1993, rep. stds. meeting in Mexico City 1993, Merit award 1990); mem. Am. Chem Soc., Soc. Plastics Engrs. Home: 708 Ravenel Rd Augusta GA 30909-1836

GRABOWSKI, ELIZABETH, healthcare administrator; b. Laskowiec, Poland, July 24, 1940; came to U.S., 1948.; d. Stanley and Marianna (Tatko) Backiel; m. John A. Grabowski; children: Elizabeth C. Taylor, Julia M. Smith, John A., Emilia A. AAD in Nursing, Memphis State U., 1975; BSN, Elmhurst Coll., 1981; MSN, U. Louisville, 1988. Clin. dir., owner Diabetes Resource Ctr., Louisville, 1989—; diabetes nurse clinician edn. dept. Humana Hosp. Audubon, Louisville, 1983-84; mem. adj. faculty U. La. Sch. Nursing, Spalding Univ. Nurse Practitioner Program, 1994—. Abstracts editor Diabetes Educator Jour., 1986—; contbr. articles to profl. jours. Chmn. adv. bd. Oldham County affiliate ARC, 1989-92, chmn. tech. adv. com. for nursing svcs. Medicaid programs, Ky., 1987-91, chmn. Ky. Nurse Recognition Banquet com., 1987-91. Recipient Hoechst-Roussel Pharms. award for clin. excellence, academic scholarship Kiwanis Internat., Clairol Found., others. Fellow ANA (Med.-Surg. Nurse of Yr. 1990), Am. Acad. Nursing; mem Ky. Nurses Assn. (state and dist. 1), Am. Assn. Diabetes Educators, Greater Louisville Assn. Diabetes Educators, Sigma Theta Tau, others. Home: 4010 Dana Rd Crestwood KY 40014-9224 Office: Diabetes Resource Ctr Inc 1001 Dupont Sq N Louisville KY 40207-4612

GRADDICK, CHARLES ALLEN, lawyer; b. Mobile, Ala., Dec. 10, 1944; s. Julian and Elvera (Smith) G.; m. Corinne Whiting, Aug. 19, 1966; children: Charles Allen, Herndon Whiting, Corinne. J.D., Cumberland Sch. Law, 1970. Bar: Ala. 1970. Clk. Ala. Supreme Ct., 1970; asst. dist. atty. County of Mobile, Ala., 1971-75, dist. atty., 1975-79; atty. gen. State of Ala., Montgomery, 1979-87; ptnr. Thorton, Farish and Gaunt, Montgomery, 1987-89, Anderson, Graddick and Nabors, P.C., Montgomery, 1989-90; dist. atty. Montgomery County, Montgomery County, Ala., 1991-93; ptnr. Graddick, Belser and Nabors, PC, Montgomery and Mobile, 1993—. Served with USNG, 1969-96. Named Outstanding Young Man of Mobile, Mobile Jaycees, 1976, State Conservationist of Yr., Ala. Wildlife Fedn.; recipient cert. appreciation Ala. Peace Officers, 1978, Appreciation award Optimists, 1978. Mem. ABA, ATLA, Ala. Bar Assn., Mobile Bar Assn., Montgomery Bar Assn., Ala. Trial Lawyers Assn., Ala. Dist. Attys. Assn., Nat. Dist. Attys. Assn., Nat. Assn. Attys. Gen. Republican. Episcopalian. Office: Graddick Belser and Nabors 138 Adams Ave Montgomery AL 36104-4224 also: Graddick Belser and Nabors 3280 Dauphin St Mobile AL 36606-4060

GRADY, BETTY FENDER, registered nurse; b. Drexel, N.C., Aug. 30, 1931; d. Lattimore and Eva (Branch) Fender; widowed, 1994; children: Shelia Ann Carlisle, Tom Jr. ADN, Western Piedmont C.C., 1974. N, N.C. Staff nurse Broughton Mental Inst., Morganton, N.C., 1974-76; night head nurse ICCU Valdese (N.C.) Gen. Hosp., 1976-78, nursing supr., 1978-83, staff nurse pediatrics and newborn nursery, 1989-95; dir. nursing Hilltop Nursing Facility, Marion, N.C., 1983-85; owner, operator children's day care Morganton, 1985-88; charge nurse Grace Ridge Health Care, Morganton, 1995—; counselor Reach to Recovery, Morganton; instr. sch. health Vahdese Gen. Hosp. Contbr. poems to books. Instr. health fairs Am. Cancer Soc., Morganton, Valdese. Mem. Order Eastern Star (conductress chpt. 269 1993, assoc. worthy matron 1994, star point). Home: 112 Falls St Morganton NC 28655

GRADY, C.P. LESLIE, JR., engineering educator; b. Des Arc, Ark., June 25, 1938; s. C. P. Leslie and Edith Claude (Booth) G.; m. Joni Jean Kellough, June 9, 1961; children: Ross Alan, Megan Suzanne. BA in Engring., Rice Inst., 1960; BSCE, Rice U., 1961, MS, 1963; PhD, Okla. State U., 1969. Registered profl. engr., Tex. Rsch. fellow Rice U., Houston, 1961-63, Okla. State U., Stillwater, 1965-68; asst. prof. Purdue U., West Lafayette, Ind., 1968-72, assoc. prof., 1972-79, prof., 1979-81, asst. dean Grad. Sch., 1980-81; prof. engring. Clemson (S.C.) U., 1981-83, R.A. Bowen prof., 1983—; cons. CH2M-Hill, Atlanta and Charlotte, N.C., 1988—, Hoechst Celanese Corp., Charlotte, 1986—. Co-author: Biological Wastewater Treatment: Theory and Application, 1980; contbr. articles to profl. jours. 1st lt. Med. Svc. Corp U.S. Army, 1963-65. Recipient Simon W. Freese award ASCE, 1989. Fellow Am. Acad. Microbiology; mem. Water Environ. Fedn. (editor Water Environ. Rsch. 1989-95), Assn. Environ. Engring. Profs. (bd. dirs.), Internat. Assn. Water Quality. Democrat. Unitarian. Home: 118 Shaftesbury Rd Clemson SC 29631-1730 Office: Clemson U Environ Sys Engring Rich Environ Rsch Lab Clemson SC 29634-0919

GRADY, THOMAS J., bishop; b. Chicago, Ill., Oct. 9, 1914; s. Michael and Rose (Buckley) G. S.T.L., St. Mary of Lake Sem., Mundelein, Ill., 1938; student, Gregorian U., Rome, 1938-39; MA in English, Loyola U., Chgo., 1944. Ordained priest Roman Cath. Ch., 1938. Prof. Quigley Prep. Sem., Chgo., 1939-45; procurator St. Mary of Lake Sem., 1945-56; dir. Nat. Shrine Immaculate Conception, Washington, 1956-67; titular bishop Vamalla, aux. bishop Chgo., 1967-74; pastor St. Hilary Ch., Chgo., 1968-74, St. Joseph Ch., Libertyville, Ill., 1974; bishop of Orlando, Fla., 1974-90; Chgo. Archdiocesan dir. seminaries and post-ordination priestly tng., 1967-74; chmn. Chgo. Archdiocesan Liturg. Commn., 1968-74; dir. program Permanent Diaconate, Chgo., 1969-74; cons. Bishops' Com. on Priestly Formation, from 1967, chmn., 1969-72; mem. Ad Hoc Com. on Priestly Life and Ministry, 1971-73; chmn. Bishops' Com. on Priestly Life and Ministry, from 1973. Address: Diocese of Orlando PO Box 1800 421 E Robinson St Orlando FL 32801-1672

GRAF, DOROTHY ANN, business executive; b. Nashville, Mar. 21, 1935; d. Henry George and Martha Dunlap (Hill) Meek; student Montgomery Coll., 1979—; m. Peter Louis Graf, Oct. 28, 1971; children—Sidney E. Pollard, Deborah Lynn Pollard, Robert George Pollard, Michelle Joy Graf. Office mgr. Pa. Life Ins. Co., Miami and Dallas, 1957-72; exec. sec. to med. dir. Pitts. Children's Hosp., 1974; sec. G.E./TEMPO, Washington, 1974-76; adminstrv. asst. to sr. v.p. Logistics Mgmt. Inst., Washington, 1976-81, dir. adminstrv. svcs., 1981—, dir. recruiting and tng., 1995—; dir. KHI Svcs., Inc. Mem. Washington Tech. Personnel Forum. Democrat. Baptist. Home: 20404 Remsbury Pl Gaithersburg MD 20879-4369 Office: 2000 Corporate Rdg Mc Lean VA 22102-7805

GRAFF, HARVEY J., history and humanities educator; b. Pitts., June 19, 1949. BA in History with honors, Northwestern U., 1970; MA in History and History of Edn., U. Toronto, 1971, PhD in History and History of Edn., 1975; cert., Newberry Libr. Inst. Instr. summer sch. Northwestern U., 1973; extramural lectr. Ont. Inst. for Studies in Edn., 1974-75; asst. to assoc. to prof. history and humanities U. Tex., Dallas, 1975—; rsch. assoc. Newberry Libr., 1980-81; vis. adj. prof. history Loyola U., Chgo., 1980; vis. prof. English and Edn., English and history summer sch. Simon Fraser U., 1980, 81; cons., reviewer NEH, 1978—, Nat. Inst. Edn., 1980—, Tex. Com. for Humanitites, 1976—; cons.-advisor Tex. local and regional hist. socs. and groups, 1976—; mem. adv. bd. Dallas Jewish Hist. Soc., 1987—; resource person Collaborative Approach to Svcs. for Elderly, U. Tex. Coun. Pres., 1977—; advisor Sta. KERA-TV, Dallas; advisor Handbook on Tex. Women, 1983—. Author: Children and Schools in Nineteenth-Century Canada/ L'école Canadienne et L'enfant au Dix-Neuvieme Siecle, 1979, rev. edit., 1993, The Literacy Myth: Literacy and Social Structure in the Nineteenth Century, 1979, rev. edit., 1991, The Legacies of Literacy, 1987, The Labyrinths of Literacy, 1987, rev. edit., 1995, Conflicting Paths: Growing Up in America, 1995, also fgn. transls., others; editor: Growing Up in America: Historical Experiences, 1987; mem. editl. bd. History Edn. Quar., 1975-79, Social Sci. History, 1994—; contbr. articles to profl. jours.; cons. editor Interchange: Quar. Rev. Edn., 1974-78, 94—. NEH fellow The Newberry Libr., 1979-80, Spencer fellow Nat. Acad. Edn., 1979-82, short-term fellow Newberry Libr., 1985-86, Am. Antiquarian Soc./NEH fellow, 1988-89; rsch. grantee U. Tex., Dallas, 1983-85, 87-89, Spencer Found., 1991, 92; recipient Critics Choice award Am. Ednl. Studies Assn., 1987. Mem. Can. Assn. Am. Studies (exec. com. 1972-75, program com. 1974), Am. Ednl. Rsch. Assn. (program com. div. F 1973), Can. Population Studies Group (steering and program coms. 1974-76), History of Edn. Soc. (nominating com. 1976, 79), Women in History Profession (coord. S.W. coordinating com. 1977-79), Social Sci. History Assn. (regional network coor. 1976-84, founding chmn. Allan Sharlin Meml. award com. 1984-85, exec. com. 1987-89), Am. Hist. Assn., Orgn. Am. Historians, Social History Soc. Home: 5315 Worth St Dallas TX 75214-5324 Office: U Tex at Dallas Sch Arts and Humanities Box 830688 Richardson TX 75083-0688

GRAGERT, STEVEN KEITH, publishing executive, researcher, writer; b. Richland, Wash., Apr. 2, 1950; s. Elmer Otto and Margie Marie (Dean) G.; m. Helen Kathleen Koons, Aug. 23, 1975. BA, Bethany Coll., Lindsborg, Kans., 1972; MA, Wichita State U., 1976; postgrad., Okla. State U., 1976-80. Asst. dir. Will Rogers Rsch. Project Okla. State U., Stillwater, 1978-81, dir., editor, 1981-83; gen. mgr. Evans Publs., Perkins, Okla., 1983-84; vis. asst. prof. Okla. Bapt. U., Shawnee, 1984-85; advt. mgr. Western Periodicals, Inc., Stillwater, Okla., 1985-86, assoc. pub., advt. dir., 1986-87, pub., pres., 1987—, also bd. dirs.; pub. Electronic House, 1993—. Editor: Letters of a Self-Made Diplomat to His President, 1976, Daily Telegrams: Volume 1, The Coolidge Years, 1926-1929, 1978, Daily Telegrams: Volume 2, The Hoover Years, 1929-1931, 1978, Daily Telegrams: Volume 3, The Hoover Years, 1931-1933, 1979, Daily Telegrams: Volume 4, The Roosevelt Years, 1933-1935, 1980, Weekly Articles: Volume 1, The Harding/Coolidge Years, 1922-1925, 1980, Weekly Articles: Volume 2, The Coolidge Years, 1925-1927, 1980, Weekly Articles: Volume 3, The Coolidge Years,. Project chair Stillwater Sister Cities Program, 1987-88; bd. dirs. Okla. Child Abuse Prevention Ctr., 1986-87. Mem. Successful Mag. Pub. Group, Western Writers Am. (patron), Western History Assn. (patron), Nat. Audubon Soc., Okla. Hist. Soc., Stillwater C. of C., Exch. Club (editor 1985-87, Nat. Newsletter award 1987), Rotary (sec. 1990-92, pres. 1992-93). Republican. Lutheran. Home: 3917 Yorkshire Dr Stillwater OK 74074-1666 Office: Western Periodicals Inc 205 W 7th Ave Ste 202 Stillwater OK 74074-4041

GRAGG, KARL LAWRENCE, lawyer; b. Watertown, N.Y., Sept. 25, 1946; s. Karl Lawrence and Pauline (Sykes) G.; m. Maureen Gilluly, Dec. 13, 1975; children: Meaghan Christina, Erika Lawrence, Jenny Camille. BS, Fla. State U., 1968; JD, U. Fla., 1974, LLM in Taxation, 1975. Bar: Fla. 1975, U.S Dist. Ct. (so. dist.) Fla., U.S. Tax Ct., U.S. Ct. Appeals (5th cir.). Assoc. Mershon, Sawyer, Johnson, Dunwoody & Cole, Miami, Fla., 1975-80, ptnr., 1980-82; ptnr. Gunster, Yoakley, Criser & Stewart, Palm Beach, Fla., 1982-84, Walker Ellis Gragg & Deaktor, Miami, 1984-86, White & Case, Miami, 1987—; adj. prof. law U. Miami, 1978-89; mem. tax com. Fla. Ho. of Reps., Tallahassee, 1983. Contbr. articles to U. Fla. Law Rev. Vol. Miami United Way, 1977-80. Mem. ABA (taxation sect.), Nat. Assn. State Bar (chmn. 1986), Am. Coll. Tax Counsel, Fla. Bar Assn. (tax sect., chmn. tax sect. 1991), Nat. Assn. Indsl. and Office Parks (bd. dirs. 1989-91), Ctr. for Health Techs., Inc. (bd. dirs. 1992—), Japan Soc. South Fla. (bd. dirs. 1990—). Office: White & Case 200 S Biscayne Blvd Ste 4900 Miami FL 33131-2310

GRAHAM, BRENDA J., nurse; b. Savannah, Ga., July 30, 1944; d. Herman James and Dotha Lee (Owens) Johnson; 1 child, La Trelle Denise Jackson. AAS, Bronx Community Coll., 1971; BS, Savannah State Coll., 1987; MEd, U. Ga., 1993. Cert. RN, Ga., N.Y., S.C. Staff nurse Athens (Ga.) Regional Med. Ctr./Hosp.; lead tchr. nursing instrn. South Coll., Savannah; dir. of nursing Pleasantview Nursing Home, Metter, Ga.; collection supr. Am. Red Cross, Savannah; program coord. Savannah (Ga.) State Coll.; retired, 1993; facilitator Athens Sickle Cell Support Group. Vol. Savannah Literacy Program, Teens Talking and Women's Christian Orgn. Mem. Savannah Women's Network, RN Innovators, Ga. Nurses Assn.

GRAHAM, BRUCE JOHN, architect; b. La Cumbre, Bogota, Colombia, Dec. 1, 1925; s. Charles Stewart and Angélica (Gómez de la Torre) G. (parents U.S. citizens); m. Jane Johanna Abend, Sept. 1, 1960; children: George, Lisa, Mara. B.F.A., B.Arch., U. Pa, 1949. Ptnr. Skidmore, Owings & Merrill, Chgo., 1949-89, Graham & Graham, Hobe Sound, Fla., 1990—; hon. prof. U. Nacional Federico Villareal, Peru, 1980; Noyes prof. Harvard U., 1985; vis. prof. U. Nebr., 1989. Chmn. bd. overseers Sch. Fine Arts, U. Pa., 1981-91, trustee, 1981—; bd. dirs. Temple Hoyne Buell Ctr., Columbia U., N.Y.C., 1984-89; pres. Chgo. Central Area Com., 1980-90; bd. dirs. Chgo. Council on Fgn. Relations, Chgo., 1983-90; mem. Urban Land Inst.; mem. adv. bd. govs. Urban Land Research Found.; mem. mem. com. on visual arts U. Chgo., 1982-92; pres. Chgo. Inst. Architecture and Urbanism, 1989-92. Recipient numerous awards for architecture. Fellow AIA; mem. Royal Inst. Brit. Architects, Royal Archtl. Inst. Can., Inst. Urbanism and Planning Peru (hon.). Clubs: Chicago, Commercial (Chgo.). Office: Graham & Graham PO Box 8589 Hobe Sound FL 33475-8589

GRAHAM, CAROL ETHLYN, insurance company administrator; b. Guthrie, Okla., Nov. 28, 1941; d. Brance Alma Woodard and Rachel Ione (Brown) Meininger; m. Morton J. Graham Dec. 14, 1965 (div. Apr. 1985); children: Brance D., Kelly L., S. Robert, M. Jeff III. AS in Civil Tech., Okla. State U.-Tech. Inst., 1978; cert. in flood plain analysis, U. Okla., 1979. Factory worker Aero Comdr., Bethany, Okla., 1963-66; legal asst. Whit Ingram Atty., Oklahoma City, 1966-75; bookkeeper Joe Roselle Atty., Oklahoma City, 1966-78; hydraulic analyst Cunningham Cons. Inc., Oklahoma City, 1978-80; premium auditor loss control Atwell, Vogel and Sterling, Dallas, 1982-83; premium auditor Mid-Continent Casualty Co., Tulsa, 1983-92, State Ins. Fund, State of Okla., 1993-94. Mem. Ins. Auditors Assn. Oklahoma City (sec. 1985-86, pres. 1986-87, 92-93, v.p. 1988-89, treas. 1989-90), Ins. Auditors Assn. of S.W., Ins. Auditors Assn. Oklahoma City (pres. 1992-93), Nat. Soc. Ins. Premium Auditors. Democrat. Home: PO Box 5074 Edmond OK 73083-5074

GRAHAM, CAROLYN JONES, elementary school administrator; b. Memphis, Jan. 28, 1957; d. Leonard and Lydia Ree (Hamer) Jones; m. Michael Graham, Nov. 19, 1988. BS in Psychology, U. Tenn., Martin, 1978, MS in Ednl. Adminstrn./Supervision, 1981. Cert. profl. tchr., Tenn. Fed. program asst. Lane Coll., Jackson, Tenn., 1979-82; prin. planner dept. ECD State of Tenn., Jackson, 1982-90; tchr. 3d grade Bolivar (Tenn.) Elem. Sch., 1990-94, asst. prin., 1994—. Sec. Hardeman County Regional Planning Commn., Bolivar, 1994—; fin. sec. NAACP, Bolivar, 1996—. Mem. NEA, ASCD, Nat. Assn. Elem. Sch. Prins., Tenn. Assn. Elem. Sch. Prins., Tenn. Edn. Assn., Hardeman Edn. Assn. (sec. 1992-96), Nat. Coun. Negro Women, Delta Sigma Theta (Jackson chpt. pres. 1994-96, Radiance Club (pres. 1984-86), Delta of the Yr. 1985, Outstanding Black Woman 1995, 96). Democrat. Baptist. Home: 19285 Highway 57E Middleton TN 38052 Office: Bolivar Elementary School PO Box 228 Bolivar TN 38008

GRAHAM, D. ROBERT (BOB GRAHAM), senator, former governor; b. Coral Gables, Flor., Nov. 9, 1936; m. Adele Khoury; children: Gwendolyn Patricia, Glynn Adele, Arva Suzanne, Kendall Elizabeth. BA, U. Fla., 1959; LLB, Harvard U., 1962. Atty.; cattle and dairy farmer; real estate developer; mem. Fla. Ho. of Reps., 1966-70, Fla. Senate, 1970-78; gov. State of Fla., Tallahassee, 1978-86; U.S. senator from Fla. Washington, 1986—; chmn. Edn. Commn. of the States, 1980-81, Caribbean/Central Am. Action, 1980-81, U.S. intergovtl. adv. council on edn.; mem. So. Growth Policies Bd., chmn., 1982-83; chmn. So. Govs.' Assn.; chmn. com. trade and fgn. affairs Nat. Govs.' Assn. Active 4-H Youth Found., Nat. Commn. on Reform Secondary Edn., Nat. Found. Improvement Edn., Nat. Com. for Citizens in Edn., Sr. Centers of Dade County, Fla.; chmn. So. Regional Edn. Bd., 1979-81. Named one of 5 Most Outstanding Young Men in Fla. Fla. Jaycees, 1971; recipient Allen Morris award for outstanding 1st term mem. senate, 1972, Allen Morris award for most valuable mem. senate, 1973, Allen Morris award for 2d most effective senator, 1976. Mem. Fla. Bar Assn. Democrat. Mem. United Ch. of Christ. Office: US Senate 524 Hart Senate Bldg Washington DC 20510*

GRAHAM, DONALD LYNN, federal judge; b. Salisbury, N.C., Dec. 15, 1948; s. Ernest Jethro and Mildred (Donald) G.; m. Brenda Joyce Savage, Sept. 27, 1969; 1 child, Sherrian Lynne. BA magna cum laude, W.Va. State Coll., 1971; JD, Ohio State U., 1974. Bar: Ohio 1974, U.S. Ct. Mil. Appeals, 1974, Fla. 1980, U.S. Dist. Ct. (so. dist.) Fla. 1980, Supreme Ct. 1980, U.S. Ct. Appeals (5th and 11th cirs.) 1981. Asst. U.S. atty. U.S. Dist. Ct. (so. dist.) Fla., Miami, 1979-84; ptnr. Raskin & Graham, Miami, 1984-91; judge U.S. Dist. Ct. (so. dist.) Fla., 1991—; instr. U. Md., Hanau, Fed. Republic Germany, 1977-78, Embry Riddle U., Homestead, Fla., 1978-79. Served to Maj., asst. staff judge adv. U.S. Army, 1974-79. Recipient Arthur S. Fleming award Washington Jaycees, 1982, Superior Performance award U.S. Dept. Justice; named One of Outstanding Young Men of Am.., 1984. Mem. Assn. Trial Lawyers Am., Nat. Bar Assn., Fed. Bar Assn. (so. Fla. pres. 1984-85, treas. 1982-83), Fla. Bar Assn., N.Y. Bar Assn., Ohio Bar Assn., NAACP, Alpha Phi Alpha. Democrat. Baptist. Office: US Courthouse Rm 1067 99 NE 4th St Miami FL 33132-2133*

GRAHAM, EVELYNE MOORE, retired school administrator, consultant; b. Bertie County, N.C., Aug. 2, 1929; d. Arthur Cotton and Evelyne (Wright) Moore; m. Walter Daniel Graham, Aug. 6,1949; children: Lynne, Julie, Walter Daniel Jr. AB, Elon Coll., 1950; MEd, U. Va., 1962; cert. advanced study, Old Dominion U., 1981. Cert. tchr., adminstr., N.C., Va. Tchr. Guildford County Schs., Greensboro, N.C., 1950-51; engring. asst. Western Electric, Burlington, N.C., 1951-52; tchr. sci., math. Isle of Wight County Schs., Smithfield, Va., 1953-55, Norfolk County Schs., Norfolk, Va., 1955-56, 59-60, Portsmouth (Va.) Pub. Schs., 1960-61, 62-63; supr. math. Chesapeake (Va.) Pub. Schs., 1963-83, asst. prin. for instrn., 1983-88; ret., 1988; ind. ednl. cons. Suffolk, Va., 1989—; adj. faculty Old Dominion U., Norfolk, 1989-92; presenter workshops, 1967-87; com. to develop minimum math. requirements Va. Dept. Edn., Richmond, 1976-77, adv. com. for spl. edn., 1980-87, mem. com. to develop curriculum materials for hand-held calculators, 1989; elem. math. extension tchr. U. Va., Charlottesville, 1967-77, ednl. cons., 1976-77; reading tutor Suffolk Literacy Coun., 1989-95. Author: Primary Coloring Book, 1976, Picture Graphing, 1976, Think-A-Grahams, 3 vols., 1985, 3 new vols., 1991; contbr. articles to ednl. publs. Troop leader Nansemond County coun. Girl Scouts U.S., 1960-70; organizer, leader Interracial and Interdenominational Youth Work Camp, Suffolk, Va., 1969-75; bd. dirs. Suffolk Red. Cross, 1989-92, mem. fin., blood coms., 1989—; vol. Suffolk Meals on Wheels, 1989-96; mem. The Prime Time Singers, 1989—; dir. jr. youth choir Bethlehem United Ch. of Christ, adult chancel choir, dir. middle sch. choir; pres. Friends of Suffolk Libr., 1989-95; chmn. Bethlehem Tent Suffolk Peanut Fest, 1992; editor newsletter Nansemond Gardens/Willowbrook Civic Assn., 1992-94; coord. Saturday Salvation Army Soup Kitchen, 1993—; Sat. lunch coord. Suffolk Habitat for Humanity, 1993—; dir. summer food program USDA, 1993. NSF scholar, 1960-61, 67-68, fellow, 1961-62. Mem. NEA (ret., life), AARP (mem. call com. Suffolk chpt., tour organizer), Organized Tidewater Coun. Tchrs. Math. (life, pres. 1964-68, exec. bd. 1968-80, 1st Ann. Svc. award 1990), Va. Assn. Supervision and Curriculum Devel. (pres. 1979-80, exec. bd. 1968-80), Nat. Coun. Suprs. Math. (charter, exec. bd. 1969-75), Am. Heart Assn. (residential chmn. Suffolk chpt. 1993), Va. Coun. Tchrs. Math. (charter, life, exec. bd. 1976-81), Va. Coun. Math. Supervision (charter, pres. 1979-81), Va. Edn. Assn. (ret., editor newsletter 1970-89, treas. dept. elem. math. 1981-95), Nat. Coun. Tchrs. Math., Va. Ret. Tchrs. Assn. (life), Chesapeake Ret. Tchrs. (v.p. 1991—), Suffolk Retired Tchrs. (v.p. 1991-96, chaplain 1996—), Delta Kappa Gamma, Phi Delta Kappa (treas. 1988-91, v.p. 1991-92, Outstanding Mem. award local chpt. 1990, Dis. award), Phi Kappa Phi (life). Home: 825 Normandy Dr Suffolk VA 23434-2907

GRAHAM, HANTFORD LEROY, publishing executive, elementary education educator; b. Centerville, N.S., Can., Aug. 16, 1918; arrived in U.S., 1919; s. Roylston Douglas and Reta Lysle (Robbins) G.; m. Maura Heloisa Napoleon, Nov. 18, 1950. AA, Boston U., 1948, BS in Edn., 1950; MEd, Mass. State Coll., 1962; EdD, U. Va., 1974. Field exec. Boy Scouts Am., Brockton, Mass., 1955-58; clinician Reading Inst. of Boston, 1958-61; reading specialist Bridgewater-Raynam Sch. Dist., 1961-67; assoc. prof. Acadia U., Wolfville, N.S., 1967-76; dir. Madison Academies Project HEW, Harrisonburg, Va., 1976-82; CEO Blue Ridge Mountains Press, Madison, 1992—. Author: Educational Psychology for Teachers, 1970, Angel at the Door, 1995; editor: Touching the Heart, 1992; contbr. articles to profl. jours. Chmn. Rappahannock-Rapidan Human Rights, Culpeper, Va., 1988-91; advisor Madison Mental Health Ctr., 1987—; historian Madison Rescue Squad, 1996—. With USAF, 1942-46. Mem. Malvern Club, Inc. (bd. dirs. 1983-85), Claflin Soc. Boston U., Corner Stone Soc. U. Va., Va. Writers Club, Cmty. Concert Assn. (bd. dirs. 1992-96). Unitarian. Office: Blue Ridge Mountains Press 33 Malvern Dr Madison VA 22727-9415

GRAHAM, HARDY MOORE, lawyer; b. Meridian, Miss., Oct. 21, 1912; s. Sanford Martin and Mary Emma (Hardy) G.; Cora Lee Poindexter, Oct. 26, 1938; children: Hardy Poindexter, Richard Newell. Student, U. So. Calif., 1932; BA, LLB, U. Miss., 1934. Bar: Miss. 1934, Tenn. 1946, U.S. Ct. Appeals (D.C. cir.) 1943, U.S. Dist. Ct. Miss. 1934, U.S. Supreme Ct. 1943, U.S. Dist. Ct. (we. dist.) Tenn. 1952. Ptnr. Graham & Graham, Meridian, 1934-43; atty. FTC, Washington, 1943-44; pvt. practice Union City, Tenn., 1946—; city judge City of Union City, 1950-58; bd. dirs., 1st v.p. Meridian Coca-Cola Bottling co., 1964—; ptnr. Union City Coca-Cola Bottling Co.; pres. Coca-Cola Coin Caterers Corp. 7-Up Bottler; pres. Tenn. Soft Drink Assn., 1963-65. Mayor City of Union City, 1950-58; pres. Union City C. of C., 1948-50, bd. dirs.; chmn. March of Dimes, Obion County Tenn., 1947, Union City Sch. Bd., 1958-66; chmn. indsl. bd. Union City, 1968—; bd. dirs. Tenn. Mcpl. League, 1950-58, pres., 1956-57; trustee Union U., Jackson, Tenn., 1st Bapt. Ch., Union City; pres. U. Tenn. Martin Devel. Com., 1970-72; mem. U. Tenn., Knoxville Devel. Coun., 1970-75, 82-85, bd. dirs. U. Miss. Found., 1987-93. Lt. USNR, 1944-46, ETO. Named Law Alumnus of Yr., U. Miss. Law Sch., 1984, Young Man of Yr., Union City, 1948; recipient Disting. Svc. award U. Tenn., Martin, 1989, U. Miss. Hall of Fame Disting. Alumnus award, 1989; Union City named Graham Park in his honor, 1986. Mem. ABA, Tenn. Bar Assn., Miss. Bar Assn., Union City-Obion County Bar Assn., (pres. 1948-49, past. bd. dirs.), Meridian Country Club, Union City Country Club, Rotary (pres. Union City 1963-64, Paul Harris fellow). Republican. Baptist. Home: 630 E Main St Union City TN 38261-3515 Office: 1915 E Reelfoot Ave Union City TN 38261-6007

GRAHAM, HOWARD LEE, SR., corporate executive; b. Monroe, Mich., May 26, 1942; s. Carl Lee and Myrtle Leota (Manis) G.; m. Bobbie Jo Hamilton; children: Kimber Lee, Howard Lee Jr., Jacquelyn Leota, John-Nathan Howard. Grad., Dake Bible Sch., Atlanta, 1960-62; student, Cen. Bible Coll., Springfield, Mo., 1964-67; DD, Internat. Sem., 1996. Debit agt. Met. Life Ins. Co., Colorado Springs, Colo., 1963-64; agt. Met. Life Ins. Co., Allen Park, Mich., 1964-67, 68; agy. mgr. Preferred Risk Life Ins. Co., Allen Park, 1968-72; agy. owner Howard Graham Ins. Agy., Taylor, Mich., 1972-85; spl. agt., rep. Prudential Ins. Co., Cleve., 1985-89; regional mgr. Primerica Fin. Svcs., Abingdon, Va., 1995—; pres. Graham Enterprises, Cleve., 1985—; CEO Graham & Graham Canvas Shoppe, Inc., 1976; nat. and regional sales leader Preferred Risk Ins. Co., Des Moines, 1969-72. Life mem. Full Gospel Bus. Men's Fellow, Detroit, 1963-85, officer, 1974-80, officer, Cleve., 1985—; active Gideons Internat., Cleve., 1963—; pres. Truth Alive, Inc., 1988—. Named Central Region Agt. of Yr., 1985; admitted to Million Dollar Round Table, 1985, Hall of Honor, 1986. Mem. Indsl. Fabrics Assn. Internat., Am. Coll., Nat. Assn. Life Underwriters, Internat. Platform Assn. Republican. Mem. Pentecostal Ch. Home: 14009 Vintage View Abingdon VA 24210-7784 Office: PO Box 1805 Abingdon VA 24212-1805

GRAHAM, JAMES A., state commissioner; b. Cleveland, N.C., Apr. 7, 1921; s. James T. and Laura G. Graham; m. to Helen Ida Kirk; children: Alice Underhill, Connie Brooks. BS, N.C. State U., 1942. Agr. tchr. Iredell County, 1942-45; supt. Upper Mountain Rsch. Sta., 1946-52; gen. mgr. Raleigh Farmers Mkt., 1956-64; owner farm N.C.; commr. N.C. Dept. Agr., Raleigh, 1964—; mem. N.C. Coun. State. Former trustee AT&T Univ., Greensboro, N.C.,past. pres.,Southern United Trade Assn., Past pres., Former bd. mem. Raleigh C. of C., bd. of Adv., Camnpbell U. Recipient Gov. award N.C. Wildlife Fedn., 1983, Spl. Svc. award Park Prodrs. Assn., 1983, Disting. Svc. award Poultry Fedn., 1983, Disting. Svc. award N.C. Crop Improvement Assn., and numerous others; named Man of Yr. Progressive Farmers Mag., 1970. Mem. Nat. Assn. Market Mgrs., N.C. Hereford Breeders Assn., Ashe County Wildlife Club (sec./treas., former pres.), Kiwanis (former pres.), Shriners, Raleigh C. of C., United Cerebral Palsy. Baptist. Office: NC Agr Dept PO Box 27647 2 W Edenton St Raleigh NC 27611*

GRAHAM, JAMES HENRY, computer science and engineering educator, consultant; b. Indpls., July 23, 1950; s. Raymond and Rosemary H. (Kiefner) G.; m. Cheryl L. Lovell, May 8, 1976; 1 child, David. BS, Rose Hulman Inst. Tech., 1972; MS, Purdue U., 1978, PhD, 1980. Registered profl. engr., Ind. Product design engr. GM, Anderson, Ind., 1972-76; grad. rsch. asst. Purdue U., West Lafayette, Ind., 1977-80; vis. asst. prof. Purdue U., West Lafayette, 1980-81; asst. prof. Rensselaer Poly. Inst., Troy, N.Y., 1981-85; assoc. prof. U. Louisville, 1985-90, prof., 1990-91, Henry Vogt endowed prof., 1991—; cons. GE, Schnectady, N.Y., 1983-85, TPX, Inc., Louisville, 1988-92. Editor: Computer Architectures for Robotics and Automation, 1987, Safety, Reliability and Human Factors in Robotic Systems, 1991. Mem. IEEE (sr. mem.), Assn. Computing Machinery, Am. Assn. Artificial Intelligence. Methodist. Office: Univ of Louisville Speed Sch-EMACS Louisville KY 40292

GRAHAM, JOHN BORDEN, pathologist, writer, educator; b. Goldsboro, N.C., Jan. 26, 1918; s. Ernest Heap and Mary (Borden) G.; m. Ruby Barrett, Mar. 23, 1943; children: Charles Barrett, Virginia Borden, Thomas Wentworth. B.S., Davidson Coll., 1938, D.Sc. (hon.), 1984; M.D., Cornell U., 1942. Asst. Cornell U., 1943-44; mem. faculty U. N.C., Chapel Hill, 1946—; Alumni Disting. prof. pathology U. N.C., 1966—, chmn. genetics curriculum, 1963-85, assoc. dean medicine for basic scis., 1968-70, coordinator interdisciplinary grad. programs in biology, 1968—, dir. hemostasis program, 1974-87; vis. prof. haematology St. Thomas's Hosp. Med. Sch., London, 1972; vis. prof. Teikyo U. Med. Sch., Tokyo, 1976; mem. selection com. NIH research career awards, 1959-62; genetics tng. com. USPHS, 1962-66, chmn., 1967-71; mem. genetic basis of disease com. Nat. Inst. Gen. Med. Scis., 1977-80; mem. pathology test com. Nat. Bd. Med. Examiners, 1963-67; mem. research adv. com. U. Colo. Inst. Behavioral Genetics, 1967-71; mem. Internat. Com. Haemostasis and Thrombosis, 1963-67; chmn. bd. U. N.C. Population Program, 1964-67; sec. policy bd. Carolina Population Center, 1972-78; cons. Environ. Health Center, USPHS, WHO, Bolt, Beranek & Newman, Inc.; mem. med. and sci. adv. council Nat. Hemophilia Found., 1972-76; hon. cons. in genetics Margaret Pyke Centre, London, 1972—. Author: Sand in the Gears, 1992, How It Was, 1896-1973, 1996; mem. editl. bd. N.C. Med. Jour., 1949-66, Am. Jour. Human Genetics, 1958-61, Soc. Exptl. Biology and Medicine, 1959-62, Human Genetics Abstracts, 1962-72, Haemostasis, 1975-80, Christian Scholar, 1958-60. Recipient O. Max Gardner award U. N.C., 1968, Disting. Svc. award U. N.C. Med. Sch., 1992; Markle scholar in med. sci., 1949-54. Mem. AMA, AAAS, Elisha Mitchell Sci. Soc. (pres. 1963), AAUP, Soc. Exptl. Biology and Medicine, Am. Soc. Exptl. Pathology, Assn. Univ. Pathologists, Am. Assn. Pathologists and Bacteriologists, Am. Soc. Human Genetics (sec. 1964-67, pres. 1972), Genetics Soc. Am., Internat. Soc. Hematology, Am. Inst. Biol. Sci., Royal Soc. Medicine (London), Med. Soc. N.C., Mayflower Soc., Sigma Xi. Democrat. Presbyterian. Home: 108 Glendale Dr Chapel Hill NC 27514-5910

GRAHAM, JOHN HAMILTON, II, customer service specialist; b. Waynesboro, Va., Mar. 30, 1960; s. John Hamilton and Joan (Clay) G. BA in Polit. Sci., Christopher Newport Coll., 1983; DD, Am. Fellowship, 1986. Dir. pub. rels. Peninsula Pilots (minor league affiliate Phila. Phillies), Hampton, Va., 1977-79, dir. broadcasting and pub. rels., 1979-81, asst. gen. mgr., 1981-85; v.p., gen. mgr. Peninsula White Sox (minor league affiliate Chgo. White Sox), Hampton, 1985-87; gen. mgr. Auburn (N.Y.) Astros Baseball Club, 1988-92; pres. Sports of the Peninsula, Hampton, 1992-94; customer svc. specialist Airborne Express, Atlanta, 1994-96; sr. agt., night ops. mgr. Airborne Express Internat., College Park, Ga., 1996—. Vice chmn. Rep. Nat. Com., 1981; vice chmn. Rep. Party Va., Hampton, 1982-92; election bd., election ofcl. Commonwealth of Va., Hampton, 1985-95; notary pub. Commonwealth of Va., Richmond, 1988—. Named Broadcaster of Yr. Carolina League, Hampton, Va., 1980, 81, 85, 87, Exec. of Yr. N.Y. Penn League, Auburn, 1991; recipient Bill Dancy award Phila. Phillies, 1987. Mem. Nat. Assn. Writers and Broadcasters, Assn. Profl. Ballplayers of Am., Moose, Am. Legion. Home: 105 Summer Glen Dr Union City GA 30291

GRAHAM, JOHN MARSHALL, French language educator; b. Owatonna, Minn., Jan. 14, 1963; s. Keith Marshall and Eileen Judith (Kjerland) G.; m. Lydia Belateche, May 15, 1990. BA summa cum laude, U. Minn., 1982; PhD, Yale U., 1988. Acting instr. Yale U., New Haven, 1985-86; asst. prof. French U. Mich., Ann Arbor, 1988-96; ind. scholar Starkville, Miss., 1996—. Contbr. articles to profl. jours. Birkelo fellow U. Minn., 1982, Whiting fellow Yale U., 1987. Mem. MLA, Am. Assn. Tchrs. French, Am. Coun. Teaching Fgn. Langs.

GRAHAM, KENT HILL, philanthropist, museum guide; b. Winston-Salem, N.C., May 16, 1937; d. Charles Gideon and Nancy Critz (O'Hanlon) Hill; m. William Thomas Graham, Feb. 1, 1958; children: William Thomas, Ashton Cannon. Student, Duke U., 1955-58, U. Hawaii, 1958. Chmn. of vols., sec., sec. to exec. bd. Forsyth County chpt. ARC, asst. to nat. chmn. vols. Am. Nat. Red. Cross, Washington; bd. dirs. Centenary United Meth. Ch. Day Care Ctr.; bd. dirs. Am. Cancer Soc., Forsyth County, Little Theatre, Child Guidance Clinic; mem. Libr. Bd. of Forsyth County, 1970-77, chmn., 1975-77; Rep. candidate for alderman West Ward, Winston-Salem, 1965; vice chmn. N.C. Battleship Commn., 1973-77; bd. dirs. Winston-Salem Debutante Com., 1984-86, pres., 1985, nominating chmn., 1986; mem. exec. bd. Historic Winston, Inc.; trustee N.C. Sch. Arts, 1986-87; mem. N.C. Sentencing and Policy Adv. Com., 1990-93, Celebration N.C. Fin. Com. Capt. N.C. Naval Militia; bd. dirs. Carolina Ballet, 1996—. Mem. Jr. League Nat. Fedn. Rep. Women, Order of the Long Leaf Pine, Twin City Garden Club (treas., 1st v.p., pres.), Garden Club Am. (zone VIII, bull. editor 1975-77, vice chmn. 1977-80, nominating com. 1979-80, water conservation coord. 1980-83). Home: 3421 Williamsborough Ct Raleigh NC 27609-6368

GRAHAM, LINDSEY O., congressman; b. Pickens County, S.C., July 9, 1955; s. E. J. and Millie Graham. BA in Psychology, U. S.C., 1977, JD, 1981. Area def. counsel Shaw AFB, 1982-84; chief prosecutor USAF Europe, 1984-88; asst. county atty. County of Oconee, S.C., 1988-92; pvt. practice, 1989—; city atty. Central, S.C., 1990-94; mem. S.C. Ho. of Reps., 1992-94, 104th Congress from 2d S.C. dist., 1995—. With USAF, 1990, Pursian Gulf; maj. S.C. Air NG, 1989—. Republican. Office: US Ho of Reps 1429 Longworth Ho Off Bldg Washington DC 20515*

GRAHAM, MICHAEL PAUL, lawyer; b. Leavenworth, Kans., May 15, 1948; s. K.L. and Norma D. (Whiteside) G.; m. Pamela Jeanne Haymes, Feb. 21, 1976; children—Sarah Kathryn, Patrick Edward. A.B., Dartmouth Coll., 1970; J.D., Harvard, 1973. Bar: Tex. 1973. Assoc., Baker & Botts, Houston, Tex., 1973-80, ptnr., 1981—. Mem. Houston Bar Assn., Houston Bar Found. Office: Baker & Botts 3000 One Shell Plz 910 Louisiana St Houston TX 77002

GRAHAM, OTTO EVERETT, JR., retired athletic director; b. Waukegan, Ill., Dec. 6, 1921; s. Otto Everett and Cordonna (Hayes) G.; m. Beverly Jean Collinge, Oct. 7, 1945; children—Duey, Sandy, David. B.A., Northwestern U., 1944. Quarterback with Cleve. Browns, 1946-55; coach Coll. All-Stars vs. Nat. Football League champions, 1958-65, 69-70; athletic dir., head football coach USCG Acad., New London, Conn., 1959-66; athletic dir. USCG Acad., 1970-85; gen. mgr., head coach Washington Redskins, 1966-68. Pres. Fellowship Christian Athletes, 1956-57; Bd. dirs. Washington YMCA, 1967—. Served with USNR, 1944-45; now capt. USCG, ret. Named All Am. in football and basketball, 1943, All Pro quarterback, 1951, 52, 54, 55; named to Coll. Football Hall of Fame, 1955, Pro Football Hall of Fame, 1965, NFL 75th Yr. Anniversary Team, 1994, NFL 75 Yr. All-Time Team, 1994. Home: 2216 Riviera Dr Sarasota FL 34232-3520

GRAHAM, RICHARD DOUGLAS, computer company executive, consultant; b. Pascagoula, Miss., July 19, 1947; s. Robert A. and Lois Mary (Dillman) G.; m. Margaret Jean Laprade (div. May 1991); 1 child, Spence D. BS in Computer Sci., La. Tech. Coll., 1968. Cert. data processor. Programmer Nat. Shawmut Bank, Boston, 1968-69; mgr. First Nat. Bank, Mobile, Ala., 1969-75, Nat. Bank Commerce, Dallas, 1976-81; regional mgr. Apple Computer, Inc., Carrollton, Tex., 1981-83; pres. Graham Cons., Inc., Carrollton, 1983—; bd. dirs First Colony Bank, The Colony, Tex. Com. mem. Jaycees, Waltham, Mass., 1969; troop leader Boy Scouts Am., Carrollton, 1985, 86. Mem. Inst. for Cert. Computer Profls., Data Processing Mgmt. Assn. Republican. Methodist. Office: Graham Cons Inc 1930 E Rosemeade Pky Ste 204 Carrollton TX 75007-2468

GRAHAM, R(ICHARD) NEWELL, soft drink bottling company executive; b. Union City, Tenn., June 15, 1947; s. Hardy Moore and Cola Lee (Poindexter) G.; m. Bettie Rene Young, Dec. 28, 1968; children: Richard, Stanford. BA, U. Miss., 1969. Operating ptnr., chief exec. officer Union City Coca-Cola Bottling Co., 1972—; sec., treas. C.C. Coin Caterers Corp., Union City, 1972-93, pres., 1993—; bd. dirs. First State Bank, Union City. Pres. Union City Arts Coun., 1978-79; mem. devel. com. U. Tenn., Martin, 1980—, vice chmn. devel. coun., 1990-93; treas. St. James Speicopal Ch., Union City, 1987—. With USN, 1969-72. Recipient Project of Yr. award Tenn. Jaycees, Nashville, 1974, Friend of Edn. award Obion County Schs., Union City, 1980. Mem. Assn. Coca-Cola Bottlers Tenn. (pres. 1989-91), Tenn. Soft Drink Assn. (bd. dirs. 1985—), Obion County C. of C. (bd. dirs. 1989—), Union City Jaycees (pres. 1975, Outstanding Young Man award 1976), Chaine des Rotisseurs (chavalier 1989—), Union City Rotary Club. Republican. Office: Union City Coca-Cola Bottling Co 1915 E Reelfoot Ave Union City TN 38261-6007

GRAHAM, SELDON BAIN, JR., lawyer, engineer; b. Franklin, Tex., Apr. 14, 1926; s. Seldon Bain and Lillian Emma (Struwe) G.; m. Patricia Gene Noah, Feb. 14, 1953; children—Seldon Bain, Kyle, Laurie. B.S., U.S. Mil. Acad., 1951; J.D., U. Tex., 1970. Registered profl. engr., Tex. Bar: Tex. 1970, U.S. Dist. Ct. (so. dist.) Tex. 1980, U.S. Ct. Appeals (5th cir.) 1983; cert. in oil, gas and mineral law Tex. Bd. Legal Specialization. Commd. 2d lt. U.S. Army, 1946; advanced through grades to col., 1979; with Office of Dep. Chief of Staff for Personnel, 1979; ret., 1979; area reservoir engr. ARCO, Okla., 1954-60; div. regulatory engr. Mobil Oil Co., Corpus Christi, 1961-67; counsel Exxon Co. USA, Houston, 1970-85. Decorated Legion of Merit. Mem. Soc. Petroleum Engrs. Methodist. Home and Office: 4713 Palisade Dr Austin TX 78731-4516

GRAHAM, SHERRIE L., sports promotions company executive; b. Zanesville, Ohio, Oct. 19, 1951; d. Virgil R. Graham and Iva L. King. BS in Behavioral Medicine, Kent State U., 1974. Cert. spl. edn./behavioral scis./speech comm. Pres. Concepts Internat., Columbus, 1970-85; mng. dir. Internat. Sports Promotions, Atlanta, 1985-96; pres. RoadRunner Pub. Rels. & Media Rels., Atlanta, 1996—; Exec. dir. James P. Meml. Found., Columbus, 1986-92. Columnist (newspaper) Women of Greater Atlanta, 1993-96. Dir. media rels. various congl. campaigns, Atlanta, 1992; govtl. affairs advisor States of Ohio and Fla. Gubernatorial Campaigns, State of Ohio Congl./Senatorial Campaigns, 1977-86; mem. Atlanta Downtown Partnership, Downtown Pub. Rels. Coun.; mem. hospitality com. Super Bowl XXVIII Host Com., 1994; vol. Atlanta Com. for Olympic Games, 1989—; vol. Nationwide Srs. Championship Bellsouth Classic Golf Tournament, Assn. for Prevention of Domestic Violence, Habitat for Humanity, mjr. com. Childhood Autistic and Ednl. Found., 1989—; media hospitality com. Peach Bowl. 1991-94. Recipient Outstanding Achievement awards League Against Child Abuse, Coun. for Exceptional Children, SCIOTO SuperFest Com. Mem. NAFE, Am. Mktg. Assn., Am. Cons. League, Kent State U. Alumni Assn. (bd. dirs., founder, past pres. 1989—), San Francisco 49ers Gold Rush Club (Atlanta). Democrat. Roman Catholic. Address: RoadRunner Pub Rels and Media PO Box 52684 Atlanta GA 30355-0684

GRAHAM, SYLVIA ANGELENIA, wholesale distributor, retail buyer; b. Charlotte, N.C., Mar. 27, 1950; d. John Wesley and Willie Myrl (Ray) White; m. James Peter Cleveland Fisher, Apr. 23, 1967 (div. Sept. 1972); 1 child, Wesley James Fisher; m. Harold Walker Graham, Sept. 14, 1972 (dec. June 1994); 1 child, Angelique Jane Graham. Cert., Naval Reserve Force Detachment Mgmt. Sch., 1985; air cargo specialist cert., Air U., 1987. Store owner Naval Air Terminal/Naval Transp. Support Unit, Norfolk, Va., 1985—; fleet liaison technician Naval Material Transp. Orgn., Norfolk, 1988-93; passenger svc. rep. Naval Transp. Support Unit Naval Material Transport Orgn., Norfolk, Va., 1996—; distbr. Blair Divsn. of Merchants, Lynchburg, Va., 1988—, Mason Shoe Co., Chippewa Falls, Wis., 1988—; driver Greater Charlotte Transp. Co., 1988—, Watkins Products, Winona, Minn., 1992—, Citizens Def. Products, St. Joseph, Mo., 1993—; dealer Creative Card Co., Chgo., 1995—, Home Showcase Products, Lynchburg, 1995—; jewelry dealer Merlite Industries, N.Y.C., 1994; dealer Creative Cards, Chgo., 1995—; mem. Nat. Safety Coun., Charlotte, 1988—, "C" team Watkins Products, Lincoln, Nebr., 1992—; sec. Popular Club Plan, Dayton, N.J., 1990—; pub. Citizens Def. Products, 1993—; sponsor The Paralyzed Vets. Am., Wilton, N.H., 1994—. Crusader Cancer Ctr. for Detection and Preventin Drive, Seattle, 1991—; blcok chmn. Easter Seal Soc., 1988—. With USN, 1991, Persian Gulf; USNR, 1992, Somolian Relief Effort; USN, 1993-94. Named Top Dealer, Home Showcase Products, Lynchburg, Va. Mem. NAFE, Nat. Enlisted Res. Assn., Naval Enlisted Res. Assn., Nat. Pk. and Conservation Assn., Nat. Trust Hist. Preservation, Direct Selling Assn., Navy League of the U.S., Libr. of Congress Assocs., Nature Conservancy. Democrat. Pentecostal. Home: PO Box 16066 Charlotte NC 28297-6066

GRAHAM, SYLVIA SWORDS, secondary school educator; b. Atlanta, Nov. 15, 1935; d. Metz Jona and Christine (Gurley) Swords; m. Thomas A. Graham, Nov. 29, 1958 (div. 1970). BA, Mary Washington Coll., Fredericksburg, Va., 1957; MEd, W. Ga. Coll., Carrollton, 1980; SEd, W. Ga. Coll., 1981; postgrad., Coll. William and Mary, 1964-67. Tchr. Atlanta pub. schs., 1957-58, Newark County pub. schs., Newark, Calif., 1960-61; tchr. history Virginia Beach (Va.) pub. schs., 1964-75, Paulding County pub. schs., Dallas, Ga., 1976—; tour dir. Paulding High Sch. trips, Far East, 1985, USSR, 1989, Australia, 1988-89. County chmn. Rep. Party, 1987-89, county chmn. for reelection of Newt Gingrich, 1982; mem. Gingrich edn. com., 1983, 88; 1st vice chmn. 6th Congl. Dist., 1989-90, chmn. 1989-90; chmn. 7th Congl. Dist., 1992-95; del. Nat. Rep. Conv., 1992. Named Star Tchr., Paulding County C. of C., Dallas, Ga., 1989. Mem. Dallas Woman's Club (pres. 1982-84, 1st v.p. 1986-88, pub. affairs chmn. 1986—, treas. for Civic Ctr. fund 1984—), Phi Kappa Phi. Republican. Baptist. Home: 204 Hart Cir Dallas GA 30132-1115

GRAHAM, TINA TUCKER, psychiatric and pediatrics nurse; b. Cherry Pointe, N.C., Jan. 16, 1962; d. Jerry Keith and Masako (Sueshita) Tucker. AAS, Shelby State Community Coll., 1985. RN, Tenn.; cert. CPR, crisis intervention, psychiat. and mental health nurse. Staff nurse newborn ICU, IMC Memphis Regional Med. Ctr., 1986-87; nurse team leader MidSouth Hosp., Memphis, 1986-87, charge nurse, 1987-89, nurse mgr. adolescent unit, 1989-90; dir. infection control/employee health/emergency responder, 1990-91; nurse mgr. child unit, acting program dir. MidSouth Hosp., Memphis, 1991-92, program dir. child svcs., 1992-93; staff nurse oper. rm. LeBonheur-Childrens Med. Ctr., Memphis, 1993—; clin. specialist ORSOS computer ops. LeBonheur-Childrens Med. Ctr., 1996—; cons. in field. Named Nurse of Yr., MidSouth Hosp., 1989. Mem. ANA, AORN, Assn. for Practitioners Infection Control, Phi Theta Kappa. Office: LeBonheur Childrens Med Ctr 50 S Dunlap St Memphis TN 38103-4909

GRAHAM, WILLIAM AUBREY, JR., real estate broker; b. Montgomery, Ala., Dec. 7, 1930; s. William Aubrey and Nina Judson (Jenkins) G.; m. Carol Fletcher, Aug. 15, 1953; children: William G., Carol Anne. BS in Bldg. Constrn., Auburn U., Ala., 1956. Lic. real estate broker, gen. contractor. V.p. Meadow Corp., Montgomery, Ala., 1956-60; pres. Graham Constrn. Co., Montgomery, 1960-65; engr. Portland Cement Assn., Orlando, Fla., 1965-69; gen. mgr. bldg. Punta Gorda Isles, Inc., Punta Gorda, Fla., 1969-72; sales mgr. Punta Gorda Isles, Inc., Punta Gorda, 1972-78; pres. Punta Gorda Realty, Inc., 1978—; chmn. bd. dirs. Southwest Fla. Bank N/A; bd. dirs. v.p. Coral Harbor Enterprises, Punta Gorda, 1978—; pres. Judson Corp., Punta Gorda, 1980—. Bd. dirs., pres. YMCA, Charlotte County, Fla., 1978-88, United Way, Charlotte County, 1979-90, Fla. Internat. Air Show, Charlotte County, 1981—; bd. dirs., v.p. Spl. Tng. and Rehab., Charlotte County, 1983—, chmn., 1990—. Mem. Nat. Assn. Realtors, Fla. Assn. Realtors, Nat. Assn. Home Builders, Charlotte County Home Builders Assn., Am. Legion, Elks, Kiwanis (bd. dirs., pres. Punta Gorda 1979—, Citizen of Yr. award 1983, Kiwanian of Yr. award 1990). Republican. Episcopalian. Home: 500 Bal Harbor Blvd Punta Gorda FL 33950-5291 Office: Punta Gorda Realty Inc 1601 W Marion Ave Punta Gorda FL 33950-3202

GRAHAM, WILLIAM ROBERT, medical educator; b. Houston, July 20, 1952; s. William George and Rudene (Gray) G.; m. Theresa Vicroy, Oct. 8, 1987; children: Erin, Stephanie, Mary Catherine, Kelly. BS, U. Houston, 1974; MD, Southwestern Med. Sch., 1981. Intern Parkland Hosp., Dallas, 1981-82, resident in internal medicine, 1982-84, chief resident, 1984-85; investigator Salk Inst., La Jolla, Calif., 1985-86; asst. prof. medicine U. Calif., San Diego, 1986-89, Baylor Coll. Medicine, Houston, 1989—; assoc. chief of medicine Ben Taub Hosp., Houston, 1990—; exec. dir. utilization rev. Ben Taub Hosp., Houston, 1992—. Contbr. chpt. to book and articles to profl. jours. Recipient Clin. Investigator award NIH, 1985. Office: Ben Taub Hosp 1504 Taub Loop Houston TX 77030-1608

GRAHAM, WILLIAM THOMAS, lawyer; b. Waynesboro, Va., Oct. 24, 1933; s. James Monroe and Margaret Virginia (Goodwin) G.; m. Kent Hill, Feb. 1, 1958; children: Ashton Cannon, William Thomas Jr. AB in Econs., Duke U., 1956; JD, U. Va., 1962. Bar: N.C. 1962, Va. 1962, D.C. 1970, U.S. Supreme Ct. 1970. Assoc. Craige, Brawley and predecessor firms, Winston-Salem, N.C., 1962-64; ptnr. Craige, Brawley, Horton & Graham, Winston-Salem, 1965-69; asst. gen. counsel HUD, Washington, 1969-70; ptnr. Billings & Graham, Winston-Salem, 1971-75; judge N.C. Superior Ct., 1975-79; pvt. practice Winston-Salem, 1981-87; commr. of banks State of N.C., Raleigh, 1987-95; counsel Patton Boggs, LLP, Raleigh, 1995—. Chmn. Forsyth County Reps., Winston-Salem, 1966-69, 73-75, George Bush for Pres., N.C., 1988. Served with U.S. Army, 1957-58. Mem. Old Town Club. Methodist. Home: 3421 Williamsborough Ct Raleigh NC 27609 Office: Patton Boggs LLP Ste 230 Brighton Hall 1101 Sister Rd Durham NC 27703

GRAHMANN, CHARLES V., bishop; b. Halletsville, Tex., July 15, 1931. Student, Assumption-St. John's Sem., Tex. Ordained priest Roman Catholic Ch., 1956. Ordained titular bishop Equilium and aux. San Antonio, 1981-82; 1st bishop Victoria, Tex., 1982-89; coadjutor biship Dallas, 1990; bishop Diocese of Dallas, Dallas, Tex., 1990—. *

GRAMM, WILLIAM PHILIP (PHIL GRAMM), senator, economist; b. Fort Benning, Ga., July 8, 1942; s. Kenneth Marsh and Florence (Scroggins) G.; m. Wendy Lee, Nov. 2, 1970; children: Marshall Kenneth, Jefferson Philip. BA, U. Ga., 1964, PhD, 1967. Mem. faculty dept. econs. Tex. A&M U., College Station, 1967-78; prof. Tex. A.&M. U., College Station, 1973-78; ptnr. Gramm & Assocs., 1971-78; mem. 96th-98th Congresses from 6th Tex. Dist.; U.S. senator from Tex., 1985—; mem. Banking, Housing, and Urban Affairs Com., Fin. Com., Budget Com., nat. Rep. Senatorial Com.; chmn., 1991-95. Contbr. articles to profl. jours., periodicals. Republican. Episcopalian. Office: US Senate 370 Senate Russell Bldg Washington DC 20510

GRAMMER, FRANK CLIFTON, oral surgeon, researcher; b. El Dorado, Ark., Aug. 12, 1943; s. Norman Alexander and Lillie Mae (Martin) G.; m. Ann Marie Beller, Feb. 8, 1964 (div. Feb. 1980); children: William Cody, Tamara Ann; m. Sandra Lanier Boyd, July 5, 1980; 1 child, Jeremy Boyd. BS, Washington U., St. Louis, 1966, DDS summa cum laude, 1968; MSD, U. Minn., 1972, PhD, 1973. Diplomate Am. Bd. Oral and Maxillofacial Surgery. Research fellow U. Minn., Mpls., 1968-73; practice dentistry specializing in oral surgery, Fayetteville, Ark., 1973—; cons. Cambridge Hosp., Minn., 1972-73; instr. U. Ark., Fayetteville, 1978-79; asst. prof. U. Tenn., Memphis, 1979-80; mem. adv. com. Am. Bd. Oral and Maxillofacial Surgery, Chgo., 1979-85; bd. govs. Antaeus Research Inst., Fayetteville, 1979-85. Editor Arkansas Dentistry, 1992—; contbr. articles to profl. jours. Recipient Research award Am. Soc. Oral Surgeons, 1973. Fellow Am. Coll. Oral and Maxillofacial Surgeons, Am. Dental Soc. of Anesthesiologists, Internat. Coll. Dentists, Am. Coll. Dentists; mem. Ark. Soc. Oral and Maxillofacial Surgeons (pres. 1982-84), Ark. State Dental Assn. (v.p. 1988-89, pres. 1990-91), N.W. Dist. Dental Soc. (pres. 1983-84). Republican. Presbyterian. Club: Fayetteville Country (pres. 1980-81, 94—). Avocations: golf, tennis, hunting. Home: 359 Fairway Ln Fayetteville AR 72701-7159 Office: PO Box 1807 Fayetteville AR 72702-1807

GRANAT, PEPI, physician; b. Miami, Fla.; m. Raul R. Cuadrado; children: R. Rolando, Gina, Eva. BS in Zoology cum laude, U. Miami, 1958, MD, 1962. Diplomate Am. Bd. Family Practice, Nat. Bd. Med. Examiners. Intern Hosp. St. Raphael, New Haven, Conn., 1962-63; fellow in internal medicine and pharmacology Yale U., New Haven, Conn., 1963-64; rsch. assoc. dept. pharmacology Yale U., New Haven, 1965; part-time emergency rm. supervising physician Jackson Meml. Hosp., Miami, 1964; rsch. assoc. pharmacology Yale U., New Haven, 1964-65; part-time sch. physician City of New Haven Dept. Health, 1965-66; asst. physician Yale U. Employee Health Clinic, 1965-66; pvt. practice Milan, Mich., 1966-67; health svc. physician U. Mich., Ann Arbor, 1967-68, U. Miami, 1968-71; pvt. practice Miami, 1969—; clin. asst. prof. dept. family practice U. Miami, 1972-95, prof., 1995—, preceptor med. students residents, 1972—, preceptor nurse practitioners program, 1975-78, clin. assoc. prof., 1977—; hosp. affiliations include South Miami Hosp., Doctors Hosp., Coral Gables, Jackson Meml. Hosp., Miami; presenter numerous seminars. Newspaper columnist Miami News, 1972-73; mem. editl. bd. Baby Times mag., South Fla. Parenting mag., Fla. Family Physicians; editor, chmn. editl. com. Miami Medicine mag.; contbr. articles to profl. jours. Advisor, participant field trips com. Girl Scouts USA, 1976; chmn. South Miami Hosp. Med. Update, 1977; grant com. United Way Found., 1977-81; sch. health lectr. Ponce de Leon Jr. H.S., 1979; mem. program steering com. Consortium for Med. Edn., U. Miami, 1979; mem., chmn. prof. edn. com. Dade chpt. Am. Cancer Soc., 1987-90, mem. breast cancer task force, 1991, 92, bd. dirs., 1988-91, mem. profl. edn. com. family practice subcom. Fla. Div., 1989-90, state level com., 1991; mem. Civic Chorale. Named Doctor of Day Fla. State Legis., 1986-90. Mem. AMA, Dade County Med. Assn. (pub. svc. com., mediation II com., med. malpractice com. chmn., spkrs. bur. chmn. Amendment 10 1988), Fla. Med. Assn., Dade County Acad. Family Physicians South, Fla. Acad. Family Physicians (legis. com., pub. rels. com., editl. com., cancer com., cancer task force, co-chmn. cancer com. 1991-93), Am. Acad. Family Physicians (nat. drugs and devices com. 1992-94), Am. Med. Women's Assn., South Dade Med. Women's Assn., Avocade and Limegrowers Assn., ZONTA Internat. Svc. Club, Beta Sigma Phi (columnist 1994). Office: 7800 S Red Rd Ste 202 Miami FL 33143-5523

GRANBERRY, EDWIN PHILLIPS, JR., safety engineer, consultant; b. Orange, N.J., Aug. 20, 1926; s. Edwin Phillips Sr. and Mabel (Leflar) G.; m. Joanne Park, June 15, 1991; children: Melissa, Edwin Phillips III, James, Jennifer, Claudia. BS, Rollins Coll., 1950; MBA, Embry Riddle Aero. U., 1985. Cert. profl. chemist. Weapons system engr. Martin Co., Orlando, Fla., 1958-62; supt. indsl. safety Guided Missiles Range div. Pan Am. World Airways, Cape Canaveral, Fla., 1962-72; mgr. indsl. hygiene/safety engring. Pratt & Whitney Aircraft, West Palm Beach, Fla., 1972-88; mgr. indsl. and systems safety engring. Chem. Systems div. United Tech. Corp., San Jose, Calif., 1988-89; pres. Granberry & Assocs. Inc., Winter Park, Fla., 1989—; adj. faculty mem. Valencia C.C., Orlando, Fla.; mem. Fla. State Toxic Substances Adv. Coun., 1984-88, Fla. State Emergency Response Commn., 1988, chmn. local emergency response planning com. region 6, 1991-92, Fla. Divsn. Safety Customer Adv. Coun. Scoutmaster Boy Scouts Am., 1946-74, dist. chmn. Wekiwa dist. Central Fla. council, 1946-74, also council commr. Served with USNR, 1944-54, PTO. Recipient Silver Beaver award, 1960. Fellow Am. Inst. Chemists; mem. Am. Welding Soc., ASTM, Am. Chem. Soc., Am. Bd. Forensic Examiners, Am. Nat. Stds. Inst., Nat. Environ. Health Assn., Nat. Fire Protection Assn., Rollins Coll. Alumni Assn. (bd. dirs. 1958-61), Am. Soc. Safety Engrs. (chmn. Gold Coast chpt. 1979-80, pres. 1981-84; regional v.p. 1984-88, 94—, v.p. divs. 1988-90, adminstr.-environ. div. 1990-92, mem. exec. com. environ. divsn. 1992—, nat. bd. dirs. 1984-90, 94—, Safety Profl. of Yr. Fla., Ga. and P.R. chpts. 1985, Safety Profl. Yr. divs. 1991), Safety Council Palm Beach County (pres. 1981-82, chmn. bd. 1983, treas. 1984). Home: 521 Langholm Dr Winter Park FL 32789-5251 Office: Granberry & Assocs Inc 2431 Aloma Ave Ste 276 Winter Park FL 32792-2566

GRANGER, HARRIS JOSEPH, physiologist, educator; b. Erath, La., Aug. 26, 1944; s. Willis Gabriel and Edith Ann (Hebert) G.; m. Ramona Ann Vice; children: Ashley, Jarrod, Brent. BS, U. S.W. La., Lafayette, 1966; PhD, U. Miss., Jackson, 1970. Asst. prof. physiology U. Miss. Med. Ctr., Jackson, 1970-74, assoc. prof. physiology, 1974-76; vis. assoc. prof. U. Calif.-San Diego, LaJolla, 1975-76; assoc. prof. dept. med. physiology Tex. A&M U., College Station, 1976-78, prof. med. physiology, 1978—, head dept. med. physiology, 1982—; dir. Microcirculation Rsch. Inst., Tex. A&M U., 1981; mem. study sect. NIH Exptl. Cardiovascular Scis. Study Sect., 1981-86, 88-93; chmn. Gordon Conf., 1982. Co-author: Circulatory Physiology II, 1975; mem. editorial bd.: Circulation Research, 1982-89, Microvascular Research, 1978-85; mem. editorial bd. Am. Jour. Physiology, 1986—, assoc. editor, 1987-93, editor, 1993—; contbr. chpts. to books, articles to profl. jours. Recipient Research Career Devel. award Nat. Heart Lung & Blood Inst., 1978-83; Disting. Achievement award in research Tex. A&M U., 1982, Merit award Nat. Heat, Lung and Blood Inst., 1987. Mem. Microcirculatory Soc. (coun. 1978-81, pres. 1989, Landis award 1992), Am. Physiol. Soc. (sec. cardiovascular sect. 1991, treas. 1992, chmn. 1993, Harold Lamport award 1978, RM Berne Disting. Lectr 1995). Home: 1403 Millcreek Ct College Station TX 77845-8352 Office: Tex A&M U Coll Medicine Microcirculation Rsch Inst College Station TX 77843

GRANGER, WESLEY MILES, medical educator; b. Tampa, Fla., Jan. 12, 1951; s. Reeves C. and Mary Jane (Parker) G.; m. Elizabeth Dianne Dunaway, June 14, 1975; children: Darah Elizabeth, John Wesley. BA, U. S. Fla., 1972; A. Deg. by Examination, U. Chgo. Hosps. and Clinics, 1972; PhD in Physiology, Med. Coll. Ga., 1983. Registered respiratory therapist; cert. respiratory therapy technician; lic. registered respiratory therapist, La. Trainee to CRTT and registry eligible therapist Univ. Community Hosp., Tampa, 1970-74; part-time staff therapist Ga. Bapt. Med. Ctr., Atlanta, 1974-76; staff therapist Emory U. Hosp., Atlanta, 1976-77; shift supr., insvc. instr. Aiken (S.C.) Community Hosp., 1977-79; grad. teaching asst. Med. Coll. Ga., 1979-81; part-time staff therapist Doctors Hosp. of Augusta (Ga.), 1979-83; instr. respiratory therapy program Univ. Ala., Birmingham, 1983-84; asst. prof. cardiopulmonary sci. La. State U. Med. Ctr., 1984-89, assoc. prof., 1989-96; respiratory therapy program dir., assoc. prof. U. Ala., Birmingham, 1996—; lectr. in field; conductor seminars in field. Contbr. articles to profl. jours. Mem. ASCD, Math. Assn. Am., Ala. Assn. Respiratory Care, La. Soc. Respiratory Cae, Soc. for Computer Simulation. Office: U Ala Sch Health Related Professions Respiratory Therapy Program 1714 9th Ave S Birmingham AL 35205-3606

GRANITZ, ADRIENNE DIANA, librarian; b. Sewickley, Pa., Nov. 10, 1946; d. Paul and Mary Ann Delores (Catizone) Hoko; m. Ronald George Granitz, Aug. 31, 1968; 1 child, Ronald George. BS, Edinboro State U., 1968; MS in Libr. Sci., Cath. U. Am., 1983. Libr. Reynolds Elem. Sch. Dist., Greenville, Pa., 1968-72; circulation libr. Piedmont Va. C.C., Charlottesville, 1974-92; libr. dir. Milliken Textile Libr., Inst. Textile Technology, Charlottesville. Mem. ALA, Va. Libr. Assn., Spl. Librs. Assn., Assn. Coll. and Rsch. Librs., Textile Info. Users Coun. Home: 1116 Holmes Ave Charlottesville VA 22901-3723 Office: ITT 2551 Ivy Rd Charlottesville VA 22903-4614

GRANO, JOAN TERESA, infection control practitioner; b. Boston, June 2, 1959; d. John J. and Mary T. (Flaherty) Cadigan; children: Rachel, Ashley. AA, AS in Nursing, St. Petersburg (Fla) Jr. Coll., 1981; BSN, U. South Fla., 1984, MSN, 1986. RN, Fla.; cert. clin. specialist in advanced med.-surg. nursing ANCC; cert. ACLS. Staff nurse, ICU relief charge nurse Largo (Fla.) Med. Ctr. Hosp., 1981-85; staff nurse, med. ICU Bay Pines (Fla.) VA Med. Ctr., 1985-89, infection ctrl. practitioner, 1989—; researcher and presenter in field. Capt. Nurse Corps, USAR. Mem. Assn. Profls. in Infection Control and Epidemiology (cert.), Fla. Practitioners in Infection Control, Sigma Theta Tau. Home: PO Box 299 Bay Pines FL 33744

GRANT, CHERI BETH HOLLMAN, obstetrical nurse, consultant; b. Vinita, Okla., Dec. 2, 1959; d. David Lyle Hollman and Patricia Gail (Conradt) Vaughan; m. Charles John Grant Jr., Aug. 14, 1982; children: Crystal Dawn, Tiffany Louise. ADN, Northeastern Okla. A&M Coll., 1982; CLE, UCLA, 1988. RN, Okla.; cert. labor support person. Nurse aide labor and delivery Craig Gen. Hosp., Vinita, 1975-81; cert. lactation educator Hillcrest Med. Ctr., Tulsa, 1982-90, coord. childbirth edn., 1987-89; staff nurse labor and delivery M&W Prodns., Tulsa, 1982—, pres., founder, 1988—, breastfeeding cons., childbirth educator, 1990—, cons., Doulas trainer, 1992—; spkr. Okla. U. Coll. Obstetrics, Tulsa, 1990—; mem. adv. bd. First Steps Labor Companions, Tulsa, 1993—; cons. Dr. Pfanstiel, Tulsa, 1991—, Am. Lung Assn., Tulsa, 1990-93. Author: A Guide to Doula Charting: Labor Support Forms, 1994. Doula vol. Doulas Northeastern of Okla., Tulsa, 1993—; candy striper vol. Craig Gen. Hosp., Vinita, 1973-75. Mem. Internat. Lactation Cons. Assn. (cert.), Internat. Childbirth Edn. Assn. (cert.), Assn. Women's Health, Obstetrics and Neonatal Nursing, Am. Soc. for Psychoprophylaxis in Obstetrics, Doula of Northeastern Okla. (v.p. 1993-96, pres. 1996—), Doulas of N.Am. (charter, cert., Okla. coord. 1993—). Democrat. Baptist. Office: M&W Prodns PO Box 14003 Tulsa OK 74159-1003

GRANT, ELIZABETH JANE THURMOND, graphic design educator, consultant; b. Jacksonville, Fla., Nov. 16, 1950; d. Lloyd Turner and Mildred Anna (Suggs) Thurmond; m. Joseph Curtis Grant, Sept. 30, 1972; children: Elizabeth Ashley, Daniel Thurmond. AA, Fla. Community Coll., Jacksonville, 1970; BS in Advt., U. Fla., 1972, MEd in Instrn. Design and Ednl. Media, 1986. Coord. merchandising Bryant Air Conditioning Co., Indpls., 1972-73; freelance designer GE, Pittsfield, Mass., 1973-74; mgr. prodn. Multi-Media Advt., Inc., Gainesville, Fla., 1974; info. specialist III, editor U. Fla. Alumni Assn., Gainesville, 1974-77; dir. mktg. and advt. The Hope Cos., real estate developers, Gainesville, 1977-80; prof. graphic design, program dir. Sante Fe C.C., Gainesville, 1980—, mem. exec. com. senate, 1981—; mem. adj. faculty pub. rels. dept. U. Fla., Gainesville, 1988-90; pres., chief exec. officer Grant, Grant & Assocs., Alachua, Fla., 1989—; contest judge Fla. Mag. Assn., Gainesville, 1988-89; pres., cons. Fla. Pub. Rels. Assn., Gainesville, 1991. Vol. Am. Cancer Soc., Vol. Action Ctr., United Way, Chris Collingsworth Fund Raise for Alachua County; troop leader Brownies, Alachua, 1987-89; v.p. Alachua Elem. Sch. PTA, 1987-90; coach Santa Fe Babe Ruth Softball, Alachua, 1987—. Recipient lst place award for menu design and direct mail, 2d place award for direct mail 4th Dist. Am. Advt. Fedn., 1978, cert. of distinction, 1980. Mem. Fla. Assn. Community Colls., Alachua County Vocat. Assn., Gainesville Advt. Fedn. (bd. dirs., treas. 1978-80), Gainesville Area Postal Customer Coun. (sec. 1979-81), Alpha Sigma Delta, Phi Theta Kappa, Kappa Delta Pi, Chi Omega. Republican. Episcopalian. Home: PO Box 2083 Alachua FL 32615-2083 Office: Santa Fe C C 3000 NW 83rd St # L-10 Gainesville FL 32606-6210

GRANT, HORACE JUNIOR, professional basketball player; b. Augusta, Ga., July 4, 1965. Grad., Clemson U. Forward Chgo. Bulls, 1988-94, Orlando Magic, 1994—. Named to NBA All-Defensive Second Team, 1993, 94. Office: Orlando Magic Orlando Arena One Magic Pl Orlando FL 32801*

GRANT, JOHN ALEXANDER, JR., engineering consultant; b. Crockett, Tex., July 13, 1923; s. John Alexander and Anne Blackburn)Lentz) G.; m. Joan Marilyn Keith, July 2, 1946; children: Linda, John, W. Keith. AS, No. Tex. Agrl. Coll., Arlington, 1942; BS, Tex. A. and M. U., 1947. Registered profl. engr., Fla., Tex., Ky., Va., Del., Gal., Md., N.C., S.C.; registered land surveyor Fla., Md., Ky. Sr. hwy. engr. Del. State Hwy. Dept., Dover, 1947-49; hwy. engr. GS9 U.S. Bur. Pub. Rds., Richmond, Va., 1949-54; asst. engring. mgr. Michael Baker, Jr., Inc., College Park, Md., 1954-55; project engr. Michael Baker, Jr., Inc., Ft. Lauderdale, Fla., 1955-58; v.p. engring. Arvida Corp., Boca Raton, Fla., 1958-61; cons. engr. John A. Grant, Jr., Inc., Boca Raton, 1961—. Bd. dirs. Boca Forum, 1988-89. Capt. U.S. Army, 1943-46. Mem. Fla. Engring. Soc. (past pres., nat. bd. dirs.), Fla. Inst. Cons. Engrs., Fla. Soc. Profl. Land Surveyors, Nat. Soc. Profl. Engrs. (hons. com. 1988), Boca Raton C. of C. (pres. 1985-86), Elks, Exch. Club of Boca Raton, 100 Club of Broward County, Royal Palm Yacht and Country Club. Home: 3211 NE 27th Ave Pompano Beach FL 33064-8109 Office: 3333 N Federal Hwy Boca Raton FL 33431-6003

GRANT, JOSEPH MOORMAN, finance executive; b. San Antonio, Oct. 30, 1938; s. George William and Mary Christian (Moorman) G.; m. Sheila Ann Peterson, Aug. 26, 1961; children: Mary Elizabeth, Steven Clay. BBA, So. Meth. U., 1960; MBA, U. Tex., 1961, PhD, 1970. Banking officer Citibank, N.Y.C., 1961-65; sr. v.p., economist Tex. Commerce Bank (N.A.) also Tex. Commerce Bancshares, Houston, 1970-73; pres., dir. Tex. Commerce Bank, Austin, 1974-75; chmn., CEO Tex. Am. Bankshares/Ft. Worth, 1986-89; pres. Tex. Am. Bank/Ft. Worth, 1976-89, chmn., CEO, 1983-89; sr. v.p., CFO Electronic Data Systems, Dallas, 1990—; bd. dirs. Heritage Media Corp., Am. Eagle Group, North Am. Energy Corp. Author: (with Lawrence L. Crum) The Development of State-Chartered Banking in Texas, 1978, The Great Texas Banking Crash, 1996. Trustee Tex. Christian U., 1989-94, So. Meth. U., 1980-89; chmn. adv. coun. Coll. Bus. Adminstrn. Found., U. Tex., Austin; trustee Edwin L. Cox. Sch. Bus. Exc. Bd., Dallas County C.C.; bd. dirs. Dallas Mus. of Art, Dallas Mus. of Natural History, North Tex. Commn., 1976-86, chmn., 1981-82; trustee Paul Quinn Coll., 1995—. Recipient Man of Yr. award Anti-Defamation League B'nai B'rith, 1988; named to Disting. Alumni, U. Tex. at Austin, Coll. Bus. Adminstrn., 1982. Mem. Ft. Worth C. of C. (past chmn.), Young Pres. Orgn. (bd. dirs. 1980-89, internat. pres. 1987-88, exec. com.), Blue Key, Ft. Worth Club, Exch. Club, Sigma Alpha Epsilon. Episcopalian. Home: 3510 Turtle Creek Blvd Apt 6C Dallas TX 75219-5543 Office: Electronic Data Systems H2-8W-30 5400 Legacy Dr Plano TX 75024-3105

GRANT, LOUISE PATRICIA, dietitian; b. Pitts., July 26, 1953; d. Thomas Arthur and Phyllis Marguarite (Heflin) Zang; m. Timothy James Grant, Sept. 13, 1975; children: Brian Timothy, Bethany Michelle. BS in Edn., Ind. U. of Pa., 1975, MS, 1982. Registered dietitian; cert. edn. specialist. Nutrition specialist Scenery Hill Manor Nursing Home, Indiana, Pa., 1975; asst. mgr. ARA Svcs., Indiana, 1975-78; dir. nutrition svc. Purchase Line Sch. Dist., Commodore, Pa., 1978-83; clin. dietitian VA Med. Ctr., Martinsburg, W.Va., 1984-88, chief, clin. sect. dietetics, 1988-89, asst. chief, dietetic svc., 1989-94; chief nutrition and food svc. VA Med. Ctr., Mountain Home, Tenn., 1994—; cons. dietitian Knott's Nursing Home, Charlestown, W.Va., 1984-87; instr. Lord Fairfax C.C., Middletown, Va., 1984-87. Mem. Am. Dietetic Assn., Am. Diabetes Assn. (Winchester chpt. pres. 1985-90, treas. 1989-89, pres. 1989-90), Va. Dietetic Assn., No. Va. Dietetic Assn., Tenn. Dietetic Assn., TCDA. Roman Catholic. Home: 813 Lazywood Dr Johnson City TN 37601-8943 Office: VA Med Ctr (Johnson City) Mountain Home TN 37684

GRANT, MIRIAM ROSENBLOUM, secondary school educator, journalist; b. Collinsville, Ala.; d. Harry M. and Rae (Rosenberg) Rosenbloum; m. Morton A. Grant, Nov. 17, 1952 (dec. 1967). AB, U. Ala., 1935; postgrad., U. Miami, 1968-69, Fla. Internat. U. Cert. tchr., Fla. Reporter Chattanooga Free Press, 1936-41, Birmingham (Ala.) Post, 1942; reporter, movie editor, drama critic Chattanooga News-Free Press, 1943-49; tchr., head journalism dept., newspaper and yearbook adviser North Miami (Fla.) Sr. High Sch., 1969-89. Recipient Disting. Svc. award Chattanooga Little Theater, 1949, Golden Medallion Fla. Scholastic Press Assn., 1987, named life member, 1990, service award Coll. Fraternity Editors Assn., 1989. Mem. AAUW, U. Ala. Nat. Alumni Assn. (coun. mem.-at-large 1960-61), Ceramic League Miami (Corr. sec. 1963-64), Women's Panhellenic Assn. Miami (Sec. 1992-93), nat. Panhellenic Editors Conf. (vice chmn. 1986-87, chmn. 1987-89), Sigma Delta Tau (nat. pres. 1950-54, editor The Torch mag. 1968—, honor key 1988, scholarship named in her honor as 1st mem. to serve 50 yrs. on sorority nat. coun. 1991, archivist 1992—, devel. com. 1996—, CFEA recognition award as editor 1993), Theta Sigma Phi, Phi Lambda Pi, Rho Lambda, Sigma Delta Chi.

GRANT, PENNY, pediatrics educator; b. N.Y.C., Dec. 19, 1959; d. Stanley Charles and Hilda (Kleinerman) G.; m. Lee Mark Cohen, Feb. 28, 1987. BA, Columbia U., 1980; MD, N.Y. Med. Coll., 1984. Diplomate Nat. Bd. Med. Examiners, Am. Bd. Pediatrics. Intern N.Y. Hosp. Cornell Med. Ctr., N.Y.C., 1984-86; resident Jackson Meml. Hosp., U. Miami, Fla.,

1986-88, dir. pediatric care network, 1989-90; pediatrician Pediatric Assocs., P.A., Hollywood, Fla., 1988-89; clin. asst. prof. dept. pediatrics U. Miami, 1989—; dir. Univ. Pediat. Assocs., Miami, 1993-95; pediatrician Bay Harbor (Fla.) Pediatrics, 1995—; med. dir. Broward County Child Protection Team, Ft. Lauderdale, Fla., 1996—. Mem. Am. Acad. Pediatrics. Office: Rub Pediatrics Ste 308 2110 Biscayne Blvd Aventura FL 33180

GRANT, PETER MICHAEL, biologist, educator; b. Erie, Pa., Feb. 23, 1953; s. Matthew Richard and Elizabeth Jane (Scheppner) G.; m. Marcia Lu McCord, Aug. 7, 1976; children: Emily Katherine, Nicholas Jacob. BS in Biology, Pa. State U., 1975; MS in Biology, North Tex. State U., 1978; PhD in Biology, Fla. State U., 1985. Asst. prof. biology Morris Coll., Sumter, S.C., 1985-88; asst. prof. biology Southwestern Okla. State U., Weatherford, 1988-93, assoc. prof. biology, 1993—, pres. faculty senate, 1996-97; adj. asst. prof. entomology Clemson (S.C.) U., 1987—. Editor: The Mayfly Newsletter, 1990—; contbr. articles to profl. jours. Chmn. Environ. Recycling and Solid Waste Task Force, Weatherford, 1991-93; vol. Vol. in Pub. Schs. program, Weatherford, 1991—; leader Cub Scouts, 1992—. Mem. AAAS, N.Am. Benthological Soc., Ecol. Soc. Am., Am. Inst. Biol. Scis., Sigma Xi. Office: Southwestern Okla State U Dept Biol Scis Weatherford OK 73096

GRANT, VIRGINIA LEE KING, nutritionist, consultant; b. Pineville, Mo., Oct. 10, 1918; d. Arthur Judson and Blanche Bell (Boyd) King; m. Weston G. Lawson, June 14, 1942 (div. Aug. 1959); children: Victoria, Robert, Weston G. Jr., Melissa; m. H. Scott Grant, Dec. 31, 1983. BS, Kans. State U., 1939; MS, U. Tenn., 1972. Registered dietitian; lic. nutritionist and dietitian. Instr. nutrition St. Joseph Hosp. Sch. Nursing, Memphis, 1957-61; instr. nutrition U. Tenn. Coll. Nursing, Memphis, 1957-61, clin. dietitian dept. medicine Diabetic Clinic, 1961-63, clin. dietitian Clin. Rsch. Ctr., 1961-65, head rsch. dietitian, 1965-73, chief rsch. dietitian, 1973-85, asst. prof. medicine, 1973-85; nutrition cons., Memphis, 1985—; nutrition cons. Rosewood Convalescent Ctr., Memphis, 1961-65. Food and nutrition columnist Comml. Appeal, Memphis, 1961-65; contbr. articles to profl. jours. Block chmn. Memphis Neighborhood Watch Program, Memphis Police Dept., 1984—. Travel grantee AMA, 1968. Mem. Am. Dietetic Assn. (career guidance com. 1967-68, Lydia J. Roberts fellow 1972-73), Tenn. Dietetic Assn. (pres. 1963, past chmn. numerous coms.), Memphis Dist. Dietetic Assn. (pres. 1961, past chmn. numerous coms., Dietitian of Yr. award 1981), Memphis Area Nutrition Coun. (pres. 1979-80). Republican. Roman Catholic. Home: 5151 Tarrytown Dr Memphis TN 38117-2125

GRANTHAM, CHARLES EDWARD, broadcast engineer; b. Andalusia, Ala., Mar. 15, 1950; s. J.C. and Geraldine (Brooks) G. Student, Enterprise State Jr. Coll., 1968-69; AA, Lurleen B. Wallace Coll., 1979; m. Sandra J. Mosley, Mar. 9, 1973; 1 child, Christopher Charles. Sales engr., draftsman S.E. Ala. Gas Co., Andalusia, 1968-70; asst. mgr., engr. Sta. WAAO, Andalusia, 1972-78; engr. Ala. Public TV, WDIQ-TV, Dozier, Ala., also chief technician Sta. WAAO, Andalusia, 1978—; South Ala. microwave engr. APTV, 1980-93; asst. dir. broadcasting ops., APTV, 1993—. Notary pub., Ala.; bd. dirs. Carolina Vol. Fire Dept., sec./treas., 1985-91; pres. Andalusia Men's Ch. Softball, 1985-86; youth dir. Cedar Grove Ch., 1987-89, deacon 1993—; pres. Andalusia High Sch. Band Boosters, 1990-91; coach Andalusia Little League, 1982-83; active Lt. Govs. Commn. on Youth and Violence, 1995-96. With inf. U.S. Army, 1970-72. Named Civitan Outstanding Young Am., 1967. Mem. I.E.E.E., I.S.C.E.T., Assn. Cert. NABER Technicians (sr. mem.), N.A.R.T.E. (master endorsement), Internat. Soc. Cert. Electronic Technicians, Am. Film Inst., Nat. Rifle Assn., Ala. State Employees Assn. (bd. dirs., pres. local chpt. 1991—), Country Music Assn., Nat. Assn. Bus. and Ednl. Radio, Soc. Broadcast Engrs., Country Music Disc Jockey Assn., Rotary Club, Phi Theta Kappa. Mem. Ch. of Christ. Home: RR 5 Box 48-w Andalusia AL 36420-9296 Office: Sta WDIQ-TV RR 2 Dozier AL 36028

GRANTHAM, JOSEPH MICHAEL, JR., hotel executive, management and marketing consultant; b. Smithfield, N.C., Aug. 23, 1947; s. Joseph Michael and Anne Laurie (Hare) G.; student Oak Ridge Mil. Inst., 1965-66, East Tenn. State U., 1966-70; m. Wilsie Moss Hartman, Nov. 3, 1973 (div. 1982); children: Molly Meade, Joseph Michael III; m. Jean Marie Scully, 1986; children: William Warner, Stewart Michael. With Grand Hotel, Mackinac Island, Mich., 1966-78, v.p. sales, 1973-74, v.p. and mgr., 1974-78; dir. resort ops., gen. mgr. Pinehurst (N.C.) Hotel and Country Club, 1978-80; pres., chmn. bd. Ind. Fin. Investments, Pinehurst, 1980—; pres., chmn. bd. Carolina Hotels, Inc., 1982—; pres., chmn. Asset Mgmt. & Mktg., Inc., 1986—. Vice chmn. No. Mich. Conv. and Visitors Bur., Mackinac Island; commr. scouting Boy Scouts Am., Pinehurst, 1978—; bd. dirs., mem. exec. com., chair legal and risk mgmt. com. Sandhills Hospice, Inc. With USNG, 1970-76. Mem. Mackinac Island C. of C. (dir. 1976-79), Mich. Lodging Assn. (dir. 1976-79), Meeting Planners Internat., Hotel Sales Mgmt. Assn. Internat., Am. Hotel and Motor Hotel Assn., N.C. Restaurant Assn., N.C. Hotel and Motel Assn., Nat. Tour Brokers Assn., Chgo. Assn. Execs., N.C. Innkeepers Assn. (dir. 1978-80), Travel Council of N.C. (dir. 1978-80), Pinehurst Bus. Guild (bd. dirs., pres. 1986), Turnaround Mgmt. Assn., Sandhills Area C. of C. (dir. 1984—), Kappa Alpha. Methodist. Lodges: Shriners (bd. dirs. Moore County club, 1982—, pres. 1986—), Masons. Home: PO Box 1479 Pinehurst NC 28374-1479 Office: 850 Linden Rd Pinehurst NC 28374-9080

GRANTHAM, ROBERT EDWARD, lawyer, educator; b. Rosedale, Miss., Apr. 18, 1944; s. Robert Oliver and Edith Evelyn (Lott) G.; m. Toni Lorraine Ray, Nov. 24, 1982; children: Heather, Robert Kendal. AA, U. Md., 1974; BS, U. Albuquerque, 1975; JD, U. Okla., 1978. Bar: Okla. 1979; cert. secondary social studies tchr. Legal intern U.S. Atty., Oklahoma City, Okla., 1975-76, Moore & Foster, Oklahoma City, Okla., 1976-77; ptnr. Shrader & Grantham, Oklahoma City, Okla., 1978-80; gen. counsel LG Williams Oil Co., Oklahoma City, Okla., 1980-82; dist. counsel Resource Inv. Cirp., Oklahoma City, Okla., 1982-84; staff atty. Stack & Barnes, Oklahoma City, Okla., 1984-86; ptnr. Wheat & Grantham, Oklahoma City, Okla., 1986-90; staff atty. Fogg, Fogg & Handley, El Reno, Okla., 1991—; prof. Redlands C.C., El Reno, Okla., 1991—. Bd. dirs. Youth & Family Svcs., El Reno, 1984-87, ARC, El Reno, 1984-87; mem. acad. achievement com. El Reno Pub. Schs., 1993—, mem. parental involvment com., 1995—, graduation rate com., 1995—; vice chmn. Mcpl. Planning Commn., El Reno, 1992—. With U.S. Army, 1962-74. Mem. Okla. Bar Assn., Okla. Bd. Bar Examiners, Canadian County Bar Assn. Democrat. Roman Catholic. Home: 921 SW 24th St El Reno OK 73036 Office: Fogg Fogg & Handley 421 S Rock Island El Reno OK 73036

GRANTHAM, SHONNETTE DENISE, mental health nurse, care facility supervisor; b. Bklyn., July 23, 1961; d. Willie Clemons and Johnice Grantham. BS, Atlantic Christian Coll., Wilson, N.C., 1983. Lead nurse O'Berry Ctr., Goldsboro, N.C., 1983-88; lead nurse Cherry Hosp., Goldsboro, 1988-89, admission screening nurse, 1989, nurse supr., 1989—; co-adminstr. Goldsboro Disciple Rest Home, 1983-90. Pres. nurses aid unit Elm Grove Ch. of Christ, Pikeville, N.C.; ch. youth hour tchr. Mem. Alpha Kappa Alpha.

GRASTY, PHILLIP ELWOOD, food bank administrator; b. Lynchburg, Va., Feb. 19, 1930; s. Reavis Bryan and Florence Elizabeth (Childress) G.; m. Audrey Maxine Campbell, Nov. 23, 1951 (dec. Feb. 1965); children: Lisa Marie, Heidi Suzanne, Aida Lori; m. Mary C. Grasty. Food ops. dir. Augusta Coop. Farm Bur., Staunton, Va., 1948-72; retail food store owner Phil's Sureway, Staunton, 1972-77; distributor auto radios Phil Grasty Enterprises, Staunton, 1977-79; dir. Bethany Home, Staunton, 1979-81; founder, exec. dir. Blue Ridge Area Food Bank, Verona, Va., 1981—. Contbr. articles and editorials to newspapers. Recipient Nat. Award for Excellence in Food Banking, Second Harvest Nat. Food Bank Network, 1988. Mem. Nat. Food Bank Networkd (pres. 1988-93), Va. Hunger Found. (bd. dirs. 1990-92), Va. Hunger Congress, Nat. Soc. Fund Raising Execs., Second Harvest Tax Incentive (chmn. 1989-92). Mem. Cornerstone Ministries. Home: PO Box 1171 Verona VA 24482-1171 Office: Blue Ridge Area Food Bank PO Box 937 Verona VA 24482-0937

GRATTON, PATRICK JOHN FRANCIS, oil company executive; b. Denver, Aug. 28, 1933; s. Patrick Henry and Lorene Jean (Johnson) G.; m Jean Marie McKinney, June 10, 1955; children: Sara, Vivian, Patrick, Lizabeth (dec.). BS in Geology, U. N.Mex., 1955, MS in Geology, 1958. Geologist Westvaco Mineral Devel. Corp., Grants, N.Mex., 1955; mining engr. Utah Internat., Denver, 1956; geologist Shell Oil Co., Roswell, N.Mex. and Tyler, Tex., 1957-62; adminstrv. asst. Delhi-Taylor Oil Corp., Dallas, 1962-64; exploration mgr., ptnr. Eugene E. Nearburg, Dallas, 1965-70; ind. geologist Dallas, 1970—; pres. Patrick J.F. Gratton, Inc., Dallas, 1976—. Contbr. articles to profl. jours. Bd. dirs. U. N.Mex. Found., 1992—. Served with USCG, 1951-53, U.S. Army, 1956-57. Named Disting. Alumnus in Geology, U. N.Mex., 1989; recipient Diplomacy and Innovation Spl. award Assn. Engring. Geologists, 1991. Mem. Am. Assn. Petroleum Geologists (v.p. S.W. sect. 1976-77, del. 1978-81, 91—, chair ho. of del. 1996—, pres. profl. affairs 1989-90, hon. life mem. profl. affairs 1993, adv. bd. divsn. environ. geoscientists 1993-96, chmn. ho. of dels. 1996—), Soc. Ind. Profl. Earth Scientists (v.p. 1976-77, pres. 1977-78, Outstanding Svc. award 1990), Tex. Ind. Producers and Royalty Owners Assn. (exec. com. 1985—), Dallas Geol. Soc. (Pub. Svc. award 1985, Profl. Svc. award 1992), Petroleum Club Dallas, Explorers Club (Tex. chpt. chmn. 1987-88), N.Y. Athletic Club. Roman Catholic. Office: 2403 Thomas St Dallas TX 75201-2037

GRAU, HAROLD JAMES, biology educator; b. Baltimore, MD, Dec. 5, 1956; s. Frank James and Flora Margaret (Strassner) G., m. Constance Theresa Bankard, Aug. 6, 1978 (div. Sept. 1990); children: Tyler Francis, Rachel Lynn; m. Michelle Lee Horner, Dec 19, 1992. BA in Biology, Towson State U., 1978; MS in Zoology, U. Okla., 1981, PhD in Zoology, 1985. Asst. prof. biology Goucher Coll, Baltimore, Md., 1985-86, Ind. U. of Pa., 1986-90, U. V.I., St. Thomas, 1990-93, Christopher Newport U., Newport News, Va., 1993—. Contbr. articles to profl. jours. and book chpts. in field. Mem. AAUP, Human Anatomy and Physiology Soc, Soc. for Coll. Sci. Tchrs., Vir. Acad. of Sci., Nat. Sci. Tchrs. Assn. Roman Catholic. Office: Christopher Newport Univ 50 Shoe Ln Newport News VA 23606

GRAUER, EVA MARIE, sculptor, artist; b. Memphis, Jan. 13, 1925; d. Otto Franklin and Mary Eva (Nichols) Lyons. Student, Southwestern Coll., Memphis, Memphis Acad. Arts. Ind. sulptor, artist, archtl. restorer, art instr. Memphis, 1955—. Sculptures represented in permanent collections including: Overbrook Acad., Nashville, St. Jude Hosp., Memphis, St. Mary's Cathedral, Memphis, numerous pvt. collections; contbr. articles to numerous publs.; contbr. art, WKNO-TV, Memphis, Memphis Brooks Mus. Showcase. Mem. Brooks Art League. Episcopalian. Home and Studio: 1261 W Perkins Rd Memphis TN 38117-6120

GRAVELIN, JANESY SWARTZ, elementary education educator; b. Cleve., Mar. 28, 1952; d. Jesse Franklin and Adele Myra (Pesek) Swartz; m. Christopher James Hof, June 15, 1974 (div. May 1988); 1 child, Zachary Christopher Hof; m. David Paul Gravelin, June 6, 1991. BS in Edn., Bowling Green State U., 1974; MEd, U. South Fla., Ft. Myers, 1985. Cert. elem., spl. edn. tchr., adminstr., supr., Fla., Ohio. Infant stimulation tchr. Wood Lane Sch., Bowling Green, 1974-76, developmentally delayed tchr., 1976-77; 1st grade tchr. Peace River Elem. Sch., Charlotte Harbor, Fla., 1978-85; 3rd grade tchr. Peace River Elem. Sch., Charlotte Harbor, 1985-90, computer edn. tchr., 1990—; yearbook advisor Peace River Elem. Sch., 1991—; com. mem. So. Assn. Colls. and Schs., 1989. Recipient Fla. Merit Tchr. award State of Fla., 1984. Mem. Phi Delta Kappa (v.p. 1994-96). Home: 21043 Cascade Ave Port Charlotte FL 33952 Office: Peace River Elem Sch 22400 Hancock Ave Port Charlotte FL 33980

GRAVELY, JANE CANDACE, computer company executive; b. Rocky Mount, N.C., Dec. 1, 1952; d. Edmund Keen and Janice Eleanor (Beavon) G.; m. Barney Ben Linthicum, July 13, 1985 (div. 1991). BS, N.C. Wesleyan Coll., 1974; MEd, Coll. William and Mary, 1980. Circulation and promotion mgr. Va. Gazette, Williamsburg, 1975-80; computer analyst, chief exec. officer Affordable Computer Systems, Rocky Mount, 1982-85, Goldsboro, N.C., 1985-95; sr. sys. analyst Nat. Tech. Group, Goldsboro, N.C., 1996—; instr. bus., math., computers Nash Tech. Coll., Rocky Mount, 1980-83; instr. math., computers N.C. Wesleyan Coll., Rocky Mount, 1983-85, instr. computers, 1985-89. Mem. NAFE, United Meth. Womens Circle (pres. 1990-91), Goldsboro C. of C. (Chamber Amb. Com. of 100, sec. 1994), Kiwanis, Goldsboro Club (2d v.p. 1994-95), Omicron Delta Kappa. Republican.

GRAVES, DANA LOUISE, elementary school educator; b. Takoma Park, Md., Mar. 15, 1948; d. John William and Patricia Eloise (langdon) Perkins; m. George William Graves, Nov. 7, 1977; 1 child, Jennifer; 1 stepchild, Michael. BA, Elon Coll., N.C., 1970. Cert. tchr. elem. edn., Va. Tchr. 5th grade Hope Valley Sch., Durham, N.C., 1971, tchr. 2d grade, 1971-72; tchr. 4th grade Alanton Elem. Sch., Virginia Beach, Va., 1972-73, tchr. 2d grade, 1973-77; tchr. 3d grade North Springfield Elem. Sch., 1978; tchr. 2d grade Hunt Valley Sch., Fairfax, Va., 1985-86, 1987—. Parent mem./helper Girl Scouts U.S., Fairfax, 1987—. Tchr. of Yr. at Alanton Elem. Sch., Virginia Beach Pub. Schs., 1976-77, Cert. of Appreciation for outstanding contbn., dedication and commitment Children and Adults with Attention Deficit Disorders of No. Va., 1994. Mem. NEA, Va. Edn. Assn., Fairfax Edn. Assn., Virginia Beach Edn. Assn., Nat. Coun. Tchrs. English, Nat. Sci. Tchrs. Assn., Greater Washington Reading Coun., Internat. Reading Assn., Va. State Reading Assn. Roman Catholic. Home: 5023 Dequincy Dr Fairfax VA 22032-2432

GRAVES, JOHN WILLIAM, historian; b. Little Rock, June 25, 1942; s. William A. and Mabel (Morehart) G. B.A. in History, U. Ark., 1964, M.A., 1967; Ph.D. in History, U. Va., 1978. Grad. teaching asst. U. Ark., 1965-66; instr. history U. S.W. La., LaFayette, 1966-68; rsch. asst. U. Va., Charlottesville, 1971-72; instr. history S.W. Tex. State U., San Marcos, 1972-77; coll. assistance migrant program, freshman studies coord., basic skills specialist, lectr. St. Edward's U., Austin, Tex., 1979-85; assoc. prof. then prof. history Henderson State U., Arkadelphia, Ark., 1985—; rep. Liberal Arts Faculty Senate, 1987-88; bd. dirs Soc. for Preservation of Mosaic Templars of Am. Bldg., Hillcrest Residents Assn., Little Rock; mem Ark. Black History Adv. Com., 1993—. Stonewall Jackson Meml. fellow Ark. History Commn., 1965, Philip Francis DuPont fellow U. Va., 1969-71. Mem. Am. Hist. Assn., So. Hist. Assn., Ark. Hist. Assn. (v.p. 1987-92, pres. 1992-96), Ark. History Coun. (Ark. sec. of state), Audubon Soc. (pres. Bastrop County Tex., 1985), Defenders of Wildlife, Environ. Def. Fund, Ark. Nature Conservancy, Nat. Trust for Hist. Preservation, Hist. Preservation Alliance Ark., Quapaw Quarter Assn., Student Senate U. Ark.(grad. sch. rep.), Tau Kappa Epsilon (pres. 1963), Phi Alpha Theta. Author: Town and Country: Race Relations in a Urban-Rural Context, Arkansas, 1865-1905, 1990 (Arkansiana award Ark. Libr. Assn. 1991); contbr. articles to profl. jours. Home: 5218 G St Little Rock AR 72205-3517 Office: Henderson State U Dept History Arkadelphia AR 71999-0001

GRAVES, KENNETH MARTIN, architect; b. Beaumont, Tex., July 6, 1943; s. Ernest Leroy and Margaret Louise (Hillyer) G.; m. Patricia Ann Edwards, Aug. 28, 1965 (div. 1978); m. Anne Brown, Jan. 26, 1991; 1 stepdaughter Elizabeth Anne Crutchfield. B. Arch., Okla. State U., 1967. Lic. architect, Tex., Okla., Mo., Fla., Ga., Ala. Architect, designer Ford, Powell & Carson, San Antonio, 1969-73; architect, ptnr. Tuggle & Graves, San Antonio, 1973-87; prin., Kenneth Martin Graves, Architect, San Antonio, 1988—. Restoration architect: Alamo Plaza, 1976, Reuter Bldg., 1980, The Commerce Bldg., 1982, Staacke-Stevens, 1983-84, Charles Ct., 1983-85, Gunn Acura Dealership Bldg. (Metal Bldg. Design award 1990), Alfred Giles House (Conservation Soc. award 1992); residence design pub. in Architectural Digest, 1981; guest house design pub. in Tex. Homes, 1984. Bd. dirs. San Antonio Soc. Performing Arts, 1982-84, Friends of McNay, San Antonio, 1983-85, Gallery of McNay, San Antonio, 1984-91, San Antonio Art League, 1991—; adv. bd. Winston Sch., 1988-90; trustee S.W. Craft Ctr., 1987-90; lay reader St. Luke's Episc. Ch., vestry, 1989-91, jr. warden, 1989, sr. warden, 1990; trustee St. Luke's Episc. Sch., 1989-90; chmn. bishop's com. for bdlg. Diocese of West Tex., 1990-91. Served to 1st lt. U.S. Army, 1967-69. Mem. AIA, Tex. Soc. Architects, Rotary. Republican. Avocations: oil painting, collecting primitive antiques, travel. Home: 121 Montclair St San Antonio TX 78209-4671 Office: 215 Broadway St San Antonio TX 78205-1923

GRAVES, MICHAEL PHILLIP, communication educator, dean; b. Berlin, N.H., Oct. 9, 1943; s. Donald Bruce Graves and Sheila Mary (Upton) Lenihan; m. Darlene Richards, June 20, 1964; children: Monica Rachael, Aaron Paul. BA, Calif. State U., L.A., 1966, MA, 1967; PhD, U. So. Calif., L.A., 1972. Instr. speech Azusa (Calif.) Pacific U., 1967-72; prof. communication arts George Fox Coll., Newberg, Oreg., 1972-87; prof. communication Regent U., Virginia Beach, Va., 1987—, chair Sch. Comm. Studies, 1989-96; assoc. dean Coll. Comm. and the Arts Regent U., Virginia Beach, 1996—; actor, dir. George Fox Coll. Theatre, Newberg, 1974-87; actor, voice over profl. Regent U., Virginia Beach, 1987-90. Founding dir. Inter-Mission touring drama troupe, 1973; producer, dir. Coyote Goes Upriver, 1985. Named for Best Publ., Religious Speech Communication Assn. Mem. So. States Comm. Assn., Speech Comm. Assn., Religious Speech Comm. Assn. (life, pres. 1995-96). Mem. Soc. of Friends. Office: Regent U Coll Comm and the Arts Virginia Beach VA 23464

GRAVES, PHILLIP JAMES, marketing professional; b. New Orleans, Oct. 25, 1955; s. Charles I. and Jane M. (Blake) G. BS in Nuclear Engring., Purdue U., 1979; MBA, Xavier U., 1985. Field engr., project mgr. GE, Oak Brook, Ill., 1979-84; engr. comml. program GE, King of Prussia, Pa., 1985-87; mgr. bus. devel. Quadrex, Oak Ridge, Tenn., 1987-88, mktg. mgr., 1988-92, dir. project svcs., 1992-93; sr. ptnr. GMA Group, Knoxville, Tenn., 1994—. Mem. Am. Mktg. Assn. (v.p. outreach, bd. dirs. 1993-94 dir. East Europe Outreach Coun., 1992-94), Am. Nuclear Soc., Exptl. Aircraft Assn., Chartered Inst. Mktg. (U.K.), European Soc. for Opinion and Mktg. Rsch., Knoxville Rugby Football Club. Office: GMA Group 432 Shelbyville Rd Knoxville TN 37922-3538

GRAVES, REBECCA O., public health nurse, consultant; b. Nashville, Jan. 25, 1941; d. Earl T. and Anna (Davis) Odom; m. Edward L. Graves, Dec. 22, 1964; children: Angela R., Alison R. BSN, Tuskegee U., 1965. RN, Tenn.; cert. intravenous therapy critical care nurse. Staff med.-surg. nurse L. Richardson Meml. Hosp., Greensboro, N.C.; coord. health svcs. Shaw U., Raleigh, N.C.; staff nurse, coord. health svcs. State of N.C., Raleigh; intravenous therapy nurse, clin. coord. IV therapy Hubbard Hosp., Nashville; pub. health nurse cons. State of Tenn., Nashville. Mem. Intravenous Nurses Soc., Tenn. Nurses Assn., Tenn. Pub. Health Assn. Home: 4111 Dalemere Ct Nashville TN 37207-1211

GRAVES, WILLIAM, architect. V.p. Lee Trevino William Graves, Inc., Dallas. Office: Lee Trevino Wm Graves Inc 16800 Dallas Pkwy Ste 180 Dallas TX 75240

GRAVING, RICHARD JOHN, law educator; b. Duluth, Minn., Aug. 24, 1929; s. Lawrence Richard and Laura Magdalene (Loucks) G.; m. Florence Sara Semel; children: Daniel, Sarah. BA, U. Minn., 1950; JD, Harvard U., 1953; postgrad., Nat. U. Mex., 1964-66. Bar: Minn. 1953, N.Y. 1956, U.S. Dist. Ct. (so. dist.) N.Y. 1956, Pa. 1968, U.S. Dist. Ct. (we. dist.) Pa. 1968, Tex. 1982, U.S. Dist. Ct. (so. dist.) Tex. 1982. Assoc. Reid & Priest, N.Y.C., 1955-61, Mexico City, 1961-66; v.p. Am. & Fgn. Power Co., Inc., Mexico City, 1966-68; atty. Gulf Oil Corp., Pitts., 1968-69, Madrid, 1969-73, London, 1973-80, Houston, 1980-82; pvt. practice London, 1982-84; prof. law South Tex. Coll., Houston, 1984—. With U.S. Army, 1953-55. Mem. Am. Soc. Internat. Law. Home: 8515 Ariel St Houston TX 77074-2806 Office: Inst Transnat Arbitration 1303 San Jacinto St Houston TX 77002-7000

GRAVOIS, JOHN REED, editor; b. Lafayette, La., Oct. 20, 1958; s. Lloyd Joseph and Wanda Joy (Reed) G.; m. Suzanne Marie Roy, Dec. 19, 1981; children: Joy Nicole, Nicholas Roy. BA in Comm. Arts, Nicholls State U., 1980; MA in Journalism, U. Mo., 1981. Reporter, sports columnist The Houma (La.) Daily Courier, 1976-80; reporter The Houston Post, 1981-89; state capitol corr. The Houston Post, Austin, 1989-90; Washington corr. The Houston Post, 1990-94, city editor, 1995; govt. affairs editor Ft. Worth Star-Telegram, 1995—; guest commentator Am.'s Talking cable t.v. network, Washington, 1993—. Founder, benefactor Clarence Doucet Meml. Journalism award Nicholls State U., Thibidaux, La., 1984—. Recipient Freedom of Info. award La. Press Assn., 1976. Roman Catholic. Home: 722 Kensington Ct Mansfield TX 76063

GRAY, ANTHONY ROLLIN, capital management company executive; b. Des Moines, Nov. 26, 1939; s. James W. and Pauline (Frink) G.; m. Janet Eicher, June 26, 1971 (div. Mar. 1987); m. Barbara Lacey Whittaker, June 14, 1991. BA, Grinnell Coll., 1961; MS, U. Iowa, 1963. Securities analyst Lincoln Nat. Life Ins. Co., Ft. Wayne, Ind., 1966-69; dir. rsch. 1st Wis. Trust, Milw., 1969-71; chief investment officer Oak Park (Ill.) Trust, 1971-74; asst. v.p. Union Cen. Life Ins. Co., Cin., 1974-79; dir. rsch. Sun Banks, Orlando, Fla., 1979-85; past pres. Sun Bank Capital Mgmt. Co., Orlando, now chmn. bd., CEO. Capt. USPHS, 1963-66. Office: Sun Bank Capital Mgmt PO Box 3786 Orlando FL 32802-3786

GRAY, ARCHIBALD DUNCAN, JR., lawyer; b. Houston, July 12, 1938; s. Archibald Duncan and Lucie (Hill) G.; m. Suzanne Curtis, July 27, 1963 (div. Nov. 1978); 1 child, Archibald Duncan III; m. Nina Carol Wheeley, June 9, 1984; children: Matthew Hill, Joseph Sharp, Michael Branch. AB with distinction, Dartmouth Coll., 1960; JD, U. Mich., 1963; LLM in Taxation, NYU, 1964. Bar: Tex. 1963, U.S. Dist. Ct. (so. dist.) Tex. 1968, U.S. Ct. Appeals (5th cir.) 1976, Colo. 1982. Assoc. Baker & Botts, Houston, 1964-72; gen. atty. Pennzoil Co., Houston, 1972-74, v.p., 1977-79; v.p. Pennzoil Producing Co., Houston, 1974-79; of counsel Ireland, Stapleton, Pryor & Pascoe, Denver, 1981; ptnr. Mayer, Brown & Platt, Denver, 1981-83; ptnr. in charge Mayer, Brown & Platt, Houston, 1983—; also sr. mgmt. com., 1992—. Mem. ABA, Colo. Bar Assn., Tex. Bar Assn., Houston Bar Assn. Republican. Methodist. Clubs: Houston Country, Houston, Cherry Hills Country (Denver), Hills of Lakeway (Austin). Home: 6046 Riverview Way Houston TX 77057-1450 Office: Mayer Brown & Platt 700 Louisiana Ste 3600 Houston TX 77002-2730*

GRAY, BOWMAN, chemist. Chemist Unipoint Industries, Inc., Thomasville, N.C. Office: 120 Transit Ave Thomasville NC 27360-8927

GRAY, CHARLES ROBERT, lawyer; b. Kirksville, Mo., Aug. 22, 1952; s. George Devon and Bettie Louise (McCormick) G.; m. Dana Elizabeth Kehr, June 1, 1974; children: Jennifer, Jessica, Marcus, Gregory, Victoria. BS, N.E. Mo. State U., 1974; JD, U. Mo., Kansas City, 1978. Bar: Mo. 1978, Va. 1993, U.S. Dist. Ct. (we. dist.) Mo. 1978, U.S. Ct. Appeals (fed. cir.) 1992, U.S. Ct. Appeals (4th cir.) 1995, U.S. Supreme Ct. 1981; cert. mediator. Pvt. practice Parkville, Mo., 1978-81; asst. pub. defender 5th Judicial Cir. Ct. Mo., St. Joseph, 1978-79; pub. defender 6th Judicial Cir. Ct. Mo., Platte City, 1981; asst. dist. counsel Army Corps of Engrs., Kansas City, 1981-82, Vicksburg, Miss., 1982-83; chief counsel space shuttle, MX missile U.S. Army, Vandenberg AFB, Calif., 1983-85; chief counsel troop support agy. U.S. Army, Ft. Lee, Va., 1985-87; fraud counsel Def. Gen. Supply Ctr. Dept. of Def., Richmond, Va., 1987-93; pvt. practice atty. Chester, Va., 1993—; owner Pvt. Jud. Svcs., Inc., Chester, 1993—; adj. prof. St. Leo Coll., Ft. Lee, 1986-91, John Tyler Coll., Chester, Va., 1994—. Mem. Selective Svc. Draft Bd., Brookfield, Mo., 1972-74; pres. Old Towne Parkville Assn., 1979-81, Chester (Va.) Youth Sports Boosters, 1989-91; den leader Boy Scouts Am., Chester, 1991—. Victor Wilson honor scholar, 1977; recipient Am. Jurisprudence award Coop-Bancroft-Whitney, 1989. Mem. ATLA, Am. Arbitration Assn. (mem. nat. panel arbitrators 1994—, mem. govt. disputes panel 1995—, mem. constrn. panel 1995—, mem. comml. panel 1995—), Def. Rsch. Inst. (approved mem. panel on mediation and arbitration), Mo. Bar Assn., Va. Bar Assn., Va. Trial Lawyers Assn. Methodist. Home: PO Drawer B Chester VA 23831 Office: Pres/Presiding Ofcl Pvt Jud Svcs PO Drawer B Chester VA 23831-0317

GRAY, CHRISTOPHER MICHAEL, management and public policy consultant, writer; b. Long Branch, N.J., Aug. 28, 1956; s. Francis Michael and Mary Louise (Donnelly) G. BA, Johns Hopkins U., 1978, MA in Modern History, 1983; Grad. student pub. policy, Duke U., 1985-86; MBA, George Mason U., 1994. Policy analyst Ray & Morris, Louisville, 1986-90; exec. dir. Ky. Vietnam Vets. Meml. Fund, 1987-88; researcher George Mason U. Bus. Sch., Fairfax, Va., 1990-92; United Nations Assn. fellow UN High Commr. for Refugees, Washington, 1992; cons. Presdl. Commn. for Assignment of Women in Armed Forces, Washington, 1992; cons. mgmt. and pub. policy. D.C., 1993—. Researcher, editor various books in field; researcher Gen. Schwarzkopf's memoirs in It Doesn't Take A Hero, 1992; contbr. articles to Global Affairs, Orbis, Policy Rev. Campaign aide Rep. Party, Ky., 1982-90, organizer, Va., 1990—. Grad. fellow Johns Hopkins U., 1980-84. Mem. Federalist Soc. Law and Pub. Policy, Soc. Advancement Mgmt., Nat. Rev.

Inst. Roman Catholic. Home: 7433 Chummley Ct Falls Church VA 22043-2938

GRAY, CLARENCE JONES, foreign language educator, dean emeritus; b. Red Bank, N.J., June 21, 1908; s. Clarence J. Sr. and Elsie (Megill) G.; m. Jane Love Little, Aug. 25, 1934; children: Frances Gray Adams, Kenneth Stewart. BA, U. Richmond, 1933, LLD, 1979; MA, Columbia U., 1934; postgrad. Centro de Estudios Historicos, Madrid, summer 1935; EdD, U. Va., 1962. Underwriter Aetna Life and Casualty, 1925-30; instr. Spanish, Columbia U., 1934-38; gen. sec., mem. exec. council Instituto de las Espanas en los Estados Unidos, 1934-39; instr., sec. dept. Romance langs. Queens Coll., N.Y.C., 1938-46 (on mil. leave 1943-46); dean students U. Richmond (Va.), 1946-68, assoc. prof. modern langs., 1946-62, prof., 1962-79, emeritus, 1979—, dean administrv. svcs., 1968-73, exec. asst. to pres., 1971-79, dean adminstrn., 1973-79, emeritus, 1979—, spl. cons. to pres., 1979-91, spl. cons. to chancellor, 1991—, editor bull., 1968-74, moderator U. Richmond-WRNL Radio Scholarship Quiz Program, mem. bd. Univ. Assos. Cons., Commn. on Colls., So. Assn. Colls. and Schs. Trustee' Inst. Mediterranean Studies. Contbr. articles to profl. jours. Served from lt. to lt. comdr., USNR, 1943-46. Recipient Nat. Alumni award for disting. svc. U. Richmond. Mem. MLA, NEA, Am. Assn. Tchrs. Spanish, Am. Assn. for Higher Edn., Newcomen Soc. N.Am., Inst. Internat. Edn. (cert. meritorius svc.), English-Speaking Union, Legion of Honor, Order of De Molay, Country Club of Va., Colonnade Club, Masons, Rotary, Phi Beta Kappa (sec. emeritus, historian), Phi Delta Kappa, Kappa Delta Pi, Omicron Delta Kappa (nat. sec. gen. council 1966-72, Disting. Svc. key 1968, nat. chmn. scholarship awards 1972-78), Alpha Psi Omega, Phi Gamma Delta (award for disting. and exceptional svc.), Alpha Phi Omega, Phi Beta Kappa Assocs. (life). Baptist. Home: Dogwood Tower P-18 1711 Bellevue Ave Richmond VA 23227-3964

GRAY, DAVID A., college educator; b. Savanna, Ill., Feb. 28, 1946; s. Lorraine Milton and Cecelia (Lawrence) G.; m. Patricia Ann Dvorak, Sept. 10, 1966; children: Stephannie, Nicole, Ragelle. BBA, U. Iowa, 1967, MA, 1969; PhD, U. Mass., 1974. Asst. prof. Western New England Coll., Springfield, Mass., 1971-73; assoc. prof. U. Tex., Arlington, 1973—, assoc. dean, 1981-86, 93-95, dept. chair, 1986-88, 90-93. Contbr. articles to profl. jours. Com. mem. United Way Tarrant County, Ft. Worth, Tex., 1992—. Mem. Acad. Mgmt., Indsl. Rels. Rsch. Assn. Office: Univ Tex 701 S West Arlington TX 76019

GRAY, DONALD LYMAN, orchard owner; b. Newkirk, Okla., Oct. 10, 1929; s. Lyman Otto and Maria Frances (Leven) G.; m. Clara Mae Groden, June 25, 1949 (dec. Feb. 1967); children: Linda, Donald, William, James, Elaine, Janet, Thomas, Robert, Michael; m. Michel Bridget Gavin, Sept. 2, 1977. Student, Okla. State U., 1968-74. Supr. Conoco, Inc., Ponca City, Okla., 1949-77; dir. Conoco Pipeline Co., Houston, 1977-85; owner, cons. Little Cabin Pecan Co., Vinita, Okla., 1985—. Co-author: (nat. computer network) Petroex, 1969; co-author Terminal Automation System, 1981. Named to Hon. Order Ky. Cols., 1976, Okla. Pecan Grower of Yr., 1989. Mem. Nat. Wool Growers Assn., Okla. Wool and Sheep Producers, Okla. Pecan Growers Assn. (offcr 1986—), Nat. Pecan Mktg. Coun., Vinita C. of C. (bd. dirs. 1990—), Okla. Route 66 Assn. (v.p.), Elks. Republican. Roman Catholic. Home: PO Box 246 Disney OK 74340-0246 Office: Little Cabin Pecan Co RR 2 Box 22 Vinita OK 74301-9183

GRAY, D'WAYNE, retired marine corps officer; b. Corsicana, Tex., Apr. 9, 1931; s. Henry Oliver and Myrtle Daisy (Lee) G.; m. Mary Joan Sobieck, Oct. 11, 1955; children: Stephen D'Wayne, Elizabeth Joan Gray Hendrickson, Theresa Mary Gray Croghan. Student, N. Tex. Agrl. Coll., 1948-49; B.A., U. Tex., 1952; M.S. in Internat. Affairs, George Washington U., 1971; postgrad., Naval War Coll., 1970-71, Harvard U., 1980. Commd. 2d lt. USMC, 1952, advanced through grades to lt. gen., 1983; combat svc. Korea, 1953, Vietnam, 1965, 71-72; asst. div. comdr. 1st Marine Div. Camp Pendleton, Calif., 1977-79; dir. plans Hdqrs. Washington, 1979-80, dir. ops. Hdqrs., 1980-81, dir. personnel mgmt. Hdqrs., 1981-83, chief of staff Hdqrs., 1983-85; comdg. gen. Fleet Marine Force, Pacific; comdr. Marine Corps Bases, Pacific, Camp H.M. Smith, Hawaii, 1985-87; ret., 1987, ind. cons., 1987-89; exec. dir. Montgomery County Revenue Authority, Rockville, Md., 1989-90; undersec. veterans affairs for benefits Dept. Vet. Affairs, Washington, 1990-93; del. Inter-Am. Def. Bd., 1980; dir. U.S. Naval Inst., 1980-85; mem. bd. govs. Uniformed Svcs. Benefit Assn. Kansas City, 1982-83, 85-88; mem. sec. of state's Adv. Panel on Overseas Security, 1984-85. Chmn. editorial bd., U.S. Naval Inst., 1980-83. Mem. maritime policy study group Ctr. for Strategic and Internat. Studies, Georgetown U., 1981-85. Decorated D.S.M., Legion of Merit with gold star and V, Bronze Star medal with V., Meritorious Svc. medal with gold star, Air medal with bronze numeral 5, Joint Svc. Commendation medal with V, Navy Commendation medal with V. Mem. Marine Corps Assn., U.S. Naval Inst., Marine Corps Hist. Found., Ret. Officers Assn. (bd. dirs. 1994—), Cath. War Vets. Roman Catholic. Home: 3423 Barger Dr Falls Church VA 22044-1202

GRAY, EDNA JANE, elementary education educator; b. Stratford, Okla., July 29, 1941; d. Cooper and Margerine (Ragland) Coles; m. Joe Carl Gray, Dec. 16, 1961; children: Carl, Scott, Marjana Gray Tharp. AS, Murray State Coll., 1961; BS, East Cen. Okla. State Coll., 1965, MEd, 1982. Cert. elem. tchr., reading specialist, jr. high sci. and social studies tchr., Okla. 4th-6th grade tchr. Connerville (Okla.) Sch., 1965-68; 2d grade tchr. Vanoss Sch., Ada, Okla., 1978-80, reading tchr., 1980—. Recipient Tchr. of Today award Masons, 1992-93. Mem. NEA, Okla. Edn. Assn., Okla. Reading Coun., Pototoc County Reading Coun., Vanoss Classroom Tchrs. Assn., Delta Kappa Gamma (rsch. com. 1991-92, auditing and fin. com. 1992—). Democrat. Mem. Pentecostal Holiness Ch. Home: RR 5 Box 219 Ada OK 74820-9336 Office: Vanoss Sch RR 5 Box 119 Ada OK 74820

GRAY, ELISE NORRIS, sculptor; b. Burkesville, Mar. 9, 1936; d. Kyle and A. Ruby (Roberts) Norris; m. Robert I. Gray, Aug. 27, 1959; children: Dean Norris, Karen Grace, Kyle Howard. BS, Western Ky. U., 1958; MS, U. Tenn., 1959; studied with Walter Yovaish and Phyllis Hammond, Westchester Art Workshop, White Plains, N.Y., 1966-70; studied at, Clay Art Ctr., Portchester, N.Y., 1971, 72; postgrad., Phyllis Hammond Studio, 1971-75; studied with Barbara Bisgyer, 1977. One-woman shows include 14 Sculptors Gallery, N.Y.C., 1979, 82, 84, 86, 89, Hudson River Mus., Yonkers, N.Y., 1983, East Gallery, Wesleyan Coll., Macon, Ga., 1992, Mus. Arts and Scis., Macon, Ga., 1995, Anlage Contemporary Art, Macon, Ga., 1996, others; exhibited in group shows at Thorpe Intermedia Gallery, Sparkill, N.Y., 1980, Mamaroneck Artist Guild, White Plains, N.Y. (sculpture award 1978, ceramics award 1979, Glickenhouse Found. award 1981), Silvermine (Conn.) Guild Artists, 1979, 82, 83, Fay Gold Gallery, Atlanta, 1990-91, Ch. Gallery, U. Ala., 1991 (award), others; represented in permanent collections GE Capital, IBM Corp., United Jersey Bank, AT&T, Eastman Pharms., Touche Ross, Inc., numerous pvt. collections; commns. include Capital Ctr., Tallahassee, 1988, Comty. U. Ch. Meml. Garden, White Plains, N.Y., 1994, Theatre Macon, 1995, Mus. Arts and Scis., Macon, 1996; works featured in various videotapes and mags. Grantee Pollock-Krasner Found., 1990-91, Ga. Coun. for Arts, 1993-94. Democrat. Unitarian. Office: Elise Gray Studio # E 501 Hillcrest Industrial Blvd Macon GA 31204-3473

GRAY, FESTUS GAIL, electrical engineer, educator, researcher; b. Moundsville, W.Va., Aug. 16, 1943; s. Festus P. and Elsie V. (Rine) G.; m. Caryl Evelyn Anderson, Aug. 24, 1968; children: David, Andrew, Daniel. BSEE, W.Va. U., 1965, MSEE, 1967; Ph.D., U. Mich., 1971. Instr. W.Va. U., Morgantown, 1966-67; teaching fellow U. Mich., 1967-70; asst. prof. Va. Poly. Inst. and State U., Blacksburg, 1971-77, assoc. prof., 1977-82, prof., 1983—; vis. scientist Rsch. Triangle Inst., N.C., 1984-85; faculty fellow NASA, 1975; cons. Inland Motors, Radford, Va., 1980, Rsch. Triangle Inst., 1987—; researcher Rome Air Devel. Ctr., N.Y., 1980-81, Naval Surface Weapons Ctr., Dahlgren, Va., 1982-83, Army Rsch. Office, 1983-86, NSF, 1991-93, ARPA, 1993—; publs. chmn. Internat. Symposium on Fault Tolerant Computing, Ann Arbor, Mich., 1985; assoc. treas., Northside Presbyn. Ch., Blacksburg, 1986—. Contbr. articles to sci. jours. Bd. deacons Northside Presbyn. Ch., Blacksburg, 1980-83; coach S.W. Va. Soccer Assn., Blacksburg, 1980-86; asst. scoutmaster Boy Scouts of Am., 1990—. Grantee NSF, Office Naval Research, NASA, Adv. Rsch. Projects Agy. Co-author: (book) Structured Logic Design With VHDL, 1993. Mem. IEEE (chpt. chmn. 1979-80), Computer Soc. of IEEE, Sigma Xi. Democrat. Achievements include research on fault tolerance, diagnosis, testing, and reliability issues for VLSI, distributed and multiprocessor computer architectures, modeling and synthesis with VHOL, modeling and design with hardware description languages. Home: 304 Fincastle Dr Blacksburg VA 24060-5036 Office: Va Poly Inst and State U Blacksburg VA 24061-0111

GRAY, GLENN RICHARD, rehabilitation nurse; b. Birmingham, Ala., Jan. 17, 1956; s. Glenn H. and Betty J. (Bedsole) Gray; m. Carolyn Diane Gray, May 26, 1984; children: Loren Michael, Patrick Ryan, Jaclyn Denise. ADN, Jefferson State Jr. Coll., 1977; BA, Corpus Christi State U., 1985, MBA, 1989. RN, Tex. Staff nurse Humana Hosp. Corpus Christi (Tex.); head nurse ICU, critical care unit Southside Community Hosp., Corpus Christi; clin. mgr. IV therapy Meml. Med. Ctr., Corpus Christi; clin. mgr. S. Tex. Occupational Health Clinic, Corpus Christi, Rehab. Hosp. of South Tex.; adminstr. McAllen County (Tex.) Kidney Ctrs. Mem. Intravenous Nurse Soc. (chmn. quality assurance com.), Phi Theta Kappa.

GRAY, GORDON HARRIS, petroleum consultant; b. Lamesa, Tex., Mar. 22, 1924; s. A. Bainard and Jessie (Harris) G.; m. Jane Britain, Oct. 11, 1981; children: Donald G., Robert L. BS in Petroleum Engring., N.Mex. Sch. Mines, 1949. Registered profl. engr., Tex., N.Mex., Okla. Engr. trainee Gulf Oil Corp., Odessa, Tex., 1949; drilling engr. Condor Petroleum Co., Abilene, Tex., 1949-51, gen. supt., 1951-55; v.p. McDonald Well Svc., Abilene, 1955-60, Caprock Gas Co., Abilene, 1960-62; pres. N.Am. Exploration Co., Abilene, 1962-84, Gray Engring. Co., Abilene, 1984—. Capt. USMC, 1942-46. Mem. Assn. Petroleum Geologists, Soc. Petroleum Engrs., MENSA. Republican. Office: Gray Engring Co 1801 Nations Bank Twrs Abilene TX 79602

GRAY, GWEN CASH, real estate broker; b. Cowpens, S.C., Oct. 24, 1943; d. Woodrow C. and Marie (Hamrick) Cash; m. Charles H. Gray, Oct. 24, 1987 ; children: Dianne Marie Young, Teena Michele Bulman. BS, Limestone Coll., Gaffney, S.C., 1984. Real estate sales rep. and mgr. ERA Miller & Gray Real Estate, Spartanburg, S.C., 1983-89, real estate sales rep., co-owner, broker-in-charge, 1989—; bd. dirs. Nations Bank Gaffney; lectr. in field. Contbr. articles to profl. jours. Advisor S.C. Peach Festival, Gaffney, 1977—, Clemson U. Extension Svc., 1987—. Named Woman of Yr. Bus. and Profl. Women, 1979, Woman of Yr. S.C. Rural Electric Coop., 1984. Mem. Am. Farm Bur., Nat. Bd. Realtors, S.C. Farm Bur., S.C. Bd. Realtors, Spartanburg Bd. Realtors (officer), S.C. Hort. Soc. (bd. dirs.), S.C. Assn. Agr. Agts. (Friend of Extension award 1986), Spartanburg Multiple Listing Svc. (bd. dirs.). Baptist. Democrat.

GRAY, HERBERT HAROLD, III, lawyer; b. Chattanooga, Apr. 5, 1953; s. Herbert H. Jr. and Mary Ellen (Parsons) G.; m. Leah Reynolds Dickie, Nov. 8, 1986; 1 child, Caroline Elizabeth. AB, U. N.C., 1975; JD, Emory U., 1978. Bar: Ga. 1978, U.S. Supreme Ct. 1982. Assoc. Powell, Goldstein, Frazer & Murphy, Atlanta, 1978-80, Varner, Stephens, Wingfield, McIntyre & Humphries, Atlanta, 1980-85; ptnr. Varner, Stephens, Humphries & White LLP, Atlanta, 1986—. Contbr. articles to profl. jours. Mem. ABA, State Bar Ga., Atlanta Lawyers Found. (trustee 1992, chmn. 1995-96), Atlanta Bar Assn., Lawyers Club (exec. com. 1986-93, pres. 1991-92), Capital City Club, Phi Delta Phi. Democrat. Episcopalian. Home: 825 Starlight Dr NE Atlanta GA 30342-2831

GRAY, J. CHARLES, lawyer, cattle rancher; b. Leesburg, Fla., Mar. 26, 1932; s. G. Wayne and Mary Evelyn (Albright) G.; m. Saundra Hagood, Aug. 18, 1955; children: Terese Ren, John Charles Jr., Lee Jerome. BA, U. Fla., 1955, JD, 1958. Bar: Fla. 1958. County atty. Orange County (Fla.), 1978-85; chmn. Gray, Harris & Robinson, P.A.; chmn. Fla. Turnpike Authority, 1965-67; city solicitor City of Orlando (Fla.), 1960-61; pres. Santa Gertrudis Breeders Internat., 1981-83. Chmn. Pres.'s Council Advisors, U. Central Fla., 1978-84; pres. U. Cen. Fla. Found., 1990-91; pres. Orange County U. Fla. Alumni Assn., Pi Kappa Alpha Alumni Assn.; past dist. v.p. U. Fla. Alumni Assn.; mem. U. Fla. Pres.'s Council; mem. Com. of 100; founding bd. dirs. Fla. Epilepsy Found.; chmn. Econ. Devel. Commn. Mid. Fla., 1987-89; mem. Fla. Econ. Devel. Adv. Coun. Mem. U. Fla. Hall of Fame. Mem. ABA, Orange County Bar Assn., Fla. Bar Assn., Fla. Blue Key, Phi Alpha Delta, Pi Kappa Alpha. Republican. Episcopalian. Clubs: University (past dir.), Citrus Club of Orlando (dir.), U. Club of Orlando. Home: 263 Bayou Cir Debary FL 32713-4000 Office: 201 E Pine St Ste 1200 Orlando FL 32801-2725

GRAY, JAMES EDWARD, gastroenterologist; b. Jonesboro, Ark., Sept. 18, 1945; s. Ben and Oma (Nunnally) G.; m. Katricia Hardin, Dec. 23, 1967 (div. 1987); children: John B., Holly E., Emily A. Gray Bresler; m. Cindy L. Carson, Nov. 4, 1988. BS, Harding U., 1966; MD, U. Mo. Sch. Medicine, 1971. Diplomate Am. Bd. Internal Medicine. Gastroenterologist Brooke Army Med. Ctr., Ft. Sam Houston, Tex., 1975-77; asst. prof. internal medicine U. Mo. Sch. Medicine, Columbia, 1977-79, U. Tex. Health Sci. Ctr., San Antonio, 1979-82; pvt. practice gastroenterology Waco, Tex., 1982—; clin. asst. prof. U. Tex. Health Sci. Ctr., 1976-77; regional med. dir. First Care, Waco, 1995—; med. dir. Brazos Valley Health Net, Waco, 1995—; asst. prof. Baylor U., Waco, 1995—. Bd. dirs. Waco Symphony Orch., 1996—. Maj. USAMC, 1973-77. Paul Harris fellow Rotary Internat. Fellow Am. Coll. Physicians; mem. AMA, Am. Coll. Gastroenterology, Am. Gastroenterol. Assn., Am. Soc. Gastroenterol. Endoscopy (membership chair 1981-84), Tex. Med. Assn., Tex. Soc. Gastroenterology & Endoscopy (v.p. 1988-90, pres. 1990-92, past pres. 1992-94, rep. Coun. Regional Endoscopists Socs. 1984-89, 94—), McLennan County Med. Soc., Am. Coll. Physician Execs. Office: Ctrl Tex Gastroenterology Cons 2911 Herring Ave Ste 211 Waco TX 76708

GRAY, JAMES LARRY, metals company executive; b. Southmayd, Tex., Dec. 17, 1932; s. Cecil Lawray and Coquese Adeline (Coe) G.; student Tex. Tech. U., 1954, So. Meth. U., 1956; MBA, Pepperdine U., 1978. Sales engr. Simplex Wire & Cable, Cambridge, Mass., 1958-63; pres. Integral Corp., Dallas, 1963—. Served with U.S. Army, 1956-58. Mem. IEEE, Sigma Alpha Epsilon. Republican. Club: Toastmasters (pres. 1966-67), Jaycees (v.p. 1969-70). Home: 3534 Fairmount St Dallas TX 75219-4703 Office: 1424 Barry Ave Dallas TX 75223-3019

GRAY, JAMES WILLIAM, city manager, public works administrator; b. Denton, Tex., Sept. 13, 1956; s. Jack William and Nancy Helen (Graham) G.; m. Marlene Elizabeth Miller, June 8, 1985; children: Janie Elizabeth, Jordan Nancy, Jill McKay. EdB in Biology, North Tex. State U., 1979; MPA, U. North Tex., 1992. State of Tex. solid waste class B lic. Tchr., coach Bowie (Tex.) Ind. Sch. Dist., 1979-80, Lewisville (Tex.) Ind. Sch. Dist., 1980-81; pres. J.W. Gray Constrn. Co., Denton, 1981-85; supt. U.S. Home, Dallas, 1985; engring. tech. City of Denton, 1986-93; interim city mgr., dir. pub. works City of Gainesville, Tex., 1993—; vice chmn. Cooke County Environ. Com., Gainesville, 1993—; mem. vice chair solid waste adv. com. Texoma Coun. Govt., Sherman, Tex., 1993-96, vice chmn., 1996—; spkr. in field. Author: Solid Waste Options, 1995, Solid Waste Options Autin, Texas, 1996. Divsn. lead United Way, Gainesville, 1993—, mem. allocations com., 1994; chmn. United Way-City of Denton, 1993. Grantee Tex. Natural Resource Conservation Commn., Austin, 1994-96, Tex. Dept. Housing and Cmty. Affairs, Austin, 1995. Mem. Kiwanis. Office: City of Gainesville 200 S Rusk Gainesville TX 76240

GRAY, KEVIN FRANKLIN, neuropsychiatrist; b. Dallas, Sept. 7, 1951; s. Joseph Jeremiah and Norma Elizabeth (Childs) G.; m. Halina Luszczynska, May 22, 1993. Student, Ind. U., 1969-72; MD, Southwestern Med. Sch., Dallas, 1976. Intern Vanderbilt U. Hosp., Nashville, 1977-78; resident in psychiatry U. Tex. Health Sci. Ctr., San Antonio, 1988-91; geropsychiatry/neurobehavior fellow UCLA, 1991-93; asst. prof. psychiatry and neurology U. Tex. Southwestern Med. Sch., Dallas, 1993—. Mem. Am. Psychiat. Assn., Am. Assn. for Geriatric Psychiatry, Am. Geriatrics Soc., Am. Neuropsychiatry Assn., Am. Acad. Neurology. Office: U Tex Southwestern Med Sch 5323 Harry Hines Blvd Dallas TX 75235-9070

GRAY, KEVIN TROY, manufacturing engineer; b. Allentown, Pa., May 28, 1963; s. Paul Revere and Nadine Bonita (McClintick) G.; m. Marlene Sue Miesel, Dec. 28, 1985; children: David Thomas, Elizabeth Victoria, Matthew Zane. BS in Aerospace Engring., Pa. State U., 1985; ME in Mech./Aerospace Engring., U. Va., 1996. Core assembly engr. Naval Nuclear Fuel divsn. Babcock & Wilcox, Lynchburg, Va., 1990-94, lead engr. for S8G fuel assemblies, 1995—; engring. mentor, designer/condr. projects for high sch. students Babcock & Wilcox in partnership with local sch. dists., 1994-96. 1st lt. USMC, 1985-89. Mem. AIAA, Am. Helicopter Soc., Res. Officers Assn., Marine Corps Assn., U.S. Naval Inst., Tau Beta Pi, Sigma Gamma Tau. Home: 132 Richeson Dr Lynchburg VA 24501 Office: Babcock & Wilcox NNFD PO Box 785 (MC 32) Lynchburg VA 24505

GRAY, MARCIA LANETTE, health, physical education and recreation educator; b. Hampton, Va., Dec. 22, 1957; d. Henry Russell and Mildred Ann (Wilson) G. BS in Edn., Longwood Coll., 1980; MEd in Counseling, Coll. of William and Mary, 1990. Cert. health, phys. edn. and recreation tchr., Va. Health, phys. edn. and recreation tchr. Forest Glen H.S., Suffolk, Va., 1980-81, Booker T. Washington Intermediate Sch., Suffolk, Va., 1981-90, John F. Kennedy Mid. Sch., Suffolk, Va., 1990-92, Kilby Shores Elem. Sch., Suffolk, Va., 1992—; head dept. Booker T. Washington Intermediate Sch., 1982-90, John F. Kennedy Mid. Sch., 1990-93, Kilby Shores Elem. Sch. 1993—. Author: Kilby's Quest, 1994, Kilby's Quest II, 1995. Coord. for sch. Jump Rope for Heart, Tidewater, Va., 1982—. Mem. Va. Assn. Health, Phys. Edn. and Recreation, Delta Psi Kappa, Kappa Delta Pi. Office: Kilby Shores Elem 111 Kilby Shores Dr Suffolk VA 23703

GRAY, MARGARET GAYLE, secondary school educator; b. Asheville, N.C., June 1, 1942; d. David Leon and Kate (Evans) McKinney; m. Frank B. Gray, Nov. 24, 1990. BA in English, Jacksonville U., 1968. Cert. English tchr., Ga. 8th grade English tchr. Paxon Jr. H.S., Jacksonville, Fla., 1968-70; 9th grade English tchr. Glynn County Jr. H.S., Brunswick, Ga., 1970-75; 9th-12th grade English tchr. Glynn Acad. H.S., Brunswick, 1975—; test ctr. supr. Ednl. Testing Svcs., Princeton, N.J., 1994—, Am. Coll. Testing, Iowa City, Iowa, 1994—. Coach oratorical contest Optimist CLub, St. Simons, Ga., 1974—. Mem. Ga. Coun. Tchrs. English, Applied Comms. Consortium. Democrat. Baptist. Home: 406 Diamondback Dr Brunswick GA 31525 Office: Glynn Acad HS 1001 Mansfield St Brunswick GA 31525

GRAY, ROBERT MCDONNELL, consulting petroleum landman; b. Port Chester, N.Y., Dec. 6, 1957; s. Julius Raymond and Julia (Kiyak) G.; m. Melinda Louise Wood Gray. BA, U. Tex., 1980. Registered land profl. Cons. Atto-Exa, Inc., Houston, 1980-81; petroleum landman Hunt Oil Co., Houston, 1981-85; owner, cons. Graylynn Properties, Houston, 1985-87; co-founder, pres. Sandstone Exploration, Inc., Houston, 1987-89; mgr. oil and gas div. Capital Fin. Group, Inc., Houston, 1989-90; asst. v.p. Bonnett Resources Corp./Bank One, Houston, 1990-92; cons. petroleum landman, Houston, 1992—. Area campaign chmn. Clayton Williams for Gov., Houston, 1990; bd. dirs. Gulf Coast Conservation Assn., West Houston, Tex., 1990—; asst. sec., bd. dirs. Mcpl. Utility Dist. 111, Ft. Bend County, Tex., 1992—. Mem. Am. Assn. Profl. Landmen, Houston Assn. Profl. Landmen, U. Tex. Ex-Students assn., Sons. of Confederate Vets. (camp #67), Velvet Fez Cigar Club, Phi Kappa Psi. Episcopalian.

GRAY, RONALD W., business executive. Dir. R&D, v.p., mgr. missle and sensor sys. divsn. Automated Sci. Group, Harvest, Ala. Office: Automated Sci Group 1555 The Boardwalk Huntsville AL 35816-1821

GRAY, SYLVIA INEZ, pallet manufacturing executive; b. Newport, Tenn., Oct. 30, 1946; d. Samuel Mitchell and Zina (Harvey) Frazier; children from previous marriage: Regina Aileen Owens, William Cluade Owens; m. Buster Doyle Gray, Jan. 5, 1984; 1 child, Samantha Nicole. Student, Walter's State Community Coll., 1981. Founder, pres. Cocke County Pallet Co., Inc., Newport, Tenn., 1985—. Chmn. Cocke County Rep. Jud. Com. 4th Dist., Tenn., 1990. Mem. Newport-Cocke County C. of C., Cocke County Rep. Women's Club (pres. 1989, treas. 1991, 93). Republican. Baptist. Office: Cocke County Pallet Co Inc 291 Chilton Rd PO Box 952 Newport TN 37821-0952

GRAY, THOMAS ALEXANDER, museum trustee; b. Winston Salem, N.C., Feb. 7, 1948; s. Bahnson and Anne Elizabeth (Pepper) G. BA, Duke U., 1970; MA (Winterthur Program), U. Del., 1974. Dir. of devel. Old Salem, Inc.,, Winston-Salem, N.C., 1974-76; chmn., bd. trustees Old Salem, Inc., 1994—; dir. Mus. of Early So. Decorative Arts, Winston-Salem, 1976-78. Trustee Old Salem, Inc., Winston-Salem, 1980—, N.C. Mus. of Arts, Raleigh, 1985—. With U.S. Navy Res., 1970-72. Recipient Cannon Cup The Hist. Preservations Soc. N.C., Inc., Raleigh, 1983. Republican. Methodist. Home: 10 West St Winston Salem NC 27101 Office: Old Salem Inc Drawer F Salem Sta Winston Salem NC 27108

GRAYDON, FRANK DRAKE, retired accounting educator, university administrator; b. Ovalo, Tex., Feb. 11, 1921; s. Alonzo Otis and Jennie Lewis (Drake) G.; m. Mary Elizabeth Galt, June 16, 1943; children: Geoffrey Galt, David Drake. BBA, Tex. Tech. Coll., 1941; MBA, Northwestern U., 1943. CPA, Tex. Pub. acct. David Himmelblau & Co., Chgo., 1942-44; lectr. in acctg. Northwestern U., Chgo., 1942-44; instr. acctg. Tex. Tech. Coll., 1944-45; chief acct. U. Houston, 1945-46; asst. prof. acctg. U. Tex., 1946-50; with fin. statement sect. Cen. Controllers Office Ford Motor Co., Dearborn, Mich., 1950-51; budget examiner Agencies of Higher Edn., Legis. Budget Bd., Austin, Tex., 1951-55; fin. planning staff Temp. Commn. on Higher Edn., Austin, Tex., 1954-55; budget dir. and prof. acctg. U. Tex. System, Austin, 1955-90, spl. counsel budget and fin., Office of the Chancellor, 1990-93; budget dir. emeritus U. Tex. System, 1993—; prof. acctg. emeritus U. Tex., Austin, 1993—. Mem. AICPAs. Home: 8158 Ceberry Dr Austin TX 78759-8743 Office: Univ of Tex System 601 Colorado St Austin TX 78701-2904

GRAYSON, SCOTT EMBRY, research manager; b. Pampa, Tex., July 3, 1962; s. Buster Xanthius Grayson and Gerry (Carruth) Caylor. BBA in Fin., U. North Tex., 1986; MPA in Acctg., U. Tex., 1989. CPA; CFP; cert. fund specialist. Tax cons. Arthur Andersen & Co., Dallas, 1989-90; cons. fin. and acctg. Calhoun & Assocs., Dallas, 1990-91; rsch. mgr. H.D. Vest Fin. Svcs., Irving, Tex., 1991—. Mem. Rep. Direction, 1993—. Mem. AICPA (personal fin. specialist), Tex. Soc. CPAs, Dallas Tex. Execs. (dir. 1993—), Rep. Club Dallas. Republican. Methodist. Home: 931 Liberty St Dallas TX 75204-5503 Office: HD Vest Fin Svcs 433 Las Colinas Blvd E Ste 300 Irving TX 75039-5522

GRAYSON, WALTON GEORGE, III, retired lawyer; b. Shreveport, La., Aug. 18, 1928; s. Walton George and Mary Alice (Lowrey) G.; m. Bennetta McEwen Purse, May 20, 1955; children: Walton Grayson IV, Mark C., Bennett P., Dwight P. AB, Princeton U., 1949; LLB, Harvard U., 1952. Bar: Tex. 1952, Dallas. Asst. counsel Gt. Nat. Life Ins. Co., Dallas, 1954-69; ptnr. Atwell Grayson & Atwell, Dallas, 1961-69, Grayson & Simon, Dallas, 1969-72; bd. dirs. Southland Corp., Dallas, 1962-87, v.p., gen. counsel, 1965-72; exec. v.p. Southland Corp., 1972-93; of counsel Simon & Twombly, 1972-84; chmn. Cityplace Devel. Corp., Dallas, 1987-93. Bd. dirs. American Trust Co., Dallas, 1995—. Served with USN, 1952-54. Mem. Tex. Bar Assn., Dallas Bar Assn., Petroleum Club, Masons. Mem. Christian Ch. Home: 10525 Strait Ln Dallas TX 75229-5424 Office: Southland Corp 2711 N Haskell Ave Dallas TX 75204-2911

GRAZIANI, N. JANE, communications executive, publisher; b. Pensacola, Fla., Apr. 25, 1958; d. Hamlet and Dolly (Fields) G. BA, La. State U., 1980, M in Journalism, 1984. Asst. editor Daily Reveille, Baton Rouge, 1978-79; with Cath. Commentator, Baton Rouge, 1979-80; bur. chief Capitol News Svc., Baton Rouge, 1981-83; adminstrv. asst. Common Cause, Baton Rouge, 1983-84; reporter Sanford (Fla.) Evening Herald, 1985; assoc. editor Inst. Internal Auditors, Altamonte Springs, Fla., 1985-86; dir. publs. Fla. Soc. Assn. Execs., Winter Park, 1986-88; dir. communications Orange County Med. Soc., Orlando, Fla., 1988-91; pub. King Publs., Orlando, Fla., 1991-92; editor Assn. Source, Casselberry, Fla., 1992-93, Car & Travel/Fla., Heathrow, 1993—; writer med. related issues Charisma mag., Lake Mary, 1989—. Team capt. March of Dimes Walk Am., Orlando, 1989. Recipient Med. Journalism award Sandoz Pharms., 1989. Mem. Soc. Profl. Journalists, Fla. Mag. Assn. (program com. 1987-89, trade show com. 1990, 91, bd. dirs. 1990-94, treas. 1991, pres. elect 1992, pres. 1993, past pres. 1994, Bronze award for Gen. Excellence 1989, Bronze award for Best Spl. Issue 1990, Bronze award for Gen. Excellence, 1994, First Place for Best Regular Editorial 1994), Ctrl. Fla. Soc. Assn. Execs. (comms. com. 1988-91), Fla.

Soc. Assn. Execs., South Atlantic Karate Assn. (1st Kyu 1985—), Internat. Shotokan Karate Fedn. Republican. Presbyterian. Office: Car & Travel 1000 Aaa Dr # 73 Heathrow FL 32746-5062

GREAR, EFFIE CARTER, educational administrator; b. Huntington, W.Va., Aug. 15, 1927; d. Harold Jones and Margaret (Tinsley) Carter. Mus.B., W.Va. State Coll., 1948; M.A., Ohio State U., 1955; Ed.D., Nova U., 1976; m. William Alexander Grear, May 16, 1952; children: Rhonda Kaye, William Alexander. Band dir. Fla. A&M High Sch., Tallahassee, 1948-51, Smith-Brown High Sch., Arcadia, Fla., 1951-56; band dir. Lake Shore High Sch., Belle Glade, Fla., 1956-60, dean of girls, 1960-66, asst. prin., 1966-70; asst. prin. Glades Central High Sch., Belle Glade, Fla., 1970-76, prin., 1976—. Bd. dirs. Palm Beach County Mental Health Assn. Recognized for outstanding achievement by Fla. Sugar Cane League, 1985; recipient Community Svc. award ElDorado Civic Club, Martin Luther King Jr. Humanitarian award Palm Beach County Urban League, 1988, Community Svc. award West Palm Br. NAACP, 1989, Ida S. Baker Disting. Black Educator Recognition award Fla. Dept. Edn., 1992. Mem. Nat. Assn. Secondary Sch. Prins. (Excellence in Edn. award 1991, Fla. Secondary Prin. of Yr. (with Burger King Corp.) 1991), Nat. Community Sch. Edn. Conf., Nat. Sch. Pub. Rels. Assn., Assn. Supervision and Curriculum Devel., Fla. Assn. Secondary Sch. Prins. (Prin. of Excellence 1991-92), Palm Beach County Sch. Adminstrs. Assn., Belle Glade Assn. Women's Clubs (pres.), Belle Glade C. of C. (chmn. beautification Com., citizen yr. 1986), Phi Delta Kappa, Alpha Kappa Alpha, Omega Psi Phi (West Palm Beach chpt. Citizen of Yr. 1990), Elite Community Club, Women's Civic Club. Office: Glades Cen High Sch 425 W Canal St N Belle Glade FL 33430-3086

GREATHOUSE, PATRICIA DODD, retired psychometrist, counselor; b. Columbus, Ga., Apr. 26, 1935; d. John Allen and Patricia Ottis (Murphy) Dodd; m. Robert Otis Greathouse; children: Mark Andrew, Perry Allen. BS in Edn., Auburn (Ala.) U., 1959, M in Edn., 1966, AA in Counselor Edn., 1975. Cert. secondary tchr., Ala., Ga. Tchr. Columbus High Sch., 1959-61, Phenix City Bd. Edn., 1957-58; tchr. pub. schs. Russell County (Ala.) Bd. Edn., Phenix City and Seale, 1961-69, 71-80, 82-83, counselor pub. schs., 1969-82, 83-93; psychometrist Russell County (Ala.) Bd. Edn., Seale, 1980-82; county psychometrist Russell County (Ala.) Bd. Edn., Phenix City, 1983-93. Editor: (ann.) Tiger Tales, 1973 (award 1980). Treas. Ladonia PTA, Phenix City, 1966-68, parliamentarian, 1987-88; leader Ladonia chpt. 4-H Club, Phenix City, 1961-80; active March of Dimes, Am. Heart Assn.; rep. Mardi Gras; tchr. Sunday Sch., Vacation Bible Sch. N. Phenix Bapt. Ch.; vol. Reach to Recovery Am. Cancer Soc., 1980—. Named Mardi Gras Queen Phenix City Moose Club, 1987, hon. life mem. Ladonia PTA, 1967, Outstanding Tchr. of Yr., 1972; recipient Silver Clover award 4-H Club, 1966, Outstanding PTA Performance award 1986-87; nominated to Tchr. Hall of Fame, 1980-81, 81-82, 82-83. Mem. NEA, AARP, Russell County Edn. Assn. (pres.-elect 1973), Ala. Edn. Assn., Ala. Pers. and Guidance Assn., Ala. Assn. Counseling and Devel., Coun. Exceptional Children, Am. Bus. Women's Assn. (pres. Phenix City charter chpt. 1986-87, Woman of Yr. 1987, Perfect Attendance award, treas. 1990-95, sec. 1995—, tri-county coun.), Daus. of Nile (pres. Phenix City club 1980-81, 83-84, Outstanding Svc. award, sec. 1994—), Ret. Tchrs. Assn. (ctrl. sr. activities ctr. 1993, sr. citizens' sec. 1993), Muscogee County Geneal. Soc., Jetettes (v.p. Phenix City club 1976, 80), Jaycettes, Order of Eastern Star (worthy matron 1981-82), Riverview Sr. Citizens, Delta Kappa Gamma (sec. 1979-80, pres. 1990-94), Kappa Iota. Democrat. Baptist. Home: 1502 Nottingham Dr Phenix City AL 36867-1941

GREAVER, JOANNE HUTCHINS, mathematics educator, author; b. Louisville, Aug. 9, 1939; d. Alphonso Victor and Mary Louise (Sage) Hutchins; 1 child, Mary Elizabeth. BS in Chemistry, U. Louisville, 1961, MEd, 1971; MAT in Math., Purdue U., 1973. Cert. tchr. secondary edn. Specialist math Jefferson County (Ky.) Pub. Schs., 1962—; part-time faculty Bellarmine Coll., Louisville, 1982—, U. Louisville, 1985—; project reviewer NSF, 1983—; advisor Council on Higher Edn., Frankfort, Ky., 1983-86; active regional and nat. summit on assessment in math., 1991, state task force on math., assessment adv. com., Nat. Assessment Ednl. Progress standards com.; lectr. in field. Author: (workbook) Down Algebra Alley, 1984; co-author curriculum guides. Charter mem. Commonwealth Tchrs. Inst., 1984—; mem. Nat. Forum for Excellence in Edn., Indpls., 1983; metric edn. leader Fed. Metric Project, Louisville, 1979-82; mem. Ky. Ednl. Reform Task Force, Assessment Com., Math. Framework, Nat. Nat. Assessment Ednl. Progress Rev. Com. Recipient Presdl. award for excellence in math. teaching, 1983; named Outstanding Citizen, SAR, 1984, mem. Hon. Order Ky. Cols.; grantee NSF, 1983, Louisville Community Found., 1984-86. Mem. Greater Louisville Council Tchrs. of Math. (pres. 1977-78, 94—, Outstanding Educator award 1987), Nat. Council Tchrs. of Math. (reviewer 1981—), Ky. Coun. Tchrs. of Math. (pres. 1990-91, Jeff County Tchr. of Yr. award 1985), Math. Assn. Am., Kappa Delta Pi, Delta Kappa Gamma, Zeta Tau Alpha. Republican. Presbyterian. Avocations: tropical fish; gardening; handicrafts; travel; tennis. Home: 11513 Tazwell Dr Louisville KY 40241 Office: Gheens Acad 4425 Preston Hwy Louisville KY 40213-2033

GRECO, ANTHONY JOSEPH, artist, educator, administrator; b. Cleve., Apr. 24, 1937; s. Joseph Anthony and Catherine C. (Corrao) G.; m. Astrida Paeglis, 1962 (div. July 1984); children: Joseph, Vivan, Regina; m. Elizabeth Vernon Shackelford, June 23, 1990. BFA, Cleve. Inst. Art, 1960, Kent State U., 1964; MFA, Kent State U., 1966. Head dept. drawing Atlanta Coll. Art, 1966-75, chmn. div. advanced studio, 1974-76, asst. to pres., 1975-76, acad. dean, 1976-82, acting acad. dean, 1985-86, prof. painting and drawing, 1988—. Solo exhbns. include Armstrong State Coll., Savannah, Ga., 1976, Javo Gallery, Atlanta, 1978, Atlanta Coll. Art Libr., 1986, Chattahoochee Valley Art Mus., LaGrange, Ga., 1992; exhibited in group shows at Auburn U., 1987, Dekalb Coun. for Arts, 1989, U. Montevallo, Ala., 1989, Fay Gold Gallery, Atlanta, 1990, McIntosh Gallery, Atlanta, 1991, 92, 93; represented in collections at Coca-Cola U.S.A., Atlanta, Chase Manhattan Bank, Summit Bank Corp., Atlanta, Kilpatrick and Cody Law Offices, Atlanta, Kent State U., Ga. State Art Commn., Atlanta, Butler Inst. Am. Art., King & Spalding Attys., Atlanta. Bd. dirs. Auditory Ednl. Clinic for Hearing Impaired, Atlanta, 1979-82; mem. adult programs adv. bd. High Mus. Art, Atlanta, 1985; mem. MARTA Coun. for the Arts, Atlanta, 1976-82, 85-86; mem. panel So. Arts Fedn., Visual Arts Dirs. Job-Alike Meeting, Atlanta, 1990. So. Arts Fedn./NEA regional fellow, 1988; recipient purchase awards and other awards for art. Office: Atlanta Coll Art 1280 Peachtree St NE Atlanta GA 30309-3502

GRECO, BARBARA RUTH GOMEZ, literacy organization administrator; b. Farifield, Calif., May 27, 1938; d. William Joseph and Ruth Marie (Fernandes) Gomez; m. Edward Fairfax Greco, Aug. 27, 1966 (div. Jan. 1995); children: Michelle, William. Assoc. degree cum laude, Lord Fairfax Community Coll., 1985; B, James Madison U., 1987. Commr. Warren County Crime Commn., Richmond, 1988; dir. mktg. and pub. rels. Wayside of Va. Inc., Strasburg, 1988; pres. Literacy Vols. Am., Warren, Va., 1988-95; dir. Literacy Vols. Am., Warren, 1988—; bd. dirs. Region 4 Literacy Coordinating Com., Harrisonburg, Va., 1989-95, Va. Literacy Coalition, Richmond, 1990; owner Moving Forward Bus. and Personal Devel. Seminars, 1995—; regional coord. World Heritage, 1996; bus. cons. Echo Ridge Nursery, Winchester, 1990; owner Barbara Greco & Assocs. Contbg. writer North Valley Bus. Jour., Winchester, 1989-93; writer and editor, 1993—. PTA chair County of Warren, 1974-78, mem. founding bd. coun. on domestic violence, 1980-88, vice-chair dem. com., 1981, pres. coun. on domestic violence, 1985-88, mem. crime commn., 1988; mem. textbook adoption com. Warren County High Sch., 1985; bd. dirs. Va. chpt. Am. Lung Assn., 1980-82; bd. dirs. United Way, 1984; Warren County coord. Patterson for State Senate, 1979; campaign coord. William A. Hall for Clk. of Ct., 1981; supr. phone bank Charles Robb Campaign, 1981; campaign treas. Michael Kitts for Town Coun., 1984; campaign vol. Gerald Lee Baliles for Gov., 1986; troop leader Girl Scouts U.S., 1970-71, area coord., 1971-72; com. mem. Warren County Strategic Planning Partnership, 1993. Mem. Shenandoah Valley Writer's Guild (past pres.), Phi Theta Kappa. Unitarian Universalist. Home: PO Box 1188 Front Royal VA 22630-1188

GRECSEK, MATTHEW THOMAS, software developer; b. Staten Island, N.Y., Nov. 17, 1963; s. Ernest Edward and Theresa Joan (Lakemann) G. Student, Rensselaer Poly. Inst., 1982-83. Software engr. IBM Corp., Boca Raton, Fla., 1983; pres., chief exec. officer Result Focused Systems Corp., Orlando, Fla., 1984-90; cons. bus. Result Focused Systems Corp., Charlotte, N.C., 1984-86, cons. software start-up, 1986-87; pres., chmn. Vi-Stat Inc. (formerly Result Focused Systems Corp.), 1990—, 1990-93; co-founder ProSkins Internat., Orlando, Fla., 1991-93; chmn. Forefront Tech. Ptnrs., Orlando, 1993—; co-founder Global Innovations Mktg., Inc., Orlando, 1990; com. chmn. Oasis Internat., 1994-95; founder, chmn. Agenetics, Inc., 1996—. Author computer software Cypher, 1984, Admissions Exec., 1985, STAR, 1986, Relocation Manager, 1988, EEO Compliance Manager, 1989, Embassy, ProCreator, ProGenitor, 1996, A-LIVE, 1996; developer Agent City (electronic workforce cmty.). Mem. Assn. for Sys. Mgmt., Better Bus. Bur., Fla. High Tech. Coun., Fla. Assn. Nomad Developers (exec. dir. 1994-95). Office: Forefront Tech Ptnrs Inc Ste 183 4630 S Kirkman Rd Orlando FL 32811-2802

GREEF, THOMAS EDWARD, arbitrator, mediator; b. Belvidere, Ill., Sept. 3, 1922; s. Hal F. and Margaret Kennedy (Means) G.; m. Hattie Elinor Greef, June 12, 1954 (div. Mar. 1988); children: Daniel A., Mary E. McDonald; m. Jean M. Lang, Nov. 11, 1988. BS, Iowa State U., 1946. Plant indsl. rels. mgr. Brunswick Corp., 1956-62, Sheller Mfg. Co., 1962-64; divsn. indsl. rels. mgr. Frye Divsn. of Pacific Industries, 1964-67, Chem. and Metals divsn. Vulcan Materials Co., 1967-73; corp. indsl. rels. mgr. Pabst Brewing Co., Milw., 1974-84; arbitrator, mediator, 1984—; adj. prof. St. Petersburg Jr. Coll., 1984-93; vis. lectr. Stetson Sch. of Law, 1991—; ednl. cons. various indsl. clients, 1981-84; permanent arbitrator U.S. Postal Svc. So. region, USPS, Nat. Assn. of Letter Carriers-UMEGA. Lt. (j.g.) USNR, 1943-46. Mem. Tampa Yacht and Country Club, Sigma Delta Chi, Psi chi. Mem. Soc. of Fed. Labor Rels. Profsl., Am. Arbitration Assn., Indsl. Rels. Rsch.Assn., Hillsborough County Bar Assn. (assoc.). Presbyterian. Home: 11200 142nd St N Largo FL 34644

GREEHEY, WILLIAM EUGENE, energy company executive; b. Ft. Dodge, Iowa, 1936; married. BBA, St. Mary's U., 1960. Auditor Price Waterhouse & Co., 1960-61; sr. auditor Humble Oil and Refining Co., 1961-63; sr. v.p. fin. Coastal Corp. (and predecessor), 1963-74; with Valero Energy Corp. (formerly LoVaca Gas Producing Co.), San Antonio, 1974—; pres., chief exec. officer Valero Energy Corp. (formerly Coastal States Gas Producing Co.), San Antonio, 1979-83, chmn. bd., 1983—, now also chief exec. officer, dir., also chmn., chief exec. officer numerous subsidiaries; pres., chief exec. officer LoVaca Gathering Co. subs., San Antonio, 1974-79. Office: Valero Energy Corp 530 Mccullough Ave San Antonio TX 78215-2104

GREEN, ALEX EDWARD SAMUEL, physicist, mechanical engineering educator; b. N.Y.C., June 2, 1919; s. Joseph Marvin and Celia (Kahn) G.; m. Freda Kaplow, June 2, 1946; children: Bruce, Deborah, Marcia, Linda, Tamara. BS in Physics, CCNY, 1940; MS, Calif. Inst. Tech., 1941; PhD, U. Cin., 1948. Exptl. physicist Calif. Inst. Tech., Pasadena, 1940-43; assoc. prof. U. Cin., 1946-53; prof. and dir. nuclear sci. Fla. State U., Tallahassee, 1953-59; mgr. space sci. lab. Convair, San Diego, 1959-63; grad. research prof. U. Fla., Gainesville, 1963—, dir. Interdisciplinary Ctr. for Aeronomy and (other) Atmospheric Scis., 1970—; cons. in field. Author: Nuclear Physics, 1995, Atomic and Space Physics, 1965, Nuclear Shell and Optical Model, 1968; editor, contbg. author: Middle Ultraviolet, 1966, Medical Waste Incineration, 1992, Defense Conversion, 1995. Served with USAF, 1944-45, Asia, Mariannas. Decorated Medal of Freedom; recipient citation for outstanding overseas service War Dept., 1945; named Outstanding Scientist of Fla., Fla. Acad. Sci., 1975. Fellow Am. Phys. Soc., Optical Soc. Am.; mem. Am. Geophys. Union, Nat. Coal Council, Order Engr. Democrat. Office: Interdis Ctr Aeronomy & Other Atmospheric Scis S311 SSRB Gainesville FL 32611-2050

GREEN, ASA NORMAN, university president; b. Mars Hill, Maine, July 22, 1929; s. Clayton John and Annie Glenna (Shaw) G.; m. Elizabeth Jean Zirkelbach Ross, May 27, 1965; 1 son, Stephen Richard Ross. A.B. cum laude, Bates Coll., Lewiston, Maine, 1951; M.A., U. Ala., 1955; LL.D., Jacksonville (Ala.) U., 1975. Research dir. Ala. League Municipalities, Montgomery, 1955-57; city mgr. Mountain Brook, Ala., 1957-65; exec. sec. Ala. Assn. Ins. Agts., 1965-66; dir. devel. Birmingham-So. Coll., 1966-71; dir. devel. and communications Dickinson Coll., Carlisle, Pa., 1971-73; pres. Livingston (Ala.) U., 1973-93; pres. emeritus Livingston U., 1993—; con. NCAA Pres.'s Commn., 1993—; instr. polit. sci. U. Ala. Ext. Ctr., Montgomery and Birmingham, 1955-57, 58-60. Author: Revenue for Alabama Cities, 1956. Served with CIC U.S. Army, 1952-54. Grad. fellow So. Regional Tng. Program in Pub. Adminstrn., 1951. Mem. Newcomen Soc. N. Am., Phi Beta Kappa. Democrat. Methodist. Office: 205 E Main St Livingston AL 35470

GREEN, CECKA ROSE, alcohol/drug abuse adminstrator; b. Okinawa, Japan, July 16, 1967; came to U.S., 1968; d. Henry Alexander and Barbara Ann (Jones) Trueblood; m. Marvin E. Green, Jr., Nov. 25, 1995. B in English, Fla. A&M U., 1991. News asst. Tallahassee Democrat, 1990-91; publs. asst. Fla. League of Cities, Tallahassee, 1991-92, dir. of publs., 1992-96; tng. coord., comm. mgr. Fla. Alcohol and Drug Abuse Assn., 1996—. Editor mag. Quality Cities, 1992-96 (award 1993, 94, 95). Mem. Fla. Mag. Assn. (bd. dirs. 1993-96), Tallahassee Soc. Assn. Execs., Delta Sigma Theta. Democrat. Presbyterian. Office: Fla Alcohol and Drug Abuse Assn 1030 E Lafayette St Ste 100 Tallahassee FL 32301-4547

GREEN, CHARLES EDWARD, minister; b. Laurel, Miss., Feb. 27, 1926; s. Edward Henry and Mattie (Miller) G.; m. Barbara Jean Self, Feb. 11, 1950; children: Michael Edward, Cynthia Jeanne Green Crider. BA, Bob Jones U., 1949; D of Theology (hon.), Evang. Sem., Petropolis, Brazil, 1978; DLitt (hon.), Calif. Grad. Sch. Theology, 1982; LLD (hon.), Oral Roberts U., 1988. Pastor Evangelistic Tabernacle, Port Arthur, Tex., 1950-52; founder, pastor Word of Faith Christian Fellowship, New Orleans, 1953—; pres. Word of Faith Coll., New Orleans, 1970—; founder, chmn. World Fellowship of Mins., 1990—; exec. bd. dirs. Church Growth Internat., Seoul, Republic of Korea, 1983—; chmn. Network Christian Ministries, New Orleans, 1985-90; regent Oral Roberts U., Tulsa, 1987—; vice chmn. Charismatic Bible Ministries, Tulsa, 1988—. Author: God's Covenants, 1976, New Testament Church, 1979, Beginning with God, 1979. Sgt. U.S. Army, 1944-46. Republican. Office: Faith Ch 13123 I 10 Service Rd New Orleans LA 70128-2633

GREEN, DON J., publisher, editor; b. Bayard, Nebr., Nov. 22, 1919; s. John Henry and Anna Marie (Sauer) G.; m. Laura Anderson Bryant, Feb. 6, 1943 (div. Feb. 1979); children: Richard Creston, Theresa Elizabeth. BA, Hastings Coll., 1949; MA in Journalism, Northwestern U., 1952. Commd. 2d lt. USAF, 1941, advanced through grades to col., 1965, ret., 1965; reporter, editor City News Bur. Chgo., Ill., 1952-63; pub. affairs officer Johnson Space Ctr., Houston, 1963-77; ret., 1977; pub., editor Blue Water Fishing News, San Marcos, Tex., 1981—; pub. affairs cons. The Salvation Army, Dallas, 1982-89; lectr. offshore fishing. Mem. Outdoor Writers Assn. Am., Tex. Outdoor Writers Assn. Republican. Episcopalian. Office: PO Box 1723 San Marcos TX 78667-1723

GREEN, DOUGLAS ALVIN, retired library director; b. Gilmer, Tex., Feb. 17, 1925; s. Arthur Elmer and Evalena (Loyless) G.; m. Clovis Wayne Elwell, Dec. 15, 1945; 1 child, Danis. BA, U. N. Tex., 1950; MA, E. Tex. State U., 1951; MS, La. State U., 1968; EdD, E. Tex. State U., 1980. Chief bibliographer U. Ark. Gen. Libr., Fayetteville, 1963-67; libr. dir. Bee County Coll., Beeville, Tex., 1968-73; chmn. learning resources Richland Community Coll., Decatur, Ill., 1973-75; libr. dir. Laredo (Tex.) State U., 1975-76; libr. dir. Ambassador Coll., Big Sandy, Tex., 1976-77, Pasadena, 1977-78; libr. dir. U. Cen. Ark., Conway, 1981-84; ret., Ark. State U., Beebe, 1990. Author: An Index to Collected Essays on Educational Media and Technology, 1982; contbg. author: The Smaller Academic Library - A Management Handbook, 1988. With USNR, 1943-46. HEA Title II scholar, 1967-68. Mem. ALA. Home: 115 Pine St Gilmer TX 75644

GREEN, ELBERT P., university official; b. Laneview, Va., June 9, 1935; s. James H. and Levallia C. (DeLeaver) G.; m. Mary M. Green, July 6, 1961; children: Mark B., Marsha B. BS, Va. State Coll., 1957; BD, Felix Adler Meml. U., Chapel Hill, N.C., 1969; MS in Edn., Troy State U., Montgomery, Ala., 1988; MBph, Am. Bible Sch., Kansas City, Kans., 1968; PhD, S.W. U., New Orleans, 1991. Cert. tchr., Ala., cert. hypnotherapist; ordained minister. 2d lt. U.S. Army, 1958, advanced through grades to maj.; ret., 1979; dir. jr. ROTC, Indianola (Miss.) City Schs., Macon County (Ala.) Schs.; dir. residence hall Tuskegee (Ala.) U. Author: Poetry Is Soul, 1988, Poetry Is Gold, 1982, The Light of the World Is Poetry, 1995; contbr. articles to newspapers. Mem. Internat. Soc. of Poets, Profl. Educators Orgn., Am. Legion, Lions Internat., Scabbard and Blade, Phi Beta Sigma, Phi Delta Kappa, Gamma Beta Phi. Home: 2910 W Martin L King Hwy Tuskegee AL 36083-3030

GREEN, GENE, congressman; b. Houston, Oct. 17, 1947; s. Garland B. and Evelyn (Clark) G.; m. Helen Lois Albers; children: Angela, Christopher. BS in Bus. Adminstrn., U. Houston, 1971; student, Bates Coll., Lee Coll. Mgr. printing co.; atty.; mem. Tex. Ho. of Reps., 1973-85, Tex. Senate, 1985-92, 103d-104th Congresses from 29th Tex. dist., 1993—; mem. econ. and ednl. opportunity com., mem. govt. reform and oversight com., mem. criminal justice bd.; mem. econ. and ednl. opportunities com. and post-secondary edn., tng. and lifelong learning and oversight and investigations subcoms., govt. reform and oversight com. and human resources and integovtl. rels. and postal svc. subcoms. Recipient Outstanding Legis. award Houston Park Police Assn., Appreciation award Dem. Nat. Com., Appreciation award Harris County Sheriff's Deputy Assn., Legis. Support award AFL-CIO, Support award Tex. Dem. Party. Mem. Baytown C. of C., Lindale Lions, Tex. Hist. Soc., Coastal Conservation Assn. Democrat. Methodist. Office: 5502 Lawndale Houston TX 77023 also: US House of Reps 1024 Longworth HOB Washington DC 20515-4329*

GREEN, GERALD, editor, consultant; b. Wilkes Barre, Pa., Mar. 3, 1923; s. Samuel and Esther G.; m. Bernice L. Green; children: Gail Green, Jeffrey Green. AS, Bucknell U. Jr. Coll., Wilkes-Barre, Pa., 1942; student, George Washington U., 1948-58. Engr. Bur. Ships, Washington, 1943-56; supr. elec. engr. Naval Air Systems Command, Arlington, Va., 1956-74; cons. Gerald Green Cons., Falls Church, Va., 1974—; Washington editor Horizon House Publs., Falls Church, Va., 1975—; editor-in-chief Elec. Warfare Digest, Springfield, Va., 1980-90; internat. speaker, U.S., U.K., France, Japan, and Israel, 1974—; conf. moderator, U.S., England, and France, 1974—. Pres. Bailey's Sch., Falls Church, Va., 1973-74, Glasgow Int. Sch., Falls Church, Va., 1974-75. Mem. AOC Elec. Def. Assn. Home and Office: 3332 Nevius St Falls Church VA 22041-1730

GREEN, HUBERT GORDON, university dean, pediatrician; b. Dallas, Tex., Oct. 31, 1938; s. Hubert Gordon and Mary Belle (Gillespie) G.; m. Jean A. Green, June 7, 1969; children: Nancy Elaine, David Gordon, Whitney Anne, Emily Erin. BA, Rice U., 1962; MD, U. Texas Southwestern, Dallas, 1968; MPH, U. California, Berkeley, 1972. Diplomate Am. Bd. Pediatrics. Intern Children's Med. Ctr., Dallas, 1968-69; resident U. Washington, Seattle, 1969-71; assoc. prof., pediatrics and biometry U. Arkansas Med. Sch., Little Rock, 1972-77; deputy dir., Divsn. Health Svcs. Delivery region VI USPHS, Dallas, 1977-83; dir. Dallas County Health Dept., 1983-90; dean U. Tex. Southwestern Allied Health Scis. Sch., Dallas, 1991—; Arkansas Children and Youth Project, (assoc. med. dir., 1972-73), Little Rock; Arkansas Children's Hosp., (med. dir., 1973-77), Little Rock; Handicapped Children's Ctr. and Child Devel. Clinic, Arkansas Dept. Health (dir., 1975-77), Little Rock; bd. dirs. Youth Impact Ctrs., Dallas, AIDS ARMS Network, Dallas; Tex.-Mex. Border Health Task Force, Tex. Contbr. articles to med. jours. Lt. USNR, 1962-64. Fellow Am. Acad. Pediat., Tex. Pub. Health Assn.; mem. AMA, APHA, Assn. Schs. Allied Health Professions, Tex. Assn. Pub. Health Physicians, Tex. Pediat. Soc., Tex. Med. Assn., Tex. Soc. Allied Health Professions, Dallas County Med. Soc., Alpha Omega Alpha. Office: U Tex Southwestern Allied Health Scis Sch 5323 Harry Hines Blvd Dallas TX 75235-9082

GREEN, JAMES FRANCIS, lawyer, consultant; b. Pittsfield, Mass., Oct. 1, 1948; s. Earl Levi and Frances Eleanor (Walshe) G.; m. Eileen Mary Kelly, July 31, 1971; children: Michael Walshe, Maura Kelly, Kelsey Kathryn. BA, St. Anselm Coll., 1970; JD, Suffolk U., 1973. Bar: Mass. 1973, U.S. Dist. Ct. Mass. 1974, U.S. Ct. Appeals (D.C. cir.) 1975, U.S. Dist. Ct. D.C. 1975, U.S. Supreme Ct. 1977, U.S. Ct. Appeals (4th cir.) 1978. Rsch. counsel Joint Com. on Jud. Reform of Joint Jud. Com. of Gen. Ct. Commonwealth of Mass., Boston, 1973-74; ptnr. Drucas, Edgerton & Green, Salem, Mass., 1974; gen. ptnr. Ashcraft & Gerel, Washington, 1975—; presdl. appointment Nat. Ad Hoc Com. on Disability. Mem. Mass. Bar Assn., Boston Bar Assn., Fed. Bar Assn. (bd. dirs. Washington chpt., 1985-86, internat. law com.), Bar Assn. D.C., D.C. Bar Assn., ABA (torts and ins. practice law sections, vice chmn. nat. com. on liaison with the judicial adminstrn.), Assn. Trial Lawyers of Am. (section chmn. nat. com. on workers compensation 1989-90), Am. Soc. Law and Medicine. Democrat. Roman Catholic. Home: 6522 Heather Brook Ct Mc Lean VA 22101-1607 Office: Ashcraft & Gerel 4900 Seminary Rd Ste 650 Alexandria VA 22311

GREEN, JAMES LARRY, legal administrator; b. Camp Atteberry, Ind., Sept. 19, 1952; s. James David and Mary (Roberts) G.; m. Kimalee Virgin, Sept. 3, 1977; 1 child, Jonathan Bradley. BA, Miss. State U., 1974; MA, U. Miss., 1977. Asst. dir. N.E. Mental Health Commn., Tupelo, Miss., 1975-80; adminstr. Winchester, Huggins, Charlton, Leake, Brown & Slater, Memphis, 1980-83; dir. adminstrn. Borod & Huggins, Memphis, 1985-88, Heiskell, Donelson, Beaman, Adams, Williams & Kirsch, Memphis, 1985-88; sr. cons. Ken Nelson & Co., Dallas, 1988-90; dir. adminstrn. Blasingame, Burch, Garrard & Bryant, Athens, Ga., 1990-95; CEO Bradley-Huggins Consulting Group, Athens, 1995—; mem. planning com., tech. adviser, and faculty Inst. on Law Firm Mgmt., Ann Arbor, Mich., 1986—. Co-author: Improving A/R Collections, 1990, Lawyers Handbook, 3d edit., Legal Secretary's Handbook; contbr. articles to profl. jours. Mem. Project Link, Memphis, 1983, Athens Homeless Shelter, 1992. Mem. ABA (assoc., vice chair com. fin. mgmt. 1985-86, chairperson com. lawyer compensation 1986-90, com. large firms 1990-94, mem. Techshow com. 1994—), Assn. Legal Adminstrs. Episcopalian. Home: 600 Kings Rd Athens GA 30606-3120 Office: Bradley-Huggins Consulting Group PC 600 Kings Rd Athens GA 30606-3120

GREEN, JAMES WYCHE, sociologist, anthropologist, psychotherapist; b. Alton, Va., Aug. 5, 1915; s. William Ivey and Mary (Crowder) G.; m. Pearl O'Neal Cornett, Mar. 2, 1940 (dec. 1982); 1 child, Margaret Lydia.; m. Arlene Borkenhagen, Mar. 26, 1983. B.S. with honors, Va. Poly. Inst., 1938, M.S., 1939; postgrad., Duke U., 1947-48; Ph.D., U. N.C., 1953; postgrad., Sch. Advanced Internat. Studies, Johns Hopkins U., 1959. Research fellow Va. Poly. Inst., 1938-39; research field supr. Va. Expt. Sta., 1939; asst. specialist program planning N.C. State Coll. Extension Service, 1939-42; v.p. Greever's, Inc., 1946; tchr. high sch., farm operator, 1946-47; asst. prof. rural sociology N.C. State Coll., 1949-54; from asso. chief to chief community devel. adv. to Govt. of Pakistan, Karachi, 1954-59; prof. rural sociology dept. Cornell U., Ithaca, N.Y., 1960; community devel. adviser to Govt. of So. Rhodesia, AID, 1960-64; chief community devel., local govt. adviser to Govt. of Peru, 1964-67; chief urban community devel. adviser to Govt. of Panama, 1967-69; prof., chmn. dept. sociology and anthropology U. N.C., Charlotte, 1969-70; chief methodology div. Bur. Tech. Assistance, AID, Washington, 1970-74; sociologist/anthropologist cons. AID, Washington, 1974-75; contractor AID, Yemen Arab Republic, 1975; pvt. practice cons., 1975—. Author: Integrative Meditation: Towards Unity of Mind/Body/Spirit, 1994; author monographs; contbr. chpts. to books and articles to profl. jours. Served from 1st lt. to capt. AUS, 1942-46; lt. col. Res. ret. 1975. Decorated Croix de Guerre with Silver Star France; Croix de Guerre with Palm Belgium; Bronze Star with cluster; named Outstanding Alumnus Hargrave Mil. Acad., 1979. Fellow Am. Anthrop. Assn., AAAS, Soc. Applied Anthropology; mem. Res. Officers Assn., Public Citizen, ACLU, Common Cause, Amnesty Internat., Omicron Delta Kappa, Alpha Zeta, Phi Kappa Phi. Democrat. Lutheran. Home and Office: 6430 Lily Dhu Ln Falls Church VA 22044-1409

GREEN, JOHN CLANCY, protective services official; b. Modesto, Calif., June 5, 1949; s. John and Edna Lee (Witt) G.; m. Emily Alice Howle, Sept. 10, 1983. Student, La. State U., New Orleans, 1974, U. Louisville, 1975-77; grad., So. Police Inst., 1992. Cert. adminstrv. officer. Newscaster/announcer WXTN Radio, Lexington, Miss., 1966, 68, WRIL FM Inc., Grenada, Miss., 1970, WWUN Radio, Jackson, Miss., 1972; pub. affairs dir. WMGO Inc., Canton, Miss., 1971; broadcaster, anchor Capitol Broadcasters Inc., Jackson, Miss., 1977-78; news dir. Mid South Communications Corp., Jackson, 1978-79; rsch. and devel. exec. Jackson Police Dept. Command

Support Office, 1973—; asset cons. Hinds Gen. Hosp., Jackson, 1975, Jackson Mcpl. Airport Authority, Jackson, 1990; media cons. Nat. Crime Prevention Inst., Louisville, 1977; exec. v.p. ops. Am. Gen. Broadcasters, Jackson, 1979; adj. prof. Jackson State U., 1990. Contbr. articles in field to profl. jours. With U.S. Army, 1971-77. Recipient Certs. of Appreciation, City of Jackson, 1974, U. Louisville, 1975,76, Jackson Police Dept., 1988, Cert. of Commendation, Jackson Police Dept., 1989, Outstanding Svc. award Hundred Club of Jackson, 1989. Fellow Miss. Inst. Arts and Letters; mem. Am. Film Inst., Internat. Narcotics Enforcement Officers Assn., Internat. Assn. Chiefs of Police, Internat. Platform Com. Assn., Planners Rsch. Officers Internat., Greater Jackson Law Enforcement Officers Assn., Miss. Law Enforcement Officers Assn., Nat. Crime Prevention Inst. Alumni Assn., Miss. Writers Club. Democrat. Baptist. Home: 1719 Lake Trace Dr Jackson MS 39211-3351 Office: Miss Dept Wildlife 2906 N State St Jackson MS 39216

GREEN, JONATHAN, fine artist; b. Gardens Corner, S.C., Aug. 9, 1955; s. Melvin and Ruth (Johnson) G. BFA, Sch. Art Inst. Chgo., 1982; DFA, U. S.C., 1996. Dir. Jonathan Green Studios, Inc., Naples, Fla., 1988—. Author: Gullah Images: Art of Jonathan Green, 1996; illustrator: Father and Son, 1992, Noah, 1994. Bd. dirs. Share Our Strength, Washington, 1993-95; v.p. bd. dirs. Collier County United Arts Coun., Naples, 1992-94; mem. bd. com. Chgo. Acad. for the Arts, 1980-85. Recipient medallion Chatham County, Savannah, Ga., 1988, Martin Luther King Humanitarian award Beaufort County, S.C., Alberta Peacock award Collier County United Arts Coun., 1996. Office: Jonathan Green Studies Inc 316 Morgan Rd Naples FL 34114-2562

GREEN, JONATHAN MITCHELL, municipal official; b. Orange, Tex., Sept. 23, 1960; s. John Floyd and Sharon Lee (Mitchell) G.; m. Shawn Elaine Oliver, June 22, 1977; children: Tye Mitchell Green, Crystal Pearl Green. Grad. h.s., Kaufman, Tex. Plant operator West Cedar Creek M.U.D., 1979-81; plant operator East Cedar Creek F.W.S.D., 1982-84, supt., 1984-90; pub. works dir. Town of Minturn, 1990-93, City of Alma, 1993—; water treatment instr. Ark. Rural Water Assn., Little Rock, 1995—, Ark. Environ. Acad., 1996; event cons. U.S. Canoe and Kayak Team, Indpls., 1991—. Mem. Am. Water Works Assn., Water Environ. Fedn., Am. Pub. Works Assn., Ark. Rural Water Assn., Ark. A.W.W. & W.E.F. (western dist. program chmn.), Ark. Water and Waste Water Mgrs. Assn., Tex. Water Utilities Assn. (program chmn. 1985-87, pres. 1989-90, Outstanding New Water Utility Profl. 1988, Outstanding Educator award 1989). Home: 623 Maple Shade Rd Alma AR 72921 Office: City of Alma 804 Fayetteville Ave Alma AR 72921

GREEN, KAREN ANN, accounting supervisor; b. Amarillo, Tex., Feb. 9, 1957; d. Stanley Dwight and Virginia Darlene (Milton) Bailey; children: Stephanie Beard, Courtney. BBA in Acctg., West Tex. A&M U., 1985. Lic. real estate, Colo. Acct. Mesa Ltd. Partnership, Amarillo, 1980-90; real estate sales assoc. Edens Realty, Brighton, Colo., 1991-93; exec. v.p., contr., bd. dirs. Colo. Grease Svc., Inc., Ft. Lupton, Colo., 1990-92; loan officer The Mortgage Broker, Ltd., Englewood, 1993; pres., owner Red Hot Enterprises, Aurora, Colo., 1993—; acct. lab. supr. Amarillo Coll. Mem. Inst. Mgmt. Accts., Grad. Realtors Inst. Republican. Home: 2335 McCormick Rd Amarillo TX 79118 Office: Amarillo Coll PO Box 447 BB415 2201 S Washington Amarillo TX 79178-0001

GREEN, KAY OWEN, special education educator; b. Meridian, Miss., Oct. 16, 1954; d. Claud Tom and Mary Joel (Green) Owen; m. James Alan Green, Mar. 12, 1983; 1 child, Katherine Joanne; stepchildren: Tena Elisabeth, Mary Jessica. Student, Auburn U., 1973-75; BS, U. Ala., Tuscaloosa, 1978; MA, U. Ala., Birmingham, 1985. Tchr. Tarrant (Ala.) High Sch., 1978-81, Midfield (Ala.) Elem. Sch., 1982-91, Vance (Ala.) Elem. Sch., 1991-93, Midfield (Ala.) Elem. Sch., 1993—. Creator/dir. Adopt-A-Grandparent prog., 1988-90. Mem. Coun. Exceptional Children, Coun. for Children with Behavior Disorders, Ala. Fedn. Children with Behavior Disorders, Ala. Coun. Exceptional Children, Ala. Edn. Assn., Midfield Edn. Assn. Baptist. Home: 12790 Bama Rock Garden Rd Vance AL 35490-9604

GREEN, LINDA GAIL, international healthcare and management consultant; b. Kalamazoo, Nov. 29, 1951; d. Jesse Floyd and Mattie Dean (Fulcher) G. BS in Nursing, Fla. State U., Tallahassee, 1974; postgrad., Nova U., Ft. Lauderdale, Fla. Staff nurse med./surg. unit St. Mary's Hosp., West Palm Beach, Fla., 1974, staff nurse coronary care, 1974-75, relief charge nurse ICU, 1975-76, asst. nursing care coord. post anesthesia recovery rm., 1976-78, insvc. instr., 1978-81, asst. dir. staff devel. and edn., 1981-83; dir. insvc. H.H. Raulerson Hosp., Okeechobee, Fla., 1983-84; adminstr. Med. Personnel Pool, Palm Beach, Fla., 1984-90; regional exec. healthcare divsn. Interim Svcs., Inc. (formerly Pers. Pool of Am.), Ft. Lauderdale, 1990-93; pres. L.G.I. Consulting/Cmty. Health Educator, West Palm Beach, 1993—; Spkr. in field. Author: Sexual Harassment in Home Healthcare, 1993; pub. Everything the Doctor Ordered. Past bd. dirs. Vinceremos Therapeutic Riding Ctr., Inc. for Physically and Mentally Challenged, 1990-95. Mem. ANA, AHA (heart walk industry leader 1994, 95), Fla. Nurses Assn., Palm Beach County Health Educators (past sec.), Palm Beach County Patient Educators (pres. 1989, Leadership and Spirit awards 1989), Royal Palm Beach Bus. Assn., Palms West C. of C. (v.p. 1987-88, Dedicated and Outstanding Svc. award 1989, Cert. of Appreciation 1986, 87), Zonta Internat. (pres. 1994-95, past v.p. Palms West chpt., del. to internat. conf., Hong Kong, 1992), Exec. Women of Palm Beaches. Office: PO Box 15301 West Palm Beach FL 33416-5301

GREEN, LINDA LOU, systems analyst; b. Cape Girardeau, Mo., Sept. 12, 1946; d. Barney Oldfield and Opal (Jeffries) G. BA, East Carolina U., 1967, MA, 1969; postgrad., U. Utah, 1969-70; grad., Naval War Coll., Newport, R.I., 1985, Command and Staff Coll., Ft. Leavenworth, Kans., 1990. Cert. in collegiate teaching. Asst. prof. history Jackson (Miss.) State U., 1970-72, Va. State U., Petersburg, 1972-74; commd. 1st lt. U.S. Army, 1974, advanced through grades to lt. col., 1991, ret., 1996; logistics engr. land systems div. Gen. Dynamics Corp., Warren, Mich., 1983-84; systems analyst Raytheon Svc. Co., Huntsville, Ala., 1984-86; pres. Green & Assocs. Inc., Huntsville, 1985-86; logistics engr., cost analyst, br. mgr. Applied Rsch. Inc., Huntsville, 1986-90; sr. ILS analyst Native Am. Svcs. Inc., Huntsville, Ala., 1990; sr. systems analyst BDM Internat. Inc., 1990; pres. Green and Assocs., Inc., Huntsville, 1990-91; sr. logistics analyst Sigmatech Inc., 1991-95; pvt. cons., 1995—; instr. U. Md., Fed. Republic Germany, 1975-77, Calhoun Community Coll., Huntsville, 1990-91; lectr. in field. Author: Study Guides for American History, 1969, The Family Tree, 1989, Logistics Engineering, 1991, The Town Crier: Descendents of Timothy and Elizabeth Trigg/Reagan, 1995, Town Crier: The Descendents of Archibald McCarver, 1996, Town Crier: The Ancestors of the Missouri Shrums, 1996. Mem. Rep. Nat. Com., Washington, 1986-91. Mem. LWV, Soc. Logistics Engrs. (bd. dirs. TVC chpt. 1992-93, chpt. Logistician of Yr. 1993, recipient Nat. Field award in Integrated Logistics Support 1994), Assn. U.S. Army (bd. dirs. Redstone, Huntsville chpt. 1988-91), Res. Officers Assn., Ret. Officers Assn., DAR, United Daus. of the Confederacy, Daus. of Union Vets. of the Civil War. Baptist. Office: Green and Assocs Inc 708 Lily Flagg Rd SE Huntsville AL 35802-3435

GREEN, MARY HESTER, evangelist; b. Oxford, N.C., May 6, 1941; d. Melvin and Martha Elizabeth (Bridges) Hester; m. Joe Lewis G., Dec. 24, 1962; children: Reginald, Renee G. Johnson, Terri Lynatta. AA in Applied Sci., SUNY, 1979; diploma in Christian Edn., Am. Bible Coll., 1984; BA in Christian Edn., City U., L.A., 1989, postgrad., 1989—; postgrad. in Christian Edn., N.C. Cen. U., 1985-86; BTh, Trinity Theol. Sem., 1993; postgrad., Shaw Div. Sch., Raleigh, N.C., 1993—; Grad. of Theology, Trinity Theol. Sem., 1994; B of Religios Edn., Christian Bible Coll., Rocky Mount, N.C., 1995; BRE, Christian Bible Coll., 1995. Charge nurse Newark City Hosp., 1967-69, Lincoln Hosp., Durham, N.C., 1974-79; team leader Duke Med. Ctr., Durham, 1969-90; part-time nurse Vets. Hosp., 1990; TV program producer Inspirational Moments, 1996—, producer TV program; instr. ARC, 1991—. Deaconess Pine Grove Ch., Creedmoor, N.C., 1971—, Sunday sch. tchr., 1972-80, mem. choir. 1970—; mem. staff Bapt. Tng. Union, 1974—, mem. scholarship com.; leader Girl Scouts U.S., 1976-79; active St. Joseph Found. Heritage Ctr., Contact Durham Inc., Nat. Coun. Women, Today's Women Orgn. Recipient Cert. Recognition YWCA, Durham, 1985, Disting. Svc. award Lincoln Hosp., 1976, Honor award Zeta Phi Beta, 1995. Mem. NAFE, Am. Soc. Notaries, Internat. Platform Assn., Century Club Winston Salem U., Masons, Order Ea. Star. Democrat. Home: 5301 Whippoorwill St Durham NC 27704-1250

GREEN, MAY CLAYMAN, early childhood educator and administrator; b. Bklyn., Apr. 8, 1923; d. Joseph and Anna (Steinger) Clayman; m. Jerome E. Bloom, Oct. 14, 1945 (div. May 1963); children: Jeffrey Clayman Bloom, Claudia J. Segal; m. Milton Green, May 10, 1963; stepchildren: Carol R. Green, Peter A. Green. BA, Adelphi U., 1944; MA, NYU, 1956; postgrad., C.W. Post Coll./Long Island U., 1978. Rsch. asst. Winston Pub. Co., Phila., 1953-55; various positions Roslyn (N.Y.) Jr. H.S., 1956-80; adminstrv. asst. to dir. Afro-Am. affairs NYU, 1971-72; owner, exec. adminstr. New Horizons Country Day Sch., Palm Harbor, Fla., 1984-96; pres. New Horizons Edn. Cons. Firm, Palm Harbor, 1996—; mem. adv. bd. St. Petersburg Jr. Coll., Tarpon Springs, Fla., 1992; pres. New Horizons Edn. Found., Palm Harbor, 1992; pres. New Horizons in Learning-Child Care Mgmt., Tarpon Springs, 1983-88; validator Nat. Acad. for Early Childhood Programs; mem. adv. bd. Cmty. Sch., Tarpon Springs, 1982-85. Pres. L.I. Riding for the Handicapped, Brookville, N.Y., 1978-80; audience devel. Fla. Orch., Tampa, 1995; mem. adv. bd. Fla. Symphony, 1995—; bd. dirs. North Suncoast Fla. Symphony, 1995-96. Recipient svc. appreciation awards Nassau County Children's Mus., 1960, Nassau County Girl Scouts, 1961, Inst. Afro-Am. Affaris, NYU, 1979, Jenkins Meml. award N.Y. State PTA, 1980, Pres.'s award Hempstead Child Care Ctr., 1962. Mem. ASCD, Nat. Tchrs. Assn., Roslyn Tchrs. (Ret.) Assn., Nat. Assn. for Edn. of Young Children. Office: New Horizons Edn Consulting Firm 2900 Maple Trce Tarpon Springs FL 34689-8518

GREEN, MICHAEL, foundation administrator; b. Niagara Falls, N.Y., Jan. 6, 1943; s. Joseph and Vivian Hughes (Egbert) G. AB in Sociology, U. Pa., 1967; MA in Polit. Sci., Temple U., 1974; MA in Environ. Planning, Calif. State U., 1980; cert. computer ops., DeAnza Coll., 1986; cert. non-profit fundraising, U. Wash., 1992, cert. documentary video prodn., 1995. Land use analyst Praeger, Kavanagh & Waterbury, N.Y.C., Camden, N.J., 1967-68; legis. analyst Guam Territorial Legis., 1970; legal counsel 23d Interiors Dist. Legislature, Stipon, TTPI, 1970; fin. analyst Assn. Am. Colls., Washington, 1971-72; environ. planner Calif. Dept. Transp., Sacramento, 1974-77; econ. analyst Inst. Internat. Law and Econ. Devel., Washington, 1977-78; econ. analyst dept. commerce Dept. Commerce U.S. V.I., St. Thomas, 1980-81; CEO Found. for Early Devel., San Francisco, Kingston and Bellingham, Wash., 1987—. Contbr. articles to profl. jours. and rsch. studies. Mem. Pacific N.W. Grantmakers Forum, Kiwanis (chmn. major emphasis Bellingham Meridian chpt. 1992-93). Republican.

GREEN, MICHAEL PRUETTE, lawyer; b. L.A., Dec. 26, 1944; s. Pruette H. and Catherine M. (Benkert) G.; m. Dorothy H. Stilmar, Aug. 10, 1974; children: Brian, Heather. BS in Engring., Northrop U., Inglewood, Calif., 1966; MS in Mgmt., Naval Postgrad. Sch., Monterey, Calif., 1972; JD with honors, Am. U., Washington, 1976. Naval officer USN, 1967-87; trial judge Charleston, S.C., 1981-84; legal counsel Nature Conservancy, Arlington, Va., 1987-89; real estate dir. Nat. Wildlife Fedn., Washington, 1989—; atty. Michael P. Green, Arlington, Va., 1987—. Author: Joint Perspectives, 1980. Asst. scoutmaster Boy Scouts Am., Arlington, 1990—. Comdr. USN, 1967-87. Mem. Va. State Bar, Fla. Bar Assn., Iowa State Bar Assn., Arlington Outdoor Edn. Assn. (pres. 1992-95, treas. 1995—). Episcopalian.

GREEN, NANCY JOYCE, librarian; b. LaFollette, Tenn.; d. Everett H. and Evelyn L. (Kidwell) Huddleston; children: Elizabeth Maria, Autumn Rebecca. Libr. LaFollette (Tenn.) Pub. Libr. Mem. PTO (pres.), Goodwill PAC. Mem. Tenn. Libr. Assn., LaFollette Book Club. Baptist. Office: LaFollette Pub Libr 205 S Tennessee Ave La Follette TN 37766-3606

GREEN, NANCY LOUGHRIDGE, higher education executive; b. Lexington, Ky.; d. William S. and Nancy O. (Green) Loughridge; BA in Journalism, U. Ky., 1964; MA in Journalism, Ball State U., 1971; postgrad. U. Ky., 1968, U. Minn., 1968. Tchr. English and publs. adv. Clark County High Sch., Winchester, Ky., 1965-66, Pleasure Ridge Park High Sch., Louisville, 1966-67, Clarksville (Ind.) High Sch., 1967-68, Charleston (W.Va.) High Sch., 1968-69; asst. publs. and pub. info. specialist W.Va. Dept. Edn., Charleston, 1969-70; tchr. journalism and publs. dir. Elmhurst High Sch., Ft. Wayne, Ind., 1970-71; adviser student publs. U. Ky., Lexington, 1971-82; gen. mgr. student publs. U. Tex., Austin, 1982-85; pres., pub. Palladium-Item, Richmond, Ind., 1985-89, News-Leader, Springfield, Mo., 1989-92; asst. to the pres., Newspaper Divsn. Gannett Co., Inc., Washington, 1992-94; exec. dir. coll. advancement Clayton State Coll., Morrow, Ga., 1994—; dir. Harte-Hanks urban journalism program, 1984; pres. Media Cons., Inc., Lexington, 1980; dir. urban journalism workshop program Louisville and Lexington newspaper pubs., 1976-82; sec. Kernel Press, Inc., 1971-82. Contbr. articles to profl. jours. Bd. dirs. Jr. League, Lexington, 1980-82, Manchester Ctr., 1978-82, pres., 1979-82; chmn. Greater Richmond Progress Com., 1986-87, bd. dirs. 1986-89; pres. Leadership Wayne County, 1986-87, bd. dirs., 1985-89; bd. dirs. Richmond Community Devel. Corp., 1987-89, United Way of the Ozarks, 1990-92, ARC, 1990-92, Springfield Arts Coun., 1990-91, Bus. Devel. Corp., 1991-92, Bus. Education Alliance, 1991-92, Caring Found., 1991-92, Cox Hosp. Bd., 1990-92, Springfield Schs. Found., 1991-92; mem. adv. bd. Ind. U. East, 1985-89, Richmond C. of C., 1987-89, Ind. Humanities Coun., 1988-89, Youth Communications Bd., 1988-92, Opera Theatre No. Va., 1992-94, Atlanta chpt. AIWF, 1995—. Recipient Coll. Media Advisers First Amendment award, 1987, Carl Towley award Journalism Edn. Assn., 1988, Disting. Svc. award Assn. Edn. Journalism and Mass Comm., 1989; named to Ball State Journalism Hall of Fame, 1988, Coll. Media Advisers Hall of Fame, 1994. Mem. Student Press Law Ctr. (bd. dirs. 1975—, pres. 1985-87, 94—, v.p. 1992-94), Assoc. Collegiate Press, Journalism Edn. Assn., Nat. Council Coll. Publs. Advs. (pres. 1979-83), Disting. Newspaper Adv. 1976, Disting. Bus. Adviser, 1984). Columbia Scholastic Press Assn. (Gold Key 1980), So. Interscholastic Press Assn. (Disting. Service award 1983), Nat. Scholastic Press Assn. (Pioneer award 1982), Soc. Profl. Journalists, Clayton County C. of C. (internat. com. chmn. 1996—).

GREEN, PETER MORRIS, classics educator, writer, translator; b. London, Dec. 22, 1924; came to U.S., 1971; s. Arthur and Olive Emily (Slaughter) G.; m. Lalage Isobel Pulvertaft, July 28, 1951 (div.); children: Timothy Michael Bourke, Nicholas Paul, Sarah Francesca; m. Carin Margreta Christensen, July 18, 1975. B.A., Cambridge U., 1950, M.A., 1954, Ph.D., 1954. Dir. studies in classics Selwyn Coll., Cambridge, Eng., 1952-53; freelance writer, journalist, translator, London, 1954-63; lectr. Greek history and lit. Coll. Yr. in Athens, 1966-71; prof. classics U. Tex., Austin, 1971—, James R. Dougherty Centennial prof., 1982—; vis. prof. classics UCLA, 1976; Mellon chair in humanities Tulane U., 1986. Fiction critic: Daily Telegraph, London, 1954-63; sr. cons. editor: Hodder & Stoughton Ltd., London, 1959-63; cons.: (Odyssey project) Nat. Radio Theatre, Chgo., 1980-81; author: The Sword of Pleasure, 1957 (Heinemann award for Lit. 1957), The Shadow of the Parthenon, 1972, Alexander of Macedon 356-323 BC: A Historical Biography, 1974, 2d edit., 1991, Classical Bearings, 1989, Alexander to Actium: The Historical Evolution of the Hellenistic Age, 1990, The Greco-Persian Wars, 1996; translator, editor: Juvenal, The Sixteen Satires, 1967, 2d edit., 1974, Ovid: The Erotic Poems, 1982, Yannis Ritsos: The Fourth Dimension, 1993, Hellenistic History and Culture, 1993, Ovid: The Poems of Exile, 1994. Served to sgt. RAF, 1943-47. NEH fellow, 1983-84; Craven scholarship Cambridge U., 1950. Fellow Royal Soc. Lit. (council 1959-63); mem. Soc. for Promotion of Hellenic Studies (U.K.), Classical Assn. (U.K.), Am. Philol. Assn., Archaeol. Inst. Am.,. Mem. Liberal Party. Club: Savile (London). Office: U Tex Dept Classics Austin TX 78712

GREEN, RACHAEL PAULETTE, librarian; b. Shreveport, La., Nov. 28, 1953; d. Harold Dayton and Carolyn Francis (Sholars) G. BA in English, La. Tech U., 1975; M in Libr. and Info. Sci., La. State U., 1986; MA in Indsl. and Orgnl. Psychology, La. Tech. U., 1993. Libr. Shreve Meml. Libr., Shreveport, 1976-78, 79-89; dept. clk. ct. Fed. Ct. House, Shreveport, 1978-79; asst. libr. La. State U., Shreveport, 1989—; mem. acad. calendar com., 1989-90, 92; mem. Noel Meml. Libr. faculty com., mem. environ. com. La. State U., Shreveport, 1991—, mem. bdlgs. and grounds com., 1991—, mem. faculty senate, 1996—, mem. faculty R&D com., 1995—. Author: The Brotherhood of Seven: A Select Bibliography of the Pre-Raphaelite Movement 1848-1914, 1995; reviewer Nat. Productivity Rev., 1994—, Am. Reference Books Annual, 1995—. Contbg. mem. Dem. Nat. Com., 1990—. Mem. ALA (reference and adult svcs. divsn.), APA (tchg. of psychology sect.), So. States Comm. Assn. Democrat. Methodist. Office: La State U Noel Meml Libr PO Box 17552 Shreveport LA 71138-0552

GREEN, SANDRA STAAP, mortgage broker, real estate appraiser; b. Washington, July 12, 1944; d. Bernard Franklin and Mary Frances (Latham) Staap; m. Charles Palmeter Martin, Nov. 4, 1978 (dec. Feb. 1980); m. Phillip Lee Green; 1 child, Mary Candace Todd. BA in Math., Randolph-Macon Woman's Coll., 1965; MBA, George Washington U., 1975. Mathematician Army Map Svc., Washington, 1965-74, Def. Mapping Agy., Washington, 1974-82; v.p., bd. dirs. Cloverleaf Corp., Warrenton, Va., 1981-86; pres., bd. dirs. Bacchus Corp., Warrenton, 1981—; real estate appraiser Appraisal Co. Key West (Fla.), Inc., 1988-91; pres. bd. dirs. Keys Mortgage Co., Key West, 1991—; treas. Wesley House, Key West, 1992-96; Lic. mortgage broker, Fla. Treas. 1st United Meth. Ch., Key West, 1990-91. Recipient Spl. Act award Army Map Svc., 1967, Def. Mapping Agy., 1974. Mem. AAUW (pres. Key West-Lower Keys chpt. 1994-96), Nat. Assn. Realtors, Fla. Assn. Realtors, Fla. Assn. Mortgage Brokers, Key West Art and Hist. Soc., Key West Woman's Club. Home: 1901 S Roosevelt Blvd #208N Key West FL 33040-4505 Office: 3314 Northside Dr Ste 210A Key West FL 33040-4171

GREEN, SHARON JORDAN, interior decorator; b. Mansfield, Ohio, Dec. 14, 1948; d. Garnet and L. Wynell (Baxley) Fraley; m. Trice Leroy Jordan Jr., Mar. 30, 1968 (dec. 1973); children: Trice Leroy III, Caerin Danielle, Christopher Robin; m. Joe Leonard Green, Mar. 13, 1978. Student, Ohio State U., 1966-67, 75-76. Typist FBI, Washington, 1968; ward clk. Means Hall, Ohio State U. Hosp., Columbus, 1970; x-ray clk. Riverside Hosp., Columbus, 1971; contr., owner T&D Mold & Die, Houston, 1988—; interior decorator, franchise owner Decorating Den, Houston, 1989-91; owner T&D Interior Decorator, Houston, 1992—. Tchr. aide Bedford Sch., Mansfield, Ohio, 1976-77, Yeager Sch., 1981-82; pres. N.W. Welcome Wagon, Houston, 1980-81, Welcome Club, El Paso, 1986-87; active North Houston Symphony, 1992—, North Houston Performing Arts, 1993—, Mus. Fine Arts, Houston, 1993—, Edn. and Design Resource Network, 1993—, The Wellington Soc. for Arts, 1994, Jr. Forum, 1995, Rep. Nat. Com., 1995—; vol. Harris County Juvenile Probation Dept., 1996. Home: 16247 Morningbrook Dr Spring TX 77379-7158

GREEN, STEPHEN LLOYD, epidemiologist; b. N.Y.C., Apr. 9, 1945; s. Sidney Lewis and Leona (Eliasberg) G.; m. Betty Sue Habel, July 14, 1972; children: Heather, Danielle, Ashley. AB, U. Pa., 1966; MD, U. N.C., 1970. Diplomate Am. Bd. Internal Medicine, subspecialty in infectious disease. Med. intern Grad. Hosp. of U. Pa., Phila., 1971; med. resident Baylor Coll. Medicine and Affiliated Hosps., Houston, 1973-75; fellow in infectious diseases dept. medicine U. N.C., Chapel Hill, 1975-77; pvt. practice Hampton Rd. Med. Specialists, Hampton; asst. prof. medicine Ea. Va. Med. Sch., Norfolk, 1978-85, assoc. prof. medicine, 1985—; lectr. in field; med. investigator Office of Chief Med. Examiner, City of N.Y., 1972; mem. staff Sentara Hampton (Va.) Gen. Hosp., Riverside Regional Med. Ctr., Newport News, v.p. internal medicine and family practice staff 1983, mem. at large exec. com., 1988; mem. staff Mary Immaculate Hops., Newport News; chmn. infection control com. Peninsula Hosp., Hampton, 1988-89; pres. MEDEV Corp., 1990; cons. VA Hosp., Mary Immaculate Hosp. Contbr. articles to profl. jours.; U.S. patent for needle resistant glove. Med. adv. bd. Va. Lung Assn., 1980; chmn. antibiotic rev. com. Colonial Va. Found. for Med. Care, 1980; bd. dirs. Physician Care, 1985; chmn. bd. Peninsula AIDS Found., 1987, pres., 1993—. Fellow ACP (Cert. of Achievement Med. Knowledge Self Assessment Program); mem. AMA (physician Recognition award 1978, 85, 88, 91), Med. Soc. Va. (Continuing Edn. award 1991), Va. Infectious Disease Soc. (charter), Outpatient Intravenous Antibiotic Therapy Assn., Infectious Diseases Soc. Am., Soc. Hosp. Epidemiologists of Am., Va. Thoracic Soc., Newport News Med. Soc., Assn. Practitioners in Infection Control, Va. Med. Soc., Hampton Med. Soc., Am. Soc. Microbiology. Office: Hampton Rd Med Specialists 2112 Executive Dr Hampton VA 23666-2402

GREEN, SUZANNE DISHEROON, language and literature educator, researcher; b. Dallas, Nov. 27, 1963; d. Fred Russell and Laurel Joan (Picou) Disheroon; m. Charles Lawrence Greeen, July 27, 1986; children: Kathryn Amanda Green, Jonathan Alexander Green. BA in English, So. Coll. S.D.A., 1985; MA in English, U. N. Tex., 1994, PhD in English, 1996. Cert. tchr., Tex. Tchr., registrar Greater Dallas Acad., 1988-89; spl. edn. tchr. Alvarado (Tex.) Mid. Sch., 1989-90, Sam Houston Jr. H.S., Irving, Tex., 1990-93; tch. fellow U. N. Tex., Denton, 1993—; instr. N. Ctrl. Tex. Coll., Gainesville, 1995—; co-dir. 8th and 9th annual conf. on linguistics and literature, 1996—; sec. Grad. Students in English Assn., 1995-96; presenter in field. Contbr. numerous articles to profl. jours. Mary Patchell scholar, 1994, 96. Mem. Am. Lit. Assn., MLA, S.-Ctrl. Modern Lang. Assn., Soc. Tech. Comm., Assn. Tchrs. Tech. Writing, Linguistic Assn. S.W., Nat. Women's Studies Assn., S.-Ctrl. Women's Studies Assn. Democrat. Home: 2136 Savannah Trail Denton TX 76205 Office: U N Tex Dept English PO Box 13877 Denton TX 76203

GREEN, THOMAS HARRIS, forestry educator; b. Mobile, Ala., Mar. 10, 1957; s. Francis W. and Marie P. (Parrish) G.; m. V. Lisa Baldwin, Aug. 26, 1978 (div. Apr. 1991); children: Ian K. Brown, James W. Green, Dylan K. Brown, Molly E. Green; m. Marcia L. Brown, July 3, 1995. BS, Auburn U., 1980, PhD, 1993. Registered forester, Ala. Forester Container Corp. of Am., Brewton, Ala., 1980-84; forestry rsch. specialist Auburn U., 1986-92; asst. prof. Ala. A&M U., Normal, 1992—. Contbr. articles to profl. jours. Mem. AAAS, Soc. of Am. Foresters. Home: 1042 Walker Ln New Market AL 35761 Office: Ala A&M Univ Carver Complex South PO Box 1208 Normal AL 35762

GREEN, WILLIAM A., sales executive, consultant; b. Columbus, Ohio, Mar. 15, 1951; s. Ralph and Vara Marie (Benner) G.; m. Mercedes A. Carrell, Feb. 18, 1972; children: William A. Jr., Brittany Erin. Student, Bliss Coll., Columbus, 1974. Dist. sales mgr. Cramer Sales Co., Cleve., 1977-80, Guaranteed Parts Co., Seneca Falls, N.Y., 1980-82; owner, mgr. Empire Parts Supply, Columbus, 1982-85; gen. mgr. McConkey Auto Parts, Waverly, Ohio, 1985-86; pres., CEO L.C.T. Sales Co., Inc., League City, Tex., 1986-93; CEO FWG Machine, Webster, Tex., 1992-95; CEO FWG Machine, 1992—; cons. TWF Distbg., Houston, 1988—, Precision Engine Rebuilders, Houston, 1989, Auto Corp of Houston, 1991-92. Youth advisor YMCA, Webster, Tex., 1986-87, Bay Area Baseball Assn., Clearlake, Tex., 1986. Mem. Greater Heights C. of C., Automotive Boosters, Livestock Show and Rodeo (life).

GREEN, WILLIAM H., lawyer, scientist; b. Gainesville, Fla., July 23, 1943; m. Diane Sue Viglione; children: Amber Wren, William H. Alexis. BS in Chemistry, U. S.C., 1963; PhD in Phys. Chemistry, 1967; JD, Georgetown U., 1973; postgrad., Cambridge (Eng.) U., 1986. Bar: Fla. 1973. NSF rsch. and tchg. asst. U. S.C., Columbia, 1963-67; NAS-NRC postdoctoral rsch. fellow Naval Rsch. Lab., Washington, 1967-68, sr. level rsch. scientist, 1968-74, head chem. spectroscopy sect., 1973-74; assoc., ptnr. Mahoney, Hadlow, Chambers & Adams, Jacksonville, Tallahassee, Miami, Fla., 1974-79; co-founder, ptnr. Hopping Green Sams & Smith, P.A and predecessor, Tallahassee, 1979—; presenter paper Internat. Environ. Conf., Russian Acad. Fed. Svc., Moscow, 1994. Contbr. articles on molecular spectroscopy, laser physics and laser induced infrared fluorescence studies of collisional energy transfer kinetics to sci. jours. Bd. dirs. Tallahassee C.C. Found., 1988—, pres., 1996; deacon Bradfordille Bapt. Ch., Tallahassee, 1994—. Fellow Royal Astron. Soc.; mem. ABA (numerous coms. and panels on environ. law), AAAS, Am. Chem. Soc., Fla. Bar (numerous coms. and panels on environ. law), Tallahassee Sci. Soc. (bd. dirs. 1989—, v.p. 1994-96), N.Y. Acad. Scis., Sigma Xi. Home: Rt 19 Box 1049 Tallahassee FL 32308 Office: Hopping Green Sams & Smith PO Box 6526 Tallahassee FL 32314-6526

GREEN, WILLIAM WELLS, civil engineer; b. Sioux City, Iowa, Nov. 26, 1911; s. Thomas William and Jessie Eadie (Wells) G.; B.S., U. Notre Dame, 1934; m. Patricia Cecille Gregory, Jan. 10, 1944; children: William Joseph, Mary Teresa. Asst. engr. Iowa Hwy. Commn., Cherokee, 1935-39; prof. civil engring. St. Edward's U., Austin, Tex., 1939-40; asst. engr. City Corpus Christi, Tex., 1940-44; asst. office county surveyor, Nueces County Tex.,

1944-54, county surveyor, 1955-94. Past mem. Tex. Bd. Registration Pub. Surveyors. Past bd. dirs. Carmelite Day Nursery; pastregional bd. dirs. Lay Carmelites. Life mem. ASCE; mem. Am. Congress Surveying Mapping, Tex. Soc. Profl. Surveyors (past bd. dirs.). Democrat. Roman Catholic. K.C. Home and Office: 3149 Topeka St Corpus Christi TX 78404-2436

GREEN, WILLIE HAROLD, mathematician, physicist; b. Miami, Fla., Oct. 5, 1940; s. Marion and Addie (Butler) G.; m. Juanita Hall, June 4, 1966; children: Kendra Y., Katrice N. BS, U. Miami, 1967, MA, 1972; cert., USAF, 1973, 74. Electronic technician AT&T, Dade County, Fla., 1965-66; postal clk. U.S. Postal Svc., Dade County, 1966-67; mathematician Dade County Sch. Bd., 1967-72, Ann Arbor (Mich.) Sch. Bd., 1972-73, NASA/KSC, Fla., 1974-84, Applications Projects, Dade County and Brevard, Fla., 1974-87, 87—. Author: Statistics A Survey, 1984, Complex Mathematical Physics, 1988, Radiation & Exponential Decay, 1989. Mem. Cocoa (Fla.) Rockledge Civic League, 1984. With U.S. Army, 1963-67. Mem. Am. Math. Soc., Math. Assn. Am., Nat. Coun. Tchrs. Math., NAACP, Alpha Phi Alpha (dean of pledges 1981-82, cert. 1982). Democrat. Home and Office: Apt 5 525 NE 63rd St Miami FL 33138

GREENBAUM, STEVEN RANDALL, mechanical engineer; b. N.Y.C., Sept. 6, 1949; s. Marvin John and Marilyn Phyllis (Kirschenbaum) G.; m. Wendezyn Faye Edlin, Dec. 26, 1971; children: Justin Michael, Health Alexander. BS, U. Tenn., 1971. Registered profl. engr., Fla. Pilot, capt. USAF, Charleston AFB, S.C., 1971-76; mgr. Ryder Truck Rental, Miami, Fla., 1976-80; ops. mgr. MCC Powers, Miami, Fla., 1980-85; energy specialist IV Sch. Bd. Broward County, Ft. Lauderdale, Fla., 1985-87; project engr. Baxter Diagnostics, Inc., Miami, 1987-93; devel. and validation engr. Corvita Corp., Miami, 1993—. Author: Introduction to the Sport of Weightlifting, 1977; composer several titles on albums. Den leader Boy Scouts of Am., Miami, 1983-87; chmn. Amateur Athletic Union, Charleston, 1973-75. Mem. ASME, NRA, Profl. Assn. Diving Instrs. (divemaster 1974—), Boat U.S. Home: 911 SE 5th Ter Pompano Beach FL 33060-8133 Office: Corvita Corp 8210 NW 27th St Miami FL 33122-1900

GREENBERG, FRANK, clinical geneticist, educator, academic administrator; b. Perth Amboy, N.J., Aug. 24, 1948. BA cum laude in Zoology, U. Mich., 1970; MMS, Rutgers U., 1972; MD, U. Pa., 1974. Cert. in pediatrics, medical genetics, Pa., N.J., Ga., Tex.; diplomate Am. Bd. Pediatrics, Am. Bd. Med. Genetics. Pediatric resident Children's Hosp. Pitts., 1974-76; pediatric resident St. Christopher's Hosp. for Children, Phila., 1976-77, fellow med. genetics, 1977-79; epidemic intelligence officer bur. epidemiology Ctrs. Disease Ctrl., Birth Defects Br., Chronic Diseases Divsn., Atlanta, 1979-81; dir. birth defects-genetics clinic, inst. molecular genetics Baylor Coll. Medicine, Houston, 1981—, dir. Maternal Serum Alpha Fetoprotein screening program, 1990—; clin. asst. prof. divsn. med. genetics Emory U. and Grady Meml. Hosp., Atlanta, 1979-81; asst. prof. dept. pediatrics Baylor Coll. Medicine, 1981-88; clin. dir. MSAFP screening program, 1981-90, asst. prof. dept. ob-gyn., 1984-88, inst. molecular genetics, 1985-88; adj. asst. prof. dept. epidemiology U. Tex., 1985—, assoc. prof. clin. genetics, inst. molecular genetics, 1988—, assoc. prof. pediatrics, 1988—; mem. profl. adv. bd. Spina Bifida Assn. Tex., 1986—, Chromosome 18 Support Group, 1991—; mem. med. adv. bd. Williams Syndrome Assn., 1986—; numerous coms. and consultations in field. Assoc. editor Birth Defects Ency., sect. editor spl. syndromes sect.; peer reviewer Agy. Toxic Substances and Disease Registry; contbr. numerous articles to profl. jours. and book chapters; reviewer numerous profl. jours. With USPHS, 1979-81. March of Dimes Med. Svc. grantee 1981-85; Biomed. Rsch. support grantee 1983-85; grantee Tex. Genetics Network, 1988—. Mem. AAAS, APHA (genetics com. maternal and child health sect. 1983—), AMA, Am. Soc. Human Genetics (social issues com. 1983-88, task force maternal serum alpha fetoprotein screening 1986), Am. Acad. Pediatrics (perinatal pediatrics sect. 1981—, genetics sect. 1991—), Am. Fedn. Clin. Rsch., Am. Coll. Med. Genetics, So. Soc. Pediatric Rsch., Tex. Genetics Soc., N.Y. Acad. Scis., Tex. Med. Assn., Tex. Pediatric Soc. (environ. health and accident com. 1986-90), Harris County Med. Soc., Houston Pediatric Soc., Teratology Soc. Office: 1529 S St NW Washington DC 20009

GREENBERG, FRANK S., textile company executive; b. Chgo., Sept. 11, 1929. PhB, U. Chgo., 1949. Asst. to pres. Charm Tred Mills, 1949, v.p., 1953, pres., 1953-59; v.p. Charm Tred Mills divsn. Burlington Industries, Inc., 1959-61; pres. Charm Tred Mills div. Burlington Industries, Inc., 1961-62; pres. Monticello Carpet Mill div. Burlington Industries, Inc., N.Y.C., 1962-70, group v.p., mem. mgmt. com., 1970-72, exec. v.p., 1972-78; pres. Burlington Industries, Inc., N.Y.C., now Greensboro, 1978-86, past chmn., CEO, also bd. dirs. Served with AUS, 1951-53. Office: Burlington Industries Inc 1345 Ave of the Americas New York NY 10105

GREENBERG, MARK I., historian; b. Montreal, Dec. 16, 1964; came to U.S., 1990; s. Charles David and Helen (Medwedeff) G. BA in History/Polit. Sci. (distinction), U. Toronto, Ont., 1988; MA in Am. History, U. Western Ont., London, 1990; PhD in Am. History, U. Fla., 1997. Teaching asst. U. Western Ont., London, 1988-90; rsch. asst. U. Fla., Gainesville, 1990-91, tchr. assoc., 1995-97; editl. asst. Fla. Hist. Quar., Gainesville, 1992-95. Contbr. articles to profl. jours. Mem. Am. Hist. Assn., Orgn. Am. Historians, Ga. Hist. Assn., So. Hist. Assn., Immigration History Soc. Office: Univ of Florida Dept History 4131 TUR Gainesville FL 32611

GREENBERG, MARVIN KEITH, chemist; b. San Antonio, Tex., Dec. 14, 1949; s. Aaron and Maureen Lois (Cohen) G. BS in Chemistry, U. Tex., San Antonio, 1977. Rsch. scientist S.W. Rsch. Inst., San Antonio, 1978-80; scientist Betz Labs., The Woodlands, Tex., 1980-85; quality control chemist Fina Oil and Chem., Deer Park, Tex., 1986-93; lab. supr. Environ. Fuel Sys., Bandera, Tex., 1994-96; chemist Chemron Inc., San Antonio, 1996—; treas. local sect. Soc. for Applied Spectroscopy, Houston, 1982-84. Contbr. articles to profl. publs. Vol. firefighter The Woodlands Fire Dept., 1982-87. Mem. Am. Inst. Chemists, Alamo Analytical Sci. Forum. Home: 8727 Huebner # 805 San Antonio TX 78240 Office: Chemron Inc 10526 Gulfdale San Antonio TX 78216

GREENBERG, RAYMOND SETH, academic administrator, educator; b. Chapel Hill, N.C., Aug. 10, 1955; s. Bernard George and Ruth Esther (Marck) G.; m. Leah Daniella Dacus, Oct. 23, 1988. BA with highest honors, U. N.C., 1976, PhD, 1983; MD, Duke U., 1979; MPH, Harvard U., 1980. Asst. prof. sch. medicine Emory U., Atlanta, 1983-86, assoc. prof., 1986-90, dep. dir. Winship Cancer Ctr., 1985-90, chair epidemiology/biostat., 1988-90, prof., dean sch. pub. health, 1990-95; v.p. for acad. affairs, provost Med. U. S.C., Charleston, 1995—; chair preventive medicine Nat. Bd. Med. Examiners, Phila., 1991-93; chair epidemiology study sect. NIH, Bethesda, Md., 1992-94; bd. sci. counselors Nat. Inst. for Dental Rsch., Bethesda, 1994—; chair adv. coun. Prudential Ctr. for Health Care Rsch., Atlanta, 1994-96; chair Harvard Adv. Com. on Electromagnetic Fields and Human Health, Boston, 1994—; adv. com. on rsch. and med. grants, Am. Cancer Soc., Atlanta, 1994-96; breast and cervical cancer early detection and control adv. com., Ctrs. for Disease Control and Prevention, Atlanta, 1996—; adv. com. on agrl. health risks, Harvard Ctr. for Risk Analysis, Boston, 1996—. Author: Medical Epidemiology, 1993, 2d edit., 1995, Epidemiologia Medica, 1995; contbr. articles to profl. jours. Bd. dirs. Am. Cancer Soc. Ga. Divsn., 1987-93. Fellow Am. Coll. Epidemiology (pres. 1990-91); mem. APHA, Am. Statis. Assn., Am. Epidemiology Soc., Soc. Epidemiol. Rsch. Democrat. Jewish. Office: Med Univ SC 171 Ashley Ave Charleston SC 29425-0001

GREENBERG, REUBEN M., protective services official. BA, San Francisco State U., 1967; M in Pub. Adminstrn., U. Calif., Berkeley, 1969, M in City Planning, 1975; grad., FBI Nat. Acad.; LLD (hon.), The Citadel Mil. Coll., 1987. Asst. prof. sociology Calif. State U., Hayward; asst. prof. polit. sci. U. N.C., Chapel Hill; undersheriff San Francisco County Sheriff's Dept.; major Savannah (Ga.) Police Dept.; chief of police Opa-Locka (Fla.) Police Dept.; chief dep. sheriff Orange County (Fla.) Sheriff's Dept.; dep. dir. Dept. Law Enforcement, State of Fla.; chief of police Charleston (S.C.) Police Dept., 1982—; instr. criminal justice Fla. Internat. U., Miami; mem. adv. bd. Nat. Inst. Corrections, 1988—, John Jay Coll. of Criminal Justice; bd. visitors Winthrop Coll., lectr. law enforcement programs in England, Jamaica, Israel, Can., Pakistan and Australia; advisor Victim Svcs. Agy., N.Y.; advisor on anti-terrorist task force to Govt. of Pakistan; numerous nat. and internat. TV appearances. guest columnist The Detroit News; contbr. numerous police-related articles to newspapers and mags. Recipient Citizenship Medal Freedom Found. at Valley Forge, 1985; named Law Enforcement Officer of Yr. State of S.C., 1983. Mem. Police Mgmt. Assn., Nat. Orgn. Black Law Enforcement Execs. (advisor domestic violence project, hate/bias crimes com.), Internat. Assn. Chiefs of Police, S.C. Law Enforcement Officers Assn. (elected officer). Office: Police Dept 180 Lockwood Blvd Charleston SC 29403-5152 also: City Hall Office of Police Chief PO Box 304 Charleston SC 29401

GREENE, CARL DAVID, academic administrator; b. Munich, Oct. 24, 1946; s. Charles Frederick and Charlotte S. (Freiman) G.; m. Anne Dorothy Sherwood, Jan. 6, 1955 (div. Feb. 1973); children: Reesha Howze, Martha Brown, Elizabeth; m. Elizabeth McFee Ice, Jan. 3, 1975; children: Mark Ice, Shahn Ice. BA, Coll. Mount St. Vincent, N.Y.C., 1968. Tchr. various schs., 1974-80; dir. recruitment South Tex. Regional Blood Bank, San Antonio, 1980-85; dir. Tex. Math. and Sci. Hotline, Austin, 1993—; exec. asst. to v.p. U. Tex. Health Sci. Ctr., San Antonio, 1986—. Author posters, brochures, slides for informal sci. edn., 1985—. Allocations panel mem. United Way, San Antonio, 1982-94; mem. animal control adv. bd. City of San Antonio, 1993—, mem. Cable TV Adv. Bd., 1995—; mem. cmty. adv. com. San Antonio Area Found., 1993—; v.p. parish coun. Our Lady of Guadalupe Cath. Ch., Helotes, Tex., 1978. Named Vol. of Yr. ARC, Brownsville, 1975. Mem. DAR, Applied Rsch. Ethics Nat. Assn. (program chair 1993—, S.W. states rep. 1993—, v.p. 1995—, cert. 1995), Tex. Soc. Biomed. Rsch. (sci. edn. com. 1990—, first disting. svc. award 1992), Scientists Ctr. for Animal Welfare (program co-chair 1994, 96), Soc. Mayflower Descendants.

GREENE, DAVID LOUIS, language professional educator, genealogist; b. Middletown, Conn., Sept. 24, 1944; s. George Louis and Margaret Elsie (Chindahl) G.; m. Elizabeth Larrabee Johnson, Nov. 1974 (div. Feb. 1986); children: Jennifer Helen, Christopher Douglas; m. Amelia Jane McFerrin, July 30, 1988; stepchildren: Elizabeth Johnson, Laura Johnson. BA, U. So. Fla., 1966; MA, U. Pa., 1967, PhD, 1974. Prof. English Piedmont Coll., Demorest, Ga., 1970—. Author: The Oz Scrapbook, 1976; editor The Am. Genealogist, 1983—. Fellow Am. Soc. Genealogists; mem. Am. Antiquarian Soc., Nat. Geneal. Soc., New Eng. Hist. Geneal. Soc., N.Y. Geneal. and Biog. Soc. Democrat. Episcopalian. Home: 299 Ostrich Dr Cleveland GA 30528 Office: English Dept Piedmont Coll Demorest GA 30535

GREENE, DOUGLAS GEORGE, humanities educator, author, publisher; b. Middletown, Conn., Sept. 24, 1944; s. George Louis and Margaret Elsie (Chindahl) G.; m. Sandra Virginia Stangland, Aug. 13, 1966; children: Eric, Katherine. BA, U. South Fla., 1966; AM, U. Chgo., 1967, PhD, 1972. Instr. history U. Mont., Missoula, 1970-71; prof. history Old Dominion U., Norfolk, Va., 1971-83; dir. Inst. Humanities Old Dominion U., Norfolk, 1983—; pub. Crippen & Landru Books, 1994—. Author: W.W. Denslow, 1976, Bibliographia Oziana, 1976, enlarged edit., 1988, St. Paul's Church, Norfolk, Virginia, 1989, John Dickson Carr: The Man Who Explained Miracles, 1995; editor: Diaries of Popish Plot, 1977, Meditations of Lady Elizabeth Delaval, 1978, The Door to Doom, 1980, enlarged edit., 1991, The Dead Sleep Lightly, 1983, The Wizard of Way Up, 1985, Death Locked in, 1987, rev. edit., 1994, Collected Short Fiction of Ngaio Marsh, 1989, enlarged edit., 1991, Fell and Foul Play, 1991, Merrivale, March and Murder, 1991; contbg. editor Espionage, 1987; contbr. articles and book revs. to profl. jours. and mags. Mem. Mystery Writers Am. Democrat. Episcopalian. Home: 627 New Hampshire Ave Norfolk VA 23508-2132 Office: Inst Humanities Old Dominion U Norfolk VA 23529-0084

GREENE, ELIOT BRUCE, public relations executive, historic conservator; b. Abilene, Tex., Sept. 12, 1958; s. Alvin Carl and Betty Jo (Dozier) G. Student, U. Tex., 1977-79. Assoc. v.p. Advanced Regional Markets Inc., Dallas, 1983-86; ptnr. Contact Conss., Inc., Dallas, 1987-92; pres. Tex. & West Co., Dallas, 1993—. Contbr. photos to S.W. Rev., Dallas Times-Herald, Tex. Monthly mag., Tex. Monthly Press. Mem. Ft. Griffin Meml. Regiment, Old Jail Art Mus., Wise County Hist. Soc., Friends of Penn Farm, Bella Vista Hist. Soc. Democrat. Office: Tex & West Co PO Box 5761 Bella Vista AR 72714

GREENE, ERNEST RINALDO, JR., anesthesiologist, chemical engineer; b. Mobile, Ala., Jan. 26, 1941; s. Ernest Rinaldo and Dorris Rolinha (Lassiter) G.; m. Lois Ellen Laura Zullig, Sept. 23, 1967; children: Laura Rolinha, Ernest Rinaldo III, Ellen Victoria, Max McKeen. BA, Rice U., 1962, BS, 1963; MA, Princeton U., 1966, PhD, 1968; MD, Washington U., St. Louis, 1981. Diplomate Am. Bd. Anesthesiology; diplomate, Nat. Bd. Med. Examiners; registered profl. engr., Ala. Tenured asst. prof. engring. U. Ala., Birmingham, 1970-84, asst. prof. anesthesiology, 1986-88; chief anesthesiology Cooper Green Hosp., Birmingham, 1986-90, VA Med. Ctr., Birmingham, 1987-90; assoc. prof. anesthesiology U. Ala., Birmingham, 1988-90; chief anesthesiology Vaughan Regional Med. Ctr., Selma, Ala., 1990-92; adjunct assoc. prof. biomed. engring. U. Ala., Birmingham, 1990—; founder, CEO Hivex, Inc.; with Anes Care, Phenix City, Ala., 1994—; reviewer (bioengring.) NSF, Washington, 1981-90; guest reviewer Anesthesiology (jour.), Phila., 1988-90. Author: Homogenous Enzyme Kinetics, 1984, Immobilized Enzyme Kinetics, 1984; (with others) New Anesthetic Agents, Devices and Monitoring Techniques, 1984, Pain Management of AIDS Patients, 1991. Mem. AIChE, Am. Soc. Anesthesiologists, Internat. Anesthesia Rsch. Soc., SAR, S.R., Soc. Colonial Wars, Gen. Soc. of War of 1812, Sigma Xi (assoc.), Tau Beta Pi, Phi Lambda Upsilon, Sigma Tau. Republican. Methodist. Office: PO Box 950 Phenix City AL 36868-0950

GREENE, GARY ALLEN, musician, educator; b. Danville, Ill., Oct. 31, 1952; s. Paul Kenneth and Ethel Wilhelmina (Hilgeman) G. BS in Music Edn. magna cum laude, U. Indpls., 1974; student, Garrett-Evang. Theol. Sem., Evanston, Ill., 1974; MusM in Music History and Lit., Butler U., 1978; PhD in Musicology, U. Md., 1987. Lic. tchr., Ill., Ind. Jr. high choral dir. Huntington (Ind.) Cmty. Schs., 1975-76; band dir. Roman Cath. elem. schs., Danville, Ill., 1976-78, Armstrong (Ill.) H.S., 1979-80; instr. Danville Area C.C., 1978-83, info. and referral officer Title XX adult edn. dept., 1981-83; grad. rsch. asst. U. Md., 1985-87; reference specialist, libr. Am. Symphony Orch League, Washington, 1987-88; asst. prof. music N.E. La. U., Monroe, 1988-95; office adminstr., sys. mgr. The Kelly Agy., 1995—; guest lectr. U. Md., 1983-87; adj. lectr. horn U. Ark., Monticello, 1995; bd. mem., v.p., pres. Danville Mcpl. Band, 1980-83; bd. mem. Monroe Symphony Orch., 1988-94; adjudicator La. Music Educators Assn., 1988-95; player rep. Monroe Symphony Orch. Bd., 1988-91, artistic adv. com., 1988-95, chair condr. search com. 1988-92, chair KEDM liaison com. 1992-95, chair negotiating com., 1992, mem. bd. devel. com. 1994-95; adjudicator La. All-State Band/Orch. contestants dist. level 1988-95, state level 1989, 94, La. Dist. Honor Band contestants N.E. dist., 1989-95; panelist Ouachita Parish grants for N.E. La. Arts Coun. Decentralized Arts Funding Program, 1995. Author: The Musical Huss Family in America, 1994, Henry Holden Huss: An American Life in Music, 1995; co-author: A Music Research Style Guide, 1993; contbr. articles to profl. jours.; author lectures, program notes, others; writer scripts KEDM broadcasts of concerts of Monroe Symphony Orch., 1991-96. Organizer of successful effort to place Danville, Ill. Pub. Libr. Bldg. on Nat. Register Historic Places, 1977-78. Recipient Bd. of Govs. award Monroe Symphony Orch., 1995; Md. fellow, 1984-87, Grad. Sch. dissertation rsch. grantee, 1986. Mem. AAUP, Am. Fedn. Musicians (Musician of Yr., Local 90, 1981), Am. Guild Organists (treas. Danville chpt. 1978-80, subdean 1981-83), Am. Musicological Soc., Coll. Music Soc., Internat. Horn Soc. (mem. editl. bd. Horn Call Ann. 1988-95), Sonneck Soc. Am. Music, Alpha Chi, Kappa Kappa Psi, Phi Kappa Phi (outstanding initiate screening com. N.E. La. U. chpt. 1993, 94), Phi Mu Alpha Sinfonia (Eta Iota chpt. adv., 1988-95), Pi Kappa Lambda. Methodist. Home: 3904 Blanks Monroe LA 71203

GREENE, GLEN LEE, JR., secondary school educator; b. Alexandria, La., Sept. 28, 1939; s. Glen Lee and Grace Lois (Prince) G. BA, La. Coll., 1960, U. N.E. La., 1967; MLIS, La. State U., 1994. Tchr. Destrehan (La.) H.S., 1964—, social studies chair, 1980—; mem. St. Charles Parish Profl. Improvement Program Com., Luling, La., 1981-85. Mem. ALA, ASCD, Nat. Coun. for the Social Studies, Phi Kappa Phi. Democrat. Baptist. Home: PO Box 203 Oak Ridge LA 71264-0203 Office: Destrehan HS 1 Wildcat Ln Destrehan LA 70047-4001

GREENE, HARRIS, author, retired foreign service and intelligence officer; b. Waltham, Mass., Oct. 22, 1921; s. Benjamin and Sara (Krongard) G. BS, Boston U., 1943; grad. student George Washington U., 1950-51; m. Charlotte Wolk, Oct. 5, 1943; children: Sharon, Deborah. Researcher, reporter Boston Herald Traveler, 1942-43; mem. U.S. Counter Intelligence Corps, U.S. Army, Salzburg, Austria, 1945-48; joined U.S. Fgn. Svc., 1949; assigned vice consul, Genoa, Italy, 1950, Rome, 1950-51, Athens, 1964-68; 1st sec. Embassy, Bern, 1969-73; with CIA, 1974-80; adj. prof. George Washington U., Washington, 1995; lectr. Soc. Milit. Hist., 1996. Author: (novels) The "Mozart" Leaves at Nine, 1960, The Flags at Doney, 1964, The Thieves of Tumbutu, 1968, Canceled Accounts, 1973, FSO-1, 1977, Inference of Guilt, 1982. With U.S. Army, 1944-48, Italy and Austria. Fellow Macdowell Colony, 1966, 71. Mem. Assn. Former Intelligence Officers, Authors Guild Assn., Cosmos Club (Washington). Home: 3671 N Harrison St Arlington VA 22207-1843

GREENE, JANELLE LANGLEY, banker; b. Tarboro, N.C., July 27, 1940; d. Romey Roscoe and Stella Louise (Keene) Langley. Student, East Carolina U., 1958-61; cert., Chowan Coll., 1961, U. Ga., 1973, Appalachian U., 1977; diploma, Inst. Fin. Edn. Savs. & Loan, 1976; cert. diploma, Grad. Sch. Savs. and Loan U., 1979. Sec., receptionist Home Savs. & Loan, Rocky Mount, N.C., 1962-67, supr. services, acctg. teller ops., 1967-74, asst. sec., 1969-74, dept. head savs. and mktg., 1974-86, v.p., corp. sec., 1974-93; dept. head non-traditional products, v.p., sec. Pioneer Savs. Bank (name formerly Home Savs. & Loan), Rocky Mount, 1986-88; sr. v.p., mgr. Pioneer Capital Investments, Rocky Mount, 1988-93; v.p. bank subsidiaries Pioneer Capital Corp., Rocky Mount, 1988-93; registered rep., agt. The Equitable, 1994-95; bus. devel. mgr. Mega Force Staffing Svcs., Rocky Mount, N.C., 1995—; asst., sec., dir. HSL Investors, Inc., Rocky Mount, 1972-86; chmn. N.C. Savs. and Loan Conf., 1977. Mem. Rocky Mt. Zoning Bd., 1977-81, YMCA, Rocky Mt., 1976-80; alumni bd. Chowan Coll., Mufreesboro, N.C., 1985—, pres. 1989-90; mem. adv. council N.E.W. Performing Arts; mem. exec. com. N.C. Wesleyan Coll.; chmn. fundraising team, United Way, 1992-93. Recipient Bronze medallion Am. Heart Assn., 1976. Mem. N.C. League Savs. Instrns. (Outstanding Svc. plaque 1977), Am. Bus. Women's Assn. (Woman of Yr., pres. 1976-77), Rocky Mount C. of C. (amb. 1976-77, 88-89, 90-92, Red Coat 1975-76, 88—, capt. amb. team 1993—), Pilot Club Internat. (gov. N.C. dist. 1986-87, coord. projects divsn. 1989-90, dir. 1989-91, treas. 1991-92, treas. 1993—), Luncheon Pilot Club (pres. Rocky Mt. chpt. 1977-78, pres.-elect 1995-96, Pilot of Yr. 1979-80, Pres. award 1982-83, 92-93, Svcs. Unltd. award 1979-80), Beta Sigma Phi (pres. 1964-65). Democrat. Baptist. Home: RR 1 Box 238 Rocky Mount NC 27803-9153 Office: Mega Force 2627 Sunset Ave PO Box 8994 Rocky Mount NC 27804

GREENE, JENNIFER, elementary school counselor; b. Angelina County, Tex., July 25, 1946; d. E.S. and Winnie F. (Morris) Scoggins; m. Foy K. Greene, Aug. 26, 1967; children: Jeff, Andy. Bs, U. Houston, 1968; MEd in Couseling, Stephen F. Austin U., 1981. Lic. profl. counselor, Tex. Tchr. West Rusk County ISD, New London, Tex.; registrar, tchr. Chapel Hill High Sch., Tyler, Tex.; elem. sch. counselor Chapel Hill ISD, Tyler, Tex.; counselor T.K. Gorman H.S. Mem. Tex. Sch. Counselors Assn., Tex. Counselors Assn., Piney Woods Counselors Assn., Delta Kappa Gamma. Home: Rte 1 Box 812 Ravenna TX 75476-9712

GREENE, JOHN JOSEPH, lawyer; b. Marshall, Tex., Jan. 19, 1946; William Henry and Camille Anne (Riley) G.; BA, U. Houston, 1969, MA, 1974; JD, South Tex. Coll., 1978. Bar: Tex. 1978, U.S. Supreme Ct., 1982. Asst. atty. City of Amarillo, Tex., 1978-79; asst. atty. Harris County, Tex., 1979-83; pvt. practice, 1983—; city atty. City of Conroe (Tex.), 1983-89, sr. asst. city atty. City of Austin (Tex.), 1990—. Capt. USAR, 1969-76. Decorated Bronze Star, Air Medal. Roman Catholic. Office: 114 W 7th St Ste 400 Austin TX 78701-3008

GREENE, SARAH M., educational administrator; b. July 30, 1945; m. James R. Greene III. BA in English, Bethune-Cookman Coll., 1967; MA, Nova U., 1981. Tchr. Bradenton (Fla.) Head Start, 1968-69, Hampton (Va.) City Schs., 1969-70, Palmetto (Fla.) Head Start, 1970-71; edn. dir. Manatee County Head Start, Bradenton, Fla., 1971-76, dir., 1976-82, exec. dir., 1983—; pres. Nat. Head Start Assn., 1982-86, exec. dir., 1991—; active Impact on Svc. Delivery Families with Substance Abuse Problems, Nat. Health/Edn. Consortium, Child Care Action Campaign. Bd. dirs. Manasota Industry Coun., Hospice Assn. and Women's Resource Ctr., Southeastern Assn. Community Action Agys.; pres. Fla. Assn. Community Action, Fla. Assn. Community Action Agys., 1979, first. v.p., 1978-79; active St. John's First Bapt. Instl. Ch., Palmetto, Fla. Recipient numerous awards and plaques. Mem. NAACP, Nat. Assn. Edn. Young Children, Head Start Rsch. Panel, Zeta Phi Beta. Office: Nat Head Start Assn 1651 Prince St Alexandria VA 22314-2642*

GREENE, STEPHEN JOSEPH, marine corps officer; b. Royal Oak, Mich., Apr. 25, 1961; s. Joseph Leroy and Lois Rhoda (Hansen) G.; m. Lori Gayle Galbraith, Oct. 21, 1978; children: Jennifer, Sheryl, Christy, Stephen Jr., Rachel. BA in History summa cum laude, The Citadel, 1988. Commd. USMC, 1989—, advanced through grades to capt.; platoon comdr. Co. C 1st Batallion 6th Marines, Camp Lejeune, N.C., 1989-91; exec. officer Weapons Co. 1st Batallion 6th Marines, Camp Lejeune, N.C., 1991-92; guard officer Marine security Force Co., Charleston, S.C., 1992-94, exec. officer, 1994—. With USMC, 1978-85. Decorated Navy Commendation medals (2). Mem. Assn. for Preservation of Civil War Battlefields, Nat. Trust for Hist. Preservation, Phi Kappa Phi, Phi Alpha Theta. Lutheran. Office: USMC 1st Bn 6th Mar 2d Mar Div MARFORLANT Camp Lejeune NC 28542

GREENE, TAMMY RENEA, early childhood educator; b. Marion, N.C., Sept. 7, 1971; d. William Lee and Betty Delores (Penix) G. AAS in Gen. Edn., Mayland C.C., 1991; BS in Edn., East Tenn. State U., 1993. Cert. early childhood edn. Waitress McDonalds, Spruce Pine, N.C., 1986-87; clk. Stamey's Video, Bakersville, N.C., 1987-90; clk., fl. supr. Family Dollar Store, Spruce Pine, 1990—; substitute tchr. Mitchell County Schs., Bakersville, 1994—. Alumni honor scholar East Tenn. State U., 1991-92, Carolyn G. Palmer ednl. scholar, 1992-93, Claudius Clemmer ednl. scholar, 1992-93, Com. of 1,000 scholar, 1992-93. Mem. Kappa Delta Pi, Phi Kappa Phi, Phi Theta Kappa. Home: Rte 1 Box 40 Bakersville GA 28705

GREENFIELD, D(AVID) TYLER, cardiothoracic surgery educator; b. Denver City, Tex., Apr. 25, 1957; s. Keller Preston and Wanda Jean (Tyler) G.; m. Anne Marie Stier, Aug. 26, 1989. BBA in Fin. summa cum laude, Baylor U., 1980; MD, U. Tex., Dallas, 1984. Diplomate Am. Bd. Surgery, Am. Bd. Thoracic Surgery. Intern in gen. surgery Med. Coll. Va. Hosps., Richmond, 1984-85, resident in gen. surgery, 1985-90, fellow in cardiothoracic surgery, 1990-92; fellow in pediatric cardiovascular surgery Hosp. for Sick Children, Toronto, Ont., Can., 1992-93; asst. prof. surgery div. cardiothoracic surgery Tulane U. Med. Ctr., New Orleans, 1993—; presenter in field. Contbr. articles to med. jours. Comdr. M.C., USNR, 1989—. Recipient David M. Hume Meml. award Med. Coll. Va. Hosps., 1990; high sch. valedictorian scholar Baylor U., 1975; merit scholar Southwestern Med. Found., 1982, 83. Fellow ACS (assoc.), Am. Coll. Cardiology, Am. Coll. Chest Physicians; mem. AMA, Am. Heart Assn., Alpha Omega Alpha, Phi Beta Phi, Alpha Chi, Omicron Delta Kappa, Beta Gamma Sigma, Gamma Beta Phi. Home: 4222 Baronne St New Orleans LA 70115-4714 Office: Tulane U Med Sch Dept Surg SL-22 1430 Tulane Ave New Orleans LA 70112-2699

GREENFIELD-MOORE, WILMA L., social worker, educator; b. Boston. BA in Social Sci., Bennington Coll., 1958; MSW, U. Calif., Berkeley; PhD Social Welfare, U. Calif., 1978; cert. in departmental leadership, Fla. State U., 1983. Lic. clin. social worker, Fla., Calif.; cert. tchr.; diplomate Am. Bd. Clin. Social Work. Teaching asst. U. Calif., Berkeley, 1964-69, teaching assoc., 1970-71; asst. prof. social svc. Calif. State Poly. U., Pomona, 1971-75, U. New Hampshire, 1976-80; asst. prof. community svcs. Fla. Atlantic U., Boca Raton, 1980-85, assoc. prof. social work, 1985—, chair Dept. Social Work, 1989-94, prof., 1996—, dir. social work student internship, 1995—; adj. prof. Barry U., 1984-88, Sylvester Inst. Aging Coll. Boca Raton, 1985-87; vis. prof. U. Wis., Green Bay, 1994-95; cons., psychotherapist, Fla., 1987—; mem. Gov.'s Task Force on Reorgn. of Social Svcs., 1996; bd. dirs. health and human svcs. bd. Dept. Health and Rehab. Svcs., Dist. IX. Contbr. chpts. to books, articles to profl. jours. Mem. adv. bd. I

Have A Dream Found., Boca Raton, 1990-92, Sr. Power News, 1990-92; mem. community rels. bd. City of Boca Raton, 1982-83; coord., mem. state adv. bd. Palm county Campaign Dukakis for Pres., 1987-88; mem. Psychol. Svcs. Coalition, Coalition Mental Health Providers State of Fla., 1985-88; bd. dirs. May Volen Sr. Ctr., Boca Raton, 1986-90, Florence Fuller Child Devel. Ctr., Boca Raton, 1986-90, Fla. Consumer Action Network, 1988-90, South Palm Beach County Migrant Coord. Coun., 1982-87; at-large del. Dem. Nat. Conv., 1988; mem. planning com. United Way Boca Raton. Grantee Fla. Atlantic U., 1981, 83, 89-91, 90-95. Mem. NASW (pres. Fla. chpt. 1986-88, Social Worker of Yr. Fla. chpt. 1983, chmn. bd. trustees PACE, 1990-94), Nat. Network Social Work Mgrs., Am. Soc. Aging, Internat. Social Welfare Conf. Inter-univ. Consortium Internat. Social Devel., Coun. Social Work Edn. Fla. Assn. Social Work Edn. Adminstrs. Home: 1400 NW 9th Ave Apt 12 Boca Raton FL 33486-1325 Office: Fla Atlantic U Social Work Dept Coll Urban and Pub Affairs 777 Glades Rd SSB 284 B Boca Raton FL 33431-0991

GREENLEAF, WALTER FRANKLIN, lawyer; b. Griffin, Ga., Sept. 21, 1946; s. Walter Helmuth and Vida Mildred (Goheen) G. B.A., Mich. State U., 1968; M.A., U. N.C., 1970, J.D., U. Ala., 1973. Bar: Ala. 1973, Fla. 1974, U.S. Dist. Ct. (no. dist.) Ala. 1973, U.S. Ct. Appeals (5th cir.) 1974, U.S. Dist. Ct. (so. dist.) Fla. 1977, U.S. Ct. Appeals (11th cir) 1981. Law clk. U.S. Dist. Ct., Birmingham, Ala., 1973-74; assoc. Sirote, Permutt, et al., Birmingham, Ala., 1975-76; assoc., then ptnr. Welbaum Guernsey, Hingston, Greenleaf, & Gregory, LLP, Miami, Fla., 1976—. Editor, Ala. Law Rev., 1972-73. Mem. ABA, Dade County Bar Assn., Am. Arbitration Assn. (panel of arbitrators), Order Coif, Phi Beta Kappa, Phi Kappa Phi, Phi Delta Phi, Omicron Delta Kappa. Home: 417 Madeira Ave Miami FL 33134-4234 Office: Welbaum Guernsey Hingston Greenleaf & Gregory LLP 901 Ponce De Leon Blvd Miami FL 33134-3073

GREENMAN, RICHARD LEONARD, physician; b. Chgo., Aug. 29, 1943; s. Albert and Gladys (Krause) G.; m. Bernadine Heller, Jul. 31, 1966; children: Benjamin, Aaron, Joshua. BA, Cornell Univ., 1964; MS, Univ. Iowa, 1965; MD, Chgo. Medical Sch., 1969. Diplomate Am. Bd. Nat Bd. Medical Examiners, Diplomate Am. Bd. Internal Medicine. Asst. prof. medicine Univ. Miami Sch. of Medicine, 1974-80, assoc. prof. medicine, 1980-92, prof. of medicine, 1992—. With USAF Res., 1973-80. Fellow ACP, Infectious Diseases Soc. of Am.; mem. Fla. Infectious Diseases Soc. (pres. 1995-96), Alpha Omega Alpha (pres. 1968). Democrat. Jewish. Office: Univ Miami Medical Sch PO Box 016960 Miami FL 33101

GREENSTREET, ROBERT WAYNE, communication educator, consultant; b. New Bedford, Mass., May 21, 1949; s. John Russell and Dora Ida (Bouchard) G.; m. Jennifer Kennis Roberts, Sept. 1, 1973; 1 child, Dacia Erin. BA cum laude, U. of the Pacific, 1971; MA, Western Wash. U., 1974; postgrad., U. Iowa, 1980-84; EdD, Okla. State U., 1996. Asst. forensics dir. Western Wash. State Coll., Bellingham, 1973-74; instr. Fresno (Calif.) City Coll., 1975-76, S.W. Tex. State U., San Marcos, 1976-79; asst. prof. Graceland Coll., Lamoni, Iowa, 1979-84, East Ctrl. U., Ada, Okla., 1984—; cons. Ada Pub. Libr., 1989, 91, Carl Albert Hosp., 1991; spkr. Okla. Pub. Health Assn., Marshall County C. of C., 1994; papers presented Internat. Conf. on Critical Thinking, 1992, Nat. Devel. Conf. on Individual Events, 1988, 90, Okla. Speech Theater Comm. Assn., 1990-93, 95, 96, Ctrl. State Comm. Assn., 1983, 92, Graceland Coll., 1981, 83, Iowa Comm. Assn., 1982, 83, Speech Comm. Assn., 1982, 93, 96, Ada Pub. Schs., 1986, 87, others; discussion facilitator Debate Watch, 1996. Asst. editor, reviewer Nat. Forensic Jour., Jour. Okla. Speech Theatre Comm. Assn., Jour. Pub. Advocacy; contbr. articles to profl. jours. Bd. dirs., pres. Ada Libr. Friends, 1991-92, 95-96; debate cons. polit. campaign, Ada, 1990; bd. dirs. Friends of Librs. Okla., 1996—. Mem. Okla. Speech Theater Comm. Assn. (bd. dirs., parliamentarian 1991-92, past pres. 1989-90, pres. 1988-89, 1st v.p. 1987, 2d v.p. 1986, planned 1988 conv., newsletter editor 1985, reviewer jour.), Speech Comm. Assn., Cross Exam. Debate Assn. (ad hoc com. on regional realignment 1987), Nat. Ednl. Debate Assn. (charter, topic com. 1994-95, 96—, stds. and practices com. 1994—), Am. Forensic Assn. (life, pres. nat. devel. conf., 1988, 90, dist. III Japan program com. 1987, chair nat. individual events tournament com. 1979, chair dist. III), Nat. Coun. Critical Thinking (presenter numerous confs.), Nat. Forensic Assn. (mem. nat. assembly 1982-84), Ctrl. States Comm. Assn. (panelist 1984, 94, 95, 96, bus. mgr. 1994—, vice chair argumentation and forensics interest group 1994-95, chair argumentation and forensics interest group 1995-96, exec. bd. 1994—, bus. mgr. 1994—), Iowa Comm. Assn. (pres.-elect 1983), Iowa Intercollegiate Forensic Assn. (v.p., host state tournament 1983), Calif. C.C. Forensic Assn. (host state championship 1975), No. Calif. Forensic Assn., Phi Rho Pi, Pi Kappa Delta. Democrat. Office: East Ctrl U Box T-4 Ada OK 74820-6899

GREENWALD, DOUGLAS, economist; b. N.Y.C., June 5, 1913; s. Max and Florence G.; m. Mildred Sachs, Oct. 23, 1979. AB, Temple U., 1934; MA, George Washington U., 1942, Ph.D., 1947; postgrad. U. Nancy (France), 1945. Market researcher Bond Mfg. Co., N.Y.C., 1934-41; statis. economist U.S. Bur. Labor Stats., Washington, 1942, 1946-47; chief statistician, chief economist, v.p. econs. McGraw-Hill Publs. Co., N.Y.C., 1947-78; cons. economist, author, N.Y.C., Fla., 1978—; dir. Standard and Poor's Intercapital Co., N.Y.C., 1974-78; cons. Congressional Budget Office, Council Econ. Advs.; U.S. Congress Joint Econ. Com., U.S. Bur. Census, U.S. Bur. Labor Stats., Dept. Commerce Office Mgmt. and Budget, Dept. Treasury, Calif. Fin. Dept. Served with AUS, 1942-46. Recipient Japanese medal Order of the Sacred Treasure, 3d class, 1985. Fellow Am. Statis. Assn., Nat. Assn. Bus. Econs.; mem. Met. Econ. Assn. (pres.), Fed. Stats. Users Conf. (chmn.), Am. Econ. Assn. Co-author: New Forces in American Business, 1958; co-author, chief editor: McGraw-Hill Dictionary of Modern Economics, 1965, 73, 83; chief editor, contbr. McGraw-Hill Ency. of Econs., 1982, 94; Concise McGraw-Hill Dictionary of Modern Economics, 1984. Home: 5790 Midnight Pass Rd Sarasota FL 34242-3062

GREENWELL, LINDA BRANHAM, social services administrator; b. Jeffersonville, Ind., July 29, 1946; d. Howard Duffy Branham and Grace (Wathen) Thompson; m. Wayne Standley, Dec. 18, 1964 (div.); 1 child, Dina; m. Stan Frager, May 18, 1980 (div.); children: Sarah, Joshua; m. J. Michael Greenwell, Aug. 20, 1996. BA in Psychology, Ind. U., 1973; MEd in Family Counseling, U. Louisville, 1995. Proof operator Citizens Fidelity Bank, Louisville, 1966-67, trainer, 1974-78; proof operator Louisville Trust Bank, 1967-68; trainer, supr. U.S. Census Bureau, Jeffersonville, 1969-71; proof operator 1st Bank Houston, 1973-74; mem. adj. faculty Continuing Sch. Edn. Ind. U. S.E., New Albany, 1979-83; hypnotechnician, counselor, v.p. Frager Assocs., Louisville, 1978-88, cons., 1979—; social worker Dept. Social Svcs., Louisville, 1988-94; Family Preservation and Reunification dir. Cmty. Action, Elizabethtown, Ky., 1994—; trainer Dept. Social Svcs., Frankfort, Ky., 1992—; cons. sports psychology Nat. Basketball Team P.R., Pan Am. Games, San Juan, 1979; presenter hypnosis workshops Sch. Dentistry U. Louisville, Clarksville, Ind., 1980, Sch. Medicine U. Louisville, 1982; tchr. time and stress mgmt. Commonwealth Life Ins., Louisville, 1983. Author: (booklets) AV Production: Directing Non-Professional Actors, 1979, A.S.T.D. Film Festival Guide, 1980. Designer training workshops Ky. Assn. for Comm. and Tech., Louisville, 1979; co-leader anorexia and bulimia group Anorexia Soc., 1980, 81; asst. to chairperson spl. events Am. Cancer Soc., Louisville, 1979, 80; vol. So. Ind. Mental Health & Guidance Clinic, Jeffersonville, 1972. Mem. Assn. to Advanced Ethical Hypnosis (cert. hypnotechnician 1980—). Jewish. Home: 4119 Brentler Rd Louisville KY 40241-1520 Office: Family Preservation 6227 N Dixie Hwy Elizabethtown KY 42701-8886

GREENWOOD, VIRGINIA MAXINE MCLEOD, real estate executive, broker; b. Ballinger, Tex., Mar. 3, 1930; d. Vernie L. and Alma (Simpson) McLeod; m. Lester Greenwood, Apr. 21, 1951 (div. May 1985), children: Virginia Leslie Pattison, Randal Lester, Sheree Lou Stiles. Student, Draughn's Bus. Sch., Wichita Falls, 1948-49; completed real estate courses, Grad. Realtors Inst., 1972. Cert. residential specialist; cert. buyer rep. Real estate agt. C. V. Perry Co., Columbus, Ohio, 1967-69, Montague, Miller and Co., Charlottesville, Va., 1970-74; sales mgr. Great Eastern Mgmt. Corp., Charlottesville, 1974-75; real estate broker Greenwood Realty Ltd., Charlottesville, 1975-93; sr. assoc. broker Coldwell Banker-Bailey Realty Co., 1993—. Mem. Monticello Area Cmty. Action Agy. adv. bd., 1988-92, Albemarle (Va.) County Rep. com., 1974-76; Albemarle County Housing adv. com., 1991-92, 94—, Thomas Jefferson Planning Dist. Housing adv. com., 1991-92. Mem. Nat. Assn. Realtors, Va. Assn. Realtors (bd. dirs. 1985-92), Charlottesville Area Assn. of Realtors (sec. 1983-84, bd. dirs. 1983-91, 2d v.p. 1988, 1st v.p. 1989, pres. 1990), Albemarle Housing Coalition. Office: Coldwell Banker Bailey Realty Co 1455 E Rio Rd PO Box 6700 Charlottesville VA 22906

GREER, HERSCHEL LYNN, JR., real estate broker; b. Nashville, June 28, 1941; s. Herschel Lynn and Mary Martha (Bradley) G.; children: Kathy, Lynn III, Bradley, Houston, Karen; m. Grace Ann Stephenson, Aug. 22, 1981; 1 stepchild, Michael Stephenson. AA, Martin Coll., Pulaski, Tenn., 1961; BS, Middle Tenn. State U., 1963. Pres., chmn. Guaranty Mortgage Co., Nashville, 1960-75; v.p., then pres. Greer Investment Co. (formerly Guaranty Realty Co.), Nashville, 1963-96; dir. Tenn. Regulatory Authority, 1996—. Vice chmn., chmn. Tenn. Bd. Edn., 1971-84; fin. chmn. Tenn. Rep. Com., Nashville, 1977; chmn. bd. trustees Martin Meth. Coll., Pulaski, Tenn., 1992—; trustee Calvary United Meth. Ch.; trustee Mid. Tenn. State U. Found., pres., 1970-71; chmn. Tenn. Housing Devel. Agy., 1985-88; bd. dirs. Nashville Ballet. Named Disting. Alumnus Middle Tenn. State U., 1987. Mem. Nashville Bd. Realtors (pres. 1975, Realtor of Yr. 1971), Tenn. Assn. Realtors (pres. 1986, Realtor of Yr. 1972), Nat. Assn. Realtors (v.p. region IV 1989), Kappa Alpha (exec. coun.). Republican. Methodist. Home: 306 Deer Park Cir Nashville TN 37205

GREER, RAYMOND WHITE, lawyer; b. Port Arthur, Tex., July 20, 1954; s. Mervyn Hardy Greer and Eva Nadine (White) Swain; m. Pamela V. Brown; children: Emily Ann, Sarah Kelly, Jonathan Collin. BA magna cum laude, Sam Houston State, 1977; JD, U. Houston, 1981. Assoc. Hoover, Cox & Shearer, Houston, 1980-83, Hinton & Morris, Houston, 1983-85; pvt. practice Houston, 1985-86; prin. Morris & Greer, P.C., Houston, 1986-90, Raymond W. Greer & Assocs., P.C., Houston, 1990—; lectr. in field. Recipient Outstanding Alumnus award, Dept. English, Sam Houston U., 1986. Mem. ABA, State Bar Tex., Houston Bar Assn., Fort Bend County Bar Assn., Rotary, Alumni Assn. (adv. bd., 2d v.p., chmn. membership com., combined charter and membership com. 1995-96, 1st v.p. 1996—), Sam Houston State U. (adv. bd., Distinguished Alumnus award 1996-97), Exch. Club Sugar Land (asst. chmn. fresh start com. 1996—). Avocations: golf, reading.

GREER, TOMMY D., marketing executive; b. 1932. With Textize Chemical Co., pres., 1950-75; founder Universal Product Dollars, 1975-80; exec. v.p. Intex Products, Inc., 1980-86; chmn. bd. dirs., CEO, co-founder Catalina Mktg. Corp., 1983—. Office: Catalina Mktg Corp 11300 9th St N Saint Petersburg FL 33716-2329*

GREGG, ANDREA MARIE, nursing administrator, educator, researcher; b. Savannah, Ga., Nov. 2, 1946; d. Walter Michael and Dorothy Marie (Coleman) Crawford; m. John Jasper Schuman Jr., July 2, 1967 (div. Aug. 1981); children: Alicia, John, Robert; m. John Franklin Gregg, Mar. 12, 1982; children: Nancy, Jay. Diploma in nursing, St. Joseph's Sch. Nursing, Savannah, 1967; BSN, Armstrong State Coll., 1976; MSN, Med. Coll. Ga., 1978; DSN in Nursing Adminstrn., U. Ala., Birmingham, 1993. RN, Ga., Fla., Ala. Staff nurse, asst. head nurse, head nurse, v.p. nursing Meml. Med. Ctr., Savannah, 1967-82; dir. nursing St. Jude's Nursing Ctr., Jacksonville, Fla., 1982-83; assoc. adminstr. patient care Nemours Children's Hosp., Jacksonville, Fla., 1983-86; asst. prof. nursing U. Fla., Jacksonville, 1986—; dir. Jacksonville urban campus Coll. Nursing, U. Fla., Jacksonville, 1995—; NIH trainee, 1988-93; cons. Nemours Children's Clinic, Jacksonville, 1991, Meml. Home Health Svcs., Savannah, 1992; statistician cons. Fla. Allergy and Immunology Soc., Jacksonville, 1993. Contbr. articles to profl. jours. Bd. dirs. Child Guidance Ctr., Inc., Jacksonville, 1994-95, chmn. bd. dirs., 1995—; bd. dirs. S.E. Ga. Health Sys. Agy., 1980-82; mem. Am. Heart Assn., Jacksonville, 1994. Mem. Nat. League for Nursing, Fla. League for Nursing (treas., bd. dirs. 1994-96), Ala. Acad. Sci., Sigma Theta Tau. Office: U Fla Coll Nursing Bldg 1 2d Fl 653 W 8th St Fl 2 Jacksonville FL 32209-6511

GREGG, BILLY RAY, seed industry executive; b. Taylorsville, Miss., Aug. 31, 1930; s. Hinds and Lillie Mae (Moore) G.; m. Mary Frances Barber, Aug. 12, 1950 (div. Jan. 1987); children: Kathryn, Patricia, Lisa; m. Orawan Chonlavorn, Dec. 20, 1988; 1 child, Nathan Paul. AA, Perkinston (Miss.) Jr. Coll., 1950; BS, Miss. State U., 1954, MS, 1956, PhD, 1968; postgrad., Wash. State U., 1957-63. Asst. prof. Wash. State U., Pullman, 1956-63; mgr. Ala. Crop Improvement Assn., Auburn, Ala., 1964-66; seed technologist Miss. State U., 1966-68; chief party/processing specialist seed improvement project U.S. AID, New Delhi, India, 1968-72; chief party and seed specialist seed project U.S. AID, Brasilia, Brazil, 1972-74; chief, seed industry devel. specialist U.S. AID, Bangkok, 1977-87; seed industry devel. specialist U.S. AID, Cairo, 1987-93; chief party and seed industry specialist IDB and GOB Agiplan Project, Brasilia, 1974-76; seed industry specialist Internat. Plant Breeders, Maringa, Parana, Brazil, 1976, Interam. Agrl. Sci. Inst., Brasilia, 1976-77; seed industry devel. specialist internat. programs Miss. State U., 1993—; cons./advisor on seed tech. matters, mgmt., quality control and industry devel. nat. govts., pvt. cos., World Bank, Interam. Devel. Bank, FAO, GTZ, U.S. AID, 1960-95. Contbr. over 480 articles to profl. jours.; author 2 books. With U.S. Army, 1950-52; ETO. Indian Soc. Seed Technologists fellow, 1987. Mem. Kiwanis Internat. (dir., Kiwanian of the Yr. 1968), Agrl. Sci. Soc. Thailand (hon.), Wash. State Crop Improvement Assn. (hon. life), Phi Kappa Phi, Sigma Xi, Phi Theta Kappa. Buddhist. Home: 1860 New Light Rd Starkville MS 39759

GREGG, DAVID, III, investment banker; b. N.Y.C., Jan. 29, 1933; s. David Gregg and Virginia (Wyckoff) Macgregor; m. May Foster Bowers, Dec. 21, 1963 (div. Apr. 1984); children: Justine Simms, David; m. Sarah Choate Massengale, Dec. 8, 1984. Assoc., Eastman Dillon Union Securities & Co., N.Y.C., 1959-67, prtnr., 1967-69; v.p. Blyth & Co., Inc., N.Y.C., 1969-72; 1st v.p. Blyth, Eastman Dillon & Co., N.Y.C., 1972-73; exec. v.p. Overseas Pvt. Investment Corp., Washington, 1973-77; dir. Pierce Internat., Ltd., Washington, 1978-85, mng. dir., 1978—; mng. dir. Pierce Investment Banking Corp., 1985—; chmn. bd. dirs. Gator Broadcasting Corp., Gainesville, Fla.; bd. dirs. So. Starr Broadcasting, Orlando, Fla., 1983-87, Trustee Calvert Tax Free Res. Fund, 1978-83; dir. 1st Variable Rate Fund, 1978-83, No. Irish Partnership U.S.A., 1990-94, No. Ireland and Border Counties Trade and Investment Coun., 1994—. Served with U.S. Army, 1955-57. Republican. Episcopalian. Clubs: Onteora (dir. 1969-72) (Tannersville, N.Y.); Chesapeake Bay Yacht (Easton, Md.); Amateur Ski of N.Y. Office: Pierce Investment Banking Corp 2200 Clarendon Blvd Ste 1410 Arlington VA 22201-3331

GREGG, LAWRENCE TERRELL, geologist; b. Ft. Worth, May 17, 1936; s. L. T. and Pearl Louise (Null) G.; m. Martha Mildred Seng, 1957 (div. 1965); children: Davis C., Thomas A., Robert F., Richard A.; m. Catherine Marie Broussard, Sept. 23, 1976. BS in Geology, Tex. A&M U., 1958, BS in Geophysics, 1958. Registered profl. geologist, Ga., Va., Tenn. Geophysicist Pan Am. Petroleum Corp., Lafayette, La., 1958-61; sr. rsch. engr. Gen. Dynamics Convair, San Diego, 1961-66; market rsch. analyst Gen. Atomic Co., San Diego, 1966-72; dir. mktg. Gulf Minerals Can. Ltd., Toronto, Ont., Can., 1972-74; mktg. mgr. Gen. Atomic Co., Atlanta, 1974-75; bus. devel. mgr. Nuclear Assurance Corp., Atlanta, 1975-83; pres., gen. mgr. Piedmont Mineral Assocs. Ltd., Atlanta, 1983-86; dir. geologic and environ. svcs. Atlanta Testing & Engring., Duluth, Ga., 1986—; adj. instr. DeKalb coll., Atlanta, 1984-90, Ga. Tech. Rsch. Inst., Atlanta, 1991-95, The Environ. Inst., Marietta, Ga., 1990-95. Capt. U.S. Army, 1957-58, Aberdeen, Md. Mem. Geol. Soc. Am., Ga. Mining Assn., Ga. Groundwater Assn. (v.p. 1984-93), Ga. Geologic Soc., Ga. Acad. Sci., Atlanta Geol. Soc., Soc. for Mining, Metallurgy, and Exploration, Am. Inst. Profl. Geologists, Am. Inst. Minerals Appraisers. Republican. Presbyterian. Home: 3915 Glencrest Ct NE Atlanta GA 30319-1893 Office: Atlanta Testing & Engring 11420 Johns Creek Pky Duluth GA 30155

GREGG, MARIE BYRD, retired farmer; b. Mount Olive, N.C., Jan. 12, 1930; d. Arnold Wesley and Martha (Reaves) Byrd; m. Robert Allen Gregg, July 11, 1953; children: Martha Susan, Kathryn Elizabeth, Kenneth Allen. BA in Elem. Edn., Furman U., 1951. Tchr. 3rd grade Greenville (S.C.) City Schs., 1951-53; med. social worker Ctrl. Carolina Rehab. Hosp., Greensboro, N.C., 1959-61; window display designer Kerr Rexall Drugs, Durham, N.C., 1960's; shop owner Something Else Antiques, Lima, Ohio, 1979-81; farm owner Mt. Olive, 1978-92. Democrat. Methodist. Home and Office: 212 Baucom Park Dr Greer SC 29650-2972

GREGG, ROY DENNIS, manufacturing company executive; b. Mt. Pleasant, Tenn., Apr. 22, 1948; s. Roy Leonard and Emma (Wells) G.; m. Carol Taylor, Dec. 28, 1968; children: Joshua Dennis, Mary Margaret. BS, U. Tenn., 1971. Sales mgr. Plantation Patterns, Inc., Birmingham, Ala., 1980-82; nat. sales mgr. Arlington House, Birmingham, 1982-85; v.p. sales dept. Arlington House and Vogue Rattan, Birmingham, 1985-87; v.p. sales and mktg. div. Sam Blount Co., Inc., Birmingham, 1987-91; pres. Cumberland Crown L.P., Chattanooga, 1991—. Mem. Parent-Tchr. Orgn., Birmingham, 1980—, Parent Advs. Down Syndrome, Birmingham, 1985—; sustaining mem. Boy Scouts Am., Birmingham, 1986—. Mem. Casual Furniture Retailers Assn., Am. Furniture Mfrs. Assn., NRA, Ducks Unltd. Republican. Methodist. Office: Cumberland Crown LP 3500 N Hawthorne St Chattanooga TN 37406-1303

GREGORIO, PETER ANTHONY, retail grocer, artist; b. Chgo., July 29, 1916; s. Frank and Teresa (Marotta) G.; grad. pub. schs., Chgo., 1942; m. Marie Blanton, Mar. 17, 1945; children—Frank Allen, Carole Teresa. Owner, operator Davis Island Supermarket, Tampa, Fla. 1949—; dir. Ellis Nat. Bank of Davis Island, Tampa 1977-78; dir. Consignment Arts Ctr., Tampa; exhibited in one man show Islands Gallery, 1976-77; group shows Am. Bicentennial, Paris, 1976, Rochester (N.Y.) Religious Art Festival, 1972, Tampa Bay Art Center, 1979, Hillsborough Art Festival, 1976, 77, 78, (award of merit) 79, (3d pl. and honorable mention) 81, (3d pl.) 82, Tampa Realistic Art Assn., 1981, Artist Alliance Guild, Tampa, 1981, Tampa Mus., 1982, Tampa Mus. Art, 1987, Le Salon des Nations a Paris, 1984; exhibited Art Inst. Chgo. (hon. mention sculpture 1982); exhibited Internat. Artists Guild, Clearwater, Fla., 1990; published in Manhattan Arts and Artists of the 1990's, 1990; represented in permanent collection Vatican Library, Rome, also numerous pvt. collections. V.p. Nat. Animal Rights, Inc., nat. hdqrs. Tampa, 1983-88. Served to capt. USAF, 1941-46. Decorated Air medal with 6 clusters; recipient award of excellence Hillsborough County Art Fair, Tampa, 1984. award of merit Tampa Hispanic Heritage Exhbn., 1987, Editor's Choice award, Outstanding Achievement award Nat. Libr. of Poetry., 1993, 94. Mem. Am., Internat. socs. artists, Graphic Soc. Roman Catholic. Home: 149 Bosphorous Ave Tampa FL 33606-3532 Office: 304 E Davis Blvd Tampa FL 33606-3731

GREGORY, ANN YOUNG, editor, publisher; b. Lexington, Ky., Apr. 28, 1935; d. David Marion and Pauline (Adams) Young; m. Allen Gregory, Jan. 29, 1957; children: David Young, Mary Peyton. BA with high distinction, U. Ky., 1956. Sec. Ky. edit. TV Guide, Louisville, summer 1956; traffic mgr. Sta. WVLK, Lexington, 1956-61; part time tchr. adult basic edn. Wise County (Va.) Sch. Bd., St. Paul, 1966-72; adminstrv. asst. Appalachian Field Svcs., Children's TV Workshop, St. Paul, 1971-74; editor, co-pub. Clinch Valley Times, 1974—; pres. Clinch Valley Pub. Co., Inc., St. Paul, 1974—; mem. mktg. com. Mountain Empire TechPrep Consortium, 1993—. Editor, text writer: The Flood of '77 in the St. Paul Area, 1977; weekly newspaper columnist Of Shoes...and Ships...and Sealing Wax, 1974—. V.p. St. Paul PTA, 1970-73; trustee Lonesome Pine Regional Libr. Bd., 1972-80, chmn., 1978-80; chmn. com. to establish br. libr. in St. Paul, opened 1975; mem. adv. bd. Pro-Art, Wise County chpt. Va. Mus. Fine Arts, 1979-86; co-leader Brownie troop Girl Scouts U.S.A., 1971-76, bd. dirs. Appalachian Coun., 1983-1995, 1st v.p., 1985-91; mem. adv. bd. Wise County YMCA, 1977-80; mem. Wise County Bd. Edn., 1975—, vice chmn., 1981-95; pres. So. Region Sch. Bds. Assn., 1987-88; mem. Va. Edn. Block Grants Adv. Com., 1981-86, Region I State Literacy Coun., 1989-91; mem. Local Vocat. Adv. Coun., 1980—, chmn., 1981—; mem. statewide planning coun. Va. Dept. Edn.; mem. Va. Coun. on Vocat. Edn., 1987-95, chmn., 1989-91; mem. exec. com. Va. H.S. League, 1984-88; past pres. Wise County Humane Soc., Inc.; bd. dirs. Va. Sch. Bds. Assn., 1979-89, pres., 1985-86; bd. dirs. Va. Literacy Found., 1987-89; bd. dir., Appalachia Ednl. Lab., 1995—; sec., treas. S.W. Va. Pub. Edn. Found. Bd., 1993—; mem. Mountain Empire C.C. Found. Bd., 1994—; mem. adv. com. Va. State Supt. Pub. Instrn., 1993-96; mem. devel. and cmty. rels. com., mem. music adv. com. Clinch Valley Coll.; mem. adv. bd. Wise Appalachian Regional Hosp., 1995—. Named Outstanding Clubwoman of Yr., St. Paul Jr. Women's Club, 1964, 66, Outstanding Citizen, S.W. Va. dist. Va. Fedn. Women's Clubs, 1968, Woman of Yr. Wise County/ Norton Dem. Women's Club, 1986; recipient Rufus Beamer award Va. Poly. Inst., 1989, William P Kanto Meml. award for contbns. to edn. Clinch Valley Coll., Mountain Empire C.C. and Wise County and Norton Pub. Schs., 1990; Ky. Broadcasters Assn. scholar, 1956; named Citizen of Yr. Wise County C. of C., 1990. Mem. Va. Press Assn. (1st place award for editorial writing 1976), Nat. Press Women, Va. Press Women, Nat. Newspaper Assn., Women in Communications, Nat. Sch. Bds. Assn. (pub. rels. com., nominating com. 1987), Mortar Bd., Delta Kappa Gamma (hon. mem. Alpha Psi chpt.), Phi Beta Kappa, Alpha Delta Pi, Chi Delta Phi, Alpha Epsilon Rho, Alpha Lambda Delta, Theta Sigma Phi. Democrat. Methodist. Home: PO Box 303 Saint Paul VA 24283-0303 Office: PO Box 817 Saint Paul VA 24283-0817

GREGORY, DANIEL KEVIN, pharmacist; b. New Orleans, Sept. 11, 1958; s. Conrad and Mildred (Knight) G.; m. Vicki Lynn Ivy, May 18, 1985; 1 child, Brandon Christopher. Student, La. State U., 1976-79; BS in Pharmacy, N.E. La. U., 1982; postgrad., La. State, 1982-84. Registered pharmacist. Pharmacist Our Lady of the Lake Regional Med. Ctr., Baton Rouge, 1982-84, pharmacist, night supr., 1985-92; cons. pharm. dir. Tau Ctr. Our Lady of the Lake Regional Med. Ctr., 1985-92; pharmacist Chem. Dependency Units of Baton Rouge, 1982-85; pharmacy supr. H.C.A. L.W. Blake Meml. Hosp., Bradenton, Fla., 1992-94; pharmacy asst. mgr. Walmart, Bradenton, 1994—; owner Darklite Graphics; artist-in-residence Eclipse Mag.; owner Darklite Graphics. Mem. La. Arts and Artist's Guild, 1988-91. Finalist Illustrators of the Future competition, 4th quar., 1990, Hon. Mention, 1991. Mem. Internat. Platform Assn., Suncoast Camera Club, Phi Delta Chi (v.p. 1980-81). Republican. Episcopalian. Home: 3108 48th Avenue Dr E Bradenton FL 34203-3928 Office: Wal Mart Pharmacy 815 44th Ave E Bradenton FL 34203-3540

GREGORY, DANIEL RICHARD, safety and environmental engineer; b. Lynn, Mass., July 31, 1958; s. Robert Francis and Arzella Pearl (Barnard) G.; m. Heather Anderson, July 21, 1990; children: Victoria Ashley, Mikayla Lynn. AT in Environ. Scis., Ft. Steila C.C., Tacoma, 1979, AAS in Bus. Adminstrn., 1980; BS in Gen. Scis., Seattle U., 1981; MS in Sys. Mgmt., Western New Eng. Coll., 1990. Cert. safety profl., cert. quality environ. profl. Veteran's affairs coord. Seattle U., 1978-81; safety engr. Raytheon (Patriot), Tewksbury, Mass., 1987-95; safety and MANPRINT mgr. Raytheon (EFOGM), Huntsville, Ala., 1995—. Bd. dirs. Camp Paul for Exceptional Needs Children, Chelmsford, Mass., 1991-95. Major USAR, 1977—. Mem. Sys. Safety Soc. (co-founder New Eng. chpt., editor newsletter 1991-93. Republican. Office: Raytheon Elec Sys 353 James Record Rd Huntsville AL 25824

GREGORY, GUS, food products executive; b. Bristol, Pa., Mar. 12, 1940; s. Charley and Mary (Chuleas) G.; m. Carol Madej, Sept. 4, 1964 (div. 1976); children: Shelley Anisa, Andi, Charly; m. Colette Barden, July 20, 1979 (div. 1994); 1 child, Nicholas. Student, Mich. State U., 1959, Fla. Internat. U., 1985. Various positions Gregory's Restaurant, Flint, Mich., 1954-60; owner Town Talk Restaurant, Flint, 1960-62; mgr. Prophet Food Svc., Flint, 1962-64; dir. Szabo Food Svc., Chgo., 1964-65, ARA Svc., Chgo., 1965-68; founder, CEO Total Food Svc. Direction, Miami, Fla., 1968—; cons. Ford Motor Co., Detroit, 1986-87, St. John Hosp., Detroit, 1986-87. Advisor Dade County Sch. Bd., Miami, 1986-88. Recipient Gov.'s award State of Fla., 1982, 84, Silver Plate award Internat. Food Svc. Mfrs., 1988, Doctorate of Food Svc. award Nat. Assn. Food Equipment Mfrs., 1993. Mem. Nat. Restaurant Assn., Fla. Restaurant Assn., Soc. for Food Mgmt. (bd. dirs., past pres.). Republican. Greek Orthodox. Office: Total Food Svc Direction 10482 NW 31st Ter Miami FL 33172-1215

GREGORY, JACKIE SUE, critical care nurse; b. Amarillo Potter County, Tex., Nov. 26, 1946; d. Albert Ray and Rosa Inez (Bryson) Horner; children: Larry, Paula, Justin. BSN, West Tex. State U., 1989; postgrad., West Tex. A&M U., 1996. RN, Tex., Okla. Staff nurse vascular ICU Baylor U. Med. Ctr., Dallas, 1991-93; adminstr. Assocs. Home Health Inc., Jacksonville,

Tex., 1994-95, Angel Home Health Inc., Malakoff, Tex., 1995-96; charge nurse, case mgr. South Plains Health Provider, Amarillo, Tex., 1996—; part-time clin. instr. Cameron U., Lawton, Okla., 1990-93. Contbr. articles to profl. jours. Vol. hospice program Vis. Nurse Assn., 1989-90. USPHS scholar, 1989. Mem. AACN, ANA, Okla. Nurses Assn., Sigma Theta Tau.

GREGORY, JEAN WINFREY, ecologist, educator; b. Richmond, Va., Feb. 13, 1947; d. Thomas Edloe and Kathryn (McFarlane) Winfrey; m. Ronald Alfred Gregory, Dec. 13, 1973. BS in Biology, Mary Washington Coll., 1969; MS in Biology, Va. Commonwealth U., 1975, postgrad. in pub. adminstrn., 1982-90; MA in Environ. Sci., U. Va., 1983. Cert. fisheries sci. Lab. specialist A Cardiovascular Div. Med. Coll. Va., Richmond, 1969-70; pollution specialist State Water Control Bd. (now Dept. Environ. Quality), Richmond, 1970-77, pollution control specialist B, 1977-81, ecologist, 1981-85, ecology programs supr., 1985-88, environ. program mgr., 1988—; adj. faculty Va. Commonwealth U., Richmond, 1978-93. Contbr. articles to profl. jours., 1972-88. Named One of Outstanding Young Women of Am., 1974; EPA fellow, Va., 1974-76. Mem. Am. Soc. Limnology and Oceanography, N.Am. Lake Mgmt. Soc., N.Am. Benthological Soc., Ecol. Soc. Am., Romance Writers Am., Sisters in Crime. Democrat. Methodist. Office: Office Water Environ Rsch Stds PO Box 10009 Richmond VA 23240

GREGORY, TERENCE VAN BUREN, clergyman; b. Atlanta, Nov. 29, 1950; s. Vic Odell and Evelyn Ora (Gardner) G.; m. Leslie Christine Lytle, July 29, 1972; children: Joshua Adam, Rachel Leigh, Matthew Jordan. BA in Bible, Antioch Bapt. Coll., 1973; MRE, Mid-Am. Bapt. Theol. Sem., 1975. Ordained to ministry So. Bapt. Conv., 1972; lic. min. Youth min. 1st Bapt. Ch., Minden, La., 1976-77, Spencer Meml. Bapt. Ch., Tampa, Fla., 1977-80; pastor Crestview Bapt. Ch., Lakeland, Fla., 1980-83; min. pastoral care 1st Bapt. Ch., Lakeland, 1983-87; pastor Seminole Bapt. Ch., Tallahassee, 1987—; del., messenger So. Bapt. Conv., Atlanta, 1990-91. Mem. Fla. Bapt. Assn. (mem. exec. com., evangelism com. 1992-94, nominating com. 1990-91, keynote speaker ann. mtg. 1994). Republican. Office: Seminole Bapt Ch 2280 W Mission Rd Tallahassee FL 32304-2627

GREGORY, THOMAS RAYMOND, management consultant; b. N.Y.C., Aug. 15, 1951; s. Thomas Henry and Dorothy Lorraine (Crowe) G.; m. Mary Jo McCormick, June 9, 1973; children: Sean, Brian, Keith. BBA in Mktg., Pace U., 1973; MBA in Food Mktg., St. Joseph's U., 1979. Dist. mgr. Nabisco Brands Inc., N.Y.C., 1973-78; brand mgr. R.J. Reynolds Industries-Del Monte Corp., San Francisco, 1978-84; v.p. mktg. Iroquois Brands Ltd., Stamford, Conn., 1984-85; Eastern sales mgr. Borden Inc., Ft. Lee, N.J., 1985-87; sr. v.p., gen. mgr. Food Enterprises, Inc., Fairfield, N.J., 1987-89; prin. The Apogee Group, Inc., Tequesta, Fla., 1989—. Mem. Am. Mktg. Assn. Roman Catholic. Clubs: Innis Arden (Old Greenwich, Conn.), Ibis (West Palm Beach, Fla.), City Club Palm Beach (North Palm Beach, Fla.), Palm Beach Yacht (West Palm Beach). Avocations: sailing, autoracing, golf. Home: 71 Cinnamon Pl Tequesta FL 33469-2111

GREGORY, VICKI L., library and information scienc educator; b. Chattanooga, Feb. 13, 1950; d. John Allen and Mary (Carter) Lovelady; m. William Stanley Gregory, Aug. 15, 1970. AB, U. Ala., 1971, MA, 1973, MLS, 1974; PhD, Rutgers U., 1987. From audio-visual libr. to head dept. sys. & ops. Auburn U., Montgomery, Ala., 1976-88; from asst. prof. to assoc. prof. U. South Fla., Tampa, 1988—. Author, editor: The State and the Academic Library, 1993; editor: A Dynamic Tradition: A History of Alabama Academic Libraries, 1991; contbr. articles to profl. jours. Mem. ALA, Assn. Coll. & Rsch. Librs., Libr. Rsch. Roundtable (sec./treas. 1994-96), Assn. Libr. and Info. Sci. Educators, Southeastern Libr. Assn. (exec. bd. 1986-88), Fla. Libr. Assn., Ala. Libr. Assn. (exec. coun. 1988-89). Office: U South Fla Sch Libr Sci CIS 1040 4202 E Fowler Ave Tampa FL 33620

GREGORY, WANDA JEAN, paralegal, court reporter, singer, musician, writer; b. Little Rock, Sept. 7, 1925; d. John Albert and Angie (Thompson) Deming; student Corpus Christi (Tex.) Jr. Coll.; m. G. C. Gregory, Jan. 15, 1945 (div.); 1 son, Rex Carleton. Ofcl. ct. reporter, Nueces County, Tex., 1959-76, 36th Jud. Dist. Ct., San Patricio, Live Oak, McMullen, Aransas and Bee Counties, Tex., 1979-82; freelance court reporter, Corpus Christi, 1976-78, 82-85, Honolulu, 1979; paralegal, sec. Edmond J. Ford, Jr., 1985-90; freelance ct. reporter, 1990—. Vocalist with dance bands and jazz combos; pvt. tchr. jazz, pop singing and ballroom dancing; a founder Tex. Jazz Festival, 1960, appeared, 1961-82, 84-86, master of ceremonies, 1983; soloist Tex. Jazz Festival Soc. Interdenominational Choir, 1975—; bd. dirs. Corpus Christi Arts Coun., 1994; incorporator Tex. Jazz Festival Soc., 1968, bd. dirs. 1992—. Mem. Tex. Jazz Festival Soc. (founder 1968, past pres., sec. 1992-94), Am. Fedn. Musicians (sec. 1993, mem. exec. bd. 1994—). Democrat. Methodist. Home and Office: 6440 Everhart Rd Apt 2D Corpus Christi TX 78413-2601

GREGORY, WILLIAM JOSEPH, editor, writer; b. Hampton, Va., Aug. 26, 1949; s. Elbert Lee and Sophronia Carol (Dayberry) G.; m. Gail Marcy Weinberg, Jan. 28, 1979; children: Amanda Carol, Harper Lee. BA in Journalism, Calif. State U. Northridge, L.A., 1980. Assoc. editor Landscape & Irrigation, L.A., 1980-81, Arbor Age, L.A., 1980-81; asst. editor The Fin. Planner, Atlanta, 1981-82; editor Swimming Pool Age, Atlanta, 1982-85, Fairways & Greens, Atlanta, 1992-93, Admissions Mktg. Report, Atlanta, 1985—, Golf Georgia, Marietta, 1993—; freelance writer, Marietta, Ga., 1985—. With USAF, 1968-71. Mem. Golf Writers Assn. of Am. (assoc.), Internat. Network of Golf, Ga. State Golf Assn. Office: Admissions Mktg Report Ste 111 3050 Presidential Dr Atlanta GA 30340

GREIGG, RONALD EDWIN, lawyer; b. Washington, June 29, 1946; s. Edwin E. and Helen Marie (Marcy) G.; m. Patricia Anne Crowe, June 5, 1968; children: Elizabeth, Rebecca. BBA, Am. U., 1969, MBA in Fin., 1971; JD, Stetson U., 1976. Registered patent atty.; bar: Fla. 1976, D.C. 1978, Va. 1985, U.S. Dist. Ct. (mid. dist.) Fla. 1976, U.S. Dist. Ct. (ea. dist.) Va. 1988, U.S. Ct. Appeals (D.C. cir.) 1979, U.S. Ct. Appeals (fed. cir.) 1982, U.S. Supreme Ct. 1980. Assoc. David E. De Serio, St. Petersburg, Fla., 1977-78, Edwin E. Greigg, Washington, 1979-82, Harris, Barrett & Dew, St. Petersburg, Fla., 1982-84; ptnr. Greigg & Greigg, Arlington, Va., 1984—. Author: A Guide to the FTC Franchise Disclosure Rule, 1979, Patent Infringement Damages, 1988. Mem. ABA, Am. Intellectual property Law Assn., Assn. Internationale pour la Protection de la Propriete Industrielle, Soc. Automotive Engrs., D.C. Bar Assn., Fla. Bar Assn., Va. Bar Assn., Washington Area Lawyers for the Arts, Inst. of Trademark Agts. (London), Internat. Trademark Assn., Phi Alpha Delta. Republican. Episcopalian. Office: Greigg & Greigg 727 23rd St S Arlington VA 22202-2441

GREINER, ELLIS CHARLES, zoology educator; b. Spokane, Wash., Apr. 3, 1944; s. Harold L. and Margaret (Dickey) G.; m. Mary Rule, Sept. 9, 1967; children: Lori, Fred, Quinn. BS in Zoology, Mont. State U., 1966; MS in Zoology, U. Nebr., 1969, PhD in Zoology, 1971. Instr. zoology Iowa State U., Ames, 1972-74; rsch. assoc. biology Meml. U., St. John's, Nfld., Can., 1974-77; asst. prof. U. Fla. Coll. Vet. Med., Gainesville, 1978-81, assoc. prof., 1981-92, prof., 1992—; parasitologist Cayman Turtle Farm, Grand Cayman, 1977, 78; vector biologist Inter Am. Inst. Coop. Agr., San Jose, Costa Rica, 1981-85, WHO/FAO, 1982-83, USDA/Office Internat. Coops. and Devel., Ctr. Am./Caribbean, 1986-92. Contbr. 12 chpts. to books, more than 130 articles to profl. jours. CPR instr. U. Fla. Coll. Vet. Medicine, 1993—. Recipient Daniels Sr. Clin. Investigator award U. Fla. Coll. Vet. Medicine, 1996; NSF summer fellow, 1970. Mem. Am. Soc. Parasitologists, Am. Assn. Vet. Parasitologists, Wildlife Diseases Assn., Soc. Vector Ecologists, Assn. Avian Vets. Office: Univ Fla Coll Vet Medicine PO Box 110880 Gainesville FL 32611-0880

GREIVELL, JULIETTE ARNOLD, painter; b. Thomaston, Ga., Nov. 1, 1933; d. Hays Lavashious and Mary Bryan (Weaver) Arnold; m. Richard Hermes Greivell; children: Juliette Hightower, Mary Bryan, John Richard. BA, U. Va., 1955; postgrad., Atlanta Art Inst., 1956, Memphis Acad. Art, 1960, U. Ga., 1961-62, Layton Sch. of Art, 1970, Alverno Coll., 1971-72. Tchr. Atlanta Art Assn., 1957-58, Upson County (Ga.) Bd. Edn., 1962-63, Cudahy (Wis.) Bd. Edn., 1972-80. Numerous one woman shows and portrait commns.; exhibited in numerous group shows, including War Meml. Art Ctr., Mils., U. Wis.-Mils., Charles Allis Mus., Milw., New Orleans Art Assn., Ga. Tech Gallery, Atlanta, Western Colo. Ctr. for the Arts, Grand Junction, Augusta Art Assn., Springfield (Mass.) Art League, Art Assn. of Harrisburg, Pa., Lake Worth (Fla.) Art League, Hoyt Inst. Art, Pa., Nat. Arts Club, N.Y.C., Chattahooche Art Guild, LaGrange, Ga., Salmagundi Club, N.Y.C., others. Recipient Best of Show award League Milw. Artists, 1984, 85, 86, Bronze award Wis. Women in the Arts Nat. Exhbn., 1984, Winsor & Newton award New Orleans Art Assn.., 1st prize Mass. Arts League, Grumbacher Gold medallion Harrisburg Art Assn., Judges Choice Dekalb Coun. for Arts and Decatur Arts Alliance, 1991, others. Mem. Atlanta Portrait Soc., Inc. (mem. of merit). Studio: Studio Pinxit 220 Cobbtown Rd PO Box 426 Thomaston GA 30286

GREMMEL, GILBERT CARL, family physician; b. Robstown, Tex., Nov. 29, 1922; s. Albert Henry and Tennie Elizabeth Gremmel; m. Helen Kistler, 1949 (div. 1965); children: Gilbert Jr., Shirley, Rebecca, Susan, Curtis, James; m. Ilse Elizabeth Schreiber Bell, Apr. 23, 1969; children: Erika Barbara, Albert Henry, Heidi. MD, U. Tex., Galveston, 1951; BA, U. Tex., San Antonio, 1978, BBA in Fin., 1982. Diplomate Am. Bd. Family Practice. Intern U.S. Army, San Antonio, 1951-52; pvt. practice Boerne, Tex., 1955-64, San Antonio, 1964-82, Sonora, Tex., 1982-86, Halletsville, Tex., 1986-88; family physician Med. Networks, Houston, 1988, Med. Clinic, Mabank, Tex., 1988-90; pvt. practice Shamrock, Tex., 1990-92, Seminole, Tex., 1992—; chief of staff Meml. Hosp., Seminole, Tex., 1995—; emergency physician S.W. Med. Assocs., Rockport, Tex., 1990—. Trustee Boerne County Line Ind. Sch. Dist., 1959-62; pres. San Antonio Community Dept. of Family Practitioners, 1980. With U.S. Army, 1943-46, 51-53. Mem. Am. Assn. Family Practitioners, Five-County Med. Soc. (v.p. 1993, pres. 1994). Republican. Home: 1409 SW 8th St Seminole TX 79360 Office: 208 NW 8th St Seminole TX 79360-3322

GRENIER, EDWARD JOSEPH, III, foundation administrator; b. Washington, May 18, 1961; s. Edward Joseph Jr. and Patricia Joan (Cederle) G.; m. Lynette Alyssa Ciervo, Sept. 21, 1991. BA in Communications, Villanova U., 1983. Fin. planner Wallace Fin. Group, Washington, 1983-85; investment broker Smith Barney, Harris Upham, Inc., Washington, 1985-88; investment cons. Legg Mason Wood Walker, Inc., Washington, 1988-90; dir. devel. Woodstock Theol. Ctr. Georgetown U., Washington, 1991-93; exec. dir. Assn. for Healthcare Philanthropy Found., Falls Church, Va., 1993-96; pres. Jr. Achievement, Bethesda, Md., 1996—. Mem. bd. advisors Columbia Lighthouse for Blind, Washington, 1988—; treas. Combined Health Appeal, Bethesda, Md., 1990-92, v.p. 1992-94, bd. dirs., pres., 1994-96, chmn. bd., 1996—; vice chmn. Davis Meml. Goodwill Industries, Washington, 1990-92, bd. dirs., 1988-92; 1996 Olympic Torch Relay Com., 1996—. Mem. Am. Soc. of Assn. Execs., Nat. Soc. for Fund Raising Execs., Nat. Family Caregivers Assn. (bd. dirs. 1991-94), D.C. Assn. for Retarded Citizens (bd. dirs. 1984-85). Home: 1602 Auburn Ave Rockville MD 20850-1144 Office: Jr Achievement 7300 Whittier Blvd Bethesda MD 20817

GRENINGER, EDWIN THOMAS, educator; b. Montoursville, Pa., Apr. 12, 1918; s. Fred R. and Martha (Cutler) G. Student Susquehanna U., 1936-38; A.B., Gettysburg Coll., 1941; M.A., Temple U., 1947; Ph.D., U. Pa., 1958; m. Jane Torbert, June 26, 1948 (dec. Mar. 1963); m. Gem Kate Taylor, Oct. 26, 1968 (dec. Apr. 1994); m. Joan Cross, Mar. 23, 1996. Instr. history Valparaiso U., 1948-49, Pa. State U., Ogontz, 1950, 52-53, Wilkes Coll., 1951-52; asst. prof. history East Tenn. State U., Johnson City, 1958-61, assoc. prof. 1961-64, prof. history, 1964-86, prof. emeritus, 1986. Writer ann. travelogue, 1963—. Mem. com. on higher edn. Synod Va., United Luth. Ch. Am., 1959-63, Southeastern Synod, 1963-77; mem. human studies subcom. Mountain Home VA Ctr., 1985; sec. ch. coun. Our Saviour, 1966-94; mem. ins. and ret. com. East Tenn. State U., 1988-91. With AUS, 1942-46. Mem. Luth. Hist. Conf., So. Hist. Assn. (European sect.), Internat. Council for Edn. of Tchrs., Lexington Group, AAUP (chpt. v.p. 1969-70, pres. 1970-72), Phi Delta Kappa, Pi Kappa Alpha, Pi Gamma Mu (treas. local chpt. 1961-86, gov. Tenn. province 1975-87). Donor Greninger prize in history Gettysburg Coll., Fred R. Greninger award in homiletics Luth. So. Theol. Sem. Author: Fifteen Days in Russia, 1966; book rev. editor Social Sci., 1961-62; editor Otey's Jour., 1994. Home: 2210 Wyndale Rd Johnson City TN 37604-7037

GRENNAN, JIM, lawyer; b. Bradford, Pa., Mar. 19, 1933; s. George Gilbert and Grace (Murray) G.; m. Patricia June Ridgway, 1954; children: Mark Tracy, Jon Gilbert. BA, U. Tulsa, 1958, LLB, 1961. Bar: Okla. 1961, U.S. Dist. Ct. 1962, U.S. Ct. Appeals (10th cir.) 1971, U.S. Supreme Ct. 1979. Adjuster claim supr. Aetna Life & Casualty Co., Tulsa and Baton Rouge, La., 1960-68; staff atty. Fireman's Fund Ins. Co., Oklahoma City, 1968-71; assoc. Don Manners, Inc., Oklahoma City, 1971-77; pres. Jim Grennan, Inc., P.C., Oklahoma City, 1977—. Author appellate briefs, 1971—. Adv. com Svcs. to Deaf & Hearing Impaired, Dept. Human Svcs., Oklahoma City, 1989. With USN, USNR, 1951-59. Mem. Okla. Trial Lawyers Assn., Okla. Bar Assn., Okla. County Bar Assn., Phi Delta Phi., Masons. Democrat. Methodist. Home: 7612 NW 25th Ter Bethany OK 73008-4926 Office: 2000 N Classen Blvd Oklahoma City OK 73106-6013

GRES, DUSTY BEVERLY SNIPES, librarian; b. West Palm Beach, Fla., May 3, 1947; d. John Etheridge and M. Merle (Williams) Snipes; m. Wright Waller Gres, Sept. 7, 1968; 1 child, Alan Kyle. BA in Edn., U. Fla., 1969; MA in Libr. Sci., U. S. Fla., 1981. Cert. libr., Ga. G-5 tchr. grades 6-8 Mango (Fla.) Bapt. Sch., 1972-78; pub. svcs. libr. Maitland (Fla.) Pub. Libr., 1981-86; dir. Maitland Pub. Libr., 1986-92, Ohoopee Regional Libr. System, Vidalia, Ga., 1992—. Sec. Centennial Com., Maitland, 1985; bd. dirs. Additions of Orange County, Orlando, Fla., 1985-91, Vidalia Kiwanis Club, 1996—; mem. Parks and Recreation Bd., Maitland, Fla., 1990-92; mem. bd. trustees Altama Art & Hist. Mus., Vidalia, Ga., 1996—, Franklinia Playhouse, Vidalia, 1996—. Mem. ALA, Nat. Storytelling Assn., Toastmasters Internat., Fla. Storytellers Guild, Kiwanis Internat., Southeastern Libr. Assn., Ga. Libr. Assn. Democrat. Presbyterian. Home: PO Box 1003 Vidalia GA 30475-1003 Office: Ohoopee Regional Libr System 610 Jackson St Vidalia GA 30474-2835

GRESHAM, ANN ELIZABETH, retailer, horticulturist executive, consultant; b. Richmond, Va., Oct. 11, 1933; d. Allwin Stagg and Ruby Scott (Faber) Gresham. Student, Peace Coll., Raleigh, N.C., 1950-52, East Carolina U., 1952-53, Penland Sch., N.C., 1953-54, Va. Commonwealth U., 1960-64. Owner, prin. Ann Gresham's Gift Shop, Richmond, 1953-56; pres., treas. Gresham's Garden Ctr., Inc., Richmond, 1955-79; v.p. Gresham's Nursery, Inc., Richmond, 1959-73, pres., treas., 1973-84; pres., treas. Gresham's Country Store, Richmond, 1964—; tchr., 1982—. Bd. dirs. Bainbridge Community Ministry, 1979, Handworkshop, 1984-89; class agt. Peace Coll., Raleigh, 1987-88, mem. alumnae council, 1987, 88—, bd. visitors, 1987-93; focus group mem. Hand Workshop, Richmond, 1983, bd. dirs., 1984-87. Mem. Midlothian Antique Dealers (treas. 1975-79), Richmond Quilt Guild (chpt. v.p. 1983-84), Nat. Needlework Assn., Quilt Inst., Am. Hort. Soc. Episcopalian. Clubs: Chesmond Women's (v.p. 1979-80), James River Woman's (Richmond) (tres. 1990-92). Home and Office: Gresham's Inc 2324 Logan St Richmond VA 23235-3462

GRESSETTE, LAWRENCE M., JR., utilities executive; b. St. Matthews, S.C., Feb. 23, 1932; s. Lawrence Marion and Florence Beech (Howell) G.; m. Felicia Arrington Gold, June 19, 1954; children: Felicia Ann Ruf, Virginia G. Spencer, L. Marion III. BS with honors, Clemson U., 1954; LLB with honors, U. S.C., 1959. Ptnr. Gressette & Prickett, St. Matthews, 1959-82; sr. v.p. S.C. Electric and Gas Co. subs. SCANA Corp., Columbia, 1983—, exec. v.p., 1983-87, vice chmn., 1987; chmn., pres., CEO SCANA Corp., Columbia, 1985—; chmn., CEO S.C. Electric & Gas Co. and other SCANA subs.; bd. dirs. Watchovia Corp., S.C. Nat. Corp., S.C. Nat. Bank, Telecom *USA, Atlanta, SouthernNet Corp., Atlanta, The Conf. Board, Palmetto Bus. Forum. Bd. dirs. Columbia C. of C., S.C. Bus. & Industry Edn. Com. Adv. Coun., S.C. Orch. Assn., Clemson U. Rsch. Found., S.C. Found. Ednl. and Econ. Excellence; trustee Clemson U., Columbia Art Assn., U. S.C. Bus. Partnership Found., Children's Trust Fund Adv. Bd., ETV Endowment of S.C., Columbia Mus. Art, Midlands Tech. Coll. Found.; campaign chmn. United Way of Midlands, 1992, group chmn., 1984, v.p. planning, 1985, 86; chmn. Midlands March of Dimes WalkAm./Teamwalk, 1985, Coun. College Pres. Blue Ribbon Com. on Higher Edn.; mem. Gov. Restructuring Com.; steering com. S.C Gov. Sch. Arts. 1st lt. inf. U.S. Army, 1954-56. Mem. ABA, S.C. Bar Assn., Edison Electric Inst., Southeastern Electric Exch., Palmetto Soc. (Columbia), Newcomen Soc. Baptist. Office: SC Electric & Gas Co 1426 Main St # 764 Columbia SC 29201-2834*

GRESSO, VERNON RIDDLE, insurance company executive; b. Charlotte, Mich., Sept. 27, 1927; s. Vernon Ruse and Bernice (Riddle) G.; m. Rae Yvonne Norlander, Aug. 29, 1955; children: Kimberly Jane, Tyler Merritt, Steven Riddle. BSBA, Wayne State U., 1951; postgrad. law sch., U. Tex., 1955-56. Dealer rep. AirKem Inc., N.Y.C., 1951-55; sales rep. Mut. Benefit Life, Houston, 1957-58, Home Life of N.Y., Houston, 1958-62; gen. agent, owner Vern Gresso & Assocs., Houston, 1962—; pres., ptnr. R.E. Lee of Houston, Inc., 1980-95, R.E. Lee of Texas, Inc., 1980-95; v.p., ptnr. R.E. Lee of Cayman, Inc., Cayman Islands, 1980—. Product designer: Co. News Jour., Contact, 1980. Coach Houston Little League, 1972-77; fin. com. Palmer Meml. Episcopal Ch., Houston, 1976; gen. Rep. Party, Houston, 1975—; leader, Boys Scouts Am., Houston, 1975-77. With USN, 1946-48, PTO. Recipient various community-related bus. awards. Mem. Crown Life Gen. Agts. Assn. (pres. 1970), Houston City Club, Brae Burn Country Club, Delta Sigma Pi. Episcopalian.

GRETSER, GEORGE WESTFALL, publisher; b. Frankfurt, Germany, Mar. 16, 1947; came to U.S., 1948; s. George Rushmore and Edythe (Westfall) G.; m. Linda J. Goff, Jan. 25, 1969; 1 child, Jennifer L. BJ, U. Tex., 1969; MBA, Keller Grad. Sch. Mgmt., Chgo., 1982. Advt. dir. Comms. Pub Corp., Denver, 1970-76; pub. Profl. Remodeling mag. Harcourt Brace Jovanovich Publs., Chgo., 1976-82; with Restaurants & Instns. mag. Cahners Pub. Co., Des Plaines, Ill., 1982-86; COO, pub. Brighton Sq. Pub., Austin, Tex., 1986-87; pub. East/West Network, N.Y.C., 1987-88; pres. ACPI pub. div. ClubCorp, pub. Pvt. Clubs mag. Assoc. Club Publs., Inc., Dallas, 1988-96; mag. mgr. L.A. Times Mag., 1996; advt. dir. Chgo. Mag., 1996—.

GRETZINGER, RALPH EDWIN, III, management consultant; b. Louisville, Sept. 7, 1948; s. Ralph Edwin Jr. and Martha Irene (Jennings) G.; m. Jewel Jean Rocker, Mar. 21, 1970; children: Ralph Edwin IV, Sarah Elizabeth. BS in Applied Math., Ga. Inst. Tech., 1970; MBA, U. Utah, 1974. Group mgr. Prudential Ins. Co., Cin., 1974-76; owner, regional office mgr. Hewitt Assocs., Lincolnshire, Ill., 1976-78, Dayton, Ohio, 1978-81, Dallas, 1981—. Trustee Child Care Partnership of Dallas, 1985-90. Served with U.S. Army, 1971-74. Mem. S.W. Pension Conf., Ga. Tech. Club of North Tex. (pres. 1986-88), Beta Gamma Sigma. Roman Catholic. Office: Hewitt Assocs 600 Las Colinas Blvd E Ste 210 Irving TX 75039-5616

GREWELLE, LARRY ALLAN, travel agency owner; b. Longview, Wash., Sept. 10, 1937; s. John Vincent and Ruth (Hansicky) G.; m. Marjorie Anne McGee, Aug. 31, 1964; 1 child, John Lawrence. AA, City Coll. San Francisco, 1961; BA, San Francisco State U., 1963; MPA, Golden Gate U., 1970. Personnel mgr. Spain Area Exch., Madrid, 1965-66, Turkey Area Exch., Izmir, 1966-68; personnel specialist Golden Gate Exch. Region, San Francisco, 1968-70, Hdqrs. U.S. Army, USAF, Dallas, 1970-72; personnel mgr. Philippine Exch., Clark AFB, 1972-74; personnel specialist Alamo Exch. Region, San Antonio, 1974-78; chief personnel Western Distbn. Region, Oakland, Calif., 1978-82; chief human resources S.E. Exch. Region, Montgomery, Ala., 1982-88; travel agy. mgr. Barry's Travel Ctr., Montgomery, 1988—. Pres. Capitol City Civitan, Montgomery, 1989-90; bd. dirs. Montgomery Area Food Bank, 1989-95, One Montgomery, 1992—, Capri Cmty. Film Soc., 1983—, pres., 1984-85; mem. Untied Way Cmty. Coun., 1993-95; bd. dirs. Internat. Assistance Project Ala., Ala. Prison Project. Sgt. U.S. Army, 1957-60. Democrat. Presbyterian. Home: 1220 Westmoreland Ave Montgomery AL 36106-2018 Office: Barrys Travel Ctr Inc 514 Cloverdale Rd Montgomery AL 36106-1855

GRIDER, KELLY VERNON, engineering executive; b. Scottsboro, Ala., May 28, 1933; s. Kelly Thomas and Mildred Anna (Morris) G.; children: Donna Deneé, Lisa Susanne, Kelly Vernon; m. Murlene Taylor, June 2, 1982. BSEE, U. Ala., 1958, MS in Engring., 1965, PhD of Elec. Engring., 1972. Registered profl. engr., Ala. Aerophysics engr. Gen. Dynamics, Ft. Worth, 1958-59; engr., sr. engr. Martin-Marietta Corp., Orlando, Fla., 1959-62; from aerospace engr. to supr. U.S. Army Missile Command, Redstone Arsenal, Ala., 1962-82; sr. exec. U.S. Army Missile Command, Redstone Arsenal, 1982—. Contbr. articles to profl. jours. With USAF, 1951-54. Recipient Presdl. Rank Meritorious Exec. award, 1992. Mem. IEEE, Am. Def. Preparedness Assn., Assn. U.S. Army, Soc. for Computer Simulation, Tau Beta Pi, Eta Kappa Nu. Office: US Army Missile Command AMSMI-RD-SS Redstone Arsenal AL 35898

GRIEDER, TERENCE, art history educator, artist; b. Cedar Rapids, Iowa, Sept. 2, 1931; s. Calvin and Florence (Peck) G.; m. Dagmar Grieder, July 9, 1972. BA, U. Colo., 1953; MS, U. Wis., 1956; MA, U. Pa., 1959, PhD, 1961. Instr. art El Dorado, Kans., 1953-54, U. Wis., Milw., 1956-57; asst. prof. art Conn. Coll., 1960-61; prof. art history U. Tex., 1961—; dir. archaeolog. project in Preceramic ruins, La Galgada, Peru, 1976-85, ruins of Pashash, Peru, 1969-73. Author: Art & Archaeology of Pashash, Peru, 1978, Origins of Pre-Columbian Art, 1982, La Galgada, Peru: A Preceramic Culture, 1989, Artist and Audience, 2d edit., 1996. Office: U Tex Dept Art & Art History Austin TX 78712

GRIEDER, THEODORE, poet, editor; b. Globe, Ariz., Feb. 25, 1926; s. Theodore and Lula (Gooch) G.; m. Lucile Leigh, June 6, 1986. BA, U. So. Calif., 1948; MA, Stanford U., 1950, PhD, 1957; MLS, U. Calif., Berkeley, 1961. Instr. La. State, Baton Rouge, 1953-55; acting instr. Stanford U., Calif., 1955-57; asst. prof. U. Nev., Reno, 1957-61; projects dir. Isaac Foot Libr. U. Calif., Santa Barbara, 1962; chief bibliographer U. Calif., Davis, 1963-66; assoc. curator NYU, N.Y.C., 1966-70, curator, 1970-81, ret., 1981; cons. AMS Press, N.Y.C., 1966-80, various N.Y. booksellers and pubs., 1966-80; cons., editor Gale Rsch., Detroit, 1970-77. Author: (poetry) I Shall Come at You, 3rd edit., 1988, The High Country, 1985, The Broken Country, 1989, Coastlands, 1994; author, editor 51 acad. vols. poetry. With USNR. Recipient Rsch. award Am. Philosophical Inst., 1965-71, Rsch. award ALA, 1976-78. Mem. MLA (life), Grolier Club, Phi Beta Kappa. Democrat. Methodist. Home: 276 Ocean Palm Flagler Beach FL 32136-4113

GRIER, BARBARA G. (GENE DAMON), editor, lecturer, writer; b. Cin., Nov. 4, 1933; d. Phillip Strang and Dorothy Vernon (Black) Grier; life ptnr. Donna J. McBride, 1972—; grad. high sch. Author: The Lesbian in Literature, 1967, (with others) 2d edit., 1975, 3d edit., 1981, 4th edit.; The Least of These (in Sisterhood is Powerful), 1970; The Index, 1974; Lesbiana, 1976; The Lesbian Home Jour., 1976; The Lavender Herring, 1976; Lesbian Lives, 1976, The Mysterious Naiad, 1994, The First Time Ever, 1995, Dancing in the Dark, 1996; editor: (with Katherine V. Forrest) The Erotic Naiad, 1992, The Romantic Naiad, 1993; pub. The Ladder mag., 1970-72, fiction and poetry editor, 1966-67, editor, 1968-72; dir. promotion Naiad Press, Reno, Nev., 1973—, treas., 1976—, v.p., gen. mgr., Tallahassee, Fla., 1980—, CEO, 1987—, pres., 1995—. Democrat. Home: RR 1 Box 3565 Alligator Point FL 32346 Office: Naiad Press Inc PO Box 10543 Tallahassee FL 32302-2543

GRIER, LEAMON FOREST, social services administrator; b. Augusta, Ga., Sept. 17, 1935; s. Gilbert Grier and Cleo Grier Norris; m. Marion Samuel Smith, Apr., 1960 (div. 1968); children: Frank O., Donald Smith, Susan Grier Bowman; m. Shirley Burroughs Graddy, June 19, 1992; children: Cheryl Cofer, Pamela N. Gordon. BA in Phys. Edn., Morris Brown Coll., 1959; postgrad., Rutgers U., 1964; MA in Community Psychology, U. D.C., 1979. Tng. officer Leadership Inst. for Community Devel., Washington, 1970-74; coll. coord. Moton Mission Edn. Opportunity Ctr., Washington, 1974-76; coord. rsch. devel. and planning, psychologist Youth Pride, Inc., Washington, 1978-81; cons. Howard U. Sch. Edn., Washington, 1981-84; tng. provider NIH, Washington, 1985—; interim exec. dir. Bethlehem Community Ctr., Inc., Augusta, Ga., 1992-93, exec. dir., 1993—; part-time prof. Voorhees Coll. Denmark, S.C., 1993—, cons. pres., 1974—; pres. Leamon F. Grier and Assocs., Washington, 1981—; field reseacher U.S. Office Edn., Washington, 1992—; program developer Laney Walker BTC, Augusta, 1991-92; evaluator Shorter Coll. Title III Program, Little Rock, 1980-86; payment adminstr. Rent Rollback Teanents Movements, Washington, 1979—; cons. mgmt. and manpower Fauquier County (Va.) Cmty. Action Agy., 1979-85. Author: Theory of Endowment Development, 1977, Roles and Responsibilities of Project Managers, 1981, Recruitment and

Admissions, 1981. Active Good Hope Bapt. Ch.; vol. Ward I Dems. Coord. Com., 1980-83, First New Horizon Bapt. Ch., Clinton, Md.; bd. dirs. Dorchester House Tenants Assn., 1979—. With U.S. Army, 1960-62. Mem. Morris Brown Coll. Alumni Assn., John M. Tutt Quarterback Club, Kappa Alpha Psi. Home: 2326 Shadowood Dr Augusta GA 30906-2936

GRIFEL, STUART SAMUEL, management engineer, consultant; b. Bklyn., May 21, 1947; s. Harry Grifel and Selma (Goldblatt) Spitalnik; m. Barbara Palermo, Nov. 27, 1977. BA with distinction, Ariz. State U., 1969; MPA, Bernard Baruch Coll. CUNY, 1978; MBA, Suffolk U., 1986. Mgmt. intern City of Kansas City, Mo., 1978; mgmt. auditor State of Mass., Boston, 1980-82; sr. methods analyst Shawmut Bank, Boston, 1983-87; mgmt. engr. A.T. Hudson & Co., Inc., Paramus, N.J., 1987-88; mgmt./indsl. engr. City of Tampa, Fla., 1988-91; sr. cons. KPMG Peat Marwick, LLP, Tampa, Fla., 1995—. Author: Performance Measurement and Budgetary Decision Making, 1993, Organizational Culture: Its Importance in Performance Management, 1994. Reader, Radio Reading Svcs. for the Blind, Tampa, 1993—. Mem. Am. Soc. Pub. Adminstrn. (exec. com. sect. on mgmt. sci. and policy analysis 1990—), Nat. Ctr. Pub. Productivity (staff assoc. 1992—), Fla. Govt. Fin. Officer's Assn. (com. mem. 1992—). Home: 15911 Farringham Dr Tampa FL 33647-1109 Office: KPMG Peat Marwick 100 N Tampa St Ste 2400 Tampa FL 33602-5809

GRIFFEY, KAREN ROSE, special education educator; b. Phila., May 15, 1955; d. Arnold and Jacqueline (Wasserman) Salaman; m. Kenneth Paul Griffey, June 18, 1988; 1 child, Jessica; stepchildren: Kristina, Joseph. BS in Elem. Edn., W. Chester U., Pa., 1977; cert. Paralegal Studies, Nat. Ctr. Paralegal Tng., Atlanta, 1986; MS in Interrelated, U. Ga., 1994. Adult habilitation program Jewish Vocat. Svc., Phila., 1977-79; instr. Phila. Sch. Sys., 1979-81; tchr. 3rd grade Fla. Sch. Sys., Fort Myers, 1981-86; paralegal Atlanta, 1986-89; tchr. Interrelated Sharp Middle Sch., Covington, Ga., 1989-91; tchr. Spl. Kindergarten Rorterdale and Fairview Elem., Covington, Ga., 1991—; tchr., liaison, bd. mem., PAC rep., bldg. rep. Tchrs. Assn. Lee County, Fort Myers, Fla., 1981-86. Tchr. liaison Senators and Reps. in Fla. Legis., Tallahassee, 1981-86; PAC bd., 1981-86; exec. bd. mem. Leadership Team. of Tchrs. Assn. Lee County, Ft. Myers, Fla., 1981-86; Bargaining Team mdm. Tchrs. Assn. Lee County, Ft. Myers, Fla., 1981-86. Recipient Svc. award for working with handicapped, Phila. Sch. Sys., 1973; Phila scholarship Phils Sch. Sys., Mayor's Sch., Phila., 1973; NEA Svc. award in Edn., NEA, Ft. Myers, Fla., 1980. Mem. Coun. for Exceptional Children, Nat. Mus. of Women in the Arts, B'Nai B'rith, Spl. Olympics, Nat. Multiple Sclerosis Soc., Kappa Delta Pi. Democrat. Jewish. Home: 65 Stone Creek Dr Covington GA 30209-9053

GRIFFIN, A. T., advertising and agricultural products executive; b. 1940. Sec., treas. Griffin & Brand Sales Agy., Inc., Hereford, Tex., 1964—, pres., 1988. Office: Griffin & Brand Sales Agency Inc PO Box 833 Hereford TX 79045*

GRIFFIN, BARBARA CONLEY, kindergarten educator, antique store owner; b. Valdosta, Ga., Mar. 29, 1955; d. Paul and Sarah Elizabeth (Ganas) Conley; children: Stephanie E., Paul E. AA in Art, Middle Ga. Coll., Cochran, 1975; EdB, Mercer U., 1977, MEd in Early Childhood, 1986. Cert. early childhood and middle grades edn. tchr., Ga. Kindergarten tchr. Houston County Bd. Edn., Perry, Ga., 1978-80; 1st grade tchr. Houston County Bd. Edn., Bonaire, Ga., 1980-87, kindergarten tchr., 1987—, faculty advisor student coun. and tchr. empowerment com., 1991-95, tchr. empowerment chmn., 1992-94; owner Timeless Treasures Antiques and Collectibles, Bonaire, Ga. Mem. PTO, 1980—, Parents Assisting With Students, 1989—; tchr. Shirley Hills Bapt. Ch.-Tng. Union, Warner Robins, Ga., 1987-91; summer missionary Inst. Caribbean Missions, Jamaica, 1992; mem. Unity Bapt. Ch., 1995—. Recipient Exemplary Svc. award Pilot Club of Houston County, Warner Robins, Ga., 1990, Tchr. of Yr. award Bonaire Elem. Sch., 1990. Mem. PAGE (state and local chpts.), Internat. Reading Assn. (state and local chpts., v.p. and pres. HOPE reading coun. 1993—), Bonaire/Kathleen Jaycettes (sec. 1979-81, Outstanding Young Woman of the Year award 1981), Warner Robins Jr. Womens Club (co-chair spl. projects 1991, corr. sec. 1993, presenter 1993 conf. children's lit., Athens). Democrat. Mem. Southern Baptist Ch. Home: 202 Williams Dr Bonaire GA 31005 Office: Bonaire Elem Sch PO Box 729 Bonaire GA 31005-0729

GRIFFIN, CHRISTOPHER OAKLEY, hospital professional; b. Memphis, Apr. 27, 1970; s. Charles Ray Griffin and Gladys Lee (Oakley) Slappey. BA in English, Miss. Coll., 1992; MA in English, Baylor U., 1996; postgrad., U. Dallas, 1995—. Tchg. asst. dept. English Baylor U., Waco, Tex., 1993-95; hosp. worker Irving (Tex.) Healthcare Sys., 1996—. Author of poetry, criticism, philosophy. Presdl. scholar Miss. Coll., Clinton, 1988-92.

GRIFFIN, EREN G., nursing educator; b. Antigua, West Indies, Jan. 30; d. John and Hilda Griffin. Diploma in nursing, Radcliffe Sch. Nursing, Oxford, Eng., 1966; diploma in dietetics, No. Poly., London, 1968; BA in Vocat. Edn., Coll. V.I., St. Croix, 1986. Nurse Radcliffe Infirmary, Oxford; therapeutic dietitian Western Meml. Hosp., Corner Brook, NF, Can.; nurse Dept. Health, Christiansted, V.I.; health occupations educator, vocat. dept. Dept. Edn., Christiansted. With Women's Royal Army Corps, 1960-63. Mem. Brit. Dietetic Assn., Am. Fedn. Tchrs. Baha'i faith.

GRIFFIN, G. LEE, banker; b. 1938. Chmn., chief exec. officer Premier Bancorp, Baton Rouge; also Premier Bank; with La. Nat. Bank, Baton Rouge, 1960—. Office: Premier Bancorp Inc 451 Florida St Baton Rouge LA 70801-1700*

GRIFFIN, GLEN J., company executive; b. 1938. BS, U. Ala., 1963. CPA. Acct. Peat, Marwick, Mitchell & Co., 1963-68; with Bruno's Inc., 1968—, exec. v.p., CFO, treas., sec., 1980-92, exec. v.p., CFO, treas., asst. sec., 1992—. Office: Bruno's Inc 300 Research Pky Birmingham AL 35211-4447*

GRIFFIN, GREGG RUSSELL, utilities supervisor; b. Waco, Tex., July 7, 1957; s. Floyd Funnell and Elizabeth (Reece) G.; m. Cynthia L. Stegall, July 5, 1980 (div.); children: Justin R., Derrick G., Morgan L. B Indsl. Engring., Ga. Tech. U., 1979. Functional engineer Houston Light & Power Co., 1979-83; distbn. engr. Tampa (Fla.) Electric Co., 1983-85, prin. engr., 1985-88, prin. engr. substation ops., 1988-91, prin. engr. load mgmt. ops., 1991-92, supr., sr. engr. load mgmt. ops., 1992-95; engr. TECOM, Inc. Interactive Sys., Tampa, 1995—. Mem. IEEE, Nat. Mgmt. Assns., Electric Coun. Fla., Power Engring. Soc., Ga. Tech. Alumni Assn. (pres. 1985-89). Republican. Baptist. Home: 6303 W Riverchase Dr Tampa FL 33637-5657 Office: TECOM Inc 702 N Franklin St Tampa FL 33602-4418

GRIFFIN, HAYNES GLENN, telecommunications industry executive; b. Charlotte, N.C., Mar. 3, 1947; s. Clarence Alonzo and Elizabeth (Shull) G.; m. Virginia Renick, Feb. 22, 1975; children: Jeffrey Taylor, Michael Jason, Carter Haynes. BA, Princeton (N.J.) U., 1969. Pres. Griffin, Glenn & Griffin Co., Amelia Island, Fla., 1968-90, v.p., 1990—; pres. Maj. Oil Co., Greensboro, N.C., 1970-86; pres., CEO, co-founder Vanguard Cellular Systems, Inc., Greensboro, 1984—; bd. dirs. Lexington Global Asset Mgrs. Inc., Geotek Comms., Inc., Ctr. for Creative Leadership; mem. U.S. Adv. Coun. on Nat. Info. Infrastructure; chmn. bd. dirs. Internat. Wireless Comm. Inc.; bd. dirs. Inter Act, Inc. Mem. nat. alumni exec. com. Princeton U., 1983-85, Greensboro Devel. Corp., 1990—; mem. alumni adv. coun. Woodberry Forest (Va.) Sch., 1990-92, trustee, 1992—; trustee Greensboro Day Sch., 1990—, former chmn. bd. Mem. Cellular Telecomms. Industry Assn. (exec. com. 1986—, chmn. 1989-90, bd. dirs.), Young Pres.'s Orgn., Greensboro Rotary. Presbyterian. Office: Vanguard Cellular Systems Inc Ste # 300 2002 Pisgah Church Rd Greensboro NC 27455

GRIFFIN, JEFFREY FARROW, surgeon; b. Dallas, 1946. MD, Tulane U., 1974. Diplomate Am. Bd. Surgery, Am. Bd. Colon and Rectal Surgery. Intern Ochsner Found. Hosp., New Orleans, 1974-75, resident in gen. surgery, 1975-79; fellow in colon and rectal surgery U. Minn., Mpls., 1979-80; now pvt. practice New Orleans; mem. staff East Jefferson Gen. Hosp., Metairie, La., So. Bapt. Hosp., La.; clin. asst. prof. medicine Tulane U. Mem. ACS, Am. Soc. Colon and Rectal Surgery. Office: 2633 Napoleon Ave Ste 915 New Orleans LA 70115-6357*

GRIFFIN, JOHN JOSEPH, JR., chemist, video producer; b. Chgo., Sept. 11, 1946; s. John Joseph, Sr. and Louise (Griswold) G.; m. Ramona Rodriguez, Apr. 19, 1969; 1 child, Marcus. BS, Tex. A&M U., 1972, MS, 1974. Lab. technician Johns-Manville, Chgo., 1964-66; chemist, rsch. chemist Dow Chemical USA, Tex. Divsn., Freeport, 1974-78; sr. chemist Soltex Polymers, Deer Pk., Tex., 1978-80; plant chemist Air Products & Chemicals, Pasadena, Tex., 1980-84; quality assurance supr. Core Lab., Chromaspec Divsn., Houston, 1984-88; plant chemist and quality assurance supr. Ga. Gulf Corp., Pasadena, Tex., 1988-95; synthesis chemist KMCO, Inc., Crosby, Tex., 1995—; propr. Petro-Star, Houston, 1995-96; propr. and owner JJ's Quality Custom Video, Houston, 1986-88; propr., prodr. Pro-Star Video Prodns., Houston, 1988—; video prodr. J. Frank Dobie and So. Houston H.S. Graduation, U. Houston Graduation, also weddings and seminars, v.p. 1996—. Pres. Kirkwood Civic Club, Houston, 1991-96, v.p. 1996—; bd. dirs. Southbelt Security Alliance, Houston, 1988—, Houston Better Bus. Bur., 1996. With USAF, 1966-70. Mem. ASTM (D-16 com. aromatic compounds and D-2 petro products and lubricants, D-2 petroleum products and lubricants), Am. Chem. Soc. Office: KMCO Inc Crosby TX 77532

GRIFFIN, KENTON GRAHAM, city administrator; b. Mt. Vernon, Ohio, May 16, 1954; s. Lawrence Eugene and Marilyn Jean (Oldham) G.; m. Candace Lee Wells, Aug. 9, 1975; children: David Lawrence, Gregory Lee, Trevor Graham. BA, Ea. Ky. U., 1976; M.Pub. Svc., Western Ky. U., 1984; postgrad., U. Louisville, 1987-90; PhD, LaSalle U., 1995. Cert. mgr., Inst. Cert. Profl. Mgrs. Asst. city mgr. City of Ocoee (Fla.), 1983-84, city mgr., 1984-86; city adminstrv. officer City of Hurstbourne, Ky., 1986-90; chief of staff Fairmount Group, Inc., Louisville, 1990-91; city mgr. City of Livingston, Mont., 1992-94; city adminstr. City of Kennewaw, Ga., 1994-96. Author: Managing Your City, 1989. Bd. dirs. Ctr. for Lay Ministries, Jeffersonville, Ind., 1988-91, YMCA, Winter Garden, Fla., 1985-86; advisor Citizens Group of United Tel., Winter Park, 1985; adult scouter Boy Scouts Am., 1976—; pres. Calvary Luth. Voters Assy., Jeffersonville, 1988-89. Mem. Am. Soc. Pub. Adminstrn. (chpt. pres. 1990-91), Internat. City Mgmt. Assn., Kiwanis (pres. 1989-90). Lutheran.

GRIFFIN, LINDA LOUISE, English language and speech educator; b. Yale, Mich., Dec. 23, 1942; d. Benjamin and Ruth (Steenbergh) Hinton; m. James Griffin, Nov. 23, 1980. BA, U. Mich., 1965, MA, 1967; postgrad., Bowling Green (Ohio) State U., 1975, U. N.C., 1985; PhD, U. South Fla., 1996. Tchr. English and speech Sandusky (Mich.) H.S.; instr. Jackson (Mich.) C.C., Terra Tech. Coll., Fremont, Ohio, Edison C.C., Naples, Fla.; frequent speaker and presenter, including harp lecture programs; mem. NEH Shakespeare Seminar, 1985; keynote speaker Collier County Tchrs. Assn. Conf., 1987. Recipient Edison C.C. Excellence in Teaching award. Mem. MLA, South Atlantic MLA, S.E. Medieval Assn., Medieval Inst., S.C. Renaissance Assn., Nat. Coun. Tchrs. English, Folger Shakespeare Libr., So. State Comm. Assn., Fla. Comm. Assn. (pres. 1989-90), Phi Kappa Phi. Home: 9781 Bobwhite Ln Bonita Springs FL 33923-4416 Office: 7007 Lely Cultural Pkwy Naples FL 34113-8976

GRIFFIN, LINNER WARD, social work educator; b. Charlotte, N.C., Apr. 24, 1942; d. Yorke Anthony and Minnie Lee (Mitchell) Ward; m. Bobby G. Griffin, July 24, 1964; children: Jannifer Lynne, Jeffrey Franklin. BA, U. N.C., Greensboro, 1964; MSW, U. N.C., 1969; EdD, U. Houston, 1985. Cert. clin. social worker, N.C. Intake/adult svcs. Guilford County Dept. Social Svcs., Greensboro, 1965-69; family counselor Family Svc. Phila., 1969-72, Cath. Welfare Bur., Trenton, N.J., 1972-74; supportive svcs. supr. Lehigh County Area Agy. on Aging., Allentown, Pa., 1974-77; project. mgr. Phila. Geriatric Ctr., 1977-80; NIMH project mgr./dir. Inst. on Aging, Temple U., Phila., 1980-82; dir. adult day care Western Mass. Hosp., Westfield, 1985-87; asst. prof. W.Va. U., Morgantown, 1987-90, East Carolina U., Greenville, N.C., 1990-95; assoc. dean for grad. studies East Carolina U., Ragsdale, N.C., 1995—; cons. Pa. Dept. Welfare/Aging, Harrisburg, 1977-82; cons. in field, 1982-85. Author, editor: (resource books) A Guide for Adult Protective Services, 10 vols., 1988-90; sr. author: Mental Health and Aging, 1983; contbr. articles and book revs. to profl. jours., chpts. to books. Bd. dirs. InTouch and Concerned, Morgantown, 1987-89; mem. Pitt County Infant Mortality Task Force, Greenville, 1990—, Ea. N.C. Poverty Com., Greenville, 1991—, Mediation Ctr. Ea. N.C., 1992—. W.Va. Adult Protective Svc. Tgn. grantee W.Va. Dept. Health and Human Resources, 1988-90. Mem. NASW, Acad. Cert. Social Workers (cert.), Am. Soc. on Aging, Assn. for Gerontology in Higher Edn., So. Gerontol. Soc. (continuing edn. tng. adv. com.). Presbyterian. Office: East Carolina U Sch Social Work 112 Ragsdale Greenville NC 27858-4353

GRIFFIN, MARY FRANCES, retired library media consultant; b. Cross Hill, Laurens County, S.C., Aug. 24, 1925; d. James and Rosa Lee (Carter) G. BA, Benedict Coll., 1947; postgrad., S.C. State Coll., 1948-51, Atlanta U., 1953, Va. State Coll., 1961; MLS, Ind. U., 1957. Tchr.-librarian Johnston (S.C.) Tng. Sch., Edgefield County Sch. Dist., 1947-51; librarian Lee County Sch. Dist., Dennis High, Bishopville, S.C., 1951-52, Greenville County (S.C.) Sch. Dist., 1952-66; library cons. S.C. Dept. Edn., Columbia, 1966-87; vis. tchr. U. S.C., 1977; bd. dirs. Greater Columbia Lit. Coun.; mem. Richland County unit Assault on Illiteracy. Recipient Cert. of Living the Legacy award Nat. Council Negro Women, 1980. Mem. ALA, Assn. Ednl. Communications and Tech. S.C., Assn. Curriculum Devel., AAUW (pres. Columbia br. 1978-80), Southeastern Library Assn. (sec. 1978-80), S.C. Library Assn. (sec. 1979), S.C. Assn. Sch. Librarians, Nat. Assn. State Ednl. and Media Personnel. Baptist. Home: PO Box 1652 Columbia SC 29202-1652 also: 1100 Skyland Dr Columbia SC 29210-8127

GRIFFIN, MARY JANE RAGSDALE, educational consultant, writer, small business owner; b. Crawfordsville, Ind., Aug. 15, 1927; d. Ira Vincent and Sophronia Burdetti (Thompson) Ragsdale; m. Walter Wanzel Griffin, Jan. 20, 1951; children: Walter Vincent, Glenn Edwin, Edwin Wanzel. BS, U. Tenn., 1949, MS, 1970, EdS, 1976, EdD, 1980. Cert. math., sci., physics, chemistry, computer programming, elem. tchr., secondary and elem. adminstr., Tenn. Pvt. tchr. piano and violin, Knoxville, Tenn., 1947-50; asst. dir. Sunshine Schoolette, Knoxville, 1954-69; tchr. sci. and math. Knox County Schs., Knoxville, 1970-74; tchr. math. methods U. Tenn., Knoxville, 1975-76; tchr. math. and computer programming Knox County Schs., Knoxville, 1977-88; freelance writer Knoxville, 1970—, real estate investor and mgr., 1975—; owner, pres. MJRG Enterprises, Knoxville, 1976—; freelance edn. cons. Knoxville, 1988—. Contbr. articles to various publs.; writer curriculum guides. Violinist Chattanooga Symphony, 1944-47; officer bd. dirs. Ossoli Circle, Knoxville, 1954-64, 89-90; poetry contest chmn. Fontinalis, 1993—, fine arts chair, 1995—; bd. dirs. Girls Club Knoxville, Inc., 1962-70; mem. Fountain City Town Hall, 1985—, Knoxville Symphony League, 1990—; tchr. adult Sunday sch., 1988—; mem. chancel choir 1st Christian Ch., Knoxville, 1949-85, bd. dirs., 1982-85; mem. chancel choir Fountain City United Meth. Ch., Knoxville, 1985-91, bd. dirs., 1993—; pres. United Meth. Women, 1993—, v.p. Knoxville Dist., 1996—. Scholar U. Chattanooga, 1947; fellow U. Tenn., 1968-70. Mem. NEA, ASCD, AAUW, Nat. Coun. Tchrs. Math. (life), Tenn. Edn. Assn. (workshop presenter 1980-88), East Tenn. Edn. Assn., Knox County Edn. Assn. (rep. 1980-85), East Tenn. Hist. Soc. (life), Ind. Hist. Soc. (life), Ky. Hist. Soc. (life), Montgomery County, Ind. Hist. Soc., Union County HIst. Soc., Gen. Fedn. Womens Clubs, Tenn. Fedn. Womens Club, Appalachian Zool. Soc. (life), Soc. for Preservation Tenn. Antiquities (life), U. Tenn. President's Club (life), Smoky Mountain Z Club, Optimists Internat. (life, local bd. dirs. 1990-92, Tenn. dist. essay contest chmn. 1990-91, 1992-93, 1993-94, Tenn. dist. 1st lady 1990-91), Sigma Phi Sigma (life, chpt. pres. U. Chattanooga 1945-47), Delta Kappa Gamma (fin. com. 1980-91), Phi Delta Theta, Kappa Delta Pi (internat. voting del. 1982, 84, 86, conf. presenter 1982), Kappa Delta (life). Home: 5213 Haynes Sterchi Rd Knoxville TN 37912-2816

GRIFFIN, MYRNA MCINTOSH, critical care nurse; b. Carrollton, Ga., May 30, 1948; d. Clifford H. and Vertie Maude (Potts) McIntosh; m. John Thomas Griffin II, June 20, 1981. Diploma, Floyd Sch. Nursing, Berry Coll., 1972. Staff nurse neonatal ICU Kennestone Hosp., Marietta, Ga.; staff nurse neonatal ICU Floyd Med. Ctr., Rome, Ga., charge nurse spl. care nursery; charge nurse neonatal ICU Gwinnett Med. Ctr., Lawrenceville, Ga. Mem. Nat. Assn. Neonatal Nurses.

GRIFFIN, O. DANIEL, JR., reporter, writer, photographer, audio engineer, videographer; b. Portsmouth, Va., Oct. 26, 1960; s. Otto Daniel Sr. and Mary Lee (Gee) G. Student, Norfolk State U., 1980-83; BS in Fin., BA in Mass Media, Hampton U., 1986. Lic. FCC. Audio engr. Sta. WOWI-FM, Norfolk, Va., 1984—, Star Prodn., Norfolk, Va., 1988—; promotion, pub. rels. rep. McDonald's, Portsmouth, Va., 1987; writer, reporter Citizens Press Am., Portsmouth, 1985—; asst. sport reporter Sta. WAVY-TV, Norfolk, 1985-86, Sta. WTKR-TV, Norfolk, 1987—, Sta. WVEC-TV, Norfolk, 1991—; owner Griffin's Photography, Audio & Video Post-Prodn. Inc., Portsmouth, 1987—, Step Above Post Prodn. Co.; writer, reporter Journal & Guide, Norfolk, 1988; audio/video/light engr. cons. Treetop Co., Portsmouth, Va., 1993—; photographer Glamour Shots, Chesapeake, Va., 1996—, The New Jour. and Guide, Norfolk, 1995—; cameraman Manor High Band, Portsmouth, 1985-88; audio engr. Hal Jackson's Talent Teens, Norfolk, 1984—; photographer Pre-Teen Pageant, Portsmouth, 1987; producer, dir. Va. Beach Joint Cable Ctr., 1990—, Quiet Storm Soundtrack, Sta. WOWI-FM, Norfolk, 1984; owner, producer, dir., writer Step Above Post Prodn. Co., Portmouth, Va., 1990—; asst. sport reporter Sta. WVEC-TV, Norfolk, 1991—; producer, dir. Va. Beach Joint Cable Ctr., 1990-91. Actor play Momma Don't; contbr. articles popular mags., 1986—. Named one of Outstanding Young Men Am., 1988. Mem. Black Filmmaker Assn., Nat. Rec. Soc. Arts and Sci., Hampton Roads Black Media Profl. Assn., Citizens Press of Hampton Roads, Norfolk State U. Alumni Band, Hampton U. Alumni Band, Yearbook Club, Newspaper Club. Baptist. Home: 1425 Horne Ave Portsmouth VA 23701-3126 Office: Sta WVEC-TV 613 Woodis Ave Norfolk VA 23510-1017

GRIFFIN, PAUL, JR., navy officer, engineer, educator; b. Aiken, S.C., Mar. 13, 1961; s. Paul and Mamie Lou (Curry) G. AS, Fla. Keys C.C., 1985; BS, Fla. A&M U., 1986, MEd, M in Applied Social Sci., 1993. Asst. produce mgr. Winn-Dixie Store, Goose Creek, S.C., 1977-79; enlisted USN, 1979—, commd. ensign, 1986, advanced through grades to lt., 1990, data systems technician, 1979-86; electrical officer USN, Mayport, Fla., 1986-88, anti-submarine officer, 1988-90; asst. prof. Fla. A&M U./USN, Tallahassee, 1990-93; chief engr. USS Stump, 1993—; master tng. specialist USN, 1992—; dept. head, perspective engring. officer, 1993; asst. safety officer USN, Mayport, 1986-88; project handclasp and cmty. rels. coord. La Guardia, Salvador, Rio de Janeiro, Puerto Ingeniero White, Valparaiso, S Am., 1994. mentor Griffin Mid. Sch., Tallahassee, 1990-92; asst. coord. Family Support Group for Desert Storm, Tallahassee, 1991; spkr., vol. Hugh O'Brien Youth Leadership Program, Tallahassee, 1991; judge Capital Regional Sci. and Engring. Fair, Tallahassee, 1992; advisor City of Tallahassee Examination of Drug and Crime Activity Project, 1992; vol., spkr. Gadsden County GED and Dropout Prevention Program, 1992-93; vol. Riley Elem. Sch. Say No To Drug's Program; others. Delores Auzenne fellow, 1992. Mem. 100 Black Men of Am. Democrat. Baptist. Home: 1607 Maize Ct Virginia Beach VA 23464-6173 Office: Uss Stump # D978 FPO AE 09587-1216

GRIFFIN, THOMAS LEE, JR., industrial and federal government specialist; b. Sumter, S.C., Feb. 10, 1929; s. Thomas Lee and Gladys (Moore) G.; m. Aileen Casey; children: Elizabeth, Leigh. BS in Engr., U.S. Naval Acad., 1952; MA, George Washington U., 1965; grad., U.S. Naval War Coll., Newport, R.I., 1965, U.S. Army War Coll., Carlisle, Pa., 1972. Commd. 2d lt. USMC, 1952, advanced through grades to col., ret., 1979; with Electronic Data Systems, Dallas, 1979-83; dir. computerized automotive maintenance systems and caterpillar accounts Electronic Data Systems, 1984-90; v.p. complex systems and govt. svcs. divsn. Electronic Data Systems, Washington, 1990-92; ret., 1993; v.p. CACI Aviation Industry and Mfg., Arlington, Va., 1993—; chief of staff Second Marine Aircraft Wing, 1977, U.S. Marine Forces Western Pacific, 1978, Marine Corps Air Base East, 1979. Chmn. pastoral rels. Franklin Community Ch., Mich. 1988-90; pres. Raceway Farms Assn., Lorton, Va., 1980-83; area dir. Boy Scouts Am., New Bern, N.C., 1979. Decorated Legion of Merit Combat V, 1966, 1969, 1979, Disting. Flying Cross, 1969. Mem. Soc. Mfg. Engrs., Automation Forum (chmn. bd. dirs.), Air Traffic Contr. Assn., U.S. Naval Acad. Alumni Assn., Assn. U.S. Army, Armed Forces Comm. and Electronic Assn., Marine Corps. Assn., Marine Corps Aviation Assn., Hancock Yacht Club, Bogue Banks Country Club. Republican. Methodist. Home: PO Box 2763 595 Forest Dunes Dr Pine Knoll Shores NC 28512

GRIFFIN, TOM FLEET, business & management educator; b. Birmingham, Ala., May 25, 1943; s. Tom Fleet Jr. and Martha (Willingham) G.; m. Paula Havard, Jan. 28, 1967; children: Martha Claire, Elizabeth Jane. BS, U. Ala., 1966, MBA, 1969, PhD, 1973. Plant chemist Goodyear Tire & Rubber Co., Gadsden, Ala., 1966-67; grad. asst. U. Ala., Tuscaloosa, 1967-72; assoc. professor Loyola U., New Orleans, 1976-79; assoc. prof. Tulane U., New Orleans, 1979-81, Southeastern La. U., Hammond, 1981-88; v.p. ops. United Dutch Publishing, Coral Springs, Fla., 1988-90; v.p. corp. product devel. United Dutch Publishing, Coral Springs, 1991; eminent scholar Auburn U., Montgomery, Ala., 1992—; Small Bus. Devel. Ctr. dir. Southeastern La. U., 1985-88. Mem. Am. Soc. Quality Control (treas. 1993—), GOAL/QPC, World Assn. Case Rsch., Mid-South Mktg. Educators, Acad. Bus., Assn. Mgmt. Office: Auburn U 7300 University Dr Montgomery AL 36117-3531

GRIFFING, CLAYTON ALLEN, retail executive; b. Pine Bluff, Ark., Oct. 20, 1940; s. Hugh Milton and Vernon Francis (Cates) G.; m. Jean Ann Lack, Nov. 21, 1962; children: C. Lance, Kimberly. B. in Ceramic Engring, Ga. Inst. Tech., 1963; M.B.A., Emory U., 1965. With Atlantic Steel Co., Atlanta, 1965-80; asst. treas. finance Atlantic Steel Co., 1969-71, treas., 1971-78, v.p. fin., 1978-80; sr. v.p. Lowe's Co. Inc., North Wilkesboro, N.C., 1980-87; exec. v.p. fin. and adminstrn. Fleming Co. Inc., Oklahoma City, 1987-88; mng. ptnr. The Griffin Group, Charlotte, N.C., 1988—; chmn. Griffon Enterprises, Inc., Charlotte, 1991—; vice chmn., trustee Fernbank, Inc.; bd. dirs. 1st Citizens Bank. Mem. Leadership Atlanta, 1972-73; founder Ga. Sci. & Natural History League; chmn. Wilkes Edn. Found.; mem. MBA regional adv. bd. Emory U.; bd. dirs. Wilkes C.C. Endowment Corp. Mem. Am. Assn. Mus. Trustees, Fin. Execs. Inst., Ga. Tech. Alumni Assn., Exchange Club (dir. 1971-72, pres. 1975-76), Emory Bus. Sch. Alumni Assn. (pres. 1975-76), Leadership Ga., Beta Gamma Sigma. Office: Griffon Enterprises Inc PO Box 470752 Charlotte NC 28247-0752

GRIFFIN-THOMPSON, MELANIE, accounting firm executive; b. Corpus Christi, Tex., Oct. 25, 1949; d. Roy Albert and Ola Emma (Hunt) G.; m. Robert Thompson; children: Maurice Dale, Donald Dwight, Merideth Thompson, Laura Thompson. BBA summa cum laude, Corpus Christi State U., 1977; MBA, Tex. A&M U., 1994. CPA, Tex.; cert. fin. planner. Sec.-treas. Roy Hunt, Inc., Corpus Christi, 1970-78, dir., 1970-82; v.p. White, Sluyter & Co., Corpus Christi, 1978-80; pres. Whittington & Griffin, Corpus Christi, 1980-82, also dir.; sec.-treas., dir. Sand Express, Inc., Corpus Christi, 1975-82; prin. Melanie Hunt Griffin & Assocs., CPAs, Corpus Christi, 1982-84; v.p. Fields, Nemec & Co., P.C., Corpus Christi, 1984—; mem. edn. and tng. task force White Ho. Conf. Small Bus., 1993; adj. prof. Tex. A&M, Corpus Christi. Contbr. articles to profl. jours. Devel. chair Am. Heart Assn., chmn. bd. 1989-90, Leadership Corpus Christi Alumni, 1982—; mem. adv. coun. Tex. A&M U., Corpus Christi. Recipient Women in Careers award YWCA, 1989, Outstanding Svc. award Corpus Christi chpt. CPA's, 1990-93. Mem. AICPA (personal fin. planning dir. small bus. taxation com. 1990-93), Tex. Soc. CPAs (bd. dirs. 1987—, v.p. 1988-89, 93-94, treas. 1995-96, pres. elect 1996-97, pres. Corpus Christi chpt. 1987-88, chmn. devel. new legis. leaders 1990-93, vice chair CPAs Helping Schs. 1994-95, Outstanding Svc. award 1990-91, Presdl. citation, pres. elect, 1996-97), Corpus Christi State U. Alumni Assn. (bd. dirs. 1987-90), Tex. State CPAs Ednl. Found. (trustee 1990-93), Exec. Women Internat. (chmn. philanthropy com. 1986-87), Corpus Christi Rotary (bd. dirs. 1996—). Home: 10817 Stonewall Blvd Corpus Christi TX 78410-2429 Office: Fields Nemec & Co PC 501 S Tancahua PO Box 23067 Corpus Christi TX 78403

GRIFFITH, CARL LESLIE, protective services official; b. Mullins, S.C., Sept. 12, 1956; s. William R. and Julia A. (Willis) G.; m. Nona E. Hunt, Jan. 12, 1980 (div. June 1986); children: Carl L. Jr., James R.; m. Lisa D. Anderson, July 21, 1987; 1 child, Charles R. AAS, U. S.C., 1976, BA, 1977; MA, Webster U., 1981. Dep. sheriff Lexington (S.C.) County Sheriff's Dept., 1978; patrolman Horry County Police Dept., Conway, S.C., 1979-81; spl. investigator S.C. Tax Commn., Columbia, 1981-83; spl. agt. U.S. Naval Intelligence, Cherry Point, N.C., 1983-86, Drug Enforcement Adminstrn., Miami, Fla., 1986—; assoc. prof. Horry-Georgetown Tech. Coll., Conway,

1981-82. Mem. Rep. Nat. Task Force, Washington, 1984. Officer USNR, 1985-92. Mem. Internat. Narcotic Officers Assn., Dade County Police Benevolent Assn., Fed. Law Enforcement Officers Assn.

GRIFFITH, MARK F., political science educator; b. Chgo., Dec. 4, 1955; s. Edgar N. and LaVerne (Hoehn) G.; m. Suzette Fraser, may 5, 1979. AA in Polit. Sci., Coll. DuPage, 1981; BA in Polit. Sci., North Cen. Coll., Naperville, Ill., 1984; MA in Polit. Sci., No. Ill. U., 1986, PhD in Polit. Sci., 1994. Assoc. prof. polit. sci. The U. West Ala., Livingston, Ala., 1990—. Contbg. author: Campaign 96: Resource Guide, 1996. Vol. Challenge 21, Tuscaloosa, Ala., 1996. Recipient Earhart fellowship Earhart Found., 1986. Mem. Ala. Polit. Sci. Assn., Am. Polit. Sci. Assn., Am. Soc. Pub. Adminstrn., Internat. Churchill Soc., Southwestern Polit. Sci. Assn., Miss. Polit. Sci. Assn. Office: Univ West Alabama Wallace Hall Livingston AL 35470

GRIFFITH, MELVIN EUGENE, entomologist, public health official; b. Lawrence, Kans., Mar. 24, 1912; s. George Thomas and Estella (Shaw) G.; m. Pauline Sophia Bogart, June 23, 1941. AB, U. Kans., 1934, AM, 1935, PhD, 1938; postgrad., U. Mich., summers 1937-40. Instr. zoology N.D. Agrl. Coll., Fargo, 1938-39, asst. prof., 1939-41, assoc. prof., 1941-42; commd. officer USPHS, 1943-71, malaria control entomologist dept. health State of Okla., 1943-51, chief malaria adviser ICA, Bangkok, Thailand, 1951-60, assoc. dir. Malaria Eradication Tng. Ctr., Kingston, Jamaica, 1960, regional malaria advisor SE Asia, AID, New Delhi, 1960-62, Near East and So. Asia, 1962-64, dep. chief malaria eradication br., Washington, 1964-67, chief, 1967-71, ret. as capt., 1971; assoc. prof. zool. scis. U. Okla., Norman, 1946-52, prof., 1952-56; cons. Office of Health, AID, Washington, 1971-75. Contbr. articles and monographs on entomology, malaria control and pub. health. Recipient citation for disting. service U. Kans., 1962. Mem. Am. Pub. Health Assn., Am. Soc. Tropical Medicine and Hygiene, Am. Soc. Limnology and Oceanography, Entomol. Soc. Am., Explorers Club, N.Y. Acad. Scis., Siam Soc., Phi Beta Kappa, Sigma Xi. Address: PO Box DG Williamsburg VA 23187-3550

GRIFFITH, RICHARD LATTIMORE, lawyer; b. Abilene, Tex., Feb. 8, 1939; s. Richard Allan and Lorayne (Lattimore) G.; m. Sarah Brewster, Feb. 16, 1963 (dec. 1979); 1 child, Grey; m. Betsy Brooks, Apr. 19, 1980. BA, U. Okla., 1961; LLB, U. Tex., 1963. Bar: Tex. 1965, U.S. Dist. Ct. (no. dist.) Tex. 1966, U.S. Ct. Appeals (5th cir.) 1981, U.S. Dist. Ct. (ea. dist.) Okla. 1976, U.S. Dist. Ct. (we. dist.) Okla. 1967. Ptnr., chmn. health law sect. Cantey & Hanger, Ft. Worth, Tex., 1965—; chmn. Health Law Sect. State Bar of Tex., 1988. Co-author: Texas Hospital Law, 1988; contbr. articles to profl. jours. 1st lt. U.S. Army, 1963-65. Fellow Am. Coll. Trial Lawyers, Tex. Bar Found. (life); mem. Am. Bd. Trial Advocates (chpt. pres. 1985, state chmn. 1995), Def. Counsel Trial Acad. (faculty), Coll. of State Bar of Tex., Internat. Assn. Def. Counsel, Def. Rsch. Inst. (bd. dirs. S.W. region), Tex. Assn. Def. Counsel (v.p. 1984-85, regional v.p. 1986-88, 92-93), Tarrant County Bar Assn., Tex. Bar Assn., Inn of Ct. (master of law). Home: 6332 Curzon Ave Fort Worth TX 76116-4604 Office: Cantey & Hanger 2100 Burnett Plaza 801 Cherry St Fort Worth TX 76102

GRIFFITH, ROBERT CHARLES, allergist, educator, planter; b. Shreveport, La., Jan. 9, 1939; s. Charles Parsons and Madelon (Jenkins) G.; m. Loretta Dean Secrist, July 15, 1969; children: Charles Randall, Cameron Stuart, Ann Marie. BS, Centenary Coll., 1961; MD, La. State U., 1965. Intern, Confederate Meml. Med. Ctr., Shreveport, 1965-66, resident in internal medicine, 1966-68; fellow in allergy and chest disease, instr. U. Va. Med. Sch. Hosp., Charlottesville, 1968-70; practice medicine specializing in allergies, Alexandria, La., 1970-72, The Allergy Clinic, Shreveport, 1972; pres. Griffith Allergy Clinic, Shreveport, 1973—; faculty internal medicine La. State U., 1972—; owner, planter Riverpoint Plantation, Caddo Parish, La. and Miller and Lafayette Counties, Ark. Bd. dirs. Caddo-Bossier Assn. Retarded Citizens, 1977-84, Access (fomerly Child Devel. Ctr.), Shreveport, 1979-85; mem. med. adv. com., spl. edn. adv. com. Caddo Parish Sch. Bd., 1977—; mem. commission on missions and social concerns First Methodist Ch., 1981-84, mem. adminstrv. bd., 1981-84; mem. med. panel for transfer Caddo Parish Sch. Bd., 1974-94; mem. adopt a flag program Confederate Meml. Mus. New Orleans; co-chair Loyola Fund Drive, 1994-95. Served to maj. M.C., U.S. Army, 1965-71. Recipient Physician of the Yr. award Shreveport-Bossier Med. Assts., 1984. Fellow Am. Coll. Asthma, Allergy and Immunology, Am. Coll. Chest Physicians (assoc.), Am. Thoracic Soc.; mem. AMA, SAR (chpt. surgeon 1994—), Am. Acad. Allergy, Asthma and Immunology, Jamestowne Soc., So. Med. Assn., La. Med. Soc., Shreveport Med. Soc. (allergy spokesman 1984—), La. Allergy Soc. (charter; past pres.), U. Va. Med. Alumni Assn. (life), Pace Soc. Am., La. State U. Med. Alumni Assn., Confederate Soc. Am., Heritage Preservation Assn., So. League (charter, sustainer), So. League La. (bd. dirs.), Mil. Order Stars and Bars, Order of So. Cross, Pub. Solicitation Review Coun., Shreveport C. of C., Kappa Alpha, Methodist. Lodges: Masons (32 degree). Clubs: Shreveport Country, Petroleum of Shreveport, Shreveport, Ambs., Cotillion, Royal, Plantation, Jesters, Les Bon Temps., Demoiselle Club. Home: 7112 E Ridge Dr Shreveport LA 71106-4749 also: Riverpoint Plantation Ida LA 71044

GRIFFITH, STEVEN FRANKLIN, SR., lawyer, real estate title insurance agent and investor; b. New Orleans, July 14, 1948; s. Hugh Franklin and Rose Marie (Teutone) G.; m. Mary Elizabeth McMillan Frank, Dec. 9, 1972; children: Steven Franklin Jr., Jason Franklin. BBA, Loyola U., New Orleans, 1970, JD, 1972. Bar: La. 1972, U.S. Dist. Ct. (ea. dist.) La. 1975, U.S. Ct. Appeals (5th cir.) 1975, U.S. Supreme Ct. 1976. With Law Offices of Senator George T. Oubre, Norco, La., 1971-75; sole practice Destrehan, La., 1975—. Served to 1st lt. U.S. Army, 1970-72. Mem. ABA, ATLA, La. State Bar Assn. (ho. of dels. 1987—), La. Trial Lawyers Assn., New Orleans Trial Lawyers Assn., Fed. Bar Assn., Lions. Democrat.

GRIFFITH FRIES, MARTHA, controller; b. Brockton, Mass., Sept. 9, 1945; d. Ishmael Hayes and Jettie L. (Dudley) Davis; m. Jack C. Griffith, May 29, 1965 (dec. June 1984); Michael S., David M.; m. Dan H. Fries, Nov. 5, 1994. Student, U. Ark., 1962-64; BA, Ball State U., 1967. Prin. Griffith Acctg. Co., Indpls., 1968-70; probate adminstr. Johnson & Weaver, Indpls., 1970-74; personnel adminstr. Hercules Inc., Houston, 1974-76; adminstr. Lapin Totz & Mayer, Houston, 1976-80; bus. mgr. Pasadena (Tex.) Citizen, 1980-84; contr. Houston Community Newspapers, 1984-88, DCI Pub., Alexandria, Va., 1989-90, Telescan Inc., Houston, 1990-93, Advolink, Inc., 1993—. Commr. Houston council Boy Scouts Am., 1983. Recipient Dist. Merit awards Boy Scouts Am., Houston, 1983. Mem. Internat. Newspaper Fin. Execs. (com. mem. 1986-89), Collier Jackson Users Group (moderator 1986-89), Nat. Assn. Female Execs. Democrat. Baptist. Address: 17218 Telegraph Creek Dr Spring TX 77379-4840

GRIFFITHS, CHARLES ROBERT, electronic and ceramic engineer; b. Attleboro, Mass., Apr. 8, 1941; s. Jennie Louise (Holske) G.; m. Hope Ellen Petersen, July 20, 1963; children: Richard, Diane, Karen. BSEE, Northestern U., 1964; MSEE, Ohio State U., 1965, PhD in Ceramic Engring., 1968. R&D engr. Signal Corps Rsch. Lab., Ft. Monmouth, N.J., 1967-68, Westinghouse R&D, Pitts., 1970-73; R&D engr. GTE Sylvania, Danvers, Mass., 1973-76, Standish, Maine, 1976-86; R&D engr. Hi-Stat Mfg. Co., Sarasota, Fla., 1986—; adj. prof. U. So. Maine, Portland, 1983-86, U.S. Fla. Sarasota, 1986-94. Patentee positive temperature coefficient thermistors. Capt. U.S. Army, 1968-70, Vietnam. Mem. Am. Ceramic Soc., Nat. Inst. Ceramic Engrs. Republican. Baptist. Office: Hi Stat Mfg 7290 26th Ct E Sarasota FL 34243-3963

GRIFFITHS, DALE LEE, marketing executive; b. Sutherland, Nebr., Nov. 25, 1954; s. William Frederick and Violet Viola (Kraft) G.; m. Sharon Lynn Raunborg, Aug. 15, 1987. BA in Journalism, U. Nebr., 1977, postgrad., 1978; postgrad., U. North Tex., 1991—. Asst. editor Collectors Media Inc., San Marcos, Tex., 1979-80; prodn. mgr. Collectors Media Inc., San Marcos, 1980-81, advt. dir., 1981-84; prodn. mgr. Respiratory Care Jour. Daedalus Enterprises, Dallas, 1984-85, prodn. mgr., 1985-86, ops. and prodn. mgr., 1986-87; mktg. mgr. Am. Assn. for Respiratory Care, Dallas, 1987-89; mktg. dir. Daedalus Enterprises-Am. Assn. Respiratory Care, Dallas, 1989—. Editor: Peak Performance USA-An Asthma Management Guide for Schools; prodr. (TV series) Professor's Rounds in Respiratory Care. Bd. dirs. William T. Cozby Pub. Libr., Coppell, 1991—, vice chmn. 1996—; chmn. press rels. Half-Cent Tax Com., Coppell, 1994. Mem. Friends of Libr. (Coppell) (pres.), Dallas-Ft. Worth Soc. Assn. Execs. Methodist.

GRIFFITTS, KEITH LOYD, oil industry executive; b. Wichita Falls, Tex., July 10, 1942; s. Loyd and Fannie (Moore) G. BS, Hardin-Simmons U., 1964; MEd, North Tex. State U., 1965. Counselor, adminstr. Dist. #6 Schs., Littleton, Colo., 1965-69; div. mgr. Westamerica Securities, Inc., Denver, 1969-71; project sales mgr. U.S. Home Corp., Denver, 1971-74; comml. real estate salesperson Wilton O. Davis & Co., Dallas, 1974-75; dir. mktg. Schneider Bakery Co., Longview, Tex., 1975-77; nat. account mktg. White Swan, Inc., Dallas, 1977-79; pres. Vantage Petroleum Resources, Inc., Dallas, 1979-82; pres., owner Western Petroleum Resources, Inc., Dallas, 1982—; v.p., mgr. corp. trust devel. 1st City Tex.-Dallas, 1984-91; lectr. North Tex. State U., 1982-86. Author, editor, pub. periodical Oil Patch, 1980-84; editor periodical Trust Trends, 1984-90. Trustee Hardin-Simmons U., Abilene, Tex., 1991—, vice chmn., chmn. bd. devel., 1987-90. Mem. North Tex. Oil and Gas Assn., Dallas and Midland Exploration Fin. Group, Tex. Ind. Prodrs. and Royalty Owners Assn., Dallas Wildcatters Club. Baptist. Home: 1089 Edith Cir Richardson TX 75080-2924 Office: 15441 Knoll Trail Ste 290 LB#2 Dallas TX 75248

GRIGEREIT, HUGH REEVES, JR., industrial relations executive; b. Benton Harbor, Mich., Oct. 29, 1930; s. Hugh Reeves and Inez Catherine (Babcock) G.; m. Ann Louise Trimble, Jan. 25, 1953; 1 child, David Hugh. BA, Mich. State U., 1952; JD, U. Notre Dame, South Bend, Ind., 1957. Cert. substance abuse counselor, employee assistance profl.; bar: Mich. 1957. Asst. to v.p. Essex Wire Corp., Ft. Wayne, Ind., 1957-59; indsl. rels. staff atty. Lincoln Nat. Life, Ft. Wayne, 1959-60; mgr. labor rels. Avco Corp., Richmond, Ind. and, Nashville, 1960-66; v.p. adminstrn. ITT Corp., Chgo., 1966-70; dir. indsl. and human rels. ITT Corp., Brussels, Belgium, 1970-75; dir. indsl. rels. ITT Corp., Providence, R.I., 1975-83; dep. dir. employee assistance program ITT Corp., Raleigh, N.C., 1983—. Actor-author-editor (film) Welcome Back, 1980. Co-chmn. Nashville Reps., 1965-66; bd. dirs. R.I. Coun. on Alcoholism, Providence, 1981-83, Alcohol Drug Coun. N.C., 1984, Gov.'s Coun. on Alcohol and Other Drug Abuse, 1989-93; mem. N.C. Commn. on Substance Abuse Treatment and Prevention, 1994—. Mem. Nat. Assn. Alcoholism and Drug Abuse Counselors, Employee Assistance Soc. N. Am., Employee Assistance Profls. Assn. Inc. Episcopalian. Office: ITT Employee Assistance Program 2920 Highwoods Blvd Ste 110 Raleigh NC 27604-1015

GRIGG, EDDIE GARMAN, minister; b. Shelby, N.C., Feb. 20, 1957; s. Gaston Theodore and Sylvia Evlyn (Davis) G.; m. Susan Wanda Ray, May 28, 1977; children: Mark Zolton, Jamie Ray, Steven Russell. BA, Gardner-Webb Coll., 1980; MDiv, Southeastern Bapt. Theol. Sem., 1985; D Ministry, Emmanuel Bapt. U., 1994, DRE, 1995. Ordained to ministry So. Bapt. Conv., 1976. Pastor Victory Bapt. Ch., Kings Mountain, N.C., 1975-79, Christian Freedom Bapt. Ch., Kings Mountain, 1979-81, Sanford Meml. Bapt. Ch., Brodnax, Va., 1981-85, Pleasant Hill Bapt. Ch., Shelby, N.C., 1985-89; sr. min. Wilson Grove Bapt. Ch., Charlotte, N.C., 1989-93; founder, pastor New Life Bapt. Ch., Charlotte, 1993—. Mem. Bapt. Metrolina Ministries Pastor's Conf. (pres. 1995-96), Bapt. Metrolina Ministries Assn. (evangelism com. 1990-93, urban ch. com. 1990-94). Republican. Office: New Life Bapt Ch 10132 Harrisburg Rd Charlotte NC 28215-7305

GRIGG, WILLIAM HUMPHREY, utility executive; b. Shelby, N.C., Nov. 5, 1932; s. Claud and Margy (Humphrey) G.; m. Margaret Anne Ford, Aug. 11, 1956; children: Anne Ford, John Humphrey, Mary Lynne. A.B., Duke U., 1954, LL.B., 1958. Bar: N.C. 1958. Gen. practice Charlotte, 1958-63; with Duke Power Co., 1963—, v.p. finance, 1970-71, v.p., gen. counsel, 1971-75; sr. v.p. legal and finance Duke Power Co., Charlotte, 1975-82, exec. v.p., 1982-90, vice chmn., 1990-94, chmn., pres., CEO, 1994—; also dir. Duke Power Co. Editor-in-chief: Duke Law Jour, 1957-58; Contbr. articles to profl. jours. Dir. NationsFunds, Inc., Aegis Ins. Svcs.; Rsch. Triangle Park Johnson C. Smith U.; bd. dirs. Found. for the Carolinas. Capt. USMCR, 1954-56. Mem. Am., N.C. bar assns. Methodist. Club: Charlotte Country. Office: Duke Power Co 422 S Church St Charlotte NC 28242-0001

GRIGGS, BOBBIE JUNE, civic worker; b. Oklahoma City, Feb. 14, 1938; d. Robert Jefferson and Nora May (Green) Fish; m. Peter Harvey Griggs, Apr. 16, 1955; children: Diana (dec.), Terry, James. Grad. high sch., Salina, Kans. Commissary rep. Family Mag., Charleston AFB, S.C., 1976—; rep. Avon Corp., Charleston, S.C., 1976—; freelance demonstrator to USAF and USN orgns. Charleston, 1976—; rep. Salute Mag., Charleston AFB, 1986—; consumer edn. counselor Air Force-Navy exchs. Oster Kitchen Appliances, Charleston, 1987-90. Contbr. World's Largest Poem for Peace, 1991, Selected Works of our Best Poets, 1992, In A Different Light, 1992. Youth advisor, Charleston AFB, 1966-78; vol. distbn. program Salvation Army; clinic vol. ARC, Charleston AFB, 1967-75, chmn. family svcs. publicity and spl. projects, 1989; clinic vol. Clara Barton award, 1972; vol. Spoleto Festival, 1989—, Twin Oaks Retirement Ctr., 1992—, Chapel SUMMOM program, 1991—; asst. coord., publicity chmn. Family Svcs., 1967-83, named vol. of quarter, 1970, 72, 74, 76, named vol. of yr., 1970; active various scouting orgns., 1967—; asst. kindergarten Sunday sch. supt. Chapel I, 1966-68; active North Charleston (S.C.) Christian Women's Club, 1988—, hosp. chmn., mem. Charleston AFB Protestant Women's Club., 1965—; tchr. Bible sch., 1984-89; vol. tutor Lambs Elem., 1992, Trident Literacy Assn. (Laubach Literacy Action cert. 1992); coun. rep. Charleston AFB parish coun., 1988—; mem. Rocketeers Actors Group, Goals 2000 com. 1993—, Barnabas Outreach program, 1991—, Clown Ministry Charleston AFB, 1993—; chairperson Helping Hands Charleston AFB, 1991—, Voyagers Sunday Sch. Class Project, Summerville Homeless Shelter Charleston AFB, 1993—, Publicity Protestant Women, 1993—; vol. Lambs Elem., 1992—, Twin Oaks Retirement Ctr., 1992—, Barnabas Outreach Com., 1991—, Military Retirees, 1994—; counselor Jr. Achievement Program, 1994; mem. Charleston Raptor Ctr., 1996, S.C. Homeless Shelter Planning com., 1995-96, Am. Indian Heritage Coun., 1996. Recipient 1,000 Hours award Air Force Times, 1971, 1st Pl. award Designer Craftsman show, 1967-71, Dedicated Svc. award Charleston AFB, 1981, Hurricane Hugo Hero award, 1989, 1st Pl. award Bake-Off Contest YMCA, 1981, Hist. Charleston Trail Hike award Cub Scouts, 1988, Family Svcs. Vol. of Quar. award, 1990, Family Svcs. 6,000 Hour award, 1990, Golden Poet award, 1991, 1992, In a Different Light award Libr. Congress, 1991; named Enlisted Wife of Yr., Charleston AFB, 1974, Family Svcs. Vol. of Quarter Charleston AFB, 1990, Family Svcs. 6000 Hour award, 1991, Outstanding Vol. Svc. award Operation Desert Shield/Storm, 1991, Family Svcs. Spl. Recognition award, 1991, Appreciation acknowledgement Pres. of U.S., 1991, First Lady Barbara Bush, 1992, Pres. of U.S., 1994, First Lady Hillary Clinton, 1994, Disting. Vol. award Charleston County Sch. Dist., 1995, Retiree Volunteer of the Quarter Charleston AFB, 1995, Vol. of Month Lambs Elem. Sch., 1995, Voting Slogan award Sec. Def., 1995. Mem. Nat. Trust Hist. Preservation, Smithsonian Inst., Charleston AFB Non-Commd. Officers' Wives Club (pres. 1971-73, publicity chmn. 1969-70, wife of month 1967, wife of quarter 1973), Rocketeers Actors Group, Friends of Dock St.-Ushers.

GRIGGS, EMMA, management executive; b. Cleveland, Ark., Feb. 8, 1928; d. James and Frazier (Byers) Wallace; m. Augusta Griggs, Mar. 20, 1954 (dec.); children: Judy A., Terri V. Grad. h.s., Chgo. Pres., CEO Burlington No. Inc., Inglewood, Calif., 1986—. Republican.

GRIGSBY, CHESTER POOLE, JR., oil and investments company executive; b. Ruston, La., Mar. 4, 1929; s. Chester Poole and Vera Aura (Lamkin) G.; B.S., La. Tech. U., 1951; postgrad. U. Ariz., 1953-54; m. Audrey Jane Tombrink, Mar. 27, 1954; children: Jayne, Chester Poole III., Julia, Diana. Acct. Hudson Gas & Oil Corp., 1955-61; gen. acctg. supr. San Jacinto Gas Processing Corp., 1961-63; v.p., treas., dir. Kinsey Corps., Shreveport, La., 1964—, Kinsey Interests, Inc., Enkay Corp., Norman Corp. Caddo, Inc., Norcad Pipeline Co., Columbia Royalty Co.; ptnr. Freestate Warehouse Co., 1972—, Freestate Circle Ltd. Mem. U.S. Tax Del. to China Citizen Amb. Program, People to People Internat. With USAF, 1951-55. CPA, La. Mem. Am. Inst. CPA's, Soc. La. CPA's, U.S. Power Squadron, Am. Legion. Home: 5721 River Rd Shreveport LA 71105-4348 Office: 401 Edwards St Ste 1805 Shreveport LA 71101-5532

GRIGSBY, RONALD, food products executive; b. 1957. Active Triple G Co., Lake Placid, Fla., 1978—, So. Farms Ltd., Lake Placid, Fla., 1990—, Samaron Properties, Inc., Winter Haven, Fla., 1986—, SFG Properties Ltd., Winter Haven, Fla., 1981—; gen. mgr. Sun Ray Farms, Lake Placid, Fla., 1981—. Office: Sun Ray Farms 4101 State Road 70 E Lake Placid FL 33852-5806

GRIGSBY-STEPHENS, KLARON, corporate executive; b. East Prairie, Mo., Feb. 15, 1952; d. Claron Grigsby and Sylvia Mae (Grigery) Oliver; m. Richard Earl Stephens, Aug. 13, 1986. Exec. asst. Quasar Petroleum Corp., Ft. Worth, 1974-80; sales mgr. ITT Life Ins. Corp., Ft. Worth, 1980-83; media buyer Boca Blue Star, Boca Raton, Fla., 1983-84; video editor Video Workshop, Pompano Beach, Fla., 1984-85; pres. Stephens Alfa Corp., Pompano Beach, 1985—. Contbr. articles to profl. jours., also numerous poems. Sgt. USAF, 1970-74. Mem. Alfa Romeo Owners Club, Challenger Ctr. (Washington, hon.). Office: 1321 S Dixie Hwy W Pompano Beach FL 33060-8520

GRIMALDI, JAMES THOMAS, investment fund executive; b. Elizabeth, N.J., Dec. 8, 1928; s. Anthony and Helen (Bernatt) G.; m. Norma Miriello, June 17, 1951; children: Patricia Ann, Pamela Gay, Donna Lynne. BS in Econs., U. Pa., 1951; MBA, Columbia U., 1955. CLU, 1964. Br. acct. Watson-Flagg Engring. Co., Paterson, N.J., 1953-56; from agt. to sr. asst. dist. mgr. Met. Life Ins. Co., Paterson, Ridgewood, N.J., 1956-61; reg. agy. dir., asst. v.p. Am. Amicable Life Ins. Co., Ft. Lauderdale, Fla., 1961-66; v.p. mktg. Inland Life Ins. Co., Chgo., 1966-69; exec. v.p. Peoples Home Life Ins. Co. Ind., 1969-71, Fed. Life & Casualty Co., Battle Creek, 1970-71; pres., chief exec. officer, also dir. Peoples Home Life Ins. Co. of Ind., 1971-74; pres., CEO, bd. dirs. Fed. Life & Casualty Co., 1971-74, Keystone Co., Boston, 1974-76, Cornerstone Fin. Svcs., Inc., Boston, 1974-76; exec. v.p. sales Keystone Custodian Funds, Inc., Boston, 1974-76; engaged in pvt. investments, 1976—; mem. faculty De Paul U., Chgo., 1969. 1st lt. USAF, 1951-53. Recipient Spl. Tribute as Outstanding Citizen, State of Mich., 1974. Mem. Sales Mktg. Execs. Internat., Am. Soc. CLU, Nat. Assn. Life Underwriters, Am. Mktg. Assn., Assn. Individual Investors, Life Assn. Mich. (pres. 1973, exec. com.), Nat. Assn. Security Dealers, Acad. Polit. Sci., U. Pa. Alumni Assn., Columbia U. Alumni Assn. Home: 4904 Sentinel Post Rd Charlotte NC 28226-7445

GRIMBALL, CAROLINE GORDON, sales professional; b. Columbia, S.C., Dec. 21, 1946; d. John and Caroline Grimball. B.A. in Polit. Sci., Converse Coll., 1968; postgrad., S.C. Law Sch., 1968-69. Asst. buyer, buyer Rich's, Inc., Atlanta, 1971-78, spl. events fashion coordinator, Columbia, S.C., 1978-83; gen. mdse. mgr. Rackes, Inc., Columbia, 1983-84, Parasol Boutique, Columbia, 1984-86; retail cons. Retail Mdsg. Service Automation, Columbia, 1986-88; sales rep. Palmetto Promotions, 1989-93; retail mdse. supr. Riverbanks Zoo & Garden, 1993—. Pres. Columbia Action Coun., 1990-92; bd. dirs. Palmetto Leadership Coun., 1991-92, Palmetto State Orch. Assn., Columbia, 1979-89, Women's Symphony Assn., Columbia, 1985; com. chmn. Columbia Action Coun., 1984-85, exec. com., 1989—. Named one of Outstanding Young Women Am., 1979, 80; recipient Community Service award Rich's, Inc., 1981. Mem. Nat. So. Colonial Dames Am., Columbia Jr. League. Democrat. Episcopalian. Club: Columbia Drama. Avocations: bridge, reading, needlepoint, tennis. Home: 4000 Bloomwood Rd Columbia SC 29205-2847

GRIMES, CRAIG ALAN, electrical engineering educator; b. Ann Arbor, Mich., Nov. 6, 1956; s. Dale Mills and Janet LaVonne (Moore) G. BS in Physics, Pa. State U., 1984, BSEE, 1984; MS, U. Tex., 1985, PhD, 1990. Engr. Applied Rsch. Labs., Austin, Tex., 1981-83; chief scientist Crale, Inc., Austin, 1985-90; rsch. scientist Lockeed Rsch. Labs., Palo Alto, Calif., 1990-92; dir. advanced materials lab. Southwall Techs., Palo Alto, Calif., 1992-94; asst. prof. dept. elec. engring. U. Ky., Lexington, 1994—; rsch. asst. U. Tex., Austin, 1985-88, teaching asst., 1987-90; cons. Eastman Kodak, San Diego, 1989, Storage Tech., Boulder, Colo., 1989, Read-Rite, Fremont, Calif., 1994, AT&T Bell Labs., Murray Hill, N.J., 1995; mem. Clark County Rural Electric Coop. Co-author: Essays on the Formal Aspects of E&M Theory, 1992, Advanced Electromagnetism: Foundation, Theory and Applications, 1995; contbr. articles to profl. jours. Active Nature Conservancy, New Braunfels, Tex., 1988-95, Austin Triathletes, 1987-90. Mem. AAAS, IEEE, Mountain View Masters, Bluegrass Masters. Home: 525 McCalls Mill Rd Lexington KY 40515 Office: U Ky Dept Elec Engring 453 Anderson Hall Lexington KY 40506

GRIMES, JAMES EDWARD, microbiologist; b. Ft. Worth, Mar. 29, 1925; s. Johnnie Edward and Ella Annie (Wiese) G.; m. Helen Martha Hahn, Dec. 12, 1929; children: Marla Yvette, Kirk Vaughn. AA, Clifton (Tex.) Jr. Coll., 1948; BA, Tex. Luth. Coll., Seguin, 1950; MA, U. Tex., 1957; PhD, Tex. A&M U., 1967. Virologist Tex. Dep. of Health, Austin, 1953-63; instr. Tex. A&M U., College Station, 1964-67, asst. prof., 1967-74, assoc. prof., 1974-87, prof. emeritus, 1987—; rsch. assoc. Tex. Vet. Med. Diagnostic Lab., College Station, 1987—. Author: (with others) Diseases of Poultry, 1991, CRC Handbook on Zoonoses, 1994; contbr. articles to profl. jours. Sgt. USAF, 1943-46, 50-51. Mem. Am. Assn. Avian Pathologists, Am. Soc. Microbiology, Assn. Avian Vets., Am. Assn. Vet. Lab. Diagnosticians, Tex. Vet. Med. Assn. (hon.), Tex. Luth. Coll. Alumni Assn. (Disting. Alumnus award 1993). Lutheran. Office: Tex Vet Med Diagnostic Lab PO Box 3040 College Station TX 77841-3040

GRIMES, JAMES GORDON, geologist; b. Kenosha, Wis., Mar. 18, 1951; s. James Gordon Bennett Jr. and Alyce Louise (Gannaway) G. BS in Earth Sci., U. Wis., Parkside, 1974; MS in Geology, Mich. Tech. U., 1977. Registered profl. geologist, Tenn. Geologist nat. uranium resource evaluation project Union Carbide Corp. Nuclear Div., Oak Ridge, Tenn., 1977-84; geol. cons. UCC-ND Mercury Task Force, Oak Ridge, 1983; geologist Lockheed Martin Energy Systems Inc., Oak Ridge, Tenn., 1984—; tech. mgr. Y-12 plant Meterol. Info. Support System, 1987—. Mem. AAAS, Am. Statis. Assn., Am. Meteorol. Soc., Am. Mgmt. Assn., Am. Water Resources Assn., Nat. Weather Assn., Geol. Soc. Am., Computer Oriented Geol. Soc., Air and Waste Mgmt. Assn., Internat. Assn. Math. Geology. Office: Lockheed Martin Energy Sys PO Box 2009 Oak Ridge TN 37831-8219

GRIMES, MARY WOODWORTH, special educational consultant; b. Huron County, Mich., Dec. 9, 1909; d. Fred Langdon and Sara Gertrude (Lowe) Woodworth; m. Ogden Edwin Grimes, June 2, 1934; children: Thomas Paul, Patricia, Mary Elizabeth, Paul Bartlett. BA, Mich. State Coll., 1933; MEd, N. Tex. State Coll., 1960; cert. in spl. edn., Tex. Women's U., 1966. Ednl. diagnostician, parent cons. in spl. edn. Carr-Farmers Branch Ind. Sch. Dist., Carrollton, Tex., to 1980; community cons., pvt. practice cons. Carrollton, 1980-90. Mary Grimes Ednl. Ctr. named in her honor, 1981. Mem. Assn. for Children With Learning Disabilities, Coun. for Exceptional Children, Assn. for Retarded Children, Tex. Ednl. Diagnosticians, PTA (life mem.), Delta Kappa Gamma. Home: 1609 Denton Dr Carrollton TX 75006-3830

GRIMES, RICHARD STUART, editor, writer; b. Wheeling, W.Va., June 28, 1939; s. Harold George and Sarah (Rebic) G.; m. Katheryn Perrine Johnson, Nov. 7, 1964; children: Sara Jane, Richard Harold, Stephen Ross. Grad., W.Va. U., 1961. Reporter Charleston (W.Va.) Daily Mail, 1964—, polit. editor, 1985—, also regular columnist; master of ceremonies TV show Underfire, Pub. TV, 1989—. Author: Old Money, New Politics, 1984; syndicated columnist in some 40 newspapers. Chmn. of bd. Meth. Ch., 1990. Sgt. U.S. Army, 1961-64. Mem. Southridge Lions Club (pres. 1994—). Republican. Home: 679 Gordon Dr Charleston WV 25314-1751

GRIMES, SIDNEY RAY, JR., research biochemist; b. Washington, July 31, 1947; s. Sidney Ray Sr. and Nancy L. (Wilkes) G.; m. Judy Kirkland Watts, June 15, 1969; children: Natalie M., Gregory T., Nathaniel J. BS in Chemistry, U. N.C., 1969, PhD in Biochemistry, 1973. Rsch. assoc. M.D. Anderson Cancer Ctr. U. Tex., Houston, 1973-75; postdoctoral fellow Vanderbilt U., Nashville, 1975-76; rsch. biochemist rsch. svc. VA Med. Ctr., Shreveport, La., 1976—; asst. prof. dept. biochemistry and molecular biology La. State U. Med. Ctr., Shreveport, 1976-87, rsch. assoc. prof. dept. biochemistry and molecular biology, 1988—. Contbr. articles to profl. jours. Grantee NIH, VA; USPHS grantee Vanderbilt U., 1976. Mem. AAAS, Am. Soc. for Cell Biology, Am. Soc. for Microbiology, Sigma Xi. Republican. Baptist. Home: 9533 Leaside Way Shreveport LA 71118-4310 Office: VA Med Ctr 510 E Stoner Ave Shreveport LA 71101-4243

GRIMES, STEPHEN HENRY, state supreme court chief justice; b. Peoria, Ill., Nov. 17, 1927; s. Henry Holbrook and June (Kellar) G.; m. Mary Fay Fulghum, Dec. 29, 1951; children: Gay Diane, Mary June, Sue Anne, Sheri Lynn. Student, Fla. So. Coll., 1946-47; BS in Bus. Adminstrn. with honors, U. Fla., 1951, LLB with honors, 1954; LLD (hon.), Stetson U., 1980. Bar: Fla. 1954, U.S. Dist. Ct. (no. and so. dists.) 1954, U.S. Ct. Appeals (5th cir.) 1965, U.S. Supreme Ct. 1972. Since practiced in Bartow, Fla.; ptnr. firm Holland and Knight and predecessor firm, 1954-73; judge Ct. Appeal 2d Dist. Fla., Lakeland, Fla., 1973-87; chief judge Ct. Appeal 2d Dist. Fla., 1978-80; chmn. Conf. Fla. Dist. Cts. Appeal, 1978-80; justice Fla. Supreme Ct., Tallahassee, 1987—, chief justice, 1994-96; chair Article V Task Force, 1994-96; mem. Fla. Jud. Qualification Commn., 1982-86, vice chmn., 1985-86; chmn. Fla. Jud. Coun., 1989-94. Contbr. articles U. Fla. Law Rev., 1951, 54. Bd. dirs. Bartow Meml. Hosp., 1958-61, Bartow Library, 1968-78; trustee Polk Community Coll., Winter Haven, Fla., 1967-70, chmn., 1969-70; bd. govs. Polk Pub. Mus., 1976—. Lt. (j.g.) USN, 1951-53. Fellow Am. Coll. Trial Lawyers; mem. ABA, Fla. Bar Assn. (bd. govs. jr. bar 1956-58, bd. dirs. trial lawyers sect. 1967-69, sec. 1969, vice chmn. appellate rules com. 1976-77, vice chmn. tort litigation rev. commn. 1985-86), 10th Cir. Bar Assn. (pres. 1966), Am. Judicature Soc., Bartow C. of C. (pres. 1964), Rotary (dist. gov. 1960-61). Episcopalian (sr. warden 1964-65, 77). Office: Fla Supreme Ct Supreme Ct Bldg Tallahassee FL 32399-1925

GRIMES, TRESMAINE JUDITH RUBAIN, psychology educator; b. N.Y.C., Aug. 3, 1959; d. Judith May (McIntosh) Rubain; m. Clarence Grimes, Jr., Dec. 22, 1984; children: Elena Joanna, Elijah Jeremy. BA, Yale U., 1980; MA, New Sch. for Social Rsch., 1982; MPhil, PhD, Columbia U., 1990. Advanced tchg. fellow Jewish Bd. Family and Childrens Svcs., N.Y.C., 1980-82; tchg./rsch. asst. Tchrs. Coll., Columbia U., N.Y.C., 1983-84; rschr., historian Youth Action Program, N.Y.C., 1984-86; psychologist Hale House for Infants, N.Y.C., 1986-89; asst. rschr. Bank St. Coll., N.Y.C., 1988; addiction program adminstr. Harlem Hosp. Ctr., N.Y.C., 1989-91; assoc. prof. and chair dept. psychology S.C. State U., Orangeburg, 1991—; adj. prof. psychology Tchrs. Coll., Columbia U., N.Y.C., 1990-91. Named Outstanding Young Women of Am., 1981. Mem. APA, Southeastern Psychol. Assn., Delta Sigma Theta, Kappa Delta Pi, Psi Chi. Democrat. Office: SC State Univ Box 7003 300 College St NE Orangeburg SC 29117-0001

GRIMM, CLAYFORD THOMAS, architectural engineer, consultant; b. Buchannon, W.Va., July 31, 1924; s. Clayford Thomas and Genevieve Fallon G.; BArchE, Cath. U. Am., 1949; m. Elide Lucy Medone, Dec. 27, 1946; 1 child, Rose Marie. Sr. lectr. archtl. engring. U. Tex., Austin, 1969-91; pres. Clayford T. Grimm, P.E., Inc., cons. archtl. engrs., Austin. Pres., Serra Club, Austin, 1970-71. Served with inf. AUS, 1944-46. Fellow ASTM (Walter C. Voss award 1994), ASCE (life); mem. The Masonry Soc. (Pres. award 1995), Constrn. Specifications Inst. (spl. award edn.), Brit. Masonry Soc., Am. Concrete Inst. Republican. Roman Catholic. Contbr. over 143 articles to profl. jours. Home: 1904 Wooten Dr Austin TX 78757-7702

GRIMM, WILLIAM THOMAS, lawyer; b. Phila., Feb. 23, 1940; s. Joseph L. and Evelyn Carstens (Gleason) G.; m. Sonja N. Lied, Jan. 17, 1977; children: Emily S., Lars J.L., Niles C.L. BA, Lafayette Coll., 1961; LLB, U. Va., 1964. Bar: N.J. 1965, N.Y. 1970, Fla. 1973, Calif. 1980. Assoc. Archer, Greiner, Hunter & Read, Camden, N.J., 1965-68; sr. assoc. Shearman & Sterling, N.Y.C., 1969-72; v.p. legal Investment Corp. of Fla., Ft. Lauderdale, 1972-75; chief counsel Westinghouse Communities, Coral Springs, Fla., 1975-86; exec. v.p. Westinghouse Communities of Ariz., Tucson, 1988-93; assoc. gen. counsel Westinghouse Electric Corp., 1991-93; freelance developer cons., mediator, arbitrator Naples, Fla., 1993—; chmn. adv. bd. Holly Inn, Pinehurst, N.C., 1986-96. Mem. Am. Arbitration Assn., Am. Assn. Corp. Counsel (assoc.), Soc. Profls. in Dispute Resolution, Assn. Bar City N.Y., Fla. Bar, Urban Land Inst. (assoc.), Fla. Acad. Cert. Mediators, Fla. Trial Lawyers (vice chair alternative dispute resolution com. 1996—), Naples Coun. on World Affairs, The Conservancy. Republican. Methodist. Office: 277 Monterey Dr Naples FL 34119-4650

GRIMSLEY, DOUGLAS LEE, psychology educator, researcher; b. San Diego, Sept. 18, 1939; s. Ralph Waldo and Anna (Gall) G.; m. Mary Beasley, Apr. 23, 1965; children: Stephen, Cynthia. BS, Fla. State U., 1961; PhD, Syracuse U., 1964. Asst. prof. Fla. State U.Tallahassee, 1964-66; sr. scientist human resources rsch. office George Washington U., Monterey, Calif., 1966-68; assoc. prof. psychology U. So. Miss., Hattiesburg, 1968-70, U. N.C., Charlotte, 1970—. Contbg. author: Thirst, 1964; contbr. articles to profl. jours. Recipient NCNB teaching award Nations Bank, Charlotte, 1965; rsch. grantee USPHS, 1964-65, State of N.C., 1971-94. Mem. Assn. for Applied Psychophysiology and Biofeedback, Sigma Xi. Office: U NC Dept Psychology Charlotte NC 28223

GRINNELL, LAWRENCE JEFFREY, systems administrator; b. Indpls., Sept. 22, 1954; s. Norman Franklin and Dorothea Cora (Nelson) G. AA, Palm Beach C.C., 1989. Ground radio comms. equipment tech. USAF, 1973-82; from product support tech. to sr. sys. adminstr. Motorola, Boynton Beach, Fla., 1982—. Recipient recognition of excellence award South Fla. Mfrs. Assn., 1994. Mem. Soc. Tech. Comm., New Eng. Hist. Geneal. Soc., R.I. Hist. Soc., Am. Radio Relay League, Grinnell Family Assn. Am. (chmn. geneal. com. 1992—), Palm Beach Macintosh User's Group (bd. dirs. 1992—), Elec. Design Assn., Motorola Tech. Communicators Assn. (steering com. 1993—). Home: 1623 16th Ln Greenacres FL 33463 Office: Motorola Inc Paging Prod 1500 Gateway Blvd Boynton Beach FL 33426

GRINNELL, PAULA C., educational researcher; b. Detroit, Nov. 16, 1945; d. Philip and Mollie (Gastman) Cameron; m. Frederick Grinnell, June 29, 1969; children: Laura, Phillip, Aviva. BA, U. Mich., 1967; MEd, Boston U., 1968; PhD, Tex. Women's U., 1980. Dir. R&D Carrollton Farmers Br. Ind. Sch. Dist.; dir. Summer Literacy Inst. U. Tex., Richardson; chair English dept. Dallas Ind. Sch. Dist.; postdoctoral fellow dept. psychology Yale U., New Haven. Author: Developing Effective Classroom Tests, Facilitating Children's Growth in Writing, Developmental Pespectives on Writing, Teaching the Learning Disabled, How Can I Prepare My Young Child for Reading?; contbr. numerous articles to profl. jours. Mem. Mayor's Task Force, Dallas, 1984; v.p. Am. Jewish Congress, Dallas; bd. dirs., program chair career and profl. women's div. Jewish Fedn. Dallas. Mem. ASCD, North Ctrl. Tex. ASCD (membership chair), North Tex. Coun. of Internat. Reading Assn. (pres.), Tex. State Coun. Internat. Reading Assn. (editor), Am. Edn!. Rsch. Assn., Nat. Coun. on Measurement in Edn. (membership com.), Nat. Coun. Tchrs. English, Phi Delta Kappa (pres. elect). Office: Carrollton Farmers Br Ind Sch Dist 1445 N Perry Rd PO Box 115186 Carrollton TX 75011

GRISCHKOWSKY, DANIEL RICHARD, research scientist, educator; b. St. Helens, Oreg., Apr. 17, 1940; s. Oscar Edward and Christine Hazel (Olsen) G.; m. Frieda Rosa Bachmann; children: Timothy and Stephanie (twins), Daniela. BS, Oreg. State U., 1962; AM in Physics, Columbia U., 1965, PhD in Physics, 1968. Postdoctoral studies Columbia U., N.Y.C., 1968-69; mem. rsch. staff IBM Watson Rsch. Ctr., Yorktown Heights, N.Y., 1969-77; sci. advisor to dir. rsch. div. IBM, Yorktown Heights, 1978; mgr. atomic physics with lasers group IBM Watson Rsch. Ctr., Yorktown Heights, 1979-83, mgr. ultra-fast sci. with lasers group, 1983-93; Bellmon chair optoelectronics Sch. Elec. and Computer Engring. Okla. State U., Stillwater, 1993—; chmn. Internat. Coun. on Quantum Electronics, 1989-93, Am. Phys. Soc./Optical Soc. Am./IEEE Joint Coun. on Quantum Electronics, 1989-93. Contbr. articles to profl. jours.; patentee in field. Recipient Boris Pregel award N.Y. Acad. of Sci., 1985. Fellow IEEE, Am. Phys. Soc. (chmn. laser sci. topical group 1993-94), Optical Soc. Am. (R.W. Wood prize 1989). Office: Okla State U Sch Elec Computer Engring Stillwater OK 74078-0321*

GRISH, MARILYN KAY, speech educator; b. Detroit, Jan. 20, 1951; d. George and Olga (Yanowsky) G.; 1 child, Christina Kay. BS, Ea. Mich. U., 1973, MA, 1974; EdD, Nova U., 1985. Speech pathologist Sch. Bd. Broward County, Ft. Lauderdale, Fla., 1974-90; adminstr. Sch. Bd. Broward County, Ft. Lauderdale, 1990—; instr. Nova Southeastern U., Ft. Lauderdale, 1990—, grant writer, 1992—; adv. bd. mem. Family and Sch. Ctr., Ft. Lauderdale, 1992-94. Supporter Broward Edn. Found., Ft. Lauderdale, 1994—, United Way, Ft. Lauderdale, 1990—, Orthodox Ch. Am., 1974—, Nova Southeastern U. Sch. & Parents Assn., 1994—. Grantee Title II Math. Sci. Project, 1992-93. Mem. Am. Speech and Hearing Assn. (hospitality com. nat. conv. 1994), Fla. ASCD (tech. jour. editor 1992—), Fla. Speech, Lang. and Hearing Assn. (publicity chairperson state conv. 1986). Democrat. Office: Nova Southeastern U 3301 College Ave Fort Lauderdale FL 33314-7721

GRISHAM, ROBERT DOUGLAS, lawyer; b. Abilene, Tex., Dec. 30, 1926; s. Thomas Franklin and Jimmie Douglas (Moore) G.; m. Justine Digby-Roberts, June 12, 1948; children: Thomas Franklin II, Cynthia Marr. BBa, Hardin-Simmons U., 1950; JD, So. Meth. U., 1954. Bar: Tex. 1954, U.S. Dist.Ct. (no. dist.) Tex. 1954, U.S. Ct. Appeals (5th cir.) 1958; cert. estate planning and probate law. Pvt. practice, Abilene, Tex., 1954-82; of counsel Glandon, Scarborough, Gravley & Leggett, P.C., Abilene, 1982—. Bd. dirs., officer Abilene Community Theater, 1954-63; pres., bd. dirs. Community Welfare Coun., Abilene, 1956-57, Pastoral Care and Counseling Ctr., Abilene, 1974-80; Abilene Coun. on Alcoholism, 1975—; sec., bd. dirs. Hendrick Med. Ctr. Found., Abilene, 1973-89; bd. dirs. Hendrick Home for Children Found., 1982-88; v.p., bd. dirs. Serenity House, Abilene, 1984—. With AUS, 1945-46. Fellow Am. Coll. Trust and Estate Counsel, Tex. Bar Found., Coll. of the State Bar of Tex.; mem. ABA, State Bar Tex., Abilene Country Club. Episcopalian. Home: 1510 Woodridge Dr Abilene TX 79605-4827 Office: Glandon Scarborough Gravley & Leggett PC 3305 N 3rd St Ste 300 Abilene TX 79603-7043

GRISHAM, THOMAS J., real estate professional; b. Lubbock, Tex., Oct. 9, 1957; s. Rufus W. and Nancy Jean (Blankenship) G.; m. Julie Ellen Thurner, July 5, 1985; children: Tyler James, Caroline Julie, Anna Catherine. BBA in Acctg., U. Miss.; MBA, U. Tex. Tax acct. Peat, Marwick, et. al., Houston, 1980-82; mng. dir. Trammell Crow, Dallas, 1983—; adv. Rollins Coll., Winter Park, Fla., 1990-93. Redevel. coun. leader Casselbery Adv. Bd., Fla., 1991-93; bd. dirs. Orange County, Orlando, Fla., 1991, Scottish Rite Hosp., Dallas, 1994—; mem. com. Presbyn. Ch., 1994—. Mem. Real Estate Coun. Republican. Home: 3700 Purdue Dallas TX 75225 Office: Trammell Crow 2200 Ross #3700 Dallas TX 75201

GRISSOM, EUGENE EDWARD, art educator, consultant, researcher, musician; b. Melvern, Kans., May 15, 1922; s. Edwin Hobart and Elizabeth Elma (Sattler) G.; m. Marjorie Jean Fanestil, Aug. 14, 1949 (div.); children: Jon F., Joni F.; m. Nancy Lorraine Day, Dec. 9, 1961. B.S. in Music, Kans. State Tchrs. Coll.-Emporia, 1948; postgrad. U. Philippines, Manila, 1945; M.F.A. in Art History and Printmaking, State U. Iowa, 1951. Instr. art Kans. State Tchrs. Coll.-Emporia, summer 1951, U. Ky., Lexington, 1951-53; asst. prof. drawing and art history U. Fla., Gainesville, 1953-60, acting chmn., 1961, chmn., 1963-78, prof. art 1978-87, prof. emeritus, ret., 1987; mem. Gainesville Community Jazz Ensemble, The New Gainesville Jazz Orch., Covenant Presbyn. Brass Quartet, 1989-93, Contemporary Jazz/Trombone 4, 1989-96; pres. Gainesville Friends of Jazz, 1985-87, Jazz at the Thomas concert series (grants adminstr. 1986-90, grantee Nat. Endowment for the Arts 1988-90); sr. grants advisor GFCJ, Inc., 1991-94; grants advisor Women in Jazz program, 1993-96. Bd. dirs., chmn. adv. com. Arts Council Alachua County, Gainesville, 1986-88; bd. dirs. Arts Assn. of Alachua County, 1988-91; mem. nat. jazz planning study The Nat. Jazz Svc. Orgn., 1990; mem. jazz adv. panel So. Arts Fedn., 1990-96; mem. art selection com. Fla. Art in State Bldgs., 1987-88; active The Harn Alliance and The Samuel P. Harn Mus. of Art, 1990-96; mem. Univ. Art Soc. U. Fla., mem. vital local cultural program panel State of Fla., 1991-92, mem. vital local cultural program on-site evaluator, 1990-91; bd. dirs. Celebration '90 & '91 U. Fla. Served with USAAF, 1943-46. Decorated Philippine Liberation ribbon with 1 Bronze Star. Founder E. E. Grissom Trombone Library, U. Fla., 1980—, co-sponsor (with Internat. Trombone Assn.) Frank Rosolino Memorial Scholarship for Jazz Trombone, 1979-96, co-founder Frank Rosolino Meml. Fund, Inc., 1994; grantee So. Arts Fedn.. Mem. Internat. Trombone Assn. (trombone choir 1976-96), Coll. Art Assn. Am., Internat. Assn. Jazz Record Collectors, Am. Fedn. Jazz Socs. (exec. sec., bd. dirs. 1985-88), Phi Mu Alpha (Sinfonia/nat. hon. music frat.). Represented in pub. and pvt. collections prints/engravings; touring exhbns. include collection etchings, Exhibits U.S.A., 1992-94. Home: 4607 Clearlake Dr Gainesville FL 32607-2238 Office: Gainesville Friends of Jazz Inc PO Box 12769 Gainesville FL 32604-0769

GRISSOM, JAMES ROGER, hematologist, oncologist; b. Jonesboro, Ark., Nov. 8, 1946. BS in Zoology, Ark. State U., 1969, MS in Biology, 1971; MD, U. Ark., 1975. Bd. cert. in internal medicine and med. oncology. Staff physician Bapt. Med. Ctr., Little Rock, 1981—, St. Vincent Infirmary, Little Rock, 1981—, Dr.'s Hosp., Little Rock, 1981—. Mem. Am. Soc. Clin. Oncology. Office: 9501 Lile Dr Ste 700 Little Rock AR 72205

GRISSOM, JERRY BRYAN, interior designer; b. Norman, Okla., Feb. 21, 1949; s. Vernon Harold and Florence Julia (Wampler) G. BA, Okla. U., 1975. Decorating cons. Sherwin Williams Co., Kansas City, Mo., 1975-77; interior designer J. Richard Blissit Assocs., Tulsa, 1977-78, 83-92; interior design instr. U. Okla., Norman, 1978-79; interior designer Day Yadon Ragland Architects, Tulsa, 1980-83, Richard F. Geary Interiors, Inc., Naples, Fla., 1992-94, Ross Design Assocs., Naples, Fla., 1994—. Sgt. USMC, 1967-70, Vietnam. Mem. Am. Soc. Interior Designers. Home: 2239 Sunset Ln Naples FL 34104-4227

GRISSOM, RAYMOND EARL, JR., toxicologist; b. Raleigh, N.C., Oct. 27, 1943; s. Raymond Earl and Edith (Ballance) G.; m. Lorraine Rankin, Aug. 11, 1974; children: Kelly Daniel, James Earl, Mary Elizabeth. 2 BS degrees with high honors, N.C. State U., 1976, PhD, 1982. Scientist N.C. Bd. Sci. and Tech., Raleigh, 1982-83; postdoctoral rsch. assoc. N.C. State U., Raleigh, 1983-87; toxicologist Environ Monitoring and Svcs., Inc., Chapel Hill, N.C., 1987-88; toxicologist Agy. for Toxic Substances and Disease Registry, Atlanta, 1988-90, sr. toxicologist, 1990—; cons. Becton Dickinson Rsch. Ctr., Research Triangle Park, N.C., 1986-87; speaker internat. symposiums, Eng., 1989, Malaysia, 1990, Can., 1993. Author book chpts., govt. documents; contbr. articles to profl. jours. Coach South Gwinnett League Basketball, Atlanta, 1990-96. Recipient citation for disting. svc. State of N.C., 1983, City of Atlanta, 1990-96. Mem. AAAS, Soc. Toxicology, Sigma Xi, Gamma Sigma Delta. Presbyterian. Home: 4959 Joy Ln SW Lilburn GA 30247-5119 Office: Agy Toxic Substances & Disease Registry 1600 Clifton Rd NE # E32 Atlanta GA 30329-4018

GRIST, ROBERT, agricultural products executive; b. 1933. With Grist Farms, Tifton, Ga., 1965-74; pres., dir. Ga. Vegetable Co., Inc., Tifton, 1974—. Office: GA Vegetable Co Inc U S Hwy 41 Tifton County Tifton GA 31794*

GRISWOLD, GEORGE, marketing, advertising and public relations executive; b. N.Y.C., Mar. 5, 1919; s. George and Isabel (Bridgman) G.; student Ecole des Beaux Arts, Fontainebleau, France, 1939; B.A., Yale U., 1941; postgrad. N.Y. U., 1947; m. Tracy Haight, May 15, 1942 (div. 1985); children: Tracy Griswold Glass, Mariana Van Rensselaer Griswold Geer, Alice Bradford Griswold Stetson; m. Joan Loosley McNamara, Mar. 11, 1986; m. Nancy Cox Holbrook, Apr. 3, 1993. Editor, Fairchild Publs., N.Y.C., 1945-46; pub. relations, operating positions long lines dept. AT&T, 1946-49, pub. relations exec., N.Y.C., 1962-79; exec. Newsweek mag., N.Y.C., 1951-55; exec. dir. pub. rels. and publs. divsn. Bell Labs., Inc., N.Y., N.J., 1955-62; pres. Litchfield Distbrs., Inc. (Conn.), 1949-52; tchr. Fairleigh Dickinson U. Grad. Sch., 1961; sr. v.p. Sheldon Satin Assocs., Inc., N.Y., 1979-83; pres. Griswold Comm. Hilton Head, S.C., 1983-89; v.p. mktg. and pub. rels., Environ. Am. Inc., Hilton Head, 1989-92. Comdr. USNR, 1941-45. Mem. Public Relations Soc. Am. (accredited), Nat. Assn. Sci. Writers, Soc. Mayflower Descs., Soc. Colonial Wars, Huguenot Soc. Am., Yale Club, S.C. Yacht Club, Piedmont Club. Home: 509 Claridge Cir Winston Salem NC 27106-6301

GRIZZARD, RICHELLE ALLENE, legal assistant; b. Sioux Falls, S.D., Nov. 6, 1948; d. Charles Richard and Barbara Shirley (Tough) Knudsen; m. John Barry Grizzard; 1 child, John Charles. BA in Polit. Sci. summa cum laude, U. North Fla., 1981, MPA, 1992. Legal sec. George W. Kent, Orange Park, Fla., 1982-84, Maness & Kachergus, Jacksonville, Fla., 1984-87; freelance legal sec. Orange Park, Jacksonville, 1987-89; legal sec. Adams, Rothstein & Siegel, Jacksonville, 1989; legal asst. Dale & Bald, P.A., Jacksonville, 1990-92; Madison/Mullis fellow Ctr. for Local Govt. Adminstrn., U. North Fla., Jacksonville, 1992; free-lance legal asst. Jacksonville, 1993-94; resource devel. specialist Agy. Approval & Devel., Inc., Jacksonville, 1993-94; legal asst. Florin, Roebig, Walker & Schloth, Jacksonville, 1995—; notary public State of Fla., 1982—. Mem., vol. tutor Learn to Read, Inc., 1995—. Mem. Am. Soc. Pub. Adminstrn., Lions (dir. 1992-94, sight chmn. 1993—, Gov.'s Achievement award 1994), Phi Theta Kappa, Pi Alpha Alpha. Democrat. Office: Florin Roebig Walker & Schloth 200 W Forsyth St Jacksonville FL 32202-4349

GRIZZLE, PATRICIA SUTTON, enterostomal therapy nurse, educator; b. Elizabethtown, Ky.; d. Charles Walter and Lucy L. (Horn) Sutton; m. Dennis D. Grizzle, 1956; children: Dennis D., Kevin P., Mary P. Grizzle Lanceta. BSN, Spalding U., Louisville, 1955; cert. enterostomal therapy, U. Kans., Kansas City, 1981. Clin. instr. Spalding U., 1956-58; dir. nursing Medifacts, Inc., Louisville, 1970-72; nurse mgr. St. Joseph Infirmary, Louisville, 1972-81; enterstomal therapy clinician Columbia Audubon Hosp., Louisville, 1981—. Mem. Wound, Ostomy and Continence Nursing Assn. (cert. enterstomal therapy nurse), United Ostomy Assn., Ky. Coun. Specialty Nurses Orgn., Spaulding U. Alumni Assn., Sigma Theta Tau (Iota Gamma chpt.).

GROCE, JAMES FREELAN, financial consultant; b. Lubbock, Tex., Nov. 24, 1948; s. Wayne Dee and Betty Jo (Rice) G.; m. Patricia Kay Rogers; 1 child, Jason Eric. BS cum laude, Tex. Tech U., 1971. Registered profl. engr., Tex. Petroleum engr. Texaco, Inc., Sweetwater, Tex., 1971-74; drilling and prodn. engr. Texaco, Inc., Wichita Falls, Tex., 1974-77; asst. dist. engr. Texaco, Inc., Midland, Tex., 1977-78; sr. prodn. engr. Bass Enterprises Prodn., Midland, 1978-81; petroleum engr. Murphy H. Baxter Co., Midland, 1981-82, Henry Engring., Midland, 1982-87; petroleum engr. Fasken Oil and Ranch Interests, Midland, 1987, mgr. engring./ops., 1987-95; fin. cons. Smith Barney, Midland, 1996—. Scoutmaster Boy Scouts Am., Midland, 1980-83, merit badge counselor, 1987; mem. Community Bible Study, Midland, 1987-93. Mem. Soc. Petroleum Evaluation Engrs. (sect. chmn. 1987), Soc. Petroleum Engrs. (sect. chmn. 1996), Nat. Assn. Corrosion Engrs., Mensa, Tex. Tech. Ex-Student Assn., Century Club, Tau Beta Pi. Presbyterian. Home: 2117 Bradford Ct Midland TX 79705-1727

GROEBER, SARA VIRGINIA, human resources executive; b. Albany, Ga., July 1, 1956; d. Thomas Roosevelt and Virginia Swallow (Colvin) Coleman; children: Caitlin Marie, Emily Louise. BS in Mktg., U. Wyo., 1977. Chief workforce planning and devel. office U.S. Army Fin. and Acctg. Ctr., Indpls., 1985-88; with legis. and external rels. dept. office dir. pers. U.S. Army, Arlington, Va., 1988, chief Army sr. exec. svc. office office asst. sec., 1988-91; dep. dir. human resources Def. Fin. and Acctg. Svc., Arlington, 1991-92, project mgr. DOD acctg. consolidation, 1992-93; project mgr. civil pers. consolidation Office of DASD, Arlington, 1993; dir. Congrl. and external rels. Office of Dep. Asst. Sec. Def., Arlington, 1993-95; dep. dir. Def. Civilian Pers. Mgmt. Svc., Arlington, 1995—. Vol. Olde Creek/Oakview Elem. Sch., Fairfax, Va., 1991—; vol. recruitment/staffing Pan Am. Games, Indpls., 1986. Recipient Hammer award V.p. of U.S., 1995, Achievement of Yr. award Assn. Govt. Accts., 1988. Home: 4876 Oakcrest Dr Fairfax VA 22030 Office: Def Civilian Pers Mgmt Svc 1400 Key Blvd Ste B200 Arlington VA 22209

GROGAN, ALICE WASHINGTON, lawyer; b. Richmond, Va., Jan. 25, 1956; d. Thomas Boyd Washington Jr. and Dorothy Jane (Smith) W.; m. Ralph Houston Grogan, Feb. 4, 1989. BS with honors, Va. Poly. Inst., 1978; JD, U. N.C., 1984. Bar: N.C. 1984, U.S. Supreme Ct. 1988. Corp. sec., atty. Piedmont Aviation, Inc., Winston-Salem, N.C., 1984-88; assoc. Womble Carlyle Sandridge & Rice, Winston-Salem, 1988-89; counsel Wachovia Corp. and Wachovia Bank of N.C., N.A., Winston-Salem, 1989—; corp. sec. Wachovia Corp., Winston-Salem, 1992—. Vol. ABCD Child Devel. Ctr., Piedmont Craftsmen, Inc. Mem. ABA (sect. bus. law corp. counsel com., fin. and securities subcom.), N.C. Bar Assn. (corp. counsel sect., sec.), Forsyth County Bar Assn., Va. Tech. Alumni Assn., U. N.C. Gen. Alumni Assn., U. N.C. Ednl. Found., Phi Kappa Phi.

GROGAN, BETTE LOWERY, steel fastener distribution executive; b. Seminole, Okla., Nov. 18, 1931; d. C.J. and Martha C. (Eakin) Lowery; m. Morris Rowell, Feb. 8, 1947 (div. Oct. 1960); children: Ronald Michael, Kathy D. Rowell Ray; m. John Kenneth Grogan, Oct. 28, 1967. Student Del Mar Coll., 1949-51, So. Meth. U., 1963-65. Sec., office mgr. Carrigan Realty, Orlando, Fla., 1958-61; dist. sec. Tektronics, Inc., Orlando, 1961-63; legal sec. Jenkens, Anson, Spradley & Gilchrist, Dallas, 1963-67; real estate broker, Dallas, 1967-77; v.p. Grogan & Co., Dallas, 1972-77; pres. Fla. Threaded Products Inc., Orlando, 1977—; dir. Women's Bus. Ednl. Council (pres. 1986, chmn. bd. 1987), Inc., Orlando, pres., 1986. Mem. Planning and Zoning Commn., Carrollton, Tex., 1972-74; bd. dirs. Jr. Achievement, Orlando, 1981-83, Healthcare Cost Containment Bd., Fla. Def. Conversion and Transition Commn., 1993—; del. Gov.'s Conf. on Small Bus., 1987, 89, 91, White House Conf. on Small Bus., Fla., 1986; sec.-treas. Cmty. Health Purchasing Alliance, State of Fla., 1993—. Named Cen. Fla. Small Bus. Person of the Yr., SBA-C. of C., 1981. Mem. Women's Bus. Ednl. Confs. Fla. (bd. dirs. 1984-85, exec. v.p. 1985-86, pres. 1986, chmn. bd. dirs. 1987), Nat. Fedn. Ind. Bus. (guardian adv. council), Fastener Assn. (bd. dirs. 1980-84), Central Fla. Leadership Council (bd. dirs. 1984—), Greater Orlando C. of C. (chairperson N.W. regional coun. 1990), Fla. Exec. Women, Better Bus. Bur. Cen. Fla. (mem. exec. com., chmn. 1989, bd. dirs. 1989), Beta Sigma Phi (pres. Orlando 1957-59), Rotary. Republican. Episcopalian. Avocations: tennis, golf, reading. Office: Fla Threaded Products Inc 3060 Clemson Rd Orlando FL 32808-3945

GROGAN, DAVID R., company executive. Pres. Toter, Inc., Statesville, N.C. Office: 841 Meacham Rd Statesville NC 28677

GROGAN, DEBBY ELAINE, home health care nurse, medical/surgical nurse; b. Roanoke, Va., Sept. 8, 1955; d. Jauquin B. and Hope Thomas (Smith) Holton; div.; children: Tina Nicole, Christopher J. (dec.). AD, South Ga. Coll., 1985. RN, Ga. Nurse's asst. Jeff Davis Hosp., Hazlehurst, Ga., 1984; staff nurse med. Coffee Regional Hosp., Douglas, Ga., 1985, head nurse 2 North Med., 1985-91; ICU staff nurse Appling Gen Hosp., Baxley, Ga., 1991-95; clin. team leader/field RN Care One Home Health, Baxley, 1994—.

GROGAN, ROBERT HARRIS, lawyer; b. Bklyn., Feb. 25, 1933: s. Robert Michael and Nora Howarth (Johnson) G. AB, Harvard U., 1955; LLB, U. Va., 1961; m. Delia Ann Grossi, Dec. 23, 1967 (div. 1982); m. Lynn D. Habian, June 20, 1987. Bar: Va., 1961, N.Y., 1962, Ill., 1977, Fla., 1986. Assoc. Milbank, Tweed, Hadley & McCloy, N.Y.C., 1961-66; counsel Anaconda Co., N.Y.C., 1966-68; assoc. Shearman & Sterling, N.Y.C., 1968-75; v.p., gen. counsel staff Citibank, N.Y.C., 1975-76; ptnr. Mayer, Brown & Platt, Chgo., 1976-81; of counsel Olwine, Connelly, Chase, O'Donnell & Weyher, N.Y.C., 1981-87, sr. v.p., dep. sr. counsel, S.E. Bank, N.A., Miami, Fla., 1987-91; sr. v.p., gen. counsel Republic Nat. Bank of Miami, Fla., 1992-96; vice chmn. exec. adv. coun. Andreas Bus. Sch. Barry U., Miami Shores, Fla., 1995—; lectr. in field. Sec., bd. dirs. 3d Equity Owners Corp., coop. housing corp., 1975-77, pres., bd. dirs., 1982-86. With U.S. Army, 1956-58. Mem. ABA, Fla. Bar, N.Y. Bar, Va. State Bar Assn., Ill. State Bar Assn., Phi Delta Phi, Harvard Club (N.Y.C), Harvard Faculty Club (Cambridge, Mass.). Contbg. author: The Local Economic Development Corporation, 1970.

GROGG, SAM, dean; b. Moline, Ill., Mar. 29, 1947; s. Samuel Luther and Hazel Ellen (Bedwell) G.; m. Linda Hougan, June 1, 1968 (div. Aug. 1979); 1 child, Brady Ellen; m. Susan Bayer, Nov. 23, 1981; 1 child, Keaton Harrison. BA in English, Western Ill. U., 1969, MA in English, 1970; PhD in English and Am. Lit., Bowling Green U., 1974. Exec. dir. nat. end. Am. Film Inst., Washington, 1974-81; exec. dir. USA Film Festival, Inc., Dallas, 1981-84; pres., CEO, exec. producer FilmDallas, Inc., Dallas and L.A., 1984-89; pres., CEO Apogee Prodns. and Magic Pictures, Inc., L.A., 1989-92; dean Sch. of Filming N.C. Sch. of The Arts, Winston-Salem, 1993—; asst. prof., instr., teaching fellow English dept. Bowling Green (Ohio) U., 1970-74; vis. prof. U. Md., College Park, 1975-77, U. Tex., Arlington, 1985-87; disting. vis. prof. Sch. of Film and TV, UCLA, 1988—. Exec. producer films The Trip to Bountiful, 1985 (nominated for 2 Acad. awards), DA, 1987

(Deauville Film Festival Coup de Coeur award); writer screenplays Ramblin Rose, 1981, Avalanche, 1982; writer, producer TV show Quiz Kids, 1980-81; editor AFI Edn. newsletter, 1977-79; gen. editor Frank Capra, 1977, Jan Kadar, 1977, Billy Wilder, 1977, Satyajit Ray, 1977; co-editor: The Popular Smithsonian, 1975, Profiles in Popular Culture, 1971-74, others. Mem. fed. interagy. com. on edn. U.S. Office Edn., 1976-78; project dir. nat. survey film and TV higher edn. Nat. Endowment for the Arts, 1976; spl. cons. Nat. Ctr. Ednl. Statistics, 1976-77; coord. nat. edn. programs Popular Culture Assn., 1973-76; mem. adv. bd. Ind. Feature Project-West, U.S. Film Festival, 1984-89, Leadership Dallas, 1983-84; bd. dirs. Ind. Feature Project-East, 1984-85. Recipient Spirit award Am. Ind. Film Arts, 1986, Luminas award Image of Women in Film, 1986; grantee Nat. Endowment for the Arts, Rockefeller Found., Atlantic Richfield Found., Oak Comm., Meadows Found., Markle Found., U.S. Office Edn., Nissan Motor Corp., others. Mem. Am. Film Inst. (chmn. internat. symposium on cinema and soc. 1977), Internat. Soc. Bus. Fellows, Acad. Motion Picture Arts and Scis. (exec. br.), Univ. Film Assn. (bd. dirs. 1978-80). Democrat. Office: N C Sch of The Arts Sch of Filming 200 Waughtown St Winston Salem NC 27127-2146

GROOMS, SUZANNE SIMMONS, music educator; b. New Orleans, Jan. 9, 1945; d. Claude Arthur and Mary Rachel (Pierce) Simmons; m. Barton Collins Grooms, May 12, 1973; children: David Barton, Michael Claude. BS, U. Tenn., 1966; M Music Edn., So. Ill. U., 1969. Cert. Suzuki tchr. instrumental music. Mem. violin sect. Knoxville (Tenn.) Symphony Orch., 1958-66; violinist St. Louis Philharmonic Orch., 1967-68; instr. Suzuki Inst., U. Wis., Stevens Point, 1970-73; violinist Amarillo (Tex.) Symphony Orch., 1973-77; dir., coordinator Suzuki string program Amarillo Coll., 1977—; violin tchr., co-founder Amarillo Area Youth Symphony. co-author: (Suzuki handbook) How To Make Your Twinkle Brighter, 1985. Bd. dirs. March of Dimes, Amarillo, 1977-79, Greater S.W. Music Festival, 1990—, Amarillo Symphony Youth Orch., Art Force, 1988-92; mem. Amarillo Jr. League, 1977-84; cir. chmn. United Meth. Ch., Amarillo. Grantee Harrington Found., 1981. Mem. Suzuki Assn. Ams., Internat. Suzuki Assn., Symphony Guild. Home: 4908 Erik Ave Amarillo TX 79106-4703 Office: Amarillo Coll PO Box 447 Amarillo TX 79178-0001

GROOVER, DEBORAH KATE, artist, educator; b. Savannah, Ga., Aug. 24, 1955; d. James Edward and Thelma Louise (Johnson) G.; m. Arnold Carlton Young, Dec. 4, 1982 (div. Aug. 1986). BS, Armstrong Coll., 1982; MFA in Ceramics, U. Ga., 1990. Ceramics instr. U. Ga., Athens, 1988-90, Ga. Dept. Corrections, Milledgeville, 1989-90; instr. Mont. House, Helena, Mont., 1991; artist in residence Archie Bray Found., Helena, 1991; ceramics instr. Athens Acad., 1991-92; ceramics instr. Penland (N.C.) Sch. Crafts, 1993-94, artist in residence, 1992-95; studio artist Tallahassee, Fla., 1995—; ceramics instr. Southwest Craft Ctr., San Antonio, Tex., St. Phillips Coll., San Antonio, 1996—; fellowship juror Nat. Endowment Arts, 1994, Mid Am. Arts Alliance. One woman shows include Archie Bray Found., Helena, Mont., 1991, Laumier Sculpture Park, St. Louis, 1995, Emily Edwards Gallery S.W. Craft Ctr., 1996; exhibited in group shows San Angelo (Tex.) Mus. Art, 1990, Ga. Mus. Art Invitational, Athens, 1990, The Archie Bray Found., Helena, 1991, Louisville Visual Arts Assn., 1992, The Hand Workshop, Richmond, Va., 1992, The Ferrin Gallery, Northampton, Mass., 1992, Groover and Zoerling Appalachianna Gallery, Bethesda, Md., 1992, The Swan Coach Gallery of Atlanta Hist. Soc., 1992, J. H. Webb Gallery, Macon, Ga., 1992, Pro Art Gallery, St. Louis, 1993, Everson Mus. Art, Syracus, N.Y., 1993, Brenau U., Gainesville, Ga., 1993, Craft Alliance Gallery, St. Louis, 1993, Kohler Art Ctr., Sheboygan, Wis., 1993, Lil St. Studios, Chgo., 1993, So. Highland Handicraft Guild, Folk Art Ctr., Blue Ridge Pkwy., Asheville, N.C., 1994, John Michael Kohler Found., Kohler, Wis., 1994, Stetson U., Deland, Fla., 1994, The Works Gallery, Phila., 1994, The Clay Studio, Phila., 1994, Albertson-Peterson Gallery, Winter Park, Fla., 1994, Miller Gallery, Cin., 1994, Clayton Gallery, Tampa, Fla., 1994, Soc. Arts and Crafts, Boston, 1995; represented in permanent collections Ga. Mus. Art, Athens, Archie Bray Found., Ga. Coun. Arts, San Diego Mus. Art, Cin. Mus. Art, The White House; works included in The N.C.E.C.A. Jour., 1992, Am. Craft Mag., 1992, Ceramics Monthly, 1992, The Potters Handbook, 1994, Hand Formed Ceramics, 1995. Vol. Dem. Nat. Party, 1976—. Visual arts fellow Nat. Endowment Arts, 1992; named to Emily's List. Mem. Nat. Coun. Ceramic Arts, Am. Craft Coun., Piedmont Craftsmen. Methodist. Home: 206 Adams St San Antonio TX 78210

GROOVER, SANDRA MAE, retail executive; b. Ft. Ord, Calif., Sept. 10, 1955; d. Ralph Hillis Jr. and Joanne (Hodges) G.; m. L. Scott Butterfield, Mar. 16, 1985 (div. July 1991). AS in Bus. Adminstrn., No. Va. C.C., Alexandria, 1983; BS in Behavioral Sci., Nat. Louis U., 1990; MBA in Mgmt. Policy and Orgnl. Behavior, Case Western Res. U., 1992—. Mgr. credit, collection Kay Jewelers Inc. (acquired by Sterling, Inc.), Alexandria, 1976-80, mgr. accounts payable, 1980-84, exec. asst. to sr. v.p., 1984-86, dir. inventory control, 1986-87, div. v.p. mdse. ops., 1987-90; v.p. distbn. Sterling, Inc., Akron, Ohio, 1990-96; v.p. mdse. support ops. Mayor's Jewelers, Inc., Coral Gables, Fla., 1996—. Mem. Gemological Inst. Am. (grad. gemologist), Mensa. Republican. Home: 20425 NE 10th Court Rd North Miami Beach FL 33179 Office: Mayors Jewelers Inc 283 Catalonia Ave Coral Gables FL 33134-6704

GROSE, JANET LYNNE, English language educator; b. Asheville, N.C., July 16, 1967; d. Jack Norman and Jane (Gooch) G. BA, Furman U., 1989; MA, U. N.C., Charlotte, 1991; PhD, U. S.C., 1995. Mgmt. assoc. S.C. Fed. Savs. Bank, Columbia, 1989; instr. Cape Fear C.C., Wilmington, N.C., 1991; lectr. U. N.C., Wilmington, 1991-92; grad. asst. U. S.C., Columbia, 1994-95; asst. prof. Union Univ., Jackson, Tenn., 1995—. Participant Meals on Wheels, Jackson, 1996. Rutledge fellow Univ. S.C. Dept. English, Columbia, 1992-93. Mem. Sigma Tau Delta, Omicron Delta Kappa. Presbyterian. Office: Union Univ Dept English Box 1832 Jackson TN 38305

GROSS, GARY NEIL, allergist, physician; b. Fort Lewis, Wash., July 25, 1944; s. Norman Harold and Dorothy Naomi (Bercie) G.; m. Elaina Wee, Mar. 23, 1974; children: Risa, Lara. BA, U. Tex., 1967; MD, Southwestern Med. Sch., Dallas, 1969; MBA, Southern Methodist U., Dallas, 1987. Diplomate Am. Bd. Internal Medicine, Am. Bd. Allergy and Clin. Immunology. Intern U. Utah Med. Ctr. Hosp., Salt Lake City, 1969-70; resident U. Utah Med. Ctr. Hosp., 1970-71; fellow Nat. Jewish Hosp., Denver, 1971-74; founding physician Dallas Allergy Clinic, Tex., 1979—; med. dir. Pharm. Rsch. and Cons., Dallas, 1992—; clin. prof. internal medicine Southwestern Med. Sch., Dallas, 1994—. Contbr to profl. jours. Bd. dirs. Am. Jewish Com., Dallas, 1990-94, Am. Lung Assn., 1978-88, Temple Emanuel Brotherhood, 1978-80. Fellow Am. Coll. Physicians, Am. Acad. Allergy Immunology (chmn. seminars com., 1987-88, chmn. pub. edn. com., 1989-90); mem. Fedn. Regional State Local Allergy Socs. (gov. reg. 5, 1992—, chmn. 1993-94), Joint Coun. Allergy Clin. Immunology (sec. bd. dirs.). Jewish. Office: 5499 Glen Lakes Dr Ste 100 Dallas TX 75231-4383

GROSS, HARRIET P. MARCUS, religion and writing educator; b. Pitts., July 15, 1934; d. Joseph William and Rose (Roth) Pincus; children: Sol Benjamin, Devra Lynn. AB magna cum laude, U. Pitts., 1954; cert. in religious teaching, Spertus Coll. of Judaica, Chgo., 1962; MA, U. Tex., Dallas, 1990. Assoc. editor Jewish Criterion of Pitts., 1955-56; publs. writer B'nai B'rith Vocat. Svc., 1956-57; group leader Jewish Community Ctrs. of Met. Chgo., 1958-63; columnist Star Publs., Chicago Heights, Ill., 1964-80; pub. info. specialist Operation ABLE, Chgo., 1980-81; dir. religious sch. Temple Emanu-El, Dallas, 1983-86; freelance writer, 1986—; columnist Dallas Jewish Life Monthly, 1992—; lectr. U. Tex., Dallas, 1994—; tchr. writing Homewood-Flossmoor (Il.) Park Dist., Brookhaven Jr. Coll., Dallas; advisor journalism program Prairie State Coll., Chicago Heights, 1978-80; adv. bd. The Creative Woman quar. publ. Governors State U., Governors Park, Ill., The Mercury U. Tex., Dallas. Bd. dirs., sec. Family Svc. and Mental Health Ctr. of South Cook County, Ill., 1965-71; active Park Forest (Ill.) Commn. on Human Rels., 1969-80, chmn., 1974-76; bd. dirs. Ill. Theatre Ctr., 1977-80, Jewish Family Svc. of Dallas, 1982-95; mem. Dallas Jewish Edn. Com., 1992-95; bd. dirs. Dallas Jewish Historical Soc., 1995—. Recipient Humanitarian Achievements award Fellowship for Action, 1974; Honor award Anti-Defamation League of B'nai B'rith, 1978; Community Service award Dr. Charles E. Gavin Found., 1978, 1st Ann. Leadership award Jewish Family Svc., 1990, Katie award Dallas Press Club, 1995. Mem. Nat. Fedn. Press Women, Tex. Press Women, Ill. Woman's Press Assn. (named Woman of Yr. 1978), Intertel (pres. Gateway Forum of Dallas 1984-85), Nat. Assn. Temple Educators, Mensa, Sigma Delta Chi, Phi Sigma Sigma. Jewish. Developed 1st community newspaper action line column, 1966. Office: 8560 Park Ln Apt 23 Dallas TX 75231-6312

GROSS, JOSEPH WALLACE, hospital administrator; b. Berwyn, Ill., June 15, 1945; married. B, Creighton U., 1968; M, U. Mo. Adminstrv. extern U. Hosp.-U. Nebr., Omaha, 1968; adminstrv. asst. Boone Hosp. Ctr., Columbia, Mo., 1971; exec. v.p. adminstrv. ops. Wausau (Wis.) Hosp. Ctr., 1971-78; pres. Luther Hosp., Eau Claire, Wis., 1978-86; pres., chief exec. officer St. Elizabeth Med. Ctr., Covington, Ky., 1986—. Mem. Ky. Hosp. Assn. (pres. 1990—). Office: St Elizabeth Med Ctr-North 401 E 20th St Covington KY 41014-1583*

GROSS, LESLIE JAY, lawyer; b. Coral Gables, Fla., July 24, 1944; s. Bernard Charles and Lillian (Adler) G.; m. Frances L. Londow, June 16, 1968; children: Jonathan Eric, Jason Marc. BA magna cum laude, Harvard U., 1965, JD, 1968. Bar: Fla. 1971, U.S. Dist. Ct. (so. dist.) Fla. 1971, U.S. Ct. Appeals (5th cir.) 1971, U.S. Tax Ct. 1971, U.S. Supreme Ct. 1971; registered real estate broker, registered mortgage broker, registered securities broker. Rsch. aide Fla. 3d Dist. Ct. Appeal, Miami, Fla., 1968-69; prof. social sci. Miami-Dade Community Coll., 1969-70; assoc. Greenberg, Traurig, et al., Miami, 1969-70, Patton, Kanner, et al., Miami, 1970-71, Fromberg, Fromberg, Roth, Miami, 1971-72; ptnr. Fromberg, Fromberg, Gross, et al., Miami, 1973-88; assoc. Thornton, David, Murray, et al., Miami, 1988-94; atty. agt. Atty.'s Title Ins. Fund, First Am. Title, Miami, 1971-94; adj. prof. U. Miami Sch. Law, 1984; lectr. seminar Nat. Aircraft Fin. Assn., 1990. Contbr. articles to profl. jours. Mem. transp. com. Greater Miami C. of C., 1984-85; v.p., pres., bd. dirs. Kendale Homeowners Assn., Miami, 1970-81; vol. Dem. candidates in state and nat. elections, Miami, 1968, 70, 72, 87, 88; mem. Vision Coun. Land Use Task Force, Miami, 1988-89; judge Silver Knight awards Miami Herald, 1987, 92, 93, 94, 95, judge spelling bee, 1987; bd. dirs. Internat. Assn. Fin. Planning, 1983-84; founding mem., bd. dirs. The Actors Playhouse, 1987—, sec., 1990—. Mem. Harvard Law Sch. Assn., Harvard Club of Miami (v.p. 1985-90, pres. 1990-94, dir. 1985—). Democrat. Jewish. Home: 10471 SW 126th St Miami FL 33176-4749

GROSS, PATRICIA LOUISE, neuropsychologist; b. Lisbon, Portugal, Feb. 29, 1952; came to U.S., 1955; d. Martin Arthur and Eva Delle (Stregevsky) G. BA magna cum laude, U. Calif., Irvine, 1974; MA, U. So. Calif., 1982, PhD, 1985. Lic. psychologist, Calif., N.C. Psychology intern Sepulveda (Calif.) VA Med. Ctr., 1983-84, L.A. Child Guidance Clinic, 1984-85; rsch. assoc. Del Amo (Calif.) Psychiat. Hosp., 1984-85; postdoctoral fellow Neuropsychiat. Inst., UCLA, 1985-86; neuropsychologist West Los Angeles VA Med. Ctr., 1986; chief neuropsychology assessment lab., geropsychologist Sepulveda (Calif.) VA Med. Ctr., 1986-89; assoc. chief neuropsychiatry clinic, 1988-89; dir. brain injury program, neuropsychologist Charlotte (N.C.) Inst. of Rehab., 1989-91; dir. med. psychology, neuropsychologist Carolinas Med. Ctr., Charlotte, 1991—; dir. neuropsychology assessment lab., 1994—. Contbr. articles to profl. jours. Mem. disaster mental health com. ARC, Charlotte, 1995—. Oakley fellow, 1980-83; Sigma Xi grantee, 1984. Mem. APA, Internat. Neuropsychol. Soc., Nat. Acad. Neuropsychology, Mecklenburg Psychol. Assn. (pres. 1994), Nat. Head Injury Found., N.C. Head Injury Found., Alzheimer's Assn. (spkr.'s bur. Charlotte 1990—, bd. dirs. 1996—), Phi Beta Kappa. Democrat. Office: Charlotte Inst Rehab 1100 Blythe Blvd Charlotte NC 28203-5814

GROSS, PATRICK WALTER, business executive, management consultant; b. Ithaca, N.Y., May 15, 1944; s. Eric T. B. and Catharine B. (Rohrer) G.; m. Sheila Eve Proby, Apr. 12, 1969; children: Geoffrey Philipp, Stephanie Lovell. Student, Cornell U., 1962-63; B in Engring. Sci., Rensselaer Poly. Inst., 1965; MSE in Applied Math., U. Mich., 1966; MBA, Stanford U., 1968. Cons. info. mgmt. operation Gen. Electric Co., Schnectady, 1965-67; sr. staff mem. Office Sec. Def., Washington, 1968-69, spl. asst., 1969-70; founder, vice chmn., prin. exec. officer Am. Mgmt. Systems, Inc., Arlington, Va., 1970—, also bd. dirs.; also bd. dirs.; chmn. bd. dirs. Medlantic Enterprises, Inc., 1988—, Baker and Taylor Holdings, Inc., 1994—, dir., 1992—, Medlantic Healthcare Group, Capital One Fin. Corp., Anthem Fin. Corp. Trustee Washington Hosp. Ctr., 1977-87, Sidwell Friends Sch., 1980-88, 92—; mem. exec. com., treas. Youth for Understanding, 1984-90, 93—, vice chmn., 1996—, Youth for Understanding Found., Germany, 1989—; mem. Econ. Policy Coun. UNA-USA, mem. Coun. on Competitiveness, Fed. City Coun., Washington, 1992—. Mem. Fgn. Policy Assn. (bd. govs., bd. dirs., mem. exec. com. 1977-86, 87—), World Affairs Coun. Washington (bd. dirs., founding vice chmn. 1980-91, chmn. 1991—), Coun. Fgn. Rels., Washington Inst. Fgn. Affairs, Internat. Inst. Strategic Studies (London), World Econ. Forum (Geneva), Coun. Excellence in Govt., Econ. Club Washington, Nat. Economists Club, Aspen Inst. Soc. Fellows, Pilgrims of U.S., Smithsonian Luncheon Group, Met. Club Washington, Chevy Chase Club, Univ. Club N.Y.C., Useless Bay Country Club (Wash.), Sigma Xi, Tau Beta Pi. Home: 7401 Glenbrook Rd Bethesda MD 20814-1327 Office: Am Mgmt Sys Inc 4050 Legato Rd Fairfax VA 22033-4003

GROSS, PAUL ALLAN, health service executive; b. Richmond, VA, Oct. 1, 1937; s. Albert and Cynthia (Saxe) G.; m. Gail Byrd, Nov. 19, 1966; children: Lorri, Garry, Randy. Student, U. Richmond, 1956-59; B.A., U. Ga., 1961; M.H.A., Va. Commonwealth U., 1964; cert. in hosp. adminstrn., U. Miami. Cert. hosp. adminstrn., Fla. Resident in hosp. adminstrn. Tampa Gen. Hosp., Fla., 1964; adminstrv. asst. Dallas County Hosp. Dist., 1964-66, asst. adminstr., 1966-69, sr. asst. adminstr., 1969-70, assoc. adminstr., 1971-72; clin. assoc. prof. hosp. med. care U. Tex. Southwestern Med. Sch., 1964-72, Sch. Allied Health Scis., Dallas, 1964-72; exec. dir. Humana Inc. Suburban Hosp., Louisville, 1972-76; v.p. Fla. region Humana Inc., Miami, 1976-81; sr. v.p. Pacific Region Humana Inc., Newport Beach, Calif., 1981-84, exec. v.p., pres. hosp. div., 1984-91, trustee acute care gen. hosps., 1983—; exec. v.p. health care svcs. Humana Inc., 1991-92, ret., 1992; prof., health adminstr. Va. Commonwealth U./Med. Coll. Va., 1992—; nat. cons. emeritus Surgeon Gen. USAF, 1987—; mem. adminstrv. and audit coms. Fedn. Am. Healthcare Systems, 1984—; vice chmn. bd. trustees MedEcon, Inc., Louisville, 1993—, also bd. dirs.; trustee St. Anthony Pub. Co., Washington; advisor KBL Healthcare Inc. Contbr. articles to profl. jours. Mem. health adv. com. Senator Paul Carpenter, Cypress, Calif., 1983; mem., asst. chmn. U.S. Selective Svc. System Local Bd. 154, Newport Beach, 1983, Bd. 113, Louisville; trustee Fedn. Am. Health Systems, 1981—; bd. assocs. U. Richmond, Va., 1990—; bd. dirs. St. Francis High Sch., Louisville, 1989-92, Louisville Zool. Found. Bd., 1989-91, chmn. investment com., 1992; mem. adv. bd. Sch. Nursing Spalding U., Louisville, 1992—; chmn. devel. bd. Jefferson County Community Coll., Kentuckiana Edn. and Work Force Com.; preceptor Fellowship Program-Education with Industry, USAF, 1986-92. With USNR, 1955-63. Recipient Humana Club award Suburban Hosp. Central Region, Louisville, 1974, 75, 76; named Outstanding Adminstr. Cen. Region Humana Inc., 1975, 76. Fellow Am. Coll. Health Care Execs. (ethics com., chmn. inv. droped sect. 1993—); mem. Am. Hosp. Assn. (hon. life, ho. of dels., regional adv. bd., chmn.-elect 1989, governing coun. sect. for health care systems 1987-89, 91—, hon. life), Tex. Hosp. Assn., Hosp. Coun. So. Calif. (chmn. multi-instnl. corp. liaison com. 1983—), United Hosp. Assn. Calif. Home: Rt 5 Box 8846 Quinlan TX 75474 Office: VCU/MCV 1008 E Clay St Richmond VA 23219-1528*

GROSS, PERLA DOLLAGA, nursing administrator, medical/surgical, oncology nurse; b. Garrita, Bani, Pangasinan, The Philippines, Nov. 22, 1951; d. Jose and Conchita A. Dollaga; m. Stewart Gross, May 21, 1988. Diploma, U. Pangasinan, 1973; BSN, Henderson State U., 1984; MSN, U. Ctrl. Ark., 1995. Charge nurse Odessa (Tex.) Med. Ctr., 1977; shift supr. maternal and child flr. Bapt. Med. Ctr., Little Rock, 1982-85, shift supr. surg. flr., 1988-91, unit supr., 1991-95; dir. med./surg. nursing, 1996—; charge nurse Coral Reef Hosp., Miami, Fla., 1985-88. Roman Catholic. Office: Bapt Med Ctr 9601 Interstate 630 Exit 7 Little Rock AR 72205-7202

GROSS, SAMSON RICHARD, geneticist, biochemist, educator; b. N.Y.C., July 27, 1926; s. Isidor and Ethel (Mermelestein) G.; m. Helen Hudi Steinmetz, Sept. 16, 1952; children—Deborah Ann, Michael Robert, Eva Elizabeth. B.A., NYU, 1949; A.M., Columbia, 1951, Ph.D. (USPHS fellow), 1953. Asst. prof. genetics Stanford U., 1956-57; asst. prof. genetics Rockefeller U., N.Y.C., 1957-60; assoc. prof. dept. microbiology and immunology Duke, Durham, N.C., 1960-65, prof. genetics and biochemistry, 1965-91, prof. emeritus genetics and biochemistry, 1991—; dir. div. genetics dept. biochemistry Duke, 1965-77, dir. univ. program in genetics, 1967-77; bd. dirs. Cold Spring Harbor Lab. Quantitative Biology, N.Y., 1967-72. USPHS Spl. fellow Weizmann Inst., 1969-70; Josiah Macy Found. fellow Hebrew U., 1977-78; John Simon Guggenheim fellow Hebrew U., 1985-86. Mem. Genetic Soc. Am., AAAS, Am. Soc. Microbiology, Am. Soc. Biol. Chemists, Phi Beta Kappa. Home: 2411 Prince St Durham NC 27707-1432

GROSS, STEPHEN RANDOLPH, accountant; b. Newark, Oct. 8, 1947; s. Edward Thomas and Frances (Randolph) G.; m. Barbara Louise Schutz, June 14, 1969 (div. Jan. 1981); children: David Randolph, Matthew Jeffrey. AB, Duke U., 1970. CPA, Ga.; cert. fraud examiner, Ga. From staff acct. to ptnr. Lester Witte & Co., Atlanta, 1970-74; ptnr. Lester Witte & Co., Chgo., 1974-79, nat. dir. tng., 1978-79, exec. com.; founder, mng. ptnr. Gross, Collins & Cress, P.C., Atlanta, 1979—; mng. gen. ptnr Van Kampen Am. Captial Exch. Fund, 1996—; trustee Common Sense Trusts, Houston, 1987, Am. Capital Income Trusts, 1993; bd. dirs. Exec. Lodging, Inc., Atlanta, Charter Bank and Trust, Marietta, Ga., Van Kampen Am. Capital Convertible Securities, Inc., Atlanta, Am. Capital Convertible Securities, Inc., Anderson Calhoun, Ltd., Component Sys. LLC, Van Kampen Am. Capital Income Trusts, Van Kampen Am. Capital Bond Fund, Inc.; treas. Henry Aaron Enterprises, Inc., Milw.; v.p. Coventry Holding Group, Inc., Decatur, Ga.; sec. Carint of NA, Milan. Active Atlanta Symphony Orch., 1975—, High Mus. Art, Atlanta, 1985—, Ga. Pub. Policy Found., 1991—. Mem. AICPA, Ga. Soc. CPA's, Cobb C. fo C. (exec. com.), Atlanta C. of C., Nat. Assn. Cert. Valuation Analysis, Assn. Cert. Fraud Examiners, Inst. Bus. Appraisers, Internat. Wine and Food Inst., Lake Arrowhead Country Club, Cherokee Town Club, Chaine des Rotisseurs (Paris), Vinings Club. Episcopalian. Home: 175 River North Dr NW Atlanta GA 30328-1111 Office: Gross Collins & Cress PC 2625 Cumberland Pky NW Ste 400 Atlanta GA 30339-3911

GROSSE, EDWARD RALPH, systems analyst; b. Altoona, Pa., June 8, 1940; s. Edward Herman and Besse (Rush) G.; 1 child, Shirley Ann. Student, Palm Beach (Fla.) Community Coll., 1986-91, So. Coll., Palm Beach, 1987. Cert. Novell engr. Field engr., ret. IBM Corp., Jacksonville, Miami, Fla., 1961-87; systems analyst IBM Corp., Boca Raton, Fla., 1989. Past pres. Okinawa Sports Car Club. With USN, 1958-61. Mem. IBM Quarter Century Club (1st v.p. 1988), Am. Radio Relay League. Republican. Roman Catholic. Home: 5374 214th Ct S Boca Raton FL 33486

GROSSETT, DEBORAH LOU, psychologist, behavior analyst, consultant; b. Alma, Mich., Feb. 16, 1957; d. Charles M. and Margaret A. (Roethlisberger) G. BS, Alma Coll., 1979; MA, Western Mich. U., 1981, PhD, 1984. Lic. psychologist, Tex.; cert. in diagnostic evaluation, Tex.; registered behavior analyst, Tex. Grad. rsch. and teaching asst. Western Mich. U., Kalamazoo, 1979-84; asst. group home supr., community outreach Residential Opportunities, Kalamazoo, 1982-84; psychologist Richmond (Tex.) State Sch., 1984-87, Shapiro Devel. Ctr., Kankakee, Ill., 1987-88; clin. coord. Monroe Devel. Ctr., Rochester, N.Y., 1988; chief psychologist Denton (Tex.) State Sch., 1989-90; dir. psychol./behavioral svcs. Ctr. for the Retarded, Houston, 1990—; behavioral cons. Ctr. for Developmentally Disabled Adults, Kalamazoo, 1984, Goodman-Wade Enterprises, Houston, 1987; instr. psychology Houston Cmty. Coll., 1985-86, U. Houston-Clear Lake, 1987, 92, 95—. Contbr. chpt. to book, articles to profl. jours. Western Mich. U. fellow, 1984. Mem. Am. Psychol. Assn., Am. Assn. on Mental Retardation, Assn. for Behavior Analysis (chair Outreach Bd. 1989-91), Tex. Assn. for Behavior Analysis (bd. dirs. 1989-91). Democrat. Presbyterian. Home: 9750 Ravensworth Dr Houston TX 77031-3130 Office: Ctr for the Retarded Inc 3550 W Dallas St Houston TX 77019-1702

GROSSMAN, LAURENCE ABRAHAM, cardiologist; b. Nashville, Sept. 21, 1916; s. Henry and Etta (Rothstein) G.; m. Dorothy Ruth Huffine, Oct. 17, 1942; children: Diane Gail Ely, Linda Marie Garfunkel, Susanne Segall, Jo Ann. BS, Vanderbilt Univ., 1937, MD, 1941. Diplomate Am. Bd. Internal Medicine. Residency Vanderbilt Univ. Hosp., Nashville, 1947; armored med. co. commander, combat command surgeon U.S. Army, 1942-46; pvt. practice cardiology and internal medicine Nashville, 1947—. Bd. dirs. Nashville City Bank, 1984-87; pres. Tenn. Heart Assn., 1956-57, Tenn. Heart Inst., 1984-89, Canby Robinson Soc., 1989-91. Decorated with Bronze Star medal with two oak leaf clusters, 1945. Fellow Am. Coll. Cardiology; mem. Vanderbilt Medical Alumni Assn. (pres. 1977-78), Tenn. Am. Coll. Cardiology (gov. 1961-64), Tenn. Soc. Internal Medicine (pres. 1957-58), Nashville & Davidson County Acad. of Medicine (pres.). Office: Saint Thomas Medical Ctr 4230 Harding Rd Ste 400 Nashville TN 37205-2013

GROSSMAN, PAUL LESLIE, sales and marketing executive; b. Bklyn., Nov. 21, 1960; s. Richard Allen and Anita (Paritsky) G.; m. Sue Ann Schermerhorn, Sept. 8, 1986; children: Ian Charles, Jessica Hope. BS, Union Coll., 1982. Mng. editor Metroland Mag., Albany, N.Y., 1982-85; creative dir. The Ambassador Group, Albany, N.Y., 1985-86, mgr. mktg. svcs., 1986-87; mgr. mktg. svcs. Kaset Inc., Tampa, Fla., 1987-89; corp. mktg. mgr. Kaset Internat., Tampa, Fla., 1989-92; dir. United Kingdom ops. Kaset Internat., Tampa, 1992—; mktg. cons. Vetcare Videos, Tampa, 1987-88, Healthcare TV Network, Tampa, 1987-88, Vet. Mktg. Svs., Tampa, 1989-92. Mem. Internat. Exhibitors Assn., Am. Mktg. Assn. (chpt. bd. dirs. 1990-91, 91-92, 92-93, Marketer of Yr. 1991). Home: 16504 Forestlake Dr Tampa FL 33624-1205 Office: Kaset Internat 8875 Hidden River Pky Tampa FL 33637-1017

GROSSO, VINCENT JOSEPH, quality systems engineering professional; b. Phila., Dec. 16, 1959; s. Vincent John and Lee Grosso; m. Caroline M. Cestone, Apr. 1990. AA in Natural Sci., Thomas Edison State Coll., Trenton, N.J., 1986, BA in Sci. and Math., 1988; MBA, Nova Southeastern U., 1995. Cert. mgr. Inst. of Cert. Profl. Mgrs. Bus. office rep. Bell of Pa., Chester, 1977-80; quality assurance engr. various nuc. power plants, Pa., N.J., Colo., 1984-89; elec. foreman Danella Constrn., Phila., 1989; supr. for a quality assurance inspection co. contracted to Three Mile Island, Middletown, Pa., 1989-90; sr. quality engr. Westinghouse Savannah River Co., Aiken, S.C., 1990-92, project quality engr., 1992, asst. to divsn. quality mgr., 1992-93, mgr. quality sys. engring., 1993—. Treas., commr. Montmorenci (S.C.) Vol. Fire Dept., 1993—. Mem. IEEE, ASME, Nat. Mgmt. Assn., Am. Nuc. Soc., Am. Soc. Quality Control. Roman Catholic. Home: 643 Old Barnwell Rd Aiken SC 29803 Office: Westinghouse Savannah River Co 742 G Aiken SC 29801

GROTE, RICHARD CHARLES, author management consultant, educator, radio commentator; b. N.Y.C., Dec. 14, 1941; s. Charles Henry and Muriel (Steele) G.; m. Jacqueline Center, May 11, 1991. BA, Colgate U., 1959; M Liberal Arts, So. Meth. U., 1992. Pers. mgr. GE, Schenectady, 1964-67; mgr. mgmt. devel. United Air Lines, Chgo., 1967-72; mgr. tng. and devel. Frito-Lay, Inc., Dallas, 1972-77; pres. Performance Systems Corp., Dallas, 1977-87; prin. Grote Cons., Dallas, 1987—; adj. prof. U. Dallas Grad. Sch. Mgmt., 1977—; commentator NPR, 1993—; reviewer Inst. Mus. Svcs., 1974-77. Author: Positive Discipline, 1985, Discipline Without Punishment, 1995, The Complete Guide to Performance Appraisal, 1996; host (film series) Respect and Responsibility, The Complete Guide to Performance Appraisal, 1996; also articles. Trustee, pres. Schaumburg (Ill.) Pub. Libr., 1969-72; bd. dirs. Shakespeare Festival Dallas, 1981-84, Dallas Opera, 1981-88; chmn. So. Meth. U. Conservatory Soc., 1988—; bd. councillors U. Dallas, 1989—. Recipient Torch award ASTD, 1979, Disting. Svc. award Malaysian Soc. for Tng. and Devel., 1984, Bapindo award Govt. of Indonesia, 1984. Republican. Office: The Madison 15851 Dallas Pky Ste 600 Dallas TX 75248-3330

GROTH, JOHN HENRY CHRISTOPHER, pastor, author; b. Waterloo, Iowa, June 26, 1954; s. Ulrich F. and Ruth E. (Kangas) G.; m. Cheryl A. Johnson, June 17, 1987; children: John Ross, Eric Samuel, Rebecca Nicole. BA, Wartburg Coll., 1976; MDiv, Wartburg Theol. Sem., 1981; STM, Trinity Luth. Sem., Columbus, Ohio, 1992. Ordained to ministry Lutheran Ch., 1982. Interim pastor St. John Luth. Ch., Preston, Iowa, 1981-82; pastor St. John Luth. Ch., Lithopolis, Ohio, 1982-88, Old St. Paul Luth. Ch., Newton, N.C., 1988-93, Eastside Luth. Bible Ch., Hickory, N.C., 1993—. Author: (book) Ritual, Legalism and Morality, 1993; editor: The Soul Winner's Log, 1996. Bd. dirs. Prison Ministry, Catawba, Maiden, N.C., 1989-93; exec. bd. dirs. Crisis Pregnancy Ctr., Hickory, N.C., 1989-93;

founder Christian Athletic Assn., Newton, 1991. Home: Eastside Luth Bible Ch 1735 24th Avenue Ct NE Hickory NC 28601-9652 Office: Eastside Luth Bible Ch 725 E 11th St Newton NC 28658

GROVE, JACK STEIN, naturalist, marine biologist; b. York, Pa., Oct. 29, 1951; s. Samuel Hersner and Myrtle Elenor (Stein) G. AS, Fla. Keys Coll., 1972; BS, U. West Fla., 1976; postgrad., Pacific Western U. Chief naturalist Galapagos Tourist Corp., Guayaquil, Ecuador, 1977-84; rsch. assoc. Sea World Rsch. Inst., San Diego, 1981—, L.A. County Mus. Natural History, L.A., 1982—; expedition leader Soc. Expeditions Cruises, Seattle, 1985-91; marine biologist, underwater photographer Eye on the World, Inc., L.A., 1986-91; assoc. investigator Nat. Fisheries Inst., Guayaquil, 1982-85; park naturalist Galapagos Nat. Park, Ecuador, 1977-85; co-founder Zegrahm Expdns., Seattle; founder Conservation Network Internat., 1994. Editor: Voyage to Adventure/Antarctica, 1985. NSF grantee, 1986. Mem. AAAS, Acad. Underwater Scis., Am. Soc. Mag. Photographers, Am. Bamboo Soc., Profl. Assn. Diving Instrs. (divemaster), U.S. Nat. Recreation and Parks Assn. (supr.). Office: 146 N Sunrise Dr Tavernier FL 33070-2524

GROVE, NORA IMOGENE, librarian; b. Van Buren County, Tenn., Oct. 3, 1926; d. D.B. and Annie Jane (Sparkman) George; m. William Murphy Grove, Apr. 26, 1947; children: Murphy, Laverne, Bobby Joe, Elaine. Libr. Burritt Meml. Libr., Spencer, Tenn. Mem. Ch. of Christ. Office: Burritt Meml Libr Hwy 30N Spencer TN 38585

GROVE, RUSSELL SINCLAIR, JR., lawyer; b. Marietta, Ga., Dec. 25, 1939; s. Russell Sinclair and Miriam (Smith) G.; m. Charlotte Mariam Glascock, Jan. 9, 1965; children—Farion Smith Whitman, Arthur Owen Sinclair. BS, Ga. Inst. Tech., 1962; LLB with distinction, Emory U., 1964; postgrad., U. Melbourne Faculty Law, Australia, 1965. Bar: Ga. 1965, U.S. Supreme Ct. 1971, U.S. Ct. Appeals (11th cir.) 1983. Assoc. Smith, Currie & Hancock, Atlanta, 1966-67; assoc. Hansell & Post, Atlanta, 1968-72, ptnr., 1972-89; ptnr. Jones, Day, Reavis & Pogue (successor merger Hansell & Post), Atlanta, 1989—; mem. adv. com. Ctr. for Legal Studies; mem. steering com. Urban Land Inst. (Atlanta dist.). Author: Word Processing and Automatic Data Processing in the Modern Law Office, 1978, Legal Considerations of Joint Ventures, 1981, Structuring Endorsements and Affirmative Insurance, 1981, Management's Perspective on Automation, 1981, Mineral Law: Current Developments and Future Issues, 1983, Drafting and the Use of Forms, 1989; co-author: The Integrated Data and Word Processing System, 1981, Georgia Partnership Law: Current Issues and Problems, 1982; (with D.E. Glass) Georgia Real Estate Forms-Practice, 1987; contbg. author: Energy Law and Transactions, 1993; editor-in-chief Jour. Pub. Law, 1963-64. Mem. Central Atlanta Progress, Inc.; bd. dirs. Caribbean Mission, Inc.; patron Atlanta Symphony Orch., High Mus. Art, Stone Mountain Highland Games. Served with USMCR, 1960-65. Mem. Internat. Assn. Attorneys Corp. Real Estate, Ga. Bar Assn. (exec. com. real property law sect., sec. 1988-89, chmn. 1990-91; chmn. legal opinions com.), Bryan Soc., U.S. Marine Corps Assn. Ga. Lawyers, Eastern Mineral Law Found., Ga. State Bar (mem. joint com. partnerhsip law UPA/ULPA), Am. Coll. Real Estate Lawyers, Ga. Oil and Gas Assn., Ga. Cattlemen's Assn., Nat. Cattlemen's Assn., Am. Scotch Highland Breeders Assn., Can. Highland Cattle Soc., Highland Cattle Soc. U.K., Lawyers of Atlanta Club, Ashford Club, Phi Delta Phi, Omicron Delta Kappa. Episcopalian. Office: Jones Day Reavis & Pogue 303 Peachtree St NE #3500 Atlanta GA 30308-3201

GROVER, ROSALIND REDFERN, oil and gas company executive; b. Midland, Tex., Sept. 5, 1941; d. John Joseph and Rosalind (Kapps) Redfern; m. Arden Roy Grover, Apr. 10, 1982; 1 child, Rosson. BA in Edn. magna cum laude, U. Ariz., 1966, MA in History, 1982; postgrad. in law, So. Meth. U., Dallas. Libr. Gahr High Sch., Cerritos, Calif., 1969; pres. The Redfern Found., Midland, 1982—; ptnr. Redfern & Grover, Midland, 1986—; pres. Redfern Enterprises Inc., Midland, 1989—; chmn. bd. dirs. Flag-Redfern Oil Co., Midland. Sec. park and recreation commn. City of Midland, 1969-71, del. Objectives for Convocation, 1980; mem., past pres. women's aux. Midland Community Theatre, 1970, chmn. challenge grant bldg. fund, 1980, chmn. Tex. Yucca Hist. Landmark Renovation Project, 1983, trustee, 1983-88; chmn. publicity com. Midland Jr. League Midland, Inc., 1972, chmn. edn. com., 1976, corr. sec., 1978; 1st v.p. Midland Symphony Assn., 1975; chmn. Midland Charity Horse Show, 1975-76; mem. Midland Am. Revolution Bicentennial Commn., 1976; trustee Mus. S.W., 1977-80, pres. bd. dirs., 1979-80; co-chmn. Gov. Clements Fin. Com., Midland, 1978; mem. dist. com. State Bd. Law Examiners; trustee Midland Meml. Hosp., 1978-80, Permian Basin Petroleum Mus., Libr. and Hall of Fame, 1989—. Recipient HamHock award Midland Community Theatre, 1978. Mem. Ind. Petroleum Assn. Am., Tex. Ind. Producers and Royalty Owners Assn., Petroleum Club, Racquet Club (Midland), Horseshoe Bay (Tex.) Country Club, Phi Kappa Phi, Pi Lambda Theta. Republican. Home: 1906 Crescent Pl Midland TX 79705-6407 Office: PO Box 2127 Midland TX 79702-2127

GROVES, NORALENE KATHERINE, elementary school educator; b. Tecumseh, Okla., Oct. 14, 1941; d. Lee Edward and Clota Meryl (Bolding) Andrews; m. Douglas M. Stewart, Jan. 27, 1962 (div. May 1975); children: Diana, Kathy, Ginger; m. Glen Wesley, Dec. 19, 1975. BS in elem. edn., East Ctrl. U., 1973, MS in learning disabilities, 1976. Cert. elem. edn. tchr., Okla. Elem. tchr. Centrahoma (Okla.) Sch., 1973-76; spl. edn. tchr. Vanoss Sch., Ada, Okla., 1976-91, elem. tchr., 1991—, chmn. staff devel., 1989-96. Pres., v.p. Ctr. Woman's Aux., Ctr. Free Will Bapt. Ch., Ada, 1986-92, women's tchr., 1987—; study chmn. Dist. Woman's Aux., Ctr. Dist., 1988-90, 94-96, 5th and 6th grade Sunday sch. tchr., 1995—; coord. spelling bee, 1992—. Recipient Controlling Worry award Dale Carnegie Inst., 1991, Dicus' Jan. Tchr. of Month, 1995. Mem. Okla. Edn. Assn., Reading Coun., Delta Kappa Gamma (rsch. com. 1992-93, 2d v.p.). Republican. Home: RR 5 Box 87 Ada OK 74820-9310

GROW, ROBERT THEODORE, economist, association executive; b. Newton, Mass., Aug. 14, 1948; s. William and Lempi (Kangas) G.; m. Anita L. Capps, Nov. 20, 1982; 1 child, Margaret Celia. BS magna cum laude, U. Mass., 1970, MS, 1973. Regional economist Southeastern Va. Planning Dist. Commn., Norfolk, 1973-80; dir. met. coord. Met. Washington (D.C.) Coun. Govts., 1980-85; exec. dir. Washington/Balt. Regional Assn., Washington, 1985-95; dir. transportation The Greater Washington Bd. Trade, 1995—; chmn. met. com. Capital Area chpt. Am. Planning Assn., Washington, 1988-89. Fellow Am. Ctr. for Internat. Leadership; mem. Am. Soc. Assn. Execs., Am. Econ. Devel. Council, Nat. Econimists Club, Southern Industrial Devel. Council, Md. Distbn. Coun., Md. Indsl. Developers Assn., Md. Internat. Trade Assn., Va. Econs. Devel. Assn., Balt. Econ. Soc. (mem. steering com. 1992), Phi Kappa Phi.

GRUBB, TODD C., human resources educator; b. N.Y.C., June 15, 1932; s. Frederick E. and Theodora A. (Todd) G.; m. Maryanne de Malleville, Sept. 20, 1952 (dec. 1989); 1 child, Jacqueline O'Brien; m. Arlene C. Newman, Aug. 24, 1990; children: Michelle Parlo, David Newman, Andrew Newman. BA, U. Calif., Santa Barbara, 1957; MPA, Syracuse U., 1971; cert., Indsl. Coll. Armed Forces, 1973; PhD, U. Louisville, 1988. Cert. sr. profl. in human resources. Dir. civilian pers. U.S. Army Interagy. Comm. Agy., Winchester, Va., 1961-62; pers. specialist Hdqrs. Dept. of Army, The Pentagon, 1962-65; dir. civilian pers. program planning U.S. Army, Europe, Germany, 1965-68; dir. civilian pers. U.S. Forces, Berlin, 1968-70; dep. dir. civilian pers. Picatinny Arsenal, Dover, N.J., 1971-75; dir. civilian pers. U.S. Army Armor Ctr., Fort Knox, Ky., 1975-80; dir. employment planning and stds. divsn. U.S. Dept. Housing and Urban Devel., Washington, 1980-82; pres. TODMAR Assocs., Sarasota, Fla., 1982-90, Todd Grubb Assocs., Tampa, Fla., 1990—; faculty U. Louisville, 1982-83; adj. asst. prof. County Coll. of Morris, Dover, 1974-75; assoc. prof. U. Sarasota, 1988-93, Fla. Inst. Tech., 1990-92, Eckerd Coll., 1992-93; asst. prof. Troy State U., 1992—. With USN, 1952-54. Named Ky. Col., Admiral of Ky. Waterways. Mem. ASPA, ASTD (Suncoast chpt. pres. 1991, pres. elect 1990, v.p. profl. devel. 1989), Fed. Exec. Assn. of Louisville (treas. 1978), Fort Knox Civil League (pres. 1979-80, v.p. 1978-79), Internat. Pers. Mgmt. Assn., Louisville Fed. Pers. Coun. (chair 1978), Nat. Spkrs. Assn. (Ctrl. Fla. chpt. pres. 1986-87, v.p. 1984-86), Sarasota Human Resources Assn. (conf. com. 1989), Phi Kappa Phi. Home: 16131 Vanderbilt Dr Odessa FL 33556-3328 Office: Troy State U Fla Region PO Box 6472 Macdill AFB FL 33608-0472

GRUBBS, DONALD RAY, educational director, educator, welder; b. Houston, Oct. 22, 1947; s. J. W. and Imo Gene (Williams) G.; Glenda Carol Nowell, Nov. 27, 1967; 1 child, Sean Lynn. EdB, Lamar U., 1974, AAS, 1983. Welder Bethlehem Steel, Beaumont, Tex., 1968-73; pipefitter, welder Pipefitters Local 195, Beaumont, 1973-86; regents instr. Lamar U., Beaumont, 1973-87, placement dir. tech. arts, 1986-87; chief instr. Am. Welding Soc., Miami, Fla., 1987—; dir. qualification and cert. Am. Welding Soc., Miami, 1988-92; welding quality mgr. Base Line Data Inc., Portland, Tex., 1993-95; dir. edn. Am. Welding Soc., Miami, 1992—; v.p. Guardian NDT, Corpus Christi, Tex., 1995—; cons. in field. Scoutmaster Boy Scouts Am., Beaumont, 1978-86. Served with USMC, 1968-70, Vietnam. Mem. Am. Welding Soc. (chmn. 1983-84, dir. edn. Miami chpt. 1992—), Tex. Jr. Coll. Tchrs. Assn. (chmn. 1980-83), Placement Assn. Tex., Lamar Ex-Students Assn. Democrat. Mem. Disciples of Christ Ch. Home: 111 Westover Dr Portland TX 78374-2310 Office: Guardian NDT PO Box 4792 Corpus Christi TX 78469

GRUBBS, RAYMOND VAN, surgeon; b. Anderson, S.C., July 23, 1946; s. Raymond Benjamin and Swanee Verbenzia (Pitts) G.; m. Caroline Clay Adams, July 3, 1965 (div.); children: Phyllis Caroline, Raymond Van. BS, Clemson (S.C.) U., 1967; MD, Med. U. S.C., 1971. Diplomate Am. Bd. Surgery, Nat. Bd. Med. Examiners. Intern Med. U. S.C., Charleston, 1971-72, resident in surgery, 1972-76; surgeon Family Surgery Ctr., Greer, S.C., 1976—; chmn. med. staff Allen Bennett Meml. Hosp., Greer, 1992-93; track surgeon NASCAR's Darlington (S.C.) Speedway, 1972—. Capt. M.C., U.S. Army, 1971-81. Fellow ACS; mem. AMA, S.C. Med. Assn., Greenville County Med. Assn., Southeastern Surg. Congress, Greater Greenville (S.C.) Physicians' Orgn (pres. 1995—). Baptist. Home and Office: Family Surgery Ctr 556A Memorial Dr Greer SC 29651

GRUBE, KARL BERTRAM, judge; b. Elmhurst, Ill., Jan. 13, 1946; s. Karl Ludwig and Gerturde (Bertram) G.; m. Mary B. Harr, May 4, 1974 (div. Aug. 1991). BSBA, Elmhurst Coll., 1967; JD, Stetson U., 1970; M in Judicial Studies, U. Nev., 1992. Asst. pub. defender State of Fla., Clearwater, 1970-73; county ct. judge State of Fla., St. Petersburg, 1977—; pvt. practice Seminole, Fla., 1973-76; city atty. City of Redington Beach, Fla., 1975-76; asst. dean Fla. Judicial Coll., Tallahassee, 1984-85; faculty mem., course coord. Nat. Judicial Coll. Contbr. articles to profl. jours. Dir. Pinellas Comprehensive Addiction Svcs., Clearwater, 1982-88. Mem. ABA (conf. chair divsn. judicial adminstrn. 1992, Dedicated Svc. award 1991), Fla. State Bar Assn., Colo. Bar Assn., Fla. Conf. County Ct. Judges (pers. 1984-85), Rolls Royce Owner's Club (editor 1982-84). Lutheran. Office: Pinellas County Ct 150 5th St N Ste 304 Saint Petersburg FL 33701-3700

GRUBER, NELSON PETER, physician, psychiatrist; b. Bklyn., Nov. 23, 1957; s. Haskell and Rosalind (Sebold) G. BA in Liberal Arts, U. Tex., Austin, 1979; MD, U. Tex. Med. Sch., Houston, 1984. Cert. psychiatry and qualifications in geriatric psychiatry Am. Bd. Psychiatry and Neurology, Inc.. Internship U. Tex. Med. Sch., Houston, 1984-85, residency, 1986-88, asst. prof. psychiatry, 1989—; assoc. prof. U. Tex. Med. Sch., 1996—; mem. pharmacy and therapeutics com. Harris County Psychiat. Ctr., 1989-91, chair safety com., 1990-93, mem. exec. com., 1991-95, mem. med. records com., 1993-94, pres. med. staff orgn., 1994-95; mem. psychiatry residency tng. com. U. Tex. Med. Sch., 1991-94, mem. faculty senate, 1993-96; mem. total quality mgmt. com. TSPP, 1994—, mem. adminstrv. psychiatry com., 1994-96. Recipient AMA Physician's Recognition award, 1989, 92, 95, Dean's Tchg. Excellence award U. Tex. Med. Sch. at Houston, 1991-96; named examiner Am. Bd. Psychiatry and Neurology, Inc., 1993. Mem. AMA, Am. Psychiat. Assn., Am. Assn. for Geriatric Psychiatry, Assn. Acad. Psychiatry, Tex. Med. Assn., Tex. Med. Found., Tex. Soc. Psychiat. Physicians, Harris County Med. Soc., Houston Psychiat. Soc., Phi Beta Kappa. Office: HCPC 2D08 2800 S Macgregor Way Houston TX 77021-1032

GRUBER, WILLIAM EDMUND, English language educator; b. Hokendauqua, Pa., Sept. 26, 1943; s. William I. and Bessie M. (Hartman) G.; m. Nancy Huntting Herrick, Oct. 21, 1968; children: Elaine Herrick, Laura Katherine, Robert Hartman. BA in English, Yale U., 1965; MA in English, U. Idaho, 1974; PhD in English, Wash. State U., 1979. Prof. English Ill. State U., Normal, 1979-80, Emory U., Atlanta, 1980—. Author: Comic Theaters, 1986, Missing Persons, 1994. Cpl. USMC, 1966-68. Mem. MLA, South Atlantic MLA. Office: Emory U English Dept Atlanta GA 30322

GRUBISICH, THOMAS JAMES, newspaper editor and publisher; b. Peoria, Ill., Dec. 31, 1936; s. Michael Bernard and Mary (Pintar) G.; m. Marilyn J. Burson, Oct. 30, 1965 (div. 1982); children: Emily, Miranda. Student, Spalding Inst., Peoria, 1950-54; BS, Marquette Univ., Milw., 1958. Copy boy New Yorker Mag., 1959; reporter Worcester (Mass.) Telegram, 1959-61; copy editor New York Post, 1961-64; reporter New York Herald Tribune, 1964-66; editor/reporter Washington Post, 1966-81; founding editor The Connection Newspapers, Reston, Va., 1981-94; exec. editor Times Community Newspapers, Reston, Va., 1995-96; resident adviser Press of Slovak Republic, Bratislava, 1996—. Author: Reston: First 20 Years 1985, op-ed articles in Washington Post and mags. Bd. dirs. Greater Reston Arts Ctr., 1992-96, Affordable Housing Opportunity Means Everyone, Fairfax County, 1992-96, Jr. League No. Va., 1995-96. Recipient In My Backyard award Fairfax United Way, 1993, Best of Reston Cmty. Svc. award Reston Interfaith and Greater Reston C. of C., 1992, Citation of Merit Fairfax Fedn. Citizens Assn., 1994; 10-yr. honoree The Women's Ctr., 1995. Mem. D.C. chpt. Soc. Profl. Journalists (Dateline award/editing, writing 1987, 91, 93, Disting. Svc. in Local Journalism award 1987), Va. Press Assn. (editl., writing 1st prize 1987), Suburban Newspapers Am. (Cmty. Svc. award 1987, editl. writing 1995), Ctr. for Fgn. Journalists (vol. faculty, 10th anniversary honoree 1995). Roman Catholic. Office: Times Community Newspapers 1760 Reston Pky Reston VA 22090-3303

GRUENDER, CARL DAVID, philosophy educator; b. Cleve., May 24, 1927; s. Charles Frederick and Charlotte S. (Freiman) G.; m. Anne Dorothy Sherwood, Jan. 6, 1955 (div. Feb. 1973); children: Reesha Howze, Martha Brown, Elizabeth Gruender, Heather Bowman, Mark Ice, Shahn Ice; m. Elizabeth McFee Ice, Jan. 3, 1975. BA, Antioch Coll., 1951; MA, U. Chgo., 1953; PhD, U. Wis., 1957. From instr. to asst. prof. Kans. State U., Manhattan, 1957-63; asst. prof. Case Inst. Tech., Cleve., 1963-67; from assoc. prof. to prof. Fla. State U., Tallahassee, 1967—. Contbr. articles to profl. jours. Campaign coord. Henry Reuss Campaign, Milw., 1954; pres. Sound Transp. Coalition, Tallahassee, 1974; co-founder Coun. Neighborhoods, Tallahassee, 1979. Recipient Grad. fellowship U. Chgo., 1950, Co-prin. Investigator award NSF, 1989. Mem. AAAS, AAUP, Am. Philos. Assn., Philosophy of Sci. Assn., History of Sci. Soc. Home: 2403 Miranda Ave Tallahassee FL 32304 Office: Fla State Univ Dept Philosophy Tallahassee FL 32306-1054

GRUENE, PETER HANS, environmental services administrator; b. El Paso, Tex., Feb. 12, 1950; m.; 2 children. BS in Chemistry, U. Fla., 1972, MS in Environ. Engring. Scis., 1974. Chemist, chief lab. svcs. sect. U.S. Army Environ. Hygiene Agy., Ft. McPherson, Ga., 1974-77; from environ. engr. to sr. environ. engr. Sonoco Products Co., Hartsville, S.C., 1977-86, dir. environ. activities, 1986-90, dir. environ. compliance and tech., 1990—. Contbr. articles to profl. jours. Active N.E. Drought Response Com., S.C., Darlington County Keep Am. Beautiful, past bd. dirs.; chmn. Hartsville Environ. Com., 1993. Mem. Carolinas Air Pollution Control Assn. (past pres.), S.C. C. of C. (tech. com. mem.), U.S. C. of C. (environ. com. mem.), Rotary (past pres.). Office: Sonoco Products Co 1 N 2nd St Hartsville SC 29550-3300

GRUENWALD, HERMANN, architecture educator; b. Augsburg, Germany, July 19, 1958; s. Hermann and Maria Gruenwald. Dipl. ing. FHA, Rudolph Diesel politechnikum, Augsburg, 1983; MArch, U. Houston, 1984; MBA, So. Meth. U., 1989; MEd, U. Okla., 1995, PhD in Adult and Higher Edn., 1995. Registered profl. architect, Okla., interior designer, bldg. designer, Tex. Designer Speidel & Ptnr. Archs., Augsburg, 1981; asst. constrn. mgr. Richard Hohenner Archs., Goegginen, Germany, 1982; teaching asst. Coll. Arch. U. Houston, 1983-84; CADO cons. Blue Tech., Houston, 1984; product mgr. WRT, Batesville, Ark., Dallas, 1984-85; CAD mgr. Tri-Steel Structures, Inc., Denton, Tex., 1985-87, R&D mgr., 1987-88, v.p., 1988-95; rsch. Coll. Arch. Okla. U., Norman, 1995—; dir. devel. Coll. Arch. Okla. U., 1995—, vis. assoc. prof., vis. assoc. prof. arch. Coll. Engring., 1995—; gust lectr. FHA-Rudolf Diesel Polytechnikum, 1995-96, Technische Universitat Berlin, 1996, Universitaet Erlangen, Germany, 1996. Author: Learning and Change in the Marketing Approach of Architects, 1995. Okla. State Dept. Health grantee, 1996; Assn. Collegiate Schs. Arch. fellow, 1995-96; Fulbright scholar, 1980-81. Mem. AIA, Am. Inst. Bldg. Designers, Internat. Facilities Mgmt. Assn., Internat. Conf. Bldg. Ofcls., Archtl. Rsch. Coun., Tex. Assn. Interior Design, Constrn. Specific Inst. Roman Catholic. Office: Okla U Coll Arch 830 Van Fleet Oval Norman OK 73019

GRUER, WILLIAM E., management consultant; b. Oak Park, Ill., Dec. 21, 1937; s. William Earle and Marguerite (Schramm); m. Jewel Susan Gourley Gruer, Nov. 15, 1958; children: Lynn, Mark. BBA, So. Meth. U., 1962; MBA, Calif. Coast U., 1979; PhD, Columbia Pacific U., 1986. Asst. mgr. personnel Mo. Pacific R.R., St. Louis, 1962-67, mgr. personnel planning, 1969-72; labor relations officer Chgo. & Eastern Ill. R.R. (now part of Union Pacific R.R. system), Chicago Heights, Ill., 1967-69; supt. personnel Monsanto Co., Cin., 1972-79, Ligonier, Ind., 1979-82; dir. personnel and risk mgmt., El Paso Products Co., Odessa, Tex., 1982-89; pres. Commerce and Emergency Ins., Odessa, Tex., 1988-89, Environ. Enterprises Inc., 1989—, Gruer & Assocs., 1990—; chmn. adv. coun. Human Resource Mgmt., U. Dallas, 1990-94. Author: Discipline, A Necessity, 1979, Career Counseling in a Changing Economy, 1984, The Just-in-Time Employee, 1991, Male vs. Female; Who is the Better Manager, 1993, Servant Leadership, 1994. Bd. dirs. Odessa Pvt. Industry Coun., 1984-89, Odessa United Way, 1987-89. With USAF, 1955-59. Mem. Am. Soc. Pers. Adminstrs. (dist. dir. 1983-88), Tex. Assn. Bus. (chmn. bd. 1985-87), Permian Basin Internat. Trade Assn. (chmn. bd. 1985-88), Permian Basin Pers. Assn. (bd. dirs., pres. 1984-85), Tex. Alliance Minority Engrs. (bd. dirs.) Cin. Pers. Assn. (bd. dirs., pres. 1978-79), Soc. for Human Resource Mgmt. (pres. Tex. State Coun. 1989-91, dir. nat. com. tng. and devel. 1991—), 40 Plus of Dallas (chmn. bd. 1991-93, profl. devel. area IV 1991—), Los Rios Country Club. Republican. Baptist. Office: 18811 Mahogany Trl Dallas TX 75252-5137

GRUM, CLIFFORD J., manufacturing company executive; b. Davenport, Iowa, Dec. 12, 1934; s. Allen F. and Nathalie (Cate) G.; m. Janelle Lewis, May 1, 1965; 1 son, Christopher J. B.A., Austin Coll., 1956; M.B.A., U. Pa., 1958. Formerly with Republic Nat. Bank, Dallas; former v.p. fin. Temple Industries, Diboll, Tex.; with Time, Inc., N.Y.C., treas., 1973-75, v.p., 1975-80, exec. v.p., 1980-83, also bd. dirs.; pub. Fortune, 1975-79; chief exec. officer Temple-Inland, Inc., Diboll, 1983—, chmn. bd., 1991—; dir. Cooper Industries, Inc., Tupperware Corp., Inc., Trinity Industries, Inc. Trustee Austin Coll. Office: Temple Inland Inc PO Drawer N 303 S Temple Dr Diboll TX 75941

GRUM, DANIEL FRANK, anesthesiologist, educator, medical administrator; b. Cleve., Oct. 18, 1947; s. Frank and Mary Rose Grum; m. Patricia Elaine Miller, Jan. 21, 1989; children: Stephen Michael, Lydia Ruth, Elise Marie. AB, Kenyon Coll., 1969; MD, Northwestern U., 1973; MBA, Memphis State U., 1992. Diplomate Nat. Bd. Med. Examiners, Am. Bd. Anesthesiology. Intern in internal medicine Cleve. Clinic Found., 1973-74; resident in anesthesiology Case Western Res. U., Cleve., 1974-76; fellowship in respiratory intensive care Northwestern U., Chgo., 1976; fellowship in cardiovascular rsch. Case Western Res. U., 1977; asst. prof. U. Hosp., Cleve., 1977-80, chief orthopedic anesthesiology, 1978-79; chief thoracic anesthesia, staff anesthesiologist Cleve. Clinic, 1980-88; assoc. prof., chief cardiac anesthesiology U. Cin., 1988-89; dir. resident edn., assoc. prof. U. Tenn., Memphis, 1989—; chief anesthesiology Regional Med. Ctr., Memphis, 1989—; cons. cardiovascular anesthesia/quality control, Memphis, 1992—; cardiopulmonary resuscitation com., Cleve. Clinic, 1984-88, rsch. projects com., 1986-88, CPR com., 1984-88; postgrad. edn., U. Tenn. Med. Sch., 1989—; chmn. clin. care com. Regional Med. Ctr., Memphis, 1989—, oper. rm. com., 1989—, chmn. pharmacy and therapeutics subocm., 1992—; spkr. in field. Contbr. articles to profl. jours. Sunday sch. tchr. Fairmount Presbyn. Ch., Cleveland Heights, Ohio, 1979-88, dir. elem. edn., 1986-88, benevolence com., 1986-88; advisor Germantown (Tenn.) Sch. Sci. Fair, 1992—. Recipient Scholarship award German Counselate, 1968. Mem. Am. Soc. Anesthesiologists, Internat. Anesthesia Rsch. Soc., Soc. Cardiovascular Anesthesiologists (bd. dirs. 1987-91, chmn. edn. com., 1989-91), Phi Beta Kappa, Beta Gamma Sigma. Office: Univ Tenn Dept Anesthesiology 877 Jefferson Ave # 023 Memphis TN 38103-2807

GRUMET, PRISCILLA HECHT, fashion specialist, consultant, writer; b. Detroit, May 11, 1943; d. Lewis Maxwell and Helen Ruth (Miller) Hecht; m. Ross Frederick Grumet, Feb. 24, 1968; 1 child, Auden Lewis. AA, Stephens Coll., 1963; student, Ga. State Coll., 1983-85. Buyer Rich's Dept. Store, Atlanta, 1963-68; instr. fashion retail Fashion Inst. Am., Atlanta, 1968-71; pres., lectr., cons. Personally Priscilla Personal Shopping Svc., Atlanta, 1971—; retail and customer svc. cons. By Priscilla Grumet, Atlanta, 1989—; instr. Cont. Edn. Program Emory U., Atlanta, 1976—; fashion merch. coord. Park Pl. Shopping Ctr., Atlanta, 1979-83; writer Altanta Bus. Mag., 1984—; cons., buyer Greers-Regensteins Store, Atlanta, 1986-87; writer Atlanta Mag., 1994—; guest lectr. Fashion Group of Am., Rancho La Puerta Resort, Tecate, Mex., 1985—; bus. cons. Atlanta Apparel Mart, 1992—; adv. bd. Bauder Fashion Col., 1986—, Atlanta Apparel Mart, 1992—; fashion panel judge Weight Watchers Internat., 1981; columnist Marquee mag., Atlanta, 1992—; lectr. on customer svc. Rhodes Furniture, Marriott Corp., So. Bell, Lady Love Cosmetics, Atlanta Retail Stores, others, 1994—; presenter profl. seminars on bus. etiquette, 1996—. Author: How to Dress Well, 1981; reporter Women's Wear Daily, 1976-90; columnist Atlanta Scene Mag.; contbr. articles to mags. and publs. including Atlanta, Seventeen, Nat. Jeweler's (Editor's Choice award The Nat. Libr. of Poetry 1995), The Old Farmer's Almanac, Bus. Seminars Profl. Etiquette. Pub. rels. dir., Atlanta Jewish Home Aux., 1986-89; admissions advisor, Stephens Coll., 1979—. Mem. Fashion Group, Inc., Women in Comm., Nat. Coun. Jewish Women, Atlanta Press Club, Buckhead Bus. Assn., Temple Sisterhood (spkr., spl. events com. 1983—). Home and Office: 2863 Careygate NW Atlanta GA 30305-2821

GRUNDER, FRED IRWIN, program administrator, industrial hygienist; b. Detroit, Aug. 17, 1940; s. Fritz and Mary Kathrine (Irwin) G.; m. Barbara Ann Ward, May 7, 1966; children: John Frederick, Robert William. BS in Engr. Physics, U. Mich., 1963, MS in Physics, 1967. Diplomte Am. Bd. Indsl. Hygiene. Rsch. assoc. U. Mich., Ann Arbor, 1960-69; chemist G.D. Clayton & Assocs., Southfield, Mich., 1969-72; lab. dir. Bethlehem (Pa.) Steel Corp., 1972-85; dir. indsl. hygiene Am. Med. Labs., Fairfax, Va., 1985-92; mgr. lab. accreditation programs Am. Indsl. Hygiene Assn., Fairfax, 1992—. Sect. editor: Methods for Biological Monitoring, 1988. Scoutmaster Boy Scouts Am., Bethlehem, 1972-84; pres. U. Mich. Club, Lehigh Valley, 1980-84; mem. toxic planning and oversight panel Chesapeake Rsch. Consortium, Solomons Island, Md., 1990-91, site visitor AIHA Lab., 1992. Mem. ASTM, Coun. Engring. and Sci. Soc. Execs., Am. Indsl. Hygiene Assn., Am. Chem. Soc., Am. Acad. Indsl. Hygiene. Democrat. Methodist. Office: Am Indsl Hygiene Assn 2700 Prosperity Ave Ste 250 Fairfax VA 22031-4320

GRUNDLEHNER, CONRAD ERNEST, information company executive, economic consultant; b. N.Y.C., Mar. 12, 1942; s. Ernest and Elise Louise (Eicks) G.; m. Marietta Ferebee Guidon, Feb. 19, 1977; children: Marietta Ferebee Karen, Guidon Steven. BS, MIT, 1964; MA, U. Pa., 1968. V.p. Simumatics, Inc., Haddonfield, N.J., 1969-72; mgr. Hay Assocs., Phila., 1973-79, Strategic Planning Assocs., Washington, 1980-82; chief economist Donoghue Orgn. Inc., Holliston, Mass., 1982-84; pres. Conrad Grundlehner Inc., McLean, Va., 1984—; bd. dirs. Conrad Grundlehner Inc., McLean, 1984—, bd. dirs., cons. economist W.E. Donoghue & Co., Inc., Holliston, Mass., 1986—. Editor: Donoghue's Mutual Funds Alamanac, 1984-86, contbg. editor: Donoghue's Mutual Funds Alamanac, 1987. 1st lt. U.S. Army, 1971. Mem. MIT Enterprise Forum, Am. Econ. Assn., Nat. Assn. Bus. Econs., MIT Club Washington. Republican. Episcopalian.

GRUNDMEYER, DOUGLAS LANAUX, lawyer, editor; b. New Orleans, Nov. 6, 1948; s. Raymond Wallace and Eva Myrl (Lanaux) G.; m. Elaine Ann Toscano, Jan. 19, 1977; 1 child, Sarah Elaine. BA, Tulane U., 1970, JD, 1976; MA in English, U. New Orleans, 1974. Bar: La. 1976, Calif. 1980, U.S. Dist. Ct. (no. dist.) Calif. 1980, U.S. Dist. Ct. (ea., mid. and we. dists.)

La. 1988, U.S. Ct. Appeals (5th cir.) 1988, U.S. Ct. Apeals (11th cir.) 1996, U.S. Supreme Ct. 1989. Sr. law clk. to presiding judge La. State Ct. of Appeal (4th cir.), New Orleans, 1976-78, 1980-88; assoc. legal editor Bancroft-Whitney Co., San Francisco, 1978-80, contract editor, 1981-92; assoc. Chaffe, McCall, Phillips, Toler & Sarpy, L.L.P., New Orleans, 1988-91, spl. ptnr., 1992-94; ptnr. Chaffe, McCall, Phillips, Toler & Sarpy, L.L.P., 1994—; contract editor Clark Boardman Callaghan, Rochester, N.Y., 1993—. Contbg. editor American Jurisprudence 2d, Criminal Law, 1981; contbg. author La. Appellate Practice Handbook, 1986. Mem. ABA, State Bar Calif., La. Bar Assn., Scribes. Democrat. Roman Catholic. Office: 2300 Energy Ctr 1100 Poydras St New Orleans LA 70163-1100

GRUPE, ROBERT CHARLES, corporate training consultant; b. Alice, Tex., Sept. 3, 1948; m. Dorothy E. Cleveland, Nov. 22, 1975; children: Amber, Robert, Elisabeth, Jonathan. BA, MBA, Calif. Coast U., 1977, PhD, 1992. Announcer Stein Broadcasting Co., Sweetwater, Tex., 1966-68; news announcer Ea. Okla. TV Co., Ada, 1969-72; announcer Anadarko (Okla.) Broadcasting Co., 1972-74; news dir. Cleveland County Broadcasting Co., Norman, Okla., 1974-75; instr. Elkins Inst., Oklahoma City, 1975-77; mng. editor Okla. World Media, Oklahoma City, 1977-78; pres., owner Quality Prodns. Inc., Oklahoma City, 1978—; job skills cons. Okla. Ovt. Industry Coun., Oklahoma City, 1989; vol. trainer U.S. Olympic Festival, Oklahoma City, 1989; mem. Total Quality Mgmt. Faculty OSU, 1990—; TV producer/host Cox Cable Pub. Programming, Oklahoma City, 1990-95; syndicated radio commentator, 1993—. Author: The Miracle of Speech, 1981, The Change, 1993, Creating The Future, 1994; contbr. articles to profl. jours. Vol. media devel. Vol. Action Com. Oklahoma City, 1991. Mem. ASTD (v.p. 1992), Internat. Assn. Bus. Communicators (v.p. 1996-97), Neuro Linguistic Programming Assocs. (v.p. 1991-92). Office: Quality Prodns Inc 4230 NW 36th St Oklahoma City OK 73112-2910

GRZESIAK, ROBERT CHARLES, therapist; b. Depew, N.Y., Feb. 2, 1948; s. Charles J. and Charlotte M. (Dzwigal) G.; m. Catherine L. Vella, Aug. 25, 1972; 1 child, Barry Robert. BA in Psychology cum laude, SUNY, Buffalo, 1971; D Clin. Hypnotherapy, Am. Inst. Hypnotherapy, Irvine, Calif., 1991; MA in Psychology, Newport U., 1993, postgrad, 1993—. Cert. hypnotherapist; registered hypnotherapist. Med. rehab. caseworker Erie County Dept. Health, Buffalo, 1971-73; supr. U.S. Dept. Commerce, Buffalo, 1973-74; foodsvc. sales mgr. Rath Packing Co., Dallas, 1974-84; food svc. sales mgr. Wilson Foods Co., Dallas, 1984—; pvt. practice therapist Arlington, Tex., 1991—. Republican. Roman Catholic. Home: 1005 Brook Hill Ct Arlington TX 76014-3353

GUANI, FILIPPO ETTORE, photographer; b. Paris, Aug. 5, 1954; s. Ermanno and Maria (Boemonte) G.; m. Santina Paterno, Feb. 8, 1992; 1 child, Alessandro Antonio. BS, Cornell U., 1980. Freelance photographer; photographic specialist Cornell U., Ithaca, N.Y., 1990—; ofcl. photographer Comitato Olimpico Nazionale Italiano, N.Y.C., fall 1990, Rieti (Italy) Festival, fall 1990.

GUBITZ, STEPHEN PAGE, university administrator; b. Glens Falls, N.Y., Mar. 6, 1935; m. Susan Steele Gubitz, Nov. 30, 1974; children: Christian, Carrie, Matthew. BA in Econs., U. Rochester, 1957; student, Harvard U., U. Wis., Northwestern U., Ind. U. V.p., credit mgr., ops. mgr., br. mgr., mktg. mgr. Marine Midland Bank, Rochester, N.Y., 1960-72; sr. v.p. mktg. RepublicBank Corp., Houston, 1972-81, sr. v.p. gen. banking group, 1981-82, sr. v.p. corp. comm., 1982-83; sr. v.p., group mgr. United Savs. Assn., Houston, 1983-84; v.p., mgr. Charter Bancshares, Inc., Houston, 1984-85; pres., COO Reliance Savs. Assn., Houston, 1986-87; mgr. banking svcs. Houston Clearing House Assn., 1987-88; dir. devel., comm. Covenant House Tex., Houston, 1989-91; dir. devel., mktg. Coll. Optometry U. Houston, 1991—. Pres., dir. Hear-Say, Inc., Houston, 1993-96; vice chmn. Cultural Arts Coun., Houston; vice chmn., bd. dirs. Tex. Arts Alliance, Houston; mem. exec. bd. Boy Scouts Am., Houston; bd. dirs. Shakespeare & Children's Theater, Family Svc. Ctr., Houston Sch. Deaf Children, Miller Theater; dir. Westbury H.S. PTA. Mem. Nat. Soc. Fund Raising Execs. (treas., bd. dirs.). Baptist. Office: U Houston 4901 Calhoun Rd Houston TX 77204-6052

GUCKERT, JANICE ELAINE, office manager; b. Ashtabula, Ohio, Oct. 15, 1958; d. Clifford Ord Earl Rice and Betty Marie (Adkins) Shears; m. John Lee Guckert, June 23, 1978; 1 child, Wayne Earl. Student, Washington State Coll., Marietta, Ohio, 1979, W.Va. U., 1996—. Cert. in adult edn., Ohio. Supr. Marietta Ophthalmology, 1980-88; sec. Camden-Clark Hosp., Parkersburg, W.Va., 1989-90; office mgr. Ohio Valley Eye Physicians and Surgeons, Vienna, W.Va., 1992—; advisor for med. assts. Washington County Adult Edn., Marietta, 1993—. Mem. Office Mgrs. Assn. Healthcare Providers (sec. 1992-95), Med. Assts. Office: Ohio Valley Eye Physicians and Surgeons 1100 9th St Vienna WV 26105-2176

GUDMUNDSSON, BRUCE I., military historian; b. Copenhagen, Mar. 5, 1959; came to U.S., 1967; s. Ivar and Barbara I. (Hannah) G.; m. Lee-Ann Louise Saedal; children: Kathleen V., Brian R. BA in History, Yale U., 1981. Historian Boston, 1985-86; case study writer Harvard U., Cambridge, Mass., 1986-89; mil. historian Quantico, Va., 1992—; dir. Inst. for Tactical Edn., Quantico, 1991—; cons. Commn. on Roles of Missions of the Armed Forces, Washington, 1994-95. Author: Stormtroop Tactics, 1989, On Artillery, 1993, On Armor, 1996; co-author: On Infantry, 1994. Candidate for mayor Town of Quantico, 1993. Capt. USMC, 1981-85, 89-92. Home: 207 Fourth Ave Quantico VA 22134 Office: 504 Broadway Quantico VA 22134

GUEDRI, TERRY TYRRELL, secondary education educator, educational consultant; b. Roanoke, Va., Mar. 31, 1954; d. William Morris Tyrrell and Marjorie Elizabeth (Andrews) Russell; m. Joseph Bernard Guedri III, July 14, 1973; children: Jenny, Beth. BS, U. Va., 1975. Genetics rschr. Med. Coll. Va., Richmond, 1985-87; tchr. biology and chemistry Chesterfield County Schs., Midlothian, Va., 1987—, crises mediation counselor, tech. trainer, 1992—, tech. cons., 1993—; head coach girls' and boys' tennis Chesterfield County Schs., Midlothian, 1994—; writer, cons. Devel. Skills Inst., U. Va., Charlottesville, 1986-87; mid. sch. sci. amb. to China, D.D. Eisenhower Found., 1993; curator Va.'s Pub. Edn. Network, 1993—; tech. instr. WCVE Pub. TV, 1994—; cons. Nat. Tchr. Tng. Inst. Author, artist: (workbook) Developmental Learning, 1987; author, editor: (textbook) Educator's Guide to the Internet, 1997; editor, artist: (textbook) Developmental Learning, 1987. Dist. chmn. Richmond Rep. Com., 1978-80; mem. Chesterfield County Planning Commn., 1980. Grantee March of Dimes, 1987, D.D. Eisenhower Found., 1993, Woodrow Wilson Inst., 1993. Mem. USTA, USPTR (tchg. pro), Va. Soc. for Tech. in Edn. (exec. bd. 1996—, cert. trainer, mentor), Alpha Delta Kappa (chaplain 1994-95).

GUERNSEY, JULIA CAROLYN, English language educator; b. Jackson, Miss., Mar. 29, 1960; d. Carl Eugene and Sue Stewart (Dunning) G. Student, U. So. Miss., Hattiesburg, 1978-80; BA summa cum laude, Millsaps Coll., Jackson, Miss., 1983; MFA, U. Ark., 1989, PhD, 1996. Grad. tchg. asst. dept. English U. Ark., Fayetteville, 1983-84, 86-94; tutor Women's Athletics, U. Ark., Fayetteville, 1993-96; Men's Athletics, 1993-95; instr./tutor Upward Bound Program, Fayetteville, 1990-93; poet in the schs., Fayetteville, 1986-89. Contbr. poetry, articles to jours. in field. Vol. Mass. Coalition for the Homeless, Boston, 1985, Operation Blessing/Silk Purse, Fayetteville, 1990-91. Mem. MLA. Democrat. Office: Auburn English Dept 9030 Haley Ctr Auburn AL 36849-5203

GUERRA, ARMANDO J., corporate professional; b. St. Clara, Las Villas, Cuba, Nov. 3, 1951; came to U.S., 1961; s. Armando and Ofelia (Bolanos) G.; m. Maria Cata, Sept. 7, 1974; children: Adrianne, Corinne, Eric. BS in Pharmacy, U. Fla., 1974. Staff pharmacist Eckerd Drugs, Miami, 1975-77; pres. Sedano's Pharmacy & Discount, Miami, 1977—; also CEO 12 brs. Sedano's Pharmacies, Miami; bd. dirs. Ready State Bank, Hialeah, Fla.; bd. dirs., v.p. Sedano's Supermarkets, Inc., Miami. Bd. dirs. ARC, South Fla. Region, Latin Bldrs. Assn.; mem. Met. Dade County Econ. Devel. Program Com. Recipient City of Hialeah Proclamation, Mayor, City of Hialeah, 1982, 86, The Merck award U. Fla., Gainesville, 1975, Dade County Proclamation, Dade County Mayor, Miami, 1986. Mem. Nat. Assn. Retail Druggists, Am. Pharm. Assn., Fla. Pharmacy Assn., Dade County Pharm. Assn., Secops Pharmacy Assn., Century 100 Club (U. Fla.). Republican. Roman Catholic.

GUERRA, CHARLES ALBERT, financial consultant and executive; b. Hialeah, Fla., Dec. 4, 1960; s. Charles M. and Elsa Guerra; m. Alicia E. Martell. AA, Miami-Dade Community Coll., 1980; BBA, Fla. Internat. U., 1982; grad., Coll. for Fin. Planning, 1986, Dale Carnegie course, 1989. CPA, Fla.; cert. fin. planner, Fla., pension plan cons.; lic. real estate agt., investment securities, life ins., health ins., disability ins. Tax auditor IRS, Miami, Fla., 1982; acct. Arthur Young & Co., Miami, 1983-85, Peat, Marwick, Mitchell & Co., Miami, 1985; fin. planner H.M. Barth & Co., Miami, 1985-86, Moring-Armstrong & Co., Miami, 1986-88; fin. svcs. cons. The New Eng. and Integrated Resources Equity Corp., Miami, 1986-89; pres., fin. cons. The Fin. Strategies Group, Miami, 1989—. Mem. AICPA, Fla. Inst. CPAs (mem. personal fin. planning com. 1988-89), Inst. Cert. Fin. Planners, Internal Assn. for Fin. Planning, Leaders Assn. of The New England. Office: The Fin Strategies Group 9240 Sunset Dr Ste 225 Miami FL 33173-3264

GUERRA, EMMA MARIA, accountant; b. Las Martinas, Cuba, Nov. 11, 1956; came to U.S., 1962; d. Herberto and Maria Emma (Ledesma) Salqueiro; m. Alfredo Guerra, June 28, 1974; children: Alfred Michael, David Christopher, Emma Cristina. BSBA with highest honors, Fla. Internat. U., 1977. CPA, Fla. Sr. acct. Deloitte, Haskins & Sells, Miami, Fla., 1977-81; v.p., chief fin. officer Union Fed. Savs. and Loan, Miami, 1981; mgr. Am. Express Co., Miami, 1981-83; pvt. practice Miami, 1983—. Mem. AICPA, Fla. Inst. CPAs. Roman Catholic. Home and Office: 10010 SW 28th St Miami FL 33165-2904

GUERRA, ROLAND, regional property manager; b. N.Y.C., Aug. 4, 1961; s. Rolando and Migdalia (Morin) G.; m. Ellen Mary De Rogatis, Oct. 20, 1979; children: Patrick James, Leslie Anne. AS, AA, Miami Dade Community Coll., 1982; student, Barry U., 1982-83; BS in Constrn. Mgmt. with highest honors, Fla. Internat. U., 1991. Lic. real estate agt., Fla; cert. gen. contractor (inactive), Fla. Property mgr. Hasco Homes, Inc., Hollywood, Fla., 1978-83; mgr. India House Inc. Wholesale Clothier, Miami, Fla., 1982-84; adminstrv. asst. Lennar Corp., Miami, 1984-87, dir. customer svc., 1987-88, asst. project supt., 1988-89, rental properties adminstr., 1989-93, regional property mgr., 1993—; mem. student honors mentor program Fla. Internat. U., 1988. Mem. Internat. Platform Soc., Phi Kappa Phi, Sigma Lamda Chi. Home: 1050 NE 107th St Miami FL 33161-7374

GUERRANT, HELEN ORZEL, artist; b. Boston, Mar. 19, 1920; d. Staley Orzel and Jo Ann Hite; m. Paul Nelson Horton (div.); m. Robert Shields Guerrant, Mar. 1, 1947; children: Somerset Orzel, David Denison, Daniel Guerin, Emerson Roy. BS, Cornell U., 1942; postgrad., U. Va., Roanoke Coll., Radford Coll., Hollins Coll., Va. Poly. Inst. Asst. geneticist Atlee Burpee Seed Co., Doylestown, Pa.; with diagnostic dept. N.Y. State Health Dept., N.Y.C.; pilot Martha Ann Woodrum Svcs., Woodrum Field, Roanoke, Va.; judge Nat. Coun. Flower Show. One woman shows include Palette Art Gallery, White House Gallery, Roanoke Fine Arts Ctr., Martinsville Fine Arts Ctr., Va. Employment Commn., Olde Eng. Frame; exhibited in group shows Valentine Mus., Richmond, Va., Empire State Bldg., N.Y.C., Reynolds Metal Co., Norfolk (Va.) Mus. Art Svc. and Art Lending, Winston-Salem (N.C.) Gallery Contemporary Art, 20th Century Gallery Contemporary Art, Williamsburg, Va., L.I. Art Show, Lynchburg Area Show, Roanoke Area Artists Show, Roanoke Coll. Ann. Shows, Wesley Found., Dominion Bank, Roanoke, Sovran Bank, United Va. Bank, Richmond, Va. Commonwealth Bankshares, Richmond, Miller and Rhoads Sidewalk Show, AAUW Heironimus Show, Roanoke Fine Arts Ctr., Lynchburg Fine Arts Ctr., Roanoke Area Shows, Lynchburg Area Shows, Radford Coll., Roanoke Coll., Bath County Regional Area Show. Active Docent Guild, Miller and Main Galleries, White House Galleries, New River Arts Coun., Arts Coun. of Blue Ridge. With USN, 1943-45. Recipient Prints Bath County Area Show award, Best Oil Bath County Regional Area Show award, Best in Show award Dogwood Festival, 1st Watercolor award Roanoke Coll. Show, Watercolor award Bath County Regional Art Show, Best in Show award Lynchburg Area Show, Watercolor award Roanoke Coll. Art Show, Watercolor award AAUW Show, Oil award Radford Coll. Show, Drawings and Graphics award Roanoke Coll. Show. Mem. Am. Legion, Va. Watercolor Soc., League of Roanoke Artists, Morning Music Club. Home: 1816 Windsor Ave SW Roanoke VA 24015-2340

GUERRERO, LILIA, school nurse; b. McAllen, Tex., Aug. 5, 1953; d. Manuel C. and Olivia (Garza) G. BSN, Tex. Woman's U., 1975; postgrad., Calif. Coll. Health Scis., 1994—. RN, Tex.; cert. sch. nurse. Emergency rm. supr. McAllen (Tex.) Med. Ctr., 1975-80; staff nurse Mission (Tex.) Hosp., 1980-85; nurse Mission Cen. Ind. Sch. Dist., 1980—; tchr., insvc. trainer Am. Cancer Soc., 1991-92. Editor newsletter Mission Pediatric Ctr., 1990-92. Past dist. pub. edn. chmn. Am. Cancer Soc.; mem. Super Saturday Asthma Day Planning Com., 1990, planning com. Epilspsy Conf., 1991; mem. adv. com. Mission Hosp. Asthma Support Group; chmn. adv. bd. Mission CISD Wellness, 1994-95. Recipient Achievement award Am. Cancer Soc. Mem. Nat. Assn. Sch. Nurses, Tex. Assn. Sch. Nurses (pres. region 1, bd. dirs. ann. conv. 1991, regional pres. 1989-91).

GUERRY, LEAH SAYE, professional society administrator; b. Shreveport, La., May 21, 1933; d. James Newton and Leah Estel (Wells) Saye; m. Jack Edwin Guerry, June 1, 1957; children: David L., Madeline Guerry. LLB, So. Meth. Univ., 1954. Bar: Tex. 1954. Briefing clk. Tex. Sup. Ct., 1955-56; editor Matthew Bender & Co., 1956-58; rsch. assoc. La. State U. Law Sch., 1964-70; exec. dir. La. Trial Lawyers Assn., Baton Rouge, 1967—; bd. dirs., exec. com. La. Indigent Defenders Bd., New Orleans, 1995—. Co-editor: Studies in Louisiana Torts Law, 1969. Bd. dirs. Friends Sch. Music La. State Univ., Baton Rouge, 1991—. Episcopalian. Office: La Trial Lawyers Assn 442 Europe St Baton Rouge LA 70802

GUEST, DONALD BRITNOR, marketing educator; b. Manchester, Lancashire, Eng., Dec. 1, 1929; came to U.S., 1973; s. Warwick Henry and Edna Elizabeth (Bagnall) G.; m. Brenda Ann Lee, May 5, 1960; children: Paul Stuart, Deborah Jane, Jane Elizabeth. BS in Prodn. Engring., Sussex (U.K.) Coll. Tech., 1969, MA in Bus. Adminstrn., 1974, PhD in Mktg., 1975. Prodn. planning engr. Centrax Ltd. Newton Abbot, Devon, U.K., 1953-57; br. mgr. Bowmaker Ltd., Bankers, London, 1957-61; mng. dir. Sussex Motors Ltd., Robertsbridge, 1961-69; mktg. mgr. Warner-Lambert Co., Sydney, Australia, 1969-73; regional gen. mgr. Warner-Lambert Co., Cen. and S.Am., Caribbean, 1973-77; sr. lectr. U. Miami, Fla., 1977-84; assoc. prof. East Carolina U., Greenville, N.C., 1984-94; prof. emeritus East Carolina U., Greenville, 1994; chair univ. teaching grants com., 1989-90; chair univ. faculty welfare com., 1990—; cons. Immugen, Inc., Miami, 1980-84, Dolfan Denny Enterprises, 1979-84, Cumulus Fibres, N.C., 1986, Landsey Co., S.C., 1987-88, Lawrence Behr Assocs., 1987—; mem. Du Pont de Nemours & Co., 1989—, U.N.X. Chem. Corp., 1989—. Contbr. articles to profl. jours. and books. Recipient Teaching Excellence award East Carolina U., 1986, Prof. of Yr. award U. Miami, 1981. Fellow Acad. Mktg. Sci. Exec.; mem. Am. Mktg. Assn. (chpt. advisor 1979-84, Outstanding Advisor award 1983, 84, advisor East Carolina U. chpt. 1992—), So. Mktg. Assn., N.C. World Trade Assn. (bd. dirs. 1987—, v.p. Coastal Plains chpt. 1989—, chair N.C. ports promotion com. 1989—), Assn. for Global Bus., Inst. for Internat. Econ. Competitiveness, Bus. Assn. for Latin Am. Studies, Commerce Club, Masons, Rotary, Shriners, Beta Gamma Sigma (treas. 1985-88, pres. 1988-89), Delta Sigma Pi (advisor 1979-84, Spotlight award 1981, 82, 83). Republican. Anglican. Home: 5354 Scattered Oaks Ct Jacksonville FL 32258-3416 Office: East Carolina U Sch Bus Dept Mktg Greenville NC 27858

GUETHLEIN, WILLIAM O., lawyer; b. Cin., May 4, 1927; s. William O. and Catherine (Sandmann) G.; m. Bette Mivelaz, Aug. 4, 1961 (dec. 1974). LLD, U. Louisville, 1950. Bar: Ky. 1950, U.S. Dist. Ct. Ky. 1954, U.S. Ct. Appeals (6th cir.) 1954. Assoc. Boehl Stopher and Graves, Louisville, 1950-60; sr. ptnr. Boehl Stopher Graves and Deindoerfer, Louisville, 1960—. Lt. USAR, 1952-60. Fellow Am. Acad. Trial Lawyers; mem. ABA, Jefferson County Bar Assn., Ky. Bar Assn., Am. Assn. Hosp. Attys. Office: Boehl Stopher & Graves Providian Ctr 400 W Market St Ste 2300 Louisville KY 40202-3349

GUETZLOE, DOUGLAS M., public relations executive; b. Tampa, Fla., June 15, 1954; s. Bruce Alan and Eleanor (Carden) G.; m. Stacey Marie Lewis, Apr. 11, 1987; children: Alexander, Jefferson. BA, Fla. State U., 1977. Pub. rels. dir. Fla. Fruit & Vegetable Assn., Orlando, 1978-81; regional dir. Fla. Med. Assn., Winter Park, 1981-83; pres. Advantage cons., Orlando, 1983—. Pres. Young Reps. of Ctrl. Fla., Orlando, 1981-90; mem. Rep. Exec. Com., Orlando, 1980—; state dir. Jack Kemp for Pres., Fla., 1988; regional coord. Buchana for Pres., Ctrl. Fla., 1992; chmn. Ax the Tax Com., Orlando, 1984; fellow Save Our State Com. Named Outstanding Rep. in Orange County, Orange County Rep. Party, 1989. Mem. SAR (pres. 1984), Fla. Pub. Rels. Assn. (v.p. 1983-85), Internat. assn. Bus. Comm. (v.p. 1981-90). Presbyterian. Office: Advantage Consultants 3660 Maguire Blvd Ste 103 Orlando FL 32803

GUFFEE, GUY KEEL, surgeon; b. Tex., Oct. 28, 1935. BA in Chemistry, U. Tex., Austin, 1958; MD, U. Tex., Galveston, 1962. Diplomate Am. Bd. Surgery. Rotating intern Parkland Meml. Hosp., Dallas, 1962-63, resident in gen. surgery, 1965-69; pvt. practice, Portland, Oreg., 1969-91. Capt. M.C., USAF, 1963-65. Fellow ACS; mem. AMA.

GUGLIELMINO, LUCY MARGARET MADSEN, education educator, researcher, consultant; b. Charleston, S.C., Feb. 20, 1944; d. Robert Allen and Margaret Webb (Rodgers) Madsen; m. Paul Joseph Gugliemino, July 31, 1965; children: Joseph Allen, Margaret Rose. BA in English magna cum laude, Furman U., 1965; MEd in English and Edn., Savannah Grad. Ctr., 1973; EdD in Adult Edn., U. Ga., 1977. Tchr. English, various pub. schs., Mass., N.J., S.C., Ga., 1965-72; vis. asst. prof. adult and cmty. edn. Fla. Atlantic U., Boca Raton, 1978-87, asst. prof., 1987-88, assoc. prof., 1988-90, prof., 1991—, chmn. dept. ednl. leadership, 1991-94, dir. Melby Cmty. Edn. Ctr., 1994—; cons. AT&T, Motorola, Westvaco, S.E. banks, 1979—; bd. dirs. South Fla. Ctr. for Ednl. Leaders, 1992—. Author: Adult ESL Instruction: A Sourcebook, 1991,; co-author: Administering Programs for Adults, 1995; author (adult form) Self-Directed Learning Readiness Scale, 1978, 3 other forms and translations into 9 other langs., 1979-94, Learning Preference Assessment (self-scoring format for business), 1991; contbr. over 70 articles, monographs to profl. jours., chpts. to books. Mem. Fla. Literacy Coalition, 1990—, Riviera Civic Assn., 1979—, Commn. on Status of Women. Recipient Tchr. of Yr. award Coll. Edn., Fla. Atlantic U., 1980, Outstanding Achievement award 1991, Presdl. Merit award, 1993; named to Fla. Adult and Cmty. Edn. Hall of Fame, Fla. Adminstrs. Adult and Cmty. Edn., 1992; numerous grants, 1979—. Mem. Nat. Cmty. Edn. Assn., Am. Assn. for Adult and Continuing Edn., Commn. Profs. Adult Edn. (chmn. self-directed learning task force 1987-88, 90-91), Fla. Adult Edn. Assn. (bd. dirs. 1989-90), AAUW, Phi Kappa Phi, Phi Delta Kappa. Episcopalian. Home: 734 Marble Way Boca Raton FL 33432-3007 Office: Fla Atlantic U ED251 777 Glades Rd Boca Raton FL 33431-6424

GUGLIUZZA, KRISTENE KOONTZ, transplant and general surgery educator; b. Siloam Springs, Ark., May 2, 1956; d. Lloyd Lawson Koontz Jr. and Helen Ruth (Camfield) Smith; m. Joseph Thomas Gugliuzza III, Sept. 3, 1989. AS, Lake Land Coll., Mattoon, Ill., 1977; BS with honors, Ea. Ill. U., Charleston, 1978; MD, U. Ill., Rockford, 1982. Diplomate Am. Bd. Surgery. Intern dept. surgery Tulane U. Med. Sch. and Affiliated Hosps., New Orleans, 1982-83, resident, 1983-87, fellow divsn. transplantation, 1987-89, instr. surgery, rsch. assoc. in surgery and transplantation, 1989-90; asst. prof. U. Tex. Med. Br., Galveston, 1990-97; assoc. clin. prof. St. Mary's Hosp., Galveston, 1997—; spl. fellow in pancreas transplantation U. Minn., Mpls., 1989; courtesy staff St. Mary's Hosp., Galveston, 1991-96; recovery surgeon La. Organ Procurement Agy., New Orleans, 1989-90; presenter in field. Contbr. articles to med. jours. Fellow ACS; mem. AMA, Am. Diabetes Assn., Galveston County Med. Soc., Tex. Med. Assn., Cell Transplant Soc., Am. Med. Women's Assn., Assn. Women Surgeons, Singleton Surg. Soc., Assn. Acad. Surgery, Transplantation Soc., Tex. Transplant Soc., Tulane Surg. Soc., Southwestern Surg. Conf., N.Y. Acad. Scis., Am. Soc. Gen. Surgeons, Am. Soc. Transplant Physicians, Tex. Surg. Soc. Office: U Tex Med Br Dept Surgery 301 University Blvd Galveston TX 77555-0542

GUIDO, MICHAEL ANTHONY, evangelist; b. Lorain, Ohio, Jan. 30, 1915; s. Mike and Julia (DePalma) G.; m. Audrey Forehand, Nov. 25, 1943. Student, Moody Bible Inst., Chgo., 1933-35. Ordained to ministry So. Bapt. Conv., 1939. Min. youth and music lst Presbyn. Ch., Sebring, Fla., 1936-38, lst Bapt. Ch., Lake Charles, La., 1939; evangelist Moody Bible Inst., 1940-50; founder, pres., speaker Guido Evangelistic Assn., Metter, Ga., 1950—; writer, speaker daily telecast A Seed from the Sower, 1972—, daily broadcaster The Sower, A Seed from the Sower, Seeds from the Sower, Your Favorite Ten, 1957—. Author: (autobiography) Seeds from the Sower, 1990; editor Sowing and Reaping mag., 1957—; daily newspaper columnist Seeds from the Sower, 1957—. Named Alumnus of Yr., Moody Bible Inst., 1982, Citizen of Yr., Kiwanis Club, Metter, 1982. Home: PO Box 508 Metter GA 30439-0508 Office: 600 N Lewis St Metter GA 30439-1428

GUIDRY, RODNEY-LEE JOSEPH, small business owner; b. Jennings, La., Nov. 20, 1935; s. Claude and Eda (Richard) G.; m. Haruko Komatsuzaki, Oct. 23, 1958; children: Emme Marie Stansbury, Emma Marie Pool. AAS, Community Coll. USAF, Lackland AFB, Tex., 1977, 79; BA, Northwestern State U., Natchitoches, La., 1978; MA, Pepperdine U., 1980. Commd. USAF, 1955; advanced through grades to sr. master sgt., 1976; ret. USAF, 1979; asst. personnel mgr. Seahorse, Inc., Morgan City, La., 1980-81; pers. dir. Acadian Marine, New Orleans, 1981; owner, cons. Rod Guidry Cons., Lafayette, La., 1980—; owner, operator Rod Guidry Ins. Ctr., Lafayette, 1982—; owner R&H Seafood Exports Ltd., Lafayette, 1990—; pres., chief exec. officer G&P Seafood Inc., Lafayette, 1990-95. Editor: USAF Retiree Newsletter, 1989-91. Sec. Retirees Activities Office, England AFB, La., 1986-88, bd. dirs., 1983—. Mem. Am. Soc. Safety Engrs. (sec. 1985-86, chmn. scholarships 1984—, Plaque 1986), VFW (life), Vietnam Vets. Am. (life, treas. 1984-88), Air Force Assn. (life), Air Commando Assn. (life), Civitan Internat. (pres. Lafayette chpt. 1989-91, sec. 1987-89), French Toastmasters. Republican. Roman Catholic. Home: 215 Fendler Pky Pineville LA 71360-4729 Office: 2229 Moss St Lafayette LA 70501-2123

GUILARTE, PEDRO MANUEL, holding company executive; b. Cuba, May 19, 1952; s. Miguel G. and Emma G.; m. Zulima Piedra, May 26, 1979. BS in Indsl. Engring., Northwestern U., 1975; MBA, Washington U., St. Louis, 1977; cert. systems dynamics MIT, 1978; m. Zulima Piedra, May 26, 1979. Market analyst Cummins Engine Co., Columbus, Ind., 1976; corp. devel. exec. FPL Group, North Palm Beach, 1977-94; pres. Cable LPI, 1989-93; internat. project mgr. ESI Energy, 1993-94, internat. power devel. cons., 1994—. Consortium for Grad. Study in Bus. fellow, 1975-77; scholar Northwestern U., 1975. Mem. Planning Execs. Inst. Republican. Methodist. Home: 6464 Woodlake Rd Jupiter FL 33458-2447

GUILL, MARGARET FRANK, pediatrics educator, medical researcher; b. Atlanta, Jan. 18, 1948; d. Vernon Rhinehart and Margaret N. (Tichenor) Frank; m. Marshall Anderson Guill III, July 6, 1974; children: Daniel Marshall, Laura Elizabeth. BA, Agnes Scott Coll., 1969; MD, Med. Coll. Ga., 1972. Diplomate Am. Bd. Pediatrics, Am. Bd. Pediatrics subbd. pulmonology, Am. Bd. Allergy and Immunology, Nat. Bd. Med. Examiners. Resident in pediatrics Kaiser Found. Hosp., San Francisco, 1976-78, fellow in allergy, 1978-79; staff physician Waipahu (Hawaii) Clinic, 1973-76; intern in internal medicine Med. Coll. Ga., Augusta, 1973, resident in pediatrics, 1974, fellow in allergy and immunology, 1979-80, from asst. prof. to prof. pediatrics, 1981—; also chief sect. pediatric pulmonology and dir. Asthma Ctr. Med Coll. Ga., Augusta, dir. Cystic Fibrosis Ctr., 1990—; spkr. in field. Host Healthwatch weekly program WJBF-TV, 1982-83; contbr. articles to profl. jours. Active Reid Meml. Presbyn. Ch.; vol. tchr. Episcopal Day Sch., 1982-85; career day participant Acad. Richmond County, 1982, 83; med. advisor Augusta Area Allergy and Asthma Support Group, 1984-86; adv. bd. East Cen. br. Am. Lung Assn. Ga., 1985—, program of work com., 1987—, bd. dirs., 1987—, program coordinating com., 1990-91, exec. bd. 1989-91, adv. bd. Asthma Ski Mates Am., 1990; med. staff Camp Breathe Easy, 1985—, med. dir. 1996. Recipient Mosby Book award, 1973; rsch. grantee BRSG, 1981-86, Del Labs., 1982, Merrell-Dow, 1983, 84, Elan Pharms., 1986, Am. Lung Assn. Ga., 1986, 87, Hollister-Stier, 1986, Fisons Corp., 1989, 91-93, 95, Med. Coll. Ga., 1989, Am. Heart Assn., 1991, Genentech, 1991-96, Miles, 1992, Clintrials, 1995. Fellow Am. Acad. Pediat., Am. Coll. Chest Physicians, Am. Acad. Allergy and Immunology, Am. Coll. Allergy, Am. Assn. Cert. Allergists; mem. Med. Assn. Ga., Richmond County Med. Soc., Allergy and Immunology Soc. Ga., S.E. Allergy Assn. (Hal Davison award 1985), Am. Assn. Clin. Immunologists and

Allergists, Ga. Thoracic Soc., Am. Thoracic Soc., Assn. for Care Asthma, Alpha Omega Alpha. Home: 2247 Pickens Rd Augusta GA 30904-4462 Office: Med Coll Ga Dept Pediatrics Augusta GA 30912

GUILLAMA-ALVAREZ, NOEL JESUS, healthcare company executive; b. Havana, Cuba, Nov. 30, 1959; came to U.S., 1966; s. Jesus Mario Guillama and Rosa Maria Alvarez Guillama; m. Elayne Z. Cueto, July 6, 1985; 1 child, Jahziel Mikhail Guillama. Student, Palm Beach C.C., Lake Worth, Fla., 1978-80; BS in Bus. Adminstrn., Pacific We. U., L.A., 1992. Cert. bldg. contractor, Fla.; lic. real estate broker, mortgage broker, gen. ins. agt. Dir. programing Teleprompter Corp., West Palm Beach, Fla., 1976-79; pres., CEO JMG Holdings Inc, Palm Beach, Fla., 1980-90; v.p. ops. Quality Care Networks, Boca Raton, Fla., 1990-95; v.p. devel. Medpartners, Inc., Birmingham, 1995; pres., CEO Met. Health Networks, Boca Raton, 1995—; vice chair Palm Beach County Adv. Bd., West Palm Beach, 1990-92; co-founder, vice chair Lake Worth Cmty. Devel. Corp., 1990-92; co-founder, dir. Project Lake Worth, 1989-92. Writer weekly column Palm Beach Latino Newspaper, 1991-92. Recipient award Leukemia Soc. Am., 1979, Chin de Plata award Todo Mag., Miami, Fla., 1978. Mem. Am. Fin. Assn., Am. Coll. Healthcare Execs. (assoc.), Med. Group Practice Assn. Office: Ste 560 51oo Town Center Circle Boca Raton FL 33486

GUILLERMIN, ARMAND PIERRE, university administrator; b. Buffalo, Nov. 23, 1936; s. Larry Rossolet and Apphia Adele (Gaskin) G.; m. Helen Louanne Rupp, May 27, 1959; children: Michelle, Lisa. BA, Bob Jones U., 1958, MA, 1960; postgrad., U. Va., Cen. Mich. U.; diploma, Harvard U. Inst Edn. Mgmt., 1983; LLD (hon.), Christian Heritage Coll., 1985; EdD, Nova Southeastern U., 1986. Dean adminstrn. So. Meth. Coll., Orangeburg, S.C., 1963-65, pres., 1965-67; ednl. mgmt. cons., 1967-73; exec. v.p. Liberty U., Lynchburg, 1973-75, pres., 1975—; advisor Tel Aviv U., 1979-80; mem. Pres.'s Nat. Adv. Coun. on Ednl. Rsch. and Improvement, 1991-94. Bd. dirs. Lynchburg Christian Acad., 1975—, United Way, Lynchburg, 1987-90, NCCJ, Lynchburg, 1986-89. Named Bicentennial Educator, Bicentennial Commn. Lynchburg, 1986. Mem. Va. State Council Higher Edn. (pvt. coll. adv. council 1975—), Am. Assn. Pres. Colls. and Univs., Assn. Evang. Sem. Pres., Assn. Christian Schs. Internat. (bd. dirs. 1986—), Greater Lynchburg C. of C. (bd. dirs. 1987-90), Kappa Delta Pi. Lodge: Rotary (bd. dirs. Lynchburg 1987-91). Office: Liberty U PO Box 20000 Lynchburg VA 24506-8001

GUILLETT, SHARRON ELAINE, nursing educator; b. Leachville, Ark., Feb. 28, 1948; d. Ralph J. and Opal Ruth (Rickard) Sanders; m. Warren V. Guillett, Nov. 17, 1981; children: Brian, Alexis, Amanda. Diploma, Harper Hosp. Sch. Nursing, Detroit, 1972; BSN, Madonna Coll., Livonia, Mich., 1982, MSN, 1989; PhD, George Mason U. Cert. in med.-surg. nursing ANA. Head nurse Harper Hosp., clin. nurse specialist in nuclear medicine; staff nurse Wm. Beaumont Hosp., Royal Oak, Mich.; instr. Madonna Coll.; nurse educator Henry Ford Health Sys., Detroit; spkr., cons. in quality assurance, leadership and caring for child with cerebral palsy. Contbr. articles to profl. jours. Mem. Mich. Nurses Assn., Mich. League for Nursing, Harper Sch. Nursing Alumni Assn. (v.p.), Sigma Theta Tau (pres. Kappa Iota chpt., rsch. grantee). Home: 14332 Compton Village Dr Centreville VA 22020

GUILLIOUMA, LARRY JAY, JR., performing arts administrator, music educator; b. Massillon, Ohio, Apr. 23, 1950; s. Larry Jay and Molly (Galob) G. BS, U. North Ala., 1972, MA, 1975; postgrad., U. Miss., 1976-78. Cert. tchr., Tex. Band dir. Phil Campbell (Ala.) H. S., 1972-76; grad. asst. U. Miss. Band, Oxford, 1976-78; asst. dir. Victoria (Tex.) H. S., 1978-81; dir. bands Harlingen (Tex.) H. S., 1981-87, McAllen (Tex.) Pub. Schs., 1991—; musician Huntsville (Ala.) Symphony Orchestra, 1970-76, Victoria (Tex.) Symphony Orchestra, 1978-81. Named Outstanding Dir. Alamo Tournament of Bands, San Antonio, 1985, Best in Class, World of Music Festival, Dallas, 1986; named to Nata. Band Dirs. Hall of Fame, Daytona Beach, Fla.; Harlingen High Sch. Big Red Cardinal Band marched in Pasadena Tournament of Roses Parade, 1987. Mem. Nat. Band Assn., Tex. Music Educators Assn. (bd. dirs, region vice chmn., region band chmn.), Tex. Band Masters Assn., Phi Beta Mu. Home: 2105 Mynah Ave Mcallen TX 78504-3808

GUILLOT, JACQUES LOUIS, internist, pediatrician; b. New Orleans, La., Apr. 11, 1965; s. Walter Louis and Blanche Marie (Jeanfreau) G.; m. Jacqueline Laure Provosty, May 4, 1990; children: Camille Elise, Corinne Adele. BS, Tulane U., 1987; MD, LSU, 1991. Diplomate Am. Bd. Internal Medicine, Am. Bd. Pediatrics. Med. resident LSU Sch. of Medicine, New Orleans, 1991-95; staff physician Lakeview Regional Med. Ctr., Mendeveille, La., 1995—. Mem. Am. Coll. Physicians, Am. Acad. Pediatrics, Phi Beta Kappa. Roman Catholic. Home: 717 N Beau Chene Dr Mandeville LA 70471 Office: Lakeview Physician Svcs 804 Heavens Dr Ste 100 Mandeville LA 70471

GUILLOTT, BARBARA FAYE, computer science and mathematics educator; b. Crowley, La., Oct. 27, 1946; d. Dallas Pierre and Nettie Mary (Meaux) G.; m. Chester Josphe Lacomb Jr., Jan. 27, 1968 (div. Jan. 1991); children: Sonya, Tara, Bart. BS, U. So. La., 1968, MS, 1986, postgrad., 1986-89; postgrad., La. State U., 1990-91. Instr. McNeese State U., Lake Charles, La., 1987-89, So. La. U., Hammond, 1990-91; computer lab. mgr. La. State U., Alexandria, 1992; instr. U. So. La., Lafayette, 1992-93, La. State U., Eunice, 1992-94. Mem. IEEE Computer Soc., Assn. Computing Machinery.

GUIN, DEBRA MAURIECE, sales executive; b. Columbus, Miss., July 27, 1953; d. Edward Lester and Ann Mauriece (Ball) G. BS in Mktg., U. New Orleans, 1980; student, The Coll. of Ins., New York, 1974-75; postgrad., U. New Orleans, 1991. Sales rep. David Fried & Assocs., Inc., New Orleans, 1977-78, R.J. Reynolds Tobacco Co., New Orleans, 1979-80; sales rep. level II 3M Co., New Orleans, 1980-82; territory mgr. Thompson Industries, New Orleans, 1983-85; sales rep. Mobil Chem. Co., New Orleans, 1985-86; acct. exec. Sara Lee Knit Products, New Orleans, 1986-92; bus. devel. mgr. Sara Lee Corp., Winston-Salem, N.C., 1992—; mem. computer tech. task force Sara Lee, 1992. Mem. Hanes Underwear Zone of Yr., 1989; mem. steering com. Sara Lee Knit Products; mentor program, vol. fundraising Covenant House, 1989—. Recipient Rookie of the Year award Hanes Underwear, 1987, Bus. Builder award Hanes Underwear, 1988. Mem. Am. Mktg. Assn., The Fashion Group Internat., Alpha Region (New Orleans, bd. dirs.), Zeta Tau Alpha. Republican. Methodist. Office: Sara Lee Corp PO Box 2760 Winston Salem NC 27102-2760

GUIN, DON LESTER, insurance company executive; b. Shreveport, La., Nov. 5, 1940; s. Lester and Ethelyn (Dumas) G.; m. Mary Ann Guin, Feb. 3, 1979. BBA in Ins., U. Ga., 1962; BS in Law, Kensington U., Glendale, Calif., 1987, JD, 1989. Bar: Calif. 1990, U.S. Ct. Appeals (5th and 9th cirs.) 1990, U.S. Dist. Ct. (no. dist.) Calif. 1990, U.S. Ct. Appeals (fed. cir.) 1991, U.S. Dist. Ct. (ea. dist.) Tex. 1991, U.S. Ct. Internat. Trade 1991, U.S. Ct. Fed. Claims 1992, U.S. Supreme Ct. 1994. Adjuster, supr. Lindsey & Newsom, Beaumont, Tex., 1963-71; mgr. Lindsey & Newsom, Port Arthur, Tex., 1968-71; asst. to pres. Lindsey & Newsom, Tyler, Tex., 1971-74, v.p. ops., 1977-84, sr. v.p., 1984—; sr. v.p. adminstrn. and legal Lindsey Morden, 1990—; sr. v.p., corp. sec. Lindsey Morden Claims Svc. Inc., Lindsey Morden Claims Mgmt., 1992-93, sr. v.p., treas. U.S. Ops., 1993—, sr. v.p., corp. treas., chief legal officer, 1995—; sr. v.p., corp. treas. and sec. Vale Nat. Training Ctrs, Inc., 1993—; sr. v.p., corp. treas, corp. sec., chief legal officer, 1995—; bd. dirs. Lindsey Morden Claims Svc., Inc., Lindsey Morden Claims Mgmt., Inc., exec. com., mgmt. com., compensation com., incentive com., Vale Nat. Tng. Ctrs., Lindsey & Newsom Inc.; trustee Lindsey and Newsom Benefit Trusts, 1990-91, plan adminstr. Lindsey Morden Profit Sharing Retirement Trust, 1994, Lindsey & Newsom Retirement Funds, 1990—; sr. v.p., corp. sec., CLO Groupe Lindsey Morden, Inc., 1996—; mem. adv. bd. Kemper Ins. Group; sr. v.p., corp. sec. Lindsey & Newsom, Vale Nat; bd. dirs. Tyler Mus. Art, chmn. pers. policy com. Author: Analysis of Garage Liability, 1972, Dishonesty Claims Handling, 1973, Casualty Reporting Manual, 1975, Sexual Harassment in the Workplace, 1986, (audio cassette) Beating the Bears of Bad Faith, 1991, (video cassette) Bad Faith and Preventing Errors and Omissions Claims, 1987. Trustee Lindsey Morden Benefit Trusts, Lindsey Morden Retirement Trusts, 1992—; dir. assoc. U. Tex Health Ctr., 1995; budget allocation panelist United Way Tyler/Smith County, Tex., 1995; bd. dirs. Tyler Mus. of Art, 1996. Mem. ABA (internat. law sect., corp. law sect.), Can. Bar Assn., Nat. Assn. Def. Counsel, Nat. Assn. Ind. Ins. Adjusters (data processing com. 1976, legis. com. 1990), Bar Assn. D.C., Bar Assn. U.S. Fed. Cir., Defense Inst. Trial Lawyers Assn. (ins. law com.), State Bar Calif. (internat. law sect., tort sect., litigation sect., labor and employment law sect.), Nat. Employee Benefit Found., Def. Rsch. Inst., Alameda County Bar Assn., Inter-Pacific Bar Assn., Italian-Am. Bar Assn., Bar Assn. 5th Fed. Cir., Optimist Club, Kiwanis Club, Sabre Club, Lawyers Club San Francisco, Ins. Soc. U. Ga. (charter mem.), Circle K-Kiwanis. Home: 17389 Hidden Valley Ln Flint TX 75762-9611 Office: Lindsey Morden Claims Svcs Inc 211 Brookside Dr Tyler TX 75711

GUIN, JUNIUS FOY, JR., federal judge; b. Russellville, Ala., Feb. 2, 1924; s. Junius Foy and Ruby (Pace) G.; m. Dorace Jean Caldwell, July 18, 1945; children: Janet Elizabeth Smith, Judith Ann Mullican, Junius Foy III, David Jonathan. Student, Ga. Inst. Tech., 1940-41; A.B. magna cum laude; J.D., U. Ala., 1947; LL.D., Magic Valley Christian Coll., 1963. Bar: Ala. 1948. Pvt. practice law Russellville; sr. ptnr. Guin, Guin, Bouldin & Porch, 1948-73; fed. dist. judge U.S. Dist. Ct. (no. dist.) Ala., Birmingham, from 1973, now sr. judge; commr. Ala. Bar, 1965-73, 2d v.p., 1969-70; Pres. Abstract Trust Co., Inc., 1958-73; sec. Iuka TV Cable Co., Inc., Haleyville TV Cable Co., Inc., 1963-73; former dir., gen. counsel First Nat. Bank of Russellville, Franklin Fed. Savs. & Loan Assn. of Russellville.; Lectr. Cumberland-Samford Sch. Law, 1974—, U. Ala. Sch. Law, 1977—. Chmn. Russellville City Planning Com., 1954-57; 1st chmn. Jud. Commn. Ala., 1972-73; mem. Ala. Supreme Ct. Adv. Com. (rules civil procedure), 1971-73; mem. adv. com. on standards of conduct U.S. Jud. Conf., 1980-87, mem. com. on Fed.-State Jurisdiction, 1982-88, mem. ad hoc com. on cameras in the courtroom, 1982-83; Rep. county chmn., 1954-58, 71-72, Rep. state fin. chmn., 1972-73; candidate for U.S. Senator from, Ala., 1954; Ala. Lawyers' Finance chmn. Com. to Re-elect Pres., 1972; former trustee Ala. Christian Coll., Faulkner U., Magic Valley Christian Coll., Childhaven Children's Home; elder Ch. of Christ. Served to 1st lt., inf. AUS, 1943-46. Named Russellville Citizen of Year, 1973; recipient Dean's award U. Ala. Law Sch., 1977. Mem. ABA (mem. spl. com. on resdl. real estate transactions 917-73), Am. Radio Relay League, Ala. Bar Assn. (com. chmn. 1965-73, Award of Merit 1973), Jefferson County Bar Assn., Fed. Bar Assn., Am. Law Inst., Ala. Law Inst. (dir. 1969-73, 76—), Am. Judicature Soc., Farrah Law Soc., Farrah Order Jurisprudence (now Order of Coif), Phi Beta Kappa, Omicron Delta Kappa, Delta Chi. Office: US Dist Ct 619 US Courthouse 1729 5th Ave N Birmingham AL 35203-2000*

GUINEE, VINCENT F., medical epidemiologist; b. N.Y.C., June 3, 1933; s. Florence V. Guinee; married, Mar. 12, 1983. BS, Fordham U., 1955; MD, Cornell U., 1959; MPH, Harvard U., 1966. Bd. cert. preventive medicine; lic. physician, Tex., N.Y. Intern St. Vincent's Hosp., N.Y.C., 1959-60, resident, 1960-61, from asst. to assoc. attending physician, 1968-72, attending physician, 1973-75, cons., 1976—; resident Bellevue and Meml. Hosp., N.Y.C., 1964-65, N.Y.C. Health Dept., 1966-67; clin. asst. dept. pediatrics Belleville Hosp., 1968-75; from clin. instr. to clin. asst. prof. dept. pediatrics NYU Med. Sch., 1968-75; assoc. prof. M.D. Anderson Cancer Ctr., Houston, 1974-92, prof., 1992; prof. epidemiology U. Tex. Sch. Pub. Health, 1975—; course dir., assoc. prof. internal medicine course dir., prof. internal medicine, Houston, 1987-95; dir. immunization program N.Y.C. Dept. Health, 1966-71, dir. bur. preventable diseases, 1968-71, hearing officer, asst. commr. program rev. and devel., 1972-74; me. audit com. M.D. Anderson Cancer Ctr., med. info. needs com., rsch. com., chmn. edn. com., 1976-77, exec. com. of med. staff; chmn. dept. patient studies U. Tex. M.D. Anderson Cancer Ctr., 1974-95; cons. tng. br. Nat. Ctr. Disease Control, 1965-71, John A. Hartford Found., 1972, Moscow Cancer Rsch. Ctr., 1979, Roswell Park Meml. Inst., 1979, Am. Joint Com. for Cancer Staging and End Results Reporting, 1977-87, Netherlands Cancer Inst., 1979, 81, Nat. Cancer Inst., 1979-81, Nat. Inst. Oncology, Budapest, 1981, ACS, 1991-95; examiner Am. Bd. Preventive Medicine, 1972-76; mem. data monitoring com. Harvard Sch. Pub. Health, 1991—, infections com. St. Vincent's Hosp., 1968-74, N.Y.C. Prison Health Care Com., 1972-73, com. on lead poisoning Nat. Rsch. Coun., 1973, Centralized Cancer Patient Data Sys., 1977-84, numerous others. Reviewer: (jours.) Lancet, Sci., Yerabook of cancer, Cancer, Am. Jour. Medicine, Tex. Medicine, Head and Neck; cons. editor Cancer Bull.; contbr. articles to med. jours., chpts. to books. Chmn. Fordham U. Coun., 1973-75; night mayor N.Y.C., 1968-74. Lt. comdr., maj. USPHS, 1961-64. Fellow ACP (joint com. nat. data resources 1974-76), APHA, Am. Coll. Cardiology (assoc.); mem. AMA (jour. reviewer), Internat. Soc. Pharmacoepidemiology, Am. Coll. Epidemiology, Am. Soc. Clin. Oncology, Am. Fedn. Clin. Rsch., S.W. Sci. Forum, Tex. Med. Assn., N.Y. Acad. Scis., N.Y. State Med. Soc., N.Y. County Med. Soc. (pub. health com. 1968-74, infant mortality com. 1973-74), Harris County Med. Soc. (pub. health com. 1989—), Sigma Xi.

GUINESS, STEVEN, sales executive; b. Brookline, Mass., May 16, 1945; s. Edwin and Ruth (Rubinoff) G.; m. Ronna Lee Dolgin, Mar. 18, 1967; children: Melissa Joy and Keith Evan. BS, U. Mass., 1966; student, U. Alaska, 1968-69. Sales assoc. McHutchinson & Co., Ridgefield, N.J., 1969-70; self-employed sales rep. Louisville, Ky., 1970-79, Atlanta, 1979—; cons. Argus, Inc., Atlanta, 1992—. Contbr. profl. publs. Served in U.S. Army, 1967-69. Mem. Southeast Men & Boys Apparel Club (dir. 1980-84), Men & Boys Apparel Club of Fla., Civil War Token Soc. Office: Atlantic Southern Sales PO Box 767002 Roswell GA 30076-7002

GUIRADO, BURT, restaurant management; b. Havana, Cuba, Jan. 15, 1955; came to U.S., 1956; s. Humberto and Riselda (Rodriguez) G.; m. Dana Lentner, Aug. 3, 1985. BS, Tulane U., 1977; MBA, U. Miami, 1992. Intern Comdr. Palace, New Orleans, 1974-77; gen. mgr. Les Jardins Restaurant, Miami, Fla., 1977-79; regional mgr. TGI Friday's, Dallas, 1979—. Republican. Roman Catholic. Home: 3470 Pine Haven Cir Boca Raton FL 33431-5404

GUIRGUIS, RAOUF ALBERT, health science executive; b. Cairo, Egypt, Aug. 25, 1953; came to U.S., 1983; s. Albert Amin Guirguis and Georgette Dahabi; m. Dana Lynn Lebo, Aug. 26, 1982 (div. June 1988); 1 child, Sandra Gene; m. Loretta Elisabeth Moschetti, July 14, 1989; 2 children. MD, Alexandria U., Alexandria, Arab Republic of Egypt, 1978; MS, Georgetown U., 1986, PhD, 1988. Intern Alexandria U. Sch. Medicine, 1979-80, navy fellow, 1980-83; rsch. assoc. Lombardi Cancer Ctr., Washington, 1983-84; rsch. fellow Nat. Cancer Inst., NIH, Bethesda, Md., 1984-86; chmn. of the bd. Antibody Resources Inc., Gaithersburg, Md., 1989-91; pres., CEO Cancer Diagnostics Inc., Rockville, Md., 1989—; chmn. of the bd. Fingerprint Biotek Inc., Rockville, 1991—; chmn., CEO Lamina Ltd., Wilmington, Del., 1991—; chmn. Comprehensive Cancer Care Ctrs. LLP, 1994—, Cancer Diagnostics Holding Co., Fairfax, Va., 1995—; cons. Nephrology Cancer Ctr., Mansura, Arab Rep. of Egypt, 1988-93; adj. assoc. prof. dept. physiology and biophysics Georgetown U. Med. Sch., Washington, 1989-93. Contbr. articles to profl. jours. Assoc. Smithsonian, Washington, 1990; mem. Kennedy Ctr., Washington, 1990, Georgetown Club, Washington, 1989; mem. Balt. Coun. on Fgn. Affairs; bd. dirs. U.S. Israel Biotech. Coun. Georgetown U. scholar, 1984-88, Saudi Minister of Health scholar, 1986-88; Nat. Coun. of Churches Rsch. grantee, 1986, Hoffmann-LaRoche Innovation Rsch. grantee, 1986. Mem. AMA (chief exec. divsn.), AAAS, Am. Math. Assn., Am. Assn. for Clin. Chemistry, Am. Soc. for Microbiology, Am. Chem. Soc., Am. Mgmt. Assn., N.Y. Acad. Sci., Soc. for Computer Simulation, IEEE Computer Soc., Sigma Xi. Republican. Coptic Orthodox. Office: Cancer Diagnostics Inc 2930 Prosperity Ave Fairfax VA 22031-2209

GULIG, PAUL ANTHONY, medical researcher, educator; b. Waco, Tex., Jan. 25, 1958; s. Leonard Charles and Barbara Jean (Smajstrla) G.; m. Mary M. Lenz, May 19, 1984; children: Christopher Paul, Kevin Scott, Scott Daniel, Brian Joseph. BS summa cum laude, Tex. A&M U., 1980; PhD, U. Tex., 1985. Grad. fellow U. Tex. Health Sci. Ctr., Dallas, 1980-85; postdoctoral fellow Washington U., St. Louis, 1985-88; asst. prof. U. Fla. Coll. of Medicine, Gainesville, 1988-93, assoc. prof., 1993—; cons. Parke-Davis Pharms., Ann Arbor, Mich., 1993, R.W. Johnson Pharm. Rsch. Inst., 1996—; speaker in field. Mem. editl. bd. Infection and Immunity, 1990—; ad hoc reviewer Infection and Immunity, 1988-90, Jour. Clin. Investigation, 1991-92, Jour. Infectious Diseases, 1992, Molecular Gen. Genetics, 1992, Molecular Microbiology, 1992-96, Microbial Pathogenesis, 1993, NIH, 1990-96, USDA, 1995-96; author numerous chpts. in books; contbr. articles to profl. jours. Mem. parish coun. Queen of Peace Cath. Ch., Gainesville, 1991-93; mem. Habitat for Humanity, Gainesville, 1992-93. Recipient grant NIH-NIAID, 1990—, numerous grants and awards Am. Heart Assn., 1989—, Rsch. grant NATO, 1993—, Jr. Faculty Rsch. grant Am. Cancer Soc., 1990-92, Rsch. grant U. Fla., 1988-89, 90, 94—; Grad. fellow NSF, 1981-84, Postdoctoral fellow Nat. Rsch. Svc. award NIH-NIAID, 1985-88. Mem. AAAS, Am. Soc. Microbiology. Home: 5025 SW 83rd Ter Gainesville FL 32608-4304 Office: U Fla Dept Molecular Genetics & Microbiology PO Box 100266 Gainesville FL 32610-0266

GULLACE, MARLENE FRANCES, systems analyst, programmer, consultant; b. Ft. Belvoir, Va., Jan. 12, 1952; d. Amerigo Francis and Martha Arlene (Wise) Guy; m. Gerald Lynn Tolley, June 26, 1970 (div. Nov. 1974); 1 child, Gerald Lynn Tolley Jr.; m. Salvatore Gullace, Nov. 19, 1976 (div. Apr. 1991). AA in Pre-Law, Cochise Coll., 1979; BA in Polit. Sci., U. Ariz., 1982; AA in Computer Sci., Bus., Chaparral Coll., 1985. Realtor, entrepreneur, inventor Sierra Vista, Ariz., 1977-84; ADP instr. Chaparral Coll., Tucson, 1985; model Barbizon, Tucson, 1986-87; clk. HUD/FHA, Tucson, 1987-88; computer programmer DOD Inspector Gen., Arlington, 1988-89; programmer analyst U.S. Army Corps of Engrs., USAF, Washington, 1989-91, Calibre Systems Inc., Falls Church, Va., 1991; cons., systems analyst/programmer EDP, Vienna, Va., 1991-93; info. engr. Ogden Profl. Svcs. (now named Anteon Corp.), Vienna, 1993-96, Orkand Corp., 1996—. Patented toy, registered trademark. Realtor assoc. Cochise County Bd. Realtors, 1977-84. Mem. IEEE, Fed. Women's Program at SBA (sec. 1976). Methodist. Home: 3327 Piney Ridge Ct Herndon VA 20171-4019

GULLEDGE, KAREN STONE, educational administrator; b. Fayetteville, N.C., Feb. 3, 1941; d. Malcolm Clarence and Clara (Davis) Stone; m. Parker Lee Gulledge Jr, Oct. 17, 1964. BA, St. Andrews Presbyn. Coll., Laurinburg, N.C., 1963; MA, East Carolina U., 1979; EdD, Nova U., 1986. Social worker Lee County, Sanford, N.C., 1963-64; tchr. Asheboro (N.C.) City Schs., 1964-67, Winston-Salem (N.C.)/Forsyth County Schs., 1967-70; research analyst N.C. Dept. Pub. Instrn., Raleigh, 1971-76, sch. planning cons., 1976-89, dir. sch. planning, 1989-95; dir. ednl. svcs. Peterson Assocs., Raleigh, 1995—; chmn. N.C. Elem. Commn. of So. Assn. Colls. and Schs., 1995; leader profl. seminars; spkr. in field. Trustee St. Andrews Coll. Recipient Outstanding Educator award, 1992. Mem. Coun. Ednl. Facility Planners (pres., chmn. 1995, Disting. Ednl. Achievement award 1994), Delta Kappa Gamma. Democrat. Home: 7405 Fiesta Way Raleigh NC 27615-3325 Office: Peterson Assocs PO Box 24118 Charlotte NC 28224

GULLEDGE, RICHARD D. (DICK GULLEDGE), security firm executive, consultant; b. Abilene, Tex., July 4, 1946; s. Tom Witt and Alice Marie (Jones) G.; m. Patricia Gwen Brassell Clark, Mar. 8, 1969 (div. Nov. 1972); 1 child, Alice Robin; m. Marilyn Parker, Aug. 22, 1982. Student, U. Tex., 1964-66, Tex. A&M U., 1973-75. Detective lt. Coll. Sta. (Tex.) Police Dept., 1973-79; chief investigator Brazos County Sheriff Dept., Bryan, Tex., 1979-88; owner Dick Gulledge Investigations, Bryan, 1988—; cons. nursing homes, 1991—. Author: Family Violence Booklet, 1986. Capt. USMC, Viet Nam, 1966-73. Decorated D.F.C., Purple Heart; named Dep. Sheriff of Yr. by VFW, Bryan, Tex., 1982. Mem. Nat. Assn. Legal Investigators. Office: Dick Gulledge Investigations PO Box 1464 Bryan TX 77806-1464

GULLEDGE, SANDRA SMITH, publicist; b. Great Lakes, Ill., July 6, 1949; d. Dennis Murrey and Olga (Grosheff) Smith. BS, Northwestern U., 1971; MA, Annenberg Sch. Communications at U. So. Calif., 1986. Columnist Camarillo Daily News (Calif.), 1971-76; editor Fillmore Herald (Calif.), 1976-78; pub. info. officer Oxnard Union High Sch. Dist. (Calif.), 1980-82; pub. info. officer Ventura County Community Coll. Dist., 1982-83; pub. rels. dir. Murphy Orgn., Oxnard, Calif., 1983-84; sr. adminstr. customer comm., editor Forum and Solutions GTE, Irving, Tex., 1988-89; sr. mktg. prog. spec. USAA Buying Svc., San Antonio, 1995—. Co-chmn. Ventura County Commn. for Women, 1981-88.

GULRICH, SILLA REMMEL, real estate executive; b. Kihelkonna, Estonia, U.S.S.R., June 21, 1934; came to U.S., 1954; d. Eduard and Tiina (Teaar) Remmel; m. Adalbert, Gulrich, Dec. 8, 1956; children: Ronald Bert, Jeffrey Bruce. Student, Marin County Jr. Coll., San Rafael, Calif., 1960. Sec. Otis Elevator, San Francisco, 1954-58; realtor Grafa Agy. & Tom Fouts, Denton, Tex., 1972-76; ind. real estate broker, 1976-86; broker, owner Century 21 Golden Triangle, Denton, 1986—. Vol. ARC, Denton, chmn. Mem. Women's Coun. Realtors, Tex. Assn. Realtors, Nat. Assn. Realtors, Tarrant County Brokers Coun. Office: Century 21 Golden Triangle 7013 S Stemmons St Denton TX 76205-2404

GUMM, JAY PAUL, media specialist; b. Durant, Okla., Nov. 29, 1963; s. Jay William and Harlene (Taylor) G. BA in Polit. Sci., Southeastern Okla. State U., 1986. LBJ Congl. intern Hon. Wes Watkins, U.S. Congressman, Washington, summer 1984; gov., chmn. bd. Okla. Intercollegiate Legislature, Inc., Oklahoma City, 1987-88; rsch. asst. Okla. Ho. of Reps., Oklahoma City, 1986-87, staff asst., 1987-90, sr. media specialist, 1990—. Recipient Presdl. scholarship Southeastern Okla. State U., 1985; named Outstanding Young Dem. in Okla., Okla. Fedn. Dem. Women, 1983, Outstanding Young Men of Am., 1986, 87, 92. Mem. Pub. Rels. Soc. Am. (bd. dirs. Oklahoma City chpt., awards of merit 1992, 93, 95, 96, Upper Case awards 1993, 94, 95, 96), Am. Soc. Legis. Clks. and Secs., Nat. Conf. State Legislatures (media rels. sect.). Home: 401 E 7th St Edmond OK 73034-4612 Office: Okla Ho of Reps State Capitol Rm B24 Oklahoma City OK 73105

GUNBERG, EDWIN WOODROW, JR., counseling psychologist, consultant, researcher; b. Sioux Falls, S.D., Nov. 13, 1950; s. Edwin Woodrow and Eileen Marie Elizabeth (Youngdahl) G.; m. Elizabeth Ann Robbins, June 5, 1976; children: Edwin Christian, Emily Elizabeth. BA, Gustavus Adolphus Coll., St. Peter, Minn., 1972; MA, George Mason U., 1975; postgrad., Va. Poly. Inst. and State U., 1975-79; PhD, U. N.D., 1981. Asst. prof. counseling U. N.D., Grand Forks, 1981-82; dir. PSYCON, Sterling, Va., 1982—; pres. MARS Assessment Tech., Inc., Sterling, 1990—; exec. v.p. United Bus. Svcs., 1996—; cons. HumRRO Internat., Inc., Alexandria, Va., 1985-91; bd. dirs. Personality Assessment System Found., 1990—. Bd. dirs. Loudoun Symphony Assn., 1994—, pres. 1996—; mem. Rep. Senatorial Inner Circle, 1989, Loudoun County Rep. Com., 1992—. Mem. Am. Assn. for Marriage and Family Therapy (clin.), Am. Psychol. Soc., Confederte Air Force (col.), Aircraft Owner and Pilot Assn., Exptl. Aircraft Assn., Mooney Aircrft Pilots Assn. Lutheran. Home: 207 Winter Frost Ct Sterling VA 20165-5821

GUNDERSEN, LAWRENCE GARFIELD, JR., historian, educator; b. Columbus, Ga., Dec. 28, 1959; s. Lawrence and Helga (Nurnburger) G.; m. Shannon Rutledge; 1 child, Claudia Blaine. BS, U. West Ala., 1988, MAT, 1989. Adj. instr. history Shaw U., Asheville, N.C., 1989; instr. history, polit. sci. Brevard (N.C.) Coll., 1990-92, Shelby State C.C., Memphis, 1992-95; asst. prof. history, polit. sci. Jackson (Tenn.) State C.C., 1995—; adj. instr. history State Tech. Inst. Memphis, 1993. With U.S. Army, 1978-82. Mem. Nat. Assn. Scholars, So. Hist. Assn., Tenn. Polit. Sci. Assn., West Tenn. Hist. Soc. Methodist. Home: 502 W Allen St Hendersonville NC 28739 Office: Jackson State Cmty Coll 2046 N Parkway Jackson TN 38301-3722

GUNDERSON, CLARK ALAN, orthopedic surgeon; b. Watertown, S.D., Aug. 27, 1948; s. Harvey Alfred and Eugenie (Tulson) G.; m. Robbie Gunderson; children: Ashley, Camille. Student, U. Minn., 1966-69; BS, U. S.D., 1971; MD, Baylor Coll. of Medicine, 1973. Diplomate Am. Bd. of Orthopaedic Surgery, 1979. Intern in gen. surgery Charity Hosp., New Orleans, 1973-74, resident in orthopedic surgery, 1974-78; chief of surgery Lake Charles (La.) Meml. Hosp., 1980-83, 90-91, sec., treas. med. staff, 1983-87, pres. med. staff, 1992-93, also trustee, 90-94; clin. assoc. prof. La. State U. Sch. of Medicine, New Orleans, 1987-90. Bd. dirs. Arthritic Found. La., 1987. Mem. AMA, ACS, Am. Acad. Orthopaedic Surgeons, La. Orthopaedic Assn. (pres. 1995-96), Calcasieu Parish Med. Soc., La. State Med. Soc., N.Am. Spine Assn., Mid Am. Orthopaedic Assn., Lake Charles Country Club (pres. 1987-89). Office: 2615 Enterprise Blvd Lake Charles LA 70601-7675

GUNDERSON, JUDITH KEEFER, golf association executive; b. Charleroi, Pa., May 25, 1939; d. John R. and Irene G. (Gaskill) Keefer; student public schs., Uniontown, Pa.; m. Jerry L. Gunderson, Mar. 19, 1971; children: Jamie L., Jeff S.; stepchildren: Todd G. (dec.), Marc W., Bookkeeper, Fayette Nat. Bank, 1957-59, gen. ledger bookkeeper, 1960-63; head bookkeeper First Nat. Bank Broward, 1963-64; bookkeeper Ruthenberg Homes, Inc., 1966-69; bookkeeper, asst. sec./treas. Pennisular Properties, Inc. subs. Investors Diversified Svcs. Properties, Mpls., 1969-72; comptr., pres. Am. Golf Fla., Inc., dba Golf and Tennis World, Deerfield Beach, 1972-89, stockholder, 1992—; sales assoc. Realty Brokers Internat., Inc., 1990; former sec., treas. Internat. Golf, Inc., now stockholder; dir. Mary Kay Cosmetics, 1993—; v.p. Am. Golf Unltd. Inc., 1995—; county committeewoman, Broward County, Fla., 1965-66; ind. agt. personal and family devel. seminars Slight Edge Enterprises, Inc., 1989-91; active Performing Arts Ctr. Energetic Resourceful Supporters. Mem. NAFE, Assn. Profl. Saleswomen, Internat. Platform Assn., Nat. Golf Found., C. of C., Beta Sigma Phi.

GUNN, FRANK MICHAEL, direct marketing professional; b. Jackson, Miss., May 26, 1956; s. Charles Warren and Sara B. (Brantley) G.; m. Grace Elisabeth Girling, Aug. 7, 1984; children: Ashley Elisabeth, Brantley Duncan. AA, Hinds Jr. Coll., 1976; BPA, U. Miss., 1977; LBJ, U. Tex., 1980; MBA, U. Va., 1987. Fin. dir. Fields for Congress, Houston, 1980; legis. asst. Senator John P. East, Washington, 1981; campaign mgr. Williams for Congress, 1982; legis. dir. U.S. Dept. Agriculture, 1983-85; prin. Gunn and Assocs., Jackson, 1987—; state rep. Jackson, Miss., 1989-91; state senator Jackson, 1991—. Co-author: Texas Energy Issues, 1990. Named Outstanding Legislator Am. Legis. Exch. Coun., 1993; recipient Leadership Jackson Jackson C. of C., 1990. Mem. NRA, Rotary, Sierra Club, Kappa Alpha. Republican. Evangelican. Office: PO Box 31613 Jackson MS 39286-1613*

GUNN, JOAN MARIE, health care administrator; b. Binghamton, N.Y., Jan. 29, 1943; d. Andrew and Ruth Antoinette (Butler) Jacoby; m. Albert E. Gunn, Jr; children: Albert E. III, Emily W., Andrew R., Clare M., Catherine A.B., Philip D. BS summa cum laude, Tex. Women's U., 1983; MSN, U. Tex., Houston, 1989. Staff nurse geriatrics St. Anthony's Ctr., Houston, 1985-86; charge nurse gero psychiatry Bellaire Gen. Hosp., Houston, 1986; head nurse gero psychiat. unit U. Tex./Harris County Psychiat. Ctr., Houston, 1986-88, asst. dir. nursing adult svcs., 1988-90, DON adult svcs., 1990-93, nurse exec., 1991-93, DON, 1993—, asst. adminstr., 1994—. Mem. Nat. Soc. Colonial Dames of the XVII Century, Daus. of Union Vets. of Civil War, Sigma Theta Tau. Roman Catholic. Home: 2329 Watts St Houston TX 77030-1139 Office: U Tex Harris County Psychiat Ctr 2800 S Macgregor Way Houston TX 77021-1032

GUNN, JOHN MARTYN, biochemistry educator; b. Wareham, Dorset, Eng., June 27, 1945; came to U.S., 1972; s. John William and Lucy Lena (Lucking) G.; m. Linda May Fisher, Feb. 26, 1977. M Biology, Inst. Biology, London, 1969; PhD, Sheffield (Eng.) U., 1972. Rsch. technician Fison's Pharms., U.K., 1963-66, Glaxo Labs., Inc., U.K., 1966-69; grad. asst. Sheffield U., 1969-72; postdoctoral fellow Temple U., Phila., 1972-76; asst. prof. Tex. A&M U., College Station, 1976-81, assoc. prof., 1981-85, prof. biochemistry, 1985—, head biochem. dept., 1989-90, 92-94; advisor NIH, 1980, 81; cons. Alcon Labs., Ft. Worth, 1991-92. Contbr. numerous articles to rsch. jours. NIH grantee, 1978-81, 80-84, 81-86. Mem. Am. Soc. Biochem. Molecular Biology, Am. Soc. Cell Biology, Biochem. Soc., soc. Exptl. Biology and Medicine. Office: Tex A&M U Biochemistry & Biophysics College Station TX 77843-2128

GUNN, KENNETH DAVID, explosives safety specialist, consultant; b. Tyler, Tex., May 28, 1940; s. Kenneth Calvin Gunn and Olivia Lucille (Boykin) Kenny; m. Roswitha Klein, Sept. 22, 1964 (div. 1985); children: James Alan, Karen Elizabeth, Stephen Matthew; m. Jutta Maria Hauser, Jan. 6, 1986 (div. 1990); m. Roswitha Klein, Nov. 11, 1991. AA in Bus. and Mgmt., U. Md., 1978, BS in Bus. and Mgmt., 1982. Enlisted USAF, advanced through grades to sr. master sgt., 1958, ret., 1986; explosive ordnance disposal specialist USAF, Vietnam, 1971-72, Volk Field, Wis., 1972-74, Spangdahlem AB, Fed. Republic of Germany, 1974-77; explosive ordnance disposal USAF, Aviano AB, Italy, 1977-80; chief explosive ordnance disposal USAF, Barksdale AFB, La., 1980-81; chief 7007th explosive ordnance disposal flight USAF, Spangdahlem AB, 1981-85; chief explosive ordnance disposal div. USAF, Patrick AFB, Fla., 1985-86; safety supr. Pan Am. World Svcs., Inc., Cape Canaveral, Fla., 1986-89; safety specialist NASA Safety, John F. Kennedy Space Ctr., Fla., 1989-90; ordnance foreman Johnson Controls World Svcs., Cape Canaveral AFS, Fla., 1990-92; explosive ordance disposal technician EOD World Svcs., Inc., 1992-93; dir. safety Spaceport Fla. Authority, 1993—; key mem. search, recovery and reconstrn. team, Space Shuttle Challenger, 1986; key mine field team leader post-war clearance, Kuwait, 1992, featured 60 Minutes. Narrator Nuclear Safety Films, 1969. Mem. AIAA, VFW (life), Air Force Assn. (life), Soc. Explosive Engrs. Republican. Home: 1680 Neptune Dr Merritt Island FL 32952 Office: Spaceport Fla Authority Cocoa Beach FL 32931

GUNN, MOREY WALKER, JR., secondary school educator, choir director, organist; b. Orangeburg, S.C., June 23, 1939; s. Morey Walker Sr. and Marjorie (Dusek) G.; m. Sheila Diane Taylor, Nov. 26, 1994. BA in Music, Furman U., 1961, MA, 1967. Cert. music edn. tchr., S.C. Band dir. Holly Hill (S.C.) High Sch., 1961-65, Orangeburg High Sch., 1965-71, Greer (S.C.) High Sch., 1971-73, Ft. Johnson High Sch., Charleston, S.C., 1973-77, Berkeley County Schs., Goose Creek, S.C., 1978-92. Mem. Nat. Rep. Senatorial Com.; deacon 1st Presbyn. Ch., 1965-71; elder James Island Presbyn. Ch., 1974-76, 78-80, choir dir., organist, 1980-94; organist St. Andrews United Meth. Ch., Orangburg, S.C., 1994—; bd. dirs. excellence in teaching award com. Charleston County Youth Symphony, 1975; bd. dirs. Charlestowne Landing Band Festival Com., 1989-90. Mem. NEA, Music Educators Nat. Conf., Am. Guild Organists, S.C. Music Educators Assn., Spertoma (bd. dirs. 1988-89), Sertoma Club (bd. dirs. 1989-90), Kiwanis Club, 1996—, Elks, Phi Mu Alpha (hon. life). Home: 980 Anchor Dr Charleston SC 29412-4930

GUNNELS, KERRY PAUL, newspaper editor, educator; b. Rising Star, Tex., July 28, 1951; s. Clyde and Jonnie Bell (Moore) G.; m. Marice Helen Richter, May 24, 1986; children: Rachel Claire, Ethan Clyde. BA, U. North Tex., 1975. Reporter Lubbock (Tex.) Avalanche Jour., 1974; reporter, city editor, mng. editor Denton (Tex.) Record-Chronicle, 1974-78; tchg. asst. U. North Tex., Denton, 1978; reporter Dallas Times Herald, 1979-80, Austin Am.-Statesman, 1981-84; instr. U. Mo., Columbia, 1984-85; dep. internat. editor Dallas Morning News, 1985—. Recipient Pulitzer prize for internat. reporting Columbia U., 1974. Mem. Soc. Profl. Journalists. Home: 2707 Roaring Springs Rd Grapevine TX 76051 Office: Dallas Morning News 508 Young St Dallas TX 75265

GUNNELS, THOMAS CURTIS, seminar company executive; b. Cameron, Tex., Aug. 1, 1929; s. Thomas Pitts and Alice (Jones) G.; m. Sue Lee Gunnels, June 3, 1959 (dec. Aug. 1965); children: Susan, Sandra; m. Frankie Regas, Aug. 16, 1970. BBA, So. Meth. U., 1954. CLU, LUTCF. Pers. mgr. State Farm Ins. Co., Murfreesboro, Tenn., 1954-58, dir. agy. tng., 1958-59; agy. mgr. State Farm Ins. Co., Knoxville, Tenn., 1959-95; CEO Seminar Co., 1995—; chmn. Nat. Conf. Christians/Jews, Knoxville, 1989-91; pres. Better Bus. Bur., Knoxville, 1973-75, Conv. Bur., Knoxville, 1970-71. Contbr. articles to profl. jours. S/Sgt. USAF, 1946-49. Named Man of the Yr., Knoxville Rotary Club, 1991, Brotherhood award, 1995, The Nat. Conf. of Christian and Jews, 1995. Mem. Knoxville Assn. Life Underwriters (pres. 1990-91, Man of the Yr. 1990). Republican. Episcopalian. Office: Tom Gunnels Seminar Co 318 Erin Dr Ste 2-b Knoxville TN 37919-6212

GUNNOE, NANCY LAVENIA, food executive, artist; b. Southside, Tenn., Jan. 7, 1921; d. Edgar Hatton and Clara Sharp (McCurdy) Thompson; m. Raymond Glen Gunnoe, Dec. 6, 1941; children: Lynn Thompson Gunnoe Sheets, Paul Randall (dec.), Joy Virginia Gunnoe Woodrum. Student, Austin Peay Coll., 1939, U. Charleston, 1973-87, 91. Cashier Kroger Co., Charleston, W.V., 1939-40; with Superior Laundry & Cleaning, Charleston, 1940-41; file clk. Hancock Oil Co., Oakland, Calif., 1942; office clk. Office Price Adminstrn., Stockton, Calif., 1943; sec.-treas. R.G. Gunnoe Farms Inc., Charleston, 1947—. Exhibited at local orgns. Mem. Nat. League Am. Pen Women, Inc., Allied Artists W.Va., Univ. Charleston Builders, Kanawha Valley Hist. and Preservation Soc., Charleston Woman's Club, Sunrise Mus. Republican. Home: 2040 Oakridge Dr Charleston WV 25311-1112 Office: 2115 Oakridge Dr Charleston WV 25311

GUNTER, BRADLEY HUNT, capital management executive; b. Norfolk, Va., Dec. 8, 1940; s. J.A. and Virginia (Whalen) G.; m. Susan Mason Hart, Dec. 27, 1962 (div. 1977); children: Bradley Hunt, Valerie Mason; m. Anne A. Macon, Nov. 7, 1985 (dec. 1994); 1 child, Bradford Macon Gunter; m. Meredith Laura Strohm, Dec. 16, 1994. BA, U. Richmond, 1962; MA, U. Va., 1963, PhD, 1969. Instr. Washington and Lee U., Lexington, Va., 1967-69; asst. prof. Boston Coll., 1969-71; corp. sec. Fed. Res. Bank, Richmond, Va., 1971-80; pres. Bartleby's Inc., Richmond, 1980-85; dir. found. rels. U. Va., Charlottesville, 1985-86; investment broker Scott and String fellow, Richmond, 1987-89; mng. dir. Scott & Stringfellow Capital Mgmt., Richmond, 1989—; cons. NEH, Washington, 1975-80. Author: Studies in The Waste Land, 1971, Guide to T.S. Eliot, 1970, Checklist of T.S. Eliot, 1969; contbr. articles to profl. jours. Vestryman St. Paul's Ch., Richmond, 1975-78; chmn. fund drive United Way, Richmond, 1980; mem. arts and scis. alumni coun. U. Va., also mem. Emeritus Soc.; bd. dirs. St. Christopher's Sch. Found., Richmond, 1981-85, Richmond Ballet, Big Bros. Richmond Inc., Va. Found. for Humanities and Pub. Policy, Elk Hill Farm; trustee St. Paul's Endowment Fund, Inc., United Way Greater Richmond; pres. Arts Coun. Richmond, Hist. Richmond Found., Poe Found. Mem. Richmond Assn. Bus. Economists, Investment Mgmt. Cons. Assn., Assn. for Investment Mgmt. and Rsch., U. Va. Alumni Assn. (chpt. pres. Richmond 1981), Va. Soc. Mayflower Descs. (bd. dirs.), Country Club Va., Colonnade Club, Focus Club, Univ. Club, Farmington Country Club, Phi Beta Kappa, Omicron Delta Kappa. Episcopalian. Office: Scott & Stringfellow Capital Mgmt 909 E Main St Richmond VA 23219-3002

GUNTER, GORDON, zoologist; b. Goldonna, La., Aug. 18, 1909; s. John O. and Joanna (Pennington) G.; B.A., La. State Normal Coll., 1929; M.A., U. Tex., 1931, Ph.D., 1945; m. Lottie G. LaCour, June 6, 1932; children: Charlotte A. Gunter Evans, Miles G., Forrest P.; m. Frances M. Hudgins, Sept. 6, 1957; children: Edmund Osbon, Harry Allen. Biologist, U.S. Bur. Fisheries, intermittently, 1931-38; marine biologist Tex. Game, Fish and Oyster Commn., 1939-45; research scientist Inst. Marine Sci., U. Tex., 1945-49, dir., 1949-55; prof. zoology Marine Lab., U. Miami (Fla.), 1946-47; sr. marine biologist Scripps Instn. Oceanography, U. Calif., La Jolla, 1948-49; dir. Gulf Coast Research Lab., Ocean Springs, Miss., 1955-71, dir. emeritus, 1971—; also prof. biology U. So. Miss., prof. zoology Miss. State U., 1956-78; adj. prof. emeritus biology U. Miss., 1979-85; area cons. Tex. Office Coordinator Fisheries, 1942-45; adv. panel comml. seafoods div. La. Commn. Wild Life and Fisheries, 1953-54; vice chmn. biology, com. treatise on marine ecology NRC, 1942-57; sci. adv. panel Gulf State Marine Fisheries Commn., mem. bd. advisors Fla. Bd. Conservation, 1956-68; prin. investigator plankton studies OTEC program, Gulf of Mex., 1978-82; mem. standing com. Gulf of Mexico Fishery Mgmt. Council. Fellow La. Acad. Scis., Internat. Oceanographic Found., Internat. Acad. Fisheries Scientists, Am. Inst. Fisheries Research Biologists, La. Acad. Scis., Explorers Club; mem. Am. Fisheries Soc. (hon.), Am. Ornithologists Union, Am. Soc. Ichthyologists and Herpetologists, Am. Soc. Limnology and Oceanography, Am. Soc. Mammalogists, Am. Soc. Naturalists, Am. Soc. Zoologists, Ecol. Soc. Am., Miss., New Orleans acads. scis., Nat. Shellfisheries Assn. (hon.), Wildlife Soc., World Mariculture Soc. (pres. 1974, hon.), Miss. Acad. Scis. (pres. 1964-65), Sigma Xi, Phi Kappa Phi. Founder editor: Gulf Research Reports, 1961-74. Author: Gunter's Archives No. 1, 1984, Gunter's Archives No. 4, 1987, No. 5, 1988, No. 6, 1989, No. 7, 1990, No. 8, 1991, No. 9, 1992, No. 10, 1992, No. 11, 1994, No. 12, 1995; contbr. over 435 articles on marine biology to profl. and popular publs. in U.S. and fgn. countries. Address: 127 Halstead Rd Ocean Springs MS 39564-5316

GUNTER, KAREN JOHNSON, government official; b. Pensacola, Fla., Jan. 7, 1948; d. Erskine DeWitt and Grace (Crutchfield) Johnson; m. Thomas A. Gunter, Aug. 25, 1975 (div. Dec. 1981). BS, U. So. Miss., 1970; MS, Fla. State U., 1976. Social svc. worker Fla. Bur. Blind Svcs., Pensacola, 1970-74; supervising counselor Fla. Bur. Blind Svcs., Tallahassee, West Palm, 1974-75; M.D. examiner Office Disability Determinations, Social Security Adminstrn., Tallahassee, 1976-80, M.D. rev. examiner, 1980-81, M.D. hearing examiner, 1981-82, M.D. examiner supr., 1982-86, area office program adminstr., 1986—; govt. official, Jafra; skin care cons. Vol. ARC. Recipient Director's citation Social Security Adminstrn., 1978, Commr.'s citation, 1988, Profl. Supr. of Quarter award Office Disability Determination, 1987. Mem. Nat. Assn. Disability Examiners (treas. 1982-85, pres. 1988-89, pres. S.E. region 1985-86, 91-92, S.E. regional dir. 1993—), Fla. Assn. Disability Examiners (pres. 1982, Examiner of Yr. 1984). Democrat. Baptist. Home: 812 Voncile Ave Tallahassee FL 32303-4683 Office: PO Box 7417 Tallahassee FL 32314-7417

GUNTER, LINDA FAITH, social studies educator, state senator; b. Binghamton, N.Y., Dec. 19, 1949; d. Walter Norman and Helen (Wolski) Hinkleman; divorced; children: Donald Tracy, Jamye Lynne. AB in Social Studies, High Point U., 1971; student, Meredith Coll., 1981, 85, N.C. Justice Acad., 1984, 85, Durham Tech. Coll., 1986. Lic. social studies edn.; lic. real estate salesman. Tchr. secondary social studies Cary (N.C.) High Sch., 1971—; mem. N.C. Senate, 1993-94. Mem. state com. Ctr. Rsch. and Devel. in Law-Related Edn., 1990, regional judge Am. Legion Oratorical Contest, 1990, nat. judge, 1993, dist. judge, 1994; edn. chair Cary Clean Cmty. Commn., 1987-90; voter registration commr., 1989-91; mem. Cary Solid Waste Mgmt. Adv. Bd., 1990-92; mem. state Dem. Exec. Com., Wake County Dem. Exec. Com., 1978—, Dem. Women, Dem. Men, Young Dems., 1987—; precinct officer Cary 4; 4th dist. Dem. elector, 1984, 88, 92, State Elector, 1996; alumni mem. N.C. Inst. Polit. Leadership. Recipient John H. Stevens Tchr. Excellence award, 1988, Am. Legion award, 1991, Vol. of Yr. award Cary Keep Am., 1991, Legislator of Yr. award Learning Disabilities Assn., 1993; Taft fellow, 1988, 95, NEH fellow, 1989. Mem. NEA, NOW, NARAL, N.C. Assn. Educators (A+ Outstanding Legislator 1994), Assn. Classroom Tchrs., Women's Polit. Caucus, Sierra Club, Delta Kappa Gamma. Democrat. Home: 1101 Highland Trl Cary NC 27511-5162

GUNTER, MICHAEL DONWELL, lawyer; b. Gastonia, N.C., Mar. 26, 1947; s. Daniel Cornelius and DeNorma Joyce (Smith) G.; m. Barbara Jo Benson, June 19, 1970; children: Kimberly Elizabeth, Daniel Cornelius III. BA in History with honors, Wake Forest U., 1969; JD with honors, U. N.C., 1972; MBA with honors, U. Pa., 1973. Bar: N.C. 1972, U.S. Dist. Ct. (mid. dist.) N.C. 1974, U.S. Tax Ct. 1975, U.S. Supreme Ct. 1979, U.S. Claims Ct. 1982, U.S. Ct. Appeals (D.C. cir.) 1985, U.S. Ct. Appeals (4th cir.) 1992. Ptnr. Womble Carlyle Sandridge & Rice PLLC, Winston-Salem, N.C., 1974—; bd. dirs. G & J Enterprises Inc., Gastonia, Indsl. Belting Inc., Gastonia. Contbr. articles to profl. jours. Coach youth basketball Winston-Salem YMCA, 1981-90; advisor Winston-Salem United Way Christmas Cheer Toy Shop, 1975; fundraiser Deacon Club Wake Forest U., also mem. exec. com., athletic coun., 1987—, v.p., pres., 1990-92; bd. dirs. Goodwill Industries, Winston-Salem, 1987—, past pres.; bd. dirs. Centenary Meth. Ch., 1980; mem. community problem solving com. United Way, 1988—; mem. Leadership Winston-Salem; mem. alumni coun. Wake Forest U. William E. Newcombe scholar U. Pa., 1972-73. Mem. ABA, So. Pension Conf., N.C. Bar Assn. (former chmn. tax sect., mem. continuing legal edn. com.), Forsyth County Bar Assn., Forsyth County Employee Benefit Coun., Winston-Salem Estate Planning Coun. (past bd. dirs.), Profit Sharing Coun. Am., ESOP Assn. Forsyth Country Club (former pres., bd. dirs.) Piedmont club, Order of Coif, Rotary (former bd. dirs. Reynolda club). Democrat. Home: 128 Ballyhoo Dr Lewisville NC 27023-9633 Office: Womble Carlyle PO Drawer 84 1600 BB&T Financial Ctr Winston Salem NC 27102

GUPTA, KAUSHAL KUMAR, internist; b. Firozpur, Punjab, India, Nov. 9, 1949; came to U.S., 1975; s. Hardayal and Lilawati (Gupta) G.; m. Meena Anand, May 23, 1978; children: Ruchi, Ajay, Nishi. MBBS, MD, Christian Med. Coll., Ludhiana, India, 1975. Diplomate Am. Bd. Internal Medicine. Rotating intern Govt. Med. Coll. and Hosp., Jodhpur, India, 1974-75, Christian Med. Coll. and Hosp., Ludhiana, India, 1974-75; rsch. assoc. dept. pharmacology Baylor Coll. Medicine, Houston, 1975-76; resident in internal medicine St. John Hosp., Detroit, 1976-79; pvt. practice internal medicine Lansing, Mich., 1979-80, Houston, 1980—; mem. utilization rev. com. Parkway Hosp., Houston, 1994; quality assurance com. Houston N.W. Med. Ctr., 1989-92; chmn. ER/ICU com. Doctors Hosp.-Airline, Houston, 1992-95. Contbr. articles to profl. jours. Mem. resource allocation and funding com. United Way, 1984; vol. physician Eastwood Health Clinic, Houston, 1985, 86; Congress key contact Am. Soc. Internal Medicine, 1993-94, ACP, 1994. Fellow ACP; mem. AMA, Tex. Med. Assn., Am. Soc. Internal Medicine, Am. Soc. Echocardiography, Mich. Med. Soc., Harris County Med. Soc., Indian Doctors Club of Houston (sec. 1988). Hindu. Home: 8015 Theisswood Rd Spring TX 77379-4637 Office: 11206 Airline Dr Houston TX 77037-1116

GURINSKY, SYLVIA, journalist; b. Miami, Fla., Oct. 3, 1968. BS in Comm., Fla. Internat. U., 1990. Editl. rschr., writer WPLG-Channel 10, Miami, Fla., 1990—. Recipient Sch. Bell award Fla. Edn. Assn., 1991, 92, 94, Fla. AP award, 1st place, 1995, 2d place, 1994, 96; Taishoff fellow. Mem. NATAS, Soc. Profl. Journalists (Miami chpt. sec. 1992-94, v.p. membership 1994—, pres.-elect 1996—).

GURLEY, STEVEN HARRISON, sales executive; b. Macon, Ga., Apr. 22, 1957; s. Harrison Wade and Louise (Forester) G.; m. Dona Ray Skelton, July 14, 1978; children: Stephanie Ray, Jonathan Steven. AA, Macon Jr. Coll., 1977; BS, Ga. Coll., 1979; cert., Cert. Med. Rep. Inst., Roanoke, Va., 1987. Med. sales rep. Adria Labs., Columbus, Ohio, 1980-81; sr. profl. sales rep. Knoll Pharms., Macon, 1981—. Democrat. Methodist. Home and Office: 5698 Charles Dr Macon GA 31210-1104

GUSDON, JOHN PAUL, JR., obstetrics and gynecology educator, physician; b. Cleve., Feb. 13, 1931; s. John and Pauline (Malencek) G.; m. Marcelle Deiber, June 6, 1956 (dec. 1979); children: Marguerite, John Phillip, Veronique; m. R. Carolyn Gallager Aycock, July, 1989. BA, U. Va., 1952, MD, 1959. Diplomate Am. Bd. Ob-Gyn. Rotating intern U. Hosps. Cleve., 1959-60, resident, 1960-64; instr. ob-gyn. Sch. Medicine, Case Western Res. U., Cleve., 1964-66, asst. prof., 1967; asst. prof. ob-gyn. Bowman Gray Sch. Medicine, Wake Forest U., Winston-Salem, N.C., 1967-70, assoc. prof., 1970-74, prof., 1974-90, prof. emeritus, 1990—; staff IHS Hosps. Contbr. articles to sci. jours., chpts. to books. Lt. USN, 1952-55, Korea. Recipient John Horsley Meml. award U. Va., Charlottesville, 1968, Pres. award South Atlantic Assn. Ob-Gyn., 1973. Fellow ACOG (Pres. award 1970, 72), Am. Assn. Immunology; mem. Am. Soc. Immunology of Reproduction (founder, pres. 1981-84), Am. Gynecol. and Obstet. Soc. Republican. Roman Catholic.

GUSTAFSON, RICHARD ALEXANDER, engineering executive; b. Winchester, Va., Oct. 10, 1941; s. Richard Oscar and Betty Alexander Gustafson; m. Jennie F. Turner, June 19, 1965; children: Richard A. Jr., David T. BSEE, The Citadel, 1963; M of Engrng., U. S.C., 1965, PhD in Engring., 1970. Lic. first class radiotelephone. Head systems design group NASA Manned Spacecraft Ctr., 1967-69, acting head real time computer complex systems sect., 1968-69; project officer, VELA Seismological Ctr., Air Force Tech. Applications Ctr., 1969-72; mem. tech. staff Tetra Tech, Inc. & Mitre Corp., 1972-73, dir. advanced rsch. directorate, 1973-75; program mgr. ocean monitoring and control divsn. Def. Advanced Rsch. Projects Agy., 1975-77, asst. dir. ocean monitoring and control, 1977-80; chief scientist advanced marine systems operation Honeywell, Inc., 1986-88, v.p. high tech. divsn. and advanced systems ctr., 1980-88; v.p. undersea systems operation Sci. Applications Internat. Corp., 1988-91; v.p. and dir. Ctr. for Monitoring Rsch. Sci. Applications Internat. Corp., Arlington, Va., 1991—. Contbr. articles to profl. jours. Home: 2645 Wild Cherry Pl Reston VA 22091-4240 Office: Ctr for Monitoring Rsch 1300 17th St N Arlington VA 22209-3801

GUSTAVSON, BRANDT, religious association executive. Pres. Nat. Religious Broadcasters. Address: 7839 Ashton Ave Manassas VA 22109

GUSTE, WILLIAM JOSEPH, JR., attorney general; b. New Orleans, May 26, 1922; s. William Joseph and Marie Louise (Alciatore) G.; m. Dorothy Schutten, Apr. 17, 1947; children: William Joseph III, Bernard Randolph, Marie Louise, Melanie Ann, Valerie Eve, Althea Marie, Elizabeth Therese, James Patrick, Anne Duchesne, John Jude (dec.). A.B., Loyola U., New Orleans, 1942, LL.B., 1943, LL.D., 1974; LL.D. (hon.) Loyola U. of the South, 1974. Bar: La. 1943. Assoc. firm Guste, Barnett & Redmann, 1943, 46-56, Guste, Barnett & Little, 1956-70, Guste, Barnett & Colomb, 1970-72; mem. La. Senate, 1968-72; atty. gen. State La., New Orleans, 1972-92; co-owner Antoine's Restaurant, New Orleans; chief counsel Housing Authority, New Orleans, 1957-71; mem. exec. working group Dept Justice, chmn., 1986, mem. nat. environment enforcement coun., 1987-92; mem. Pres.'s Commn. on Organized Crime, 1983-86. Pres. New Orleans Cancer Assn., 1960-62; nat. pres. United Cancer Council, 1965-67; pres. Met. Crime Commn., 1956-57, Assn. Cath. Charities, 1960-62; chmn. Juvenile Ct. adv. com. Orleans Parish, 1961-63; mem. City New Orleans Street Paving Study Com., 1965-66; Trustee Xavier U., 1967-72, also chmn. bd. lay regents. Served with AUS, 1942-46, ETO. Named Outstanding Young Man City New Orleans, Nat. Jr. C. of C., 1951, comdr. Mil. and Hospitaller Order St. Lazarus of Jerusalem, 1978; recipient John F. Kennedy Leadership award Young Dems. La. State U., 1973; No. La. Polit. Action League award, 1975; Gautrelet award Springhill Coll., 1976; Housing Man of Yr. award Nat. Housing Conf., 1976; Nat. Penology award Am. Prison Ministry, 1979; Pelican award Ecology Center, 1980; Silver Torch award Anti-Defamation League; B'nai B'rith, 1980. Mem. Am. Assn. Small Bus. (dir.), Nat. Assn. Housing and Redevel. Ofcls. (dir.), Am. Judicature Soc., Legal Aid Bur., Am., La., New Orleans bar assns., St. Thomas More Cath. Lawyers Assn., Young Men's Bus. Club of Greater New Orleans (hon. life), Internat. House, Blue Key, Sigma Alpha Kappa, Phi Alpha Delta (hon.). Democrat. Roman Catholic. Clubs: Pickwick, Bienville.

GUSTIN, ANN WINIFRED, psychologist; b. Winchester, Mass., 1941; d. Bertram Pettingill and Ruth Lillian (Weller) G.; B.A. with honors in Psychology, U. Mass., 1963; M.S. (USPHS fellow), Syracuse U., 1966, Ph.D., 1969. Registered psychologist, Sask.; lic. psychologist, Ga.; Diplomate Am. Bd. Med. Psychotherapists. Research asst., psychology trainee U. Mass., Tufts U., Harvard U., Syracuse U., 1961-66; psychology intern VA, Canandaigua, N.Y., 1967-68; asst. prof. psychology U. Regina (Sask., Can.), 1969-74, assoc. prof. psychology, dir. counseling services, head clin. tng., 1974-78; pvt. practice psychology, Carrollton, Ga., 1978—, Atlanta, 1980—; staff tng. cons. Frobisher Bay Dept. Social Services, N.W. Territories, Can., 1979-80; cons. staff Tanner Hosp.; ancillary staff West Paces Ferry Hosp.; psychiat. cons. Social Security Adminstrn., Ga. Dept. Human Resources, 1980—. Membership chmn. Carroll County Mental Health Assn., 1979-81; mem. nat. mental health disaster response team ARC. Fellow Ga. Psychol Assn. (exec. divsn. lic. psychologists 1986-91, 92—, Nat. Red Cross disaster mental health team 1991—); mem. Am. Psychol. Assn., Can. Psychol. Assn., Sask. Psychol. Assn. (mem. exec. council 1971-72, registrar 1972-73), Nat. Assn. Disability Examiners, Ga. Assn. Disability Examiners. Office: 107 College St Carrollton GA 30117-3136 also: One Decatur Town Ctr 150 E Ponce De Leon Ave Ste 46 Decatur GA 30030-2553

GUSZ, JOHN ROBERT, general surgeon; b. Trenton, N.J., Sept. 28, 1958; s. John Fred and Barbara Ann G.; m. Mindy Kline, Apr. 20, 1985; children: Nicolle, Daniel. BS, West Point, 1980; MD, Rutgers Med. Sch., 1984. Surgeon Ireland Army Cmty. Hosp., Fort Knox, Ky., 1989-90, Reynolds Army Cmty. Hosp., Fort Sill, Okla., 1990, 475th MASH, Asia, 1991; chief gen. surgery, chief dept. surgery Ireland Army Cmty. Hosp., 1991—; surgeon Robinson Meml. Hosp., Ravenna, Ohio, 1996—. Fellow Am. Coll. Surgeons; mem. So. Am. Gastrointestinal Endoscopic Surgeons. Home: 6231 Paderborne Dr Hudson OH 44236

GUTELIUS, EDWARD WARNER, marketing professional; b. Pitts., Dec. 28, 1922; s. Edward N. Gutelius and Ruth (Warner) Skinner; m. Dorothy Payne, Apr. 29, 1944 (div. Dec. 1991); children: Edward Warner, Paul, D.L. Josepha S., April; m. Lynn Curtis, May 12, 1994. Student, U. Pitts., 1943, Case Western Res. U., 1945-46; BBA, La Salle Extension U., 1965. Asst. mgr., sales promotion Gen. Electric, Cleve., 1946-48; advt. sales promotion mgr. lighting div. Sylvania Electric, N.Y.C., 1952-59; v.p., mktg. devel. mgr. Fuller, Smith & Ross, N.Y.C., 1952-59; dir. new products Gen. Food, White Plains, N.Y., 1959-68; v.p. mktg. Borden Dairy Svcs., N.Y.C., 1968-70; pres., mktg. cons. Edward W. Gutelius & Assocs., N.Y.C. and Miami, Fla., 1971—; broker Richard Bertram & Co., Miami; yacht broker, 1974-95. Contbr. articles to profl. jours. Active bd. edn. Tarryton, N.Y., 1958-61;

chmn. bd. Second Ch. of Christian Sci., 1975, bd. dirs., 1984-86, 91-93; chmn. Hurricane Relief Fund., 1992. 2d lt. USAAF, 1943-45. Mem. Am. Mktg. Assn. (program chmn. Miami chpt. 1978-79), Adms. of Fla. (v.p.). Republican. Christian Science Practitioner. Home and Office: PO Box 816 Kent CT 06757

GUTH, JAMES DONALD, commanding officer; b. Hays, Kans., Aug. 31, 1951; s. Francis Donald and Dorothy Rae (Dorman) G.; m. Barbara Frances Lenau, June 1, 1974; children: Gretchen Christine, Brendon Michael. BA in Chemistry, Benedictine Coll., Atchison, Kans., 1973; postgrad., Duke U. Marine Lab., 1973. Flag lt. Submarine Group Six, Charleston, S.C.; chemistry, radiol. asst., main propulsion asst. USS Boone (SSBN-629), Charleston, S.C., 1976-79; chief engr., shift engr., tng. officer Nuclear Power Tng. Unit, Ballston Spa, N.Y., 1981-84; mem. Nuclear Power Examining Bd., Norfolk, Va., 1984-86; exec. officer USS Pasadena, Groton, Conn., 1986-89; force nuclear power office Comdr. Submarine Force, U.S. Atlantic Fleet, Norfolk, 1989-91; commanding officer USS Atlanta, Norfolk, 1992—. Water safety instr., trainer ARC, Kansas, Okla., 1967-75; den leader, scoutmaster Boy Scouts Am., Virginia Beach, Va., 1984-89. Recipient Meritorious Svc. medal, Navy Commendation medal, Navy Achievement medal. Mem. U.S. Naval Inst., U.S. Submarine League, Nat. Eagle Scout Assn., Tidewater Striders. Roman Catholic. Home: 5489 Hargrove Blvd Virginia Beach VA 23464-2333 Office: USS Atlanta (SSN 712) FPO AE Norfolk VA 09564-2392

GUTH, JAMES LEE, political science educator; b. Racine, Wis., Feb. 24, 1946; s. Karle Peter and Vernice Viola (Ludtke) G.; m. Cydelle Annette Dukleth, Aug. 26, 1967; children: Bradley, Karen, Eric, Gary. BS, U. Wis., 1966; PhD, Harvard U., 1973. Teaching fellow Harvard U., Cambridge, Mass., 1968-70; instr. Bowdoin Coll., Brunswick, Maine, 1972-73; asst. prof. Furman U., Greenville, S.C., 1973-78, assoc. prof., 1979-84, prof. polit. sci., 1984—, chair polit. sci. dept., 1988-91, chair univ. faculty, 1987-89; manuscript referee/reviewer in field; appeared on various TV programs, CBS, ABC, PBS, CNN, and various local stas. Co-editor: The Bible and the Ballot Box: Religion in the 1988 Election, 1991; contbr. articles to profl. publs., polit. analysis to newspapers. Polling cons. Dorn for Gov. Com., 1974; polling dir. Mann for Congress Com., S.C., 1974, 76. Grantee NEH, 1977, 90, 88, NSF, 1978-79, Am. Polit. Sci. Assn., 1985, Soc. for Sci. Study of Religion, 1988, Lilly Endowment/Christian Ch. (Disciples of Christ, 1988, Pew Charitable Trusts, 1989, 91, Lilly Endowment/Inst. for Study of Am. Evangelicals, 1992, Ctr. for Study of Am. Protestantism, Lilly Endowment, 1983-85. Mem. Am. Soc. Polit. Assn. (chair panels, editor Religion and Politics newsletter 1989—, mem. various panels), Assn. for Sociology of Religion (mem. panel 1990), Soc. for Sci. Study of Religion (convenor panel 1990), Acad. Polit. Sci., Agrl. Hist. Soc., Religious Rsch. Assn., Midwest Polit. Sci. Assn., S.C. Polit. Sci. Assn. (exec. com., treas. 1977-78), So. Polit. Sci. Assn. (sect. chair, program com. 1982, mem. various coms.). Republican. Baptist. Home: 5 Pecos Dr Greenville SC 29609-1114 Office: Furman U Dept Polit Sci Greenville SC 29613

GUTHRIE, DONNA MORTER, English language and journalism educator; b. Buena Vista, Va., Jan. 21, 1940; d. Robert Lewis and Hilda Meriweather (Daniel) Morter; m. Kenneth Lee, June 1, 1963 (div. May 1973); children: Benjamin Lewis Cook, David Crawford Cook, Daniel Lee Cook, Elizabeth Meriweather Cook; m. Gary Grant Guthrie, Nov. 1, 1975; 1 child, Gary Grant Jr. BA in Philosophy, Religion and English magna cum laude, Greensboro Coll., 1962. Cert. tchr. English and journalism, Va. Dir. Christian edn. South Roanoke Meth. Ch., Roanoke, Va., 1962-64; ins. claims sec. Davis & Stephenson, Inc., Roanoke, 1964-67; tchr. 4th grade Sontag (Va.) Elem. Sch., 1967-68; tchr. English Andrew Lewis H.S., Salem, Va., 1968-69; tchr. 6th grade Boones Mill (Va.) Elem. Sch., 1970-71; exec. sec. Continental Homes, Inc., Boones Mill, 1972-77; with drafting dept., bookkeeper Peerless Drafting & Sales, Boones Mill, 1978-82; tchr. English Franklin County Mid. Sch., Rocky Mount, Va., 1982-85; tchr. English and journalism Franklin County H.S., Rocky Mount, 1985—; tchr. trainer supervision and evaluation Franklin County Pub. Schs., Rocky Mount. Advisor: (yearbook) Animo, 19876— (6 1st pl. awards), (newspaper) The Eagle, 1989— (yearly awards), (lit. mag.) The Mind's Eye, 1989—. Participant Leadership 2000/C. of C., Rocky Mount, 1993; councilwoman Boones Mill Town Coun., 1990-94, 96—. Mem. NEA, Franklin County Edn. Assn. Methodist. Home: PO Box 65 Boones Mill VA 24065-0065 Office: Franklin County H S 506 Pell Ave Rocky Mount VA 24151-1141

GUTHRIE, HUGH DELMAR, chemical engineer; b. Murdo, S.D., May 11, 1919; s. John Arlington and Farol Venus (Smith) G.; m. Elizabeth Anne Harris, Mar. 4, 1950; children: Katherine Farol, Gretchen, Mary Melissa, Elizabeth Lenore, Emily Jo. BSChemE with highest distinction, State U. Iowa, 1943. Jr. engr., engr., group leader Shell Devel. Co., San Francisco, 1943-52; technologist, sr. technologist, asst. dept. mgr. Shell Oil Co., Wood River, Ill., 1952-56; staff engr., group leader Shell Oil Co., N.Y.C., 1956-60; dept. mgr. Shell Oil Co., Wood River, 1960-62; asst. mgr. to mgr. mktg. Shell Oil Co., N.Y.C., 1962-70; from dept. mgr. to sr. staff Shell Oil Co., Houston, 1970-76; div. dir. ERDA, Dept. Energy, Washington, 1976-78; dir. Energy Ctr., Stanford Rsch. Inst., Menlo Park, Calif., 1978-80; v.p. licensing, mgr. tech. assessment Occidental Rsch. Corp., Irvine, Calif., 1980-83; v.p. licensing, mgr. rsch. planning Cities Svc., Tulsa, 1983-86; dir. extraction divsn. Morgantown (W.Va.) Energy Tech. Ctr. Dept. Energy, 1987-92, gen. engr. products tech. mgmt., mgr. gas products, 1992—; cons. Hugh D. Guthrie & Assocs., Tulsa, 1986-87; mem. adv. bd. U. Iowa, U. Calif., Berkeley, Tulsa U., U. Tex., U. Pitts., W.Va. U. Former sr. warden Episcopal chs., Conn., Ill., Tex. Fellow AIChE (pres. 1969, chair Assembly of Fellows 1990-92, chair mgmt. divsn. 1991, chair membership campaign found. 1992—, Founder's award 1974, F.J. Van Antwerpen award 1986, Robert L. Jacks Meml. award 1992); mem. AAAS, Am. Chem. Soc., Soc. Petroleum Engrs., N.Y. Acad. Scis., Sigma Xi, Tau Beta Pi, Phi Lambda Upsilon, Omicron Delta Kappa. Republican. Home: 901 Stewart Pl Morgantown WV 26505-3688 Office: Dept Energy Morgantown Energy Tech Ctr 3610 Collins Ferry Rd Morgantown WV 26505-2353

GUTHRIE, JOHN CRAVER, insurance agency owner; b. Bryan, Tex., Mar. 4, 1946; s. Claude Edward and Verle (Craver) G.; m. Miriam Florence Chapman, Apr. 29, 1969 (div.); children: Cheryl Denise, John Craver Jr.; m. Margot Elizabeth French, July 29, 1978. ASBA, St. Petersburg Jr. Coll., 1975. Gen. mgr. Pier Restaurants, Greenville, S.C., 1968-69; dept. mgr. Bellas Hess Dept. Stores, Clearwater, Fla., 1970-74; advt. rep. Clearwater Sun, 1974-76, St. Petersburg (Fla.) Times, 1976-81, Suncoast News, New Port Richey, Fla., 1981-82; inst. agt. Fergueron & Assoc., St. Petersburg, Fla., 1982-84; owner John Guthrie Agy., Inc., Largo, Fla., 1984—. Pres. Bicentennial Sertoma Club, Largo, 1987; sr. warden Holy Spirit Episcopal Ch., Safety Harbor, 1989; treas. Forestbrook Homeowners Assn., Largo, 1989; trustee St. Paul's Sch., Inc., Largo, 1990; mem. ch. sch. com. Episcopal Ch., St. Petersburg, 1990-94; bd. dirs. Lakeside Homeowner's Assn., 1994-97. Recipient award Leatherneck Mag., 1975, Challenger award Nationwide Ins. Co., Columbus, 1986, Exec. award, 1986, Life Exec. award, 1987. Fellow Life Underwriters Assn. Office: John Guthrie Agy Inc 1110 E Bay Dr Largo FL 33770-2533

GUTHRIE, JOHN ROBERT, physician, writer; b. Spartanburg, S.C., Mar. 8, 1942; s. Clarence L. and Rosa Jane (Thackston) G.; m. Natasha K. Guthrie, Sept. 18, 1993; 1 child, Alexi; children from previous marriage: Luke, Asia, Jason, Elizabeth. BS, Mercer U., 1969; MA, Duke U., 1971; DO, Chgo. Coll. Osteo. Medicine, 1979. Diplomate Am. Bd. Osteopathic Medicine and Surgery. Sci. and math. tchr. Mebane (N.C.) Med. Sch., 1969-71; instr. sci. N.C. Community Coll., 1971-75; intern Dr.'s Hosp., Atlanta, 1979-80; physician with family practice assoc. Spartanburg, S.C., 1980-82; med. dir. The Guthrie Clinic, PA, Spartanburg, 1982—; patient care com. Spartanburg Regional Med. Ctr., 1982-84; faculty student liaison com. Chgo. Coll. Osteo. Medicine, 1978-79; med. cons. CBS-TV, Spartanburg, 1985-88; CEO, med. dir. The Agy. for Internat. Understanding. Author: The Dynamic Action Diet Fat Gram and Calorie Counter, 1993, The Dynamic Action Diet, 1994; contbr. articles to profl. jours., poetry and prose to various publs. Bd. dirs. Spartanburg Parents Who Care, 1984-85, Spartanburg Teen Ctr., 1984-85; v.p. S.C. Osteo. Med. Assn., 1980-81, 85, pres., 1986-87; 7th grade Royal Amb. group leader First Bapt. Ch., Spartanburg, 1985, childrens com., 1983-84. With USMC, 1961-65, comdr. M.C., USNR, 1982-88. Grantee NSF, 1971. Mem. Am. Soc. Bariatric Physicians, Spartanburg County Med. Assn., Acad. Am. Poets, Am. Physicians Poetry Assn., Carolina Country Club. Baptist. Office: The Guthrie Clinic PA 216 Beechwood Dr Spartanburg SC 29307

GUTIERREZ, ELIA GARZA, elementary school educator; b. Corpus Christi, Tex., Oct. 30, 1932; d. J.M. and Maria (Garcia) Garza; m. Albert A. Gutierrez, June 1, 1958; children: Alynn Ann Riley, Alda Alia Thompson, Alban Albert, Alane Alexandra. BS, Tex. Women's U., 1957; MA, Tex A&I U., 1980. Cert. elem. tchr., Tex., cert. elem. prin., Tex., cert. bilingual educator. Tchr. Corpus Christi Ind. Sch. Dist., 1957—; educator specialist bilingual edn. and ESL Corpus Christi Ind. Sch. Dist., 1957—. Mem., vol., social chmn. Sts. Cyril and Methiodus Sch. Bd., 1978, 79; v.p. Corpus Christi Classroom Assn., 1980-82; pres. Corpus Christi Assn. Bilingual Edn., 1982-83, 88-89; mem. Friends of the Librs., 1958—, pres., 1995; mem. Town Hall of Corpus Christi, Preperative Corpus Christi Area Tchrs. Credit Union; mem., vol. guide info. desk Tex. State Aquarium; vol. tutor Drop-out Program; mentor YWCA Teen Moms; chair program activities on sch. sites Am. Heart Assn.; appointee Corpus Christi Pub. Librs. Bd., 1994-95; Coastal Bend coun. Govt. Area Agy. on Aging; pres. adv. bd. Ret. and Sr. Vol. Program, 1994-95. Recipient Award of Distinction, Tex. Assn. Bilingual Edn., 1987, Award of Distinction, Twentieth Century Teach Award, 1993; named Lauchoch Literacy Action Distiing. Tutor, Leadership Corpus Christi, 1991-92. Mem. AAUW (corr. sec.), NEA, LWV (v.p. program study action), Nat. Assn. Female Execs., Tex. State Tchrs. Assn. (bd. dirs. ret. tchrs., Tchr. of Yr.), Tex. Women's U. Alumni Assn. (past pres., v.p. 1994—), Corpus Christi Retired Tchr. Assn. (bd. dirs., chair awards, rep. Corpus Christi Tchrs. Fed. Credit Union), Bay Area Female Exec. Assn., Sceptre Club (pres. 1971-87), Neuces County Hist. Soc., Friends of Corpus Christi Librs. (bd. dirs. 1991—, pres. 1995), Hispanic Women's Network Tex. (pres. Corpus Christi chpt. 1994-95), Hispanic Network Tex. (pres. 1994-95), Hispanic Geology Soc., Schoenslatt Club, Town Club, Beta Sigma Phi (Girl of Yr. 1978, 79, 90), Lambda Psi (preceptor). Home: 6233 Pebble Beach Dr Corpus Christi TX 78413-3126

GUTIERREZ, GUADALUPE SALVADOR, elementary school educator; b. San Antonio, Feb. 3, 1954; s. Francisco T. and Maria (Sandoval) G.: m. Martha Ann Moncivals, Aug. 3. 1985. BA, Our Lady of the Lake U., 1976; MS, Tex. A&I U., 1991. Cert. bilingual educator, ESL tchr., sch. adminstrs., Tex. Youth counselor San Antonio Neighborhood Youth Orgn., 1976; pub. sch. tchr. Edgewood Ind. Sch. Dist., San Antonio, 1976-77, San Antonio Ind. Sch. Dist., 1977—; pers. interviewer Gerstenhaber, Jacks & Co., San Antonio, 1983-85. Den leader Boy Scouts Am., San Antonio, 1988-90; mem. divsn. aerospace edn. CAP. Mem. NEA (conv. del. 1976—),Tex. State Tchrs. Assn. (conv. del. 1976—, San Antonio Tchrs. Coun. (faculty rep. coord. 1982-84, chair membership com. 1984-86, bd. dirs. 1986-90, mem. consultation team 1992—, mem. budget and fin. com. 2989, 92), San Antonion Conservation Soc. (assoc.). Democrat. Roman Catholic. Home: 351 Cosgrove San Antonio TX 78210

GUTIERREZ, JOSE RAMON, bank executive; b. Havana, Cuba, Sept. 8, 1936; came to U.S., 1960; s. Jose Ramon and Maria Concepcion (Mendieta) G.; m. Rosa Maria Jones, Mar. 3, 1942; 1 child, Carlos Victor. Student, U. Havana, 1954-60; BBA cum laude, U. Miami, 1967. Credit mgr. Ford Motor Credit Co., Miami, Fla., 1967-69; gen. mgr. Peruvian ops. Chrysler Fin. Corp., 1969-71; v.p. loans Amerifirst Fed., 1971-79; pres., real estate broker Union Mgmt. Realty Corp., 1979-81; pres., lic. mortgage broker UMA Mortgage Co., 1979-81; exec. v.p. Commercebank, N.A., Miami, 1980-88, mem. exec. com., 1980-88, also bd. dirs., bd. sec.; sr. lending officer, pres. and CEO Ponce de Leon Fed. Savs. and Loan Assn., Coral Gables, Fla., 1988-92; sr. lending officer, pres. and CEO Popular Bank Fla., Coral Gables, 1992—, chmn. loan com., 1992—. Ashe scholar U. Miami. Mem. Nat. Assn. Rev. Appraisers and Mortgage Underwriters (sr., registered mortgage underwriter), Beta Gamma Sigma, Phi Kappa. Office: Popular Bank Fla 2 Alhambra Plz Ste 100 Coral Gables FL 33134-5202

GUTMAN, LUCY TONI, school social worker, educator, counselor; b. Phila., July 13, 1936; d. Milton R. and Clarissa (Silverman) G.; divorced; children: James, Laurie. BA, Wellesley Coll., 1958; MSW, Bryn Mawr Coll., 1963; MA in History, U. Ariz., 1978; MEd, Northwestern State U., 1991, MA in English, 1992; postgrad., U. So. Miss., 1992—. Cert. Acad. Cert. Social Workers, La. Bd. cert. social worker, sch. social work specialist, Nat. Bd. Cert. Counselor; diplomate in clin. social work; cert. secondary tchr., La. Social worker Phila. Gen. Hosp., 1963-65; sr. social worker Irving Schwartz Inst. Children and Youth, 1965-66; sr. psychiat. social worker Child Study Ctr. Phila., 1966-68; chief social worker Framingham (Mass.) Ct. Clinic Juvenile Offenders, 1968-72; cons. Nashua (N.H.) Community Coun., 1969-72; dir. clinic, supr. social work Tucson East Community Mental Health Ctr., 1972-74; coord. spl. adoptions program Cath. Social Svcs. So. Ariz., Tucson, 1974-75; social worker Met. Ministry, 1983; supr. social work Leesville (La.) Mental Health Clinic, 1984; sch. social worker Vernon Parish Sch. Bd., Leesville, 1984—; adj. instr. English, sociology, Am. and European history Northwestern State U., Ft. Polk, La., 1984—; part-time counselor River North Psychol. Svcs., Leesville, 1989-92; presenter ann. conf. NASW, 1987, 88, La. Sch. Social Workers Conf., 1986, 87, La. Spl. Edn. Conf., 1988, La. Conf. Tchrs. English, 1991, 94, So. Assn. women Historians, 1994. Contbr. articles to profl. jours. Nat. Soc. Colonial Dames scholar, 1978-79; fellow Pa. State, 1961-62, NIMH, 1962-63. Mem. NASW, AACD, MLA, LWV, Am. Coll. Pers. Assn., Acad. Cert. Social Workers (diplomate), Bus. and Profl. Women Assn., Am. Legion Aux., So. Hist. Assn., So. Assn. Women Historians, Gamma Beta Phi, Phi Alpha Theta. Home: 2004 Allison St Leesville LA 71446-5104

GUTMAN, RICHARD EDWARD, lawyer; b. New Haven, Apr. 9, 1944; s. Samuel and Marjorie (Leo) G.; m. Jill Leslie Senft, June 8, 1969 (dec.); 1 child, Paul Senft; m. Rosann Seasonwein, Dec. 10, 1987. AB, Harvard U., 1965; JD, Columbia U., 1968. Bar: N.Y. 1969, U.S. Ct. Appeals (2d cir.) 1969, U.S. Dist. Ct. (so. and ea. dists.) N.Y. 1975, U.S. Supreme Ct. 1982, Tex. 1991. Assoc. Parker Chapin & Flattau, N.Y.C., 1968-72, Marshall Bratter Greene Allison & Tucker, N.Y.C., 1972-76, 78; ptnr. Bartel Engelman & Fishman, N.Y.C., 1976-78; counsel Exxon Corp., N.Y.C., 1978-90; Dallas, 1990-91; asst. gen. counsel Exxon Corp., Dallas, 1992—; pres. 570 Park Ave Apts., Inc., N.Y.C., 1984-89, past bd. dirs. Fellow Am. Bar Found.; mem. ABA (fed. regulation securities com., vice chmn. 1995—), Am. Law Inst., N.Y. State Bar Assn. (exec. com. 1983-86, 93—, securities regulation com. 1980—, chmn. 1993—), Assn. of Bar of City of N.Y. (securities regulation com. 1980-81, 83-86), Dallas Bar Assn., Coll. of the State Bar of Tex., N.A.M. (corp. fin. and mgmt. com.), Harvard Club (N.Y.C., admissions com. 1983-86, chmn. 1985-86, nominating com. 1986-87, bd. dirs. 1988-91, v.p. 1990-91).

GUTMANN, MYRON PETER, history educator; b. Chgo., Nov. 4, 1949; s. Walter Martin and Myrtle (Stein) G.; m. Barbara Caine Stein, June 18, 1970; 1 child, Robert. AB, Columbia U., 1971; PhD, Princeton U., 1976. Asst. prof. history U. Tex., Austin, 1976-82; assoc. prof. history U. Tex., 1982-88, prof. history, 1988—. Author: War and Rural Life in the Early Modern Low Countries, 1980, Towards the Modern Economy, 1988. ACLS fellow, 1983. Mem. Am. Hist. Assn. (Gershoy award chair 1993), Population Assn. Am. Office: Dept History U Tex Austin TX 78712

GUTMANN, REINHART BRUNO, clergyman, social worker; b. Munich, Bavaria, Germany, May 1, 1916; came to U.S., 1942, naturalized, 1946; s. Franz and Berta G.; m. Vivian Carol Brunke, Oct. 7, 1944; children: Robin Peter Edward, Martin Francis. Student, History Honours Sch., Manchester U., Eng., 1936-38; M.A. in Social Scis, St. Andrews U., Scotland, 1939; postgrad., Coll. of Resurrection, Eng., 1939-41, Coll. Preachers, Washington, 1948, 52, U. Wis., summer, 1951, St. Augustine's Coll., Eng., 1964. Ordained deacon Ch. of Eng., 1941, ordained priest, 1942; curate St. Michael's Parish, Golders Green, London, 1941-42; rector St. Mark's Parish, Green Island, N.Y., 1944-45, St. Andrew's Parish, Milw., 1952-54; chaplain and mem. faculty Hoosac (N.Y.) Sch., 1943-45; founder, exec. dir. Neighborhood House and Episcopal City Mission, Milw., 1945-60; part-time priest-in-charge St. Peter's Mission, North Lake, Wis., 1958-60; exec. dir. Friendship House, Washington, 1960-62; cons. Indian Social welfare Exec. Council of Episcopal Ch., N.Y.C., 1962-64; exec. sec. div. community services Exec. Council of Episcopal Ch., 1964-68, exec. for social welfare and field services, 1968-71; part-time priest-in-charge St. Thomas of Alexandria, Pittstown, N.J., 1968-75; hon. asst. priest St. Martin's Ch., Pawtucket, R.I., 1980; mgr. spl. projects Human Resources Adminstrn., N.Y.C., 1971-72, spl. asst. to asst. adminstr., 1972-73, dir. mgmt. office community services, 1973, spl. asst. to dep. adminstr. social services, 1973-75; nat. exec. dir. Foster Parents Plan, Inc., Warwick, R.I., 1975-82; pres. Cedar Brook Cons., Inc., 1982-86, ret., 1987. Chmn. dept. Christian social relations Province of Midwest, Episcopal Ch., 1954-60; chmn. social edn. and action Nat. Fedn. Settlements, 1960-62; hon. canon All Saints Cathedral, Milw., 1971; founder Silver Spring Neighborhood Ctr., Milw., 1958. Mem. Acad. Cert. Social Workers, Nat. Assn. Social Workers. Democrat.

GUTTERSON, JANET MIRIAM, assessor; b. Brockton, Mass., Mar. 9, 1939; d. Axel Harold and Jennie Alberta (Ellmes) Anderson; m. Donald E. Cooper, May 25, 1962 (dec. 1966); m. Lyman P. Gutterson Jr., May 4, 1968; children: Melody Gutterson-Russell, Freya Diane. BS, Bridgewater State Coll., 1961; MS, Stetson U., 1990. Tchr. Montverde (Fla.) Acad., 1961-62; with pers. office South Shore Nat. Bank, Quincy, Mass., 1964-72; program coord. Lake County Bd. Commrs., Tavares, Fla., 1977-81; counselor State of Fla., Eustis, 1982-85; area supr. Green Thumb Program, Jacksonville, Fla., 1985-86; exec. dir. Lake County Family Health Coun., Eustis, 1986-93; assessor Lakeside Alternatives, Orlando, 1995—; bd. dirs. Haven Inc., Leesburg, Fla., 1983-89; founding dir. Lake County Child Adv. Coun., Tavares, 1987-88. Mem. Lake County Svc. League, Leesburg, 1986-93; mem. adv. bd. Lake Sumter Community Coll., 1987-88. Recipient Service award Fla. Choices, 1985. Mem. LWV, U.S. Pony Club (Altoona, Fla., sec. 1980-86). Republican. Episcopalian. Home: 2470 Eastland Rd Mount Dora FL 32757-2406 Office: Lakeside Alternatives 995 Kennedy Blvd Orlando FL 32810-6139

GUTTMAN, JON SHELDON, magazine editor, historian; b. Flushing, N.Y., Jan. 3, 1951; s. Paul Dennis and Lee Ann (Sterling) G. BA, SUNY, Albany, 1973, MA, 1975. Artist Divisional Ad Comp, Northvale, N.J., 1975-81, Dynamic Graphics, Nanuet, N.Y., 1981, 1983-84, Courier Life, Bklyn., 1981-82; sales mgr. First Investors, Hartsdale, N.Y., 1982-83; art dir. Custombook, Inc., Tappan, N.Y., 1985-86; recruiter N.Y. Army N.G., Valhalla, 1986-88; sr. editor, rsch. dir., writer Cowles History Group (formerly Empire Press), Leesburg, Va., 1988—; writer Sea Classic Internat. and Windsock Internat., Hemel Hempstead, Herts, Eng., 1987, Albatross Prodns., Ltd., Berkhamsted, Herts, Eng., 1989—. Editor, co-author: Desert Storm, 1992; author: Nieuport 28, 1992, Defiance at Sea, 1995, Martin Kitten, 1996; contbg. editor, author (jour.) Over the Front, 1989—. Staff sgt., Va. Army N.G., 1988—. Mem. League of World War I Aviation Historians (Thornton D. Hooper award 1988, 91), Cross and Cockade Internat., Loudon County Civil War Roundtable (bd. dirs.). Democrat. Jewish. Home: 125U Club House Dr SW Apt 11 Leesburg VA 20175-4223 Office: Cowles Enthusiast Media 741 Miller Dr SE Ste D-2 Leesburg VA 20175

GUY, L(EONA) RUTH, medical educator; b. Kemp, Tex., Mar. 17, 1913; d. Henry Luther and Minnie Elizabeth (Murphy) G. AB, Baylor U., 1934, MS, 1949; PhD, Stanford (Calif.) U., 1953. Rsch. fellow NOOO Stanford U., 1951-53, teaching asst., 1951; with U. Tex. Southwestern Med. Sch., Dallas, 1962-82, prof., 1977-82, prof. emeritus, 1982—; assoc. dir. Parkland Meml. Hosp. Blood Bank, Dallas, 1953-78; cons. VA Hosp., Dallas, 1960-80, Temple, 1964-80; vis. prof. to Far East, China Med. Bd. of N.Y., N.Y.C., 1969-70. Author: (with others) Modern Blood Banking and Transfusion Practices, 1982; editor: Technical Manual, 1966; contbr. numerous articles to profl. jours. Bd. dirs. Dallas Repertory Theater, Dallas, 1983-89. Named Disting. Alumnus Baylor U., 1994; inducted into Tex. Women's Hall of Fame, Gov.'s Commn. for Women, 1989. Fellow Am. Soc. Clin. Pathologists (hon., assoc., Disting. Svc. award 1989); mem. Bus. and Profl. Women's Club Dallas (pres. 1970-71), Baylor Women's Coun. (Woman of Distinction award 1988), Baylor Heritage Club (pres. Dallas chpt. 1991-92), Zonta (pres. Dallas chpt. 1961-62, Spirit of Zonta award 1994). Baptist. Home: 5455 La Sierra Dr Dallas TX 75231-4176

GUY, SHARON KAYE, state agency executive; b. Nashville, Apr. 5, 1958; d. Dallas Hearold and Elizabeth Jean (Towns) Gregory; 1 child, Anthony Lee. Grad. high sch., Chgo. Clk. Pub. Health dept. State of Tenn., Nashville, 1979-84, office mgr. Health Facilities commn., 1984-92; asst. Legis. Svcs., Nashville, 1992-95; rep. State Ins., Nashville, 1995—; acct. Bryant Guy Constrn., Nashville, 1984—. Blood drive coord. ARC, Nashville, 1984—; campaign vol. United Way, Nashville, 1984—; vol. State Community Coll., 1990—, Nashville Tech., 1991—. Baptist. Home: 121 Candle Woods Dr Hendersonville TN 37075 Office: Andrew Jackson State Office Bldg Ste 1400 Andrew Jackson Bldg Nashville TN 37243-0295

GUZZETTA, PHILIP CONTE, JR., pediatric surgeon, educator; b. Great Lakes Naval Base, Ill., July 7, 1946; s. Philip Conte and Ann (Suchomel) G.; m. Cathleen Elizabeth Kah, Aug. 16, 1969; children: Angela Anne, Philip Conte III. BS in Biology, Marquette U., 1968; MD, Med. Coll. Wis., 1972. Diplomate Am. Bd. Surgery, Pediatric Surgery. Attending surgeon Children's Nat. Med. Ctr., Washington, 1981-92; chief clin. dept. surgery Children's Med. Ctr. Dallas, 1992—; from asst. prof. to prof. surgery George Washington U., Washington, 1981-92; prof. surgery U. Tex. Southwestern, Dallas, 1992—, chmn. pediatric surgery divsn., 1992—. Contbr. articles to profl. jours., chpt. in book. Maj. U.S. Army, 1977-79. Mem. ACS, Am. Pediatric Surg. Assn., Soc. Univ. Surgeons, Am. Soc. Transplant Surgeons, Am. Assn. Pediatrics, Parkland Surg. Soc. Office: Children's Med Ctr Dallas 1935 Motor St Dallas TX 75235

GWALTNEY, JAVY RUDOLPH, III, computer operations consultant; b. Goldsboro, N.C., May 10, 1961; s. Javy Rudolph Gwaltney Jr. and JoAnn (Sloan) Cavenaugh; m. Holly Marie Greer, June 28, 1988; children: Javy Rudolph IV, Sloan Brantley Gwaltney. AS in Computer Sci. Tech., Abraham Baldwin Agr. Coll., 1984; M in Orgnl. Mgmt., So. Wesleyan U., 1993. Programmer II U. Ga., Athens, 1984-85; ops. mgr. VNA of Greater Bamberg, S.C., 1985—; propr. JRG Programming Svcs., Bamberg, 1985—; pres., chief exec. officer G&W Micro-Specialties, Inc., Bamberg, 1988-92. Mem. Bamber County C. of C. (bd. dirs. 1987-92, pres. 1989-90), S.C. Home Care Assn. (bdir. dirs. 1991-94, treas. 1993-94), Phi Theta Kappa Honor Soc. (pres. 1983-84), Phi Beta Lambda (treas. 1983-84), Alpha Beta Gamma Honor Soc. Home and Office: PO Box 1051 Bamberg SC 29003-0651

GWATHMEY, JOE NEIL, JR., broadcasting executive; b. Brownwood, Tex., Jan. 4, 1941; s. Joe Neil and Grace Christine (Henry) G.; m. Linda Sue Sams, Aug. 22, 1965; children: Sara Lynn, David Alan. BA, Howard Payne Coll., 1963; postgrad., U. Denver, 1963-64, George Washington U., 1964-65. Sta. mgr. Sta. KUT-FM, Austin, 1965-71; various mgmt. positions Nat. Pub. Radio, Washington, 1971-83, v.p., 1983-88; pres. Tex. Pub. Radio, San ANtonio, 1988—; bd. dirs. Devel. Exchange, Inc., Washington. Review panel chair United Way Bexar County, San Antonio, 1994, 95; adv. coun. mem. Coll. Fine Arts Univ. Tex., Austin, 1990-93. Recipient Edward R. Murrow award Corp. Pub. Broadcasting, 1988. Mem. Rotary. Democrat. Protestant. Home: 2926 Meadow Cir San Antonio TX 78231-1720 Office: Tex Pub Radio 8401 Datapoint Dr Ste 800 San Antonio TX 78229-5925

GWAZDAUSKAS, FRANCIS CHARLES, animal science educator, dairy scientist; b. Waterbury, Conn., July 25, 1943; s. Francis Julian and Agnes Eva Gwazdauskas; m. Judy Keller, Mar. 20, 1971; children: Jennifer, James (dec.), John, Peter. BS in Animal Sci., U. Conn., 1966; MS in Dairy Sci., U. Fla., 1972, PhD in Animal Sci., 1974. Asst. prof. dairy sci. Va. Polytechnic Inst. and State U., Blacksburg, 1974-80, assoc. prof. dairy sci., 1980-86, prof. dairy sci., 1986—; cons. PPL (Pharm. Proteins Ltd.), Blacksburg, 1992—. Contbr. articles to profl. jours. Treas. Troop 706, Boy Scouts Am., Blacksburg, 1991-94; treas. Blacksburg High Athletic Boosters, 1990—. Sgt. U.S. Army, 1967-68, Vietnam. Recipient award for rsch. excellence Va. Poly. Inst. and State U. Alumni Assn., 1995, David R. and Magaret Lincicome endowed professorship, 1996, Pharmacca/Upjohn Physiology Rsch. award Am. Dairy Sci. Assn., 1996. Office: Va Polytechnic Inst State U Dept Dairy Sci Blacksburg VA 24061-0315

GWIN, JAMES ELLSWORTH, librarian; b. Chattanooga, Mar. 1, 1947; s. Madison Taylor and Juanita Elizabeth (Wallace) G.; m. Sheena Margaret Mackenzie, Oct. 5, 1985; children; Colleen Mackenzie, Elizabeth Maureen. AB, U. Tenn., 1969; M Library, Emory U., 1970; MPA, Va.

Commonwealth U., 1984. Instr., cataloger U. Chattanooga, 1970; asst. prof., asst. head U. Tenn., Chattanooga, 1972-75; head bibliographic svc. U. Richmond, Va., 1975-85, acting univ. librarian, 1985-86, acting dir. LRC, 1986, dir. tech. svc., 1987—; acting univ. libr. U. Richmond, Va., 1990-91, 96-97. Editor Terminal Talk, 1980-81. Dir. Cen. Va. Union List of Serials Project, 1990—. 1st lt. U.S. Army, 1971-72. Lyndhurst Found. grantee, Chattanooga, 1974-75. Mem. ALA, Am. Soc. Pub. Adminstrn., Assn. Coll./Rsch. Libraries (chmn. Va. chpt. 1986), Va. Libr. Assn. (2d v.p. 1992-93), Phi Kappa Phi, Pi Alpha Alpha. Democrat. Episcopalian. Home: 1232 Windsor Ave Richmond VA 23227-3743 Office: U Richmond Boatwright Meml Libr Richmond VA 23173

GWIN, JOHN MICHAEL, marketing educator, consultant; b. Montgomery, Ala., June 21, 1949; s. Emmett Brindley Jr. and Irma Rebecca (Watkins) G.; m. Pamela Jane Blair, Sept. 7, 1970; children: Colin Blair, Connor Brindley. BBA, Auburn U., 1971; MBA, U. Ga., 1973; PhD, U. N.C., 1979. Fiscal officer U. Ga., Athens, 1971-73; ops. mgr. Bedsole & Gwin Inc., Fairhope, Ala., 1973-75; instr. Faulkner Coll., Bay Minette, Ala., 1975-76; research asst. U. N.C., Chapel Hill, 1976-78, vis. lectr., 1978-79; asst. prof. Ind. U., Bloomington, 1979-81; asst. prof. U. Va., Charlottesville, 1981-83, assoc. prof., 1983—, mktg. area coord., 1990-93, dir. Ctr. for Entrepreneurial Studies, 1992—; Fulbright prof. Trinity Coll., Dublin, Ireland, 1986-87;, vis. prof., 1993; exec. educator numerous U.S. firms, 1981—; cons. numerous internat. and U.S. firms, 1983—; invited lectr. Sorbonne, U. Paris, Alsace Inst., Strasbourg, France, 1987. Inventor LaMaze Timer and audio text. Sesquicentennial Research Assoc., U. Va., 1986-87, 93-94; named Outstanding Young Man Am., U.S. Jr. C. of C., 1976. Mem. Am. Mktg. Assn. (conf. coord. Cen. Va. chpt. 1986), So. Mktg. Assn., Acad. Mktg. Sci., Japan-Va. Soc. Planning Forum, Colonnade Club. Episcopalian. Home: 824 King William Dr Charlottesville VA 22901-0618 Office: U Va 226 Monroe Hall Charlottesville VA 22903-2438

GYIMAH-BREMPONG, KWABENA, economics educator; b. Kintampo, Ghana, July 24, 1949; came to U.S., 1975; s. Yaw Agyekum and Akua Nyarkoh; m. Rose Nyanor, July 24, 1974; children: Akua, Adwoa. BA, U. Cape Coast, 1974; PhD, Wayne State U., 1981. Lectr. econs. U. Cape Coast, Ghana, 1974-75; vis. asst. prof. econs. Allegheny Coll., Meadville, Pa., 1980-81; asst. prof. econs. New Coll. U. So. Fla., Sarasota, 1981-88; from assoc. prof. econs. to prof. econs. Wright State U., Dayton, Ohio, 1988-94; prof. econs. U. So. Fla., Tampa, 1994—; chief analyst Elliot Berg Assocs., Alexandria, Va., 1986-87; fellowship panelist NSF, Washington, 1995—. Mem. Am. Econs. Assn., Ea. Econs. Assn., So. Econs. Assn., Am. Statis. Assn., African Fin. & Econs. Assn. (co-founder, com. chair 1991—), Phi Beta Gamma.

HAAS, EDWARD LEE, business executive, consultant; b. Camden, N.J., Nov. 9, 1935; s. Edward David and Mildred (Wynne) H.; m. Maryann Lind, Dec. 27, 1958; children: John Eric, Gretchen Lind Theodore. BA, LaSalle U., 1958. Mgr. systems devel. RCA Corp., Cherry Hill, N.J., 1966-71; mgr. computer tech. svcs. Gencorp, Akron, Ohio, 1971-74; sr. mgr. computer applications R & D Ernst & Young LLP, Cleve., 1974-75; dir. nat. systems group Ernst & Young LLP, 1976-77, chief info. officer, nat. dir. software products, 1977-80, nat. ptnr., 1978-82, cons. ptnr., 1983-95; ind. mgmt. cons., 1996—. 1st lt. arty. U.S. Army, 1958-59. Mem. Data Processing Mgmt. Assn., Assn. Systems Mgmt., Assn. Inst. for Cert. Computer Profls., Plantation Country Club, Union League of Phila. Republican. Roman Catholic.

HAAS, GILBERT GEORGE, JR., reproductive endocrinologist; b. Cody, Wyo., Sept. 29, 1948; s. Gilbert and Mary Francis (Murray) H.; m. Mary Beth Haas, Nov. 27, 1976; children: Shane Gregory, Ashley Martin Murray, Tyler Emory, Benjamin Patrick. BA, U. Okla., 1970; MD, Baylor U., 1973. Diplomate Am. Bd. Ob-Gyn., with spl. competence in reproductive endocrinology. Intern Baylor Coll. Medicine Affiliated Hosps., Houston, 1973-74; resident U. Tenn. Ctr. for Health Scis., Memphis, 1974-77; fellow in reproductive endocrinology and infertility U. Pa. Sch. Medicine, Phila., 1977-79, asst. prof., 1979-84; assoc. prof. U. Okla. Health Scis. Ctr., 1984-90, tenured prof., 1990-96, chief sect. reproductive endocrinology, 1984—; pvt. practice Oklahoma City, 1996—; cons. Splty. Labs. Inc., Santa Monica, Calif., 1992-93; designated physician Family Hospice of Greater Okla. City Okla. Meml. Hosp.; spl. reviewer biochem. endocrinology study sect. NICHD NIH, 1993, divsn. scientific rev. study sect., 1993. Mem. editl. bd. Am. Jour. Reproductive Immunology, 1988-93, Jour. Andrology, 1990-93, Fertil Steril, 1988-94; ad hoc editor for numerous sci. jours.; contbr. articles to profl. jours. Mem. vestry St. Paul's Episc. Ch., 1990-93; asst. troop leader Boy Scouts Am., Edmond, Okla., 1991-94. Grantee in field. Fellow Am. Coll. Ob.-Gyn.; mem. Am. Fertility Soc., Am. Soc. Andrology (mem. exec. coun. 1990-93), Am. Soc. for Immunology of Reproduction (pres. 1992-93), Soc. for Study of Reproduction, Soc. Reproductive Endocrinologists, Soc. Reproductive Surgeons, Okla. City Obstetrics and Gynecology Soc. (pres. 1989-90), Pacific Coast Fertility Soc. (hon.), Fla. Obstetric and Gynecologic Soc. (hon.). Office: 1000 N Lincoln Blvd Ste 300 Oklahoma City OK 73104

HAAS, GREGORY GEORGE, mechanical engineer; b. Phila., Mar. 3, 1949; s. Joseph J. and Edith (LaBelle) H.; m. Sharon M. Mahaffey, May 4, 1996; M.E., Temple U., 1973. Prodn. mgr. Bruce Industries, Inc., Phila., 1973-76; supt. woodworking Dunning Industries, Inc., Greensboro, N.C., 1976-80; East Coast sales mgr. Ind. Moulding Co., Lexington, N.C., 1980-82; dir. mfg. Advanced Technology Inc., 1982-88; owner The Better Button Bur., 1985-91, Gregory's Discount Jewelry, 1991—, Ltd. Prodn., mktg. inventions, Two-Bit Video, operator amusement and vending machines. Inventor specialized machinery for lighting, woodworking and picture frame industry. Home: 6306 Roblyn Rd Greensboro NC 27410-4038 Office: PO Box 19303 Greensboro NC 27419

HAAS, ROBERT CHARLES, municipal official; b. Paris, Tex., June 16, 1949; s. Rutherford Ethridge and Frances Alberta (White) H.; m. Elizabeth Joann Schaible, June 28, 1975; children: Deborah Ann, Daniel Joseph. BA, Dallas Bapt. U., 1971; MPA, North Tex. State U., 1974. Health inspector City of Irving, Tex., 1972-74, adminstrv. asst., 1974-80, purchasing administrator, 1980-82, purchasing dir., 1982-95, purchasing mgr., 1995—. Mem. Nat. Inst. Govt. Purchasing, Nat. Purchasing Inst., Nat. Assn. Purchasing Mgmt., Tex. Purchasing Mgmt. Assn. (bd. dirs. 1986-89, 92-95, pres. 1990-91, newsletter editor 1990-95, Most Valuable Contrbn. award 1993). Home: 2212 Spanish Trail Irving TX 75060 Office: City of Irving 825 W Irving Blvd Irving TX 75060

HAAS, ROBERT DONNELL, flight instructor, airline transport pilot, lawyer; b. Ft. Worth, Nov. 28, 1953; s. Albert Donnell and Shirley (Tucker) H.; m. Dawn Elaine Wallace, Jan. 9, 1975 (div. June 1976); m. Barbara Anne Sonnemann, July 4, 1981 (div. Mar. 1989); m. Linda Marie Roberson Shinall, July 28, 1995; 1 stepchild, Amber Dawn. Student, U. Tex., 1971-72, Tarrant County Jr. Coll., Ft. Worth, 1975-76; B of Profl. Studies, Memphis State U., 1988, JD, 1990. Bar: U.S. Dist. Ct. (we. dist.) Ky.; cert. comml. aviator. Night supr. Tex. Leisure Chair, Inc., Ft. Worth, 1972-76; prin. Memphis Parts House, Inc., Memphis, 1976-86; pilot, dir. of flight standards Exec. Charter of Memphis, 1986-88; principal Haassong Prodn. Enterprises and Haastronix, Ltd. Corp., Ft. Worth and Memphis, 1975—; with sales dept., purchasing agt., of counsel Preferred Engine Parts, Inc., 1987—; head acctg. exec., of counsel Weiss Auto Parts Co., Inc., Memphis, 1993—; flight instr. Metro Flying Sch., Olive Branch, Miss., 1985-90, Lazy Eight Flight Ctr., Memphis, 1985-88. Author: (poems) Songs of Feeling, 1975, Portraits of Love, 1976, Girls of My Dreams, 1987. Mem. ABA, Future Aviation Profls. Am., Aircraft Owners and Pilots Assn., World Future Soc., Assn. Trial Lawyers Am., Tenn. Trial Lawyers Assn., Tenn. Bar Assn., Sherby County Bar Assn., Phi Delta Phi. Republican. Jewish. Home: PO Box 751084 Memphis TN 38175-1084

HABER, JENNIFER RIEBEN, English language educator; b. Phila., Oct. 9, 1972; d. Carl Richard and Susan Jean (Jones) Rieben; m. Michael B. Haber, June 1, 1996. BA in Eng. Lit., U. Fla., 1994; MA in Eng. Lit., U. Ctrl. Fla., 1996. Tchr. freshman writing U. Ctrl. Fla., Orlando; tutor UCF, Orlando; dir. Career Resource Ctr., Gainesville, Fla. Mem. MLA, Phi Kappa Phi. Home: 10848 Glen Cove Ctr #105 Orlando FL 32817

HABER, MARIAN WYNNE, journalism educator, writer; b. N.Y.C., Aug. 23, 1936; d. Louis and Sara Pauline (Ingber) Feit; m. Sheldon Jay Wynne, June 14, 1959 (dec. Sept. 1963); children: Susan Wynne Ghotbi, Robert Warren; m. Julian Stuart Haber, Aug. 21, 1983. AA, U. Fla., 1956; BA, U. Miami, 1958, diplomate, 1972; PhD, U. North Tex., 1987. Newspaper reporter Hollywood (Fla.) Sun-Tattler, 1958-59, Coral Gables (Fla.) Times, 1963-69, Miami (Fla.) News, 1969-70; staff writer Miami Beach Visitor and Conv. Authority, 1972-82; instr. journalism Tex. Christian U., Ft. Worth, 1982-84, Tex. Wesleyan U., Ft. Worth, 1984-89, 93—; mem. faculty U. Tex., Arlington, 1985-94, vis. asst. prof. journalism, 1990-91; presenter Newspaper in Edn., Ft. Worth Star-Telegram, 1991-94, 96, Journalism and Mass Comm. Symposium, Corpus Christi, Tex., 1991, U. S.C., Charleston, 1991, Nat. Conf. on Teaching and Learning, Jacksonville, Fla., 1991; book reviewer Journalism Educator, 1991-92, Coll. Media Rev., 1984, Jour. Ednl. Comm., 1984, Coll. Press Rev., 1984, Nursing Homes mag. Contbg. writer: Cut Your Spending in Half, 1994; contbr. articles to profl. publs. Recipient scholarships U. North Tex., U. Miami. Mem. Assn. Women Journalists, Assn. Journalism Educators and Mass Comms., Soc. Profl. Journalists. Home: 2821 Amber Dr S Fort Worth TX 76133-6455

HABER, PAUL, health psychologist, educator; b. Yonkers, N.Y., Jan. 30, 1936; s. Herbert Hubert and Sylvia Martha (Kliger) H.; m. Marsha Last, June 29, 1957 (dec. 1994); m. Donna Rudman, Feb. 18, 1996; children: Kara Edin Haber Stevens, Robert Jacobs. BA in Psychology, St. Thomas U., Miami, Fla., 1978; MA in Counseling, Goddard Coll., Plainfield, Vt., 1979; PhD in Health Psychology, The Union Inst., Cin., 1981. Pres., dir. Stress Inst., Inc., Miami, 1978-94; pres. Stress Inst., Inc., Boulder, Colo., 1994—; co-founder, former v.p. and project dir. Child Assault Prevention Project of South Fla., Inc., Miami, 1984, cons., 1984—; faculty coord., co-creator child abuse and literacy graduate sch. curriculum, 1994—; course cons. Masters psychology program Regis U., Denver, 1995—; adj. prof. various ednl. instns., including St. Thomas U., U. Miami, Miami-Dade C.C., Union Inst., 1978-89. Writer, moderator 11-part TV series on child abuse, 1985-86; author: Health, Stress and Type A Behavior, 1984-86; co-author: The Stress Reduction Workbook, 1987, Protecting Your Child, 1988; creator The Stop Smoking Program, Refocusing, 1989. Active Fla. Com. for Prevention of Child Abuse, 1989—, Fla. Ctr. for Children and Youth, 1989—, Fla. Ctr. for Children and Youth, 1989—. Recipient Nat. Sony Innovator award, 1969. Fellow Am. Inst. Stress; mem. ACA, Am. Orthopsychiat. Assn., Am. Profl. Soc. on the Abuse of Children, Assn. Transpersonal Psychology, Assn. Psychol. Type, Inst. Noetic Sci., Phi Theta Kappa.

HABERER, JOHN HENRY, JR., minister; b. Queens, N.Y., Feb. 16, 1955; s. John H. and Maureen (Hastings) H.; married; children: David, Kelly. BA magna cum laude, Roberts Wesleyan Coll., Rochester, N.Y., 1976; MDiv cum laude, Gordon-Conwell Theol. Seminary, South Hamilton, Mass., 1982; D of Ministry, Columbia Theol. Seminary, Decatur, Ga., 1989. Ordained to ministry Presbyn. Ch., 1984. Asst. mgr. Christian Ctr. Bookstore, Allendale, N.J., 1976-79; dir. of worship First United Ch., Swampscott, Mass., 1979-82; dir. of family ministries New Covenant Ch., Pompano Beach, Fla., 1982-84; sr. minister Trinity Presbyn. Ch., Satellite Beach, Fla., 1984-94, Clear Lake Presbyn. Ch., Houston, 1994—; bd. dirs., chmn. Spl. Gathering, Inc., Cocoa, Fla., 1987-93; mem. evangelism commn. Fla. Coun. Chs., Orlando, 1989-91; chmn. Brevard-Indian River Counties Presbyn. Mission Conf., Satellite Beach, 1989-92, chmn. long-range planning com. Presbytery Coordinating Coun., Cen. Fla. Presbytery, Orlando, 1985-90; bd. dirs. Aids Alliance of Bay Area, 1994—. Contbr. articles to profl. jours. Vol. chaplain Brevard Pub. Schs., Satellite Beach, 1984-94; mgr. Little League Baseball, Satellite Beach, 1984-88; founder, dir. Mustard Seed Coffeehouse, Ramsey, N.J., 1971-79. Recipient Good Will award for 1990, City of Satellite Beach City Coun., 1990; named to Outstanding Young Men of Am., 1986. Mem. Presbyns. for Renewal, Evangel. Tchr. Tng. Assn. Republican.

HABERMAN, RICHARD EDWARD, city administrator; b. Oakland, Calif., Nov. 6, 1946; s. Elmer Jack and Ruth Marie (Weaver) H.; m. Elizabeth Ann Walters, June 6, 1969 (div. Dec. 1981); m. Diana Louise Blaine, Feb. 5, 1983; 1 child, Haley Rae. BPA magna cum laude, U. Ark., 1991, MPA, 1995. Field underwriter Met. Ins. Co., Hayward, Calif., 1971-76; mfrs. rep. Allgood Industries, Inc., Hayward, 1978-86; purchasing agt. Baldwin Piano & Organ Co., Fayetteville, Ark., 1986-87; materials mgr. Hydrotec Internat., Siloam Springs, Ark., 1988-90; adminstrv. intern City of Fayetteville, 1992-94; city adminstr. City of Barling, Ark., 1994—; subcoms. chair Gen. Plan Revision Task Force, Hayward, 1984-85. Res. police officer San Leandro (Calif.) Police Dept., 1975-77; vol. firefighter Wheeler (Ark.) Fire Dept., 1991-93. Wtih USN, 1966-70. Mem. ASPA, Internat. City Mgmt. Assn., Ark. City Mgmt. Assn. (v.p. 1992—, scholar 1992), Beta Gamma Sigma, Phi Kappa Phi, Golden Key. Republican. Baptist. Home: 3135 N Hughmount Rd Fayetteville AR 72704 Office: City of Barling 304 Church St Barling AR 72923

HABGOOD, JOHN FRISBIE, city administrator; b. St. Petersburg, Fla., Feb. 27, 1943; s. Douglas V. and Alice M. (Sanders) H.; m. Mary Kay Struthers, Dec. 18, 1965; children: Kenneth C., Richard T. BS in Forestry, U. Fla., 1966, MBA, 1972. Strong mayor City of St. Petersburg, Fla., 1972—; mgr. zoning and subdivsns. City of St. Petersburg, 1972-79, dir. econ. devel., 1979-85, asst. dep. city mgr. community devel. & fiscal mgmt., 1985-90, internal svcs. adminstr., 1990—; trustee St. Petersburg Police Pension Bd.; past pres. First Fla. Govtl. Fin. Commn. Bd. mem. ARC; past bd. mem. biracial com. Community Alliance; soccer referee; coach, league commr. Youth Soccer and Baseball; active Suncoast Tiger Bay Club; deacon Maximo Presbyn. Ch. Capt. USAF, 1966-70. Decorated Bronze star. Mem. Internat. City Mgrs. Assn., Am. Inst. Cert. Planners, Fla. Redevel. Assn. (past pres.), Leadership St. Petersburg, Govt. Fin. Officers Assn., St. Petersburg Cert. Devel. Corp. (past dir.). Home: 4084 48th Ave S Saint Petersburg FL 33711-4606

HABITO, RUBEN LEODEGARIO FLORES, religion educator; b. Cabuyao, Laguna, Philippines, Oct. 2, 1947; came to U.S., 1989; s. Celestino and Faustina (Flores) H.; m. Maria Dorothea Reis, Apr. 18, 1990. MA, Tokyo U., 1975, DLittC, 1978; STL, Sophia U., Tokyo, 1978. Ordained priest Roman Cath. Ch., 1976. Lectr. Sophia U., 1978-85, assoc. prof., 1985-89; prof. Perkins Sch. Theology, So. Meth. U., Dallas, 1989—; authorized Zen tchr., 1988; dir. Maria Kannon Zen Ctr., Dallas. Author: Total Liberation, 1989, Healing Breath, 1993. Mem. Japanese Cath. Coun. for Justice and Peace, Tokyo, 1978-89. Mem. Sanbo Kyodan Religious Found., Japanese Assn. for Religious Studies, Am. Acad. Religion, Assn. Asian Studies, Japanese Assn. Indian and Buddhist Studies. Office: So Meth U Perkins Sch Theology Dallas TX 75275-0133

HACKEMAN, CALVIN LESLIE, accountant; b. Hanover, N.H., Oct. 6, 1953; s. Leslie B. and Myrtle (Gallup) H.; m. Amy Jo Weissman, May 7, 1978; children: Peter Jonathan Rodger, William Robert Stephan. BS cum laude, Am. U., 1975. CPA, Va. Staff acct. Grant Thornton, Washington, 1975-77, sr. acct., 1977-79, audit supr., 1979-81, mgr. audit, 1981-84, dept. head quality assurance, 1983-84, account mgr., 1984-87, audit ptnr., 1987-89, ptnr.-in-charge, McLean, Va., 1989-95, ptnr.-in-charge govt. contractor industry, 1987—. Sec. Manassas Downtown Revitalization Action Com., 1982-85, chmn., 1985-86; chmn. spl. events com. Hist. Manassas, Inc., 1986-87; vice chmn. for Reston (Va.) Bd. Commerce Trade Expo '87, chmn. 1988; bd. dirs. Reston (Va.) Bd. Commerce, 1987, pres.-elect, 1990-91, pres., 1991-92; pres. Greater Manassas Jaycees, 1983-84, chmn. bd. dirs., 1984-86; mem. exec. com. George Mason U. Entrepreneurial Inst., chmn. Grants and Contracts Com., 1988-91, Profl. Svcs. Coun., mem. com., 1989—, chmn., mem. svcs. com., 1990—, bd. dirs. ann. conf. com., 1990—, chmn. 1990-92; trustee Va. Jaycee Found., 1986-93, pres. 1988-89, bd. dirs., 1989-91; bd. dirs. City of Manassas Sch. Ednl. Found., 1993—, v.p., 1995—; mem. City of Manassas Bus. Coun., 1995—, vice chmn. 1996—. Mem. AICPAs, Va. Soc. CPAs, Am. U. Alumni Assn., Prince William County-Gtr. Manassas C. of C. (chmn. seminar com. 1986-87, bd. dirs. 1987-95, 96—, v.p. membership and programming 1987-88, v.p. govtl. rels. 1988-89, v.p. econ. and community devel. 1989-90, sec., treas. 1990-92, pres.-elect 1992-93, pres. 1993-94, past pres. 1994-95), Stretch Glass Soc. (treas. 1993—), Va. Jaycees (sec.-treas. 1984-85, v.p. fin. adminstrn. 1985-87), Va. Jaycees Life Mem. Assn., Jaycees Internat. Senate (life, Va. liaison 1988-93), Phi Kappa Phi, Omicron Delta Kappa. Home: 8865 Olde Mill Run Manassas VA 22110-6132 Office: Grant Thornton LLP Accts Mgmt Cons 2070 Chainbridge Rd Ste 375 Vienna VA 22182-2536

HACKER, ANTHONY WAYNE, private investigator; b. Ardmore, Okla., Mar. 26, 1956; s. George Harry and Helen Yvonne (Clemmons) H.; 1 child, Richard Lawrence; m. Jennifer Louise Raynor, Apr. 28, 1987; children: Heather Nicole, Ashley Elizabeth, Dalton Wayne. Diploma, Coll. of Police Sci., Fairfield, Ala., 1976. Bounty hunter U.S.A., 1980-84; owner S.F.P. Photography, Houston, 1989—; ops. mgr. Ranger Security, Inc., Houston, 1984—. Press photographer Internat. Freelance Photographer mag. With USMC, 1974-78. Baptist. Home: 5810 Arthington St Houston TX 77053-3004 Office: Ranger Security Inc 16157 Cairnway Dr # 204 Houston TX 77084-3541

HACKER, MARK GREGORY, training and development executive; b. N.Y.C., Apr. 17, 1961; s. George L. and Joan L. (Lake) H. BA in Comm., U. Denver, 1984, MA in Comm., 1988. Cable TV dir. Am. Cablevision, Littleton, Colo., 1983-84; gen. mgr. Screenplay Video, Littleton, 1984-86; corp. comm. specialist Jones Intercable, Englewood, Colo., 1987-88; mgr. tng. and employee comm. Pace Membership Warehouse, Englewood, 1988-94; sr. mgr. mgmt. devel. Wal-Mart Stores, Bentonville, Ark., 1994—. Mem. Univ. Park Cmty. Coun., Denver, 1991-94, mem. alumni mentoring program U. Denver, 1991-94. Mem. ASTD (pres.-elect NW Ark. Chpt. 1995-96, pres. 1996—), Nat. Trust for Hist. Preservation, Mountain States Employer's Coun., U. Denver Grad. Sch. Alumni Assn., Beta Theta Pi (v.p. alumni assn. 1985-89). Home: 6209 Callaway Pl Alta Loma CA 91737-6904 Office: Sam's Club Divsn Wal-Mart Stores Inc 608 SW 8th St Bentonville AR 72712-9139

HACKER, SHELLEY GORDON, oil and chemical company manager; b. Hereford, Tex., Feb. 24, 1956; s. Wendlin and Joe and Evelyn Jeane (Benson) H.; m. Shawn Ruth Mumbach, Oct. 26, 1985. BA in Microbiology, Tex. Tech U., 1978, MSChemE, 1981. Registered profl. engr., Tex. Constrn. supt. Hacker Constrn., Nacogdoches, Tex., 1978-79; rsch. asst. Tex. Tech U, Lubbock, 1979-81; process engr. II FINA Oil & Chem., Big Springs, Tex., 1981-84; process engr. III FINA Oil & Chem., Dallas, 1984-87; sr. process engr. FINA Oil & Chem., Deer Park, Tex., 1987-89; mgr. terminal ops. FINA Oil & Chem., Dallas, 1989-91; area mgr. OMS OMS FINA Oil & Chem., Big Spring, 1991-93, tech. mgr., 1993-94, sr. mktg. advisor, 1994—. Vol. Big Spring State Hosp. Mem. AIChE, Am. Soc. Quality Control, Tex. Tech. Engring. Alumni of the Metroplex (sec. 1989-91), Rotary, Toastmasters. Office: FIHA Oil & Chem 8350 N Central Expy Dallas TX 75206-1625

HACKETT, EDWARD VINCENT, investment company executive; b. N.Y.C., Jan. 17, 1946; s. Edward Vincent and Gladys Theresa (O'Connell) H. BA, Fordham U., 1967; MBA, Columbia U., 1969. CPA, N.Y.; registered gen. securities rep. Cons. Irving Trust Co., N.Y.C., 1968; mgr. cons. svcs. Arthur Young & Co., N.Y.C., 1969-78; dir. mgmt. svcs. Insilco Corp. Group, Meriden, Conn., 1978-84; v.p. ops., COO, CFO Coatings div. Insilco Corp., Tampa, Fla., 1984-86; pres. mid-Atlantic div. Insilco Corp., Tampa, 1986-90; exec. v.p., COO Coronado Paint Co., Edgewater, Fla., 1990-92, bd. dirs.; fin. advisor Dean Witter Reynolds, Tampa, 1992-96; sr. investment officer Baybridge Fin. Group, Tampa, 1996—. Editor Productivity News, 1984. Capt. U.S. Army, 1969-71. Mem. AICPA, Fla. Inst. CPAs, Nat. Mktg. Assn., Columbia Alumni Assn. (v.p.), Ivy League Club (treas.), Tampa Rotary Club (benefactor). Home: 3301 Bayshore Blvd Unit 1007 Tampa FL 33629-8843 Office: Baybridge Fin Group 201 N Franklin St Ste 2350 Tampa FL 33602

HACKMAN, GWENDOLYN ANN, private duty nurse; b. Phila., Mar. 22, 1932; d. Stanley Heaney and Joy Hayes (Sands) H. Diploma, Phila. Gen. Hosp. Sch. Nursing, 1953; postgrad., La. State U., Tulane U. RNC, La.; cert. gerontol. nurse. Staff nurse pediatrics Phila. Gen. Hosp., 1953; staff nurse premature ctr. Charity Hosp., New Orleans, 1953-55, head nurse premature ctr., 1955; asst. instr. fundamentals of nursing, 1956-57; asst. instr. med. surg. nursing Touro Infirmary Sch. Nursing, 1957-60; rsch. assoc. maternal and child health sect. Tulane U., New Orleans, 1965-67; pvt. duty nurse New Orleans, 1955, 60-65, 67—. Mem. ANA, Nat. League for Nursing, New Orleans Dist. Nurses Assn., Nat. Gerontol. Assn., La. State Nurses Assn. (profl. practice com. 1962-63, 2d vice chmn. pvt. duty sect. 1962-66, chmn. 1968-69, bd. dirs. 1966), New Orleans Dist. Nurses Assn. (chmn. pub. rels. com. 1962, chmn. pvt. duty sect. 1962-67, bd. dirs. 1962-67), DAR. Home: 1460 Henry Clay Ave New Orleans LA 70118-6062

HACKNEY, VIRGINIA HOWITZ, lawyer; b. Phila., Jan. 11, 1945; d. Charles Rawlings and Edith Wrenn (Pope) Howitz; m. Barry Albert Hackney, Feb. 15, 1969; children: Ashby Rawlings, Roby Howison, Trevor Pope. BA in Econs., Hollins Coll., 1967; JD, U. Richmond, 1970. Bar: Va. 1970. Assoc. Hunton & Williams, Richmond, Va., 1970-77, ptnr., 1977—; pres. Am. Acad. Hosp. Attys. Chgo., 1992-93. Mem. agy. evaluation com. United Way of Greater Richmond, 1981-86; sustainer Jr. League of Richmond. Named Outstanding Woman in field of law, YWCA, Richmond, 1981. Mem. ABA (bus. law sect. 1984—, forum com. on health law 1982—), Am. Acad. Hosp. Attys. (bd. dirs. 1988-94, pres. 1992-93), Va. State Bar (long range planning com. 1985-90, chmn. standing com. lawyer discipline 1986-90, exec. com. 1988-90). Office: Hunton & Williams Riverfront Plz East Tower 951 E Byrd St Richmond VA 23219-4074

HADDAD, FRED, lawyer; b. Waterbury, Conn., Sept. 14, 1946; s. Fred Melad and Nancy Anne (Crean) H.; m. Julia Hester, Aug. 2, 1980; 1 dau., Allison Hester; children by previous marriage: Tonja, Tristan, Matthew. Student U. Conn., 1964; BA, U. New Haven, 1971; JD, U. Miami (Fla.), 1974. Bar: Fla. 1974, U.S. Dist. Cts. (so. and mid. dists.) Fla. 1975, U.S. Cts. Appeals (4th, 5th, 6th, 10th, 11th cirs.) 1975, U.S. Supreme Ct. 1977, U.S. Dist. Ct. (we. dist.) Tenn. 1982. Ptnr. Sandstrom & Haddad, Ft. Lauderdale, Fla., 1974-83; pvt. practice, Ft. Lauderdale, 1983—. Mem. Nat. Assn. Criminal Def. Lawyers, Fla. Bar (criminal law, reverse sting coms.), Broward County Criminal Def. Attys. Assn., Fed. Bar Assn. (exec. com.), Nat. Fla. Criminal Def. Attys. Assn., Assn. Trial Lawyers Am., Assn. Criminal Def. Lawyers, Broward County Bar Assn. Democrat. Office: Ste 2612 One Financial Plz Fort Lauderdale FL 33394

HADDAWAY, JAMES DAVID, retired insurance company official; b. Louisville, July 25, 1933; s. Charles Montgomery Jr. and Viola (Sands) H.; m. Myrna Lou Harris, June 5, 1954; children: Peggy Ann, Robert Marshall, Susan Gayle. BS in Commerce, U. Louisville, 1960; MBA, Xavier U., 1973. Cert. adminstrv. mgr. (life); cert. purchasing mgr. (life); accredited personnel mgr.; sr. profl. human resources (life). Ins. cons. Met. Life Ins., Louisville, 1955-59; supt. Byck Bros. & Co., Louisville, 1959-61; dir. purchasing Liberty Nat. Bank, Louisville, 1961-63; v.p. and mgr. gen. services adminstrn. Citizens Fidelity Bank, Louisville, 1963-79; asst. v.p. and mgr. human resources Ky. Farm Bur. Ins. Co., 1979-95. Founder, chmn. emeritus Kentuckiana Expn. of Bus. and Industry, 1973-85. Served with U.S. Army, 1953-55. Named Boss of Year, Louisville chpt. Nat. Secs. Assn., 1978, 79. Mem. Adminstrv. Mgmt. Soc. (nat. dir. 1979-81), Nat. Assn. Purchasing Mgmt. (dir. nat. affairs 1970-71), Adminstrv. Mgmt. Soc. Louisville (pres. 1975-76, bd. dirs. 1976-92), Adminstrv. Mgmt. Soc. Found. (charter), Purchasing Mgmt. Assn. Louisville (pres. 1969-70), Louisville Soc. Human Resource Mgmt. (pres. 1983-84, chmn. strategic planning com. 1989, chmn. reorganization com. 1992, Professional Excellance award 1993), Conf. Casualty Ins. Cos. (chmn. nat. personnel conf. com. 1983), Nat. Eagle Scout Assn. (life), Soc. Human Resource Mgmt. (chmn. conf. com. region 9, 1984, dist. dir. for Western Ky. 1984, v.p. region 9 1985-86, Ky. coun. chmn. 1986), Nat. Assn. Ind. Insurers (mem. personnel com. 1987-95), Ky. C. of C. (benefits com., 1987-88, chmn. banking and ins. health and welfare sub-com. project 21, 1988), Hon. Order Ky. Cols., Am. Assn. of Individual Investors (life), Am. GO Assn., Louisville Soc. for Advancement Mgmt. (charter, pres. 1993-94, dir. 1994-95). Clubs: U. Club Louisville (charter), Wally Byam Caravan Internat. (pres. Ky. unit 1993, chmn. long range planning com. 1994, 2d v.p. region 5 1996—), Good Sam Recreational Vehicle, Bass Anglers Sportsman Soc. (life), Am. Legion. Lodges: Masons, Shriners. Baptist. Home: 4015 Wimpole Rd Louisville KY 40218-4735

HADDEN, JOHN WINTHROP, immunopharmacology educator; b. Berkeley, Calif., Oct. 23, 1939; s. David Rodney Hadden; m. Elba Mas, July 31, 1964; children: John W. II, Paul J. BA, Yale U., 1961; MD, Columbia U., 1965. Asst. prof. pathology U. Minn., Mpls., 1972-73; assoc. prof.

Cornell Grad. Sch., N.Y.C., 1973-82; assoc. mem., dir. lab. immunopharmacology Sloan-Kettering Meml. Cancer Inst., N.Y.C., 1973-82; prof. medicine, dir. div. immunopharmacology U. South Fla., Tampa, 1982—. Assoc. editor Internat. Jour. Immunopharmacology, 1978-86, editor, 1986—; editor 10 textbooks; contbr. chpts. to books, more than 250 articles to profl. jours. Mem. Am. Assn. Immunologists, Internat. Soc. Immunopharmacologists (v.p. 1982-85, pres. 1985-88), Tampa Yale Club (v.p. 1986-91). Home: 824 S Orleans Ave Tampa FL 33606-2939 Office: Univ S Fla Med Coll 12901 Bruce B Downs Blvd Tampa FL 33612-4742

HADDIX, ROBERT ALLEN, architect; b. Tucson, Ariz., Mar. 10, 1964; s. David Abner and Geneva Mae (Williams) H.; m. Kimberly Ann Christensen, Aug. 24, 1991. BArch, U. Ariz., 1988. Lic. profl. architect, Utah, Ariz. Civil engring. draftsman S.W. Engrs. & Planners, Tucson, 1983-84; archtl. technician Henningson, Durham, Richardson, Dallas, 1984-85; archtl. draftsman Aros & Goldblatt Architects, Tucson, 1985-86, Burlini/Silberschlag Ltd., Tucson, 1986-87; architect USAF-Hill AFB Utah, Clearfield, 1988-93; hist. preservation officer, architect Barksdale AFB, La., 1993-95; chief contract constrn. planning Kadena Air Base, Okinawa, Japan, 1995—. Active Nat. Trust for Hist. Preservation. Capt. Civil Engring. Squadron, USAFR, 1993-95. Mem. AIA. Republican. Presbyterian. Office: 718 CES/CECDP Unit 5261 APO AP 96367-5261

HADDOCK, RONALD WAYNE, oil company executive; b. St. Elmo, Ill., July 29, 1940; s. Clarence and Marie (Price) H.; m. Sandra Sue Thomas, Sept. 1957; children: Roni Sue Haddock Campey, Mark Tayler, Rick Wayne. BMechE, Purdue U., 1963. With Exxon Corp., 1963-86; various tech. staff, mgmt. positions Baton Rouge Refinery, 1963-71; specialties econs. coordinator, adminstrv. mgr., planning mgr. Refining Dept. Houston hdqrs., 1971-75; ops. mgr., refinery mgr. Baytown Refinery, 1975-78; corp. planning mgr. then v.p. for refining Houston hdqrs., 1978-81; exec. asst. to chmn. Exxon Corp. Hdqrs. N.Y.C., 1981-82; v.p., dir. Esso Eastern Houston hdqrs., 1982-85; exec. v.p., COO FINA, Inc., Dallas, 1986-88; pres., CEO Fina, Inc., Dallas, 1988—; also bd. dirs. FINA, Inc., Dallas. Mem. Long Range Strategy Task Force, Pub. Comm. Task Force, Dallas Citizens Coun., Dallas Morning News Energy Bd., Dallas United Bd.; chief execs. Round Table; bd. dirs., exec. com. Dallas Opera. Mem. Am. Petroleum Inst. (pub. policy com., budget com., chmn. strategic planning oversight group), Nat. Petroleum Refiners Assn. (bd. dirs.), Ind. Producers Assn., Am. Petrochem. Industry Founders Club, North Dallas Chamber, Dallas C. of C. (bd. dirs., compensation and benefits com.), FINA Found., 25 Yr. Club Petroleum Industry, Energy Club. Methodist. Clubs: Energy, Petroleum (Dallas). Office: FINA Inc 8350 N Central Expy Dallas TX 75206-1625*

HADDOX, JOHN HERBERT, philosophy educator; b. Pawnee, Okla., Aug. 9, 1929; s. Charles Hugh and Mary Madeleine (Webb) H.; m. Maria del Carmen Mendoza, Sept. 6, 1954; children: Christina, John Jr., Charles, Thomas, Margaret, Raissa, Grace, Madeleine, Richard, Robert. BA, U. Notre Dame, 1954, MA, 1955, PhD, 1958. From asst. prof. to assoc. prof. U. Tex., El Paso, 1957-67, prof., 1968—. With U.S. Army, 1951-53. Ziegler fellow in human rights Samuel E. Ziegler Found., 1982. Democrat. Roman Catholic. Home: 2711 Radford El Paso TX 79903-1228 Office: U Tex Box 628 El Paso TX 79968

HADEN, CHARLES H., II, federal judge; b. Morgantown, W.Va., Apr. 16, 1937; s. Charles H. and Beatrice L. (Costolo) H.; m. Priscilla Ann Miller, June 2, 1956; children: Charles H., Timothy M., Amy Sue. BS, W.Va. U., 1958, JD, 1961. Ptnr. Haden & Haden, Morgantown, W.Va., 1961-69; state tax commr. W.Va., 1969-72; justice Supreme Ct. Appeals W.Va., 1972-75, chief justice, 1975; judge U.S. Dist. Ct. No. and So. Dists. W.Va., Parkersburg, 1975-82; chief judge U.S. Dist. Ct. (so. dist.) W.Va., 1982—; mem. W.Va. Ho. of Dels., 1963-64; asst. prof. Coll. Law, W.Va. U., 1967-68; mem. com. adminstrn. probation system Jud. Conf., 1979-86. Mem. Bd. Edn., Monongalia County, W.Va., 1967-68. Fellow Am. Bar Found.; mem. ABA, W.Va. Bar Assn., W.Va. State Bar Assn., Am. Judicature Soc. Office: US Dist Ct PO Box 351 Charleston WV 25322-0351*

HADLEY, CHARLES DAVID, JR., political science educator, researcher; b. Springfield, Mass., June 5, 1942; s. Charles David and Caroline (Filip) H.; m. Mary Turner, Feb. 7, 1970 (div. 1980); 1 child, Nathaniel. BA in Polit. Sci., U. Mass.-Amherst, 1964, MA in Polit. Sci., 1967; PhD in Polit. Sci., U. Conn., 1971. Instr., U. New Orleans, 1970-71, asst. prof., 1971-74, assoc. prof., 1974-86, prof., 1986-90, rsch. prof., 1990—, asst. to chmn., dept. polit. sci., 1971-75, coordinator grad. studies, dept. polit. sci., 1975-76, asst. dean Coll. Liberal Arts, 1976-79, dir. internship program dept. polit. sci., campus coordinator City Hall internship program, 1982-88, univ. internship coord., 1988-90, dir. Austrian student program, 1992—; asst. prof. polit. sci. Inst. for Social Inquiry, U. Conn., 1973-74; vis. prof. Inst. Für Politikwissenschaft Universität Innsbruck, Austria, 1987; cons. pub. opinion poll, State Rep. Candidate Vinturella, 1983, Title Research Corp., New Orleans, 1983, Ednl. Testing Service, Princeton, N.J., 1971, 91—, Commn. on Human Rights and Opportunities, Conn., 1973; mem. govt. and politics test devel. com. Coll. Bd., N.Y.C., 1993—; co-investigator report Conn. Bank & Trust Co., 1972. Author: (with Everett C. Ladd, Jr.) Political Parties and Political Issues: Patterns in Differentiation Since the New Deal, 1973; Transformations of the American Party System: Political Coalitions from the New Deal to the 1970s, 1975, 2d edit. 1978; co-editor: Political Parties in the Southern States: Party Activists in Partisan Coalitions, 1990, Southern State Party Organizations and Activists, 1995; mem. editorial bd. Am. Rev. Politics, 1992-93, co-editor, 1994-95, editor, 1995—; editl. bd. Jour. Politics, 1977-88; mem. editorial adv. bd. Campaigns & Elections Mag., 1993—, Nat. Forum, 1994—; contbr. chpts. to books, articles to publs.; panelist, speaker profl. confs. in field. Bd. dirs. Irish Channel Neighborhood Assn., 1976-78, 80-86, pres. 1983, 84, 85; bd. dirs. Children's Community, 1979-81; room parent John Dibert Elem. Sch., 1981-82, sch. site planning com., 1982-83, organizer Friends of Dibert Library, 1983, mgmt. team, 1983-86; mem. alumni admissions council U. Mass., Amherst, 1980—; mem. adv. council and reelection steering com. state Rep. Mary Landrieu, 1980-88; mem. Neighborhood Council Preservation Resource Ctr., 1981-84; mem. credit com. U. New Orleans Fed. Credit Union, 1982-85; participant leadership forum Met. Area Com., 1984, mem. Met. Area Com., 1985—; deacon, elder governing bd. St. Matthew United Ch. Christ, 1984-94, new minster search com., 1986-87; bd. dirs. Human Services On Cable, 1985-91, Back Bay Mission, Biloxi, Miss.; asst. coach Lakeview Soccer Club, 1988-89. Recipient Career Achievement award U. New Orleans Alumni Assn., 1991, Scholar award South Ctrl. region Phi Kappa Phi, 1994; NEH younger humanist fellow, 1973; faculty research fellow U. Conn., summer 1972; predoctoral research grantee, U. Conn. Research Found., 1969-70, summer fellow, 1970; summer research tng. grantee U. Conn. to Inter-Univ. Consortium for Polit. Research, 1968; Phi Kappa Phi scholar-in-residence Southeastern La. U., 1988. Mem. Am. Polit. Sci. Assn. (sec.-treas. polit. orgns. and parties sect. 1989—), So. Polit. Sci. Assn. (exec. council 1978-81, rec. sec. 1984-85, v.p. 1989-90, pres. 1992-93), Com. for Party Renewal (exec. com. 1984—), Midwest Polit. Sci. Assn., New Eng. Polit. Sci. Assn., U. Mass. New Orleans Club (mem. steering com. 1994—), Pi Sigma Alpha, Omicron Delta Kappa, Phi Kappa Phi (U. New Orleans chpt. pres. 1991—, nat. fellowship com. 1995—). Congregationalist. Home: 3117 Constance St New Orleans LA 70115-2301 Office: Dept Polit Sci U New Orleans New Orleans LA 70148

HADLEY, PAMELA LYNN, adolescent counselor; b. Independence, Kans., Nov. 19, 1963; d. Billy Eugene and Mary Sue (Younger) Reed; m. Joe B. Hadley, Sept. 23, 1995; children: Garett Chase, Tanner Keith. BS, U. Tex., Arlington, 1987. Cert. alcohol and drug abuse counselor, compulsive gambling counselor; lic. chem. dependency counselor. Phys. therapy asst. Dr. James Elbaor, Arlington, 1980-83; supr. cashiers Target, Arlington, 1983-84; unit sec. Mansfield (Tex.) Community Hosp., 1984-85; sec. Willow Creek Hosp., Arlington, 1986-87, ednl. tester, 1987-89, student assistance counselor, 1989-90; case mgr., counselor Oak Grove Treatment Ctr., Burleson, Tex., 1990-91; drug edn. specialist Mansfield Ind. Sch. Dist., 1991-94; juvenile detention officer Tarrant County, Ft. Worth, 1994; case mgr. All Saints Episc. Hosp., Hurst, Tex., 1994—; cons. ednl. tester Carpenter & Assocs., Arlington, 1988-90, Mind Time, Arlington, 1989, Willow Creek Hosp., Arlington, 1989-90, Oak Grove Treatment Ctr., Burleson, 1990. Coach Mansfield Pee-Wee Cheerleading, 1986-90, coach adult volleyball; vol. Dallas Intertribal Ctr., 1990, Project Charlie, Kids Safe Saturday, 1990-91, AIDS Outreach Ctr., 1994, Horizons Tng. Mem. NAFE, Tex. Assn. Alcohol and Drug Abuse Counselors, Tarrant County Assn. Alcohol and Drug Abuse Counselors, Tex. Assn. Student Asst. Profls. Republican. Home: 1025 NCR 810 Alvarado TX 76009

HADLEY, RALPH VINCENT, III, lawyer; b. Jacksonville, Fla., Aug. 20, 1942; s. Ralph V. and Clare (Cason) H.; m. Carol Fox Hadley, Sept. 18, 1993; children: Graham Kimball, Christopher Bedell, Blair Vincent. BS, U. Fla., 1965, JD, 1968. Bar: Fla. 1968, Calif. 1972. Assoc. Kurz, Toole, Taylor & Moseley, Jacksonville, 1968-69; asst. atty. gen. State of Fla., Orlando, 1972-73; ptnr. Davids, Henson & Hadley, Winter Garden, Fla., 1973-80; sr. ptnr. Hadley & Asma, Winter Garden, 1980-89, Parker, Johnson, Owen, McGuire, Michaud, & Hadley, Orlando, 1989-91, Owen & Hadley, Orlando, 1991-94, Hadley, Gardner & Ornstein, P.A., Winter Park, Fla., 1994-95; Swann, Hadley & Alvarez, P.A., Winter Park, 1995—; vice chmn. bd. dirs. Tucker State Bank, Winter Garden, 1981-88; vice chmn. bd. dirs., sec. Tucker Holding Co., Jacksonville, 1984-88; bd. dirs. BankFIRST, BankFIRST Capital Corp. Bd. dirs. Orange County Dem. Exec. Com., Orlando, 1974-81, Spouse Abuse, Inc., Orlando, 1975-81. Lt. comdr. USN, 1969-72, Vietnam. Recipient award of merit Orange County Legal Aid Soc., 1987, Disting. Svc. award Judge J.C. Jake Stone Legal Aid Soc., 1989, Pres. Pro Bono Svc. award Fla. Bar, 1992. Mem. ABA, Fla. Bar Assn., Calif. Bar Assn., Orange County Bar Assn. (legis. chmn. 1979, 82), Am. Inn of Ct. (master), Winter Park C. of C. (bd. dirs. 1979-80), West Orange C. of C. (bd. dirs. 1979-82), Rotary. Presbyterian. Office: 1031 W Morse Blvd Winter Park FL 32789-3715

HADY, THOMAS FRANK, economist, retired government administrator; b. Brookings, S.D., Apr. 30, 1933; s. Frank Thomas and Alice (Sundstrom) H.; m. Marilyn Nelson, June 6, 1959; children: Susan, Frank. BA magna cum laude, U. Minn., 1955, PhD, 1961. Economist Econ. Rsch. Svc., USDA, Washington, 1962-64, leader farm tax and rural govt. group, 1964-65, chief community facilities br., 1965-73, chief community resources br., 1973-85, chief nat. economy and history br., 1985-93. Contbr. chpts. to book; author monographs, more than 60 articles. 1st lt. USAF, 1960-62. Mem. Am. Econ. Assn., Am. Agrl. Econ. Assn. (various coms.), Minn. Hist. Soc., Phi Beta Kappa, Delt Sigma Rho.

HAEMMERLEIN, BOB, company executive. Project mgr. The Kevin Tucker Group Inc.

HAERER, DEANE NORMAN, marketing and public relations executive; b. N.Y.C., Feb. 14, 1935; s. Frederick Sidney and Florence Agnes (Jackson) H.; m. Polly Ann Dunn, Feb. 24, 1961; children: Jennifer A., Heather J. AA, Boston U., 1955, BS, 1957, cert. achievement U. Iowa, 1979. Account exec. pub. rels. and advt. Charles Abbott Assos., Inc., N.Y.C., 1957-60; dir. alumni, community and ch. rels. Iowa Wesleyan Coll., 1960-61; tech. editor J.I. Case Co., Burlington, Iowa, 1961-64; dir. publs., asst. dir. pub. rels. Drake U., 1964-68; v.p. pub. rels. account supr. Thomas Wolff Assocs., Des Moines, 1968; dir. sch.-community rels. Des Moines Pub. Sch. System, 1968-74; dir. mktg. communications and corp. pub. rels. Stanley Cons., Inc., Muscatine, Iowa, 1974-78, dir. corp. pub. rels. and mktg. svcs., 1978-82; dir. mktg. svcs. Howard Needles Tammen & Bergendoff, Kansas City, Mo., 1982-84; dir. corp. mktg. Robert E. McKee, Inc., 1984-88, pres., chief exec. officer Haerer, Stoltz & Assocs., Inc., Dallas, 1988-90; prin., mgmt. cons. Haerer & Assocs. Inc., Dallas, 1990-95; v.p. corp. mktg. Price Consulting, Inc., Dallas, 1995—; guest lectr. Sch. Journalism, Drake U., 1970-74, U. Iowa, 1974-78. Bd. dirs. Heart of the Hawkeye coun. Camp Fire Girls, Des Moines, 1969-72. Recipient 1st place publ. award Univ. div. Mid-Am. Conf., Am. Coll. Pub. Rels. Assn., 1965, 66; nat. awards outstanding ednl. publs. Nations Schs. and Sch. Mgmt. mags., 1972, 73. Mem. Pub. Rels. Soc. Am. (accredited; charter mem., co-founder, past pres. and dir. Iowa chpt.; charter mem., co-founder, del. assembly, past chpt. dirand v.p. Quad Cities chpt.), Nat. Sch. Pub. Rels. Assn., Acad. Am. Educators, Soc. Mktg. Profl. Svcs., Am. Mktg. Assn., Tex. Indsl. Devel. Coun., So. Indsl. Devel. Coun., Pub. Rels. Soc. Am., Soc. Am. Mil. Engrs. Nat. Alumni Coun. of Boston U. Contbr. articles profl. publs. Home: 17 Cypress Ct Trophy Club TX 76262-8763

HAFNER, JOSEPH A., JR., food company executive; b. San Bernadino, Calif., Oct. 9, 1944; s. Joseph Albert and Mary Florence (McGowan) H.; m. Merrill Hafner; children: John Michael, Daniel Stephen, Caroline Elizabeth. A.B. cum laude, Dartmouth Coll., 1966; M.B.A. with high distinction, Amos Tuck Sch. Bus. Adminstrn., 1967. C.P.A. Intern Latin Am. Cornell U.-Ford Found., Lima, Peru, 1967-69; sr. cons. Arthur Andersen & Co., Houston, 1969-71; controller C/A div. Riviana Internat., Inc., Guatemala City, Guatemala, 1972-73; treas., v.p. fin. Riviana Internat., Inc., Houston, 1973-77; v.p. Riviana Foods Inc., Houston, 1977-81, pres., chief operating officer, 1981-84, pres., chief exec. officer, 1984—, dir., 1985—; bd. dirs. Tex. Commerce Bank-Houston. Recipient C.P.A. Gold medal Ark. State Bd. Pub. Accountancy, 1969. Mem. AICPA, Coun. on Fgn. Rels. Office: Riviana Foods Inc 2777 Allen Pky Houston TX 77019-2141

HAGAN, JOHN JOSEPH, health care executive; s. John Joseph Sr. and Helen Olga H.; m. Mary Lou Alliano, Nov. 5, 1977; children: Cheryl Lynn, Melissa Ann. BBA in Mktg., UCLA, 1972, MBA in Fin., 1976. Med. diplomate U.S. Gov. H.H.S. Dept., Washington. Pres. Internat. Hosp. Corp., L.A., 1976-85; chmn. The Hagan Group, Inc., Orlando, Fla., 1985-92; pres., CEO Life Care Med. Products, Inc. (formerly Northridge Home Health Care), St. Petersburg, Fla., 1992—; health care cons. various internat. hosps., 1985—. Author: Health Care in Developing Nations, 1990. 1st lt. USMC, 1964-68, Vietnam. Fellow Internat. Hosp. Consortium (chmn. 1985-92).

HAGAR, JAMES THOMAS, retail executive; b. Nashville, Jan. 11, 1950; s. Thomas Cecil and Lydia Pauline (Spicer) H. AS, Cumberland U., 1973; BA, U. Tenn., 1975. Buyer Davidson's Dept. Stores, Atlanta, 1975-78; ter. mgr. DuCommon Metals, Corpus Christi, Tex., 1978-82; franchise field dir. Workbench Furniture, Inc., N.Y.C., 1982-89; dir. training Expressions Custom Furniture, New Orleans, 1990-93; dir. retail ops. Rowe Furniture Corp., McLean, Va., 1993—; desktop pub.; design cons.; mgmt. lectr. U. New Orleans, 1990—. Author, editor: Professional Selling Techniques, 1990. Vol. New Orleans AIDS Task Force, 1990, Buddy Roemer for Gov., New Orleans, 1991; mem. Wyes Pub. Broadcasting, New Orleans, 1990; co-chmn. Lamar Alexander for Gov., Montgomery County, Tenn., 1978. 1st lt. USMC, 1969-72. Mem. Citizens for Airline Safety, Greenpeace, Am. Soc. Training and Devel. Republican. Home: 6299 Walkers Croft Way Alexandria VA 22315-5212 Office: Rowe Furniture Corp 1650 Tysons Blvd Ste 710 Mc Lean VA 22102

HAGAR, ROBERT MONTEL, chief executive officer, business owner; b. Pauls Valley, Okla., Apr. 21, 1942; s. Robert Henry and Flora Magnolia (Gentry) H.; m. Catherine K. Kovar, Feb. 8, 1978 (div. Apr. 1990). Grad. high sch., Centrahoma, Okla. Delivery pilot Max Conrad Aviation, Lock Haven, Pa., 1961-64; chief pilot, owner Flight Precision Inc., Phoenix, 1963-69; test pilot Bomark Industries, L.A., 1964-71; chief pilot PMC, Corp., Chgo., 1967-81; pres., owner Bomina Corp., Phoenix, 1969-87; chief exec. officer, owner Hagar Industries Corp., Boston, 1972—; founder Control Data Corp., Vancouver, B.C., Can., 1984—; dir. Aviation Aero. Rsch., Helsinki, Finland, 1977—; bd. dirs. Aerospace Cons., London; CEO, owner Paragon Group, Christchurch, New Zealand, 1995—. Author: Aviation Thermodynamics, 1973; owner, inventor COB interrelational system; inventor relational systems. Mem. Aero. Soc. S.Am. Democrat. Roman Catholic. Home: PO Box 1320 Edmond OK 73083-1320 Office: Hagar Industries Corp PO Box 1320 Edmond OK 73083-1320

HAGBERG, VIOLA WILGUS, lawyer; b. Salisbury, Md., July 3, 1952; d. William E. and Jean Shelton (Barlow) Wilgus; m. Chris Eric Hagberg, Feb. 19, 1978. BA, Furman U., Greenville, S.C., 1974; JD, U. S.C., 1976; LLM, U. Tulsa, 1978; DOD Army Logistics Sch. honor grad. basic mgmt. def. acquisition, def. small purchase, advanced fed. acquisition regulation, Fort Lee, Va., 1981-82. Bar: Okla. 1978, Va. 1979, U.S. Ct. Appeals (4th cir.) 1979. With Lawyers Com. for Civil Rights, Washington, 1979; pub. utility specialist Fed. Energy Regulatory Commn., Washington, 1979-80; contract specialist U.S. Army, C.E., Ft. Shafter, Hawaii, 1980-81; contract officer/supervisory contract specialist Tripler Army Med. Ctr., Hawaii 1981-83; supervisory procurement analyst and chief policy Procurement Div. USCG, Washington, 1983; contracts officer and chief Avionics Engring Contracting Br., 1984; procurement analyst office of sec. Dept. Transp., 1984-85; contracting officer Naval Regional Contracting Ctr., Long Beach, Calif., 1985-87; chief acquisition rev. and policy, Hdqrs. Def. Mapping Agy., Washington, 1987-92, dir. acquisitions, Fairfax, Va., 1992-93, dir. acquisition policy, 1994-96;dir. procurement Dept. of Def. policy tech. and legislated programs Nat. Mapping and Imagery Agy., 1996—. Mem. ABA (law student div. liaison 1977-78), Nat. Contract Mgmt. Assn., Va. State Bar Assn., Okla. Bar Assn., Phi Alpha Delta, Kappa Delta Epsilon. Home: 9810 Meadow Valley Dr Vienna VA 22181-3215 Office: Nat Mapping and Imagery Agy (PCP) 8613 Lee Hwy Fairfax VA 22031-2130

HAGE, GEORGE CAMPBELL, social studies educator, minister, and counselor; b. Huntington, W.Va., Nov. 12, 1944; s. Campbell Joseph and Martha (George) H.; m. Ellen Elaine Harner, July 1, 1972; 1 child, Shauna Kristin. BA, Marshall U., 1971; BRE, Washington Bible Coll., 1971; MEd, U. N.C., Greensboro, 1984, EdD, 1990. Diplomate Am. Coll. Counselors, Nat. Acad. Forensic Counseling; lic. tchr., N.C.; cert. criminal justice specialist; lic. profl. counselor, N.C.; ordained to ministry Christian Ch. (Disciples of Christ), 1982. Religious educator, 1971—; tchr. adult and continuing edn. Forsyth Tech. C.C., Winston Salem, N.C., 1979-85; min. New Hope Christian Ch., Winston Salem, N.C., 1982-88; rsch. asst. Sch. Edn. U. N.C., Greensboro, 1986-89; social studies tchr. Guilford Tech. C.C., Greensboro, 1986-88, Carver High Sch., Winston Salem, 1988-89; min. South Pk. Christian Ch., Reidsville, N.C., 1988-89; social studies tchr. Forsyth Tech. C.C., Winston Salem, 1990—; social worker/therapist Children's Home, Inc., Winston Salem, 1989-92; min. Trinity Christian Ch., 1991-92; social worker/therapist Elon Homes for Children, 1993; family therapist Host Homes of Cath. Social Svcs., Winston Salem, 1993—. Author: (booklet) The Seed Within You, 1976, A Symbolic Analysis of the Dimensions of Holiness in American Culture and Curriculum: Toward a Symbolic Synthesis of Wholeness, 1990; author poems (winner of George Herbert Meml. Poetry Competition 1982); composer booklet: Rhapsodia Fantaa: A Musical Design for an Autobiographical Theory of Curriculum, 1986; art works in temperas and oils. Recipient Editor's Choice award Nat. Libr. Poetry, 1996; named Poet of Yr. Internat. Soc. Poets, 1996. Fellow ACA, Assn. Lic. Profl. Counselors N.C., Nat. Assn. Forensic Counselors, N.C. Counseling Assn., Am. Assn. Christian Counselors, Nat. Coun. Social Studies (presdl. appointee adv. com. religion 1986-90), Winston-Salem Profl. Piano Tchrs. Assn.; mem. Internat. Soc. Poets, Chi Alpha Omega.

HAGERSON, LAWRENCE JOHN, healthcare consultant; b. Lakewood, Ohio, Dec. 30, 1931; s. John Lawrence and Ruth Evelyn (Watson) H.; m. Shirley Lorraine Carter, July 2, 1955; children: Nancy Lynn, Tracy Ann, Laura Jane. BS in Econs., U. Pa., 1954, postgrad. in Economics, 1957-59. Cons. John Price Jones Co., N.Y.C., 1960-62, U.S Agy. for Internat. Devel. Southeast Asia, 1970-74; asst. to chancellor U. Calif., Santa Barbara, 1962-63, U. Mo., Kansas City, 1967-70; cons. Asia Found., Singapore, Malaysia, 1964-67; exec. v.p. Mid. Am. Health Edn. Consortium, Kansas City, 1970-78; dir. bus. and devel. Inst. Logopedics, Wichita, Kans., 1978-88; dir. devel. The Conservancy, Naples, Fla., 1988-90. Mem., officer Kans. City Civic Orchestra Bd., 1976-78; bd. dirs. Greater Kans. City Urban Coalition, 1969-70. Served to lt. USN, 1954-56. Mem. Nat. Soc. Fund Raising Execs. (nat. bd. dirs. 1984-88). Republican. Presbyterian. Avocation: golf. Home: 4260 Hawaii Blvd Naples FL 33962-3730

HAGERTY, POLLY MARTIEL, financial analyst, construction executive; b. Joliet, Ill., Aug. 17, 1946; d. George Albert and Gene Alice (Roush) Jerabek; m. Theodore John Hagerty, Feb. 12, 1972. BS in Elem. Edn., Midland Luth. Coll., 1968; MEd in Early Childhood Edn., U. Ill., 1977; MBA in Fin., U. Tex., 1986. Elem. tchr. Madison Heights (Mich.) Sch. Dist., 1968-70, Taft Sch. Dist., Lockport, Ill., 1970-72; systems clerk U.S. Army, The Pentagon, Washington, 1972-74; psychology aide Psychology Clinic U. Ill., Urbana, 1974-75; elem. tchr. Champaign (Ill.) Sch. Dist., 1975-77; with recruitment Standard Oil of Ohio, Cleve., 1977-78; v.p. NCNB Texas-Houston, 1981-88, Citibank, Tucson, 1988-92; substitute tchr. Austin (Tex.) Ind. Sch. Dist., 1993-94; fin. analyst MK Devel. Inc., Austin, 1994—; co-owner Hagerty Constrn. Co., Austin, 1994—. Pres. Christus Victor Luth. Ch., League City, Tex., 1985-88, Luth. Ch. of the Foothills, Tucson, 1990-92; treas. Holy Cross Luth. Ch., Austin, 1996—. Recipient Golden Circle Sales and Svc. award, 1991. Mem. NAFE, AAUW, U. Ill. Alumni Club. Republican. Lutheran. Home: 7403 Callbram Ln Austin TX 78736-3119 Office: 7200 N Mo Pac Expy Ste 400 Austin TX 78731-2562

HAGGARD, WILLIAM HENRY, meteorologist; b. Woodbridge, Conn., Nov. 20, 1920; s. Howard Wilcox and Josephine Cecelia (Foley) H.; m. Blanche Woolard, Mar. 21, 1944 (div. May 1967); children: William Henry Jr., Robert H.; m. Martina Wadewitz, Oct. 1, 1967. BS in Physics, Yale U., 1942; cert. in profl. meteorology, MIT, 1942; MS in Meteorology, U. Chgo., 1946; postgrad., Fla. State U., 1958-59. Instr. meteorology N.C. State U., Raleigh, 1946-47; rsch. meteorologist U.S. Weather Bur., 1947-48; forecaster USWB Nat. Airport, 1949-50; instr. U.S. AID, Washington, 1950-51; staff weather rsch. project U.S. Navy, Norfolk, Va., 1951-54; chief adv. svcs. br. U.S. Weather Bur., Washington, 1954-59, asst. chief Office of Plans, 1960-61; dep. dir. Nat. Weather Records Ctr., Asheville, N.C., 1961; dir. Nat. Climatic Ctr., Asheville, 1963-75; pres. Climatol. Cons. Corp., Asheville, 1976—; mem. weather com. U.S. Power Squadron, Raleigh, N.C., 1988—. Contbr. articles to tech. jours., 1947-96. Bd. dirs. ARC, Asheville, 1965-70, United Way, Asheville, 1964-70. Capt. USN, 1942-45, with Res. 1951-54. Recipient Tech. Adminstr. award NOAA, Washington, 1970. Fellow Am. Meteorol. Soc. (cert. cons. meteorologist, bd. dirs. pvt. sector meteorology sect. 1989-92, mem. cert. cons. meteorologist bd. 1983-88), Nat. Coun. Indsl. Meteorologists (pres. 1988-89, bd. dirs. 1987-90, 94-96, sec., treas. 1994-96). Republican. Presbyterian. Office: Climatological Cons Corp 150 Shope Creek Rd Asheville NC 28805-9795

HAGGIS, LEWANNA STROM, principal, author, consultant; b. Youngstown, Ohio, Aug. 6, 1924; d. Charles Benjamin and Pearl (Simon) Strom; m. Arthur G. Haggis, Apr. 7, 1944; children: Lynda Lee, Arthur G. III, Richard Charles, Douglas Hood, Pamela Sue. BA, Youngstown Coll., 1946. Adminstr. top secret plans Office Dep. Chief Staff Mil. Ops. Dept. of the Army, The Pentagon, 1962-63; v.p. Haggis Assocs. Inc., Washington and Hollywood, Fla., 1964-71, Ednl. Cons. Inc., Washington and Hollywood, 1966—; v.p., prin. Atlantis Pvt. Schs., Inc., Hollywood, Fla., 1971—; bd. dirs., v.p. Atlantis Pub. Co., Hollywood, 1978—, Atlantis Rsch. Inst., Inc., Hollywood, 1981—; bd. dirs., vice chair. Atlantis-Lewart Group, Inc, Hollywood, 1988—; chmn. USO 1st Ann. Armed Forces Week Svc. Award, Ft. Lauderdale, Fla., 1990. Co-author: (books 1 and 2) Atlantis Beginning Language & Number Development Pro, 1981, (7 vols.) Atlantis Basic Spelling, 1982, (7 vols.) Atlantis Basic Arithmetic, 1982, EDU-CARE, The New School Concept, 1991. Founder, bd. dirs. USO Greater Ft. Lauderdale, Fla., 1988—; bd. dirs. Philharmonic Soc. Ft. Lauderdale, 1986—, Broward County chpt. Freedoms Found., Valley Forge, 1984—; active The Opera Guild, Inc., Ft. Lauderdale, 1985—, Rep. Senatorial Inner Circle, Washington, 1985—; bd. dirs. Protestant Parish Chapel, Patrick AFB, 1994—. Recipient USO Founding Dirs. award, USO Greater Ft. Lauderdale, 1988, Y-100 and Mobile Message award, 1990, USO Disting. Svc. award, 1991, Army Wife Extraordinaire award, 1995. Mem. ASCD, Assn. of U.S. Army (corp. mem., chmn. Fla. Gulf Stream chpt. JROTC medal awards com. 1986-96, Cert. of Appreciation 1996), Ret. Officers Assn., Army Wives Group (chmn. 1995—), Broward County Child Care and Kindergarten Assn., Officers Wives Club, North Arlington Newcomers Club (v.p. 1961-62). Republican. Lutheran. Home: 620 Verbenia Dr Indian Harbour Beach FL 32937-2533

HAGLER, ROBYN L., education educator; b. Birmingham, Ala., Feb. 20, 1959; d. Gene D. and Margaret A. (Duffey) H. BS, U. Montevallo, 1981, MEd in Secondary Edn., 1982, EdS in Secondary Edn., 1991. Part-time faculty mem., grad. asst. U. Montevallo, Ala., 1981-82, assoc. prof. edn., 1988—; tchr. Russellville (Ala.) H.S., 1982-85, Pelham (Ala.) H.S., 1987-88; rehab. specialist Ala. State Dept. Edn., Birmingham, 1985-87; faculty athletic rep. U. Montevallo, 1992—; bd. dirs. No. Ala. divsn. Nat. Safety Coun., Birmingham, 1994-96, sec., 1992-96. Vol. coord. 4-H Club, Ala., 1991—; instr. Ala. program Motorcycle Safety Found., 1989—. Mem. Am. Driver and Traffic Safety Edn. Assn. (mem. exec. southeast region 1993-96, pres. southeast region 1994-95, mem. com. 1992, 95), Assn. Driver Educators for the Disabled. Methodist. Home: PO Box 11 Montevallo AL 35115 Office: U Montevallo Sta 6740 Shelby St Montevallo AL 35115

HAGOOD, M. FELTON, surgeon; b. Marietta, Ga., Oct. 18, 1941; s. Murl Miller and Mary Evelyn (Jones) H.; m. Martha Addie James, June 20, 1965; children: Gregory Felton, Robert Miller, Richard James. MD, Emory U., 1966. Diplomate Am. Bd. Surgery. Am. Bd. Colon & Rectal Surgery. Intern U. Va. Hosp., Charlottesville, 1966-67, surg. resident, 1967-68; med. officer Charleston Naval Hosp. U.S. Navy, 1968-70; resident gen. surgery Med. U. S.C., 1970-73; fellow colon & rectal surgery Ochsner Found. Hosp., New Orleans, 1973-74; pvt. practice-colon & rectal surgery Kennestone Hosp., Marietta, 1974—. past pres. Am. Cancer Soc., 1978. Lt. cmdr. USNR, 1968-70. Mem. Cobb County Med. Soc. (pres. 1993-94), Kiwanis Club, Phi Beta Kappa, Alpha Omega Alpha. Methodist. Home: 577 Keeler Woods Dr Marietta GA 30064-2043 Office: Surg Assocs of Marietta 790 Church St Ste 500 Marietta GA 30060-7290

HAGOOD, SUSAN STEWART HAHN, clinical dietitian; b. Balt., May 31, 1953; d. Paul Gilbert and Phyllis Jeanette (Mann) Hahn; m. Thomas Richard Hagood, Jr., Nov. 25, 1978; 1 child, Margaret Foster. BS, Western Ky. U., 1975; MS, Ga. State U., 1992. Registered and lic. dietitian. Dietetic trainee U. Hosp., Jacksonville, Fla., 1975-76; clin. dietitian VA Med. Ctr., Lake City, Fla., 1976-80; in-service and staff devel. dietitian VA Med. Ctr., Lake City, 1980-85; clin. specialist Clayton Gen. Hosp., Riverdale, Ga., 1985-88; grad. teaching asst. Ga. State U., 1991; ambulatory care dietitian VA Med. Ctr., Atlanta, 1992—. Pres. Lake City (Fla.) Hist. Preservation Bd., 1982-83; chmn. youth adv. com. Columbia County 4-H, Lake City, 1981-84; vol. instr. Tech. Assistance Health Resource Group, Lake City, 1982-84; co-chmn. Com. for Restoration Columbia County Hist. Mus., 1983-84; bd. dirs. Clayton County unit Am. Heart Assn., 1987-88; mem. Dekalb unit nutrition and cancer work group Am. Cancer Soc., 1993—; leader Avondale-Decatur svc. unit Girl Scouts U.S.A., 1993—. Mem. Am. Dietetic Assn., Atlanta Dist. Dietetic Assn., Atlanta English Speaking Union, DAR, Colonial Dames Am., Colonial Dames XVII Century, Phi Upsilon Omicron, Alpha Xi Delta. Republican. Presbyterian. Home: PO Box 982 Decatur GA 30031-0982 Office: VA Medical Ctr 1670 Clairmont Rd Decatur GA 30033

HAGOOD, THOMAS RICHARD, JR., publisher; b. Charlotte, N.C., Sept. 16, 1954; s. Thomas Richard and Donna Gwendolyn (Williams) H.; m. Susan Stewart Hahn, Nov. 25, 1978; 1 child, Margaret Foster. BA, Davidson Coll., 1976; MDiv, Columbia Theol. Sem., 1996. Editor Columbia Publs., Inc., Decatur, Ga., 1976-88, publisher, 1988—. Scoutmaster Boy Scouts of Am., Lake City, Fla., 1982-85; pres. Columbian Countians, Lake City, 1982-85; mem. Govt. Study Com., Columbia County, Fla., 1984; elder Presbyn. Ch., Atlanta. Recipient Silver Beaver award North Fla. coun. Boy Scouts Am., 1986. Mem. English Speaking Union, Lake City Rotary (bd. dirs. 1982-85). Home: PO Box 982 Decatur GA 30031-0982

HAGOOD, WESLEY OLAN, management consultant; b. Annapolis, Md., Nov. 16, 1954; s. James Melvin and Eva Carol (Suit) H.; m. Denise Joane Lee, Dec. 18, 1976; children: Katherine, Mark, Kelley, Paul. BS in Math Edn., U. Md., 1977; MA in Edn., Bowie State U., 1982. Cert. advanced profl. tchr., Md. Math instr. Anne Arundel County Pub. Schs., Annapolis, Md., 1977-84; asst. programmer analyst IIT Rsch., Annapolis, 1984-85; course mgr. Ford Aerospace, Hanover, Md., 1985-87; mgr. Price Waterhouse, Washington, 1987-89; sr. assoc. Booz-Allen & Hamilton, McLean, Va., 1989—; founder Math Doctors, Annapolis, 1987, Anne Arundel County Tutoring Svc., Annapolis, 1988. Author: Presidential Sex, 1995. Sunday sch. tchr. New Hope Chapel, Annapolis, 1995. Home: 110 Boyd Dr Annapolis MD 21403

HAGY, TERESA JANE, elementary education educator; b. Bristol, Va., Nov. 1, 1950; d. Don Houston and Mary Garnett (Yeatts) Hagy. AA in Pre-Edn., Va. Intermont Coll., 1970, BA in Elem. Edn., 1972; MEd, U. Va., 1976, postgrad.; postgrad., Radford U. Cert. tchr., Va., Tenn. Tchr. 1st and 4th grades St. Anne's Demonstration Sch., Bristol, Va., 1972-75; tchr. 1st, 3d, 4th, 5th and 6th grades Washington Lee Elem. Sch., Bristol, 1975—; clin. instr. edn. Va. Intermont Coll., Bristol, 1972-75; coordinator gifted and talented program Bristol Schs., 1980-82; condr. workshops; developer tests to evaluate reading progress. Pres. women's circle Cen. Christian Ch., Bristol, Tenn., also v.p. women's fellowship, libr. chmn., mem. ch. choir, dir. music for Bible Sch., Sunday sch. tchr. 3d and 4th grades, 1979—. Recipient numerous edn. awards; named Tchr. of Yr., S.W. Va. Reading Coun., 1994, Tchr. of Quarter, Bible Sch., 1992. Mem. NEA, AAUW (sec. 1976-79, v.p. 1981-86), Va. Edn. Assn., Bristol Edn. Assn. (sec. 1978-80, chmn. Am. Edn. Week 1993, v.p.-membership chair 1994-95, faculty rep. 1996, sch. renewal steering com. sch. staff com. chmn. 1994—), Va. State Reading Assn., U. Va. Alumnae Assn., Va. Intermont Coll. Alumni Assn. (nat. pres. 1987-89), U. Va. Alumni Assn., Delta Kappa Gamma (chpt. v.p. 1986-88, pres. 1988-90, coordinating coun. chmn. 1990-92), Nat. Trust for Hist. Preservation, Phi Theta Kappa. Republican. Home: 820 Virginia Ave Bristol TN 37620-3935 Office: Washington Lee Elem Sch Washington Lee Dr Bristol VA 24201

HAHN, CATHY ANN CLIFFORD, sales executive; b. Celina, Ohio, June 6, 1947; d. William Eugene and Kathleen (McNally) Clifford; m. John Hahn (div.). BS, U. Dayton, 1969. Sales rep. J.T. Baker Instruments, Bridgeport, Conn., 1972-76, E.I. duPont de Nemours & Co., Dallas, 1976-81; new bus. developer E.I. duPont de Nemours & Co., Wilmington, Del., 1981-83, sr. tng. designer, 1983-84, sales tng. mgr., 1984-85; ter. mgr., trainer E.I. duPont de Nemours & Co., Dallas, 1985-94; v.p. Planet Cadillac Clothing Co., Plano, Tex., 1994-95; owner Metaluna Ltd. Co., Dallas, Tex., 1996—. Vol. Am. Cancer Soc., Dallas, 1986—. Home and Office: 5217 Old Shepard Pl Plano TX 75093-5002

HAHN, KEITH WORDEN, physiatrist; b. Ft. Lauderdale, Fla., Feb. 11, 1959; s. Theodore Wallace and Virginia (Kennedy) H.; m. Carol Blankenburg, Aug. 8, 1993. BA in Chemistry, Emory U., 1981; MD, U. South Fla., 1985. Diplomate Am. Bd. Physical Medicine and Rehab. Intern The Med. Ctr., Columbus, Ga., 1985-86; resident Univ. Tex., Dallas, 1986-89; med. dir. Lakeshore Rehab. Hosp., Birmingham, Ala., 1989-90; rehab. physician Tampa VA Hosp., 1990—. Active Nature Conservancy, Winter Park, Fla., 1989—, Covenant House, NYC, 1994—. Mem. Am. Acad. Physical Medicine and Rehab. (assoc.). Republican. Episcopalian. Home: 18311 Cypress Stand Cir Tampa FL 33647

HAHN, STANLEY ROBERT, JR., lawyer, financial executive; b. Louisville, Dec. 8, 1946; s. Stanley Robert and Dorothy Dodd (Moseley) H.; children from previous marriage: Laura, Valerie, Kathy; (div.). BBA in Fin., Ga. State U., MBA; LLM in Litigation, Atlanta Law Sch., JD. Bar: Ga. 1983, U.S. Dist. Ct. (no. dist.) Ga. 1983, U.S. Ct. Appeals (11th cir.) 1983, U.S. Ct. Apppeals (4th cir.) 1985, U.S. Supreme Ct. 1986. Mgr. credit White-Westinghouse Corp., Atlanta, 1975-77; mgr. fin. Am. Can Co., Greenwich, Conn., 1977—; pvt. practice Atlanta, 1983—; bd. dirs. HDC Investments Inc., Atlanta 1984—, Interest Unltd. Inc., Atlanta, 1985—. Mem. Assn. MBA Execs., Assn. Trial Lawyers Am., Nat. Assn. Credit Mgmt. Baptist. Club: Atlanta CB (pres. 1982-84). Home and Office: Ste 110 5865 Jimmy Carter Blvd Norcross GA 30071-4608

HAHN, THOMAS JOONGHI, accountant; b. Seoul, Korea, Apr. 12, 1955; came to U.S., 1979; s. Sang Jin and Seong Soon (Hong) H.; m. Linda Young Kim, May 26, 1984; children: Gina K., Michael J., Catherine S. BS, U. Md., 1982. CPA, CFP. Jr. acct. VerKenteren, Anerbach & Olson, CPAs, Silver Springs, Md., 1982-83; sr. acct. Chough, Oh & Co., CPAs, Silver Springs, 1983-85; ptnr. Lee & Hahn, CPAs, Falls Church, Va., 1985-87; prin. Thomas J. Hahn, CPA, Falls Church, 1987—; bd. dirs. STG, Inc., Fairfax, Va. Host weekly radio talk show, 1996—. Recipient Svc. award Posung H. S. Alumni Assn. of Greater Washington Area, 1992. Mem. AICPA, Va. Soc. CPAs. Roman Catholic. Office: Thomas J Hahn CPA 7777 Leesburg Pike Ste 305N Falls Church VA 22043-2403

HAHN, THOMAS MARSHALL, JR., forest products corporation executive; b. Lexington, Ky., Dec. 2, 1926; s. Thomas Marshall and Mary Elizabeth (Boston) H.; m. Margaret Louise Lee, Dec. 27, 1948; children: Elizabeth Hahn McKelvy, Anne Hahn Clarke. BS in Physics, U. Ky., 1945; PhD, MIT, 1950; LLD (hon.), Seton Hall U., 1976, Fla. So. Coll., 1986, U. Ky., 1990; PhD (hon.), Va. Poly. Inst., 1987; HHD (hon.), Presbn. Coll., 1989. Physicist U.S. Naval Ordinance Lab., 1946-47; rsch. asst. MIT, Cambridge, 1947-50; assoc. prof. physics U. Ky., Lexington, 1950-52, prof., 1952-54; prof., head dept. physics Va. Poly. Inst. and State U., Blacksburg, 1954-59, pres., 1962-75; dean arts and scis. Kans. State U., Manhattan, 1959-62; exec. v.p. chems. Ga.-Pacific Corp., Atlanta, 1975, exec. v.p. pulp, paper and chems., 1975-76, pres., 1976-82, pres., COO, 1982-83, pres., CEO, 1983-84, chmn. bd., pres., CEO, 1984-85, chmn. bd., CEO, 1985-93, bd. dirs., 1985-93, chmn. bd. dirs., 1993, hon. chmn. bd. dirs., 1993—; bd. dirs. Norfolk So. Corp., Coca-Cola Enterprises, Am. Paper Inst., chmn. 1982-83, Sun Trust Banks, Trust Co. Bank of Ga.; former chmn. N.Y. Stock Exchange Listed Co. Adv. Com.; exec. com. Nat. Coun. Pulp and Paper Industry on Air and Stream Improvement. Pres. So. Assn. Land Grant Colls. And State Univs., 1965-66; chmn. Va. Met. Area Study Commn., 1966-68, Va. Cancer Crusade ; bd. visitors Air U., 1966-69, Ferrum Jr. Coll.; bd. dirs. Atlanta Arts Alliance, Bus. Coun. Ga., Cen. Atlanta Progress, Keep Am. Beautiful Inc.; mem. adv. bd. Atlanta chpt. Boy Scouts Am.; former chmn. capital funds campaign Atlanta Area Svcs. for Blind, 1984; bd. visitors Callaway Gardens; mem. Atlanta Action Forum, Carter Ctr. Emory Univ. Bd. Councilors, nat. adv. bd. and campaign team greater Atlanta Salvation Army; former campaign chmn. Ga. chpt. Am. Diabetes Assn., 1985-86, United Way of Met. Atlanta Inc., 1987; Ga. chmn. U.S. Savs. Bond Program, 1985-87; trustee Emory U., Inst. Paper Chemistry, Robert W. Woodruff Arts Ctr., Emory U. (adv. coun.), Clark Atlanta U. With USN, 1945-46. Named Chief Exec. Officer of Yr. for forest products and lumber industry Wall Street Transcript, 1984-86, 88-91, Papermaker of Yr., Paper Trade Jour., 1984, PaperAge Mag., 1989, Chief Exec. Officer of Yr., Forest Products and Paper Industry, 1986, 89, Outstanding Alumnus of Ky. U. Ky., 1991, Top 10 Best Exec., Gallagher Report, 1986, 88; recipient Outstanding Citizen Va. award Toastmasters Internat., 1966, Outstanding Profl. Contbns. award Va. Citizens Planning Assn., 1970, Corp. Leadership award MIT, 1976, Silver and Bronze CEO awards Fin. World Mag., 1990, Ky. Advocates for Higher Edn. award U. Ky., 1991. Fellow Am. Phys. Soc., U. Ky.; mem. The Conf. Bd., Pres.'s Export Coun., Atlanta C. of C. (dir., past chmn.), Phi Beta Kappa, Sigma Xi, Omicron Delta Kappa. Republican. Methodist. Clubs: Piedmont Driving, The Links, Shenandoah, Capital City, Ocean Reef, Commerce. Office: Ga-Pacific Corp 133 Peachtree St NE Atlanta GA 30303*

HAHNE, C. E. (GENE HAHNE), computer services executive; b. Savannah, Ga., Sept. 21, 1940; s. Charles Eugene and Hortense (Kavanaugh) h.; m. Brenda Wike, Nov. 25, 1983; children: Gregory, Christopher, David, Stephanie. BS in Indsl. Mgmt., Ga. Inst. Tech., 1963. Sales mgr. Shell Oil Co., Cleve., 1969-72; head office rep. Shell Oil Co., Houston, 1973-75, mgr. tng., human resources and products, 1979-93; mgr. tng. and recruiting Shell Chem., Houston, 1976-78; CEO, chmn. bd. dirs. Intercom, The Woodlands, Tex., 1993—; mem. adv. coun. U. Houston, 1984-85, curriculum com., 1990-92; chair mktg. com. Houston C.C., 1987-90; speaker in field Europe, Can., S.Am., U.S. Author: Management Handbook, 1981, Training Handbook, 1986, Sales Training Handbook, 1991, Training and Development Handbook, 1995; contbr. articles to profl. jours. Mem. bus. and industry coun. Houston C.C., 1986—; mem. adv. coun. Tex. A&M U., College Station, 1985-88; chair fundraising com. Brookwood Cmty., Houston, 1986-88; bd. dirs. Interact, Houston, 1983, U. Tex., Austin, 1984-85, H.R. Comm. Recipient Speaker's award United Way, 1988, Pres. award Houston Community Coll., 1987, Tex. Vocat. Excellence award, 1990. Mem. ASTD (nat. bd. treas. 1981-86, Gordon M. Bliss award 1989, Torch award 1987, Lifetime Recognition award 1989, Disting. Contbn. to Cmty./Nation award 1984, James Ball award 1981), World Future Soc., Sales and Mktg. Execs. of Houston (bd. dirs. 1986-88), Soc. for Human Resource Mgmt. Republican. Home: 20210 Atascocita Lake Dr Humble TX 77346-1659

HAID, STEPHEN DONALD, health facility administrator; b. St. Louis, Oct. 4, 1951; s. William Riley and Sarah Felicia (Accardo) H.; m. Jamie Sue Blaine Haid, Apr. 27, 1985; children: Cristin Jennifer, Michael Stephen. BA, U. Mo., 1973; MS, Tex. Woman's U., Denton, 1992. Cert. transplant procurement coord. Rsch. assoc. Jewish Hosp. St. Louis, 1971-74; life sci. tech. III Stanford (Calif.) U. Med. Sch., 1974; supr. Organ Procurement Washington U. Sch. Medicine, St. Louis, 1974-82; mgr. recovery svcs. S.W. Organ Bank, Dallas, 1982-88; dir. organ procurement Organ Recovery Systems, Inc., Dallas, 1985-87; exec. dir. S.W. Organ Bank, Dallas, 1987—, Organ Recovery Systems, Inc., Dallas, 1987—; treas. Organ Recovery Systems, Inc., 1995—; editl. adv. bd. Nephrology News and Issues, Scottsdale, Ariz., 1991—; editl. bd. Jour. Transplant Coord., Mpls., 1991—. Contbr. articles to profl. jours.; numerous presentations in field. Sec. S.W. Soccer Club, DeSoto, Tex., 1991-92; mem. Tex. Organ Procurement Com., Austin, Tex., 1995. Recipient High Scholastic Achievement award Phi Kappa Phi Honor Soc., Denton, Tex., 1990-91; named Inductee Phi Kappa Phi Honor Soc., Denton, Tex., 1991. Mem. Assn. Organ Procurement Orgn., N.Am. Transplant Coord., Internat. Soc. HEart Transplantation, Am. Mgmt. Assn., Tex. Transplantation Soc., Rotary. Office: Organ Recovery Systems Inc 3500 Maple Ave Ste 800 Dallas TX 75219-3903

HAIGHT, CAROL BARBARA, lawyer; b. Buffalo, May 3, 1945; d. Robert H. Johnson and Betty R. (Walker) Hawkes; m. H. Granville Haight, May 28, 1978 (dec. Nov. 1983); children: David Michael, Kathleen Marie. BSW summa cum laude, Widener U., Chester, Pa., 1980, BA in Psychology summa cum laude, 1980; JD cum laude, Widener U., Wilmington, Del., 1984. Assoc. Pepper, Hamilton & Scheetz, Phila., 1985-88, Hodgson, Russ, Andrews, Woods & Goodyear, Buffalo, 1988-90; pvt. practice Boca Raton, Fla., 1990—; arbitrator Am. Arbitration Assn., 1988—, mediator, 1989—, mediation instr.; founding dir. Mediation Ednl. Svc.: Coun. for Marriage Preservation and Divorce Resolution, Inc., 1992. Contbr. article to profl. jours. Mem. ABA (com. on adr), Pa. Bar Assn., Fla. Bar Assn., Phi Kappa Phi, Phi Alpha Delta, Phi Gamma Mu. Republican. Episcopalian. Home: Braemar Isle Townhouse 9 4744 S Ocean Blvd Highland Beach FL 33487-5343 Office: 370 Camino Gardens Blvd Ste 300 Boca Raton FL 33432-5817

HAIK, RICHARD T., SR., federal judge; b. 1950. BS, U. Southwestern La., 1971; JD, Loyola U., New Orleans, 1975. Assoc. Haik & Broussard, 1975-79; ptnr. Haik, Broussard & Haik, 1979-81, Haik, Haik & Minvielle, 1981-84; judge La. State Dist., New Iberia, 1984-91; dist. judge U.S. Dist. Ct. (we. dist.) La., 1991—. With USAR, 1978-81; USNG, 1971-78. Mem. ABA, La. Bar Assn., Iberia Parish Bar Assn., La. Dist. Judge's Assn. (exec. com. 1988-91), Nat. Coun. Juvenile and Family Ct. Judges (steering com. alcohol and substance abuse). Office: US Dist Ct Fed Bldg 705 Jefferson St Ste 213 Lafayette LA 70501-6936*

HAILE, L. JOHN, JR., journalist, newspaper executive; b. Cleveland, Tenn., Mar. 20, 1945; s. Loyd Johnson and Pearl Edith (Gilliland) H.; m. Gwen Marie Jones, Sept. 4, 1965; children: Philip Alan, John Christopher. B.A., Vanderbilt U., Nashville, 1967; M.S. in Journalism, Boston U., 1969. Polit. reporter The Nashville Tennessean, 1966-79; dep. mng. editor The Orlando Sentinel, Fla., 1979-81, assoc. editor, 1981-85, editor, 1985—; juror Pulizer Prize Com., 1992-93. Nat. Endowment Humanities Profl. Journalism fellow, 1975-76. Mem. Am. Soc. Newspaper Editors, Fla. Soc. Newspaper Editors. Office: The Orlando Sentinel 633 N Orange Ave Orlando FL 32801-1300*

HAILS, ROBERT EMMET, aerospace consultant, business executive, former air force officer; b. Miami, Fla., Jan. 20, 1923; s. Daniel Troy and Jean (Burke) H.; m. Ethel Fitzgerald Gayle, Mar. 2, 1957; children: Robert Emmet Jr., Merrily G., Florence T. Hails Patton, Laura Hails Smith. BS in Aero. Engring., Auburn U., 1947; MS in Indsl. Engring., Columbia U., 1950; postgrad., C&CS Air U., 1955; postgrad. AMP, Harvard U. Sch. Bus., 1965. Enlisted USAAF, 1942, commd. 2d lt., 1944, advanced through grades to lt. gen., 1974, combat pilot Pacific Theater, 1944-45; assigned to SAC, 1947-48; inspector gen. Hdqrs. USAF, 1950-53; program devel. officer Marcel Dassault Mystere IV Jet Aircraft, French Air Force Am. embassy, Paris, 1953-55; air staff project officer F-104/F-105 aircraft HQ USAF, 1956-60; comdr. procurement dist. USAF, San Francisco, 1960-62; mil. asst. for weapons systems acquisition Office Sec. AF, 1962-66; system program dir. Joint USAF/USN A-7D Aircraft Engring., Devel., Test & Prodn., AF Systems Cmmd., 1966-68; dep. chief staff maintenance engring. Air Force Logistics Command, 1968-71; comdr. Def. Pers. Support Ctr. Def. Log. Agy., Phila., 1971-72; comdr. Air Logistics Ctr. USAF, Warner Robins AFB, Ga., 1972-74; vice comdr. Tactical Air Command Langley AFB, Va., 1974-75; dep. chief staff systems and logistics Hdqrs. USAF, Washington, 1975-77; ret. USAF, Washington, 1977; mgmt. cons. Atlanta, 1978-80; sr. v.p. internat. ops. LTV Corp., Dallas, 1980-84; pres. Hails Assocs. Inc., Macon, Ga., 1984—; mem. sci. bd. Loral Corp., Macon, Ga. Regional exec. Boy Scouts Am.; mem. Auburn U. Alumni Engring. Coun.; bd. advisors Wesleyan Coll. Decorated DSM with 2 oak leaf clusters, legion of Merit with 2 oak leaf clusters, Air medal with 2 oak leaf clusters; Order of Nat. Security (Korea). Mem. AIAA, Air Force Assn., Daedalians, Auburn U. SPADES, Army-Navy Country Club (Arlington, Va.), Idle Hour Golf and Country Club, Omicron Delta Kappa, Sigma Alpha Epsion. Roman Catholic. Office: PO Box 5290 Macon GA 31208-5290

HAIMAN, ROBERT JAMES, newspaper editor, journalism educator; b. Norwich, Conn., May 6, 1936; s. Albert and Letta (Cone) H.; m. Elizabeth Royce Greenlaw, Sept. 26, 1964 (div. Aug. 1996); 1 child, Robert Greenlaw. Student, U. Conn., 1953-55; BS, U. Fla., 1957. Reporter St. Petersburg (Fla.) Times, 1958-60, copy editor, 1962-63, nat. editor, 1964-66, mng. editor, 1966-76, exec. editor, 1976-83; pres., mng. dir. Poynter Inst. Media Studies, 1983—; bd. dirs. Times Pub. Co., St. Petersburg; trustee Fla. InterAm. Scholarship Found.; mem. minority mgmt. task force Inst. Journalism Edn. Mem. pres. round table Eckerd Coll.; trustee Poynter Inst. Media Studies, St. Petersburg; mem. Pulitzer Prize jury, 1977, 90, 91, 96; internat. adv. bd. Inst. Advancement Journalism, Johannesburg, South Africa. Mem. Pres.'s coun. U. Fla., U. South Fla.; chmn. campus adv. bd. U. South Fla., 1989-91; mem. journalism adv. bd. Knight Found., Inst. Current World Affairs, Hanover, N.H., Tampa Bay Com. Coun. on Fgn. Rels.; trustee Bayfront Ctr. Found.; elder Presbyn. Ch. With USMC, 1961. Named Disting. Alumnus, U. Fla., 1988. Mem. AP Mng. Editors Assn. (pres. 1982), Am. Soc. Newspaper Editors (dir. 1992—), Internat. Press Inst. (Vienna), Interam. Press Assn., Racquet Club, St. Petersburg Yacht Club, Dragon Club, Quarterback Club, Golden Triangle Club, Soc. Profl. Journalists. Democrat. Home: Isla Key # 103 5155 Isla Key Blvd S Saint Petersburg FL 33715-1687 Office: 801 3rd St S Saint Petersburg FL 33701-4920

HAIMO, MICHAEL JAY, colon and rectal surgeon; b. Mt. Vernon, N.Y., May 30, 1941; s. Alan and Sylvia (Schrier) H.; m. Kathalyn Feuer; children: Adam, Barry. BA, Brandeis U., 1963; MD, SUNY, Bklyn., 1967. Intern Boston City Hosp., 1968; resident Hartford (Conn.) Hosp., 1972; gen. surgeon Plantation, Fla., 1977-82; fellow colon and rectal surgery Dallas, 1982-83; colon and rectal surgeon Tamarac, Fla., 1983—. Major U.S. Army, 1973-75. Fellow Am. Soc. Colon and Rectal Surgeons; mem. AMA, Fla. Soc. Colon and Rectal Surgeons (sec. 1990-95, 95-97), Broward County Med. Soc., Fla. Med. Soc. Office: 7421 N University Dr Fort Lauderdale FL 33321-2977

HAINES, DUANE E., neuroscience educator, academic administrator; b. Springfield, Ohio, May 4, 1943; s. Lester Lee and Marjorie (Herr) H.; m. Gretchen Clubb, July 1, 1983; children: Kristian, Aaron. BA, Greenville Coll., 1965; MS, Mich. State U., 1967, PhD, 1969. Instr. Mich. State U., East Lansing, 1968-69; asst. prof. Med. Coll. Va., Richmond, 1969-73; assoc. prof. W.Va. U. Sch. Medicine, Morgantown, 1973-78, prof., 1978-85, assoc. chair, 1982-85; prof. and chair U. Miss. Med. Ctr., Jackson, 1985—. Author: Neuroanatomy, An Atlas of Structures, Sections and Systems, 4th edit., 1995; assoc. editor Jour. Med. Primatology, 1977-95; mem. editl. bd. Anat. Record, 1985—, Metabolic Brain Disease, 1992—; neuroanatomy cons. Stedman's Medical Dictionary, 26th edit., 1994; contbr. rsch. papers to profl. jours. Named Ronneberg lectr. Denison U., 1992. Fellow Royal Anthropol. Inst.; mem. Am. Assn. Anatomists, Am. Assn. Phys. Anthropology, Neurosci. Soc., Inst. Brain Rsch. Orgns., Sigma Xi. Office: U Miss Sch Medicine 2500 N State St Jackson MS 39216-4500

HAINES, HELEN DRAKE, diversified manufacturing and service company assistant controller; b. Chattanooga, Apr. 2, 1943; d. Charles Barry and Madelyn Lenis (Garner) Neill; m. Stanley Alan Haines, Dec. 20, 1987; BA in Math., Fla. State U., 1966; MBA in Acctg., Ga. State U., 1977. Acctg. clk. Ga. Dept. State, 1962-66; accountant Modern Foods, Inc., Winter Haven, Fla., 1970-72; Staff acct. Nat. Service Industries, Inc., Atlanta, 1972-73, acctg. supr., 1974-75, mgr. corp. acctg., 1975-81, mgr. fin. planning and analysis, 1981-82, asst. to treas., 1982-83, asst. controller, 1983-90, asst. v.p. and asst. controller fin. reporting, 1991—. C.P.A., Ga. Mem. Am. Inst. CPA's, Ga. Soc. CPA's. Republican. Episcopalian. Home: 1690 Pineford Ct Stone Mountain GA 30088-4125 Office: Nat Svc Industries 1420 Peachtree St NE Atlanta GA 30309-3002

HAINES, KENNETH H., television broadcasting executive; b. Spokane, Sept. 5, 1942; s. Kenneth A. and Helen Elizabeth (Evans) H.; m. Stephanie Marie Phelps, Nov. 23, 1981; 1 child, Avery Jordan. BA, Dakota Wesleyan U., 1964; MA, U. Wyo.; MS, Troy State U., 1970; EdD, Va. Tech., 1976. News dir. KORN TV, Mitchell, S.D., 1962-64; sta. mgr. KUWR Radio, Laramie, Wyo., 1965-67; gen. mgr. KLME Radio, Laramie, 1967-68; instr. flight ops. U.S. Army, Ft. Rucker, Ala., 1968-70; from dir. radio, tv, film to dir. pub. affairs, univ. rels. Va. Tech., Blacksburg, 1970-81; from dir. network ops. to exec. v.p. Raycom Sports, Charlotte, N.C., 1981—; bd. dirs. Charlotte Sports Commn. Named reporter of yr. UPI, 1967; recipient golden award Coun. Support Higher Edn., 1978. Mem. Am. Assn. Agriculture Writers, Am. Coll. Pub. Rels. Assn. (exceptional achievement award 1974), Va. Press Assn., Coun. for Advancement & Support of Edn. (pres. univ. faculty club 1980-82), Charlotte C. of C., Phi Kappa Delta., Pi Delta Epsilon. Home: 1909 Carmel Rd Charlotte NC 28226 Office: Raycom Sports 412 East Blvd Charlotte NC 28233

HAINES, PHILIP A., pharmacist; b. Binghamton, N.Y., Nov. 18, 1958; s. George Joseph and Mary Margaret (Moore) H.; m. Karen Mary Palmer, Aug. 21, 1984; children: Erin, Michelle, Bridget. BS in Pharmacy, Mass. Coll. Pharmacy, Boston, 1981. Lic. pharmacist, Fla., Mass. Pharmacist Mass. Gen. Hosp., Boston, 1981-84; IV pharmacist St. Vincent's Med. Ctr., Jacksonville, Fla., 1984-89; clin. pharmacy coord. Integrated Pharmacy Solutions, Jacksonville, 1989-96, asst. dir. pharmacy, 1996—. Editor Pharmacy and Therapeutics newsletter, 1989—. Mem. Am. Soc. Health Sys. Pharmacists. Republican. Roman Catholic. Home: 13400 Mossy Cypress Dr Jacksonville FL 32223 Office: Integrated Pharmacy Solutions 1200 Riverplace Blvd Ste 301 Jacksonville FL 32207-9046

HAINSWORTH, MELODY MAY, information professional, researcher; b. Vancouver, B.C., Can., May 13, 1946; m. Robert John Hainsworth, Jan. 6, 1968; children: Kaleeg William, Shane Alan. BA with honors, Simon Fraser U., Vancouver, 1968; MLS, Dalhousie U., Halifax, N.S., Can., 1976; PhD, Fla. State U., Tallahassee, 1992. Libr. Dept. Edn. of Tanzania, Mbeya, 1969-72, Dept. of Edn. of Zambia, Mwinilunga, 1972-74; law libr., deptl. libr. Dept. of Atty. Gen. of N.S., Halifax, 1975-77; regional libr. Provincial Ct. Librs. Dept. of Atty. Gen. of Alta., Calgary, 1977-80, So. Alta. Law Soc. libr., 1980-89; dir. librs. Keiser Coll., Tallahassee, 1992-93; v.p. info. resources and svcs. Internat. Coll., Naples, Fla., 1993—; adj. instr. Sch. Libr. and Info. Studies, Fla. State U., Tallahassee, 1990-91; speaker in field; active Women's Polit. Caucus. Author monographs; contbr. articles to profl. jours. Pres. Naples Free Net, 1993—; co-chair adv. com. com. on edn. and tech. Fla. State Bd. Ind. Colls. and Univs., 1993—; pres. Pvt. Coll. and Univ. Libr. Consortium Bd., 1995—; founding mem. Pub. Access to the Law of Fla., 1990—; mem. adv. bd. paralegal program Ft. Lauderdale Coll., Tallahassee, 1990-92; mem. exec. bd. Calgary Legal Guidance, 1985—, vice chmn., 1988-89, hon. life mem.; tech. grant com. Collier County Edn. Found., 1994—. Student Leader Bursaries Simon Fraser U. scholar, 1966-68; H.W. Wilson scholar Dalhousie U., 1974; Fla. State U. grad. asst., 1989-90. Mem. Spl. Librs. Assn (chair 1994—), North Fla. Libr. Assn., Fla. State, Ct. and County Librs. Assn., Tallahassee Law Librs. Assn., Fla. Libr. Assn., Assn. Libr. and Info. Sci. Edn., Alta. Legal Archives Soc. (hon. life), Collier County Bar Assn., Tempo, Naples Press Club. Office: Internat Coll 2654 Tamiami Trl E Naples FL 34112-5707

HAIRALD, MARY PAYNE, vocational education educator, coordinator; b. Tupelo, Miss., Feb. 25, 1936; d. Will Burney and Ivey Lee (Berryhill) Payne; m. Leroy Utley Hairald, May 31, 1958; 1 child, Burney LeShawn. BS in Commerce, U. Miss., 1957, M in Bus. Edn., 1963; postgrad., Miss. Coll.,

1964, Miss. State U., 1970, U. So. Miss., 1986-88, 90. Bus. edn. tchr. John Rundle High Sch., Grenada, Miss., 1957-59; youth recreation leader City of Nettleton, Miss., summers 1960-61; tchr. social studies Nettleton Jr. High Sch., 1959-70; tchr.-coord. coop. vocat. edn. program Nettleton High Sch., 1970—; area mgr. World Book, Inc., Chgo., 1972-84; local coord. Am. Inst. for Fgn. Study, Greenwich, Conn., 1988—; instr. bus. Itawamba C.C., Tupelo, 1975-80; sponsor Coop. Vocat. Edn. Club, Nettleton, 1970—; advisor DECA, Nettleton, 1985—; apptd. adv. coun. mem. Miss. Coop. Edn.-State Dept. Edn. Editor advisor State DECA Newsletter, 1987-92; contbr. articles on coop. edn. to newspapers. Co-organizer Nettleton Youth Recreation Booster Club; fundraiser Muscular Dystrophy Assn.; Sunday sch. tchr. coll. and career class Nettleton United Meth. Ch. Recipient 1st place Nat. Newsletter award Nat. DECA, 1988, 89, 90, 92, Excellence in Supervision award Am. Inst. for Fgn. Study, 1992; named Star Tchr., Miss. Econ. Coun., 1978, 95, Dist. II DECA Advisor of Yr., Miss. Assn. DECA, 1990, 93, Nat. DECA Hall of Fame charter mem., 1996. Mem. AAUW (charter), Am. Vocat. Assn. (Region IV Coop. Vocat. Edn. Tchr. of Yr. 1985, Region IV Mktg. Edn. Tchr. of Yr. 1988, Region IV New and Related Svcs. Tchr. of Yr. 1996, Region IV Outstanding Vocat. Tchr. of Yr. 1996), Coop. Work Experience Edn. Assn., Miss. Assn. Vocat. Educators (dist. sec.), Miss. Assn. Coop. Vocat. Edn. Tchrs. (v.p. 1980-83, pres. 1983-84, Miss. Tchr. of Yr. 1984, 87, d5), Miss. Assn. Mktg. Educators (Dist. II Tchr. of Yr. 1993, 94), Mktg. Edn. Assn., Nettleton Ladies Civitan Club (charter), Phi Delta Kappa. Democrat. Methodist. Home: PO Box 166 Nettleton MS 38858-0166

HAIRE, WILLIAM J., healthcare executive; b. Hillsdale, Mich., Aug. 19, 1944; s. John Monroe and Virginia H.; m. Salene B. Haire; children: Jennifer, Gregory. BA, Austin Coll., 1966; MHA, Trinity U., 1969. Adminstrn. resident Presbyn. Hosp. of Dallas, 1969-70, asst. adminstr., 1970-73; asst. adminstr. Presbyn. Hosp. Ctr., Albuquerque, 1973-76; adminstr. Kaseman Presbyn. Hosp., Albuquerque, 1976-79; regional adminstr. Presbyn. Healthcare Svc., Albuquerque, 1979-86; pres., CEO Capital Hill Hosp., Washington, 1986-89; exec. v.p. Presbyn. Healthcare System, Dallas, 1989—; bd. dirs. Dallas/Ft. Worth Hosp. Assn., 1991—, Capital Hill Assn. Merchants/Profls., Washington, 1987-89, D.C. Hosp. Assn., 1986-89; mem. adv. bd. Healthcare Risk Mgmt. Cert. Program, Chgo., 1985—. Chair United Way-Healthcare divsn., Washington and Dallas, 1987-91. Mem. Am. Hosp. Assn., Am. Coll. Healthcare Execs., Tex. Hosp. Assn. Office: Presbyn Hosp Dallas 8200 Walnut Hill Ln Dallas TX 75231-4402*

HAIST, CHARLES FREDERICK, systems engineer; b. Hershey, NE, Apr. 3, 1936; s. William Mitchell and Edna Lillian (Johnson) H.; m. Gwendolyn Jane (Polly) Chandler, Jan. 30, 1959; children: Erika Gabrielle, Christopher Frederick. BSEE, Okla. State U., 1962. Jr. engr. IBM, Owego, N.Y., 1962, assoc. engr., 1963; sr. assoc. engr. IBM, Huntsville, Ala., 1964-72; adv. engr. IBM, Boca Raton, Fla., 1971-72, devel. engr., 1973; v.p. ops. Fred Chandler & Enterprises, Winnfield, La., 1973-74; sr. subsys. mgr. U.S. Boosters, Inc., Huntsville, 1974-84; dir. advanced engring. Singer Link, Houston, 1984-86; dir. acquisition mgmt. CAE-Link, Houston, 1987-89, sr. sys. engr., 1990—; mem. Coun. Def. Sys. Industry Assn., 1965-69. Co-author: Program Management Manual, 1989; editor: An Hypothesis for Total Systems Management, 1967. Scoutmaster Boy Scouts Am., Huntsville, 1976; com. mem. Lunar Rondevous Festival, Clear Lake City, Tex., 1994. With USAF, 1955-59. Mem. Nat. Mgmt. Assn. (pres. Link chpt. 1994-95, bd. dirs. 1987-88), Nat. Coun. Systems Engring. (charter), Masons, Scottish Rite. Republican. Episcopalian. Home: 539 Shadylawn St Shoreacres TX 77571-7254 Office: HTI Link 2224 Bay Area Blvd Houston TX 77058-2008

HAJEK, FRANCIS PAUL, lawyer; b. Hobart, Tasmania, Australia, Oct. 21, 1958; came to U.S., 1966; s. Frank Joseph and Kathleen Beatrice (Blake) H. BA, Yale U., 1980; JD, U. Richmond, 1984. Bar: Va. 1984, U.S. Dist. Ct. (ea. dist.) Va. 1984, U.S. Ct. Appeals (4th cir.) 1986. Law clk. to presiding magistrate U.S. Dist Ct., Norfolk, Va., 1984-85; assoc. Seawell, Dalton, Hughes & Timms, Norfolk, 1985-87, Weinberg & Stein, Norfolk, 1987-89, Wilson & Hajek, Virginia Beach, Va., 1989—, I'Anson-Hoffman Am. Inn of Ct. Mem. ABA, Assn. Trial Lawyers Am., Va. Bar Assn., Norfolk-Portsmouth Bar Assn. (chmn. exec. com. young lawyer's sect. 1990-91). Roman Catholic. Home: 2116 Windward Shore Dr Virginia Beach VA 23451 Office: Wilson & Hajek PO Box 5369 Virginia Beach VA 23455

HALBARDIER, SHERYL LINETTE, social studies educator, counselor; b. San Antonio, Sept. 13, 1948; d. Edward William and Barbara (Hensley) Halbardier; m. John Sterling Thompson, May 14, 1979 (div. Mar. 1982). BS in Elem. Edn., U. Tex., 1970; postgrad., Our Lady of the Lake Coll., San Antonio, 1981—; student, U. Paris, 1969. Lic. chem. dependency counselor, Tex. Substance abuse prevention specialist Edgewood Ind. Sch. Dist., San Antonio, 1986-90; rsch. asst. Univ. Health Scis./U. Tex. Health Sci. Ctr., San Antonio, 1990-92; tchr. social studies and sci. Dallas Ind. Sch. Dist., 1992-94; owner, counselor Co-A-Tots, San Antonio, 1994—; Mem. adv. bd. on writing fed. grants Edgewood Ind. Sch. Dist., 1986-88, Ark. County Youth Support Ctr., Rockport, Tex., 1989. Author: Co-A-Tots, 1996. Job coach for mentally retarded Alamo Hts. Manor, San Antonio, 1995-96; aide Rep. Task Force, Washington, 1980-96. Our Lady of the Lake U. fellow, 1990. Mem. Women in Bus., Tex. Com. on Alcoholism and Drug Abuse. Roman Catholic. Home and Office: 101 Arcadia Pl # 209 San Antonio TX 78209

HALBREICH, JEREMY L., newspaper publishing executive. Pres. and gen. mgr. The Dallas Morning News. Office: The Dallas Morning News Communications Center PO Box 655237 Dallas TX 75265*

HALBROOK, RITA ROBERTSHAW, artist, sculptor; b. Greenville, Miss., May 22, 1930; d. William Daniel and Artye Loree (Robinson) R.; m. David McCall Halbrook, Oct. 1, 1949; children: Ann L. Peden, D. M. Jr., Tina H. Donahoo, Andrew L. BFA, Delta State U., 1982. Bd. dirs. Miss. Art Colony, Utica, 1977-80, publicity dir., 1977-84. One-woman shows include Miss. ETV Studios, Jackson, 1985, Gulf South Gallery, McComb, Miss., 1987, State Capitol Rotunda, Jackson, State Dept. Agr. and Miss. Arts Commn., 1988, New Stage Theatre, Jackson, 1992, The Courthouse Racquet Club Galleries, Jackson, 1992; two-woman show Pegasus Gallery, Miss. State U., 1986; exhibited in group shows at Cottonlandia Mus., Greenwood, Miss., 1987, 93, Miss. Mus. Art, Jackson, 1989, 93, Gov.'s Mansion, Southeastern Crafts Conf., Jackson, 1991, Miss. Mus. Art, Jackson, Wiregrass Mus. Art, Dothan, Ala., 1993, Cork Gallery, Avery Fisher Hall, Lincoln Ctr. Pla., N.Y.C., 1994, others; commd. artist Delta Catfish Mus., Belzoni, Miss., 1993, St. Therese's Cath. Ch., Jackson, 1996, others; represented in collections Delta State U., Ernst and Whinney, Tatung, Inc. (Taiwan), Citizens Bank Yazoo City, former Pres. and Mrs. George Bush, The White House; subject in publs.: (books) Mississippi Artsts, 1977, Of Arts and Artists, 1980, Artists of the South, Vol. I, 1992, (newspaper) The Clarion Ledger-Jackson Daily News, 1985. Mem. county com. Miss. Republicans, 1963-69, inter-agy. coun. Partners in Health and Nutrition, 1989—, parish coun. All Saints Cath. Ch.; bd. dirs. Helping Hands Humphreys County, 1991—. Recipient Best in Show and Second award Miss. Art Colony, 1986, Best in Show, Nat. League Am. PEN Women, 1987, 95. Mem. Nat. League Am. Pen Women (pres. Delta, Miss. br. 1996—), Craftsmen's Guild Miss. (exhibiting, bd. dirs. 1993-96), Profl. Artists League Miss., Ofcl. Miss. Women's Club, Delta State U. Alumni Assn. (Disting. 1993). Democrat. Home: 501 Cohn St Belzoni MS 39038-3703 Studio: 301 Hayden St Belzoni MS 39038

HALDEN, MARTHA ANN, pediatrics nurse, educator; b. Dallas, July 22, 1933; d. Ollie and Nona I. (Lavender) Gouger; m. William J. Halden, Oct. 23, 1954; children: William J., Sue Halden Albe, Daniel L., Mary Beth Sherman. Student, So. Meth. U., 1950-51; diploma, Meth. Hosp. of Dallas, 1954. RN. Pediatric nurse physician's office, Austin, Tex., Dallas. Mem. Tex. Nurses Assn.

HALE, ALBERT SPENCER, JR., radiologist; b. Salem, Va., Nov. 19, 1933; s. Albert Spencer and Julia Caldwell (Meyer) H.; m. Lorraine Helen Decker, June 7, 1958; children: David W., Sharon M., Stephen M., Michael A. BS, Wake Forest U., 1954; MD, Bowman Gray Sch. Medicine, Winston-Salem, N.C., 1958. Diplomate Am. Bd. Radiology., Am. Bd. Nuclear Medicine. Intern Grady Meml. Hosp., Atlanta, 1958-59; resident in radiology Bowman Gray Sch. Medicine, 1961-64; advanced through grades to col. USAF, 1959-89; chief profl. svcs. 517th Med. Group, Pease AFB, N.H., 1959-61; chief radiology svc. USAF Hosp. Carswell, Ft. Worth, 1964-67, USAF Hosp. Clark, Clark Air Base, The Philippines, 1967-69, USAF Acad. Hosp., Colo. Springs, Colo., 1969-74; chmn. dept. radiology Wilford Hall USAF Med. Ctr., Lackland AFB, Tex., 1974-89; chief radiology dept. Tex. Ctr. for Infectious Disease, San Antonio, 1990—. Fellow Am. Coll. Radiology; mem. Soc. Nuc. Medicine, Radiol. Soc. N.Am. Home: 5303 Chancellor St San Antonio TX 78229

HALE, ARNOLD WAYNE, religious educator, army officer, clergyman, psychotherapist; b. Colome, S.D., Sept. 2, 1934; s. Archiebald William and Alvena Lucille (Williams) H.; m. Mary Alice Mauricio, Nov. 30, 1962; 1 child, Alexander; children by previous marriage: Colleen, Zola; stepchildren: Charles, Marlow. BA, U. S.D., 1959; MEd, Our Lady of the Lake U., 1971, MEd, 1973; BS, U. State of N.Y., Albany, 1976; AA, Austin Comm. Coll., 1979; ministerial cert. Gospel Ministry Inst., 1981; DD (hon.), Gospel Ministry Ctr., 1981; diploma ministerial studies, Berean Coll., 1983; ThD, Reeves Christian Seminary, 1984, D of Ministry, 1990; PhD, Christian Bible Coll., 1994. Ordained to ministry Gospel Ministry Ctr. Full Gospel Ch. in Christ, Victory New Testament Fellowship Internat., 1983. Infantryman, U.S. Army, 1953-55, commd. lt., 1959, advanced through ranks to maj., 1973, served in various staff and mgmt. positions with Med. Service Corps, 1959-67, med. adviser Mil. Assistance Command, Vietnam, 1967-68, ednl. tng. officer, U.S. Army Med. Tng. Ctr., Ft. Sam Houston, Tex., 1968-73, hosp. comdr., Ft. Campbell, Ky., 1973-75, med. adviser Tex. Army N.G., Austin, 1975-77, ret., 1977; librarian Thorndale/Milano Independent Sch. Dists., Milam County, Tex., 1977-78; instr. psychology Austin Community Coll., 1977-79; librarian, dist. test adminstr. Austwell-Tivoli Ind. Sch. Dist., Tex., 1979-81; adult probation officer Travis County (Tex.), 1981-82; founding min.-counselor Chaplain Biblio Edn. Counseling Ministry, 1983—. Decorated Bronze Star; recipient Duke of Paducah award, 1975, Experienced Pastoral Counselor award Inst. Experienced Pastoral Counselors, 1981, Commemorative medal of honor Am. Biog. Inst., 1985, Appreciation plaque Messengers of Great King, 1994, Faithful Svc. cert., Trinity Ch. of Assemblies of God, 1996, Appreciation cert., Ministries United, 1996, Order of Merit, Nat. Rep. Senatorial Com., 1996. Mem. ALA (bibliotherapy discussion group), NEA, Am. Pers. and Guidance Assn., Christians United for Israel, Am. Assn. Christian Counselors, PTL Club, Nat. Chaplains Assn., Internat. Platform Assn., Tex. Jr. Coll. Tchrs. Assn., CAP (maj., med. advisor, chaplain), Ret. Officers Assn. (life), N.G. Assn. Tex. (life), Mil. Order World Wars, Assn. U.S. Army, U.S. Armor Assn., Inst. of Experienced Pastoral Counselors (diplomate advanced Christain pastoral counselor), Internat. Assn. of Christian Pastoral Counselors (diplomate 1987), United Assn. of Christian Counselors Internat. (diplomate), Full Gospel Biblio Counseling Ministry Soc. (diplomate 1989), Am. Acad. Clin. Family Therapists (supervising clin. therapist), Christian Assn. Psychol. Studies, Am. Assn. Marriage and Family Therapy (clin. mem.), Am. Legion (life), VFW (life). Club: Masons (Fed. Republic West Germany). Lodge: Lions. Home: 10412 Firethorn Ln Austin TX 78750-1733

HALE, CHARLES DENNIS, education educator; b. L.A., Jan. 27, 1954; s. Roland Keith Sr. and JoAnne (Steel) H.; m. Dilna Maria Victor, Sept. 10, 1977. BS, U. So. Miss., 1977; MA in Health Edn., U. Fla., 1982, EdS, 1986, EdD, 1989. Health edn. cons. Dist. Health Program Office, Gainesville, Fla., 1982-85; edn. specialist Alachua County Health Dept., Gainesville, 1985-87; project mgr. Family Resource Ctr., Gainesville, 1987; health educator U. Fla., Gainesville, 1988-89; assoc. prof., dept. chair St. Leo (Fla.) Coll., 1989-94; coord. acad. programs, assessment and evaluation U. Ga., 1994-96; assoc. prof., dir. grad. studies in edn. St. Leo (Fla.) Coll., 1996—. Contbr. articles to profl. publs. Recipient 5 grants. Mem. Am. Assn. for Higher Edn., Am. Ednl. Rsch. Assn., Assn. Continuing Higher Edn., Assn. for Instnl. Rsch., Assn. for Study of Higher Edn., Nat. Coun. Measurement in Edn. Roman Catholic. Office: Saint Leo Coll MC 2005 PO Box 6665 Saint Leo FL 33574

HALE, CHRISTOPHER ALLEN, music director; b. Sylacauga, Ala., Aug. 12, 1959; s. Albert Jones and Mary Elizabeth (Atkins) H. BA Music, Miles Coll., Fairfield, Ala., 1991. File clk. U.S. Immigration Svc., Detroit, 1975-77; outside sales coord. Allnet Comm., Detroit, 1984-88; music dir. Miles Coll., Fairfield, 1989-96, Bethel AME Ch., Tallahassee, Fla., 1996—. Composer (song): Hallelujah It Is Done, 1991. Home: 201 W Harrison St #10 Tallahassee FL 32301 Office: Bethel AME Church 501 W Orange Ave Tallahassee FL 32310

HALE, D. CURTIS, commercial artist, painter, writer; b. Wichita Falls, Tex., Dec. 29, 1951; s. Don Mathew and Iva Lee (Pennington) H.; children: Don Wesley, Charity LaRae, Nicholas Gabriel Eugene. Student, Bartlesville Wesleyan Coll., 1970-71, Covenant Found. Coll., 1972-73; AA, Tulsa Jr. Coll., 1975; postgrad., U. Mo., 1977-78. Display artist Renberg's, Tulsa, 1971-72; artist, draftsman Mayhill Publs., Knightstown, Ind., 1972-73; draftsman Williams Bros. Engring., Tulsa, 1974-76; sta. agt. Ozark Air Lines, St. Louis, 1976-78; black/white art dept. supr. Accelerated Christian Edn., Lewisville, Tex., 1978-80; tchr. Bible Fellowship Learning Ctr., Tulsa, 1981-82; art dir. The Family Workshop, Tulsa, 1981-82; free-lance artist, writer Graphic Holiness, Stuart, Fla., 1980-89; v.p. comm. Phoenix Mgmt., Stuart, 1984-89. Contbg. writer, art dir. (mag.) Cornerstone for Youth, 1981-85. Bd. dirs. Community Bible Chapel, Stuart, 1987-89; founder, bd. dirs. Victory Children's Home, Ft. Pierce, Fla., 1987-89; sec., treas. Svc. Orgn./Media Assistance, Stuart, 1987-89. Republican. Home and Office: 2115 W 41st St Tulsa OK 74107-6703

HALE, FORD R., JR., retired accountant; b. Nacogdoches, Tex., Apr. 28, 1918; s. Ford Rutland and Valeta (Windham) H.; m. Ellen Murray, June 18, 1944; children: Ford R. III, Margaret Murray. BA in Acctg., Stephen F. Austin State U., 1939; postgrad., Tex. A&M U., 1939-40; MBA in Acctg., Northwestern U., 1941. CPA, Tex., Okla. Instr. acctg. Tex. A&M U., College Station, 1941-44; acct. Oil Well Supply Co., Dallas, 1944-45; staff acct. W.O. Ligon & Co. CPAs, Dallas, 1945-47, ptnr., 1947-55; ptnr. Dranguet, Foote & Co. CPAs, Dallas, 1955-57, Ford R. Hale & Co. CPAs, Dallas, 1958-74; sr. ptnr. Hale & Co. CPAs, Dallas, 1975-82; ret. Dallas, 1982-; cons., Tyler, Tex. Contbr. articles to profl. jours. Mem. Am. Inst. CPAs (hon., 40-year award 1988), Tex. Soc. CPAs (exec. com. 1968-69, v.p. 1970-71, trustee ednl. found., pres. 1975-77, Hurst fellow 1979), Chapparral Club, Summit Club. Republican. Methodist. Home and Office: 1548 Tanglewood Dr E Lindale TX 75771-5149

HALE, JUDY ANN, education educator; b. Tuscaloosa, Ala., Oct. 16, 1955; d. Rogene Bae and Berta Inez (Smelley) Hale. BA, David Lipscomb U., 1978; MEd, Ala. A&M U., 1989; PhD, Miss. State U., 1994. Art tchr. grades 7-8 Scottsboro (Ala.) Jr. High, 1978-81; headstart tchr. Bridgeport (Ala.) Elem. Sch., 1983-84, tchr. grade 1, 1984-87; migrant tchr. grades K-6 Stevenson (Ala.) Elem. Sch., 1987-89, kindergarten tchr., 1989-91; tchg. asst. Miss. State U., Starkville, 1991-94; asst. prof. Jacksonville (Ala.) State U., 1994—; owner, operator The Art Studio, Scottsboro, 1981-83; presenter in field. Mem. beautification coun. C. of C., Scottsboro, 1983; mem., v.p. Doctoral Student's Assn., Starkville, 1991-94. Faculty Rsch. grantee Jacksonville State U., 1994-96. Mem. AAUW (sec. 1987-89, pres. 1989-91), DAR, Am. Assn. for Edn. Young Children, Mid South Ednl. Rsch. Assn., Ala. Assn. for Young Children, Phi Delta Kappa (historian 1993-94). Office: Jacksonville State Univ Ramona Wood Bldg 700 Pelham Rd N Jacksonville AL 36265-1602

HALE, LANCE MITCHELL, lawyer; b. Roanoke, Va., Oct. 14, 1956; s. Ralph M. and Ruby A. (Akers) H.; m. Terry Lynn Sprouse; children: Christina Nicole, Laura Michelle, Layna Maribeth. BSBA, U. Va., 1979, MS in Acctg., 1981; JD, N.Y. Law Sch., 1984. Bar: Va. 1984, N.J. 1984; CPA, Va. Staff acct. Robert M. Mussleman, CPA, Atty. at Law, Charlottesville, Va., 1979-81; CPA Schapiro, Wisan & Krassner, P.C., N.Y.C., 1982-84; ptnr. King, Fulghum, Snead & Hale, P.C., Roanoke, 1984-89; pvt. practice Lance M. Hale Esquire, P. C., Roanoke, 1989—. Bd. dirs. estate planning coun. Ferrum Coll., Va., 1988. Mem. Am. Trial Lawyers Assn., Va. Trial Lawyers Assn., Va. Soc. CPAs, First Latvian/Am. Trade Conf., Phi Alpha Delta, Beta Alpha Psi. Home: 1048 Maywood Dr Vinton VA 24179-3714 Office: PO Box 1721 Roanoke VA 24008-1721

HALE, LEONARD PETER, III, instrumentation and electrical engineer; b. Cuero, Tex., Nov. 29, 1945; s. Joe Karbosky and Geneva (Hale) Johnson. AAS in Elec. Engring., Tex. State Tech. Inst., 1972; BS in Elec. Engring. Technology, U. Houston, 1976. Lic. radio telephone operator FCC. Electronics technician Tektronix, Houston, 1972-77; elec. engr. Daniel Industries, Houston, 1977-85, Morco, Inc., Corpus Christi, Tex., 1985-86; instrumentation engr. Ebasco Engring., Houston, 1986; elec. engr. S.W. Tube, Sandsprings, Okla., 1987; R&D technician T.D. Williamson, Tulsa, 1987-88; controls technologist Parsons SIP, Houston, 1988-89; instrumentation and elec. engr. Elf Atochem, Houston, 1989—. Sgt. USAF, 1965-69, Vietnam. Mem. Instrument Soc. of Am., VFW (trustee), Moose. Republican. Home: 1512 Allston Houston TX 77008 Office: Elf Atochem NA 2231 Haden Rd Houston TX 77015

HALE, MARIE STONER, artistic director; b. Greenwood, Miss.. Student in Piano, U. Miss., Hattiesburg; studied with Richard Ellis, Christine du Boulay, Jo-Anna Kneeland, David Howard. Tchr. Ellis/du Boulay Sch., Chgo., Jo-Anna Kneeland Imperial Studios, Palm Beach County, Fla.; co-founder Ballet Arts Found., West Palm Beach, Fla., 1973-86; co-founder, artistic dir. Ballet Fla., West Palm Beach, 1986—. Office: Ballet Fla 500 Fern St West Palm Beach FL 33401-5726

HALE, NANCY ANNETTE, kindergarten educator; b. Paris, Tex., Sept. 6, 1959; d. William Richard and Ruby Lee (Davidson) Bills; m. Roy Wayne Hale, May 6, 1983; 1 child, Christopher Wayne. BA in Elem. Edn., U. Tex., San Antonio, 1986, MEd in Early Childhood Edn., 1995. Cert. elem. tchr., early childhood specialist, kindergarten team leader, supr., Tex. Presch. tchr. Adventure Presch., San Antonio, 1986-87; 1st grade tchr. Bob Hope Elem. Sch. S.W. Ind. Sch. Dist., San Antonio, 1987-89, 1st grade tchr. Hidden Cove Elem. Sch., 1989-91, kindergarten tchr. Hidden Cove Elem. Sch., 1991—; mem. Districtwide Improvement Coun. S.W. Ind. Sch. Dist., 1990-91, instnl. coord., 1992-93, site-based mgmt. com., 1992-93, social studies instrnl. coord., 1992-93, dist. curriculum design com., 1996-98, campus improvement com., 1996-97, kindergarten team leader, 1996—, dist. curriculum designer, 1996—, mentor tchr., 1996, campus improvement com., 1996—. Mem. Neighborhood Watch, Atascosa, Tex., 1988—; sec. Macdona Heights Homeowners Assn. Mem. NEA, ASCD, ATPE, Nat. Assn. for Edn. of Young Children, Tex. Tchrs. Assn., Kindergarten Tchrs. Tex. Baptist. Home: 10925 Kelly Rd Atascosa TX 78002-3728

HALE, PAUL NOLEN, JR., engineering administrator, educator; b. Galveston, Tex., Dec. 5, 1941; s. Paul Nolen Hale and Margaret (Wentzel) Carroll; m. Frances Anne Andrews, Jan. 26, 1968; children: Tammy Lynn, Eric Timothy. BS in Indsl. Engring., Lamar Tech., Beaumont, Tex., 1965; MS in Indsl. Engring., U. Ark., 1966; PhD in Indsl. Engring., Tex. A&M U., 1970. Registered profl. engr., La., Tex. Asst. prof. indsl. engring. La. Poly. Inst., Ruston, 1966-67, Tex. A&M U., College Station, 1970-71; from asst. prof. to prof. indsl. engring. La. Tech. U., Ruston, 1971-84, head dept. indsl. engring., 1982-84, head dept. biomed. engring., 1984-85, 87—, dir. rehab. engring. ctr., 1984—; spl. tech. asst. Western Electric, Shreveport, La., 1966; safety cons. Continental Can Co., Hodge, La., 1972; v.p. C.H.& D. Tech. Cons., Ruston, 1967—; pres. Mgmt. Support Corp., Ruston, 1973—; keynote speaker Conf. of Assn. Driver Educators for Disabled, Ky., 1988; standards com. adaptive driving devices, Soc. Auto. Engrs., 1984—; adv. com. bioengring. div. NSF, 1989-92; program evaluator bioengring. Accreditation Bd. Engring. and Tech., 1990—. Author: (with others) Hazard Control Information Handbook, 1983, Ergonomics in Rehabilitation, 1988; editor: Rehabilitation Technical Services, 1989; co-editor: (proceedings) Technology for the Next Decade, 1989; mem. editorial bd. Assistive Tech., 1988—. Pres. Wesley Chapel Water System, Ruston, 1972-82; mem. Mayor's Com. for Disabled, Ruston, 1985-88; adminstrv. bd. Trinity Meth. Ch., Ruston, 1984-87; bd. dirs. Safety Coun. Greater Baton Rouge, 1984-87. Recipient Meritorious Svc. award Gov.'s Conf. for Handicapped, La., 1984. Fellow Am. Inst. Med. and Biol. Engring.; mem. Biomed. Engring. Soc. (bd. dirs., student affairs com. 1989-91, soc. affairs com. 1991-93), RESNA (bd. dirs.), Coun. of Chairs of Biomed. Engring. (chair 1992-93). Home: 3978 Hwy 818 Ruston LA 71270-9804 Office: La Tech U PO Box 3185 Ruston LA 71272

HALE, THOMAS MORGAN, professional services executive; b. Syracuse, N.Y., Nov. 29, 1936; s. Thomas Morgan and Ruth Ingrid (Stangeland) H.; m. Marilyn Johnson, June 12, 1959 (div. Aug. 1980), m. Linda Diana Pappas, Feb. 12, 1981; Children: Rodney, Kenneth, Timothy, Marilee. BS, Fla. State U., 1959; MA, U. Houston, 1967; DPA, George Mason U., 1990; diploma, Nat. War Coll., D.C., 1980. Commd. ensign USN, 1959, advanced through the grades to capt., 1983; served on destroyers, ops. officer USS Sampson, 1963-65; assoc. prof. naval sci. Tex. A&M U., 1965-67; chief staff officer, comdr. Destroyer Squadron Five, 1967-71; with Bur. of Naval Personnel, 1971-74; comdg. officer USS Paul, 1974-76; staff, chief naval ops., chmn. Joint Chiefs of Staff, 1976-83; ret. USN, 1983; sr. mgr. RCI, Vienna, Va., 1983-87, v.p., 1987-96, divsn. gen. mgr., 1992-96, sr. v.p., 1996—; qualified expert witness Federal Dist. Ct. System. Contbr to profl. jours. Recipient Legion of Merit award Sec. of the U.S. Navy, 1983. Mem. U.S. Naval Inst. (life), The Retired Officer's Assn. (life), The Tower Club (life), Army Navy Country Club. Methodist. Home: 3783 Center Way Fairfax VA 22033-2602 Office: RCI 1952 Gallows Rd Vienna VA 22182-3823

HALE, W. THOMAS, golf club executive; b. 1946. With Ernst & Young, Tampa, Fla., 1968-74, Fla. Mining & Materials, Tampa, 1974-79, Arvida, Jacksonville, Fla., 1979-92; with Myrtle Beach (S.C.) Golf Club, 1992—, pres. Office: Myrtle Beach Golf Club 1203 48th Ave N Ste 200 Myrtle Beach SC 29577

HALE-ROBINSON, LORRAINE AUGUSTA, musician; b. Balt., Md., Apr. 20, 1948; d. LeRoy Mitchell and Emma Augusta (Collenberg) H.; m. David Jacobs, Oct. 29, 1969; (div. June, 1974); 1 child, Karen Marcia; m. Johnie Graves, Aug. 31, 1979. Cert., Peabody Inst. of Music, Balt., 1966; Student, Western Md. Coll., Westminster, 1969; BA, E Carolina U., Greenville, 1977; MA, Carolina U., Greenville, 1983. Nat. Guild of Piano Tchrs. Cert. Dir. music MCAS Chapel Cherry Point, N.C., 1971-74; instr. English E. Carolina U., Greenville, 1977-79; dir. music Christ Episc. Ch., New Bern, N.C., 1974-81; English, music instr. Craven Community Coll., New Bern, N.C., 1977-82; English instr. N.C. Wesleyan, New Bern, 1986; dir. music St. Andrew Luth. Ch., 1982-87; tchr. Arendell Parrott Acad., Kinston, N.C., 1988; music, English instr., 1974—; musician, actress Cabaret Players, New Bern, N.C., 1983-89; music editor Composers Music Co., New Bern, N.C., 1987—; lectr. English lang. East Carolina U., 1990—. Composer Various Handbell Music at Dir.'s Workshop, 1989; contbr. articles to profl. jours. Sec. E. Carolina Chap. Am. Guild of Organists New Bern N.C. 1985-87; Active Craven County Bicentennial Com. New Bern N.C. 1985-88, Women's Forum New Bern N.C. 1988--. Teaching fellow English Dept. E. Carolina U. Greenville 1977-78. Mem. Delta Omicron Profl. Music Frat., Phi Kappa Phi, Sigma Tau Delta, Guild of Organists, N.C. Composers Alliance, Occasional Gourmet. Republican. Lutheran. Office: Lorraine Hale Music 212 Metcalf St New Bern NC 28562-5608

HALEY, CAIN CALMES, computer consultant; b. Greensville, S.C., Apr. 4, 1952; d. Julius French and Melville Cain (Calmes) H.; m. John Francis Blakeslee, Jr., Oct. 24, 1983. BA, U. S.C., 1974, MA, 1975. Sch. psychologist Allendale (S.C.) County Sch., 1976-77; sch. psychologist, tchr. Beaufort (S.C.) County Sch., 1977-80; editor South World Mag., Hilton Head, S.C., 1980-82; mgr. Acctg./Mgmt. Svcs., Hilton Head, S.C., 1982-83, Computer Gazebo, Hilton Head, 1983-84; owner, prin. Entre Computer Ctr., Hilton Head, 1984-92, Calcom Ventures, Hilton Head, 1987—; ptnr. Robbins & Haley, Atlanta, 1990-92; adv. to bd. dirs. Dunes Mktg. Group, Hilton Head, 1984-86. Mem. Hilton Head Planning Commn., 1987—; bd. dirs. Gov.'s Council Vocat. Edn., Hilton Head, 1987—. Mem. LWV (chmn. 1986-87), Profl. Women (pres. 1985-86), Hilton Head C. of C. (chmn. com. 1986-87), Nat. Assn. Female Execs., Zonta. Office: Calcom Ventures 52 New Orleans Rd Hilton Head Island SC 29928-4722

HALEY, ELLIOTT CLARKE, JR., neurologist, educator; b. Front Royal, Va., Oct. 14, 1949; children: Patrick Robert, Andrew Clarke, Kellen Emily. BA in Chemistry, U. Va., 1971; MD, Tulane U., 1975. Resident in internal medicine U. Va. Med. Ctr., 1975-78, resident in neurology, 1979-82, chief resident in neurology, 1981-82; mem. med. staff Richmond Meml.

Hosp., 1978-79; cerebrovascular rsch. fellow Cerebral Blood Flow & Met. Lab. Mass. Gen. Hosp.-Harvard Med. Sch., 1983-84; rsch. asst. prof. neurology U. Va., Charlottesville, 1982-83, asst. prof. neurology, 1984-90, asst. prof. neurosurgery, 1988-90, assoc. prof. neurology and neurosurgery, 1990-96, prof., 1996—, co-dir. comp. stroke program, dir. neurovascular lab., 1984—; med. dir. neurol. spl. care unit U. Va., 1985-89, acting med. dir. neurancy neuro ICU, 1988-90, med. dir. stroke unit, 1991—; cons. and lectr. in field. Ad hoc reviewer Jour. Neurosurgery, 1990—, Neurosurgery, 1991—, Stroke, 1990-91, mem. editl. bd., 1991—; contbr. articles to med. jours., chpts. to books. Fellow Stroke coun. Am. Heart Assn.; mem. ACP, Am. Acad. Neurology, Am. Neurol. Assn., Am. Soc. for Neurol. Investigation, Va. Neurol. Soc., Albemarle County Med. Soc., Phi Beta Kappa, Alpha Omega Alpha. Office: U Va Med Ctr Dept Neurology PO Box 394 Charlottesville VA 22902-0394

HALEY, JEANNE ACKERMAN, preschool director; b. Dayton, Ohio, June 26, 1953; d. Harold John and Florence Mary (Jacobs) Ackerman; m. James Francis Haley, Feb. 28, 1975; children: J. Michael, Jason, Jamie. AB, Miami JAcobs Jr. Coll., 1972; BBA, Ft. Lauderdale Coll. Bus., 1974. Sec. to pres. Fla. Atlantic U., Boca Raton, 1974-76; tchrs. aide Meth. Early Childhood Edn., Boca Raton, 1974-83; substitute tchr., tchrs. aide Mint Hill Presbyn. Ch. Presch., Charlotte, N.C., 1984-86; tchr. St. James Episcopal Presch., Warrenton, Va., 1987-93; dir. St. John Presch. and Extended Care Program, Warrenton, Va., 1993-96, St. John Presch. Program and Parish Sch. of Religion Program, 1993—; adminstrv. asst. to propertors The Inn at Little Washington (Va.), 1993. Chairperson Diocesan Com. on Extended Day Programs, Diocesan Com. on Pre-Schs., organizer, dir.'s com., Diocese of Arlington, Va.; leader, organizer Boy Scouts Am., Charlotte, N.C., Warrenton, 1984—, asst. dist. commr., Warrenton, 1991-93, com. mem. troop 175, 1992— (Dist. award Merit 1992, Key Three award 1991); leader, organizer Girl Scouts U.S. Nat. Capital, Washington, 1991-94; v.p. Friends of Libr. Bd., Deerfield Beach, Fla., 1975-83. Mem. Assn. Childhood Edn. Internat., Nat. Assn. for Edn. of Young Children, Fauquier Cmty. Child Care Network (charter), Nat. Assn. Child Care Profls. Roman Catholic. Office: Saint John Presch 285 Winchester St Warrenton VA 22186

HALEY, PATRICIA ANN, psychiatric therapist, school counselor, administrator; b. Waxahachie, Tex., Jan. 17, 1951; d. Bob A. and Gertie M. (Graham) H. BA, Tex. Woman's Univ., 1973, postgrad. in deaf edn., 1978; MEdin counseling and student svcs., U. North Tex., 1994. Tchr. Ennis (Tex.) Ind. Sch. Dist., 1985-93; counselor Ferris (Tex.) Ind. Sch. Dist., 1994—; psychiat. therapist HCA Med. Ctr., Columbia-Midway Park Hosp.; owner Graham Comms., Waxahachie. Editor (poetry) Family Tributes, 1989, Therapeutic Poetry, 1990, Heroes and Heroines, 1991; contbg. poet (cassette) The Sound of Poetry, 1993. Fellow AAUW (interviewee cable TV show 1994); mem. ACA, Tex. Counseling Assn. (Edn. Endowment award 1996), Poetry Soc. of Tex., Tex. Play Therapy Assn., Tex. Sch. Counselors Assn., Kappa Delta Pi, Phi Delta Kappa, Pi Lambda Theta.

HALFACRE, ROBERT GORDON, landscape architect, educator; b. Newberry, S.C., June 22, 1941; s. Edwin Harvey and Lela (Ruff) H.; m. Carolyn F. Halfacre, Jan. 24, 1963 (div. Jan., 1980); children: Angela, Robert. BS, Clemson U., 1963, MS, 1965; PhD in Horticulture, Va. Poly. Inst., 1968; MLA, N.C. State U., 1973. Registered landscape architect, S.C. Asst. prof. N.C. State U., Raleigh, 1968-71, assoc. prof., 1971-74; assoc. prof. horticulture Clemson (S.C.) U., 1974-79, prof., 1979-90, Alumni disting. prof., 1990—; landscape architect Landscape Archtl. Svcs., Clemson, 1977—; mem. Planning Commn. City of Clemson, 1990-93; pres. faculty senate, Clemson U., 1989-90, bd. visitors, 1992-94, chmn. grievance bd., 1996-98. Author: Carolina Landscape Plants, 1971, Keep 'em Growing, 1972, Fundamentals of Horticulture, 1975, Horticulture, 1979, Plant Science, 1987, Landscape Plants of the Southeast, 5th edit., 1989. Dir. Horticulture Gardens, Clemson U., 1974-77; pres. bd. dirs. Daniel H.S. P.T.A., Clemson, 1985-86; chmn. United Way Campaign, Clemson U., 1996-97. Recipient Silver Seal award Nat. Coun. State Garden Clubs, 1984, Helen S. Hull award, 1979, Sigma Xi Rsch. award, 1968, Outstanding Tchr. award N.C. State U., 1970. Mem. Am. Soc. Landscape Architects, Am. Soc. for Hort. Sci. (L.M. Ware Outstanding Tchr. award So. region 1982, Julian C. Miller rsch. award 1968). Republican. Lutheran. Home: 136 Riverpoint Dr Clemson SC 29631 Office: Clemson U 164 Poole Agrl Ctr Clemson SC 29634

HALFEN, DAVID, publishing executive; b. Newark, July 23, 1924; s. Abraham and Rachael (Sudit) H.; m. Geneviève Alberte Martin, Jan. 15, 1948; children: Daniel, William, Alexandre Anthony. BS with high honors, U. Wis., 1948; Diploma in French Civilization with high honors, U. Paris, 1949, PhD with highest honors, 1954. From asst. to chief cost acct. Atlas Constructors, Morocco, 1952-54; from asst. editor to editor-in-chief Hart Pub. Co., N.Y.C., 1954-56, 58-62; fgn. affairs editor Scholastic mag., N.Y.C., 1956-58; from field editor to v.p., gen. mgr. Coll. divsn. Scott, Foresman and Co., Glenview, Ill., 1962-78, v.p., gen. mgr. Lifelong Learning divsn., 1978-87, ret., 1987; chmn. adv. com. USN Courses at Sea Program, 1987-92; sr. assoc. Middlesex Rsch. Ctr., Bethesda, Md., 1991-93; vol. exec. Internat. Exec. Svc. Corps, Zimbabwe, 1993, cons., 1994-96. Author: La Plume: Revue Symboliste 1889-1899, 1954. Host sister Cities program Destin, Fla., Gilles St. Croix, France, 1996. With AUS, 1943-46, PTO.

HALICZER, JAMES SOLOMON, lawyer; b. Ft. Myers, Fla., Oct. 27, 1952; s. Julian and Margaret (Shepard) H.; m. Paula Fleming, Oct. 3, 1987. BA in English Lit., U. So. Fla., 1976, MA in Polit. Sci., 1978; JD, Stetson U., 1981. Bar: Fla. 1982. Assoc. Conrad, Scherer & James, Ft. Lauderdale, Fla., 1982-86, ptnr., 1988—; assoc. Bernard & Mauro, Ft. Lauderdale, 1985-86; shareholder Cooney, Haliczer, Mattson, Lane, Blackburn, Pettis & Richards, Ft. Lauderdale, 1992-96, Haliczer, Pettis & White, P.A., Ft. Lauderdale, Fla., 1996—. Mem. ABA, Fla. Bar Assn., Broward County Bar Assn., Assn. Trial Lawyers Am., Def. Rsch. Inst., Am. Acad. Healthcare Attys., Phi Kappa Phi, Pi Sigma Alpha, Omicron Delta Kappa. Democrat. Methodist. Office: Haliczer Pettis & White PA 101 NE 3rd Ave Fort Lauderdale FL 33301

HALL, ANNA CHRISTENE, federal agency administrator; b. Tyler, Tex., Dec. 18, 1946; d. Willie B. and Mary Christene (Wood) H. BA in Polit. Sci., So. Meth. U., 1969. Clk.-stenographer Employment and Tng. Adminstrn., U.S. Dept. Labor, Dallas, 1970, fed. rep., 1970-80; program analyst U.S. Dept. Labor, Washington, 1980-84, div. chief, 1984-87, exec. asst., 1987-88; office dir. U.S. Dept. Labor, Dallas, 1988—. Recipient Outstanding Performance award U.S. Dept. Labor, 1972, 73, 74, 79, 95, Meritorious Achievement award, 1986. Mem. Partnership for Employment and Tng., Nat. Honor Soc. Democrat. Presbyterian. Home: 2304 Hunters Run Dr Dallas TX 75232-4146 Office: US Dept Lab ETA 525 Griffin St Rm 315 Dallas TX 75202

HALL, ATLEE BURPEE, researcher; b. Talking Rock, Ga., Feb. 5, 1911; s. Thomas Sanford and Betulia Queen (Lambert) H.; m. Rhonwyn Fay Blevins, Apr. 9, 1933; children: Kilmer Lanier, Gloria Joyce, Rebecca Lou, Andrea Faith. Grad. high sch. Postmaster U.S. Postal Svc., Ider, Ala., 1935-56; elec. mechanic NASA, Huntsville, Ala., 1956-66; rschr. pvt. practice, Arab, Ala., 1966—. Author: Goodness and Mercy, 1989, Crossword Puzzle Dictionary, 1993, (booklets) Nature Study Calendar, 1972, Primitive Baptist Statistics, 1974. Home: 1427 Fenton Rd Arab AL 35016-4629

HALL, BENNETT FREEMAN, minister; b. Macon, Ga., Nov. 30, 1914; s. Charles McDonald and Mary Elizabeth (Lyon) H.; m. Mae Elizabeth Wells, June 2, 1937; children: Mari, Laura, Louise, Ben. Student, Bryan U., 1934-36; AB, Stetson U., 1938; ThM, So. Bapt. Theol. Sem., 1943; postgrad., Jewish Theol. Sem., 1968-71; ThM, Princeton Theol. Sem., 1975; DMin, Drew U., 1979. Ordained to ministry Bapt. Ch., 1936. Pastor Falmouth (Ky.) Bapt. Ch., 1942-44, First Bapt. Ch., Titusville, Fla., 1944-49, Bay Haven Bapt. Ch., Sarasota, Fla., 1950-53, Southside Bapt. Ch., Bradenton, Fla., 1954-67, Somerset Hills Bapt. Ch., Bernardsville, N.J. (Now in Basking Ridge, N.J.), N.J., 1967-79, First Bapt. Ch., Lexington, Ky., 1982-85; trustee Bapt. Bible Inst., Fla., 1949-59; mem. state mission bd. Fla. Bapt. Conv., 1957-59; dean, tchr. extention dept. Stetson U., 1960-64; evangelist Jamaica Crusade, 1966; missions com. Met. N.Y. Bapt. Assn., 1968-72, chmn. constn. and credentials com., 1972-77; tchr., sem. extension Met. N.Y. Assn., 1976-78; adv. bd. Cumberland Coll., Williamsburg, Ky., 1982-91. Chmn. ARC, Titusville, 1944-46; mem. Mental Health Orgn., Bradenton, 1964-66. Home: 293 S Main St Winchester KY 40391-2471

HALL, BEVERLY ADELE, nursing educator; b. Houston, Aug. 19, 1935; d. Leslie Leo and Lois Mae (Pesnell) H. BS, Tex. Christian U., 1957; MA, NYU, 1961; PhD, U. Colo., 1974. RN, Tex., N.Y. With Ft. Worth (Tex.) Dept. Health, 1957-59; asst. prof. U. Mass., Amhurst, 1961-65; chief nurse N.Y.C. Med. Coll., 1965-67; asst. prof. U. Colo., Denver, 1967-70; assoc. prof. U. Washington, Seattle, 1974-80; prof., chmn. dept. U. Calif., San Francisco, 1980-84; Denton Cooley prof. nursing U. Tex., Austin, 1984—; mem. grad. faculty Sch. Biomed. Sci. U. Tex., Galveston; pres. med. svcs. Bd. Dir. Project Transitionss; mem. NIH Study Group. Author: Mental Health and the Elderly, 1985 (Book of Yr.); mem. editl. rev. bd. Advances in Nursing, Archives Psychiat. Nursing, Qualitative Health Rsch., Rsch. in Nursing and Health, Nursing Outlook, Jour. Profl. Nursing, Jour. of the Am. Psychiat. Nurses Assn.; contbr. articles to profl. jours., chpts. to books. Served to capt. U.S. Army, 1962-66. Recipient Tex. Excellence Teaching award U. Tex. Ex-Students Assn., 1994. Fellow Am. Acad. Nursing (governing bd., mem. fellowship selection com.), Am. Coll. Mental Health Adminstrn.; mem. ANA (divsn. gerontological practice), Coun. Nurse Rschrs., Am. Inst. Life Threatening Illness and Loss, So. Nursing Rsch. Soc. Home: 8401 Mesa Doble Ln Austin TX 78759-8028 Office: U Tex 1700 Red River St Austin TX 78701-1412

HALL, BILLY RAY, JR., political scientist; b. Marlin, Tex., Jan. 6, 1967; s. Billy Ray and Linda Joyce (Whitlow) H. BA, Baylor U., 1990, MA, 1990; PhD, Tex. A&M U., 1995. Sales agt. Baylor Athletic Ticket Office, Waco, Tex., 1985-90; rsch. asst. pub. policy project Tex. A&M U., College Station, 1990-92; editl. intern Jour. Politics, College Station, 1993-94; project supr. Policy Agendas in Congress Project Tex. A&M U., College Station, 1993-95; Baylor Law Sch., 1996—. Contbr. chpts. to books. Mem. Acad. Polit. Sci., Am. Polit. Sci. Assn., Ctr. for Study of Presidency, So. Polit. Sci. Assn., Century Club, Ctrl. Tex. Baylor Alumni Assn. (bd. dirs.). Baptist. Home: 1916 Redbud Rockdale TX 76567 Office: Tex A&M U Dept Polit Sci College Station TX 77843

HALL, BONLYN GOODWIN, librarian; b. Middlebury, Pa., June 28, 1936; d. Gordon E. and Marjorie A. (Gee) Goodwin; m. James H. Hall Jr., May 25, 1957 (div. Sept. 1977); children: Jonathan, Christopher. BS, U. N.C., 1961; MLS, SUNY, Geneseo, 1975; MusM, U. Md., 1983. Music libr. U. Richmond, Va., 1976—. Mem. Music Libr. Assn. (com. chair 1975—), Sonneck Soc. Am. Music, Va. Libr. Assn. Unitarian. Office: Parsons Music Libr Modlin Ctr for Arts U Richmond Richmond VA 23173

HALL, COLIN DAVID, neurologist; b. Chester, Eng., May 11, 1941; came to U.S., 1969; s. David and Olive (Blanch) H.; m. Valerie Gordon, Sept. 22, 1961 (div. Dec. 28, 1989); children: Russell, Steven, Michael. MBChB, Aberdeen (Scotland) U., 1966. Diplomate Am. Bd. Electrodiagnostic Medicine, Am. Acad. Neurology. House officer Aberdeen Gen. Hosps., 1966-69; resident in neurology U. N.C., Chapel Hill, 1969-72, asst. prof. neurology and medicine, 1973-77, assoc. prof. neurology and medicine, 1977-82, prof. neurology and medicine, 1982—, also vice chair neurology, 1986—, interim chair neurology, 1995; rschr. in AIDS and neuromuscular disease U. N.C., Chapel Hill, 1992—. Mem. editl. bd. Jour. Neuro-AIDS, Jour. Neurovirology; ad hoc referee numerous jours.; ad hoc examiner Am. Bd. Neurol. Surgery; contbr. numerous articles to profl. jours. Mem. numerous NIH peer rev. coms. Fellow Am. Neurol. Assn.; mem. AMA, Am. Assn. Electrodiagnostic Medicine, Am. Assn. Electromyography and Electrodiagnosis, N.C. Med. Assn., N.C. Neurol. Assn., Orange-Durham County Med. Soc., N.C. Soc. Neuroscis. Office: Univ NC Dept Neurology Chapel Hill NC 27599

HALL, DENNIS SANFORD, sales executive; b. Washington, June 6, 1947; s. Dennis Daniel and Laura (Hurlock) H.; m. Christine Marion Legge, Nov. 1, 1969 (div. Nov. 1982); children: Dennis Sanford Jr., Christopher Daniel, Mary Katherine; m. Kathleen Daryl Sheehan, Apr. 13, 1985. BA in History, George Mason U., 1995. Driver Parker-Thomas Glass, Fairfax, Va., 1969-70; mgr. House of Glass, Alexandria, Va., 1970-71; gen. mgr. DDK & Assocs., Fairfax, Va., 1972—; mgr. McQuinn Sporting Goods, Arlington, 1972-74, Sports Unltd., Arlington, 1975-79, Neal Olkewicz's Sport Ctr., Springfield, Va., 1983-87, Cellular Phone Stores, Fairfax, 1988-90. Author: Expressions from Within, 1969-90; co-author: Dedicated To Serve a Nation, 1992. With U.S. Army, 1967-69, Vietnam. Mem. VFW, Nat. Football Found. & Hall of Fame, Disabled Am. Vets., Ea. Assn. Intercollegiate Football Ofcls., Ea. Coll. Athletic Counf., Vietnam Vets. Am., No. Va. Football Ofcls. Assn. (bd. dirs. 1972—, Dedicated Svc. award 1990). Methodist.

HALL, DOROTHY J., credit union executive; b. 1931. Pres., sec., treas., dir. Va. Credit Union, Inc., Richmond, 1957—. Office: Va Credit Union Inc 7500 Boulder View Dr Richmond VA 23225-4046*

HALL, DOUGLAS LEE, computer science educator; b. San Antonio, Feb. 5, 1947; s. Robert Arthur and Thelma (Stischer). AA in Foreign Lang., San Antonio Coll., 1967; BA in Spanish, U. Tex., 1969; MEd in Bilingual Edn., Pan Am. U., 1977; PhD, N. Tex. State U., 1987. Tchr. Edgewood Ind. Sch. Dist., San Antonio, 1969-73, Brownsville (Tex.) Ind. Sch. Dist., 1973-74, 76-78; precious metals specialist Nu-Metals, Inc., Dallas, 1974; tchr. DPC Am. Sch., Dubai, UAE, 1975-76; tng. dir. ABDick, San Antonio, 1978-79; bilingual tchr. Dallas Ind. Sch. Dist., 1979-82; computer cons. Taylor Mgmt. Systems, Dallas, 1982-83; lectr. in field N.Tex. State U., Denton, 1984-86; grad. advisor St. Mary's U., San Antonio, 1986—, chair dept. computer sci., 1990—, pres. faculty senate, 1992-93; dir. Deutscher Volkstanzverein, San Antonio, 1987—; asst. dir. San Antonio Folk Dance Fest, 1986—; advisor St. Mary's U. Chpt. Assn. for Computing Machinery, 1989—. Contbr. articles to profl. jours. Docent Inst. Texan Cultures, San Antonio, 1989—; pres. Crown Hill Pk. Homeowners, San Antonio, 1986-89; del. 1st U.S.-Japan Grassroots Summit, 1991. Named Tchr. of Yr., Brownsville Ind. Sch. Dist. 1974, 77, Outstanding Elem. Tchr. 1974, Disting. Grad. Faculty Mem. 1991-92. Mem. NEA, IEEE, ACM, Tex. State Tchrs. Assn., Am. Assn. Artificial Intelligence. Home: 515 Marquis St San Antonio TX 78216-5217 Office: Saint Mary's U One Camino Santa Maria San Antonio TX 78228-8524

HALL, DWAYNE ALLEN, investment broker; b. Winston-Salem, N.C., Dec. 11, 1958; s. R. Claxton and Alice Lea (Hart) H.; m. Angela Petree Hall, Aug. 20, 1983; children: Landon Allen, Skyler Petree. BA in Econs., Wake Forest U., 1981; cert., Am. Coll., 1991. Cert. fin. Planner Coll. of Fin. Planning, 1988, CLU Am. Coll., 1991; ChFC, Am. Coll., 1995. Sales rep. R.J. Reynolds Tobacco Co., Winston-Salem, 1981-83; agt. Pilot Life Ins. Co., Winston-Salem, 1983-84; account exec. Consol. Planning, Inc., Charlotte, N.C., 1984—, sales mgr., 1987-92, v.p., 1992—; sr. v.p., 1994—; v.p. exec. com. Guardian Life Ins. Co. Am., N.Y.C., 1990—. Vol. fundraiser Wake Forest Deacon Club, Winston-Salem, 1983-89; bd. dirs. Arbor Run Homeowners Assn., 1992—, Exch. Club/Child Abuse Ctr., 1994. Mem. Internat. Assn. Fin. Planning, Nat. Assn. Securities Dealers, Nat. Assn. Life Underwriters, Inst. Cert. Fin. Planners, Am. Soc. Chartered Life Underwriters and Chartered Fin. Cons., Million Dollar Round Table, Wake Forest Alumni Assn. (pres. class of 1981). Republican. Methodist. Office: 370 Knollwood St Ste 300 Winston Salem NC 27103-1834

HALL, GAY PATTERSON, nurse midwife; b. Long Beach, Calif., Feb. 26, 1937; d. John James III and Rhueybelle (Alter) Patterson; m. Steven A. Ahlf, Sept. 23, 1962 (div. 1972); 1 child, Rhueybelle Anne; m. Mortimer Joseph Hall, Nov. 17, 1979; step children: Jennifer, Janelle, Michael. BSN, Columbia U., 1961; MSN, Cath. U. Am., 1968. RN N.Y., Pa., Fla. Commd. capt. USAF, 1975, advanced through grades to col., 1993; staff nurse U.S. Pub. Health Svc., Dillingham, Alaska, 1961-62; charge nurse med. ward Hosp. Bella Vista, Mayaguez, P.R., 1963; pub. health nurse Pa. Dept. Health, Harrisburg, 1964-66; pvt. duty nurse Homemakers Upjohn Inc., Harrisburg, 1973; clin. nurse Perry Health Ctr., Loysville, Pa., 1973-75; dir. USAF nurse-midwifery clin. program Georgetown U., Washington, 1989-94; chief ob-gyn and pediatrics 6th Med. Group Hosp., MacDill AFB, Fla., 1994-95; ret., 1995; advanced nurse practitioner Guidance Clinic of Mid. Keys., Marathon, Fla., 1996—; adj. faculty nurse-midwifery program Georgetown U. Sch. Nursing, 1980-84, 89-94; cons., spkr. in field. Contbr. articles to profl. jours. Mem. ACOG (com. obstetric practice 1994—), Am. Coll. Nurse-Midwives (chmn. clin. practice com. 1991-94, head teller nominating com. 1983, 90, fin. com. 1981-83), USAF Assn. (life), Ret. Officers Assn., Uniformed Nurse Practitioners Assn., Air Force Assn. Republican. Eastern Orthodox. Home: 721 W Indies Dr Ramrod Key FL 33042

HALL, GEORGANNA MAE, elementary school educator; b. St. Louis, June 4, 1951; d. George Winfred and Judith Lou (Wheatley) H. BS in Edn., Stephen F. Austin U., 1973; MS in Edn., U. Houston, 1979. Cert. elem., early childhood and kindergarten edn. tchr., Tex.; cert. mid mgmt. adminstr. Elem. educator Lamar Consol. Ind. Sch. Dist., Rosenberg, Tex., 1973-94; part-time campus coord. Houston C.C., 1994; exec. dir. Sylvan Learning Ctrs. Pasadena (Tex.) Ind. Sch. Dist., 1994—; mem. Smith Elem. Improvement Task Force, Richmond, Tex., summers 1988-90, active mem., summer 1991. Mem. choir St. John's Meth. Ch., Richmond. Mem. Tex. Classroom Tchrs. Assn., Nat. Assn. for the Edn. Young Children, Assn. Curriculum and Supervision, Celebration Ringers, Delta Kappa Gamma, Sigma Kappa. Home: 5009 Holt St Bellaire TX 77401-5724 Office: Sylvan Learning Ctrs 100 Jackson Ave Pasadena TX 77506-2213

HALL, HOUGHTON ALEXANDER, electrical engineering; b. Kingston, Jamaica, W.I., Aug. 17, 1936; came to U.S., 1985; s. James Alexander and Clarice Viola Hall; m. Grace Yvonne Anglin, Feb. 22, 1964; children: Andrew Geoffery, Christine Elizabeth. BS, U. W.I., Kingston, 1958, diploma in chem. tech., 1959, diploma in mgmt., 1977. Registered profl. engr., Fla.; chartered engr. Great Britain. Elec. engr. Jamaica Pub. Svc. Co., Kingston, 1960-84; dir. R&D Ministry of Sci., Tech. and the Environ., Kingston, 1984-85; elec. engr. Electric Dept. City of Tallahassee, 1985-90; supr., substation engring. Electric Dept., City of Tallahassee, 1990—. Fellow Fla. Engring. Soc.; mem. IEEE (sr.), NSPE, Inst. Elec. Engrs., Tallahassee Sci. Soc. (charter pres. 1989—), Fla. Acad. Scis. (chmn. engring. sect.). Baptist. Home: 4335 Sherborne Rd Tallahassee FL 32303-7607 Office: City of Tallahassee 2602 Jackson Bluff Rd Tallahassee FL 32304-4408

HALL, JAMES BRYAN, gynecological oncologist; b. Dayton, Ohio, Nov. 24, 1946; s. Mitchell Z. and Moyne L. H.; m. Edith Miller, Mar. 22, 1975; children: James B. Jr., William B. AB, Taylor U., 1969; MD, Med. U. S.C., 1974. Diplomate Am. Bd. Ob-Gyn., Oncology. Rotating intern Miami Valley Hosp., Dayton, 1974-75; resident in ob-gyn. Wright State U.-Miami Valley Hosp., 1975-78, chief resident in ob-gyn., 1977-78; fellow in gynecologic oncology, asst. in gynecology Mass. Gen. Hosp., Boston, 1978-80; pvt. practice Charlotte, N.C., 1988-95; instr. ob-gyn. Harvard U., Boston, 1978-80; dir. gynecologic oncology, dept. ob-gyn. Carolinas Med. Ctr., 1980—, coord. med. student clerkship, 1982-87, acting dir. dept. ob-gyn., 1987-88, assoc. prof., 1986-88; asst. prof. U. N.C., Chapel Hill, 1980-86, assoc. prof., 1986-88, clin. prof., 1995—; spkr. at profl. confs. Contbr. numerous articles to med. jours. Fellow Am. Coll. Ob-Gyn.; mem. Soc.Gynecologic Oncology, Charlotte Gynecol. and Obstetrical Soc. (sec.-treas. 1984-86, v.p. 1986-87, pres. 1987-88), Am. Cancer Soc. (bd. dirs. Mecklenburg County chpt., chmn. profl. edn. com., exec. com.), AMA, N.C. Med. Soc., Assn. Profs. of Gynecologists and Obstetricians, James H. Nelson Jr. Oncology Soc. Republican. Evang. nondenominational. Office: Cancer Ctr Carolinas Med Ctr 100 Blythe Blvd Charlotte NC 28232

HALL, JAMES GRANVILLE, JR., history educator; b. Phila., Aug. 22, 1917; s. James Granville and Jane Margaret (Moorehead) H.; m. Eva Mae Woodruff, June 1946; 1 child, Evelyn Alison. AB, George Washington U., 1950; cert., Georgetown U., 1951; postgrad., U. Colo., Colorado Springs, 1965-67; MA, Va. State U., 1972. Commd. 2nd lt. U.S. Army, 1943; transferred to USAF, 1948, advanced through ranks to lt. col., 1961; aircraft controller U.S. Army, Panama, U.S., 1943-50; various assignments, 1950-64; comdr. dir. staff officer, weapons staff officer NORAD, 1964-67; comdr. MDC, King Salmon, 1968, Air Def. Sector, King Salmon, Alaska, 1967-68; dir. ops. 5th Tactical Control group, comdr. 605th Tactical Control Squadron, Clark Air Base, The Philippines, 1969-71; chief control & environ. 20th Air Div., Ft. Lee, Va., 1971-72; retired USAF, 1972; faculty history and govt. Austin (Tex.) C.C., Austin, 1973-93; participant Mid. East Seminar, Fgn. Svc. Inst., U.S. Dept. State, Washington, 1953; lectr. civic and garden clubs, Tex., 1974—. Author: Men's Garden Club Show and Judges Handbook, 1980; contbr. articles to profl. jours. Pres. Kiwanis club, Opheim, Mont., 1960; organizer, leader Girl Scouts Am., Opheim, 1959-60; pres. Little League, Itazuke, Japan, 1961-63; bd. dirs. Colo. Springs Opera Assn., 1967; mem. Austin Lyric Opera, 1987—; guest expert TV and radio garden shows, Austin, 1976—; polit. worker, Austin, 1974—. Decorated Meritorious Svc. medal, Joint Svcs. Commendation medal, Air Force Commendation medal, Am. Campaign medal, World War II Victory medal, Nat. Def. Svc. medal with 1 Bronze Star, Vietnam Svc. medal with 1 Bronze Star, Armed Forces Expeditionary medal, Combat Readiness medal with 1 Bronze Oak Leaf Cluster, Air Force Reserve medal, Air Force Outstanding Unit Citation, Master Weapons Dir. Badge; recipient Philippine Presidential Unit Citation for Humanitarian Svc., 1970-71. Mem. Nat. Chrysanthemum Soc. (awards chmn. 1986-91, accredited judge 1976-85, master judge 1986—), S.W. Chrysanthemum Region (organizer, pres. 1981-82), Capitol Area Chrysanthemum Soc. (pres. 1975), Men's Garden Club (pres. 1977), Men's Garden Club Am. (nat. schs. and judges chmn. 1979-81, accredited judge 1976—). Republican. Episcopalian. Home and Office: Halls Greenhouse 12503 Utah Cir Manchaca TX 78652-3535

HALL, JAMES RANDAL, lawyer; b. Augusta, Ga., Nov. 9, 1958; s. James Marcus and Gary Patricia (Ross) H.; m. Mary Suzanne Crowder, Dec. 19, 1981; children: Mary Catherine, Elizabeth Hinson. BA, Augusta Coll., 1979; JD, U. Ga., 1982. Bar: Ga. 1982, U.S. Dist. Ct. (no. dist.) Ga. 1982, U.S. Tax Ct. 1983, U.S. Dist. Ct. (so. dist.) Ga. 1984. Assoc. Sanders, Mottola, Haugen & Goodson, Newnan, Ga., 1982-84; ptnr. Avrett & Hall, Augusta, 1984-85; gen. counsel, v.p., sec. Bankers First Corp., Augusta, 1985—; corp. v.p., gen. counsel, sec. Bankers First Corp.; lectr. Inst. Fin. Edn., Augusta, 1989—; treas. Bankers First Com. for Quality Govt., Augusta, 1988—. Bd. dirs., ex-officio Augusta Port Authority, 1987-88; chmn. Augusta So. Nats. Inc., 1987-88, Evang. com. Trinity Meth. Ch., Augusta, 1989-91; bd. dirs. Richmond County Consumer Adv. Bd., Augusta, 1988-89; bd. dirs. Augusta Coalition for Children and Youth, 1991-93, pres. 1993-94. Mem. ABA (savings instn. subcom.), Augusta Bar Assn., Am. Corp. Counsel Assn., State Bar Ga. (corp. counsel com., legal econs. com., arrangements for meetings com.), Assn. Fin. Svcs. Holding Co. (holding cos. law com. 1987—), Leadership Augusta (bd. dirs. 1991-93), Lions (pres. Augusta chpt.), Phi Delta Phi. Home: 519 Winchester Dr Augusta GA 30909-3235 Office: Bankers First Corp 1 Tenth St Augusta GA 30901-1295*

HALL, JERRY FRANK, retired journalist; b. Childress, Tex., Mar. 12, 1934; s. Frank J. and Lottie Mae (Wolf) H.; m. Dorothy Sue Leveritt, Feb. 17, 1956; children: Clifford Frank, Jennifer Leigh Zant. BJ, U. Tex., 1956. Reporter Borger (Tex.) News Herald, 1952-53; editor Daily Texan, Austin, 1953-56; reporter, photographer Rock Hill (S.C.) Evening Herald, 1958-59; from info. asst. to asst. v.p. pub. rels. Southwestern Bell Tel. Co., various locations, 1959-86; ptnr. Jaderry Enterprises, Dallas, 1986-89; cons. Tex. Tel. Assn., 1990-91; freelance writer, Wimberley, Tex., 1990—. Author: Hello, Texas, 1991; author, illustrator: I Love a Farmers Market, 1987. dir. Kans. City (Mo.) Philharm., 1975-76; mem. prime time com., Kans. City, 1975-76, Bicentennial com., Kans. City, 1975-76. Served in U.S. Army, 1956-58. Mem. Pub. Rels. Soc. Am. (dir. 1975-76), Soc. Profl. Journalists, U. Tex. Ex-Students Assn. (pres. St. Louis chpt. 1963), TLC Birding Soc. (v.p. 1996-97). Home: 707 Cypress Creek Rd Wimberley TX 78676-3656

HALL, J(OHN) DANIEL, II, asset management consultant; b. Elkin, N.C., Jan. 21, 1947; s. John D. and Thelma (Waddell) H.; children: John D. III, Adam W. BA in Acctg., Wingate Coll., 1967; BS, East Tenn. State U., 1970, MBA, 1972. Pres. Hall, Sledge & Co., Knoxville, Tenn., 1975-78; 1st v.p., mgr. pub. fin. EF Hutton & Co., Atlanta, 1978-84; sr. v.p., mgr. pub. fin. EF Hutton & Co., N.Y.C., 1984-86; dir. investment banking 1st Boston Corp., N.Y.C., 1986-89; v.p. Kidder, Peabody & Co., Inc., Atlanta, 1990—. Editor: Public Finance Directory & Resource Guide, 1984. Mem. internat. bd. overseers Wingate Coll.; officer, mission pilot Atlanta Squadron One, Civil Air Patrol. Recipient Deal of Yr. award Instnl. Investor mag., 1983. Mem. Aircraft Owners and Pilots Assn., N.Y. Bond Club, Atlanta Bond Club, Atlanta Peachtree Rotary Club (charter mem.), Cherokee Town and Country Club, Sigma Phi Epsilon Alumni (pres. Atlanta area 1989-90).

Home: 77 E Andrews Dr NW Atlanta GA 30305-1370 Office: Kidder Peabody & Co 1201 W Peachtree St NW Ste 3500 Atlanta GA 30309-3400

HALL, JOHN THOMAS, lawyer; b. Phila., May 14, 1938; s. John Thomas and Florence Sara (Robinson) H.; m. Carolyn Park Currie, May 26, 1968; children: Daniel Currie, Kathleen Currie. AB, Dickinson Coll., 1960; MA, U. Md., 1963; JD, U. N.C., 1972. Bar: N.C. 1972. Chmn. dept. speech Mercersburg (Pa.) Acad., 1960-63, U. Balt., 1963-69; research asst. N.C. Ct. Appeals, Raleigh, 1972-73, dir. pre-hearing research staff, 1974-75, asst. clk., marshall, librarian, 1980-81; counsel Dorothea Dix Hosp., Raleigh, 1974; asst. dist. atty. State of N.C., Raleigh, 1975-80, 81-83; pvt. practice Raleigh, 1973-74, 83—; mem. faculty King's Bus. Coll., Raleigh, 1973-75, N.C. Bar Assn., 1987—; undercover inmate Cen. Prison Duke Ctr. on Law and Poverty, Durham, N.C., 1970. Mem. Raleigh Little Theatre, Theatre in the Park, Raleigh; charter mem. Wake County Dem. Men's Club, 1977—. Named Best Actor, Raleigh Little Theatre, 1975, 77, 80, 82, 85, 86, 93. Mem. ABA, N.C. Bar Assn. (bd. dirs. The Lawyers of N.C. 1986-89), Wake County Bar Assn. (bd. dirs. 1986-89, vice chmn. exec. com. 1986-87), 10th Jud. Dist. Bar Assn. (bd. dirs. 1986-89, chmn. grievance com. 1987-90), N.C. Acad. Trial Lawyers, Wake County Acad. Criminal Trial Lawyers (v.p. 1986-87), Scottish Clan Gunn Soc., Neuse River Valley Model R.R. (Raleigh). Roman Catholic. Office: PO Box 1207 Raleigh NC 27602-1207

HALL, JOHN WESLEY, JR., lawyer; b. Watertown, N.Y., Jan. 28, 1948; s. John Wesley and Mary Louise (Hodge) H.; children: Justin William, Mark Daniel. BA, Hendrix Coll., 1970; JD, U. Ark., 1973. Bar: Ark. 1973, D.C. 1975, Tenn. 1988, Nev. 1993, N.Y., 1996, U.S. Dist. Ct. (ea. and we. dists.) Ark. 1973, U.S. Ct. Appeals (8th cir.) 1973, U.S. Ct. Appeals (5th cir.) 1976, U.S. Supreme Ct. 1976, U.S. Ct. Appeals (fed. cir.) 1988, U.S. Ct. Appeals (6th cir.) 1991, U.S. Ct. Appeals (9th cir.) 1995; cert. criminal trial adv. Nat. Bd. Trial Advocacy, 1981. Dep. pros. atty., Little Rock, 1973-79, head career criminal div., 1978-79; trial advocacy instr. Ark. Prosecuting Attys. Assn., 1977-79; law clk. Ark. Supreme Ct., 1974; pvt. practice law, Little Rock, 1979—; adj. prof. sch. law, grad. sch. criminal justice U. Ark., Little Rock, 1985, 88, 91; speaker to lawyer and police groups. Author: Search and Seizure, 1982, 2d edit., 1991, 93, Professional Responsibility of the Criminal Lawyer, 1987, 2d edit., 1996; Trial Handbook for Arkansas Lawyers, 1986, 2d edit. 1993; editor, author: Arkansas Prosecutor's Trial Manual, 1976-77; Arkansas Extradition Manual, 1978; editor (with B. Scheck and P. Neufield) DNA: Understanding, Controlling, and Depleting the New Evidence of the 90's, 1990; contbr. articles to profl. jours. Mem. Am. Bd. Criminal Lawyers, Ark. Bar Assn. (ho. of dels. 1976-79), Nat. Assn. Criminal Def. Lawyers (life, bd. dirs. 1989-95), Assn. Profl. Responsible Lawyers, Ark. Assn. Criminal Def. Lawyers (pres. 1987-89). Episcopalian. Home: 12920 Southridge Dr Little Rock AR 72212-1633 Office: 523 W 3rd St Little Rock AR 72201-2228

HALL, JOHNNIE CAMERON, pathologist; b. Nashville, Nov. 30, 1958; s. Johnnie Claiborne and Mary Pauline (Roark) H. BS in Biochemistry, David Lipscomb Coll., 1980; MD, U. Tenn., 1984. Diplomate Nat. Bd. Med. Examiners, Am. Bd. Pathology. Intern U. Tenn., Memphis, 1984-85, resident in pathology, 1986-88; surg. pathology fellow U. Tenn./Bapt. Meml. Hosp., Memphis, 1988; pathologist Pathology Group of Midsouth (formerly Midsouth Path. Group), Memphis, 1989—; co-med. dir. Bapt. Regional Lab., Memphis, 1991-93; med. dir. Bapt. Regional Lab. Specialist Technologist Sch., Memphis, 1991-93; devel. coun. Freed-Hardeman U., 1993—; spkr. in field. Contbr. articles to profl. jours. Active Rep. Presdl. Task Force, Washington, 1990—, Nat. Taxpayers Union, Washington, 1990—. Fellow Coll. Am. Pathologists, Am. Soc. Clin. Pathologists; mem. AMA, Am. Soc. Microbiology, U.S. and Can. Acad. Pathologists, Tenn. Med. Assn., Memphis-Shelby County Med. Soc. (medicolegal com. mem.). Republican. Mem. Church of Christ. Home: 8375 Westfair Dr Germantown TN 38139-3259 Office: Midsouth Pathology Group 899 Madison Ave # 270 Ue Memphis TN 38103-3405

HALL, JOYCE TURNER, utility company administrator; b. Atlanta, Sept. 1, 1948; d. Joseph C. and Hazel (Wilkins) Turner; m. Larry B. Hall, Aug. 16, 1969; children: Lamont D., Lisa D. BA in Spanish and Secondary Edn., Clark Coll., Atlanta, 1970. Mgmt. trainee Sears, Atlanta, 1970-71, dept. mgr., 1971-72, asst. mdse. mgr. so. terr., 1972-77; supr. Oglethorpe Power Corp., Tucker, Ga., 1979-88, buyer II, 1988-93, sr. buyer, 1993-96; sr. buyer Ga. Transmission Co., Tucker, 1996—; exec. on loan to Ga. Minority Supplier Devel. Coun. for Oglethorpe Power Corp., 1993. Mem. NAACP. Recipient Youth Motivation commendation Nat. Alliance Bus., 1983; Communication Techniques award Eileen M. Higgins & Assocs., 1983. Mem. Nat. Assn. Purchasing Mgmt., Purchasing Mgmt. Assn. of Ga., Clark Coll. Alumni Assn., Alpha Kappa Alpha. Democrat. Roman Catholic. Home: 3467 Blazing Pine Path Decatur GA 30034-4843 Office: Ga Transmission Co 2100 E Exchange Pl Tucker GA 30085

HALL, JUANITA JUSTICE, librarian; b. Olive Hill, Ky., Mar. 6, 1927; d. Lee Roye and Mary Opal (Phillips) Justice; m. John D. Hall (dec. Jan. 1994); 1 child, Diane. AB in Edn., Morehead State U., 1967, MA in Edn., 1973; MSLS, U. Ky., 1970. Libr. Camden Carroll Libr., Morehead (Ky.) State U., 1966-69, head of cataloging, 1969—. Mem. ALA. Home: Rt 4 Box 281 Olive Hill KY 41164 Office: Camden Carroll Libr Morehead State U University Blvd Morehead KY 40351

HALL, KENNETH KELLER, federal judge; b. Greenview, W.Va., Feb. 24, 1918; s. Jack and Ruby (Greene) H.; m. Geraldine Tabor, Apr. 6, 1940; 1 son, Kenneth Keller Jr. JD, U. W.Va., 1948. Bar: W.Va. 1948. Practiced law Madison, W.Va., 1948-52; mem. firm Garnett & Hall, 1948-53; mayor City of Madison, 1950-52; pvt. practice, 1969-70; judge 25th Jud. Cir. Ct. W.Va., Madison, 1953-69; adminstrv. law judge Social Security Adminstrn., Charleston, W.Va., 1970-71; judge U.S. Dist. Ct. for So. Dist. W.Va., Charleston, 1971-76, U.S. Ct. Appeals (4th cir.), 1976—. Com. mem. Budget Com. of Jud. Conf., 1989-92. With USNR, 1942-45. Recipient Silver Beaver award Boy Scouts Am., 1962, Outstanding Fed. Appellate Judge award Assn. Trial Lawyers Am., 1985. Mem. ABA, W.Va. Bar Assn., W.Va. Jud. Assn. Baptist. Office: US Ct Appeals 2100 Federal Bldg Charleston WV 25301

HALL, LAWRIE PLATT, consumer products executive, public, community and government relations executive, consultant; b. Balt., Mar. 26, 1942; d. William Henry and Virginia (Stein) Pitcher. AB in Fine Arts, Goucher Coll., Balt., 1960; Cert. Middle Mgmt., Simmons Grad. Sch., Boston, 1977. With Hutzlers Dept. Stores, Balt., 1964-66; pub. rels. asst. The Balt. Mus. Art, 1966-68; pub. info. officer U. Balt., 1969-70; pub. rels. dir. Balt. Assn. for Retarded Citizens, 1971; advt. supr., pub. rels. asst. Sierra Pacific Power Co., Reno, Nev., 1972-74; dir. local govt. rels. to dir. we. state and local rels. Atlantic Richfield Co., L.A., 1974-79; group exec. govt. affairs Greater Cin. C. of C., 1980-81; owner Pitcher Platt & Assocs., 1981-90; exec. dir. Crime Commn., Orlando, Fla., 1982-83; staff dir. Office of Mayor City of Orlando, 1983-88; pub. rels. and community affairs dir. Tupperware Home Parties U.S., Orlando, 1988-90; dir. external affairs Tupperware Worldwide, Orlando, 1990-94, Tuperware U.S., INc., Orlando, 1994—. Bd. dirs. Sta. WMFE, pub. broadcasting, Orlando, 1987-90, Metro Orlando Urban League, 1984-89, Cen. Fla. Women's Resource Ctr., 1984-87, vice-chmn., 1986, 87; mem. bd. Heart of Fla. United Way, campaign chmn. Osceola County, 1992; bd. dirs. Cultural Alliance Cen. Fla., 1988-90, chmn., 1990, Boys and Girls Clubs Ctr.. Fla., 1994—, mktg. com., 1994—; chmn. Arts Svcs. Coun., Inc., 1990-91, Chamber Found., 1994—; mem. Leadership Orlando, 1982—, Orange Blossom Trail Devel. Bd. Orlando and Orange County, 1990-93, Leadership Fla., 1987-88. Mem. Pub. Rels. Soc. Am., Am. Assn. Polit. Cons., Fla. Exec. Women, Fla. Women's Network (bd. dirs. 1994—), Greater Orlando C. of C. (bd. dirs. 1990-91), Fla. C. of C. (bd. dirs. 1990—), Kissimmee-Osceola C. of C. (bd. dirs. 1988—), Citrus Club. Democrat. Office: Tupperware PO Box 2353 Orlando FL 32802-2353

HALL, LUCINDA GENEVIEVE LONG, public relations executive, writer; b. Chattanooga, Dec. 28, 1941; d. Virgil Elbert and Genevieve Cora (Green) Long; m. Charles Louis Hall, Oct. 25, 1964 (div. Sept. 1979); children: Charles Christopher, Gregory Louis. BSJ, U. Tenn., 1963. Reporter, substitute soc. editor, copy editor, proofreader Enid (Okla.) Morning News and Daily Eagle, 1965-66; sr. editorial asst. youth publs. United Meth. Pub. House, Nashville, 1966-68; freelance writer, editor Nashville, 1968-73; assoc. editor NIADA Newsletter, Nashville, 1972-73; editor Tenn. Realtor and Touring Tenn., Nashville, 1972-76; publs. editor Holder Kennedy Pub. Rels., Nashville, 1968-79, acct. exec., publs. editor, 1979-84, sr. account exec., 1984-86, sr. v.p., 1990-92; owner, pres. Lucinda Hall Pub. Rels., Brentwood, Tenn., 1992—. Co-author: Nashville Tourguide, 1974; contbr. articles to profl. jours. Chair comm. com. Brentwood United Meth. Ch., 1982-88, mem. coun. ministries, 1982-88, 89-93, mem. adminstrv. bd., 1982-88, 89-93, chair religion and race comm., 1989-93, mem. various coms.; chair publicity com. Mid. Tenn. chpt. Am. Diabetes Assn., 1982-84, bd. dirs., 1983—, pres., 1984-85, bd. dirs. Tenn. affiliate, 1984-90, chair publicity com., 1984-85, chair pers. com., 1985-86, v.p., 1986-87, chair nominating com., 1986-88, chair bd. dirs.-elect, 1987-88, chair bd. dirs., 1988-89; project PENCIL coord. Adopt-a-Sch. Program for Antioch High Sch., Nashville, 1983-85; mem. publicity adv. coun. Mid. Tenn. chpt. Boy Scouts Am., 1985; mem. adult and community edn. adv. coun. Glencliff Comprehensive High Sch., 1988—; mem. publicity com. Brentwood Pearfest, 1988-90; publicity chair of benefit dinner Exch. Clubs Ctr. Prevention Child Abuse Mid. Tenn., Nashville, 1990; mem. Williamson County Econ. Showcase Com., Franklin, Tenn., 1992-93; active Nashville Symphony Guild, 1992—, mem. edn. com., 1993-94; bd. dirs. Combined Health Appeal Tenn., 1992—; vp. Combined Hlth. Appeal of Tenn., 1996; mem. adv. bd. dirs. Parents Reaching Out; mem. pub. rels. com. Mid. Tenn. chpt. Multiple Sclerosis Soc., 1993—. Recipient Citizen Leadership award Tenn. Community Edn. Assn., 1991, Parthenon award of merit Pub. Rels. Soc. Am., 1991, Excellence award Consol. Paper Inc., 1993, Addy award Nashville Advt. Fedn., 1994, Amer. Advertising Federation, Nashville Chapt., Citation of Excellence, 1996. Mem. Internat. Assn. Bus. Communicators (v.p. internal comms. 1982-83, chair nominating com. 1988-90, v.p. external comms. 1990-91, v.p. profl. devel. 1991-92, pres.-elect 1992-93, pres. Nashville chpt. 1993-94, sr. del. to Dist. 2, 1994—, Vintage Excellence Award 1978, 80, Silver Quill Award of Excellence 1981, 83, Gold Pen Award of Merit 1983, 86, 88, 92, 93, Gold Pen award of Excellence 1984, 96, Gold Pen Award of Recognition 1988, 91, 93), Soc. Profl. Journalists, Brentwood C. of C. (mem. econ. devel. com. 1993—), Sigma Kappa (v.p. Nashville chpt. 1968-69, pres. 1969-71, nat. alumnae province officer 1977-79), mem. Nashville Advertising Federation, public relations chair, 1994—. Mem. United Methodist Ch. Home: 1440 Columbine Cir Brentwood TN 37027-6920 Office: Lucinda Hall Pub Rels 5115 Maryland Way Brentwood TN 37027-7512

HALL, MARCEL SCOTT, nurse; b. Big Spring, Tex., Mar. 12, 1926; d. Nathan Graves and Nora Essie (Long) Scott; m. James W. Hall, Oct. 11, 1945 (div.); children: Deborah, Beviely, Rebekah. AS, Galveston (Tex.) Coll., 1981. Cert. Luback tchg. instr., Luboack Literacy; cert. poll mgr., cert. adminstr. CPR, cert. adminstr. first aid., Charleston County Election Commn. Nurse asst. Tex. Woman's Hosp., Houston, 1979; hosp. tech. asst. John Sealy Hosp., Galveston, Tex., 1979-81; nurse St. Francis Xavier Hosp., Charleston, S.C., 1981—. Mem. Neighborhood Safety, Charleston, 1981—. Mem. ANA, Nurses Svc. Orgn., S.C. Nurses Assn., Phi Sigma Alpha. Republican. Mem. Ch. of Christ. Home: 1734 Wambaw Ave Charleston SC 29412-2913 Office: St Francis Xavier Hosp 135 Rutledge Ave Charleston SC 29401-1338

HALL, MARILYN M., occupational health nurse; b. Bay City, Mich., Mar. 1, 1941; d. Oscar and Esther (Kolb) Pfannes; m. Harold D. Hall, June 5, 1965; children: Veronica Hall Henley, Gregory H. Diploma in nursing, Saginaw (Mich.) Gen. Hosp., 1962. RN, Ala., S.C.; cert. occupational health nurse-specialist; cert. in pulmonary function testing, audiometrics. Occupational health nurse GM, Athens, Ala., MeMC Materials Inc., Spartanburg, S.C. Mem. Patnership for Nursing, S.C., 1990-92. Mem. Am. Assn. Occupational Health Nurses, S.C. Assn. Occupational Health Nurses, Saginaw Gen. Hosp. Sch. Nursing Alumni Assn. Home: 312 Tearose Ln Simpsonville SC 29681-5847

HALL, MARY BETH, special education educator, writer; b. Bellevue, Ky., Sept. 8, 1961; d. Robert Arthur and Sue Ann (Geoslen) Ruschell; m. C.A. Hall; Apr. 1, 1989; children: A.C. Hall, B.M. Hall. BS in Spl. Edn., Ea. Ky. U., 1985, MS in Recreation and Parks Adminstrn., 1987. Cert. tchr. Ky. Tchr. Kenton County Bd. Edn., Erlanger, Ky., 1985—; cons. self employed, 1990—; coll. instr. No. Ky. U., Highland Heights, Ky., 1990-94; columnist Ky. Post Newspaper, Covington, Ky., 1996—. Author: The Silly Book, 1995. Grantee; TOPS grant Kenton County Bd., Erlanger, Ky., 1990. Baptist. Office: River Ridge Primary 2772 Amsterdam Rd Covington KY 41017

HALL, MARY HUGH, secondary school educator; b. Sumter, S.C., Apr. 15, 1937; d. Hughson Perry and Virginia Dare (Owens) Matthews; m. James Wallace Hall Sr., July 2, 1960; 1 child, James Wallace Jr. BA in Social Studies and French, Columbia Coll., 1959; postgrad., West Ga. Coll., 1975-79. Tchr. Arlington (Ga.) Schs., Inc., 1959-61; tchr., chair French dept. Douglas County H.S., Douglasville, Ga., 1965—; mem. steering com. West Ga. Alliance, Carrollton, 1992—. Recipient Outstanding Officer award Jaycees, 1970, 71. Mem. NEA, Douglas County Assn. Educators, Ga. Assn. Educators. Home: 4679 Bedford Pl Douglasville GA 30135

HALL, MICHAEL BISHOP, chemistry educator; b. Phila., Oct. 21, 1944; s. William and Virginia Hall; m. Carolyn Virginia Dale, Aug. 26, 1967; 1 child, Whitney Devon. BS, Juanita Coll., Huntingdon, Pa., 1966; PhD, U. Wis., 1971. Rsch. asst. chemistry dept. U. Wis., Madison, 1968-71, rsch. assoc., 1973-74; Assn. Elec. Industry fellow in chemistry U. Manchester, Eng., 1971-72; asst. prof. chemistry dept. Adelphi U., 1974-75; asst. prof. chemistry dept. Tex. A&M U., College Station, 1975-80, assoc. prof., 1980-83, grad. advisor, 1982-84, prof., 1983—, head chemistry dept., 1986-94; vis. assoc. Clare Hall U. Cambridge, Eng., 1982; lectr. various univs. and orgns. Contbr. articles to profl. jours. Grantee NSF, 1987—, Robert A. Welch Found., 1988—, Cornell Nat. Supercomputer Facility, 1989—, Cray Rsch., Inc., 1989-93, Tex. A&M U., 1991-92. Mem. Am. Chem. Soc., Sigma Xi, Alpha Chi Sigma, Phi Lambda Upsilon. Office: Tex A&M U Dept Chemistry College Station TX 77843

HALL, MICHAEL DALE, middle school educator, small business owner; b. Corona, Calif., Aug. 17, 1956; s. Marion Eugene and Shirley Loraine (Wells) H.; m. Patricia Jean Webb, July 17, 1993. BS, Ball State U., 1979, MA, 1983, cert. tchr., 1991; postgrad., Tex. A&M U., 1995—. Reporter, photographer The Greensburg (Ind.) Daily News, 1979-80, The Holmes County Farmer Hub, Millersburg, Ohio, 1980-81; chief photographer Cmty. Pubs., Bentonville, Ark., 1985-86; reporter, photographer The So. Sentinel, Ripley, Miss., 1987; owner, operator Freedom Photography, Ripley, 1987; mfr. display furniture Cubicon, Inc., Ripley, 1987-89; tchr. English Brownsville Ind. Sch. Dist., 1991—; adj. instr. English U. Tex., Brownsville, 1993-95; owner, operator Check Points Specialty Sales, Brownsville, 1994—. Contbg. author: Outstanding Poets of 1994, Best Poems of 1995, Best Poems of the 90's, 1996; author, pub.: (pen name Elias Tobias) (Post Card Series) Love Notes, 1995. Creator, sponsor GT Club Faulk Mid. Sch., Brownsville, 1995—, tchr., photographer ESL Saturday Acad., 1994-95; co-sponsor Fellowship of Christian Athletes, Brownsville, 1994; creator, editor Ball State Lit. Found., Muncie, Ind., 1989-91. Recipient Editors Choice awards Nat. Libr. Poetry, Owings Mills, Md., 1993, 94, 95; United Meth. Ch. scholar, Nashville, 1989-91; named Jaycee of Yr., Millersburg Area Jaycees, 1981. Mem. Nat. Specialty Merchants Assn., Assn. Tex. Profl. Educators, Tex. Mid. Sch. Assn., Internat. Soc. Poets (disting.), Kappa Tau Alpha. Democrat. Methodist. Home: Apt 256 4200 Boca Chica Blvd Brownsville TX 78521

HALL, MILES LEWIS, JR., lawyer; b. Fort Lauderdale, Fla., Aug. 14, 1924; s. Miles Lewis and Mary Frances (Dawson) H.; m. Muriel M. Fisher, Nov. 4, 1950; children: Miles Lewis III, Don Thomas. A.B., Princeton U., 1947; J.D., Harvard U., 1950. Bar: Fla. 1951, U.S. Supreme Ct., 1972, U.S. Ct. Appeals (11th cir.), U.S. Dist. Ct. Since practiced in Miami; ptnr. Hall & Hedrick, Miami, 1953—; dir. Gen. Portland, Inc., 1974-81. Author: Election of Remedies, Vol. VIII, Fla. Law and Practice, 1958. Pres. Orange Bowl Com., 1964-65, dir., 1950—, sec., treas. 1984-86; vice-chmn., dir. Dade County (Fla.) ARC, 1961-62, chmn., 1963-64, dir., 1967-73; nat. fund cons. ARC, 1963, 66-68, trustee, 1985—; pres. Ransom Sch. Parents Assn., 1966; chmn. South Fla. Gov.'s Scholarship Ball, 1966; mem. exec. bd. South Fla. council Boy Scouts Am., 1966-67; citizens bd. U. Miami, 1961-66; mem. Fla. Council of 100, 1961—, vice chmn., 1961-62; mem. Coral Gables (Fla.) Biltmore Devel. Com., 1972-73; mem. bd. visitors Coll. Law, Fla. State U., 1974-77; bd. dirs. Coral Gables War Meml. Youth Ctr., 1967—, pres., 1969-72; bd. dirs. Salvation Army, Miami, 1968-83, Fla. Citizens Against Crime 1984-89; bd. dirs. Bok Tower Gardens Found. Inc., 1987-90, 92—, sec., 1987-88, 91—; trustee St. Thomas U., 1990-96, vice chmn., 1993-96; trustee Fla. Supreme Ct. Hist. Soc., 1988—, v.p., 1991-92, pres., 1993-95. 2d lt. USAAF, 1943-45. Fellow Am. Bar Found., Fla. Bar Found.; mem. ABA (Fla. c-chmn. membership com. sect. corp. banking and bus. law 1968-72), Dade County Bar Assn. (dir. 1964-65, pres. 1967-68), Fla. Bar Assn., Am. Judicature Soc., Miami-Dade County C. of C. (v.p. 1962-64, dir. 1966-68), Harvard Law Sch. Assn. Fla. (dir. 1964-66), Cottage Club, Harvard Club, The Miami Club (v.p., dir. 1989-91, pres. 1990-91), Princeton Club So. Fla. (past pres.), Alpha Tau Omega. Methodist. Home: 8134 SE Hall Dr Arcadia FL 34266 Office: Hall & Hedrick 25 SE 2nd Ave Ste 1105 Miami FL 33131-1605

HALL, PAMELA BRIGHT, school health nurse; b. Pasquotank County, N.C., Nov. 23, 1955; d. Erna Dare and Virginia Lee (Edwards) Bright; m. Randy Byrd Hall, Apr. 6, 1975; children: Alton Paul, Randy Byrd. AS, Coll. of the Albemarle, Elizabeth City, N.C., 1987; BSN, E. Carolina U., 1994. Cert. CPR instr., AHA; cert. sch. health nurse, Nat. Bd. Sch. Nurses. Pub. health nurse Albemarle Home Care, Elizabeth City, 1988-89; staff nurse ICU Albemarle Hosp., Elizabeth City, 1987-95; sch. health nurse Elizabeth City-Pasquotank Sch. Sys., 1994—; mem. Pasquotank County Rescue Squad, 1985-88. Recipient Captains award Pasquotank County Rescue Squad, 1986. Home: 1191 Consolidated Rd Elizabeth City NC 27909-7897

HALL, PAUL V., company executive; b. 1943. With Am. Cyanamid, Andersonville, Ga., 1965-69; v.p. ops. Mullite Co. of Am., Andersonville, 1969—. Office: Mullite Co of Am Off State Hwy 49 Andersonville GA 31711

HALL, PIKE, JR., lawyer; b. Shreveport, La., May 27, 1931; s. Pike and Hazel (Tucker) H.; m. Anne Oden Hall, Dec. 24, 1951; children: Brevard Hall Knight, Pike III. BA, La. State U., 1951, JD, 1953. Bar: La. 1953. Asst. city atty. City of Shreveport, 1954-58; elected mem. Caddo Prish Sch. Bd., Shreveport, 1964-70; judge 2d Cir. Ct. Appeal, Shreveport, 1971-85, chief judge, 1985-90; assoc. justice Supreme Ct. La., 1990-94; counsel Blanchand, Walker, O'Quin & Roberts, Shreveport, 1994—; past chmn. La. Conf. of Ct. Appeal Judges; past bd. govs., vice chmn. La. Jud. Coll.; chmn. La. Jud. Bugetary Control Bd., 1992-94. Mem. adminstrv. bd. First United Meth. Ch., Shreveport. Mem. ABA, La. State Bar Assn. (past bd. govs., past Ho. of Dels.), Shreveport Bar Assn., Order of Coif. Democrat. Home: 1018 Delaware St Shreveport LA 71106-1402

HALL, RALPH CARR, lawyer, real estate consultant; b. Chicago, Ill., Mar. 28, 1928; s. Rupert Irving and Pauline Martha (Prime) H.; m. Barbara Fordyce, Jan. 21, 1950; children: Brett C., Brian C., Judson P., Trudy A. LLB, Tulsa U., 1952. Bar: Okla. 1952, Tex. 1974. V.P. Hall Investment Co., Tulsa, 1948-58; pres. Realty Constrn. Co., Tulsa, 1958-61; real estate investment rep. Am. Oil Co., Birmingham, Ala., 1961-63; div. real estate mgr. Kroger Co., Nashville and Charlotte, N.C., 1963-66; v.p., real estate counsel H.E.B. Properties, Corpus Christi, Tex., 1966-85; pvt. practice, Corpus Chirsti, 1985—; real estate cons., 1985—; mediator Nueces County Dispute Resolution Ctr., 1994—. Pres., bd. dirs. Goodwill Ind. South Tex., Corpus Christi, 1969-88; planning commr. City of Corpus Christi, 1990-95. Mem. Tex. Bar Assn., Nueces County Bar Assn., Corpus Christi Pistol and Rifle Club (pres. bd. dirs. 1980). Republican. Episcopalian. Office: PO Box 8364 Corpus Christi TX 78468-8364

HALL, RALPH MOODY, congressman; b. Fate, Tex., May 3, 1923; s. Hugh O. and Maude Hall; m. Mary Ellen Murphy, Nov. 14, 1944; children: Hampton, Brett, Blakeley. Student, U. Tex., Tex. Christian U., So. Meth. U.; LL.D., So. Meth. U. Bar: Tex. County judge Rockwall County, Tex., 1950-62; mem. Tex. Senate, 1962-72; past pres., chief exec. officer Tex. Aluminum Corp.; past gen. counsel Tex. Extrusion Co., Inc.; past organizer, chmn. bd. Lakeside Nat. Bank of Rockwall; chmn. bd. Bank of Crowley; past chmn. bd. dirs. Lakeside News, Inc.; chmn. bd. Linrock Inc.; pres. Crowley Holding Co.; mem. 97th-104th Congresses from 4th Tex. dist., Washington, D.C., 1980—; mem. commerce com., mem. sci. com., ranking minority mem. space sub-com. Served with USNR, 1942-45. Mem. Am. Legion, VFW. Methodist. Lodge: Rotary (past pres.). Office: US Ho of Reps 2236 Rayburn Hob Washington DC 20515•

HALL, ROBERT ALAN, financial company executive; b. Montgomery, Ala., Oct. 30, 1958; s. Mack Luverne and Miriam (Johnston) H. BS in Commerce and Bus. Adminstrn., U. Ala., 1981. CPA, Ala., cert. internal auditor. Sr. acct. Jackson and Thornton, CPAs, Montgomery, 1981-83; sr. auditor Vulcan Materials Co., Birmingham, Ala., 1983-86, supr. internal audit, 1986-87; mgr., fin. and adminstrn. Saudi Arabian Vulcan Ltd., Jubail, Saudi Arabia, 1987-90; spl. assignments analyst Vulcan Materials Co., 1990-91; contr., treas., asst. sec. Harbert Internat. Constrn. Inc., Birmingham, Ala., 1991-95, v.p., CFO, 1995—; presdl. appointee White House Conf. on Small Bus., 1995; profl. adv. bd. Sch. Accountancy/U. Ala., 1991—. Charter mem. Rep. Presdl. Task Force, Washington, 1984-86; presdl. appointee White House Conf. Small Bus., 1995. Recipient presdl. achievement award Pres. Ronald Reagan, 1983, Cert. of Appreciation, Gov. of Ala., 1988; named hon. citizen City of L.A., 1984, hon. asst. atty. gen. State of Ala., 1984; named one of Outstanding Young Men of Am., 1986. Mem. AICPA, Ala. Soc. CPA's, Am. Businessmen's Assn. Saudi Arabia (bd. dirs. 1988-90), U. Ala. Sr. Execs. Club., Coll. Commerce, Young Republicans, Hon. Order Ky. Cols., Civitans. Republican. Baptist. Home: 416 Old Brook Cir Birmingham AL 35242-5337 Mailing Address: PO Box 531390 Birmingham AL 35253-1390

HALL, ROBERT H., research director; b. Washington, Nov. 7, 1944; s. Harwood Vassar and Ruth Reuman (Carter) H.; m. Jennifer E. Miller; 1 child, Cecelia Jane. BA, Rhodes Coll., 1966; MA, Columbia U., 1970. With Inst. for So. Studies, Durham, 1970—, founding editor quar. jour. Southern Exposure, exec. dir., 1974-84, rsch. dir. Author: The Democracy Index, 1993, Who Owns North Carolina?, 1986; editor: Environmental Politics: Lessons from the Grassroots, 1987; co-author: The Green Index: State-by-state Guide to the Nation's Environmental Health, 1991. Founding bd. dirs. N.C. Coastal Fedn., Workplace Reform Coalition, N.C., Southerners for Econ. Justice, Fund for So. Communities. Named Tar Heel of the Week Raleigh NEWS and Observer, 1990; recipient Nancy Reynolds Sabbatical Z. Smith Reynolds Found., 1991; MacArthur fellowship J.D. & C.T. MacArthur Found., 1992. Office: Inst for So Studies PO Box 531 Durham NC 27702-0531

HALL, RONALD E., retired oil company executive; b. 1933. With Shell Oil Co., Houston, 1958-83, Gulf Oil Co., Houston, 1983-85; pres., CEO Citgo Petroleum Corp., Houston, 1985-96; chmn. Citgo Refining and Chems., Tulsa, Okla., 1987-96. Office: Citgo Petroleum Corp PO Box 3758 6100 S Yale Ave 12th Fl Tulsa OK 74136

HALL, SIDNEY GUY, retired orthodontist; b. Danville, Va., Dec. 31, 1924; s. Sidney Glenn and Nellie Amelia (Oakley) H.; m. Helmi Maria Wirta, Aug. 25, 1945; 1 child, Jonathan Guy Hall. BS in Biology, Lynchburg Coll., 1951; DDS, Med. Coll. Va., 1952; MS in Orthodontics, U. Montreal, Can., 1965. Lic. dentist, orthodontist. From asst. prof. operative dentistry to assoc. prof. Med. Coll. Va. Sch. Dentistry, Richmond, 1952-62; pvt. practice Lynchburg, Va., 1965-90; retired, 1990. Active Comty. Concert Band, Lynchburg, 1968. Mem. ADA, Am. Assn. Ret. Persons, Am. Assn. Orthodontists, Piedmont Dental Assn., Va. Dental Assn., Lynchburg Dental Soc. (pres.), Va. Assn. Orthodontists, Amateur Radio Club, Antique Auto Club, Am. Legion (bd. dirs. Lynchburg comty. concerts 1975-93), Psi Omega, Omicron Kappa Upsilon. Republican. Lutheran. Home: 2207 Mimosa Dr Lynchburg VA 24503-4307

HALL, TELKA MOWERY ELIUM, educational administrator; b. Salisbury, N.C., July 22, 1936; d. James Lewis and Malissa (Fielder) Mowery; m. James Richard Elium III, June 20, 1954 (div. 1961); 1 child, W. Denise Elium Carr; m. Allen Sanders Hall, Apr. 15, 1967 (div. 1977). Student, Am. Inst. Banking, 1955-57, Mary-Hardin Baylor Coll., Waco, Tex., 1957; BA, Catawba Coll., Salisbury, 1967; MEd, Miss. U. for Women, Columbus, 1973;

EdS, Appalachian State U., 1975; postgrad., U. N.C., Greensboro, 1977; EdD, U. N.C., Chapel Hill, 1990. Cert. early childhood, intermediate lang. arts and social studies tchr., curriculum specialist, adminstr., supr., supt., N.C.; notary pub., N.C. Bookkeeper, teller Citizens & So. Bank, Spartanburg, S.C., 1955-56; bookkeeper 1st Nat. Bank, Killeen, Tex., 1956-58; bookkeeper, savs. teller Exchange Bank & Trust Co., Dallas, 1958-61; acct. Catawba Coll., 1961-65; floater teller bookkeeping and proof depts. Security Bank & Trust Co., Salisbury, 1965-68, 71; tchr. Rowan County Sch. System, Salisbury, 1967-70, 71-72, 1973-82; asst. prin. North Rowan Elem. Sch., Spencer, N.C., 1982-94; asst. prin. Rockwell (N.C.) Elem. and China Grove Elem. Schs., 1994-96, ret., 1996; part time asst. prin. of curriculum China Grove Elem., 1996—; receptionist H & R Block, Salisbury, 1979-83; Chpt. I reading tchr. Nazareth Children's Home, Rockwell, N.C., 1979-81. Author: The Effect of Second Language Training in Kindergarten on the Development of Listening Skills. Mem. Salisbury Cmty. Chorus, 1951-52, Hist. Salisbury Found., Inc., Salisbury Concert Choir, 1981-83; foreperson Rowan county grand jury, 1991; pianist Franklin Presbyn. Ch., Salisbury, 1952-55, choir dir., 1975-87; past pres. Women of Ch., Sunday Sch. tchr., sec., 1979-80, deacon, 1980-83, elder, 1991-92, 96-99, clk. of session, 1992, choir mem., 1947—, hand-bell choir 1996—; cons. Dial HELP, Salisbury, 1981-83; charter mem. bd. dirs. Old North Salisbury Assn., 1980—. Civitan Music scholar, 1954, Kiwanis Acad. scholar, 1966, Catawba Coll. Acad. scholar, 1965-67, Mary Morrow Ednl. scholar N.C. Assn. Educators, 1966. Mem. AAUW (v.p. 1985-87, 91-93), ASCD, N.C. Assn. Sch. Adminstrs., N.C. Assn. Educators, Tarheel Assn. Prins. and Asst. Prins., U. N.C. Gen. Alumni Assn., Rowan County Prins. Assn., Sci. Alliance (Rowan County, charter), Salisbury Hist. Assn., Kappa Delta Pi, Theta Phi (pres. 1992-93). Home: 1626 N Main St Salisbury NC 28144-2928 Office: China Grove Elem 514 Franklin St China Grove NC 28023

HALL, WARD MILES, show producer, writer; b. Trenton, Nebr., June 21, 1930; s. Glenn Kenneth Hall and Opal Irene (Miles) Kaske. DDiv, Universal Coll., Chgo. Performer Dailey Bros., Gonzalez, Tex., 1946-49, Frisco Follies, New Orleans, Tampa, 1949-50; mgr., owner Hall and Leonard Show, Cin., 1951-64, Ward Hall Shows, Gibsonton, Fla., 1965-68; sec.-treas., mgr. World Attractions, Inc., Gibsonton, 1969-85; president Wondercade Inc., Gibsonton, 1969-85; sec.-treas., mgr. Hall & Christ, Inc., Gibsonton, 1965-89; pres., producer Froman Prodns., Inc., Gibsonton, 1968-80; v.p., mgr. Christ Hall Inc., Gibsonton, 1990—; bd. dirs. Internat. Ind. Showmen's Assn., Gibsonton, Fla., 1968-79. pres., 1974-75; v.p. East Bay C. of C., Gibsonton, Fla., 1977, bd. dirs. 1976-77. Author: (books) Gypsy No More, 1961, Struggles and Triumphs of a Modern Day Showman, 1981, My Very Unusual Friends, 1991; author and composer: (musical) Saigon Doll, 1995; producer, dir. Magic on Parade, Mexico City, 1976, Wonderglade Can. and U.S., 1975-83, Circus Blues, Carnegie Hall, 1995. Recipient award Royal Am. Shrine Club, Tampa, Fla., Smithsonian Instn., Washington, 1980; named Internat. Showman, New Eng., Showmans Assn., Boston, 1976. Mem. Internat. Showmens Assn., Showmans League of Am., Circus Fans of Am. (Creative Contbn. award 1995), Circus Hist. Soc. Home: PO Box 907 Gibsonton FL 33534

HALL, WILLIAM, minister; b. Buffalo, Ill., Oct. 25, 1914; s. Frederick Charles and Martha Ann (Fletcher) H.; m. Mary Lu Randall, June 26, 1938; children: David Randall, Bruce Fletcher, Sarah Wynne. BS in Edn., U. Ill., 1936; BD, Yale Div. Sch., 1941. Ordained to ministry Disciples of Christ, 1941. Missionary rural areas Bilaspur Dist., Madhya Pradesh, India, 1945-52; dir. gen. ch. program, missionary edn. dept. United Christian Missionary Soc., Indpls., 1953-56; assoc. prof. Brite Div. Sch., Tex. Christian U., Ft. Worth, 1957-80; ret. Brite Div. Sch., TCU, 1980. Author: Mission Follow New Frontiers, 1958, Beliefs and Consequences, 1964, Six Hundred Million Neighbors, 1968. Home: 2825 Merida Ave Fort Worth TX 76109-1727

HALL, WILLIAM DAVID, municipal official; b. Chillicothe, Ohio, Aug. 4, 1943; s. Harry William and Mary Naomi (Trainer) H.; m. Mary Ann Horton, June 17, 1964; children: Barbara Ann, William David Jr., Cheryl Lynn, Scott Michael. Student, Ohio U., 1961-62, Texarkana C.C., 1962-63. Mng. editor, sports editor Texarkana (Tex.) Gazette, 1962-68; news dir., gen. mgr. Sta. KTFS-AM/FM Radio, Texarkana, 1968-86; mng. ptnr. ASAP Printing, Texarkana, 1986-88; emergency mgmt. coord. City of Texarkana, 1988—; adj. instr. Divisn. Emergency Mgmt. State of Tex., 1992—; chmn. 911 Adv. Com., Texarkana, 1995; liaison local emergency planning com., Texarkana, 1991—; instr. Ark. Police Dept., Texarkana, 1992—; bd. mem., coord. Four States CISM Team, Texarkana, 1992—. Coach, mgr. Dixie Baseball, Texarkana, 1976—; chair govt. and civic affairs Boy Scouts Am., Texarkana, 1995—, mem. dist. com., 1995—; mem., liaison Bowie County Fire Assn., Texarkana, 1990—. Recipient APME award AP, 1986. Mem. Emergency Mgmt. Assn. Tex. Home: 2211 Flower Acres Rd Texarkana TX 75501 Office: City of Texarkana PO Box 1967 Texarkana TX 75501

HALL, WILLIAM LLOYD, surgeon; b. Wichita Falls, Tex., Aug. 25, 1925; s. Lloyd Lorenso and Frankie (Hodges) H.; M.D., Southwestern Med. Coll., 1947; student N. Tex. State U., 1942-44; m. Ann Carolyn Short, July 11, 1947 (div. 1976); children: Marc William, Michael Steven, Lisa Merenith, Jay Jonathan. Intern George Washington U. Hosp., 1947-48; resident Gt. Lakes Naval Hosp., 1948-49, Baylor U. Hosp., 1953-56; practice occupational medicine, Dallas, 1991—; chief surgery S.W. Dallas Hosp., 1986—. Served as lt. M.C., USN, 1948-53. Diplomate Am. Bd. Surgery. Mem. Am., Tex. med. assns., Dallas County Med. Soc. Home: 1419 Yakimo Dr Dallas TX 75208-2546 Office: 5414 Forest Ln Dallas TX 75244

HALLANAN, ELIZABETH V., federal judge; b. Charleston, W.Va., Jan. 10, 1925; d. Walter Simms and Imogene (Burns) H. U. Charleston, 1946; JD, W.Va. U., 1951; postgrad. U. Mich., 1964. Atty. Crichton & Hallanan, Charleston, 1952-59; mem. W.Va. State Bd. Edn., Charleston, 1955-57, Ho. of Dels., W.Va. Legis., Charleston, 1957-58; asst. commr. pub. instns. Charleston, 1958-59; mem., chmn. W.Va. Pub. Service Commn., Charleston, 1969-75; atty. Lopinsky, Bland, Hallanan, Dodson, Deutsch & Hallanan, Charleston, 1975-84; judge U.S. Dist Ct. (so. dist.) W.Va., 1983—. Mem. W.Va. Bar Assn. Office: US Dist Ct PO Box 2546 Beckley WV 25329*

HALLAS, GAIL, healthcare and nursing home consultant, executive; b. Jamaica, Mar. 21, 1942; m. David J. Hallas, Oct. 28, 1976; children: Jeff, Wendi, Staci, Nicole (dec.), Laura. AS with honors, RN, St. Petersburg Jr. Coll., 1975; BS, U. State of N.Y., 1979; MA, Columbia Pacific U., 1980, PhD in Edn. and Psychology, 1982. Lic. RN, Tex., N.C.; cert. regional long term care ombudsman, N.C. Regional long term care ombudsman Region D Coun. of Govts., Boone, N.C., 1983-85; psychiat. RN in charge New River Mental Health, Psychiat. Inpatient Unit, Banner Elk, N.C., 1985-87; DON svcs. ARA Living Ctrs., Spring Br. Healthcare Ctr., Houston, 1987-88; dir. of edn. Tex. Health Care Assn., Austin, 1988; owner The Hallas Group, St. Petersburg, Fla., 1988—, Benchmark Books, St. Petersburg, 1988—; trainer on Ams. with Disabilities Act to numerous cos.; ADA trainer U.S. EEOC; guest lectr. Northwestern La. U., U. N.Mex. Coll. Law, Albuquerque, Am. Health Care Assn., Am. Assn. Homes and Svcs. for Aging, Am. Coll. Health Care Adminstrs., Am. Hosp. Assn., Am. Ambulance Assn., numerous other nat., state and local orgns. and facilities. Author: How To Recruit and Retain Staff in Long Term Care, How To Manage and Supervise Your Workplace to Comply with the Americans with Disabilities Act, How To Prevent Mistakes During Surveys: 5 Secrets Nobody Ever Told You, Final Rule Survival Workbook and Teaching Text, Beyond Surviving the Final Rule: Going for the Gold Superior Rating at Your Facility, How to Prepare for and Implement the Americans with Disabilities Act, also others; editor: Recording for the Blind; contbr. articles to profl. jours. Active Fla. Assn. Community Rels. Profls.; bd. advocacy, support group people with disabilities; Family Network on Disabilities; Tex. Med. Assn. Task Force on Nursing Shortage; Tex. Legis. Task Force on AIDS; Gov.'s Task Force Post-Secondary Med., Dental, Allied Health Edn., testimonial on nursing shortage, Austin; Internat. Platform Assn.; adv. com. AIDS Tex. Health Care Assn.; divsn. LTC paperwork reduction com. Tex. Dept. Health/Tex. Dept. Human Resources; speakers bureau AIDS Svcs., Austin; adv. bd. Spencer Inst., divsn. Fischer Ednl. System; Watauga Opportunities; bd. dirs. Elisabeth Kubler-Ross Hospice; advocacy group Gray Panthers, Pinellas County, Fla.; Gov.'s Task Force on Women's Rights, testimonial, rights of women in nursing, Tampa; adj., life mem. Disabled Am. Vets. Auxiliary; mem. faculty Nat. Judicial Coll., U. Nev., Reno. Nominated for Gerontol. Nurse of Yr. award, 1978; named Outstanding Young Women of Am., 1979; recipient VFW award, 1981, Susan B. Anthony award, 1981, Apple From the Tchr. award, 1982. Mem. ANA (cert. gerontol. RN, cert. nurse adminstr.), Am. Soc. for Assn. Execs. (cert. edn. dir.), Am. Mgmt. Assn., U.S. C. of C., Pinellas Braille Group, Nat. Assn. Self-Employed, Parent to Parent, Nat. Assn. Female Execs., Am. Soc. Assn. Execs., Fla. Vets. Fgn. War, Fla. Am. Legion, Soc. Profl. and Exec. Women, AAUW, Houston Orgn. Nurse Execs., Houston Area Dirs. of Nursing Assn.

HALLBAUER, ROSALIE CARLOTTA, business educator; b. Chgo., Dec. 8, 1939; d. Ernest Ludwig and Kathryn Marquerite (Ramm) H. BS, Rollins Coll., 1961; MBA, U. Chgo., 1963; PhD, U. Fla., 1973. CPA, Ill.; cert. mgmt. acct., cost analyst, profl. estimater. Assoc. prof. acctg. Fla. Internat. U., Miami, 1972—. Mem. Am. Acctg. Assn., Am. Woman's Soc. CPAs, Ill. Soc. CPAs, Inst. Mgmt. Accts., Acctg. Historians Soc., Beta Alpha Psi, Pi Gamma Mu. Office: Fla Internat Univ N Miami Campus 3000 NE 145th St Miami FL 33181-3612

HALLENBERG, NANCY LEE, school administrator; b. Toledo, Feb. 13, 1941; d. Wallace John and Elizabeth Jane (Manley) Corban; m. James Edward Hofferberth, Aug. 26, 1961 (div. 1984); children: Matthew James, Wendy Lee, John Edward; m. Harvey Raymond Hallenberg, Feb. 14, 1986. BS in Edn., Ohio State U., 1962; MEd in Reading, George Mason U., Fairfax, Va., 1977; postgrad., U. Md., 1978, Ohio State U., 1979, 84. Lectr./asst. George Mason U., Fairfax, 1976-77; tchr. St. Joseph Montessori Sch., Columbus, Ohio, 1979-80; lead tchr., Erdkinder project St. Joseph Montessori Sch., 1980-84; elem. prog. coord. Inst. Advanced Montessori Studies, Silver Spring, Md., 1984-87; elem. intern coord. Inst. Advanced Montessori Studies, 1984-87; reading specialist City of Manassas pub. schs., Va., 1985-86; Montessori ednl. cons. Hallenberg & Hallenberg Cons., Lake Worth, Fla., 1984—; lectr./tchr. trainer Inst. for Adv. Montessori Studies, Silver Spring, 1983-91; co-dir. The Claremont Sch., Annandale, 1986-92; co-dir., elem. course coord. Claremont Ctr. for Advanced Montessori Studies, Boca Raton, 1992—; dir. Claremont Montessori Sch., Boca Raton, 1992—; rschr. in field; writer, dir., tchr. Montessori programs for secondary level students; adj. prof. Barry Univ., Miami; guest lectr. Houston Montessori Tng. Ctr., Houston; intern coord., lectr. Claremont Ctr. for Advanced Montessori Studies, 1992—. Contbr. articles to profl. jours. Vol. tchr. gifted children Fairfax County pub. schs., 1977-78. Grantee, The Washington Post, 1985-86. Mem. Am. Montessori Soc., Lake Charleston Homeowner's Assn., Phi Delta Kappa, Kappa Delta Pi. Office: Claremont Montessori Ctr 2450 NW 5th Ave Boca Raton FL 33431-8205

HALLER, ROBERT HENRY, endodontist, USAF officer; b. Suffern, N.Y., July 16, 1957. BA, Bucknell U., Lewisburg, Pa., 1979; DDS, U. Md., 1983. Cert. in Endodontics, Wilford Hall Med. Ctr., San Antonio, 1994. Commd. 2d lt. USAF, 1980; advanced through grades to lt. col., 1983; resident in gen. practice USAF Med. Ctr., Wright-Patterson AFB, Ohio, 1983-84; general dental officer USAF 833d Med. Group, Holloman AFB, N.M., 1984-88, USAF 416th Med. Group, Griffiss AFB, N.Y., 1988-92; resident in endodontics USAF Wilford Hall Med. Ctr., Lackland AFB, Tex., 1992-94; endodontic dental officer USAF 6th Med. Group, MacDill AFB, Fla., 1994—; endodontist Shea Specialty Group, Largo, Fla., 1995—; chmn. computer steering group USAF 6th Dental Squadron, MacDill AFB, 1995—, radiology officer, 1994—. Contbr. articles to profl. jours. Mem. Nat. Democratic Com., Washington, 1996; youth dir. United Meth. Ch., N.M. and N.Y., 1984-92. Fellow Acad. of Gen. Dentistry; mem. ADA, Am. Assn. Endodontists, U.S. Amateur Ballroom Dancers Assn., Tai Chi Soc., Hillsborough County Dental Assn. (mem. com. 1994—). Democrat. Methodist. Home: 1102 Belladonna Dr Brandon FL 33510 Office: USAF 6th Dental Squadron 8415 Bayshore Blvd Tampa FL 33621

HALLETT, DEAN ALLAN, insurance company executive; b. Meriden, Conn., Sept. 22, 1959; s. Eugene Ruel and Frances (Melvin) H.; m. Rebecca Lynn Harwood, July 21, 1988; 1 child, Ian Paul. BS, U. New Haven, 1986; postgrad., U. West Fla., 1986-87. Mgr. regional sales Golden Rule Ins., Indpls., 1988-93; pres. Hallett Inst. Svcs., Deerfield Beach, Fla., 1993—. With USCG, 1979-86. Mem. Nat. Assn. Life Underwriters, Nat. Assn. Health Underwriters (v.p. Palm Beach chpt. 1989), Masons (lodge meridian 77). Republican. Office: Hallett Ins Svcs Inc Ste 300 6120 Cherokee Dr Milton FL 32570-6507

HALLILA, BRUCE ALLAN, welding engineer; b. Washington, D.C., Nov. 2, 1950; s. Esko Ensio and Gertrude Naomi (Tilley) H.; m. Pamela Joan Guerin, Dec. 18, 1982; children: Gregory Michael Decedue, April Patrice, Andrew Allan, Joshua Scott. BSME, BS in Welding Engrng., LeTourneau U., 1974. Welding engr. Chgo. Bridge & Iron Co., Houston, 1975-77, Avondale Shipyards, Inc., New Orleans, 1977-80; asst. shipbuilding supt. Avondale Shipyards, Inc., 1980-82; steel supt. Halter Marine, Inc., New Orleans, 1982; welding supt. Bell Halter, Inc., New Orleans, 1982-84; sr. welding engr. Avondale Industries, Inc., New Orleans, 1984-86; chief welding engr. Avondale Industries, Inc., 1986—; vice chmn. welding com. Ogden Corp., N.Y.C., 1984-86; welding cons. Gas Tech. Cons., Inc., Metairie, La., 1990—; CWI test proctor Am. Welding Soc., Miami, 1979—; welding industry cons. State of La VoTech Welding Coun., Metairie, 1982—; panel mem. welding R & D, Maritime Adminstrn. Mem. com. troop 33 Boy Scouts Am., 1991—. recipient Gov.'s award State of La., Baton Rouge, 1982. Mem. Am. Welding Soc. (dist. 9 dir. 1994—, D3 com., Proposer award 1982, Dist. Meritorious award 1987, 92, named Disting. Mem. 1989), Am. Bur. Shipping (spl. com. on materials and welding), Delta Sigma Psi. Republican. Home: 8725 Carriage Rd New Orleans LA 70123-3605 Office: Avondale Industries Inc PO Box 50280 New Orleans LA 70150-0280

HALL-KELLY, KATHY B., small business owner, columnist, speaker; b. Gretna, Va., July 4, 1957; d. James C. Hunt; children from previous marriage: Barry, Fayola, Ewan; m. Ronald E. Kelly, Aug. 27, 1993; 1 child, Veronica Nia. Cert. med. technician, Bronx C.C., 1977; cert. in TV prodn./radio, Foothill Coll., 1981; AA in Comm., Elizabeth Seton Coll., 1982-84. Prodn. asst. WNYW-TV, N.Y.C., 1984-85; computer asst. mgr. Computer Ctr. 1, Middletown, N.Y., 1985-87; advt. rep. Hudson Valley Black Press, Newburgh, N.Y., 1987-88; with ctrl. reservations divsn. Cablevision, Inc., Middletown, 1988-91; on-air reporter Presentation Power, Orlando, Fla., 1991-92; real estate timeshare salesperson Westgate Resort, Kissimmee, Fla., 1992-93; radio talk show host, prodr. CNN/Sta. WPRD, Orlando, 1992-94; with ctrl. reservations-customer svcs. divsn. Walt Disney World, Orlando, 1995—; motivational spkr. Orange County Dept. Juvenile Corrections, Orlando, 1994; art show coord. Multicultural/Black History, Orlando, 1995—. Author: Building a Better You, 1996; columnist African-American Steps: Towards Positive Art, 1996. Mem. Nat. Writers Assn. Office: Building a Better You PO Box 560607 Orlando FL 32856

HALLLWELL, LEIGH FRANCES, artist, writer; b. Framingham, Mass., Mar. 4, 1947; d. Leonard Francis and Rena Louise (Aptt) Herrick; m. Roger Zants Youmans, Aug. 12, 1967 (dec. Dec. 1974); m. Thomas Britton Hallowell, Dec. 24, 1975 (div. July 1981). Student, Clark U., 1965-67. Sec. svc. ctr., corr., desktop pub. Fla. Power & Light, Juno, 1981-91, shareholder svcs. rep., 1992-95; ISO 9001 asst. Pratt & Whitney, West Palm Beach, Fla., 1995-96. Home and Office: 13573 49th St N Royal Palm Beach FL 33411

HALLOCK, ANN HAYES, Italian language and literature educator; b. Los Angleles, May 13, 1941; d. Marshall Hayes and Dorothy Hallock. BA, Stanford U., 1963; MA, Middlebury Coll., 1968; PhD, Harvard U., 1974. Asst. prof. Italian U. Calif., Riverside, 1969-72; asst. prof. Italian Tulane U., 1972-78, assoc. prof., 1978—; reviewer NIH, Washington, 1978, Inst. of Internat. Edn., Washington, 1994—. Author: Michelangelo The Poet, 1978; asst. to editor Forum Italicum, 1968-72; contbr. articles to profl. jours. including Neophilologus, Italica, also others. Elder Presbyn. Ch., 1976—; ct. apptd. spl. advocate, New Orleans, 1992—; sec. Broadmoor Improvement Assn., New Orleans, 1995, pres., 1996. Recipient Cultural Achievement award Italian Cultural Soc., 1977, Medal of Merit Italian Rep., 1977; named Goodwill Amb. of La. Lt. Gov. of La., 1977. Mem. Am. Assn. of Univ. Profs., Am. Assn. of Tchrs. of Italian. Republican. Presbyterian. Home: 3500 Upperline St New Orleans LA 70125 Office: Tulane U Dept French & Italian New Orleans LA 70118

HALLOWELL, BRUCE ALLEN, health facility administrator; b. Camden, N.J., Aug. 27, 1958; s. Edward Duboise and Ruth Ann (McNabb) H.; m. Marilyn Elizabeth Cohen, Aug. 9, 1981; children: Ryan Louis, Samantha Elizabeth, Matthew Bruce. B of Health Sci., Fla. Atlantic U., 1980; MSW (hon.), Barry Coll., Miami, Fla., 1982; MBA, Tampa (Fla.) Coll., 1992. Charge auditor Blue Cross & Blue Shield, Miami, 1980-83; installation dir. Shared Medical, Miami, 1983-86; sr. installation rep. Gerber Alley & Co., Wellesley, Mass., 1986; project mgr. Tampa Gen. Hosp., 1986-89; sr. cons. Ernst & Young, Washington, 1989-90; dir. patient accts. Morton Plant Mease Health Care, Clearwater, Fla., 1990—; Mem. adv. bd. SSI Software, Mobile, Ala., 1993-96, Hospital Cost Cons., Pleasanton, Calif., 1994-96. Contbg. editor HFMA Fla., Miami, 1993-96; contbr. articles to profl. jours. Supr. Palm Bay Cmty., Tampa, 1996; cons. Jewish Family Svc., Tampa, 1992, Crisis Ctr., Tampa, 1991. Recipient Receivable Mgr. of Yr., Aspen Pub., 1983, 95. Mem. Healthcare Fin. Mgmt. (membership chmn. 1996, Advance award 1995), Fla. Hospital Assn. (founding), Patient Fin. Svcs. (founding). Home: 5803 Cay Cove Tampa FL 33615 Office: Morton Plant Mease 818 Milwaukee Ave Dunedin FL 34698-7031

HALMOS, PETER, investment company executive; b. Budapest, Hungary, July 4, 1943; came to U.S., 1951; s. George Anthony and Clara (Sacher) H.; m. Vicki Carol Knight, Dec. 31, 1978; children: Nicholas, Gregory. BS, MBA, U. Fla., 1969; postgrad., Harvard U., 1976. Chmn. bd. Safecard Svcs., Inc., Ft. Lauderdale, Fla., 1969-90; v.p. High Plains Capital Corp., Laramie, Wyo., 1978-92, chmn., 1992—; chmn., chief exec. officer Credit Ln. Corp., 1990—; exec. mgmt. cons. Safecard Svcs., Inc., 1990-92; chmn., CEO Privacy Protection Svcs., Inc., 1993—, Passport Ins. Co., Inc., 1990—; mng. ptnr. Halmos Trading and Investment Co., 1978—; chmn. Continuity Mktg. Corps., 1993—. Trustee Palm Beach (Fla.) Day Sch., 1988-91, Halmos Found., Inc., 1986—, chmn. 1984—; bd. dirs. Pinecrest Sch., Ft. Lauderdale, 1985-92; trustee Preservation Found., Palm Beach, 1988—, Palm Beach Community Chest United Way, 1988-92, Am. Cancer Soc., Palm Beach, 1988—. Independent. Episcopalian. Home: 315 Clarke Ave Palm Beach FL 33480-6126

HALPER, EDWARD CHARLES, philosophy educator; b. Barberton, Ohio, Sept. 28, 1951; s. Robert and Audrey (Buckwold) H.; m. Jaroslava Tausinger, Aug. 19, 1979; children: Yehuda, Daniel, Aaron. BA, U. Chgo., 1973; MA, Columbia U., 1975; PhD, U. Toronto, Ont., Can., 1980. Asst. prof. philosophy Gustavus Adolphus Coll., St. Peter, Minn., 1980-84; asst. prof. U. Ga., Athens, 1984-87, assoc. prof., 1987-92, prof., 1992—; presenter various univs. and philos. confs. Author: One and Many in Aristotle's Metaphysics: The Central Books, 1989, Form and Reason: Essays in Metaphysics, 1993; contbr. articles to philosophy jours. Mem. Am. Philos. Assn., Metaphys. Soc. Am., Soc. for Ancient Greek Philosophy. Office: Dept Philosophy Peabody Hall U Ga Athens GA 30602

HALPERIN, EDWARD CHARLES, physician; b. Somerville, N.J., Nov. 15, 1953; s. Irving M. and Ruth (Jacobs) H.; m. Sharon F. Rosenblatt, Sept. 6, 1981; children: Rebecca, Jennifer, Alison. BS, U. Pa., 1975; MD, Yale U., 1979. Diplomate Am. Bd. Radiology. Intern Stanford (Calif.) U. Hosp., 1979-80; resident Mass. Gen. Hosp., Boston, 1980-83; asst. prof. Duke U., Durham, N.C., 1983-85, assoc. prof., 1985-93, prof., 1993-96, L.R. Prosnitz prof. and dept. chmn., 1996—. Author: Pediatric Radiation Oncology, 1989, 2d edit., 1994. Recipient Career Devel. award Am. Cancer Soc., 1986; fellow Am. Coun. on Edn., 1992. Office: Duke Med Ctr Box 3085 Durham NC 27710

HALPERN, PETER JAY, marketing professional; b. N.Y.C., Dec. 25, 1951; s. Seymour Theodore and Bernice Helen (Rogoff) H.; m. Catherine M. Daley, Aug. 23, 1971 (div. 1974). BA, U. Conn., 1974; MS, Rensselaer Poly. Inst., 1988. Bus. analyst Hartford Life Ins. Co., Simsbury, Conn., 1978-88; sr. market rsch. analyst Sun Trust Bank, Ft. Lauderdale, Fla., 1988-89; exec. dir. product devel. John Alden Life Ins. Co., Miami, Fla., 1989-95; dir. corp. product devel. analysis Physician Corp. Am., Miami, 1995—. Chair audience devel. com. Joan Lehman Mus. Contemporary ARt, North Miami, Fla., 1994-96. Mem. Greater Miami Shores C. of C. (bd. trustees). Home: 109 NE 104th St Miami Shores FL 33138

HALPIN, JAMES F., business executive; b. 1950. Officer Zayres Store Corp., Chgo. and Boston, 1971-90, Child World Inc., Avon, Mass., 1971-90, BJ's Wholesale Club, Inc., Natick, Mass., 1971-90, Home Base Inc., Fullerton, Calif., 1990-93; pres., CEO Compusa Inc., Dallas, 1993—. Office: Compusa Inc 14951 Dallas Pky 10th Dallas TX 75240

HALSETH, MICHAEL JAMES, medical center administrator; b. Bagley, Minn., Nov. 3, 1944; s. Alden Edmore and Christine (Knutson) H.; m. Jill Gwendolyn Utter, Feb. 18, 1967; children: Keith Henry, Holly Lynn, Katherine Jean. BS, Cailf. State U., 1967; MS, U. N.D., 1971. Indsl. engr., dir. pers. St. Agnes Hosp., Fresno, Calif., 1971-75; resident mgr. systems engrng. McDonnell Douglas Automation, San Francisco, 1975-76; dir. mgmt. engrng. Providence Meml. Hosp., El Paso, Tex., 1976-77; assoc. dir. All Sts. Episcopal Hosp., Ft. Worth, 1977-82; adminstr., chief oper. officer U. Va. Med. Ctr., Charlottesville, 1982-89, interim exec. dir., 1989-90, exec. dir., 1990—. Cpt. USAF, 1967-71. Mem. Am. Coll. Healthcare Execs., Va. Hosp. Assn., Univ. Hosp. Consortium (bd. dirs. 1985-95). Office: U Va Med Ctr PO Box 148 Medical Center Charlottesville VA 22908*

HALSEY, BRENTON SHAW, paper company executive; b. Newport News, Va., 1927. BS in Chem. Engrng., U. Va.; postgrad., Inst. of Paper Chemistry. V.p. planning Albemarle Paper Co., 1955-66; pres., gen. mgr. Interstate Bag. Co., 1966-68; co-founder James River Corp. of Va., Richmond, 1969, chmn., CEO, now chmn., dir.; dir. Dominion Bankshares, Dominion Nat. Bank, Westmoreland Coal Co. Office: James River Corp of Va PO Box 2218 Richmond VA 23217-2218

HALSEY, WILLIAM, artist, educator; b. Charleston, S.C., 1915; m. Corrie McCallum. Student U. S.C., 1932-34, Boston Mus. Sch. Fine Arts, 1935-39, U. Mex., 1939-41, doctorate fine arts (hon.) Coll. Charleston, 1995. Instr. Boston Mus. Fine Arts Sch.; dir. Telfair Acad. Sch., Savannah, Ga., Gibbes Art Gallery Sch., Charleston, S.C.; artist-in-residence Castle Hill Found., Ipswich, Mass., Mus. Sch., Greenville County Mus., S.C.; instr. to asst. prof. to artist-in-residence Coll. Charleston, 1965-84. One-man shows include: Bertha Schaefer Gallery, N.Y., Berkshire Mus., Pittsfield, Mass.; Norton Gallery, West Palm Beach, Fla., Mint Mus. Art, Charlotte, N.C., Greenville County Mus. Art, Greenville, S.C., Columbia Mus. Art., S.C., SECCA, Winston-Salem, N.C., Spoleto Festival, USA; exhibited in group shows: Met. Mus. N.Y., Boston Mus. Fine Arts, Whitney Mus. Am. Art, Mus. Modern Art, N.Y.C., Bklyn. Mus., Jewish Mus., N.Y., Chgo. Art Inst., Pasadena Art Inst., Birmingham Mus., Ringling Mus., Sarasota, Fla., Palazzo Venezia, Rome; represented in permanent collections at Balt. Mus., NAD, Nat. Collection of Am. Art, Ind. U., Ga. Mus., Greenville County Mus., Gibbes Art Gallery, Columbia Mus., S.C. State Art Commn., S.C. Nat. Bank, C&S Nat. Bank, First Fed. Savs. & Loan Assn., Springs Mills; executed mural in Berkshire Mus., Pittsfield, Mass., Balt. Hebrew Congl. Temple, Balt., Md., Beth Elohim Synagogue Tabernacle, Charleston; decorations and paintings in Dock St. Theatre, Charleston; portraits in Simons Fine Arts Ctr., Coll. of Charleston, Charleston County Court Room, Dock St. Theatre. Author: (with Corrie McCallum) A Travel Sketchbook, 1971, Maya Jour., 1976. James W. Paige fellow, 1939-41; Pepsi-Cola fellow, 1948; Hughes Found. fellow, 1950-51; grantee S.C. Com. for Humanities, 1982, Coll. of Charleston, 1982; fine arts gallery at Coll. of Charleston named in his honor, 1984.

HALSTEAD, WARREN WAYNE, aviation consultant; b. Hutchinson, Kans., Apr. 20, 1921; s. Galen Foster and Alice Cleo (Psikal) H.; m. Thora Waters, May 27, 1955; 1 child, Gail Lynne Halstead Capp. BS, U. Tulsa, 1950; grad., AFSQ Offcke, 1951; MS, U. Tex., 1955; grad., Air Command and Staff Coll., 1961, Indsl. Coll. Armed Forces, 1966, Army War Coll., 1969; AA, U. D.C., 1977. Unit comdr. U.S. Army, New Orleans, 1941-43; combat pilot U.S. Army, 1943-44; flight comdr. officer Air Force, 1949-51, unit comdr. adminstrn., 1950-53; 1st lt. USAF, 1947; U.S. Army, 1943-44; advanced through grades to col. USAF, 1968, ret., 1975; airplane mechanic U.S. Army, New Orleans, 1941-43; combat pilot, 1990—, unit comdr. adminstrn., intelligence, R & D, staff, asst. to inspector gen. syss. command; assoc. prof. U. D.C., 1977-90; aviation cons., 1990—; FAA rated pilot ATP, CFII. 2nd lt. U.S. Army, 1941-47. Decorated Air Medal with 5 clusters U.S. Army, 1945, Disting. Flying Cross USAF, 1953; recipient Pistol trophy Army War Coll., Carlisle, Pa., 1969. Mem. Profl. Aircraft Maintenance

Assn., Aircraft Owners & Pilots Assn. Home and Office: 1622 Woodmoor Ln Mc Lean VA 22101

HALTER, EDMUND JOHN, mechanical engineer; b. Bedford, Ohio, May 10, 1928; s. Edmund Herbert and Martha (Demske) H.; student Akron U., 1946-48; B.S. in Mech. Engring., Case Inst. Tech., Cleve., 1952; M.S. in Mech. Engring., So. Meth. U., 1965; m. Carolyn Amelia Luecke, June 29, 1955; children—John Alan, Amelia Katherine, Dianne Louise, Janet Elaine. Flight test engr., analyst Chance Vought Aircraft, Dallas, 1952-59; chief research and devel. engr. Burgess-Manning Co., Dallas, 1959-68; engring. specialist acoustics Vought div. LTV Aerospace Corp., Dallas, 1968-69; mgr. continuing engring. Maxim Silencer div. AMF Beaird, Inc., Shreveport, La., 1969-72; chief research and devel. engr. Burgess-Manning div. Burgess Industries, Dallas, 1972-79; chief engr. Vibration & Noise Engring. Corp., Dallas, 1979-92, v.p. engring., 1993—; cons. Organizer Citizen Noise Awareness Seminar, Irving, 1977. Mission ptnrs., coord. Nothern Tex., Nothern La. Synod of Evang. Luth. Ch. Am. Served with USNR, 1946-49. Registered profl. engr., Tex., Ohio; cert. fallout shelter analyst. Mem. Inst. Environ. Scis. (pres. S.W. chpt. 1977-78), Indsl. Silencer Mfrs. Assn. (chmn. 1975-77), Acoustical Soc. Am., Nat., Tex. socs. profl. engrs., ASME. Republican. Lutheran. Contbr. articles to profl. jours. Patentee in field. Home: 200 Hillcrest Ct Irving TX 75062-6900

HALTER, H(ENRY) JAMES, JR. (DIAMOND JIM HALTER), retail executive; b. Fernandina, Fla., Feb. 28, 1947; s. Henry James and Grace (Bealey) H.; m. Wanda O'Quinn, Mar. 15, 1970; children: Jennifer, John, Elizabeth, Amelia. BS in Mgmt., Valdosta State Coll., 1970. Sales mgr. Southwestern Co., Nashville, 1969; collection mgr. Fla. Title & Mortgage Co., Jacksonville, 1970-72; appraiser Richard Hamilton & Assocs., Jacksonville Beach, 1972-74; exec. v.p. Developers Investors Svc. Corp., Jacksonville, 1975-78; pres. A-Coin and Stamp Gallery, Inc., Jacksonville, 1978-81; ptnr. Jacksonville Precious Metals, 1981, Sidetrack Video Arcade Chain, Ga., 1982-84; pres. Diamond House Corp., Valdosta, Ga., 1985—, J-Mart Jewelry Outlets, Inc., Tifton, Ga., 1988—; chmn. bd. J-Mart Jewelry Outlets, Inc., 1990-91; pres. K&H Ltd., Valdosta, 1992-94; exec. dir. Soc. for Legalization of Drugs, Valdosta, 1994—; bus. cons., 1996—. Author: May I Help You, 1988. Bd. dirs. Park Ave. United Meth. Ch., Valdosta, 1986-88, Alapaha coun. Boy Scouts Am., 1982—; mem. Alumni Bd. Valdosta State U.; youth spkr. Atlanta Com. for the Olympic Games, selected local hero torch bearer Olympic Games, Atlanta, 1996; co-author Olympic Awareness Award for 1996 Olympic Games, 1994-95; mem. Ga. Small Bus. Task Force. Recipient Addy award, 1980, 83, God and Svc. nat. award Meth. Ch. and BSA, Cmty. Hero Torch Bearer, Coca Cola Olympic Torch Relay, 1996; named Adm. in Ga. Navy, 1983, Outstanding Ga. Citizen, 1990. Mem. Nat. Speakers Assn., Toastmasters, Sertoma, Vigil Honor, Order of the Arrow, Rotary, Sigma Iota (pres. charter), Alpha Phi Omega. Home and Office: PO Box 3647 Valdosta GA 31604-3647

HALTER, KYLE WILLIAM, marketing professional; b. Port Arthur, Tex., Sept. 12, 1959; s. Joseph Franklin Sr. and Peggy Ann (Kile) Thompson; m. Ruby Kathryn Warner, Sept. 7, 1979; children: Jason Kendall, Lindsay Kile. Degree in Mortuary Sci., Commonwealth Coll., 1978-79. Cert. embalmer, funeral dir.; lic. life & health ins. agent. Life guard Pompano Club, Port Neches, Tex., 1975-76; emergency med. tech. Clayton-Thompson Ambulance, Groves, Tex., 1976-79; funeral dir. Clayton-Thompson Funeral Home, Groves, Tex., 1979-85; owner Acoustic Restoration Tech., Port Neches, Tex., 1983-85; agent Mission Life Ins. Co., Houston, Lafayette La., 1984-85; regional sales dir. Mission Life Ins. Co., Lafayette, La., 1985-86, state sales dir., 1986-89; sr. sales dir. La., Fla., Ark., Tenn., Tex., Miss., Ala., Mission Life Ins. Co., 1989—; sec., CEO Cycle Bag Inc., Lafayette, 1991—; mem. bd. dirs. ARC, Port Arthur Tex., 1979-85, CPR, First Aid Instr., 1975-85. Inventor Reusable Recycling Bag, 1991. Mem. La. Funeral Sales Club (pres. 1994-95, Salesman of Year award 1994-95), Fla. Funeral Sales Club, Tex. Funeral Sales Club, Mis. Funeral Sales Club, Evening Optimist Internat. Home: 305 Oak Coulee Dr Lafayette LA 70507-4819 Office: Mission Life Ins Co 9235 Katy Fwy Houston TX 77024-1522

HALTOM, ELBERT BERTRAM, JR., federal judge; b. Florence, Ala., Dec. 26, 1922; s. Elbert Bertram and Elva Mae (Simpson) H.; m. Constance Boyd Morris, Aug. 19, 1949; 1 dau., Emily Haltom Olsen. Student, Florence State U., 1940-42; JD, U. Ala., 1948. Bar: Ala. 1948. Practiced in Florence, 1948-80; mem. firm Bradshaw, Barnett & Haltom, 1948-58, Haltom & Patterson, 1959-80; judge U.S. Dist. Ct. (no. dist.) Ala., Huntsville & Birmingham, 1980-91; sr. judge U.S. Dist. Ct. (no. dist.) Ala., Florence, 1992—; bar commr. 11th Jud. Cir. Ala., 1976-80. Mem. Ala. Ho. of Reps., 1954-58; mem. Ala. Senate, 1958-62; candidate lt. gov. Ala., 1962; mem. Ala. Democratic Exec. Com., 1966-80. Served with USAAF, 1943-45. Decorated Air medal with four oak leaf clusters. Fellow Internat. Soc. Barristers, Am. Coll. Trial Lawyers; mem. ABA, Ala. Bar Assn., Am. Legion, VFW, Florence Rotary Club, Phi Gamma Delta, Phi Delta Phi. Methodist. Office: US Dist Ct US PO and Courthouse 210 N Seminary St Florence AL 35630-4759

HALUSHKA, PERRY VICTOR, physician, medical educator; b. Chgo., June 4, 1941; married with three children. BS with honors, U. Ill., Chgo., 1963; PhD, U. Chgo., 1967, MD with honors, 1970. Cert. Nat. Bd. Med. Examiners, Am. Bd. Internal Medicine. Teaching asst. in pharmacology U. Chgo., Ill., 1967-68; med. intern, jr. asst. resident medicine Grady Meml. Hosp., Atlanta, 1970-71, 71-72; rsch. assoc. in pharmacology Nat. Heart and Lung Inst., NIH, Bethesda, Md., 1972-74; asst. prof. pharmacology and medicine Med. U. S.C., Charleston, 1974-77, assoc. prof. pharmacology and medicine, 1978-81, prof. pharmacology and medicine, 1981—, attending physician Med. U. Hosp., 1974—, attending physician Charleston County Hosp., 1974—, attending physician Charleston VA Hosp., 1974—, dir. divsn. clin. pharmacology, 1990—; mem. grad. tng. com. dept. pharmacology Med. U. S.C., Charleston, 1974—, chmn. pharmacy & therapeutics com. Med. U. Hosp., 1974-77, mem. postdoctoral tng. com., 1976—, chmn. postdoctoral tng. com., 1976-87, assoc. program dir. Gen. Clin. Rsch. Ctr., 1978-82, 83-87, gen. clin. rsch. ctr. adv. com., 1978-87, rsch. com. dept. medicine, 1979—, hon. vis. cons. Hammersmith Hosp., 1982-83, univ. rsch. com., 1985—, others; VA med. rsch. svc. merit rev. bd. on cardiovascular studies NIH, 1978-81, numerous others; Ann. Pfizer lectr. in clin. pharmacology, 1981, 82, 84, 85; Burroughs-Wellcome-Wm. N. Creasy vis. professorship, 1990; Gordon Wilson lectr. Am. Clin. and Climatological Assn., 1993. Patentee in field. With USPHS, 1972-74. Recipient Merck award, 1963, U. Chgo. fellowship, 1963-64, USPHS Predoctoral fellowship, 1964-67, Med. Sch. scholarship U. Chgo., 1967-70, Pharm. Mfrs. Assn. Found. award, 1969, Pharm. Mfrs. Assn. Found. Faculty Devel. award in clin. pharmacology, 1975, 77, Ralph Colp award for best surg. paper Mt. Sinai Jour. Medicine, 1982, Fogarty Sr. Internat. fellowship, 1983, Burroughs Wellcome Scholar in Clin. Pharmacology, 1984-89, Faculty Excellence award for teaching U. Kans., 1985, Golden Apple award, 1989, 94. Mem. AAAS, Am. Fedn. Clin. Rsch., Am. Soc. Pharmacology and Exptl. Therapeutics (exec. com. Clin. Pharmacology Divsn. 1983-85, 87-93), So. Soc. for Clin. Investigation, Am. Soc. for Clin. Pharmacology and Therapeutics, N.Y. Acad. Scis., Am. Soc. for Clin. Investigation, Coun. for High Blood Pressure Rsch., Am. Soc. Renal Biochemistry and Metabolism, Shock Soc., Rho Chi, Alpha Omega Alpha. Office: Dept Pharmacology Med Univ S C Charleston SC 29425

HALVORSON, WILLIAM ARTHUR, economic research consultant; b. Menomonie, Wis., June 26, 1928; s. George Henry and Katherine Eileen (Dietsche) H.; m. Patricia Janet von Trebra, Dec. 27, 1951; children: Robert, James, Janet, Audrey, Katherine. Student Stout Inst., 1945-46, U. Mich., 1948; B.B.A., U. Wis., 1950, M.B.A., 1951. Registered investment advisor. Asst. group actuary N.Y. Life Ins. Co., N.Y.C., 1951-56; cons. actuary Milliman & Robertson, Inc., San Francisco, 1956-61, Milw., 1961-83, exec. v.p., 1972-81; founder Halvorson Research Assocs., econ. and investment research cons., 1983—; gen. ptnr. HRA Partnership Ltd., 1992-96. Contbg. author: Group Insurance Handbook, 1965; pub. of investment letter. Served with AUS, 1946-47. Recipient Alumni award Menomonie High Sch., 1945. Fellow Soc. Actuaries (v.p. 1973-75, pres. 1977-78); mem. Wis. Actuarial Club (pres. 1964-65), Am. Acad. Actuaries (sec. 1971-73, pres. 1981-82), Beta Gamma Sigma, Phi Kappa Phi, Chi Phi. Roman Catholic. Clubs: Watertown Golf, Wyndemere Country (Naples Fla.). Home: 2550 Windward Way Naples FL 34103 Office: 2900 14th St N Naples FL 34103-4501

HALWIG, J. MICHAEL, allergist; b. Denver, Apr. 15, 1954; s. John Philip and Hilda (Fuggis) H.; m. Nancy Diane Graupman, June 14, 1975; children: Courtney Elizabeth, J. Christopher. BA, Johns Hopkins U., 1975; MD, Northwestern U., Chgo., 1980. Diplomate Am. Bd. Allergy and Immunology, Am. Bd. Internal Medicine. Intern in internal medicine Northwestern U. Meml. Hosps., Chgo., 1980-81, resident in internal medicine, 1981-83; allergy fellowship Northwestern U. Med. Sch., Chgo., 1983-85; practice medicine specilizing in allergy, asthma, immunology Atlanta, 1985—; instr. Northwestern U. Med. Sch., Chgo., 1984-85, admissions amb., 1989—; clin. asst. prof. Emory U. Sch. Medicine, 1989—. Bd. dirs. Am. Lung Assn., Douglas County, Ga., 1994—, med. dir., 1994—, chmn. pediat. lung sects., 1994—, chmn. spkrs. bur., 1994—; bd. dirs. Am. Lung Assn. Ga., 1996—. Fellow Am. Coll. Allergy, Asthma and Immunology (allergy practice and practice guidelines com. 1992—), Am. Acad. Allergy, Asthma and Immunology; mem. AMA, Med. Asthma and Allergy Found. of Am. (founding mem., bd. dirs. 1996—, bd. dirs. Ga. chpt. 1994—, med. dir. 1994—, chmn. med. adv. com. 1995—), Med. Assn. Ga. (rep. Coun. on Legislation 1989—), Allergy, Asthma and Immunology Soc. Ga. (pres. 1993-95, v.p. 1991-93, program chmn. 1991-93, co-chmn. third party payors com. 1992—), So. Med. Assn., Cobb County Med. Assn., Douglas County Med. Soc., Joint Coun. on Allergy and Immunology. Presbyterian. Office: Ste 404 1700 Hospital South Dr Austell GA 30001-8116

HALWIG, NANCY DIANE, banker; b. Rochester, N.Y., Sept. 17, 1954; d. Norman Charles and Elizabeth Marie (Callemyn) Graupman; m. John Michael Halwig, June 14, 1975; children: Courtney Elizabeth, John Christopher. BA in Elem. Edn. with honors, Goucher Coll., 1975; M. Mgmt. in Fin., Northwestern U., 1979. Br. adminstrv. mgmt. trainee Md. Nat. Bank, Balt., 1975-76; comml. banking officer Am. Nat. Bank Chgo., 1976-80; v.p. relationship mgr. Citicorp USA-Chgo., 1980-85; v.p., team leader Citicorp N.Am., Atlanta, 1985-89, v.p. region credit officer, 1986-90; v.p., regional mgr. Kredietbank-Atlanta, 1990-95; regional v.p. Bank of Am., FSB, Atlanta, 1995-96, sr. v.p., 1996—; mem. contbns. com. Citicorp, Chgo., Atlanta, 1984-90; sec., bd. dirs. S.E. Cobb Allergy and Asthma, P.C. Mem. fin. com. Big Bros./Big Sisters, Atlanta, 1987-91; mem. leadership forum Scottish Rite Hosp., Atlanta, 1988-92; contbns. contact Scitrek Mus., Atlanta, 1988-90, mem. pres.'s coun., 1990-91; mem. steering com. N.W. Ga. Girl Scouts Friendship Ctr., 1993, mem. Friendship Circle, 1996; troop treas. Girl Scouts U.S., 1994-96; sustainer Atlanta Women's Fund, 1995-96. Named one of Atlanta Women to Watch, Atlanta Bus. Chronicle, 1988. Mem. Fin. Women Internat. (Paragon Cir., futures com. 1996—), Nat. Assn. Bank Women (found. trustee 1984-85, treas. found. 1985-86, bd. dirs. and chmn. fin. com. 1987-88, chmn. task force on child care financing alternatives, restructuring task force 1988-89, nat. conf. program chmn. 1991-92), Aux. Am. Coll. Allergy, Asthma & Immunology, Women's Fin. Exch. (founding bd. dirs.), Atlanta C. of C. (bd. advisors), Atlanta Venture Forum, Assn. Corp. Growth, Northwestern Univ. Club of Atlanta, Phi Beta Kappa. Republican. Home: 4400 Woodland Brook Dr NW Atlanta GA 30339-5365 Office: Bank of Am FSB 1230 Peachtree St Ste 3600 Atlanta GA 30309

HAM, CLARENCE EDWARD, university administrator; b. Wink, Tex., Dec. 27, 1936; s. Clarence Joseph and Edwina Olive (Brantley) H.; m. Joyce Suzella Travis, Apr. 20, 1962; children: Patricia Lynn, John Joseph, Duane Michael, Christina Diane. BA, Baylor U., 1959; MEd, Tex. Technol. Coll., 1965; PhD, U. Tex., Austin, 1969. Cert. supt., prin., secondary tchr. Elem. prin. Perrin (Tex.) County Line Sch. Dist., 1960-62; h.s. prin. Cotton Ctr. (Tex.) Ind. Sch. Dist., 1962-66; supt. schs. Orange (Tex.) Common Sch. Dist. #1, 1967-68, Bay City (Tex.) Ind. Sch. Dist., 1969-74, Killeen (Tex.) Ind. Sch. Dist., 1974-88; dep. supt. for instrn. Fort Bend Ind. Sch. Dist., Sugar Land, Tex., 1989-92; dean sch. edn. U. Mary Hardin-Baylor, Belton, Tex., 1992—. Contbr. articles to profl. jours. Named Outstanding Adminstr. of Yr. Tex. Classroom Tchrs. Assn., 1984. Mem. Nat. Assn. of Federally Impacted Schs. (pres. 1987-88, area v.p., bd. dirs. 1980-87), Am. Assn. of Sch. Adminstrs., Tex. Assn. of Sch. Adminstrs., Assn. of Tchr. Educators, Phi Delta Kappa (pres. Ctrl. Tex. chpt. 1981-82, Educator of Yr. 1984, Kappan of Yr. 1995-96). Baptist. Home: 213 Turtle Creek Dr Belton TX 76513-2167 Office: Univ of Mary Hardin-Baylor PO Box 8017 Belton TX 76513

HAMBERGER, ARTHUR DONALD, radiation oncologist; b. Bronx, June 23, 1945; s. Reuben Isaac and Ethel (Platzker) H.; m. Ester Zilberman, Nov. 19, 1968; children: Leora, Sigalit Ethel. Student, Cornell U., 1965; MD, Albert Einstein Coll., 1969. Diplomate Am. Bd. Radiology, Am. Bd. Internal Medicine. Intern, resident Bronx Mcpl. Hosp. Ctr., 1969-72; fellow in radiotherapy M.D. Anderson Cancer Ctr., Houston, 1972-75, from asst. prof. to assoc. prof. radiotherapy, 1975-82, dir. residency tng. program, 1980-82, chmn. edn. com., 1981-82; med. dir. radiotherapy Meml. City Med. Ctr., Houston, 1982-91; med. dir. radiation therapy Meml. Healthcare Syst., Houston, 1991—. Contbg. author: Textbook of Radiotherapy, 1980; contbr. articles to med. jours. Mem. AMA, Am. Coll. Radiology, Am. Soc. Therapeutic Radiology and Oncology, Am. Soc. Clin. Oncology, Am. Cancer Soc. (chmn. patient svc. com. 1989-92, v.p. 1989-91, pres. 1991-93, fellow 1974-75). Jewish. Home: 8711 Stable Crest Blvd Houston TX 77024-7032 Office: Radiation Oncology Assocs 1631 North Loop W # 150 Houston TX 77008

HAMBLEN, KAREN, art educator. PhD, U. Oreg., 1981. Prof. art edn. La. State U., Baton Rouge, 1985—; vice chmn. art com. Nat. Bd. Profl. Tchg. Stds., 1990—; reviewer, cons. Getty Ctr. for Edn. in Arts, 1991-94. Sr. editor Studies in Art Edn., 1991-93; contbr. articles to profl. jours. Mem. NEA (Manuel Barkan award 1984, Mary Rouse award 1985, June McFee award 1995).

HAMBLIN, DANIEL MORGAN, economist; b. Kansas City, Kans., Oct. 7, 1942; s. Enright Morgan and Helen Ruth (Cain) H.; m. Rebecca Menn, Dec. 6, 1969 (div. Aug. 1988); children: Caroline Helen, David Thorpe; m. Judith Killen, Nov. 21, 1990 (div. Mar. 1992). BA in Maths., U. Kans., 1972, BA in Econ. with hon., 1972; PhD in Applied Econs., SUNY, Buffalo, 1979. Systems engr. Smoot Co., Kans. City, 1968-70; asst. prof. econs. U. Wis., Parkside Kenosha, 1977-80; rsch. assoc. Oak Ridge (Tenn.) Nat. Lab., 1980-82, leader demand analysis group, 1982-86; project mgr. Battelle Columbus (Ohio) Div., 1986-89; pres Dan Hamblin & Assocs., Inc., Conway, Ark., 1989—; mgr. competitive assessment hydro-carbon substitutes for coke in ironmaking Gas Rsch. Inst., 1994—; assessor econ. benefit and mortality risks of corn pesticides Ciba-Geiby Corp., 1992-94. Editor, co-author natural gas utility integrated resource planning rev. Gas Rsch. Inst., 1992—; contbr. (book chpts.) Forecasting U.S. Electricity Demand, 1985, Energy Sources: Conservation and Renewables, 1985. With USN, 1961-65. Mem. AAAS, Am. Econ. Assn., Am. Statis. Assn., Ops. Rsch. Soc. Am., Internat. Assn. Energy Econs., Iron and Steel Soc., Am. Legion. Democrat. Episcopalian. Home: 16 Ironwood Dr Conway AR 72032-3626 Office: 915 Oak St Ste 106 Conway AR 72032-4371

HAMBLIN, J. ANTHONY, medical/surgical nurse; b. Calhoun City, Miss., Sept. 19, 1959; s. O.D. and Robbie Doris (Ingram) H. AS, N.W. Miss. Jr. Coll., 1979; BA, U. Miss., 1989; AAS, Holmes C.C., Grenada, Miss., 1992. RN, Miss.; ANCC; ACLS; TNCC, PALS, Neonatal Resuscitation, Emergency Nurses Assn.; cert. Med.-Surg. Nurse, Emergency Nurse. Staff nurse Grenada Lake Med. Ctr., 1992—. Mem. Miss. Nurses Assn., Phi Mu Alpha Sinfonia.

HAMBOURGER, ROBERT MICHAEL, philosophy educator; b. Evanston, Ill., Sept. 10, 1944; s. Walter Elmer and Reva (Casler) H.; m. Lynda Horhota, Feb. 13, 1972; children: Elizabeth Ann, Michael Stuart, Timothy Robert. BA, U. Chgo., 1969; PhD, Rockefeller U., 1976. Instr. U. Wis., Madison, 1971-75, asst. prof., 1975-77; asst. prof. Northwestern U., Evanston, Ill., 1979-82; assoc. prof. philosophy N.C. State U., Raleigh, 1982—; vis. asst. prof. NYU, 1973-74, UCLA, 1977-78, Stanford U., Palo Alto, Calif., 1978, U. Minn., Mpls., 1978-79. Contbr. articles to profl. jours. Bd. dirs. Episcopal Housing Ministry, Inc., Raleigh, 1991—. Mem. Am. Philos. Assn., Soc. Christian Philosophers, Hume Soc. Home: 2509 Kenmore Dr Raleigh NC 27608-1419 Office: NC State U PO Box 8103 Raleigh NC 27695

HAMBRICK, ARLENE, school system administrator, minister; b. Chgo., Nov. 8, 1945; children: Ronald T., Anthony C. BS, Chgo. State U., 1971; MDiv, Chgo. Theol. Sem., 1981; EdD, U. Mass., 1993. Spl. edn. tchr. Chgo. Pub. Schs., 1971-81, Boston Pub. Sch., 1981-93; dir. elem. and mid. sch. Bluefield (Va.) Coll., 1993—; sr. mgr. Appalachia Ednl. Lab., Charleston, W.Va., 1996—; mem. Mercer County Pub. Sch. Bd., Bluefield, 1992—, Tazewell (Va.) County Pub. Sch. Bd., 1993—. Contbr. articles to profl. jours. Chair, founder Attleboro, Mass. Civil Rights Commn., 1991-93. Mem. AAUW, NAACP, Assn. of Tchr. Educators (del. 1994—). Home: 4 Chilton Manor Circle Charleston WV 25314

HAMBRIGHT, ROBERT JOHN, lawyer; b. Beaumont, Tex., Mar. 28, 1956; s. James William and Edna Ann (Eaheart) H.; children: Rosemary, Phoebe. BBA, BA, So. Methodist U., Dallas, Tex., 1978, JD, 1981. Bar: Tex. 1981, U.S. Dist. Ct. (ea. dist.) Tex. 1982, U.C. Ct. Appeals (5th cir.) 1984, U.S. Tax Ct. 1983, U.S. Supreme Ct. 1986. Assoc. Orgain, Bell & Tucker, L.L.P., Beaumont, Tex., 1981-87, ptnr., 1987—. Contbr. articles to profl. jours. Mem. ABA, State Bar of Tex. (Chmn. Labor and Employment Law Section, 1986-87). Home: 296 Ridgeland St Beaumont TX 77706-4511 Office: Orgain Bell & Tucker LLP 470 Orleans St Beaumont TX 77701-3000

HAMDY, RONALD CHARLES, geriatrician; b. Alexandria, Egypt, July 31, 1946; came to U.S., 1985; s. Charles and Mary Hamdy; m. Eleanor Gertrude Hamdy, Aug. 19, 1977; children: Conrad, Gerard, Ronan. MB, ChB with honours, U. Alexandria, 1968, DM, 1971. Rotating intern U. Alexandria, 1968-69; resident in internal medicine Al-Gomhouriya Gen. Hosp., Alexandria, 1969-70; resident registrar internal medicine U. Alexandria Main Teaching Hosp., 1970-72; sr. ho. officer geriatric and internal medicine Farnborough (Eng.) Hosp., Kent, 1972-73; registrar in geriatric medicine Bromley (Eng.) Group of Hosps., Kent, 1974; sr. registrar in geriatric medicine King's Coll. Group Hosps., London, 1975-77; consulting physician St. John's Hosp. Richmond (Eng.), Twickenham & Roehampton Health Authority, 1977-85; chmn. dept. clin. gerontology, ethics rsch. com. Richmond (Eng.), Twickenham & Roehampton Health Authority, Eng., 1981-85; prof. internal medicine, Cecile Cox Quillen prof. geriatric medicine, head divsn. gerontology East Tenn. State U., Mountain Home, 1985—, Cecile Cox Quillen prof. geriatric medicine, head divsn. gerontology, 1990—; chief geriatrics VA Med. Ctr., Mountain Home, 1985-88, assoc. chief of staff geriatric and extended care, 1988—; hon. sr. lectr. geriatric medicine St. George's Hosp. Med. Sch., U. London, 1981-85; planning team for elderly Wandsworth Health Care, 1982-85; med. dist. initiated peer rev. orgn. VA Hosps., Dist. 8, 1986-89; vis. prof. Health Care for Elderly, U. London, 1991-93; Burroughs Wellcome vis. prof. geriatric medicine Royal Soc. Medicine, 1994-95; co-chmn. pharmacy and therapeutics com. VA Med. Ctr., Johnson City, Tenn., chmn. adverse drug reaction com.; chmn. program com. Coll. Medicine Continuing Med. Edn., East Tenn. State U.; mem. Gov.'s task force on Alzheimer's Disease, Tenn., task force on edn., prevention and detection of osteoporosis; mem. advisor to pub. guardian 1st Tenn. Devel. Dist.; adv. bd. Colonial Hill Health Care Ctr., Johnson City, Golden J-55, Johnson City Med. Ctr. Hosp., Inc.; sr. health adv. com. 1st Tenn. Regional Health Office; adj. clin. prof. divsn. clin. nutrition and psychiatry East Tenn. State U. Author: Diuretic Therapy in the Older Patient, 1978, Paget's Disease in Bone, Assessment and Management, 1981, Geriatric Medicine: A Problem Oriented Approach, 1984; editor: (with J. Turnbull, M. Lancaster, L. Norman) Alzheimer's Disease: A Handbook for Caregivers, 1990, 2d edit., 1994; mem. editl. adv. bd. Revs. Clin. Gerontology, South Med. Jour., Geriatria; reviewer for med. jours.; contbr. chpts. to books, articles to profl. jours. Fellow ACP (com. geriatrics 1987-90, chmn. com. geriatrics MKSAP IX 1991-94), Royal Coll. Physicians; mem. Am. Geriatrics Soc. (membership com., reviewer jour., ann. meeting planning com. 1993), Gerontol. Soc. Am., Royal Coll. Surgeons, So. Med. Assn. (vice-chmn. coun. 1995-96, chmn. coun. 1996-97, editor geriatric medicine sect. Dial-Access program, from assoc. councilor to councilor state Tenn., chmn. adv. com. sci. activities, reviewer jour.), So. Assn. Geriatric Medicine (pres. 1990-92), Tenn. Med. Assn. (reviewer jour.), Tenn. Geriatrics Soc. (founding), Brit. Med. Assn., Brit. Geriatrics Soc., Bone and Mineral Soc., Alzheimer's Assn. (pres. bd. dirs. N.E. Tenn. chpt. 1990-91). Office: Ea Tenn State U Coll Medicine Box 70429 Johnson City TN 37614

HAMEL, DAVID CHARLES, health and safety engineer; b. Plattsburgh, N.Y., Feb. 19, 1953; s. Charles Joseph and Helena Mary (Tormey) H. BS, Fla. Inst. Tech., 1977. Cert. paramedic, Fla.; cert. safety mgr.; WSO-CSM. Sr. safety engr. United Space Boosters, Kennedy Space Ctr., Fla., 1977-81; safety and health supr. STC Documation, Inc., Palm Bay, Fla., 1981-82, Martin Marietta Corp., Ocala, Fla., 1983; adminstr. safety, health and environ. affairs Hughes Aircraft Co., Titusville, Fla., 1983-86; pres. Pi Assocs. Inc., Orlando, Fla. and Cary, N.C., 1986—; tchr. Nat. Safety Council, Brevard Safety Council, Cocoa, Fla., 1978-84, U. Fla., 1987-91; cons. Continental Shelf, Inc., Tequesta, Fla., 1976-77. Emergency med. technician Harbor City Vol. Ambulance Squad, Melbourne, Fla., 1974-81, paramedic, 1981-91. Recipient Group Achievement award NASA, 1979, Cert. of appreciation, NASA, 1979, 81. Mem. Am. Soc. Safety Engrs. (treas. 1980-81), Am. Indsl. Hygiene Assn., World Safety Orgn., N.Y. Acad. Scis. Avocations: skiing, horseback riding, hiking, camping.

HAMEL, JOSEPH DONAT, minister; b. Rumford, Maine, Aug. 9, 1923; s. Donat Henry and Ethel Louise (Kennison) H.; m. Jean Marie Rowsey, Aug. 7, 1949; children: JoAnne, John, Janet. BE, Ashland U., 1949, DD (hon.), 1972; MRE, Ashland Theol. Sem., 1951. Ordained to ministry Brethren Ch., 1950. Pastor Lanark (Ill.) Brethren Ch., 1951-53, South Bend (Ind.) Brethren Ch., 1953-60; pastor Sarasota (Fla.) 1st Brethren Ch., 1960-88, pastor emeritus, 1988—. Chaplain Fla. State Fireman's Assn., 1962—, Sheriff Dept. Sarasota County, 1960—, Police Dept., Sarasota, 1960—, Fire Dept., Sarasota, 1960—. With USAAF, 1943-45; lt. col. USAF Aux., 1961-86, Ret. Recipient Freedom award Sertoma Club, 1964; named Evangelical of Yr., Manasota Ministerial, 1975, Citizen of Yr., Fraternal Order Police, Sarasota, 1980. Mem. Military Chaplains, Nat. Fellowship Christian Firefighters, Nat. Religious Broadcasters (founder, speaker The Brethren Hour), VFW. Home: 605 Caruso Pl Sarasota FL 34237-4721

HAMEL, LEE, lawyer; b. N.Y.C., Oct. 1, 1940; s. Herman and Jessie Blanche (Mapes) H.; m. Carole Ann Holmes, Dec. 30, 1965; children: Todd Leland, Stuart Russell. BA, Duke U., 1962; JD, U. Tex., 1967. Bar: Tex. 1967, U.S. Ct. Appeals (5th and 11th cirs.) 1968, U.S. Ct. Mil. Appeals 1968, U.S. Dist. Ct. (so. dist.) Tex. 1968, U.S. Supreme Ct. 1971, U.S. Tax Ct. 1979, U.S. Dist. Ct. (we. dist.) Tex. 1984, U.S. Dist. Ct. (ea. dist.) Tex. 1994. Asst. U.S. atty. U.S. Dist. Ct. (so. dist.) Tex., Houston, 1968-71, chief Corpus Christi divsn., 1970-71; owner Lee Hamel & Assocs., Houston, 1971-74, 90—; ptnr. Dickerson, Hamel, Early & Pennock, Houston, 1974-88, Hamel & Rouner, Houston, 1988-89; instr. Nat. Inst. for Trial Advocacy, 1986—. Former trustee St. Luke's Hosp., Houston, St. James Home for Aged, Baytown; former dir. exec. bd. Episcopal Diocese of Tex.; pres. St. Francis Endowment Fund, 1993-94; former councilman Hunters Creek Village, Tex. Comdr. USN, 1962-64, USNR, ret. 1993. Fellow Coll. of State Bar of Tex., Houston Bar Found., State Bar Tex.; mem. ABA (litig. sec., white collar crime com., bus. sec., chair health care fraud subcomittee), FBA, Houston Bar Assn., Houston Vol. Lawyers Assn. (bd. dirs.). Episcopalian. Office: Lee Hamel & Assocs 333 Clay Ste 777 Houston TX 77002

HAMES, CARL MARTIN, educational administrator, art dealer, consultant; b. Birmingham, Ala., July 12, 1938; s. William Geda and Mary Anna (Martin) H. BA, Birmingham So. Coll., 1958; MA, Samford U., 1971, MS, 1980. Cert. tchr. in English, History and Spanish; cert. sch. adminstr. Tchr. Birmingham Pub. Schs., 1958-64; tchr. Birmingham U. Sch., 1964-69, asst. headmaster, 1969-75; coll. counselor The Altamont Sch., Birmingham, 1975-91, dean of students, 1975-89, asst. headmaster, 1989-91, headmaster, 1991—; dir. Town Hall Gallery, Birmingham, 1965—; chmn. Birmingham Nat. Coll. Fair, 1995, 96. Writer poetry. Ethnic heritage chmn. Birmingham Hist. Soc., 1989—; active Birmingham Mus. Art, 1958-92; com. ann meeting Am. Hort. Soc., 1991. Recipient Silver Bowl awards in drama, visual arts Birmingham Festival of Arts, Disting. Alumnus award Birmingham-So. Coll., 1993, 1st Pl. Hackney prize for poetry State of Ala.; named Barton Hill Head Instr. in the Humanities the altamont Sch., 1986, named a Gem of Birmingham Black & White newspaper, 1996;. Mem. Nat. Coun. Tchrs. English, Ala. Assn. Ind. Schs. (bd. dirs. 1991—, chmn. biennial conf. 1994), Nat. Assn. Coll. Admissions Counselors (chmn. Nat. Coll. Fair Sept. 1995), So. Assn. Coll. Admissions Counselors (chmn. Coll. Fair 1994), Birmingham Bot. Soc., Birmingham Art Assn. (editor), Birmingham Mus. Art (editor), The Club, Phi Delta Kappa. Democrat. Roman Catholic. Home: 3963

Montclair Rd Birmingham AL 35213-2414 Office: The Altamont Sch PO Box 131429 Birmingham AL 35213-6429

HAMILTON, BOBBY WAYNE, small business owner; b. Kingsport, Tenn., May 25, 1946; s. Charles Robert and Juanita Faye (McClellan) H.; m. Wanda Jean Tankersley, June 7, 1969; children: Rachel Susanne, Bobby Steven. Grad. high sch., Kingsport. Chem. operator Tenn. Eastman Co., Kingsport, 1965-76, prodn. records clk., 1976-86, prodn. records and cost clk., 1986-91, prodn. records cost analyst, 1991; sr. prodn. records cost analyst Tenn. Eastman Co., 1992-96; coin dealer B.W. Hamilton Coins, Kingsport, 1972—; mfg. SAP specialist Eastman Chemical Co., Kingsport, 1996—; cons., authenticator B.W. Hamilton Coins, Kingsport, 1972—. Mem. Am. Numismatics Assn., Numismatics Internat., Nat. Assn. Investors Corp., Liberty Seated Coin Club, Blue Ridge Numismatic Assn. Republican. Club: Model City Coin (Kingsport). Home: 430 Chesterfield Dr Kingsport TN 37663-2980 Office: Tenn Eastman Co Kingsport TN 37662

HAMILTON, CARL HULET, academic administrator; b. Morris, Okla., Sept. 30, 1934; s. Alva H. and Olah E. (Pryor) H.; m. Gloria Joyce Gore, Sept. 3, 1954; children: Ray, Carla Jo, Deanna Jean. ThB, Southwestern Coll., 1956; BA, Oklahoma City U., 1957; MA, U. Tulsa, 1962; PhD, U. Ark., 1968. English tchr. Southwestern Coll., Oklahoma City, 1957-60; editor Oral Roberts Evangelistic Assn., Tulsa, 1960-62; English tchr., editor Oral Roberts U., Tulsa, 1966-68; acad. dean, 1968-75; provost Oral Roberts U., Tulsa, 1975-84; adminstr. World Evangelism, San Diego, 1984-86; chief of staff Feed the Children, Oklahoma City, 1986-88; provost, chief acad. officer Oral Roberts U., 1989—. Mem. Tulsa Met. C. of C., Rotary. Republican. Methodist. Home: 2660 E 75th St Tulsa OK 74136-5565 Office: Oral Roberts U 7777 S Lewis Ave Tulsa OK 74171-0003

HAMILTON, CLYDE HENRY, federal judge; b. Edgefield, S.C., Feb. 8, 1934; s. Clyde H. and Edwina (Odom) H.; children: John C., James W. B.S., Wofford Coll., 1956; J.D. with honors, George Washington U., 1961. Bar: S.C. 1961. Assoc. J.R. Folk, Edgefield, 1961-63; assoc., gen. ptnr. Butler, Means, Evins & Browne, Spartanburg, S.C., 1963-81; judge U.S. Dist. Ct. S.C., Columbia, 1981-91, U.S. Ct. Appeals (4th cir.), Richmond, Va., 1991—; reference asst. U.S. Senate Library, Washington, 1958-61; gen. counsel Synalloy Corp., Spartanburg, 1969-80. Mem. editorial staff Cumulative Index of Congl. Com. Hearings, 1935-58; bd. editors George Washington Law Rev., 1959-60. Pres., Spartanburg County Arts Council, 1971-73; pres. Spartanburg Day Sch., 1972-74, sustaining trustee, 1975-81; past mem. steering com. undergrad. merit fellowship program and estate planning council Converse Coll., Spartanburg; trustee Spartanburg Methodist Coll., 1979-84; mem. S.C. Supreme Ct. Bd. Commrs. on Grievances and Discipline, 1980-81; del. Spartanburg County, 4th Congl. Dist. and S.C. Republican Convs., 1976, 80; mem., past chmn. fin. com. and adminstrv. bd. Trinity United Meth. Ch., Spartanburg, trustee, 1980-83. Served to capt. USAR, 1956-62. Recipient Alumni Disting. Svc. award Wofford Coll., 1991. Mem. S.C. Bar Assn., Piedmont Club (bd. govs. 1979-81), John Belton O'Neall Am. Inn of Ct. (founding mem., pres. 1987-88). Office: US Ct Appeals 4th Cir 1901 Main St Columbia SC 29201-2443*

HAMILTON, DAGMAR STRANDBERG, lawyer, educator; b. Phila., Jan. 10, 1932; d. Eric Wilhelm and Anna Elizabeth (Sjöström) Strandberg; A.B., Swarthmore Coll., 1953; J.D., U. Chgo. Law Sch., 1956; J.D., Am. U., 1961; m. Robert W. Hamilton, June 26, 1953; children: Eric Clark, Robert Andrew Hale, Meredith Hope. Admitted to Tex. bar, 1972; atty., civil rights div. U.S. Dept. Justice, Washington, 1965-66; asst. instr. govt. U. Tex.-Austin, 1966-71; lectr. Law Sch. U. Ariz., Tucson, 1971-72; editor, researcher Assoc. Justice William O. Douglas, U.S. Supreme Ct., 1962-73, 75-76; editor, research Douglas autobiography Random House Co., 1972-73; staff counsel Judiciary Com., U.S. Ho. of Reps., 1973-74; asst. prof. L.B. Johnson Sch. Pub. Affairs, U. Tex., Austin, 1974-77, assoc. prof., 1977-83, prof., 1983—, assoc. dean, 1983-87; vis. prof. Washington U. Law Sch., St. Louis, 1982; vis. fellow Univ. London, 1987-88, vis. prof. U. Maine Portland, 1992. Mem. Tex. Bar Assn., Am. Law Inst., Assn. Pub. Policy Analysis and Mgmt., Kappa Beta Phi (hon.), Phi Kappa Phi (hon.). Democrat. Quaker. Contbr. to various publs. Home: 403 Allegro Ln Austin TX 78746-4301 Office: U Tex LBJ Sch Pub Affairs Austin TX 78712

HAMILTON, DAVID EUGENE, minister, educator; b. Pyeng Yang, Korea, Jan. 21, 1929; m. Marilyn Long Hamilton; children: Beth Jean Hamilton Stanton, Rebecca Sue Hamilton Vierling, Sarah Ruth Hamilton Goeglein, Jill Linette Hamilton Martin. AB in Theology, Gordon Coll., 1950; BD, Gordon Div. Sch., 1953; ThM, Columbia Theol. Seminary, Decatur, Ga., 1960, Fuller Theol. Seminary, 1983. Ordained to ministry Presbyn. Ch. of U.S., 1954. Asst. to pastor McIlwain Presbyn. Ch., Pensacola, Fla., 1954-55; founding pastor Fairfield Presbyn. Ch., Pensacola, 1956-60; pastor El Presbiterio del Pacifico ch., Teloloapan, Mexico, 1964-66, Northside Presbyn. Ch., Burlington, N.C., 1972-76; moderator Pacific Presbytery of the PCA; dir. Bible Inst., Telolapan; missionary Mexico; dean of students, dir. field edn. Westminster Theol. Seminary, Escondido, Calif., 1984-87; min. to srs. Ind. Presbyn. Ch., Memphis, 1987—; involved numerous ch. and missionary endeavors, including coord. ch. planting team in Quito, Ecuador, 1977-81, dir. Cosecha dept., Radio Sta. HCJB, establisher Family Counseling ministry, leader weekly Bible studies; organizer Gideon camp to distribute Bibles in Acapulco; interim pastor Covenant Presbyn. Ch., Bakersfield, Calif., 1982, others. Office: Ind Presbyn Ch 4738 Walnut Grove Rd Memphis TN 38117-2524

HAMILTON, DEBORAH, educational administrator; b. Amory, Miss., Sept. 13, 1951; d. Kearney and Ernestine (Ausbon) H. AS, N.W. Ala., 1969-71; BS, U. Ala., 1973-75, MA, 1975-76. Statistician med. rcds. N.W. Ala. Mental Health Ctr., Hamilton, 1971-73; student, rsch. asst. U. Ala., Tuscaloosa, 1973-76, rsch. assoc. Ctr. for Bus. and Econ. Rsch., 1977-84; asst. dir. Ctr. Bus. and Econ. Rsch. U. Ala., 1984—; part-time instr. C & BA U. Ala., 1977-81. Editor: (book) Economic Abstract of Alabama, 1995, (annual book) Alabama Economic Outlook, 1986—, (biannual mag.) Focus, 1991-95. Mem. Assn. for U. Bus. & Econ. Rsch., Soc. of Rsch. Adminstrs. Methodist. Office: Ctr for Bus and Econ Rsch Box 870221 Tuscaloosa AL 35487

HAMILTON, EDWARD DOUGLAS, protective services official; b. Lebanon, Ky., May 18, 1951; s. Edward Tony and Martha Lillian (Salsman) H.; m. Melanie Snider, Sept. 21, 1973 (div. Mar. 1976); m. Judy Ann Sloan, Mar. 22, 1980; children: Carol Ann, Taylor, Chris. A in Police Adminstrn., U. Louisville, 1988, B in Police Adminstrn., 1991; AA, Jefferson C.C., Louisville, 1990. Police officer Louisville Divsn. Police, 1971-78, police sgt., 1978-87, police lt., 1987-89, police asst. chief, 1989-90, police capt., 1990, chief of police, 1990—; mem. SWAT team Louisville Divsn. Police, mem. honor guard, mem. bomb squad; mem. regional adv. com. U.S. Dept. Edn.-S.E.R.C.; mem. adv. bd. Commonwealth of Ky. Crime Commn.; bd. dirs. Louisville Police Officers Credit Union, Commonwealth of Ky. Corrections Commn. Mem. coun. Salvation Army Adult Rehab. Program; mem. exec. com. Ky. Derby Fesitval, Child Advocacy Ctr.; mem. exec. com. law enforcement torch run Ky. Spl. Olympics; mem. com. Atty. Gen.'s Task Force Domestic Violence; mem. exec. bd. Area Wide Alcohol & Drug Rehab., Edn. & Enforcement; bd. dirs. Jefferson County Office Women, Bingham Child Guidance Ctr., Louisville and Jefferson County Crime Commn. Mem. Nat. Conf. Christians and Jews (bd. dirs.), Ky. Assn. Chiefs of Police (v.p.), Internat. Assn. Chiefs of Police, Fraternal Order Police (lodge 6), Leadership Louisville, Louisville Police Commdg. Officers Club (pres.), Alpha Phi Sigma. Home: 4611 Southern Pky Louisville KY 40214-1422 Office: Louisville Divsn Police 633 W Jefferson Louisville KY 40202-2735*

HAMILTON, GORDON STOKES, mechanical engineer, consultant; b. Miami, Fla., June 5, 1932; s. Lewis Stokes and Beatrice (Yearout) H.; m. Wanda Lee Littleton, Feb. 23, 1974. AB in Physics, Berea Coll., 1954; BSME, Va. Polytech. Inst., 1956. Cert. profl. ski instr. Tchg. asst. Va. Polytech. Inst., Blacksburg, 1954-55; various positions Norfolk & Western Rlwy. Co., Roanoke, Va., 1956-82; equip. maintenance engr. Norfolk So. Rlwy., Roanoke, 1982-91; R.R. cons. mech. engring. Assn. Am. R.R.s and various cos., Roanoke, 1991—; ski instr. Snowshoe Mountain Resort, W.Va., 1993—. With U.S. Army, 1956-58. Home and Office: 5202 Carriage Dr Roanoke VA 24018-2214

HAMILTON, HOWARD LAVERNE, zoology educator; b. Lone Tree, Iowa, July 20, 1916; s. Harry Stephen and Gertrude Ruth (Shibley) H.; m. Alison Phillips, Dec. 22, 1945 (dec. 1972); children: Christina Helen, Phillips Howard, Martha Jayne; m. Elizabeth Burnley Bentley, June 18, 1975; children: Elizabeth Marshall, Catherine Randolph. B.A. with highest distinction, State U. Iowa, 1937, M.S., 1938; postgrad., U. Rochester, 1938-40; Ph.D., Johns Hopkins U., 1941. Asst. prof. to prof. zoology Iowa State U., 1946-62, acting head, 1960-61, chmn. dept. zoology and entomology, 1961-62; prof. biology U. Va., 1962-82, prof. emeritus, 1982—. Author: Lillie's Development of the Chick, 1952; cons. editor, McGraw-Hill Ency. Sci. and Tech., 1962-78; mng. editor: The Am. Zoologist, 1965-70; Author: (with Viktor Hamburger) Citation Classic: A Series of Normal Stages in the Development of the Chick, 1951. Served to capt. Med. Adminstrv. Corp., AUS, 1941-45, to col. USAR, 1945-69. Mem. Am. Soc. Zoologists, Am. Soc. Naturalists, Soc. Developmental Biology, Internat. Inst. Devel. Biology, Am. Inst. Biol. Sci., Nat. Soc. Ams. of Royal Descent (pres. gen. 1974-80, hon. life pres. gen. 1980—), SAR (nat. exec. com., pres. Va. Soc. 1979-80, registrar gen. 1980-82, pres. gen. 1982-83, Minuteman award and Gold Good Citizenship medal), Order of Three Crusades 1096-1192 (historian gen. 1976-83, 1st v.p. gen. 1983—), Assn. Preservation Va. Antiquities, Va. Hist. Soc. Club: Farmington Country. Home: Jumping Branch Farm 1906 Garth Rd Charlottesville VA 22901-8829 Office: U Va Dept Biology Gilmer Hall Charlottesville VA 22901

HAMILTON, JACKSON DOUGLAS, lawyer; b. Cleve., Feb. 5, 1949; m. Margaret Lawrence Williams, Dec. 19, 1971; children: Jackson Douglas Jr., William Schuyler Lawrence. BA, Colgate U., 1971; JD, U. Pa., 1974. Bar: Calif. 1974, U.S. Dist. Ct. (cen. dist.) Calif. 1974, U.S. Tax Ct. 1978, U.S. Ct. Claims 1984, U.S. Ct. Appeals (6th and 11th cirs.) 1988, N.C. 1991, U.S. Supreme Ct. 1991. Ptnr. Kadison, Pfaelzer, Woodard, Quinn & Rossi, L.A., 1986-87, Spensley, Horn, Jubas & Lubitz, L.A., 1987-91, Roberts & Stevens, Asheville, N.C., 1991—; adj. prof. law U. San Diego, 1981, Golden Gate U., San Francisco, 1981-85, U. N.C., Asheville, 1994; cons. Calif. Continuing Edn. Bar, 1983-84, select com. on sports Calif. Senate, 1983-85. Editor Entertainment Law Reporter, 1979—; contbr. articles to profl. jours. Mem. ABA (tax sect., internat. law sect.), Los Angeles County Bar Assn. (tax sect., internat. law sect.). Republican. Episcopalian. Office: BB & T Bldg Asheville NC 28802

HAMILTON, JACQUELINE, art consultant; b. Tulsa, Mar. 28, 1942; d. James Merton and Nina Faye (Andrews) H.; m. Richard Sanford Piper, Jan. 2, 1968 (div. June 1976). BA, Tex. Christian U., 1965; grad., Stockholm U., 1967; postgrad., Harvard U., 1972-73, Tufts U., 1971, Rice U., 1982-83, Houston C.C., 1986-87. Pvt. practice art cons. Houston, 1979—. Contbr. articles to profl. publs. Active Cultural Arts Council of Houston. Mem. Assn. Corp. Art Curators, Nat. Assn. Corp. Art Mgmt., Rice Design Alliance, Tex. Arts Alliance, The Houstonian Club, The Forum Club, L'Alliance Francaise, Swedish Club. Presbyterian. Office: PO Box 1483 Houston TX 77251-1483

HAMILTON, JOHN KENNEDY, state treasurer. Treas. State of Ky., Frankfort. Office: State Treas Office Capitol Annex Rm 183 Frankfort KY 40601

HAMILTON, JOYCE MARIE, adult education educator; b. San Antonio, Tex., June 13, 1950; d. Robert Taylor and Gladys Genevieve (Briggs) Hamilton; 1 child, Gabriel Emile. BA, U. Tex., 1975, BS, 1977, MEd, 1979; postgrad., Va. Commonwealth U., 1996—. Cert. clin. reading specialist; cert. tchr. with adult edn. endorsement, Va. Adult edn. tchr. Austin (Tex.) State Hosp., 1979-82; devel. studies instr. Austin C.C., 1982-88; study lab. coord., athletic dept. U. Tex., Austin, 1986-88; regional adult edn. specialist Spotsylvania County Schs., Spotsylvania, Va., 1988-90, regional adult edn. coord., 1990—; chair adult literacy com. Rappahannock Reading Coun., Fredericksburg, Va., 1993-95. Task force leader Fredericksburg Area Task Force for Learning Disabled Adults, 1991—; den leader Cub Scouts, Falmouth, Va., 1991-93. Recipient Vol. award Austin Assn. for Children and Adults with Learning Disabilities, 1986, Exemplary Svc. award Rappahannock Reading Coun., 1996. Mem. AAUW (v.p. 1991-92, gender equity chair 1992-93), Va. Assn. for Adult and Continuing Edn. (v.p. 1994-95, bylaws chair 1995-97), Delta Kappa Gamma (sec. 1994-95, v.p. Beta Eta chpt. 1996-98), Phi Delta Kappa. Quaker (attender). Office: Spotsylvania Vocat Ctr 6703 Smith Station Rd Spotsylvania VA 22553-1803

HAMILTON, LAURA ANN, social worker; b. Cordele, Ga., Nov. 16, 1939; d. Herbert Williams and Janie LaVerne (Lumpkin) Hamilton; student Valdosta State Coll., 1957-58; B.S., Fla. State U., 1961, M.S.W., 1965; postgrad. U. Ga., 1961-62, U. Chgo., summer 1967, W. Ga. Coll., 1969, Ga. State U., 1970; postgrad. U. Tex.-Arlington, 1985-88; PhD, 1988. Vis. tchr. Crisp County Schs., Cordele, 1961-63; social service worker Social Service Dept., Milledgeville (Ga.) State Hosp., 1963; med. social worker Crippled Children's Svc., Birmingham, Ala., 1964; psychiat. social worker Fla. State Hosp., Chattahoochee, 1965, Milledgeville State Hosp., 1965-66; cons. for social work projects ESEA Title I, Ga. Dept. Edn., Atlanta, 1966-68, ESEA Title III, 1968-71; cons. program evaluations and audits Robert Davis Assos., Inc., Atlanta, 1971-72; chief Div. Planning, Evaluation, Monitoring & Analysis, S.C. Dept. Social Svcs., Columbia, 1973-76; regional dir. social svcs. Regions 01 and 02, Tex. Dept. Pub. Welfare, Lubbock, 1976-77; partner Kaye Fleming Boutique and Bridal Corner, Ft. Worth, 1978-83; pvt. practice social work, Ft. Worth, Tex., 1978—; dir. Tarrant County Dept. Human Svcs., Ft. Worth, 1985-91; dep. dir. Richmond (Va.) Dept. Social Svcs., 1991-96, dir. Forsyth County, dept Social Svc., 1996—; field supr. Kirschner Assos., Inc., Albuquerque, 1972, 73; evaluator for edn. professions devel. act project Waycross (Ga.) City Schs., 1972, W. Ga. Ednl. Service Center, Carrollton, 1972; program auditor Clarke County Schs., Atlanta, 1972; instr. Human Resource Center, U. Tex., Arlington, 1977-79; lectr. in field. Mem. Acad. Cert. Social Workers, Am. Pub. Welfare Assn., Am. Soc. Pub. Adminstrn., Nat. Assn. Social Workers. Address: 1111 Cypress Cir Winston Salem NC 27106 Office: Forsythe County Dept Social Svcs Winston Salem NC 27127

HAMILTON, LORRAINE REBEKAH, adult education consultant; b. York, Pa., Jan. 17, 1960; d. Robert Stephen Sheely and Emma Estella (Taylor) Ford; m. Ronald Dana Hamilton, Apr. 14, 1990. Diploma in Drafting and Design Tech., Cumberland-Perry Tech. Sch., Mechanicsburg, Pa., 1978; BS in Psychology, U. Houston, 1992, MA in Gen. Behavioral Scis., 1994. Drafter aluminum products Capitol Products, Camp Hill, Pa., 1978-81; drafter oil field equipment Continental Emsco, Houston, 1981-82; coll. prof. Coll. of the Mainlaind, Texas City, Tex., 1983-87; contract drafter/piping Astech Svcs., Houston, 1985-86; computer specialist Amoco Oil Co., Texas City, 1986-92; ind. cons. Sage Learning Method, 1994—; owner Synergy Sys., 1994-95, E-Three, 1996—; founder EntertaiNET Networking Party, 1996—. Convenor Women's Studies Student Assn., Houston, 1994; treas., forum rep. NOW, Houston, 1992; vol. Landmark Edn. Corp., Houston, 1992-94. Mem. Omicron Delta Kappa. Home: PO Box 22653 Houston TX 77227-2653

HAMILTON, MARIAN ELOISE, housing authority official; b. Salt Lake City, Mar. 21, 1931; d. Frederic William and Kathryn Eloise (Core) Wrathall; m. Stanley Keith Hamilton, Feb. 2, 1951 (dec. 1983); children: Edmond Scott, Perri Collette, Deena Kathryn. Student U. Utah, 1949-51, U. Calif.-Santa Barbara, 1951-52, U. Mont., 1952-53. Cert. pub. housing mgr. Field exec. Cross Timbers Girl Scouts, Denton, Tex., 1971-76; camp dir. Camp Kadohadacho, Pottsboro, Tex., 1971-75; acting dir. Wesley Pre-Sch., Denton, 1976-78; field dir. 1st Tex. Council, Campfire, Ft. Worth, 1979-81; housing mgr. Denton Housing Authority, 1981-88, exec. dir., 1988—; cons. on shared housing Tex. Agy. on Aging, Austin, 1984—; area rep. City of Denton Land Use Com., 1986-88; bd. dirs. Denton County Extension Svc., 1991-94, Denton Affordable Housing Coalition, 1995—; mem. City of Denton Housing Task Force, 1991-94, Dallas Mus. Fine Arts; mem. adv. bd. Martin Luther King, Jr. Recreation Ctr.; mem. human subjects rev. com. Tex. Woman's U.; founder Tex. Woman's U. CARES. Recipient Fred Moore award Denton chpt. NAACP, 1990, Women Working Together award Morse St. Bapt. Ch., 1995; named Citizen of Yr. Nat. Assn. Social Workers, 1991. Mem. Nat. Assn. Housing and Redevel. Ofcls. (8 Merit awards), Am. Assn. Homes for Aging, Nat. Coun. on Aging, Nat. Assn. Female Execs., First Tex. Coun. of Camp Fire (bd. dirs. SuRaHa, Flame award), Kimbell Mus. Fine Arts, Signature Home Health (mem. review com.), Austin Writer's League, Dallas Mus. Art, Altrusa Internat. (v.p.). Democrat. Avocations: writing, travel, reading. Home: 900 Sierra Dr Denton TX 76201-8742 Office: Denton Housing Authority 308 S Ruddell St Denton TX 76205-6329

HAMILTON, NANCY RICHEY, critical care nurse, educator; b. Alexandria, La., Oct. 8, 1950; d. Allen M. and Beryl M. (Price) Richey; m. James G. Hamilton, July 15; 1 child, April Michele. BS, Northwestern State U., Natchitoches, La., 1972; postgrad., U. Md., 1973-74; ADN, Hinds Jr. Coll., Raymond, Miss., 1983; BSN, Northwestern State U., 1994. RN Tenn., N.C., La.; cert. ACLS instr., TNCC, intensive and coronary care. Charge nurse Jefferson Meml. Hosp., Jefferson City, Tenn., St. Mary's Med. Ctr., Knoxville, Tenn.; asst. head nurse Duke U. Med. Ctr., Durham, N.C.; tchr. biology high sch., 1972-75; asst. head nurse, emergency rm. St. Frances Cabrini Hosp., Alexandria, critical care instr.; insvc. dir./supr. Huey Long Med. Ctr., Pineville, La., area mgr. critical care, critical care educator. Mem. AACN, Tenn. Nurses Assn., N.C. Nurses Assn.

HAMILTON, NANETTE LOUISE, librarian; b. Lae, Papua New Guinea, Jan. 6, 1969; d. Robert Lee and Shirley Ann (Carroll) Litteral; m. James Alexander Hamilton, Dec. 31, 1988. BA, Wheaton Coll., 1989; MLIS, U. S.C., 1995. Head tech. svcs. Columbia (S.C.) Internat. Univ., 1991—. Tutor Cook County Jail, Chgo., 1986-88. Mem. Am. Theol. Libr. Assn. Office: Columbia Internat U 7435 Monticello Rd Columbia SC 29230

HAMILTON, PATRICK JOSEPH, city official; b. Denver, Nov. 22, 1936; s. Raymond Whittier and Elizabeth Agnes (Slattery) H.; m. Margaret Alice Maddern, June 8, 1957 (div.); children: Denise, Stephen, Diane, Donna, Lisa, Michael; m. G. Jean Croucher, July 18, 1987. BA, Washburn U., 1961. Programmer/analyst Procter & Gamble, Cin., 1961-66; gen. supr. fiscal sys. LTV Electrosys./E-Sys., Greensville, Tex., 1966-73; exec. dir. South Tex. Computer Ctr., Edinburgh, 1973-75; data processing mgr. City of Wichita Falls, Tex., 1976-79; cons. Tres Sys., Inc., Dallas, 1979-83, Actron Info. Data Sys., Arlington, Tex., 1983-87; dir. info. svcs. Dallas Ctrl. Appraisal Dist., 1987-92; technology svcs. mgr. City of Arlington, 1992—. Author/editor/pub.: A System for Playing Roulette, 1981. With USNR, 1954-62. Mem. Tex. Assn. Govt. DAta Processing MGrs. (sec.-treas. 1989-90, v.p. 1990-91, pres. 1991-92, plaques 1990, 91, 92), Govt. Mgmt. Info. Sci. Assn. (v.p. 1989-93, pres. 1993-94, exec. dir. 1994-95, plaque 1994). Home: 8050 Slide Rock Rd Fort Worth TX 76137 Office: City of Arlington 101 W Abram St Arlington TX 76004

HAMILTON, PAUL MARTIN, psychologist; b. Albia, Iowa, Aug. 19, 1952; s. George Alan Hamilton and Shirley Lee (Martin) Martin; m. Kathleen Denise Allen Hamilton, June 8, 1974; children: Jason, John. BS, U. Houston, 1972, MA, 1977; postgrad., Fielding Inst., Santa Barbara, Calif., 1989—. Lic. psychol. assoc. Tex. State Bd. Examiners of Psychologists. Psychol. assoc. R.F. Sarmiento, PhD, Houston, 1977-81; staff psychologist children's outpatient svcs. Mental Health Mental Retardation Authority of Harris County, Houston, 1978-81; psychol. assoc. Alan T. Fisher, PhD, Corpus Christi, Tex., 1981-89, Associated Psychologists, Corpus Christi, 1987-89, Joseph J. Horvat, PhD, Corpus Christi, 1987—; bd. dirs. Profl. Counseling Ctr., Aransas Pass, Tex., 1988-90. Editor (newsletter) The Psychol. Assoc., 1979-84. Coun. mem. Aransas Pass City Coun., 1986-92, mayor pro tempore, 1988-89; bd. dirs. Coastal Bend Found., Aransas Pass, 1987-92, Aransas Pass C. of C., 1984-86. Named Outstanding Psychol. Assoc., The Psychol. Assoc. newsletter, 1980. Mem. Am. Soc. Clin. Hypnosis (student mem.), Nueces County Psychol. Assn., Tex. Psychol. Assn. (assoc.), Am. Psychol. Assn. (assoc.). Methodist. Home: 954 S 11th St Aransas Pass TX 78336-3810 Office: Joseph J Horvat PhD 4646 Corona St # 150 Corpus Christi TX 78411-4320

HAMILTON, PETER SCOTT, management consultant; b. Denton, Tex., Mar. 15, 1945; s. F. Sidney and Lucia Mary (Rushing) H.; m. Carolyn B. Hamilton, Apr. 12, 1968; children: Jaina, Blake, Darren. MS, U. North Tex., 1968, PhD, 1983. Mgr. Jon Pierce Inc., Ft. Worth, 1976-81; pres. Hamilton and Assocs., Denton, Tex., 1981-92, Hamilton Assocs., Inc., Denton, 1992-95; v.p. Profiles Internat., Waco, Tex., 1995—. 1st lt. U.S. Army, 1969-72. Office: Profiles Internat 5205 Lake Shore Dr Waco TX 76710

HAMILTON, ROBERT BROOKS, lawyer; b. Houston, Mar. 3, 1936; s. Brooks Hamilton and Doris Truitt Moye; m. Judy Claire Beeson, June 8, 1956; children: Terry, Kay, Robbie, Jenny. BS, U. Houston, 1958; JD, So. Meth. U., 1963. Bar: Tex. 1963. Servicing agt. Hand & Assocs., Houston, 1956-58; account exec. Wickenden & Assocs., Ft. Worth, Tex., 1958-60; cons. A.S. Hansen, Dallas, 1960-66; ptnr. Abney & Burleson, Dallas, 1966-69; pres. Benefit Tech., Dallas, 1969-76; founder Hamilton & Assocs., Dallas, 1976—. Trustee State Bar of Tex. Benefit Trust, Austin, 1985-91, Tom Hughes Found., Dallas, 1986—, St. Philips Sch., 1992—. Mem. Tex. Bar Assn., Dallas Bar Assn., Order of the Barons. Home: 6809 Mossvine Cir Dallas TX 75240-7951 Office: Hamilton & Assocs 12900 Preston Rd Ste 500 Dallas TX 75230-1321

HAMILTON, ROBERT WOODRUFF, law educator; b. Syracuse, N.Y., Mar. 4, 1931; s. Walton Hale and Irene (Till) H.; m. Dagmar S. Strandberg, June 2, 1953; children: Eric Clark, Robert Andrew, Meredith Hope. BA, Swarthmore Coll., 1952; JD, U. Chgo., 1955. Bar: D.C. 1956, U.S. Ct. Appeals (D.C. cir.) 1960, U.S. Supreme Ct. 1965. Law clk. to justice Tom Clark U.S. Supreme Ct., Washington, 1955-56; assoc. Gardner, Morrison & Rogers, Washington, 1956-64; assoc. prof. law U. Tex., Austin, 1964-67, prof., 1967—, Minerva House Drysdale Regents chair in law; research dir. U.S. Admin. Conf., Washington, 1972-73; vis. prof. U. Pa., U. Minn., Washington U., St. Louis, others; mem. rev. panel on new drugs HEW, Washington, 1974-77. Author: Texas Practice, vols. 19 and 20, 1973, Cases on Corporations, 1975, 5th rev. edit., 1994, Cases on Contracts, 1984, 2d rev. edit., 1992, Nutshell on Corporations, 1980, 4th rev. edit., 1996, Cases on Corporate Finance, 1984, 2d rev. edit., 1989, Fundamentals of Modern Business, 1990, Money Management for Lawyers and Clients, 1993. Chmn. bd. dirs. U. Coop. Soc., Austin, 1989—; elected mem. Westlake Hills (Tex.) City Coun., 1969-72; chmn. zoning commn. Westlake Hills, 1983-87. Rsch. grantee U. Tex., 1970, 84, 92. Mem. ABA (reporter), Am. Law Inst., Tex. Bar Assn. (partnership com., corp. laws com.), Order of Coif. Democrat. Office: U Tex Law Sch 727 E 26th St Austin TX 78705-3224

HAMILTON, SCOTT ERIC, computer software engineer, communications executive; b. Peoria, Ill., Oct. 31, 1948; s. Merle C. and Virginia L. H.; m. Martha J. Ross, July 21, 1981 (div. Apr., 1993). BS, U. Nebr., 1971. Engr. Nebr. ETV Commn., Lincoln, 1969-72; engr., analyst Pub. Broadcasting Svc., Washington, 1972-73; mgr. Litton Systems, College Park, Md., 1973-77, Satellite Bus. Systems, McLean, Va., 1977-84; sr. cons. GE, Rockville, Md., 1984-89; dir. Advanced TV Test Ctr., Alexandria, Va., 1989-94; pres. Pyxis Corp., Fairfax, Va., 1993—; dir. engring. Fox Animation Studios, Phoenix, 1995—; mem. tech. adv. bd. Commtex Corp., Crofton, Md., 1989-91. Author: Handbook of Standard Resistor, Capacitor, Inductor Ratios, 1988. Capt., communications officer CAP, Washington, 1984—; pres. Home Owners Assn., Crofton, Md., 1979-81. Mem. IEEE Computer Soc., Assn. for Computing Machinery, Audio Engring. Soc. Republican. Lutheran. Home and Office: 3104 E Camelback Rd Ste 624 Phoenix AZ 85016

HAMILTON, SUSAN OWENS, transportation company executive, lawyer; b. Birmingham, Ala., Aug. 7, 1951; d. William Lewis and Vonnette (Wilson) Owens; m. M. Raymond Hamilton, June 8, 1974. BA, Auburn U., 1973; JD, Samford U., 1977. Bar: Ala., Fla. Claim agt. Seaboard System R.R. and predecessor cos., Birmingham, Ala., 1977-78; atty. Seaboard System R.R. and predecessor cos., Louisville, 1978-80, claims atty., 1980-81; asst. gen. atty. Seaboard System R.R. and predecessor cos., Jacksonville, Fla., 1981-83, asst. gen. solicitor, 1983-84, gen. mgr. freight claim services, 1984-85; asst. v.p. casualty prevention Chessie System R.R.'s, Balt. and Jacksonville, 1985-86; asst. v.p. freight damage prevention and claims CSX Transp., Jacksonville, 1986-87, asst. v.p. adminstrv. svcs., 1987-90, sr. asst. v.p. adminstrv. svcs., 1990-95; v.p., gen. counsel CTI, a Unit of CSX, 1995—. Vice chair fund distbn. com., United Way of N.E. Fla., 1991-93, chmn., 1993-94, mem. exec. com., 1992—, chmn. bd. dirs., 1996—; mem. Gator Bowl Com., 1993—, Gator Bowl officer, 1995—. Mem. ABA, Jacksonville Bar Assn., Bus. and Profl. Women (pres. Jacksonville chpt. 1984-85),

Fla. Bus. and Profl. Women (Outstanding Young Career Woman 1982), Uptown Civitan (bd. dirs. Jacksonville club 1982-84, v.p., pres. elect. 1993, pres. 1993-94). Methodist. Home: 12154 Hidden Hills Dr Jacksonville FL 32225-3653 Office: 500 Water St Jacksonville FL 32202-4422

HAMILTON, THOMAS ALLEN, insurance agent, registered representative; b. Oklahoma City, July 7, 1947; s. Vernon Carlton and Hazel (Margie) H.; children: Travis Matthew, Heather Lynne. BBA Mktg. and Mgmt., Okla. U., 1969. Dept. mgr. J.C. Penney, Oklahoma City, 1969-71; spl. agt. CNA Ins., Oklahoma City, 1971-74; group cons. Mass. Mut. Ins. Co., Oklahoma City, 1974-79, qualified plan cons.; bus./estate ins. cons. Mass Mut. Ins. Co., Oklahoma City, 1979-93; ins. investment cons. Sun Fin. Group, Oklahoma City, 1993-95; ind. agt., rep., 1996—; owner Advantage Golf Southwest, Oklahoma City. Past chmn. troop 177 Boy Scouts Am., Oklahoma City, 1987-88. Mem. Nat. Assn. Life Underwriters, Mass. Mut. Agts. Assn. (past pres., sec. agts., rep.), Am. Bus. Clubs, Oklahoma City Art Mus., Bapt. Med. Ctr. Okla. Found., Oklahoma City Ski Club. Republican. Baptist. Home and Office: 6500 Dulane Cir Oklahoma City OK 73132-2005

HAMILTON, THOMAS PERCY, preventive medicine physician, military officer; b. Buffalo, July 11, 1932; s. James Alexander and Charlot Clara (Krathwohl) H.; m. Elsie Marie Myers, Apr. 2, 1971; children: Stephen, Patricia, Beverly, Susan. BS, Case-Western Res. U., 1954; MD, SUNY, Buffalo, 1957; MPH, U. Mich., 1969. Diplomate Am. Bd. Preventive Medicine, Pub. Health Adminstrn.; lic. MD, Calif., Ga., Mich., Nev., N.J., Pa. Internship U.S. Naval Hosp., Charleston, S.C., 1958; sr. med. officer, squadron flight surgeon U.S. Navy, various locations, S.C., N.J., 1958-61; regional flight surgeon FAA, Atlanta, 1961-62; family practitioner Levittown (Pa.) Med. Ctr., 1962-63; staff physician, asst. med. dir. Rutgers U., New Brunswick, N.J., 1963-64, 64-66; dir. health dept., cons. in local health adminstrn. various health depts., Adrian, Detroit, Lansing, Mich., 1966-71; dir. health and human svcs., health officer various counties, Santa Ana, Pasadena, L.A., Calif., 1971-84; dep. comdr. U.S. Army Aeromed., med. staff officer Health Svcs. Command, Ft. Rucker/Sam Houston, Ala., Tex., 1984-86, 88-89; chief preventive medicine svc., dep. comdr., comdr. Brooke Army Med. Ctr., Fort Sam Houston, 1989-90, 90-92; prof. and chief preventive medicine, ret. Army Med. Dept. Ctr. and Sch., Fort Sam Houston, 1992-93, 93—; assoc. clin. prof. community and environ.medicine U. Calif., Irvine, 1972—; asst. clin. prof. dept. preventive medicine U. So. Calif., 1977—; asst. clin. prof. dept. family medicine Loma Linda U., 1983—; residency dir. preventive medicine L.A. and Riverside County Health Depts., 1979-84; acad. chair continuing med. edn. Health Officers Assn. of Calif., 1977-84. Contbr. numerous articles to profl. jours. Fellow Am. Coll. Preventive Medicine, Am. Pub. Health Assn.; mem. Am. Coll. Physician Execs., Assn. U.S. Army, Assn. Army Flight Surgeons, Calif. Med. Assn., Res. Officers Assn., Riverside County Med. Assn., The Ret. Officers Assn.

HAMILTON, WILLIAM JOSEPH, osteopath; b. Beech Grove, Ind., July 20, 1940; married; 3 children. BS in Biol. Scis., Purdue U., 1962; MA in Biology, Ball State U., 1963; DO, Coll. Osteo. Medicine and Surgery, 1972. Diplomate Am. Bd. Psychiatry and Neurology. Intern St. Mary's Med. Ctr., Evansville, Ind., 1972-73; resident in neurology Med. Coll. Ga., Augusta, 1973-76, asst. prof. neurology, 1976-81; staff neurologist VA Med Ctr., Augusta, 1976-82; assoc. prof. neurology Med. Coll. Ga., Augusta, 1981-82, acting chief, assoc. prof. medicine, 1981-83, assoc. prof. neurology, 1982-83, dir. residency tng. program in neurology, 1983; pvt. practice Joplin, Mo., 1984-85; assoc. prof. dept. neurology Coll. Medicine U. South Ala., Mobile, 1985-89, prof., chief adult neurology, 1989—, med. advisor dept. physical therapy Coll. Allied Health, 1991—; cons. neurologist VA Med. Ctr., Augusta, 1982-83; mem. med. coll. admissions com. U. South Ala., medicine/family practice com., task force network com., med. staff quality assurance com., drug utilization and evaluation com., Univ. faculty grievance com., curriculum com., appointments, promotions, and evaluations com.; dep. examiner Ala. Bd. Med. Examiners, 1991-93. Contbr. articles to profl. jours. Recipient Pfizer Pharm. award, 1972, Geriatric Medicine Acad. award Nat. Insts. on Aging, NIH, 1981, 82, 83, 84, grant Sandoz Pharms., 1988, Co-investigator award Miles Inc., 1988-91, Co-investigator Nat. Inst. Neurol. Disorders and Stroke, 1991-94, Co-investigator Abbott Labs., 1992—. Mem. Am. Acad. Neurology, Am. Acad. Osteo. Neurologists and Psychiatrists (v.p. 1988-89, pres. 1989-90), Ala. Osteo. Med. Assn., Stroke Coun., Psi Sigma Alpha. Home: 105 Mcmillan Ave Daphne AL 36526-4435 Office: Univ South Ala Dept Neurology 2451 Fillingim St Rm 1007 Mobile AL 36617-2238

HAMILTON, WILLIAM OLIVER, physics educator, researcher; b. Lawrence, Kans., Sept. 5, 1933; s. Francis C. and Bernraine (Winegar) H.; m. Mary Helen Kelson, June 23, 1956; children: Eric William, Christopher David, Ann Elizabeth. BS, Stanford U., 1955, PhD, 1963. Asst. prof. Stanford (Calif.) U., 1965-70; assoc. prof. La. State U., Baton Rouge, 1970-77, prof., 1977—; vis. prof. U. Rochester (N.Y.), 1977-78; cons. in field. Contbr. over 50 articles to profl. jours. Lt. USN, 1955-58. NSF Postdoctoral fellow, 1963-65, Vis. fellow U. Western Australia, 1987; Rsch. grantee, NSF, 1970—. Mem. AAAS, Am. Phys. Soc., Am. Assn. Physics Tchrs. Office: La State U Dept Physics Baton Rouge LA 70803

HAMILTON-KEMP, THOMAS ROGERS, organic chemist, educator; b. Lebanon, Ky., May 13, 1942; s. Thomas Rogers and Catherine Rose (Hamilton) K.; m. Lois Ann Groce, Sept. 13, 1980. AA, St. Catharine Coll., 1962; BA, U. Ky., 1964, PhD in Chemistry, 1970. Mem. faculty U. Ky., Lexington, 1970—, asst. prof. natural products chemistry, 1970-75, assoc. prof., 1975-85, prof., 1985—. Rschr. on isolation, identification and biol. effects of natural compounds including antimicrobials; contbr. articles to profl. jours. Mem. AAAS, SAR, Am. Chem. Soc., Am. Soc. Hort. Sci., Sigma Xi, Gamma Sigma Delta, The Filson Club. Democrat. Roman Catholic. Home: 2025 Williamsburg Rd Lexington KY 40504-3015 Office: U Ky Agrl Sci Ctr N # N 308 Lexington KY 40546

HAMLETT, ROBERT BARKSDALE, systems engineer; b. Richmond, Va., Nov. 3, 1949; s. Thomas Coleman and Kathleen Pendleton (Snow) H.; m. Linda Lane Moody, June 24, 1972 (div. Dec. 1982); 1 child, Sarah Barksdale; m. Karen Ann Carwile, Jan. 19, 1985; children: John Coleman, Robert Barksdale Jr. BS in Physics cum laude, Hampden-Sydney Coll., 1972. Programmer United Va. Bank, Richmond, 1972-74, systems programmer, 1975-78, systems programming officer, 1979-82, mgr. tech. support, 1983-84; account systems engr. IBM Corp., Richmond, 1984-87, adv. systems engr., 1987-93; advisory svcs. specialist IBM Corp., Richmond, Va., 1993—. Clk. Grace Bapt. Ch., Richmond, 1986-88. Home: 5223 Willane Rd Glen Allen VA 23060-5352 Office: IBM Corp 1051 E Cary St Richmond VA 23219-4029

HAMLIN, EDWIN CLIBURN, account executive; b. Eden, N.C., Nov. 17, 1961; s. James Henry and Odessa (Strong) H.; m. DeWanna Thomas, Feb. 16, 1986; children: Erran, Catherine. B Bus. Adminstrn. and Acctg., Catawba Coll., 1984. Corp. mgmt. assoc. dept. corp. tng. Wachovia Corp., Winston-Salem, N.C., 1984-85, loan adminstrn. rep. dept. gen. loan adminstrn., 1985-86; sr. analyst dept. asset-based finances Wachovia Bank, Winston-Salem, 1986-87, asst. v.p., corp. lending officer, 1987-90, mgr. corp. tng. and devel., 1990-91; account exec. Supermarket Info. Systems Inc., Winston-Salem, 1991-95, sales cons., 1995—; instr. Living Well Fitness Ctr., 1988-89. Chmn. bd. trustees Cleveland Avenue Christian Ch. Disciples of Christ, 1991, deacon, 1992—, chmn. ofcl. bd., 1992-94; vol., team leader United Way, March of Dimes, Piedmont Team Walk, 1984-93; v.p. Griffin Elem. Sch. PTA, 1992-94. Home: 1791 Greencedar Ln Winston Salem NC 27127-7355 Office: Supermarket Info Systems Inc 4045 University Pky Winston Salem NC 27106-3360

HAMM, GEORGE FRANCIS, university president; b. Rapid City, S.D., June 26, 1931; s. Michael and Mae E. (Howard) H.; m. Jane Sigler, Aug. 29, 1958; children—Jean Marie, Gregory F., Robert Joseph, Daniel G. (dec.). B.A., S.D. State U., 1953; M.A., U. Wyo., 1958, Ph.D., 1961. Asst. prof. Ariz. State U., 1962-63, dean students, 1963-69, v.p. student affairs, 1969-81; prof. psychology U. Tex., Tyler, 1981—, pres., 1981—; mem. academic planning com. Inst. for Advanced Strategic and Polit. Planning, Jerusalem, Israel, 1985. Chmn. internat. bd. Sister Cities Internat., Washington; bd. dirs. E. Tex. Hosp. Found., Tyler, 1982; bd. dirs. Fiesta Bowl, Tempe, Ariz., 1978-81; bd. trustees St. Edwards U., Austin, Tex., 1982-87. Served with U.S. Infantry, 1954-56. Named Outstanding Young Man Yr. Jr. C. of C., Ariz., 1964; recipient Highest Civilian award U.S. Air Force, 1967; Disting. Alumnus award S.D. State U., 1983; Southwestern Internat. Bus. fellow, 1987. Mem. Tex. Assn. of Atlantic Council, Am. Assn. State Colls. and Univs., Nat. Assn. State Univ. and Land Grant Colls. (exec. com. 1979-81, chmn. council on student affairs 1976-78), Phi Kappa Phi, Omicron Delta Kappa, Psi Chi. Roman Catholic. Home: 9438 Cherokee Trl Tyler TX 75703-5445 Office: U Tex 3900 University Blvd Tyler TX 75799-0001*

HAMMAD, ALAM E., international business consultant, educator; b. Cairo, Egypt, Sept. 24, 1943; s. Mohammad Attia H.; m. Dyannoelle Elizabeth, Jan. 19, 1978; 1 child, Adam. BA in Commerce, Cairo Poly. Inst., 1965; MS in Mktg., La. State U., 1971; D of Bus. Adminstrn., George Washington U., 1977. Advisor Min. State & Gov. of Dhofar, Salalah, Oman, 1977-79; advisor Min. Petroleum & Minerals, Muscat, Oman, 1979; head planning Min. Agr. & Fisheries, Muscat, Oman, 1979-83; pres., founder Pyramex Fin. Internat., Va., 1983-84; chmn. MicroAge Computers Corp., Va., 1984-86; prof., lectr. George Washington U., Washington, 1984-88; pres., found Pizza Club, Inc., Va., 1987—; contractor, builder, internat. cons., 1984—; vis. prof. George Washington U., 1988-90; chmn. found. com. Oman Nat. Fisheries Co., 1980-81, Oman Bank Agr., 1981-82; bd. dirs. Oman Sun Farms Co., 1979, Oman Devel. Bank, 1979-83; pres. Am. Global Pub., 1992—; pub. policy expert The Heritage Found., 1996—; writer Okaz Saudi Newspaper, 1996—. Author: Development of Agriculture and Fisheries in Oman, 1981, Agriculture, Animal Wealth, Water Resources and Fisheries of Oman, 1987, Islamic Banking: Theory and Practice, 1989; Encyclopedia of Computer Terms, English-Arabic, 1994; Dictionary of Computer Terms, English-Arabic, 1994; contbr. articles to profl. jours. Mem. found. com. Sultan Qaboos U., 1981-86; pres. Info. Security Found., 1991-93, chmn. pub. affairs, exec. vice chmn. Alexandria Rep. City Com., 1st vice chmn.; pres. Nat. Arab-Am. Rep. coun.; mem. George Washington Dist. Com., Boy Scouts Am.; bd. visitors, trustee George Mason U., 1994—, vice rector, 1996—; mem. Campaign for Honest Change, Empower Am., Rep. Nat. Com., Com. for a Safe Va., Heritage Found.; commr. Alexandria Indsl. Devel. Authority, 1996—; mem. Nat. Policy Coun., Nat. Alumni Found., Northern Va. Rep. Bus. Forum, Com. for a Safe Va. Campaign for Honest Change, Empower Am., Rep. Nat. Com. Decorated Order of Sultan Qaboos. Mem. Assn. Governing Bds. Univs. and Colls., Acad. Internat. Bus., Friendship Vets. Fire Engine Assn., Beta Gamma Sigma. Home: 819 S Fairfax St Alexandria VA 22314-4311

HAMMARBACK, JAMES ARVID, molecular biologist. BS, U. Minn., Mpls., 1980, PhD, 1986. NIH fellow Worcester Found. Exptl. Biology, Shrewsbury, Mass., 1986-89, rsch. assoc., 1989-91; asst. prof. Bowman Gray Sch. Medicine, Winston-Salem, N.C., 1991—. Recipient Bacaner Basic Sci. award Minn. Med. Found., Mpls., 1986. Mem. Am. Soc. Cell Biology. Office: Bowman Gray Sch Medicine Medical Center Blvd Winston Salem NC 27157-1010

HAMMARTH, RAYMOND JEAN, state commission administrator; b. Rockville Center, N.Y., Oct. 1, 1949; s. Raymond and Marie (Dorothee) H.; m. Bertie Love Ferrell, Mar. 29, 1984. AA, Suffolk Coll., 1969; BA, SUNY, Stony Brook, 1971; MPA, W.Va. Coll. Grad. Studies, 1978. Culinary guide Le Pompon Rouge, Bay Shore, N.Y., 1965-66; grocery mgr. Food Fair/ Pantry Pride, Phila., 1966-72; social worker Angel Guardian Home, Mineola, N.Y., 1972-73; field rep. W.Va. Human Rights Commn., Charleston, 1973-74, investigations supr., 1974-77, sect. chief investigations, 1977-79, mgr., 1979-84; investigator II Tex. Commn. Human Rights, Austin, 1984-88, unit supr., 1988—; arbitrator Better Bus. Bur., Austin, 1984—. Committeeman Islip Town Dem. Party, Bay Shore, 1971-73; Del. Travis County Dem. Convention, Austin, 1984. Roman Catholic. Home: 122 Park South Dr Kyle TX 78640-9718 Office: Tex Commn on Human Rights PO Box 13493 Austin TX 78711

HAMMER, JANE AMELIA ROSS, advocate; b. Charlotte, N.C., Apr. 9, 1916; d. Otho Bescent and Lucy (Harris) Ross; m. Philip Gibbon Hammer, Aug. 27, 1937; children: Philip Jr., Thomas Ross, Michael Levering. AB, U. N.C., 1936, MA, 1937; postgrad., Radcliffe Coll., New Eng. Conservatory, 1938-39. Charter mem. N.C. Symphony, 1933-36; mem. faculty philosophy Spelman Coll., Atlanta, 1946-58. Violinist Symphony String Quartet, N.C., 1933-36, Atlanta Symphony, 1947-52, Friday Morning Music Club Orch. at Kennedy Ctr., Washington, 1975-82; author: Protector: A Life History of Richard Cromwell, 1996; editor: Logic for Living, Lectures of H.H. Williams, 1951; editor, pub.: Origin of Belief (H.H. Williams), 1972; contbr. articles to profl. jours. Dir. tng. programs Overseas Edn. Fund LWV, Washington, 1962-63, mem. registration and voting projects staff Edn. Fund LWV, 1964-65, mem. spl. projects com., 1970-75, advisor natural resources com. LWV of Fla., Palm Harbor, 1990-92, bd. dirs. LWV Atlanta and State of Ga., 1942-61, pres. LWV of North Pinellas County, Fla., 1989-90; appointed pub. rep. mem. com. for feasibility study of health of residents of Pinellas County, U.S. Dept. Energy and Fla. Dept. Health and Rehab. Svcs., 1991-94; chmn. OASIS Coalition for Integration of Pub. Schs., Atlanta, 1960-61; mem. bd. overseers Dag Hammerskjold Coll., Columbia, Md., 1968-71; pres. FMMC Music Club Inc., Washington, 1973-74, trustee found., 1968-71; treas. H.W. Philos. Soc., Washington and Fla., 1975—; mem. women's com. Washington Performing Arts Soc., 1974—; mem. Pres. Clinton's Nat. Steering Com., 1995-96; mem. Nat. Women's Dem. Club. Named 500 Environ. Achiever, Friends of UN Environ. Programme, 1987. Mem. Friday Morning Music Club (Washington), The Social List (Washington), Bethesda (Md.) Country Club, Chi Omega (Epsilon Beta). Presbyterian. Home: 521 Holly Rd Edgewater MD 21037-3846

HAMMERLI, ANGELA MITCHELL, dance educator; b. Lafayette, La., Jan. 27, 1950; d. George and Angelina (Mannuccia) M.; m. Edwin Vincent Hammerli, June 12, 1972; children: Nathaniel Hawthorne, Walt Whitman. BFA in Dance, Stephens Coll., 1970; MA in Edn., U. Mo., 1972; postgrad., Nicholls State U., 1976-84. Tchr. phys. edn. various parochial schs., New South Wales, Australia, 1972-73; assoc. prof. dance Nicholls State U., Thibodaux, La., 1973—; head artists and lectures com. Nicholls State U., 1989—; cons. Leighton Health Club, Thibodaux, 1983-84; mem. dance panel La. Div. of Arts, 1991, 92, 94; mem. Lt. Gov.'s Task Force for the Arts, 1993; creative movement specialist. Choreographer numerous local mus. prodns.; columnist Daily Comet newspaper, 1985-89. Pres. Thibodaux Service League, 1985, Thibodaux Friends of the Libr., 1985, Bayou Lafourche Arts Coun., 1988—; active child abuse prevention Thibodaux pub. schs., pres., 1990—; organizer, producer Children's Theater Summer Workshops, 1982-87; guest speaker health and child abuse topics numerous civic groups; tchr. CPR Thibodaux ARC, 1975—; bd. dirs. Thibodaux Playhouse, 1984—, La. Coun. on Child Abuse, Am. Lung Assn., River Parish Coun., 1986-87; chair artists and lectures com. Nicholls State U., 1988—. Recipient Presdl. award for teaching excellence, 1996; named to Outstanding Young Women of Am., 1978, 81, Outstanding Young Women in Thibodeaux, Thibodeaux Jaycees, 1985, Dance Educator of Yr., La., 1994; La. Divsn. Arts grantee, 1991, 92, 93, 94, La. Endowment of Arts grantee, 1993. Mem. AAHPERD, La. Assn. Health, Phys. Edn. and Dance (chair dance performance, chair elect 1990-91, v.p. elect dance sect.), New Orleans Coun. Dance, Delta Kappa Gamma (contbg. author The Delta Kappa Gamma Bull., 1989). Home: 618 Saint Phillip St Thibodaux LA 70301-3236 Office: Nicholls State U PO Box 2038 Thibodaux LA 70301

HAMMERSCHMIDT, JOHN PAUL, retired congressman, lumber company executive; b. Harrison, AR, May 4, 1922; s. Arthur Paul and Junie (Taylor) H.; m. Virginia Sharp; 1 child, John Arthur. Student, The Citadel, U. Ark., Okla. State U. Chmn. bd. Hammerschmidt Lumber Co., Harrison, 1946-84; mem. 90th-102d Congresses from 3d Ark. Dist., 1967-93; mem. Pub. Works and Transp. Com., 1967-93, ranking mem., 1987-93; mem. V.A. Com., 1967-93, ranking mem., 1973-86; bd. dirs. 1st Fed. Bank of Ark.; bd. dirs. Dillard's Dept. Store, Southwestern Energy Co.; bd. trustees U. of the Ozarks; mem. adv. bd. Winrock Internat.; chmn. N.W. Ark. Coun.; state chmn. Ark. Citizen of Yr. Com.; mem. Presdl. Commn. on Aviation Security and Terrorism; mem. Claude and Mildred Pepper Found., 1989-90 (PVA Speedy award), Bd. Rev., Met. Washington Airports Authority, 1987-92. Chmn. Ark. Republican Com., 1964-66; mem. Rep. Nat. Finance Com., 1960-64, nat. Rep. committeeman from, Ark., 1976-80; mem. Harrison City Coun., 1948, 60, 62. Served as pilot USAAF, World War II, CBI. Decorated Air medal with 4 oak leaf clusters, D.F.C. with 3 oak leaf clusters, 3 Battle Stars, The China War Meml. medal, Meritorious Svc. award VFW Congl. award, Silver Helmet award, Nat. Order Trenchrats Legis. Svc. award, Award for Life Svc. to Vets.; named. Ark. Citizen of Yr., 1991, Ark. Aerospace Found. Hall of Fame, 1991. Mem. Ark. Lumber Dealers Assn. (past pres.), Midwest Lumbermens Assn. (past pres.), Harrison C. of C. (named Man of Yr. 1965), Am. Legion. Presbyn. (ordained elder, deacon). Lodges: Masons (33 degree-Grand Cross), Shriners, Jesters, Elks, Rotary (past pres. Harrison).

HAMMERT, DOROTHY SAVAGE, investment company executive; b. Hartshorne, Okla.; d. Eugene Bertrand and Lillian Vivian (Graves) Savage; m. Walter Scott Hammert Jr., Sept. 2, 1972; children: Diane Welker, Cindy Heinze, Warren, June. BA in English, U. Okla., 1951. Cert. profl. sec. Sr. sec. Stanolind Oil and Gas Co., Oklahoma City, Okla., 1951-58, Pan Am. Petroleum Corp., Oklahoma City, Okla., 1963-67; exec. sec. to chmn. of bd., chief exec. officer Benham-Blair and Affiliates, Oklahoma City, Okla., 1967-81; dist. mgr., area ednl. cons. World Book Ednl. Products, Oklahoma City, Okla., 1987-95; owner Practical Publishing Co., Oklahoma City, Okla., 1991—. Author: Rights are Responsibilities, 1991. V.p. Oklahoma City chpt. Freedoms Found. at Valley Forge, 1991-92; pres. Okla. Mother's Assn., 1996. Named Sec. of Yr. Nat. Secs. Assn., 1979, Okla. Mother's Assn. Mother of Yr., 1994. Mem. Am. Bus. Women's Assn. (yearbook chmn. 1991), Synergy Bus. Group (pres. 1987-88, 94-95), Women's Bus. Network (membership chmn. 1991), Joie de Vie Club (pres. 1993-94), Psi Psi Psi (pres. 1979-80, 93-95), Alpha Chi Omega (sect. chmn. 1987-88). Republican. Episcopalian. Home: 1616 Westminster Pl Oklahoma City OK 73120-1230 Office: Practical Pub Co 1616 Westminster Pl Oklahoma City OK 73120-1230

HAMMES, THERESE MARIE, advertising, public relations and marketing executive; b. Chgo., Mar. 27, 1955; d. Howard John and Lorna Marie (Jeans) H. BFA with honors, U. Miami, Coral Gables, Fla., 1976; MBA in Internat. Bus., St. Thomas U., Miami, 1992. Lic. real estate broker, Fla., 1985—. Pres. Hammes Advt. Agy., Coral Gables, Fla., 1978—; pres., broker Hammes Realty Mgmt. Corp., Coral Gables, 1986—; pres. Pro-Motion Media, Inc., Coral Gables, 1990-92; external bank dir. 1st Fla. Savings, FSB, 1990-93; v.p. Ponce de Leon Devel. Assn., Coral Gables, 1990-91, bd. dirs. One-woman shows include U. Miami, Fla., 1975; juried art show Lowe Art Mus., 1976, Internat. Erotic Art Show, Miami Beach, 1995; mem. home enthusiast panel Home & Gardens Remodeling Ideas mag. Bd. dirs. Young Dems., Dade County, 1982-86; del. Fla. Dem. Conv., 1995; landlord, Dade County Dem. Party, 1995—; mem. fin. com. Dade County Dem. Party Exec. Com., 1995; trustee Miami Youth Mus., 1990-94, bd. dirs., 1994—; mem. Leadership Miami, 1988—, mem. exec. com., co-chair commn., 1990—, chair pub. rels. and comm. com., 1991-93; bd. dirs. Crime Stoppers, 1992—. Named Miss Minn. Coun. of State Socs., 1975, Valley Forge Freedom Found. scholar, 1971; recipient Fla. award for mktg. excellence in best print campaign Best Corp. Campaign, Best Print Ad, Best Spl. Event, Best Collateral, 1989, 1991 Up and Comer award for advt. Price Waterhouse/South Fla. Mag., 1991. Mem. Nat. Assn. Women Bus. Owners (pub. rels. chmn. 1985-89), Builders Assn. South Fla. (editor, publisher 1986-87), Advt. Fedn. Greater Miami, Coral Gables C. of C., Greater Miami C. of C., Orange Key, Alpha Lambda Delta. Democrat. Home: 460 Hardee Rd Coral Gables FL 33146-3555 Office: Hammes Advt Inc 896 S Dixie Hwy Coral Gables FL 33146-2604

HAMMETT, THERESA CLAIR HOY, elementary school educator; b. Bklyn., Apr. 29, 1946; d. Birchard Clair Hoy and Philomena (Gaete) Davis; m. Thomas Gordon Hammett; 1 stepchild, Shelly Hammett; 1 child, Steven James. BS in Edn., St. Thomas Aquinas Coll., 1968; MA in Edn. and Adminstrn., Montclair (N.J.) State U., 1973; AS in Sociology, So. Okla. Jr. Coll., 1978. Cert. tchr. Tchr. social studies East Orange (N.J.) Bd. Edn., 1968-69, 70-72; tchr. Adult Basic Edn., East Orange, 1970-71; tchr. reading Denville (S.C.) Bd. Edn., 1969-70, Northfield (N.J.) Bd. Edn., 1972-74; part-time cons. Stockton State Coll., Pomona, N.J., 1973; substitute tchr. Dobbs Ferry (N.J.) Bd. Edn., 1974-75; prin. community edn. and recreation Bordentown Twp. (N.J.) Bd. Edn., 1975-76; substitute tchr. Oklahoma City Coll., 1979, tchr. English for the fgn. born, 1982-83; tchr. high sch. equivalency and ESL Adult Sch., Trenton; tchr. Blessed Sacrament Sch., Trenton, N.J., 1983-87; substitute tchr. Hillsborough County Bd. Edn., Tampa, Fla., 1988-89; tchr. Dunbar Elem. Sch., Tampa, 1989—; chair edn. dept. Study of Extended Sch. Ctr., East Orange, 1970-71, Community Com. Needs Assessment, Northfield, 1973-74; participant adult edn. think tank project U. Md., College Park, 1972-74; instr. adult basic edn., East Orange, 1971, high sch. equivalency, ESL Trenton Adult Sch., 1983. Active Dem. com. Right to Vote Blacks, Columbia, S.C., 1969; pres. Women's Auxilary Hamilton Little Lads Baseball League; counselor Kinderkamp YMCA, 1984; den mother Cub Scouts, 1985-87; initiator Cath. Ch. Bible Alive, Hamilton and St. Raphael, N.J., 1986. Grantee, 1974-75; recipient Disting. Svc. award Planning Sociology Club, 1978. Mem. NAFE, AAUW, ASCD, Ladies Guild. Roman Catholic. Home: 12008 Stone Crossing Cir Tampa FL 33635-6226

HAMMON, NORMAN HAROLD, fundraising counsel and development consultant; b. McAlester, Okla., Dec. 26, 1952; s. Duane E. and Mary Maxine (Donley) H.; m. Sheryl L. Martin, 1994. AA in Sociology, Tulsa Jr. Coll., 1974; BSW, U. Okla., 1977, MSW, 1978; ed. grantwriting tng. program, Funding Ctr., Oklahoma City, 1984; peer adv. program cons. tng., Mid Am. Arts Aliance, Kansas City, Mo., 1993. Presentance investigator Mcpl. Ct., Tulsa, 1971-72; exec. dir. Open Line Crisis Ctr., Tulsa, 1970-74; asst. dir. Number Nyne Crisis Ctr., U. Okla., Norman, 1978-83; bus. mgr., co-founder Street Players Theatre, Norman, Okla., 1980-85, devel. dir., 1985-88; cons. fund raising, devel. and planning Hammon & Assocs., Norman, 1985—; cons. profl. orgns., including Jazz in June Ann. Festival, 1988, Okla. Shakespeare in the Park, 1990—, Sta. KGOU Pub. Radio, I. Okla., 1990, others; condr. workshops and seminars various non-profit orgns., 1994—; advisor funding devel., proposal writer various non-profit orgns., 1978—; prodr., bus. mgr. 2X4 Prodns., Norman. Contbr. articles to area newspaper, profl. publs. Human rights commr. City of Norman, 1978-81, mem. arts roundtable for design of arts grants program, 1980; mem. City Coun., Norman, 1981-83; co-designer ind. artists/emerging orgns. grant program Norman Arts and Humanities Coun., 1981, chair Roundtable, 1986; project assistance panelist/evaluator State Arts Coun. Okla., 1986-89, mem., 1991—; trainer/cons. client svcs. delivery team Support Ctr. of Okla. City. Recipient Mayor's Proclamation in Appreciation for Svc., City of Norman, 1988. Mem. Okla. Cmty. Theatre Assn. (bd. dirs. 1989, mem. cons.-in-residence program, condr. seminars 1987, 89, Officer of Yr. 1989). Democrat. Mem. Christian Ch. (Disciples of Christ). Office: Hammon & Assocs PO Box 2356 Norman OK 73070-2356

HAMMON, WILLY ERNST, III, physical therapist, educator; b. Paul's Valley, Okla., Nov. 17, 1950; s. Willy Ernst Jr. and Frances (Witten) H.; m. Marilyn Gardner Newell, July 19, 1969; children: Shonna Marie, Billy Ernst IV, John Michael, Stephen James. BS, U. Okla., 1973. Registered phys. therapist. Pvt. practice N.W. Phys. Therapy, Oklahoma City, 1973-74; phys. therapist Norman (Okla.) Mcpl. Hosp., 1974-76; clin. specialist phys. therapist U. Hosp., Oklahoma City, 1978-80, dir. physs. and occupational therapy, 1980—; spl. instr. phys. therapy U. Okla. Health Scis. Ctr., 1978—, clin. instr., 1990—; adj. clin. coord., phys. therapy Wichita (Kans.) State U., 1984—. Reviewer jours.; contbr. articles to profl. jours. Okla. Lung Assn. grantee, 1978. Mem. Am. Phys. Therapy Assn. Home: 1628 Rolling Stone Dr Norman OK 73071-1431 Office: U Hosp 800 NE 13th St Oklahoma City OK 73104-5006

HAMMOND, ANNA JOSEPHINE, nurse practitioner; b. Cumberland, Md., Sept. 16, 1938; d. Ernest Morton and Helen Grace (Hamilton) Wolford; m. Harold Allan Hammond, Oct. 3, 1959; 1 child, Norma Lee. Diploma, Sacred Heart Hosp. Sch. Nsg., 1959; postgrad., U. Md., 1979. RN, Md.; cert. nurse practitioner. Office nurse Ralph W. Ballin, MD, Cumberland; staff nurse Sacred Heart Hosp., Cumberland, 1963-67, head nurse ICU, critical care nurse, 1967-70, nurse practitioner emergency dept., 1978-90; nurse practitioner Seton Med. Clinic, 1990-93, Hampshire Meml. Hosp. and Elk Garden Rural Health Clinic, 1993—. Mem. ANA, Md. Nurses Assn., Coun. Nurse Practitioners, Am. Acad. Nurse Practitioners, Sacred Heart Hosp. Alumni Assn. Home: 5 Lakeside Loop Ridgeley WV 26753-9730

HAMMOND, C(LARKE) RANDOLPH, healthcare executive; b. Anniston, Ala., July 3, 1945; s. Clarke MacAlpin and Edna Odell (Webb) H.; m. Carolyn Jane Milam, Oct. 26, 1974; children: Chadwick, Kyle, Amanda. BS in BA, U. So. Miss., 1968; M.Health Adminstrn., U. Ala., Birmingham, 1978. CPA, Ark. Asst. adminstr., controller Helena (Ark.) Hosp., 1971-74; asst. adminstr. S. Highlands Hosp., Birmingham, 1974-77; adminstr. Brookwood Health Svcs., Rocky Mt., N.C., 1977-79; v.p. ops. Brookwood Health Svcs., Birmingham, 1979-81; pres., CEO Medlab, Birmingham, 1981-88; asst. v.p. Hoffman-LaRoche, Birmingham, 1988-90; sr. v.p.. Roche Biomed. Lab., Birmingham, 1988-90; v.p. Jemison Investment Co., Birmingham, 1990-92; CEO, pres. Textile Resource & Mktg., Dalton, Ga., 1990-92; COO, sr. v.p. ops. Diagnostic Health Corp., Birmingham, 1992-94; sr. v.p. ops. Healthsouth Corp., 1994-95; pres., CEO Monitor MEDX, Inc., 1996—; bd. dirs. Med Occ, Birmingham, Ala., Kustem Threads, Birmingham, Puckett Labs., Hattiesburg, Miss., Touch & Know, Altanta. Pres. Diabetes Trust Fund, Birmingham, 1989, bd. dirs., 1984-89; chmn. deacons Valleydale Bapt. Ch., Birmingham, 1983, strategic planning com., 1983; chmn. bd. Liberty Recreation Ctr., Inc., Pensacola, 1989—. With USN, 1968-70. Mem. Am. Assn. Health Care Execs., Health Fin. Mgmt. Assn., U. Ala. Health Adminstrs. Alumni Soc. (pres. 1989), U. Ala. Alumni Assn. (bd. dirs. 1988-90), The Club, The Summit Club, N. River Yacht Club, Inverness Country Club, Greystone Country Club. Republican. Baptist. Home: 1011 Greymoor Rd Birmingham AL 35242-7210 Office: Monitor MEDX Inc Perimeter Park One S #315N Birmingham AL 35243

HAMMOND, CLAUDE ELLIS, university public relations administrator; b. Louisville, June 3, 1959; s. Claude Ellis and Pauline Margaret (Nederman) H.; m. Nancy Kathleen Ross, Oct. 21, 1989; children: claude Ellis III, Zachary James, Molly Kathleen. BA in Journalism, U. Ky., 1981. Ptnr. Hammond of Ky., Louisville, 1981-84; mng. editor The Kentucky Jour., Lexington, 1984-86; editor, pub. Georgetown (Ky.) News and Times, 1986-89; assoc. Dick M. Blue Pub. Rels., Lexington, 1989-90; dir. pubs. Berea (Ky.) Coll., 1990—; cons. Claude Hammond & Hassocs., Lexington, 1992—. Editor The Berea Alumnus, 1990—; editor: May I Say a Few Words?, 1995; author newspaper col.: Hammond on Kentucky, 1986-88; narrator, editor videos. Adv. bd. Project Future Hope, Lexington, 1995—; bd. dirs. CASE-Ky., Louisville, 1994—; regional del. Fayette County Rep. Party, Lexington, 1992, 96; bd. dirs. Scott County Rep. Party, Georgetown, 1986-89; pub. rels. advisor Autism Soc. Am., Lexington chpt., 1995—. Recipient Key to the City of Georgetown, 1989, Model of Achievement award Scott County Govt., Georgetown, 1989, news story awards Ky. Press Assn., 1986-89. Mem. The Patristic Soc., Chestnut St. Irregulars (pres. 1995—). Christian Ch. Home: 2596 Millbrook Dr Lexington KY 40503 Office: Berea College Publications Dept CPO 2316 Chestnut St Berea KY 40404

HAMMOND, GLENN BARRY, SR., lawyer; b. Roanoke, Va., Sept. 3, 1947; s. Howard Reichard and Billie (Cromer) H.; m. Vickie McComb, Dec. 29, 1973; 1 child, Glenn Barry II. BA, Va. Mil. Inst., 1969; MBA, So. Ill. U., 1974; JD, U. Richmond, 1978; BS elec. engring., Nova Coll., 1995. Bar: Va. 1979, U.S. Dist. Ct. (we. dist.) Va. 1979, U.S. Ct. Appeals (4th cir.) 1981, U.S. Ct. Mil. Appeals 1989, Air Force Ct. Mil. Rev. 1989, U.S. Supreme Ct., 1992. Assoc. Wilson, Hawthorne & Vogel, Roanoke, 1978-79; pvt. practice Roanoke, 1979-80, 86—; atty., advisor to chief adminstrv. law judge Social Security Adminstrn., HHS, Roanoke, 1980-86; ptnr. Wooten & Hart P.C., 1995—; pres. LCH Broadcasting Group, Inc. Roanoke, also bd. dirs. Editor: Psychiatry in Military Law, 1988. Sr. vice comdr. Mil. Order World Wars, Roanoke, 1981. Col. JAGC, USAF, 1969-75, Res. 1975—. Mem. Nat. Orgn. Social Security Claimants Reps., Masons. Office: 707 S Jefferson St SW Roanoke VA 24016-5122

HAMMOND, KAREN SMITH, marketing professional, paralegal; b. Baton Rouge, Dec. 20, 1954; d. James Wilbur Smith and Carolyn (May) Carper; m. Ralph Edwin Hammond, Dec. 17, 1985. Student, La. State U., 1973-75, Colo. Women's Coll., 1976; BJ, U. Colo., 1978; cert. paralegal, U. Tex., 1981. Newspaper reporter Lakewood (Colo.) Sentinel, 1978; paralegal Office U.S. Atty. No. Dist. Tex.; sales rep. Arlington Citizen Jour. newspaper, 1979-80; legal asst. Oscar H. Mauzy Atty.-at-Law, Dallas, 1981; editor Ennis (Tex.) Press, 1981-82; sales rep. VEU Subscription TV, Dallas, 1983-84; comml. account rep. U.S. Telecom, Dallas, 1984; with The Movie Channel/Showtime, 1985; mktg. rep. Allnet Comm., Dallas, 1985-87, ChemLawn Svcs. Inc., Plano, Tex., 1992, Accuroof, 1994, Diversified Info. Svcs., Plano, 1994, Elite Roofing, Plano, 1994—; owner Smith, Hammond & Assocs., Dallas, 1986; advt. sales rep. Legal Asst. Today Mag., 1987; sales rep. Telecable Inc., Richardson, Tex., 1988-91; account exec. Brewer Comm., Carrollton, Tex., 1988-89, Plano (Tex.) Cellular, 1989-90; triex agt. Pkwy. Pontiac, Dallas, 1983-86; free lance writer Dallas Metro mag., 1991—. Bus. writer Mid-Cities Daily News, 1981. Campaign mgr. Mark Bielamowicz for Mayor, Cedar Hill, Tex., 1979; active campaigns Martin Frost for U.S. Congress, Dallas, 1978, Jimmy Carter for Pres., Ft. Worth, 1980, Ann Richards for Gov., Tex., 1990; vol. Clinton/Gore Re-election Campaign, 1996, Collin County Dem. Party. Mem. NAFE, Women in Comms. (fin. com. 1979), Dallas Assn. Legal Assts., Soc. Profl. Journalist, Dallas C. of C. Democrat. Home: 3500 Hillridge Dr Apt 118 Plano TX 75074-4367 Office: Elite Roofing 1209 Ave N Plano TX 75074

HAMMOND, MARGARET, lawyer; b. Winterville, N.C., June 2, 1949; d. Hoyt and Mary Hammond. BS, N.C. A&T State U., 1971; MA, Atlanta U., 1983; JD, Loyola U., New Orleans, 1984. Bar: La. 1984, U.S. Dist. Ct. (ea. dist.) La. 1987. Instr. polit. sci. N.C. A&T State U., Greensboro, 1973-76, So. U., New Orleans, 1979-82; edn. cons. Edn. Services and Programs Inc., New Orleans, 1982-84, Loyola U., New Orleans, 1982-84; asst. dist. atty. Parish of Orleans, New Orleans, 1984-86; staff atty. Orleans Indigent Defender Program, New Orleans, 1986-92; pvt. practice New Orleans, 1986—. Ford Found. fellow, 1971-73, Earl Warren Found. fellow, 1981-84. Mem. ABA, La. Bar Assn., Sorority Inc., Alpha Kappa Alpha. Democrat. Office: One Poydras Plaza Ste 2100 New Orleans LA 70113

HAMMOND, MARY SAYER, art educator; b. Bellingham, Wash., Oct. 1, 1946; d. Boyd James and Jacqueline Anna (Thurston) Sayer; m. Lester Wayne Hammond, Aug. 26, 1967 (div. Feb. 1972); m. Wiley Devere Sanderson, Jan. 13, 1983. BFA in Art Edn., U. Ga., 1967, MFA in Photo Design, 1977; PhD in History of Photo/Art Edn., Ohio State U., 1986. Art supr. Madison County Pub. Schs., Danielsville, Ga., 1968-71; art instr. U. Ga., Athens, 1971-73, instr. photo design, 1975-76; instr. in art edn. North Ga. Coll., Dalonega, 1975; instr. in art Valdosta (Ga.) State Coll., 1976-77, asst. prof. art, 1979-80; asst. prof. art, Am. Studies George Mason U., Fairfax, Va., 1980-87, assoc. prof. art, Am. Studies, 1987-94, prof. art, Am. studies, 1995—, dir. divsn. art studio; adminstrv. assoc. Ohio State U., Columbus, 1978-79, tchg. assoc., 1977-78; co-dir. Saturday program U. Ga., 1966-76, tchg. asst., 1974. Photographs represented in permanent collections at Ctr. for Creative Photography, Ariz., Internat. Mus. Photography, N.Y.C., Nat. Gallery of Art, Washington, Nat. Mus. Women in Arts, Washington. Treas. Faculty Senate of Va., 1991-96. Grantee Fulbright Hays Commn., 1973-74; travel grantee Samuel H. Kress Found., 1986, George Mason U., 1993, 91—; photographer's fellow NEA, 1982-84. Mem. Soc. Photo Edn. (mid-Atlantic bd. dirs. 1990—), Phi Kappa Phi (hon.). Office: George Mason U MS1C3 Art Studio Fairfax VA 22030-4444

HAMMOND, NICOLAS JOHN, computer executive; b. Nottingham, Eng., Aug. 3, 1964; came to U.S. 1986; s. Michael John and Paul Christine (Barsby) H. BA, Cambridge (Eng.) U., 1986, MA (hon.), 1990. Mgr. Pafec, Inc., Atlanta, 1986-89; custom engring. mgr. Secureware, Inc., Atlanta, 1989-96; pres. Intelligent Shopping, Inc., Atlanta, 1996—, NJH Security Consulting Inc., Atlanta, 1996—. Author: How to Solve the Rubik's Cube in 37 Seconds, 1981. Treas. Young Careers, Atlanta, 1991-92, vice chair edn., 1992-93, chmn.-elect, 1993-94, chmn., 1994-95. Mem. Ga. Field Hockey Assn. (pres. 1992-96).

HAMMOND, PATRICIA FLOOD, lawyer; b. Racine, Wis., Aug. 29, 1948; d. Francis James Flood and Shirley (Osterholt) Erickson; children: Bradley D. Mortensen, Erin N. Mortensen. Student, Wis. State U., Oshkosh, 1966-69, Alverno Coll., West Allis, 1973-74. Bar: Va.1985, U.S. Dist. Ct. (ea. dist.) Va. 1988. Br. dir. Am. Heart Assn., Manassas, Va., 1977-85; attorney Manassas, Va., 1985—; ptnr. Smith, Hudson, Hammond and Alston, Manassas, Va.; mem. VBA-VSB joint com. on alternative dispute resolution. Contbr. articles to newspapers. Mem. ABA, ACLU, ATLA, Nat. Abortion and Reproductive Rights Action League, Va. State Bar Assn., Prince William County Bar Assn. (treas., pres. 1991). Democrat. Episcopalian. Office: Smith Hudson Hammond & Alston 9403 Grant Ave Manassas VA 22110-5509

HAMMOND, RALPH CHARLES, real estate executive; b. Valley Head, Ala., Feb. 1, 1916; s. William Bleve and Alice Corina Jane (Holleman) H.; student Snead Jr. Coll., 1938-39, Berea Coll., 1940-41; AB, U. Ala., 1945; DLitt, Livingston U., 1992; m. Myra Leak, June 20, 1954; children—James, Ben. Press sec. to gov. Ala., Montgomery, 1946-50, exec. sec., 1955-59; gen. rep. ARC, Greensboro, N.C., 1950-54; mayor of Arab (Ala.), 1963-69; pres. City Ctr., Inc., Arab, 1959—. Commr. from Ala., U.S. Study Commn. S.E. River Basins, 1958-64; bd. dirs. Ala. Tb Assn., 1956-83, pres., 1972-74; hon. Christmas Seal chmn., Ala. Served with AUS, 1941-45. Commd. Poet Laureate of Ala., 1991—; Paul Harris fellow Rotary Internat., 1992. Mem. Ky. Hist. Soc., Phillip Hamman Family Assn. Am. (pres. 1972-78), Ala. Poetry Soc. (pres. 1981-84, Ala. Poet of Yr. 1985), Ala. Writers' Conclave (pres. 1987-89), Nat. Fedn. State Poetry Socs. (treas. 1985-86, 2d v.p. 1990-92, 1st v.p. 1993-94, pres. 1994-96). Democrat. Methodist. Lodge: Masons. Author: My GI Aching Back, 1945; Ante Bellum Mansions of Alabama, 1951; Philip Hamman, Man of Valor, 1976; Song of Appalachia, 1982; How High the Stars, 1982; Upon the Wings of the Wind, 1982; One Golden Apple a Day, 1983; Collected Poems, 1983; Wisdom Is, 1984; Edging Through the Grass (Book of Yr. Ala. Poetry Soc.), 1985; editor: Alabama Poets: A Contemporary Anthology, 1989, A Blossoming of Sonnets, 1990, Upper Alabama-Poems Out of Light (George Washington Honor medal Freedoms Found. Valley Forge 1993, Book of Yr. award Ala. Poetry Soc. 1993), Crossing Many Rivers-Poems Along the Way, 1995 (Book of Yr. award Ala. Poetry Soc. 1995); contbr. short stories and feature articles to jours., mags.; poems pub. in 40 jours. Home: 1280 Guntersville Rd Arab AL 35016 Office: PO Box 486 Arab AL 35016-0486

HAMMOND, (GALE) THOMAS, art educator, printmaker artist; b. Lumberton, N.C., Sept. 27, 1939; s. Chalmers Eason and Mamie (Cribbs) H.; m. Mary Alice Sellars, June 28, 1941; children: Phillip Thomas, Laura Alice. BS, East Carolina U., 1962, MA in Edn., 1964; diploma in art, Chgo. Acad. Fine Art, 1959. Tchr. art New Hanover Pub. Schs., Wilmington, N.C., 1962-64; instr. art Western Carolina U., Cullowhee, N.C., 1964-66, asst. prof., 1967, 68; asst. prof. James Madison U., Harrisonburg, Va., 1966, 67, Greensboro (N.C.) Coll., 1968-70; prof. U. Ga., Athens, 1970—. Exhibited in group shows at Mus. Modern Art, Antwerp, Belgium, Fransmasereel Ctr., Belgium; represented in permanent collection Met. Mus. Art, N.Y.C., 1982. Mem. So. Graphics Coun., Boston Printmakers, Print Consortium. Democrat. Office: U Ga Sch Art Jackson St Athens GA 30602-4102

HAMMOND, VERNON FRANCIS, school administrator; b. Grand Rapids, Mich., Sept. 27, 1931; s. Rodney Clyve and Wylida Helen (Bonner) H.; m. Anne Louise Seeley, Dec. 10, 1954; children; Michelle, Milissa, Milanie, Michael. BA, Bob Jones U., 1959, MA, 1960; postgrad., Butler U., 1968-69, Pepperdine U., 1969-72; MEd, Lynchburg Coll., 1975. Cert. ednl. adminstrn. Tchr., coach, vice prin. Cen. Bapt. Schs., Anaheim, Calif., 1963-68; tchr. Indpls. Christian Acad., 1968-69; tchr., coach Faith Bapt. Schs., Canoga Park, Calif., 1969-72; prin. Lynchburg (Va.) Christian Acad., 1972-75, Bethany Christian Sch., Troy, Mich., 1975-84, Heart to Heart Christian Acad., Phoenix, 1984-88; administr. Temple Christian Schs., Lakeland, Fla., 1989—, girls' basketball coach, 1990—; girls head basketball coach Temple Christian Sch., 1990-96; instr. Ind. Bapt. Coll., Indpls., 1968-69, Lynchburg Bapt. Coll., 1973-75; sec.-treas. Mich. Assn. Christian Schs., Troy, 1982-83; bd. dirs. Western Fellowship Christian Schs., Phoenix, 1985-88; conv. spkr. Christian Edn. Assn., S.E., Pensacola, Fla. Del. Mich. Rep. Conv., 1980, 82; precinct del. Mich. Rep. Party, Troy, 1980-84; precinct leader Ariz. Rep. Party, Phoenix, 1986-89; bd. dirs. Bethany Villa, Troy, 1975-84. With USN, 1951-55. Coach of Fla. Christian Conf. State Championship Basketball Team, 1993-94. Mem. adv. bd. Sketch Erickson Nat. Ministries, Lakeland, Fla., 1995—. Office: Temple Christian Schs 4210 Lakeland Highlands Rd Lakeland FL 33813-3113

HAMNER, CHARLES, company executive. Pres. N.C. Bio-Tech. Ctr., Research Triangle Park, N.C. Office: PO Box 13547 Research Triangle Park NC 27709

HAMNER, LAWRENCE RAEBURN, JR., bank executive; b. Union County, Ky., Dec. 1, 1916; s. Lawrence Raeburn and Bessie Kathryn (O'Nan) H.; m. Callie Boyd Harris, Jan. 29, 1947; children: Callie Ann Hamner Anderson, Lawrence Raeburn III. BBS, So. Meth. U., 1949. Trust officer Republic Nat. Bank, Dallas, 1950-57; exec. v.p., trust officer Amarillo (Tex.) Nat. Bank, 1958-81, ret. Bd. dirs., past chmn. Craig Found., Amarillo, Mullins Found., Amarillo, McCarley Found., Amarillo; bd. dirs., past pres. Cal Farley's Boys Ranch and Girls Town, Amarillo, 1962—; bd. dirs. United Fund, Amarillo, 1964-66, ARC, Amarillo, 1965-69; bd. stewards Polk St. United Meth. Ch., Amarillo, 1970-80. 1st lt. USMC, 1942-46. Republican. Home: 3200 Milam Amarillo TX 79109

HAMNER, ROBERT DANIEL, English language educator, writer, literary critic; b. Northport, Ala., Jan. 16, 1941; s. Robert F. and Margaret Louise (Atkins) H.; m. Carol Ann Elmore, Aug. 24, 1963; children: Jared Robert, Ryan Fernando. BA, Wayland U., 1964; MA, U. Tex., 1966, PhD, 1971. Asst. prof. English, Wayland U., Plainview, Tex., 1968-70; prof. Hardin-Simmons U., Abilene, Tex., 1971—, Minnie Stevens Piper prof., 1996; Fulbright prof. U. Guyana, Georgetown, 1975-76; external examiner grad. degrees U. N.B., Can., 1985—, U. W.I., Cave Hill, Barbados, 1987—, U. Cape Town, South Africa, 1989—. Author: V.S. Naipaul, 1973, Derek Walcott, 1981, 2d edit., 1993; editor: Critical Perspectives on V.S. Naipaul, 1977, Joseph Conrad: Third World Perspectives, 1990, Critical Perspectives on Derek Wolcott, 1993. Mem. MLA, Assn. Caribbean Studies, Caribbean Studies Assn., Joseph Conrad Soc. Am., Joseph Conrad Soc. Gt. Britain, Soc. Etude Pays du Commonwealth. Office: Hardin-Simmons U HSU Box 15195 Abilene TX 79698

HAMON, DAVID WILLIAM, organizations analyst; b. Denver, Dec. 27, 1955; s. Carrol Eugene and Alice Marie (Skidmore) H.; m. Mabel Rosa Emerson, Mar. 1, 1982; children: Alexandra E., Caitlin N. B in Edn., Colo. State U., 1978; MA, Northeastern U., 1988. Aide-de-camp European Exch. Svc., Munich, 1979-82; company cmdr. U.S. Army, Ft. Lewis, Wash., 1982-85; asst. prof. Northeastern U., Boston, 1985-88; dir. logistics U.S. Army, Livorno, Italy, 1988-91; battalion exec. officer NATO Armor Divsn., Mannheim, Germany, 1991-94; chief current ops. UN-HQ Dept. Peacekeeping, N.Y.C., 1994-95; sr. policy analyst ANSER Inst., Arlington, Va., 1995—. Mem. UN Assn., Soc. Logistic Engrs., Polit. Scis. Acad., Masons, Toastmasters. Republican. Roman Catholic. Home: 1108 Blackbeard Dr Stafford VA 22554 Office: ANSER Inst 1215 Jefferson Davis Hwy Arlington VA 22202

HAMONTREE, GEORGE SAMUEL, III, military officer; b. Ft. Worth, Dec. 24, 1963; s. George Samuel Hamontree Jr. and Carolyn Sue Amburn; m. Dennie Ann Hall, July 4, 1995; 1 chile, Hannah Marie. BA, West Tex. State U., Canyon, 1989; MBA, Embry-Riddle Aero. U., Daytona Beach, Fla., 1994. Cert. comml. rotary wing. instrument. Capt. U.S. Army, 1986—; infantry platoon leader E-Co. 2-142 Infantry, Wellington, Tex., 1987-88; liaison officer HHB 1-36th Field Artillery, Augsburg, Germany, 1989-91; asst. ops. officer HHC 2-101st Aviation Regt., Ft. Campbell, Ky., 1991-93; with flight sch. D Co. 1-14th Aviation Rgt., Ft. Rucker, Ala., 1993-94; logistics officer-in-command Combat Aviation Tng. Brigade, Ft. Hood, Tex., 1994-96; comdr. D. Co. 1-4 Aviation Regt., Ft. Hood, 1996—. Decorated Overseas Ribbon U.S. Army, Germany, 1991, 4 army achievement medals, 2 army commendation medals, 1 Nation Def. Svc. medal; decorated Germany Efficiency Badge (silver), German Army, Augsburg, 1990, German Sportsmanship Badge, 1990; named Outstanding German-Am. Soldier U.S. Army Europe and Fed. Republic Germany, Grafenwoehr, Germany, 1989-90, 90-91; named to order of St. Barbara, 81st German Field Arty., Kempten, Germany, 1991. Mem. Army Aviation Assn. Am., N.G. Assn. Tex., Lambda Chi Alpha Alumni Assn. Republican. Home: 2101 Beretta Dr Killeen TX 76542 Office: D Co 1-4 Aviation Rgt Fort Hood TX 76544

HAMPARES, KATHERINE JAMES, retired foreign language educator; b. Grand Rapids, Mich., May 24, 1932; d. James E. and Chresanthe (Giannakekee) H. BA cum laude, U. Mich., 1955, MA cum laude, 1956; PhD, Columbia U., 1968. Tchr. Spanish Ottawa Hills High, Grand Rapids, Mich., 1958-60; prof. Spanish Jersey City State U., 1960-67, NYU, N.Y.C., 1967-69, Finch Coll., N.Y.C., 1969-72, Baruch Coll., CUNY, N.Y.C., 1972-89; ret., 1989; pres. Winning Internat. Strategies, Fla., N.Y., 1990—. Author 5 Spanish textbooks; co-author: 2 textbooks; contbr. articles to profl. jours. Recipient various scholarships and grants; Fulbright fellow, 1964. Mem. MLA (life), Am. Assn. Tchrs. Spanish and Portuguese (life), Sigma Delta Pi (emeritus). Home: 4121 NE 31st Ave Lighthouse Point FL 33064

HAMPTON, CAROL MCDONALD, religious organization administrator, educator, historian; b. Oklahoma City, Sept. 18, 1935; d. Denzil Vincent and Mildred Juanita (Cussen) McDonald; m. James Wilburn Hampton, Feb. 22, 1958; children: Jaime, Clayton, Diana, Neal. BA, U. Okla., 1957, MA, 1973, PhD, 1984. Postulant Episcopal Diocese of Okla., 1996. Tchg. asst. U. Okla., Norman, 1976-81; instr. U. of Sci. and Arts of Okla., Chickasha, 1981-84; coord. Consortium for Grad. Opportunities for Am. Indians, U. Calif., Berkeley, 1985-86; trustee Ctr. of Am. Indian, Oklahoma City, 1981—; vice chmn. Nat. Com. on Indian Work, Episc. Ch., 1986; field officer coun. Native Am. Ministry, 1986-94, sec., co-chmn., advising elder, prin. elder 1994-96; field officer for Congl. Ministries, 1994—; mem. nat. coun. Chs. Racial Justice Working Group, 1990—, co-convenor, 1991-93, convenor, 1993-95; officer Multicultural Ministries, 1994—. Contbr. articles to profl. jours. Trustee Western History Collections, U. Okla., Okla. Found. for the Humanities, 1983-86; mem. bd. regents U. Sci. and Arts Okla., 1989-95; bd. dirs. Okla. State Regents for Higher Edn., mem. adv. com. on social justice; mem. World Coun. of Chs. Program to Combat Racism, Geneva, 1985-91; bd. dirs. Caddo Tribal Coun., Okla., 1976-82; accredited observer Anglican Consultative Coun. 4th World Conf. on Women, 1995. Recipient Okla. State Human Rights award, 1987; Francis C. Allen fellow, Ctr. for the History of Am. Indian, 1983. Mem. Western History Assn., Western Social Sci. Assn., Orgn. of Am. Historians, Am. Hist. Assn., Okla. Hist. Soc., Assn. Am. Indian Historians (founding mem. 1981—). Democrat. Episcopalian. Club: Jr. League (Oklahoma City). Avocation: travel. Home: 1414 N Hudson Ave Oklahoma City OK 73103-3721 Office: Episcopal Ch Congl Ministry 924 N Robinson Ave Oklahoma City OK 73102-5814

HAMPTON, CHARLES EDWIN, lawyer, mathematician, computer programmer; b. Waco, Tex., Oct. 22, 1948; s. Roy Mizell and Hazel Lucretia (Cooper) H.; m. Cynthia Torrance, Sept. 14, 1968; children: Charles Edwin Jr., Adam Ethan. Student Baylor U., 1967, Rice U., 1967-68; BA with highest honors, U. Tex., Austin, 1971, JD with high honors, 1977; MA (NSF fellow 1971-74), U. Calif., Berkeley, 1972, Candidate in Philosophy in Math., 1975. Bar: Tex., 1977, U.S. Dist. Ct. (we. dist.) Tex., 1979, U.S. Dist. Ct. (no. dist.) Tex., 1980, U.S. Ct. Appeals (5th cir.) 1986. Rsch. asst. U. Calif., 1974-75; briefing atty. to justice Tex. Supreme Ct., 1977-78; assoc. Law Offices Don L. Baker, P.C., Austin, 1978-81; legal counsel Office Ct. Adminstrn., Tex. Jud. Coun., Austin, 1981; staff atty. Supreme Ct. Tex., Austin, 1981—; assoc. Rinehart & Nugent, 1984-87; mem. vis. com. dept. math. U. Tex. at Austin, 1987-95. Del. Travis County Dem. Conv., 1978, 80, 82, 84, 86, 88, 90, 92. Moody Found. scholar. Mem. ABA, State Bar Tex., Travis County Bar Assn., Chancellors, Order of Coif, Phi Beta Kappa, Phi Kappa Phi, Phi Delta Phi. Mem. Ch. of Christ. Lodge: Lions. Office: PO Box 164191 400 W 15th St Ste 600 Austin TX 78716

HAMPTON, JAMES WILBURN, hematologist, medical oncologist; b. Durant, Okla., Sept. 15, 1931; s. Hollis Eugene and Ouida (Mackey) H.; m. Carol McDonald, Feb. 22, 1958; children: Jaime, Clay, Diana, Neal. BA, U. Okla., 1952, MD, 1956. Intern U. Okla. Hosps., 1956-57; also resident; instr. to prof. U. Okla., Oklahoma City, 1959-77, clin. prof. medicine, 1977—, mem. admissions bd., 1965—, subcom., 1985-95, head hematology/oncology, 1972-77; head hematology rsch. Okla. Med. Rsch. Found., Oklahoma City, 1972-77; dir. cancer program and med. oncology Bapt. Med. Ctr., 1977-85, med. dir. Cancer Ctr. S.W., 1985-94, Troy and Dollie Smith Cancer Ctr., 1994—; AOR network oncologist, 1995—; cons. NIH, Biomed. and Nat. Cancer Inst.; vis. prof. Karolinska Inst., Stockholm; vis. scientist U. N.C., 1966-67; pres. Stewart Wolf Soc., 1990-92; founder Robert Montgomery Bird Soc., 1973—, pres., 1996—. Contbr. over 100 articles to profl. jours. Chmn. network Cancer Prevention and Control for Am. Indians/Alaska Natives Nat. Cancer Rsch. Inst., 1990—; mem. Intercultural Cancer Coun., 1996—; bd. dirs. Heritage Hills, Oklahoma City, 1972-90, initiator Hospice of Ctrl. Okla., 1982-89, Hospice of Okla. County, 1990—, Am. Cancer Soc., mem. at large, nat. bd. dirs., 1990-96, mem. com. task force on Cancer in the Socio-economically Disadvantaged, 1990—, chmn. Okla. divsn. svc. and rehab. com., 1988-91; chair Okla. Pain Initiative, 1996; co-chmn. Save St. Paul's Episcopal Cathedral com., 1983, chmn. bishop's Okla. com. on Indian work, mem. province VII Indian com., alt. del. Diocesan conv. for Okla., 1991-95, mem. adv. com. Office Minority Health NIH, 1996—, others. NIH Career Devel. Award., 1966-76. Fellow ACP; mem. Am. Fedn. Clin. Rsch. (pres. midwest sect. 1970-71), Ctrl. Soc. Clin. Rsch. (assoc. editor Jour. Lab. and Clin. Medicine 1975-76), Okla. County Med. Soc. (editor bull. 1981—, bd. dirs. 1989-91), Internat. Soc. Thrombosis and Hemostasis, Assn. Am. Indian Physicians (pres. 1978-79, 88-89); Am. Physiol. Soc., Assn. Am. Pathologists, Am. Soc. Hematology, Am. Soc. Clin. Oncology, So. Soc. Clin. Investigation, Am. Psychosomatic Soc., English Speaking Union. Clubs: Oklahoma City Golf and Country, Blue Cord, Faculty House, Chaine des Rotisseurs. Home: 1414 N Hudson Ave Oklahoma City OK 73103-3721 Office: Troy and Dollie Smith Cancer Ctr Baptist Med Ctr 3300 NW Expressway St Oklahoma City OK 73112-4999

HAMPTON, MARGARET FRANCES, international trade and finance professional; b. Gainesville, Fla., May 12, 1947; d. William Wade and Carol Dorothy (Maples) H.; m. Kenneth Lee Kauffman (dec.); 1 child, Robert Lee. BA in French summa cum laude, Fla. State U., 1969; postgrad. U. Nice (France), summer 1969; MBA in Fin. (Alcoa Found. fellow), Columbia U., 1974. Fin. analyst, economist Bd. of Govs. of Fed. Res. System, Washington, 1974-75; v.p. corp. fin. Mfrs. Hanover Trust Co., N.Y.C., 1975-76; v.p., dir. corp. planning and fin., asset and liability mgmt. and strategic planning coms. Nat. Bank of Ga., Atlanta, 1976-81; sr. v.p. corp. planning and devel. Bank South Corp., Atlanta, 1981-85; mng. ptnr. Hampton Mgmt. Cons., Atlanta, 1985—; pres., bd. dirs. Accent Enterprises, Inc., Atlanta, 1993—; pres., CEO Accent Global Mktg., Inc., Atlanta, 1993—; registered rep. Rockwell Investments, Inc., Evergreen, Colo., 1994-96, offshore commodities trader, 1995—; broadcast affiliate The People's Network, 1995; v.p. Internat. Friendship City, 1996—. Nat. trustee Leukemia Soc. Am., 1986-90; trustee Ga. chpt. Leukemia Soc., 1980-94, treas., 1981-82, 1st v.p., 1982-84, sec., 1991-92, hon. bd. dirs.; dir. Combined Health Appeal Ga., 1991—, sec., 1992—. Named Trustee of Yr., Leukemia Soc., 1982, 85; recipient Gold Key, Fla. State U. Hall of Fame. Mem. Planning Execs. Inst., Atlanta Venture Forum, Am. Inst. Banking, Inst. of Fin. Edn., Am. Fin. Assn., Downtown Atlanta C. of C., (govt. affairs subcom. 1976-77) Atlanta C. of C. (high tech. task force 1982-83), Ga. Women's Forum (sec./treas., bd. dirs. 1985-86), Ga. Exec. Women's Network (sec. 1982-83, dir. 1982-84), Bus. and Tech. Alliance, Mortar Bd., Alliance Française, Kappa Sigma Little Sisters (pres., treas., sweetheart), Phi Beta Kappa, Beta Gamma Sigma, Phi Kappa Phi, Alpha Lambda Delta, Pi Delta Phi, Alpha Delta Pi. Episcopalian. Clubs: Women's Commerce (charter mem., steering com. 1985-86), Northside Athletic, Oxford (life).

HAMPTON, MARTIN JUSTUS, financial planner; b. Barbourville, Ky., Sept. 18, 1952; s. Ernest A. and Ethel Ellen (Martin) H.; m. Sandra Kay Zigos, July 24, 1971; 1 child, Ryan Christopher. BBA, Ea. Ky. U., 1974; M in Acctg., Va. Polytech. Inst., 1976. CPA, Ky., Tenn. Acct. Dent K. Burk Assocs., Grundy, Va., 1976-77, Webb, Cloyd, Hamilton & Corbett, Corbin, Ky., 1977-81; ptnr. Corbett, Hampton & Bray, Corbin, 1981-86; shareholder Eskew & Gresham, Corbin, 1986-87; pres. Martin J. Hampton, Louisville, 1987—; registered rep. Alexander Investment Svcs., Louisville, 1991-94, MFI Investments Corp., Louisville, 1994—. Bd. dirs. Rotary Club, Corbin, 1988; chmn. Rep. Com., Oldham County, Ky., 1992-94. Mem. AICPA, Internat. Assn. Fin. Planning, Inst. Cert. Fin. Planners, Am. Acctg. Assn., Ky. Soc. CPA (dir. 1984-86, chmn. SE Ky. chpt. 1984-85), Tenn. CPA Soc. Baptist. Home: 125 Mount Mercy Pl Pewee Valley KY 40056-9006 Office: MFI Investments Corp 2000 Waterfront Plz Louisville KY 40202

HAMPTON, RALPH CLAYTON, JR., pastoral studies educator, clergyman; b. Blanchard, Okla., Dec. 13, 1934; s. Ralph Clayton Sr. and Ida Lucille (Jackson) H.; m. Margaret Ann Evans, Aug. 22, 1958; children: Laura Ann, Clayton Lee, Kenneth Michael. AA, Diablo Community Coll., Pleasant Hill, Calif., 1955; BA, Free Will Baptist Bible Coll., Nashville, 1958; MA, Winona Lake (Ind.) Sch. Theology, 1961; MDiv, Covenant Theol. Sem., St. Louis, 1970; postgrad., Trinity Evang. Div. Sch., Deerfield, Ill., 1981-84. Ordained to ministry Bapt. Ch., 1962. Dir. Christian svc. Free Will Bapt. Bible Coll., Nashville, 1958-63, mem. faculty, 1958-68, 70—, chmn. dept. Christian ministries, 1975—, dean Grad. Sch., 1986—; pastor Oakwood Free Will Bapt. Ch., Woodlawn, Tenn., 1962-65, Rock Springs Free Will Bapt. Ch., Charlotte, Tenn., 1966-68, Cross Timbers Free Will Bapt. Ch., Nashville, 1975-78; asst. moderator Nat. Assn. Free Will Baptists, Nashville, 1982-87, moderator, 1987—, mem. exec. com., 1982—. Author: Adult Bible Studies in Old Testament—Teachers edit., 1971-78; contbr. articles to denominational mags. Office: Free Will Baptist Bible PO Box 50117 Nashville TN 37205-0117

HAMPTON, THOMAS EDWARD, real estate appraiser, consultant; b. Tuscaloosa, Ala., June 24, 1943; s. William Edward and Winnie Rivers (Wallace) H.; m. Susan Judd Linder, July 14, 1979; children: Virginia Rivers, Laura Elizabeth. BS in Bus. Adminstrn., U. So. Miss., 1970. Cert. gen. real estate appraiser, Tenn. Staff appraiser Fla. Dept. Transp., Clearwater, 1971-74; appraiser C.F. Erickson, MAI, Clearwater, 1974-76; v.p. Barnhill & Hampton, Clearwater, 1976-78; ind. fee appraiser Thomas E. Hampton, Clearwater, 1978-80; asst. v.p., chief appraiser First Fedn. Savs. and Loan, Tullahoma, Tenn., 1980-81; owner, appraiser, cons. Hampton Appraisal Svcs., Tullahoma, 1981—; adj. instr. St. Petersburg Jr. Coll., Clearwater, 1977-79, Motlow State Community Coll., Tullahoma, 1980, 84, 85; pres. Appraisal Inst. Nashville-Mid. Tenn. chpt., 1992. Bd. dirs., v.p. Assn. to Revitalize Community Heritage, Tullahoma, 1984-86. Served to sgt. Spl. Forces, U.S. Army, 1964-67, Panama Canal Zone. Named Eagle Scout, Nat. Coun. Boy Scouts Am., Yazoo City, Miss., 1959; Aide de Camp, Gov.'s Staff, State of Tenn., Nashville, 1985. Mem. Soc. Real Estate Appraisers (chmn. pub. relations com. 1976-78, chmn. admissions com. 1984, edn. com. 1980-82, profl. practice com. 1988-90, assoc. instr., bd. dirs. Nashville chpt. #78 1989, 90, sr. real property appraiser, sr. residential appraiser), Am. Inst. Real Estate Appraisers (chmn. roster com. local chpt. 1984, edn. com. local chpt. 1981-83), chmn. Franklin County (Tenn.) Bd. Equalization, Internat. Right of Way Assn. (local chpt. newsletter editor 1982, chmn. edn. com. 1983, chmn. membership com. 1984, Pres.'s Sphere award 1983, 84), Coffee Franklin County Bd. Realtors (affiliate), Real Estate Educators Assn., Tenn. Real Estate Educators Assn., U. So. Miss. Alumni Assn. (life), Nat. Eagle Scout Assn. (life), Pi Sigma Epsilon (Outstanding Member award-mktg. 1969). Republican. Presbyterian. Lodges : Masons, Rotary (Paul Harris fellow), Scottish Rite. Avocations: history, golf. Home and Office: 2623 Lancaster Ct Murfreesboro TN 37129-6534

HAMRICK, BILL ALLEN, principal, retired; b. Brownwood, Tex., Sept. 23, 1925; s. William Rufus and Gladys Myril (Elms) H.; m. Mary Edith Loyd Hamrick, May 27, 1949; children: Billy Don, Jerry Neal. BA, Howard Payne Coll., Brownwood, Tex., 1950; MEd, U. Houston, 1963. School administration. Prin. and coach Bangs I.S.D., Bangs, Tex., 1950-51; coach and A.D. Round Rock I.S.D., Round Rock, Tex., 1951-52, Angleton I.S.D., Angleton, Tex., 1952-59, Rosenberg I.S.D., Rosenberg, Tex., 1959-63, Athens I.S.D., Athens, Tex., 1963-67, Carroll High Corpus Christi I.S.D., Corpus Christi, Tex., 1967-76; asst. prin. Martin Jr. High, Corpus Christi, Tex., 1976-78, King High Sch., Corpus Christi, Tex., 1978-80; prin. Wynn Seale Jr. High, Corpus Christi, Tex., 1980-85, W.B. Ray High Sch., Corpus Christi, Tex., 1985-95; retired, 1995; pres. Corpus Christi Coaches Assn., Corpus Christi Prin. Assn., Corpus Christi, Tex.; bd. dirs. Tex. High Sch. Coaches Assn., Austin, Tex. Fellowship I.D.E.A. Kitering Found., Columbus. Mo., Tex. A&M Found., College Station. Mem. Tex. Assn. of Secondary Prin., Corpus Christi Prin. Assn., Parent and Tchrs. Assn. Democrat. Methodist. Home: 54 Townhouse Ln Corpus Christi TX 78412-4269 Office: Corpus Christi Ind Sch Dist 1002 Texan Trl Corpus Christi TX 78411-2530

HAMRICK, LESLIE WILFORD, JR., metallurgy supervisor; b. Charleston, W.Va., Dec. 26, 1946; s. Leslie Wilford and Olive Marie (Means) H.; m. Margaret C. Hamrick, Sept. 20, 1970 (div. Jan. 1976); m. Mary Lee Smathers, Aug. 6, 1978; 1 child, Hannah Chance. BA, U. Charleston, 1969. Shift coord. FMC, South Charleston, W.Va., 1973-79; maint. supr. Foote Mineral Co., Graham, W.Va., 1979-86; maint. foreman Ravenswood (W.Va.) Aluminum, 1986-92, metallurgy supr., 1992—. Author: Hating Hugh, 1991 (2d place award 1991), Wozzek's Price, 1990 (2d place award 1992); (short story) Reconciliation, 1992 (3d place award 1993). Trustee Point Mountain/Hamrick Reunion, 1995. With USN, 1969-73. Republican. Home: RR 2 Box 157AAA Ravenswood WV 26164-9794

HAMRICK, RITA GALE, elementary school educator; b. Chattanooga, Sept. 27, 1951; d. Thomas Austin and Alma Lucille (Horne) Hamrick; m. Bill R. Hilliard, Jan. 11, 1974 (div. Aug. 1980); stepchildren: Terri Feraghat, Renee Beaumont; m. James Kamenik, June 27, 1981 (div. Feb. 1994). BS in Band and Choral Music Edn., U. Tenn., Chattanooga, 1975, elem. and spl. edn. endorsement, 1981, MEd in Spl. Edn., 1984; postgrad., W. Ga. Coll., 1986-87; cert. edn. specialist, U. Ala., 1996; postgrad., Walker Tech. C.C., 1996—. Cert. tchr. spl. edn., Ga., band and choral music, spl. edn., Tenn. Tchr. spl. edn. Chattanooga City Schs., 1981-83, Walker County Schs., Lafayette, Ga., 1983-93; dir., owner Sterling Learning Ct., Ft. Oglethorpe, Ga., 1991-93; tchr. partial hospitalization program for adults Cumberland Hall Psychiat. Hosp., 1993-94; music tchr. Daisy Elem. Sch., Chattanooga, 1994—; founder, dir. Sterling Learning Found., Ft. Oglethorpe, 1992-93. Singer Rita G. Hamrick Southern Belle album, 1995. Pres. Bradley County Rep. Women, Cleveland, Tenn., 1976; leader Girl Scouts U.S.A., Chattanooga, 1981-82; mem., choir soloist, dir. youth handbells St. Timothy's Episcopal Ch., Signal Mountain, Tenn. Named Hon. Sgt. at Arms Tenn. Ho. of Reps., Nashville, 1975. Mem. NEA, Nat. Story League, Tenn. Edn. Assn., Hamilton County Edn. Assn., Tenn. Aquarium, Ladies Oriental Shrine N.Am., Order of Amaranth (life, royal matron 1978-79, grand musician 1992-93), Kappa Delta Pi. Episcopalian. Home: 3503 Lockwood Cir Chattanooga TN 37415-5203 Office: Daisy Elem Sch 620 Sequoyah Access Rd Soddy Daisy TN 37379

HAN, CHINGPING JIM, industrial engineer, educator; b. Shanghai, People's Republic China, Aug. 24, 1957; came to U.S., 1983; s. Bao-San Zhang and Xiao-xian Han; m. Man-xia Maria Zhang, Feb. 22, 1982; children: George, Elaine. PRC, BSME, Dalian Inst. Tech., Dalian, 1982; MS in Indsl. Engring., Pa. State U., 1985, PhD, 1988. Project coord. Nat. Forge Co., Irvine, Pa., 1988; asst. prof. mfg. systems engring. Fla. Atlantic U., Boca Raton, 1988-93; assoc. prof. and assoc. dir. mfg. systems engring. Fla. Atlantic U., Boca Rabon, 1993—; cons. Nat. Forge Pa., KDS, Deerfield Beach, Fla., Motorola, Inc., Boynton Beach, Fla., Ford Motor Co., Livonia, Mich., Xerox Co., Webster, N.Y. Contbr. articles to profl. jours., procs. Grantee NSF, 1990-94, Material Handling Rsch. Ctr., 1990-94. Mem. Soc. Mfg. Engrs., N.Am. Mfg. Rsch. Inst., Inst. Indsl. Engrs., Inst. Mgmt. Scis. Home: 19571 Black Olive Ln Boca Raton FL 33498-4827 Office: Fla Atlantic Univ 500 NW 20th St Boca Raton FL 33431-6415

HANAHAN, JAMES LAKE, insurance executive; b. Burlington, Iowa, Aug. 27, 1932; s. Thomas J. and Clarice P. (Lorey) H.; BS, Drake U., 1955; postgrad. George Williams Coll., 1956; m. Marilyn R. Lowe, Dec. 27, 1952; children: Bridget Sue Bahlke, Erin Rose Savage. Phys. dir. Monmouth (Ill.) YMCA, 1955-56; with community relations staff Caterpillar Tractor Co., Peoria, Ill., 1956-57; rep. Conn. Gen. Life Ins. Co., Des Moines, 1957-59, asst. mgr., 1959-63, mgr. group ins. ops., Tampa, Fla., 1963-80; pres., chief exec. officer WHP, First In Employee Benefits Inc., 1980-91, J & H Cons. Group Inc., 1980-81; v.p. An Cons., 1991—; instr. C.P.C.U. courses; seminar leader C.L.U. workshop; cons. ins. seminar Fla. State U. Bd. dirs. West Coast Employee Benefit Coun., Tampa Sports Found., Jr. Achievement, Tampa Bay Acad., Meml. Hosp. Tampa; bd. dirs., past pres. Pinellas Emergency Mental Health Services; mem. Hillsborough County Health Council. Recipient Double D award Drake U., 1978, PEMHS Community Svc. award, 1991. Mem. Sales Mktg. Execs. Tampa (past pres., Exec. of Yr. 1982), Nat. Risk Mgmt. Soc., Greater Tampa C. of C., Minerat Soc. U. Tampa, Tampa Sports and Recreation Council (bd. dirs.), Self Ins. Assn. Am., Pinellas Econ. Devel. Coun., Health Ins. Inst. Am., Profl. Benefit Adminstrs. Assn., Com. of 100, Phi Sigma. Democrat. Roman Catholic. Clubs: 7th Inning (chmn.), Nat. D (Drake U.) (v.p., dir.), Innisbrook Country Resort, Pres.'s Assn. Home: 6659 Garden Palm Ct New Port Richey FL 33655

HANCE, DOUGLAS JAMES, JR., aerospace research engineer, consultant; b. Corpus Christi, Tex., Apr. 10, 1946; s. Douglas James and Jamie Louise (Pate) H.; m. Cheri Lynn Allen, Dec. 24, 1979 (div.); 1 child, Douglas James III. BS in Aerospace Engring., U. Tex., Arlington, 1969, postgrad., 1989-93; postgrad., USAMC Intern Tng. Ctr., Texarkana, Tex., 1974-76. Engr.-in-tng., Tex. Aerodynamics engr. Bell Helicopter Co., Hurst, Tex., 1968; flight test engr. Gen. Dynamics, Ft. Worth, 1970-71; buyer Lone Star Army Ammo Plant, Texarkana, 1972-74; indsl. engr. U.S. Army Materiel command, Texarkana, 1974-75; constrn. asst. William H. Briggs Co., Texarkana, 1976-81; mech. engr. USAF Air Logistics Ctr., Oklahoma City, 1981; constrn. estimator Calvin Carter Constrn., Texarkana, 1984-86; grad. tchg. asst. U. Tex., Arlington, 1990; engr. cons., disc aircraft inventor Hanssadyne Aerosci., Wake Village, Tex., 1993—; cons. Sequoia Environ. Constrn., Wake Village, 1994—; engr. assoc. Aero. Engring. Cons., Arlington, 1991—. Co-prodr.: (TV prodn.) It Came From Malton, 1992; featured interviewee on radio programs. Mem. reunion com. 1950 Texarkana Citizen Marines, 1995; mem. Bapt. Singles Sunday Sch., 1995—. Mem. Internat. Legion of Intelligence, Tau Beta Pi (charter), Alpha Chi. Office: Hanssadyne Aerosci PO Box 1062 Nash TX 75569

HANCE, JAMES HENRY, JR., bank executive; b. St. Joseph, Mo., Sept. 16, 1944; s. James Henry Sr. and Kathryn (Lichty) H.; m. Beverly Vaughan Smith, May 20, 1960; children: Samantha, Lindsay, Meredith, Blair. BA in Econs., Westminster Coll., Fulton, Mo., 1966; MBA in Fin., Washington U., St. Louis, 1968. CPA. Ptnr. Price Waterhouse, Phila. and Charlotte, N.C., 1968-85; chmn. bd. Consolidated Coin Caterers Corp., Charlotte, 1985-86; exec. v.p., chief acctg. officer NCNB Corp., Charlotte, 1987-88; CFO, vice-chmn. Nationsbank Corp., Charlotte, N.C., 1988—; bd. dirs. Nationsbank of Tenn., D.C., Md., Charlotte, N.C. Bd. dirs. Microelectronis Ctr. N.C., Research Triangle Park, 1988; trustee Presbyn. Hosp. and Presbyn. Hosp. Health Svcs. Corp., Charlotte, 1989, Charlotte County Day Sch., 1990; mem. acctg. and fin. commn. Bank Adminstrn. Inst., Rolling Meadows, Ill., 1989. Fellow Soc. Internat. Bus. Fellows. Republican. Presbyterian. Office: Nationsbank Corp Nationsbank Corp Ctr 100 N Tryon St Fl 58 Charlotte NC 28202-4000*

HANCOCK, JAMES HUGHES, federal judge; b. 1931. B.S., U. Ala., 1953, LL.B., 1957. Bar: Ala. Ptnr. firm Balch, Bingham, Baker, Hawthorne, Ward & Williams, Birmingham, Ala., 1957-73; judge U.S. Dist. Ct. (no. dist.) Ala., Birmingham, 1973—. Mem. Ala. Bar Assn. *

HANCOCK, JOHN C., pharmacologist; b. Lockwood, Mo., Aug. 20, 1938; s. Daniel L. and Cordelia O. (Chandler) H. BS, U. Mo., Kansas City; MS, U. Tex., Galveston, 1965, PhD, 1968. Instr. U. Conn., Storrs, 1968-69; asst. prof. U. Conn., Farmington, 1969-71, La. State U., New Orleans, 1971-73; assoc. prof. La. State U., 1973-77; prof. East Tenn. State U. Coll. Medicine, Johnson City, 1977—, dep. chair, 1985—; peer rev. panel Am. Heart Assn., Tenn., 1991—; presenter in field. Author (software) Autonomic Pharmacology; contbr. articles to profl. jours. Grantee NIH. Mem. Am. Soc. Pharmacol. Exptl. Therapeutics, Neurosci./Am. Heart Assn., Soc. Exptl. Biology and Medicine, Soc. Neuroscience (Applachian chpt.), Sigma Xi.

HANCOCK, MARK MATTHEW, photojournalist, journalist; b. Vina del Mar, Chile, June 20, 1965; came to U.S., 1965; s. William Heman and Majorie Ellen (Davis) H.; m. Stephanie Kaye Burdine, Oct. 28, 1995. A in Arts & Sci., Richland Coll., Dallas, 1993; BS in Photojournalism, East Tex. State U., 1995. Collection coord. G.E. Capitol Corp., Richardson, Tex., 1989-93; photojournalist Plano, Tex., 1995; staff photojournalist DFW Suburban Newspapers, Richardson, 1996, The Dallas Morning News, 1997—; staff writer, photographer The Richland Chronicle, Dallas, 1992-93; news editor, photographer The East Texan, 1993-94, editor-in-chief, 1995. Sgt. U.S. Army, 1984-88, Conus. Rayburn Mayo scholar East Tex. State U., 1993; journalism grantee, 1994. Mem. Soc. Profl. Journalists (v.p. 1995-96), Nat. Press Photographers Assn. (1st place award 1996), Phi Theta Kappa. Home: 30 Lucy Ln Wylie TX 75098 Office: The Richardson News 409 Belle Grove Dr Richardson TX 75080-5203

HANCOCK, PATRICIA ANN, artist; b. Columbia, S.C., Apr. 1, 1956; d. William Edwards and Joan Marie (Moore) H. Student, Queens Coll., 1973-75; BFA, U. Ga., 1979; postgrad., Va. Commonwealth U., 1980-81. Art tchr. Thornwell Sch., Clinton, S.C., 1979-80. Author, illustrator: Rupert, The Fantastic Flamingo, 1989; exhibited works in C&S Bank Show, 1991, 92. Mem. Jr. League. Presbyterian.

HANCOCK, SANDRA OLIVIA, secondary and elementary school educator; b. Jackson, Tenn., Oct. 22, 1947; d. Carthel Leon and Thelma (Thompson) Smith; m. Jerome Hancock, Aug. 1, 1969; children: Casey Colman, Mandy Maria. BS, U. Tenn., 1969, MS, 1973; grad. safety seminar, Universal Cheerleaders Assn., 1989. Cert. educator. Educator Lexington (Tenn.) High Sch., 1969-70, Clarksburg (Tenn.) High Sch., 1970-78, 83-90, Dresden (Tenn.) Jr. H.S., 1994-95; instr. Camden (Tenn.) Elem. Sch., 1995—; instr. Very Spl. Arts Festival, Carroll County, Tenn., 1994; GED instr. Contbr. poetry to various publs. Cub scout leader Boy Scouts Am., Clarksburg, 1982-84; assoc. mem. St. Labre Indian Sch. and Home Arrow Club, Ashland, Mont., 1988-89; former vol. March of Dimes; vol. Leukemia Soc. Am.; mem. fund raising com. Project Graduation, Huntingdon H.S., 1992-95; dir. presch. 1st United Meth. Ch., Huntingdon, 1992-93; art edn. asst. Huntingdon Spl. Sch. Dist., 1993-94. Recipient various poetry awards. Mem. NEA, Tenn. Edn. Assn., Benton County Edn. Assn., Benton County Reading Assn., U.S. Olympic Assn., Nat. Cheerleaders Assn. (Superior Advisor Performace award 1988), Am. Assn. Cheerleading Coaches and Advisors, Jackson Writer's Group (rec. sec. 1993-94), Poetry Soc. Tenn. (rec. sec. 1993-94, guest spkr. 1994), Haiku Soc. Am., Phi Delta Kappa (N.W. Tenn. chpt. sec. 1993-94). Republican. Home and Office: 435 Timber Ln Huntingdon TN 38344-1625 Office: Camden Elem Sch 208 Washington St Camden TN 38320

HAND, LOIS FLEMING, medical technologist; b. Lakeland, Fla., July 18, 1953; d. Louis Alfred and Mary Lee (Burnett) Fleming; m. John Screven Hand, Feb. 22, 1992. BS in Med. Tech., Jacksonville U., 1976; diploma in med. tech., Bapt. Meml. Hosp., Jacksonville, Fla., 1976. Lab. mgr. Madison County Meml. Hosp., Madison, Fla., 1976-89; med. technologist, supr. hematology John D. Archbold Meml. Hosp., Thomasville, Ga., 1990—. Mem. Thomasville Landmarks Inc., Thomasville Entertainment Found., Thomasville Arts Guild. Mem. Am. Soc. Clin. Pathologists (assoc., registrant), Nat. Soc. DAR (2d v.p. 1993-96), UDC, Colonial Dames 17th Century, Daus. Am. Colonists, Magna Carta Dames, Nat. Geneal. Soc., Alpha Delta Pi. Republican. Episcopalian. Home: 312 E Jefferson St Thomasville GA 31792-5107 Office: John D Archbold Meml Hosp Gordon At Mimosa Thomasville GA 31792

HAND, WILLIAM BREVARD, federal judge; b. Mobile, Ala., Jan. 18, 1924; s. Charles C. and Irma W. H.; m. Allison Denby, June 17, 1948; children: Jane Connor Hand Dukes, Virginia Alan Hand Hollis, Allison Hand Peebles. BS in Commerce and Bus. Adminstrn., U. Ala., 1947, JD, 1949; LLD (hon.), U. Mobile, 1990. Bar: Ala. 1949. Assoc. Hand, Arendall, Bedsole, Greaves & Johnston, Mobile, 1949-71; chief judge, then sr. judge U.S. Dist. Ct. (so. dist.) Ala., Mobile, 1971—. Chmn. Mobile County Rep. Exec. Com., 1968-71. Served with U.S. Army, 1943-46. Decorated Bronze Star medal. Mem. Am., Fed., Ala., Mobile bar assns. Methodist. Office: US Dist Ct US Courthouse 113 Saint Joseph St # 7 Mobile AL 36602-3606*

HAND, WILLIAM LEE, physician; b. Cartersville, Ga., Jan. 23, 1937. BS, Davidson Coll., 1958; MD, Emory U., 1962. Instr. medicine Emory U. Sch. Medicine, Atlanta, 1965-66, asst. prof. medicine, 1970-74, asst. prof. preventive medicine & cmty. health, 1970-74, assoc. prof. medicine, 1974-79, co-dir. divsn. infectious disease dept. medicine, 1975-81, dir., 1981-93, prof. medicine, 1979-94; staff mem. Wilford Hall USAF Hosp., Lackland AFB, Tex., 1966-68; USPHS fellow infectious diseases U. Tex. Southwestern Med. Sch., Dallas, 1968-70; clin. investigator VA Hosp., Atlanta, 1971-74, acting assoc. chief of staff R&D, 1974, 76; chief infectious disease sect. VA Med. Ctr., Decatur, 1975-90; chief infectious disease svc. Grady Meml. Hosp., Atlanta, 1981-94; prof., regional chmn. Tex. Tech U. Health Sci. Ctr., El Paso, 1994—. Office: Texas Tech U Health Scis Ctr 4800 Alberta Ave El Paso TX 79905

HANDEL, RICHARD CRAIG, lawyer; b. Hamilton, Ohio, Aug. 11, 1945; s. Alexander F. and Marguerite (Wilks) H.; m. Katharine Jean Carter, Jan. 10, 1970. AB, U. Mich., 1967; MA, Mich. State U., 1968; JD summa cum laude, Ohio State U., 1974; LLM in Taxation, NYU, 1978. Bar: Ohio 1974, S.C. 1983, U.S. Dist. Ct. (so. dist.) Ohio 1975, U.S. Dist. Ct. S.C. 1979, U.S. Tax Ct. 1977, U.S. Ct. Appeals (4th cir.) 1979, U.S. Supreme Ct. 1979; cert. tax specialist. Assoc. Smith & Schnacke, Dayton, Ohio, 1974-77; asst. prof. U. S.C. Sch. Law, Columbia, 1978-83; ptnr. Nexsen, Pruet, Jacobs & Pollard, Columbia, 1983-87, Moore & Van Allen, Columbia, 1987-88, Nexsen Pruet Jacobs & Pollard, Columbia, 1988-89; chief tax policy and appeals S.C. Tax Commn., Columbia, 1989-95; chief coun. Policy S.C. Dept. of Revenue, Columbia, 1995—; adj. prof. U. S.C. Sch. Law, 1990—. Contbr. articles to legal jours. bd. dirs. Friends of Richland County Pub. Libr. Served with U.S. Army, 1969-70, Vietnam. Gerald L. Wallace scholar, 1977-78; recipient Outstanding Law Prof. award, 1980-81. Mem. ABA (com. State and Local Taxes, vice chair com. tax procedures 1993-94), S.C. Bar Assn., Order of Coif. Office: SC Tax Commn PO Box 125 301 Gervais St Columbia SC 29214-0702

HANDELSMAN, MICHAEL, Hispanic studies educator; b. Weehawken, N.J., May 11, 1948; s. Jay and Betty (Feinstein) H.; m. Maria Victoria Suarez, June 18, 1971; children: Leah, Alysa. AB, Gettysburg (Pa.) Coll., 1970; MA, U. Fla., 1973, PhD, 1976. Asst. prof. Spanish U. Tenn., Knoxville, 1976-82; assoc. prof. Spanish U. Tenn., 1982-89, prof. Spanish, 1989—. Author: El modernismo en las revistas ecuatorianas, 1981, En torno al verdadero Benjamín Carrión, 1989. Fulbright scholar, Ecuador, 1987. Mem. Am. Assn. Tchrs. of Spanish and Portuguese, Latin Am. Studies Assn., Southeastern Coun. Latin Am. Studies (pres. 1992), Tenn. Fgn. Langs. Tchrs. Assn. (bd. dirs. 1991-94). Home: 8908 Neartop Dr Knoxville TN 37923 Office: U Tenn Knoxville TN 37996

HANDLEY, LEON HUNTER, lawyer; b. Lakeland, Fla., Sept. 9, 1927; s. Driskle Hubert and Mamie (Denmark) H.; m. Mary Virginia Wolfe, May 2, 1953; children: Leon Hunter, Mary Ellen, Laura Catherine, Leann Virginia; BSBA with honors, U. Fla., 1949, JD, 1951. Bar: Fla. 1951, U.S. Dist. Ct. (so. dist.) Fla. 1952, U.S. Dist. Ct. (mid. dist.) Fla. 1962, U.S. Supreme Ct. 1956, U.S. Ct. of Appeals (5th cir.) 1960, U.S. Ct. Appeals (11th cir.) 1981; pres. Gurney & Handley, Orlando, Fla., 1951—; bd. dirs. Beneficial Savs. Bank, chmn.; bd. dirs. Orlando/Tampa, Cracker Groves Inc., Orlando, 1964—; v.p., bd. dirs. So. Indsl. Savs. Bank, Orlando, Mine & Mill Supply Co., Lakeland, 1966—, Claude H. Wolfe, Inc., Orlando, 1969—; gen. counsel, life dir., past pres. Cen. Fla. Fair; chmn. bd. trustees Sta. WMFE-TV. Pres. Chesley Magruder Charitable Trust; elder Presbyn. Ch. Warrant officer U.S. Maritime Svc., 1945-46, ETO; sgt. U.S. Army, 1946-48, Korea; capt. USAFR, 1949-59. Fellow Am. Coll. Trial Lawyers; mem. ABA, Am. Bd. Trial Advocates (Fla. Trial Lawyer of Yr. 1996, advocate), Orange County Bar Assn. (past pres. sta. jr. bar sect., bd. govs. 1959-60), Fedn. Ins. and Corp. Counsel, Internat. Assn. Def. Counsel, Assn. Def. Trial Attys., Trial Attys. Am., Am. Judicature Soc., Pres.'s Coun. (founder U. Fla. chpt.), Citrus Club, Orlando Country Club, Univ. Club, Masons (grand orator Fla. 1982, 86) K.T., Shriners, Scottish Rite (33d degree, insp. gen. hon. 1979), Rotary (pres. Orlando chpt. 1984, Paul Harris fellow), Travelers' Century Club, Fla. Blue Key (pres. 1951), Phi Delta Phi, Alpha Tau Omega (prs. U. of Fla. chpt. 1951), Phi Kappa Phi, Alpha Kappa Psi, Beta Gamma Sigma. Republican. Avocations: jogging, handball. Home: 1621 Spring Lake Dr Orlando FL 32804-7111 Office: Gurney & Handley 225 E Robinson St Ste 450 Orlando FL 32801-4321

HANDLY-JOHNSON, PATRICIA, school administrator, school psychologist, educational consultant; b. Bryn Mawr, Pa., Feb. 20, 1950; d. Robert Shanaman and Raye (Piland) Handly; m. Michael Lane Johnson, Sept. 14, 1991. BA in Child Devel., Conn. Coll., 1972; MA in Clin. Psychology, George Mason U., 1979. Cert. profl. tchr., sch. psychologist, Va., elem. prin., Pa. Elem. tchr. St. Agnes Sch., Alexandria, Va., 1972-74; tchr. Lordswood Jr. Mixed Sch., Chatham, Eng., summer 1973; elem. tchr. Fairfax County (Va.) Pub. Schs., 1974-78, sch. psychologist, 1978-84; lectr. in psychology No. Va. C.C., Woodbridge, 1978-84; sch. psychologist The Carol Morgan Sch., Santo Domingo, Dominican Republic, 1984-88, elem. sch. prin., 1988-91; ednl. cons. Houghton Mifflin Co., Boston, 1992; asst. prin. St. John's Sch., San Juan, P.R., 1992-96; adminstr. and co-trainer Prin.'s Tng. Ctr. for Internat. Leadership, summers 1994-96; co-prin. Escuela Campo Alegre, Caracas, Venezuela, 1996; adv. bd. Instructor mag., N.Y.C., 1980-81; presenter in field. Vice pres. bd. dirs. Sacred Music Soc., Santo Domingo, 1985-88; mem. Coro Sinfonico de Puerto Rico, Newcomers Club, Puerto Rico. Recipient acad. scholarship Conn. Coll., 1971-72. Mem. ASCD, Internat. Reading Assn., Sailing Assn. (sgt.-at-arms 1984-89). Episcopalian.

HANDY, LORETTA RAYMORÉ, entertainer, minister; b. Mobile, Ala., Jan. 31, 1941; d. Levernon Raymoré and Lillian Charletta Harrison Mitchell; m. Arthur Lee Williams, Sept. 1959 (div. 1963); children: Darryl, Michael, Tony; m. Eddie Louis Handy, June 29, 1971; 1 child, Dejuan. Cert. in Bus. Adminstrn., Ala. Banking Inst., 1980. Entertainer The Esquire Band, Mobile, 1962-63, Otis Redding Band, Mobile, 1963-68; ins. cons. Atlanta Life Ins., Mobile, 1969-71; long distance operator South Ctrl. Bell, Mobile, 1971-77; new accounts cons. Ctrl. Bank, Mobile, 1977-81; dir. Mary Kay Cosmetics, Mobile, 1981-84; supr. Shaklee Products, Mobile, 1984-85; fin. planner Prudential Ins. Co., Mobile, 1985-88; agt. United Ins. Co., Mobile, 1988-90; cons. Ctrl. Bank, Mobile, 1977-81; asst. pastor Browns Temple Ch., Bogalusa, La., 1986-90; TV personnel/singer Son-lite Broadcasting, Mobile, 1989—. Author: (autobiography) Woman Who Lived Twice, 1989; rec. artist (album/single) "Second Chance" Back to the Altar, 1990, (single) Missing You, Baby Cakes; voice trainer; gospel singer Ameka Records, 1990—. Min. AOH Ch. of God, Mobile, 1983—; campaigner City Coun. Women, Mobile, 1994-95. Mem. Women's Aglow of Am., ASCAP Music Assn., 2d Chance Outreach Ministry (founding mem., v.p 1996—), Also Helping Hands Ministry (pres. 1991-95, Cert. of Achievement), TBN Ministries (min., singer 1989—). Democrat. Pentecostal. Office: 2d Chance Outreach and Ministries PO Box 850851 Mobile AL 36685-0851

HANDY, ROBERT TRUMAN, association administrator; b. Portland, Oreg., May 1, 1941; s. Royal Sheppard and Eloise (Yeager) H.; m. Linda Rose Andreas, Aug. 26, 1967 (div. 1976); 1 child, Heather Andreas Handy; m. Janet Lee Ward, Jan. 14, 1979; stepchildren: Christopher W. Ward, Elizabeth Leigh Ward. BS in History, Polit. Sci., Portland State U., 1969, MA in Am. Diplomatic History, 1971. Dir. community svcs. Coll. of the Mainland, Texas City, Tex., 1972-74, dir. internat. programs, 1975-76; founder and exec. dir. Gulf Coast World Affairs Coun., 1976-84; exec. dir. Houston World Trade Assn., 1984-88; pres. Devel. Resources Internat., Houston, 1988—; exec. dir. Brazoria County Hist. Mus., Angleton, Tex., 1992—; adj. faculty Alvin (Tex.) C.C., 1994—. Pub., editor Jour. Fgn. Affairs; internat. editor In Between Mag.; book reviewer Houston Chronicle; contbr. articles to profl. jours. including Angleton Times, Images mag. Bd. dirs. Galveston County Community Action Coun., Galveston, Tex., 1973, La Marque (Tex.) Aid and Guidance Coun., 1979; mem. La Marque Econ. Devel. Coun., 1980; del. European Community Visitors Program, Belgium, Fed. Republic Germany, France, Eng., 1981; chmn. Galveston County Coun. of Chambers, 1988; appointee European Community "Team 1992", 1989. With USN, 1959-62. Mem. Brazosport C. of C. (chmn. internat. com. 1992-93), Am. Assn. Museums, Am. Assn. State & Local Hist., Angleton C. of C. Democrat. Home: 2910 Frostwood Cir Dickinson TX 77539-4207 Office: 100 E Cedar Courthouse Sq Angleton TX 77515

HANDY, WILLIAM TALBOT, JR., bishop; b. New Orleans, Mar. 26, 1924; s. William Talbot Sr. and Dorothy Pauline (Pleasant) H.; m. Ruth Odessa Robinson, Aug. 11, 1948; children—William Talbot III (dec.), Dorothy D. Handy Davis, Stephen Emanuel, Mercedes Handy Cowley. Student, Tuskegee U., 1940-43; B.A., Dillard U., 1948, LL.D. (hon.), 1981; M.Div., Gammon Theol. Sem., 1951; S.T.M., Boston U., 1952; DD, Cen. Meth. Coll., 1991. Ordained to ministry United Meth. Ch., 1949, consecrated bishop, 1980. Pastor Newman Meth. Ch., Alexandria, La., 1952-59; pastor St. Mark Meth. Ch., Baton Rouge, 1959-68; pub. rep. Meth. Pub. House, Nashville, 1968-70; v.p. pers. svc. United Meth. Pub. House, Nashville, 1970-78; dist. supt. Baton Rouge-Lafayette dist. United Meth. Ch., 1978-80; bishop Mo. area United Meth. Ch., St. Louis, 1980-92; bishop in residence U. Meth. Ch., Nashville, 1993—; interim dir. The Mission Resource Ctr., Atlanta, 1992; vis. Arthur J. Moore prof. Evangelism Candler Sch. Theol., Atlanta, 1993-94; mem. exec. com. Gen. Bd. Publ., Nashville, 1988-92. Chmn. sibcom. on voting rights U.S. Commn. on Civil Rights, 1959-68; mem. mayor's biracial adv. com. La. Adv. Com., Baton Rouge, 1965-66; Golden Heritage life mem. NAACP, 1971; chmn. bd. trustees Gammon Theol. Sem., Atlanta, 1990-94, St. Paul Sch. Theology, Kansas City, Mo., 1980-92, Interdenominational Theol. Ctr., Atlanta, 1990-93; bishop in residence Meml. United Meth. Ch., 1992—; vis. chaplain United Meth. Pub. House, 1996—; adj. advisor Theol. Sch., Drew U.; vis. regional dir. DMin. Projects Drew U. Theol. Sch., 1996—. Mem. Masons (33 degree).

HANEKE, DIANNE MYERS, education educator; b. San Francisco, Feb. 23, 1941; d. Wayne and Dorothy (Johnson) Myers; m. John Paul Haneke, Apr. 10, 1965; children: Mark, Debra, Julie. BA in Social Sci., Edn., So. Calif. Coll., 1964; MS in Edn., SUNY, Albany, 1971, cert. advanced studies, 1990, doctoral student, 1990—. Cert. elem., social studies and reading tchr., N.Y. Reading specialist Greenville (N.Y.) Elem. Sch., 1971-72, 84-85, Durham (N.Y.) Elem. Sch., 1972-74, Cairo (N.Y.) Durham Schs., 1979-82, 86-89; counselor Capital Area Christian Counseling, Delmar, N.Y., 1980-81; instr. psychology Columbia Greene Community Coll., Hudson, N.Y., 1982-83; reading specialist Hunter (N.Y.)-Tannersville Schs., 1985-86; instr. of edn. and reading Mt. St. Mary Coll., Newburgh, N.Y., 1990-92; adj. prof. of reading edn. Concordia U. at Austin, Tex., 1993—. Author: A Woman After God's Own Heart, 1982, A View From the Inside: An Action Plan for Gender Equity in New York State Educational Administration, 1990. Instr. water safety ARC, 1978-91; host parents Youth for Understanding, 1984-85, 88-89; leader, resource person Girl Scouts Am., 1978-90. Myers-Haneke Edn. scholar So. Calif. Coll., 1971—; recipient Alumnus of Yr. award So. Calif. Coll., 1979, Disting. Contbr. award So. Calif. Coll. Alumni Assn., 1988, Disting. Svc. award So. Calif. Coll. Edn. Dept., 1988, So. Calif. Coll. Alumni Assn., 1994. Mem. ASCD, Am. Ednl. Rsch. Assn., Assn. Tchr. Educators, Capital Area Reading Coun., Christian Educators' Assn. Internat., Coll. Reading Assn., Nat. Reading Conf., Internat. Coun. Tchrs. English, Tex. State Reading Assn., Delta Kappa Gamma, Phi Delta Kappa. Republican. Office: Concordia Univ Austin Edn Div 3400 Interstate 35 N Austin TX 78705-2799

HANEY, ARTHUR JOHN, art educator, academic administrator; b. Niagara Falls, N.Y., Oct. 28, 1942; s. Frederick John and Jeannette (Czypinski) H.; m. Gail Rabold, June 5, 1976; 1 child, Danielle. Student, East Carolina U., 1965-67; BFA, Syracuse U., 1971; MFA, Alfred U., 1973. Ins. agt. Met. Life Ins. Co., Raleigh, N.C., 1964-65; draftsman Carrier Airconditioning Corp., Syracuse, N.Y., 1967-68; artist Syracuse Newspapers, 1968-71; prof. Sch. Art East Carolina U., Greenville, 1973—, asst. dean, 1983—. Artist (fused glass) Internat. Exhbn. Glass, Kanazawa, Japan, 1990, Westmoreland Art Nats., Youngwood, Pa., 1990, Hot Glass 1990, Ft. Wayne, Ind., 6th Ann. Greater Mid-West Internat., Warrensburg, Mo., 1991. Sgt. U.S. Army, 1961-64. Recipient 1st prize Beaufort County Arts Coun., Washington, N.C., 1990, honorable mention Lake Worth (Fla.) Art League, 1990, 2d pl. Bemidji (Minn.) Community Arts Coun., 1991. Mem. Greenville Mus. Art, Glass Art Guild, Atlanta, Art Enthusiasts East Carolina (bd. dirs. 1987—), Designs for Special Needs Populations (bd. dirs. 1986-89), Carolina Designer Draftsmen (bd. dirs. 1977-78, pres. 1978-80), Am. Legion. Democrat. Roman Catholic. Home: RR 8 Box 766 Greenville NC 27834-8870 Office: East Carolina U Sch Art E 5th St Greenville NC 27858-4353

HANFORD, AGNES RUTLEDGE, financial adviser; b. Far Rockaway, N.Y., Aug. 26, 1927; d. Warren Day and Agnes Beatrice (Kane) H. Grad., Convent of Sacred Heart Prep. Sch., N.Y.C.; BA in English, French, Newton Coll., 1950. Asst. clk. rules com U.S. Ho. of Reps., Washington, 1953-56; account exec. W.E. Hutton & Co., N.Y.C., 1956-74; fin. cons. Thomson McKinnon Securities, N.Y.C., 1974-80, Tampa, Fla., 1980-89; fin. adviser Prudential Securities, Inc., Tampa, 1989-94. Mem. Hillsborough County Rep. Exec. Com., Tampa, 1980-93, Women's Econ. Coun., N.Y.C., 1979-80, Tampa Mus. Art, 1980-93, Friends of Plant Park, 1995—, Tampa Bay History Ctr., 1995—; mem. adv. coun. U. South Fla. Contemporary Art Mus., 1996—. Mem. Women's Nat. Rep. Club (mem. bd. govs. 1970-75, v.p. 1975-76), Tampa Yacht and Country Club, Lawrence Beach Club. Roman Catholic. Home: 4141 Bayshore Blvd Tampa FL 33611

HANFORD, GRAIL STEVENSON, writer; b. Far Rockaway, N.Y., Apr. 10, 1932; d. Warren Day and Agnes Beatrice (Kane) Hanford. BA, Smith Coll., 1954. Reporter Tustin (Calif.) News, 1955; newspaper editorial asst. The Register, Santa Ana, Calif., 1955; assoc. editor Am. Mercury Mag., N.Y.C., 1956-59; freelance writer N.Y.C., 1959-60; editor Royal Ins. Cos., N.Y.C., 1960-62; book editor/copy editor Am. Legion Mag., N.Y.C., 1962-75; sr. editor Am. Legion Mag., Washington and Indpls., 1976-82; asst. editor Am. Legion Mag., Indpls., 1982-83; sr. writer Writers For Bus., Indpls., 1983-88, Tampa, Fla., 1988—. Contbr. articles to profl. jours. Bd. dirs. Cathedral Sch. of St. Mary, Garden City, N.Y., 1967-71, pres. Alumna Assn., 1967-69; bd. dirs. Hort. Soc. Indpls. Mus. of Art, 1981-86; pres. Smith Coll. Club Indpls., 1982-84. Mem. Fla. Motion Picture and TV Assn., Nat. Book Critics Cir., Indpls. Press Club (bd. dirs. 1980), Am. News Women's Club, West Fla. Smith Coll. Club (v.p. 1992-94, v.p. 1996—), Ivy League Club of Tampa Bay (bd. dirs. 1989-96, sec. 1990, v.p. 1991). Republican. Roman Catholic. Office: Writers For Bus 4141 Bayshore Blvd Tampa FL 33611-1800

HANISEE, MARK STEVEN, employee benefits professional; b. Logansport, Ind., Dec. 23, 1958; s. William Bernard and Nancy (Thomas) H.; m. Patricia Jean Lauria, Jan. 7, 1989. BS, Fla. So. Coll., 1981. Account exec. Canon, Tampa, Fla., 1981-83; group sales exec. John Alden Life Co., Tampa, 1983-85; group account exec. State Mut. Cos., Tampa, 1985-89; sr. account exec., v.p. sales Bankers Risk Mgmt. Svcs., Inc., St. Petersburg, Fla., 1989-93; ptnr. Pension Investors Corp., Inc., 1993-94; sales exec. Sedgwick Noble Lowndes, 1994—; pres. Tampa Bay Group Ins. Assn., 1993. Mem. Leadership Hillsborough, 1996, Tiger Bay Club, 1996. Mem. Internat. Assn. Fin. Planning (bd. dirs. 1989-92), Employee Benefit Coun., Health Underwriters, Life Underwriters, Tampa C. of C. (health care task force com.), West Tampa bus. Alliance (bd. dirs.), Krewe Sant'Yago (com. chmn. 1990-91, sec., bd. dirs. 1992-93, grand marshall night parade 1994, large exec. bd.), Lincoln Club (sec. 1995), Merry Makers Club, Tampa Club, Rough Riders, Masons. Republican. Roman Catholic. Home: 4208 N Albany Ave Tampa FL 33607-6504 Office: Pension Investors Corp 3820 Northdale Blvd Ste 102-b Tampa FL 33624-1863

HANKINS, BARRY GENE, historian, university institute director; b. Bossier City, La., Oct. 27, 1956; s. Robert James and Shirley Ruth (Jackson) H.; m. Jennifer Ann Stubbs, May 1978; children: Dixon Jackson, Johanna Marie. BA in Religion, Baylor U., 1978, MA, 1983; PhD in History, Kans. State U., 1990. Tchr. history Vanguard Coll. Prep. Sch., Waco, Tex., 1986-90; asst. prof., then assoc. prof. history La. Coll., Pineville, 1990-96; assoc. dir. J.M. Dawson Inst. Ch.-State Studies, Baylor U., Waco. Contbr. articles to profl. jours. Vol. Habitat for Humanity, Alexandria, La., 1991—; tchr. Sunday sch. Emmanuel Bapt. Ch., Alexandria, 1993—. Mem. Conf. on Faith and History, Phi Alpha Theta, Phi Kappa Phi. Office: Baylor Univ JM Dawson Inst Ch-St Study Box 97308 Waco TX 76798-7308

HANKINSON, HARRIETTE FOSTER, amusement company executive; b. Atlanta, Feb. 25, 1942; d. Walter Price and Harriette Louise (Moore) Foster; m. Donald Dean Hankinson, Dec. 2, 1966; children: Donald Dean Jr., Philip Scott, Andrea Elaine. B in Liberal Arts in Journalism, U. Ga., 1963; postgrad., Clayton State Coll., 1994. Advt. copywriter Rich's Dept. Stores, Atlanta, 1963-65; rsch. asst. indsl. devel. dept. Atlanta C. of C., 1965-67; rsch. assoc. Atlanta Region Met. Planning Commn., 1967-69; v.p., sec. Phoenix Amusements, Inc., Riverdale, Ga., 1982—. Mem. Profl. Secs. Internat., Nat. Soc. DAR (state regent 1990-92, NSDAR speakers staff 1989-90, 92-95, state vice regent 1988-90, state 2nd vice regent 1986-88, state chaplain 1984-86, state treas. 1982-84, state corr. sec. 1976-78, state outstanding jr. 1978), Jamestown Soc., Nat. Soc. Descendants Early Quakers, Nat. Soc. Descendants Ancient Planters, Daus. of Am. Colonists, Daus. Colonial Wars State Ga., U.S. Daus. 1812, United Daus. Confederacy, Dames Ct. of Honor (hon. life pres. Ga. 1990, state pres. 1988-90), Freedoms Found. at Valley Forge (rec. sec. Atlanta chpt. 1981-83), Continental Soc. Daus. Indian Wars, First Families Ga., Ga. Fedn. Women's Clubs, Magna Charta Dames, Colonial Order of Crown, Descendants Order of Garter, Plantagent Soc., United Daus. of Confederacy, Order Descendants of Ancient Planters, Descendants of Early Quakers. Episcopalian. Home: 170 Dix Leon Dr Fairburn GA 30213-3606

HANKS, JACKSON RAYBURN, lawyer; b. Palestine, Tex., Dec. 16, 1951; s. Jack Holcomb and Jacquelyn R. Hanks; m. Helen Ann Reeves, Dec. 29, 1979; children: Susanna Holcomb Hanks, Frances Brewer Hanks, Lucy Garrison Hanks. BBA, U. Tex., Austin, 1974; JD, U. Houston, 1977. Bar: Tex.; bd. cert. farm and ranch real estate and residential real estate Tex. Bd. Legal Specialization. Personal trust officer Tex. Commerce Bank, Houston, 1977-78; pvt. practice Palestine, 1978—; exec. bd. East Tex. Coun. of Govt., Kilgore, 1993—. Mayor of Palestine, 1989—; vestryman, former sr. warden St. Philip's Episcopal Ch.; former headmaster St. Philip's Episcopal Ch. Discovery Sch.; former dir. Friends of the Palestine Pub. Libr., Inc.; past drive chmn. Anderson County chpt. Am. Cancer Soc.; past chmn. profl. divsn. United Way campaign; past bd. dirs. Associated Charities; bd. dirs. ARC; pres. Palestine Libr. Meml., Inc.; mem. exec. bd. East Tex. Coun. on Govts., bd. dirs., 1990—; chmn. Palestine Area Fund Communities Found. Tex.; mem. Tex. Mcpl. League Legis. Policy Com. Pub. Safety, 1993-94, vice-chair, 1994; active Tex. Mcpl. League Resolutions Com., 1994. Paul Harris fellow Palestine Rotary Club, 1992; recipient Road Hand award Tex. Dept. of Transp., 1991. Mem. State Bar of Tex., Anderson County Bar Assn. (past pres.), Tex. Bar Assn. (sect. on real estate, probate and trust law, sect. on oil, gas and mineral law, former mem. dist. 2-C grievance com., past chmn.), Palestine C. of C. (past dir., v.p. legis. divsn.),. Episcopalian. Office: 601 E Lacy St Palestine TX 75801-3012

HANLON, PHILLIP ROLLINS, anesthesiologist; b. Balt., Mar. 2, 1950; s. C. Rollins and Margaret (Hammond) H.; m. Mary Charlene Henry, Sept. 10, 1977; children: Matthew, Lindsey, Christopher, Angela. BA, Duke U., 1971; MD, Johns Hopkins U., 1975. Diplomate Am. Bd. Anesthesiology. Intern Charity Hosp., New Orleans, 1975-76; resident Shands Tchg. Hosp., Gainesville, Fla., 1976-78; pvt. practice Anesthesia Assocs., Panama City, Fla., 1978-84; asst. prof. U. So. Ala., Mobile, 1984-87; assoc. prof. U. So. Ala., 1987-91; pvt. practice Anesthesia Svcs. PC, Mobile, 1991—. Mem. AMA, Am. Soc. Anesthesiologists, Ala. State Soc. Anesthesiologists (pres. 1989), Mobile County Med. Soc. Home: 1200 Savannah Dr Mobile AL 36609-5128 Office: Anesthesia Svcs PC 201 Cox St Mobile AL 36604-3302

HANNA, EMMA HARMON, architectural designer, business owner, official; b. Sharpsville, Pa., Apr. 29, 1939; d. James McKarney Supplee and Anne (Woods) Thompson; m. William Hayes Harmon, Sept. 1, 1962 (div. 1984); 1 child, James McKarney Harmon; m. Hugh Allen Hanna, Mar. 21, 1992. BArch, Kent (Ohio) State U., 1962. Drafter W.H. Harmon Architects, Orlando, Fla., 1970-73; pres., owner The Plan Shop, Inc., Orlando and Palm Bay, Fla., 1973-87, The Plan Place, Inc., Palm Bay, 1987—; pres. Engrng. & Design Concepts, Palm Bay, 1986—; vice chmn. Palm Bay Utility Corp.; vice chmn. substance abuse program Broken Glass, Valkaria, Fla. Mem. coun. City of Palm Bay, 1989-91, dep. mayor, 1991-92; treas. League of Cities, Brevard County, Fla., 1989-92, East Ctrl. Fla. Planning Coun., Orlando, 1989-90; mem. Federated Rep. Women, South Brevard County, 1989-91; mem. exec. com. Brevard County Reps.; mem. Panther Athletic Assn. bd. Fla. Inst. Tech., 1990—, pres., 1995-96; mem. open campus adv. coun. Brevard C.C., Holmes Regional Hosp. Devel. Coun., 1991—. Mem. Home Builder and Contractors Brevard County (assoc., bd. dirs. 1993—, 2nd v.p. 1994-95, Assoc. of Yr. 1995), Bldg. Ofcls. Assn. Brevard County (assoc., Assoc. of Yr. 1989), Drafters Guild (organizer), Palm Bay C. of C., Greater South Brevard C. of C. (mem. govt. affairs com., bd. dirs. 1991-93), Exch. Club (chpt. pres., charter pres.), Zonta Club Melbourne. Home: 1482 Meadowbrook Rd NE Palm Bay FL 32905-5007 Office: The Plan Place 1398 Palm Bay Rd NE Palm Bay FL 32905-3837

HANNA, FRANK JOSEPH, credit company executive; b. Douglas, Ga., Apr. 20, 1939; s. Frank Joseph and Josephine (Nahoom) H. m. Vail Deadwyler, Sept. 15, 1960; children: Frank, Lisa, David. BBA, U. Ga., 1961. Credit mgr. Sears, Roebuck & Co., Atlanta, 1961-63, Gen. Motors Corp., Atlanta, 1963-65; gen. mgr. Rollins Acceptance Corp., Atlanta, 1965-81; with Credit Claims & Collections, 1981-90, First Fin. Mgmt. Corp., 1990-93, Worldwide Capital, Inc., Atlanta, 1993—; real estate developer, 1968. Office: Two Ravinia Dr Ste 1750 Atlanta GA 30346

HANNA, LEE ANN, critical care nurse; b. Little Rock, June 16, 1961; d. David Lee and Betty Lou (Pope) Redmond; m. Anthony Warren Hanna, June 18, 1986; children: Thomas Dale, Katherine Elizabeth. AS in Nursing, Belmont Coll., 1980; BSN, Union U., 1983; MSN, Vanderbilt U., 1993. RN, Tenn. Mgr. CQI/edn. Am. Transitional Hosp., Nashville; instr.: ACLS, BCLS and PALS; lectr. in field. Mem. AACCN (cert.).

HANNA, PETE M., executive steel company; b. 1936. Various executive positions Hanna Steel Co., Fairfield, Ala., 1960-1984; chmn. bd., CEO Hanna Steel Co., Fairfield, 1984—. Office: 3812 Commerce Ave Fairfield AL 35064-1440

HANNA, TERRY ROSS, lawyer, small business owner; b. Wadsworth, Ohio, May 17, 1947; s. Harry Ross and Geraldine (Frensley) H.; m. Max Anna Hindes, Jan. 20, 1968; children: Travis, Taylor, Molly. BBA, U. Okla., 1968, JD, 1972; LLM, NYU, 1973; MA in Bibl Studies, Dallas Theol. Sem., 1988. Bar: Okla. 1972, U.S. Tax Ct. 1974, U.S. Ct. Appeals (10th cir.) 1979, U.S. Supreme Ct. 1989; CPA, Okla. Mem. McAfee & Taft, Oklahoma City, 1972-80; pres. P 356 Inc., Oklahoma City, 1980—; of counsel Crowe & Dunlevy, Oklahoma City, 1987—; owner Mo Jo Video, 1995—; spl. lectr. Oklahoma City U. Sch. Law, 1974-75. Editor Okla. U. Law Rev., 1970-72. Mem. internat. com. Boy Scouts Am., 1988—; dir. U.S. Found. for Internat. Scouting, Irving, 1989—. Baden-Powell fellow World Scout Found., 1988—; recipient Silver Beaver award Boy Scouts Am., 1988. Mem. Okla. Bar Assn. (pres. taxation sect. 1978-79), Sports Lawyers Assn., Order of Arrow (lodge advisor 1989—), Kappa Sigma (chpt. advisor 1974-75), Phi Delta Phi (magister 1972). Republican. Mem. Christian Ch. Home: 621 NW 41st St Oklahoma City OK 73118-7027 Office: Crowe & Dunlevy 1800 Mid America Towers Oklahoma City OK 73102

HANNA, VAIL DEADWYLER, critical care nurse; b. Atlanta, Jan. 28, 1942; d. George B. and Dorothy (Heffernan) Deadwyler; children: Frank, Lisa, David. ADN, Kennesaw (Ga.) Jr. Coll., 1976; BSN, Ga. State U., Atlanta, 1983; MAudent, Ga. Sch. Profl. Psychology, 1996. RN, Ga. Staff nurse ICU, recovery room Cobb Gen. Hosp., Austell, Ga., 1976-84; staff nurse ICU, recovery room St. Joseph's Hosp., Atlanta, 1984-87, clin. mgr. coronary care unit, 1987-89; post anesthesia care unit staff nurse St. Joseph's Hosp., 1991-92; staff nurse adolescent unit CPC Parkwood Behavioral Health Care, 1994-95; staff nurse Charter Peachford Hosp., 1995—; psychometrist, 1995—. Chmn. quality assurance coun. St. Joseph's Hosp., 1988-89, chmn. nursing staff, 1988-89. Cert. of Commendation, Kennesaw Jr. Coll., 1976, Evangeline Lane Founder's award, 1983. Mem. ANA, AACN, APA, ACA, LPCA, Ga. Nurses Assn., Am. Heart Assn., Golden Key, Northside Women's Club, Phi Kappa Phi, Mu Rho Sigma. Home: 4621 Sharon Valley Ct Dunwoody GA 30338-5953

HANNAH, JOHN HENRY, JR., judge; b. 1939; 1 child, John III. BS, Sam Houston State U., 1966; postgrad., South Tex. Sch. Law, 1970. Mem. Tex. Ho. of Reps., 1967-73; pvt. practice Lufkin, Tex., 1971-73; dist. atty. Angelina County, Tex., 1973-77; atty. Hannah & Welch, Lufkin, 1977-81; U.S. atty. Ea. Dist. Tex., 1977-81; prin. John Hannah Law Office, 1981-91; sec. of state State of Tex., Austin, 1991-94; dist. judge U.S. Dist. Ct. (ea. dist.), Tyler, 1994—; legal counsel Common Cause, Austin, 1975. Served USN, 1961. Grad. Tchg. fellow Sam Houston U., 1965-66. Mem. Am. Bd. Trial Advocates, State Bar Tex., Tex. Dist. and County Attys. Assn., Tex. Trial Lawyers Assn., Tex. Criminal Def. Lawyers Assn., Phi Gamma Mu. Office: US Dist Ct Ea Dist Tex 221 W Ferguson Rm 100 Tyler TX 75702*

HANNAH, JOHN ROBERT, SR., accountant; b. Monroe, La., Aug. 11, 1939; s. Robert Ruskin Hannah and Berta (Gilliland) Nelson; m. Elizabeth Girdner, Dec. 26, 1965; children: Allison, John Robert Jr. BS, La. State U., 1960. CPA, Tex. Acct. Arthur Young & Co., Houston, 1960-70, Peters & Smith, Midland, Tex., 1970-71; ptnr. Hannah & Trott, Midland, 1971-72; contr. Western States Producing Co., San Antonio, 1972-73; v.p. fin. Sommers Drug Stores Co., San Antonio, 1973-77; pvt. practice acctg. San Antonio, 1987—; ptnr. Peters, Anders & Hannah, San Antonio, 1978-86; seminar speaker Bexar County Med. Soc., San Antonio, 1981. Fin. chmn. YMCA, San Antonio, 1975-82, chmn., 1982-83; adminstr. Bible Study Fellowship, San Antonio, 1977-83; bd. dirs. Morningside Ministries, 1991, Christian Ministry Assistance, 1992, treas. Lt. USN, 1961-65. Mem. Am. Inst. CPA's, Tex. Soc. CPa's, Fin. Execs. Internat., Execs. Internat. Club (San Antonio, pres. 1975-76). Methodist. Home: 102 Castleoaks Dr San Antonio TX 78213-2303 Office: 800 Navarro St Ste 210 San Antonio TX 78205-1725

HANNERS, JOHN, theatre educator; b. Hemel Hempstead, Eng., Sept. 28, 1945; s. Deon D. and Ruth (Ambrose) H.; m. Louella Denham, Jan. 27, 1968; children: Lisa, Michael. BS, Ea. Ill. U., Charleston, 1972; MA, Ind. State U., 1974; PhD, Mich. State U., 1979. Grad. asst. Ind. State U., Terre Haute, 1972-74; tchr., football coach Griffith (Ind.) H.S., 1974-77; actor Mich. Performing Arts Co., East Lansing, 1977-79; prof., chair Allegheny Coll., Meadville, Pa., 1977-92; prof., dept. head East Tex. State U., Commerce, 1992—. Author: (book) It Was Play or Starve, 1993; (plays) Moscow Nights, 1982, Juba!, 1984, Shakespeare X2, 1988, The Importance of Being Oscar, 1989; author, contbr. Biog. Dictionary Am. Sports, Ency. U.S. Popular Culture; contbr. articles to profl. jours.; actor, playwright, dir.; exhibited in group shows at NEH, St. Paul, 1987, 90, Pa. Coun. Arts, 1985, Pitcairn-Crabbe Found., Allegheny Coll.,1 985. Mem. Round Table, Meadville, Pa., 1987-92; mem. United Way Fund Dr., Meadville, 1984, 86, 88; mem. downtown improvement com., Meadville, 1986-91. Sgt. USAF, 1966-70. Mem. Am. Soc. Theatre Rsch., Speech Comm. Assn., S.W. Theatre Assn., Assn. Theatre in Higher Edn., Assn. Comm. Adminstrn., Tex. Ednl. Theatre Assn. Home: Rt 2 Box 225 Commerce TX 75428 Office: East Tex State U 102 Performing Arts Ctr Commerce TX 75429

HANNON, MICHAEL, investment banker; b. Youngstown, Ohio, June 13, 1947; s. Patrick Edward and Elizabeth (Lienau) H.; m. Doris Hallford, Nov. 6, 1987; children: Michael Beringer, Tyler. BA in Economics, N.C. State Univ., Raleigh, 1971. With U.S. Leasing Corp., San Francisco, 1971-75, ITEL Corp., San Francisco, 1976-77, Security Pacific Leasing, San Francisco, 1978-79, Gould Financial, Rolling Meadows, Ill., 1979-80; v.p. Amvest Leasing, Charlottesville, Va., 1981; founder, chmn. Hannon Armstrong & Co., Alexandria, Va., 1981—; bd. dirs. Offshore Sci. Corp., Alexandria, Gen. Offshore Corp., Ft. Lauderdale, Fla., Corp. Incentive Travel, Alexandria, System Fin. Group, Miami, Fla.; founder Meier Mitchell & Co., San Francisco, 1983-84, Delta Cement Corp., Georgetown, S.C., 1987-88; chmn., founder Heritage Pointe Builders, Inc., Wilmington, N.C., 1993. Mem. Sigma Alpha Epsilon. Republican. Roman Catholic. Office: 112 S Alfred St Alexandria VA 22314-3061

HANOLD, R. C. FREDERICK, III, entrepreneur; b. Decatur, Ala., Oct. 12, 1940; s. R.C. Frederick Jr. Hanold and Thelma Estelle (Jones) Sandifer; m. Floy Frances Shaffer, Feb. 17, 1963 (div. May 1982); children: Maylon Turner, R.C. Frederick IV. BS in Chemistry, Coll. of Charleston, 1963. Process engr. Aerovox Corp., Myrtle Beach, S.C., 1963-67; lab. technician Raybestos Manhattan, North Charleston, S.C., 1962-63; process engr. Gen. Instrument, Tazewell, Va., 1967-68; process engr. Union Carbide Corp., Simpsonville, S.C., 1968-70, mgr. process engring., 1970-73, sr. devel. engr., 1973-75; exporter precious metals, 1975-81, owner motels,, 1981—. Patentee in field. Home and Office: PO Box 847 Simpsonville SC 29681

HANRAHAN, LAWRENCE MARTIN, healthcare consultant; b. Cin., Mar. 9, 1961; adopted s. Robert Donald and Mary Francis (Doran) H.; s. Barry Wright and Kathryn Regina Kinkaid. AB in Chemistry, Miami U., 1983; MD, U. Cin. Coll. Medicine, 1988; MBA, U. Tex. Grad. Sch. Bus., Austin, 1992. Founder, owner Landscaping group, Cin., 1975-85; chief ultrasound tech., instr., rsch. assoc. The Good Samaritan Hosp. Peripheral Vascular Lab., Cin., 1983-84; instr., technologist The Christ Hosp. Clin. Vascular Lab., Cin., 1986; tech. cons., instr. Biosound, Inc., Indpls., 1983-89; surg. rsch. fellow divsn. surgery Boston U. Sch. Medicine; peripheral vascular technologist, instr. Seton Med. Ctr., Austin, 1991; summer assoc. health care ops. Deloitte & Touche, Houston, 1991, cons. health care ops., 1991-92, sr. cons., 1992-94, mgr. health care ops., 1994—; assoc. healthcare provider cons. William M. Mercer, Inc., Atlanta, 1995—; founder, chmn., pres. CORE Med. Techs., Inc., 1992—; treas. Miami Med. Edn. and Devel., Miami U., 1975-79; com. mem. Disting. Lecture Series, U. Tex. Sch. Bus., Austin; founding pres. Tex. Bus. Hall of Fame Found. Scholarship Alumni Assn., 1992-93; bd. dirs., exec. com., 1992-95. Contbr. 10 articles to profl. jours.; co-inventor 2 U.S. patents. Finalist ACS resident competition, 1990, San Diego State U. Entrepreneurship competition; winner New Eng. Surg. Soc. resident competition, 1990; Tex. Bus. Hall of Fame Found. scholar, 1991, Abell-Hanger Endowed presdl. scholar, 1991. Mem. AMA, Soc. for Vascular Tech., Tex. Med. Assn., Mass. Med. Soc., Harris County Med. Soc., Med. Student Surgical Soc., Beta Theta Pi Frat.

HANRATTY, CARIN GALE, pediatric nurse practitioner; b. Dec. 31, 1953; d. Burton and Lillian Aleskowitz; m. Michael Patrick Hanratty, May 22, 1983; 1 child, Tyler James. BSN, Russell Sage Coll., 1975; postgrad., U. Calif., San Diego, 1980. Cert. CPR instr.; cert. NALS; cert. specialist ANA. PNP day surgery unit Children's Med. Ctr., Dallas, 1981-85; clin. mgr. pediatrics Trinity Med. Ctr., Carrollton, Tex., 1985-86; pediatric drug coord. perinatal intervention team for substance abusing women and babies Parkland Meml. Hosp., Dallas, 1990—. Guest talk show Morning Coffee, Sta. KPLX-FM, various TV programs. Rep. United Way, 1988—, blood donor chair Parkland Hosp., 1990—, chair March of Dimes, 1992—; bd. dirs., med. cons. KIDNET Found. Mem. ARC (profl., life), Nat. Assn. PNPs (v.p. Dallas chpt. 1982-83), Tex. Nurses Assn. Office: Parkland Meml Hosp PNP 5201 Harry Hines Blvd Dallas TX 75235-7708

HANS, JAMES S., English language educator; b. Elgin, Ill., May 6, 1950; m. Hilma Ross, Aug. 17, 1974; 1 child, Heather Anne. BA in English Lit., So. Ill. U., 1972, MA in English Lit., 1974; PhD in Modern Lit. and Theory, Washington U., 1978. Faculty So. Ill. U., Edwardsville, 1972-74, Washington U., St. Louis, 1974-78, Kenyon Coll., 1978-82; faculty Wake Forest U., Winston-Salem, N.C., 1982—, prof. English; editorial cons. SUNY Press, John Benjamins' Cultural Ludens series; cons. Tool Tech. Pub. Co.; advisor The Kenyon Rev., 1979-82; resident dir. Kenyon/Exeter Program, Exeter, Eng., 1980-81; dir. Poetry Circuit of Ohio, 1979-80. Author: The Play of the World, 1981, Imitation and the Image of Man, 1987, The Question of Value: Thinking Through Nietzsche, Heidegger and Freun, 1989, The Value(s) of Literature, 1990, The Value(s) of Literature, 1990, The Fate of Desire, 1990, The Origins of the Gods, 1991, Cotextual Authority and Aesthetic Truth, 1992, The Mysteries of Attention, 1993, The Golden Mean, 1994; The Site of Our Lives: The Self and the Subject from Emerson to Forecast, 1995. Office: Wake Forest Univ Dept English Winston Salem NC 27106

HANSARD, WILLIAM NEY, environmental scientist, consultant; b. Clarksville, Tenn., Dec. 27, 1951; s. David Grayson and Estelle Bell (Hart) H.; married; 1 child, Grayson Ney. BS in Biology, Austin Peay State U., 1974; postgrad., Vanderbilt U., 1988—. Registered environ. assessor, Calif.; registered profl. environmentalist, Tenn.; cert. hazardous materials mgr.; cert. environ. trainer. Chemist AWARE, Inc., Nashville, 1974-75, sr. ops. specialist, 1975-80; pres. Hansard & Assoc., Nashville, 1980-84; mgr. City Manchester, Tenn., 1984-86; project mgr. Eckenfelder, Inc., Nashville, 1986-90; dir. Summitt Environ. Group, Nashville, 1990-91; pres. Environ. Mgmt. Svcs., Inc., Nashville, 1991—. Developed bioremediation techs. and othr environ. techs., energy rsch. and devel.; contbr. articles to profl. jours. Mem. Creek Indian Tribe, Eufaula, Okla., 1951. Mem. Am. Water Works Assn., Nat. Environ. Tng. Assn., Tenn. Water and Wastewater Assn., Water Pollution Control Fedn., Inst. Hazardous Materials Mgmt., Masons (32 degree).

Episcopalian. Home and Office: Environ Mgmt Svcs Inc 5655 Valley View Rd Brentwood TN 37027-4688

HANSBERGER, WILLIAM LYLE, manufacturing executive; b. Worthington, Minn., Dec. 22, 1921; s. Floyd Lester and Edith May (Vail) H.; m. Constance Benna, Aug. 20, 1944 (div. 1962); children: Thomas, Gerald, Patricia; m. Clytee Smith, Nov. 29, 1985; children: Lisa, Joey, Susan. Student, Dunwoody Inst., 1942, IBM, 1944. Engr. trainee IBM, Chgo. and Endicott, N.Y., 1942-45; design engr. Nat. Acoustic Products, Chgo., 1944-46; owner Hansberger Tool & Die, Chgo., 1946-47; owner, founder Sportsmans Golf (Ram Golf), Chgo., 1948; pres. Sportsmans-Ram Golf, Chgo., 1948-70; v.p. mfg. and rsch. Ram Golf, Chgo., 1970-75, 91—; v.p., chmn. bd. Ram Golf, Pontotoc and Melrose Park, Ill., 1980-90, Melrose Park, Ill., 1980-90; v.p. mfg. and rsch. Colgate, Pontotoc, Miss., 1975-80; also bd. dirs. Ram Golf, Chgo.; owner and exec. v.p. Hansberger Precision Golf, Pontotoc, Miss., 1993—. Edn. advisor Itawamba Jr. Coll., Fulton, Miss., 1982; advisor external research adv. com. Miss. State U., Starkville, 1990-95; pres. Rotary, Pontotoc, 1970, N.E. Emergency Med. Svcs. Coun., Pontotoc, 1978; bd. dirs., Miss. Health Coun., Pontoc, 1976. Mem. Young Pres. Orgn. (elected mem. Chgo. chpt.). Office: Hansberger Precision Golf PO Box 300 Pontotoc MS 38863-0300

HANSCOM, FRED ROBERT, III, transportation executive; b. Washington, Apr. 11, 1942; s. Fred Robert and Elise (McCary) H.; m. Karen Ann Walborn, Aug. 18, 1974 (div. Dec. 1976). BSCE, Va. Poly. Inst., 1968, MSCE, 1970; postgrad., U. Md. Registered profl. engr., Va., Calif. Hwy. design engr. Arlington (Va.) County Govt., 1968-69; hwy. rsch. engr. Va. Hwy. Rsch. Coun., Charlottesville, 1969-72; sr. transp. rsch. engr. BioTech., Inc., Falls Church, Va., 1972-81; dir. Transp. Rsch. Corp., Haymarket, 1981—. V.p. Bull Run Mountain Civic Assn., Haymarket, 1982. Fellow Inst. for Transp. Engrs. (Pres.'s award 1975); mem. ASCE, Inst. Transp. Engrs. (exptl. traffic control device com.), Human Factors Soc., Nat. Forensic Ctr., Transp. Rsch. Bd. (com. on motorist info. systems, com. on methodology for evaluation hwy. improvements, tech. rev. panel truck size and weight, nat. com. uniform traffic control devices). Democrat. Baptist. Home and Office: 2710 Ridge Rd Haymarket VA 22069-1645

HANSEL, PATSY J., library director; m. James J. Govern. BA in History, U. N.C. Charlotte, 1970; MA in History, Wake Forest U., 1972; postgrad., U. N.C. Chapel Hill, 1972-73, MS in Libr. Sci., 1974. Libr. Warren Regional Planning Corp., Manson, N.C., 1974-75; dir. Onslow County Pub. Libr., Jacksonville, N.C., 1975-82; asst. dir. Cumberland County Pub. Libr. and Info. Ctr., Fayetteville, N.C., 1982-89; dir. Williamsburg (Va.) Regional Libr., 1989—; adj. instr. mgmt., sch. libr. and info. sci. N.C.C.U., 1988-90. Mem. editorial bd. (jour.) Am. Librs., 1988-90. Mem. curriculum adv. com. sch. libr. sci. U. N.C. Chapel Hill, 1980, pub. libr. devel. com. Va. State Libr. and Archives Bd., 1993. Mem. Va. Pub. Libr. Dirs. Assn. (pres. 1992-93), Va. Libr. Assn. (chair region III 1991-92, coun. 1991-92, editor jour. 1991-92), N.C. Libr. Assn. (pres. 1987-89, pub. libr. editor, assoc. editor and editor N.C. librs.), N.C. Pub. Libr. Dirs. Assn. (founding 1980, sec. 1980-81). Office: Williamsburg Regional Libr 515 Scotland St Williamsburg VA 23185-3625

HANSEL, STEPHEN ARTHUR, holding company executive; b. Long Branch, N.J., Aug. 13, 1947; s. Paul George and Helen (Stephens) H.; m. Sarah Holyfield, Nov. 16, 1985; children: Alexander, Nicholas; children by previous marriage: Derek, Andrew, Paula. B.A., Wesleyan U., 1969; M.B.A., Darden Sch. Bus. Adminstrn., 1971; cert. Advanced Mgmt. Program, Harvard Bus. Sch. Pres., CEO Hibernia Corp., Hibernia Nat. Bank, New Orleans; Bd. dirs. The Bankers Roundtable, World Trade Ctr. Founder, pres. Found. for Pulmonary Hypertension, Inc.; trustee Wesleyan U., New Orleans Mus. of Art; mem. greater New Orleans bus. coun. Republican. Office: Hibernia Corp PO Box 61540 313 Carondelet St New Orleans LA 70130-3109

HANSEL, WILLIAM, biology educator; b. Vale Summit, Md., Sept. 16, 1918; s. John W. and Helen M. (Sperlein) H.; m. Milbrey Downey, Aug. 16, 1942; children: Barbara, Kay. MS, Cornell U., 1947, PhD, 1949. Asst. prof. Cornell U., Ithaca, N.Y., 1949-52, assoc. prof., 1952-61, prof., 1961-90, Liberty Hyde Bailey prof., 1983-90, chmn. physiology dept., 1978-83; Gordon D. Cain prof. La. State U., Baton Rouge, 1990—; scientific adv. Merck, Sharp and Dohme, Rahway, 1980-85, Smith, Kline, Beecham, Westchester, Pa., 1986-91. Author: Genetic Engineering of Animals, 1990; contbr. over 300 articles to profl. jours. Maj. U.S. Army, 1941-46, ETO. Fellow AAAS; mem. Soc. Study Reprodn. (pres. 1976), Am. Physiol. Soc., Endocrine Soc., Soc. Exptl. Biology and Medicine (treas. 1975), Gamma Sigma Delta, Sigma Xi, Phi Kappa Phi. Office: Pennington Biomed Rsch Ctr B-1047 Baton Rouge LA 70808

HANSELMAN, RICHARD WILSON, entrepreneur; b. Cin., Oct. 8, 1927; s. Wendell Forest and Helen E. (Beiderwelle) H.; m. Beverly Baker White, Oct. 16, 1954; children: Charles Fielding, II, Jane White. BA in Econs, Dartmouth Coll., 1949. V.p. merchandising RCA Sales Corp., Indpls., 1964-66, v.p. product planning, 1966-69, v.p. product mgmt., 1969-70; pres. luggage div. Samsonite Corp., Denver, 1970-73, pres. luggage group, 1973-74, exec. v.p. ops., 1974-75, pres., 1975-77; sr. v.p. Beatrice Foods Co., Chgo., 1976-77, exec. v.p., 1977-80; pres., chief operating officer, dir. Genesco Inc., Nashville, 1980-86, chief exec. officer, 1981-86, pvt. investor, corp. dir., 1986—; bd. dirs. Becton Dickinson and Co., Arvin Industries, Gryphon Holdings Inc., Bradford Funds, Inc., Found. Health Corp., Imco Recycling Inc., BEC Group Inc., Wollin Products, Inc. Trustee Com. for Econ. Devel. Served with U.S. Army, 1950-52. Mem. Belle Meade Country Club, Union League, Chgo. Club, Golf Club of Tenn., Phi Kappa Psi. Office: 3017 Poston Ave Nashville TN 37203-1313

HANSEN, B(OBBY) J., management consultant, real estate investor and developer; b. Newton, Kans., Jan. 30, 1926; s. Clarence Nielsen and Blanche Eleanore (Andrews) H.; children: Cherokee E. Stock, Jody K. Abbott, Christopher Nielsen (dec.), Mimi E. Heldreth, Nicole M. Nickols. BS, U. So. Calif., 1949; MA Pub. Adminstrn., Am. U., 1966. Cert. sailbd. instr. U.S. Sailing Assn., Internat. Yachting Fellowship Rotarians, dingy sailboat sailor Brit. Royal Yachting Assn., internat. open water diver Brit. Sub-Aqua Club, Profl. Assn. Diving Instrs. Pres. Trak-Life Inc., Portland, Oreg., 1957-59; staff specialist Lockheed Missile & Space Co., Sunnyvale, Calif., 1959-61; program mgr. Ops. Research Inc., Silver Spring, Md., 1961-62; exec. v.p. Computer Dynamics Corp., Silver Spring, 1961-65; sr. v.p., cons. for U.S. Dept. Def. in Vietnam, John I. Thompson & Co., Washington, 1965-68; pres. Decision Research Corp., Washington, 1968-70; chmn., mem. Commn. on Change-in-Govt., county exec. Prince William County, Manassas, Va., 1970-71; county adminstr. Wythe County, Wytheville, Va., 1971-73; city mgr. Marion, Va., 1973-77; mgr. Williams Crane & Rigging Inc., Wytheville, 1977-80; prin. adminstr. and investors coordinator Royal Commn. Jubail (Saudi Arabia)-Yanbu, 1980-83; div. mgr. Al-Rushaid Investment Co., Dammam, Saudi Arabia, 1983-85; investor Hansen Assocs., Wytheville, 1985—; owner Surfun Co., InTech Internat. & Tax Shak; adj. faculty professorial lectr. Wytheville Community Coll., Am. U., New River Community Coll., Golden Gate U., Jubail, Saudi Arabia; guest lectr. fgn. affairs dept. Bluefield State U.; mem. adv. bd. ADP, No. Va. Community Coll.; boat safety coord. Southwest Va., Dept. Game and Inland Fisheries. Author: Practical Program Evaluation and Review Technique, 1962; guest editor Government Exec. Mag.; former columnist Southwest Va. Enterprise, columnist Smith County News; patentee in field. Mem., former chmn. small bus. adminstrn. coun. Met. Washington SBA, tech. adv. com. Claytor Lake, Va.; bd. dirs. No. Va. Police Acad.; founder, chmn. Master Swimming, Kingdom of Saudi Arabia; founder Va. Master Swimming Assn., 1st pres., 1979-80; mem. Spencer London UK Master Swim Team, Nat. Sr. Broadsailing Coun.; former pres. Va. Mt. Rogers affiliate Nat. Alliance for Mentally Ill, 1990-91; mem. Am. Businessmen's Alliance, Kingdom of Saudi Arabia; mem. Consumer Adv. Coun. SW Va., Mental Health Inst. Ensign USNR, 1943-47, lt., 1951-53, Korea, capt., 1966-67, Vietnam. Mem. FI-ABCI-Fedn. Internationale des Professions Immobilieres, International Platform Assn., Am. Inst. for Mgmt., Am. Mgmt. Assn., Nat. Assn. Real Estate Appraisers (sr.), Coll. Real Estate Appraisers, Armed Forces Mgmt. Assn. (past v.p.), Def. Orientation Conf. Assn., United Inventors and Scientists, Associated Gen. Contractors, Am. Waterworks Assn., Internat. City Mgrs. Assn., Internat. Platform Assn., English Speaking Union, Nat. Assn. County Adminstrs., Am. Soc. Pub. Adminstrs., Nat. Security Indsl. Assn., Am. Arbitration Assn. (nat. panel arbitrators), Naval Res. Officer's Assn., VFW (life mem.), SAR, Am. Legion (life, China Post 1), DAV (life), Nat. Space Club, U.S. Sailing Assn., U.S. Windsurfing Assn., U.S. Waterpolo Assn. (player), Brit. Amateur Swimming Assn., Danish Brotherhood in Am., Evergreen Country Club (Haymarket, Va.), Evansham Swim & Racquet Club (Wythe County), Va. Masters Assn. (pres. 1976-77), Chantilly Country Club (Va.), Rotary (former chmn. sr. olympics), Moose, Confederate Air Force of Am. (col.), Nat. Aviation Club, Beta Gamma Sigma (Beta of U. So. Calif. chpt.), Kappa Mu Epsilon (math. hon.), Sigma Nu, Phi Sigma Epsilon. Methodist. Home: PO Box 777 Wytheville VA 24382-0777

HANSEN, ELISA MARIE, art historian; b. Sarasota, Fla., July 14, 1952; d. Gotfred and Barbara (Ham) Hansen; m. Flemming Sogaard, 1987; children: Inga Marie, Anna Sofia. BA in Art History, Fla. State U., 1974; MA in Art History, So. Meth. U., 1982; MA, U. So. Fla., 1984. Edn. specialist Pinellas County Art Coun., Clearwater, Fla., 1977-78; curator of edn. Mus. Fine Arts, St. Petersburg, Fla., 1978-80; asst. prof. Eckerd Coll., St. Petersburg, 1985-88, adj. prof., 1988—; dir. adult and acad. programs, acting curator The John & Mable Ringling Mus. Art, Sarasota, 1989-95; adj. instr. Ringling Sch. Art and Design, 1992—. Contbr. articles and book reviews to profl. jours. Mem. Am. Assn. Mus., Coll. Art Assn. Republican. Lutheran.

HANSEN, ERIK DENSLOW, accountant; b. Miami, Fla., Oct. 30, 1940; s. Erik Oluf and Hester (Denslow) H.; m. Carol Ann Wheeler, Oct. 23, 1965. BSBA, U. Tampa, 1965. Cert. tax prof.; enrolled agent; accredited tax advisor; cert. practitioner of taxation, 1990. Asst. mgr. Winn-Dixie Stores, Miami, Tampa, Fla., 1956-65; jr. acct. Bigham & Carter, Tampa, 1965-66; sr. acct. Hansen & Pearson, CPAs, Hendersonville, N.C., 1969-75; ptnr. Costerisan, Engle & Hansen, Hendersonville, 1975-77; house parent Cope House, Brevard, N.C., 1974-78; v.p. bd. Denslow, Inc., Clermont, Fla., 1987—; pres., acct. Star Sapphire Co., Inc., Brevard, 1972—. Treas. Transylvania County Substance Abuse Task Force, Brevard, 1989-91; prs. Sapphire (N.C.) Whitewater Cmty. Club, 1969-75. With U.S. Army, 1966-68. Mem. Nat. Soc. Tax Profls. (pres. 1986-91, instr.), Nat. Assn. Tax Practitioners, Nat. Soc. Pub. Accts., N.C. Soc. Accts., Rotary (pres. Brevard 1985-86, treas. 1986—), Elks (acct. Brevard), Optimists (pres. Brevard 1977). Republican. Mem. Ch. of Christ. Home: 202 S Caldwell St Brevard NC 28712-3604 Office: Star Sapphire Co Inc 202 S Caldwell St Brevard NC 28712-3604

HANSEN, HAROLD JOHN, art educator; b. Chgo., June 18, 1942; s. Harold Melbourne and Florence Marion (O'Connell) H.; m. Martha Dianne Lyon, May 8, 1965; children: Daniel Charles, Susan Elziabeth. BFA, U. Ill., 1964; MFA, U. Mich., 1966. Instr. art Kendall Sch Design, Grand Rapids, Mich., 1966-69; asst. prof. art Ferris State Coll., Big Rapids, Mich., 1969-70; asst. prof. art U. S.C., Columbia, 1970-75, assoc. prof., 1975-86, prof. art, 1986—, faculty asst. to the dean, 1990-93, assoc. chair dept. art, 1995—. One-man shows include 12 N.Am. Artists, Buenos Aires, 1987-88, The Goodall Gallery, Columbia, 1988, The Portfolio Gallery, Columbia, 1989, Mus. York County, Rock Hill, S.C., 1992, Mus. Kershaw County, Camden, S.C., 1992, Anderson County Arts Ctr., 1996, numerous others. S.C. Arts Commn. and NEA grantee, 1975; S.C. Humanities Coun. grantee, 1995. Mem. Archaeology Soc. S.C. (v.p. 1988-89), Guild S.C. Artists (treas. 1989-93, sec./treas. 1974-75), S.C. Watercolor Soc. (bd. dirs. 1988—). Office: U SC Dept Art Columbia SC 29208

HANSEN, JOHN HENRY, secondary school teacher; b. Okla. City, May 19, 1966; s. John Henry and Donna (Joplin) H. BA in Letters, U. Okla., 1989; MA in Classics, U. Cin., 1992. Translator, researcher History of Sci. Collections U. Okla., Norman, 1992-93; adj. prof. Latin U. Ctrl. Okla., Edmond, 1993; tchr. Latin Westmoore H.S., Okla. City, 1993—, Moore (Okla.) H.S., 1994-95. Louise Taft Semple fellow U. Cin., 1990-92; Philip Nolan scholar, U. Okla., 1988. Mem. PHi Beta Kappa. Office: Westmoore HS 12613 S Western Ave Oklahoma City OK 73170

HANSEN, KENNETH D., lawyer, ophthalmologist; b. Seattle, Mar. 26, 1947; s. George R. and Elaine D. (Jacobsen) H.; m. Barbara Caleen, Oct. 8, 1976; 1 son, David Scott. BS in Psychology, U. Wash., 1969, JD, 1972, MD with honors, 1976. Bar: Wash. 1972, Mich. 1977, Ill. 1984, D.C. 1986, U.S. Supreme Ct. 1981. Diplomate Am. Bd. Ophthalmology. Legal counsel Assn. Wash. Bus., Olympia, 1972-73; asst. atty. gen. State of Wash., Seattle, 1973-74; v.p., gen. counsel Northwest Med. Rsch. Found. Seattle, 1976-86; pres. Internat. Health Found., 1986—; intern medicine U. Mich. Hosp., Ann Arbor, 1977, resident in ophthalmology, 1978-80; sr. med. staff Henry Ford Hosp., Detroit, 1981-82; dir. ophthalmology Carbondale Clinic, Ill., 1983-86, chmn. dept. surgery, gen. counsel, 1984-86; clin. asst. prof. ophthalmology and med. humanities So. Ill. U., Carbondale 1983-86; clin. asst. prof. ophthalmology U. Md., Balt., 1986—; med.-legal adv. com. U. Mich. Hosp. System; cons. Nat. Def. Med. Coll., China; charter coun. mem. practicing physicians adv. coun. to Sec. of U.S. Dept. Health and Human Svcs., 1992—; internat. med.-legal lectr. Assoc. editor Trauma, 1995—. Recipient U. Wash. Med. Thesis Award, Gold Medal Egyptian Med. Syndicate, 1986; William Wallice Wilshire Meml. scholar; Anna C. Dunlap Meml. scholar; Grad. Research fellow, 1975—; recipient Red Rose award Soc. Rsch. Adminstrs., 1989. Fellow Am. Coll. Legal Medicine (jud. council, model statutes com., Pres's. award 1989), Internat. Coll. Surgeons; mem. ABA, AMA, Wash. State Bar Assn. Mich. Bar Assn., Ill. Med. Soc. (med.-legal council), Ill. Bar Assn., Mich. Med. Schs. Council Deans (med.-legal adv. com.), Mich. Ophthalmology Soc. (research award 1981), Am. Acad. Ophthalmology, D.C. Bar Assn., Phi Delta Pi, Phi Eta Sigma, Pi Sigma Epsilon. Baptist. Assoc. editor Wash. Law Rev., 1971-72; contbr. articles to legal and med. profl. jours., publs. Home: 6501 Bright Mountain Rd Mc Lean VA 22101-1701 Office: 4601 Fairfax Dr Ste 100 Arlington VA 22203-1546

HANSEN, PETER JAMES, reproductive physiologist, researcher; b. Oak Park, Ill., Nov. 23, 1956; s. Peter Aloysious and Cathleen Ann (Forristal) H.; m. Nancy Ann Donovan, Mar. 15, 1980; 1 child, Meghan. BS, U. Ill., 1978; MS, U. Wis., 1980, PhD, 1983. Postdoctoral rsch. assoc. U. Fla. Dept. Biochemistry and Molecular Biology, Gainesville, 1983-84; asst. prof. U. Fla. Coll. Vet. Medicine, Gainesville, 1984-86; asst. prof. U. Fla. Dairy Sci. Dept., Gainesville, 1986-89, assoc. prof., 1989-93; prof. dairy and poultry sci. U. Fla., Gainesville, 1993—; mem. panel USDA CSRS Competitive Grants Animal Sci. Rev. Panel, Washington, 1990, 93, 94, 95, panel mgr., 1995. Contbr. articles to profl. jours. NIH postdoctoral fellow, 1984. Mem. Am. Dairy Sci. Assn. (Young Scientist award 1991), Soc. Study Reprodn., Am. Soc. Animal Sci. (Young Sci. award so. sect. 1994), Am. Soc. Reproductive Immunology. Democrat. Roman Catholic. Home: 3519 NW 27th Ter Gainesville FL 32605-2224 Office: Univ Fla PO Box 110920 Gainesville FL 32611-0920

HANSEN, ROBERT CARL, JR., naval officer; b. Kenosha, Wis., Mar. 7, 1954; s. Robert Carl Sr. and Billie Jean (Rixey) H.; m. Peggy Lynn Morris, Dec. 17, 1977; children: Erica Carol, Kelsey Jean. BS in Ocean Engring. with distinction, U.S. Naval Acad., 1977; MS in Internat. Rels., Troy State U. (Europe), 1993. Commd. ensign U.S. Navy, 1977, advanced through grades to comdr., 1992; combat info. ctr. officer USS Barbey, San Diego, 1978-80; officer programs mgr. Navy Recruiting Command, Iowa City, Iowa, 1980-82; flight tng. officer fighter squadrons, Naval Air Sta. Miramar, Calif., 1983-90; staff officer Cincusnaveur London, Washington, 1990-93. Dir edn., confirmation instr. Holy Spirit Luth. Ch., Centreville, Va., 1994—. Decorated Meritoroius Svc. medal, Naval Commendation medal, others. Mem. Tailhook Assn., U.S. Naval Acad. Alumni Assn. (life), VFW (life), Assn. Naval Aviation (life), Mensa, Heritage Found. Republican. Home: 13625 South Springs Dr Clifton VA 22024 Office: Navy Internal Programs Office CGN 701E 1111 Jefferson Davis Hwy Arlington VA 22202-1111

HANSON, DAVID ALAN, software engineer; b. Great Lakes, Ill., Nov. 23, 1956; s. John Berry and Roberta (Sargent) Sizemore; m. Dianna Lynn Hixson, May 20, 1989; stepchildren: Stanley Bob Capps, Jon Allen Capps. BS, U. So. Miss., 1978, MS, 1980. Programmer USDA/Miss. State U., Starkville, Miss., 1979-80; engr. Automated Warehouse, Tex. Ins., Dallas, 1980-83; evening instr. Dallas Community Coll. Dist., 1981-90; software engr. FSAS Systems E-Systems, Dallas, 1983-85, sr. software engr., instr. tng. dept., 1985-90; sr. software engr., lead engr. Spl. Systems E-Systems, Greenville, Tex., 1990-94; sr. software engr. Electrospace, Richardson, Tex., 1994-95, Tex. Instruments Aircraft Traffic Radar, McKinney, 1995—. Author: (tech. manuals) Introduction to C Language, 1985, Introduction to UNIX O.S., 1986, The Ada Language, 1986, Advance C Language, 1987, Advance Ada, 1988. Mem. Tex. Rep. Party, Dallas, 1986-89, PTA, Sulphur Springs, Tex., 1990-91, Dallas, 1989-90, Civil Air Patrol, Miss., 1972-83; cadet leader Civil Air Patrol, Dallas, 1988-90; asst. leader Boys Scouts Am., 1988-90. Recipient scholarship Air Force ROTC, U. So. Miss., 1976, assistantship dept. computer sci., 1978, Billy Mitchell award Civil Air Patrol, Gulfport, Miss., 1973, Amelia Earhart award, 1975. Mem. EEA (Sulphur Springs chpt.), Toastmasters (sec. 1990-91, pres. 1991-93), Sulphur Springs Theatre Group. Lutheran. Home: 729 Church St Sulphur Springs TX 75482-4422 Office: Texas Instruments Mc Kinney TX 75070

HANSON, HENRY ORAN, computer company executive, consultant; b. Luling, Tex., May 2, 1952; s. Oran Raymond and Ruth (Davidson) H.; m. Olivia Anne Bryant, Aug. 12, 1977 (div. Oct. 1993); children: Oran Henry, Noel Bryant. Student, U. Houston, 1972-75, Stanford U., 1979, U. Calif., Berkeley, 1980-81. Tape libr. Tex. Instruments, Houston, 1970, engring. technician, 1971-76; system analyst Tex. Instruments, Dallas, 1976-79; system analyst Intel Corp., Santa Clara, Calif., Austin, Tex., 1979-84; engring. mgr. DSC Comm. Corp., Plano, Tex., 1985-88; product mgr. Tandem Computers, Plano, 1989-91; sr. product line mgr. No. Telecom, Inc., Richardson, Tex., 1991-93; founder, pres. Hantech Systems Int'l, Inc., Luling, Tex., 1993—; cons. Tex. Elks Found. for Handicapped Children, Ottine, Tex., 1981-89, MCI Comm., Richardson, 1993—. Author: (seminar) International Communications Forum on Intelligent Networks, 1992. Deacon Disciples Christian Ch., Plano, 1990—; co-founder, bd. dirs. Hanson Found. for Human Advancement, Luling, 1993—. Mem. IEEE, Assn. for Computing Machinery. Office: Hantech Systems Int'l Inc 220 E Crockett St Luling TX 78648-2404

HANSON, LOWELL KNUTE, seminar developer and leader, information systems consultant; b. Langford, S.D., Sept. 28, 1935; s. Hans Jacob and Katherine Sofie (Hoines) H.; m. Mary Lou Heeney, Oct. 24, 1964; children: Victoria Lynn Hanson Wheeler, Thomas Lowell, Ronald Richard. BSEE, S.D. Sch. Mines and Tech., 1961. Cert. Cisco trainer. Field engr. supr. Control Data, Sunnyvale, Calif., 1961-62; mgr. systems test Control Data, Mpls., 1962-69; mgr. product mgmt. Control Data, France, 1969-71; mgr. test and integration Control Data, Mpls., 1971-74; communications cons. Control Data, Republic of South Africa, 1974-76; prin. applications engr. Control Data, Mpls., 1976-85; prin. systems engr. Martin Marrietta, Washington, 1986; pres. Viking Svcs., Centreville, Va., 1986—; LAN seminar dir. The Am. Inst., N.Y., 1987, 89; dir. and cons. Bus. Comm. Rev., Hinsdale, Ill., 1990-93, Am. Rsch. Group, 1993—. Author, presenter Trouble Shooting LANs seminar, 1988, Hands on LAN, 1990, Maintaining and Trouble Shooting Novell LANs, 1990. Pres. Homeowner Assn., Maple Grove, Minn., 1983-84. Fellow IEEE; mem. Toastmasters (pres. Maple Grove chpt. 1981-82, Capital area gov. 1986, Toastmaster of Yr. Maple Grove chpt. 1983, past pres. worldwide 84, Club of Yr. 84 Toastmasters). Republican. Office: Viking Svcs 6418 Overcoat Ln Centreville VA 22020

HANSON, RONALD WINDELL, cardiologist, lawyer, physicist; b. Jeffersonville, Ind., Apr. 30, 1947; s. Erwin D. and Bernice (Windell) H. BS summa cum laude, Ariz. State U., 1968, MS, 1969, PhD in Physics, 1972; MD, U. Ala., 1977, JD, Birmingham Sch. Law, 1995. Diplomate Am. Bd. Internal Medicine, Am. Bd. Cardiovascular Diseases. Asst. prof. physics U. Ala., 1972-74; resident in internal medicine and cardiology Good Samaritan Hosp., Phoenix, 1977-82; practice medicine specializing in cardiology, Gadsden, Ala., 1982—; pvt. law practice, 1995—. Served to lt. col. CAP. Fellow Am. Coll. Cardiology, Am. Coll. Angiology, Soc. for Cardiac Angiography and Interventions; mem. ABA, Nat. Health Lawyers Assn., Ala. Bar Assn., Phi Eta Sigma, Phi Kappa Phi. Office: 300 Med Ctr Dr Ste 500 Gadsden AL 35903-1156

HANSON, VICTOR ARTHUR, surgeon; b. Syracuse, N.Y., May 5, 1933; s. Victor Arthur Sr. and Dorothy (Burns) H.; m. Mary Diane Nadijcka, Sept. 13, 1985. AB, Princeton U., 1955; MD, U. Pa., 1959. Diplomate Am. Bd. Surgery. Intern then resident, instr. surgery U. Pa. Hosp., Phila., 1964-69, chief resident, 1968-69; instr. surgery SUNY, Syracuse, N.Y., 1969-71, asst. prof. surgery, 1971-78, clin. asst. prof. surgery, 1978-80; asst. prof. surgery Thomas Jefferson U., Phila., 1980-88; pvt. practice Syracuse, 1969-80; dir. rsch. VA Med. Ctr., Wilmington, Del., 1983-87; pvt. practice Wilmington, Del., 1987-90; staff surgeon Kaiser-Permanente, Atlanta, 1990-96; pvt. practice Atlanta, 1996—. Contbr. articles to profl. jours. Lt. USN, 1961-64, Vietnam. Grantee Am. Heart Assn., 1975, FDA, 1988. Fellow ACS; mem. AMA, Med. Assn. Ga., Med. Assn. Atlanta. Home: 3875 W Nancy Creek Ct Atlanta GA 30319

HANZAK, GARY A. JOHN, credit and leasing executive; b. Cleve., June 21, 1957; s. Richard and Amelia Maria (Sarna) H.; m. Veronica Lee Myers, Sept. 28, 1980 (div. Feb. 1987); m. Frances Watson Peay Herring, Aug. 11, 1990; 1 child, Heather Deniese. AAS summa cum laude., J. Sargeant Reynolds Coll., 1991. Dept. mgr. Progressive Cos., Cleve., 1979-85; pres. Com Pro, Richmond, Va., 1984-85; state contract adminstr. Copy Systems Inc., Richmond, 1985-86; recovery mgr. Freedlander Mortgage, Richmond, 1986-88; credit-leasing mgr. Copy Van Inc., Richmond, 1988—; mem. Alco Capital Resource Task Force, 1993. Author (corp. newsletter) Leasing Leader. Vol. Virginia Aveni Election Campaign, Cleve., 1974, YMCA Camp for the Deaf, Cleve., 1976. Recipient achievement award Dun & Bradstreet, 1990, Ace award, 1993. Mem. Pres. Club. Roman Catholic. Office: PO Box 6819 Richmond VA 23230-0819

HAPNER, ELIZABETH LYNN, lawyer, writer; b. Cleve., May 15, 1957; d. William Ralph Hapner and Anita F. (Thomas) Gillen; 1 child, Kyle William. BA in English, U. Fla., 1978, JD, 1980. Bar: Fla. 1981, U.S. Dist. Ct. (mid. dist.) Fla. 1986. Atty. Pub. Defender's Office, Bartow, Fla., 1981, State Atty.'s Office, Tampa, 1981-86; prin./pres. Elizabeth L. Hapner, P.A., Tampa, 1986—; dir. DUI Counterattack Sch., Tampa, 1985—, Prevention, Rehab., Edn. Program, Inc., Tampa, 1990—; adv. Children's Bd Task Force for Judiciary, Tampa, 1991-93. Author: Texas Probate Manual, 1983, Georgia Probate, 1985, Virginia Probate, 1987, Florida Juvenile Procedure, 1986, Florida Civil Procedure, 1990. Mem. Hillsborough County Democratic Adv. Coun., 1988—; trustee Carrollwood Recreation Dist., 1989-91; chair sr. pastor nom. com., Forest Hills Presbyn. Ch., 1989-91, 93-94, elder, 1995—; active mem. Jr. League of Tampa, Inc. Named Victim's Voice, Hillsborough County Victim Assistance Coun., 1991; recipient Pro Bono Svc. award Guardian Ad Litem's Office, Tampa, 1989-95. Mem. ABA, Fed. Bar Assn., Nat. Assn. Female Execs., Internat. Platform Assn., Fla. Bar Assn. (juvenile ct. rules com. 1991—, chair 1994-95, family law special needs of children com. 1992—, chair 1996—, bar fee arbitration com., 1989—, family law juvenile com. 1993—, vice chair 1995—), Fla. Acad. Trial Lawyers, Hillsborough County Bar Assn., Mensa. Democrat. Presbyterian. Home: PO Box 272998 Tampa FL 33688-2998 Office: 101 S Franklin St Ste 100 Tampa FL 33602-5327

HARAGAN, DONALD ROBERT, university administrator, geosciences educator; b. Houston, Apr. 15, 1936; s. Donald William and Mary (Thompson) H.; m. Willie Mae O'Berry, July 2, 1966; children—Shannon Lea, Shelley Jo. B.S., U. Tex., 1959, Ph.D., 1969; M.S., Tex. A & M U., 1960. Registered profl. engr., Tex. Research asst. Tex. A & M U., College Station, 1959-60; research scientist U. Tex., Austin, 1960-66, instr., 1966-69; asst. prof. Tex. Tech. U., Lubbock, 1969-72; assoc. prof. Tex. Tech U., Lubbock, 1972-78, prof. geosci., 1978—, dept. chmn., 1972-77, 80-83, interim dean, 1985, interim v.p., 1985-86, v.p. for acad. affairs and research, 1986-88, exec. v.p., provost, 1988—; interim pres. Tex. Tech. U., Lubbock, 1996, pres., 1996—. Contbr. articles in field to profl. jours. Mem. Am. Soc. Civil Engrs., AAAS, Am. Meteorol. Soc., Am. Water Resources Assn., Tex. Acad. Sci. Home: 6914 Nashville Dr Lubbock TX 79413-6002 Office: Tex Tech U Office of Provost Lubbock TX 79409

HARBECK, WILLIAM JAMES, real estate executive, lawyer, international consultant; b. Glenview, Ill., Dec. 16, 1921; s. Christian Frederick and Anna (Gaeth) H.; m. Jean Marie Allsopp, Jan. 20, 1945; children: John, Stephen, Timothy, Mark, Christopher. B.A., Wabash (Ind.) Coll., 1947; J.D., Northwestern U., 1950. Bar: Ill. 1950. Land acquisition atty. Chgo. Land

Clearance Commn., 1950-51; regional real estate dir. Montgomery Ward & Co., Chgo., 1951-68; asst. to pres., dir. corp. facilities Montgomery Ward & Co., 1968-70, v.p., dir. facilities devel., 1970-81; v.p. Montgomery Ward Devel. Corp., 1972-81; pres., chief exec. officer Montgomery Ward Properties Corp., 1974-81; pres. William J. Harbeck Assocs., 1981—; bd. dirs. Randhurst Corp., 1972-81, mem. exec. com., 1975-79. Mem. editorial bd. profl. jours.; contbr. articles to profl. jours. Bd. dirs. Chgo. Lawson YMCA, 1973-89, chmn. devel. com., 1979-89, mem. exec. com., 1985-89; bd. dirs. Greater North Michigan Ave Assn., Chgo., 1979-81; chmn. constrn. com. Chgo. United, 1979-81; co-chmn. Chgo. Bus. Opportunities Fair, 1980-81; mem. real estate com. Chgo. Met. YMCA, 1982-89, chmn. Bldg. Task Force, 1985-90; mem. pres.'s coun. Concordia Coll., River Forest, Ill., 1969-87, mem. bd. regents, 1987-96, mem. strategic planning com., 1989-91; trustee Concordia U. Found., 1996—; mem. planning com. Inst. for Philanthropic Mgmt., 1985-89; youth Bible and Bethel instr. Redeemer Luth. Ch., Highland Pk., Ill., 1965-89, congregation pres., 1968-70, 85-87, chmn. ch. growth com., 1982-89; mem. Eternal Shepherd Luth. Ch., Salem, S.C., 1990—, bd. elders, 1991-96, chmn., 1993-96; trustee Luth. Ch. Mo. Synod Found., 1975-76, 81-90, bd. mems., 1992—, mem. Synodical mission study commn., 1974-75, mem. dist. rsch. and planning com., 1981-90, mem. task force on synodical constn. by-laws and structure, 1975-79; bd. mems. Luth. Ch. ext. fund, 1989-92; mem. rsch. and planning com. No. Ill. Dist. Luth. Ch. Mo. Synod, 1984-89; nat. mem. Luth. Ch. Ext. Fund. Bd., 1991-94; sponsor Luth. Chs. for Career Devel., 1979-88; corp. chmn. U.S. Bond drive, Chgo., 1976; chief crusader Chgo. Crusade Mercy, 1976-78; divsn. chmn. Chgo. Cerebral Palsy campaign, 1977-78. Lt. (j.g.) USNR, 1942-46. Mem. Ill. Bar Assn., Internat. Coun. Shopping Ctrs. (bd. dirs. 1972-78, exec. com. 1975-78, govt. affairs com. 1977-89, awards com. 1980-83, urban com. 1980-83, lectr. 1969-89), Luth. Layman's League, Alpha Sigma Kappa, Phi Alpha Delta. Home and Office: 23 Eastern Point Keowee Harbours Salem SC 29676

HARBER, LORETTA MICHELE, retired corporate executive; b. Amarillo, Tex., Dec. 15, 1954; d. James Frank and Lillian Hatfield; 1 child, John Steven II; m. Franklin Douglas Harber, Jan. 9, 1980; stepchildren: Franklin D., Christina. AA, Hillsborough C.C., 1996. Pres. Balloonies, Inc., Tampa, Fla., 1984-93. Contbr. articles to profl. jours., 1987. Founder Italian Children Cultural Group, Tampa, 1986; pres. Sml. Bus. Networking, Tampa, 1987-88; bd. dirs. L'Unione Italiana, Tampa, 1988-89. Recipient appreciation Sml. Bus. Networking, 1987, Paolo Longo medal L'Unione Italiana, 1989. Mem. Nat. Assn. Balloon Artists (cert. master balloon artist), Small Bus. Network (pres. 1987-88), Leadership Brandon Alumni, Las Damas de St. Yago (liaison bd. dirs. 1995—), Italian Club (bd. dirs. 1988-89). Democrat. Roman Catholic. Home: PO Box 562 Valrico FL 33594-0562

HARBER, PATTY SUE, librarian; b. Vidalia, Ga., Nov. 12, 1955; d. Hugh Linton Harber and Estelle (Risner) Harber Knight. BA in English, Charleston (S.C.) So. U., 1977; M.Librarianship, Emory U., 1978. Cert. libr. Ga. Young adult libr. Moultrie-Colquitt County Libr., Moultrie, Ga., 1978-81; asst. dir. pub. svcs. West Ga. Regional Libr., Carrollton, 1981-82; head cataloging dept. main libr. Mercer U., Macon, Ga., 1985-89; head tech. svcs., sys. adminstr. Bartram Trail Regional Libr., Washington, Ga., 1990—. Reviewer books Voice of Youth Advocates, 1982-85. Mem. ALA, Internat. Sirsi Users Group (swap and shop coord. 1994—, pub. libr. spl. interest group leader 1994-96, program chmn. 1996—), Pilot Club of Washington (Ga.). Baptist. Home: 307 W Liberty St Washington GA 30673 Office: Bartram Trail Regional Library 204 E Liberty St Washington GA 30673

HARBIN, JOHN PICKENS, oil well company executive; b. Waxahachie, Tex., July 17, 1917; s. Elijah Pickens and Mary Joy (Beale) H.; m. Dorothy Lee Middleton, Dec. 13, 1920; children: Linda Ann Harbin Robuck. Student, Trinity U., San Antonio, 1935-37; BBA, U. Tex., 1939. Acct. Carter Oil Co., Tulsa, 1939-40, Creole Petroleum, Venezuela, 1940-42, 45-48; controller Halliburton Co., Duncan, Okla., 1948-59; v.p. fin. Halliburton Co., Duncan and Dallas, 1959-62; v.p. fin. and dir. Halliburton Co., Dallas, 1962-67; sr. v.p. fin., dir. Halliburton Co., 1967-72, chmn. bd., chief exec. officer, 1972-83; ret.; bd. dirs. Lone Star Techs., Dallas, chmn. bd., CEO, 1989—. Pres., trustee Boy Scout Cir. Ten Coun. Found., Dallas, 1967—; elder Highland Park Presbyn. Ch. Named to Tex. Bus. Hall of Fame, 1994. Mem. Am. Petroleum Inst. (hon. dir. 1983—), PEtroleum Equip. Suppliers Assn. (bd.dirs. 1965—, pres. 1974), Tex. Rsch. League (bd. dirs., past chmn. 1978-79), Southwestern Med. Found. (trustee 1975—), Navy League of U.S., Dallas Petroleum Club (past pres. and dir.), Brook Hollow Golf Club, Dallas Country Club (past dir.), The Brook Club, Beta Alpha Psi. Home: 4816 Lakeside Dr Dallas TX 75205-3121 Office: Lone Star Techs Ste 500 5501 Lyndon B Johnson Fwy Dallas TX 75240-6202 also: 3838 Oak Lawn Ave Ste 908 Dallas TX 75219-4510

HARBORDT, CHARLES MICHAEL, forest products executive; b. Houston, Apr. 8, 1942; s. Charles and Mary Lydia (Shumard) H.; m. Jackie Ward, June 23, 1960; children: Michelle, Katherine, Julie. BS, Stephen F. Austin U., Nacogdoches, Tex., 1963; MS, So. Meth. U., 1965; PhD, Tex. A&M U., 1970. Cert. environ. profl., Nat. Assn. Environ. Profls., Nat. Registry Environ. Profls.; registered environ. profl., environ. assessor. Assoc. chemist Texaco, Inc., Bellaire, Tex., 1965-67, sr. chemist, 1970-71; environ. dir. Temple Industries, Diboll, Tex., 1971-75; environ. dir. Temple-Eastex Inc., Diboll, 1975-80, energy, environ. and individual hygiene dir., 1980-90; v.p. Temple-Inland Forest Products Corp., Diboll, 1990—, Temple-Inland, Diboll, 1996—; mem. oper. com. Nat. Coun. Air and Stream Improvement, 1994—, chmn. chem. health effects and mgmt., 1994-97. V.p. United Fund, Lufkin, Tex., 1976; mem. adminstrn. bd. Lufkin Meth. Ch., chmn. bd. trustees, 1989-91, bd. trustees, 1996—; chmn. career edn. com. Lufkin High Sch., 1980-86. Robert A. Welch Found. fellow, 1963-65, Stephen F. Austin U. Disting. alumnus, 1994. Fellow Am. Inst. Chemists; mem. Am. Hardboard Assn. (chmn. environ. com. 1982-85, chmn. environ. com. 1983-85), TAPPI, Air Pollution Control Assn., Water Pollution Control Fedn., Diboll Jaycees, Angelina County (Tex.) C. of C. (bus. com. 1979, mem. edn. coun. 1984), Phi Kappa Phi, Phi Lambda Upsilon. Office: Temple Inland Inc PO Drawer N Diboll TX 75941

HARBOUR, PATRICIA ANN MONROE, poet; b. Winchester, Ind.; d. Cecil James and Opal (Crouse) Monroe; m. James Claude Harbour, July 29, 1972; children: Eric Arif Monroe Khan, Reneé Ann Monroe Harbour. A in Bus., Ball State U., 1956. Typist Lincoln Life Ins. Co., Ft. Wayne, Ind., 1957; office sec. Lincoln Life Ins. Co., Dallas, 1957; legal exec. sec. Russell E. Wise Law Firm, Union City, Ind., 1958-63; sales assoc., sr. sales assoc. Palais Royal (SRI Retailers, Inc.), Katy, Tex., 1993, sr. sales assoc., cosmetician, cons., 1994; instr. tap dancing, swimming. Contbr. poems World of Poetry (honorable award 1991), Sparrowgrass Poetry Forum, Inc., 1992, The Poetry Center Anthology, Arcadia Poetry Anthology (honorable award 1992), On the Threshold of a Dream. Vol. III (Outstanding Poets of 1994: Nat. Libr. of Poetry, Editor's Choice Outstanding Achievement award 1994). Mem. Internat. Soc. Poets (Poet of Merit award, 1992, 93), Sigma Sigma Sigma. Home: 310 Buckeye Dr Katy TX 77450-1633

HARBOUR, ROBERT RANDALL, state agency administrator; b. Oklahoma City, Dec. 13, 1949; s. Robert Roy and Anna Belle (Boatner) H.; m. Patti Rae Levine, Apr. 4, 1981; children: Ann Joelle, Robert Daniel. BA in Pub. Adminstrn., U. Ctrl. Okla., 1975. Clk. Okla. Dept. Human Svcs., Oklahoma City, 1974-76; interviewer Okla. Employment Security Commn., Oklahoma City, 1976-80, sr. interviewer, 1980-89, local office mgr. I, 1989-93, trainer, mgr. I, 1993—, tng. program writer, presenter, 1993—; job search workshop presenter, employment svc. programs presenter Okla. Employment Security Commn., Oklahoma City, 1987-93; facilitator job fair Gov.'s Coun. Small Bus., Oklahoma City, 1990, Mayor's Employer Adv. Coun., Oklahoma City, 1992, Oklahoma City C.C., 1991. Contbr: (workbook) Job Search Workshop Workbook, 1989; writer: (tng. programs) State-Mandated Manager Training Program, 1993, Non-Supervisory Employee Training Program, 1993, New Employee Training Program, 1993. Recipient Spl. Merit award Mil. Order Purple Heart, Oklahoma City, 1991, Career Day Program Appreciation award Pvt. Industry Coun., Oklahoma City, 1991, Honorable Mention award ASTD Tng. Manual, 1994. Mem. ASTD (Honorable Mention for tng. manual ctrl. Okla. chpt. 1994, Honorable Mention award for program design ctrl. Okla. chpt. 1995), Internat. Assn. Pers. in Employment Svc., Nat. Forensic League, Internat. Platform Assn. Democrat. Home: 1740 Carlisle Rd Oklahoma City OK 73120-1117 Office: Okla Employment Security Commn 2401 N Lincoln Blvd Oklahoma City OK 73105-4402

HARBUCK, EDWIN CHARLES, insurance agent; b. Shreveport, La., Mar. 5, 1934; s. Charles Adam and Elsie (Owens) H.; m. Delores Threlkeld, June 10, 1955; children: Jonathan S., Edwin Seth, Christopher L., Charles Adam II. BS, Centenary Coll., 1956. CLU. Vice pres., gen. mgr. Harbuck Sporting Goods, Inc., Shreveport, 1958-63; agt. Prudential Ins. Co. of Am., Shreveport, 1963—. Chmn. bd. trustees First Bapt. Ch. Sch., Shreveport, 1978; mem. La. State Civil Svc. Commn., 1981-93; chmn. Centenary Coll. Gt. Tchrs. Scholar Campaign, Shreveport, 1992-93; campaign chmn. United Way N.W. La., Shreveport, 1989, pres., 1993; trustee Centenary Coll. La., 1990; v.p. La. Civil Svc. League, 1994—. Recipient Monte M. Lemann Pub. Svc. award La. Civil Svc. League, New Orleans, 1985, Clyde E. Fant Meml. award for Cmty. Svc., 1994; named Shreveport Outstanding Young Man, Jaycees, 1962, Outstanding Young Men in Am., U.S. Jaycees, Washington, 1970. Mem. Chartered Life Underwriters (pres. Shreveport chpt. 1976), Tax Inst. Arklatex, Estate Planning Coun., Shreveport Assn. Life Underwriters, Million Dollar Roundtable (life), Shreveport Club, Pierremont Oaks Tennis Club. Baptist. Home: 4364 Richmond Ave Shreveport LA 71106-1418 Office: Harbuck & Ridley 400 Travis St Ste 808 Shreveport LA 71101-3111

HARDAGE, PAGE TAYLOR, health care administrator; b. Richmond, Va., June 27, 1944; d. George Peterson and Gladys Odell (Gordon) Taylor; m. Thomas Brantley, July 6, 1968; 1 child, Taylor Brantley. AA, Va. Intermont Coll., Bristol, 1964; BS, Richmond Profl. Inst., 1966; MPA, Va. Commonwealth U., Richmond, 1982. Cert. tchr. Competent toastmaster, dir. play therapy svcs. Med. Coll. Va. Hosps., Va. Commonwealth U., Richmond, 1970-90; dir. Inst. Women's Issues, Va. Commonwealth U., Va., Richmond, 1986-91; adminstr. Childhood Lang. Ctr. at Richmond, Inc., 1991—; bd. dirs. Math. and Sci. Ctr. Found., Richmond, Emergency Med. Svcs. Adv. Bd., Richmond. Treas. Richmond Black Student Found., 1989-90, Leadership Metro Richmond Alumni Assn.; bd. dirs. Richmond YWCA, 1989-91; group chmn. United Way Greater Richmond, 1987; bd. dirs. Capital Area Health Adv. Coun.; commr. Mayors Commn. of Concerns of Women, City of Richmond. Mem. NAFE, ASPA, Adminstrv. Mgmt. Soc., Internat. Mgmt. Coun. (exec. com.), Va. Recreation and Park Soc. (bd. dirs.), Va. Assn. Fund Raising Execs., Rotary Club of Richmond. Unitarian. Office: Childhood Lang Ctr at Richmond Inc 4202 Hermitage Rd Richmond VA 23227-3755

HARDAWAY, ANFERNEE DEON (PENNY HARDAWAY), professional basketball player; b. Memphis, July 18, 1972. Grad., Memphis State U. Guard, forward Orlando Magic, 1993—. Appeared in film Blue Chips, 1994. Named to Newcomer of Yr. in the BMC, 1992-93, NBA All-Rookie First Team, 1993, Eastern Conf. All-Star Team, 1994-95, 95-96, All NBA First Team, 1995, Dream Team III, 1996; Nat. H.S. Player of Yr. award Paracle Mag., 1990-91; 1st team All Am. Memphis State U., 1992-93; honored by retiring of Jersey at Memphis State U., 1994. Office: Orlando Magic Orlando Arena One Magic Pl Orlando FL 32801*

HARDCASTLE, VALERIE GRAY, philosophy educator; b. Frederick, Md., Nov. 3, 1963; d. Robert Hugh and Sherry Dean (Gray) Walker; m. Gary Lockwood Hardcastle, July 22, 1989; children: Kiah, Cheshire, John Quinton. AB in Philosophy with high distinction, U. Calif., Berkeley, 1986; MA in Philosophy, U. Houston, 1987; PhD in Cognitive Sci. and Philosophy, U. Calif., San Diego, 1994. Teaching fellow dept. philosophy U. Houston, 1986-87; reader dept. philosophy U. Calif., San Diego, 1988-91, teaching asst. humanities program, 1988-90, writing instr. summer bridge program, 1989; asst. prof. philosophy Va. Poly. Inst. and State U., Blacksburg, 1992—; lectr. in field. Contbr. articles to profl. jours. Eagle scholar, Mary Gibbs Jones scholar, Nat. Merit scholar, Phi Beta Kappa Alumni scholar, 1982-83; fellow AAUP Ednl. Found., McDonnell-Pew Found. for Cognitive Neurosci. Rsch., U. Calif.-San Diego, San Diegan Minority fellow U. Houston, 1990-91; Va. Poly. Inst. and State U. grantee, 1992-94. Mem. Am. Philos. Assn., Brain and Behavior Assoc., Cognitive Neurosci. Soc., Internat. Soc. for History, Philosophy and Social Studies in Biology, Philosophy of Sci. Assn., Soc. for Philosophy and Psychology, So. Soc. for Philosophy and Psychology, Va. Philos. Assn., Golden Key, Phi Beta Kappa. Office: Va Poly Inst and State Univ Dept Philosophy Blacksburg VA 24061-0126

HARDEE, LUELLEN CARROLL HOOKS, school psychologist; b. Dublin, N.C., May 19, 1948; d. Charlie Lee Thomas and Mary Lou (Lewis) Carroll; m. Richard Eugene Hooks Jr., Dec. 20, 1969 (div. Jan. 1986); m. Jasper Ronald Hardee, Apr. 29, 1995. BS in Speech Pathology and Audiology, East Carolina U., 1969; MEd in Counseling, U. N.C., 1978; PhD in Sch. Psychology, N.C. State U., 1989. Speech pathologist, audiologist Robeson County Schs., Lumberton, N.C., 1970-71, Rowan County Schs., Salisbury, N.C., 1971, Stanly County Schs., Albemarle, N.C., 1971-78; counselor exceptional children, psychologist Montgomery County Schs., Troy, N.C., 1978-81; psychol. asst. Lions Clinic for the Blind N.C. State U., Raleigh, 1981; coord. psychol. svcs. Brunswick County Schs., Southport, N.C., 1981-83; psychology instr. Carteret Community Coll., Morehead City, N.C., 1984; part-time sch. psychologist Carteret County Schs., Beaufort, N.C., 1985-87, sch. psychologist, 1989—; speech pathologist Stanly County Headstart, Albemarle, summers 1971-73, dir., 1973-76, coord. handicapped children programs, summer 1977. Solicitor Cancer Fund Drive, Albemarle, 1977-78; mem. com. N.C. Azalea Festival, Wilmington, 1981—; hostess Hospice-Festival of Trees, Beaufort, 1989; bd. dirs. Carteret County Domestic Violence Program, 1992—, chair fashion show, 1993-95, chair edn. com., 1994-96; mem. Carteret Residents for Excellence in Edn., 1990-95, Carteret County Child Rev. and Child Protection Teams, 1990—, chair, 1992-93. Mem. NCSPA (treas. 1990-92). Home: 104 Rattan Ln Morehead City NC 28557-9677 Office: Carteret County Bd Edn 107 Safrit Dr PO Box 600 Beaufort NC 28516

HARDEGREE, GLORIA JEAN FORE, health services administrator; b. Atlanta, July 18, 1940; d. Lee Harrison and Corine Joan (Atkinson) Fore; m. Guy H. Hardegree Jr., Jan. 23, 1960; children: Pamela Jean Reas, Sherrie Etta Drew. Diploma in nursing, Crawford W. Long Hosp., 1971; BS, Coll. St. Francis, 1982; M in Counseling, Liberty U. RN, Ga.; cert. occupational health nurse; cert. case mgr. Occupational health nurse Dobbs House Inc., Dallas, 1974-75, AT&T, Atlanta, 1974; occupational health nurse Ga. Power Co., Atlanta, 1976—, coord. Wellness Program. Recipient Schering award, 1987, Nurse of Yr. award, Med. Products S.E., 1991. Mem. Ga. Assn. Occupational Health Nurses (recording sec., Nurse Yr. award, 1987), Atlanta Assn. Occupational Health Nurses. Office: Southern Co Bin 10013 333 Piedmont Ave NE Atlanta GA 30308

HARDEN, DOYLE BENJAMIN, import-export company executive; b. Banks, Ala., Oct. 15, 1935; s. J.C. and Gladis C. (Romine) H.; m. Elvira Harden; children: Janet Denice, Misty Lyn, Dusty Lyn, Wesley Doyle, Crystal Elvira. Student pub. schs. Salesman, Gordon Foods, Atlanta, 1955-64; pres. Kwik Shop Markets, Columbus, Ga., 1964-73, Exportaciones Chico, S.A., Juarez, Mex., 1973-76, Chico Arts, El Paso, Tex., 1976—, Transp. Interoceanica, S.A., Honduras, C.Am., 1975-80. Office: 1045 Humble Pl El Paso TX 79915-1008

HARDEN, GAIL BROOKS, elementary school educator; b. Fulton County, Ga., Feb. 7, 1950; d. Dorsey D. and Gippie C. Brooks; m. Jack H. Harden, July 14, 1978; children: Kevin G. Jackson, Jeremy J., Erin B. BS, Brenau Coll., Gainesville, Ga., 1974; MEd, U. Ga., 1978; EdS, West Ga. Coll., 1991. Cert. reading specialist, Ga. Tchr. Barrow County Schs., Winder, Ga., 1974-78; with Sand Hill Sch., Carrollton, Ga., 1980—, coord. elem. testing, 1988-89; dir. Sand Hill after-sch. program Carroll County Schs., Carrollton, Ga., 1989-90; coord. elem. testing Sand Hill Sch., tech. coord., 1992—. Named Tchr. of Yr., Sand Hill Sch., 1986. Mem. Internat. Reading Assn., Christian Educators Assn. Internat. Home: 340 Laurel Rd Carrollton GA 30117-8847 Office: Sand Hill Sch 45 Sandhill School Rd Carrollton GA 30116-9736

HARDEN, PATRICK ALAN, journalist, news executive; b. Twickenham, Eng., Aug. 13, 1936; s. Ernest William and Annie Ceridwen (Jones) H.; m. Connie Marie Graham, Nov. 2, 1963; children: Marc Graham, Ceri Marie. Cert. in journalism, Ealing (Eng.) Tech. Coll., 1957. With UPI, 1960-78; regional exec. UPI, London, 1968-69; European picture mgr. UPI, London and Brussels, 1969-72; regional exec. UPI, Detroit, 1973-75; gen. mgr. UPI Can. Ltd., Montreal, 1976-78, UP Can., Toronto, 1979-82; dir., sec. UP Can., 1979-82; treas. UPI Can. Ltd.; gen. mgr. Edmonton (Alta.) Sun, 1982-84, pub., 1984-92; v.p. Toronto Sun Pub. Corp., 1989-94; v.p., bur. chief Washington, 1992-94; Washington columnist Toronto Sun Pub. Corp., 1994—. Mem. senate U. Alta, 1991-92. Recipient Merit award City of Edmonton, 1992. Mem. Can.-Am. Bus. Coun., Nat. Press Club.

HARDESTY, STEPHEN DON, secondary education educator; b. Oak Park, Ill., Feb. 23, 1945; s. Donald A. and Corinne M. (Wilson) H.; m. Linda C. Shafer, Aug. 2, 1968; 1 child, Heather Anne. BA in Geology, U. South Fla., 1967; postgrad., U. Mo., 1968; MS in Bus., Rollins Coll., 1977. Cert. tchr., Fla. Tchr. earth sci. and math. Maitland (Fla.) Jr. High Sch., 1968-69; tchr. earth, life and physical scis., geography Conway Jr. High Sch., Orlando, 1969-87, chmn. sci. dept., 1981-87; adj. instr. earth sci., astronomy, meteorology Valencia C.C., 1977—; tchr. earth and environ. sci., astronomy, dual enrollment geology Dr. Phillips Sr. High Sch., Orlando, 1987—; tchr. for tchr. inservice insts. in earth scis. Orange County Schs./Valencia C.C., 1982-88; instr. summer inst. in oceanography/hist. geology Valencia C.C.; mem. earth/space scis. middle/jr. sect. State Ednl. Frameworks Com., 1985; chmn. earth/space scis. State Ednl. Materials Coun., 1986-88; mem. earth/space scis. sr. high and middle/jr. sects. State Course Performance Standards Com., 1986-87; mem. earth/space sci. sect. State Tchr. Cert. Writing Team, U. South Fla., 1987-89, State Tchr. Cert. Specialization Validation Team, 1987-88, mem. State Minimum Performance Statdards in Sci. Writing and Review Coms., 1987-88; mem. State Tchr. Cert.-Passing Score Com. Earth Sci., U. Ctrl. Fla., 1989; mem. student performace test writing team Fla. State U., 1989-90; owner, tartan weaving instr. Caithness Shuttle Crafts. Past pres. Greenview Homeowners Assn., Orlando. Mem. Nat. Assn. Geology Tchrs. (Fla. Earth Sci. Tchr. of Yr. 1992), Nat. Earth Sci. Tchrs. Assn., Soc. Econ. Paleontologists and Mineralogists, Fla. Assn. Sci. Tchrs., Fla. Earth Scis. Tchrs. Assn., St. Andrews Soc. Ctrl. Fla. (past pres.), Scottish-Am. Soc. Ctrl. Fla. (past chmn. bd.), Clan Gunn Soc. North Am. (past pres.). Republican. Office: Dr Phillips High Sch 6500 Turkey Lake Rd Orlando FL 32819-4718*

HARDIN, CLYDE DURHAM, federal senior executive scientist; b. Fort Worth, Tex., May 26, 1925; s. Elbert Fant and Mabel Bradley (Clyde) H.; m. Carolyn Chaney, Sept. 4, 1948; children: Clyde D., Charles K., Clifton D. BS in physics, math., Wake Forest Univ., 1948; postgrad., Univ. Md., 1950-58. Physicist/elec. sci. group leader Nat. Bureau of Standards, Washington, 1948-53; rsch. sect. chief Diamond Ordance Fuze Labs., Washington, 1953-58; lab. chief U.S. Army Harry Diamond Labs., Washington, 1958-69; cons. to sci. adv. mil. assistance commdr. MACV, Saigon, 1967-68; spl. asst. to asst. sec. army R&D for SEAsia Dept. of Army, Washington, 1969-72; dir. U.S. Def. RDTE Group Seoul, Korea, 1972-73; dir. U.S. Army EW Lab USA Electronics Command, Ft. Monmouth, N.J., 1973-79; assoc. tech. dir., to tech. dir. USA Electronics R&D Command, Adelphi, Md., 1979-81; cons. in def. electronics Clyde D. Hardin COns., Rockville, Md., 1981-86; army mem. Joint Svc. Adv. Group Lincoln Labs, Lexington, 1960-65; army scientific adv. panel Dept. Army, Washington, 1969-71; army chmn. EW panel Def. Tech. Coord Paper, Washington, 1976-77; dir. working group NATO Long Range Study of Surveillance, 1971. Contbr. article to profl. jour.; patentee in field. Chmn., bd. trustees Unitarian Ch. Rockville, 1958-61; co-founder, trustee Citizens for Good Govt., 1953-64; pres., co-founder Twinbrook Swimming Pool Corp., Rockville, 1955-56; pres. Rockville Little Theatre Rockville, 1960-61; pres. Rockville Civic Assn. With U.S. Navy, 1943-46. Decorated SecDef. Medal for Meritorious Civil Svc. Dept. Defense, Washington, 1973, Army Medal for Merit. Svc., Sec. of Army, Washington, 1971, Korea Presdl. Cheonsu medal, Seoul, 1976, Disting. Svc. award City of Rockville, 1956. Fellow IEEE (life, chmn. sav sect.); mem. Am. Def. Preparedness Assn. (fire control rep.), Assn. Old Crows (tech. adv.), Assn. U.S.Army, Habitat for Humanity, The Landing Club.

HARDIN, DALE WAYNE, retired law educator; b. Peoria, Ill., Sept. 9, 1922; s. James P. and Lucille Maureen (Elgin) H.; m. Sandra L. Gorzen, July 3, 1939; children: Bradley J., Stacy K. Nolen, Rebecca M., J. Scott Keaton. AB in Polit. Sci., George Washington U., 1949, JD, 1951. Bar: Va. 1951, D.C. 1951, U.S. Dist. D.C. 1951, U.S. Ct. Appeals (D.C. cir.) 1951. Assoc. Mills & Partridge, Washington, 1951; spl. agent FBI, Washington, 1951-54; fin. counsel ICC, Washington, 1954-55, legis. counsel, 1955-64, presdl. appointee as commr., 1967-77, vice chmn., acting chmn. agy., 1971-73, chmn. rates divsn., 1975-77; Presdl. appointee, mem. Adminstrv. Conf. U.S., 1969-72; dir. dept. transp. and comm. U.S. C. of C., Washington, 1964-66; v.p. govt. affairs Overmeyer Co., Washington, 1966-67; spl. counsel Am. Trucking Assn., Washington, 1967; assoc. prof. polit sci. S.W. Tex. State U., San Marcos, Tex., 1977-89; assoc. prof. emeritus S.W. Tex. State U., 1989—, acting dean sch. liberal arts., 1986-87, chmn. dept. home econs., 1990-92; gen. counsel Transp. Assn. Am., Washington, 1959; moderator 14th Ann. Seminar, State Bar Tex., 1982, moderator profl. devel. program gen. paralegal skills, 1988, standing com. on legal assts., 1988—; chmn. Tex. forum IV Conf. Legal Asst. Educators, 1985, chair forum VII, 1988; presenter papers in field. Bus. sec. George Washington U. Sch. Law Rev., 1951. With USMC, 1942-46, PTO, 2nd lt. Res. Mem. Nat. Assn. Regulatory Utility Commns., Interstate Commerce Commn. Practitioners, Soc. Former Spl. Agents FBI. Fed. Bar Assn., Va. State Bar., D.C. Bar, Phi Delta Phi. Home: 2203 Onion Creek Pky Unit 3 Austin TX 78747-1600

HARDIN, DONALD WAYNE, standards and industrial manufacturing engineer; b. Ponca City, Okla., Dec. 29, 1950; s. Jack Paul and Louvona Bell (Gingerich) H.; m. Linda S. Bright, Feb. 28, 1976; children: Robert D., Jenny G. AS magna cum laude, No. Okla. Coll., 1985; postgrad., Okla. State U., 1986-90. Cert. systems engr. Prodn. planner Smith Gruner, Ponca City, Okla., 1978-82; assoc. indsl. engr. Smith Internat., Inc., Ponca City, Okla., 1982-85, stds. engr., 1985—. Tng. dir. Sunset Bapt. Ch., Ponca City, 1980-84, chmn. pers. com., 1989-91, chmn. recreation com., 1991-94; coach, asst. coach children's baseball, football, basketball and soccer, Ponca City, 1982-89; coach, pitcher Ponca City Softball Assn., 1972—. Mem. Inst. Indsl. Engrs. (sr.). Home: 2036 Mary St Ponca City OK 74601-1908 Office: Smith Internat Inc 1405 N Waverly St Ponca City OK 74601-2135

HARDIN, ELIZABETH ANN, academic administrator; b. Charlotte, N.C., Nov. 21, 1959; d. William Gregg and Ann (Astin) H. BBA magna cum laude, U. Ga., 1981; MBA, Harvard U., 1985. Spl. project coord. NCNB Corp., Charlotte, 1981-82, investment officer, 1982-83; cons. Booz, Allen & Hamilton, Atlanta, 1985-86; asst. placement dir. Harvard U. Bus. Sch., Boston, 1986-87, dir. MBA program adminstrn., 1987-89, acting placement dir., 1988-89; mgr. employment Sara Lee Hosiery, Winston-Salem, N.C., 1990-92, mfg. mgr., 1992-93; dir. product devel. Sara Lee Hosiery, Winston-Salem, 1993-94; mng. cons. Info. Sci. Assocs., Charlotte, N.C., 1994-95; assoc. vice chancellor for bus. planning U. N.C., Charlotte, 1995—; cons., developer adminstrv. policy guide Chelsea (Mass.) Pub. Schs., 1989-90. Mem. adv. bd. Harvard Non-Profit Fellowship, 1986—; chmn. Harvard Non-Profit Mgmt. Fellowship, 1989-96; active AIDS Action Com. Mass., Holy Comforter, Charlotte; mem. total quality edn. task force N.C. Bus. Com. on Edn., 1992-93; troop leader Girl Scouts U.S.A.; mem. Leadership Charlotte, 1996—. Fellow State Farm Co. Found., 1980, Delta Gamma Found., 1983. Mem. Assn. for Corp. Growth (bd. advisors 1996—), Harvard Bus. Sch. Assn., Phi Kappa Phi, Delta Gamma (pres. alumnae Charlotte 1982-83). Republican. Office: U of NC at Charlotte Charlotte NC 28223

HARDIN, HAL D., lawyer, former U.S. attorney, former judge; b. Davidson County, Tenn., June 29, 1941. B.S., Middle Tenn. State U., 1966; J.D., Vanderbilt U., 1968; attended State Jud. Coll., Reno, 1976. Bar: Tenn. 1969, D.C. 1983, Tex. 1990, U.S. Ct. Claims, U.S. Tax Ct., U.S. Ct. Mil. Appeals, U.S. Supreme Ct. Fingerprint technician FBI, 1961; dir. St. Louis Job Corps Ctr., 1968; asst. dist. atty. Nashville, 1969-71; pvt. practice, 1971-75; presiding judge Nashville Trial Cts., 1976-77; U.S. atty. Middle Dist. Tenn., 1977-81; practice law Nashville, 1981—; instr. govt. Aquinas Coll., Tenn. State Coll., 1975-76; adj. prof. fed. sentencing Nashville Sch. Law, 1994. Bd. dirs. Leadership Nashville, 1983, Capital Case Resource Ctr., 1988-95; vol. Peace Corps, Colombia, South America, 1963-65. Named one of Best Lawyers in Am., 1993-96. Mem. ABA, Nat. Assn. Criminal Def. Attys., Nashville Bar Assn. (bd. dirs. 1983-85, v.p. 1985), Tenn. Bar Assn. (gen.

counsel 1982-90), D.C. Bar, Tex. Bar Assn., Tenn. Criminal Def. Attys., Am. Bd. Trial Advs. (sec. Tenn. chpt. 1987, nat. bd. dirs. 1988-89, pres. Tenn. chpt. 1990), Master Inns of Ct. Office: 219 2nd Ave N Ste 300 Nashville TN 37201-1618

HARDIN, HILLIARD FRANCES, microbiologist; b. Columbia, S.C., Dec. 12, 1917; d. Lawrence Legare and Addria Eugenia (Chreitzberg) H. AB, Duke U., 1939, MA, 1949, PhD, 1953. Bacteriologist Bowman Gray Sch. of Medicine, Winston-Salem, N.C., 1941-42; instr. Med. Sch. Duke U., Durham, N.C., 1948-53; from instr. to asst. prof. Med. Sch. U. Ark., Little Rock, 1954-58; rsch. assoc. Sch. of Medicine Duke U., 1958-63; chief mycology tng. unit C.D.C., Atlanta, 1963-68; dir. microbiology dept. VA Hosp., Little Rock, 1968—. With USNR, 1942-45. Mem. N.Y. Acad. Scis., Med. Mycology Soc. Am., Am. Bus. Women's Assn. (v.p. 1986-87, pres. 1987-88, Top 10 of the Yr. 1988). Republican. Methodist. Home: 301 Kings Row Dr Apt 401 Little Rock AR 72207-4169

HARDIN, JAMES EDMOND, executive recruiter; b. Elizabethton, Tenn., Aug. 23, 1937; s. Crawford Edmond and Laura Evelyn (Peters) H.; m. Marilyn Jaye Frye, Jan. 2, 1960; children: Gregory Stephen, David Philip. BS, Lincoln Meml. U., 1959; degree in chem. engring. (hon.), U. Miss., 1972. Lab. technician Am. Bemberg Corp., Elizabethton, 1959-60; human resources rep. Monsanto, Pensacola, Fla., 1961-69; S.E. recruiting mgr. Monsanto, Atlanta, 1969-73; profl. recruiting mgr. Monsanto, St. Louis, 1973-77; mgr. employment Philip Morris USA, Richmond, Va., 1977-94; S.E. region mgr. recruiting Philip Morris USA, Atlanta, 1994-95; mgr. exec. recruiting Philip Morris USA, N.Y.C., 1995—. Asst. scoutmaster Boy Scouts Am., Richmond, 1984-85. Mem. So. Coll. Placement Assn. (chmn. new membership), Va. Coll. Placement Assn. (pres.), Midwest Coll. Placement Assn., S.W. Coll. Placement Assn. Republican. Methodist. Office: Philip Morris USA 120 Park Ave New York NY 10017

HARDIN, JAMES MICHAEL, health sciences educator, researcher; b. Mobile, Ala., Mar. 14, 1956; s. James Morris and Willonese (Howell) H.; m. Anna Kathryn Chism, May 19, 1984; 1 child, David Michael. BA in Math.-Philosophy magna cum laude, U. West Fla., 1978; MS in Rsch. Design and Stats., Fla. State U., 1981; MA in Maths., U. Ala., 1984, PhD in Applied Statis., 1985. Math. statis. Freeman Math. Lab., Eglin AFB, Fla., 1979-81, 1984-86; asst. prof. statis. Miss. State U., Mississippi State, 1986-88; asst. prof. biostatis. U. Ala., Birmingham, 1988-91, assoc. prof. biostatis., 1991—, dir. Biostatistics Core, dir. Rsch. and Data Analysis Core, 1991—, scientist AIDS Ctr., 1991—, preceptor Caries Rsch. Program, Sch. Dentistry, 1992—, assoc. prof. nutrition scis., preventive medicine, 1993—, assoc. prof. health info. mgmt., 1993—, scientist Ctr. for Aging, 1993—; assoc. prof. counseling, human svcs. and founds. U. Ala., 1993—, assoc. prof. gerontology and geriatric medicine, 1994—; dir. rsch. and data analysis core Civitan Internat. Ctr., U. Ala., 1991—, biostatistics core Head Start Nat. Rsch. Evaluation Team, Civitan Internat. Ctr., 1991—; dep. dir. CARDIA Coord. Ctr., NHLBI, NIH, 1991-93; scholar U. Ala.-Birmingham Ctr. for Health Risk Assessment and Disease Prevention, Sch. Pub. Health, 1991—, dir. Computer Resources Lab., 1990-93; assoc. scientist Comprehensive Cancer Ctr., U. Ala., 1988—; adj. asst. prof. math. and statistics U. W. Fla., Pensacola, 1985-86. Contbr. articles to profl. jours. Mem. Am. Statis. Assn., Am. Math. Soc., Biometric Soc., Inst. Math. Statistics, Philosophy of Sci. Assn., Soc. for Indsl. and Applied Math., Phi Kappa Phi, Phi Sigma. Baptist. Home: 624 Olde Towne Ln Alabaster AL 35007-9190 Office: U Ala Birmingham 1719 6th Ave N Rm 252 Birmingham AL 35203-2014

HARDIN, JAMES ORAN, retired biochemist; b. Grant, Ala., Sept. 27, 1923; s. William Robert and Gertha Lee (Key) H.; m. Katherine Mackie, Dec. 29, 1947; children: Carolyn Sue, Ruth Ann. BS in Agrl. Edn., Auburn U., 1949, Ms in Animal Nutrition, Biochemistry, 1951. With E.I. Dupont DeNumors Co., Childersburg, Ala., 1942-43; mgr. ingredient divsn. Ralston Purina Co., St. Louis, 1951-62; asst. prof. U. Md., College Park, 1962-64; dir. rsch. Wilson Inc. Poultry Divsn., Federalsburg, Md., 1964-70; v.p. Nutrient Products Co., Kilarnock, Va., 1970-75; dir. rsch., quality control Standard Products Co., Kilarnock, 1975-86; retired, 1987; mem. nutrition coun. Am. Feed Mfg. Assn., Arlington, Va., 1965-85; cons. several feed companies. Author: Hardin USA, Vols. 1-4; pub. quar. newsletter; pub., editor family newsletter. Asst. chmn. Dem. Com., Nottoway County, Va., 1992-96. With U.S. Army, 1943-1946. Recipient Meritorious Unit award, two Bronze Indian Arrowheads, Volunteer Worker awards Piedmont Geriatric Hosp., Burkeville, Va., 1987-96. Baptist. Home and Office: Rt 1 Box 2290 Crewe VA 23930

HARDIN, JAMES W., botanist, herbarium curator, educator; b. Mar. 31, 1929. BS, Fla. So. Coll., 1950; MS, U. Tenn., 1951; PhD, U. Mich., 1957. Instr. U. Mich., 1956-57; from asst. prof. to prof. N.C. State U., Raleigh, 1957-86, prof., 1968-96, emeritus prof., 1996—, curator herbarium, 1957-96; vis. prof. Mountain Lake Biological Sta. U.Va., summers 1962, 64, 83, U. Okla. Biological Sta., summers 1967, 70; mem. exec. com. Flora Southeastern U.S., 1966—; endangered species com. N.C. Dept. Natural & Econ. Resources, 1973-74, natural areas adv. com., 1973-79; mem. plant conservation sci. com. N.C. Dept. Agriculture, 1980—, chmn. 1987—; mem. endangered species com. N.C. Wildlife Resources Commn., 1976-78, N.C. State Mus. Natural Hist., 1975-78; pres. Highlands Biological Station, Inc., 1963-69, trustee, 1958-69, sec., 1960-63; invited symposium speaker. Author: Human Poisoning, 1974, Textbook of Dendrology, 1996; editor ASB Bull., 1980-86; mem. editorial com. Am. Jour. Botany, 1964-66; mem. editorial bd. Brittonia, 1964-67, Brimleyana, 1975—; reviewer jours. in field. Trustee Highlands Biol. Found., 1976—. Mem. Am. Soc. Plant Taxonomists (pub. policy com. 1976-78, editorial bd. 1964-67, editor-in-chief Systematic Botany 1985-91, pres. elect 1991-92, pres. 1992-93, past pres. 1993-94, Cooley award 1958), Southern Appalachian Botanical Club (v.p. 1959-60, pres. 1964-65, Bartholomew award 1994), Botanical Soc. Am. (editorial com. 1964-66, chair southeastern sect. 1968-69), Assn. Southeastern Biologists (Meritorious Teaching award 1991, chmn. local arrangements 1966, 77, v.p. 1968-69, pres. 1970-80, editor 1980-86), Internat. Assn. Plant Taxonomy, Soc. Economic Botany (chmn. local arrangements 1979), Torrey Botanical Club, Coun. Biology Editors (reference style com. 1986-89), Gamma Sigma Delta (sec.-treas. N.C. chpt. 1972-73), Phi Kappa Phi, Sigma Xi (exec. com. N.C chpt. 1962-63, sec. 1965-66, treas. 1966-67, v.p. 1967-68, program chmn. 1968-69, pres. 1969-70). Office: N C State Univ Dept Botany Raleigh NC 27695-7612

HARDIN, JOHN ARTHUR, history educator; b. Louisville, Sept. 18, 1948; s. Albert A. and Elizabeth (Hansbro) H.; m. Maxine Randle, Dec. 22, 1973; 1 child, Jonathan Rico. BA in History, Bellarmine Coll., 1970; MA in History, Fisk U., 1972; PhD in History, U. Mich., 1989. Instr. Ky. State U., Frankfort, 1972-74, 74-78, asst. prof., 1978-84; asst. prof. Ea. Wash. U., Cheney, 1984-90; assoc. prof. black studies Ea. Wash. U., 1990-91; assoc. prof. history Western Ky U, Bowling Green, 1991—; lectr. U. Louisville, 1972, 73, 74, 75, 79; vis. asst. prof. U. Ky., 1980-81; mem. Ky. Hist. Preservation Rev. Bd., Frankfort, 1983-84; mem. pub. adv. com. Ky. Hist. Soc., Frankfort, 1983-84; mem. adv. bd. Filson Club History Quarterly Pub., 1989-92. Author: Onward and Upward: Centennial History of Kentucky State University 1886-1986. Pres. Kiwanis of Frankfort, 1983-84. Mem. Nat. Coun. for Black Studies (regional v.p. 1987-88), Ky. Assn. Tchrs. of History, Ky. Assn. of Blacks in Higher Edn., Phi Alpha Theta History Honor Soc., Phi Beta Sigma. Home: 2424 Tipperary Way Bowling Green KY 42104-4558 Office: Western Ky U Dept History Bowling Green KY 42101

HARDIN, MARK, thoroughbred horse breeder; b. Washington, DC, Mar. 10, 1930; s. Taylor Scott Hardin and Nancy (Hale) Bowers; m. Katherine Ida Guiff, Nov. 15, 1952; children: Rosalie Janelle Hardin Morton, Norah Kathrine Hardin Lind, MaryWelby Scott Hardin Watkins. Student, U. Va., 1951-52. Owner Ctrl. Va. Gas Co., Charlottesville, Va., 1966-73; co-owner Newstead Farm, Upperville, Va., 1977-83; owner Rockburn Farm, Marshall, Va., 1983—. With U.S. Army, 1949-51. Mem. Va. Thoroughbred Assn. (bd. dirs. 1980—). Home: 2224 Crenshaw Rd Marshall VA 22115

HARDIN, MELANIE ANNE, ophthalmic technician; b. Memphis, Nov. 7, 1971; d. David Wyatt McNeil and Carolyn Anne (Buchanan) Crawford; m. Gary Everett Hardin II, Feb. 15, 1991; children: Joel Everett, Jacob Alexander. Student, Carson Newman Coll., 1990-92, 96—. Ophthalmic technician Morristown (Tenn.) Regional Eye Ctr., 1989—. Republican. Baptist. Office: Morristown Regional Eye Ctr 735 Mcfarland St Morristown TN 37814-3977

HARDIN, PAUL, III, law educator; b. Charlotte, N.C., June 11, 1931; s. Paul and Dorothy (Reel) H.; m. Barbara Russell, June 8, 1954; children: Paul Russell, Sandra Mikush, Dorothy Holmes. AB, Duke U., 1952, JD, 1954; LHD (hon.), Clemson U., 1970; LLD (hon.), Coker Coll., 1972; LittD (hon.), Nebr. Wesleyan U., 1978; LLD (hon.), Adrian Coll., 1987, Monmouth Coll., 1988; HHD (hon.), Wofford Coll., 1989; LLD (hon.), Rider Coll., 1990; LHD (hon.), Duke U., 1994. Bar: Ala. 1954. Practiced in Birmingham, 1954, 56-58; asst. prof. Duke Law Sch., 1958-61, assoc. prof., 1961-63, prof., 1963-68, univ. trustee, 1969-74, 1995—; pres. Wofford Coll., Spartanburg, S.C., 1968-72, So. Methodist U., Dallas, 1972-74, Drew U., Madison, N.J., 1975-88; chancellor U. N.C., Chapel Hill, 1988-95, prof. law, 1995—; vis. prof. U. Tex., summer 1960, U. Pa., 1962-63, U. Va., 1974; dir. Smith Barney mut. funds, Italy Fund, Inc. Author: (with Sullivan, others) The Administration of Criminal Justice, 1966, (with Sullivan) Evidence, Cases and Materials, 1968; contbr. articles to profl. jours. law revs. Chmn. Human Relations Com., Durham, N.C., 1961-62; mem. gen. conf. United Meth. Ch., 1968, 76, 80, 84; pres. Nat. Assn. Schs. and Colls. of United Meth. Ch., 1984; chmn. Nat. Commn. on United Meth. Higher Edn., 1975-77. Served with CIC, AUS, 1954-56. Mem. Carnegie Found. for Advancement Teaching (bd. dirs.), Order of Coif, Phi Beta Kappa.

HARDIN, THOMAS JEFFERSON, II, investment counsel; b. Richmond, Va., Jan. 19, 1945; s. Nathaniel Arnold and Margaret Fatio (L'Engle) H.; m. Catherine Merrifield Hoar, Feb. 24, 1968 (div. Sept. 1991); children: Maria L'E., T. Jefferson III. Student, Ga. State U., 1965; BS in Commerce, Washington and Lee U., 1967; MBA in Fin., Emory U., 1971. Security analyst J.C. Bradford & Co., Nashville, 1971-72; v.p., sr. security analyst N.C. Nat. Bank, Charlotte, 1972-79; v.p., dir. Forsyth Twine & Cordage Co., Charlotte, 1979-82; v.p., sr. security analyst Interstate Securities Corp., Charlotte, 1982-84; v.p., dir. rsch. Portfolio Capital Mgmt. Inc., Charlotte, 1984-85; pres. ATIM, Inc. (formerly A.T. Investment Mgmt., Inc.), Charlotte, 1985—; bus. mgr. M-B Ltd. Partnership, 1993—; co-mgr. Russelville Mgmt. LLC, 1996—; participant Fin. Analysts' Fedn. Rockford Sem., Ill., 1973, Ctr. Rsch. SEcurities Pricing U. Chgo., 1975-76, AIMT sem. Chgo., 1992; exec. dir. Alliance for Clean Energy, Washington, 1985-89. V.p., dir. Barclay Downs Homeowners Assn., Charlotte, 1977-78, Foxcroft Homeowners Assn., Charlotte, 1982-86; mem. chpt. svcs. com., support group leader, peer counselor Multiple Sclerosis Soc., Charlotte, 1987-94. 1st lt. U.S. Army, 1967-69. Named Master Forest Mgr., N.C. Agrl. Extension Svc., 1987. Fellow Assn. Investment Mgmt. Rsch.; mem. Am. Forestry Assn. (life), N.C. Soc. Fin. Analysts, Mecklenburg Forestry Assn. (chmn. 1988-91), Bald Head Island Club, Piedmont Driving Club, Washington and Lee Alumni Assn., Emory Grad. Bus. Assn. Home: 1976 Ferncliff Rd Charlotte NC 28211-2704 Office: ATIM Inc 725 Providence Rd Ste 217 Charlotte NC 28207-2248

HARDING, ANN CAROL, painter; b. Mpls., Mar. 16, 1942; d. Forest Quinlan and Agnes Mathilda (Garmer) H.; m. Sidney Richardson Garrett, Mar. 25, 1983. BA, U. Minn., 1966; MFA, U. Cin., 1971. Grad. asst. U. Cin., 1970-71; instr. Thomas More Coll., Lakeside Park, Ky., 1971; lectr. in fine arts U. Cin., 1971-73; instr. La. State U., Baton Rouge, 1973-76, asst. prof., 1976-80, assoc. prof., 1980-86, prof., 1986-93, prof. emerita, 1993—. one-person exhbns. include Rainbow Galleries, Cannon Beach, Oreg., 1977, Friend's Gallery Mpls. Inst. Fine Arts, 1981, La. State U. Union Art Gallery, Baton Rouge, 1981, Clark Hall Gallery Southeastern La. U., Hammond, 1982, West Baton Rouge Mus., Port Allen, 1983, Mario Villa Gallery, New Orleans, 1985, Duplantier Gallery, New Orleans, 1987, Still-Zinsel Contemporary Fine Art, New Orleans, 1991, Cason Gallery, Baton Rouge, 1993; 2-person exhbns. include La. Arts Alliance Old Bogan Fire Sta. Gallery, Baton Rouge, 1985, Mario Villa Gallery, 1983, Park Ctrl. Gallery, Springfield, Mo., 1976, La. State U. Union Art Gallery, 1973; numerous juried exhbns. including Houston Ctr., 1976, Ball State U. Art Gallery, Muncie, Ind., 1978, El Paso Mus. Art, 1978, Okla. Art Ctr., 1979, Abilene Fine Arts Mus., Tex., 1981, Contemporary Arts Ctr., New Orleans, 1982, Mint Mus., Charlotte, N.C., 1981, 83, Butler Inst. Am. Art, Youngstown, Ohio, 1981, 82, 84, Tampa Mus., 1985, St. Hubert's Giralda Animal Art Nat. Exhbn., Madison, N.J., 1988, 89, Art Festival Atlanta, 1989; invitational group exhbns. include Sandra Zahn Oreck Gallery, New Orleans, 1978, West Baton Rouge Mus., 1980, 82, 93, New Century Gallery, New Orleans, 1981, Fine Art Gallery Delgado C.C., New Orleans, 1982, Southeastern Ctr. for Contemporary Art, Winston-Salem, 1987, So. Ill. U. Mus., Carbondale, 1983, Masur Mus. Art, Monroe, La., 1988, Forum Gallery, Mpls., 1988, others; pub. collections include Graphic Packaging Corp., Phila., Rhone-Poulenc Rorer Pharm. Corp., Phila., Ochsner Ctr. for Cosmetic Surgery, New Orleans, Burrus Investments Corp., New Orleans, Sterling Drug Corp., Phila., Luth. Brotherhood, Mpls., Ala. Power Co., Birmingham, Tudor Enterprises, Baton Rouge, Freeport-McMoRan Corp., New Orleans, Kestenbaum Equipment Supply Co., L.I. City, N.Y., City Nat. Bank, Baton Rouge, Morgan Resources, Ltd., Baton Rouge, Minn. Mut. Life, St. Paul, Am.-Italian Renaissance Found. Mus., New Orleans, Pan Am. Life, New Orleans, 3-M Corp., Mpls., La. State Art Collection, Ark. Arts Ctr., Little Rock, U. Cin., IDS Corp., Mpls. Recipient Sabbatical Rsch. grant La. State U., 1980, 86-87, Visual Arts fellowship La. State Art Coun., 1985, Artist fellowship Southeastern Ctr. for Contemporary Art, 1981, Rsch. Coun. grant La. State U., 1977, Full Tuition fellowship and scholarship U. Cin., 1969-71, numerous art awards.

HARDING, BARRY, school system administrator, educational consultant; b. Lumberton, N.C., 1952; s. Stephen and Berlie Mae (Brewington) H.; m. Cheryl Ann Blanks, Nov. 19, 1978; children: Laura Beth, Stephen Barry. BS in Elem. Edn., Pembroke (N.C.) State U., 1975, MA in Ednl. Adminstrn., 1978; EdS, East Carolina U., Greenville, N.C., 1983; EdD, S.C. State Coll., Orangeburg, S.C., 1990. Tchr. grades 4-6 Allenton Sch., Lumberton, bldg. prin., 1978-79; prin. Pembroke Middle Sch., 1979-83, Green Grove Elem. Sch., Fairmont, N.C., 1983-89, Peterson Elem. Sch., Red Springs, N.C., 1989-93; asst. supt. adminstrn. Pub. Sch. Robeson County, 1993—; mem. N.C. Sch. Improvement Panel, 1995-96; local and state cons. to schs. and civic orgns.; speaker in field; presenter Internat. Reading Assn., 1995. Author: The Saddletree Church of God Organizational Handbook-"Who We Are", 1st edit., 1992, 2nd edit., 1995. People to People del. to China, 1988; selected as mem. The Z. Smith Reynolds Found. Inc. N.C.; mem. laymens bd. N.C. Ch. of God, 1994—. Recipient Disting. Educator award Charles F. Kettering Found., 1983, award for sch. improvement project N.C. Inst. Govt., 1986, Prin. of Yr. Pub. Schs. of Robeson County Wachovia, 1992, others. Mem. Nat. Assn. Elem. Sch. Adminstrs., N.C. Assn. Sch. Adminstrs., Tarheel Prins. Assn., Robeson County Prins. Assn. (pres. 1986), Phi Delta Kappa, Kappa Delta Pi. Home: 107 Camellia Ln Lumberton NC 28358-8101

HARDING, MAJOR BEST, state supreme court justice; b. Charlotte, N.C., Oct. 13, 1935; m. Jane Lewis, Dec., 1958; children: Major B. Jr., David, Alice Harding Sanderson. BS, Wake Forest U., 1957; LLM, U. Va., 1995; LLD (hon.), Stetson U., 1991; LLM in Jud. Process, U. Va., 1995. Bar: N.C. 1959, Fla. 1960. Staff judge adv. hdqrs. Ft. Gordon, Ga., 1960-62; asst. county solicitor Criminal Ct. of Record, Duval County, Fla., 1962-63; pvt. practice law, 1964-68; judge Juvenile Ct., Duval County, 1968-70; judge 4th Jud. Cir. of Fla., 1970-74, chief judge, 1974-77; justice Supreme Ct. of Fla., Tallahassee, 1991—; supervisory judge Family Mediation Unit, 1984-90; mem. Matrimonial Law Commn. and Gender Bias Study Commn.; chair Fla. Ct. Edn. Coun., past mem. Jud. Conf.; 1st dean New Judges Coll., 1975, faculty mem. in probate and juvenile areas, until 1979; dean Fla. Jud. Coll., 1984-92, mem. bench-bar commn. Bd. dirs. Legal Aid Assn., Family Consultation Svc., Daniel Meml. Home; past pres. Rotary Club of Riverside, Jacksonville, Fla., Rotary Club of Tallahasee; chmn. U.S. Constn. Bicentennial Commn., Jacksonville; past mem., deacon, elder St. John's Presbyn. Ch.; commr. Gen. Assembly Presbyn. Ch. U.S., 1971; mem. Christ Presbyn. Ch., Tallahasee. Recipient Award for Outstanding Contbn. to Field of Matrimonial Law Am. Acad. Matrimonial Lawyers, 1986. Mem. ABA, The Fla. Bar, N.C. State Bar Assn., Chester Bedell Inn of Ct. (past pres), Scabbard and Blade, Tallahassee Am. Inn of Ct., Tallahassee Bar Assn., Sigma Chi, Phi Delta Phi. Office: Supreme Ct of Fla 500 S Duval St Tallahassee FL 32399-6556

HARDING, MARGARET TYREE, minister; b. Lynchburg, Va., May 28, 1951; d. Aubrey Nathaniel and Audrey (Riley) Tyree; m. William R. Harding, Sep. 11, 1993. BA, Averett Coll., 1978; MDiv, Southeastern Bapt. Theol. Sem., Wake Forest, N.C., 1981. Ordained to ministry So. Bapt. Conv., 1982. Min. youth Moffett Meml. Bapt. Ch., Danville, Va., 1976-78, West Main Bapt. Ch., Danville, 1979-81; min. edn. and youth North Run Bapt. Ch., Richmond, Va., 1981-84; min. edn., youth and adminstrn. Grandin Ct. Bapt. Ch., Roanoke, Va., 1984—. Contbr. articles to profl. jours. Devotional officer Jr. Women's Club, Madison Heights, Va., 1971-75; alumni rep. Averett Coll., Danville, 1984—, mem. mins. adv. com., 1991; usher Mill Mountain Theater, Roanoke, Va., 1990—. Mem. Religious Edn. Assn. U.S. and Can. (bd. dirs. 1991), Va. Bapt. Gen. Assn. (gen. bd. 1989—), Va. Bapt, Religious Assn. (pres. 1989), So. Bapt. Religious Edn. Assn. (asst. sec. 1994-95), Roanoke Area Religious Edn. Assn. (pres. 1991). Home: 3613 Martinell Ave SW Roanoke VA 24018 Office: Grandin Ct Bapt Ch 2660 Brambleton Ave SW Roanoke VA 24015-4306

HARDISTER, DARRELL EDWARD, insurance executive; b. Davidson County, N.C., Sept. 17, 1934; s. George Herbert and Myrtle Rosa (Parrish) H.; m. Miriam Smith; children: Debra Sue, Pamela Louise, Myrtle Darlene. Grad., Am. Coll. CLU, ChFC, LUTCF. Asst. mgr. Correct Craft Boat Co., Titusville, Fla., 1952-57; sales rep. Napa/Stradley's Motor Supply, Titusville, 1957-59; sales rep., mgr. Peninsular Life Ins. Co., Brevard County, Fla., 1959-64; owner, mgr. D.E. Hardister, CLU & Assocs., Titusville, 1964—; speaker at convs. in field. Contbr. articles to profl. publs. and company publs. Pres. North Brevard County Devel. Com., 1979, 80; mem. Gov.'s Adv. Coun., Fla.; pres. Titusville High Choir Parents Assn., 1979-83; past advisor Fla. Theater Restoration Com., Titusville; past chmn. bd. dirs. North Brevard YMCA; past mem. Brevard County Zoning Bd. Recipient Key to City of Titusville; Paul Harris Fellow. Mem. Nat. Assn. Life Underwriters, North Brevard Assn. Life Underwriters (pres. 1969-70, bd. dirs.), Rotary (pres. local chpt. 1976-77, Paul Harris Fellow), Lions (pres., sec. local chpt. 1961, 64). Republican. Baptist. Home: 3305 Royal Palm Ct Titusville FL 32780-5648 Office: Hardister Eads & Assocs 3305 Royal Palm Ct Titusville FL 32780-5648

HARDMAN, DANIEL CLARKE, accountant; b. Gadsden, Ala., Aug. 10, 1954; s. Edgar Paul and Juanette Lorena (Hall) H.; m. Elwanda Denise Holland, June 6, 1976; children: Benjamin M., Adam L. BS with honors, Jacksonville State U., 1976. CPA, Ala. Acctg. mgr. Ernst & Whinney, Birmingham, Ala., 1976-81; prin. Hardman, Guess, Frost & Cummings, P.C., Birmingham, 1981—; bd. dirs. Exec. Techs., Inc., Birmingham. Dist. commr. Boy Scouts Am., Birmingham, 1982-84; bd. dirs. Highlands Day Sch.; chmn. tax com. Bus. Coun. Ala., 1986—. Mem. Am. Inst. CPA's, Ala. Soc. CPA's, Nat. Assn. Accts. (bd. dirs. Ala. 1981), Birmingham C. of C. (pres.' com. 1981). Republican. Methodist. Club: Exchange (bd. dirs. Birmingham 1986). Home: 5200 Meadow Brook Rd Birmingham AL 35242-3312 Office: Hardman Guess et al 2120 16th Ave S Ste 300 Birmingham AL 35205-5046

HARDRICK, CHARLES M., airport executive. Dir. of ops. Jacksonville Internat Airport, Fla. Office: Jacksonville Intl Airport PO Box 3005 Jacksonville FL 32206-0005*

HARDY, ASHTON RICHARD, lawyer; b. Gulfport, Miss., Aug. 31, 1935; s. Ashton Maurice and Alice (Baumbach) H.; m. Katherine Ketelsen, Sept. 4, 1959; children: Karin H. Wood, Katherine B. BBA, Tulane U., 1958, JD, 1962. Bar: La., 1962, FCC, 1976. Ptnr. Jones, Walker, Waechter, Poitevent, Carrere & Denegre, New Orleans, 1962-74, 76-82; gen. counsel FCC, Washington, 1974-76; ptnr. Fawer, Brian, Hardy, Zatzkis, New Orleans, 1982-86, Hardy & Popham, 1986-88; ptnr. Walker, Bordelon, Hamlin, Theriot & Hardy, New Orleans, 1988-92, Hardy & Carey, New Orleans, 1992—; gen. counsel La. Assn. Broadcasters, 1976-86, Greater New Orleans Assn. Broadcasters, 1976—, La. Assn. Advt. Agys., 1982-86; lectr. in field; advance rep. to Pres. U.S., 1971-74. Sec. bd. dirs. New Orleans Mission, 1989—; bd. dirs. Met. Crime Commn. New Orleans, 1993—, United Christian Charities, 1993—. Lt. USN, 1958-60. Mem. La. Bar Assn. (del. ho. of dels. 1987-92), FCC Bar Assn., Nat. Religious Broadcasters (bd. dirs. S.W. chpt. 1994—), Christian Legal Soc., Metairie Country Club (pres. 1986), Communications Club. Republican. Evangelical Christian. Home: 306 Cedar Dr Metairie LA 70005-3902 Office: Hardy & Carey Ste 255 111 Veterans Memorial Blvd Metairie LA 70005-3030

HARDY, HARVEY LOUCHARD, lawyer; b. Dallas, Dec. 2, 1914; s. Nat L. and Winifred H. (Fouraker) H.; m. Edna Vivian Bedell, Feb. 14, 1948; children: Victoria Elizabeth Hardy Pursch, Alice Anne Hardy Gannon. Bar: Tex. 1936, U.S. Dist. Ct. (so. and we. dists.) Tex. 1946, U.S. Ct. Appeals (5th cir.) 1946, U.S. Supreme Ct. 1949. First asst. dist. atty. Bexar County, San Antonio, 1947-50, acting dist. atty., 1950-51; city atty., San Antonio, 1952-53, Castle Hills, Tex., 1959-96, Leon Valley, Tex., 1967—, Roma, Tex., 1973-96, Helotes, Tex., 1984—, Fair Oaks Ranch, Tex. 1986—; legal advisor bd. trustees Firemen and Policemen's Pension Fund of San Antonio, 1956—; legal advisor Grey Forest Utilities, 1986—. Served to 1st lt. inf. U.S. Army, 1941-45. Decorated Bronze Star with cluster. Fellow Tex. Bar Found.; mem. Nat. Inst. Mcpl. Legal Officers, Tex. Bar Assn., San Antonio Bar Found., Tex. Assn. City Attys., San Antonio Bar Assn. Methodist. Home: 215 Atwater Dr San Antonio TX 78213-3321

HARDY, KENNETH JAMES, rheumatologist, educator; b. New Orleans, July 14, 1946. BS, La. State U., 1968, MS, 1973, MD, 1980; PhD, U. Tex., 1977. Diplomate Am. Bd. Internal Medicine and Rheumatology. Med. rsch. technologist dept. physiology La. State U., New Orleans, 1968-71, instr. in biology, zoology and physiology labs., grad. rsch. assoc. biochemistry sect., 1971-73, rsch. assoc. sect. rheumatology, 1976-80; predoctoral rsch. assoc. dept. biochemistry Vanderbilt U. Sch. of Medicine, Nashville, 1973-76; resident in internal medicine U. Calif. Sch. of Medicine, Davis, 1980-83; fellow in rheumatology, immunology, molecular immunogenetics U. Calif. Sch. of Medicine, San Francisco, 1983-86, asst. investigator sect. rheumatology and immunology, 1986; asst. prof. depts. medicine, microbiology and immunology, asst. investigator Howard Hughes Med. Inst., Baylor Coll. of Medicine, Houston, 1986-90; asst. prof. dept. cell biology Baylor Coll. of Medicine, Houston, 1989-90; assoc. prof. dept. medicine/rheumatology, scientist multipurpose arthritis ctr. U. Ala., Birmingham, 1990-93; prof. medicine, dir. divsn. rheumatology/molecular immunology U. Miss. Med. Ctr., Jackson, 1993—; biologist depts. human cytogenetics, virology and cell biology Gulf South Rsch. Inst., New Orleans, 1968-71; rsch. cons. dept. biol. scis. U. New Orleans, 1976-80, sch. of medicine, 1980-83; courtesy physician VA Hosp., Martinez, Calif., 1980-83; cons. Hoefer Sci. Instruments, Inc., 1983-86, Meth. Hosp. and Harris County Hosps., 1986-89; chief physician VA Hosp., Birmingham, 1991, Jackson, 1993—; originator, co-dir. satellite treatment of arthritis and rheumatism program U. Ala., Birmingham, 1991-93, originator, rsch co-dir. rheumatology at Healthsouth Hosp. program, dir. molecular divsn., cytokine core program; dir. rheumatology fellowship tng. program U. Miss. Med. Ctr., Jackson, 1993—; referee various sci. jours.; lectr. in field. Contbr. articles to profl. jours., chpts. to books; patentee automated perfusion chamber. Predoctoral fellow, Welsh Found. scholar U. Tex., 1973-76; Predoctoral Summer fellow Vanderbilt Med. Ctr., 1976-80; fellow Greater New Orleans Cancer Soc., 1972; ARA Sr. Rheumatology scholar Merck, Sharp & Dohme, 1986; recipient Investigator award Arthritis Found., 1987, J.V. Satterfield Arthritis Investigator award Nat. Arthritis Found., 1988, Merit Rev. award VA, 1992. Fellow ACP, Fellow Am. Coll. Rheumatology; mem. AAAS, Am. Assn. Immunologists, Am. Fedn. Clin. Rsch., Ams. for Med. Progress Internat. Soc. Interferon Rsch. (Sci. Excellence award 1987, 88), Internat. Soc. Rheumatic Therapy, Ala. Rheumatic Disease Soc., Ankylosing Spondylitis Assn., Beta Beta Beta.

HARDY, LINDA LEA STERLOCK, media specialist; b. Balt., Aug. 15, 1947; d. George Allen and Dorothy Lea (Briggs) Sterlock; m. John Edward Hardy III, Apr. 25, 1970; 1 child, Roger Wayne. BA in History, N.C. Wesleyan Coll., 1969; MEd in History, East Carolina U., 1972, MLS, 1990. Cert. tchr., N.C. History tchr. Halifax (N.C.) County Schs., 1972-83, learning lab tchr., 1983-91, computer lab tchr., 1990-95; media specialist Nash-Rocky Mount (N.C.) Schs., 1995—; part-time history instr. Nash C.C., 1993. Mem. AAUW (pres. Rocky Mount br. 1993-95, Named Gift award 1987), Bus. and Profl. Women (pres. Rocky Mount chpt. 1986-87, 90-91, treas. 1992—, sec.-treas. dist X 1989-90, state election chmn. 1989-90, 93-95, Girl Friday award 1981, Woman of Yr. award 1986), Nat. Assn. Educators, N.C. Assn. Educators, Nash/Rocky Mount Assn. Educators (raculty rep. 1995—), Phi Delta Kappa, Pi Gamma Mu. Republican. Methodist. Office: Nash-Rocky Mount Schs Benvenue Mid Sch 1571 Benvenue Rd Rocky Mount NC 27804-1846

HARDY, ROBERT BASKERVILLE, city planner; b. Columbus, Miss., July 5, 1919; s. Robert Orgain and Mary Paine (Chapman) H.; m. Anne Wight Cazort, 1941; children: Robert Orgain, Jane Cazort, Sarah McIntosh, John Cazort. BS in Bus., Miss. State U., 1941; postgrad., Air U., 1952. Commd. 2d lt. U.S. Army, 1941; advanced through grades to lt. col. USAF, 1960, ret., 1967; city planner, exec. dir. Comprehensive Planers, Inc., West Point, Miss., 1967-88; v.p. Tupelo (Miss.) Tool and Die, Inc., 1990—. State senator State of Miss., Jackson, 1972-76. Named King of the Pilgrimage, Jr. Aux., Columbus, 1993. Mem. Kiwanis, Sigma Alpha Epsilon. Republican. Episcopalian. Home: The Cedars 1305 Military Rd Columbus MS 39701-3607

HARDY, SALLY MARIA, retired biological sciences educator; b. San Juan, P.R., June 12, 1932; d. Obdulio Roberto Cordero and Maria Teresa (Judice) Perez; m. Anthony Michael Hardy, Apr. 22, 1962; children: Ricardo Antonio, Maria Isabel. BS, Midland Coll., Fremont, Nebr., 1952; MS, Fordham U., 1956, PhD, 1958. Tech. asst. Postgrad. Hosp., N.Y.C., 1952-54; tchr. Ursuline Acad., N.Y.C., 1957-58; asst. prof. Marymount Manhattan Coll., N.Y.C., 1957-62, 67-68, Queensborough Community Coll., CUNY, 1967-69; rsch. assoc. Am. Mus. Natural History, N.Y.C., 1967-73; assoc. prof. Bergen Community Coll., Bergen, N.J., 1969-70, Rutgers U., Piscataway, N.J., 1970-79; prof. biol. scis. La. State U., Shreveport, 1979-88; ret., 1988; mem. minority com. Grad. Record Exam. Bd., 1976-79; cons. Office Tech. Assessment, U.S. Ho. of Reps., 1985-87. Mem. editorial bd. Jour. Allied Health Professions, 1983-86; contbr. articles to profl. publs. Pres. Hispanic Youth Civic Assn., N.Y.C., 1954-57, PTA, Mendham, N.J., 1972-74; mem. Mendham Borough Bd. Edn., 1973-77, Mendham Borough Bd. Health, 1979; mem. Emerald Isle Vol. Rescue Squad, 1994, cons. program eval. and devel., 1994—. Recipient Faculty Merit award Rutgers U., 1978, Nuestro award Hispanic mag., 1978, award Assn. for Advancement Chicanos and Native Ams. in Sci., 1982. Mem. AAAS (chmn. Office Opportunities in Sci. 1979-85), N.Y. Acad. Scis., Assn. for Puerto Ricans in Sci. and Engring. (pres. 1981-84, bd. dirs. 1984-87), Sigma Xi, Pi Epsilon, Lambda Tau. Roman Catholic. Home: PO Box 4173 Emerald Isle NC 28594-4173

HARDY, THOMAS CRESSON, insurance company executive; b. Hoisington, Kans., 1942; s. C.C. and Delia Hardy; children—Jay C., Glenn W. B.A., U. Kans., 1963; M.B.A., Wharton Sch., U. Pa., 1965. CLU, CPCU, FLMI. With Exxon Corp., N.Y.C., 1965-69; treas. Keene Corp., N.Y.C., 1969-73; exec. v.p. fin. Fidelity Union Life Ins. Co., Dallas, 1973-79; (co. acquired by Allianz of Am. 1979); v.p. Allianz of Am.; pres. Allianz Investment Corp., Dallas, 1979-82; pres., chief exec. officer Gt. Am. Res. Ins. Co., 1983-88; exec. v.p., COO Provident Life & Accident Ins. Co., Chattanooga, 1988-94; bd. dirs. 1st Tenn. Bank of Chattanooga. Bd. dirs., pres. Chattanooga Symphony & Opera Assn.; bd. dirs. exec. com. Chattanooga Allied Arts; mem. U. Kans. Bus. Sch. Adv. Bd.; bd. visitors Berry Coll. Mem. Fin. Execs. Inst. (chpt. pres., nat. bd. dirs.), Firemark Cir. Am. (pres., dir.). Home: 216 Stephenson Ave Lookout Mountain TN 37350-1323

HARDY, WILLIAM MCDONALD, JR., clergyman, physician assistant; b. Madisonville, Tex., Feb. 7, 1957; s. William McDonald and Frankie Beatrice (Bell) H.; m. Kathryn Joyce Phillips, Jan. 19, 1980; children: Karen R., Karla J., Kimberly A., Klarissa D. Student, Tex. A&M U., 1975-77; BS, Howard U., 1980; CME, U. Okla., 1991. Lic. Okla. Bd. Med. Examiners. Physician asst. John A. Kenney M.D., Washington, 1980-82; D.C. Dept. of Correction, Lorton, Va., 1982, Fed. Prison Hosp., El Reno, Okla., 1982-89, Okla. Army Nat. Guard, Midwest City, Okla., 1983-89, VA Medical Ctr., Oklahoma City, 1989—; physician asst. in psychiatry VA Med. Ctr., 1983; instr. CPR Emergency Care, ARC, Edgewater, Md., 1982; admissions officer VA Hosp., patient referral coord., clinical instr., 1992—. Contbr. articles to Am. Jour. Psychiatry. Vol. ARC; vice chmn. Citizens' Participation Com., 1989; bd. dirs. Lincoln Terrace Neighborhood Assn., Okla City, 1991; emergency medical svc. Huntsville Police dept., 1975, EMT Madisonville County Hosp., 1976-77. Recipient Cert. of Appreciation AMC, 1987, Cert. of Commendation Okla. Army Nat. Guard, 1983, Cert. of Svc. U.S. Army, 1983, Letter of Commendation D.C. Dept. Corrections, 1982; named Outstanding Young Men of Am. U.S. Jaycees, 1983. Office: VA Hosp 921 NE 13th St Oklahoma City OK 73104-5007

HARE, ELEANOR O'MEARA, computer science educator; b. Charlottesville, Va., Apr. 6, 1936; d. Edward King and Eleanor Worthington (Selden) O'Meara; m. John Leonard Ging, Feb. 4, 1961 (div. 1972); 1 child, Catherine Eleanor Ging Huddle; m. William Ray Hare, Jr., May 24, 1973. BA, Hollins Coll., 1958; MS, Clemson U., 1973, PhD, 1989. Rsch. asst. cancer rsch. U. Va. Hosp., Charlottesville, 1957-58; rsch. specialist rsch. labs. engring. sci. U. Va., Charlottesville, 1959-64; tchr. Pendelton (S.C.) High Sch., 1964-65; vis. instr. dept. math. Clemson (S.C.) U., 1974-79, instr. dept. computer sci., 1979-83, lectr. dept. computer sci., 1983-90, asst. prof. dept. computer sci., 1990—. Contbr. articles to profl. jours. Bd. dirs. LWV of the Clemson Area, 1988-96; chmn. nursing home study LWV of S.C., 1988-92; oboe and English horn player Anderson (S.C.) Symphony, 1980—. Fellow Inst. Combinatories and its Applications; mem. AAUP, Assn. for Computing Machinery. Office: Clemson U Dept Computer Sci Clemson SC 29634-1906

HARE, KIMBERLY DAWN, communications director; b. Petersburg, Va., Sept. 16, 1970; d. Wayne Curtis and Judith Ann (Caldwell) H. BA, Ouachita Bapt. U., 1993, secondary tchg. cert. in journalism, 1993. Sales rep. Russellville (Ark.) Courier Dem., 1990, Hollingsworth Advt., Arkadelphia, 1993; asst. to dir. publs. Ouachita Bapt. U., Arkadelphia, 1991-92; office mgr. Advantage Advt., Arkadelphia, 1991-92; reporter, promotional asst. Bap. State Conv. of Ind., Indpls., 1992; dir. comms. Dallas Bapt. U., 1993—; workshop leader Walsworth Pub. Co., Marceline, Mo., 1991; judge, asst. to exec. dir. Ark. H.S. Press Assn., Little Rock, 1989-91. Sunday sch. tchr. 3d St. Bapt. Ch., Arkadelphia, 1991-93; vol. Ronald McDonald House, Ft. Worth, 1993; mem. women's adv. bd. Dallas Bapt. U., 1993-94; singles publicity coord. Glenview Bapt. Ch., Ft. Worth, 1993-95. Republican. Office: Dallas Bapt U 3000 Mountain Creek Pkwy Dallas TX 75211-9299

HARE, RUFUS DWIGHT, education educator; b. Pikeville, N.C., Feb. 3, 1947; s. Rufus and Fannie Agnes (Edmundson) H.; m. Laura Jayne Whitman, Mar. 28, 1986; children: Lee Carpenter, Daniel, Nathan. BA in Early Childhood Edn., U. N.C., 1975, PhD in Philosophy, 1985. Tchr. Durham County Schs., Durham, N.C., 1975-79; rsch. asst. U. N.C., Chapel Hill, 1979-1984; from asst. to assoc. prof. N.E. La. U., Monroe, 1985-89; assoc. prof. Coll. Edn. Miss. State U., Mississippi State, 1990-93, prof. Coll. Edn., 1993—, coord. grad. programs, 1995—; evaluator Upper Cumberland and Cmty. Health Agy. Tng. Resource Ctr., Cookeville, Tenn. 1995—, Cmty. Counseling Svc. Rural Health Outreach, Columbus, Miss., 1994—. Co-Author: Meta-Ethnography, 1988. Sgt., USMC, 1968-72, Vietnam. Grantee team mem. Miss. Off. Children Youth, Jackson, Miss., 1990, rsch. devel. Miss. State U., Starkville, Miss., team mem. U.S. Dept. Commerce grant, 1995. Mem. Am. Ednl. Studies Assn., Am. Edn. Rsch. Assn., Phi Delta Kappa. Home: 209 North Montgomery Starkville MS 39759 Office: Dept of Curriculum and Instrn Box 9705 311 Allen Hall Miss State U Mississippi State MS 39762-9705

HARELL, GEORGE S., radiologist; b. Vienna, Austria, Apr. 27, 1937; came to U.S., 1940; s. Isidore and Zinaida (Hilferding) Silbermann; m. Carol Deane Wright, Mar. 21, 1970; children: Mark, Ben. AB, Oberlin Coll., 1959; MD, Columbia U., 1963. Resident in radiology Med. Sch., Stanford (Calif.) U., 1967-71, asst. prof., 1971-78, assoc. prof., 1978-82; radiologist dept. radiology East Jefferson Gen. Hosp., Metairie, La., 1982-84, chmn. dept. radiology, 1984-94; clin. prof. radiology Tulane U., New Orleans, 1987—; project officer NIH, Washington, 1965-67. Author: (chpt.) The Oesophagus, 1986, 92. Lt. comdr. USPHS, 1963-65. James C. Picker Found. grantee, 1972-74, NIH grantee, 1977-80, 82-85, Am. Heart Assn. grantee, 1981-83. Mem. Soc. Computed Body Tomography/Magnetic Resonances, Soc. Gastrointestinal Radiologists, Phi Beta Kappa. Office: East Jefferson Gen Hosp 4200 Houma Blvd Metairie LA 70006-2970

HARGRAVE, ROBERT WARREN, hair styling salon chain executive; b. Meridian, Miss., Sept. 15, 1944; s. George Herbert and Clara (Gibson) H.; m. Janeice Stodghill, Dec. 23, 1967; 1 child, Jennifer Lyn. Student, Tyler Jr. Coll., 1963-65; BS, Baylor U., 1967; postgrad., East Tex. State U., 1968. Lic. nursing home adminstr., Tex. Nursing home adminstr. ARA-Nat. Living Ctrs., Waco, Tex., 1969-71; dir. personnel and spl. programs ARA-Nat. Living Ctrs., Houston, 1971-75; exec. v.p. ARA-Geriatrics, Colo., Tex, 1975-79; founder, owner 16 hair styling salons San Antonio Enterprises, Inc., 1979—; tchr. nursing home adminstrn., McLennan Community Coll., Waco, 1970, mem. steering com. to establish nursing home license program, 1970; mem. Nat. Bd. Salon Franchises, Cutco Insustries, Inc., N.Y.C., 1985-87, pres. Direct Licensees' Assn., 1991-92; adv. com. Tex. Cosmetology Commn., 1994—. Mem. adv. bd. cosmetology dept. South San High Sch., 1987—, adv. coun. for career and tech. edn. N. East Ind. Sch. Dist., 1994—. Mem. Am. Salon Assn., Tex. Salon Assn., San Antonio Salon Assn., Tex. Nursing Home Assn. (chpt. pres. 1970), Colo. Health Care Assn. (del. for nat. fire safety 1978), Am. Health Care Assn., Nat. Parks and Recreation Assn., Nat. Therapeutic Recreational Soc., Gideons Internat. Office: San Antonio Enterprises Inc 4221 Centergate St San Antonio TX 78217-4802

HARGRAVE, RUDOLPH, justice; b. Shawnee, Okla., Feb. 15, 1925; s. John Hubert and Daisy (Holmes) H.; m. Madeline Hargrave, May 29, 1949; children: Cindy Lu, John Robert, Jana Sue. LLB, U. Okla., 1949. Bar: Okla. 1949. Pvt. practice Wewoka, Okla., 1949; asst. county atty. Seminole County, 1951-55; judge Seminole County Ct., 1964-67, Seminole County Superior Ct., 1967-69; dist. judge Okla. Dist. Ct., Dist. 22, 1969-79; assoc. justice Okla. Supreme Ct., Oklahoma City, 1979, former vice chief justice, former chief justice, justice, 1979—. Mem. Seminole County Bar Assn., Okla. Bar Assn., ABA. Democrat. Methodist. Lodges: Lions; Masons. Office: Okla Supreme Ct 202 State Capital Bldg Oklahoma City OK 73105*

HARGRODER, CHARLES MERLIN, retired journalist; b. Franklin, La., Sept. 5, 1926; student La. State U., 1943-47. Writer, Baton Rouge Morning Adv., 1947-50, Monroe (La.) Morning World, 1952-53; exec. asst. to gov. La., 1953-56; pub. rels. sec. to Congressman Hale Boggs, 1956-57; regional rep. Inter-Industry Hwy. Safety Com., 1957-58; writer New Orleans Times-Picayune, 1959-88, polit. writer, columnist, 1961-88. With U.S. Army, 1950-52. Home: 217 S Ardenwood Dr Baton Rouge LA 70806-4323

HARGROVE, GAIL ANNETTE, educational administrator; b. Washington, Oct. 30, 1940; d. Benny Hill Hargrove and Allie Lee Lovelady; m. Joseph Gayle Henderson, May 12, 1962 (div.); children: Monica Lee, Stanley James, Molly Marie. BS, La. State U., 1962, Masters degree, 1970. Cert. tchr., Level A Evaluator. Tchr. East Baton Rouge Parish, 1967-70; dir., IASA, Title I Dept. Corrections, Baton Rouge, 1970—; specialist Libr. Power Project, Baton Rouge, 1995-96; mem. adv. coun. Spl. Sch. Dist. #1, Baton Rouge, 1994-96. Evaluator Libr. Power Vols. in Pub. Schs., Baton Rouge, 1993-94; mem. com. United Way of Greater Baton Rouge, 1993. Mem. Am. Correctional Assn., Correctional Ednl. Assn., La. Assn. Sch. Adminstrs. of Federally Assisted Programs, Lions (Downtown Baton Rouge club), Delta Kappa Gamma. Office: Dept Pub Safety & Corrections 504 Mayflower St Baton Rouge LA 70802-6419

HARGROVE, ROY BELMONT, III, stockbroker; b. Farmville, Va., Sept. 2, 1958; s. Roy Belmont Jr. and Margaret Ann (Heaton) H.; m. Cynthia Ann Metcalf, Aug. 9, 1980; children: Roy B. IV, Katherine Allyn. BS, Lynchburg Coll., 1980, MBA, 1985. CFP. Account exec. Wheat First Securities, Williamsburg, Va., 1980-86, investment officer, 1986-88, v.p., investment officer, 1988-94; sr. v.p. Wheat First Butcher Singer, Williamsburg, 1994—, br. mgr. Williamsburg office, 1996—. Trustee Endowment, Williamsburg Bapt. Ch., 1990—, chmn. ofcl. bd., 1988, Sunday sch. tchr., 1990—; founding bd. dirs., past chmn. Hospice Support Care of Williamsburg, 1982-91, 95—; fundraiser Am. Cancer Soc., Williamsburg, 1992—; mem. local com. Kingsmill chpt. Ducks Unltd., 1982-90; bd. dirs. Williamsburg Landing Retirement Cmty., 1996—; mem. budget and fin. com. Kingsmill Cmty. Svc. Assn., 1996—; bd. dirs. Williamsburg Landing, 1996—. Mem. Kiwanis, Kingsmill KCSA (mem. budget and fin. com. 1996—). Home: 104 Thomas Cartwright Williamsburg VA 23185-8904 Office: Wheat First Butcher Singer 161 John Jefferson Sq # B Williamsburg VA 23185-5640

HARGROVE, S. KEITH, mechanical engineer, educator; b. Alexandria, La.; s. Joseph and Jessie Hargrove Moody. BS in Mech. Engring., Tenn. State U., 1985; MS in Engring., U. Mo., Rolla, 1987; PhD, U. Iowa, 1993. Mfg. engr. Gen. Electric Co., Syracuse, N.Y., 1987-88, Erie, Pa., 1988-89; rsch. engr. Nat. Inst. Standards and Tech., Gaithersburg, Md., 1991-93; asst. prof. mech. engring. Tuskegee (Ala.) U., 1993—. Editor MESA Newsletter, 1992; contbr. articles to profl. jours. Named to Outstanding Young Men in Am., 1988, 89; CIC doctoral fellow, 1989-93, GM fellow, 1983-85. Mem. Am. Prodn. and Inventory Control Soc., Inst. Indsl. Engrs. (assoc.), Am. Soc. Engring. Mgmt., Nat. Tech. Assn., Soc. Mfg. Engrs., Inst. Indsl. Engrs. (assoc.). Democrat. Office: Tuskegee U Dept Mech Engring Tuskegee AL 36088

HARING, ROBERT WESTING, newspaper editor; b. Salem, Mo., Nov. 13, 1932; s. Arthur S. and Martha I. (Westing) H.; m. Jo M. Houser, June 1, 1957 (dec. Nov. 1991); children: Robert A., Joel B., Jon G.; m. Carolyn Scudder, May 20, 1995. AA, Kansas City (Mo.) Jr. Coll., 1951; BJ, BA in History, U. Mo., 1954. Reporter So. Illinoisan, Carbondale, Ill., 1954-55, city editor, 1957-59; writer AP, Little Rock, 1959-61; corr. AP, Tulsa, 1961-64; asst. bur. chief AP, Columbus, Ohio, 1964-67; bur. chief AP, Newark, 1967-71; exec. AP, N.Y.C., 1971-75; Sunday editor Tulsa World, 1975-81, exec. editor, 1981-95. Chmn. Goodwill Industries, Tulsa, 1990-94; bd. dirs. River Parks Authority, Tulsa, 1985-93; pres. Tulsa Zoofriends, 1994-96; chmn. Tulsa Mentoring Coun., Tulsa Lit. Coalition, 1996—; initiated price earnings ratio in newspaper stock tables, 1973. With U.S. Army, 1955-57. Home: 7023 E 66th St Tulsa OK 74133-1804 Office: Tulsa World PO Box 1770 315 S Boulder Ave Tulsa OK 74103

HARKER, HELEN CONNIE, medical/surgical nurse; b. Santa Monica, Calif., Feb. 4, 1955; d. Adolph Gil and Helen Florence (Stewart) Araujo; m. James Andrew Harker III, June 26, 1982; 1 child, Jennifer Ann Alexis. RN, Orangeburg (S.C.) Reg. Hosp., 1982; diploma med. office asst., Cen. Piedmont Community Coll., Charlotte, N.C., 1975. Med. office asst. Florence Neurol., Florence, S.C.; med. sec. Coleman Aimer Hosp., Darlington, S.C.; staff nurse Presbyn. Hosp., Charlotte, N.C.; staff nurse II McLeod Reg. Med. Ctr., Florence; nurse mgr. plastics, ENT, gynecology McLeod Regional Med. Ctr., Florence, S.C., 1985—; info. analyst, resource appt. scheduling, computer svcs. McLeod Regional Med. Ctr., 1992-94; nursing analyst, 1994—, home health nurse, 1994-95. Home: 3850 Pine Needles Rd Florence SC 29501-8522 Office: 555 E Cheves St Florence SC 29506

HARKEY, ROBERT SHELTON, lawyer; b. Charlotte, N.C., Dec. 22, 1940; s. Charles Nathan and Josephine Lenora (McKenzie) H.; m. Barbara Carole Payne, Apr. 2, 1983; 1 child, Elizabeth McKenzie. BA, Emory U., 1963, LLB, 1965. Bar: Ga. 1964, U.S. Dist. Ct. (no. dist.) Ga. 1964, U.S. Ct. Appeals (1st, 5th, 7th, 9th and 11th cirs.) 1964-86, U.S. Supreme Ct. Assoc. Swift, Currie, McGhee & Hiers, Atlanta, 1965-68; atty. Delta Air Lines, Atlanta, 1968-74, gen. atty., 1974-79, asst. v.p. law, 1979-85, assoc. gen. counsel, v.p., 1985-88; gen counsel, v.p., 1988-90; gen. counsel, sr. v.p. Delta Air Lines, Atlanta, 1990-94, gen. counsel, sr. v.p., sec., 1994—. Unit chmn. United Way, Atlanta, 1985; trustee Woodruff Arts Ctr., 1995—; bd. visitors Emory U., 1996—. Mem. ABA (com. gen. counsels), Air Transport Assn. (chmn. law coun. 1996—), State Bar Ga. (chmn. corp. counsel sect. 1992-93), Atlanta Bar Assn., Corp. Counsel Assn. Greater Atlanta (bd. dirs. 1990), Commerce Club. Presbyterian. Office: Delta Air Lines Hartsfield Atlanta Internat Airport Atlanta GA 30320

HARKIN, DANIEL JOHN, controller; b. Bradenton, Fla., Mar. 29, 1955; s. John Lewis and Stella Marie (Durand) H.; m. Theresa Ann Ford; children: Erin Kathleen, Shaun Ford. BBA, Fla. Atlantic U., 1975. CPA, Fla. Controller Vis. Home Health Svc., Boca Raton, Fla., 1975-78; CPA Cherry Bekaert & Holland, Ft. Lauderdale, Fla., 1978-85; controller Griffin Bros. Co., Inc., Davie, Fla., 1985-90, L.W. Rozzo, Inc., Pembroke Pines, Fla., 1990—. Contbr. articles to profl. jours. Fla. univ. faculty scholar Fla. Atlantic U., 1972-75. Mem. AICPA, Fla. Inst. CPAs (mem. com. 1980-91, adv. com. MAS 1990-91, speaker 1984), Nat. Assn. Accts., Nat. Inst. Tax Profls., Smithsonian Instn., Inst. Mgmt. Accts., Greenpeace, Roscicrucian Order AMORC. Roman Catholic. Home: 1834 SW 21st St # 2 Fort Lauderdale FL 33315-1833 Office: L W Rozzo Inc 17200 Pines Blvd Hollywood FL 33029-1505

HARKINS, ANNA MARIE, JR., cardiologist, preventive medicine physician; b. Ft. Worth, Oct. 22, 1943; d. Maurice Alexander Sr. and Anna Marie (Boyd) . BS in Chemistry, Tex. Christian U., 1965; postgrad., MIT, 1964-65; MA, PhD in Phys. Chemistry, Duke U., 1970; DO, Tex. Coll. Osteo. Medicine, Ft. Worth, 1980. Diplomate Nat. Bd. Osteo. Examiners, Am. Bd. Internal Medicine; cert. ATLS, ACLS; lic. physician, Tex., Ariz. Welch postdoctoral fellow Tex. Woman's U., Denton, 1970; postdoctoral fellow dept. biochemistry U. Tex. Southwestern Med. Sch., Dallas, 1971; fellow in phys. chemistry U. Calif., San Francisco, 1972; intern Dallas Osteo. Hosp., 1980-81; resident in internal medicine U. Mo., Kansas City, 1981-84; fellow in cardiology Baylor Coll. Medicine, Houston, 1984-87; physician Med. Care Clinic, Sun City, Ariz., 1987-88; sole practitioner cardiology and internal medicine Pasadena, Tex., 1989—; chair cardiology sect. Bayshore Hosp., 1993—; staff privileges Meml. S.E. Hosp., Houston, Meth. Hosp., Houston, others. Fellow Am. Coll. Cardiology; mem. AMA, Am. Coll. Cardiology, Ariz. Angioplasty Soc., Sigma Xi. Office: 901 E Curtis # 38 Pasadena TX 77502

HARKLEROAD, JO-ANN DECKER, special education educator; b. Wilkes-Barre, Pa., Oct. 22, 1936; d. Leon Joseph Sr. and Beatrice Catherine (Wright) Decker; m. A. Dwayne Harkleroad; 1 child, Leon Wade. AS, George Washington U., 1960, BS in Health, Phys. Edn. and Recreation, 1968, MA in Spl. Edn. and Ednl. Diagnosis and Prescription, 1969, also postgrad. Recipient Appreciation cert. Fairfax County (Va.) Police Dept., 1987, Meritorious Svc. medal Pres. Com. on Employment of People with Disabilities, 1988. Instr. Cath. U. Am., Washington, 1960-61; tchr. Bush Hill Day Sch., Franconia, Va., 1961-63; ednl. diagnostician Prince William County Schs., Manassas, Va., 1969-71, supr. title I, 1971-72; writer, editor Sta. WNVT-TV, Fairfax, Va., 1980-82; dir. spl. edn. Highland County Schs., Monterey, Va., 1987-90. Author: (novel) Horse Thief Trail, 1981, 83, 86; columnist op-ed page The Recorder; radio broadcaster Sta. WVMR, Frost, W.Va. Elder Presbyn. Ch., McDowell, Va., Clifton, Va.; former mem. comm. com. Shenandoah Presbytery; dir. McDowell Presbyn. Ch. Choir; rotating dir. Highland County Cmty. Choir; pres. Highland County Pub. Libr. Bd. Home: Windy Ridge Farm HCR 33 Box 60 Mc Dowell VA 24458

HARKNESS, MARY LOU, librarian; b. Denby, S.D., Aug. 19, 1925; d. Raleigh Everette and Mary Jane (Boyd) Barker; m. Donald R. Harkness, Sept. 2, 1967. B.A., Nebr. Wesleyan U., 1947; A.B. in L.S, U. Mich., 1948; M.S., Columbia U., 1958. Jr. cataloger U. Mich. Law Library, 1948-50; asst. cataloger Calif. Poly. Coll., 1950-52; asst. cataloger, then head cataloger Ga. Inst. Tech., 1952-57; head cataloger U. S.Fla., Tampa, 1958-67; dir. libraries U. S.Fla., 1967-87, dir. emeritus, 1987—; cons. Nat. Library Nigeria, 1962-63. Bd. dirs. Southeastern Library Network, 1977-80. Recipient Alumni Achievement award Nebr. Wesleyan U., 1972. Mem. Am., S.E., Fla. library assns., Fla. Women's Alliance, Athena Soc. Democrat. Mem. United Ch. Christ. Home: 13511 Palmwood Ln Tampa FL 33624-4409

HARKNESS, R. KENNETH, restaurant chain executive; b. Warren, Ohio, Aug. 22, 1949; s. Roy K. and Yvonne D. (Howitt) H.; m. Marianne Loprete, Sept. 28, 1974; 1 child, Austin Blaine. BS in Bus., Rutgers U., 1972, MBA in Acctg., 1973. Pres., chief exec. officer N.Y. Sub Inc., Dallas, 1974-81, 85—, Fox Hunt Realty, Inc., Far Hills, N.J., 1981-85, Kenco Restaurants, Inc., Dallas, 1987—. Mem. University Park Master Plan Com. Mem. Nat. Restaurant Assn., Tex. Restaurant Assn., Rep. Inner Circle. Episcopalian. Office: NY Sub Inc 3411 Asbury St Dallas TX 75205-1844

HARKRADER, SUE ROBERTSON, secondary school educator; b. Christiansburg, Va., Jan. 7, 1941; d. Franklin Mitchell and Ivory Opal (Bell) R.; m. Robert McLean Harkrader, Dec. 23, 1962; children: Robert Ashley, Mary Beth. BS in Edn., Radford (Va.) Coll., 1963. Classroom tchr. Pulaski (Va.) County Schs., 1963-66, Ashe County Schs., Jefferson, N.C., 1966-67, Elizabeth City (N.C.)-Pasquotank Schs., 1967-70, Washington City (N.C.) Schs., 1970-71, Pamlico Community Sch., Washington, 1974-75; tchr. ceramics and crafts Pitt C.C., Greenville, N.C., 1975-81, reading aide, 1981-84; tchr. crafts Winston-Salem, N.C., 1985-88; tchr. asst. autistic class Forsyth County Schs., Winston-Salem, 1988; tchr. asst. self-contained autistic trainable mentally handicapped classroom South Park High Sch., Winston-Salem, 1988-90, tchr.; ind. craft tchr. Winston-Salem, 1989-90; tchr. TMH/autistic/self-contained class South Park High Sch., 1990-94, TMH socialization tchr., 1994-95, TH acad. tchr., 1995—; cmty. based vocat. trainer for TMH, 1995—; subs. tchr. Winston-Salem/Forsyth County Schs., 1985—. mem. editorial bd. Pro Ed Mag. Rep. election judge, Winston-Salem, 1986-87; rep. commr. spl. registration, Winston-Salem, 1987—; mem. youth com. Calvary Bapt. Ch. Mem. NEA, Forsyth Assn. of Classroom Tchrs., Coun. for Exceptional Children (v.p., presenter Pacific-RIM internat. conf. 1992, pres. 1993—), Twin City Civitan, Beta Sigma Phi (pres. 1986-87, sec. city coun. 1988, v.p. city coun. 1992-93, pres. city coun. 1993—, Pledge of Yr. 1986, Woman of Yr. 1987, 88, chpt. pres. 1994—), Ayden Golf and Country Club (pres. ladies ass. 1976-77), Jonestown Swim and Tennis Club (v.p. socials). Baptist. Home: 4731 Chippendale Way Winston Salem NC 27103-5201

HARLEY, AL BOYCE, JR., psychiatrist; b. Sylvania, S.C., Sept. 20, 1932; s. A. Boyce and Bertie T. (Flythe) H.; m. Sidney Martin, Aug. 16, 1958; children: Al B. III, Charles T.M., Kayreth W. BS, The Citadel, 1955; MD, Med U SC, 1959; PhD, Christian Bible Coll., 1987. Diplomate Am. Bd. Medical Psychotherapist. Intern Greenville (S.C.) Gen. Hosp., 1959-60; resident in psychiatry Eastern State Hosp., Williamsburg, Va., 1960-62; chief resident Medical U. S.C., Charleston, 1962-63; chief NP Svc. 3rd Army Headquarters, Atlanta, 1965; chmn. psychiatry dept. McLeod Regional Medical Ctr., Florence, S.C., 1965—. Co-author: Group Psychotherapy For Parent of Disturbed Children, 1966. Lt. col. Aid de Camp Gov. State Ga., 1964. Capt. U.S. Army, 1963-65. Life fellow Am. Psychiat. Assn.; mem. Assn. Mil. Surgeons, Christian Assn. Psychol. Studies. Republican. Presbyterian. Home: 1111 Wisteria Dr Florence SC 29501-5763 Office: 151 W Pine St Florence SC 29501-4711

HARLEY, RUTH, artist, educator; b. Phila., July 24, 1923; children: Peter Wells Bressler, Tori Angela. Student, Pa. State U., 1941; BFA, Phila. Coll. Art, 1945; postgrad., U. N.H., 1971, Hampshire Coll., 1970. Former instr. Phila. Mus. Art, 1946-59; former art supt. Ventnor (N.J.) City Bd. Edn., 1959-61; art tchr. The Print Club, Phila., Allens Lane Art Ctr., Phila., Suburban Ctr. Arts, Lower Merion, Pa., Radner (Pa.) Twp. Adult Ctr., 1949-59, Atlantic City Adult Ctr., 1959-60. One-woman shows include Dubin-Lush Galleries, Phila., 1956, Pa. Acad. Fine Arts, Phila., 1957, Contemporary Art Assn., Phila., 1957, Vernon Art Exhbns., Germantown, Pa., 1958, Detroit Inst. Arts, 1958, Phila. Mus. Art, 1957, 59, Moore Inst., Phila., 1962-68, Greenhill Galleries, Phila., 1974, Phila. Civic Ctr., 1978, Natal Rio Grande du Norte, Brazil, 1979, Galerie Novel Esprit, Tampa, Fla., 1992-95, Mind's Eye Gallery, St. Petersburg, Fla., 1993; exhibited in various group shows, including Group 55, Phila., 1955, Print Club, Phila., 1955, Nat. Tours 1956-59, Pa. Acad. Fine Arts, 1957, Vernon Art Exhbns., 1958, Detroit Inst. Arts, 1958, Phila. Mus. Art, 1959, Moore Inst., 1962, Phila. Civic Ctr. Mus., 1975, Galerie Nouvel Esprit Assemblage Russe, 1992, Kenneth Raymond Gallery, Boca Raton, 1992-93, Mind's Eye Gallery, 1993, Polk Mus. Art, Lakeland, Fla., 1993, Don Roll Gallery, Sarasota, Fla., 1994-95, Las Vegas (Nev.) Internat. Art Expo, 1994, Heim Am. Gallery, Fisher Island, Fla., 1996, Galerie Nouvel Esprit, 1996; represented in permanent collections at U. Villanova (Pa.) Mus., Temple U. Law Sch., Pa., Woodmere Mus., Phila.; included in Art in America Ann. Guide, 1993-97; 1973 photo sculpture commd. through Phila. Re-Devel. Authority. Address: PO Box 433 Melrose FL 32666-0433

HARLIN-FISCHER, GAYLE C., elementary education educator; b. Fort Worth, Mar. 27, 1950; d. Noble Eugene and Myrtle Mildred (Aycock)

Chandler; m. Roger William Harlin, May 23, 1979 (div. 1987); children: Jesse Chandler Harlin, Laura Claire Harlin; m. Terry Wayne Fischer, Mar. 18, 1990. BS in Edn., U. Ga., 1973; MS in Edn., U. Okla., 1990, postgrad., 1991-94. Cert. tchr., Tex., Okla.; cert. elem. prin. Okla. Tchr. Cobb County Dist., Marietta, Ga., 1973-75; tchr. of emotionally disturbed Spring Br. Acad., Houston, 1976-78; 4th grade tchr. Aldine Sch. Dist., Houston, 1979-81; tchr. of emotionally disturbed Mid-Del Schs., Midwest City, Okla., 1979-81; 3d grade tchr. Mid Del Schs., Midwest City, Okla., 1989—; 6th and 8th grade tchr. Norman (Okla.) Sch. Dist., 1988-89; trainer behavioral mgmt. Mid-Del Schs., 1990-95; chmn. adminstrv. com. Okla. Commn. on Tchr. Preparation, Oklahoma City, 1991-95. Mem. NEA, ASCD, Coun. for Exceptional Children, Coun. for Children with Behavioral Disorders, Coun. Adminstrs. in Spl. Edn., Okla. Assn. Colls. Tchr. Edn. (presenter winter conf. 1993), Assn. Classroom Tchrs., Okla. Edn. Assn. Home: 6028 SE 104th St Oklahoma City OK 73165-9606

HARLLEE, MARY BETH, social worker; b. Statesville, N.C., Apr. 20, 1946; d. Zimmie Edward and Anna Beth (Morrison) Tharpe; m. Thomas Cannon Harllee, Nov. 12, 1972. AA, Mitchell Jr. Coll., 1966; BA, Catawba Coll., 1968; MEd, U. N.C., Charlotte, 1977; MSW, U. S.C., Columbia, 1990. Lic. social worker, N.C., S.C. Child welfare specialist City of Danville, Va., 1968-72; personnel cons. Golden Door, Charlotte, 1972-74; reading specialist, program coord. Learning Found., Charlotte, 1974-76; human svcs. asst. City of Charlotte, 1977-87; svc. rep. Kelly Svcs., Charlotte, 1987-88; social worker S.C. State Hosp., Columbia, 1989-90, Harris Psychiat. Hosp., Anderson, S.C., 1990—; dir. Project Cope, Hartsville, S.C., 1995—; adj. prof. Coke Coll., Hartsville, S.C., 1995—. Chair social com. N.C. Literacy Bd., Charlotte, 1984-88; mem. gov.'s Adv. Bd. Alzheimer's Assn. Named Social Worker of Yr. Dept. Health and Environ. Control, Florence, S.C., 1992, 95. Mem. Nat. Assn. Clin. Social Workers, Dem. Women Charlotte. Democrat. Office: Harris Psychiat Hosp PO Box 2907 Anderson SC 29622-2907

HARMAN, JO ANN SNYDER, secondary school educator; b. Lahmansville, W.Va., Aug. 30, 1940; d. Lloyd Neil and Eva Lucretia (Parker) Snyder; m. Robert L. Harman, June 17, 1962; children: Kenton Snyder, Brenton Robert. BA summa cum laude, Fairmont (W.Va.) State Coll., 1962; MA, W.Va. U., 1986. Cert. in gifted edn., French, English. Sec. tchr. Fairfax (Va.) County Bd. Edn., 1962-64; adult edn. instr. Shepherd Coll., Petersburg, W.Va., 1986—; sec. tchr. Grant County Bd. Edn., Petersburg, W.Va., 1964—; pres. Petersburg High Sch. Faculty Senate; coord., instr. summer program gifted and talented students Collegiate Acad. of Learning; presentor insvc. sessions and profl. programs on writing, creativity, and gifted edn.; dir. numerous student trips; mentor new tchrs.; invited participant Pearl S. Buck Centennial Celebration, China; selected pilot program for French book for Am. Schs. Libraire Hachette, France; mem. North Ctrl. Evaluation Team; participant confs. in field; tchr., mentor, supr.; supervising tchr. for student tchrs. from France. Contbr. articles to profl. jours. Sponsor Nat. Honor Soc. and French Club; mem. and clk. of session Petersburg Presbyn. Ch.; originator tribute for Pearl S. Buck Centennial, 1991. Recipient Presdl. citation from W.Va. Gov.'s Honors Acad., Tchr. Achievement award Ashland Oil, 1992; named Grant County Tchr. of Yr., 1996 W.Va. Tchr. of Yr.; 9 mini-grants for edn. Mem. NEA, ASCD, W.Va. Edn. Assn., Grant County Edn. Assn., Nat. Coun. Tchrs. English, W.Va. Assn. for Gifted, Internat. Platform Assn., Nat. Assn. Student Activity Advisors, World of Poetry, Order Eastern Star (past grand officer and grand rep.), Delta Kappa Gamma, Kappa Delta Pi, Pi Lambda Theta. Home: HC 84 Box 26 Lahmansville WV 26731-9701

HARMER, DON STUTLER, physics and nuclear engineering educator; m. Carolyn Wood, 1952 (div. 1964); children: Diana H. Brown, Katherina H. Lucey, Nancy H. Wiggers; m. Lee DeLoache, Dec. 22, 1965; children: David Stutler, Muffin Louise Blakeney, Jonathan Aubrey. Student, USN Electronics Schs., Great Lakes, Ill. and Washington, 1946-47; BS in Chemistry cum laude, George Washington U., 1952; PhD in Nuclear Chemistry, UCLA, 1956; postgrad., N.C. State U., 1960. Postdoctoral fellow Brookhaven Nat. Labs., Upton, N.Y., 1956-59; prof. physics and nuclear engrng. Ga. Inst. Tech., Atlanta, 1959—; cons. on solar neutrino experimental physics rsch. Brookhaven Nat. Labs., 1959-67; cons. computer systems design Digital Equipment Corp., Maynard, Mass., 1967-76; cons. hardware and software design, systems tng. CompuCom Inc., Atlanta, 1986-89; performed experimental rsch. on blood coagulation and in vitro tagging Ferst Rsch. Ctr., Atlanta, 1960-67; designed and implemented numerous on-line computer data acquistion and control systems. Contbg. author (textbook) Introduction to Computer Technology and Interfacing, 1970; contbr. more than 80 articles on physics and computer systems to profl. jours.; patentee in field. With USN, 1946-48, USNR, 1948-53. Recipient Outstanding Mentor award, 1992; named Faculty Mem. of Yr., 1992-93. Fellow Am. Inst. Chemists, Am. Inst. Physics, Am. Nuclear Soc., Southeastern MGT Register (past pres.), Peachtree MG Registry, MG Car Club, Sigma Nu. Episcopalian. Home: 3926 Harts Mill Ln NE Atlanta GA 30319-1854

HARMER, ROSE, marriage and family therapist, mental health counselor; b. Kirkland Lake, Ont., Can., Dec. 9, 1939; came to U.S. 1976, naturalized 1984.; d. John and Tyyne (Nykanen) Spillenaar; m. Montford Oakes, Sept. 3, 1960 (div. 1972); children: Sandra, Nancy; m. Robert Elswood Harmer, July 27, 1973; stepchildren: Joanne, Michael. BA summa cum laude, U. S. Fla., 1986, MA in Counseling, 1986; Cert., Ashland Theol. Sem., 1983, 87. Cert. rehab. counselor; lic. marriage and family therapist; lic. mental health counselor. Intern S.W. Addiction Svcs., Ft. Myers, Fla., 1985, S.O.L.V.E. Maternity Home, Ft. Myers, Fla., 1986; therapist and cons. Counseling & Growth Ctr., Ft. Myers, Fla., 1987-89; psychotherapist in pvt. practice Cape Coral, Fla., 1987—; founder, dir. Genesis III Counseling Ctr., Ft. Myers, 1990—. Rotary scholar, 1983, 84, 85; recipient award John Price Found., 1986. Mem. Am. Assn. Counseling & Devel., Am. Assn. Marriage and Family Therapy, Nat. Bd. Certified Counselors. Mem. Assemblies of God. Home: 1516 SW 53rd Ln Cape Coral FL 33914-7490 Office: Genesis III Counseling Ctr 5264 Clayton Ct Ste 3 Fort Myers FL 33907-2112

HARMON, DAVID EUGENE, optometrist, geneticist; b. Greeneville, Tenn., July 27, 1951; s. Carl Eugene and Kathryn Elizabeth (Colyer) H.; m. Kimberly Denise Brooks. BS, U. Tenn., 1973, MS, 1975; PhD, U. Ga., 1978; OD, New Eng. Coll. Optometry, 1989. Fellow U. Ga., Athens, 1978, U. Fla., Gainesville, 1979; vis. asst. prof. So. Ill. U., Carbondale, 1980-82; asst. prof. Clemson (S.C.) U., 1982-85, assoc. prof., 1985; internist VA Hosp., Boston, 1988, Children's Hosp., Boston, 1988-89, Dimock Community Health Ctr., Boston, 1989; eye specialist Morristown, Tenn., 1989—; geneticist Morristown, 1989—; genetic cons. Nigerian Govt., 1980—. Contbr. articles to profl. jours. Mem. Sunday sch. Trinity United Meth. Ch., Greeneville, 1954—; sch. rep. New Eng. Coll. Optometry, 1987. Recipient Breeder Al-Am. Dairy Animal award Am. Guernsey Cattle Club, 1973. Mem. Am. Optometric Assn., Am. Dairy Assn., Am. Soc. Animal Sci., Tenn. Optometric Assn., So. Coun. of Optometrists, Holstein Assn. Am., Sigma Xi, Alpha Zeta. Home and Office: 131 N Henry St Morristown TN 37814

HARMON, (LOREN) FOSTER, art consultant; b. Judsonia, Ark., Nov. 5, 1912; s. Alfred Roscoe and Mae (Foster) H.; m. Martha Rowles Foster, July 25, 1943. Student, Ind. U., 1930-32, Ohio U., 1932-33; BA, U. Iowa, 1935, MFA, 1936; DFA (hon.) Ohio U., 1992. Dir. Univ. and Exptl. Theatre, Ind. U., Bloomington, 1936-42; pub. relations mgr. Sta. WKBN Broadcasting Co., Youngstown, Ohio, 1943-48; owner, developer, dir. Pine Shores Park, Sarasota, Fla., 1950-54 v.p., dir. Players, Sarasota, 1955-57; pub. relations dir. Ringling Mus. Art, 1958-59; dir. Oehlschlaeger Galleries, Sarasota, 1961-70; v.p. Vandium Tool Co., Athens, Ohio, 1954-64; founder, owner, dir. Harmon Gallery, Naples, Fla., 1964-79; owner, dir. Foster Harmon Galleries Am. Art, Sarasota, 1979-93; bd. trustees, advisor Ohio U. Mus. Am. Art, Fla. Artists Group Mus. and Gallery, 1974-87; founder Foster and Martha Harmon Am. Art Study Ctr. and Archives Ohio U., 1995. Active Ringling Mus. Coun., 1957—; trustee Ringling Sch. Art, Sarasota, 1981—; bd. dirs. Asolo State Theater 1982-89, Sarasota Opera Assn., 1983—, Van Wezel Performing Arts Hall Found., 1987—, Players, 1989—. Recipient cert. of merit Ohio U., 1970. Mem. Am. Ednl. Theatre Assn. (founder), Am. Fedn. Arts, Sarasota Art Assn. (pres. 1959-60), Fla. League Arts, Smithsonian Inst., Archives Am. Art, Sarasota Arts Council, St. Armands Assn. (pres. 1957-58), Internat. Platform Assn. Methodist. Clubs: Sarasota Yacht, Univ. (Sarasota). Home: 1255 N Gulfstream Ave Apt 1102 Sarasota FL 34236-8905

HARMON, GARY LEE, English language educator; b. Aurora, Nebr., Aug. 16, 1935; s. Vyrle Martin and Esther Irene (Koberstein) Uehling; m. Susanna Marie Pollock, Apr. 10, 1939 (div. Mar. 1984); children: Thomas Thorburn, James Matthias, Nathan Martin; m. Deborah Sinton Gray Harmon, May 9, 1995. BA, Hastings (Nebr.) Coll., 1956; MAT, MA, Ind. U., 1960, PhD, 1966. Men's counselor Ind. U., Bloomington, 1957-59, tchg. asst., 1959-60; instr. Flint (Mich.) C.C., 1960-64; chair divsn. langs. and lit. Morehead (Ky.) State U., 1966-67; chair divsn. lang., lit. and philosophy Stephens Coll., Columbia, Mo., 1967-71; prof. lit. and English U. North Fla., Jacksonville, 1971—, chair dept., 1971-79. Co-author: Write Now: Substance, Strategy and Style, 1972, Scholar's Market: Periodicals Publishing Literary Scholarship in English, 1974; editor/author: Film and Gender: Myth, Power and Change, 1996. Treas., mem. Film Inst. Jacksonville, 1973-85. Mem. MLA, Am. Culture Assn., Popular Culture Assn. (v.p. 1979-81, Leadership award 1984), Popular Culture Assn. of the South (pres. 1977-78), Am. Culture Assn. of the South (exec. sec. S.E. region 1983-87, Leadership award 1984), Fla. Coll. English Assn. Episcopalian. Home: 2815 Sylvan Ln N Jacksonville FL 32157 Office: University of North Florida Saint Johns Bluff Blvd Jacksonville FL 32724

HARMON, JANE ELLEN, occupational therapist, writer; b. Muskegon, Mich.; d. Robert Junior and Edith (Boven) H. BS in Occupational Therapy, Western Mich. U., 1974; postgrad., Cleve., 1997. Registered occupational therapist; licensed occupational therapist, Tex.; cert. CPR/BCLS instr.-trainer. From vol. to staff therapist Hackley Hosp., Muskegon, 1972-75; head occupational therapy dept. Mercy Hosp., Muskegon, 1975-79; pvt. practice, 1976-79; with Mary Free Bed Hosp. & Rehab. Ctr., Grand Rapids, 1979; free-lance writer, 1979—; cons. Tri-City Health Ctr./Hosp., Dallas, 1993. Author: At Home with MS, 1996; contbg. writer Inside MS, 1996; contbr. articles to profl. jours.; contbg. editor, cons. Occupational Therapy Forum, 1993-95. Active Arthritis Vol. Action Com., 1975-79; founder Vols. Against Multiple Sclerosis Mich. chpt. Nat. Multiple Sclerosis Soc., 1973 (recipient Individual Vol. of the Yr. award, 1994), co-chair Govtl. Rels. Com., mem. profl. adv. com. North Tex. chpt., mem. patient svc. com., MS Tex. CAN, 1996—; mem. HIV/AIDS Com. Bethel Ch., Dallas, 1992—, prayer chain coord., 1990-96, editor Bethel News, 1989-90; editor, cage bird cons. pet-facilitated therapy program Baylor Inst. for Rehab., Dallas, 1992-93; founder, dir. Project HAVEN Dallas Cage Bird Soc., 1991-93; vol. Dallas Ctr. for Ind. Living, 1990—; liaison Classis Pella Com. on Disability Concerns; founder, dir. Ecology Ministries, 1987—; rep. com. disability concerns Classis Pella, Christian Reformed Ch. N.Am., 1994—; bd. dirs. Northeast Tex. chpt. Am. Parkinson Disease Assn., 1996—; mem. Greater Dallas/Ft. Worth chpt. Myasthenia Gravis Found., 1994—; mem., editor Dallas County CLASS adv. bd., 1996—; resource person MS & Degenerative Neurol. Diseases, 1991—. Mem. Tex. Occupational Therapy Assn., Environ. Health Assn. Dallas, Am. Occupational Therapy Assn., Write Shop Writer's Assn., Rehab. Engring. and Assistive Tech. Soc. N.Am. Office: 14232 Marsh Ln Ste 320 Dallas TX 75234-3865

HARMON, JOHN LAFAYETTE, retired petroleum engineer; b. Hillsboro, Tex., June 24, 1929; s. John Lee and Winnie Kate (Stallings) H.; m. Lucile Gracy, Dec. 23, 1949 (div. June 1973); m. Bettye Sue McKinney, June 21, 1974; children: John C., David L., Christopher L. BS in Geology, U. Tex., 1952. Rsch. engr. Midstates Petroleum, Abilene, Tex., 1952-54; geol. engr. Kent Waddell & Co., Abilene, Tex., 1954-55, Connally Oil Co., Abilene, Tex., 1955-63; engr., owner J.L. Harmon & Assocs., Abilene, Tex., 1963-86; engr., drilling supr. Texland Petroleum, Inc., Lubbock, 1986-95. Contbr. articles to profl. jours. Mem. Soc. Petroleum Engrs. (sr., 25-yr. club). Republican. Episcopalian. Home: 4901 Fairway Ct Granbury TX 76049

HARMON, MELINDA FURCHE, federal judge; b. Port Arthur, Tex., Nov. 1, 1946; d. Frank Cantrell and Wilma (Parish) Furche; m. Frank G. Harmon III, Oct. 16, 1976; children: Mary Elizabeth, Phelps, Francis. AB, Harvard U., 1969; JD, U. Tex., 1972. Bar: Tex. 1973, U.S. Dist. Ct. (so. dist.) Tex. 1974, U.S. Dist. Ct. (no. dist.) Tex. 1975, U.S. Dist. Ct. (ea. dist.) Tex. 1978, U.S. Ct. Appeals (5th and 11th cirs.) 1981, U.S. Supreme Ct. 1982, U.S. Ct. Claims 1987. Law clk. to presiding judge U.S. Dist. Ct. (so. dist.) Tex., Houston, 1973-75; atty. Exxon Co., Houston, 1975-88; judge 280th Jud. Dist. Ct. Tex. State Trial Ct., ctrl. jurisdiction, 1988-89; judge U.S. Dist. Ct. (so. dist.) Tex., Houston, 1989—. Mem. Tex. Bar Assn., Houston Bar Assn., Harvard Radcliffe Club. Roman Catholic. Office: US Dist Ct US Courthouse 515 Rusk St Ste 9114 Houston TX 77002-2605*

HARMON, WILLIAM RUTH, poet, English language educator; b. Concord, N.C., June 10, 1938; s. William Richard and Virginia Ruth (Pickerel) H.; m. Lynn Frances Chadwell, Dec. 21, 1965 (div. July 1984); children: Sally Frances, William Richard II; m. Anne Margretta Wilson, May 7, 1988; 1 child, Caroline Ruth. AB, U. Chgo., 1958, AM, 1968; MA, U. N.C., 1968; PhD, U. Cin., 1970. Instr. U. N.C., Chapel Hill, 1970-71, asst. prof., 1971-73, assoc. prof., 1973-77, prof., 1977-94, J.G. Hanes prof., 1994—. Author of five books of poetry, 1970-85. Lt. USNR, 1960-67. Recipient Lamont Poetry award Acad. Am. Poets, 1970, William Carlos Williams award Poetry Soc. Am., 1985. Democrat. Office: Univ NC English Dept CB # 3520 Chapel Hill NC 27599-3520

HARMONY, BARBARA HELEN, educational administrator, environmental educator; b. Newark, Feb. 8, 1943; d. Israel David and Marjorie (Robinson) Weiss; 1 child, Ben. BA, Goddard Coll., 1964. Field rep. Scandinavian Seminar, 1964-66; cmty. organizer Citizens Com. Pub. Edn., 1967; trainer Temple U., 1968, Western Cmty. Action Tng., 1969; dir. tng. & career devel. Hoboken Model Cities, 1970-74; dir. Ctr. 21st Century Edn., 1974-79; Coord. Water Ctr., Eureka Springs, Ark., 1979—, Lifelong Learning, Eureka Springs, Ark., 1989—. Author: Back to the Vineyard; co-author: Aquaterra Metaecology and Culture; publ.: We All Live Downstream. Home: Rte 7 720 Eureka Springs AR 72632

HARMS, BLAIRE MICHELE, army officer; b. Berkeley, Calif., June 9, 1967; d. Richard William Harms and Julie Ann (Olsen) Steinmetz; m. Stuart Michael Hirstein, June 25, 1994; 1 child, Austin Xavier. BA in Internat. Rels. summa cum laude, Calif. State U., Chico, 1990; grad., Army Mil. Intelligence Sch., 1991; postgrad., Syracuse Univ., 1994—. Commd. 2d lt. U.S. Army, 1990, advanced to capt., 1995; platoon leader Hdqs. Co. U.S. Army, So. Korea, 1991, Ground Suveillance Platoon, 1991-92; asst. chief intelligence prodn. sect. U.S. Army, Ft. Bragg, N.C., 1992-93, bn. intelligence officer, Aviation Battalion, 1993-94, intelligence analyst, 1994-95, exec. asst. to comdr., spl. ops. command, 1995-96, co. comdr., 1996—. First aid and CPR instr., lifeguard ARC; coord. patient ministry Womack Army Med. Ctr. Phi Epsilon Phi scholar. Mem. Acad. Polit. Sci., Assn. U.S. Army, Wilson Ctr. Assocs., Ariz. Honors Acad., Scabbard and Blade, Phi Kappa Phi, Sigma Iota Rho, Omicron Delta Epsilon, Phi Eta Sigma. Republican. Roman Catholic. Home: 5840 Conservation Ct Fayetteville NC 28314

HARNER, DAVID PAUL, development administrator; b. Morgantown, W.Va., Dec. 27, 1943; s. Clarence Vincent and Lillian Yvonne (Utt) H.; m. Patty Elaine Bentley, June 5, 1964; children: David Paul II, Jennifer Nicole. BA, Fla. So. Coll., Lakeland, 1965; MEd, U. Miss., 1972, PhD, 1973. Tchr. Polk County (Fla.) Schs., 1968-71; asst. prof. edn., supr. student tchrs. Centennary Coll. La., 1973-76, asst. prof., dean student svcs., 1976, v.p., dir. budget and planning, assoc. prof. edn., 1977-78; mgr. Shreveport C. of C., 1978-80; dir. devel. Loretto Hts. Coll., 1980-83; dir. Ctr. for Ednl. Rsch. Shreveport C. of C., 1978-80; realtor, broker Pyramid Realty and Mortgage Corp., 1983-85; broker, owner Harner Real Estate, Winter Haven, Fla., 1985-89; assoc. dir. Iowa State U. Found., Ames, 1989-92; pres. Christopher Newport U. Ednl. Found., Newport News, Va., 1993-96; v.p. for devel. univ. rels. Christopher Newport U., Newport News, 1993-96; regional dir. devel. Fla. regional office The Nature Conservancy, Altamonte Springs, 1996—; adj. prof. Polk C.C., 1985-89; cons. Caddo Parish Schs., Shreveport, La., 1974-79, Lexa-Barton Sch. Dist., Barton, Ark., 1979, Webber Coll., Babson Park, Fla., 1988, Habitat for Humanity, Winter Haven, 1988-89. Editor: (tabloid) Shreveport Jour., 1979; contbr. articles to profl. jours. Bd. dirs. United Way of Va. Peninsula, Hampton, 1993-96; mem. La. Priorities Com., Baton Rouge, 1978-79. Served with mil. intelligence U.S. Army, 1966-68, Vietnam. Decorated Bronze Star; recipient numerous awards. Mem. ASCD, Assn. Governing Bds., Coun. for Advancement and Support of Edn. (award of merit for ednl. fund-raising 1992), Am. Assn. Sch. Adminstrs., Coun. Ednl. Facility Planners Internat., Nat. Orgn. on Legal Problems in Edn., Warwick Rotary Club, Kappa Delta Pi, Phi Delta Kappa, Omicron Delta Kappa. Methodist. Office: The Nature Conservancy 222 S Westmonte Dr Ste 300 Altamonte Springs FL 32714-4269

HARNESS, WILLIAM WALTER, lawyer; b. Ottumwa, Iowa, Apr. 14, 1945; s. Walter W. and Mary E. (Bukowski) H.; m. Carolyn Margaret Barnes, Jan 4, 1969; children: Matthew William, Michael Andrew. BA, U. Iowa, 1967; JD, Cleve. State U., 1974. Bar: Ohio 1975, U.S. Dist. Ct. (no. dist.) Ohio 1975, D.C. 1976, U.S. Dist. Ct. D.C. 1976, U.S. Ct. Appeals (D.C. cir.) 1976, U.S. Ct. Appeals (5th cir.) 1981, U.S. Dist. Ct. (we. dist.) N.C. 1979, U.S. Ct. Appeals (1st cir.) 1980, U.S. Ct. Appeals (4th cir.) 1981, U.S. Ct. Appeals (11th cir.) 1981. Mem. labor rels. staff Monogram Industries, Cleve., 1970-75; asst. counsel Nat. Treasury Employees Union, Washington, 1975-77, nat. counsel, Atlanta, 1977—; lectr. Emory U., Atlanta, 1978—; participant various seminars Ga. State U. Pres. Spring Mill-Kingsborough Ct. Corp., Atlanta. Served to 1st lt. U.S. Army, 1967-70. Mem. ABA (com. on fed. labor-mgmt. 1981-84), D.C. Bar Assn. (bd. dirs.), Soc. Fed. Labor Relations Profls., Indsl. Relations Research Assn. Home: 1285 Mile Post Dr Atlanta GA 30338-4756 Office: Nat Treasury Employees Union 2801 Buford Hwy NE Ste 430 Atlanta GA 30329-2137

HARP, JOHN ANDERSON, lawyer; b. Helena, Ark., Nov. 30, 1950; s. Bert Seth and Mary Eleanor (Jolley) H.; m. Jane Van Cleave, Apr. 26, 1980; children: Anderson, Elizabeth, William, Hamilton. BA, Am. U., Washington, 1973; JD, Mercer U., Macon, Ga., 1980. Bar: Ga., Ala. Ptnr. Taylor, Harp & Callier, Columbus, Ga., 1985—; with Office of Asst. Sec. for Def., The Pentagon, 1996—. Co-author: Litigating Head Trauma Cases, 1991; bd. editors Neurolaw Letter, 1991—, IATROGENICS, 1992-93, Topics in Spinal Cord Injury Rehab., 1994—; contbr. articles to profl. jours. Mem. Mayor's Com. for Persons with Disabilities, Columbus, Ga., 1994-96. Col., USMCR, 1995—. Mem. ABA, ATLA, Ga. Bar Assn., Ala. Bar Assn., Nat. Spinal Cord Assn. (bd. dirs. 1987-95), Mercer U. Law Sch. Alumni Assn. (bd. dirs. 1994—). Office: Taylor Harp & Callier 233 12th St Ste 900 Columbus GA 31901-2449

HARP, RENO SHEFFER, III, lawyer; b. Balt., Nov. 27, 1931; s. Reno Sheffer Jr. and Ruth (Cline) H.; m. Patricia Stewart, Oct. 15, 1993; children: Reno Sheffer IV, Anne H. Vaeth. BA, Washington and Lee U., 1954, JD, 1956. Bar: Va. 1954, U.S. Dist. Ct. (ea. and we. dists.) Va. 1954, U.S. Supreme Ct. 1960. Asst. atty. gen. Atty. Gen.'s Office, Richmond, Va., 1956-70; dep. atty. gen. Atty. Gen.'s Office, Richmond, 1970-78; counsel Jud. Inquiry and Rev. Com., Richmond, 1978—. Home: 509 Matoaka Rd Richmond VA 23226-2118 Office: Jud Inquiry & Rev Com PO Box 367 Richmond VA 23203-0367

HARPER, CHRISTINE JOHNSON, psychiatric clinical nurse, administrator; b. Tyler, Tex., June 26, 1952; d. Reinhold P. and Alice G. (Levingston) Johnson; m. James H. Harper, Sept. 4, 1982; 1 child, Timothy Wright. BSN, U. Tex., 1974; MS, U. Tex., Tyler, 1981; MSN, Tex. Woman's U., 1992. RN, Tex.; cert. clin. nurse specialist in psychiat. mental health. Instr. Tyler Jr. Coll., 1976-87; sr. lectr. U. Tex., Tyler, 1987-91, adj. nursing faculty, 1994—; clin. specialist Rusk (Tex.) State Hosp., 1992-94, dir. nursing svcs., 1994—. Mem. Tex. Nurses Assn. (bd. dirs. dist. 19, ho. of dels., past pres., Exemplary Leadership in Tex. Nursing award 1988), Am. Psychiat. Nurses Assn. (Tex. rep. 1995), Sigma Theta Tau (chmn. nominations Iota Nu chpt.). Home: PO Box 921 Rusk TX 75785-0921

HARPER, JAMES LEO, real estate appraiser, consultant; b. Nashville, Mar. 26, 1925; s. Porter Carney and Annie Mai (Follis) H.; m. Jo Ann Criswell, Oct. 1, 1949; 1 child, Virginia Harper Griffin. BA, Vanderbilt U., 1949; JD, Nashville YMCA Night Law Sch., 1955. Bar: Tenn. Engring. asst. City of Nashville, 1949-51; in sales W.H. Criswell Co., Nashville, 1951-53; in sales and prodn. WSIX TV & Radio, Nashville, 1953-55; ptnr. Harper-Freeman & Co., Nashville, 1960-70; owner James L. Harper & Assocs., Nashville, 1970-88; ptnr. Harper-Maes & Assocs., Nashville, 1988-95, James L. Harper & Assoc., Nashville, 1995—; bd. dirs. Union Planters Nat. Bank, Memphis. Chmn. Com. on Zoning Ordinance, Nashville, 1966-70; mem. Tenn. Real Estate Commn., Nashville, 1966-69; commr. Nashville Airport Authority, 1970-78; chmn. Com. on Tax Exempt Property, Nashville, 1984. With USN, 1943-46, PTO. Mem. Nashville Bd. Realtors (pres. 1963), Nat. Assn. Realtors (bd. dirs. 1969-71, 75-77, regional v.p. 1974, chmn. com. on real estate econs. and rsch. 1977), Tenn. Assn. Realtors (pres. 1964, Realtor of Yr. 1965), Appraisal Inst. (pres. Mid-Tenn. chpt. 1969, regional v.p. 1973, chmn. govt. rels. com. 1980, vice chmn. div. publs. 1981), Am. Soc. Real Estate Counselors (edn. com. 1967-70, chmn. rsch. com. 1975, bd. govs. 1977-79), Rotary Club of Nashville. Home: Two Whitehall 3701 W End Ave Nashville TN 37205-2461 Office: James L Harper & Assocs 401 Union St Fl 6 Nashville TN 37219-1708

HARPER, JAMES ROLAND, JR., lawyer; b. El Paso, Tex., June 27, 1918; s. James R. and Clara Belle (Deason) H.; m. Nancy Graves, Mar. 25, 1946; children: Stephen R., Thomas D., James R. III. AB, U. Tex., El Paso, 1940; JD, Northwestern U., 1951. Bar: Ill. 1951, Ga. 1956, U.S. Ct. Appeals (5th cir.) 1960, U.S. Ct. Appeals (1st cir.) 1966, U.S. Ct. Appeals (4th cir.) 1967, U.S. Supreme Ct. 1969, U.S. Ct. Appeals (11th cir.) 1981; CPA, Ga. Acct. El Paso Natural Gas Co., 1940-41; instr. acctg. Sch. Commerce, Northwestern U., Chgo., 1946-53; sr. atty. appellate, staff asst. to regional counsel Office of Chief Counsel, IRS, Atlanta, 1953-60; pvt. practice Atlanta, 1960—; trial lawyer, of counsel Chamberlain, Hrdlicka, White, Williams & Martin, Atlanta, 1986-88; ptnr. Johnson, Harper, Daniel & Ward, 1966; named ind. counsel under a sealed appt. pursuant to Title 28 USCA 591-598 to investigate the fin. affairs of a presdl. appointee U.S. Dept. Justice, Washington, 1987-88. Contbg. author: New Frontiers of the Trial Lawyer, 1969, Master Advocates Handbook, 1986. Capt. USMC, 1941-46, Col. Res. ret. Decorated bronze star with combat badge. Fellow Internat. Soc. Barristers (bd. govs. 1981-87); mem. Fed. Bar Assn. (chpt. pres. 1966), Marine Corps Res. Officers Assn. (dist. dir. 1962). Presbyterian. Home: 4355 Brookview Dr NW Atlanta GA 30339-4608 Office: Chamberlain Hrdlicka White Williams & Martin 233 Peachtree St NE Ste 1400 Atlanta GA 30303-1507

HARPER, JANE WALKER, educational administrator; b. Warren, Ohio, Aug. 10, 1946; d. Thomas C. and Julia M. (Reyes) Walker; m. Elmer A. Harper, June 20, 1970; children: Allison, Kasie, Timothy. BA, Stetson U., 1968; MA, Rollins Coll., 1976; EdS, Stetson U., 1994. Cert. elem tchr., guidance counselor, reading tchr., ednl. leadership. Tchr. Lake County Schs., Tavares, Fla., program specialist; presenter in field. Mem. ASCD, Internat. Reading Assn., Fla. Reading Assn., Fla. Assn. State and Fed. Ednl. Program Adminstrs., Reading Suprs. Fla., Lake County Reading Assn., Phi Delta Kappa. Home: 27839 Lisa Dr Tavares FL 32778-9706

HARPER, JANET SUTHERLIN LANE, educational administrator, writer; b. La Grange, Ga., Apr. 2, 1940; d. Clarence Wilner and Imogene (Thompson); m. William Sterling Lane, June 28, 1964, (div. Jan. 1981); children: David Alan, Jennifer Ruth; m. John F. Harper, June 9, 1990. BA in English and Applied Music, LaGrange Coll., 1961; postgrad., Auburn U., 1963; MA in Journalism, U. Ga., Athens, 1979. Music and drama critic The Brunswick News, Brunswick, Ga., 1979—; info. asst. Glynn County Schs., Brunswick, 1979-82; adj. prof. Brunswick Coll., Ga., 1981-87; dir. pub. info. and publs. Glynn County Schs., Brunswick, 1982—; media relations Ga. Assn. of Ednl. Leaders, 1983—. Contbg. editor Ga. Jour., 1981-84; editor, writer GAEL Conf. Jours., 1987-89. Organist St. Simons United Meth. Ch., 1981—; pres. Jekyll Island Music Theater Bd., 1994—. Recipient award of excellence in sch. and community rels. Ga. Bd. Edn., 1984, 92, Edn. Leadership award, Ga., 1989. Mem. Nat. Sch. Pub. Rels. Assn. (Golden Achievement award 1985, 2 awards 1988, 90, 3 awards 1991, 92, 94), Ga. Sch. Pub. Rels. Assn. (Disting. Svc. award 1991), Brunswick Press-Advt. Club (award of excellence in pub. rels. 1992), Brunswick Golden Isles C. of C., Mozart Soc., Phi Delta Kappa, Phi Kappa Phi, Sigma Delta Chi. Office: Glynn County Schs 1313 Egmont St Brunswick GA 31520-7244

HARPER, JEWEL BENTON, pharmacist; b. Springfield, Tenn., Nov. 14, 1925; s. William Henry and Violet Irene (Benton) H.; m. Josephine Cook,

Feb. 12, 1953; children: Pamela Jewel, Karen Jo. BS, Austin Peay State U., 1948, BS, Samford U., 1950, Command and Gen. Staff Officer Course diploma U.S. Army Command and Gen. Staff Coll., 1968; cert. pharmacist, Tenn. Pharmacist Battlefield Pharmacy, Nashville, 1950-52, VA Hosp., Nashville, 1952-63, Lexington, Ky., 1963-67, Durham, N.C., 1967-76, Manchester, N.H., 1976-82, Vanderbilt U., Nashville, 1982-86, Nashville Meml. Hosp., 1986-91. Served to col. Med. Service Corps, USAR, 1944-85. Recipient Hosp. Adminstrn. Diploma, Acad. Health Scis., 1970, Nat. Security Mgmt. Diploma, Indsl. Coll. Armed Forces, 1973, Logistics Exec. Devel. Diploma U.S. Army Logistics Mgmt. Ctr., 1977. Mem. Assn. Mil. Surgeons U.S., Am. Pharm. Assn., Am. Soc. Hosp. Pharmacists, Res. Officers Assn. U.S. (pres. chpt. 1962-63, sec. 1970-73, dept. surgeon 1977-82), Assn. of U.S. Army, The Mil. Order of World Wars, The Retired Officers Assn., , Am. Legion, The Gideons Internat., Lambda Chi Alpha, Kappa Psi. Republican. Baptist. Avocations: country music, deep sea fishing, horticulture. Home and Office: 503 Cunniff Ct Goodlettsville TN 37072-3003

HARPER, MARSHA LEA, special education educator; b. St. Charles, Mo., Feb. 5, 1969; d. Donald Clay and Floy Wanella (Gentry) Roark; m. Lance Howard Harper, June 12, 1993. BS in Edn., Troy (Ala.) State U., 1992. Tchr. varying exceptionalities W.W. Irby Elem. Sch., Alachua, Fla., 1992-95; tchr. early childhood transition W.W. Irby Elem. Sch., 1995—; mem. faculty sch. adv. coun. Alachua, 1993—. Mem. PTA, Alachua, 1992—. Mem. ASCD, Coun. for Exceptional Children, Phi Delta Kappa. Mem. Ch. of Christ. Home: 4640 SW 57th Dr Gainesville FL 32608

HARPER, MARY SADLER, banker; b. Farmville, Va., June 15, 1941; d. Edward Henry and Vivien Morris (Garrett) Sadler; m. Joseph Taylor Harper, Dec. 21, 1968; children by previous marriage: James E. Hatch III, Mary Ann Hatch Czajka. Cert. Fla. Trust Sch., U. Fla., 1976. Registered securities rep., Fla., gen. securities prin., fin. and ops. prin., options prin., mcpl. securities prin. Dep. clk. Polk County Cts., Bartow, Fla., 1964-67; rep. Allen & Co., Lakeland, Fla., 1967-71; with First Nat. Bank, Palm Beach, Fla., 1971-89, sr. v.p., 1984-86, sr. v.p. S.E. Bank N.A., Palm Beach, 1986-89; pres., CEO Palm Beach Capital Svcs., Inc., 1986-88, mng. dir. Investment Svcs., Palm Beach Capital Svcs. Div., 1988; v.p. investments, trustee J.M. Rubin Found., Palm Beach, 1983—; sr. v.p. investment div. Island Nat. Bank & Trust Co., 1989—; chmn., dir., pres. CEO Island Investment Svcs., Inc., Palm Beach, 1989—, also bd. dirs.; mem. adv. coun. Nuveen, 1987-96. Mem. adv. panel Palm Beach County YWCA, 1984—; Jupiter Hosp. Found.; life mem. June Beach Civic Assn. Mem. YWCA (adv. panel 1985, endowment com. 1990-93), Nat. Assn. Securities Dealers (registered dist. com. mem. 1995—), Fin. Women Internat., Fla. Securities Dealers Assn., Exec. Women of Palm Beaches (mem. fin. com. 1985-92), Internat. Soc. Palm Beach (treas., trustee 1986—), Jupiter Hosp. Med. Assn. (pres.'s club 1989—), Loxahatchee Hist. Soc. (bd. dirs. 1991-93, chmn. devel. com. 1992-93), Sebring, Fla. Hist. Soc. (life), Jupiter/Tequesta C. of C. (assoc.), United Daus. of Confederacy, Gov.'s Club, Pub. Securities Assn. (exec. rep.), Jonathans Golf Club, Rotary (Palm Beach found. com. 1990—, bd. dirs. 1992, 93-94), Lighthouse Gallery Art (life), Norton Gallery Art (patron). Democrat. Baptist. Avocations: reading, history. Home: 630 Ocean Dr Apt 103 Juno Beach FL 33408-1916 Office: Island Investment Svcs Inc Island Nat Bank Palm Beach 180 Royal Palm Way Palm Beach FL 33480-4254

HARPER, PAULA, art history educator, writer; b. Boston, Nov. 17, 1938; d. Clarence Everett and Maura (Lee) Fish. BA in Art History magna cum laude, Hunter Coll., 1966, MA in Art History, 1968; postgrad., U. N.Mex., 1968-69; PhD in Art History, Stanford U., 1976. Dancer Munt-Brooks Modern Dance Co., N.Y.C., 1963-65; teaching fellow U. N.Mex., 1968-69; asst. prof. Calif. Inst. Arts, Valencia, 1971-72; dir. Hunter Arts Gallery CUNY, 1977-78; vis. asst. prof. Mills Coll., Oakland, Calif., spring 1979, 80-81, Stanford (Calif.) U., 1979-80; assoc. prof. art history U. Miami, Coral Gables, Fla., 1982—; art critic Miami News, 1982-88; frequent lectr. mus., art galleries and univs.; project advisor TV series on Camille Pissarro, PBS Channel 10, St. Thomas, V.I., 1992—. Author: (with R.E. Shikes) Pissarro: His Life and Work, 1980 (transl. into French, German, and Romanian), Daumier's Clowns, 1981; author (catalogues) "Powerplay" Paintings by Judy Chicago, 1986, Contemporary Sculpture from the Martin Z. Margulies Collection, 1986, Visions from Brazil-The Drawings of Paolo Gomes Garcez, 1993; contbr. articles to profl. jours., books, exhbn. catalogues. Bd. trustees Ctr. for Fine Arts, Miami, 1990-93; mem. Art in Pub. Places Com., Miami Beach, 1991—. Recipient Film Inst. fellowship CUNY, 1966, Tuition fellowship Hunter Coll., 1966-67, Ford Found. grant Stanford U., 1969-73, Rsch. grant French govt., 1973-74, Rockefeller Found. Residency at Bellagio, 1991, Ailsa Mellon Bruce Vis. Sr. fellowship, CASVA, Nat. Gallery of Art, 1990-91. Mem. Coll. Art Assn. (founder Women's Caucus for Art 1972, pres. N.Y. chpt. 1977-78, nat. adv. bd. 1977-80), Internat. Assn. Art Critics, Soc. Mayflower Descs., Foundlings Club, Art Table.

HARPER, SANDRA STECHER, university administrator; b. Dallas, Sept. 21, 1952; d. Lee Roy and Carmen (Crespo) Stecher; m. Dave Harper, July 6, 1974; children: Justin, Jonathan. BS in Edn., Tex. Tech. U., 1974; MS, U. N. Tex., 1979, PhD, 1985. Speech/reading tchr. Nazareth (Tex.) High Sch., 1974-75; speech/English tchr. Collinsville (Tex.) High Sch., 1975-77, Pottsboro (Tex.) High Sch., 1977-79; communication instr. Austin Coll., Sherman, Tex., 1980-82; rsch. asst. U. N. Tex., Denton, 1982-84; vis. instr. communication Austin Coll., Sherman, 1985; asst. prof. communication McMurry Coll., Abilene, Tex., 1985-89; assoc. prof. comm. McMurry U., Abilene, Tex., 1989-95, dean Coll. Arts and Scis., 1990-95; v.p. for acad. affairs Oklahoma City U., 1995—; asst. dir. NEH univ. core curriculum project McMurry U., Abilene, Tex.; critic judge Univ. Interscholastic League, Austin, 1980-93; mem. adv. bd. Univ. Rsch. Consortium, Abilene, 1990-95. Contbr. articles to profl. jours.; author: To Serve the Present Age, 1990; co-author U.S. Dept. Edn. Title III Grant. Planner TEAM Abilene, 1991; del. Tex. Commn. for Libr. and Info. Svcs., Austin, 1991; chair Abilene Children Today: Life and Cmty. Skills Task Force, 1994-95. Named Outstanding Faculty Mem., McMurry U., 1988, Outstanding Adminstrv., 1993; Media Rsch. scholar, Ctr. for Population Options, 1989. Mem. Internat. Communication Assn., Speech Communication Assn., So. Speech Communication Assn., Film and Video Assn., Council Coll. of Arts and Sciences. Democrat. Roman Catholic. Office: Oklahoma City U 2501 N Blackwelder Oklahoma City OK 73106

HARPER, SHIRLEY FAY, nutritionist, educator, consultant; b. Auburn, Ky., Apr. 23, 1943; d. Charles Henry and Annabelle (Gregory) Belcher; m. Robert Vance Harper, May 19, 1973; children: Glenda, Debra, Teresa, Suzanna, Cynthia. BS, Western Ky. U., 1966, MS, 1982. Cert. nutritionist and lic. dietitian, Ky. Dir. dietetics Logan County Hosp., Russellville, Ky., 1965-80; cons. Western State Hosp., Hopkinsville, Ky., 1983-84, instnl. dietetic adminstr., 1984-88; dietitian Rivendell Children's Psychiat. Hosp., Bowling Green, Ky., 1988-90; instr. nutrition Western Ky. U., Bowling Green, 1990-92; cons. Auburn (Ky.) Nursing Ctr., 1976-95, Belle Meade Home, Greenville, Ky., 1980—, Brookfield Manor, Hopkinsville, Ky., 1983—, Sparks Nursing Ctr., Central City, Ky., 1983—, Muhlenberg Cmty. Hosp., Greenville, 1989—, Russellville (Ky.) Health Care Manor, 1978-83, 92—, Westlake Cumberland Hosp., Columbia, Ky., 1993—, Franklin-Simpson Meml. Hosp., Franklin, Ky., 1993—; nutrition instr. Madisonville (Ky.) Cmty. Coll., 1995—. Mem. regional bd. dirs. ARC of Ky., Frankfort, 1990-96; vice chair ARC of Logan County, 1992-93, chmn., 1993-96; bd. dirs. Logan County ARC United Way, 1993—; co-chair adv. coun. devel. disabilities Lifeskills, 1992-93, adv. coun. Lifeskills Residential Living Group Home, 1993—, human rights adv. coun., 1994—; chair Let's Build our Future Campaign; nutrition del. Citizen Am. Program to USSR, 1990; adv. chair for vocat. edn., Russellville; mem. adv. coun. for home econs. and family living, We. Ky. U., 1990-93; bd. dirs. ARC of Logan County for United Way, 1993—. Recipient Outstanding Svc. award Am. Dietetic Assn. Found., 1993, Outstanding Svc. award Barren River Mental Health-Mental Retardation Bd., 1987, Svc. Appreciation award Logan-Russellville Assn. for Retarded Citizens, 1987, Internat. Woman of Yr. award for contribution to Nutrition and Humanity, Internat. Biographical Assn., 1993-94, World Lifetime Achievement award Am. Biographical Inst., 1995; inaugurated Lifetime Dep. Gov., Am. Biographical Rsch. Bd., 1995, Pres.'s award ARC of Logan County, 1996. Mem. Am. Dietetic Assn., Nat. Nutrition Network, Ky. Dietetic Assn. (pres. Western dist. 1976-77, Outstanding Dietitian award 1984), Bowling Green-Warren County Nutrition Coun., Nat. Ctr. for Nutrition and Dietetics (charter), Ky. Nutrition Coun., Logan County Home Economist Club (sec. 1994-95, v.p. 1995-96, pres. 1996-97), Internat. Biog. Assn., Internat. Platform Assn., Gerontol. Nutritionist, Oncology Nutrition, Diabetes Care and Edn., Dietitians in Nutrition Support, Dietitians in Gen. Clin. Practice, Cons. Dietitians in Health Care, Dietetic Educators of Practice Nutrition, Edn. of Health Profls., Nutrition Rsch. and Nutrition Edn. for Pub. Practice Groups, Phi Upsilon Omicron (pres. Beta Delta alumni chpt. 1994-96). Home and Office: 443 Hopkinsville Rd Russellville KY 42276-1286

HARPER, WILLIAM THOMAS, III, psychologist, educator; b. Newport News, Va., Sept. 10, 1956; s. William Thomas Jr. and Queen Vastie (Wilson) H. BS in Psychology, Va. State U., 1978, MEd in Counseling, 1980; cert. in teaching, Coll. William and Mary, 1987; postgrad., Old Dominion U., 1990—. Cert. tchr., Va. Edn. specialist, counselor U.S. Army, Arlington, Va., 1984-85; counselor Hampton (Va.) U., 1980-82, asst. supr. testing, dir. student support svcs., 1982-88; asst. to prin., home sch. coord. Hampton City Schs., 1988-89; dir. transition programs Norfolk (Va.) State U., 1989—; v.p. devel. AmChest Diversified Inc., Hampton, 1990—; crisis counselor Va. State U., Petersburg, 1978-80; counselor ManPower Tng. Svcs., Newport News, Va., 1980; rsch. assoc. Ea. Va. Med. Sch.-The Med. Coll. of Hampton Roads, Norfolk, Va.; rsch assoc Health Promotions 1st Med. Group, USAF, Langley AFB, Hampton, Va.; exec. v.p. rsch. grants and devel. Lott Cary Hist. Found. Inc.; rsch. bd. advisors Am. Biog. Inst.; mental health technician, counselor Vets. Adminstrn. Med. Ctr., Hampton, Va.; tchr. Christopher Newport U. Excel Program. Spl. Olympic vol. Sarah Boswell Hudgins Regional Ctr., Hampton, 1983—; advisor Psi Chi Nat. Honor Soc., Hampton, 1986; v.p. rsch., grants and devel. Lott Cary Hist. Soc. Exec. Bd.; v.p. r&d The Lott Cary Hist. Found. Recipient Disting. Svc. award peer counselors Hampton U., 1982, U.S. Army Svc. award, 1985, Va. Coll. Pers. Assn. award, 1981, 85, Community Svc. award Kappa Alpha Psi, 1986, Edn. Achievement award, 1986, Va. State U. Alumni award, 1985, Historically Black Coll. Program Counselor Achievement award, 1985, Psi Chi Honor Soc. Achievement award, 1986, Leadership Devel. Tng. Achievement award Howard U., 1983, 85, 86, Hampton VA Med. Ctr. award, 1990, 91, Nat. Black Male Conf. Achievement award, 1990, 91, Black Am. Doctoral Rsch. award, 1991-92, Recognition awards Christopher Newport Coll., 1985-86, Boys Club of Greater Hampton Roads, 1987, 88, 89, 90, City of Alexandria Dept. Human Svcs., 1987, 88, Fraternal Order Police Hampton, Mayor of City of Newport News, 1990, 91, Bd. Govs. Coll. of William and Mary/Internat. Platform Assn., 1990, 4th Nat. Black Student Leadership Devel. 1990-91, Va. Alcohol Safety Action Program, 1990, 91, Commonwealth of Va. Ho. of Dels., 1991, others; Old Dominion U. grad. scholar, 1983, 85, Hampton U. Mobile Oil scholar, 1985. Mem. AACD, Nat. Assn. Black Psychologist, Nat. Assn. Alcoholism & Drug Abuse Counselors, Va. Assn. Alcoholism & Drug Abuse Counselors, Va. Assn. Adminstrs. in Higher Edn., Va. Assn. Black Psychologists (chmn. com.), Va. Assn. Black Psychologists, Peninsula Literacy Coun. (counselor), Internat. Platform Assn. (bd. govs. 1990), Kappa Alpha Psi. Democrat. Baptist. Home: 1042 44th St Newport News VA 23607-2313 Office: Norfolk State U 2401 Corprew Ave Norfolk VA 23504-3907

HARPRING, LINDA JEAN, critical care nurse; b. Louisville, Ky., Mar. 28, 1956; d. James Phillip and Ellabelle Jean (Crowder) Anderson; m. Jerel Patrick Harpring, June 13, 1992; children: Bradley, Vanessa, Frances, Joseph, Ashley. BSN, U. Louisville, 1989, postgrad. RN, Ky. Staff nurse Audubon Regional Med. Ctr., Louisville, 1989-90; nurse clinician Visiting Nurses Assn. Louisville, 1990—; staff nurse Southwest Hosp., Louisville, 1990—; rsch. coord. electrophysiology-cardiology U. Louisville, 1993-94. Mem. alumni bd. govs. U. Louisville Sch. Nursing, 1988—. Mem. Sigma Theta Tau. Home: 7308 Cardinal Hill Rd Louisville KY 40214-4104

HARPSTER, JAMES ERVING, lawyer; b. Milw., Dec. 24, 1923; s. Philo E. and Pauline (Daanen) H. PhB, Marquette U., 1950, LLB, 1952. Bar: Wis. 1952, Tenn. 1953; dir. info. svcs. Nat. Cotton Council Am., Memphis, 1952-55; dir. public rels. Christian Bros. Coll., 1956; mgr. govt. affairs dept. Memphis C. of C., 1956-62; exec. v.p. Rep. Assn. Memphis and Shelby County, 1962-64; individual practice law, Memphis, 1965; ptnr. Rickey, Shankman, Blanchard, Agee & Harpster, and predecessor firm, Memphis, 1966-80, Harpster & Baird, 1980-83; pvt. practice, Memphis, 1984—. Mem. Shelby County Tax Assessor's Adv. Com., 1960-61; editor, asst. counsel Memphis and Shelby County Charter Com., 1962; mem. Shelby County Election Commn., 1968-70; mem. Tenn. State Bd. Elections, 1970-72, sec., 1972; mem. Tenn. State Election Commn., 1973-83, chmn., 1974, sec., 1975-83; a founder Lions Inst. for Visually Handicapped Children, 1954, chmn. E. H. Crump Meml. Football Game for Blind, 1956; pres. Siena Student Aid Found., 1960; bd. dirs. Memphis Public Affairs Forum; mem. Civic Rsch. Com., Inc., Citizens Assn. Memphis and Shelby County; Republican candidate Tenn. Gen. Assembly, 1964; v.p. Nat. Council Rep. Workshops, 1967-69; pres. Rep. Workshop Shelby County, 1967, 71, 77, 78, Rep. Assn. Memphis and Shelby County, 1966-67; chmn. St. Michael the Defender chpt. Catholics United for the Faith, 1973, 75, 89-92. With USAAF, 1942-46. Mem. Tenn. Bar Assn., Wis. Bar Assn., Am. Immigration Lawyers Assn., Navy League U.S., Cardinal Mindszenty Found., Am. Security Coun., Am. Legion, Latin Liturgy Assn. Roman Catholic. Home: 3032 E Glengarry Rd Memphis TN 38128-2984 Office: 100 N Main St Ste 3217 Memphis TN 38103-0532

HARR, SHELDON JAY, rabbi; b. Youngstown, Ohio, Sept. 5, 1946; s. Aaron A. and Arlene (Levy) H.; m. Fern J. Harr, Aug. 30, 1969; children: Elizabeth (dec.), Bryan. BA, U. Cin., 1968; B. Hebrew Letters, Hebrew Union Coll., 1971, MA, 1973; D, Emory U. Ordained rabbi, 1973. Asst. rabbi Temple Israel, West Palm Beach, Fla., 1973-76; sr. rabbi Temple Kol Ami, Plantation, Fla., 1976—; pres. Jewish Nat. Fund, S.E. Fla., Ft. Lauderdale. Vice chmn. Urban League of Broward County, Ft. Lauderdale, 1988-90; mem. bi-racial com. Sch. Bd. of Broward County, 1987-89; chaplain Police Dept. of Davie, Fla., 1988—, Police Dept. of Plantation, Fla., 1990—. Mem. NCCJ (bd. dirs. 1986—), Ctrl. Conf. Am. Rabbis (v.p. S.E. region), Jewish Fedn. Ft. Lauderdale (bd. dirs., Outstanding Rabbi of Yr. 1990-91), West Broward Religious Leaders Fellowship (pres. 1985-87), Union Am. Hebrew Congregations (bd. dirs. S.E. region). Office: Temple Kol Ami 8200 Peters Rd Fort Lauderdale FL 33324-3201

HARRAL, JOHN MENTEITH, lawyer; b. Ancon, Panama Canal Zone, June 25, 1948; s. Brooks Jared and Sara (Mumma) H.; m. Marjorie Van Fosson, Aug. 15, 1970; children: Alyse, Jessica. BBA, U. Miss., 1971, JD, 1974. Bar: Miss. 1974, U.S. Dist. Ct. (so. dist.) Miss. 1974, U.S. Ct. Appeals (5th cir.) 1977. Law clk. to Judge J.P. Coleman, U.S. Ct. Appeals (5th cir.), New Orleans, 1978-79; ptnr. White & Morse, Gulfport, Miss., 1979-92, Eaton & Cottrell, P.A., Gulfport, Miss., 1993—; mem. Miss. Gov.'s Jud. Nominating Com., 1990-93. Chmn. Episc. Svcs. for Aging, Mississippi Gulf Coast, 1981-85, also bd. dirs.; bd. dirs. Make-A-Wish Found. Miss.; pres. Gulfport Excellence, 1991—; bd. dirs., exec. com. Christmas in April, Harrison County, 1994—, pres., 1995-96; bd. dirs. Meadows Discovery Ctr., 1996—; lay eucharistic min. St. Mark's Episcopal Ch., Gulfport, 1980, chalice bearer, vestryman, sr. and jr. warden, Sunday sch. tchr. Lt. JAGC, USNR, 1974-78. Mem. ABA, Miss. Bar Assn. (bd. dirs. young lawyers divsn. 1982-84, commr. 1991-94), Harrison County Bar Assn. (pres. young lawyers sect. 1982, v.p. 1986, pres. 1987-88), Gulf Coast Law Inst. (bd. dirs. 1993—), Gulfport C. of C. (bd. dirs. 1995-97, chmn. elect 1996), Miss. Coast C. of C. (bd. dirs. 1994-96), Bayou Bluff Tennis Club, Gulfport Yacht Club. Republican. Home: 12 Old Oak Ln Gulfport MS 39503-6210 Office: Eaton & Cottrell 1310 25th Ave Gulfport MS 39501-1931 also: 205 S Beach Dr Bay Saint Louis MS 39520

HARRELD, MICHAEL N., banker; b. 1944. BA, U. Louisville, 1966, JD, 1969. With PNC Bank Ky., Inc., Louisville, 1969-89, pre., 1969—; chmn. bd. Louisville Cmty. Found. Office: PNC Bank 500 W Jefferson St Louisville KY 40202-2823*

HARRELL, BENJAMIN CARLTON, columnist, retired editor; b. Mamie, N.C., Oct. 1, 1929; s. Taylor Smith Jr. and Nellie Augusta (Gallop) H.; m. Audrey Jeanine Tarkenton, Apr. 26, 1952; children: Melissa Ann, Sheila Lynn. Student, U. N.C., 1947-49. Reporter Daily Advance, Elizabeth City, N.C., 1950-52, 53-56, Goldsboro (N.C.) News-Argus, 1956-57; reporter Durham (N.C.) Sun, 1957-64, state editor, 1964-65, asst. city editor, 1965-69, city editor, 1969-72, mng. editor, 1972-90; assoc. editor Herald-Sun, Durham, 1991-96, editor emeritus, columnist, 1996—, columnist, 1996—. 2d lt. U.S. Army, 1952-53. Mem. Am. Soc. Newspaper Editors. Office: Herald Sun 410 Argonne Dr Durham NC 27704-1428

HARRELL, CHARLES LYDON, JR., lawyer; b. Norfolk, Va., Oct. 22, 1916; s. Charles Lydon Sr. and Ethel Theresa (Toone) H.; m. Martha de Weese Guild, Feb. 5, 1943 (dec. March 1991); children: Charles Lydon III, John Morgan, Marshall Guild, DeWeese Toone; m. Lynn Aikens Johnson, July 13, 1993. BA, Randolph-Macon Coll., 1938; LLB, U. Richmond, 1941. Bar: Va. 1940, U.S. Dist. Ct. (ea. dist.) Va. 1946, U.S. Bankruptcy Ct. (ea. and we. dist.) Va. 1946, U.S. Ct. Appeals (4th cir.) 1947, U.S. Ct. Internat. Trade 1950, U.S. Supreme Ct. 1952. Ptnr. Harrell & Landrum, Norfolk, 1947-76; pvt. practice, Norfolk, 1987—; commr. in chancery Cir. Ct. Princess Anne County, 1950-76, City of Norfolk, 1955-77; spl. justice Princess Anne County, 1952-65. Mem. health care consumer coun. Naval Hosp., Portsmouth, 1980—; mem. adminstrv. bd. Ghent United Meth. Ch., 1950—, tchr. Bible class, 1966—, master, mem. com. Boy Scouts of Am., Sea Scouts; mem. Coun. of Ministries, 1955-88, chmn. Commn. on Meth. Ch., 1971-76; co-founder, chmn., pres. bd. dirs. Ghent Venture, Inc.; chmn., Norfolk Seaman's Soc., 1970-80, bd. dirs., 1990—, v.p.; bd. dirs. Handicaps Unltd. of Va., legis. chmn., legal advisor; vol. prayer counsellor Christian Broadcast Network, 1977—; co-founder, bd. dirs. Va. Assn. of Blind, 1977—; dir. Norfolk Interfaith Coalition for the Elderly, Tidewater Christian Outreach Project; pres. Mobility on Wheels, Inc., 1980-83, bd. dirs., 1977—; mem. com. for therapeutic recreation of handicapped people City of Norfolk, 1991—; co-founder, v.p., dir. New Life Devel.; pro bono counsel Tidewater Legal Aid Soc., 1989—. Comdr. USN, 1962. Decorated 9 campaign medals, 4 combat stars; recipient Cross Mil. Svc., UDC. Mem. ABA, Norfolk-Portsmouth Bar Assn., Va. State Bar Assn. (Lawyers Helping Lawyers), Va. Bar Assn., Jud. Soc., Christian Legal Soc., Am. Legion, VFW, Jr. C. of C., Jesus to the World Evangelistic Assn. (co-founder, bd. dirs., v.p., chmn. bd.), Masons, Shriners, Kiwanis, Ret. Officers Assn., The Fleet Res., Tin Can Sailors Assn., Mine Warfare Assn., The Caine Mutineers, McNeil Law Soc., Phi Beta Kappa, Omicron Delta Kappa (sec. Tidewater Alumni chpt.), Tau Kappa Alpha. Home and Office: 1302 Westover Ave Norfolk VA 23507-1026

HARRELL, HENRY HOWZE, tobacco company executive; b. Richmond, Va., Sept. 18, 1939; s. Theron Rice and Susan Howze (Haskell) H.; m. Jean Covington Camp, Feb. 7, 1970; children—Susan Hampton, Shelby Madison. A.B., Washington and Lee U. V.p. Universal Leaf Tobacco Co., Inc., Richmond, 1974-81, sr. v.p., 1981-82, exec. v.p., 1982-86, pres., 1986-88, pres., chief exec. officer, 1988-91; chmn., chief exec. officer Universal Corp. (formerly Universal Leaf Tobacco Co., Inc.), 1991—; dir. Universal Corp.; bd. dirs. Jefferson Bankshares Inc., Charlottesville, Va.; mem. bd. visitors James Madison U., Harrisonburg, Va. Mem. Forum Club, Commonwealth Club, Phi Beta Kappa, Omicron Delta Kappa. Republican. Episcopalian. Clubs: Country of Va., Deep Run Hunt (bd. dirs. 1981-83). *

HARRELL, INA PERRY, maternal/women's and medical/surgical nurse; b. Gates County, N.C., Dec. 26, 1930; d. Willie Lee and Willa Maris (Tinkham) Perry; m. Reuben Brooks Harrell, Dec. 19, 1954; children: Brooks Lee, David Austin. Diploma in nursing, Norfolk Gen. Hosp., 1952; diploma in obstetrics, Providence Lying-In Hosp., 1953. RN, N.C., Va.; cert. obstet. labor and delivery nurse, in CPR, admissions assessment nurse. Office nurse Dr. Bruce J. Franz, Asheville, N.C.; head nurse labor and delivery room and obstetrics unit Meml. Mission Hosp., Asheville; staff nurse obstetrics unit, labor and delivery room Norfolk (Va.) Gen. Hosp.; staff nurse St. Joseph's Hosp., Asheville. Mem. Nat. Bapt. Nurses Fellowship, N.C. Nurses Assn., Norfolk Gen. Hosp. Alumni Assn.

HARRELL, KAREN LEIGH SASSER, secondary school educator; b. West Palm Beach, Fla., Apr. 15, 1954; d. Fred Douglas and Wilma Leigh (Prophitt) Sasser; m. Ronnie Michael Harrell, Jan. 17, 1976; children: Eric Michael, Jennifer Anne Harrell Beverly, Kathryn Leigh. AS, Palm Beach Jr. Coll., Lake Worth, Fla., 1975; BS, Auburn U., Montgomery, 1985, MEd, 1993; Cert. in Spanish, U. Ala., 1986. Tchr. Tallapoosa County Bd. Edn., Dadeville, Ala., 1985-89, Benjamin Russell H.S., Alex City, Ala., 1989—. Facilitator Bldg. Leadership Team, Alex City, 1994—; pres., sec. Tchr. Adv. Bd., Alex City, 1991-94; mem. Ala. Reunion Com., 1989, WWII Comm. Com., Alex City, 1995-96, Alex City Arts Coun., 1989. NEH fellow, 1991, Sunbelt fellow, 1992; Pacer scholar, 1985-86. Mem. NEA, Ala. Edn. Assn., Am. Assn. Tchrs. Spanish and Portuguese, Nat. Coun. Tchrs. English, Ala. Coun. Tchrs. English, Alpha Kappa Delta. Baptist. Home: 4258 Madwind Rd Jackson Gap AL 36861 Office: Benjamin Russell High School 225 Heard Blvd Alexander City AL 35010

HARRELL, LIMMIE LEE, JR., lawyer; b. Jackson, Tenn., Aug. 15, 1941; s. Limmie Lee Sr. and Mary Benthal (Nowell) H.; m. Betsy D. Harrell; children: Limmie Lee III, Mary Kimberley. BS, Memphis State U., 1963, JD, 1966. Bar: Tenn. 1966, U.S. Dist. Ct. (we. dist.) Tenn. 1968, U.S. Supreme Ct. Ptnr. Harrell & Harrell, Attys., Trenton, Tenn., 1966—; chmn. bd. dirs. Bank of Commerce, Trenton. Pres. Gibson County Young Dems., Trenton, Tenn., 1968. Named one of Outstanding Young Men in Am. Mem. ABA, Tenn. Bar Assn., Gibson County Bar Assn., Assn. Trial Lawyers Am., Tenn. Trial Lawyers Assn., Memphis State Alumni Assn. (pres. 1984-85). Baptist. Club: Pinecrest Country Club (Trenton, Tenn.) (pres. (2) terms). Lodges: Elks (exalted ruler 1971-72), Moose. Home: 300 Rosemont Dr Trenton TN 38382-3116 Office: Harrell & Harrell Attys Court Sq Trenton TN 38382-1862

HARRELL, LINDY ELLYSON, neurologist; b. Arlington, Va., Oct. 5, 1950; d. Leighton Earnest and Virginia Dick (Blackwell) Harrell; m. T. Steven Barlow, July 24, 1976. BA, U. Miami, Fla., 1971; MD, U. Miami, 1977; MS, U. Mass., 1973, PhD, 1974. Med. intern Duke U., Durham, N.C., 1977-78, resident in neurology, 1978-81, geriatric fellow, 1981-83; asst. prof. neurology U. Ala., Birmingham, 1983-87, assoc. prof., 1987-91, prof., 1991—, dir. Alzheimer's Disease Ctr., 1991—, dir. Memory Disorders clinic, 1984—, sr. scientist Ctr. for Aging, 1983—. Assoc. editor So. Med. Jour., 1990—; contbr. numerous articles to profl. jours. Bd. dirs. Alzheimers Ctrl. of Ala., Birmingham, 1992—. Recipient Busse Rsch. award Geriatric Assn., 1995; named Best Dr. in Am. Southeast region Woodward/White, Inc., 1995, 96; grantee VA, 1984—, Nat. Inst. Aging, 1991—. Mem. AMA, Am. Neurol. Assn., Am. Acad. Neurology, So. Med. Assn., Med. Assn. State of Ala. Office: Univ of Alabama Sparks Ctr 454 Birmingham AL 35294

HARRELL, ROY HARRISON, JR., minister; b. San Angelo, Tex., July 13, 1928; s. Roy Harrison and Melinda (Garza) H.; m. Iris Ann Keeton, Dec. 15, 1951 (div. Aug. 1982); children: Amy Sue Dopson, Patrick Roy, Paula Ann; m. Iva Helen Odeen Dunton, Apr. 21, 1990. BA, Hardin Simmons U., 1949; MDiv, SW Bapt. Theol. Sem., 1956. Ordained to ministry So. Bapt. Conv., Aug. 1946. Campus min. Draughns Bus. Coll., Ft. Worth, 1952-53; youth min. Polytechnic Bapt. Ch., Ft. Worth, 1953-56; campus min. Tex. Wesleyan Coll., Ft. Worth, 1953-56; instr., asst. prof. Religion, campus min. Baylor U., Med. Ctr., Dallas, 1956-62; campus min. Baylor U., Waco, Tex., 1962-68; asst. pastor U. Bapt. Ch., Abilene, Tex., 1969, Pk. Cities Bapt. Ch., Dallas, 1970-82; pastor Ross Ave. Bapt. Ch., Dallas, 1983-95; retired 1995; pres. East Dallas Coop. Parish, 1991-92. Contbr. articles to profl. jours. Bd. dirs. United Way Met. Dallas, 1992—, exec. com. 1996-97; mem. exec. com. East Dallas Coop. Parish Coun., 1985-95; advisor Dallas Mus. Art Youth Crime Commn., Dallas County Crime Commn., Dallas Pub. Schs. Religious Cmty. Task Force; mem. chapel com. Thanksgiving Sq., 1991—, chair, 1995—, chair Dallas Observance of Nat Day of Prayer Breakfast, 1996. Mem. Dallas Pastors Assn. (sec.-treas. 1990-91, v.p. 1991-92, pres. 1992-94), Rotary Club Dallas. Home: 3521 Villanova St Dallas TX 75225-5008

HARRELL, WANDA FAYE, retail executive; b. Littlefield, Tex., June 3, 1942; d. Woodrow Wilson and B. Florence (Adams) Frazier; m. William Robert Harrell, Dec. 10, 1959; children: Wesley Roger, Debra Lanette. Bookkeeper Harrell Bldg. Supply, Inc., Anton, Tex., 1963-81, v.p., 1981—, also sec., mem. bd. dirs. Author: Under the Rainbow: The Harrells, 1986, Pot's of Gold, Harrell's Cookin 1990; editor, author (ch. bulletin) The Anton Herald, 1973; writer: The Anton Tale Spinner, 1994. Sec., treas., life and charter mem. Anton Mus. Assn., 1986—. Mem. S.W. Hardware Assn., Hardware Wholesalers Assn., Tex. Genealogy Assn., Ark. Genealogy Assn., Genealogy Helper of Iowa, Anton Jr. Home Demonstration (pres. 1974-76),

Garden Club (Anton), Hockley County Home Demonstration Levellaland, Tex., chmn. 1976, Littlefield Ex-Students Assn., Cotter and Co., Inc. Democrat. Mem. Ch. of Christ. Clubs: Anton Jr. Home Demonstration (pres. 1974-76), Garden (Anton); Hockley County Home Demonstration (Levelland, Tex.) (chmn. 1976). Home: 208 Duggan Anton TX 79313 Office: Harrell Bldg Supply Inc 213 Lawrence Ave Anton TX 79313 also: Harrell Bldg Supply Inc 2481 E Highway 114 Levelland TX 79336-9236

HARRELL, WILLIAM EDWARD, JR., orthodontist; b. Columbus, Ga., Dec. 18, 1948; s. William Edward and Mimi (Milner) H.; m. Joyce Tatum Jackson, Dec. 21, 1974; children: Sara Tatum, William Edward III. BS, U. Ala., Tuscaloosa, 1971; DMD, U. Ala., Birmingham, 1975; cert. in orthodontics, U. Pa., 1977. Diplomate, Am. Bd. Orthodontists. Pvt. practice orthodontics/TMJ Alexander City, Ala., 1977—; orthodontic/TMJ instr. Normandie Study Group for Temporomandibular Joint Disfunction, Montgomery, Ala., 1981-86; lectr. temporomandibular joint disorders; chmn. NASA Project Lazar for State of Ala., 1990—; prin. investigator/researcher on three-dimensional x-ray and video imaging NIH. Mem. Ala. Assn. Orthodontists (sec.-treas. 1988-89, v.p. 1989-90, pres. 1990-91), Am. Assn. Orthodontists, So. Assn. Orthodontists (chmn. new mem. com. 1986-90, bd. dirs. 1995—), Coll. Diplomates Am. Bd. Orthodontists, Dental Soc. Ala. (v.p., then pres. 9th dist. 1986-88), Am. Bd. Orthodontists, Ala. Assn. Orthodontists, ADA, 9th Dist. Dental Assn. State of Ala., Am. Equilibration Soc., Farrar-Norgaard Radiol. Soc., Royal Soc. Medicine, Found. for Orthodontic Rsch. Methodist. Home: 379 Auburn Dr Alexander City AL 35010-2904 Office: 125 Alison Dr Alexander City AL 35010-4408

HARRELSON, CLYDE LEE, secondary school educator; b. Baton Rouge, Nov. 20, 1946; s. Hezzie Clyde and Marguerite Lucille (Tucker) H. BA, Southeastern La. U., 1968; MA, La. State U., 1974, EdS, 1980; postgrad., So. U., Baton Rouge. Cert. social studies and English tchr., prin., supr., La. Tchr. English, East Baton Rouge Parish Sch. Bd., 1970—, McKinley Mid. Magnet Sch., Baton Rouge, 1982—; mem. Mid. Sch. Lang. Arts Curriculum Com. Mem. Arts Coun. Greater Baton Rouge, Found. for Hist. La., La. Preservation Alliance, Nat. Trust for Hist. Preservation, Colonial Williamsburg Found., NCCJ, Cmty. Assn. for Welfare Sch. Children, La. Dem. Com., Nat. Dem. Com. Mem. NEA, ASCD, Nat. Coun. Tchrs. English, La. Coun. Tchrs. English, East Baton Rouge Coun. Tchrs. English, East Baton Rouge Parish Dem. Exec. Com., La. Assn. Educators, East Baton Rouge Parish Assn. Educators, Kiwanis, Phi Delta Kappa. Episcopalian. Home: 3710 Prescott Rd Baton Rouge LA 70805-5055

HARRELSON, WALTER JOSEPH, minister, religion educator emeritus; b. Winnabow, N.C., Nov. 28, 1919; s. Isham Danvis and Mabel (Rich) H.; m. Idella Aydlett, Sept. 20, 1942; children: Marianne McIver, David Aydlett, Robert Joseph. Student, Mars Hill (N.C.) Coll., 1940-41, Litt.D. (hon.), 1977; A.B., U. N.C., 1947, Litt.D. (hon.), 1994; B.D., Union Theol. Sem., 1949, Th.D., 1953; postgrad., U. Basel, Switzerland, 1950-51, Harvard, 1951-53; D.D. (hon.), U. of South, 1974, Christian Theol. Sem., 1992. Instr. philosophy U. N.C., 1947; ordained to ministry Baptist Ch., 1949; tutor asst. Union Theol. Sem., 1949-50; prof. Old Testament Andover Newton Theol. Sch., 1951-55; dean, assoc. prof. Old Testament U. Chgo. Div. Sch., 1955-60; prof. Old Testament Div. Sch., Vanderbilt U., Nashville, 1960-75; chmn. grad. dept. religion Div. Sch., Vanderbilt U., 1962-67, dean, 1967-75, Disting. prof. Hebrew Bible, 1975-90, prof. emeritus, 1990—, dir. Lilly Ministry Project, 1990-94; interim dean Disciples Div. House, 1993-94; prof. Wake Forest U., 1994-96, adj. prof. Divinity Sch., 1996—; dir. Ecumenical Inst. Advanced Theol. Studies, Jerusalem, 1977-78, 78-79; vice-chmn. transl. com. Rev. Standard Version of the Bible; vis. prof. Brite Div. Sch. Tex. Christian U., 1992, Boston Coll., 1991, 93. Author: Jeremiah, Prophet to the Nations, 1959, Interpreting the Old Testament, 1964, From Fertility Cult to Worship, 1969, 80, The Ten Commandments and Human Rights, 1980, (with Rabbi R.M. Falk) Jews and Christians: A Troubled Family, 1990, (with Bruce M. Metzger and Robert C. Dentan) The Making of the New Revised Standard Version of the Bible, 1991, (with Rabbi R.M. Falk) Jews and Christians: In Pursuit of Social Justice, 1996; co-author, editor: Teaching the Biblical Languages, 1967; editor, contbr.: Israel's Prophetic Heritage, 1962; editl. chmn. Religious Studies Rev., 1974-80; assoc. editor Mercer Dictionary of the Bible, 1990; assoc. editor Mercer Commentary on the Bible, 1995. Dir. project to film Ethiopian Manuscripts, NEH, 1972-84; bd. dirs. Dead Sea Scrolls Found., 1991—, Planned Parenthood Assn., Nashville; active ch. rels. com. U.S. Holocaust Meml. Coun. Traveling fellow Union Theol. Sem., 1949; Am. Coun. Learned Socs. fellow, 1950-51, 70; exch. fellow U. Basel, 1950-51; Fulbright rsch. scholar, Rome, 1962-63; Harvie Branscomb Disting. prof. Vanderbilt U., 1977-78, Alexander Heard Disting. Svc. prof., 1985-86; NEH fellow, Rome, 1983-84; recipient Thomas Jefferson prize, 1987-88, Alumni/ae award Vanderbilt U., 1989, Festschrift, Justice and the Holy, 1989. Mem. NAS (mem. ethics com. Inst. Medicine), Soc. for Values in Higher Edn. (pres. 1972-74), Soc. Bibl. Lit. (pres. 1972), Am. Acad. Religion, Cath. Bibl. Assn., Phi Beta Kappa. Home: 708 E Moore St Southport NC 28461-4029

HARRER, GUSTAVE ADOLPHUS, librarian, educator; b. Durham, N.C., Dec. 30, 1924; s. Gustave Adolphus and Florence Caroline (Wagner) H.; m. Elizabeth Varnado, Sept. 3, 1948; children—Elizabeth Ida, Kathryn Florence, Hugh, Thomas. A.B., U. N.C., 1948, M.A., 1950, Ph.D. in Germanic Langs, 1953; M.S. in L.S. (Katherine L. Sharp fellow), U. Ill., 1954. Asst. prof. German and Latin Millsaps Coll., 1949-51; asst. order librarian U. Tenn. Libraries, 1954-55, assoc. order librarian, 1955-57; chief acquisition librarian Stanford Libraries, 1957-58, asst. dir. for central services, 1958-60; dir. libraries Boston U., 1960-68, U. Fla., Gainesville, 1968-84; Disting. Service prof. bibliography U. Fla., 1985-93, emeritus, 1994—; bd. dirs. Southeastern Library Network, 1974-77, vice chmn., 1976-77; mem. OCLC Users Council, 1978-81. Contbr. articles to profl. jours. Served with AUS, 1943-45, maj. Res. ret. Faculty fellow Fund for Advancement Edn., 1951-52; fellow Carnegie Project Advanced Library Adminstrn. Rutgers U., 1958; Am. Coun. Learned Socs. Linguistic Inst. fellow, summer 1948. Mem. ALA (life), Assn. Research Libraries (dir. 1973-76), Assn. Caribbean U. and Research Libraries (exec. council 1973-76, pres. 1977-78, hon. life mem.). Home: 2815 NW 29th St Gainesville FL 32605-2707

HARRIMAN, MALCOLM BRUCE, software developer, healthcare consultant; b. Sandusky, Ohio, Feb. 25, 1950; s. Robert Byron and Catherine (Nicolson) H.; m. Carla J. Holgren, Sept. 19, 1971 (div. Mar. 1980); m. Suzan Gwen Alexander, June 27, 1980 (div. Dec. 1985); 1 child, Sasha Bryn; m. Alysa Ellen Gelband, Apr. 19, 1986; children: Sarah Ashley, Catherine Nicole. BA, Antioch Coll., 1976; MA, U. Md., 1980. Child care worker Ft. Wayne (Ind.) Children's Home, 1971-72; adolescent program supr. Taylor Manor Hosp., Ellicott City, Md., 1972-76; program coord. child and adolescent svcs. Horizon Hosp, Clearwater, Fla., 1981-82, mktg. specialist, 1983-86; v.p., prin. ptnr. Am. Residential Ctrs., Tampa, Fla., 1986-89; pres., prin. ptnr. Continuum Psychiat. (formerly Am. Residential Ctrs.), 1989-95; exec. dir., COO Tampa Bay Acad., Riverview, Fla., 1988-94; chmn. bd., 1994-96; pres., chief exec. officer HealthExpert Systems, Inc. (formerly HealthWare, Inc.), 1989—; assoc. dept. psychiatry U. South Fla. Med. Sch., Tampa, 1980-81; mem. severely emotionally disturbed network project adv. coun. Pinellas County, Fla., 1985-86. Mem. corp. adv. bd. Behavioral Healthcare Tommorrow jour., 1994—. Gubernatorial appointee Project Freeway Task Force, HRS Dist. V, Fla., 1985-86; mem. adv. bd. Behavioral Informatics Tomorrow, Inst. Behavioral Healthcare, San Francisco, 1993—; mem. adv. com. Cognitive Rehab. Inst. Tampa, Fla., 1993-94. Mem. ASTM, Am. Health Info. Mgmt. Assn., Am. Med. Info. Assn., Am. Assn. Children's Residential Ctrs. (sci. com.), Nat. Assn. Psychiat. Treatment Ctrs. for Children (bd. dirs. 1989-95), Assn. for Ambulatory Behavioral Healthcare (outcome task force 1993—, cons. bd. dirs. 1994—), Nat. Assn. for Healthcare Quality, Nat. Alliance for Mentally Ill, Suncoast C. of C. (edn. com., del. youth svcs. adv. coun. 1982-86), Assn. Mental Health Adminstrs., Soc. for Computer in Psychology, Computer Based Patient Record Inst., Healthcare Info. and Mgmt. Systems Soc. Republican. Presbyterian. Office: HealthExpert Sys 6200 W Courtney Campbell Cswy Tampa FL 33607-1486

HARRINGTON, BETTY BYRD, entrepreneur; b. Longview, Tex., July 11, 1936; d. William Henry Byrd and Minnie Lee Tidwell; 1 child, Randy Lee Harrington. AA, Cedar Valley DCCCD, Dallas, 1988. Adminstrv. asst. Conf. Coun. on Ministries United Meth. Ch., Dallas, 1983-86; pres., actress, model, entertainer Kathy King Entertainment Agy., DeSoto, Tex., 1956—; pres. Gateway to Success/Resume Writing and Career Counseling, DeSoto, Tex., 1987—; Career Devel. and Placement, 1982—. Author: The Dallas Dazzler, Job Search and Interview Techniques, (poetry) She Has Been Faithful, 1996, Pity the Children, 1996. Mem. AFTRA, AGVA, DeSoto C. of C., Greater Dallas C. of C. Republican. Baptist. Home and Office: 1338 E Parkerville Rd De Soto TX 75115-6421

HARRINGTON, BRUCE MICHAEL, lawyer, investor; b. Houston, Mar. 12, 1933; s. George Haymond Harrington and Doris (Gladden) Maginnis; m. Anne Griffith Lawhon, Feb. 15, 1958; children: Julia Griffith, Martha Gladden, Susan McIver. B.A., U. Tex., 1960, J.D. with honors, 1961. Bar: Tex. 1961, U.S. Dist. Ct. (so. dist.) Tex. 1962, U.S. Ct. Appeals (5th cir.) 1962, U.S. Supreme Ct. 1973. Assoc. Andrews & Kurth and predecessor firm, Houston, 1961-73, ptnr., 1973-84; dir. Offenhauser Co., Houston, Allied Metals, Inc., Houston. Trustee St. John's Sch., Houston, 1981-92, chmn. bd., CEO, 1986-92; chmn. bd. Covenant House, Tex., 1991-95; trustee St. Luke's Episcopal Hosp., Tex. Med. Ctr., Houston, 1983-86; bd. dirs. YMCA Bd. Mgmt., Am. Cancer Soc., 1992-94, Ctr. for Hearing and Speech, 1993, chmn. bd., 1995—; vice chmn. Gateway Found., 1993-95; mem. adv. com. Assn. Governing Bds. of Colls. and Univs., 1991—. Mem. ABA, Nat. Assn. Ind. Schs. (chmn. trustee com.), Ind. Schs. Assn. S.W. (chmn. trustee com., bd. exec. com.), Tex. Bar Assn., Houston Bar Assn., The Mil. and Hosp. Order of St. Lazarus, The Venerable Order of St. John (U.K.), The Order of Saints Maurice and Lazarus (Savoy), Houston Country Club, Petroleum Club, Houston Club, Phi Delta Phi, Order of Coif. Republican. Episcopalian. Home: 3608 Overbrook Ln Houston TX 77027-4128

HARRINGTON, GEORGE FRED, aviation consultant; b. Killingly, Conn., July 29, 1923; s. George Whitman and Beatrice Evelyn (Sheldon) H.; m. Ruth Lydia Saarinen, June 7, 1947; children: Joanne Ruth, George Lauri, Julie Ann. BS, U.S. Mil. Acad., 1947; MBA, Harvard U., 1957; grad., Armed Forces Staff Coll., 1961, Indsl. Coll. of Armed Forces, 1967. Commd. 2d lt. USAF, 1947, advanced through grades to col., 1968, ret., 1977; mgr. market devel. Beech Aircraft, Washington, 1978-81; gen. mgr. internat. div. Beech Aircraft, Wichita, 1981-82, v.p., 1982-85; cons. Gen. Aviation, Arlington, Va., 1986—; cons. in field. Dir. Collingwood Libr. & Mus. on Americanism, Mt. Vernon, Va. Decorated D.S.M., Legion of Merit with oak leaf cluster. Mem. Air Force Assn., Retired Officers Assn., Harvard Bus. Sch. Club of Washington (pres. 1988-89), Masons, Shriners, Nat. Sojourners. Republican. Methodist. Home and Office: 1300 Crystal Dr # 304 Arlington VA 22202-3234

HARRINGTON, HERBERT H., accountant; b. Meadville, Pa., Sept. 19, 1946; s. Herbert H. and Sara R. (Rogers) H. BA, Kent State U., 1969; postgrad., Memphis State U., 1975; MS in Criminal Justice, Dyersburg State U., 1977. CPA, Tenn. Transp. dir. West Tenn. Easter Seal Soc., 1972-75; compt. So. Trucking, Inc., 1976-77; acct. Cen. So., Inc., 1978-79; compt. Wonder div. ITT Baking Corp., 1980-84; contr. N. Fla. Transport, 1985-86; fin. con. Computa-Tax, Inc., 1986—; pres. H&H Enterprises, Inc., Covington, 1989—; CEO Tenco, Inc., Burlison, Tenn., 1995—; cons. computer and acctng. software, Covington, 1973—. Author 3 textbooks on acctg. procedures and practice. Served with USN, 1963-81. Mem. Covington C. of C. Republican. Episcopalian. Lodges: Lions, Good Fellows, Optimists, Rotary. Home and Office: PO Box 402 Covington TN 38019-0402

HARRINGTON, JAMES CHARLES, lawyer; b. May 16, 1946; s. Alden G. and Mary I. (Johnson) H.; m. Rebecca Flores, May 6, 1972. BA in Philosophy, Pontifical Coll. Josephinum, 1968; MA in Philosophy, U. Detroit, 1970, JD, 1973. Bar: Tex. 1973, U.S. Dist Ct. (so., no., ea. and we. dists.) Tex., U.S. Ct. Appeals (5th cir.), U.S. Supreme Ct., 1975. Atty., dir. South Tex. Project, Austin, 1973-83; legal dir. Tex. Civil Liberties Union Found. Inc., Austin, 1983-90; columnist Texas Lawyer, Austin, 1988-95; atty. Advocacy Inc., Austin, 1993-95; legal dir. Tex. Civil Rights Project, Austin, 1990—; adj. prof. Law U. Tex., Austin, 1986—, St. Mary's U., Austin, 1990—, St. Edwards's U., Austin, 1991, 92; prof. dept. English U. Salamanca (Spain), 1989; mem. State Bar Com. on Legal Representation for Those on Death Row, 1991—; chmn. panel on law and ethics task force on AIDS Tex. Dept. of Health; dir. ADA Nat. Backup Ctr., 1995—; lectr. in field. Contbr. articles to profl. jours. Mem. ABA (Judge John Wisdom Pub. Svc. and Professionalism award 1990), State Bar of Tex., Capitol Area Mexican-Am. Lawyers. Office: Tex Civil Rights Project 2212 E MLK Blvd Austin TX 78702-1344

HARRINGTON, JOAN KATHRYN, counselor; b. Harvey, Ill., Dec. 21, 1934; d. Roy W. and Thelma (Hedlund) H. BA, Gordon-Barrington Coll., 1967; MPS, Alliance Theol. Sem., 1984; MEd, William Paterson State U., 1986; PhD, So. Calif. Grad. Sch. Theology, 1995. Cert. counselor; ordained Bapt. min. Rural Bible tchr. New Eng. Fellowship Evangs., Boston, 1960-62; co-dir. Children's Haven Inc., East Douglas, Mass., 1962-78; dir. edn. Calvary Gospel Ch., Newark, 1975-80; min. edn. Northside Community Chapel, Paterson, N.J., 1980-85; dir. guidance Eastern Christian High Sch., North Haledon, N.J., 1985-87; counselor Passaic County C.C., Paterson, 1987-89; counselor activities, social svcs. Palm Shores Retirement: The Colonnade, St. Petersburg, Fla., 1989-91; mental health therapist sr. support svcs. Suncoast Ctr. for Cmty. Mental Health, St. Petersburg, Fla., 1990-93; prof., asst. dean students St. Petersburg Theol. Sem., 1992—; urban coord. Africa Inland Mission, Newark, Paterson, 1975-82; vis. prof. Alliance Theol. Sem., Nyack, N.Y., 1986-88; min. parish witness First Bapt. Ch., Paterson, 1987-89; min. counseling Am. Bapt. Ch. of Beatitudes, St. Petersburg, 1990—; clin. dir. Life Mgmt. Counseling Svcs., 1994—. Author: (poetry) Deep Rivers, 1981; script writer, producer Haven Radio Club, 1962-78. Family Selection com. Habitat for Humanity, Paterson, 1985; bd. dirs. Urban Ministries of A.I.M., Newark, Children's Haven, Inc. (clk. 1962-77); mem. Paterson Clergy Assn., Paterson, 1980-85. Mem. ACA, Am. Assn. Christian Counselors, Assn. Specialists in Group Work, Am. Mental Health Counselor's Assn., Assn. for Spiritual, Ethical and Religious Values in Counseling, Nat. Assn. Alcoholism and Drug Abuse Counselors, Christian Assn. Psychol. Studies, Pi Lambda Theta. Democrat. Home: 5220 Brittany Dr S Apt 801 Saint Petersburg FL 33715-1537 Office: Am Bapt Ch Beatitudes 300 S Duncan Ave Ste 283 Clearwater FL 34615-6412 also: 300 Duncan Ave S Ste 293 Clearwater FL 34615

HARRINGTON, JOHN NORRIS, ophthalmic plastic and reconstructive surgeon, educator; b. Dallas, Oct. 1, 1939; s. Marion Thomas and Ruth Evelyn (Norris) H.; m. Elizabeth Hunt, June 20, 1964; children: Thomas Wesley, Clinton Hunt. BA, Tex. A&M U., 1961, BS, 1964; MD, U. Tenn., Memphis, 1966. Diplomate Am. Bd. Ophthalmology. Intern Letterman Gen. Hosp., San Francisco, 1966-67; resident in ophthalmology Scott and White Clinic, Temple, Tex., 1970-73; fellow in ophthalmic plastic and reconstructive surgery U. Calif., San Francisco, 1973-74; plastic and reconstructive surgeon Tex. Ophthal. Plastic, Reconstructive & Orbital Surg. Assoc., Dallas, 1974—; clin. prof. ophthalmic plastic and reconstructive surgery U. Tex. Southwestern Med. Ctr., Dallas, 1974—; chief staff Mary Shiels Hosp., Dallas, 1986-88; active staff, dir. ophthalmic plastic and reconstructive surgery Baylor U. Med. Ctr., Dallas, active staff dept. oncology Baylor-Sammons Cancer Ctr. Mem. editorial bd. Ophthalmic Plastic and Reconstructive Surgery Jour.; contbr. chpts. to textbooks; contbr. articles to med. jours. Mem. Univ. Park Citizens League, Dallas, 1976-82; pres. Highland Park High Sch. Dads Club, Dallas, 1982-83; sec. bd. deacons Park Cities Bapt. Ch., Dallas, 1981. Maj. M.C., U.S. Army, 1966-70, Vietnam. Decorated Bronze Star. Fellow ACS, Am. Soc. Ophthalmic Plastic and Reconstructive Surgery (sec. 1991-93, v.p. 1994, pres.-elect 1995, pres. 1996, del. to AMA 1995—), Am. Acad. Ophthalmology (bd. counselors 1991-94, Honor award 1989); mem. AMA, Tex. Med. Assn., Dallas Acad. Ophthalmology (pres. 1986). Office: 2731 Lemmon Ave Ste 304 Dallas TX 75204-2831

HARRINGTON, MARK GARLAND, oil company executive, venture capitalist; b. San Antonio, Mar. 5, 1953; s. Lloyd Hampton and Gray (Dugger) H.; divorced; 1 child, Alexandra Beall. BBA in Fin., U. Tex., 1976, MBA, 1977. Assoc. U.S. Trust Co. N.Y., N.Y.C., 1977-78, Carl H. Pfozheimer & Co., N.Y.C., 1978-81; ptnr. Carl H. Pfozheimer & Co., 1981-85; pres., CEO Harrington & Co. Internat., Houton, 1986—; founder, dir. HCO Energy Ltd., Calgary, 1987—; chmn., CEO HarCor Energy, Inc., L.A., 1987—; bd. dirs. Jefferson Gas Systems, Washington. Dir. Third St. Music Sch., N.Y.C., 1978-89, Found. for New Am. Music, L.A., 1986—. Mem. Ind. Petrol Assn., Petroleum Exploration Soc. N.Y., Brook Club N.Y., Racquet and Tennis Club (N.Y.), Coronado Club (Houston). Mem. Unity Ch. Office: HarCor Energy Inc Ste 2220 Five Post Oak Park Houston TX 77027

HARRINGTON, PATSY ANN, geriatrics nurse; b. Jackson, Tenn., Sept. 1, 1948; d. Tommy Andrew and Hattie Mae (Moody) Mullins; m. Joseph Randall Harrington, June 3, 1966; children: Gina C. Harrington Parham, Pamela Gail Harrington. ADN, U. Tenn., Martin, 1983; cert., U. Tenn., Knoxville, 1991. Cert. CEN, ACLS, PALS, BLS instr. Am. Heart Assn.; cert. CPR and First Aid instr. ARC; cert. gerontol. nurse. Nurse CCU and emergency rm. Bapt. Meml. Hosp., Huntingdon, Tenn., 1983-84, emergency rm., CCU nurse, 1988-91; emergency rm., recovery rm. and shift supr. Benton County Hosp., Camden, Tenn., 1984-87; tchr. LPN class Benton County Vocat. Sch., Camden, 1987-91; emergency rm. nurse Henry County Med. Ctr., Paris, Tenn., 1991; DON Hillhaven Convalescent Ctr., Huntingdon, 1991—. Med. team leader Disaster Team, Hollow Rock, Tenn., 1990-92; girl scout leader Girl Scouts Am., Hollow Rock, 1976-81; softball coach Little League, Hollow Rock, 1980-81; pres. PTA, Hollow Rock, 1979; chmn. Cystic Fibrosis Fundraising, Hollow Rock, 1979-81. Mem. ANA (bd. dirs. 1989-91), Tenn. Nurses Assn., Emergency Nurse Assn., Am. Cancer Assn., Tenn. Health Care Assn. Democrat. Baptist. Home: Massey Dr PO Box 414 Hollow Rock TN 38342-0414 Office: Hillhaven Convalescent Ctr 635 High St Huntingdon TN 38344-1703

HARRINGTON, THOMAS BARRETT, judge; b. Alexandria, La., Feb. 15, 1936; s. Robert Lee and Clara (Barrett) H.; m. Elizabeth Wheeler; children: Thomas Barrett Jr., Mary Kathryn Harrington Peltier. BS, La. State U., 1958; JD, Tulane U., 1962; grad., Nat. Coll. Criminal Def. Lawyers, 1978. Asst. dist. atty. 15th Jud. Dist., 1970-72; city judge Crowley, 1983—; judge pro tempore 15th Jud. Dist. Ct., Acadia, Lafayette and Vermilion Parish, 1983. Mem. ABA, La. State Bar Assn., Fed. Bar Assn., Assn. Trial Lawyers Am., La. Trial Lawyers Assn. Office: PO Box 225 Crowley LA 70527-0225

HARRINGTON, THOMAS KEVIN, transportation planner; b. Ridley Park, Pa., Jan. 23, 1969; s. Thomas Patrick and Maureen Mary (Muldowney) H.; m. Claire Moya Hebeler, July 25, 1992. BS in Sys. Engring., U. Va., 1990; M in Regional Planning, U. N.C., 1996. Assoc. Barton-Aschman Assocs., Inc., Washington, 1990-94, Cary, N.C., 1994—. Grad. fellow Inst. Transportation Rsch. and Edn., 1995-96. Mem. Am. Planning Assn. Office: Barton-Aschman Assocs Inc 401 Harrison Oaks Blvd Cary NC 27513

HARRIS, ANNE RUTH, volunteer services administrator; b. Houston, Jan. 27, 1944; d. John Willie Harris and Erma Lee (Rogers) Harris/Phillips. BA in Music, Tex. So. U., 1966, MS in Sociology, 1974. Cert. tchr., Tex. Grad. student intern Tex. So. U., Houston, 1972-74; caseworker ARC, Houston, 1974-77, asst. dir. social svcs., 1977-82; vol. coord. Tex. Youth Commn., Houston, 1982-85; vol. svcs. adminstr. Houston Pub. Libr., 1985—. Mem. planning com. Gov.'s Vol. Conf., Austin, Tex., 1992-94, Internat. Conf. on Vol. Adminstrn., 1992-93; mem. Project Blueprint Leadership program United Way of Tex. Gulf Coast, Houston, 1990; pres. Cmty. Vol. Youth Coun., Houston, 1992-94; adv. bd. Vol. Ctr. Family Matters, Houston, 1992-94; mentor for student athlete U. Houston Athletic Program, 1992—; bd. dirs. Lighthouse of Houston, 1990—; pres. Houston Network Coun. Recipient Woman of Excellence award Fedn. Houston Profl. Women, 1994, Best Dressed Houston award Fashion Statement Inc., 1994, Diamond Key award Nat. Women of Achievement, 1994, Humanitarian award Tex. So. U. Sch. Social Work, 1988. Mem. Houston Assn. Vol. Adminstrs. (adv. coun., pres. 1988-89, Joan Hanlon Meml. award 1989). Baptist. Home: 9042 Lawncliff Ln Houston TX 77040 Office: Houston Public Library 500 McKinney Houston TX 77002

HARRIS, ANNIE RENE, elementary school educator; b. Eden, Miss., Aug. 20, 1946; d. Tommie L. and Rosetta (Tolbert) H. BS in Edn., Jackson (Miss.) State Coll., 1968, MS, 1972, EdS, 1974; EdD, Ind. U., 1983. Cert. elem. tchr., Miss. Elem. tchr. Jackson Pub. Schs.; asst. prof. edn. Ky. State U., Frankfort, Western Ky. U., Bowling Green; elem. tchr. Atlanta Pub. Schs.; guest lectr. home econs. dept. Indiana Univ., Bloomington, 1982-83. Leadership team chairperson E.L. Connally Sch., Atlantic Pub. Schs. Olympics com.; chair Red Cross and March of Dimes for E.L. Connally Elem. Sch.; rep. Am. Heart Fund; mem. PTA. Recipient Outstanding Elem. Tchr. Am. award, 1975, Finer Womanhood award Nat. Coun. Negro Women, 1980, Disting. Svc. citation United Negro Coll. Fund, 1979-80, others. Mem. NEA, Nat. Soc. Study of Edn., Coun. for Exceptional Children.

HARRIS, BAYARD EASTER, lawyer; b. Washington, July 22, 1944; s. Edward Bledsoe and Grace (Childrey) H.; m. Rebecca Bond Jeffress, June 10, 1967; children: Nicholas Bayard, Nathan Bedford (dec. 1989), Ellen Coley. AB in History, U. N.C., 1966; JD cum laude, U. S.C., 1973. Bar: Va. 1974, U.S. Dist. Ct. (we. dist.) Va. 1974, U.S. Ct. Appeals (4th cir.) 1974, U.S. Supreme Ct. 1982. Assoc. Woods, Rogers, Muse, Walker & Thornton, Roanoke, Va., 1973-79, ptnr., 1979-85; ptnr. Woods, Rogers & Hazlegrove, Roanoke, 1985-90; pres. Ctr. for Employment Law, Roanoke, 1991—; mem. Transp. Safety Bd., 1992-96. Comments and rsch. editor U. S.C. Law Rev., 1972-73. Chpt. chmn. ARC, Roanoke Valley, 1985-87, chmn. ea. ops. hdqrs., 1988-91. Lt. USNR, 1966-70. Recipient Clara Barton award ARC Roanoke Valley chpt., 1986. Mem. ABA (labor and employment sect. 1974—), Va. Bar Assn. (labor and employment com. and sect. 1974—), Rotary. Republican. Episcopalian. Office: The Ctr for Employment Law 2965 Colonnade Dr Roanoke VA 24018-3541

HARRIS, BELINDA JEAN, librarian; b. Roanoke, Va., Apr. 13, 1955; d. Kimbrough Settle and Louise Virginia (Croye) H. BA in History, Roanoke Coll., 1977. Asst. libr. Roanoke Times and World News, Va., 1978-84; libr. Roanoke Times, 1984—. Vol. Roanoke Valley Therapeutic Riding, 1992—. Mem. Spl. Librs. Assn., Investigative Reporters and Editors, Inc., N.Am. Riding for Handicapped Assn. Methodist. Office: Roanoke Times 201 Campbell Ave SW Roanoke VA 24011-1105

HARRIS, BRUCE EUGENE, financial analyst; b. Zanesville, Ohio, Jan. 14, 1950; s. Harold Eugene and Ruth A. (Harbaugh) H.; m. Linda Elaine Vess, Mar. 6, 1971. BS in Acctg., Ohio State U., 1974; MBA, U. Houston, 1991. Payroll, pers. clk. Peabody Coal Co., New Lexington, Ohio, 1970-72; auditor Boykin Enterprises, Columbus, Ohio, 1973-74; cost acct. Ashland Chem. Co., Dublin, Ohio, 1974-76; acct. Ohio State U., Columbus, 1976-78; systems analyst Gulf Oil Corp., Houston, 1978-81; cons. Deloitte Haskins & Sells, Houston, 1981-82; systems mgr. Info. Svc. Internat. div. Mars, Inc., Houston and Los Angeles, 1982-88; owner Brulyn Mmgt. Group, 1988-92; mgr. integration svcs. McLane Co. Inc./M-Group, Temple, Tex., 1992—. Mem. Data Processing Mgmt. Assn. (cert.), Mensa, Friends of Temple Pub. Libr., Air Force Mus. Found. Roman Catholic. Home: 606 W Zenith Ave Temple TX 76501-1353 Office: M Group 4001 Industrial Blvd PO Box 549 Temple TX 76503

HARRIS, CHARLES EDGAR, retired wholesale distribution company executive; b. Englewood, Tenn., Nov. 6, 1915; s. Charles Leonard and Minnie Beatrice (Borin) H.; m. Dorothy Sarah Wilson, Aug. 20, 1938; children: Charles Edgar, William John. Pres., chmn., CEO H.T. Hackney Co., Knoxville, Tenn., 1972-83; ret.; former chmn. bd., chief exec. officer, dir. various corps. in Tenn., Ky., N.C., and Ga.; former bd. dirs. Park Nat. Bank, 1st Am. Nat. Bank Knoxville; dir. U.S. Indsl. Coun. Former bd. dirs. Downtown Knoxville Assn., Greater Knoxville Smoky Mountain coun. Bou Scouts Am., Met. YMCA, Knoxville, United Way Knoxville; mem. budget com. 1982 World's Fair, Knoxville; deacon, trustee Ctrl. Bapt. Ch., Knox County Assn. Bapt.; mem. exec. bd. Tenn. Bapt. Conv., Nashville; assoc. chmn. Layman's Nat. Bible Week, Washington; trustee Carson Newman Coll., Jefferson City, Tenn.; dir. Tenn. Taxpayers Assn.; dir. Religious Heritage of Am., St. Louis; bd. dirs. Tenn. Bapt. Children's Homes. Recipient Outstanding Community Leadership award Religious Heritage Am., Red Triangle award and Silver Triangle award YMCA. Mem. Greater Knoxville C. of C. (bd. dirs., Outstanding Corp. Citizenship award), Nat. Assn. Wholesalers-Distbrs., LeConte Club (charter), Knoxville Execs. Club (bd. dirs.), Rotary (officer, bd. dirs.). Home: 7914 Gleason Dr Unit # 1071 Knoxville TN 37919-5477

HARRIS, DANIEL FREDERICK, biomechanical analyst, educator; b. Pitts., Nov. 11, 1944; s. Frederick C. and Elizabeth May (Donley) H. BA, W.Va. U., 1966, MA, 1972, postgrad., 1986; postgrad., Yale U., 1990. Instr. photographic and computer graphics Greenville (S.C.), 1987-96; clin. researcher in motion analysis St. Francis Hosp., Greenville, 1991-95, clin. and indsl. rsch. in applied ergonomics, human factors and motion analysis, 1993—; instr. photography Greenville Tech. Coll., 1992, dept. head Visual Arts Inst., 1995—; adj. instr. art history U. S.C., Spartanburg, 1987-91; mem. S.C. Curriculum Congress, 1991—; cons. Motion Analysis Corp., Calif., 1991—; presenter in field. Named Tchr. of Yr. Monongalia County, W.Va., 1981. Mem. Phi Delta Kappa. Presbyterian. Home: 205 Springvale Dr Mauldin SC 29662-1622

HARRIS, DELMARIE JONES, elementary education educator; b. New Orleans, Mar. 16, 1947; d. Ralph and Ruth Lena (Ackerson) Jones; m. Hosey W. Williams (div. 1974); children: Hosey Willie, Sabrena Michelle; m. Ronald Andrew Harris, Mar. 7, 1978; 1 child, Rene Andrea. Student, Southern U., New Orleans, 1967-70; BA, Southern U., 1971. Tchr. St. Mary of Angels, New Orleans, La., 1971-73, J.F. Gauthier Elem. Sch., Poydras, La., 1973—; grade chmn. J.F. Gauthier steering com. bull. 741, 1987, language arts textbook adoption rep., 1992-93; recorder St. Bernard Parish Discipline Dress Code Adoption Com., 1988-90, math. rep., 1990, primary tchr.; mem. com. to rewrite curriculum for math. State of La., 1996. Mem. NEA, Nat. Coun. Tchrs. Math., Internat. Reading Assn., La. Assn. Educators, St. Bernard Assn. Educators. Democrat. Roman Catholic.

HARRIS, DOUGLAS CLAY, newspaper executive; b. Owensboro, Ky., Oct. 9, 1939; s. Marvin Dudley and Elizabeth (Adelman) H. BS, Murray State U., 1961; MS, Ind. U., 1964, EdD, 1968; grad. advanced mgmt. program, Harvard U., 1987. Counselor, asst. to dean of students Ind. U., Bloomington, 1965-68; mgmt. appraisal specialist United Air Lines, Elk Grove Village, Ill., 1968-69; dir. manpower div. Computer Age Industries, Washington, 1969; area personnel dir. Peat Marwick Mitchell & Co., N.Y.C., 1969-72; v.p. personnel Knight-Ridder, Inc., Miami, Fla., 1972-85, v.p., sec., 1986—. Served to capt. U.S. Army, 1961-62. Mem. APA, Inst. CFP's, Internat. Assn. Fin. Planners, Fla. Psychol. Assn., Southeastern Psychol. Assn. Democrat. Home: Baypoint 580 Sabal Palm Rd Miami FL 33137-3374 Office: 1 Herald Plz Miami FL 33132-1609

HARRIS, EARL DOUGLAS, state agency administrator; b. Athens, Ga., Apr. 9, 1947; s. Roland Russell and Martha Sue (Davis) H.; m. Jean Wright, Dec. 26, 1975; children: Jeannette, Stephanie. BSAE, U. Ga., 1970, MBA, JD, 1973. Bar: Ga. 1973, U.S. Dist. Ct. (mid. dist.) Ga. 1973, U.S. Ct. Appeals (5th cir.) 1973, U.S. Ct. Claims 1977, U.S. Tax Ct. 1977, U.S. Patent Office 1977, U.S. Customs Ct. 1977, U.S. Supreme Ct. 1977, U.S. Ct. Customs and Patent Appeals 1980, U.S. Ct. Internat. Trade 1981, U.S. Ct. Appeals (5th, 11th cir., and federal ct. of Appeals) 1981. Sole practice of law and patent law, Watkinsville, Ga., 1973-76, 1986-92; city atty. Town of Bogart, 1974-75, 85-90; sr. ptnr. Harris & Rice, Watkinsville, 1977-78; mem. Harris, Rice & Alford, P.A., Watkinsville, 1978-80; ptnr., pres. Harris & Alford, P.A., Watkinsville, 1980-85; Ga. asst. commr. agr., 1992— mem. Ga. State Olympic Law Enforcement Commd., 1996; pres. Fed. Title Corp., 1978-90; county atty. Oconee County, Ga., 1978-80; atty. Town of Bishop, 1980-89; corp. sec. Lawlog Corp., 1980-90. Bd. dirs. The Oconee Enterprise, Inc., 1987-93, Clarke County unit Am. Cancer Soc., 1970-72; mem. Oconee County Dem. Exec. Com., 1976-94, treas., 1976-82; pres., trustee N.E. Ga. Presbytery, 1987-91; trustee Masonic Children's Home Ga., 1985-89; trustee Gen. Counsel Ga. Scottish Rite Found., Inc., 1989—; pres., chmn. bd. dirs., Georgia Masonic Charities Found., Inc., 1996; Served with USCMR, 1965-68; with USAF, 1968. Mem. Western Cir. Bar Assn., Gridirion Secret Soc., AGHON Soc. (pres.), U. Ga. Agrl. Alumni Assn. (pres. young alumni div. 1975-76, dir. at Large, 1996), Oconee County C. of C. (dir., sec. 1976-78), Masons (33 degree Scottish Rite, Past Grand Master of Masons in Ga.) Order of Eastern Star (past patron), Societas Rosicruciana In Civitatibus Foederatis (VIII grade), Shriners, KT, Tall Cedars of Lebanon, Royal Order of Scotland, Red Cross of Constantine, Knights of York Grand Cross of Honor, York Rite Coll., Blue Key, Sphinx, Omicron Delta Kappa, Sigma Iota Epsilon, Alpha Zeta. Presbyterian (ruling elder). Home: 1230 Allgood Rd Athens GA 30606-5371 Office: Agriculture Bldg Capital Sq Rm 209 Atlanta GA 30334-2001

HARRIS, ED JEROME, retired judge; b. May 19, 1920; m. June Brickson, Mar. 25, 1945; children: Edward J., Ann Harris Jones. Grad., Southwestern U., Georgetown, Tex., 1941; LLB, JD, U. Wis., 1948; MA, So. Meth. U., 1949. Cert. mediator. Sr. ptnr. Harris, Martin, Carmona, Cruse, Micks & Dunten, 1956-77; mem. Tex. Ho. of Reps., Austin, 1962-77; state dist. judge, 1977-93, ret., 1993. Del. Dem. Nat. Conv., N.Y.C., 1976; councilman, Galveston City, 1961-63; mem. adminstrv. bd. Moody Meml. First United Meth. Ch.; admiral Tex. Navy. Recipient 1st Ann. Independence award North Galveston County Dems., 1991. Mem. Am. Judges Assn., Coll. State Bar Tex., Wis. Bar Assn., Tex. Bar Assn., Galveston County Bar Assn., Navy League, Ret. Officers Assn., VFW, U. Wis. Alumni Assn., Judiciary Tex. Coll. Advanced Jud. Studies, Galveston Coffee Club, Galveston Rifle and Pistol Club, Kiwanis, Eagles, Knights of Momus.

HARRIS, ELIZABETH HALL, writer, English language educator; b. Ft. Worth, Nov. 27, 1944; d. William David and Elizabeth M. Hall; m. Warwick Paul Wadlington, Feb. 18, 1995. BS with honors, Carnegie Inst. of Tech., 1965; MA, Boston U., 1967; PhD, Stanford (Calif.) U., 1976. Asst. prof. U. Tex., Austin, 1976-83, assoc. prof., 1983—. Author: The Ant Generator, 1991 (John Simmons short fiction award 1991); contbr. short stories to publs. Rsch. inst. fellowship U. Tex. at Austin, 1994; named 100 Other Disting. Short Stories of the Yr. 1985, 1986. Episcopalian. Office: Univ Tex Dept English Austin TX 78712

HARRIS, ERNEST CLAY, SR., marketing consultant, engineer; b. Georgetown, Ky., Feb. 6, 1939; s. Lee Ernest and Virginia R. (Haskins) H.; m. Lenora White, June 24, 1961; 1 child, Ernest Clay Jr. Engring. degrees, U. Cinn., 1961, U. Ky., 1975; grad. in Bus. Mgmt., U. Ky., 1977. Quality rep. R&D lab. IBM Corp., Lexington, Ky., 1968-73, product engr., 1973-74, mfg. engr., 1974-75, quality engr., 1975-79, devel. engr., 1979-81; mfg. engr. IBM Corp., Charlotte, N.C., 1981-93; cons. engr., mktg. cons. Harris & Assocs., Charlotte, 1993—. Mem. Dem. Nat. Com., Washington., 1993. Sgt. U.S. Army, 1961-63. Mem. NSPE (Top Team scholar 1992), Am. Soc. Quality Control (treas. 1978). Baptist. Home: 5521 Cutshaw Ct Charlotte NC 28215-2409

HARRIS, GARY MARCEL, theater educator; b. Kingsport, Tenn., Apr. 2, 1953; s. Charles Luther and Yvonne (Stoefs) H.; m. Carole Fagan, Apr. 28, 1979; 1 child, Joshua. BFA, U. of the South, 1975; MA in Speech and Theater, U. Tenn., 1980, MFA in Theater, 1981. Asst. prof. Vanderbilt U., Nashville, Tenn., 1981-88; assoc. prof. Austin Peay State U., Clarksville, Tenn., 1988-95, Palm Beach Atlantic Coll., West Palm Beach, Fla., 1995-96; asst. prof. Lyon Coll., Batesville, Ark., 1996—; guest artist Leysin (Switzerland) Am. Sch., 1993. Designer, tech. dir. of sets, lighting, and costumes for over 100 theatrical prodns. Tchr., drama ministry Holy Trinity Episc. Ch., West Palm Beach, 1996; guest spkr. Rotary, Clarksville, Tenn., 1994; bd. dirs. Mockingbird Pub. Theatre, Nashville, 1994-95. Named one of Outstanding Young Men Am., 1988; recipient 1st Night award Middle Tenn. Theatre Alliance, 1995. Mem. Southeastern Theatre Conf., U.S. Inst. for Theatre Technology (orgnl. mem.). Democrat. Home: 485 S 23d St Batesville AR 72501 Office: Lyon Coll Box 2317 Batesville AR 72503-2317

HARRIS, GEORGE BRYAN, lawyer; b. Columbia, S.C., July 8, 1964; s. A. Bryan and Beverly Gaye (Bennett) H. BA, U. Ala., 1986; JD, U. Va., 1989. Bar: Ala. 1989, U.S. Dist. Ct. (no., mid., and so. dists.) Ala. 1990, U.S. Ct. Appeals (11th cir.) 1990, D.C. 1991, U.S. Ct. Appeals (5th cir.) 1992, U.S. Supreme Ct. 1993, London Ct. Internat. Arbitration 1995, U.S. Dist. Ct. (no. dist.) Tex. 1996. Ptnr. Bradley, Arant, Rose & White, Birmingham, Ala., 1996—; spl. asst. atty. gen. for environment State of Ala., Montgomery, 1990-92. Mem. Birmingham Bar Assn., U. Va. Law Alumni Assn., U. Ala. Alumni Assn., Birmingham Mon. Morning Quarterback Club, Delta Tau Delta (v.p., bd. dirs. chpt. 1991-94). Methodist. Office: Bradley Arant Rose & White 2001 Park Place Ste 1400 Birmingham AL 35203

HARRIS, GLENDA STANGE, medical transcriptionist, writer; b. Jacksonville, Fla., Jan. 11, 1954; d. Robert Lee and Wynelle (Jowers) S.; m. David Michael Harris Sr., Aug. 11, 1973; children: David Michael Jr., Mason Andrew. AA, Fla. Jr. Coll., Jacksonville, 1980. Asst. adminstr. Primary Health Care Ctr., Orange Park, Fla., 1980-83; med. transcriptionist, exec. sec. Ctr. for Plastic and Reconstructive Surgery, Orlando, Fla., 1984-90; med. transcriptionist Fayette Med. Clinic, Fayetteville, Ga., 1991—. Author: (newspaper column) Grand Slam News, 1991-94. Republican. Methodist. Home: 135 Mark Ln Fayetteville GA 30214-7202 Office: Fayette Med Clinic 101 Yorktown Dr Fayetteville GA 30214-1568

HARRIS, HOLLIS WARD, electrical engineer; b. Amarillo, Tex., Dec. 23, 1910; s. Harve Henry and Naomi Florence (Hagar) H.; m. Ellen Iola Fox, Nov. 24, 1930 (dec. July 1960); children: Robert G., Wilma Colleen; m. Aline Ola Waldron, Jan. 25, 1961. AS, Ea. N.Mex. U., 1939; BS, N.Mex. State U., 1941; postgrad., U. Mo., 1941-42. Registered profl. engr., Tex., Okla., N.Mex., Kans., Ariz. Instr. engring. U. Mo., Columbia, 1941-42; prof. elec. engring. U. Wyo., Laramie, 1942-43; engr. Carl C. Cox, Cons., Amarillo, 1944-45; cons. engr. Amarillo, 1945-82; trustee Hollis & Aline Harris Trusts, Amarillo, 1982—. Mem. Truth in Spending Com., Amarillo, 1991—. Mem. IEEE (life), Tex. Soc. Profl. Engrs. (dir., chmn. Panhandle chpt. 1950, nat. dir. 1961-62, Outstanding Engr. 1954). Republican. Methodist. Home: 1110 Clyde Amarillo TX 79106

HARRIS, JACK HOWARD, II, consulting firm executive; b. Chgo., Mar. 22, 1945; s. Jack Howard and Myrtice Geneva (Dickson) H.; m. Barbara Beck Czika, Jan. 1, 1983; children: Jack, William, T. Patrick; stepchildren: Joseph C. Czika, Brad D. Czika. AB, U. Chgo., 1966; MPh, George Washington U., 1984. Chief China desk Air Force Intelligence, U.S. Air Force, Washington, 1971-74; dir. policy studies BDM Corp., Washington, 1974-78; sr. assoc. Booz-Allen and Hamilton, Washington, 1979; corp. v.p., govt. ops. Sci. Applications, Inc., Washington, 1980-85; exec. v.p., CFO The Harris Group, Inc., Washington, 1985-95; pres. Ctr. for Nat. Program Evaluation, Washington, 1988-94; v.p. Corp. & Polit. Comms., Inc., 1995—. With USAF, 1967-71. Mem. Air Force Assn., Am. Legion, DAV, VFW, Internat. Platform Assn., Phi Gamma Delta. Home and Office: 911 Challedon Rd Great Falls VA 22066-1727

HARRIS, JAMES HAROLD, III, lawyer, educator; b. Texarkana, Tex., Apr. 26, 1943; s. James Harold Jr. and Mildred (Freeman) H. BA, Dartmouth Coll., 1964; JD, Vanderbilt U., 1967. Bar: Tenn. 1967, U.S. Dist. Ct. (mid. dist.) Tenn. 1967, U.S. Ct. Appeals (6th cir.) 1967. Asst. dean Vanderbilt U. Sch. Law, Nashville, 1971; atty. Met. Govt. Nashville, Nashville, 1972-75; ptnr. Harris & Leach, Nashville, 1975-87, Harris & Baydoun, Nashville, 1987-90; counsel Wyatt, Tarrant, Combs, Gilbert & Milom, Nashville, 1990-93, Gordon, Martin, Jones & Harris, Nashville, 1994—. Capt. USNR, 1967—. Mem. ABA, Tenn. Bar Assn., Nashville Bar Assn., Nashville Entertainment Assn. (legal counsel). Home: 103 Burlington Ct Nashville TN 37215-1843 Office: Gordon Martin Jones & Harris PA 49 Music Sq W Ste 600 Nashville TN 37203-3230

HARRIS, JAMES HERMAN, pathologist, neuropathologist, consultant, educator; b. Fayetteville, Ga., Oct. 19, 1942; s. Frank J. and Gladys N. (White) H.; m. Judy K. Hutchinson, Jan. 30, 1965; children: Jeffrey William, John Michael, James Herman. BS, Carson-Newman Coll., 1964; PhD, U. Tenn.-Memphis, 1969, MD, 1972. Diplomate Am. Bd. Pathology; sub.-cert. in anatomic pathology and neuropathology. Resident and fellow N.Y.U.-Bellevue Med. Ctr., N.Y.C., 1973-75; adj. asst. prof. pathology N.Y. U., N.Y.C., 1975-83; asst. prof. pathology and neuroscis. Med. Coll. Ohio, Toledo, 1975-78, assoc. prof., 1978-82, dir. neuropathology and electron microscopy lab., 1975-82; cons. Toledo Hosp., 1979-82, assoc. pathologist/neuropathologist, dir. electron microscopy pathology lab., 1983-91, mem. courtesy staff, 1991—, mem. overview com., credentials com., appropriations subcom. medisgroup, interqual task force; chmn. clin. support services com., vice chmn. med. staff quality rev. com.; cons. neuropathologist Mercy Hosp., 1976-93, mem. courtesy staff, 1993—, U. Mich. dept. pathology, 1984-93; cons. med. malpractice in pathology and neuropathology; mem. AMA Physician Rsch. and Evaluation Panel; mem. ednl. and profl. affairs commn., exec. council Acad. Medicine; mem. children's cancer study group Ohio State U. satellite; chmn. tech. and issues subcom. of adv. com. Blue Cross, mem. task force on Cost Effectiveness N.W. Ohio; chmn. med. necessity appeals com. Blue Cross/Blue Shield; adv. bd. PIE Mut. Ins. Co. Chmn. steering com. Pack 198, Boy Scouts Am.; chmn. fin. com., dir. bldg. fund campaign First Baptist Ch., Perrysburg, Ohio; faculty chmn. Med. Coll. Ohio United Way Campaign; mem. adv. com. Multiple Sclerosis Soc. NW Ohio. Recipient Outstanding Tchr. award Med. Coll. Ohio, 1980; named to Outstanding Young Men Am., U.S. Jaycees, 1973; USPHS trainee, 1964-69, postdoctoral trainee, 1973-75; grantee Am. Cancer Soc., 1977-78, Warner Lambert Pharm. Co., 1978-79, Miniger Found., 1980, Toledo Hosp. Found., 1985, Promedica Health Care Found., 1986. Mem. Am. Profl. Practice Assn., Am. Pathology Found., Am. Soc. Law and Medicine, Coll. Am. Pathologists, Lucas County Acad. Medicine (bar acad. liaison com.), Ohio State Med. Assn. (fed. key contact), Med. Assn. Ga., Am. Assn. Neuropathologists (profl. affairs com., awards com., program com., constitution com.), Internat. Acad. Pathologists, Ohio Soc. Pathologists, Coll. Am. Pathologists, EM Soc. Am., Sigma Xi. Author med., sci. papers; reviewer Jour. Neuropathology and Exptl. Neurology. Republican. Avocations: tennis, real estate rehabilitation, bldg. developer, gardening, white water rafting. Home and Office: 9105 Nesbit Lakes Dr Alpharetta GA 30202-4028

HARRIS, JOHN ROBERT, secondary education educator; b. Fort Worth, Tex., Dec. 4, 1953; s. Gary Carlisle and Charlotte (Perkins) H.; m. Juanita Canada, Jan. 28, 1989; 1 child, Owen Myles Alasdair. BA in English, U. Tex., 1974, MA in classics, 1978, PhD in comparative literature, 1984. Cert. tchr., Tex. Asst. prof. English U. Tex., Tyler, 1985-88, Berry Coll., Rome, Ga., 1988-90, Belmont (N.C.) Abbey Coll., 1990-92; assoc. prof. English Union U., Jackson, Tenn., 1993—. Contbr. articles to profl. jours. Mem. Am. Conference for Irish Studies, Conference on Christianity and Literature, So. Comparative Literature Assn., The Vergilian Soc. Presbyterian. Home: 52 Ginger Ln Bells TN 38006 Office: Union U Box 1837 Jackson TN 38305

HARRIS, JOHN WOODS, banker, lawyer; b. Galveston, Tex., Sept. 23, 1893; s. John Woods and Minnie (Hutchings) H.; m. Eugenia Davis, June 14, 1917 (dec.); children: Eugenia (Mrs. Archibald Rowland Campbell, Jr.), Anne (Mrs. Donald C. Miller) (dec.), Joan (Mrs. Alvin N. Kelso), Florence (Mrs. Marshall McDonald, Jr.) (dec.). LLB, U. Va., 1920. Bar: Tex. 1920. Practiced as atty. and mng. agt. oil, farm, ranch properties in Tex., 1922-95; dir. Hutchings Sealy Nat. Bank; chmn. exec. com., chmn. bd., chmn. emeritus First Hutchings Sealy Nat. Bank (merged into First Internat. Bancshares, merged into InterFirst Corp., merged into NCNB Corp.), Galveston, 1960-74; dir., mem. exec. com. InterFirst Bank Galveston N.A.; pres. Hutchings Joint Stock Assn., 1936-87; dir. Galveston Corp., Cotton Concentration Co., Gulf Transfer Co., Tex. Fiberglas Products Co. Sr. v.p. Sealy and Smith Found. for John Sealy Hosp., 1938-85, mem. fin. com., chmn. land com.; pres. bd., trustee, trustee emeritus Rosenberg Libr., 1934-83, Galveston Orphans Home; founder, pres. Galveston Found.; bd. dirs., v.p., chmn. fin. com. George Ball Charity Fund; trustee Galveston Ind. Sch. Dist., 1927-30; sr. adv. U.S. Congl. Adv. Bd.; life mem. Naval Aviation Mus. Found., Inc. Aviator USN, 1918. Named Rabbi Henry Cohen Humanitarian of Yr., 1981; $1,000,000 awarded to the John Woods Harris Chair in Surgery at the U. of Tex. presented in his honor by The Sealy & Smith Found. and The Bd. of Regents of the U. of Tex., 1986. Mem. Am. Judicature Soc., Early and Pioneer Naval Aviators Assn., Sons of Republic Tex., Am. Legion, Order of the Daedalians (life), Galveston Artillery Club, The Yacht Club (Galveston), Delta Kappa Epsilon. Episcopalian. Home: 2603 Avenue O Galveston TX 77550 Office: 801 NationsBank Tex 2200 Market St Galveston TX 77550-1530

HARRIS, JOSEPH LAMAR, state agency administrator; b. Pensacola, Fla., Mar. 26, 1951; s. Joseph Erlis and Mazie Lois (Plant) H.; m. Elizabeth Gail Golden, Dec. 15, 1973; children: Heather Brooke, Brandon Lamar. AA in Bus., Pensacola Jr. Coll., 1971; BA in Acctg. magna cum laude, U. W. Fla., 1973. CPA, Fla., Ala. Staff acct. Touche Ross and Co., Atlanta, 1974-75; div. acct. Gulf Power Co., Pensacola, Fla.; field auditor U.S. Dept. Health, Edn., and Welfare Audit Agy., Montgomery, Ala., 1975-77; budget analyst II Ala. State Budget Office, Montgomery, 1977-82, budget analyst III, 1982-85, budget analyst IV, 1985-87; acting budget officer, dep. state budget officer State of Ala., Montgomery, 1987-88, dep. state budget officer, 1987—; bd. dirs. Ala. Gov.'s Legis. First Reading Com., Montgomery; bd. dirs. Ala. Bd. Pub. Accountancy, sec.-treas. 1989-94; chmn. state adv. group Ala. Mgmt. Improvement Program, Montgomery, 1987-89; mem. adv. coun. to govtl. acct. and auditor tng. program Auburn U. Recipient Cert. of Appreciation, Office of the Gov. State of Ala., 1987. Mem. AICPA, Ala. Soc. CPAs (state legis. com. 1981—), Assn. Govt. Accts. (chpt. treas. 1975-77), Govt. Fin. Officers Assn. Ala., Nat. Assn. State Budget Officers, Ala. State Employees Assn., Nat. Assn. State Bds. Accountancy (govt. rels. com. 1990-93). Mem. Assembly of God Ch. Home: 6032 Meridian Ln Montgomery AL 36117-2789 Office: Exec Budget Office Rm 237 Ala State House Montgomery AL 36130-2610

HARRIS, JOYCE FAYE, elementary education educator; b. Drummond, Okla., Feb. 22, 1912; d. David Samuel and Pearl (Joyce) Harris; m. Samuel Smith Kendrick, Aug. 8, 1939 (dec. Dec. 1944); 1 child, Patricia Joyce; m. John Henry Glass, Mar. 8, 1946 (dec. 1973); 1 child, William John; m. Theodore Ted Anderson, Oct. 14, 1979 (dec. Sept. 1989). Student, Sullins Coll.; BS, U. Okla., 1933. Tchr. Nome (Alaska) H.S., from 1935, Kodiak (Alaska) H.S., Halsey (Oreg.) Schs., Creslane (Oreg.) Elem. Sch., to 1976. Mem. DAR, Kappa Kappa Gamma. Republican. Home: PO Box 155 Drummond OK 73735

HARRIS, LEE CHARLES, health and nursing educator; b. Hiseville, Ky.; s. George Lee and Grace (Twyman) H. BS in Biology, Ky. State U., 1954; grad. in nursing, Freedmen's Hosp. Sch. Nursing, Washington, 1957; MS, EdD, U. Ky., 1965, 86; MPH, Johns Hopkins U., Balt., 1974. RN, Ky. Sch. nurse Lincoln Inst., Lincoln Ridge, Ky., 1958-59; staff nurse Cleve. Clinic Found. Hosp., 1960-61; pub. health nurse Detroit City Health Dept., 1961-63; health edn. cons. Ky. State Dept. Health and Human Svcs., Frankfort; assoc. prof., dir., coord. continuing nurses edn. nursing Ky. State U., Frankfort, dir., assoc. dir. dept. nursing, 1968-73, 80—, media ctr. coord. dept. nursing, 1976-77, dir. freshman studies, 1977-80, asst. v.p. acad. affairs, 1990-92; nat. and internat. lectr. and presenter in field. Named Centennial Outstanding Alumni, Disting. Alumni, Nat. Assn. Equal Opportunity in High Edn.; U. Ky. doctoral fellow, 1980-81, others. Mem. ANA, Ky. Nurses Assn., Nat. League for Nursing, Ky. Pub. Health Assn., Order Ea. Star (Mispah chpt.), Chi Eta Phi, Alpha Kappa Alpha (25 yr. honoree). Baptist. Home: 238 Missouri Ave Frankfort KY 40601-3034

HARRIS, LOUIS SELIG, pharmacologist, researcher; b. Boston, Mar. 27, 1927; s. Max Selig and Pearl (Oppochinski) H.; m. Ruth Irma Schaufus, Aug. 22, 1952; 1 child, Charles Allan. BA, Harvard U., 1954, MA, 1956, PhD, 1958. Sect. head, sr. rsch. biologist Sterling-Winthrop Rsch. Inst., Rensselaer, N.Y., 1958-66; lectr. in pharmacology Albany (N.Y.) Med. Coll., 1959-66; from assoc. prof. to prof. U. N.C., Chapel Hill, 1966-73; Harvey Haag prof. Med. Coll. Va./Va. Commonwealth U., Richmond, 1972—, chmn. pharmacology, toxicology dept., 1972-92; acting assoc. dir. Nat. Inst. on Drug Abuse, Rockville, Md., 1987-88; Sterling Drug vis. prof., 1983; mem. com. on problems of drug dependence NAS/NRC, 1973-77; mem. Com. on Problems of Drug Dependence, Inc., 1977-93, chmn., 1990-92; hon. prof. Beijing Med. U., People's Republic of China, 1990—. Editor: (monograph) NIDA Monographs, Proceedings, Committee on Problems of Drug Dependence, 1979—; author chpts. in books. Recipient Hartung Meml. award U. N.C., 1981, Univ. Excellence award Med. Coll. Va./Va. Commonwealth U., 1984, Outstanding Faculty award, 1984, Nathan B. Eddy award Com. on Problems of Drug Dependence, 1985, Abe Wikler award Nat. Inst. on Drug Abuse, 1991, Gov.'s award on Drug Abuse Rsch., 1992, Presdl. medallion Va. Commonwealth U., 1993. Fellow Am. Coll. Neuropsychopharmacology, Coll. Problems Drug Dependence; mem. AAAS, AAUP, Am. Soc. Pharmacology and Exptl. Therapeutics, Am. Chem. Soc., Am. Assn. for Med. Sch. Pharmacology, Am. Pain Soc. (charter 1977), Am. Pharm. Assn., Am. Soc. for Clin. Pharmacology and Therapeutics, Assn. Harvard Chemists, Elisha Mitchell Sci. Soc., Internat. Narcotic Enforcement Officers Assn., Soc. for Neurosci., Internat. Soc. Biochem. Pharmacology, Internat. Soc. for Study of Pain, Collegium Internationale Neuro-Psychopharmacologicum, Va. Acad. Sci., Harvard Club Boston, Cosmos Club Washington. Home: 7830 Rockfalls Dr Richmond VA 23225-1049 Office: Va Commonwealth U PO Box 980027 Richmond VA 23201-0027

HARRIS, LUCY BROWN, accountant, consultant; b. Ft. Smith, Ark., Feb. 25, 1924; d. Joseph Real and Lucy (McDonough) Brown; m. Clyde B. Randall, June 10, 1944 (div. Aug. 1970); children: Clyde B. III, Bradford, Sara, Lucy, Mark R.; m. Mack C. Harris, Aug. 1, 1980. Student, Holton Arms Jr. Coll., 1943, U. Mo., 1944; BA, U. Ark., 1970; grad., U. Tex., 1982. CPA. Comptroller Rebmar, Inc., Dallas, 1974-78; acctg. mgr. Republic Bank, Dallas, 1978-80; ptnr. Lucy B. Harris Ltd. Co., CPAs, Dallas, 1981—; cons. Discipleship Counseling Svcs., Dallas, 1987-90. Mem. Better Bus. Bur.; bd. dirs. Ethel Daniels Found., Dallas, 1987-90, NAWBO. Mem. AICPA, Nat. Assn. Women Bus. Owners, Tex. Soc. CPAs, CPA Club, Jr. League of Dallas, Brookhollow Golf Club, Kappa Alpha Theta. Episcopalian. Office: 3710 Rawlins St Ste 810 Dallas TX 75219-4237

HARRIS, LYNDON F., priest; b. Gaffney, S.C., June 3, 1961; s. Wallace Greer and Annie Laura (Murph) H.; m. Kirsten Whitney Rutherford, Apr. 19, 1986; 1 child, Margaret Kirsten. BA in Philosophy, Wofford Coll., 1983; MDiv, U. of South, 1990; postgrad., Gen. Theol. Sem., N.Y.C., 1995—. Ordained deacon Episcopal Ch., 1990, priest, 1991. Prodn. mgr. Milliken and Co., Spartanburg, S.C., 1983-87; asst. rector St. Alban's Episcopal Ch., Lexington, S.C., 1990-91, Episcopal Ch. of Advent, Spartanburg, 1991—; Episcopal chaplain Wofford Coll., Converse Coll., Spartanburg, 1991-95; interim rector St. Paul's Episcopal Ch., Spring Valley, N.Y., 1996—; chaplain St. Hilda's and St. Hughes Episcopal Sch., N.Y.C., 1996—; coord. Jr. High Ministry, Diocese of Upper S.C., Columbia, 1990—, standing com., 1992—, pres., 1995, vice chair ecumenical commn., 1993—; tutor Gen. Theol. Sem., 1996—. Bd. dirs. Vols. Am., Spartanburg, 1993—; mem. human rels. group Shared Hope in People, 1992—; active Let's Stop the Violence. Recipient award for excellence in Bibl. studies Am. Bible Soc., 1990; Coll. of Preachers/Washington Nat. Cathedral fellow, 1994. Mem. Assn. Religion and Intellectual Life. Office: Gen Theol Sem 175 9th Ave New York NY 10011

HARRIS, LYTTLETON TAZWELL, IV, property management and publishing executive; b. Baton Rouge, Aug. 7, 1940; s. Lyttleton Tazwell and Marjorie Fleming (Windsor) H.; m. Venita Walker VanCaspel, Dec. 26, 1987. BBA, U. Miss., Oxford, 1962; MS, La. State U., 1963. Product mgr. Scott Paper Co., Phila., 1968-71; mktg. mgr. Wm. B. Reily & Co., New Orleans, 1971-72; mktg. dir. Blue Plate Foods, Inc., New Orleans, 1972-74, Dallas Fed. Savs., 1974-77; v.p. First Magnolia Fed. Savs., Hattiesburg, Miss., 1977-81; pres. S.W. Mgmt. & Mktg. Co., Houston, 1982—; v.p. Innerview Pub. Co., Houston, 1984-86; mng. editor Money Dynamics Letter Pub. Co., Houston, 1985-91; gen. mgr. Diamond V Ranch of Bernardo, Tex., 1990—. V.p. Nat. Kidney Found. of Miss., Jackson, 1980-82; bd. dirs. Nat. Kidney Found. S.E. Tex., Houston, 1983-88, Boy Scouts Am., Hattiesburg, 1980-82; vol. Big Bros. of Dallas, 1975-77. With USAR, 1963-68. Mem. Inst. Real Estate Mgmt., Internat. Assn. Fin. Planning, Am. Mktg. Assn., Sales and Mktg. Execs. (pres. 1982), Nat. Gavel Soc., Nat. Congress of Patriotic Orgns., Soc. Colonial Wars, Mil. Order Stars and Bars, Order of Three Crusades, Huguenot Soc., Order Founders and Patriots of Am. (gov. Tex. chpt. 1987-91, Meritorious Svc. award 1990, gov. gen. 1992-94), U. Miss. Alumni Assn., Sons of Confederate Vets., Soc. Ams. of Royal Descent, SAR, Houston Racquet Club, Univ. Club, Sigma Alpha Epsilon, Delta Sigma Pi. Republican. Methodist. Office: Southwest Mgmt & Mktg 6524 San Felipe St Ste 102 Houston TX 77057-2611

HARRIS, MARJORIE JANE, religious studies educator; b. Roanoke Rapids, N.C., Oct. 22, 1951; d. Jesse Parker Taylor and Myrtle Jane H. BA, Meredith Coll., 1974; MDiv, Southeastern Bapt. Theol. Sem., Wake Forest, N.C., 1981; MA, U. N.C., 1988, PhD, 1994. English educator Baptist Fgn. Mission Bd., Kaohsiung, Taiwan, 1974-76; English and history educator J.V. Martin Jr. H.S., Dillon, S.C., 1976-78; residence dir. Peace Coll., Raleigh, N.C., 1979-81; grad. tchg. asst. U. Va., Charlottesville, 1982-84; assoc. pastor Univ. Bapt. Ch., Chapel Hill, N.C., 1984-85; grad. asst. U. N.C., Chapel Hill, 1985-90; asst. prof. religion Hendrix Coll., Conway, Ark., 1990-96, assoc. prof. religion, 1996—; assoc. Bapt. campus minister, U. N.C.,

1985-87, instr. religion, 1989-90; mentor Edn. for Ministry Univ. of the South, Sewanee, Tenn., 1992—. Vestry St. Peter's Episcopal Ch., Conway, 1994—; bd. dirs. Steel Ctr. for the Study of Religion & Philosophy, Conway, 1991—. Mem. AAUP (treas. Hendrix Coll. chpt. 1993—), Am. Acad. Religion, Am. Soc. Ch. History. Democrat. Home: 4220 Raleigh Dr Conway AR 72032 Office: Hendrix Coll Dept Religion 1600 Washington Ave Conway AR 72032

HARRIS, MARVIN, anthropology educator; b. Bklyn., Aug. 18, 1927; s. Irving and Sadie (Newman) H.; m. Madeline Grove, Jan. 25, 1953; children: Robert Eric (dec.), Susan Lynn. BA, Columbia U., 1948, PhD, 1953. From asst. prof. anthropology to prof. anthropology Columbia U., N.Y.C., 1953-80, chmn. dept. anthropology, 1963-66; grad. rsch. prof. U. Fla., Gainesville, 1980—; lectr. Fgn. Svc. Inst., U.S. Dept. State, 1965-67, U. Colo. NSF summer inst., 1970; vis. disting. prof. Ctrl. Wash. State Coll., 1968-69; Snider Bequest lectr. U. Toronto, 1980; dir., exec. sec. Columbia-Cornell-Harvard-Ill. summer field studies program, 1965-66; McMurrin prof. U. Utah, 1984; cons. UN Fund Population Activities, 1983-84, McKinsey and Co. Global Inst., 1991-92; cons. family rsch. project Bronx State Hosp., 1968; prin. investigator Videotape Study Urban Domiciles, 1967-74; rschr. in field, 1950— including Color-Race Categories, Brazil, 1992; presenter papers in field. Author: Town and Country in Brazil, 1956, The Nature of Cultural Things, 1964, Patterns of Race in the Americas, 1964, The Rise of Anthropological Theory, 1968 (designated a citation classic Inst. Sci. Rsch. 1992), Culture, Man, and Nature, 1971, Culture, People, Nature, 6th edit., 1992, Cows, Pigs, Wars, and Witches, 1974, paper, 1991, Cannibals and Kings, 1977, Cultural Materialism, 1979, paper, 1980, America Now, 1981, paper, 1982 reissued as Why Nothing Works, 1988, Cultural Anthropology, 1983, 4th edit., 1993, Good To Eat, 1985, reissued as Sacred Cow and the Abominable Pig, 1987, Our Kind, 1989, (with Charles Wagley) Minorities in the New World, 1958, (with co-edits. M. Fried and R. Murphy) War: The Anthropology of Armed Conflict and Aggression, 1968, (with Eric Ross) Death, Sex, and Fertility, 1987, (with Eric Ross, co-editor) Food and Evolution, 1987, paper, 1990, (with Thomas Headland and Kenneth Pike co-editors) Emics and Etics: The Insider/Outsider Debate, 1990, Cultural Anthropology, 4th edit., 1992. NSF grantee. Mem. AAAS, Am. Anthrop. Assn. (chmn. Gen. Anthropology divsn. 1991, Disting. Lectr. award lifetime exemplary scholarship 1991). Home: 1511 NW 38th St Gainesville FL 32605-4807 Office: U Fla Dept Anthropology Gainesville FL 32611

HARRIS, MARY B., home economics educator; b. Vanceville, La., Dec. 27, 1933; d. John Sidney and Bettie Clara (Merritt) Barnes; m. Robert Edward Harris, Sr., Dec. 31, 1950; children: Robert Jr., John, George. BS, NE La. U., 1970; MEd, Northeast La. U., 1972; EdD, Okla. State U., 1975. Cert. home economist, provisional vocat. homemaking tchr., job specific home econs., Tex.; cert. type B vocat. home economist, prin., La. Grad. asst. NE La. U., 1971-72, Okla. State U., 1972-74; home econs. tchr. Waterproof (La.) High Sch., 1967-70; prof. home econs. Sam Houston State U., Huntsville, Tex., 1975—; presenter workshops, seminars; cons. in field. Contbr. articles to profl. jours. Participant African/Am. Cross-Cultural Study Tour of Sierra Leone (West Africa, funded by AAUW). Sex Equity grantee, Teen Responsibility grantee, Title Twelve grantee. Mem. Am. Assn. of Family and Consumer Scis., Am. Vocat. Assn., AAUW, Phi Delta Kappa, Delta Kappa Gamma, Kappa Omicron Nu, Phi Upsilon Omicron. Baptist. Home: 224 Westridge Dr Huntsville TX 77340-8917 Office: Sam Houston State Univ Dept Consumer Services Fashion & Design Academic Bldg 2 Huntsville TX 77341

HARRIS, MAXINE, administrative assistant; b. Timpson, Tex., Jan. 24, 1950; d. Willie Copeland and Rosa Bell (Witherspoon) Pass; m. Travis Wade Harris, Oct. 11, 1968; 1 child, Tarisa Rose. Student, Panola Jr. Coll., 1976, LeTourneau U., 1986. Ptnr. Harris Constrn., Gary, Tex., 1973-91; contrs. asst. Drew Woods, Inc., Carthage, Tex., 1980-91; adminstrv. asst. child care licensing State of Tex., Tyler, 1992—; notary pub., Tex. Mem. United Trekkers of Planet Earth (founder, pres., pub. newsletter The Voice). Home: PO Box 470 Winona TX 75792

HARRIS, MELBA IRIS, secondary school educator, state agency administrator; b. Cullman, Ala., Aug. 8, 1945; d. Karl and Leona Christine (McDowell) Budweg; m. James Allen Harris, Apr. 17, 1965 (div. June 1981); 1 child, James Allen II. BS in Home Econs., U. Ala., 1970, MA in Elem. Edn., 1977, EdS, 1982; BS in Elem. Edn. magna cum laude, St. Bernard Coll., 1975. Instr. Cullman (Ala.) City Schs., 1966-68, Ft. Payne (Ala.) City Schs., 1974—; curriculum developer Ala. State Dept. Edn., Montgomery, 1987-89; aerospace edn. coordinator Ala. State Dept. Aeronautics, Montgomery, 1987-89. V.p. Ft. Payne Civettes, 1979. Recipient commendations Ala. Gov. George C. Wallace, 1985, 86, Gov. Guy Hunt, 1987, Ft. Payne City Coun., 1987, Ft. Payne City Bd. Edn., 1987, Civil Air Patrol Albertville Composite Squadron, 1987, Ala. State Bd. Edn., 1987; recipient Ala. State Excellence in Edn. award Fed. Aviation Adminstrn., 1987, Stewart G. Potter award Nat. Aircraft Distbrs. and Mfrs. Assn., 1988, Nat. Frank G. Brewer Meml. Airospace Edn. award Civil Air Patrol, 1989, Aviation Edn. Excellence award Nat. Gen. Aviation Mfrs. Assn., 1989, NEWEST award NASA, 1995; named A. Scott Crossfield Nat. Aerospace Educator of Yr., 1987, The Nat. Aerospace Edn. Tchr. of Yr., 1987; Christa McAuliffe fellow, 1987, Tchr. of Yr. Meml. award, 1991; named to Ala. Aviation Hall of Fame, 1991. Mem. NEA, NSTA, Ala. Edn. Assn. (state aerospace edn. coord. 1992—), Ft. Payne Edn. Assn. (pres. 1985-86), Air Force Assn. (life), Ala. Aviation Assn., Exptl. Aircraft Internat. (maj. achievement award 1988), Exptl. Aircraft Chpt. 683 (sec., treas. 1987, pres. 1988), Internat. Ninety-Nines, Inc., Kappa Delta Pi. Home: PO Box 1174 Fort Payne AL 35967-1174 Office: Forest Ave Sch 101 Forest Ave SW Fort Payne AL 35967-1954

HARRIS, MICHELLE KAYE, advertising executive, publishing executive; b. S.C., Jan. 29, 1971; d. Wilbur Franklin Maddox and Nena Kaye Queen; m. Charles Richard Harris, Dec. 17, 1994. BA, W. Ga. Coll., 1993. Mktg. rep. U. Comms., Inc., Cornelia, Ga., 1994-96; co-owner, advtsg. dir. The Tri-County Jour., Buena Vista, Ga., 1996—. Mem. Marion County/Buena Vista (Ga.) C. of C. Republican. Baptist. Home: PO Box 850 215 S Broad St Buena Vista GA 31803 Office: The Tri-County Jour PO Box 850 215 S Broad St Buena Vista GA 31803

HARRIS, MIRIAM KALMAN, writer, educator, consultant; b. Houston, Sept. 30, 1942; d. Philip Kalman and Frances Aileen Levy Kalman Rose; m. Stanley R. Harris, Feb. 21, 1965; children: Pepi Eileen, Earl Kalman. BA, U. Tex. at Dallas, Richardson, 1980, MA, 1985, PhD, 1997; student, U. Tex. Southwestern Health, Houston, 1962. Instr. English, women's studies and humanities various colls. in Dallas area, 1983-90; dir. Battered Women's Emergency Intervention Project, Parkland Hosp., Dallas, 1988-90; vis. prof. Sheridan Coll., Brampton, Ont., Can., 1992; tchg. asst. instr. U. Tex. Dallas, Richardson, 1995—; writing cons. and editor Write Now, Dallas; founder, dir. Women's Learning Ctr., Dallas, 1984-88. Cntbr: The Unpredictable Adventure by Claire Myers Spotswood Owens, 1993; contbr. chpt. to anthology: All Sides of the Subject: editor, Teresa Iles; author articles on women's issues. Treas., Cabbages and Kings Theater, Dallas, 1990-95; chair lit. com. Second Story Theater, Dallas, 1991-95; mem. Lawyers Against Domestic Violence, Dallas, 1988-90. AAUW Am. fellow, 1996—; Jordan Arts scholar, 1995; Ky. Found. for Women grantee, 1988. Mem. MLA, South Central MLA, South Ctrl. Women's Studies Assn. (editor 1992-96), Nat. Women's Studies Assn. (editor, comms. chair 1992-96, chair Jewish Caucus 1992-96). Jewish. Office: U Tex at Dallas PO Box 830688 Richardson TX 75083-0688

HARRIS, NICHOLAS ROBERT, army officer; b. Batavia, N.Y., Apr. 28, 1960; s. Robert Lee and Mary Elizabeth (Criticos) H.; m. Karen Canella Adams, May 18, 1985; children: Adam, Ethan, Logan. BS in Polit. Sci., Radford U., 1982. Commd. U.S. Army, 1982, advanced through grades to maj., 1994; troup exec. officer 4th Squadron, 12th Cavalry Regiment, Ft. Polk, La., 1985-86; action officer Dir. Combat Developments, Ft. Knox, Ky., 1986-87; sr. class advisor B Troop 2d Squadron, 12th Cavalry Regiment, Ft. Knox, 1988-89, squadron exec. officer, 1989-90; chief cavalry asst. Readiness Group Knox, Ft. Knox, 1990-91; commandant of cadets Bowling Green (Ohio) State U., 1991-95; ops. officer U.S. Army Forces Command, Atlanta, 1995—. V.p. Down Syndrome Assn. of Atlanta, 1995—. Named Hon. Ky. Col., Gov. of Ky., 1989, Order of St. George, 1989. Fellow Panthers Partnership for Excellence (chmn. 1996—). Republican. Greek Orthodox. Home: 203 Kentwood Dr Peachtree City GA 30269

HARRIS, OREN, retired federal judge; b. Belton, Ark., Dec. 20, 1903; s. Homer and Bettie Lee (Buloock) H.; m. Ruth Ross, May 9, 1934; children: Carolyn Marie, James Edward. BA, Henderson State U., 1929; LLB, Cumberland U., 1930; LLD (hon.), Ouachita State U., 1988. Bar: Ark. 1930, U.S. Supreme Ct. 1943. Dep. pros. atty. Union County, Ark., 1933-36; pros. atty. 13th Jud. Circuit, 1936-40; mem. 77th-89th congresses from 4th Dist. Ark.; chmn. com. on interstate and fgn. commerce, chmn. spl. investigatory com. on regulatory agys., judge U.S. Dist. Ct. for Eastern and Western Dists. Ark., 1966-76, sr. judge, 1976-92; ret., 1992; mem. budget com. Fed. Judiciary, 1973-85; mem. Jud. Conf. U.S., 1971-74. Del. Democratic Nat. Conv., 1944, 52, 56, 60. Recipient Saturday Rev. award, 1960; Public Service award Air Freight Forwarders Assn., 1960; award of merit Air Traffic Control Assn., 1962; Disting. Public Service citation Western Ry. Club, 1962; Joint Chiefs of Staff Nat. Transp. award Nat. Def. Transp. Assn., 1962; Presdl. citation Pioneer Nat. Broadcasting Assn., 1963; Presdl. citation APHA, 1963; Albert Lasker Svc. award, 1964; George Washington award Good Govt. Soc., 1965; Oren Harris Chair of Transp. established at U. Ark., 1970. Mem. Am. Bar Assn., Ark. Bar Assn., Ark. Bar Found., Sigma Alpha Epsilon. Baptist. Clubs: Lions (Ark. dist. gov. 1939-40), Jaycees (life), Masons (33 deg.), Shriners, K.P. Home: 510 Brookside Dr Little Rock AR 72205-1694

HARRIS, PATRICIA LEA, librarian; b. Hanau, Fed. Republic Germany, Oct. 2, 1952; came to U.S., 1954; d. Harvey J. and Laurielea A. (Huth) H. BS in Edn., Wright State U., 1973; MLS, La. State U., 1975. Reference libr. Greene County Dist. Libr., Xenia, Ohio, 1975-78; br. head Greene County Dist. Libr., Fairborn, Ohio, 1978-79; devel. cons. State Libr. of Ohio, Columbus, 1979-83; pub. libr. cons. La. State Libr., Baton Rouge, 1983-84; asst. dir. for devel. Va. State Libr., Richmond, 1984-87; state libr. N.D. State Libr., Bismarck, 1987-91; dir. Ala. Pub. Libr. Svc., Montgomery, 1992—; sec. Ohio Coun. of Info. and Referral Providers, 1976-79. Mem. Citizens Adv. Coun. on Adult Basic Edn., Bismarck, 1988-90, Western Coun. State Librs., 1987-91; bd. dirs. N.D. Coalition on Adult Literacy, 1987-89; mem. N.D. Hist. Records Adv. Bd., Bismarck, 1987-91; mem., chief officer State Libr. Agys., 1987—. Mem. ALA, SE Libr. Assn., Ala. Libr. Assn. Democrat. Roman Catholic. Office: Ala Pub Libr Svc 6030 Monticello Dr Montgomery AL 36117-1907

HARRIS, RICHARD EARL, pharmacist; b. Florence, S.C., Dec. 22, 1922; s. Robert Prescott and Pauline (Burns) H.; m. Audrey Miner, July 7, 1946; children: Terry Robert, Sara Dee Harris Kerr, Paula Jean Harris Fleming, Mary Kathryn Harris Jones, Richard Kirk. AA, U. Fla., 1942, BS in Pharmacy, 1947, PD, 1980. Pharmacist, ptnr. Grant-Harris Drug Store, Clermont, Fla., 1950-68; pharmacist, mgr. Eckerd Drugs #116, Clermont, 1968-89; pres. R. Harris Enterprises, Inc., Clermont, 1988—; cons. pharmacist State of Fla., Clermont, 1947-96. Author: Yesterday's Remedies for Today's Ills, 1991, My Dad's Sayings, 1994, Fishin' Tips 'N' Tales, 1994, Much Ado About Many Things, 1995. Bd. trustees South Lake Meml. Hosp., Clermont, 1989-96. Capt. USMCR, 1942-46, PTO. Decorated Bronze Star, USMC, PTO, 1945, Purple Heart with gold star, USMC, PTO, 1945, Pres. Unit citation, U.S., PTO, 1945. Mem. Lions Internat. (pres. 1955). Methodist. Home: 448 W Juniata St Clermont FL 34711-2235

HARRIS, RICHARD FOSTER, JR., insurance company executive; b. Athens, Ga., Feb. 8, 1918; s. Richard Foster and Mai Audli (Chandler) H.; m. Virginia McCurdy, Aug. 21, 1937 (div.); children: Richard Foster, Gaye Karyl Harris Law; m. Kari Melandso, Dec. 29, 1962. BCS, U. Ga., 1939. Bookkeeper, salesman 1st Nat. Bank, Atlanta, 1936-40; agt. Vol. State Life Ins. Co., Atlanta, 1940-41; asst. mgr. N.Y. Life Ins. Co., Atlanta and Charlotte, N.C., 1941-44; mgr., agt. Pilot Life Ins. Co., Charlotte and Houston, 1944-63; mgr., agt. bus. planning div.; city agy. Am. Gen. Life Ins. Co., Houston, 1963—; bd. dirs. Fidelity Bank & Trust Co., Houston, 1965-66, mem. bd. business devel., Sterling Bank, Upper Kirby Br., 1996. Chmn. fund drive Am. Heart Assn., Charlotte, Mecklenburg County, 1958-59, chmn. bd., 1959-61; gen. chmn. Shrine Bowl Promotion, Charlotte Shriners, 1955; v.p., bd. dirs. Myers Park Meth. Ch. Men's Class, 1956-59, bd. stewards, Charlotte, 1959-61; bd. dirs. Houston Polit. Action Com., 1982—; charter mem. Rep. Presdl. Task Force, pres., 1981-90; at large del. Rep. Nat. Convention Planning Platform, Houston, 1992; co-chmn. Christian Community Service Ctr., 1984-90; mem. First Tuesday Group, Houston, 1985—; tchr. Mens's Bible class St. John the Divine Ch., 1963-93; founder Episcopal High Sch., Houston, 1984. Recipient Pres.'s Cabinet award Am. Gen. Life Ins. Co., 1964-67, 69, 71, 77-83, Disting. Salesman award Charlotte Sales Exec. Club, 1955, 57-59, Bronze Medallion award Am. Heart Assn., 1959, Nat. Quality awards, 1965-92, The Rep. Presdl. Legion of Merit award, 1992; named Adm. of Tex. Nav. Gov. of Tex., 1989. Mem. Assn. Advanced Life Underwriters, Am. Soc. CLUs, Nat. Assn. Life Underwriters, SAR (mem. bd. Business Devel., Sterling Bank, chpt. 5 Tex. 1974—, Good Citizenship award 1991), Life Underwriters Polit. Action Com. (life), Houston Estate and Fin. Forum, English Speaking Union, Mensa Internat., Houston Assn. Life Underwriters, Lone Star Leaders Club, Tex. Leader's Round Table (life), Million Dollar Round Table (life), Tex. Assn. Life Underwriters, Am. Security Council (nat. adv. bd. 1979—), Houston Club, 100 Club, Deerwood Club, Forum Club of Houston, Pachyderm Club, Campaigner Club, Tex. Circle Club, Kiwanis (bd. dirs. 1979—), Masons (32 degree), Shriners, Sertoma (life, v.p. bd. dirs. Charlotte chpt.), Royal Order Jesters. Episcopalian. Home: 2701 Westheimer Rd 6E Houston TX 77098-1243 Office: Am Gen Life Ins Co Wortham Tower 2727 Allen Pky Ste 104 Houston TX 77019-2100

HARRIS, RICHARD FOSTER, III, lawyer; b. Charlotte, N.C., Apr. 10, 1942; s. Richard Foster and Frances Virginia (McCurdy) H.; m. Jacqueline Kaplan; children—Richard Foster, IV, John Walter Rodney. A.B. in English, Duke U., 1964; J.D., U. N.C., Chapel Hill, 1967. Bar: N.C. 1967, U.S. Dist. Ct. (we. dist.) N.C. 1971, U.S. Ct. Appeals (4th cir.) 1973. Assoc. Eugene C. Hicks III, Charlotte, 1968-70; ptnr. Hicks, Harris & Sterrett and predecessor Hicks & Harris, Charlotte, 1970-81; sole practice, Charlotte, 1982—. Served with Air N.G., 1967-73. Mem. ABA, N.C. State Bar, N.C. Bar Assn. (Outstanding Young Lawyer award 1977, chmn. Young Lawyers Sect. 1977-78), Assn. Trial Lawyers Am., N.C. Acad. Trial Lawyers, Mecklenburg County Bar Assn. (chmn. young lawyers sect. 1976-77). Democrat. Presbyterian. Club: Myers Park Country (Charlotte). Home: 329 Cherokee Pl Charlotte NC 28207-2301 Office: 757B Providence Rd Charlotte NC 28207-2245

HARRIS, RICHARD JOHN, medical librarian; b. Bournemouth, Dorset, U.K., Aug. 15, 1948; came to U.S., 1960.; s. I. Gwyn and Margaret (Taylor) H.; m. Colleen Kay Tuttle, Nov. 15, 1987. BA, Glassboro (N.J.) State Coll., 1971; MLS, Rutgers U., 1975; PhD, Old Dominion U., 1996. Tech. svcs. coord. Eastern Va. Med. Sch. Libr., Norfolk, 1975-88; sys. coord. Eastern Va. Med. Sch. Libr., 1985—. Mem. Med. Libr. Assn., Med. Tech. Assn., Pi Alpha Alpha. Office: Eastern Va Med Sch Libr PO Box 1980 Norfolk VA 23501

HARRIS, RICHARD LEONARD, automotive executive, entrepreneur; b. Huntington, N.Y., Feb. 8, 1963; s. Joseph Maurice and Shirley Mae (Everson) H.; m. Diane Annete Barrett, Oct. 26, 1991 (div. Jan. 1994). Student, U. Colo., 1980-82, Farmingdale Coll., 1981-82, SUNY, Stony Brook, 1982-83. Mgr. Jekylls Hidels Leather, Huntington, N.Y., 1981-82; dist. mgr. Houston Hat & Boot, Cromwell Heights, Pa., 1982-83; regional mgr. Phila. Trunk Co., Cromwell Heights, Pa., 1983-84; sales mgr. Duracraft Products, Babylon, N.Y., 1984-85; asst. sales mgr. Excel Ind. Inc., Chgo., 1985-86, Am. Automotive Mfg., Ronkonkoma, N.Y., 1986-87; exec. v.p., shareholder Allstate Replacement Parts, Inc., Orlando, Fla., 1986-87, pres., CEO, 1987—; pres., CEO, The R.G. Coffman Co., Inc., Orlando, 1991-92, Magnum Entertainment, Inc., Orlando, 1990—, Nat. Automotive Distbn. Inc., Orlando, 1993—; v.p., shareholder Empire Equities, Inc., Orlando, 1992—. Composer songs, 1978—, including Let the Music Flow, I Think I'm in Love. Sponsor Perot '92, Orlando, 1992. Mem. ASCAP, Profl. Musicians Union, Automotive Parts and Rebuilders Assn., Automotive Aftermarket Industry Week, No. Fla. PGA, Marriott Execs. Club. Republican. Home: 1205 43rd St Orlando FL 32839-1328 Office: Allstate Replacement Parts 1333 Pine Ave Orlando FL 32824-7941

HARRIS, ROBERT ALAN, JR., physician; b. Shreveport, La., June 15, 1950; s. Robert A. and Hannah G. Harris; m. Dianna Donnell, June 26, 1977; children: Robert III, Ashley Anne. BA cum laude, Vanderbilt U., 1972; MD, U. Tex. Southwestern, 1976. Diplomate ACP. Intern Baylor Coll. of Medicine, Houston, 1976-77, resident, 1977-79; attending physician Presbyn. Hosp., Dallas, 1979-93; chief internal medicine North Dallas Rehab. Hosp., Dallas, 1987-93; pvt. practice Dallas, 1979—. Contbr. articles to Jour. AMA, Archives in Internal Medicine. Fellow ACP;. Office: 9900 N Central Expy Ste 225 Dallas TX 75231-3301

HARRIS, ROBERT LEE, environmental engineering educator; b. Hollister, Mo., July 18, 1924; m. Peggy Louise Sellers; children: Linda Harris, James Andrew, Robert Jonathan. BSChemE magna cum laude, U. ARk., 1949; MS in Environ. Engring., Harvard U., 1954; PhD in Environ. Scis. and Engring., U. N.C., 1972. Cert. indsl. hygienist. Jr. engr. divsn. indsl. hygiene USPHS, Cin., 1949-50, asst. engr. environ. health ctr., 1950-52; engr. divsn. spl. health svcs. USPHS, Washington, Louisville, Cin., 1952-57; engr. divsn. occupational health USPHS, Salt Lake City, 1957-60; chief engring. sect. divsn. occupational health USPHS, Cin., 1960-64, chief field investigations Nat. Air Pollution Control, 1964-68; dir. Bur. Abatement and Control USPHS, Durham, N.C., 1968-70; assoc. prof. environ. engring. U. N.C. Sch. Pub. Health, Chapel Hill, 1973-75, prof., 1976-89, prof. environ. engring. emeritus dept. environ. scis. and engring., 1990—; Mem. safety and occupational health study sect. Nat. Inst. Occupational Safety and Health, 1978-82; mem. adv. bd. Environ. Sci. and Tech., 1980-82, mem. N.C. Environ. Mgmt. Commn., 1981-87; mem. N.C. Radiation Protection Commn., 1982-87; mem. bd. sci. counselors Nat. Inst. Occupational Safety and Health, 1984-87; mem. acrylonitrile adv. panel Nat. Cancer Inst./Nat. Inst. Occupational Safety and Health, 1987—; cons. reproductive health study, sci. adv. panel Semicondr. Industry Assn., 1988-92; mem. adv. panel Environ. Health Scis. Rsch. Ctr., Coll. of Medicine, U. Iowa, 1989—, sci. adv. bd., subcom. nonionizing electric and magnetic fields, EPA, 1990—, epidemiology rev. bd. E.I. du Pont de Nemours & Co., 1991—; chmn. com. low-level radioactive waste siting N.C. Acad. Scis., 1988-89, chmn. sci. adv. bd. toxic air pollutants N.C. Dept. Environ., Health and Natural Resources, 1990-92; mem. adv. com. energy-related epidemiologic rsch. CDC, 1992—. Mem. editorial bd. Applied Occupational and Environ. Hygiene, 1985—; contbr. articles to profl. jours. Fighter pilot U.S. Army, 1943-45. Recipient Outstanding Paper award Mich. Indsl. Hygiene Soc., 1965. Mem. Am. Conf. Govtl. Indsl. Hygienists (Meritorious Achievement award 1991), Am. Acad. Indsl. Hygiene (Henry F. Smyth award 1985), Am. Inds. Hygiene Assn. (Cummings Meml. award 1994), Brit. Occupational Hygiene Soc., N.C. Acad. Scis., Soc. Occupational and Environ. Health (governing coun. 1977-80), Sigma Xi, Tau Beta Pi (Spl. Svc. award 1971), Delta Omega, Omicron Delta Kappa, Alpha Chi Sigma. Home: 4620 Fernham Pl Raleigh NC 27612-5612 Office: U NC-Chapel Hill Sch Pub Health CB# 7400 Rosenau Hall Chapel Hill NC 27599-7400

HARRIS, ROGERS S., bishop; b. Anderson, S.C., 1930; s. Wilmot Louis and Sara Sanders Harris; m. Anne Marshall Stewart, 1953; children: Rebecca Susan, Frances Elizabeth, Katherine Anne. BA, U. of South, 1952, BD, 1957, STM, 1969; DMin, Va. Theol. Sem., 1977. Served various churches The Epis. Ch., Diocese of Upper S.C.; suffragan Bishop Diocese of Upper S.C., 1985-89; bishop Diocese of Southwest Fla., 1989-97; pres. Province IV Episcopal Ch., 1994-97. Lt. USMC, 1952-54. Address: PO Box 491 Saint Petersburg FL 33731-0491

HARRIS, ROLAND ARSVILLE, JR., college official; b. Portsmouth, Va., July 25, 1930; s. Roland Arsville Sr. and Odelle (Thomas) H.; m. Helen Beatrice Johnson, Oct. 12, 1956; children: Roland Arsville III, Benjamin Christopher. BA, Paine Coll., 1971; MEd, U. Ga., 1972; PhD, U. Tenn., 1981. Enlisted U.S. Army, 1948, advance through grades to sgt. 1st class, 1968; from instr. to asst. prof. Knoxville (Tenn.) Coll., 1972-76, dir. institutional rsch. and planning, 1976-85, Title III coord., 2nd officer-in-charge, 1985-87, chief adminstrv. officer, 1987-88; exec. v.p., chief operating officer, 1995-96, acting pres., 1996—; exec. dir. instnl. advancement Stillman Coll., Tuscaloosa, Ala., 1988-92. Hearing examiner U.S. Civil Svc. Merit award, Knoxville, 1985; mem. Tuscaloosa Tourism Adv. Com., 1989; loaned exec. United Way, Tuscaloosa, 1990, team capt., 1991. Mem. Am. Sociol. Assn., Optimists Internat., Phi Beta Sigma, Sigma Pi Phi. Democrat. Baptist. Home: 802 Wildview Way Knoxville TN 37920-7605

HARRIS, RONNA S., artist, educator; b. L.A., July 25, 1952; d. James and Janet (Marcuson) H.; divorced, 1990; 1 child, Claire Morgan. Student, San Francisco Art Inst., 1973; BA in Drawing, Calif. State U., Northridge, 1974; MFA in Painting, U. Calif., Santa Barbara, 1977. Tchg. asst. U. Calif., Santa Barbara, 1976-77; instr. art Humboldt State U., Arcata, Calif., 1977-78; asst. prof. Saddleback Coll., Mission Viejo, Calif., 1978; asst. prof. dept. art and art history U. Miami, Coral Gables, Fla., 1985-89; asst. prof. dept. art Newcomb Coll., Tulane U., New Orleans, 1989-92, assoc. prof., 1992—; scenic artist ABC-TV, NBC-TV, Universal Studios, L.A., Disney Studios, L.A., 1979-85; dir. vis. artist program Humboldt State U., 1977-78; undergrad. advisor, grad. advisor U. Miami, 1985-89, coord. found. drawing program dept. art and art history, 1988-89; grad. advisor Tulane U., 1989-91, freshman advisor art dept. Newcomb Coll., 1990-91, 92, 93, grad. coord. dept. art Newcomb Coll., 1993-94; juror art exhbns. at Miami-Dade County Pub. Schs., 1986, Fla. Internat. U., Miami, 1987, Royal Poinciana Fiesta, City of Miami, 1988, Broward Art Guild, 1988, Plantation Jr. Woman's Club, 1988, Ann. Deerfield Beach Festival of Arts, 1989; lectr., slide presenter Fla. Internat. U., 1987, U. Mass., Amherst, U. Colo., 1991; mem. panel, slide presenter Slidell Cultural Ctr., Calif., 1991. One-woman shows include U. Calif., Santa Barbara, 1977, Herbert Palmer Gallery, Beverly Hills, Calif., 1979, 84, New Gallery, Coral Gables, 1985, O.K. South Gallery, Miami Beach, Fla., 1987, Sculpture Space Gallery, South Miami, Fla., 1987, Gellert Fine Arts Gallery, Bay Harbor Islands, Miami, 1988, Phyllis Morris Gallery, L.A., 1989, Newcomb Gallery, Tulane U., 1990, Still-Zinsel Gallery, New Orleans, 1990, 92, 94, 96; exhibited in group shows at numerous galleries and mus., most recently Still-Zinsel Gallery, 1990, 91, 92, 93, 94, 95, 96, Alexander F. Milliken Gallery, N.Y.C., 1990, U. Colo., 1991, Capricorn Gallery, Bethesda, Md., 1991, Contemporary Art Ctr., New Orleans, 1992, Newcomb Gallery, 1990, 93, 94, Pensacola (Fla.) Art Mus., 1993, Louisiana Women Artists, Baton Rouge, 1994; represented in permanent collections at New Orleans Arts Coun., S.E. Bank, Fla., Interloom, Inc., Atlanta, Jacksonville (Fla.) Art Mus., various individuals; contbr. revs., articles and works to publs. in field. Recipient Anna Arnold Bing award UCLA, 1975, 1st pl., Best of Show award Santa Barbara County Fair, 1977, finalist Am. Acad. in Rome, 1977, Cert. of Excellence, Internat. Art Competition, Scarsdale (N.Y.) Art Soc., 1987, many others. Home: 4111 Vincennes Pl New Orleans LA 70125 Office: Tulane Univ Newcomb Art Dept New Orleans LA 70118

HARRIS, SAMUELLA ROSALYN, mathematics educator; b. Medford, Oreg., Dec. 15, 1940; d. Harry Franklin Bartol and Dollie Doris Lantz; m. Walter Robert Harris, Dec. 21, 1962; children: Sandra Harris Briggs, Scott. BA in Edn., Ctrl. Wash. U., 1962; MA in Math., U. Tex., Dallas, 1985. Tchr. math. Battle Ground (Wash.) Pub. Schs., 1962-63, Minot (N.D.) Pub. Schs., 1963-66, Ft. Worth Ind. Schs., 1975-76, Garland (Tex.) Ind. Sch. Dist., 1976—. Mem. NEA, Nat. Coun. Tchrs. Math., Tex. State Tchrs. Assn., Tex. Coun. Tchrs. Math., Garland Edn. Assn., Greater Dallas Coun. Tchr. Math. Lutheran. Office: North Garland H S 2109 W Buckingham Rd Garland TX 75042-5031

HARRIS, SHELLEY FOLLANSBEE, contracts administrator; b. Quantico, Va., Oct. 20; d. Lawrence Peyton and June Maynard (Trout) H. Student, Western Carolina U., 1967-69; BS in Fine Arts, Towson State U., 1973. Surgeon's asst. Drs. Bennett, Johnson & Eaton, P.A., Balt., 1979-82; pers. adminstr., human resources specialist Legent, Vienna, Va., 1983-88; pers. cons. Snelling & Snelling, Vienna, 1988-89; acct. exec. Forbes Assocs., Inc., Annandale, Va., 1989-90; spl. projects adminstr. for dep. gen. counsel, contracts and legal divsn. Electronic Data Systems Corp., Herndon, Va., 1991—. Vol. scuba instr. asst., EDS Mentor Program, In Touch-EDS Friends of Viet Nam Vets, emergency rm. vol. Reston Hosp.; team capt. Walk for Wealth; cmty. rels. ambassador Bowl for Bus. Jr. Achievement; active Holiday LINCS family project, Holiday 1994-96. Recipient regional awards for paintings, regional and nat. awards for sales and mktg., also awards for community contbns. Mem. Artist's Equity. Episcopalian. Home: 851 Dogwood Ct Herndon VA 22070-5446

HARRIS, STANLEY LOUIS, JR., advertising agency executive; b. Newark, May 7, 1948; s. Stanley Louis and Terrace Marie (Steiner) H.; m. Linda Ruth Berger, May 29, 1969; children: Samantha Joy, Scott Jason. B.S., Boston U., 1970. Creative supr. J.C. Penney, Inc., N.Y.C., 1970-72; copy group head Dancer, Fitzerald, Sample Advt. Agy., N.Y.C., 1972-79; copy supr. SSC&B Advt. Agy., N.Y.C., 1978-79; sr. writer Group 3hree Advt. Agy., Fort Lauderdale, Fla., 1979-80; pres. Harris, Drury Advt. Agy., Fort Lauderdale, 1980-84; creative ptnr. Harris Drury Cohen Advt., Ft. Lauderdale, 1984—. V.p. Ramat Shalom Synagogue, 1990-92. With U.S. Army, 1969-75. Mem. Fort Lauderdale Advt. Fedn., Broward C. of C. (editorial com. 1984), Hollywood C. of C., South Broward Bus. Club. Avocations: music, fitness, antiques. Office: Harris Drury Cohen 1901 W Cypress Creek Rd, 6th Fl Fort Lauderdale FL 33309-1864*

HARRIS, VERA EVELYN, personnel recruiting and search firm executive; b. Watson, Sask., Can., Jan. 11, 1932; came to U.S., 1957; d. Timothy and Margaret (Popoff) H.; student U. B.C. (Can.), Vancouver; children—Colin Clifford Graham, Barbara Cusimano Page. Office mgr. Keglers, Inc., Morgan City, La., 1964-67; office mgr., acct. John L. Hopper & Assocs., New Orleans, 1967-71; office mgr. Elite Homes, Inc., Metairie, La., 1971-73; comptroller Le Pavillon Hotel, New Orleans, 1973-74; controller Waguespack-Pratt, Inc., New Orleans, 1974-76; adminstrv. controller Sizzler Family Steak Houses of So. La., Inc., Metairie, 1976-79; dir. adminstrn. Sunbelt, Inc., New Orleans, 1979-82, sec., dir., 1980—; exec. v.p. Corp. Cons., Inc., 1980-83, pres., 1984-86; pres. Harris Personnel Resources, Arlington, Tex., 1986—, Harris Enterprises, Arlington, 1986—, Harris Personnel Resources Health Staff, Arlington, 1990—; exec. dir. Nat. Sizzler Franchise Assn., 1976-79. Mem. NAFE, Am. Bus. Women's Assn., La. Assn. Personnel Consultants (treas. 1985-86), Indep. Recruiters Group, Soc. Exec. Recruiters. Home: 3110 Waterside Dr Arlington TX 76012-2123 Office: Harris Personnel Resources 2201 N Collins St Ste 260 Arlington TX 76011-2653

HARRIS, WARREN WAYNE, lawyer; b. Houston, Nov. 5, 1962. BBA, U. Houston, 1985, JD, 1988. Bar: Tex. 1988, U.S. Ct. Appeals (5th cir.) 1989, U.S. Ct. Appeals (fed. cir.), U.S. Dist. Ct. (so., no., ea. and we. dists.) Tex. 1990, U.S. Supreme Ct. 1991; bd. cert. civil appellate law Tex. Bd. Legal Specialization. Briefing atty. Tex. Supreme Ct., Austin, 1988-89; ptnr. Porter & Hedges, L.L.P., Houston, 1989—. Editor-in-chief: Houston Lawyer mag., 1991-92; assoc. editor: The Appellate Advocate, 1992—; editor: Pocket Parts, 1993-95, The Appellate Lawyer, 1994—. Fellow Tex. Bar Found. (dist. 4 nominating com. 1994—), Houston Bar Found.; mem. ABA (litigation sect. appellate practice com. 1990—, tort and ins. practice sect. appellate advocacy com. 1990—), Fed. Bar Assn. (appellate law and practice com. 1992—), State Bar Tex. (appellate practice and adv. sect. 1988—, chair pro bono com. appellate practice and adv. sect. 1995—, bar jour. com. 1990-92), State Bar Coll. (bd. dirs. 1994-95), State Bar Pro Bono Coll., Tex. Young Lawyers Assn. (bd. dirs. 1994—, TYLA sect. bar jour. com. 1993—, com. chair 1994-95, local affiliates com. 1993—, co-chair com. 1995—, voter edn. com. 1995—, co-chair com. 1995—), Houston Bar Assn. (Pres.' award 1994, Houston lawyer com. 1989-93, com. chair 1991-92, CLE com. 1992—, co-chair cmty. affairs com. 1993-94, chair spkrs.' bur. 1994-95, treas. appellate practice sect. 1995—, coun. appellate practice sect. 1993-95), Houston Young Lawyers Assn. (sec. 1994—, bd. dirs. 1993-94, outstanding com. chair 1992-93, mem. com. 1992-94, chair com. 1992-93, chair publicity and publ rels. com. 1993—, outstanding young lawyer com. 1993—, chair Pocket Paris com. 1993-95), Houston Lawyer Referral Svc. (trustee 1994-95, chair mem. com. 1994-95), Stages Repertory Theatre (pres. 1994-95, bd. dirs. 1994—, chair 1994-95, exec. com. 1994—, WineFest com. 1993—, com. chair 1994—), Order of Barristers, Order of Barons, Phi Delta Phi (life). Republican. Office: Porter & Hedges LLP 700 Louisiana St Fl 35 Houston TX 77002

HARRIS, WILLIAM ELGIE, art educator; b. Charlotte County, Va., Jan. 28, 1951; s. Eli William and Juanita (Johnson) H.; m. Theresa Elizabeth Mitchell, Aug. 1993. BA, N.C. Cen. U., 1973; M in Art Edn., Va. Commonwealth U., 1985; PhD, Ohio State U., 1996. Elem. tchr. art Richmond (Va.) Pub. Schs., 1975-83, secondary tchr. art, 1983-88; grad. tchr. asst. dept. art edn. Ohio State U., Columbus, 1988-93; asst. prof. Old Dominion U., Norfolk, Va., 1993-95; prin., cons. Harris & Assocs. Art Edn., Norfolk; cons. Ohio-Partnership for the Visual Arts, Columbus, 1989-93, Columbus Mus.-Minority Outreach Com., 1989, Art for Cmty. Expression, Columbus, 1990, Art Appreciation-Upward Bound, Wittenberg Coll., Ohio, 1990; juror The Arts Com., Inc., Columbus, 1990, Ft. Hayes Met. Edn., Ctr., Columbus, 1990; juror-arts and letters Delta Sigma Theta, Inc., Columbus, 1989; moderator gallery talk Martin Luther King, Jr. Ctr., Columbus, 1990. Author: Elijah Pierce: More Than A Preacher in Wood, 1993. Chair Com. on Minority Concern, 1986-87. Recipient J.E. Grigsby award, 1985. Mem. NEA, ACA, Nat. Art Edn. Assn., N.C. Ctrl. U. Alumni Assn., Ohio State U. Alumni Assn., U.S. Soc. for Edn. Through Art. Baptist. Home and Office: 8725 Roswell Rd Ste O-224 Dunwoody GA 30350-1898

HARRIS, WILLIAM HAMILTON, academic administrator; b. Fitzgerald, Ga., July 22, 1944; m. Wanda Filmore; children: Cynthia, Bill. BA, Paine Coll., 1966; MA, Ind. U., 1967, PhD, 1973; LLD (hon.), Paine Coll., 1991. Instr. history Paine Coll., Augusta, Ga., 1967-69, pres., 1982-88; assoc. instr. history Ind. U., Bloomington, 1969-71, lectr. in history, 1972-73, asst. prof. history, 1973-77, acting affirmative action officer, 1977-78, assoc. prof. history, 1977-81, prof. history, 1981-82, dir. CIC Minorities Fellowship program, 1977-82, assoc. dean. grad. sch., 1979-82; pres. Paine Coll., 1982-88, Tex. So. U., Houston, 1988-93, Ala. State Univ., Montgomery, 1994—; vis. prof. history Ind. U., 1993-94; bd. dirs. Tex. Commerce Bank; mem. exec. com. Coun. Pres.'s Tex. Pub. Colls. and Univs., 1991. Author: Keeping the Faith, 1977, The Harder We Run, 1982. Bd. dirs. Augusta Jr. Achievement, 1983-86, Ga.-Carolina coun. Boy Scouts Am., 1986-88, Leadership Ala., 1996—, Am. Coun. on Edn., 1986-90, Montgomery Metro YMCA, Montgomery Area United Way, v.p.; bd. visitors Air Univ. of USAF; trustee Greater Houston Partnership, 1989-93, mem. exec. com., 1990-93; vice chmn. Coun. Pres. of Ala. Pub. Univs., 1995—. Am. Coun. Learned Socs. fellow, 1979-80, Fulbright professorship U. Hamburg, Germany, 1978-79, So. Fellowships Fund fellow, 1970-71; recipient Paine Coll. Alumni award, 1984-85; named Disting. Son of Fitzgerald Ga. Centennial Observance, 1996. Mem. Am. Coun. Edn. (bd. dirs. 1986-88), United Negro Coll. Fund, Inc. (bd. dirs. 1984-88, vice chmn. instl. and individual mems. 1986-88, chmn. 1988), Ednl. Testing Svc. (bd. trustees 1985-91, chmn. 1988), Lilly Endowment Inc., Open Fellowships, Assn. for Study of Afro-Am. Life and History (pres. 1986-89), Nat. Assn. Equal Opportunity in Higher Edn. (bd. dirs. 1985-88), Nat. Assn. Ind. Colls. and Univs. (bd. dirs.), Nat. Assn. Colls. and Schs. of United Meth. Ch. (mem. exec. bd.), Ind. U. Alumni Assn. (Disting. Alumni Svd. award 1991), Paine Coll., L.L.D., 1991, Montgomery Area C. of C. (bd. dirs.). Office: Ala State Univ Office of the Pres 915 S Jackson St Montgomery AL 36104-5732

HARRIS, WILLIAM MCKINLEY, SR., urban planning educator, consultant; b. Richmond, Va., Oct. 29, 1941; s. Rosa M. (Minor) H.; m. Jessie Mathews, 1996; children: Rolisa H. Smith, Dana, Melissa. BS, Howard U. 1964; M Urban Planning, U. Wash., Seattle, 1972, PhD, 1974. Physicist AEC, Richland, Wash., 1968-70; research fellow Battelle Seattle, 1970-73; asst. prof. Western Wash. State U., Bellingham, 1973-74, Portland State U., Oreg., 1974-76; prof. urban planning U. Va., Charlottesville, 1976—; headmaster Sci. St. Sch., 1990—; tech. advisor Mennonite Econ. Devel. Project, Chgo., 1982-85; chmn. Indsl. Devel. Authority, Charlottesville, 1983-85. Mem. Charlottesville Planning Commn., Charlottesville Bd. of Zoning Appeals, 1992-96, T.J. United Way, 1990-96, Devel. Tng. Inst., 1989-95; cons. Westhaven Resident Mgmt. Corp., 1994-95; del. leader People to People to China, 1992-94. Narrator: (movie) Blacks in Oregon, 1975; author: Black Community Development, 1976. Site reviewer Planning Adv. Bd., Washington, 1985; bd. dirs. Charlottesville Mediation Ctr., 1985. Recipient Community Service award Albina Lions Club, 1975; vis. scholar Cornell U., 1985. Mem. Am. Inst. Cert. Planners, Am. Planning Assn. (editorial bd. jour. 1985, leader planning team Greensboro N.C. 1995-96), Assn. Study Afro-Am. Life and History, Community Devel. Soc. (pres. Va. chpt. 1983-84), Assn. Voluntary Action Scholars, AIA (team leader Cleve.). Episcopalian. Club: Charlottesville Anglers (bd. dirs. 1984). Lodge: Masons. Avocations: handball; reading. Office: U Va Campbell Hall Charlottesville VA 22903

HARRIS-OFFUTT, ROSALYN MARIE, psychotherapist, counselor, nurse anesthetist, educator, author; b. Memphis; d. Roscoe Henry and Irene Elnora (Blake) Harris; 1 child, Christopher Joseph. R.N., St. Joseph Catholic Sch. Nursing, Flint, Mich., 1965; B.S. in Wholistic Health Scis., Columbia-Pacific U., 1984, postgrad., 1985—. RN; cert. registered nurse in anesthesia; nat. bd. cert. addiction counselor; cert. psychiat. nursing Kalamazoo State Hosp.; lic. profl. counselor, N.C.; cert. detoxification acupuncturist; Staff nurse anesthetist, clin. instr. Cleve. Clinic Found., 1981-82; pvt. practice psychiat. nursing and counseling; Assoc. Counselor in Human Services, Shaker Heights, Ohio, 1982-84; ind. contractor anesthesia Paul Scott & Assocs., Cleve., 1984, Via Triad Anesthesia Assocs., Thomasville, N.C., 1984-85; sec. Cons., Psychology and Counseling, P.A., pvt. practice psychiat. nursing and counseling, Greensboro, N.C., 1984-86, pvt. practice psychiat. nursing, counseling and psychotherapy UNA Psychol. Assocs., 1986—, staff cons. Charter Hills Psychiat. Hosp. in Addictive Disease, 1991—; nat. resource cons. Am. Assn. Nursing Anesthetists on Addictive Disease; cons. Ctr. for Substance Abuse Prevention, also adviser to assoc. and clin. med. dir. Ctr. Substance Abuse Prevention. Co-sponsor adolescent group Jack and Jills of Am., Inc., Bloomfield Hills, Mich., 1975; co-sponsor Youth of Unity Ctr., Cleveland Heights, Ohio, 1981-84; vol. chmn. hospitality Old Greensboro Preservation Soc., 1985; bd. dirs. Urban League, Pontiac, Mich., 1972; apptd. mem. gov's. coun. on alcohol and other drug abuse State of N.C., 1989—, gov's. coun. women's issues of addiction, 1991—; apptd. advisor to assoc. clin., med. dir. Ctr. for Substance Abuse Prevention, Dept. Health and Human Svcs. U.S., 1991—, nat. speakers bureau, 1991—, cons.; apptd. legis. com., mental health study commn. on child and adolescent substance abuse State of N.C., 1992—; lay speaking min. United Meth. Ch.; mem. Triad United Meth. Native Am. Ch. Mission . Columbia-Pacific U. scholar, 1983. Contbr. chpt. to book, also articles and columns in health field. Fellow Soc. Preventive Nutritionists; mem. Am. Assn. Profl. Hypnotherapists (registered profl. hypnotherapists, adv. bd.), Am. Assn. Nurse Anesthetists (cert.), Nat. Alaska Native Am. Indian Nurses Assn., Assn. Med. Educators and Rsch. in Substance Abuse, Nat. Acupuncture Detoxification Assn., Am. Assn. Counseling and Devel., Assn. for Med. Edn. and Rsch. in Substance Abuse, Am. Assn. Clin. Hypnotists, Am. Assn. Wholistic Practitioners, Am. Nurse Hypnotherapy Assn. (state pres. 1992—), Am. Nurse Assn., Am. Holistic Nurses Assn. (charter mem.), Guilford Native Am. Assn., Negro Bus. and Profl. Women Inc. (v.p., parliamentarian 1961-83), Oakland County Council Black Nurses (v.p. 1970-74), Assn. Med. Educators (researcher substance abuse, ad hoc com. mem. cultural diversity 1994—), Zeta Phi Beta (Nu Xi Zeta chpt. 2d anti-basilevs 1992-93). Republican. Avocations: music, nature, reading, Egyptian history, metaphysics. Office: UNA Psychol Assocs 620 S Elm St Ste 371 Greensboro NC 27406-1371

HARRISON, ARNOLD MYRON, chemist; b. Pitts., Sept. 25, 1946; s. Robert Myron and Irma (Arnold) H.; divorced. AB, Princeton U., 1968; MS, U. Chgo., 1970, PhD, 1975. Chemist Union Carbide Tech. Ctr., South Charleston, W.Va., 1975-80, project scientist, 1980-85, rsch. scientist, 1985-90, sr. rsch. scientist, 1990—; chmn. bd. Travel Agy., South Charleston, 1993—. Contbr. articles to profl. jours.; patentee in field. Mem. AAAS, Am. Chem. Soc., Sigma Xi. Presbyterian. Office: Union Carbide Tech Ctr 3200 Kanawha Tpke South Charleston WV 25303

HARRISON, BRYAN GUY, lawyer; b. Norman, Okla., Nov. 22, 1963; s. Danny Guy and Judith Kay (Dalke) H.; m. Kathleen Hazel Cody, May 8, 1993. BS, Lehigh U., 1986; JD, Emory U., 1989. Bar: Tex. 1989, Ga. 1991. Assoc. Shank, Irwin, Conant, Lipshy & Casterline, Dallas, 1989-90; trial atty. antitrust div. U.S. Dept. Justice, Dallas, 1990-91; assoc. Morris, Manning & Martin, Atlanta, 1991—. Office: Morris Manning & Martin 3343 Peachtree Rd NE Atlanta GA 30326-1022

HARRISON, EARLE, former county official; b. Rainsville, Ala., May 20, 1903; s. Robert Lee and Sarepta Ophelia (Hansard) H.; m. Joan Mary Jackson, Jan. 24, 1942. AB, Northwestern U., 1929, postgrad. in bus. adminstrn., 1942; LLB, Chgo.-Kent Coll. Law, 1935. With Marshall Field & Co., Chgo., 1929-68; div. operating mgr. Marshall Field & Co., 1958-60, v.p. operations, 1960-64, v.p., treas., 1964-68; bd. dirs. Credit Bur. Cook County, 1949-69, pres., 1958-69; mem. bd. suprs., chmn. planning and zoning com. Lake County, Ill., 1970—; cons. finance and adminstrn. to hosps. and health care instns. Commr. Northeastern Ill. Planning Commn., 1970—; pres. Northeastern Ill. Plan Commn., 1973, now mem. exec. com.; ret. pres., bd. dirs. Family Fin. Counseling Svc. Greater Chgo.; bd. dirs. Condell Meml. Hosp., Libertyville, Ill., 1971—, adminstr., 1973—, pres., 1975-78, bus. cons., 1978—. Mem. Phi Delta Phi. Home: 150 Cottage Ln Carrollton GA 30117-6200

HARRISON, J. FRANK, JR., soft drink company executive; b. 1930. With Coca Cola Bottling Co., Charlotte, N.C., 1973—, now chmn. bd. dirs., chmn. exec. com. Office: Coca-Cola Bottling Co Consol PO Box 31487 Charlotte NC 28231-1487*

HARRISON, JAMES HARVEY, JR., information systems specialist; b. Shelbyville, Tenn., Sept. 13, 1927; s. James Harvey and Mary Berniece (Orr) H.; m. Dolores May Hanson, Nov. 23, 1957; children: James Harvey III, Elizabeth Ann. BS, Mid. Tenn. State Coll., 1950, USN Postgrad. Sch., 1963; MSTM, Am. U., 1975, postgrad., 1978. Commd. ensign USN, 1950, advanced through grades to comdr., ret., 1972; program mgr. electronics lab. USN, San Diego, 1963-64; exec. officer U.S.S. Maddox USN, San Francisco, 1964-66; fleet computer combat systems USN, Virginia Beach, 1966-69; dir. mgmt. info. systems CINC USN Europe USN, London, 1969-72; test and evaluation of R&D systems-software systems engr. Raytheon Svc. Co., Washington, 1972-77; program mgr. Intern. Systems Div. Sperry, Washington, 1978-83, dir. ops., 1983-87, mktg. mgr., 1987-91; pres., CEO Proposals Plus Inc., 1991-95; ret., 1995; chmn. adv. com. Budget and Fiscal Affairs, Alexandria, Va., 1985--. Commr. Boy Scouts Am., London, 1969-72, Alexandria, 1972-78; mem. Alexandria Sch. Bd., 1979-83, Nat. Counc. Edn. Rsch., 1983-89. Mem. Nat. Security Industry Assn., Navy League, Am. Def. Preparation Assn., Ret. Officer's Assn., Soc. Mgmt. Info. Systems, Data Processing Assn., Va. C. of C., Ind. C. of C. Home: 303 Aspen Pl Alexandria VA 22305-1703

HARRISON, JAMES OSTELLE, ecologist; b. Harrison, Ga., June 17, 1920; s. James Drew and Marie (Mills) H.; m. Katherine Deal, Jan. 12, 1942 (div. 1970); m. Joyce Rape, Mar. 21, 1971; children: Michael James, Juliet. BA, Mercer U., 1949; MS, U. Ga., 1953; PhD, Cornell U., 1962. Assoc. entomologist United Fruit Co., Palmar Sur, Costa Rica, 1956-62; asst. prof. biology Mercer U., Macon, Ga., 1962-64, assoc. prof., 1964-67, prof., 1967-85, prof. emeritus, 1986—; columnist Macon Telegraph, 1976-80; editorial assoc. Seabreeze Mag., St. Simons Island, Ga., 1985—; ecol. cons. Avland Devel. Co., Macon, 1970-71. Contbr. articles to profl. jours. Chmn. Area Water Quality Adv. Com., Macon, 1979-82, City Energy Adv. Com., Macon, 1979-80; pres. Ocmulgee Monument Assn., Macon, 1981-83. Capt. USAAF, 1942-47, North Africa, ETO. Mem. Nat. Audubon Soc., Nat. Wildlife Fedn. Republican. Baptist. Home: 1179 Matthews Pl Macon GA 31210-3425 Office: Mercer U 1400 Coleman Ave Macon GA 31207-1000

HARRISON, JAMES RICHARD, business management educator; b. Stillwater, Okla., Apr. 20, 1947; s. Charles Arthur and Mary Beatrice (Huggins) H. BS in Math. with high honors, U. Okla., 1969, BS in Physics, 1976; PhD in Bus., Stanford U., 1986. Vice pres. acad. affairs Assoc. Students of U. Calif., Berkeley, 1972-73, exec. dir. grad. student assn., 1976-78; v.p. Siren Records, San Francisco, 1976-78; asst. prof. Bus. U. Ariz., Tucson, 1983-85; asst. prof. mgmt. U. Tex., Dallas, 1985-91, assoc. prof. mgmt., 1991—, assoc. dean sch. Mgmt., 1991-95; dir. Russian Inst. U. Tex., Richardson, 1993-96; referee various acad. jours., 1980—; co-coord. St. Petersburg (Russia) Internat. Consortium of Univs., 1993-95. Contbr. articles to profl. jours. Active Dallas County Dem. Party, Dallas, 1990—, precinct chair, Dallas, 1990—. Recipient Teaching Excellence award Halliburton Corp., 1990. Mem. AAAS, Acad. Mgmt., Strategic Mgmt. Soc., Am. Sociol. Assn., European Assn. of decision Making, St Petersburg Acad. of Engring., Phi Beta Kappa. Home: PO Box 831327 Richardson TX 75083-1327 Office: U Tex Dallas Sch Mgmt/JO5I PO Box 830688 Richardson TX 75083

HARRISON, JAMES WILBURN, gynecologist; b. Martin, Tenn., Mar. 23, 1918; s. Woodie and Georgia Harrison; m. Babs Wise Dudley, Jan. 29, 1948; children: James Wilburn Jr., James Michael, Babs Suzanne, Linda Denise. Student, U. Tenn., Martin, 1936-37, U. Tenn., Knoxville, 1937-38; MD, U. Tenn., Memphis, 1941; grad., U.S. Army Staff Coll., Ft. Leavenworth, Kans., 1972. Diplomate Am. Bd. Ob-gyn. Asst. resident Brooke Gen. Hosp., Ft. Sam Houston, Tex., 1947; chief surgery Saturn Hosp., Clark AFB, Philippines, 1948-49; resident, sr. resident Letterman Gen. Hosp., San Francisco, 1949-51; advanced through grades to coll. U.S. Army, ret., 1954; chief staff St. Michael Hosp., Texarkana, Ark., Wadley Regional Med. Ctr., Texarkana, Tex., So. Clinic, Texarkana, Ark.; asst. clin. prof. ob.-gyn. U. Ark. Coll. Medicine, Little Rock. Chmn. Bowie County Child Welfare Bd.; mem. N.E. Tex. Mental Health Bd. Decorated Army Commendation medal, Legion of Merit. Fellow ACS (life), ICS (life), Am. Coll. Ob-gyn. (life), Assn. Mil. Surgeons U.S. (life), Tex. Soc. Ob-gyn. (life); mem. AMA (life), Tex. Med. Assn., Northridge Country Club (founding), Alumni Assn. U.S. Army Command and Gen. Staff Coll. Methodist. Home: 4009 Pecos St Texarkana TX 75503-2857

HARRISON, JIM RUSH, JR., minister of music; b. Jackson, Tenn., Apr. 26, 1969; s. Jim Rush and Juanita (Clarke) H. BA, Union U., Jackson, Tenn., 1991. Lic., 1989; cert. ordination, 1991. Music interim Grace Bapt. Ch., Jackson, Tenn., 1987; ch. music intern First Bapt. Ch., Jackson, Tenn., 1990; min. of music/youth West Shiloh Bapt. Ch., Stantonville, Tenn., 1988-91; min. music/youth First Bapt. Ch., Livingston, Tenn., 1991—; exec. bd. Overton County Teen Ctr., Livingston, Tenn., 1993—; music dir. Riverside Bapt. Assn., Livingston, Tenn., 1993—. Mem. Gospel Music Assn. Republican. Southern Baptist. Office: First Baptist Church 708 E Main St Livingston TN 38570-1650

HARRISON, LOWELL HAYES, historian, educator; b. Russell Springs, Ky., Oct. 23, 1922; s. Chester A. and Cecil Mae (Hayes) H.; m. Elaine M. Maher, Dec. 23, 1948. AB, Western Ky.U., 1946; MA, NYU, 1947, PhD, 1951; postgrad., London Sch. Econs., 1951-52. Instr. history NYU, 1947-50; assoc. prof. history West Tex. State U., Canyon, 1952-57, prof. history, dept. head, 1957-67, chmn. div. social scis., 1962-67; prof. history Western Ky.U., Bowling Green, 1967-88, prof. emeritus, 1988—; vice chair editl. bd. U. Press Ky., Lexington, 1968-88; mem. Ky. Hist. Properties Adv. Commn., Frankfort, 1987-90, Ky. Oral History Commn., Frankfort, 1976-81, Perryville Battlefield Commn., 1993—. Author: John Breckinridge, 1969, Civil War in Kentucky, 1975, George Rogers Clark and the War in the West, 1976, The Antislavery Movement in Kentucky, 1978, Western Kentucky University, 1987, Kentucky's Road to Statehood, 1992; co-editor: A Kentucky Sampler, 1977; editor: Kentucky's Governors, 1792-1985, 1985; assoc. editor: The Kentucky Encyclopedia, 1992. Active City Commn., Canyon, 1958-61. With U.S. Army, 1943-45, ETO. Fulbright scholar, 1951-52; recipient Pub. Svc. award Pub. Rels. Soc., 1986. Mem. Orgn. Am. Historians, So. Hist. Assn., Filson Club History Soc., Ky. Hist. Soc., Panhandle-Plains Hist. Soc. (co-editor 1957-67), Soc. for Historians of Early Am. Republic, Phi Alpha Theta, Phi Kappa Phi. Democrat. Methodist. Home: 704 Logan Way Bowling Green KY 42101-2952 Office: Western Ky U Cherry Way # 238 Bowling Green KY 42101-2814

HARRISON, LUCIA GUZZI, foreign languages educator; b. Bergamo, Italy, Aug. 16, 1958; came to U.S., 1987; d. Ernesto Giuseppe and Livia Rosa (De Franco) Guzzi; m. Robert Wesley Harrison, Jr., Apr. 27, 1991; 1 child, Nicholas. BS and Laurea, U. Verona, 1986; MA, U. Ky., 1990, PhD, 1995. Tchg. asst. U. Ky., Lexington, 1988-93; coord. basic Spanish La. State U., Baton Rouge, 1994-96; asst. prof. Southeastern La. U., Hammond, 1996—; vis. asst. prof. Eastern Ky. U., Richmond, 1988; instr. cmty. edn. U. Ky., Lexington, 1992; dir. studies abroad Ky. Inst. Internat. Studies, Italy, 1988-92. Mem. MLA, North Atlantic MLA, La. Classic Assn., Am. Assn. Tchrs. Spanish and Portuguese, Sigma Delta Pi, Phi Sigma Iota. Roman Catholic. Office: Southeastern La U Dept Fgn Langs PO Box 719 Hammond LA 70402

HARRISON, MARY, religious organization executive. CPE program mgr. Assn. of Bapt. Chaplains. Office: Cen Bapt Hosp 1740 Nicholasville Rd Lexington KY 40503-1424

HARRISON, OTTO R., oil industry executive; b. July 18, 1935; m. Kay Pearson; children: Matthew, Douglas, Michael, Lori. BS, U. Tex., 1959. CEO Exxon Pipeline, 1992—. Office: Exxon Pipeline 800 Bell St Houston TX 77002-7426

HARRISON, PATRICIA GREENWOOD, historian; b. Monticello, Ark., Jan. 2, 1937; d. Howard Walter and Lorene (Stewart) Greenwood; m. Edward Lindsay Harrison, Aug. 7, 1960; children: Gregory Edward, Rebecca Lindsay, Laura Patricia. BS, Henderson State Coll., 1959; MA, So. Meth. U., 1964; postgrad., U. Wis., 1965-67; PhD, Tulane U., 1994. Instr. history Eastfield Coll., Dallas, 1968-73, Richland Coll., Dallas, 1972-74, U. South Ala., Mobile, 1977-86, Spring Hill (Ala.) Coll., 1979—; book rev. editor Gulf Coast Hist. Rev., Mobile, 1985-87. Author: Women in Mobile during World War II, 1986, The Development of Gulf Shores, Alabama: An Interview with Erie Hall Meyer, 1986. So. Meth. U. fellow, 1962-64. Mem. AAUW, Am. Hist. Assn., So. Hist. Assn., Ala. Assn. Historians, So. Assn. Women Historians, Oral History Assn., Phi Alpha Theta. Methodist. Home: 6409 Sugar Creek Dr S Mobile AL 36695-2926 Office: Spring Hill Coll Dept History Mobile AL 36608

HARRISON, RICHARD DEAN, minister, counselor; b. Gaffney, S.C., Oct. 15, 1952; s. Wiley H. and Georgia Ann (Earwood) H.; m. Sandra Kay Parris, Oct. 16, 1970; children: Kathryn Hope, Richard Dean Jr. BA, U. S.C., 1973, MAT, 1975; MDiv, So. Bapt. Theol. Sem., 1986, DMin, 1990. Ordained to ministry So. Bapt. Conv., 1985. Pastor English Bapt. Ch., Stephensport, Ky., 1985-87, Rehoboth Bapt. Ch., Gaffney, 1987-92; counselor Cherokee Mental Health and Counseling Ctr., Gaffney, S.C., 1992—. Chaplain Gaffney Jaycees, 1977-79, Asbury-Rehoboth Vol. Fire Dept., Gaffney, 1989—; bd. dirs. Piedmont Community Action Agy., Spartanburg, S.C., 1979-81. Mem. Breckinridge Bapt. Assn. (exec. com. 1985-87), Broad River Bapt. Assn. (exec. com., dir. Sunday sch. 1987-92). Home: 117 Stacy Dr Gaffney SC 29341-1433 Office: Cherokee Mental Health and Counseling Ctr 125 E Robinson St Gaffney SC 29340-2444

HARRISON, RICHARD MILLER, physiologist, researcher, educator; b. Pineville, Ky., Apr. 8, 1939; s. Roy Miller and Pauline (Boswell) H.; m. Joanna Schafer, Aug. 11, 1962; children: Brian Glen, Byron Greg. BA, U. Ky., 1962; MS, Mich. State U., 1971, PhD, 1973. Scientist Mead Johnson Rsch. Ctr., Evansville, Ind., 1963-69; rsch. asst. Endocrine Rsch. Unit Mich. State U., East Lansing, 1969-73; rsch. scientist Tulane U. Regional Primate Rsch. Ctr., Covington, La., 1973—; assoc. prof. Sch. of Medicine Tulane U., New Orleans, 1976—; lectr. Tulane U., Covington, 1990—. Author: (play) My Brother's Keeper, 1993; editor: Animal Laparoscopy, 1980. Deacon, tchr. First Bapt. Ch., Covington, 1976—; mem. Sex Edn. Rev. Com., St. Tammany Parish, 1986—. Mem. Am. Soc. Andrology (chair by-laws com. 1978-80, chair program 1980-81, v.p. 1980-81, pres. 1981-82, chair membership com. 1982-84, chair local chpt. 1988-89), Am. Soc. Reproductive Medicine (assoc. chair session mgmt. 1990—), Soc. for Study of Reprodn. (local arrangements com. 1972, session chmn. 1982), Internat. Study of Andrology (orgn. com. 1981, session chmn. 1981, rep. to assembly 1985), Soc. for Study of Fertility, Am. Soc. Primatologists (historian), Internat. Primatological Soc. Republican. Baptist. Home: 327 Robinhood Rd Covington LA 70433 Office: Tulane Regional Primate Rsch Ctr 18703 Three Rivers Rd Covington LA 70433-8915

HARRISON, RICHARD WAYNE, lawyer; b. Marfa, Tex., June 23, 1944; s. George Willis and Mildred Irene (Rooks) H.; Teresa Green, Jan. 14, 1981; children: Michelle, Breck, Shawn, Victoria. AA with honors, Schreiner Inst., Kerrville, Tex., 1964; BBA, U. Tex.-Austin, 1966, JD, 1968. Bar: Tex. 1968, U.S. Dist. Ct. (ea. dist.) Tex. 1968, U.S. Dist. Ct. (so. dist.) Tex. 1973, U.S. Dist. Ct. (we. dist.) Tex. 1974, U.S. Supreme Ct. 1975, U.S. Ct. Appeals (5th cir.) 1977, U.S. Dist. Ct. (no. dist.) Tex. 1983, U.S. Ct. Fed. Claims, 1987. Ptnr. Florence & Harrison, Hughes Springs, Tex., 1968-69; sole practice Hughes Springs, Tex., 1969-73; asst. atty. gen. Atty. Gen.'s Office of Tex., Austin, 1973-74, chief tax div., 1974-76, spl. asst. atty. gen., 1976-78; ptnr. McGinnis, Lochridge & Kilgore, Austin, Tex., 1978-87, ptnr. Jones, Day,

Reavis & Pogue, Austin, 1987-94, Harrison & Rial, L.L.P., Austin, 1994—. Precinct chmn. Cass County Dem. Com., 1969-73; pres. Hughes Springs Indsl. Found., 1970; Cass County chmn. Salvation Army, 1970-72; area coordinator Lloyd Bentsen for Senate Com., 1970; chmn. Hughes Springs United Fund Drive, 1972; mem. Austin Convocation Cursillo Steering Com., 1983-86, chmn., 1985-86; sr. warden St. Luke's-on-the-Lake Episcopal Ch., 1984. Fellow Tex. Bar Found.; mem. State Bar of Tex. (mem. fed. jud. com. 1980-83, bar jour. com. 1980-83), Travis County Bar Assn., Cass County Bar Assn. (past pres.), Schreiner Coll. Former Student Assn. (bd. dirs. 1985-88), trustee, treas. St. Andrews Episcopal Sch., Austin. Democrat. Clubs: Austin, Horseshoe Bay Country, Barton Creek Country. Lodge: Masons. Home: 6603 W Courtyard Dr Austin TX 78730-5052 Office: Harrison & Rial LLP 410 Congress Ave Ste 100 Austin TX 78701-3620

HARRISON, ROSCOE CONKLIN, JR., special projects administrator; b. Belton, Tex., Sept. 20, 1944; s. Roscoe Conklin Sr. and Georgia Dell (Moore) H.; m. Sandra Kay Smitha, Aug. 27, 1966; 1 child, Corinne Michelle. AA, Temple Jr. Coll., 1965; postgrad., Prairie View A&M U., 1965-66, U. Mary Hardin Baylor, 1966-67. Radio announcer KTEM Radio, Temple, Tex., 1960-64; reporter Temple Daily Telegram, 1966-67, San Antonio Express-News, 1967-68; assoc. editor Jet Mag., Chgo., 1968-69; reporter, bur. chief KCEN-TV, Temple, 1970-77; dep. press sec. Tex. Atty. Gen. John Hill, Austin, 1977-79; reporter KTBC-TV, Austin, 1979; pub. affairs dir. KCEN-TV, Temple, 1979-93; assoc. dir. spl. projects Scott and White Hosp., Temple, 1993—; adv. coord. Scott and White Hosp., Temple, 1993—. Bd. dirs. Ctrl. Tex. United Way, Temple, 1993—, Cultural Activities Ctr., Temple, 1992—, Temple Jr. Coll. Found., 1991—. Recipient Pub. Affairs Programming award Tex. Assn. Broadcasters, 1977; named Communicator of Yr., Bell County Comms. Profls., 1988, Broadcaster of Yr., Tex. Farmers Union, 1992. Mem. Nat. Assn. Health Svcs. Execs., PRSA, Soc. Profl. Journalists, Masons. Democrat. Baptist. Home: 3806 Wendy Oaks Dr Temple TX 76502-2862 Office: Scott and White Meml Hosp 2401 S 31st St Temple TX 76508-0001

HARRISON, SAMUEL HUGHEL, lawyer; b. Atlanta, Jan. 12, 1956; s. Gresham Hughel and Leslie (Powell) H.; m. Margaret Mary Carew, June 24, 1978; 1 child, Peter James. Student, Mercer U., 1974-75; BA magna cum laude, Washington & Lee U., 1978; JD cum laude, U. Ga., 1981. Bar: Ga. 1981, U.S. Dist. Ct. (no. dist.) Ga. 1981, U.S. Ct. Appeals (11th cir.) 1981, U.S. Dist. Ct. (mid. dist.) Ga. 1985. Ptnr. Harrison & Harrison, Lawrenceville, Ga., 1981-86, 87—; solicitor state ct. Gwinnett County, Lawrenceville, 1986. Vestryman St. Edward the Confessor Episcopal Ch., Lawrenceville, 1983-86; coun. del. Episcopal Diocese of Atlanta, 1986, 88; mem. Gwinnett County Bd. Registrations and Elections, 1991—; mem. exec. com. Gwinnett Dems., 1991—; asst. scoutmaster Boy Scouts Am. Mem. Ga. Bar Assn. (mock trial com. young lawyers sect. 1987-88), Ga. Assn. Criminal Def. Lawyers, Nat. Assn. Criminal Def. Lawyers. Democrat. Office: Harrison & Harrison 151 W Pike St # 88 Lawrenceville GA 30245-4929

HARRISON, STEPHEN EARLE, manufacturing executive; b. Little Rock, May 25, 1941; s. Richard G. and Edwin R. (McDaniels) H.; m. Donie Evelyn Brown, Aug. 5, 1960; children: Stephen Brian, Angela Eve. Grad. high sch., Joe T. Robinson, Pulaski County, Ark. Purchasing Welsco Inc., Little Rock, 1959-64, corp. sec., 1964, corp. sec., treas., 1964-80, pres., 1980-85, owner, pres., CEO, chmn. bd., 1985-89, chmn. bd. and CEO, 1977-94; chmn. E'Meritous, 1996—; bd. dirs., a founder Airgas Inc., Del. Recipient Leonard Parker Poole Safety award Compressed Gas Assn., Washington, 1986, 93, Fleet award for safety, 1989, 91. Mem. Internat. Oxygen Mfg. Assn. (pres. 1975-76), Nat. Welding Supply Assn., Compressed Gas Assn. Office: Welsco Inc 9006 Crystal Hill Rd North Little Rock AR 72113-6693

HARRISON, THOMAS, television executive; m. Kathy Harrison. BS in Telecom., Oral Roberts U.; MA in Journalism and Mass Media, U. Okla., 1992. Ops. mgr. Sta. KSOH-AM, Little Rock, 1978-79; sta. mgr. Sta. KJIL-FM, Oklahoma City, Okla., 1979-81; owner DYR Agy., Oklahoma City, 1981-83; corp. mktg. dir. Arrow Printing Co., Inc., Tulsa, 1983-87; v.p., gen. mgr. Sta. KXTD-AM, Broken Arrow, Okla., 1987-89; gen. mgr. KDOR-TV, Tulsa, 1989—; guest Trinity Broadcasting Network, 1980; interviewer, reporter tng. session U.S. Jaycees, 1989; actor nationally-syndicated Christian TV drama/comedy Fire by Nite, 1990; guest speaker undergrad. classes Northeastern State U., 1990, U. Tulsa, 1991; guest speaker grad. class U. Okla., 1990; actor missions comml. Teen Mania Mins., 1992; appeared on various talk programs, Tulsa. Designer ofcl. logo Coweta (Okla.) C. of C., 1985; mem. Encore Coun., Okla. Sinfonia, Tulsa, 1990-92; bd. dirs. Tulsa Inner-City Ministries, 1991-95, sec., 1992-95; mem. Tulsa Employers Adv. Coun., Okla. State Employment Svcs., 1992—; tchr. adult continuing edn. Broken Arrow Pub. Schs. Grad. scholar Tulsa Press Club. Mem. Kappa Tau Alpha. Office: KDOR-TV 17 2120 N Yellowood St Broken Arrow OK 74012-9101

HARRISON, THOMAS W., company executive; b. 1953. BS in Acctg., Lamar U., 1975. With Tex. Bank Beaumont, 1974-76; contr. Bella Constrn., Beaumont, 1985-86; exec. v.p. Allco, Inc., Beaumont, 1986—. Office: Allco Inc 6720 College St Beaumont TX 77707-3309

HARRISON, VIRGINIA FLORENCE, retired anatomist and educator, philanthropist; b. St. Louis, Mar. 15, 1918; d. George Benjamin and Florence Gertrude (McManus) H.; m. William Hector Marsh, Dec. 1, 1963 (dec. Dec. 1986); m. George William Elliott, Oct. 27, 1991; stepchildren: Carolyn Frances Roberts, George William II, Robert Bonner (dec. Apr. 1995), Cathrine Susan Dimino. BS, U. Wis., 1940, PhD, 1959; MA, Columbia U., 1944. Lectr. Columbia U., N.Y.C., 1943-46; asst. prof. Mary Washington Coll. of U. Va., Fredericksburg, 1946-48; asst. prof. Oreg. State U., Corvallis, 1948-50, assoc. prof., 1950-59; instr. Army Med. Acad./Brooks Army Med. Ctr., San Antonio, 1959-60, assoc. prof., 1960-64; vis. prof. U. Wash., Seattle, 1961; lectr. U. Tex. Med. Sch., Galveston, 1962-64, Hadassah Med. Sch., Hebrew U. of Jerusalem, 1965; lectr. grad. sch. U. Wis., Madison, 1964; pvt. practice stock market investment lectr. Washington, 1969-84, pub. stock market letter, 1969-84; cons. U. Tex. Med. Sch., 1962-64, U.S. Pentathlon Team, San Antonio, 1960-64, Dentists for Treatment of Pain from Muscular Tension, San Antonio, 1960-64; bd. visitors Sch. of Edn. U. Wis., Madison. Contbr. articles to profl. jours. Bd. visitors Sch. Edn., U. Wis., Madison. Recipient Civilian Meritorious Svc. award U.S. Civil Svc., 1965; Amy Morris Homans fellow, 1958; hon. fellow U. Wis., 1956, 58, 59. Fellow AAH-PERD, Tex. Acad. Sci.; mem. Am. Assn. Anatomists divs. Fedn. Am. Socs. for Exptl. Biology, Cosmos Club, Achievement Rewards Coll. Scientists, Inc. (v.p. 1973-74, 78-80, bd. dirs. 1974-75, 76-78, 80-85, 87-89), Hospitality Info. Svc., Lake Bancroft Woman's Club. Home: 6333 Cavalier Corridor Falls Church VA 22044-1301

HARRISON, WALTER THOMAS, JR., accounting educator, chair; b. Elizabeth City, N.C., Apr. 25, 1945; s. Walter Thomas and Billie Page Harrison; m. Nancy Lee Brown, Apr. 18, 1970; children: Will, Emily. BBA, Baylor U., 1967; MS, Okla. State U., 1968; PhD, Mich. State U., 1976. Projects asst. to fin. v.p. SMI, Inc., Waco, Tex., 1965-67; cons. SMI, Inc., Brussels, 1968; staff acct. Price Waterhouse & Co., Dallas, 1968-70; instr. of acctg. Cleve. (Tenn.) State Community Coll., 1970-72; teaching asst., rsch. asst., instr. Mich. State U., 1972-75; asst. prof. U. Tex., 1976-81, assoc. prof., 1982-85; vis. assoc. prof. Stanford U., 1981-82; prof., KPMG Peat Marwick-Thomas L. Holton chair in acctg. Baylor U., 1985—; cons. Grupo Alfa Indsl., Monterey, Mexico, 1981, dept. of controller State of Tex., 1984. Contbr. numerous articles to profl. jours.; co-author coll. textbooks; ad hoc reviewer Acctg. Rev., 1979-86, Acctg. Edn., 1994. Grantee Ernst & Young Tax Rsch. Found., 1989. Mem. Am. Acctg. Assn. (mem. fin. acctg. stds. subcom. 1977, fin. acctg. stds. com. 1985-87, chair 1986-87, co-chair acctg. edn. sect. 1987-88, mem. teaching/curriculum devel. award com. 1990-91), AICPA, Beta Alpha Psi, Beta Gamma Sigma (pres. Delta of Tex. chpt. 1989-90). Mem. Evangel. Free Ch. Office: Baylor U Hankamer Sch Bus Dept Acctg Waco TX 76798

HARRISON, WILLARD W., chemist, educator; b. McLeansboro, Ill., July 28, 1937. BA, So. Ill. U., 1958, MA, 1960; PhD, U. Ill., 1964. Asst. prof. chemistry U. Va., 1964-69, assoc. prof. chemistry, 1969-74; vis. sci. Max-Planck Inst. for Plasmaphysics, Munich, West Germany, 1975-76; chmn. dept. chemistry U. Va., 1978-81; sr. rsch scholar Fulbright-Hayes U. Paris, 1981; vis. scholar dept. chemistry Stanford U., 1982; assoc. provost foe acad. support U. Va., 1982-86; vis. scholar dept. geology Stanford U., 1987-88; prof. chemistry U. Va., 1974-88; dean, Coll. Liberal Arts and Scis. U. Fla., 1988—. Recipient Lester W. Strock award Soc. for Applied Spectrscopy, Frederick, Md., 1993. Office: Univ of Florida Dean Liberal Arts & Scis 2014 Turlington Hall Gainesville FL 32611*

HARRISON, WILLIAM OLIVER, JR., lawyer, small business owner; b. Corpus Christi, Tex., Oct. 16, 1945; s. William Oliver and Nell Betty (Anderson) H.; m. Cathy Lynn Williams, Dec. 1, 1984. BA, Tex. Christian U., 1967; JD, U. Tex., 1970. Atty. Wood, Burney, Nesbitt and Ryan, Corpus Christi, 1971-75; sole practice Corpus Christi, 1975-78; ptnr. Harrison, Stone and Jordan, Corpus Christi, 1978-84; state rep. Tex. House of Reps., 1979-81, 83-85; ptnr. Parkinson and Assocs., Austin, Tex., 1983—; sec., treas. CompuPrint, Inc., Austin, Tex., 1983-86, Cooper's Alley Restaurant and Saloon, Inc., Corpus Christi, 1983-86; pres. Lighthouse Bar and Grill Inc., Corpus Christi, 1984—, chmn., chief exec. officer, 1987—; ptnr. Heard Goggan Blair Williams and Harrison, Houston, 1984-88; sole practice, 1989—. Bd. dirs. Corpus Christi C. of C., Cerebral Palsy Found., 1982-83; selection chmn. Leadership Corpus Christi, 1981-82, adv. com., 1989-90; mem. steering com. Goals for Corpus Christi; mem. Corpus Christi Conv. and Tourist Bur., LWV, Leadership Corpus Christi Alumni, Govtl. Commn. on Efficiency and Economy, 1986; chmn. Long Range Planning Heart of Corpus Christi, 1989-90, Downtown Revitalization Dist., 1991-92; v.p. Regional Transit Authority, 1991, bd. dirs, 1990, chmn., 1991-95; mem. govtl. affairs com. C. of C., 1991, vice chmn., 1992, chmn., 1993. Cpl. U.S. Army, 1964-70. Named one of Outstanding Young Men of Am., U.S. Jaycees, 1978. Mem. ABA, Houston Bar Assn., County Bar Assn., Nat. Restaurant Assn., Tex. Restaurant Assn. Democrat. Mem. Disciples of Christ Ch. Office: 214 Bayridge Dr Corpus Christi TX 78411-1212

HARRISON, WILLIAM TIMOTHY, college administrator; b. Royston, Ga., Apr. 30, 1961; s. Vernon Paul and Mary Helen (Ware) H.; m. Rebecca Lynn Sutphin, Jan. 5, 1985. BA in Religion, Emmanuel Coll., 1984; MDiv, Erskine Seminary, 1990; postgrad., U. Ga., 1995—. Pastor Royston (Ga.) Pentecostal Holiness Ch., 1990-95; resident dir. Emmanuel Coll., Franklin Springs, Ga., 1987-91, asst. dean of students, 1991-92, dir. admissions, 1993—. Republican. Home: PO Box 394 1 King St Franklin Springs GA 30639

HARROP, GEORGE BERT, construction executive; b. Manhattan, Kans., Feb. 21, 1939; s. G.B. Harrop and Miriam Falk; m. Valberta Berel, June 22, 1961; children: Rachel, David, Sarah, Susan. BS in Hotel Mgmt., Cornell U. Ptnr. Stone Constrn., Houston, 1961-85; pres. Harrop Constrn., Houston, 1985-95, chmn., CEO, 1995—; bd. dirs. AGC, Houston, Sterling Bank, Houston. Mem. Whitehall Club. Office: Harrop Constrn Co Inc 10190 Old Katy Rd # 350 Houston TX 77043

HARRYMAN, RHONDA L., education educator; b. Perry, Okla., Apr. 1, 1954; d. Otis Issac Jr. and Jeanette Roberta (Creacy) Shelley; m. Gilbert Wayne Harryman, Mar. 19, 1978. BS in Edn. cum laude, U. Ctrl. Okla., 1975, M in Spl. Edn., 1979; postgrad., Okla. State U., 1992—. Cert. learning disabilities, mentally handicapped, physically handicapped, emotional disturbance, elem. sch. adminstrs., Okla. Asst. workshop coord. for trainable mentally handicapped, physically handicapped Edmond (Okla.) ARC, 1974-76; instr. educable mentally handicapped, physically handicapped, emotionally disabled Edmond Pub. Schs., 1976-77, instr. spl. edn., emotionally disabled, educable mentally handicapped, physically handicapped, visually and hearing impaired, 1977-91; univ. coord., supr. practicums, instr. spl. edn. U. Ctrl. Okla., Edmond, 1992—; edn. advisor tchrs. undrepresented populations in Shawnee, Okla. Three Feathers Assn., Norman, Okla. 1983; pvt. teaching, parent counseling learning disabilities, 1982-87; part-time instr. spl. edn. Okla. Christian U., 1992—, mem. tchr. edn. adv. coun.; co-moderator New Eng. Joint Conf. Specific Learning Disabilities, Boston, 1991; edn. rep. Okla. Joint Conf. Juvenile Justice; edn. del. Okla. Japan-Am. Grassroots Coun., Tokyo, 1991; conducted workshops, presented insvcs., speaker in field. Editorial rev. bd. Teaching Resources, Dayton, Ohio. Counselor Edmond Youth Advocacy Bd.; mem. Gov.'s Round Table on Edn. and Bus., Edmond Juvenile Crime Commn.; sponsor Ala-Teen, Boys Ranch Town. Named Okla. Tchr. of Yr. by Okla. State Dept. Edn., 1992. Mem. Orton Dyslexia Soc., Coun. Exceptional Child, Kappa Delta Pi. Home: 2104 Running Branch Rd Edmond OK 73013-6646 Office: U Ctrl Okla Dept Curriculum and Spl Education 100 N University Dr Edmond OK 73034*

HARSHMAN, EDWARD JAY, physician, author; b. N.Y.C., Nov. 26, 1955; s. Richard Renville and Mary Ashley Cooper (Hewitt) H.; m. Marcia Ellen Greenberg, Jan. 26, 1986 (div. Mar. 1995). Student, Haverford (Pa.) Coll., 1973-75; BA in Ext. Studies, Harvard U., 1978; postgrad., Columbia U., 1979-80; MD, N.J. Med. Sch., Newark, 1985; MBA in Health Care Adminstrn., Baruch Coll., N.Y.C., 1989. Intern St. Barnabas Med. Ctr., Livingston, N.J., 1985-86; house-call physician N.Y.C., 1986-88; dir. rsch. 32B-32J Welfare Fund, N.Y.C., 1989-92; pres. AMCE, Inc., N.Y.C., 1993. Author: Fantastic Lat. Think. Puz., 1996; contbr. articles to profl. jours.; prodr. weekly TV series: Dr. Harshman's Medical Cost Control, 1993. Bd. dirs. Bridge the Gap, Inc., Jacksonville, 1996—. Mem. Internat. Soc. for Philos. Enquiry, Mensa. Republican. Episcopalian.

HART, FAY MARIA MITCHELL, counselor, mediator; b. Greer, S.C., Nov. 28, 1935; d. George Arthur and Agnes Grace (Burdett) Mitchell; m. E. Kemp Hart, Sept. 19, 1973 (dec.); 2 stepchildren. BA, Lander Coll., 1957; MA, Furman U., 1965; specialist degree, U. S.C., 1979, postgrad., 1991. Lic. profl. counselor, mediation specialist, S.C.; nat. cert. counselor. Choral dir. Hollis Jr. High Sch., Greenville, S.C., 1957-65; tchr. history, instrnl. TV researcher Greenville County (S.C.) Sch. Dist., 1966-67; asst. prin. Sevier Mid. Sch., Greenville, 1968-70, dean guidance, 1970-79; dir. guidance Pelham Road Elem. Sch., Greenville, 1979-88; counselor dir. Blue Ridge Mid. Sch., Greenville, 1988-90; pvt. practice Profl. Counseling Svc., Greenville, 1987—; mediator specialist, Greenville, 1989—; elem. cons. Clemson U., Furman U., 1987—; parenting tng. supr., 1979—; supr. trainer S.C. Mediators, Columbia, 1990-91, mem. adv. bd., 1990—. Author: The Teaching of Phonics Through Song, Art and Work, 1965; contbr. articles to profl. jours. Guardian ad litem, Greenville, 1987—; sec. Greenville Foster Care Rev. Bd., 1990—; mem. Greenville Mental Helath Coun., 1980—; chmn. B.B. Foster Care Rev. Bd. S.C., 1993—; S.C. rep. for religious and spiritual values, 1993—. Scholar Lander Coll.; grantee, 1979. Mem. S.C. Counselors Assn. (publicity dir., exec. coun. 1993-94, awards 1988-91). Baptist. Home and Office: Batesville Rd PO Box 978 Taylors SC 29687-0978

HART, FRANK, company executive. Pres. MCNC. Address: 3021 Cornwallis Rd Research Triangle Park NC 27709

HART, GERRY KEITH, computer engineer; b. Independence, La., Nov. 5, 1964; s. James Alexander and Georgia Mae (Tillery) H. BS, Southeastern La. U., 1986; MS, Ala. A&M U., 1995. Computer sci. instr. Rutledge Coll., New Orleans, 1988-89; computer programmer/analyst SEMA Corp., New Orleans, 1989; computer engr. U.S. Army Signal Ctr., Ft. Gordon, Ga., 1989-91, U.S. Army Missile Command, Redstone Arsenal, Ala., 1991—. Roman Catholic. Home: 6620 Old Mason Pike NW #910 Huntsville AL 35806-2154

HART, HERBERT MICHAEL, military officer; b. St. Louis, Oct. 19, 1928; s. Herbert Malcolm and Helen Genevive (Quigley) H.; m. Teresa Keating, Oct. 13, 1958; children: Bridget, Erin, Bret, Tracy, Megan, Michael, Patrick. BS in Journalism, Northwestern U., 1951. Commd. 2d lt. USMC, 1951, advanced through grades to col., 1972; infantry platoon, co. and bn. comdg. officer USMC, Republic of Korea, 1952, 53, Vietnam, 1969-70; Arab, Israeli, Persian plans officer U.S. Strike Command, Mid. East and Tampa, Fla., 1967-69; head profl. edn. Dept. Navy, Washington, 1977-78; head hist. br. Marine Corps. Hqrs., Washington, 1973-77, dep. dir. pub. affairs, 1978-80, dir. pub. affairs, 1980-81, ret., 1981; dir. pub. affairs Res. Officers Assn. of U.S., Washington, 1982-94; cons. office of History U.S. Army Corps Engrs., 1981—; mem. adv. bd. ad hoc com. Nat. Park Svc., 1985—; mem. com. on Cemeteries and Memls. VA, 1987-92; mem. coun. advisors Nat. Parks and Conservation Assn., 1992—. Author 9 mil. history books; editor ROA Nat. Security Report, 1983-94; mem. editorial bd. Mil. History mag., 1983—. Decorated 2 Purple Heart medals, 2 Legion of Merit medals; recipient Award of Merit Am. Assn. State and Local History, 1976, Cultural Achievement award Sec. of Interior, 1979, Conservation Svc. award Sec. Interior, 1986. Fellow Co. Mil. Historians; mem. Potomac Westeners (pres. 1974-75, 84-85), Res. Officers Assn. U.S. (life), Marine Corps Res. Officers Assn. (life), Marine Corps Combat Corres. Assn. (life), Marine Corps Hist. Found. (charter, bd. dirs. 1983-87), Assn. U.S. Army, Nat. Pk. Svc. Employee and Alumni Assn. (life), VFW (life), Am. Legion (life), Mil. Order Purple Heart (life), Civil War Trust (charter mem.), Ret. Officers Assn. (life), 1st Marine Divsn. Assn. (life), 3rd Marine Divsn. Assn. (life), Coun. Am. Mil. Past. (co-founder 1966, exec. dir. 1971—), Western History Assn. (charter), Nat. Assn. Uniformed Svcs. (life), Coast Def. Study Group, Naval and Maritime Corrs. Circle, State Hist. Soc. S.D. (life), Ft. Adams, R.I. Trust (charter), Ft. Douglas, Utah, Mus. Assn. (life), Civil War Fortifications Study Group (charter), Friends of Ft. Davis, Tex. (life), Battlefield Preservation Coalition (dir. 1991—), Friends of Ft. Ward, Va. (charter), Friends of Manassas Battlefield, Va. (charter), Nat. Trust Hist. Preservation, Theodore Roosevelt Assn., Va. Hist. Soc., Order of Indian Wars (companion), Apollo Soc. (bd. dirs. 1983-87), Am. Civil Def. Assn. (bd. advisors 1991—), Soc. Mil. History (trustee 1978-83), Mil. Order of Carabao, K.C., Soc. Profl. Journalists, Theta Xi (life). Republican. Roman Catholic. Home and Office: PO Box 1151 Fort Myer VA 22211-1151

HART, LAURIE ELLEN, education educator; b. Ames, Iowa, Feb. 14, 1948; d. Arthur E. and Mary Lois (Lane) H. Student, U. Madrid, 1968-69; BS in Math., Purdue U., 1971; MA in Math. Edn., U. Tex., 1977; PhD in Curriculum-Instrn. in Math. Edn., U. Wis., 1981. Tchr. math. Nova Mid. Sch., Ft. Lauderdale, Fla., 1971, Twin Lakes High Sch., Monticello, Ind., 1971-72, 72-74, Austin (Tex.) High Sch., 1976; freelance tchr. English, Madrid, 1972; teaching asst. math. dept. U. Tex., Austin, 1974-75; project asst. dept. curriculum and instrn. U. Wis., Madison, 1976-77, 78-79, grad. asst., rsch. asst., project assoc., 1976-81, hon. fellow, 1991; asst. prof. dept. elem. edn. U. Ga., Athens, 1981-86, assoc. prof., 1986—; vis. asst. prof. dept. math. Mich. State U., East Lansing, 1985; presenter in field, 1979—; speaker nat., state and local profl. meetings; condr. tchrs. workshops; book manuscript reviewer HarperCollins Pub., summer 1992; proposal reviewer NSF; referee Elem. Sch. Jour., Jour. for Rsch. in Math. Edn., Am. Ednl. Rsch. Jour., Rev. Ednl. Rsch., Rsch. in Mid. Level Edn. Assoc. editor, mem. editorial bd. Jour. for Rsch. in Math. Edn., 1982-87; contbr. articles and abstracts to profl. jours., chpts. to books. Grantee Nat. Inst. Edn., 1979-81, U. Ga. Coll. Coll. Edn., summers 1982, 85, 86, 91, faculty rsch. grantee U. Ga., 1982, 84, U.S. Dept. Edn., 1992-94, Ga. Initiative in Math. and Sci., 1992-97. Mem. Am. Ednl. Rsch. Assn. (co-chmn. rsch. in math. edn. spl. interest group 1985-87), Psychology of Math. Edn., Nat. Coun. Tchrs. Math., Nat. Mid. Sch. Assn., Internat. Group for Psychology of Math. Edn., Ga. Coun. Tchrs. Math., Ga. Mid. Sch. Assn. Home: 295 University Dr Athens GA 30605-1437 Office: U Ga Dept Elem Edn 427 Aderhold Hall Athens GA 30602-0001

HART, PHILLIP, credit union executive; b. 1944. With Tulsa Mcpl. Credit Union, 1965-76; with Tulsa Fed. Employees Credit Union, 1977—, pres., bd. dirs. Office: Tulsa Fed Employees Cr Un 9323 E 23rd St Tulsa OK 74129*

HART, RICHARD WESLEY, religious organization administrator, pastor; b. Greensboro, N.C., Feb. 21, 1933; s. Shelly Monroe and Virginia (Boaz) H.; m. 1954; (div. May, 1969); m. Barbara Jean Ruddock, Aug. 30, 1980 (dec. Sept.); children: Richard Wesley Jr., Larry Earl, Howard Clayton, . BDiv, Toccoa Falls (Ga.) Coll., 1951; DDiv, Evang. Christian Sem., 1966. Regional dir. Am. Evang. Christian Chs., Fontana, Calif., 1958-66; pres. Evang. Christian Chs., San Bernardino, Calif., 1966-83; founder, dir. Reidsville (N.C.) Urban Ministry, 1983—. Mem. Rep. Nat. Com., Washington, 1991—; establisher AGAD Scholarship Fund, 1992. Mem. Am. Vets. Home and Office: 2125 Smith St Reidsville NC 27320-6513

HART, ROGER LOUIS, accounting consultant; b. Elkhorn, Wis., May 30, 1944; s. Donald John and Margaret Ellen (Thorpe) H.; m. Margaret Elizabeth Scarborough, Oct. 20, 1990; children: Anna Elizabeth, Laura Margaret. BA, Rhodes Coll., 1965; MA, Princeton U., 1968, PhD, 1970; MPA, U. N.C., 1994. Assoc prof. History LeMoyne-Owen Coll., Memphis, 1970-73; vis. asst. prof. History Rhodes Coll., Memphis, 1973-74; fgn. svc. officer U.S. Dept. State, Washington, 1975-87; legis. asst. U.S. Ho. Reps., Washington, 1987-89; vis. asst. prof. History N.C. State U., Raleigh, N.C., 1989-91; asst. to v.p. Self-Help Credit Union, Durham, N.C., 1992-93; policy analyst Office of State Planning State of N.C., Raleigh, 1994-95; acctg. cons. Non-Profit Fiscal Mgmt. Svc., Chapel Hill, N.C., 1995—. Author: Redeemers, Bourbons and Populists, 1975; contbr. articles to profl. jours. Recipient Sinclaire Lang. award Am. Fgn. Svc. Assn., 1985. Mem. Sierra Club (exec. com. N.C. chpt. 1992—, treas. 1995—). Democrat. Home: 209 Wood Cir Chapel Hill NC 27514-2421 Office: Non-Profit Fiscal Mgmt Svc PO Box 3451 Chapel Hill NC 27515

HART, THOMAS HUGHSON, III, lawyer; b. Montgomery, Ala., Aug. 19, 1955; s. Thomas H. and Nora A. (McDonald) H.; m. Jane Elizabeth Morgan, Aug. 4, 1979; children: Morgan Elizabeth, Katherine MacDonald, Mary MacQuarrie, Teresa Jane, Thomas MacGregor. BA in Polit. Sci., Furman U., 1977; JD, U. S.C., 1980. Bar: S.C. 1980, U.S. Dist. Ct. S.C. 1981, U.S. Ct. Appeals (4th cir.) 1981, U.S. Ct. Appeals (11th cir.) 1982, U.S. Ct. Appeals (10th cir.) 1985, U.S. Supreme Ct. 1987, U.S. Ct. Appeals (8th cir.) 1990, U.S. Ct. Appeals (3d cir.) 1991, V.I., 1991. Assoc. Blatt and Fales, Barnwell, S.C., 1980-83; ptnr. Ness, Motley, Loadholt, Richardson & Poole, P.A., Barnwell, 1983-90, Brady, Hart & Jacobs, Christiansted, V.I., 1990-93; ptnr. Alkon, Rhea & Hart, Christiansted, 1993—. Editor S.C. Law Rev., 1978-80. Baruch scholar Furman U., Greenville, S.C., 1973-77; James Verner scholar U. S.C. Law Sch., 1978, Paul Cooper scholar, 1979. Mem. ABA, S.C. Trial Lawyers Assn. (bd. govs.), Assn. Trial Lawyers Am., S.C. Bar Assn., V.I. Bar Assn., Barnwell County C. of C. (bd. dirs.). Roman Catholic. Home: 2 Boetzburg Christiansted VI 00820-4516 Office: 2115 Queen St Christiansted VI 00820-4835

HART, VALERIE GAIL, writer; b. Detroit, May 6, 1936; d. Royal Allen and Elsa Adele (Freeman) Oppenheim; m. Robert Fredric Hart, Mar. 29, 1959; children: Alexandra H. Bosshardt, Gregory S., Katherine. Student, U. Mich., 1954-59, Cite-Universite, Cordon Bleu Cooking Sch., 1970. Tchr. Eng. Dexter (Mich.) Shc., 1958-59; co-owner Imports For the Trade, 1962-95; tchr. cooking, etiquette classes, 1965—. recorded children's books for the blind, 1948; recorded books Univ. Miami Recording For The Blind, 1960-65; food editor Panax, 1977-82; editor ZAGAT, 1992, 95; author: The New Tradition Cookbook, 1988, A Trilogy of Children's Stories: Strangers, The Prize, The Table Tangles of Tommy and Ted, 1996, Special Occasions, 1997; writer Social Mag.; contbr. articles to mags. Tutor freshman Eng. blind pre-coll. students Lighthouse for the Blind, N.Y.C., 1959; leader Girl Scouts Am., Miami Beach, 1967-69; pres. sponsors Mus. Sci., 1975-77, tchr. cooking mus. benefit, 1975-79, past bd. trustees; pres. Parents' Assn. Ransom-Everglades Sch., 1976-77; bd. dirs. March of Dimes, 1976—, chair gourmet gala, 1980, 85; bd. dirs. Children's Psychiat. Ctr., 1980-95; chmn. judges kahlua bake-off contest FBO Project Newborn, 1986-96; chmn. auction, ball St. Francis Hosp., red ribbon day Dade County Schs. Healthy Foods Recipe Contest; tchr. cooking benefit Mt. Dora Ctr. For The Arts; vol. Hospice, Leesburg, 1995; mem. vestry, lay reader, chalice bearer All Souls' Episc. Ch., 1982—. Inducted into Chaine des Rotisseurs, 1981; honored by Gastronome Mag., honored Outstanding Couple, Am. Cancer Soc., 1996; recipient Outstanding Woman award Miami Ballet Soc., 1985. Mem. Surf Club, Mount Dora Yacht Club. Republican. Episcopalian. Home: 6849 S Clayton Mount Dora FL 32757-7024 Office: Downtowne Mount Dora dba Renaissance 411 N Donnelly St Mount Dora FL 32757

HART, VIRGINIA WADE, elementary education educator; b. Rolla, Mo., Nov. 20, 1943; d. Clifford Neil and Nellie Z. (Jaggers) Wade; m. Edward F. Hart, Oct. 12, 1968 (div. June 1994); children: Edward S., Clifford T., James R., Deborah J., Sarah E. BA in Sociology, Mary Washington Coll., Fredericksburg, Va., 1965; MA in Elem. Edn., Adelphi U., Garden City, N.Y., 1973; MA in Reading, U. Ala., Birmingham, 1988, student, 1990. Cert. in elem. edn., reading, early childhood edn., Ala. Tchr. 1st grade Nassakegg Elem. Sch., Setauket, N.Y., 1966-68, Blue Point (N.Y.)-Bayport Schs., 1968-69; ednl. outreach Discovery Place Children's Mus., Birmingham, 1986-87; tchr. developmental kindergarten Hall Kent Elem. Sch., Birmingham, 1989-90, tchr. kindergarten, 1990-91, tchr. 2d grade, 1991—; clin. master tchr. U. Ala., Tuscaloosa, 1993—; mem. curriculum adv. com.

Hoover Pub. Sch., 1989-91. Bd. dirs. Grace House Ministries, Fairfield, Ala., 1993-96. Mem. Internat. Reading Assn., Nat. Coun. Tchrs. English, Whole Lang. Umbrella, Nat. Sci. Tchrs. Assn., Kappa Delta Pi. Baptist. Office: Hall Kent Elem Sch 213 Hall Ave Homewood AL 35209

HARTE, HOUSTON HARRIMAN, newspaper, broadcasting executive; b. San Angelo, Tex., Feb. 15, 1927; s. Houston and Caroline Isabel (McCutcheon) H.; m. Carolyn Esther Hardig, June 17, 1950; children: Houston Ritchie, David Harriman, Sarah Elizabeth. B.A., Washington and Lee U., 1950. Partner Snyder (Tex.) Daily News, 1950-52, editor, 1952-54; with Des Moines Register and Tribune, 1954-56; pres. San Angelo Standard, Inc., 1956-62; v.p. Express Pub. Co., San Antonio, 1962-66; pres. Express Pub. Co., 1966-72; chmn. bd. Harte-Hanks Communications, Inc., 1971—. Pres., bd. dirs. San Angelo Symphony, 1960; v.p. Concho Valley coun. Boy Scouts Am., 1960-62; bd. vistors USAF Acad., 1965-69; bd. regents East Tex. State U., 1970-81; trustee Stillman Coll., 1976—, Washington and Lee U., 1981-92; chmn. bd. trustees Tex. Presby. Found., 1985-88. With USNR, 1945-46. Democrat. Presbyterian. Office: Harte-Hanks Communications 200 Concord Plaza Dr San Antonio TX 78216-6943

HARTFORD, SHAUN ALISON, pediatrics nurse, educator; b. Houston, Mar. 30, 1962; m. Mark M. Danney; children: Angela, Nicholas. BSN, U. Tex. Health Sci. Ctr., San Antonio, 1984; MSN, U. Tex., San Antonio, 1988. Cert. pediatric nurse Nat. Assn. Pediatric Nurse Practitioners and Nurses. Staff nurse, pediatrics Santa Rosa Health Care Corp., San Antonio, 1985-89; mem. faculty Bapt. Meml. Hosp. System Sch. Profl. Nursing, San Antonio, 1989—. Mem. Am. Diabetes Assn. (Patient Edn. award 1994, Champions for Life award 1996), Am. Assn. Diabetes Educators, Sigma Theta Tau.

HARTL, WILLIAM PARKER, oil company executive; b. Boston, May 9, 1935; s. Emil Martin and Elizabeth (Parker) H.; m. Judith Ford, Feb. 9, 1985. BA, Boston U., 1964. Exec., Ashland Oil Europe, Inc., Geneva, 1968-72, dir. fin. communications Ashland Oil, Inc. (name changed to Ashland Inc. 1995), N.Y.C., 1972-94; v.p. investor rels., 1994—; dir. Communications Strategy Group Inc., Boston. Bd. dirs. Jr. Achievement, Ashland, Ky; mem. adv. bd. Salvation Army, Ashland. Served to maj. USA, 1956-63, ETO. Recipient Disting. Svc. award Investment Edn. Inst., 1981, Nat. Assn. Investment Clubs, 1979. Mem. Am. Mgmt. Assn., Nat. Investor Rels. Inst. (chmn. bd. 1977-78), Fin. Communications Soc. (pres. 1983), Sr. Investor Rels. Roundtable (chair), Investor Rels. Assn. (pres. 1991-92), Petroleum Investor Rels. Assn. (pres. 1995—), Pub. Rels. Soc. Am., Internat. Assn. Bus. Communicators, Am. Petroleum Inst., Nat. Alumni Coun. Boston U., Met. Club N.Y.C. (bd. govs. 1993—), Columbian Lodge. Republican. Methodist. Office: Ashland Inc PO Box 391 Ashland KY 41105-0391

HARTLEY, CRAIG SHERIDAN, dean, mechanical engineering educator; b. Quantico, Va., Dec. 9, 1937; s. Cleo Stancil and Velva Marie (Grayson) Bowers; m. Cornelia Margaret McMann, June 7, 1958; children: Margaret Ann, Katherine Jeanne, David Brian. BMetE, Rensselaer Poly. Inst., 1958; MS, Ohio State U., 1961, PhD, 1965; MFA, U. Fla., 1980. Registered profl. engr., Ala., Fla., La., N.Y. Project engr. USAF Materials Lab., WPAFB, Ohio, 1959-66; postdoctoral fellow NSF, 1965-66; prof. materials sci. and engring. U. Fla., Gainesville, 1966-80; chair materials sci. and engring. SUNY, Stony Brook, 1980-82; assoc. dean engring. La. State U., Baton Rouge, 1982-86; program dir. NSF, Washington, 1986-87; chair materials sci. and engring. U. Ala., Birmingham, 1987-90; dean engring. Fla. Atlantic U., Boca Raton, 1990—; program dir. Nat. Sci. Found.; cons. Materials Cons., Inc., Gainesville, 1975-90, Brookhaven (N.Y.) Nat. Lab., 1980-82, NSF, Washington, 1987—. Contbr. articles to jours. Acta Metallurgica Et Materialia, Exptl. Mechanics, Philos. Mag., Jour. Applied Physics. Pres. Gainesville Little Theatre, 1967-69, Fla. Theatre Conf., 1977-79. Capt. USAF, 1959-62. Grantee NSF, 1966-69, 82-85, Office of Naval Rsch., 1967-69, AEC, 1973-79, Nuclear Regulatory Commn., 1976-79, Army Rsch. Office, 1983-86. Fellow AAAS, ASM Internat.; mem. ASME, The Metall. Soc. (mining, metals and materials sect., chmn. edn. and profl. affairs com. 1990-92), Am. Soc. Engring. Edn., Soc. Exptl. Mechanics. Unitarian. Office: Nat Sci Found 4201 Wilson Blvd Arlington VA 22230

HARTMAN, CAROL OLIVER, investment banker; b. Long Beach, Calif., July 28, 1964; d. Charles Edmond and Mary Elizabeth (Althaus) Oliver; m. Craig S. Hartman, Feb. 22, 1992. BA in Econs., Claremont McKenna Coll., 1986. Assoc. managed investment dept. Sutro & Co. Inc., San Francisco, 1986-88; fin. analyst Dean Witter Capital Markets, Inc., L.A., 1988-89; dir. devel. Am. Diabetes Assn., Oakland, Calif., 1990-92; exec. dir. Children's Hosp. Branches, Inc., Berkeley, Calif., 1993; in instnl. fixed income sales, capital markets Oppenheimer & Co. Inc., Houston, 1994—. Mem., com. chmn. San Francisco Spinsters, 1989-91; bd. dirs. East Bay Svcs. Devel. Disabled, Concord, Calif., 1992-93; former mem. vol. coun. San Francisco Symphony. Mem. Nat. Soc. Fund Raising Execs., Claremont McKenna Coll. Alumni Assn. (chpt. pres. San Francisco 1990-94). Republican. Roman Catholic. Office: 333 Clay St Ste 4700 Houston TX 77002-4103

HARTMAN, DOUGLAS COLE, lawyer; b. Richmond, Va., Jan. 7, 1950; s. Joseph David and Lillian Marie (Gannon) H.; m. Christine C. Coile, May 3, 1980; children: Kimberly, Jonathan, Kelly. BBA, Univ. Miami, Coral Gables, 1972, JD, 1975. Bar: Fla. 1975, U.S. Dist. Ct. (so. dist.) Fla. 1977, U.S. Ct. Appeals (5th and 11th cirs.) 1977. Asst. state atty. State Attys. Office 11th Jud. Cir., Miami, 1974-79; assoc. Offices of Eugene Spellman, Miami, 1979-80; ptnr. Dean & Hartman, P.A., Miami, 1980-90; mng. ptnr. Hartman & cornely, P.A., Miami, 1990—; bd. dirs. Fla. Assn. Criminal Def. Attys., Miami, 1982-86; mem. Fla. Bar Criminal Rules Com., Tallahassee, 1980-81, Dade County Bar Assn. Criminal Com., Miami 1984-85. Mem. ch. coun. Christ the King Luth. Ch., Miami, 1991-95, pres. ch. found., 1994-96. Hon. mem. Dade County Police Benevolent Assn., Miami, 1980. Home: 1000 Pine Branch Dr Fort Lauderdale FL 33326-2840 Office: Hartman & Cornely PA 10680 NW 25th St Ste 200 Miami FL 33172-2108

HARTMAN, JAMES AUSTIN, retired geologist; b. Lanark, Ill., Jan. 29, 1928; s. Llewelyn John and Gladys Mae (Doyle) H.; m. Zoe Marie Wiley, June 16, 1951; children: Victoria Lynn, Lester James. BS, Beloit (Wis.) Coll., 1951; MS, U. Wis., 1955, PhD, 1957. Cert. petroleum geologist. Geologist Reynolds Jamaica (W.I.) Mines, Jamaica, W.I., 1951-53, Union Carbide Ore Co., Parimaribo, Surinam, 1956-57; various positions Shell Oil Co., New Orleans, 1957-86; cons. New Orleans, 1986-94; ret., 1994. Bd. mgmt. YMCA, Metairie, 1972-74; pres. Jefferson Com. for Better Schs., Metairie, 1961-63, pres. Westgate PTA, Kenner, La., 1964-65. With U.S. Army, 1946-47. Union Carbide Rsch. fellowship U. Wis., 1954-56. Mem. Am. Assn. Petroleum Geologists (hon., sec. 1981-83, Disting. Svc. award 1985), New Orleans Geol. Soc. (hon., 2d v.p. 1975-76, pres.-elect 1984-85, pres. 1985-86, Outstanding Mem. 1977), Gulf Coast Assn. Geol. Socs. (hon., v.p. 1987, pres. 1988), Sigma Xi. Republican. Episcopalian. Home: 4512 Newlands St Metairie LA 70006-4138

HARTNETT, THOMAS ROBERT, III, lawyer; b. Sioux City, Iowa, July 19, 1920; s. Thomas R. and Florence Mary (Graves) H.; m. Betty Jeanne Dobbins, Mar. 3, 1943; children: Thomas Robert Joseph, Jeanine Elizabeth, Dennis Edward, Glenn Michael. Student Trinity Coll., 1937-39; LLB, U. So. Calif., 1948. Bar: Tex. 1948, U.S. Dist. Ct. (no. dist.) Tex. 1949, U.S. Ct. Appeals (5th cir.) 1954, (10th cir.) 1955, (11th cir.) 1983, U.S. Supreme Ct. 1957. Sole practice law, Dallas, 1948-88; of counsel Hartnett Law Firm, Dallas, 1988—. Served with USAAF, 1939-45. Mem. State Bar Tex., Dallas Bar Assn. Republican. Roman Catholic. Home: 5074 Matilda St 224 Dallas TX 75206-4268 Office: 4900 Thanksgiving Tower 1601 Elm St Dallas TX 75201-7254

HARTON, MERLE CARTER, JR., writer; b. Deland, Fla., Mar. 26, 1950; s. Merle Carter and Gladys (Geranis) H.; m. Kathy Haase, May 18, 1974; children: Kristen, Erik, Kiel, Lara. BA, U. South Fla., 1972; MA, McMaster U., 1976, PhD, 1987. Tutor in philosophy McMaster U., Hamilton, Ont., Can., 1974-80; rsch. editor Historic New Orleans Collection, 1980-84; exec. dir. Tulane Med. Alumni Assn., New Orleans, 1984-87; instr. Delgado C.C., 1987-89; adminstr. Urol. Inst. New Orleans, 1987-92; mem. editorial bd. Thomas Reid Papers, 1982-87, TulaneMedicine, 1984-87, Healthcare New Orleans, 1991-92. Author: Signor Faranta's Iron Theatre, 1982 (nominated Bernard Hewitt award for outstanding rsch. in theatre history 1982); editor: Thomas Reid Papers; contbr. to Back Porch, Paper Dance News and Satire; contbr. articles to profl. jours.; reviewer Bookscapes. Recipient travel grants. Mem. Phi Kappa Phi. Home: 129 Beau Pre Dr Mandeville LA 70471-1527

HARTSELL, MICHAEL REED, nurse; b. Knoxville, Tenn., Nov. 21, 1958; s. James Reed and Maxine (Snow) H.; m. Robin Renee Williams, June 5, 1982; 1 child, Nathaniel Reed. Diploma, East Tenn. Bapt. Hosp., 1981. RN, Tenn. Staff nurse East Tenn. Bapt. Hosp., Knoxville, 1981-82; staff nurse open heart unit U. Tenn. Hosp., Knoxville, 1982-86, hyperbaric nurse specialist, 1986-87, hyperbaric nursing supr., 1987—. Editor: Baromedical Nurses Assn. Newsletter, 1988—. Recipient Dist. II Leadership award Tenn. Nursing Assn., 1981. Mem. Baromed. Nursing Assn. (pres. 1994-95), Undersea Hyperbaric and Med. Soc. (assoc.). Office: U Tenn Meml Hosp 1924 Alcoa Hwy Knoxville TN 37920-1511

HARTSOCK, PAMELA ANN, English language educator; b. Berwyn, Ill., Mar. 20, 1968; d. James Albert and Elizabeth Ann (Holub) Masden; m. Craig Anthony Hartsock. BA, Ea. Ill. U., Charleston, 1990, MA, 1991; postgrad., U. Mo., 1991—. Instr. English, Ea. Ill. U., 1990-91; instr. English, U. Mo., Columbia, 1992-95, acad. advisor, 1995; instr. English, St. Leo Coll., Hampton, Va., 1996—. Mem. MLA, Soc. Early Americanists, Am. Lit. Assn., Soc. 18th Century Studies, Nat. Coun. Tchrs. English, Friends Benjamin Franklin Soc. Democrat. Lutheran.

HARTT, GROVER, III, lawyer; b. Dallas, Apr. 12, 1948; s. Grover Jr. and Dorothy June (Wilkins) H. BA, So. Meth. U., 1970, LLM in Tax, 1986; JD, Tex. Tech U., 1973. Bar: Tex. 1973, U.S. Dist. Ct. (no. dist.) Tex. 1974, U.S. Dist. Ct. (we. dist.) Tex. 1975, U.S. Ct. Appeals (5th cir.) 1975, U.S. Supreme Ct. 1976. Law clk. to presiding justice Ct. Criminal Appeals Tex., Austin, 1973-75; atty. Hartt and Hartt, Dallas, 1975-79; atty., advisor Office Spl. Counsel U.S. Dept. Energy, Dallas, 1979-80, dep. chief counsel, 1981-83; trial atty. tax divsn. U.S. Dept. Justice, Dallas, 1983-86, dep. atty.-in-charge tax divsn., 1986-95, asst. chief southwestern region civil trial sect. tax divsn., 1995—. Contbg. author: Collier on Bankruptcy. Mem. ABA, Tex. Bar Assn., Dallas Bar Assn. Office: US Dept Justice Tax Div 717 N Harwood St Ste 400 Dallas TX 75201-6506

HARTUNG, PATRICIA MCENTEE, therapist; b. Syracuse, N.Y.; d. James Henry and Frances Julia (Yehle) McEntee; m. Duane James Hartung, July 30, 1960; children: James Joseph, Tamara Ann, John Patrick, Jennifer Lynn. BS, LeMoyne Coll., 1957; MSW, Boston U., 1959. Diplomate Am. Bd. Examiners in Clin. Social Work; lic. social worker, Fla. Social worker Dept. of Pub. Welfare/Child Welfare Div., Bay Shore, N.Y., 1959-60, Dept. Pub. Welfare/Alcohol Rehab. Prog., Omaha, 1961; cons./social worker Carnegie Gardens Nursing Home, Melbourne, Fla., 1970-72; parent educator Brevard Community Coll., Cocoa, Fla., 1968-74; therapist Circles of Care, Rockledge, Fla., 1974-81; program dir. Circles of Care, Titusville, 1981-93, therapist, 1981—; adv. com. When Entering New Directions I, Cocoa, 1988-93; mem. Family Svc. Planning Team, Titusville, 1991-93. Mem. NASW, AAUW (Cen. Brevard chpt., v.p. membership 1991-93, pres. 1993-95), Fla. Alcohol and Drug Assn., Acad. Cert. Social Workers. Democrat. Roman Catholic. Office: Circles of Care 6700 S US # 1 Titusville FL 32780

HARTWIG, RICHARD ERIC, political science educator; b. N.Y.C., Dec. 14, 1942; s. Helmut Arthur and Anna Beata (Erickson) H.; 1 child, Sophie Anne. Student, U. Hamburg, Germany, 1962-63; BS in Govt. and German, So. Ill. U., 1965; student, U. La Plata, Argentina, 1966; MA in Polit. Sci., U. Wis., 1967, PhD, 1980. Charles E. Culpepper fellow Wesleyan U., 1981-82; asst. prof. Ill. State U., 1982-85; assoc. prof. Troy State U., Europe, 1985-86; from asst. to assoc. prof. Valdosta (Ga.) State Coll., 1986-90; Fulbright fellow U. Monterrey, Mex., 1990-91; prof. Tech. Inst. (ITE SM), Monterrey, Mex., 1991-93; chair dept. Tex. A&M U., Kingsville, 1994—; instr. Vanderbilt U., Nashville, 1971-72; vis. asst. prof. Coe Coll., Iowa, 1973, 74, Coll. Charleston, S.C., 1978-79, Tex. A&I Univ., 1980-81; lectr. Marquette U., 1977; vis. instr. Iowa State U., 1978; cons. World Bank Transp. Dept. 1983-84; reviewer for NEH grants. Author: Roads to Reason: Transportation, Administration and Rationality in Colombia, 1988; co-producer Nicaragua Jour., Pub. Radio, 1990 (Citation for Excellence Overseas Press Club 1991); contbr. articles to profl. jours., book revs for Am. Polit. Sci. Rev., Am. Rev. of Pub. Adminstrn., Nelson Hall Pubs. Recipient Woodrow Wilson fellowship 1965-66, 1967-68, Rotary Internat. fellowship, 1966-67, NSF traineeship 1989, Fulbright Hayes Dissertation fellowship, 1970. Office: Tex A&M U Kingsville Polit Sci Dept Kingsville TX 78363

HARTWIG, ROBERT PAUL, economist; b. Providence, Mar. 26, 1964; s. Robert Joseph and Rachel Aileen (Morin) H.; m. Laura Michelle Warner, May 19, 1990; 1 child, Jordan Alexander. BA in Econs. cum laude, U. Mass., 1986; MS in Econs., U. Ill., 1988, PhD in Econs., 1993. Instr. econs. U. Ill., Urbana-Champaign, 1986-89, rsch. asst. Bur. Econ. and Bus. Rsch., 1988-91, project coord. Bur. Econ. and Bus. Rsch., 1989-91; statistician Directorate for Epidemiology U.S. Consumer Product Safety Commn., Washington, 1991-93; sr. economist, instr. Nat. Coun. on Compensation Ins., Boca Raton, Fla., 1993—; adj. prof. econs. Fla. Atlantic U., 1996—; econ. cons. Office of Pres. of U. Ill., Urbana, 1990-91, Aerosol Industry Devel. Assn., Niles, Ill., 1990-91, Office of Atty. Gen. of State of Ill., Springfield, summer 1989. Contbr. articles to profl. jours. Mem. Am. Econ. Assn., Am. Risk and Ins. Assn. Office: Nat Coun Compensation Ins 750 Park Of Commerce Dr Boca Raton FL 33487-3621

HARTY, JOHN, III, humanities educator; b. Memphis, Aug. 11, 1945; s. John Jr. and Lorraine (Gardener) H. BS, U.S. Naval Acad., 1968; MA, U. Richmond, 1976; PhD, U. Md., 1985. Faculty J. Sargeant Reynolds C.C., 1975, East Carolina U., 1976-77, U.S. Naval Acad., 1977-82; faculaty Montgomery Coll., 1985, U. Fla., Gainesville, 1986-89, No. Mich. U., 1989-90, Alice Lloyd Coll., Pippa Passes, Ky., 1991—. Author: Tom Stoppard: A Casebook, 1988, James Joyce's Finnegans Wake: A Casebook, 1991; guest editor Abstracts of English Studies, Vol. 26 supplement, James Joyce Quar., 1983; contbr. articles to profl. jours. EPDA fellow for English tchrs., Western Carolina U., 1976, NEH fellow, 1987, N.E. MLA summer fellow, 1987, NEH summer fellow, 1991; U.S. Naval Acad. Rsch. Coun. grantee, 1979, 80, 81. Office: Alice Lloyd Coll Humanities Dept Pippa Passes KY 41844

HARTZLER, GENEVIEVE LUCILLE, physical education educator; b. Hammond, Ind., June 19, 1921; d. Lewis Garvin and Effie May (Orton) H. BS in Edn., Ind. U., 1944; MEd, U. Minn., 1948. Tchr. phys. edn. Griffith (Ind.) Pub. Schs., 1944-45, Northrup Collegiate Sch., Mpls., 1945-47; supr. student tchrs., 1947-79; tchr. phys. edn. Marquette (Mich.) Pub. Schs., 1948-50, Albion (Mich.) Pub. Schs., 1951-56; tchr. phys. edn. Jackson (Mich.) Pub. Schs., 1957-79, coord., project dir., tchr., coach, 1979-83; chair equity workshop Jackson Pub. Schs., 1979-83; chair various convs., 1964-70. Mem. Am. Heart Assn., Jackson, 1977-83; mem., chair Women in Mgmt., Jackson, 1981-83; mem. Bus. and Profl. Women, Jackson, 1980-90. Recipient Honor awards Young Women's Christian Assn. and Mich. Divsn. Girls and Women's Sports. Mem. AAHPERD, NEA, Mich. Assn. Health, Phys. Edn. and Recreation (Honor award), Mich. Edn. Assn. (Women's Cultural award), Delta Kappa Gamma (Woman of Distinction award). Home: 703 Bay Meadows Cir Lady Lake FL 32159-2285

HARVARD, ASHLEY WHEELER, primary school educator; b. Birmingham, Ala., Oct. 22, 1971; d. John Paul and Janet Kay (Heptinstall) Wheeler; m. Lucius Bryant Harvard III, July 30, 1994. BS in Early Childhood Edn. cum laude, Auburn U., 1994. Cert. tchr., Ga. 1st grade tchr. Garrison-Pilcher Elem. Sch., Thomasville, Ga.; intern U. Ky. Consortium for Overseas Tchg., Christchurch, New Zealand, 1994. Mem. NEA, Ala. Assn. for Early Childhood Edn., Assn. for Childhood Edn. Internat. Republican. Presbyterian. Home: 5163 US Hwy 19 S Thomasville GA 31792 Office: Garrison-Pilcher Elem Sch Rt 2 Box 2 Hall Rd Thomasville GA 31792

HARVARD, BEVERLY JOYCE BAILEY, police chief; b. Macon, Ga., Dec. 22, 1950; d. Arcelious and Irene (Perkins) Bailey; m. Jimmy C. Harvard, 1972; 1 child: Christa. BA, Morris Brown Coll., 1972; MS, Ga. State U., 1980. Cert. FBI Nat. Acad. Police officer Police Bur. City of Atlanta, crime analysis officer Police Bur., exec. protection officer Police Bur., dep. chief of police, spl. asst. to commr. dept. pub. safety, dir. pub. affairs dept. pub. safety, chief of police, 1994—; commr. Commn. Accreditation for Law Enforcement Agys., 1991; bd. dirs. Met. Atlanta ARC, 1991, Coun. on Battered Women, 1991; trustee Leadership Atlanta, 1991; adv. bd. dir. Big Bros./Big Sisters, 1986—, Atlanta Victim/Witness Assistance Program, 1985—. Named Outstanding Atlantan, 1983, Alumna Yr., Morris Brown Coll., 1985, Bronze Woman Yr., Iota Phi Lambda, 1986, Woman Achiever Atlanta YWCA; recipient Trailblazer award for Law Enforcement City of Atlanta. Mem. Internat. Assn. Chiefs Police (tng. com. Ga. chpt.), Nat. Orgn. Black Law Enforcement (chmn. program), Bus. System Planning Team, Ga. State U. Alumni Assn. (bd. dirs. Atlanta chpt.), Delta Sigma Theta (parliamentarian). Office: Police Svcs City Hall 9th Fl 675 Ponce De Leon Ave NE Atlanta GA 30308-1807

HARVEY, BILLY DALE, landman; b. Greenville, Tex., Sept. 9, 1950; s. William Powell and Etta Dell (Wright) H.; m. Lana Lee Duncan, Aug. 27, 1972 (div. May 1991); children: Bradley Dexter, Ryan Jeremy. BBA, U. Tex., 1972. Cert. Profl. Landman. Landman Shell Oil Co., various cities, 1972-78, Mitchell Energy Corp., The Woodlands, Tex., 1978—. V.p. Shenandoah (Tex.) Home Owners Assn., 1981. Mem. Am. Assn. Petroleum Landmen, North Houston Assn. Petroleum Landmen (dir. 1984-85), Houston Assn. Petroleum Landmen, Woodland Lions Club (pres. 1990-91), Alpha Kappa Psi (pledge trainer 1971-72), Chi Phi (sec. 1970-71, Best Mem. award 1971). Methodist. Office: Mitchell Energy Corp PO Box 4000 The Woodlands TX 77387-4000

HARVEY, DANIEL RICHARD, minister; b. Franklin, Pa., Aug. 27, 1930; s. Richard H. and Dorothy E. (Winder) H.; m. Lois V. Meyers, Mar. 7, 1953; children: Deborah, Stephen, Rebecca, Timothy, Rachel. BA, John Brown U., 1952; postgrad., Moody Bible Inst., 1953-54, Burnside-Ott Aviation, 1970-71. Ordained to ministry Trans World Radio Ch., 1956. Pastor Christian and Missionary Alliance, Siloam Springs, Ark., 1949-52, Urbana, Ill., 1953-55; missionary Trans World Radio, various locations, 1956—; evangelist, 1992—; chaplain Guam Dept. Pub. Safety, Agana, 1975-82, Lakeland, Fla. Police Dept., 1991—; chmn. bd. dirs. Chaplaincy Corps, 1991-93; civilian chaplain USN, Agana, 1975-82. Bd. dirs. ARC, Agana, 1976-82. Named to Ancient Order of Chammori, Govt. of Guam, 1982; recipient citation Comdr. Naval Forces Marianas, USN, 1982. Home: 4818 Leisurewood Ln Lakeland FL 33811-1592 Office: Trans World Radio PO Box 8700 Cary NC 27512-8700

HARVEY, DREAMA JOYCE, operating room nurse; b. Kanawha County, W.Va, Dec. 18, 1945; d. Alex A. and Myrtie L. (Young) Birchfield; m. Kenneth L. Blankenship, June 12, 1964 (div. Feb. 1991); children: Kenneth L. II, Helena Gail; m. Ronald E. Harvey, June 2, 1994. Lic. Practical Nurse, Cabell County Career Ctr., Huntington, W.Va., 1975; diploma, St. Marys Sch. Nursing, Huntington, 1980. Cert. in perioperative nursing. Staff nurse Huntington Hosp., 1980-82; nurse clinician II Cabell Huntington (W.Va.) Hosp., 1982—. Mem. Assn. Operating Room Nurses (past sec. local chpt.).

HARVEY, HERSCHEL AMBROSE, JR., glass and marketing company executive; b. Steubenville, Ohio, Sept. 16, 1929; s. Herschel Ambrose and Josephine (Bernert) H.; BSBA, U. Notre Dame, 1951; postgrad. Mich. State U., 1958; m. Thelma F. Freeman, July 4, 1974; children: Herschel A. III, Debra, H.R. Indsl. engr. Uniroyal, N.Y.C., 1951-53; indsl. rels. mgr. Brunswick Co., Chgo., 1956-64; pres. Harvey Industries, Inc., Clarksburg, W.Va., 1964-90, Hersh Harvey Assocs., Inc., Georgetown, S.C., 1974—, Harvey Glass, Inc., Georgetown, S.C., 1986—. Bd. dirs. Am. Cancer Soc. Lt. USNR, 1953-56. Mem. VFW (life), Am. Ceramic Soc., Alumna Club Sorin Soc. U. Notre Dame. Republican. Roman Catholic. Home: DeBordieu Colony 3 Prospect Ct W Georgetown SC 29440-7106 Office: Hersh Harvey Assocs Inc PO Box 1099 Georgetown SC 29442-1099

HARVEY, HILDA RUTH, special education educator; b. Kingsville, Tex., Sept. 6, 1950; d. Nicolas Guerra and Maria de Jesus (Sanchez) Montalvo; m. Steve Allen Harvey, Oct. 20, 1978 (div. Nov. 1991); children: John, Kristy. BA, Tex. Wesleyan Univ., 1982; cert., Univ. Mary Hardin Baylor, 1985. Cert. secondary edn. educator. Tchr. adult edn. Ctrl. Tex. Coll., Killeen, 1985-86; tchr. homebound Fort Worth Ind. Sch. Dist., 1986-87, psychoednl. instr., 1987-91, adult ESL instr., 1988-90; spl. educator Killeen (Tex.) Ind. Sch. Dist., 1991—; fgn. lang. chmn. Manor Mid. Sch., Killeen, Tex., 1995—; cons. Fort Worth Ind. Sch. Dist., 1990-91. With USAF, USAFR, U.S. Army Res., 1975—. Recipient Outstanding Coach-Girls Softball Dependent Youth Activity Ctr., 1983. Fellow ASCD; mem. AAUW, Tex. State Tchrs. Assn., Disabled Am. Vets., Century Club, Sigma Delta Pi. Republican. Southern Baptist. Office: Manor Mid Sch 1700 S WS Young Dr Killeen TX 76543

HARVEY, J. ERNEST, JR., agricultural company executive; b. Abbeville, Ga., Sept. 15, 1935; married; 2 children. Student, Abraham Baldwin Agrl. Coll., 1954-56; BSA in Agronomy, U. Ga., 1960, MS in Genetics, 1962, PhD in Agronomy, 1967. Rsch. asst. grass breeding Coastal Plains Experiment Sta, Tifton, Ga., 1960-61, asst. agronomist peanut breeding, 1962-65; dir. peanut seed rsch. Gold Kist Peanuts, divsn. Gold Kist Inc., Ashburn, Ga., 1967-69; dir. agronomic rsch. Gold Kist Inc., Ashburn, 1970-80; dir. rsch. AgrTech Seeds, Inc. subs. Gold Kist Inc., Ashburn, 1981—. Contbr. articles to sci. publs.; patentee in field. With U.S. Army, 1956-57. Mem. Am. Soc. Agronomy (Ga. sect.), Am. Genetics Assn., Am. Peanut Rsch. and Edn. Assn., Crop Sci. Soc. Am., Ga. Soybean Assn., Ga. Crop Improvement Assn. (dir., chmn. peanut commodity com., chmn. seed cert. com.). Office: PO Box 644 Ashburn GA 31714-0644

HARVEY, JAMES E., graphic communications executive; b. Buffalo, Nov. 12, 1962; s. Roger K. and Carol Ann (Siegel) H.; m. Susan Barbara Harvey, June 6, 1987; 1 child, Eric James. BA, SUNY, Buffalo, 1985. Mktg. specialist Volt Info. Scis., Inc., Bethesda, Md., 1987-88; mktg. mgr. Volt Info. Scis., Inc., Chantilly, Va., 1988-90, bus. devel. mgr., 1990-93; dir. spectrum ops. Graphic Comm. Assn., Alexandria, Va., 1993-95; v.p. Graphic Comm. Assn., 1995—; mem. CALS Electronic Publishing Com. Capt. USAR, 1981-92. Mem. Soc. Automobile Engrs. (job task force 1992-94), Graphic Comm. Assn., Tech. Assn. Graphic Arts, Am. Nat. Standards Inst. (IT2 and IT8 coms.), Com. for Graphic Arts Tech. Specifications, Digital Printing Coun., Specifications for Web Offset Printing, Gen. Requirements for Applications in Comml. Offset Lithography Com., Industry Policy and Direction Com. Home: 1908 Harcourt Ave Crofton MD 21114-2104 Office: Graphic Comm Assn 100 Daingerfield Rd Alexandria VA 22314-2888

HARVEY, JAMES MATHEWS, JR., instructional media producer, columnist; b. Detroit, Dec. 5, 1964; s. James M. and Leotha (Frazier) H. BS, Troy State U., 1987. Media assoc. Ctr. for Environ. Rsch., Troy, Ala., 1987-88; producer, dir. Coop. Extension Svc. (became Coop. Extension Sys. 1995), Auburn, Ala., 1988—. Dir. videos including: Nature's Way, 1988, Red Drum: A Struggle for Survival, 1989, Pond Management, 1991; slide series including: Nature's Way, 1988, Beach Mice and Their Habitat, 1989; dir., editor Safety in the Logging Woods series, 1989-95, Forestry in Alabama, 1993, Small Business Resources Series, 1995, Adult Education Principles for Loggers, 1996, Multiple Use Management, 1996; assoc. producer, dir. Extension Today, 1990; assoc. producer satellite programs Principles of Parenting and State of Our Environment, 1991, White-Tailed Deer Management, 1991-92, Residential Landscaping, 1992, Small Business Resources, 1994, Wildlife Damage Management, 1995, Alabama Forest Resources Today, 1996; creator, producer Ala. 4-H Congress Video, 1990—, 4-H Performing Arts Video, 1993-94; prodr., dir. Street Trees and Sewing Update for Entrepreneurs, 1994, Tax Fraud Prevention, 1995; guest columnist The Messenger, 1993—. Mem. agrl. adv. com. Pike County H.S., Brundidge, Ala., 1983-95, pres. 1995—; bd. dirs. Pike County Agrl. Complex Bd. Mem. Assn. Ednl. Communications and Tech., Troy State U. Journalism Alumni Assn., So. Region Ext. Video Prodrs. Baptist. Office: Ala Coop Extension Sys Duncan Hall Anx Auburn AL 36849-5634

HARVEY, KIM LYLE, chemical engineer; b. New Orleans, Dec. 8, 1953; s. Lyle Henry and Ruth Lorraine (Loutzenheiser) H.; m. Margarita R. Bensussan, June 1, 1973; children: Michael, Ryan, Kevin, Scott. BSChemE, Tulane U., 1976. Registered prof. engr. in chem. & environ. engring. Process engr., project engr. Taft Plant Union Carbide, Hahnville, La., 1976-

85; environ. compliance engr. Taft Plant Union Carbide, Hahnville, 1985—. Cub Scouts pack master Boys Scouts Am., Harahan, La., 1986-88, asst. Scout master, Luling, La., 1989—; soccer coach St. Charles Parish Recreation, Luling, 1992. Mem. La. Chem. Assn. (solid waste com. 1985—). Office: Union Carbide Taft Plant PO Box 50 Hahnville LA 70057-0050

HARVEY, LEIGH KATHRYN, lawyer; b. Abilene, Tex.; d. Jasper Elliott and Kathryn E. (McDaniel) H.; m. Bert Gubbels, Oct. 1983 (div. 1993). BA cum laude, U. Tex., 1971, JD, 1974. Bar: Tex. 1975. Asst. atty. City of San Angelo, Tex., 1974-77; asst. dist. atty. County of Fort Bend, Richmond, Tex., 1978; pvt. practice various cities, Tex., 1977—. Bd. dirs. Tom Green County Community Action Council, San Angelo, 1975-77, pres. 1976; vol. judge bd. advs. U. Tex. Law Sch., Austin, 1980; mem. Met. Austin 2000, 1982; mem. vestry St. Mary's Episcopal Ch., Lampasas, Tex., 1989-91. Recipient Young Careerist award Dist. 7 Bus. and Profl. Women's Club, 1977. Mem. ABA, Tex. Bar Assn. (legal forms com. manual for Real Estate Transactions rev. edit. 1986-92), Travis County Bar Assn., Bell Lampasas Mills County Bar Assn. (sr. citizen project 1986). Episcopalian. Office: PO Box 926 Lampasas TX 76550-0926

HARVEY, PETER MARSHALL, podiatrist; b. Lubbock, Tex., Nov. 12, 1941; s. Marshall and Betty (Compton) H.; B.S., Tex. Tech. U., 1962; grad. Ill. Coll. Podiatric Medicine, 1966; m. Sue Kadane, Feb. 1, 1981; children by previous marriage—Jason, Jacob; stepchildren—Chris Robertson, Jill Robertson, Brent Robertson. Intern, Community Hosp., Lubbock, Tex., 1966-67; practice podiatry specializing in foot surgery, Wichita Falls, Tex., 1967—; bd. dirs. Podiatry Ins. Co. Am. Mem. Am. Podiatry Med. Assn. (Tex. del. to ho. of dels. 1985—), Tex. Podiatry Med. Assn. (dir. 1975—, pres. 1982-83, Svc. award 1978), Am. Coll. Foot Surgeons (assoc.). PICA (chmn. claims com. 1984—). Republican. Office: 1612 10th St Wichita Falls TX 76301-4307

HARVEY, WALTER H(AYDEN), hematologist, medical oncologist; b. Shreveport, La., Feb. 12, 1949; s. Max Richard and Marion Lee (Polk) Campbell; m. M. Constance Mock, 1996; children: Merry Lee, Lexie Carl, Erica Dawn. BS, Ea. Tenn. State U., Johnson City, 1971; DO, Kirksville Coll. Osteo. Medicine, Kirksville, Mo., 1976. Diplomate Am. Osteo. Bd. Internal Medicine, Med. Oncology, Hematology. Rsch. chemist Beecham Pharms. Rsch. Divsn., Bristol, Tenn., 1971-72; intern Riverside Hosp. of Wichita (Kans.), 1976-77, resident in internal medicine, 1977-79; fellow jr. faculty Am. Cancer Soc.-M.D. Anderson Cancer Ctr., Houston, 1979-80; fellow in hematology and med. oncology Brooke Army Med. Ctr., San Antonio, 1980-82, dir. bone marrow transplant program, 1983-87; chief divsn. hematology and oncology Darnall Army Hosp., Ft. Hood, Tex., 1982-83; dir. bone marrow transplant lab., clin. rsch. U. Tex. Med. Br., Galveston, 1987-91; pvt. practice clin. rsch. Ft. Myers, Fla., 1991-93; clin. rschr. Hematology/Oncology Assocs. S.W. Fla., Naples, 1993—. Maj. M.C., U.S. Army, 1980-87. Recipient Army Svc. Ribbon, 1982, Army Commendation Medal, 1983, Meritorious Svc. medal, 1987, Def. Svc. Medal Desert Shield, 1990. Mem. AMA, AAAS, Internat. Soc. for Hematotherapy and Graft Engrng., Am. Osteo. Assn., Am. Coll. Osteo. Internists, Assn. Mil. Osteo. Physicians and Surgeons, Assn. Mil. Surgeons U.S., S.W. Oncology Group, Am. Soc. Clin. Oncology, Pediat. Oncology Group, Am. Soc. Hematology, Am. Soc. for Blood and Marrow Transplantation, So. Med. Assn., So. Assn. for Oncology (founder), Fla. Soc. Clin. Oncology, Lee County Med. Soc., Collier County Med. Soc., Am. Cancer Soc. (chmn. lung cancer task force 1991-94), Leukemia Soc. Am. (mem. exec. com. 1993-94), Leukemia Soc. Am. (mem. adv. com. 1994—). Office: Hematology/Oncology Assocs SW Fla 671 Goodlette Rd N Ste 200 Naples FL 34102-5615

HARVEY, WILLIAM GIPSON, JR., physician; b. Tulsa, June 10, 1925; s. William Gipson and Bernice Cole (Johnson) H.; m. Willie Maude Weeks, Aug. 22, 1949; children: Gayle Allison, John Robert, Jan Elizabeth, Paul William. BS, Okla. Bapt. U., Shawnee, 1949; MD, U. Okla., 1953. Pvt. practice Beaver, Okla., 1961-90; physician Med Plus, Oklahoma City, 1990—. With USN, 1943-46. Republican. Baptist. Home: 8320 NW 107th St Oklahoma City OK 73162

HARVEY, WILLIAM ROBERT, university president; b. Brewton, Ala., Jan. 29, 1941; s. Willie D. C. and Mamie Claudis (Parker) H.; m. Norma Baker, Aug. 13, 1966; children: Kelly Renee, William Christopher, Leslie Denise. BA, Talladega Coll., 1961; EdD, Harvard U., 1971. Asst. to dean Harvard U. Grad. Sch. Edn., 1969-70; adminstrv. asst. to pres. Fisk U., Nashville, 1970-72; v.p. student affairs/dir. planning Tuskegee (Ala.) Inst., 1972-75, v.p. adminstrv. services, 1976-78; pres. Hampton (Va.) U., 1978—; owner Pepsi-Cola Bottling Co., Houghton, Mich., 1987—, also bd. dirs.; dir. Signet Bank, Richmond, Va., Blue Cross Blue Shield Va., Va. Air and Space-Hampton Rds. History Ctr., Internat. Guaranty Ins. Co., Am. Coun. Edn. Contbr. articles to profl. jours. Bd. dirs. United Way, Peninsula Econ. Devel. Council; mem., vice-chmn. President's nat. adv. council ESEA; mem. Harvard U. Alumni Council.; trustee Va. Mus. Fine Arts, Va. Hist. Soc. Served with U.S. Army, 1962-65. Woodrow Wilson Martin Luther King fellow, 1968-70; Woodrow Wilson Found. intern fellow, 1970-72; Harvard U. Higher Edn. Adminstrv. fellow, 1968-70. Mem. Am. Council Edn., Am. Assn. Higher Edn., Nat. Assn. Equal Opportunity in Higher Edn., Va. Assn. Higher Edn., Peninsula C. of C. (dir.), Omega Psi Phi. Baptist. Office: Hampton U Office of Pres Hampton VA 23668

HARVILL, MELBA SHERWOOD, university librarian; b. Bryson, Tex., Jan. 22, 1933; d. William Henry and Delta Verlin (Brawner) Sherwood; m. L. E. Harvill Jr., Feb. 2, 1968; children: Sherman T. III, Mark Roling. BA, North Tex. State Coll., 1954; MA, North Tex. State U., 1968, MLS, 1973, PhD, 1984. Tchr. Graham (Tex.) Ind. Sch. Dist., 1966-68; reference libr. Midwestern U., Wichita Falls, 1968-73; dir. librs. Midwestern State U., Wichita Falls, 1973—; presenter in field. Vol. Boy Scouts Am., Wichita Falls, 1969-74, Conv. and Visitors Bus. Falls Fifty, 1993—; vol. Wichita Falls Sr.-Jr. Forum, 1978—, mem. exec. bd. girls club, ways and means com., sec., asst. treas.; chmn. United Way, Midwestern State U., 1975-76; mem. talent coordinating com. Wichita Falls Centennial Celebration; mem. U. North Tex. Advancement Adv. Coun.; vol. Conv. and Vis. Bur., Lone Stars, 1993—; bd. dirs. YWCA Wichita Falls, 1987-94, pres. bd. dirs., 1989-91, 94-95; grad. Leadership Wichita Falls, 1990. Recipient Svc. award Sr.-Jr. Forum, Wichita Falls United Way Community Svc. award, 1975, Svc. award YWCA Bd. Dirs., 1991; named Met. BPW Woman of Yr., 1980. Mem. ALA, LWV (program v.p., pres. 1991-92), Tex. Libr. Assn. (mem. planning com., mem. membership com., mem. legis. com., mem. rsch. and grants com., chairperson dist VII, chairperson adminstrn. round table), Tex. Coun. State U. Librs. (sec.-treas. 1990-92), Wichita Falls Rotary North (sec. 1993—), U. North Tex. Alumni Assn. (bd. dirs. 1992-94), Phi Alpha Theta, Pi Sigma Alpha, Phi Delta Phi, Gamma Theta Upsilon, Alpha Chi, Beta Phi Mu, Phi Delta Kappa. Democrat. Home: 4428 BUS 287J Iowa Park TX 76367 Office: Midwestern State U 3410 Taft Blvd Wichita Falls TX 76308-2095

HARVILL-DICKSON, CLARA GEAN, medical facility administrator; b. Humphrey, Ark., Nov. 9, 1940; d. Clarence Lee and Lillian Pearl (Vanlandingham) Harvill; widowed; 1 child, Cynthia Summer. BS, Rollins Coll., 1987. Supr. Orlando (Fla.) Regional Med. Ctr., 1968-70; exec. sec. Gilmer-Uricchio Orthopaedic Assocs., Orlando, 1970-72; dir. clinic Orlando Orthopaedic Ctr., 1972—. Mem. adv. bd. Webster Sch., Orlando, 1983—; tchr. Sunday sch. and youth activities 1st United Meth. Ch., Orlando. Mem. Med. Group Mgmt. Assn., Med. Office Mgrs. Assn. (founding pres. 1972-76), Bones, Human Resource Soc. Republican. Home: 1254 Saint Tropez Cir Orlando FL 32806-5552 Office: Orlando Orthopaedic Ctr 100 W Gore St Ste 500 Orlando FL 32806-1049

HARWELL, DAVID WALKER, retired state supreme court chief justice; b. Florence, S.C., Jan. 8, 1932; s. Baxter Hicks and Lacy (Rankin) H.; divorced; children: Robert Bryan, William Baxter. LL.B., J.D., U. S.C., 1958; HHD (hon.), Frances Marion U., 1987. Bar: S.C. 1958, U.S. Dist. Ct. S.C. 1958, U.S. Ct. Appeals 1964, U.S. Supreme Ct. 1961. Circuit judge 12th Jud. Ct. S.C., 1973-80; justice S.C. Supreme Ct., 1980-91, chief justice, 1991-94; ret., 1994; spl. counsel Nelson, Mullins, Riley and Scarborough; pres. Resolute Systems of S.C., 1994—. Mem. S.C. Ho. of Reps., 1962-73. Served with USNR, 1952-54. Mem. Am. Bar Assn., Am. Trial Lawyers Assn., S.C. Bar Assn., S.C. Trial Lawyers Assn. (Portrait and Scholarship award 1986). Presbyterian. Office: PO Box 2459 Myrtle Beach SC 29578-2459

HARWELL, LINDA MARYANN, nursing educator; b. Detroit, Mar. 24, 1953; d. John F. and Marjorie A. (Near) Logan; m. Charles L. Harwell, Aug. 2, 1975; children: Amy, Megan, Shawn. BSN, No. Mich. U., 1975; MEd in Adult Edn., U. Ark., 1984; MNSc, U. Ark. for Med. Scis., 1989. RN, Ark. Instr. in nursing edn. VA Med. Ctr., Fayetteville, Ark.; instr. dept. nursing U. Ark., Fayetteville; dir. area health edn. ctr. N.W. U. Ark. for Med. Scis., Fayetteville. Mem. Ark. Nurse's Assn. (pres. Dist. 9 1985-86, 88-89), Gamma Xi chpt. Sigma Theta Tau. Home: 1318 San Miguel Dr Springdale AR 72762-2142

HARWOOD, STEVEN J., nuclear medicine physician, consultant; b. N.Y.C., Sept. 6, 1942; s. Ferd C. and Anita J. (Steinberg) H.; m. Sandra C. Pfeffer, June 4, 1967; children: Jay Benjamin, Beth Ann, Michelle Denise. BS, Carnegie-Mellon U., 1964; MS, U. Wis., 1967, PhD, 1970; MD, U. Ala., 1975. Diplomate Am. Bd. Pathology, Am. Bd. Nuclear Medicine. Resident in nuclear medicine, clin. pathology U. Ala., Birmingham, 1975-77; staff physician Univ. Hosp., Augusta, Ga., 1977-80; assoc. prof. radiology, pathology U. S.C. Med. Sch., Columbia, 1980-81; chief nuclear medicine svc. Bay Pines (Fla.) VA Med. Ctr., 1981—; adj. clin. prof. pathology Med. Coll. Ga., 1977-80; clin. asst. prof. radiology U. So. Fla., Tampa, 1986—; prin. investigator grantee using monoclonal antibodies for detection of cancer and bone infection, 1985—; pathology cons. State of Fla., Pub. Health Lab., 1994—; presenter papers nat. and internat. meetings in field. Contbr. more than 100 papers, book chpts. in field. Founder Tampa Bay Symphony, Seminole, Fla., 1987—, v.p., 1987—; spl. advisor VA Nat. Med. Music Group, Washington, 1991—; coun. mem. Southeast chpt. Soc. Nuc. Medicine, 1994—. Mem. Nat. Assn. VA Chiefs of Nuclear Medicine (coun. mem.), Soc. Nuc. Medicine, Clin. Ligand Assay Soc., Rotary Club Seminole (Paul Harris fellow). Jewish. Office: Nuclear Medicine Svc Bay Pines VA Med Ctr Bay Pines FL 33504

HASEMAN, JOSEPH KYD, biostatistician, researcher; b. Sheffield, Ala., July 20, 1943; s. Joseph Fish and Margaret Truella (Kyd) H.; m. Mary Janelle Hood, Nov. 25, 1972; children: David, Ashley. BS in Math. cum laude, Davidson Coll., 1965; PhD in Biostats., U. N.C., 1970. Rsch. math. statistician Nat. Inst. Environ. Health Scis., Research Triangle Park, N.C., 1970—; mem. working group Internat. Agy. for Rsch. on Cancer, 1986, 87. Assoc. editor Shorter Comm., Biometrics, 1979-84; bd. editors Environ. Health Perspectives, 1980—; mem. editorial bd. Fundamental and Applied Toxicology, 1986-92; contbr. articles to profl. jours. Pres. Tarheel Swimming Assn., Raleigh, N.C., 1990-91; officer Longbow coun. YMCA Indian Guides/Princesses, Raleigh, 1991. Recipient Dir.'s award NIH, 1983. Fellow Am. Statis. Assn.; mem. Biometric Soc., Soc. Toxicology, Genotoxicity and Environ. Mutagen Soc., Phi Beta Kappa. Democrat. Methodist. Home: 2408 Ferguson Rd Raleigh NC 27612-6904 Office: Nat Inst Environ Health Sci PO Box 12233 Research Triangle Park NC 27709

HASIUK, CYNTHIA LEE, nurse practitioner, psychotherapist; b. Hartford, Conn., Oct. 8, 1950; d. Leslie Eugene and Joan Lee (Carrington) Stevens; m. Walter Hasiuk, Aug. 13, 1976. LPN, Mesa (Ariz.) Community Coll., 1972; ADN, Mohegan Community Coll., Norwich, Conn., 1977; BSN, U. Hartford, 1984; MA in Counseling, St. Joseph Coll., 1987. Cert. adult nurse practitioner, advanced practice RN. Adult nurse practitioner Dr. Edward Sawicki, Internist, Willimantic, Conn., 1983-88, U. Conn., Storrs, 1988-91; advanced practice RN Hartford Hosp., 1991-92; pvt. practice in psychotherapy Amston, Conn., 1987—; advanced practice RN Health Care Ptnrs. of Conway, Conway, S.C., 1992—; supr. tng. transactional analysis, 1989-92; healing touch practitioner Healing Touch Workshop-Level I, II-A, II-B and III-A. Mem. ANA, S.C. Nurses Assn., Iota Upsilon (v.p. 1989-90), Sigma Theta Tau. Home: 521 Blythewood Walk Little River SC 29566-7656

HASKELL, PAUL GERSHON, law educator; b. Boston, Mar. 31, 1927; s. David Israel and Leah (Paris) H.; m. Sarah Potter Evarts, Jan. 22, 1955; children: Peter, Thomas, John. AB, Harvard U., 1948, LLB, 1951. Bar: N.Y. 1952. Assoc. Kelley, Drye, Newhall & Maginnes, N.Y.C., 1951-56, White & Case, N.Y.C., 1956-59; asst. gen. counsel The Houston Corp., St. Petersburg, Fla., 1959-60; resident counsel, asst. treas. Ednl. Testing Service, Princeton, N.J., 1960-62; prof. law Georgetown U., Washington, 1962-67, Case Western Res. U., Cleve., 1967-79; prof. law U. N.C., Chapel Hill, 1979-83, Graham Kenan prof. law, 1983-91, William R. Kenan prof. law, 1991—. Co-author: Preface to Estates In Land and Future Interests, 1966, 2d edit., 1984; author: Preface to the Law of Trusts, 1975, Preface to Wills, Trusts and Adminstration, 1987, 2d edit. 1994; contbr. articles to profl. jours. Bd. dirs. Cleve. Fair Housing Inc., 1967-70; trustee Harvard Club of Cleve., 1976-79. Served with USN, 1945-46. Am. Coll. Trust and Estate Counsel fellow. Mem. ABA (spl. com. to revise standards for legal edn. 1970-73, sect. on legal edn. and admissions to bar 1973-76, standing com. on legal assts. 1976-80), N.C. Assn. Scholars (chmn., bd. dirs. 1994—). Republican. Home: 1805 Rolling Rd Chapel Hill NC 27514-7505 Office: The Univ of NC Sch of Law Chapel Hill NC 27514

HASPEL, ARTHUR CARL, podiatrist, surgeon; b. Bklyn., May 18, 1945; s. Ephriam and Sophie (Rabinowitz) H.; m. Anna Kiperman, Feb. 2, 1969; children: Mark Steven, Alan Charles. BS, L.I. U., 1967; D of Podiatric Medicine, Ohio Coll. Podiatric Medicine, 1972. Cert. Am. Bd. Ambulatory Foot Surgery, Am. Bd. Quality Assurance and Utilization Rev. in Podiatric Medicine, Am. Podiatric Med. Specialties Bd. in Surgery and Podiatric Medicine, Am. Acad. Pain Mgmt. Practice medicine specializing in podiatry Chgo., 1972-77, Hallandale, Fla., 1977—, Miami Shores, Fla., 1990-94; lectr. in field. Author HMOs- Long Term Effects, 1986, (with others) Lions and Retinitis Pigmentosa, 1982, Procedural Podiatric Service Codes, 1986. Bd. govs. Hillel Community Day Sch., 1980-82; mem. land acquisition and devel. com. Beth Torah Congregation, 1986; active Am. Red Magen David for Israel (charter 1st v.p. South Broward profl. chpt. 1980, 1st v.p. 1980—, fin. sec. 1980—, southeastern U.S. steering com. 1980-82), Highland Lakes Homeowners Assn. Fellow Acad. Ambulatory Foot Surgery (trustee, 1984-89, 91-93, mem. profl. standards com., research and devel. com., seminars com., ins. com., pres. Region IX, 1981-85, sec.-treas. 1979-81, mem.-at-large 1978-79, mem. adv. bd. 1985—, seminar coordinator 1979-85, chmn. statewide referral service, coordinator continuing med. edn. State of Fla. 1979-85), Am. Assn. Hosp. Podiatrists, Am. Podiatric Circulatory Assn., Am. Soc. Podiatric Medicine; mem. Am. Coll. Foot and Ankle Surgeons, Fla. Podiatric Med. Assn. (pres. 1990-91, 1st v.p. 1989-90, v.p. 1988-89, treas. 1987-88, sec. 1986-87, exec. com. sec. 1986-87, exec. bd. 1986, chmn. banner com. 1981, 86, chmn. pub. health com., 1982, co-chmn. membership com., 1983, 84, 85, mem. sci. and surg. program com. 1984—, chmn. sunshine com. 1986, chmn. profl. standards rev. orgn. 1982), Broward County Podiatric Med. Assn. (co-chmn. legis. appreciation night 1979-81, sec. 1981-83, sec. May Day com., sec. continuing med. edn. cert., March of Dimes Walk-a-Thon, health fairs, ethical advt. com.), Am. Podiatric Circulatory Assn., Am. Podiatric Med. Assn., Ill. Podiatry Assn., Fla. Podiatric Med. Assn. (del. to Am. Podiatric Med. Assn. 1989-93), Am. Pub. Health Assn., Ohio Coll. Podiatric Medicine Alumni Soc., Hallandale C. of C., Lions (charter treas. Fla. community hearing bank 1979, treas. 1979-82, 83-85, pres. 1982-83, v.p. 1985-87, exec. dir. 1983-84, mem. exec. com. 1979-84, TV and radio liaison 1982-84, bd. dirs. Hallandale club 1978-80, treas. 1978-80, charter treas. dist. 35A for Retinitis Pigmentosa 1980, treas. 1980-82, mem. exec. com. 1980-82, co-chmn. state com. on deaf and hearing impaired, multiple dist. 35, sec. Fla. Lions deaf profject 1980-82), Optimists (soccer coach, tee ball coach), Kappa Tau Epsilon. Office: 1105 E Hallandale Beach Blvd Hallandale FL 33009-4431

HASS, JOSEPH MONROE, automotive executive; b. Syracuse, N.Y., July 28, 1955; s. Joseph Monroe and Susan Faith (Betts) H.; m. Lisa Michelle Palmer, Aug. 14, 1982. BS in Secondary Edn., Tenn. Temple U., 1977. Diesel mechanic Cummins Engines Tenn., Chattanooga, 1978-81; mgr. tng. Cummins Engines Tenn., Nashville, 1981-85; svc. fl. foreman Cummins Cumberland, Nashville, 1985-86, CompuChek technician, 1986-87, fleet systems support engr., 1987-89, tech. advisor, instr., 1989-90, dir. devel., 1990—. Mem. ASTD, Internat. Platform Assn., Am. Assn. Individual Investors, Citizens Against Govt. Waste. Office: Cummins Cumberland 706 Spence Ln Nashville TN 37217-1144

HASSAN, HOSNI MOUSTAFA, microbiologist, biochemist, toxicologist and food science educator; b. Alexandria, Egypt, Sept. 3, 1937; came to U.S., 1961; s. Mousfafa Hosni and Sania M. (El-Hariri) H.; m. Awatif El-Domiaty, July 12, 1961 (div. May 1983); children: Jehan, Suzanne; m. Linda C. McDonald, Dec. 16, 1992; 1 child, Nora. BSc, Ain Shams U., Cairo, 1959; PhD, U. Calif., Davis, 1967. Asst. prof. Cairo High Polytech. Inst., 1968-70; assoc. prof. U. Alexandria, 1970-72; vis. prof. McGill U., Montreal, 1972-74; rsch. assoc. biochemistry Duke U. Med. Ctr., Durham, N.C., 1975-79; assoc. prof. McGill U. Med. Sch., Montreal, 1979-80; assoc. prof. N.C. State U., Raleigh, 1980-84, prof., 1984-93, prof., head microbiology dept., 1993—. Mem. editorial bd. Free Radicals in Biology and Medicine, 1984—; author: (chpts.) Enzymatic Basis of Toxicology, 1980, Biological Role of Copper, 1980, Advances in Genetics, 1989, Stress Responses in Plants, 1990, FEMS Microbiol. Reviews, 1994; author, co-author over 100 rsch. publs. fellow NIH, 1967, Fulbright sr. fellow, Paris, 1987-88; NIH-NSF grantee N.C. State U., 1982, 83-93. Fellow Am. Inst. Chemists, Sigma Xi; mem. Am. Soc. Biol. Chemists and Molecular Biology, Am. Soc. for Microbiology (pres.-elect and pres. N.C. chpt. 1993-95). Democrat. Home: 2637 Freestone Ln Raleigh NC 27603-3950 Office: NC State U Microbiology Dept 4515 Gardner Hall Box 7615 Raleigh NC 27695-7615

HASSAN, KHAN MAMNOON, librarian; b. Fatehpur, India, May 4, 1941; came to U.S., 1970; s. Masroor Hasan and Bilqis Fatima (Zaman) Khan; m. Jan Marian Payne, June 30, 1973; children: Kiran Elizabeth, Jay Tariq. BS, U. Karachi, Pakistan, 1963, MS, 1965; diploma in edn., U. Western Ontario, London, 1970; MLS, SUNY, Geneseo, 1971. Lectr. in charge dept. geology Urdu Coll., Karachi, 1965-67; quality control asst. Johns-Manville Mining and Trading, Timmins, Ont., Can., 1968-69; high sch. libr. Salmon River Cen. Schs., Ft. Covington, N.Y., 1971-72, Walton (N.Y.) Cen. Schs., 1972-73; asst. libr. for media and reference Alfred (N.Y.) State Coll., 1973-77; asst. libr. Idaho State U., Pocatello, 1977-83; dir. learning resources Piedmont Va. C.C., Charlottesville, Va., 1983-96; coord. instl. rsch. Piedmont Va. C.C., Charlottesville, 1996—; pres. Idaho Ednl. Media Assn., Pocatello, 1981-82, Friends of 10, Pocatello, 1980-81. Author: The Unknown Angel, 1989; contbr. articles to publs. Bd. dirs. Clean Community Commn., Charlottesville, 1988-92; pres. Leadership Charlottesville Alumni Assn., 1989-90. Edn. fellow Province of Ont., 1969-70; recipient Cornerstone award Leadership Charlottesville Alumni Assn., 1991; fellow Acad. C.C. Leadership, Advancement, Innovation and Modeling, 1993-95. Mem. Va. Ednl. Media Assn., Assn. for Ednl. Communication and Tech. (internat. div. adv. bd.), Toastmasters Internat. (Club Toastmaster of Yr., 1982, Area Gov. of Yr. 1984-85, Disting. Svc. award 1989, pres. Blue Ridge Club 1985, mentor for State Farm Ins. Co. 1988). Office: Piedmont Va Community Coll 501 College Dr Charlottesville VA 22902-7589

HASSAN, SAYED MOHAMMED, analytical chemist; b. Cairo, Oct. 18, 1944; came to U.S., 1988; s. Mohammed Hassan Ali; m. Souad Ali Shaaban, July 12, 1973; children: Wael, Ghada, Hany. B Pharmacy and Pharm. Chemistry, U. Cairo, 1966, M Pharm. Sci., 1973, PhD in Pharm. Sci., 1975. Drug control analyst Nile Co. for Pharms., Cairo, 1966-67, Drug Control and Rsch. Ctr., Cairo, 1967-74; asst. lectr. to prof. and head dept. analytical chemistry Faculty of Pharmacy, Al-Mansoura, Egypt, 1974-88; prin. rsch. chemist DynCorp/U.S. EPA, Athens, Ga., 1988-95; mgr. chem. instrumentation dept. crop and soil scis. Coll. Agrl. and Environ. Scis., U. Ga., Athens, 1996—; cons. Nat. Orgn. Drug Control and Rsch., Cairo, 1976-88, Kahira Co. for Chem. and Pharm. Industries, Cairo, 1987-88. Contbr. articles, revs. to profl. jours. Recipient Abdul Hameed Shoman award Shoman Found., Jordon, 1984. Mem. AAAS, Am. Chem. Soc., N.Y. Acad. Scis., Assn. Ofcl. Analytical Chemists, Egyptian Biochem. Soc., Chem. Soc. Egypt, Pharm. Soc. Egypt, Sigma Xi.

HASSEL, RUDOLPH CHRISTOPHER, English language educator; b. Richmond, Va., Nov. 16, 1939; s. Rudolph Christopher and Helen Elizabeth (Poehler) H.; m. Sedley Louise Hotchkiss, June 16, 1962; children: Bryan Christopher, Paul Sedley. BA, U. Richmond, 1961; MA, U. N.C., 1962; PhD, Emory U., 1968. English instr. Mercer U., Macon, Ga., 1962-65; asst. prof. Vanderbilt U., Nashville, 1968-73, assoc. prof., 1973-85, prof., 1985—; dir. grad. studies English dept. Vanderbilt U., 1974-81, dir. undergrad. studies, 1991; mem. exec. com. Folger Inst., Washington, 1986-95; cons. State of Tenn., Nashville, 1987-93; cons. for various univ. presses and profl. jours. Author: Renaissance Drama and the English Church Year, 1979, Faith and Folly in Shakespeare's Romantic Comedies, 1980, Songs of Death, 1987; contbr. articles to Shakespeare Quar. and others. Mem. choir Christ Episcopal Ch., Nashville, 1974-95, outreach vol., 1974—, vestryman, 1980-83; vol. United Way, Vanderbilt U., 1980—, Habitat for Humanity. Woodrow Wilson Found. fellow, 1962; Emory U. fellow, 1965; Folger Libr. fellow, 1976; Am. Philol. Soc. fellow, 1986. Mem. MLA, Shakespeare Assn. Am., Malone Soc. New Variorum Editor, South Atlantic MLA, Christianity and Lit. Soc., Phi Beta Kappa, Omicron Delta Kappa. Home: 107 Pembroke Ave Nashville TN 37205-3728 Office: Vanderbilt U PO Box 129-B Nashville TN 37235-0129

HASSELL, JOHN FLEMING, III, business consulting company executive; b. Charleston, S.C., Mar. 18, 1949; s. John Fleming Jr. and Caroline Lebby (Smith) H.; m. Jane Iredell White, Aug. 27, 1966; children: John Fleming IV, Thomas Lynch, Emily Fleetwood. BA, U. S.C., 1969. Specialist employment and tng. Robert Bosch Corp., Summerville, S.C., 1973-75; asst. v.p. govtl. affairs and econ. devel. S.C. Pub. Svc. Authority, Moncks Corner, S.C., 1975-80; exec. asst. to exec. dir. S.C. State Ports Authority, Charleston, S.C., 1980-86; assoc. dir. S.C. State Devel. Bd., Columbia, 1986-87; dir. Charleston Trident Devel. Bd., Charleston, 1987-88; pres. Hassell & Co. Ltd., Charleston, 1988—; mem. adv. bd. Sch. Bus. Coll. Charleston, 1992—; chmn. Maritime Assn. of Pt. of Charleston, 1994—, The Port is Your Future, Charleston, 1992—; founding mem., v.p. East Asia Inst., Charleston, 1992—; gen. chmn. 20th S.C. Internat. Trade Conf., Charleston, 1993; chmn. emeritus S.C. World Trade Ctr., Charleston, 1992. Contbr. articles to profl. jours. and newspapers. Sec., trustee The Charleston Mus., 1988—; mem. Charleston County Aviation Authority, 1990-94. With U.S. Army, 1970-71. Mem. SAR, Assn. of Enterprises and Industries of Spain (hon. bd. Washington bur. 1992—), Rotary Club of Charleston (pres. 1992-93, Paul Harris fellow 1994), Beta Gamma Sigma. Episcopalian. Home: 44 Savage St Charleston SC 29401-2410 Office: Hassell & Co Ltd PO Box 687 Charleston SC 29402-0687

HASSELL, LEROY ROUNTREE, SR., state supreme court justice; b. Aug. 17, 1955. BA in Govt. and Fgn. Affairs, U. Va., 1977; JD, Harvard U., 1980. Bar: Va. Former ptnr. McGuire, Woods, Battle and Boothe; now justice Supreme Ct. of Va.; former mem. Va. gen. assembly task force to study violence on sch. property. Former mem. adv. bd. Massey Cancer Ctr.; mem. policy com., former chmn. Richmond Sch. Bd., ; former bd. dirs. Richmond Renaissance, Inc., richmond chpt. ARC, Garfield childs Fund, Carpenter Ctr. for Performing Arts, St. John's Hosp., Legal Aid Ctrl. Va.; vol. Richmond Pub. Schs., Hospice vol.; bd. dirs. Va. State conf. of Christians and Jews; elected sch. bd. chmn. 4 terms. Recipient Liberty Bell award 1985, 86, Black Achievers award, 1985-86, Outstanding Young Citizen award Richmond Jaycees, 1987, Outstanding Young Virginian award Va. Jaycees, 1987; one of youngest persons to both serve on the Richmond Sch. Bd. and to serve as bd. chmn. Mem. Va. Trial Lawyers Assn., Assn. Trial Lawyers Am., Va. Assn. Def. Attys., Old Dominion Bar Assn., Va. Bar Assn. Office: Supreme Ct of Virginia PO Box 1315 Richmond VA 23210-1315

HASSELL, MORRIS WILLIAM, judge; b. Jacksonville, Tex., Aug. 9, 1916; s. Alonzo Seldon and Cora Lee (Rainey) H.; m. Mauriete Watson, Sept. 3, 1944; children: Morris William, Charles Robert. AA, Lon Morris Coll., 1936; JD, U. Tex., Austin, 1942. Bar: Tex. 1941, U.S. Dist. Ct. 1948, U.S. Supreme Ct. 1973. County atty. Cherokee County, Tex., 1943-47; mem. Norman Hassell Spiers & Thrall of Rusk and Jacksonville, Tex., 1948-78; sr. judge 2d Jud. Dist. Tex., 1978—; chmn. bd. Swift Oil Co., 1964-77, H & I Oil Co., 1968-77; dir. First State Bank, Rusk, Tex., 1959-78. Mayor, City of Rusk, Tex., 1959-63, 73-78; trustee Rusk Ind. Sch. Dist., 1967-73; chmn. bd. trustees, chmn. exec. com. Lon Morris Coll., Jacksonville; chmn. bd. trustees Tex. conf. United Methodist Ch.; vice-chmn. bd. trustees Lakeview Meth. Assembly; trustee Tex. ann. conf. United Meth. Found. Recipient Disting. Alumnus award Community Svc. U. Tex. Law Sch., 1994. Mem. State Bar Tex., ABA; fellow Tex. Bar Found., Am. Bar Found. Democrat. Lodges: Kiwanis (lt. gov. 1964), Masons, Odd Fellow. Home: 1300 Copeland St

Rusk TX 75785 Office: Second Jud Dist Ct PO Box 196 Rusk TX 75785-0196

HASSIG, SUSAN ELIZABETH, health research administrator, epidemiologist; b. Mpls., Feb. 27, 1956; d. Frank Joseph and Kathryn Ann (Tinker) H.; 1 child, Elizabeth Anne. BA, St. Mary's Coll., 1977; MPH, Tulane U., 1985, DrPH, 1987. Cert. med. technologist. Med. technologist North Meml. Hosp., Mpls., 1978-80; vol. Peace Corps, Thailand, 1980-82; epidemiologist, analyst pulmonary medicine Tulane U., New Orleans, 1985; epidemiologist La. Dept. Health; AIDS epidemiologist Tulane U., New Orleans, 1985-87; epidemiologist, researcher Tulane U. and Project SIDA, Kinshasa, Zaire, 1988-89; evaluation scientist AIDSTECH project Family Health Internat., Rsch. Triangle Pk., N.C., 1990-91; assoc. dir. evaluation AIDSCAP project Family Health Internat., Arlington, Va., 1991-95, sr. assoc. office of dir. AIDSCAP project, 1995—; cons., adj. faculty Tulane U., New Orleans, 1990—; instr. Sch. Pub. Health, U. N.C., Chapel Hill, 1991; cons. Nat. Acad. Scis., Washington, 1992; reviewer NIH, Bethesda, Md., 1991—. Author, editor: Tools for Evaluation, 1991. Vol. No. Va. Dem. Com., Arlington, 1991; vol., capt. AIDS Walk, Whitman Walker Clinic, Washington, 1992-93. Mem. APHA, Soc. for Epidemiol. Rsch., Internat. AIDS Soc., Delta Omega (Nat. Merit award 1988). Office: Family Health Internat AIDSCAP Project 2101 Wilson Blvd Ste 700 Arlington VA 22201-3062

HASTIE, JOHN DOUGLAS, lawyer; b. Guthrie, Okla., Dec. 9, 1939. BA, U. Okla., 1961, LLB, 1964. Bar: Okla. 1964. Atty. Hastie McCutcheon Maye and Kirschner, Oklahoma City, 1974—; adj. prof. Coll. of Law U. Okla., 1982-90; adviser and lectr. in field. Contbr. articles to profl. jours. Capt. U.S. Army, 1964-66. Mem. ABA, Okla. Bar Assn., Oklahoma County Bar Assn., Assn. of Bar of City of N.Y., Am. Coll. Real Estate Lawyers, Anglo-Am. Real Property Inst., Am. Law Inst., Am. Coll. Mortgage Attys. Office: Hastie McCutcheon & Maye 300 MidFirst Plz 501 Northwest Expy Oklahoma City OK 73118

HASTINGS, CHESTER RAN, education educator, director student services; b. San Antonio, Tex., Oct. 29, 1928; s. Albert C. and Flora B. (Ballard) H.; m. Elva J. Davidson, Aug. 27, 1960; children: Terri Lynn, Stephen, Allison Anne. BS, S.W. Tex. State U., 1949, MEd, 1955; PhD, U. Tex., 1964. Lic. profl. counselor, Tex. Tchr. social studies Harlandale H.S., San Antonio, Tex., 1945-54, Alamo Heights Jr. H.S., San Antonio, 1954-55, Armed Forces Dependent Schs., Germany and Japan, 1955-58, Brackenridge H.S., San Antonio, 1958-60; dir. guidance and student svcs. Del Mar Coll., Corpus Christi, Tex., 1961-66; dean and v.p. McLennan C.C., Waco, Tex., 1966-88; prof. edn. adminstrn. Sch. Edn., Baylor U., Waco, Tex., 1988—; dir. student svcs. program and collegiate scholars of practice doctoral progam; mem. summer seminar in acad. adminstrn. Tex. Assn. Colls., San Antonio and Coll. Sta., Tex., 1967; mem. Nat. com. of Coll. Placement and Guidance Exams. Coll. Bd., Princeton, N.J., 1969-70; mem. com. on sch. and coll. practice So. Assn. of Schs. and Colls., Atlanta, 1969-72; adv. com. Area Agy. on Aging, Waco, Tex., 1987-88, Tex. Higher Edn. Coord. Bd. Affirmative Action Com., Austin, 1984-86. Pres. N.W. Rotary Club, Waco, Tex., 1977-78; v.p. and charter mem. Eastside Rotary Club, Waco, 1967-69; bd. trustees The Art Ctr., Waco, 1980-88, chair edn. adv. com. Heart of Tex. Private Industry Coun., Waco, 1986-88; administrator Founds. in Edn. U. Tex., Austin, 1959. Recipient Nat. Def. Edn. Act fellowship in guidance and counseling, U. Tex., Austin, 1969, fellowship in Jr. Coll. Adminstrn. Kellogg Found., 1960-61, 1962-63. Mem. ASCD, Am. C.C. Assn., Am. Counseling Assn., Am. Coll. Pers. Assn., Tex. Counseling Assn., Phi Delta Kappa (pres. Baylor chpt. 1990-91). Home: 504 Kiowa Waco TX 76706 Office: Baylor U Sch Edn Waco TX 76748

HASTINGS, EVELYN GRACE, retired elementary school educator; b. Seguin, Tex., May 25, 1938; d. Ed Howard Coleman and Mae Stella (King) Haywood; m. Marvin Hastings, Oct. 9, 1982. BS, Tex. Luth. Coll., 1960; MA, U. Tex., San Antonio, 1985. Cert. tchr., Tex. Tchr. Seguin (Tex.) Ind. Sch. Dist., 1962-94, Vogel Elem. Sch., Sequin, 1991-94; retired, 1994; sec. Guadalupe County Tchr.'s Meeting, Seguin, 1962-65, Juan Seguin Sch. PTA, 1969. Historian, corr. sec. Tex. Women's Conv. Ch. of our Lord Jesus Christ, 1961-69, internat. treas. IFAE; treas. Tex. Armor Bears Young Peoples Union, 1960-63, pres., 1963-65, 68-70; sec. Tex. Sunday Sch. Assn., 1960-63, asst. supt., 1968-70, state supt., 1970-74; local missionary pres., fin. sec. Rufuge Ch.; state supr. Tex. Jr. Conv., 1970—; Sunday supr. Lighthouse Ch., 1975—; state missionary v.p. Tex.-Okla. Conv. Ch. of Our Lord Jesus Christ of Apostolic Faith. Recipient Cert. of Outstanding Svc. Nat. Youth Congress Ch. of Our Lord Jesus Christ, 1968, Cert. of Appreciation, Tex.-Okla. Conv. of the Ch. of Our Lord Jesus Christ of The Apostolic Faith, 1989, Outstanding Svc. Plaque, 1981, Tchr. of Yr. Plaque Seguin-Guadalupe County C. of C., 1990; inducted into The Internat. Sunday Sch. Hall of Fame of the Ch. of Our Lord Jesus Christ of the Apostolic Faith, 1990. Mem. AAUW (sec. 1968-70), NEA, Tex. State Tchrs. Assn. (minority del. 1982) Seguin Educators Assn. Democrat. Home: 950 Elsik St Seguin TX 78155-6756

HASTINGS, JOHN PARIS, librarian; b. Mascoutah, Ill., Nov. 27, 1948; s. Don and Mary Fae (Davis) H. BA in English Lit., U. Okla., 1969, MLS in Libr. Sci., 1973. Cert. libr., Tex. Claims authorizer U.S. Social Security Adminstrn., Kansas City, Mo., 1969-71; periodicals libr. Southwestern U., Georgetown, Tex., 1973-76; pub. libr. cons. Big Country Libr. Sys., Abilene, Tex., 1976-78; dir. libr. svcs. Paris (Tex.) Pub. Libr., 1978-84; catalog libr. Tex. A&M Internat. U., Laredo, 1984—. Mem. Tex. Libr. Assn. (chair nat. libr. week com. 1979). Democrat. Office: Texas A&M International Univ Rm KL215E 5201 University Blvd Laredo TX 78041

HASTINGS, MARY LYNN, real estate broker; b. Carthage, N.Y., Jan. 16, 1943; d. Floyd Albert and Mary Frances (Schack) Neuroth; m. Ronald Anthony Casel, Nov. 28, 1963 (div. Nov. 1977); children: Mark, Steven, Glen; m. Charles F. Hastings, Apr. 27, 1991. Grad. Harper Method, Rochester, N.Y., 1961. Lic. real estate broker. Owner M. L. Salon, Rochester, N.Y., 1962-72; specialty tchrs.-aide Broward County, Ft. Lauderdale, Fla., 1973-77; office mgr. Broward County Voter Registration, Margate, Fla., 1977-82; real estate salesperson Pelican Bay, Daytona Beach, Fla., 1982-84, broker, 1984—, broker; owner Mary Lynn Realty, 1989—. Mem. adv. bd. Dem. Club, Margate, Fla., 1977-82. Mem. Nat. Assn. Realtors, Fla. Home Builders Assn., Nat. Home Builders Assn., Daytona Beach Home Builders Assn., Daytona Beach Bd. Realtors, Ft. Lauderdale Bd. Realtors, Nat. Assn. Women in Constrn. (v.p. 1988-89, pres.-elect 1989—, pres. 1990—), NAFE, Sales and Mktg. Council. Avocations: travel, dancing, theater, real estate investments. Democrat. Roman Catholic. Home: 1301 Beville Rd Daytona Beach FL 32119 Office: Mary Lynn Realty 1301 Beville Rd Ste 20 Daytona Beach FL 32119-1503

HASTINGS, RONNIE JACK, secondary school educator; b. Ranger, Tex., Apr. 8, 1946; m. Sylvia Louise Hastings, July, 1968; children: Dan, Chad. BS in Physics, Tex. A&M U., 1968, PhD in Physics, 1972. Teaching asst. dept. physics Tex. A&M U., 1966-72, rsch. asst. Cyclotron Inst., 1968-70; regional sci. advisor U. Tex., Austin, 1972-73; instr. physics and advanced math. Waxahachie (Tex.) High Sch., 1973—, chmn. dept. sci., curriculum developer, coord., 1973-85, 95—, dir. computer svcs., 1975-88; bd. dirs. nat. Ctr. Science Edn.; adj. asst. prof. dept. physics Tex. Woman's U., 1975-84; instr. Navarro Jr. Coll., 1975-84; mem. Nat. Supercollider Edn. Consortium, 1989-91; mem. Tex. State Textbook Com. Secondary Edn., Secondary Sci., 1990, 91, 92; mem. biology sect., Tex. secondary sci. textbook com., 1990, chemistry sect. 1992, chmn. physics sect. , 1991; mem. Tex. Science Adv. Com., 1990, 91; instr., master tchr. Superconducting Supercollider's First Summer Inst. Physics and Physical Science Tchrs., 1993; v.p. Tex. Coun. Science Edn.; mem. edn. subcom. Com. Sci. Investigation of Claims of Paranormal; participant tchr. space program NASA; chair edn. pubs. task force Nat. Ctr. Science; presenter numerous seminars. Contbr. articles to profl. jours. Recipient Recognition of Achievement and Contributions to Science Edn. Tex. State Senate, 1988. Mem. AAAS, Am. Assn. Physics Tchrs. (Excellence in Physics teaching award Tex. sect. 1988), Nat. Assn. Geology Tchrs. (pres. Tex. sect. 1987-88), Tex. Acad. Sci., Sci. Tchrs. Assn. Tex., North Tex. Skeptics (co-founder, pres. 1980-84, tech. advisor 1985—), Sigma Xi (Outstanding Secondary Schs. Tchr. award Tex. A&M chpt. 1986), Phi Kappa Phi, Sigma Pi Sigma. Office: Waxahachie High Sch 1000 Dallas Hwy N Waxahachie TX 75165

HAST-LANSDELL, JOAN EILEEN, cellular communications company manager; b. Denver, Jan. 6, 1955; d. Bernard Arthur and Erma Ann (Pospisil) H.; married. Student, U. Denver, 1973-74, Goethe Inst., Munich, 1974-75; BA in Internat. Affairs, U. Colo., 1983, postgrad., 1983-85, MS in Telecommunications, 1985. Owner, mgr. Celebrity Slickers Custom Jackets, Boulder, Colo., 1978-80; monogram specialist Custom Monogramming, Denver, 1981; summer intern in telecommunications Horizon House Pub., Dedham, Mass., 1983; office mgr. Universal Fuels Oil Co., Denver, 1983-84; sr. engr. GTE-Midwestern Telephone Ops., Fort Wayne, Ind., 1985-86; network adminstr. GTE-Info. Bus., Indpls., 1987-88; adminstrv. mgr. engring. assoc. devel. program GTE Svc. Corp., Stamford, Conn., 1988-89, mgr. advanced network planning GTE Mobile Communications, Houston, 1989-91; mgr. Tech. Planning Internat., Atlanta, 1991-96; mgr. internat. mktg. support GTE Svc. Corp., 1996—. Advisor Jr. Achievement, Fort Wayne, 1985-86; vol. Fort Wayne Zoo, 1985. Research grantee U. Colo. Dept. Telecommunications, Honolulu, 1984, Las Vegas, 1984. Mem. U. Colo. Alumni Assn. Avocations: foreign languages, traveling, art, scuba diving. Office: 245 Perimeter Center Pky NE Atlanta GA 30346-2304

HASTY, LINDA HESTER, business educator; b. Shelbyville, Tenn., Nov. 16, 1946; d. John Thomas and Alma Keith (Turner) Hester; m. Doyle Edwin Hasty, June 16, 1968; children: Darin Edwin, Derek Thomas. BS in Bus. Edn., Mid. Tenn. State U., 1968, M in Bus. Edn., 1979; EdD in Higher Edn., Nova Southeastern U., 1994. Cert. profl. sec., cert. mgr., elem. tchr. bus., cert. mgr. Tchr. English West Jr. High Sch., Tullahoma, Tenn., 1968-71; instr. office systems tech. Motlow State Community Coll., Tullahoma, Tenn., 1978-83, asst. prof., 1983-87; assoc. prof. Motlow State Community Coll., Tullahoma, 1987-95; prof. Motlow State C.C., Tullahoma, 1995—; cons. effective writing Arnold Engring. Devel. Ctr., Arnold AFB, Tullahoma, 1982—, Tenn. Corrections Acad., Tullahoma, 1985-90, Tullahoma Utilities Bd., 1990. Mem. AAUP, Nat. Bus. Edn. Assn., So. Bus. Edn. Assn. (conv. treas. 1982), Tenn. Bus. Edn. Assn. (exec. bd. 1982-85), Am. Tech. Edn. Assn. (Teaching Excellence award 1981). Baptist. Home: 412 Riverbend Country Club Shelbyville TN 37160 Office: Motlow State Cmty Coll Dept Edn Tullahoma TN 37388-8100

HATCH, DONALD JAMES (JIM HATCH), business leadership and planning executive; b. Live Oak, Fla., May 23, 1933; s. Albert James and Grace (Peeples) H.; m. Marilyn Blackmon Hatch, June 11, 1953; children: Rebecca, Melanie, Lynn, Donald J. Jr. BPE, U. Fla., 1955. Col. USMC, 1955-80; dir. Intelligence Systems System Planning Corp., Rosslyn, Va., 1980-86; advanced systems engr. RCA, Rosslyn, Va., 1986-88; advanced systems mktg. GE Aerospace, Arlington, Va., 1988-93; advanced systems bus. planning Martin Marietta, Arlington, Va., 1993-94; pres. Bus. Leadership and Planning, Jacksonville, Fla., 1994—. Author: Marine Corps Master Intelligence Plan, 1982. Recipient Bronze Star Sec. Navy, 1966, Legion of Merit Sec. Navy, 1970, 80, Gen. Mgrs. award GE Govt. and Comm. Sys., Camden, N.J., 1993. Mem. Marine Corps Cryptologic Assn. (pres.), Naval Cryptologic Vets. Assn., Armed Force Comm. Electronics Assn., U. Fla. Blue Key (Hall of Fame 1955), Nat. Mil. Intelligence Assn., Rotary. Episcopalian. Home: 15331 Cape Dr N Jacksonville FL 32226-1266

HATCH, ROBERT NORRIS, JR., banking executive; b. Norfolk, Va., Oct. 28, 1952; s. Robert Norris Hatch and Helen Tierney; divorced; 1 child, Robert Norris Hatch III. BA in Bus. and Econs., Emory and Henry Coll., 1975; MSBA in Bus. and Fin. with honors, Radford U., 1982. Sr. credit analyst Dominion Bank, N.A. (now First Union), Roanoke, Va., 1975-80; western region credit mgr., regional comml. lending officer Nations Bank, Richmond, Va., 1980-83; v.p. corp. banking Charleston (W.Va.) Nat. Bank (mem. Key Centurion Bancshares), 1983-85, sr. v.p. corp. banking/credit adminstrn., 1985-89, exec. v.p. corp. banking and trust groups, 1990-93; regional sr. credit officer Key Centurion Bancshares, Inc., 1990-93; exec. v.p. Bank One W.Va. Charleston, NA, 1993-94; state sr. v.p., chief credit officer Banc One West Va. Corp., 1994—. Bd. dirs. Salvation Army; vice-chmn. Boy Scouts Am. Fundraising; fundraiser Riverfront Park Project, Spirit of the Valley. Mem. Charleston Regional C. of C. and Devel. (bd. dirs.), Berry Hills Country Club (past pres.), Phi Kappa Phi, Delta Mu Delta. Office: Banc One WVa Corp 1000 5th Ave Huntington WV 25701-2203

HATCH, WILLIAM G. (BILL), management consultant; b. Milw., Mar. 16, 1959; s. William R. and Sevia V. Hatch. BSBA, U. Fla., 1981, MBA, 1982. Cert. mgmt. cons.; cert. fraud examiner. Fin. cons. JK Fin. Corp., Tampa, 1983-85; mgr. Ernst & Whinney, CPAs, Tampa, 1985-89; exec. cons. Peterson Cons., L.P., Atlanta, 1989-93; mgr. litigation and claims Coopers & Lybrand, L.L.P., Tampa, 1993—. Co-author: Proving and Pricing Construction Claims, 1996. Mem. The Tampa Connection, 1994-95. Mem. Assn. Cert. Fraud Examiners (treas. 1996—), Hillsborough County Bar Assn., Omicron Delta Kappa, Beta Gamma Sigma. Democrat. Methodist. Home: 719 Spencer Ave Clearwater FL 34616 Office: Coopers & Lybrand LLP 101 E Kennedy Blvd Ste 1500 Tampa FL 33602-5147

HATCHER, BRUCE ALDERMAN, entertainment event company executive; b. Morganton, N.C., Apr. 24, 1960; s. Norris Clark Jr. and Nancy Evelyn (Gordon) H.; m. Debra Jean Nay, May 21, 1988. BA in Bus. Mgmt., N.C. State U., 1982, BA in Econs., 1983. Cert. facility exec. Bus. officer mgr., athletic dept. N.C. State Univ., Raleigh, 1983-84, athletic box office supr., 1984-86, athletic controller, 1986-88, stadium/coliseum dir., 1986-91; pres. Entertainment Event, Hatcher Prodns. Inc., Raleigh, 1991—; exec. dir. Stadium and Coliseum Mgmt.; prodr. Land of Fantasy Holiday Light Display, 1993, 94. Events promoter The Rolling Stones, Pink Floyd, The Who, Paul McCartney, The Grateful Dead, NFL Exhibition Game. Fundraiser Alzheimers Assn., Raleigh, 1990, Diabetes Assn., Raleigh, 1990. Recipient Against the Odds award The Nat. Pub. T.A & P, Raleigh, 1988. Mem. Interanat. Assn. Auditorium Mgrs., Carolina Bldg. Mgrs. (pres. 1990). Methodist. Home: Hatcher Event Mgmt Corp 1205 Castlemoor Ct Raleigh NC 27606-3462 Office: Capital Club Bldg 16 W Martin St Ste 1008 Raleigh NC 27601-2931

HATCHER, JAMES MITCHELL, principal; b. Erwin, Tenn., Aug. 19, 1950; s. James Walter and Delorese Kathleen (Callahan) H.; m. Ernestine Buchanan, Nov. 18, 1967; 1 child, Christopher Scott. BS, East Tenn. State U., 1972, MEd, 1983; EdD in Ednl. Adminstrn., 1994. Cert. tchr., adminstr. and supr., supt. of schs. Corrective therapist McGuire VA Hosp., Richmond, Va., 1973—; tchr. Unicoi County Bd. Edn., Erwin, 1973-84, prin., 1984—. Mem. Unicoi County Polit. Action Com., Erwin, 1973—, Tenn. Polit. Action Com., Nashville, 1973—, PTA, Erwin, 1982; deacon Bapt. Ch. Fellow Tenn. Edn. Assn., NEA; mem. Unicoi County Edn. Assn. (pres. 1981-82, negotiator 1979-83, rep. to Tenn. Edn. Assn. 1980-82), Unicoi County Prins. Assn. (v.p. Erwin chpt. 1986-87, pres. 1987-88). Home: RR 1 Box 50A Erwin TN 37650-9108 Office: Unicoi Elem Sch 300 Massachusetts Ave Unicoi TN 37692-9707

HATCHER, ROBERT DEAN, research scientist, geology educator; b. Madison, Tenn., Oct. 22, 1940; married; 2 children. BA, Vanderbilt U., 1961, MS, 1962; PhD, U. Tenn., 1965. Registered profl. geologist Ga., Tenn., S.C.; registered engring. geologist S.C. Teaching asst. Vanderbilt U., Nashville, 1960-62, U. Tenn., Knoxville, 1962-65; asst. prof. geology Clemson (S.C.) U., 1966-70, assoc. prof. geology, 1970-76, prof. geology, 1976-78; prof. geology Fla. State U., Tallahassee, 1978-80, U. S.C., Columbia, 1980-86; prof. geology and disting. scientist U. Tenn./Oak Ridge Nat. Lab., Knoxville/Oak Ridge, 1986—; part-time geologic mapping S.C. Divsn. Geology, 1966-82, N.C. Divsn. Mineral Resources, 1974-80, Ga. Geol. Survey, summer, 1970, Humble Oil and Refining Co., New Orleans, 1965-66, Tenn. Divsn. Geology, 1961-64; cons., lectr. in field; reviewer/evaluator geology depts. and programs SUNY-Birmingham, 1984, U. Tenn., Chattanooga, 1984, Rutgers U., 1991, SUNY, Geneseo, 1995, Indian Geol. Survey, 1995, U. Ala., 1995; rev. panel NSF, 1982, 85, 95; mem. NAS Bd. RAdioactive Waste Mgmt., 1990—; mem. nuclear reactor safety com. NRC; mem. Nat. Coop. Geologic Mapping Program Adv. Com., 1994—; mem. rev. panel Ednl. Geologic Mapping Program, 1995—. Co-author: Physical Geology: Principles, Processes and Problems, 1976, Laboratory Manual for Structural Geology, 1990, The U.S. Appalachian and Quachita Orogens, 1990; author: Structural Geology: Principles, Concepts and Problems, 1990, 2d edit., 1995; editor: GSA Bull, 1981-88; co-editor: Contributions to the Tectonics and Geophysics of Mountain Chains, 1983, GSA Centennial Articles from Volume 100 of the GSA Bulletin, 1990, others; contbr. numerous articles to profl. jours. Grantee NSF, 1968-70, 70-72, 76-78, 78-79, 79-87, 89-92, Clemson U. Faculty Rsch. Fund, 1972, Duke Power Co., 1974-75, Westinghouse Elec. Corp., 1974-75, Nuclear Regulatory Commn., 1978-79, Dept. Energy, 1993. Fellow AAAS, Geol. Soc. Am. (chmn. exec. com. 1991-92, pres. 1992-93, exec. dir. search com. 1993-94, numerous other coms.), Geol. Assn. Can.; mem. Am. Geol. Inst. (pres.-elect 1994-95, pres. 1995-96), Am. Assn. Petroleum Geologists, Am. Geophys. Union, Carolina Geol. Soc., East Tenn. Geol. Soc., Ga. Geol. Soc., Sigma Xi. Office: U Tenn Dept Geol Scis 306 G & G Bldg Knoxville TN 37996-1410

HATCHER, WILLIAM WAYNE, retired clergyman and church executive; b. W.Va., Feb. 9, 1925; s. Daniel Grey and Dola Margaret (Allen) H.; m. Ruth Mary Dickey, Aug. 25, 1949; children: William Wayne Jr., Nancy Colleen, Sharon Ruth, Richard Allen, Martha Lois, John Calvin. BA, King Coll., Bristol, Tenn., 1950; MDiv, Columbia Theol. Sem., Decatur, Ga., 1953. Ordained to ministry Presbyn. Ch., 1953. Pastor Graham Presbyn. Ch., Bluefield, Va., 1953-57, Mt. Hope (W.Va.) Presbyn. Ch., 1957-60, Westminster Presbyn. Ch., Monroe, La., 1960-65; exec., presbyter Red River Prsbytery, Ruston, La., 1965-70; exec., moderator Presbytery of Pines, Arkadelphia, Ark., 1970-84, Presbytery of Fayetteville, N.C., 1984-89, Presbytery of Coastal Carolina, Wilmington, N.C., 1989-91; ret., 1991; mem. exec. bd. Presbyn. Ch. U.S., 1971-73. Trustee Davis Stuart Sch., Lewisburg, W.Va., 1957-60, Evergreen Sch., Minden, La., Ark. Coll., Batesville, 1976-78, Presbyn. Sch. Christian Edn., Richmond, Va., 1974-80, Austin (Tex.) Theol. Sem., 1967-88; county chmn. ARC, Mt. Hope, 1958. With USN, 1943-45, PTO. Democrat. Home: 3222 Jura Dr Fayetteville NC 28303

HATCHETT, EDWARD BRYAN, JR., auditor, lawyer; b. Glasgow, Ky., Aug. 8, 1951; s. Edward Bryan and Leona Katherine (Azbill) H.; m. Judie Etta James, Aug. 3, 1973; children: Catherine Wade, Elizabeth Black, James Edward Bryan. BA, Centre Coll., Danville, Ky., 1973; JD, U. Louisville, 1976; diploma Nat. Grad. Trust Sch., Northwestern U., 1980; diploma Stonier Grad. Sch. Banking, U. Del., 1986; diploma Ky. Mgmt. Inst., Western Ky. U., 1988. Bar: Ky. 1976. Editorial asst. Dept. Agr., Washington, 1971; edn. rsch. asst. Ky. Legis. Rsch. Commn., Frankfort, 1972; law clk. Dept. Law, City of Louisville, 1973-76; pvt. practice Glasgow, 1978-88; v.p., trust officer New Farmers Nat. Bank, Glasgow, 1980-88, sec., 1986-88; asst. gen. counsel Ky. Dept. Fin. Instns., Frankfort, 1977, commr., 1988-94, dir. securities divsn., 1992-94; auditor pub. accts. Commonwealth Ky., 1996—; chmn. Ky. Fin. Instns. Bd., Frankfort, 1988-94; bd. dirs. Commonwealth Preservation Advs., Inc., Frankfort; pres. Barren County Bar Assn., Glasgow, 1988, Estate Planning Coun. So. Ky., Bowling Green, 1988. Gov.'s appointee Ky. Heritage Coun., Frankfort, 1985-88; pres. Mammoth Cave Area 4-H Found., Glasgow, 1981; lay reader Ch. of the Ascension, 1988—. Named nat. pub. speaking champion Future Farmers Am., 1970. Mem. N.Am. Securities Adminstrs. Assn., Frankfort Rotary Club. Democrat. Episcopalian. Home: 454 Chinook Trl Frankfort KY 40601-1602 Office: Coll of Bus & Public Admin 144 Capitol Annex Frankfort KY 40601

HATCHETT, JOSEPH WOODROW, federal judge; b. Clearwater, Fla., Sept. 17, 1932; s. John Arthur and Lula Gertrude (Thomas) H.; children: Cheryl Nadine, Brenda Audrey. A.B., Fla. A. and M. U., 1954; J.D., Howard U., 1959; J.D. certificate mil. judge course, U.S. Naval Justice Sch., Newport, R.I., 1973. Bar: Fla. 1959, U.S. Ct. Appeals (5th and 11th cirs.). Pvt. practice Daytona Beach, 1959-66; asst. U.S. atty. Dept. Justice, Jacksonville, Fla., 1966-70; U.S. magistrate U.S. Cts., Jacksonville, 1971-75; justice Supreme Ct. Fla., Tallahassee, 1975-79; judge U.S. Ct. Appeals (11th cir.), Tallahassee, 1979—; Cooperating atty. N.A.A.C.P. Legal Def. Fund, 1960-66; gen. counsel Masons of Fla., 1963-66; cons., mem. staff dept. urban renewal, Daytona Beach, 1963-66, spl. asst. to city atty., 1964; Mem. com. selection for Jacksonville Naval Res. Officer Tng. Corps, 1971. Contbr. articles to profl. jours. Mem. John T. Stocking Meml. Trust, med. sch. scholarships, 1961-66; Co-chmn. United Negro Coll. Fund of Volusia County, Fla., 1962; bd. dirs. Jacksonville Opportunities Industrialization Center, 1972-75. Served to 1st lt. AUS, 1954-56, Germany. Recipient Mary McCloud Bethune medallion for community service Bethune-Cookman Coll., 1965, medallion for human relations, 1975. Mem. Am., Nat., Fla., Jacksonville, D. W. Perkins, Fed. bar assns., Am. Judicature Soc., Nat. Council Fed. Magistrates, V.F.W., Omega Psi Phi. Baptist (trustee). Club: Fla-Jax (Jacksonville) (Man of Year 1974). Home: PO Box 981 Tallahassee FL 32302-0981 Office: US Ct Appeals 11th Circuit PO Box 10429 Tallahassee FL 32302-2429

HATFIELD, JACK KENTON, lawyer, accountant; b. Medford, Okla., Jan. 26, 1922; s. Loate L. and Cora (Walsh) H.; m. D. Ann Keltner, Dec. 5, 1943 (dec. Sept. 1988); children: Susan Kathryn Hatfield Bechtold, Sally Ann Hatfield Clark. BS in BA, Phillips U., Enid, Okla., 1947; BA, Phillips U., 1953; LLB, Oklahoma City U., 1954, JD, 1967. Bar: Okla. 1954; CPA 1954. Pvt. practice, Enid, Okla., 1954-58; with Dept. Interior, Tulsa, 1958-77; pvt. practice, Tulsa, 1977—. Mem. ABA, Okla. Bar Assn., Tulsa Co. Bar Assn., Am. Inst. CPA's, Okla. Soc. CPA's. Club: Petroleum. Home: 4013 E 86th St Tulsa OK 74137-2609 Office: 7060 S Yale Ave Ste 601 Tulsa OK 74136-5739

HATFIELD, JAMES ALLEN, theater arts educator; b. Marion, Ind., May 1, 1953; s. Frederick Marion and Mary Josephine (Murray) H.; m. Teresa Faye House, Mar. 28, 1977; 1 child, Edward Everett. BS, Ball State U., 1974, MA, 1975; PhD, Wayne State U., 1981. Asst. prof. Oakland U., Rochester, Mich., 1978-83; assoc. prof. Jackson (Miss.) State U., 1983-86; assoc. prof., chmn. theater dept. Butler U., Indpls., 1986-90; assoc. prof., dir. theater dept. U. Tex., Tyler, 1990—; mem. Performance evaluation com. Miss. Arts Commn., Jackson, 1983-86; vice-chair Tex. Kennedy Ctr./Am. Coll. Theatre Festival, 1992-95, state chair, 1996—. Dir., designer: (operas) Lost in the Stars, 1987, The Marriage of Figaro, 1988, The Merry Widow, 1989, The Great Soap Opera, 1990; (plays) My Sister in This House, 1988 (Am. Coll. Theatre Festival nomination), Another Antigone, 1991 (Am. Coll. Theatre Festival N.E. Tex. Cert. of Excellence), The Doctor in Spite of Himself, 1991, Thymus Vulgaris, 1991, Antigone, 1992, Habeas Corpus, 1992, The Norman Conquests, 1992, Getting Married, 1993, Anatol, 1993, Old Times, 1993, La Ronde, 1994, As You Like It, 1994, You Never Can Tell, 1994, Oleanna (Am. Coll. Theatre Festival Critics Choice Cert. of Excellence), 1994, Oleanna, 1995, KC/ACTF Region VI Production, Later Life, 1995 The Heiress, 1995, 3 Courtelines, 1995, Lettice & Lovage, 1995, Best of Friends, 1996, Phaedra, 1996, Octavia, 1996, Mrs. Klein, 1996; (mus. theater prodns.) Candide, 1987, Sunday in the Park With George, 1988, Marry Me a Little, 1989 (Am. Coll. Theatre Festival Nomination), Two by Two, 1993. State chmn. Kennedy Ctr./Am. Coll. Theatre Festival, 1996—. Recipient medal of excellence in lighting Am. Coll. Theatre Festival, 1978, Outstanding Tchg. award U. Tex. Chancellor's Coun., 1993. Mem. AAUP, Am. Fedn. Musicians, Assn. for Theatre in Higher Edn., U.S. Inst. for Theatre Tech., Ind. Theatre Assn., Speech Communication Assn., Assn. Communication Adminstrn., Soc. Stage Dirs. and Choreographers, Tex. Ednl. Theatre Assn., Tex. U.S.I.T.T., Am. Alliance for Theatre and Edn., South West Theatre Assn. Office: U Tex Dept Theater 3900 University Blvd Tyler TX 75799-0001

HATFIELD, JOEL THANE, music educator, minister; b. Kansas City, Mo., Apr. 15, 1964; s. Jimmie LeRoy and Martha Marie (Lunn) H.; m. Dianna Virginia Phillips, Apr. 21, 1990. BS, William Jewell Coll., 1988; M in Ch. Mus. cum laude, Midwestern Bapt. Theol. Sem., 1992. Lic. gospel ministry, 1988. Bus. mgr. Liberty (Mo.) Symphony Orch., 1984-85; minister of mus. & youth Providence Bapt. Ch., Kansas City, Mo., 1986-89; minister of music First Bapt. Ch., Oak Grove, Mo., 1989-90; mus. asst. First Bapt. Ch., N. Kansas City, Mo., 1990-91; prof. voice & ch. music Prairie Bible Coll., Three Hills, Alta., Can., 1991-93; exec. bd. Blue River-Kans. City Bapt. Assn., 1989-90; mem. subcom. governance, adminstrn. Am Assn. Bible Colls., coll. acad. com. Prairie Bible Coll., 1992-93; messenger Clay-Platte Bapt. Assn., Kans. City, 1985-89, music minister's coun., 1988-89; treas. Northwest Mo. Regional Symphony Orch. Conf., 1984-85; chmn. religious affairs com. Midwestern Bapt. Theol. Sem., 1989-90, com. chapel/spiritual devel., 1989-90, com. missions and special lectrs., 1990-91; worship leader Prairie Tabernacle Congregation, 1991-92, mem. worship com. 1992; seminar leader worship, ch. music; vocal soloist for recitals, concerts. Asst. scoutmaster, other offices Boy Scouts of Am. Troop 320, Liberty, Mo., 1981-85. Recipient resolution recognizing svc. City Coun. Liberty, Mo. 1982.

Mem. The Hymn Soc. of the U.S. and Can., Alberta Choral Fedn., So. Bapt. Ch. Music Conf., Nat. Eagle Scout Assn., Phi Mu Alpha Sinfonia (pres. Kappa Mu chpt. 1984-85, treas. Kappa Mu chpt. 1983-84). Baptist.

HATFIELD, MARGARET CLARK, biology educator; b. Waycross, Ga., July 19, 1968; d. William Duke and Aundry Eloise (Music) Clark; m. John Mark Hatfield, June 24, 1995. AS in Biology, 1987; BS in Biology, Ga. Southwestern, 1989; MS in Biology, Ga. Coll., 1991. Cert. tchr. T-5, Ga. Instr., tchg. asst. Ga. Coll., Milledgeville, 1989-91; asst. prof. biology Ga. Southwestern Coll., Americus, 1991-92; rsch. asst. U. Ga., Athens, 1992-94; biology instr. Truett McConnell Coll., Walkinsville, Ga., 1994; sci. tchr. Ware Co. H.S., Waycross, Ga., 1994—. Mem. AAAS, Nat. Sci. Tchrs. Assn., Ga. Sci. Tchrs. Assn., Am. Soc. for Microbiology. Methodist. Home: 1604 Moss Creek Rd Waycross GA 31501-4184

HATFIELD, WILLIAM KEITH, minister; b. Detroit, Dec. 26, 1951; s. William Grant and Marquita (Ratliff) H.; m. Sharon Jean, Aug. 26, 1972; children: Sarah, Elisabeth, Matthew, Charity, Jonathan, Joshua. BA, Bapt. Bible Coll., 1976. Ordained to ministry Beacon Bapt. Ch., 1976. Assoc. pastor Brown Ave. Bapt. Ch., Springfield, Mo., 1974-76; pastor Bible Bapt. Ch., South Haven, Mich., 1976-79, Golden Gate Bapt. Ch., Tulsa, 1979-85, Charity Bapt. Ch., Tulsa, 1985—; prof. O.T. Survey Mingo Bible Inst., 1987—; mem. bd. advisors Moral Majority, Tulsa, 1981—; pres. Dynamics for Living, Inc. Author: Dynamics for Living, A Heart for God, When God Empties You; columnist Tulsa Tribune, 1983—; host Dynamics for Living radio program; host TV show Dynamics for Living, 1982-83, 85—. Spokesman Oklahomans for Life, 1983-85, Tulsans for Life, 1983-85. Republican. Home: PO Box 691050 Tulsa OK 74169-1050 Office: Charity Bapt Ch 13350 E 21st St Tulsa OK 74134

HATGIL, PAUL PETER, artist, sculptor, educator; b. Manchester, N.H., Feb. 18, 1921; s. Peter and Katina (Karkadou) H.; m. Katherine Haritos. BS, Mass. Coll. of Art, 1950; MFA, Columbia U., 1951. Instr. art U. Tex., Austin, 1951-54, asst. prof., 1954-56, assoc. prof., 1956-67, prof., 1967—, from instr. in art to prof., 1951-85; design curator Archer M. Huntington Gallery U. Tex. Mus., Austin, 1965-68; prof. emeritus U. Tex., Austin, 1985—; vis. instr. Columbia U. (summer) 1958; designed and installed Tex. Pavilion Exhbn., N.Y. World's Fair; ccord. for Gov. John Connolly's Exhbn. of Art and Conf. on the Arts; aux. edn. officer Dist. 8 U.S. Coast Guard, 1965-74. Author: (autobiography) Apostolos, The Immigrant's Son, 1990; (book) Contemporary Encaustic Painting, 1994; contbr. numerous articles and papers to profl. jours.Internat. and Nat. exhbns. include: 42 annual faculty exhbns. U. Tex., Austin, 2d, 3d, 4th Internat. Invitational Exhbn. of Ceramic Art Smithsonian Mus., Washington, 2d, 3d and 7th Nat. Decorative Arts Exhbns., Wichita, Kans., Internat. Invitational Exhbn. of Ceramic Art Iowa State U., Ceder Rapids; in numerous nat. and internat. mus. and private collections including St. Paul's Luth. Ch., U. Tex. Bus. Administrn. Bldg., Huston Tillotson Coll., Seguin Luth. Coll., U. Tex. Faculty Club. Served with U.S. Army Air Force, 1943-45, PTO. Recipient Estelle Grey Meml. prize in art, Margaret Flowers prize in art, White Mus., San Antonio, Wolff and Marx prize in art, Dallas Mus. of Fine Arts; purchase prizes Dallas Mus. of Art, Laguan Gloria Mus. Austin; grantee U. Tex. Mem. Am. Hellenic Ednl. and Progressice Assn., Am. Legion. Home: 2203 Onion Creek Pky Unit 7 Austin TX 78747-1648

HATHAWAY, AMOS TOWNSEND, retired naval officer, educator; b. Pueblo, Colo., Dec. 5, 1913; s. James Amos and Nina (North) H. B.S., U.S. Naval Acad., 1935; postgrad. U.S. Naval War Coll., 1947-48; M.A. in Teaching, Duke U., 1965-66; m. Marianne Langdon Train, June 10, 1937 (dec. Dec. 1972); children: Joan Langdon, Marianne Train, Melinda North (dec.), Barbara Spencer, Sarah Townsend; m. Gay Johnson Blair, Jan. 2, 1979. Commd. ensign USN, 1935, advanced through grades to capt., 1954; exec. officer, navigator destroyer minesweeper Zane, Guadalcanal, 1942; command destroyer Heermann, Battle off Samar, 1944; mem. faculty U.S. Naval Acad., 1945-47, U.S. Naval War Coll., 1951-53; mem. war staff Gen. MacArthur, Korea, 1948-50, writer theater logistic plan Inchon Landing, 1950; exec. officer cruiser St. Paul, 1950-51; command Destroyer Div. 92, 1953-54, command attack transport Okanogan, 1958-59; command cruiser Rochester, 1959-60; mem. joint staff Joint Chiefs of Staff, 1961-63, dir. logistic plans Office Chief of Naval Ops., 1963-65, ret., 1965; asst. prof. math. and computer sci. The Citadel, Charleston, S.C., 1966-79. Decorated Navy Cross, Legion of Merit (2), Bronze Star (2). Mem. Math. Assn. Am., U.S. Naval Acad. Alumni Assn., U.S. Naval Acad. Athletic Assn. (bd. dir. 1945-47), U.S. Naval Inst., Kappa Delta Pi. Club: Army Navy (Washington). Home: 11 Sayle Rd Charleston SC 29407-7517 also: PO Box 5463 Charlottesville VA 22905-5463

HATHAWAY, CHARLES E., academic administrator. BS in Physics, Tex. A&M U., 1958; PhD in Physics, U. Okla., 1965. Mem. faculty dept. physics Kans. State U., Little Rock, 1965-81; dept. head Kans. State U., 1971-81; dean Coll. Sci. and Engring. U. Tex., San Antonio, 1981-86; v.p. acad. affairs Wright State U., 1986-93; chancellor U. Ark., Little Rock, 1993—. Founder, sr. editor Met. Univs.: An Internat. Forum. Mem. Ark. Sci. and Tech. Authority, 1995—. Woodrow Wilson fellow U. Okla. Mem. Ark. Sci. and Tech. Authority. Office: U Ark Little Rock Office of Chancellor 2801 S University Ave Little Rock AR 72204-1000

HATHCOCK, JOHN EDWARD, vocalist; b. Memphis, Sept. 6, 1955. BA in Psychology, Memphis State U., (now U. Memphis), 1986; studied with Dr. David Williams, U. Memphis; studied with Ethel Maxwell, 14 yrs. Singer, performer, composer opera and sacred classical music; pres. Position Prodns., 1988-90; pres., founder Soaring Spirit Music, 1996—. Author: Seasons of Wonder, 1995; patentee in field. Mem. Bellevue Choir, 1991-92, Christian Coalition, 1996—; life mem. Rep. NAt. Com., 1996—, Nat. Rep. Senatorial Com., 1996—. Recipient Mr. Wheelchair Am. award, 1990, Man of Yr. award Happi Internat. Talent, Trailblazer award City of Memphis, 1990. Mem. Gospel Music Assn. (profl.), Beethoven Club (dir. pub. rels. 1993), Internat. Platform Assn., Heritage Found. Baptist. Home: 4285 Powell Ave Memphis TN 38122-2634

HATTEM, ALBERT WORTH, physician; b. High Point, N.C., May 20, 1951; s. Henry Albert and Stella Jane (Penfield) H.; m. Deborah Elaine Bellew, Nov. 9, 1974. BA, U. S.C., 1985, MD, 1989. Diplomate Nat. Bd. Med. Examiners. Officer McColl (S.C.) Police Dept., 1970-71; mgr. Norris Ambulance Svc., Spartanburg, S.C., 1971-72; spl. events mgr. Coca-Cola Co., Spartanburg, 1972-73; tng. officer, paramedic Emergency Med. Svcs., Spartanburg, 1973-76; tng. coord. emergency med. svcs. divsn. S.C. Dept. Health, Columbia, 1976-83; intern U. Tenn. Med. Ctr., Knoxville, 1989-90, resident in ob-gyn., 1990-93; obstetrician-gynecologist Paradise Valley Women's Care, Las Vegas, Nev., 1993-94; med. dir. Russellville (Ky.) Women's Ctr., 1995—; clin. assoc. prof. Vanderbilt U. Sch. Nursing. Mem. faculty S.C. Heart Assn., Columbia, 1981-89; adv. coun. S.C. Emergency Med. Svcs., Columbia, 1983-89. Fellow ACOG (jr.), ACS (assoc.); mem. AMA (v.p. student sect. 1985-86), Am. Med. Student Assn. (chpt. v.p. 1985-86), Am. Fertility Soc., Soc. Laparoscopic Surgeons, Am. Assn. Gynecologic Laparoscopists, N.Am. Menopause Soc., Logan County Med. Soc., Logan County Health Bd., Hon. Order Ky. Colonels. Office: Russellville Women's Ctr PO Box 596 Russellville KY 42276-0596

HATTEN, ROBERT RANDOLPH, lawyer; b. Charlottesville, Va., Jan. 27, 1948; s. John Quackenbush and Mary Lou (Payne) H.; m. Anne Meredith Sherman, Aug. 14, 1970 (div. Jan. 9181); children: Catharine Cary, Anne Meredith; m. Shirley Kaye Ambrose, Feb. 21, 1981; 1 stepchild, Christopher Hilton. BA, Hampden-Sydney Coll., 1969; JD, Washington & Lee U., 1972. Bar: Va. 1972, U.S. Dist. Ct. (ea. dist.) Va. 1973, U.S. Ct. Appeals (4th cir.) 1973, U.S. Supreme Ct. 1982. Law clk. U.S. Dist. Ct. (ea. dist.) Va., Norfolk, 1972-73; assoc. Patten & Wornom, Newport News, Va., 1973-75; ptnr. Patten, Wornom & Watkins, Newport News, 1976—; bd. dirs. Asbestos Health Claimants Com., Johns Manville Bankruptcy Region, N.Y.C., 1983-89; mem. MDL Steering Com., 1991—. Contbr. articles to profl. jours. Bd. dirs. Peninsula Big Bros. Assn. Hampton Va., 1974-79; chmn. Newport News League of Downtown Churches, 1978; bd. trustees Lexington (Ky.) Theol. Sem., Hampden-Sydney Coll., 1994—. Mem. ATLA (mem. key congl. liaison, spl.), Am. Bd. Trial Advocates, Va. Trial Lawyers Assn. (bd. govs. 1985-91, spl. award for courageous advocacy 1987), Newport News Bar Assn. Democrat. Club: James River Country (Newport News). Home: 9 Hopemont Dr Newport News VA 23606-2116 Office: Patten Wornom & Watkins 12350 Jefferson Ave Ste 360 Newport News VA 23602-6956

HATTON, QUINDELL LOUISE, poet; b. Suffolk, Va., Sept. 2, 1953; d. Wilbert Thomas Jordan Sr. and Elsie Louise (Mann) Porter; m. Burt Hatton Jr., Sept. 4, 1979; 3 children. Poet Southeastern Va. Art Assn., Norfolk, 1995—. Author: A Message in a Rhyme, 1995, A Message in a Rhyme II, 1995, Fill it Up With Grace, 1996, Journey Toward Jesus 96, 1995. Home: 7702 Orcutt Ave Newport News VA 23605

HAUBER, FREDERICK AUGUST, ophthalmologist; b. Pitts., July 3, 1948; s. Michael H. and Cecilia (Azinger) H.; m. Cathy Lu Rosellini, Aug. 3, 1981; children: Elizabeth Alexandra, Natalia Fredericka. BS in Microbiology cum laude, U. Pitts., 1970; MD, U. Tenn., 1974. Intern U. South Fla., Tampa, 1975, resident in ophthalmology, 1982; pvt. practice Pasco Eye Inst., New Port Richey, Fla., 1983—; asst. clin. prof. U. South Fla., Tampa, 1984—; rechr., spkr. in field, 1990—; cons. Optimed, Inc. Contbr. articles to profl. jours. Advisor health care cost containment com., Tarpon Springs, Fla., 1988; founder Pasco County Diabetes Assn.; mem. bd. counsellors U. Tampa. Fellow ACS, Am. Acad. Ophthalmology; mem. Southeastern U.S. Debate Soc. Office: Pasco Eye Inst 5347 Main St New Port Richey FL 34652-2506

HAUBERG, ROBERT ENGELBRECHT, JR., lawyer; b. Jackson, Miss., Oct. 26, 1943; s. Robert Engelbrecht and Robbie Mae (Bowen) H.; m. Claudia Carithers; children: Greta, Patrick, Michael. BA, U. Miss., 1965; MA, Yale U., 1967, JD, 1970. Bar: N.Y. 1971, U.S. Dist. Ct. (so. dist.) N.Y. 1971, U.S. Ct. Appeals (2d cir.) 1971, D.C. 1974, U.S. Dist. Ct. D.C. 1974, U.S. Ct. Appeals (D.C. cir.) 1974, U.S. Supreme Ct. 1974, U.S. Ct. Appeals (5th cir.) 1988, U.S. Dist. Ct. (no. dist.) Tex. 1989, U.S. Dist. Ct. (so. dist.) Miss. 1989, Miss. 1991, U.S. Dist. Ct. (no. dist.) Miss. 1991. Assoc. Donovan, Leisure, Newton & Irvine, N.Y.C., 1970-73; asst. U.S. atty. U.S. Dept. Justice, Washington, 1973-76, trial atty., 1976-79, asst. chief, 1979-86, sr. trial atty., 1986-90, sr. litigation counsel Dallas Bank Fraud Task Force, 1990-91; ptnr. Watkins, Ludlam & Stennis, Jackson, Miss., 1991—. Contbr. numerous articles to profl. jours. Mem. ABA (mem. anti-trust, criminal justice, litigation sects.), D.C. Bar Assn., Miss. Bar, Internat. Bar Assn., Yale Law Sch. Assn. (D.C. pres. 1986-87, exec. com. 1987-88, 93—), Beta Theta Pi. Episcopalian. Home: 4656 Calnita Pl Jackson MS 39211-5801 Office: 633 N State St Jackson MS 39202-3300

HAUENSTEIN, GEORGE CAREY, life insurance executive; b. Hattiesburg, Miss., May 8, 1936; s. George Jacob Jr. and Earline (Allsup) J.; m. Marjorie Rutland, Aug. 27, 1960; children: Ruth Hauenstein Austin, George Jacob III. Student, Miss. State U., Starkville, 1954-56; BS, U. So. Miss., 1961. CLU. Prin. G. Carey Hauenstein & Assocs., Laurel, Miss., 1962—. Contbr. articles to numerous profl. publs.; spkr. profl. convs. and symposia. Mem. Jones County Econ. Devel. Authority, Laurel; bd. dirs. Miss. Easter Seal Found., 1966, Laurel Community Concert Assn., 1990—; chmn. dist. xi Am. Heart Assn. 1964-65; ruling elder Evang. Presbyn. Ch.; bd trustees French Camp Acad. Served to Sgt. U.S. Marine Corps, 1956-58. Otho Smith fellow U. Miss., 1989; named to Hall of Fame The New England, 1982. Me. Nat. Assn. Life Underwriters, Am. Soc. CLU and CFC, Internat. Ins. Soc., Assn. for Advanced Life Underwriting, Miss. Estate Planning Coun., Miss. Assn. Life Underwriters (pres. 1964-65), Million Dollar Round Table (exec. com. 1986-90, pres. 1989), Miss. Chpt. CLU (dir. 1991).

HAUG, JAMES CHARLES, business and management educator; b. Nashua, N.H., Dec. 3, 1948; s. Charles Louis and Doris A. (Lynch) H.; m. Mary Theresa Dowley, Dec. 19, 1970; children: Michele, Emily, Brian, Matthew, Jonathan, Mary Louise. Student, Manhattan Coll., Bronx, 1966-68; BS, Columbia U., 1970; MBA, U. Calif., Berkeley, 1971; DBA, George Washington U., 1981. Registered profl. engr., Calif. Commd. ensign USN, 1971, advanced through grades to lt. comdr., 1981; activity customer engr. Navy Pub. Wks. Ctr., Oakland, Calif., 1974-75; asst. pub. wks. officer Naval Rsch. Lab., Washington, 1975-77; facilities planning officer Naval Data Automation Command, Washington, 1977-80; pub. wks. officer Naval Air Sta., South Weymouth, Mass., 1980-82; facilities planning instr. Naval Civil Engring. Officer Sch., Port Hueneme, Calif., 1982-85; dir. contracts group Naval Air Sta., Pensacola, Fla., 1985-88; asst. officer in chg. Navy Broadway Complex Project, San Diego, 1988-91; ret.; asst. prof. Troy State U., Pensacola, 1991-92; coord. MS in Mgmt. program Troy State U., Norfolk, Va., 1992—; vis. prof. U. San Diego, 1991-92; mem. adv. com. San Diego ext. U. Calif., 1989-91. Contbr. articles to profl. jours. Chmn. adv. bd. on spl. edn. Hampton (Va.) City Schs., 1994-96; scoutmaster Boy Scouts Am., San Diego, 1991; treas. Early Childhood Ctr., Alexandria, Va., 1978-80. Mem. Alpha Pi Mu, Tau Beta Pi, Beta Gamma Sigma. Roman Catholic. Home: 60 Chowning Dr Hampton VA 23664-1755 Office: Troy State Univ PO Box 15218 Norfolk VA 23511-0218

HAUGHT, JAMES ALBERT, JR., journalist, newspaper editor; b. Reader, W.Va., Feb. 20, 1932; s. James Albert and Beulah (Fish) H.; m. Nancy Carolyn Brady, Apr. 22, 1958; children: Joel, Jacob, Jeb, Cassie. Student, Morris Harvey Coll., 1950-52; part-time, W.Va. State Coll., 1960-63. Apprentice printer Charleston Daily Mail, 1951-53; reporter Charleston Gazette, 1953—, varied positions as night and weekend city editor, music and film critic, govt., schs., suburban, religion and investigative reporter, 1970-82, assoc. editor, 1983-92, editor, 1992—. Author: Holy Horrors, 1990, Science in a Nanosecond, 1990, The Art of Lovemaking, 1992, Holy Hatred, 1994, 2000 Years of Disbelief, 1996. Recipient award Headliners Club, 1971, 1st Ann. Consumer Writing prize Nat. Press Club, 1973, Nat. Hwy. Safety Writing award Uniroyal Tire Co., 1975, First Amendment award Sigma Delta Chi, 1977, Merit award ABA, 1977, Consumer Writing prize Nat. Press Club, 1979, 83, Spl. award Religion Newswriters Assn., 1980, Health Journalism award Am. Chiropractic Assn., 1981, 83, First Amendment award People for Am. Way, 1986, Nat. award for edn. reporting Edn. Writers Assn., 1989, Hugh M. Hefner First Amendment award Playboy Found., 1989, Benjamin Fine award for edn. reporting Nat. Assn. Secondary Sch. Prins., 1990. Democrat. Unitarian. Home: 15 KH Lake Shore Dr Charleston WV 25313 Office: Charleston Gazette 1001 Virginia St E Charleston WV 25301-2835

HAUKE, KATHLEEN ARMSTRONG, writer, editor; b. Kalamazoo, Mich., Aug. 27, 1935; d. Robert J. and Katherine E. (Gall) Armstrong; m. Richard L. Hauke, Sept. 20, 1958; children: Katy DuGarm, Nellie Ohr, Andrew M., Henry J. BA Journalism, U. Mich., 1958; MA in English, U. R.I., 1962, PhD in English, 1981. Teaching asst. English U. R.I., Kingston, 1976-81; instr. Hopkinsville (Ky.) C.C., 1984; asst. prof. Morris Brown Coll., Atlanta, 1986-91; vis. prof. Emory U., Atlanta, 1985; part-time instr. Ga. State U., Atlanta, 1986-88; vis. lectr. U. Nairobi, Kenya, 1988-89; lectr. Spelman Coll., Atlanta, 1994—. Editor: Dark Side of Hopkinsville, 1991; editor (newsletter) Citizens to Advance Negro Edn., 1969-71; contbr. articles to profl. jours. Grantee NEH, 1984. Mem. MLA, Coll. Lang. Assn., Langston Hughes Soc. Democrat. Roman Catholic. Home: 456 Mcgill Pl NE Atlanta GA 30312-1070

HAUMSCHILD, MARK JAMES, pharmacist; b. West Bend, Wis., Apr. 6, 1951; s. James Harlow and Helen Marie (Bohn) H.; m. Mary Jo Snider, Oct. 15, 1976; 1 child, Ryan James. BA in Chemistry, Fla. Atlantic U., 1973; BS in Pharmacy, U. Fla., 1976; MS in Mgmt., U. South Fla., 1982; PharmD, Mercer U., 1984. Cert. nuclear pharmacist; cert. nutritional support pharmacist. Continuing edn. instr. St. Petersburg (Fla.) Jr. Coll., 1977-81; staff pharmacist Morton F. Plant Hosp., Clearwater, Fla., 1976-78, nuclear pharmacy coordinator, 1978-83, clin. pharmacist, 1984-86, resident, 1984-85; ctr. mgr. Foster Infusioncare, St. Petersburg, 1986-88; gen. mgr. Healthinfusion Inc., St. Petersburg, 1988-95; pres. Pharm D. Cons., Largo, Fla., 1984—; regional dir. ops.-Fla. UPC Health Network, Clearwater, Fla., 1995—; adj. instr. Coll. Pharmacy, U. Fla., Gainesville, 1980-86. Mem. Am. Soc. Hosp. Pharmacists, S.W. Soc. Hosp. Pharmacists, Am. Pharm. Assn. (cert. in nuclear pharmacy), Soc. Nuclear Pharmacy, Am. Coll. Hosp. Adminstrs., SW Fla. Soc. Hosp. Pharmacists (cert. nuclear pharmacist), Beta Gamma Sigma, Phi Kappa Phi. Republican. Home: 12494 104th Ter Largo FL 34648-3407 Office: UPC Health Network 13920 58th St N Ste 1011 Clearwater FL 34620-3770

HAUPTLI, BARBARA BEATRICE, environmental specialist; b. Glenwood Springs, Colo., Sept. 20, 1953; d. Frederick James and Evelyn June (Rood) H.; m. Curtis Scott Bostian, July 4, 1992. BBA, Western State Coll., 1975. Contract specialist USA-TACOM, Warren, Mich., 1981-86; contract buyer Martin Marietta Orlando (Fla.) Aerospace, 1986; purchasing expediter Moog, Inc., Clearwater, Fla., 1986-89; subcontract adminstr. Olin Ordnance, St. Petersburg, Fla., 1989-91; sr. subcontract adminstr. Olin Ordnance, 1991-93; reimbursement specialist Tod. K. Allen, Inc., 1993—. Mem. Nat. Contract Mgmt. Assn.

HAUSCHILD, DOUGLAS CAREY, optometrist; b. Manchester, Conn., Oct. 3, 1955; s. Vernon Francis and Barbara Gwendolyn (Rose) H.; 1 child, Chelsea Anna. BA in Biology magna cum laude, Wesleyan U., 1977; OD, New Eng. Coll. Optometry, 1981. Clinician Boston Eye Clinic, 1978-81; assoc. Drs. Todd, Todd & Hauschild, Hendersonville, N.C., 1981-84; owner, optometrist Weaverville (N.C.) Eye Assocs., 1984—, Asheville (N.C.) Eye Care Assocs., 1985—; clinician Walter Reed Army Med. Ctr., 1980, West Roxbury VA Med. Ctr., 1981, Newenco Pediatric/Geriatric Sply. Clinic, 1981; nominee Buncombe County Bd. of Health. Contbr. health articles to newsletters. Mem. Henderson County Bd. Health, 1983-85; actor Asheville Community Theatre, 1988—; instr. phys. edn. Evangel. Chapel Christian Acad., Asheville, 1985-86; mem. Bent Creek Bapt. Ch. Choir, Soloist; leader Bent Creek Bapt. Ch. Care Group, 1987-91; choir mem., soloist St. Eugene's Roman Cath. Ch., 1992—. Mem. Am. Optometric Assn., So. Coun. Optometrists, N.C. State Optometric Soc., Mtn. Dist. Optometric Soc., Am. Pub. Health Assn., Lions (past pres.), KC, Elks, Beta Sigma Kappa, Delta Tau Delta. Republican. Office: Weaverville Eye Assocs PO Box 1628 Weaverville NC 28787-1628

HAUSE, EDITH COLLINS, college administrator; b. Rock Hill, S.C., Dec. 11, 1933; d. Ernest O. and Violet (Smith) Collins; m. James Luke Hause, Sept. 3, 1955; children—Stephen Mark, Felicia Gaye Hause Friesen. B.A., Columbia Coll., S.C., 1956; postgrad. U. N.C.-Greensboro, 1967, U. S.C., 1971-75. Tchr. Richland Dist. II, Columbia, 1971-74; dir. alumnae affairs Columbia Coll., 1974-82, v.p. alumnae affairs, 1982-84, v.p. devel., 1984-89, v.p. alumnae rels., 1989—. Named Outstanding Tchr. of Yr., Richland Dist. II, 1974. Mem. Columbia Network for Female Execs., Council for Advancement and Support Edn., Nat. Soc. Fund Raising Execs., S.C. Assn. Alumni Dirs. (pres. 1995-97). Republican. Methodist. Home: 92 Mariners Pointe Rd Prosperity SC 29127-9386 Office: Columbia Coll Alumnae Office Columbia SC 29203

HAUSMAN, BRUCE, lawyer; b. N.Y.C., Mar. 4, 1930; s. Samuel and Vera (Kuttler) H.; m. Jeanne Epstein, June 8, 1952 (div. Oct. 1992); children: Robert Lloyd, Arlene; m. Amy Kadin, Dec. 12, 1992. BA, Brown U., 1951; MS, Columbia U., 1952; postgrad., N.Y. Law Sch., 1979. Bar: N.Y. 1980. Dir. Belding Real Estate Corp., Corticelli Real Estate Corp., 1960-63; pres., dir. Va. Dyeing Corp., 1962-64; div. mgr. M. Hausman & Sons, Inc. (named changed to Belding Hausman Fabrics Inc.), 1952-64; ptnr. Kastex Corp., L.A., 1964; regional sales mgr. Belding Heminway Co., Inc., 1965; pres., dir. contract knitting divsn. Mozzil Knits Inc., 1969-73; exec., adminstrv. officer apparel fabric divsn. Belding Heminway Co., Inc., N.Y.C., 1966-73, exec. asst. to chmn. bd., 1973-74, group pres. home furnishings divsn., 1975-79, corp. v.p., 1979; corp. counsel Belding Heminway Co., Inc., 1980-85; sr. vice chmn. Belding Heminway Co., Inc., N.Y.C., 1980-86, chmn. exec. com., 1981-86, cons., 1987-88, sr. v.p., 1988-92; ret., 1993; exec. adminstrv. head Belding Hausman Fabrics Inc., 1975-79; adminstrv. officer Va. Dyeing Corp., Belding Corticelli Fiberglass Fabrics Inc.; pres. M.K. Leasing Corp., 1974; bd. dirs. Plastigone Techs., Inc., chmn. compensation com., mem. audit com., 1992—; mem. exec. com. Daltex Med. Scis., Inc., 1993, pres., CEO, 1995—. Bd. overseers Parsons Sch. Design, 1975-91; trustee, mem. exec. com. Beth Israel Med. Ctr., N.Y.C., 1976-93, hon. trustee, 1993—; trustee, mem. exec. com. Beth Israel Nursing Home, 1991-93, hon. trustee, 1994—. Named Man of Yr., Fabric Salesmens Guild, Inc., 1972. Mem. Textile Salesmen's Assn. (bd. govs., Man of Yr. award 1987), Textile Distbrs. Assn. (gov. 1979, v.p. 1982, sec. 1983-87), Am. Arbitration Assn., NCCJ (bd. dirs. 1974-88).

HAUSS, EDWARD EARL, nurse legal consultant; b. Salina, Kans., Dec. 23, 1955; s. Edward A. and Fannie Mae (Nichols) H.; m. Frances L. Harbour, Sept. 5, 1981; children: Christopher, John, Nicholas, Benjamin. BSN, U. Tex., Arlington, 1977. CNOR. Staff nurse Harris Meth.-Ft. Worth, Tex., 1977-78; asst. supr. Harris Meth.-Ft. Worth, 1978-82; legal nurse cons. Law Firm of Darrell Keith, P.C., Ft. Worth, 1982—. Mem. Assn. Oper. Rm. Nurses, Am. Assn. Legal Nurse Cons., Legal Assts. Div.-State Bar Tex., Ft. Worth Paralegal Assn. Office: Law Firm Darrell Keith PC 201 Main St Ste 1400 Fort Worth TX 76102-3118

HAVEN, MARTHA BILLIE, school system administrator; b. Chatsworth, Ga., Sept. 12, 1928; d. James B. and Maud A. (Whitener) Butler; m. Robert E. Morrison, Feb. 26, 1949 (dec. June 18, 1967); children: Pamela Elizabeth Morrison, Robert Michael Morrison, Martha Diana Morrison; m. Wendell Lee Haven, Mar. 18, 1972. BS, North Ga. Coll., 1953; MA Edn. Specialist, George Peabody Coll., 1964. From classroom tchr. to asst. supt. Murray County Bd. Edn., Chatsworth, 1955—. Recipient appreciation award Am. Heart Assn., 1984, Ga. State Supt. Schs., 1984. Mem. Nat. Assn. Educators, Ga. Assn. Curriculum/Instrn., Ga. Assn. Educators (appreciation award 1984), Murray County Assn. Educators, Delta Kappa Gamma. Baptist. Home: PO Box 275 111 Colonial Hills Dr Chatsworth GA 30705 Office: Murray County Sch Sys 100 Magnolia Dr Box 40 Chatsworth GA 30705

HAVENS, JAN, artist; b. Norfolk, Va., May 7, 1948; d. Barry DeWitt Havens; 1 child, Christine. BS, Barton Coll., 1970; MA, Vanderbilt U., 1973. One-woman shows include Cheekwood Bot. Gardens, Nashville, 1980, S.E. Ctr. for Contemporary Art, Winston-Salem, N.C., 1983, Zimmerman/Saturn Gallery, Nashville, 1991; group exhbns. include Renwick Gallery, Washington, 1981, Mid. Tenn. State U., 1982, Elizabeth Fortner Gallery, Santa Barbara, Calif., 1983, Bloomingdale's, N.Y.C., 1984, Dirkson Senate Office Bldg., Washington, 1985, Hand Workshop, Richmond, Va., 1986, Metro Arts Commn., Nashville, 1987, 91, Vanderbilt U., Nashville, 1990, Farmington Valley Arts Ctr., Avon, Conn., 1991, Blue Spiral Gallery, Asheville, N.C., 1993; represented in permanent collections; contrb. photos, articles to profl.& popular mags. Mem. So. Highland Handicraft Guild, Piedmont Craftsmen. Home and Office: 1121 Graybar Ln Nashville TN 37204-3214

HAVENS, MURRAY CLARK, political scientist, educator; b. Council Grove, Kans., Aug. 21, 1932; s. Ralph Murray and Catherine Clara (Clark) H.; m. Agnes Marie Scharpf, July 5, 1958 (dec. 1969); children—Colin Scott, Theresa Agnes. B.A., U. Ala., 1953; M.A. (Woodrow Wilson fellow 1953-54), Johns Hopkins U., 1954, Ph.D., 1958. Postdoctoral fellow Brookings Instn., Washington, 1958-59; asst. prof. polit. sci. Duke U., 1959-61; from asst. prof. to prof. U. Tex., Austin, 1961-73; vis. lectr. U. Sydney (Australia), 1966; prof. polit. sci. Tex. Tech U., Lubbock, 1973—; chmn. dept. Tex. Tech U., 1975-83. Author: City Versus Farm?, 1957, The Challenges to Democracy, 1965, The Politics of Assassination, 1970, Assassination and Terrorism, 1975, Texas Politics Today, 1995; book rev. editor Jour. Politics, 1971-83; contbr. numerous articles to profl. jours. Served with AUS, 1954-56. Mem. Am. Polit. Sci. Assn., So. Polit. Sci. Assn., Southwestern Polit. Sci. Assn. (pres. 1983-84), AAUP, Phi Beta Kappa. Home: 7408 Topeka Ave Lubbock TX 79424-2216 Office: Tex Tech Univ Dept Polit Sci Lubbock TX 79409-1015

HAVNER, KERRY SHUFORD, civil engineering and solid mechanics educator; b. Huntington, W.Va., Feb. 20, 1934; s. Alfred Sidney and Jessie May (Fowler) H.; m. Roberta Lee Rider, Aug. 28, 1954; children: Karen Elese Smith, Clark Alan, Kris Sidney. BSCE, Okla. State U., 1955, MS, 1956, PhD, 1959. Registered prof. engr., Okla. Stress analyst Douglas Aircraft Co., Tulsa, 1956; from instr. to asst. prof. civil engring. Okla. State U., Stillwater, 1957-62; sr. stress and vibration engr. Garrett Corp., Phoenix, 1962-63; sect. chief solid mechs. rsch. missile/space systems divsn. McDonnell-Douglas Corp., Santa Monica, Calif., 1963-68; lectr. civil engring. U. So. Calif., L.A., 1965-68; from assoc. prof. to prof. civil engring. N.C. State U., Raleigh, 1968-82, prof. civil engring. and materials sci., 1982—; sr. vis. dept. applied math. and theoretical physics U. Cambridge, 1981, 89. Author: Finite Plastic Deformation of Crystalline Solids, 1992; contbg. author:

Mechanics of Solids, The Rodney Hill 60th Anniversary Volume, 1982; contbr. articles to Jour. Applied Math. and Physics, Jour. of Mechs. and Physics of Solids, Acta Mechanica, Procs. Royal Soc., others; bd. editors Mechs. of Materials, Internat. Jour. Plasticity. 1st lt. U.S. Army, 1961. Rsch. grantee NSF, 1971, 74, 76, 78, 81, 83, 87, 91, 94; vis. fellow Clare Hall, 1981; recipient Melvin R. Lohmann medal Okla. State U., 1994. Fellow ASCE (sec. engring. mechs. divsn. 1983-85, chmn. 1987-88, chmn. engring. mechs. adv. bd. 1990-91, chmn. TAC-CERF awards com. 1991-94; assoc. editor Jour. Engring. Mechs. 1981-83), Am. Acad. Mechanics (assoc. editor Mechanics, 1991—); mem. ASME, Soc. Engring. Sci., Soc. Indsl. and Applied Math., Sigma Xi. Democrat. Methodist. Home: 3331 Thomas Rd Raleigh NC 27607-6743 Office: NC State U Dept Civil Engring Box 7908 Raleigh NC 27695

HAWASH, RALPH R., obstetrician, gynecologist; b. Assylet, Egypt, Feb. 3, 1931; came to U.S., 1966; s. Rafeil and Louise (Hawash) H.; children: Amy, Vena, Graham John. MB, BChir, U. Cairo, 1955; MB, BS, U. London, 1962. Former mem. staff N.W. Met., London, Radcliffe Infirmary, U. Oxford, Eng., Wayne State U., Detroit; pvt. practice Detroit and Houston, 1966—; mem. staff Houston N.W. Med. Ctr., Cypress Fairbanks Med. Ctr., Houston. Fellow ACS, Am. Coll. Obstetricians/Gynecologists, Am. Coll. Fertility; mem. Royal Coll. Obstetricians/Gynecologists. Republican. Christian Orthodox. Office: 800 Peakwood Dr Ste 7E Houston TX 77090-2904

HAWES, WILLIAM KENNETH, communication educator; b. Grand Rapids, Mich., Mar. 6, 1931; s. William Kenneth and Cora Elizabeth (Tibble) H.; m. Ella Margaret Plant, Aug. 13, 1961 (div. Apr. 1985); children: William III, Robert Ernest. AB, Eastern Mich. U., 1955; MA, U. Mich., 1956, PhD, 1960. Teaching asst. U. Mich., Ann Arbor, 1956-57; instr. English and speech Eastern Mich. U., Ypsilanti, 1956-60; asst. prof., mgr. KTCU Tex. Christian U., Ft. Worth, 1960-64; vis. assoc. prof., mgr. WUNC U. N.C., Chapel Hill, 1964-65; assoc. prof., mgr. KUHF U. Houston, 1965-76, prof., 1976—; admissions bd. Biomed. Program, Sch. Allied Health Scis., U. Tex. Health Sci. Ctr., Houston, 1974-95. Author: The Performer in Mass Media, 1976, American Television Drama, 1986, Television Performing, 1991, Ante La Camera, 1993, Public Television: America's First Station, 1996; contbg. author: Understanding Radio, 1967, 85, La Radio: Une Carriere, 1970, Understanding Television, 1978, Television Station Management and Operations, 1989; editor: Pornography Cinema Community Standards, 1975, 82, 93; prodr., creator TV series including Video Workshop, 1967—; film guest Fed. Republic of Germany, 1981. With USAF, Mich. Air NG, 1949-54. Recipient Avery Hopwood award U. Mich., 1957; grantee U. Houston and/or NEH, 1982, 83, 86, 87, 91; named to U. Houston London Program, 1984, 94. Mem. Am. Film Inst. Home: Parc V-902 3600 Montrose Blvd Houston TX 77006-4658 Office: U Houston Sch of Comm Houston TX 77204-4072

HAWK, CHARLES SILAS, computer programmer, analyst; b. Tulsa, Mar. 8, 1953; s. Samuel Shumway and Patricia Lee (Livingston) H.; m. Emelia Elizabeth Presley. BS in Zoology, U. Tex., 1980. Cons. Med. Systems, Houston, Dallas, 1982-87, Mfg. Systems, Dallas, 1987-89, The Hawk Group, Dallas, 1987—. Del. Tex. Rep. Conv., Houston, 1984. Active St. George's Episcopal Ch. Commd. USNR, 1984. Grantee Merit scholarship U. Tex., 1974. Mem. AAAS, IEEE, N.Y. Acad. Scis., Tau Kappa Epsilon, Mason. Mem. Christian Ch. Home and Office: 1655 Randolph Pl Apt # 1 Memphis TN 38120-4358

HAWK, JOHN CHRISMAN, III, surgeon; b. Charlottesville, Va., Jan. 26, 1947; s. John Chrisman Jr. and Nancy Dinwiddie H.; m. Frances Anne Solley, May 30, 1970; children: Anne, James, John, Robert. BS cum laude, Davidson Coll., 1967; MD, Vanderbilt U., 1971. Diplomate Am. Bd. Surgery. Intern Mass. Gen. Hosp., Boston, 1971-72; from asst. resident to chief resident in surgery Harvard Med. Sch., Boston, 1972-76; clin. fellow in surgery Harvard Med. Sch., 1976; surgeon, v.p. Charleston (S.C.) Surg. Assoc., P.A., 1978-90; clin. instr. in surgery Med. U. S.C., 1978-82; asst. clin. prof. surgery Med. U. S.C., Charleston, 1982—; surgeon, pres. Charleston (S.C.) Surg. Assoc., p.a., 1991—; asst. in surgery Mass. Gen. Hosp., 1976; clin. instr. in surgery; active staff Roper Hosp., Charleston, 1978—, St. Francis Xavier Hosp., Charleston, 1978—, East Cooper Cmty. Hosp., Mt. Pleasant, S.C., 1985—. Deacon First Presbyn. Ch., Charleston, 1980-82, chmn., 1982, elder, 1985-87, 92-95, ch. sch. tchr., 1989-96; Charleston unit pres. Am. Cancer Soc., 1982-85, chmn. profl. edn. com. S.C. divsn., 1984-86, v.p., 1985-87, pres., 1987-88; med. adv. com. Carolina Lowcountry ARC Blood Svcs., 1979-89, Hospice Charleston, 1986—; fundraising com. Trident United Way Physicians, 1986, 94. Recipient Disting. Svc. award Am. Cancer Soc., 1985. Fellow ACS; mem. AMA (del. 1992—), S.C. Med. Assn. (chmn. bd. 1988-90, bd. trustees 1985—, pres. 1991-92, chmn. HIV/HBV safety network policy panel 1992—), S.C. Coll. Surgeons, S.C. Surg. Soc., S.C. Oncology Soc., S.C. Med. Assn., Southeastern Surg. Congress, Charleston County Med. Soc. (long-range planning com. 1979, health svcs. rev. com. 1981-84, nominations and pub. policy com. 1981-86, exec. com. 1985—), Charleston County Med. Soc., Rotary (bd. dirs. 1994-96). Alpha Omega Alpha. Presbyterian. Home: 992 Equestrian Dr Mount Pleasant SC 29464-3615 Office: Charleston Surgical Assoc 125 Doughty St Ste 660 Charleston SC 29403-5731

HAWK, SAMUEL SILAS, broadcast engineer, announcer; b. Tulsa, Sept. 2, 1954; s. Samuel S. and Patricia Lee (Livingston) H.; m. DeEtta M. Geller, Mar. 1, 1980; 1 child, Samuel Jr. Assoc. degree in journalism, Tulsa Jr. Coll., 1975; BS in Telecommunications, Oral Roberts U., 1978. Broadcaster various radio stas., Okla., 1972-74; community rels. dir. Sta. KWEN-FM, Tulsa, 1974-76; owner, operator Hawk Prodns., Tulsa, 1976—; news anchor Sta. KVOO, Tulsa, 1976-77; prodn. dir. Stas. KAKC, KBEZ-FM, Tulsa, 1977-79, Sta. KXXO, Tulsa, 1979-80; asst., chmn. bd. Telex Computer Products, Tulsa, 1979-80; broadcaster, chief announcer/audio engr. Sta. KJRH-TV, Tulsa, 1980-89; talk show host The Talk of Tulsa Sta. KTRT, Tulsa, 1991-94; owner-operator The Computercenter, Tulsa, 1988-94; network specialist Bank of Okla., Tulsa, 1994—. Mem. Green Country Computer Assn. (electronic communcations officer 1985-88, systems operator, editor monthly jour.), Tulsa Computer Soc. (bd. dirs. 1982-84, editor monthly jour.). Home: 511 N Wilson St Sand Springs OK 74063-6742 Office: Hawk Prodns Co PO Box 114 Tulsa OK 74101-0114

HAWKE, PAUL HENRY, historian; b. Canton, Ohio, Mar. 9, 1958; s. Richard Carl and Sara (Hemming) H.; m. Gaynel O. Allen, May 2, 1987; children: Cailean Stewart, Angela J. Viney. BA in History, Geography, Mary Washington Coll., 1982; student, Temple U., 1983, U. Ark., 1984-85; MA in History and Heritage Preservation, Ga. State U., 1993. Park tech. Petersburg (Va.) Nat. Battlefield, 1978-81; intern Fredericksburg (Va.) and Spotsylvania Nat. Mil. Park, 1981-82; park ranger Independence Nat. Hist. Park, Phila., 1982-83; park historian Pea Ridge (Ark.) Nat. Mil. Park, 1983-85; historian Southeast Regional Office, Atlanta, 1985-95; S.E. coord. Am. Battlefield Protectio Program, Atlanta, 1991-95, Civil War sites adv. commn. staff, 1991-93; coord. Nat. Historic Landmarks Program, Atlanta, 1986-95; chief interpretation and resources mgmt. Shiloh (Tenn.) Nat. Mil. Park, 1995—. Contbg. author: Civil War Battlefield Guide, 1991; editor The Parapet: Newsletter of the Civil War, 1992—; asst. editor, author: Jour. of Civil War Fort Study Group, 1994. Water safety chmn. Am. Nat. Red Cross, Benton County, Ark., 1984-85, water safety instr., Canton, Ohio, 1975-80, Fredericksburg, Va., 1980-82, small craft safey inst., Benton County, Ark., 1984-85, Canton, 1975-80. Named Ky. Col., Gov. of Ky., 1992. Mem. Civil War Fortification Study Group (sec., treas.), Caost Def. Study Group, Assn. of Nat. Park Rangers, Assn. for Preservation of Civil War Sites, Nat. Trust for Hist. Preservation, Civil War Trust, Soc. of Mil. Historians. Home: Rt 10 Box 128 5000 N Harper Rd Corinth MS 38834 Office: Nat Park Svc Shiloh Nat Mil Park Rt 1 Box 9 Shiloh TN 38376

HAWKINS, AUDREY DENISE, academic administrator, educator; b. Marshall, Tex., Apr. 13, 1958; d. Oscar and Mattie D. Rand. BA in History magna cum laude, Wiley Coll., 1978; MEd in Guidance and Counseling, Prairie View A & M, 1979; postgrad., East Tex. State U., 1994, South Tex. Coll. Law, 1983-85. Cert. secondary social sci. tchr., Tex. Tchr. social studies Marshall (Tex.) Ind. Sch. Dist., 1979-80; counselor East Tex. Ednl. Opportunity Ctr., Longview, 1980-83, counselor, specialist fin. aid, 1988-92; aide law libr. South Tex. Coll. Law, Houston, 1983-84; asst. dir. fin. aid, instr. bus. law, constl. law Wiley Coll., Marshall, Tex., 1985-87; paralegal specialist EPA, Dallas, 1987-88; paralegal Devel. Planning and Rsch. Assocs., Dallas, 1987-88; asst. dir. Mach III/student support svcs. East Tex. State U., Commerce, 1992-94; dir. Ednl. Talent Search Program Paris (Tex.) Jr. Coll., 1994—; participant numerous seminars, confs. Contbr. article to Women in Higher Edn., 1994. Mem. staff Nat. Student Leadership Congress, 1992. Mem. Tex. Assn. Student Spl. Svcs. Programs, Tex. Assn. Student Fin. Aid Adminstrs., S.W. Assn. Student Assistance Programs, Phi Alpha Delta, Alpha Kappa Alpha, Alpha Kappa Mu. Democrat. Mem. Ch. Christ. Home: 506 S Callum St Marshall TX 75670-4934

HAWKINS, BRENDA L., psychologist. BS in Secondary Edn., Frostburg (Md.) State Coll., 1972; MS in Counseling and Guidance, Ind. U., 1977, EdD counseling & counselor edn., 1981. Lic. psychologist, Ga.; cert. counselor, clin. hypnotherapist. Grad. asst. counseling and counselor edn. Ind. U., Bloomington, 1977-80, intern, acting counselor ctr. for human growth/career ctr., 1980-81; counselor SUNY, Fredonia, 1981-83; psychologist Karuna Counseling, Atlanta, 1984-87; asst. prof., psychologist dept. psychiatry Emory U., Atlanta, 1988-93; pvt. practice, 1985—; speaker in field; mem. profl. adv. task force CPC Parkwood Hosp., Atlanta, 1992. Contbr. articles and revs. to profl. jours. Mem. speakers bur. Mental Health Assn. Met. Atlanta, 1983—; group facilitator Adult Survivors of Phys. and Emotional Child Abuse Ga. Coun. on Child Abuse, Atlanta, 1990-91; counselor, trainer paraprofls. Women's Crisis Svc., Bloomington, 1975-77. Scholar Md. Congress Parents and Tchrs., 1968-72, Md. Senatorial scholar, 1968-72, Delta Theta Tau nat. counseling scholar, 1977-80. Mem. Am. Psychol. Assn., Am. Soc. for Clin. Hypnosis, Assn. for Women in Psychology, Atlanta Hypnosis Soc., Ga. Psychol. Assn., Internat. Soc. for Study of Dissociation, ACA, Assn. for Specialists in Group Work, Pi Lambda Theta. Office: 2520 Windy Hill Rd Ste 203 Marietta GA 30067

HAWKINS, DEBORAH CRAUN, community health nurse; b. Atlanta, Feb. 13, 1941; d. Adolph F. and Suzanne (Catchings) Spear; m. Hugh M. Hawkins Jr.; children: Kimberley Ann, Susan Elizabeth. BSN, U. Va., 1962, MS in Nursing, 1981. Cert. in nursing adminstrn., advanced. Pub. health nurse supr. Va. Dept. Health, Charlottesville, 1975-85; pub. health nurse mgr. Va. Dept. Health, Culpeper, 1985-96. With Nurse Corps, USN, 1961-63, lt. comdr. USNR. Mem. Va. Nurses Assn., Va. Pub. Health Assn., Sigma Theta Tau. Home: 2312 Banbury St Charlottesville VA 22901-1823

HAWKINS, ELINOR DIXON (MRS. CARROLL WOODARD HAWKINS), retired librarian; b. Masontown, W.Va., Sept. 25, 1927; d. Thomas Fitchie and Susan (Reed) Dixon; AB, Fairmont State Coll., 1949; BS in Libr. Sci., U. N.C., 1950; m. Carroll Woodard Hawkins, June 24, 1951; 1 child, John Carroll. Children's libr. Enoch Pratt Free Libr., Balt., 1950-51; head circulation dept. Greensboro (N.C.) Pub. Libr., 1951-56; libr. Craven-Pamlico Libr. Svc., New Bern, N.C., 1958-62; dir. Craven-Pamlico-Carteret Regional Libr., 1962-92; storyteller children's TV program Tele-Story Time, 1952-58, 63—; bd. dirs. Triangle Bank of New Bern. Mem. New Bern Hist. Soc., 1973—, Tryon Palace Commn., 1974—; mem. adv. bd. Salvation Army. Authority. Mem. N.C. Assn. Retarded Children, Pilot Club (pres. 1957-58, v.p. 1962-63). Baptist. Home: PO Box 57 Cove City NC 28523-0057

HAWKINS, FALCON BLACK, JR., federal judge; b. Charleston, S.C., Mar. 16, 1927; s. Falcon Black Sr. and Mae Elizabeth (Infinger) H.; m. Jean Elizabeth Timmerman, May 28, 1949; children: Richard Keith, Daryl Gene, Mary Elizabeth Hawkins Eddy, Steely Odell II. BS, The Citadel, 1958; LLB, U. S.C., 1963, JD, 1970. Bar: S.C. bar 1963. Leadingman electronics Charleston (S.C.) Naval Shipyard, 1948-60; salesman ACH Brokers, Columbia, S.C., 1960-63; from assoc. to sr. ptnr. firm Hollings & Hawkins and successor firms, Charleston, 1963-79; U.S. dist. judge Dist. of S.C., Charleston, 1979—, chief judge, 1990-93, sr. status, 1993—. Served with Mcht. Marines, 1944-45, with AUS, 1945-46. Mem. Jud. Conf. 4th Jud. Circuit, ABA, S.C. Bar Assn., Charleston County Bar Assn., Am. Trial Lawyers Assn., S.C. Trial Lawyers Assn., Carolina Yacht Club, Hibernian Soc. Charleston, Masons. Democrat. Methodist. Office: Hollings Jud Ctr PO Box 835 Charleston SC 29402-0835

HAWKINS, HUNT, English language educator; b. Washington, Dec. 23, 1943; s. Edward Russell and Hermione Helen (Hunt) H.; m. Elaine Yvonne Smith, Sept. 4, 1976; children: Samuel Hunt, Amelia Anne Elaine. BA, Williams Coll., 1965; MA, Stanford U., 1969, PhD, 1976. Tchr. Kurasini Coll., Dar Es Salaam, Tanzania, 1966-67; instr. Tex. So. U., Houston, 1968-70; asst. prof. U. Minn., Mpls., 1977-78; asst. prof. Fla. State U., Tallahassee, 1978-83, assoc. prof., 1983-94, prof., 1994—. Poet: The Domestic Life, 1994 (Starrett prize 1992); contbr. articles to profl. jours. Fellow Woodrow Wilson Found., 1965-66, Fla. Arts Coun., 1993-94; grantee NEH, 1982. Mem. MLA, South Atlantic MLA (chair English V sect. 1981-82, chair English lit. other than Brit. or Am. lit. 1991-92, chair exec. com. grad. English coop. 1987-88), Joseph Conrad Soc., Coll. Lang. Assn., Mark Twain Cir., Phi Beta Kappa. Democrat. Office: Fla State U Dept English Tallahassee FL 32306

HAWKINS, IDA FAYE, elementary school educator; b. Ft. Worth, Dec. 28, 1928; d. Christopher Columbus and Nannie Idella (Hughes) Hall; m. Gene Hamilton Hawkins, Dec. 22, 1952; children: Gene Agner, Jane Hall. Student Midwestern U., 1946-48; BS, N. Tex. State U., 1951; student Lamar U., 1968-70; MS, McNeese State U., 1973. Tchr. DeQueen Elem. Sch., Port Arthur, Tex., 1950-54, Tyrrell Elem. Sch., Port Arthur, 1955-56, Roy Hatton Elem. Sch., Bridge City, Tex., 1967-68, Oak Forest Elem. Sch., Vidor, Tex., 1968-91, ret. 2d v.p. Travis Elem. PTA, 1965-66, 1st v.p., 1966-67; corr. sec. Port Arthur City coun. PTA, 1966-67; Sunday sch. tchr. Presbyn. Ch., 1951-53, 60-66. Named Tchr. of Yr., Oak Forest Elem., 1984-85. Mem. NEA, Tex. State Tchrs. Assn., Am. Psychol. Assn. Home: 6315 Central City Blvd Apt 619 Galveston TX 77551-3807

HAWKINS, J. MICHAEL, housing development administrator; b. Newport News, Va., June 3, 1962; s. Jerry Morris and Patricia Gay (McClaugherty) H. BA, Coll. William and Mary, 1984; MPA, Old Dominion U., 1993. Lic. firefighter III. Dep. coord. emergency mgmt. City of Newport News, Va., 1984-85; ops. mgr. Pearle Vision Ctr., Hampton, Va., 1985-90; chief planner Office of Human Affairs, Newport News, 1991-92; home program coord. Newport News Redevel. and Housing Authority, 1992-94, mgr. home program, 1994—. Mem. svc. team explorer program Boy Scouts Am., Newport News, 1994. Mem. Internat. City Mgmt. Assn. (affiliate), Am. Soc. Pub. Adminstrn., Am. Planning Assn., USCG Aux. Home: 113 Deal Dr Newport News VA 23602-1610 Office: Newport News RHA PO Box 77 227 27th St Newport News VA 23607

HAWKINS, JANICE EDITH, medical/surgical clinical nurse specialist; b. Greer, S.C., Sept. 12, 1950; d. Theron Gibson and Christine Edith (Bright) H. Diploma, Greenville (S.C.) Gen. Hosp. Sch. Nursing, 1971; BSN, Med. U. of S.C., 1974; MN, Emory U., 1977. RN, Ga.; CS; cert. nutrition support nurse. Staff nurse Emory U. Hosp., Atlanta, 1974-76; instr., staff nurse Med. U. of S.C., Charleston, 1978-79; instr. nursing edn., staff nurse Wilford Hall Med. Ctr. Lackland AFB, San Antonio, 1979-83; clin. nurse specialist med.-surg./nutrition support VA Med. Ctr., Decatur, Ga., 1983—; affiliate faculty BCLS Am. Heart Assn., 1989—; presenter in field. Contbr. chpts. to books and articles to profl. jours. Lt. col. USAF, 1979-83, USAFR, 1983—. Mem. ANA (chairperson coun. clin. nurse specialists 1989-91, chairperson coun. nurses in advanced practice 1991-92, task force to delineate the substructure of the Congress Nursing Practice 1990-91), Nurses Orgn. Vets. Affairs, Am. Soc. Parenteral and Enteral Nutrition (nurses com., stds. com. 1988-90, 96—, nominating com. 1992), Res. Officers Assn., Ga. Soc. Parenteral and Enteral Nutrition (bd. dirs. 1992-94), Ga. Nurses Assn. (cabinet on govtl. affairs 1989-93, chairperson 1995—), Sigma Theta Tau. Home: 1750 Clairmont Rd # 21 Decatur GA 30033-4030

HAWKINS, JEFFREY WILLIAM, pulmonary physician; b. Salt Lake City, Dec. 1, 1947; s. Clarence Richard and Billie Loraine H.; m. Susan Marie Harding, Oct. 26, 1992. BSChemE, U. Utah, 1971; MD, U. South Ala., 1979. Diplomate Am. Bd. Internal Medicine. Attending pulmonary physician Norwood Clinic, Birmingham, Ala., 1986—; dir. respiratory care Carraway Meth. Med. Ctr., Birmingham, 1986—, dir. sleep lab, 1986—. Capt. U.S. Army Chem. Corps., 1971-73. Fellow Am. Coll. Chest Physicians; mem. AMA, Am. Thoracic Soc., Am. Soc. Critical Care Medicine, Am. Soc. Sleep Disorders. Home: 2714 Old Trce Birmingham AL 35243-2030

HAWKINS, JOHN, department store executive. V.p., treas. Dillard Dept. Stores, Inc., Little Rock. Office: Dillard Dept Stores Inc PO Box 486 Little Rock AR 72203

HAWKINS, LINDA PARROTT, school system administrator; b. Florence, S.C., June 23, 1947; d. Obie Lindberg Parrott and Mary Francis (Lee) Evans; m. Larry Eugene Hawkins, Jan. 5, 1946; 1 child, Heather Nichole. BS, U. S.C., 1969; MS, Francis Marion Coll., 1978; EdS in Adminstrn., U. S.C., 1994. Tchr. J.C. Lynch High Sch., Coward, S.C., 1973-80; tchr. Lake City (S.C.) High Sch., 1980-89, coord. alternative program, 1989-90, asst. prin., 1990-95; assoc. prin. Lake City H.S., 1994-95; chair dept. Lake City H.S., 1980-89; mem. Williamsburg Tech. Adv. Coun., Kingstree, S.C., 1985-90; mem. adv. coun. Florence-Darlington (S.C.) Tech., 1981-87; co-chair Florence-Darlington-Marion counties preparation for the technologies consortia steering com.; co-chmn. allied health adv. com., 1990-93; spkr., presenter leadership workshops. Editor: Parliamentary Procedure Made Easy, 1983; contbr. articles to profl. jours. State advisor Future Bus. Leaders of Am., Columbia, S.C., 1978-86; treas. S.C. State Women's Aux., 1983-93; sec.-treas. J.C. Lynch Elem. Sch. PTO. Named Outstanding Advisor S.C. Future Bus. Leaders of Am., 1985, Tchr. of Yr., S.C. Bus. Edn. Assn., 1988-89, Secondary Tchr. of Yr., Nat. Bus. Edn. Assn., 1989-90, Educator of Yr. S.C. Trade & Indsl. Edn. Assn., 1993, S.C. Asst. Prin. of Yr., 1995. Mem. Profl. Secs. Internat., Nat. Bus. Assn. (S.C. chpt. membership dir. 1986-89, so. region membership dir. 1989-92, secondary program dept. dir. 1991-92), S.C. Bus. Edn. Assn. (jour. editor 1985-86, v.p. for membership 1986-87, treas. 1987-88, pres. elect 1988-89, pres. 1989-90), Am. Vocat. Assn., S.C. Vocat. Assn. (parliamentarian 1985-86, v.p. 1989-90, treas. 1991-92), Internat. Soc. Bus. Educators, Lake City C. of C., Kappa Kappa Iota, Delta Kappa Gamma. Democrat. Baptist. Office: Lake City High Sch PO Drawer 1569 Lake City SC 29560-1157

HAWKINS, LIONEL ANTHONY, life insurance company executive; b. Jackson, Miss., June 20, 1933; s. Lionel A. and Ruth (Hanna) H.; m. Anne Giesecke, June 29, 1958; children: Lionel A. III, John Randall, Hollie A. Miezio. Student, U. Tex., Arlington, 1951-54, George Washington U., 1957-59. Ins. agt., asst. mgr. Mut. Ins. of N.Y., Washington, 1959-63; regional supr. and mgr., agy. mgr. Kansas City (Mo.) Life Ins., 1963-69, gen. agt., 1971-73; agy. dir. Jefferson Nat., Indpls., 1969-70, Allied Life Ins., Birmingham, Ala., 1970-71; agy. dir., regional v.p. Mut. Trust Life Ins., Oakbrook, Ill., 1973-87; field v.p., dir. agys. Am. Gen. Life Ins. Co., Oakbrook Terrace, Ill., 1987-92; regional v.p. Fidelity and Guaranty Life Ins. Co., Plano, Ill., 1993-94; ins. cons., 1994—. Mem. Merit Commn. Kendall County Sheriff's Dept., Ill., 1993-94. 1st lt. U.S. Army, 1955-59. Mem. Nat. Assn. Life Underwriters, Gen. Agts. and Mgrs. Assn., Western Agy. Officers Assn. (bd. dirs. 1983-87). Democrat. Home and Office: HCR 64 Box 386D Flippin AR 72634

HAWKINS, MICHAEL LAWRENCE, trauma surgeon; b. Tampa, Fla., Sept. 22, 1943; s. Eustice Lawrence Jr. and Marjorie Evelyn (Hayes) H.; 1 child, Jennefer Beth; m. Deborah Ann Ostrowski, Aug. 4, 1984; children: Michelle Leann, Jeffrey Michael. Student, Emory U., 1961-64, MD, 1968. Diplomate Am. Bd. Surgery; cert. ACLS, Ala.; cert. Advanced Trauma Life Support instr., Okla., Ark., Tex., Tenn. Intern Naval Hosp., Great Lakes, Ill., 1968-69; resident in gen. surgery Naval Hosp., Portsmouth, Va., 1969-73; mem. staff Naval Hosp., Corpus Christi, Tex., 1973-76, chief surgery, 1974-76; mem. staff Baxter County Regional Hosp., Mountain Home, Ark., 1976-85, chief surgery, 1976-79; trauma fellow Carraway Meth. Med. Ctr., Birmingham, Ala., 1985-86; chief trauma and surg. cirtical care svc., med. dir. Med. Coll. Ga., Augusta, 1990—, prof. surgern and anesthesiology, 1991—; mem. regional trauma com. EMS Region VI, Ga., 1987—; state faculty Advanced Trauma Life Support, Ga., 1989—, regional faculty, 1992—; abstractor Surgery of Gyn/Ob., 1989—; dir. surg. ICU, cons. VA Med. Ctr., Augusta, 1990-93; chmn. Ga. Com. on Trauma, 1992—; adv. coun. and com. Dept. Human Resources, 1992—; state trauma cons. Ga. Dept. Human Resources, 1993—; lectr. in field. Author: (with H.L. Laws) Advanced in Trauma, Vol. 2, 1987; (with others) Modern Perspectives in Trauma Surgery, 1990; editor newsletter Trauma Time, 1987—; reviewer jours.; contbr. numerous articles to profl. jours. Comdr. USN, 1964-76. Grantee Dept of Navy, 1986, Kendall-McGaw Labs., 1989, Biomed. Rsch. Support grantee, 1991. Mem. ACS (regional com. on trauma 1989—), AMA, Am. Assn. Surgery Trauma, Am. Soc. Parenteral and Enteral Nutrition, Am. Burn Assn., So. Surg. Assn., Ea. Assn. Surgery Trauma (program com. 1993—, charter), Southwestern Surg. Congress, So. Med. Assn., Ga. Surg. Soc., Richmond County Med. Soc., Soc. Internat. Surgery, William H. Moretz Surg. Soc. Republican. Presbyterian. Home: 2721 Kipling Dr Augusta GA 30909-2019 Office: Med Coll Ga 1120 15th St # 4411 Augusta GA 30901-3157

HAWKINS, OTHA CARLTON, management educator, consultant; b. Roxboro, N.C., Nov. 4, 1952; s. Jasper Warren and Betty Musette (Evans) H.; m. Myra Louise Rogers, Nov. 19, 1976 (div. Feb. 1994); children: Laura Michelle, Heather Valeta, Benjamin Jared. A in Indsl. Mgmt., Edgecombe C.C., Tarboro, N.C., 1984; BS in Bus. Mgmt., Shaw U., 1986; MBA, Calif. Pacific U., 1987; postgrad., N.C. State U., 1996. Cert. ISO-9000 trainer; ASQC cert. trainer, APICS. Pub. info. officer Buncombe County, Asheville, N.C., 1972-75; advance man Congl. Club, Raleigh, N.C., 1976; store mgr. The Singer Co., Syosset, N.Y., 1977-81; supr. Glenoit Mills, Tarboro, N.C., 1982-85; quality/prodn. mgr. Lions Svcs., Charlotte, N.C., 1985-88; planner Copes-Vulcan, Charlotte, 1989-90; ops. mgmt. dept. head Alamance C.C., Graham, N.C., 1990—; co-owner Stds. and Compliance Co., Burlington, N.C., 1993—. Treas. Buncombe County Young Reps., Asheville, 1973-75. Mem. AAUP, APICS (chpt. 85/40 pres. 1994, chair edn. Burlington/Alamance chpt. 1995—), Am. Soc. Quality Control, State Employees Assn., Phi Theta Kappa. Baptist. Home: 703-C Trail 2 Burlington NC 27215 Office: Alamance C C PO Box 8000 Graham NC 27253

HAWKINS, PHILLIP LEE, Christian Science practitioner; b. Oklahoma City, Feb. 16, 1926; s. Charles Bartow and Norma Gladys (Thompson) H.; m. Cora May Nickell, May 29, 1965; children—Valerye Kirsten, Allyson Kelly, Phillip Lee II. With various oil cos., Tulsa, 1949-62; asst. supr. travel Cities Service, Tulsa, 1962-68; mgr. corp. travel, meetings coordination Conoco, Inc., Houston, 1968-85; cons. Hawkins and Assocs., Houston, 1985-86; cons. Harper Travel Internat., Houston, 1985-86, Internat. Tours., Inc., Tulsa, 1985-86; practitioner Christian Science, 1987—; cons. Lynda's Travel, Siloam Springs, Ark., 1994. Active Assn. Retarded Citizens, 1979—. Mem. Tex. Passenger Traffic Assn. (life), Nat. Passenger Traffic Assn. (hon.), Nat. Passenger Traffic Assn. (bd. dirs. 1979-83), Conn. Westchester Passenger Traffic Assn. (pres., chmn. 1974-77), Del. Inst. Travel Mgrs., Internat. Bus. Travel Assn., Soc. Co. Meeting Planners. Christian Scientist. Home and Office: 16434 W Spring Valley Rd Gravette AR 72736-9634

HAWKINS, ROBERT A., college administrator; b. Anabelle, W.Va., Aug. 21, 1924; s. Lawrence R. Hawkins and Grace O. (Lauer) Glover Hawkins; B.A., Abilene Christian Coll., 1948, M.A., 1967; Ed.D., Tex. Tech U., 1974; m. Nina Jo Milton, June 6, 1943; children: Paul C., Sheila Ann. Adminstr. youth camps, 1949-64; tchr., adminstr. Denver schs., 1953-56; instr. Abilene (Tex.) Christian Coll., 1965-68; instr., registrar Lubbock (Tex.) Christian Coll., 1968-74; dir. guidance Midland (Tex.) Coll., 1974-83, dir. testing, 1982-87, instr. behavioral and social sci. depts., 1974-87. Recipient Outstanding Tchr. award Lubbock Christian Coll., 1971. Mem. Am., Tex., Permian Basin personnel and guidance assns., Jr. Coll. Student Personnel Assn. Tex., Tex. Jr. Coll. Tchrs. Assn., Phi Kappa Phi, Alpha Chi. Author, translator: Bible Student's New Testament; The Power of God, The Grace of Giving and Living; contbr. articles to profl. jours. Home and Office: Ste 3436 6110 W Pleasant Ridge Rd Arlington TX 76016-4307

HAWKINS, SCOTT ALEXIS, lawyer; b. Des Moines, Nov. 24, 1954; s. Alexis Merrill and Rosemary Kathryn (Carney) H. BS, Drake U., 1977, JD, 1981. Bar: Iowa 1982, U.S. Dist. Ct. (no. dist.) Iowa, Tex. 1983, U.S. Dist. Ct. (no. and we. dists.) Tex., U.S. Ct. Appeals (5th cir.) Tex. 1988. In house counsel Internat. Housing Systems Inc., Dallas, 1982-84; assoc. Durant & Mankoff, Dallas, 1984-85; ptnr. Hawkins & Hawkins, Dallas, 1985—. Gen.

counsel Wednesday's Child Benefit Corp., Dallas, 1987-88; pres., gen. counsel Hunger Solutions, Inc., a non-profit orgn., 1989. Mem. ABA, State Bar Tex. Office: Hawkins & Hawkins 5747 Ridgetown Cir Dallas TX 75230-2657

HAWKS, BARRETT KINGSBURY, lawyer; b. Barnesville, Ga., July 13, 1938; s. Paul K. and Nettie Glenn (Barrett) H.; m. Kathleen C. Pafford, Apr. 3, 1965. B.B.A., Emory U., 1960, LL.B., 1963; LL.M., Harvard U., 1964. Bar: Ga. Clk. Supreme Ct. Ga., 1963; Assoc. Gambrell, Russell, Moye & Richardson (now Smith, Gambrell & Russell), Atlanta, 1961-65; assoc. Sutherland, Asbill & Brennan, Atlanta, 1965-70; ptnr. Sutherland, Asbill & Brennan, 1970-82, 93—, Paul, Hastings, Janofsky & Walker, 1982-93. Pres. Brookwood Hills Assn., Atlanta, 1978; mem. Piedmont Park Adv. Com., Atlanta, 1980-83. Served to lt. comdr. USN. Mem. ABA (mem. coun. pub. utility, transp. and comms. law sect.), State Bar Ga. (bd. govs. 1981-88), Atlanta Bar Assn., D.C. Bar Assn., Emory Law Sch. Alumni Assn. (pres.), Capital City Club, Highlands Country Club. Presbyterian. Home: 3835 Club Dr Atlanta GA 30319-1109 Office: Sutherland Asbill & Brennan 999 Peachtree St NE Atlanta GA 30309-3964

HAWLEY, HAROLD PATRICK, educational consultant; b. Paducah, Ky., Jan. 8, 1945; s. Mathew Mark and Mae (Herndon) H.; m. Lucrecia Thomas, Aug. 27, 1983; children: Cherise, Charlotte. AA, Paducah Jr. Coll., 1965; BA, U. Ky., 1968; MS, Ind. U., New Albany, 1974; EdD, Ind. U., Bloomington, 1977; postgrad., Mary Baldwin Coll., 1988. 5th liaison to adjutant gen. U.S. Army, Ft. Carson, 1970, Bien Hoa, Vietnam, 1969-70; English tchr. Southwestern Consol. Schs., Hanover, Ind., 1971-73; asst. prin. Whitewater Consol. Sch., Lyons, Ind., 1978-80; assoc. prof., dir. secondary edn. Birmingham (Ala.) - So. Coll., 1980-86, chmn. freshman seminar, 1988-95; 1988-95 Ga. Dept. Edn., Atlanta, 1988-95; evaluator So. Assn. Schs. and Colls., 1988—; ednl. cons. Ga. Dept. Edn., Atlanta, 1988-95; adj. prof. Ind. U., Bloomington, 1975-80, Samford U., 1980-84, Auburn U., 1987, U. Ala., Gadsen, 1984-85, Brenau U., Gainesville, Ga., 1988—; cons. Ford Ednl. Found., Parker H.S., Birmingham, Ala., 1981-85, Christina Acad., Cornerstone, Baton Rouge, 1983-84, Happy Valley Elem., Fairview Elem. Schoolwide Project, 1995, Walker County Curriculum Specialist, 1995—; tech. advisor Polk County Schoolwide Projects, 1995; ednl. cons. Ga. Dept. Edn., Atlanta, 1988-95; coord. 9th Dist. Schs. of Excellence, Ga., 1988-92; team leader sch. improvement teams Ga. Dept. Edn., Calhoun, 1995; numerous ESEA Instrnl. Confs., Ga., 1993-94; presenter ESEA Instrnl. Conf., Statesboro, 1994, Carrolton, Ga., 1995; dir. 1st State Remedial Edn. Conf., Lafayette, Ga., 1994; dir. 1st statewide instrnl. conf. ESEA, 1995-96; participant Inst. for Comm. Seminars, Birmingham So. Coll., 1983-86; tech. advisor Floyd County Schoolwide Project, 1995—, Dade County Schoolwide Project, 1996; student tchr. supr. Covenant Coll., Chattanooga, 1996—; dir. Title I Northwest Ga. Instrnl. Conf., 1996; ednl. cons. AD/HD, 1995—. Author: (with Don Manlove) Classroom Climate Teacher-Student Relations, Expectancy Effects, 1976; rsch. asst. (with Floyd Coppedge) Binford Middle School Project, Bloomington, Ind., 1976, Individual Instrn. Project, 1975, Lebanon High Sch. Project, 1975-76, Katherine Hamilton Rsch. Project, New Albany, Ind., 1974 (with Carol Lewis). Bd. dirs. Boys Club of Am., Paducah, Ky., 1963-65; tech. adv. Polk County Consolidated Schs., 1995-96, Dade County Consolidated Schs., 1995; internat. prof. Reinhardt Coll./Brenau Coll. Collaboration, 1995—. Basketball scholar, 1965, rsch. scholar AD/HD; Spenser grantee, 1981, Mellon grantee, 1985; grad fellow Okla. State Sch. Supt.,1975-77, Nat. Study Sch. Evaluation fellow Ind. U., 1977; named to Goals 2000 Ga. State Panel, 1994, others. Mem. Ga. Com. Leaders Assn., Internat. Platform Assn., Phi Delta Kappa.

HAWLEY, JOHN L., JR., mental health facility administrator, psychologist; b. Naha, Okinawa, Apr. 2, 1953; naturalized citizen, 1953; s. John L. and Hazel M. (Kinny) H.;m. Cythia Lea Hibbs, Aug. 2, 1975 (div. Jan. 1984); m. Mary Ellen Duzan, Feb. 29, 1992. BA, George Mason U., 1975, MA, 1977; PhD, U. Tenn., 1982. Lic. psychologist, Va. Psychologist Alexandria (Va.) Community Mental Health Ctr., 1980-81, N.W. Community Mental Health Ctr., Reston, Va., 1981-85, Family Counseling Ctr., Reston, 1983-85, Springwood Psychiat. Inst., Leesburg, Va., 1985—; clin. dir. Reston Counseling Ctr., 1985—. Recipient Univ. Svc. award George Mason U., 1975. Mem. APA, Va. Psychol. Assn., Va. Acad. Clin. Psychologists, U. Tenn. Pres.'s Club. Office: Reston Counseling Ctr 131 Elden St Ste 206 Herndon VA 22070-4810

HAWLEY, PHILLIP EUGENE, investment banker; b. Tecumseh, Mich., Dec. 9, 1940; s. Paul P and Vadah Arlene (Lawhead) H.; m. Linda Darlene Miller, Feb. 14, 1957; children—Pierre Lee, Paul Marvin, Danny Parke, David Eugene, Martin Edward. Student in mgmt. Yale U., 1959-63; BSBA, Northwestern Coll., Tulsa, 1980. With Credit Bur. Fort Myers, Inc., Fla., 1956—, chmn. bd., regional mgr., Credit Bureau Internat. Corp., Ft. Myers, Fla., 1993—; pvt. investigator Transworld Investigators, Inc., 1964, now v.p.; mgr., founder real estate co. (now Gold Coast Develop. Corp.), 1965, pres.; pres. Phillip Hawley Investment Banking Co.; bd. dirs. Caribbean Industries Internat. Corp., Future Investment Corp. Co-founder, bd. dirs. Collier-Lee Wrestling Assn., 1974—. Named Outstanding Speaker, Fla. Collectors Assn., 1967; Outstanding Individual, Fla. Fedn. Young Republicans, 1971; recipient Presdl. Sports award, 1979. Author: Law And It's Alternative to Chaos, 1958; The Happiest Man in the World, 1970; The Best Buys In Fort Myers, 1982. Mem. Fla. Collectors Assn., Am. Collectors Assn., Assn. Credit Burs. Am., Med.-Dental Hosp. Burs. Am., Fla. Assn. Mortgage Brokers, Fla. Assn. Pvt. Investigators. Republican. Mem. Nazarene Ch. Clubs: Gideons Internat., Collier Lee Wrestling Assn.; Am. Numismatic Assn. Home: 6535 Winkler Rd Fort Myers FL 33919-8167 Office: Credit Bureau Internat Corp 13300 S Cleveland Ave Ste 242 Fort Myers FL 33907-3871

HAWTHORNE, F(LOYD) DONALD, publishing company executive; b. Melrose Park, Ill., Dec. 16, 1931; s. Floyd and Clara Louise (Cheney) H.; m. Marilyn Fant Fausett, Aug. 27, 1951; children: Benjamin Floyd, Marcus Daniel, Jonathan Fant, Rebecca Lynn. BA, Furman U., 1951; BTh, So. Bapt. Seminary, 1954. Ordained to ministry Bapt. Ch., 1954. Pastor Chestnut Ridge Bapt. Ch., Laurens, S.C., 1954-56; owner, operator Noah's Ark Book Attic, Greenwood, S.C., 1954—; mfrs. rep. Floyd Fausett & Co., Atlanta, 1956-61, Donald Hawthorne & Assoc., Greenwood, 1961-71; pres., v.p. Attic Press, Inc., Greenwood, 1961—; rural mail carrier U.S. Postal Svc., Hodges, S.C., 1971-93. Pres. Greenwood Hist. Soc., 1973-76; v.p. Community Theatre, Greenwood, 1979-80, pres., 1980-81. Office: Attic Press Inc 1502 Highway 246 N Greenwood SC 29649-9643

HAY, BETTY JO, civic worker; b. McAlester, Okla., June 6, 1931; d. Duncan and Kathryn Myrtle (Albert) Peacock; m. Jess Thomas Hay, Aug. 3, 1951; children: Deborah Hay Spradley, Patricia Lynn Daibert. BA, So. Meth. U., 1952. Bd. dirs. White House Preservation Fund, 1980-87, Nat. Parents as Tchrs., 1991-94; bd. dirs. Nat. Mental Health Assn., 1978-87, pres., 1986, mem. fin. com. and child adolescent com., 1978-79, mem. resource devel. com., 1980-83; v.p. fundraising Mental Health Assn. Tex., 1980, bd. dirs., 1974-90, pres., 1983-84; bd. dirs. Mental Health Assn., Dallas County, 1972-88, pres., 1981-82; bd. dirs. United Way Met. Dallas, 1983-94, treas., 1989; bd. dirs. Assn. Higher Edn. North Tex., 1980-82, vice chmn., 1982-83, chmn., 1984-85; mem. adv. bd. Sch. Social Work, U. Tex., Arlington, 1983-94; mem. Nat. Commn. on Children, 1989-92, Dallas Coun. on World Affairs, Woman's Div., March of Dimes Aux., 1982—; bd. dirs. Baylor Coll. Dentistry, 1987-94. mem. exec. com., 1989, vice chmn., 1992; mem. Tex. Commn. on Children and Youth, 1994-95; pres. Tex. Mental Health Found., 1982—; many past involvements in charitable orgns. Address: 7236 Lupton Cir Dallas TX 75225-1737

HAY, RICHARD CARMAN, retired anesthesiologist; b. Queens, N.Y., June 9, 1921; s. Richard Carman and Frances Pauline (Woodbury) H.; B.S., U. Vt., 1944, M.D., 1946; m. Martha Fambrough, Mar. 2, 1957; children: Richard C., William W., Anne H., Sandra L., Bradford T., Holly K. Practice medicine, specializing in anesthesiology, Houston; ret., 1994. Served with M.C., U.S. Army, 1948-50. Mem. AMA, Tex. Med. Soc., Harris County Med. Soc., Am. Soc. Anesthesiologists, Tex. Soc. Anesthesiologists. Republican. Baptist. Office: 1102 Deerfield Rd Richmond TX 77469-6574

HAYDEN, JOHN KELLY, historian; b. N.Y.C., May 10, 1962; s. James S. and Ann (Kelly) H.; m. Laura Ann Endicott, May 1, 1992. BA, Georgetown U., 1984; MA, U. Va., 1988, PhD, 1991. Legal asst. Williams & Connolly, Washington, 1984-86; instr. dept. history U. Va., Charlottesville, 1990, asst. dean faculty arts and scis., 1991-92; lectr. Piedmont Va. C.C., Charlottesville, 1988-92; asst. prof. history Southwestern Okla. State U., Weatherford, 1992—; mem. alumni admissions program Georgetown U., Washington, 1993—. Leopold Schepp Found. grantee, 1983-84, 86-87, 88-90; rsch. travel grantee Gt. Britain, 1989. Mem. AAUP, N. Am. Conf. Br. Studies, Soc. for French Hist. Studies, Am. Hist. Assn., Phi Beta Kappa. Democrat. Roman Catholic. Office: Southwestern Okla State U Social Scis 100 Campus Dr Weatherford OK 73096

HAYDEN, LINDA C., school librarian; b. Hazard, Ky.; d. Walter H. and Nancy Catherine (Gott) Combs. BA, Coll. of William and Mary, 1966; MA in Teaching, Spalding U., 1976, postgrad., 1987. Cert. elem. and early childhood edn. tchr., Ky. Tchr. York County Pub. Schs., Poquoson, Va., 1966-67; asst. coord. children's svcs. Louisville Free Pub. Library, 1969-74; tchr. Ursuline Spl. Edn. Ctr., Louisville, 1975-79; tchr., owner Multi-Handicapped Tutoring, Louisville, 1979-80; tchr. J-Town Presch., Inc., Jeffersontown, Ky., 1983-84; therapist Pine Tree Villa Nursing Home, Louisville, 1982-84; asst. prin., tchr. Brown's Lane Acad., Louisville, 1984-86; tchr. Jefferson County Pub. Schs., Louisville, 1986-94; librarian Ky. State U., 1994—. Vol. tutor ESL with refugees, 1990-91. Mem. ASCD, Amnesty Internat., Internat. Soc. for Tech. in Edn., Leadership Edn. Alumni Assn., Pi Lambda Theta. Democrat.

HAYDEN, MICHAEL ALLEN, technology educator; b. Danville, Ill., July 9, 1958; s. Walter Irven and Gladys Delphia (Reed) H.; m. Emilse Teresa Camacho, Feb. 16, 1990. BS, Ea. Ill. U., 1983, MS, 1984; PhD, Iowa State U., 1989. Cert. sr. indsl. technologist; cert. quality engr. Instr. Vermillion Occupational & Tech. Edn. Ctr., Danville, 1983-84, Danville Area Community Coll., 1984-85; teaching asst. Iowa State U., Ames, 1985-89; asst. prof. U. So. Colo., Pueblo, 1989-91; assoc. prof. Miss. State U., Miss. State, 1991—; cons. to indsl. tech. industries, 1984—, pub. schs. and univs., 1989—. Contbr. articles, poems and short stories to profl. jours. With USAF, 1976-78. Mem. ASTD, SAR, Soc. Mfg. Engrs., Am. Soc. Quality Control, Nat. Assn. Indsl. Tech., Internat. Tech. Edn. Assn. (coms.).

HAYES, BRENDA JOYCE, school counselor; b. Hempstead, Tex., Oct. 21, 1953; d. Roy Clayton and Carrie Mae (Toliver) Thompson; m. Roland Anthony Hayes, Oct. 21, 1972 (div. 1979); children: Teahon Shanta, Nyoka Demestre, Anthony Sharod, Kevin Bernard Thomas (dec.). BS in Elem. Edn., Prairie View A&M U., 1978, degree in guidance and counseling, 1982. Resource tchr. Magnolia (Tex.) High Sch., 1978-79; migrant tchr. Navasota (Tex.) Elem. Sch., 1979-80; mental health mental retardation tchr. Brenham (Tex.) State Sch., 1980-81, supervising tchr., 1981-82; Title I math. tchr. Hempstead Elem. Sch., 1982-83, math. coord., 1983-84, 3d grade tchr., 1984-86; mental health mental retardation tchr. Jewel Banks-Alamo Elem. Sch., Galveston, Tex., 1986-88; 3d grade tchr. Alamo Elem. Sch., 1988-94, counselor, 1994—; tutorial tchr. Galveston Housing Authority, 1993-96, West Point Bapt. Ch., Galveston, 1995-96. Sunday sch. tchr. West Point Bapt. Ch., 1988-96. Mem. Tex. State Tchrs. Assn. Democrat. Home: PO Box 643 Galveston TX 77553

HAYES, CHARLES AUSTIN, economist, consultant; b. Norlina, N.C., Nov. 4, 1946; s. Clarence Holt and Eleanor Mitchell (Spain) H.; m. Margaret Jackson Perkinson, Dec. 19, 1970; 1 child, Elizabeth Warren. BSBA, East Carolina U., 1972, MA in Edn., 1974. Instr. in bus. Isothermal Community Coll., Forest City, N.C., 1972-73, Wilson (N.C.) Tech. Coll., 1973-74; county mgr., indsl. developer Warren County, Warrenton, N.C., 1974-78; prin. Warrenton Ins. & Real Estate, 1978-86; pres. Moore County Econ. Devel. Corp., Pinehurst, N.C., 1986-96; pres., CEO Rsch. Triangle Regional Partnership, N.C., 1996—; adj. faculty mem. Sandhills Community Coll., 1987—. Author: Managing Financial and Marketing Rural Economics Development. Adv. bd. Cape Fear Area Consortium of Small Bus. Tech. and Devel. Ctr.; mem. friends of children com. Bapt. Children's Home, 1986—; ex officio dir. Pinehurst Area Conv. and Vis. Bur., 1988—. With U.S. Army, 1968-69, Vietnam. Recipient Disting. Svc. award, Warren County, N.C., 1977. Mem. N.C. Indsl. Assn. (pres. 1978-79), Am. Econ. Devel. Coun., So. Indsl. Devel Coun., Sandhills C. of C. (ex officio), Pinehurst Country Club, Rotary (Sandhills, N.C.) (bd. dirs. 1989—). Office: Research Triangle Regional Partnership PO Box 80756 Raleigh NC 27623

HAYES, DAVID VAUGHN, construction equipment company executive; b. Jacksonville, Fla., July 16, 1954; s. Carrol Joseph and Mary Lou (Floyd) H.; m. Suzanne Louise Pinel, Aug. 4, 1984; children: David Vaughn Jr., Nicholas Pinel. AA, Fla. Jr. Coll., 1975; postgrad., Rollins Coll. Lic. real estate sales assoc., Fla., gen. contractor, Fla., underground utility contractor, Fla., pub. utilities contractor, N.C., S.C.; lic. pvt. pilot. Project coord. CH2M Hill Cons. Engrs., Gainesville, Fla., 1977-84; exec. v.p. Allen's Environ. Equipment, Longwood, Fla., 1984-95; fed. and internat. divsn. mgr. Wharton-Smith, Inc., Lake Monroe, Fla., 1995—. Author mag. article Water Management District Policies. Mem. Friends of Bob Graham, Fla., 1989-91; pres. Fla. Leaders Coun., Ctrl. Fla., 1991-92; chmn. Environ. Protection Com., Orange County, Fla., 1988—; mem. Well Drillers Adv. Bd., Orange County, 1988—; mem. Utility Adv. Bd., Winter Park, Fla., 1989-90; mem. Environ. Adv. Bd., Winter Park, 1986-89. Mem. Am. Water Works Assn., Water Pollution Control Fedn., Leadership Orlando Class of 1996, Country Club of Orlando. Republican. Office: Wharton-Smith Inc 750 County Rd 15 Lake Monroe FL 32747

HAYES, GORDON GLENN, civil engineer; b. Galveston, Tex., Jan. 2, 1936; s. Jack Lewis and Eunice Karen (Victery) H. BS in Physics, Tex. A&M U., 1969. Registered profl. engr., Alaska, Tex. Rsch. technician Shell Devel. Co., Houston, 1962-68; rsch. assoc. Tex. Trans. Inst., College Station, 1969-71, asst. rsch. physicist, 1971-74, assoc. rsch. physicist, 1974-80; traffic safety specialist Alaska Dept. Transp. & Pub. Facilities, Juneau, 1981-83, state traffic engr., 1983-85, traffic safety standards engr., 1985-90; owner Alaska Roadsafe Cons., Juneau, 1990-92; owner Hayes Highway Consulting, Carson City, Nev., 1992-93, Livingston, Tex., 1993—. Author of numerous pubs. in the hwy. safety field; producer of numerous documentary films in the hwy. safety field. Petty officer USN, 1953-57. Mem. ASCE, Nat. Com. on Uniform Traffic Control Devices (signs tech. com.) Inst. Transp. Engrs., Mensa. Home: RR 1 Box 1499N Livingston TX 77351-9720

HAYES, JACK IRBY, historian; b. Danville, Va., Aug. 13, 1944; s. Jack Irby and Minnie Lee (Conner) H.; m. Bernadine Joy Arnn, June 5, 1966; children: Emily Wilson, Julia Arnn. BS in History, Hampden-Sydney Coll., 1966; MA in History, Va. Poly. Inst. and State U., 1968; PhD in History, U. S.C., 1972; BS in Bus., Averett Coll., 1987. Dir. continuing edn. U. S.C., Columbia, 1972-74; asst. prof. history Averett Coll., Danville, 1974-77, assoc. prof., 1977-82, prof., 1982-90, W.C. Daniel prof. history and polit. sci., 1990—, chmn. dept. history, 1976—; adj. prof. grad. sch. Va. Poly. Inst. and State U., Blacksburg, 1977-79; archival cons. Dibrell Bros., Inc., Danville, 1990-91; mem. So. Assn. Colls. and Schs.; vis. accreditation com. Gardiner-Webb Coll., Salem Coll., Tusculum Coll., Meredith Coll., Lindsay-Wilson Coll., Wesleyan Coll., Ga., Covenant Coll., 1986-96. Author: A History of Averett College, 1984. Pres. citizens adv. bd. Salvation Army, Danville, 1989-92; mem. bd. trustees Hughes Home for Children, Danville, 1982-89, v.p. bd. trustees, 1988-89; bd. dirs. The Womack Found., Danville, 1982-88, v.p. bd. dirs., 1988; bd. dirs. Danville Mus. Fine Arts and History, 1994—; active Danville Dem. Com., 1980—. Grantee Va. Found. for Humanities and Pub. Policy, Charlottesville, 1976-80, Commn. on Bicentennial of U.S. Constn., Washington, 1989, 90; Westmoreland Davis Meml. Found. fellow, 1967-68, Seminar for Hist. Adminstrs. fellow, Colonial Williamsburg, Va., 1967; named one of Outstanding Young Men of Am., 1977. Mem. Orgn. Am. Historians, So. Hist. Assn., Assn. for Preservation of Va. Antiquities (life), Kiwanis (lt. gov. div. 2 capital dist. 1991-92, pres. Danville club 1989), German Club Danville. Presbyterian. Home: 245 Linden Dr Danville VA 24541-3523 Office: Averett Coll 420 W Main St Danville VA 24541-3612

HAYES, JUDY DIANE, medical/surgical and ophthalmological nurse; b. Atlanta, Mar. 17, 1961; d. Coley Walter and Clorece (Markham) H. Student, Tift Coll., Forsyth, Ga., 1979-81; BSN, Med. Coll. Ga., 1983. Camp nurse Camp Pinnacle Woman's Missionary Union of Ga., Atlanta; staff nurse postpartum Piedmont Hosp., Atlanta, staff nurse preceptor med.-surg. unit, 1984-91, charge nurse on med.-surg. unit, 1991—; vol. missionary nurse to Rio de Janeiro, 1985, to Mombassa, Kenya, 1988. Vol. missionary nurse to Panama, 1993. Mem. Nat. Bapt. Nursing Fellowship (v.p. Ga. chpt. 1991, pres.-elect 1992, pres. Ga. chpt. 1993-95, chmn. nominating com. 1996—), Sigma Theta Tau.

HAYES, K. WILLIAM, secondary school educator; b. Holyoke, Mass., Mar. 11, 1943; s. O. William and Helen Marion (McGrath) H.; m. Phyllis Marie Bichard, Aug. 1, 1964 (div. 1989); children: Heather M. (dec.), Russell William. Student, U.S. Mil. Acad., 1962-63; BA, St. Mary's U., San Antonio, 1964, MA, 1971; student, Dept. Army Insp. Gen. Course, 1975; cert. law enforcement, Mil. Police Officer Course, 1983. Commd. 2nd lt. U.S. Army, 1964, advanced through grades to lt. col., 1980; officer Hdqrs. 2nd Armored Div., Ft. Hood, Tex., 1964-66, Hdqrs. 4th Army, Ft. Sam Houston, Tex., 1966; prin. Antonian High Sch., San Antonio, 1966-69; prof. Tex. Mil. Inst., San Antonio, 1969-76; instr. San Antonio Coll., 1971-78; with ops./investigations U.S. Army, Ft. Sam Houston, 1976-79; with sales Franklin Watts Pub. Co., N.Y.C., 1979-80; educator Leesburg (Fla.) High Sch., 1980—; cons. social studies The Coll. Bd., Tex., 1973-76; advisor Lake County Sheriff's Dept., Tavares, Fla., 1980—; instr. counterinsurgency, terrorism and counterterrorism C&GSC, 1983-88; ops. officer Fed. Emergency Mgmt. Agy., 1988. Co-author: Death Row: 1994; contbr. articles to profl. jours.; rschr. on capital punishment; presenter papers at profl. confs. Named Tchr. of Yr. Valley Forge Freedoms Found., 1970; recipient Ednl. Rsch. award Nat. Endowment for the Humanities, 1976, Fla. Social Studies Tchr. of Yr. Fla. Coun. for Social Studies, 1994. Mem. Orgn. Am. Historians, Fla. Hist. Soc. (sustaining), Res. Officer Assn. (life), Am. Legion, Nat. Coun. for the Social Studies, Fraternal Order of Police, HMH Scholarship (chmn.), Youth Exch. Found. (chmn.), Optimist Club (bd. dirs. 1976-79), Lions. Republican. Home: PO Box 492257 Leesburg FL 34749-2257

HAYES, KEVIN GREGORY, university administrator; b. Jamestown, N.Y., May 14, 1941; s. Francis Joseph and Mary Blanche (Driscoll) H.; m. Marilyn Jane Dougherty, Dec. 7, 1968; children: Tracy Lynn Hayes Schaeffer, Brendan Paul Hayes. AA in Humanities, Jamestown C.C., 1966; BA in English, Allegheny Coll., 1968; MA in Journalism, Pa. State U., 1974; EdD, Okla. State U., 1995. Broadcaster James Broadcasting Co., Jamestown, 1959-63, 65-66; program dir. Regional Broadcasters, Meadville, Pa., 1966-69; asst. radio-TV editor Pa. State U., University Park, 1969-71, assoc. publs. editor, 1971-75, publs. editor, 1975-80, asst. dir. agrl. comm., 1980-83, interm dir., 1983-84; info. specialist, chief of party Swaziland Cropping Systems Rsch. and Extension Tng. Project, 1984-87; asst. dir. agrl. comms. Pa. State U., University Park, 1987-88; prof., head agrl. com.. Divsn. of Agrl., Okla. State U., Stillwater, 1988-94, prof., distance edn. coord., 1994—. Author: On Coming Home, 1979, Distance Learning Policies in Postsecondary Education, 1996. With U.S. Army, 1963-65. Recipient Pioneer ACE award Agrl. Communicators in Edn., 1976. Mem. KC (grand knight 1990-92, dist. dep. 1992—), Phi Kappa Phi, Kappa Tau Alpha, Epsilon Sigma Phi. Democrat. Roman Catholic. Home: 1123 S Mansfield St Stillwater OK 74074 Office: Okla State U 103 PIO Bldg Stillwater OK 74078

HAYES, LAURA JOANNA, psychologist; b. Winnebeau, N.C., Mar. 26, 1943; d. Victor Wilson and Pansy Lorraine (Springsteen) Hayes; m. Jerry Allen Gladson, June 20, 1965 (div. Mar. 1992); children: Joanna Kaye, Paula Rae. BA, So. Coll., 1965; MEd, U. Tenn., Chattanooga, 1977; EdD, Vanderbilt U., 1985. Lic. psychologist, Ga. Psychol. intern Lakeshore Mental Health Inst., Knoxville, Tenn., 1985-86; counselor, psychologist Tara Heights Enterprises, Atlanta, 1986—; psychologist, owner Assoc. Psychol. Svcs., Inc., Ringgold, Ga., 1990—. Mem. APA, Christian Assn. for Psychol. Studies, Ga. Psychol. Assn. Democrat. Home: 327 Homestead Cir Kennesaw GA 30144-1335 Office: Assoc Psychol Svcs Box 700 5476 Battlefield Pkwy Ringgold GA 30736

HAYES, MICHAEL BERNARD, sales executive; b. State College, Pa., Aug. 1, 1958; s. John Robert and Elizabeth (Dooley) H.; m. Jamie Ann Wood, Aug. 26, 1989. BS in Quantitative Bus. Analysis, Pa. State U., 1980; student, U. Cologne, Fed. Republic of Germany, 1980. Mgmt. sci. analyst Pennzoil Co., Houston, 1981-83, sr. mgmt. sci. analyst, 1983-84; applications engr. Spectragraphics Corp., San Diego, 1984; graphics systems specialist Precision Visuals, Inc., Houston, 1985; sales rep. Precision Visuals, Inc., Dallas, 1986-89, account mgr., 1989-90, sr. account mgr., 1991-93; dist. sales mgr. Visual Numerics, Dallas, 1994—. Member Houston Proud, 1984. Mem. Pa. State U. Alumni Club (v.p. Dallas chpt. 1987-89, pres. 1990, bd. dirs. 1991—). Office: Visual Numerics 3710 Rawlins St Ste 1100 Dallas TX 75219-4275

HAYES, NEIL JOHN, lawyer; b. N.Y.C., Nov. 16, 1951; s. John T. and Marion G. (Watson) H.; m. Rebecca A. Wisner, Dec. 8, 1985. BA, Villanova U., 1973; JD, Stetson U., 1981. Bar: Fla. 1982, U.S. Dist. Ct. (so. and mid. dists.) Fla. 1982, U.S. Supreme Ct. 1986. Detective Mt. Laurel (N.J.) Police Dept., 1974-79; law clk. to chief judge Fla. 5th Dist. Ct. Appeals, Daytona Beach, 1982-83; assoc. Jones & Foster P.A., West Palm Beach, Fla., 1983-88, Bobo, Spicer & Ciotoli, West Palm Beach, 1988-89; pvt. practice West Palm Beach, 1989—. Assoc. editor Stetson U. Law Rev., 1981. Mem. ABA, Fla. Bar Assn., Palm Beach County Bar Assn., Palm Beach County Claims Assn., Fla. Def. Lawyers Assn., Tuscawilla Club. Roman Catholic. Home: 2558 Lochmore Rd West Palm Beach FL 33407-1304 Office: 4365 Northlake Blvd Palm Beach Gardens FL 33410

HAYES, PATRICIA ANN, university president; b. Binghamton, N.Y., Jan. 14, 1944; d. Robert L. and Gertrude (Congdon) H. BA in English, Coll. of St. Rose, 1968; PhD in Philosophy, Georgetown U., 1974. Tchr. Cardinal McCloskey High Sch., Albany, N.Y., 1966-68; teaching asst. Georgetown U., Washington, 1968-71; instr. philosophy Coll. of St. Rose, Albany, 1973-75, instr. bus., spring 1981, adminstrv. intern to acad. v.p., 1973-74, dir. admissions, 1974-78, dir. adminstrn. and planning, 1978-81, v.p. adminstrn. and fin., treas., 1981-84; pres. St. Edward's U., Austin, Tex., 1984—; bd. dirs. Tex. Bus./Edn. Coalition. Bd. dirs. Sta. KLRU Pub. TV, United Way, Seton Med. Ctr. Mem. Nat. Assn. Ind. Colls. and Univs. (mem. com. on financing higher edn.), Assn. Cath. Colls. and Univs., Ind. Colls. and Univs. Tex., So. Assn. Colls. and Schs. (mem. commn. on colls.). Roman Catholic. Office: St Edwards U Office of the President 3001 S Congress Ave Austin TX 78704-6489

HAYES, REBECCA ANNE, communications professional; b. Princeton, Ky., June 3, 1950; d. James Luther and Margaret Anne (Sparks) H. AA, Midway Coll., 1970; AB, U. Ky., 1972; MEd, U. Louisville, 1974. Educator Jefferson County Bd. Edn., Louisville, 1972-78; mgmt. asst. S. Cen. Bell, Louisville, 1978-80, engr., 1980-82; engr. AT&T, Tucker, Ga., 1983-84, asst. staff mgr., 1984-87, systems cons. bus. markets group, 1987-88; staff mgr. hdqrs. BSD sales ops. AT&T, Bridgewater, N.J., 1988-90; staff mgr. BC Systems AT&T, San Francisco, 1990-91; CFO Bus. Comms. Systems Lucent Techs., Columbia, S.C., 1991—. Advisor Career Explorers South Ctrl. Bell, Louisville, 1979-80; mem. Columbia Mus. of Art. Mem. NAFE, Ky. Hist. Soc., U. Ky. Alumni Assn. (life), Columbia Mus. Art, Friends of the S.C. State Mus., Greater Columbia C. of C., Phi Theta Kappa. Democrat. Roman Catholic. Office: Lucent Techs 1201 Main St Columbia SC 29201-3200

HAYES, VERNON HOLGATE, retired design engineer; b. Preston, Lancashire, Eng., Oct. 8, 1915; came to U.S., 1923; s. Henry and Veronika Annie (Hauser) H.; m. Bernice Elizabeth Kalmen, Oct. 15, 1948; children: Roger Martin, Kenneth Alan. Student, Wayne U., 1938-46, U. Minn., 1951-58. Mechanic Becker Motor Co., Springerville, Ariz., 1949; bldg. designer Hitchcock & Estabrook, Mpls., 1949; machine designer Continental Machines, Inc., Savage, Minn., 1950-54; topographic draftsman Cardarelle & Assocs., Eden Prairie, Minn., 1954; machine designer Bemis Rsch. Lab., Mpls., 1954-56; devel. engr. Univac/Sperry Rand Corp., Hopkins, 1956-62; project engr. Honeywell Corp., Hopkins, Minn., 1962-64, G.T. Schjeldahl Co., Northfield, Minn., 1964-65; design engr. Thermo King corp., Bloomington, Minn., 1965-66; rsch. engr. Pako Corp., Golden Valley, Minn., 1966-71; engrng. tech. writer MTS Systems Corp., Hopkins, Minn., 1971-73, ret., 1974. Author: Say-Write English Alphabet Improved 20,000 Percent Over A-B-C English, 1989, TOPON Optimum Thought Code Improved 9,000,000 Percent Over A-B-C English, 1993; contbr. articles to profl. jours.; inventor in field. Mem. hist. commn. Val Verde County, Tex., 1978—. Cpl. U.S.

Coast Artillery, 1940-43. Mem. ASME, Honewywell Engrs. Club (sr.), Standards Engrs. Soc. Home: 309 Ohio St Del Rio TX 78840-2857

HAYGOOD, DAVID LOUIS, pet care professional, entrepreneur; b. Atlanta, Jan. 19, 1955; s. James Louis and Betty Jane (Bowers) H. BBA, U. Ga., 1977. CPA, Va. Acct. Matson Driscoll & Dam Co., Atlanta, 1978-80, Dulles Gateway Kennels, Ltd., Chantilly, Va., 1980-88, Kennesaw (Ga.) Pet Ctr., 1988—; pres. pet care profl. Haygood Enterprises, Inc., Kennesaw, 1988—. Mem. AICPA, Va. Soc. CPAs. Home and Office: 2139 N Cobb Pky Kennesaw GA 30152-3627

HAYHOE, GEORGE FREDERICK, III, technical communication consultant; b. Washington, Dec. 18, 1949; s. George F. Jr. and Phyllis A. (Houston) H. BA maxima cum laude, LaSalle U., 1972; MA, Cath. U. Am., 1973; PhD, U. S.C., 1979. Asst. prof. Va. Polytech. Inst. and State U., Blacksburg, 1977-84; cons. Presearch Inc., Merryfield, Va., 1984-87, Am. Computer Profls., Columbia, S.C., 1987-89; prin. tech. editor Westinghouse Savannah River Co., Aiken, S.C., 1989-95; pres. George Hayhoe Assocs., Aiken, 1995—. Contbr. articles to profl. jours. Fellow Soc. for Tech. Comm. (assoc., editor Tech. Comm. 1995—, Disting. Chpt. Svc. award 1995); mem. IEEE (sr., Best Paper award 1989). Office: George Hayhoe Assocs 194 Aberdeen Dr Aiken SC 29803

HAYMORE, CURTIS JOE, environmental consultant; b. L.A., June 9, 1951; s. George Blinn and Lela (Ayers) H.; m. Mary Janice Maucher, Sept. 8, 1973 (div.); 1 child, John Andrew; Paula Robbyne Perry. BA in Econs., U. Calif., Santa Barbara, 1974; MP in Environ. Planning, U. Va., 1978. Rsch. assoc. Nat. Econ. Rsch. Assoc., Inc., Washington, 1974-78; economist U.S. Econ. Devel. Adminstrn., Washington, 1978; economist/program analyst U.S. EPA, Washington, 1978-83; project mgr. ICF, Inc., Fairfax, Va., 1983-88; divsn. dir. Labat-Anderson, Inc., Arlington, Va., 1988-89; pres. Environomics, Inc., Vienna, Va., 1989-91; v.p. Sociotech. Rsch. Applications, Inc., Arlington, 1991—; adj. instr. U. Va., Charlottesville, 1982-92; commr. Arlington County Planning Commn. Author: (book chpt.) Environmental Risk Management, 1991, 95; editor: The Wills and Woes of W.O., 1993; contbr. articles to profl. jours. Bd. dirs. Belvedere Sch. PTA, Annandale, Va., 1986-88; mem. Dem. Com., Arlington, 1975; bd. dirs. Northern Va. Ethical Soc., 1994-95, Nat. Capital Area Skeptics, 1994-95, Jeb Stuart High Sch. PTA, 1994-95. Mem. Soc. for Risk Analysis (pres. Nat. Capital Area chpt. 1991). Democrat. Home: 6310 Columbia Pike Falls Church VA 22041-1204 Office: Sociotech Rsch Applic Inc 1100 Wilson Blvd Arlington VA 22209-2297

HAYNES, ADA FAYE, sociology educator; b. Altamont, Tenn., Aug. 24, 1961; d. Joe & Margaret (Meeks) H.; m. Barry S. Stein, May 13, 1991; child: Alana. BS, Tenn. Tech. U., 1983, MA, 1986; PhD, Fla. State U., 1992. Instr. Tenn. Tech. U., Cookeville, 1989-1993, asst. prof., 1993—. Author: The Ideal Workplace, 1996, Poverty in Central Appalachia, 1997. Chair Upper Cumberland Dismas, Cookeville, 1992-94, co-chair 1995-96; CookevilleUNICEF, 1991-92. Grantee Raskob, 1993, United Thank Offering, N.Y.C., 1994, Tenn. Housing Devel., 1995. Mem. So. Sociol. Assn., Mid-So. Sociol. Assn, Tenn. Assn. for Devel. Edn. (liaison 1994-96). Office: Tenn Tech Univ Box 5052 Cookeville TN 38506

HAYNES, CHERYL ETTORA, healthcare industry marketing representative; b. Washington, Oct. 13, 1948; d. Joseph Harvey Jr. and Rosalie Elizabeth (Brown) F.; m. Leon Haynes Jr., Feb. 15, 1988 (dec. Feb. 1989); 1 child, Aisha Nia Ruffin-Haynes. BS, Wayland Bapt., 1991; MA, Webster U., 1993. Clk. typist Dept. Def., Battle Creek, Mich., 1971-76, USDA, Howell, Mich., 1976-78; acctg. tech. dept. mgmt. and budget State of Mich., Lansing, 1978-80; enlisted U.S. Army, 1980; served as med. lab. tech. Walter Reed Army Med. Ctr., Washington, 1981-84; student adv. lab. Acad. Health Scis., St. Sam Houston, Tex., 1984-85; med. lab. non-commd. officer dept. pathology Brooke Army Med. Ctr., Ft. Sam Houston, 1985-87, 89-91; med. lab. non-commd. officer 121st Evacuation Hosp., Seoul, Republic of Korea, 1987-88, 41st Combat Support Hosp., Ft. Sam Houston, 1988-89; mgr. Supply Ctr. Logistics div., Ft. Sam Houston, 1991-94; faculty Wayland Bapt. U., 1994—; mktg. rep. Consolidated Care Crew Home Health Agy., Inc., San Antonio, 1995—. Mem. Nat. Coun. Negro Women, Washington, 1966-70, Bapt. Tng. Union, Washington, 1975-70. Mem. Am. Coll. Healthcare Execs., Nat. Assn. Health Svc. Execs. Home: 6868 Columbia Rdg Converse TX 78109-3419 Office: North Star Healthcare Mgmt Ste 200 7550 IH IOW San Antonio TX 78229

HAYNES, EDWARD SHELDON, history educator; b. Roanoke, Va., Oct. 16, 1948; s. Sheldon Elias and Laurie (Arbuckle) H.; m. Elaine S. Bardes, Aug. 7, 1971 (div. Apr. 1991); 1 child, Usha; m. Paula Levin Mitchell, June 6, 1994. AB, Duke U., 1970, AM, 1972; MPhil, Jawaharlal Nehru U., 1975; PhD, Duke U., 1975. Vis. instr. history Kans. State U., Manhattan, 1975-76; vis. scholar South Asian studies Skidmore Coll., Saratoga Springs, N.Y., 1976-77; adj. asst. prof. history SUNY, Albany, 1977-78; asst. prof. history U. N.Iowa, Cedar Falls, 1978-80; from asst. editor to mng. editor Duke U. Press, Durham, N.C., 1982-83; rsch. assoc. history Duke U., 1983-87; assoc. prof. history Winthrop U., Rock Hill, S.C., 1987—; cons. N.Y. State Edn. Dept., Albany, 1978-82; dir. pre-major adv. ctr. Winthrop U., 1988-93. Co-editor: Guide to Buddhist Religion, 1981, Guide to Islam, 1983, Guide to Chinese Religion, 1985. Assoc. dir. Carolinas Com. on U.S.-Arab Rels., Rock Hill, 1993-96, dir., 1996—. Fulbright-Hays fellow, 1988, Joseph Malone fellow, 1992, 93, Am. Inst. Indian Studies rsch. fellow, 1980, 85, NEH summer seminar fellow, 1980, Shell Cos. Found. fellow, 1973-74, numerous others. Mem. AAUP (pres. Winthrop U. chpt. 1992—), Am. Hist. Assn., Assn. Asian Studies, Rajasthan Study Group (sec. 1987-91), South Atlantic States Assn. Asian & African Studies. Office: History Dept Bancroft Hall Winthrop U Rock Hill SC 29733

HAYNES, GARY R., anesthesiologist; b. Jan. 21, 1952; m. Debra Kurtock. BS in Biology and Chemistry with honors, Ill. Coll., Jacksonville, 1974; MS in Exptl. Pathology, U. Cin., 1977; PhD in Pathology, Case Western Res. U., Cleve., 1984, MD, 1986. Diplomate Am. Bd. Anesthesiology; cert. BLS, ACLS; lic. physician S.C. Resident in anesthesiology Med. U. S.C., Charleston, 1986-90, chief resident dept. anesthesiology, 1990, asst. prof. dept. anesthesiology, 1990—, dir. obstetrical anesthesia, 1990—, assoc. prof., ambulatory anesthesia, 1995—; cons. Health Care Analysis, Cleve., 1985-86; teaching asst. dept. pathology Case Western Res. U. Sch. Medicine, 1979-83; lectr. in field. Mem. manuscript rev. bd. Hosp. Physician, 1993—; contbr. articles and abstracts to profl. jours. .sher First Scots Presbyn. Ch., 1987—, Sunday sch. tchr., 1987-88; mem. S.C. Art Assn., The Gibbs Art Mus., The Preservation Soc. of Charleston; class agt. for Class of '74 Ill. Coll. Alumni Assn., 1974—. Grantee Glaxo, 1991-92, 92-93, 93—, Bayer, 1996—. Mem. AAAS, Am. Soc. Anesthesiologists, Am. Acad. Pain Mgmt., Am. Soc. Regional Anesthesia, Soc. for Obstetrical Anesthesia and Perinatology (panel moderator and com. on local arrangements 1992), So. Med. Assn., S.C. Soc. Anesthesiologists, S.C. Med. Assn. (Doctor of the Day program), Charleston County Med. Soc. (health legis. com., pres rels. com.), Phi Alpha. Office: Med Univ of South Carolina Dept Anesthesiology 171 Ashley Ave Charleston SC 29425

HAYNES, KAREN SUE, university president, social work educator; b. Jersey City, July 6, 1946; d. Edward J. and Adelaide M. (Hineson) Czarnecki; m. James S. Mickelson; children: Kingsley Eliot, Kimberly Elizabeth, David. AB, Goucher Coll., 1968; MSW, McGill U., 1970; PhD, U. Tex., 1977. Cons. Inst. Nat. Planning, Cairo, 1977-78; asst. prof. Ind. U., Indpls., 1978-81, assoc. prof., 1981-85; prof. social work U. Houston, 1985-95, dean, 1985-95, pres., 1996—; pres. Ind. Coalition Human Services, Indpls., 1984-85. Author: Sage Publications, 1984; Longman, 1986, 91, 93, 96, Springer, 1989, also articles. Mem. Nat. Assn. Social Workers, Council Social Work Edn., Internat. Assn. Schs. Social Work, Nat. Alliance Info. and Referral (pres. 1983-87), Leadership Houston, 1986, Leadership Tex., 1990, Leadership Am., 1996. Avocation: poetry. Office: U Houston-Victoria 2506 Red River Victoria TX 77901

HAYNES, MICHAEL STEWARD, pulmonologist, critical care specialist; b. Muskogee, Okla., June 9, 1949; s. Edgar Steward and Thelma Ethel Haynes; m. Suzanne Tennyson; children: Patrick, Katie, Lauren, Jenna. BS in Biochemistry, Okla. State U., 1970; MD, U. Okla., 1974. Diplomate Am. Bd. Internal Medicine, Am. Bd. Pulmonary Medicine, Am. Bd. Critical Care. Intern and resident in internal medicine Parkland Meml. Hosp., Dallas, 1974-77, chief resident in internal medicine, 1976-77, fellow in pulmonary medicine, 1977-79; co-founder Augusta (Ga.) Diagnostic Assn., 1979—; assoc. med. dir. respiratory therapy U. Hosp., 1979-80; med. dir. respiratory therapy St. Joseph Hosp., 1981-86, Humana Hosp., 1989; med. dir. Augusta Tech. Sch., 1980-87; presenter Ga. State Respiratory Therapy Conv., 1988, 89, 90, 93, Tri-State Respiratory Therapy Conv., 1982, 86, Aiken County Hosp., Jefferson County Hosp., Burke County Hosp., McDuffie County Hosp., St. Joseph Hosp., Atlanta Repiratory Symposium, 1988, Ga. Soc. Respiratory Care, 1987, 88, Med. Coll. Ga., 1989. Pres.-elect Am. Lung Assn. Ga., 1988-89, bd. dirs., 1984—, mem. exec. com., 1987—, pres., 1989-90, dir. fin., 1988-89; pres. East Ctrl. br. Ga. Lung Assn., 1983-93; judge Ga. Swim Assn., Atlanta, 1993—. Recipient Profl. Svc. award Ga. Lung Assn., 1984, Community Svc. award Am. Lung Assn. of Ga., 1987, Outstanding Young Investigator award Tex. Thoracic Soc., 1979; grantee Am. Socs. Exptl. Biology, 1979, Am. Fedn. Clin. Rsch., 1979. Fellow Am. Coll. Chest Physicians, Am. Thoracic Soc.; mem. ACP, Ga. Thoracic Soc. (exec. com. 1990—, bd. dirs. 1979—, sec.-treas. 1995—), Soc. for Critical Care Medicine, Sigma Xi, Alpha Omega Alpha, Phi Kappa Phi. Home: 3645 Pebble Beach Dr Martinez GA 30907-9088 Office: U Med Assocs Ste 1000 1303 D'Antignac Augusta GA 30901

HAYNES, ROBERT VAUGHN, retired university official, historian; b. Nashville, Nov. 28, 1929; m. Martha Farr, Dec. 25, 1952; children: Catherine Anne, Carolyn Alice, Charles Allen. B.A., Millsaps Coll., 1952; M.A., Peabody Coll., 1953; Ph.D., Rice U., 1959. Mem. faculty U. Houston, 1956-84, prof. history, 1967-84, acting dir. Afro-Am. studies, 1969-71, interim dir. libraries, 1976-78; dir. libraries U. Houston central campus, 1978-80, assoc. provost, 1980-81, dep. provost, 1981-84; v.p. acad. affairs Western Ky. U., Bowling Green, 1984-96; vis. prof., Black studies cons. U. Ala., 1970; dir. Inst. Cultural Understanding, 1971; mem. adv. planning com. Tex. Conf. on Library and Info. Services, 1978-79. Author: A Night of Violence: The Houston Riot of 1917, 1976, The Natchez District and the American Revolution, 1976; editor: The Houston Rev., 1981-84; Contbr. articles to profl. jours. Mem. Houston United Campus Christian Life com., 1973-81; chmn. ch. and soc. com. Synod of Tex., Presbyn. Ch. U.S.A., 1970-73; treas. Houston Com. on the Humanities, 1978-79. Served with USAF, 1950-51. Danforth asso., 1969; Carnegie fellow, 1952-53; Nat. Endowment Humanities fellow, 1973. Mem. Am. Hist. Assn., Orgn. Am. Historians, So. Hist. Assn., Miss. Hist. Soc., Inst. Early Am. History and Culture, Tex. Assn. Coll. Tchrs. (past chpt. pres.), Phi Kappa Phi (past pres.). Democrat. Office: Western Ky U Office of VP Acad Affairs Bowling Green KY 42101

HAYNIE, TONY WAYNE, corporate lawyer; b. Houston, Sept. 26, 1955; m. Mary E. Steward, Sept. 1, 1978. BA, U. Okla., 1978; postgrad., Boston U., Heidelberg Br., Fed. Republic Germany, 1980-81; JD, U. Tulsa, 1984; MBA, Okla. State U., 1993. Bar: Okla. 1985, U.S. Dist. Okla. 1985, U.S. Ct. Appeals (10th cir.) 1987, U.S. Supreme Ct. 1990. Assoc. Conner & Winters, Tulsa, 1984-90, ptnr., 1991-92, shareholder, 1992—; pres., CEO The Colonneh Co., Tulsa, 1991—; arbitrator N.Y. Stock Exch., 1991—. 1st lt. U.S. Army, 1978-82. Mem. ABA (sect. bus. law and litig., chair subcom. on expert witness on trial evidence com. of litig. sect. 1991-94), Am. Inns of Ct. (barrister Hudson-Hall-Wheaton chpt. 1996—), Okla. Bar Assn., Okla. Bar Found., Tulsa County Bar Assn., Tulsa County Bar Found., Phi Delta Phi. Democrat. Methodist.

HAYS, CHARLES WILFRED, medical epidemiologist, public health educator; b. Kansas City, Mo., Oct. 9, 1938; s. Wilfred Beneville and Alice Alleta (Magoffin) H.; m. Catherine Marie Gerritz, Dec. 29, 1968; children: Catrina Chalise, Christa Marie. BA, Oreg. State U., 1963; MD, U. Kans., 1967; MPH, Harvard U., 1969, MS, 1973. Diplomate Am. Bd. Preventive Medicine. Rsch. fellow dept. pharmacology Stanford U. Med. Sch., Palo Alto, Calif., 1962; rsch. fellow dept. physiology U. Kans. Med. Sch., 1964; intern Med. Ctr. Hosp. Vt., Burlington, 1967-68; resident in gen. preventive medicine Harvard Sch. Pub. Health, 1968-69, 71-72; med. epidemiologist malaria program Ctr. for Disease Control, Kathmandu, Nepal, 1969-71; teaching fellow dept. prevention and social medicine Harvard Med. Sch., 1972-73; asst. dean U. Mass. Med. Sch., 1973-75, asst. prof. dept. family and community medicine, 1973-76, acting dean students, 1975-76, assoc. prof. dept. family and community medicine, 1976-82; state epidemiologist and dir., Bur. Epidemiology and Disease Prevention Pa. Dept. Health, 1982-85; med. officer programming and tng. unit malaria action programme WHO, 1985-89, med. officer operational rsch. unit, divsn. ctrl. of tropical diseases, 1990-92; med. epidemiologist Indian Health Svc., Oklahoma City area, 1992—; cons. curriculum devel. project Harvard U., Boston, Insect Control and Rsch. Bur. Inc., Balt., Minority Student Admissions Project of Orkand Corp., Silver Springs, Md., Pub. Affairs Rsch. Ctr., Clark U., Worcester, Mass.; adj. lectr. health studies, health planning and adminstrn. program Pa. State U., 1983-86, clin. assoc. prof. medicine, 1983-86; adj. assoc. prof. epidemiology U. Pitts., 1983-87; vis. assoc. prof. biostats. and epidemiology U. Okla. Coll. Pub. Health, 1992—; presenter in field. With U.S. Army, 1956-59, Korea. Recipient Meritorious award U.S. Agy. Internat. Devel., 1972. Mem. APHA (cons. internat. health programs divsn.), Am. Assn. History Medicine, Am. Coll. Preventive Medicine, Phi Eta Sigma, Phi Kappa Phi. Democrat. Lutheran. Office: Oklahoma City Area Indian Health Svc 3625 NW 56th St Oklahoma City OK 73112-2001

HAYS, DONALD OSBORNE, retired government official; b. New Braintree, Mass., June 5, 1907; s. Edward Christopher and Grace Theresa (Osborne) H.; m. Mary Katherine Jackson Oliver, Aug. 30, 1937. Student, Middlebury Coll., 1925-27; B.A., U. Colo., 1929; M.A., Columbia U., 1937, postgrad., 1942; postgrad., Am. U., 1951. Tchr. English, head dept. English, pub. schs. of Colo., Pa., 1929-38; head English dept., sr. master Woodmere (L.I.) Acad., 1938-42; mgmt. analyst, asst. dir., mgmt. and planning staff Spl. Services, VA, 1946-51; asst. dir. budget and mgmt. div. NPA, 1951-53; asst. dist. commr. for adminstrn. IRS, Balt., 1953; asst. regional commr. for adminstrn. IRS, Boston, 1953-54, Phila., 1954-57; asst. to dir. Bur. Fgn. Commerce, Dept. Commerce, Washington, 1957-61, Bur. Internat. Commerce, 1961-63; dir. overseas personnel div. Office Fgn. Comml. Services, 1963-68, dir. performance evaluation div., 1968-70; dir. performance evaluation Fgn. Comml. Services Staff, 1970-75; asst. to dir. support services Office of Internat. Mktg., Bur. Internat. Commerce, 1975; Dept. Commerce mem. 13th and 16th Fgn. Service Officer Selection Bd. Dept. State, 1959, 62; dep. examiner Bd. Fgn. Service Examiners, 1960-74. Active numerous civic orgns. Served from lt. (j.g.) to lt. comdr. USNR, 1942-46; staff Comdr. Fourth Fleet 1943-44, Recife, Brazil; contact negotiator, electronics div. Bur. Ships, also staff Navy Manpower Survey Bd. 1944-46. Mem. Cum Laude Soc., SAR (past pres. D.C. soc.), Diplomatic and Consular Officers Ret., Alpha Sigma Phi, Kappa Phi Kappa, Washington Met. Club. Episcopalian (jr. warden 1968-73). Home: 200 Dominican Dr Apt 3212 Madison MS 39110

HAYS, FRANKLIN ERNEST, minister, chaplain; b. Invokern, Calif., Aug. 8, 1947; s. Franklin Burley and Eileen Pauline (Munsterman) H.; m. Peggy Kay Specie, Nov. 4, 1968 (div. Jan. 1972); m. Marsha Ann Van Etten, Aug. 27, 1983; children: Noel, Robert, Shelley, Jane. BS, San Jose (Calif.) State U., 1971; MS in Divinity, Golden Gate Theology Seminary, 1977; MS of Theology, U. Chgo., 1983. Ordained to ministry Evangelical Luth. Ch., 1978. Pastor Chapel Hills, Mill Valley, Calif., 1977-78; enlisted U.S. Navy, 1978; chaplain Fleet Religious Support Actvity U.S. Navy, Norfolk, Va., 1978-80, Credo Great Lakes, Chgo., 1980-82, 3rd Marine Div., Okinawa, Japan, 1982-83, U. Chgo., 1983-84, Naval Air Sta., Alameda, Calif., 1984-86, Naval Mec Det, San Francisco, 1986-88, CNRA-8, Oakland, Calif., 1988-89, Comdr. Logistics Group One, 1989-90, Resource Bd., Norfolk, Va., 1990-93; comdr. Amphibious Group 2, 1993-95; pres. Armed Forces Staff Coll., 1995—. Named One of Outstanding Young Men Am. U.S. Jaycess, 1979. Lodges: Lions, Elks, Kiwanis. Home: 1492 Five Forks Rd Virginia Beach VA 23455-4245 Office: 6500 Hampton Blvd Norfolk VA 23508-1200

HAYS, HOLLY MARY, editor, freelance photojournalist; b. L.A., Nov. 28, 1952; d. Herschel Martin and Mary Catherine (Miller) H. Cert. in art history, Fla. State U., 1971; cert. in computer sci., Fla. Atlantic U., 1979; BS in Journalism, U. Fla., 1974. Layout editor Ind. Fla. Alligator, Gainesville, 1974; reporter Gainesville Sun, 1974; computer specialist Gilbert Law Printing, Gardena, Calif., 1975; copy editor Hartford (Conn.) Courant, 1976-78; mech. artist CRC Press, Inc., Boca Raton, Fla., 1980-85; asst. editor Fla. Living mag., Gainesville, 1986-92, mng. editor, 1993-94, editor-in-chief, 1994-95; asst. editor Ga. Living mag., Gainesville, 1989-91; owner Cross Creek Wilderness Safaris, 1995—; writer Womans World Mag., Englewood, N.J., 1987-89; writer, photographer Fla. Sportsman Mag., Miami, 1988. Vol. Marjorie K. Rawlings State Hist. Site, Cross Creek, Fla., 1987—. Master capt. U.S. Coast Guard. Mem. Outdoor Writers Am., Internat. Group for Hist. Aircraft Recovery (expedition mem.). Republican. Home and Office: PO Box 96 Lochloosa FL 32662-0096

HAYS, MARY KATHERINE JACKSON (MRS. DONALD OSBORNE HAYS), civic worker; b. Flora, Miss.; d. Rufus Lafayette and Ada (Collum) Jackson; student U. Miss., 1925-26, Millsaps Coll., 1926-27, 43-44; grad. Clark Bus. Sch., 1934; student Columbia U., 1935, Strayer Bus. Coll., 1951; m. Halbert Puffer Oliver, Aug. 9, 1927 (dec. 1934); m. 2d, Donald Osborne Hays, Aug. 30, 1937. Sec. to pres. McCullough Box and Crate Co., Pharr, Tex., 1934-36; sec. to field supr. Miss. Unemployment Compensation Commn., 1936-37; rep. Homes of Tomorrow, 1940 N.Y. World's Fair; sec. to head interior design Lord & Taylor, N.Y.C., 1940; sales dept. Knabe Piano Co., N.Y.C., 1941-43. Active, Little Theatre, Wilkes Barre, Pa., 1937-39; charter mem. and incorporator Conf. State Socs., Washington, 1952; vol. worker Am. Cancer Soc., Washington, 1957; mem. Center City Residents Assn., Phila., 1956; mem. women's com. Nat. Symphony Assn., vol. worker USO, 1945-48, symphony sustaining com. drives, 1957; mem. women's com. Corcoran Gallery Art, Washington, 1957-62; mem. Pierce-Warwick Adoption Assn. of Washington Home for Foundlings; vol. Washington Heart Assn., 1959-66; mem. Nat. Capital Area chpt. United Ch. Women, 1957-72; mem. D.C. Episcopal Home for Children, 1961-86, D.C. Salvation Army Aux., 1962—. Mem. Miss. State Soc. D.C. (sec. 1950-53), Miss. Women's Club D.C., DAR (vice regent chpt. 1970-72, regent chpt. 1972-74, vice chmn. D.C. com. celebration Washington's birthday 1972-76, state libr. 1974-76, state officers club 1976—), chpt. chmn. DAR Svc. for Vet. Patients Com., 1986-88, 90-95, UDC (chpt. historian 1982-84, 86—, chaplain 1984-86), Johnstone Clan Am. (exec. coun. 1976-81, nat. chmn. membership com. 1976-81), First Families of Miss., Women's Club of Flora, Miss. Episcopalian. Club: The Washington. Home: 200 Dominican Dr Apt 3212 Madison MS 39110

HAYS, ROBERT WILLIAM, communications consultant, educator, writer; b. Atlanta, Oct. 17, 1925; s. Calvin Samuel and Elizabeth (Green) H.; m. Rebecca Copeland, June 15, 1950; children: Michael, David, William. Student, Duke U., 1943-44; AB summa cum laude, Presbyn. Coll. S.C., 1947; MEd, Emory U., 1957. Comml. mgr. Sta. WSFT-AM, Thomaston, Ga., 1947-48, Sta. WLBG, Clinton, S.C., 1948; co-owner Clinton Plastic Co., 1948-49; instr. English So. Tech. Inst. (now So. Polytechnic State U.), Chamblee, Ga., 1950-51; supr. of tng. course devel. Lockheed Aircraft Corp., Marietta, Ga., 1951-52; asst. prof. So. Tech. Inst. (now So. Polytechnic State U.), Chamblee, Ga., 1952-57; head English dept. So. Tech. Inst. (now So. Polytechnic State U.), Marietta, 1953-73, assoc. prof., 1958-60, prof., 1960-85, prof. emeritus, 1985—; cons. in communications, Marietta, 1965—. Author: Pacific Parodies, 1947, Principles of Technical Writing, 1965, Practically Speaking in Business, Industry and Government, 1969, Guide to Technical Writing, 1970, (with others) Getting Your Message Across, 1981; published many poems; contbr. numerous articles to profl. jours. Served to lt. (j.g.) USNR, 1943-46. Hixson fellow Kiwanis, 1996; recipient Arthur Williston award, 1967, Internat. Tech. Communications Conf. Honor, 1980, 83, Cmty. Svc. award King Ctr., 1994, 95. Fellow Soc. for Tech. Communication (life, Disting. award 1983); mem. Assn. for Bus. Communication. Home: 3360 Trickum Rd Marietta GA 30066-4683

HAYS, STEELE, state supreme court judge; b. Little Rock, Mar. 25, 1925; s. L. Brooks and Marion (Prather) H.; m. Peggy Wall, July 12, 1980; children: Andrew Steele, Melissa Louise, Sarah Anne. B.A., U. Ark., 1948; J.D., George Washington U., 1951. Bar: Ark. 1951. Adminstrv. asst. to Congressman Brooks Hays, 1951-53; practice in Little Rock, 1953-79; mem. firm Spitzberg, Mitchell & Hays, 1953-79; circuit judge 6th Jud. Circuit Ark., Little Rock, 1969-70; judge Ark. Ct. Appeals, 1979-81; assoc. justice Ark. Supreme Ct., 1981-95; ret., 1995; chmn. Bd. Law Examiners, 1968-70. Mem. Ark. com. U.S. Civil Rights Commn.; Del. Presbyn. Ch. Consultation on Ch. Union, 1968-70; Trustee Presbyn. Found. Mem. ABA, Ark. Bar Assn. (past sec.-treas.), Sigma Chi, Delta Theta Phi. Home: 12 Deerwood St Conway AR 72032-6113

HAYS, WILLIAM GRADY, JR., corporate financial and bank consultant; b. Covington, Ga., July 9, 1927; s. William Grady and Ella Maude (Wofford) H.; m. Emily Ann Holcombe, Aug. 1, 1954; children: Woodfrin Grady, Steven Gregory, William Danfield. B.S., U. Ga., 1949; M.Litt., U. Pitts., 1950. Pres. First So. Corp., Atlanta, 1955-57; v.p. Comml. Trust Co., 1957-59; pres., chief exec. officer Comml. Acceptance Corp., 1959-74; fin. cons. William G. Hays & Assocs., Inc., 1974—; cons., chief exec. officer N.Am. Acceptance Corp., 1974—; cons. Kaleidoscope, Inc., 1979—, Speir Ins. Agy., Inc., 1982—; CEO United Am. Fin. Corp., Knoxville, Tenn., 1983—; cons. Banque Nationale De Paris, Nat. Westminister Bank, PLC, United Bank of Kuwait, PLC, Security Pacific Nat. Bank, First Nat. Bank of Boston; trustee Beacon Fin. Group, Inc., 1986; cons. Micro Mart, Inc., 1987; examiner World Bazzar Franchise Corp., 1992; spl. master Hannover Corp. Am., 1991; spl. agt. Diversified Growth Corp., 1989; trustee Internat. Trading Inc., 1993, Aledo Fin. Svcs., Inc., 1985. Contbr. articles to profl. jours. Mem. Kappa Delta Pi. Republican. Presbyterian. Clubs: Cherokee Town and Country, Univ. Yacht. Home: 2755 Normandy Dr NW Atlanta GA 30305-2822 Office: William G Hays & Assocs Inc 1422 W Peachtree St NW Ste 218 Atlanta GA 30309-2940

HAYTON, RICHARD NEIL, retired military officer, writer, publisher; b. Pine Bluff, Ark., Nov. 25, 1916; s. Richard Raymond and Ruth Naomi (Owens) H.; m. Virginia Ann Ridenour, Apr. 18, 1943 (dec. July 1994); children: Richard Neil Jr., Stephen Brian; m. Bertha Tellez, May 10, 1996; 1 child, Louann Vinci. BS, U. Md., 1955; MA in Govt., George Washington U., 1956. Commd. 2d lt. USAF, 1942; advanced through grades to maj. USAF, Fla., 1960—; ret. USAF, 1960; freelance writer, pub. Fla., 1960—. Author: (pen name Thomas Starling) The King and the Cat, 1975, The Garlic Kid, 1978, Jethrow's Cabin, 1982, Peter Paladine of the Great Heart, 1995. Office: Spindrift Press PO Box 2222 Cocoa FL 32923-2222

HAYWOOD, B(ETTY) J(EAN), anesthesiologist; b. Boston, June 1, 1942; d. Oliver Garfield and Helen Elizabeth (Salisbury) H.; m. Lynn Brandt Moon, Aug. 29, 1969 (div. Aug. 1986); children: Kaylin, Kris Lee, Kelly, Kasy R. BSc, Tufts U., 1964; MD, U. Colo., 1968; MBA, Oklahoma City U., 1993. Intern Wilford Hall AFB, San Antonio, Tex., 1968-69; resident in pediatrics U. Ariz., Tucson, 1971-72, resident in anesthesiology, 1972-74; dir. anesthesia dept. Pima County Hosp., Tucson, 1975-76; staff anesthesiologist South Community Hosp., Oklahoma City, 1977—; staff anesthesiologist Moore (Okla.) Mcpl. Hosp., 1981-94, chief of anesthesia, 1990-94; staff anesthesiologist St. Anthony Hosp., Oklahoma City, 1982—; chief of ethics com. S.W. Med. Ctr., 1996—. Bd. dirs. N.Am. South Devon Assn., Lynnville, Iowa, 1978-86, Found. Surgery Affiliates; mem. med. com. Planned Parenthood Okla., 1992—. Lt. col. USAFR, 1968—. Mem. AMA, NAFE (co-dir. Oklahoma City chpt. 1996—), World South Devon Assn. (U.S. rep. 1985, 88—), Tufts U. Alumni Assn. (rep.), Chi Omega (treas. 1963-64). Republican. Presbyterian. Home: 6501 Hunting Hill Oklahoma City OK 73116-3523

HAYWOOD, CHARLES FOSTER, finance educator; b. Ludlow, Ky., Apr. 7, 1927; s. Charles Adam and Julia Morton (Strode) H.; m. Josephine Richards (div.); children: Julia Elizabeth, Mary Josephine, Charles Ransome, John Watson; m. Judith Lynn Milburn, June 14, 1986; stepchildren: Piper Holladay, Noelle Holladay. BA, Berea Coll., 1949; MA, Duke U., 1950; PhD, U. Calif., 1955. Rsch. economist Am. Bankers Assn., N.Y.C., 1954-55; asst. prof. econ. Tulane U., New Orleans, 1955-57; provost, chair banking U. Miss., Oxford, 1958-63; dir. rsch. Bank Am., San Francisco, 1963-65; dean, prof. econ. U. Ky., Lexington, 1965-75, prof. econ., fin., 1975-89; nat. city bank prof. fin., 1989—; chmn. Colembe Assn., Inc., Washington, 1967-77; cons. Am. Bankers Assn., Washington, 1970-94; vice chmn. bd. dirs. Bank of Lexington, 1972-90; sec. devel. Commonwealth Ky., Frankfort, 1973-75; dir. Pittston Co., Richmond, Va., 1980—, ctr. bus. and econ. rsch. U. Ky., Lexington, 1990-94. Author: (monograph) Commercial Banking: An Industry, 1980, Economic Significance of Equine Industry in Kentucky, 1991,

Economic Impact of Toyota Industry, 1992. With U.S. Army, 1946-48, Japan. Earhart Found. fellow, 1953-54. Mem. Phi Beta Kappa, Phi Kappa Phi. Democrat. Methodist. Home: 2120 Ridgecane Ct Lexington KY 40513 Office: Gatton Coll Bus Econ Univ Ky Lexington KY 40506

HAYWOOD, JOHN WILLIAM, JR., engineering consultant; b. Savannah, Ga., Mar. 10, 1955; s. John William Sr. and Elizabeth (Williams) H.; m. Carol Johnice Staton, Jan. 15, 1976 (div. 1985); children: Venus Roshone, Maurice Antonio. BS in Mech. Engring. Tech. cum laude, Savannah State Coll., 1979; MS in Tech. summa cum laude, Pitts. State U., 1980. Aircraft foreman Grumman Aircraft Corp., Savannah, 1977-80; sr. mfg. engr. Superior Accessories Co., Parsons, Kans., 1980-81; sr. mech. engr. Martin Marietta Aerospace, Orlando, Fla., 1981-85; mem. tech. staff Rockwell Internat., Duluth, Ga., 1985-86; sr. mfg. engr. Boeing Airplane Co., Wichita, Kans., 1986-87; engring. cons. Sverdrup Tech. Inc., Elgin FB, Fla., 1987-90; pvt. practice engring. cons. Raritan, N.J., 1990-92; pvt. practice contract engring. Savannah, Ga., 1992—; cons. TP Cons., Oakland, N.J., 1990-91; mgr. environ. and indsl. engring. N.J. Inst. Tech., Newark, 1991-92; safety cons. N.Am. Contract Engring. Svcs., Tigard, Oreg., 1993-94; environ. mgr. Chatham County Dept. of Pub. Health, Savannah, Ga., 1995-96. Contbr. numerous articles to profl. jours. Teacher Macedonia Bapt. Ch., Savannah, 1991—; mentor Ramah Jr. Acad., Savannah, 1991—. With USAF, 1973-77. Mem. Minority Engrs. Coun., Nat. Tech. Assn. Republican. Home and Office: 1809 Vassar St Savannah GA 31405-3864

HAYWOOD, THEODORE JOSEPH, physician, educator; b. Monroe, N.C., Feb. 13, 1929; s. Jesse Beman and Mary (McDonald) H.; m. Nancy Hume Ferguson, Dec. 21, 1959; children: Elizabeth Linscott, Keene McDonald, Mark Shepard. B.S., The Citadel, 1948; M.D., Vanderbilt U., 1952. Diplomate: Am. Bd. Pediatrics, Am. Bd. Allergy and Immunology. Pvt. practice allergy Houston, 1958—; mem. staff Tex. Children's Hosp., 1958—, mem. active staff Pediatrics, 1963—; mem. faculty Baylor U. Coll. Medicine, 1958—, clin. assoc. prof. pediatrics and allergy, 1977—; mem. faculty U. Tex. Grad. Sch. Biomed. Scis., 1960—, adj. assoc. prof. allergy, 1969—. Served with M.C. AUS, 1955-57. Fellow Am. Coll. Allergists, Am. Acad. Allergy and Immunology, Am. Acad. Pediatrics, Am. Acad. Psychoanalytic Medicine; mem. Sigma Xi. Republican. Episcopalian. Club: River Oaks Country (Houston). Home: 2923 Ferndale Pl Houston TX 77098-1117 Office: 6969 Brompton St Houston TX 77025-1611

HAZARD, CHRISTOPHER WEDVIK, international business executive; b. N.Y.C., Aug. 9, 1943; s. Herbert Ray and Ellen Clausine (Wedvik) H.; m. Sally Grace Woodruff, Sept. 1, 1966; children: Mark Alexander, Julie Lynne. BA, Ohio State U., 1965; MPA, U. Colo., 1973; postgrad., U. Pa. Officer USAF, 1965-86; near east region dir. ops. Def. Security Assistance Agy., Washington, 1982-86; exec dir. internat. mktg. United Def. Ltd. Partnership, Arlington, Va., 1986—. Pres. M. Vernon Citizens Assn., Alexandria, Va., 1984-85; mem., 1982—. Recipient Def. Superior Svc., Sec. of Def., 1986, Joint Svc. Achievement, Dept. of Def., 1984; decorated Air Force Meritorious Svc. medal. Home: 9399 Mt Vernon Cir Alexandria VA 22309-3218

HAZARD, SHERRILL JOHN, III, business team leader; b. Syracuse, N.Y., Sept. 29, 1958; s. Sherrill John Jr. and Merle Charolette (Pabst) H.; m. Marcella Joan Thesing, Jan. 12, 1985; children: Sherill John IV, Mary Frances. BS in Pulp & Paper/Chem. Engring., U. Maine, Orono, 1980; MS in Mech. Engring., Naval Postgrad. Sch., 1987. Cert. engr.-in-tng., cert. naval command-at-sea. Project engr. Westyaco, Luke, Md., 1980-81; commd. surface line officer USN, 1982, advanced through grades to lt. comdr., ret., 1992; damage control asst., main propulsion asst. USN-USS Brewton, Pearl Harbor, Hawaii, 1982-85; chief engr. USN-USS Elrod, Charleston, S.C., 1988-90, USN-USS Charleston, Norfolk, Va., 1990-92; project engr.-mech. James River Corp.-Naheola Mill, Pennington, Ala., 1992-94; prodn. engr.-bleaching James River Corp.-Naheola Mill, Pennington, 1994-96; bus. team leader Pulp Dryer, 1996—. Patentee in field. Recipient Navy Achievement medals USN, 1985, 89, Navy Commendation medals USN, 1990, 91. Mem. NRA, Am. Mgmt. Assn., USN League, Tech. Assn. Pulp and Paper Industry, Delta Upsilon. Republican. Lutheran. Home: 276 Dogwood Cir Meridian MS 39305-9669 Office: James River Corp Naheola Mill HC 66 Box 315 Pennington AL 36916-9499

HAZELETT, PRISCILLA SUE, writer; b. Logan, W.Va., Aug. 11, 1947; d. Ralph Vernon and Enid Patsy (Rogers) H. BS in Gen. and Natural Scis., U. Charleston, 1971; postgrad., Marshall U., 1976-79. Playground dir. Charleston (W.Va.) Parks and Recreation, 1967-71; tchr. Kanawha Co. Schools, Charleston, 1971-77, Houston Ind. Sch. Dist., 1981-83; owner Gemini Trucking Co. D & R Coal Co., Huntington, 1977-79; nicotine analyzer Brown & Williamson Tobacco, Lexington, Ky., 1979-80; self employed writer South Point, Ohio, 1983-84; pathology clk. St. Joseph Hosp., Lexington, 1985-89; residential counselor Bluegrass Assn. Mentally Ill., Lexington, 1991-92; substitute tchr. Fayette County Schs., Lexington, 1992; writer self-emp., Morristown, Tenn., 1992—. Author: Native Am. Proetry and Proetics, 1996; Jehovah's Mistress, 1980. Mem. exec. bd. Sierra Club, 1986; team leader God's Pantry, Lexington, 1988; mem. adv. bd. Raven Run Friends, Lexington, 1988; reading and printing poet Working Class Kitchen, Lexington, 1988-89. Named Vol. of Yr. Sierra Club, 1986. Mem. Poetry Soc. Am., W.Va. Writers Club, Chi Beta Phi, Kappa Delta Pi. Democrat. Home: 100 Cherrywood Dr Frankfort KY 40601

HAZELIP, HERBERT HAROLD, academic administrator; b. Bowling Green, Ky., Aug. 3, 1930; s. Herbert and Maggie Marie (Ferguson) H.; m. Helen Frances Royalty, Mar. 23, 1956; children: Patrick Harold, Jeffrey Alan. AA, Freed-Hardeman Coll., Henderson, Tenn., 1948; BA, David Lipscomb Coll., Nashville, 1950; MDiv, So. Bapt. Theol. Sem., 1958; PhD, U. Iowa, 1967. Ordained to ministry Ch. of Christ, 1947. Minister Cen. Ch. Christ, Owensboro, Ky., 1950-53, Taylor Blvd. Ch. Christ, Louisville, 1954-64, Cen. Ch. Christ, Cedar Rapids, Iowa, 1964-67, Highland St. Ch. Christ, Memphis, 1967-86; dean, prof. Harding U. Grad. Sch. Religion, Memphis, 1967-86; pres. David Lipscomb U., Nashville, 1986—. Author: Discipleship, 1977, A Devotional Guide to Bible Lands, 1979, Anchors in Troubled Waters, 1981, Lord, Help Me When I'm Hurting, 1984, Happiness in the Home, 1985, Questions People Ask Ministers Most, 1986, Jesus: Our Mentor and Model, 1987, Becoming Persons of Integrity, 1988, Anchors for the Asking, 1989. Mem. Rotary. Office: David Lipscomb U 3901 Granny White Pike Nashville TN 37204-3951

HAZEN, CHARLES MELVILLE, mathematics educator; b. N. Girard, Pa., May 25, 1941; s. Charles Edward and Gladys Estelle (Miller) H. BS, Edinboro State Coll., 1962; MAT, Jacksonville U., 1973. Tchr. Kenton City Schs., Ohio, 1963-67; tchr. math. Episc. High Sch., Jacksonville, 1967-95, chmn. dept. math., 1973-93, sr. master, 1985-95, rsch. dir., 1993-95; adj. prof. math. Jacksonville U., 1995—. Designer computer programs for acad. office. Layreader Episc. Ch. various locations, 1962—, mem., clk. vestry Ch. of the Good Shepherd, Jacksonville, 1981-84, 87; mem. Cummer Gallery Art, Jacksonville Art Mus., Riverside Avondale Preservation Assn. Recipient Chaplains award Jacksonville Episcopal High Sch., 1976. Mem. Nat. Council Tchrs. Math., Math. Assn. Am., Kenton Edn. Assn. (sec. 1964-65, pres. 1965-67), Nat. Assn. Railroad Passengers, Nat. Ry. Hist. Soc., Nat. Model Railroad Assn. (life), Gateway Model Railroad Club (past sec., treas., pres.), Jacksonville Episc. High Sch. Alumni Assn. (hon.) Democrat. Avocations: model railroading; photography; singing; travelling. Home: 474 Laurina St Jacksonville FL 32216-9164 Office: Jacksonville U Dept Math 2800 University Blvd N Jacksonville FL 32211-3321

HAZLETT, JOHN DOWNTON, English language educator; b. Mason City, Iowa, July 13, 1949; s. Charles Junior and Diana Nancy (Downton) H.; m. Diana Maury Robin, Apr. 1, 1972 (div. 1978). BA cum laude, Coe Coll., 1971; MA, U. Iowa, 1981, PhD, 1984. Editor U. Calif., Berkeley, 1980-85; instr. Contra Costa Coll., San Pablo, Calif., 1983-85; Fulbright lectr. U. Complutense de Madrid, Spain, 1985-87; asst. prof. U. New Orleans, 1987-91, assoc. prof., 1991—, coord. grad. studies English dept., 1994—, dir. faculty exch. programs in Spain, 1991-96; vis. prof. U. Salamanca, Spain, 1991-92. Contbr. articles to profl. jours. Tchg. Rsch. fellow U. Iowa, Iowa City, 1972-76; Faculty Exch. grantee Spanish Consulate of New Orleans, 1991. Mem. MLA, Am. Studies Assn., The Autobiography Soc. Office: Dept English Univ New Orleans New Orleans LA 70148

HAZUDA, HELEN PAULINE, sociologist, educator; b. San Francisco, Oct. 20, 1943; d. Alexander William and Dolores Underwood (Green) H.; children: Ann Elizabeth Richter, Sean. BA in Sociology and Philosophy, Incarnate Word Coll., 1965, MA in Edn. and History, 1968; PhD in Sociology, U. Tex., 1975. Asst. prin. Incarnate Word H.S., San Antonio, 1967-71; discipline head for curriculum, instrn., dir. bilingual edn. Our Lady the Lake U., San Antonio, 1976-79; asst. prof. clin. medicine in medicine and psychiatry U. Tex. Health Sci. Ctr., San Antonio, 1980-88, assoc. prof. medicine dept. medicine and psychiatry, 1988-96, prof. medicine dept. medicine and psychiatry, 1996—; del. Gov's White House Conf. Children and Youth, Austin, 1970; admissions com. med. sch. U. Tex. Health Sci. Ctr., San Antonio, 1986-91, med. humanities curriculum planning com., 1989-91, tech. adv. panel for clin. and epidemiological rsch., 1991—; doctoral dissertation com. Sch. Nursing, 1992-93, adj. asst. prof. medicine and psychiatry, 1979-80; lectr. Incarnate Word Coll., San Antonio, 1971-72; cons. San Luis Valley Health and Aging Study/U. Colo. Health Sci. Ctr., Denver, 1992—; mem. nat. adv. panel RMC Rsch. Corp., 1977-81; mem. ad hoc study section NIH, 1988, mem. clin. applications and prevention adv. com. divsn. epidemiology and clin. applications Nat. Heart, Lung and Blood Inst., 1991-94, chair behavioral medicine working group, 1993-94, task force on rsch. in epidemiology and prevention cardiovascular disease, 1993-94; reviewer grants and proposals; mem. working group on epidemiology of hypertension in Hispanic-Ams., Native Ams., and Asian/Pacific Islanders-Ams., 1993-94; co-chair NHLBI Conf. socioeconomic status and cardiovascular health and disease, 1995; cons. McDonnell-Douglas Automation Co., St. Louis, 1969-78, Devel. Assocs., 1975-77; speaker and presenter in field. Contbr. articles to profl. jours. Panelist San Antonio Cmty. Symposium on the Changing Role Women in Personal and Profl. Life, 1976; resource person Leadership San Antonio, 1976; co-chair Working Women in Am.: Where Are They and Why are They There?, 1976-77; judge Hobby Middle Sch. Sci. Fair, San Antonio, 1984, John Jay H.S. Sci. Fair, San Antonio, 1987, Alamo Area Regional Sci. Fair, San Antonio, 1987; alumnae bd. dirs. Incarnate Word H.S., San Antonio, 1986-89; pledge vol. Womens Faculty Assn., San Antonio, 1991. U.S. Seminar on the Epidemiology and Prevention Cardiovascular Disease fellow, Lake Tahoe, Calif., 1983; instl. rsch. grantee U. Tex. Health Scis. Ctr./Hogg Found. for Mental Health, Austin, 1981-82; grantee Am. Heart Assn., 1983-84, Morrison Trust Found., 1986-87, NIH, 1979—, Nat. Cancer Inst., 1985-89. Mem. Am. Sociol. Assn., Soc. for Behavioral Medicine, Am. Diabetes Assn., Soc. for Epidemiol. Rsch., Am. Heart Assn. (mem. coun. on cardiovasc. epidemiology), Acad. Behavioral Medicine Rsch., Phi Kappa Phi, Kappa Gamma Phi, Alpha Chi, Alpha Lambda Delta. Office: U Tex Health Sci Ctr Dept Medicine/Epidemiology 7703 Floyd Curl Dr San Antonio TX 78284-7873

HAZY, JEFFREY LEE, metal products executive; b. Miami, Fla., July 10, 1961; s. Joseph Hazy and Sandra (Rutledge) Overbeck; m. Carol Mae Gross, Jan. 2, 1981; children: Elizabeth Rae, Allison Jean, Jonathan Lee. BS in Indsl. Engring. Tech., Southern Tech., 1983; MBA, Ind. U, 1993. Indsl. engr. McCrackin Industries, Atlanta, 1984-86; mfg. engr. Leslie-Locke, Atlanta, 1986-91; quality assurance mgr. Sun Metal Products, Warsaw, Ind., 1991-93; plant mgr. Sun Metal Products, Warsaw, 1993-95; v.p. ops. Sun Metal Products, Warsaw, Ind., 1995—. Mem. Warsaw C. of C. (edn. coun.), Kiwanis. Republican. Roman Catholic. Office: Ga Displays Inc 218 Seaboard Rd Fitzgerald GA 31750

HAZZARD, MARY ELIZABETH, nurse, educator; b. Evansville, Ind., Mar. 2, 1941; d. John Waven and Lucille Elizabeth (Theobold) H.; 1 child, Mary Lucille. BSN, Nazareth Coll., 1963; AM, NYU, 1965, PhD, 1970. Staff nurse Caldwell County War Meml. Hosp., Princeton, Ky., 1962, staff nurse supr., 1963, 65; asst. nurse St. Joseph's Hosp., Louisville, 1962-63; teaching fellow NYU, 1966, instr., 1966-68; nursing sister-in-charge Meru (Kenya) Dist. Hosp., 1966; asst. prof. U. Va. Sch. Nursing, Charlottesville, 1968-70, assoc. prof., 1970-74, dir. learning resources, 1971-74; assoc. prof. Sangamon State U., Springfield, Ill., 1974-79; prof. Western Ky. U., Bowling Green, 1979—; head dept. nursing Western Ky. U., Bowling Green, 1979-96; adj. assoc. prof. U. Ky., Lexington, 1983-94; curriculum cons. MacMurray Coll., Jacksonville, Ill., 1978, U. Louisville, 1981; pres. So. Coun. on Collegiate Edn. in Nursing, 1993-95. Author: Review of Med-Surg Nursing, 1976, Nursing Outline Series: Critical Care Nursing, 1978; also articles; mem. edit. rev. bd. Health Care for Women Internat., 1984—. Pres. So. Coun. on Collegiate Edn. in Nursing, 1993-95. Fellow Am. Acd. Nursing; mem. ANA, Ky. Nurses Assn. (pres. 1986-87), Ky. League for Nursing (bd. dirs. 1980-83), Ky. Acad. Sci., Ky. Assn. Baccalaureate and Higher Degree Programs (sec. 1986-87), Ky. Cols., Sigma Theta Tau, Pi Lambda Theta. Democrat. Roman Catholic. Office: Western Ky U Dept Nursing Bowling Green KY 42101

HAZZARD, WILLIAM RUSSELL, geriatrician, educator; b. Ann Arbor, Mich., Sept. 5, 1936; s. Albert Sidney and Florence Bernice (Woolsey) H.; m. Ellen Bennett Friedman, June 10, 1961; children: Susan Lovejoy Roque, Russell Holden, Rebecca Cornell Oliver, Daniel Bennett. AB, Cornell U., 1958, MD, 1962. Diplomate Am. Bd. Internal Med. Resident in internal medicine U. Wash. Sch. Med. and Affiliated Hosps., Seattle, 1966-67, fellow in endocrinology and metabolism, 1965-66, 67-69; from instr. to prof. medicine U. Wash., Seattle, 1969-82, dir. Northwest Lipid Rsch. Clinic, 1972-78; investigator Howard Hughes Med. Inst., U. Wash., Seattle, 1972-80; prof. medicine, assoc. dir. dept. medicine Johns Hopkins Med. Instns., Balt., 1982-86, dir. ctr. on aging, 1983-86; prof., chmn. dept. internal med. Bowman Gray Sch. Medicine of Wake Forest U., Winston-Salem, N.C., 1986—; dir. J. Paul Sticht Ctr. on Aging of Wake Forest U., Winston-Salem, N.C., 1987—. Editor: Principles of Geriatric Medicine and Gerontology, 1984, 89, 93; contbr. over 100 articles to jours. in field. Lt. USNR, 1963-65. Fellow ACP; mem. Inst. Medicine of NAS, Am. Geriatrics Soc. (bd. dirs. 1988—, pres. 1993), Assn. Profs. Medicine, Gerontol. Soc. Am. (chmn. clin. med. sect. 1984), Am. Heart Assn. (Coun. on Arteriosclerosis), Am. Fedn. Clin. Rsch. (mem. emeritus), Am. Soc. Clin. Investigation (mem. emeritus), Assn. Am. Physicians, AM. Clin. and Climatol. Assn., Nat. Inst. on Aging (aging rev. com. 1990-94, Geriatric Medicine Acad. award 1980). Home: 5200 Riverwest Rd Lewisville NC 27023-8121 Office: Bowman Gray Sch of Medicine Dept Internal Medicine Winston Salem NC 27157

HE, CHAOYING, molecular biologist, researcher; b. Yiyang, Hunan, China, July 6, 1958; came to U.S., 1987; s. Guong Yao He and Simei Nie; m. Xianghong Rong, Jan. 1, 1984; children: Judy, Wendy. MD, Human Med. U., Changsha, Hunan, 1982, PhD in Toxicology, 1985. Rsch. assoc. Human Med. U., 1985-87; postdoctoral Nat. Cancer Inst., Frederick, Md., 1987-88; postdoctoral NIH, Research Triangle Park, N.C., 1988-91, rsch. assoc., 1991-93, sr. rsch. assoc., 1993—. Contbr. articles to profl. jours. Home: 4831 Highgate Dr Durham NC 27713-9301 Office: NIH 111 Alexander Ave Durham NC 27705

HEACKER, THELMA WEAKS, retired elementary school educator; b. Lakeland, Fla., Nov. 27, 1927; d. Andrew Lee and Stella Dicy (Hodges) Weaks; m. Howard V. Heacker, Aug. 21, 1947; children: Victor, Patricia, Paula, Jonathan, Johannah; m. V.L. Brown, Mar. 31, 1991. BA, Carson-Newman Coll., Jefferson City, Tenn., 1949; MA, Tenn. Technol. U., 1980; postgrad., U. Tenn. Cert. elem. and secondary tchr., Tenn.; cert. secondary tchr., Ga. Elem. tchr. Hamblen County Pub. Schs., Morristown, Tenn., 1949; secondary tchr. Morgan County-Coalfield High Sch., Coalfield, Tenn., 1986-87, Roane County-O. Springs High Sch., Oliver Springs, Tenn., 1949-71; elem. tchr. Morgan County-Petros-Joyner Sch., Oliver Springs, 1975-93. Named Tchr. of Yr., 1986. Mem. NEA, Tenn. Edn. Assn., Ea. Tenn. Edn. Assn., Morgan County Edn. Assn., RCTA, HCTA. Home: 102 Ulena Ln Oak Ridge TN 37830-5237 Office: Petros Joyner Elem Sch Petros-Joyner Rd Oliver Springs TN 37840-9700

HEACOCK, DONALD DEE, social worker; b. Anthony, Kans., Feb. 21, 1934; s. C.W. and Thelma Olive (Hilton) H.; m. Margaret Newberry, Sept. 4, 1953; children: Teresa Ellen, Mark Dee. AB, Washburn U., 1956; BD cum laude, United Sem., 1959; MSW, Barry Coll., 1971. Ordained priest Episcopal Ch., 1965; diplomate in clin. social work. Parish minister St. John's Ch., Clinton, Mich., 1961-66; chaplain, Margarita, Canal Zone, 1966-69; tchr. Christ Ch. Acad. Secondary Sch., Colon, Panama, 1966-69; counselor South Fla. Neighborhood Youth Corp., Miami, 1969-70; chief social service, instr. pediatric comprehensive health care program U. Miami, 1971-72; asst. dir. Alpha House, Dade County, Fla. and field supr. Barry Coll., 1972-73; marriage and family therapist Psychiatric Assocs., Shreveport, La., 1973-75; pvt. practice social work, Shreveport, 1975—; dir. Holy Cross Child Placement Agy., Inc., 1984; lectr. sociology Centenary Coll., 1981-88. With USAF, 1959-61. Mem. Am. Assn. Marriage and Family Therapy, Nat. Assn. Social Workers, Acad. Cert. Social Work, Phi Kappa Mu, Phi Gamma Mu. Lodge: Masons. Home: 748 Thora Blvd Shreveport LA 71106-1824 Office: 929 Olive St Shreveport LA 71104-2103

HEAD, CLARENCE MCMAHON, environmental scientist; b. San Diego, Apr. 3, 1935; s. Clarence McMahon Sr. and Susanna (Sprague) H.; m. Jacqueline Byars Smith, July 17, 1976. BS in Ceramic Engring., Ga. Inst. Tech., 1957, MS in Ceramic Engring., 1965; PhD in Environ. Geography, U. Ga., 1975. Registered profl. engr., Ga., Fla. Sr. mfg. rsch. engr. Lockheed-Ga. Co., Marietta, 1962-68; assoc. prof. So. Tech. Inst., Marietta, 1968-78; assoc. prof. civil and environ. engring. Ctrl. U. Fla., Orlando, 1978—; established joint Am.-Siberian Environ. Rsch. Inst., 2 Fla. legis. funded environ. rsch. insts. Author: Geologic Perspective of Florida, 1982, Shaping the Florida Platform, 1983, Winter Park Sinkhole Investigation, 1983, Face of Florida, 1990; contbr. articles to profl. jours., including Plastic Tech., Lockheed Quar., also conf. procs., reports in field. Capt. USN, 1957-59. Edward Orton Jr. Found. fellow, 1959-61, Fulbright fellow Agy. for Internat. Devel., Russia, 1993; grantee Engring. Inst. Environ. Scis., 1980, Jammal & Assocs., 1981, 83, Fla. Dept. Ins., 1982, All State Ins., 1982, Fla. Dept. Natural Resources, 1982, 88, 89, 91, Orange County Commn., 1983, Fla. STAR Program, 1985, Wekiva Resources Coun., 1989, U.S. EPA, 1992-93. Mem. Assn. Am. Geographers (sec.-treas. environ. sect. 1991-96), Am. Soc. Engring. Educators (newsletter editor internat. divsn. 1994-95). Office: U Ctrl Fla Civil Engring Dept Orlando FL 32816

HEAD, ELIZABETH SPOOR, mycology consultant; b. Galveston, Tex., July 10, 1928; d. Robert Newcomb and Bernice Lillian (Lumley) Spoor; m. Foy Paul Head, Feb. 23, 1952; children: Robert Paul, Phillip Lee, Elisabeth Anne. Student, North Tex. State U., 1945-47, U. Tex. Med. Br., Galveston, 1947-48; BS in Health Care Scis. with high honors, U. Tex., Galveston, 1984. Cert. med. technologist. Med. technologist, lab dir. dept. dermatology U. Tex. Med. Br., Galveston, 1948-91; ret., 1991; mycology cons. dept. dermatology U. Tex. Med. Br., Galveston, 1992—. Contbr. articles to profl. jours., chpts. to books and presentations at nat. and internat. meetings. Mem. Altar Guild, Trinity Episcopal Ch., Galveston. Mem. Am. Soc. Med. Technologists, Galveston Dist. Soc. Med. Technologists (pres. 1976-77), Internat. Oleander Soc. (pres. 1978-82, corr. sec. 1985—, editor newsletter Nerium News 1986—), Galveston Hist. Found., Friends of Moody Gardens (pres., chmn. bd. 1990-92), Wednesday Lit. Club (pres. 1995-97). Home: 4610 R 1/2 Galveston TX 77551 Office: U Tex Med Br Dept Dermatology Galveston TX 77555

HEAD, GREGORY ALAN, mechanical engineer, consultant; b. Dallas, Mar. 2, 1955; s. A. Lee and Georgia M. Head. BSME, Brigham Young U., 1981; MS in Engring. Mgmt., U. Alaska, Anchorage, 1988; postgrad., U. Tex., Arlington, 1990—. Registered profl. engr., Tex. Engr. tech. Hercules Aerospace, Inc., Salt Lake City, 1978-79, LTV Aerospace Inc., Dallas, 1979-80; engr. Hercules Aerospace Inc., Sale Lake City, 1980-82, CMH-Vitro, Anchorage, 1982-84; petroleum engr. Arco Alaska, Anchorage, 1984-87; cons. FAH World Wide Photographers, Anchorage and Dallas, 1987—; sr. v.p. systems divsn. D.C. Systems, Denton, Tex., 1988-94; pres. D.C. Systems, Denton, 1994—; cons. Alaska Mountaineering Assn., Anchorage, 1990—; capt. Arctic Adventurers, 1988—. Author: Arctic Lands and Uses, 1989. Missionary, Ch. of Jesus Christ of Latter Day Saints, Washington, 1975-77; mem. Mountain Rescue Team, Anchorage, 1989-96; emergency med. technician State of Alaska, 1987—. Named Photographer of the Yr., FAH Worldwide Photo, Inc., 1990. Mem. ASME, Nat. Geog. Soc., Nat. Assn. Pvt. Entrepreneurs, Am. Soc. Profl. Photographers, Brigham Young U. Football Alumni Assn., Suzuki Moto Cross Team. Republican. Office: DC Systems Tex 1800 N Carroll Blvd # C Denton TX 76201-3031

HEAD, JONATHAN FREDERICK, cell biologist; b. Syracuse, N.Y., Nov. 23, 1949; s. Arthur Everard and Lillian Myrtle (Hendra) H.; m. Priscilla Catherine Tambone, July 28, 1984; 1 child, Catherine Elizabeth. BS in Zoology, Syracuse U., 1971; MA in Biology, Bklyn. Coll., 1977; PhD in Biology, Fordham U., 1985. Rsch. asst. Naylor Dana Inst. Disease Prevention/Am. Health Found., Valhalla, N.Y., 1974-78, Cornell U. Med. Coll., N.Y.C., 1978; rsch. asst. Mt. Sinai Sch. Medicine, N.Y.C., 1978-84, rsch. assoc., 1984-86, rsch. asst. prof., 1986-87; dir. tumor cell biology Ctr. Clin. Scis./Internat. Clin. Labs., Nashville, 1986-89; pres. Mastology Rsch. Inst., Baton Rouge, 1989—; adj. asst. prof. Tulane U. Sch. Medicine, New Orleans, 1989—; adj. prof. Delta State U., Cleveland, Miss., 1992—; researcher and lectr. in field of cancer. Contbr. articles, abstracts and chpts. to sci. publs. Mem. State of La. Adoption Cmty. Adv. Bd., 1992-95. Mem. AAAS, Am. Assn. Cancer Rsch., Am. Soc. Clin. Oncology, Soc. Biol. Therapy, European Soc. Med. Oncology. Methodist. Home: 6144 Hagerstown Dr Baton Rouge LA 70817-3917 Office: Mastology Rsch Inst 1770 Physicians Park Dr Baton Rouge LA 70816-3222

HEAD, MARK D., insurance and employee benefit broker; b. Dallas, Apr. 24, 1958; s. Claude D. III and Mariam Joyce H. Student, Richland Coll., 1979, 80, 83. Assoc. Baldwin Fin. Group, 1981-88; owner Mark D. Head Ins., 1989-91; pres. MDH Benefits Corp., 1992—. Mem steering com. Anita N. Martinez Ballet Forklorico, 1995; mem. steering com. Positive Parents Dallas, 1982-87; mem. adv. com. DISD Bus. and Mgmt. Ctr., 1982-87; mem. edn. com. Goals for Dallas, 1985-87; campaign treas. David Childs, 1995. Mem. Nat. Assn. Life Underwriters, Nat. Assn. Health Underwriters, Tex. Assn. Health Underwriters, Tex. Assn. Life Underwriters (bd. dirs. Dallas assn. 1986-87, chair LUPAC, bd. dirs. 1994—, chair health and employee benefits, chair pub. rels. 1995—), Dallas Assn. Health Underwriters, Dallas Estate Planning Coun., Dallas Jaycees (bd. dirs. 1982-84, mem. fin. com. 1984, dir. comm. 1984), World Future Soc., Internat. Platform Assn. Office: MDH Benefits Corp 5307 E Mockingbird Ste 800 Dallas TX 75206

HEAD, WILLIAM CARL, lawyer, author; b. Columbus, Ga., Mar. 4, 1951; s. Louis Bernice and Betty June (Vickery) H.; m. Sandra Earle, Sept. 3, 1972 (div. 1979); m. Kathleen Crenshaw, Aug. 8, 1981 (div. 1988); 1 stepchild, Stephanie A. Hansen; m. Kris L. Foreman, Feb. 14, 1990; 1 child, Lauren Ansley. BA cum laude, U. Ga., 1973, JD, 1976. Bar: Ga. 1976, U.S. Dist. Ct. (mid. dist.) Ga. 1976, U.S. Ct. Appeals (5th and 11th cirs.) 1979, S.C. 1990. Ptnr. Galis, Timmons, Andrews & Head, Athens, Ga., 1977-79, Andrews & Head P.C., Athens, 1979-82; pvt. practice Athens, 1982-85; ptnr. McDonald, Head, Carney & Haggard, Athens, 1985-88; real estate developer Athens, 1979-88; regent Nat. Coll. DUI Def., Inc. Author: The Georgia DUI Defense Trial Practice Manual, 1996, Handling License Revocations and Suspensions in Georgia, 1993; co-author: 101 Ways to Avoid A Drunk Driving Conviction, 1991. Pres. Joseph Henry Lumpkin Found., Inc., Athens, 1979; chmn. Bridge the Gap seminar, Atlanta, 1980. Awardee Athens-Clarke Heritage Found. Inc., Athens, 1983. Mem. ABA, Ga. Bar Assn., S.C. Bar Assn., Assn. Trial Lawyers Am., Ga. Trial Lawyers Assn., Def. Drinking Drivers Network (founder), Order of Barristers, U. Ga. Pres.'s Club. Democrat. Baptist. Home: 6115 Spalding Bluff Ct Norcross GA 30092

HEAD, WILLIAM IVERSON, SR., retired chemical company executive; b. Tallapoosa, Ga., Apr. 4, 1925; s. Iverson and Ruth Britain (Hubbard) H.; m. Mary Helen Ware, June 12, 1947; children: William Iverson, Connie Suzanne Head Toohey, Alan David. BS Ga. Inst. Tech., 1949; D of Textile Engring. (hon.), World U., 1983; PhD in Indsl. Mgmt., Columbia Pacific U., 1988. Textile engr. Tenn. Eastman Co., Kingsport, 1949-56, quality control-mfg. sr. textile engr., 1957-67, dept. supt., 1968-74; supt. acetate yarn dept., mem. bus. team, chems. div. Eastman Kodak Co., Kingsport, 1975-85; info. officer U.S. Naval Acad., 1983—; mem. adv. bd., rsch. assoc. Point One Adv. Group, Inc., 1988—. Patentee textured yarns tech. in U.S., Great Britain, Fed. Republic of Germany, Japan and France. Capt. USNR, 1943-83. Decorated Navy Commendation medal, Selective Svc. System Meritorious Svc. medal, 1980. Mem. Internat. Soc. Philos. Enquiry (pers. cons. 1978-79, v.p. 1979-80, sr. rsch. fellow and internat. pres. 1980-85, diplomate and trustee 1986—, chmn. bd. trustees 1987—, Whiting Meml. award 1993), Prometheus Soc., Internat. Platform Assn., Naval Res. Assn., Assn. Naval Aviation, Mil. Order World Wars, Res. Officers Assn. (pres. Tenn. dept. 1981-82, nat. councilman 1991—, nat. coun. steering com. 1993—), Ret.

Officers Assn., VFW, Mensa (pres. Upper East Tenn. 1976-79), Sons of Revolution, Internat. League of Intelligence. Unitarian. Home and Office: 4035 Lakewood Dr Kingsport TN 37663-3374

HEAD, WILLIAM PACE, historian, educator; b. Miami, Oct. 15, 1949; s. Downer Pace and Ella Marguerite (Crittenden) H.; m. Randee Lynne Geiger, June 6, 1975; children: Matthew Brian, Evan Zachery. AS Bus., Miami-Dade C.C., 1969; PhD History, Fla. State U., 1980, BA History, 1971; MA History, U. Miami, 1974. Asst. prof. history U. Ala., Huntsville, 1981-84; historian USAF, Robins AFB, Ga., 1984—; chief Office of History WR-ALC USAF, 1996—; adj. prof. history Fla. State U., Tallahassee, 1980-81, Macon (Ga.) Coll., 1985—; site dir. Ala. Heritage Festival, Ala. Humanities Coun., Huntsville, 1981; hist. advisor WMAZ-TV Robins at Fifty, 1991, Ga. Pub. TV, The State of War: Ga. in WWII, Atlanta, 1994. Author: America's China Sojourn, 1983, Yenan, 1983, Reworking the Workhorse: The C-141B, 1984 (Best in AF 1985), Every Inch a Soldier, 1995 (Best in AF 1996), Tet Offensive, 1996; editor: Looking Back at the Vietnam War, 1993, Eagle in the Desert, 1996; assoc. editor Asia, Jour. of Third World Studies, 1985—. Mem. Houston County Dem. Com. Coun., Warner Robins, Ga., 1990—; active little league baseball, Warner Robins City League, 1992—; hist. judge, Ga. Hist. Day/Ga. Humanities Coun., Atlanta, 1988—. Recipient Spl. Commendation award Ala. State Senate, Huntsville, 1986, Air Force Spl. Achievements award, 1994; Fla. State U. grad. fellow, 1977. Mem. Assn. Third World Studies (nom. com. chmn. 1989—), Ga. Assn. Historians (pubs. com. 1984—), Soc. Mil. History, Soc. Hist. Fed. Govt., Phi Kappa Phi. Democrat. Methodist. Home: 111 Chantilly Dr Warner Robins GA 31088-6329 Office: USAF-Warner Robins ALC 955 Robins Pky Robins AFB GA 31098-2423

HEADEN, CAROL MARY SKINNER, university administrator; b. Lithgow, N.S.W., Australia, Dec. 6, 1960; d. Craig P. and Mary Skinner; m. Mark S. Headen, July 4, 1987 (div.). BA, Calif. Bapt. Coll., 1982; MA, Azusa Pacific U., 1987. Cert. tchr., calif., N.C. Resident dir. Pitzer Coll./Claremont Colls., Claremont, Calif., 1985-86; fin. aid counselor Azusa (Calif.) Pacific U., 1986-87; tchr. kindergarten St. Francis of Assisi Sch., Jacksonville, N.C., 1987-88; tchr. jr. high art Trexler Jr. H.S., Richlands, N.C., 1988-89; residence life coord. Seattle Pacific U., 1989-93; graphic artist/events coord. Events West, Mill Valley, Calif., 1993; area coord. residence life The U. Memphis, 1994-95; asst. v.p. student svcs. Union U., Jackson, Tenn., 1995—. Named to Outstanding Young Woman of Am., 1982. Mem. Nat. Assn. Student Pers. Adminstrs., Assn. Christians in Student Devel., So. Assn. Coll. Student Affairs (new profls. com. 1995—). Baptist. Office: Union University 2447 Us Highway 45 Byp Jackson TN 38305-2002

HEADLEY, ALLAN DAVE, chemistry educator; b. St. James, Jamaica, May 10, 1955; came to the U.S., 1974; s. Allan Constantine and Eleanor Elizebeth (Dixon) H.; m. Fay Rose Marie Francis Keane, June 6, 1987; children: Micah A, Jahmela I. BA, Columbia Union Coll., 1976; PhD, Howard U., 1982. Lectr. U. W.I., Mona, Jamaica, 1983-87, U. Calif., Irvine, 1987-89; asst. prof. Tex. Tech U., Lubbock, 1989-95; assoc. prof. Tex. Tech. U., Lubbock, Tex., 1995—. Grantee NSF, 1991, 94. Mem. Am. Chem. Soc. Office: Texas Tech U Dept Chemistry Lubbock TX 79409

HEADLEY, JOHN MILES, history educator; b. N.Y.C., Oct. 23, 1929; s. Peter Sanford Ross and Beatrice Sontag (Miles) H. BA summa cum laude in history, Princeton U., 1951; MA in History, Yale U., 1953, PhD in History, 1960. Tchr. Oakwood Sch., Poughkeepsie, N.Y., 1955-56; instr. history U. Mass., Amherst, 1959-61; instr., then asst. prof. U. B.C., Vancouver, 1962-64; asst. prof. history U. N.C., Chapel Hill, 1964-66, assoc. prof., 1966-69, prof. history, 1969—; lectr. in field. Author: Luther's View of Church History, 1963, Responsio ad Lutherum, Complete Works of St. Thomas More, Vol. V, 1969, Medieval and Renaissance Studies, Vol. 3, 1968, The Emperor and his Chancellor: A Study of the Imperial Chancellery under Gattinara, 1983, San Carlo Borromeo: Catholic Reform and Ecclesiastical Politics in the Second Half of the Sixteenth Century, 1988; contbr. articles to profl. jours. With Signal Corps U.S. Army, 1953-55. Jr. Sterling fellow, 1958-59, Guggenheim fellow, 1974; Inst. for Rsch. in Social Sci., U. N.C. grantee, 1966, U. Rsch. Coun., 1972, ACLS grantee, 1977, others. Fellow Southeastern Inst. of Medieval and Renaissance Studies (chmn. 1967), Am. Soc. for Reformation Rsch. (mem. coun. 1970, chmn. nominating com. 1973, pres. 1978-80), Renaissance Soc. Am. (adv. coun. 1972), Phi Beta Kappa. Office: Univ of NC Dept History 500 Hamilton 070A Chapel Hill NC 27599-3195

HEALEY, DAVID LEE, investment company executive; b. Pomona, Calif., Dec. 13, 1950; s. Robert Lincoln Sr. and Bernice (Mayes) H.; m. Barbara Petty, June 24, 1995; children: Paul Marcus, Elaina Rose. BS, U. Tulsa, 1978, postgrad. in law, 1979-80; cert., N.Y. Inst. Fin., 1980. Sales mgr. Magnavox, Tulsa, 1978-80; dir. tng. First State Fin., Tulsa, 1980-81; asst. v.p. Prudential-Bache Securities, Tulsa, 1981-86, E.F. Hutton, Tulsa, 1986-91, Paine Webber, Inc., Tulsa, 1991—; sales cons., Tulsa, 1981—. Judge Miss Teen USA pageant, 1984; chair endowment fund adv. com. Tulsa YWCA. Sgt. USAF, 1974-78. Mem. Internat. Assn. Fin. Planners (bd. dirs. 1984), Toastmasters Internat. (speakers bur.). Republican. Baptist. Home: RR 1 Box 108 Inola OK 74036-9603 Office: Paine Webber 321 S Boston Ave Ste 1010 Tulsa OK 74103-3322

HEAP, DENISE ELAINE, writer, accountant; b. Houston, Nov. 30, 1954; d. John A. Jr. and Joyce M. (Light) H. BA in Math, German, Tex. Christian U., 1977. Cert. tchr., Tex. Sr. acct. Lingen Oil and Gas, Houston, 1981-84; sec., treas., contr. ITAG Exploration, Inc., Houston, 1984-89; owner, pres. Translations Verbatim, Houston, 1989-95; acct. Corr Ocean, Inc., Houston, 1994—; chmn. Tex. Christian U. Links, Houston, 1982-95. Editor Word of Mouth newsletter, 1992-95, Round Top Patchwork newsletter, 1996. Mem. German Am. C. of C., Houston, 1990-95; pianist Round Top (Tex.) Bapt. Ch., 1996—. Recipient Fulbright fellowship U. Augsburg, Germany, 1977-78. Mem. Fulbright Assn. (life), Inst. Internat. Edn. and Consular Corps. (vol. 1982—). Home: 7824 Waldeck Cemetery Rd Round Top TX 78954

HEARN, SHARON SKLAMBA, lawyer; b. New Orleans, Aug. 15, 1956; d. Carl John and Marjorie C. (Wimberly) Sklamba; m. Curtis R. Hearn. BA magna cum laude, Loyola U., New Orleans, 1977; JD cum laude, Tulane U., 1980. Bar: La. 1980, Tex. 1982; cert. tax specialist. Law clk. to presiding judge U.S. Ct. Appeals Fed. Cir., Washington, 1980-81; assoc. Johnson & Swanson, Dallas, 1981-84, Kullman Inman Bee & Downing, New Orleans, 1984—. Recipient Am. Legion award, 1970. Mem. ABA, La. State Bar Assn., Tex. State Bar Assn., Dallas Women Lawyers Assn. Democrat. Roman Catholic. Home: 44 Swallow St New Orleans LA 70124-4404 Office: Kullman Inman Bee & Downing 615 Howard Ave New Orleans LA 70130-3917

HEARN, THOMAS K., JR., academic administrator; b. Opp, Ala., July 5, 1937; s. Thomas H. Hearn; m. Laura Walter; children: Thomas K., William Neely, Lindsay. B.A. summa cum laude, Birmingham-So. Coll., 1959; B.D., Baptist Theol. Sem., 1963; Ph.D. (NDEA fellow), Vanderbilt U., 1965. Instr. Birmingham-So. Coll., summers 1964-65; asst. prof. Coll. William and Mary, 1965-68, assoc. prof., 1968-74; prof. philosophy U. Ala., Birmingham, 1974-83, chmn. dept. philosophy, 1974-76, dean Sch. Humanities, 1976-78, v.p. Univ. Coll., 1978-83; pres. Wake Forest U., Winston-Salem, N.C., 1983—. Contbr. articles to profl. jours. Recipient Thomas Jefferson Teaching award, 1970; summer grantee Nat. Found. Humanities, 1967; summer fellow Council Philos. Studies, 1968; fellow Coop. Program in Humanities, 1969-70; faculty summer grantee Coll. William and Mary, 1970, 72, 73. Mem. AAUP, So. Soc. Philosophy, Psychology (exec. council 1974-77 Jr. award), Soc. Philosophy Religion (pres. 1974-75), Am. Philos. Assn., David Hume Soc., Newcomen Soc. N.Am., Phi Beta Kappa, Omicron Delta Kappa, Phi Kappa Phi. Home: 1000 Kearns Ave Winston Salem NC 27106-5824 Office: Wake Forest U Office of President Winston Salem NC 27109*

HEARNE, CAROLYN FOX, art and history educator, artist; b. Brownwood, Tex., June 15, 1945; d. Marshal D. and Lena May (Parson) Fox; m. Roy Nicholas Hearne, Apr. 14, 1968; children: Jason Nicholas, Angela Della. BA in Spanish, Art, So. Meth. U., 1967; MA in Fine Arts, U. Tex., Tyler, 1985. Astrology lady, commls. K-BUY Radio, Ft. Worth, 1970-71; decorator, exec. dir. Holiday Inns, Inc., Houston, 1971-73; exec./bilingual sec. Kennecott Copper Corp., Houston, 1973-74; owner Fox-Hearne Studio, Kilgore, Tex., 1977—; art/music, history tchr. LeTourneau U., Longview, Tex., 1988—; co-chmn. LeTourneau Fine Arts Week, Longview, 1992—; demonstrator, lectr. mus. and art groups, Longview and Tyler, 1979—; judge East Tex. art groups, Longview, Kilgore, and Henderson, 1990—; invited participant Master Artists Workshop, L.I. U., 1990. Prin. works include book cover, Gory Days, 1987, bronze sculpture, Frontier Spirit, 1983 (Citation 1983), sculpture for dedication, Gussie Nell Davis, 1983, commnd. A Race Against Time, 1978 (Spl. award 1978), model for catalogue, TV commls. for Strictly Petites, 1987—; exhbns. incl. Tex. Art Gallery, 1990-92. Bd. dirs. Kilgore Hist. Preservation Found., Kilgore, 1989—, past sec., past pres.; chmn. art fest Kilgore Improvement and Beautification Assn., 1981-86; chmn. Kilgore Civic Ball, 1980; decorator Jr. League Charity Ball, Longview, 1992; pres. Kilgore Garden Club, 1982-83; chmn. Theatre Restoration Kilgore, 1989-92; life mem. Tex. PTA, 1978—; bd. dirs., 1st v.p. Longview Art Mus., 1994—, exhbns. and acquisitions chmn., 1995-97. Recipient 5 Citation awards East Tex. Classics, 1981, Outstanding Achievement award Artitudes mag., 1989. Mem. East Tex. Fine Arts Assn. (pres. 1981-83, Top Citation award 1984), Tex. Fine Arts Assn., LeTourneau Faculty Orgn., Coterie Club (pres. 1990). Republican. Presbyterian. Home: 8 Briar Ln Kilgore TX 75662-2201 Office: LeTourneau Univ Mobberly Ave PO Box 7001 Longview TX 75607-7001

HEARN-HAYNES, THERESA, lawyer; b. Chgo., Feb. 27, 1954; d. Gustia L. and Johnnie Hearn; m. Emil P. Haynes, Dec. 20, 1985 (dec. Apr. 1990); children: Dominique, Ashley, Alexis; m. William Murphy, 1994; 1 child, William Ivory Murphy. BS, U. Ill., 1975; MS, U. Iowa, 1980; JD, South Tex. Coll. Law, 1986. Ordained to ministry, Ch. of Yahvah Ala Hay, 1991. Pvt. practice Spring, Tex., 1986—, gubernatorial candidate for Tex., 1989—. Author: 20th Century Slavery in America. Chairperson Senatorial dist. 18, Fort Bend County, Tex., 1988; v.p. Southside Community Improvement Assn., Houston, 1985; active African-Am. Legal Def. Fund, 1994; bd. dirs. Harris County Coop. Resources, 1994. Named Hon. Tuskegee alumni, 1994. Mem. Trial Lawyers of Am., Landowners Assn. (bd. dirs. 1984—), Wild Heather Civic Club. Office: PO Box 1495 Spring TX 77383-1495

HEATH, BRENT ALAN, electrical engineer; b. Midland, Tex., May 3, 1960; s. James Allen and Loretta T. (Dobbs) H.; m. Dawn Lin Ambrose, May 29, 1982. BSEE, Okla. State U., 1983. Registered profl. engr., Tex. Elec. engr. Southwestern Pub. Svc. Co., Lubbock, Tex., 1983-89; elec. engr. Lubbock Power & Light, 1989-91, substation ops. supervising engr., 1991—; mem. plat com. City of Lubbock, 1984-89; pres. Heath Engring. and Tech. Help, Lubbock, 1991-92. Loaned exec. United Way of Lubbock, 1986; chmn. Bacon Heights Bapt. Ch., 1989-92, Fourth on Broadway Com., Lubbock, 1992-96. Mem. IEEE, Tex. Soc. Profl. Engrs. (treas. 1992, sec. 1993, 2d v.p. 1994, 1st v.p. 1995, pres. 1996, Young Engr. Yr. award South Plains chpt. 1993), Lubbock Amateur Radio Club (treas. 1991-95), Caprock Repeater Club, Nat. Elec. Contractors Assn., Aircraft Owners and Pilots Assn., Exptl. Aircraft Assn. Mem. IEEE, Tex. Soc. Profl. Engrs. (treas, 1992, sec. 1993, 2d v.p. 1994, 1st v.p. 1995, Young Engr. Yr. award South Plaines chpt. 1993), Lubbock Amateur Radio Club (treas. 1991-95), Caprock Repeater CLub, Nat. Elec. Contractors Assn., Aircraft Owners and Pilots Assn., Exptl. Aircraft Assn. Republican. Home: 9502 York Ave Lubbock TX 79424-4853 Office: Lubbock Power and Light PO Box 2000 Lubbock TX 79457-0001

HEATH, CHERYL DELORES, librarian; b. Lubbock, Tex., Jan. 23, 1970; d. Thelma Oscar and Ella Louise (Lockett) H. BS, Jarvis Christian Coll., Hawkins, Tex., 1992. Housekeeper Wildflower Inn Restaurant, Hughes Springs, Tex., 1994; substitute tchr. Linden (Tex.) Elem. Sch., 1994; libr. Jarvis Christian Coll., 1994—. Democrat. Baptist. Home: PO Drawer G Hawkins TX 75765 Office: Jarvis Christian Coll Olin Libr Comm Ctr E Hwy 80 Hawkins TX 75765

HEATH, FRANK BRADFORD, dentist; b. Houston, Dec. 11, 1938; s. Robert Bradford and Maudie H. (Sweeney) H.; m. Heide J.M. Schmidt, Aug. 20, 1965; children: Dirk Alan, Shannon Erika, Kent Bradford. BA, Sam Houston State U., 1961; DDS, U. Tex., Houston, 1965. Pvt. practice dentistry, Houston, 1967—. Served as capt. U.S. Army, 1965-67. Fellow Acad. Gen. Dentistry, Acad. Dentistry Internat.; mem. ADA, Houston Dist. Dental Soc., Tex. Dental Assn., Delta Tau Delta, Xi Psi Phi. Republican. Methodist. Home: 12904 W Shadow Lake Ln Cypress TX 77429-5907 Office: 12337 Jones Rd Ste 322 Houston TX 77070-4845

HEATH, JINGER L., cosmetics executive; b. 1952. Homemaker, 1973-81; part-time interior decorator, cons. Dallas; chmn. bd. Beauticontrol Cosmetics Inc., Carrollton, Tex. Office: Beauticontrol Cosmetics Inc 2121 Midway Rd Carrollton TX 75006

HEATHERLEY, MELODY ANN, nursing administrator; b. Dallas, Apr. 15, 1957; d. Harold Ray and Barbara Ann (Roebuck) Jones; m. James Lawrence Heatherley, July 21, 1982. BSN, U. Tex., Arlington, 1979; postgrad., Amber U. RN, Tex., Fla. Surg. nurse St. Paul Hosp., Dallas, 1979, Mesquite (Tex.) Meml. Hosp., 1979-80; charge nurse All Saints Hosp.-Main, Ft. Worth, 1980-87; house supr., charge nurse All Saints Cityview Hosp., Ft. Worth, 1987-88; staff nurse ICU, critical care coord. Hosp. Corp. Am. Med. Plz. Hosp., Ft. Worth, 1986-89; staff nurse ICU, CCU Harris Meth. Hurst, Euless, Bedford, Bedford, Tex., 1989-91; staff nurse rehab. unit Harris Meth. HEB, Bedford, 1991; charge nurse surg. ICU, cardiovascular recovery Humana Hosp.-Lucerne, Orlando, Fla., 1991-93, relief house supr., 1991-93; divsn. supr. nursing adminstrn. St. Paul Med. Ctr., Dallas, 1993-94; adminstrv. supr Baylor Med. Ctr. Ellis County, Waxahachie, Tex., 1994—. Mem. AACN, ANA, NAFE, Assn. Rehab. Nurses, Tex. Orgn. Nurse Execs., Tex. Nurses Assn. Episcopalian. Office: Baylor Med Ctr Ellis County Waxahachie Campus 1405 W Jefferson St Waxahachie TX 75165-2231

HEATON, JANET NICHOLS, artist, art gallery director; b. Miami, Fla., May 27, 1936; d. Wilmer Elwood and Katherine Elizabeth (Rodgers) Nichols; m. Wendell Carlos Heaton, Apr. 14, 1956; children: Benjamin Nichols Heaton, Nancy Elizabeth Breedlove. Student, Fla. State U., 1954-56. Artist Heaton's Studio & Gallery, Lake Park, Fla., 1976—, dir., 1979—. Exhibited in group shows at Leight Yawkey Woodson Art Mus., Wausau, Wis., 1988-89, 91-93, 95, 96, Norton Gallery Art, West Palm Beach, Fla., 1989, Mt. Kenya Safari Club, Kenya, East Africa, 1989, Prestige Gallery, Toronto, Can., 1989, Kimball Art Ctr., Park City, Utah, 1990-91, Grand Cen. Gallery, N.Y.C., 1990, Gallery Fine Arts, Ft. Myers, Fla., 1990, Cornell Fine Art Mus., Winter Park, Fla., 1990, Cen. Park Zoo Gallery, N.Y.C., 1991, Norton Art Gallery, Palm Beach, Fla., 1992, The Art League Marco Island, Fla., 1993, 96, Washington State Hist. Soc. Mus., Tacoma, 1993, Leigh Yawkey Woodson Art Mus., Wausau, 1993, Old Sch. Sq. Cultural Arts Ctr., Delray Beach, Fla., 1993, 94, The Salmagundi Club, N.Y.C., 1994, J.N. Bartfield Galleries, N.Y.C., 1994, Pt. Royal Gallery, Naples, Fla., 1994, Brookfield Zoo, Chgo., 1994, Ward Mus. Wildfowl Art, Salisbury, Md., 1995, Easton (Md.) Waterfowl Festival, 1995, Sarasota (Fla.) Visual Art Ctr., 1995, Art League Maro Island, Fla., 1996, Shenandoah Art Ctr., North Wainsboro, Va., 1996, Wendell Gilley Mus., Southwest Harbour, Maine, 1996; represented in permanent collections Leigh Yawkey Woodson Art Mus., State House, Nairobi, Kenya; numerous pvt. collections; subject numerous art jours. Mem. Soc. Animal Artists, Pastel Soc. Am., Fla. Watercolor Soc., Outdoor Writers Assn. Am., Catherine Lorillard Wolfe Art Club, Inc. Home: 11680 Lake Shore Pl North Palm Beach FL 33408 Office: Heatons Studio and Gallery 1169 Old Dixie Hwy Lake Park FL 33403-2311

HEATWOLE, HAROLD FRANKLIN, ecologist; b. Waynesboro, Va., Dec. 2, 1932; s. Elmer Jason and Fannie Ruth (Martin) H.; m. Audry Ann Yoder, June 11, 1955; children: Eric Karl, Miguel Andrés. BA in Botany, Goshen Coll., 1955; MS in Zoology, U. Mich., 1958, PhD in Zoology, 1960; DSc, U. New Eng., Australia, 1981; PhD in Botany, U. Queensland, Australia, 1987. Instr. U. Mich., Ann Arbor, 1959-60; asst. prof. U. P.R., Rio Piedras, 1960-63, assoc. prof., 1963-66; sr. lectr. U. New Eng., Armidale, Australia, 1966-71, assoc. prof., 1971-91; prof., head dept. N.C. State U., Raleigh, 1991-96, prof., 1991—; pres. Great Barrier Reef Com., Australia, 1980-82, Australian Coral Reef Soc., Australia, 1982-83, Australian Soc. Herpetologists, Australia, 1977-78. Author: Reptile Ecology, 1976, A Coral Island, 1981, Community Ecology of a Coral Cay, 1981, Ecology of Reptiles, 1989, Dieback Death of a Landscape, 1987, Sea Snakes, 1988, Energetics of Desert Invertebrates, 1995; contbr. 230 rsch articles to profl. jours. Fellow Inst. of Biology (cert. biologist), Australian Inst. of Biology, Explorers Club, Phi Beta Kappa. Office: NC State U Dept Zoology Raleigh NC 27695-7617

HEAVNER, JAMES E., anesthesiology educator, pharmacologist; b. Cumberland, Md., Apr. 25, 1944; s. Douglas Balange and Grace E. (Frantz) H.; m. Betsey Clark, Sept. 10, 1967; children: Matthew James, Kori Rae, Benjamin Douglas. DVM, U. Ga., 1968; PhD, U. Wash., 1971. Diplomate Am. Coll. Vet. Anesthesiologists. Rsch. fellow in anesthesiology U. Wash., Seattle, 1968-71, acting asst. prof. anesthesiology Anesthesia Rsch. Ctr., 1971-72, asst. prof. anesthesiology, 1972-75, assoc. prof. anesthesiology, 1975-80; chief pharmacology and toxicology FDA, Beltsville, Md., 1980-82; assoc. prof. Health Sci. Ctr. Sch. Medicine Tex. Tech. U., Lubbock, 1983-87, prof. anesthesiology and physiology, 1987—, dir. Anesthesia Rsch., 1983—; vis. prof. dept. physiology and pharmacology vet. sch. U. Ga., 1971, inst. chem. def. AUS, Aberdeen Proving Ground, Md., 1984, Tex. A&M U., College Station, 1990, others; vis. scientist physiology U. Edinburgh, Scotland, 1978; adj. prof. Va.-Md. Regional Coll. Vet. Medicine, Va. Tech., Blacksburg, 1980-82; with vet. pathology sect. Armed Forces Inst. Pathology, Washington, 1967, Rocky Gorge Animal Hosp. and White Oak Vet. Clinic, Laurel, Md., 1968; neurology and anesthesia cons. Green Lake Animal Hosp., Seattle, 1974-80; relief vet. Vivarium, U. Wash., 1976-77; chmn. vis. scientist program dept. anesthesiology health scis. ctr. Tex. Tech. U., 1983-93; mem. edn. com. 1983—, assoc. dir. oper. rm. stat lab., 1983—, oper. rm. respiratory monitoring sys. supr., 1983—, assoc. dir. respiratory therapy blood gas lab., 1983-93, editor dept. newsletter, 1983—, coord. ann. pain symposium, 1983—, coord. didactic program pain fellowship, 1992—; mem. various coms.; cons. Finland Sch. Vet. Medicine, Helsinki, 1986, MEDIC, 1992; mem. ad hoc animal resources rev. com. facilities improvements applications NIH, 1990; lectr., presenter in field. Author: (with others) Capnography in the Operating Room, 1985, Methods of Animal Experimentation, 1986, Technical Manual of Anesthesiology: An Introduction, 1989; assoc. editor Vet. Anesthesia, 1974-78, mem. editl. rev. bd., 1978-85; guest columnist Soundoff, 1980; sci. editor Lab. Animal Sci., 1990—; contbr. more than 100 articles to profl. jours.; manuscript reviewer various profl. jours.; inventor respiratory monitor, method of treating epidural lesions and epidural catheter sys. for treating epidural lesions. Judge Puget Sound Sci. Fair, 1971; trustee St. John's United Meth. Ch., 1985—; bd. dirs. Rush Pool, 1988-90, pres., 1988, 89. Recipient spl. award for work with anesthesia and lab. animals Hildegard Doerenkamp/Gerhard Zibinden-Stiftung, 1988; spl. fellow NIH, 1971-72, Fulbright fellow, 1986, fellow Am. Scandinavian Found., 1986; grantee Bristol Labs., 1986, Raven Press, 1987, Siemens-Elema, 1987—, Anaquest Equipment, 1989, Olympus, 1989—, Inst. for Nutritional Scis., 1990, Medtronic, 1993, 94, also others. Mem. AVMA, AAAS, Am. Soc. Anesthesiologists, Am. Vet. Med. Assn., Tex. Pain Soc. (trustee 1989—, chmn. edn. com. 1989—, editor newsletter 1989—, program chmn. 1989—, sec. 1992—), Am. Soc. Vet. Anesthesiologists (treas. 1971-72, ad hoc com. on manpower status 1972, ad hoc com. on welfare of rsch. animals 1985), Am. Soc. Regional Anesthesia (newsletter com. 1992—), Am. Coll. Vet. Anesthesia (mem. sci. planning com. 1976-79, mem. continuing edn. com. 1977-79, mem. exam. com. 1980-82, mem. ad hoc com. animal rsch. 1985, examiner 1988), Am. Soc. Pharmacology and Exptl. Therapeutics, Brit. Brain Rsch. Assn. (hon.), Tex. Anesthesia Soc., Seattle Vet. Med. Assn. (chmn. rsch. and regulatory chpt. 1971, sec. 1972-73, pres.-elect 1974, pres. 1975, trustee 1977), Mid-Atlantic Soc. Toxicology, Western Pharmacology Soc., Internat. Assn. Study Pain (mem. subcom. refresher courses com. edn. 1993—), Internat. Anesthesia Rsch. Soc., Internat. Brain Rsch. Orgn., Digital Equipment Computer Users Soc., Soc. Neuroscience, Phi Zeta, Alpha Zeta, Gamma Sigma Delta. Office: Tex Tex U Health Sci Ctr 3601 4th St Rm 1 C258 Lubbock TX 79430-0001

HEBERT, CHRISTINE ANNE, elementary education educator; b. Waltham, Mass., Aug. 31, 1953; d. Alfred Lionel and Virginia Eugenia (Nogas) Mellor; m. Dennis Armand Hebert, Dec. 18, 1976; 1 child, Kirsten Erica. BS in Early Childhood Edn., Wheelock Coll., Boston, 1975; MS in Spl. Edn., Coll. of William & Mary, Williamsburg, Va., 1985. Cert. elem. tchr., learning disabled, emotional disturbances. Title I aide Fryeburg (Maine) Pub. Schs., 1975-76; title I tutor Conway (N.H.) Pub. Schs., 1976-77; presch. tchr. Elmendorf AFB, Anchorage, 1978-80; counselor, caregiver Intermission/Parent Resource Ctr., Anchorage, 1980-81; residential counselor Group Home for MR Adults, Bridton, Maine, 1983-84; tchr. learning disabled Norfolk (Va.) Pub. Schs., 1985-90; tchr. elem. Norfolk Pub. Schs., 1990—, lead tchr. sci., 1992—; tchr. magnet sch. math. and sci. Norfolk, 1995—; tutor Learning Resource Ctr., Virginia Beach, Va., 1986-89; inclusion tchr., 1993-95; mem. NASA Tchr. Enhancement Inst., summer 1994. Recipient Norfolk Sch. Bell award, 1994, 95; faculty scholar Coll. William and Mary, 1984-85. Mem. ASCD, NSTA, Internat. Reading Assn., Audubon Soc., Optimists (pres. Bayside chpt. 1996-97), Childhood Edn. Internat., Kappa Delta Pi.

HEBERT, LEO PLACIDE, physician; b. Houma, La., Oct. 27, 1940; s. Leo Placide and Ethel (Trosclair) H.; m. Carolyn Mae St. Amant, Aug. 2, 1969; children: Anne-Marie, Catherine, Elizabeth (dec.), Leo, Maria, Julie. BS, U. Southwestern La., 1963; MD, La. State U., New Orleans, 1965. Lic. physician, La. Physician, internist in pvt. practice Thibodaux, La., 1971—; chief of staff Thibodaux Hosp., 1978. Mem. com. of 100, La. State U. Sch. Medicine. Capt. USAF, 1966-68. Mem. Am. Soc. Internal Medicine, La. Med. Soc., LaFourche Parish Med. Soc., U. Southwestern La. Alumni Assn., U. Southwestern La. Found., Ragin Cajun Club-U. Southwestern La., Phi Kappa Phi, Alpha Omega Alpha. Roman Catholic. Home: 207 E Plater Dr Thibodaux LA 70301-5609 Office: 1101 Audubon Ave Thibodaux LA 70301-4957

HEBERT, LEONARD BERNARD, JR., contractor; b. Jeanerette, La., Aug. 8, 1924; s. Leonard B. Sr. and Katherine R. (Rader) H.; m. Hilda Girard, Nov. 28, 1946 (div. 1980); children: Suzanne Lynne, Andre Lane, Yvette Ann; m. Catherine Kempa, June 14, 1984. BE, Tulane U., 1944. Registered civil engr., La., Miss. Field engr. Humble Oil & Refining Co., Houston, 1946-48; exec. v.p. Gurtler-Hebert & Co., Inc., New Orleans, 1948-72; chief exec. officer, pres. Leonard B. Hebert Jr., & Co., Inc., New Orleans, 1972—; chief exec. officer Profl. Constrn. Svcs. Inc., New Orleans, 1972-95; pres. Greater New Orleans Sci. and Engr. Fair, 1986-92. Lt. USNR, 1944-46. Republican. Roman Catholic. Office: PO Box 26245 7933 Downman Rd New Orleans LA 70186-1296

HEBERT, ROBERT D., academic administrator; b. Abbeville, La., Nov. 14, 1938; married. BA, U. Southwestern La., 1959; MA, Fla. State U., 1961, PhD, 1966. Asst. prof. history Miss. State U., 1962-69, assoc. prof. history, 1969-76; prof. McNeese State U., 1976—, v.p. acad. affairs, 1980-87, pres., 1987—. Office: McNeese State U Office of President Lake Charles LA 70609

HECHLER, KEN, state official, former congressman, political science educator, author; b. Roslyn, N.Y., Sept. 20, 1914; s. Charles Henry and Catherine Elizabeth (Hauhart) H. AB, Swarthmore Coll., 1935; AM, Columbia U., 1936, PhD, 1940; LittD (hon.), U. Charleston, 1988; HHD (hon.), W. Va. Inst. Tech., 1988. Lectr. govt. Barnard Coll., Columbia Coll., N.Y.C., 1937-41; research asst. to Judge Samuel I. Rosenman, 1939-50; research asst. on Pres. Roosevelt's pub. papers, 1939-50; sect. chief Bur. Census, 1940; personnel technician Office Emergency Mgmt., 1941; adminstrv. analyst Bur. of Budget, 1941-42, 46-47; spl. asst. to Pres. Harry S. Truman, 1949-53; research dir. Stevenson-Kefauver campaign, 1956; adminstrv. aide Senator Carroll of Colo., 1957; mem. 86th-94th Congresses from 4th W.Va. dist., 1959-77; sec. state WV, 1996, State of WV, 1996; mem. Sci. and Tech. Com. 86th to 94th Congresses from 4th W.Va. Dist., chmn. Energy (Fossil Fuels) Subcom.; mem. Joint Com. on Orgn. of Congress, 1965-66, NASA Oversight Subcom. (U.S. Congress); asst. prof. politics Princeton U., 1947-49; prof. polit. sci. Marshall U., Huntington, W.Va., 1957, 82-84; sec. of state State of W.Va., 1984—; sci. cons. U.S. House Com. on Sci. and Tech., 1978-80; radio, TV commentator Sta. WHTN, Huntington, 1957-58, Sta. WWHY, 1978; adj. prof. polit. sci. U. Charleston (W.Va.), 1981; keynote spkr. Harry Truman lecture ser. USAF Acad., 1995. Author: Insurgency: Personalities and Politics of the Taft Era, 1950, The Bridge at Remagen, 1957, rev. edit., 1993, West Virginia Memories of President Kennedy, 1965, Toward the Endless Frontier, 1980, The Endless Space Frontier, 1982, Working with Truman, 1982, rev. edit., 1996; weekly columnist Cabell Record, Hampshire Rev., Elk River and Little Kananha News, W.Va. Hillbilly, 1990—. Bd. dirs. W.Va. Humanities Found., 1982-84; del. Democratic Nat. Conv., 1964, 68, 72, 80, 84. Served to maj. AUS, 1942-46; served to col. Res. Decorated Bronze Star; named W.Va. Son of Yr., W.Va. State Soc. of D.C., 1969, W.Va. Speaker of Yr., W.Va. U., 1970; recipient Conservation award Nat. Audubon Soc., 1973, Mother Jones award W.Va. Environ. Coun., 1995; subject of biography by Dr. Charles H. Moffat, Ken Hechler: Maverick Public Servant, 1987; Smithsonian Instn. lectr. on 50th Anniversary of Pres. Truman, 1995. Mem. Am. Polit. Sci. Assn. (assoc. dir. 1953-56), Civitan, Am. Legion, VFW, DAV. Democrat. Episcopalian. Lodge: Elks. Home: 917 5th Ave Huntington WV 25701-2028 Office: State Capitol Bldg 1 Ste 157-K 1900 Kanawha Blvd E Charleston WV 25305-0770

HECHT, ALAN, retired physician, insurance company executive; b. N.Y.C., May 4, 1925; s. Abraham Louis and Susan (Rubin) H.; m. Corrinne Marie Mahre, June 11, 1953 (div. May 1979); 1 child, James Lee; m. Gabriele Rodrigues, June 30, 1979. BA, Sarah Lawrence Coll., 1949; MD, Washington U., 1953. Diplomate Am. Bd. Ins. Medicine. Staff physician outpatient dept. VA Hosp., Richmond, Va., 1957-59; pvt. practice Richmond, 1959-70; staff physician Beth Sholem Home for Aged, Richmond, 1959-79; chief physician Richmond City Nursing Home, 1962-79; chief disability evaluation clinic Richmond Dept. Welfare, 1963-74; assoc. med. dir. Fidelity Bankers Life Ins. Co., 1970-79, v.p., med. dir., 1979-91; med. cons. Teamsters Health and Welfare Fund, Richmond, 1980-92; clin. assoc. in medicine Med. Coll. Va., Richmond, 1957-91; pres. Physicians Svc. Assocs., P.C., Richmond, 1970-79. Vol. med. cons. Richmond Cmty. Action Program Sr. Ctr., 1967-70; vol. med. advisor for initial licensure and certification Chesterfield County (Va.) Nursing Home, 1969-70. With U.S. Army, 1943-46. Mem. AMA (Physicians Recognition award 1981, 84, 87, 91), Am. Acad. Ins. Medicine, So. Med. Assn., Richmond Acad. Medicine. Home: 2212 Merrymount Dr Suwanee GA 30174

HECHT, KARL EUGENE, bank software company specialist; b. Clovis, N.Mex., Aug. 5, 1956; s. Harold and Mary (Byerly) H.; m. Candace Dawn Downey, Aug. 18, 1978; children: Jonathan David, Joshua Caleb. Student, N.Mex. State U., 1974-76, So. Meth. U., 1988. Compliance officer Citizens Bank, Clovis, N.Mex., 1979-93; trust officer Citizens Bank, Clovis, 1985-93; acct. mgr. BancTec, Inc., Dallas, 1994—; instr. Clovis C.C., 1982-93. Mem. Am. Bankers Assn. (corp. trust assocs. 1989-90), Ind. Bankers Assn. N.Mex., N.Mex. Am. Inst. Banking (bd. dirs.), Lions (pres. 1988), Bright Hopes Found. (bd. dirs. 1989-90). Republican. Home: 3117 Fairgate Dr Carrollton TX 75007-3953 Office: BancTec Inc 4435 Spring Valley Rd Dallas TX 75244-3704

HECHT, NATHAN LINCOLN, state supreme court justice; b. Clovis, N.Mex., Aug. 15, 1949; s. Harold Lee and Mary Loretta (Byerly) H. BA, Yale U., 1971; JD cum laude, So. Meth. U., 1974. Bar: Tex. 1974, D.C. 1975, U.S. Dist. Ct. D.C. 1975, U.S. Dist. Ct. (no. and we. dists.) Tex. 1976, U.S. Ct. Appeals (D.C. cir.) 1975, U.S. Ct. Appeals (5th cir.) 1976, U.S. Supreme Ct. 1979. Law clk. to judge U.S. Ct. Appeals (D.C. cir.), 1974-75; assoc. Locke, Purnell, Boren, Laney & Neely, Dallas, 1976-80, ptnr., 1981; dist. judge 95th Dist. Ct., Dallas, 1981-86; justice Tex. 5th Dist. Ct. Appeals, 1986-89, Texas Supreme Ct., Austin, 1989—. Contbr. articles to profl. jours. Bd. visitors So. Meth. U., Dallas, 1984-87; trustee Children's Med. Found., Dallas, 1983-89; bd. dirs. Children's Med. Ctr. North, Dallas, 1985-89; elder Valley View Christian Ch., Dallas, 1981—. Lt. USNR, 1971-79. Named Outstanding Young Lawyer of Dallas, Dallas Assn. of Young Lawyers, 1984. Fellow Tex. Bar Found., Am. Bar Found.; mem. ABA, Dallas Bar Assn., D.C. Bar Assn., Am. Law Inst. Republican. Office: Tex Supreme Ct Box 12248 Capitol Sta Austin TX 78711

HECK, JOEL CHRISTOPHER, career officer; b. Carroll, Iowa, Oct. 2, 1959; s. John Merlin and Carmen Joann (Rasmussen) H.; m. Ivette Falto, June 6, 1991; children: Joel Jr., Brittany N. BS in Econs., USAF Acad., Colo. Springs, Colo., 1983; MS in Sys. Tech., Naval Post Grad. Sch., Monterey, Calif., 1989. Cert. acquisition profl., dept. def. Commd. 2d lt. USAF, 1983, adv. through grades to maj.; mgr. spaceflight operations Space & Missile Sys. Divsn., L.A., 1982-84, flight oper. officer, space shuttle, 1984-86, mgr. solid rocket motors, 1986-87; test mgr. space sys. Airforce Oper. Test Ctr., Albuquerque, 1989-91; orbital test flight dir. Brilliant Pebbles Program, Washington, 1992-93; dep. dir. BMC3 Ballistic Missile Def. Orgn., Washington, 1993-94; exec. officer Dep. Theater Missile Def., Washington, 1994-95; staff officer U.S. Forces Korea, Seoul, 1995—; mil. adv. Aviation Week Magazine, 1986-87. Mem. Air Force Assn., Assn. Grad. USAF Acad., Army/Navy Country Club (bd. govs.). Home: 1714 Armour Ln Redondo Beach CA 90278 Office: Air Command & Staff Coll Maxwell AFB Montgomery AL 36112

HECKENBACH, IDA EVE, modern languages educator; b. Lafayette, La., Sept. 13, 1962; d. John Heckenbach and Jeanne Ann (Pitre) Soileau; m. François Havel-Gentil, May 10, 1992; children: Leyla, Guillaume. BA, U. S.W. La., 1986, MA, 1992. Program asst. Dept. Edn. (La.)/Codofil, Lafayette, 1988-91; instr. French Episcopal Sch. of Acadiana, Cade, La., 1991-94; fellow U. S.W. La., Lafayette, 1994—. Co-editor: Feux Follets, Lafayette, 1991-93; contbr. articles to profl. jours.; author various book revs. Rep. Graduate Sch. Orgn., Lafayette, 1994-95, rep. to grad. coun. and grad. appeals, 1996—. Master's fellow U. S.W. La., 1989-90; Doctoral fellow U. S.W. La., 1994—. Mem. Am. Assn. of Tchrs. of French, Women in French, Société des Professeurs Français et Francophones D'Amérique (summer scholar 1995), Modern Language Assn., Pi Delta Phi (pres. 1989-90), Phi Kappa Phi. Home: 108 Faculty Dr Lafayette LA 70506 Office: U SW La Dept of MODL PO Box 43331 Lafayette LA 70504

HECKER, RICHARD BERNARD, osteopathic physician, anesthesiologist; b. Chgo., July 3, 1951; s. Melvin Ralph and Magdalen Louise (Kiernan) H.; m. Kelly Ann Spence, Nov. 9, 1988. BS in Biology, BA in Psychology, St. Martin's Coll., Lacey, Wash., 1981; DO, U. Osteo. Medicine and Health Scis., Des Moines, 1986. Diplomate Am. Bd. Anesthesiology, Am. Osteo. Bd. Anesthesiology. Various positions med. dept. to chief warrant officer U.S. Army, U.S., Okinawa, Germany, 1972-81; commd. 2d lt. U.S. Army, 1982, advanced through grades to maj., 1991, retired, 1997; intern Brooke Army Med. Ctr., Ft. Sam Houston, Tex., 1986-87, residency, 1987-90, postgrad. fellow critical care medicine, 1990-91, anesthesiologist, 1990—, invensivist, pain mgmt. specialist, dir. post-anesthesia care units, 1991—, dir. surg. ICU 42-A, 1991; dir., mem. affiliate faculty ACLS program Am. Heart Assn., 1991—; cons. Am. Osteo. Bd. Anesthesiology; regional med. dir. Critical Air Medicine, Inc., San Diego. Contbr. articles to profl. jours. Mem. Am. Soc. Anesthesiologists, Soc. Critical Care Medicine. Republican. Roman Catholic. Office: Anesthesia Practice Group 1017 N Main Ste 225 San Antonio TX 78212

HECKLER, JOHN MAGUIRE, stockbroker, investment company executive; b. Meriden, Conn., Nov. 11, 1927; s. George Ernest and Mary Catherine (Maguire) H.; m. Sheryl Jean Bills, Nov. 30, 1985; children: Belinda West Mulliken, Alison Anne, John Maguire. AB, Fairfield U., 1951; postgrad. Fordham U., 1951-53, Harvard U., 1953-54. Exec. Maguire Homes, M. W. Maguire, 1954-62; instl. salesman Harris Upham & Co., Boston, 1962-68; resident mgr. Middendorf, Colgate & Co., Boston, 1968-70; founder, chmn., CEO Boston Instl. Svcs., Inc., 1971-92; chmn. Spur Publs., Inc., 1989-94; founder, chmn., CEO Independence Instl. Securities & Co., L.P., Middleburg, Va., 1994—; del. White House Conf. on Small Bus., 1995; mem. N.Y. Stock Exch., 1970-93. Campaign asst. Congressman Bradford Morse, 1960. Served with USCG, 1945-47. Republican. Episcopalian. Clubs: Harvard (Washington), Piedmont (Va.) Hunt.

HECKLER, WALTER TIM, association executive; b. Kimberley, Republic South Africa, Jan. 30, 1942; s. Walter Martin and Mavis Joyce (Cardinal) H.; m. Renée Anne Tamborello, Dec. 16, 1984; children: Cindy, Mark, Timothy, David, Chelsea. BS in Biology, Lamar U., Beaumont, Tex., 1963. Chief rsch. technician M.D. Anderson Cancer Inst., Houston, 1963-69; rsch. asst. Salk Inst. Biol. Studies, La Jolla, Calif., 1969-70; dir. tennis Westwood Country Club, Houston, 1970-75; gen. mgr. Chancellors Racquet Club, Houston, 1975-82; chief exec. officer U.S. Pro Tennis Assn., Houston, 1982—. Mem. Am. Soc. Assn. Execs., U.S. Profl. Tennis Assn. (pres. 1980-82), Profl. Assn. Diving Instrs. Office: US Profl Tennis Assn World Hdqrs 1 USPTA Centre 3535 Briarpark Dr Houston TX 77042-5235

HECKLEY, TERESA JOANN, health facility administrator; b. Blue Earth, Minn., May 8, 1956; d. Milton and Kathryn (Grise) Rauenhorst; m. Gregg Heckley, June 28, 1986; children: Laura Ann, Nicole Kristina. BS, Coll. St. Teresa, 1978; MS in Nursing, U. S. Fla., 1990. Cert. critical care registered nurse, advanced cardiac life support instr., basic cardiac life support instr. Staff nurse med./surg. Vets. Hosp., Tampa, Fla., 1978-79, staff nurse intensive care, 1979-86, nurse mgr. surgery unit, 1986-89, nurse mgr. coronary care unit, 1989—. Mem. Am. Assn. Critical Care Nurses, Sigma Theta Tau, Phi Kappa Phi.

HECTUS, CHARLES THOMAS, lawyer; b. Newburgh, N.Y., Feb. 19, 1949; s. Joseph and Catherine Alma (Ringlehan) H.; m. Rebecca Ann Torres, Dec. 1970 (div. 1978); m. Karen Lynn Kutz,Aug. 27, 1983; children: Jamie Elizabeth, Joseph Edward Alexander. BA in Psychology, Manhattan Coll., 1972; JD, U. Louisville, 1978. Bar: Ky. 1978, U.S. Dist. Ct. (we. dist.) Ky. 1980, U.S. Dist. Ct. (ea. dist.) Ky. 1981, U.S. Ct. Appeals (6th cir.) 1980, U.S. Supreme Ct. 1982, Ind. 1987, U.S. Dist. Ct. (so. dist.) Ind. 1988. Asst. pub. advocate Dept. Pub. Advocacy, Frankfort, Ky., 1978-80; asst. pub. defender Jefferson Dist. Pub. Defender, Louisville, 1980; ptnr. Gittleman, Bleidt & Barber and predecessor firm, Louisville, 1980-83, 1983-89; ptnr. Williams & Wagoner, Louisville, 1990—; bd. dirs. Ky. Assn. Criminal Def. Attys., Frankfort, 1987-91. Mem. ABA, Assn. Trial Lawyers Am., Ky. Bar Assn., Ky. Acad. Trial Attys., Ky. Acad. Justice (pres. 1985), Louisville Bar Assn., Ind. Bar Assn. Home: 11207 New Stone Ct Louisville KY 40223-2654 Office: Williams & Wagoner 101 Bullitt Ln Ste 202 Louisville KY 40222-5429

HEDDINGER, FREDERICK MARTIN, SR., publisher; b. Wilkinsburg, Pa., Jan. 31, 1917; s. William McKinley and Helen Cecelia (Kimmel) H.; m. Lillian M. Beatty, Sept. 7, 1940; 1 child, Frederick Martin Jr. Student, Duquesne U., 1937-46. With Westinghouse Electric, E. Pitts., 1941-52, contract mgr., Pitts., 1952-54, asst. plant mgr., Youngwood, Pa., 1955-64; pres., founder Pa. Electronics Tech., Inc., Pitts., 1964-69; exec. dir. Pa. Sch. Bds. Assn., Harrisburg, 1970-82, sec., trustee Ins. Trust, 1971-82; pres., pub. Martin Frederick Inc., Surfside Beach, S.C., 1982—; trustee Pa. Sch. Employees Retirement System, 1970-82. Pres. Wilkinsburg Sch. Bd., 1951-69; vestryman Zion Lutheran Ch., 1975-82; life mem. N. Huntingdon Twp. Vol. Fire Co.; lectr. Dickinson Law Sch. Forum. Named Paul Harris fellow Rotary Internat., 1986. Mem. IEEE, Am. Assn. Sch. Adminstrs., Am. Soc. Assn. Execs., Nat. Orgn. Legal Problems in Edn., Pa. Soc., SCORE, Republican. Methodist. Club: Litchfield Country (Pawleys Island, S.C.). Lodge: Rotary, Shriners, Omar Temple. Co-inventor series electronic games, 1968, Big Mouth trash bag; author: Handbook on Public Sector Collective Bargaining, 1971; mng. editor School Law Digest, 1970-82; pub. Kwik-Fax Books, 1983—.3 . Office: Martin Frederick Inc PO Box 14613 Myrtle Beach SC 29587-4613

HEDGECOUGH, REBECCA J., nurse; b. Dayton, Ohio, Dec. 17, 1963; d. Opie L. and Margaret L. (Henry) Hedgecough; 2 children, Jaime Nicole, Jordan Nicholas. LPN, Livingston (Tenn.) Tech., 1983; ASN, SUNY, Albany, 1991. RN, Tenn.; cert. ACLS, Tenn.; CCRN. Critical care nurse Cookeville (Tenn.) Gen. Hosp., 1983-91, CCRN cardiac cath. lab., 1994—; nurse cardiology Dr. J.B. Arnstine, Cookeville, 1991-93. Recipient Cmty. Leadership award Am. Biog. Inst., 1986, Internat. Biog. Achievement award, 1984, Tenn. Gov.'s award for Vocat. Edn., 1983. Mem. AACN (cert.), Coun. Cardiovascular Nursing, Am. Heart Assn., Am. Kennel Club, Upper Cumberland Kennel Club (sec.). Mem. Ch. of God. Home: 969 Indian Hills Rd Cookeville TN 38506 Office: Cookeville Gen Hosp 142 W 5th St Cookeville TN 38501-1760

HEDGEMAN, LULAH M., secondary education educator; b. Memphis, Jan. 30, 1938; d. A.B. and Joanne (Wells) McEwen; m. Herbert L. Hedgeman, Sept. 1962 (div. 1967); 1 child, Denita J. BA, Fisk U., 1959; MusM, Memphis State U., 1970; cert., No. Ill. U., 1976; DFA (hon.), Rhodes Coll., 1991. Tchr. Melrose Jr. High Sch., Memphis, 1960-63, Chgo. Pub. Schs., 1963-66, Hamilton High Sch., Memphis, 1966-70, Treadwell High Sch., Memphis, 1970-76, Overton High Sch., Memphis, 1976—. Mem. Opera Memphis Guild, 1974—, NAACP, 1970—, Memphis Symphony Guild, 1976—; music cons. Miss. Blvd. Christian Ch., Memphis, 1989. Named Most Outstanding Condr. World Music Festivals, 1982, Most Outstanding Performing Arts Tchr. The Disney Co., 1990; recipient Gov's. award NARAS, 1991, Mr. Holland award, 1996. Mem. NARAS (asst. condr. All-Am. h.s. grammy jazz choir 1994, Mr. Holland award 1996), NEA, Memphis Edn. Assn., tenn. Edn. Assn., Tenn. Music Educators Assn. (bd. dirs. 1970), Nat. Black Music Caucus (bd. dirs. 1990), West Tenn. Vocal Assn. (pres. 1968-70), Am. Choral Dirs. Assn. (pres. Tenn. chpt. 1980-82), Music Educators Nat. Conf., Rotary (Tchr. Excellence award Memphis chpt. 1984), Delta Sigma Theta (Arts and Letters award 1991), Kappa Delta Pi. Office: Overton Performing Arts High Sch 1770 Lanier Ln Memphis TN 38117-7006

HEDGES, BOBETTE LYNN, business administrator; b. Glendale, Calif., Aug. 12, 1959; d. Robert LeRoy Newman and Charolette Joan (Kirk) Garris; m. Michael Glenn Hedges, July 4, 1981 (div. May 1992); children: Michael Glenn, Matthew Stephen. Corp. dir., sec.-treas. Hoss Discount Aluminum & Builders, Okeechobee, Fla., 1985—; corp. dir., v.p. Taylor Creek Motors, Inc., Okeechobee, 1994—, Brahma Bull Restaurant, Okeechobee, 1994—. Author poetry. Mem. bus. adv. com. Okeechobee County Sch. Bd., 1995-96; speaker ABWA, 1990, Indian River Com. Coll., 1990, Trinity Assembly of God, 1990. Named Miss Alaska Nat. Teenager, 1976. Mem. Assembly of God Ch. Office: Brahma Bull Restaurant 2405 Highway 441 SE Okeechobee FL 34974-7325

HEDGES, JEAN KYLE, educator; b. Big Stone Gap, Va., Jan. 11, 1930; d. Robert Swanson and Vera Sue (Hampton) K.; m. Lewis Charles Hedges, Sept. 11, 1954; children: L. Kyle, S. Blair, Susan H., R. Hampton. BA, Mary Baldwin Coll., 1951; postgrad. studies, U. Va., 1970. Cert. tchr., Va. Tchr. Fairfax County Schs., Falls Church, Va., 1951-53, Alexandria, Va., 1953-54; subst. tchr. Arlington County Schs., Arlington, Va., 1972-75; sect. supr. County Treas. Office, Arlington, 1975-87; substitute tchr. Arlington County Schs., Arlington, 1987-93. Mem. Ashton Heights Civic Assn., 1965—; pres. Maury Sch. PTA, Arlington, Va., 1970-71; v.p. Ashton Heights Civic Assn., Arlington, 1973-74, 92-93; asst. chief election officer Ashton Heights Precinct, Arlington, 1987—; pres. Women's Conf. for Arlington Symphony, 1990, 93-94; coord. FISH, North Arlington, 1989—; docent Arlington Hist. Soc., 1990—. Mem. AAUW, DAR. Republican. Methodist. Home: 415 N Monroe St Arlington VA 22201-1737

HEDRICK, DAVID WARRINGTON, lawyer; b. Jacksonville, Fla., Oct. 25, 1917; s. Frederic Cleveland and Edith (Warrington) H.; m. June Nicholson, Apr. 23, 1949 (div. 1991); children: John Warrington, Stephen Brian; m. Sherra M. Hedrick, Jan. 31, 1992. BA with honors, U. Fla., 1940, JD with honors, 1947. Bar: Fla. 1947, U.S. Supreme Ct. 1962. Assoc. LeRoy B. Giles, 1947-52; ptnr. Giles, Hedrick & Robinson, Orlando, Fla., 1953-92, David W. Hedrick Atty., 1992—; dir. Indsl. Devel. Commn. of Mid-Fla., 1978-79, First Fed. Savs. and Loan Assn., 1963-79; dir., sec. Comint Corp., 1966-84; pres. Attys. Title Services, 1963-64, Sharaconcept, Inc., 1987—. Legal counsel, bd. dirs. Central Fla. Council Boy Scouts Am., 1970—; bd. dirs. Holiday Hosp. of Orlando, 1966-69; mem. Orange County Human Planning Council, pres., 1973-75, bd. dirs., 1973-89; mem. Orlando Mayor's Interracial Adv. Commn., 1967; chmn. United Appeal Drive of Orange County (Fla.), 1967, pres., 1970, chmn. bd. dirs., 1971, chmn. social planning com., 1973-76, legal counsel, 1975—; chancellor Diocese of Central Fla., Orlando, 1970-90. Capt. AUS, 1941-46; ETO; to col. USAR, 1946-67. Decorated Bronze Star; Belgian Fourragere. Recipient Disting. Eagle Scout award Boy Scouts Am., 1972, Silver Beaver award, 1976. Mem. Orange County Bar Assn. (pres. 1959-60, past pres. council 1976—), ABA, Fla. Bar, Am. Judicature Soc., Am. Legion, VFW, Fla. Blue Key, Assn. of U.S. Army, Res. Officers Assn., Phi Kappa Phi, Phi Delta Phi, Alpha Tau Omega. Democrat. Episcopalian. Clubs: Country of Orlando, Univ. (Orlando), River (Jacksonville), Kiwanis of North Orlando. Home: 1112 Eastin Ave Orlando FL 32804-6308 Office: David W Hedrick Atty at Law 135 W Central Blvd Ste 1100 Orlando FL 32801-2436

HEDSTROM, SUSAN LYNNE, maternal women's health nurse; b. Dowagiac, Mich., Jan. 17, 1958; d. Clinton J. and Gloria Anna (Hyink) Moore. ADN, Southwestern Mich. Coll., 1978. RN, Mich., Ind., Calif., Ga., Fla. Staff nurse obstetrics unit Lee Meml. Hosp., Dowagiac, Mich., 1979-81, Meml. Hosp., South Bend, Ind., 1981-90; with MRA Staffing Systems, Inc., Ft. Lauderdale, Fla., 1990-93; staff nurse traveler MUSC, Charleston, S.C., 1990-91; nurse Desert Hosp., Palm Springs, Calif., 1991, Ind. U. Hosp., Indpls., 1992, Valley Med Ctr., Fresno, Calif., 1992; staff nurse post partum/nursery Tallahassee Meml. Regional Med. Ctr., 1993-95, asst. head nurse post partum, 1995—. Mem. Am. Women's Health, Obstetrics and Neonatal Nurses. Office: Tallahassee Meml Reg Hosp Magnolia Dr & Miccosukee Rd Tallahassee FL 32308

HEESCHEN, BARBARA ANN, retired music critic; b. Gary, Ind., Dec. 22, 1931; d. William George and Irene Elizabeth (Enterline) Stuhlmacher; m. Jerry Parker Heeschen, Sept. 30, 1956; children: William Andrew, Paul Richard, James Matern. BA magna cum laude, Hanover Coll., 1953; postgrad., Union Theol. Sem., 1956; MusM, Cen. Mich. U., 1977. Sec. to supt. Presyn. Schs., Cardenas, Cuba, 1953-54; press staff World Coun. Chs., Evanston, Ill., 1954; dir. christian edn. 1st Presbyn. Ch., Champaign, Ill., 1954-56; instr. piano, harpsichordist, dir. youth choir Meml. Presbyn. Ch., Midland, 1963-82; accompanist, asst.dir. Canzona di Musica; instr. music theory Delta Coll., Midland, 1975-76; dir. Chancel choir Aldersgate United Meth. Ch., 1982-91; music critic Midland Daily News, 1987-92; instr. Northwood Inst., Midland, 1991; dir. Bay Chorale, Bay City, Mich., 1988; piano tchr.; lectr. in field. Sec. bd. dirs. Midland Music Soc., 1961-65, mem., 1971-77; bd. dirs. Midland Ctr. for Arts, 1971-77, asst. sec. bd. dirs., 1974-75; mem. Saginaw Valley Arts Coun., 1963-64; mus. dir. for Teenage Musicals, 1969, 70, other mus.; publicity chmn. Sugnet Sch. Parent-Tchr. Orgn., 1971-73; mem. Midland Piano Quartet, 1986-91. Recipient Citizenship award DAR, Nat. Honor Soc., Hanover Coll. Alumni award, 1953; named Midland Musician of Yr. Music Soc. & Midland Symphony Orch. of Midland Ctr. for Arts, 1982. Mem. PEO, Nat. Guild Piano Tchrs. (bd. judges), Mich. Music Tchrs. Assn. (cert., asst. chmn. jr. high activities 1972-74, concerto chmn. 1985-89, rep. Mich. youth arts coun. 1985-89), Midland Music Tchrs. Assn. (v.p. 1966-70, 80-82, pres. 1982-84, student activities chmn. 1978-80), Midland Community Concert Soc. (bd. mgrs.), Alpha Delta Pi, Twentieth Century Club. Home: 244 Lakeside Dr Crossville TN 38558-7065

HEESTAND, DIANE ELISSA, educational technology educator, medical educator; b. Boston, Oct. 9, 1945; d. Glenn Wilson and Elizabeth (Martin) H. BA, Allegheny Coll., 1967; MA, U. Wyo., 1968; edn. specialist, Ind. U., 1971, EdD, 1979. Asst. prof. communication Clarion (Pa.) State Coll., 1971; asst. prof. learning resources Indiana U. of Pa., 1971-72; asst. prof. communication U. Nebr. Med. Ctr., Omaha, 1972-74; assoc. prof. learning resources Tidewater Community Coll., Virginia Beach, Va., 1975-78; ednl. cons. U. Ala. Sch. Medicine, Birmingham, 1978-81; dir. learning resources, assoc. prof. med. edn. Mercer U. Sch. Medicine, Macon, Ga., 1981-88; asst. dean ednl. devel. and resources Ohio U. Coll. Osteopathic Medicine, 1989-90; assoc. prof. clin. med. edn., dir. biomed. communications U. So. Calif. Sch. Medicine, L.A., 1990-95, acting chair dept. med. edn., 1992-95; dir. office ednl. devel. U. Ark. for Med. Scis., Little Rock, 1995—; cons. Lincoln (Pa.) U., summer, 1975; vis. fellow Project Hope/China, Millwood, Va., summer, 1986. Author (teleplay) Yes, 1968 (award World Law Fund 1968); producer, dir. (slide tape) Finding a Way, 1980 (1st Pl. award HESCA 1981, Susan Eastman award 1981). Grantee Porter Found., 1984. Mem. Health Scis. Comm. Assn. (bd. dirs. 1982-86, pres.-elect 1987-88, pres. 1988-89, Spl. Svc. award 1990), Assn. Ednl. Comm. and Tech. (pres. media design and prodn. div. 1985-86), Assn. Biomed. Comm. Dirs. (bd. dirs. 1993-95). Republican. Unitarian Universalist.

HEFFERNAN, JOHN WILLIAM, retired journalist; b. Stockbridge, Hants., Eng., Oct. 21, 1910; came to U.S., 1946; s. John and Alice Ann (Edwards) H.; m. Edith Curry, Oct. 12, 1948 (dec. Feb. 1990); 1 stepchild, Anthony Edward; m. Martha Powell Hensley, Apr. 25, 1992. Student, Clarks Coll., Eng., 1924-26. Sub-editor Central News, London, 1929-34; sub-editor Press Assn., London, 1934-36, sports reporter, 1936-39; fgn. corr. Reuters, N.Y.C., 1946, fgn. corr. for UN, 1946-57; chief corr. Reuters, Washington, 1957-76; ret., 1976. Pres. Gasparilla Island Conservatoin and Improvement Assn., Boca Grande, Fla., 1994. Maj. Brit. Army, 1941-46. Decorated Comdr. Order of Brit. Empire, 1969. Mem. Nat. Press Club (pres. 1969), UN Corr. Assn. (pres. 1956), Overseas Press Club. Home: PO Box 687 Boca Grande FL 33921

HEFFLEY, JAMES DICKEY, nutrition counselor; b. Collinsville, Tex., Jan. 12, 1941; s. Floyd F. and Bessie C. (Dickey) H.; m. Betty E. Dozier, Dec. 22, 1963; children: James M., Jon R., David D., Sara E., Anna C. BS, Abilene Christian U., 1964; PhD, U. Tex., 1970. Cert. clin. nutritionist. Rsch. asst., then rsch. assoc. Clayton Found. Bich. Inst., Austin, Tex., 1965-74; lab. supr. Ctr. for Better Health, Austin, 1984—; dir. Nutrition Counseling Svc., Austin, 1974—; cons. Tex. Sch. for Blind, Austin, 1972-74, Tex. Gov.'s Commn. on Aging, Austin, 1976. Contbr. articles to profl. jours. Mem. Internat. Acad. Nutrition and Preventive Medicine (pres. 1994—), Internat. and Am. Assn. Clin. Nutritionists (pres. 1991-95), Clin Nutrition Cert. Bd. (chmn. 1996—). Office: Nutrition Counseling Svc 3913 Medical Pky Ste 101 Austin TX 78756-4016

HEFLIN, HOWELL THOMAS, senator, lawyer, former state supreme court chief justice; b. Poulan, GA, June 19, 1921; s. Marvin Rutledge and Louise D. (Strudwick) H.; m. Elizabeth Ann Carmichael, Feb. 23, 1952; 1 son, Howell Thomas. AB, Birmingham So. Coll., 1942; JD, U. Ala., 1948, LLD (hon.); LLD (hon.), U. No. Ala., Samford U., Tuskegee U., Del. Law Sch., Widener Coll., Troy State U., Ala. Christian Coll., Tuskegee U., Livingston U., Ala. A&M U., Ala. State U., Stillman Coll.; DHH (hon.), Birmingham So. Coll., 1980; DHL (hon.), Talledega Coll. Bar: Ala. 1948. Practiced in Tuscumbia; sr. ptnr. firm Heflin, Rosser and Munsey; chief justice Supreme Ct. Ala., 1971-77; chmn. Nat. Conf. Chief Justices, 1976-77; mem. U.S. Senate from Ala., Washington, 1979-96; mem. judiciary com., agr. com.; Ala. A&M U.; bd. dirs. Meth. Pub. House, 1952-64; lectr. U. Ala., 1946-48, U. North Ala., 1948-52; Tazewell Taylor vis. prof. law Coll. William and Mary, 1977. Mem. Ala. Edn. Commn., 1957-58; chmn. Colbert County A.R.C., 1950; Ala. field dir. Crusade for Children, 1948; pres. Ala. Com. Better Schs., 1958-59; chmn. Tuscumbia Bd. Edn., 1954-64, Ala. Tenure Commn., 1959-64; pres. U. Ala. Law Sch. Found., 1964-66; co-chmn. NCCJ, Tri-Cities area, 1949-70; chmn. Brotherhood Week; bd. dirs., v.p. Nat. Center for State Cts., 1975-77; trustee Birmingham So. Coll.; hon. pres. Troy State U. Served to maj. USMC, 1942-46. Decorated Silver Star, Purple Heart; recipient Ala. Citizen of Yr. award Ala. Cable TV Assn., 1973, 82; Outstanding Alumnus award U. Ala. and Birmingham So. Coll., 1973; Herbert Lincoln Harley award Am. Judicature Soc., 1973; Justice award, 1981; Ala. Citizen of Year award Ala. Broadcasters Assn., 1975; mem. Ala. Acad. Honor; named Outstanding Appellate Judge in U.S. Assn. Trial Lawyers Am., 1976; recipient Highest award Am. Judges Assn., 1975, Thomas Jefferson award Ala. Press Assn., 1979; Inst. Human Relations award, 1980; Silver Chalice award Am. Council on Alcoholism, 1980; Disting. Am. award Nat. Football Found. and Hall of Fame; Warren E. Burger award Inst. Ct. Mgmt.; Leadership award Am. Security Council, 1985-87; Leadership award Southeastern Soc. Am. Forresters, 1986, Taxpayers Hall of Fame, 1987, Patriotic Civilian award U.S. Army, 1987, Henry Jackson Senatorial Leadership award, 1987, Golden Plow award Am. Farm Bur., Outstanding Svc. to Sci. award Nat. Bio-med. Rsch. Assn., 1992, Werner Von Braun award Nat. Sci. Coun., 1992; named Progressive Farmer's 1993 Man of Year in agrl., Disting. Svc. award Nat. Rural Electric Coop. Assn, Recipient of the Helen Keller, Outstanding Public Svs., award, Am. Found. for the Blind, 1996, Nat. Public Svs. award, Am. Heart Assn., 1996, John B. Medacaris award, Am. Defense Assn., 1996. Fellow Internat. Acad. of Law and Scis., Internat. Acad. Trial Lawyers, Internat. Soc. Barristers, Am. Coll. Trial Lawyers; mem. ABA, Ala. Law Inst. (v.p.), Ala. Bar Assn. (pres. 1965-66), Colbert County Bar Assn. (past pres.), Ala. Bar Found. (past pres.), Am. Judicature Soc. (v.p. 1977-79), Ala. Law Sch. Alumni Assn. (past pres.), Ala. Trial Lawyers Assn. (pres.), Nat. Assn. Biomedical Rsch. Assn. (Outstanding Pub. Svc. award, Nat. Veterans award), VFW, Am. Legion, 40 and 8, DAV, Third Marine Div. Assn., Order of Coif, Omicron Delta Kappa, Phi Delta Phi, Tau Kappa Alpha, Lambda Chi Alpha. Methodist. Office: PO Box 228 Tuscumbia AL 35674

HEFLIN, RUTH JANELLE, English language educator; b. Pratt, Kans., June 19, 1963; d. Charles Albert and Mary Rosella (Mallonee) H.; m. James Paul Cooper, Oct. 27, 1989; 1 child, Harland J.P.C. Cooper. BA, Kans. State U., 1985, MA, 1988; postgrad., Okla. State U., 1992—. Tchg. asst. Kans. State U., Manhattan, 1986-88, adj. instr., 1988-89; adj. instr. U. Kans., Lawrence, 1989-90, William Jewell Coll., Liberty, Mo., 1990-91, Kansas City (Kans.) C.C., 1990-92, U. Mo., Kansas City, 1990-92; tchg. assoc. Okla. State U., Stillwater, 1992—; fiction editor Touchstone Mag., Manhattan, 1986-87; photo journalist for ROTC, U.S. Army, Fort Riley, Kans., 1986; presenter in field. Pres. Student Assn. of Grad. Students in English, Manhattan, 1987-88; co-chair rsch. com. Kansas City (Kans.) C.C., 1991-92; voting mem. Adj. Instrn. Com., Kansas City, 1991-92. Recipient First Place for Fiction, Coll. Woman Mag., 1985; Steve Kraisinger scholar 4-H, Pratt, Kans., 1981-82; Second Century scholar Kans. State U., Manhattan, 1981-82. Mem. MLA, Assn. for Study of Am. Indian Lits., Soc. for Cinematic Study, English Grad. Student Assn. (chair professionalism com. 1995, chair hosting com. 1996). Office: Okla State U 205 Morrill Hall Stillwater OK 74075

HEFNER, TERRY THOMAS, soil conservationist; b. Magnolia, Ark., Aug. 1, 1949; d. Sam Terrell and Ann (Keese) Thomas; m. Joe B. Hefner, Aug. 14, 1982; children: Thomas Carroll, Joseph Terrell. BS, So. Ark. U., 1972. Clk.-typist USDA, Denton, Tex., 1970; soil conservationist GS-9 USDA, Waco, Tex., 1978-80; soil conservationist USDA, Ballinger, Tex., 1980-83; soil conservationist GS-11 USDA, Snyder, Tex., 1983-87, 94—, dist. conservationist, 1987-94; mil. personnel clk. Hdqrs. 3rd ROTC Region, Ft. Riley Kans. at So. Ark. U., Magnolia, Ark., 1972-78; clk.-typist Hdqrs. III Corp., Ft. Hood, Tex., 1978; charter com. mem. Fed. Women's Program, Temple, Tex., 1986-90. Recipient Cert. Merit USDA, 1981, 83, 88. Mem. Soil and Water Soc. Am. (bd. dirs. 1983-84, pres.-elect 1992, pres. 1993), Nat. Assn. conservation Dists., Orgn. of Profl. Employees of Dept. Agr., Am. Quarter Horse Assn., Am. Bus. Women's Assn. Methodist. Home: PO Box 1295 Snyder TX 79550-1295 Office: USDA Soil Conservation Svc 5309 Big Springs Hwy Snyder TX 79549-6347

HEFNER, W. G. (BILL HEFNER), congressman; b. Elora, Tenn., Apr. 11, 1930; s. Emory James and Icie Jewel (Holderfield) H.; m. Nancy Louise Hill, Mar. 23, 1952; children: Stacye, Shelly. Grad. high sch. Mem. 94th-104th Congresses from 8th N.C. dist., Washington, D.C., 1975—; leadership adv. group mem., mem. appropriations com., subcom. on mil. constrn. (ranking mem.), subcom. on nat. security, leader on textile trade issues; former owner Sta. WRKB radio, Kannapolis, N.C. Former profl. entertainer with Harvesters Quartet; former performer weekly gospel show, Sta. WXII-TV, Winston-Salem, N.C.; also appeared on Sta. WBTV, Charlotte, N.C., Sta. WRAL-TV, Raleigh, N.C., Sta. WGHP-TV, High Point, N.C., Sta. WBTW-TV, Florence, S.C. Mem. bd. visitors U.S. Mil. Acad., 1982—; mem. Dem. Congl. campaign com. Office: US Ho Reps 2470 Rayburn Bldg Washington DC 20515-0005

HEFNER, WILLIAM JOHNSON, JR. (W. JOHN HEFNER, JR.), oil and gas industry executive; b. Oklahoma City, July 29, 1952; s. William Johnson and Eloise (Wallace) H.; m. Deborah Seyan Raulston, Nov. 23, 1979; children: Margaret Leigh, Virginia Lynn. BA in Journalism, U. Okla., 1980; MBA, Oklahoma City U., 1983. Reporter city desk The Daily Oklahoman, Oklahoma City, 1978-79; field landman Gerald D. Whitfield, Oklahoma City, 1980, W.W. Blair, Oklahoma City, 1980-81; field landman, in-house landman T.S. Dudley Land Co., Oklahoma City, 1981-82; landman, part owner Arbuckle Enterprises, Inc., Oklahoma City, 1984-88; mng. ptnr. Hefner Co., Oklahoma City, 1986-93, Hefner Prodn. Co., Oklahoma City, 1986-93; leasing agt. First Resource Realty, Inc., Oklahoma City, 1987; leasing agt., property mgr. Alquest Property Corp., Oklahoma City, 1987-88; pres. Hefner Corp., Oklahoma City, 1988-93, Hefner Co., Inc., Oklahoma City, 1994—. Bd. dirs. Hist. Preservation, Inc., 1982—, mem. trees, parks and beautification com., 1983-85, 88-89, 95, chmn. trees, parks and beautification com., 1986, mem. projects com., 1986, 89, 91, 94, mem. enforcement com., 1984-85, 88, mem. long range planning com., 1988-89, mem. oil and gas com., 1991, mem. fin. and budget com., 1989, 1st v.p., 1988, 2d v.p., 1989, mem. assoc. bd., 1992, chmn. pub. rels. com., 1992; reporter, editor The Heritage Hills Herald, 1987-89, vice-chmn., 1993—; participant Heritage Hills Housetour, 1982, 87, 93; assoc. bd. dirs. Okla. Med. Rsch. Found., 1988-92, mem. fin. and investment com., 1991, exec. com., 1991—, bd. dirs., 1992—; bd. dirs. Lyric Theatre, 1990-92, adv. bd. dirs., 1992—; bd. dirs. Deaconess Hosp., 1991—, mem. exec. com., 1993—, 2d v.p., 1994—; bd. dirs. Deaconess Health Care Corp., 1994—; mem. devel. com. Casady Sch., 1994—, co-chair leadership circle, 1994; active Leadership Oklahoma City Class XI, 1993; vestry mem. St. Paul's Cathedral, 1990-92, mem. Usher's Guild, 1988—; bd. dirs. Children's Med. Rsch., 1992-94; bd. dirs. Okla. Heritage Assn., 1994—, mem. com. of 100, 1993—; active Downtown Now, 1989—, Oklahoma City Art Mus., 1985—, Omniplex Sci. Mus. Oklahoma City, 1990—, U. Okla. Found., Norman, 1990—, YMCA, 1988-94, Com. of 100, 1993—. Mem. Ind. Petroleum Assn. Am., Okla. Ind. Petroleum Assn., Chafing Dish Soc., Okla. Hist. Soc., Petroleum Club, Oklahoma City Golf and Country Club (stockholder 1986—), Magna Charta Barons (Somerset chpt.), Lotus Club, Kiwanis Club Oklahoma City (bd. dirs. 1993-94, co-chmn. interclub com. 1993). Republican. Episcopalian. Home: 319 NW 18th St Oklahoma City OK 73103-1903 Office: Hefner Co Inc PO Box 2177 Oklahoma City OK 73101-2177

HEGGEN, IVAR NELSON, lawyer; b. Tulsa, Sept. 22, 1954; s. Ivar George Lewis and Marley L. (Whitson) H.; m. Caroline Ann Driscoll, Dec. 20, 1976 (div. 1980); children: Kristin Dominique. BS, Charter Oaks Coll., 1979; JD cum laude, U. Houston, 1983. Bar: Tex. 1983, U.S. Ct. Appeals (5th cir.) 1987, U.S. Ct. Appeals (11th cir.) 1994; cert. in personal injury and civil trial law Nat. Bd. Trial Advocates. Assoc. Dibrell & Greer, Galveston, Tex., 1983-86, Schmidt & Matthews, Houston, 1986-87, Hornbuckle & Windham, Houston, 1987-89; pvt. practice, Houston, 1989—. Mem. ABA, Tex. Bar Assn., Coll. of State Bar Tex., Houston Bar Assn., Tex. Trial Lawyers Assn. (lectr.), Order of the Baron. Home: 422 W 15th St Houston TX 77009 Office: Ste 200 440 Louisiana St Houston TX 77002

HEGGERS, JOHN PAUL, surgery, immunology, microbiology educator; b. Bklyn., Feb. 8, 1933; s. John and May (Hass) H.; m. Rosemarie Niklas, July 30, 1977; children: Arn M., Ronald R., Laurel M., Gary R., Renee L., Annette M. BA in Bacteriology, Mont. State U., 1958; MS in Microbiology, U. Md., 1965; PhD in Bacteriology and Pub. Health, Wash. State U., 1972. Diplomate Am. Bd. Bioanalysis. Med. technologist U.S. Naval Hosp., St. Albans, N.Y., 1951-53; bacteriologist Hahnemann Hosp., Worcester, Mass., 1958-59; commd. 2d lt. U.S. Army, 1959, advanced through grades to lt. col., 1975; mem. staff dept. bacteriology 1st U.S. Army Med. Lab., N.Y.C., 1959-60; chief clin. lab. U.S. Army Hosp., Verdun, France, 1960-63; chief virology and rickettsiology div. dept. microbiology 3d U.S. Army Med. Lab., Ft. McPherson, Ga., 1965-66; instr. bacteriology Basic Lab. Sch., Ft. McPherson, 1965-66; chief diagnostic bacteriology 9th Med. Lab., Saigon, Vietnam, 1966-67; chief microbiology div. dept. pathology Brooke Gen. Hosp., Ft. Sam Houston, Tex., 1967-69; chmn. dept. microbiology U.S. Army Sch. Med. Tech., Ft. Sam Houston, 1967-69; instr. bacteriology evening div. San Antonio Jr. Coll., 1969; lab. scis. officer Office Surgeon Gen., Washington, 1972-74; microbiologist spl. mycobacterial disease br. div. geog. pathology Armed Forces Inst. Pathology, Washington, 1973; spl. asst. to dir. Armed Forces Inst. Pathology, 1973-74; chief clin. rsch. lab. clin. rsch. svc. Madigan Army Med. Ctr., Tacoma, 1974-76, asst. chief clin. investigation svc., 1976-77; instr. immunology, parasitology and mycology Clover Park Vocat. Tech. Inst., 1976-77; ret., 1977; assoc. prof. dept. surgery U. Chgo., 1977-80, prof., 1980-83; prof. surgery Wayne State U., Detroit, 1983-88; prof. surgery, microbiology and immunology U. Tex. Med. Br., 1988—; dir. clin. microbiology Shriners Burn Inst., Galveston, Tex., 1988—. Author: Current Problems in Surgery, 1973, Quantitative Bacteriology, 1991; contbr. articles to profl. jours.; contbg. editor: Jour. Am. Med. Tech., 1972—. Pres. Aloe Rsch. Found., 1989-92, vice-chmn. 1992-95. Decorated Bronze Star; Legion of Merit; recipient cert. of appreciation A.C.S., 1969, cert. appreciation Armed Forces Inst. Pathology, 1974, Valley Forge Honor cert. Freedoms Found., 1974 Fisher award in med. tech., Fisher Scientific, Am. Med. Techs., 1968, 82, Gerard B. Lambert award, 1973, Ednl. Found. Rsch. award Am. Soc. Plastic and Reconstructive Surgery, 1978, Alumni Achievement award Wash. State Univ., 1993, Disting. Alumni award U. Mont., 1994. Fellow N.Y. Acad. Sci., Am. Acad. Microbiology, Royal Soc. Tropical Medicine and Hygiene, Am. Geriat. Soc.; mem. Nat. Registry Microbiologists (chmn. exec. coun. 1976-79), Am. Soc. Microbiology (chmn. com. tellers 1974-75), Wash. Soc. Am. Med. Technologists (pres. 1975-77), Wash. Soc. Med. Tech. (chmn. sect. microbiology sci. assembly, dir. 1975-77), Assn. Mil. Surgeons U.S. (life), Am. Soc. Clin. Pathologists (assoc.), Am. Med. Technologists (disting. svc. award 1975, exceptional merit award 1976, nat. dir. 1979-80, nat. sec. 1980-82, nat. v.p. 1982-84, Technologist of Yr. 1983), Am. Burn Assn. (Pres.'s continuing edn. award 1981, chmn. rsch. com., At Large award 1986, Robert B. Lindberg award 1991, 92, Curtis P. Artz Disting. Svc. award 1996), Plastic Surgery Rsch. Coun., Surg. Infection Soc. (charter), Ill. State Soc. Med. Technologists (v.p. 1979), AVMA, Internat. Soc. for Burn Injuries, VFW (life), VVA (life), Masons (32d degree), Shriners, Sigma Xi. Office: Shriners Burns Inst 815 Market St Galveston TX 77550-2725

HEGSTROM, WILLIAM JEAN, mathematics educator; b. Macomb, Ill., Oct. 21, 1923; s. Carl William and Thelma (Canavit) H. Student Western Ill. U., 1941-42; B.Sc., Rutgers U., 1949, Ed.M. 1952; MA in Teaching, Purdue U., 1964; postgrad. U. Fla., 1961, Fla. Atlantic U., 1965-68; EdD, U. Miami, 1971; m. Grace Ann Paladino, May 3, 1944; children: Elizabeth Louise, William Jean II, Jean (Mrs. Carl Zimbro). Tchr. jr. h.s., South Plainfield, N.J., 1949-52, high sch., Bernardsville, N.J. 1952-54, Oak St. Sch., Bernard's Twp., N.J., 1954-55, high sch., Summit, N.J., 1955-58, jr. h.s., Delray Beach, Fla, 1958-65; chmn. math. dept. John I. Leonard H.S., Lake Worth, Fla., 1965-68, dir. Palm Beach County rsch. project, 1966-68; adj. prof. Fla. Atlantic U., 1965-69, assoc. prof., 1969-70; counselor coord. John Leonard Adult Ctr., Lake Worth, 1965-68; supr. rsch. and evaluation Palm Beach County Sch. Bd., West Palm Beach, Fla., 1970-74; adj. prof. Palm Beach Jr. Coll., 1981-88, Palm Beach Atlantic Coll., 1984-86, asst. prof., 1986-87; Palm Beach Atlantic Coll., 1984-87; cons. math. prof. Palm Beach County Sch. Bd., 1985-87, ret., 1987. With USAAF, 1942-46. Mem. NEA, Nat. Assn. Investors Corp., Am. Assn. Individual Investors, Phi Delta Kappa. Contbr. articles to profl. jours. Home: 225 NE 22nd St Delray Beach FL 33444-4221

HEGWOOD, ELIZABETH Z., nurse educator and manager; b. Gardner, Mass., Feb. 13, 1941. Student, Johnson County Vocat. Nursing, Cleburne, Tex., 1971; BSN, U. Tex., Austin, 1986. Cert. emergency med. technician, BLS, ACLS. Staff nurse Stephenville (Tex.) Gen. Hosp., 1983, Lea Regional Hosp., Hobbs, N.Mex., 1983; staff nurse med.-surg. unit South Austin Community Hosp., Austin, Tex., 1983-86; staff nurse on neuro-respiratory unit Dallas Meth. Med. Ctr., 1986-87; staff nurse post cardiac unit Mary Washington Hosp., Fredericksburg, Va., 1987-89; staff nurse and night shift supr. Summers County Hosp., Hinton, W.Va., 1990-94; edn. coord. Summers County Appalachian Regional Hosp., 1994-96, edn. coord., ICU mgr., 1996—. Founder Follow the Sun Ministries. Founder Fellow the son Ministries; Mem. Phi Theta Kappa.

HEIBERG, WILLIAM LYTLE, defense industry executive; b. West Point, N.Y., June 29, 1938; s. Elvin Ragnvald and Evelyn (Lytle) H.; m. Louisa O'Meara Heiberg, Oct. 31, 1967; children: William L. Jr., James F., Harriet A. BS, U.S. Military Acad., West Point, N.Y., 1961; MA in Internat. Rels., Columbia U., 1967. Mil. command and staff positions U.S. Army, 1961-79; internat. staff officer SHAPE, Brussels, Belgium, 1979-81; sr. rsch. fellow Nat. Def. U., Washington, 1981-82; dir. Washington office U.S. Ctrl. Command Pentagon, Washington, 1982-83, systems mgr. cannons and missiles, 1983-85; dir. Combat Devel. U.S. Army Field Artillery Ctr., Fort Sill, Okla., 1985-87; dir. Army Programs Burdeshaw Assocs., Ltd., Bethesda, Md., 1987-89; mgr. Army programs LTV Aerospace and Def., Washington, 1989-90; mgr. regulatory compliance oversight LTV Aerospace & Def., Dallas, 1990-92, Loral Vought Sys. Corp. merger LTV Aerospace & Def., Dallas, 1992-96, Lockheed Martin Vought merger Loral Vought Sys. Corp., Dallas, 1996—. Author: Spain's Role in NATO, 1982. Col. U.S. Army, 1982-87. Recipient Two Bronze stars, Legion of Merit, U.S. Army, Vietnam, Washington, 1967, 87, diploma Nat. War Coll., Washington, 1982. Mem. U.S. Army field Artillery Assn., Assn. graduates U.S. Mil. Acad. Home: 4127 Cross Bend Dr Arlington TX 76016-3813 Office: Lockheed Martin Vought PO Box 650003 Dallas TX 75265-0003

HEIDE, JOHN WESLEY, engineering executive; b. Chgo., Sept. 14, 1946; s. Frederick Bernard Heiner-Heide and Eleanor Francis (Tuttle) Heide; m. Patricia Ann Lynn, Aug. 5, 1967 (div. Jan. 1973); children: John Wesley, Joseph Edward; m. Karen Lois Johnson, Jan. 24, 1976; children: Johanna Karin Marie, Nicholas Bernard. AA, Phoenix Jr. Coll., 1972; BS, Ariz. State U., 1975. Quality assurance engr. Tex. Instruments, Dallas, 1969-70, ITT Courier, Tempe, Ariz., 1975-79; sr. project engr. GTE Comms., El Paso, 1979-83, Telxon Corp., Houston, 1983-87; engrng. mgr. United Techs., Niles, Mich., 1987-91, Automotive Industries, Midland, Tex., 1991-94; divsn. quality assurance mgr. Pec Golden Triangle Plastics, El Paso, Tex., 1994-95; mgr. quality control Elcom, Inc., El Paso, Tex., 1995—; instr. engring. Houston C.C., 1984-85. Author: Reflections, 1990, Scan-It, 1991, A Step Beyond the Fog, 1992, How Cheap Is Cheap, 1993. Candidate for mayor, El Paso, 1980, 82, 84; candidate for State Rep., Berrien Springs, Mich., 1990. With USMC, 1965-69, Vietnam. Mem. NSPE, Soc. Plastics Engrs., Inst. Indsl. Engring. (v.p. 1982-83), Soc. Mfg. Engrs. (sr.), Am. Soc. Quality Control. Republican. Lutheran. Home: 2604 Lake Spier El Paso TX 79936 Office: Elcom Inc 20 Butterfield Trail El Paso TX 79906

HEIDGERD, FREDERICK CAY, lawyer; b. Sewickley, Pa., Sept. 27, 1950; s. Diederich W.F. and Margaret (Ozburn) H.; m. Sarah H. Beck, Jan. 16, 1976; children: Rebecca, Rachel, Christian. BA, Wake Forest U., 1972; JD, U. Fla., 1975. Bar: Ga. 1975, Fla. 1976, U.S. Dist. Ct. (mid. dist.) Fla. 1981, U.S. Dist. Ct. (so. dist.) Fla. 1977, U.S. Ct. Appeals (5th and 11th cirs.) 1981, U.S. Supreme Ct. 1980. Assoc. Haynsworth, Baldwin & Miles, Greenville, S.C., 1976, Cabot, Wenkstern & Casteel, Ft. Lauderdale, Fla., 1976-78; from assoc. to ptnr. Lunny, Tucker & Heidgerd, Ft. Lauderdale, Fla., 1978-82; ptnr. Heidgerd, Martin & Bennis, P.A., Ft. Lauderdale, Fla., 1982—; mem. traffic ct. rev. com. Fla. Supreme Ct., Tallahassee, 1980-89. Mem. law rev. U. Fla. Law Sch., 1975. Pres. Broward County Citizens Safety Coun., Inc., Ft. Lauderdale, Fla., 1981-83; mem. planning and zoning bd. City of Deerfield Beach, Fla., 1979-81. Carswell scholar Wake Forest U., 1968-72. Mem. Broward County Bar Assn. (sec., treas., exec. com. young lawyers sect. 1980-84), Kiwanis (pres. Ft. Lauderdale southside club 1994-95). Office: Heidgerd Martin & Bennis PA 800 SE 3rd Ave Ste 300 Fort Lauderdale FL 33316-1152

HEIDISH, LOUISE ORIDGE-SCHWALLIE, transportation specialist, marketing professional; b. Cin., May 21, 1938; d. Leslie Jacob and Louise (Oridge) Schwallie; m. William Edward Heidish, Sept. 2, 1961; children: Sara Louise, Amy Jean. BA in History, Denison U., 1960; MA in History, Miami U., Oxford, Ohio, 1962; MS in Urban Studies, Ala. A&M U., 1994. Secondary tchr. Fox Chapel Sch. Dist., Pitts., 1962-69; part-time instr. U. Ala., Huntsville, 1976-78; substitute history tchr. City of Huntsville Schs., 1977-79; dir. comm. svcs. Heidish Enterprises, Huntsville, 1979-83; transp. specialist City of Huntsville, 1981—; regional 5 state coord. AAUW and NEH, Huntsville, 1981-83. Author: Biography: Alexander Long 1816-86, 1962, Marketing Ride Sharing, 1994. Mem., project chair Huntsville Symphony Orch. Guild, 1974—; bd. dirs. Huntsville-Madison County Sr. Ctr., 1980-86, sec. 1981, v.p. 1982, pres. 1983; bd. dirs. Huntsville High Sch. PTA, 1983-88, v.p. 1985-86, pres. 1986-88; com. chmn. Panoply of the Arts Festival, Huntsville, 1985-87. Mem. AAUW (local pres. 1979-81, state v.p. 1981-83, regional coord. 1981-83), Pub. Rels. Coun. No. Ala. (newsletter editor 1993, conf. treas. 1994, coun. treas. 1995, coun. sec. 1996), S.E. Assn. for Commuter Transp. (regional conf. chair 1995, chpt. treas. 1996), Kappa Kappa Gamma (alumnae officer, local pres., regional officer 1958—). Presbyterian. Office: Pub Transp City Huntsville 100 Church St SW Huntsville AL 35801-4908

HEIDLER, CECILE E., public health nurse; b. Cleve.; d. James Joseph and Anna (Novak) H. Diploma, Mercy Coll., Detroit, 1944; BSN, Western Res. U., 1951; MSN, Wayne U., 1955; MPH, U. Mich., 1961. RN, Fla., Ohio. Dir. nursing Maria Manor Health Care, St. Petersburg, Fla.; coll. nurse, instr., counselor St. John Coll., Cleve.; staff instr., supr. Div. Health City of Cleve.; staff nurse Little Sisters of the Poor, Cleve.; ret.; prefect, lay consultor Secular Franciscan Order. Bd. dirs., mem. coms. ARC; mem. Five Towns Women's Club, Gt. Lakes Club, Choristers, Sr. Care and Seniority orgns.; hospice vol. Fed. Nurse Traineeship U. Mich. Mem. Am. Assn. Ret. Persons, Ohio Nurses Assn. (Greater Cleve. dist.), Cleve. Diocesan Coun. Cath. Nurses (pres.), Wayne State U. Nurse Scholars Soc., Holy Cross Cath. Women's Club.

HEIDT, JOHN HARRISON, priest; b. Madison, Wisc., Apr. 5, 1932; s. George Homer Heidt and Lilliam Frances Couchman; m. Katherine J. Preston, Aug. 1, 1964; children: Michael, Elizabeth, Christopher, Katherine Marie, Teresa. AB, Yale U., 1954; BD, Nashotah Seminary, 1957, MDiv, 1963; BLitt, Oxford U., 1967, PhD, 1975. Curate Christ Episcopal Ch., New Haven, Conn., 1957-59; rector St. Mary's Episcopal Ch., Pitts., 1959-61, St. Barnabas Episcopal Ch., Denton, Tex., 1961-64; asst. chaplain Keble Coll., Oxford, England, 1964-67; chaplain U. Wisc., Milw., 1967-70; instr. theology Marquette U., Milw., 1970-72; editor Christian World Newspaper, Oxford, 1978-80; vicar SS Philip & James C of E, Cheltemham, England, 1980-96; rector Christ Ch., Dallas, 1996—; com. chmn. Am. Ch. Union, N.Y., 1959-72; exec. Ch. Union, London, 1972-85, Cost of Conscience, London, 1990-96; oblate Alton Abbey, 1991—; coun. chmn. Diocese Forward in Faith, Gloucester, U.K., 1993-96; del. Am. Anglican Congress, 1996; lectr. Anglican Sch. of Theology, 1996. Author: Believe It or Not, 1993; editor: (weekly newspaper) Christian World, 1979-80; co-editor: (periodical) Church Theological Rev., 1969-72; contbr. articles to profl. jours. Councilor Up Hatherley Coun., England, 1990-93; mem. Assn. for Treatment of Young Offenders, England, 1985-95; chmn. Manhattan Trust for Young People at Risk, England, 1991-93; trustee Canterbury Episcopal Sch., 1996, Anglican Sch. Theology, 1996—. Mem. Soc. of the Holy Cross. Episcopalian. Home: 204 Rosemont Ave Dallas TX 75208 Office: Christ Episcopal Ch 534 W 10th St Dallas TX 75208

HEIENS, RICHARD ALLEN, education foundation executive; b. Alton, Ill., Aug. 6, 1940; s. Richard Alvin Heiens and Dorthey Verleen (Johnson) Depew; m. Gabriella Maria Sau, July 20, 1963; children: Marina, Deborah, Richard, Michael. BBA, Washington U., 1974; PhD, Kennedy-Western U., 1990. Social worker ARC, Republic of Vietnam, 1968-69, Munich, German Democratic Republic, 1969-70; internal auditor ARC, St. Louis, 1970-74; bus. mgr. ARC, Miami, 1974-76, asst. div. mgr., 1976-78, dep. mgr., 1978-82, exec. dir., 1982-85; exec. dir. Archdiocese Edn. Found., Miami, 1985-87, Our Lady of Lourdes Acad. Found., Miami, 1987—; pres. South Fla. Crack Ctrs., Inc., Miami, 1986—. Decorated Cross of Gallantry (Vietnam); recipient U.S. Civilian Service in Vietnam medal, 1969. Mem. Nat. Soc. Fund Raising Execs. (cert.). Republican. Roman Catholic. Lodge: Rotary (Miami). Office: Lourdes Acad Found 5525 SW 84th St Miami FL 33143-8322

HEIFETZ, CARL LOUIS, microbiologist; b. Somerville, N.J., Mar. 9, 1935; s. Samuel and Frances Mildred (Potter) H.; m. Sandra Feld, June 28, 1959; children: Jodee Beth, Terry Jay. BS, U. Md., 1957, MS, 1960, PhD, 1964. Registered pharmacist Bd. Pharmacy, Md., 1958. Assoc. rsch. bacteriologist Parke-Davis Pharm. Rsch., Detroit, 1964-68; rsch. microbiologist Parke-Davis Pharm. Rsch., 1968-70, rsch. scientist, 1970-76, rsch. assoc., 1976-78, sr. rsch. assoc., 1978-83; sect. dir. Parke-Davis Pharm. Rsch., Ann Arbor, Mich., 1983-90; dir. infectious diseases Parke-Davis Pharm. Rsch., 1990-92; pres. Micro Doc Cons., Inc., Palm Harbor, Fla., 1992—; clin. prof. med. microbiology and immunology U. South Fla. Med. Sch., 1992—; clin. prof. assoc. health Ea. Mich. U., Ypsilanti, 1986—, adj. prof. biology, 1986—. Editor: New Generation of Quinolones, 1990, Diagnostic Microbiology and Infectious Diseases, 1989-94; contbr. articles to profl. jours.; inventor, patentee in field. Pres. Evergreen Trails Homeowners Assn., Southfield, Mich., 1978; Rep. precinct del., Mich., 1978-80. Fellow Am. Acad. Microbiology; mem. Am. Soc. Microbiology (pres. Mich. br. 1986-87, chmn. div. A 1990-91, councilor 1990-92, alt. 1988-90, councilor Fla. br. 1994—), Brit. Soc. Antimicrobial Chemotherapy, Inter-Am. Soc. Chemotherapy, Sigma Xi, Rho Chi. Republican. Jewish. Office: Micro Doc Cons Inc 5490 Salem Square Dr S Palm Harbor FL 34685-1138

HEIL, HOLLY ANN, public relations practitioner, consultant; b. West Palm Beach, Fla., Nov. 30, 1967; d. Robert John and Phyllis Ann (Duerr) H. BS in Pub. Rels., U. Fla., Gainesville, 1994. Pub. rels., media liaison U.S. Water Polo, Ft. Lauderdale, Fla., 1994—; pub. rels. dir., media comms. Internat. Swimming Hall of Fame, 1994—; media liaison Atlanta Olympic Games for Atlanta Com., 1996. editor, designer, reporter (newsletter) Internat. Swimming Hall of Fame Headlines, 1994—.

HEIL, MARY RUTH, former counselor; b. Westerville, Ohio, June 8, 1921; d. George Walter and Bertha Ellen (Shrodes) H. BS in Edn., Ohio State U., 1944; MEd, Wayne State U., 1956; cert. advanced study, Western Carolina U., 1987; cert. theol. edn., U. South, 1987. Cert. counselor, tchr., Ohio, Ky., Mich., Fla., N.C. Tchr. 7th grade Cheshire (Ohio) Sch., 1942-43; tchr. biology, English Ohio Soldiers' and Sailors' Orphans' Home, Xenia, 1943-47; tchr. 7th grade Lakeview High Schs., Winter Garden, Fla., 1947-48; tchr. English, journalism Pine Mountain (Ky.) Settlement Sch., 1948-49; field and established camp dir. Columbus (Ohio) and Franklin County Girl Scouts, 1949-50; tchr. Mary Lyon Jr. High Sch., Royal Oak, Mich., 1950-56, 57-62, Coston Secondary Modern Girls' Sch., Greenford, Middlesex, Eng., 1956-57; tchr. English West Henderson High Sch., Hendersonville, N.C., 1962-65, guidance counselor, 1965-86. Chmn. Mayor's Com. Employment of Handicapped, Hendersonville, 1972-74; v.p. Mountain Ramparts Health Planning Bd., Asheville, N.C., 1972-76, Western Carolina Health Systems Agy. Bd., Morganton, N.C., 1976-82; bd. dirs., sec., com. chmn., Henderson County Disput Settlement Bd., 1989-95; exec. com., bd. dirs. Western Carolina Presbyn. Retirement Com., 1987-94; active Henderson County Coun. Women, Hendersonville, 1994-96, treas.; mem.-at-large Pisgah coun. Girl Scouts U.S., 1994—, chair 1995—. Named Civitan Citizen of Yr. Civitan Club, Hendersonville, 1986, Woman of Achievement Hendersonville, Bus. and Profl. Women's Club, 1978; recipient award Galludent U., Washington, 1986; named to Hon., Order Ky. Cols., 1988. Mem. NEA, ACA, Royal Oak Edn. Assn. (pres. 1954-56), N.C. Assn. Educators (pres. dist. 1970-72), Henderson County Mental Health Assn. (bd. dirs. 1965-74), Alpha Delta Kappa (N.C. 1st v.p. 1978-80, state pres. 1980-82, S.E. region grand v.p. 1987-89). Democrat. Episcopalian. Home: RR 6 Box 137 Hendersonville NC 28792-9428

HEILIG, TERRY LEN, economic development executive; b. Council Bluffs, Iowa, Feb. 15, 1947; s. Donald G. and Vera Ruth (Buck) H.; m. Claire Kay Knudsen, June 2, 1968; children: Amy Jo, Christopher Scott. BS, Iowa State U., 1969. Zone mgr. Ford Motor Co., Omaha, 1972-79; pres. Terry Ford Lincoln/Mercury, Inc., Perry, Iowa, 1979-87; tech. trans. dir. Rural Enterprises, Inc., Durant, Okla., 1987-89; exec. dir. McAlester (Okla.) Econ. Devel. Svc., 1989—; mem. Gov.'s Indsl. Team, Oklahoma City, 1990—; bd. mem. adv. com. Kiamichi Area Vocat. Tech. Sch., 1990—; pres. S.E. Okla. Econ. Devel. Assn., Planning and Avc. Com., 1989—, Ea. Okla. State Coll., 1990—, Rural Devel. Program, 1990—; team. mem. Govs. Econs. Devel., 1990—; apptd. vice-chmn. Okla. Film Adv. Bd., 1992—; pres. Okla. Econ. Devel. Coun., 1994. Mem. Elks, Perry, 1981, Kiwanis, Perry, 1981. Sgt. USNG, 1970-78. Recipient Disting. Svc. citation Ford Motor Co., Dearborn, Mich., 1983, 1st Pl. Radio Addy award Advt. Profls. of Des Moines, 1986, Sec. of Commerce salutation State of Okla., Oklahoma City, 1990. Mem. Nat. Bus. Incubator Assn. (sec. 1990—), Okla. Bus. Incubator Assn. (pres. 1990-91), Okla. City Econ. Roundtable, Southeastern Okla. Econ. Devel. Assn. (bd. mem. 1989—, pres.). Lutheran. Home: RR 5 Box 207 Eufaula OK 74432-9138 Office: McAlester Econ Devel Svcs 100 S Main St Mcalester OK 74501-5364

HEILKER, PAUL, English language educator; b. Bethpage, N.Y., Aug. 20, 1962; s. Vincent dePaul and Mary Catherine (Wood) H.; Aileen Murphy, May 27, 1989; 1 child, Elijah Aaron. BA in English, SUNY, Stony Brook, 1985; MA in English, Colo. State U., 1988; PhD in Rhetoric and Composition, Tex. Christian U., 1992. Asst. prof. English Loyola U., Chgo., 1992-94; asst. prof. English Va. Tech., Blacksburg, 1994—, dir. writing program, 1994—; Textbook reviewer Allyn & Bacon, Harbrace, St. Martin's Press, Prentice-Hall, Houghton-Mifflin, 1995—. Author: The Essay: Theory and Pedagogy, 1996; co-author, co-editor: Keywords in Composition Studies, 1996; contbr. articles to profl. jours. Mem. parish coun. St. Jude's Roman Catholic Ch., Christiansburg, Va., 1996. Mem. MLA, South Atlantic MLA, Nat. Coun. of Tchrs. of English, Conf. on Coll. Composition and Communication. Democrat. Roman Catholic. Office: Va Tech English Dept Blacksburg VA 24061

HEILMAN, E. BRUCE, academic administrator; b. La Grange, Ky., July 16, 1926; s. Earl Bernard and Nellie (Sanders) H.; m. Betty June Dobbins, Aug. 27, 1948; children—Bobbie Lynn, Nancy Jo, Terry Lee, Sandra June, Timothy Bruce. BS, Vanderbilt U., 1950, MA, 1951; PhD, Peabody Coll., 1961; postgrad., U. Tenn., U. Omaha, U. Ky.; LLD (hon.), Wake Forest U., 1967, Ky. Wesleyan Coll., 1980, James Madison U., 1986, U. Richmond, 1986; DHum. (hon.), Campbell Coll., 1971; LLD; LHD (hon.), Bridgewater Coll., 1991; DHL, DPS, Campbellsville Coll., 1995. Instr. bus. Peabody Coll., Vanderbilt U., 1950-51, bursar, 1957-60, adminstrv. v.p., 1963-66; instr. accounting Belmont Coll., Nashville, 1951-52; auditor Albert Maloney Co., Nashville, 1951-52; asst. prof. accounting, bus. mgr. Ky. Wesleyan Coll., 1952-54; treas. Georgetown (Ky.) Coll., 1954-57, Georgetown (Ky.) Coll. (Louisville Housing Project), 1954-57; coordinator higher edn. and spl. schs. Tenn., 1960-61; v.p., dean Ky. So. Coll., Louisville, 1961-63; prof. ednl. adminstrn. Peabody Coll. Vanderbilt U., Nashville, 1963-66; pres. Meredith Coll., Raleigh, N.C., 1966-71; pres. U. Richmond, Va., 1971-86, chancellor, 1986—, chancellor, interim chief exec. officer, 1987-88; bd. dirs. Cooperating Raleigh Colls., 1967-71; cons. indsl. studies in edn. and adminstrn., 1954—; dir., cons. long range planning confs. Fund Advancement Edn., 1960—; cons. acad. Ednl. Study Task, 1964-65; mem. Wake County-Raleigh City Sh. Merger Study Com., 1969; adv. com. N.C. Dept. Pub. Instrn., 1970; bd. dirs. Fidelity Bankers Life Ins. Co., A.H. Robins Co., Richmond, Ctrl. Fidelity Bank, Fidelity Fed. Savs. Bank, Bapt. Theol. Sem., Richmond; mem. adv. bd. Sta. WLEE Radio-TV; chmn. Cardinal Savs. and Loan Assn., Fast Fox, Inc., Office Am., Richmond, Direct Med. Inc., Cordell Med., Va. Escrow & Title co. The Phoenix Corp.; trustee, chmn. bd. advisors, mem. exec. com., devel. coms. Campbellsville (Ky.) Coll; instnl. cons. adv. bd. Paine Webber, Inc. Author: (with others) Sixty College Study, 1954; also booklets and articles. Chmn. blood com. for edn. ARC, 1971; mem. Nashville Urban Renewal Coordinating Com., 1965-66; ann. giving chmn. for N.C. Peabody Coll. Vanderbilt, U., 1970-72; mem. Friends of HOME, 1974—; chmn. trustee orientation com. N.C. Bapt. Conv., 1961; mem. edn. commn. So. Bapt. Conv.; mem. bd. advisors Bapt. Hosp. Sch. Nursing, Nashville, 1956-60, 64—; mem. com. Met. Gen. Hosp. Sch. Nursing, 1965-68; mem. Federated Arts Coun. Richmond, 1975—, Robert Lee coun. Boy Scouts Am., 1975—; mem. devel. adv. bd. Va. Ctr. Performing Arts, 1980; bd. dirs. Bill Wilkerson Speech and Hearing Ctr., Nashville, 1963-64, Bapt. Theology Sem., Richmond, 1964, N.C. Symphony, United Fund Wake County, 1968-71, N.C. Mental Health Assn., 1969-71, Wake County Mental Health Assn., 1969-71, Va. Thanksgiving Festival, 1972, Richmond Pub. Libr., Richmond chpt. NCCJ, Ba. Inst. Sci. Rsch., 1971—, Leadership Metro Richmond, 1980—; hon. dir. Richmond Ballet, 1971; bd. govts. United Givers Fund Richmond, 1971; trustee Inst. Mediterranean Studies, 1972—, E.R. Patterson Ednl. Found., 1972—, U. Richmond, 1973-86; bd. govs. Marine Corps. Assn., 1990; pres. Marine Mil. Acad., 1964, exec. v.p. bd., 1979—, chmn. bd. trustees, 1994, pres. bd. trustees, 1994—, bd. dirs. USMC Def. Bat., Chairman, Marine Corps. U. bd. of trustees, Quantico, Va., Nat. Def. Univ. Found., So. Sem. Found., Bapt. Theol. Sem., Richmond, Va.; mem. adv. bd., chmn. devel. com., bd. dirs. Marine Hist. Found.. Served with USMCR, 1944-47. Recipient award Owensboro (Ky.) Jr. C. of C., 1953; Agrl. and Industry Service award U. Nashville, 1961; Outstanding Civic and Ednl. award Raleigh, 1970; Distinguished Salesman award Richmond, 1972, Disting. Alumni award Campbellsville Coll. and Peabody Coll. Vanderbilt U., Distinguished Citizen of Oldham County (Ky.) award, Va. Assn. Future Farmers Am. award, 1976, Disting. Citizen award Meredith Coll., 1977; named Ky. Col., 1969; Paul Harris Rotary fellow, 1970; Reverse Exchange Eisenhower fellow to Peoples Rep. of China, 1987; named Hon. Pres. Sino-Am. Cultural Soc., 1988. Mem. Internat. Assn. Univ. Pres.'s (N. Am. council 1976—), Nat. Fedn. Bus. Officers, Nat. Fedn. Bus. Officers Cons. Service, So. Assn. Colls. Women (pres. 1969), Nat. Soc. Lit. and the Arts, So. Univ. Conf., Sino Am. Soc. (hon. pres.), Am. Council Edn., Tenn. Edn. Assn., Ky. Ednl. Buyers Assn., Am. Assn. Pres.'s Ind. Colls. and Univs., Ky. Assn. Acad. Deans, Peabody Alumni Assn. Vanderbilt U. (exec. com), Nat., So. assns. coll. and univ. bus. officers, Assn. Governing Bds. Univs. and Colls., Coll. and Univ. Personnel Assn., Internat. Platform Assn., Nashville, Raleigh, Richmond, Va. chambers commerce, Nat. Assn. Ind. Colls. and Univs., Navy League U.S., Marine Corps League, Council Ind. Colls. in Va. (pres. 1974-76), Va. Found. Ind. Colls., Assn. Va. Colls., Assn. So. Bapt. Colls. and Schs. (pres. 1976), N.C. Found. Ch.-Related Colls., Assn. Am. Colls., So. Assn. Colls. and Schs. (trustee 1977), Phi Beta Kappa, Pi Omega Pi, Kappa Phi Kappa, Kappa Delta Pi, Delta Pi Epsilon, Omicron Delta Kappa, Beta Gamma Sigma, Lambda Chi Alpha (Achiever award 1993), Va. Bapt. Hist. Soc., English-Speaking Union, Newcomen Soc. N. Am. Democrat. Baptist (deacon). Clubs: Rotary (Raleigh) (bd. advisers Raleigh 1966-71), Execs. (Raleigh) (v.p., dir. 1971), City (Raleigh); Downtown (Richmond); The Club, Forum. Home: 4700 Cary Street Rd Richmond VA 23226-1703 Office: President's Office University of Richmond Richmond VA 23173*

HEIM, CHARLES WILLIAM, JR., fund raising executive; b. New Orleans, Dec. 31, 1941; s. Charles William Sr. and Leona Mary (O'Dowd) H.; m. Barbara Cohen; children: Laura F., Michael C., Mark B. BS, U. So. Miss., 1965; MEd, Loyola U., 1969. Cert. tchr. social studies, Miss. Tchr., coach Lakewood Sch., New Orleans, 1965-73; dir. alumni/devel./pub. rels. Tulane U., New Orleans, 1973-75, dir. planned gifts program, 1975-77; asst. to exec. dir., dir. devel. Ohio Valley Med. Ctr., Wheeling, W.Va., 1977-80; dir. devel. Alton Ochsner Med. Found., New Orleans, 1981-85, v.p., dir. divsn. devel., 1985—; advisor Girl Scout Coun. S.E. La., St. Paul's Sch., Covington, La., Dominican H.S., New Orleans, Comty. Arts Ctr., New Orleans, Cath. Found., New Orleans, Archdiocese of New Orleans, others. Mem. editl. adv. bd. City Bus. Cubmaster pack 183 Boy Scouts Am.; bd. dirs. Isidore Newman Sch. Dad's Club, Mt. de Chantal Visitation Acad., Wheeling, W.Va., Wheeling Symphony Soc.; mem. parent ann. giving campaign Jesuit H.S., mem. pres.'s adv. coun.; bd. trustees U. So. Miss. Found.; vol. Leadership Tng. Ctr.; mem. adv. com. Wheeling Country Day Sch. Recipient ECHO award for direct mail excellence Direct Mktg. Assn., 1983. Fellow Assn. for Healthcare Philanthropy (chair nat. conf. 1985, regional dir. del. 1986, chmn. 1989, mem. exec. com. 1987-90, dean devel. primer 1992-94, mem. ednl. found. bd. 1992-95, chmn. ednl. found. bd. 1993, 94, Harold J. Seymour award 1992); mem. Nat. Soc. Fundraising Execs. (bd. dirs. La. chpt. 1983-87, pres. La. chpt. 1985, nat. bd. dirs. 1984-85, Outstanding Fundraising Exec. La. chpt. 1986), Assn. Am. Med. Colls., New Orleans Sports Found., Jesuit High Sch. New Orleans Alumni Assn., U. So. Miss. Alumni Assn., The Touchdown Club (pres. 1993-94, New Orleans), Plimsoll Club (New Orleans). Roman Catholic. Office: Alton Ochsner Med Found 3850 N Causeway Blvd Ste 1860 Metairie LA 70002-1752

HEIMBERG, MURRAY, pharmacologist, biochemist, physician, educator; b. Bklyn., Jan. 5, 1925; s. Gustav and Fannie (Geller) H.; children by previous marriage: Richard G., Steven A.; m. Anna Frances Langlois Knox, July 12, 1964; stepchildren: Larry M. Knox, David S. Knox. BS, Cornell U., Ithaca, N.Y., 1948, MNS, 1949; PhD in Biochemistry (NIH fellow), Duke, 1952; MD, Vanderbilt U., 1959. NIH Postdoctoral fellow in biochemistry Med. Sch. Washington U., St. Louis, 1952-54; research asso. physiology Med. Sch. Vanderbilt U., 1954-59, asst. prof. to prof. pharmacology, and asst. prof. medicine, 1959-74; prof., chmn. dept. pharmacology, prof. medicine U. Mo., 1974-81; prof. and chmn. dept. pharmacology, prof. medicine, endocrinology and metabolism U. Tenn., Health Sci. Ctr., Memphis, 1981-96; Van Vleet prof. pharmacology U. Tenn., Memphis, 1986-96; Disting. prof. pharmacology and medicine U. Tenn., 1996—; Cons. NSF, NIH; cons., established investigator Am. Heart Assn.; attending physician U. Tenn. Hosps.; dir. lipid metabolism clinic U. Tenn. Med. Group. Contbr. numerous articles to profl. jours. Served with inf., AUS, 1943-45, ETO. Decorated Purple Heart, Bronze Star; recipient Lederle Med. Faculty award; research grantee. Fellow AAAS; mem. Am. Soc. Biol. Chemistry and Molecular Biology, Am. Soc. Pharmacology and Exptl. Therapeutics, Endocrine Soc., Am. Heart Assn., Am. Diabetes Assn., So. Soc. Clin. Investigation. Home: 105 Devon Way Memphis TN 38111-7711 Office: U Tenn Dept of Pharmacology 115 Crowe 874 Union Ave Memphis TN 38103-3514

HEIMBINDER, ISAAC, construction company executive, lawyer; b. Bklyn., May 15, 1943; s. David and Evelyn (Brown) H.; m. Sheila Marie Mooney, Aug. 3, 1970; children: Susan, Daniel, Erin, Michael. BS in Bus., Am. U., 1965; JD, NYU, 1968. Atty. Debevoise and Plimpton, N.Y.C., 1969-72; corp. counsel U.S. Home Corp., Clearwater, Fla., 1973-77; v.p. legal affairs U.S. Home Corp., Houston, 1977-79, chief fin. officer, 1979-86, pres. chief operating officer, 1986—. Mem. N.Y. Bar Assn., Fla. Bar Assn., Tex. Bar Assn., Urban Land Inst., Order of Coif, Omicron Delta Kappa. Home: 2 Glendenning Dr Houston TX 77024-6827 Office: US Home Corp 1800 West Loop S Houston TX 77027-3210

HEIMBOLD, MARGARET BYRNE, publisher, educator, consultant; b. Tullamore, Ireland, June 24; came to U.S., 1966, naturalized, 1973; d. John Christopher and Anne (Troy) Byrne; m. Arthur Heimbold, Feb. 26, 1984; 1 child, Eric Thomas Gordon. BA, Queens Coll. Recipient cert. Dale Carnegie, 1977, Psychol. Corp. Am., 1981, Wharton Sch., 1983, Stanford U., 1989. Group advt. mgr. N.Y. Times, N.Y.C., 1978-85; pub. Am. Film, Washington, 1985-86, v.p., pub. Nat. Trust for Hist. Preservation, Washington, 1986-90; pres. Summerville Press, Inc., Washington, 1990—; pub. Metro Golf, 1992—; advisor Mag. Pubs. Bd. dirs. Anchor Ctrs. Ireland; bd. trustees Nat. Mus. Women in Arts. Mem. NAFE, Am. Soc. Assn. Execs., Women's Econ. Alliance, Soc. Nat. Assn. Publs. (chmn. editl. com., bd. dirs.), D.C. Preservation League. Avocations: golf, writing, volunteering.

HEIMBUCH, JOSEPH WILLIAM, marketing educator; b. Teaneck, N.J., Mar. 13, 1931; s. Joseph William and Helen Ann (Spiza) H.; m. Margaret Ellen Boulton, Oct. 17, 1956 (div. Nov. 1979); children: Elaine Margaret, Virginia Louise, Elizabeth Ann. BS in Engring., U.S. Mcht. Marine Acad., 1952; MBA, Duquesne U., 1960; PhD, Fla. Internat. U., 1995. Sr. mktg. cons. Westinghouse Electric Corp., Pitts., 1952-61; ind. bus. unit mgr. IBM Corp., Bethesda, Md., 1961-65; chief oper. officer Tracor Marine, Miami, Fla., 1965-68; sr. staff advisor Racal/Milgo, Miami, 1968-83; dir. spl. projects Mylex Corp., Miami, 1983-86; vol. Peace Corps, Honduras, 1986-88; lectr. mktg. Fla. Internat. U., Miami, 1989-93; asst. prof. mktg. Fla. Meml. Coll., Miami, 1993—. Co-editor: Seafood Marketing Manual, 1988. Lt. USN, 1953-55. Fellow Acad. Mktg. Sci.; mem. Am. Mktg. Assn. Home and Office: 7256 Jacaranda Ln Hialeah FL 33014

HEIN, JERRY MARVIN, paper coating scientist, consultant, chemist; b. Appleton, Wis., May 14, 1933; s. Martin Richard and Helen (Tennie) H.; m. Mary Ann Kaeser, Aug. 30, 1958; children: Jeffrey M., Gregory M., Christopher M., Julie M. BS in Chemistry, U. Wis., 1960. Chemist Inst. of Paper Chemistry, Appleton, 1959-61, Stein-Hall, Inc., N.Y.C., 1961-63, Nat. Cash Register, Dayton, Ohio, 1963-65; sr. chemist Potlatch Corp., Cloquet, Minn., 1965-80; sr. scientist Dry Branch (Ga.) Kaolin Co., 1980—; cons. Jerry Hein Cons. Svc., Appleton, 1983—; instr. U. Minn.-St. Paul, spring 1985. Patentee in field. Vice chmn. County Young Reps., Appleton, 1959; facilitator Welsch Ctr., Duluth, Minn., 1973-78; deliverer Meals-on-Wheels, ARC, Appleton, 1990-91. Mem. Tech. Assn. of the Pulp and Paper Industry (div. chmn. 1991-92, Plaque 1992, reviewer mag. 1982-83, seminar instr. 1984-87, past chmn. coating binders com., past chmn. coating basestock com., coating conf. chmn. 1989). Home: 1507 Lorain Ct Appleton WI 54914-3356 Office: Dry Branch Kaolin Co RR 1 Box 468D Dry Branch GA 31020-9799

HEINDL, PHARES MATTHEWS, lawyer; b. Meridian, Miss., Dec. 14, 1949; s. Paul A. and Leila (Matthews) H.; m. Linda Ann Williamson, Sept. 21, 1985; children: Lori Elizabeth, Jesse Phares, Jared Matthews. BS in Chem. Engring., Miss. State U., 1972; JD, U. Fla., 1981. Bar: Fla. 1981, Calif. 1982, U.S. Dist. Ct. (cen. dist.) Calif. 1983, U.S. Dist. Ct. (mid. dist.) Fla. 1983; bd. cert. civil trial lawyer Fla. Bar. Assoc. Lafollette, Johnson et al, L.A., 1982-83, Sam E. Murrell & Sons, Orlando, Fla., 1983-84; pvt. practice Orlando, Fla., 1984-93, Altamonte Springs, Fla., 1993—; bd. cert. civil trial lawyer. Precinct coord. Freedom Coun., Orlando, 1986. Mem. Fla. Bar Assn., Calif. Bar Assn., Seminole County Bar Assn., ATLA, Christian Legal Soc. (past pres. Ctrl. Fla.), Fla. Acad. Trial Lawyers, Workers Compensation Rules Com. Republican. Mem. Assembly of God Ch. Home: 2415 River Tree Cir Sanford FL 32771 Office: 222 S Westmonte Dr Ste 208 Altamonte Springs FL 32714-4269

HEINEMAN, FREDERICK K. (FRED HEINEMAN), congressman; b. New York, N.Y., Dec. 28, 1929; m. Linda Heineman; 6 children. BBA in Mgmt., St. Francis Coll., 1970; M in Criminal Justice, John Jay Coll., 1975. From patrolman to dep. chief insp. N.Y.C. Police Dept., 1955-79; chief of police City of Raleigh, N.C., 1979-94; mem. 104th Congress from 4th N.C. dist., 1995—; mem. jud. and banking coms. Active Triangle Challenge in Support of DARE, Wake County Child Protection Team, North Carolinians Against Race and Religious Violence. With USMC, 1951-54. Mem. Nat. Exec. Inst., N.C. Assn. Chiefs of Police, N.C. Police Execs. Assn., Internat. Assn. Chiefs of Police. Office: US House Reps 1440 Longworth Washington DC 20515-3304

HEINICKE, RALPH MARTIN, biotechnology company executive; b. Hickory, N.C., Sept. 3, 1914; s. Martin John and Lydia Sophia (Kurth) H.; m. Sarah Anne Hall, July 31, 1944; 1 child, Mark. BS, Cornell U., 1936; PhD, U. Minn., St. Paul, 1950. Agr. chemist Shell Oil Co., N.Y.C., 1939-43; tech. advisor Jintan-Dolph, Osaka, Japan, 1962-86; assoc. faculty U. Hawaii, Honolulu, 1950-86; chemist Pineapple Rsch. Inst., Honolulu, 1950-55; dir. rsch. Dole Co., Honolulu, 1955-72; v.p. Biol. Control Systems, Honolulu, 1981-86; pres. Biotech. Resources Inc., Clarksville, Ind., 1990-94; cons. various drug cos., 1972—. Inventor, patentee on xeronine; inventor, patentee (pending) on cytoline. Master sgt. U.S. Army, 1942-45, CBI. Democrat. Home and Office: Biotechnology Resources Inc. 1124 Rostrevor Cir Louisville KY 40205-1742

HEINRICH, RANDALL WAYNE, lawyer, investment banker; b. Houston, Nov. 29, 1958; s. Albert Joseph Sr. and Beverly June Earles; m. Linda Carol Cheek, June 6, 1993; 1 child, Angela Leigh. BA, Baylor U., 1980, postgrad., 1981; postgrad., Rice U., 1981-82; JD, U. Tex., 1985. Bar: Tex. 1985. Assoc. Baker & Botts, Houston, 1985-87, Chamberlain, Hrdlicka, White, Williams & Martin, Houston, 1987-91, Norton & Blair, Houston, 1991-92; of counsel Gillis & Slogar, Houston, 1992—; mng. dir. Baytree Investors, Houston, 1993—. Mem. dirs.' circle Houston Grand Opera, 1991, The Arts Symposium, 1991, Center Stage, Alley Theater, Houston, 1992—, Houston Entrepreneurs' Forum, 1990—; bd. dirs. The Cadre, 1991-92; pres. Exchange Club of Bayou City, 1992-93. Mem. ABA (YLD securities law com. 1993—, vice chmn. 1994-95), NASD Pool Securities Arbitrators, Am. Arbitration Assn. (mem. nat. panel neutrals), Houston Bar Assn., Forum Club Houston, Phi Delta Theta. Republican. Baptist. Home: 2614 Fairway Dr Sugar Land TX 77478-4017 Office: Gillis & Slogar 1000 Louisiana St Ste 6905 Houston TX 77002-5014

HEINS, MARY FRANCES, educational administrator, nun; b. Galveston, Tex., Nov. 12, 1927; d. George and Rosella (Eckenfels) H. BA, Dominican Coll., 1954; MEd, Lamar U., 1973. Joined Dominican Sisters, Roman Cath. Ch., 1946. Tchr. parochial schs. Tex. and Calif., 1948-68; tchr., head sci. dept., asst. prin. Kelly High Sch., Beaumont, Tex., 1968-80; co-prin., then prin. St. Pius X High Sch., Houston, 1980-84; tchr., adminstrv. asst., computer coord., sci. fair coord. Galveston Cath. Sch., 1986-89; tchr., head sci. dept. O'Connell Jr. High Sch., Galveston, 1984-86; prin. O'Connell High Sch., Galveston, 1989—; mem. Goals for Beaumont Edn. task force Beaumont C. of C., 1979-80. Mem. interfaith com. Galveston Hist. Found., 1990; mem. ch. involvement com. City-wide Conf. on Youth Violence. Recipient O'Connell Booster of Yr. award, 1995-96. Mem. Nat. Cath. Edn. Assn., Lamar U. Alumni Assn., World Future Soc., Sci. Tchrs. Assn. Tex. (Outstanding Tchr. 1980), Galveston C. of C. (edn. com. 1990-91), Galveston Garden Club (2d v.p.), Delta Kappa Gamma (chpt. achievement award 1990, pres. 1988-90). Democrat. Roman Catholic. Home: 2210 Avenue M Galveston TX 77550-4730 Office: O'Connell High Sch 1320 Tremont St Galveston TX 77550-4513

HEINZ, DOLLIE WOOLEY, secondary education educator; b. New Orleans, Apr. 20, 1940; d. Howard Francis Sr. and Odalie Stephanie (Mire) Wooley; m. Gregory Scott Heinz, Feb. 10, 1973 (div. 1994); children: Howard Jack, Eric Tyson. BS, St. Mary's Dominican Coll., 1964; MST, Loyola U., New Orleans, 1976, postgrad., 1985. Tchr. Rosaryville High Sch. Jr. Coll., Ponchatoula, La., 1963-64, St. Agnes, Baton Rouge, 1964-66, Holy Ghost, Hammond, La., 1966-68, Rosaryville Jr. Coll., Ponchatoula, La., 1966-68, Ridgewood Preparatory Schs., Metairie, La., 1968-70, East Jefferson High Sch., Metairie, 1970-78, Mandeville (La.) High Sch., 1978-82; tchr. math. Covington (La.) High Sch., 1982—, head math. dept., 1988—; judge state sci. fair La. State U., Baton Rouge, 1990. Pres. Covington Kaycettes, 1980-84, 88-89; state liaison dist. officer La. Kaycee Aux., Inc., 1984-85. Named Family of Yr., KC, Covington, 1981, 92, Sister of Yr., Covington Kaycettes, 1984-85; grantee NSF, 1970-75, QSM, 1994, SLU, 1994-95, AMT, 1995. Mem. Nat. Coun. Tchrs. Math., La. Assn. Tchrs. Math., Greater New Orleans Tchrs. Math., Baton Rouge Area Coun. Tchrs. Math. Republican. Roman Catholic. Office: Covington High Sch 73030 Lion Dr Covington LA 70433-0934

HEINZ, TONI SUE, irrigation company executive; b. Elizabeth, N.J., Oct. 3, 1951; d. William Ralph LaPorte and Sarafina (DiBlasio) Jones; m. Jacob Edward Heinz, Dec. 26, 1980; 1 child, Tiffany Sara. Gen. mgr. Sunnyland Irrigation, West Palm Beach, Fla., 1980—. Contbr. poems and prayers to books and mags. Mem. Nat. Assn. Women in Constrn. Democrat. Roman Catholic. Home: 1406 Victoria Dr West Palm Beach FL 33406-5833 Office: Sunnyland Irrigation 3114 45th St Ste 7 West Palm Beach FL 33407-1945

HEINZE, MARVIN H., naval officer; b. Cheverly, Md., Sept. 10, 1957; s. Peter H. and Mary Agnes (Summers) H.; m. April M. Fenton, May 18, 1982. BS in Architecture, U. Va., 1980; MS in Mech. Engring., Naval Postgrad. Sch., Monterey, Calif., 1988. Lic. blaster, Calif. Commd. ensign U.S. Navy, 1979, advanced through grades to comdr., 1994; nuclear weapons officer, comdr. Naval Surface Force U.S. Pacific Fleet, Coronado, Calif., 1989-91; exec. officer Explosive Ordnance Disposal Mobile Unit 5, Subic Bay, Philippines, 1991-93; fleet ops. officer, comdr. 3d Fleet, Coronado, 1993-96; comdr. officer Explosive Ordnance Disposal Mobile Unit 2, Norfolk, Va., 1996—. Commr. Boy Scout Am., 1980-91. Decorated Meritorious Svc. medal, Navy Commendation medal (2), Navy Achievement medal (2), Mil. Star of Merit. Mem. Internat. Assn. Bomb Technicians and Investigators, U.S. Naval Inst. Office: EOD Mobile Unit TWO 2520 Midway Rd Norfolk VA 23521-3324

HEISER, ROLLAND VALENTINE, former army officer, foundation executive; b. Columbus, Ohio, Apr. 25, 1925; s. Rudolph and Helen Cecile H.; BS, U.S. Mil. Acad., 1947; MS in Internat. Affairs, George Washington U., 1965; m. Gwenne Kathleen Duquemin, Feb. 26, 1949; children: Helen Heiser Sanford, Charlene Heiser Wolff. Commd. 2d lt. U.S. Army, 1947, advanced through grades to lt. gen., 1976; served in Europe, Korea, Vietnam; army planner, Washington, 1973-74; comdr. 1st Armored div., Ger., 1974-75; chief of staff U.S. Army Europe, 1975-76; chief staff U.S. European Command, 1976-78; pres. New Coll. Found., Sarasota, Fla., 1979—; dir. Sun Trust Bank/Gulf Coast, Sarasota. Mem. Sarasota Com. 100. Decorated D.S.M. with oak leaf cluster, Def. Superior Service medal, Legion of Merit (3), Bronze Star, others. Mem. Ret. Officers Assn., Sarasota County C. of C. Republican. Episcopalian. Clubs: Univ., Ret. Officers of Sarasota (past pres., dir.), Masons. Home: 4104 Las Palmas Way Sarasota FL 34238-4532 Office: New Coll Found 5700 N Tamiami Trl Sarasota FL 34243-2146

HEISERMAN, RUSSELL LEE, electronics educator; b. Oklahoma City, Dec. 25, 1930; s. Mack Russell Heiserman and Helen Fay (Sills) Landon; m. Alberta Elizabeth Nardi, Aug. 17, 1956 (div. June 1990); children: Thomas Scott, Alan Steven (dec.), Mary Christa. Cert. in electronics tech., Okla. A&M U., 1954; BS in Physics, Okla. State U., 1960, MS in Physics, 1962, EdD in Tech. Edn., 1978. Cert. sr. electronics engring. technician, Nat. Inst. for Certification. Sr. R & D technician Airpax, Inc., 1954-56; electronics technician Labko Sci., Stillwater, Okla., 1956-58, 59; physicist Naval Ordnance Lab., White Oak, Md., summer 1960; rsch. assoc. dept. physics, NDEA grad. fellow Okla. State U., Stillwater, 1960-62, asst. prof., head electronics dept. Tech. Inst., 1962-66; pres. sch. divsn., v.p. Hickok Tchg. Sys., Boston, 1966-74; prof. electronics and computer tech. Okla. State U., Stillwater, 1984-90; assoc. prof. tech. dept. McNeese State U., Lake Charles, La., 1990—; mem. faculty coun. Coll. Engring., Architecture and Tech., Okla. State U., 1982-84, chmn., sec., 1983-84; pres. QTEK, Inc., 1981-90; mem. adv. coun. Seminole (Okla.) Jr. Coll., 1976-83; regional project coord. Am. Coun. Edn., Washington, 1971-91; tech. writer, ednl. product developer Interplex Electronics, Inc., New Haven, 1983-88; programs advisor assigned to ADNOC Career Devel. Ctr., Internat. Gas Tech., Abu Dhabi, United Arab Emirates, 1988-90; cons. in field. Author: Electronics Curriculum Guide, 1963, Introduction to Electrochemical Systems, 1981, Basic Electricity, 1982, Microcomputer Troubleshooting, 1984, (with Thomas Scott Heiserman) Introduction to Microcomputers, 1986; co-author: Introduction to Amplifiers, 1968, Introduction to Electronic Devices, 1968, Digital Electronics, 1987; contbg. author entry on electronics Career Opportunities Ency., 1969; contbg. author Energy Management Handbook, 1982; tech. editor, project mgr. John Wiley & Sons Pubs., 1982-83; cons. editor McGraw Hill Book Co., 1966-76; reviewer SRA Pubs., 1975-84; contbr. articles to profl. publs.;. With U.S. Army, 1950-52, Japan and Korea. Mem. Am. Soc. Engring. Edn. (tech. edn. sect., session chmn. joint nat. conv. with Coll. and Industry Edn. Conf. 1986), Okla. Tech. Soc. (life, bd. dirs. 1976-80, editor jour. 1976-80, cons./presenter workshops on early identification of drop-outs 1978-80),Phi Kappa Phi (mem. membership com. Okla. State U. chpt. 1980-88), Sigma Pi Sigma (pres. physics honor soc. 1958-59), Tau Iota Epsilon (pres. Sch. Tech.'s honor soc. Okla. State U. chpt. 1953-54). Home: 216 Aqua Dr Lake Charles LA 70605-4462 Office: McNeese State Univ Dept Tech PO Box 91780 Lake Charles LA 70609-1780

HEISS, FREDERICK WILLIAM, political science educator, public administrator, policy researcher; b. Kansas City, Mo., Mar. 3, 1932; s. William and Sophia Else (Schmid) H.; m. Patricia Jane Stark, June 19, 1958 (div. May 1982); children: William Frederick, Scott Evan, Kerrel Kae; m. Carol Mae Knox, Jan. 9, 1983; 1 child, Brac Seaton. BSBA, U. Denver, 1958; MPA, U. Colo., 1968, PhD, 1973. Adminstr. City and County Denver, 1958-70; asst. prof. U. Colo., Boulder, 1973-78, assoc. prof., 1978-85; dir. Denver Urban Obs. U. Colo., Denver, 1970-82, dir. MPA grad. program, 1982-85; chmn. dpet. pub. adminstrn. Va. Commonwealth U., Richmond, 1985-91, prof., 1991—; dir. met. study Nat. Acad. Pub. Adminstrn., Washington, 1974-76; dir. sci. tech. NSF, Denver, 1976-78, nat. chmn. sci. and tech. transfer, 1977-78; cons. U.S. Civil Svc. Commn., Utah, 1975; dir. Capital Area Study and Program, Richmond, 1987-93; vis. prof. Huanghe U., Henan, China, 1989. Author: Urban Research and Urban Policy, 1975; contbr. articles to profl. jours. Keynote speaker League of Women Voters, Denver 1975, Pres. Carters Urban Conf., Denver, 1977; dir. regional governance Capital Area Assembly, Richmond, 1990-94. With Air Corps, USN, 1953-55, Korea. Grantee HUD, 1972-83, Dept. of Energy, 1979-82. Fellow Beta Theta Pi; mem. ASPA. Home: 14198 Mill Creek Dr Montpelier VA 23192-2837 Office: Va Commonwealth U Dept Polit Sci & Pub Admin 923 W Franklin St Richmond VA 23284-9008

HEIT, RAYMOND ANTHONY, civil engineer; b. Norfolk, Va., Sept. 12, 1936; s. Lawrence H. and Cecelia H. (Klauke) H.; m. H. Carlee Langford, Oct. 25, 1969; children: Christopher C., Amy C. Degree in civil engring., U. Cin., 1959. Assoc. prof. Tex. A&M U., Galveston, 1967-68; project mgr. Union Carbide Corp., Texas City, Tex., 1967-68; prin. Raymond A. Heit, Cons. Engrs., Houston, 1968-74; dir. engring. stds. Brown & Root, Inc., Houston, 1974—. Fellow ASCE; mem. Constrn. Specifications Inst. Home: 1609 Cranway Dr Houston TX 77055-3116 Office: Brown & Root Inc PO Box 3 Houston TX 77001-0003

HEITZ, EDWARD FRED, freight traffic consultant; b. Chgo., May 18, 1930; s. Fredo and Hildur (Olson) H.; m. Gaymae Woodrow Heitz, Apr. 28, 1960; children: Merry, Ted. Student, Northwestern U., Chgo., 1950-55. Registered I.C.C. practitioner. Supr. transp. rsch. Internat. Minerals and Chem. Corp., Chgo., 1946-58; asst. freight traffic mgr.-rate rsch. C.&.N.W.Ry., Chgo., 1958-64; traffic mgr. U.S. Dept. Agriculture, Washington, 1964-78; agriculture transp. analyst Fed. R.R. Adminstrn., Washington, 1978-82; freight traffic cons. Falls Church, Va., 1982-96; ret., 1996; Arbitrator Am. Arbitration. Assn., 1991—. Commr. Boy Scouts Am., Fairfax County, Va., 1974-77; chmn. Community Action Agy. County of Fairfax, 1975-77; v.p. Coun. of Fairfax PTAs, 1975; deacon Arlington Ch. of Christ, Falls Ch. Ch. of Christ; mem. Fairfax Com. of 100.

HEIZER, RUTH BRADFUTE, philosophy educator; b. Knoxville, Tenn., Oct. 8, 1933; d. George Archibald and Margaret Eleanor (Smith) Bradfute; m. James Lee Heizer, Aug. 3, 1956; children: John Philip, Mark Russell, Virginia Ruth. BA, Baylor U., 1954; MRE, So. Baptist Theol. Sem., 1957; MA, U. Ky., 1965; PhD, Ind. U., 1971; postgrad., Oxford (Eng.) U., 1980-81, 89. Tchr. Jefferson County Pub. Schs., Louisville, 1956-58; secondary tchr. Gallatin County Pub. Schs., Warsaw, Ky., 1959-60, 61; teaching assoc. dept. philosophy Ind. U., Bloomington, 1965-67; from instr. to assoc. prof. Georgetown (Ky.) Coll., 1967-83, prof., 1983—, chair dept. of philosophy, 1981—; vis. prof. philosophy Baylor U., Waco, Tex., 1979, 84; tchr. oral English Jiangnan U., Wuxi, China, summers 1990, 91, Yantai U., China, summer 1994, Inst. for Advanced Qualification of Workers of Edn., Kazan, Russia, summer, 1995. Author: Bradfute Beginnings, 1988; co-author: Women, Philosophy, & Sport, 1983, Contemporary Essays on Greek Ideas, 1987. Deacon Faith Bapt. Ch., Georgetown. Recipient NEH summer stipend, 1973. Mem. AAUW, Am. Philos. Assn., So. Soc. Philosophy and Psychology, Ky. Philos. Assn. (pres. 1973-74), Bapt. Assn. Philosophy Tchrs. (pres. 1988-89), Omicron Delta Kappa (Baylor Woman of Merit award 1980). Republican. Home: 910 Second Ave SW Apt 16 Jamestown ND 58401-4611

HEJL, JAMES GEORGE, principal; b. Caldwell, Tex., Nov. 21, 1939; s. Henry Walter and Annie Rosie (Krenek) H.; m. Patsy Anne Drury, June 8, 1962; children: Sandra Diane, Janice Elaine, David James. MusB, U. Tex., 1962; MusM, U. Mich., 1968; postgrad., Iowa State U., 1976-77, U. Houston-Clear Lake, 1989-93. Cert. secondary tchr., sch. adminstr., Tex. Band dir. W.B. Travis High Sch., Austin, Tex., 1962-68; music supr. Westlake High Sch., Austin, 1969-70; asst. dir. bands U. Tex., Austin, 1970-75; dir. bands Buena Vista Coll., Storm Lake, Iowa, 1975-78, Miss. State U., Starkville, 1978-83; music supr. Angleton (Tex.) Ind. Sch. Dist., 1983-90; asst. prin. Angleton High Sch., 1990-91, prin., 1991—; band cons. Tex., Iowa, Mo., Nebr., Minn., Ohio, Ala., Tenn, Miss.; judge Tex. State Solo-Ensemble contest, 1975, Tex. State Marching contest, 1980. Condtr. Miss. Music Educators All-State Band, 1980; creator marching band drill Scott Joplin on Parade, 1974. Named Adminstr. of the Yr., Tex. Assn. Journalism Educators, 1993; named to Outstanding Young Men in Am., 1976; music supervision fellow U. Mich., 1968. Mem. Tex. Assn. Secondary Sch. Prins. Democrat. Presbyterian. Home: 701 Milton St Angleton TX 77515-3421 Office: Angleton Ind Sch Dist 1201 W Henderson Rd Angleton TX 77515-2801

HEJTMANCIK, MILTON RUDOLPH, medical educator; b. Caldwell, Tex., Sept. 27, 1919; s. Rudolph Joseph and Millie (Jurcak) H.; B.A., U. Tex., 1939, M.D., 1943; m. Myrtle Lou Erwin, Aug. 21, 1943; children: Kelly Erwin, Milton Rudolph, Peggy Lou; m. 2d, Myrtle M. McCormick, Nov. 27, 1976. Resident in internal medicine U. Tex., 1946-49, instr. internal medicine, 1949-51, asst. prof., 1951-54, assoc. prof., 1954-65, prof. internal medicine, 1965-80, dir. heart clinic, 1949-80, dir. heart sta., 1965-80; chief of staff John Sealy Hosp., 1957-58; chief staff U. Tex. Hosps., 1977-79; prof. medicine Tex. A&M Coll. Medicine, 1981-82; cardiologist Olin E. Teague VA Hosp., Temple, Tex., 1981-82, VA Clinic, Beaumont, Tex., 1982-86. Served from 1st lt. to capt., M.C., AUS, 1944-46; ETO. Recipient Ashbel Smith Outstanding Alumnus award U.Tex. Med.Br., 1991, Titus Harris Disting. Svc award, 1992. Diplomate in cardiovascular diseases Am. Bd. Internal Medicine. Fellow ACP, Am. Coll. Chest Physicians, Am. Coll. Cardiology; mem. Am. (fellow council clin. cardiology), Tex. (pres. 1979-80), Galveston Dist. (pres. 1956) heart assns., AMA (Billing's Gold medal 1973), Am. Fedn. Clin. Research, AAAS, Tex. Acad. Internal Medicine (gov. 1971-73, v.p. 1973-74, pres. 1976-77), N.Y. Acad. Scis., Tex. Club Cardiology (pres. 1972), Galveston County (pres. 1971), Tex. (del. 1972-80) med. assns., Am. Heart Assn. (pres. Tex. affiliate 1979-80), Phi Beta Kappa, Sigma Xi, Alpha Omega Alpha, Phi Eta Sigma, Mu Delta, Phi Rho Sigma. Contbr. articles to profl. jours. Home: 500 N Spruce St Hammond LA 70401-2549

HELBURN, ISADORE B., arbitrator, mediator, educator; b. Cin., Aug. 14, 1938; s. I.B. and Jeanette (Greenburg) H.; m. Judith Dee Horwitz, Aug. 21, 1960; children: Graham D., Robin L. Holt. BS with honors, U. Wis., 1960, MS, 1962, PhD, 1966. Mem. faculty U. Tex., Austin, 1968—, prof. indsl. relations Grad. Sch. Bus., 1979-92; contract prof. Area Estudios de Postgrado, U. Carabobo, Valencia, Venezuela, summer 1974; mem. arbitration panels Fed. Mediation and Conciliation Service, 1972—, Am. Arbitration Assn., 1974—, Nat. Mediation Bd., 1983—. Author: (with others) Total Group Productivity Motivation in Business, 1961, Progress Sharing at American Motors, 1964, Manpower, Employment and Income, A Statistical Profile of Texas, 1969, Public Employer-Employee Relations in Texas: Contemporary and Emerging Developments, 1971, (with others) Local Option Recognition and Bargaining: The Texas Fire Fighter and Police Experience, 1976; contbr. articles to profl. jours. and chpts. to books. Served to capt. U.S. Army, 1966-68. Recipient Jack G. Taylor Teaching Excellence award U. Tex., Austin, 1970. Mem. Nat. Acad. Arbitrators, Indsl. Rels. Rsch. Assn. Jewish. Home: 5914 Highland Hills Dr Austin TX 78731-4057

HELD, JOHN, JR., artist; b. N.Y.C., Apr. 2, 1947; s. Lawrence and Selma (Solomon) H.; m. Paula Barber; children: Amanda, Nathaniel. BA, Syracuse U., 1969, MLS, 1971. Librarian Mid York Libr. Sys., Utica, N.Y., 1975-81, Dallas Pub. Libr., 1981-95; dir. Modern Realism Gallery, Dallas, 1982—; curator Stamp Art Gallery, San Francisco, 1995-96, Nat. Art Mus., Havana, Cuba, 1995. Author: Mail Art: An Annotated Bibliography, 1991. grantee Estonian Art Soc., 1990. Home: 1903 McMillan Ave Dallas TX 75206 Office: Stamp Art Gallery PO Box 410837 San Francisco CA 94141

HELD, MICHAEL JOSEPH, broadcasting executive; b. St. Louis, July 24, 1948; s. Lawrence E. and Thelma (Mockler) H.; m. Marie Constance Fehlig, Aug. 29, 1969; children: Heather, Kristen, Aubrey, Carrie. BSBA, Rockhurst Coll., 1971. Account exec. Sta. KCTV-TV, Kansas City, Mo., 1971-77, MMT Sales, Chgo., 1977-81; br. mgr. MMT Sales, St. Louis, 1981-89; v.p., regional group mgr. MMT Sales, Chgo., 1989-95; gen. sales mgr. Sta. WCBD-TV, Charleston, S.C., 1996—. Benefit chmn. Off the Street Club, Chgo., 1977-81. Mem. Broadcast Ad Club Chgo., Chgo. Broadcast Rep. Assn. (pres. 1994, 95, exec. v.p., sec.-treas.).

HELFRICK, ALBERT DARLINGTON, electronics engineering educator, consultant; b. Camden, N.J., June 10, 1945; s. Eugene G. and Irma (Darlington) H.; m. Toni Venezia, May 6, 1989; children: A. Karl, Rachel. BS, Upsala Coll., East Orange, N.J., 1969; MS, N.J. Inst. Tech., 1973; PhD, Clayton (Mo.) U., 1988. Registered profl. engr., N.J. Sr. rsch. engr. Singer-Kearfott Div., Little Falls, N.J., 1969-72; sr. engr. Kay Elemetrics, Pine Brook, N.J., 1972-77; sr. project engr. Cessna Aircraft, Boonton, N.J., 1977-84; prin. engr. RFL Industries, Boonton, 1984-89; cons. engr. Boonton, 1989-92; prof. electronics engring. Embry-Riddle Aero. U., Daytona Beach, Fla., 1992—; mem. com. Radio Tech. Commn. for Aeros., Washington, 1980-85, 93—; mem. adj. faculty Upsala Coll., 1972-73, Kean Coll. N.J., 1979-81, Fairleigh Dickinson U., 1986-87. Author: Practical Repair and Maintenance of Communications Equipment, 1983, Modern Aviation Electronics, 1984, 2d edit., 1994, Electronic Instrumentation and Measurement Techniques, 1985, Modern Electronic Instrumentation and Measurement Techniques, 1990, Electrical Spectrum and Network Analyzers, 1991, Practical Aircraft Electronic Systems, 1994; also 60 articles. Bd. dirs. Aircraft Electronics Assn. Edn. Found. Sgt. U.S. Army, 1969-71, Vietnam. Recipient award RF Design mag., 1988. Fellow AIAA (assoc.), Radio Club Am. (bd. dirs. 1989-90, 92-94, sec. 1990-91); mem. IEEE (sr.). Home: 2925 Betty Dr Deland FL 32720-1945 Office: Embry-Riddle Aero U 600 Clyde Morris Blvd Daytona Beach FL 32114

HELGUERO, GRACE (GRACIELA HELGUERO), language educator; b. N.Y.C., June 5, 1957; d. Isidro U. and Fanny (Dominguez) H.; m. Massimo Benini. BA, St. John's U., N.Y.C., 1979; MA, NYU, 1982; postgrad., NYU, Spain, 1985; PhD, ABD, NYU, 1989. Internat. sales asst. Merrill Lynch Pierce Fenner & Smith, N.Y.C., 1980-82; acct. exec., asst. regional dir. Latin Am. Drexel Buraham Lambert, N.Y.C., 1982-84; fin. asst., computer work Citibank Corp., Queens, N.Y., 1984-85; lang. tchr. Stranahan High Sch., Ft. Lauderdale, Fla., 1985-87; tchr. Spanish, moderator St. John's Preparatory, Astoria, N.Y., 1987-90; tchr. Spanish and tennis Forest Hills (N.Y.) High Sch., 1989-90; Spanish tchr. St. Andrews Sch., Boca Raton, 1991; tchr. Spanish/English, translator Lang. Exchange, Boca Raton, 1991; tchr., adminstr. asst. Fla. Lang. Ctr., Ft. Lauderdale, 1992-95; Spanish tchr., coord. Donna Klein Jewish Acad., 1995-96; AP instr. in Spanish Pope John Paul II H.S., 1996—; mem. program com. Broward ESOL Coun. Conf., Ft. Lauderdale, 1993-94; adj. prof. Spanish Broward C.C., 1995—; adj. prof. ESOL, Fla. State U., 1994—; presenter in field. Editor: (book reviewer) Broward Network TESOL, 1992, Broward ESOL Network, 1994, (lesson plan tips) Broward ESOL Network, 1993; editorial staff mem.: BEC Network Newsletter. Active pub. rels. AMIGOS, Queens, N.Y., 1980. Mem. MLA, TESOL (chair hospitality com. Gulf Conf. 1994), Broward ESOL Coun. (pvt. inst. rep. 1994—), Assn. Tchrs. Spanish and Portuguese, Inst. of Cervantes, Sigma Delta Pi, Kappa Delta Pi. Democrat. Home: 6350 W Longboat Ln Apt D101 Boca Raton FL 33433-8082 also: Via Giovanni XXIII n 19/3, 40037 Pontecchio Marconi Sasso Marconi, Bologna Italy Office: Broward CC Central Campus Modern Fgn Lang Davie FL 33314

HELLAND, GEORGE ARCHIBALD, JR., manufacturing company executive, former government official, management consultant; b. San Antonio, Nov. 28, 1937; s. George Archibald and Ruth (Gorman) H.; m. Josephine Howell, June 9, 1962 (div. 1989); children: Jane Elizabeth, Thomas Gorman; m. Antonia Scott Day, Nov. 24, 1990. BS in Mech. Engring., U. Tex., 1959; MBA with distinction, Harvard U., 1961. Registered profl. engr., Tex. With Cameron Iron Works, Inc., Houston, 1961-77, asst. sales mgr., 1963, dist. sales mgr., 1964, dist. sales mgr., U.K., Africa, 1965, product mgr., 1966, plant mgr., Leeds, Eng., 1967, mgr. oil tool products, 1968, v.p., 1969-75, exec. v.p., 1975-77; with Weatherford Internat., Inc., Houston, 1977-79; v.p. Weatherford Internat., Inc., 1977, pres., chief exec. officer, dir., 1978-79; pres. McEvoy Oilfield Equipment Co. (name changed to Sii McEvoy div. Smith Internat., Inc. 1980), Houston, 1979-85; pres. McCall Industries, Inc., Houston, 1986-87, bd. dirs.; gen. mgmt. cons., 1987-90; dep. asst. sec. of energy for export assistance U.S. Dept. Energy, Washington, 1990-93; v.p. Dreser Industries, Inc., Houston, 1993—; pres. Lockwood Corp., Gering, Nebr., 1986-87; chmn. bd. dirs. SIE Internat., Inc., Ft. Worth; prin. Innova Ptnrs., 1988-90. Bd. dirs. Jr. Achievement Internat., Briarwood Sch., Houston, Eurasia Found., Washington; trustee S.W. Rsch. Inst.; mem. exec. com. Jr. Achievement of S.E. Tex.; trustee Eurasia Found., Washington. Recipient Five Outstanding Young Texans award Tex. Jr. C. of C., 1972; named Outstanding Young Houstonian Houston Jr. C. of C., 1972; Disting. Grad. Sch. Engring. U. Tex., 1977. Mem. ASME, Am. Inst. Mining, Metall. and Petroleum Engrs., Am. Petroleum Inst. (bd. dirs.), Inst. Gas Engrs. (U.K.), Tex. Soc. Profl. Engrs., Am. Wellhead Equipment Assn. (pres. 1967), Petroleum Equipment Suppliers Assn. (pres. 1976-77), Houston C. of C., Tau Beta Pi, Phi Eta Sigma, Pi Tau Sigma, Sigma Nu, Friars Soc. Presbyterian. Home: 2622 W Lane Dr Houston TX 77027-4914 Office: Dreser Industries Inc PO Box 6504 Houston TX 77265-6504

HELLERSTEIN, NINA SALANT, French literature and language educator; b. N.Y.C., Mar. 29, 1946; d. Allan and Martha (Cantor) Salant; m. Walter Hellerstein, Aug. 31, 1970; children: Michael, Margaret. BA, Brown U., 1968; MA, U. Chgo., 1969, PhD, 1974. Adj. asst. prof. Baruch Coll. CUNY, N.Y.C., 1974-75; vis. asst. prof. Vassar Coll., Poughkeepsie, N.Y., 1975-76; instr. Rosary Coll., River Forest, Ill., 1976-78, Roosevelt U., Chgo., 1976-78; asst. prof. U. Ga., Athens, 1978-83, assoc. prof. French literature and language, 1983-92, prof., 1992—, acting head dept. Romance langs., 1992-3. Author: Mythe et Structure Dans Les 'Cing Grandes Odes', 1990; mem. editorial bd. South Atlantic Rev., 1990-93; contbr. articles to profl. jours. Grantee Ford Found., 1968-72, U. Ga., 1982, 91. mem. MLA, MADD, Am. Assn. Tchrs. French, Paul Claudel Soc. (v.p. 1978-79, sec.-treas. 1979-80, pres. 1981-82), Handgun Control, Inc., Societe Paul Claudel, Assn. des Amis de la Fondation St. John Perse. Jewish. Office: U Ga Dept Romance Langs Athens GA 30602

HELM, ALETHA ANN, human resources specialist; b. Charleston, W.Va., Apr. 14, 1957; d. John William and Juanita G. (McCoy) H.; 1 child, Jasmine Leigh. Student, Marshall U., 1975-80; BS in Mgmt. & Fin., W.Va. State U., 1989; M Human Resources, U. Charleston, 1995. Personal banker, new accts. counselor Magnet Bank, Charleston, W.Va., 1983-87; acctg. analyst Eastern Am. Energy, Charleston, 1988-95; benefits acct., office mgr. Light of the World, Decatur, Ga., 1995—. Vol. tchr. Horace Mann Jr. High Sch., Chamberlain Elem. Sch.; active Kanawha Players Charleston, Charleston Light Opera Guild. Office: Light of the World 2135 Shamrock Dr Decatur GA 30032

HELM, GARY STEWART, minister; b. Athens, Tenn., Apr. 13, 1956; s. Grant Lee and Dessie Virginia (Thompson) H.; m. Debra Y. Taylor Mayberry, July 21, 1972 (div. 1978); 1 child, Brandi Daina Mayberry; m. Debra Yvonne Taylor Helm, Dec. 22, 1986; children: Sarah Elizabeth Helm, Michael Dale Helm. BA, Mo. Bapt. Coll., St. Louis, 1980; MDiv, Southeastern Bapt. Theol. Sem., Wake Forest, N.C., 1987; postgrad., Tenn. Tech. U., 1974-77, So. Bapt. Theol. Sem., 1981-83. Ordained to ministry, 1983. Summer missionary Teton Resort Ministries, Jackson Hole, Wyo., 1979; pastoral intern Kirkwood Bapt. Ch., St. Louis, 1980; pastoral supervised minister First Bapt. Ch., Spring Hope, N.C., 1986; mission pastor Harquahala Bapt. Ch., Buckeye, Ariz., 1983-84; pastor Bethlehem Bapt. Ch., Dillwyn, Va., 1987-93, Nomini Bapt. Ch., Montross, Va., 1993—; religion instr. Rappahannock C.C., Warsaw, Va., 1995.; participant messenger The Bapt. Fellowship, Atlanta, 1990—; mem. So. Bapt. Religious Edn. Assn., Ft. Worth, 1987-90; cons. values-based tactical planning for religious orgns., 1996—; field supr. Bapt. Theol. Sem., Richmond, Va., 1996—. Literacy tutor Buckingham County Literacy Coun., Dillwyn, 1990; chaplain Harquahala Fire Dist., Buckeye, 1983. Mem. James River Bapt. Assn. (mission vol. 1990), Associated Sunday Sch. Improvement and Support Team (dir.), Bapt. Committed to the So. Bapt. Conv. Home: PO Box 1336 Montross VA 22520-1336 Office: Nomini Bapt Ch PO Box 186 Montross VA 22520-0186

HELMERICH, PEGGY VARNADOW, actress; b. Columbia, Miss., Mar. 18, 1928; d. Leon A. and Minnie Lee (Roper) Varnadow; m. Walter H. Helmerich III, Nov. 24, 1951; children: Walter H. IV, Dow Zachary, Matthew Galloway, Hans Christian, Jonathan David. BA, Northwestern U., 1948. Actress: (radio) WWL, New Orleans, 1948-49; (films) Woman in Hiding, , 1949, Undertow, 1949, Sleeping City, 1949, Reunion in Reno, 1950, You Never Can Tell, 1950, Bright Victory, 1951, I Want You, 1951, Harvey, 1951; (Screen Dirs. Playhouse) One Way Passage, 1950. Trustee Tulsa County Libr. Commn., 1975—, Okla. State Arts. Coun., 1989—; bd. dirs. Pro America, 1975—, Philbrook Art Ctr., 1980—, Gilcrease Mus., 1982-88, Woman's Bd. Northwestern U., 1986—, Okla. Found. for Excellence, 1986—, Tulsa Garden Ctr., 1988—. Recipient Am. Libr. Assn.'s Trustee citation, Tulsa, 1985, Citizen's Recognition award, Okla. Libr. Assn., 1985, Medici award, Tulsa Ballet Theatre, 1985; named Outstanding Philantrophist, Nat. Soc. Fund Raising Execs., 1985, Tulsa Headliner, Tulsa Press Club, 1987. Republican. Methodist. Home: 2121 S Yorktown Ave Tulsa OK 74114-1425

HELMS, JESSE, senator; b. Monroe, NC, Oct. 18, 1921; s. Jesse Alexander and Ethel Mae (Helms) H.; m. Dorothy Jane Coble, Oct. 31, 1942; children: Jane (Mrs. Charles R. Knox), Nancy (Mrs. John C. Stuart), Charles. Student, Wingate (N.C.) Jr. Coll., Wake Forest Coll. City editor Raleigh (N.C.) Times, 1941-42; news and program dir. Sta. WRAL, Raleigh, 1948-51; adminstrv. asst. to U.S. senators Willis Smith and Alton Lennon, 1951-53; exec. dir. N.C. Bankers Assn., 1953-60; exec. v.p., vice chmn. Capitol Broadcasting Co., Raleigh, 1960-72; U.S. senator from N.C., 1973—; chmn. Agriculture, Nutrition and Forestry subcom. on Mktg., Inspection & Product Promotion, Com. on Fgn. Relations; mem. Rules & Adminstrn. Com., Republican Policy Com.; chmn. bd. Specialized Agrl. Publs., Inc., Raleigh, 1964-72; mem. Raleigh City Council, 1957-61. Bd. dirs. N.C. Cerebral Palsy Hosp., Durham, United Cerebral Palsy N.C., Wake County Cerebral Palsy and Rehab. Center, Raleigh, Camp Willow Run, Littleton, N.C.; former trustee Campbell Coll., Wingate Coll., Meredith Coll., John F. Kennedy Coll. Served with USNR, 1942-45, World War II. Recipient Freedoms Found. award for best TV editorial, 1962, for newspaper article, 1973, So. Bapt. Nat. award for Service to mankind, 1972; Gold medal VFW; Conservative Congressional award, 1976; Liberty award Am. Econ. Council, 1978; Disting. Public Service award Public Service Research Council, 1978; Watchdog of Treasury award; Guardian of Small Bus. award; named Man of Yr. Women for Constl. Govt., 1978; Legislator of Yr. award Nat. Rifle Assn., 1978, Taxpayer's Best Friend award Nat. Taxpayer's Union, 1993; other awards. Republican. Baptist (deacon). Clubs: Rotary (past pres. Raleigh), Raleigh Executives (past pres.), Masons (32 degree). Office: US Senate 403 Dirksen Senate Bldg Washington DC 20510

HELMSTETTER, WENDY LEE, librarian; b. Port Arthur, Ont., Can., Aug. 31, 1947; came to U.S., 1960; d. Estyn Lloyd and Vera Gertrude (Derwa) Edwards; m. Glenn Charles Grisetti, June 17, 1967 (div.); 1 child, Lee Glenn Grisetti; m. Charles Edward Helmstetter, July 1, 1988. BA in Psychology summa cum laude, SUNY, Buffalo, 1985; MLS, U. South Fla., 1994. Adminstrv. asst. to libr. dir. Roswell Pk. Cancer Inst., Buffalo, 1973-89; reference libr. Fla. Inst. Tech., Melbourne, 1994—. Bd. dirs. Friends of Evans Libr., Melbourne, 1996—. Mem. ALA (membership com.), Assn. Coll. and Rsch. Librs. (instrn. sect., policy com., sci. and tech. sect., univ. librs. sect.), Reference and User Svcs. Assn., Southeastern Libr. Assn., Spl. Librs. Assn., Fla. Libr. Assn., Libr. Assn. Brevard (continuing edn. com.), Phi Kappa Phi, Beta Phi Mu, Alpha Sigma Lambda. Home: 854 Hawksbill Island Dr Indian Harbor Beach FL 32937 Office: Fla Inst Tech 150 W University Blvd Melbourne FL 32901

HELOISE, columnist, lecturer, broadcaster, author; b. Waco, Tex., Apr. 15, 1951; d. Marshal H. and Heloise K. (Bowles) Cruse; m. David L. Evans, Feb. 13, 1981. B.S. in Math. and Bus, S.W. Tex. State U., 1974. Owner, pres. Heloise, Inc. Asst. to columnist mother, Heloise, 1974-77, upon her death took over internationally syndicated column, 1977; author: Hints from Heloise, 1980, Help from Heloise, 1981, Heloise's Beauty Book, 1985, All-New Hints from Heloise, 1989, Heloise: Hints for a Healthy Planet, 1990, Heloise from A to Z, 1992, Household Hints for Singles, 1993, Hints for All Occasions, 1995; contbg. editor Good Housekeeping mag., 1981, Speaker for the House; co-founder, 1st co-pilot Mile Pie in the Sky Balloon Club. Mem. Good Neighbor Coun. Tex.-Mex.; sponsor Nat. Smile Week. Recipient Mental Health Mission award Nat. Mental Health Assn., 1990, The Carnegians Good Human Rels. award, 1994. Mem. AFTRA, SAG, Women in Comm. (Headliner 1994), Tex. Press Women, Internat. Women's Forum, Women in Radio and TV, Confrerie de la Chaine des Rotisseurs (bailli San Antonio chpt.), Ordre Mondial des Gourmets De'Gustateurd de U.S.A., Death Valley Yacht and Racket Club, Zonta. Home: PO Box 795000 San Antonio TX 78279-5000 Office: care King Features Syndicate 235 E 45th St New York NY 10017-3305

HELPERT-NUNEZ, RUTH ANNE, clinical social worker, psychotherapist; b. Rosebud, Tex., Jan. 7, 1956; d. Otto Henry and Lorene Margaret (Hoelscher) Helpert; m. J.W. Will Nunez. BS with high honors in Social Work, U. Tex., Austin, 1978, MS in Social Work, 1981. Lic. master social worker-advanced clin. practitioner; lic. marriage and family therapist, Tex. Student intern Child Protective Svcs. Tex. Dept. Human Svcs., Austin, 1978; child protective svcs. specialist Tex. Dept. Human Svcs., Killeen and Belton, 1979-80; grad. student intern Austin Child Guidance Ctr., 1981; caseworker Heart of Tex. Region Mental Health Mental Retardation, Waco, Tex., 1981-83; child protective svcs. specialist Tex. Dept. Human Svcs., Austin, 1983-84; caseworker DayGlo Family Treatment program Austin-Travis County Mental Health Mental Retardation Ctr., 1984-88; therapist, clin. social worker Anthony W. Arden, Ph.D & Assocs., Bryan, Tex., 1989-90, Thomas Edwards, Ph.D., P.C., Bryan, 1990-95; therapist/clin. social worker Brazos Valley Cmty. Action Agy.-Family Health Svcs.: Psychology Svcs., Bryan, 1996—; clin. vol. Scotty's House Child Advocacy Ctr., 1992—; field instr. U. Houston Grad. Sch. Social Work, 1995—. Bd. dirs. Toy Libr., College Station, Tex., 1989; mem. spkrs. bur. Child Advocacy Resource and Edn. Coalition, 1989-92, v.p., 1991. Mem. NASW (diplomate, qualified clin. social worker, chmn. Brazos Valley unit 1990-94, bd. dirs. Tex. chpt. 1990-94, exec. com. 1993-94, chmn. profl. stds. com. 1993-94), Acad. Cert. Social Workers, Phi Kappa Phi, Phi Theta Kappa. Democrat. Home: 10004 Edge Cut-Off Rd Hearne TX 77859

HELSLEY, ALEXIA JONES, archivist; b. Louisville, Ky., Sept. 9, 1945; d. George Alexander and Evelyn (Masden) J.; m. Terry Lynn Helsley, Oct. 11, 1969; children: Cassandra Keiser, Jacob Henry. BA in History, Furman U., 1967; MA in History, U. S.C., 1974; cert., Modern Arcives Inst., Washington, 1978, S.C. Exec. Inst., Columbia, 1996. Archival asst. S.C. Dept. Archives and History, Columbia, 1988-96, archivist I, 1969-72, asst. reference archivist, 1972-76, supr. reference and rsch., 1976-88, dir. pub. programs divsn., 1988—; historian Am. Lodging Resources, Inc. Author: Harbison: an Historical Sketch, 1986, First Baptist Church of Irmo: Historical Overview, 1992, Researching Family History: A Workbook, 1992, The 1840 Revolutionary Pensioners of Henderson County, North Carolina; co-author: S.C. Court Records, 1993, The Changing Face of S.C. Politics, 1993; contbr. articles to profl. jours. Chair social and recreation com. Harbison Cmty. Assn., Columbia, S.C., 1984-89; trustee S.C. Hall of Fame, Myrtle Beach, 1988—; vice-chair Columbia Quincentennial Commn. S.C., 1989-93; 1st v.p. Richland Sertoma, Columbia, 1996—. Named to Hon. Order of Ky. Cols. Mem. Henderson County Geneal. and Hist. Soc. (charter, chair spl. projects 1993—), Joseph McDowell Nat. Soc. DAR, Soc. Am. Archivists (chair reference, access, outreac sect. 1981-83), S.C. Hist. Assn. Baptist. Home: 1 Northpine Ct Columbia SC 29212 Office: SC Dept Archives History 1430 Senate St Columbia SC 29201

HELTMAN, ROBERT FAIRCHILD, distribution executive; b. Lakewood, Ohio, May 11, 1934; s. Fairchild Long and Sarah Agnes (Fleck) H.; m. Melody Elaine Valentine, Feb. 14, 1992; children: Ken, Kathy, Daniel, Kim, Karen, David, Kerri, Summer. BS, Oberlin Coll., 1956. Mktg. & exec. staffing mgr. GE Co., 1960-88; pres. Leading Edge Products & Svcs. Co., Hendersonville, N.C., 1988—. Inventor Ultimate Hiking Staff; contbr. articles to mags. Treas., pres. Homeowner's Assn., Palatine, Ill.; chmn. bd. dirs. Erie (Pa.) City and County Librs.; pres. Adv. Coun. on Vocat. Edn. Pa. Mem. Masons. Republican. Lutheran. Office: Leading Products & Svcs 106 Dogwood Dr Hendersonville NC 28791-9076

HELTON, KAREN JOHNSON, college administrator; b. Cin., May 20, 1947; d. James C. and Ruth (Lee) Payne; m. Malcolm Helton, June 29, 1995; children: Terence, Traci, Tina. BA, Ohio U., 1969; MSW, Atlanta U., 1976; postgrad., U. Mich., 1978, Tex. A&M U., 1992. Social worker Hamilton County, Cin., 1969-74; dir. planning LeMoyne-Owen Coll., Memphis, 1976-82; fed. programs officer Mary Holmes Coll., West Point, Miss., 1982-85; v.p. devel. Tex. Coll., Tyler, 1985-87; asst. to pres. Wiley Coll., Marshall, Tex., 1987—. Chmn. Higher Edn. and Campus Ministry, 1992-94. Recipient Disting. Svc. award U.S. Dept. Edn., 1996. Mem. NAFE, Zonta (pub. rels. com. 1989-92), Zeta Phi Beta (3d v.p. 1990-94). Democrat. Methodist. Home: 4807 S Washington St Marshall TX 75670 Office: Wiley College 711 Wiley Ave Marshall TX 75670

HELTON, MARGARET SUSAN YOUNG, enterostomal therapy nurse, surgical nurse; b. Pulaski, Va., Dec. 6, 1942; d. Fred Eugene and Mary Evans (Zentmeyer) Y.; m. Leon Gavin Helton, Dec. 4, 1967 (div. Sept. 1995); children: John Gavin, Eric Scott, Virginia Lee. Student, King Coll., 1961-63; diploma in nursing, Stuart Circle Hosp., Sch. for Nurses, 1966; BSN, Mobile Coll., 1980; diploma in enterostomal therapy, Emory U., 1988. Cert. enterostomal therapy nurse. Staff nurse Stuart Circle Hosp, Richmond, Va., 1966-67; camp nurse Camp Mt. Shenandoah, Milboro Springs, Va., 1967; staff nurse mil. USAF, Sewart AFB, Tenn., 1967-68; staff nurse med.-surg. Mobile (Ala.) Gen. Hosp., 1968; operating room nurse Doctors Hosp., Mobile, 1972-73; recovery room nurse Mobile Infirmary Med. Ctr., 1981-82, outpatient surgery nurse, 1982-88, enterostomal therapy nurse, 1988-90; home health enterostomal therapy nurse Saad's Healthcare Svcs., Mobile, 1990-96; cons., educator in home health Infirmary Home Health Agy., Mobile, 1996—; cons., educator in field; mem. wound mgmt. team. 1st lt. USAF, 1967-68. Mem. Mobile Coll. Nursing Honor Soc. (charter), Stuart Circle Hosp. Sch. for Nurses Alumnae Assn., Mobile Ostomy Assn., Mobile Area Enterstomal Therapy Nurses (pres. 1992—), Wound, Ostomy and Continence Nurses Soc. (past del. nat. conf. S.E. region). Episcopalian. Home: 517 Grand Ave Fairhope AL 36532 Office: Infirmary Home Health 2559 Emogene St Mobile AL 36606

HELTON, MAX EDWARD, minister, consultant, religious organization executive; b. Conasauga, Tenn., Nov. 24, 1940; s. Herman Marshall and Nellie Gladys (Haddock) H.; m. Jean Bateman, June 8, 1962; children: Elaine, Melanie, Crista, Becky. BA, Tenn. Temple U., 1963; DD (hon.), Hyles-Anderson Coll., 1973. Ordained minister Bapt. Ch., 1963. Sr. pastor Koolau Bapt. Ch., Kaneohe, Hawaii, 1964-71; exec. v.p. Hyles-Anderson Coll., Crown Point, Ind., 1971-77; sr. pastor Grace Bible Ch., White Plains, N.Y., 1977-83, West Park Bapt. Ch., Bakersfield, Calif., 1983-86; pastor outreach program Grace Bapt. Ch., Glendora, Calif., 1986-88; pres. Motor Racing Outreach, Harrisburg, N.C., 1988—. Author: Thirty Qualities of Leadership, 1975; contbr. articles to profl. jours.; keynote speaker Commonwealth Youth Day, Cayman Brac, B.W.I., 1964. Dep. sheriff Lake County (Ind.) Sheriff Dept., Crown Point, 1974-77; mem. adv. bd. legis.

N.Y., Albany, 1980-82, sch. bd. Bakersfield Christian Sch. Dist., 1985-86; bd. dirs. N.C. Racing Hall of Fame Mus., Sports Outreach Am. Mem. Internat. Sports Coalition, Conservative Bapt. Assn. (cons. 1983—, chmn. fellowship com. 1985-87), Nat. Assn. for Stock Car Auto Racing. Republican. Office: Motor Racing Outreach Hwy 29 Harrisburg NC 28075-9402

HELTON, NORMA JEAN, special education educator; b. Mentor, Tenn., Dec. 26, 1930; d. Carlyle and Mildred Nancy (Clemens) Robbins; m. Albert Layman Helton Jr., Dec. 29, 1950; children: Stanley Joseph, Patricia Faith Helton Ross, Anthony Lyndon. AA in Social Studies, Antelope Valley Coll., 1958; BS in Edn., Athens Coll., 1965, MAT, 1970; EdD in Curriculum and Instrn., Highland U., 1975. Cert. tchr., Ala., Tenn. English and bus. edn. tchr. Huntsville (Ala.) City Schs., 1965-70; spl. edn. tchr. Jackson County Schs., Scottsboro, Ala., 1971-72, Hollywood, Ala., 1975-77; adult edn. tchr. Jackson County Schs., Hollywood, 1975-77; spl. edn. supr. Jackson County Schs., Scottsboro, 1977-91, mental retardation svc. dir., 1992-93; tchr. corps team leader Ala. A&M U., Normal, 1972-74; spl. edn. tchr. Blount County Schs., Maryville, Tenn., 1974-75; part-time min. United Meth. Ch., Ala., 1987—. Mem. Coun. for Exceptional Children, Ala. Edn. Assn., NEA, Ret. Tchrs. Assn., ASCD. Democrat. Home: 117 Stacy Cir Huntsville AL 35811

HEMBERGER, GLEN JAMES, university band director, music educator; b. Boulder, Colo., Jan. 18, 1962; s. James Frank and Jacqueline Ann (Kent) H.; m. Linda Dawn Thomas, June 3, 1989. BME, U. Colo., 1985, MMus, 1989. Cert. music tchr., Colo. Dir. bands Thornton (Colo.) Sr. High Sch., 1985-87; grad. asst. U. Colo. Bands, Boulder, 1987-89; assoc. dir. bands, mem. music edn. faculty U. R.I., Kingston, 1989-92; assoc. dir. bands Okla. State U., Stillwater, 1992—; clinician R.I. Music Educators' State Conv., 1992, summer music camp U. Wis., 1993, Chinese ARmed Police Band, Beijing, 1996, Nat. Taiwan U. Wind Orch., Taipei and Hong Kong, 1996, Beijing Band Dirs. Assn., 1996, U. S.D. Band Festival, 1996; adjudicator Colo. Bandmasters Judging Assn., Denver, 1984-89, N.E. Scholastic Band Assn., Boston, 1989-90; guest condr. high schs., honor bands, clinics, 1984—, USCG Band, Charter Oak H.S. Honor Band, R.I. Jr. High All-State Band, Comty. Bands., 1991—, Okla. Secondary Sch. Activities Assn. music workshop, 1993, 94, Okla. Mozart Internat. Music Festival, 1995, 96, Classic Bowl Honors Marching Band, 1996; founder So. New Eng. H.S. Honor Band, 1991. Contbr. articles to profl. jours. Mem. Olympic All-Am. Marching Band, L.A., 1984. Mem. Coll. Band Dirs. Nat. Assn. (mem. jour. staff, nat. athletic band adv. coun., clinician nat. conv. 1995), Okla. Bandmasters Assn., Internat. Assn. Jazz Educators, Music Educators Nat. Conf., World Assn. for Symphonic Bands and Ensembles, Okla. Music Educators Assn. (clinician state conv. 1995), Big Twelve Band Dirs. Assn., Phi Mu Alpha Sinfonia, Kappa Kappa Psi, Tau Beta Sigma. Home: 1503 S Berkshire Dr Stillwater OK 74074-1613 Office: Okla State U 220 Seretean Ctr Stillwater OK 74078-4077

HEMINGWAY, BETH ROWLETT, author, columnist, lecturer; b. Richmond, Va., May 6, 1913; d. Robert Archer and Evelyn Lucille (Doggett) Rowlett; B.Mus., Hollins Coll., 1934; m. Harold Hemingway, Apr. 2, 1938; children—Ruth Hartley, Martha Scott. Writer, Richmond-Lifestyle mag.; columnist Artistry in Bloom, Richmond Times-Dispatch; author: A Second Treasury of Christmas Decorations, 1961; Flower Arrangement with Antiques, 1965; Christmas Decorations Say Welcome, 1972; Antiques Accented by Flowers, 1975; Beth Hemingway's No Kin to Ernest, 1980; Holidays with Hemingway, 1985; lectr. numerous states, also Australia, 1966, Eng., 1977. Vol., Hermitage Meth. Home, 1977-79. Mem. Nat. League Am. Pen Women, Va. Writers Club, Richmond Hort. Assn., Va. Fedn. Garden Clubs (book rev. chmn.), Richmond Council Garden Clubs (flower arrangement chmn.), Clay Spring Garden Club (pres. 1953-55), Barton Garden Club (pres. 1959-61, 74). Republican. Methodist. Home: 1900 Lauderdale Dr Apt E-103 Richmond VA 23233-3942

HEMINGWAY, RICHARD WILLIAM, law educator; b. Detroit, Nov. 24, 1927; s. William Oswald and Iva Catherine (Wildfang) H.; m. Vera Cecilia Eck, Sept. 12, 1947; children: Margaret Catherine, Carol Elizabeth, Richard Albert. B.S. in Bus, U. Colo., 1950; J.D. magna cum laude (J. Woodall Rogers Sr. Gold medal 1955), So. Meth. U., 1955; LL.M. (William S. Cook fellow 1968), U. Mich., 1969. Bar: Tex. 1955, Okla. 1981. Assoc. Fulbright, Crooker, Freeman, Bates & Jaworski, Houston, 1955-60; lectr. Bates Sch. Law, U. Houston, 1960; assoc. prof. law Baylor U. Law Sch., Waco, Tex., 1960-65; vis. assoc. prof. So. Meth. U. Law Sch., 1965-68; prof. law Tex. Tech U. Law Sch., Lubbock, 1968-71, Paul W. Horn prof., 1972-81, acting dean, 1974-75, dean ad interim, 1980-81; prof. law U. Okla., Norman, 1981-83, Eugene Kuntz prof. oil, gas and natural resources law, 1983-92, Eugne Kuntz prof. emeritus oil, gas & natural resources law, 1992—. Author: The Law of Oil and Gas, 1971, 2d edit., 1983, lawyer's edit., 1983, 3d edit., 1991, West's Texas Forms (Mines and Minerals), 1977, 2d edit., 1991, 85; contbg. editor various law reports, cases and materials. Served with USAAF, 1945-47. Mem. Tex. Bar Assn., Scribes, Order of Coif (faculty), Beta Gamma Sigma. Lutheran. Home: 1411 Greenbriar Dr Norman OK 73072-6858 Office: U Okla Law Sch Norman OK 73019

HEMMI, CHRISTIAN OTTO, electrical engineer; b. Archer City, Tex., June 1, 1940; s. Otto Christian and Alice (Weinzapfel) H.; m. Eva Ann Garza, Jan. 29, 1983; children: Christian Otto Jr., Eva Ann. BSEE, U. Tex., Arlington, 1962; MSEE, U. Tex., Austin, 1964, PhD in Elec. Engring., 1966. Registered profl. engr., Tex. Rsch. assoc. Elec. Engring. Rsch. Lab., U. Tex., Austin, 1962-66; sr. mem. tech. staff def. systems and equipment group Tex. Instruments Inc., Dallas, 1966—; conf. presenter in field. Contbr. articles to profl. jours.; patentee bifocal pillbox antenna system, scanning antenna with extended off-broadside capability, amplitude modulation scanning antenna system, antenna pattern roll stblzn. Mem. IEEE (sr.), Eta Kappa Nu, Tau Beta Phi. Home: 2213 Newcastle Cir Plano TX 75075-3326

HEMMINGHAUS, ROGER ROY, energy company executive, chemical engineer; b. St. Louis, Aug. 27, 1936; s. Roy Geroge and Henrietta E.M. (Knacht) H.; children: Sheryl Ann, Susan Lynn, Sally Ann; m. Dorotyh O'Kelly, Aug. 18, 1979; children: R. Patrick, Kelley Elizabeth, Roger Christian. Student, Purdue U., 1954-56; B.S. in Chem. Engring., Auburn U., 1958; grad. cert., Bettis Reactor Engring., Pitts., 1959; postgrad., La. State U., 1963-66. Various tech. and mgmt. positions Exxon Co. U.S.A., Baton Rouge, 1962-66, Benicia, Calif., 1967-70, Houston, 1970-76; refinery gen. mgr. C.F. Industries, East Chicago, Ind., 1976-77; pres. Petro United Inc., Houston, 1977-80; v.p. planning United Gas Pipe Line, Houston, 1980-82, United Energy Resources, Houston, 1982-84; v.p. corp. planning and devel. Diamond Shamrock Corp. (name changed to Maxus Energy Corp., 1987), Dallas, 1984-85, past exec. v.p.; pres. Diamond Shamrock Refining & Mktg., San Antonio, 1985—; now also chmn., chief exec. officer Diamond Shamrock Refining & Mktg.; dir. InterFirst Bank, San Antonio. Adviser Jr. Achievement, Baton Rouge, 1956-66; pres. congregation Lutheran Ch., Baton Rouge, 1965, Moraga, Calif., 1969; chmn. indsl. div. United Crusade, Solano County, Calif., 1970; assoc. gen. chmn. United Way, Tex. Gulf Coast, 1983-84. Served to lt. USN, 1958-62. Mem. Am. Chem. Soc., Am. Inst. Chem. Engrs., Naval Architects and Marine Engrs., Am. Petroleum Inst., San Antonio C. of C. (dir.), Tau Beta Pi, Phi Lambda Upsilon, Phi Kappa Phi, Kappa Alpha. Clubs: Fair Oaks Country; Plaza, Petroleum (San Antonio). Office: Diamond Shamrock R&M Inc 9830 Colonnade Blvd San Antonio TX 78269

HEMPFLING, GREGORY JAY, mechanical engineer; b. Terre Haute, Ind., Sept. 7, 1961; s. John G. and Sandra (Sutton) H. BSME, Rose-Hulman Inst. Tech., Terre Haute, Ind., 1983; M in Engring. Mgmt., George Washington U., Washington, 1991. Asst. engr. Cherne Contracting Corp., New Washington, Ind., 1983-84; engr. I Newport News Shipbuilding, 1984-86; engr. II Newport News (Va.) Shipbuilding, 1986-89, engring. supr., 1989-93, engring. dept. mgr., 1994-95, LPD-17 design mgr., 1995-96, Electric Boat br. mgmr., 1996—; chmn. Industry Rels. Com. (ea. Va. sect.), 1990-92. Mem. ASME (chmn. industry rels. com. 1990-92, rep. Peninsula Engring. Coun. 1992-93), SAE (Marine Vehicle Systems panel 1989—), Soc. Naval Architects and Marine Engrs., Am. Mgmt. Assn., Naval Submarine League. Home: 559 Kristy Ct Newport News VA 23602-9025 Office: Newport News Shipbuilding 4101 Washington Ave Newport News VA 23607-2734

HEMPFLING, LINDA LEE, nurse; b. Indpls., July 28, 1947; d. Paul Roy and Myrtle Pearl (Ward) H. Diploma Meth. Hosp. Ind. Sch. Nursing, 1968; postgrad. St. Joseph's Coll. Charge nurse Meth. Hosp., Indpl., 1968; staff nurse operating room Silver Cross Hosp., Joliet, Ill., 1969; charge nurse operating room Huntington (N.Y.) Hosp., 1969-73; night supr. oper. rm., post anesthesia care unit Hermann Hosp., Houston, 1973-76; unit. mgr., purchasing coord. oper. rms., 1976-83; RN med. auditor, quality improvement and tng. coord. Nat. Healthcare Rev., Inc., Houston, 1984—. Future Nurses Am. scholar, 1965, Nat. Merit scholar, 1965. Mem. Assn. Oper. Rm. Nurses, Tex. Med. Auditors Assn., Nat. Med. Cost Containment Assn. Office: 6565 Fannin MS MBI-04 Houston TX 77030

HEMPHILL, JEAN HARGETT, college dean; b. Pollocksville, N.C., Aug. 21, 1936; d. Robert Franklin and Frances (Hill) Hargett; m. Raymond Arthur Hemphill, Feb. 28, 1964; 1 child, Gerald Franklin. BS, East Carolina U., 1958; MEd, U. Nev.-Las Vegas, 1968; student N.C. State U., 1993. Sec.-treas. Five Points Milling Co., Inc., New Bern, N.C., 1968-77; instr. Craven C.C., New Bern, 1973-80, dean service techs., 1980—; mem. New Bern-Craven County Tech. Prep, steering com. New Bern-Craven County Sch., 1990-95; supervisor rep. curriculum improvement project N.C. C.C. Sys., 1992-96; mem. Craven County Schs. Sch.-to-Work Curriculum Com., 1996—. Scholarship chmn. continuing edn. div. Woman's Club, New Bern, 1981—, treas. continuing edn. div., 1986—. Mem. N.C. Assn. C.C. Instrnl. Adminstrs., Phi Kappa Phi. Democrat. Methodist. Office: Craven Community Coll 800 College Ct New Bern NC 28562-4900

HENARD, ELIZABETH ANN, controller; b. Providence, Oct. 9, 1947; d. Anthony Joseph and Grace Johanna (Lokay) Zorbach; m. Patrick Edward Mann, Dec. 18, 1970 (div. July 1972); m. John Bruce Henard Jr., Oct. 19, 1974; children: Scott Michael, Christopher Andrew. Student, Jacksonville (Fla.) U., 1966. Sec. So. Bell Tel.&Tel., Jacksonville, 1964-69; office mgr. Gunther F. Reis Assocs., Tampa, Fla., 1969-71; exec. sec. Ernst & Ernst, Tampa, 1971-72; exec. sec. to pres. Lamalie Assocs., Tampa, 1972-74; exec. sec. Arthur Young & Co., Chgo., 1975; adminstrv. asst. Irving J. Markin, Chgo., 1975; contr., v.p., corp. sec. Henard Assocs., Inc., Dallas, 1983-92. Mem. Dallas Investors Group (treas. 1986-91), Tampa Palms Country Club. Republican. Roman Catholic. Home: 15705 Mifflin Ct Tampa FL 33647-1120

HENCH, JANE GILBERT, retired cultural organization administrator; b. Chgo., Mar. 19, 1920; d. John Ashley and Jeannette Julia Gilbert; m. Miles Ellsworth Hench, Dec. 11, 1945 (div. Mar. 19, 1990); children: Virginia Ellen, Carol Hench Valentine, Thomas Gilbert. BA, Lawrence Coll., 1941; MA, Northwestern U., 1945; postgrad., Richmond (Va.) Profl. Inst. Tchg. asst. Lawrence Coll., Appleton, Wis., 1940-41; dir. test divsn. svc. Sci. Rsch. Assocs., Chgo., 1941-43; personnel dir. Johnson & Johnson Co., Chgo., 1944-45; counselor Sch. Grad. Studies U. Mich., Ann Arbor, 1946-48; organizer, dir. Old Dominion Symph. Coun., Richmond, 1960-75; dir. state svcs. Va. Chamber Orch., Alexandria, 1975-82; tchr. part-time ENSWP War Time night classes, Chgo., 1942-44; cons. Va. Cultural Devel. Commn., 1965-66; freelance cons., Chgo., 1945. Contbr. article to Music Educator's Jour. Chief election judge electoral bd. Reveille United Meth. Ch., Richmond, 1987-93, mem. adminstrv. bd., historian, 1988—. Recipient Outstanding Vol. Svc. award Richmond Symphony, 1964, United Way, 1965; named Woman of Yr. Fairfax (Va.) Symphony. Mem. Am. Symphony Orch. League (organizer women's coun. 1963), Nat. Soc. Lit. and Arts, Mil. Officers' Wives Club (sec. 1980-85), Alpha Chi Omega, Phi Beta Kappa. Republican. Methodist. Home: 2113 Hanover Ave A Richmond VA 23220-3427

HENDEL, ROBERT CHARLES, surgeon; b. New Haven, Conn., Aug. 6, 1946; s. James Norman and Jane Elizabeth (Seabury) H.; m. Kathleen Dienhoffer, Sept. 11, 1976. BS in Physics, MIT, 1968; MD, U. Conn., 1972. Diplomate Am. Bd. Surgery. Intern SUNY Upstate Med. Ctr., Syracuse, N.Y., 1972-73, resident in surgery, 1973-77; surgeon USN Hosp., Guatanamo Bay, Cuba, 1977-79, Transylvania Community Hosp., Brevard, N.C., 1979—; med. dir. Transylvania Hospice, brevard, 1989—. Fellow ACS, Soc. Am. Gastrointestinal Endoscopic Surgeons, Am. Soc. Gen. Surgeons. Office: Transylvania Community Hosp Med Park Dr Bldg 1 Brevard NC 28712

HENDERSON, ALBERT JOHN, federal judge; b. Canton, Ga., Dec. 12, 1920; s. Albert Jefferson and Cliffie Mae (Cook) H.; m. Jenny Lee Medford, Feb. 24, 1951; children—Michael John, Jenny Lee. LL.B., Mercer U., 1947. Bar: Ga. bar 1947. Practiced law Marietta, Ga., 1948-60; judge Juvenile Ct. Cobb County, Ga., 1953-60, Superior Ct. Cobb County, 1961-68, U.S. Dist. Ct. for No. Dist. Ga., Atlanta, 1968-76; chief judge U.S. Dist. Ct. for No. Dist. Ga., 19[illegible]-79; judge U.S. Circuit Ct. of Appeals for 5th Circuit, 1979-81; judge U.S. Circuit Ct. Appeals for 11th Circuit, 1981-86, sr. judge, 1986—; asst. solicitor gen. Blue Ridge Jud. Circuit, 1948-52. Chmn. Cobb dist. Atlanta council Boy Scouts Am., 1964. Served with AUS, 1943-46. Fellow Am. Bar Found.; mem. ABA, FBA, Am. Judicature Soc., State Bar Ga., Atlanta Bar Assn., Cobb Jud. Bar Assn., Lawyers Club Atlanta, Old War Horse Lawyers Club. Office: US Ct Appeals 11th Circuit 56 Forsyth St NW Atlanta GA 30303-2205*

HENDERSON, ARCHIBALD, III, lawyer; b. Houston, Mar. 2, 1955; s. Archibald and Helen Claire (White) H.; m. Luisa Loera, Mar. 9, 1996. BA, Rice U., 1977; MA, UCLA, 1979, PhD, 1983; JD, U. Houston, 1986. Bar: Tex. 1986. Rsch. assoc. in med. jurisprudence Inst. for Med. Humanities/ U. Tex. Med. Br., Galveston, 1986-88; pvt. practice Houston, 1988-93; ptnr. Bolivar, Henderson & Assocs., Houston, 1993—. Contbr. articles to profl. jours. Mem. State Bar of Tex., MLA. Episcopalian. Home: 8003 Highmeadow Houston TX 77063-4719 Office: Bolivar Henderson & Assocs 2419-A South Blvd Houston TX 77098-5109

HENDERSON, ARVIS BURL, data processing executive, biochemist; b. Abilene, Tex., Oct. 24, 1943; s. Arvis Vernon and Aubra Lee (Patton) H.; m. Mary Ann Pickett, Mar. 17, 1966 (div. Sept. 1983); 1 child, Michelle Rene; m. Jo Nell Hartsell, July 2, 1985 (dec. May 1996). AA, San Angelo Coll., 1964; BA, U. Tex., 1966; MAS, So. Meth. U., 1969; PhD, U. Tex. Health Sci. Ctr., 1976. Postdoctoral fellow U. Tex., Austin, 1976-80; dir. rsch. lab. Instrumentation Specialities Co., Lincoln, Nebr., 1980-81; asst. prof. pediatrics U. Tex. Health Sci. Ctr., Houston, 1981-84; dir. sci. computing S.W. Found. for Biomed. Rsch., San Antonio, 1984-91; assoc. v.p. info. tech. U. Tex., San Antonio, 1991-96; vice provost for computing and info. tech. U. Tex., Arlington, 1996—. Contbr. articles on biomed. research to profl. jours., chpts. to books. Chmn. Alamo Area Quality Workforce Planning Com., 1990-92; active Class XII Gov. Exec. Devel. Program, 1993. Recipient Research Service award NIH, 1976-79; fellow U. Tex., 1976-80, Clayton Found. Biochemistry Inst., 1980. Mem. NIH spl. study sect. 9, Data Processing Mgmt. Assn., Assn. Systems Mgmt., Assn. for Computing Machinery. Republican. Baptist. Home: 5309 Farragut Dr Arlington TX 76018 Office: U Tex PO Box 19118 Arlington TX 76019-9118

HENDERSON, BRUCE B., psychology educator; b. Pitts., Apr. 21, 1950; s. David and Janet (Getty) H.; m. Judith E. Storr, Aug. 16, 1972; children: Heidi, Robert, Holly. BA in Psychology, Bucknell U., 1972, MA in Psychology, 1975; PhD in Child Psychology, U. Minn., 1978. Tchr. presch. handicapped Cen. Susquehanna Intermediate Unit, Lewisburg, Pa., 1972-74, dir. presch. handicapped, 1974-75; instr. psychology Bucknell U., 1974-75, U. Minn., Mpls., 1977-78; asst. to full prof. Western Carolina U., Cullowhee, N.C., 1978—; evaluation cons. Warren Wilson Coll., Swannanoa, N.C., 1986-88; adj. prof. Sch. of Social Work, U. N.C. Chapel Hill, Asheville, 1987, 89, 91-93, 96; seminar leader N.C. Ctr. for Advancement of Tchg., Cullowhee, 1987—. Editor/author: (book) Curiosity and Exploration, 1994, Teaching Critical Thinking in Psychology, 1986; contbr. articles to profl. jours. Trustee Black Mountain, N.C. Children's Home, 1990—; elder Presbyn. Ch., Sylva, N.C., 1993—. Recipient Influences on Children's Curiosity award Spencer Found., 1980-82, Young Scholar award Found. for Child Devel., 1984. Mem. Soc. for rsch. in Child Devel., Am. Psychol. Assn., Phi Kappa Phi. Home: Box 216 Cullowhee NC 28723 Office: Dept Psychology Western Carolina Univ Cullowhee NC 28723

HENDERSON, CHARLES WILLIAM, health and medical publishing executive; b. Fitzgerald, Ga., July 20, 1949; s. Ashton Leven Henderson Jr. and Frances Ethel Fortson. Cert. in health and WCI, Emory U., 1971; BA in Journalism and Mass Comms., U. Ga., Athens, 1971. Exec. editor Business Atlanta Mag., Atlanta, 1971; columnist Atlanta Mag., 1972; writer Atlanta Jour./Constitution, Atlanta, 1972; staff corr. Bur. Nat. Affairs, Inc., Washington, 1973-74; editor-pub. Buckhead Atlanta, 1975-76; dir. cmty. affairs divsn. City of Atlanta Dept. Cmty. and Human Devel., 1976-77; dir. pub. rels. and comms. Nat. Bank of Ga., Atlanta, 1977; publicist New World Pictures, L.A., Atlanta, 1977, TriStar Pictures, L.A., Atlanta, 1977-79; v.p. TriStar Studios, L.A., Atlanta, 1979; exec. v.p., exec. prodr. Henderson-Crowe Prodns., Inc., Atlanta, 1980-84; publisher, editor-in-chief C.W. Henderson, Publisher, Atlanta, 1984—; featured spkr. Internat. Newsletter Conf., Washington, 1996. Editor-in-chief: (periodicals) AIDS Weekly, 1985—, AIDS Weekly Plus, 1985—, Cancer Weekly, 1988—, Cancer Rschr. Weekly, 1988—, Cancer Biotech. Weekly, 1988—, Vaccine Weekly, 1993—, Blood Weekly, 1993—, TB Weekly, 1993—, Health Letter on the CDC, 1994—, Gene Therapy Weekly, 1994—, Disease Weekly, 1994—, Hepatitis Weekly, 1995—, Malaria Weekly, 1995—, Antiviral Weekly, 1996—, Immunotherapy Weekly, 1996—, Emerging Pathogen Weekly, 1996— (interactive database) NewsFile, 1996—; publisher (book) AIDS Therapies, 1988. Cited by Billboard Mag. as Co-Founder First Nationwide Video Music Programming on Cable TV, 1980; cited by Arbitron TV Ratings as exec. producer of Highest Rated Syndicated Musical Variety Program 0f 1984; cited by USA Today as One of Six Who Made a Difference on the Impact of AIDS, 1985; cited by N.Y. Times as World's Largest Producer Weekly Health Info., 1995; recipient Eagle Scout award Boy Scouts Am., 1963, Fiftieth Anniversary award Order of the Arrow, 1964, Top Pub. Rels. Mktg. Campaign award News Analysis Inst. Over 100 Club, 1979. Mem. AP, Internat. AIDS Soc., Assn. for Continuing Med. Edn., Newsletter Publishers Assn., U. Ga. Alumni Assn., Journalism Alumni Assn. of the Univ. of Ga., Phi Kappa Theta. Home: PO Box 5528 Atlanta GA 30307 Office: CW Henderson Publisher PO Box 5528 Med Ctr II Atlanta GA 31107

HENDERSON, DAVID ALLEN, lawyer; b. Japan, Feb. 18, 1948; s. Frank David and Pauline Elizabeth (Patton) H. BA, Miami U., Oxford, Ohio, 1970; LLB, U. Cin., 1974. Bar: Calif. 1974, U.S. Ct. Appeals (9th cir.) 1975, U.S. Dist. Ct. (no. dist.) Calif. 1976, U.S. Dist. Ct. (ea. dist.) Calif. 1978, U.S. Supreme Ct. 1978, D.C. 1980, N.Y. 1981, U.S. Ct. Appeals (D.C. cir.) 1982, Ariz. 1983, U.S. Dist. Ct. Ariz. 1983, U.S. Dist. Ct. Tex. 1996. Law clk. to presiding justice U.S. Ct. Appeals (9th cir.), San Diego, 1974-75; adj. prof. U. San Diego Coll. Law, 1975; assoc. Pillsbury, Madison & Sutro, San Francisco, 1975-79, Chadbourn, Park, Whiteside & Wolfe, N.Y.C. and Washington, 1981-82; dep. gen. counsel Pres.'s Council on Wage and Price Stability, Washington, 1979-81; ptnr. Brown & Bain, Phoenix and Palo Alto, Calif., 1983-93, Fish & Richardson, Menlo Park, Calif., 1993-95, Jenkens & Gilchrist, Dallas, 1995—; mem. adv. bd. St. Francis Meml. Hosp., 1978—, Ctr. Nat. Policy, Washington, 1981—, Corp. Pub. Broadcasting, Washington, 1969-70; counsel to Alfred Kahn, inflation advisor to Pres., Washington, 1979-81; superior ct. judge pro tem Maricopa County, Ariz. Editor in chief U. Cin. Law Rev., Jour. World Intellectual Property and Trade Forum. Mem. ABA (litigation and anti-trust sects.), Order of Coif, St. Francis Yacht Club (San Francisco). Office: Jenkens & Gilchrist 1445 Ross Ave Dallas TX 75202

HENDERSON, GEORGE ERVIN, lawyer; b. Pampa, Tex., June 7, 1947; s. Ervin L. and Elizabeth (Yoe) H.; m. Linda L. Dalrymple, Aug. 22, 1970; children: Andrew, Elizabeth. BA, Tex. Christian U., 1969; JD, Yale U., 1972. Bar: Tex. 1972, U.S. Dist. Ct. (so. dist.) Tex. 1974, U.S. Dist. Ct. (we. dist.) 1978. Assoc. Fulbright & Jaworski, Houston and Austin, 1972-79; ptnr. Fulbright & Jaworski, Austin, 1983—, Sneed & Vine, Austin, 1979-82; adj. instr. law U. Tex., Austin, 1983-85. Contbr. articles to profl. jours. Mem. S. Tex. Youth Soccer Assn. Rules Com., 1993-96, Greater Austin Soccer Coalition. Capt. USAR, 1972-78. Mem. ABA, Tex. Bar Assn. (chmn. corp. banking and bus. law sect. 1983), State Bar of Tex (chmn. corp. banking and bus. law sect. 1985-88), Tex. Assn. Bank Counsel (pres. 1985-86), Travis County Bar Assn. (bankruptcy law sect., chmn. 1988-89), San Antonio Bankruptcy Bar Assn., Uniform Comml. Code Com., Austin Yacht Club, Met. Club, Capital Soccer Club (pres. 1993-95). Office: Fulbright & Jaworski 600 Congress Ave Ste 2400 Austin TX 78701-3248

HENDERSON, GERALDINE THOMAS, retired social security official, educator; b. Luling, Tex., Jan. 7, 1924; d. Cornelius Thomas and Maggie (Keyes) Thomas; m. James E. Henderson, Feb. 9, 1942 (dec. Apr. 1978); children—Geraldine, Jessica, Jennifer. BS, Fayetteville State U., 1967. Tchr. Cumberland County Schs., Fayetteville, N.C., 1966-67, Fayetteville City Schs., 1967-68; with Social Security Adminstrn., Fayetteville, 1968-87; substitute tchr. Cumberland County Sch. System, 1987—; claims rep. Pres. Fayetteville State U. Found., 1981-82; pres. NAACP, Fayetteville br., 1983-86. DeaconColl. Heights Presbyn. Ch., 1965-79, ruling elder, 1980-91; bd. dirs. Fayetteville Art Coun., 1984—, Cumberland County United Way, 1983—, chmn. div. corp. mission Fayetteville Presbytery, 1986, mem. personnel review bd. City of Fayetteville, 1987—; inductee Nat. Black Coll. Alumni Hall of Fame, 1988; bd. dirs. Habitat for Humanity, Fayetteville, N.C., 1989, Share, Heart of the Carolinas, 1991; moderator Presbytery of Coastal Carolina, 1989; vice chair Cape Fear Food Bank, 1991. Recipient Life Membership Chmn. award NAACP Nat. Conv., Chgo., 1994, Essence of Freedom award NAACP State Conf., Goldsboro, N.C., 1995. Mem. LWV, Nat. Assn. Equal Opportunity in Higher Edn. (disting. alumni 1989), Legion Aux. (treas. 1981-83), Zeta Phi Zeta (Woman of Yr. 1984), Omega Psi Phi (Citizen of Yr. 1985). Democrat. Presbyterian. Avocations: creative dress design; gardening; travel.

HENDERSON, HARRIET, librarian; b. Pampa, Tex., Nov. 19, 1949; d. Ervin Leon and Hannah Elizabeth (Yoe) H. AB, Baker U., 1971; MLS, U. Tex., 1973. Sch. libr. Pub. Sch. System, Pampa, Tex., 1971-72; city libr. City of Tyler, Tex., 1973-80, City of Newport News, Va., 1980-84; dir. librs. and info. svcs. City of Newport News, 1984-90; dir. Louisville Free Pub. Libr.; del. White House Conf. Librs. and Info. Svcs.; bd. mem. Tex. Libr. Systems Act Adv. Bd., 1979-80. Budget panel chmn. Peninsula United Way, Hampton, Va., 1984-85; mem. bd. Peninsula coun. Boy Scouts Am., 1982-84, Peninsula Womens Network, Newport News, 1983-85; mem. Leadership Louisville, 1991—, Alliant Health System Adult Oper. Bd., 1991—; mem. adv. com. dept. edn. Spalding U., 1991—; diaconate Hidenwood Presbyterian Ch., Newport News, 1983-85; del. White House Conf. Librs. and Info. Svcs., 1991. Recipient Tribute to Women in Bus. and Industry, Peninsula YWCA, Newport News, 1984. Mem. ALA, Ky. Libr. Assn. (vice chair pub. libr. sect. 1994), Va. Libr. Assn. (chmn. legis. com. 1981-84, v.p. 1985, pres. 1986), Rotary Club Louisville (chair youth svc. com. 1994—), Jr. League Louisville. Office: Louisville Free Pub Libr Office of Dir 301 York St Louisville KY 40203-2205

HENDERSON, HOWARD MICHAEL, federal agency administrator, mediator; b. Atlanta, Mar. 14, 1943; m. Shirley C. Henderson, Dec. 20, 1969; 1 child, Quentin Anthony. BA in Sociology, Morehouse Coll.; MA in Journalism and Pub. Rels., U. Ga.; AS in Comml. Music, Recording Industry, Ga. State U. Pub. info. specialist City of Atlanta, 1977-78; sr. pub. info. specialist Employees Retirement System State of Ga., 1978-81, sr. pub. info. specialist dept. human resources, 1981-84; cert. mediator Neighborhood Justice Ctr., Atlanta, 1987—; pub. affairs specialist EPA, Atlanta, 1984—; part-time instr. evening program Ga. State U., Atlanta, 1989—; mem. adv. bd. comml. music recording Ga. State U. Author: Meditations in the Privy, 1978, (poems) The Bitter, The Sweet, and The Inbetween, 1981, Sex, Racism, and Other Reflective Tidbits, 1987, Mid-Life Crisis, 1990, 91, In My Poetic Nakedness You Will See..., 1992, My Saint Emma Years 1957-61, 1994; contbr. articles to profl. jours. Life mem. APEX Mus.; former mem. Dekalb County Cmty. Rels. Commn.; mem. citizens adv. com. State of Ga. Senate Music/Recording Industry. With USN, 1965-69, USCG, 1969-72. Recipient Outstanding Young Men in Am. award. Mem. NAACP (life), Nat. Acad. Recording Arts & Scis., Soc. Profls. in Dispute Resolutions (assoc.), Am. Legion, Kappa Alpha Psi (life). Office: EPA 345 Courtland St NE Atlanta GA 30308-3420

HENDERSON, JAMES RONALD, industrial real estate developer; b. Columbus, Nebr., Dec. 2, 1947; s. Bill and Roeburta (Hamrick) H.; m. Jamey Lee Blevins, June 30, 1972 (div. Mar. 1993); children: Benjamin James, Katrin Lee, Joseph Marion. BSBA, Okla. State U., 1970. Commd. 2d lt. USAR, 1970, advanced through grades to maj., 1987, ret., 1992;

appraiser Dorchester Cos., Tulsa, 1970-72; devel. mgr. Wolf Point Properties, Tulsa, 1972-82; v.p. Mager Mortgage Co., Tulsa, 1972-78; mktg. dir. Tulsa Port of Catoosa, Okla., 1987-89; pres. J. Ronald Henderson Real Estate, Tulsa, 1978—, Henderson Exploration Co., Tulsa, 1982—; mng. dir. Wolf Point Indsl. Pky. Owners Assn., Tulsa, 1984—. Organizer, incorporator Tulsa Charity Fight Night, Inc., 1993; organizer N.E. Okla. Econ. Devel. Assn., 1988. Maj. USAR ret. Mem. Nat. Assn. Indsl. and Office Pks. (pres. Tulsa chpt. 1990), Propeller Club Port of Catoosa (pres. 1987). Southern Baptist. Office: Henderson Cos 1643 E 15th St Tulsa OK 74120-6044

HENDERSON, JOSEPH H., cardiologist; b. Atlanta, Mar. 7, 1960; s. Joseph Clarence and Mary (Houston) H.; m. Cynthia Brooks, July 24, 1982; children: Sarah Elizabeth, Hannah Elizabeth. BS in Biology, Furman U., Greenville, S.C., 1982; MD, Med. Coll. Ga., 1986. Diplomate in Internal Medicine and Cardiology. Resident in internal medicine Greenville Meml. Hosp., Greenville, 1986-89; fellow in cardiology U. S.C., Columbia, 1989-92; invasive cardiologist Edgewood Cardiology, Greenville, 1992—. Fellow Am. Coll. Cardiology. Office: Edgewood Cardiology 14 Edgewood Dr Greenville SC 29605

HENDERSON, KAYE NEIL, civil engineer, business executive; b. Birmingham, Ala., June 10, 1933; s. Ernest Martin and Mary (Head) H.; BS, Va. Mil. Inst., 1954; BA with honors, U. South Fla., 1967; m. Betty Jane Belanus, June 26, 1954; (div.); children: David Scott, Alan Douglas, Helen Kaye. Registered profl. engr., Fla. Mgmt. trainee Gen. Electric Co., Schenectady, 1954; sales engr. Fla. Prestressed Concrete, Tampa, 1956-57; field engr. Portland Cement Assn., Tampa, 1957-63; gen. mgr. residential and comml. sales Tampa Electric Co., 1963-66; v.p. Watson & Co., architects and engrs., Tampa, 1966-69; v.p. Reynolds, Smith & Hills, architects, engrs. and planners, Jacksonville, Fla., 1969-78, sr. v.p., 1978-86, dir., 1976-86; sec. transp. State of Fla., 1987-89; pres., CEO Old World Svc., Inc., bd. dirs. Stavros Ctr. Econ. Edn. Vice chmn. Temple Terrace Planning and Zoning Bd., 1962-67; pres. Guidance Center Hillsborough County, 1969; mem. adv. bd. Multi-State Transp. System, 1976-82; mem. Duval County Republican Exec. Com., 1970-72; bd. dirs. Salvation Army Home and Hosp. Coun., 1964-69; mem. found U. South Fla., Fla. Taxwatch; 1st lt. USAF, 1954-56. Recipient Service awards Greater Tampa C. of C., 1964-66; named Outstanding Young Man of Tampa Jr. C. of C., 1965; Outstanding Young Man of Am., U.S. Jr. C. of C., 1967; Boss of Year award Am. Bus. Women's Assn., 1978. Mem. Fla. Engrng. Soc., Timuquana Country Club, River Club, Rotary (dir. 1984-85, Paul Harris fellow 1987), Phi Kappa Phi (life), Tau Beta Pi. Republican. Presbyterian. Home and Office: 4227 Water Oak Ln Jacksonville FL 32210-5843

HENDERSON, LARRY RAY, banker; b. Buford, Ga., May 28, 1950; s. James William and Ann (Turner) H.; m. Pamela Sharon Puckett, July 20, 1974; children: Lisa M., Jennifer L. BS, Middle Tenn. State U., 1973. Asst. branch mgr. Pub. Finance, Covington, Ga., 1974-75; credit officer 1st Nat. Bank of Atlanta, 1975-78; branch mgr. 1st Comml. Bank, Buford, Ga., 1978-83; COO, exec. v.p., dir. Peoples Bank & Trust, Buford, 1984—; bank dir. Peoples Bank & Trust, Buford, 1983—. 1st Lt. U.S. Army, 1974. Mem. Buford Lions (pres. 1989). Republican. Baptist. Home: 2492 Doc Hughes Rd Buford GA 30519-4227 Office: Peoples Bank & Trust 1899 Buford Hwy Buford GA 30518-3672

HENDERSON, MARCUS TERRELL, financial counselor; b. Nashville, Tenn., Dec. 16, 1966; s. Samuel and LeLia Mai (Allen) H.; m. Sunji Michelle Beasley, Sept. 29, 1990; children: Justin Manning, Shifra LeLia, Mystique Michelle, Marcus Terrell Jr. BS in Bus., Tenn. State U., 1988. Fin. transfer counselor Envoy Corp., Nashville, 1987-88; fin. and ins. mgr. Beaman Automotive Group, Nashville, 1988-89; fin. counselor Henderson Fin. Group, Nashville, 1989—; cons. John Hancock Fin. Svcs., Nashville, 1989—; bd. dirs. Lloyd C. Elam Meharry Mental Health Adv. Bd., Nashville. Treas., asst. budget dir. St. John AME Ch. Steward Bd., Nashville, 1992—; asst. dir. Nashville's Rm. in the Inn, 1987—; mem. Million Dollar Round Table Found., Park Ridge, Ill., 1994. Recipient Nat. Quality award Life Ins. Mktg. and Rsch. Assn., 1992-94, Assoc. of Yr. award Gen. Agts. and Mgrs. Assn., 1992. Fellow Life Underwriter Tng. Coun. (Nat. Quality award 1992-94); mem. Nat. Assn. Securities Dealers, Nat. Assn. Life Underwriters, Internat. Assn. Fin. Planning, Million Dollar Round Table (qualifying mem., programs com. 1992—), John Hancock Pres. Club. Republican. Office: Henderson Fin Group 3200 W End Ave Ste 303 Nashville TN 37203-1319

HENDERSON, NANCY CARR, dietitian, medical transcriber, writer; b. Pearisburg, Va., Apr. 11, 1939; d. Allen Paris and Nannie Amanda (Woodyard) Carr; m. Ander Burnell Henderson, Apr. 14, 1962; children: Randall Craig, Gina Andrea. BS, W.Va. Wesleyan Coll., 1961. Intern Hines VA Hosp., Chgo., 1965-66; part-time instr. nutrition Fla. Jr. Coll., Jacksonville, 1966-68; chief dietitian Meth. Hosp., Jacksonville, 1969-74; cons. dietitian St. Alban's Psychiat. Hosp., Radford, Va., 1975-80; clin. dietitian Montgomery County Hosp., Blacksburg, Va., 1980-82; food svc. dir. Battlefield Park Home, Petersburg, Va., 1984-86; cons. dietitian Rappahannock Gen. Hosp., Kilmarnock, Va., 1990-92; clin. dietitian South Hill (Va.) Community Health Ctr., 1992-93; telemarketer Rep. Party Va., Richmond, 1985-93; preceptor of 1st minority food svc. supr. Duval Med. Ctr., Jacksonville, 1966-67. Mem. Am. Dietetic Assn. Home: 313 Giles Ave Dublin VA 24084

HENDERSON, REXFORD STEPHEN, reporter; b. Long Beach, Calif., Mar. 31, 1952; s. Rexford Rees and Amelia Julia (Stefkovic) H. Student, Lawrence U., 1970-74; BA, U. Nebr., 1978; MBA, U. South Fla., Tampa, 1995. Editor Columbus (Nebr.) Telegram, 1978-81; reporter Odessa (Tex.) American, 1981-82, San Angelo (Tex.) Standard-Times, 1982-87, Tampa Tribune, 1987—. Home: 1407 S Lorenzo Ave Apt 4 Tampa FL 33629-6273

HENDERSON, RICHARD MARTIN, chemical engineer; b. Winston-Salem, Dec. 12, 1934; s. Billy Martin and Marion Lucille (Dunn) H.; m. Patricia Lucille Green, Dec. 27, 1958 (div. 1978); children: Marian Patricia, Richard Martin; m. Janice Lee Ferris, Apr. 3, 1981. BBA, Wake Forest U., 1957. Cert. quality engr. Jr. chem. engr. R.J. Reynolds Tobacco Co., Winston-Salem, 1957-58, asst. chem. engr., 1958-65, product devel. group leader, 1965-66, devel. sect. head, 1966-80, div. mgr., 1981—. Pres. Y Men's Club of Winston-Salem, 1989, Moravian Music Found., Winston-Salem, 1983; active United Way of Forsyth County, 1958—, Winston-Salem Arts Coun., 1958—. With Signal Corps, U.S. Army, 1960-61. Recipient Merit award, Moravian Music Found., 1984; Ky. Col. Mem. Am. Soc. for Quality Control (founding dir./sr. mem.), Forsyth Country Club. Republican. Moravian. Home: 717 Mitch Dr Winston Salem NC 27104-5127 Office: RJ Reynolds Tobacco Co 401 N Main St Winston Salem NC 27101-3818

HENDERSON, ROBB ALAN, minister; b. Wilkes Barre, Pa., Mar. 21, 1956; s. Robert Alan and Mary (Gallup) H.; m. Norma Jean Davis, Nov. 26, 1994; children: Jason Allyn, Gareth Kent. BA in Theology, King's Coll., Wilkes Barre, 1981; MDiv, Lancaster Theol. Sem., 1985; D Ministry, Bethany Theol. Sem., 1990. Ordained to ministry United Meth. Ch. as deacon, 1986, as elder, 1988. Pastor Luzerne (Pa.) United Meth. Ch., 1985-88, Carverton United Meth. Ch., Wyoming, Pa., 1988—, St. Paul's United Meth. Ch., Scranton, Pa., 1993-94; owner R&R Bus Line, Luzerne, 1990—; chmn. interreligious and ecumenical affairs com. Coun. of Chs., 1989—; bd. dirs. Wyoming Valley Coun. of Chs.; safety dir., dispatcher First Class Coach Co., St. Petersburg, Fla. Chaplain Mt. Zion Vol. Fire Dept., Mt. Zion, Harding, Pa.; mem. Wilkes Barre Dist. Coord. Coun., 1988—. Mem. Masons (chaplain Kingston lodge 1989), Irem Temple. Home and Office: 2821 14th St N Saint Petersburg FL 33704-2512

HENDERSON, SALATHIEL JAMES, minister, clergy; b. Key West, Fla., June 15, 1944; s. James Joseph and Merlice Yvone (McIntosh) H.; m. Mary Louise Henderson, June 28, 1969; children: Salathiel James II, Shane Jamal. Diploma, LaSalle Extension U., 1977; AA, St. Leo Coll., 1987, BA, 1988. Ordained to ministry Bapt. Ch. 1989. Deacon Antioch Bapt. Ch., Hampton, Va., 1980-87, assoc. min., 1987—; vol. chaplain Hospice unit VA Med. Ctr., Hampton, Va., 1987—; substitute tchr. Hampton City Schs., 1991-95, adminstrv. asst., 1995—; sr. fed. supply cataloger Mason & Hanger Svcs., Inc., NASA/Langley AFB, Va., 1988-91; dir. Christian Edn., Antioch Bapt. Ch., 1986—, mem. fin. com., 1984-94, spiritual advisor Youth Usher Bd., 1984-90, sec. Ministerial Staff, 1991-94; dir. Bereavement Ministry, Antioch Bapt. Ch., Hampton, 1988—; cubmaster Cub Scouts Am., Antioch Bapt.-Hampton, 1990-95; chartered scouting rep. Antioch Bapt., 1995—; sec. Hampton Ministers' Coalition, 1992-94; v.p. Ministers' Coalition for Hampton & Vicinity, 1994—. Mem. Hampton U. Min.'s Conf., 1990—; co-chmn. publicity com. Peninsula United Clergy Coun,. 1994—; vol. Am. Heart Assn., 1992—. With USAF, 1962-85. Mem. NAACP, DAV (life), Am. Assn. Christian Counselors, Masons. Democrat. Home and Office: 607 Allendale Dr Hampton VA 23669-1621

HENDERSON, WILLIAM EUGENE, education educator; b. Miami, Fla., Sept. 9, 1947; s. William Bartow and Evelyn Mildred (Stansell) H. BA in Polit. Sci., Acctg., U. South Fla., 1967; MS in Guidance, Counseling, Barry U., 1971, EdS in Sch. Psychology, 1976, MBA in Mgmt., Fin., 1981; postgrad., Fla. State U., Northwestern U., U. Miami. Cert. tchr., prin., sch. psychologist, Fla. Tchr. Dade County Pub. Schs., Miami, 1968-75, dept. chair, 1975-82, subject area coord., 1982-83, asst. prin., 1983-89, assoc. intern prin., 1989—; adj. prof. Nova U., Ft. Lauderdale, Fla., 1983-90, Barry U., Miami Shores, Fla., 1987—; assessment cons. Fla. Dept. Edn., Tallahassee, 1979-83, Ednl. Testing Svc., Princeton, N.J., 1981-82. Author: S.O.S. Sourcebook, 1985; author curriculum materials; editor, curriculum reviewer Harcourt Brace Jovanovich, Orlando, Fla., 1985-86. Named Outstanding Econs. Educator Fla. Coun. Econ. Edn., 1981, 82, 93, Outstanding Secondary Social Studies Tchr. Dade County Coun. Social Studies, 1982, Outstanding Exceptional Student Edn. Adminstr., Coun. Exceptional Children, 1988, 89, 90. Mem. Nat. Coun. Social Studies, Coun. Exceptional Children, Dade Assn. for Sch. Adminstrs., Phi Alpha Theta. Office: North Miami Sr H S 800 NE 137th St Miami FL 33161

HENDLEY, DAN LUNSFORD, retired university official; b. Nashville, Apr. 26, 1938; s. Frank E. and Mattie (Lunsford) H.; m. Patricia Fariss, June 18, 1960; children: Dan Lunsford, Laura Kathleen. B.A., Vanderbilt U., 1960; grad., Stonier Grad. Sch. Banking, Rutgers U., 1969; postgrad., Program Mgmt. Devel., Harvard, 1972. With Fed. Res. Bank Atlanta, 1962-73, v.p., officer in charge Birmingham br., 1969-73; v.p., exec. v.p. AmSouth Bancorp, 1973-77; exec. v.p. First Nat. Bank Birmingham, 1976-77, pres., 1977-79, chmn. bd., chief exec. officer, 1979-83; pres., chief operating officer Am South Bank, N.A., 1983-90, also dir.; v.p. bus. affairs Samford U., Birmingham, Ala., 1991-94; ret., 1994. Trustee Children's Hosp. With Tenn. Air N.G., 1961-67. Mem. Kiwanis, Mountain Brook Club, Shoal Creek Club, The Club. Baptist. Home: 3258 Dell Rd Birmingham AL 35223-1318

HENDON, MARVIN KEITH, psychologist; b. Miami, Fla., Oct. 18, 1960; s. James William and Esther (Holts) H.; m. Deborah Faye Moore, Mar. 17, 1990. BA, U. Fla., 1980, MS, 1982, PhD, 1985. Lic. psychologist Fla. Psychologist Psylab Psychol. Svc., Sarasota, Fla., 1986-87; pvt. practice psychology Sarasota, Fla., 1987—; psychol. cons. Child Protection Team, Sarasota, 1988—; outpatient therapist Mental Health Resource Ctr., Jacksonville, 1984-86; therapist U. Counseling Ctr, U. Fla., Gainesville, 1979-83; adj. prof. Manatee Community Coll., 1985. Columnist Insights into Human Behavior, 1987. Adv. bd. One Ch. One Child, 1990—; mem. sch. bd. Westcoast Sch. for Human Devel., 1987—. Republican. Office: 240 N Washington Blvd Sarasota FL 34236-5929

HENDREN, JIMM LARRY, federal judge; b. 1940. BA, U. Ark., 1964, LLB, 1965. With Little & Enfield, 1968-69; pvt. practice Bentonville, Ark., 1970-77, 79-92; chancellor, probate judge Ark. 16th Chancery Dist., 1977-78. Served to lt. comdr. JAGC, USN, 1965-70, USNR, 1970-83. Mem. ABA, Ark. Bar Assn. Office: US Dist Ct PO Box 1586 Fort Smith AR 72902-1586

HENDREN, JO ANN, small business owner; b. Maryville, Tenn., Feb. 26, 1935; d. Sidney W. and Myra (Hutto) Burns; m. R. Neil Southern, July 17, 1954, (div. Mar. 1973); children: Robert Neil Jr., Joel Burns, Myra Ann; m. James E. Hendren (June 10, 1976). Student, Va. Intermont, Bristol, 1952-53; student in home econs., U. Tenn., 1953-54. Asst. mgr. Hallmark Cards & Gifts, Maryville, 1977-84; owner, mgr. Hideaway Cottages, Townsend, Tenn., 1980—; gov. task force Tourism and the Arts, 1986-87. Bd. dirs. Blount County Hist. Trust, 1986-88; mem. Friends of Christy, the Musical, 1995, 96. Mem. Townsend C. of C., Blount County C. of C., Nature Conservancy. Republican. Episcopalian. Home and office: 102 Oriole Ln Maryville TN 37803

HENDREN, LEE EDWARD, journalist, publisher; b. Columbus, Ohio, May 14, 1959; s. Elmer Wilson and Frances Irene (Rob) H. Student, Bowling Green State U., 1977-80, Orangeburg-Calhoun Tech. Coll., 1992. Pub., editor, founder The Gahanna (Ohio) Ind. News, 1973-75; govt. and edn. reporter The Rocky Fork Enterprise, Gahanna, 1975-76; reporter, proofreader The Tri-Cmty. News, Gahanna, 1976-77; founder, pub., editor The Bull./Kohl Daily Bull., Bowling Green, Ohio, 1978-79; police, fire, gen. assignments Rocky Fork Enterprise, Gahanna, 1979-80; news editor, mng. editor, editor The Holly Hill (S.C.) Observer, 1980-86, news editor, 1988-93; staff writer, govt. The Enquirer-Jour., Monroe, N.C., 1986-88; staff writer The (Seneca) Jour./Tribune, The (Clemson) Messenger, S.C., 1993; copy editor, staff writer The Times and Dem., Orangeburg, S.C., 1994—. Founder, pub., editor The Joyful Single Newsletter, 1995—; freelance writer for numerous newspapers. Active Dem. Party, Orangeburg County, S.C., 1994—. Recipient various awards S.C. Press Assn., others. Mem. J.U.S.T. Singles, Writers Ink, Breakfast Club of S.C. Christian. Office: The Times and Dem 1010 Broughton St Orangeburg SC 29115

HENDRICKS, AILEEN ALANA, theatre educator, director, actress; b. Bronx, N.Y., Jan. 20, 1940; d. Edwin Vincent and Mary Frances (Taaffe) H.; m. Robert William Wenck, Jan. 3, 1960 (Apr. 21, 1993); children: August William II, Robert William Jr.; m. Donald Luke Couvillion, Mar. 26, 1994. BA, Tex. A&M U., 1971, MA, 1974; PhD, La. State U., 1988. Instr. Tex. A&M U., College Station, 1974-747; inst. speech & theatre Nicholls State U., Thibodaux, La., 1988-89; asst. prof. theatre, speech McNeese State U., Lake Charles, La., 1989-90; tchr. drama Mid. Sch. East Baton Rouge, La., 1990-91; from instr. to asst. prof. speech, theatre and English So. Univ., Baton Rouge, 1991—. Sec. bd. dirs. Greater Boston Interfaith Sponsoring Com. Mem. Am. Soc. for Theatre Rsch., Black Theatre Network, Southwest Theatre Assn., Assn. for Theatre in Higher Edn., Women and Theatre Program, Southeastern Theatre Conf., Coll. Lang. Assn., Phi Kappa Phi. Democrat. Roman Catholic. Unitarian Universalist. Office: So Univ Dept Visual Arts So Br Post Office Baton Rouge LA 70813

HENDRICKS, IDA ELIZABETH, mathematics educator; b. Roanoke, Va., Aug. 13, 1941; d. Samuel Jarboe and Nannie Virginia (Needy) Hodges; m. William Hampton Hendricks, Aug. 10, 1963; 1 child: William Hodges. BS in Math. & BA in Secondary Edn., Shepherd Coll., 1963; MA in Devel. Studies/Leadership Edn., Appalachian State U., 1992, cert. devel. edn. specialist, 1988. Faculty Harpers Ferry (W.Va.) High Sch., 1963-72, Jefferson High Sch., Shanandoah Junction, W.Va., 1972-78; mem. math. faculty, devel. math. specialist, adminstr. Shepherd Coll., Shepherdstown, W.Va., 1981-94; ret., 1994; creator, implementor devel. math. program Shepherd Coll.; tutor. Contbr. articles to profl. jours. Elder, organist, supt. Sunday sch., mem. Christ Reformed Ch., Shepherdstown, 1950—; organist Shepherdstown Presbyn. Ch., 1957—. Mem. AAUW (past treas.), Nat. Assn. Devel. Edn., W.Va. Assn. Devel. Edn. (sec. 1993—, v.p. 1994-95), W.Va. Coun. Tchrs. Math., Shepherdstown Hist. Soc. Home: PO Box 123 Shepherdstown WV 25443-0123

HENDRICKS, JAMES W., lawyer, real estate executive; b. Palisades, Park, N.J., Mar. 31, 1924; s. William R. and Grace W. (Womack) H.; m. Frances E. Earls, Feb. 24, 1945; children: Rickey Lynn, Janet Leigh, Barbara Louise, James W. Jr. BS, Ohio State U., 1947; JD, Columbia U., 1949. Bar: Ky. 1949. Assoc. Bullitt, Dawson & Tarrant, Louisville, 1949-54; ptnr. Marshall, Cochran, Heyburn & Wells, Louisville, 1957-67; individual practice law, Louisville, 1968—; owner Holiday Inn, Key Largo, Fla., African Queen; ptnr. Holiday Manor, Inc.; pres. Key Largo Holiday Harbour, Key Largo Marine Tours and related cos. Served with USMC, 1943-46. Fellow Am. Bar Found. (life); mem. ABA, Ky. Bar Assn., Louisville Bar Assn., Am. Judicature Soc. Presbyterian. Clubs: Ocean Reef, Harmony Landing, Cat Cay, Jefferson, Louisville Boat, Key Largo Angler's. Home: 49 Spadefish Ln Key Largo FL 33037-5226 Office: 6401 Upper River Rd Harrods Creek KY 40027

HENDRICKS, RANDAL ARLAN, lawyer; b. Kansas City, Mo., Nov. 18, 1945; s. Clinton H. and Edith T. (Anderson) H.; m. Suann Rose, June 1, 1965 (div. 1976); children: Kristin Lee, Daehne Lynn; m. Jill Edith Duke, Mar. 22, 1982; 1 child, Bret Larson-Hendricks. Student, U. Mo.-Kansas City, 1963-65; BS with honors, U. Houston, 1968, JD with honors, 1970. Bar: Tex. 1970, U.S. Dist. (so. dist.) Tex. 1970, U.S. Tax Ct. 1985. Assoc. Baker & Botts, Houston, 1970-71; pvt. practice, Houston, 1971—; ptnr. Hendricks Sports Mgmt., Houston, 1977-81; pres. Hendricks Mgmt. Co., Inc., Houston, 1981—. Author: Inside the Strike Zone, 1994. Dir. profl. div. Excellence Campaign, U. Houston, 1971; bd. dirs. Cypress Creek Christian Ch., Spring, Tex., 1979-85; expert witness U.S. Senate Subcom. on Antitrust and Monopoly, 1972; mem. pub. adv. com. Houston/Harris County Sports Facility, 1995—. Mem. Houston Bar Assn., Assn. Reps. Profl. Athletes (bd. dirs. 1978-88, mem. at large 1978-79, treas. 1979-80, v.p. 1980-81, pres. 1981-82, chmn. ethics com. 1978-80, chmn. baseball com. 1981-88), Sports Lawyers Assn. (bd. dirs. 1992—), Order of Barons (chancellor 1969-70), Phi Kappa Phi, Phi Delta Phi. Home: 417 Timberwilde Ln Houston TX 77024-6927 Office: 400 Randal Way Ste 106 Spring TX 77388-8908

HENDRICKSON, HARVEY SIGBERT, accounting educator; b. Mpls., July 23, 1928; s. Sigbert and Hilma M. (Johnson) H.; m. Rosanne C. Maddy, Aug. 18, 1962; children: Mary, Erik, Elise. BBA, U. Minn., 1957, MBA, 1962, PhD, 1963. CPA, Minn. Inst. U. Minn., Mpls., 1958-61, vis. assoc. prof., 1969; asst. prof. acctg. SUNY, Buffalo, 1963-68; assoc. prof. acctg. Fla. State U., Tallahassee, 1968-69; asst. dir. exams Am. Inst. CPAs, N.Y.C., 1970-72; chmn. fin., acctg. div. Fla. Internat. U., Miami, 1972-77, prof. acctg., 1972—; acad. acctg. fellow Office of Chief Acct. SEC, Washington, 1980-81; cons. acctg., fin. reporting, and budgeting, expert witness, Miami, 1973—. Author: (with others) The Accounting Primer, 1972; editor: Relevant Accounting Concepts and Applications: The Writings and Contributions of C. Rufus Rorem, 1991; editor: (with others) The Accounting Sampler, 1967, 72, 76, 86; mem. editorial bd. The Acctg. Rev., 1976-82, book rev. editor, 1984-87; contbr. articles to profl. jours. Active Dade County Pub. Schs., mem. South Area adv. com. 1973-76, chmn. 1973-74; bd. dirs. South Fla. Assn. Accts. Pub. Interest, 1976-80, chmn. 1976-77. Sgt. U.S. Army, 1951-52, Korea. Ford Found. predoctoral fellow, 1961-62, Arthur Andersen and Co. Found. doctoral dissertation fellow, 1961-63; Haskins and Sells Found. scholar, 1957. Mem. AICPA, Am. Acctg. Assn. (SEC liaison com. 1981-83, 85-86, chmn. S.E. region exec. planning com. 1977-82, chmn. 1978-79), Fin. Execs. Inst. (pres. South Fla. chpt. 1991-92, chmn. acad. rels. com. 1983-95, sec. 1988-92, chmn. mem. 1988-94, bd. dirs. 1988-96), Beta Alpha Psi, Beta Gamma Sigma. Democrat. Home: 7865 SW 158 Terr Miami FL 33157-2330 Office: Fla Internat U Sch Acctg Miami FL 33199

HENDRICKSON, JEROME ORLAND, trade association executive, lawyer; b. Eau Claire, Wis., July 25, 1918; s. Harold and Clara (Halverson) H.; student Wis. State Coll., 1936-39; J.D., U. Wis., 1942; m. Helen Phoebe Harty, Dec. 27, 1948 (dec. Oct. 1988); children—Jaime Ann, Jerome Orland. Bar: Wis., 1942, U.S. Supreme Ct., 1955; sole practice, Eau Claire, 1946; sales and advt. mgr. Eau Claire Coca-Cola Bottling Co., Inc., 1947-48; exec. sec. Eau Claire Community Chest, 1948-49; in charge dist. office Am. Petroleum Inst., Kansas City, Mo., 1950-53, Chgo., 1953-55; exec. dir. Nat. Assn. Plumbing-Heating-Cooling Contractors, 1955-64; sec. Joint Apprentice Text, Inc., 1955-64; exec. v.p. Cast Iron Soil Pipe Inst., Washington, 1964-74; pres. Valve Mfrs. Assn., McLean, Va., 1975-80; exec. v.p. Plumbing and Piping Industry Coun., Inc., 1981-90, ret. Treas., Wis. Community Chest, 1948-49. Treas., All-Industry Plumbing & Heating Modernization Com., 1956-57; co-sec. Joint Industry Program Com., 1958-64. Served to lt. USNR, 1943-46. Mem. ABA, Wis. Bar Assn., Am. Soc. Assn. Execs., Washington Soc. Assn. Execs, Wis. State Soc. Washington (pres. 1966-68), Nat. Conf. Plumbing-Heating-Cooling Industry (chmn. 1967-69), NAM, U. Wis. Alumni Assn., U. Wis. Law Sch. Alumni Assn. Washington (pres. 1970-74), C. of C. of U.S., Gamma Eta Gamma (pres. Upsilon chpt. 1941-42). Episcopalian. Mason (32 deg., Shriner). Clubs: Washington Golf and Country, Internat. (Washington). Home and Office: 4621 33rd St N Arlington VA 22207-4407

HENDRICKSON, WILLIAM GEORGE, business executive; b. Plainview, Minn., May 31, 1918; s. Clarence and Hildegarde (Heaser) H.; m. Virginia M. Price, Sept. 1, 1942; children: Robert, Thomas, Donald, Julie Ann. BS, St. Mary's Coll., Winona, Minn., 1939; MS, U. Detroit, 1941; PhD, U. Wis., 1946; D Humanities, St. Mary's U., Winona, Minn., 1991. Scientist Wis. Alumni Research Found., Madison, 1946-54, dir. devel., 1954-61; v.p. Ayerst Labs. div. Am. Home Products Corp., N.Y.C., 1961-67, exec. v.p., 1967-69; group v.p. Am. Home Products Corp., N.Y.C., 1969-80; chmn. emeritus bd. St. Jude Med., Inc., St. Paul; bd. dirs. emeritus Rsch. Corp. Techs., Tucson, chmn. bd. dirs. IntelliNet, Naples, Fla. Mem. Am. Chem. Soc., N.Y. Acad. Scis., Country Club N.C., Quail Creek Country Club, Sigma Xi. Republican. Roman Catholic.

HENDRIX, ALBERT RANDEL, social services administrator; b. Batesville, Miss., Aug. 17; s. Howard Roy Sr. and Marjorie Corine (Oliphant) H.; m. Sandra June Reynolds, July 15, 1973; children: Jo Ellen, Sarah Elizabeth, Albert Randel Jr., Sandra Louise. BA, U. Miss., 1968, MEd, 1971; PhD, U. So. Miss., 1979. Grants coord. Ellisville (Miss.) State Sch., 1971-75; dir. North Miss. Retardation Ctr., Oxford, 1975-86; exec. dir. Miss. Dept. Mental Health, Jackson, 1986—; adj. instr. health care adminstrn. U. Miss. Pharmacy Sch., 1977—, acting asst. prof. spl. edn., dept. of curriculum and instrn. Sch. Edn., 1979-87; instr. human svcs. technician program Itawamba Jr. Coll., Fulton, 1981-83; dir. div. of mental retardation, dept. mental health, Jackson, Miss., 1981-82; adv. bd. Congress of Advocates for the Retarded, 1978—. Exec. dir. Miss. Arts Fair for the Handicapped, 1980—; adv. bd. U. Miss. Sch. Edn. (bd. dirs. 1989—), Jackson State U. Sch. Liberal Arts, 1986—; bd. dirs., adv. bd. Jackson State U. Sch. Social Work, 1990—; social work adv. bd. U. So. Miss., 1987-90; v.p. U. Miss. Health Coun., 1986-89; adv. coun. Foster Grandparent Program, Oxford, Miss., 1975-89; mem. Govs. Coun. on Aging, 1976-80. With U.S. Army, 1968-70. Mem. Phi Theta Kappa, Phi Kappa Phi, Phi Delta Kappa. Office: Miss Dept Mental Health 1101 Robert E Lee Bldg Jackson MS 39201*

HENDRIX, DENNIS RALPH, energy company executive; b. Selmer, Tenn., Jan. 8, 1940; s. Forrest Ralph and Mary Lee (Tull) H.; m. Jennie L. Moore, Dec. 28, 1960; children—Alisa Lee, Natalie Moore, Amy Louise. BS, U. Tenn., 1962; MBA, Ga. State U., 1967. CPA, Ga. Staff acct., cons. Arthur Andersen & Co., Atlanta, 1962-65; faculty Ga. Inst. Tech., 1965-67; sr. cons. Touche, Ross & Co., Memphis, 1967-68; pres. United Foods, Inc., Memphis, 1968-73; asst. to pres. Tex. Gas Transmission Corp., Owensboro, Ky., 1973-75, pres., 1976-83, chief exec. officer, 1978-83; vice chmn. CSX Corp., 1983-84; exec. v.p., dir. Halliburton Co., Dallas, 1984-85; pres., COO, dir. Tex. Ea. Corp., Houston, 1985-86, CEO, pres., dir., 1986-89; CEO, chmn. bd. Panhandle Ea. Corp., Houston, 1990-95, chmn., 1995—; bd. dirs. Tex. Commerce Bancshares, Tex. Med. Ctr., M.D. Anderson Cancer Ctr. Outreach Corp. Bd. dirs. Nat. Jr. Achievement, U. Tenn. Devel. Coun., Greater Houston Partnership Bd., chmn., 1995, The Robert A. Welch Found., Harris County Children's Protective Svcs. Fund., Baylor Coll. Medicine; campaign chmn. United Way of Tex. Gulf Coast, 1993; mem. Mus. Fine Arts Houston, Ctr. for Strategic and Internat. Studies. Mem. Am. Petroleum Inst. (bd. dirs.), Interstate Natural Gas Assn. Am. (bd. dirs., chmn. 1994), Nat. Petroleum Coun. (vice chmn. 1995), Burning Tree Club, Ramada Club, Houston Ctr. Club, River Oaks Country Club, Forum Club (bd. dirs.), Eldorado Country Club, Castle Pines Club. Presbyterian. Office: Panenergy Corp. PO Box 1642 5400 Westheimer Ct Houston TX 77251-1642

HENDRIX, ROBERT ANDREW, otolaryngologist; b. Louisville, Sept. 16, 1951; s. John Gilbert and (Stigall) H.; m. Karen Elizabeth Bessey, May 24, 1980; children: Andrew Stephen, Erika Kristen, Allan Scott. Student, U. Saarlandes-Karl Ruprecht U., Germany, 1971-72; BS with honors in Math., Purdue U., 1973, postgrad., 1973-74; MD, U. Ky., 1978. Diplomate Am. Bd. Otolaryngology (task force on new materials 1991-94). Surg. intern Baystate Med. Ctr.-Tufts U., Springfield, Mass., 1978-79; postgrad. in surgery Med. Coll. Wis., Milw., 1979-80; resident in otolaryngology-head and neck surgery Ohio State U., Columbus, 1980-83; asst. prof., assoc. prof. U. Pa. Sch. Medicine, Phila., 1983-92, dir. med. edn. dept. otorhinolaryngology, head-neck surgery, 1985-92, acting chmn. dept., 1990-91, med. dir. Smell and Taste Ctr., 1990-91; chief otolaryngology svc. Phila. VA Med. Ctr., 1989-92;

pvt. practice, Matthews, N.C., 1992—; mem. courtesy staff Carolinas Med. Ctr., 1992—, mem. vol. tchg. staff, 1994-95; mem. active staff Mercy Hosp., Mercy Hosp. South, Presbyn. Hosp.; courtesy staff Univ. Hosp. (all Charlotte); reviewer rsch. proposals Pa. Lions Hearing Rsch. Found., Inc., 1990-91. Contbr. articles and abstracts to med. jours., chpts. to books. Am. Cancer Soc. grantee, 1988-89. Fellow Am. Laryngol. Rhinol Otological Soc., ACS, Am. Acad. Otolaryngolgoy-Head and Neck Surgery (task force on new materials 1991-94, home study course faculty 1994-99), Am. Soc. for Head and Neck Surgery, Am. Acad. Facial Plastic and Reconstructive Surgery; mem. IEEE, Soc. Univ. Otolaryngologists-Head and Neck Surgeons, Acoustical Soc. of Am., Apple Programmers and Developers Assn., Mecklenburg County Med. Soc., Alpha Epsilon Delta. Home: 2108 Peterborough Ln Charlotte NC 28270-9749 Office: Matthews Ear Nose & Throat & Comm Disorders 101 1352 Matthews Township Pky Matthews NC 28105-4600

HENDRIX, SUSAN CLELIA DERRICK, civic worker; b. McClellanville, S.C., Jan. 19, 1920; d. Theodore Elbridge and Susan Regina (Bauknight) Derrick; m. Henry Gardner Hendrix, June 5, 1943; children: Susan Hendrix Redmond, Marilyn Hendrix Shedlock. BA, Columbia Coll., 1941; MA, Furman U., 1961; EdD (hon.) Columbia Coll., 1985. Cert. tchr., S.C. Tchr. Whitmire Pub. Schs., 1941-43, Greenville Pub. Schs., S.C., 1944-46, 58-63, dir. Reading clinic, 1965-68; counselor Greenville Pub. Schs., 1963-65; supr. Greenville County Sch. Dist., S.C., 1965-68, dir. pub. rels., 1968-83; grad. instr. Furman U., 1967-69; cons. Nat. Seminar on Desegregation, 1973. Author: (with James P. Mahaffey) Teaching Secondary Reading, 1966; Communicating With the Community, 1979, History of Robert Morris Class, 1995; editor: Communique, 1968-83; mem. United Meth. Conf. editl. and revision com. Book of Discipline, 1996; contbr. articles to profl. jours. and mags. Chmn. bd. trustees Columbia Coll., 1969-70; chmn. Greenville County Rehab. Bd., S.C., 1974-76; vice chmn. bd. Jr. Achievement, Greenville, 1978-79; chmn. S.C. Commn. on Women, Columbia, 1982-88; pres. United Meth. Women, Buncombe St. Ch., Greenville, 1956-57; mem. adminstrv. bd. Buncombe St. Ch., 1968—, bd. trustees, 1980-88, lay del. to S.C. Ann. Conf., 1986—; mem. United Meth. Ch. Southeastern Jurisdictional Coun. on Ministries, 1984-88; chmn. S.C. Conf. Coun. on Ministries United Meth. Ch., 1980-88, del. gen. conf., 1980, 84, 88, 92; mem. S.C. Conf. Commn. Comm., 1995—, S.C. Conf. Budgeting Task Force, 1996—, Columbia Coll. Strategic Planning Com., 1996—; mem. Bd. Global Ministries United Meth. Ch., 1972-80, mem. commn. study of ministry, 1984-92, mem. gen. ch. coun. ministries, 1988-96, mem. gen. conf. agys. staff and site location com., 1988—, rschr. missions project, West Africa, 1986, chmn. com. legis., 1992-96, chmn. com. on inter-agency legis, 1992-96, mission agy. site location com., 1993-96, structure com., 1992-96. Recipient Medallion Columbia Coll., 1980, Alumnae Disting. Svc. award Columbia Coll., 1983, Disting. Achievement award Women's History Week, Greenville, 1984, S.C. Woman of Achievement award, 1988. Mem. S.C. PTA (life), Columbia Coll. Alumnae Assn. (life), Democratic Women, S.C. Women in Govt. (bd. dirs. 1985-87), Alpha Delta Kappa (pres. 1970-72, 90-91). Home and Office: 309 Arundel Rd Greenville SC 29615-1303

HENDRY, ROBERT RYON, lawyer; b. Jacksonville, Fla., Apr. 23, 1936; s. Warren Candler and Evalyn Marguerite (Ryon) H.; children by previous marriage: Lorraine Evalyn, Lynette Comstock, Krista Ryon. BA in Polit. Sci., U. Fla., 1958, JD, 1963. Bar: Fla. 1963. Assoc. Harrell, Caro, Middlebrooks & Wiltshire, Pensacola, Fla., 1963-66; assoc. Helliwell, Melrose & DeWolf, Orlando, Fla., 1966-67, ptnr., 1967-69; ptnr., pres. Hoffman, Hendry, Parker & Smith and predecessor Hoffman, Hendry & Parker, Orlando, 1969-77, Hoffman, Hendry & Stoner and predecessor, Orlando, 1977-82, Hendry, Stoner, Sims & Sawicki, Orlando, 1982-88, Hendry, Stoner, Townsend Sawicki & Brown, 1988-92, Hendry, Stoner, Sawicki & Brown, 1992—. Author: U.S. Real Estate and the Foreign Investor, 1983; contbr. articles to profl. jours. Mem. Dist. Export Council, 1977-91, vice chmn., 1981; chair Fla. Export Coun., 1995—; bd. dirs. World Trade Ctr. and predecessor, Orlando, 1979-89, pres., 1980-82, 84; chmn. Fla. Gov.'s Conf. on World Trade, 1983; chmn. Fla. coun. on internat. edn., 1993-96; mem. internat. fin. and mktg. adv. bd. U. Miami Sch. Bus., Fla., 1979-90, Commn. on Internat. Edn., 1986-88; mem. Metro Orlando Internat. Bus. Coun., 1994-96, Metro Orlando Internat. Affairs Commn., 1995—. Lt. U.S. Army, 1958-60, capt. Army N.G., 1960-70. Mem. Fla. Coun. Internat. Devel. (bd. dirs. 1972-85, chmn. 1977-79, adv. bd. 1985-95, chmn. emeritus 1991—, vice chair 1995—), Fla. Bar (vice chmn. internat. law com. 1974-75, chmn. com. 1976-77, mem. exec. coun. internat. law sect. 1982—), Fla. Assn. Voluntary Agys. for Caribbean Action (bd. dirs. 1987—, pres. 1989-91, past pres. 1991—), Orange County Bar Assn. (treas. 1971-74), Soc. Internat. Bus. Fellows, Brit.-Am. C. of C. (bd. dirs., sec. 1984-85), Univ. Club. Office: Hendry Stoner Sawicki & Brown PA 200 E Robinson St Ste 500 Orlando FL 32801-1956

HENEGAN, JOHN CLARK, lawyer; b. Mobile, Ala., Oct. 14, 1950; s. Virgil Baker and Marie (Fife) Gunter; m. Morella Lloyd Kuykendall, Aug. 5, 1972; children: Clark, Jim. BA in English and Philosophy, U. Miss., 1972, JD with honors, 1976. Bar: Miss. 1976, U.S. Dist. Ct. (no. dist.) Miss. 1976, N.Y. 1978, U.S. Dist. Ct. (so. dist.) N.Y. 1979, U.S. Ct. Appeals (5th and 11th cirs.) 1982, U.S. Ct. Appeals (2nd cir.) 1984, U.S. Dist. Ct. (so. dist.) Miss. 1984, U.S. Ct. Appeals (fed. cir.) 1995, U.S. Supreme Ct. 1995. Law clk. to judge U.S. Ct. Appeals (5th cir.), N.Y.C., 1976-77; atty. Dewey, Ballantine, Bushby, Palmer & Wood, N.Y.C. and Washington, 1977-81; exec. asst., chief of staff to Gov. William Winter Jackson, Miss., 1981-84; atty. Butler, Snow, O'Mara, Stevens & Cannada, PLLC, Jackson, 1984—; lectr. U. Miss. Ctr. for Continuing Legal Edn., 1985, 87, Miss. Jud. Coll., Oxford, 1982; mem. lawyers adv. com. U.S. Ct. Appeals for 5th Cir. Jud. Conf., 1991-93. Editor-in-chief Miss. Law Jour., 1976; editor Miss. Lawyer, 1985; contbr. articles to legal jours. Bd. dirs. Mississippians for Ednl. Broadcasting, Jackson, 1983-90, North Jackson Youth Baseball, Inc., 1991-97, Parents for Pub. Sch. of Jackson; co-pres. Chaistain Mid. Sch. Parent Tchrs. Students Assn., 1995-96; mem. Miss. Ethics Commn., Jackson, 1984-87; del. Hinds County Dem. Conf., 1988; mem. Miss. Dem. Fin. Coun., 1988, Hinds County Dem. Exec. Com., 1989-92; Sunday sch. supt. Covenant Presbyn. Ch., 1989-90, elder, 1996—, deacon, 1991-96, moderator of diaconate, 1993-94. Mem. ABA, Miss. Bar Assn. (chmn. Law Day U.S.A. 1983), Miss. Def. Lawyers Assn., Miss. Law Jour. Alumni Assn. (bd. dirs. 1985—), Fed. Bar Assn., 5th Cir. Bar Assn., Jackson C. of C., Am. Inns of Ct. (barrister Charles Clark chpt. 1991-93, Phi Kappa Phi, Phi Delta Phi, Omicron Delta Kappa. Home: 2441 Eastover Dr Jackson MS 39211-6727 Office: Deposit Guaranty Plz Ste 1700 Jackson MS 39201-2374

HENIGSON, ANN PEARL, freelance writer, songwriter, lyricist; b. N.Y.C., Jan. 20, 1946; d. Leo and Lillian Shires; m. David Henigson, Oct. 23, 1988 (dec. July 1993); stepchildren: Helaine, Kenneth, Keith. Student, U. Miami, Fla., 1964-68, Miami-Dade Jr. Coll. Author: (song/poem) American Flag, 1986, pub. in Congressional Record, 1990, Dreamin' Reality, 1986, Parents, 1986, Miss Liberty, 1986, Eternal Love, 1986, (Looking at You) Face of Love, 1986, Book Without a Cover, 1986, 8 Days of Hanukkah, 1986, Songwriter, 1986, Hanukkah Sing Along, 1988, Oh Baby, Oh Baby, 1991, Hold Me Tight, 1995, Democracy, Democracy, (Freedom, Freedom) 1995, and numerous others; (cartoons/drawings) Ducks/Birds, 1988. Activist, lobbyist; candidate bd. govs. State of Fla., (non-attorney) 1993; 1st female usherette Temple Israel of Greater Miami High Holy Day Svcs.; mem. Civic League Miami Beach, 1976-89; patron Temple Emanu-El Cultural Series, 1989-90; mem. Friends of Bass Mus., 1991; del. nat. Dem. party, 1970s. Mem. ASCAP, Soc. Profl. Journalists, Quill and Scroll, Tiger Bay Club, 1974-91, Sigma Delta Chi. Home: Hallandale Fla.

HENINGTON, DAVID MEAD, library director; b. El Dorado, Ark., Aug. 16, 1929; s. Bud Henry and Lucile Check (Scranton) H.; m. Barbara Jean Gibson, June 2, 1956; children—Mark David, Gibson Mead, Paul Billins. B.A., U. Houston, 1951; M.S. in L.S, Columbia U., 1956. Young adult libr. Bklyn. Pub. Libr., 1956-58; head lit. and history dept. Dallas Pub. Libr., 1958, asst. dir., 1962-67; dir. Waco (Tex.) Pub. Libr., 1958-62, Houston Pub. Libr., 1967-95. Served with USAF, 1951-55. Council on Library Resources fellow, 1970-71; recipient Liberty Bell award Houston Bar Assn., 1976. Mem. ALA, AIA (hon. mem. Tex. chpt.), Am. Mgmt. Assn., Tex. Libr. Assn. (Libr. of Yr. 1976, Disting. Svc. award 1993), Philos. Soc. Methodist. Home: 6225 San Felipe St Houston TX 77057-2809 Office: PO Box 540363 Houston TX 77254-0363

HENKE, SHAUNA NICOLE, police dispatcher, small business owner; b. San Bernardino, Calif., Oct. 25, 1966; d. Gary Duane and Pamela Denyne (Duke) H. BA, U. San Francisco, 1988. Cert. police officer std. and tng. dispatcher, Calif. Pub. rels. dir. Sta. KUSF Radio, San Francisco, 1986; theater and recreational asst. Hamilton Field Recreation, Novato, Calif., 1986-89; morning asst., newswriter Sta. KTID Radio, San Rafael, Calif., 1987-88; dispatcher Warren Security, San Rafael, Calif., 1988-89; pub. safety dispatcher Twin Cities Police Dept., Larkspur/Corte Madera, Calif., 1989-94; family svc. worker Head Start, Bogalusa, La., 1994-95; police dispatcher Mandeville (La.) Police Dept., 1995-96, Bogalusa (La.) Police Dept., 1996—; co-owner Time After Time Designs. Named Outstanding Young Woman, Outstanding Young Women of Am., 1987. Mem. Marin Emergency Dispatchers Assn. (hon. bd. dirs.), S.E. La. Dispatcher's Assn. (pres.), S.E. La. Dispatcher's Assn. Office: Bogalusa Police Dept 202 Arkansas Ave Bogalusa LA 70427

HENKIN-BOOKMAN, JEAN PATRICIA, editor, writer, literary agent; b. Queens, N.Y., Feb. 17, 1948; d. Shepard Paul and Marian Margaret (Guerin) Henkin; m. Giuseppe Porcaro, June 10, 1969 (div. July 1982); children: Carmine Anthony, Elizabeth; m. Henry Charles Bookman, Dec. 30, 1982. BA in English, R.I. Coll., 1992, MEd in ESL, 1993. Cert. secondary English tchr., Va. presenter in field; former mem. planning com. on integration acad. and vocat. instrn. R.I. Dept. Edn.; founder As Long As You Believe Fund for Children. Editor, contbr. Harvest mag., 1982; contbr. poetry to various publs. Panel mem. program for children DARE, Hawaii; prodr., performer weekly children's radio show; sci. monitor high sch. sci. fair; English tutor Hood Meml. Ch., Providence; co-sponsor Cookout for People, 1993; organizer Just for Children Holiday Celebration, 1993; bd. dirs. Chesapeake (Va.) Mus., 1994-95. Recipient 1st place award Poetry Unltd., Tex., 1988, 2d place award for short story USAF, 1987; named R.I. Poet of Yr., 1993, 94. Mem. Nat. Coun. Tchrs. English, New Eng. Assn. Tchrs. English, Order Ea. Star, Phi Theta Kappa, Kappa Delta Phi.

HENLEY, J. SMITH, judge; m. Dorothy Henley; children: Jane K., Wordna S. Henley Deere; Referee in bankruptcy, Western Dist. Ark., 1943-45 assoc. gen. counsel, FCC, 1954-56; dir. Office of Adminstrv. Procedure, Dept. Justice 1956-58; judge U.S. Dist. Cts. (ea. and we. dists.) Ark., 1958-75; judge, U.S. Ct. Appeals (8th cir.), Harrison, Ark., 1975-82, sr. judge, 1982—; mem. Judicial Conf. Subcom. on Supporting Personnel, 1975-77, Adv. Com, on Appelate Rules, 1978-84. Mem. ABA, Am. Judicature Soc., Ark. Bar Assn. Office: US Ct Appeals 200 Federal Bldg Harrison AR 72601

HENLEY, LILA JO, school social worker, consultant, retired; b. Winter Haven, Fla., Feb. 9, 1936; d. Harold James and Hazel Louise (Collier) Selman; m. James Wilson Henley, Jr., Feb. 2, 1968; 1 child, Joy Selman. BA, Tenn. Temple U., 1961; MSW, Ind. U., Indpls., 1967; EdD, Nova U., 1988. Lic. clin. social worker, Ga. Social worker Douglas County Dept. Family Svcs., Douglasville, Ga., 1961-62, Cobb County Dept. Family Svcs., Marietta, Ga., 1963-66; dir. mental health Cobb County Health Dept., Marietta, 1967-68; social worker Atlanta Pub. Schs., 1969-93, retired, 1993—; cons. Garden Terr. Nursing Home, Douglasville, 1968-70, various ch. youth groups, Douglasville, 1973—. Adv. bd. State of Ga. Sch. Social Work, 1970-85; vol. Mental Health Assn., 1970-73. Mem. NEA, NASW, Acad. Cert. Social Workers, Nat. Guild of Hypnotists, Parent Teacher Assn. Baptist. Home: 6240 River Ridge Dr Douglasville GA 30135-6148

HENLEY, VERNARD WILLIAM, banker; b. Richmond, Va., Aug. 11, 1929; s. Walter Abraham and Mary Ellen (Crump) H.; m. Pheriby Christine Gibson, June 14, 1958; children: Vernard William, Wade Gibson, Adrienne Christine. B.S., Va. State Coll., 1951; LHD, Va. State U., 1992. Teller, cashier Mechanics & Farmers Bank, Durham, N.C., 1951-52, 54-58; v.p. Consol. Bank & Trust Co., Richmond, 1958-71; pres., trust officer Consol. Bank & Trust Co., from 1971; chmn. bd., chief exec. officer, trust officer J. Sargeant Reynolds Community Coll. Edn. Found., Inc., 1984-92; bd. govs. Consumer Adv. Coun., Fed. Res. Bd., 1979-83; mem. Deferred Compensation Bd., 1982-87; bd. dirs. Retail Mchts. Assn. Greater Richmond, 1986; mem. Joint. Subcom. to study Capital Area Water Authority, Commonwealth of Va., 1994. Mem. Downtown Devel. Commn., 1984-85, gen. vocat. edn. adv. council Richmond Pub. Schs., 1975-78; dist. commr. Robert E. Lee council Boy Scouts Am., 1964-69; vice chmn. adv. com. Vol. Service Bur., 1964-69; asst. treas. Richmond chpt. ARC, 1968-69; bd. mgmt. North br. YMCA Met. Richmond, 1975-79; commr. Va. Housing Devel. Authority, 1972-83, chmn., 1980-83; bd. dirs. Richmond Community Hosp., 1970-83, Inst. Bus. and Community Devel., 1966-69, Richmond Met. Authority, 1966-69, Human Services Planning div. United Way Greater Richmond, 1970-72, Church Hill Econ. Devel. Corp., 1971-75, Central Ednl. TV, 1971-81, Richmond Meml. Hosp., 1970, Children's Hosp., 1975-85, Richmond Met. Blood Services, 1975-83, Atlantic Rural Exposition, 1976, Pvt. Industry Council Richmond, 1983-85, Federated Arts Council Richmond, 1979-85, Richmond Meml. Hosp. Found., 1980—, Richmond Renaissance, Inc., 1982—, Va. Coun. Econ. Edn., 1993; mem. Premier Edn. Coun. U.S.; bd. dirs. Maymont Found., 1973, pres., 1983-84, mem. exec. and fin. coms.; bd. dirs. Project AID-SIR, 1979-80, Cities in Schs. Found. of Va., 1989, Va. Housing Found., vice chmn. apptd. by gov., 1989; mem. adv. bd. Black Mus., 1984, The Arts Council of Richmond, Inc., 1986; mem. Gov's Econ. Adv. Council, 1982-85; adv. council Salvation Army Boys Club, 1970—; Va. Council on Econ. Edn., 1985, trustee Richmond Meml. Hosp., 1970—, Va. Mus. Fine Arts, 1983, mem. exec., exhibition and fin. coms.; trustee Va. Union U., 1984, mem. exec. com., chmn. fin. com., past chmn. audit com.; trustee St. Paul's Coll., Lawrenceville, Va., 1976-84, bd. assocs., 1984; trustee J. Sargeant Reynolds Coll. Found., 1984; mem. nat. corp. com. United Negro Coll. Fund, 1975—; vice chmn. audit com. City of Richmond, 1983-85, chmn. 1986-88; mem. Richmond Police Meml. Found., 1985, debt policy com. City of Richmond; trustee univ. fund Va. Commonwealth U., 1986, Historic Richmond Found., 1986 ; mem. adv. bd. Sch. Social Work Va. Commonwealth U., 1985-88. Served to 1st lt. AUS, 1952-54. Decorated Bronze Star; recipient Order of Merit Boy Scouts Am., 1967; Man and Boy award Boys Club, 1969; Citizenship award NAACP, 1974; Citizenship award Astoria Beneficial Club, 1976; Brotherhood award Richmond chpt. NCCJ, 1979; Quest for Success award for Black Entrepreneurs Am., Miller Brewing Co. and Philip Morris Co., 1986. Mem. Am. Inst. Banking, Bank Adminstrn. Inst., Am. Banking Assn. (minority lending com. comml. lending divsn. 1976-79, exec. com. 1992-94, legis. com. 1988, 93—, fed. govt. rels. com. 1995—, bd. dirs. 1994—), Va. Bankers Assn. (bd. dirs. 1986-88, pres.-elect 1992, pres. 1993-94), Ctrl. Richmond Assn. (dir. 1971-72), Old Dominion Bar Assn. (lay mem., bd. dirs.), Ind. Order St. Luke (trustee 1970-88), Kiwanis, Owens & Minor, Inc. (bd. dirs. 1993), Alpha Phi Alpha, Alpha Beta Boule, Sigma Phi. Home: 1728 Hungary Rd Richmond VA 23228-2335 Office: Consol Bank & Trust Co PO Box 26823 Richmond VA 23261

HENN, SHIRLEY EMILY, retired librarian; b. Cleve., May 26, 1919; d. Albert Edwin and Florence Ely (Miller) H.; AB, Hollins Coll., 1941; MS, U. N.C., 1966; m. John Van Bruggen, July 14, 1944 (div. May 1947); 1 child, Peter Albert (dec.). Libr. asst. Hollins (Va.) Coll., 1943-44, 61-64, reference libr., 1965-84, ret., 1984; advt. mgr. R.M. Kellogg Co., Three Rivers, Mich., 1946-47; exec. sec. Hollins Coll. Alumnae Assn., 1947-55; real estate salesman Fowlkes & Kefauver, Roanoke, Va., 1955-61. Pres. Soc. for Prevention Cruelty to Animals, 1959-61, 69-72, bd. dirs., 1972-81; donor Mary Williamson award in Humanities Hollins Coll., 1947—; endowed fund for purchase books children's lit. collection Fishburn Libr. Hollins Coll., 1986-93; donor, patron Women's Ctr. Hollins Coll., 1993—, Scholarship Aids, 1994, Children's Lit. Masters Program, 1993-95; active Nat. Trust for Historic Preservation, 1994—, Roanoke Valley Hist. Soc., 1984—, Roanoke Valley Hist. Mus., Roanoke Valley Sci. Mus., Cystic Fibrosis Found., 1995—, Nat. Audubon Soc., 1995—, MADD, 1995—; donor Va. Tech. Found. for restoration Hotel Roanoke, 1992—; ptnr. Spl. Olympics, 1995—. Recipient Rath award, 1984, Critical Scholarship award, 1995, Creative Achievement award, 1995—. Mem. ALA, MADD, Am. Alumni Council (dir. 1952-54, dir. women's activities 1952-54), Va. Libr. Assn., Nat. DAR (libr. Nancy Christian Fleming chpt. Roanoke 1977-84, regent 1984-88, chair Good Citizenship award 1990-92, Am. Essay awards 1991—), Poetry Soc. Va. Clubs: Quota Internat. (chpt. pres. 1958-60) (Roanoke), Antique Automobile Club Am., Roanoke Valley Antique Auto Club, Roanoke Valley Mopar Club, Children's Lit. Assn., Am. Mus. Nat. History, Blue Ridge Zool. Soc., Cystic Fibrosis Found., Poetry Soc. Va., Nat. Audubon Soc. Author, illustrator: Adventures of Hooty Owl and His Friends, 1953; editor: Hollins Alumnae Bull., 1947-56. Avocations: collecting teddy bears, antique French and English plates, bells, pewter. Home: 6915 Tinkerdale Rd Roanoke VA 24019-1530

HENNECY, BOBBIE BOBO, English language educator; b. Tignall, Ga., Aug. 11, 1922; d. John Ebb and Lois Helen (Gulledge) Bobo; student, Wesleyan Conservatory, 1943-44; AB summa cum laude, Mercer U., Macon, Ga., 1950; postgrad. Oxford (Eng.) U. English-Speaking Union Scholar, 1961; MA, Emory U., 1962; postgrad. Cambridge U., Eng., 1987; m. James Howell Hennecy, Dec. 28, 1963; 1 child, Erin. Sec. Tattnall Sq. Bapt. Ch., 1943-48; sec., adminstrv. asst. to pres., instr. Mercer U., 1950-61, instr. English, 1961-76, asst. prof., 1976-89, emeritus assoc. prof. and adj. prof., 1989—; founder Tattnall Sq. Acad., Macon, 1968, sec. acad. corp., 1968-73, dir., 1968-78; Bobbie Bobo Hennecy scholarship named in her hon. Tattnall Sq. Acad., Mercer U.; NDEA fellow Emory U., 1962; named outstanding Psi Gamma Chi Omega, 1995. Mem. AAUW (chpt. v.p. 1959, pres. 1964), AAUP, MLA, S. Atlantic MLA, So. Comparative Lit. Assn., Am. Comparative Lit. Assn., Internat. Comparative Lit. Assn., Nat. Assn. Tchrs. English, Ga. Assn. Tchrs. English, English Speaking Union, LWV, Collegiate Press (adv. bd.), Am. Acad. Poets, Pres. Club of Mercer U., YWCA (life), Mid. Ga. Art Assn., Hereditary Register, Soc. Genealogists London, Nat. Soc. So. Dames, Nat. Soc. Magna Charta, UDC (pres. 1994-96), DAR (registrar 1980-82), Daus. of 1812, Descendants, Colonial Clergy, Daus. of Am. Colonists, Jamestowne Soc., Colonial Dames XVII Century (chpt. 1st v.p. 1988-91), Colonial Order of the Crown (descendants of Charlemagne), Ams. of Royal Descent, Mid. Ga. Hist. Soc., Coosa County Ala. Hist. Soc., Friends of the Cannonball House, Cardinal Key, Sigma Tau Delta, Sigma Mu (pres., v.p., sec.-treas.), Phi Delta (advisor), Phi Kappa Phi, Alpha Psi Omega, Chi Omega (alumnae pres. 1953, advisor 1953-83). Baptist. Home: 1347B Adams St Macon GA 31201-1515

HENNELLY, KAY ELIZABETH, travel agency executive; b. Shreveport, La., Nov. 13, 1951; d. Edward Bell Jr. and Dorothy Elizabeth (Hughes) Howard; m. James M. Hennelly, Aug. 9, 1983; children: Julie, Christopher. Student, N.E. La. U., 1969-72, La. State U., Shreveport, 1970, Richland Coll., Dallas, 1978. Pres. Alur World Travel Ctr., Inc., Dallas, 1989—. Baptist. Home: 5910 Excalibur Dr Garland TX 75044-3636 Office: Alur World Travel Ctr Inc 4144 N Central Expy Ste 285 Dallas TX 75204-2102

HENNESSEY, AUDREY KATHLEEN, computer researcher, educator; b. Fairbanks, Apr. 4, 1936; d. Lawrence Christopher and Olga Virginia (Strandberg) Doheny; m. Gerard Hennessey, Mar. 10, 1963; children: Brian, Kate. BA, Stanford U., 1957; HSA, U. Toronto, Ont., Can., 1968; PhD, U. Lancaster, Eng., 1982. Asst. dir. European sales Univ. Soc., Heidelberg, Fed. Republic Germany, 1959-61; landman's asst. Union Oil Co. Calif., Anchorage, 1962; system analyst No. Telephones, New Lisheard, Can., 1962-63; adminstr. group pension Mfgs. Life Ins., Toronto, 1963-65; instr. office systems Adult Edn. Ctr., Toronto, 1965-68; lectr. office systems Salford Coll. Tech., Lancashire, Eng., 1968-70; sr. lectr. data processing Manchester (Eng.) Polytechnic, 1970-79; lectr. computation U. Manchester, Eng., 1979-82; assoc. prof. computer sci. Tex. Tech. U., Lubbock, 1982-86, assoc. prof. info. systems, 1987-94, prof. info. systems, 1994—; dir. Inst. for Studies of Organized Automation, Lubbock, 1987-95; pres. ISOA Inc., 1994—; dir. Internat. Ctr. Informatics Rsch., 1996—; vis. instr. Fed. Law Enforcement Tng. Ctr., Glynco, Ga., 1984-88; adj. prof. West Tex. A&M U., Canyon, 1994-95, U. Alaska, Anchorage, 1995, U. Tex., Dallas, 1995—. Author: Computer Applications Project, 1982; editor procs.: Office Document Architecture Internat. Symposium, English version, 1991; contbr. articles to profl. jorus.; patentee in field. Organizer Explorer Scouts Computer Applications, Lubbock, 1983-85. Recipient various awards Tex. Instruments, 1982-86, 94-95, Xerox Corp., 1985, Halliburton, 1986, Sys. Exploration, 1987, State of Tex., 1988-93, 96—, Knowledge-based Image Analysis award USN Space Sys., 1991—, Immunization Tracking Sys. award Robert Wood Johnson Found., 1993, Leica, 1994—, Sematech ADC awards, 1994. Mem. IEEE, Soc. Mfg. Engrs., Assn. Computing Machinery, Data Processing Mgmt. Assn. (pres. chpt. 1989, Disting. Info. Sci. award 1992), Sigma Xi Rsch. Soc. (chpt. pres. 1996-97). Office: ICIR-Tex Tech U MS #2101 Tex Tech U Lubbock TX 79409 also: OICIR 1221 W Campbell Rd Ste 231 Richardson TX 75080

HENNEY, FREDERIC ALLISON, English language educator; b. Washington, Oct. 5, 1929; s. Frederic Allison and Elizabeth Christine (Fries) H.; m. Carolee Josephine Wells, June 16, 1951; children: Valerie Jocelyn Henney Vincent, Frederic Allison Jr., Cynthia Alexandra Henney Fisher. BS in Mil. Engrng., U.S. Mil. Acad., 1951; MA in English, U. N.C., 1958; EdD in Higher Edn. Adminstrn., Coll. William and Mary, 1977. Lic. pilot single and multi-engine land aircraft. Commd. 2d lt. USAF, 1951, advanced through grades to lt. col., 1967, edn. and tng. staff officer, pilot, 1951-71; asst. prof. English USAF Acad., Colorado Springs, Colo., 1958-62; dir. student svcs. Rappahannock C.C., Glenns, Va., 1973-74; coord. evening programs Thomas Nelson C.C., Hampton, Va., 1974-79, asst. to pres., 1979-82, prof. English, 1982—; pub. Aton press, Grafton, Va., 1989—; judge speech and forensics contests, Colo., 1960-62, Va., 1974—. Editor: Calbert and His Adventures, 1990, Tac and Tuk, 1993, A No-Frills Survival Guide for the WordPerfect 5.1(R) Illiterate, 1993, Using All of MS-Works 3.0 (R), 1993. Mem. York County (Va.) Rep. Com., 1978-85. Mem. Air Force Assn., Southeastern Conf. English in Two-Year Coll., Kappa Delta Pi. Episcopalian. Home: 407 Wormley Creek Dr Yorktown VA 23692-4215 Office: Thomas Nelson CC 1 Thomas Nelson Dr Hampton VA 23666-1433

HENNIG, BERNHARD, nutritional science educator; b. Saalfeld, Germany, Apr. 7, 1952; came to U.S., 1972; s. Karl Dietrich and Anneliese Hennig; m. Marsha Jean Moran, Jan. 27, 1978; children: Paul Dietrich, Karl Bernhard, Andrea Jean. BA in Biochemistry, San Francisco State U., 1977; MS in Nutrition, Colo. State U., 1979; PhD in Nutrition, Iowa State U., 1982. Registered dietitian; cert. nutritionist, Ky. Rsch. asst. dept. food sci. and nutrition Colo. State U., Ft. Collins, 1977-79; teaching asst. dept. food and nutrition Iowa State U., Ames, summer 1981, rsch. asst., 1979-82; postdoctoral scholar Nat. Heart Lung and Blood Inst., NIH Cardiovascular Ctr., Coll. Medicine, U. Iowa, Iowa City, 1983-84; asst. prof. Grad.Ctr. Toxicology U. Ky., Lexington, 1987-89, assoc. prof., 1989-95, prof., 1995—, assoc. prof., then prof. nutritional scis. grad. faculty, 1989—, asst., then assoc., then prof. dept. nutrition and food sci., 1984—; assoc. Ctr. Membrane Scis., U. Ky., 1992—; cons. dietitian NIH Cardiovascular Risk Reduction Study, 1987-89; dir. grad. studies U. Ky., Lexington, 1987-91, 93—; vis. scholar Inst. Molecular Biology, Salzburg, Austria, 1991; ad hoc reviewer USDA Nat. Rsch. Initiative Competitive Grants Program, 1993, 94; NIH postdoctoral rschl fellow, 1983-84. Mem. editl. bd. Jour. Optimal Nutrition, 1992, Jour. Applied Nutrition, 1991, Jour. Am. Coll. Nutrition, Nutritional Rsch.; ac hoc reviewer Am. Jour. Cardiology, Cancer Rsch., Diabetes, Jour. Am. Coll. Nutrition, Jour. Applied Nutrition, Jour. Nutritional Biochemistry, Jour. Lab. and Clin. Medicine, Jour. Lipid Rsch., Jour. Trace Elements in Exptl. Medicine, Nutrition Rsch., Lipids, Toxicology and Applied Pharmacology; contbr. articles to profl. jours., chpts. to books. Vol. Am. Heart Assn., Lexington chpt., 1988, 89, 90, 92, 93. Rsch. grantee NIH, Nat. Dairy Coun., Nat. Live Stock and Meat Bd., Ky. Heart Assn., Ky. Beef Cattle Assn., NSF, U. Ky. Fellow Am. Heart Assn. Coun. Arteriosclerosis; mem. AAAS, Am. Coll. Nutrition (awards com. 1994, membership com. 1994, coun. mem. cardiovascular/hypertension sect. 1992—, editorial bd. Jour. 1991, Clintec award lecture 1993, Borden award 1993, Grace A. Goldsmith award 1995), Internat. Soc. Trace Element Rsch. in Humans, Am. Home Econs. Assn., Am. Inst. Nutrition, Am. Dietetic Assn., Ky. Dietetic Assn., Bluegrass Dietetic Assn., N.Y. Acad. Scis. Home: 1953 Bellefonte Dr Lexington KY 40503-2038 Office: U Ky Dept Nutrition & Food Sci 204 Funkhouser Bldg Lexington KY 40506

HENNIG, CHARLES WILLIAM, psychology educator; b. Queens, N.Y., May 7, 1949; s. Charles Joseph and Evelyn Mary (Gerstel) H.; m. Mary Christina Shamrock, Jan. 9, 1982; 1 child, Brian Steve. BA, SUNY, Buffalo, 1971; MS, Tulane U., 1976, PhD, 1978. Grad. teaching asst. Tulane U., New Orleans, 1974-78; vis. asst. prof. psychology U. Okla., Norman, 1978-79, Centre Coll. Ky., Danville, 1979-80; asst. prof. Salem (W.Va.) Coll., 1980-83, assoc. prof., 1983-88, prof., 1988-89, chair psychology, 1983-89; prof., chair psychology McMurry U., Abilene, Tex., 1989—; bd. dirs. African Elephant Rsch. and Survival Ranch, Abilene, 1990-96, Client Advocacy Coun., Abilene, 1996—. Contbr. articles to profl. jours. Vol. United

Way of Abilene, 1990—; mem. Abilene Zool. Soc., 1990—. With U.S. Army, 1972-74. Mem. APA, Am. Psychol. Soc., Animal Behavior Soc., Psychonomic Soc., Midwestern Psychol. Assn., Southeastern Psychol. Assn., Abilene Psychol. Assn. (sec.-treas. 1990-91, 94-95, pres. 1992-93, 96-97), Psi Chi. Republican. Roman Catholic. Home: 4701 Stonehedge Rd Abilene TX 79606-3429 Office: McMurry U Psychology Dept PO Box 86 Abilene TX 79604-0086

HENNIGAN, GEORGE R., chemicals executive. B in Elec. Engring. summa cum laude, Ariz. State U., M in Bus. Adminstrn. and Syss. Mgmt. Cert. profl. logistician. Pilot USAF, 1954-79, advanced through ranks to col.; maintenance mgr., then mfg. mgr., mktg. mgr. Kerr-McGee Chem. Corp., Oklahoma City, 1979-91, pres., CEO, 1991—. Mem. Internat. Soc. Ligisticians, Tau Beta Pi, Eta Kappa Nu. Office: Kerr-McGee Chem Corp Kerr-McGee Ctr Oklahoma City OK 73102

HENNIGER, DAVID THOMAS, lawyer; b. Cuyahoga Falls, Ohio, Dec. 12, 1936; s. Herman Harrison and Wilma (Weeks) H.; m. LaRayne Virginia Kerlin, Apr. 9, 1965; children: Mark, Jill, Matthew, Michael. AA, St. Petersburg Jr. Coll., 1957; BS summa cum laude, Fla. So. Coll., 1959; JD cum laude, Stetson U., 1965. Bar: Fla. 1965, U.S. Dist. Ct. (mid. dist.) Fla. 1965, U.S. Ct. Appeals (5th cir.) 1966, U.S. Supreme Ct. 1971, U.S. Ct. Appeals (11th cir.) 1981. Diplomate Nat. Bd. Trial Advocacy. Assoc. Masterson, Lloyd, Sundberg & Rogers, St. Petersburg, Fla., 1965-75; ptnr. Lloyd and Henniger, P.A., St. Petersburg, 1975-84; assoc. Greene and Mastry, P.A., St. Petersburg, 1984-91; coll. atty. St. Petersburg Jr. Coll.; instr. Stetson Coll. Law, Gulfport, Fla., 1972-73; St. Petersburg Jr. Coll., 1968-73; pres. St. Petersburg Legal Aid Soc., 1976. Pres. Christian Arbitration Ctr., St. Petersburg, 1987—; v.p. Christian Businessmen's Com., 1981-82; chmn. sch. adv. com. Dixie Hollins High Sch., Kenneth City, Fla., 1985-86, pres. Parent Tchrs. Student Assn., 1987-88. Mem. ABA, Fed. Bar Assn., Am. Judicare Soc., Assn. Trial Lawyers Am., Fla. Trial Lawyers Soc., Am. Arbitration Assn. (panel arbitrators 1977-88), Christian Legal Soc. (treas. St. Petersburg 1984—). Home: 5862 32nd Ave N Saint Petersburg FL 33710-1837 Office: St Petersburg Jr Coll PO Box 13489 Saint Petersburg FL 33733-3489

HENNING, DOROTHY ANN, special education educator; b. Miami, Fla., Oct. 1, 1947; d. Abraham Kearney and Dorothy Marilyn (Ebanks) H. BA in Exceptional Child Edn., U. So. Fla., Tampa, 1977; MA in Mental Retardation, 1993. Cert. tchr., Fla. Tchr. Hillsborough County Sch. Bd., Tampa, 1977—; mem. Curriculum Revision Com., Dept. Exceptional Child Edn., Tampa, 1991-92; mem. Textbook Adoption Com., Hillsborough County Sch. Dist., 1994-95. Named Tchr. of Month, WTSP Channel 10 Bus. and Edn. Adv. Bd. St. Petersburg, Fla., 1993, Tchr. of Yr., Caminiti Exceptional Child Ctr., Tampa, 1994-95. Mem. AAUW, Coun. on Exceptional Children (MR divsn.), U. So. Fla. Alumni Assn., Phi Kappa Phi. Democrat. Baptist. Office: Caminiti Exceptional Child Ctr 2600 W Humphrey St Tampa FL 33614-1825

HENRIOTT, DORIS SUSAN, technology and publications services educator; b. Fairbanks, Alaska, May 12, 1944; d. Robert Alexander and Norma Helen (Blanchard) MacDonald; m. James Edward Henriott, May 15, 1965; children: Gena L., A. Paul, Donald E., Linda M. Student, U. Md., London, 1962-64. Cert. tchr., vocat. edn., bus., data processing, Fla. Records mgmt. Orange County Pub. Schs., Orlando, Fla., 1977-81; tchr. tech. and software Technology Publs., Orlando, Fla., 1981-94; coord. Instrl. Tech. Resource Ctr. Orange County Pub. Schs., Orlando, Fla., 1982-94, coord. tech. publs., 1982—; co-owner Henriott Enterprises, Apopka, Fla., 1986—; records/forms liaison Orange County Pub. Schs., Orlando, 1982-92, tng./devel. liaison, 1989-91; cons. Winter Garden (Fla.) Bapt. Ch. Sch., 1988-90; design cons. Apple Computer, Inc., Fla. Edn. div., Tampa, 1988, instr. tech., 1991—. Author, editor Instrnl. Tech. newsletter INTEC News, Tech. Svcs. Newsletter. Mem. North Orange County Improvement Assn., Apopka, 1979-87. Recipient Better Than Ever cert. Orange County Pub. Schs. Found., 1988, plaque Orange County League Mid. Schs., 1989, Walker Mid. Sch., Orlando, 1989, Vocat. Indsl. Clubs Am., Orlando, 1990, Ptnr. in Edn. plaque Colonial 9th Grade Ctr., 1991, plaque Westridge Mid. Sch., 1991-93. Mem. Nat. AppleWorks Users' Group, Nat. Assn. Desktop Pubs., Orange County Reading Coun., Fla. Assn. Ednl. Data Systems, Print Shop Users' Group. Home: 4523 Ondich Rd Apopka FL 32712 Office: Orange County Pub Schs PO Box 271 Orlando FL 32802-0271

HENRY, ANN RAINWATER, education educator; b. Okla., Nov. 2, 1939; d. George Andrew and Opal Norma (Cohea) Rainwater; m. Morriss M. Henry, Aug. 1, 1964; children: Paul, Katherine, Mark. BA, U. Ark., 1961, MA, 1964, JD, 1971. Bar: Ark. 1971. Pvt. practice law Fayetteville, Ark., 1971-72; instr. Coll. Bus. Adminstrn. U. Ark., Fayetteville, 1976-78, asst. prof., 1978-84, assoc. prof., 1984—, asst. dean, 1984-86, assoc. dean, 1986-89, faculty chair, 1989-91. Bd. dirs. City of Fayetteville, 1977-83, 91-92, McIlroy Bd., Fayetteville, 1986—; chmn. cert. com. Ark. Tchrs. Evaluation, 1984-85; mem. Ark. Local Svcs. Adv. Bd., 1980-88, Ark. Gifted and Talented, 1989—, Ark. State Bd. Edn., 1985-86. Mem. Ark. Alumni Assn. (bd. dirs., asst. treas. 1989-93), Fayetteville C. of C. (bd. dirs. 1983-85), Ark. Bar Assn. (chmn. ethics com. 1986-87). Democrat. Methodist. Home: 2465 Township Common Dr Fayetteville AR 72703-3568 Office: U Ark BA 204 Fayetteville AR 72701

HENRY, CAROLYN SUE, educator, family therapist; b. Newton, Kans., Jan. 31, 1955; d. Harold Dwight and Averil Jean (Hawes) H. BS in Social Studies Edn., Okla. Christian Coll., 1976; MS in Counseling, Okla. State U., 1977; MS in Child and Family Studies, U. Tenn., 1981, PhD in Family Studies, 1984. Lic. marital and family therapist, Okla.; cert. family life educator. Dir. career planning/placement Pepperdine U., Malibu, Calif., 1977-80; counselor Project Talent Search, Knoxville, Tenn., 1980, Douglass Cherokee Econ. Authority, Morristown, Tenn., 1985; asst. prof. Child Devel. & Family Rels. S.D. State U., Brookings, S.D., 1985-88, acting dept. head CDFR, 1987-88; asst. prof. FRCD Okla. State U., Stillwater, 1988-93; assoc. prof. FRCD Dept. Family Rels. and Child Devel., Stillwater, 1993—, interim head FRCD, 1995—; pres. Okla. Coun. on Family Rels., 1993-94; co-chair, rural focus group Nat. Coun. on Family Rels., Mpls., 1991-92; cons. S.D. Health Dept., 1986. Editl. bd. Family Relations, 1994-96; contbr. articles to profl. jours. Mem. Cooperative Extension Adv. Bd., Southeastern Okla., 1995; spl. edn. task force State of S.D., 1987. Recipient Lela O'Toole Rsch. award Okla. Family and Cons. Scis. Assn., 1995. Mem. Nat. Coun. on Family Rels. (co-chair rural focus group 1991-93), Am. Assn. for Marriage and Family Therapy, Am. Assn. of Family and Consumer Scis., Soc. for Rsch. on Adolescence, Okla. Coun. on Family Rels (pres. 1993-94, treas. 1989-90, New Prof. of Yr. 1990). Mem. Ch. of Christ. Office: Okla State U FRCD Dept Stillwater OK 74078

HENRY, DAVID EUGENE, artist, educator; b. Rome, Ga., Dec. 10, 1946; s. Eugene Edenfield Henry and Mattie Mae (Bannister) Riggins. BArch, Ga. Inst. Tech., 1970; M.Visual Arts, Ga. State U., 1972. Faculty Eckerd Coll., St. Petersburg, Fla., 1976-77; faculty art tchr. Am. Coll. for Applied Arts, Atlanta, 1996—. One-man shows include Banks-Hailey Gallery, Albany, 1974, Travis and Co. Gallery, Atlanta, 1992, Douglas County Cultural Arts Ctr., Douglasville, Ga., 1995; exhbns. include 23d Southeastern exhbn. High Mus. Art, Atlanta, 1969, Ga. Artists Invitational exhbn., 1972, 3d Biennial Tweed Mus. Internat. Exhbn., 54th Nat. Painting exbhn. Ogunquit (Maine) Art Ctr.; murals at Ga. Tech., Atlanta Area Tech. Sch., St. Petersburg Bayfront Mcpl. Civic Ctr. Recipient First Prize in painting Arts Festival of Atlanta, 1975, Purchase award Piedmont Exhbn., Mint Mus., 1972; winner mural competition Nat. Endowment for Arts, St. Petersburg, 1977; Nat. Endowment for Arts grantee, 1974-76. Office: The American College for Applied Arts 3330 Peachtree Rd NE Atlanta GA 30326

HENRY, DAVID HOWE, II, former diplomat and international organization official; b. Geneva, N.Y., May 19, 1918; s. David Max and Dorothy (Buley) H.; m. Margaret Beard, Nov. 16, 1946; children: David Beard, Peter York, Michael Max, Susan. Student, Hobart Coll., 1935-37, Sorbonne, 1937-38; A.B., Columbia U., 1939; student, Russian Inst., 1948-49, Harvard U., 1944-45, Nat. War Coll., 1957-58. Ins. agt., 1939-41; mem. fgn. service Dept. State, 1941-71; assigned Dept. State, Montreal, 1941-42, Beirut, 1942-44, Washington, 1944-45, 48-52, 57-66, 70, Moscow, 1945-48, 52-54, Vladivostok, 1945-46, Berlin, 1955-57; acting dir. Office Research and Intelligence Sino-Soviet bloc, 1958-59; dir. dept. polit. affairs Nat. War Coll., 1959-61; dep. dir. Office Soviet Affairs, 1961-64, dir., 1964-65; mem. Policy Planning Council, 1965-66; dep. chief of mission Am. embassy, Reykjavik, Iceland, 1966-69; information systems specialist, 1970; polit. and security council affairs UN, N.Y.C., 1971-78. Mem. Kappa Alpha. Presbyterian. Club: Rotarian. Home: 2551 SW Brookwood Ln Palm City FL 34990-4752

HENRY, DEBORAH BORAN, librarian; b. Pottsville, Pa., Mar. 28, 1951. BA, Regis Coll., Weston, Mass., 1973; MS, U. Del., 1981; MA, U. S. Fla., 1987. Oceanographer Nat. Oceanic and Atmospheric Adminstrn., Miami, 1980-86; corp. libr. TECO, Tampa, 1988; asst. univ. libr. U. S. Fla., St. Petersburg, 1988—; program coord. Multiformat Periodicles, 1996, Teaching the Internet workshop, 1996; mem., cataloguer steering com. and coun. Blessed Trinity Ch. Libr., St. Petersburg, 1994—. Contbg. author: Trace Metals in Seawater, 1983, Humic Substances in Soil, Sediment and Water, 1985; editor: (newsletter) Poynter Libr. Newsletter, 1995—; contbr. articles to profl. jours. (winner NOAA/ERL Disting. Authorship award 1984 for 1983 article in Marine Chemistry). Mem. Assn. of Coll. and Rsch. Librs. (pres. Fla. chpt. 1996-97, v.p. 1995-96), Fla. Libr. Assn. (acad. caucus vice-chair 1995-96, acad. caucus chair 1996-97), Suncoast Info. Specialists (pres. 1990-91, 93-94, v.p., program chair 1989-90), Phi Kappa Phi, Beta Beta Beta. Office: Univ South Fla 140 Seventh Ave South Saint Petersburg FL 33701

HENRY, FLOREEN BARGER, foreign language educator; b. Ft. Worth, Tex., Apr. 26, 1954; d. Robert Lindsey and Jurhee Mozella (Moose) Barger; m. Gary William Henry, Feb. 26, 1977; children: Bryan, Ashley, Dustin Williamson. BA in Fgn. Langs., U. Tex., Arlington, 1977, MA in French, 1985. Cert. secondary tchr. of French and Spanish, ESL endorsement, Tex. Intensive English instr. English Lang. Inst. U. Tex., Arlington, 1985-86, lectr. French, Spanish, ESL, 1986-89, Lang. Acquisition Ctr. asst. Dept. Fgn. Langs./Linguistics, 1988-89; instr. French and ESL, N.E. Campus Tarrant County Jr. Coll., 1986; instr. French and ESL, South Campus Tarrant County Jr. Coll., Ft. Worth, 1989-90, instr. French and ESL, chmn. dept. fgn. langs., 1990-91, instr. French and ESL, chmn. dept. comm. arts, 1991—; lectr. in field. Contbr. articles to profl. jours.; newsletter editor various non-profit orgns. including Tarrant Aero Assn. Mem. North Tex. Higher Edn. Authority, 1992-94, exec. dir., 1993-94; former bd. dirs. Arlington Orgn. for Parent Edn., Arlington Gifted and Talented; vol. Parenting Guidance Ctr., 1985—; cub scout leader/asst. leader Boy Scouts Am.; Soviet space vol. Ft. Worth Mus. of Sci. and History; active Arlington Ind. Sch. Dist. SERVA, 1983—, PTA, 1983—; rm. mother/asst. C.C. Duff Elem. Sch., 1983—; mem., vol. St. Albans Episcopalian Ch., 1981—. Mem. Am. Coun. on Teaching Fgn. Langs., Assn. of Depts. of Fgn. Langs., Linguistic Assn. of Can. and U.S., Am. Assn. Tchrs. French, North Tex. Assn. Tchrs. French, Internat. Assn. Learning Labs., South Ctrl. Region of Internat. Assn. Learning Labs., Computer Assisted Learning and Instrn. Consortium, Tex. Fgn. Lang. Assn., Tex. Humanities Alliance, South Ctrl. Modern Lang. Assn., U. Tex.-Arlington Macintosh Users Group (charter), U. Tex. Arlington Alumni Assn., Tex. TESOL (region V), Southwestern Theatre Assn., Phi Sigma Iota. Democrat. Office: Tarrant County Jr Coll 5301 Campus Dr Fort Worth TX 76119-5926

HENRY, JOHN DUNKLIN, hospital administrator; b. Atlanta, Dec. 23, 1937; married. B, Emory U., 1957; Cert. Health Adminstrn., 1962, 64, 66. Adminstrv. asst. Crawford Long Hosp. Emory U., Atlanta, 1964, adminstrv. resident, 1963-64, asst. dir., 1964-73, asst. adminstr., 1973-77; assoc. adminstr. Crawford Long Hosp., Atlanta, 1977-84, adminstr., CEO, 1984—. Home: 2054 Imperial Dr NE Atlanta GA 30345-3436 Office: Crawford Long Hosp 550 Peachtree St NE Atlanta GA 30365*

HENRY, LORETTA M., writer; b. Gould, Mich., May 21, 1942; d. Sigvard Strom and Florence Loretta (McNeill) Tremblay; m. Richard Lee Denton, Jan. 20, 1980 (wid. Mar. 1985); stepchildren: Dale Carter Henry, Brian Henry; m. Delbert L. Henry, July 4, 1989. Color print technician Van's Camera and Processing, Lansing, Mich., 1960-64, Lynn's Processing Lab., Lansing, Mich., 1964-66; color movie film technician Capitol Film Svcs., Lansing, 1966-68; part-time photographer Olan Mills, Lansing, 1960-73; real estate broker Graham Realty, Lansing, 1973-84; owner coin laundry Laundry Mat, Haslett, Mich., 1974-83; owner rental units, flooring store, D&D Plumbing, Lansing, 1973-85, D&D Mechanical, Lansing, 1976-85, Denton Harbor Marina, Haslett, 1979-87, Denton Harbor Amusements, Haslett, 1979-85; pres. Delton Swartz Investments, 1980-87, Foxden, Inc., Haslett, Mich. and, Ky., 1985—; Author: (craft book) Braided Wire Jewelry, 1995. Mem. Moose, Eagle's. Home: PO Box 40 Utica KY 42376 Office: Foxden Inc 3721 Vanover Rd Utica KY 42376-9737

HENRY, MARGARET ANNETTE, activities director; b. Cleve., Oct. 9, 1953; d. Charles Jacob Bing and Jacqueline Mildred (Fulton) Wilson; m. Hugh David Reynolds, Aug. 20, 1974 (div. June 1982); m. Philip Lawrence Henry, Apr. 16, 1994. BA in Sociology, Lee Coll., 1974; MA in Christian Edn., Sch. of Theology, 1988; postgrad., Ga. State U., 1993—. Verifier, supr. Harrison Co., Norcross, Ga., 1977-84; file clk. Fisher & Phillips, Atlanta, 1984-89; proofreader O.D. Resources, Atlanta, 1989-91; activities dir. Tucker (Ga.) Nursing Ctr., 1991-94; dir. activities/social svcs. Country Gardens Sr. Living, Norcross, Ga., 1994—. Vol. Big Bros./Big Sisters, 1979-82, The Open Door Community Soup Kitchen, 1990—; camp counselor Mission Ch. of God, 1979-82; vol. monthly chapel svcs. Atlanta Union Mission, 1990; nursing home visitor, 1984, 87—. Mem. Pentecostal Church. Home: 3937 Hancock Cir Doraville GA 30340-4276 Office: Country Gardens Sr Living 600 Holcomb Bridge Rd Norcross GA 30071

HENRY, MARY LOU SMELSER, elementary education educator; b. Russellville, Ala., Mar. 2, 1953; d. Jessie Clifton and Margie Lou (Willingham) Smelser; m. Don M. Henry, Aug. 26, 1972; children: Aaron, Nathan. BS, Middle Tenn. State U., 1975; MA, Tenn. Tech. U., 1986; student, N.W. Ala. State Jr. Coll., 1971-72. Cert. elem. tchr., secondary tchr. history and sociology, Tenn., Ala. Substitute tchr. Warren County Bd. Edn., McMinnville, Tenn., 1979-82; tchr. LaPetite Acad., McMinnville, 1982-83; tchr. 2d grade Grundy County Bd. Edn., Altamont, Tenn., 1983—. Coord. Drug Awareness Task Force, 1990-92; mem. Grundy County Edn. Assn. Recipient Tchr. of Yr. award 1987-88, Trophy award 4H, 1988-91. Mem. NEA, Grundy County Edn. Assn. (sec. 1989-90, chmn. pub. rels. 1990-91, rep. North Elem. 1990-91, editor Tchr. Times 1989-91, pres. 1993-94, chair grievance com. 1994-95), Tenn. Edn. Assn. (Cert. of Appreciation 1991, women status com. 1994-96). Home: 212 Forest Dr Mc Minnville TN 37110-2333

HENRY, NANCY SINCLAIR, middle school educator; b. Alexandria, Va., Aug. 4, 1940; d. John Wilson and Margaret Lucille (Bryant) Sinclair; m. James Russell Henry, June 21, 1969; 1 child, Ryan Sinclair. BA in Elem. Edn., Coll. William and Mary, 1962; MA in Edn., Instrn. & Curriculum, Lynchburg Coll., 1997. Cert. tchr., Va. Primary tchr. Alexandria Pub. Schs., 1962-69, 70-73, Louisa County Pub. Schs., Louisa, Va., 1969-70; presch. tchr. St. Paul's Nursery and Day Sch., Alexandria, 1973-81; elem. and mid. tchr. Bedford County Pub. Schs., Bedford, Va., 1981—, math.-coop. learning cons., 1988—; cons. learning ctrs. Alexandria Pub. Schs., 1970-73; cons. math. and coop. learning Appomattox County Schs., Appomattox, Va., 1989, 90, 91, Bedford County Schs., 1990-96, mentor, 1996—. Vol. James Earl Carter U.S. Presdl. campaign, Alexandria, 1976; pres. Bookmark Club, Bedford, 1987-88, Bedford Hist. Soc., 1989-90; trustee Bedford Regional Libr., 1988-96. Named Tchr. of Yr. Bedford County Mid. Sch., 1990-91; grantee Va. Commn. on Fine Arts, 1989-90. Mem. NEA, Nat. Coun. Tchrs. Math., Nat. Mic. Sch. Assn., Va. Edn. Assn., Piedmont Area Reading Coun., Va. Reading Assn., Bedford County Edn. Assn. (Tchr. of Month 1991), Phi Kappa Delta, Alpha Delta Kappa. Episcopalian. Home: 1096 Meadowbrook Dr Bedford VA 24523-3020 Office: Bedford Mid Sch Longwood Ave Bedford VA 24523-3402

HENRY, NICHOLAS LLEWELLYN, college president, political science educator; b. Seattle, May 22, 1943; s. Samuel Houston and Ann (Connor) H.; m. Muriel Bunney; children: Adrienne Richardson, Miles Houston. B.A., Centre Coll. Ky., 1965; M.A., Pa. State U., 1967; M.P.A., Ind. U., 1970, Ph.D., 1971. Asst. to dean Coll. Arts and Scis.; instr. Ind. State U., 1967-69; vis. asst. prof. U. N.Mex., 1971-72; asst. prof. polit. sci. U. Ga., 1972-75, assoc. prof., 1975-78, prof., 1978-87, dir. Ctr. Pub. Affairs, 1975-80, dean Coll. Pub. Programs, 1980-87; prof., pres. Ga. So. U., Statesboro, 1987—. Author or editor 12 books; contbr. numerous articles to profl. jours. Recipient Author of Yr. award Assn. Sci. Jours.; named One of 100 Most Influential People in Ga., Ga. Trend, 1994. Fellow Nat. Acad. Pub. Adminstrn. Office: Ga So U Office of President Statesboro GA 30460-8033

HENRY, PATRICIA ANN, nutrition coordinator, dietitian; b. Monongahela, Pa., Jan. 18, 1957; d. Frank Robert and Beverly Ann (Zanardelli) H.; m. Paul David Lewandowski, Oct. 17, 1992. BS, W.Va. U., 1978; MEd, U. Houston, 1993. Registered and lic. dietitian. Clin. dietitian ARA Food Svcs., Elkins, W.Va., 1978-80, HNW Med. Ctr., Houston, 1980-81; nutrition coord. Tomball (Tex.) Regional Hosp., 1981—; cons. Barbour County Ctr., Belington, W.Va., 1978-80, Internal Medicine Assn., Tomball, 1984—; spkr. Am. Heart Assn., Houston, 1983-86, program chair, 1995-96. Nursery coord. St. Simon and Jude Cath. Ch., Woodlands, Tex., 1984—; mem. BBB, Houston, 1986. Mem. Am. Dietetic Assn., Tex. Dietetic Assn. (pub. rels. conv. chair 1988-89), Tall Pines Dietetic Assn. (founder, pres. 1982-83, treas. 1984-86, bylaws chair 1991-94, pub. rels. chair 1994-95, v.p. 1995-96), Diabetes Care and Edn. Sports and Cardiovascular Nutritionists. Republican. Roman Catholic. Home: 3206 Windgap Ct The Woodlands TX 77380-2451 Office: Tomball Reg Hosp 605 Holderrieth Blvd Tomball TX 77375-6445

HENRY, PETER YORK, lawyer, mediator; b. Washington, Apr. 28, 1951; s. David Howe II and Margaret (Beard) H.; children: Ryan York, Zachary Price, Chance Nagdorn; m. Deidra B. Hagdorn, May 1995; 1 child, Chance Hagdorn Henry; stepchildren: Nathan Hebert, Christopher Hebert. B.B.A., Ohio U., 1973; J.D. St. Mary's U., San Antonio, 1976. Bar: Tex. 1976. Sole practice, San Antonio, 1976—. Mem. ATLA, Tex. Bar Assn., Tex Trial Lawyers Assn., San Antonio Trial Lawyers Assn. (bd. dirs. 1989-90), San Antonio Bar Assn., Phi Delta Phi. Home: 7642 Bluesage Cv San Antonio TX 78249-2541 Office: 224 Casa Blanca St San Antonio TX 78215-1232

HENRY, RANDOLPH MARSHALL, real estate broker, company executive; b. Houston, Jan. 23, 1946; s. Marshall Gambrell and Merriem Rue (Evans) H.; m. Janis Kay Frank, Apr. 5, 1979; children: Vernon Clark, Clark Marshall. BA, So. Meth. U., 1968; Diploma in Hist. Studies, Cambridge (Eng.) U., 1969; MBA, U. Pa., 1971. Lic. real estate broker. Asst. to pres. Surfcoat Inc., Houston and Fairbanks, Alaska, 1971-72; mgr. Gerald D. Hines Interests, Houston, 1972-75; pres. The Randolph Henry Co., Houston, 1975—, EcoPoly, Inc.; pres. MGP Mgmt. Inc., Houston, 1976-87; adv. dir. Tex. Commerce Bank, Houston, 1982—; v.p., bd. dirs. Brazos Mgmt. Co., 1976-90, Skyline Condominium Corp., 1983-90; bd. dirs. Pvt. Sector Initiatives, Houston; mem. adv. com. New Founds. for Neighborhoods. Mktg. network Houston Econ. Devel. Coun., 1987—; chmn. Post Oak Sch., Houston, 1987-89; founding pres. City of Post Oak Assn., 1974-75; Rep. precinct chmn., Houston, 1979; adminstrv. bd. Chapelwood Meth. Ch., 1987. Mem. Wharton Alumni Assn., Houston C. of C. (aviation com.). Methodist. Club: Univ. Home: 640 Pifer Rd Houston TX 77024-5434 Office: 5858 Westheimer Rd Ste 703 Houston TX 77057-5647

HENRY, ROBERT H., federal judge, former attorney general; b. Shawnee, Okla., Apr. 3, 1953. BA, U. Okla., 1974, JD, 1976. Atty. Henry, West, Still & Combs, Shawnee, Okla., 1977-83, Henry, Henry & Henry, Shawnee, 1983-87; mem. Okla. Ho. of Reps., 1976-86; atty. gen. State of Okla., Oklahoma City, 1987-91; dean, prof. law. Law Sch. Okla. City U., 1991-94; judge U.S. Ct. Appeals (10th cir.), Oklahoma City, 1994—; mem. Nat. Conf. Commrs. on Uniform State Law. Mem. Okla. Bar Assn., Am. Coun. Young Polit. Leaders, Nat. Assn. Attys. Gen. (chmn. state constl. law adv. com., vice-chmn. civil rights com.). Office: US Ct Appeals 10th Cir 200 Northwest 4th St Oklahoma City OK 73102

HENRY, ROBERT LEE, association executive; b. Lewisburg, W.Va., Mar. 25, 1934; s. Thomas Wilson and Marguerite McClung (Ruckman) H.; m. Sally Joy Moore, Sept. 7, 1958; children: Thomas Wilson, Timothy Glen, Jacob Mathew. BS in Civil Engring., W.Va. U., 1958; MS in Civil Engring., Iowa State U., 1963; PhD in Civil Engring., N.C. State U., Raleigh, 1971. Registered profl. engr., Tex., Colo., Miss. Indsl. engr.-in-tng. fabricated steel divsn. Bethlehem Steel Co., Pitts., 1958-59; grad. tchg. asst. Iowa State U., Ames, 1961-62, grad. rsch. asst., 1962-63; grad. tchg. asst. N.C. State U., Raleigh, 1967-68, grad. rsch. asst., 1968-70; asst. prof. civil engring. U. Miss., Oxford, 1964-73, assoc. prof., 1973-77, asst. dean engring., dir. Engring. Expt. Sta., 1977; adj. assoc. prof. civil engring. dept. U. Tex., Arlington; head structural engring. dept. Lawrence D. White & Assocs., Ft. Worth, 1977; chief engr. Tex. Testing Labs., Inc., Dallas, 1977-83; cons. Wiss, Janney, Elstner Assocs., Inc., Irving, Tex. & Northbrook, Ill., 1983-87; v.p., br. mgr., head assessment of existing structures dept. Maxim Engrs., Inc., Ft. Worth, 1987-89; sr. cons. Bowen Structures, Bedford, Tex., 1990-92; nat. sec.-treas. Chi Epsilon, U. Tex., Arlington, 1992—; structural engring. cons., forensic engr., Colleyville and Bedford, Tex., 1992—. Contbr. articles to profl. jours. Precinct capt. Republican party, Tarrant County, Tex., 1996. Capt. C.E. U.S. Army, 1958-66. Recipent Stanford E. Thompson award ASTM, 1965. Fellow Am. Concrete Inst. (com. chmn., pres. N.E. chpt. 1986, Sophus Thompson award 1991), ASCE (dir. Ft. Worth br. 1982, 96), Chi Epsilon (supreme councillor S.W. dist., exec. sec.). Republican. Mem. Metroplex Covenant Ch. Home: 3510 Fox Glen Dr Colleyville TX 76034 Office: Chi Epsilon U Tex Arlington Box 19316 Arlington TX 76019-0316

HENRY, STEPHEN LEWIS, state official, orthopedic surgeon, educator; b. Owensboro, Ky., Oct. 8, 1953; s. Virgil Lewis and Wanda (Harper) Henry. BS, We. Ky. U., 1976; MD, U. Louisville, 1981. Diplomate Am. Bd. Orthopaedic Surgery. Intern gen. surgery U. Louisville Med. Ctr., 1981-82, resident, 1982-86, instr. orthopedic surgery, 1986—; lt. gov. State of Ky., 1995—; clin. investigator Richards Med. Co., Memphis, 1986—; athletic physician football teams U. Louisville, 1987—, Seneca High Sch., 1987—, Ky. State Football Championships, 1986—. Editor: Sports Medicine; contbr. abstracts and articles to profl. jours., chpts. to books. Treas. Louisville Tyler Park Neighborhood Assn., 1983-88, pres., 1988-89. Recipient best paper award So. Med. Assn., 1985, best clin. rsch. award U. Cin., 1986, outstanding resident rsch. award U. Louisville, 1988, Edwin G. Bovill rsch. award Orthopaedic Trauma Assn., 1989, Bell award for outstanding vol., Louisville, 1989, Presdl. recognition Nat. Vol. Week, The White House, 1989; named Outstanding Young Leader in Ky., 1988, One of 10 Outstanding Young Ams., U.S. Jaycees, 1989, Bell award, 1989, Jefferson award, 1989, Owensboro award for excellence, 1990, Lawrence-Grever award, 1990; grantee Richards Med. Co., 1986, Dept. Navy, 1989. Mem. Jefferson County Med. Soc., So. Orthopedic Assn., Ky. Med. Assn., U. Louisville House Staff Assn. (com. on health, phys. edn. and med. aspects of sports 1987—). Democrat. Home: 1361 Tyler Park Dr Louisville KY 40204-1539 Office: 700 Capitol Ave Frankfort KY 40601-3410

HENRY, WILLIAM CHARLES, manufacturing company administrator; b. Monroe, La., Dec. 30, 1961; s. William and Catherine (Lewis) Staten; m. Jacqueline Rochelle Profit, Aug. 11, 1984; children: Jasmine, William II, Jade. BS in Electronics Tech., Grambling (La.) State U., 1984. Systems engr. Telos Corp., 1993-95; facilitator Ethicon, Inc., San Angelo, Tex., 1995—. Sec. Pan Hellenic Coun., Lawton, Okla., 1995-96. With U.S. Army, 1984-93. Mem. Psi Upsilon (v.p. Omega Psi Phi 1994-95, chaplain 1993-94). Baptist. Home: 3878 Old Post Road San Angelo TX 76904 Office: Ethicon Inc 3348 Pulliam St San Angelo TX 76904-4403

HENRY, WILLIAM OSCAR EUGENE, lawyer; b. Ocala, Fla., Mar. 30, 1927; s. Jesse Dawson and Alice M. (Johnson) H.; m. Bobbie Moorhead, May 9, 1952; children: Carol Ann, Robert Dawson, Jean Elizabeth. BS in Journalism, U. Fla., 1950, JD, 1952. Bar: Fla. 1952; cert. cir. mediator Supreme Ct. Fla., tax lawyer Fla. Bd. Legal Specialization. Newspaperman The Marion Sun, Ocala, 1952-53; assoc. Holland, Bevis, McRae & Smith, Bartow, Fla., 1953-55; ptnr. Holland and Knight (and predecessor firms), Bartow, Lakeland and Orlando, Fla., 1955—; bd. dirs. Consol.-Tomoka Land Co., Daytona Beach, Fla.; arbitrator, mem. panel Am. Arbitration Assn. Contbr. articles to profl. jour. Legis counsel Office of Gov. of Fla., Tallahassee, 1963; bd. dirs. U. Fla. Found., Inc., 1977-87, Holland and Knight Found., Lakeland, 1982—; v.p. Ctrl. Fla. coun. Boy Scouts Am., 1990-95; trustee Fla. Bar Found. Endowment Fund, 1991—. Recipient Disting. Eagle Scout award, 1990, Silver Beaver award, 1992; named Outstanding Past Pres. Vol. Bar Assn. award Fla. Coun. Bar Assn. Pres., 1991-92. Fellow Am. Bar Found., Am. Coll. Trusts and Estates Coun., Am. Coll.

Tax Coun., Am. Judicature Soc., Nat. Health Lawyers Assn., Fla. Bar Found. (bd. dirs. 1983-89, pres. 1988-89); mem. ABA (ho. of dels. 1984-89, 93—), Fla. Bar (pres. 1983-884, Fla. Outstanding Tax Atty. award 1986), U. Fla. Nat. Alumni Assn. (bd. dirs., pres. 1968, Disting Alumnus award 1972), Univ. Club, Citrus Club, Elks, Sigma Alpha Epsilon (pres. Fla. Upsilon alumni 1993—). Methodist. Home: 560 S Osceola Ave Orlando FL 32801-3900 Office: Holland & Knight 92 Lake Wire Dr Lakeland FL 33815-1510

HENSCHEL, D. BRUCE, chemical engineer, environmental researcher; b. Alameda, Calif., Feb. 13, 1945; s. George E. and Maxine P. (Schmagran) H.; m. Ann Blattmann, June 20, 1970; children: Brian A., Cheryl C. BSChemE with honors, U. Calif., Berkeley, 1966; MSChemE, MIT, 1967. Registered profl. engr., N.C. Assoc. engr. Unocal (Union Oil Co.), Rodeo, Calif., 1966; rsch. engr. U.S. EPA, Research Triangle Park, N.C., 1967-80, sr. rsch. engr., 1980—. Author: (manual) Radon Reduction Techniques for Detached Houses, 1986, 3d edit., 1993; contbr. articles to profl. jours. Recipient Bronze medals EPA, 1978, 83, 94, Gold medal 1987. Mem. AIChE, Internat. Soc. Indoor Air Quality and Climate, Phi Beta Kappa. Office: US EPA MD-54 Research Triangle Park NC 27711

HENSEL, JOHN ERIC, sales executive, educator; b. Phila., Apr. 17, 1963; s. Joseph Peter and Alice Marie (Rhindernict) H. BSBA in Mktg. and Sales, S.E. Mo. State U., 1986. Sales rep., trainer Dale Carnegie & Assoc., Inc., St. Louis, 1986-87; hosp. rep. ethicon divsn. Johnson & Johnson, Indpls., 1988-89, Lanier Worldwide, St. Louis, 1989-92; nat. sales trainer Lanier Worldwide, Atlanta, 1992-93; healthcare sales rep. Milner Bus. Products, Atlanta, 1993—; pres., CEO Hensel Enterprises Sales & Motivational Training, Atlanta, 1993—. Contbr. articles to profl. jours. Mem. Ga. Spkrs. Assn., Sales and Mktg. Execs., Toastmasters, Atlanta Rowing Cir., St. Louis Rowing Club (bd. dirs. 1991-92), Sigma Chi (bd. dirs. 1990—, leadership tng. bd. 1992—, chpt. advisor 1986—).

HENSLEY, ALLAN LANCE, security consultant, litigation support specialist; b. San Jose, Dec. 6, 1944; s. Orville and Isabel (Garcia) H.; m. Margaret Anne Shelley, Aug. 13, 1966; children: Janet E., David A., Susan E. BA in Edn., Seattle U., 1966; MA in Police Sci. and Adminstrn., Sam Houston State U., Huntsville, Tex., 1973. Cert. protection profl. V.p. security Macy's, Atlanta, 1976-92; pres. Hensley & Assoc. Security Mgmt. Cons. Group, Marietta, 1992—; instr. Johnson County Community Coll., Overland Park, Kans., 1981-84. Capt. U.S. Army, 1966-76, USAR, 1976-89, ret. Decorated Bronze Star (2), Purple Heart, Silver Star. Mem. Am. Soc. Indsl. Security, Am. Correctional Assn., Internat. Assn. Chiefs of Police, Canterbury Golf Club. Republican. Roman Catholic. Home and Office: 1454 Oak Springs Dr Marietta GA 30066-3969

HENSLEY, JOHN CLARK, religious organization administrator, minister; b. Sullivan County, June 16, 1912; s. Truman and Ivan (Moddrell) H.; m. Margaret Sipes, Nov. 24, 1946; children: Gary, Clark, Dana. Ordained to ministry So. Bapt. Conv., 1930. Pastor Moberly and Kansas City, Mo., 1935-46, Nashville and Pulaski, Tenn., 1947-58; supt. missions Hinds County Bapt. Assn., Jackson, Miss., 1958-66; exec. dir. Christian Action Commn. Miss. Bapt. Conv., Jackson, 1966-82, exec. dir. emeritus, 1982—, cons. family life, 1982-90, rec. sec., 1982-90; assoc. prof. Cen. Bapt. Theol. Sem., 1943-46. Author: The Pastor as Educational Director, rev. edit., 1950, My Father is Rich, 1956, In the Heart of the Young, 1952, Behaving at Home, 1972, Help for the Single Parents and Those Who Love Them, 1973, Coping With Being Single Again, 1978, Preacher Behave! Pointers on Ministerial Ethics, 1978, Good News for Todays Single, 1985, The Autumn Years, 1987, The Pastor in Family Ministry, 1990. Pres. bd. CONTACT, 1973—; trustee Radio and TV Commn. So. Bapt. Conv., 1980-88; mem. Gov. Miss. Com. Alcohol Abuse and Alcoholism, 1972—; mem. bd. Am. Coun. Alcohol Problems, 1972—; trustee Hannibal, Mo. LaGrange Coll., 1939-45. Recipient Disting. Svc. award for leadership in Christian ethics Christian Life Commn., 1975, Disting. Svc. award Family Ministry Bapt. Sunday Sch. Bd., 1988, Brooks Hays Christian Citizenship award, 1992, Ctrl. Bapt. Theol. Sem. Alumnus of the Yr. award, 1996. Mem. Nat. Coun. Family Problems, Southeastern Coun. Family Problems, Miss. Couns. Family Problems, Am. Judicature Soc., Am. Acad. Polit. Assn., Am. Assn. Sex Educators and Counselors. Home: 130 Caribbean Cv Clinton MS 39056-6136

HENSLEY, STEPHEN ALLAN, insurance executive; b. Portsmouth, Va., July 29, 1950; s. Theodore Allen and Lillie Mae (Costner) H. BA, U. W. Fla., 1976. Mgr. Carlyle & Co. Jewelers, Killeen, Tex., 1977-83; owner L.T., Ltd. Property, Killeen, 1983—; claims specialist State Farm Ins., San Antonio, 1985—; disaster rep. State Farm Fire & Casualty Ins. Co., San Antonio, 1989—; investigator State Farm Life Ins. Co., 1986—. Univac focus group Brasenose Coll., Oxford, England, 1993; contbr. articles to profl. jours. Active Friends of KNCT-TV, Belton, 1985—, Viva Les Arts Societe, Killeen, 1988—. Decorated Knight Grand Comdr., Order of the Commonwealth, Can., 1990, Knight Grand Cross, Order of St Joseph, B.C., 1994, Count, Order of the Sursum Corda, Belgium, 1991, Baron, Sovereign of Order von Liechtenstein, 1991, Keeper of the Tomes Principality of St. Michel de Clermont, 1991, Adm., Tex. Navy, 1991, Knight Comdr., Mil. and Chivalric Order of Sword of Eng., 1996. Mem. U.S. Golf Assn., Lake Belton Yacht Club.

HENSLEY, STEPHEN RAY, academic administrator; m. Mary Ann Deines; children: Scott, Walt, Rick. BS in Phys. Edn., Kans. State U.; MS in Natural Sci., Okla. State U., EdD in Sci. Edn. Tchr. sci. and math. Hoxie (Kans.) high Sch., 1964-67; instr. biology Ft. Hays (Kans.) State Coll., 1971-73; assoc. prof. biology Black Hills State Coll.; asst. prof. Northwestern Okla. State U., 1973-78, v.p. acad. affairs, 1978-90; pres. Western Okla. State Coll., Altus, 1990—; mem. team Nat. Coun. Accreditation Tchr. Edn., 1984-87; evaluation team Okla. State Regents, 1986-87, Tchr. Edn. State Dept. Edn., 1983-84; temporary dir. Enid Higher Edn. Ctr., 1989; author grants, presenter in field. Mem. Phi Delta Kappa (pres. Cimarron chpt. 1987, advisor 1988). Home: 4019 Colorado St Texarkana TX 75503-2724 Office: Western Okla State Coll 2801 N Main St Altus OK 73521-1310

HENSLEY, SUSAN ELEANORE, communications and language educator; b. Estherville, Iowa, Nov. 23, 1946; d. William Sherman and Eleanore Marion (Haverland) Burho; m. Wayne Edward Hensley, Feb. 21, 1995; children: Andrew Martin, Frederick. BA in Speech and Drama, Mary Washington Coll., Fredericksburg, Va., 1968; MEd in Comm., U. Va., 1971; postgrad., Va. Poly. Inst. and State U., 1980-89. Cert. tchr. speech, English and drama, Va. Tchr. Roanoke City Schs., 1968-71; sales mgr. World Book, 1977-78; tchr. pub. speaking Va. Poly. Inst. and State U., Blacksburg, 1978-80; tutor homebound Montgomery County Schs., 1982-85; instr., forensics coach Radford U., 1985-86; instr. dept. comms., 1986, 88, 93; tchr. pub. speaking Radford U., 1988-89, 93-96; instr., pronunciation expert for royal Thai scholars Va. Poly. Inst. and State U., 1990—; rsch., cons. Grad. Sch., Va. Poly. Inst. and State U., 1990-94. Dir., writer, costumes, lights and makeup for original theatre prodns. Dir. pub. rels. Montgomery County Christmas Store, Blacksburg, 1988-92. SCHEV gantee, 1990-94. Mem. TESOL. Methodist. Office: Radford University Grad Sch 7A Speech Comms Radford VA 24141

HENSON, GLENDA MARIA, newspaper writer; b. Marion, N.C., June 17, 1960; d. Douglas Bradley and Glenda June (Crouch) H. BA in English cum laude, Wake Forest U., 1982. Reporter Ark. Dem., Little Rock, 1982-84; bur. reporter Tampa Tribune, Crystal River, Fla., 1984; statehouse reporter Ark. Gazette, Little Rock, 1984-87; bur. chief Ark. Gazette, Washington, 1987-89; editorial writer Lexington (Ky.) Herald-Leader, 1989-94; editorial writer, columnist The Charlotte (N.C.) Observer, 1994—. Mem. Wake Forest Presdl. Scholarship Com., Ky., 1992, Wake Forest Bd. Visitors, 1995—; Pulitzer Prize juror, 1994, 95. Recipient Pulitzer prize, 1992, Walker Stone award Scripps Howard Found., 1992, award Ky. Press Assn., 1992, N.C. Press Assn., 1995, Leadership award Duke U., 1995, Nat. Headliner award, 1996; named Wake Forest Woman of Yr., 1992. Mem. Soc. Profl. Journalists (Sigma Delta Chi award 1991, Green Eyeshade award Atlanta chpt. 1992), Nat. Conf. Editorial Writers, Omicron Delta Kappa. Home: 1527 Cleveland Ave # B Charlotte NC 28203-4515 Office: The Charlotte Observer PO Box 549 Raleigh NC 27602

HENSON, HENRY PAUL, protective services official; b. Norfolk, Va., Apr. 9, 1931; s. Charles Minton and Beulah Lee (Harden) H.; m. Jane Octavia Flowers, Dec. 22, 1966; 1 child, Marian Elizabeth. Diploma, FBI Nat. Acad., 1972, Northwestern U., 1975, Nat. Exec. Inst., Quantico, Va., 1987; AA in Law Enforcement, Old Dominion U., 1973, BA in Sociology, 1978. With Norfolk Police Dept., 1954—, sgt., 1964-71, lt., 1971-84, capt., 1984-85, chief of police, 1985—; notary pub. Va. Notary Pubs., Norfolk, 1985—. Mem. Tidewater Alcohol Safety Program, Norfolk, 1988-89. Mem. Internat. Assn. Chiefs of Police, Va. Assn. Chiefs of Police, Hampton Rds. Chiefs of Police (v.p. 1988-89), FBI Nat. Acad. Assocs., Fraternal Order of Police (sec. local chpt. 1964-66), Law Enforcement Officers Fellowship (Norfolk chpt.), Lions (mem. eye bank com. 1985—). Baptist. Office: Norfolk Police Dept 206 Monticello Ave PO Box 358 Norfolk VA 23510

HENSON, HOWARD KIRK, lawyer; b. Chgo., Apr. 28, 1956; s. Howard I. and Constance M. (Evanhoff) H. BA, Ga. State U., 1979; JD, U. Ga., 1982. Bar: Ga. 1982, U.S. Dist. Ct. (no. dist.) Ga. 1983, U.S. Dist. Ct. (mid. dist.) Ga. 1986. Pvt. practice Atlanta, 1982-86; of counsel Corlew, Smith & Wright, Atlanta, 1984-86; house counsel Am. States Ins. Co., Atlanta, 1986-88; atty. Amoco Corp., Atlanta, 1988-95; pvt. practice Atlanta, 1995—. Mem. ABA, State Bar Ga., Atlanta Bar Assn. Home: 4615 Lake Forrest Dr NE Atlanta GA 30342-2537 Office: 3690 N Peachtree Rd Ste 250 Atlanta GA 30341

HENSON, JOHN DENVER, international management consulting firm executive; b. Fairmont, W.Va., Feb. 28, 1921; s. Denver Clair and Achsa Elizabeth (Martin) H.; m. Jitka Dondova, Feb. 14, 1947 (div. Jan., 1962); children: John Donda, Mark Denver; m. Lydia Cuan-Perez, June 3, 1966. Student Liberal Arts, Phoenix Coll., 1940-42; student Fin., Econs., Am. U., Biarritz, France, 1945; student pharmacy, U. New Mex., 1946-47; grad. cert. Internat. Trade, Am. Grad. Sch. Internat. Mgmt, 1948. Commd. 2d lt. U.S. Army, 1942, advanced through ranks to capt., 1946, active duty., 1942-46, 49-58; wartime svc. U.S. Army, ETO and Korea; lt. col. AUS; asst. gen. svcs. officer Internat. Coop. Adminstrn., Kabul, Afghanistan, 1959-61; chief supply mgmt. br., sr. supply mgmt. advisor to Cambodian Govt. Internat. Coop. Adminstrn., Phnom Penh, Cambodia, 1961-64; chief procurement mgmt. br. Agy. for Internat. Devel. State Dept., Saigon, Vietnam, 1964-66; chief office of Korea/Vietnam affairs Agy. for Internat. Devel. State Dept., Seoul, Korea, 1966-68; dep. chief supply mgmt. divsn. U.S. AID, State Dept., Jakarta, Indonesia, 1968-71; chief E. Asia Bur. comml. import programs, dep. Cambodia desk officer AID, Washington, 1971-72; chief procurement mgmt. divsn., sr. supply mgmt. advisor to Vietnamese govt. U.S. AID Saigon, 1972-75; chief logistics divsn. Bangkok, Thailand, 1975; pres. J.D. Henson & Assocs. Internat. Mgmt. Cons., Miami, Fla., 1976—; sr. v.p. U.S. Gulf Holdings Corp., Fla. and Guyana, 1995—; pres. Here Comes Grandma, Inc., Miami, 1996—; pres. Nat. Industries and Consol. Energy Corp., Dallas and Miami, 1987-91; v.p. internat. ops. Diversified Internat. Directions, Inc., Miami and Costa Rica, 1984-87, Miami, 1986-88; bd. dirs. Mandel Enterprises, Inc., Miami, Zane Internat. Mktg., Inc., Miami, House of Cuan, Inc. Oriental Imports, Miami; dir. internat. affairs U.S. Gulf Holdings Corp., Fla. and Guyana, 1995—; v.p., sec., treas. Sabrine Ballroom Shoes, Inc., Miami, 1991—; spl. advisor to Sec. Commerce, State of Fla., Miami, 1987-92; exec. guest lectr. U. Miami Grad. Sch. Internat. Bus., Miami, 1978—. Mem. Founding Task Force, The Beacon Coun., Miami, 1985; spl. advisor to Fla. Vol. Orgn. Internat. Commerce Execs., Miami, 1987-92; dir. Internat. Ctr. Fla. (now World Trade Ctr.), Miami, 1978—; v.p., dir. Fla. Exporters and Importers Assn., 1978-86; asst. to civilian aide to Sec. of War for Ariz., 1940-42; founder, 1st commdr. citizens military tng. camps, Assn. the U.S., Ariz., 1940-42; chmn. Maricopa County C.M.T.C. War Dept., 1940-42; observer Rep. Nat. Conv., Chgo., 1944; del. Ariz. Rep. State Conv., Phoenix, 1946, 48; chmn. Govs. Coord. Com. for Civic and Vet. Orgns., 1946-48, adv. bd. Miami Dade C.C. Endowment Found., 1987—; pres. Cambodia Gourmat Soc., Phnom Penh, 1963. Recipient medaille de la France Liberées, French Ministry of Vets. Affairs, Perigueux, France, 1955, Vietnam Civilian Svc. medal U.S. Dept. State, Washington, 1966, Chong My Boi Tinh Pub. Svc. medal Pres. Vietnam, Siagon, 1974, Vietnam Spl. Svc. medal Office of Prime Min., Saigon, 1975, Pres.'s E awards for Export Promotion, U.S. Dept. Commerce, Washington, 1981, 83. Mem. VFW (life mem., judge advocate Ariz. 1946-47, nat. membership com. 1979-80, 80-81), Fla. Coun. of Internat. Devel., Am. Health Industries World Trade Assn. (v.p., sec., treas., bd. dirs. 1983—), World Trade Ctr., Am. Fgn. Svc. Assn., Health Coun. South Fla., Mil. Order of World Wars (life), Res. Officers Assn. (life), Ret. Officers Assn. (life), Nat. Assn. Ret. Fed. Employees (life), Am. Philatelic Soc. (life), Soc. IndoChina Philatelists, Fla. C. of C. (internat. devel. com. 1991-94), Alliance Francais, The Chosin Few, Am. Legion (life), Asia-Am. Assn., Elks. Republican. Unitarian-Universalist. Office: JD Henson & Assocs Internat Mgmt Cons 12265 S Dixie Hwy Ste 907 Miami FL 33156-5260

HENSON, JOHN ELY, accountant; b. Olney, Ill., Nov. 5, 1947; s. Harry Mayfield and Vesta Lois (Ely) H.; m. Susan A. Able, Nov. 17, 1973; children: Emily Susan, John Ely II. Student, Graceland Coll., 1965-67; BS, Murray State U., 1970. CPA, Ky., Tenn., Fla. Supr. Delloite Touche & Co., Louisville, 1970-75; comptroller Arnold Cos., LaFollette, Tenn., 1975-76; ptnr., shareholder Carr, Mynatt & Henson, CPAs, Oak Ridge, Tenn., 1976-85; pvt. practice acctg. Zephyrhills, Fla., 1985—; bd. dirs. First Nat. Bank of Pasco. Pres. Little League, Zephyrhills, 1989; treas. Reorganized Ch. Jesus Christ Latter day Saints, Zephyrhills, 1986—, Zephyr Youth Soccer, Zephyrhills, 1987-91, Dave Dunaway for Congress Com., LaFallotte, 1980-82; pres. Zephyrhills Youth Basketball, 1989-94; bd. mem. Zephyrhills Hist. Preservation com., 1989—; chmr. Zephyrhills adv. com., 1994-95; treas. East Pasco Habitat for Humanity, 1994—. Mem. AICPA, Nat. Soc. Pub. Accts., Fla. Inst. CPAs, Tenn. Soc. CPAs (state tax liaison 1982-85), Ky. Soc. CPAs, Kiwanis (pres. Zephyrhills chpt. 1989-90, bd. dirs. Oak Ridge, Tenn. chpt. 1983-85). Home: 5734 Elaine Dr Zephyrhills FL 33541-1965 Office: 38145 5th Ave Zephyrhills FL 33541-4974

HENTGES, DAVID JOHN, microbiology educator; b. LeMars, Iowa, Sept. 18, 1928; s. Romaine Francis and Geneva Mae (Kruger) H.; m. Kathleen Edwina Mullan, Dec. 28, 1957; children: Stephen Edward, Kathleen Marie, Margaret Ann. BS, U. Notre Dame, 1953; MS, Loyola U., Chgo., 1958, PhD, 1961. Asst. prof. Creighton U. Sch. Medicine, Omaha, 1964-67, assoc. prof., 1967-68; assoc. prof. U. of Mo. Sch. of Medicine, Columbia, 1968-72, prof., 1972-81, interim chmn., 1976-79; prof., chmn. Tex. Tech. U. Sch. Medicine, Lubbock, 1981-96, vice provost for rsch., dean grad. sch. biomed. scis., 1996—, assoc. dean basic scis., 1996—. Editor: Human Intestinal Microflora, 1983, Medical Microbiology, 1986—, Microbiology and Immunology, 2d edit., 1995; regional editor Microbial Ecology in Health and Disease, 1987—; editorial bd. Infection and Immunity, 1983-92; contbr. chpts. to books and articles to profl. jours. Lay gen. chmn. Diocesan Cath. Appeal, Lubbock, 1989, steering com., 1985—. Named Knight Comdr., Order of the Holy Sepulchre, 1995. Fellow Am. Acad. of Microbiology; mem. Am. Soc. Microbiology, Assn. for Gnotobiotics, Soc. for Microbial Ecology and Disease (pres. 1987-89), Serra Internat. (dist. gov. 1987-88, Serran of Yr. 1988), Sigma Xi. Republican. Roman Catholic. Home: 4601 88th St Lubbock TX 79424-4107 Office: Tex Tech U Health Sci Ctr Rsch and Grad Programs Lubbock TX 79430

HENTSCHEL, HILARY GEORGE, physicist, educator; b. Tel-Aviv, Israel, Jan. 13, 1951; s. Cedric Eberhardt and Eva (Bolgar) H. BSc with 1st class honors, Univ. Coll., London, 1972; PhD, Cambridge U., 1978. Postdoctoral asst. Stuttgart (Germany) U., 1978-81; postdoctoral fellow Weizmann Inst., Rehovot, Israel, 1981-83, MIT, Cambridge, Mass., 1983-85; cons. Dowell Schlumberger, Tulsa, 1986-87; sr. rsch. assoc. Cambridge U., 1988-89; assoc. prof. physics Emory U., Atlanta, 1990—. Contbr. over 50 articles to profl. jours. Fellow Cambridge Philos. Soc.; mem. AAAS, Am. Phys. Soc., Royal Soc. Chemistry, Inst. of Physics. Office: Emory University Dept of Physics Atlanta GA 30322

HEPKER, ROBERT EUGENE, environmental executive; b. Cedar Rapids, Iowa, Jan. 25, 1949. BS in Edn., N.E. Mo. State U., 1971; BS in Environ. Health, East Tenn. State U., 1975; MA in Mgmt., Ctrl. Mich. U., 1984; MS in Safety, No. Ill. U., 1985. Indsl. hygienist Deere & Co., 1980-82; indsl. hygiene mgr. Unocal, 1982-87; safety dir. Morton Chems., 1987-89; safety and environ. mgr. Motorola, 1989-93; environ. mgr. MagneTek, Nashville, 1993—. Lt. col. USAF, 1971-95. Office: MagneTek 26 Century Blvd Nashville TN 37214-3644

HEPNER, JOHN CARSON, librarian; b. Harlingen, Tex., Sept. 28, 1946; s. James Matthews and Marjorie Alice (Knowles) H.; m. Virginia Pauline McHenry, Oct. 18, 1969 (div. Aug. 1981); 1 child, John David. AA, Tex. Southmost Coll., Brownsville, 1967; BA, U. Tex., 1970, MLS, 1974. Reference libr. Blagg-Huey Library Tex. Woman's U., Denton, 1974—, adj. instr., 1991-92. Compiler (book) AHE CD-ROM Directory, 1989, CD-ROM Directory and Online Database Services Directory, 1992; section editor, reviewer Tex. Reference Sources, 1993. Mem. ALA, Reference and User Svcs. Assn. (mem. various coms. and couns., bd. dirs.), Assn. Coll. and Rsch. Librs. (mem. various coms.), Tex. Libr. Assn. (mem. various coms.). Democrat. Home: PO Box 507 Denton TX 76202-0507 Office: Blagg Huey Libr Box 425528 Denton TX 76204-3528

HEPP, ROBERTA ANN, primary education educator; b. Bowman, N.D., May 12, 1940; d. Leslie Arthur and Olga Borghild (Tollefsrud) DeFoe; m. Jerry Phillip Hepp, Apr. 6, 1973; children: Steven Ray, Kevin Patrick. BA, St. Scholastica, Duluth, Minn., 1963; BS, Mary Coll., Bismarck, N.D., 1965; student, U. Dayton, 1970-72. Tchr., second grade St. Joseph's Sch., Dickinson, N.D., 1965-68; tchr., first grade Cathedral Sch., Bismarck, 1968-72; tchr., first/second grades Progressive Sch., Fairview, Okla., 1974-81; headstart tchr. Fairview Pub. Schs., 1973; kindergarten tchr. Kingman Ind. Sch. Dist., Norwich, Kans., 1983-85; tchr., fourth grade Springtown (Tex.) Ind. Sch. Dist., 1986-89, tchr., first grade, 1989—. Den leader Boy Scouts Am., Longhorn Coun., 1986-88, roundtable commr., 1988-90, dist. advancement chmn., 1992—. Named Tchr. of Yr., Progressive Sch., Fairview, 1979. Mem. Assn. Tex. Profl. Educators. Republican. Mennonite.

HERB, F(RANK) STEVEN, lawyer; b. Cin., Nov. 9, 1949; s. Frank X. and Jean M. (Zurcher) H.; m. Jean L. Jeffers, June 21, 1971; children: Tracy Lynn, Jacquelyn Anne. BS, Bowling Green U., 1971; JD, U. Cin., 1974. Bar: Ohio 1974, Fla. 1978. Assoc. Connaughton Law Offices, Hamilton, Ohio, 1974; jud. adv., chief of civil law USAF, Tyndall AFB, Fla., 1975-78; mng. ptnr. Nelson Hesse, Sarasota, Fla., 1979—. Author: (with others) Bennedicts on Admiralty, 1996; contbr. chpts. to books. Bd. dirs. Brock Wilson Found., Sarasota, 1983-92, Riegels Landing Assn., Sarasota, 1986-90; dir., vice chmn. Siesta Key Utilities Assn.; mem. govt. rels. com. Nat. Marine Mfrs. Assn. Capt. JAGC USAF, 1975-78. Decorated USAF Meritorious Svc. medal. Mem. Ohio Bar Assn., Fla. Bar Assn. (chmn. 12th Jud. cir. unauthorized practice of law com. 1986-93, fee arbitration com. 12th jud. cir. 1996—), Sarasota Bar Assn., Def. Rsch. Inst., The Field Club, Am. Boat and Yacht Coun. Republican. Roman Catholic. Office: Nelson Hesse 2070 Ringling Blvd Sarasota FL 34237-7002

HERBEL, LEROY ALEC, JR., telecommunications engineer; b. Ft. Carson, Colo., July 24, 1954; s. LeRoy Alec and Mabel Bertha (Huffman) H. BS, S.W. Mo. State U., 1976; MEd, Ga. So. U., 1978; MS in Telecommunications, Golden Gate U., 1987, MBA, 1990; student, Southern U., 1996. Asst. mgr. toy dept. Dillard's Dept. Store, Springfield, Mo., 1971-76; material controller GTE of the South, Durham, N.C., 1979-80; asst. prof. mil. sci. Army ROTC, U. N.H., Durham, 1982-85; tech. instr. Northern Telecom Inc., Raleigh, N.C., 1988-91; sr. engr. No. Telecom Inc., Raleigh, N.C., 1991-93; field engr. mgr. Western Wireless Corp., Bellevue, Wash., 1994-95; switch supr. Palmer Wireless (CellularOne), Ft. Myers, Fla., 1995—; adj. prof. DeKalb (Ga.) C.C., 1978-79, N.C. Wesleyan Coll., Rocky Mount, 1991. Scoutmaster Troop 213 Boy Scouts Am., Cary, N.C., 1990-93, asst. dist. commr. Dan Beard dist., 1992—, mem. merit badge staff Nat. Jamboree, 1993. Capt. U.S. Army, 1980-88; maj., USAR, 1988—. Recipient Scoutmaster award of merit Boy Scouts Am., 1991, Disting. Leadership citation Boy Scouts Am., 1991, Scoutmaster Key award Boy Scouts Am., 1992, Dist. Order of Merit Boy Scouts Am., 1994, Boy Scout Commr. Key award, 1995. Mem. Telephone Pioneers of Am., Phi Delta Kappa. Office: Palmer Wireless Corp 7001 Chatham Center Dr Ste 400 Savannah GA 31405-1342

HERBELIN, KAREN, survey and certification specialist, dietitian; b. Ft. Worth, Dec. 1, 1954; d. Ted and June Herbelin. BS in Home Econs., Kans. State U., 1978; MS in Adminstrn., Ctrl. Mich. U., 1992. Registered dietitian; cert. long term care facility surveyor. Therapeutic dietitian USPHS Hosp., San Francisco, 1978-79; dep. dir. dietetics USPHS Hosp., Boston, 1979-80; clin. dietitian Gallup (N.Mex.) Indian Med. Ctr., 1980-85; nutrition cons. Health Care Fin. Agy., Dallas, 1985-90, survey and cert. program rev. specialist, 1991—; staffing officer II Div. of Commd., Rockville, Md., 1990-91; chair com. dietetic profl. group USPHS, 1993—. Contbr. articles to profl. jours. Comdr. USPHS, 1978—. Recipient Achievement ward USPHS Commd. Corps, 1990, Commendation medal, 1994, Isolated Hardship award USPHS, 1983. Mem. Dallas Dietetic Assn. (legis. com. 1992). Office: Health Care Fin Adminstrn 1200 Main St Ste 1940 Dallas TX 75202-4348

HERBENER, MARK BASIL, bishop; b. Chgo., Jan. 2, 1932; s. Otto Berthold and Elsbeth Marie (Mueller) H.; m. Donna Fay Gergens, Apr. 25, 1958; children: Matthew, Jenny Pickett. Student, Concordia Coll., Milw., 1949-51; BA, Concordia Sem., St. Louis, 1953, theol. diploma, 1956. Ordained to ministry Luth. Ch.-Mo. Synod, 1956, Evang. Luth. Ch. in Am., 1978. Intern St. John Luth. Ch., Durand, Wis., 1954-55; pastor Messiah Luth. Ch., Richardson, Tex., 1956-61, Mt. Olive Luth. Ch., Dallas, 1961-87; bishop No. Tex.—No. La. synod Evang. Luth. Ch. in Am., Dallas, 1987—; co-chair Dallas Interfaith Task Force, 1981-86; v.p. Greater Dallas Cmty. of Chs., 1983-85; dir. Dallas region NCCJ, 1983-86; pres. Tex. Conf. Chs., 1995—; fellow Thanks-giving Sq. Pres. Dallas Opportunities Industrialization Ctr., 1983-85; co-convenor Martin Luther King Jr. Inst., Dallas, 1986-87; v.p. Greater Dallas Cmty. Rels. Commn., 1987; convenor Jewish-Christian-Muslim Dialogue, Dallas, 1990; co-chair Tex. Jewish-Christian Forum, 1992-95; chair chapel com. Thanks-Giving Square, 1992-95. Recipient Disting. Ch. Svc. award Tex. Luth. Coll., 1987, A. Maceo Smith award Dallas African-Am. Mus., 1987; named Peacemaker of Yr., Dallas Peace Ctr., 1987. Mem. Tex. Conf. Chs. (pres. 1995—), Dallas Com. on Fgn. Rels., Dallas Pastors Assn. (chmn. 1978-80). Democrat. Office: Evang Luth Ch in Am No Tex—No La Synod PO Box 560587 Dallas TX 75356-0587 also: 1530 River Bend Ste 105 Dallas TX 75247

HERBERT, ADAM WILLIAM, JR., university president; b. Muskogee, Okla., Dec. 1, 1943; s. Addie (Hibler) H.; m. Karen Y. Lofty, Apr. 1980. BA, U. So. Calif., 1966, MPA, 1967; PhD, U. Pitts., 1971. Instr., asst. prof., coord. acad. programs Ctr. Urban Affairs Sch. Pub. Adminstrn., U. So. Calif., L.A., 1969-72; assoc. prof., chmn. urban affairs program div. environ. and urban systems Va. Poly. Inst. State U., Blacksburg, 1972-75, prof., dir. North Va. programs, Ctr. for Pub. Adminstrn. and Policy, 1978-79; White House fellow/spl. asst. sec. HEW, Washington, 1974-75; spl. asst. to under sec. HUD, Washington, 1975-77; prof., dean Fla. Internat. U., Miami, 1979-87, assoc. v.p. for acad. affairs, chief acad. officer North Miami campus, 1985-88, v.p., chief adminstrv. officer, 1987-88; pres. U. North Fla., Jacksonville, 1988—. Bd. dirs. N.E. Fla. chpt. ARC, 1989; trustee Sta. WJCT, Channel 7/Stereo 90, Jacksonville, 1989; bd. mem. Mazda Gator Bowl Assn., Jacksonville, 1989. Jessie Smith Noyes fellow, 1967-68. Mem. Nat. Assn. Sch. Pub. Affairs and Adminstrn. (chair com. on peer rev./accreditation), Am. Soc. for Pub. Adminstrn., Nat. Conf. Minority Pub. Adminstrs., Jacksonville C. of C. (bd. govs. 1989), Phi Kappa Phi. Office: U North Fla 4567 Saint Johns Bluff Rd S Jacksonville FL 32224-2646

HERBERT, AMANDA KATHRYN, special education educator; b. Cleve., Apr. 10, 1948; d. Ralph Earle and Nina Kathryn (Burkey) Herbert; m. John Davis Reeves, June 26, 1971 (div. 1978). Student, Coll. of Wooster, Ohio, 1966-68; BA, Defiance Coll., 1971; MEd, Lynchburg Coll., 1982. Cert. tchr., Va. Elem. tchr. Napoleon (Ohio) City Schs., 1970-72; substitute tchr. Juvenile Boys Correction Ctr., Maumee, Ohio, 1972-73; Title I reading tchr. Defiance City Schs., 1973-76, tchr. 4th grade, 1976-78; tchr. 4th to 6th grades Platte Valley Schs. RE3, Ovid, Colo., 1978-81; tchr. elem. and secondary spl. edn. Amherst County (Va.) Schs., 1982—; tchr. Camp Little Indian, Defiance, 1967-77. Contbr. to book. Deacon, elder First Presbyn. Ch., Defiance, 1973-78; singer Defiance Community Choir, 1972-77; actor, singer Fine Arts Ctr., Lynchburg, Va., 1983—; mem. choir Parkland United Meth. Ch., Lynchburg, 1982—. Mem. NEA, Coun. for Exceptional Children (div. learning disabilities), Va. Edn. Assn., People to People Citizen Ambassador Program to Peoples' Rep. China, Amherst Edn. Assn., Alpha Chi. Methodist. Office: Amherst County High Sch Old Rt 29 Amherst VA 24521

HERBERT, JAY ANDREW, assembly engineering professional. Student, U. Wis., Stout, 1980; BSME with honors, U. Wis., 1986; student, GE Mfg. Mgmt. Program. Elec./mech. technician tool engring. Eastman Kodak Co., Kodak Apparatus Divsn., 1982, mfg. engr. consumer products, 1983, design engr. copy products, 1984, rsch. engr. engring. tech. lab., 1985; new product/quality engr. GE Co., Plastics Bus. Group, Selkirk, N.Y., 1986; utilities project engr. GE Co., Plastics Bus. Group, Selkirk, 1986-87; supr. stockrooms GE Co. Constrn. Equip. Bus. Switchgear Operation, Burlington, Iowa, 1987; mfg./process control engr. GE Co. Constrn. Equip. Bus. Switchgear Operation, Burlington, 1987-88; process control engr. GE Co. Appliances, Decatur, Ala., 1988-90; assembly engring. mgr. United Technologies: Carrier Scroll Compressor Ops., Arkadelphia, Ark., 1990—. Bd. advisor Shelby Dodge Automobile Club; dir. Internat. Viper Registry. Mem. Tau Beta Pi, Pi Tau Sigma, Triangle. Office: Scroll Techs One Scroll Dr Arkadelphia AR 71923-8813

HERBERT, WILLIAM NORMAN PARKE, obstetrician, gynecologist, administrator; b. Greensboro, N.C., June 28, 1946; s. Andrew William and Madaline (Cates) H.; m. Marsha Turner, Mar. 3, 1973; children: Turner, Coleman. BA in Biology, Elon Coll., 1968; MD, Wake Forest U., 1972. Diplomate Am. Bd. Ob-Gyn. Asst. prof. dept. ob-gyn U. N.C., Chapel Hill, 1978-84, assoc. prof. dept. ob-gyn, 1984-90, prof. dept. ob-gyn, 1990-92; prof., dir. dept. ob-gyn Duke Univ. Med. Ctr., Durham, N.C., 1992—, F. Bayard Carter prof. ob-gyn, 1996—. Author/co-author numerous articles and book chpts. Recipient Outstanding Spkr. award Am. Assn. Clin. Chemisty, Inc., 1988, 89, 91, 92, 93, 94, 95. Fellow Am. Coll. Ob-Gyn. (vice chair N.C. chpt. 1995—, mem. com. 1993—), Assn. Profs. Ob-Gyn. (program chair, dir., com. mem. 1993—, sec., treas. 1994); mem. N.C. Ob-Gyn. Soc. (pres. 1993-94), Soc. Perinatal Obs., Alpha Omega Alpha, Beta Beta Beta. Office: Duke Univ Med Ctr Trent Dr Box 3967 Durham NC 27710

HERBOLSHEIMER, LAWRENCE FREDERICK, entrepreneur; b. LaSalle, Ill., July 25, 1950; s. George Leonard and Texie (Tilton) H. BA in Econs., Ill. Wesleyan U., 1972; MBA, Harvard U., 1980. Dir. cabinet office The White House, Washington, 1983-85; dep. adminstr. NASA, Washington, 1985-91; ptnr. Ballston Ptnrs., Arlington, Va., 1985-93; v.p. Montgomery Foods, Bethesda, Md., 1983—; CEO United Pacific Holdings, Ltd., Washington, 1991—; pres. Adsumma Group, Inc., Arlington, Va., 1991—; chmn. Sunway Techs., Inc., Beijing, 1995—. Co-author: Doing Business in China-The Contemporary Chinese Puzzle, 1982. Bd. dirs. Found. for Critical Care, Washington, 1992—. Republican. Home: 1431 Cedar Ave Mc Lean VA 22101

HERBST, CHARLES ARTHUR, JR., general surgeon, educator; b. Atlanta, Jan. 22, 1941; s. Charles A. Sr. and Edith Fay (Hart) H.; m. Gloris Rosemary Norton, Aug. 15, 11964; children: Edith Ann, Randolph Norton. BS, Miss. Coll., 1963; MS, U. Miss., 1972, MD, 1967. Diplomate Nat. Bd. Med. Examiners. Intern in surgery U. Va. Hosp., Charlottesville, 1967-68; asst. to chief resident in surgery U. Miss. Med. Ctr., Jackson, 1968-72; rsch. fellow div. gastroenterology U. Fla., Gainesville, 1972-73; asst. prof. surgery U. N.C. Sch. Medicine, Chapel Hill, 1973-78, assoc. prof. surgery, 1978-91, prof. surgery, 1991—; mem. surgery staff U. N.C. Hosps., Chapel Hill, 1973—; surg. cons. Watts Hosp., Durham, N.C., 1973-77, Dorothea Dix Hosp., Raleigh, N.C., 1975-78, Durham County Gen. Hosp., Durham, 1977-87; assoc. chief-of-staff Quality Asurance, 1989-95; cons. diagnostic and therapeutic tech. program AMA, 1991—; mem. clin. evaluative scis. specialty coun. U. Hosp. Consortium, 1990-93; mem. numerous hosp. and state coms.; dir. edn. programs; vis. prof. U. Miss., 1985, New Hanover Meml. Hosp., annually, 1973—. Contbr. numerous articles, abstracts to profl. jours., chpts. to books; presenter in field. Mem. Crohn's and Colitis Found. of Am., 1990—; deacon, tchr. First Baptist Ch., Durham. Grantee Am. Cancer Soc. Fellow ACS, Am. Cancer Soc., Southeastern Surg. Congress, So. Surg. Assn.; mem. Am. Gastroenterol. Assn., So. Med. Assn., Nathan A. Womack Surgica Soc., Collegium Internationale Chirurgiae, Soc. for Surgery of Alimentary Tract, Soc. Am. Gastrointestinal Endoscopic Surgeons. Republican. Office: U NC Dept Surgery CB7210 Chapel Hill NC 27599

HERD, CHARMIAN JUNE, singer, actress; b. Waterville, Maine, June 1, 1930; d. Samuel Braid and Jennie May (Lang) Herd; B.A., Colby Coll., 1950; postgrad. Boston U., 1951, EdM, U. Maine, 1965; ednl. cert. No. Conservatory, Bangor, Maine, 1954; also study voice with Roger A. Nye. Dir. music State Sch. for Girls, Hallowell, Maine, 1950-51; head English, French, dramatics depts. St. George High Sch., Tenants Harbor, 1951-52; dir. music pub. schs. Albion and Unity, 1952-54, Troy, Freedom, Maine, 1953-54; dir. music pub. sch. system Belgrade, Maine, Waterville Jr. High Sch., 1954-55; dir. vocal music Waterville Jr. and Sr. high schs., 1954-58; head English and dramatics depts. Besse High Sch., Albion, 1959-62; tchr. French, Skowhegan Jr. High Sch., 1962-63; tchr. French, English, Skowhegan Sr. High Sch., 1963-69; tchr. French, Lawrence Sr. High Sch., Fairfield, Maine, 1969-71, chmn. drama and speech dept., 1972-79; instr. dramatics U. Maine, Farmington, 1969-70; tchr. conversational French, Skowhegan Adult Edn. Sch., 1963-69, drama instr., 1965-69; dance asst. Plaza Studio; producer, appeared in role of Vera, Mame, Waterville; soloist various churches, Maine, 1951—; mus. dir. children's sect., performing mem. Theater at Monmouth, Maine, 1970—, mem. exec. bd., 1976—, sec. bd. trustees, 1977—; performing mem. Augusta Players, Camden Civic Theatre, Portland Lyric Theatre, Waterville Players, Titipu Choral Soc., Waterville Community Ballet, Choral Arts Soc., Portland, Maine, 1980—, Treasure Coast Opera Soc., Ft. Pierce, Fla., 1986—, Riverside Theatre Co., Vero Beach, Indian River Ctr. for Arts, New Lyric Opera, Port St. Lucie, Fla.; theatre chmn. ann. Maine Festival Arts, Bowdoin Coll., 1978—; soloist Vero Beach Chorale Soc., 1986—, numerous club, ch., conv., coll. concerts, oratorios; performing mem. Vero Beach Solo Gates, Encore Alley Theatre, 1987-91, Esprit des Amis, Vero Beach, Ft. Pierce City Ballet, Fla.; treas. Coast Opera Co., Ft. Pierce, Fla., 1986—, New Lyric Opera, Port Saint Lucie, Fla., 1995—; hostess, prodr. TV show Lively Arts of the Treasure Coast with Charmian Herd, Ft. Pierce, Fla., 1994—. Bd. dirs. Opera New Eng., 1980—, Portland Lyric Theatre, 1982—Mem. Waterville Friends Music, DAR, Waterville Theatre Guild (charter mem., pres. 1967——), Vero Beach Theatre Guild (Fla.), Encore Alley Theatre, Vero Beach, Waterville Bus. and Profl. Women's Club (program chmn. 1957-58, v.p. 1958-59, pres. 1959-61, chmn. drama dept. 1961, drama and music chmn. 1961—), Fla. Profl. Theatre Assn., Ednl. Speech and Theatre Assn. Maine (mem. exec. bd., pres. 1972-74), Maine Profl.-Community Theatre Assn. (mem. organizing com.), Actors Equity Assn., Albion-Burnham Tchrs. Club (sec. 1960-61), NEA, Maine Tchrs. Assn., New Eng. Theatre Conf. (exec. bd. 1976—, 1st v.p. 1976-77, conf. chmn. 1977), Theatre Assn. Maine (membership chmn. 1972-73, 2d v.p. 1973-74, exec. bd. 1972—, exec. sec. 1975—, state pres. 1976—), Internat. Platform Assn., Nat. Assn. Tchrs. of Singing (sec. Maine chpt. 1980—), St Lucie Cultured Affairs Assn., Fla., 1996— Pine Tree Post Card Club (exec. bd., Spring show chmn. 1979-80, pres. 1982-84), Maine Hist. Soc., Bay State Post Card Club, R.I. Post Card Club. Club: Cecilia (Augusta, Maine). Composer sacred music: Babylon, 1959, The Greatest of These is Love, 1961, Pan; Keep Not Thy Silence, O God, Remember Now Thy Creator, Slow, Slow, Fresh Fount, A Witch's Charm, Hymn to God the Father. Avocations: acting, singing, oil painting, collecting opera and operetta scores. Home and Office: 601 Seaway Dr E 2 Fort Pierce FL 34949

HERD, JOANNE MAY BEERS, intravenous therapy nurse, educator; b. Nazareth, Pa., Nov. 28, 1934; d. Robert Albert and Marguerite (Small) Beers; m. Robert Von Steuben Herd, Oct. 25, 1958; 1 child, Scott Robert. Diploma, Allentown (Pa.) Hosp., 1955. Cert. intravenous nurse. Asst. instr. sci. Allentown Hosp., 1956-57, recruitment dir., 1957-58; staff nurse Tidewater Blood Bank Svcs., ARC, Norfolk, Va., 1959-60; staff nurse Virginia Beach (Va.) Gen. Hosp., 1979-86, staff educator, 1986—; intravenous nurse educator, cons. Pharmacy Care Plus, Norfolk, Va., 1991—. Designer intravenous nurse emblem lapel pin, mobile teaching unit. Mem. League Intravenous Therapy Edn., Intravenous Nurses Soc. (chmn. Ea. Va. chpt. 1983-85, pres. elect 1993-94, pres. 1994-95, presdl. advisor 1995-96), Tidewater Assn. Continuity of Care, Allentown Hosp. Alumni Assn. (life).

HERENDEEN, CAROL DENISE, dietitian; b. Cleve., Dec. 10, 1955; d. Charles Ralph and Betty Ann (Simashkevich) Dunlap; m. Norman James Herendeen, June 30, 1979; children: Seth Ryan, Eric Kyle. AA, Lakeland Community Coll., 1976; BS, Kent State U., 1978. Lic. dietitian, Fla. Dietary supr. U. Hosps., Cleve., 1978-79, St. Luke's Hosp., Cleve., 1979; trainee Lake County Hosps., Willoughby, Ohio, 1980, Case Western Res. U., Cleve., 1980; clin. dietitian Lakeland (Fla.) Regional Med. Ctr., 1980-87; renal dietitian Watson Clinic, Lakeland, 1987—; cons. Pasco County Nursing and Rehab. City, Dade City, 1981-84, City of Lakeland Employee Fairs, 1985, 87, 91, 92, Sta. WLKF-AM, Lakeland, 1989-91, Polk County Schs., Winter Haven, Fla., 1990; speaker diabetes and cardiac programs Watson Clinic, Lakeland, 1989-91, others. Mem. Am. Dietetic Assn. (registered, renal dietitians practice group), Am. Diabetes Educators Assn. (cert.), Am. Heart Assn. (CPR cert.), Cypress Dietetic Assn. (sec. 1987-88, pres. elect 1988-89, pres. 1989-90, chair nominating com. 1990-91, 91-92, membership 1991, 92), Nat. Kidney Found. (coun. renal nutrition 1981—), Fla. Coun. Renal Nutrition (sec. 1983-84, treas. 1987-89, pres. elect 1989-90, pres. 1990-91, chair nominating com. 1991-92). Methodist. Office: Watson Clinic 1550 Lakeland Hills Blvd Lakeland FL 33805-3204

HERKE, ROBERT, SR., chemist, researcher; b. Subotica, Yugoslavia, Sept. 8, 1932; came to U.S., 1969; s. Antal and Julianna (Konkol) H.; m. Eva Csala, Sept. 1, 1951; 1 child, Robert. Chem. engr., Coll. Chemistry, Zrenjanin, 1964; Grad. chem. engr., U. Novi Sad, 1969. Tchr. Techj. High Sch., Zrenjanin, Yugoslavia, 1950-62; lab. mgr. Zitoproduct, Zrenjanin, 1962-64; prof. Tech. High Sch. and Jr. Coll., Zrenjanin, 1964-69; quality control technician Kraft Foods, Chgo., 1969-70; chemist Blommer Chocolate, Chgo., 1970-72; chemist, scientist Witco Corp., Chgo. and Houston, 1972—. Specialist in surfactants; patentee and author in field. Past mem. Yogoslavian Aeronautical Soc.; past. mem., treas. Serbian Chem. Soc. in Zrenjanin. With Yugoslav Army, 1952-53. Named sailplane champion of Serbia, Yugoslavia, 1960. Mem. Am. Chem. Soc., Am. Sci. Soc., Am. Oil Chemist Soc. Home: 3278 Hunters Glen Dr Missouri City TX 77459-3616 Office: Witco Corp 3200 Brookfield Dr Houston TX 77045-6610

HERMAN, JERRY R., not for profit foundation executive; b. Chgo., Aug. 25, 1947; s. Roy A. and Rasa Lee (Clayton) J. BS, U. Tenn., 1976, MS, 1982; EdD, East Tenn. State U., 1995. Cert. career level III supervisor Tenn. Dept. Edn. Spl. edn. tchr. Hawkins County Schs., Rogersville, Tenn.; spl. edn. tchr. Sevier County Schs., Sevierville, Tenn., supervisor spl. edn.; exec. dir. The Dollywood Found., Pigeon Forge, Tenn. Bd. dirs. Health Improvement Coun., Sevierville, 1994—, Sevierville Housing Authority, 1994—, Head Start HUD Adv. Bd., Pigeon Forge; mem. Dropout Adv. Coun., Sevierville, 1989—; mem. Foster Care Review Bd., Sevier County, 1984—; mem. State Commn. Nat. & Cmty. Svc., 1993—, vice chair, 1996, chair, 1997. Mem. Rotary, Masons. Office: The Dollywood Found 1020 Dollywood Ln Pigeon Forge TN 37863-4113

HERMAN-GIDDENS, GREGORY, lawyer; b. Birmingham, Ala., Aug. 8, 1961. BA, U. N.C., 1984; JD, Tulane U., 1988; LLM in Estate Planning, U. Miami, 1993. Bar: N.C. 1988, U.S. Dist. Ct. (mid. dist.) N.C. 1988, Fla. 1992. Assoc. N. Joanne Foil, Atty. at Law, Durham, N.C., 1988-92, Catalano, Fisher, Gregory & Crown, Chartered, Naples, Fla., 1993, Northen, Blue, Rooks, Thibaut, Anderson & Woods, L.L.P., Chapel Hill, N.C., 1994-96; pvt. practice Chapel Hill, 1996—. Mem. Chapel Hill Bd. Adjustment, 1989-92; bd. dirs. Friends of Chapel Hill Sr. Ctr., 1994, vice chair, 1996—; bd. dirs. Orange County adv. Bd. on Aging, 1994—; treas. Orange County Literacy Coun., Carrboro, N.C., 1994—; mem. nat. com. on planned giving N.C. Planned Giving Coun. Mem. ABA (mem. coms. on stds. of tax practice and tax practice mgmt. of tax sect., mem. coms. on lifetime and testamentary charitable gift planning and planning for execs. and profls. of real property, probate and trust sect. 1996—), N.C. Bar Assn. (mem. elder law com., law and aging com. 1994—, vice-chair 1995-96, mem. career devel. com. 1990-91, elder law com. 1995—), Fla. Bar (out of state mem. rels. com. 1994-96), Nat. Acad. Elder Law Attys., Durham/Orange Estate Planning Coun., Orange County Kiwanis (Orange County quality of life and stress mgmt. com. 1996—), Phi Beta Kappa, Psi Chi. Office: 100 Europa Dr Ste 271 Chapel Hill NC 27514

HERMANN, NAOMI BASEL, librarian, interior decorator; b. N.Y.C., Feb. 12, 1918; d. Alexander and Rebecca (Deinard) Basel; m. Henry I. Almour, June 26, 1938 (dec.); 1 child, Jay Alexander; m. Stanford Leland Hermann, Dec. 20, 1951. BS in Edn., NYU, 1937, MS in Psychology, 1939; MLS, Columbia U., 1963; postgrad., Vassar Coll., Cornell U., Hunter Coll. Newspaper reporter Times Picayune, New Orleans, 1935; tchr. gifted children N.Y.C. Schs., 1946-58; libr. supr. 22 elem., jr. and sr. high schs., N.Y.C., 1958-72; libr. Brandeis High Sch., 1972-75; interior decorator, pvt. practice, N.Y.C., 1946—; instr. Children's Literature, N.Y.C. Bd. Edn., 1969-73; libr. examiner, N.Y.C. Bd. of Edn., 1967-72. Pres. Hadassah, N.Y.C., 1939-41, life mem.; life mem. Coun. Jewish Women, 1974—; charter mem. Eleanor Roosevelt Fund for Women and Girls; established adult library Temple Beth El, Boca Raton, Fla. Mem. AAUW (pres. Boca Raton chpt. 1987-89), Boca Raton Noontime Ladies Club (pres.). Home: 550 S Ocean Blvd Boca Raton FL 33432-6264

HERMANSEN, JOHN CHRISTIAN, computational linguist; b. Athens, Greece, Oct. 21, 1949; s. John Theodore and Lois Ann (Shope) H.; m. Sharyl Lynn Miner (div. 1994); children: John Theodore, Janet Lois. BA in Speech, BA in Linguistics, Pa. State U., 1975; PhD in Computational Linguistics, Georgetown U., 1985. Propr. CompAssociates, Inc., Washington, 1974-78; lectr., univ. fellow computational linguistics Georgetown U., Washington, 1980-83, dir. Lang. Processing Ctr., Sch. Langs. and Linguistics, 1982-85; artificial intelligence rsch. scientist Planning Rsch. Corp., McLean, Va., 1985-88, computational linguistics cons., 1988-90; cons. knowledge engring. Sterling Software, Inc., McLean, Va., 1991-95; lead scientist linguistics analysis team State Dept. CLASS Project, Lang. Analysis Systems, Inc., Herndon, Va., 1986—; computational linguistics cons. Ctr. for Applied Linguistics, Washington, 1985-94; CEO Lang Analysis Systems, Inc., Herndon, Va., 1991—. Co-author: Southeast Asia Refugee Testing Report, Vols. I and II, 1985, Report on the Evaluation of Kenya Radio Language Arts Project, 1985, PAKTUS Version 1 User's Guide, 1986, Building NLU Systems in the PAKTUS Environment: Developer's Introduction, 1987, Message Processing Systems: Evaluation Factors, 1987, Meronomy, Word Experts and Prepositional Phrase Attachment in PAKTUS, 1989, Techniques in Multilingual Name Searching, 1989, The Automated Templating System for Database Update from Unformatted Message Traffic, 1995; contbr. articles to profl. jours.; patentee in field. Mem. IEEE, Assn. for Computational Linguistics, Internat. Assn. Knowledge Engrs., Soc. for Psychology and Philosophy, Data Adminstrn. Mgmt. Assn. Home: 12012 Robin Dr Catharpin VA 22018-1307 Office: Lang Analysis Systems Ctr for Innovative Tech 2214 Rock Hill Rd Herndon VA 22070

HERMES, MOTHER THERESA MARGARET, prioress; b. Hallettsville, Tex., Sept. 30, 1906; d. Anthony Thomas and Teresa (Drysee) H. BA, U. Tex., 1930. Novice Discalced Carmelite Nuns, New Orleans, 1934-36; foundress Discalced Carmelite Nuns, Lafayette, La., 1936, directress of novices, 1936-48, prioress, 1948-82, 85—; organizer, coord. St. Teresa Assn., Lafayette, 1978; organizer, counselor Carmelite Guild, 1950—. Collaborator Satutes/St. Teresa's Assn., 1979. Recipient Papal medal Pope John Paul II, Lafayette, 1990, Jerusalem Cross, Patriarch Maximos V Hakim, Lafayette, 1991, Mission Cross Rev. Giovanni Salerno, Lafayette, 1990. Home: 1250 Carmel Ave Lafayette LA 70501-5299 Office: Discalced Carmelite Nuns 1250 Carmel Ave Lafayette LA 70501-5211

HERNANDEZ, DANIEL ARTHUR, elementary school educator; b. Galveston, Tex., Dec. 8, 1945; s. Reyes and Irene (Unzueta) H.; m. Bettye Ann Sing, Aug. 4. 1972; children: Angelica Dana, Mishael Stephen. BA in Music Edn., Howard Payne U., 1969; M of Ch. Music, Southwestern Sem., 1973; postgrad., Sam Houston State U., 1977-78, 1981-84, Tex. Woman's U., 1981, U. Tex., Arlington, 1979. Cert. music tchr., Tex. Minister music, youth Rocky Creek Bapt. Ch., Brownwood, Tex., 1967-69; tchr. elem. music Galveston (Tex.) ISD, 1969; minister music, youth First Bapt. Kennedale, Tex., 1971-72, Pleasant Glade Bapt. Ch., Grapevine, Tex., 1972-74; tchr. elem. music Birdville ISD, Ft. Worth, Tex., 1974—; clinician Chorister's Guild, Ft. Worth 1981, Edn. Service Ctr., Region XI, Ft. Worth 1981, 84. Deacon Birdville Bapt. Ch., Ft. Worth, 1975, dir. young musicians choir, 1977-91; founder Snow Hts. Soundbusters Boys' Choir; mem. exec. bd. Tex. Boys' Choir, Ft. Worth, 1985; pres. Walton Band Friends, 1992-93. With U.S. Army, 1969-71, Vietnam. Decorated with Bronze Star, Air medal. Named Outstanding Young Men Am., U.S. Jaycees, 1982. Mem. NEA (chmn. Region XI elem. music 1978), Tex. Tchrs. Assn. (chmn. elem. music 1978), Tex. Music Educators Assn. (regional chmn. 1979-80, nominating com. 1980-82, mem. agenda com. 1986, clinician region X, 1982), Kodaly Educators Tex. (clinician 1980), Orgn. Am. Kokaly Educators, Ft. Worth Arts Council, S.W. Vietnam Vets. (charter), Phi Mu Alpha (charter mem. Nu Omega chpt.). Home: 6909 Mccoy Dr Fort Worth TX 76148-2318 Office: Glenview Elem Sch 3900 Norton Dr Fort Worth TX 76118-5205

HERNANDEZ, GILBERTO JUAN, accountant, auditor, management consultant; b. Havana, Cuba, July 12, 1943; came to U.S., 1960; s. Gilberto E. and Zoila M. (Mendez) H.; m. Maria-Elena Diaz Lugo, Jan. 19, 1968 (div. 1971); 1 child, A. Patrick; m. Maria-Carmen Marcet, Dec. 23, 1972; children: Martin J., David J., Thomas J. BBA, Pace U., 1968. CPA, N.Y., Fla. Auditor sr. Arthur Andersen & Co., N.Y.C., Tampa, Fla., 1968-73; v.p., treas. Coaxial Comms., Inc., Sarasota, Fla., 1973-81; tax mgr. Laventhol & Horwath, Tampa, Fla., 1981-83; ptnr. Valiente, Hernandez & Co., CPAs, Tampa, 1983—. Commr. City of Tampa Housing Authority, 1981-95; treas., bd. dirs. Ybor City Devel. Corp., Tampa, 1988—; vice-chmn. Tampa Bay Econ. Devel. Corp., 1990—; active City of Tampa Mayor's Hispanic Adv. Coun., 1984-96. Mem. AICPA, N.Y. State Soc. CPAs, Fla. Inst. CPAs (bd. dirs. West Coast chpt. 1992—, chmn. com. on unauthorized practice of pub. accountancy 1993-94, Outstanding Chmn. of Yr. 1994), Nat. Assn. Housing and Redevel. Ofcls. (bd. govs. 1988-94), Govt. Fin. Officers Assn., Fla. Assn. Govt. Fin. Officers, Ybor City C. of C. (v.p., bd. dirs. 1986—), Ybor City Rotary Club (pres. 1990-91). Office: Valiente Hernandez & Co PA 918 E Busch Blvd Tampa FL 33612-8542

HERNANDEZ, JOSE YOLANDO BALASTAS, physician, surgeon; b. Manila, Philippines, Dec. 30, 1938; came to U.S., 1964; s. Panblo Manio and Leoncia (Balastas) H.; m. Minerva Cuaorante, Dec. 17, 1966; children: Jay, Myra, Maureen. MD, U. St. Thomas, Manila, Philippines, 1962. Diplomate Am. Bd. Surgery, Am. Bd. Colon-Rectal Surgery, Internat. Bd. Proctology. Fellow Am. Soc. Colon Rectal Surgeons, Am. Soc. Abdominal Surgeons, Internat. Coll. Surgeons, Internat. Acad. Proctology, InterAm. Coll. Physicians and Surgeons, Southeastern Surgical Congress, Soc. Philippine Surgeons in Am.; mem. AMA, Am. Gastroent., Endoscopic Surgeons, Coll. Internat. Chirurgiae Digestuae. Roman Catholic,. Home and Office: 3053 Carlow Cir Tallahassee FL 32308

HERNANDEZ, LINDA LUREE WELCH, physician; b. Lansing, Mich., Sept. 18, 1952; d. Richard Dale and Muriel Ruth (Frye) Welch; m. Harry Hernandez, June 16, 1979; children: Sarah Luree, Gabriel Aaron, Harry Jr. BS, Mich. State U., 1974, DO, 1978. Diplomate Am. Bd. Osteo. Family Practioners; cert. Am. Acad. Pain Mgmt. Intern Grand Rapids (Mich.) Osteo. Hosp., 1978-79; asst. prof. dept. family medicine Mich. State U. Coll. Osteo. Medicine, East Lansing, 1979-82, fellow in primary medicine edn., 1981; pvt. practice San Antonio, 1982—. Missionary physician to Romania, Travis Park United Meth. Ch., San Antonio, 1991; clin. preceptor for missionary trip to Mexico Christian Med. & Dental Soc., 1994. Recipient cert. of recognition Cristo Rey Clinic, Lansing, 1982, El Buen Pastor Meth. Ch., San Antonio, 1988, 89; named Sunday's Woman, San Antonio Light, 1989. Fellow Am. Acad. Disability Evaluating Physicians; mem. Am. Osteo. Assn., Am. Oseo. Coll. Family Practitioners, Tex. Osteo. Med. Assn., Tex. Coll. Family Practitioners, Mich. Assn. Osteo. Physicians, Mich. Assn. Osteo. Family Practitioners,Am. Osteo. Coll. Rheumatology, Am. Acad. Med. Ethics, Am. Osteo. Acad. of Sclerotherapy, Am. Assn. Orthopedic Medicine. Office: 1339 Fair Ave San Antonio TX 78223-1437

HERNANDEZ, ROBERTO REYES, secondary school educator; b. Juarez, Chihuahua, Mex., Apr. 30, 1950; came to U.S., 1953; s. Felipe de Jesus and Juanita (Reyes) H.; m. Joanne Dora Richard; adopted children: Rosellor, Ledores, Joetta, Harriett, Barbara, Richard, Ray. AA in Edn., El Paso C.C., 1976; BS in Psychology, U. Tex., El Paso, 1978, BE in Secondary Edn., 1981, BS in Biology, 1982, MS in Biology, 1986; grad. sci. fellow, Baylor Coll. Medicine, 1984-85. Cert. secondary edn. teacher, Tex. Pharmacy technician Southwestern Gen. Hosp., El Paso, 1974-79, William Beaumont Army Med. Ctr. U.S. Civil Svc., Ft. Bliss, Tex., 1979-81; tchr. life and earth sci. Houston Ind. Sch. Dist., 1984-85; tchr. phys. sci., anatomy, physiology, phys. sci., biology Socorro Ind. Sch. Dist., El Paso, 1981-84; tchr. phys. sci., biology, astronomy, chemistry, computer sci. and GED Ysleta Ind. Sch. Dist., El Paso, 1985—; instr. English El Paso C. C., spring, 1986; grad. asst. interdisciplinary edn. Tex. A & M U., summer, 1989, 90; mem. evaluation team So. Assn. of Accreditation, El Paso, 1984; mem. textbook adoption team Tex. Biology Textbook Adoption Com., El Paso, 1983-84. Pres. Tex. Student Edn. Assn., El Paso, 1980-81; vol. instr. ESL Western Paso Del Norte Hotel, El Paso, 1990; den leader Wolf and Bear Cub Scout Pack 201, 1994-95. Mem. NEA, Tex. State Tchrs. Assn., Bow and Arrow Sci. Club (faculty sponsor 1985—), Ysleta Tchrs. Assn. (area rep.), Vista Hill Lions Club (lion tamer 1992-94, Leo advisor 1993-97, editor newsletter 1993-95, 2d v.p. 1994-95, dir. 1995-96). Home: 10310 Kellogg St El Paso TX 79924-2902 Office: Ysleta High Sch 8600 Alameda Ave El Paso TX 79907-6104

HERNDON, ALICE PATTERSON LATHAM, public health nurse; b. Macon, Ga.; d. Frank Waters and Ruby (Dews) Patterson; m. William Joseph Latham, July 21, 1940 (dec. Apr. 1981); children: Jo Alice Latham Miller, Marynette Latham, Lauruby Cathleen Beach; 1 adopted child, Courtney Marie Herndon; m. Sidney Dumas Herndon, Apr. 26, 1985. diploma, Charity Hosp. Sch. Nursing, New Orleans, 1937; student George Peabody Coll. Tchrs., 1938-39; BS in Pub. Health Nursing, U. N.C., 1954; MPH, Johns Hopkins U., 1966. Staff pub. health nurse assigned spl. venereal disease study USPHS, Darien, Ga., 1939-40; county pub. health nurse Bacon County, Alma, Ga., 1940-41; USPHS spl. venereal disease project, Glynn County, Brunswick, 1943-47; county pub. health nurse Glynn County, 1949-51, Ware County, Waycross, 1951-52; pub. health nurse supr. Wayne-Long-Brantley-Liberty Counties, Jesup, 1954-56 dist. dir. pub. health nursing Wayne-Long-Appling-Bacon-Pierce Counties, Jesup, 1956-70; dist. chief nursing S.E. Ga. Health Dist., 1970-79, organizer mobile health services, 1973—. Exec. dir. Wayne County Home Health Agy., 1968-80; exec. dir. Ware County Home Health Agy., 1970-79, mem. exec. com., 1978-85; mem. governing bd. S.E. Ga. Health Systems Agy., 1975-82; mem. governing bd. Health Dept. Home Health Agy., 1978—, also author numerous grant proposals. Bd. dirs. Wayne County Mental Health Assn., 1959, 60, 61, 81, 82, Wayne County Tb Assn., 1958-62; a non-alcoholic organizer Jesup group Alcoholics Anonymous, 1962-63; mem. adv. coun. Ware Meml. Hosp. Sch. Practical Nursing, Waycross, Ga., 1958; mem. Altar Guild, St. Paul's Episc. Ch., 1979-86, vestrywoman, 1981-82; mem. Altar Guild St. Marks Episcopal Ch., Brunswick, Ga., 1994—. Recipient recognition Gen. Service Bd., Alcoholics Anonymous, Inc. Fellow APHA; mem. ANA, 8th Dist. (pres. 1954-58, sec. 1958-60, dir. 1960-62, 1st v.p. 1962), Ga. Nurses Assn. (exec. bd. 1954-58, program rev. continuing edn. com. 1980-86, Dist. 21 Excellence in Nursing award 1994), Ga. Pub. Health Assn. (chmn. nursing sect. 1956-57), Ga. Assn. Dist. Chiefs Nursing (pres. 1976). Contbr. to state nursing manuals, cons. to Home Health Svc. Agys. Home: 192 Bluff Dr Brunswick GA 31523

HERNDON, ANNE HARKNESS, sales executive; b. Knoxville, Tenn., July 21, 1951; d. Alexander Jones and Mary Belle (Lothrop) Harkness; m. David S. Egerton, Apr. 21, 1972 (div. 1979); children: David, Mary; m. Morris Herndon, Nov. 26, 1993. Student, Agnes Scott Coll., Decatur, Ga., 1969-71, U. Tenn., 1971-73. Mktg., advt. mgr. Volunteer Realty, Knoxville, 1975-77; adminstrv. asst. nat. sales Creative Displays, Knoxville, 1977-81; salesperson Sta. WJXB Radio, Knoxville, 1981-86, sales mgr., 1988—; sales and mktg. mgr. Cellular One, Knoxville, 1986-87; cons. nat. ourdoor advt. Berkline Corp., Morristown, Tenn., 1978-81, Knoxville C. of C.; speaker nat. convs. Contbr. articles to profl. jours. Bd. dirs. Knoxville Polit. Action Com., Knoxville Arts Coun., Knoxville Beautification Bd., Boy Scouts Fin. Com.; com. mem. Dogwood Arts Festival, United Way. Recipient Pres.'s award South Ctrl. Comm. Corp., 1991, 92, 93. Mem. Ad Club. Republican. Presbyterian. Home: 605 Westborough Rd Knoxville TN 37909-2132 Office: WJXB 1100 Sharps Ridge Knoxville TN 37917-7122

HERNDON, CATHY CAMPBELL, artist, art educator; b. Richmond, Va., Sept. 25, 1951; d. Kenneth Holcomb and Grace (Brooks) Campbell. BS in Art and Drama, Radford (Va.) Coll., 1973; MS in Art Edn., Va. Commonwealth U., 1980. Art cons., tchr. Hanover County Schs., Ashland, Va., 1973-76; art tchr. Stafford County Schs., Stafford, Va., 1976-86, artist, signmaker Woodford, Va., 1986-92; artist, tchr. Fredericksburg (Va.) City Schs., 1992—; neon artist, mixed media constrn. artist; artist, tchr. Rappahannock Security Ctr., Fredericksburg, 1989-91; artist, tchr. Fredericksburg Ctr. for Creative Arts, 1984—, curator, 1991-94, bd. dirs., 1984—; exchange tchr. Kingston U., Eng., 1995—. One-person shows include Fredericksburg Ctr. for Creative Arts, 1986, Southside Va. C.C., Alberta, 1992, Art First Gallery, Fredericksburg, 1992, 94, Shenandoah Valley Art Ctr., Waynesboro, Va., 1993, Geico Corp. Hdqs., Fredericksburg, 1994, others; exhibited in group shows at Exposure Unltd., Fredericksburg, 1985—, Art in Greece, Helios, 1992, Montross Galleries, Fredericksburg, 1992, Va. Ctr. Creative Arts, Sweetbriar, Rocquebrune, France, 1995; executed various murals. Historian, Fredericksburg Sister City Assn., 1992—. Recipient numerous awards for works; named Best in Show, Hanover Arts Festival, 1995. Mem. Nat. Art Edn. Assn., Washington Projects for the Arts, Va. Mus. Fine Arts, Va. Watercolor Soc. Home: PO Box 7955 408 Frederick St Fredericksburg VA 22401 Office: FCCA 813 Sophia St Fredericksburg VA 22401-5823

HERNDON, DONNA RUTH GROGAN, educational administrator; b. Murray, Ky., Aug. 14, 1942; d. E. Leon and Virgil (Childress) Grogan; m. Clarence W. Herndon Jr., Jan. 31, 1963; children: Melissa Herndon Graves, Roger Allan (dec.). BS summa cum laude, Murray State U., 1960; MA, Western Ky. U., 1975. Tchr. biology Calloway County H.S., Murray, 1964-66, dir. project COPE, 1978-81; coord. of vols. Army Cmty. Svc., Berlin, 1972; vol. supr. Army Cmty. Svc., Ft. Knox, Ky., 1974-75; mayor Van Voorhis Cmty., Ft. Knox, 1975-76; plant mgr. Lin-Val Garden Ctr., Penn Hills, Pa., 1977; admissions rep. Art Inst. Pitts., 1978; dir. alumni affairs Murray State U., 1981-92; coord. Family Resource Ctr., Calloway County Schs., Murray, 1992—. Bd. dirs., co-founder CHAMP, Murray, 1986-93; rep. edn. Ky. Juvenile Justice Commn., 1982-92; mem. adv. coun. dept. social work Murray State U., mem. adv. bd. Coll. Industry and Tech.; mem. rural health adv. bd. U. Ky.; bd. dirs. Murray United Way; founder, chairperson Calloway United Benevolent Svcs. Network; bd. dirs. Murray-Calloway C. of C., 1993-96, Leadership Ky. Found. Recipient Recognition award Murray State U. Black Alumni, 1989, Humanitarian of Yr. award Murray Rotary Club, 1994; named Vol. of Yr., United Way of Ky., 1993; Donna Herndon scholarship established Murray State U. Student Alumni Assn., 1988; state winner Ky. Fedn. Women's Clubs Poetry Contest. Mem. Ky. Alliance for Exploited and Missing Children (bd. dirs. 1982-92), Ky. Ctr. Pub. Issues (bd. dirs. 1990-92), Nat. Coun. for Advancement and Support Edn. (achievement award 1984, bronze award 1987, Dist. III Outstanding Advisor award 1992), Nat. Assn. Parents and Tchrs. (hon. life), Leadership Ky. (bd. dirs. 1990-95), Leadership Ky. Alumni Assn. (trustee 1989-95), Murray Woman's Club. Mem. Ch. of Christ. Office: Calloway County Schs Family Resource Ctr 1169 Pottertown Rd Murray KY 42071-9104

HERNDON, RHONDA DIANNE, dietitian; b. Milan, Tenn., Aug. 28, 1960; d. William Jennings Jr. and Avinell (Sproles) H. AA, St. Petersburg Jr. Coll., 1980; BS, Fla. State U., 1982, MS, 1986. Project asst. Leon County Coop. Extension Svc., Tallahassee, 1985-87; area program mgmt. specialist dept. edn. State of Fla., Tallahassee, 1987-89, adult care food program coord. dept. edn., 1989-92; dietary svcs. supr. Heritage Health Care Ctr., Tallahassee, 1992; pub. health nutrition cons. Fla. Dep. Corrections., 1992-95; pub. health nutritionist supr. Leon County WIC Program, Tallahassee, 1995—. Mem. Am. Dietetic Assn.

HERNDON, ROBERT EDWARD, construction executive; b. Saltville, Va., Jan. 23, 1943; s. Clyde Morris Herndon and Pauline (Dawson) Plumb; m. Margaret Lynn Ziegler Fonda, Aug. 28, 1965 (div.); 1 child, Robert Edward Jr.; m. Sharon Hughes Styles, Sept. 27, 1990. BSBA, Old Dominion U., 1977; MA in Orgnl. Mgmt., Tusculum Coll., 1991; cert. in elec. design, Newport News (Va.) Shipbldg. Apprentice Sch., 1968. Electrician Newport News (Va.) Shipbldg., 1961-63, elec. design apprentice, 1963-68, apprentice instr., 1968-71, constrn. supr., 1971-77, mktg. adminstr., 1978-81, constrn. supt., 1981-88, 92; plant mgr. Greeneville (Tenn.) Industries, Inc., 1988-92, trade mgr., 1992-94; postdoctoral fellow George Wash. U., Washington, 1993—; plant mgr. Premier Mfg. Corp., Henderson, Tenn., 1995—. Chmn. adv. coun. Greeneville-Greene County Ctr. for Tech., 1990-92; exec. bd. dirs. U.S.S. Greenville, 1989-91; bd. dirs. Greene County Jr. Achievement, 1990-91. 1st sgt. USAR, 1968-95. Mem. Spl. Forces Assn., Greeneville-Greene County Mfg. Assn. (chmn. 1991-92), May Club, Propeller Club U.S. Republican. Baptist. Home: 608 Gatling Point Pky Smithfield VA 23430-2302 Office: Premier Mfg Corp 867 Premier Way Henderson TN 38340-1265

HERNDON, WALLACE EUGENE, JR., human resources manager; b. Hopkinsville, Ky., June 12, 1945; s. Wallace Eugene Sr. and Cornelia (Edwards) H.; m. Jane Macomber, Aug. 16, 1969; children: Bradford Colby, Jane Allison. BS in Pers. Mgmt., U. Ky., 1963; postgrad., W.Va. U., 1967-69. Employee and community rels. specialist GE, Memphis, 1969-72; employee and community rels. mgr. GE, Jefferson, Ohio, 1972-76; hourly rels. specialist GE, Murfreesboro, Tenn., 1977; human resources mgr. The Drackett Co., Franklin, Ky., 1977-93; corp. human resource mgr. Fruit of the Loom, Bowling Green, Ky., 1993—. Bd. dirs. Franklin-Simpson Arts Coun., 1987-89, United Way So. Ky., Bowling Green, 1991-93, Franklin-Simpson Literacy Coun., 1983-86, Franklin-Simpson Sch. Cmty. Partnership Com., 1985-88. Recipient Outstanding Community Vol. award Bristol-Myers Squibb, 1992; named Ky. Outstanding Vol. of Yr., United Way Ky., Louisville, 1992. Mem. Soc. Human Resource Mgmt., So. Ky. Pers. Assn., Franklin Pers. Assn. (pres. 1980-81), U. Ky. Nat. Alumni Assn. (bd. dirs. 1991-96), U. Ky. Logan-Simpson-Warren County Alumni Club (pres. 1985-86), Franklin-Simpson C. of C. (bd. dirs. 1981-83), Rotary (v.p. Franklin club 1988-89, Paul Harris fellow 1992). Methodist. Home: 206 Hastings Dr Franklin KY 42134-9138

HERRERA, CATHERINE MARIA, lawyer, documentary film maker, photographer; b. Omaha, July 27, 1965; d. Henry Richard and Diana (Watson) H. BA, U. So. Calif., 1989, JD, 1992. Fed. jud. law clk. to chief judge U.S. Fed. Ct. Sys., El Paso, Tex., 1992-93; cons. Mexico City, 1993—; translator Mexican internat. property laws, Mexico City, 1993—. Author: Screaming Underwater, 1996; dir, prodr. (documentary films) Alphabet People, 1993 (award 1995), From the Same Family, 1996. Fulbright fellow U.S. Govt., 1993. Democrat. Office: PO Box 3067 Laredo TX 78044-3087

HERRERA, GUILLERMO ANTONIO, pathologist; b. Havana, Cuba, Mar. 16, 1952; came to U.S., 1967; s. Guillermo S. and Olga (Del Castillo) H.; m. Elba A. Turbat, Dec. 23, 1972; 1 child, Marlene F. Student, U. Miami, 1970; MD cum laude, U. P.R., 1975. Diplomate Am. Bd. Pathology, cytopathology added qualification bd.; lic. physician Fla., N.Mex., Ala., Miss., La. Intern categorical pathology Brooke Army Med. Ctr., Ft. Sam Houston, Tex., 1975-76, resident pathology, anatomic and clin., 1975-79, chief resident, 1978-79; asst. prof. dept. pathology Sch. Medicine and Dentistry U. Ala., Birmingham, 1982-87, scientist II Nephrology Rsch. and Tchr. Ctr. Sch. Medicine, 1982-88, dir. nephropathology Schs. Medicine and Dentistry, 1987-88, assoc. prof. dept. pathology, 1987-88, prof. pathology, head surg. pathology, 1991-95, sr. scientist Comprehensive Cancer Ctr., 1991-95; prof., chmn. dept. pathology medicine and cell biology La. State U.-Shreveport Sch. Medicine, Jackson, 1996—; head surg. pathology, attending pathologist VA Hosp., Birmingham, 1991-95; acting med. dir. Sch. Cytotech. U. Ala., Birmingham, 1991-93, faculty mem. Grad. Sch., 1991-95; sr. scientist, co-dir. EM Core Facility Comprehensive Cancer Ctr. Ala., 1991-95; chmn. dept. pathology La. State U., Shreveport, 1996—; assoc. pathologist Palm Beach Pathology, Good Samaritan Hosp., West Palm Beach, Fla., 1988-89; faculty Grad. Sch. U. Miss., 1989-91; cons. pathologist VA Hosp., Jackson, 1990-91; attending pathologist, head surg. pathology VA Hosp., Birmingham, 1991-95; acting med. dir. Sch. Cytotech., U. Ala., Birmingham, 1991-93, acting head cytopathology, 1991-93, faculty mem. Grad Sch., 1991-95; sr. scientist Comprehensive Cancer Ctr. Ala., co-dir. EM Core facility, 1991-95; prof., chair dept. pathology La. State U., Shreveport, 1996—. Mem. editl. bd. Ultrastructural Pathology and Pathology Case Revs, 1995—; manuscript reviewer Applied Pathology, Diagnostic Cytopathology, Am. Jour. Medicine, Am. Jour. Kidney Diseases, Archives Pathology and Lab. Medicine, Ultrastructural Pathology, Stain Tech. and Histochemistry, Am. Jour. Clin. Pathology, Pathobiology, Human Pathology, Cancer, Kidney Internat., Pathology Rsch., Practice and Annals of Saudi Medicine, Am. Jour. Pathology; contbr. articles to profl. jours., chpts to books. Maj. M.C., U.S. Army, 1974-82, col. USAR, 1988—. Grantee U. P.R., 1972-75, Brooke Army Med. Ctr., Ft. Sam Houston, 1978-79, U. Ala., Birmingham, 1983-86, 87-88, Universita Degli Studi di Milano, 1984, VA, 1986—, Nat. Cancer Inst., 1991—, NIH, 1992—, Ala. Kidney Found., 1992-93. Mem. Internat. Acad. Pathology, Am. Soc. Clin. Pathology, Armed Forces Soc. Lab. Scientists, Electron Microscopy Soc. Am., Soc. Ultrastructural Pathology (sec. 1988-91, tras. 1991—), Am. Soc. Nephrology, Arthur Purdy Stout Soc. Surg. Pathologists, Tex. Electron Microscopy Soc., Birmingham Soc. Pathologists (v.p. 1987-88). Roman Catholic.

HERRERA, MARY CARDENAS, education educator, music minister; b. Sugar Land, Tex., Feb. 21, 1938; d. Jose Chavez and Juanita (Lira) Cardenas; m. Saragosa Martin Herrera, Sept. 20, 1960 (dec.); children: Michael (dec.), Patricia Ann Zagrzecki, Aaron Martin, Katherine Ann Nava. Grad., Patricia Stevens Bus. Sch., 1960; student, Houston C.C., 1991, 92. Sec. William Penn Hotel, Houston, 1959-66; payroll clk. Peakload, Inc., Houston, 1967-69; acctg. clk. Am. Gen., Inc., Houston, 1970-73; nurse asst. Ft. Bend Ind. Sch. Dist., Stafford, Tex., 1973-88; tchr.'s asst. Ft. Bend Ind. Sch. Dist., Sugarland, Tex., 1988—; numerous offices Holy Family Cath. Ch., Missouri City, Tex., 1981-90, Hispanic choir dir., 1981-89; Hispanic choir dir. Notre Dame Cath. Ch., 1990-91; Hispanic del. Galveston-Houston Diocese, 1987-89; regional del. Encuetro Diocesceno Conf., San Antonio, 1983, 84, 85; dir., coord. Diocesan Hispanic Choir, 1982-86, music workshops, 1982-88. Songwriter in field. Mem., tchr. PTO, 1973—; mem. Holy Family Hispanic Com.; mem. choir Iglesia del Pueblo, Pasadena, Tex., 1991, 92, asst. Sunday sch. tchr., 1992-93, coord. monthly Women's Praise Gathering, 1994—; music minister local prayer groups Houston area, 1990—. Mem. Women's Aglow (praise and worship music minister Pasadena chpt. 1988-90), Nat. Assn. Pastoral Musicians, Iglesia del Pueblo. Democrat. Home and Office: 4506 Ludwig Ln Stafford TX 77477-5219

HERRES, ROBERT TRALLES, insurance company executive; b. Denver, Dec. 1, 1932; s. F. Williard and Edna Margaret (Tralles) H.; m. Shirley Jean Snecker, Apr. 16, 1957; children: Julie, Michael, Jennifer. BS, U.S. Naval Acad., 1954; M.S. in Elec. Engring., Air Force Inst. Tech., 1960; M.P.A., George Washington U., 1965. Commd. lt. U.S. Air Force, 1954, advanced through grades to full gen., 1984; ret., 1990; pres. property and casualty ins. divsn. United Svcs. Automobile Assn., San Antonio, 1990; vice chmn., COO, pres. United Svcs. Automobile Assn., San Antonio, TX, 1992; chmn., pres., CEO United Svcs. Automobile Assn., 1993. Vice chmn. Nat. Jr. Achievment; bd. dirs. A.F. Acad. FAlcon Found., U.S. Naval Acad. Found., USO's World Bd. Govs., Atlantic Coun. U.S., Trinity U. Decorated Def. DSM, DSM Legion of Merit with 1 oak leaf cluster; bronze star medal, air medal, others. Office: United Svcs Automobile Assn USAA Bldg 9800 Fredericksburg Rd San Antonio TX 78288-0001

HERRICK, JOHN DENNIS, financial consultant, former law firm executive, retired food products executive; b. St. Paul, Oct. 8, 1932; s. Willard R. and Gertrude (O'Connor) H. BA, Univ. St. Thomas, 1954; MBA (hon.), U. Laval. Field auditor Gen. Mills, Inc., Mpls., 1954-59; acctg. supr. Gen. Mills, Inc., Kankakee, Ill., 1959-61; adminstrv. mgr. Gen. Mills, Inc., Chgo., 1961-62; mgr. auditing Gen. Mills, Inc., Mpls., 1962-65; mgr. new bus. devel. Gen. Mills, Inc., 1965-66; dir. adminstrn. and controller Smiths Food Group (subs.) Gen. Mills, Inc., London, 1966-68; pres. Gen. Mills Cereals Ltd., Toronto, Ont., Can., 1969-71; chmn. bd., pres., chief exec. officer Gen. Mills Canada, Inc., Toronto, Ont., Can., 1971-86; chief operating officer Borden & Elliot, Toronto, 1986-89; cons. Palm Beach Gardens, Fla., 1989—; past chmn. Grocery Products Mfrs. of Can., Toronto; dir. CP Express & Transport, Toronto. Pres. Jr. Achievement Can., Toronto, 1970-71; past chmn. Toronto Area Indsl. Devel. Bd.; past pres., mem. coun. Bd. Trade Met. Toronto; past chmn. Emmanuel Convalescent Found., Toronto; past pres. Am. Club; past vice-chmn. Nat. Theater Sch. Can., Montreal; past chmn. Toronto Harbour Commn.; bd. dirs., pres. Cath. Charities Palm Beach; bd. dirs. Pub. Voice for Food and Health Policy, Washington; mem. pres.'s coun. U. St. Thomas; chmn.'s adv. bd. Rep. Nat. Com.; pres. J.D. Herrick Found. Capt. USAF, 1954-57. Recipient Queen's Silver Jubilee medal, 1978; decorated comdr. Knights of Holy Sepulchre, Order of St. John, Order of Polonica Restituta. Mem. Can. C. of C. (past chmn., gov.), Beefeater Club, Empire Club, Royal Can. Yacht Club, Lambton Golf and Country Club, N.Y. Athletic Club, Old Port Yacht Club, Loxahatchee Club, Internat. Platform Assn., Palm Beach Roundtable, Accademia Italiana Della Cucina Club, K.C., Capital Hill Club (Washington), Princiana Club (Palm Beach, Calif.). Roman Catholic. Home: 15100 Palmwood Rd Palm Beach Gardens FL 33410 Office: PO Box 31828 Palm Beach Gardens FL 33420

HERRIN, FRANCES E., critical care nurse; b. Blairsville, Ga., Mar. 27, 1930; d. George W. and Iris C. (Tramell) Anderson; widowed; children: Naguyalti, Warren. AA, L.A. Trade Tech. Coll., 1973; postgrad., Calif. State U., 1973, Chapman Coll., 1987. RN, Calif.; ACLS, Calif. Nurse emergency rm. Oak Ridge (Tenn.) Hosp., 1950-57; staff nurse Cen. Rec. Hosp., L.A., 1958-68; charge nurse Hollywood Pres. Hosp., L.A., 1970-74; coronary care nurse Kaiser Permanent Med. Ctr., Fontana, Calif., 1974-90; nurse in med. unit De Kalb Med. Ctr., Decatur, Ga., 1992—; pediat. care nurse PSA Home Health, 1995-96. Mem. Hosp. Christian Fellowship (pres.), Black Nurses Assn. (quality assurance com.).

HERRIN, JOSEPH RICHARD, real estate developer; b. Shreveport, La., Aug. 14, 1923; s. Joseph Richard Sr. and Ophelia Madlin (Mullikin) H.; m. Helen Richbourg, Nov. 9, 1940; children: Susan, Joe, Bo, William. Grad., Gulf Coast Mil. Acad., Gulfport, Miss., 1941. Dist. mgr., asst. v.p. Herrin Motor Lines, Inc., Shreveport, 1941-50; v.p., pres. Herrin Transp. & Whse. Co., Inc., Shreveport, 1950-75; owner Cattle Farm, Marshall, Ark., 1968-85; pres. Herrin Feed and Farm Supply, Inc., Marshall, 1970-75, Mid-States Industries, Inc., Shreveport, 1973-75, Am. Internat. Dec. Svcs. Inc., Little Rock, 1969—, H.C.H. Inc., Little Rock, 1985—, CHR, Inc., 1996—; cons. internat. trade and bus., 1985—. Author: A Note to Mr. American, 1965 (Freedom Found. award 1965), inventor Desk Mover, 1955, All Surface Wheel, 1959. Sec., treas. Nat. Aero. Assn., Shreveport, 1946; pilot CAP, Shreveport, 1946; gov. committeeman La. Peace Officers Devel. Commn., Baton Rouge, 1963, La. Intern. Rels. Commn., Baton Rouge, 1960; dist. lay leader La. Conf. United Meth. Ch., Baton Rouge, 1973-74. Mem. Nat. Def. Exec. Res., Citizens Democracy Corps Inc., Southwest Transp. and Whse. Assn. (bd. dirs. 1950-58), La. Motor Transp. Assn. (pres. HHG divsn. 1962-63), Am. Trucking Assn. (exec. com. 1964-66), SCORE/ACE (pres. 1978-79, chmn. 1996), Pres. Club, Indsl. Devel. Com. (bd. dirs. 1960-63), Amb. Club (bd. dirs. 1961-76), Jaycees, Lions, Optomist, Masons, York and Scottish Rites, Shrine. Office: PO Box 5662 Shreveport LA 71135-5662

HERRING, DAVID M(AYO), engineer; b. Rockport, Tex., Jan. 18, 1929; s. James Clark and Edith Esther (Sneed) H.; m. Nell Adams, Sept. 10, 1955; children: Clark, John, Scott. BS, U. Tex., Austin, 1955, MS in Structures, 1960. Cons. engr. W.P. Moore & Co., Houston, 1955; constrn. engr. Chgo. Bridge & Iron Co., Ltd., Caracas, Venezuela, 1956, supt., 1957, asst. mgr. ops., 1958-60, mgr. ops., 1960-64; mgr. internat. ops. Western Hemisphere CBI Co., Oak Brook, Ill., 1964-68, asst. mgr. CBI Nuc. Co., Memphis, 1968-72; constrn. mgr. S.E. div. CBI Co., Birmingham, Ala., 1973-78; pres., dir. Sea-Con Svcs. Inc., New Iberia, La., 1978-87 ; dir. Thermal Designs Inc., Houston, Atlantic Sea-Con, Gloucester, Mass., Sea-Con Svcs., Ltd., Yarmouth, Eng., cons., 1991—. Dir. Rockport Art Ctr and several non-profit orgs. Inventor world's largest revolving derrick. Contbr. articles to profl. jours. Served with C.E., U.S. Army, 1950-52, Korea. Mem. Offshore Pipeline Contractors Assn. (founding chmn.), Nat. Ocean Industries Assn., ASCE (Featured Engr. award 1971), Assn. Diving Contractors (bd. dirs. 1980-87), Colegio de Ingeneros, Arquetectos and Agrimensores de P.R., Chi Epsilon, Tau Beta Pi. Episcopalian. Office: 1691 N Fulton Beach Rd Rockport TX 78382

HERRING, GROVER CLEVELAND, lawyer; b. Nocatee, Fla., Dec. 9, 1925; s. Joseph I. and Martha (Selph) H.; m. Dorothy L. Blinn, Apr. 17, 1947; children: Stanley T., Kenneth Lee. JD, U. Fla., 1950. Bar: Fla. 1950. Assoc. Haskins & Bryant, 1950-52; sole practice West Palm Beach, Fla., 1952-60, 64—; ptnr. Blakeslee, Herring & Bie and predecessor firm, 1953-60, Warwick, Paul & Herring, 1964-70, Herring & Evans now Arnstein & Lehr, 1970-95, Baldwin & Herring, West Palm Beach, Fla., 1995—; atty. City of Atlantis, Fla., City of West Palm Beach, 1960-63, Town of Ocean Ridge, Fla., 1953-61, 64-66, Village of Royal Palm Beach, Fla., 1964-72, Town of South Palm Beach, Fla., 1966-72; spl. master-in-chancery 15th Jud. Cir. Palm Beach County, 1953-54; judge ad litem Mcpl. Ct., West Palm Beach, 1954-55; bd. dirs. Lawyers Title Services Inc., West Palm Beach. Contbr. legal articles to profl. revs. Active PTA, Family Service Agy., Palm Beach County Mental Health Assn.; chmn. profl. sect. ARC, 1960; mem. Charter Revision Com. West Palm Beach, 1960-65, Palm Beach County Resources Devel. Bd., 1959—, Dem. Exec. Com., 1965-70; apptd. mem. Govtl. Study Commn. by Fla. Legis.; bd. dirs. Community Chest. Served with USNR, 1944-46. Mem. ABA, Palm Beach County Bar Assn. (treas. 1960), John Marshall Bar Assn., Fla. Bar Assn., Am. Judicature Soc., Lawyers Title Guaranty Fund (field rep. 1955-60, 64—), East Coast Estate Planning Council, Nat. Inst. Mcpl. Law Officers, Law-Sci. Acad., Assn. Trial Lawyers Am. (assoc. editor 1960—), Lawyers Lit. Club, Nat. Mcpl. League, U. Fla. Law Ctr. Assn., World Peace Through Law Ctr., Fla. Sheriff's Assn. (hon.), U. Fla. Alumni Assn., VFW, Am. Legion, West Palm Beach C. of C., Civic Music Assn., Palm Beach County Hist. Soc. (pres. 1969-72), New Eng. Hist. Geneal. Soc. Boston. Clubs: West Palm Beach Country (hon.); Airways (N.Y.C.). Lodges: Eight Oaks River, Masons (32 deg.), Elks, Moose. Home: 3515 N Australian Ave West Palm Beach FL 33407-4511 Office: Baldwin & Herring Ste G 1675 P B Lakes Blvd West Palm Beach FL 33401

HERRING, LEONARD GRAY, marketing company executive; b. nr. Snow Hill, N.C., June 18, 1927; s. Albert Lee and Josie (Sugg) H.; m. Rozelia Sullivan, June 18, 1950; children: Sandra Grey, Albert Lee II. BS, U. N.C., 1948. With Dun & Bradstreet, Inc., Raleigh, N.C., 1948-49, H. Weil & Co., Goldsboro, N.C., 1949-55; pres., chief exec. officer Lowe's Cos., Inc., North Wilkesboro, N.C., 1955—; also bd. dirs.; bd. dirs. First Union Corp., Charlotte, N.C.; mem. Lowe's Cos. Inc. Employee Stock Ownership Plan mgmt. com.; mem. bd. vis. U. N.C., Davidson Coll. Trustee Pfeiffer Coll., Misenheimer, N.C. Mem. Chi Psi. Democrat. Methodist. Home: 310 Coffey St North Wilkesboro NC 28659-3249 Office: Lowe's Cos Inc PO Box 1111 North Wilkesboro NC 28659-1111

HERRING, LUCILLE M., retired community health nurse; b. Gaston, Ind., Jan. 29, 1914; d. Frank and Edna J. (Jackson) Melvin; m. Edward O. Herring, Apr. 13, 1947 (dec. Aug. 1991); 1 child, Richard E. Diploma in nursing, Ind. U., Indpls., 1935; student, St. Peter Jr. Coll., 1995—. RN. Field supr. So. Home Care, St. Petersburg, Fla., 1988-95; retired, 1995. Vol. math. dept. St. Peter Jr. Coll. Recipient Sr. Citizens award Kiwanis Club of Boca Ciega, 1989, Dr. Frist Humanitarian award. Mem. Ind. U. Alumni Assn. (life), Sigma Theta Tau.

HERRING, ROBERT ALEXANDER, III, management educator; b. Washington, Apr. 5, 1946; s. Robert Alexander, Jr. and Alice Catherine (Fisk) H.; m. Gail Millians, Feb. 14, 1971; children: Aimee Caroline, David Bradford. BA in Math/Psychology, U. Miss., 1969; MA in Correctional Counseling, Chapman Coll., 1975; MBA in Mgmt., Fla. State U., 1981, PhD in Mgmt., 1987. Commd. ens. USN, 1969-79, advanced through grades to lt., 1979; gunnery officer USS Robert L. Wilson (DD-847) USN, Norfolk, Va., 1969-71; adminstrv. asst. to officer in charge Assault Craft Unit 1 WESTPAC DET USN, Subic Bay, Philippines, 1971-72; engring. officer Assault Craft Unit 1 USN, Coronado, Calif., 1972-73; dir. counseling and assistance ctr. Naval Air Sta. USN, Lemoore, Calif., 1973-76; treatment unit mgr. Naval Drug Rehab. Ctr. USN, San Diego, 1976-78, asst. to rehab. officer Naval Drug Rehab. Ctr., 1978-79; grad. teaching asst. Fla. State U., Tallahassee, 1980-85; instr., then asst. prof. mgmt. Old Dominion U., Norfolk, Va., 1985-91; asst. prof. mgmt. Radford (Va.) U., 1991—; exec. officer/comdg. officer Pers. Mobilization Team 1208, USNR, Tallahassee, 1981-85, comdg. officer Pers Mobilization Team 3106, Norfolk, 1986-88; navy ops officer U.S. Atlantic Command, DET 206, Norfolk, 1988-93; comdg. officer Fleet Support Tng. Unit 3206, Richmond, Va. Chmn. drug adv. coun. Kings County, Hanford, Calif., 1975-76. Commdr. USNR, 1979-95. Recipient Best Case award Southeast Case Rsch. Assn., 1993. Mem. AAUP, Acad. Mgmt., Soc. Human Resources Mgmt., Employee Assistance Profls. Assn., Naval Reserve Assn., Officers' Christian Fellowship. Republican. Methodist. Home: 101 Hidden Valley Dr Radford VA 24141 Office: Radford U Coll Bus and Econs Box 6954 Radford VA 24142

HERRING, SUSAN CATHERINE, linguistics educator; b. Springfield, Mass., May 27, 1955; d. John Woodbridge and Eileen Vera (Bradt) H. BA in French, SUNY, Potsdam, 1976; MA in Linguistics, U. Calif., Berkeley, 1982, PhD in Linguistics, 1991. Instr. French U. Calif., Berkeley, 1981-84, instr. linguistics, 1986-88; instr. Tamil Stanford (Calif.) U., 1989; asst. prof. linguistics Calif. State U., San Bernardino, 1989-92; assoc. prof. linguistics U. Tex., Arlington, 1992—, acting dir. program in linguistics, 1993, 95; asst. dir. program in linguistics, 1995—; vis. scholar South Asia program Cornell U., summer 1994, dept. modern langs., summer 1996; presenter in field to univs., profl. meetings and confs.; panel organizer. Editor: Computer-Mediated Communication: Linguistic, Social, and Cross-Cultural Perspectives, 1996, Computer-Mediated Discourse Analysis, 1996, (with John C. Paolillo) UTA Working Papers in Linguistics, Vol. 1, 1994; contbr. articles to profl. jours. Fgn. lang. area studies fellow U. Calif., 1981-82, 84-86, 87-88, Am. Inst. Indian Studies Tamil lang. fellow, 1983-84; Fulbright-Hays doctoral grantee, 1986-87, Affirmative Action grantee Calif. State U., 1990, 92, grantee NEH, 1994, faculty rsch. grantee U. Tex., Arlington, 1994. Mem. Linguistic Soc. Am., Internat. Linguistics Assn., Internat. Soc. for Hist. Linguistics, Internat. Pragmatics Assn., Internat. Inst. Tamil Studies, Indian Linguistics Assn., Dravidian Linguistics Assn., Comm. Inst. for Online Scholarship, Soc. Text and Discourse. Office: U Tex Program in Linguistics Box 19559 Arlington TX 76019

HERRING, WILLIAM ARTHUR, artist; b. El Paso, Feb. 18, 1948. BA in Internat. Rels. and S.Am. History, Tex. A&M U., 1971; investor financed spl. studies, Mexico City, Ruins of Xochicalco, 1987, Paris, London, Venice, 1988, southwestern U.S., 1989. Artist-in-residence Ysleta Ind. Sch. Dist., El Paso, 1983, 85; pres. Knickerbocker Artists U.S.A., 1992—; represented by Joan Cawley Galleries, Scottsdale, Ariz. and Santa Fe; drawing instr. El Paso Mus. Art, 1983; cons. to the schs. Eastland and Breckenridge, Tex., 1985; spl. studies drawing instr. Jan Herring Summer Sch. Art, Cloudcroft, N.Mex., 1973-86; spl. guest artist commd. Coors World Finals Rodeo, El Paso, 1989; guest instr. Parson's Sch. Design, N.Y.C., 1990; master of ceremonies awards banquet 43d Grand Internat. Ann. Open Juried Exhbn., Knickerbocker Artists-USA, Washington, 1993; hon. chmn. awards banquet Internat. Dance Theatre, 1993; juror Pastel Soc. SW 12th Ann. Juried Exhbn., Dallas, 1993. One-man shows include Fox Libr., Ea. N.Mex. U., Portales, 1985, Centennial Mus., U. Tex. El Paso, 1986, Marlin Design Internat., Houston, 1986, Jan Herring Gallery, Clint, Tex., 1988, 89, Tex. Commerce Bank, El Paso, 1988, Joan Cawley Gallery, Santa Fe, 1993, Palmer's Gallery 800, Hot Springs Nat. Park, Ark., 1993, (also guest instr.) Redwood Art Workshops, Crescent City, Calif., 1993, Mid-So. Watercolor Soc., Little Rock, 1993, numerous others; two-man show Dos Pajaros Gallery, El Paso Internat. Airport, 1987; mother and son exhbn. Iman Galleries, San Angelo, Tex., 1988; two-person exhbn. Studio W Galleries, El Paso, 1991; exhibited in group shows at Chamizal Nat. Meml. Mus., El Paso, 1983, The McAllen (Tex.) Mus. Fine Art, 1986, Rio Bravo Watercolor Soc. and El Paso Mus. Art Tri-State Agua Media Exhbn., El Paso, 1987, El Paso Mus. Art, 1988, PS Gallery, Goshen, Conn., Massey Fine Art Gallery, Santa Teresa, N.Mex., 1993, numerous others, (Herring family exhbns.) (ann.) The McCloud Gallery, 1982-86, Iman Galleries, 1984-85, Jan Herring Gallery and Studio, Clint, 1992, others; numerous juried exhbns. and pub., pvt. and corp. collections; cover artist The Physician, 1986, El Paso Art Assn. 1987 Yearbook, Southwest Guide, 1988; author: The Wonderful Madness of Becoming A Horse of A Different Color, 1994; guest columnist El Paso Times, 1992; subject numerous newspaper and mag. articles and revs., including Southwest Art Mag., 1994. Featured artist El Paso Parade of Homes, Jessup Homes, El Paso, 1988; ofcl. artist Christmas commn. Bank of Ysleta, El Paso, 1988-89, El Paso Internat. Amigo Airsho, El Paso, 1989, El Paso State Capitol Days, 1989, El Paso Symphony Assn. 60th Anniversary Celebration, 1990, Hospice El Paso, 1990, 93; bd. dirs. SW Mus. Cultural History. Recipient Best of Show award and Mus. Purchase prize El Paso Mus. Art, 1987, William Hollingsworth award Miss. Watercolor Soc., 1987, Muriel Alvord award Hudson Valley Art Assn., 1988, Gold medal for Watercolor El Paso Art Assn., 1988, Honor award for Watercolor, Acad. Artists Assn., 1988, Travelling Show award Ky. Watercolor Soc., 1989, Merit award Digicon Graphics, Inc., 1990, hon. mention NW Pastel Soc., 1990, Purchase prize Mithoff Advt., Inc. and El Paso Disposal, Inc., 1990, Gold medal, Grumbacher award and Purchase prize The Marriot Hotel,

1991. Mem. Pastel Soc. Am. (Bd. Dirs. award 1990, Travelling Show award 1991, West Coast award 1992), Am. Artist Profl. League, Acad. Artists Am., Niagara Frontier Watercolor Soc., Knickerbocker Artists, Rio Bravo Watercolor Soc. (Best of Show award 1987), The Salmagundi Club (hon., open ceremony demonstrations artist 1990, guest exhibitor 1991, 92).

HERRINGTON, DALE ELIZABETH, lay worker; b. Logansport, La., Feb. 1, 1913; d. Charles Ross and Ola Delnorte (Tillery) Currie; m. Cecil Doyle Herrington, June 25, 1939; 1 child, Jo Earle Herrington Hartt. BS, Stephen F. Austin Univ., 1932, MA, 1948, MEd, 1948. Cert. tchr., Tex. Min. edn. First Bapt. Ch., Garrison, Tex., 1947-81, organist, 1947—, lay worker, 1947—, tchr. Sunday sch. Bible, 1947—, woman's missionary union dir., 1990-92; tchr. Garrison Pub. Schs., 1940-76; dir./asst. dir. Vacation Bible Sch., Garrison, 1950-92; vol. local newspaper, nursing home and sch., city libr., ch. libr. Named Mother of Yr., First Bapt. ch., Garrison, 1988, Citizen of Yr., Garrison, 1992. Mem. Nat. Ret. Tchrs. Assn., Tex. Ret. Tchrs. Assn. (life), Stephen F. Austin Alumni Assn. (life), Lions (Sweetheart), Heritage Soc., Genealogy Soc., Order Eastern Star (past Matron, organist), Delta Kappa Gamma. Home: 319 N Avenue A Garrison TX 75946

HERRINGTON, DAVID MCLEOD, cardiologist, educator; b. Seattle, Feb. 15, 1957; s. Robert and Margaret (McLeod) H.; m. Deirdre Achtellik, Nov. 26, 1983; children: Daniel, Kristen. BS in Math., Davidson (N.C.) Coll., 1979; MD, U. N.C., 1983; MHS in Epidemiology, Johns Hopkins U., 1989. Lic. physician, N.C., Md. Intern Johns Hopkins Hosp., Balt., 1983-84, resident, 1984-86, fellow various divsns., 1986-90; asst. prof. cardiology Bowman Gray Sch. Medicine, Winston-Salem, N.C., 1990-95, assoc. prof., 1995—; dir. SHAC Clinic, U. N.C. Sch. Medicine, Chapel Hill, 1980-81, dir. CROP Lunch, 1980-81; mem. FDA adv. com. on use of QCA in Angiography, Bethesda, Md., 1991, NIA adv. com. on Conf. on DHEA and Aging, 1992; chmn. cardiovascular endpoints com. Asymptomatic Carotid Atherosclerosis Study, 1993—; rapporteur cardiovascular working group NIH Workshop on Menopause, Bethesda, 1993; mem. NIA ad hoc rev. com., 1994. Editl. cons. Am. Jour. Medicine, Am. Jour. Cardiology, Am. Jour. Epidemiology and Prevention, Arteriosclerosis and Thrombosis, Catheterization and Cardiovascular Diagnosis, Controlled Clin. Trials, Circulation, Exptl. Gerontology, IEEE Transactions on Biomed. Engring., New Eng. Jour. Medicine, Transactions on Med. Imaging, Williams and Wilkins; contbr. articles to profl. jours., chpts. to books. Bd. dirs. Sem. Ridge Neighborhood Assn., Lutherville, Md., 1988-90; mem. Leadership Circle, United Way, Winston-Salem, N.C., 1991—. Recipient Andrew W. Mellon Found. fellowship award in clin. epidemiology, 1986-88, Hartford Geriatric Acad. Initiative fellowship award, 1992; granteeNat. Rsch. Svc., 1986-88, Nat. Am. Heart Assn., 1991-94, Wyeth-Ayerst, 1992-99, NIH, 1994-99. Fellow Am. Coll. Cardiology; mem. Am. Heart Assn. (fellow coun. on epidemiology and prevention 1995), Am. Fedn. Clin. Rsch. (young faculty award So. sect. 1991), N.Y. Acad. Scis. Office: Bowman Gray Sch Medicine Med Ctr Blvd Winston Salem NC 27157

HERRINGTON-BORRE, FRANCES JUNE, sign language school director; b. Austin, Tex., June 14, 1935; d. George Wilmas Neill and Mildred Lucille (Alexander) Williamson; m. Harold M. Herrington, June 6, 1953 (dec. Dec. 1978); children: Harold M. Jr. (dec.), Cheryl Anne Herrington; m. Thomas Raymond Borre, Apr. 5, 1985. Student, U. Tex., 1967-71. With Tex. Dept. Human Services, Austin, 1961-90, adminstrv. technician, 1967-71, field rep., 1971-81, asst. personnel dir., 1981-88, labor relations dir., 1988-89, judge adminstrv. law, 1989-90; free-lance profl. interpreter for deaf, 1964—; dir. Austin Sign Lang. Sch., 1964—; legis. liaison symposium Deaf and Hard-of-Hearing Texans, 1991—; cons. in field; project dir. Gov.'s Office, 1980. Gov.'s appointee Joint Adv. Com. on Ednl. Services to Deaf, Austin, 1976-78; chmn. Tex. Commn. for Deaf Bd. Eval. of Interpreters, 1981-84; chmn. Tex. State Agy. Liaisons to Gov.'s Commn. for Women, 1985. Recipient Tex. Rehab. Commn. Merit award, 1977, Gov.'s citation, 1978; co-recipient Lyndon B. Johnson award Tex. Assn. for the Deaf and the Gallaudet U. Regional Ctr., 1992; named An Outstanding Woman Central Tex., AAUW, 1982, Significant and Meritorious Service to Mankind award Capitol Sertoma Club, 1976, Disting. Service as Adv. and Interpreter award Dal-Tar Lions Club, 1977. Mem. Nat. Assn. of Deaf (Golden Hand award 1987), Tex. Assn. of Deaf (Service citation 1967, Vol. Svc. award 1971, 91-93, Interpreter of Decade award 1981, Presdl. citation for Outstanding Svc. to symposium on deafness 1989, Friendship award 1994, Gratitude for Vol. Svcs. award 1993-95, Appreciation award 1996), Nat. Registry Interpreters for Deaf, Tex. Soc. Interpreters for Deaf (pres. 1969-70), Austin Interpreters for Deaf. Mem. Ch. of Christ. Home: 2404 Laramie Trl Austin TX 78745-3664

HERRMANN, JOHN, editor, journalist; b. Berkeley, Calif., May 17, 1931; s. John Phillip Herrmann and Roberta Louise (Neuwohner) Liberto; m. Dolores Mae Arvin, Sept. 15, 1956 (div. 1965); children: Deborah Autsen, Linda West, Kathryn Anne Topper; m. Andrea Bess Watson, May 25, 1968 (div. 1993). BA, San Francisco State U., 1960, MA, 1961; MFA, U. Iowa, 1964. Founding editor Chrysalis Review, San Francisco, 1959-63; sect. head InfoWeek, Manhasset, N.Y., 1982-83; assoc. editor Mgmt. Technology Mag., N.Y.C., 1983-84; mng. editor Direct Mktg. Mag., Garden City, N.Y., 1984-85; asst. editor Health Systems Rev. Mag., Little Rock, 1985-88, exec. editor, 1988—; dir. creative writing U. Mont., Missoula, 1963-66; asst. prof. English, U. N.Y., Oswego, 1966-69; vis. prof. English Pahlavi U., Shiraz, Iran, 1969-70; writer-in-residence Cedar Crest Coll., Allentown, Pa., 1971-78; lectr. creative writing U. Ark., Little Rock, 1989-93. Author: Summer Will Rise and Other Stories, 1975, Office Automation, 1984. With USN, 1951-54. Recipient Hart Crane award in poetry Am. Weave Press, 1969; named to Roll of Honor, Best Am. Short Stories, 1973; Residency grantee Edward MacDowell Colony, Peterborough, N.H., 1968, Yaddo, Saratoga Springs, N.Y., 1968, 69. Mem. Assoc. Writing Programs. Democrat. Home: 2410 Bobtail Cutoff Libby MT 59923-9404

HERRO, JOHN JOSEPH, software specialist; b. Watertown, Wis., Oct. 3, 1945; s. Alexander Chris and Lyla Victoria H.; m. Beverly Lynn Franz, June 26, 1976; children: Carla Lynn, Brian Peter, Emily Anne. BS, Ill. Inst. Technology, Chgo., 1967; MS, Ill. Inst. Technology, 1968, PhD, 1973. Electronic engr. Motorola, Inc., Schaumburg, Ill., 1968-71; assoc. engr. Ill. Inst. Technology Rsch. Inst., Chgo. and Dayton, Ohio, 1972-75; tech. staff Logicon, Inc., Dayton, 1975-77; systems analyst Cin. Electronics Corp., 1977-78; sr. software engr. GE Co., Cin., 1978-86; staff software engr. Grumman Aerospace, Melbourne, Fla., 1986-88, Harris Corp., Palm Bay, Fla., 1988-89; software specialist Golden Enterprises, Inc., Melbourne, 1989—; pres. Software Innovations Technology, Palm Bay, 1988—; tchr. SUNY at Binghamton, 1985-86, Fla. Inst. Technology, Melbourne, 1988-89. Author: ADA Tutor, 1988. Recipient Spl. Fellowship Ill. Inst. Technology, 1969, Traineeship NSF, 1971. Mem. Tau Beta Pi, Sigma Xi, Sig-ADA, Four Sigma Soc. Roman Catholic. Home: 1083 Mandarin Dr NE Melbourne FL 32905-4706

HERRON, EDWIN HUNTER, JR., energy consultant; b. Shreveport, La., June 7, 1938; s. Edwin Hunter and Helen Virginia (Russell) H.; B.S. in Chem. Engring., Tulane U., 1959, M.S., 1963, Ph.D. (NSF fellow, 1963-64), 1964; m. Frances Irvine Hunter, June 27, 1959; children—Edwin, David, Ashley. Rsch. engr. Exxon Rsch. & Engring. Co., Linden, N.J., 1959-61; sr. rsch. engr. Exxon Prodn. Rsch. Co., Houston, 1964-66; corp. planning advisor Esso Europe, London, Eng., 1966-74; fin. analyst Exxon Corp., N.Y.C., 1974-78; v.p. Gruy Petroleum Tech., Inc., McLean, Va., 1978-84; pres. Petro-Analysis Inc. (name changed to Hunter Trading Co. Inc.), 1984—; pres. Petroleum Equities, Inc., 1987—; dir. petroleum projects CORE Internat., Inc., 1989—; pres. Petroleum Holdings, Inc., 1993—. Recipient Levey award, Tulane U., 1970. Mem. Soc. Petroleum Engrs., Am. Inst. Chem. Engrs., Sci. Rsch. Soc., Soc. Tulane Engrs., Tau Beta Pi. Contbr. articles to profl. publs.

HERRON, JAMES MICHAEL, lawyer; b. Chgo., May 4, 1934; s. J. Leonard and Sylvia H.; m. Sara J. Czaja; children: Kathy Lynn, Tracy Ellen, Andrew Ross. A.B., U. Mo., Columbia, 1955; postgrad., Northwestern U., 1958-59; J.D., Washington U., 1961; postgrad., Harvard Bus. Sch., 1982. Bar: Mo. 1961, Ohio 1971, Fla. 1975. Asst. gen. counsel, asst. sec. May Dept. Stores Co., St. Louis, 1961-70; assoc. counsel Federated Dept. Stores, Inc., Cin., 1970-71; v.p., sec., gen. counsel Kenton Corp., N.Y.C., 1971-73; gen. counsel Ryder System, Inc., Miami, Fla., 1973-74, v.p., sec., gen. counsel, 1974-78, sr. v.p., sec., gen. counsel, 1978-79, exec. v.p., gen. counsel, from 1979, sec., 1983-86, now sr. exec. v.p., gen. counsel; bd. dirs. ATA Litigation Ctr., Fiduciary Trust Internat. for the South. First v.p., bd. dirs. exec. com. Fla. Grand Opera, chmn. corp. devel. com., 1981-82, pres., 1989-93, vice chmn., 1993—; bd. dirs. Am. Cancer Soc., 1985-87; chmn. bd. dirs. New World Sch. of the Arts, 1995—; mem. Washington U. Sch. Law Nat. Coun. With USMC, 1955-58. Mem. ABA, Mo. Bar Assn., Bar Assn. Met. St. Louis, Assn. of Bar of City of N.Y., Am. Soc. Corp. Secs., Fla. Bar Assn., Dade County Bar Assn. Club: Royal Palm Tennis (dir.). Home: 2891 Seminole St Miami FL 33133-3234 Office: Ryder System Inc PO Box 020816 3600 NW 82nd Ave Miami FL 33102-3682

HERSHATTER, ANDREA SILVER, university official; b. N.Y.C., Jan. 19, 1960; d. K. David and René Eileen (Kirsch) Silver; m. Bruce Warren Hershatter, Oct. 1, 1983; children: Jessica René, Justin Ross. BS in Mgmt., Tulane U., 1981; MBA, Duke U., 1983. Promotions and mktg. dir. WBAG, The Village Cos., Burlington, N.C., 1983-84; asst. dir. admissions and fin. aid Fuqua Sch. Bus. Duke U., Durham, N.C., 1984-86, assoc. dir. admissions, 1986-87; dir. admissions and student affairs Emory Bus. Sch. Emory U., Atlanta, 1988-90, asst. dean Emory Bus. Sch., 1990-94, assoc. dean for acad. programs Goizueta Bus. Sch., 1994-96, assoc. dean undergrad. edn., 1996—, adj. instr., rep. grad. mgmt. admissions coun., chmn. MBA curriculum task force; mem. reaccreditation task force So. Assn. Colls. and Schs., Am. Assn. Collegiate Schs. Bus.; trustee Grad. Mgmt. Admissions Coun., 1996—; mem. bd. trustees nominating group, rsch. adv. group GMAC; MBA/MPH curriculum rep. Rollins Sch. Pub. Health, FLAS scholarship selection com. Soviet programs, Emory U., mem. career svcs. adv. bd.; advisor MBA Enterprise Corps. and Free Mkt. Devel. Adv. Program., mem. MBA roundtable steering com. Editor-in-chief Emory Bus. Mag., 1993, contbg. editor, 1993—. Pres. Mt. Paran Neighborhood Assn., Atlanta, 1991-94. Democrat. Jewish. Home: 4400 Mount Paran Pky NW Atlanta GA 30327-3722 Office: Emory Univ Goizueta Bus Sch Atlanta GA 30322

HERSHBERGER, CARRIE LEE, program developer; b. Erie, Pa., Mar. 4, 1946; d. Jerome Denile and Ruth Marie (Driscoll) Krill; m. Joel Lindsey Stafford, Aug. 18, 1973 (div. Aug. 1980); 1 child, Patricia Lynn; m. Edmund G. Hershberger, Nov. 25, 1982; 1 child, Kathryn Marie. BS in Edn., Edinboro U., 1968, MA, 1969. Tchr. McDowell High Sch., Erie, 1969-73; various civil service positions, Ft. Sill, Okla., 1973-84; tng. developer, analyst Telos Fed. Systems, Lawton, Okla., 1984-87, Telos Systems Devel. div. Info. Systems, McLean, Va., 1987-88; Loudoun County Pub. Schs., Va., 1988-91, Consolidated Tech. Svcs., Sterling, Va., 1992-95, KC Resources, Cabin John, Md., 1995, NGA, 1996—; adjunct faculty No. Va. C.C., 1988—. Contbr. articles to profl. jours. Democrat. Roman Catholic. Club: Artillery. Home: 21162 Morning Way Sterling VA 20164-4634 Office: Telos Systems Devel Info Systems 1500 Planning Research Dr Mc Lean VA 22102-5001

HERSHBERGER, KENNETH ERNEST, fundraiser, public relations and marketing; b. Butler, Pa., Feb. 7, 1943; s. Ernest Wilmer and Gladys Ruth (Smith) H.; m. Susan Jane Kiernan, June 16, 1973 (div. Oct. 1989); children: David Hugh, Leah Elizabeth. BA in Comms., Pa. State U., 1961-65. Mgr. campus rels. Pa. State U., University Park, 1976-78; dir. comty. rels. devel. The Cornwall (N.Y.) Hosp., 1978-82; pres. Hersh Comms., Inc., Cornwall, 1982-83; dir. mktg. and community rels. St. Luke's Hosp., Newburgh, N.Y., 1983-86; mktg. dir., sales mgr. The Evening News, Newburgh, 1986-88; mktg. dir. Mich. HealthSource, Petoskey, 1988-89; referral devel. mgr. Chestnut Ridge Hosp., Morgantown, W.Va., 1990; mktg. cons. Splty. Care Psychiat. Svcs., Inc., Boardman, Ohio, 1991; profl. rels. rep. Belmont Pines Hosp., Youngstown, Ohio, 1991; community rels. rep. St. Joseph's/Parkside Ctr. for Behavioral Medicine, Hosp., Parkersburg, W.Va., 1991-94; devel. dir. W.Va. Edn. Fund, Charleston, 1994; v.p. Straight Wire Orthodontic Studies, Inc., St. Mary's, W.Va., 1994-95; dir. devel. Parkersburg (W.Va.) Cath. Schs., 1995—; 2d vice chmn. auction com. SW Resources, Inc.; CQI com. mem. St. Joseph's Hosp., publicity com., chmn. Christmas Carolling, organizer line dancing lessons. V.p. for programs Cmty. Svc. Coun. of Greater Parkersburg; mem. memership and comml. devel. coms. C. of C. of Mid-Ohio Valley; active Planned Approach to Cmty. Health; bd. dirs., liaison with United Way Wood County Assn. for Mental Health; legis. reform com. Wood County Commn. on Crime, Delinquency and Correction. Mem. ASTD (former v.p. membership), Nat. Assn. of Mental Health Info. Officers (fellows program), Nat. Assn. Health Care Mktg., W.Va. Soc. Healthcare Mktg. Planning and Pub. Rels. (pres.), Employee Assistance Resource Network, W.Va. Assn. for Counseling (conf. exhibits chmn.), W.Va. State Health Edn. Coun., Rotary Club of Parkersburg, Sierra Club, KC, Am. Legion Post 15. Republican. Roman Catholic. Home: 2803 Fairview Ave Parkersburg WV 26104-2201 Office: Parkersburg Catholic Schs Development Office 3201 Fairview Ave Parkersburg WV 26104

HERSHENSON, MIRIAM HANNAH, librarian; b. Springfield, Mass., July 23, 1944; d. David and Thelma (Wasserman) Ratner; m. Frank J. Hershenson, July 7, 1968; children: Trent M., Scott D. AB, Syracuse U., 1966; MS, Simmons Coll., 1967; postgrad., Nova U., 1987-89. Cert. tchr., librarian, Mass. Media specialist Quincy (Mass.) Pub. Schs., 1967-71, Virginia Beach (Va.) Pub. Schs., 1982-84, Portsmouth (Va.) Pub. Schs., 1984; regional children's coord. Broward County Libr., Ft. Lauderdale, Fla., 1985-88, br. liaison, 1988-89, br. librarian, 1989-93, regional br. supr., 1993—. Mem. ALA, Fla. Libr. Assn. (caucus chair 1990-91), Broward County Libr. Assn. (pres. 1994-95), Hadassah (life, chpt. pres. 1983-84), Nat. Coun. Jewish Women (life), Jewish Women Internat. (life), Brandeis Univ. Women (life). Office: Ft Lauderdale Libr 1300 E Sunrise Blvd Fort Lauderdale FL 33304-2802

HERSKOVITZ, S(AM) MARC, lawyer; b. Munich, Jan. 1, 1949; came to U.S., 1949; s. Max and Bella (Mappen) H.; 1 child from previous marriage, David Michael; m. Barbara Hobbs, Nov. 28, 1990; 1 child, Daniel Max. BA, Pa. State U., 1970; MS in Edn. with high honors, So. Ill. U., 1974; JD with honors, Fla. State U., 1987. Bar: Fla. 1987, U.S. Dist. Ct. (mid. dist.) Fla. 1988, U.S. Ct. Appeals (11th cir) 1988. Agy. mgr. Sun Personnel Svcs., Inc., Sarasota, Fla., 1978-80; claims adjuster Allstate Inc. Co., Lake Worth, Fla., 1980-84; sr. atty. Fla. Dept. Ins., Tallahassee, 1987—. Mem. ABA, Assn. Trial Lawyers Am., Phi Kappa Phi. Democrat. Jewish. Home: 707 Lothian Dr Tallahassee FL 32312-2858 Office: Fla Dept Ins 612 Larson Bldg Tallahassee FL 32399-0333

HERTENSTEIN, MYRNA LYNN, publishing executive; b. Detroit, July 19, 1937; d. Bernard Franklin and Alice Agnes (Stewart) Aller; m. George Ronald Hertenstein, June 21, 1958 (div. July 1979); children: Dale Ronald, Robert Mark. AS in Bus., Wayne State U., 1957; student, Huntingdon Coll., 1980-84. Departmental sec. Sch. of Bus. Wayne State U., Detroit, 1957-59; county and vol. coord. Montgomery (Ala.) Area Coun. on Aging, 1977-80; admissions counselor Coastal Tng. Inst., Montgomery, 1981-83; rural volunteerism coord. State of Ala., Montgomery, 1983-84; account exec. Ala. Bus. Rev., Montgomery, 1984-85, Sta. WRJM-FM, Montgomery, 1985-86; asst. local sales mgr. Sta. WCOV-TV Fox Affiliate, Montgomery, 1986-90; owner, assoc. pub. TRAVELHOST of Cen. Ala., Montgomery, 1990—; mem. Dirs. of Vols. in Agys., Montgomery, 1978-82, Montgomery County Health Coun., 1979-81, Area Agy. on Aging Adv. Coun., Montgomery, 1981-83, Pres.' Coun. Montgomery, 1983, 84; asst. to instr. Dale Carnegie & Assocs., Montgomery, 1978-83. Editor (newsletter) Montgomery Area Coun. on Aging, 1978-80; dir., writer (commls.) Sta. WCOV-TV, 1986-90; writer (commls.) Sta.WRJM-FM, 1985-86. Mem. adminstrv. coun. Whitfield United Meth. Ch., Montgomery, 1977, coord. Meals-on-Wheels, 1978-86; mem. pub. rels. coun. First United Meth. Ch., Montgomery, 1992-94, vice chmn. comms., 1996—; den leader, coach Boy Scouts Am., Bellevue, Nebr., 1969-71; editor Capitol Jr. Woman's Club. Montgomery, 1975-82; pres. Parents Without Ptnrs., 1983-85; bd. dirs. Arthritis Found., 1992—, vice chair 1995, chair Ala. chpt. exec. com., 1996; mem. dance com. Ala. Dance Theatre, 1996—. Recipient Emerging 30 award Montgomery Area C. of C., 1992, small business of yr. award, 1994, corp. vol. of yr. award Voluntary Action Ctr., Montgomery, 1992, award Montgomery Com. for Arts, 1993. Mem. Pub. Rels. Coun. Ala., Ala. Travel Coun., Montgomery Restaurant Assn., Montgomery Hotel/Motel Assn. (bd. dirs. 1992-94), Sales and Mktg. Execs. (editor newsletter 1995—), Montgomery Assn. Bus. Communicators, Montgomery Advt. Fedn. (bd. dirs. 1985-92, 96—), Montgomery C. of C. (vice chmn. ambs. 1992, chmn. ambs. 1993, chmn. advt. promotions and publs. 1994, hospitality devel. and mktg. task force 1995—, chmn. spl. projects com. 1996), Montgomery Civitans. Home: 3005 Baldwin Brook Dr Montgomery AL 36116-3803 Office: Travelhost of Cen Ala PO Box 20666 Montgomery AL 36120-0666

HERTH, KAYE ANN, nursing educator, academic administrator, hospice nurse; b. Oak Park, Ill., Sept. 9, 1945; d. Donald J. and Martha A. (Kent) Huron; m. Leonard A. Herth, June 18, 1971; children: Wendy Joye, Randy Scott. BSN, No. Ill. U., 1968; MS, U. Minn., 1973; PhD, Tex. Woman's U., 1987. Mem. faculty U. Tex., Houston, 1978-85; mem. grad. faculty U. Okla., Tulsa, 1986-88, No. Ill. U., DeKalb, 1988-93; prof., chmn. dept. nursing Ga. So. U., Statesboro, 1993—. Contbr. articles to profl. jours. Grantee Am. Cancer Soc., No. Ill. U. Fellow Am. Acad. Nursing; mem. Midwest Nursing Soc., Gerontol. Soc. Am., Sigma Theta Tau (Pres.'s Pillar award, disting. scholar).

HERTZ, ARTHUR HERMAN, business executive; b. Bklyn., Sept. 10, 1933; s. Edwin Carl and Blanche H.; Stephen R., Andrew P. B.B.A., U. Miami, Fla., 1955, postgrad., 1955-56. Acct. Aetna Mortgage Co., Miami, Fla., 1955; acct. Wometco Enterprises, Inc., Miami, 1955-60, controller, v.p., 1960-64, sr. v.p., 1964-71, exec. v.p., treas., chief fin. officer, 1971-81, chief ops. officer, 1981-84, chmn., chief exec. officer, 1985—; exec. v.p., chief ops. officer WEI Enterprises Corp., Miami, 1984-85; exec. v.p. Wometco Broadcasting Co., Inc., Miami, 1984-85; bd. dirs. Spec's Music, Inc. Past pres. Orange Bowl Com.; mem. City of Miami Off St. Parking Authority, Fla. Tourism Commn.; trustee U. Miami, 1979, Dade County Pub. Health Trust. Mem. AICPA, Fla. Inst. CPAs, Greater Miami C. of C. (gov. 1975-78), Iron Arrow, Phi Kappa Phi, Omicron Delta Kappa, Phi Eta Sigma. Home: 610 Fluvia Ave Coral Gables FL 33134-7016 Office: Wometco Enterprises Inc PO Box 141609 Coral Gables FL 33114-1609

HERTZ, KENNETH THEODORE, health care executive; b. Jackson Heights, N.Y., Aug. 19, 1951; s. Irwin R. and Dorothy S. H. B.A. in Spl. Studies, SUNY, Fredonia, 1974; cert. med. and dental practice mgmt., Loyola U., 1992. Gen. mgr. Cape Cod Symphony, West Barnstable, Mass., 1974-75; mng. dir. Tulsa Philharm., 1975-78; pres., gen. mgr. Atlanta Ballet, 1979-89; instr. continuing edn. Oglethorpe U.; dir. Atlanta Great Artists Series, 1989-90, Atlanta Arts Devel. Svcs., 1989-90; exec. dir. New Orleans Symphony, 1990-91; adminstr. M.D. Care, Inc., New Orleans, 1991-95; dir. acquisitions and network devel. Tenet Healthcare, New Orleans, 1995-96, area mgr. practice ops., 1996—; mem. dance panel City of Atlanta, 1983-89, Ga. Coun. for Arts, 1984-88, NEA, 1985-87; dir. Dance/USA, 1985-89; mem. adv. bd. cert. program in med./dental practice mgmt. Loyola U., 1993—; mem. Pres.'s Adv. Coun., De La Salle H.S., 1993—. Chmn. Atlanta C. of C. Cultural Programming Task Force, 1987-89, Atlanta C. of C. "Arts Alive,", art celebration, 1986; former chmn. Ga. Profl. Arts Caucus, 1983-85; former bd. dirs. Am. Jewish Com., Atlanta, 1987, Big Bros./Big Sisters, Atlanta, 1988-89, Arts Festival Atlanta, BVA, Atlanta, 1986-90, Bus. Vols. for the Arts, Atlanta; bd. dirs. New Orleans Ballet Assn., 1996—. Mem. Midtown Bus. Assn. (dir. 1984-89), Ga. Citizens for Arts, Am. Symphony Orch. League, Alpha Phi Omega.

HERTZBERG, BARBARA SPECTOR, academic radiologist; b. N.Y.C., Nov. 22, 1956. BS, Cornell U., 1977; MD, Duke Sch. of Medicine, 1980. Diplomate Nat. Bd. Med. Examiners, N.C.; bd. cert. in diagnostic radiology. Internship FAHEC Family Practice Program, Fayetteville, N.C., 1980-81; residency diagnostic radiology Duke U. Med. Ctr., Durham, N.C., 1981-85; fellowship Thomas Jefferson U. Hosp., Phila., 1985-86; asst. prof. dept. radiology Duke U. Med. Ctr., Durham, 1986-92, asst. prof. dept. ob-gyn., 1990—, assoc. prof. dept. radiology sect. ultrasound, 1992—; lectr. in field; quality assurance com. Dept. Radiology, Duke U. Med. Ctr., 1986-91, residents evaluation and adv. com., 1991—, med. ctr. awards coms., 1992—, continuing med. edn. com., 1993—; reviewer Investigative Radiology, 1992—, Radiology, 1994—. Mem. editl. bd. The Radiologist, 1992—; contbr. articles and abstracts to profl. jours., chpts. to books. Phi Kappa Phi fellow, 1977; recipient award for excellence in teaching Duke Radiology Residents, 1989, 94. Fellow Am. Inst. Ultrasound in Medicine (chmn. edn. com. 1993-95, covention program com. 1993—, info. media com. 1993-95, bd. govs. 1996—, accreditation commn. 1995—, nominating com. 1994), Soc. Radiologists in Ultrasound (chairperson rsch. com. 1994—); mem. N.C. Med. Soc. (ho. dels. 1992—), Radiol. Soc. N.Am. (audiovisual com. 1996—), Am.Roentgen Ray Soc., Am. Coll. Radiology (chair rsch. & tech. assessment ultrasound com. 1995—, ultrasound commn. 1995—, rsch. and tech. assessment com. 1995—, ultrasound stds. and accreditation com. 1993—), Durham Orange County Med. Soc. Office: Duke Univ Med Ctr Dept Radiology Box 3808 Durham NC 27710

HESS, AMY MORRIS, law educator; b. N.Y.C., Sept. 11, 1947; d. Bernard H. and Ruth Katharine (Batchker) Morris; divorced; 1 child, Carlos Alberto. BA, Barnard Coll., 1968; JD, U. Va., 1971. Bar: N.Y. 1973, Va. 1975, Tenn. 1985. Assoc. Kelley Drye & Warren, N.Y.C., 1971-75; ptnr. Carwile & Hess, Charlottesville, Va., 1976-80; vis. asst. prof. Coll. of Law U. Tenn., Knoxville, 1979-80, assoc. prof., 1981-90, prof., 1990—; assoc. prof. U. Colo. Law Sch., Boulder, 1980-81; vis. prof. U. Mo. Law Sch., Columbia, 1989-90, U. Tex. Sch. Law, summer 1991; mem. Tenn. joint com. Uniform Probate Code, 1995—. Successor author: Bogert on the Law of Trusts and Trustees, 1995—; co-author: Virginia Forms, Vol. I, Civil Litigation, 1978, 89 replacement vol. and ann. supplements; contbr. articles to profl. publs., chpt. to book. Risk mgr. Children's Internat. Summer Village, Knoxville, 1990-93; mem. endowment fund com. Tennessee Valley Unitarian Universalist Ch., 1993-94. Recipient Outstanding Tchr. award U. Tenn. Alumni Assn., 1994, Bass, Berry & Sims award for outstanding svc. to legal profession, 1994; grad. fellow AAUW, 1970-71. Mem. ABA (assoc. editor Real Property, Probate and Trust jour. 1989—, chmn. taxation subcom. on significant devels. 1991-95, taxation subcom. on grantor trusts 1995—, vice chmn. probate and trust com. on income taxation of estates and trusts 1989—), Tenn. Bar Assn., Tenn. Lawyers' Assn. for Women, Knoxville Bar Assn., LWV, Phi Kappa Phi (U. Tenn. chpt. exec. com., 1993-98, pres. 1996-97). Unitarian. Home: 6916 Quail Dr Knoxville TN 37919-5930 Office: U Tenn Coll Law 1505 W Cumberland Ave Knoxville TN 37996-1800

HESS, EDWIN JOHN, oil company executive; b. Newark, Nov. 9, 1933; s. Harry E. and Victoria (Bienkowski) H.; m. Barbara Claire Gernert, June 29, 1957; children: Susan Lynn, Cheryl Lee, Nancy Jean, Cynthia Ann, Edwin John. Mech. engr., Stevens Inst. Tech., 1955; MBA, Harvard U., 1957. Engr. Exxon Co., U.S.A., Linden, N.J., 1957-60; with supply mktg. dept. Houston, Midland, Tex. and Los Angeles, 1960-72; retail bus. mgr. Houston, 1972-74; dep. dept. mgr. N.Y.C., 1974-78, v.p. mktg., 1978-81, sr. v.p., 1981-85; exec. v.p. Exxon Internat. Co., 1985-86; v.p. petroleum products Exxon Co. Internat., 1986-87, sr. v.p., 1988-89; v.p. environ. and safety Exxon Corp., 1990-92, sr. v.p., 1993—. Mem., trustee Edwin A. Stevens Soc. com. Stevens Inst. Tech.; trustee Com. for Econ. Devel., The Sci. Pl., Dallas; bd. dirs., Execs. com. Nat. Action Coun. for Minorities in Engring., Jr. Achievement Dallas, Inc.; trustee, mem. exec. com. U.S. Coun. for Internat. Bus. With U.S. Army, 1959. Recipient Alumni Achievement award Stevens Inst. Tech., 1980, Stevens Honor award, 1993. Mem. Am. Petroleum Inst., Lakeside Country Club, Bent Tree Country Club, Dallas Petroleum Club, The Hills of Lakeway Club. Republican. Presbyterian. Office: Exxon Corp 5959 Las Colinas Blvd Irving TX 75039-2298

HESS, GEORGE FRANKLIN, II, lawyer; b. Oak Park, Ill., May 13, 1939; s. Franklin Edward and Carol (Hackman) H.; m. Diane Ricci, Aug. 9, 1974; 1 child, Franklin Edward. B.S. in Bus., Colo. State U., 1962; J.D., Suffolk U., 1970; LL.M., Boston U., 1973. Bar: Pa. 1971, Fla. 1973, U.S. Tax Ct. 1974, U.S. Dist. Ct. (so. dist.) Fla. 1975. Assoc. Hart, Childs, Hepburn, Ross & Putnam, Phila., 1970-72; instr. Suffolk U. Law Sch., Boston, 1973-74; ptnr. Henry, Hess & Hoines, Ft. Lauderdale, Fla., 1974-79; sole practice George F. Hess, II, P.A., (merged with Mousaw, Vigdor, Reeves, Heilbronner & Kroll., Rochester, N.Y., 1981, name now Mousaw, Vigdor, Reeves & Hess), Ft. Lauderdale, 1979-94; sole practice George F. Hess II PA, 1995—. Bd. dirs. Children's Home Soc., Ft. Lauderdale, 1985-89 , Nadeau Charitable Found., 1985—; Served to lt. USNR, 1963-66. Mem. ABA, SAR, Fla. Bar Assn., Broward County Bar Assn., Phi Alpha Delta. Episcopalian. Clubs: Lauderdale Yacht, U.S. Navy League. Home: 2524 Castilla Is Fort Lauderdale FL 33301-1505 Office: George F Hess II PA 333 N New River Dr E Fort Lauderdale FL 33301-2241

HESS, JANICE BURDETTE, nursing administrator; b. LaGrange, Ga., July 4, 1946; d. Carl Alton and Bennetta Felton (Hipp) Burdette; m. John Randall Hess, Aug. 19, 1966; children: Heather Bennetta, Laurie Ellen. Diploma, Orange Meml. Sch. Nursing, Orlando, Fla., 1967; certificate nurse practitioner, Brigham Young U., 1976; BSN cum laude, So. Missionary Coll., Collegedale, Tenn., 1980; MS in Nursing, U. Fla., 1984. Cert. nurse practitioner in adult health; cert. in nursing adminstr. ICU staff nurse West Volusia Meml. Hosp., Deland, Fla., 1967-69; dir. health svcs., nurse practitioner coll. health Stetson U., Deland, 1969-85; coord. nursing, nurse practitioner adult health & amb. care VA Outpatient Clinic, Daytona Beach, Fla., 1985-95; clin. dir., nurse practitioner family health svcs. Munroe Regional Health Systems, Ocala, Fla., 1995—; nurse practitioner, adj. faculty U. Fla., Orlando, 1991—. Mem. adv. com. grad. nursing program U. Ctrl. Fla.; mem. adv. com. Head Start Marion County. Mem. Fla. Nurses Assn., VA Ambulatory Care Nurse Network, Ctrl. Fla. Advanced Coun. Nursing (pres., editor newsletter), Sigma Theta Tau. Home: 865 N Summit Ave Lake Helen FL 32744-2002

HESSAMFAR, ELAHE, communications executive. V.p. chief info. officer Turner Broadcasting Sys., Atlanta. Office: Turner Broadcasting Sys 1 CNN Ctr Box 105366 Atlanta GA 30348-5366

HESSE, NANCY JANE, gas company executive; b. Quincy, Ill., Nov. 2, 1948; d. John William and Geraldine Elaine (Ossian) H. BA, U. Ill., 1970; MEd, U. Memphis, 1971; M of Mgmt., Northwestern U., 1980; JD, Loyola U., 1996. Program dir. Memphis State U., 1970-75; regional mgr. SEI Info. Tech., Chgo., 1975-80, mgr. cons. ops. sect., 1980-83, mgr. devel. projects, 1983-85, mgr. adminstrn. and fin., 1985-87; dir. adminstrn. Laventhol & Horwath, Chgo., 1987-90; treas. Hesse Gas Co., Houston, 1991—. Bd. dirs. YWCA Met. Chgo., 1983-89. Office: Hesse Gas Co 6524 San Felipe Ste 129 Houston TX 77057

HESTAND, JOEL DWIGHT, minister, evangelist; b. Henrietta, Tex., May 23, 1939; s. Dee Lathell and Jack Fern (Gamble) H.; m. Carolyn Somers, June 12, 1959; children: Paul Daniel, Joe Randall. Student, Odessa (Tex.) Coll., 1963-66; Diploma, Brown Trail Sch. Preaching, Ft. Worth, Tex., 1968-70, Sunset Sch. Missions, Lubbock, 1973; BTh, Trinity Theol. Sem., 1988. Evangelist Ch. of Christ, various locations, 1968—; missionary Tanzania, E. Africa, 1973-75, Chimala Mission and Hosp., Mbeya, Tanzania, 1994-95; police chaplain Naperville (Ill.) Police Dept., 1977-83; ednl. dir. Rockford (Ill.) Christian Camp, 1977-82, bd. dirs., 1977-82; instr. Fishers of Men Evangelism, Frankfort, Ky., 1984—. With USAF, 1957-66. Republican. Office: Myrtle Ave Ch of Christ 134 Myrtle Ave Frankfort KY 40601-3114

HESTER, BRUCE EDWARD, library media specialist, lay worker; b. Clarksville, Tenn., June 26, 1956; s. Edward Vaughan and Mabel Sarah (Chandley) H. BS, Middle Tenn State U., 1978; MEd, Trevecca Nazarene Coll., 1987. Cert. elem. tchr., cert. secondary tchr. and libr., Tenn. Tchr. Met.-Davidson County Schs., Nashville, 1993—; adj. faculty-vol. State C.C., Gallatin, Tenn., 1993—; choir dir. First Christian Ch., Dover, Tenn., 1983—, Sunday sch. tchr., deacon, 1988-93, chmn. bd. dirs., 1989-93; dir. Stewart County Cmty. Choir, 1987-89. Co-chmn. Stewart County Rep. Party, 1986-89. Recipient Vol. Svc. award Cystic Fibrosis Found., 1984, Mayor's Acts of Excellence award, 1994; named E. Middle Sch. Tchr. of Yr., 1996. Mem. NEA, Tenn. Edn. Assn., Tenn. Assn. Sch. Librs., Tenn. Assn. Mid. Schs., Met. Nashville Edn. Assn. (East Mid. Sch. Tchr. of Yr. 1995). Mem. Disciples of Christ Ch. Home: 1724 Valley Rd Clarksville TN 37043-4537 Office: East Mid Sch 110 Gallatin Rd Nashville TN 37206-3217

HESTER, JAMES HERBERT, JR., minister; b. Clovis, N.Mex., July 6, 1948; s. James Herbert and Sybil Eileen (Upton) H.; m. Cynthia Rose Boal, June 6, 1969; children: Corrie Ellen, Cassie Laine. BA, U. N.Mex., 1972; MDiv, Southwestern Bapt. Theol. Sem., Ft. Worth, 1975; D Ministry, Luther Rice Internat. Sem., Jacksonville, Fla., 1978. Ordained to ministry So. Bapt. Conv., 1969. Pastor Highland Bapt. Ch., Albuquerque, 1975-78, Parkland Bapt. Ch., Clovis, 1978, Killarney Bapt. Ch., Winter Park, Fla., 1978-86, 1st Bapt. Ch., Lake Worth, Fla., 1986-92, Colonial Bapt. Ch., Memphis, 1992—; pres. So. Bapt. Pastor's Conf., Albuquerque, 1977-78; chmn. com. on order of bus. Fla. Bapt. Conv., 1982-86, Palm Lake Bapt. Assn., 1986-91; chmn. credentials com. So. Bapt. Conv., Orlando, 1985-86. Judge Mother of Yr. award, N.Mex., 1977; chaplain football team U. Ctrl. Fla., Orlando, 1985-86; bd. dirs. So. Fla. fellowship Christian Athletes, 1986-92; trustee Palm Beach Atlantic Coll., West Palm Beach, Fla., 1989-91; bd. religious affairs Union U., Jackson, Tenn., 1993-96. Republican. Home: 2540 Crewe St Memphis TN 38119-7922 Office: Colonial Baptist Church 1503 Colonial Rd Memphis TN 38117-6503

HESTER, LINDA HUNT, university dean, counselor; b. Winston-Salem, N.C., June 16, 1938; d. Hanselle Lindsay and Jennie Sarepta (Hunt) H. BS with honors, U. Wis., 1960, MS, 1964; PhD, Mich. State U., 1971. Lic. ednl. counselor, Wis. Instr. health and phys. edn. for women U. Tex., Austin, 1960-62; asst. dean women U. Ill., Urbana, 1964-66; dean of women, asst. prof. sociology and phys. edn. Tex. Woman's U., Denton, 1971-73; rsch. assoc. bur. higher edn. Mich. Dept. Edn., Lansing, 1969-70; counselor Dallas Challenge and Dallas Ind. Sch. Dist., 1989-90. Bd. dirs. Dallas Opera, 1986—; Stradivarious mem. Dallas Symphony, 1991—; assoc. mem. Dallas Mus. Art, 1991—. Fellow coll. edn. Mich. State U., 1968. Mem. Am. Counseling Assn., Am. Coll. Pers. Assn., Nat. Assn. Women in Edn., Brookhaven Country Club, Delta Kappa Gamma, Alpha Lambda Delta. Republican. Presbyterian. Home and Office: 7606 Wellcrest Dr Dallas TX 75230-4857

HESTER, ROSS WYATT, business forms manufacturing company executive; b. Amarillo, Tex., Aug. 23, 1924; s. Wyatt Langford and Nettie Estelle (Horne) H.; m. Elizabeth Ruth Hobbs, May 28, 1948 (div. Aug. 1984); children: Sherry Gail, Randal Ross, Debra Renee, Stephen Keith, Jeffry Wyatt. BA, Austin Coll., Sherman, Tex., 1947. Vice pres. Hester's Office Supply, Inc., Lubbock, Tex., 1947-60; pres. Caprock Bus. Forms, Inc., Lubbock, 1960-90, chmn. bd., 1990-96; ret., 1996. Trustee Austin Coll., 1987—. With USAAF, 1943-46, CBI. Recipient Disting. Alumnus award Austin Coll., 1984. Mem. Printing Industry Assn. Tex. (pres. 1988-89). Republican. Presbyterian. Office: Caprock Bus Forms Inc 1211 Avenue F Lubbock TX 79401-4224

HETHCOCK, WENDELL HAROLD, private school educator, principal; b. Mercedes, Tex., Dec. 12, 1938; s. William Cleo and Mary Myrtle (Robison) H.; m. Laura Catherine Meyer, July 3, 1965; children: William, Denise, Laurie. BS, S.W. Tex. State U., San Marcos, 1961, MA, 1964. Cert. tchr., counselor, adminstr., Tex. Tchr. sci. San Marcos Bapt. Acad., 1962-64; assoc. dean students S.W. Tex. State U., San Marcos, 1964-65; adminstr. Gary Job Corps, San Marcos, 1965-69; guidance counselor San Marcos Bapt. Acad., 1969-71, dir. guidance, 1971-78, prin., 1978-96, exec. adminstr., 1996—. Mem. Tex. Assn. Secondary Schs. Principals., Masons, Rotary Club, Phi Delta Kappa (sec.-treas. 1974-76, v.p. 1976-77, pres. 1977-78). Baptist. Home: 1509 Hamilton St San Marcos TX 78666 Office: San Marcos Bapt Acad 2801 Ranch Rd # 12 San Marcos TX 78666

HETHERWICK, GILBERT LEWIS, lawyer; b. Winnsboro, La., Oct. 30, 1920; s. Septimus and Addie Louise (Gilbert) H.; m. Joan Friend Gibbons, May 31, 1946 (dec. Aug. 1964); children: Janet Hetherick Pumphrey, Ann Hetherwick Lyons Winegeart, Gilbert, Carol Hetherwick Sutton, Katherine Hetherwick Hummel; remarried Mertis Elizabeth Cook, June 7, 1967. BA summa cum laude, Centenary Coll., 1942; JD, Tulane U., 1949. Bar: La. 1949. With legal dept. NorAm Energy Corp., Shreveport, La., 1949-53; dir. Blanchard, Walker, O'Quin & Roberts, Shreveport, 1953—. Mem. Shreveport City Charter Revision Com., 1955; Shreveport Mcpl. Fire and Police Civil Svc. Bd., 1956-92, vice chmn., 1957-78, chmn., 1978-88. Served with AUS, 1942-46. Recipient Tulane U. Law Faculty medal, 1949. Mem. ABA, La. Bar Assn., Shreveport Bar Assn. (pres. 1987), Fed. Energy Bar Assn., Order of Coif, Phi Delta Phi, Omicron Delta Kappa. Episcopalian. Home: 4604 Fairfield Ave Shreveport LA 71106-1432 Office: Bank One Tower Shreveport LA 71101

HETRICK, CHARLES BRADY, county official; b. Linton, Ind., Jan. 16, 1932; s. Norman Charles and Emma (Klinger) H.; divorced; children: Keith Charles, David Kent, Steven John. BA, Ind. U., 1953; MPA, U. Mich., 1957. Adminstrv. asst., asst. to city mgr., asst. city mgr. City of Park Ridge (Ill.), 1956-68; exec. dir. Miami Valley Coun. Govts., Dayton, Ohio, 1968-69; cons. to pres., div. mgr., dir. corp. planning Dayton Progress Corp., 1969-71, 73-74; exec. v.p., gen. mgr. Ft. Worth Area C. of C., 1971-73; sr. assoc. Louis A Allen Assocs., Inc., Palo Alto, Calif., 1974-75; econ. devel. coord. State of Wis., Madison, 1975-76; asst. county mgr. Volusia County, Daytona Beach and Deland, Fla., 1975-80; county adminstr. Rock County, Janesville and Beloit, Wis., 1980-84, Charleston County, Charleston, S.C., 1984-85, Hernando County, Brooksville, Fla., 1985—. Contbr. articles on mcpl. problems and urban affairs to various publs. 1st lt. U.S. Army, 1953-55. Recipient resolution S.C. Ho. of Reps. and Senate, 1985; U. Mich. Met. Community fellow, 1955-56. Mem. Internat. City Mgmt. Assn., Am. Soc. for Pub. Adminstrn. Home: PO Box 1778 Brooksville FL 34605-1778 Office: Hernando County Govt 20 N Main St Rm 460 Brooksville FL 34601-2817

HETTINGER, STEVE, mayor. Mayor Huntsville, Ala., 1988—. Office: Mayor's Office 308 Fountain Cir SW Huntsville AL 35801-4240

HETTRICK, GEORGE HARRISON, lawyer; b. Piney River, Va., Aug. 15, 1940; s. Ames Bartlett and Frances Caryl (O'Brian) H.; m. Ann Fontaine Hutter, June 15, 1963; children: Heather White Hettrick Brugh, Edward Lord; m. Helen Kay MacDonald, Dec. 29, 1990. BA, Cornell U., 1962; JD, Harvard U., 1965. Bar: Va. 1965. Assoc. Hunton & Williams, Richmond, Va., 1965-73, ptnr., 1973—; ptnr. in charge Church Hill Neighborhood Law Office Hunton & Williams, 1990—, chmn. Community Svc. com.; dir. Richmond Community Hosp., 1992—. Contbr. articles to profl. jours. Spl. counsel Gov. of Va., Richmond, 1971-72; vice chmn. bd. dirs. Va. Port Authority, Norfolk, 1970-75, former commr., vice chmn.; pres. bd. trustees Va. Episcopal Sch., Lynchburg, 1978-81; mem. Va. State adv. com. Neighborhood Assistance Program; past dir., chmn. Peter Paul Devel. Ctr., Inc.; bd. dirs. Richmond Cmty. Hosp., Free Clinic for Substance Abuse, Charity Family Life, Richmond Better Housing Coalition. Capt. U.S. Army, 1966-68. Mem. ABA, Va. Bar Assn. (chmn. substance abuse com. 1995—, Lawyers Helping Lawyers), Va. State Bar, Richmond Bar Assn. Republican. Episcopalian. Home: 6350 Memorial Dr Sandston VA 23150-6307 Office: Hunton & Williams 951 E Byrd St Richmond VA 23219-4040

HEUER, MARTIN, temporary services company executive; b. Algoma, Wis., Oct. 16, 1934; s. Orland Fred and Gertrude Mayme (Zimmerman) H.; m. Rita Mae Prokash, Oct. 27; children: Martin Joseph, Ronald James. AA, SUNY, 1973, AS, 1975. Commd. 2d lt. C.E., U.S. Army, 1954, advanced through grades to lt. col., 1968; flight comdr., adminstrv. and maintenance officer 1st Aviation Co., Fort Riley, 1958-61; with 937th Engr. Aviation Co., Panama, Lima, Peru, 1961-65; maintenance officer 174th Aviation Co., Vietnam, 1966; adj. 14th Combat Aviation Bn., 1966-67; dir. systems, curriculum and spl. projects div. Army Primary Helicopter Sch., Fort Wolters, Tex., 1967-69; aviation advisor Wis. Army N.G., West Bend, 1969-70; airfield comdr. Cu Chi Army Airfield, Vietnam, 1970; adj. 165th Combat Aviation Group, Vietnam, 1970-71; engr. advisor Wis. N.G., Eau Claire, 1971-73; mgr., area mgr. Manpower Temp. Services, 1973-76; exec. v.p. Aide Services, Inc. and KARI Services, Inc., Tampa, Fla., 1976-80, pres., chmn., 1980—; pres., chmn. Capitol Services, Inc., Tallahassee, 1982-86; pres. bd. dirs. Fort Wolters Fed. Credit Union, 1967-69; chmn. bd. Digital Control Corp., Seminole, Fla., 1981—. Pres., Seminole High Sch. Band Boosters, 1974-79, v.p. Vietnam Helicopter Pilots Assn., 1996—, Pinellas County Band Boosters, 1977-78; bd. dirs. Seminole High Sch. Booster Assn., 1975-79, pres., 1978-79. Decorated Legion of merit with 1 oak leaf cluster, Bronze star medal with 3 oak leaf clusters, Air medal with 3 oak leaf clusters; recipient First Band Booster Pres. award Seminole High Sch., 1979, Service to Mankind award Sertoma, 1980. Mem. Assn. Manpower Franchise Owners (dir. 1980-82, 83-86, treas. 1981-82, chmn. 1984-86), Assn. U.S. Army (chmn. bd. govs. 1981-82, asst. state v.p. Suncoast chpt. and Fla., 1981-82, state v.p. 1982-84, chmn. chpt. communications com. nat. adv. bd. 1982-86, mem. corp. adv. council 1985-90, Fla. exec. council 1985-90, bd. dirs. Sun Coast chpt. 1994—), Army Aviation Assn. Am., Air Force Assn., Soc. Am. Mil. Engrs., Res. Officers Assn., Retired Officers Assn., Future Farmers Am. Alumni Assn., Nat. Assn. Temp. Svcs. (treas./sec. Fla. chpt. 1991-94), Vietnam Helicopter Pilots Assn. (bd. dirs. Fla. chpt. 1993—). Republican. Club: Runaway Bay (Tex.) Country. Office: Ste 102 5402 Beaumont Center Blvd Tampa FL 33634-5202

HEUER, ROBERT MAYNARD, II, opera company executive; b. Detroit, Nov. 27, 1944; s. Robert Maynard and May Elizabeth (Quinn) H. Student, Capital U., 1963-64; B.A., Wayne State U., 1976. Youth dir. Grace Lutheran Ch., Detroit, 1964-66; costume designer, prodn. mgr. U. Windsor, Ont., Can., 1967-69; program coordinator Detroit Youtheatre, Detroit Inst. Arts, 1970-71; mng. dir. Mich. Opera Theatre, Detroit, 1971-79; prodn. dir. Fla. Grand Opera (formerly Greater Miami Opera), 1979-83; asst. gen. mgr. Greater Miami (Fla.) Opera, 1984-85, gen. mgr., CEO, 1986—. Mem. Performing Arts Ctr. Found. Greater Miami. Recipient Grand Decoration of Honor Republic of Austria, 1990. Mem. Opera Am. (bd. dirs.), Greater Miami C. of C. Home: 547 Navarre Ave Coral Gables FL 33134-4231 Office: Fla Grand Opera 1200 Coral Way Miami FL 33145-2927

HEUSER, OSCAR EDWARD, marketing professional; b. Ardmore, Okla., Nov. 25, 1922; s. George John Heuser and Velma Violenta (Deardorff) Connell; m. Mary Bolin White, Jan. 27, 1945; children: Ronald Wayne, Debra Leigh. BS in Bus., Okla. City U., 1976, MEd, 1978, MBA, 1979. Announcer and newscaster KSWO Radio, Lawton, Okla., 1941-42; flight instr. Page Aviation/Cimarron Field, Yukon, Okla., 1943-44; copywriter Lowe Runkle Co., Oklahoma City, 1952-55; exec. v.p. Long Runkle Co., Oklahoma City, 1972-81, pres., 1981-87; vice-chmn. Runkle-Moroch Co., Oklahoma City, 1987-88; chmn., CEO Mid-America Mktg. Comms., Oklahoma City, 1988-96; exec. dir. Sales and Mktg. Execs. Internat. Acad., Oklahoma City, 1993-96; trustee, exec. dir. sales and mktg. execs. Internat. Acad. of Achievement, Oklahoma City, 1992-96; bd. dirs. Epworth Villa Retirement Comm., Oklahoma City; adj. faculty Okla. City U., 1980-96; guest participant Nat. Security Seminar, Army War Coll., Carlisle Barracks, Pa., 1995. State chmn. Okla. Com. for Employer Support of the Guard and Res., Office of the Asst. Sec. of Def., Okla. and Arlington, Va., 1994-96. Capt. USAF, 1944-52, ETO; lt. col. USAFR. Named Outstanding Young Man of Oklahoma City, Okla. Jaycees, 1954; recipient George Washington Honor medal Freedom's Found., 1994, Friend of Immunization award Okla. State Dept. Health, Oklahoma City, 1996. Mem. Rotary (Paul Harris fellow 1980, gov. dist. 5750 1991-92), Okla. Sales and Mktg. Execs. Assn. (past bd. dirs. 1989-96). Office: Mid-Am Mktg Comms and Debronco Inc Ste 284 5500 N Western Ave Oklahoma City OK 73118 *Died Dec. 3, 1996.*

HEUSINKVELD, PAULA RAE, foreign language educator, writer; b. Kingfisher, Okla., Nov. 21, 1945; d. George Richard and Emma Louise (Becker) H. BA in Spanish, Ctrl. Coll., Pella, Iowa, 1968; MA in Spanish, U. Wis., 1969, PhD in Spanish, 1979. Grad. teaching asst. U. Wis., Madison, 1968-69, 70-73, grad. teaching asst., 1975-79; Spanish instr. Alma (Mich.) Coll., 1969-70; Spanish, French instr. Greensboro (N.C.) Day Sch., 1973-75; asst. prof. Spanish St. Olaf Coll., Northfield, Minn., 1979-82; asst. prof. Spanish, French Clemson U., Clemson, S.C., 1982-88; assoc. prof. Spanish Clemson U., 1988—; editl. cons. for fgn. lang. texts Holt/Rinehart, Harper & Row, Houghton-Mifflin, D.C. Heath, John Wiley & Sons, Simon-Schuster, 1990—; dir. Clemson U. summer study program in Mexico, 1984—; presenter in-svc. workshops, seminars, lectrs. sch. dists. in St. Louis, Mpls., Dallas, others, 1985—. Author: Inside Mexico: Living, Traveling and Doing Business in a Changing Society, 1994; contbr. articles to profl. jours. Mem. AAUW, Am. Assn. Tchrs. Spanish and Portuguese, Am. Coun. on the Teaching Fgn. Langs., So. Conf. on Lang. Teaching (exec. bd., Outstanding Fgn. Lang. post-secondary Tchr. award 1994). Democrat. Unitarian-Universalist. Home: 3037 Creekside Dr Seneca SC 29672 Office: Dept Languages Clemson U 717 Strode Tower Clemson SC 29634-1515

HEVENER, FILLMER, JR., English language educator, writer, portrait artist; b. Churchville, Va., May 14, 1933; s. Fillmer Sr. and Estie (Harper) H.; m. Celia Achenbach, Aug. 27, 1954; children: Dennis Lyle, Yolanda Mae. BA, Columbia Union Coll., 1954; MA, James Madison U., 1957; EdD, U. Va., 1973. Cert. tchr., Va. Secondary English tchr. State of Va., 1954-55, Shenandoah Valley Acad., New Market, Va., 1955-57; tchr. ESL Bugema Missionary Coll., Kampala, Uganda, 1957-58; secondary English tchr. State of Mich., 1958-60; asst. prof. English Frostburg (Md.) State Coll., 1960-64, LaSierra Coll., Riverside, Calif., 1965-66; assoc. prof. English edn. Longwood Coll., Farmville, Va., 1966-92; owner Fillmer Hevener Studio-Gallery, Farmville, Va., 1995—; cons. student tchrs. Longwood Coll., Farmville, Va.; pres., owner Fillmer Hevener Studio, Inc., Farmville, 1992—. Author: Successful Student Teaching: A Handbook for Elementary and Secondary Student Teachers, 1981, Hot Tips for Student Teachers, 1985, Technical Writing: A Theoretical Basis, 1991, Tithing: Not Required After the Cross, 1993; contbr. articles to profl. publs.; one-man shows include Richmond (Va.) Pub. Libr., Appomattox (Va.) Pub. Libr., Jefferson Hotel Gallery, Richmond; portraits exhibited at Mayflower Hotel Gallery, Washington, New England Fine Arts Inst., Boston Trade Ctr., Chateau Elan Gallery, Braselton, Ga.; commd. portraits include H. Ross Perot, Gen. Douglass MacArthur, Gen. Robert E. Lee, Pres. George Bush, Pres. Bill Clinton, Pres. J.F. Kennedy, Will Rogers, Pres. Thomas Jefferson, Sir Winston Churchill, Pres. Abraham Lincoln, Pres. Woodrow Wilson, Stone Mountain (Ga.) carving. Mem. bd. regents Gen. Conf. Seventh Day Adventists, 1977-80; supr. Buckingham County (Va.). 1984-87; pres. Lower Francisco Fire Assn., Buckingham County, 1981—; vice chair Crossroads Mental Health Svcs., Va., 1985-87; elected sec. Ctrl. Va. Fine Arts Assn., 1993-94, 94—. Mem. ASCD, Va. Conf. English Educators (chmn. 1988-90), Nat. Coun. Tchrs. English, Va. Assn. Tchrs. English, Univ. Profs. for Acad. Order, Internat. Platford Assn., Am. Culture/Popular Culture Assn. (presenter 1990). Home and Office: RR 2 Box 1425 Farmville VA 23901-9502

HEVNER, ALAN RAYMOND, educator, consultant; b. Marion, Ind., Dec. 9, 1950; s. Raymond Leland and Pauline Honora (Roach) H.; m. Susan Nichols, July 13, 1985; 1 child, Caitlin Marie. BS, Purdue U., 1973, MS, 1976, PhD, 1979. Asst. prof. U. Minn., Mpls., 1979-81; prof. U. Md., College Park, 1981-94; chmn. Info. Sys. Dept. U. Md., 1987-93; prof. U. South Fla., 1994—; endowed chair Salomon Bros. Dist. Tech.; eminent scholar U. Fla. Sys. Author: Principles of Information Systems Analysis and Design, 1986; contbr. articles to profl. jours. Lt. U.S. Army, 1973-75. Mem. Computer Soc. of IEEE (Cert. of Appreciation 1985), Assn. Computing Machinery, Assn. Info. Systems, Inst. Ops. Rsch. and Mgmt. Sci. Christian (Disciples of Christ). Home: 15703 Cheston Ct Tampa FL 33647 Office: Info Systems College of Business Admin University of South Florida Tampa FL 33620-7800

HEWETT, ARTHUR EDWARD, real estate developer, lawyer; b. Dallas, Oct. 16, 1935; s. Arthur Elton and Clara Mae (Wagoner) H.; m. Helen Yvonne Barry, May 20, 1959; children: Julie, Matthew, Clara. B.B.A., So. Methodist U., 1957, LL.B., 1965. Bar: Tex. 1965. Asst. to exec. v.p. Diversa, Inc., Dallas, 1960-61; asst. to pres. RichPlan Corp., Dallas, 1961-62; ptnr. Vial, Hamilton and Koch, 1965-69; founder, mng. ptnr. firm Hewett Johnson Swanson & Barbee, 1970-80; pres., chief executive officer Thompson Realty Corp., Dallas, 1980-83; pres., chief exec. officer Republic Property Group, Inc., 1983—. Served to lt. USNR, 1957-60. Mem. Tex. Bar Assn., Bohemian Club (San Francisco), Park City Club. Presbyterian. Home: 3550 Granada Ave Dallas TX 75205-2236 Office: Republic Property Group 8th Fl Lockbox 3 8440 Walnut Hill Ln Dallas TX 75231-3833

HEWITT, OTTO D., III, lawyer; b. Hillsboro, Tex., Oct. 21, 1946; s. Otto D. Jr. and Marguerite (Porter) H.; m. Sunny N. Martin, Aug. 1970; children: Heather Eleanor, Heidi Elizabeth. BA, Baylor U., 1969, JD, 1980. Bar: Tex. 1980, U.S. Dist. Ct. (so., ea. and we. dists.) Tex. 1981, U.S. Ct. Appeals (5th cir.) 1983, U.S. Ct. Appeals (10th cir.) 1988, U.S. Supreme Ct. 1984. Staff atty. Ct. Appeals, Eastland, Tex., 1980-81; assoc., firm officer McLeod, Alexander, p.c., Galveston, Tex., 1981-91; participating atty. Davenport Law Firm, Alvin, Tex., 1991-94; owner, lawyer Hewitt Law Firm, Alvin, Tex., 1994—; adj. prof. civil rights and constitutional law Baylor Law Sch., Waco, Tex., 1990—. Contbr. articles to profl. jours. law enforcement officer State of Calif., 1970-78; law grad. asst. Gov.'s War Against Crime Commn., 1980; pres. AFSCME, AFL-CIO, 1975-78, sec. 1972-75; vice-chmn. Merced County Dem. Cen. Com., Calif., 1972-78; commnr. Mcpl. Airport Commn., Atwater, Calif., 1977-78. Sgt. USAF, 1969-72. named one of Outstanding Young Men of Am., 1978, Boss of Yr. Galveston Legal Secretaries Assn., 1985, 90. Mem. Tex. Bar Assn., Tex. Bar Found., Tex. Indian Bar Assn., Galveston Bar Assn., Brazoria County Bar Assn., 5th Cir. Bar Assn. (founding mem.), Assn. Civil Trial and Appellate Specialists, Coll. State Bar Tex., Southeastern Cherokee Confederation (cert. mediator state and fed. cts.). Office: Hewitt Law Firm 1600 E Hwy 6 Ste 302 Alvin TX 77511

HEYBURN, JOHN GILPIN, II, federal judge; b. 1948; m. Martha Keeney, 1976. BA, Harvard U., 1970; JD, U. Ky., 1976. Ptnr. Brown, Todd & Heyburn, Louisville, 1976-92; fed. judge U.S. Dist. Ct. (we. dist.), Louisville, 1992—; mem. budget com. Jud. Conf. U.S. Cts. Bd. dirs. Kentuckians for Jud. Improvement, 1975-76; mem. budget com. Jud. Conf.of U.S., 1994—; chair Jefferson County Crime Commn.; mem. vis. com. U. Ky., 1980; active Leadership Louisville Found. With USAR, 1970-76. Mem. ABA, Ky. Bar Assn., Louisville Bar Assn., U. Ky. Coll. Law Alumni Assn., Louisville Com. Fgn. Rels. Office: US Dist Ct 601 W Broadway St Louisville KY 40202-2238

HEYDRICK, LINDA CAROL, consulting company executive, editor; b. Pomona, Calif., July 25, 1947; d. Robert Bruce and Wanda Georgine (Wellman) Middough; m. Stephen R. Bova, Jan. 20, 1968 (div. May 1981); children: Karen E., Lori L.; m. Allen L. Heydrick, Mar. 15, 1995. Student, El Camino Coll., Gardena, Calif., 1965-66. Sec. TRW, Inc., Manhattan Beach, Calif., 1967-68, USAF NCO Clubs, Mildenhall, Eng., 1968-70; adminstrv. asst. Prudential-Bache Securities, N.Y.C., 1970-73, Tex. Instruments, Inc., Dallas, 1980-83; asst. to pres. Acclivus Corp., Dallas, 1983-85, mgr. design and prodn., 1985-88, mgr. ops., 1988-89, v.p. ops., 1989—; cons. Digital Equipment Corp., Boston, 1984-89, internat. translations of books, audiotapes and videotapes. Editor: (books and videotapes) BASE for Sales Performance, 1984, Acclivus Sales Negotiation, 1985, The New BASE for Sales Excellence, 1989, Major Account Planning and Strategy, 1993, rev., 1996, Building on the BASE (award for best new tng. products Human Resource Exec.), 1993. Organizer Meals on Wheels, Denton, Tex., 1977; editor, pub Denton Bible Ch., 1993—. Mem. ASTD, Instructional Systems Assn., Nat. Soc. for Performance and Instrn., Soc. for Aplied Learning Tech., Soc. for Accelerative Learning and Tchg., Internat. Listening Assn., Womens Ctr. Dallas. Republican. Home: 3301 Santa Monica Denton TX 76205-8245 Office: Acclivus Corp 14500 Midway Rd Dallas TX 75244-3109

HEYEN, MELANIE STONE, newspaper editor, educator; m. R.V. Wehrle; 1 child, Chris; m. Curtis D. Heyen. Student, La. State U., 1978-80, 85; BA, La. Tech. U., 1991. Editl. asst., designer Social Register Mag., Shreveport, La., 1977-78; state desk editor, reporter The Times, Shreveport, 1978-82; editor, pub. rels. dir. ArtBeat SR Arts Coun., Shreveport, 1982-83; lifestyles, news editor Bossier Press-Tribune, Bossier City, La., 1984; bur. reporter, soc. editor The Times, Shreveport, La., 1984-91; editor The Ruston (La.) Daily Leader, La., 1991—; adj. instr., intern supr. La. Tech. U., Ruston, 1988—, lectr. 1990-96; lectr. Grambling State U., 1994-96. Designer: (mag.) Forests and People, 1980; author, photographer (mag.) River Cities, 1982-84 (cover 1983); author: Shreveport Mag., 1983. Bd. dirs. Am. Diabetes Assn. La. (N.W. Affiliate) 1986-88; fund raiser St. Jude Children's Hosp., Ruston, La., (ESA chpt.), 1991-92. Recipient award of excellence NEA, Baton Rouge, La., 1993, 94, 95., La. Assn. Educators, 93, 94, 95; grantee Gannett Found., 1989-91. Mem. Nat. Assn. Press Women, La. Press Women (v.p. 1995—, 10 1st pl. awards), Assoc. Press, La., Miss. (v.p., bd. dirs., 5 1st pl. awards 1992-95), La. Press Assn. (13 1sts 1991—). Office: The Ruston Daily Leader 208 W Park Ave Ruston LA 71270

HEYER, ANNA HARRIET, retired music librarian; b. Little Rock, Aug. 30, 1909; d. Arthur Wesley and Harriet Anna (Gage) H. A.B., B.Mus., Tex. Christian U., 1930; B.S. in L.S., U. Ill., 1933; M.S. in L.S., Columbia U., 1939; M.Mus. in Musicology, U. Mich., 1943. Elem. sch. music tchr. Ft. Worth Pub. Schs., 1931-32; high sch. librarian, 1934-38; cataloguer library, U. Tex.-Austin, 1939-40; music librarian, asst. prof. L.S., N. Tex. State U. (name now U. N. Tex.), Denton, 1940-65, librarian emeritus, 1976; cons. music library materials Tex. Christian U., Ft. Worth, 1965-79; ret., 1979. Author: A Check-List of Publications of Music, 1944; A Bibliography of Contemporary Music in the Music Library, North Texas State College, 1955; Historical Sets, Collected Editions and Monuments of Music: A Guide to

Their Contents, 1957, 2d edit., 1969, 3d rev. edit., 1980; contbr. articles to profl. publs. Recipient citations for contbn. to music librarianship Music Library Assn., 1980, to music librarianship in Tex., 1983. Mem. ALA, Tex. Library Assn., Music Library Assn., AAUW, DAR. Mem. Disciples of Christ Ch. Clubs: Altrusa, Woman's Club Ft. Worth, Colonial Country. Home: 5334 Premier Ct Fort Worth TX 76132-4016

HIATT, JANE CRATER, arts agency administrator; b. Winston-Salem, N.C., May 26, 1944; d. Howard Rondthaler Jr. and Irene (Sides) Crater; m. K.W. Everhart Jr. (div. June 1973); m. Wood Coleman Hiatt, May, 1978; 1 child, Jonathan David. BA, U. N.C., 1966; MA, Wake Forest U., 1972. Eng. tchr. Winston-Salem (N.C.)/Forsyth County Schs., 1966-70; exec. dir. Tenn. Com. for the Humanities, Nashville, 1973-77; cons. various ednl. and cultural agys. Ocean Springs, Miss., 1978-80; asst. dir. Miss. Humanities Coun., Jackson, Miss., 1981-85; exec. dir. Arts Alliance of Jackson and Hinds County, Miss., 1985-89, Miss. Arts Commn., Jackson, 1989-95; participant Arts Leadership Inst. of Humphrey Inst. for Pub. Affairs, Mpls., 1986, Leadership, Jackson, 1987. Co-editor Peoples of the South, 1976; exec. producer (TV series) The South with John Siegenthaler, 1976; host, reporter Miss. Ednl. TV, Jackson, 1981-87. Mem. Miss. Econ. Coun., 1986-87, Miss. R & D Coun., 1984-88; pres. Mental Health Assn. of Hinds County, Jackson, 1986; treas. Miss. for Ednl. Broadcasting, 1987, 88, 89, Premier Class Leadership, Jackson, 1987, 88. Recipient Heritage award City of Biloxi, 1984. Mem. Nat. Assembly of Local Arts Agys., Nat. Coun. on Arts, Nat. Assembly State Arts Agys. (bd. dirs. 1992-95, 2d v.p. 1995), So. Arts Fedn. (bd. dirs. 1989-95), Miss. Ctr. for Nonprofits (vice chmn., bd. dirs. 1993—), Pub. Edn. Forum (bd. dirs. 1993—), Greater Jackson Found. (bd. dirs. 1996—), Phi Beta Kappa. Home: 507 Roses Bluff Dr Madison MS 39110-9690

HIATT, MABEL STRADER, real estate investment executive; b. Greensboro, N.C., Dec. 22, 1921; d. Demetrius Anderson and Jessie Irene (Stack) Strader; m. John Thomas Hiatt, Oct. 5, 1940 (div. June 1972); children: John T. Jr., Bruce Demetrius. BS in Home Econs., U. N.C., Greensboro, 1941; student, King's Bus. Coll., Greensboro, 1942, Dance Educators Am., N.Y.C., 1951-90. Sec. Page Yarn Co., Greensboro, 1942-43; home decorator Hiatt Homes, Inc., Greensboro, 1945-70; owner Mabel Hiatt Ballroom Dance Studio, Greensboro and High Point, N.C., 1951—; instr. of children Temple Emanuel, Greensboro, 1952-69; owner Hiatt Investment Co., Greensboro, 1975—. Dance awards Jaycees, Greensboro/Winston-Salem. Mem. Dance Educators of Am. (numerous awards), Terpsichore Dance Club (dance chmn. 1955, 86, treas. 1991), Blue Bonnet Garden Club (pres. 1970, blue ribbons 1969), Greensboro Pks. and Recreation Social Club (tchr. 1974-77), Parents without Partners (tchr. 1974-78). Republican. Methodist. Home and Office: 4003 W Friendly Ave Greensboro NC 27410-5645

HIBBERT, WILLIAM ANDREW, JR., surgeon; b. Pensacola, Fla., June 15, 1932; s. William Andrew and Blanche Marie (Blair) H.; children: Andy III, Blair, Reb Stuart. BS, U. of South, 1953; MD, Emory U., 1957. Diplomate Am. Bd. Surgery, recert., Am. Bd. Colon and Rectal Surgery, recert. Intern, Duval Med. Center, U. Fla., Jacksonville, 1957-58; resident in gen. surgery Grady Meml. Hosp., Emory U., Atlanta, 1958-62; fellow in colon-rectal surgery Ochsner Found. Hosp., New Orleans, 1962-63, Baylor U. Med. Center, Dallas, 1964-65; practice medicine specializing in colon-rectal surgery, Austin, Tex., 1965—; mem. staff St. David, Seton, Brackenridge hosps.; instr. Tulane U. Med. Sch., New Orleans, 1962-64; sr. surgeon gen. surgery svc. USPHS, 1963-64; cons. U. Tex. Student Health Center. Bd. govs. Shrine Burn Hosp., Galveston, Tex.; past chmn. bd. trustees Ben Hur Shrine Temple; past vol. People to People; med. amb. to China and Russia. Chmn. fin. bd., bd. dirs. Austin Scottish Rite Learning Ctr. Fellow ACS, Am. Soc. Colon and Rectal Surgeons, Am. Soc. Gastrointestinal Endoscopists, Am. Soc. Laser Surgery, Soc. of Am. Gastrointestinal Endosopic Surgeons, Internat. Soc. Univ. Colon and Rectal Surgeons, Southwestern Surg. Congress; mem. Tex. Med. Assn., Tex. Colon-Rectal Soc. (past pres.), mem. Pan Am. (past chmn. colon-rectal sect.), So. Med. Assn. (past sect. chmn.), Pan Pacific Surg. Soc., Tex. Soc. Gastrointestinal Endosopists, Royal Soc. Medicine (hon.). Club: Austin Rotary Downtown (Paul Harris fellow). Lodges: Masons, Shriners (potentate 1985, past. gov. imperial shrine Burn Hosp., past chmn. rsch. com., past rep. Imperial Council Shrine North Am.), Royal Order of Jesters (past dir.), Order of DeMolay (Legion of Honor), Scottish Rite (Knight Comdr.). Contbr. articles to med. jours.; past assoc. editor So. Med. Jour. Office: 4208 Medical Pky Austin TX 78756-3310

HIBBITTS, MARIAN HAYES, family nurse practitioner; b. Honolulu, May 1, 1959; d. Marcus A. and Martha E. (Jones) H. BSN, Valdosta (Ga.) State U., 1982; MS, Ga. State U., 1995. RN, FNP, Ga.; cert. BLS instr., BLS instr.-trainer. Staff RN/charge nurse South Ga. Med. Ctr., Valdosta, 1982-87; DRG coord., with infection control and social svcs. units Berrien County Hosp., Nashville, Ga., 1985-87; staff RN/charge nurse Gwinnett Med. Ctr., Lawrenceville, Ga., 1987—; staff nurse Med. Plus Dunwoody Med. Ctr., Lawrenceville, Ga., 1992-96; occupational nurse practitioner CIBA Vision, Norcross, Ga., 1996—; customer svc. rep. Nursing Home Svcs. Group, 1989-91. Camp nurse Ga. Bapt. Assn., 1983-92. Mem. ANA (cert. med.-surg. nurse), Am. Assn. Occupational Health Nurses, Ga. Nurses Assn. Home: 1431 Providence Way Lawrenceville GA 30245-4351

HIBEL, EDNA, artist; b. Boston, Jan. 13, 1917; d. Abraham Bert and Lena (Rubin) H.; m. Theodore Plotkin, Jan. 7, 1940; children: Jon, Andy, Richard. Student, Boston Mus. Sch. of Fine Arts, 1938, 41-42; study abroad, Boston Mus. Sch. of Fine Arts, Mexico, 1939; DHA(hon.), U. for Peace UN, 1988; LHD, Mt. St. Mary's Coll., 1988, Eureka Coll., 1995. Pvt. art tchr. Boston, 1957-58; art dir. Edna Hibel Gallery, Boston and Palm Beach, Fla., 1960—, owner, mgr., 1960—; curator Hibel Mus. of Art, Palm Beach, Fla., 1977—; prime organizer First Boston Arts Festival, 1954; judge statewide art competition, Tenn., 1983, Frances Hook Found. Scholarship Competition, Wis., 1985. Artist Soc. of the Little Flower, Darien, Ill., 1985-87; artist Lake Kezar Cookbook, Cordon Blue award, 1982; artist, author several art books; TV prodn.; Hibel's Russian Palette, on location in the Soviet Union, 1990, shown on PBS stas. across U.S.; commn. by Found. for Nat. Archives to Commemorate 75th Anniversary of ratification of 19th amendment to U.S. Constitution granting women the universal right to vote, 1995. Active Hibel Mus. Art. Recipient Woman of Yr. award State of N.J., 1979, Presdl. award Arts for the Handicapped, 1985, Spirit of Life award City of Hope, 1984, 94, Humanitarian of Yr. award, Boy's Town, Italy, 1994; Ruth B. Sturtevant traveling fellow Boston Mus. Sch. Fine Arts, 1939. Fellow Royal Soc. of Art, World Acad. of Art and Sci. (first painter to be elected as such), Edna Hibel Soc. Democrat. Jewish. Lodge: B'nai B'rith (hon. founder Edna Hibel unit 1986). Office: Hibel Museum of Art 150 Royal Poinciana Plz Palm Beach FL 33480-4045

HICKEY, BOBBY RAY, underwriting assistant; b. Louisville, Apr. 13, 1960; s. Virgle Ray and Doris Jean (Adams) H. Student, U. Louisville, 1990. Various positions Kroger, Louisville, 1980-87; student asst. U. Louisville, 1987-91, libr. asst. I, 1991-95; mail courier Ky. Farm Bur. Ins., Louisville, 1995, underwriting asst., 1995—; auto underwriting dept. rep. to safety com. Ky. Farm Bur., 1996. Neighborhood rep. Environ. Health Task Force, Louisville, 1996; neighborhood rep. Family Health Ctrs., Louisville, 1986—, vice chmn., 1991—, chairperson nominating com., 1994—. Recipient William O. Cowger award Jefferson County Rep. Party, Louisville, 1986, Mayor's citation City of Louisville, 1990, 96, Cert. of Recognition, Jefferson County Commr., 1996. Mem. Toastmasters (v.p. pub. rels. Ky. Farm Bur. chpt. 1996). Roman Catholic. Office: Ky Farm Bur Ins 9201 Bunsen Pkwy Louisville KY 40220-3792

HICKEY, JOHN HEYWARD, lawyer; b. Miami, Fla., Dec. 18, 1954; s. Weyman Park Hickey and Alice Joan (Heyward) Brown. BA magna cum laude, Fla. State U., 1976; JD, Duke U., 1980. Bars: Fla. 1980, U.S. Dist. Ct. (so. dist) Fla. 1980, U.S. Dist. Ct. (mid. dist.) Fla. 1982, U.S. Ct. Appeals (5th cir.) 1982, U.S. Ct. Appeals (11th cir.) 1983, U.S. Supreme Ct. 1985. Trial lawyer Smathers & Thompson, Miami, 1980-85; trial lawyer Hornsby & Whisenand P.A., Miami, 1985—, ptnr., 1988; ptnr. Hickey & Jones, Miami, 1988—; lectr. securities litigation Internat. Assn. Fin. Planners, 1989, 90, Fla. Inst. CPAs, 1990, Flood Ins. Conf., Columbus, Ohio, 1991, Scottsdale, Ariz., 1992, Orlando, Fla., 1993; lectr. admiralty law, Fla. Bar, 1994. Contbg. author: Fla. Bar Jour., 1990. Interviewer of prospective undergrads. Duke U. Alumni Adv. Com., 1984—; arbitrator Miami Marine Arbitration Coun. Mem. ABA (litigation mgmt./econs. com. 1986—, comml. transactions and banking com. 1986—), Fla. Bar (chmn. grievance com. 1986-89, lectr. Bridge the Gap seminars 1984-85, jud. evaluation com. 1985, chmn. 11th cir. fee arbitration com. 1991—, cert. civil trial lawyer 1990, admiralty law com., family law com., lectr. admiralty law 1994), Dade County Bar Assn. (media rels. com. 1982-83, membership com. 1982-83, legal edn. com. 1983-84, cir. ct. com. 1983-84, dir. 1984-86, chmn. young lawyers sect. meetings and programs com. 1985-86, chmn. young lawyers sect. sports com. 1984-85, exec. com. 1985—, chmn. profl. arbitration subcom. 1986—, cert. of merit 1985, 88, 89, 91, 921, 93, bd. dirs. 1990-93, chmn. banking and corp. litigation com. 1990, 91, 92, chmn. civil litigation com. 1992-93, exec. com. 1992-93), Greater Miami C. of C., Coral Gables C. of C., Propellor Club of U.S. (Miami divsn.), Marine Coun. So. Fla., Southeastern Admiralty Law Inst., Maritime Law Assn., Miami Marine Arbitration Coun., Phi Beta Kappa. Office: Hickey & Jones 1401 Brickell Ave Ste 800 Miami FL 33131-3501

HICKEY, JOSEPH MICHAEL, investment banker; b. Greensburgh Pa., June 6, 1940; s. Joseph Michael and Margaret (Nelson) H.; m. Suzanne Klempay, July 2, 1970. BS, Ind. U. Pa., 1963. Sales rep. 3M Co., St. Paul, Minn., 1967-69; account exec. Hornblower & Weeks, Hemphill, Noyes, Cleve., 1970-75; pres. Prescott, Ball & Turben, 1976-88; dist. chmn. Nat. Assn. Security Dealers, 1979-81; mem. mktg. com. SIA, N.Y.C., 1982-86, mem. regional firms com., 1989; chmn. bd. Carnegie Capital Mgmt. Co., Cleve., 1983-86; pres. J.W. Charles Group, 1988-90; chmn. Pierman Golf Co., North Palm Beach, Fla., 1991-92; pres. Greyfriar Capital Corp., North Palm Beach, Fla., bd. vis. U. Dallas Grad. Sch. of Mgmt., 1995—. Capt. U.S. Army, 1963-67. Mem. Kirtland Country Club (Willoughby, Ohio), Loxahatchee Club (Fla.), Castle Pines Golf Club (Castle Rock, Colo.), Lost Tree Club (Fla.).

HICKMAN, CHERYL ANN, health facility administrator, pediatric nurse; b. Charleston, W.Va., May 8, 1950; d. Joseph Francis and Lucille Mae (Thomas) Geueke; m. Reginald Kirk Hickman, Apr. 23, 1977; children: Sarah Marie, Kimberly Ann, Elizabeth Diane. ADN, Prestonsburg (Ky.) C.C., 1974; BSN, Morehead State U., 1993; postgrad., LaSalle U., 1994. RN, Ky.; cert. ACLS, BLS provider, PALS provider and instr., neonatal resuscitation provider and instr. Staff nurse/head nurse med. surg. unit Pikeville (Ky.) Meth. Hosp., 1974-75, head nurse CCU, 1975-78, house supr., asst. DON svcs., 1978-90, unit mgr. pediatrics and level II neonatal ICU, 1990-91, unit mgr. level II neonatal ICU, transport coord., 1991-92, dir. children's svcs., 1992—. Home: 107 Elm St Pikeville KY 41502-1196 Office: Pikeville Meth Hosp US 911 S Bypass Rd Pikeville KY 41501

HICKMAN, ELIZABETH PODESTA, retired counselor, educator; b. Livingston, Ill., Sept. 30, 1922; d. Louis and Della (Martin) Podesta; BE summa cum laude, Eastern Ill. State U.; MA, George Washington U., 1966; postgrad. U. Chgo., 1945, U. Va., 1964-66, (fellow) Northeastern U., 1967-68; EdD (Exxon Found. grantee, Raskob Found. grantee), George Washington U., 1979; m. Franklin Jay Hickman, Mar. 17, 1944 (dec.); children: Virginia Hickman Hellstern, Franklin. Tchr. public schs., Ill., Ohio, Va., Naples, Italy, 1944-64; dir. coll. transfer guidance Marymount Coll. of Va., Arlington, 1964-67, dir. Counseling Center, 1974-81, assoc. dean counseling and residence life, 1981-84; community counselor div. Mass. Employment Security, Newton, 1968-69; tchr. English conversation, Fuchu, Japan, 1969-73; placement dir., career counselor Coll. Great Falls (Mont.), 1973-74; assoc. researcher George Washington U., 1986; lectr. Far East di v. U. Md., Fuchu, 1971-73; spl. adv. Internat. Ranger Camps, Denmark and Switzerland, 1974-81; spl. cons. Internat. Quaker Sch., Wekhoven, Netherlands, 1959-63; mem. steering com. Pres.'s Com. on Employment of Handicapped, 1974-95. Vol., ARC, 1967-78, Family Services, 1954-75, White House Agy. Liaison, 1986—, Kennedy Ctr. Adminstrn., Washington, 1984—. Served with WAVES, 1943-44. Recipient Disting. Alumnus award Eastern Ill. U., 1984. Lic. counselor, Va. Mem. Brent Soc., Rose Soc. Potomac, Ill. Soc., Italian Am. Soc., Marymount Univ. Angels Soc., Women's Com. Nat. Symphony Orch., Washington Opera Guild, Delta Epsilon Sigma, Pi Lambda Theta. Roman Catholic. Home: 4708 38th Pl N Arlington VA 22207-2915

HICKMAN, HUGH VERNON, science educator, researcher; b. Washington, June 3, 1947; s. Jack Wallis Hickman and Mary Cecelia (Regar) McCoy. BSEE, U. South Fla., 1984, PhD, 1989. Entrepreneur, 1969-80; vis. prof. elec. engring. U. South Fla., Tampa, 1989-90; vis. prof. computer sci. Eckerd Coll., St. Petersburg, Fla., 1990-91; prof. physics Hillsborough Community Coll., Tampa, 1991—. Contbr. articles to profl. jours. Mem. AAAS, IEEE, Am. Assn. Physics Tchrs., Am. Phys. Soc., Ye Mystic Krewe of Gasparilla, Phi Kappa Phi. Republican. Roman Catholic. Home: 5010 W Dante Ave Tampa FL 33629-7513 Office: Hillsborough Community Coll PO Box 30030 Tampa FL 33630-3030

HICKMAN, MARGARET CAPELLINI, advertising agency executive; b. Hartford, Conn., Sept. 21, 1949; d. Anthony Serafino Capellini and Mary Magdelan (Budash) Zanardi; m. Richard Lonnie Hickman, Nov. 6, 1982; children: Wilder A., Langdon B. BA, U. Conn., 1971. Mktg. asst. Advo Sys., Inc., Hartford, 1971-72, mktg. analyst, 1972-75; mktg. asst. Cinamon Assocs. Inc., Brookline, Mass., 1975-77, prodn. supr., 1977-81, v.p. prodn., 1981-84, v.p. client svcs., 1984-85; dir. client svcs. Bozell, Jacobs, Kenyon & Eckhardt, Boston, 1985-86, v.p. client svcs. Cinamon Assocs., 1986; ptnr. Hickman & Hickman, Merritt Island, Fla., 1987; prodn. mgr. Direct Mktg. Agy., Stamford, Conn., 1988-90; v.p. prodn. Martin Direct, Glen Allen, Va., 1990-96; v.p. prodn. Martin Agy., Richmond, Va., 1996—. Mem. Direct Mktg. Assn. (past sec., treas., v.p.), Cape Ann Child Devel. Programs (past dir.), Ctrl. Fla. Direct Mktg. Assn. (past mem.), Am. Legion Aux. Democrat. Roman Catholic. Home: 10717 Wellington St Fredericksburg VA 22407-1272

HICKMAN, RICHARD LONNIE, advertising executive; b. Atlanta, Oct. 18, 1950; s. Lonnie C. and Dean (Wilder) H.; m. Margaret Mary Capellini, Nov. 6, 1982; children: Wilder Anthony, Langdon Bond. BA, U. S.C., 1973, MA, 1973. V.p. mktg. Mowbray Pub., Providence, 1977-80; pres. Indianhead Advt., Gloucester, Mass., 1980-87; v.p., dir. prodn. Barry Blau & Ptnrs., Fairfield, Conn., 1987-89; pres. Oxford Direct, Boston, Va., 1990-92; v.p. new bus. NAIM, Fredericksburg, Va., 1993-94, exec. v.p., 1994; v.p. DiMark Va., 1994-95; dir. market devel. Harte-Hanks Direct Mktg., Fredericksburg, 1995—. Author: The Four Color Primer, 1983, The Direct Mail Package from Hell, 1989, Credit Card Retention in a Shark's Feeding Frenzy, 1994; inventor in field. Active Rep. Nat. Com. Sgt. U.S. Army, 1969-71. Mem. VFW, Direct Mktg. Assn., Direct Mktg. Assn. Washington, Internat. Platform Soc., Ednl. Funding Group (chair 1992—), Am. Legion. Republican. Episcopalian. Home and Office: 10717 Wellington St Fredericksburg VA 22407-1272

HICKMAN, TERRIE TAYLOR, administrator; b. Rapid City, S.D., Dec. 2, 1962; d. William Adrian and Carolyn Gene (Habben) T. BS, Okla. State U., 1985; MEd, Cen. State U., 1988. Mktg. dir. Tealridge Manor, Edmond, Okla., 1989-90; owner Oxford Pointe Jazzercize, Edmond, Okla., 1989-90; adminstr. Retirement Inn at Quail Ridge, Oklahoma City, Okla., 1991-92, Country Club Square, Edmond, 1992-93; planner Areawide Aging Agency, Oklahoma City, 1992—; co-chmn. Okla. Bus. and Aging Leadership Coalition, newsletter Networker editor; presenter in field; adv. coun. sr. companion planning com. State of Okla. Conf. on Aging. Co-editor Sage Age; contbr. articles to various pubs. Co-chmn. media hosting party Olympic Festival, Norman, Okla., 1989; co-coord. jazzercize for hope Benefit for Hope Ctr., Edmond, The McGruff Safe House Program, Stillwater, Okla.; com. chmn. Coalition for Elderly Concerns, Oklahoma City; vol. Stillwater Domestic Violence Shelter, Payne County Employment Svcs., Stillwater; mem. renter's adv. bd. Okla. State U. Student Senate. Mem. Women in Bus., Edmond Area C. of C., Okla. Bus. and Aging Leadership Coalition, Phi Kappa Delta, Alpha Gamma Delta, Sigma Phi Omega. Republican. Lutheran.

HICKOX, GARY RANDOLPH, pulp and paper engineer; b. Waycross, Ga., Oct. 16, 1952; s. Everett Lloyd and Alma (Douglas) H. BCE with high honors, So. Tech. Inst., Marietta, Ga., 1975. Registered profl. engr., Ga., Ala., N.Mex., Tex., Colo., Miss., La. Engr. technologist Internat. Paper Co., Mobile, Ala., 1975-79, project engr., 1979-81, design engr., 1981-85, dept. engr., 1985-89, sr. dept. engr., 1989-93, acting mgr. design-paper group, 1993, 94, sr. engring. Corp. Tech. Ctr., 1994, process software devel. engr., 1995; sr. engr. paper group corp. tech. Internat. Paper Co., Mobile, 1996—. Mem. ASCE, TAPPI (project officer finishing div.-winding 1989-90, sec. 1990-91, vice chmn. 1991—, tech. cons. to instrn. videos and manuals 1991), Ducks Unltd., Rocky Mountain Elk Found., Safari Club Internat., NRA (life), Colo. Bowhunters Assn. (life), United Bowhunters N.Mex. (life), U.S. Shooter Devel. Fund (com. 1984, inner cir.), Tau Alpha Pi.

HICKS, C. THOMAS, III, lawyer; b. N.Y.C., Sept. 14, 1945; s. Charles Thomas and Jeane (Merritt) H.; m. Susan Massie, Dec. 30, 1967; children: Melissa, Merritt. BSCE, Va. Tech. U., 1967; JD, U. Ga., 1970; LLM in Tax, Georgetown U., 1975. Bar: Ga. 1970, Va. 1972, D.C. 1981. Assoc. Booth, Prichard & Dudley, Fairfax, Va., 1975-78; ptnr. Wickwire, Gavin & Gibbs, P.C., Vienna, Va., 1978-83, Shaw, Pittman, Potts & Trowbridge, Washington, 1983—. Judge advocate USMC, Washington, 1971-75; co-founder, dir. No. Va. Transp. Alliance, McLean, Va., 1987, gen. counsel, 1987—. Mem. Va. Bar Assn. (mem. bus. law coun.), Va. State Bar (bus. law sec. bd. governors, sec.), Fairfax Bar Assn., Nat. Assn. Bond Counsel, Va. Assn. Comml. Real Estate (pres. 1991—, co-founder, dir.), NAIOP (pres., dir. Va. chpt. 1990), Greater Washington Bd. Trade, Fairfax County C. of C. Home: 8110 Georgetown Pike Mc Lean VA 22102-1415 Office: Shaw Pittman Potts & Trowbridge 1501 Farm Credit Dr Ste 4400 Mc Lean VA 22102-5004

HICKS, CLAUDE ALVIS, retired children's home administrator; b. Hockley County, Tex., Aug. 2, 1932; s. Alvis L. and Ethyl (Basham) H.; m. Jenny Lynn Cargile, Feb. 18, 1956. BS, Hardin-Simmons U., 1955, MEd, 1964. Lic. child care adminstr. Dir. promotion So. Bapt. Radio & TV Communications, Ft. Worth, 1965-66; dir. student aid and placement Hardin-Simmons U., Abilene, Tex., 1957-65; pres., chief exec. officer Hendrick Home for Children, Abilene, 1966-94; ret., 1994; bd. dirs. NCNB Bank Adv. Bd., Abilene. Past dist. gov. Rotary Internat. Dist. 579, Abilene. awded Disting. Citizen of Abilene, Dyess AFB Mil. Affairs Com., 1978, Disting. Alumni, Hardin-Simmons U., 1980. Mem. Tex. Assn. Execs. of Homes for Children, Nat. Assn. of Homes for Children. Baptist.

HICKS, DAVID LANE, computer systems analyst; b. Harlingen, Tex., Sept. 5, 1962; s. Jerry Lane and Yvonne Lane (Shaw) H. BS in Computer Sci., Angelo State U., San Angelo, Tex., 1984; MCS, Tex. A&M U., 1985, PhD, 1993. Computer operator Angelo State U., 1982-84; micro computer cons. several area businesses, San Angelo, 1983-84; programmer, grad. asst. Tex. A&M U., College Station, 1984-86, systems analyst Computer Svc. Ctr., 1986-88, worksta. specialist Super Computer Ctr., 1988-89, rsch. assoc. HyperMedia Rsch. Lab., 1989-93; sys. analyst Computing and Info. Svcs. Ctr., College Station, 1993-95; guest rschr. GMD-IPSI, Darmstadt, Germany, 1995—; presenter at workshops and corp. meetings. Author tech. reports and rsch. papers. Dancer in spl. event Brazos Valley Symphony Orch., Tex. A&M U., 1992. Omar E. Hunter scholar, 1983-84, Carr Acad. scholar, 1982-84, Shell Oil Co. doctoral fellow, 1991-92. Mem. ACM (Spl. Interest Group on Hypertext; v.p. Angelo State U. chpt. 1983-84), Alpha Chi, Epsilon Delta Pi (pres. Angelo State U. chpt. 1983-84), Phi Kappa Phi. Home: 10004 Preston Vineyard Dr Frisco TX 75034-8070 Office: Tex A&M U Computer Sci Dept HyperMedia Rsch Lab College Station TX 77843

HICKS, HAROLD EUGENE, chemical engineer; b. Mpls., Jan. 20, 1919; s. Julius and Della (Beebe) H.; m. Ruth Esther Nelson, Oct. 4, 1941 (dec. Mar. 1989); children: Barbara H. Young, Charlotte H. Silvia, David H., Douglas E.; m. Virginia C. Hobson, Mar. 31, 1990. B Chem. Engring., U. Minn., 1941; postgrad., U. Del., 1946-47. Chemist Hercules Powder Co., Wilmington, Del., 1941, rsch. chemist, 1941, 46-50; prodn. supr. Hercules Powder Co., Hattiesburg, Miss., 1950-64; plant mgr. Hercules Powder Co., Chicopee, Mass., 1964-66; plant mgr. Hercules Inc., Franklin, Va., 1966-68, Brunswick, Ga., 1968-76, Louisiana, Mo., 1978-80; tech. advisor Dawood-Hercules, Lahore, Pakistan, 1976-78; vol. exec. Internat. Exec. Svc. Corp., 1986-94. Mem. county cos. Glynn County; dir. St. Mark's Towers. Maj. U.S. Army, 1941-46, ETO; dir., Pine Belt Savings & Loan Assn, Hattiesburg, Miss., 1958-64, dir., 1st Nat. Bank of Brunswick, Ga., 1969-76, pres., The Book Shop, Inc., Brunswick, Ga., 1991—. Mem. AIChE (emeritus), Am. Chem. Soc. (emeritus), Rotary. Methodist. Home: 133 Shore Rush Dr Saint Simons GA 31522

HICKS, HERALINE ELAINE, environmental health scientist, educator; b. Beaufort, S.C., Sept. 27, 1951; d. Heral and Ophelia Lillie (Albergottie) H. BA, Ohio Wesleyan U., 1973; MS, Atlanta U., 1978, PhD, 1980; postgrad., U. N.C., 1980-84. Rsch. assoc. Chapel Hill Dental Rsch. Ctr. U. N.C., 1980-81; NIH postdoctoral fellow Chapel Hill Dental Rsch. Ctr. Chapel Hill Dental Rsch. Ctr. and Dept. Surgery, 1982-84; guest scientist Naval Med. Rsch. Inst., Bethesda, Md., 1985-87; asst. prof. Chapel Hill Sch. Dentistry U. N.C., 1985-88; prof., dir. electron microscopy Morris Brown Coll., Atlanta, 1988-90; sr. environ. health scientist, dir. Cts. for Disease Control and Prevention/Agy. for Toxic Substances and Disease Registry, Atlanta, 1990—; program dir. Gt. Lakes Human Health Effects Rsch. Program, Agy. for Toxic Substances and Disease Registry; mem. health profls. task force adv. bd. Internat. Joint Commn., Washington, 1995—. Author: (chpt.) Development and Diseases of Cartilage and Bone Matrix, 1987, Birth Defects and Reproductive Disorders, 1993; contbr. articles to profl. jours. Predoctoral traineeship NIH, 1977-79, Barnett F. Smith award for outstanding achievement Atlanta U., 1978; Acad. scholar Ohio Wesleyan U., 1969-73, Josiah Macy Jr. scholar Woods Hole Marine Biol. Lab., 1979, Tuition scholar Atlanta U., 1979-80; postdoctoral fellow NIH, 1982-84, Notable Alumnus of Clark U., 1995; named one of Outstanding Young Women of Am., 1980. Mem. Am. Soc. for Cell Biology (Young Investigator fellowship 1990), Teratology (Young Investigator fellowship 1987), Microscopy Soc. Am., Biology Honor Soc., Beta Kappa Chi. Presbyterian. Office: Ctrs for Disease Control and Prevention Mail Stop E29 1600 Clifton Rd NE Atlanta GA 30333

HICKS, JUDITH M., secondary education educator; b. Henderson, Ky, Mar. 4, 1941; d. Richard Weir and Genevieve Evelyn (LeMaster) Martin; m. Otis Allen Hicks, Dec. 28, 1963; children: Scott Allen, Jennifer Lynn, Eric Christopher. BS, Western Ky. U., 1963, MS, 1986. Tchr. Owensboro (Ky.) Ind., 1963-65; tchr. Owensboro Cath. H.S., 1965-66, 71—, chair English dept., 1990-96; tchr. Daviess County Schs., Owensboro, 1967-68. Mem. Nat. Coun. Tchrs. Eng., Assn. Supervision Curriculum Devel. Office: Owensboro Cath High Sch 1524 W Parrish Ave Owensboro KY 42301

HICKS, ROBIN KLINE, marketing research professional; b. Harrisonburg, Va., Dec. 22, 1959. Grad., Art Instrn. Schs., Mpls., 1979; BS in Math., James Madison U., 1982; postgrad., Burke Inst., Cin. Asst. v.p. Dominion Bankshares Corp., Roanoke, Va., 1982-93; pres. R.K. Hicks Mktg. Rsch. & Bus. Planning, Elkton, Va., 1993—. Active Flint Hill Bapt. Ch., Moneta, Va., Valley Christian Ctr., Roanoke, Mount Olivet United Ch. of Christ, Elkton, Va. Mem. Rutherford Inst. Home and Office: RR 2 Box 338B Elkton VA 22827-9643

HIERS, MARY A., museum director. Dir. Fernbank Science Ctr., Atlanta, Ga. Office: Fernbank Science Center 156 Heaton Park Dr NE Atlanta GA 30307-1318

HIETT, CHANLEY JOSEPH, publishing executive; b. Cedartown, Ga., Apr. 12, 1947; s. James William and Clara Maynell (Littlefield) H.; m. Patsy Ann Tong, Oct. 22, 1970; children: Jeffrey Joseph, Michael Ethan, Elizabeth Ann. BBA, Ga. State U., 1969. Mgr. advt. Houston Home Jour., Perry, Ga., 1971-72, asst. editor, 1972-78; editor South Fulton Recorder, Fairburn, Ga., 1978-80; Sunday editor Clayton News-Daily, Jonesboro, Ga., 1980-81, mng. editor, 1981-84, exec. editor, 1984-86, interim pub., 1989-91; pub. Henry Herald, McDonough, Ga., 1986—. Dir. so. met. chpt. ARC, Jonesboro, 1986-88; dir. Henry commn. Bicentennial of U.S. Constn., McDonough, 1988-89; chmn. adv. com. Odyssey Counseling Ctr. Henry County, McDonough, 1988—; bd. dirs. Henry Arts Alliance, 1991—, sec., 1991-94; bd. dirs. Henry Prevention Alliance, 1991. Recipient Media award Ga. Hosp. Assn., 1976, Sharecropper award Ga. Farm Bur., 1989, Merit award Ga. Soil and Water Conservation Soc., 1991; co-recipient Ga. Earth Team of Yr. award Soil Conservation Svc., 1990. Mem. Ga. Press Assn. (chmn. editl. seminar 1983, advt. com. 1989, circulation com. 1991, chmn. circulation com. 1993, Pres.'s award), Ky. Press Assn. (judge newspaper contest 1991), Rotary (chmn. pub. rels. 1990-93), Henry C. of C. (bd. dirs. 1988-89, accreditation com. 1988-89). Mem. Ch. of Christ. Office: Henry Herald 32 Macon St Mc Donough GA 30253-3223

HIGBIE, PATRICIA D., assistant principal; m. William Charles Higbie, Aug. 10, 1969; children: Linda, Laura, Leslie, Lisa. BA, CUNY, N.Y.C.; MEd, U. N.C., Charlotte, 1986. Tchr. Gaston County Schs., Gastonia, N.C., asst. prin., dir. summer enrichment program, 1993-95; tchr. Charlotte-Mecklenburg Schs. Recipient Fulbright-Hayes award U.S. Govt.; Gaston County Schs. mini-grantee, 1995. Mem. ASCD, AAUW, N.C. Assn. Edn. Home: 1993 Hickory Cove Ln Denver NC 28037

HIGBY, EDWARD JULIAN, safety engineer; b. Milw., June 9, 1939; s. Richard L. Higby and Julie Ann (Bruins) O'Kelly: m. Frances Ann Knoodle, 1959 (div. 1962); 1 child, Melinda Ann Mozader. BS in Criminal Justice, Southwestern U., Tucson, 1984. Tactical officer Miami Police Dept., Fla., 1967-68; intelligence officer Fla. Div. Beverages, 1968-72; licensing coord. Lums Restaurant Corp., Miami, 1972-73; legal asst. Walt Disney World, Lake Buena Vista, Fla., 1973-78; loss control cons. R.P. Hewitt & Assocs., Orlando, Fla., 1978-79; safety coord. City of Lakeland, Fla., 1979-94. Author: Safety Guide for Health Care, 1979. Councilman City of Bay Lake, 1974-76, mayor, 1975-76; active Fla. League of Cities, 1974-76, Tri-County League of Cities, 1974-76, Orange County Criminal Justice Coun., 1974-78, Ctrl. Fla. Safety Coun., 1978-79; bd. dirs. Greater Lakeland chpt. ARC, 1980-86, chmn. bd. dirs., 1983-84, 85-86, chmn. health svcs., 1980-86; mem. budget com. United Way Ctrl. Fla., 1983-85; bd. dirs. Tampa Area Safety Coun., 1983-92, pres. 1990-91; bd. dirs. Imperial Traffic Safety Coun., 1983-89; mem. Polk County Disaster Coordination com., bd. dirs., 1984-92; Local Emergency Planning com., 1987-92, 94—; bd. dirs. Employers Health Care Group Polk County, 1987-89, Parent Resources and Info. on Drug Edn., 1989-92; bd. dirs. ARC Polk County chpt., 1990-92, 94-96, coord. Mass Care, 1994-95, chmn. Health and Safety, 1994-95, chmn. Risk Mgmt., 1995-96; active ARC Disaster Svcs. Human Resources Sys., 1994—; mem. Fla. Adv. Com. Arson Prevention, Local Emergency Planning Com., State of Fla., 1987-92, 94—, Fla. Disaster Mortuary Team, 1995—. With U.S. Army, 1963-64. Named Vol. of Yr., Greater Lakeland chpt. ARC, 1983-84. Mem. World Safety Org., Fla. Sheriffs Assn. (hon. life), Internat. Assn. Identification (life, Fla. divsn., Russian divsn.), NRA (life), Nat. Found. Mortuary Care, Automatic Fire Alarm Assn., Disaster Emergency Response Assn. (life), U. Fla. Nat. Alumni Assn. (life), Fla. Pub. Health Assn., Fla. Fedn. Safety, Am. Soc. Safety Engrs. (mem. regional oper. com. 1983-85, 88-90, profl. devel. conf. com. 1983, 85, chpt. bd. dirs. 1983-87, chpt. pres. 1984-85, v.p. profl. devel. region VIII 1988-90, Safety Profl. of Yr. 1984-85, Albert G. Mowson award 1995-96), Heartland Safety Soc. (life, pres. 1982-83, 94-95), Fla. Citrus Safety Assn. (pres. 1981-83), Nat. Fire Protection Assn., Am. Indsl. Hygiene Assn. (Fla. chpt.), Fire Marshals Assn. N.Am., Soc. Fire Protection Engrs. (bd. dirs. Fla chpt. 1994—), So. Health Assn., Fla. Affiliation of Ins. Safety Reps., Internat. Critical Incident Stress Found., Critical Incident Stress Debriefers Fla., Nat. Assn. Search and Rescue, Fla. Funeral Dirs. Assn., Fla. Emergency Preparedness Assn., Fla. Assn. Code Enforcement, Internat. Assn. Arson Investigators, Fla. Cracker Cattle Assn. (life), Harley Owners Group (life), Am. Motocycle Assn. (life). Republican. Club: Lakeland Rifle and Pistol. Avocations: hunting, fishing.

HIGDON, LINDA HAMPTON, congressional staff; b. Athens, Tenn., Mar. 14, 1951; d. Homer G. and Lula Sue (Stiles) Hampton; m. Donald Wayne Higdon, Dec. 20, 1973. BA, Tenn. Wesleyan Coll., Athens, 1973; MPA, U. Tenn., 1985. Cert. Am. Soc. Pub. Adminstrs., Knoxville, Tenn. Tchr. McMinn Co. Schs., Etowah, Tenn., 1973-75; dist. staff asst. U.S. Rep. John Duncan Jr., Athens, Tenn., 1975—; adjunct instr. Tenn. Wesleyan Coll., Athens, 1985-86. Former pres., publicity chmn., vice chmn., McMinn Co. Young Rep., Athens, Tenn.; former pres. McMinn Co. Women, Athens, Tenn., 1990-92. Named Miss Tenn. Young Rep. State Yr-Fed, Nashville, 1972; recipient Lincoln award McMinn Co. Young Rep. Club, Athens, Tenn., 1992. Mem. ASPA. Republican. Methodist. Home: Kirkwood Est Englewood TN 37327 Office: US Rep John Duncan Jr 6 W Madison Ave Athens TN 37303-4252

HIGDON, SHIRLEY A., medical/surgical nurse; b. El Paso, Tex., Feb. 28, 1953; d. Raymond J. and Beatrice H. Tarang; 1 child, Adam D. Higdon. Diploma, Tex. Ea. Sch. Nursing, Tyler, 1982; AS in Nursing, Tyler Jr. Coll., 1981; BS, U. Tex., Tyler, 1990. Sch. nurse Tyler Ind. Sch. Dist.; staff nurse Tyler Square Ambulatory Ctr.; staff and charge nurse Mother Frances Hosp., Tyler; utilization rev./admissions nurse Med. City Hosp., Dallas. Mem. ANA, Tex. Nurses Assn. (program chair), Sigma Theta Tau.

HIGGINBOTHAM, PATRICK ERROL, federal judge; b. Ala., Dec. 16, 1938. Student, U. Ala., 1956, Arlington State Coll., 1957, North Tex. State U., 1958, U. Tex., 1958; B.A., U. Ala., 1960, LL.B., 1961; LLD (hon.), So. Meth. U., 1989. Bar: Ala. 1961, Tex. 1962, U.S. Supreme Ct. 1962. Assoc. to ptnr. Coke & Coke, Dallas, 1964-75; judge U.S. Dist. Ct. (no. dist.) Tex., Dallas, 1976-82, U.S. Ct. Appeals (5th cir.), Dallas, 1982—; adj. prof. So. Meth. U. Law Sch., 1971—, adj. prof. constl. law, 1981—; conferee Am. Assembly, 1975, Pound Conf., 1976; bd. suprs. Inst. Civil Justice Rand. Contbr. articles, revs. to profl. publs.; note editor: Ala. Law Rev., 1960-61. With USAF, 1961-64, JAG. Named Outstanding Alumnus U. Tex., Arlington, 1978, One of Nation's 100 Most Powerful Persons for the 80's Next Mag.; recipient Dan Meador award U. Ala. Fellow Am. Bar Found.; mem. ABA (chmn. com. to compile fed. jury charges antitrust sect., mem. coun. antitrust sect., bd. editors Jour. chair appellate judges conf. 1989—), Dallas Bar Assn. (dir., chmn. cons. legal aid civic affairs), Dallas Bar Found. (bd. dirs.), Am. Law Inst., S.W. Legal Found., am. Judicature Soc. (bd. dirs., trustee), Nat. Jud. Coun. State and Fed. Cts., Dallas Inn of Ct. (pres. pres. 1988-89, 96—, chair adv. com. on civil rules jud. conf. U.S. 1993—), Farrah Law Soc., Order of Coif (hon.), Bench and Bar, Omicron Delta Kappa. Office: US Ct Appeals 13E1 US Courthouse 1100 Commerce St Dallas TX 75242-1027

HIGGINBOTHAM, PRIEUR JAY, city official, writer; b. Pascagoula, Miss., July 16, 1937; s. Prieur Jay and Vivian Inez (Perez) H.; m. Alice Louisa Martin, June 27, 1970; children: Jeanne-Felicie, Denis Prieur, Robert Findlay. BA, U. Miss.; postgrad. Am. U., CCNY. Asst. clk. Miss. Ho. of Reps., Jackson, 1955-58; tchr. Mobile County Pub. Schs., Ala., 1962-73; head local history Mobile Pub. Libr., 1973-83; dir. Mobile Mcpl. Archives, 1983—. Author: Old Mobile, 1977 (ALA prize 1978); Fast Train Russia, 1983; 13 other books, articles; contbg. editor The Citizen Diplomat, Gainesville, Fla., 1985—; adv. editor, contbr. Encyclopedia Britannica, 1989—; editl. dir. Gulf Coast Hist. Rev., 1984—; book reviewer Library Jour., N.Y.C., 1985—; bd. dirs. Ala. Records Commn., 1984—. Pres. Mobile Soc. for Soviet-Am. Understanding, 1982-88; chmn. Mobile Com. on Fine Arts, 1985—, Soc. Mobile-Rostov-on-Don, 1988-94; exec. bd. Mobile Internat. Festival, 1984-86, Neighborhood Improvement Coun., 1974-79; pres. Soc. Mobile-La Habana, 1993—; chmn. Mobile Tricentennial Commn., 1994—; pres. Friends of Freedom, 1995—. Served with USAR, 1956-62. Recipient Gen. L. Kemper Williams award La. Hist. Assn., 1977, award of Merit, Miss. Hist. Soc., 1979, Gilbert Chinard prize, Franco-Am. Soc., Duke U., 1979, Elisabeth Gould award Mobile Hist. Devel. Commn., 1981. Mem. Soc. Am. Archivists, Smithsonian Soc., Nat. Geog. Soc., Authors League, Am. Com. on East-West Accord, Sister Cities Internat. Democrat. Methodist. Avocations: tennis; painting; music. Home: 60 N Monterey St Mobile AL 36604-1348 Office: Mobile Mcpl Archives 457 Church St Mobile AL 36602-2304

HIGGINS, ROBERT HALL, chemistry educator; b. Warren, Ohio, Dec. 9, 1942; s. Ralph Odell and Kathryn Georgia (Hall) H.; m. Janice Lee Boyd, July 26, 1965 (div. Aug. 1977); m. Chae Yong Kim, Dec. 29, 1982 (div. Sept. 1990); children: Jamie Lynn, Chi Ae Lee, John David, Yong Hyun Lee. BS, Ohio U., 1965, MS, 1967; PhD, U. Nebr., 1971. Instr. Doane Coll., Crete, Nebr., 1968-70; rsch. assoc. U. Nebr., Lincoln, 1971-72; rsch. chemist Dorsey Labs., Lincoln, 1972-74; rsch. assoc. U. Colo., Boulder, 1974-75; asst. prof. chemistry Fayetteville (N.C.) State U., 1976-82, assoc. prof., 1982-95, prof., 1995—. Contbr. articles to profl. jours. Grantee NIH, 1984, 1989, 94. Office: Fayetteville State U 1200 Murchison Rd Fayetteville NC 28301-4298

HIGGINSON, JERRY ALDEN, JR., bank executive; b. Mt. Vernon, Ill., July 21, 1957; s. Jerry Alden Sr. and Beverly Joyce (York) H.; m. Leah Jane Murray, June 11, 1983; children: Sara Elisabeth, Jon Patrick Alden. BA, Graceland Coll., Lamoni, Iowa, 1979; postgrad., So. Ill. U., 1979; M in Fin. and Banking, So. Meth. U., 1988. Trust officer, asst. cashier Salem (Ill.) Nat. Bank, 1979-80; trust officer MidAm. Bank and Trust, Carbondale, Ill., 1980-82; v.p., city mgr. NationsBank Tex., San Antonio, 1982—; instr. Am. Inst. Banking, San Antonio, 1984—; mem. Estate Planners Coun., San Antonio, 1982—; mem. faculty Palo Alto Community Coll., 1989-90. Pres. San Antonio Symphony Soc., 1985-86; treas., pres. San Antonio Clean and Beautiful Com., 1986-87, pres. bd. dirs., 1987-89; pres. bd. trustees San Antonio Area Found., 1986-90; bd. dirs. Beautify San Antonio, 1987—, pres., 1988-89; bd. dirs. Keep Tex. Beautiful, Inc.; bd. dirs. Mental Health Assn. Tex., 1989-90, chmn., 1991—, treas., 1992—, v.p., bd. dirs. , treas. 1992—, past pres.; pres. Keep San Antonio Beautiful Inc., 1986-89; mem. bd. vol. Alamo Area Coun. Boy Scouts Am., 1990; bd. dirs. San Antonio Jr. Achievement, 1990, San Antonio Botanical Soc., 1992—, Planned Giving Coun. San Antonio, 1993—, treas., 1993—, Mission Rd. Devel. Ctr.; chmn. Koehler Found., 1991—; mem. adv. bd. Salvation Army, San Antonio, bd. dirs.; mem. devel. bd. Our Lady of Pillar, 1992—. Mem. Symphony Soc. San Antonio, San Antonio Baroque Music Soc., San Antonio Conservation Soc., San Antonio Bot. Soc. (bd. dirs. 1992—), Knife and Fork Club San Antonio (bd. dirs. 1990-91, v.p. 1991-92, pres. 1992—), The Witte Mus. (bd. 1994—), The Salvation Army (adv. bd. 1994—). Republican. Mem. Reorganized Ch. Jesus Christ of Latter-day Saints.

HIGGS, DAVID WAYNE, state agency administrator; b. Chgo., Dec. 14, 1962; s. Bobby Gene and Judy Marie (Connelly) H.; m. Janet F. Moore, May 28, 1988; 1 child, Michael David. BS, Murray State U., 1985; grad., Ky. Dept. Corrections Basic Acad., 1994. Sta. mgr. Thomas Broadcast Engring., Central City, Ky., 1985-86; ops. mgr. Rough River Broadcasting, Leitchfield, Ky., 1986-87; city adminstr., city clk. City of Central City, Ky., 1987-94; fiscal mgr. Dept. Corrections, Commonwealth of Ky., Central City, 1994—; mem. Ky. Indsl. Devel. Coun. Pres. Central City Mainstreet, 1990-92; chmn. Central City Christmas Parade, Inc., 1988—; mem. Muhlenberg County 911 Bd., Greenville, Ky., 1991—; sec.-treas. Muhlenberg County Zoning Commn., Greenville, 1991—, Central City Bd. of Zoning Adjustments, 1991—; bd. dirs. Pennrile Area Devel. Dist., 1988—, Muhlenberg County Big Bros./Big Sisters Inc.; asst. scoutmaster Central City troop Boy Scouts Am.; active Central City Tourism Commn., 1991-94. Mem. Ky. City Mgrs. Assn., Ky. Mcpl. Clks. Assn., Central City-Muhlenberg C. of C. (pres. 1991), Alpha Epsilon Rho. Democrat. Baptist. Home: 1104 Perkins St Central City KY 42330-2161 Office: Commonwealth of Ky Green River Correc Complex 1200 River Rd Central City KY 42330-3008

HIGGS, ELIZABETH WAYNE, anthropology educator; b. Evansville, Ind., Aug. 20, 1953; d. Emmett Wayne and Frieda Louise (Lee) H. BA, Harding U., 1974; MEd, Miss. State U., 1976; MA, U. Ga., 1979; PhD, U. Fla., 1990. Tchg. asst. in anthropology U. Fla., Gainesville, 1981, rsch. asst. Latin Am. Studies Ctr., 1981-82; Fulbright scholar U.S. Info. Agy., Washington, 1983-84; adj. faculty mem. in social scis. U. Evansville, Ind., 1986; lectr. in sociology U. Ala., Huntsville, 1990-91; mem. adv. bd. Cultural Arts Coalition, Gainesville, 1991-94; hist./folk arts coord. Fla. Dept. of State, White Springs, 1991-94; adj. instr. in anthropology U. North Fla., Jacksonville, 1993-94; temp. asst. prof. anthropology Valdosta (Ga.) State U., 1994—. Editor Fla. Jour. of Anthropology, 1980-81; contbr. articles, revs. to profl. jours. Recipient Appreciation award for outstanding support of performing, lit. and visual arts in African Am. cmty. Cultural Arts Gainesville, 1993, 94; Humanities scholar Fla. Humanities Coun., 1993, Ga. Humanities Coun., 1996. Mem. Am. Anthropol. Assn., L.Am. Studies Assn., So. Anthropol. Soc. (judge grad. student papers 1994-95), Assn. for Feminist Anthropologists, Soc. for Applied Anthropology. Home: 1710 Azalea Dr Valdosta GA 31602 Office: Valdosta State U Sociology/Anthropology Dept 1500 N Patterson St Valdosta GA 31602-3847

HIGGS, J. JEFFREY, retired physician and medical director; b. Jersey City, Nov. 23, 1919; s. Joseph J. and Margaret S. (Edmonds) H.; m. Julia Bertha Smith, Apr. 9, 1944 (div. 1977); children: Gregory David, Maggie Higgs Blackburn; m. Geraldine Agnes Sherman, Dec. 28, 1978. BA, Lincoln (Pa.) U., 1939; MD, Howard U., 1943. Rotating intern Harlem Hosp., N.Y.C., 1943-44; resident in internal medicine Provident Hosp., Balt., 1944-45; staff physician Tewksbury (Mass.) State Hosp., 1945-46; mcpl. physician St. Croix, Christiansted, V.I., 1946-48; attending family practice physician Huntington (N.Y.) Hosp., 1948-68, emergency physician, 1968-75; staff physician Union Carbide Corp., Texas City, Tex., 1978-84, med. dir., 1984-90; counselor N.Y. State chpt. Am. Coll. Emergency Physicians, 1960s and 70s; bd. dirs. Alcoholism Referral project U. Tex. Med. Br., Galveston, 1986. Past pres. local chpt. NAACP, Huntington, 1950s; chmn. Huntington Housing Authority, 1960s; bd. dirs. Suffolk County br. ARC, 1960s, other civic activities. Fellow Am. Coll. Occupational and Environ. Medicine; mem. Galveston County Med. Soc. (life). Home: 18647 Cape Charles Ln Houston TX 77058-4204

HIGH, MELVIN C., police chief. Chief Norfolk (Va.) Police Dept. Office: Office of the Police Chief 206 Monticello Ave Norfolk VA 23510-2301

HIGH, TIMOTHY GRIFFIN, artist, educator, writer; b. Memphis, Tenn., Mar. 10, 1949; s. Warren Barrett and Jo Ellen (Wise) H.; m. Cynthia Spikes, Aug. 10, 1973. BFA, Tex. Tech U., 1973, MA, 1975; MFA, U. Wis., 1976. Assoc. prof. U. Tex., Austin, 1976—; visual artist drawings, serigraphs, papermaking, monoprints, monotypes, installation sculpture. Numerous one-man shows including Amarillo (Tex.) Art Ctr., 1993; represented in permanent collections including Art Inst. Chgo., Bklyn. Mus., Mus. Fine Art, Boston, Met. Mus. Art, N.Y.C., Fogg Mus., Cambridge, Mass., Mus. Fine Art, Houston. Travel fellow Ford Found., Peruvian Andes, 1978; individual artist fellow Nat. Endowment Arts, 1989. Mem. So. Graphics Coun. (conf. coord. 1988-89), Austin Christian Arts Fellowship (pres. 1994-96), Coll. Art Assn., Nat. Assn. Scholars (panelist conv. 1993), Tex. Fine Arts Assn., Austin Visual Artists Assn. Address: care/Terra Rosa Studio 2308 Lawnmont Ave Austin TX 78756-1915 Office: Univ of Tex Austin Dept Art & Art History Austin TX 78712

HIGHLAND, MARTHA ELLEN, retired education educator, consultant; b. Lexington, Ky., June 3, 1934; d. William Thomas and Lyda Bruce (Wilson) H.; foster children: Barbara O. Noe, Teresa O. McKenzie, Debby O. Hodges, Joseph Owens. AA, Cumberland Jr. Coll., 1955; BA in Edn., U. Ky., 1958; MA in Edn., U. Louisville, 1981. Cert. tchr., Ky. Tchr. Jefferson County Bd. Edn., Louisville, 1958-59, Ft. Knox (Ky.) Dependent Schs., 1959-65; tchr. Louisville City Schs., 1965-66, reading specialist, 1966-75; reading specialist Jefferson County Sch. System, Louisville, 1975-89, remedial specialist in reading and math., 1989-91; ret., 1991; substitute tchr., vol. Jefferson County Bd. Edn., Louisville, 1991—; faculty rep. Jefferson County Tchrs. Assn., 1981-91. Nominated Disney Tchr. of Yr., 1989. Mem. ASCD, Am. Bus. Women's Assn. (sec. 1989-92, v.p. 1988-89, 92-93, Woman of Yr. 1990). Home: 126 Stevenson Ave Louisville KY 40206-3125

HIGHSMITH, ANNA BIZZELL, executive secretary; b. Richmond, Va., May 31, 1947; d. John Lee and Jacquelyn Frances (Miller) Bizzell; m. Jack Francis Starkey, Jan. 25, 1970 (div. Apr. 1972); 1 child, Mary Cathereine; m. Lemuel Martin Highsmith, May 25, 1974; 1 child, Lemuel Tayloe. Student, N. Fla. Jr. Coll., 1965-66, Armstrong State Coll., 1966-71. Sec. Seaboard Coastline RR, Savannah, Ga., 1966-76; sec., bookkeeper Highsmith Enterprises, Savannah, 1976—; Centennial Olympic vol. Yachting-Sports Info. Desk, Olympic Village, Savannah, Ga., 1996. Pres., chmn. of bd. Ballet South, Inc., Savannah, 1982-89, bd. dirs., advisor to pres., 1989—. Mem. Nat. Assn. Women in Constrn. (bd. dirs. 1982-87, 90-92, v.p. 1987-88, pres. 1989-90, 90-91, 94-95), Rinky Dink Sailing Club (sec., editor newsletter 1990-93, liaison 1989-93, prin. race officer 1993, cert. club race officer 1994), Geechee Sailing Club (editor newsletter 1990-91, sec. 1993), Savannah Yacht Club.. Republican. Episcopalian. Home: 519-A Whitfield Ave Savannah GA 31406-8207 Office: Highsmith Enterprises 615 Stiles Ave Savannah GA 31401-5322

HIGHSMITH, JASPER HABERSHAM, sales executive; b. Waycross, Ga., Dec. 3, 1940; s. Jasper H. and Linda (Weatherly) H.; m. Constance Orr Fitzgibbons, Aug. 26, 1963 (div. 1969); m. Linda Inez Diaz, Aug. 25, 1979; children: Richard, Eric, Jason. BBA, U. Ga., 1963. Engring. assoc. Western Electric Co., Atlanta, 1964-66; engr. No. Electric Co., Montreal, Que., Can., 1966-68, Gen. Telephone Co., Tampa, Fla., 1969-74; staff engr. No. Telecom, Inc., Tampa, 1974-76, regional mgr., 1977-85, dir. sales, 1986-94; v.p. eastern ops. Goldfield Telecom Inc., Tampa, 1994—. Mem. IEEE, U.S. Telephone Assn., Ind. Telephone Pioneers Assn. (mem. adv. coun. mfrs. chpt. 1987-88), Nat. Telephone Coop. Assn., Telephone Assns. of Ga., Fla., N.C., S.C., Tenn., and Ala., Treasure City Jaycees (v.p. 1969, pres. 1971), Orgn. for the Protection and Advancement of Small Telephone Cos., Phi Delta Theta. Methodist. Home: 13714 Halliford Dr Tampa FL 33624-6903 Office: Goldfield Telecom Inc 8902 N Dale Mabry Hwy Ste 117 Tampa FL 33614-1579

HIGHSMITH, SHELBY, federal judge; b. Jacksonville, Fla., Jan. 31, 1929; s. Isaac Shelby and Edna Mae (Phillips) H.; m. Mary Jane Zimmerman, Nov. 25, 1972; children—Holly Law, Shelby. A.A., Ga. Mil. Coll., 1948; B.A., J.D., U. Kansas City, 1958. Bar: Fla. 1958. Trial atty. Kansas City, Mo., 1958-59, Miami, Fla., 1959-70; circuit judge Dade County, Fla., 1970-75; sr. ptnr. Highsmith, Strauss, Glatzer & Deutsch, P.A., Miami, 1975-91; judge U.S. Dist. Ct. (so. dist.) Fla., Miami, 1991—. Chief legal adviser Gov.'s War on Crime Program, 1967-68; spl. counsel Fla. Racing Commn., 1969-70; mem. Inter-Agy. Law Enforcement Planning Counsel of Fla., 1969-70. Served to capt. AUS, 1949-55. Decorated Bronze Star. Fellow Internat. Soc. Barristers; mem. ABA, Dade County Bar Assn., Bench and Robe, Torch and Scroll, Kendale Lakes Country Club, Wildcat Cliffs Country Club, (Highlands, N.C.), Omicron Delta, Phi Alpha Delta. Republican. Methodist. Office: Fed Justice Bldg 99 NE 4th St Rm 1027 Miami FL 33132-2138

HIGHSMITH, WANDA LAW, retired association executive; b. Cleveland, Mo., Oct. 25, 1928; d. Lloyd B. and Nan (Sisk) Law; student U. Mo., 1954-56; 1 child, Holly. Legal sec., firms in Mo. and D.C., until 1960; various staff positions Am. Coll. Osteopathic Surgeons, 1960-72, asst. exec. dir., conv. mgr., Alexandria, Va., 1974-94; ret., 1994. Mem. NAFE, Profl. Conv. Mgmt. Assn., Washington Soc. Assn. Execs., Am. Soc. Assn. Execs. Republican. Methodist. Home: 4835 Martin St Alexandria VA 22312-1838

HIGHT, JOE IRVIN, editor; b. Guthrie, Okla., July 14, 1958; s. Wilber Eugene and Pauline Ruth (Kingston) H.; m. Nannette Louise Bloch, Sept. 20, 1986; children: Elena Nicole, Elyse Christine. BA, U. Cen. Okla., 1980. From sports editor to mng. editor Guthrie Daily Leader, 1980-81; reporter, wire editor Shawnee (Okla.) News-Star, 1981-82, city editor, 1983-84; reporter Lawton (Okla.) Constn., 1982-83; from reporter to cmty. editor, asst. mng. editor The Oklahoman, Oklahoma City, 1985—; freelance writer USA Today, 1987. Bd. dirs., spokesman Red Andrews Christmas Dinner for Poor, Oklahoma City, 1985-95; bd. dirs. Okla. Archdiocese Young Adults, Oklahoma City, 1985-86; bd. dirs. Chelsea Sta. Neighborhood Assn., Edmond, Okla., pres., 1992-93, 95-96, v.p., 1993-94; mem. pastoral coun. St. John's Cath. Ch., Edmond, 1987-91, chmn. planning commn.; mem. Okla. Youth Arts Hon. Adv. Coun., 1992-93; mem. outreach com. Ctrl. Okla. 2020, 1993-94; parade marshal Celebrating Our Future Parade, 1994; mem. comm. com. Ctrl. Okla. Citizens League, 1995—; grad. Leadership Oklahoma City, 1995. Recipient E.K. Gaylord award Okla. Gridiron Club, 1979, Sweepstakes trophy Okla. Press Assn., 1984, Carl Rogan award AP, 1986, 95, gov.'s commendation, 1991, 1st Excel award Internat. Assn. Bus. Communicators, 1994; named Outstanding Vol., Okla. Archdiocese Young Adults, 1985, Red Andrews Christmas Dinner, 1987. Mem. Soc. Profl. Journalists. Democrat. Office: The Oklahoman PO Box 25125 Oklahoma City OK 73125-0125

HIGHTOWER, JACK ENGLISH, former state supreme court justice and congressman; b. Memphis, Tex., Sept. 6, 1926; s. Walter Thomas and Floy Edna (English) H.; m. Colleen Ward, Aug. 26, 1950; children—Ann, Amy, Alison. B.A., Baylor U., 1949; JD, 1951; LLM, Univ. Va., 1992. Bar: Tex. 1951. Since practiced in Vernon; mem. Tex. Ho. of Reps., 1953-54; dist. atty. 46th Jud. Dist. Tex., 1955-61; mem. Tex. Senate, 1965-75, pro tempore, 1971; mem. 94th-98th Congresses from 13th Tex. Dist., 1975-85; 1st asst. atty. gen. State of Tex., 1985-87; justice Texas Supreme Ct., Austin, 1988-95; ret., 1996. Mem. Tex. Law Enforcement Study Commn., 1957; del. White House Conf. Children and Youth, 1970; alt. del. Democratic Nat. Conv., 1968; bd. regents Midwestern U., Wichita Falls, Tex., 1962-65; trustee Baylor U., 1972-81, acting gov., 1971; trustee Wayland Bapt. Univ., Plainview, Tex., 1991—, Tex. Bapt. Children's Home, 1959-62, Tex. Scottish Rite Hosp. Children, 1991—, Human Welfare Commn.; bd. dirs. Bapt. Standard, 1959-68. With USNR, 1944-46. Named Outstanding Dist. Atty, Tex., Tex. Law Enforcement Found., 1959, Disting. Alumnus, Baylor U., 1978; recipient Knapp-Porter award Tex. A&M Univ., 1980. Mem. Tex. Dist. and County Attys. Assn. (pres. 1958-59), Scottish Rite Ednl. Assn. Tex. (exec. com. 1990—), Tex. Supreme Ct. Historical Soc. (pres. 1991—), Tex. Bar. Found. (fellow 1992), SAR, U.S. Supreme Ct. Historical Soc., Tex. State Historical Soc., Masons (grand master Tex. 1972), Lions (pres. Vernon 1961).

HIGHTOWER, JOHN BRANTLEY, arts administrator; b. Atlanta, May 23, 1933; s. Edward A. and Margaret (Kimzey) H.; m. Martha Ruhl, Feb. 25, 1984; children: Amanda, Matthew. BA in English, Yale U., 1955; DFA, Calif. Coll. Arts and Crafts. Asst. to pub. Am. Heritage Pub. Co., Inc., N.Y.C., 1961-63; exec. asst. N.Y. State Coun. Arts, N.Y.C., 1963-64, exec. dir., 1964-70; dir. Mus. Modern Art, N.Y.C., 1970-72; pres. Am. Coun. Arts, N.Y.C., 1972-74; pres. South St. Seaport, 1977-83, dir., vice chmn., 1983-84; exec. dir. Richard Tucker Music Found., 1977-89, Maritime Ctr. at Norwalk, 1984-89; dir. planning and devel. for the arts U. Va., 1989-93; pres., CEO The Mariners' Mus., Newport News, Va., 1993—; exec. com. WHRO, Norfolk; chmn. exec. dir. coun. Hampton Rds. Arts Alliance; exec. com., Coun. Am. Maritime Mus.; founder, chmn. Advs. for Arts, 1974-77; instr. arts mgmt. Wharton Sch., U. Pa., 1976-77, New Sch., 1976-77; cultural advisor Rockefeller Mission to Latin Am., 1969; vis. critic in arts adminstrn. Grad. Sch. Drama, Yale U., 1972-77; chmn. Planning Corp. for Arts, Urban Arts Corps. Bd. dirs. N.Y. State Coun. on Arts, Poets and Writers, Inst. Art and Urban Resources. Capt. USMCR, 1955-63. Fulbright fellow; recipient N.Y. State award, 1970. Mem. Century Assn. (N.Y.C.), 1805 Club (London). Home: 1600 Chesapeake Ave Hampton VA 23661-3128

HILBRINK, WILLIAM JOHN, violinist; b. Cleve., June 16, 1928; s. William and Caroline (Theil) H.; m. Patricia Anne Schultz, Aug. 6, 1955; children: Mark David, Holly Lee. B of Music Edn., Baldwin-Wallace Coll., 1955; MusM, U. Rochester, 1960. Cert. tchr. Tchr. strings, orch. Cleve. Pub. Schs., 1955-57; tchr. strings, dir. orch. MacMurray Coll., Jacksonville, Ill., 1958-62; tchr. violin, viola, string pedagogy, theory U. N.C., Greensboro, 1962-67; tchr. strings, grades 1-12, dir. orch. Fairfax (Va.) County Schs., 1967-83; asst. condr., assoc. concertmaster Fairfax Symphony Orch., 1977-84; ops. mgr. Fairfax (Va.) Symphony Orch., 1983-84; founder, 1st violinist Fairfax String Quartet, 1983—; orch. condr. MacMurray Coll. Community Orch., Jacksonville, 1958-62; founding mem. Collegium Musicum, Jacksonville, 1960-62; concertmaster Springfield (Ill.) Symphony Orch., 1962; 1st violinist Piano Trio, String Quartet, U. N.C., Greensboro, 1962-67; freelance violinist Washington area, 1977—. Reviewer of concerts, Civic Music Assn., 1960-62; violinist in several hundred concerts and recitals, 1958—. Organizer, condr. Fairfax All-County Orch., 1977-78; organizer Washington Met. area Spl. Olympics Orch., 1979; mem. music com. Fairfax United Meth. Ch., 1990—; music contractor for several choral groups, Washington; adjudicator for numerous festivals, Va. and Md. Recipient scholarship Eastman Sch. Music, 1957-58, Suzuki Inst., 1966. mem. Am. Fedn. Musicians. Home: 5112 Forsgate Pl Fairfax VA 22030-4507

HILBURG, ALAN JAY, crisis management consultant; b. N.Y.C., May 7, 1948. BFA, N.Y. Inst. Tech., 1970. Publicity mgr. NBC-TV, N.Y.C., 1970-74; communications and mktg. dir. Jr. Achievement, N.Y.C., 1974-76; v.p. mktg. Michaels-Stern, N.Y.C., 1976-77; sr. v.p., gen. mgr. Burson-Marsteller, Cleve., 1977-84; pres. Bloom, Dallas, 1984-87, Alan Hilburg & Assocs., Irving, Tex., 1987—; cons. Nat. Inst. Dental Rsch., Washington, 1980, Nat. Cancer Inst., Washington, 1982-83; vis. instr. Ohio U., Athens, 1982-83, Northwestern U., U. Tex.. Co-chmn. Young Republicans, N.Y.C., 1976; chmn. long range planning mktg. subcom. United Way, Cleve., 1983. Recipient Clio awards, 1979, 81, Silver Anvil award, 1975, 80, 82. Mem. Pub. Rels. Soc. Am. (chmn. found. com. 1982-83), Nat. Acad. TV Arts and

Scis. Republican. Clubs: City, Univ. (Cleveland). Office: 1090 Vermont Ave NW Washington DC 20005-4905 also: Alan Hilburg & Assocs 5215 N O'Connor Blvd Ste 200 Irving TX 75039-3732

HILBURN, ANDREA L., principal; b. Williamston, S.C., Sept. 25, 1949; d. Frederick and Ruth Mildred (Royal) Leverett; m. Glenn W. Hilburn Sr., Nov. 14, 1970; children: Lisa Nichol, Glenn W. II. BS in Edn., U. North Tex., 1971; MEd in Spl. Edn., East Tex. State U., 1978. Trainable mentally retarded tchr. Dallas Ind. Sch. Dist., 1980-85, vocat. adjustment coord. counselor, 1985-89, asst. prin., 1989-91, dean of instrn., 1991-96, prin., 1996—; cons. Spl. Edn., Dallas, 1980-85. Active Girls Scouts Am., Boy Scouts Am. Mem. Dallas Assn. Sch. Adminstrs., Phi Delta Kappa, Delta Sigma Theta. Methodist. Home: 6760 Talbot Pkwy Dallas TX 75232 Office: Nat Assn Elem Princ 1615 Duke St Washington DC 22314-3483

HILBURN, JOHN CHARLES, geologist, geophysicist; b. Dallas, Sept. 16, 1946; s. William Grant and Catherine (Thorwald) H.; 1 child, John C. Jr. BS in Geol. Scis., U. Tex., Austin, 1978. Mfg. mgr. Scorpio, Inc., Austin, 1972-74; rsch. engr., scientist U. Tex., Austin, 1974-78; corp. v.p. Reeves, Inc., Houston, 1978-79; mgr. acqusitions S.A.M. Western Geophys. Corp., Houston, 1979-80; sr. mktg. geophysicist GECO Geophys. Co., Inc., Houston, 1980-85; pres. John Hilburn & Assocs., Inc., Austin, 1985—. Mem. Soc. Exploration Geophysicists, European Assn. Exploration Geophysicists, Can. Soc. Exploration Geophysicists, Am. Assn. Petroleum Geologists, Geol. Soc. Am. Home and Office: 6302 Mountainclimb Dr Austin TX 78731-3908

HILDEBRAND, DON, science foundation executive. Pres. Rhone Merieux, Inc. Address: 115 Transtech Dr Athens GA 30601

HILDEBRAND, DONALD DEAN, lawyer; b. Emden, Ill., Aug. 9, 1928; s. Henry John and Ethel Paulena (Weimer) H.; m. Jewell Howell, Jan. 4, 1959. BA, Ill. Wesleyan U., 1950; JD, Vanderbilt U., 1955; postgrad., U. Ill., U. Nev.; nat. advocacy cert., U. Nev. Nat. Coll. Advocacy, 1984. Bar: Tenn. 1957, U.S. Dist. Ct. (mid. dist.) Tenn. 1957, U.S. Supreme Ct. 1980. Claims rep. State Farm Mut. Ins., Nashville, 1957-62; pvt. practice, Nashville, 1962—; advocate Tenn. chpt. Am. Bd. Trial Advocates, sec., 1990—. Prodr., host (local TV show) Law: Cases & Comment, 1989-95. Rep. candidate for Tenn. Supreme Ct., 1973. With U.S. Army, 1952-54, Korea; col. Tenn. Def. Force, 1984—. Mem. Tenn. Bar Assn., Tenn. C. of C. (chmn. mil. affairs com. 1978-82), Am. Legion (state comdr. 1970-73, post comdr. 1978, Shriners (life, Legion of Honor 1982). Methodist. Home: 132 Hardingwoods Pl Nashville TN 37205-3612 Office: 214 3d Ave Nashville TN 37201

HILDENBURG, SYDNEY LEIGH, elementary education educator; b. Freeport, Tex., Dec. 21, 1971; d. Kenneth Ray and Phyllis Kay (Davlin) Gerdes; m. Christopher Wayne Hildenburg, Dec. 18, 1992. BS in Elem. Edn., U. Houston, 1994. Tchr. 4th grade Angleton (Tex.) Ind. Sch. Dist., 1994—. Mem. Tex. Classroom Tchrs. Assn. (Angleton chpt.), Alpha Chi. Presbyterian.

HILENSKI, LULA LAIL, research scientist; b. Gastonia, N.C., Dec. 5, 1947; d. Julius Loyd and Anna Catherine (Huffstickler) Lail; m. Ferdinand Alexi Hilenski, June 6, 1970; children: Mary Catherine, Jesse Lail. BA, Pfeiffer Coll., 1970; MA in Coll. Teaching, U. Tenn., 1974, PhD, 1980. Rsch. asst. prof. dept. zoology U. Tenn., Knoxville, 1981-83, rsch. assoc. dept. microbiology, 1985; rsch. assoc. Harvard Med. Sch., Boston, 1983-84; rsch. assoc. dept. pathology U. S.C., Columbia, 1988-91; rsch. scientist Ga. Inst. Tech. Sch. Mech. Engring., Atlanta, 1994—. Contbr. articles to sci. jours. Fellow U. Tenn. Grad. Sch., 1977; grantee NSF, 1989, S.C. and Ga. affiliates Am. Heart Assn., 1989. Mem. AAAS, Am. Soc. for Cell Biology, Sigma Xi, Phi Kappa Phi. Office: Ga Inst Tech Sch Mech Engring Atlanta GA 30332

HILER, MONICA JEAN, reading and sociology educator; b. Dallas, Sept. 3, 1929; d. James Absalom and Monica Constance (Farrar) Longino; m. Robert Joseph Hiler, Nov. 1, 1952; children: Robert, Deborah, Michael, Douglas, Frederick. BA, Agnes Scott Coll., Decatur, Ga., 1951; MEd, U. Ga., Athens, 1968, EdS, 1972, EdD, 1974. Social worker Atlanta Family and Children's Services, 1962-63; tchr. Hall County pub. schs., Ga., 1965-67; mem. faculty Gainesville Jr. Coll., Ga., 1968-87, prof. reading and sociology 1975-87, chmn. devel. studies program, 1973-85, acting chmn. div. social scis., 1986-87, prof. emeritus reading and sociology, 1987—; cons. So. Regional Edn. Bd., 1975-83, Gainesville Coll., 1987-95; apptd. spl. advocate Juvenile Ct. Union County, Ga., 1994-96. Mem. ASCD, Internat. Reading Assn., Ga. Sociol. Assn., Gainesville Music Club, Phi Beta Kappa, Phi Delta Kappa, Phi Kappa Phi. Avocations: piano, painting, sewing.

HILGENKAMP, KATHRYN DARLINE, physical education educator, health education educator; b. Denver, Nov. 5, 1952; d. LeRoy C. and Darline L. (Callaway) Thoms; m. James D. Hilgenkamp, July 25, 1987; children: Jessica Erin, Whitney Jayne, Colton James, Devin Corinne. BS in Edn., U. Nebr., Lincoln, 1977; MS in Edn., Southern Ill. U., Carbondale, 1980; EdD, U. Nebr., Lincoln, 1987. Teaching asst. So. Ill. U., Carbondale, Ill., 1977-78; patient edn. cons. Lincoln (Nebr.) Med. Edn. Found., 1978; dir. health occupations McCook Community Coll., McCook, Nebr., 1980-82; evaluation cons. High Plains Emergency Med. Svcs., North Platte, Nebr., 1980-82; instr. grad. asst. U. Nebr., Lincoln, 1982-87; affiliate faculty Peru (Nebr.) State Coll., 1986-89; health edn. coord. Mem. Community Hosp., Blair, Nebr., 1989-90; asst. prof. Creighton U., Omaha, Nebr., 1990-93; adj. faculty U. Nebr., Omaha, 1994-95; asst. prof. La. Tech. U., Ruston, 1995—; wellness coord. Saint Elizabeth Cmty. Health Ctr., Lincoln., 1983-84; instr. trainer Am. Heart Assn., Blair, Nebr., 1990—, EMT-A instr. Nebr. EMS, 1980—, governing bd. Greater Nebr. Health Systems Agency, Grand Island, Nebr., 1979-82. Author: Emergency Health Care, 1987, Nebraska EMT Skills Guide, 1986. CPR instr. Am. Heart Assn., Am. Red Cross, Blair, Nebr., 1980—. Recipient 2nd pl. Student Rsch. award, Soc. Prospective Med., Atlanta, Ga., 1987; Enhancement grantee Nebr. Alliance Health, Phys. Edn., Recreation and Dance, Lincoln, Nebr., 1991, State of La., 1996. mem. APA, AAHPERD, Am. Assn. Lifestyle Counselors (cert.), Nat. Wellness Assn., Nebr. Alliance Health, Phys. Edn., Recreation and Dance. Office: La Tech U Health and Phys Edn Dept PO Box 3176 Ruston LA 71272

HILL, ALTON MCKIVER, university official, small business owner; b. Germanton, N.C., July 22, 1939; s. Gabe Kenner and Trevor Erlene (Kiser) H.; m. Sandra Gail Midkiff, Dec. 30, 1962 (div. July 1968); m. Cathy Ann Poindexter, Sept. 30, 1968; children: Allison Michelle Hill Newsome, Alton McKiver II. AS in Electronic Tech., Sprayberry Acad., Chgo., 1959; AA in Bus. Mgmt., U. Del., 1961; AA in Law Enforcement Tech., U. Louisville, 1980. Cert. campus enforcement officer, cert. N.C. State Bur. Investigation. Owner, operator Hill's Electronics, Winston-Salem, N.C., 1959-61, Melodie Mobile Vending Co., Winston-Salem, 1965-70; br. mgr. Family Fin. Corp., Winston-Salem, 1961-65; spl. police officer City of Winston-Salem, 1970-72; adminstr. campus law enforcement and campus pub. safety Wake Forest U., Winston, Salem, 1972—; chief of police Wake Forest U., Winston, 1977-79, dir. pub. safety, 1979-96, cons., supr. univ. police, 1986—; instr. N.C. Justice Acad., 1982-83; co-owner wholesale and retail miniature craft bus. Contbr. poetry to various publs. Zoning rep., spkr. Stanleyville Neighborhood Assn., Winston-Salem, 1973-75; hwy. zoning rep., spkr. Wake Forest U., City of Winston-Salem and Raleigh, N.C. Dept. Trans., 1978-84; instr., vol. N.W. chpt. ARC, 1990—. Mem. Internat. Assn. Campus Law Enforcement Adminstrs., N.C. Assn. Campus Law Enforcement Adminstrs. (sec., v.p. 1979-91, pres. 1981-82, Membership Achievement award 1983), Kernersville Arts and Crafts Guild (bd. dirs. 1994—). Democrat. Baptist. Home: 735 Lacock Ave Rural Hall NC 27045 Office: Wake Forest U Police PO Box 7686 Wingate Rd Winston Salem NC 27109

HILL, BARBARA ANN, academic administrator, consultant; b. Wallace, Idaho, Feb. 5, 1944; d. Raymond Wallace and Anna May 9Krause) Johnson; m. John M. Hill, June 14, 1969; 1 child, Katherine Alison. BA, U. Ill., 1965; MA, U. Washington, Seattle, 1967, PhD, 1975. Asst. prof. Holyoke (Mass.) Community Coll., 1970-76; lectr. in English Smith Coll., Northampton, Mass., 1972-74, asst. dir. acad. ctr., 1974-76; lectr. in English Goucher Coll., Towson, Md., 1976-77; assoc. and asst. prof. English Hood Coll., Frederick, Md., 1977-83; assoc. dean of the faculty Barnard Coll., Columbia U., N.Y.C., Md., 1983-86; provost Denison U., Granville, Ohio, 1986-90; pres. Sweet Briar (Va.) Coll., 1990—, prof. English, 1995; mem. Am. Coun. on Edn. Fellow, exec. com. 1980-81, 88-91, 95—. Edit. bd.: Liberal Education, 1987-95. Mem. Econs. and Employment Subcom. Lynchburg C. of C. Vision 2001, 1991-93, Amherst C. of C., Va., 1990-93, Am. Coun. on Edn., Commn. on Leadership Devel., 1991-94; bd. dirs. Employee Asst. Program, 1992-95, Centra Health, Va., 1994—; Danforth Found. Assn., 1980-85. Fellow Am. Coun. Edn., 1979-80, Danforth Found., 1980-85. Mem. Am. Coun. on Edn., Commn. on Govt. Rels., Mortarboar, Phi Beta Kappa. Home: Sweet Briar House Sweet Briar VA 24595 Office: Sweet Briar Coll Office of the President Sweet Briar VA 24595

HILL, BARRY MORTON, lawyer; b. Wheeling, W.Va., Sept. 13, 1946; m. Jacqueline Sue Jackson, Aug. 12, 1967 (div. Mar. 1988); children: Jackson Duff, Brandy; m. Lisa C. Wien, Jan. 7, 1989; 1 child, Gbriel Hunter. BS in Journalism, W.Va. U., 1968, JD, 1977. Bar: W.Va. 1977, U.S Dist. Ct. (no. and so. dists.) W.Va. 1977, Ohio 1978, U.S. Dist. Ct. (no. dist.) Ohio 1978, U.S. Ct. Appeals (3d, 4th, 6th and D.C. cirs.) 1984, U.S. Supreme Ct. 1984, U.S. Ct. Appeals (2d and 11th cirs.) 1986, Pa. 1986, U.S. Ct. Appeals (5th, 7th and 10th cirs.) 1988; cert. civil trial specialist Nat. Bd. Trial Adv. mem. W.Va. Pattern Jury Instrn. Panel, 1986; mem. exec. com. for rev. jury selection U.S. Dist. Ct. (no. dist.) W.Va.; mem. W.Va. Bar Civil Procedure Rules Rev. com., 1987; draftsman Interprofl. Code for Attys. and Physicians W.Va., 1987-88; adj. prof. Saba U. Sch. of Medicine, 1994—. Founding sponsor Civil Justice Found. Served to 1st lt. U.S. Army, 1969-71. Mem. ABA (regional editor torts and ins. practices sect. of newsletter 1987-88), Assn. Trial Lawyers Am. (sec. Pres.' coun. 1987-88, key person com., 1987-88, Pres.' coun. study com. 1988—, ins. practices com. 1988—), Am. Bd. Profl. Liability Attys. (diplomate), Ohio Acad. Trial Lawyers, Pa. Trial Lawyers Assn., W.Va. Trial Lawyers Assn. (pres. 1987-88, Outstanding mem. 1984), So. Trial Lawyers Assn. (bd. govs. 1988—). Democrat. Office: Gompers McCarthy et al 320 Penco Rd Weirton WV 26062-3813

HILL, BEATRICE ZAROBINSKI, home care services regional director; b. N.Y., Jan. 2, 1946; d. Alfred Harold and Mona Adele (Nelson) Zarobinski; children: Joseph, Fredrick, Michael. Grad. practical nurse, Lindsey Hopkins Tech. Coll., Miami, Fla., 1970; ADN, Miami Dade Community Coll., 1980; BSN, U. of the State of N.Y., Albany, 1985; MS in Healthcare Adminstrn., Cen. Mich. U., 1990. With constrn. health svcs. adminstrn.; staff surg. nurse U. Miami Hosp. and Clinics; nursing supr. Total Care Home Health Agy., Miami; adminstrv. supr. Moore Regional Hosp., Pinehurst, N.C.; regional dir. St. Joseph Hosp. Home Health Agy., N.C.; regional ops. dir. interim health care Richmond County Home Health; instr. profl. patient program U. Miami; assoc. prof. clin. nursing Cen. Carolina Community Coll., Sanford, N.C. Mem. ANA. Home: PO Box 57 Hoffman NC 28347-0057

HILL, BRYCE DALE, school administrator; b. Seminole, Okla., Mar. 5, 1930; s. Charles Daniel and Ollie (Nichols) H.; B.S., East Central State Coll., 1952, M.Teaching, 1957; postgrad. U. Okla., 1959-70; profl. adminstrs. certificate, 1969; m. Wilma Dean Carter, Aug. 16, 1956; children: Bryce Anthony, Brent Dale. Tchr. pub. schs., New Lima, Okla., 1952-56, supt. pub. schs., 1956-95; owner New Lima Gas Co., 1958-82. Chmn. bd. dirs. Seminole County chpt. ARC, 1969-90; v.p. bd. dirs. Redland Community Action Program, 1968-71; mem. Seminole County Bd. Health, 1985-95, v.p., 1986-88, chmn., 1988; mem. Seminole County Rural Devel. Council, edn. leader com. Okla. Farmers Union, 1990-93, exec. com. Okla. Commn. for Ednl. Leadership, 1993-95; v.p., bd. dirs. Okla. Assn. Acad. Competition, 1991-95, Okla. Commn. Ednl. Leadership, 1993-95; chmn. Seminole County Democratic Central Com., 1962-64, 70-95. Named to Seminole Jr. Coll. Hall of Fame, 1995. Mem. NEA, Okla. Edn. Assn. (Friend of Edn. award 1996), Am. Assn. Sch. Adminstrs., Okla. Assn. Sch. Adminstrs. (exec. com. 1976-78, 79-81, bd. dirs. 1979-81, 93-95, Dist. 8 Adminstr. of Yr. 1983, 94, Lifetime Achievement award 1996), Orgn. Okla. Rural Schs. (bd. dirs. 1986-92, pres. 1993-94), Seminole County Tchrs. Assn. (pres. 1964-65, 71-72, 79-80, 90-91), Seminole County Sch. Adminstrs. Assn. (chmn. 1969-70, 93-95), Seminole County Schoolmasters Club (pres. 1963-64, 69-70, 77-78), Seminole County Ret. Tchrs. Assn. (pres. 1996—), Seminole Hist. Soc. (v.p. 1971-73, 74-76), Okla. Assn. Svc. Impact Schs. (bd. dirs. 1987-95). Baptist. Home: 33 Swquoyah Blvd Shawnee OK 74801

HILL, CAROLYN GREGG, lawyer; b. Boston, June 4, 1936; d. David Almus and Virginia (Thompson) G.; m. Richard H. Rawls, June 15, 1957 (dec. Jan. 1967); children: Margaret Gregg Rawls Gifford, Richard Gregg; m. Victor Gerald Hill Jr., May 6, 1967; 1 child, Victor Gerald Hill III. BA, Wellesley Coll., 1958; JD, Oklahoma City U., 1969, MBA with high honors, 1977. Bar: Okla. 1969, U.S. Dist. Ct. (we. dist.) Okla. 1971, U.S. Ct. Appeals (10th cir.) 1977, U.S. Supreme Ct. 1981, U.S. Dist. Ct. (no. dist.) Miss. 1986, U.S. Ct. Appeals (5th cir.) 1987, U.S. Dist. Ct. (so. dist.) Ill. 1987, U.S. Dist. Ct. (ea. and we. dists.) Ark. 1987, U.S. Ct. Appeals (7th cir.) 1988, U.S. Dist. Ct. (so. dist.) Tex. 1988, U.S. Ct. Appeals (3rd and 8th cirs.) 1989, U.S. Dist. Ct. (ea. dist.) Okla. 1991. Sr. counsel litigation Kerr-McGee Corp., Oklahoma City, 1969-91; of counsel Andrews Davis Legg Bixler Milsten & Price, Oklahoma City, 1991—; pres. Carvill Co., Nichols Hill, Okla., 1977—. Founding editor: (book) Digest of Petroleum Marketing Act Decisions, 1978—; assoc. editor (monthly) Okla. Bar Jour., 1980-85. Mem. Okla. County Bar Assn. (chmn., founding editor The Briefcase 1974), Nat. Soc. Colonial Dames of Am. (pres. Okla. chpt. 1978-79, sec., treas). Office: Andrews Davis Legg Bixler Milsten & Price 500 W Main St Oklahoma City OK 73102

HILL, DAVID WAYNE, geologist; b. Brenham, Tex., May 20, 1954; s. Charles Bethel Hill and Anita Joyce (Myrow) King; m. Gay Ann Weaver, Aug. 21, 1976; children: Jennifer L., Samantha M. BS, Tex. A&M U., 1976; MS, U. Tex., 1993. Engr. Dresser Industries, Victoria, Tex., 1976-91; project mgr., geologist Tex. Natural Resource Conservation Commn., Austin, 1994—; instr. Austin C.C., 1994—. Coord. Martin Luther King Commemorative March, Round Rock, Tex., 1994, 95, 96. Mem. Nat. Ground Water Assn., Soc. Petroleum Engrs., Am. Inst. Hydrology (student chpt. v.p. 1992, 93), Phi Kappa Phi. Home: 1104 St Williams Round Rock TX 78681 Office: TNRCC PO Box 13087 MC136 12100 Park 35 Austin TX 78711-3087

HILL, DELINDA JEAN, medical/surgical nurse, enterostomal therapy nurse; b. Okmulgee, Okla., Jan. 11, 1957; d. Robert Winfield and Phillis Lucille (Locker) Davis; m. Stanton Robert Hill, Nov. 26, 1976. AAS in Nursing with honors, Tulsa Jr. Coll., 1979; BSN with high honors, Langston U., 1990; MS, U. Okla., 1996. Cert. med.-surg. nurse, ANCC, cert. enterostomal therapy nurse. Enterostomal therapy nurse clin. specialist Hillcrest Med. Ctr., Tulsa, 1979—; mem. skin integrity task force Hillcrest Med. Ctr. Mem. Sigma Theta Tau (Beta Delta chpt. at large). Office: Hillcrest Med Ctr 1120 S Utica Tulsa OK 74104

HILL, ELIZABETH REESE, elementary education educator; b. Montgomery, Ala., Sept. 4, 1962; d. Owen Nelson and Betty (Stoudenmire) Reese; m. John Brant Hill. BS in Family and Child Devel., Auburn U., 1984; BS in Elem. Edn., Auburn U., Montgomery, 1986; MEd in Elem. Edn., Troy State U., 1990; Ednl. Specialist, Auburn U., 1994. Tchr. Montgomery County Bd. Edn.-MacMillan Sch., 1986-88, Montgomery County Bd. Edn.-Forest Ave. Sch., 1988-89, Montgomery County Bd. Edn.-Fitzpatrick Sch., 1989—. Mem. Kappa Delta Pi, Delta Kappa Gamma, Omicron Delta Kappa, Gamma Beta Phi. Baptist. Home: 914 Meriwether Rd Pike Road AL 36064 Office: Fitzpatrick Elem Sch 4055 Fitzpatrick Blvd Montgomery AL 36116-4820

HILL, ERIC VON KRUMREIG, aerospace engineer, educator; b. Iowa City, Iowa, Nov. 5, 1946; s. Fosdick Emerson and Nellie Roberta (Clawson) H.; m. Marilynn Sue Eagan, Aug. 17, 1968 (div. Sept. 1984); children: Rachael Alane, Nathaniel Eldon, Matthew Alexander, Jeremiah James, Brendan Michael, Benjamin Charles; m. Susan Barbara Croon Adams, Mar. 31, 1991; 1 stepchild, Renee Suzanne Adams. BS in Aerospace Engring., U. Okla., 1970, PhD in Mech. Engring., 1980. Asst. prof. mech. engring. Clemson (S.C.) U., 1981-82; assoc. scientist, quality project engr. Thiokol Corp., Brigham City, Utah, 1982-85; asst. prof. mech. engring. U. Denver, 1986; assoc. prof. aerospace engring. Embry-Riddle Aero. U., Daytona Beach, Fla., 1986-93; prof. aerospace engring., 1993—; vis. asst. prof. mech. engring. U. Okla., Norman, 1980-81; cons. FAA Transp. Safety Inst., Oklahoma City, 1976-78, Dunegan/Endevco corp., San Juan Capistrano, Calif., 1980, Physical Acoustics Corp., Princeton, N.J., 1995-96, NASA Michoud Test Facility, New Orleans, 1995; chief F-111 Data Analysis sect. Oklahoma City Air Logistics Ctr., Tinker AFB, 1974-75. Contbr. articles to profl. jours. Asst. scoutmaster Boy Scouts Am., Daytona Beach, 1989-90, scoutmaster, Brigham city, Utah, 1983, Mantua, Utah, 1983,84, New Smyrna Beach, Fla., 1995-96. Capt. USAF, 1967-75, USAF res. Decorated Air Force Commendation medal (2); Air Force Inst. Tech. scholar, 1968-70. Mem. ASTM, Am. Soc. for Nondestructive Testing, Acoustic Emission Working Group, Sigma Gamma Tau. Republican. Mormon. Home: 3041 Turnbull Bay Rd New Smyrna Beach FL 32168-5437 Office: Embry-Riddle Aero U Dept Aerospace Engring Daytona Beach FL 32114-3900

HILL, EULA VERTNER, former state agency administrator; b. Americus, Ga., Aug. 16, 1928; d. Oscar Thomas and Eula Vertner (Forrest) Harrell; m. Jefferson Perry Hill, Nov. 28, 1946 (dec. Oct. 1985); 1 child, Robert Perry. Ed. Southwestern Coll., Americus, Ga. Cert. tchr., Ga. 6th and 7th grade tchr. Plains (Ga.) Sch., 1946-47; buyer, office mgr. Belk's Dept. Store, Americus, 1949-60; sales assoc., 1992-94; field service mgr. Ga. Dept. Labor, Americus, 1961-90; assoc. owner Walmart, Albany, Ga., 1990-92. V.p., organizer Inter-Agy. Coun., 1970-90; active Ga. Coun. on Aging, 1964-74; organizer Americus unit Ga. Heart Assn., 1975; adv. bd. Ga. Dept. Human Resources, 1976-78; chmn. bd. advisors for bus. edn. South Ga. Tech. Inst., 1973-90; mem. career devel. bd. Ga. Southwestern Coll., Americus. Recipient Cert. of Appreciation Kiwanis Club of Americus, 1985. Mem. NAFE, Acad. Women in Mgmt., Internat. Assn. Personnel in Employment Security (chmn. profl. standards com. 1986-87, Ga. chpt. activities chmn. 1987-88, exec. com. 1987-90), Americus-Sumter County Bus. and Profl. Women (founder), Lions Club. Democrat. Methodist. Home: 138 Highway 27 E Americus GA 31709-9117

HILL, GRACE LUCILE GARRISON, education educator, consultant; b. Gastonia, N.C., Sept. 26, 1930; d. William Moffatt and Lillian Tallulah (Tatum) Garrison; m. Leo Howard Hill, July 24, 1954; children: Lillian Lucile, Leo Howard Jr., David Garrison. BA, Erskine Coll., 1952; MA, Furman U., 1966; PhD, U. S.C., 1980. Lic. sch. psychologist, S.C. Tchr. Bible, Clinton (S.C.) Pub. Schs., 1952-53; tchr. English Parker High Sch., Greenville, S.C., 1953-55; elem. tchr. Augusta Circle Sch., Greenville, 1955-57; tchr. homebound children Greenville County Sch. Dist., Greenville, 1961-64, psychologist, 1966-77; adj. prof. grad. studies in edn. Furman U., Greenville, 1977—, U. S.C., Columbia, 1982—; ednl. cons. Ednl. Diagnostic Svcs., Greenville, 1980—; exec. dir. Camperdown Acad., Greenville, 1986-87; cons. learning disability program Erskine Coll., Due West, S.C., 1978—. Contbr. articles to profl. jours. Pres. Lake Forest PTA, Greenville, 1970-71; pres. of Women A.R. Presbyn. Ch., Greenville, 1973-75, adult Bible tchr., 1978—; sec. bd. trustees Erskine Coll., 1982-88; bd. dirs. Children's Bur. S.C., Columbia, 1981-87, YWCA, Greenville, 1984-88; bd. advisors for adoption S.C. Dept. Social Svcs., Columbia, 1987-92. Recipient Order of the Jessamine, Greenville News award, 1994-95. Mem. Am. Edn. Rsch. Assn. (southeastern rep. 1982-84, editor newspaper for SIG group 1982-83), Jean Piaget Soc., Assn. for Supervision and Curriculum Devel., Orton Dyslexia Soc. (pres. Carolinas br. 1984-88), Ea. Ednl. Rsch. Assn., S.C. Psychol. Assn., Order of the Jessamine, Delta Kappa Gamma. Democrat. Home and Office: 28 Montrose Dr Greenville SC 29607-3034

HILL, HAROLD NELSON, JR., lawyer; b. Houston, Apr. 26, 1930; s. Harold Nelson and Emolyn Eloise (Geeslin) H.; m. Betty Jane Fell, Aug. 16, 1952; children: Douglas, Nancy. B.S. in Commerce, Washington and Lee U., Lexington, Va., 1952; JD, Washington & Lee U., 1981; LL.B., Emory U., 1957, JD, 1986. Bar: Ga. 1957. Assoc., then partner firm Gambrell, Harlan, Russell, Moye & Richardson, 1957-66; asst. atty. gen. Ga., 1966-68; exec. asst. atty. gen., 1968-72; partner firm Jones, Bird & Howell, 1972-74; assoc. justice Supreme Ct. Ga., 1975-82, chief justice, 1982-86; ptnr. Hurt, Richardson, Garner, Todd & Cadenhead, Atlanta, 1986-92, Judicial Resolutions Inc., Atlanta, 1993-94; of counsel Long, Aldridge & Norman, Atlanta, 1994-95. Served with AUS, 1952-54. Fellow Am. Bar Found.; Mem. Am. Law Inst., State Bar Ga., Lawyers Club Atlanta, Old War Horse Lawyers Club. Methodist.

HILL, HELEN KATHERINE, librarian, educator; b. Ponca City, Okla., May 27, 1961; d. Kendall Patrick and Lois Anne (Larrabee) H., Dona Jean Barker (stepmother) H.; 1 child, Alexandra. BA in Maths., Tex. Christian U., 1983; MA in Libr. Sci., Tex. Woman's U., 1987. Libr. asst. Va. Tech. U., Blacksburg, 1983-85; asst. prof. libr. svcs. Northeastern State U., Tahlequah, Okla., 1987—. Trainer, product sales mgr. Lake-Wood Girl Scout Coun., Cherokee county, Okla., 1987—; foster parent Dept. Human Svcs., Tahlequah, 1990. Recipient Title IIB fellowship U.S. Office Edn., 1985-86. Mem. ALA (co-chair GLTF 1986-88, Olofson award 1986), AAUW, Nat. Women's Studies Assn., Mountain Plains Libr. Assn., Okla. Libr. Assn., Phi Beta Kappa. Office: Northeastern State U John Vaughan Libr Tahlequah OK 74464-2398

HILL, HULENE DIAN, accountant; b. Salisbury, N.C., Mar. 17, 1948; d. Hulon Clive and Matie Cordelia (Plyler) H.; m. Ed Adkins; 1 child, Daren Steven Starnes. BS in Acctg., U. N.C., Charlotte, 1971. CPA, N.C., S.C. Staff acct. Peat, Marwick Mitchell & Co., Charlotte, 1971-74; sr. tax acct. Arthur Andersen & Co., Charlotte, 1974-76; tax mgr. Ernst & Young (formerly Clarkson, Harden & Gantt), Columbia, 1976-79; ptnr. Deloitte & Touche, Charlotte, 1979-92; v.p. tax Hodge, Steward & Co., P.A., Raleigh, N.C., 1992—. Recipient Hon. Mention as Bus. Woman of Yr. Shearson Lehman and Queens Coll., 1986, 89, 90, 91; named Acct. of Yr. Acad. Women Achievers YWCA, 1985. Mem. AICPA, Women Execs. (pres. 1987-88), Univ. N.C. Charlotte Athletic Found. (v.p. 1986-87), U. N.C. Charlotte Alumni Assn. (pres. 1985-86), Beta Alpha Psi (Acct. of Yr. U. N.C. chpt. 1985). Republican. Roman Catholic. Home: 204 Rosehaven Dr Raleigh NC 27609-3880 Office: PO Box 41168 Raleigh NC 27629-1168

HILL, I. KATHRYN, professional certification agency administrator; b. Phila., Apr. 6, 1950; d. Joseph Anthony and Irma Lorraine (Walther) Piehs; m. John Patrick McElwain, May 17, 1969 (div. Aug. 1979); children: John Charles, Brian Patrick; m. David Terence Hill, Sept. 27, 1980. BA, Widener Coll., 1979; MEd, Temple U., 1982. Cert. secondary tchr., Pa. Translator, transcriber Sci-Tech, Inc., Phila., 1970-77; tchr. West Chester (Pa.) East High Sch., 1978, Garnet Valley Jr.-Sr. High Sch., Concordville, Pa., 1979; asst. to dir. Nat. Bd. Med. Examiners, Phila., 1980-81, evaluation program asst., 1981-82, evaluation program assoc., 1982-84, sr. program assoc., 1984-85; asst. exec. v.p. Fedn. State Med. Bds., Ft. Worth, 1985-86, asst. exec. v.p., exec. dir. of the examination bd., 1986-94, sr. v.p., exec. dir. examination bd., 1995-96; exec. v.p. Nat. Commn. on Cert. of Physician Assts., Atlanta, 1996—. Editor: FLEX/SPEX Guidelines, 1985, 87, 90, FLEX/SPEX Info. Bull., 1987-94; co-editor Fedn. Exchange, 1986-95; contbr. articles to profl. jours. Mem. Am. Ednl. Rsch. Assn., Nat. Coun. on Measurement in Edn., Assn. of Am. Med. Colls. Republican. Lutheran. Office: NCCPA 6849-B2 Peachtree Dunwoody Atlanta GA 30328

HILL, JAMES CLINKSCALES, federal judge; b. Darlington, S.C., Jan. 8, 1924; s. Albert Michael and Alberta (Clinkscales) H.; m. Mary Cornelia Black, June 7, 1946; children: James Clinkscales, Albert Michael. BS in Commerce, U. S.C., 1948; JD, Emory U., 1948. Bar: Ga. 1948, U.S. Supreme Ct. 1969. Assoc. Gambrell, Russell, Killorin & Forbes, Atlanta, 1948-55, ptnr., 1955-63; ptnr. Hurt, Hill & Richardson, Atlanta, 1963-74; judge U.S. Dist. Ct. (no. dist.) Ga., 1974-76, U.S. Cir. Ct. (5th cir.), Atlanta, 1976-81, U.S. Cir. Ct. (11th cir.), Atlanta, 1981-89; sr. U.S. cir. judge U.S. Ct. Appeals, Atlanta, 1989—; chmn. com. on appellate ednl. programs Fed. Jud. Ctr.; mem. com. on intercir. assignments Jud. Conf. U.S. With USAAF, 1943-45. Fellow Am. Coll. Trial Lawyers, Am. Bar Found. (life); m. ABA, Am. Law Inst., World Assn. Judges, State Bar Ga., Atlanta Bar Assn., Am. Judicature Soc., Lawyers Club Atlanta (life), Old War Horse Lawyers. Republican. Baptist. Office: US Ct Appeals PO Box 52598 Jacksonville FL 32201-2598 also: US Court Appeals 11th Circuit 56 Forsyth St NW Atlanta GA 30303-2205

HILL, JAMES ROBERT, accountant; b. Marshalltown, Iowa, Jan. 20, 1960; s. James Ralph and Darlene Shirley (Kaufmann) H.; m. Debra Sue

Wantz, May 11, 1985; children: Bradley James, Kayla Marie, Erica Kristi. BA in Acct. and Systems Mgmt., Cen. Coll., Pella, Iowa, 1982. Livestock acct. Swift Ind., Marshalltown, Iowa, 1982-83, departmental acct., 1983-86; acctg. supr. Swift Ind., St. Joseph, Mo., 1986-88; plant contr. Monfort (formerly Swift Ind.), St. Joseph, 1988-89; acctg. mgr. Jet Stream Plastic Pipe Co., Siloam Springs, Ark., 1990—. Trustee, mem. fin. com. ACTS Free Meth. Ch., also treas.; cmty. edn. adv. bd. mem.; bd. dirs. United Way of Benton County; chmn. pack com., den leader Boy Scouts Am. Mem. Inst. Mgmt. Accts., Jaycees (treas. Gladbrook, Iowa chpt. 1984, Jaycee of Yr. Gladbrook chpt. 1985, v.p. 1986, state finalist Brownfield award 1983, dist. dir. 1991, pres. Siloam Springs chpt. 1992-93, 94-95, Dist. Dir. of Quarter 1991, Number 5 Dist. Dir. in U.S. 1991-92, Number 1 Local Pres. 2d quarter 1992-93, Internat. senator). Home: 136 Highland St Siloam Springs AR 72761-4910 Office: Jet Stream Plastic Pipe Co PO Box 190 Siloam Springs AR 72761-0190

HILL, JOHN EDWARD, JR., investment banker, small business owner; b. Amarillo, Tex., Nov. 26, 1927; s. John Edward Sr. and Laura Ann (Jones) H. BS, MIT, 1948. Student test engr. GE, Lynn, Mass., 1945-46; traffic contr. Navy Search Lights High Voltage Testing Lab., Pittsfield, Mass., 1946-47; assoc. instrumentation engr. Phillips Chem. Co., Bartlesville, Okla., 1948-55; surveyor, acct. John E. Hill, Amarillo and San Luis, Colo., 1957-70; co-executor Estate of John E. Hill, Amarillo, 1970-72; asst. mgr. Laura A. Hill, Amarillo, 1972-77; executor Estate of Laura A. Hill, Amarillo, 1977-79; pres. J.E. Hill Investment Co., Inc., Amarillo, 1980-90; prin. J.E. Hill Investment Co., Amarillo, 1990—; dir. San Acacio Land Co., Le Veta, Colo., 1980-91. Inventor coal treatment process, anti-missile device, activated chem. reaction. Mem. ASME (assoc.), ASTM, AIChE.

HILL, JOHN SYLVESTER, allergist, immunologist; b. Charleston, W.Va., 1948. MD, U. W.Va., 1974. Diplomate Am. Bd. Allergy and Immunology, Am. Bd. Internal Medicine. Intern Charleston (W.Va.) Area Med. Ctr., resident in internal medicine; fellow in allergy and immunology Virginia Mason Clinic, Seattle; now with St. Joseph Hosp., Lexington, Ky. Mem. Ky. Med. Assn. Office: 1725 Harrodsburg Rd Lexington KY 40504-3628

HILL, JOSEPHINE CARMELA, realtor; b. Tulsa, Feb. 27, 1932; d. Raphael and Jennie (Ferro) C.; m. Billy Gene Hill, Aug. 10, 1957; children: Patricia Ann, Barbara Jo. BEd, Chgo. State U., 1954; postgrad., Southwestern State U., 1957-58, Tulsa U., 1962. Cert. tchr.; lic. real estate broker; cert. residential specialist; cert. in referral and relocation. Clk. typist part-time Glidden Paint Co., Chgo., 1954-57; tchr. Chgo. Pub. Schs., 1954-57, Clinton (Okla.) Pub. Schs., 1958-59; sales rep. and bookkeeper Hill's Drug Shop, Tulsa, 1962-74; realtor assoc. Carriage Co. Realtors, Tulsa, 1974-77; broker assoc. John Hausam Realtors, Tulsa, 1977-87, 95—, J. Menger Elite Realtors, Tulsa, 1987-95, John Hausam Realtors, Tulsa, 1995—; mem. adv. bd. Tulsa Jr. Coll., 1991-93; divsn. v.p. Womens coun. Realtors Referral and Relocation,1993. Contbr. articles to profl. jours. Mem. St. Francis Hosp. Aux., Tulsa, 1986—; mem. exec. bd. March of Cimes, 1991-96. Mem. Nat. Assn. of Realtors (realtors active in politics 1990-91, polit. calling network 1988-91, Outstanding award 1990, Svc. award), Women's Coun. of Realtors (regional v.p. 1991, state chpt. pres. 1988, gov. 1989), Okla. Assn. of Realtors (mem. legis. com. 1988—, Okla. State Mem. of Yr. 1990, Mem. of Yr. local chpt. 1990, bd. dirs. 1993-94, mem. edn. com. 1994), Greater Tulsa Assn. of Realtors (vice chair realtors polit. action com. 1991, mem. profl. stds. com. 1992-96, mem. profl. bylaws com. 1992, bd. dirs. 1992-94, treas. 1994, sales assoc. of yr. 1991, chmn. fin. and budget 1994, mem. exec. com. 1993, 94), Women's Coun. of Realtors, Real Estate Sales Assocs., Omega Tau Rho. Roman Catholic. Office: John Hausam Realtors 6550 E 71st St Tulsa OK 74133-2754

HILL, KATHRYN VIERECK, library administrator; b. Joliet, Ill., Oct. 25, 1963; d. Wayne R. and Patricia A. (Knaack) Viereck; m. Randal E. Hill, Dec. 27, 1986. BA in English and History, No. Ill. U., 1985, MA in English, 1987; MLIS, U. Tex., 1991. Instr. No. Ill. U., Dekalb, 1987-89; reference libr. Deer Park (Tex.) Pub. Libr., 1991-95, asst. libr. dir., 1996—. Mem. ALA, Tex. Libr. Assn., Beta Phi Mu. Office: Deer Park Pub Libr 3009 Center St Deer Park TX 77536

HILL, KENNETH CLYDE, clergyman; b. Kingsport, Tenn., Mar. 22, 1953; s. Hubert Clyde and Erma Lee (Harless) H.; m. Janet Reynolds, Oct. 15, 1976; children: Matthew Joseph, Timothy Aaron, Lydia Rebekah. BS in Speech, History, East Tenn. State U., 1974; MS in Speech, Ind. State U., 1976; BA in Bibl. Studies, Bapt. Christian Coll., 1986; M. Religious Edn., Manahath Sch. Theology, 1989. Ordained to ministry Evang. Meth. Ch., 1982. Pastor Crestwood Bapt. Ch., Ft. Wayne, Ind., 1980-81; pres., chief exec. officer Appalachian Ednl. Communication Corp., Bristol, Tenn., 1981—; pulpit supply various ch. congregations Ind., Tenn., 1981-82; deacon Evang. Meth. Ch., Kingsport, Tenn., 1982-86, elder, 1986—; chmn. Publs. Bd. of the Evang. Meth. Ch., Kingsport, 1986—; sec. Gen. Conf. Evang. Meth. Ch., Kingsport, 1990—; gen. dir. Siloam Internat., Inc., 1993—; v.p. Southwest Radio Ch. of the Air, Inc., 1993—; gen. dir. Mission Field Task Force, Santiago, Chile, 1991, 93, 95-96; bd. dirs. Bancroft Gospel Ministry, Kingsport, 1984—, Manahath Sch. Theology, Hollidaysburg, Pa., 1986-93, 95—; chmn. Servant Ministries, Kingsport, 1990-91; mem. Mission Field Task Force, Blantyre, Malawi, 1989. Author: Reconstructionism: Is It Scriptural, 1989, (with Keith Walsworth) What's Next? 1993, (with others) Why I Still Believe We Live in the Last Days—Nuclear Proliferation, 1993, (with Joan B. Collins) Constitution in Crisis, 1994, (with Bill Usselton) Constitution Conspiracy, 1994, (with Jim Nicholls) Reflections on the Fairness Doctrine, 1994, (with Jose Holowaty and N.W. Hutchings) International Christian Broadcasting from South America, 1995; editor: A Classic Christmas, 1995; prodr. (video) The Temple Mount, 1993, Petra in History and Prophecy, 1993, The Revived Roman Empire, 1993, 25 Messianic Signs, 1993; contbr. articles to profl. jours. Disaster vol. ARC, 1986—; bd. dirs. Radio Reading Svcs. Corp., Kingsport, 1989-90; vol. World Reach, Inc., Honduras, 1986-91. Mem. Delta Sigma Rho, Tau Kappa Alpha. Home: 4045 Weaver Pike Bluff City TN 37618-2030 Office: Appalachian Ednl Comm Corp PO Box 2061 Bristol TN 37621-2061

HILL, LA JOYCE CARMICHAEL, marketing professional; b. Tifton, Ga., Nov. 14, 1952; d. Ralph Eugene and Vista Eloise (Dooley) Carmichael; m. Bobby Wayne Hill, Jan. 1, 1972. AS, Abraham Baldwin Agrl. Coll., Tifton, 1971. With R.E. Carmichael Co. Inc., 1970-89, sec./treas., 1978-88, pres., chmn. bd., 1988-89; gen. mgr. J & B Power Equipment, Inc., 1989-95; v.p. J&B Power, 1995—. Mem. Chula Charge United Meth. Women (sec.-treas. 1986—), Tifton Exch. Club (pres. 1994-95). Methodist. Home: PO Box 947 Tifton GA 31793-0947

HILL, LARKIN PAYNE, real estate company data processing executive; b. El Paso, Tex., Oct. 30, 1954; d. Max Lloyd and Jane Olivia (Evatt) H. Student Coll. Charleston, 1972-73, U. N.C., 1973. Lic. real estate broker, N.C. Sec., property mgr. Max L. Hill Co., Inc., Charleston, S.C., 1973-75, sec., data processor, 1979-82, v.p. adminstrn., 1982—; resident mgr. Carolina Apts., Carrboro, N.C., 1975-77; sales assoc., Realtor, Southland Assocs., Chapel Hill, N.C., 1977-78; cons. specifications com. Charleston Trident Multiple Listing Service, 1985. Bd. dirs. Charleston Area Arts Coun., 1992-93. Mem. Royal Oak Found., Scottish Soc. Charleston (bd. dirs. 1989-91), Preservation Soc., Charleston Computer Users Group, N.C. Assn. Realtors, Spoleto Festival USA (chmn. auction catalog com. 1990-92); co-chair Beaux Arts Ball, Sch. Arts. Republican. Methodist. Avocations: reading, crossword puzzles, Am. Staffordshire Terriers, T'ai Chi. Home: 7 Riverside Dr Charleston SC 29403-3217 Office: Max L Hill Co Inc 824 Johnnie Dodds Blvd Mount Pleasant SC 29464

HILL, LESLEY SUSAN, university official; b. Robstown, Tex., Aug. 31, 1948; d. Dudley B. and Leslie M. (Jones) Gregory; m. Roy D. Hill, Nov. 29, 1968; 1 child, Sarah Catherine. AA in Music with honors, Del Mar Coll., 1968; BA in Music cum laude, U. Houston, 1976, MBA, 1985. Coord. acad. affairs Coll. Social Scis. U. Houston, 1980-85; dir. ops. Ctr. for Pub. Policy U. Houston, 1985-87, staff assoc., Office of the Sr. V.P./Acad. Affairs, 1991-92, ops. officer divsn. distance and continuing edn., 1992—, also dir. continuing edn., 1992—; chmn., co-founder The Neighborhood Program, Inc., 1987—; project coord. Harris County Community Devel. Block Grant, 1992-93; cons. Houston Coun. on Alcoholism and Drug Abuse, Houston Harris County Cmty. Partnership Project, 1993-94; chmn. Tex. Dept. Criminal Justice Parole Divsn. Cmty. Participatory Coun., 1995—; vol. cons. Aldine Y.O.U.T.H., 1993-94; spkr. in field. Editor: When You Buy Your Home in Houston, 1989; weekly columnist Houston Chronicle, 1989-92; co-author: Neighborhood War on Drugs Manual, 1990; co-host (weekly radio talk show) Cmty. Spotlight, 1989-90. Bd. dirs. Camden Park Homeowners Assn., 1986-96, chmn. comm., 1986-92, pres., 1988-91, CCUCA delegate, 1988—; v.p. comm. UH Women's Interest Network, 1986-90, chmn. nominating com. 1989, pres. 1990-91; active United Way Inter-Agy. Info. and Referral Sys., 1987-91, Nat. Assn. Neighborhoods, 1990-91; gala com. mem. Houston Read Commn., 1988-89; adv. coun. bd. dirs. Greater Houston Preservation Alliance, 1989-92, Greater Eastwood Cmty. Devel. Corp., 1990; bd. dirs. Houston Proud Found., Inc., 1990-93, sec. to bd., 1990, bd. dirs. exec. com., 1991-92; bd. dirs. Cypress Creek United Civic Assns., 1988—, v.p. pub. rels., 1990-91, pres. 1991-94; steering com. Citizen's Planning and Neighborhood Assn., 1988-89; sec. neighborhood subcom. Houston Crackdown, 1989-91; mem. adv. com. Market Square Pk. Project, 1990-91; sec. adv. bd. Houston Harris County Cmty. Partnership, 1991-95, mem. spl. programs com., 1991—; co-organizer, mem. steering com. Citizen's forum Citizens for a Liveable Houston, 1991; pres., bd. dirs. Harris County Mcpl. Utility Dist. #150, 1992-96. Mem. Nat. Univ. Continuing Edn. Assn., Tex. Assn. Cmty. Svc. and Continuing Edn., Cmty. Assns. Inst., Inc. (nat. bd. trustee, pub. sector trustee 1990-93, pub. sector com. 1991-92, long-range planning com. 1991—, Greater House chpt. bd. dirs. 1987-91, edn. com. 1987-91, broadcast com. 1989-91, others), Tex. Neighborhoods Together, Inc. (bd. dirs. 1992—, co-chmn. legis. action com., v.p. edn. 1995—), U. Houston Sch. Music Alumni Assn. (v.p. comm. 1987-88, pres. 1988-89, 91-92, 92-93, 93-94, others). Office: Univ House 4800 Calhoun Rd Houston TX 77004-2610

HILL, LOIS JANE, nutritionist, dietitian; b. Hardinsburg, Ky., Feb. 8, 1949; d. James Wilburn and Cecilia Lorena (Flood) Bland; m. Don W. Hill, Aug. 9, 1948. BS, U. Ky., 1971. Registered dietitian, Ky. Intern Miami Valley Hosp., Dayton, Ohio, 1972; renal, surgical dietitian U. Ky. Med. Ctr., Lexington, 1972-75; instr. dialysis tng. program Dialysis Clinic, Inc., Lexington, 1975—, renal dietitian, 1975-83, sr. renal dietitian, 1980-91, nutrition svcs. supr., 1991—; renal dietitian Nephrology Assocs., Lexington, 1980-87; mem. med. rev. bd. End State Renal Disease Network #17, Lexington, 1984-87; chair Ky. Bd. Dietitians and Nutritionists, 1989-93, Ky. Bd. Licensure and Cert. for Dietitians and Nutritionists, 1994-96; cons. in field. Author: (with others) Lifetime Weight Control, 1977. Bd. dirs. Nat. Kidney Found. of East Ky., Lexington, 1981-86, Kidney Found. Ctrl. Ky., Lexington, 1986-93. Named Women of Achievement YWCA, Lexington, 1989. Mem. Am. Dietetic Assn. (editl. bd. renal practice group 1983, chmn. renal practice group 1986-87, chmn. clin. nutrition divsn. 1992-96), Ky. Dietetic Assn. (pres. 1978-79, lobbyist 1984-85, Ky. Outstanding Dietitian 1986, del. 1988-91), Bluegrass Dietetic Assn. (Outstanding Yount Dietitian 1978). Democrat. Roman Catholic.

HILL, MARIE See DAVIS, MAGGIE

HILL, MAX LLOYD, JR., realtor; b. Belleville, Ill., Aug. 15, 1927; s. Max L. and Leora (Jacobs) H.; student Purdue U., 1944-47; B.S., U.S. Naval Acad., 1951; postgrad. Harvard Law Sch., 1955-56; m. Jane Olivia Evatt, June 23, 1951; children—Larkin Payne, Max Lloyd III, Naomi Evatt. Sales engr. indsl. equipment Indsl. Welding Supplies, Inc., 1957-59; real estate salesman Simmons Realty Co., Inc., Charleston, S.C., 1959-63; pres. Max L. Hill Co., Inc., realtors, Charleston, 1964—; pres. Re/Max Realty Svcs., Inc., 1992—; lectr. S.C. Realtor's Inst., 1967-73, U. S.C. Sch. Gen. Studies and Extension, 1962-64. Pres. Greater Charleston YMCA, 1965-67; mem. Charleston Planning and Zoning Commn., 1969-74; mem. Charleston Zoning Bd. Adjustment, 1971-74; sec. Charleston County Bd. Assessment Control, 1972-75; bd. dirs. Edn. Found., 1966-74, Charleston Symphony Orch., 1980-88, pres. 1985-86; bd. dirs. Carolina Art Assn., 1979-83, bd. dirs. Ashley Hall Sch., 1973-87; adv. bd. Coll. Charleston Sch. Bus., 1992—; bd. vis. Charleston So. U., 1992—. Served with AUS, 1945-46, USNR, 1946; to 1st lt. USAF, 1951-55. Mem. Nat. Assn. Realtors (dir. 1976-84, 86-88, 89—, v.p. coms. 1981, regional v.p. 1982), Nat. Assn. Realtors (disting. svc. award 1989), Berkeley C. of C. (pres. 1990-91), S.C. Assn. Realtors (dir. 1966—, pres. 1976), Greater Charleston Assn. Realtors (pres. 1970), Charleston Trident C. of C. (dir. 1981-85), St. Andrews Soc., New Eng. Soc., Phi Gamma Delta. Methodist (ofcl. bd. 1964-76). Mason. Clubs: Carolina Yacht, Charleston, Seabrook Island. Home: 109 Tradd St Charleston SC 29401-2422 Office: 824 Johnnie Dodds Blvd Mount Pleasant SC 29464

HILL, OLIVER WHITE, SR., lawyer, consultant; b. Richmond, Va., May 1, 1907; s. William Henry White Jr. and Olivia (Lewis) White-Hill; m. Beresenia Ann Walker, Sept. 5, 1934; children: Oliver White Hill, Jr. AB, Howard U., 1931, JD, 1933; LLD (hon.), St. Paul's Coll., 1978, Va. State U., 1982, Va. Union U., 1988, U. Richmond; LHD (hon.) Va. Commonwealth U., 1991. Bar: Va. 1934, U.S. Dist. Ct. (ea. dist.) Va. 1939, U.S. Ct. Appeals (4th cir.) 1940, U.S. Dist. Ct. (we. dist.) Va. 1947, U.S. Supreme Ct. 1950. Sole practice, Roanoke, Va., 1934-36, Richmond, Va., 1939-43, 59-61; ptnr. Hill, Martin & Robinson, Richmond, 1943-55, Hill Martin & Olphin, Richmond, 1955-59; asst. to commr. FHA, Washington, 1961-66; asst. to asst. sec. Mortgage Credit and Fed. Housing Commn., Washington, 1966; ptnr. Hill, Tucker, & Marsh, Richmond, 1966—; dir. HTM, Inc., Richmond; mem. President's Commn. on Govt. Contract Compliance, Washington, 1951-53, Commn. on Constl. Revision for Commonwealth of Va., U. Va., 1968-69, Va. State Bar Disciplinary Bd., 1976-82. Bd. dirs. Richmond br. NAACP, 1940-61 (Outstanding Svc. award 1992), Richmond Urban League, 1950-61; mem. City Council, Richmond, 1948-50, Richmond Citizens Assn., 1950-54, Richmond City Dem. Com., 1956-61, 67-72, Va. Regional Med. Program, 1969-76; chmn. legal com. Va. State Conf. of NAACP, 1940-61. Staff sgt. U.S. Army, 1943-45, ETO. Recipient Chgo. Defender Merit award, 1949, Howard U. Alumni award, 1950, Nat. Publ. Assn. Russwurm award, 1952, Disting. Service award Delver Women's Club, 1954, Va. State Conf. of NAACP award, 1957, Ann. Conv. award NAACP, 1964, Disting. Service award Va. Tchrs. Assn., 1964, Francis Ellis Rivers award NAACP Legal Def. and Edn. Fund, 1976, Charles Hamilton Houston Medallion of Merit award Washington Bar Assn., 1976, Outstanding Pub. Service award The Moles, 1977, Disting. Service award Va. Union U. Am. Black Soc. Workers, 1978, John Mercer Langston Outstanding Alumnus award Howard U. Student Bar Assn., 1980, William Robert Ming Advocacy award NAACP, 1980, Appreciation award Va. State U., 1981, William P. Robinson Meml. award Democratic Party Va., 1981, Alumnus of Yr. award Howard U. Alumni Assn., 1981, Disting. Service award Va. State U., 1981, Distinguished Scholar award Oliver W. Hill Pre-Law Assn. of U. Va., 1983, award Commn. on Women and Minorities in Legal System Va. State Bar, 1987, Citizen of the Yr. award Alpha Kappa Alpha, 1992, Pro Bono Publico award ABA standing com. on lawyer's pub. svc. responsibility, 1993, Justice Thurgood Marshall award commn. for opportunities in the profession, 1993; citation for Disting. Legal Service, Richmond chpt. Frontiers of Am., 1954, Cert. of Appreciation, Assn. for Study of Afro-Am. Life and History, 1974, Brotherhood citation NCCJ, 1982, Thomas Jefferson Pub. Svc. award Richmond chpt. Pub. Rels. Soc. Am., 1995. Fellow Am. Coll. Trial Lawyers, Old Dominion Bar Assn. Found. (pres. 1985—), Va. Bar Found.; mem. Old Dominion Bar Assn. (pres. 1941-43, 46-56, recipient numerous awards), Va. Bar Found., Richmond Bar Assn. (Hill-Tucker Pub. Svc. award 1989), Nat. Bar Assn. (C. Francis Stradford award 1959, Wiley A. Branton Symposium award), NAACP (legal def. fund The Simple Justice award 1986), George C. Marshall Found. (bd. dirs. 1989-94), Evolutionary Change Inc. (bd. dirs. 1990—), Strong Men and Women Excellence in Leadership award Va. and N.C. Power Co. 1992, Lewis F. Powell Jr. Pro Bono award Va. State Bar 1992, Harry L. Carrico Professionalism award; Friend of Edn. award Va. Edn. Assn. 1992; Apex Museum tribute Atlanta Ga. 1992, Va. Senate commendation 1992, NAACP Branches hall of fame Va. State Conference 1992. Sigma Pi Phi (grand sire archon 1964-66), Omega Psi Phi (Omega Man of Yr. 1957), Omicron Delta Kappa. Baptist. Home: 3108 Noble Ave Richmond VA 23222-2528 Office: Hill Tucker & Marsh 509 N 3rd St Richmond VA 23219-1323

HILL, PETER M., sporting company executive. CEO Billy Casper Golf Mgmt., Inc. Address: Ste 980 1919 Gallows Rd Vienna VA 22182

HILL, ROBERT FOLWELL, JR., information systems specialist; b. High Point, N.C., July 24, 1946; s. Robert Folwell Sr. and Antilee (Dinkins) H.; Cynthia Hightower, Mar. 5, 1971 (div. Dec. 1977); 1 child, Robert Folwell III; m. Linda Kay Frier Balfour, June 7, 1978. BS in Computer Sci., N.C. State U., 1971. Supr. quality control Mac Panel Computer Tape Co., High Point, N.C., 1965-68; computer programmer U. N.C., Wilmington, 1972-74; programmer, analyst Gen. Adminstrn. U. N.C., Chapel Hill, 1974-79, dir. info. systems Gen. Adminstrn., 1979—. Pres. Triangle chpt. Nat. Found. for Ileitis and Colitis Rsch., Triangle Park, N.C., 1983, treas., 1984, v.p., 1985-88; pres. Crohn's and Colitis Found. Am., 1989-91, v.p. membership, 1991—; spl. registrar Orange County Bd. Elections, Hillsborough, N.C., 1984; mem. exec. com., mem.-at-large N.C. Vol. Health Agys., 1990, sec., 1991; bd. mem. Combined Health Appeal of N.C., 1991-95, treas. 1993-95. Recipient Mary Ann Mobley Vol. Leadership award, 1996. Mem. Data Processing Mgmt. Assn., N.C. Assn. Instnl. Rsch., State Employees Assn. N.C., Coll. and Univ. Sys. Exch., Nat. Assn. Stock Car Auto Racing, Toastmasters Internat. Democrat. Home: 203 Northwood Dr Chapel Hill NC 27516-1122 Office: U NC Gen Adminstrn PO Box 2688 Chapel Hill NC 27515-2688

HILL, RONALD CHARLES, surgeon, educator; b. Parkersburg, W.Va., Sept. 4, 1948; s. Lloyd E. and Margaret (Pepper) H.; m. Lenora Jane Rexrode, June 12, 1971; children: Jeffrey, Mandy. BA, W.Va. U., 1970, MD, 1974. Lic. physician W. Va., N.C.; diplomate Am. Bd. Surgery (recert.), Am. Bd. Thoracic Surgery. Intern dept. of surgery Duke U. Med. Ctr., Durham, N.C., 1974-75; resident in surgery Duke U., Durham, N.C., 1974-85, rsch. assoc., 1976-79, tchg. scholar, 1984-85; asst. prof. surgery W.Va. U., Morgantown, 1985-90, assoc. prof., 1990-96, prof. surgery, 1996—; cons. VA Med. Ctr., Clarksburg, W.Va., 1985—; dir. surg. rsch. dept. surgery W.Va. U., 1986-88, student coord. dept. surgery, 1986—; mem. ad hoc com. Merit Rev. Bd. for Cardiovasc. Studies, VA, Washington, 1988-90. Contbr., co-contbr. numerous book chpts. and articles to profl. publs. Mem.-at-large adminstrv. bd. Drummond Chapel Unified Meth. Ch., Morgantown, 1987-89, 93-95. Recipient Lange Med. Book award, 1971, 73, 74, Merck Med. Book award, 1974, Roche Med. award, 1972, Sowers award Duke U., 1992. Fellow ACS, Southeastern Surg. Congress, Assn. Acad. Surgery, Sabiston Soc., Am. Coll. Cardiology, Am. Coll. Chest Physicians, Am. Coll. Angiology, So. Thoracic Surg. Assn., Soc. Thoracic Surgeons; mem. Am. Heart Assn., (v.p., pres. elect, pres. W. Va. affiliate 1994-96), Soc. Univ. Surgeons, Am. Assn. Thoracic Surgery, Internat. Surg. Soc., So. Surg. Assn., W. Va. Med. Assn., Mended Hearts, Lakeview Country Club, Pines Country Club, Phi Beta Kappa, Alpha Omega Alpha, Alpha Epsilon Delta. Republican. Home: 10 Flegal St Morgantown WV 26505-2240 Office: WVa U Med Ctr Dept of Surgery Medical Center Dr Morgantown WV 26506

HILL, SUSAN SLOAN, safety engineer; b. Quincy, Mass., June 1, 1952; d. Ralph Arnold and Grace Elenore (Sloan) Crosby; m. William Loyd Hill, Dec. 16, 1973 (div. July 1982); m. William Joseph Graham, Sept. 10, 1983 (div. Feb. 1985). Assoc. Sci. in Gen. Engring., Motlow State C.C., Tullahoma, Tenn., 1976; BS in Indsl. Engring., Tenn. Technol. U., 1978. Intern, safety engr. Intern Tng. Ctr., U.S. Army, Red River Army Depot, Tex., 1978-79, Field Safety Activity, Charlestown, Ind., 1979, system safety engr. Comm.-Electronics Command, Ft. Monmouth, N.J., 1979-84, gen. engr., 1984-85; chief system safety Arnold Air Force Sta., USAF, Tullahoma, 1984; system safety engr. U.S. Army Safety Ctr., Ft. Rucker, Ala., 1985-91; medically retired; ind. cons. system safety, 1991—; founder Fibromyalgia Support Group; leader Arthritis Found. Support Group; active Arthritis Found. Recipient 5 letters of appreciation U.S. Army. Mem. NAFE, Assn. Fed. Safety and Health Profls. (regional v.p. 1980-84), Soc. Women Engrs., Nat. Safety Mgmt. Soc., Am. Soc. Safety Engrs., System Safety Soc., Order Engr. Republican. Episcopalian. Avocations: bowling, needlework, sewing, cooking, golf. Home and Office: PO Box 1075 Tullahoma TN 37388-1075

HILL, THOMAS HARRY, music education educator; b. Nashua, N.H., Mar. 19, 1925; s. William Baker and Mae Belle (Jones) H.; m. Ruth Elizabeth Caswell, July 20, 1946; children: Donna, Janet, Wendy. Student, New Eng. Conservatory, Boston, 1942, 46; MusB, Boston U., 1949, MusM, 1955; D Mus. Arts, Cath. U. Am., 1970. Supr. music Dighton (Mass.) Pub. Schs., 1949-50; head music dept. Bangor (Maine) Pub. Schs., 1950-54; tchr. music Arlington County Pub. Schs., Arlington, Va., 1954-63; asst. prof. Am. U., Washington, 1963-72; assoc. prof. music edn. George Mason U., Fairfax, Va., 1972-95; chmn. com. on music edn. Nat. Music Coun., 1975-78; cons. Richmond (Va.) Pub. Schs., 1968-70; co-dir. youth concert study U.S. Office Edn., Washington, 1966-68. Author: Arundo Donax Class Woodwind Method, 1987; also articles. Pres. Fairfax Symphony Orch., 1961-62; pres. No. Va. Youth Symphony, 1972-73, hon. mem. bd. dirs., 1975; condr. City of Fairfax Band, 1971-93. Lt. USNR, 1943-46, 53-54. Danforth assoc. Danforth Found., 1976-80. Mem. Music Educators Nat. Conf. (nat. chmn. history spl. rsch. interest group 1988-90), Coll. Music Soc., Coll. Band Drs. Nat. Assn., Internat. Double Reed Soc., Va. Music Educators Assn. (chmn. coll. sect. 1981-83). Mem. United Ch. of Christ.

HILL, WILLIAM VICTOR, II, retired army officer, secondary school educator; b. Carlisle, Pa., Dec. 14, 1936; s. William Victor and Frances Ellen (Swanson) H.; m. Doris Ann Cox, Nov. 11, 1961; children: William Victor III, David C., Stephanie C. Hill Trede. BBA, Tex. A&M U., 1959; MPA, U. Mo., Kansas City, 1972; diploma, Command and Gen. Staff Coll., 1969, Air War Coll., 1982. Lic. realtor. Commd. 2d lt. U.S. Army, 1959, advanced through grades to col.; tank bn. comdr. 2d Bn., 13th Armor, Ft. Knox, Ky., 1976-78; prof. mil. sci. Sam Houston State U., Huntsville, Tex., 1979-81; insp. gen. 5th U.S. Army, Ft. Sam Houston, Tex., 1982-85; ret. U.S. Army, 1987; dir. army Jr. Res. Officers Tng. Corps South San Antonio (Tex.) Ind. Sch. Dist., 1988-95; sr. Army instr. South San Antonio H.S., 1988—. Author army materials. Decorated Legion of Merit, Bronze Star medal, Combat Inf. badge, Airborne-Ranger, others. Mem. U.S. Armor Assn. Home: 3208 Bent Bow Dr San Antonio TX 78209-3518 Office: South San Antonio High Sch JROTC 2512 Navajo St San Antonio TX 78224-1298

HILLEARY, VAN, congressman; b. Rhea County, Tenn., June 20, 1959. BS in Bus. Adminstrn., U. Tenn., 1981; JD, Samford U., 1990. With SSM Industries, Inc., 1984-86, dir. planning and bus. devel., 1992—; mem. 104th Congress from 4th Tenn. dist., 1995—. With USAF, 1981-82, Persian Gulf; with USAFR, 1991-92. Decorated 2 U.S. Air medals, Nat. Svc. medal, Kuwaiti Liberation medal. Mem. Am. Legion, Sigma Chi. Republican. Presbyterian. Office: US Ho of Reps 114 Cannon House Off Bldg Washington DC 20515-4204

HILLER, GEORGE MEW, financial advisor, investment manager, lawyer; b. Washington, July 21, 1956; s. William Eugene and Vera Ellen (Mew) H.; m. Marie Naomi Aliceaacosta, Mar. 24, 1979; children: George Mew Jr., Danielle Celeste, Emory Durell. BBA in Bus. Mgmt., Tex. A&M U., 1977, MBA in Fin., 1978; JD, Emory U., 1982, LLM in Taxation, 1986. Bar: Ga., 1982; CFP. Prin. Hiller & Assocs., Attys. at Law, Atlanta, 1985—; owner George M. Hiller Cos., Atlanta, 1985—. Author: Christian Financial Concepts Will Kit, 1993; contbg. author (booklet): Estate Planning Addendum Christian Financial Concepts, Gainesville, Ga., 1992—; co-author (textbook chpt.) Developing a Personal Portfolio in Real Estate, 1988; contbr. articles profl. jours. Mem. State Bar of Ga., Inst. Cert. Fin. Planners, The Atlanta Soc. Republican. Home: 1165 Clifton Rd NE Atlanta GA 30307-1229 Office: George M Hiller Cos 3414 Peachtree Rd NE Ste 1110 Atlanta GA 30326-1167

HILLERY, ROBERT CHARLES, naval engineer, management consultant; b. Waltham, Mass., May 3, 1953; s. Robert Parker Hillery; m. Diane Christine Kelly, Aug. 5, 1989; children: Kathleen, Kristen, Matthew. BA in Marine Transp., Mass. Maritime Acad., Buzzards Bay, 1975; MA in Internat. Rels., Salve Regina Coll., Newport, R.I., 1988; MA in Strategic Studies, Naval War Coll., Newport, 1991. Commd. ensign U.S. Navy, 1977, advanced through grades to comdr., 1990; exec. officer USS Charles F. Adams, Mayport, Fla., 1988-90; head enlisted engring. assignments U.S. Navy Bur. of Pers., Washington, 1990-92, head sea spl. programs, 1992-95; tech. advisor Navy Pers. R & D Ctr., San Diego, 1990-95; mem. membership bd. Surface Navy Assn., Arlington, Va., 1990-95; comdg. officer Fleet Surveillance Support Command, 1995—; mgmt. info. sys. cons. Pers. Sys. Ctr. Naval Analysis, 1991; prin. rschr. Navy Enlisted Pers. Assignment model, 1990-95. Contbr. articles to profl. jours. Recipient George Washington Honor medal Freedoms Found. at Valley Forge, 1979; MIT fellow, 1991. Mem. U.S. Naval Inst. Office: CO FSSC 1298 Olympic Ave Chesapeake VA 23322-4098

HILLEY, JOSEPH HENRY, lawyer; b. Birmingham, Ala., June 29, 1956; s. Howard Guy and Ruby Josephine (Mann) H.; m. Joy Elaine Fitzgerald, Aug. 11, 1984. BA, Asbury Coll., 1978; MDiv, Asbury Theol. Sem., 1984; JD, Cumberland Sch. Law, 1988. Bar: Ala. 1988, Ga. 1988, U.S. Dist. Ct. (no. dist.) Ala. 1988, U.S. Tax Ct. 1988, U.S. Ct. Appeals (11th cir.) 1993, U.S. Supreme Ct. 1995. Sports photographer World Wide News Svc., 1978-84; law clk. Gen. Counsel to Sec. of Def., Washington, 1987; assoc. Redden, Mills and Clark, Birmingham, Ala., 1988—; coord. capital campaign Asbury Coll., Wilmore, Ky., 1989-91. Author: (screenplays) Wake Up, 1994, Union Town, 1995. Mem. Pinnelas County Dem. Exec. Com., St. Petersburg, Fla., 1984; trustee Woodlawn United Meth. Ch., Birmingham, 1988, mem., 1987—. Named to Dean's List, Cumberland Sch. of Law, 1985-88, 86-88, Nat. Dean's List, 1985-88. Mem. ABA, Ala. Bar Assn., Ga. Bar Assn., Birmingham Bar Assn., Bar of U.S. Tax Ct., Phi Alpha Delta. Democrat. Methodist. Office: 729 Frank Nelson bldg Birmingham AL 35203

HILLIS, DAVID MARK, zoology educator; b. Copenhagen, Dec. 21, 1958; came to U.S., 1960; s. William Daniel and Argye Idell (Briggs) H.; m. Ann Marie Mackie, Aug. 16, 1980; children: Ereckson Briggs, Jonathan Daniel. BS, Baylor U., 1980; MA, U. Kans., 1983, MPh, 1984, PhD, 1985. Asst. prof. U. Miami, Coral Gables, Fla., 1985-87, U. Tex., Austin, 1987-90; assoc. prof. U. Tex., 1990-92, Alfred W. Roark Centennial prof., 1992—. Editor Molecular Systematics, 1990, 96, Systematic Zoology Jour., 1988-90, Systematic Biology Jour., 1990-92. Recipient Presdl. Young Invstigator award NSF, 1987. Mem. AAAS, Am. Assn. Ichthyologists and Herpetologists (bd. govs. 1988-93, 95—), Soc. Systematic Biologists (pres. 1993-94), Herpetologists League (assoc. editor 1987-89). Home: 2609 Westover Rd Austin TX 78703-1225 Office: U Tex Dept Zoology 2400 Speedway Austin TX 78712

HILLIS, JOHN DAVID, television news executive, producer, writer; b. Washington, Dec. 28, 1952; s. Willard E. and Holly M. (Shacklett) H.; m. Catherine H. McQuaig, Nov. 21, 1975; children: Faith Courteney, David Esten, Elizabeth Nicole. AB in Journalism, U. Ga., 1975. Film editor Sta. WSB-TV, Atlanta, 1973-74, asst. producer, 1974-76, news producer, 1976; exec. news producer Sta. KOTV-TV, Tulsa, 1976-79; news producer Sta. WRAL-TV, Raleigh, N.C., 1979-80; news producer Cable News Network, Inc., Atlanta, 1980-81, exec. producer, Newswatch, 1981-83, exec. producer, 1983-84, spl. events producer, 1984; news dir. Cablevision Systems Corp., Woodbury, N.Y., 1984-86; gen. mgr. Rainbow News 12 Co., Woodbury, 1986-89; pres., CEO Allnewsco, Inc., Washington, 1989—, Newschannel 8 Cable Svc., Springfield, Va., 1991—. Contbr. articles to profl. jours. Recipient Radio Newscast award Ga. AP Broadcasters, 1973, TV Newscast award Okla. AP Broadcasters, 1978, TV Series award News Acad. Cable Programming, 1985. Mem. NATAS (bd. govs. Washington chpt.), Soc. Profl. Journalists, Radio TV News Dirs. Assn., Nat. Press Club, Assn. Regional News Channels (founder, chmn. 1993), Nat. Cable T.V. Assn. (satellite network com.). Methodist. Office: Newschannel 8 7600 Boston Blvd # D Springfield VA 22153-3136

HILLMAN, PEARL ELIZABETH, minister; b. Lincoln, Kans., Sept. 2, 1907; d. Isaiah Marine and Estelle Belle Elizabeth (Masterson) Turner; m. Lester Robert Hillman (dec. July 1973); children: Bernice, Lois, Robert, Roberta, Durward, Donald. BS, Nazarene Bible Coll., 1980; MDiv, Asbury Theol. Sem., 1985. Ordained to ministry Ch. of the Nazarene, 1994. Min. Ch. of Nazarene, Crockett, Tex., 1987—; tchr., bd. dirs. Mt. Hope Ch. of Nazarene, Jacksonville, TEx., 1973-75, steward, del., 1973-79; pres. missionary Kiowa West of Colorado Springs, Colo., 1976-79, tchr. asst. Nicholasville (Ky.) Nazarene, 1982-85. Author: (devotions) Oral Roberts, 1990, Woman Alone mag., 1993, New Horizon, 1993. Mem. Ministerial Assn. Home and Office: Ch of Nazarene 505 S 4th St Crockett TX 75835-2713

HILLMAN, TOMMY, food products company executive; b. 1936. Arkansas Tech., 1963. Vice chmn., dir.,then chmn bd. dirs. Riceland Foods, Inc., Stuttgart, Ark., 1985—. Office: Riceland Foods Inc 2120 S Park Ave Stuttgart AR 72160-6822*

HILLS, LEE, foundation administrator, newspaper executive, consultant; b. Granville, N.D., May 28, 1906; s. Lewis Amos and Lulu Mae (Loomis) H.; m. Leona Hass, Dec. 25, 1933 (div. 1944); 1 child, Ronald L.; m. Eileen Whitman, June 7, 1948 (dec. 1961); m. Argentina Schifano, Oct. 31, 1963. Attended, Brigham Young U., 1924-25, U. Mo., 1927-29; LLB, Okla. City Univ., 1934; hon. degree in Bus. Adminstrn., Cleary Coll., 1958; LLD (hon.), Eastern Mich. U., 1969; LHD (hon.), U. Utah, 1969, U. Mo., 1988; D. in Journalism (hon.), U. Miami, Fla., 1986. News/edit. exec. Scripps-Howard Newspapers, Cleve., Indpls., Okla. City, 1933-41; mng. editor Miami (Fla.) Herald, 1942-51; exec. editor, pub. Miami Herald and Detroit Free Press, 1951-79; pres. Knight Newspapers, 1967-73; chmn., chief exec. officer Knight-Ridder, Inc., Miami, 1973-81; trustee, vice chmn., chmn. John S. & James L. Knight Found., Miami. Co-author: Facsimile, 1949. Trustee Am. Fedn. Arts, N.Y.C., Ctr. Fine Arts, Miami, Fla.; life trustee Detroit Inst. Arts.; pres. Detroit Arts Commn., 1966-80. Recipient Maria Moors Cabot Gold Medal for disting. contbn. to inter-Am. rels. Columbia U., N.Y.C., 1946, Disting. Svc. Journalism, U. Mo., Columbia, 1950, 63, Pulitzer Prize in Journalism, 1950, 56, William Allen White Found. award journalistic merit U. Kans., 1983; named to Hall of Honor U. Mo. Sch. Journalism, 1959, Okla. Journalism Hall of Fame, 1973; first inductee Comm. Hall of Fame, Brigham Young U., 1992; named in his honor Lee Hills Hall U. Mo. Sch. Journalism, 1992, Lee Hlls Journalism fellowship Stanford U. within Knight Fellowship Program, 1992, Lee Hills Award Disting. Career Svc. to Detroit Theater, 1986. Home: Bay Point 4450 Banyan Ln Miami FL 33137-3302 Office: John & James Knight Found One Herald Plz 6th Fl Miami FL 33132-1693

HILSON, DIANE NIEDLING, nursing administrator; b. Balt., May 28, 1956; d. John William and Marlyn Elaine (Weber) Niedling; m. James Earl Hilson, Sept. 18, 1982 (div.); children: James Ross, Katherine Michelle. BSN, Med. Coll. of Ga. Sch. Nursing, 1977, MSN, 1990. RN, Ga. Staff nurse, RN CCU St. Joseph Hosp., Augusta, Ga.; charge and staff nurse ICU Med. Coll. of Ga. Hosp., Augusta, nurse mgr. med./surg. unit. Recipient Nurses Make a Difference award Am. Hosp. Assn., 1985, Excellence in Nursing award, 1994. Mem. Ga. Nurses Assn., Sigma Theta Tau. Home: 3632 Bermuda Cir E Augusta GA 30909 Office: Med Coll of Ga 1120 15th St Augusta GA 30912-0004

HILT, DIANE ELAINE, middle school educator, computer specialist; b. Gadsden, Ala., Jan. 3, 1944; d. William Edward and Adele Helen (Plasman) Frantz. BS, Jacksonville (Ala.) State U., 1965; MEd, Ga. State U., 1972; cert. 6th yr. specialist in adminstrn., Troy State U., 1996. Cert. adminstr., supr., tchr. math, Ala., Ga. Actuarial clk. Life Ins. Co. Ala., Gadsden, 1965-66; tchr. Trinity Pvt. Sch., Columbus, Ga., 1968-69, Phenix City (Ala.) Sch. Sys., 1969-71; tchr. mid. grades Post Dependent Schs., Ft. Benning, Ga., 1970-82, chairperson dept. math., 1973-85, coord. curriculum, 1980-84, instr. staff devel., 1985—, tchr. math. grade 7, 1991-96, tchr. math. grade 8, 1996—; chairperson negotiation contract com. Post Dependent Schs., Ft. Benning, Ga., 1993—, mediation trainer, 1994, mem. salary negotiations team, 1995, faculty rep., 1992; owner computer bus., 1984-85; active Tchr. in Space Program NASA, 1985; sch. sys. rep. to survey Rand Corp., 1987; pres. Fla. Instrnl. Computing Conf. for Computer Using Educators, 1988, North Cook Ednl. Svc. Ctr., St. Charles, Ill., 1990, Ga. Tech. Conf., Columbus; liaison Nat. Coun. Tchrs. Math. and Chattahoochee Coun. Tchrs. Math., 1996. Contbr. to curriculum guide, 1969, vignette to text book. Sec. PTA, 1979-80, Columbus Cmty. Concerts, 1983; usher Springer Theater, Columbus, 1984. Mem. NEA (del. 1978-79), ACA, Nat. Coun. Tchrs. Math. (guest spkr. 1979, 70), Profl. Assn. Ga. Educators, Ga. Coun. Tchrs. of Math., Benning Edn. Assn. (sec. 1973-77, v.p. 1992), Fed. Edn. Assn., Rotary (pres. Columbus chpt. 1975-76). Methodist. Home: 4151 Anglin Rd Unit 19A Columbus GA 31907

HILTON, CLAUDE MEREDITH, federal judge; b. Scott County, Va., Dec. 8, 1940; s. Claude Swanson and Edna (Fletcher) H.; m. Joretta Cabaniss, June 16, 1963; children: John, Rachel. BS, Ohio State U., 1963; JD, Am. Univ., 1966. Bar: Va. 1966, U.S. Ct. Appeals (4th cir.) 1967, U.S. Supreme Ct. 1981. Dep. clk. of cts. Arlington County, Va., 1964-66, asst. commonwealth atty., 1967-68, commonwealth atty., 1974; sole practice Arlington, 1967-85; judge U.S. Dist. Ct. (ea. dist.) Va., Alexandria, 1985—; asst. commonwealth atty., Arlington, 1967-68, commonwealth atty., 1974; dep. clk. ct., Arlington, 1964-66; commr. in chancery U.S. Ct. Appeals (4th cir.), 1976-85; bd. govs. criminal law sect. Va. State Bar, 1979-84, chmn., 1982-83, mem. ins. com., 1981-85. Mem. ABA, Va. Bar Assn., Arlington County Bar Assn. Republican. Methodist. Lodges: Masons, Alexandria Lodge of Perfection, Kena Temple. Home: 3912 N Upland St Arlington VA 22207-4642 Office: US Courthouse 401 Courthouse Sq Alexandria VA 22314-5799*

HILTON, DEANIE HERMAN, human resources executive, telecommunications manager; b. Hickory, N.C., Mar. 23, 1947; d. Ruel Franklin and Daisy (Loftin) Herman; m. Kenneth James Massagee, Aug. 19, 1967 (div. 1976); 1 child, Amy Celeste; m. William Glenn Hilton, May 18, 1996. Diploma, Catawba Valley Community Coll., 1966, student, 1979, 89; student, Clemson U., 1988. Accounts receivable clk. Hickory Springs Mfg. Co., Hickory, N.C., 1966-68, cashier, 1968-72, sec., v.p. mfg., 1972-79, pers. adminstr., 1979-81, sr. pers. rep., 1981-83, human resources adminstr., 1983—. Bd. dirs. Flynn Christian Fellowship Houses, Hickory, 1989-92; vol. ARC, Hickory, 1989—. Named Outstanding Young Woman Hickory Jaycettes, 1981. Mem. NAFE, Piedmont Personnel Assn., Am. Bus. Women's Assn. (sec., 1981-82, pres. 1982-83, Woman of Yr. 1982, 89), Foothills Exchange of Am. Bus. Women's Assn. (chmn. 1983), Outstanding Bus. Woman of Catawaba County (chmn. 1988). Lutheran. Home: 3226 21st Ave NE Hickory NC 28601-7933 Office: Hickory Springs Mfg Co 235 2nd Ave NW Hickory NC 28601-4950

HILTON, JAMES ARTHUR, clergy member; b. Salem, Ind., June 6, 1937; s. Walter Francis and Bernice Frye (Dawalt) H.; m. Carolyn June Sprecher, June 19, 1960; children: Mark Alan, Holly Anne Hamer. BA, Butler U., 1959; MDiv, Christian Theol. Sem., 1962; DMin, Emory U., 1979. Ordained to ministry Christian Ch., 1963. Pastor First Christian Ch., Rensselaer, Ind., 1963-73; sr. pastor Tropical Sands Christian Ch., Palm Beach Gardens, Fla., 1973-87, Fairview Christian Ch., Lynchburg, Va., 1987-90, First Christian Ch., Tampa, Fla., 1990-96, Ctrl. Christian Ch., Clearwater, Fla., 1996—; dir. Global Mission, Christian Ch., 1990-93; v.p. Christian Ch., Indianapolis, 1972; chmn. New Congregation Com., Christian Ch., Orlando, Fla., 1982-86. Author: Congregational Administration, 1979, God's Word Interpreted, 1992. Mem. adv. bd. Planned Parenthood, Palm Beach, Fla., 1985-86; congl. witness on sch. prayer U.S. Congress, 1995; trustee Lexington Theol. Sem., 1996—. Recipient Neighbor award St. Joseph's Coll., Rensselaer, 1973, Brotherhood award B'nai B'rith, Palm Beach, 1985. Mem. Rotary Club. Home: 1714 Emerald Dr Clearwater FL 34616

HILTON, THEODORE CRAIG, computer scientist, computer executive; b. Oakland, Calif., June 14, 1949; s. Theodore Caldwell and Maxine (Donnelly) H.; m. Peggy Estes, May 21, 1990; children from a previous marriage: Christopher, Kelly, Clark. BS in Internat. Rels., Occidental Coll., 1972; BS, Calif. Inst. Tech., 1972; MS in Computer Sci., N.Y. Inst. Tech., 1980. Ptnr., founder Cen. Data Corp., L.A., 1971—, CEO, 1988—; engr. RSK, L.A., 1972-73; prof. Lake (Fla.) Coll., 1981-85, dept. chmn., 1983-85; prin. rsch. invest. U.S. Dept. Def., L.A., 1985-88; chmn. Interlink World-Wide, 1996—; chmn., CEO E-City Corp., 1996—; bd. dirs. TBS S.A., Versailles, France, Interlink Corp., S.E. Data Comms.; U.S. presenter SOLE Internat. Conv., 1991, CALS presenter, 1995; chmn. Interlink Worldwide, 1996—; chmn., CEO E-City Corp., 1996—. Creator: (computer systems) Broadcast Management System, 1972, ICSS, 1974, EBook, 1993, Quality Assurance System, 1994; patentee Autonomous Network Smart Labels, filterable ditigal advertising, internat database mgmt. sys.; contbr. over 57 articles to profl. jours. Mem. IEEE, IEEE Computer Soc., Am. Mgmt. Assn., Logistics Engrs. Soc., Data Processing Mgmt. Assn., N.Y. Acad. Scis., Rotary (Paul Harris fellow). Office: Cen Data Corp 145 N Church St Spartanburg SC 29306-5163

HIMELBLAU, JACK JOSEPH, Latin-American literature and culture educator; b. Chgo., Feb. 6, 1935; s. Jonas David and Sarah (Grika) H.; divorced; children: Robert Enrique, Vanessa Ann. BA, U. Chgo., 1958, MA, 1959; PhD, U. Mich., 1965. Asst. prof. U. Mich., Ann Arbor, 1965-72; assoc. prof. Columbia U., N.Y.C., 1969-72, Mills Coll., Oakland, Calif., 1972-76; prof. U. Tex., San Antonio, 1976—. Author: Alejandro O. Deustua: Philosophy in Defense of Man, 1979, Quiche Worlds in Creation: The Popol Vuh as a Narrative Work of Art, 1989, The Indian in Spanish America: Two Centuries of Removal, Survival and Integration, 1993, The Indian in Spanish America: Centuries of Removal, Survival, and Integration. A Critical Anthology Vol. I: The Discovery and The Colonial (Pre-Republican) Years, 1994, Vol. II: Republican and Post-Republican Periods, 1995; contbr. numerous articles to profl. jours. Ford Found. postdoctoral fellow, 1966-67. Mem. MLA, Am. Assn. Tchrs. Spanish and Portuguese, Extranjero e la Academia Venezolana de la Lengua (corr., corr. de la real Española 1995). Home: 9834 John Rolfe Dr San Antonio TX 78230-3212

HIMMELFARB, ELLIOTT HARVEY, radiologist; b. N.Y.C., Nov. 20, 1942; s. Hyman and Sarah (Blimkin) H.; m. Cynthia G. Friedman, June 14, 1990; children: Eric, Cara. MD summa cum laude, SUNY, Bklyn., 1966. Diplomate Am. Bd. Radiology. Med. intern VA Hosp., Bklyn., 1966-67; 1st resident radiology Kings County Hosp., Bklyn., 1967-69; chief resident radiology Bklyn. Cumberland Med. Ctr., 1969-70; instr. radiology SUNY, Bklyn., 1970, asst. prof. radiology, 1970-71; attending radiologist St. Josephs Hosp., Far Rockaway, N.Y., 1971-73, Long Beach (N.Y.) Meml. Hosp., 1971-73; assoc. prof. radiology U. Tenn. Med. Ctr., Memphis, 1973-76; dir. radiology Williamson Med. Ctr., Franklin, Tenn., 1976—. Lt. comdr. USN, 1966-83. Republican. Home: 802 Franklin Rd Brentwood TN 37027-5912

HINDLE, PAULA ALICE, nursing administrator; b. Cambridge, Mass., Feb. 26, 1952; d. Edward Adam and Geraldine Ann (Donahue) H. BSN, Fitchburg State Coll., 1974; MSN, Duke U., 1980; MBA, Simmons Coll., 1988. Staff nurse Mt. Auburn Hosp., Cambridge, Mass., 1974-75; staff nurse U. Hosp., Boston, 1975-77, head nurse, 1977-79; staff nurse Duke U. Med. Ctr., Durham, N.C., 1979-80, clin. instr., 1980-81, area mgr., 1981; nurse leader, clin. dir. New Eng. Med. Ctr., Boston, 1981-87; cons. Ctr. for Nursing Case Mgmt., Boston, 1984-87; v.p. nursing Faulkner Hosp., Boston, 1987-94; v.p. nursing and support svcs. Alexandria (Va.) Hosp., 1994—; mem. adv. com. Regis Coll. Nursing, 1993; mem. planning and resource com. Simmons Coll., 1993-94; mem. affiliate faculty George Mason U., 1994-95. Active Am. Heart Assn. Mem. Am. Orgn. Nurse Execs., Va. Orgn. Nurse Execs., Mass. Orgn. Nurse Execs. (treas. 1991-93), Humane Soc., Simmons Coll. Grad. Sch. Mgmt. Alumni Assn. (bd. dirs. 1991-93, pres. 1992-93), Sigma Theta Tau. Democrat. Roman Catholic. Home: 5908 Munson Ct Falls Church VA 22041-2444 Office: Alexandria Hosp 4320 Seminary Rd Alexandria VA 22304-1500

HINDMAN, DAVID MEREDITH, minister; b. Richmond, Va., Dec. 17, 1950; s. Neville Millard and Hilda Addison (Mitchell) H.; m. Betty Jane Figg, Jan. 29, 1972 (div. 1981); 1 child, Jonathan; m. Terrell Linkous, Aug. 22, 1982; children: Benjamin, Grace. BA, Randolph-Macon Coll., 1972; DMin, Union Theol. Seminary, 1976; MA, Presbyn. Sch. of Christian Edn, 1984, EdD, 1995. Assoc. pastor Westhampton United Meth Ch., Richmond, 1976-78; pastor, administrator Asbury-Parkside Cmty. Ministries, Portsmouth, Va., 1978-81; pastor Lebanon United Meth. Ch., Hanover, Va., 1981-84, Asbury United Meth. Ch., Newport News, Va., 1987-88; dir. Wesley Found./The Coll. of William and Mary, Williamsburg, Va., 1988—; bd. diaconal ministry, mem. Va. Conference, United Meth. Ch., Richmond, 1997—; mem. coord. com. Nat. Campus Ministers Assn., Banner Elk, N.C., 1995—. Pres., bd. dirs. Meals on Wheels, Inc., Portsmouth, 1980. Mem. Religious Edn. Assn., Christian Educators Fellowship, Assn. of Profs. and Researchers in Religious Edn. Methodist. Office: Wesley Found 526 Jamestown Rd Williamsburg VA 23185

HINDS, ANN M., programmer, systems analyst; b. Denver, Oct. 4, 1949; m. Robert Hinds, Aug. 26, 1978; 1 child, Michelle. BBA/Bus. Info. Systems with honors, Eastern N.Mex. U., 1982. Sr. programmer, analyst CrediCard Systems Inc., Amarillo, Tex., 1989-90; programmer, analyst AMI Investment Corp., Amarillo, 1988-89; programmer Pioneer Corp., Amarillo, 1983-84; programmer analyst Amarillo Hardware Co., 1990-91; programmer/analyst Am. Quarter Horse Assn., Amarillo, 1991—. Advisor student chpt. Eastern N.Mex. Univ., 1983-84, chmn. fund raising, social chmn., 1989-90. Mem. DPMA. Home: 2510 6th Ave Canyon TX 79015-4176 Office: Am Quarter Horse Assn 1600 Quarter Horse Dr Amarillo TX 79104-3406

HINE, JONATHAN TRUMBULL, JR., university administrator, translator; b. Norfolk, Va., Aug. 3, 1947; s. Jonathan Trumbull Hine and Carrie Louise Curtis; m. Carol Ann Snyder, Dec. 29, 1970; 1 child, Daniel Edward. BS in Italian, U.S. Naval Acad., Annapolis, Md., 1969; MPA, U. Okla., 1982. Cert. rsch. adminstr. Commd. ensign USN, 1965, advanced through grades to lt. comdr., 1976, ret., 1989; profl. translator, 1961—; rsch. analyst U.S. Naval War Coll., Newport, R.I., 1988-89; adminstr. physics dept. U. Va., Charlottesville, 1989-95, assoc. dir. housing, 1995—; owner Scriptor Svcs., Charlottesville, 1984—. Translator: Fundamentals of Naval Strategy, 1990; contbr. articles and book revs. to mags. and profl. jours. Vet. scouter Boy Scouts Am., Italy, R.I., Va., 1986—. Decorated Navy Commendation medal, 1982, 86, 89; recipient Cross of St. George, Episcopal Ch., 1988. Mem. Am. Translators Assn. (accreditation), Soc. Rsch. Adminstrs., Am. Evaluation Assn. (student mem.), U.S. Naval Inst. (Silver medal 1986). Episcopalian. Office: Scriptor Svcs Ste 106 977 Seminole Trail Charlottesville VA 22901-2824

HINER, GLADYS WEBBER, psychologist; b. Mt. Park, Okla., Mar. 10, 1907; d. Santford and Erie Emma (Rose) Webber; m. Wayman Hiner, Aug. 11, 1927 (dec. Mar. 1967); children: Waynel Cook, Sandra Homer. BS, U. Okla., 1934, MS, 1955, PhD, 1962; HHD (hon.), Wagon Wheel Found., McCloud, Okla., 1973. Bd. cert. devel. psychologist. Tchr. Okla. City Pub. Schs., 1953-61; dir. Dale Rogers Tng. Ctr., Okla. City, 1962-63; prof. Okla. City U., 1963-72, Rose State Coll., Okla. City, 1972-86; cons. Wagon Wheel Sch. McLoud, Okla., 1962-82, pvt. practice, Okla. City, 1986—. Supr. Sunday Sch. Trinity Baptist Ch., Okla. City, 1940-72; bd. dirs. Okla. State Assn. for Mentally Retarded Children, 1963-67, Youth and Child Coun. Okla. U. Med. Sch., 1966-69, Bridge Builders, Okla. City; Dem. state del., 1986. Fellow Okla. Psychol. Assn., Am. Assn. on Mental Deficiency; mem. The Acad. Ret. Profls., Okla. Hist. Soc., DAR, Colonial Dames, Psi Chi, Phi Theta Kappa. Home: 800 S Canadian Trails Dr Ap Norman OK 73072-7627

HINES, BETTY TAYLOR, women's center administrator; b. El Paso, Aug. 23, 1927; d. Harold Baldwin and Mary Agnes (Baldwin) Taylor; m. H. Andrew Hines, Jan. 29, 1950; children: Andrew T., Bettina L., Daniel A., D.E.G. AS in Liberal Arts, Grossmont Coll., El Cajon, Calif., 1968; B of Applied Arts and Sci. in Sociology, East Tex. State U., Texarkana, 1990, MS in Counseling Psychology, 1995. Classified advt. clk. L.A. Times, 1961-63; with Realty World Brokers, Calif., 1976-82; sexual assault counselor, adv./vol. Domestic Violence Prevention, Inc., Texarkana, Tex., 1983-89; exec. dir. Bi-State Women's Ctr., Texarkana, 1989—; mem. steering com. Women's Involvement, Texarkana, 1988—; Goodwill amb. Ladies Aux. Fleet Res. Assn., 1993-94. Recipient Christine Nelson award YWCA, 1992, Leadership Texarkana Wilbur award in human rels., 1994; named Woman of Yr., Am. Bus. Women's Assn., 1994. Mem. SCORE. Office: Bi-State Women's Ctr Inc 124 W Broad St Texarkana TX 75501-5609

HINES, JESSICA, art educator, artist; b. St. Louis, Nov. 4, 1958; d. Lee Granger and Frances Josephine (Drake) H.; m. Mazhar Hajossein, June 24, 1989. BFA in Photography, Washington U. St. Louis, 1982; MFA in Photography, U. Ill. Champaign-Urbana, 1984. Instr. photography U. Ill. Champaign-Urbana, 1983-84; assoc. prof. Ga. So. U., Statesboro, 1984—; image maker lectr. SE regional conf. Soc. Photographic Edn., Charlotte, N.C., 1986; tchr. and co-tchr. workshops Rochester (N.Y.) Inst. Tech., 1990; lectr. workshop Va. Intermont Coll., Bristol, 1991. One-woman shows include Elgin (Ill.) C.C., 1985, Duke U., 1986, St. Louis C.C./Meremec Gallery, 1988, Nexus Contemporary Art Ctr., Atlanta, 1988, Exhibit A Gallery, Savannah (Ga.) Sch. Art and Design, 1989, Market Place Gallery, Seattle, 1991, Ga. Coun. Arts, Carriage Works Gallery, Atlanta, 1993, Hollins Coll., Roanoke, 1995, Butcher Gallery, Concord Coll., Athens, W.Va., 1996, Lamar Dodd Gallery, U. Ga., Athens, 1996; two-woman show Women's Studio Workshop-A Ctr. for the Visual Arts, Rosendale, N.Y., 1986; exhibited in group shows at Artemisia Gallery, Chgo., 1983, U. Fla., Gainsville, 1984, Fine Art Ctr., Salem Coll., Winston-Salem, 1985, Ctrl. Wash. U., Sarah Spurgeon Gallery, Ellensburg, 1987, European City of Culture Festival and Glasgow (Scotland) Sch. Art, 1990, Sawtooth Galleries, Assoc. Artists, Winston-Salem, 1990 (Alternative Media Excellence award), 91, The Forum Gallery, Jamestown (N.Y.) C.C., 1991, Rockford (Ill.) Coll., 1991, New Visions Gallery Contemporary Art, 1992, Ga. So. U., 1993, Brewton Parker Coll. Gallery, Mt. Vernon, Ga., 1994, Barton Coll., Gallery, Wilson, N.C., 1994, Crealde Sch. Art, Winter Park, Fla., 1994, Ga. State Capitol, Atlanta, 1994, Creative Arts Guild, Dalton, Ga., 1995, Washington U., St. Louis, 1995, San Guiseppe Art Gallery, Cin., 1995, High Mus. Art, Atlanta, 1995, Ctr. Visual Arts U. Toledo, Ohio, 1995, Rocky Mount Ctr. for Arts, Wilson, N.C., 1996; represented in permanent collections Ohio U., Athens, 1984, Erie (Pa.) Art Mus., 1984; numerous pvt. collections. Grantee Ga. Coun. Arts, 1992, Ga. So. U., 1992, 94, 96, travel grantee Ga. So. U., 1985, 86; recipient Merit award Southeast Juried Art Exhbn., Savannah, 1995. Office: Ga So U Art Dept L B 8032 Statesboro GA 30458

HINES, JONATHAN S., internist; b. Chgo., July 28, 1958; s. David Winslow and Ann (Irwin) H.; m. Jean Domonique Lavney, Aug. 23, 1986; children: Molly Jordan, Emily Kathryn. BFA, U. Tex., 1982; MD, Baylor Coll. Medicine, 1992. Intern Baylor Coll. Medicine, Houston, 1992-93, resident in internal medicine, 1993-95, chief resident, 1995-96. Contbr. articles to med. jours. Vol. Caritas Free Clinic, Austin, Tex., 1986-88. Recipient award for excellence in clin. practice Syntex Co., 1993; named Outstanding Medicine Resident, Houston Acad. Medicine, 1995. Mem. ACP, AMA.

HINES, PEGGY DALE, middle school educator; b. Nashville, Dec. 10, 1937; d. Perry and Mary Alberta (Grandstaff) Dale; children: John Bery Jr., Suzanne Hines Berens. BS, George Peabody Coll., Nashville, 1965, MA, 1975, EdS, 1976; postgrad., Tenn. State U. Cert. biology, gen. sci. tchr., 1-12 reading specialist, elem. sch. adminstr., 1-8 sch. adminstrn., career ladder III, Tenn. Tchr. Haywood Elem. Sch., Nashville, 1966-70; tchr. Ford Greene Mid. Sch., Metro Nashville Bd. Edn., 1970-83; tchr. Wharton Mid. Sch., Nashville, 1983-84; tchr. John Early Mid. Sch. Metro Nashville Bd. Edn., 1984—. Mem. NEA, Tenn. Edn. Assn., Met.-Nashville Edn. Assn., Nashville Middle Sch. Assn., Phi Delta Kappa (sec. chpt. 1987-89, v.p. programs 1990-91, pres. 1991-92). Office: John Early Mid Sch 2013 25th Ave N Nashville TN 37208-1305

HINES, RUTH E., retired postal worker; b. Starke, Fla., Jan. 8, 1958; d. Waiscel and Cora Mobley (Allen) Hines; m. Bernard Green, Dec. 31, 1980 (div. Nov. 1991); children: Drew, Quinton, Bernadette; m. 12/14/93. Diploma, Bradford-Union Vo-Tech. Sch., Starke, 1977. Air traffic contr. FAA, Oklahoma City, 1986-87; letter sorting machine clk. U.S. Postal Svc., Gainesville, Fla., 1987-93. Author: The Racist, 1992, (poetry) The Dark Side of the Moon. With U.S. Army, 1980-84. Democrat. Baptist.

HINES, SUSAN CAROL, English language educator; b. Atlanta, Aug. 6, 1965; d. William Walter and Gretchen Ann (Heers) H. BA, U. Alaska, 1987; MA, U. B.C., Vancouver, Can., 1989; postgrad., Ga. State U., 1990—. Sessional lectr. U. B.C., 1989-90; instr. English, Ga. State U., Atlanta, 1990-93, Mid. Ga. Coll., Cochran, 1993—; instr. English, George Soros Found., Prague, Czech Republic, 1991-92, DeKalb Coll.-Gwinnett, Lawrenceville, Ga., 1990-91, DeKalb Coll.-North, Dunwoody, 1992-93; founder TransText. Contbr. articles to profl. jours. Grantee Ga. Humanities Coun., 1995, NSF, 1996. Mem. MLA, Friends Casa Guidi. Home: RR 1 Box 158 Chester GA 31012-9764 Office: Middle Ga Coll Dept English Cochran GA 30314

HINESLEY, J. HOWARD, superintendent. Supt. Pinellas County Schs., Largo, Fla. Recipient State Finalist for Nat. Supt. of Yr. award, 1993. Office: Pinellas County Schs PO Box 2942 Largo FL 34649-2942

HINES-MARTIN, VICKI PATRICIA, nursing educator; b. Louisville, Aug. 18, 1951; d. William Adolphus Hines and Mary Iris Bailey; m. Kenneth Wayne Martin, Dec. 30, 1978; 1 child, Michelle Hines Martin. BSN, Spalding Coll., 1975; MA in Edn., Spalding U., 1983; MSN, U. Cin., 1986; PhD, U. Ky., 1994. Cert. clin. specialist in adult psychiat. mental. Staff nurse Norton Hosp., Louisville, 1978-81; instr. critical care Sts. Mary & Elizabeth Hosp., Louisville, 1981-82; asst. chief nursing svcs. VA Med. Ctr., Cin., 1983-85; nursing instr. Jefferson Community Coll., Louisville, 1985-87; head nurse mgr. VA Med. Ctr., Louisville, 1987-88; asst. prof. nursing Ind. U. S.E., New Albany, 1989-95, U. Ky., Lexington, 1995—; bd. dirs. Seven Counties Mental Health Svcs.; mem. steering com. on practice parameters Ky. Health Policy Bd. Contbr. articles to profl. jours. Nurses Scholar/Fellow, Lucy Zimmerman scholar, 1982, Estelle Massey Osborne Meml. scholar, 1983-84, trainee U. Cin., 1983, grad. scholar, 1983; named to Outstanding Young Women of Am., 1986; recipient Rsch. award Ky. Nurses Found., 1992, Nursing Excellence award Jefferson County Ky., 1995, Psychiatric Mental Health Nurse of the Year Ky. Nurses Assn., 1995; Elizabeth Carnegie scholar, 1991, Am. Nurses Found. scholar, 1992; Fellow U. Ky., 1988, grad. fellow, 1992,; postdoctoral fellowship in Health Policy ANA Ethnic Minority fellowship program, 1996. Mem. ANA (minority clin. fellow 1991-93), Ky. Nurses Assn. (mental health coun. sec. 1986-88, psych. mental health nurse of yr. award 1995), Kyanna Black Nurses, Inc. (co-founder, past pres.), Nat. Black Nurses Assn., Soc. Edn. and Rsch. Psychiat. Nursing, Sigma Theta Tau. Office: Univ of Kentucky College of Nursing 537 CON Lexington KY 40536

HINGERTY, BRIAN EDWARD, biophysicist, researcher; b. Bklyn., July 30, 1948; s. Lee Clarence and Claire Ada (Merenda) H. BS, Bklyn. Coll., 1969; MA, Princeton U., 1971, PhD, 1974. NSF postdoctoral fellow Max Planck Inst. for Exptl. Medicine, Gottingen, Fed. Republic Germany, 1974-75; NIH postdoctoral fellow MRC Lab. of Molecular Biology, Cambridge, England, 1975-78; rsch. staff Oak Ridge (Tenn.) Nat. Lab., 1978—; cons. NYU, 1976—; shared faculty U. Tenn., Knoxville, 1981—. Contbr. numerous articles to scholarly and profl. jours. Eugene Wigner fellow, 1978-81. Fellow Am. Physical Soc.; mem. Biophysical Soc., Am. Crystallographic Assn., Phi Beta Kappa, Sigma Xi, Pi Mu Epsilon. Office: Oak Ridge Nat Lab PO Box 2009 MS-8077 Oak Ridge TN 37831-8077

HINKELMANN, KLAUS HEINRICH, statistician, educator; b. Bad Segeberg, Germany, June 6, 1932; came to U.S. 1966; s. Emil F. and Elly (Meincke) H.; m. Christa G., July 29, 1966; 1 child, Christoph. PhD, Iowa State U., 1963. Rsch. assoc. Inst. for Forest Genetics, Schmalenbeck, Germany, 1960; sci. asst. U. Freiburg, Germany, 1964-66; assoc. prof. Va. Poly. Inst. and State U., Blacksburg, 1966-72, prof. statistics, 1972—, head dept. statistics, 1982-93. Editor: Design of Experiments, Statistical Models and Genetic Statistics, 1984; co-author: Design and Analysis of Experiments, 1994; editor Biometrics, 1990-93, Current Index to Statistics, 1995—. Fellow AAAS, Am. Statis. Assn. Office: Va Poly Inst and State U Dept Statistics Blacksburg VA 24061-0439

HINKLE, JEFFREY WAYNE, religious writer, speaker; b. Dallas, 1964; s. Robert and Linnie H. BBA in Fin., U. Tex. Arlington, 1987. Owner Lone Star Lawn Care, Dallas, 1987-92; entrepreneur Dallas, 1992-93, Christian motivator, writer, 1994—; lay Christian spkr. Lover Lane United Meth. Ch., Dallas, 1994; spkr., rschr., Dallas, 1994—. Author: (book) The Fulfillment of You: A Spiritual Perspective, Test Version, 1995. asst. treas. (Adult Sunday Sch.) Lover Lane United Meth. Ch., Dallas, 1993; vol. food bank coord., Metrocrest Svc. Ctr., Carrollton, Tex., 1993-94. mem. Conf. Cross Country Championship Team, U. Tex. Arlington, 1985, Letterman. Mem. Peale Ctr. for Christian Living.

HINKLE, WILLIAM PAUL, mechanical and electrical engineer, consultant; b. Thomasville, N.C., Sept. 24, 1921; s. William Alphus and Julia Ida (Snider) H.; m. Dora Nell Workman, July 15, 1950; children: Paula Yvonne, William Lynn. BS in mech. engring., N.C. State U., 1943; postgrad., Citadel Coll., Charleston, S.C., 1944-45; postgrad. engring. cert., Western Electric Grad. Sch., Princeton, N.J., 1967-69. Registered profl. engr., N.C.; land surveyor, N.C.; pesticide applicator, N.C. Naval architect Charleston Navy Yard, 1943-46; mech. planning engr. AT&T Techs., Greensboro, N.C., 1946-75; profl. engr., cons. Thomasville (N.C.) Svc., 1976—; pres. Thomasville Golf Course, 1976—. Autor: "G" Factor Designs, 1960, Electical Shielding, 1963; inventor: magnetic trim strips, cabinet mounting frames. Instr. pub. speaking Boy Scouts Am., Winston-Salem, N.C., 1973. Mem. IEEE (sr. life mem., del. 1966-67, publicity chmn. 1965-70, Exec. Com. award 1968), ASME (life, Carolina chmn. 1971-72, Dist. Chmn. award 1972, Ann. Handbook award 1943), NSPE (exec. com. 1964-67, Exec. Com. award 1967), Am. Congress Surveying and Mapping, Nat. Soc. Profl. Surveyors, Toastmasters Internat. (disting., club pres. 1965, 73, dist. area gov. 1967-68, Disting. Toastmaster award 1969, Gov. of Yr. 1968, Hall of Fame award 1968). Methodist. Home: 1524 Lexington Ave Thomasville NC 27360-3329 Office: Thomasville Golf Course 1515 Lexington Ave Thomasville NC 27360-3328

HINKLEY THOMPSON, CAROL JOYCE, philanthropy consultant, motivational speaker; b. Detroit, Oct. 28, 1939; d. Carl O. and Vivial Louise (Hoover) Hinkley; m. Keith Francis MacKechnie Thompson, Oct. 5, 1962 (div. Aug. 1979); children: Kathryn M. Thompson Timms, Gregory R., Rebecca E. Thompson Cecin, Gwendolynne Thompson Lyon, Monica Clare. Student, Mercy Coll. Sch. Nursing, Detroit, 1960-62; BS magna cum laude, Tex. Woman's U., Denton, Tex., 1988. Office nurse Miller & Shore, Boston, 1962; pvt. perinatal educator Cambridge, Dallas, Tulsa, Mass., 1965-90; S.W. regional dir. Am. Soc. Psychoprophylaxis in Obs., Inc., Dallas, 1967-71; exec. dir. Family Life Info. Ctr., Dallas, 1973-81; mgr., co-founder Dallas Chamber Orch., 1979-82; major gifts officer U. North Tex., Denton, 1989-92; pvt. cons. nationwide, 1992—; chmn., exec. producer LORAC, Inc., Dallas, 1994—. Author: Childbirth Today: Prepared and Positive, 1978; columnist Grapevine Sun, 1980-81; contbr. articles to profl. jours. Originator, lobbyist for passage Child Safety Act U.S. Congress, Washington, 1965-66; co-founder Stop the Hwy., Tulsa, 1966, Family Life Info. Ctr., Dallas, 1973; trustee Family Counseling and Children's Svcs., Big Bros., Big Sisters; founder Project-Abandoned Mother and Child, Dallas, 1978, Leadership Dallas. Mem. AAUW, Internat. Platform Assn., Nat. Soc. Fund Raising Execs., Internat. Trade Assn., Dallas, Ind. Colls. Advancement Assn., The Dallas 40, Dallas Coun. World Affairs, Univ. Ind., Ctr. on Philanthropy, Greater Dallas Hispanic C. of C. (trustee). Office: LORAC Inc 5025 B Winder North Richland Hills TX 76180

HINMAN, ALAN RICHARD, health facility administrator, epidemiologist; b. New Orleans, Mar. 23, 1937; s. E. Harold and Katharine Ellen (Fradenburgh) H.; m. Donna Virgene Graham, Dec. 21, 1959 (div. 1962); m. Lucy Winkler Householder, May 30, 1965; children: Johanna Mary, Katharine Emily. BA, Cornell U., 1957; MD, Western Res. U., 1961; MPH, Harvard U., 1969. Intern in internal medicine Cleve. Met. Hosp., 1961-62, resident, 1962-64, chief resident, 1964-65; with USPHS, 1965-69, 77-96; advanced through grades to asst. surgeon gen., 1988; epidemic intelligence svc. officer Ctr. for Disease Control, Calif. State Dept. Health, 1965-66; regional evaluation officer Malaria Eradication Program, Ctr. for Disease Control, Atlanta, 1966-67, San Salvador, El Salvador, 1967-68; asst. chief viral diseases br. Epidemiology Program, Ctr. for Disease Control, Atlanta, 1969-70; dir. Bur. Epidemiology, N.Y. State Dept. Health, Albany, 1970-71; asst. commr. epidemiology and preventive health svcs. N.Y. State Dept. Health, 1971-75; asst. commr., dir. Bur. Preventive and Med. Svcs., Tenn. Dept. Pub. Health, Nashville, 1975-77; dir. Divsn. Immunization Ctr. for Prevention Svcs., Ctr. for Disease Control, Atlanta, 1977-88; coord. Nat. Vaccine Program Office of Asst. Sec. for Health, 1987-90; asst. surgeon gen. USPHS, 1988-96; dir. Nat. Ctr. for Prevention Svcs. Ctrs. for Disease Control, 1988-95; sr. advisor to dir. Ctrs. for Disease Control and Prevention, 1995—; sr. cons. pub. health programs Task Force Child Survival and Devel., Atlanta, 1996—; adj. asst. prof. preventive and cmty. medicine Albany Med. Coll., Union U., 1970-75; adj. asst. prof. pub. health Rensselaer Poly Inst., 1971-75; assoc. clin. prof. dept. preventive medicine Vanderbilt U., 1975-77; clin. asst. prof. dept. cmty. medicine Divsn. Healthcare Svcs., U. Tenn., 1975-77; clin. asst. prof. dept. family and cmty. health Meharry Med. Coll., 1975-77; clin. assoc. prof. dept. preventive medicine-cmty. health Emory U. Sch. Medicine, Atlanta, 1978-90; vis. prof. Case Western Res. U. Sch. Medicine, 1984; adj. prof. Emory U. Sch. Pub. Health, 1990—; vis. lectr. Shanghai 1st Med. Coll., 1981; sr. cons. for pub. health programs, The Task Force for Child Survival and Devel., 1996—. Contbr. over 250 articles to profl. jours. Decorated D.S.M.; recipient Indian Health Svc. Dir. Spl. Excellence award, 1992. Fellow ACP, APHA (mem. gov. coun. 1975-77, mem. program devel. bd. 1984-86, mem. nominating com. 1984-86, chair 1985-86, chair-elect epidemiology sect. 1985-87, chair sect. 1987-89, past chair 1989-91, mem. exec. bd. 1991-95, spkr. governing coun. 1995—), Am. Acad. Pediat., Am. Coll. Epidemiology (mem. exec. bd. 1990-94, v.p. 1991-92, pres. 1992-93), Am. Coll. Preventive Medicine (regent 1974-75, 77-81, v.p. for pub. health 1975-76); mem. AMA, Am. Epidemiol. Soc., Am. Soc. Tropical Medicine and Hygiene, Am. Venereal Disease Assn. (bd. dirs. 1972-75, sec.-treas. 1975-77), Assn. Tchrs. Preventive Medicine, Infectious Diseases Soc. Am., Internat. Epidemiol. Assn., Physicians for Social Responsibility, Soc. Epidemiol. Rsch., Soc. Med. Decision Making. Home: 2194 Creek Park Rd Decatur GA 30033-2714

HINMAN-SWEENEY, ELAINE MARIE, aerospace engineer; b. Lincoln Park, Mich., Nov. 18, 1960; d. John Edward and Florence Emelie (Langouse) H.; m. Joseph Lee Sweeney, May 24, 1992. BS in Aero. Engring., U. Mich., 1983; MS in Aerospace Engring., U. Tenn., 1989; PhDME, Vanderbilt U., 1993. Engr. Marshall (Ala.) Space Flight Ctr. NASA, 1983-94, Oceaneering Space Sys., Houston, 1995—; mem. Global Environ. Inst. Curriculum Devel. Com.; mem. Masters of Space studies curriculum planning working group Internat. Space U., 1993. Safety diver Neutral Bouyancy Simulator, Extravehicular Mobility Unit suit, 1987. Recipient performance award NASA, 1987, 90-93, tech. innovation award, 1989, cert. of appreciation, 1988. Mem. AIAA (sr., space ops. support tech. com. 1991—, Outstanding Young Aero. Engr. of Yr. award 1986), Soc. Mfg. Engrs. Robotics Internat. (chmn. 1989-90, sec. 1987, mem. nat. adv. bd. 1994-96, chmn. nat. adv. bd. 1996, Outstanding Engr. award 1988). Home: 2703 Shady Ln Webster TX 77598-6001 Office: Oceaneering Space Sys 16665 Space Center Blvd Houston TX 77058-2253

HINNANT, CLARENCE HENRY, III, health care executive; b. Richmond, Va., June 7, 1938; s. Clarence Henry Jr. and Billie Louise (Chewning) H.; m. Barbara Ann Livingston, June 10, 1966 (div. Feb. 1971); children: C.H. IV, W.W. Tuck. BS, Va. Poly. Inst. and State U., 1961; BS magna cum laude, Med. Coll. Va., 1981. Math. tchr. Hopewell (Va.) High Sch., 1961-64; staff mem. Harper & Row Pub., N.Y.C., 1964-67; stockbroker Merrill Lynch & Co., Richmond, Va., 1967-71; pres. Lancaster Corp., White Stone, Va., 1971-81; v.p., treas. Westminster Canterbury, Lynchburg, Va., 1981-89; pres. Westminster Canterbury of Blue Ridge, Charlottesville, Va., 1989—; faculty Am. Coll. Healthcare Adminstrn., Washington, 1982-84. Contbr. articles to profl. jours. Rep. del. to State Conv., Richmond, 1973. Fellow Am. Coll. Healthcare Adminstrs.; mem. Va. Assn. Non-Profit Homes for Aging (bd. dirs. 1983-84), S.R., Country Club of Va. (Richmond), Rotary. Republican. Episcopalian. Home: 407 Key West Dr Charlottesville VA 22911-8423 Office: Westminster Canterbury Blue Ridge 250 Pantops Mountain Rd Charlottesville VA 22911

HINNANT, HILARI ANNE, educator, educational consultant; b. Coral Gables, Fla., Mar. 23, 1953; d. William Walker and Margaret Elizabeth (Ennis) H.; m. M. Greg Miller. BS in Edn., U. Ga., 1974; MS in Edn., Fla. Internat. U., 1976. Art tchr. Banyan Elem. Sch. Dade County, Miami, 1974-79; tchr. Hilliard (Fla.) Sr. High Sch., 1979-80, Callahan (Fla.) Jr. High Sch., 1980-81; tchr. Duval County Pub. Schs., Jacksonville, Fla., 1981-83, Jacksonville, 1982-83; tchr. The Am. Sch., Hamburg, West Germany, 1983-84, Brevard County Pub. Schs., Rockledge, Fla., 1984-86; clin. experience facilitator U. Wis., LaCrosse, 1987-88; tchr. Sarasota County Pub. Sch., Sarasota, Fla., 1988-90; asst. dir., exploratorium specialist Ednl. Rsch. Ctr. for Child Devel. U. South Fla., Tampa, 1990-91; dir. cen. and VA brs. YMCA Child Care, Milw., 1991-92; ednl. coord. Portage (Wis.) Project transition grant Coop. Edn. Svc. Agy. # 5, 1992-93; project transition grantee Coop. Svc. Agy. # 5, 1992-93; instr. child care & devel. Madison (Wis.) Area Tech. Coll., 1993-94; ednl. cons., 1994—; tchr. Bedford County Pub. Schs., 1994-96, Prince Williams Public Schs., 1996—; illustrator, writer Brevard County Maths. Curriculum Guide Rockledge; presenter Nat. Headstart Tng. Conf., 1993—. Author poems; contbr. numerous articles to profl. jours. Selby grantee, 1989. Mem. Nat. Assn. for Edn. Young Children, So. Early Childhood Assn., Midwest Assn. for Edn. Young Children (conf. presenter 1992, 93), Kappa Delta Pi (presenter internat. convocation 1988), Phi Delta Kappa (past pres. Sarasota-Bradenton chpt. 1989, rsch. grantee 1996), Delta Gamma. Democrat. Roman Catholic. Home: The Westbury 16140 Henderson Ln Montclair VA 22026-1755

HINOJOSA, ALMA ALICIA, pharmaceuticals executive; b. Roma, Tex., Dec. 5, 1953; d. Isidro and Silvina (Solis) H. BS, U. Tex., 1978, BA, 1976. From staff pharmacist to mgr. nuclear pharmacist Nuclear Pharmacy Inc., San Antonio, 1978-86; nuclear pharmacist Diagnostic Medicine, Inc., San Antonio, 1986-89; nuclear sales specialist Siemens Med. Sys., Dallas, 1990—. Roman Catholic. Home: 7706 Braeburn Valley Dr Houston TX 77074 Office: Siemens Med Sys 12705 S Kirkwood #210 Stafford TX 77477

HINOJOSA, EMILIO ALFREDO, community development director; b. San Francisco, Oct. 28, 1939; s. Emiliano and Ruby (Williams) H. Diplomatic scis., U. Nat. Autonoma Mexico, 1960-64; B in Diplomatic Scis., U. Nat. Autonoma Mex., 1964. Cultural attache Mexican Consultate Gen., Chgo., 1960-61; pub. rels. dir. Viana Enterprises, Mexico City, 1965-67; press and info. cons. Embassies of India and Australia, Mexico City, 1968-70; ptnr., editor-in-chief Deporte Grafico, Mexico City, 1970-74; owner, mgr. VV Health Spa, Cuernavaca, Mexico, 1974-84; community devel. dir. Sahuaro Girl Scout Coun., Tucson, 1986-92, San Antonio (Tex.) Area Coun. Girl Scouts, 1992—; v.p. Am. Football Collegiate League, Mexico City, 1971-73; adv. bd. Latin Am. Study Ctr., U. Ariz., 1990. Author: (weekly column) The News, 1970-74; prodr., writer: (daily radio talk show) Grupo Orfeon, 1971-73; contbr. cultural articles to newspapers. Adv. bd. mem. Pio Decimo Neighborhood Ctr., Tucson, 1987-89; adv. bd. mem. cultural heritage com. Tucson (Ariz.)-Pima Arts Coun., 1990-92; mem. Hispanic Emphais Task Force, Boy Scouts Am., 1992; mem. Hispanic Profl. Action Com., Tucson, 1988-92, chmn. mem. com., 1991, 92; mem. Rep. Nat. Com., 1994, 95, 96; bd. dirs. Southwest Mental Health Ctr., 1996—. Recipient Outstanding Svc. to the Cmty. award Cmty. Devel. Block Grant Program, South Tucson, Ariz., 1990, St. Elizabeth Ann Seton award Diocese of Tucson, Ariz., 1991, St. Agnes medal for outstanding leadership Archdiocese of San Antonio, 1996; named Emilio Hinojosa Day in State of Ariz., Gov. of Ariz., Phoenix, 1992. Mem. Patronato Cultural Hispano (bd. pres. 1996—), Mexican Cultural Found. (charter mem., v.p. 1989), Guadalupe Cultural Arts Ctr. Republican. Roman Catholic. Office: Girl Scouts Am San Antonio Area Coun 10443 Gulfdale St San Antonio TX 78216-4130

HINOJOSA, FEDERICO GUSTAVO, JR., judge; b. Edinburg, Tex., Apr. 16, 1947; s. Federico Gustavo and Zulema (Trevino) H.; m. Yolanda Silva, 1970 (div. 1977); 1 child, Cynthia; m. Magdalena Garza, Oct. 30, 1992. BA, Pan Am. U., 1969; JD, U. Houston, 1977. Bar: Tex. 1977, U.S. Dist. Ct. (so. dist.) Tex. 1977, U.S. Ct. Appeals (5th cir.) 1980, U.S. Supreme Ct. 1980. Assoc. Clark, Lowes & Carrithers, Houston, 1977-79; ptnr. Clark & Hinojosa, Houston, 1979-81; child support atty. Tex. Dept. Human Resources, McAllen, 1981-83; asst. dist. atty. Hidalgo County, Edinburg, 1983-84; assoc. Atlas & Hall, McAllen, 1984-87; ptnr. Lewis, Pettitt & Hinojosa, McAllen, 1987-91; justice Tex. Ct. Appeals for 13th Dist., Corpus Christi, 1991—. Sgt. USAF, 1970-74. Mem. State Bar Tex., Mexican-Am. Bar Tex., Mexican-Am. Bar Assn. Coastal Bend (dir. 1993-94), Hidalgo County Bar Assn. (dir. 1986-90). Democrat. Office: 13th Ct Appeals 100 N Closner Edinburg TX 78539

HINOJOSA, RICARDO H., federal judge; b. 1950. BA, U. Tex., 1972; JD, Harvard U., 1975. Judge U.S. Dist. Ct. (so. dist.) Tex.; law clk. to presiding justice Tex. Supreme Ct., 1975-76; assoc. Ewers & Toothaker, McAllen, Tex., 1976-83; judge U.S. Dist. Ct. (so. dist.) Tex., McAllen, 1983—. Office: US Dist Ct 1701 W Bus Hwy 83 Ste 1011 Mcallen TX 78501*

HINSHAW, CHESTER JOHN, lawyer; b. Sacramento, Mar. 10, 1941; s. Chester Edward and Gertrude Lorraine (Miller) H.; m. Karen Forbes Breakey, Feb. 19, 1977. AB, Stanford U., 1963; JD, U. Calif., Berkeley, 1966. Bar: Calif. 1966, U.S. Dist. Ct. (no. dist.) Calif. 1967, U.S. Ct. Appeals (9th cir.) 1967, N.Y. 1968, U.S. Dist. Ct. (so. dist.) N.Y. 1972, U.S. Dist. Ct. (ea. dist.) N.Y. 1974, U.S. Ct. Appeals (2d cir.) 1974, U.S. Dist. Ct. (no. dist.) N.Y. 1980, U.S. Dist. Ct. (ea. dist.) Mich. 1982, U.S. Dist. Ct. (no. dist.) Tex. 1983, Tex. 1984, U.S. Ct. Appeals (5th cir.) 1984, U.S Supreme Ct. 1991. Assoc. Chadbourne & Parke, N.Y.C., 1967-74, ptnr., 1974-83; ptnr. Jones, Day, Reavis & Pogue, Dallas, 1983—; lectr. U. Calif. Berkeley, 1966. Mem. ABA, Tex. Bar Assn., Calif. Bar Assn. Office: Jones Day Reavis & Pogue PO Box 660623 2001 Ross Ave Dallas TX 75201

HINSHAW, DONALD GRAY, music publisher; b. Boonville, N.C., Aug. 23, 1934; s. Evan Willard and Rosella (Sizemore) H. BA in Music, Davidson Coll., 1955; M of Sacred Music, New Orleans Sem., 1958. Music tchr. Jonesville (N.C.) Pub. Sch., 1955-56; music dir. First Bapt. Ch., Wilson, N.C., 1958-64; prof. of music Barton Coll., Wilson, 1959-64; mgr. Ligett & Myers, Durham, N.C., 1964-67, La Perla, Manila, Phillipines, 1967-68; choral editor Carl Fisher, Inc., N.Y.C., 1968-75; pres., chief exec. officer Hinshaw Music, Inc., Chapel Hill, N.C., 1975—, Hindon Pubs. Inc., Chapel Hill, 1975—, Chapel Hill Music, Inc., 1980—. Composer, Arranger, Editor: 28 titles vocal and choral music, 1965—. Treas. Ch. Music Pubs. Assn., 1980-82; trustee Westminster Choir Coll., Princeton, N.J., 1982-86; nat. winner Take Pride in Am., Washington, 1988. Named Col. Commonwealth of Ky., 1971. Mem. ASCAP, SESAC, Nat. Music Pubs. Assn., Am Choral Conductors Assn., Broadcast Music, Inc., Phi Mu Alpha Singonia. Office: Hinshaw Music Inc PO Box 470 Chapel Hill NC 27514-0470

HINSON, DONALD ROY, clinical nurse specialist; b. Jacksonville, Fla., Nov. 6, 1952; s. Murphy Roy and Mable Eugenia (Barber) H.; m. Agnelia Gonzalez, Jan. 17, 1974; 1 child, Daniel Roy. BS, Pan Am. U., Edinburg, Tex., 1980; MS, U. Pacific, 1984, U. S.C., 1988; SciD, U. S.C., 1992. RN, Tex., Calif.; cert. tchr., Tex., Calif. Tchr. spl. edn. PSJA High Sch., Pharr, Tex., 1980-81, Kate Griffin Elem. Sch., Stockton, Calif., 1981-84; cognitive rehab. therapist Dept. Spl. Svcs., Columbia, S.C., 1984-89; clin. nurse specialist Health South, Columbia, 1989—; lectr. neurobiology Richland Dist. II, Columbia, 1984-89; pvt. practice Columbia, 1992. Co-author: Techniques for Accelerated Cognitive Development, 1983; author: Fundamentals of Cognitive Rehabilitation for Learning Disabilities, 1986, Neurobiology Fundamentals for Educators, 1990. Charter pres. St. John Neumann PTO, Columbia, 1987; unit commr. Boy Scouts Am., Columbia, 1988. With USN, 1972-78. Fellow Assn. Cognitive Rehab. Practitioners (treas. 1990); mem. S.C. Nurses Assn., South Ebert Found. for Learning Disabilities, The N.Y. Acad. of Scis. Republican. Roman Catholic. Home: 102 Halling Dr Columbia SC 29223-6520

HINTON, AGNES WILLOUGHBY, nutritionist, university administrator; b. Vicksburg, Miss., May 8, 1946; d. Walter Robert and Tressie Jewel (Hollingsworth) Willoughby; m. Thomas Monroe Hinton, June 3, 1967; children: Thomas Montgomery, Angela Renee. BS, Miss. U. for Women, 1967; MS, U. Tenn., 1968; PhD, U. Ala., Birmingham, 1996. Lic. dietitian Miss. Dept. Health. Pub. health nutritionist Balt. County Dept. Health, Towson, Md., 1968-70; chief dietitian Mercy Hosp., Vicksburg, Miss., 1970-73; cons. dietitian various nursing homes, Miss., 1975-78; cons. nutritionist Miss. State Dept. Health, Hinds and Rankin Counties, 1976-78; coord. nutrition svcs. Miss. State Dept. Health, Jackson, 1978-80, dir. nutrition svcs., 1980-91; fellow cancer control U. Ala., Birmingham, 1991-93; dir. community health advisor network Freedom from Hunger, Jackson, 1993-96; acting dir. and vis. asst. prof. Ctr. Cmty. Health, U. So. Miss., Hattiesburg, 1996—; nutrition cons. Region IV Headstart program, Atlanta, 1992. Recipient Mary Egan award APHA, 1991, Catherine Cornell award, 1996, Felix Underwood award Miss. Pub. Health Assn., 1991, award for outstanding svcs. to reduce hunger and malnutrition ADA, 1994. Mem. Am. Dietetic Assn. (registered dietitian, nominating com. 1989, polit. action com. 1990, legis. and pub. policy com. 1989-90, Outstanding Svc. award 1989, 90, 92), Assn. State and Territorial Pub. Health Nutrition Dirs. (sec. 1987-89, bd. dirs. 1989-91, pres. 1990-91, Excellence in Svc. award 1988, 90, 91), Miss. Dietetic Assn. (sec. 1979-91, chmn. coun. on practice 1981-82, nominating com. 1990-93, Outstanding Dietitian 1988). Republican. Baptist. Home: 14 Tranquility Bay Petal MS 39465 Office: University of Southern Mississippi Ctr for Cmty Health PO Box 5122 Hattiesburg MS 39406-5122

HINTON, BARBARA LORRAINE, corporate tax assistant; b. Tuscaloosa, Ala., Jan. 6, 1951; d. Percyville and Irene (Prewitt) Burns; m. Donald Edward Hinton, Feb. 24, 1973; children: Vincent Dwayne, Randall Lamont. BA in Bus. Adminstrn., Stillman Coll., 1973; attended, U. Ala., Birmingham, 1983, U. Ala., Tuscaloosa, 1988. Office mgr. The Selma Project, Tuscaloosa, 1972-73; sec., clerk Gulf States Paper Corp., Tuscaloosa, 1973-78, gen. acct., 1978-94, tax asst., 1994—. grad. mem. Leadership Tuscaloosa, 1987-88; mem. steering com. Leadership Tuscaloosa, 1989, 90; mem. bd. dirs. Big Brothers/Big Sisters, 1991-94. Mem. Leadership Tuscaloosa Alumni Assn., Inst. Mgmt. Accts. (named Mem. of Yr. 1991-92, Perfect Attendance award 1988-96, v.p. comm. 1990-91, v.p. adminstrn. 1991-92, pres. 1992-93, chmn. 1993-94, v.p. mktg. 1994-95). Methodist.

HINTON, DAVID OWEN, retired electrical engineer; b. Guilford County, N.C., May 12, 1938; s. George Owen Hinton and Barbara Elizabeth (Greeson) Wilder; m. Thelma Marie Arrington, Jan. 26, 1963; 1 child, David Scott. BSEE, N.C. State U., 1965. Electronics officer USN Destroyer, Norfolk, Va., 1965-67; naval flight officer Patrol Squadron, Brunswick, Maine, 1967-70; aircraft maintenance officer USN Rsch. Lab., Patuxent River, Md., 1970-72; project officer Health Effects Rsch. Lab. U.S. EPA, Research Triangle Park, N.C., 1972-79, dep. dir. Human Exposure & Field Rsch. Divsn., 1992; dir. Quality Assurance and Tech. Support Divsn., Research Triangle Park, N.C., 1993-95; ret., 1995; sr. scientist So. Rsch. Inst., Chapel Hill, N.C., 1995—; mem. Air Sampling Instruments Com., Cin., 1976-84; chmn. Electronics Tech. Adv. Com., Durham, N.C., 1981-85. Author: (with others) Air Sampling Instruments for Evaluation of Atmospheric Contaminants, 1983; contbr. papers, articles to profl. jours. Capt. USPHS, 1977-95, ret. Recipient Nat. Def. medal USN, 1972, Commendation medal USPHS, 1986, Bronze medal U.S. EPA, 1988. Mem. Internat. Soc. Exposure Analysis, Am. Conf. Govt. Indsl. Hygienists, Soc. Am. Inventors, Commd. Officers Assn. (sec., treas. 1988), Navy Res. Assn. (life), Res. Officers Assn. (life). Home: 115 Meadow Run Clayton NC 27520

HINTON, NORMAN WAYNE, information services executive; b. Maysville, Ky., Mar. 8, 1944; s. Eugene Fay and Julia Lafelle (Dalton) H.; m. Juanita Ann Smith, Nov. 16, 1968; children: Janis Renee, Brian Wayne. BA in Bus. Adminstrn., Centre Coll. Ky., 1966. Programmer, systems analyst Union Cen. Life Ins., Cin., 1966-70, Electronic Data Systems Corp., Dallas, 1970—. Bd. dirs. S.E. La. chpt. ARC, New Orleans, 1991-92, Orleans Svc. Ctr., 1990-92; chmn. emergency svcs. commn. Info. and Referral Ctr. of Collin County, 1994—, vice chmn., 1995-96, chmn., 1996—; mem. Tulane U. Coll. Bus. Adv. Bd., New Orleans, 1989-92; mem. Dallas-Ft. Worth Ch. coun. Ch. of God Internat., 1994-96, treas., 1995, pres., 1996. Fellow Life Office Mgmt. Assn., Am. Mgmt. Assn.; mem. Los Rios Country Club, Am. Quarter Horse Assn., Assn. Ky. Cols., Sigma Alpha Epsilon. Office: care EDS 5400 Legacy Dr Plano TX 75024-3105

HINTON, SUSAN FRAZIER, elementary education educator; b. Lebanon, Tenn., Dec. 13, 1951; d. Henry Edward and Frances (Fuston) Frazier; m. Jerry Lee Hinton, 1993; children: Troy E. Hinton, David L. Hinton, Rance Kelly Jr. BS, Belmont U., Nashville, 1972; Master's degree, Ala. A&M U., 1974, EdS, 1976. Cert. elem. tchr., Ala.; reading specialist, Ala. Dir. migrant edn. Morgan County Sch. Sys., Decatur, Ala., 1986-89, elem. tchr., 1972-86, 1989—; cons., chmn. So. Assn. Colls. and Univs., 1993—. Vol. Hospice of Am., Huntsville, Ala., 1992—, 4-H Clubs of U.S., Morgan County, 1989-96; organist Smithville (Tenn.) First Bapt. Ch., 1995-96; active Friends of Libr. Assn., Marshall County, Ala., 1994-96, Huntsville Hosp. Assn., 1993-96, Morgan County Mental Health Assn., 1992-96. Mem. NEA (del. 1986, mem. pub. rels. com., Ala. Educator of Yr. 1986, Morgan County Tchr. of Yr. 1996), Ala. Edn. Assn. (del., mem. various commns.), Morgan County Edn. Assn. (pres. 1972, 76). Democrat. Home: 10073 Union Grove Ave Union Grove AL 35175

HINTON, TROY DEAN, civil engineer; b. Floydada, Tex., Jan. 5, 1959; s. James Henry and Olive Nan (Gross) H.; m. Kim Lanette Bertrand, May 30, 1981; children: Kyle, Bradley. BS in Agr. Engring., Tex. Tech U., 1981. Registered profl. engr., Tex. Engring. assoc. West Tex. Consultants, Inc., Odessa, Tex., 1981-84, Amarillo, Tex., 1984-85; engr. West Tex. Consultants, Inc., Odessa, 1985-88, Corlett, Probst & Boyd, Inc., Wichita Falls, Tex., 1989—. Deacon Faith Bapt. Ch., Wichita Falls, Tex. Mem. NSPE, ASCE, Tex. Soc. Profl. Engrs. (sec. treas. 1992-93, Mathcounts coord. North Ctrl.

Tex. chpt. 1992-96, v.p. 1993-94), Water Environ. Fedn. Office: Corlett Probst & Boyd Inc 1912 Kemp Blvd Wichita Falls TX 76309-3960

HINTZ, ROBERT LOUIS, transportation company executive; b. Chgo., May 25, 1930; s. Louis A. and Gertrude V. (Herman) H.; m. Gloria Mae Safbom, Nov. 12, 1955; children—Cary, Leslie, David, Erin. BS in Bus. Adminstrn. magna cum laude, Northwestern U., 1960, MBA, 1965. With Chessie System Inc., from 1963; internal audit officer C.&O. Ry., Cleve., 1963-65; staff asst. to v.p. C.&O. Ry.-B.&O. R.R., Cleve., 1965-68, asst. to v.p., 1968-70; compt. C.&O. Ry.-B.&O. R.R., Balt., 1970-72; asst. to pres. parent co. C.&O. Ry.-B.&O. R.R., Cleve., 1972-74, v.p. corp. svcs., 1974-76, v.p. fin., 1976-78, sr. v.p.-fin., 1978-80; sr. v.p. fin. CSX Corp., Richmond, Va., 1980-83, exec. v.p., 1983-88, ret.; chmn., CEO, CSX Energy Corp., Richmond, 1985-88, ret., Sea-Land Corp., Edison, N.J., 1986-88; pres., CEO, CSX Properties Group, 1985-88; chmn., CEO R.L. Hintz & Assocs., 1989; bd. dirs. Scott & Stingfellow Fin., Inc., Chesapeake Corp., Reynolds Metals Co., Ashland Coal Co. Chmn. St. Joseph's Villa; bd. dirs. Christian Children's Fund. With USAF, 1950-54. Mem. Fin. Execs. Inst., Commonwealth Club, Country Club Va. Roman Catholic. Home and Office: 10002 Walsham Ct Richmond VA 23233-5401

HIPP, LESLIE CAROL, nuclear energy industry executive; b. Newberry, S.C., Aug. 25, 1951; s. Carol M. and Doris (Kunkle) H.; m. Sarah Grayson, June 5, 1992. B in Engring., U. S.C., 1985. Cert. lead auditor Am. Nat. Standards Inst. Insp. VC Summer Nuclear Sta., Jenkinsville, S.C., 1974-76; supr. civil inspectors VC Summer Nuclear Sta., Jenkinsville, 1976-79, coord. site mgmt., 1979-82, quality assurance engr., 1982-87, design engr., 1987-88, supr. procurement quality engring., 1988-92, mgr. procurement and materials, 1992—; steering com., mem. Nuclear Utility Procurement Issues Com., S.E. Region, 1991; mem. Nuclear Material Mgmt. Exch., 1993. Past pres. Newberry (S.C.) Jaycees, 1979; com. mem., sponsor Ducks Unltd., Newberry, 1993; mem. pub. rels. com. Newberry (S.C.) County Sch. Dist., 1994. Named one of the Outstanding Young Men of Am., 1979. Mem. ASME, NRA, Amity Lodge. Methodist. Home: PO Box 451 Newberry SC 29108-0451 Office: VC Summer Nuclear Sta PO Box 88 Jenkinsville SC 29065-0088

HIPPLE, JAMES BLACKMAN, financial executive; b. Pierre, S.D., Oct. 14, 1934; s. James B. and Leola Margaret (Blackman) Hipple; m. Jeanette Pellerin, May 10, 1958; children: Carolyn Jean, Leah Margaret. CPA, La., Tex.; cert. data processor; cert. internal auditor. Jr. auditor Tex. Ea. Corp., Shreveport, La., 1957-60, auditor, 1960-63, sr. auditor, 1963-66, supr. internal auditing, 1966-67; supr. auditing, corp. planning and devel. Tex. Ea. Corp., Houston, 1967-68, asst. treas., 1968-70, asst. treas., asst. sec., 1970-76, treas., 1976-81, comptroller, 1981-87, v.p., controller, 1987-88; v.p., chief fin. officer Panhandle Eastern Corp., Houston, 1988—, sr. v.p. fin., 1989, sr. v.p., chief fin. officer, 1990—. Mem. AICPA, La. Soc. CPAs, Tex. Soc. CPAs, Fin. Execs. Inst. (treas. 1986-87, sec. 1987-88, pres. 1990, nat. bd. dirs. 1991-93), Inst. Internal Auditors, Tax Research Assn. Houston and Harris County (bd. dirs. 1986-88). Office: Panhandle Eastern Corp 5400 Westheimer Ct Houston TX 77056-5310

HIPPS, LARRY CLAY, clergyman, evangelistic association executive; b. Huntsville, Ala., Aug. 11, 1953; s. William B. and Clara M. (Yance) H.; m. Cathy Ann Dees, Mar. 22, 1975; children: Betsy Ann, Allison Renee, Jonathan Clay. BS, Ala. A&M U., 1975; MinM, Internat. Bible Inst. and Sem., 1983, MinD, 1984. Ordained minister Bapt. Ch., 1975. Dir. ministry Flint River Bapt. Ch., Huntsville, 1973-76; assoc. pastor West Rome Bapt. Ch., Rome, Ga., 1976-80, Broadway Bapt. Ch., Memphis, 1980-87; pres. Bring Them In Evangelist Assn., Inc., Memphis, 1976-88, Houston, 1988—; pres. BTI Home Bus. Dirs. Inst., Memphis and Houston, 1984-89. Author: Bring Them in Sunday School Lesons, 1980, BTI Bus Director Manual, 1981, BTI Bus Captain's Handbook, 1987; pub., editor Bring Them In Mag., 1975—; pub. Puppet UpDate mag., Tulsa, 1978. Mem. Nation Wide Bus Ministry Assn. (pres. 1978-79). Republican. Office: Bring Them In 11323 Hughes Rd Houston TX 77089-4637

HIPPS, OPAL SHEPARD, dean, nursing educator; b. May 16, 1938; d. Leon Earl and Georgia (Gould) Shepard; m. Gary Melvin Hipps, May 3, 1959; children: Gary Melvin Jr., Julia Maria Hipps Vasquez. BSN, U. N.C., 1960, MSN, 1964; EdD, U. S.C., Columbia, 1976. Instr. U. N.C. Scg. Nursing, Chapel Hill, 1962, 66-67, Watts Hosp. Sch. Nursing, Durham, N.C., 1964-65, Greenville (S.C.) Gen. Hosp. Sch. Nursing, 1966, 68-69; instr., asst. to assoc. prof. Clemson (S.C.) U. Coll. Nursing, 1969-79, prof., dean, 1987—; prof., dean Baylor U. Sch. Nursing, Waco and Dallas, Tex., 1979-85, East Tenn. State U. Sch. Nursing, Johnson City, 1986-87; mem. adv. com. State Bd. Nursing, Columbia, S.C., 1988-92, policy coun. S.C. Recruitment and Retention Ctr., Columbia, 1988-92; mem. nominating com. So. Coun. on Collegiate Edn. for Nursing, 1995. Bd. dirs. Hospice of the Foothills, Seneca, S.C., 1989-91, Pickens (S.C.) County Free Med. Clinic, 1992-94. Fellow Am. Acad. Nursing; mem. Am. Assn. Colls. Nursing (rep. 1979-95, bd. dirs. 1988-90), Nat. League Nursing (mem. exec. com. 1989-91, chair-elect exec. com. 1991-93, chair 1993-95, bd. govs. 1993-95), Clemson C. of C. (bd. dirs. 1989-92), Phi Kappa Phi, Sigma Theta Tau (charter 1978). Democrat. Southern Baptist. Home: 232 Stonehaven Way Seneca SC 29672-9132 Office: Clemson U Sch Nursing 438 Edwards Hall Clemson SC 29634-1703

HIPSCHER, JEROME JAY, host, educator, writer, actor; b. Bklyn., May 9, 1932; s. Charles and Helen (Blumberg) H.; m. Joan Miller, Nov. 6, 1960; children: Hara, Phillip, Marla. AA, Queensboro C.C., 1978; BA, Fla. Internat. U., 1984, Masters, 1986; cert., Inst. Children's Lit., 1996, Writers Digest Sch., 1995. Spl. delivery technician U.S. Postal Svc., Jamaica, N.Y., 1959-89; tchr. Broward County, Fla., 1990-92, Dade County, Fla., 1989-92; writer Orlando, Fla., 1992—; attraction host Walt Disney World, Orlando, Fla., 1995—, Universal Studios, Orlando, Fla., 1991—; exec. officer Am. Postal Workers Union, Jamaica, 1959-76; exec. dir. Jamaica Bay Coun., Queens, N.Y., 1974-78; actor Screen Actor Guild, Miami, Fla., 1984-92; student senator Fla. Internat. U., Miami, 1984-86. Author: Stickywick, 1994, Abuse Trilogy, 1994, (poems) Daddy, 1995 (Pres. award 1995). Lobbyist Crime in the St. bill; adv. cmty. coun., founder, lobbyist Gateway East Nat. Park. With U.S. Army, 1950-52, Korea. Recipient N.Y.C. Mayor's Youth award, 1976, Comprehensive Ednl. Tng. Act grant U.S. EPA, 1977-78, Pres.'s EPA award White House, 1978, U.S. EPA Spl. award, 1976. Mem. K of Pythians, AARP (founding pres. Southwest Orlando chpt. 1996). Home: 11249 Bonwit Ct Orlando FL 32837

HIRSCH, JEFFREY ALLAN, lawyer; b. Chgo., June 14, 1950; s. Leo Paul And Dorthy (Seidman) H.; m. Lennie Sue Henderson, June 16, 1979; children: Lea, Ashley. BSBA, U. Fla., 1972, JD with honors, 1975. Bar: Fla. 1975, U.S. Dist. Ct. (so. and mid. dists.) Fla. 1975. Assoc. Swann & Glass, Coral Gables, Fla., 1975-76, Glass, Schultz, Weinstein & Moss, Coral Gables, 1976-80; ptnr. Holland & Knight, Ft. Lauderdale, Fla., 1980-93; prin. shareholder Greenberg, Traurig, Hoffman, Lipoff, Rosen & Quentel, P.A., Ft. Lauderdale, Fla., 1993—; exec. dir. Govtl. Research Ctr., Gainesville, Fla., 1975. Active Leadership Broward, Ft. Lauderdale, 1986—, Leadership Fla., 1994—. Mem. ABA, Fla. Bar Assn., Broward County Bar Assn. Office: Greenberg Traurig Hoffman Lipoff Rosen & Quentel PA 515 E Las Olas Blvd Ste 150 Fort Lauderdale FL 33301-2268

HIRSCH, JOE ELBE, surgeon; b. Shamrock, Md., Mar. 7, 1925. MD, Tulane U., 1949. Diplomate Am. Bd. Colon and Rectal Surgery, Am. Bd. Surgery. Intern Charity Hosp., New Orleans, 1949-50, resident gen. surgery, 1952-54; resident gen. surgery VA Hosp., Wadsworth, 1954-56; fellow colon and rectal surgery St. Mary's Hosp.-FB Campbell, Kansas City, 1958-59; with Bapt. Med. Ctr., Kansas City, Mo. Mem. ACS, JCMS. Office: PO Box 5191 Pineville LA 71361-5191

HIRSCH, LAURENCE ELIOT, construction executive, mortgage banker; b. N.Y.C., Dec. 19, 1945; s. S. Richard and Lillian (Avenet) H.; m. Susan Judith Creskoff, Dec. 23, 1967; children: Daria Lee, Bradford Richard. BS in Econs., U. Pa., 1968; JD cum laude, Villanova U., 1971. Bar: Pa. 1972, Tex. 1973. Assoc. Wolf, Block, Schorr & Solis Cohen, Phila., 1971-73; assoc. Bracewell & Patterson, Houston, 1973-76, ptnr., 1976-78; pres. Southdown, Inc., Houston, 1977-85, CEO, 1984-85; pres. Centex Corp., Dallas, 1985—, CEO, 1988—, also chmn. bd. dirs., 1991—; chmn. Centex Constrn. Products, Inc., Dallas, 1994—; bd. dirs. Envoy Corp., Comml. Metals, Inc.; trustee The Blackrock Group; adv. dir. Heidelberger Zement, A.G. Mem. bd. cons. Villanova U. Law Sch.; mem. undergrad. exec. bd. U. Pa. Wharton Sch. With USAR, 1968-75. Office: Centex Corp PO Box 199000 3333 Lee Pky Dallas TX 75219-5111

HIRSCH, MILTON CHARLES, lawyer; b. Chgo., Sept. 10, 1952; s. Charles Ira and Beverly Ruth (Kelner) H.; m. Ilene Lonnie Schreer, Feb. 16, 1986. BA, U. Calif., San Diego, 1974; MS, DePaul U., 1979; JD, Georgetown U., 1982. Bar: Fla. 1982, U.S. Dist. Ct. (so., mid. dists.) Fla. 1983, U.S. Dist. Ct. (no. dist.) Fla. 1985, U.S. Ct. Appeals (5th and 11th cirs.) 1983, U.S. Tax Ct. 1983, U.S. Ct. Claims 1983, U.S. Supreme Ct. 1988. Acct. Arthur Young & Co., CPAs, Chgo., 1977-79; asst. state atty. Office State Atty., Miami, Fla., 1982-84; assoc. Finley, Kumble, Wagner, Heine, Underberg, Manley et al., Miami, 1985-87; pvt. practice Miami, 1987—; adj. prof. Nova U. Law Sch., Ft. Lauderdale, Fla., 1988, 94, 95. Author: Florida Criminal Trial Procedure; contbg. editor Jour. Nat. Assn. Criminal Def. Attys., 1987—; contbr. articles to profl. jours. Mem. ABA (litigation sect.), Nat. Assn. Criminal Def. Lawyers, Fla. Bar Assn.), Fla. Criminal Def. Attys. Assn. (former pres., Presdl. award for Disting. Svc. 1987-88). Office: 9130 S Dadeland Blvd Ste 1702 Miami FL 33156-7858

HIRSCHFELD, ROBERT M.A., psychiatrist; b. Alexandria, La., Feb. 9, 1943. BS, MIT, Cambridge, 1964; MD, U. Mich., Ann Arbor, 1968; MS, Stanford (Calif.) U., 1972. Diplomate Am. Bd. Psychiatry & Neurology. Rsch. scientist NIMH, Rockville, Md., 1972-77, head depression sect., clin. rsch. br., 1977-78, chief ctr. for studies of affective disorders, Clin. Rsch. Branch, 1978-85, chief mood, anxiety & personality disorders rsch. branch, Divsn. Clin. Rsch., 1985-90; Titus Harris disting. prof. & chair, Dept. Psychiatry & Behavioral Scis. U. Tex. Med. Branch, Galveston, 1990—; mem. bd. dirs. Am. Suicide Found., N.Y., 1991—, v.p. 1995—; mem. bd. dirs. Anxiety Disorders Assn. Am., Washington D.C., 1990—, Nat. Depressive & Manic Depressive Assn., Chgo., 1989—. Recipient Adminstr's. award for meritorious achievement ADAMHA, 1979, Commd. Corps. Outstanding Svc. medal, 1987, Commendation medal Pub. Health Svc., 1990, Gerald Klerman award for panic disorder World Psychiatric Assn., 1993, Jan Fawcett Humanitarian award Nat. Depressive and Manic Depressive Assn., 1996. Fellow Am. Psychiat. Assn., Am. Coll. Psychiatry, Am. Coll. Neuropsychiatry; mem. Am. Assn. Chmn. Dept. of Psychiatry (chair rsch. com.). Office: U Tex Med Branch 301 University Blvd Galveston TX 77555

HIRSH, BERNARD, supply company executive, consultant; b. Seguin, Tex., July 18, 1916; s. Samuel and Sarah (Marks) H.; m. Johanna Charlotte Cristol, Feb. 14, 1941 (dec. Jan. 1977); children: Richard, Robert, Terry, Cristy; m. Beatrice Castelle, Feb. 11, 1978. BA, U. Tex., 1939, LLB, JD, 1939. Bar: Tex. 1939. Claims rep. Handley Claim Svc., Dallas, 1939-41; spl. agt. War Food Adminstrn., U.S. Govt., Dallas, 1941-44; pres. Milliners Supply Co., Dallas, 1945-82, chmn. bd., 1982-85, chmn., owner, 1985—. Pres. Temple Emanu-El Brotherhood, Dallas, 1960-62, Temple Emanu-El, Dallas, 1970-72, Nat. Fedn. Temple Brotherhoods, N.Y.C., 1974-76; chancellor Jewish Chautauqua Soc., N.Y., 1970-72. Mem. Dallas Bar Assn., State Bar Tex., Columbian Country Club. Office: Milliners Supply Co 911 Elm St Dallas TX 75202-3164

HIRSH, CRISTY J., school counselor; b. Dallas, Oct. 3, 1952; d. Bernard and Johanna (Cristol) H. BS in Early Childhood and Elem. Edn., Boston U., 1974; MS in Spl. Edn., U. Tex., Dallas, 1978; MEd in Counseling and Student Svcs., U. North Tex., 1991. Nat. cert. counselor; lic. profl. counselor, Tex.; cert. tchr., Tex., Mass. Dir., learning specialist Specialized Learning, Dallas, 1981-93; counselor, mem. adj. faculty Eastfield Coll., Mesquite, Tex., 1992-95; counselor Grapevine (Tex.)-Colleyville Ind. Sch. Dist., 1995—; mem. adj. faculty Richland Coll., Dallas, 1991-92. Mem. Am. Counseling Assn., Coun. for Exceptional Children, Coun. for Learning Disabilities, Pi Lambda Theta, Phi Delta Kappa. Office: VISTA Alternative Campus care 3051 Ira E Woods Ave Grapevine TX 76051

HIRSH, EUGENE HAROLD, gastroenterologist; b. Sept. 12, 1947; m. Frieda Hirsh; children: Joshua, Benjamin, Julie. BS, Cornell U., 1968; MD, SUNY, Buffalo, 1975. Diplomate Am. Bd. Internal Medicine. Intern, resident Emory U. Affiliated Hosps., Atlanta, 1975-78, specialty tng., 1978-80; pvt. practice, Atlanta, 1980—; assoc. clin. prof. Emory U. Sch. Medicine, Atlanta, 1983—; staff physician St. Joseph's Hosp., chief gastrointestinal sect., 1995-97; mem. staff Northside Hosp., chief gastrointestinal sect., 1995-97; mem. staff West Paces Ferry Hosp., chief medicine, 1985; mem. staff Shallowford Hosp. Contbr. articles to profl. jours. Fellow ACP, Am. Coll. Gastroenterology; mem. AMA, Med. Assn. Ga., Med. Assn. Atlanta, Am. Soc. Gastrointestinal Endooscopy, Ga. Gastroent. Soc., Am. Gastroent. Assn. Home: 7395 Wildercliff Dr NW Atlanta GA 30328-1145 Office: Gastroenterology Cons PC #270 5669 Peachtree Dunwoody Rd Atlanta GA 30342

HIRST, NANCY HAND, retired legislative staff member; b. L.A., Feb. 24, 1926. BA magna cum laude, Stanford U., 1947. Staff dir. Spl. Subcom. on Traffic Safety, Washington, 1957-58; legis. asst., speechwriter Rep. John C. Watts, 1962-71; adminstrv. aide to chmn. Ho. Com. on Edn. and Labor, Washington, 1975-77. Contbr. photographs to Rio Rimac, Ency. Britannica, 1965. Trustee Va. Mus. Fine Arts, Richmond; active Va. Bd. Historic Resources; chmn. Citizens Adv. Coun. on Furnishing and Interpreting the Exec. Mansion, 1988-93; active 175th Anniversary Commn. for Va.'s Exec. Mansion, 1987-88; trustee Am. Friends of Attingham Summer Sch., G.B., 1988-91; chmn. Woodlawn Plantation Coun., 1974-86; trustee, v.p., pres. Woodlawn Found., 1987-88; bd. visitors George Mason U., 1982-90; mem. Stanford in Washington Coun.; vice chair Mid-Atlantic region Stanford Centennial. Mem. Phi Beta Kappa. Home: 1001 Basil Rd Mc Lean VA 22101-1819

HISE, KENNETH WINFORD, retired finance educator; b. Henrietta, Tex., Sept. 21, 1927; s. Marion Kenneth and Bessie Frances (Palmer) H.; m. Franca Maria Kersevany, Feb. 22, 1948; children: Mary Frances, Kenneth Neal, Thomas Wayne, Kevin Michael. BS, U. Md., 1963; MS, Fla. State U., 1968; EdD, Nova U., 1975. Prof. econs. Valencia C.C., Orlando, 1968-90, dir. banking program, 1985-90, ret., 1990; adj. prof. econs. Fla. Inst. Tech., Orlando, 1984—, Nova U., 1987—; adj. faculty Orlando metro campus Webster U., 1990—, faculty coord., 1991-93. Maj. U.S. Army, 1945-67. Decorated Bronze Star. Mem. Am. Econ. Assn., Am. Inst. Banking (charter, ednl. dir. 1975-93), Fla. Assn. C.C. (hon. life), Ret. Officers Assn., Rotary Internat., Elks. Home: 320 Spring Lake Hills Dr Altamonte Springs FL 32714-3427

HISEY, LYDIA VEE, educational administrator; b. Memphis, Tex., July 10, 1951; d. Murray Wayne Latimer and Jane Kathryn (Grimsley) Webster; m. Gregory Lynn Hisey, Oct. 4, 1975; children: Kathryn Elizabeth, Jennifer Kay, Anna Elaine. BS in Edn., Tex. Tech U., 1974, MEd, 1990. Cert. tchr., mid-mgmt., Tex.x. Tchr. phys. edn. Lubbock (Tex.) Ind. Sch. Dist., 1975-79, tchr., 1982-91, asst. prin., 1991-95, prin., 1995—. Recipient Way-To-Go award Lubbock Ind. Sch. Dist., 1989, Impact II grantee, 1991. Mem. Tex. Elem. Prins. and Suprs. Assn., Delta Kappa Gamma, Phi Delta Kappa. Baptist. Home: 4613 94th St Lubbock TX 79424-5015

HISS, SHEILA MARY, librarian; b. Evanston, Ill., May 7, 1949; d. Bernard F. and Mary Cecelia (Schubert) H.; m. John D. Hales Jr., Oct. 16, 1976; children: Christina Marie, John D. III. BA in History, Mundelein Coll., 1971; MLS, Ind. U., 1973; postgrad., Florence (Italy) Study Ctr., 1986, Fla. State U. Libr. art and music dept. Jacksonville (Fla.) Pub. Libr., 1974-76; asst. libr. North Fla. Jr. Coll., Madison, 1977-91; dir. libr. svcs. North Fla. C.C., Madison, 1991—; mem. adv. bd. Coll. Ctr. for Libr. Automation, Tallahassee, Fla., 1991—, mem. exec. com., 1994-96. Contbr. articles to profl. jours. Leader Girl Scouts U.S., Live Oak, Fla., 1994-96. Mem. ALA, Fla. Libr. Assn., Beta Phi Mu. Roman Catholic. Home: 13337 CR 136 Live Oak FL 32060 Office: North Fla Cmty Coll 1000 Turner Davis Dr Madison FL 32340

HITCHCOCK, BION EARL, lawyer; b. Muscatine, Iowa, Oct. 9, 1942; s. Stewart Edward and Arlene Ruth (Eichelberger) H.; m. Adele Berry, June 11, 1966 (div. 1996); children: Collin William, Amber Leigh. BSSE, Iowa State U., 1965; JD, U. Iowa, 1968. Bar: Iowa 1968, Okla. 1968, U.S. Ct. Customs and Patent Appeals 1973, U.S. Ct. Appeals (fed. cir.) 1982. Atty., Phillips Petroleum Co., Bartlesville, Okla., 1968-69, 73-76; mgr. licensing Phillips Petroleum Co. Europe-Africa, Brussels, 1977-80, sr. patent counsel Phillips Petroleum Co., Bartlesville, 1980-84, assoc. gen. patent counsel, 1984—. Bd. dirs. Bartlesville Symphony Orch., 1973-77, 80-91, pres., 1975-77, 82-84, bd. dirs. Bartlesville Allied Arts and Humanities Council, 1976-77, 80-86, 1st v.p., 1982-83; mem. Govt. and Fin. Goals for Bartlesville Com., 1974-75; bd. dirs. Bartlesville Community Concert Assn., 1982-90, Okla. Assn. Symphony Orchs. 1983-88. Lt. JAGC, USN, 1969-73. Mem. ABA, Okla. Bar Assn. (dir. patent trademark and copyright sect. 1980-86, sec. 1982-83, vice chmn., 1983-84, chmn. 1984-85), Iowa Bar Assn., Washington County Bar Assn. (pres. 1981-82), Am. Intellectual Property Law Assn., Am. Judicature Soc., Am. Corp. Counsel Assn., Fed. Cir. Bar Assn., Licensing Execs. Soc., Eta Kappa Nu. Home: 1227 Misty Lake Ct Sugar Land TX 77478 Office: Phillips Petroleum Co 236 PLB Bartlesville OK 74004

HITCHCOCK, CHERYL HODGES, former middle school educator, business owner; b. Macon, Ga., Oct. 22, 1953; d. Ostell and Eddie Mae Hodges; m. Leon Hitchcock Jr., Aug. 30, 1975 (div. 1981); 1 child, Michael Dennard. BS in Bus. Edn., Ft. Valley State Coll., 1975; postgrad., Ga. Southwestern Coll., 1975-76; MS in Bus. Edn., U. Tenn., 1979. Cert. tchr., Ga. Sec. divsn. sci. and math. Ft. Valley (Ga.) State Coll., 1975-76; sec. Union Carbide Corp., Oak Ridge, Tenn., 1976-79; instr. CETA, Knoxville, Tenn., 1978-79, Crandall Coll., Macon, 1979-83; owner, mgr., operator Superior Secretarial Svcs., Macon, 1983—; dir., instr. Superior Secretarial Inst., Macon, 1985-86; tchr. Mary Persons High Sch. Monroe County Bd. Edn., Forsyth, Ga., 1988-89; tchr. Miller Mid. Sch. Bibb County Bd. Edn., Macon, 1989-94; instr. Ga. Employer's Assn., Macon, 1986-87, Macon Tech. Inst., 1989—; condr. workshop on profl. devel. for secs. Mercer U., 1985; coord. tutorial/self-esteem program Miller Mid Sch., 1991-94. Former mem. supt.'s adv. coun. Bibb County Bd. Edn.; mem. activities com. Mentor's Project of Bibb County, 1992-93; typist Unionville Improvement Assn.; mem. Networking for Women in Bus. Recipient Computer Tech. Tchr. of Yr. cert. for innovative use of computers, Outstanding Svc. award Future Bus. Leaders Am. Mem. NEA, Bibb Assn. Educators, Macon C. of C., Delta Pi Epsilon. Democrat. Baptist. Home: 1795 Anthony Rd Macon GA 31204-5903 Office: 1795 Anthony Rd Macon GA 31204-5903

HITCHCOCK, DENISE THORNBURG, public relations executive; b. Des Moines, Sept. 22, 1951; d. V. Duane and Marcella Mae (Shearer) Thornburg; m. Harold Francis Link, Oct. 6, 1973 (div. Mar. 1980); m. Stanley Edward Hitchcock, Sept. 21, 1985; children: Scott Austin T., Dennis Walker T. (dec.). BA in Journalism, U. Wis., 1973. On-air/promotions mgr. WMTV (NBC), Madison, 1973-74; promotion-on-air writer pub. rels. WLWC/WCMH (NBC), Columbus, Ohio, 1974-76; promotion mgr. on-air Warner Cable QUBE, Columbus, 1976-78; franchise mgr. Warner Amex Cable, Mpls., St. Paul, 1978-81; dir. franchising so. Calif. United Cable TV, L.A., 1981-83; mktg. coord. L.A. (Calif.) Olympic Organizing Com., 1983-84; nat. promotion mgr. Woman to Woman Golden West Broadcasting, L.A., 1983-84; v.p. new media divsn. Merrill & Assocs. Mktg. and Pub. Rels., L.A., 1985; pres. Hitchcock Enterprises, Inc., Castalian Springs, Tenn., 1985—; corp. sec., head pub. rels. Americana TV Network, Inc., Branson, Mo., 1994—; mktg. and pub. rels. cons. Nashville Conv. Ctr., 1985-86; corp. sec. Americana TV Network, Inc., Branson, 1993—; mem. internat. curriculum rev. com. Forum for Sport and Event Mgmt. and Mktg., George Washington U., Washington, 1994-95. Prodr.: Bush Inagural Tribute to the First Lady, Washington, 1989; co-prodr.: Nashville (Tenn.) Summer Lights Festival, 1991. Met. regional com. mem. arts coun. Met. Govt., Mpls., St. Paul, 1979; bd. mem. Task Force on Women's Drug Abuse, L.A., 1981-85, Wynnewood Hist. Site, Castalian Springs, 1988-91, Assn. for the Preservation of Tenn. Antiquities, Gallatin, Tenn., 1989-91. Recipient The Johnson Found. grant Work-Study UN, N.Y., 1972, Addy for Best News Campaign, Madison (Wis.) Ad Coun., 1974, ACE for Best Nat. Documentary Nat. Cable TV Assn., Washington, 1980. Mem. Pub. Rels. Soc. Am. (accredited pub. rels., membership chair local chpt. 1989, 90, Parthenon Merit award 1987).

HITCHENS, DUNCAN, company executive. V.p. rsch. Lynntech, Inc. Address: Ste 105 7610 Eastmark Dr College Station TX 77840

HITCHINGS, OWEN LYMAN, sports association executive, jewelry executive; b. Corvallis, Oreg., July 19, 1937; s. Edward Leroy and Dorothy Frances (Owen) H.; m. Clemmie Baham, Aug. 15, 1958; children—Monica Rene, Kim Louise, Terri Lynne, Lisa Marie. B.B.A., Columbia Coll., Mo., 1975. Commd. officer U.S. Air Force, 1961, advanced through ranks to maj., 1971; comdr. detachment 409 U.S. Air Force Recruiting Office, Oklahoma City, 1974-76, 552 CAMS Squadron, Tinker AFB, Okla., 1976-77; command pilot, 1977; ret., 1977; salesman Bob Moore Cadillac, Oklahoma City, 1977-78; mgr., appraiser Midwest Jewelers, Oklahoma City, 1978-83; utility svs. supr., telecommunication mgr. City of Midwest City, Okla., 1983-92; advisor Black and Black Investment, Oklahoma City, 1978—, Mcpl. Electric Systems of Okla., Midwest City, 1985, Post Office Adv. Bd., Oklahoma City, 1985. Contbr. articles to profl. jours. Donor mem. Smithsonian Instn., 1985, Okla. Aviation and Space Mus., 1985; mem. Friends of the Air Force Mus.; golf course club house asst., Midwest City Mcpl. Golf Course, 1993—. Decorated 14 awards for valor. Mem. KC, Air Force Assn., Ret. Officers Assn., Gemological Inst. Am., Air Commando Assn., Order of Daedalians (flight capt. 1985—, service award 1979, recruiting award 1978), Vietnam Vets. Am., Disabled Am. Vets. Republican. Roman Catholic. Club: Vietnam Vets. Lodge: Rotary. Avocations: public speaking; golf; bowling; flying; collecting art. Home: 5025 Federal Ct Oklahoma City OK 73135-3003 Office: Mcpl Golf Course City of Midwest City 3210 Belaire Dr Oklahoma City OK 73110-3900

HITCHMAN, CAL MCDONALD, SR., secondary education educator; b. Houston, July 9, 1948; s. Robert McDonald and Isabel Mary (Shugert) H.; 1 child, Cal McDonald Jr. BA, Houston Bapt. U., 1972. Cert. vocat./tech. edn. mktg. Tex. Auditor, pers. adminstr., tng. coord. Rice Food Markets, Inc., Houston, 1968-76; tchr., coord. Houston (Tex.) Ind. Sch. Dist., Sterling High Sch., 1976-80; dir. edn. Airco Tech. Inst., Houston, 1980-81; tchr., coord. Houston (Tex.) Ind. Sch. Dist., Sterling High Sch., 1981-91, Houston (Tex.) Ind. Sch. Dist., Sam Houston High Sch., 1991—. Named Outstanding Young Men of Am., 1975, 77. Mem. Am. Vocat. Assn., Mktg. Educators Tex., Mktg. Edn. Assn., DECA (profl. div.), DECA Tex. Assn. (dist. dir. mktg. edn. 1990—), sec., v.p. 1987-90), Metrodet, Tex. Adv. Coun. for Mktg. Edn./DECA, 1990— (chair 1995-96), Kappa Alpha Order. Methodist. Home: 923 Gober St Houston TX 77017-4116 Office: Houston Ind Sch Dist Sam Houston H S 9400 Irvington Blvd Houston TX 77076-5224

HITE, JESSIE OTTO, art museum director; b. San Antonio, Apr. 4, 1947; d. Driscoll Arthur Otto, Jr. and Ruth Corinne (Meyer) Wilson; m. Gerron Stephen Hite, Mar. 16, 1985; 1 child, Catherine Carter. BS, U. Tex., 1969, MA, 1981. Teacher Austin Community Nursery, 1972-78; asst. curator Archer M. Huntington Art Gallery, Austin, 1979-82, asst. dir., 1982-89, acting dir., 1989-93, dir., 1993—; peer panelist rev. City Austin Cultural contracts, 1994—; juror City Austin/Art Pub. Places, 1994. Mem. Am. Assn. Mus., Assn. Art Mus. Dirs., Art Mus. Devel. Assn., Tex. Assn. Mus., Mus. Mgmt. Inst. Office: U Tex Archer M Huntington Art Gallery 23d & San Jacinto Sts Austin TX 78712-1205

HITES, BECKY E., financial executive; b. Oceanport, N.J., Sept. 24, 1964; d. Robert William and Beatrice Everritt (Beck) H. BBA in Econs., West Ga. Coll., 1986; MBA in Fin., Ga. State U., 1992. Pers. asst. The Robinson-Humphrey Co., Inc., Atlanta, 1986-88, rsch. asst., 1988-89, analyst asst., 1989-92, sr. analyst asst., 1992-95, fin. analyst, 1995-96; corp. fin. mergers and acquisitions Kurt Salmon Assocs., Atlanta, 1996—; guest lectr. MBA program Ga. State U., 1995. Patron Ga. Shakespeare Festival, 1986—; vol. Com. to Elect Paul Coverdell, 1992, mem. Atlanta Young Reps., 1990—, Atlanta Hist. Soc., Atlanta High Mus. Art. Mem. Atlanta Soc. Fin. Analysis, Assn. for Investment Mgmt. and Rsch. (program com. ann. conf. 1996), Inst. Chartered Fin. Analysts (Cert. of Achievement 1993-95), Assn. of Women in Metal Industries (Atlanta chpt. program chair 1995-96, treas. 1997—), Atlanta Econs. Club, Nat. Assn. of Bus. Economists, Beta Gamma Sigma, Omicron Delta Kappa. Baptist. Office: Kurt Salmon Assocs Ste 900 1355 Peachtree St NE Atlanta GA 30309-0900

HITT, JOHN CHARLES, university president; b. Houston, Dec. 7, 1940; s. John Charles and Mary W. (Green) H.; m. Martha Ann Halsted, Dec. 23, 1961; children: John Charles, Sharon Aileen. A.B. cum laude, Austin Coll., 1962; M.S. (Danforth fellow, NSF fellow), Tulane U., 1964, Ph.D. (Danforth fellow, NSF fellow), 1966. Cert. psychologist, Tex. Asst. prof. psychology Tulane U., 1966-69; assoc. prof. psychology Tex. Christian U., Ft. Worth, 1969-77; assoc. dean of univ. Tex. Christian U., 1972-77; v.p. Tex. Christian U. Research Found., 1974-77; dean Grad Sch. Tex. Christian U., 1975-77; v.p. acad. affairs Bradley U., Peoria, Ill., 1977-87; provost Bradley U., 1981-87; v.p. acad. affairs, prof. psychology U. Maine, Orono, 1987-92, interim pres., 1991-92; pres. U. Cen. Fla., Orlando, 1992—; bd. dirs. Quad Cities Grad. Study Ctr., 1985-87, Space Coast Devel. Commn., 1992—. Orlando Regional Health Care Sys., 1992—; bd. trustees EDUCOM, 1993—; adv. bd. World Trade Ctr., 1993-94, Orlando Sci. Ctr., 1992—; bd. dirs. Seminar on Acad. Computing, 1984-88, chmn. bd. dirs., 1986-87; chair task force distance learning State U. Sys. of Fla., 1993; pres.'s commn. NCAA, 1993—; nat. adv. bd. Ctr. for the Study of Sports in Soc., 1994—. Mem. bd. coeditors Psychological Research, 1973-77; editl. bd. TQM in Edn., 1993—; editl. adv. bd. Met. Univs., 1993—; contbr. articles in psychology and neurosci. to scholarly jours. Chmn. com. on social scis. Austin Coll. 125th Anniversary Commn., 1973-77; charter mem. Austin Coll. Bd. Edn. Visitors, 1976-80; Tex. Christian U. rep. Leadership Ft. Worth, 1973-74; program chmn. Forum Ft. Worth, 1976-77; mem. Tarrant County United Way Budget Com., 1975-77, Forward Ft. Worth, 1976-77, Econ. Devel. Commn. Mid-Fla., Found. Orange County Pub. Schs., Fla Info. Resource Network; chmn. loaned exec. program Heart of Ill. United Way, 1979, chmn. edn. unit, 1980, bd. dirs. 1983-87; bd. dirs. Greater Peoria YMCA, 1980-84, SunBank, 1992—, mem. community adv. council St. Francis Med. Ctr., Peoria, 1984-87; bd. dirs. Inst. Phys. Medicine and Rehab., Peoria, 1981-87, pres. bd. dirs., 1986-87, Heart of Fla. United Way, 1993—; v.p. Penobscot Valley United Way, Bangor, Maine, 1989-92; trustee Bangor YWCA, 1991-92; vestry St. John's Episcopal Ch., Bangor, 1990-91. Mem. APA, AAAS, Psychonomic Soc., Soc. for Neurosci., Am. Assn. Higher Edn., Peoria Area C. of C. (bd. dirs. 1986-87), Greater Orlando C. of C., Winter Park C. of C., Fla. Assn. of Colls. and Univs. (bd. dirs.), Sigma Xi, Alpha Chi, Psi Chi, Phi Kappa Phi, Beta Gamma Sigma, Omicron Delta Kappa. Home: 2242 Westminster Ter Oviedo FL 32765-7501 Office: U Ctrl Fla PO Box 160002 Orlando FL 32816-0002

HITTLE, JAMES D., writer, business consultant; b. Bear Lake, Mich., June 10, 1915; s. Harry F. and Margaret Jane (McArthur) H.; m. Edna Jane Smith, Dec. 9, 1939 (dec. 1969); children: Harry McArthur, James Richard; m. Patricia Ann Herring, Sept. 5, 1970. B.A., Mich. State U., 1937; M.S. in Oriental History and Geography, U. Utah, 1952. Commd. 2nd lt. USAR cav., 1937; resigned USAR, 1937; directly commd. 2nd lt. USMC, 1937, advanced through grades to brig. gen., 1958, legis. asst. to comdt., 1952-58; asst. to sec. def. legis. affairs, 1958-60, ret., 1960; dir. nat. security and fgn. affairs VFW, 1960-67; syndicated columnist Copley News Service, 1964-69; mil. commentator MBS, 1964-69; dir. DISC, Inc., 1960-67; spl. counsel Senate Armed Services Com., 1968-69; cons. House Armed Services Com., 1968-69; founder, dir. D.C. Nat. Bank, 1965-69; asst. sec. navy for manpower and res. affairs, 1969-71; sr. v.p. govt. affairs Pan Am. World Airways, Washington, 1971-73; cons. to adminstr. VA, 1973-77; cons. to pres. Overseas Pvt. Investment Corp., 1974-75; participant comml. air mgmt. survey S.E. Asian Transp. and Communications Commn., 1975; cons. Gleason Assocs. Inc., 1974-90, LTV Aerospace and Def. Corp., 1975-88, Marriott Corp., 1975—, KMS Industries, Inc., 1985-90; comdt. U.S. Marine Corps, 1979-81; sec. U.S. Navy, 1981-82; counselor to Sec. of Navy, 1982-87; mem. adv. com. USN Postgrad. Sch. 1983-87, 89-94. Author: History of the Military Staff, 1949; also articles; editor: Jomini's Art of War, 1945; columnist: Navy Times, 1974-95, N.Y. Times Regional Newspapers, 1993-95. Bd. dirs. Stafford County (Va.) Indsl. Devel. Authority, 1974-88, 90-96, vice chmn., 1993-96; vice chmn. Belleau Woods U.S. Mil. Cemetery Meml. Day Svcs., 1978—. Decorated Legion of Merit with combat V, Purple Heart, Medal of Combat Merit France, Cross of Chevalier, Mil. Order European Vets.; recipient Alfred Thayer Mahan award Navy League U.S., 1960, Scroll of Honor, 1967, silver medal City of Paris, 1961, gold medal, 1972, George Washington award Freedom Found., 1967, 69, Selective Svc. Sys. Disting. Svc. award, 1971, U.S. Navy Civilian Disting. Svc. award, 1971, 87, Meritorious Pub. Svc. citation U.S. Marine Corps, 1981, Outstanding Alumnus award Mich. State U., 1987, Disting. Alumni award Coll. Arts and Letters, 1994, Commemorative medal China duty, Republic of China, Commemorative medal Murmansk convoy svcs., Russian Fedn. Mem. VFW, Am. Legion, Brit. Legion (hon.), La. State Hist. Soc. (hon. life), Mil. Order World Wars, Clan MacArthur Soc. Am., Navy League, U.S. Marine Corps League (legis. com. 1980-82), Battleship Assn. U.S., 1st Marine Div. Assn. (life), 3d Marine Div. Assn. (life), Co. Mil. Historians, Mil. Order of Carabao, China-Burma-India Vets. Assn., China Marine Assn., Sons of Union Vets. of Civil War, Sons of the Revolution, Naval and Maritime Correspondents Circle, USS Washington Reunion Group, Army-Navy Club of Washington (pres. 1983-87, pres. emeritus 1988—), Phi Kappa Phi, Phi Kappa Delta. Address: 3137 14th St S Arlington VA 22204-4330

HITTNER, DAVID, federal judge; b. Schenectady, N.Y., July 10, 1939; s. George and Sophie (Moskowitz) H.; children: Miriam, Susan, George. BS, NYU, 1961, JD, 1964. Bar: N.Y. 1964, Tex. 1967. Pvt. practice, Houston, 1967-78; judge Tex. 133d Dist. Ct., Houston, 1978-86, U.S. Dist. Ct. (so. dist.) Tex., Houston, 1986—. Author 2 books; contbr. articles to profl. jours. Mem. Nat. coun. Boy Scouts Am. Capt., paratrooper U.S. Army, 1965-66. Recipient Silver Beaver award Boy Scouts Am., 1974, Silver Antelope award Boy Scouts Am., 1988, Samuel E. Gates award Am. Coll. Trial Lawyers. Mem. ABA (merit award), State Bar Tex. (Outstanding Lawyer in Tex. award), Houston Bar Assn. (president's and Dirs.' award), Am. Law Inst., Am. Judicature Soc., Masons (33d degree). Office: US Courthouse 515 Rusk St Ste 8509 Houston TX 77002-2603

HITZMAN, DONALD OLIVER, microbiologist; b. Milw., Dec. 2, 1926; s. Walter John and Irene (Smith) H.; m. Mary Elizabeth Neumann, Aug. 20, 1952; children: Murray W., Daniel C. AB, Carleton Coll., Northfield, Minn., 1948; MS, U. Ill., 1950, PhD, 1954. Resident microbiologist Texaco Co., Long Beach, Calif., 1951; sr. rsch. assoc. Phillips Petroleum Co., Bartlesville, Okla., 1954-85; v.p. rsch. Geo-Microbial Tech., Inc., Ochelata, Okla., 1985—. Contbr. articles to sci. publs. With USAAF, 1944-45. Fulbright scholar, Australia, 1951. Mem. Soc. Microbiology, Soc. Indsl. Microbiology, Am. Chem. Soc. Republican. Episcopalian. Office: Geo-Microbial Tech East Main St Ochelata OK 74051

HIXON, ANDREA KAYE, healthcare quality specialist; b. Clifton Forge, Va., Jan. 15, 1955; d. Leon Malcolm and Mary Ruth (Bowyer) Whitmer; m. Charles L. Hixon Jr., Sept. 11, 1976. ADN, Frederick (Md.) Community Coll, 1974; BSN, George Mason U., Fairfax, Va., 1981; MS, U. Md., Balt., 1986. Cert. profl. for healthcare quality, 1993. Staff ambulatory care VA Med. Ctr., Martinsburg, W.Va., 1974-82; nursing home adminstr. VA Med. Ctr., 1982-86; quality assurance coord. nursing James A. Haley VA Hosp., Tampa, Fla., 1987-93; coord. med. ctr. CQI Program, Tampa, 1993—. Mem. Am. Assn. Spinal Cord Injury Nurses, Nat. Assn. for Healthcare Quality. Home: 2610 Bridle Dr Plant City FL 33567-6742

HIXSON, DORIS KENNEDY, secondary education educator; b. Sweetwater, Tenn., Mar. 24, 1944; d. Warren Harding and Orinda Eugenia (Wood) Kennedy; m. Virgil Lee Hitson, Dec. 31, 1963 (dec. July 1973); m. Luther Terrell Hixson, Feb. 14, 1974; children: Rindi, Elaine, Liana. Student, Less-McRae Jr. Coll., 1962-63, Vanderbilt U., 1963-64; BA in English, Tenn. Wesleyan Coll., 1967; postgrad., U. Tenn., Chattanooga, 1983-85; MA in Liberal Studies, Hollins Coll., 1985. Secondary English tchr. Cleveland (Tenn.) City Schs., 1967—; faculty rep. United Tchg. Profession, Cleveland, 1976-86, Tchrs. Study Coun., Cleveland, 1983-87; English instr. Cleveland (Tenn.) State C.C., 1986-89. Bd. dirs. YMCA, Cleveland, 1978-81; pres. SNB Women's Book Club, Cleveland, 1992-94; chmn. Christian edn., 1995-96, Sunday Sch. supt. Wesley Meml. Meth. Ch., Cleveland, 1994-96. Fellow in Bible Lit. NEH, Bloomington, Ind., 1977, fellow in Lit. of Alienation NEH, Hollins, 1983, fellow in English Romantics NEH, Chgo., 1987, fellow in Holocaust Lit. NEH, Boston, 1993. Mem. Nat. Coun. Tchrs. English, Tenn. Coun. Tchrs. English, United Tchg. Profession (rep. 1976-86), Delta Kappa Gamma (rec. sec. 1987-90, parliamentarian 1990-94). Home: PO Box 8 Calhoun TN 37309 Office: Cleveland High 850 Raider Dr NW Cleveland TN 37312-3724

HIXSON, ELMER L., engineering educator. Prof. Dept. Electrical Engring. U. Tex., Austin. Recipient Fellow Mems. award Am. Soc. Engring. Educators, 1992. Fellow Acoustical Soc. Am.; mem. IEEE (life), Inst. for Noise Control Engring. (founding mem.). Office: U Tex Dept Elec & Computer Engring Austin TX 78712

HIXSON, NATHAN HANKS, retired military officer; b. Breezewood, Pa., Dec. 15, 1913; s. Ernest Amos Hixson and Jennie Augusta Hanks; m. Mary Frances Williamson, Mar. 5, 1948; children: Glenn Williamson, Pauline Frances. AB, Temple U., 1935; MBA, U. Pa., 1952; grad., U.S. Army War Coll., 1962. Asst. credit mgr. Julius Garfinkel & Co., Washington, 1937-41, 1945-47; commd. 2nd lt. U.S. Army, 1941-45, advanced through grades to col., 1960, ret., 1969; battery comdr. U.S. Army, various, Europe, 1941-45; chief machine records unit U.S. Army, Ft. McPherson, Ga., 1947-48; chief various brs. U.S. Army, Washington, 1948-69; comdt. Adjutant Gen.'s Sch. U.S. Army, Ft. Benjamin Harrison, Ind., 1966-69; instr. George Washington U., Washington, 1958-61, Maryland U., Taegu, Republic of Korea, 1963-64. Scout master Boy Scouts Am., Ft. McPherson, 1947; coord. charitable fund raising U.S. Army War Coll., 1962. Decorated D.S.M., Bronze Star with oak leaf cluster; Disting. Svc. award, Republic of China. Republican. Methodist. Home: Apt B116 733 Plantation Estates Dr Matthews NC 28105-9143

HIXSON, STANLEY G., computer technology, speech, language educator; b. Chgo., Nov. 25, 1947; s. George Samuel and Alice Elizabeth (Domino) H.; m. Alice Jean Ray, May 25, 1975; children: Polly Alice, Jay Stanley, Christa Renee, Michael Wayne. BA, William Jewell Coll., Liberty, Mo., 1969; MS, Cen. Mich. U., 1986; postgrad., U. Kans. Dir. comm. and retail mktg. Successful Living, Inc., Mpls., 1975-78; pres. LightShine Comm., Shawnee Mission, Kans., 1979-91; editor-in-chief Successful Living, Inc., Mpls.; pub. affairs specialist U.S. Army C.E., Kansas City, Mo., 1983-84; instr. leadership, speech and lang. U.S. Army Command and Gen. Staff Coll., Ft. Leavenworth, Kans., 1984-91; sr. tng. instr. total quality leadership Naval Supply Sys. Command, Washington, 1991-92; dir. quality and process improvement Bur. of Naval Pers., Washington, 1992-94; pres. Great Ideas! in Edn., Alexandria, Va., 1994—; adj. prof. William Jewell Coll., 1989-90; presenter computer tech., leadership, mktg. and mgmt. seminars, 1973—. Author: Research and Study Skills, 1989, Implementing Total Quality Leadership in the U.S. Navy, 1992, Professional Graphics Presentation, 1995, Intermediate and Advanced Relational Database Management Using MS Access, 1996; co-author: Effective Staff Communications, 1985, 89, Visions and Revisions, 1981, Total Quality Leadership: Customers, Teams and Tools, 1992. With USAF, 1969-73. Recipient Achievement cert. Dept. Army, 1988, Outstanding Svc. award Successful Living, Inc., 1979, 81-82, 84. Mem. Fed. Info. Coun., Washington Deming Study Group, Navy Total Quality Leadership Advocates Network, Genealogy Club (Loudon County, Va.), Assn. Philippe Du Trieux, Alpha Phi Omega (life). Home: 5211 Leeward Ln Alexandria VA 22315-3944

HLAD, GREGORY MICHAEL, psychometrist, assessment services coordinator; b. McKeesport, Pa., Feb. 14, 1947; s. Michael Gregory Jr. and Helen Delores (Harman) H.; m. Carol Ann Huzinec, July 15, 1972; 1 child, Kristen. BEd, U. Miami, Coral Gables, 1969; MEd, Calif. (Pa.) State U., 1974. Cert. tchr., Fla., Pa.; cert. work evaluator; cert. occupational specialist. Tchr. Wilkinsburg (Pa.) Sch. Dist., 1969-79; asst. prof. Pasco-Hernando Community Coll., New Port Richey, Fla., 1979-83; occupl. specialist Pasco-Pvt. Industry Coun., Fla., 1983-93; assessment coord. Workforce Devel. Authority, Ocala, Fla., 1993-96, Pasco-Hernando C.C., New Port Richey, Fla., 1996—; cons. Xerox Ednl. div. New Haven, 1977-79, Pasco-Hernando Community Coll., 1983—, mem. learning lab. adv. com., 1985-86; v.p. Ednl./Psychol. Assessments Inc. Mem. budget adv. com. Safety Harbor (Fla.), 1986-87. Recipient Cert. of Appreciation Dept. of Corrections, 1982, Appreciation of Service award Boy Scouts Am., 1986. Home: 39 Friendship Ct Safety Harbor FL 34695-2644 Office: Pasco-Hernando CC 10230 Ridge Rd New Port Richey FL 34654-5129

HLAVAY, JAY ALAN, geologist, analyst; b. Pitts., Sept. 30, 1956; s. Joseph and Margaret Marie (Danjou) H.; m. Sandra Kay Yoho, July 15, 1978 (div. Apr. 1985); m. Cayce Avril Martin, Sept. 26, 1992; 1 child, Joseph Martin. Student, Rutgers U., 1979; BS in Geology magna cum laude, U. Pitts., 1983, MBA, 1989. Geologist RSC Energy Corp., New Philadelphia, Ohio, 1983-85; dist. geologist Carless Resources Inc., New Philadelphia, 1985-89; gen. mgr. What on Earth, Pitts., 1989-90; prin. OPUS Energy Cons. Svcs., Coraopolis, Pa., 1990-92; exploration fin. analyst Union Pacific Resources, Ft. Worth, 1991-92, Austin chalk analyst, 1992-93, controller Gulf of Mexico/Other Profit Ctr., 1993-95; controller Gulf Coast Profit Ctr., Ft. Worth, 1996, project mgr. fin. ops., 1996—. Navy ROTC scholar, 1974; recipient Appreciation award Tuscarawas Valley Desk and Derrick Club, 1985, 86, 87; recipient West Allegheny Sch. Dist. Disting. Alumni award, 1988. Mem. Am. Assn. Petroleum Geologists (co-chmn. fin. com. S.W. sect. ann. conv. 1993), Pitts. Assn. Petroleum Geologists, Sigma Gamma Epsilon. Home: 1106 Ascott Ct Arlington TX 76012-5360 Office: Union Pacific Resources PO Box 7 Fort Worth TX 76101-0007

HLOZEK, CAROLE DIANE QUAST, securities company administrator; b. Dallas, Apr. 17, 1959; d. Robert E. and Bonnie (Wootton) Quast. BS, Tex. A&M U., 1982, BBA, 1982. CPA, Tex. Internal auditor Brown & Root Inc., Houston, 1982-84; asst. contr. Wilson Supply Co., Houston, 1984-86, sr. acctg. supr., Hydro Conduit Corp., Houston, 1986-87; fin. analyst Am. Capital, Houston, 1989-94; dir. adminstrn. CFO Am. Gen. Securities, Inc. 1994—. chmn. bd. dirs. On Our Own Inc. 1987-91. Mem. MENSA, Houston Zool. Soc., Tex. Soc. CPAs, Houston Livestock Show and Rodeo. Lutheran. Home: 15405 Mauna Loa Ln Houston TX 77040-1344 Office: Am Gen Securities Inc 2727 Allen Pky Ste 290 Houston TX 77019-2115

HO, HIEN VAN, pediatrician; b. Hue, Thuathien, Vietnam, Aug. 1, 1947; came to U.S., 1982; s. Vinh Van Ho and Te (Thi) Truong; m. Huong Xuan Diep, Aug. 2, 1972; children: Hoa, Hieu, Hiep, Stephen Huy. MD, Saigon U., 1972. Diplomate Am. Bd. Pediatrics. Resident in pediatrics Georgetown U. Hosp., Washington, 1983-86; chief resident Arlington Hosp., Va., 1985-86; pediatrician Seven Corners Pediatrics, Falls Church, Va., 1986—; instr. Georgetown U. Hosp., 1986. First lt. Republic of Vietnam Army, 1972-75. Fellow Am. Acad. Pediatrics; mem. AMA, N.Y. Acad. Scis., Vietnamese Med. Assn. Home: 10001 Robindale Ct Great Falls VA 22066-1848 Office: Seven Corners Pediatrics 6079 Arlington Blvd Falls Church VA 22044-2707

HO, MIN-CHUNG, computer scientist; b. Taipei, Taiwan, Sept. 29, 1963; came to U.S., 1989; s. Ling-Hsu and Yin-Chin (Chang) H.; m. Fei Wen, Aug. 23, 1991. BS in Electrophysics, Nat. Chiao Tung U., Taiwan, 1985; MS in Electronic Engring., Nat. Chiao Tung U., 1987; MSEE, U. Calif., San Diego, 1991; PhD in Elec. Engring., U. Calif., 1995. Rsch. asst. U. Calif., San Diego, 1990-95; rsch. asst. Rockwell Internat. Sci. Ctr., Thousand Oaks, Calif., 1993; mem. tech. staff Texas Instruments, Dallas, 1995—; engring. cons. Alphax, Mt. Laurel, N.J., 1996. Contbr. articles to profl. jours. 2d lt. Taiwanese Army. Mem. IEEE. Office: Texas Instruments 13588 N Central Expwy Dallas TX 75243

HOADLEY, IRENE BRADEN (MRS. EDWARD HOADLEY), librarian; b. Hondo, Tex., Sept. 26, 1938; d. Andrew Henry and Theresa Lillian (Lebold) Braden; m. Edward Hoadley, Feb. 21, 1970. BA, U. Tex., 1960; AMLS, U. Mich., 1961, PhD, 1967; MA, Kans. State U., 1965. Cataloger Sam Houston State Tchrs. Coll. Library, Huntsville, Tex., 1961-62; head circulation dept. Kans. State U. Library, Manhattan, 1962-64; grad. asst. U. Mich. Dept. of Library Sci., 1964-66; librarian gen. adminstrn. and research Ohio State U. Libraries, Columbus, 1966-73; asst. dir. libraries adminstrv. services Ohio State U. Libraries, 1973-74; dir. of libraries Tex. A&M U. Library, College Station, Tex., 1974-92; dir. Evans Libr. Capital Campaign, 1993-95; dir. Higher Edn. Act Inst. Quantitative Methods in Librarianship, Ohio State U., summer 1969; instr. inst. U. Calif. at San Diego, 1970, summer; Mem. steering com. Gov's. Conf. on Library and Info. Services, Ohio, 1973-74, joint chairperson, 1974; mem. adv. com. Library Services and Constrn. Act Cuyahoga County Pub. Library, Cleve., 1973. Author: (with others) Physiological Factors Relating to Terrestrial Altitutes: A Bibliography, 1968; Editor: (with Alice S. Clark) Quantitative Methods in Librarianship: Standards, Research, Management, 1972; chair editorial adv. bd. National Forum, 1992—; contbr. (with Alice S. Clark) articles to profl. jours. Co-chair program com. Tex. Conf. Librs. and Info. Svcs., 1989-91. Recipient Scarecrow Press award for libr. lit., 1971, Disting. Alumnus award Sch. Libr. Sci., U. Mich., 1976; named Assn. Coll. and Rsch. Librs. Acad. Rsch. Libr. of Yr. 1994. Mem. ALA (coun. 1990-94, legis. com. 1990-92), Am. Librs. (edtl. bd., Ohio Libr. Assn. (chmn. constn. com. 1967-68, chmn. election tellers com. 1969, asst. gen. chmn. local conf. com. 1969-70, sec. 1970-71, v.p., pres.-elect 1971-72, pres. 1972-73, bd. dirs. 1970-75), Tex. Libr. Assn. (com. on White House conf. 1975-77, vice chmn., chmn. coll. and univ. divsn. 1977-78, exec. bd. 1978-81, legis. com. 1987-89, chair nominating com. 1994, Tex. Libr. of Yr. 1994), Assn. Rsch. Librs. (bd. dirs. 1978-81, search com. for exec. dir. 1980, stats. com. 1991-93, Acad. Libr. of Yr. 1994), Midwest Fedn. Libr. Assns. (exec. bd. 1973-74, chairperson program com. 1974), Online Computer Libr. Ctr. (pres. User's Coun., 1983-84, 84-85, trustee 1984-90, chmn. pers. and compensation com. 1987-89), Tex. Conf. Librs. and Info. Svcs. (co-chair program com.), Coll. and Rsch. Librs. (edtl. bd. 1991-96), Phi Kappa Phi (chair nat. forum com. 1993-96), Phi Alpha Theta, Pi Lambda Theta, Beta Phi Mu, Phi Delta Gamma. Home: 5835 Raymond Stotzer Pky College Station TX 77845-8060

HOAG, DAVID ALAN, academic administrator, fundraising consultant; b. Lakewood, Ohio, Sept. 22, 1963; s. John Ellis and Patricia Jane (Gregg) H.; m. Joanna Lynn Butts Hoag, June 21, 1986; children: Jamie Elizabeth, Joni Nicole. BS in Edn., Asbury Coll., Wilmore, Ky., 1986; MS in Sports Adminstrn., U. Ky., 1990; cert. achievement, Ind. U. Ctr. on Philanthropy, Indpls., 1990. Acad. grad asst. U. Ky. Athletics Assn., Lexington, 1986-87; dir. Application and Data Processing Bluegrass State Games, Frankfort, Ky., summer 1987; asst. dir. admissions Asbury Coll., Wilmore, Ky., 1987-90; coord. for Acad. and Compliance Asbury Coll. Athletic Dept., Wilmore, Ky., 1987-90; dir. Advancement, mgr. Second Century Campaign Asbury Coll., Wilmore, Ky., 1990-95; part time fundraising cons. pvt. practice, Wilmore, Ky., 1993-96; v.p. coll. advancement Greenville (Ill.) Coll., 1996—. Recipient awards for cross-country and track and field Nat. Assn. Intercollegiate Athletics, 1983, 85. Mem. Nat. Sic. Fundraising Execs., Coun. for Advancement Support of Edn. Republican. Home: 10 Trails End Rd Greenville IL 62246-1074 Office: Greenville Coll 1 Macklem Dr Wilmore KY 40390-1152

HOAGLAND, JENNIFER HOPE, accountant; b. N.Y.C., Nov. 29, 1955; d. John Joseph and Winifred Adele (Strohmann) Vetter; m. John Grinnell Hoagland, Jr., Jan. 24, 1983; 1 child, John Grinnell III. BS in Acctg., Case We. Res. U., 1977; postgrad., U. Tex., El Paso, 1989—. CPA, Tex.; cert. internal auditor; cert. in mgmt. acctg. Rsch. analyst Predicasts, Inc., Cleve., 1977-79; internal auditor El Paso Electric Co., 1979-80; acct. Exxon Corp., Houston, 1980-81; sr. acct. Colton, Starr, Pena & Co., El Paso, 1981-83, Paul J. Ellenburg Corp., El Paso, 1983-85; dir. of acctg. Life Mgmt. Ctr., El Paso, 1985—. Mem. AICPA, Inst. Mgmt. Accts. Office: Life Mgmt Ctr 8929 Viscount Blvd El Paso TX 79925-5823

HOAGWOOD, TERENCE ALLAN, English language and literature educator; b. Shirley, Mass., Jan. 23, 1952; s. Thomas Earl and Barbara Elaine (Thomas) H.; m. Kimberly Hoagwood; 1 child, Hilary Ruth. BA with honors, U. Md., 1972; MA, Am. U., 1973; postgrad., U. Fla., 1974; PhD, U. Md., 1979. Vis. asst. prof. English Vassar Coll., Poughkeepsie, N.Y., 1979-80; professorial lectr. Am. U., Washington, 1981; asst. prof. English Pa. State U., Altoona, 1981-84, W.Va. U., Morgantown, 1984-86; assoc. prof. Tex. A&M U., College Station, 1986-90, prof., 1990—; mem. adminstrv. bd. Victorian Poetry, 1985-86; mem. editorial bd. Studia Mystica, 1986-92. Author: Prophecy and the Philosophy of Mind: Traditions of Blake and Shelley, 1985, Skepticism and Ideology: Shelley's Political Prose and Its Philosophical Context from Bacon to Marx, 1988, Secret Affinities, 1989, Byron's Dialectic: Skepticism and the Critique of Culture, 1993, A.E. Housman Revisited, 1995, Politics, Philosophy and the Production of Romantic Texts, 1996; editor: Sir William Drummond's Academical Questions, 1984, Mary Hays's The Victim of Prejudice, 1990, Charlotte Smith's Beachy Head and Other Poems, 1993; co-editor: Cornish Ballads and Other Poems, 1994, Sappho and Phaon, 1995, Denzil Place, 1996; contbr. articles and revs. to profl. jours. Mem. MLA, Internat. Assn. Univ. Profs. English, N.Am. Soc. for Study of Romanticism, Assoc. Writing Programs, Conf. on Christianity and Lit., Southeastern Nineteenth-Century Studies Assn., Keats-Shelley Assn., Byron Soc., Coll. English Assn., Ellen Glasgow Soc., N.E. MLA, South Atlantic MLA, Washington Romanticists Group, Interdisciplinary Group for Hist. Lit. Study, Phi Kappa Phi, others. Office: Tex A&M U Dept English College Station TX 77843-4227

HOANG, HUNG MANH, information systems analyst, consultant; b. Hanoi, Vietnam, July 6, 1954; came to U.S., 1975; s. Frank Dinhue and Dianne (Nguyen) H.; m. Candice Kim Truong, Apr. 6, 1986; 1 child, Judy Anh. BSME, Tex. A&M U., 1982; postgrad., Sch. Engring. and Logistics, 1987; MS in Software Engring., Monmouth Coll., 1988. Mech./electronics engr. Dept. Army, Texarkana, Tex., 1984-88, Ft. Monmouth, N.J., 1984-88; programmer/analyst Computer Scis. Corp., Houston, 1988-89; engr. specialist McDonnell Douglas Space Systems Co., Houston, 1989-91; info. sys. analyst Texaco Inc., Houston, 1991-95; consulting database adminstr. Brown and Root Inc., Houston, 1995-96; software engr. Landmark Graphics Corp., Houston, 1996—. Sec. gen. Phat Quang Temple, South Houston, 1984; com. mem. Vietnamese-Am. Space Tech. Assn., Houston, 1991; pres. Vietnamese-Am. Student Assn., Tex. A&M U., College Station, 1981-83, spring 1983. Mem. IEEE, Assn. Computing Machinery, Phi Theta Kappa. Home: 8723 Kalewood Dr Houston TX 77099-1520 Office: Landmark Graphics Corp 15150 Memorial Dr Houston TX 77079-4304

HOBBS, CATHERINE LYNN, English language and literature educator; b. Guymon, Okla., Feb. 13, 1951; d. Dan Stewart and Betty Jean (Ray) H. m. Cecil L. Peaden, Mar. 23, 1975 (div. Feb. 15, 1994). BA in Journalism, U. Okla., 1973; MA in Modern Letters, U. Tulsa, 1983; PhD in English, Purdue U., 1989. Instr. Rogers State Coll., Tulsa, Okla., 1983-84; vis. lectr. comms. U. Tulsa, 1984-85; teaching asst. English dept. Purdue U., West Lafayette, Ind., 1985-89; asst. prof. English Ill. State U., Normal, 1989-92; asst. prof. English dept. U. Okla., Norman, 1992-95, assoc. prof., 1995—; mem. bd. history of rhetoric discussion group, 1993—. Editor: Nineteenth-Century Women Learn to Write, 1995; mem. editl. bd. jour. Genre, 1992—; contbr. articles to profl. jours. NEH fellow, 1990, 93. Mem. AAUW, MLA, Am. Soc. Eighteenth Century Studies, Internat. Soc. History of Rhetoric, Nat. Coun. Tchrs. of English, Rhetoric Soc. Am., Soc. Critical Exch., Tchrs. for Democratic Soc., Phi Kappa Phi. Democrat. Office: U Okla English Dept Norman OK 73019

HOBBS, RALPH LEE, textile consultant; b. Alamo, Ga., June 18, 1921; s. Charles Augustus and Rachel May (Griffin) H.; m. Vivian Aileen Lineberger, Apr. 18, 1942 (dec. June 1952); m. Dorothy Louise Julian, Mar. 20, 1954; children: Mary Lauren, Harriet Louise. BS in Textile Engring., N.C. State U., 1949; student, Harvard U., 1969-70. Rsch. engr. Uniroyal, Inc., Winnsboro, S.C., 1949-64; rsch. and devel. mgr. Uniroyal, Inc., Winnsboro, 1964-83; pres. Whitfield Products, Inc., Cohutta, Ga., 1983-87; textile cons. Hobbs & Assocs., Winnsboro, 1987—. Author: Hobbs & Related Families, 1976, Vol. II, 1986; Fate of 2 Wagon Trains of Gold, 1986, Descendants of Benjamin Hobbs, 1996. Founder, chmn. We The People of Fairfield County, 1992—. With USMC, 1942-46. Mem. Am. Retired Officers Assn. (Hon. Brevit Col. 1986). Episcopalian. Home and Office: Rt 4 Box 318 H Winnsboro SC 29180

HOBSON, DOUGLAS PAUL, psychiatrist; b. Louisville, July 22, 1952; s. Charles Paul and Stella Mae (Billings) H.; m. Vicki Lyn Hoofnel, Dec. 18, 1976; children: Zachary, Lucas. BA, U. Louisville, 1974, MD, 1978; MA, Baylor U., 1983. Diplomate Am. Bd. Psychiatry and Neurology. Resident in psychiatry Yale U. Sch. Medicine, New Haven, 1978-82; fellow in psychosomatic medicine Mass. Gen. Hosp., Boston, 1982-83; dir. psychiatry residency Med. Coll. Ga., Augusta, 1983-87, St. Louis U., 1987-89; regional med. officer Dept. of State, Abidjan, Cote d'Ivoire, 1989-91, Vienna, Austria, 1991-95; asst. prof. psychiatry U. Louisville, 1995—. Contbr. articles to profl. publs. Named Ky. Col., Hon. Order of Ky. Cols., 1974. Mem. AMA, Acad. Psychosomatic Medicine, Internat. Soc. Polit. Psychology. Republican. Mem. Ch. of God. Office: Louisville VA Med Ctr Dept Psychiatry 800 Zorn Ave Louisville KY 40206-1433

HOCHEL, SANDRA STROOPE, speech communication educator, researcher; b. Stanton, Tex., June 7, 1946; d. Clarence Julius and Bonnie Estelle (Winter) Stroope; m. Robert Charles Hochel, Aug. 17, 1969; children: Robin, Ryan. BA, U. Tex. El Paso, 1968; MA, Purdue U., 1970, PhD, 1973. Asst. prof. U. S.C., Aiken, 1974-79, chair divsn. arts & letters, 1979-84, dir., bachelor of interdisciplinary studies, 1984-90, prof., 1985—. Contbr. articles to profl. jours. Mem. So. Comm. Assn., Speech Comm. Assn., Carolinas Speech Comm. Assn. (v.p. 1984-85, pres. 1985-86). Democrat. Mem. Unitarian Universalist Ch. Office: U SC at Aiken 171 University Pky Aiken SC 29801-6309

HOCHMAN, MARCELO L. J., facial plastic surgeon; b. Buenos Aires, Sept. 14, 1959; came to U.S., 1977; s. Isaac M. and Marta R. Hochman; div.; children: Joseph Alexander, Adam Martinez. BA in Biology with honors, U. Tex., 1981; MD, U. Tex., San Antonio, 1985. Diplomate Am. Bd. Otolaryngology. Intern Stanford (Calif.) Med. Ctr., 1985-86, resident, 1986-90; fellow Wash. U., St. Louis, 1990-91, U. Ark., Little Rock, 1990-91; asst. prof., dir. facial plastic reconstructive surgery Med. U. of S.C., Charleston, 1991—, assoc. prof., depts. dermatology and otolaryngology, 1991—. Contbr. to profl. jours. Recipient John Orlando Rowe Outstanding Rsch. award, 1992, Investigator Devel. award, 1992. Fellow Am. Acad. Facial Plastic and Reconstructive Surgery; mem. Alpha Omega Alpha, Am. Acad. Otolaryngology, Am. Soc. Dermatology Surgery, Am. Cleft Palate Cranial Facial Assn. Jewish. Office: Med U SC Otolaryn Sect Facial Pl Sur 171 Ashley Ave Charleston SC 29425-0001

HOCHSTRASSER, DONALD LEE, cultural anthropologist, community health and public administration educator; b. Taylorsville, Ky., June 10, 1927; s. Emil John and Mary E. (Schad) H.; m. Marie Emlen, Apr. 9, 1960; 1 child, Letitia Cope; stepchildren—Eloise Q. Hatch, Laura A. Hatch. B.A., U. Ky., 1952, M.A., 1955; postgrad. (univ. fellow) Northwestern U., 1955-56; Ph.D. in Anthropology, U. Oreg., 1963; M.P.H., U. Calif.-Berkeley, 1969. Research asst. dept. rural sociology U. Ky., Lexington, 1954-55, instr. dept. anthropology, 1956-57, 1959-60, instr. dept. community medicine, 1961-63, asst. prof., 1963-66, assoc. prof., 1966-73, prof., 1973-80, assoc. dir. Ctr. Developmental Change, 1970-73, prof. community health Coll. Allied Health, prof. anthropology Coll. of Arts and Scis., prof. pub. adminstrn. Grad. Ctr. Pub. Adminstrn., 1980—; teaching fellow dept. anthropology U. Oreg., Eugene, 1957-58, instr., 1958-59, NSF research fellow, 1960-61; USPHS spl. research fellow Sch. Pub. Health, U. Calif.-Berkeley, 1968-69; chmn. state family planning rev. com. Ky. State Comprehensive Health Planning Council, 1972-74; mem. state family planning task force Council Health Services, Ky. State Dept. Human Resources, 1974-78; cons., adv. numerous orgns.; vis. scholar dept. adminstrv. and social health scis. Sch. Pub. Health, U. Calif.-Berkeley, 1979; dir. Bluegrass Regional Birth Planning Council, Inc., Lexington, 1978-81, Lexington Planned Parenthood, Inc., 1982-89; mem. adv. coun. Ctr. of Creative Living/Adult Care Program of Lexington-Fayette County Health Dept., 1989. Mem. Union of Concerned Scientists, Am. Farmland Trust, Wilderness Soc. Served with USN, 1946-47. Grantee pub. health, family planning, sickle cell anemia, Tb control and occupational health-risk factors. Fellow Am. Anthrop. Assn., Soc. Applied Anthropology; mem. Soc. Med. Anthropology (founding), Am. Pub. Health Assn. (founding mem. population sect.), Assn. Tchrs. Preventive Medicine, AAAS, AAUP, Phi Beta Kappa, Sigma Xi, Alpha Kappa Delta, Delta Omega. Democrat. Clubs: Univ. Faculty, Alumni. Contbr. numerous articles to profl. publs. Home: 953 Holly Springs Dr Lexington KY 40504-3119 Office: Univ Ky Med Ctr 208A Annex 2 Lexington KY 40536

HOCKER-HATCHETT, NANSI, investigative journalist, writer; d. Elwood and Mildred L. (Cutteridge) Hatchett; m. Jerry G. Hocker, Aug. 23, 1963 (div. June 1977); children: Angela M., Jocinda S., Shellie R. Contbr. poetry to anthologies. Mem. Internat. Soc. Poetry, Nat. Libr. Poetry, World of Poetry Press, Life Study Fellowship, Humane Soc. (award), Coun. for Mentally Ill. Episcopalian. Home: 1201 N Chowning Apt 8 Edmond OK 73034-5059

HOCKETT, SHERI LYNN, radiologist; b. Cleburne, Tex., Apr. 20, 1953; d. Dale and Rosamond (Prater) Hockett; BA, So. Meth. U., 1974; MD, Southwestern Med. Sch., 1978; m. David Alexander Campbell, Apr. 22, 1978; children: Courtney Michelle, Jonathan David. Resident diagnostic radiology St. Paul Hosp., Dallas, 1978-81, chief resident, 1980-81; fellow, 1981-82; chmn. dept. radiology Baylor Med. Ctr. Garland, Tex. Diplomate Am. Bd. Radiology. Mem. Am. Assn. Women Radiologists, Am. Coll. Radiology, Radiol. Soc. N.Am., Tex. Radiol. Soc., AMA, Dalls-Ft. Worth Radiol. Soc. Office: 2300 Marie Curie Dr Garland TX 75042-5706

HOCOTT, JOE BILL, chemical engineer, educator; b. nr. Big Flat, Ark., Sept. 19, 1921; s. Jeiks Edmonds and Frances Clara (Berry) H.; B.S., U. Ark., 1945; M.S., Okla. State U., 1951. Insp. Maumelle Ordnance Works, U.S. Army Ordnance Dept., Little Rock, 1942-43; head sci. dept. Joe T. Robinson High Sch., Little Rock, 1945-46; instr. chemistry U. Tulsa, 1946-47; teaching fellow Okla. A. and M. Coll., Stillwater, 1947-49; research chem. engr. Deep Rock Petroleum Corp., Cushing, Okla., 1950, Kerr-McGee Oil Corp., Stillwater, 1951; chem. engr. cons. Joe Bill Hocott, Little Rock, 1952-55, 63—; med. technician U. Ark. Med. Center, Little Rock, 1955-56, research asso., 1956-57, instr. internal medicine, 1957-62; head chemistry dept. Little Rock Central High Sch., 1963-66; head sci. dept. Met. Vocat.-Tech. High Sch., Little Rock, 1967-73. Asst. scoutmaster Boy Scouts Am., 1945-46, troop committeeman, 1945-46, 57-58, neighborhood commr., 1969-70. Bd. dirs. Ark. Jr. Sci. and Humanities Symposium, 1965-75, asst. dir., 1972. Mem. Am. Inst. Chem. Engrs., Nat. Soc. Profl. Engrs., Ark., Ark. Jr. (dist. dir. 1966-70) acads. sci., Sigma Xi, Phi Lambda Upsilon, Unitarian. Home: 1010 Rice St Little Rock AR 72202-4536

HODAPP, SHIRLEY JEANIENE, curriculum administrator; b. Uniontown, Pa., July 10, 1934; d. James Sylvester and Nellie Mae (Kennedy) Amos; children: Holly Hodapp Vining, Curtis, David, Gordon. BS in Elem. Edn., Otterbein Coll., 1956; MEd, Wright State U., 1973; EdS, U. Toledo, 1990. Cert. elem. tchr., local supt., Ohio. Tchr. 3d grade Elyria (Ohio) City Schs., 1955-56; tchr. 2d grade Beavercreek Local Schs., Xenia, Ohio, 1956-57; tchr. elem. Xenia City Schs., 1965-73; ednl. facilitator Wright State U., Dayton, Ohio, 1973-74; adminstr. Marion S. Kinsey PreSch., Xenia, 1974-79; adminstr. elem. Northeastern Local Schs., Defiance, Ohio, 1979-85; supr. elem. Defiance County Bd. Edn., 1985-92, dir. curriculum and related svcs., 1992-94; nat. cons. ITE Ednl. Consulting, 1995—; adj. prof. Defiance Coll., 1985-93, U. Toledo, 1989, N.W. Tech. Coll., Archbold, Ohio, 1989-90, Bowling Green State U., 1994; dir. Little Gnat Kindergarten Readiness program, Babson Park Elem. Sch., 1996—; cons. in field. Author: Learning About Our World-Germany, 1993, Integrated Thematic Experiences, Implementation Guide, 1994; author and editor: Solving The Puzzles of Early Childhood, 1986, Integrated Thematic Experiences, Vol. I, 1993; contbr. articles to profl. jours. Chmn. Tng. Ohio's Parents for Success Program, Defiance County, 1989-92; mem. Early Childhood Intervention Collaborative, Defiance County, 1988-92, Four County Early Childhood Adv. Coun., Archbold, 1986-90; host Ohio Coop. Ext. Svc. Internat. Exch. Program, Defiance, 1990; chmn. Defiance 2000 Sch. Readiness Fair, 1994; coord. Lake Wales Pub. Libr. Time to Rhyme Presch. Summer Program, 1995; bd. dirs. Lake Wales Cmty. Theatre, 1995—; presch. planning com. Babson Park Elem. Sch., 1995—; corr. sec. Fla. Fedn. Music Clubs, 1995—; vol. dir. Little Gnat Program, Babson Park Elem. Sch. Martha Holden Jennings grantee; named Early Childhood Advocate of Yr., Defiance Assn. for Edn. Young Children, 1988, Leader of Lang. Arts Support Groups in Ohio, Ohio Dept. Edn., 1990. Mem. ASCD, AAUW, Nat. Coun. Tchrs. Social Studies, Nat. Coun. Tchrs. Math., Nat. Assn. for Edn. of Young Children, Polk Coun. for Edn. of Young Children, Assn. Childhood Edn. Internat., Nat. Fedn. Music Clubs. Home: 48 W Johnson Ave Lake Wales FL 33853

HODEL, RICHARD EARL, mathematics educator; b. Winston Salem, N.C., Sept. 24, 1937; s. Earl M. HOdel and Winnifred Groth; m. Margaret Jones, Jan. 3, 1970; children: Richard Groth Jones, Katherine Kennedy. BS, Davidson Coll., 1959; PhD, Duke U., 1962. 1st lt. U.S. Army, Ft. Sill, Okla., 1963-65; asst. prof. math. Duke U., Durham, N.C., 1965-70, assoc. prof. math., 1970—. Author: An Introduction to Mathematical Logic, 1995. Home: 1614 Woodburn Rd Durham NC 27705

HODGE, ANN F., environmental company executive; b. Los Angeles, Aug. 17, 1949; d. Harry Carl and Violet (Howard) Calhoun; m. Thomas Michael Sanders (div. Feb. 1971); 1 child, Richard Dean; m. Robert David Hodge, May 15, 1982. B.A., UCLA, 1976. Legal administr. Cossack & Artz, Los Angeles, 1972-80; paralegal Manatt, Phelps, Rothenberg & Tunney, Los Angeles, 1980-82; tech. writer Galler Assocs., Houston, 1982-83; paralegal Mayor, Day & Caldwell, Houston, 1983-85; divisional v.p. ext. affairs Browning-Ferris Industries, Houston, 1985—; cons. non-profit groups, Houston, 1984—. Contbr. articles to profl. jours. Bd. dirs. Odyssey House. Mem. Pub. Affairs Council (bd. dirs.), Tex. Coun. on Workforce and Econ. Competitiveness, Am. Diabetes Assn. (bd. dirs.), Leadership Am. (past pres.), Leadership Tex. (bd. dirs.). Club: Forum. Lodge: Jobs Daughters (honored queen 1966-67). Avocations: reading, traveling, politics. Office: Browning Ferris Industries 10th fl 580 Westlake Park Blvd Fl 10 Houston TX 77079-2662

HODGE, DONALD RAY, systems engineer; b. Springfield, Mo., Aug. 22, 1939; s. William Orin Jr. and Ruth Mildred (Jones) H. BS, Drury Coll., 1961; MS, U. Wis., 1963, PhD, 1968. Analyst Ctr. for Naval Analysis U. Rochester, Arlington, Va., 1968-71; staff mem. NAS, Washington, 1971; ops. rsch. analyst Dept. Army, Washington, 1971-73; sr. scientist The BDM Corp., Vienna, Va., 1973-77; sr. project engr. TRW, Fairfax, Va., 1977-88; sr. scientist Jaycor, Vienna, 1988-89; exec. staff Computer Scis. Corp., Falls Church, Va., 1989-96; pres. D.R. Hodge & Assocs., Alexandria, Va., 1996—; panel moderator Internat. Command Ctr. Facilities Interoperability, Honolulu, 1987. Contbr. to Van Nostrand's Scientific Encyclopedia, 1976. Recipient Disting. Alumni award Drury Coll., Springfield, Mo., 1980. Mem. IEEE, Ops. Rsch. Soc. Am., Am. Phys. Soc., Mil. Ops. Rsch. Soc. (chmn. tactical command and control workshop). Home: 2907 Farm Rd Alexandria VA 22302-2411 Office: D R Hodge & Assocs 2907 Farm Rd Alexandria VA 22302

HODGE, DOROTHY WILSON (SCOTTIE HODGE), gallery executive; b. Darlington, S.C., Oct. 21, 1940; d. Julian Walter and Elizabeth (Wilson) H. BS, Winthrop Coll., 1961; MA, Furman U., 1973. Band dir. S.C. Pub. Schs., 1961-73; musician S.C., 1961-78; owner, dir. Tempo Gallery, Greenville, S.C., 1975—; visual art cons. Greenville, 1975—; lectr. in field. Exhibited in group shows at Charlotte Open Exhbn., N.C., 1980, 81, Tempo Gallery, S.C., 1980, 83, 93, Curators Choice Exhbn., Greenville Mus., 1981, Francis Marion Coll., S.C., 1983; contbr. articles to profl. jours. Event chairperson Art in the Park, Greenville, 1992—. Recipient Heart in Arts award Greenville Metro. Arts Coun., 1993. Mem. Upstate Visual Arts (bd. dirs. 1991—), S.C. Watercolor Soc. (co-founder 1977—). Office: Tempo Gallery Art and Frame 125 W Stone Ave Greenville SC 29609-5523

HODGE, MARY GRETCHEN FARNAM, manufacturing company distributor, manager and executive; b. DeFuniak Springs, Fla., Sept. 24, 1943; d. Thomas Dewey and Mary Catherine (Mixon) Farnam; m. Spessard L. Hodge, Apr. 28, 1962; children: Jennifer Robin, Monica Leigh Hodge Schulz, Stephanie Lea Hodge Glascock. Student, Orlando Coll.; grad., Citizens' Police Acad., Maitland, Fla., 1996. Adminstrv. asst. The Cameron and Barkley Co., Orlando, Fla., 1961-68, office mgr. Machine Tool div., 1975-76; mgr. Frazer Machinery and Supply Co., Orlando, 1976—, sec.-treas., 1988—. Pioneered effort to establish parent support groups for gifted edn., Seminole County, 1979; sec. Parent of Gifted Edn., Seminole County, 1980-87; mem. adv. bd. Exceptional Student Edn., Seminole City, Fla., 1980-87; chairperson Maitland (Fla.) Centennial Founders Bd., 1985; tour guide Orlando Opera Guild, Winter Park, Fla., 1985; celebrity waitress Leukemia Soc. Am., Orlando, 1986; co-chairperson Project Graduation Lyman High Sch., Seminole County, 1986-87; chairperson Alzheimers Resource Auction Dinner, Winter Park, 1987, 88, pres., bd. dirs. 1988-89, ex-officio bd. dirs. 1989-90, 96—; bd. dirs. Maitland Civic Ctr., 1983-86, v.p., 1993-94, pres. 1994-95, 95-96, ex-officio, 1996—; v.p. Maitland Woman's Club, 1994-95, 95-96, 96-97, mem. Cultural Corridor Com., Maitland, 1994, 95, 96; bd. dirs. non-profit Showcase Group, Maitland Hist. Soc.; co-chair Am. Heart Assn. Lock-up Vol., 1995-96; vol. Golden Orch. and Chorus Aux., Maitland/So. Sem. C. of C., Over the Rainbow Auction, 1995, 96. Recipient appreciation plaque Dividends, Seminole City, 1974-75, cert. appreciation Maitland Civic Ctr., 1986, Alzheimer Resource Ctr., Winter Park, 1987, Pres.'s Gavel, 1989, 96, Northam award, 1995. Mem. Am. Machine Tool Ditbrs., Soc. Mfg. Engrs., Maitland Woman's Club (several offices 1970—). Democrat. Methodist.

HODGE, RAYMOND DOUGLAS, minister; b. Charlotte, N.C., Dec. 5, 1951; s. George Washington Hodge and Mary (Allen) Maloy; m. Gale Lynn Baldwin, Aug. 11, 1972; children: Raymond Douglas Jr., Randolph Daniel. Student, Carson-Newman Coll., 1968, Lee Coll., 1970-71; MA, Ch. of God Sch. Theology, 1992. Ordained to ministry Ch. of God., 1979. Evangelist Ch. of God in S.C., Mauldin, 1972-73; pastor Chs. of God, N.C. and Tenn., 1974-79, Dandridge (Tenn.) Ch. of God, 1979-84, Paragon Mills Ch. of God, Nashville, 1984-85, South Haven Ch. of God, Maryville, Tenn., 1985-94, Spring Creek Ch. of God, East Ridge, Tenn., 1994—; bd. dirs. State Bd. Evangelism, Chattanooga, State Bd. Youth and Christian Edn., Chattanooga; chmn. Ministerial Exam. Bd., Nashville, 1984-85; spkr. on daily radio program Life in the Spirit, 1978; adj. faculty Lee Coll., Cleveland, Tenn., 1992—. Recipient Merit award Vision Found., 1978. Republican. Home: 1005 Spring Creek Rd East Ridge TN 37412-3911 Office: South Haven Ch of God 1005 Spring Creek Rd East Ridge TN 37412-3911

HODGES, ALLEN ARTHUR, plastics film company executive; b. Saginaw, Mich., May 3, 1955; s. Arthur G. and Elizabeth (Flynn) H.; m. Sonia Marie Sharp, July 10, 1976; children: Rebekah, Rachel, Ruth, Lydia. BS in Acctg., Bob Jones U., 1977. CPA, S.C. Mgr. Ernst & Young, Greenville, S.C., 1977-85; ptnr. Stair, Hodges & Co., CPAs, Greenville, 1985-89; corp. contr. JPS Textile Group, Inc., Greenville, 1989—; converter, distbr. Interfilm Holdings, Inc., Piedmont, S.C. Mem. AICPA, S.C. Assn. CPAs, Civitan Club of Greenville (treas. 1988-96), pres., dir., 1993-94). Office: Interfilm Holdings Inc PO Box 1128 Piedmont SC 29673

HODGES, DEVON LEIGH, English language educator; b. Santa Monica, Calif., Feb. 23, 1950; m. Kenneth M. and Shirley A. (Davis) Wolfe; m. Eric V. Swanson, Dec. 15, 1978; children: Tristan, Cecily. BA, Reed Coll., Portland, Oreg., 1969; student, U. Calif. Berkeley, 1972; MA, SUNY Buffalo, 1977; PhD, 1979. Asst. prof. George Mason U., Fairfax, Va., 1981-96; assoc. prof., 1986-92, prof., 1992—. Author: Renaissance Fictions of Anatomy, 1985, Nostalgia and Sexual Difference, 1987, From Klein to Kristeva, 1992. Bd. dirs. Rwanda Children's Fund, Arlington, Va., 1996—. Fellow Nat. Endowment to the Humanities, 1996, Visiting Pembroke, 1983-84. Mem. MLA, Phi Beta Kappa. Office: English Dept George Mason U Fairfax VA 22030-4444

HODGES, EDWIN CLAIR, company executive; b. Montgomery, Kans., July 9, 1940; s. Charles E. and Mary R. (Marvel) H.; m. Rebecca Carlisle; children: Mark E., Elaine L., Kelly M., Cheri E. Greer, William H. Edelen III. BA, U. Kans., 1964. Commd. 2nd lt. U.S. Army, 1964, advanced through grades to maj., 1974; with Adv. Team 33, Republic Vietnam, 1968; ret. U.S. Army, 1985; founder Q-Sys. Internat., Inc. (formerly Genesis Con., Ltd. Inc.), Arlington, Tex., 1985-88, pres., chmn. bd., CEO, 1988—; chief force devel., test and evaluation, U.S. Army, Ft. Knox, Ky., 1974, chief operational test and evaluation, 1976, exec. office dir. chief Requirements team for Armored Gun System, 1980-83; security asst. officer, Ankara, Turkey, 1983-85. Contbr. articles and reports profl. jours. Mem. Masons (32), Knights of Malta. Republican. Office: Q-Systems Internat Inc 1148 107th St Arlington TX 76011-3109

HODGES, ELIZABETH SWANSON, educational consultant, tutor; b. Anoka, Minn., Apr. 7, 1924; d. Henry Otto and Louise Isabel (Holiday) Swanson; m. Allen Hodges, June 27, 1944; children: Nancy Elizabeth, Susan Kathleen, Jane Ellen, Sara Louise. BA cum laude, Regis Coll., Denver, 1966; postgrad., U. No. Colo., 1966-79, Valdosta State U., 1979-81. Cert. secondary edn., hosp./homebound, learning disabilities, Colo., Ga., Ariz. Vol. emergency St. Anthony's Hosp., Denver, 1960-64; v.p., tutor St. Elizabeth's Adult Tutorial, Denver, 1964-69; hosp./homebound tchr. Liberty County Sch. System, Hinesville, Ga., 1979-87; ednl. tutor Colo. River Indian Tribes, Parker, Ariz., 1986-87; vol. Twin Cities Community Hosp., Templeton, Calif., 1987-89, Guardian Ad Litem Cir. Ct. 5th Dist. Fla., 1992—, Munroe Regional Med. Ctr., Ocala, Fla., 1991-92; cons., tutor Sylvan Learning Ctr., Ocala, 1990—. Reporter Trinity Triangle Newsletter, Ocala, 1992—. Mem. AAUW (chmn. internat. affairs 1991-92). Democrat. Roman Catholic. Home and Office: 4544 SE 13th St Ocala FL 34471-3241

HODGES, JAMES H., state legislator; married; 2 children: Luke, Sam. BBA, U. S.C., 1979, JD, 1982. Rep. Dist. 45 (Lancaster County) S.C. House of Reps., 1986—, chmn. house judiciary com., 1992-94, chmn. joint com. judicial screening, 1993-94, minority leader of house, 1995—; sec., gen. counsel The Springs Co. Named. Legislator of Yr., S.C. C. of C., 1993; recipient Compleat Lawyer Silver medallion U. S.C. Sch. of Law, 1994. Mem. Phi Beta Kappa. Office: PO Drawer 460 104 E Springs St Lancaster SC 29720

HODGES, JAMES STEPHEN, community development missionary; b. Whitinsville, Mass., Jan. 7, 1953; s. James Bartlett and Margaret Isabelle (Livingston) H.; m. Diantha Lois Inglis, Nov. 30, 1974; children: Hope Bethany, Joy Anna, Sarah Grace. BA with honors, Earlham Coll., 1974; MDiv, Union Theol. Sem., Richmond, Va., 1980. Coord. Richmond Peace Edn. Ctr., 1980-84, coord. nonviolence projects, 1985-87; missionary prof. Pai Chai U., Taejon, Republic of Korea, 1987-89; cmty. organizer Ctr. for Cmty. Action, Lumberton, N.C., 1989-91; dir. cmty. devel. Jubilee Project, Sneedville, Tenn., 1991—; rschr. Christian Inst. for Study Justice and Devel., Seoul, 1987-89; mem. Appalachian devel. com. United Meth. Ch., 1992—; pres. Clinch Powell Sustainable Devel. Initiative, Abingdon, Va., 1995—; sec. Sneedville-Hancock Cmty. Ptnrs., 1995—; mem. bd. U. Tenn. Cmty. Partnership Ctr., Knoxville, 1995—. Contbr. chpt. to book. Bd. dirs. Hancock Edn. Boosters Assn., Sneedville, 1992; trustee Nolichucky Regional Libr. Morristown, Tenn., 1995—. Mem. Nat. Bus. Incubation Assn. Office: Jubilee Project 123 Jockey St Sneedville TN 37869

HODGES, JOT HOLIVER, JR., lawyer, business executive; b. Archer City, Tex. Nov. 16, 1932; s. Jot Holiver and Lola Mae (Hurd) H.; m. Virginia Cordray Pardue, June 11, 1955; children—Deborah, Jot, Darlene. BS, BBA, Sam Houston State U., 1954; JD, U. Tex.-Austin, 1957. Bar: Tex., U.S. dist. ct. (so. dist.) Tex., U.S. Ct. Appeals (5th cir.). Asst. atty. gen. State of Tex., 1958-60; chmn. bd. Presidio Devel. Corp.; bd. dirs., gen. counsel First Nat. Bank of Missouri City; organizer, founder 3 banks, several corps. and ltd. partnerships. Capt. U.S. Army. Methodist. Club: Houston Contbr. articles to legal, med., pharm. and hosp. jours. Home: 3527 Thunderbird St Missouri City TX 77459-2445 Office: 3660 Hampton Dr Ste 200 Missouri City TX 77459-3044

HODGES, LENORE SCHMID, dietitian; b. Hammond, Ind., Mar. 26, 1938; d. Merle D. and Juanita F. (Keplinger) Schmid; m. Robert Ray Hodges; children: Cheryl Fraser, Charles, Chris, Caryl McEndree. BS in Home Econs., Andrews U.; MS, Ind. U., 1974; PhD, U. Nebr., 1982. Registered dietitian, Ohio, lic. dietitian, Fla. Asst. prof. Union Coll., Lincoln, Nebr., 1974-83; asst. dir. nutritional svcs. Fla. Hosp., Orlando, 1983—; adj. prof. dietetics program Andrews U.; tchr. nutrition Fla. Hosp. Coll. Health Scis.; mem. adv. bd. diabetes program Fla. Hosp., 1990—. Appearances TV, radio regarding nutrition; speaker, writer in field. Mem. Am. Dietetic Assn., Fla. Dietetic Assn., East Ctrl. Dietetic Assn., Seventh-Day Adventist Dietetic Assn. (past pres.), Sigma Xi. Office: Fla Hosp Nutritional Svcs 601 E Rollins St Orlando FL 32803-1248

HODGES, MITCHELL, computer executive; b. Fayetteville, N.C., Mar. 10, 1959; s. Eddie Jr. and Phyliss Marie (Dill) H.; Ilene Michelle Cohen; m. Aug. 16, 1986. BS in Philosophy, Randolph-Macon Coll., 1981; MS in Info. Systems, Nova U., 1992. Applications engr. Anderson Jacobson, Inc., Gaithersburg, Md., 1983-85; programmer, installer Baxter Travenol Corp., Reston, Va., 1985-86, sr. product engr., 1986-87; sr. engr. Baxter systems div. The Compucare Co., Reston, 1987-88; PC coord. Racal-Datacom, Sunrise, Fla., 1988-92; mgr. global electronic messaging W.R. Grace & Co., Boca Raton, Fla., 1992-95; with TransQuest, Atlanta, 1995—. Mem. Alpha Psi Omega (chpt. pres. 1980-81), Theta Chi (chpt. chaplan 1979-80), Omnicron Delta Kappa. Republican. Home: 976 Oakleigh Manor Ct Powder Springs GA 30073

HODGES, RALPH B., state supreme court justice; b. Anadarko, Okla., Aug. 4, 1930; s. Dewey E. and Pearl R. (Hodges) H.; m. Janelle H.; children: Shari, Mark, Randy. B.A., Okla. Baptist U.; LL.B., U. Okla. Atty. Bryan County, Okla., 1956-58; judge Okla. Dist. Ct., 1959-65; justice Okla. Supreme Ct., Oklahoma City, 1965—. Office: Okla Supreme Ct 244 State Capital Bldg Oklahoma City OK 73105

HODGES, THOMPSON GENE, librarian; b. Clinton, Okla., Jan. 30, 1913; s. Kiah and Allie Lee (Thompson) H.; m. Claire Surbeck, June 19, 1935 (dec. 1979); 1 son, Thompson Gene (dec. 1995); m. Dorothea Arnold Ray, 1980. B.S., U. Okla., 1934, M.L.S., 1955; B.D., McCormick Theol. Sem., Chgo., 1939. Ordained to ministry Presbyn. Ch., 1939; minister supply Ch. of Scotland, 1939; pastor Pawhuska and Lawton, Okla., 1939-47; aquisitions librarian U. Okla., 1955-58; dean library services Central State U., Edmond, Okla., 1958-76; dean emeritus Central State U., 1976—; library cons. Univ. Microfilms, 1977; vis. prof. bibliography U. Okla., 1980-81; library cons. Moderator Tulsa Presbytery, 1943. Mem. ALA, Southwestern Library Assn., Okla. Library Assn. (pres. 1965-66), Okla. Ednl. Assn., Kappa Sigma, Beta Phi Mu, Kappa Kappa Psi. Home and Office: 415 Macy St Norman OK 73071-5024

HODGES, ERIN MARIE, statistics educator; b. Pitts., Nov. 12, 1960; d. Edwin E. and Justine J. (Plazak) H. BS in Econs., U. Dayton, 1981; MA in Econs., U. Pitts., 1987; MS in Stats., Temple U., 1989, PhD in Stats., 1995. Econ. rsch. analyst Mellon Bank, NA, Pitts., 1981-85; programmer Techalloy Co., Inc., Rahns, Pa., 1985-86; programmer analyst The Linpro Co., Berwyn, Pa., 1986-87, Jones Apparel Group, Bristol, Pa., 1987-88; programming cons. various cos., Phila., 1988-89; teaching asst. Temple U., Phila., 1990-92, adj. instr., 1992-94, group leader grad. asst. tng. workshop, 1992; asst. prof. U. Houston-Downtown, 1994—; spkr. Temple U.-Rutgers U. Stats. Day, Brunswick, N.J., 1988; presenter Statis. Sci. Conf., Rider U. Lawrenceville, N.J., 1995. Contbr. articles to profl. jours., including Jour. Statis. Sci., Linear Algebra and Its Applications. Fellow Temple U., 1988-90, grantee, 1994. Mem. Am. Statis. Assn. (presenter winter meeting Raleigh, N.C. 1995), Soc. Indsl. and Applied Math., Inst. Math. Stats. (presenter 4th matrix workshop McGill U., Montreal Que., Can. 1995), Intertel Internat., Mensa. Democrat. Roman Catholic. Home: 9449 Briar Forest Dr Apt 3544 Houston TX 77063-1048 Office: U Houston-Downtown One Main St Houston TX 77002

HODGSON, REGINALD HUTCHINS, JR., corporate executive; b. Atlanta, Mar. 10, 1939; s. Reginald Hutchins and Dorothy (Roberts) H.; m. Sigrid Lund, June 6, 1961 (div. 1974); children: Dorothy Louise, Edward Lund; m. Janice Crook, Dec. 4, 1976; children: Daniel Clayton Patrick, Matthew Benjamin. BA in Econs., Kenyon Coll., 1961; MBA, Harvard Bus. SCh., 1968. Trainee Coca-Cola Co., Toronto, Canada, 1961-63; dist. mgr. Coca-Cola Export, Johannesburg, S. Africa, 1963-66; mktg. mgr. Coca-Cola Export, London, 1968-73; region mgr. Coca-Cola, U.S.A., Atlanta, 1973-74; area mgr. Coca-Cola, U.S.A., San Francisco, 1974-75, Chgo., 1975-79; v.p. Coca-Cola Far East, Hong Kong, 1980-84; pres. Paradise Foods Inc., Atlanta, 1984—. Mem. fin. com. Holy Innocents Episcopal Ch., Atlanta, 1991; mem. Blue Ribbon com. to assure quality growth for North Fulton County; team capt. YMCA Ptnrs. with Youth Campaign, 1996. Mem. Rotary (dir. cmty. svc. Roswell East chpt. 1992—, pres.-elect 1993-94, pres. 1994-95). Republican. Episcopalian. Home: 6435 Westchester Pl Cumming GA 30130

HODNICAK, VICTORIA CHRISTINE, pediatric nurse; b. Detroit, Dec. 29, 1960; d. Roderick Lewis and Beverly Caroline (Backus) Turner; m. Mark Michael Hodnicak, Sept. 20, 1986; children: Christopher Alan and Matthew Lewis (twins). ADN, Henry Ford C.C., Dearborn, Mich., 1982. RN, Mich., Tenn. Charge nurse, surg. nurse Harper Grace Hosp., Detroit, 1982-86; neonatal nurse St. John Hosp., Detroit, 1986; home care nurse, coord. med. mgmt. Bloomfield Nursing Svcs., Clawson, Mich., 1986-88; coord. pediatric endocrine growth study So. Health Sys., Memphis, 1988-92; nurse specialist, growth study coord. U. Tenn. Med. Group/St. Jude Children's

Rsch. Hosp., Memphis, 1992—; home care pediatric nurse Personal Pediatric Nursing Profls., Pontiac, Mich., 1987-88; staff nurse Nancy Kissick's Profl. Nursing Svc., Mt. Clemens, Mich., 1988. Inventor Growth Hormone new dose form, 1991, Hydrocortisone dose and stress dosing card, 1990; contbr. articles to profl. jours. Mem. Pediatric Endocrinology Nursing Soc. (membership com. 1992), Endocrine Nursing Soc., Human Growth Found., Neurofibromatosis Found., Turner Syndrome Soc., MAGIC Found. Lutheran. Office: Univ Tenn Med Group 50 S Dunlap St Memphis TN 38103-4909

HOE, RICHARD MARCH, insurance and securities consultant, writer; b. Plainfield, N.J., June 16, 1939; s. Arthur James Hoe and Marjorie (Vandergrift) Beeson; m. Lynne Hovell, Sept. 26, 1964; children: Joshua Blake, Susan Brooke, Seth Jamieson. Student, Pace U., 1964-67, U. Tenn., 1976. CLU. Asst. to controller, fleet mgr., asst. purchasing agt. Hoe & Co. Inc., Bronx, N.Y., 1964-66; pres. OJS Mfg. Co., Bklyn., 1966-68, Fresh Impressions Inc., N.Y.C., 1968; agt. Fidelity Mut. Life, N.Y.C., 1968-72; asst. mgr. Fin. Life, N.Y.C., 1972-73; brokerage mgr. Am. Life N.Y., N.Y.C., 1973-75; exec. Provident Life & Accident Ins. Co., Chattanooga, 1975-78; mgr. Jefferson Standard, Tulsa, 1978-81; pres. Hoe & Co. Inc., Tulsa, 1981-93; fin. planner, Tulsa, 1968—, designer, cons., 1978—; lectr. project bus. Tulsa Pub. Schs., 1983, 85, cons., 1984-86; lectr. in field; founder employee and exec. benefit plans, residual split-dollar, money purchase flexible spending plans, pvt. sector social security alternative portable plans, satellite split-dollar, satellite supplemental pensions, lifetime income nontaxable retirement plans, balanced funding plans. Columnist (monthly) Broker World, 1985-86, 89—, Probe, Life Assn. News; contbr. articles to profl. jours., novelist. Chmn. fund raising Grimes Elem. Sch., Tulsa Pub. Schs., 1984-87; mem. gifted and talented com. Tulsa Pub. Schs., 1982; bd. dirs. Nat. ALS Found., N.Y.C., 1971-82. Fellow Life Underwriter Tng. Coun. (moderator 1979-86); mem. Reach Across Divs., Am. Soc. CLUs (student devel. chmn. 1990, mem. chmn. 1991, advt. and pub. rels. 1992-93), Tulsa Estate Planning Forum, Nat. Okla. Multiple Sclerosis Soc. (chmn. 150 tour com. 1992), Rotary Club of Will Rogers. Republican. Episcopalian. Home and Office: 5843 E 50th St Tulsa OK 74135-6885

HOEFER, MARGARET J., librarian; b. Bklyn., July 28, 1909; d. Thomas A. and Margaret Emma (Skillin) Ford. BS, Kans. State Coll., 1932; MA, Colo. State Coll., 1939; BLS, U. Denver, 1943. Tchr., Smith Ctr. High Sch., Kans., 1934-38; head English dept. Iola (Kans.) Sr. High Sch., 1939-43; head circulation dept. Topeka Pub. Libr., 1943-44; libr. Pueblo (Colo.) Jr. Coll., 1944-46; bookmobile libr. U.S. Army, Nurnberg, Germany, 1946-48; dir. SCAP Civil Info. and Edn. Libr., Osaka, Japan, 1948-50; comd. libr. PHILCOM & 13th Air Force, Clark AFB, Manila, 1950-51; staff libr. Cen. Air Def. Force, Kansas City, Mo., 1951-53; county libr., Carroll County, Md., Westminster, 1958-62; head libr. Woodlawn Jr. High Sch., Balt., 1962-63; head reference svcs. Smithtown (N.Y.) Libr., 1963-65; dir. Emma S. Clark Meml. Libr., Setauket, N.Y., 1965-67; reference libr. Nassau Community Coll., Garden City, N.Y., 1967-69; asst. prof. libr. sci. Suffolk County Community Coll., Selden, N.Y., 1969-72; libr. Golden Hills Acad., Ocala, Fla., 1972-74; reference libr. Melbourne (Fla.) Pub. Libr., part-time, 1975-78; corp. libr. Harris Corp., Melbourne, 1980-85. Mem. Palm Bay Community Assn., 1976—; v.p., membership com. Brevard Assn. for Advancement of Blind, 1975-90; archivist Sebastian Inlet Dist., Melbourne, Fla., 1977-87; mem. Brevard County Libr. Bd., 1977-81, pres., 1979; mem. Friends of the Palm Bay (Fla.) Library, 1980—, pres., 1981-82; cert. tutor Literacy, English for Speakers of Other Langs., Literacy Coun. South Brevard, 1985—; cons. librs. Brevard Art Ctr. and Mus., South Brevard Women's Ctr. Recipient 1st Ann. award for svc. to Fla. librs. Coun. for Fla. Librs., 1981. Mem. AARP, Greater Palm Bay Area Sr. Ctr. Assn., Retired Sr. Vol. Persons. Republican. Home: 3251 Edgewood Dr NE Palm Bay FL 32905-5931

HOEH, DAVID CHARLES, urban planning consultant; b. Boston, Dec. 1, 1937; s. Robert Yetter and Priscilla (Smith) H.; m. Sandra Juliema Unterman, Feb. 9, 1963 (div. Feb. 1983); children: Christoper D., Jeffrey D., Jonathan R.; m. Brigid Sullivan, May 18, 1985; 1 child, Julia P.S.; 1 stepchild, Ryan S. Flynn. BA, U. N.H., 1960; AM, Boston U., 1966; PhD, U. Mass., 1978. Cmty. planning technician N.H. State Planning Project, Concord, 1963-65; cmty./regional planner N.H. Office Planning and Rsch., Concord, 1965-67; assoc. dir. Pub. Affairs Ctr. Dartmouth (N.H.) Coll., 1967-69; regional planner Planners Collaborative, Norwich, Vt., 1969-72; asst. prof. Sch. Architecture U. Wis., Milw., 1972-74, asst. prof. dept. urban planning, 1974-77, vis. scholar, assoc. Planning and Design Inst., 1993-94; exec. dir. Parkwest Redevel. Task Force, Milw., 1977-82; pres. Planning and Design Partnership, Milw., 1981-86, Hoeh, Schroeder, Piwoni, Inc., Milw., 1986-88; v.p. Corradino Group, Louisville, 1993-94; sr. supervising planner Parsons Brinckerhoff, Louisville, 1994-95; cons. planner Louisville, 1995—. Author: 1968-McCarthy-New Hampshire, 1995; contbr. chpt. to: Introduction to Urban Planning-Environmental Planning, 1977; contbr. articles to profl. publs. Dem. congl. nominee 2nd Dist. N.H., 1968; candidate Milw. Bd. Alderman, 1989; elected del., del. chairperson Dem. nominating convs., N.H. and Chgo., 1968. Mem. Am. Polit. Sci. Assn., Am. Planning Assn. (Wis. chpt. editor 1980-81), Am. Inst. Cert. Planners (cert.), Am. Soc. for Pub. Adminstrn. (pres. Milw. chpt. 1986-87). Home: 1755 Cherokee Ter Louisville KY 40205-1336

HOEL, ROBERT FREDRICK, JR., construction executive, civil engineer; b. St. Louis, Apr. 14, 1949; s. Robert F. Sr. and LaVerne (Schaller) M. BSCE, U. Mo., 1971. Registered profl. engr., Mo., Fla. Project mgr. Hoel-Steffen Constrn. Co., St. Louis, 1971-79; project dir. Sverdrup Corp., St. Louis, 1979-82; regional mgr. Vector Constrn. Co., Orlando, Fla., 1982-84; sr. project mgr. Fed. Constrn. Co., St. Petersburg, Fla., 1984-87; dir. ops. Brown & Root Bldg. Co., St. Petersburg, Fla., 1987—. Mem. Mo. Soc. Profl. Engrs., Fla. Engring. Soc., Mo. Athletic Club. Roman Catholic. Home: 4909 SW 5th Pl Cape Coral FL 33914-6501 Office: Brown & Root Bldg Co 5830 142nd Ave N Clearwater FL 34620-2819

HOELLERICH, VINCENT L., anesthesiologist; b. Plainfield, N.J., Oct. 4, 1956; m. Karen Simon. BSChemE with distinction, Iowa State U., 1979; MD with high distinction, U. Nebr., 1983. Diplomate Am. Bd. Anesthesiology; lic. physician, N.C., Md. Surg. intern, then resident in anesthesiology Johns Hopkins U., Balt., 1983-86; physician Fallston (Md.) Hosp., 1984-86; assoc. staff anesthesiology Mass. Eye & Ear Infirmary, Boston, 1986-87; couresty staff anesthesiology Goddard Meml. Hosp., Stoughton, Mass., 1986-87; pvt. practice Raleigh (N.C.) Anesthesia Assocs./Critical Healty Sys., Inc., Raleigh, N.C., 1987—; fellow Mass. Gen. Hosp., 1986-87; mem. staff Rex Hosp., med. dir. respiratory therapy, 1990-96; mem. staff Raleigh Cmty. Hosp.; fellow surgery Johns Hopkins U., 1983-84, fellow anesthesiology, 1984-86, Harvard Med. Sch., 1986-88; assoc. clin. prof. anesthesiology Duke U. Med. Ctr., 1988-89; adj. assoc. prof. U. N.C., Greensboro, 1992—; cons. Project Hope, Peoples Republic of China, 1987; med. dir. Raleigh Sch. Nurse Anesthesia, 1990-94, pres., 1994—; lectr. in field. Contbr. articles to profl. jours. Triangle scholar, 1977-79, Regents scholar, 1980-83, Bookmeyer scholar, 1981-83, Nellie House Craven scholar, 1982-83. Mem. AAAS, AMA, Am. Soc. Anesthesiologists (subcom. critical care medicine 1990-91), Am. Soc. Critical Care Anesthesiologists (bd. dirs.), Am. Med. Student Assn., Internat. Anesthesia Rsch. Soc., Nebr. Med. Assn., N.C. Med. Soc., N.C. Soc. Anesthesiologists (chmn. memberhsip com. 1994-96), Wake County Med Soc., Alpha Omega Alpha, Tau Beta Pi, Omega Chi Epsilon, Phi Kappa Phi. Home: 4038 JS Raboteau Wynd Raleigh NC 27612-5329 Office: PO Box 18139 Raleigh NC 27619-8139

HOERTER, SAM SPALDING, transportation executive; b. Montgomery, Ala., Jan. 12, 1955; s. George Joseph and May LaMotte (Smith) H.; m. Nancy Sue Shaffer, July 12, 1980; 1 child, Joseph Adam. B.S. in Aviation Mgmt., Auburn U., 1978; M.B.A., U. Ala.-Birmingham, 1983. Accredited airport exec. Adminstrv. asst. Birmingham Mcpl. Airport (Ala.), 1975-77, airport ops. mgr., 1978-83; exec. dir. Gulfport-Biloxi Regional Airport (Miss.), 1983-86; dir. airports Charleston County Aviation Authority, Charleston, S.C., 1986—; instr. airport mgmt. and mktg. Embry-Riddle Aero. U.; aircraft accident investigator, Nat. Transp. Safety Bd. Bd. dirs. Coastal Carolina council Boy Scouts Am. Mem. Am. Assn. Airport Execs. (sec. S.E. chpt.), Southeastern Airport Mgrs. Assn., Miss. Airports Assn. (v.p., past bd. dirs.), Gulfport C. of C. (past bd. dirs.). Roman Catholic. Contbr. articles to publ. in field. Office: Charleston Cty Aviation Authority Charleston Internat Airport 5500 International Blvd Charleston SC 29418-6900

HOETH, KATHLEEN ANN, librarian; b. Fort Monmouth, N.J., May 21, 1958; d. Robert Harold and Patricia Ann (McGuire) Fairbrother; m. William Patrick Hoeth, Aug. 21, 1977; 1 child, Robert William. BA in Polit. Sci. cum laude, SUNY Albany, 1979, MLS, 1981. Libr. reference St. John's U., S.I., N.Y., 1981-83; info. specialist FIND/SVP, N.Y.C., 1983-84; libr. N.Y. Pub. Libr., S.I., 1984-89; libr. reference Lee County Libr. Sys., Fort Myers, Fla., 1989-91; asst. dir., dep. dir. Lee County Libr. Sys., Fort Myers, 1991—. Mem. ALA, Fla. Libr. Assn., SW Fla. Libr. Network (organizing com., chair exec. com. 1991). Democrat. Roman Catholic. Office: Lee County Libr Sys 2050 Lee St Fort Myers FL 33901-3933

HOFER, CHARLES WARREN, strategic management, entrepreneurship educator, consultant; b. Phoenixville, Pa., Nov. 11, 1940; s. Charles Emil and Alice May (Howard) H.; m. Judith Racella Millner, Oct. 22, 1980. BS in Engring. Physics summa cum laude, Lehigh U., 1962; MBA in Mktg. with distinction, Harvard U., 1965, MS in Applied Math., 1966, D in Bus. Policy, 1969. Research asst. Harvard Bus. Sch., Boston, 1965-66; asst. prof. Northeastern U., Boston, 1968-69; vis. lectr. Singapore Inst. Mgmt., 1969-70; asst. prof. Northwestern U., Evanston, Ill., 1970-75; assoc. prof. Northwestern U., 1975-76; vis. assoc. prof. Stanford (Calif.) U., 1976-77, Columbia U., N.Y.C., 1978, NYU, 1978-80; vis. prof. U. Calif., Riverside, 1980; regents prof. strategy, entrepreneurship U. Ga., Athens, 1981—; vis. chair in entrepreneurship Rutgers U., 1988; lectr. Chgo. C. of C., 1976-78; Donald W. Riegle campaign cons., Flint, Mich., 1968-72; vis. lectr. Ga. Tech., 1993; lectr. Nova U., 1981-96, Ga. State U., 1995-96. Author: Toward a Contingency Theory of Business Strategy, 1975 (ranked 16th in world Acad. Mgmt. survey 1985), Strategy Formulation: Analytical Concepts, 1978 (ranked 30th in world Acad. Mgmt. survey 1985); co-author: Strategic Management: A Casebook in Policy and Planning, 1980, 84; co-editor: Strategic Management: A New View of Business Policy and Planning, 1979 (ranked 6th in world Acad. Mgmnt. survey 1985); editor: Strategic Planning Management, 1987-90; and others. Baker scholar Harvard U., 1965; NSF fellow, 1962-63, Ford Found. fellow, 1966-67; recipient Rsch. award U. Ga., 1990, Leavey award Freedoms Found. Valley Forge, 1991, Coleman Entrepreneurship Mentor award Acad. Mgmt., 1992, Internat. Hall Fame Entrepreneur award Inventors Club Am., 1992, Williams A. Owens Rsch. award U. Ga., 1993, Sargent Americanism award Soc. Mfg. Engrs., 1994. Fellow U.S. Assn. Small Bus. and Entrepreneurship (chmn. corp. entrepreneurship div. 1989-90, v.p. devel. 1990-92, Nat. Model Entrepreneurship Program award 1991, Disting. Entrepreneurship Educator of Yr. award 1992); mem. Acad. Mgmt. (chmn. policy div. 1977-78, chair awards com. 1993-95, membership chmn. 1995-96, First Outstanding Contbns. entrepreneurship divsn. award 1989), Strategic Mgmt. Soc. (charter), Decision Scis. Inst. (chmn. policy track 1985-86), Inst. Mgmt. Scis., Am. Econ. Assn., Harvard Bus. Sch. Club Atlanta, Harvard Club Ga., Phi Beta Kappa, Phi Eta Sigma, Pi Mu Epsilon, Tau Beta Pi, Sigma Iota Epsilon, Beta Gamma Sigma. Lutheran. Home: 4445 Stonington Cir Atlanta GA 30338-6621 Office: U Ga Mgmt Dept Terry Coll Bus Athens GA 30602

HOFF, GERHARDT MICHAEL, lawyer, insurance company executive; b. Vienna, Austria, June 12, 1930; came to U.S., 1951, naturalized, 1955; s. Erich Theodor and Vilma (Frank) Klockenhoff; m. Lisa Decristoforo, June 1, 1970; children: Michael, Elisabeth, Anne-Christine. Student, U. Munich Law Sch., Fed. Republic Germany, 1948-51, Columbia U., 1951-52; LL.B., NYU, 1958; LL.M. in Taxation, Emory U., 1982; C.L.U., 1961. Bar: Mass. 1959, D.C. 1968, Ga. 1984. With Mass. Mut. Life Ins. Co. and Variable Annuity Life Ins. Co., 1958-67; v.p. Variable Annuity Life Ins. Co. Am., Washington, 1967-68; mem. staff fin. services group ITT Corp., 1968-69; pres. ITT Hamilton Life Ins. Co., also ITT Variable Annuity Ins. Co., St. Louis, 1970-72, Sun Life Ins. Co. Am., Balt., 1972-78, 81-83; chief exec. officer Sun Life Ins. Co. Am., 1978-83; pres. Sun Life Group Am., Inc., Atlanta, 1978-83; chmn. law practice Bus. Planning Corp. Am., Atlanta, 1983—; founder (with Lisa Hoff) Cities in Color, Inc., 1985—. Served with AUS, 1955-57. Decorated Commendation ribbon with pendant. Mem. Am. Soc. C.L.U.'s, ABA. Presbyterian. Clubs: Cherokee Country, Capital City (Atlanta). Office: 12 Braemore Dr NW Atlanta GA 30328-4844

HOFF, TIMOTHY, law educator, priest; b. Freeport, Ill., Feb. 27, 1941; s. Howard Vincent and Zillah (Morgan) H.; m. Virginia Nevill; children: Brian Charles, Morgan Witherspoon; stepchildren: Guy Baker, Katherine Baker. A.B., Tulane U., 1963, J.D., 1966; student U. London, 1961-62; LL.M., Harvard U., 1970. Bar: Fla. 1967, Ala. 1973, U.S. Dist. Ct. (mid. dist.) Fla. 1967. Assoc., Williams, Parker, Harrison, Dietz & Getzen, Sarasota, Fla., 1966-69; asst. legal editor The Fla. Bar, 1969; asst. prof. U. Ala., 1970-73, assoc. prof., 1973-75, prof. law, 1975-93, Gordon Rosen prof., 1993—; cons. Ala. Law Inst.; reporter Ala. Adminstrv. Procedure Act, 1977—; ordained priest Episcopal Ch. V.p., founding dir. Hospice of West Ala.; founding dir. Community Soup Bowl, Inc.; Episc. priest assoc. Canterbury Chapel U. Ala.; rector St. Michael's Episc. Ch., Fayette, Ala. Recipient Hist. Preservation Service award, 1976. Mem. ACLU, Maritime Law Assn. U.S., AAUP, Council on Religion and Law, Episc. Soc. for Ministry in Higher Edn., Phi Beta Kappa, Order of Coif, Omicron Delta Kappa, Eta Sigma Phi. Democrat. Club: University. Author: Alabama Limitations of Actions, 1984, 2d edit., 1992, Forms for Civil Trial Practice, 1991; contbr. articles to profl. jours. Home: 2601 Lakewood Cir Tuscaloosa AL 35405-2727 Office: U Ala Law Sch 101 Paul W Bryant Dr E Box 870382 Tuscaloosa AL 35487-0382

HOFFBERG, ALAN MARSHALL, accountant; b. Chgo., Apr. 15, 1940; s. Nathan and Evelyn Ruth (Zelensky) H.; m. Janet C. Glunts, Aug. 7, 1966; children: Amy, Donna, Wendy. BSc in Acctg., DePaul U., 1962; postgrad. DePaul Law Sch., 1961-63; MBA with honors, Roosevelt U., 1966. CPA, Ill., N.Y.; cert. systems profl., FAA priv. pilot, 1993; cons. Ernst & Young, N.Y.C., 1966-69; Adminstrv. v.p. Williams & Co., N.Y.C., 1969-80, Williams Real Estate Co., Inc., N.Y.C., 1969-80; pres. Info. Resource Mgmt. Inc., N.Y.C., 1980-93; pres., IRM Inc. Longwood, Fla. 1993—; pres., DIVExpeditions, Longwood, Fla., 1993—. Author: Fortran IV, 1975, 2d edit., 1980, Apple Supplement, 1980, (chpt.) Handbook of Management for the Growing Business, 1986. Contbr. articles to profl. publs. Treas. Broadview Police Pension Fund (Ill.), 1961, trustee, 1961-65; pres. Wantagh Scholarship Fund Inc. (N.Y.), 1978, treas., 1977; bd. dirs., treas., cons. Sabal Point Cmty. Svcs. Assoc., Longwood, Fla., 1994—. Mem. Am. Inst. CPAs, N.Y. State Soc. CPAs (chmn. coms.), Assn. for Systems Mgmt. (pres., v.p., treas., merit award 1975, achievement award 1976, disting. service award 1979), Am. Soc. for Psychoprophylaxis in Obstetrics (treas. L.I. chpt. 1975), pilot for Angel Flight of Fla., mem. S. Seminole Flying Club (dir., sec.). Jewish. Scuba instr. (cert.). Home: 414 Twisting Pine Cir Longwood FL 32779-2634 Office: IRM Inc PO Box 917750 Longwood FL 32791-7750

HOFFMAN, CARL H(ENRY), lawyer; b. St. Louis, May 28, 1936; s. Carl Henry and Anna Marie (Remlinger) H.; m. Pamela L. Polk, May 8, 1971 (div. Novl 1982); children: Kurt M., Jennifer K. BS, St. Louis U., 1958; postgrad., U. Mex., Mexico City, 1958, U. Nev., 1960-61, Tex. Technol. Coll., 1961-62; JD, Washington U., St. Louis, 1966. Bar: Mo. 1966, Fla. 1969, U.S. Supreme Ct. 1970; cert. civil trial adv. Nat. Bd. Trial Advocacy. Pilot Eastern. Airlines, Inc., Miami, Fla.; assoc. Spencer & Taylor, Miami, Fla., 1969-70; pvt. practice, Miami, 1970-80; ptnr. Hoffman & Hertzig, P.A., Coral Gables, Fla., 1980—. Capt. USAF, 1958-63. Mem. ABA, ATLA, Fla. Bar (cert. civil trial lawyer, jud. evaluation com., chmn. aviation com.), Fla. Acad. Trial Lawyers, Am. Jurisprudence Soc., Greater Miami C. of C. (trustee). Office: Hoffman & Hertzig PA 241 Sevilla Ave Ste 900 Coral Gables FL 33134-6600

HOFFMAN, DONALD RICHARD, pathologist, educator; b. Boston, Aug. 25, 1943; s. William Maurice and Laura (Rodman) H.; m. Valeria Anne Mossey, Oct. 24, 1971; children: Anthony Horatio, Maria Lauren, Avram Joseph. AB, Harvard, 1965; PhD, Calif. Inst. Technology, 1970. Asst. prof. pediatrics U. So. Calif. Sch. Medicine, L.A., 1971-75; assoc. prof. pathology Creighton U. Sch. Medicine, Omaha, 1975-77, East Carolina U. Sch. Medicine, Greenville, N.C., 1977-82; prof. pathology and lab. medicine East Carolina U. Sch. Medicine, Greenville, 1982—; adv. com. U.S. Dept. Health and Human Svcs., FDA Allergenic Products, Rockville, Md., 1990-94. Mem. editorial bd. Jour. Allergy Clin. Immunology, 1988-93, Immunochemistry, 1974-77; contbr. articles to profl. jours. Fellow Am. Acad. Allergy and Immunology; mem. Am. Assn. Immunologists, Protein Soc., N.Y. Acad. Scis., AAAS. Office: E Carolina U Sch Medicine Dept Pathology/Lab Medicine Greenville NC 27858

HOFFMAN, FRED L., human resources professional; b. Wauseon, Ohio, Mar. 13, 1953; s. Lowell Max and Annabell (Whitmire) H.; m. Diane Patricia Pope, Sept. 2, 1975; Brandon C. BSBA, Bowling Green U., 1975. Asst. mgr. indsl. rels. Colonial Press div. Sheller-Globe Corp., Clinton, Mass., 1975-76; dir. human resources Leece-Neville div. Sheller-Globe Corp., Gainesville, Ga., 1976-88; v.p. human resources Golder Assocs., Atlanta, 1988—; bd. dirs. Hoffman-Rettig Foods, Inc., Maquoketa, Iowa, Golder Assocs. Corp., Atlanta. Guest columnist BG News, 1971-75. State dir. pub. rels. Ohio League of Coll. Reps., Columbus, 1974, 75; lt. col. aide-de-camp gov.'s staff Gov. Joe Frank Harris, Atlanta, 1983-91. Recipient disting. svc. award Bowling Green State U., 1975. Mem. Atlanta C. of C., Soc. Human Resources Mgmt., Antaen Soc. (pres. 1974-75), Pres.'s Club Bowling Green State U., Omicron Delta Kappa, Phi Delta Theta. Home: 235 Parian Run Duluth GA 30155 Office: Golder Assocs Corp 3730 Chamblee Tucker Rd Atlanta GA 30341-4414

HOFFMAN, IRA ELIOT, lawyer; b. Highland Park, Mich., Jan. 3, 1952; s. Maxwell Mordecai and Leah (Silverman) H.; m. Ruth Felsen, Aug. 19, 1975 (div. 1981); 1 child, Daniel Gideon; m. Meredith Lippman, Dec. 17, 1988; 1 child, Lauren Samantha. BA, U. Mich., 1973; MSc in Econs., London Sch. Econs., 1975; JD cum laude, U. Miami, 1983. Bar: Fla. 1983, U.S. Ct. Appeals (D.C. cir.) 1984, D.C. 1985, Md. 1991, U.S. Ct. Appeals (10th cir., 4th cir) 1992, U.S. Dist. Ct. (D.C. dist.) 1992, U.S. Dist. Ct. Md., 1992, U.S. Ct. Appeals (fed. cir.) 1994. Tchr. London Sch. Econs., 1975-77; rsch. assoc. Shiloah Ctr. Mid. East Studies, Tel Aviv U., 1978-80; staff atty. FTC, Washington, 1983; law clk. U.S. Ct. Appeals (D.C. cir.), Washington, 1983-84; assoc. Fried, Frank, Harris, Shriver & Jacobson, Washington, 1984-86, 87-88; counsel Ministry of Def. Mission to the U.S., Govt. of Israel, N.Y.C., 1986-87; counsel to vice chmn. U.S. Internat. Trade Commn., Washington, 1988-89; assoc. Howrey & Simon, Washington, 1989-91; pres. Israel Housing Investors, Inc., Rockville, Md., 1990-92; v.p. H.P.F. Prefab Constrn., Ltd., Givatayim, Israel, 1991-92; of counsel Savage & Schwartzman, Balt., 1992-94, McAleese & Assocs., P.C., McLean, Va., 1995—. Translator: The Emergence of Pan-Arabism in Egypt, 1980; contbr. articles to profl. jours. Spl. counsel Nat. Sudden Infant Death Syndrome Found., Landover, Md., 1984-86; hon. counsel to chmn. Nat. Holocaust Meml. Coun., Washington, 1985. Mem. ABA. Jewish. Office: McAleese & Assocs PC Ste 820 8201 Greensboro Dr Mc Lean VA 22102

HOFFMAN, KARLA LEIGH, mathematician; b. Paterson, N.J., Feb. 14, 1948; d. Abe and Bertha (Guthaim) Rakoff; BA, Rutgers, U., 1969; MBA, George Washington U., 1971, DSc in Ops. Research, 1975; m. Allan Stuart Hoffman, Dec. 26, 1971; 1 son, Matthew Douglas. Ops. research analyst IRS, Washington, 1970-72; research asst. George Washington U., 1972-75; asso. professorial lectr., 1978-85; NSF postdoctoral research fellow Nat. Acad. Sci., Washington, 1975-76; mathematician Nat. Bur. Standards, Washington, 1976-84; vis. assoc. prof. ops. research U. Md., spring 1982; assoc. prof. systems engring. dept. George Mason U., 1985-86, assoc. prof. ops. research and applied stats., 1986-89, prof. ops. research, 1990—, disting. prof. 1989; mng. ptnr. Optimization Software Assocs.; cons. to govt. agys., airline, telecom. and def. industries. Recipient Applied Rsch. award Nat. Inst. Stds. and Tech., 1984, Silver medal U.S. Dept. Commerce, 1984. Mem. Ops. Research Soc. Am. (sec.-treas. computer sci. tech. sect. 1979-80, vice chmn. sect. 1981, chmn. sect. 1982, vis. professorial lectr. 1980—, chmn. tech. sect. com. 1983-86, council 1985-88, chmn. Lanchster Prize com. 1989, treas. 1993-94), Inst. Ops. Rsch. and Mgmt. Sci. (treas. 1995-96, pres.-elect 1997), Math. Programming Soc. (editor newsletter 1979-82, chmn. com. algorithms 1982-85, council 1985-88, exec. com. 1986-88, chmn. mem. com. 1988-89). Contbr. articles to profl. jours.; assoc. editor Internat. Abstracts of Ops. Research, The Math. Programming Jour., Series B, The Ops. Research Soc. Jour. on Computing, Jour. Computational Optimization and Applications. Home: 6921 Clifton Rd Clifton VA 22024-1525

HOFFMAN, LARRY J., lawyer; b. N.Y.C., Aug. 20, 1930; s. Max and Pauline (Epstein) H.; m. Deborh E. Alexander, Oct. 2, 1954; children: Lisa, Ken, Heidi, Mark. AA, U. Fla.; JD, U. Miami. Bar: Fla. 1954. Pres., mng. dir. Greenberg, Traurig, Hoffman, Lipoff, Rosen & Quentel, P.A., Miami, 1968—, mng. shareholder, 1989—. Mem. ABA, Fla. Bar Assn., Dade County Bar Assn. Office: Greenberg Traurig 1221 Brickell Ave Miami FL 33131-3224*

HOFFMAN, MAUREANE RICHARDSON, pathologist and researcher; b. Los Alamos, N.Mex., Apr. 21, 1957; d. Marvin M. and Darleane C. (Christian) Hoffman; m. Stephen G. Richardson, Mar. 21, 1981. BS in Animal Sci. with high honors, N.Mex. State U., 1976; MD, PhD, U. Iowa, 1982. Diplomate Am. Bd. Pathology; lic. physician, N.C. Resident in pathology Duke U., Durham, N.C., 1982-85, asst. prof. dept. pathology, 1985-87; asst. prof. pathology, assoc. dir. transfusion svc. U. N.C., Chapel Hill, 1987-91, adj. asst. prof. dept. medicine, 1993—; asst. prof. pathology Duke U., 1991-95; assoc. prof. pathology, 1995—; asst. prof. immunology Duke U., 1994—, assoc. prof. pathology, 1995—; staff physician lab. svc. VA Med. Ctr., Durham, 1991-92, dir. hematology lab. svc., 1992—; program specialist in pathology Health Svcs. and Rsch. Adminstrn., VA, 1992-94. Contbr. numerous articles to profl. jours., chpts. to books. Recipient Young Investigators Merit Travel award Internat. Soc. on Thrombosis and Hemostasis, 1991, Young Investigators Travel award Am. Heart Assn., Coun. on Thrombosis, 1992; N.Mex. State U. scholar, 1973-76, Am. Soc. Animal Sci. scholar, 1976; grantee United Way of N.C., 1985-86, Am. Cancer Soc., 1985-86, VA Rsch. Career Devel. Program, 1985-88, USPHS, 1988-89, Jr. Faculty Devel. Award/U. N.C. at Chapel Hill, 1989, Univ. Rsch. Coun., 1989-90, Dept. Vets. Affairs, 1992-93, NIH, 1991—, 1992—. Mem. IEEE, Am. Assn. Blood Banks, Am. Assn. Pathologists, Am. Fedn. Clin. Rsch., Am. Soc. Clin. Pathologists, Am. Soc. Hematology, N.Y. Acad. Sci., N.C. Assn. Blood Bankers (bd. dirs. 1991), Soc. for Free Radical Rsch., Soc. for Leukocyte Biology. Home: 5408 Sunny Ridge Dr Durham NC 27705-8552 Office: Duke University Dept Pathology Durham NC 27705

HOFFMAN, MICHAEL ROBERT, physician; b. Youngstown, Ohio, Feb. 2, 1946; s. John Rath Hoffman and Sally Jane Conroy; m. Gail Marie Sittmann, June 1, 1968; children: G. Ryan, Jonathan, W. Jeffrey, Erin. BS, Carnegie Tech., 1968; MBA, Clemson U., 1972; MD, Med. U. S.C., 1976. Diplomate Am. Bd. Ob-Gyn. Intern Greenville (S.C.) Hosp., 1976, resident, 1977-79; owner, dir. Ctr. Reproductive Surgery and Medicine, Greenville, S.C., 1980—. Bd. dirs. Ctr. State Theatre, Greenville, S.C., 1982-86, 92—, Greenville (S.C.) Civic Chorale, 1987. Kellogg Found. fellow, 1983-85. Fellow Am. Coll. Ob-Gyn.; mem. Am. Fertility Soc. (mem. session mgmt. com. 1993—), S.C. Soc. Ob-Gyn., S.C. Med. Assn., Soc. Reproductive Surgeons. Republican. Roman Catholic. Office: Ctr Reproductive Surgery & Medicine 10 Enterprise Blvd Greenville SC 29615-3534

HOFFMAN, MICHAEL WILLIAM, lawyer, accountant; b. Bowling Green, Ohio, Feb. 5, 1955; s. Oscar William and Marie Louise (Carlson) H.; m. Lynne Ellen Steele, Aug. 31, 1975; children: Megan, Jessica, Kristine, Robert. BA in Acctg. summa cum laude, Bowling Green State U., 1976; JD, U. Toledo, 1981. Bar: Ohio 1981, Ga. 1983; CPA, Ga., Ohio. Acct. Ernst & Whinney, Toledo, 1976-81; acct., ptnr. Touche Ross & Co., Atlanta, 1981-86; v.p. Profl. Svcs. Network Inc., Atlanta, 1986; assoc. Chamberlain, Hrdlicka, White, Johnson & Williams, Atlanta, 1986-89; ptnr. Somers & Altenbach, Atlanta, 1989-91; atty. Hoffman & Assocs., Atlanta, 1991—; organizing dir. Paces Bank & Trust Co., Atlanta; speaker in field. Author: RIA's U.S.A. News for the Inbound Investor, 1983. Treas. Friendship Force Internat., 1984. Recipient Leadership award Boy Scouts Am., 1986. Mem. ABA, AICPA, State Bar Ga. (fiduciary law and tax sects.), State Bar Ohio, Ga. Soc. CPAs (Atlanta chpt. estate and gift tax com., ins. adv. com.), Cobb C. of C., Bowling Green State U.-Atlanta Alumni Assn. (prs. 1988-90), Atlanta Country Club, Serra. Republican. Roman Catholic. Home: 535 Willow Knolls Dr Marietta GA 30067-4647 Office: Ste 210 6075 Lake Forest Dr Atlanta GA 30328

HOFFMAN, MITCHEL SCOTT, gynecologic oncologist; b. West Palm Beach, Fla., Dec. 21, 1956; m. Sylvia Orrantia, Sept. 11, 1982; children:

David Benjamin, Emily Ann. BS in Biology, Emory U., 1978; MD, U. South Fla. Diplomate Am. Bd. Obstetrics and Gynecology, Am. Acad. Pain Mgmt.; lic. physician, Fla. Resident ob-gyn. Tampa (Fla.) Gen. Hosp., 1981-85; fellow in gynecologic oncology U. South Fla., Tampa, 1985-87, prof. divsn. gynecologic oncology, 1991—, dir. med. student edn. in ob-gyn., 1987—; dir. Colposcopy and Tumor Clinic at Genesis Clinic, 1987—; physician H. Lee Moffitt Cancer Ctr., Tampa; lectr. in field. Jour. peer reviewer Gynecologic Oncology, 1991—, Obstetrics and Gynecology, 1993—, Cancer, 1993—, Jour. of Reproductive Medicine, 1993—; contbr. numerous articles and abstracts to profl. jours., chpts. to books. South Atlantic assn. Obstetricians and Gynecologists John R. McCain Student fellow, 1980. Fellow ACOG, ACS; mem. AMA, Fla. Med. Assn., Fla. Soc. Clin. Oncology, So. Assn. Oncology, Soc. Gynecologic Oncologists, Hillsborough County Med. Assn., Assn. of Profs. of Gynecology and Obstetrics, Fla. Physicians Assn., Fla. Obstetric and Gynecologic Soc. (Award for Outstanding Achievement in study of ob-gyn. 1981), N.Y. Acad. Sci., European Soc. Gynecologic Oncology. Office: 4 Columbia Dr Ste 500 Tampa FL 33606-3589

HOFFMAN, MITCHELL WADE, corporate executive; b. Newport News, Va., Sept. 27, 1954; s. Joseph and Sarah (Goldberg) H.; m. Patrice Lynn Bare, Dec. 2, 1978; 1 child, Loren Kimberly. BA in Psychol., U. Va., 1975; MBA, Coll. Wm. and Mary, 1978; MS in Fin., Va. Commonwealth U., 1988. Cert. purchasing mgr., Nat. Assn. Purchasing Mgmt. Sr. buyer Harvey Hubbell Inc., Christiansburg, Va., 1978-79; agt. purchasing Ingersoll Rand Inc., Roanoke, Va., 1979-82; supr. distbn. HoN Industries Inc., Richmond, Va., 1983; agt. capital purchasing Brockway Inc., Richmond, 1983-88; ops. fin. analyst Philip Morris, Inc., Richmond, 1988—; adj. prof. fin. Va. Commonwealth U., 1988—. Mem. Nat. Assn. Purshasing Mgmt., Nat. Assn. Fin. Mgmt., Alpha Iota Delta, Beta Gamma Sigma, Phi Kappa Phi. Home: 4218 Brixton Rd Chesterfield VA 23832-7764

HOFFMAN, NELSON MILES, JR., retired academic administrator, consultant; b. Phila., June 10, 1920; s. Nelson Miles and Sara (Suiter) H.; m. Marjorie Anne Mendenhall, Dec. 3, 1942; children: Nelson III, Michael, Elizabeth, George, Joseph. BA, Asbury Coll., 1942; MA, U. Kans., 1947, PhD, 1964. Ednl. missionary Meth. Ch., India, 1947-57; pastor Meth. Ch., Williamsburg, Kans., 1958-60; prof. history Emory-at-Oxford, Ga., 1960-63; dean acad. affairs Fla. So. Coll., Lakeland, 1963-68; v.p. acad. affairs W.Va. Wesleyan Coll., Buckhannon, 1969-70; headmaster Pennington (N.J.) Sch., 1970-78; pres. Midway (Ky.) Coll., 1978-85; v.p. Capital Formation Counselors, Belleair Bluffs, Fla., 1988—; chmn. edn. com. N.J. Meth. Conf., Pennington, 1972-78; pres. Ky. Ind. Coll. Assn., Midway, 1982-84. Author: American Indian Policy of the Continental Congress, 1947, Godfrey Barnsley, 1805-1873, British Cotton Factor in the South, 1964. Lt. USN, 1942-46, ETO. Recipient Alumni "A" award Asbury Coll., Wilmore, Ky., 1992. Mem. Lions Club, Kiwanis, Rotary. Republican. Methodist. Home: 19152 Grenelefe Ct Fort Myers FL 33903-6607

HOFFMAN, RONALD, historical institute administrator, educator; b. Balt., Feb. 10, 1941; s. Emanuel and Ethel (Lubin) H.; m. Sandra Zalma Rudman, Aug. 28, 1965; children: Maia, Barak. AA, Balt. C.C., 1963; BA, George Peabody Coll., 1964; MA, U. Wis., 1965, PhD, 1969. Asst. prof. history U. Md., College Park, 1969-74, assoc. prof., 1974-92, prof., 1992-95; dir. Inst. Early Am. History and Culture, Williamsburg, Va., 1992—; prof. Coll. William and Mary, Williamsburg, 1993—; cons. Office Sec. Def., Washington, 1975—; symposia dir. U.S. Capitol Hist. Soc., Washington, 1977-93. Author: A Spirit of Dissension, 1973; co-author: The Pursuit of Liberty: A History of the American People, 1983; co-editor: Diplomacy and Revolution, 1971, Sovereign States in an Age of Uncertainty, 1982, Slavery and Freedom in the Age of the American Revolution, 1983, Arms and Independence: The Military Character of the American Revolution, 1983, An Uncivil War: The Southern Backcountry during the American Revolution, 1985, Peace and Peacemakers: The Treaty of 1783, 1985, The Economy of Early America: The Revolutionary Period, 1763-1790, 1989, We Call Overcome: Martin Luther King, Jr., and the Black Freedom Struggle, 1990, To Form a More Perfect Union: The Critical Ideas of the Constitution, 1992, Religion in a Revolutionary Age, 1994, Of Consuming Interests: The Style of Life in the Eighteenth Century, 1994, The Transforming Hand of Revolution, 1996; contbr. articles to hist. publs. 3d class petty officer USNR, 1959-61. Fellow Ford Found., 1967, Eleutherian Mills-Hagley Found., 1978; grantee NEH, 1977, Nat. Hist. Publs. and Records Commn., 1979—. Mem. Am. Hist. Assn., Orgn. Am. Historians, Assn. Documentary Editing, So. Hist. Assn., Va. Hist. Soc., Md. Hist. Soc. Democrat. Jewish. Home: 201-B Palace Green St Williamsburg VA 23185 Office: Inst Early Am History and Culture PO Box 8781 Williamsburg VA 23187

HOFFMANN, FRANK WILLIAM, library science educator, writer; b. Geneva, N.Y., May 2, 1949; s. Frank Anton and Lydia Mae (Mayer) H.; m. Ann Black, Jan. 5, 1980. BA, Ind. U., 1971, MLS, 1972; PhD, U. Pitts., 1977. Libr. Memphis Pub. Libr., 1972-74; grad. asst. Grad. sch. Libr. & Info. Sci. U. Pitts., 1974-77; libr. Woodville State Hosp., Carnegie, Pa., 1976-78; prof. Sam Houston State U., Huntsville, Tex., 1979—; part-time reference libr. Carlow Coll., Pitts., 1974-76, Northland Pub. Libr., Pitts., 1976-78; adj. prof. La. State U., 1980, U. Houston, 1985-88, U. Tex., Brownsville, 1996—; editor Haworth Press, Binghamton, N.Y., 1990—. Author: The Literature of Rock, vol. 1, 1981 (Best Acad. Book, Choice Mag. N.Y.C. 1981), vol. 2, 1986, vol. 3, 1995, Popular Culture and Libraries, 1984, Intellectual Freedom & Censorship, 1988 (Best Acad. Book, Choice Mag. N.Y.C. 1988), Encyclopedia of Fads, vol. 1, 1990, vol. 2, 1991, vol. 3, 1992, vol. 4, 1993, American Popular Culture, 1995, Library Collection Development Policies, 1996; editor: Popular Culture in Libraries, 1995, Popular Culture Sourcebook, 1990—; reviewer jours. in field; contbr. articles to profl. jours. Bd. trustees Montgomery County Pub. Libr. Sys., Conroe, Tex., 1990—; lay rep. Houston Area Librs., 1990—; automation consortium mem. North Harris C.C.- Montgomery Librs., Houston, 1994—. Mem. ALA, Spl. Libr. Assn. (Tex. chpt. bd. dirs. 1979-89), Popular Culture Assn., Beta Phi Mu. Democrat. Home: 30 E Shadowpoint Cir The Woodlands TX 77381 Office: Sam Houston State U Dept Libr Sci Box 2236 Huntsville TX 77341

HOFFMANN, MANFRED WALTER, consulting company executive; b. Bklyn., Apr. 21, 1938; s. Hermann Karl and Emilie (Talmon) H.; BS, Cornell U., 1960; MEd, Temple U., 1972, PhD, 1977; m. Barbara Ann Kenvin, Aug. 5, 1961; children: Lisa Joy, Lauren Kimberly, Kurt William. With Sun Oil Co., 1967-71, mgr. mktg. devel., Rosemont, Pa., 1971-72, mgr. tng., 1973-77, dir. orgn. and mgmt. devel., 1977-79; dir. human resources and adminstrn. Sun Prodn. Co., Dallas, 1979-83; dir. world wide human resources Sun Exploration & Prodn. Co., 1983-90; pres. Gyroscopic Mgmt. Inc., 1989—; lectr. Grad. Sch., U. Tex., Dallas, 1979—. Pres., PTA, bd. mem. Beechwood Sch., 1975-77; cons. exec. com. Orgns. Industrialization Congress Am., 1975-79; bd. dirs. Job Opportunity for Youth, 1980-81; bd. dirs. Dallas SER, 1986—. Served with USMCR, 1956-62. Mem. Am. Soc. Tng. and Devel., Am. Soc. Pers. Adminstrn., Dallas C. of C., Tex. Assn. Bus. Republican. Episcopalian. Home: 1316 Lakewood Dr Mc Kinney TX 75070-5222

HOFFMANN, MARY ANNE, music company executive, consultant; b. New Orleans, May 29, 1931; d. Elsnert Joseph and Lilly Marie (Bourgeois) DeLaune; m. Charles Lindy Hoffmann, June 1, 1952. B Music Edn., Southwestern La. U., 1951; postgrad., La. State U., Columbia U., U. Southwestern. Tchr. music Winnie(Tex.)-Stowell Elem. and Jr. H.S.; substitute tchr. New Orleans Parish Schs., 1958; pvt. tchr. piano Sacred Heart Acad., New Orleans, 1858; tchr. vocal music Thibodaux (La.) Schs., 1958-64; v.p. Hofman Music, Thibodaux, 1958—; mem. adv. bd. for artists and lects. Nicholls State U., 1993—; mem. adv. bd. Sta. KTLN-FM, New Orleans, 1995—. Mem. rev. bd. Cancer Ctr., Thibodaux Hosps., 1995—; state chmn. music in hosps. and nursing homes, 1995-97. Recipient award for highest hours put in nursing homes Nat. Fedn. Music Clubs. Mem. Thibodaux Music Club. Home: 625 Lagarde St Thibodaux LA 70301-3429

HOFSTEAD, JAMES WARNER, laundry machinery company executive, lawyer; b. Jackson, Tenn., Feb. 3, 1913; s. Harry Oliver and Agnes Lucile (Blackard) H.; m. Ellen Frances Bowers, Dec. 27, 1940; 1 child, Eda Lucile. AB, Vanderbilt U., 1935, LLB, 1938. Bar: Tenn. Pvt. practice law; v.p., chmn. bd. dirs. United Tel. Co., 1969—; pres., dir. Wishy Washy, Inc., Nashville, 1946—; pres., dir. Wishy Sales Inc., 1959—. Capt. USMC, 1942-45. Mem. SAR (nat. committeeman, state pres. emeritus, nat. trustee), Vanderbilt Bar Assn. (pres. emeritus), So. Srs. Golf Assn., Soc. of the Cincinnati, English Speaking Union (chmn.), Soc. Colonial Wars (past gov. Tenn., deputy gov. gen.), C. of C., Belle Meade Country Club, 200 Club, Exch. Club, Eccentric Club (London), Gasparilla 48 Club, Cumberland Club (charter), Sons of Confederate Vets., Sigma Chi. Methodist. Home: 215 Deer Park Cir Nashville TN 37205-3324 Office: 3729 Charlotte Pike Nashville TN 37209-3734

HOGAN, ADEN ELLSWORTH, JR., city government administrator; b. Fredonia, Kans., July 31, 1951; s. Aden Ellsworth Sr. and Maxine Ruth (Buchanan) H.; m. Debra Ann Ford, July 26, 1969 (div. Apr. 1982); 1 child, Michael Troy; m. Denna Marie Moore, Dec. 9, 1982. AA with honors, Mesa State Coll., Grand Junction, Colo., 1985, BBA cum laude, 1987; MPA, U. Colo., 1992. Engrng. technician City of Dodge Dept. Engrng., Dodge City, Kans., 1970-77; prodn. mgr. Gingery Assn. Inc., Engrs., Grand Junction, 1978-84; planner Mesa County Govt., Grand Junction, 1984-85, dir. risk and fleet mgmt. div., 1985-92; dir. risk mgmt. City of Okla. City, 1992-95; asst. to city mgr. City of Oklahoma City, 1995-96; town adminstr. Town of Parker, Colo., 1996—; regional rep. N.W. Colo. Transp. Task Force, Glenwood Springs, 1988-91; mem. Gov.'s Round Table for Local Transp. Needs, Denver, 1989-92; bd. dirs. Colo. club Classics, Ltd., Grand Junction; mem. response team for Okla. City bombing, 1995; mem. Kans. Hunter Safety Inst. Author: (manual) Fleet Policies and Procedures, 1989, Safety Manual, 1989, A View From the Top-Management Perspectives of Risk Management, 1995. Speaker Grand Junction Helicopter Ops. Task Force, 1986; instr. Kans. Hunter Safety Program, Dodge City, 1974-77; chmn. S.W. Kans. Ducks Unltd., Dodge City, 1974-77, Grand Junction Bd. Adjustment and Appeals, 1986-90. Named to Hon. Order of Buffalo, Kans. Fish and Game Hunter Soc., 1976; Colo. Gen. Assembly scholar, 1986-88. Mem. USTA (life), Pub. Risk Mgrs. Assn. (seminar presenter 1993-94), Internat. City Mgrs. Assn., Ducks Unltd. (chmn. 1975-78), Horizon Tennis Club (bd. dirs., pres. Grand Junction chpt. 1989-91). Republican. Home: 19663 A East Mann Creek Dr Parker CO 80134 Office: 20120 E Main St Parker CO 80134-7334

HOGAN, ARTHUR JAMES, portfolio manager; b. Boston, Dec. 30, 1940; s. Arthur James and Marie Romula (Daigneau) H.; m. Ellen Ann LaCour, Feb. 8, 1962. AB, U. Ala., 1961, MA, 1968. Chartered fin. analyst. Tchr. Muscogee County Sch. System, Columbus, Ga., 1964-66; tchr. Taylor County Sch. System, Butler, Ga., 1966-69, project dir., 1969-79; dir. Supplemental Edn. Svcs., Butler, 1970-80; program developer Columbus Coll., 1974-76; owner, cons. Arthur Hogan Cons. Svc., Butler, 1976-81; systems developer Register Data Systems, Warner Robins, Ga., 1981-82; officer, cons. Resource Devel. Corp., Charleston, S.C., 1982-86; owner, mgr. Arthur J. Hogan and Assoc., Charleston, 1986—; adj. prof. Limeston Coll., Charleston, 1989—, Charleston So. U., 1990—. Contbr. articles to profl. jours. Mem. Exec. Adv. Bd. Charleston So. U., 1991—. Lt. U.S. Army, 1961-63. Named Outstanding Planner Money mag., 1987. Fellow Fin. Analyst Fedn.; mem. Am. Inst. CFA, Ea. Fin. Assn., Fin. Mgmt. Assn., Navy League of U.S., Concerned Boaters (pres. 1995—). Home: 25 Sothel Ave Charleston SC 29407-7319 Office: PO Box 201 Charleston SC 29402

HOGAN, CECIL EVERETT, security company executive; b. Memphis, Dec. 6, 1947; s. Joseph L. and Doris G. Hogan; m. Peggy Darlene Thorn, June 15, 1968; children: Terri Darlene, Christina Lynn, Joseph Randolph. Student, Memphis State U., 1965-66. Cert. instr. Nat. Burglar & Fire Alarm Assn. Nat. Tng. Sch., 1986—. Draftsman Security Title Co., Memphis, 1967, Am. Realty Svc. Corp., Memphis, 1968-73; exec. v.p. Devel. Design Inc., Memphis, 1973-76, Protection Unlimited Inc., Memphis, 1976-81; pres., owner Security Cons., Inc., Memphis, 1981—; mem.-at-large Alarm Industry Rsch. and Edn. Found. False Alarm Coalition, 1992—. Pres. Frayser Jaycees, Memphis, 1980-81; life mem. Rep. Presdl. Task Force, Washington, 1984—. Named Jaycee of the quarter Tenn. Jaycees, 1980, Jaycee of Yr., Frayser Jaycees, 1980, Col. of the Vol. Corps., Tenn. Jaycees, 1982. Mem. Am. Soc. for Indsl. Security, Nat. Burglar & Fire Alarm Assn. (bd. mem. 1988—), Tenn. Burglar & Fire Alarm Assn. (bd. mem. 1981—, pres. 1983-84, 92). Baptist. Home: 2128 Swinnea Rd Nesbit MS 38651-9712 Office: Security Cons Inc 3158 Broad Ave Memphis TN 38112-3104

HOGAN, DANIEL JAMES, dermatologist, educator; b. Baie Comeau, Que., Can., Feb. 15, 1953; came to U.S., 1989; s. John Vincent and Georgette (Burgess) H.; m. Lorea Ann Hogan, May 20, 1975; children: Gregory Sean, Matthew Charles. MD cum laude, Dalhousie U., Halifax, N.S., Can., 1976. Lic. physician Fla. Rotating intern Ottawa (Ont.) Civic Hosp., 1976-77; resident in internal medicine Ottawa Gen. Hosp., 1977-78; resident in dermatology Royal Victoria Hosp., Montreal, 1978-81; fellow in occupl. dermatology U. Cin., 1981-82; asst. prof. dermatology U. Sask. (Can.), 1982-86, assoc. prof. dermatology, 1986-89; assoc. prof. dermatology U. Miami (Fla.), 1990-93; asst. chief dermatology VA Med. Ctr., Miami, Fla., 1992-93; chief dermatology Bay Pines (Fla.) VA Med. Ctr., 1993—; prof. dept. medicine, pediatrics and pub. health U. South Fla., 1993-96; prof. Dept. Medicine and Pediatrics LSU Med. Coll. Ctr., Shreveport, La., 1996—. Editor: Occupational Dermatology, 1994; contbr. articles to profl. jours. Fellow Am. Contact Dermatology Soc. (v.p., bd. dirs. 1990-92, exec. com. 1991-92); mem. Can. Dermatol. Assn. (Barney Usher award 1985), Am. Acad. Dermatology (task forces environ. and occupational dermatology, contact dermatology), Alpha Omega Alpha. Home: 1231 Remington Cir Shreveport LA 71106 Office: Dermatology Medicine LSU Medical Ctr 1501 Kings Hwy Shreveport LA 71130-3932

HOGAN, JOHN DONALD, college dean, finance educator; b. Binghamton, N.Y., July 16, 1927; s. John D. and Edith J. (Hennessy) H.; m. Anna Craig, Nov. 26, 1976; children—Thomas P., James E. A.B., Syracuse U., 1949, M.A., 1950, Ph.D., 1952. Registered prin. Nat. Assn. Securities Dealers. Prof. econs., chmn. dept. Bates Coll., Lewiston, Maine, 1953-58; dir. edn. fin. research State of N.Y., 1959, chief mcpl. fin., 1960; staff economist, dir. research Northwestern Mut. Life Ins. Co., Milw., 1960-68; v.p. Nationwide Ins. Cos., Columbus, Ohio, 1968-76; dean Sch. Bus. Adminstrn. Central Mich. U., Mt. Pleasant, 1976-79; v.p. Am. Productivity Ctr., Houston, 1979-80; pres., chmn., chief exec. officer Variable Annuity Life Ins. Co., Houston, 1980-83; sr. v.p. Am. Gen. Corp., Houston, 1983-86; dean, prof. fin. Coll. Commerce U. Ill., Champaign, 1986-91; dean, prof. fin. and econs. Coll. Bus. Adminstrn. Ga. State U., Atlanta, 1991—; bd. dirs. Covenant Med. Ct., Champaign, 1986-92, Sinfonia da Camera, Champaign, Ga. Coun. on Econ. Edn., Pvt. Industry Coun. Author: American Social Legislation, 1965, U.S. Balance of Payments and Capital Flows, 1967, School Revenue Studies, 1959, Fiscal Capacity of the State of Maine, 1958, American Social Legislation, 1973; editor: Dimensions of Productivity Research (2 vols.), 1981; contbr. articles to jours., abstracts to profl. meetings. Bd. dirs. Goodwill Industries, Columbus, 1972-76, chmn. capital fund drive, 1974-75; mem. Houston Com. on Fgn. Rels., 1980—, Chgo. Coun. on Fgn. Rels., 1986—, Chgo. com., 1987—. Served with U.S. Army, 1944-46, ETO; capt. (ret.) USAR. Maxwell fellow Syracuse U., 1950-52; recipient Best Article award Jur. Risk and Ins., Alumni Appreciation award U. Ill., 1991, 1964; Maxwell Centennial lectr. Maxwell Grad. Sch., Syracuse U., 1970. Mem. Acad. Mgmt., Am. Econ. Assn., Inst. Mgmt. Scis., Nat. Assn. Bus. Economists, Nat. Tax Assn. (dir. 1981-85, treas., exec. com. 1988—), Inst. Rsch. in Econs. of Taxation (dir. 1984—), Columbus C. of C. (chmn. econ. policy com. 1972-76), Phi Kappa Phi, Beta Gamma Sigma, Columbus Athletic Club, Heritage Club (Houston), Univ. Club (Chgo.), Lincolnshire Fields Country Club (Champaign), Commerce Club (Atlanta), World Trade Club (Atlanta, bd. dirs. 1993—). Clubs: Columbus Athletic; Heritage (Houston); University (Chgo.), Lincolnshire Fields Country (Champaign); Commerce Club (Atlanta). Office: Ga State U Coll Bus Adminstrn University Pl Atlanta GA 30303

HOGGARD, WILLIAM ZACK, JR., amusement park executive; b. Albuquerque, Dec. 2, 1951; s. William Zack Sr. and Geneva Ruth (Garner) H.; m. Sandra K. Walker (div. 1989); children: Steven Wayne, Amanda Danielle; m. Deborah M. Deal, 1992; children: Roxanne A., Katrina K. Asst. mgr. Lone Star Amusements, Amarillo, Tex., 1969; gen. mgr. Golden Spread Amusements, Hedley, Tex., 1969-72; booking agt. Monte Young Shows, Provo, Utah, 1972; independent concessionaire Gene Ledel Shows, Ft. Worth, Tex., 1973; concession mgr. Schaffer Shows Unit 2, Dallas, 1974, Pearson Enterprises, Ft. Worth, 1975-76; gen. agt., concession mgr. Aero Space Shows, Dallas, 1977-80; western sales mgr., operating engr. Pretzel Ride Inc., Shiloh, N.J., 1981; broker, distributor of amusement rides, carnival operator Joshua, Tex., 1982—; chief exec. officer Phoenix Amusements (President's Park Amusement Park), Carlsbad, N.Mex., 1991-93; amusement ride inspector Beckman Ins. Agy., Brookfield, Wis., 1993—; loss control cons. Allied Speciality Ins. Co., St. Petersburg, Fla., 1985—, State Bd. of Ins., Austin, Tex., 1985—; cons. engr. Eli Bridge Co., Inc. Jacksonvil le, Ill., 1985-89, Pretzel Ride, Inc., Shiloh, N.J., 1981—; cons. Amusement Ride Safety Act 1982, State of Oklahoma. Carnival organizer and fund raiser, fair bds., numerous civic orgns., Tex., N.Mex. and Okla., 1969-89; CEO Phoenix Amusements (dba Presidents Park Amusement Park), Carlsbad, N.Mex, 1991-92; pres., CEO Hoggard Amusement Industries Inc., 1996—. Mem. Tex. Assn. Fairs and Expositions, Okla. Assn. Fairs and Festivals, Outdoor Amusement Bus. Assn., Nat. Assn. Amusement Ride Safety Officials, Lone Star Showmen's Club. Home and Office: PO Box 952 Joshua TX 76058-0952

HOHN, DAVID, physician; b. Tucson, 1942. MD, U. Ill., 1970. Intern Rush-Presbyn. St. Luke's Hosp., Chgo., 1970-71; resident in gen. surgery U. Calif., San Francisco, 1971-78; v.p. patient care M.D. Anderson Cancer Ctr.- U. Tex., Houston, 1993—. Mem. AAS, ACPE, AFCR, ASCO, SIS, SSO. Office: U Tex MD Anderson Cancer Clinic PO Box 43 1515 Holcombe Blvd Houston TX 77030

HOINES, DAVID ALAN, lawyer; b. St. Paul, Oct. 18, 1946; s. Arnold H. and Patricia (Olson) H.; m. Bonnie K. Smith, June 4, 1983. BA, Calif. State U., San Jose, 1969; JD, Santa Clara U., 1972; LLM in Taxation, Boston U., 1973. Bar: Fla. 1975, Calif. 1975, U.S. Dist. Ct. (so. dist.) Fla. 1975, U.S. Dist. Ct. (no. dist.) Calif. 1980, U.S. Dist. Ct. (mid. dist.) Fla. 1984, U.S. Dist. Ct. (ctrl. dist.) Calif. 1990, U.S. Ct. Claims 1980, U.S. Tax Ct. 1975, U.S. Ct. Appeals (fed. cir.) 1990, U.S. Ct. Appeals (4th cir.) 1985, U.S. Ct. Appeals (5th cir.) 1978, U.S. Ct. Appeals (9th cir.) 1980, U.S. Ct. Appeals (11th cir.) 1981, U.S. Supreme Ct. 1980; cert. civil trial lawyer, Fla. Pvt. practice Ft. Lauderdale, Fla., 1975—; adj. instr. Nova U. Ctr. for Study of Law, 1977. Author: Taxman and the Textbook, The Ripon Forum, 1972. Mem. ABA, ATLA, Broward County Bar Assn., Hundred Club of Broward County, Tau Delta Phi. Office: 1290 E Oakland Park Blvd Fort Lauderdale FL 33334-4443

HOJJATIE, BAHRAM, mechanical engineer, educator, researcher; b. Boroojerd, Iran, May 6, 1954; came to U.S., 1977; s. Ali and Batool Hajjatie; m. Homa Hooshmand, Dec. 29, 1990; 1 child, Sara Ladan. MSME, Miss. State U., 1980; PhD in Engrng. Mechanics, Mech. Engrng., U. Fla., 1990. Registered profl. engr., Fla., Ga. Grad. rsch. asst. dept. mech. engrng. Miss. State U., Starkville, 1977-80; test engr. Jacksonville (Fla.) Electric, 1981-84; engr. II U. Fla. Health Sci. Ctr., Gainesville, 1984-89; asst. scientist in dental biomaterials, materials sci. and engrng. U. Fla., 1990-93; assoc. engr. Inst. Paper Sci. and Tech., Ga. Tech., Atlanta, 1993—; reviewer Jour. Dental Rsch., 1989—, Jour. Implantology, 1992; engrng. cons. on heat transfer, fluid mechanics, material behavior and finite element analysis, Fla. and Ga., 1985—; instr. math. and stats. Fla. Jr. Coll., 1984-85; instr. math. and sci. Santa Fe C.C., Gainesville, 1985; investigator rsch. projects NIH, 1988-92. Contbr. numerous articles on thermal stress analysis, heat transfer, fluid mechanics, biomechanics and paper making tech. Recipient rsch. devel. award U. Fla., 1992, 93. Fellow ASME (award 1992); mem. TAPPI, Am. Soc. Exptl. Mechs. Office: Ga Inst Tech Inst Paper Sci and Tech 500 10th St NW Atlanta GA 30318-5714

HOKE, ALEXANDER PEABODY, life underwriter, financial consultant; b. Hartford, Conn., Dec. 9, 1949; s. Marshall Peabody and Frances Marion (Beardsley) H.; children; Hannah Margaret, Marshall Peabody III. BA, Gettysburg Coll., 1972. Chartered fin. cons., CLU. Mgrs. asst. First Nat. Bank Boston, 1972-77, trust assoc., 1978-79; trust rep. Old Colony Bank, Springfield, Mass., 1979-81; life ins. agt. Northwestern Mut. Life, Springfield, 1981-85, Atlanta, 1985-94; life ins. agt. Mass. Mutual Life, Atlanta, 1994—. Bd. dirs. Bay Village Neighborhood Assn., 1972-78, Mental Health Assn. Greater Springfield, 1982-85, Metro Atlanta Serenity House, 1990—, Arcadia Wildlife Found., 1992—, Child Devel. Ctr. at Ctrl., 1992-94; v.p., bd. dirs. Springfield Preservation Trust, 1979-85; participant Springfield Leadership Inst., 1980; pres., v.p., bd. dirs., mem. Inman Park Neighborhood Assn., Inc., Atlanta, 1986—; v.p., bd. dirs. Inman Park Coop. Presch., 1990-91; elder Ctrl. Presbyn. Ch., 1992—; docent, mem. Atlanta Hist. Soc., 1985—; tourguide, mem. Atlanta Preservation Ctr., 1986—, mem. coun., 1988-90; fundraiser Am. Heart Assn., 1976; mem. Atlanta Clean City Commn., 1988-96. Mem. Nat. Assn. Life Underwriters, Am. Soc. CLU's, Atlanta Assn. Life Underwriters, Atlanta Assn. CLU's, Atlanta Estate Planning Coun., Atlanta Exec. Network, Nat. Trust Hist. Preservation, Ga. Trust Hist. Preservation, Soc. for Protection N.H. Forests, Kiwanis (bd. dirs. Atlanta chpt. 1994—). Home: 156 Waverly Way NE Atlanta GA 30307-2568 Office: Mass Mutual Life Ste 2300 245 Peachtree Center Ave NE Atlanta GA 30303-1224

HOLBERG, RALPH GANS, JR., lawyer; b. Mobile, Nov. 5, 1908; s. Ralph G. and Lillian (Frohlichstein) H.; m. Amelia Schwarz, Feb. 16, 1938; children: Ralph G. III, Robert S. J.D., U. Ala., 1932. Bar: Ala. 1932. Since practiced in Mobile; now sr. counsel Holberg and Holberg P.C. Contbr. articles to hist. and profl. jours. Pres. Mobile Bay Area chpt. ARC, 1954-55; chmn. Southeastern area council, 1957-58; life bd. dirs. emeritus Mobile Bay Area chpt., Ala. nat. v.p., 1960-61, mem. nat. bd. govs., 1965-68, 68-71; chmn. bd. Mobile County Bd. Pensions and Security, 1947-77; bd. dirs. Mobile Gen. Hosp., 1963-67, chmn., 1965-67; mem. Ala. State Docks Adv. Bd., 1962-69, 3d Army Area Adv. Com., Gov. Ala. Com. Adult Edn. Negroes, 1949; chmn. Mobile Pub. Library Bd., 1954-55; past appeal agt. local selective service bd.; pres. Estate Planning Council Mobile, 1971-72; pres. Hon. Fellows Mobile Coll., 1972-73; mem. nat. adv. council Nat. Multiple Sclerosis Soc., 1973-87; alt. Mobile Hist. Devel. Commn., 1973-76; pres. Old Shell Rd. PTA, 1954-55; pres., Ala. Jr. C. of C., 1935; mem. bd. Mobile Community Chest and Council, 1965-71; trustee Mobile YWCA, 1978-80; bd. dirs. Gordon Smith Ctr., 1973-85. Served to lt. USNR, 1944-46. Recipient Disting. Svc. Key, Mobile Jaycees, 1938, J.N. Carmichael Meml. award 1984; named Mobilian of Yr., 1963; ann. vol. svcs. award named in his honor Mobile Bay Area chpt. ARC, 1986. Fellow The Am. Coll. Trust and Estate Counsel; mem. ABA, Ala. Bar Assn., Mobile Bar Assn. (pres. 1942), VFW, Ala. Hist. Assn. (exec. com. 1981-85), Ala. Jud. Coll. Faculty Assn. (hon.), SCV, Am. Legion (post comdr. 1947-48), Mobile Jaycees (pres. 1934), Mobile Area C. of C. (dir. 1962-65, 71-74, 81), Mobile Hist. Preservation Soc. (dir. 1974-77), Mobile's Azalea Trail (pres. 1934-35), Navy League (judge advocate Mobile council 1979-92), Am. Council Judaism (nat. adv. bd. 1955-85), Spring Hill Ave. Temple (pres. 1947-48), Mobile Exch. Club (charter, pres. 1938), Internat. Trade Club, Touchdown Club (past mem. bd.), Country Club of Mobile, Rotary (hon. Mobile club 1989), Zeta Beta Tau (pres. Psi chpt. 1932). Home: 217 Berwyn Dr W Apt 215 Mobile AL 36608-2125 Office: Commerce Bldg 118 N Royal St Ste 804 Mobile AL 36602-3600

HOLBROOK, FRANK MALVIN, lawyer; b. Atlanta, Mar. 26, 1952; s. James David and Mary Linda (Fambrough) H.; m. Julie Melissa Holley, Aug. 30, 1975; children: Holley Marie, James Clinton. AA with honors, Brevard Community Coll., Cocoa, Fla., 1972; BS cum laude, Fla. State U., 1974; JD cum laude, U. Ga., 1979. Bar: Ga. 1979, Miss. 1979, U.S. Dist. Ct. (no. and so. dists.) Miss. 1979, U.S. Ct. Appeals (5th cir.) 1979, U.S. Ct. Appeals (11th cir.) 1982. Assoc. Fuselier, Ott & McKee, Jackson, Miss., 1979-83; assoc. Thompson, Alexander & Crews, Jackson, 1983-85, ptnr., 1985-95; v.p., shareholder Edmonson, Biggs, Mozingo & Holbrook P.A., Jackson, Miss., 1995—. Mem. ABA, Fed. Bar Assn. (pres. Miss. chpt. 1991-92), Miss. State Bar Assn., State Bar Ga., Hinds County Bar Assn. Republican. Methodist. Office: Edmonson Biggs Mozingo & Holbrook PA PO Box 865 Jackson MS 39205-0865

HOLCOMB, ALICE WILLARD POWER, diversified investments executive; b. Franklin County, Ga., Sept. 11, 1922; d. William McKinley and Flora Sarah (Cash) Cantrell; m. Fleming Mitchell Power, May 6, 1941 (dec. Sept. 1967); children: Susan Cantrell, Fleming Michael; m. George Waymon Holcomb, June 4, 1982. Student, Toccoa (Ga.) Falls Coll., 1939-40; BS, Perry Bus. Sch., 1941. Owner Power Poultry Co., Toccoa, 1950-61, Fleming Mitchell Power Properties, Toccoa and Athens, Ga., 1962—, Power's (retail shops), Athens, 1968-85; ptnr. Power Constrn. Co., Athens, 1972—, Athens Indsl. Electric, Athens, 1973—. Active Ga. Hist. Soc. Mem. DAR. Republican. Baptist. Home and Office: 199 Avalon Dr Athens GA 30606-3234

HOLCOMB, CARAMINE KELLAM, volunteer worker; b. Painter, Va., Jan. 23, 1941; d. Emerson Polk and Amine (Cosby) Kellam; m. Isaac Somers White, Nov. 25, 1961 (div. 1975); children: Kellam White, Caramine White, Virginia Somers White; m. Harry Sherman Holcomb III, May 12, 1979. AA, St. Mary's Coll., Raleigh, 1960; Cert., Richmond Bus. Coll., Va., 1961. Bd. dirs. Kellam Energy, Inc., Belle Haven. Va., 1980—, AUto Plus, Inc., Belle Haven, 1980-89, Shore Stop, Inc., Bele Haven, 1981-89. Contbr. articles to profl. jours. Trustee Northampton-Accomack Meml. Hosp., Nassawadox, Va., 1986—, v.p. aux., 1986-88, pres., 1988-90, sec. bd. trustees, 1989-91, vice chmn., 1991-94, chair, 1994-96; bd. dirs. Ea. Shore Hist. Soc., Onancock, Va., 1987-92; bd. dirs. Med. Soc. Va. Alliance, Richmond, 1984-94, v.p., 1989-91, pres., 1992-93; treas. E. Polk Kellam Found., 1991—. Mem. AMA Alliance Bd. (ERF com. 1994, AMA-ERF com. chmn. 1994-95), Med. Soc. Va. Trust, Garden Club Ea. Shore (pres. 1973-75, 85-87, field dir. 1995—). Home: PO Box 40 Franktown VA 23354-0040

HOLCOMB, CONSTANCE L., sales and marketing management executive; b. St. Paul, Oct. 28, 1942; d. John E. Holcomb and Lucille A. (Westerdahl) Hope. BS, U. Minn., 1965; MA in Intercultural Edn., U. of the Americas, Puebla, Mex., 1975. Rsch. analyst U.S. Dept. Def., Washington, 1965-66; br. gen. mgr. Berlitz Lang. Schs., Mexico City, 1966-68; pres., gen. mgr. Centro Lingüistico, Puebla, 1968-72; gen. mgr., prof. Lang. Ctr. Am. Sch. Found., Puebla, 1972-74; assoc. prof., dir. lang. programs U. of the Americas, Puebla, 1974-76; prof., dean faculty of langs. Nat. Autonomous U. Mex., Mexico City, 1976-78; dir. sales & mktg. Longman Pub. Co., N.Y.C., 1978-80, dir. internat. sales & mktg., 1980-84; mng. dir. ESL Pub. Div. McGraw-Hill Book Co., N.Y.C., 1984-85; dir. mktg. mgmt. McGraw-Hill Tng. Systems and Book Co., N.Y.C., 1985-86; dir. mktg. electronic bus. McGraw-Hill Book Co., N.Y.C., 1986-87; info. industry mgmt. cons., career mgmt. cons., ind. contractor, N.Y.C., 1987-91; mktg. cons. Sarasota, Fla., 1991—; v.p. MexTESOL, Mexico City, 1977-78. Editor: English Teaching in Mexico, 1975; contrb. articles to profl. jours. Bd. trusteess, devel. com. mem. John and Mable Ringhive Mus., 1993—. Mem. Assn. Am. Pubs. (com. chmn. internat. div. 1980-84, exec. com. 1980-84), Info. Industry Assn., Nat. Assn. Women Cons., Am. Soc. Profl. and Exec. Women. Office: 3555 Mistletoe Ln Longboat Key FL 34228-4103

HOLCOMB, GORDON ERNEST, plant pathology educator; b. Monroe, Wis., July 6, 1932; s. Ernest Holcomb Jr. and Florence (Henneman) Hefty; m. Alice Harriet Duff, Jan. 25, 1964; children: Janette Lynn, Amy Florence. BS, U. Wis., Platteville, 1959; PhD, U. Wis., Madison, 1966. Asst. prof. La. State U., Baton Rouge, 1965-70, assoc. prof., 1970-78, prof. dept. plant pathology, 1978—. Contbr. sci. articles to profl. jours. Tchr. Operation Upgrade, Baton Rouge, 1972-73; judge La. State Sci. and Engring. Fair, Baton Rouge, 1980—, Internat. Sci. and Engring. Fair, San Antonio, 1979. With USAF, 1951-55, Korea. Recipient Davd Feathers award Am. Camellia Soc., 1981, 82. Mem. AAAS, Am. Phytopathol. Soc. (mem. various coms.), Am. Inst. Biol. Scis., La. Acad. Scis., Sigma Xi. Office: La State Dept Plant Pathology & Crop Physics Baton Rouge LA 70803

HOLCOMB, HOMER SIMMONS See GARRETT, LEE

HOLCOMB, LYLE DONALD, JR., retired lawyer; b. Miami, Fla., Feb. 3, 1929; s. Lyle Donald and Hazel Irene (Watson) H.; m. Barbara Jean Roth, July 12, 1952; children: Susan Holcomb Davis, Douglas J., Mark E. BA, U. Mich., 1951; JD, U. Fla., 1954. Bar: U.S. Supreme Ct. 1966, U.S. Ct. Appeals (5th and 11th cirs.) 1981. Ptnr. Holcomb & Holcomb, Miami, 1955-72; assoc. Copeland, Therrel, Baisden & Peterson, Miami Beach, Fla., 1972-75; ptnr. Therrel, Baisden, Stanton, Wood & Setlin, Miami Beach, 1976-85; ptnr. Therrel Baisden & Meyer Weiss, Miami Beach, 1985-93; pvt. practice, Tallahassee, Fla., 1993-95; mem. organizing bd. Econ. Opportunities Legal Svcs. Program (now Legal Svcs. of Greater Miami, Inc.), 1965-75; organizing pres. So. Fla. Migrant Legal Svcs. Program (now Fla. Rural Legal Svcs.), 1966-68. Mem. exec. coun. So. Fla. coun. Boy Scouts Am., 1958-93; past pres. Miami chpt., past counselor state soc. Huguenot Soc. Fla. Served with USNR, 1947-53. Recipient Silver Beaver award So. Fla. coun. Boy Scouts Am., 1966. Fellow Am. Coll. Trust and Estate Counsel, 1980-94, Acad. Fla. Probate and Trust Litigation Attys.; mem. Dade County Bar Assn. (dir. 1960-71, sec. 1963-71), Miami Beach Bar Assn. (pres. 1980), Estate Planning Council Greater Miami., Soc. Mayflower Descs. (past pres. Miami club, past counselor state soc.), SAR (past pres. Miami chpt.), Univ. Yacht Club. Republican. Mem. United Ch. of Christ. Home: 3538 Killarney Plaza Dr Tallahassee FL 32308-3491

HOLCOMB, MILDRED GENEVA COMRIE, elementary education educator; b. New London, Conn., Sept. 22, 1941; d. Wendell Silas and Florence Marjorie (Gallup) Comrie; m. Michael Alan Holcomb, Dec. 22, 1973. BS, Ea. Nazarene Coll., 1963; MA, U. Conn., 1968; MS, U. Houston, Clear Lake, Tex., 1983. Cert. elem. edn. tchr., Tex. Tchr. 2d grade Ledyard (Conn.) Sch. Dist., 1963-68; tchr. 1st and 2d grades Mt. Vernon (Ohio) Sch. Dist., 1968-72; tchr. 4th grade Sheldon Ind. Sch. Dist., Houston, 1972-75; tchr. K-2d Pasadena (Tex.) Ind. Sch. Dist., 1976-83; tchr. kindergarten Sheldon Ind. Sch. Dist., Houston, 1985—. Vol. Nixon polit. campaign, Houston, 1972; organist Open Fellowship Ch. of the Nazarene, Houston, 1987-88, Broadway Ch. of the Nazarene, Houston, 1988-89, Pasadena Ch. of the Nazarene, 1980-81, Crosby Ch. of the Nazarene, 1994—; v.p. Pasadena Ind. Sch. Dist. PTO, 1979-80; pres. Parkway Elem. Sch. PTO, Houston, 1993-94; founder Parkside C.H.A.T.S. miniworkshops, 1990—. Named Tchr. of Yr., Parkway Elem. Sch., 1990-91. Mem. Assn. Tchrs. and Profl. Educators, Sheldon Educators Assn. Republican.

HOLCOMBE, FORREST DOUGLAS, business administration educator, retired naval officer; b. Newark, Ohio, Apr. 26, 1947; s. Forrest Wendell and Dorothy May (Lewis) H.; children: Kristen Annette Holcombe Seeley, Jeremy Douglas; m. Sharon Louise Conwell, Dec. 18, 1993. BS, Ohio State U., 1969, PHD in Orgnl. Behavior, 1982; MBA, U. West Fla., 1977. Commd. USN, 1969, advanced through grades to lt. commdr., 1987; naval flight officer, tactical coord. patrol squadron 5 USN, Jacksonville, Fla., 1970-73; naval flight officer instr. tng. squadron 10 USN, Pensacola, Fla., 1973-77; teaching assoc. Ohio State U., Columbus, 1977-81; asst. prof. mgmt. Marshall U., Huntington, W.Va., 1981-83; student aerospace exptl. psychologist USN Aerospace Med. Inst., Pensacola, 1983-84, head operation support divsn., 1984-87; head human factors br. USN Safety Ctr., Norfolk, Va., 1987-90; head human factors divsn. USN Biodynamics Lab., New Orleans, 1990-94; ret., 1994; asst. prof. bus. adminstrn. Lubbock Ctr. Wayland Bapt. U., Lubbock, Tex., 1994—; sr. scientist McWane & Co., Inc., Arlington, Va., 1994—; adj. instr. Franklin U., Columbus, 1978-79; adj. prof. U. West Fla., Pensacola, 1984-85, Troy State U., Pensacola, 1986-87; orgnl. cons. various cos., 1981-83. Editor Aeromedical Newsletter, 1988-90. Schoenbaum fellow Ohio State U., 1979. Mem. NRA, Nat. Acad. Mgmt., Ret. Officers Assn., Ohio State U. Alumni Assn., Phi Kappa Phi. Office: Wayland Baptist Univ Lubbock Ctr 4601 83rd St Lubbock TX 79424

HOLDAR, ROBERT MARTIN, chemist; b. Ozark, Ark., Feb. 10, 1949; s. Luther and Francess Ethyl (Briscoe) H.; m. Barbara Jean Sobczak, Jan. 5, 1985; children: Luther Edward, William Thomas, Frank King, Samuel Robert. BS in Chemistry, U. Ark., 1976; MS in Chemistry, Tex. A&M U., 1979; MBA, U. Dallas, 1996. Chemist Parkem Indsl. Svcs., LaPorte, Tex., 1979-80, Mohawk Labs div. NCH Corp., Irving, Tex., 1980—. Patentee in field. Chmn. Zoning Bd. Adjustments, Irving, 1991-95; mem. Local Emergency Planning Commn., Dallas, 1991-93; mem. bd. amortizations and appeals City of Irving, 1994. With USAF, 1968-73. W.K. Noyce scholar U. Ark., 1975. Mem. Am. Chem. Soc., Nat. Assn. Corrosion Engrs., Am. Soc. Lubrication Engrs. (chmn. North Tex. sect. 1982-83), Irving Rep. Club (editor 1989-92, 94—, treas. 1992-94), Irving Noon Toastmasters (pres. 1983, Accomplished Toastmaster award 1986). Home: 2816 Brockbank Dr Irving TX 75062-4523 Office: NCH Corp Mohawk Labs 2730 Carl Rd Irving TX 75062-6405

HOLDEN, JANELL M., geriatrics nurse; b. N.C., Apr. 28, 1950; d. Arnold D. and Evelyn E. (Taylor) Pait; m. Gary B. Holden, Apr. 6, 1972; children: Jeremy, Joseph. LPN, New Horizons Tech. Ctr., 1989. Relief charge nurse James River Convalescent Ctr., Newport News, Va., 1989; charge nurse, supr. Northampton Convalescent Ctr., Hampton, Va.

HOLDER, BEN R., protective services official; b. Dawson, Ga.; s. Leroy H.; m. Louise Grooms, Nov. 3, 1966; children: Rodney A., Kia Q. AA in Police Sci. and Adminstrn., Hillsborough C.C., Tampa, 1977; BA in Criminology, St. Leo Coll., 1989. Avaition mechanic USAF, Tampa, 1966-70; welder F.R. Strelow, Inc., Tampa, 1970-73; patrol officer Tampa Police Dept., 1973-75, vice detective, 1975-79, sgt., 1979-84, lt., 1984-86, capt., 1986-91, maj., 1991-93, police chief, 1993—. Mem. FACP, Internat. Assn. Chiefs Police. Office: Office of the Police Chief 1710 N Tampa St Tampa FL 33602-2648

HOLDER, EUGENE PAUL, clinical pharmacist, researcher; b. Beaumont, Tex., Sept. 1, 1954; s. Eugene Ellsworth and Leonie Mae (Mellen) H.; m. Cheryl Diane Jaggers, Aug. 6, 1977. BS in Chemistry, Sam Houston State U., Huntsville, Tex., 1979, MS in Chemistry, 1981; BS in Pharmacy, U. Tex., 1991; PharmD, U. Tex./U. Tex. HSC, Austin/San Antonio, 1994. Registered pharmacist, Tex. Instr. chemistry McLennan C.C., Waco, Tex., 1981-82, North Harris County Coll., Houston, 1987-88; rsch. scientist Betz Labs., Inc., The Woodlands, Tex., 1983-88; pharmacist Bapt. Med. Ctr., San Antonio, 1991-92; clin. pharmacist Bexar County Hosp. Dist., San Antonio, 1992-93; rsch. coord. U. Tex., Austin, 1989-91, clin. instr. pharmacy, 1994-95, resident in drug info. and internal medicine, 1994-95, course coord. PharmD class, 1992-93; clin. specialist Adult Medicine/Infectious Diseases Dept. Scott & White Meml. Hosp., Temple, Tex., 1995—; asst. prof. medicine Tex. A&M U. Health Sci. Ctr., Temple, 1995—; clin. asst. prof. pharmacy U. Tex., Austin, 1995—; cons. Jaggers and Assocs., Rison, Ark., 1988—; asst. prof. medicine Tex. A&M U. Health Sci. Ctr., Temple, 1995—; clin. asst. prof. pharmacy U. Tex., Austin, 1995—. Patentee in field. Vol. paramedic Cypress Creek Emergency Med. Svc., Houston, 1986-88; instr. CPR and first aid ARC, Houston and Conroe, Tex., 1986-88. Mem. Am. Soc. Hosp. Pharmacists, Am. Pharm. Assn., Am. Coll. Clin. Pharmacy, Am. Chem. Soc., Tex. Soc. Hosp. Pharmacists, N.Y. Acad. Scis., Golden Key, Alpha Chi, Rho Chi. Office: Scott and White Meml Hosp Dept Pharmacy/Clin Div 2401 S 31st St Temple TX 76508-0001

HOLDER, HOWARD RANDOLPH, SR., broadcasting corporation executive; b. Moline, Ill., Nov. 14, 1916; s. James William and Charlotte (Brega) H.; m. Clementi Lacey-Baker, Feb. 21, 1942; children: Janice Clementi Holder Collins, Susan Charlotte Holder, Marjory Estelle Holder, Howard Randolph, Jr. BA, Augustana Coll., 1939. With radio stas. WHBF, Rock Island, Ill., 1939-41, WOC, Davenport, Iowa, 1945-47, WINN, Louisville, 1947, WRFC, Athens, Ga., 1948-1956; pres. Clarke Broadcasting Corp., 1956-91, chmn., 1991—, WGAU and WNGC, Athens, 1956—, KVML and KZSQ, Sonora, Calif.,1987—, KVRQ, Atwater, Calif., 1995—, KLOQ and KFMK, Merced, Calif., 1996—; mem. adv. bd. U. Georgia Coll. Journalism and Mass Communication, 1973-78, sec. 1973-74; pres. Mid-West Ga. Broadcasting, Inc., 1965-68, bd. dirs. AP Broadcasters Inc., 1983-91. Author: Escape to Russia, 1995. Chmn. adv. bd. Salvation Army, 1962-63, life mem., 1952—; chmn. Athens Parks and Recreation Bd., 1952-62; chmn. Cherokee dist. Boy Scouts Am., 1966-67, bd. N.E. Ga. council, 1950—; regent for life Nat. Eagle Scout Assn., 1989; mem. adv. bd. Clarke County Juvenile Ct., 1960-72; chmn. region IV Ga. div. Am. Cancer Soc., 1968; bd. dirs. Athens Crime Prevention Com., 1960-70; mem. Georgians for Safer Hwys., 1970; mem. adv. bd. Athens-Clarke County ARC, 1950-70; trustee Ga. Rotary Student Fund, Inc., 1969-90, trustee emeritus, 1990—; mem. Model Cities Policy Bd., 1970-71, Ga. Criminal Justice Coordinating Com.; mem. Ga. Productivity Bd., 1984-85; mem. bicentennial alumni activities com. U. Ga., 1982; co-pres. Friends U. Ga. Mus. Art, 1973-75; state bd. advisors Ga. Mus. Art, 1984—; sec. adv. bd. Henry W. Grady Coll. Journalism U. Ga. adv. coun., 1990-92; mem. adv. group views for the nineties U. Ga., 1989-92; mem. fine arts task force, adv. com. for evaluation v.p. for svcs., U. Ga., 1989; mem. adv. com. Ga. Commn. for Nat. Bicentennial, 1976; bd. dirs. Rec. for the Blind, 1977-83, Athens Symphony, 1981-85, Quality Growth Task Force N.E. Ga., 1989-91; mem. Ga. Gov.'s Jail/Prison Overcrowding Com., 1982; mem. svcs. adv. coun. UGA, 1990—; mem. WWII Commemorative Com., 1993-95; bd. dirs. Lyndon House Arts Ctr. Found., 1995—. Served with AUS, 1941-46, ETO, maj. USAR ret. Decorated Bronze Star with valor insignia; named Boss of Yr., Athens Jr. C. of C., 1959, Broadcaster-Citizen of Yr., Ga. Assn. Broadcasters, 1962, Ga. Assn. Broadcasters Hall of Fame, 1993, Employer of Yr., Bus. and Profl. Women's Club, 1969, Athens Citizen of Yr., Rotary Club, 1971, Athens Citizen of Yr., Athens Woman's Club, 1971; recipient Silver Beaver award Boy Scouts Am., 1973, Inspiration award Athens Community Coun. on Aging, 1990, Advt. Silver medal Am. Advt. Fedn., Liberty Bell award Athens Bar Assn., 1977, Robert Stolz medaille, 1973, Nat. DAR medal of Honor, 1983, cert. of Merit United Daus. of the Confederacy, 1983, Disting. Citizen award Ga. Dept. Labor, 1994, George Washington Patriotic Achievement award Soc. of Cin. in the State of Ga., 1996; H. Randolph Holder Day proclaimed by the City of Athens, 1989; Paul Harris fellow, 1978, Will Watt fellow, 1984, Hue Thomas fellow, 1989. Mem. Res. Officers Assn. (pres. Athens chpt. 1962), Am. Ex-prisoners War (life), Ga. Assn. Broadcasters (pres. 1961), Athens Area C. of C. (pres. 1970), Ga. AP Broadcasters (pres. 1963), Augustana Coll. Alumni Assn. (bd. dirs. 1973-76; Augustana Outstanding Achievement award 1973), Golden Quill, Gridiron, Sigma Delta Chi, Alpha Psi Omega, Alpha Delta Sigma, Di Gamma Kappa (Ga. Pioneer Broadcaster of Yr. award 1971, 91, Lamplighter award, 1993), Phi Omega Phi (pres.1938-39), Touchdown Club (Athens) (pres. 1963-64), Rotary (pres. Athens Club 1957-58, gov. dist. 692, 1969-70, Rotary internat. pub. rels. com. 1987-90, W. Lee Arrandale Vocat. Excellence award 1992) Home: 383 Westview Dr Athens GA 30606-4635 Office: Clarke Broadcasting Corp 850 Bobbin Mill Rd Athens GA 30606-4208

HOLDER, KATHLEEN, elementary education educator; b. Peoria, Ill., Jan. 19, 1942; d. Clifford B. and Margaret Anne (Bowker) Bourne; m. James Sherman Holder, Dec. 29, 1962; children: Laurie Lynn, Cheryl Anne. BS, Bradley U., 1965; MEd, Regents Coll., 1981; postgrad., SUNY, Cortland, 1990-91. Cert. elem. tchr., Ky., N.Y., Ga.; cert. tchr. ages birth-6 yrs., Am. Montessori Soc. Tchr. St. Philomena Sch., Peoria, Ill., 1962-63, Garfield Sch., Danville, Ill., 1964-67, St. David's Sch., Willow Grove, Pa., 1972-74, St. Austin Sch., Mpls., 1974-75, Knoxville (Tenn.) City Schs., 1977-79, Chenango Forks (N.Y.) Schs., 1985-92, Fayette County Schs., Lexington, Ky., 1992-96, Glynn County Schs., Brunswick, Ga., 1996—; team coord. sci. impact project SUNY, Cortland, 1987-90, presenter tchrs. teaching tchrs., 1988, sci. insvc. workshops for tchrs. Fayette County Schs., 1994-96 Glynn Co. Schs., Brunwick, Ga., 1996; team coord. Broome-Tioga Boces Coop. Regional Curriculum Devel. Project, Binghamton, N.Y., 1989;. Author: Science Curriculum Resource Guide K-3, 1989. Hoyt Found. grantee, 1988. Mem. Nat. Reading Assn., Knoxville Reading Assn. (treas. 1978-79), Delta Zeta (Sec. 1977-79, Rose of Honor 1979), Sigma Alpha Iota. Methodist. Home: 96 Marsh Oak Dr Brunswick GA 31525

HOLDER, RICHARD GIBSON, metal products executive; b. Paris, TN. BA, Vanderbilt U., 1953. With Reynolds Metals Co., Richmond, Va., 1953—, various mgmt. positions, 1953-78, v.p., gen. mgr. flexible packaging divsn., 1978-80, v.p., gen. mgr. flexible packaging & consumer products divsn., 1980-83, v.p. mill products divsn., 1983-84, exec. v.p., fabricating ops., 1984-86, exec. v.p., COO, 1986-88, pres., COO, 1988-92, chmn., CEO, 1992-96, also bd. dirs.; bd. dirs. CPC Internat., Inc., Englewood Cliffs, N.J., Universal Corp., Richmond, Va. Office: Reynolds Metals Co 6601 W Broad St Richmond VA 23230-1701

HOLDER, SUSAN LEWIS, state agency administrator; b. Clayton, N.Mex., Dec. 27, 1952; d. Jack W. and Mary Alice Lewis; m. Terry S. Holder, Oct. 1, 1975; children: Chance, Shanna, Tiffany. BS, Eastern N.Mex. U., 1974; MS, Tex. Tech U., 1976; EdD, N.Mex. State U., 1990. Home svc. advisor South Plains Electric Coop., Lubbock, 1975-76; county extension agent Tex. Agr. Extension, Claude, 1976-77; housing specialist N.Mex. Coop. Extension, Las Cruces, 1977-80, 4-H specialist, 1985-89; housing and home furnishing specialist Okla. State U., Stillwater, 1980-81; real estate broker, owner H&L Realty, Tucumcari, N.Mex., 1981-85; instr. Tucumcari Area Vocat. Sch., 1981-85; 4-H program leader, dept. chair N.Mex. Coop. Extension, Las Cruces, 1989-91; state leader 4-H youth devel. Miss. Coop. Extension, 1991—; assoc. prof. edn. leadership Miss. State U., 1991—; mem. Nat. 4-H Shooting Sports Com., 1995, chmn. Youth Issues, 1995, chmn. So. Region Congress, 1995. Contbr. articles to profl. jours. including Jour. of Extension, Housing and Society. Dir. Home Econ. Assn., N.Mex., Tex., Okla., 1970-85. Beor Wolfe fellow Tex. Tech U., 1974-75, Farm Found. fellow, 1980-81, Costello Trust fellow, 1988. Mem. Miss. 4-H Club Found. (exec. sec. 1991-95). Office: Miss Coop Extension Svc Extension Dr Box 9601 Mississippi State MS 39762

HOLDER, SUSAN MCCASKILL, computer company executive, small business owner; b. Tulsa, July 8, 1956; d. Allan Murdock McCaskill and Kathryn Irene (Padgett) Dolan; m. Robert Newton Holder, Jr., Nov. 30, 1985; children: Tara Susan, Abigail Megan. BA in Bus. Mgmt., Upsala Coll., East Orange, N.J., 1978; MBA in Fin., Fairleigh Dickinson U., 1985. Comml. underwriter State Farm Ins. Cos., Wayne, N.J., 1978-81, svc. supr., 1981-83; adminstrn. mgr. Digital Equipment Corp., Piscataway, N.J., 1983-85; project mgr. Digital Equipment Corp., Princeton, N.J., 1985-87, area adminstrv. svcs. mgr., 1987-88, area adminstrv. support mgr., 1988-89; bus. analyst U.S. Hdqrs. Digital Equipment Corp., Alpharetta, Ga., 1989-91, Westboro, Mass., 1989-91; project mgr. U.S. Desktop Svcs., Digital Equipment Corp., Alpharetta, 1991-92; co-owner Basket Innovations, Inc., Roswell, Ga., 1992-94; co-owner, tng. cons., corp. officer Asphodel Assocs., Inc., Roswell, 1994—. Mem. pastor-parish rels. Christ United Meth. Ch., Roswell, Ga., 1990-91, chair pastor-parish rels., 1992, mem. nurture com., tchr. Sunday sch. elem. grades, 1990—. Mem. AAUW (br. sec. Point Pleasant, N.J. 1986-89), Internat. Soc. for Performance Improvement. Home: 1810 Azalea Springs Trl Roswell GA 30075-1857 Office: Asphodel Assocs Inc Ste 203-231 4651 Woodstock Rd Roswell GA 30075-1640

HOLDER, TIMOTHY WAYNE, physician; b. Lynwood, Calif., June 30, 1961; s. David Earl and Frances Ann (Bayer) H.; m. Kaia Lynn Synnestvedt, Aug. 12, 1989. BA in Biology, U. Dallas, 1983; MD, U. Tex., Houston, 1987. Resident physician Meml. Med. Ctr., Corpus Christi, Tex., 1987-90; physician Med. Arts Clinic, Mexia, Tex., 1990-92, Parkview Med. and Surg. Clinic, Mexia, 1992—; mem. profl. adv. bd. Spl. Reports TV, Knoxville, Tenn., 1991-93. Vol. physician Tex. Dept. Health, Groesbeck, Tex., 1991—. Mem. Am. Acad. Family Physicians (Mead Johnson award 1989), Christian Med. and Dental Soc., Tex. Med. Assn. (del. 1991—), Tex. Acad. Family Physicians (com. mem. 1991-94), Limestone County Med. Soc. (pres. 1991-94). Roman Catholic. Office: Parkview Med Clinic 408 E Tyler St Mexia TX 76667-3620

HOLFELDER, LAWRENCE ANDREW, pediatrician, allergist; b. Bklyn., June 7, 1939. MD, Albany Med. Coll., 1965. Diplomate Am. Bd. Pediats., Am. Bd. Allergy and Immunology. Intern St. Vincent's Med. Ctr., N.Y.C., 1965-66, resident, 1966-68, fellow in allergy and immunology, 1972; fellow in allergy and immunology U. Chgo. Hosps., 1970-71; now pvt. practice Tampa, Fla.; mem. staff St. Joseph's Hosp., Tampa; clin. prof. pediats. in allergy U. So. Fla. Mem. Am. Acad. Allergy and Immunology. Office: Harrelson Med Arts Bldg 3709 W Hamilton Ave Ste 1 Tampa FL 33614-4015

HOLIEN, KIM BERNARD, historian; b. Bad Cannstadt-Stuttgart, Germany, Mar. 10, 1948; (parents Am. citizens); s. Maurice Joel and Margaret Alice (Wild) H. BS, Bethel Coll., 1970; MA, George Mason U., 1984. With Dept. State, Washington, 1971-73; adjudicator GAO, Washington, 1975-76; with Nat. Archives, Washington, 1977-79; mil. historian Dept. Army, Washington, 1979—; historian Nat. Guard Bur., 1984; officer First North-South Brigade, Inc., 1974-84. Author: Battle at Ball's Bluff, 1985, 2d edit., 1989; asst. editor The Sharpshooter, 1974-79; editor Clarion's Call, 1980-83, ann. rev. N.G. Bur., 1984. Recipient Letter of Commendation, Dept. State, 1971, Disting. Svc. award Va. div. Sons of Confederate Vets., 1980, Outstanding Svc. award, 1980, Outstanding Svc. award and Spl. Svc. award, 1981 (all Dept. Army), Comdr.-in-Chief's award Sons Confederate Vets., 1982, Comdr.'s award Sons Union Vets., 1982, cert. of achievement U.S. Army Ctr. Mil. History, 1984, Found. award Loudoun County Pub. Libr., 1989, also letters of commendation/appreciation Dept. Army, Sec. Def., 1983, spl. svc. award Chief of Mil. History, 1986, ofcl. commendation, 1988, letter of commendation Army Materiel Command, 1992, Commanding Gen.'s Medal for superior work, Cert. Recognition Commanding Gen. Army Materiel Command, Army Material Command Chief of Staff's medal for superior work, Command Sgt. Maj.'s medal for superior work Army Materiel Command, Sesquicentennial medal for Disting. Alumni Svc. Bethel Coll. Mem. Am. Hist. Assn., Co. of Mil. Historians, D.C. Civil War Round Table (past pres.), Am. Mil. Inst., No. Va. Assn. of Historians (bd. dirs. 1979-81, 83-84), Alexandria Civil War Round Table (past pres.), Sons of Norway, Bethel Coll. Alumni Assn. (bd. dir.), Heritage of Honor (pres.), Friends of Ft. Ward (bd. dirs. 1990—). Lutheran.

HOLLAND, AMY JEANETTE, psychiatrist; b. High Point, N.C., Jan. 25, 1964; d. Jefferson Dewey and Mary Esther (Marsh) H.; m. Dana Neal Martin, July 14, 1990; 1 child, Bradley Neal Holland Martin. BS magna cum laude, Wake Forest U., 1986; MD, East Carolina U., 1991. Cert. med. technologist. Med. technologist Humana Hosps., Greensboro, N.C., 1986-87; intern U. N.C. Hosps., Chapel Hill, 1991-92, resident in psychiatry, 1992-94; fellow in child psychiatry Emory U. Hosps., Atlanta, 1994—. Mem. AMA, Am. Psychiat. Assn. (author, presenter poster nat. mtg. 1991), Am. Assn. Psychiatry and the Law, Ga. Med. Soc., Ga. Psychiat. Assn., Ga. Coun. on Child and Adolescent Psychiatry, Am. Acad. Child and Adolescent Psychiatry. Office: Emory U Hosps Dept Child Psychiatry Atlanta GA 30322

HOLLAND, CHARLES EDWARD, medical products corporate executive; b. Pottstown, Pa., Aug. 31, 1940; s. Charles Edward and Ethel Viola (Ludwig) H.; m. Linda Beth VandeBerg, Nov. 20, 1982. Student, Messiah Coll., 1962-63; BS in Biology and Chemistry, Albright Coll., 1966; PhD in Zoology, Rutgers U., 1974. Clin. lab. technician Reading Hosp., West Reading, Pa., 1962-66; rsch. assoc. dept. biochemistry St. Louis U. Sch. Medicine, 1972-75; rsch. assoc. dept. pharmacology and surgery U. Ill.Med. Ctr., Chgo., 1975-77; clin. project mgr. Am. Critical Care (Am. Hosp. Supply), McGraw Park, Ill., 1977-81; asst./assoc. dir. clin. rsch. Glaxo Inc., Research Triangle Park, N.C., 1981-84; dir. planning and project mgmt. Glaxo Inc., Research Triangle Park, 1984-86, dir. human resources, 1986-87, dir. strategic planning, 1987-88, dir. dermatology bus. expansion, 1988-89, dir. dermatology bus. and product devel., 1989-91, group dir. dermatology bus. and product devel., 1991-95; pres. XPharm, Inc., Chapel Hill, N.C., 1996; sr. dir. corp. licensing Searle, Skokie, Ill., 1996—; mem. indsl. adv. bd. Pharmacotherapy jour., 1986—, Geriatric Medicine jour., 1986-89; bd. trustees Glaxo Bus. Sch., 1986-89, chmn. 1986-88. Contbr. articles to profl. jours. USPH fellow Rutgers U., 1966-71; grad. teaching fellow Rutgers U., 1971-72; NIH fellow St. Louis U. Sch. Medicine, 1973-75, U. Ill., 1975-77. Mem. Project Mgmt. Inst. (editor newsletter 1986-87), AAAS, Nat. Psoriasis Found., Soc. Investigative Dermatology, Am. Acad. Dermatology, Lic. Exec. Soc., Am. Cont. Dermatology Soc., N.Y. Acad. Sci., Sigma Xi.

HOLLAND, CHARLOTTE SUE, counselor; b. Durham, N.C., Feb. 24, 1937; d. Charles Henry and Maybelle (Dowdy) H. BA in Religion, Lynchburg Coll., 1959; M in Religious Edn. cum laude, Lexington Theol. Seminary, 1966. Lic. profl. counselor, Va.; nat. cert. counselor; cert. clin. mental health counselor. Dir. news bur. Lynchburg Coll., 1958-62, Lexington (Ky.) Theol. Seminary, 1962-65; min. Christian edn. Va. Assn. Christian chs., Richmond, 1965-68; min. assoc. Euclid Christian Ch., Lynchburg, 1968-74; adj. prof. Lynchburg Coll., 1977, 89—; assoc. prof. social sci. Cen. Va. Community Coll., Lynchburg, 1974-81, 92-94; dir. emergency mental health cons. svcs. Lynchburg (Va.) Gen. Hosp. div. Centra Health, Inc., 1981-91; owner Creative Counseling Svcs., Forest, Va., 1991—. Active Complete Count Com., Lynchburg, 1990, Civil Rights Blue Ribbon Com., Lynchburg, 1989-90, Lic. Profl. Counselor Bd., Richmond, 1983-86; chmn. drug and alcohol counselors cert. com., 1985. Named one of Outstanding Young Women Am., 1967, one of Community Leaders Am., 1971; recipient Acad. Women award YWCA, 1986. Mem. Internat. Assn. Transactional Analysis, Am. Counseling Assn., Va. Counselors Assn., Lynchburg Counselors Assn., Women's Resource Ctr., AARP, Chi Sigma Iota. Democrat. Home: 1414 Ashbourne Dr Lynchburg VA 24501-5345 Office: Creative Counseling Svc PO Box 587 Forest VA 24551-0587

HOLLAND, GENE GRIGSBY (SCOTTIE HOLLAND), artist; b. Hazard, Ky., June 30, 1928; d. Edward and Virginia Lee (Watson) Grigsby; m.

George William Holland, Sept. 22, 1950; 3 children. BA, U. S. Fla., 1968; pupil of Ruth Allison, Talequah, Okla., 1947-48, Ralph Smith, Washington, 1977, Clint Carter, Atlanta, 1977, R. Jordan, Winter Park, Fla., 1979, Cedric Baldwin Egeli Workshop, Charleston, S.C., 1984. Various clerical and secretarial positions, 1948-52; news reporter, photographer Bryan (Tex.) Daily News, 1952; clk. Fogarty Bros. Moving and Transfer, Tampa and Miami, Fla., 1954-57; tchr. elem. Schs., Hillsborough County, Fla., 1968-72; salesperson, assoc. real estate, 1984—; owner, operator antique store, 1982-87. One-woman and group shows include Tampa Woman's Clubhouse, 1973, Cor Jesu, Tampa, 1973, bank, Monks Corner, S.C., 1977, Summerville Artists Guild, 1977-78, Apopka (Fla.) Art and Foliage Festival, 1980, 81, 82, Fla. Fedn. Women's Clubs, 1980, 81, 82; numerous group shows, latest being: Island Gifts, Tampa, 1980-82, Brandon (Fla.) Station, 1980-81, Holland Originals, Orlando, Fla.; represented in permanent collections including Combank, Apopka, also pvt. collections. Vol. ARC, Tampa, 1965-69, United Fund Campaign, 1975-76; pres. Mango (Fla.) Elem. Sch. PTA, 1966-67; pres. Tampa Civic Assn., 1974-75; vol. Easter Seal Fund Campaign, 1962-63; art chmn. Apopka Art & Foliage Festival, 1990; deaconness Ctrl. Christian Ch. of Orlando, 1992-94, chmn. bible study 1993-94; deaconness First Christian Ch. of Tampa, 1996—. Recipient numerous art awards, 1978-82. Mem. AARP (parlimentarian Apopka chpt.), Internat. Soc. of Artists, Coun. of Arts and Scis. for Cen. Fla., Fedn. Women's Clubs (pres. Hillsborough County 1974-75, v.p. Tampa Civic 1974-75), Meth. Women's Soc. (sec. 1976-77), Nat. Trust Hist. Preservation, Nat. Hist. Soc., Fla. Geneal. and Hist. Soc. (bd. dirs. 1996—), Am. Guild Flower Arrangers, The Nat. Grigsby Family Soc. (mem. SW chpt., assoc. sec. 1991-92, corp. sect. 1992-96, dir. 1995—), Internat. Inner Wheel Club (past chmn. dist. 696, pres. Tampa 1972-73), Musicale Club (1st v.p. bd. incorporators Tampa 1974-75), Apopka Woman's Club (pres. 1981-82, bd. dir. 1983-85, Woman of Yr. 1991, 92), Apopka Tennis Over 50's Group Club (pres. 1988-90), Federated Garden Club Plant City Fla. (conservation chmn.). Home: 1001 W Mahoney St Plant City FL 33566-4437 also: PO Box 2213 Plant City FL 33564-2213

HOLLAND, JOHN BEN, clothing manufacturing company executive; b. Scottsville, Ky., Mar. 26, 1932; s. Elbridge Winfred and Lou May (Whitney) H.; m. Margaret Irene Pecor, Jan. 31, 1954; children: John Sandra, Robert. BS in Acctg., Bowling Green U., 1959. With Union Underwear Co., Inc., Bowling Green, Ky., 1961—, v.p. adminstrn., 1972-74, vice chmn., 1975, chmn., chief exec. officer, 1976-96; ret., 1996, cons., 1996—; bd. dirs. Louisville, Dollar Gen. Corp., Fruit of the Loom, Inc. Bd. dirs. Ky. Coun. Econ. Edn., Louisville, 1981-90, Ky. Advocates for Higher Edn. Inc., 1985-93, Ky. C. of C., 1987-88, Camping World Inc., Associated Industries of Ky., Ireland-Am. Econ. Adv. Bd., Tech. Corp. Inc.; chmn. corp. coun. Western Ky. U., devel. steering com. Mem. Bowling Green-Warren County C. of C. (bd. dirs. 1981-85), Am. Arbitration Assn. (panel 1985-93). Office: Fruit of the Loom Inc PO Box 90015 Bowling Green KY 42102-9015

HOLLAND, LYMAN FAITH, JR., lawyer; b. Mobile, Ala., June 17, 1931; s. Lyman Faith and Louise (Wisdom) H.; m. Leannah Louise Platt, Mar. 6, 1954; children: Lyman Faith III, Laura. BS in Bus. Adminstrn, U. Ala., 1953; LLB, 1957. Bar: Ala. 1957. Assoc. Hand, Arendall & Bedsole, Mobile, 1957-62; ptnr. Hand, Arendall, Bedsole, Greaves & Johnston, 1963-94, mem., 1995—. Mem. Mobile Hist. Devel. Com., 1965-69, v.p., 1967-68; bd. dirs. Mobile Azalea Trail, Inc., 1963-68, chmn. bd., 1963-65; bd. dirs. Mobile Mental Health Ctr., 1969-76, v.p., 1972, pres., chmn. bd., 1973; bd. dirs. Mobile chpt. ARC, 1975-89, 91—, vice chmn., 1975-77, exec. vice chmn., 1978-80, chmn., 1980-82; bd. dirs. Deep South coun. Girl Scouts U.S., 1965-77, Gordan Smith Ctr. Inc., 1973, Bay Area Coun. on Alcoholism, 1973-76, Comty. Chest, Coun. of Mobile County, Inc., 1976-81; bd. dirs. Greater Mobile Mental Health-Mental Retardation, 1975-81, pres., 1975-77; mem. exec. com. Mobile Estate Planning Coun., 1988—, pres., 1994-95. 1st lt. USAF, 1953-55; lt. col. Res. ret. Mem. ABA, Mobile County Bar Assn., Ala. State Bar (chmn. sect. corp., banking and bus. law 1978-80), Am. Counsel Assn., Am. Coll. Trust and Estate Counsel, Am. Coll. Trust and Estate Counsel Found. (bd. dirs. 1990-96), Ala. Law Inst. (coun. 1978—), Pi Kappa Alpha, Phi Delta Phi. Baptist (deacon, ch. trustee 1968-73, chmn. trustees 1971-73). Clubs: Athleston (Mobile); Country Club of Mobile, Bienville. Lodge: Lions (Mobile). Home: 610 Burlington Ct Mobile AL 36608-3839 Office: Hand Arendall PO Box 123 Mobile AL 36601-0123

HOLLAND, MICHAEL JAMES, financial executive; b. Syracuse, N.Y., Apr. 6, 1955; s. Robert Francis and Elaine H.; m. Lorraine DePaola, Aug. 1987. BS in Mktg., Syracuse U., 1977, postgrad. in acctg., 1978-83. With M. Lichtman & Co., Liverpool, N.Y., 1977-83, asst. controller, 1979-83; v.p. fin., v.p. mktg. Chadwick Bay Wine, 1983-84; pres., chief exec. officer Eastern Data Analysts, Syracuse, 1984—; mgr. Coopers & Lybrand, Syracuse, 1986-90; owner, operator M.J.H. Cons. Co., Syracuse, 1979—; sr. mgr. Arthur Andersen, Miami, Fla., 1990-93; pres. Mas Corp., Hollywood, Fla., 1993—. Contbr. ednl. articles to Leisure Time Inc. monthly. Republican. Roman Catholic. Office: Mas Corp 3800 S Ocean Dr Ste 212 Hollywood FL 33019-2915

HOLLAND, NORMAN NORWOOD, English language educator; b. N.Y.C., Sept. 19, 1927; s. Norman Norwood and Harriette (Breder) H.; m. Jane Kelley, Dec. 17, 1954; children: Kelley, John. BS, MIT, 1947; LLB, Harvard U., 1950, PhD, 1956; cert. in psychoanalysis, Boston Psychoanalytic Inst. Instr., assoc. prof. MIT, Cambridge, 1955-66; McNulty prof. English SUNY, Buffalo, 1966-83; prof. assoc. U. Paris, 1971-72, 85; Marston-Milbauer eminent scholar U. Fla., Gainesville, 1983—; cons. various pubs., 1960—, Pres's. Coun. on Obscenity, 1971, Can. Coun., 1980. Author: The First Modern Comedies 1959, The Shakespearean Imagination, 1964, Psychoanalysis and Shakespeare, 1966, The Dynamics of Literary Response, 1968, Poems in Persons: An Introduction to the Psychoanalysis of Literature, 1973, 5 Readers Reading, 1975, Laughing: A Psychology of Humor, 1982, The I, 1985, The Brain of Robert Frost: A Cognitive Approach to Literature, 1988, Holland's Guide to Psychoanalytic Psychology and Literature-and-Psychology, 1990, The Critical I, 1992, Death in a Delphi Seminar, 1995. Am. Couns. Learned Socs. fellow, 1974-75, Guggenheim Found. fellow, 1979-80. Mem. Am. Acad. Psychoanalysis (sci. assoc.), Boston Psychoanalytic Soc., Modern Lang. Assn. (div. exec. com. 1975-81). Democrat. Office: U Fla Dept English Gainesville FL 32611

HOLLAND, OWEN BRYAN, medical educator; b. Galveston, Tex., Feb. 23, 1942; m. Carolyn Stephenson; 2 children. BA summa cum laude, U. Tex., 1963; MA, U. Tex., Galveston, 1965, MD, 1968. Diplomate Am. Bd. Internal Medicine; lic. physician, Tex. Rsch. assoc. health svcs. USPHS Hosp., Balt., 1969-71; resident in internal medicine Parkland Meml. Hosp., Dallas, 1971-73; NIH rsch. fellow U. Tex. Southwestern Med. Ctr., Dallas, 1973-75, asst. prof. internal medicine, 1975-80; assoc. prof. internal medicine U. Tex. Med. Br., Galveston, 1980-85, divsn. dir., 1988-91, Raymond L. Gregory prof. medicine, 1988—. Mem. editoral bd. Jour. Clin. Endocrinology and Metabolism, 1986-90; reviewer jours.; contbr. numerous articles to profl. jours. and abstracts. Merit scholar U. Tex. Med. Br., 1963-68; Life Ins. Med. Found. fellow, 1966-68; grantee NIH, VA, Am. Heart Assn. Fellow ACP, Am. Heart Assn. (coun. high blood pressure rsch.); mem. Am. Fedn. Clin. Rsch., So. Soc. Clin. Investigation, Endocrine Soc., Sigma Xi, Alpha Omega Alpha. Home: 2824 Dominique Dr Galveston TX 77551-1569 Office: U Tex Med Br Dept Internal Medicine Galveston TX 77555

HOLLANDER, LUELLA JEAN, public relations executive, educator; b. Stonewall County, Tex., July 29, 1935; d. Eugene Debs and Ella (Letz) Vanderworth; m. Byron D. Hollander, June, 1980 (div. Apr. 1989). BA in Advt. Art, North Tex. State U., 1956; MEd, U. Cen. Okla., 1992. Graphic designer, yearbook cons. Taylor Pub. Co., Dallas, 1957-89; mng. editor Ninety-Nines, Inc., Oklahoma City, 1980-86, Okla. Living Mag., Oklahoma City, 1985-86; adj. instr. U. Cen. Okla. (formerly Cen. State U., Edmond, 1987-92; mgr. express pers. svcs. Franchise Comms., Oklahoma City, 1990—. Producer graphics History of Ninety-Nines, 1979, Heartline Newsletter, 1991— (Black Gold award 1991, Addy award 1991, Clarion award 1992). Bd. dirs. Okla. Air Space Mus., Oklahoma City, 1990-96, sec., 1992-96, Omniplex, 1996—. Mem. Women in Comms., Inc. (v.p. programs 1984, v.p. mem. retention 1992), Soc. Profl. Journalists, Ninety-Nines Inc. (bd. dirs. 1988-90, internat. sec. 1990-92, pub. rels. cons. 1988-91, internat. pres. 1992-94, immediate past pres. 1994-96), World Aerospace Edn. Orgn., Aircraft Owners and Pilots Assn., Freedom of Info. Okla., Kappa Tau Alpha. Republican. Home: PO Box 12458 Oklahoma City OK 73157-2458

HOLLAWAY, ERNEST LEE, III, journalist, public relations consultant; b. Ft. Benning, Ga., Sept. 16, 1942; s. Ernest Lee Jr. and Ida Nelle (Daily) H.; m. Elizabeth Ann Paine, July 11, 1964 (div. May, 1983); children: Lori Elizabeth Daily, Victoria Lynn; m. Sharon Lee Richards, Dec. 7, 1985; 1 stepchild, John-Paul Wood. BA, Ouachita Bapt. U., 1964; M in Religious Edn., Southwestern Bapt. Theol. Sem., 1966; MA in Journalism, U. Mo., 1968. Asst. editor Ambassador Life Brotherhood Commn., Memphis, 1968-70, editor Crusader, 1970-77; dir. comms. Sem. Extension, Nashville, 1977-92; pres. Editworks, Nashville, 1992—; dir. seminars, confs. Christian Life Commn., Nashville, 1995-96; mem. sem. pub. rels. group Inter-Sem. Conf., Nashville, 1977-92. Author: David: Shepherd, Musician, King, 1977, Donald Orrs: Missionary Duet, 1983; editor: Hayford Bible Handbook, 1995, Has Democracy Had Its Day?, 1996. Bd. dirs. Nashville Adult Literacy Coun., 1983—, Tenn. Literacy Coalition, Nashville, 1983-96. Recipient Sequoyah award Tenn. Hist. Commn., Nashville, 1991. Mem. Nashville Adult Literacy Coun. (pres. 1984-86), Tenn. Literary Coalition (pres. 1986-88, 90). Mem. So. Bapt. Ch. Home: 5049 McLendon Dr Antioch TN 37013 Office: Christian Life Commn SBC 901 Commerce St Ste 550 Nashville TN 37203-3629

HOLLEMAN, CURT PAUL, librarian; b. Grand Rapids, Mich., Jan. 22, 1944; s. Paul Willard and Florence Edith (Kraay) H.; m. Ruth Elaine Sagendorf, Aug. 9, 1945; 1 child, Joshua Peter. BA, Hope Coll., 1965; MA, U. Kans., 1967; MLS, U. Tex., 1973. Tchg. fellow U. Kans., Lawrence, 1965-67; instr. lit. Park Coll., Parkville, Mo., 1967-70; tchg. asst. U. Tex., Austin, 1970-72; reference libr. So. Meth. U., Dallas, 1973-75, asst. dir. libraries collection dept., 1975-89, assoc. dir. libraries collection dept., 1989-93, dir. libraries for collection mgmt. and devel., 1993—; mem. inst. faculty Collection Mgmt. and Devel. Inst., ALA, San Antonio, 1985. Contbr. articles to profl. publs. Mem. sch. bd. St. John's Episcopal Sch., Dallas, 1986-89. Mem. Phi Kappa Phi, Beta Phi Mu. Home: 11311 Lanewood Cir Dallas TX 75218

HOLLEMAN, GARY LAYNE, writer; b. Memphis, Nov. 19, 1947; s. Garland A. and Laverna L. (Wilkins) H.; m. Kathleen M. Milmoe, Oct. 2, 1992. BS in Marine Biology, Fla. Atlantic U., 1982. Author: Demon Fire, 1995, Howl-O-Ween, 1996.

HOLLEMAN, SANDY LEE, religious organization administrator; b. Celina, Tex., June 6, 1940; d. Guy Lee and Gustine (Kirby-Sheets) Luna; m. Allen Craig Holleman, June 5, 1959. Cert., Eastfield Coll., 1979. With Annuity Bd. So. Bapt. Conv., Dallas, 1958—, mgr. personnel, 1983-85, dir. human resources, 1985-91, v.p. human resources, 1991—. Mem. Am. Mgmt. Soc. (dir. salary surveys local chpt. 1986—, v.p. chpt. svcs. 1987—), Dallas Soc. Human Resource Mgmt., Soc. Human Resource Mgmt., Diversity Club Dallas (program chmn. 1976, v.p. 1977), Order Ea. Star, Daus. of Nile. Baptist. Home: 4524 Sarazen Dr Mesquite TX 75150-2348 Office: Annuity Bd So Bapt Conv 2401 Cedar Springs Rd Dallas TX 75201-1407

HOLLEMAN, VERNON DAUGHTY, physician, internist; b. Brownwood, Tex., Oct. 1, 1931; s. Vernon Edgar and Olene Nollie (Reece) H.; m. Shirley Eyvonne Roberts, April 26, 1961; children: Richard, Joel, Douglas. BA in Chemistry and Biology, Howard Payne Coll., Brownwood, 1953; MD, Baylor U., 1958. Mem. med. staff Santa Fe Meml. Hosp, 1962-83; pres. med. staff Santa Fe Meml. Hosp., 1979-83; mem. med. staff Scott and White Hosp., 1962—; asst. chief physician Santa Fe Employees Hosp. Assn., 1962-85, med. dir., 1985—; intern Scott and White Clinic and Hosp., Temple, Tex., 1958-59, resident in internal medicine, 1959-62; dir. div. gen. internal medicine Santa Fe Ctr., Temple, Tex., 1985—; assoc. prof. internal medicine Tex. A&M Coll. Medicine, Temple, 1982—; adj. faculty clinician Ohio Coll. of Podiatric Medicine, Cleveland, 1982-86. Illustrator: Aesculapian, 1957; contbr. photography to books, including Colorados Biggest Bucks and Bulls, Boone and Crocket Books, Awesome Antlers, Records of North American Mule Deer; author: articles on health, preventive medicine, and numerous others. Bd. dirs Santa Fe Meml. Found. Recipient Centennial award Santa Fe Meml. Found., 1991. Mem. Nat. Assn. Retired and Vet. Railway Employees (hon. life), AMA, Am. Socc. Internal Medicine, Tex. Med. Assn., Tex. Med. Found., Am. Heart Assn. (cardiopulmonary coun.), Am. Assn. Ry. Physicians, World Med. Assn., Tex. Diabetes and Endocrine Soc., N.Y. Acad. Scis., So. Med. Assn. (life), Am. Coll. Occupational Medicine, Am. Acad. Pain Mgmt. (diplomate), Boone and Crockett Club (charter assoc.), Alpha Chi, Phi Chi. Baptist. Office: Scott and White Clinic 600 S 25th St Temple TX 76504-5371

HOLLER, ADLAI CORNWELL, JR., minister; b. Orangeburg, S.C., Mar. 21, 1925; s. Adlai Cornwell and Miriam (Fair) H.; m. Elizabeth Cobb, June 4, 1949; children: Suzanne Elizabeth, Adlai Stephen, Stephanie Elwood. AB, Wofford Coll., 1947; MDiv, Duke U., 1952; D of Ministry, Columbia Sem., 1987. Lic. marriage and family therapist, profl. counselor; nat. bd. cert. counselor. Mil. pilot USAAF, 1943-46; chaplain USAF, various cities, 1952-82; minister of counseling Bethany United Meth. Ch., Summerville, S.C., 1982-87; pres. Pyramid Counseling Svcs., Inc., Summerville, S.C., 1992—; bd. dirs. Medicine and Ministry Conf., Kanuga, N.C., 1983-92; dir. Charleston (S.C.) Dist. Pastoral Counseling Ctr., 1987—; mem. Bd. Ordained Ministry, Columbia, 1980-88. Author: Ministry to Flying Students, 1957, Training Laity for Counseling, 1987. Mem. ACA, Am. Assn. for Marriage and Family Therapy (clin. mem., approved supervisor), Am. Assn. Christian Counselors, Daedalians, DAV, Rotary. Methodist. Home: 112 Old Dominion Dr Charleston SC 29418-3012 Office: Pyramid Counseling Svcs Inc 1810 Old Trolley Rd # B Summerville SC 29485-8224

HOLLEY, CYRUS HELMER, management consulting service executive; b. Chgo., June 14, 1936; s. Cyrus Howell and Elizabeth Fay (Helmer) H.; m. Shirley Marquitta Cannon, Aug. 31, 1957; children—Barrett Cannon, Russell William. B.S. in Chem. Engring., Tex. A&M U., 1957. Registered profl. engr.,. Vice pres. indsl. chems. BASF Wyandotte Corp., Parsippany, N.J., 1976-79; sr. v.p. minerals & chem. div. Engelhard Corp., Edison, N.J., 1979-81, v.p., exec. v.p., 1981-83, v.p., pres., chief operating officer metals div., 1983-84, sr. v.p., pres. chem. div., 1984-85, exec. v.p., chief operating officer, 1985-91; pres. Mgmt. Cons. Svcs., Grapevine, Tex., Iselin, N.J., 1991—; CEO Oakmont Enterprises, Inc., 1993—; dir. Atlantic Energy, Inc., 1990—, Hexcel Corp., 1991-94, UGI Corp., 1990—, Kerns Oil & Gas, 1995—. Contbr. articles to profl. jours. Trustee Bloomfield (N.J.) Coll., 1988—; dir. Nat. Assn. Ptnrs. in Edn., 1990-95, Tex. Assn. Ptnrs. in Edn., 1991—, N.J. Assn. Ptnrs. in Edn., 1991—, Tex. Bus. & Edn. Coalition, 1992-96; chair Ind. Coll. Fund. N.J., 1990-92. Mem. AICE. Republican. Presbyterian. Office: Mgmt Cons Svcs 1701 W Northwest Hwy Grapevine TX 76051-8105

HOLLEY, EDWARD GAILON, library science educator, former university dean; b. Pulaski, Tenn., Nov. 26, 1927; s. Abe Brown and Maxie Elizabeth (Bass) H.; m. Robbie (Bobbie Lee) Gault, June 19, 1954; children: Gailon Boyd, Edward Jens, Beth Alison, Amy Lin Holley. BA magna cum laude, David Lipscomb Coll., Nashville, 1949; MA, George Peabody Coll., 1951; PhD, U. Ill., 1961. Asst. libr. David Lipscomb Coll., 1949-51; mem. staff U. Ill., 1951-62, libr. edn., philosophy and psychology libr., 1957-62; dir. librs. U. Houston, 1962-72; dean Sch. Libr. Sci. Sch. Library Sci., U. N.C. at Chapel Hill, 1972-85, prof., 1985-89, William Rand Kenan, Jr. prof., 1989-95; prof. emeritus U. N.C. at Chapel Hill, 1996—; vis. lectr. U. Wis., Madison, summer 1968; vis. prof. North Tex. State U., summer 1970, UCLA, fall 1986; mem. adv. coun. libr. resources U.S. Office Edn., 1968-71; cons. various librs. Tex., Ill., S.C. bd. higher edn., NEH, U.S. Dept. Edn. Author: Charles Evans, American Bibliographer, 1963, Raking the Historic Coals, 1967, (with Don Hendricks) Resources of Texas Libraries, 1968, ALA at 100, 1976, Resources of South Carolina Libraries, 1976; co-author: The Library Services and Construction Act, 1983; contbr. articles to profl. jours. Trustee Disciples of Christ Hist. Soc., 1973-85; mem. governing bd. U. N.C. Press, 1975-95, chmn., 1989-93; trustee OLC, Inc., 1985-94, chmn., 1989-92. Lt. USNR, 1953-56. Coun. on Libr. Resources fellow, 1971. Mem. ALA (pres. 1974-75, chmn. pub. bd. 1972-73, Scarecrow Press award 1964, Melvil Dewey medal 1983, Lippincott award 1987), Tex. Libr. Assn. (pres. 1971), Southea. Libr. Assn. (Rothrock award 1992), N.C. Libr. Assn. (Disting. Svc. award 1995), Assn. Coll. and Rsch. Librs. (editor monographs 1969-72, Rsch. Libr. of Yr. award 1988), Spl. Librs. Assn. (hon.), Phi Kappa Phi, Kappa Delta Pi, Beta Phi Mu (pres. 1984-86, award 1991). Democrat. Mem. Ch. of Christ. Address: 1508 Ephesus Church Rd Chapel Hill NC 27514-2551

HOLLEY, EDWARD JENS, librarian; b. Champaign, Ill., Apr. 23, 1959; s. Edward Gailon and Robbie Lee (Gault) H.; m. Mary Mae Robison, July 30, 1983; children: Melody Mae, Faith Robison. BA magna cum laude, Furman U., 1981; MSLS, U. N.C., 1983; postgrad., U. S.C., 1985-87. Intern U.S. EPA Libr., Research Triangle Park, N.C., 1982-83; asst. reference libr. U. S.C., Columbia, 1983-88, interlibr. loan libr., 1988-93; head resource sharing Clemson (S.C.) U., 1993—; mem. Phi Beta Kappa exec. com. U. S.C., 1987-90, chairperson U.S.C. System Interlibr. Loan Com., 1990-93; mem. interlibr. loan oversight com. Assn. of Southeastern Rsch. Librs., 1993—. Co-author: Religion in the American Experience, 1620-1900, 1993, Religion in the American Experience, Twentieth Century, 1995; contbr. to Dictionary Am. Literacy Characters 1900; editor libr. newsletter Reflections, 1989-91. Margaret Kalp fellow U. N.C., Chapel Hill, 1981-82. Mem. ALA, Assn. Coll. and Rsch. Librs., Reference and Adult Svcs. Divsn. (mem. coll. devel. computer-based methods com. 1993-95, mem. bibliographies and indexes com. history sect. 1993—), Fellowship of Christian Librs. and Info. Specialists (mem. exec. com. 1988-95, editor newsletter 1988-95), S.C. Libr. Assn. (sec. coll. and univ. sect. 1985-86, mem. editl. com. 1986-88, mem. interlibr. loan com. 1989-90), Piedmont Libr. Assn. Office: RM Cooper Libr Clemson Univ Box 343001 Clemson SC 29672

HOLLEY, TAMMY D. FENNELL, critical care nurse; b. Rockmart, Ga., Mar. 29, 1967; d. Ira Eugene and Barbara Ann (Sprayberry) Fennell; m. Jonathan Olin Holley, Dec. 23, 1989; children: Jonathan Olin Adam, Jacob Emery Aaron. ASN, Floyd Coll., Rome, Ga., 1987. Cert. ACLS. Med.-surg./telemetry unit nurse Paulding Meml. Med. Ctr., Dallas, Ga., 1986-88; staff nurse, relief charge nurse CCU Floyd Med. Ctr., Rome, Ga., 1988—, CCU charge nurse, utilization rev. nurse, 1994—. Home: 930 Lowery Rd Rockmart GA 30153-3416

HOLLIDAY, PATRICIA RUTH MCKENZIE, evangelist; b. Jacksonville, Fla., Nov. 17, 1935; d. Robert Irving and Leona Adele (Bell) McKenzie; student Massey Bus. Coll., 1969, Luther Rice Sem., 1976; DD, Southeastern Theol. Sem., 1986, ThD, 1989; m. Jan. 20, 1965; children—Connie, Katheryn, Alexander. Sec., Delta Drug Corp., Jacksonville, 1965—; pres. Microfilm Center, Jacksonville, 1974—; pres. Miracle Outreach Ministry, Jacksonville, 1974—; pastor Mircle World Outreach, Jacksonville; prof. Southeastern Theol. Sem., Jacksonville, Fla., 1992—. Sec.. Four Found., Inc.; Republican candidate for Fla. Ho. of Reps., 1972; mem. Fla. Republican. Com., 1976-80; lobbyist Fla. Legislature, 1978-80; hostess Pat Holliday TV Show, Jacksonville. Clubs: Minutewomen of Fla. (founder), Univ., Women, Ponte Vedra Women's. Author: Holliday for the King, 1978, Be Free, 1979, Only Believe, 1980, Born Anew, 1981, The Walking Dead, 1982, Anointing Power, 1982, Signs, Wonders and Reactions, 1984, Dealing with Heresies, 1986, Marriage Answers, 1992, Solitary Satanist, 1993, Entertaining Angels of Light, 1993, The Plan: Ascended Masters, 1994, The New World Aftershock, 1994; columnist Christian Courier. Home: 9252 San Jose Blvd Apt 2804 Jacksonville FL 32257-9205

HOLLIDAY, PETER OSBORNE, JR., dentist; b. Macon, Ga., July 9, 1921; s. Peter Osborne and Martha Elizabeth (Riley) H.; m. Mary Lucille Dozier, Nov. 12, 1949; children: Peter III, Lucy, Lindsay, Mary. DDS, Emory U., 1945; postgrad., U. Mich., 1947-48. Pvt. practice dentistry Macon, 1947—; mem. Gov. Carter's Dental Adv. Com., Atlanta, 1972. Head dental div. United Givers Fund, Macon, 1956; mem. bicycle com. Macon-Bibb County Planning & Zoning Commn., 1995—. With USNR Dental Corps, 1945-47, China. Fellow Am. Coll. Dentists, Internat. Coll. Dentists (dep. regent for Ga. 1983-85); mem. ADA (alt. del. 1978), Ga. Dental Assn. (sec.-treas. 1971-76, v.p. 1977, pres. 1978-79), Ga. Acad. Dental Practice (charter), Hinman Dental Soc., Ctrl. Dist. Dental Soc. (pres. 1963, Dentist of Yr. 1962), Pierre Fauchard Acad., League of Am. Wheelmen, So. Bicycle League. Democrat. Unitarian. Home: 744 Forest Hill Rd Macon GA 31210-4202 Office: Holliday Dental Assocs 360 Spring St Macon GA 31201-6739

HOLLIEN, HARRY FRANCIS, speech and communications scientist, educator; b. Brockton, Mass., July 16, 1926; s. Henry Gregory and Alice Bernice (Coolidge) H.; m. Patricia Ann Milanowski, Aug. 26, 1969; children: Karen Ann, Kevin Amory, Keith Alan, Brian Christopher, Stephanie Ann, Christine Ann. B.S., Boston U., 1949, M.Ed., 1951; M.A., U. Iowa, 1953, Ph.D., 1955. Asst. prof. Baylor U., 1955-58, U. Wichita, 1958-62; asso. prof. speech U. Fla., Gainesville, 1962-68; prof. U. Fla., 1968—, prof. linguistics, 1976—, prof. criminal justice, 1979—, assoc. dir. communication scis. lab., 1962-68, dir., 1968-75; dir. Inst. Advanced Study of Communication Processes, 1975—, assoc. dir. linguistics, 1989-91; vis. prof. Inst. Telecommunications and Acoustics, Wroclaw Tech. U., Poland, 1974; adj. prof. Juilliard Sch. Music, N.Y.C., 1973-84; rsch. assoc. Gould Research Lab., 1958; vis. sci. Speech Transmission Lab., Royal Inst. Tech., Stockholm, 1970, U. Trier, Fed. Republic of Germany, 1987; fencing coach U. Iowa, 1953-55; mem. communication sci. study sect. NIH, 1963-67; mem. neurobiology merit rev. bd. VA, 1969-74; pres. Hollien Assocs., 1966—; cons. in field. Author: Current Issues in Phonetic Sciences, 1978, Acoustics of Crime, 1990; assoc. editor Jour. Speech and Hearing Rsch., 1967-69; editor The Phonetician, 1975-92, Jour. Voice, 1987—; mem. edtl. bd. Jour. Comm. Disorders, 1980-91, Jour. Rsch. in Singing, 1980-83, Jour. Phonetics, 1982-85, Studia Phonetica Posnan, 1985—, Speech, Language and the Law, 1993—. Chmn. bd. Unitarian Fellowship, Waco, Tex., 1956-58; chmn. bd. Wild Animal Retirement Village, 1981-90. Served with USN, 1944-46; with USNR, 1946-75. Recipient Garcia/Sandoz prize Internat. Assn. Logopedics and Phoniatrics, 1971, Gould award Wm. and Harrett Gould Found., 1975, Gutzmann medal Union European Phoniatrists, 1980; NIH career fellow, 1965-70, Fulbright scholar, 1987. Fellow Am. Speech and Hearing Assn., AAAS, Acoustical Soc. Am., Internat. Soc. Phonetic Scis. (pres. 1989—, sec.-gen. 1975-89, exec. v.p. 1983-89, Kay Elemetrics prize 1987, S. Smith prize 1991), Am. Acad. Forensic Sci. (John R. Hunt award 1988), Inst. Acoustics; mem. Am. Assn. Phonetic Scis. (pres. 1973-75, editor 1976-79, exec. com. 1979-82), Am. Assn. Underwater Scis., Acad. for Forensic Application of Communication Scis. (editor 1975-80, exec. com. 1976-93, mem. sci. coun. 1975-76, chmn. 1985-93), Japan Soc. Phonetic Scis. (hon. v.p. 1989—), World Congress Phoneticians (permanent coun.), Voice Found. (sci. bd., merit awards 1981, 93), Internat. Assn. Forensic Phonetics, Fla. Acad. Scis., Sigma Xi. Republican. Home: 229 SW 43rd Ter Gainesville FL 32607-2270 Office: U Fla Inst Advanced Study Comm Processes 50 Dauer Hall Gainesville FL 32611

HOLLIEN, PATRICIA ANN, small business owner, scientist; b. N.Y.C., May 11, 1938; d. Leon and Sophia (Biernacki) Milanowski; m. Harry Hollien, Aug. 26, 1969; children: Brian, Stephanie, Christine. AA, Sante Fe Jr. Coll., 1969; ScD (hon), Marian Coll., 1983; student, U. Fla., 1977—. Rsch. asst. Marineland Rsch. Labs., 1965-69; co-owner, exec. v.p. Hollien Assocs., 1969—; owner, dir. Forensic Communication Assocs., Gainesville, Fla., 1981—, The Eden Group, Gainesville, 1995—; vis. assoc. Royal Inst. Spl. Transmission Lab., Stockholm, 1970, Wroclaw Tech. U., Poland, 1974; asst. in research Inst. Advanced Study Communication Scis. U. Fla., 1977-83, assoc. in research, 1983—; adj. asst. prof. Communication Sci. Lab., N.Y., 1982—. Co-author: Current Issues in the Phonetic Sciences, 1979; editor The Phonetician, 1991—; contbr. articles to profl. jours. Bd. dirs. Ann. Retirement Village, Waldo, Fla., 1981-93. Fellow Am. Acad. Forensic Scis., Internat. Soc. Phonetic Scis. (coun. reps. 1983—); mem. Am. Assn. Phonetic Scis., Acad. Forensic Application of the Comm. Sci., Internat. Assn. Forensic Phonetics (sec. gen. 7th ann. congress 1995). Home: 229 SW 43rd Ter Gainesville FL 32607-2270 Office: Forensic Communication Assocs PO Box 12323 Gainesville FL 32604-0323

HOLLIN, SHELBY W., lawyer; b. Varilla, Ky., July 29, 1925; s. Herbert and Maggie Hollin; m. Martha Jane Fisch, Nov. 27, 1948; children—Sheila K, Henry T., Richard G., Roberta E., Nathan W., Jacob C. B.B.A., St. Mary's U., 1965, J.D., 1970. Bar: Tex. 1969, U.S. Supreme Ct. 1974, U.S. Claims, 1978, U.S. Ct. Appeals 1981, Ky. 1990. Sole practice, San Antonio, 1969—; mem. nat. bd. advisors Am. Biog. Inst. Served with USAF, World War II. Decorated Air medal, Air Force Commendation medal with oak leaf cluster; recipient award for fighting discrimination Govt. Employed Mejures,

1981, others. Mem. Tex. State Bar, San Antonio Bar Assn., Res. Officers Assn. (life), Air Force Assn. (life), VFW (life), DAV (life), Am. Legion, Mil. Order World Wars. Baptist. Home and Office: 7710 Stagecoach Dr San Antonio TX 78227-3430

HOLLINGER, CHARLOTTE ELIZABETH, medical technologist, tree farmer; b. Meadville, Miss., June 29, 1951; d. John Fielding and Irene Elizabeth (Mullins) H. BS in Biology, U. So. Miss., 1973. Cert. med. Technologist ASCP. Staff med. technologist U. Miss. Med. Ctr., Jackson, 1974-76, Grady Hosp., Atlanta, 1976, Atlanta ARC, 1976-78; staff med. technologist I Emory U. Hosp., Atlanta, 1978-85, staff med. technologist II, 1985-88, asst. chief technologist, 1988-94; del. Blood Bank Del. to People's Republic China, People-to-People, Seattle, 1988. Supporter numerous civic orgns. Mem. Am. Assn. Blood Banks, Am. Soc. Clin. Pathologists, NOW, Forest Farmers Assn., Habitat for Humanity, People for Ethical Treatment Animals, People-to-People, Miss. Forestry Assn., Cousteau Soc., Ga. Pub. TV, U. So. Miss. Alumni Assn., Delta Zeta, Pi Tau Chi. Roman Catholic. Home: 2490 Silver King Dr Grayson GA 30221-1470

HOLLINGSWORTH, J. SELWYN, sociology educator; b. Dresden, Tex., Dec. 20, 1939; s. Clyde and Alma Vera (Clark) H. AA, Navarro Coll., 1960; BS, Tex. A&M U., 1962, MS, 1964; PhD, U. Fla., 1970. Rsch. assoc. U. Fla. Ctr. for Latin Am. Studies, Gainesville, 1968-69; asst. prof. sociology U. Ala., Tuscaloosa, 1969-75, assoc. prof. sociology, 1975—. Fulbright scholar U. Guadolajara, Mex., 1978-79. Mem. Am. Sociol. Assn., So. Sociol. Assn., Southeastern Conf. Latin Am. Studies, Ala.-Miss. sociol. Assn. (sec. 1976, pres. 1994—, Disting. Svc. award 1992), Sociol. Costarriecene de Demografia, So. Demographic Assn. Democrat. Baptist. Home: 3204 Ontario Dr Northport AL 35476-1948 Office: U Ala PO Box 870219 Tuscaloosa AL 35487-0219

HOLLINGSWORTH, MARTHA LYNETTE, secondary school educator; b. Waco, Tex., Oct. 9, 1951; d. Willie Frederick and Georgia Cuddell (Bryant) J.; m. Roy David Hollingsworth, Dec. 31, 1971; children: Richard Avery, Justin Brian. A.A., McLennan Community Coll., 1972; B.B.A., Baylor U., 1974, MS in Ednl. Administrn., 1992. Tchr., Connally Ind. Sch. Dist., Waco, 1974—; with Adult Edn. Night Sch., 1974-78; chairperson for Area III leadership conf. Vocat. Office Careers Clubs Tex., Waco, 1985—; active Lakeview Little League Booster Club, 1985—. Mem. PTA (hon. life), Vocat. Office Edn. Tchr.'s Assn. Tex., Assn. Tex. Profl. Educators (v.p. local chpt. 1988-90), Future Homemakers Am. Area VIII (hon.), Tex. Future Farmers Am. (hon.), Delta Kappa Gamma. Baptist. Office: Connally Vocat Dept 715 N Rita St Waco TX 76705-1140

HOLLINS, WILLIAM JOSEPH, II, cardiologist, educator; b. Camden, S.C., June 23, 1955. BS magna cum laude, U. S.C., 1977; MD, Med. U. S.C., 1981. Diplomate Am. Bd. Internal Medicine, Am. Bd. Cardiovascular Disease; lic. physician, S.C., N.C. Intern in internal medicine Bowman Gray Sch. Medicine/N.C. Bapt. Hosp., Winston-Salem, N.C., 1981-82, resident in internal medicine, 1982-84; fellow in cardiology Med. U. S.C., Charleston, 1984-86; pvt. practice cardiovascular medicine Columbia (S.C.) Cardiovascular Clinic PA, 1986—; clin. asst. prof. medicine Sch. Medicine U. S.C., Columbia, 1986-91, clin. assoc. prof. medicine, 1991—; dir. dept. cardiac diagnostics Richland Meml. Hosp., Columbia, 1991—, med. dir. mobile critical care unit Heart Ctr., 1992; mem. staff Providence Hosp., Columbia, 1986—, Bapt. Med. Ctr., Columbia, 1986—, Lexington Med. Ctr., Columbia, 1986—; presenter in field. Contbr. articles to profl. jours. Fellow Am. Coll. Cardiology; mem. AMA, ACP, Am. Coll. Chest Physicians, Am. Heart Assn. (med. rep. Richland Meml. Hosp. 1992-93), Phi Beta Kappa, Alpha Omega Alpha, Omnicron Delta Kappa, Phi Beta Sigma. Home: 20 Heathwood Cir Columbia SC 29205-1939 Office: Columbia Cardiovascular Clinic PA One Medical Park Ste 420 Columbia SC 29203

HOLLIS, MARY FERN CAUDILL, community health nurse; b. Augusta, Ga., Mar. 13, 1942; d. Robert Paul and Fern (Alderton) Caudill; children: Harry N. III (dec.), Mary Melissa, H. Newcombe IV. B in Music Edn., U. Louisville, 1964; AS in Nursing, Tenn. State U., 1980; postgrad., Nashville Tech. Inst., 1987—. RN, Tenn. Staff nurse oncology and med.-surg. units St. Thomas Hosp., Nashville, 1981-82; staff oncology nurse Alive Hospice, Nashville, 1982-83; scheduling coord. HCA Parkview Med. Ctr., Nashville, 1987-88; nurse, staff relief coord. Partners Home Health, Nashville, 1989-90; nursing supr. Kimberly Quality Care Staffing, Nashville, 1991-92; RN coord. on call MedPartners Nursing Svc. of Mid. Tenn., Nashville, 1994-95; profl. vocal soloist; tchr. piano, music edn., music theory, voice. Author: Out of My Suffering: Reflections of a Hospice Nurse, 1984. Mem. Music Tchrs. Nat. Assn. (profl. cert. music edn. and voice), Tenn. Music Tchrs. Assn., Nashville Area Music Tchrs. Assn., Am. Coll. Musicians, Nat. Guild Piano Tchrs., Sigma Alpha Iota, Gamma Phi Beta.

HOLLIS, PAUL RICHARD, JR., wholesale/retail business owner; b. Shreveport, La., May 7, 1943; s. Paul Richard Sr. and Kathryn R. Hollis; m. Gloria Lea Gardner, June 18, 1966; children: Kathryn M., Susan E. B-SChemE, Okla. State U., 1966; MBA, U. Tex., Odessa, 1974. Process engr. Phillips Petroleum Co., Oklahoma City, 1966-70; gas-gaso engr. Phillips Petroleum Co., Houston, 1970-72; supr. treating and environ. engring. Phillips Petroleum Co., Odessa, 1972-76; group system devel. coord. Phillips Petroleum Co., Bartlesville, Okla., 1976-77; Shidler (Okla.) area engring. supr. Phillips Petroleum Co., 1977-81, Shidler area mgr., 1981-84; Lindsay area mgr. Phillips Petroleum Co., Oklahoma City, 1984-86; staff dir. oil and gas pricing Phillips Petroleum Co., Bartlesville, 1986-92; owner, pres., CEO Crown Enterprises, Bartlesville, 1992—. Patentee in field. Mem. Jaycees (bd. dirs. Oklahoma City chpt. 1966-68, State of Okla. 1969, v.p. Bartlesville chpt. 1976-77), Bartlesville Optimist Club (key mem., bd. dirs. 1992-93, v.p. 1993-94, pres. 1994-95). Republican. Methodist. Home: 4621 Rolling Meadows Rd Bartlesville OK 74006-5529

HOLLIS, REGINALD, archbishop; b. Eng., July 18, 1932; emigrated to Can., 1954; s. Jesse Farndon and Edith Ellen (Lee) H.; m. Marcia Crombie, Sept. 7, 1957; children—Martin, Hilda, Aidan. B.A., Cambridge U., Eng., 1954; M.A., Cambridge U., 1958; B.D., McGill U., Montreal, 1956; D.D. (hon.), U. South, 1977, Montreal Diocesan Theol. Coll., 1975. Ordained to ministry Anglican Ch. as deacon, 1956, as priest, 1956. Chaplain Montreal Diocesan Theol. Coll.; also chaplain to Anglican students McGill U., 1956-60; asst. St. Matthias Parish, Westmount, Que., 1960-63; incumbent St. Barnabas Ch., Roxboro, Que., 1963-66; rector St. Barnabas Ch., 1966-71, Christ Ch., Beaurepaire, Que., 1971-74; dir. parish and diocesan services Diocese Montreal, 1974-75, bishop, 1975-90; archbishop of Montreal Met. of the Ecclesiastical Province of Can., 1989-90; asst. bishop Diocese of Ctrl. Fla., Orlando, 1990-94; episc. dir. Anglican Fellowship of Prayer, 1990-94; rector St. Paul's Ch., New Smyrna Beach, Fla. Author: Abiding in Christ, 1987. Home: 831 Evergreen St New Smyrna Beach FL 32169-2903 Office: PO Box 1559 New Smyrna Beach FL 32170-1559

HOLLIS, TIMOTHY MARTIN, bank executive; b. Marietta, Ga., Nov. 13, 1962; s. Milton Joel and Mary Syvila (Skanner) H. BSBA in Mgmt., Shorter Coll., 1986. Lead foreman attractions Six Flags Over Ga., Atlanta, 1982-85; desk supr. front desk Wyndham Hotel Co., Atlanta, 1986-87; personal banker C&S/Sovran Corp., Atlanta, 1987-90, sr. personal banker, 1990-91; asst. br. mgr., banking officer NationsBank of Ga., N.A., Atlanta, 1991-92, banking ctr. mgr., 1992-95; sales mgr. First Union Nat. Bank Ga., Atlanta, 1995—. Treas., mktg. chairperson, fin. com., bd. trustees Choral Guild of Atlanta, 1991; mem. Buckhead Young Reps., Atlanta, 1989-92; bd. dirs. Artcare, Inc., Atlanta, 1991-94; docent, vol., mem. Friends of Zoo Atlanta; mem. steering com. First Night Atlanta, 1993-95, 1994 class Atlanta Midtown Leadership Program, Atlanta Midtown Alliance, 1992—, Human Rights Campaign Fund, 1992—, GAPAC, 1993-95; mem. adv. bd. Atlanta Exec. Network, 1993-96, Joining Hearts, Inc., 1994—; steering com. Aids Walk Atlanta, 1995—; bd. dirs. Positive Impact, 1996—; co-chair Young Profls. of Atlanta Exec. Network, 1996—. Mem. Atlanta Track Club (vol.). Baptist. Home: 28 Finch Trail Atlanta GA 30308 Office: First Union Nat Bank Ga 1605 Monroe Dr Atlanta GA 30324

HOLLMANN, MARK WILLIAM, orthopaedic surgeon; b. Waukegan, Ill., May 3, 1958; s. Kenneth John and Nancy Jane Hollmann; m. Stacia Lynne Murphy, May 23, 1992. Student, Edison C.C., Ft. Myers, Fla., 1976-79; BA in Math., So. Meth. U., 1981; MD, U. Tex., Dallas, 1985. Lic. physician, Fla. Fellow in sports medicine and knee surgery Jewett Orthopaedic Clinic, Winter Park, Fla., 1991-92; intern dept. orthopaedic surgery Univ. Hosp./U. Fla., Jacksonville, 1985-86, resident, 1986-90; mem. staff Fla. Hosp., Orlando, 1991—, West Volusia Meml. Hosp., DeLand, Fla., 1991—, Fish Meml. Hosp., DeLand, 1991—; prin. Orthopaedic Assocs. West Volusia, P.A., DeLand, 1993—; team physician Stetson U., DeLand, 1991—; presenter profl. confs. and meetings, 1983-91. Contbr. articles to med. jours. Vol. team physician Jacksonville Sports Medicine Program, 1986-90. Named All-Am. Basketball Player, 1979. Mem. AMA, Fla. Med. Assn., So. Med. Assn., So. Orthopaedic Assn., Citrus Orthopaedic Assn., Kappa Mu Epsilon. Republican. Lutheran. Home: 310 W Minnesota Ave Deland FL 32720-3350 Office: Orthop Assocs W Volusia PA 740 W Plymouth Ave Deland FL 32720-3282

HOLLOCKER, CHARLES PETER, computer company executive; b. Chgo., Dec. 25, 1950; s. Peter Nicholas and Maybelle (Stewart) H.; m. Cynthia Lee Dungan, Sept. 17, 1977; children: Raymond Charles, Paul Joseph. BS, Northwestern U. Tech. Inst., 1980, M in Engring. Mgmt., 1984. Mem. staff. AT&T Network Systems and Bell Labs., Naperville, Ill., 1980-86; mem. mgmt. staff No. Telecom, Inc., Nashville, 1987-89, DSC Comm. Corp., Inc., Plano, Tex., 1989-94; dir. of quality Tandem Telecom, Plano, Tex., 1995—, cert. quality systems lead auditor, ISO 9000, 1995—; examiner Malcolm Baldridge Nat. Quality Award, 1992, Tex. State Quality Award, 1993. Contbr. articles to profl. jours. Sgt. USAF, 1970-75. NSF grantee, 1983-84. Mem. IEEE (sr., reviewer articles 1984—), Am. Soc. Quality Control (sr., publ. mgmt. bd. 1987—, standing rev. bd. 1987—), Quality Assurance Inst. (cert. quality analyst, rev. bd. 1986—), Software Qualtiy System (registration com. 1992—, chair software qualified auditor cert. 1991—), Assn. Software Engring. Excellence, Phi Theta Kappa. Office: DSC Comm Corp Inc 1000 Coit Rd Plano TX 75075-5802

HOLLOMAN, HARRY HUNTER, civil engineer; b. Ft. Benning, Ga., Oct. 9, 1957; s. Robert A. and Jane H.; m. Marilyn Sue Baggett; children: John William, Harry Joseph. BS in Civil Engring., Auburn U., 1980; MBA, Columbus Coll., 1984. Project mgr. Chris R. Sheridan & Co., Macon, Ga., 1984-87; prin. Hole, Montes & Assocs., Naples, Fla., 1987—. Author (religious texts) Gifts of the Spirit, 1992, Lessons from the Cross, 1994. Sec., bd. trustees E. Naples (Fla.) United Meth. Ch., 1991-93; mem. Lely Elem. Sch. PTA, Naples, 1991—; chmn. Hispanic Mission Adv. Bd., Naples, 1992—; precinct committeman Collier County Rep. Exec. Com., Naples, 1992—; pres., sec. Collier County Young Reps., 1993, 94; mem., engring. advisor Meth. Bd. of Ch. Relocation, Ft. Myers, Fla., 1993—; chmn. launch com. United Meth. Ch., Collier County, 1996; v.p. Collier County Coun. of PTA's, 1996; newsletter com. mem. Boy Scout Troop 707. Named Young Rep. of Yr., Collier County Young Reps., Naples, 1992—, Outstanding Vol., Lely Elem. Sch. PTA, Naples 1993. Mem. ASCE, Am. Water Works Assn., Am. Concrete Inst., Fla. Engring. Soc. (Project of Yr. Caloosa chpt. 1991, 93). Republican. Home: 166 Pinehurst Cir Naples FL 33962-8329 Office: Hole Montes & Assocs Inc 715 10th St S Naples FL 34102-6725

HOLLOWAY, BRIAN RAY, English language educator; b. N.Y.C., Mar. 23, 1952; s. Harold Ray and Hazel Lorraine (Galbo) H.; m. Kathleen Mary Hough, May 12, 1978; 1 child, Rachel. BA in English, U. Mo., 1974, MA in English Lit., 1975; PhD in English Lit., U. Ill., 1981. Mem. humanities faculty Parkland Coll., Champaign, Ill., 1988-94; assoc. prof. Coll. of W.Va., Beckley, 1994—; advisor Omicron Psi Honorary Soc. Presenter in field; advisor The Mountain Whispers pub. Recipient stipend for rsch. NEH-W.Va. Humanities Coun., 1996, NIF Conf. scholarship W.Va. Humanities Coun., 1996. Mem. MLA, W.Va. Shakespeare and Renaissance Assn., John G. Neihardt Found., 16th Century Studies Conf. Office: Coll of W Va Dept English PO Box AG Beckley WV 25802

HOLLOWAY, EDWARD OLIN, human services manager; b. Rochester, N.Y., July 3, 1944; s. Charles Robert and Chrystal Gertrude (Darling) H.; m. Hama Elizabeth Farris, Dec. 23, 1967. AA, Palm Beach Jr. Coll., Lakeworth, Fla., 1964; BA, Lenoir Rhyne Coll., 1967; MS in Pub. Health, U. N.C., 1975. From sanitarian I to sanitarian supr. I Palm Beach County Health Dept., West Palm Beach, Fla., 1969-73; from emergency med. svcs. coord. to exec. dir. dist. IX Health Planning Coun., Inc., West Palm Beach, 1975-89; sr. health and human svcs. planner bd. county commrs. Palm Beach County Dept. Community Svcs., West Palm Beach, 1989—; faculty Pub. Health Physician Residency Program, 1990—; steering com. Fla. Atlantic Univ. Inst. Govt., 1992—, vice chmn., 1994. Chmn. dist. 9 adv. coun. Dept. Helath and Rehab. Svcs., West Palm Beach, 1990-92; pres. Fla. Assn. Health Planning Agys., Inc., 1984-89; mem. planning unit steering com. Leadership Palm Beach County, 1991; chmn. health care dist. feasibility subcom. Palm Beach County, 1989-90; mem. Palm Beach County data collection com. Health and Human Svcs. Planning Assn., 1992—; mem. Interagy. Planning Group, 1994—; mem. Palm Beach Gardens Cmty. H.S. Adv. Com., 1994—. With U.S. Army, 1967-69, Vietnam. Decorated Bronze Star, Purple Heart, Army Commendation medal, Cross of Gallantry (Vietnam); recipient Outstanding Svc. award Fla. Assn. Health Planning Agys., 1989, Outstanding Achievement award Bd. County Commrs. Palm Beach County Citizens Adv. Com. on Health and Human Svcs., 1995; planning grantee Regional Emergency Med. Svcs., 1975. Mem. ASPA (chpt. 102 coun. mem. 1989—), APHA, Nat. Environ. Health Assn., U. N.C. Sch. Pub. Health Alumni Assn. (bd. dirs. 1994—). Democrat. Lutheran. Office: Bd County Commrs Palm Beach Dept Community Svcs 810 Datura St West Palm Beach FL 33401-5204

HOLLOWAY, HARRY ALBERT, political science educator; b. Seattle, Aug. 28, 1925; s. Albert Cecil and Elizabeth Maude (Hall) H.; m. Jean Gretchen Connorton, June 21, 1951 (div. 1972); children: Linda, Diana, Scott; m. Virginia Carol, June 30, 1974; stepchildren: Robert, Chris Ryan. BA, U. Wash., 1949; MS in Econs., London Sch. Econs., 1954; PhD, Cornell U., 1958. From instr. to asst. prof. U. Tex., Austin, 1957-62; assoc. prof. U. Okla., Norman, 1962-67, prof., 1967-91, retired, 1991. Author: Politics of Southern Negro, 1969, (with others) Pubic Opinion: Coalitions, Elites and Masses, 1980, Party and Factional Division in Texas, 1964; sr. author: Bad Times for Good Ol' Boys: The Oklahoma County Commisssioner Scandel, 1993. Rockefeller Found. grantee, 1963-64. Mem. AAUP (pres. local chpt. 1990), Okla. Polit. Sci. Assn. Home: 1029 W Imhoff Rd Norman OK 73072-7550 Office: U Okla Dept Polit Sci 455 W Lindsey St Rm 205 Norman OK 73019-0535

HOLLOWAY, JAMES GLEN, marketing opinon and media researcher; b. San Antonio, Tex., July 20, 1936; s. Ralph Preston and Lucille Katherine (Hillyer) H.; m. Mary Carol Shackelford Maddock, Apr. 5, 1958 (div. Dec. 1977); children: Julie, Jamie, Jason, Preston; m. Margaret Jane Bauscher, Aug. 12, 1978. BBA in mktg., Southern Meth. U., 1959; MA in communication, U. Pa., 1967. Sales rep. Svc. Bur. Corp. IBM, Dallas, 1960-62; project dir. Belden Assocs., Dallas, 1962-65, v.p., 1967-78; owner Action Sports Svc., Dallas, 1978-80; sr. project dir. Dr Pepper Co., Dallas, 1980-82; rsch. mgr. Southwest Rsch. Inc., Dallas, 1982-84; rsch. mgr., v.p. Savitz Rsch. Ctr., Dallas, 1984-91; pres. Holloway Con. Group, Dallas, 1991-93, 94; rsch. project dir. Audience Rsch. & Devel., Dallas, 1993-94. Mem. Am. Mktg. Assn. Home: 5334 Emerson Ave Dallas TX 75209-5004

HOLLOWAY, THOMAS EDWARD, investor; b. Trenton, N.J., Mar. 23, 1951; s. Thomas Elmer and Betty Lou (Nolen) H.; m. Debra Jean Beard, May 26, 1979. BA in Broadcast Journalism, U. S.C., 1973, postgrad., 1976; postgrad., U. Va., 1980, N.C. State U., 1983. Svc. mgr. Clearwater Pool Svc., Columbia, S.C., 1976-77; asst. mgr. Record Bar, Inc., Columbia, 1978-79; mgr. Record Bar, Inc., Savannah, Ga, 1979-81; inventory mgr. corp. hdqs. Record Bar, Inc., Durham, N.C., 1982-84; sr. account exec. Cable Adnet, Raleigh, N.C., 1985-93. Bd. dirs. Mental Health Assn. Ctrl. Carolina, 1988-93, golf tournament dir., 1989, 90. Recipient Comms. award Mental Health Assn. Ctrl. Carolina, 1990, 92. Mem. Am. Mktg. Assn. (program dir. Triangle chpt. 1989-90, comms. dir. 1990-92). Home: 7 Trotwood Dr Columbia SC 29209-4813

HOLLOWAY, WILLIAM JUDSON, JR., federal judge; b. 1923. A.B., U. Okla., 1947; LL.B., Harvard U., 1950; LLD (hon.), Okla. City U., Oklahoma City, 1991. Ptnr. Holloway & Holloway, Oklahoma City, 1950-51; atty. Dept. Justice, Washington, 1951-52; assoc., ptnr. Crowe and Dunlevy, Oklahoma City, 1952-68; judge U.S. Ct. Appeals (10th cir.), Oklahoma City, 1968—; past chief judge U.S. Ct. Appeals 10th Cir., 1984-91. Mem. ABA, Fed. Bar Assn., Okla. Bar Assn., Oklahoma County Bar Assn. Office: US Ct Appeals 10th Cir PO Box 1767 Oklahoma City OK 73101-1767

HOLLOWELL, JAN BENNETT, adult education educator; b. Valdosta, Ga., Nov. 11, 1951; d. Charles Leonard Bennett and Mitzi Brewton Driggers; m. Monte Jerry Hollowell, Nov. 19, 1972; children: Jerel Brett, Matt Jared. BS in Edn., Ouachita Bapt. U., Arkadelphia, Ark., 1973; MEd, U. Tex., El Paso, 1978. Cert. in adult edn., Ala., elem. edn., Tex., Ark.; cert. reading specialist, Ala., Ark., Tex. Elem. tchr. Pforzheim (West Germany) Elem. Sch., 1974-75; basic skills instr. Edn. Ctr., Ft. Bliss, Tex., 1978; Title I lang arts English tchr. El Paso Ind. Sch. Dist., 1978-80; GED/adult basic edn. instr. Region XIX Edn. Ctr., Wichita Falls, Tex., 1980-83; tutor The Reading Ctr., Huntsville, Ala., 1983; adult edn. instr. North Ala. Skills Ctr., Huntsville, 1984-88; mgr. Individualized Prescribed Instrn. Lab. J.F. Drake State Tech. Coll., Huntsville, 1988—. Mem. ASCD, NEA, Ala. Edn. Assn., Am. Vocat. Assn., Internat. Reading Assn., Drake Edn. Assn., Vocat. Indsl. Clubs Am. (advisor). Baptist. Office: JF Drake State Tech Coll 3421 Meridian St N Huntsville AL 35811-1544

HOLLY, ELLISTINE PERKINS, music educator; b. Grenada, Miss., Aug. 12, 1934; d. Addison Lampton and Anna Pearl (Powell) Perkins; m. Donald Beall, June 10, 1960 (div. June 1966); 1 child, Donna Camille; m. Kermit Wells Holly, Jr., Dec. 23, 1979. BA in Music and Piano, Fisk U., Nashville, 1955; M Music Edn., Ind. U., 1960; MusM, U. Mich., 1972, PhD, 1978. Tchr. Middleton Sr. High Sch., Tampa, 1955-58; instr. music Mary Holmes Jr. Coll., West Point, Miss., 1960-61; tchr. Jefferson Jr. High Sch., Pontiac, Mich., 1961-68; grad. asst. U. Mich., Ann Arbor, 1972-74; counselor Sch. Music, U. Mich., Ann Arbor, 1975-76; assoc. prof. music Jackson (Miss.) State U., 1976—; vis. lectr. U. Paris, 1989, Institut du Monde Anglophone, Universite de Paris, 1989; reviewer travel grants Nat. Endowment for Humanities, 1986-87. Performing soloist Opera South Co., Jackson State U., 1983-85, U. Mich. Chamber Choir, U.S. Cultural Team to Russia, Germany, Spoleto, Italy, Opening Ceremonies Internat. Ballet Competition, Jackson, 1986, 90; editor, compiler: Biographies of Black Composers an Songwriters, 1989; contbr. articles to prol. jours. Mem. Jackson Arts Alliance, 1985—. Faculty rsch. scholar NEH, Harvard U., 1982, Chgo., 1985, Newberry Libr., Chgo., 1987, Ford Found., U. Miss., Oxford, 1987. Mem. Music Educators Nat. Conf., Nat. Assn. Tchrs. Singing (pres. Miss. chpt. 1984-87), Ctr. Black Music Rsch., Nat. Links, Inc., Miss. Hist. Soc., Sonneck Soc., Coll. Music Soc. (bd. dirs. so. region), Harmonica Music Club Inc. (pres. 1983-85), Delta Sigma Theta. Home: 261 Northgate Blvd Jackson MS 39206-2618

HOLLYFIELD, JOHN SCOGGINS, lawyer; b. Harlingen, Tex., Aug. 20, 1939; m. Penny Pounds, Dec. 27, 1962; children: Jon Scott, Courtney. Bar: Tex. 1968;. Assoc. Fulbright & Jaworski, Houston, 1968-75, ptnr., 1975—. Lt. USNR, 1961-65. Recipient Pres.'s award Houston Bar Assn., 1986. Mem. ABA (coun. real property sect. 1986-93, sec. 1993-94, vice chair real property divsn. 1994-96, chair elect 1996—), Am. Coll. Real Estate Lawyers (pres. 1990-91), Anglo-Am. Real Property Inst. (gov. 1986—). Office: Fulbright & Jaworski LLP 1301 Mckinney St Houston TX 77010

HOLMAN, DARRELL EDWARD, programmer/analyst, cost accountant; b. Gastonia, N.C., Aug. 11, 1965; s. Alvin Joe and Jane (Summitt) H. BA in Math., Belmont Abbey Coll., 1988; MBA, Queens Coll., 1993. System mgr. S.E. Huffman, Clover, S.C., 1988-89, software engr., 1989-91; bus. systems analyst Schrader Automotive, Monroe, N.C., 1991-93, cost acct., 1993-95; programmer/analyst Green Point Mortgage, Charlotte, N.C., 1995—. V.p. MBA Student Assn., Queens Coll., Charlotte, N.C., 1992-93; mem. Mint Mus. Art, Charlotte, 1992, 93, Friends of Belmont (N.C.) Abbey Libr., 1991, 92, 93. Mem. Am. Math. Assn.

HOLMAN, WILLIAM EARL, lobbyist, consultant; b. Greensboro, N.C., Sept. 27, 1956; s. Earl Eugene Jr. and Janice (Morgan) H.; m. Stephanie Bass, Aug. 15, 1985. B in Biology, N.C. State U., 1978. Lobbyist N.C. Pub. Transp. Assn., Raleigh, 1990—, Am. Planning Assn., Raleigh, 1985—, Sierra Club, Raleigh, 1981—, Conservation Coun. N.C., Raleigh, 1979—; cons. N.C. Wildlife Fedn., Raleigh, 1989, N.C. Alternative Energy Corp., Raleigh, 1983. Dir. issue campaign N.C. Toxics Agenda, 1984, Safe Drinking Water, 1988, Outstanding Resource Water, 1989; mem. Gov.'s Waste Mgmt. Bd., Raleigh, 1982-87, State Parks Study Commn., Raleigh, 1984, Hazardous Waste Study Commn., Raleigh, 1983-84. Recipient Citizen award Ind. Newspaper, 1987, Joseph LeConte award N.C. chpt. Sierra Club. Mem. N.C. Acad. Scis., Conservation Coun. N.C. (bd. dirs. 1982—), N.C. Wildlife Fedn. (bd. dirs. 1985—), Triangle Land Conservancy (bd. dirs. 1984-86), Clean Water Fund N.C. (bd. dirs. 1984—), Phi Kappa Phi. Democrat. Presbyterian. Office: 1024 Washington St Raleigh NC 27605-1258

HOLMBERG, JAMES JOHN, curator; b. Louisville, Feb. 15, 1958; s. John Joseph and Wilma Ann (Becker) H.; m. Ruthe Ann Pfisterer, Sept. 25, 1982; children: Elisabeth Marie, Aaron Becker, Emily Samantha. BA, U. Louisville, 1980, MA, 1985. Project archivist U. Louisville, 1981-82; from manuscript asst. to curator manuscripts The Filson Club Hist. Soc., Louisville, 1982—; history instr. U. Louisville, 1986—, Bellarmine Coll., Louisville, 1992—; dir. Nat. Lewis & Clark Bicentennial Coun., Seattle, 1995—. Mem. Soc. Am. Archivists, Lewis & Clark Trial Heritage Found., Louisville Civil War Roundtable, Ky. Coun. on Archives, Louisville Hist. League. Republican. Episcopal. Home: 8511 Glaser Rd Louisville KY 40291 Office: The Filson Club Hist Soc 1310 S 3d St Louisville KY 40208

HOLMES, BARBARA DEVEAUX, college president; b. Miami, Fla., Nov. 26, 1947; d. Robert Eugene and Lula Mae (Stewart) Deveaux; m. Roosevelt Leon Holmes, June 19, 1970; children: Michael, Courtney. BA, Stetson U., 1969, MEd, 1972; PhD, U. Conn., 1974. Tchr. English, Seabreeze Sr. High Sch., Daytona Beach, Fla., 1969-72; dir. instnl. rsch. and planning Fayetteville (N.C.) State U., 1974-77, asst. to chancellor, 1977-79; dir. rsch. and planning Mo. Dept. Higher Edn., Jefferson City, 1979-81; v.p. adminstrv. svcs. Hillsborough Community Coll., Tampa, Fla., 1981-85; provost No. Va. Community Coll., Annandale, 1985-89; provost, v.p. acad. affairs Va. State U., Petersburg, 1989-90; pres. Milw. Area Tech. Coll., 1990—. Mem. Greater Milw. Com., Pvt. Industry Coun.; bd. dirs. Sinai Samaritan Med. Ctr. Fellow U. Conn. Grad. Sch., 1971-74. Mem. Am. Assn. Community and Jr. Colls., Nat. Coun. on Black Am. Affairs, Presidents Roundtable, Tempo, Rotary. Home: PO Box 10411 Conway AR 72033-2003

HOLMES, BARRY TREVOR, business and cross cultural development consultant; b. Letchworth, England, Sept. 23, 1933; came to U.S., 1985; s. Edwin George and Marian (Jones) H.; children from previous marriage: Katharine, Alison, Joanne; m. Sherie Shortridge Bell, Mar. 27. 1992; 1 child, Kelly Campbell Shortridge. Diplomat U.K., 1950-92; bus. and cross cultural devel. cons. Atlanta, 1992—; bd. dirs. Br. Am. Bus. Group, Atlanta, 1994—. Capt. Br. Army, 1953-55. eem. Atlanta C. of C. (internat. com. 1994—), Atlanta Rotary, English Speaking Union (pres. 1996—). Presbyn. Home: 3751 Haddon Hall Rd NW Atlanta GA 30327

HOLMES, CLAIRE COLEMAN, real estate broker; b. Ruston, La., Sept. 14, 1931; d. Eusel Monroe and Mabel Claire (Cahoon) Coleman; m. Major Joe Holmes, Dec. 20, 1951; children: George David, Claire Anne de Noble, William Gray. BA cum laude, U. Ark., 1952. Tchr. Pulaski (Ark.) County Spl. Sch. Dist., 1952-53, Pine Bluff (Ark.) Sch. Dist., 1953-55; real estate salesman Sullivant-Cross Realty, Pine Bluff, 1979-83; legal sec. Joe Holmes, Atty., Pine Bluff, 1985-91; real estate broker C & J, Inc., Pine Bluff, 1985—. Mem. DAR, Soc. Mayflower Descendants, Jr. League, Pine Bluff Duplicate Bridge Club, Am. Contract Bridge League, Nat. Audubon Soc., Three Rivers Audubon Soc. Home: 22 S Pines Dr Pine Bluff AR 71601 Office: C & J Inc 22 Southern Pines Dr Pine Bluff AR 71603-6934

HOLMES, COLE E., graduate admissions administrator; b. San Antonio, Nov. 10, 1960; s. Coley E. and Sue S. Holmes. BS in Edn., U. Tex., 1984; MA in Human Svcs., St. Edward's U., 1992; postgrad., U. Tex., 1996—. Tchr. Klein Ind. Sch. Dist., Spring, Tex., 1984-85; dir. student affairs Dobie Ctr., Austin, 1985-86; admission counselor St. Edward's U., Austin, 1987-89, asst. dir. admission, 1989-90, asst. dir. alumni rels., 1991-93, dir. grad. admissions, 1993—. Recipient Cactus Goodfellow award U. Tex., 1983. Mem. Tex. Assn. Coll. Admission Counselors, Nat. Assn. Grad. Admission Profls.

(conf. com. mem. 1995), St. Andrew's Presbyn. Ch. Democrat. Presbyterian. Office: Saint Edwards Univ 3001 S Congress Austin TX 78704

HOLMES, FRANK RANDALL, university administrator; b. McKenzie, Tenn., July 11, 1948; s. William Randall and Margaret Louise (Moyer) H.; m. Maria Alexander Holmes, Dec. 16, 1967; children: Alexander, Yancey, Margaret. BA in Polit. Sci., U. Memphis, 1975. Field svc. coord., asst. alumni dir. Memphis State U., 1975-76; exec. dir. Tex. A&I Alumni Assn., Kingsville, Tex., 1976-80; dir. devel. Millsaps Coll., Jackson, 1980; dir. ann. support, interim dir. devel. U. Houston, 1980-82; gen. mgr. Gray-Walker, Inc., Houston, 1982-84; exec. v.p. U. Houston Alumni Assn., 1984-95; assoc. v.p. for advancement/alumni U. Memphis, 1995—; spkr./presenter Coun. for Advancement and Support of Edn. Dist. IV, 1990-95, Coun. of Alumni Assn. Execs., 1992-94. Baseball mgr. Collierville (Tenn.) Youth Athletic Assn., 1996. Named to Outstanding Young Men of Am., 1979. Mem. Coun. for Advancement and Support of Edn. (mem. comm. on alumni 1995, bd. dirs. dist. IV 1994), Highland Hundred, U. Memphis Soc., U. Memphis Alumni Assn., Windyke Country Club, Omicron Delta Kappa. Republican. Episcopalian. Home: 1211 Wincreek Dr Collierville TN 38017 Office: University of Memphis The Alumni Ctr Memphis TN 38152-0001

HOLMES, HARRY DADISMAN, health facility administrator; b. Houston, Aug. 8, 1944; s. Harry newton and Ruth Eleanor (Dadisman) H.; m. Patricia Ann Hunt, Aug. 23, 1969; children: Hillary Hunt, Ashley Elizabeth. BA, Rice U., 1966; MA, La. State U., 1968; PhD, U. Mo., 1973. Asst. prof. urban devel. U. Tenn., Knoxville, 1973-76; asst. to exec. v.p. Tex. Med. Ctr., Inc., Houston, 1976-80; dir. govt. affairs, orgnl. liaison U. Tex. System Cancer Ctr., Houston, 1980-90, asst. to pres., 1981-90; assoc. v.p. gvtl. rels. U. Tex. M.D. Anderson Cancer Ctr., Houston, 1990—; mem. Cancer Ctrs. Adminstrs. Forum, 1994—; mem. select com. on pub. issues Greater Houston Hosp. Coun., 1983—; mem. exec. adv. bd. White, Petrov and McHone, 1987—; mem. pub. rels. adv. coun. Tex. Med. Ctr., 1985—; chair South Tex. Legis Conf., 1995, 97; founder Biotech. Assn., 1986. Mem. adminstrv. bd. St. Luke's Meth. Ch.; mem. Mayor's Task Force on Pvt. Sector Initiatives for Houston, 1981-82, Houston C.C. Found. Bd., 1992—, Greater Houston Partnership State and Fed. Com., 1989—; mem. U. Tex. Tex./Mex. Border Health Task Force, 1989—, exec. com., 1989—; pres. Higher Edn. Fin. Corp., 1989—; mem. Rice U. Fund Coun., 1991-94, Nat. Cancer Ctrs. Task Force, 1991—; mem. exec. bd. Leadership Houston, 1983-86, Houston Ctr. for Humanities, 1983-86; mem. govt. rels. com. Greater Houston Hosp. Coun., 1985—; mem. com. Harris County Sesquicentennial, 1986, Instnl. Task Force on Oncology in Chile, 1986-87; exec. com. Instnl. Strategic Planning Com., 1986—; pub. issues com. Engring. Coun. Houston, 1986; divsn. chmn. United Way of Houston, 1983; com. to evaluate the status of minority and women faculty, faculty adminstrs. and adminstrv. staff U. Tex., M.D. Anderson Cancer Ctr., 1990. White fellow U. Mo., 1972. Mem. Houston C. of C. (co-chmn. govt. rels. com. 1982-83), Rice U. Alumni Assn. (exec. bd., chmn. publs. com. 1982-83), Phi Alpha Theta. Home: 5642 Cedar Creek Dr Houston TX 77056-2310 Office: U Tex MD Anderson Cancer Ctr 1515 Holcombe Blvd Houston TX 77030-4009

HOLMES, JULIA FAYE, librarian; b. Meridian, Miss., May 12, 1950; d. Bilbo and Claudia (Morris) Rodgers; m. William Porter Holmes, Dec. 20, 1969; children: Tanya, Tiffani, Tristan. BS, U. So. Miss., Hattiesburg, 1982, MS in Libr. Sci., 1990; Grad., Leadership Jackson County, 1992. Libr. asst. Jackson-George Regional Libr., Pascagoula, Miss., 1972-74, pub. svcs. asst., 1974-76, serials clk., 1978-80, interlibr. loan clk., 1980-83, reference coord., 1983-86, mgr. reference dept., 1986—; br. mgr. Moss Point (Miss.) Libr., 1995—. Contbr. articles to libr. jours. Mem. Dem. Exec. Com., Pascagoula, 1988—, 4-H Club Adv. Coun., Pascagoula, 1984—, Foster Care Rev. Bd., Pascagoula, 1985—; pres. East Park Elem. PTA, Moss Point, Miss., 1976-80; mem. NAACP, 1988—; mem. Jackson-George Regional Libr. Sys., Jackson County Civic Action Com., Policy Coun., 1992—; bd. dirs., sec. Jackson County Arts Coun., 1992—; grant review panelist Miss. Arts Commn., 1994—; bd. trustees Moss Point City Libr. Bd., 1985-95. Black Pride in Art grantee Miss. Arts Commn., 1991, Black History Program grantee Miss. Arts Commn., 1993, Black So. Voices grantee Miss. Humanities Coun., 1993. Mem. ALA (Black Caucus 1991—, membership com. 1991-94), Miss. Libr. Assn. (membership com., scholar com., libr. edn. com., Black Caucus v.p. 1994—, SRS Outstanding Citizen Outstanding Achievement, 1996), Libr. Instrn. Roundtable (Jackson, sec. 1991-92, v.p. 1993-94, 96-97, pres. 1993-96), Beta Phi Mu (v.p. chpt. 1993-94, pres. 1994-95), Delta Sigma Theta (Town Involved in Getting Everyone to Read Something com. 1996—, sec. 1986-87, 87-88, v.p. 1990-91, 94-95). Home: 4013 Charles St Moss Point MS 39563-5456 Office: Moss Point City Libr 4401 McInnis Ave Moss Point MS 39563

HOLMES, MARJORIE ROSE, author; b. Storm Lake, Iowa; d. Samuel Arthur and Rosa (Griffith) H.; m. Lynn Mighell, Apr. 9, 1932; children—Marjorie Mighell Croner, Mark, Mallory, Melanie Mighell Dimopoulos; m. George P. Schmieler, July 4, 1981. Student, Buena Vista Coll., 1927-29, D.Litt. (hon.), 1976; B.A., Cornell Coll., 1931. Tchr. writing Cath. U., 1964-65, U. Md., 1967-68; mem. staff Georgetown Writers Conf., 1959-81. Free-lance writer short stories, articles, verse for mags. including McCall's, Redbook, Reader's Digest; bi-weekly columnist: Love and Laughter, Washington Evening Star, 1959-75; monthly columnist: Woman's Day, 1971-77; author: World By the Tail, 1943, Ten O'Clock Scholar, 1946, Saturday Night, 1959, Cherry Blossom Princess, 1960, Follow Your Dream, 1961, Love is a Hopscotch Thing, 1963, Senior Trip, 1962, Love and Laughter, 1967, I've Got to Talk to Somebody, God, 1969, Writing the Creative Article, 1969, Who Am I, God?, 1971, To Treasure Our Days, 1971, Two from Galilee, 1972, Nobody Else Will Listen, 1973, You and I and Yesterday, 1973, As Tall as My Heart, 1974, How Can I Find You God?, 1975, Beauty in Your Own Back Yard, 1976, Hold Me Up a Little Longer, Lord, 1977, Lord, Let Me Love, 1978, God and Vitamins, 1980, To Help You Through the Hurting, 1983, Three from Galilee—The Young Man from Nazareth, 1985, Writing the Creative Article Today, 1986, Marjorie Holmes' Secrets of Health, Energy and Staying Young, 1987, The Messiah, 1987, At Christmas the Heart Goes Home, 1991, The Inspirational Writings of Marjorie Holmes, 1991, Gifts Freely Given, 1992, Writing Articles From the Heart, 1993, Second Wife, Second Life!, 1993, Still by Your Side-How I Know a Great Love Never Dies, 1996; contbg. editor Guideposts, 1977—; bd. dirs. The Writer, 1975—. Bd. dirs. Found. Christian Living, 1975—. Recipient Honor Iowans award Buena Vista Coll., 1966, Alumni Achievement award Cornell Coll., 1963, Woman of Achievement award Nat. Fedn. Press Women, 1972; Celebrity of Yr. award Women in Communications, 1975; Woman of Yr. award McLean Bus. and Profl. Women, 1976; award Freedom Found. at Valley Forge, 1977; gold medal Marymount Coll. Va., 1978. Mem. Am. Newspaper Women's Club, Nat. Fedn. Press Women, Author's Guild, Washington Nat. Press Club. Home: Lake Jackson Hills 8681 Cobb Rd Manassas VA 22111

HOLMES, PAUL HERMON (TONY HOLMES), federal agency official; b. Nashville, Mar. 30, 1939; s. Dennis Hawkins and Fransena (Cooper) H.; m. Bonnie Marie McIntyre, Sept. 5, 1965; 1 child, Alison Cooper. BS, U. Tenn., 1965, MA, 1971. Tchr. polit. sci. U. Tenn., Knoxville, 1968-70; editor, writer TVA, Knoxville, 1971-74, asst. Washington rep., Washington, 1974-78, asst. chief Citizen Action Office, Knoxville, 1978-84, chief mgmt. services, land and econ. resources, 1984-88, mfg. devel. specialist, 1988-91, comm. specialist, 1991—. Contbr. articles to newspapers and mags. Served with U.S. Army, 1957-60, Korea, Japan. Ford Found. grantee, 1968-70. Mem. SAR, Sons of Confederacy, Nat. Geneal. Soc., Tenn. Hist. Soc., East Tenn. Hist. Soc., West Tenn. Hist. Soc., Nat. Press Club, East Tenn. Assn. Preservation of Friends (Quaker) History, Sigma Delta Chi, Phi Kappa Phi, Delta Gamma Sigma. Avocations: writing, genealogy, reading, fishing, gardening. Home: 1025 Stagecoach Ln Friendsville TN 37737-2009 Office: TVA Office Community Partnerships 2048 Old City Hall Knoxville TN 37902

HOLMES, PAUL KINLOCH, JR., private investor; b. Lindsay, Okla., July 6, 1915; s. Paul Kinloch and Kathryn (Price) H.; m. Virginia Turner Harrison, Oct. 9, 1946; children: Virginia Holmes Brown, Paul Kinloch III. BA, U. Ark., 1937, JD, 1939. Bar: Ark., 1939. Sole practice Newport, Ark., 1939-41; owner P. K. Holmes Co., Newport, 1946-84, Personal Investments, Newport, 1984-93; chmn. bd. Newport Fed. Savs. Bank; trustee Lyon Coll., 1978-96. Dist. gov. Rotary Internat. Cen. Ark., 1958; pres. Ark. Retail Merchants, 1959, Univ. Ark. Alumni Assn., 1967; legis. House of Reps. State of Ark., 1971; del. Ark. Constnl. Conv., 1980. Capt. U.S. Army, 1942-46, ETO. Decorated Purple Heart and Silver Star, U.S. Army, 1945; recipient Silver Beaver award Boy Scouts Am., 1972. Mem. Newport (Ark.) Indsl. Devel. (pres. 1962—), Newport (Ark.) C. of C. (pres. 1966), Newport (Ark.) Country Club (pres. 1968), Newport (Ark.) Rotary Club (pres. 1947-48. Democrat. Presbyterian. Home: 1 Country Club Rd Newport AR 72112-4001 Office: 107 Hazel St Newport AR 72112-3309

HOLMES, ROBERT WAYNE, service executive, consultant, biological historian; b. Brush, Colo., July 16, 1950; s. George William Jr. and Reba Mary (Sandel) H. BA, Western State Coll., 1972. Exec. Rose Exterminator Co., San Francisco, 1986-92; founder, owner BFE Cons., 1992—. Author: The Killing River. Mem. Smithsonian Instn., Washington, 1986, Sta. KRMA-TV-PBS, Denver, 1987, Ft. Morgan (Colo.) Heritage Found., 1988, Ctr. for Study of Presidency, Wilson Ctr., Nat. Mus. Am. Indian, Nat. Trust for Hist. Preservation, 1994-95. Mem. AAAS, N.Y. Acad. Scis., Acad. Polit. Sci., Wilson Ctr. Assoc. Ctr. for Study of the Presidency, Am. Mus. Natural History, Nat. Trust for Hist. Preservation, Denver Mus. Natural History, Nat. Mus. Am. Indian, Nature Conservancy, FPCN, SoAm. Explorers Club.

HOLMES, ROBIN ENYCE, secondary education educator; b. Savannah, Ga., Oct. 7, 1969; d. Melvin Winters and Leola (Bennett) H. BA, Armstrong State, Savannah, 1993. Cert. secondary tchr. Tchr. Groves H.S., Garden City, Ga. Mem. Ga. Counsel Tchrs. Eng., Ga. Assn. Educators. Baptist. Home: 8415 Elmhurst Rd Savannah GA 31406 Office: Groves HS 100 Wheathill Rd Garden City GA 31408-1642

HOLMES, ROSCETTE YVONNE LEWIS, educational administrator, consultant; b. Portland, Oreg., Dec. 1, 1944; d. Roscoe Warfield and Burnadine (Langston) Lewis; BS, Tex. So. U., 1965, MS, 1970, EdD, 1991; cert. in adminstrn. and supervision U. Houston, 1979; cert. mediator family, civil, and adolescent; m. Johnny Mason Holmes, Jr., July 28, 1971; children—Roderick Earl, Andriette Yvonne. With Houston Ind. Sch. Dist., 1965-96, sch. tchr. E.O. Smith Jr. H.S., 1965-69, tchr. biology, coord. sch. sci. fair, sponsor student coun. Madison Sr. H.S., 1970-74, sci. content team mem. Emergency Sch. Aid Act, 1974-76, staff devel. specialist for tchr. tng. in sci., English, math, and social studies, 1976-78, instrnl. specialist for sci. Area I, 1978-81; asst. prin. Hogg Middle Sch., 1981-84, dir. chpt. 1, 1984-90; asst. prin. Fleming Fine Arts Middle Sch., 1990-96; owner, pres., CEO Roscette's Diversified Svcs. & Assocs., cons. for devel. needs; cons. Prairie View, Tchr. Corp, Peace Corps, 1976-78; cons. Ednl. Leadership Inst., Prescription Learning Inc.; ednl. cons. North Forest Ind. Sch. Dist; mem. Tex. Adv. Coun., dept. human resources Adv. Bd. Region II-Tex, vice-chairperson Tex. Adv. Coun. Social Work Cert. NSF ednl. grantee, 1968-70. Mem. ASCD, Houston Profl. Adminstrs., Expt. in Internat. Living, Top Ladies of Distinction, Inc. (Houston chpt.), Delta Sigma Theta (voter registration, Sch. after Sch. Project, hypertension screening, v.p., dean of probates, 1967, v.p., 1980-81, com. chmn., pres. Suburban Houston-Ft. Bend Alumnae chpt. 1981-83, voting del. to nat. conv. 1981, del. regional conv. 1982, nat. membership intake trainer Delta Sigma Theta Sorority Inc. Southwest Region), Phi Delta Kappa. Democrat. Episcopalian. Home: 7919 Oakington Dr Houston TX 77071 Office: 7919 Oakington Dr Ste D Houston TX 77071-2018

HOLMES, SANDRA EILEEN KILGORE, nurse; b. Florence, Ala., Feb. 23, 1942; d. William Austin and Kathryn Elizabeth (Threet) Kilgore; m. Milton Mapes Holmes, June 16, 1962; 1 child, Kathryn Ann-Elizabeth Holmes Glass. Diploma in Nursing, U. Ala. Hosp. Sch. Nursing, 1963; BSN, Sanford U., 1989. RN, Ala. Head nurse U. Ala. Hosp., Birmingham, 1969-71; staff nurse Bapt. Med. Ctr.-Montclair, Birmingham, 1971-75, coord. patient care, 1975-89, coord. outpatient diabetes edn., 1989-93, internal nurse auditor, 1993-95; audit coord. Bapt. Health Sys., 1995-96, supr. auditing and patient reps. combined bus. office, 1996—. Mem. Ala. Assn. Diabetes Educators (state v.p. 1990-91, pres. 1991-92), Ala. Med. Auditors Assn. Republican. Baptist. Home: 612 Tambay Dr Birmingham AL 35217-1035 Office: Montclair Bapt Med Ctr 800 Montclair Rd Birmingham AL 35213-1908

HOLMES, SHERIE BELL SHORTRIDGE, lawyer; b. Detroit, Mar. 27, 1956; d. Milton Harold and June Marie (Demarse) Bell; m. Wayne Hall Shortridge, Apr. 17, 1986 (div. 1992); 1 child, Kelly Campbell Shortridge; m. Barry T. Holmes, Mar. 27, 1992. BA, Emory U., 1976, JD, 1980. Bar: Ga. 1980, U.S. Dist. Ct. (no. dist.) Ga. 1981, U.S. Ct. Appeals (11th cir.) 1982. Assoc. Swift, Currie, McGhee & Hiers, Atlanta, 1980-83, Powell, Goldstein, Frazer & Murphy, Atlanta, 1984-1990, Jones, Day, Reavis & Pogue, Atlanta, 1994—; mem. adj. faculty Nat. Ctr. Paralegal Tng., Atlanta, 1984. Active Jr. League Atlanta, 1988—, Twigs, Atlanta, 1990-92, English Speaking Union, 1991—, Friends of Zoo Atlanta, 1988—; bd. dirs. Southeastern Savoyards Light Opera Co., Atlanta, 1990—, chmn. bd. dirs., 1993—. Mem. ABA, Atlanta Bar Assn. Presbyn. Home: 3751 Hadden Hall Rd NW Atlanta GA 30327-2629 Office: 3500 One Peachtree Ctr 303 Peachtree St Atlanta GA 30308

HOLMES, SUZANNE MCRAE, nursing supervisor; b. Birmingham, Ala., June 23, 1952; d. Paul Bickman and Mabel E. (Tyler) McRae; m. Bryan Thomas Holmes, Jan. 14, 1989; 1 child, Meredith Rae. ADN, Jefferson State Coll., Birmingham, 1988. RN, Ala.; cert. BCLS instr. Staff nurse burn unit The Children's Hosp., Birmingham, 1988-89; staff nurse dept. medicine The Kirklin Clinic at U. Ala.-Birmingham, 1989-90, head nurse gen. medicine clinic, 1990-91, head nurse allergy clinic, 1991—; facilitator and spkr. on nursing edn. at asthma workshops Rorer Pharms., Collegeville, Pa., 1994—; mem. faculty Genecom, N.Y.C., 1994—; operator 1-800 Allergy Info. Svc., 1991-92. Editor Allergy Update, 1991-92. Mem. Am. Coll. Allergy and Immunology, Am. Acad. Allergy, Asthma and Immunology. Presbyterian. Office: The Kirklin Clinic Allergy Clinic 2d Fl 2000 6th Ave S Birmingham AL 35233-2110

HOLSAPPLE, CLYDE WARREN, decision and information systems educator; b. Raleigh, N.C., Nov. 1, 1950; s. Van Warren and Jeanne (Rickert) H.; m. Carol Eades; children: Christiana, Claire. BS in Math., Purdue U., 1972, MS in Computer Sci., 1975, PhD in Mgmt., 1977. From asst. prof. to assoc. prof. bus. adminstrn. U. Ill., Urbana, 1978-83; vis. asst. prof. mgmt. Purdue U., West Lafayette, Ind., 1977-78, from assoc. prof. to prof. mgmt., 1983-89; prof. decision sci. and info. systems U. Ky., Lexington, 1988—, Rosenthal endowed chair in mgmt. info. systems, 1988—, chmn. dept. decision sci. and info. systems, 1993-94; adj. prof. U. Tex., Austin, 1989—. Co-author: Foundations of Decision Support Systems, 1981, Micro Database Management, 1984, Manager's Guide to Expert Systems, 1986, The Information Jungle, 1988, Operations Research and Artificial Intelligence, 1994, Decision Support Sustems: A Knowledge-Based Approach, 1996; assoc. editor Jour. Orgnl. Computing and Electronic Commerce, Ablex Corp., Norwood, N.J., 1990—, Mgmt. Sci., Providence, 1991—; area editor Decision Support Systems, Amsterdam, 1992—; contbr. over 100 articles to profl. jours. Recipient Pres.'s Acad. award Purdue U., 1970, 71, 72, Computer Educator of Yr. award Internat. Assn. for Computer Info. Systems, 1993. Mem. IEEE, Internat. Soc. for Decision Support (co-founder, co-dir. 1989—), Assn. for Computing Machinery, Inst. for Operations Rsch. Mgmt. Scis., Assn. for Info. Systems, Decision Sci. Inst., Phi Beta Kappa, Phi Kappa Phi. Office: U Ky Gatton Coll Bus & Econs Lexington KY 40506

HOLSCHER, ROBERT F., county official. Dir., ceo Kenton County Airport Bd, Hebron, Ky., 1961—. Office: Kenton County Airport Bd 2939 Terminal Hebron KY 41048

HOLSHOUSER, CLAIRE K., anesthesiologist; b. San Antonio, Mar. 9, 1955; d. Robert and Shirley (Fisher) K.; m. John H.S. Holshouser; children: John H. Clayton, Thomas. BA, Wellesley Coll., 1977; MD, U. Tex. Health Sci. Ctr., 1981. Resident in anesthesiology U. Tex. Health Sci. Ctr., San Antonio, 1981-84; fellow in pediatric anesthesiology Hosp. for Sick Children, Toronto, Ont., Can., 1984; staff S.W. Tex. Meth. Hosp., San Antonio, 1985—; pvt. practice San Antonio, 1985—. Bd. dirs. Friends of the McNay Mus., San Antonio, 1987-89; mem. Jr. League of San Antonio. Mem. AMA, Am. Soc. Anesthesiologists, Tex. Soc. Anesthesiologists (alt. del. 1990-92), Tex. Med. Assn., Bexar County Med. Assn. Office: 8401 Datapoint Dr San Antonio TX 78229-5925

HOLT, EDWIN JOSEPH, psychology educator; b. Shreveport, La.; s. James S. and Sammie L. (Draper) H.; m. Essie Williams; children: Lisa Michelle, Rachelle Justine. BA, Cen. State U., Wilberforce, Ohio, 1958; MS, Ind. U., 1962; EdD, U. Ark., 1972; postgrad., U. Tenn., 1976. Cert. lic. profl., La. Tchr. Caddo Parish Sch. System, Shreveport, 1959-67, guidance counselor, 1967-68, asst. prin., 1968-71, prin., 1971-74, dir. spl. services, 1974-80, asst. supt., 1980-90; now assoc. prof. psychology La. State U., Shreveport, 1990—; adj. asst. prof. La. State U., Baton Rouge, 1972, N.E. La. U., Monroe, 1973, La. Tech. U., Ruston, 1974, Grambling (La.) State U., 1974-84. Vice-pres. N.W. La. United Way, 1987; dir. Summer Youth Program, Trinity Bapt. Ch., 1980-90; activie Shreveport Clean Community Commn., 1981-85, Shreveport Youth Enrichment Program, 1986-90, La. Parental Involvement Task Force, 1987, Shreveport Task Force on Housing, 1984, Caddo Community Coun. of Parents and Educators, 1984-90; bd. dirs. Am. Heart Assn., 1991-92, Norwella Coun. Boy Scouts Am., 1983-87; fin. chmn. Carver br. YMCA Bd. Mgmt., 1983-88; cultural arts chmn. Caddo Dist. PTA Bd. Mgrs., 1981-90. Nat. Sci. Found. fellow, So. Fund fellow, NDEA fellow; recipient Nat. Council of Negro Women's award, 1984, 85, Nat. Univ. Women's Council award, 1984, 85. Mem. NEA, ACA, La. Edn. Assn., Am. Assn. Sch. Adminstrs., Caddo Assn. Educators, Kappa Delta Pi, Sigma Pi Phi. Baptist. Home: 208 Plano St Shreveport LA 71103-2057 Office: La State U Dept Psychology One University Pl Shreveport LA 72225

HOLT, ELBERT HILTON, JR., insurance company executive; b. Richmond, Va., June 16, 1954; s. Elbert Hilton and Dorothy (Patterson) H.; m. Rebecca Mason Tyus, Feb. 14, 1982; children: Kathleen Hilton, John Harrison. BS, Va. Commonwealth U., 1978. CLU. Sales mgr. Fin. Design Corp., Richmond, 1979-82; sales mgr. Paul Revere Ins. Group, Richmond, 1983-90, asst. gen. mgr., 1990—; cons., life ins. mktg. specialist for advanced estate and bus. planning Paul Revere Ins. Group, Worcester, Mass., 1993—. Mem. Am. Soc. CLU's and ChFC's, Nat. Assn. Life Underwriters, Nat. Assn. Health Underwriters (registered). Baptist. Home: 2221 Castlebridge Rd Midlothian VA 23113-4010 Office: Paul Revere Fin Group 9100 Arboretum Pky Ste 290 Richmond VA 23236-3471

HOLT, J. DARRIN, corporate executive; b. Sanford, N.C., Dec. 27, 1964; s. James Strickland and Alice Faye (Mitchell) H.; m. Rebecca Anne Waters, June 22, 1996. BS in Civil Engring., N.C. State U., 1988, MS in Civil Engring., 1990, PhD in Civil Engring., 1994. Engr.-in-tng. N.C. Draftsman Carolina Aquatech Pools, Sanford, N.C., 1982-84; engr.'s asst. N.C. Dept. Transp., Raleigh, 1986-88; tchg. asst. N.C. State U., Raleigh, 1988-91, rsch. assoc., 1991-94; v.p., sr. analyst FDH, Inc., Raleigh, 1994—; cons. FDH, Inc., 1994—; prin. investigator for a rsch. project N.C. State U., Raleigh, 1993. Co-developer, inventor: Pile Testing Technology, N.C. Dept. Transp., 1993; co-author: Pile Testing by Dispersive Wave Methods, 1994, others. Dep. fire chief Fairgrounds Fire Dept., Raleigh, 1987—, vol. firefighter, 1982-87. Mem. ASCE, Transp. Rsch. Bd., Fairgrounds Fire Dept., Pi Mu Epsilon, Chi Epsilon. Baptist. Home: 1908 Sunset Dr Raleigh NC 27608 Office: FDH Inc PO Box 33037 Raleigh NC 27636

HOLT, JACK WILSON, JR., state supreme court chief justice; b. Harrison, Ark., May 18, 1929; s. Jack Wilson and Mary Margaret (Spikes) H.; divorced; children: Kelley, Candace. J.D., U. Ark., 1952. Bar: Ark. 1952, U.S. Dist. Ct. (ea. and we. dists.) Ark. 1952, U.S. Ct. Appeals (8th cir.) 1954, U.S. Supreme Ct. 1954. Dep. prosecuting atty. 16th Jud. Dist., Little Rock, 1955-60; chief asst. atty. State of Ark., Little Rock, 1960-62; atty. gen. State of Ark., 1962; sole practice law Little Rock, 1962-80; chief justice Ark. Supreme Ct., Little Rock, 1985—. Fellow Am. Bar Found., Am. Judicature Soc., Conf. Chief Justices, Am. Coll. Trial Lawyers; mem. ABA, Ark. Bar Assn. (Golden Gavel awrd 1976), Pulaski Bar ASsn., William Overton Inns of Ct. Democrat. Methodist. Lodge: Lions (v.p. 1980). Home: 4208 Fairview Rd Little Rock AR 72227 Office: 813 West Third St Little Rock AR 72201

HOLT, MILO, retired printer; b. Siler City, N.C., May 30, 1927; s. Robert Eugene Holt and Elizabeth Albertine Amick; divorced; 1 child. Grad. high sch., Siler City. With Siler City Mills, 1952-63, Chatham News, Siler City, 1963-73; printer N.C. State U., Raleigh, 1986-91; ret., 1991. With USN, 1947-51. Mem. Old Time Western Film Club (pres. 1971—). Home: Box 142 Siler City NC 27344

HOLT, PHYLLIS ANN, medical/surgical nurse; b. Sapporo, Hokkaido, Japan, Sept. 8, 1949; d. Raymond Edward and Janet Gaynor (Bolt) Flournoy; m. Fred Elliot Holt, Dec. 17, 1967; children: John Elliot, Patricia Ruth Holt Coleman. ADN, Austin Peay State U., 1973. RN Tenn. Charge nurse Parkview Hosp., Nashville, 1973-74; primary care staff nurse Vanderbilt U. Med. Ctr., Nashville, 1975-78; nurse Cmty. Health Svcs., Nashville, 1980-88, 92—; charge nurse Jennie Stuart med. Ctr., Hopkinsville, Ky., 1988-92; oncology nurse physician's office, Nashville, Hopkinsville, Ky., 1992-94. Home: 2181 Hwy 76 Adams TN 37010-8917

HOLT, ROBERT EZEL, data processing executive; b. Red Bay, Ala., May 8, 1957; s. Robert E. Sr. and Ruby (Weathers) H.; m. Elizabeth Ann Simmons, May 19, 1978; children: Robert E. III, James Michael. AA, N.E. Community Coll., 1977; BS, Miss. State U., 1980. Operator, programmer Watkins, Ward & Stafford, CPA, West Point, Miss., 1978-81; computer programmer Gen. Tire Corp., Inc., Columbus, Ohio, 1981-83; programmer, analyst Arvin Industries, Inc., Starkville, Miss., 1983-84; analyst, data processing mgr. Data Systems Mgmt., Inc., Columbus, Miss., 1984—; data processing cons., West Point, 1983. Deacon, chmn. Calvary Bapt. Ch., West Point, 1990-91; mem. West Point Follies, 1991. Recipient Deacon Cert., Calvary Bapt. Ch., West Point, 1986. Democrat. Baptist. Home: RR 3 Box 273 West Point MS 39773-9718 Office: Data Systems Mgmt Inc Ste 300 Court Square Towers Columbus MS 39701-5733

HOLT, TERESA JAN, community health nurse; b. Birmingham, Ala., Dec. 25, 1957; d. Coy Eugene and Elizabeth Jeanette (Vann) Estes; m. Thomas G. Holt, Oct. 7, 1977. AAS in Nursing, Wallace State C.C., Hanceville, Ala., 1986; BBA, Faulkner U., 1994. Staff nurse in surg. ICU Walker Regional Med. Ctr., Jasper, Ala., 1986-87; staff nurse in cardiovascular intensive care U. Ala. Hosp., Birmingham, 1987-88, circulating RN for cardiovascular oper. rm., 1987-88; staff devel. coord. with dept. edn. 1st Am. Home Care, Inc. (formerly ABC Home Health Svcs.), Cullman, Ala., 1988—; owner, founder Jan Holt and Assocs., 1992—. With Army N.G., 1982-84.

HOLTON, GRACE HOLLAND, accountant; b. Durham, N.C., Sept. 14, 1957; d. Samuel Melanchthon and B. Margaret (Umberger) H. BS in Math., Univ. N.C., Greensboro, 1978; MBA, Univ. N.C., Chapel Hill, 1984; M.Acctg. Sci., U. Ill., 1993. CPA N.C.; cert. mgmt. acct. Indsl. engr. Burlington Industries, Inc., Mayodan, N.C., 1978-79; plant indsl. engr. Burlington Industries, Inc., Stoneville, N.C., 1979-80; methods indsl. engr. Blue Cross and Blue Shield of N.C., Durham, 1980-82; fin. analyst R.J. Reynolds, Inc., Winston-Salem, N.C., 1984-85; accounting cons. Ryder Truck Rental, Inc., Miami, Fla., 1985-88; controller Ryder Jacobs (div. Ryder Distbn. Resources), Jessup, Md., 1988-90; grad. asst. in acctg. U. Ill., Urbana, 1990-93; contr. Salem NationaLease, Winston-Salem, N.C., 1993-94; dir. fin. Chapel Hill-Carrboro City Schs., 1994—. KPMG-Peat Marwick scholar, 1991-92. Mem. AICPAs, Inst. Mgmt. Accts., N.C. Soc. CPAs. Democrat. Methodist.

HOLTON, J(ERRY) THOMAS, concrete company executive; b. Middletown, Ohio, June 7, 1932; s. Joseph Walton and Elizabeth (Fagaly) H.; m. Annie Lou Dearborn, Sept. 26, 1958; children: Elizabeth, Luanne, Ruth, Catherine, J. Thomas Jr. BSE, Princeton U., 1954; MBA, Harvard U., 1959. V.p. Sherman Concrete Pipe Co., Birmingham, Ala., 1959-66, pres., 1966-74; pres. Sherman Industries, Birmingham, 1974-84; pres., chmn. Sherman Internat. Corp., Birmingham, 1984—; dir. Fed. Res. Bank Atlanta, Robin-Morton Corp., KSA, Inc., Sciotoville, Ohio, The Shaw Group Ltd., Halifax, N.S. Pres. coun. U. Ala. Birmingham, 1984-92; mem. exec. bd. Boy Scouts Am., Birmingham, 1985—; chmn., Salvation Army, Birmingham; elder Briarwood Presbyn. Ch., Birmingham, 1968—. Lt. comdr. Civil Engring. Corp. USN, 1954-57. Mem. Birmingham Country Club, Shoal Creek, The Club, Summit Club. Home: 10 Ridge Dr Birmingham AL 35213-3632 Office: Sherman International Inc 1400 Urban Center Dr Ste 200 Birmingham AL 35242-2500

HOLTZ, MARY HESTON, realtor, retired fashion coordinator; b. Rochester, N.Y., Mar. 13, 1926; d. Charles Ellis and Jane (Bechtle) Heston; m. Edward D. Kostic, Nov. 1946 (div. 1953); 1 child, Lynne Patricia Gillam; m. F. Richard Holtz, Dec. 30, 1961 (dec. 1967); m. Beverlee R. Demeritt, June 13, 1970 (div. 1979). Student, Miami U., 1944-46, U. Rochester, 1957. Photographic model Eastman Kodak, Rochester, N.Y., 1947-55; statistician Eastman Kodak, Rochester, 1956-57, fashion coord., 1958-61, ret., 1961; realtor Maggie Anderson and Assocs., Palm City, Fla., 1993—. Del. Rep. State Conv., Fla., 1990; bd. dirs. Planned Parenthood, Stuart, Fla., 1988-92, Riverbend Condo Assn., Stuart, 1989-91, 92-93, Foxboro Homeowners Assn., 1994-96. Mem. Indian River Plantation Club (bd. dirs., steering com. 1989-91), Rochester Yacht Club, Delta Delta Delta. Republican. Episcopalian. Home: 1904 SW Springfield Ct Palm City FL 34990-4796 Office: 1249 SW 27th St Palm City FL 34990

HOLTZ, NOEL, neurologist; b. N.Y.C., Sept. 13, 1943; s. Irving and Lillian H.; m. Carol Sue Smith, June 9, 1968; children: Pamela Wendy, Aaron David, Daniel Judah. BA, NYU, 1965, MD, U. Cin., 1969. Diplomate Am. Bd. Psychiatry and Neurology. Intern Cin. Gen. Hosp., 1969-70; resident in internal medicine and neurology Emory U., Atlanta, 1970-71, 73-76; pvt. practice medicine specializing in neurology, Marietta, Ga., 1977—; mem. faculty Emory U. Coll. Medicine, Atlanta, 1977—, asst. prof. dept. neurology, 1977—, assoc. prof., 1987; mem. staffs Kennestone Hosp.; dir. neurodiagnostics unit; mem. staff Grady Meml. Hosp.; cons. Ga. Med. Care Found. Neurology. Co-author: Conceptual Human Physiology, 1985. With USN, 1971-73. Mem. Am. Acad. Neurology, Ga. Neurol. Soc. (sec.-treas., pres. 1990-92), Alpha Omega Alpha. Office: 522 North Ave Marietta GA 30060-1125

HOLTZAPPLE, JOHN CROFT, museum director; b. York, Pa., May 26, 1958; s. John Wesley and Mary Grace (Croft) H. BA in History summa cum laude, U. Del., 1980; MA in History Mus. Studies, SUNY, Cooperstown, 1982. Interpreter, curatorial asst. Carl Sandburg Home Nat. Hist. Site, Flat Rock, N.C., 1982; lead interpreter Hist. Rugby (Tenn.), Inc., 1983; dir. James K. Polk Ancestral Home, Columbia, Tenn., 1984—. Mem. Phi Beta Kappa, Phi Kappa Phi, Phi Alpha Theta. Lutheran. Office: James K Polk Ancestral Home 301 W 7th St Columbia TN 38401-3132

HOLTZMAN, GARY YALE, administrative and financial executive; b. N.Y.C., Aug. 7, 1936; s. Abram and Pearl (Kashetsky) H.; m. Alice A. Lang, Sept. 5, 1958; children: Bruce, Sheri, Michele. BBA, CCNY, 1958. Exec. v.p. control and ops. Jordan Marsh Co., Miami, Fla., 1967-87; sr. v.p. ops. and stores L. Luria & Sons Inc., Miami, 1987-93; exec. dir. Mar Jewish Community Ctr., Greater Miami, Fla., 1993-95; TSR-Social Security Adminstrn., 1995—; bd. advisers Universal Nat. Bank. Bd. dirs. Dade County Safety Coun., Miami, 1978-85, Jewish Cmty. Ctr. Greater Miami, 1983-88, Fla. Bus. Roundtable, 1975-80, Anti-Defamation League of B'nia B'rith, 1983-87; bd. advisers Opportunities Industrialization Ctr., 1982-84; pres. Michael Ann Russell Jewish Cmty. Ctr., 1984-86, bd. dirs., 1980—; life bd. dirs. Temple Beth Torah Adath Yeshurun, 1969-75, 96—, Temple B'nai Aviv, 1984-86; active Miami Jewish Fedn.; com. chmn. United Way of Dade County. Lt. U.S. Army, 1958-59; capt. USAR, 1959-65. Recipient Americanism award Anti-Defamation League, 1983; recipient Adath Yeshurun Man of Yr. award, 1978. Mem. Greater Miami C. of C., Fla. Retail Fedn. Democrat. Home: 2019 Cove Ln Fort Lauderdale FL 33326-2336

HOLUTIAK-HALLICK, STEPHEN PETER, JR., retired military officer; b. N.Y.C., May 3, 1945; s. Stephen and Hope (Kukura) H.; m. Ann Marie Bazycki, July 29, 1972; children: Larissa Ann, Christine Michelle, Stephen Michael III. BA in Russian, Penn State U., 1967; MA in Slavic Studies, U. Manitoba, Winnipeg, Can., 1969; AS in Bus. Mgmt., C.C. of Allegheny County, 1977; MBA in Internat. Bus., Mercer U., 1992; Cert. in Russian Area Studies, Pa. State U. With USAR, 1967-95, advanced through grades to lt. col., active duty, 1970-71, 85-95; translator, interpretor, mgr. Russian translation dept. Pullman-Swindell, Inc., Pitts., 1972-76; inspector mech. engring. dept. Robert W. Hunt, Co., Pitts., 1977-79; adminstr., procurement svcs. KHD, Humboldt of Wedag, N.Y.C., Montreal, Atlanta, 1979-82, adminstr., project mgmt. svcs., 1982-84, mgr. expediting and sub-contracts adminstrn., 1984-85; staff intelligence officer Forces Command Hdqs., U.S. Army, 1985-90; asst. prof. mil. sci. Clemson (S.C.) U., 1990-92; mem. INF. Treaty inspection team U.S. Army, 1988, inspector gen. 95th Divsn., 1992-95; adj. instr. Park Coll., Tinker AFB, Okla., 1993-95, Am. Coll., Atlanta; pres. TATO's Choice. Author: Slavic Topohymic Atlas of the United States, Vol. I, Ukrainian, 1982, Dictionary of Ukrainian Surnames in the United States, 1994; mem. editl. com. Ridnychkana, 1986-92, chmn., 1993-95; contbr. articles to profl. jours. Organizer, benefactor St. Andrew's Ukrainian Orthodox Mission parish, Atlanta. Decorated Army Commendation medal (3), Meritorious Svc. meda. (3); recipient Danforth Leadership award, 1963, Wasyl Swystun prize of Ukrainian Studies, U. Man., 1967-68, grad. assistantship, 1968-69, Cert. of Appreciation, DAV, 1985-95, Am. Soc. Blind, 1985; Senatorial grantee Pa. State U., 1963-67, Eagle Scout Boy Scouts Am., 1961. Mem. Res. Officers Assn. of U.S., Am. Security Coun. (U.S. Congl. adv. bd.), Atlanta Com. of Fgn. Rels., Am. Name Soc., Can. Soc. for Study of Names, Ga. Hist. Soc. Home: 2755 Kenwood Ct Duluth GA 30136

HOLYOAK, WILLIAM HARDING, machine tool company executive; b. Lybrook, N.Y., July 6, 1937; s. Arthur Lesley and May Anne (Harding) H.; m. Blossom Polo, July 15, 1961; children: Pamala Lynne, John Scott, Jeffrey Todd. BSME, U.S. Mcht. Marine Acad., 1959; postgrad., Trinity Coll., Hartford, Conn., 1963. Project engr. Spencer Turbine Co., Windsor, Conn., 1961-67; products mgr. Waterbury Farrell div. Textron, Cheshire, Conn., 1967-78; v.p., chief exec. officer Am. Feintool, Blue Ash, Ohio, 1978-81; pres. T-Drill Industries Inc., Norcross, Ga., 1981—; bd. dirs. T-Drill Holdings; speaker profl. seminars, 1981—. Contbr. articles to profl. jours. Bd. dirs. Scandinavian-Am. Soc., Atlanta, 1992-93, Finnish Am. C. of C., 1992-94, pres., 1992-94. Mem. ASHRAE, Fabricator Mfrs. Assn., Soc. Mfg. Engrs., Soc. Naval Architects and Engrs. Republican. Methodist. Office: T-Drill Industries Inc 1740 Corporate Dr Norcross GA 30093-2928

HOLZER, TAMERA LEE-PHILLIS, middle school educator; b. Chillicothe, Ohio, Apr. 8, 1961; d. William Lee and Betty Lou (Reeder) Phillis; m. Timothy John Holzer, July 1, 1989; 1 child, Jordyn Elizabeth Lee. AA, Mich. Christian, 1981; BA in Elem. Edn., Harding U., 1983; MA, The Ohio State U., 1989; degree in ednl. adminstrn. and supervision, Ga. State U., 1995, specialist degree in ednl. adminstrn., 1995. Elem. tchr. Prairie Lincoln Elem. Sch., Columbus, Ohio, 1983-89; tchr. Pinckneyville Middle Sch., Norcross, Ga., 1989-92, tchr. Quest, 1992—; county mem. Tchrs. as Leaders, Norcross, 1990—, OBE Strategic Team, Norcross, 1991-94, Tech. Subgroup, Norcross, 1992; chairperson Interdisciplinary Task Force, Norcross, 1991; freelance writer in field. Upreach leader Campus Ch. of Christ, Norcross, 1991-94. Named 1992 Coach of Yr., Gwinnett County. Mem. ASCD, Am. Ednl. Rsch. Assn. Republican. Home: care Kim Eagle 7936 Morris Rd Hilliard OH 43026-9747 Office: Pinckneyville Middle Sch 5440 W Jones Bridge Rd Norcross GA 30092-2021 also: 10 Wallace St, Greenwich Point NSW 2065, Australia

HOMESLEY, HORACE EDWARD (NICHOLAS S. SOKOLNIKOV), writer; b. Jacksonville, Ala., July 9, 1928; s. Horace Edward and Ethel Euphene (Couch) H.; m. Sara Grace Walker, Dec. 16, 1945; children: Angela Barbara, Dennis Edward, Michael Wayne, Timothy Paul, Katrina Darlene. BS in Math. and Chemistry, Jacksonville State U., 1951; MS in Math. and Physics, U. Fla., 1957, Oak Ridge Inst. Nuclear Studies, 1958; PhD in Polit. Sci. and Ops. Rsch., Nova Southeastern U., 1984. Enlisted U.S. Army, 1947, advanced through grades to maj., 1958; tech. dir. Exec. Office Pres., Washington, 1961-66; rsch. dir. Booz Allen and Hamilton, St. Louis, 1966-71; dir. Systems Analysis Office, Leavenworth, Kans., 1972-73, Systems Analysis, St. Louis, 1973-76; spl. asst. to asst. sec. Dept. Commerce, Washington, 1976-77; spl. asst. to chief staff U.S. Army, Washington, 1977-78; dir. Systems Analysis and Info. Mgmt., St. Louis, 1978-88; cons. Presdl. Task Force, Washington, 1989—; seminar speaker Sokolnikov Inc., Pamana City Beach, 1988—; missionary Ind. Christian Chs. Internat., Spur, Tex., 1990—. Author: The Sturm-Liouville Oscillation Theorems, 1957, A History of U.S. Army Squads and Platoons, 1970, Operational Readiness of U.S. Military Equipment, 1984, Preachers' Kids, 1986. Dir. Native Am. Program, St. Louis, 1980-88. Maj. U.S. Army Res. ret. Decorated Silver Star, Bronze Star; recipient Exceptional Civilian Svc. award Dept. Def., 1988; fellow U. Fla., 1955-57. Mem. Nat. Acad. Polit. Soc., Am. Indian Soc., Fla. Writers Assn., VFW, U. Fla. Alumni Club, Jacksonville State U. Alumni Club, Nova U. Alumni Club, Kappa Delta Pi. Home: 1106 E Washington St Thomasville GA 31792-4719 Office: Sokolnikov Inc 233 13th St Panama City Beach FL 32413-4439

HOMESTEAD, SUSAN E. (SUSAN FREEDLENDER), psychotherapist; b. Bklyn., Sept. 20, 1937; d. Cy Simon and Katherine (Haas) Eichelbaum; m. Robert Bruce Randall, 1956 (div. 1960); 1 child, Bruce David; m. George Gilbert Zanetti, Dec. 13, 1962 (div. 1972); m. Ronald Eric Homestead, Jan. 16, 1973 (div. 1980); m. Arthur Elliott Freedlender, Apr. 1, 1995. BA, U. Miami-Fla., 1960; MSW, Tulane U., 1967. Diplomate Am. Bd. Clin. Social Work; Acad. Cert. Social Workers, 1971, LCSW, Va., Calif. Psychotherapist, cons., Richmond, Va., 1971—, Los Altos, Calif.; pvt. practice, Homestead Counseling, Richmond, Piedmont Psychiatric Ctr., P.C. (formerly Psychol. Evaluation Rehab. Cons., Inc.), Lynchburg, Va., 1994—; cons. Family and Children's Svcs., Richmond, 1981—, Richmond Pain Clinic, 1983-84; Health Internat. Va., P.C., Lynchburg, 1984-86, Franklin St. Psychotherapy & Edn. Ctr, Santa Clara, Calif., 1988-90; pvt. practice, 1971—; Santa Clara County Children's Svc., 1973-75, 86-88; co-dir. asthma program Va. Lung Assn., Richmond, 1975-79, Loma Prieta Regional Ctr.; chief clin. social worker Med. Coll. Va., Va. Commonwealth U., 1974-79; field supr. 1980 Census, 1981-87. Contbr. articles to profl. jours. Active Peninsula Children's Ctr., Morgan Ctr., Coun. for Community Action Planning, Community Assn. for Retarded, Comprehensive Health Planning Assn. Santa Clara, Mental Health Commn., Children and Adolescent Target Group Calif., Women's Com. Richmond Symphony, Va. Mus. Theatre, mem. fin. com. Robb for Gov.; mem. adv. com. Va. Lung Assn.; mem. steering com. Am. Cancer Soc.(Va. div.), Epilepsy Found., Am. Heart Assn. (Va. div.), Cen. Va. Guild for Infant Survival. Mem. NASW, Va. Soc. Clin. Social Work, Inc. (charter mem., sec. 1975-78), Internat. Soc. Communicative Psychoanalysis & Psychotherapy, Am. Acad. Psychotherapists, Internat. Soc. for the Study of Dissociation, Am. Assn. Psychiatric Svcs. for Children.

HON, RALPH CLIFFORD, retired arbitrator, educator; b. Jonesboro, Ark., Jan. 29, 1903; s. Earl Augustus and Mary Oma (Little) H.; m. Hazel McLain, July 14, 1930. Student Central Methodist Coll., 1920-23; AB, U. Ill., 1924; MA, Harvard U., 1926; PhD, U. N.C., 1930; postgrad. Am. U., 1928-29. Prof. econs. and bus. adminstrn. Nebr. Wesleyan U., Lincoln, 1929-31, Southwestern at Memphis, 1931-73; vis. prof. Duke U., Durhan, N.C., 1941-43; sr. fin. analyst SEC, Phila., 1943-46; arbitrator, 1955-86; prof. emeritus Rhodes Coll., Memphis, 1973—. Mem. Nat. Acad. Arbitrators, So. Econ. Assn. (past pres. 1941-42). Home: 1760 Jackson Ave Memphis TN 38107-4550 Office: Rhodes Coll 2000 N Parkway Memphis TN 38112-1624

HONAHAN, H(ENRY) ROBERT, motion picture theatre executive; b. N.Y.C., June 26, 1937; s. Henry Walter and Mary (Kovac) H.; children: Sara Anne, Robert Jeremiah. BBA, U. San Jose; postgrad., UCLA, 1968. Div. mgr. Loews Theatres, Los Angeles, 1968-73; gen. mgr. ABC Theatres, San Francisco, 1971-73, asst. to pres., 1973-76; asst. to pres. United Artists Communications, San Francisco, 1976-80; v.p. Honahan Entertainment, Ft. Lauderdale, Fla.; cons., motion picture exec. producer Ft. Lauderdale, 1981-88; pub. Honahan Newsletter, Ft. Lauderdale, 1988—; pres., CEO Famous Artists Movie Entertainment, Hollywood, Fla. Author: Basic Theatre Operation, 1967; exec. producer (films) The World Without Me, 1996, Race to Triumph, 1996, (TV movie) The Dave Lindsey Story, 1996. Recipient Citizen Community Svc. award City of Los Angeles, 1972, Best Subject Live Action award Ft. Lauderdale Film Festival, Film Prodr. of Yr. award, 1992. Office: Honahan Entertainment Group Maj Motion Picture Prodns 2001 NW 9th Ave Fort Lauderdale FL 33311

HONEA, NANCE, artist, educator; b. Tampa, Fla., Feb. 4, 1945; d. Hiram James and Vadie Kathryn (Fleming) H.; m. Thomas T. Bragg, Jr., Aug. 16, 1964 (div. 1973); children: Elisabeth Paige, Kristen Fleming. Student, Mercer U., 1963-64, Emory U., 1978, Art Students League, N.Y.C., 1995. Adminstrv. asst. for leukemia rsch. Emory U., Atlanta, 1973-80; owner Honea Fine Art Studio, Stone Mountain, Ga., 1980—; instr. portrait workshops, 1982—; instr. portrait painting Spruill Ctr. for Arts, Atlanta, 1985—, Internat. Workshop, Italy, 1996; instr. portrait painting Atlanta Coll. Art, 1993—, advisor Shute scholarship fund, 1993—; resident portrait painter Grand Hotel, Mackinac Island, Mich., 1981, The Lodge at Vail, Colo., 1982. One-woman shows Ga. Inst. Tech. Art Gallery, Atlanta, 1979, Am. Nat. Bank, Chattanooga, 1983, Hunter Mus. Art, Chattanooga, 1983, Macon (Ga.) Little Theater, 1988, Picasso Cafe, Atlanta, 1988, Brown & Spiegel, Atlanta, 1991; exhibited in group shows Birmingham (Ala.) Mus. Art, 1978, North Tex. State U. Art Gallery, Denton, 1979, Asheville (N.C.)) Mus., 1983, Shenandoah Coll. and Conservatory, Winchester, Va., 1985, Bellarmine Coll., Louisville, 1985, George Walter Vincent Smith Art Mus., Springfield, Mass., 1986, Macon Mus. Arts and Scis., 1986, Okla. Art Ctr., Oklahoma City, 1986, North Arts Gallery, Atlanta, 1988, Portrait Soc. Ann., 1987—, SE Pastel Soc. Internat., 1989, 90, 92, 96, Ritz-Carlton Hotel, Atlanta, 1988, Ga. Mountains Srt Mus., Gainesville, 1992, So. Bell Ctr., Atlanta, 1993, Atlanta Coll. Art, 1996, Am. Coll. Art, Atlanta, 1996, Avery Gallery, Marietta, 1996, also others; represented in over 200 corp. and pvt. collections throughout U.S. and fgn. countries. Recipient Best in Show awards La. Tech U., 1984, 1st merit award, 1986; purchase award Ga. Coun. for Arts, 1986, also others; named Artist of Yr. Atlanta br. Nat. League Am. Pen Women, 1995. Mem. Nat. Mus. Women in Arts (charter), So. Watercolor Soc., Pastel Soc. Am., Ga. Watercolor Soc. (merit award 1984), Ky. Watercolor Soc., Portrait Soc. Atlanta (charter, pres. 1985-87, exec. bd., bd. dirs., merit mem. 1991—), Ala. Watercolor Soc. (juried mem.), Southeastern Pastel Soc. (Mem. of Excellence award 1992, Merit award 1992, Honorable Mention 1990, 96), Alpha Delta Pi. Studio: 361 Navarre Dr Stone Mountain GA 30087

HONEA, T. MILTON, gas industry executive; b. 1933. Pres., CEO Ark.-La. Gas Co. (divsn. Arkla, Inc.), 1984-91; exec. v.p. Arkla, Inc., 1991-92; vice chmn. bd. NorAm Energy Corp., Houston, 1992, chmn., CEO, 1992—, also bd. dirs.; also pres. NorAm Energy Corp., Houston, TX. Office: Noram Energy Corp 1600 Smith St Houston TX 77002

HONEYCUTT, RODNEY LEE, biologist, educator; b. Houston, Tex., Aug. 5, 1948; s. Max Erwin and Neta (Still) H.; m. Dierdre Anne Hale, Aug. 1, 1970; children: Heather Anne, Morgan Lee. BA, U. Tex., 1970; MS, Tex. A & M U., 1978; PhD, Tex. Tech. U., 1981. Environ. cons. Stearns-Roger, Inc., Denver, 1975-77; rsch. asst. Tex. Tech. U., Lubbock, 1977-81; rsch. fellow Australian Nat. U., Canberra, Australia, 1981-83; postdoctoral fellow U. Mich., Ann Arbor, 1983-84; assoc. prof. Harvard U., Cambridge, Mass., 1984-89; prof. Tex. A & M U., College Station, 1989—; program officer NSF, Washington, 1992-93. Assoc. editor: Jour. of Evolution, 1989-92, Molecular Biology and Evolution, 1994—, Jour. of Heredity, 1995—; contbr. chpts. to books and articles to profl. jours. Sgt. U.S. Army, 1970-72, Vietnam. Recipient 17 grants NSF, 1985-93. Fellow Willi Hennig Soc.; mem. Am. Soc. Mammalogy, Soc. for the Study Evolution, Soc. Systematic Biology, Soc. for Molecular Biology and Evolution. Office: Tex A & M Univ 210 Nagle Hall College Station TX 77840-1434

HONKANEN, JARI OLAVI, electrical engineer; b. Uurainen, Finland, June 3, 1964; came to U.S., 1988; s. Eero Olavi and Aino Inkeri (Kuusisto) H. MS, Helsinki U. Tech., Finland, 1989; MBA, So. Meth. U., 1993. Engr. Ericsson Network Sys., Richardson, Tex., 1988-91, sr. engr., 1991-94; sr. software engr. Sprint, Irving, Tex., 1994-95, DSC Comms. Corp., Plano, Tex., 1995; pres. Odin TeleSystems Inc., Dallas, 1995—; also bd. dirs. Odin Telesystems, Inc., Dallas. Sgt. Finnish Air Force, 1983-84. Mem. IEEE, Assn. Computing Machinery, Beta Kappa Sigma. Office: Odin TeleSystems Inc PO Box 59686 Dallas TX 75229

HONNAS, CLIFFORD M., equine orthopedic surgeon; b. Nogales, Ariz., Sept. 19, 1958; s. Donald E. and Carolyn (Pine) H.; m. Lorie Ann Robinson, Jan. 2, 1982; children: Audre, Mollie, Henre, Cheri, Kenny. Student, U. Ariz., 1976-80; BS, Colo. State U., Ft. Collins, 1981, DVM, 1984. Diplomate Am. Coll. Vet. Surgeons; lic. in Colo., Ariz., Tex., Calif. Large animal medicine intern Coll. Vet. Medicine, Tex. A&M U., College Station, 1984-85; resident in equine surgery Sch. Vet. Medicine, U. Calif., Davis, 1985-88; asst. prof. equine surgery Sch. Vet. Med., Vet. Clin. Scis., La. State U., Baton Rouge, 1988-89, Tex. Vet. Med. Ctr., Coll. Vet. Medicine, Tex. A&M U., College Station, 1989—. Contbr. numerous articles to profl. jours.; presenter in field. Recipient grants. Mem. AVMA, Vet. Orthopedic Soc., Am. Coll. Vet. Surgeons, La. Acad. Vet. Practice, Calif. Vet. Med. Assn., Am. Assn. Vet. Clinicians, Tex. Soc. for Biomed. Rsch., Bluebonnet Area Vet. Med. Assn., Colo. State U. Alumni Assn., Phi Zeta, Alpha Zeta. Office: Tex A&M U Coll Vet Med Tex Vet Med Ctr Dept Large Animal Med/Surg College Station TX 77843-4475

HONNER SUTHERLAND, B. JOAN, advertising executive; b. N.Y.C., Oct. 23, 1952; d. William John and Mary Patricia (Edwards) H.; m. Donald J. Sutherland, Oct. 3, 1987; children: Chelsea Lauren, Whitney Devon. Student, Endicott Coll., 1970-71. Art dir. Kerrigan Studio, Darien, Conn., 1971-73, Foote Cone and Belding, Phoenix, 1973-77; sr. art dir. Foote Cone and Belding, Chgo., 1977-81; v.p., assoc. creative dir. J. Walter Thompson, Chgo., 1982-86; v.p., exec. art dir. BBDO Chgo., 1986-91; creative dir. Knautz & Co., Sarasota, Fla., 1992-93; co-owner X-L Advt., Sarasota, Fla., 1993-94; owner Beyond Design, Sarasota, 1994—; cons. J. Walter Thompson, Toronto and San Francisco, 1983-84; owner Fla. Antiques, Geneva, Ill., 1986-90. Introduced Discover card, 1985. Tchr. elem. sch. art; mem. Southside Sch. PTA Bd., Sarasota, 1996—. Recipient 1st pla. TV local campaign WGN, 6th dist. Addy, 1980, Kemp. Corp. Addy, 1990; Best Internat. TV campaign Pepsi Clio, 1985. Roman Catholic. Home: 4941 Commonwealth Dr Sarasota FL 34242-1421

HOOD, EDWARD EXUM, JR., retired electrical manufacturing company executive; b. Boonville, N.C., Sept. 15, 1930; s. Edward Exum and Nellie (Triplett) H.; m. Kay Transou, Dec. 30, 1950; children: Lisa Kay, Molly Ann. M.S. in Nuclear Engring., N.C. State U., 1953. Registered profl. engr., Ariz. Powerplant design engr. Gen. Electric Co., 1957-62, mgr. supersonic transport engine project, 1962-67, v.p., gen. mgr. comml. engine div., from 1968, v.p., group exec. internat. group, 1972-73, v.p., group exec., power generation group, 1973-77, sr. v.p., sector exec. tech. systems and materials sector, from 1977, vice-chmn. and exec officer, 1979-93, also bd. dirs. Served with USAF, 1952-56. Fellow AIAA; mem. Nat. Acad. Engring., Aerospace Industries Assn. (chmn. 1981). Home: 11674 Lake House Ct North Palm Beach FL 33408-3311 Office: GE PO Box 8300 260 Long Ridge Rd Stamford CT 06904

HOOD, MARY BRYAN, museum director, painter; b. Central City, Ky., July 5, 1938; d. Irving B. and Mary Louise (Anderson) Cayce; m. Ronnie L. Hood, Oct. 16, 1960. Student Ky. Wesleyan Coll., 1956-59, 68-73. Exec. dir. Owensboro Arts Commn., Ky., 1974-76; founding dir. Owensboro Mus. Fine Art, 1976—. Author/editor exhbn. catalogues. Mem. exec. com. Ky. Citizens for Arts, 1980-86, Owensboro Arts Commn., 1977—, Owensboro Bicentennial Commn., 1990—, Ky. Arts Commn., 1974-76; bd. dirs. Japan/Am. Soc. Ky., 1987-89, Owensboro Symphony, 1975-76, Owensboro Area Mus., 1970-72, Theatre Workshop Owensboro, 1968-70; chair Owensboro Mayor's Arts Com., 1970-75; me. Cmty. Appearance Planning Bd., 1988-92, Davies County Bicentennial Commn., 1990-92, Owensboro Bicentennial Commn., 1996; mem. steering com. Yr. of the Am. Craft, Ky., 1991-93, Mayor's Adv. Coun. on Arts, 1996. Mary Bryan Hood Day named in her honor, Owensboro, 1974. Mem. Southeastern Mus. Conf., Am. Assn. Mus., Ky. Assn. Mus. (pres. 1980-82). Office: Owensboro Mus Fine Art 901 Frederica St Owensboro KY 42301-3052

HOOD, OLLIE RUTH, health facilities executive; b. San Francisco, Nov. 26, 1947; d. Rodger Brown and Lucile Brooks (Reid); m. McKinley Hood, Aug. 27, 1969 (div. 1987); children: Antoinette Brown, Kirk Stewart, Seancy Hood. BA, San Francisco State U., 1971. Asst. sec., v.p. Weyerhauser Mortgage Co., L.A., 1971-80; asst. supr. Plaza Mortgage Co., L.A., 1980-84; data entry supr. Western Standard Truck, L.A., 1984-85; mgr. Kaiser Hosp., San Francisco, 1985-92; with Emory Clinic, Atlanta, 1995—. Patentee in field. Mem. Calif. Assn. Hosp. Admitting Mgrs., Nat. Assn. Hosp. Admitting Mgrs., NAFE, Kaiser Permanente Club (2d v.p. 1987), Nat. Assn. Women (v.p. 1989—). Jehovah's Witness. Home: PO Box 87117 College Park GA 30337-0117

HOOD, ROBERT HOLMES, lawyer; b. Charleston, S.C., Oct. 5, 1944; s. James Albert and Ruth (Henderson) H.; m. Mary Agnes Burnham, Aug. 5, 1967; children: Mary Agnes, Elizabeth, Robert Holmes Jr., James Bernard. BA, U. of the South, 1966; JD, U. S.C., 1969. Bar: U.S. Supreme Ct. 1969, S.C. 1969, U.S. Dist. Ct. S.C. 1969, U.S. Ct. Appeals (4th cir.) 1969. Asst. atty. gen. State of S.C., Columbia, 1969-70; ptnr. Sinkler, Gibbs & Simons, Charleston, 1970-85; prin. Hood Law Firm, Charleston, 1985--. Mem. Assn. Def. Trial Attys. (pres. 1985-86), Am. Bd. Trial Advs. (diplomate), Internat. Assn. Def. Counsel (state chmn. 1987—), Def. Rsch. and Trial Inst. (bd. dirs. 1987-90), Fedn. Ins. and Corp. Counsel, S.C. Def. Trial Attys. Assn. (pres. 1980-81). Episcopalian. Office: 172 Meeting St Charleston SC 29401-3126

HOOD, RONALD CHALMERS, III, historian, writer; b. Florence, Ala., Apr. 2, 1947; s. Ronald Chalmers II and Elizabeth Woods (Craig) H.; m. Lucile O'Connor, Dec. 20, 1969; children: Ronald Chalmers IV, Reed Cathleen. BS, U.S. Naval Acad., 1969; MA, U. Maine, Orono, 1972; PhD, U. Md., 1979. Commd. 2d lt. USMC, 1969, advanced through grades to capt., 1973, resigned, 1982; historian, writer Johns Hopkins U., Balt., 1982—, George Mason U., Fairfax, Va., 1982—, U. Md., College Park, 1982—; lectr. Smithsonian Instn., Washington, 1988; speaker Conf. on Strategic Studies, Washington, 1985; co-chair Muscle Shoals Revisited Conf. on Future of Tenn. Valley, 1993. Author: (history monograph) Royal Republicans, 1985; co-author: (mil. history) Military Effectiveness, 1987, Body, Mind, Spirit: 75 Years of Camp Hazen YMCA, 1995; contbr. editorial columns to Washington Post, Potomac News, articles to profl. jours. Asst. scoutmaster Boy Scouts Am., Woodbridge, Va., 1989—; advisor County Sch. Bd., Prince William County, Va., 1991; instr. ARC, Prince William County, 1982—. Samuel Eliot Morison fellow U. Maine, Orono, 1971-72, Grad. Sch. fellow U. Md., 1975. Mem. AAUP, Writers' Ctr., Smithsonian Instn., Nat. Geographic Soc.

HOOD, WILLIAM WAYNE, JR., lawyer; b. Tulsa, July 22, 1941; s. William Wayne and Alys (Charles) H.; m. Nancy Raynolds; children—W. Wayne III, Kristina L. B.A., U. Okla., 1963; LL.B., U. Tulsa, 1966. Bar: Okla. 1966, U.S. Dist. Ct. (no. dist.) Okla. 1966; diplomate Am. Coll. Matrimonial Trial Lawyers. Sole practice, Tulsa, 1966-70; pub. defender Tulsa County, 1966-68; ptnr. Hood & Lindsey, Tulsa, 1970-87; partner Hood, Thornbrugh and Raynolds, 1989—. Served to maj. JAGC, USAR, 1966-84. Fellow Am. Acad. Matrimonial Lawyers (v.p. 1985-88, pres. Okla. chpt. 1991-93), Internat. Acad. Matrimonial Lawyers (bd. govs. Am. chpt. 1987-91); mem. Okla. Bar Assn. (dir. continuing legal edn.-family law 1980-84, chmn. family law sect. 1975-77, 80-82), Tulsa County Bar Assn. (exec. com. 1979). Republican. Roman Catholic. Office: Hood Thornbrugh & Raynolds 1914 S Boston Ave Tulsa OK 74119-5222

HOOGENBOOM, GERRIT, agricultural engineer; b. Monster, Netherlands, Dec. 19, 1955; came to U.S., 1981; s. Gerrit and Christina Margaretha (van Duijker) H.; m. Carol Jo Wilkerson, Dec. 16, 1984. MSc, Agrl. U., Wageningen, Netherlands, 1981; PhD, Auburn U., 1985. With Scottish Horticultural Rsch. Inst., 1977-78; vis. scientist Volcani Ctr., Bet Dagan, Israel, 1979; grad. rsch. asst. Auburn (Ala.) U., 1981-85; postdoctoral rsch. assoc. U. Fla., Gainesville, 1985-89; asst. prof. dept. biol. and agrl. engring. U. Ga., Griffin, 1985-95, assoc. prof., 1995—; cons. Winrock Internat., New Delhi, India, 1990. Contbr. articles to Can. Jour. Forest Rsch., Agrl. Sys., Agronomy Jour., Agr. and Fgn. Meteorology, Trans. Am. Soc. Agrl. Engrs. Mem. Am. Soc. Agrl. Engrs., Am. Soc. Plant Physiology, Crop Sci. Soc. Am., Soil Sci. Soc. Am., Am. Soc. Agronomy (Step award 1994), Soc. Computer Simulation (sr.), Sigma Xi. Episcopalian. Home: 500 Chatfield Way Marietta GA 30064 Office: U Ga 1109 Experiment Sta Griffin GA 30223-1731

HOOGLAND, ROBERT FREDERICS, lawyer; b. Paterson, N.J., Apr. 3, 1955; s. Robert J. and Lucretia H.; m. Diane Wood, Sept. 21, 1983 (div. Mar. 1985). BA, U. Fla., 1976; MBA, Rollins Coll., 1977; JD, U. Fla., 1982. Bar: Fla. 1983, U.S. Dist. Ct. (mid. dist.) Fla. 1989. Assoc. Giles, Hedrick & Robinson, Orlando, Fla., 1983-89; ptnr. Hoogland & Durket, P.A., Longwood, Fla., 1989-92, Robert F. Hoogland, P.A., Altamonte Springs, Fla., 1992—. Pres. Southbrooke Condominiums, Orlando, 1985—. Mem. ABA, Fla. Bar Assn., Orange County Bar Assn., Seminole County Bar

Assn., Winter Park C. of C., Phi Delta Phi. Republican. Roman Catholic. Home: 139 Olive Tree Cir Altamonte Springs FL 32714-3240 Office: PO Box 160021 Altamonte Springs FL 32716-0021

HOOK, CORNELIUS HENRY, insurance agency owner; b. St. Paul, Mar. 29, 1929; s. Cornelius Henry and Lois Bethel (Blaisdell) H.; m. Zuane Gordon Napier, Dec. 27, 1951 (div. 1979); children: Cornelius Henry III, Thomas Colin, Stephen Napier; m. Lucy Ellen Smith, Dec. 26, 1987. BA, U. Minn., 1951; grad. Language Sch., Fgn. Svc. Inst., 1969. Comd. officer USAF, 1951, advanced through grades to lt. col., 1971; with USAFR, 1972-89, ret., 1989; account exec. Alexander & Alexander, Atlanta, 1971-73; owner Hook Ins. Agy., Atlanta, 1973—. Com. chmn. Northside Kiwanis Club, Atlanta, 1971-73. Decorated Master Badge, Vietnam Svc. medal. Mem. Profl. Ins. Assn., Res. Officers Assn., Masons (32 degree), Beta Theta Pi. Presbyterian.

HOOK, HAROLD SWANSON, insurance company executive; b. Kansas City, Mo., Oct. 10, 1931; s. Ralph C. and Ruby (Swanson) H.; m. Joanne T. Hunt, Feb. 19, 1955; children: Karen Anne, Thomas W., Randall T. BS in Bus. Adminstrn., U. Mo., 1953, MA in Acctg., 1954; grad., So. Meth. U. Inst. Ins. Mktng., 1957; postgrad., NYU, 1967-70; LLD (hon.), U. Mo., 1983, Westminster Coll., 1983. CLU, FLMI. Mem. faculty U. Mo. Sch. Bus., 1953-54; asst. to pres. Nat. Fidelity Life Ins. Co., Kansas City, Mo., 1957-60, dir., 1959-66, adminstrv. v.p., 1960-61, exec. v.p., investment com., 1961-62, pres., exec. com., 1962-66; sr. v.p. U.S. Life Ins. Co., N.Y.C., 1966-67, dir., 1967-70, exec. v.p., mem. exec. com., 1967-68, pres., 1968-70; pres. Calif.-Western States Life Ins. Co., Sacramento, 1970-75, chmn., 1975-79, sr. chmn., 1979-91, also bd. dirs.; mem. exec. com. Am. Gen. Corp., Houston, 1975—, pres., 1975-81, chmn., chief exec. officer, 1978-96, also bd. dirs., chmn., 1996—; founder, pres. Main Event Mgmt. Corp., Sacramento, 1971—; bd. dirs. PanEnergy Corp., Houston, Sprint Corp., Kansas City, Mo., Cooper Industries, Inc., Houston, Chase Manhattan Corp., N.Y.C., Manhattan Bank, N.Y.C., Tex. Commerce Bank Nat. Assn. Houston. Founder, mem. Naval War Coll. Found.; trustee, chmn. fin. com. Baylor Coll. Medicine, Houston; vice chmn. coun. overseers Jesse H. Hones Grad. Sch. Adminstrn., Rice U., Houston; pres. nat. exec. bd. Boy Scouts Am., 1988-90, now mem. nat. adv. coun. Boy Scouts Am., mem. adv. bd. Sam Houston Area coun.; bd. dirs. Tex. Rsch. League, Soc. for Performing Arts, Houston, Greater Houston Partnership (formerly Houston C. of C.). Recipient Citation of Merit U. Mo. Alumni Assn., 1965, Faculty-Alumni award U. Mo., 1978; Silver Beaver award Boy Scouts Am., 1974, Disting. Eagle Scout award, 1976, Silver Antelope award, 1989, Silver Buffalo award, 1990; Chief Exec. Officer award Fin. World mag., 1979, 82, 84, 86; named Man of Yr., Delta Sigma Pi, 1969, Outstanding Chief Exec. Officer in Multiline Ins. Industry, Wall Street Transcript, 1981-87. Fellow Life Mgmt. Inst.; mem. Mgmt. Exec. Soc., Philos. Soc. Tex., Tex. Assn. Taxpayers (bd. dirs.), Nat. Assn. Life Underwriters, Houston Assn. Life Underwriters, Forum Club (bd. govs. 1983-93), River Oaks Country Club, Petrolum Club, Econ. Club N.Y.C., Eldorado Country Club, Rotary, Beta Gamma Sigma (dirs. table 1976, nat. honoree 1984). Presbyterian. Office: Am Gen Corp 2929 Allen Pky Houston TX 77019-2197 also: PO Box 3247 Houston TX 77253-3247

HOOKER, RENÉE MICHELLE, postanesthesia and perinatal nurse; b. Kansas City, Mo., June 26, 1965; d. Roland Edward and Loretta Mae (Rathbun) Woods; m. Joel Thomas Hooker, Sept. 17, 1988; children: Andrew, Catherine, Rebekah. BSN, U. Kans., 1987. RN, Tex., Calif.; cert post anesthesia nurse, inpatient obstetric nurse ANCC; cert. ACLS, neonatal resuscitation. Staff med.-surg. nurse Desert Hosp., Palm Springs, Calif., 1987-88; staff nurse neonatal ICU Santa Rose Children's Hosp., San Antonio, 1988; staff obstetrics nurse, supr. post anesthesia care unit McKenna Meml. Hosp., New Braunfels, Tex., 1988—. Mem. Assn. Women's Health, Obstet. and Neonatal Nursing, Tex. Assn. Post Anesthesia Nurses, Am. Soc. Post Anesthesia Nurses, Assn. Oper. Room Nurses. Republican. Roman Catholic. Office: McKenna Meml Hosp 143 E Garza New Braunfels TX 78130

HOOKS, VANDALYN LAWRENCE, former elementary school educator; b. Dyersburg, Tenn., Feb. 26, 1935; d. James Bridges and Mary Lucille (Anderson) Lawrence; m. Floyd Lester Hooks, June 15, 1952; children: Lawrence James, Steven Lester. BA, Ky. Wesleyan U., 1967; MA, Western Ky. U., 1970, Edn. Specialist, 1976; postgrad. U. Tenn., 1975. Tchr., Owensboro Bd. Edn., Ky., 1967-71, adminstr., 1976-85; dir. career experience Western Ky. U., Bowling Green, 1971-73; dir. career edn. Owensboro Daviess County Sch. Dist., elem. tchr., 1967-71, elem. prin. 1974-78, 83-85, adminstr., elem. prin. dir. career experience, 1976-85; curriculum developer Career Experience Voc. Edn., Frankfort, Ky., 1971-76; cons. Motivation Workshop, Bowling Green, 1971-76, Decision and Goal Setting, 1971-76. Editor: Ky. Assn. Elem. Prin. Jour., 1977-81; editor, pub. Ednl. Alert, 1985-90, A Crash Course In Ednl. Reform, 1989, A Dangerous Liaison A Tax Exempt Foundation and Two Teacher Unions, 1990, The Alphabet Books, 1991, Caution! Change Agents at Work, 1992, A System for Control PPBS, 1994; contbr. articles to profl. jours. Organizer, Ky. Council for Better Edn., Owensboro, 1984; legis. advisor Eagle Forum, leadership forum, Washington, 1985, 86-87, 88-92; Rep. legis. researcher . Recipient Presdl. award, Ky. Wesleyan Coll., 1966. Mem. Concerned Edn. of Am., Nat. Council for Better Edn., Pro Family Forum, Eagle Forum, Plymouth Rock Found., Nat. Council Christian Educators. Republican. Baptist. Address: 1302 Waverly Pl Owensboro KY 42301-3683

HOOKS, VENDIE HUDSON, III, surgeon; b. Metter, Ga., Nov. 1, 1948; s. Vendie Hudson Jr. and May (Jones) H.; m. Carolyn Anderson Braithwaite, Nov. 1, 1974; children: Hudson, Susanna, David, Katherine. BS, U. Ga., 1970; MD, Med. Coll. Ga., 1974. Diplomate Am. Bd. Surgery, Am. Bd. Colon and Rectal Surgery. Intern surgery Med. Coll. Ga. Hosps., Augusta, 1974-75; resident gen. surgery Med. Coll. Ga. Hosps., 1975-78, chief resident gen. surgery, 1978-79; G.I. surgery fellow gen. infirmary U. Leeds (Eng.), 1979-80; colon and rectal surgery fellow U. Minn. Hosps., 1982-83; asst. prof. surgery, asst. chief sect. GI surgery Med. Coll. Ga., Augusta, 1980-85; dir. colon/rectal surgery clinic Med. Coll. Ga., 1980-85; attending in surgery VA Hosp., Augusta, 1980-85; asst. clin. prof. surgery Med. Coll. Ga., Augusta, 1985-94; assoc. clin. prof. surgery, 1994—; staff surgeon Univ. Hosp., Augusta, 1985—, St. Joseph Hosp., Augusta, 1985—; attending colon/rectal surgery endoscopy Univ. Hosp., Augusta, 1986—; dir. Southeastern Familial Polyposis Registry; bd. dirs. Richmond-Columbia County unit Am. Cancer Soc., v.p. medicine, 1985-91; mem. Ethicon Colon and Rectal Adv. Panel, 1988, Panel Specialist-Surgery, Vocat. Rehab., 1980—; mem. interview com. for med. sch. admissions Med. Coll. Ga., 1981-82, 84-85, mem. tissue com., 1983-85; chmn. familial polyposis registry com. U. Hosp. Augusta, 1986—; assoc. examiner Am. Bd. Colon and Rectal Surgery, 1995, 96. Co-author: Textbook of Gastroenterology, 1984, Clinical Management of Gastrointestinal Cancer, 1984; contbr. articles to profl. jours.; book reviewer and abstractor in field; reviewer Gastrointestinal Endoscopy, 1985-88. Recipient Continuing Med. Edn. award Am. Soc. Colon and Rectal Surgeons, 1984, 87, Spl. award for colorectal cancer control Am. Cancer Soc., 1987, Cert. of Appreciation, Am. Cancer Soc., 1991-92, Award of Excellence, Am. Cancer Soc., 1992-93; grantee Am. Soc. Hosp. Pharmacists, 1981, Smith Kline & French Labs., 1981, Merck Sharp & Dohme, 1984. Fellow ACS, Southeastern Surg. Congress, Am. Soc. Colon and Rectal Surgeons; mem. AMA (Physician Recognition award 1984-89, 1990-93, 93-96), Med. Assn. Ga., Richmond County Med. Soc., So. Med. Assn., Moretz Surg. Soc., Assn. for Acad. Surgeons, Ga. Gastroenterologic and Endoscopy Soc., Am. Soc. for Gastrointestinal Endoscopy, Soc. Am. Gastrointestinal Endoscopic Surgeons, Ga. Surg. Soc., Piedmont Soc. Colon and Rectal Surgeons (pres. 1992-94), Soc. Surgery Alimentary Tract, Phi Beta Kappa, Phi Kappa Phi. Methodist. Office: Colon and Rectal Surgery Assocs PC 820 Saint Sebastian Way Ste 7C Augusta GA 30901-2641

HOOPER, CARL GLENN, civil engineer, software writer; b. Granville, N.Y., Apr. 6, 1936; s. W. Glenn and Alma (Osborne) H.; m. Priscilla Anne Hall, June 15, 1957; children: Martin Eric, Diane Elizabeth, Lynn Louise, Charles Douglas, Julie Anne. BSCE, Norwich U., 1958. Registered profl. engr., Vt., Fla., Ga., N.C., S.C. Mng. ptnr. Hooper Constrn. Co., Palm Coast, Fla., 1960—; town auditor Town of Poultney (Vt.), 1964-67; pres. Hooper Constrn. Products Corp., Granville, N.Y., 1969-76; project dir. Briley, Wild & Assocs., Ormond Beach, Fla., 1977-88; dir. community svcs., city engr. City of Daytona Beach Shores (Fla.), 1988-96; pres. Bent Tree Software Inc., Palm Coast, Fla., 1990—. Author computer programs for personal fin. and real estate program, others. lst lt. C.E., U.S. Army, 1958-60. Mem. ASCE. Republican. Methodist. Home and Office: 2 Cameo Ct Palm Coast FL 32137-8155

HOOPER, EDNA ROSIER, insurance company executive; b. Augusta, Ga., July 12, 1926; d. Allen Lester Sr. and Edna Earl (Trader) Rosier; m. Thomas Calvin Hooper, Nov. 25, 1948. Cert. property and casualty ins. agt. Clk.-typist Brookley AFB, Mobile, Ala., 1945-49; teletype operator U. Miss., Oxford, 1950-53; traffic mgr. WSGN Radio Sta., Birmingham, Ala., 1953-54; claims processor Wilkie, Johnson, Norton, Birmingham, 1954-55; sec. B.P.O.E., Dothan, Ala., 1955-57; counselor Long's Pers. Svc., Mobile, Ala., 1959-61; exec. sec. to v.p. and CEO Stonewall Ins. Co., Mobile, 1961-62, Morrison Assurance Co., Mobile, 1962-81; v.p., reins. asst. sec., treas. Am. Resources Ins. Co., Mobile, 1981-93; ret., 1993. Baptist. Home: 2208 Dogwood Ct N Mobile AL 36693-3211

HOOPER, PERRY OLLIE, judge; b. Birmingham, Ala., Apr. 8, 1925; s. Ernest J. and Mary Lou (Perry) H.; m. Marilyn Yost, May 16, 1953; children: Perry O. Jr., Walter, Conwell, John. BS, U. Ala., 1950, LLB, 1953. Bar: Ala. 1953, U.S. Dist. Ct. (so. dist.) Ala. 1953. Pvt. practice Montgomery, Ala., 1953-64, 83—; probate judge Montgomery County, Montgomery, 1964-76; cir. ct. judge State of Ala., Montgomery, 1975-83, presiding cir. judge, 1978-83, chief justice Supreme Ct., 1995—. Mem. Nat. Republican Com., 1972-96. Presbyterian. Home: 3191 Thomas Ave Montgomery AL 36106-2425 Office: 300 Dexter Ave Montgomery AL 36104-3741

HOOPER, WILLIAM EDWARD, broadcast journalist; b. Tampa, Fla., Mar. 10, 1964; s. Dennis William and Doris Jean (Burkhart) H. Student, U. Tenn., 1984-87; degree cert., Profl. Acad. Broadcasting, Knoxville, Tenn., 1988. Traffic reporter K-Trans, Knoxville, 1987-93; news dir. Sta. WNOX-FM, Knoxville, 1988-90, Sta. WWZZ-FM, Knoxville, 1991-93; news reporter Sta. WKXT-TV, Knoxville, 1993-96; writer, host Tennesse Chronicles Tenn. Pub. Television System, 1996—; host, writer Radio Appalachia, Knoxville, 1987-92, Celebrate Knoxville, 1991, WKXT's Tenn. Bicentennial Minute, 1995; feature writer Foothills mag., Knoxville, 1993; host, producer Viewpoint Talkshow, 1994-96. Author: (broadcast reports) Public Access Denied: Tennessee Statute 40-23-116; syndicated columnist Banjo Newsletter, 1981. Treas. Knoxville Juvenile Diabetes Assn., 1989. Recipient Cert. of Appreciation, Knoxville Transit Co., 1993, Cert. of Merit, Tenn. Hist. Commn., So. Journalism award 1996, Tenn. Jefferson Davis Media award 1996, Cert. of Appreciation City of Knoxville, 1996, Robert E. Lee Media award Sons of Confederate Veterans Tenn. Divsn., 1996, Merit award Tenn. Gov., 1996, Cmty. Svc. award Knox County Commn., 1996, Horace V. Wells Cmty. Svc. award East Tenn. Soc. Profl. Journalists, 1996, Cert. of Merit, Tenn. Hist. Commn., 1996. Mem. Soc. Profl. Journalists (1st pl. award for radio feature reporting Atlanta chpt. 1990, Investigative Reporting award Atlanta chpt. 1994, TV-Feature Reporting award 1995, TV Deadline News award 1995, So. Journalist award 1996), Investigative Reporters and Editors, Masons (historian Knoxville 1990—, Meritorious cert. 1991, 92). Office: Sta WKXT-TV 6432 Papermill Rd Knoxville TN 37919-4812

HOOTMAN, HARRY EDWARD, retired nuclear engineer, consultant; b. Oak Park, Ill., June 5, 1933; s. Merle Albert and Rachel Edith (Atkinson) H.; m. Linda P. Smith, Nov. 23, 1963; children: David, Holly, John. BS in Chemistry, Mich. Technol. U., 1959, MS in Nuc. Engring., 1962; LLB , LaSalle Extension U., 1971. Registered profl. engr., S.C. Rsch. assoc. Argonne (Ill.) Nat. Lab., 1959-62; process engr. Savannah River Plant, Aiken, S.C., 1962-65; rsch. assoc. reactor physics group, nuclear engring. div. Savannah River Lab., Aiken, 1965-87; with New Reactor Devel. Group, 1987-92, adv. engr. Planning, Studies and Analysis, 1992-95; ret., 1995; cons. transuranic waste disposal and incineration, radioisotope prodn., separation and shielding; instr. Math. and Engring. Dept. U. S.C., Aiken, 1979-80, 90-94. Inventor alpha waste incinerator. Bd. dirs. Central Savannah River Area Sci. and Engring. Fair, Inc., Augusta, Ga., 1972-91. Served to sgt. USAF, 1953-57. Mem. Am. Acad. Environ. Engrs., Nat. Soc. Profl. Engrs. (local chmn. 1978-79), Am. Nuclear Soc. (local chmn. 1979-80), Am. Phys. Soc., Sigma Xi. Baptist. Home: 820 Brandy Rd Aiken SC 29801-7281

HOOVER, BETTY-BRUCE HOWARD, private school educator; b. Wake County, N.C., Mar. 20, 1939; d. Bruce Ruffin and Mary Elizabeth (Brown) Howard; m. Herbert Charles Marsh Hoover, Sept. 3, 1961; children: David Andrew, Howard Webster, Lorraine VanSiclen. B.A., Wake Forest U., 1961; M.A., U. S. Fla., 1978. Tchr. English, Greensboro Sr. High Sch., N.C., 1961-62, Lindley Jr. High Sch., Greensboro, 1963, Berkeley Prep. Sch., Tampa, Fla., 1976—, chmn. English dept., 1977-85, dir., dean upper div., 1984—, chmn. curriculum com., 1982-86 . Author: Resources in Education, 1992. Pres., Suncoast Midshipmen Parents Club, Tampa Bay Area, 1983-84. Mem. Assn. Supervision Curriculum Devel., Nat. Council Tchrs. English, Sociedad Honoraira Hispanica, The Nat. Coun. States, Wake Forest U. Alumni Assn., DAR, Hillsborough County Bar Aux., Cum Laude Soc. (sec. 1981—), Nat. Honor Soc., Phi Beta Kappa, Phi Sigma Iota, Sigma Tau Delta, Kappa Kappa Gamma. Republican. Episcopalian. Avocations: sewing; gardening. Home: 4504 W Beachway Dr Tampa FL 33609-4234 Office: Berkeley Preparatory Sch 4811 Kelly Rd Tampa FL 33615-5020

HOOVER, DEBORAH, critical care, medical and surgical nurse; b. Bay St. Louis, Miss., Apr. 1, 1958; d. Donald Terence and Mary Mauvereen (Graham) Ball; m. Harold Hoover, Jan. 16, 1982; children: Harold Ryan, Carolyn Mauvereen. BSN, Miss. Coll., Clinton, 1991; LPN, Jones Jr. Coll., Ellisville, Miss., 1980; AA, Jones Jr. Coll., 1982. Pvt. duty nurse Upjohn Health Care, Baton Rouge, 1984; charge nurse Zachary (La.) Manor Nursing Home, 1984; staff nurse Hinds Gen. Hosp., Jackson, Miss., 1982-83, Jones County Community Hosp., Laurel, Miss., 1979-82; 3-11 supr. Clinton (Miss.) Country Manor, 1983-84, 85-86; charge nurse Tracehaven Nursing Home, Vicksburg, Miss., 1986-87; staff nurse Vicksburg (Miss.) Med. Ctr., 1987-91; nurse mgr. ICU Vicksburg Med. Ctr., 1991—, nurse mgr. emergency rm., 1992—, asst. chief nursing officer, critical care coord., 1994, critical care and emergency dept. dir., 1996—. Mem. AACN, ANA, Miss. Nurses Assn., Student Nurses Assn., Emergency Nurses Assn., Miss. Coll. Nursing Honor Soc., Vicksburg Bus. and Profl. Women's Club, Lions, Sigma Theta Tau, Alpha Chi. Baptist. Home: 120 Post Oak Ln Vicksburg MS 39180-7686

HOOVER, JIMMIE HARTMAN, librarian; b. Board Camp, Ark., Nov. 5, 1930; s. James Thomas and Alice Victoria (Peters) H.; m. Lillian Elaine Fitzgerald, Jan. 2, 1959. Student Coll. Ozarks, 1948-49; BA, Ark. Poly. Coll., 1952; MS, La. State U., 1958. With La. State U. Library, Baton Rouge and New Orleans, 1958-84, head order dept., Baton Rouge, 1965-67, head bus. adminstrn. and govt. documents dept., 1968-84, mem. faculty Sch. Library Sci., 1972-73, affiliate faculty Grad. Sch. Library Sci., 1974-81, 87; head reference East Baton Rouge Parish Library, 1984-86; assoc. info. rsch. Baton Rouge, 1984—; dir. Centroplex Br. Libr., br. mgr., 1991—. Served with Security Service, USAF, 1952-56. Mem. La. (bus. mgr. bull. 1964-65), Southwestern library assns., ALA, Spl. Libraries Assn. (nat. govt. info. service com. 1969-71), Am. Legion. Author: (with J. Norman Heard) Bookman's Guide to Americana, 6th edit., 1970, 7th edit., 1977; editor Spl. Libraries Assn. Ark., Miss. and La. chpt. Bull., 1970, La. Library Assn. Coll. Sect. Bull., 1968-80; govt. documents reviewer Reference Service Rev., 1973-81. Home: 1815 Myrtledale Ave Baton Rouge LA 70808-2871

HOOVER, PAUL WILLIAMS, JR., lawyer; b. Little Rock, Feb. 27, 1942; s. Paul Williams and Mary Elizabeth (Lasley) H.; m. Barbara Josephine Rogers, Sept. 6, 1969; 1 child, Josephine Lasley. BS, U. Ark., Little Rock, 1965; JD, U. Ark., 1969; LLM, NYU, 1970. Bar: U.S. Dist. Ct. (ea. dist.) Ark. 1969. Assoc. partner Fulk, Lovette & Mayes, Little Rock, 1970-73; mng. ptnr. Hoover Dougherty & Kooistra, Little Rock, 1973—; Dir. Met. Nat. Bank, Little Rock, 1983—. Bd. dirs. Ark. Diabetes Assn., 1974-78, Quapaw Area Boy Scouts Coun., 1976-80, Ark. Symphony Orch., 1986-89, Florence Crittendon Home, 1994. Mem. ABA, Ark. Bar Assn., Pulaski County Bar Assn., Rotary Club #99 (Little Rock), Fifty for Future, Country Club of Little Rock. Methodist. Home: 5 Edgehill Rd Little Rock AR 72207-5443 Office: Hoover Dougherty & Kooistra 11th Floor 111 Center 11th St Little Rock AR 72201-4402

HOPE, GEORGE MARION, vision scientist; b. Waycross, Ga., Jan. 24, 1938; s. George Marion and Jessie Candler (Norman) H.; m. Dorothy Marie Hendrix, Aug. 4, 1956; 1 child, Steven Richard. AB, Mercer U., 1965; MA, U. Fla., 1967, PhD, 1971. Asst. prof., rsch. assoc. U. Louisville, 1972-80; assoc. rsch. scientist U. Fla., Gainesville, 1980—; dir. low vision svc. U. Fla. Eye Ctr., U. Fla. Coll. Medicine, 1980—; co-dir. low vision clinic Dept. Ophthalmology U. Louisville, 1972-79. Contbr. numerous articles to profl. jours. Nat. Eye Inst. NIH grantee, 1975-78, 83-87. Mem. AAAS, Assn. Rsch., Vision and Ophthalmology (placement svc. 1972-84), Sigma Xi. Office: U Fla Ctr Low Vision PO Box 100284 Gainesville FL 32610-0284*

HOPE, MARGARET LAUTEN, civic worker; b. N.Y.C.; privately educated; 1 son, Frederick H., III. Mem. ball coms. various charity fund raising events. Mem. Jr. League N.Y.C., Everglades Club, Sailfish Club (Palm Beach), Women's Nat. Rep. Club (N.Y.C.), St. James Club (London). Address: Box # 601 236 Dumbar Rd Box 601 Palm Beach FL 33480-3715

HOPF, JAMES FREDRIK, lawyer; b. Taipei, Taiwan, Taiwan, Dec. 21, 1961; s. William H.; m. Julie Carole Bunch, May 22, 1982; children: Christopher James, Benjamin Thomas, Maggie Elizabeth. BA, Campbell U., N.C., 1983; JD, U. N.C., 1986. Bar: N.C. 1986, U.S. Dist. Ct. (mid. and ea. dists.) N.C. 1986, U.S. Ct. Appeals (4th cir.) 1988. Assoc. Smith, Anderson, Blount, Dorsett, Mitchell & Jernigan, Raleigh, 1986-90, Law Offices of Marvin Blount, Jr., Greenville, N.C., 1990-95; pvt. practice Law Offices of James F. Hopf, Greenville, 1995-96; ptnr. Barefoot & Hopf, L.L.P., Greenville and Raleigh, 1996—. Mem. ABA, ATLA, N.C. Bar Assn., N.C. Acad. Trial Lawyers, Order of Barristers, Omicron Delta Kappa, Phi Kappa Phi. Baptist. Office: 1694 E Arlington Blvd Ste E Greenville NC 27858

HOPKINS, B(ERNICE) E(LIZABETH), artist; b. Marinette, Wis., Mar. 7, 1926; d. George John and Hazel Aseneth (La Sage) Hohnberger; m. Arthur Stanford Hopkins, June 4, 1954; children: Kerry Gail Hopkins Stratton, Arthur Stanford Jr., Susan B. Hopkins Flessas. Student, Maryville Coll., Tenn., 1945-46. Lab. technician Boren Clinic, 1946-48, St Josephs Hosp., 1948-51, Marinette (Wis.) Med. Clinic, 1951-54; artist/promotion Northridge Lakes, 1972-83. Charter mem. LeMoyne Gallery, Tallahassee, Vis. Arts Ctr. N.W. Fla., Panama City. Mem. Pastel Soc. Am. (charter, master pastelist), Pastel Soc. N.W. Fla. (charter), Optimists Internat. (bd. dirs. Panama City Beach chpt. 1992-96). Republican. Presbyterian.

HOPKINS, DAVID LEE, medical manufacturing executive; b. Marietta, Ohio, Nov. 5, 1937; s. David Russel and Bonnie Grace (Adams) H.; m. Marcia Loretta Hopkins, Oct. 12, 1957; children: Tamara, Theresa, Tracey, David, Heidi, Wendy, Jeremy. Student, U. Dayton, 1955-57, Lorain (Ohio) C.C., 1959; BS, Ohio State U., 1960. Sales mgr. Am. Hosp. Supply, Columbus, Ohio, 1957-75; divsn. mgr. Baxter Healthcare, Stone Mountain, Ga., 1975-80; owner Hosp. Sterile Products, Stone Mountain, Ga., 1980-84; owner Angio Systems, Inc., Ducktown, Tenn., 1984—, also chmn. bd.; bd. dirs. Dalore, Inc., Ducktown, Ashfield Med., Cumbernauld, Scotland. Elder His Kingdom First Ministries. Mem. Rotary (pres. 1968-87, bd. dirs. 1990-91, Presdl. Citation 1987, Paul Harris fellow 1988), Copper Basin Area C. of C. (bd. dirs., pres.). Office: Angio Systems Inc PO Box 760 7 Hopkins Pl Ducktown TN 37326

HOPKINS, EDWARD JOHN, lawyer; b. Newark, Oct. 22, 1952; s. Edward Francis and Mary Dorothy (Cullen) H.; m. Nancy Theresa Moran, Oct. 9, 1957; 1 child, Meaghan Elizabeth. BS, Jersey City State Coll., 1990; JD cum laude, St. Thomas U. Sch. Law, 1992; LLM cum laude, U. Fla., 1994. Bar: Fla. 1993. Detective lt. Newark Police Dept., 1974-90; sr. atty. E.J. Hopkins & Assocs., Clearwater, Fla., 1993—; adv. bd. St. Thomas Sch. Law, Miami, 1992—; honor com. U. Fla. Coll. Law, Gainesville, 1993-94. Mem. Fraternal Order Police, Patrolmen's Benevolent Assn., U. Fla. Alumni Assn., K. of C., Shillelagh Club, Emerald Soc. Roman Catholic. Office: EJ Hopkins & Assocs 2420 Enterprise Rd Ste 207 Clearwater FL 34623-1703

HOPKINS, GEORGE MATHEWS MARKS, lawyer, business executive; b. Houston, June 9, 1923; s. C. Allen and Agnes Cary (Marks) H.; m. Betty Miller McLean, Aug. 21, 1954; children: Laura Hopkins Corrigan, Edith Hopkins Collins. Student, Ga. Tech., 1943-44; BSChemE, Ala. Poly. Inst., 1944; LLB, JD, U. Ala., 1949; postgrad., George Washington U., 1949-50. Bar: Ala. 1949, Ga. 1954; registered patent lawyer, U.S.; registered profl. engr., Ga.; Can. qualified deep-sea diver. Instr. math. U. Ala., 1947-49; assoc. firm A. Yates Dowell, Washington, 1949-50, Edward T. Newton, Atlanta, 1950-62; ptnr. firm Newton, Hopkins and Ormsby (and predecessor), Atlanta, 1962-87; sr. ptnr. Hunt, Richardson, Garner, Todd & Cadenhead, Atlanta, 1987-91; ptnr. Hopkins & Thomas, 1991-95; ret., 1996; spl. asst. atty. gen. State of Ga., 1978; chmn. bd. Southeastern Carpet Mills, Inc., Chatsworth, Ga., 1962-77, Thomas-Daniel & Assocs., Inc., 1981-85, Eastern Carpet Mills, Inc., 1983-87; asst. dir. rsch., legal counsel Auburn (Ala.) Rsch. Found., 1954-55; spl. asst. atty. gen. State of Ga., 1978; chmn. bd. S.E. Carpet Mills, Inc., Chatsworth, Ga., 1962-77, Thomas-Daniel & Assocs., Inc., 1981-85, Ea. Carpet Mills, Inc.; dir. Xepol Inc. Served as lt., navigator, Submarine Service USNR, 1944-46, 50-51. Mem. ABA, Ga. Bar Assn. (chmn. sect. patents 1970-71), Atlanta Bar Assn., Am. Intellectual Property Law Assn., Am. Soc. Profl. Engrs., Submarine Vets. World War II (pres. Ga. chpt. 1977-78), Phi Delta Phi, Sigma Alpha Epsilon, Atlanta Lawyers Club, Phoenix Soc., Cherokee Town and Country Club, AtlantaSoc. Episcopalian. Home: 795 Old Post Rd NW Atlanta GA 30328-4758

HOPKINS, KAREN MARTIN, cytologist, educator; b. Summerville, S.C., Aug. 29, 1945; d. McLeod Sanchez and Leonell (Knight) Martin; m. Douglas James Hopkins, Feb. 12, 1966; children: Douglas Joel, Elizabeth April, Jonathan Martin. Cert. in cytology, Med. U. S.C., Charleston, 1966; BS, U. Tex. Med. Ctr., 1989; MA, U. Tex., 1992. Instr. cytology Med. U. S.C., Charleston, 1966-67; cytologist, supr. Med. Lab. Svcs., Dallas, 1968-70; cytologist Internat. Clin. Labs., Dallas, 1971-74; sr. cytologist Dallas Pathology Assocs., 1974-87; rsch. fellow U. Tex. S.W. Med. Ctr., Dallas, 1989-90; tng. and devel. coord. Olympus Corp., Dallas, 1991-93; instr., mgmt. and staff devel. Children's Med. Ctr. Dallas, 1993—; dir. orgn. support & client svcs. M3 The Healthcare Learning Co., Irving; cons. Tex. Med. Assn., Austin, 1990. Mem. editl. bd. Jour. Allied Health; contbr. articles to profl. jour. Bd. dirs. Thelma Boston Home for Handicapped Foster Children, Dallas, 1980-82; v.p., program chair Carrollton (Tex.)-Farmers Branch Assn. for Gifted and Talented, 1982-90; pres., v.p., projects chair Children's Found. of Episcopal Diocese of Dallas, 1971-89; neighborhood chair United Way, Dallas., 1989-90. Mem. ASTD (co-chair program com. 1994, v.p. 1995, pres.-elect 1995), Am. Coll. Healthcare Execs., Am. Soc. Healthcare, Edn. and Tng. (editl. bd., 25th anniversary com. 1994-95), Tex. Soc. Cytology, Beta Sigma Phi (pres. 1975, 87, v.p. 1974, treas. 1990, Woman of Yr. 1978, 87), Alpha Eta. Republican. Office: The Healthcare Learning Co Director M3 5215 N O'Connor Blvd # 760 Irving TX 75039

HOPKINS, LINDA ANN, school psychologist; b. Bristol, Va., Aug. 23, 1937; d. James Robert and Trula Mae (Mink) Broce; AB, King Coll., 1959; MA, East Tenn. State U., 1977, postgrad., 1977-79; postgrad. Radford U., 1978-79, U. Va., 1980-89; m. James Edwin Hopkins, Oct. 8, 1960; children: James Edwin, David Lawrence. Nat. cert. sch. psychologist. Social worker Washington County Welfare Dept., Abingdon, Va., 1959-61; social worker Bristol (Va.) Welfare Dept., 1963-65, Washington County Welfare Dept., 1965-68, Bristol Meml. Hosp., 1968-72; psychologist Washington County Public Schs., Abingdon, 1978-87; pvt. practice sch. psychology, Abingdon, 1987-91; sch. psychologist Georgetown (S.C.) Dist. Pub. Schs., 1991—; adj. prof. East Tenn. State U., 1989-91. Active Pawleys Island Rescue Squad Midway Fire Dept., Swamp Fox Players Mem. Nat. Assn. Sch. Psychologists, Phi Kappa Phi. Methodist. Home: 64 Osprey Way Georgetown SC 29440-8504 Office: Georgetown County Pub Sch Dist 305 Front St Georgetown SC 29440-3733

HOPKINS, MURIEL-BETH NORBREY, lawyer; b. Fredericksburg, Va., June 29, 1951; d. Maurice D. and Grace (Hill) Norbrey; m. L. David Hopkins, Dec. 28, 1973; children: David, Michelle. BA cum laude, Wake Forest U., 1973; JD, Coll. William and Mary, 1977. Bar: Va. 1977, N.C. 1984. Assoc. Tucker & Marsh Law Firm, Richmond, Va., 1977-78; asst. atty. gen. Commonwealth of Va., Richmond, 1978-80; asst. U.S. atty. U.S. Dept. Justice, Richmond, 1980-82, Shreveport, La., 1982-83; mgr. small bus. group Winston-Salem (N.C.) C. of C., 1985; asst. counsel Wake Forest U.,

Winston-Salem, 1985—; adj. prof. sch. law Wake Forest U., 1986; bd. dirs. Carolina Medicorp, Inc., 1989. Sec. Sawtooth Ctr. Visual Design, Winston-Salem, 1987-88; mem. Bus. & Tech. Ctr., Winston-Salem, 1987-88, Carolina Medcorp. Inc., 1989; mem. campaign cabinet United Way, 1989; bd. dirs. Urban League, Richmond, Va., 1980-82, Winston-Salem, 1985-89, Brenner Children's Hosp., 1992—, Tanglewood Found., 1993—; chmn. fundraiser United Negro Coll. Fund, 1992, 94. Mem. ABA (assoc. editor young lawyer's affiliate outreach pub.), Winston-Salem/Forsyth County Bar Assn. (exec. com. 1987-88), N.C. Bar Assn. (cle com.), The Links, Jack & Jill, N.C. Assn. Black Lawyers, Nat. Bar Assn. (continuing legal edn. com.). Baptist. Office: Wake Forest U PO Box 7656 Winston Salem NC 27109-7656

HOPKINS, PATRICIA ANNE (TRACY), advertising agency executive; b. Evanston, Ill., May 19, 1943; d. Robert John and Vivian Noreen (Van Wormer) Whalen; m. James L. Favri, June 13, 1970 (div. Aug. 1980); m. Grahame Rodger Hopkins, May 12, 1989. BFA, Marymount Coll., 1965. Exec. v.p. The Bloom Agy., Dallas, 1978-81; pres. Hopkins & Assoc., Dallas, 1981-82; pres., owner Underline, Inc., Dallas, 1982-89; exec. v.p. Strategic Promotions/The Strategic Group, Dallas, 1989-94, pres., 1994-96; prin. MBRK/The Strategic Group, Dallas, 1996—. V.p. comm. Dallas Womens Found., 1990-94, pres. 1996-97, Dallas Opera Guild, 1992-93; pres. Lone Star Coun., Camp Fire, Dallas, 1995-96. Recipient Matrix award Women in Comm., Dallas, 1983, Hall of Fame, 1995, Tops awards Dallas Advt. League, Mktg. Excellence award Mktg. Comm., 1982, Pro Comm award Bus./Profl. Advt. Assn. Mem. Assn. Promotion Mktg. Agencies Worldwide, Promotion Mktg. Assn., Mktg. Comm. Execs. Internat. (pres. 1984-85). Office: MBRK The Strategic Group 3100 Monticello Dr 6th Fl Dallas TX 75205

HOPKINS, ROBERT HOWARD, JR., internist, pediatrician, medical educator; b. Batesville, Ark., Apr. 28, 1962; s. Robert Howard and Susan Jane (Patterson) H. BS in Biology, Davidson Coll., 1984; MD, Med. Coll. Ga., 1989. Resident in pediatrics and internal medicine U. Ark., Ark. Childrens Hosp., 1989-93, asst. prof. medicine, 1993—. Fellow Am. Acad. Pediatricians; mem. Am. Coll. Physicians. Presbyterian. Home: 415 North Monroe St Little Rock AR 72205

HOPKINS, SALLYE F., women's health nurse; b. Waco, Tex., Jan. 17, 1928; d. Gerald P. and Birdie Mae (Peters) Ferguson; m. Aeron Hopkins, Aug. 22, 1950 (dec.); children: Cathy (dec.), Eddie, Beth. Diploma, Hillcrest Meml. Hosp., 1948; student, Baylor U. Health nurse Tri-County Health Nurse, Newton, Tex.; shift supr., labor/delivery Hillcrest Med. Ctr., Waco; dir. nurses Merryville (La.) Gen. Hosp.; staff nurse Newton (Tex.) County Meml. Hosp., 1990. Baptist. Home: PO Box 12 Newton TX 75966-0012

HOPKINS, SHARON MATTOX, orthodontist; b. Burbank, Calif., July 29, 1953; d. James David and Barbara (Duncan) Mattox; divorced; 1 child, James Ashley. AB, Westeyan Coll., 1975; DDS, Emory U., 1979, cert. in orthodontics, 1981. Pvt. practice in orthodontics Douglasville, Ga., 1981—; med. staff Inner Harbour Hosp., Douglasville, 1981—. Mem. ADA, Am. Assn. Orthodontists, West Ga. Dental Study Club (pres. 1984-85).

HOPKINS, SIDNEY WAYNE, agriculturist; b. Borger, Tex., Apr. 27, 1958; s. Wayne Franklin and Loyce Jayne H.; m. Holly Beth White, July 25, 1981; children: Bradley Wayne, Bethany Gayle. BS in Entomology, Tex. A&M U., 1980, M of Agriculture in Entomology, 1983, PhD in Entomology, 1993. Cert. profl. crop cons.; cert. entomologist, cert. crop adv. Ext. agt. entomologist Tex. Agriculture Ext. Svc., Sinton, 1980-83; prin. Hopkins Agriculture Svcs., Portland, Tex., 1983—; spkr. Beltwide Cotton Conf., New Orleans, 1984, San Diego, 1994, San Antonio, 1995, Agriculture Chem. Co., 1984—. Contbr. articles to profl. jours. Youth basketball coach YMCA, Portland and Corpus Christi, Tex., 1988—; youth baseball coach Gregory/Portland Little League Assn., 1988—; softball umpire alt. San Patricio Girls Softball Assn., 1990-95; judge at area sci. fairs, Tex., 1983—. Mem. Entomological Soc. Am. (cert.), Nat. Alliance Ind. Crop Cons., Tex. Agrl. Crop Cons., Weed Sci. Soc. Am., Century Club. Republican. Methodist. Home and Office: Hopkins Agrl Svcs 1801 Oak Ridge Dr Portland TX 78374-2909

HOPKINS, WILLIAM B., golf course management group executive. BS in Turfgrass Mgt., Auburn U. Class A PGA profl. Head profl. Amelia Links, Amelia Island Plantation; dir. golf Magnolia Point Country Club, Green Cove Springs, Fla.; head profl. Wade Hampton Golf Club, Cashiers, N.C.; from project mgr. to gen. mgr. River's Edge Golf Club, Fayetteville, Ga.; project mgr. Champions Club, Fayetteville, Ga.; mktg. dir., staff adminstr. Champions Club, Atlanta; pres. Riverside Golf Mgmt. Co., Jacksonville, Fla. Office: Riverside Golf Group Inc 111 Riverside Ave Ste 330 Jacksonville FL 32202-4929

HOPKINS, ZORA CLEMONS, training and development specialist; b. Burleson County, Tex., Nov. 19, 1945; d. Otto and Rubie Lee (Sams) Clemons; children: Thean, Aikia. BA in Elem. Edn., Incarnate Word Coll., San Antonio, 1968; MA in Early Childhood Edn., East Tex. State U., 1974; MEd in Ednl. Adminstrn., Prairie View A&M U., 1979. Tchr. Dallas Ind. Sch. Dist., 1968-88, staff trainer, 1988-89, specialist III, 1989-92, specialist in tng., 1992-94; vice prin. Roger Q. Mills Elem. Sch., Dallas Ind. Sch. Dist., 1994—; curriculum writer Dallas Ind. Sch. Dist., 1987-89, monitor for sch. improvement plan, 1989-92; revision team mem. Texas Assessment Academic Skills Test State of Texas, 1992. Advisor Oratorical Club, Dallas, 1987—; counselor Ch. of Christ Youth Club, Dallas, 1970—, mem. site based decision making team, 1993; vol. tutoring program, Dallas, 1988—; organizer Neighborhood Beautification, Dallas and Cedar Hill, Tex., 1987—; mem. adv. com. infusion multicultural edn. Cedar Hill Ind. Sch. Dist. Mem. ASCD, Internat. Reading Assn., Nat. Assn. for Young Children, Nat. Staff Devel. Coun. Tex. Staff Devel. Coun., Tex. Assn. Adminstrs. and Suprs. of Programs for Young Children, Phi Delta Kappa. Home: 218 N Waterford Oaks Dr Cedar Hill TX 75104-2324 Office: Roger Q Mills Elem Sch 1515 Lynn Haven Ave Dallas TX 75216-1323

HOPPE, LEA ANN, elementary education educator; b. Birmingham, Ala., Mar. 20, 1959; d. George Carson and Annie Merle (Carleton) Jones; m. David Thomas Hoppe, Nov. 21, 1983; children: Kathryn Ann, Emily Louise. BS in Edn., Samford U., Birmingham, 1981; MA in Edn., U. Ala., Tuscaloosa, 1986. Cert. tchr., Ala. Reading tutor Pearson's Reading & Math. Ctr., Birmingham, 1979-81; kindergarten tchr. Scottsboro (Ala.) City Schs.-Brownwood, 1981-86; pre-kindergarten tchr., ctr. dir. First Bapt. Learning Ctr., Scottsboro, 1986-89; kindergarten tchr. Covenant Weekday Kindergarten, Huntsville, Ala., 1990-95, Randolph Sch., Huntsville, 1995—; chmn. bd. dirs. First Bapt. Child Devel. Ctr., Huntsville, 1992—; conf. leader Samford U., Birmingham, 1993, Farley Elem. Parents Orgn., Huntsville, 1994. Author: (children's activity books) A Child For All Seasons: Volume 1, 1994, Volume 2, 1994. Children's choir dir. First Bapt. Ch., Huntsville, 1991—, children's Sunday Sch. tchr., 1993—. Mem. Nat. Assn. Edn. Young Children, So. Early Childhood Assn., Ala. Assn. Young Children, Delta Omicron (life), Kappa Delta Pi, Kappa Delta Epsilon, Pi Gamma Mu, Omicron Delta Kappa. Republican. Baptist. Home: 2911 Barcody Rd Huntsville AL 35801 Office: Randolph Sch 1005 Drake Ave SE Huntsville AL 35802-1036

HOPPE, WILLIAM CHARLES, military officer; b. Fort Carson, Colo., Feb. 17, 1961; s. William Henry and Phylis Jean (Weston) H.; m. Deanna Michelle Foster, July 4, 1987; children: Ashley Michelle, Sean Patrick, Christopher Ronald. BS in Gen. Engring., U.S. Mil. Acad., West Point, 1983; MS in Computer Sci., Naval Postgrad. Sch., Monterey, Calif., 1992. Commd. 2d lt. U.S. Army, 1983, advanced through grades to maj., 1995; platoon leader U.S. Army Berlin (Germany) Brigade, 1984-87; co. comdr. Co. B 5th Battalion, 16th Infantry, Fort Riley, Kans., 1987-90; with U.S. Army Info. Systems, Fairfax, Va. Mem. IEEE (assoc.), Am. Assn. Artificial Intelligence, VFW (life), Am. Legion, KC (charter mem., recorder, chancellor 4 deg.). Republican. Roman Catholic. Home: 10412 Forney Loop Fort Belvoir VA 22060-1842

HOPPER, ARTHUR FREDERICK, biological science educator; b. Plainfield, N.J., Sept. 7, 1917; s. Arthur Frederick and Catherine (Hoenig) H.; m. Amy Patricia Hull, Dec. 28, 1940 (dec. Nov. 1982); children: Arthur Frederick, Geoffrey Victor, Christopher James, Gregory Lorton; m. Patricia Ann Vennett, Sept. 6, 1986. AB, Princeton U., 1938; MS, Yale U., 1942; PhD, Northwestern U., 1948. Instr. Northwestern U., Evanston, Ill., summer 1948; asst. prof. Wayne U., Detroit, 1948-49; asst. prof. to prof. Rutgers U., New Brunswick, N.J., 1949-80, dir. biol. scis. grad. program, 1973-75; rsch. assoc. Brookhaven (N.Y.) Nat. Lab., 1961-68; visiting prof. U. Liège Med. Sch., Belgium, 1967-68; prof. emeritus Rutgers U., New Brunswick, 1980—; rsch. assoc. Detroit Cancer Inst., 1948-49; scientist aboard Columbia U. R/V "Vema", summer, 1955, 58; vis. investigator Battelle N.W., Richland, Wash., summer 1970, Jackson Meml. Lab., Bar Harbor, Maine, summers, 1971, 73. Author: Foundations of Animal Development, 1st ed. 1979, 2nd ed. 1985; contbr. articles to profl. jours. Chmn. troop 53 Boy Scouts Am., Bedminster, N.J., 1953-58; v.p., pres. Bedminster Bd. Edn., 1957-63; coach, mgr. Far Hills Little League Baseball, 1954-56; pres. Somerset County Bd. Edn., Somerville, N.J., 1960-63; coord. radiology def. Somerset County, 1959-63; bd. dirs. Palm Beach County Kidney Assn., Lake Worth, Fla., 1988-90, mem. med. adv. bd., 1993—. 1st lt. USAAF, 1943-46; lt. col. USAFR, 1946-68. Rsch. grantee NSF, USPHS, Am. Cancer Soc., Lalor Found, Rutgers U. Rsch. Coun., 1950-80. Mem. AAAS, Soc. Integrative and Comparative Biology, Soc. Devel. Biologists, Sigma Xi. Home: 231 Cocoanut Row Palm Beach FL 33480-4132

HOPPER, MARGARET SUE, academic administrator, educational diagnostician, consultant; b. New Gulf, Tex., Feb. 8, 1937; d. Thomas Clinton and Margaret Evelyn (McDaniel) Letts; m. Rufus Denman Hopper Jr., Apr. 7, 1955; children: Lloyd Wade, Nancy Marie. BS, Sam Houston State U., 1960, MEd, 1973. Cert. reading specialist, ednl. disgnostician, tchr. of mentally retarded and learning disabled elem. students, elem. edn. tchr. Tchr. Jarrell (Tex.) Ind. Sch. Dist., 1960-67; tchr. Lohn (Tex.) Ind. Sch. Dist., 1967-68, Brady (Tex.) Ind. Sch. Dist., 1968-70; tchr. Huntsville (Tex.) Ind. Sch. Dist., 1970-78, spl. edn. tchr., 1978, edn. diagnostician, 1978-80; pre-lab. student tchr. Sam Houston State U., 1971-78; edn. diagnostician Carrollton (Tex.)-Farmers Branch Ind. Sch. Dist., 1980-85, instructional diagnostician, 1985-88, instructional facilitator, 1988-91, edn. diagnostician, 1991-92; pvt. practice as ednl. cons., diagnostician, tchr. appraiser, 1992-94; inclusion specialist Huntsville, 1994-95; supr. student tchrs. Sam Houston State U., 1995—; mem. Bd. Registry-Diagnostician #0522, Houston, 1984—. Mem. Tex. Ednl. Diagnostician's Assn., Tex. State Tchr.'s Assn., Tex. Retired Tchr.'s Assn. (legis. com. 1995), Alpha Chi. Methodist. Home and Office: PO Box 1536 Huntsville TX 77342-1536

HOPPER, VANESSA J., oncological nurse; b. Port Hueneme, Calif., Feb. 6, 1955; d. Richard E and Ruth Ellen (Ober) Bird; m. Bennie J. Hopper, Jr., Dec. 8, 1984; 1 child, Bennie J. III. BSN, U. Tex., San Antonio, 1978. RN, Tex.; cert. in ACLS; cert. oncology nurse. Staff nurse Met. Gen. Hosp., San Antonio; head nurse S.W. Oncology Assocs., P.A., San Antonio, 1982-95; nurse South Tex. Oncology and Hematology, P.A., San Antonio, 1995-96; nurse mgr. Tex. Oncology, P.A., San Antonio, 1996—. Mem. Oncology Nurses Soc. (cert.). Home: 5915 Woodridge Cv San Antonio TX 78249-3115 Office: Tex Oncology PA Ste 720 7940 Floyd Curl Dr San Antonio TX 78229

HOPPES, LOWELL ELLARD, cartoonist; b. Alliance, Ohio, July 4, 1913; s. Wilson William and Forrest Rebecca (Stamp) H.; m. Lucille Elsie Rardon (dec.); children: Bruce Michael, Jenny Lynn. Freelance cartoonist; currently presenting a new type of cartoon humor for mags. Contbr. 39,500 cartoons to mags. worldwide, including Colliers, Post, New Yorker, Cosmo, Esquire, Farm Journal, Nation's Biz, King Features. Mem. United Comml. Travelers. Home: 642 Calle Del Otono Sarasota FL 34242-1958

HOPPLE, JEANNE M., adult nurse practitioner; b. Pitts., Nov. 2, 1955; d. John Andrew and Esther Ruth (Seitz) Dettis; m. William H. Hopple II, May 21, 1977; children: Mary Christine, Melissa Jeanne, Matthew John. BSN, U. Pitts., 1977; MSN, U. South Fla., 1993. RN, Fla.; cert. adult nurse practitioner, cardiovascular clin. specialist, case mgr. in cardiovascular surgery, critical care nurse. Staff nurse CCU, med. ICU S.W. Fla. Regional Med. Ctr. and Healthpark Med. Ctr.-Lee Meml. Hosp., Ft. Myers; clin. educator angioplasty and med. critical care S.W. Fla. Regional Med. Ctr., Ft. Myers, cardiac patient educator; edn. specialist in med. nursing, dept. ednl. svcs. Lee Meml. Hosp., Ft. Myers; clin. specialist, acute care practitioner, case mgr. Charlotte Regional Med. Ctr., Punta Gorda, Fla., 1995—. Mem. AACCN (past local treas.), Fla. Nurses Assn., Advanced Practice Nursing Coun. S.W. Fla., Masters RN Group, Sigma Theta Tau. Home: 23381 Van Buren Ave Port Charlotte FL 33980 Office: Charlotte Regional Med Ctr 809 E Marion Ave Punta Gorda FL 33950-3819

HOPPMANN, RICHARD ANTHONY, physician; b. Charleston, S.C., Aug. 20, 1950; s. Harry Joseph and Dorothy Gadsen (Couturier) H.; m. Anne Griffin Harman, May 331, 1975; children: Emily, Karla, Nicholas. BS, U. S.C., 1972; MS, U. Ga., 1978; MD, Med. U. S.C., 1982. Diplomate Am. Bd. Internal Medicine, subspeciality rheumatology. Resident internal medicine East Carolina U. Sch. Medicine, Greenville, N.C., 1982-85; rheumatology fellow Bowman Gray Sch. Medicine, Wake Forest U., Winston-Salem, N.C., 1985-87; ast. prof. medicine East Carolina U. Sch. Medicine, Greenville, 1987-90; chief rheumatology med. svcs. Dorn Vets. Hosp., Columbia, S.C., 1990—; assoc. prof. medicine, dir. divsn. allergy, immunology U. S.C. Sch. Medicine, Columbia, 1990—. Mem. editorial bd. Med. Problems of Performing Artists, 1992—; contbr. articles to profl. jours. Recipient VA Commendation-Profl. Leadership, 1993. Fellow ACP, Am. Coll. Rheumatology; mem. AMA, Internat. Arts Medicine Assn., Nat. Assn. VA Physicians and Dentists, Performing Arts Medicine Assn. (mem. policy com.), S.C. Rheumatology Assn. Home: 6042 Hampton Leas Ln Columbia SC 29209-1963 Office: U SC Sch Medicine Med Libr Bldg Columbia SC 29208

HOPSON, MARY LOUISE CARSTENS, marketing consultant; b. Alexandria, La., Nov. 17, 1956; d. Carl Rand and Sally Randolph (Pitts) Carstens; m. David Carlisle Hopson, Apr. 17, 1982; 1 child, Stuart Randolph. BA in Journalism, La. State U., 1978. Corp. law cert. The Phila. Inst., 1978. Corp. legal asst. Tex. Instruments Inc., Dallas, 1979-81; mgr. corp. legal affairs Natural Resource Mgmt. Corp., Dallas, 1981-84; mgr. bus. devel. Haynes & Boone, Dallas, 1984-90; dir. practice devel. Calhoun, Gump, Spillman & Stacy, Dallas, 1990-93; pvt. practice profl. svcs. mktg. cons. Dallas, 1993—; free-lance writer, 1993—; lectr. in field. Contbr. articles to profl. jours. Mem., bd. dirs. Dallas Tex. Exes, 1987-94, Ctr. for Nonprofit Mgmt., Dallas, 1988-89. Mem. Nat. Law Firm Mktg. Assn. (bd. dirs. 1989-90), Profl. Svcs. Mktg. Assn. (dir. 1987-89, founder 1987), Jr. League Dallas, Chi Omega Alumnae Orgn. Republican. Episcopalian. Office: Suite 102 LB184 6110 E Mockingbird Lane Dallas TX 75214

HOPTON, JANICE, elementary school principal. Prin. Skyway Elem. Sch., Opa Locka, Fla. Office: Skyway Elem Sch 4555 NW 206th Ter Opa Locka FL 33055-1248

HORAHAN, EDWARD BERNARD, III, lawyer; b. Drexel Hill, Pa., Dec. 30, 1951; s. Edward Bernard and Ann Veronica (Schneeweis) H.; m. Rebecca Joy Fusco, Mar. 13, 1976; 1 child, Elizabeth Joy. BA, LaSalle Coll., Phila., 1973; JD, Yale U., 1976. Bar: D.C. 1976. Staff atty. office of gen. counsel SEC, Washington, 1976-78; staff atty. office of solicitor, plan benefits security div. U.S. Dept. Labor, Washington, 1978-80; assoc. Arter & Hadden, Washington, 1980-84; ptnr. Parker, Chapin, Flattau & Klimpl, Washington, 1984-88, Stroock & Stroock & Lavan, Washington, 1988-93; propr. Law Offices of Edward B. Horahan III, Washington, 1993-96; counsel Groom and Nordberg, Chtd., McLean, 1996—. Mem. ABA. Office: Ste 600 888 16th St NW Washington DC 20006

HORD, ALLEN HENRY, medical educator; b. Louisville, Sept. 4, 1957; s. Charles Richard and Jessie (Boles) H.; children: Emilly Manning, Jane Lyle; m. Terry Lynn Haber, Jan. 8, 1994; 1 child, Cheryl Ann. BA, Vanderbilt U., 1979; MD, U. Ky., 1983. Diplomate Am. Bd. Anesthesiology, Am. Bd. Pain Medicine. Resident Emory U. Sch. of Medicine, Atlanta, 1986, asst. prof., 1987—, dir. divsn. pain medicine, dept. anesthesiology, 1994—. Editor: Acute Pain: Mechanisms and Management, 1992, (monograph) Analgesia Advances, 1993. U. Cin. fellow, 1987. Office: Emory U Hosp Dept Anesthesiology 1364 Clifton Rd NE Atlanta GA 30322

HORKAN, ALICIA M., nursing educator; b. Cin., Oct. 3, 1953; d. William B. Moody and Lu Alice (Gibson) Pope; m. George A. Horkan III, June 11, 1988; children: Amy Morgan, Lisa Kent. ADN, ABAC, Tifton, Ga., 1985; BSN, Ga. Southwestern Coll., 1990; MSN, Valdosta State U., 1993. RN. From asst. nurse mgr. dialysis to nurse mgr. critical care Colquitt Regional Med. Ctr., Moultrie, Ga., 1985-90; cardiac rehab. Palmyra Med. Ctrs., Albany, Ga., 1990-92; instr. Valdosta (Ga.) State U., 1992—; adv. bd. Care One Colquitt Co., Moultrie, 1995—. Bd. dirs. Am. Heart Assn., 1995. Recipient nurses alumni award Ga. Southwestern Coll. Sch. Nursing, 1990. Mem. Am. Assn. Critical Care Nurses, Emergency Nurses Assn., Sigma Theta Tau. Home: PO Box 1931 Moultrie GA 31776 Office: Valdosta State U 1300 N Patterson St Valdosta GA 31601-3925

HORKOWITZ, SYLVESTER PETER, chemist; b. Lansford, Pa., Sept. 7, 1921; s. Simeon and Mary (Leshefka) H.; m. Olga Assaf, Sept. 12, 1964. Student, Kans. State Coll., Pittsburg, 1948-51. Chemist Spencer Chem. Co., Pittsburg, 1946-51; chief chemist Spencer Chem. Co., Vicksburg, Miss., 1951-56; rsch. mgr. Spencer Chem. Co., Orange, Tex., 1956-61; v.p. Spencer Chem. Far East, Tokyo, 1961-65; chem. mgr. Far East Gulf Oil Corp., Tokyo, Singapore, Bangkok, 1965-72; cons. chemist New Orleans, 1972—; cons. chemist New Orleans, 1972—; bd. dirs.; chmn. A-Jin Chem. Co., Pusan, Republic of Korea, 1965-68; adv. bd. Pertamina Gulf, Djakarta, Indonesia, 1969-71; bd. dirs. chmn. Gulf Plastics-Singapore. Contbr. articles to profl. jours. With U.S. Army, 1942-46. Mem. ASTM, Am. Oil Chemists Soc., Soc. Plastics Engrs., Am. Chem. Soc. Republican. Byzantine Catholic Ch. Home and Office: 5700 Ruth St Metairie LA 70003-2330

HORN, ANDREW WARREN, lawyer; b. Cin., Apr. 19, 1946; s. George H. and Belle (Collin) H.; m. Melinda Fink; children: Lee Shawn, Ruth Belle. B.B.A. in Acctg., U. Miami, 1968, J.D., 1971. Bar: Fla. 1971, Colo. 1990, U.S. Dist. Ct. (so. dist.) Fla. 1972, U.S. Tax Ct. 1974. Ptnr. Gillman & Horn P.A., Miami, Fla., 1973-74; pvt. practice Miami, 1974—. Active civic coun. Children's Hosp., Miami. Recipient Am. Jurisprudence award Lawyers Coop. Pub. Co., 1970. Mem. ABA, Fla. Bar, Assn. Trial Lawyers Am., Acad. Fla. Trial Lawyers.

HORN, GEOFFREY MICHAEL, writer, editor; b. N.Y.C., Nov. 22, 1944; s. Louis and Elizabeth (Laderman) H.; m. Marcia Luise Davidson, June 25, 1967; children: David, Michael. AB, Columbia Coll., 1965; BA, St. Johns Coll., Cambridge, Eng., 1967, MA, 1972. Editor Macmillan Inc., N.Y.C., 1968-75; writer, editor, 1975—; project editor Behrman House, West Orange, N.J., 1976—; sr. editor Funk and Wagnalls New Ency., Mahwah, N.J., 1984—; exec. editor Worldmark Press, N.Y.C., 1980-84. Author: (with Arthur Cavanaugh) Bible Stories for Children, 1980, Barron's Book Notes: The Old Testament, 1986, (with Abba Eban) Heritage: Civilization and the Jews, 1984; contbr. articles to profl. publs. E.J. Kellett fellowship Columbia U., 1965. Mem. Phi Beta Kappa. Jewish. Home and Office: Rt 1 Box 95 Ferrum VA 24088

HORN, JOSEPH ROBERT, IV, priest; b. Selma, Ala., Oct. 9, 1953; s. Joseph Robert III and Jean Elizabeth (Haden) H.; m. Martha Holmes McGougan, July 9, 1977; children: Martha Legare, Joseph Robert V. BA in English, Coll. of Charleston, 1976; MDiv, Va. Theol. Sem., 1981. Ordained deacon Episcopal Ch., 1981, ordained priest, 1982. Vicar St. Matthias Episc. Ch., Summerton, S.C., 1981-84; assoc. rector Christ Ch., Savannah, Ga., 1984-88; rector Episc. Ch. of Holy Spirit, Lafayette, La., 1988-95, St. Paul's Episc. Ch., Foley, Ala., 1995—; bd. dirs., v.p. Victorous Ministry Through Christ, Winter Park, Fla.; registrar Bishop's Scholar Program, Diocese of S.C., 1982-84, Commn. on Youth, 1981-84; co-chair Youth Commn., Diocese of Ga., 1987-88, edn. for ministry mentor; bd. dirs. Family Life of Savannah, Savannah Care Ctr.; mem. exec. com. Diocese of Western La., 1993-95; mem. Commn. on Personal Spiritual Growth Diocese of Ctrl. Gulf Coast, 1996—. Author: A Mis-Used Label, The Living Church, 1991. Home: 1712 Burtonwood Dr Foley AL 36536 Office: Saint Paul's Episc Ch PO Box 1745 Foley LA 70598-0085

HORN, LEWIS MARTIN, business analyst; b. Bklyn., May 28, 1965; s. Charles and Fay (Zuckerman) H.; m. Jerrel Ruth Bond, July 25, 1992. AA, Broward Community Coll., 1987; BS, Calif. State U., Dominguez Hills, 1993. Cardmember svcs. rep. Am. Express Co., Fort Lauderdale, Fla., 1984-87; sr. cost acct. Am. Comml. Inc., Carson, 1987-92; ind. cons. L.M. Horn & Assocs., Gardena, Calif., 1992-93; cardmem. svcs. rep. Am. Express Co., Ft. Lauderdale, Fla., 1993-95; bus. analyst Am. Express Co., Ft. Lauderdale, 1995—. Author: (computer software) Vic Autodialer, 1984, Comnet BBS, 1985, InterStore, 1992, JV, 1992. Mem. Nat. Assn. Rocketry, Am. Radio Relay League, Nature Conservancy. Democrat. Home: 6314 Ocean Dr Margate FL 33063-7023 Office: Am Express 777 American Expy Fort Lauderdale FL 33337

HORN, PATRICIA SOLOMON, technology curriculum facilitator; b. Quincy, Fla., Oct. 17, 1944; d. Thomas William and Mary Margaret (Lecky) Solomon; m. Phillip W. Horn Jr., May 14, 1965; children: Phillip W. III, Thomas W. BA, Jacksonville U., 1965; MEd, U. North Fla., 1988-91, EdD, 1996. Cert. elem. tchr., Fla. Tchr. 2d and 3d grades Newberry (Fla.) Sch., 1965-68; tchr. kindergarten Dept. of Def. Schs. Overseas, Madrid, Spain, 1969-79, Lackawanna Elem. Sch., Jacksonville, Fla., 1979-85; tchr. kindergarten, sch. improvement chair Webster Sch., St. Augustine, Fla., 1987-93; facilitator for integrated curriculum and tech. St. Johns County Sch. Dist., St. Augustine, Fla., 1993—; technology cons. Fulbright Commn., Egyptian Ministry Edn., 1996. Contbr. chpts. to Handbook of Literacy Assessment and Evaluation, and articles to profl. jours. Den leader Cub Scouts Am., Jacksonville, Fla., 1978-84; bd. dirs. Boy Scouts Am., Jacksonville, 1979-84; pres., sec. St. Johns County Med. Aux., 1987-94; bd. dirs. Childbirth and Parenting Edn. Assn. (1991-94), mem. Tech. Resource Com. for Fla. Accountability Commn., Tallahassee, 1994. Mem. ACSD (Tech. Futures Commn. 1994-95), Fla. League Tchrs. (charter, adv. bd. 1992—), Fla. Assn. Computers in Edn. (Fla. Instrnl. Tech. Tchr. of Yr. award 1994), Internat. Reading Assn., Internat. Soc. for Tech. in Edn. (Internat. Tech. Tchr. of Yr. award 1994, cons. to Fulbright Commn. of the Middle East and Egyptian Ministry of Edn. 1996), Nat. Coun. Tchrs. English and Lang. Arts, Alpha Delta Kappa, Phi Kappa Phi. Democrat. Roman Catholic. Home: 6 Versaggi Dr Saint Augustine FL 32084-6926 Office: Saint Johns County Sch Dist 40 Orange St Saint Augustine FL 32084-3633

HORNBACK, BERT GERALD, English language educator, writer; b. Bowling Green, Ky., Dec. 22, 1935; s. Vernon Theodore and Mary Elizabeth (Borrone) H. AB, U. Notre Dame, Ind., 1957, AM, 1961; attended, Trinity Coll., Dublin, Ireland, 1961-62; PhD, U. Notre Dame, Ind., 1962-64. Lt. U.S. Marine Corps., 1957-60; instr. in English U. Notre Dame, 1963-64; instr. in English U. Michigan, Ann Arbor, 1964-65, asst. prof. English, 1965-70, assoc. prof. English, 1970-74, prof. English, 1974-92; vis. prof. English Univ. Coll., Dublin, 1990-91; prof. humanities Bellarmine Coll., Louisville, Ky., 1992—; dir. Ctr. for the Advancement of Peripheral Thought, Ann Arbor, 1982—; dir. Honors Program Bellarmine Coll., Louisville, 1993—. Author: (books) Noah's Architecture: A Study of Dickens, 1972, The Hero of My Life: Essays on Dickens, 1981, Middlemarch: A Novel of Reform, 1988, King Richard the Catsup, 1971; actor: Recreation of Charles Dickens' Readings From His Novels, 1974—. Chmn. Teach-In Against The War in Iraq, Ann Arbor, 1990, Lectures Against The War in Vietnam, Ann Arbor, 1967-70; mem. Campaign for Nuclear Disarmament, London, 1961—. Mem. English-Speaking Union (v.p. Ky. branch 1994—, scholarship coord. 1994—), Ctr. for the Advancement of Peripheral Thought (founder, dir. 1982—), Dickens Soc. Am. (dir., v.p., pres. 1970—), Dickens Fellowship (sec. Ann Arbor branch 1979-86), Soc. Bremen Scholars. Mem. Neopolitan Catholic Ch. Home: 1701 Trevilian Way Louisville KY 40205 Office: Bellarmine Coll Newburg Rd Louisville KY 40205

HORNBERGER, ROBERT HOWARD, psychologist; b. Trenton, N.J., Jan. 26, 1933; s. Jennings Howard and Leah Margaret (Lewis) H.; m. Anne Deshon Lyman, June 11, 1958; children: Lynn Diane, Todd Lyman. BA, Amherst Coll., 1954; MA, U. Iowa, 1957, PhD, 1957. Lic. psychologist, Fla.; cert. Family Mediator, Fla. Instr. to assoc. in med. psychology U. Nebr. Coll. Medicine, Omaha, 1958-62; staff psychologist Nebr. Psychiat. Inst., Omaha, 1958-62; chief psychologist Drs. Young, Wigton & Aita, Omaha, 1962-65; dir. Eastern Maine Guidance Ctr., Bangor, 1965-68; assoc. dir. The Counseling Ctr., Bangor, 1968-69; lectr. in psychology U. Maine,

Orono, 1966-69; dir. psychology tng. VA Med. Ctr., Gainesville, Fla., 1969-81; asst. to assoc. adj. prof. U. Fla., Gainesville, 1969—; staff psychologist VA Med. Ctr., Gainesville, 1981—; bd. advisors Fla. Mental Health Inst., Tampa, 1987-95; psychologist pvt. practice, Gainesville, 1976-85, 90—. Contbr. articles to profl. jours. Founder, 1st pres. Sugarfoot Cmty. Improvement Assn., 1972; pres. Mental Health Assn. Alachua County, Gainesville, 1981, Mental Health Assn. Fla., Tallahassee, 1987, Planned Parenthood Nebr., Omaha, 1963; comdr. Gainesville Power Squadron, 1995-96. Mem. Fla. Psychol. Assn. (pres. north ctrl. chpt. 1996). Democrat. Unitarian. Home: 4056 NW 23rd Cir Gainesville FL 32605-2683 Office: DVA Med Ctr Psychology Svc # 116B Gainesville FL 32608

HORNE, KENNETH CHESTER, minister; b. Woonsocket, R.I., Apr. 26, 1946; s. Kenneth Chester and Pauline Frances (Randall) H.; m. Jean Elizabeth Kelley, Aug. 5, 1969; children: Jonathon David, Sean Michael, Jennifer Kathleen. BA in Geology, U. Va., 1968; MBA, Coll. William and Mary, 1971; MDiv, Southeastern Bapt. Theol. Sem., Wake Forest, N.C., 1976; DDiv, Shenandoah Coll., Winchester, Va., 1990. Ordained minister United Meth. Ch. Asst. plant mgr. Craddock-Terry Shoe Corp., Dillwyn, Va., 1971-73; deacon United Meth. Ch., Boydton, Va., 1974-77, elder, 1977; dir. Highland Larger Parish United Meth. Ch., Highland County, Va., 1977-79; co-dir./co-founder Soc. of St. Andrew, Big Island, Va., 1979—; adv. bd. Breedlove Dehydrated Food, Inc., Lubbock, Tex., 1993—. Prodr./performer worship music: Occasional Songs, 1989, Prepare the Way of the Lord, 1986; co-author: A Hungry Word/A Responsive Church, 1981. Coord. Gunstock Creek Coop., Big Island, Va., 1980-81; exec. bd. Bedford Christian Ministries Assocs., 1985-92; vice chmn. Bedford Against Nuclear Dumping, 1986; com. chmn. Va. Congress on Hunger, 1986—, Rural Va. Coalition, 1989—; chmn. agrl. mission United Meth. Vols. in Mission, 1989—; mem. Traveling Musicians Workshop; chmn. environ. concerns Va. Bd. Ch. and Soc., 1991—; bd. dirs. Bedford Area YMCA, 1990-91, Food Chain, 1995—. With U.S. Army, 1968-71. Named one of "100 Real Hero's" for civic contbns. Maxwell House Coffee, Inc., Nashville, 1992; recipient Letter of Commendation Pres. Ronald Reagan, 1985. Mem. Internat. Platform Assn. Home: RR 5 Box 192 Bedford VA 24523-9333 Office: Society of Saint Andrew PO Box 329 State Rt 615 Big Island VA 24526

HORNE, LITHIA BROOKS, finance executive; b. Troy, N.C., Nov. 2, 1951; d. Tom Stewart and Anne Grace (Ward) Brooks; 1 child, Leslie Grace Hahn. AS in Bus. Adminstrn. Acctg., Wingate U., 1972. Cert. govtl. acctg. and fin. reporting, county adminstrn., acctg. and fiscal control, budgeting and fin. planning, effective mgmt.; cert. local govtl. fin. officer. Fin. officer Stanly County, Albemarle, N.C., 1972-86; dir. fiscal ops. Brunswick County, Bolivia, N.C., 1986—. Participant conf. Nat. Assn. Counties, Anaheim, Calif., 1988-89, Miami, Fla., 1990-91, legis. conf. NACO, Washington, 1987-88, GFOA Nat. Conf., Orlando, Fla., 1992-93, 1995-96. Named N.C. Outstanding Fin. Officer, 1991-92. Mem. Govt. Fin. Officers Assn., N.C. Assn. County Finance Officers (sec.-treas. 1988-89, 2nd v.p. 1989-90, 1st v.p. 1990-91, pres. 1991-92, chmn. legis. com. 1992-93, mem. nom. com. 1994—), N.C. Cash Mgmt. Trust (chmn., adv. bd. 1987-88), NAFE, Nat. Assn. County Finance Officers and Treasurers, Carolinas Assn. Govt. Purchasers. Home: PO Box 249 Bolivia NC 28422-0249

HORNE, MARK J., lawyer; b. Mobile, Ala., June 20, 1960; s. Herbert Boyd and Vivian (Shofner) H.; m. Suzanne Underberg, Oct. 4, 1986. BS in Polit. Sci. and Criminology, Fla. State U., 1983; JD, Stetson U., 1986. Bar: Fla. 1987, U.S. Dist. Ct. (Mid. dist.) 1987. Assoc. Kosto & Rotella PA, Jacksonville, Fla., 1987-90; pvt. practice atty. Jacksonville, 1991—. Home: 12876 Plummer Grant Rd Jacksonville FL 32258-4109

HORNE, THOMAS LEE, III, entrepreneur; b. Athens, Ga., Dec. 21, 1950; s. Thomas Lee and Roberta Eldridge (Brunby) H.; m. Karen Blair, 1972 (div. 1980); m. Skeater Jane Doster, 1982 (div. 1985). BA, Stetson U., 1972. Mechanic Durham Motors, New Orlrans, 1973-74; parts man Ferguson Pontiac, Daytona Beach, Fla., 1976-80; salesman Noels Salvage, Orlando, Fla., 1980-84; owner, mgr. Dourphous Enterprises, Orlando, 1980—; pres. Brumby Enterprises, Franklin, La., 1992—; mgn. ptnr. Horne Partnership, Franklin, 1992—; trustee Brumby Family Trust, Franklin, 1985—; treas. Riggs Land Corp., Franklin, 1992—. Mem. Loyal Order Moose. Libertarian. Unitarian. Office: Dourphous Enterprises PO Box 5349 225 Main St Unit 12 Destin FL 32540-0189 also: Dourphous Enterprises 1803 Crown Way PO Box 547881 Orlando FL 32541 also: Aycock Horne 519 Main St PO Box 999 Franklin LA 70538

HORNER, CARL STUART, English language educator; b. Cleve., Apr. 24, 1945; s. Carl S. Jr. and Dorothy Alberta Straub (Kurtz) H.; m. Helane Marie Turner, June 11, 1969; children: Carmen Marie, Holly Kristin. BA in English, Ea. Ky. U., 1968; MA in English, Ind. U., 1972; PhD in English, Fla. State U., 1989. Tchr. English Little Miami H.S., Morrow, Ohio, 1968-71, Bolles Sch., Jacksonville, Fla., 1973-78; sales rep., dir. pub. rels. Sta. WKDF-WKDA, Nashville, 1979-82; chairperson dept. English Brentwood Acad., Nashville, 1982-85; assoc. prof. English, dir. creative writing Flagler Coll., St. Augustine, Fla., 1989—; dir. Flagler Coll. Colloquium, 1989—, Flagler Coll. Writers' Workshop, 1989—; co-dir. St. Augustine Writers' Conf., 1996—. Author: The Boy Inside the American Businessman, 1992; contbr. poem to: (anthology) North of Wakulla, 1989; contbr. poetry and revs. to lit. publs.; editor: Flagler Rev., 1989—. Mem. MLA, South Atlantic MLA, Phi Kappa Phi, Sigma Tau Delta. Republican. Presbyterian. Office: Flagler Coll Dept English PO Box 1027 Saint Augustine FL 32085

HORNER, JOHN EDWARD, former college president; b. Passaic, N.J., Dec. 12, 1921; s. William Joseph and Cardera Estelle (Bissell) H.; m. Anne Catherine Evans, Aug. 16, 1952; children: Joanne Horner Woerner, Jefrey John, heather Horner Hohlt, Scott Edward. AB cum laude, Drew U., 1943; AM, Columbia U., 1947; PhD, Ohio State U., 1955; LLD (hon.), Ind. U., 1978, Drew U., 1971, Ind. State U., 1979, Wabash Coll., 1978, Hanover Coll., 1986; LittD (hon.), Morehead State U., 1975, Heidelberg Coll., 1990. Tchr. English, coach baseball, football Morristown (N.J.) H.S., 1945-49; instr. Latin and English Drew U., Madison, N.J., 1950-52; asst. prof., dir. athletics Kans. Wesleyan U., Salina, 1952-53; adminstrv. asst. Ohio State U., Columbus, 1954-56; asst. to pres., dean grad. sch. U. Omaha, Nebr., 1956-58; pres. Hanover (Ind.) Coll., 1958-87, pres. emeritus, 1987—; cons./examiner North Ctrl. Assn., Chgo., 1956-87. Contbr. articles to profl. jours., chpts. to books. Chmn. Ind. State Scholarship Commn., Indpls., 1977-79; pres. Presbyn. Coll. Union, Phila., 1963-64; ruling elder Presbyn. Ch., Hanover, 1967—; chmn. bd. dirs. Historic Madison, Inc., 1981-87; pres. Ind. State Libr. and Historic Bd., Indpls., 1974-87; chmn. Ind. State Student Assistance Commn., 1977-79. With USAAF, 1943-44. Named Sagamore of the Wabash, Gov. of Ind., 1964, 79, 83, Ky. Col., 1967; Phi Beta Kappa fellow, 1943; Fulbright scholar, 1949-50. Mem. Am. Assn. Pres. of Pvt. Colls. and Univs. (pres. 1978-80). Republican. Presbyterian. Home: Pebble Creek 706-A Constitution Dr Durham NC 27705

HORNER, MARGO ELIZABETH, municipal official; b. Norfolk, Va., Aug. 14, 1947; d. Samuel Watson II and Elizabeth (O'Connell) H. BA in History, Old Dominion U., 1970, MA in History, 1973; cert. legal asst., Georgetown U., 1974; MS in Mgmt., Nat.-Louis U., 1993. Legis. aide to Del. Warren G. Stambaugh Va. Gen. Assembly, Richmond, 1978; sr. legis. and corp. paralegal Kirkpatrick & Lockhart, Washington, 1974-82; legis. analyst Nat. Fedn. Ind. Bus., Washington, 1982-84; acct. exec. Johnston and Lemon, Washington, 1984-85; editor Bur. Nat. Affairs, Washington, 1986-87; dep. commr. revenue Office the Commr. Revenue, Arlington, Va., 1987—; legal asst. adv. bd. Georgetown U.; writer, cons. in field. Pres. Nat. Capital Paralegal Assn., Washington, 1976-78; bd. dirs. Nat. Fedn. Paralegal Assn., Washington, 1976-78; chmn., vice chmn., sec., ARC, 1978—; chmn. Election Officials Adv. Com., Washington Met. Coun. Govts.; chmn. Arlington Com. 100, 1990-91, Arlington County Dem. Com., 1987-91, 8th Dist. Dem. Com., Va., 1993, Arlington Electoral Bd., 1982-87; mem. Va. Electoral Bd. Assn., 1982-87; mem. 10th Dist. Dem. Com. 1987-91; com. Status of Women, 1976; exec. com. United Way; mem. steering com. Va. Dem. Party, 1993; active Sheriff's Office Citizen's Advisement Com., Arlington, 1987—; vice-chmn., sec. Arl Com. 100; mgmt. Vets. Meml. YMCA, Arlington, 1978—; bd. vis. George Mason U., 1993; com. mem. Va. Gov. Commn. on Campaign Reform, Govt. Accountability and Ethics, 1992; bd. dirs. Sister City Assn., Arlington, 1993, treas. 1995—; sec., dir. Fairlington Civic Assn., Del., Arl. Civic Fed., 1994—. Named Outstanding Young Woman of Am., 1979, Outstanding Young Woman of Va., 1979, Outstanding Young Dem., 1981, 84, Arlington (Va.) Outstanding Young Dem., 1991, Outstanding Dem., 1993, Arlington County Govt. Exceptional award, 1994. Mem. AAUW (life), Women in Govt. Rels., '94 Leadership Am., Am. Polit. Items Collectors. Roman Catholic. Home: 3057 S Buchanan St # B-2 Arlington VA 22206-1515 Office: Office the Commr Revenue #1 Courthouse Pla 2100 Clarendon Blvd Ste 200 Arlington VA 22201-5445

HORNSBY, BRUCE RANDALL, composer, musician; b. Richmond, Va., Nov. 23, 1954; s. Robert Stanley and Lois (Saunier) H.; m. Kathy Yankovich, Dec. 31, 1983. BA, U. Miami, Coral Gables, Fla., 1977. Recording artist; albums include The Way It Is, 1986 (double platinum award, gold award Eng., Platinum award Can., gold award Germany, gold award Australia), Scenes from the Southside, 1988 (platinum award, gold award Eng., platinum award Can.), A Night on the Town, 1990 (gold award Can., silver award Eng.), Harbor Lights, 1993 (gold award), Hot House, 1995; composer numerous songs including The Way It Is (Song of Yr. ASCAP 1987), Mandolin Rain, Jacob's Ladder, Every Little Kiss, Valley Road, Look Out Any Window, Defenders of the Flag, On the Western Skyline, The End of Innocence, Across the River, Lost Soul, Fields of Gray, Rainbow's Cadillac, Walk in the Sun, Spider Fingers; performed on records by Bob Dylan, The Grateful Dead, Rock and Roll Hall of Fame Concert Album, Tin Cup soundtrack, Bonnie Raitt, Bob Seger, Squeeze, Cowboy Junkies, Huey Lewis, Nitty Gritty Dirt Band, Chaka Khan, others. Recipient Best New Artist Grammy award, 1986, Best Bluegrass Rec. Grammy award, 1989, Best Pianist Keyboard Mag., 1987, 88, 89, 90, 91, 93; Best Song of Yr. Grammy nomination, 1989, Record of Yr. Grammy nomination, 1989, Best Performance by a Duo or Group Grammy nomination, 1990, Best Original Score Emmy award, 1987, Best Pop Instrumental Grammy award for "Barcelona Mona" with Branford Marsalis, 1994, Best Pop Instrumental Grammy nomination for "Star Spangled Banner" with Branford Marsalis, 1995, Best Pop Instrumental Grammy nomination for "Song B", 1995, Best Song Written for a Motion Picture "Love Me Still" with Chaka Khan Grammy nomination, 1995; winner Best Beyond album Downbeat Reader's Poll, 1994. Home: PO Box 3545 Williamsburg VA 23187-3545

HORNSBY, (E.C.) SONNY, judge. Chief justice Ala. Supreme Ct., Montgomery, 1989—. Office: Judicial Bldg 300 Dexter Ave Montgomery AL 36104-3741

HOROWITZ, DAVID HARVEY, dermatologist; b. New Haven, Jan. 13, 1945; s. Philip and Frances Gertrude (Spivack) H.; m. Katarina Bracker Biggs, May 1, 1971 (div. May 1976); m. Shirley Griggs Daniels, May 1, 1983; children: Joseph, Michael, Brian. BA in Chemistry, Emory U., 1966; MD, Meharry Med. Coll., 1970. Resident U. Cinn. Med. Ctr., 1973, fellow, 1974; asst. prof. Meharry Med. Sch., Nashville, 1974-75; pvt. practice Nashville, 1975—; clin. asst. prof. internal medicine Meharry Med. Sch., 1975—; asst. prof. divsn. dermatology Vanderbilt U. Med. Ctr., 1992—. Maj. U.S. Army, 1970-76. Home: 219 Brook Hollow Rd Nashville TN 37205-3503 Office: 1916 Patterson St Nashville TN 37203-2120

HOROWITZ, JUDITH ANNE, dean; b. Rochester, N.Y., June 25, 1937; m. Donald L. Horowitz; children: Marshall, Karen, Bruce. AB in English, Syracuse U., 1959, AM in English and Am. Lit., 1962. Lectr., professorial lectr. English edn. sch. edn. Am. U., Washington, 1972-81, dir. planning and evaluation, 1978-79, co-dir. African educators program, 1978-80, dir. tchr. edn., 1979-81; internat. advisor Fuqua sch. bus. Duke U., Durham, N.C., 1983-91, dir. internat. programs, 1991-93, internat. advisor sch. law, 1981-86, asst. dean internat. studies, 1986-89, assoc. dean internat. studies, 1989—; assoc. dir. summer program gifted and talented students sch. edn. Am. U., 1980; mem. accreditation rev. team Nat. Assn. State Dirs. Tchr. Edn. and Cert., 1981; mem. Fuqua sch. admissions com. law sch., 1989-94, mem. coun. internat. ctrs. and programs, 1992—; mem. subcom. admissions to bar N.C. State Bar, 1989-90; mem. selection panel Benjamin Franklin and Edmund S. Muskie Fellowship Program Law, 1992—; vis. scholar Canterbury U. Sch. of Law, New Zealand. 1995-96; speaker, cons. in field. Contbr. articles to profl. jours. Scholar N.Y. State Regents, Syracuse U. Mem. Nat. Assn. Fgn. Student Affairs, Assn. Am. Law Schs. (mem. exec. com. sect. grad. law programs fgn. law grads. 1987-88, 90-93, chair 1988-89, chair various sessions at ann. meetings 1989, 92, 93). Office: Duke U School Law Durham NC 27708

HOROWITZ, PAUL MARTIN, photographer, electronic technician; b. Phila., Nov. 18, 1936; s. Ben and Reba Horowitz; m. Paula Rose Horowitz, Jan. 1, 1978. Grad. in Electronics, Radio Electronic Inst., Phila., 1960; grad. in Photography, N.Y. Inst. Photography, 1962. Cert. engr., photographer. Photographer, real estate investor; technician GE, RCA, IBM. Author: Florida Oar Bust, 1990, The Condo Commandos, 1994; author (screenplay) The Condo Commandos, 1996; co-author (with Paula Rose Horowitz) 2 novels, 1 screenplay. With U.S. Army, 1956-58. Mem. Profl. Photographers Inc. Home: 8849 Old Kings Rd S Jacksonville FL 32257

HOROWITZ, SUSAN AMY, pathologist and cytopathologist; b. Jersey City, Jan. 2, 1957; d. Leo and Nona Joyce (Huberman) H. BS with honors summa cum laude, Tulane U., 1978; MD with honors, Baylor Coll. of Medicine, 1982. Diplomate Am. Bd. Pathology. Intern in internal medicine Baylor Coll. Medicine, Houston, 1982-83; resident in dermatology U. Miami, Fla., 1983-84; resident in pathology U. South Fla., Tampa, 1985-89, fellow in cytopathology, 1989-90; pathologist, med. dir. Roche Biomed. Labs., Inc. (now Lab Corp. of Am., holdings), Clearwater, Fla., 1990-95; pathologist and med. dir. Hernando County Lab., Inc., Springhill, Fla., 1992—; pathologist Lab Corp. of Am., Tampa, Fla., 1995—; clin. asst. prof. pathology U. South Fla., Tampa, 1990-94, voluntary faculty in pathology, 1994—. Mem. AMA, Am. Med. Women's Assn. (Achievement award 1982), Coll. Am. Pathologists, Am. Soc. Clin. Pathologists, Am. Soc. Cytology, Fla. Med. Assn., Fla. Soc. Pathologists, Pinellas County Med. Soc., Fla. West Coast Assn. Pathologists. Office: Lab Corp of Am holdings 5610 W La Salle St Tampa FL 33607-1770

HORSBURGH, BEVERLY, law educator; b. Albany, N.Y., June 5, 1942; d. Isadore and Frances Drapkin; m. Donald Horsburgh; children: Elizabeth, Lawrence. BA, Smith Coll., 1964; JD, U. Miami, 1987. Bar: Fla. 1988. Assoc. prof. St. Thomas U. Sch. Law, Miami, 1988—. Contbr. articles to profl. jours. Mem. ABA (family law sect.), Fla. Bar Assn. (gender equality subcom.), Assn. Am. Law Schs. (women in legal edn. sect.).

HORTON, DONNA ALBERG, technical writer; b. Newport, Ky., Sept. 2, 1935; d. Donald Hyatt and Virginia Margaret (Bauer) Mincey; m. Frederick Albert Alberg, July 16, 1962 (div. 1980); children: Stephanie Alberg Obringer, Jenee, Nicole Alberg; m. William Michael Horton, Sept. 29, 1985. Student, Cin. Conservatory of Music, 1953; BA, Ea. Ky. U., 1957, 60, MA, 1961; postgrad., U. South Fla., 1981. Cert. tchr. Fla., Ky. Tchr. Flint (Mich.) Pub. Sch. System, 1957-59; head dept. art Titusville High Sch., Brevard County, Fla., 1961-63; tchr. Toledo (Ohio) Pub. Schs., 1964-68; feature writer St. Petersburg (Fla.) Times, 1978-79; instr. spl. edn. Pinellas County (Fla.) Pub. Schs., 1979-82; tech. writer, computer specialist MAV/Strategic div. Honeywell Inc., Clearwater, Fla., 1982—; lectr. in field; profl. tech. speaker and comml. writer; symposia speaker. Contbg. writer Cin. Times Star, 1949-53, Richmond Register, 1953-61, Titusville Star Advocate, 1961-63, Toledo Blade, 1964-68; author children's plays: Holiday Presentation, 1957-59; contbr. articles to profl. jours. Mem. Flint Community Chorus, 1957-59; head vols. Largo (Fla.) Pub. Libr., 1975-79; mem. Messiah Choir, Clearwater, 1988-89. Mem. Soc. Logistics Engrs. (sr., treas. 1983-85, workshop organizer), Profl. Tech. Writers Assn., Sigma Xi Mu (chpt. pres. 1954-57), Alpha Chi Epsilon. Democrat. Roman Catholic. Home: 3717 Mckay Creek Dr Largo FL 34640-4515 Office: Honeywell Inc 13350 Us Highway 19 N Clearwater FL 34624-7226

HORTON, FINIS GENE, management services company executive; b. Batesville, Ark., Jan. 3, 1953; s. Allie George and Zelda (Brooks) H. BA, Ark. Coll., 1974; postgrad., Ark. State U., 1974-75, U. Cen. Ark., 1976. Asst. v.p., cost mgr. Worthen Bank, Little Rock, 1975-81; contr. First Fed. Bank of Morrilton, Ark., 1981-82; bank auditor Superior Fed. Bank, Little Rock, Ft. Smith, Ark., 1982-91; mng. dir. Audit Svcs. Group, Little Rock, Ark., 1991-95; pres., owner Corp. Bus. Svcs., Little Rock, 1991—; bd. dirs. Corp. Bus. Svcs. Am. Inc. Mem. Nat. Fin. Assocs., Kiwanis (pres. Little Rock 1978-79, bd. dirs. 1979-81). Home: 5 Palmer Dr Conway AR 72032-9484 Office: PO Box 1352 Conway AR 72033-1352

HORTON, FRANCIS KNAPP, manufacturing executive, industrial engineer; b. Atlanta, Oct. 2, 1944; s. John Gibson and Jennie Hazleton (Knapp) H.; m. Charlotte Anne Reele, June 11, 1966 (dec. July 1989); children: David Alexander, Amy Reele. BS in Indsl. Engring., Ga. Inst. Tech., 1966, MS in Indsl. Engring., 1967; postgrad., U. Ala., 1991—. Indsl. engring. supr. Tenneco/Newport News (Va.) Shipbuilding Dry Dock Co., 1968-72; mgr. advanced mfg. engring. Tenneco-Westinghouse Offshore Power Systems, Jacksonville, Fla., 1972-75; sr. engring. supr. Gen. Dynamics Elec. Boat Div., Groton, Conn., 1975-77; prin. engr. Teledyne-Brown Engring., Hunstville, Ala., 1977-78; chief engr. Automatic Screw Products, Decatur, Ala., 1978-92; v.p. Automatic Screw Products, 1993—; judge Decatur pub. schs., jr. coll. sci. fairs. Mem. Am. Assn. Lab. Accreditation, Soc. Mfg. Engrs., Am. Soc. Quality Control, River City Kiwanis. Office: Automatic Screw Products PO Box 1608 709 2d Ave SE Decatur AL 35602

HORTON, FREDERICK TYRON, JR., child psychiatrist; b. Durham, N.C., Feb. 26, 1943; m. Virginia Reynolds; 2 children. BS in Zoology, N.C. State U., 1966; MD, Med. Coll. of Va., 1970. Diplomate in psychiatry and child psychiatry Am. Bd. Psychiatry and Neurology; diplomate Nat. Bd. Med. Examiners; lic. physician, Va., Tenn. Intern Vanderbilt U. Hosp., Nashville, 1970-71, resident in psychiatry, 1971-73, fellow in child psychiatry, 1973-75; asst. prof. child psychiatry Vanderbilt U. Sch. Medicine, 1975-77, asst. clin. prof., 1977-92, assoc. clin. prof., 1992—, dir. tng. divsn. child psychiatry, 1976-77; pvt. practice child psychiatry Nashville, 1977—; cons. Westminster Individualized Teaching Ctr., Nashville, 1978-79; staff psychiatrist Centennial Med. Ctr., St. Thomas Hosp., Vanderbilt U. Hosp., Psychiat. Hosp. at Vanderbilt; mem. grievance com. Nashville Acad. Medicine, 1981-83. Contbr. articles to profl. jours. Fellow Am. Acad. Child and Adolescent Psychiatry, Am. Psychiat. Assn.; mem. AMA (Physician's Recognition award 1979, 82, 85, 88, 91, 94), Tenn. Psychiat. Assn. (mem. ins. com. 1979-81, ethics com. 1977-82)), Tenn. Acad. Child and Adolescent Psychiatry, Tenn. Med. Assn., Phi Sigma Soc. Office: 4535 Harding Rd Ste 102 Nashville TN 37205-2120

HORTON, GRANVILLE EUGENE, nuclear medicine physician, retired air force officer; b. Jean, Tex., July 2, 1927; s. James Granville and Etna (Boyle) H.; B.A., Tex. Technol. Coll., 1950; M.D., U. Tex., 1954; m. Mildred Helen Veale, June 13, 1953; children: Linda Kay, Kevin Bruce, Carson Scott. Intern, Detroit Receiving Hosp., 1954-55; tng. in radioactive isotope techniques Oak Ridge Inst. Nuclear Studies, 1958; practice medicine, Weslaco, Tex., 1955-56, Outlar-Blair Clinic, Wharton, 1956-72; dir. dept. nuclear medicine Nightingale Hosp., El Campo, Tex., 1973-75; mem. staff Horton Med. Clinic, El Campo, 1972-75; part-time research assoc. radioisotope dept. Meth. Hosp., Houston, 1961-66; mem. med. adv. com. and sec. med. staff Caney Valley Meml. Hosp., Wharton, 1956-72; clin. dir. Wharton County TB Assn., 1957-67; commd. lt. col. U.S. Air Force, 1975; postgrad. U.S. Air Force Sch. Aerospace Medicine, 1975; chief aeromed. services Brooks AFB, Tex., 1976-82. Bd. dirs. Wharton County div. Am. Cancer Soc., pres., 1960-61; dir. 8th dist. Tex., Citizens Com. for Hoover Report, 1957-58. Served with USN, 1946-47. Fellow Am. Coll. Angiology (state gov. 1979), Am. Coll. Nuclear Medicine; mem. Am. Coll. Emergency Physicians, Wharton C. of C. (dir., v.p. 1960-61), Am., Tex. (ho. of dels. 1959-61) med. assns., Soc. Nuclear Medicine, Tex. Assn. Physicians Nuclear Medicine, AAAS, Law Enforcement Officers Tex. (asso.), Am. Nuclear Soc., Tex. Med. Found., El Campo C. of C., Phi Chi. Republican. Episcopalian. Lodge: Elks. Contbr. articles to med. publs. Home: 15102 Oakmere St San Antonio TX 78232-4623 Office: Occupational Med Clinic 2200 Mccullough Ave San Antonio TX 78212-3751

HORTON, JERRY SMITH, minister; b. Columbus, Miss., Oct. 6, 1941; s. William Robert and Sarah Elizabeth (Smith) H.; m. Patricia Jan Taylor, May 30, 1964; children: Thomas Christian, William Andrew. AA, Wood Jr. Coll., 1963; BA in Edn., U. Miss., 1968; MDiv, Emory U., 1972. Ordained to ministry United Meth. Ch., 1973. Min. various chs. in Miss. and Ga., 1962-72; assoc. min. Southaven (Miss.) 1st United Meth. Ch., 1972-74; min. Minor Meml. United Meth. Ch., Walls, Miss., 1974-81; parish dir. Iuka (Miss.) 1st United Meth. Ch., 1981-84; min. Belzoni (Miss.) 1st United Meth. Ch., 1984-91, Fulton (Miss.) 1st United Meth. Ch., 1991-92, Holly Springs (Miss.) 1st United Meth. Ch., 1992-95, Long Beach (Miss.) 1st United Meth. Ch., 1995—; mem. bd. diaconal ministries No. Miss. Conf., United Meth. Ch., 1972-74, mem. commn. on equitable salaries, 1981-90, conf. ins. com., 1990-94; head chaplain vol. chaplaincy program in local hosp. Bd. dirs. Habitat for Humanity, Marshall County; active Vol. Chaplaincy Program in local hosp., North Miss. chpt. Emmaus Walk Cmty. in Miss., Citizen Vols. Against Crime, 1994 Class Competitive Cmty. Program, Marshall County; trustee Rust Coll., 1992-95; trustee Internat. Seamen and Trucker Ctr., Gulfport, 1996—. Named one of Outstanding Young Men of Am., Internat. Jaycees, 1976, Top Evangelistic Pastor of Conf., 1981; honored with Spl. Proclamation, Mayor of Iuka; Estaral scholar. Mem. Rotary. Office: 1st United Meth Ch 208 Pine St Long Beach MS 39560-6041

HORTON, JOHN ERNEST, motion picture industry consultant; b. Davenport, Iowa, Jan. 3, 1919; s. Leroy Francis and Beatrice Olga (Abramson) H.; m. Drucie Snyder, Jan. 26, 1950; children: Evlyn Spencer, Elizabeth Snyder, Jon Dru. B Pub. Adminstrn., U. Mo., 1940. Location mgr. Warner Bros. Pictures, Burbank, Calif., 1946-48; chief motion pictures Dept. Army and Dept. Def., Washington, 1948-50; mil. aide to Pres., The White House, Washington, 1949-50; Washington rep. Universal Pictures Co., 1950-55; prodn. exec., prodr. Universal Pictures Co., Universal City, Calif., 1955-59; cons. to motion picture industry John E. Horton Assocs., Washington, 1959—; v.p., bd. dirs. Doremus and Co., Washington, 1971-80; cons. to def. industry Ryan Aero./Continental Motors, Washington, 1965-72; cons. Univ. Support Svcs., Washington, 1987—; Washington rep. Alliance Motion Picture and TV Prodrs., 1987-95. Chmn. pub. rels. U.S. Olympic com., 1968-72; cons. on pub. affairs Pres.'s Coun. on Pub. Fitness and Sports, Washington, 1973-90; co-chmn. 21st Century Fund, Harry S. Truman Libr. Inst., Independence, Mo., 1993-96; trustee Charleston Mus., 1992—, v.p. bd. trustees; bd. dirs. Harry S. Truman Libr. Inst., 1996—. Lt. col. inf. U.S. Army, 1940-46, MTO. Recipient commendation res. forces policy bd. Dept. Def., 1956, cert. of achievement Dept. Army, 1961. Mem. Acad. Motion Picture Arts and Scis., Met. Club, Burning Tree Club (Bethesda, Md.), Seabrook Island Club, Phi Gamma Delta. Episcopalian. Home: 3108 Up Da Creek Johns Island SC 29455-6075 Office: 1301 K St NW Ste 725 East Washington DC 20005-3317

HORTON, MADELINE MARY, financial planner, consultant; b. Chgo., Mar. 1, 1939; d. James P. and Priscilla Mary (Caruso) Fiduccia; m. Richard J. Dickman, July 7, 1962 (div. 1981); children: James Earl, Suzanne Dickman Noel; m. Larry B. Horton, June 30, 1984 (dec. 1993). BA in Math. cum laude, Rosary Coll., River Forest, Ill., 1960; MS in Math., U. Miami, Coral Gables, Fla., 1962; postgrad., U. Va., 1974-78. Cert. fin. planner. Instr. in math. U. Miami, Coral Gables, 1962-63, Miami Dade C.C., 1964-65, St. Patrick's High Sch., 1968-69; prin. Dickman Deductions, Charlottesville, Va., 1974-77; instr. devel. math. Piedmont Community Coll., Charlottesville, Va., 1974-78; health affairs planner U. Va. Med. Ctr., Charlottesville, 1978-80; zone mgr. Investors Diversified Svcs., Inc., Charlottesville, 1980-83; fin. cons. Merrill Lynch, Charlottesville, 1983-86; mgr., fin. cons. Prudential-Bache Securities, Inc., Charlottesville, 1986-87; investment broker Wheat First Securities Inc., Charlottesville, 1987; pres., fin. cons., founder Horton Fin. Svcs. Inc., Charlottesville, 1987—. Humor columnist Charlottesville Daily Progress, 1971; featured in article Va. Bus. monthly mag., 1988. Mem. Internat. Mgmt. Coun. (sec. Charlottesville chpt. 1986-88, v.p. 1988-89), Inst. Cert. Fin. Planners, Internat. Platform Assn., Kappa Gamma Pi. Republican. Roman Catholic. Home: 3346 Arbor Terrace Charlottesville VA 22901-7227 Office: Horton Fin Svcs Inc 1160 Pepsi Pl Ste 300 Charlottesville VA 22901-0807

HORTON, ODELL, federal judge; b. Bolivar, Tenn., May 13, 1929; s. Odell and Rosa H.; m. Evie L. Randolph, Sept. 13, 1953; children: Odell, Christopher. AB, Morehouse Coll., 1951; cert., U.S. Navy Sch. Journalism, 1952; JD, Howard U., 1956; HHD (hon.), Miss. Indsl. Coll., 1969; LLD (hon.), Morehouse Coll., 1983. Bar: Tenn. 1956. Pvt. practice law Memphis, 1957-62; asst. U.S. atty. Western Dist. Tenn., Memphis, 1962-67; dir. div. hosp. and health services City of Memphis, 1968; judge Criminal Ct. Shelby County, Memphis, 1969-70; pres. LeMoyne-Owen Coll., Memphis, 1970-74; commentator Sta. WREC-TV (CBS), Memphis, 1972-74; judge U.S. Dist. Ct. (we. dist.) Tenn., 1980—, chief judge, 1987; mem. Jud. Conf. of U.S. Com. on Defender Svcs.; chair com. to establish a Death Penalty Resource Ctr., Nashville. Bd. mgrs. Meth. Hosp., Memphis, 1969-79; bd. dirs. Family Svc. Memphis, United Negro Coll. Fund, N.Y.C., 1970-74. With USMC, 1951-53. Recipient Disting. Alumni award Howard U., 1969, L. M. Graves Meml. Health award Mid-South Med. Ctr. Coun., Memphis, 1969, Bill of Rights award West Tenn. chpt. ACLU, 1970, Disting. Service award Mallory Knights Charitable Orgn., 1970, Disting. Service award Smothers Chapel C.M.E. Ch., 1971, Outstanding Citizen award Frontiers Internat., 1969, Ralph E. Bunche Humanitarian award Boy Scouts Am., 1972, Outstanding Educator and Judge award Salem-Gilfield Bapt. Ch., 1973, Spl. Tribute award A.M.E. Ch., 1974, United Negro Coll. Fund award, 1974, Humanities award Citizens Com. Coun. of Memphis, 1969, Shelby County Penal Farm award, 1974, Disting. Service award LeMoyne-Owen Coll., 1974, Disting. Service award Lane Coll., 1977, Dedicated Community Service award Christian Meth. Episc. Ch., 1979. Mem. NAACP, ABA (sr., chair conf. fed. trial judges, jud. adminstrn. divsn., chair exec. com. nat. conf. fed. trial judges 1994-95). Office: 957 Fed Bldg 167 N Main St Memphis TN 38103-1816

HORTON, THOMAS MARK, futures and options trader, commodity consultant; b. San Angelo, Tex., Dec. 14, 1952; s. Lee Bascom and Mary Jane (Nash) H.; m. Shannon Green, July 18, 1987 (div. Sept. 1990). BS, Tex. A&M U., 1975. Self employed rancher San Angelo, 1976; v.p. Rolling Plains Prodn. Credit Assn., Childress, Tex., 1976-79, Western Prodn. Credit Co., Guymon, Okla., 1979-80, Agrow Credit Corp., Amarillo, Tex., 1980; account exec. Procom Co., Inc., Chgo., 1981; ptnr. Hennessey & Assocs., Chgo., 1981-85; account exec. Linnco Futures, Inc., Chgo., 1985; pres., futures cons., advisor commodities Horton Futures Advisory, Inc., Amarillo, 1985—; ptnr. Green-Horton & Assocs., Amarillo, 1987-89; fin. cons. Procom Co., Inc., 1981, Shearson-Lehman-Hutton, Amarillo, 1989-90, Merrill Lynch, Pierce, Fenner & Smith, Amarillo, 1990—; tech. analyst Hales Cattle Letter, 1989—. Mem. Civic Ctr. for Performing Arts, Chgo., 1983-85, Newberry Libr., Chgo., 1984-85, Lone Star Ballet, Amarillo, 1986-88, Panhandle Plains Hist. Mus., 1991—; patron Amarillo Symphony, 1988-89. Served to 1st lt. U.S. Army, 1975-76. Mem. Chgo. Mercantile Exch., Chgo. Rice & Cotton Exch., Nat. Futures Assn., Trout Unltd., Ducks Unltd., Exec. Club. Methodist. Home: 6303 Gainsborough Amarillo TX 79106 Office: Horton Futures Adv PO Box 892 Amarillo TX 79105-0892

HORTON, WILFRED HENRY, mathematics educator; b. Newark, Nottingham, Eng., May 27, 1918; s. Henry and Alice M. (Spence) H.; m. Margaret E. Haskard; children: Richard, Sheila, David, Jennifer. BSc in Math. with honors, U. Coll., Nottingham, 1940; Engr., Stanford U., 1959. With De Havilland Aircraft Co., Hatfield, Eng., 1940-45, Percival Aircraft, Luton, Eng., 1945-50; sr. sci. officer Royal Aircraft Establishment, Farnborough, Eng., 1950-54, prin. sci. officer, 1954-57; assoc. prof. Stanford (Calif.) U., 1959-67; prof. Ga. Inst. Tech., Atlanta, 1967-84; prof. emeritus U. System Ga., 1985—; cons. various orgns. Contbr. articles to profl. jours. and encys.

HORTON, WILLIAM ALAN, structural designer; b. Ft. Benning, Ga., Dec. 29, 1955; s. William Howard and Edith Marjorie (Amick) H.; m. Laurie Lynn Sewell, Sept. 6, 1986. AAS, Midlands Tech. Coll., 1975; BS, David Lipscomb U., 1980. Sr. drafter Nat. Convenience Stores, Inc., Houston, 1981-87, Morris and Assocs., Inc., Houston, 1987-88; sr. designer Fluor Daniel, Inc., Sugar Land, Tex., 1988—. Judge skill olympics Vocat. Indsl. Clubs Am., Houston, 1990, San Antonio, 1991. Mem. Church of Christ.

HORVAT, VLADIMIR, physicist, research scientist; b. Zadar, Croaţia, Jan. 23, 1958; s. Stanislav and Blaženka (Kostelnik) H.; m. Leonarda Šimićev, Dec. 20, 1980; children: Darijana, Oliver. BS in Physics, U. Zagreb, Croatia, 1980, MS in Physics, 1984, PhD in Physics, 1988. Teaching and rsch. asst. U. Zagreb, 1981-89; postdoctoral rsch. assoc. Tex. A&M U., College Station, 1989-92, asst. rsch. scientist, 1992—. Contbr. sci. papers to conf. procs., profl. jours. Mem. Am. Phys. Soc. Roman Catholic. Office: Tex A&M Univ Cyclotron Inst College Station TX 77843-3366

HORVATH, CAROL MITCHELL, home health administrator; b. Cleve., Aug. 7, 1940; d. Ralph Douglas and Hazel (Carpenter) Mitchell; m. William R. Horvath, Aug. 2, 1958; children: Kenneth R., Rosalie C. Stallcup. AS, Tulsa Jr. Coll., 1977, AD Nursing, 1977; BS in Profl. Arts, St. Joseph Coll., 1992; MPH, Okla. U., 1995. Cert. Gerontological Nurse. Cons. home health McCurtain Meml. Hosp., Idabele, Okla., 1989; dir. home health Okla. Home Health, Cleveland, Okla., 1980-1985; regional adminstr. Okla. Home Health, Cleveland, 1985-96; home health adminstr. Cleveland Area Hosp., 1985-96; dir. Helping Hands Program COEDD Grant Program for Aging, 1990-96; CPR instr. trainer AHA, 1990-91; nursing cholesterol trainer, 1990-96, home health nursing aide instr., 1990-96; cons. home health Mission Hill Hosp., Shawnee, Okla.; dir. home health East Tex. Med. Ctr., Mt. Vernon, 1996—. Mem. profl. adv. com. Area Agy. on Aging; active Cleve. Sch. Edn. coalition, Elderly Edn. coalition, Health Promotion coalition, Okla. Bus. and Aging Leadership coalition. Mem. Home Health Assn., Rehab. Assn., Am. Heart Assn., Pawnee County Svc. Network, Am. Coll. Healthcare Execs., Pub. Health Assn., Okla. Nurses Assn., Okla. Health and Welfare Assn. Home: 113 Oak St Mount Vernon TX 75457 Office: East Tex Med Ctr Mt Vernon Home Health Box 477-500 Hwy 37 South Mount Vernon TX 75457-3033

HORVATH, JOHN, JR., English language educator. BA in English, Peabody Coll. of Vanderbilt U.; MA in English, Fla. State U., PhD in Am. Lit. Purdue U., 1980-86; Assoc. prof. Am. Lit. Tougaloo (Miss.) Coll., 1990—, chair dept. English, 1992—, chair Commn. on Writing and the Humanities, 1991-92; Rsch. asst. to dir. Am. studies Purdue U., 1980-86; vis. instr. Fla. A&M U., 1979-80; presenter in field. Author: I Am a Child, 1971, Cain's Country: A Volume of Oral Poetry, 1977, Calumet Border Crossing, 1979, The Certain Uncertainty of the Text: Essays on Literature as Conflict/Controversy, 1989; contbr. numerous poems, articles to profl. publs.; editor Tougaloo College Faculty Handbook, 1992. Bush Faculty Devel. grantee, 1992-93. Office: Tougaloo Coll Dept English Tougaloo MS 39174

HOSEY, SHERYL LYNN MILLER, university health facility administrator; b. Phila., May 15, 1968; d. Roger Lee and Janice Catherine (Myers) M.; m. John William Hosey, July 8, 1994. AA, Bucks County C.C., Newtown, Pa., 1989; BFA summa cum laude, Va. Commonwealth U., 1992. Cert. secondary sch. tchr., Va., Pa. Instr. drama Va. Commonwealth U., Richmond, 1989-92; program support technician Va. Commonwealth U./Med. Coll. Va., Richmond, 1992—; proofreader, editor. Mem. NEA, Va. Edn. Assn., Theatre Edn. Assn., Nat. Coun. Tchrs. English, Va. Assn. Tchrs. English, Phi Kappa Phi. Home: 1430 Floyd Ave Richmond VA 23220-4618 Office: Med Coll Va GI Divsn Sect Nutrition PO Box 980711 1200 E Broad St Richmond VA 23298-0711

HOSEY, TERRY ANNETTE, medical/surgical nurse, post critical care nurse; b. Laurel, Miss., June 2, 1948; d. R.C. and Virginia (Collins) Clark; m. Phillip M. Hosey, June 24, 1966; children: Terry Michael, Kimble Wayne, Phillip David. ADN, Houston Community Coll., 1983; BSN, U. Tex., Houston, 1990. RN, Tex. Asst. head nurse Meth. Hosp., Houston; relief charge nurse Midland (Tex.) Meml. Hosp.; staff nurse, team leader Meml. Care System, Houston; case mgr. Slidell Meml. Hosp. Home Health; DON Paradigm Med. Svcs., Abita Springs, La.; case mgr., nurse Network Home Health, Inc., Lafayette, La.; mem. panel content experts NCLEX-RN Rev., 1988. Mem. ANA, La. Nurses Assn., Tex. Nurses Assn. (bd. dirs.). Home: 502 Constitution Dr Maurice LA 70555

HOSEY, VICTOR PHILLIP, photojournalist; b. Connelsville, Pa., Aug. 10, 1950; s. Victor Flavel and Betty Mae (Lawson) H.; m. Susana Maria de La Cruz, Jan. 9, 1973; 1 child, Victor Travis. AA, Del Mar Coll., 1974; postgrad., Austin C.C., 1977-79, U. Tex., 1980-81. Ind. photojournalist, 1968—; owner, operator SCUBATEXAS! World Hdqrs., Austin, 1981-90, TEXpeditions UNlimited Travel Videos, Lockhart, Tex., 1986-96; substitute tchr. Lockhart Ind. Sch. Dist., 1988-94, vol. spkr., 1993—; videographer local weddings, Lockhart, 1991—. Author, pub.: SCUBATEXAS! Dive Guide Book, 1983; contbr. to book: Book of Texas Lists, 1981, also to various newspapers and mags. Umpire, asst. coach Lockhart Little League, 1993; fin. sponsor KUT-FM Radio Project 2000, U. Tex., Austin, 1995. Mem. Internat. Assn. of Air Travel Couriers, Nat. Space Soc. Mem. LDS Ch. Home and Office: 406 N Blanco Lockhart TX 78644

HOSKIN, SANDRA RUBLE, medical equipment company executive, nurse; b. Chgo., Apr. 21, 1935; d. Robert Adrian and Hallie Jane (Pence) Ruble; m. Ronald Alan Budgett, Dec. 30, 1960 (div. 1973); 1 child, Laura Adrianne; m. James William Hoskin, May 20, 1974. RN, Ill. Masonic Hosp., Chgo., 1957; BSA, Coll. of St. Francis, 1979; MBA, Houston Bapt. U., 1983. RN, Ind., Tex. Staff, head nurse Meml. Hosp., South Bend, Ind., 1960-72; dir. nursing Carlysle Nursing Home, South Bend, 1972-78, Healthwin Hosp., South Bend, 1978-80; surgical supr. The Meth. Hosp., Houston, 1980-82; relief supr. Polly Ryon Hosp., Richmond, Tex., 1982-84; pres. Am. Med. Equipment Co., Houston, 1984—; pres., CEO Am. Med., Inc., 1993—; pres. Sandy's Med. Warehouse, Inc., 1992—. Named one of Houston's Top 50 Women-Owned Bus. Owners, 1995, 96. Mem. Am. Quarter Horse Assn., Nat. Assn. Med. Equipment Dealers, Tex. Assn. Med. Equipment Dealers, Internat. Tex. Longhorn Assn. Republican. Methodist. Home: Running S Ranch PO Box 69 Dobbin TX 77333 Office: Am Med Equipment Co 1841 Old Spanish Trl Houston TX 77054-2001

HOSKINS, KATY GARREN, secondary school educator; b. El Paso, Tex., Nov. 17, 1966; d. John Franklin and Patricia Louise (McDaniel) Garren; m. Curt William Kuykendall Hoskins, Sept. 17, 1988. BS in Range Sci., Tex. A&M U., 1988; MEd, Sul Ross State U., 1994—. Lic. tchr. spl. edn.; cert. profl. counselor, profl. spl. edn. counselor, K-12 spl. edn., secondary lang. arts, secondary reading, secondary history, secondary life/earth sci., secondary art. Rsch. asst. I.E. duPont, Inc., Dallas, 1988; tchr. Culberson County Ind. Sch. Dist., Van Horn, Tex., 1989—; presenter multicultural edn. Tex. Edn. Agy., Austin, 1991; presenter Tex. culture Hardin-Simmons U., Abilene, 1994. Author: A Cultural Approach to Environmental Studies, 1991, Regions of Texas Trans-Pecos, 1994. Plant identification team coach Culberson County 4-H Club, Van Horn, 1990—; soil conservation svc. vol. USDA, Van Horn, 1992—; cancer crusade chmn. Am. Cancer Soc., Van Horn, 1991-93. Named Conservationist of Yr. High Point Soil & Water Dist., Van Horn, 1991, Tchr. of Yr. Culberson County Ind. Sch. Dist., Van Horn, 1992-93; recipient Leadership Appreciation award Culberson County 4-H Club, Van Horn, 1992, 93, 94. Mem. ASCD, Trans-Tex. Heritage Assn. (edn. com. 1991—), Soc. Range Mgmt. (past edn. com.), Inst. Tex. Culture. Republican. Episcopalian. Home: 101 Ranch Van Horn TX 79855 Office: Culberson County Ind Sch Dist Van Horn Jr High Sch 4th & Crockett Sts Van Horn TX 79855

HOSKINS, MABLE ROSE, secondary education educator, English language educator; b. Natchez, Miss., May 23, 1945; d. Johnny and Josephine (Jones) Reynolds; m. Charles Hoskins, Dec. 23, 1973 (div. Dec. 5, 1989). BA in English, Jackson State Coll., 1967; MED, Miss. State U., 1979, Ednl. Specialist, 1982. Tchr. English Natchez (Miss.) Pub. Schs., 1968-70, Quitman (Miss.) Consol. Schs., 1971-81, Meridian (Miss.) Schs., 1981—; bd. dirs. Pub. Employee's Retirement Sys., Jackson, 1988-92, Meridian Bonita Lakes Authority. Co-author: (teaching units) Miss. Writers Teaching Units for Secondary English, 1988; consulting editor: (book) Mississippi Writers-An Anthology, 1991. Newsletter editor, co-editor Assn. of Meridian Educators, 1988-92; mistress of ceremonies Alpha Kappa Alpha Sorority, Meridian, 1985-90; Children's Discovery, vol. coord. Meridian Coun. for the Arts, 1990. Named S.T.A.R. tchr. Miss. Econ. Coun., 1980, Tchr. of Yr., Meridian Pub. Schs., 1988, 94, finalist Miss. Hall of Master Tchrs., 1994. Mem. NEA, Miss. Assn. Educators (Mem. of Yr. 1988, bd. dirs. 1990-93), Miss. Coun. Tchrs. English, Nat. Coun. Tchrs. English, Phi Kappa Phi, Phi Delta Kappa. Baptist. Home: 1409 37th Ave Meridian MS 39307-6004 Office: Meridian H S 2320 32nd St Meridian MS 39305-4657

HOSKINS, SARA LYNN, pediatrics critical care nurse; b. Houston, Dec. 7, 1962; d. Fred John and Sharlie Ann (Ross) H. BSN, West Tex. State U., 1987. RN, Tex.; cert. pediatric advanced life support instr. and provider, ACLS provider, ICU transport team nurse. Clin. asst. NW Tex. Hosp., Amarillo; staff nurse III Scott and White Hosp., Temple, Tex., U. Tex. Med. Br., Galveston, Tex., 1993—; nurse clinician III Children's Hosp.-U. Tex. Med. Br., Galveston, 1993—. Friends in Nursing scholar. Mem. AACCN. Home: 10105 Schaper Dr Galveston TX 77554-8027

HOSKINSON, CAROL ROWE, middle school educator; b. Toledo, Mar. 10, 1947; d. Webster Russell and Alice Mae (Miller) Rowe; m. C. Richard Hoskinson, June 8, 1969; 1 child, Leah Nicole. BS in Edn., Ohio State U., 1968; MEd, Ga. State U., 1972. Tchr. Whitehall City Schs., Columbus, Ohio, 1968-69; tchr. DeKalb County Schs., Decatur, Ga., 1969-74, Mt. Olive (N.J.) Twp. Schs., 1974-75, DeKalb County Schs., Decatur, 1975-79; Fulton County Schs., Atlanta, 1991—; substitute tchr. DeKalb County Schs., Decatur, 1980-91, Fulton County Schs., Atlanta, 1989-91. Pres. Esther Jackson PTA, Roswell, Ga., 1988-89; treas. Women of the Ch., Roswell, 1983-84; chairperson local sch. adv. Esther Jackson, Roswell, 1989-91; del. Women and Constn. Conv., Atlanta, 1988; mem. Supt.'s Adv. Com.; local sch. adv. Holcomb Bridge Mid. Sch.; active Chattahoochee H.S. Booster Club; corr. sec. Chattahoochee H.S. PTSA, v.p. Cheers Club; VIP dedicated hostess Olympic Games, Atlanta, 1996. Named Vol. of Yr. Fulton County Schs., 1988-89. Mem. AAUW (v.p. Atlanta chpt. 1970-89, edn. scholarship honoree 1984, 86), Atlanta Lawn Tennis Assn., Roswell Hist. Soc., Roswell Hist. Preservation Commn., Ga. Sci. Tchrs. Assn., Nat. Mid. Sch. Assn., Zoo Atlanta, High Mus. Art, Ga. PTA, Ohio State Alumni Assn., Ga. State Alumni Assn., Profl. Assn. Educators. Democrat. Presbyterian. Home: 1670 Branch Valley Dr Roswell GA 30076-3007

HOSLEY, MARGUERITE CYRIL, volunteer; b. Houston, July 29, 1946; d. Frederick Willard and Marguerite Estella (Arisman) Collister; m. Richard Allyn Hosley II, July 18, 1968; children: Richard A. III, Sean Frederick, Michelle Cyril. BS in Edn., U. Houston, 1968; postgrad., Tex. A&M U., 1970-71. Cert. tchr., Tex. Tchr. Sharpstown High Sch., Houston, 1968-69, Bryan (Tex.) High Sch., 1969-71; ins. asst. Farmers Ins., Stafford, Tex., 1981-83; adminstrv. asst., fin. asst. Christ United Meth. Ch., Sugarland, Tex., 1984-92; mem. Planning and Zoning Commn. City of Sugarland, 1995—. Pres. bd. dirs. Ft. Bend Boys Choir, 1984-85; docent Bayou Bend Collection and Gardens, Houston Mus. Fine Arts, 1994—; bd. dirs. Am. Cancer Soc., 1990—; pres. Am. Cancer Soc. League, 1993-94; mem. Lone Staar Stomp com. Ft. Bend Mus. Assn., 1991-96; parent vol. Ft. Bend Ind. Schs., 1980-94; raffle chmn. Ft. Bend Drug Alliance Gala, 1989; newsletter chmn. Am. herat Asn. Guild, 1990-91, v.p., 1992-93. Named Ft. Bend Outstanding Woman, Ft. Bend County, 1992. Mem. Houston Ladies' Tennis Assn. (team capt.), Ft. Bend Mus., Sweetwater Country Club (bd. govs. 1990-93), Sweetwater Women's Assn. (treas. 1985-87, pres. 1987-88), Friends of Casa (charter mem.), Aggie Moms Club, Chi Omega Alumnae. Republican. Methodist. Home: 427 W Alkire Lake Dr Sugar Land TX 77478-3527

HOSMANE, NARAYAN SADASHIV, chemistry educator; b. Gokarn, Karnatak, India, June 30, 1948; came to U.S., 1976, naturalized citizen, 1993; s. Sadashiv Ganapati and Lalita (Kurse) H.; m. Sumathy Rao, May 6, 1976; children: Suneil Narayan, Nina Narayan. BS, Karnatak U., Dharwar, India, 1968, MS, 1970; PhD, Edinburgh (Scotland) U., 1974. Rsch. asst. Queen's U. of Belfast (No. Ireland), 1974-75; rsch. scientist Lambeg (No. Ireland) Indsl. Rsch. Inst., 1975-76; rsch. assoc. Auburn (Ala.) U., 1976-77, U. Va., Charlottesville, 1977-79; asst. prof. Va. Poly. Inst. and State U., Blacksburg, 1979-82; asst. prof. So. Meth. U., Dallas, 1982-86, assoc. prof., 1986-89, full prof., 1989—; chemist cons. Vertically Integrated Tech., Inc., Dallas, 1990—; invited speaker in field; chmn. 1st Boron-USA (BUSA-I) Workshop, 1988. Author: (with others) Boron Chemistry, 1980, Advances in Boron and the Boranes, 1988, Advances in Organometallic Chemistry, 1990, Electron Deficient Boron and Carbon Clusters, 1991, Pure and Applied Chemistry, 1991, Chemical Reviews, 1993; (jour.) Cluster Sci.; contbr. over 100 peer rev. sci. articles to profl. jours. including Jours. of Am. Chem. Soc., Inorganic Nuclear Chemistry. Recipient Camille and Henry Dreyfus Scholar award, 1994, Mother-India Internat. Rsch. award for outstanding contbn. to field of chemistry, 1994; grantee So. Meth. U., 1983-84, Rsch. Corp., 1983-85, Petroleum Rsch. Fund, 1984—, NSF, 1985—, Tex. Higher Edn. Corrdinating Bd., 1994—; Welch grantee, 1985—. Fellow Royal Soc. Chemistry, Am. Inst. Chemists; mem. Am. Chem. Soc. Soc., Soc. of Sigma Xi (Outstanding Rsch. award 1987). Home: 2802 Pear Tree Ln Garland TX 75042-5635 Office: Southern Meth U Dept Chemistry Airline Rd Dallas TX 75275

HOSTETLER, THEODORE JAN, library director; b. Canton, OH, Feb. 7, 1951; s. Garrison and Arline Doris (Conrad) H.; m. Sue Ellen Berry, Nov. 28, 1975; children: Libby Anne, Timothy Jan, Daniel Richard. BA, Bluffton Coll., 1973; MA, U. Iowa, 1974. Cataloger Iowa Wesleyan Coll., Mt. Pleasant, Iowa, 1974-75; reference libr. Iowa Wesleyan Coll., Mt. Pleasant, 1975-78; circulation head U. S. Fla., Tampa, 1978-79; head access svcs. Syracuse (N.Y.) U., 1979-89, U. Calif., Davis, 1987-93; libr. dir. Randolph-Macon Woman's Coll., Lynchburg, Va., 1993—; mem. bd. trustees Ctrl. N.Y. Libr. Resources Coun., Syracuse, 1986-88, Mountain Valley Libr. Assn., Sacramento, Calif., 1991-93. Editor-author (periodical) The Library and Undergraduate Education, 1995. Sec. bd. trustees Woodland (Calif.) Pub. Libr., 1991-92, chair, 1992. Mem. Am. Libr. Assn., Va. Libr. Assn. (mem. intellectual freedom com. 1993—). Democrat. Methodist. Office: Randolph Macon Woman's Coll Lipscomb Libr 2500 Rivermont Ave Lynchburg VA 24503

HOTCHNER, KIRBY ROSS, osteopath; b. St. Louis, May 25, 1954; s. Selwyn Ross and Beverly June (Novack) H.; m. Cynthia Mercedes Rodriguez, June 30, 1990; children: Gabriel Dominique, Alexis Sofia. BA, Washington U., 1976; DO, U. Osteo. Medicine, Des Moines, 1981. Bd. cert. in pain mgmt. Osteopath pvt. practice Chgo., 1982-83; assoc. prof. U. Osteo. Medicine, Des Moines, 1983-90; physician group practice Comprehensive Health Ctr., Miami, Fla., 1990-92; assoc. prof. Nova Southwestern U., North Miami Beach, Fla., 1992—. Mem. Am. Osteo. Assn., Am. Acad. of Osteopathy. Home: 735 SW 21st Rd Miami FL 33129-1337

HOUCHARD, MICHAEL HARLOW, organization executive; b. Long Beach, Calif., Oct. 4, 1935; s. Harold Harlow and Michella (Mehle) H.; m. Merry Carol Filek, May 5, 1962; 1 child, Christina Carol. B. in Bus., U. Fla., 1962; M., U. Utah, 1975. Asst. mgr. W.T. Grant Co., St. Petersburg, Fla., 1962; with Fla. Indsl. Commn., Miami, 1962-65, U.S. Dept. Labor, Atlanta, 1965-91; fed. rep. Manpower Adminstrn., Atlanta, 1965-69; exec. asst. Manpower Adminstrn., 1969-75; assoc. regional adminstr. Employment & Tng. Adminstrn., Atlanta, 1975-76; exec. asst. Employment & Tng. Adminstrn., 1976-83, asst. regional adminstr., 1984-87, regional adminstr., 1987-91; ret., 1991; assoc. dir. Alliance for Employee Growth and Devel. Inc., Atlanta, 1991—. Mem. Am. Legion, Conyers, Ga., 1988-89. With USN, 1954-58. Mem. Southeastern Employment & Tng. Assn., Internat. Assn. Personnel in Employment Security, Great Dane Club Mid-South (pres. 1968-70), Conyers Kennel Club (pres. 1984-85). Home: 3250 Gees Mill Rd NE Conyers GA 30208-1438 Office: Alliance Employee Growth & Devel Inc 2635 Century Pky NE Ste 120 Atlanta GA 30345-3112

HOUCHEN, CONSTANCE ELAINE, nursing administrator; b. Jamaica, W.I., Aug. 25, 1941; d. Leslie Percival and Olive Isabelle Lobban; m. Dave Houchen; children: Trevor, Adrian, Diedre. AAS, N.Y.C. Community Coll., 1968; BSN, CCNY, 1977; MSN, U. Fla., 1996. Supr. Hollis Park Gardens Nursing Home, Queens, N.Y., 1974-78; operating room nurse VA Med. Ctr., Northport, N.Y., 1979-81; operating room nurse VA Med. Ctr., Gainesville, Fla., 1981-85, night supr., 1986-95, head nurse, 1995—. Mem. F.O.N.E., Sigma Theta Tau. Home: 4 Lake Ct Ocala FL 34472-2718

HOUCHIN, JOHN FREDERICK, SR., human services administrator; b. Oak Park, Ill., Nov. 1, 1945; s. O. Boyd and Mary Ruth (Schroke) H.; m. Bette Louise Arnold, July 9, 1969; children: John Jr., David Locke. AA, Kemper Mil. Sch. & Coll., Boonville, Mo., 1966; BS, Ohio State U., 1968; EdD, U. Mass., 1987. Prog. dir. Cuyahoga County Assn. Retarded Citizens, Cleve., 1973-75; resdl. dir., asst. supt. Ohio Dept. Mental Health & Retardation, Braodview Devel. Ctr, Broadview Hts., Ohio, 1975-80; reg. mental retardation coord. Mass. Dept. Mental Health, Region IV A, Watertown, Mass., 1980-83; dir. devel. svcs. Mass. Dept. Mental Health, Belchertown State Sch., 1983-86; asst. reg. dir. Conn. Dept. Retardation, Region 6, Waterford, 1986-91; CEO G.B. Cooley Svcs. for Retarded Citizens, West Monroe, La., 1991—; lectr. in field. Contbr. book: Supported Employment Implementation, 1988. State adv. coun. Conn. Dept. Rehab. Svcs., Hartford, 1988-91; regional adv. coun. Region 8 Office Mental Retardation, 1992-94, chmn., 1993; mem. Monroe Beautification Bd., 1996—; mem. Twin Cities Mayors Com. on Disabled, 1994—. Capt. U.S. Army, 1969-72. Mem. Internat. Platform Assn., Internat. Freelance Photographer Assn., Monroe C. of C., N.E. La. Camera Club (pres. 1993-94). Episcopalian. Office: GB Cooley Svcs 364 Cooley Rd West Monroe LA 71291-8800

HOUGH, AUBREY JOHNSTON, JR., pathologist, physician, educator; b. Little Rock, July 20, 1944; s. Aubrey Johnston and Thelma Willeen (Miller) H.; m. Linda Ann Yaeger, June 10, 1968; children: Charles Prentiss, Robert Page. BA, Hendrix Coll., 1966; MD, Vanderbilt U., 1970. Diplomate Am. Bd. Pathology. Resident dept. pathology Vanderbilt U., Nashville, 1970-72, chief resident, 1974-75, asst. prof. dept. pathology, 1975-78, asst. prof. dept. orthopedics, 1977-78, assoc. prof. depts. pathology and orthopedics, 1978-80; prof. and vice chmn. dept. pathology U. Ark. for Med. Scis., Little Rock, 1980-81, prof., chmn. dept. pathology, 1981—; clin. assoc. Nat. Inst. Arthritis & Metabolic Disease, Bethesda, Md., 1972-74; chief of staff U. Ark. Hosp., Little Rock, 1986-88; pres. Ark. Acad. Pathology, Little Rock, 1982-86, Coun. of Dept. Chmn. U. Ark. Coll. of Medicine, Little Rock, 1987-88; mem. pathology test com. Nat. Bd. Med. Examiners, 1989-92, chmn., 1993-95, comp II com., 1992-95; mem. Nat. Bd. Med. Examiners, 1996—; mem. residency rev. com. for pathology Accreditation Coun. Med. Edn., 1990-96. Author: Tumors of the Adrenal Gland, 1987; contbr. numerous articles on orthopedic diseases to profl. jours, chpts. to books; assoc. editor Human Pathology, 1988—; editorial bd. Am. Jour. Pathology. Alumni fund rep. Hendrix Coll., Conway, Ark., 1983-86; chmn. Shideler Chemistry Edn. Endowment, 1991—. Served as surgeon USPHS, 1972-74. Basic Sci. Grantee Nat. Inst. Gen. Med. Studies, 1978, Altheimer Found., 1984, Nat. Inst. Arthritis, 1988; recipient Dirs. Commendation VA, 1980, Disting. Service award U. Ark., Little Rock, 1985. Fellow Coll. Am. Pathologists (field inspector 1977-88); mem. AMA, AAUP, Internat. Acad. Pathology, Am. Soc. Clin. Pathologists, Am. Assn. Pathology, Assn. Clin. Scientists (Brown Meml. lectr 1986), Arthur Purdy Stout Soc., Commd. Officers Assn., Assn. Pathology Chmn. (mem. publ. affairs com. 1985—, chmn. 1993-96), Orthopedic Rsch. Soc., History of Medicine Assocs. (bd. dirs. 1986-88), Assn. Am. Med. Colls. (mem. coun. academic soc. Washington 1985-89). Democrat. Clubs: Bapt. Med. Dental (Memphis) (program chair 1983-84). Home: 23 Lorine Cir Little Rock AR 72205-2530 Office: U Ark for Med Scis 4301 W Markham Slot 517 Little Rock AR 72205

HOUGH, DONALD LEE, computer consultant; b. San Francisco, Dec. 29, 1951; s. Wallace Marvin Hough and Annie Virginia Knight; m. Monica Lynne Norman, June 14, 1975; children: Justin Todd, Megan Blair. Student, Northeastern Okla. State U., 1970-72. Programmer 1st Nat. Bank and Trust Co., Tulsa, 1977-84, Amoco Oil Co., Tulsa, 1984-86; cons. Computer Task Group, Tampa, Fla., 1986-88, Am. Airlines, Dallas, 1988-89, IBM, Dallas, 1989—. Author: Rapid Delivery, Incremental Development: Methods for Responsive Application Development, 1993, Rapid Delivery: An Evolutionary Approach for Application Development, 1993. Mem. Assn. for Sys. Mgmt., Data Adminstrn. Mgmt. Assn., Assn. for Computing Machinery. Office: IBM Corp 1605 Lyndon B Johnson Fwy Dallas TX 75234-6034

HOUGHLAND, SARAH ROBERTS, museum administrator; b. Indpls., June 30, 1943; d. Donald Birdell and Sally (Robards) Roberts; m. David Edwin Kranbuehl, July 2, 1966 (div. Apr. 1984); children: Katherine, Donald; m. Wright B. Houghland, May 4, 1985. BA, DePauw U., 1965; MS, U. Wis., 1970. Tchr. English and History Lincolnwood (Ill.) schs., 1965-66; tchr. Oregon (Wis.) Jr. High Sch., 1966-69, Williamsburg-James City Schs., Williamsburg, Va., 1970-71, 82-86; dir. devel. rsch. and writing Colonial Williamsburg, 1987—. Author: (guide) In and Around Williamsburg with Children, 1978. Sec. Williamsburg Electoral Bd., 1980-82; pres. Williamsburg LWV, 1975-77; bd. dirs. United Way, 1985—; pres. Friends of

Williamsburg Libr., 1991-93, Williamsburg Libr. Found., 1994—. Mem. Am. Assn. Museums, Am. Prospect Rsch. Assn., S.E. Mus. Conf., Phi Beta Kappa. Presbyn. Office: Colonial Williamsburg PO Box 1776 Williamsburg VA 23187-1776

HOUGHTALING, PAMELA ANN, public relations executive; b. Catskill, N.Y., July 8, 1949; d. Stanley Kenneth and Mildred Edythe (Fyfe) H. BA, Princeton U., 1971; cert. Russian Inst., Columbia U., 1976, M in Internat. Affairs, 1974. Internat. rels. analyst Libr. of Congress, Washington, 1974-75, U.S. GAO, Washington, 1976-77; pub. affairs specialist IBM Corp., Washington, 1977-81; sr. external programs analyst IBM World Trade Americas/Far East Corp., North Tarrytown, N.Y., 1981-82; mgr. labor affairs/bus. practices U.S. Coun. Internat. Bus., N.Y.C., 1982-84; communications specialist-advt. IBM Corp., Boca Raton, Fla., 1984-86; staff communications specialist IBM Corp., White Plains, N.Y., 1986-88; communications cons., 1988-90; sr. mktg. specialist Wang Labs., Bethesda, Md., 1990-93; pub. rels. dir. STG Mktg. Comm., 1993-94; mgr. mktg. comm. Cable & Wireless, Inc., Vienna, Va. 1994-95; tech. comms. cons., 1995—. Mem. Am. Mktg. Assn., Armed Forces Comms. and Electronics Assn.

HOUGHTON, PHYLLIS SUE, vocational school educator; b. Yale, Okla., Nov. 27, 1935; d. Roland Joe and Mary T. (Lawhon) Cleveland; m. Sammy Lee Houghton, June 2, 1958; 1 child, Malinda Lee Houghton Helton. BS in Bus. Edn., U. Ctrl. Okla., 1958; MS in Bus. Edn., Okla. State U., 1968. Cert. tchr., Okla. Bus. tchr. Piedmont (Okla.) H.S., 1958-59, 60-61; elem. tchr. Sapulpa (Okla.) Pub. Schs., 1961-62; vocat. bus. tchr. Sapulpa H.S., 1962—; chair dept. bus. Sapulpa H.S., 1979—. Contbg. author: Business Bulletin Board Ideas, 1985; contbr. chpts. to books. Mem. NEA, Am. Vocat. Assn., Okla. Edn. Assn., Okla. Bus. Edn. Assn., Pi Omega Pi, Delta Pi Epsilon. Democrat. Baptist. Home: 1616 Glendale Rd Sapulpa OK 74066 Office: Sapulpa H S 3 S Mission Sapulpa OK 74066

HOUK, JAMES TITUS, writer, educator; b. Baton Rouge, La., Feb. 26, 1955; s. J.T. Jr. and Elmaid Mary (Ducote) H.; m. Lynne Bernice Hollister, July 4, 1980; children: Jacob Alexander, Ethan Benjamin. BS in Math., La. State U., 1982, MA in Anthropology, 1986; PhD in Anthropology, Tulane U., 1992. Cert. tchr., La. Instr. La. State U., 1990-91, Tulane U., New Orleans, 1990-91; acting asst. prof. La. State U., 1991-92; writer, ind. scholar, 1992—; with Energy Mgmt. Dept., Baton Rouge, 1996—. Author: Spirits, Blood, and Drums, 1995; contbr. articles to profl jours. Fulbright grant Coun. for Internat. Exch. of Scholars, 1988; fellowship Tulane Grade Sch., 1986. Mem. AAUP, Am. Anthropological Assoc., Mu Sigma Rho. Home: 12531 Coursey Blvd # 1089 Baton Rouge LA 70816 Office: Energy Mgmt Dept 2875 Michelli Baton Rouge LA 70805

HOULIHAN, PATRICIA POWELL, financial planner; b. Emporia, Va., Dec. 16, 1947; d. John Cyrus and Hazel Wright (Hines) Powell; m. Dennis Finley Houlihan, Oct. 13, 1973; children: Sean Finley, Ryan Patrick. BS, U. Richmond, 1969. Cert. and lic. fin. planner. Tchr. math. Fairfax County Schs., McLean, Va., 1970-74; fin. planner Cavill & Co., Washington, 1985—; panelist TV Washington Forum on Fin. Planning, Fairfax, Va., 1987-89, TV Money Watch, Washington, TV the Money Makers, PBS, Video Fin. Planning, The Internat. Found. of Employee Benefit Plans; TV host The Fin. Advisers, PBS, 1991-92; adj. prof. Coll. Fin. Planning, George Washington U. Pres. Homeowners Assn., Oakton, Va., 1984; treas. Navy Elem. PTA, Fairfax, 1984; chmn. Creative Playground Project, Fairfax, 1982. Recipient Disting. Svc. award Va. Congress Parents and Tchrs., 1985. Mem. Internat. Assn. Fin. Planning, CFP Bd. Stds. (lic., job analysis task force, practice stds. task force, item writing com., chair-elect 1996). Methodist. Office: Cavill & Co 3200 Pommel Ct Oakton VA 22124-2316

HOUSE, FREDRICK CRISLER, allergist, immunologist; b. Atlanta, 1941. MD, Med. Coll. Ga., 1968. Diplomate Am. Bd. Allergy & Immunology, Am. Bd. Internal Medicine. Intern Meml. Hosp., Savannah, Ga., 1968-69; resident Med. Coll. Ga., Augusta, 1969-71, asst. clin. prof. medicine; fellow in allergy and immunology Walter Reed Army Med. Ctr., Washington, 1972-74; with U. Hosp., Augusta. Fellow Am. Acad. Allergy and Immunology, Med. Assn. Ga., Southeastern Allergy Assn. Office: 3646 Wheeler Rd Augusta GA 30909-6519

HOUSE, NAOMI GERALDINE (GERRY HOUSE), school system administrator; b. Patrick Springs, Va., Aug. 23, 1947; d. Robert L. and Edna (Hopper) Hagwood; m. Lee A. House Jr., July 4, 1970; children: Lee A. III, Jennifer Renee. BS, N.C. A&T State U., 1969; MS, So. Ill. U., 1973; edn. specialist, U. N.C., 1985, EdD, 1988. Adminstrv. asst. to supt. Chapel Hill (N.C.)-Carrboro Schs., 1976-79, prin. elem. sch., 1980-81, asst. supt., 1981-85, acting fin. dir., 1984, supt., 1985-92; supt. Memphis City Schs., 1992—; assoc. edn. Harvard U., Cambridge, Mass., 1994—. Contbr. articles to profl. jours. Mem. bd. vis. sch. edn. U. N.C., Chapel Hill, 1992-98; trustee Goals Memphis, 1992-98; bd. dirs. So. Edn. Found., Atlanta, 1992—, Free the Children, Memphis, 1992—, Girls Inc., Memphis, 1993, Nat. Civil Rights Mus., Memphis, 1993—, Christian Bros. U., Memphis, 1994—. Recipient Leadership award Triangle Roundtable Consortium, 1992; named Role Model for Women, Women Edn., 1992, one of Exec. Educator 100, Exec. Educator Mag., 1993, Communicator of Yr., Pub. Rels. Soc., 1993. Mem. ASCD, Am. Assn. Sch. Adminstrs. (mem. global edn. com. 1992), Nat. Sch. Bds. Assn., Phi Delta Kappa (editor newsletter), Kappa Delta Pi. Home: 2221 Hickory Crest Dr Memphis TN 38119-6847 Office: Memphis City Schs 2597 Avery Ave Memphis TN 38112-4818

HOUSE, STEPHEN EUGENE, information systems consultant; b. Pueblo, Colo., July 18, 1951; s. Floyd Eugene and Jewell (Brame) H.; m. Cheryl Virginia Ashby, Mar. 15, 1975; children: Deborah Lynne, Mark Stephen. BS in Bus. Info. Systems, West Coast U., 1992. Programmer Calif. Sch. Employees Assn., San Jose, 1976-79; programmer/analyst Marysville (Calif.) Joint Unified Sch. Dist., 1979-80; tech. lead Mervyns, Hayward, Calif., 1980-85, Lucky Stores, Inc., Dublin, Calif., 1985-87; project lead Northrop, Pica Rivera, Calif., 1987-92; tech. cons. Computer Profls. Inc., Charlotte, N.C., 1992—.

HOUSER, CINDY L., middle school educator, counselor; b. Moab, Utah, June 3, 1954; d. John Richardson Wilcox and Jean B. (Blackman) Stevens; m. Brennon L. Pepper, Aug. 3, 1972 (div. Aug. 1983); children: Angela Page, Joshua L.; m. Clifford F. Houser, Mar. 22, 1989. BS in Edn., U. Tex., Tyler, 1981. Counselor Interventions, Dallas, 1992; math tchr. Hogg Mid. Sch., Tyler, 1993—. Grantee Tyler Found., 1996. Republican. Home: 2725 Old Jacksonville Tyler TX 75701

HOUSER, JAMES COWING, JR., painter, art educator; b. Dade City, Fla., Nov. 12, 1928; s. James C. and Martha (Futch) H.; m. Constance Woodward; children: James Jackson, Katrina J. BS, Ringling Sch. of Art, 1949; BFA, Fla. So. Coll., 1951; postgrad., Art Inst. Chgo., 1952; MFA, U. Fla., 1953. Exhibited at Grand Ctrl. Moderns Gallery, N.Y.C., 1966—; represented by Rudolph Galleries, Woodstock, N.Y., Coral Gables Fla., 1964-90, Gallery Camino Real, Boca Raton, Fla., 1972—, David Findlay Galleries, N.Y.C., 1974-84, Sherry French Gallery, N.Y.C., 1985; sr. instr. art Ky. Wesleyan Coll., Owensboro, 1954-60, art chmn., 1964-70, dir. art gallery, 1974-91; art instr. Palm Beach C.C.; artist Notre Dame U., 1970; Cornell U., NYU, 1971: judge local and nat. art competitions; lectr. in field. Author: Color for the Artist, 1975, video texts; one man shows include Brevard Community Coll., Cocoa, Fla., 1973, Valencia Community Coll., Orlando, Fla., 1974, David Findlay Galleries, N.Y.C., 1976, 78, 81, 83, Northwood Inst., 1986, Palm Beach Community Coll., 1988, numerous others in U.S. and Europe; exhibited in group shows at Dept. State Spl. Exhbn., Washington, 1967—, Major Fla. Artist Invitational Exhbn., Sarasota, Fla., 1981-92, North Miami Mus. and Art Ctr., North Miami, Fla., 1985, South Fla. Invitational Exhbn., 1991, Ft. Lauderdale Mus. Art, Men's Art Northwood U., West Palm Beach, Fla., 1994. Mem. selection com. Palm Beach Coun. Arts, 1987; mem. art. rev. bd. scholarship awards Palm Beach Post-Times, 1982-87. Recipient Merit award Ft. Lauderdale Mus., 1974, Atwater Kent award 1977, 89, Akston Found. award 1977, Philip Hulitar award 1982, Four Arts award 1992, 93, Soc. Four Arts, West Palm Beach. Republican. Methodist. Home and Office: 8338 SE Coconut St Hobe Sound FL 33455-2911

HOUSER, JOHN EDWARD, lawyer; b. Richmond, Va., Dec. 24, 1928; s. Aubrey Alphin and Winnifred (Savage) H.; m. Elizabeth Rives Pollard, Apr. 1, 1967; children—Allen Rives Cabell Lybrook, Andrew Murray Lybrook. B.S., U. Va., 1959, LL.B., 1959. Bar: Fla. 1959, U.S. dist. ct. (so. and mid. dists.) Fla. 1959, U.S. Ct. Appeals (5th cir.) 1963, U.S. Supreme Ct. 1970, U.S. Ct. Appeals (11th cir.) 1981. Assoc., Jennings, Watts, Clarke & Hamilton, Jacksonville, Fla., 1959-61, Howell, Kirby, Montgomery & Sands, Jacksonville, 1961-63; ptnr. Howell & Houser, Jacksonville, 1963-65; sole practice, Jacksonville, 1965—; lectr. on Long shore and Harbor works Comp. Act Loyola U., 1979, 88; dir. William P. Polythress & Co., Richmond, Neal F. Tyler & Sons, Jacksonville. Active Jacksonville U. Council, Jacksonville Symphony Assn., Fla. Hist. Soc., Jacksonville Hist. Soc., Cummer Gallery of Art, Jacksonville Art Mus.; mem. English-Speaking Union, dir., 1970-79, pres., 1974-78, nat. regional chmn., 1973-76, nat. dir., 1976-81; hon. sec. Live Oak Hounds; subscriber Exmoor Foxhounds; active Thomasville Landmarks, dir., 1991—, Thomasville Arts Guild, Thomasville Cultural Ctr., Thomas County Hist. Soc. Served with AUS, 1953-57. Mem. Internat. Assn. Indsl. Accident Bds. and Commns., Maritime Law Assn., Southeastern Admiralty Law Inst., Jacksonville Claimsmen Assn., Atlanta Claimsmen Assn., ABA, Jacksonville Bar Assn., Fla. Bar, Fla. Def. Scl. Assn., Am. Judicature Soc., Am. Arbitration Assn., Ga. Trust for His. Preservation, Nat. Trust Hist. Preservation, Fla. Inst. Pub. Affairs, Navy League, Jacksonville Assn. Def. Counsel, Def. Research Inst., Theta Delta Chi, Sigma Nu Phi. Clubs: Rotary Internat., River, Fla. Yacht, University (Jacksonville), Deerwood, Ponte Vedra River, Exchange, German, Ye Mystic Revellers, Univ., Princeton of N.Y., Glen Arven, Commonwealth (Richmond, Va.); 2300. Office: PO Box 873 Jacksonville FL 32201-0873

HOUSTON, BRIAN CHRISTOPHER MICHAEL, small business owner; b. Kitchener, Ont., Canada, Dec. 27, 1938; came to the U.S., 1968; s. Brian F.C. and Patricia E. (Jones) H.; m. Carol A. Donnan, Feb. 9, 1964 (div. 1978); children: Adrienne Elizabeth, Kelly Patricia; m. Heather S. Duncan, Dec. 29, 1978. BSME, Air Force Coll., 1957; grad., Staff Command Coll., London, 1970, Staff War Coll., London, 1972, Police Acad., Hamilton County, Ohio, 1973; AA in Document Analysis, Lion Acad., 1991. Pres., CEO Pegasus Group Holdings Inc., Herndon, Va., 1979—, K. Investigations Inc., Herndon, 1983—; cons. Chemform Co., Fort Lauderdale, Fla., 1976-79; chief instr., dir. Twin Oaks Ski Club, Middleton, Nova Scotia, 1963-65; cons. Washington Rsch. Bur., 1981-86. Lt. col. Royal Marines, 1965-79; with Royal Can. Airforce, 1957-65, ret. Recipient Bronze medallion Royal Life Saving Soc., 1963. Mem. NRA (life), Am. Soc. Tooling and Mfg. Engrs., Soc. Mfg. Engrs. (sr. mem.), Internat. Assn. Counter Terrorism and Security Profls., Am. Soc. for Indsl. Security, Masons, Harley Owners Group (life), N.Am. Hunting Club (life), Silver Wings Fraternity (life). Republican. Episcopalian. Home: 1207 Sunrise Ct Herndon VA 22070 Office: K Investigations Inc 1252 Elden St Ste # 107 Herndon VA 22070

HOUSTON, JAMES GORMAN, JR., state supreme court justice; b. Eufaula, Ala., Mar. 11, 1933; s. James Gorman and Mildred (Vance) H.; m. Martha Martin, Dec. 3, 1955; children: Mildred Vance, J. Gorman III. BS, Auburn U., 1955; LLB, U. Ala., 1956, JD, 1969. Bar: Ala. 1956. Law clk. to chief justice Ala. Supreme Ct., Montgomery, 1956-57; ptnr. Houston & Martin, P.C., Eufaula, 1960-85; assoc. justice Ala. Supreme Ct., Montgomery, 1985—; county atty. Barbour County, Clayton, Ala., 1961-79. Contbr. numerous opinions to So. Reporter; contbr. articles to profl. jours. Mayor pro tem, alderman City of Eufaula, 1964-70; pres. Heritage Assn., Eufaula, Ala., 1979-82. 1st lt. JAGC, USAF, 1957-60. Named Citizen of Yr., City of Eufaula, 1979; recipient Alumni Achievement in Humanities award Auburn Univ., 1993. Fellow Am. Bar Found.; mem. ABA, Ala. Bar Assn., Ala. State Bar (examiner 1979-82, disciplinary commn. 1984-85, state bar commr. 1982-85), Barbour County Bar Assn. (pres. 1975), Eufaula C. of C. (pres. 1974). Democrat. Methodist. Office: Ala Supreme Ct 300 Dexter Ave Montgomery AL 36104-3741

HOUSTON, KELLI ANNE, software engineering specialist; b. Cin., Mar. 24, 1964; d. Kenneth Arthur Schweikhart and Arlene Dawn (Bakie) Shokes; m. Robert Kevin Houston, June 24, 1989; 1 child, Katherine Lauren. BS in Computer Sci., U. South Fla., Tampa, 1987; MS, Johns Hopkins U., 1993. Software engr. E-Systems, ECI Divsn., St. Petersburg, Fla., 1985-89, Raytheon Svc. Co., Rockville, Md., 1990-93; software engring. specialist Rational Software Corp., McLean, Va., 1993—. Mem. IEEE, Assn. Computing Machinery. Republican. Episcopalian. Home: 7701 Barnum Rd Bethesda MD 20817 Office: Rational Software Corp 8000 Westpark Dr 5th fl Mc Lean VA 22102

HOUSTON, MARCUS CLARENCE, physician; b. Jackson, Tenn., Aug. 14, 1948; s. Rupert Roosevelt and Mary Ruth (Jones) H.; m. Ellen Samms, May, 1971 (div. 1980); children: Helen Ruth, Marcus James; m. Keatha Parsons, May 7, 1983; children: John Marcus, Martha Kelly. BA in Chemistry summa cum laude, Southwestern U., Memphis, 1970; MD, Vanderbilt U., 1974. Diplomate Nat. Bd. Med. Examiners, Am. Bd. Internal Medicine. Resident, intern U. Calif. Hosps., San Francisco, 1974-77; chief resident in medicine Vanderbilt U. Med. Ctr., Nashville, 1977-78, asst. prof. medicine, 1978-89, assoc. prof. medicine, 1989-90, med. dir. coop. care ctr., 1983-90, chief, clin. sect., divsn. of internal medicine, 1987-90, co-dir. med. intensive care, 1978-90, assoc. clin. prof. medicine, 1990—; chief of hypertension St. Thomas Med. Group, Nashville, 1990—; adv. bd. Health Trac Hypertension, 1990; mem. Nat. Bur. for Info. on Coronary Heart Disease Risk, Conn., 1990—. Author: Treatment of Hypertensive Urgencies and Emergencies, 1985, (handbook) Handbook of Anthypertensive Therapy, 1986; reviewer, contr. Facts and Formulas Handbook, 1984; reviewer, editor: Change of Seasons: Sodium-Living, 1985; editorial cons. Chest, 1979—; editorial bd. for protocols Strategies From Experts in Cardiology, 1990—. Fellow ACP (Tenn. chpt. sec. 1987-90); mem. Am. Heart Assn., Am. Thoracic Soc., Am. Soc. Hypertension, Inter-Am. Soc. Hypertension, Internat. Soc. Hypertension, S.E. Consortium Hypertension Ctrs., Nashville Acad. Medicine, Am. Soc. Internal Medicine. Republican. Methodist. Office: St Thomas Med Group 4230 Harding Rd Ste 400 Nashville TN 37205-2013

HOUSTON, ROBERT LEE, defense systems manufacturing company executive; b. Little Rock, Jan. 14, 1953; s. David and Versie Mae (Houston) Johnson; m. Rosemary Harris, Sept. 28, 1978; children: Meagan Nicole, Robert Rashad. BS, Grambling State U., 1976; MBA, Liberty U., Lynchburg, Va., 1993. Mfg. analyst FMC Corp., Cedar Rapids, Iowa, 1977-79, supr., 1979-82; team mgr. FMC Corp., Aiken, S.C., 1982-84, shift mgr., 1984-87, mfg. mgr., 1987-89, bus. mgr., 1989-92, mfg. mgr., 1992—. Bd. dirs. United Way, Aiken, 1989-92, Jr. Achievement, Aiken, 1993—. Mem. Rotary (bd. dirs. 1990—). Home: 633 Chestnut Ct Aiken SC 29803-5805 Office: FMC Corp 15 Windham Blvd Aiken SC 29801-9384

HOUSTON, SHIRLEY MAE (MRS. THOMAS H. HOUSTON), court reporter; b. Jasper, Tex., Oct. 4, 1938; d. Walter Louis and Effie Marie (Hulett) Gordon; student U. Houston, 1957, South Tex. Jr. Coll., Houston, 1958; grad. Robert Krippner Sch. Reporting, 1965; m. Thomas Harold Houston, Aug. 3, 1957. Various secretarial positions, 1956-65; ct. reporter, owner Houston Reporting Svc., 1965—; owner H-R-S, 1975—; v.p. Tradewinds Indsl. Park, Inc., 1974-83, dir., 1984—; ptnr. Houston Video Svc., 1977—; dir. Skate City USA, Inc., 1980—, pres., 1987—; owner Houston Litigation Support Svc., 1986—, Depositions Unltd., 1995—. Vol. juvenile counselor; advisor Houston C.C., 1976-78, Alvin C.C., 1980-84. Registered profl. reporter, cert. shorthand reporter, cert. legal video specialist. Recipient Tex. Spl. Recognition award Tex. Hall of Fame, Houston Ct. Reporters Disting. Svc. award. Fellow Acad. Profl. Reporters; mem. Nat. Ct. Reporters Assn. (co-chmn. Tex. fundraising com. 1991-92, chmn. Tex. presdl. reception 1992-93, Disting. Svc. award 1995, pres.'s banquet chmn. 1993-94, pres.'s banquet com. 1994-95, chmn. disting. svc. award com. 1995-96), Nat. Ct. Reporters Found. (chmn. adv. com. 1994-95), Greater Houston Ct. Reporters Assn. (pres. 1975, chmn. tech. com. 1986-87, disting. svc. award 1983), Nat. Shorthand Reporters Assn. (state chmn. membership com. 1977-78, dir. 1979-80, placement com. 1980-82, chmn., 1990-92, dir. ins. com. 1982-84, membership com. 1990-91, co-chmn. word processing com. 1981-83, chmn. videotape com. 1985, mem. 1986, mem. alt. techs. com. 1988-89, seminar instr. nat. conv. 1978, 79, 81, 82, 83, 84, fund-raising task force 1986-88, chmn. videotape com. 1987-88, nat. membership award 1980, Disting. Svc. award 1995), Tex. Shorthand Reporters Assn. (advt. chmn. conv. 1967, dir. 1978-80, spl. advisor to bd. dirs. 1988, state liaison to state bar of Tex. 1986-88, chmn. mktg. and pub. rels. 1987-88, mem. nominating com. 1989—, co-chmn. This is Your Life 1989-93, vice chmn. cost, efficiency and delay com., disting. svc. award 1987, seminar instr. 1985, 86, 87, 88, 89, advisor conv. and budget com., 1991-92, chmn. task force for exec. dir. 1992-93, chmn. ethics task force 1993-96, mid-yr. seminar com. 1995-96), Reporters Coop., Inc. (sec. 1986-87, v.p. 1987-88, pres. 1988-89, treas. 1993-94), Nat. Shorthand Reporters Assn. (placement chmn. 1990-91), Nat. Assn. Legal Secs., Tex. Assn. Legal Secs., Greater Houston Legal Secs. Assn. (dir. 1969), Tex. Ct. Reporters Assn. (Spl. Recognition award 1990, Fellow Tex. Hall of Fame 1990, chmn. conv. 1991—, advisor to conv. chmn. 1992-93), Legal Assts. Assn., DAR, Soc. for Technol. Advancement of Reporters (conv. chmn. 1984, bd. dirs. 1984-87, treas. 1987-88, seminar instr. 1986, 87, chmn. conv. 1988, membership com. 1992-93, star 1992—), Jr. League of Houston. Baptist. Club: Cotillion (Houston). Address: 1111 Fannin St Ste 1400 Houston TX 77002-6923

HOUSTON, SUSAN JEANNINE HUDSON, writer; b. South Boston, Va., Dec. 20, 1961; d. Shirley Eldridge and Lois Dean (Clayton) Hudson. BA, U. N.C., 1984. Features editor The Daily Tar Heel, Chapel Hill, N.C., 1982; state news reporter The News and Observer, Raleigh, N.C., 1983-84; features writer The Fayetteville (N.C.) Observer, 1984-89; writer, editor Dept. Army, John F. Kennedy Spl. Warfare Ctr. Sch., Ft. Bragg, N.C., 1989-91; freelance writer Fayetteville, 1991-94; pub. info. officer N.C. Dept. Commerce, 1994-95; arts editor The Independent Weekly, Durham, N.C., 1995—. Bd. mem. N.C. Cath. newspaper, Raleigh, 1988-90. Westinghouse family scholar Westinghouse Elec. Corp., 1980, Scripps-Howard journalism scholar Scripps-Howard Found., 1980, C.A. "Pete" Knight scholar Charlotte (N.C.) Observer, 1983, James M. Johnston scholar U. N.C., Chapel Hill, 1980-84; recipient writing awards N.C. Press Women, 1986-88; emerging artists grantee Arts Coun. Fayetteville/Cumberland County, 1993. Home: PO Box 13763 Research Triangle Park NC 27709

HOUTS, LARRY LEE, osteopathic medicine educator; b. Three Rivers, Mich., Oct. 1, 1942; s. Elmer S. and Hilma M. (Pulver) H.; m. Karen Anne Priddle, Apr. 28, 1973; children: Willem Paul, Carrie Rena. BA in Zoology, Rockford (Ill.) Coll., 1964; MS in Biology, Fla. State U., 1966; PhD, SUNY, Albany, 1976; DO, West Va. Sch. Osteo. Medicine, 1986. Instr. Winthrop Coll., Rock Hill, S.C., 1966-69; rsch. assoc. VA Hosp., Albany, N.Y., 1974-76; asst. prof. Bethany (W.Va.) Coll., 1976-81, Wheeling (W.Va.) Coll., 1981-82; intern Garden City (Mich.) Osteopathic Hosp., 1986-87; resident in internal medicine Garden City Hosp.; pvt. practice, Three Rivers, Mich., 1988-95; assoc. prof. family practice W.Va. Sch. Osteo. Medicine, Lewisburg, 1995—; cons. East Cen. Coll. Consortium, Alliance, Ohio, 1979; presenter, lectr. in field. Coun. mem. Town Council, Bethany, W.Va., 1978-80; elder 1st Presbyn. Ch., Three Rivers, 1989. Mem. Sigma Sigma Phi Osteo. Honor Soc., Sigma Xi. Office: WVa Sch Osteo Medicine Clinic 400 N Lee St Lewisburg WV 24901

HOUX, SHIRLEY ANN, personal and business services company executive, consultant, researcher; b. Claremore, Okla., Nov. 1, 1931; d. George Warren and Alta Zena (Starkweather) Pritchard; m. William Dean Munson, June 1, 1951 (div. June 1962); children—Debra Kay, Diana Sue, Donna Lynn; m. Leonard Houx, June 22, 1963 (div. Oct. 1989); 1 child, David Leonard. Student in bus. Okla. State U., 1949-50. Sec. Jack Gordon, P.A., Claremore, Okla., 1947-48; sec., personnel mgr. Gulf Oil Corp., Tulsa, 1950-51; exec. sec. to wing comdr. U.S. Air Force, Cocoa Beach, Fla., 1951-53; exec. sec. to gen. counsel Houston So., P.A., Stillwater, Okla., 1957-60; exec. sec. to exec. v.p. and sr. v.p. Williams Cos., Tulsa, 1962-64; owner, chief exec. officer Hallmark Exchange, Inc., Tulsa, 1981—; cons. small bus., Tulsa, 1981—; mem. small bus. adv. bd. Tulsa Jr. Coll., 1983—. Author: (drama) Wedding Rehearsal for the Bride of Christ, 1985. Contbg. editor The Chronicle, 1984. Co-creator, producer foot health program, 1967 (Am. Podiatry Assn. Outstanding award 1968); creator, advt. campaign for Cystic Fibrosis Found.: I'm One...Be One, 1978. Pres. women's aux. Okla. Podiatry Assn., Tulsa, 1966-82; sec.-treas. Okla. bd. examiners Okla. Podiatry Assn., 1969-76; nat. audio-visual chmn. women's aux. Am. Podiatry Assn., 1976; pres. Tulsa Cerebral Palsy Assn., 1977, Cystic Fibrosis Found. Aux., Tulsa, 1979. Named Miss Claremore, Claremore Bus. and Profl. Women, Okla., 1949; recipient Two-Star award Pure D'Lite Co., 1982. Mem. Nat. Assn. Female Execs. Democrat. Avocations: fashion design; the arts; writing.

HOWARD, ALEX T., JR., federal judge; b. 1924. Student, U. Ala., 1942, U. Ala., 1946, Auburn U., 1942-44; JD, Vanderbilt U., 1950. U.S. probation officer Mobile, Ala., 1950-51; ptnr. Johnstone, Adams, Howard, Bailey & Gordon, Mobile, 1951-86; U.S. commr. U.S. Dist. Ct. (so. dist.) Ala., 1956-70; judge U.S. Dist. Ct. (so. dist.) Ala., Mobile, 1986—, chief judge, 1989-94; assoc. editor Am. Maritime Cases for Port of Mobile. Served to 2d lt. U.S. Army, 1943-46. Mem. ABA, Internat. Soc. Barristers, Internat. Assn. of Ins. Counsel, Maritime Law Assn. of U.S., Southeastern Admiralty Law Inst. (dir. 1978-80), Ala. Bar Assn., Ala. Def. Lawyers Assn. (dir. late 1950's), Mobile Bar Assn. (pres. 1973). Office: US Courthouse 113 Saint Joseph St Mobile AL 36602-3606

HOWARD, ALEX WAYNE, financial consultant; b. N.Y.C., May 2, 1946; s. Joel and Marjorie Howard; m. Paulette May Traylor, Oct. 18, 1987. BS in Fin., NYU, 1970, MBA in Econs., 1975. Cert. chartered fin. analyst. V.p. Standard Rsch. Cons., N.Y.C., 1972-81; 1st v.p. Rotan Mosle, Inc., Houston, 1981-85; v.p. Allied Capital Co., Houston, 1985-88; mng. dir. Kemper Securities Group, Inc. (formerly Lovett, Underwood, Neuhaus & Webb, Inc.), Houston, 1988-91; dir., owner Howard Frazier Barker Elliott, Inc., Houston, 1991—. Contbr. articles to profl. publs. Mem. allocations com. Gulf Coast Campaign United Way, Houston, 1989-91; bd. dirs. Odyssey House Tex., Inc., 1992—. Mem. Am. Soc. Appraisers, Assn. Investment Mgmt. and Rsch., Plaza Club (gov. 1990-92). Office: Howard Frazier Barker Elliott Inc 815 Walker St Ste 1447 Houston TX 77002-5716

HOWARD, ANGELA KAY, lawyer, accountant; b. Tripoli, Libya, May 29, 1964; d. Laydell Ronnie and Thelmarie (Harris) H. BS magna cum laude, Va. State U., 1986; JD, DePaul U., 1989. Bar: Ill. 1989, U.S. Dist. Ct. (no. dist.) Ill. 1989, D.C. 1991. Bank compliance officer, bank secrecy officer Jefferson Nat. Bank, Charlottesville, Va. Mem. ABA, Ill. Bar Assn., Chgo. Bar Assn., D.C. Bar, Nat. Assn. Black Accts. Home: 601 Jefferson Dr E Palmyra VA 22963 Office: Jefferson Nat Bank 123 E Main St Charlottesville VA 22902-5223

HOWARD, BARBARA ANN, obstetrical/gynecological nurse practitioner; b. Palestine, Tex., Nov. 22, 1952; d. Pink and Pearlene Delois (Green) Sanders; m. Troy W. Simmons (div.); 1 child,Troy W. Jr.; m. Gardner B. Howard, Jr., Dec. 23, 1978; 1 child, Tiri Chantréal. AS in Nursing, Tarrant County Jr. Coll., Fort Worth, Tex., 1975; Nursing Practitioner Women's Health, U. Tex Southwestern Med. Sch., Dallas, 1992. RN, Tex.; cert. ob-gyn. nurse practitioner. Student nurse emergency room and ICC Ft. Worth Osteopathic Hosp., Ft. Worth, Tex., 1973-75; supr. emergency room Newburn Meml. Hosp., Jacksonville, Tex., 1975-77; part time staff nurse Newburn Meml. Hosp., Jacksonville, 1979-80; staff for labor and delivery Doctor's Meml. Hosp., Tyler, Tex., 1977-79; staff nurse med.-surg. Woman's Hosp. of Tex., Houston, 1982-84; nurse, PMS counselor Women's Health Inst. Baylor U., Houston, 1984-89; ob-gyn. nurse practitioner, cons. Smith County Health Dist. and Family Care Ctr., Tyler, 1990-95; pvt. practice, Henderson, Tex., 1995—; counselor PMS Support Group, Houston, 1984-89; 1st v.p. Women's Hosp. Employee Adv. Bd., Houston, 1984-88; cons. Smith County Health Dist., Tyler, 1990—. Mem. Spkrs. Bur., Women's Hosp. Tex., Houston, 1985-90; mem. Houston Regional Coun. for Alcohol and Drug Abuse, 1984-86; cons. on teen pregnancy Jr. League Tyler, 1995-97. Mem. Tex. Nursing Assn., Tex. Nurse Practitioners Assn., East Tex. Black Nurses Assn., Teenage Parent Program Adv. Com., Nat. Black Leadership Initiative Against Cancer, Profl. Black Womens Assn. Baptist. Home: 10778 County Road 2219 Tyler TX 75707-9794 Office: 815 N Marshall Henderson TX 75652

HOWARD, BERNARD EUFINGER, mathematics and computer science educator; b. Ludlow, Vt., Sept. 22, 1920; s. Charles Rawson and Ethel (Kearney) H.; m. Ruth Belknap, Mar. 29, 1942. Student Middlebury Coll., 1938-40; B.S., MIT, 1944; M.S., U. Ill., 1947, Ph.D., 1951. Staff mem. Radiation Lab, MIT, Cambridge, 1942-45; asst. math. U. Ill., Champaign-

Urbana, 1945-49; sr. mathematician Inst. Air Weapons Rsch., U. Chgo., 1951, asst. to dir. Inst. for Systems Rsch., 1952-56, assoc. dir., 1956-60, assoc. dir. Labs. for Applied Sci., 1958-60; dir. Sci. Computing Ctr. U. Miami, Coral Gables, Fla., 1960-64, prof. math. and computer sci., 1960-91, prof. emeritus, 1991—, assoc. faculty Grad. Sch. of Internat. Studies, 1996—; chmn. bd. dirs. Sociocybernetics, Inc.; exec. sec. Air Force Adv. Bd. Simulation, 1951-54; cons. Systems Rsch. Labs, Inc., Dayton, Ohio, 1963-67, acting dir. math. scis. div., 1965; cons. Variety Children's Rsch. Found., Miami, 1964-66, Fla. Power & Light Co., Miami, 1968, Shaw & Assocs., 1964-75; vis. fellow Dartmouth Coll., Hanover, N.H., 1976; co-investigator Positron Emission Tomography Ctr., U. Miami Dept. Neurology/Mt. Sinai Med. Ctr., 1981-84. Creator Parabolic-Earth Radar Coverage Chart, 1944; co-creator: (with Henry W. Kunce) Sociocybernetics, 1971, Optimum Curvature, 1964, Optimum Torsion, 1974, (with J.F.B. Shaw) Principles in Highway Routing, (with James M. Syck) Twisted Splines, 1992. Chmn. bd. dirs. Blue Lake Assn., Inc., Miami, 1969-96, chmn. emeritus 1996—. Am. Soc. Engring. Edn.-Office of Naval Research fellow Naval Underwater Systems Ctr., 1981, 82. Mem. Am. Math. Soc., Soc. Indsl. and Applied Math. (treas. S.E. sect. 1964), Am. Phys. Soc., Assn. Computing Machinery (chpt. chmn. 1969-70), IEEE, AAUP (chpt. sec. 1974-91), Sigma Xi, Phi Kappa Phi, Pi Mu Epsilon, Alpha Sigma Phi, Alpha Epsilon Lambda. Home: 7320 Miller Dr Miami FL 33155-5504 Office: U Miami Sci Computing Ctr Coral Gables FL 33124

HOWARD, BILL OSBORNE, small business owner; b. Mooresville, N.C., Jan. 31, 1930; s. Ray Henry and Ollie Louise (Miller) H.; m. Ann Blanton, Aug. 13, 1950; children: Deborah Howard, Michael Ray. BA, Gardner Webb U., 1960. Detail rep. Ives Labs., Columbia, S.C., 1963-75; salesperson, mgr. Bio-Med, Columbia, 1975-79; pres. Howard's Courier Svc., Inc., Spindale, N.C., 1990—. Republican. Methodist. Home: 279 H Creekside Oak Springs Rutherfordton NC 28139 Office: Howard's Courier Svc 116 Arnett St Rutherfordton NC 28139

HOWARD, CAROL SPENCER, librarian, journalist; b. Great Bend, Kans., 1944; d. Thomas Glendon and Margaret Merle (Jackson) Spencer; m. William Neal Howard, Dec. 31, 1977 (div. July 1987); 1 child, Morgan William. BA in Journalism, English and Edn., Baylor U., 1967; MLS, U. Tex., 1974. Cert. libr. City desk reporter Waco (Tex.) News-Tribune, 1965-67; guest editor Mademoiselle mag., N.Y.C., 1966; womens' news reporter Houston Post, 1969; libr. Austin Ind. Sch. Dist., 1974-86, 91—, San Antonio Ind. Sch. Dist., 1989-90, Del Valle (Tex.) Ind. Sch. Dist., 1990-91; children's book reviewer Austin Am. Statesman, 1984-90; freelance journalist, children's lit. cons. Contbr. articles to profl. jours. Fellow U. Tex., 1973-74. Home: PO Box 5875 Austin TX 78763-5875

HOWARD, CHARLENE, community health nurse, administrator; b. Beaumont, Tex., Dec. 29, 1949; d. Henry and Hattie Mae (Cruse) Collins; m. Edward C. Howard, Oct. 21, 1989; children: Wednesday, Edward V. III. Diploma, Bapt. Hosp. Sch. Nursing, Beaumont, 1974; BSN, Lamar U., Beaumont, 1983. Cert. women's health advanced nurse practitioner; recert. Head nurse Women's and Children's Hosp., Beaumont; clin. supr. Port Arthur (Tex.) Health Dept., asst. DON; DON Grayson County Health Dept., Sherman, Tex. Mem. Tex. Pub. Health Assn.

HOWARD, CLARICE HARDEE, special education educator; b. Baxley, Ga., May 29, 1962; d. Frank D. and Beth (Fulghum) Hardee; m. Jarrett Mayes Howard, June 24, 1989. BS in Edn., U. Ga., 1984; MEd, Ga. State U., 1989; Edn. Specialist Degree, West Ga. Coll., 1993. Tchr. mentally handicapped Glynn County Middle Sch., Brunswick, Ga., 1984-86, Lee St. Elementary Sch., Jonesboro, Ga., 1986-87, Richards Middle Sch., Lawrenceville, Ga., 1987, Flat Rock Middle Sch., Fayetteville, Ga., 1990-91; tchr. handicapped presch., presch. coord., spl. edn. dir.'s adminstrv. asst. Oak Grove Elem. Sch., 1991—; conductor workshops in field. Youth counselor St. Simons Meth. Ch., 1985-86, vacation Bible tchr.; active Boy Scouts Am., Handicapped, 1986-89. Named Atlanta Jour. Honor Tchr., 1991, P.L.A.C.E. Educator of Yr., 1996. Mem. ASCD, Coun. for Exceptional Children, Assn. for Severely Handicapped. Home: 120 Chesterfield Ct Fayetteville GA 30214-1785

HOWARD, DAGGETT HORTON, lawyer; b. N.Y.C., Mar. 20, 1917; s. Chester Augustus and Olive Ree (Daggett) H.; m. Patricia McClellan Exton, Sept. 1950; children: Daggett Horton Jr., Jeffrey, David, Patricia. B.A. magna cum laude, Yale U., 1938, J.D., 1941. Bar: N.Y. 1942, D.C. 1961. Legal staff Root, Clark, Buckner & Ballantine, N.Y.C., 1941-43, Lend Lease Adminstrn., Fgn. Econ. Adminstrn., 1943-44; exec. asst. to spl. counsel to Pres. White House, 1945; legal adviser on WWII Allied war settlements, developing Marshall Plan Dept. State, 1945-47; internat. atty. on world-wide civil aviation bilateral agreements, asst. chief internat. and rules div. CAB, 1947-52; assoc. gen. counsel Dept. Air Force, 1952-56, dep. gen. counsel, 1956-58; Dept. Def. rep. on world-wide military base negotiations, 1952-58; 1st gen. counsel FAA, 1958-62; partner Cox, Langford & Brown, Washington, 1962-66, Howard, Poe & Bastian, Washington, 1966-83; partner Howard & Law, Washington, 1983-88, atty.-at-law, real estate syndicator, 1988—; exec. v.p. Realty Growth Mgrs., Inc., 1990—; co-author, counsel L'Enfant Plaza Complex; spl. counsel for Amtrak acquistion of N.E. corridor. Mem. bd. editors Yale Law Jour.; co-author, counsel, advisor L'Enfant Plaza Project, 1963-88. Past mem. policy com. Daniel and Florence Guggenheim Aviation Safety Ctr.; past corp. mem. Children's Hosp. D.C. Ensign USNR, 1938-41. Recipient Exceptional Civilian Service award Dept. Air Force, 1958; Disting. Service award FAA, 1962. Mem. ABA, Washington Bar Assn., Corby Ct., Fed. Bar Assn., Yale Law Sch. Assn., Yale Club, Met. Club, Chevy Chase Club, Phi Beta Kappa, Alpha Sigma Phi. Home: 4319 Cathedral Ave NW Washington DC 20016-3560 Office: Maple Profl Park Birch Bldg Ste C 301 Maple Ave W Vienna VA 22180

HOWARD, DEAN ALLEN, purchasing agent; b. Bartlesville, Okla., Apr. 5, 1966; s. Eudean and Patricia (Allen) H. Student, Tex. Tech U., Lubbock, 1987-90, Stephen F. Austin State U., 1992. Purchasing specialist Tex. Legis. Coun., Austin, 1992-93; purchasing mgr. Tex. Ho. of Reps., Austin, 1994—. Mem. Nat. Assn. Purchasing Mgrs., Theta Chi. Republican. Mem. Ch. of Christ. Home: 6506 Valley Ridge Ct Austin TX 78746 Office: Tex Ho of Reps 105 W 15th St Austin TX 78701

HOWARD, ELSIE STERLING, marketing executive; b. Phila., June 30, 1946; d. Julian Alexander and Reba (Shaffer) S.; m. Eugene Jay Howard, Mar. 9, 1969; children: Heidi, Elizabeth. BA, U. Pa., 1968. Mgr. spl. events Miami Heart Assn., Miami Beach, Fla., 1986-91; mktg. cons. Temple Beth Sholom, Miami Beach, 1991-92, Women's Healthcare Svc., Miami Beach, 1992-93; spl. events cons. Sylvester Comp. Cancer Ctr., Miami, Fla., 1991-92; pres. Sterling Pub. Rels., Miami Beach, 1993—; bd. dirs. Bankers Trust Co. of Fla., Children's Home Soc., 1996—. Active Citizens Commemorative Coin Adv. Com., U.S. Mint, 1994—; founding mem. Trustees' Coun. of Penn Women, 1986—, chair, 1994—; assoc. trustee U. Pa., 1987-91, founding mem. pres.'s coun., 1983—, so. regional alumni trustee, 1991—, overseer Sch. of Veterinary Medicine, 1992—, dir. Inst. Contemporary Arts, 1991—, trustee, 1990—, pres. Gen. Alumni Soc., 1995—; mem. Commn. on Status of Women, City of Miami Beach, 1992—, vice chair, 1993; founding mem. devel. coun. Sylvester Comprehensive Cancer Ctr., U. Miami Sch. Medicine, 1993—, chair spl. events task force, 1993—, vice chair devel. coun., 1995—; mem. Police Sub-Com. Task Force, City of Miami Beach, 1993—. Recipient Ivory Lady award NFIC, 1986, Women of Charity award Am. Cancer Soc., 1986, Love and Hope Rose award Juvenile Diabetes, 1985. Mem. Am. Numismatic Assn. (Pres. award 1995), Brickell Ave. Literary Soc., U. Pa. Gen. Alumni Soc. (mem. exec. com. 1991—), U. Pa. Dade Alumni Club (founding pres. 1982-85, secondary sch. chmn. 1988-90), U. Pa. Faculty Club, Westview Country Club, Foundlings Club. Democrat. Home: 4825 Lakeview Dr Miami FL 33140

HOWARD, GENE CLAUDE, lawyer, former state senator; b. Perry, Okla., Sept. 26, 1926; s. Joe W. and Nell L. (Brown) H.; m. Belva J. Prestidge, Dec. 28, 1979; children: Jean Ann Howard, Joe Ted, Belinda Janice. LL.B., U. Okla., 1951. Bar: Okla. 1950, U.S. Ct. Mil. Appeals 1956, U.S. Supreme Ct. 1956. Ptnr. Howard & Widdows, Tulsa, 1952—; mem. Okla. Ho. of Reps., 1958-62; mem. Okla. Senate, 1964-82, pres. pro tem, 1974-81; bd. dirs. Roseland Oil and Gas, Inc., Local Am. Bank; trustee Phila. Mortgage Trust; mem. exec. com. Coun. State Govts., 1976-82; chmn. Okla. State and Edn. Employees Group Ins. Bd. Pres. Okla. Jr. Democrats, 1954; del. Dem. Nat. Conv., 1964; mem. So. Growth Policy Bd., 1972-76. Served with U.S. Army, 1944-46, PTO, lt. col. USAF, 1961-62. Mem. Okla. Bar Assn., Tulsa County Bar Assn. (Outstanding Young Atty. 1953), Phi Delta Phi. Mem. Christian Ch. (Disciples of Christ). Home: 2404 E 29th St Tulsa OK 74114-5619 Office: Howard & Widdows PC 2021 S Lewis Ave Tulsa OK 74104

HOWARD, GEORGE, JR., federal judge; b. Pine Bluff, Ark., May 13, 1924. Student, Lincoln U., 1951; B.S., U. Ark., J.D., 1954; LL.D., 1976. Bar: Ark. bar 1953, U.S. Supreme Ct. bar 1959. Pvt. practice law Pine Bluff, 1953-77; spl. assoc. justice Ark. Supreme Ct., 1976, assoc. justice, 1977; justice U.S. Ct. Appeals, Ark., 1979-80; U.S. dist. judge, Eastern dist. Little Rock, 1980—; Mem. Ark. Claims Commn., 1969-77; chmn. Ark. adv. com. Civil Rights Commn.. Recipient citation in recognition of faithful and disting. svc. as mem. Supreme Ct. Com. of Profl. Conduct, 1980, disting. jurist award Jud. Coun. Nat. Bar Assn., 1980, Wiley A. Branton Issues Symposium award, 1990; voted outstanding trial judge 1984-85 Ark. Trial Lawyers Assn.; inducted Ark.'s Black Hall of Fame, 1994; recipient keepers of the spirit award Univ. Ark., Pine Bluff, 1995, quality svc. award Ark. Dem. Black Caucus, 1995. Mem. ABA, Ark. Bar Assn., Jefferson County Bar Assn. (pres.). Baptist. Office: US Dist Ct PO Box 349 Little Rock AR 72203-0349

HOWARD, HERBERT HOOVER, broadcasting and communications educator; b. Johnson City, Tenn., Nov. 7, 1928; s. Bonnie Robert and Laura Elizabeth (Crumley) H.; m. Alpha Sells Day, Nov. 16, 1956; 1 child, Joseph David. BS, E. Tenn. State U., Johnson City, 1952, MS, 1955; cert., U. N.C., 1959; PhD in Mass Communications, Ohio U., 1973. Announcer, program dir. Sta. WJHL-AM-FM-TV, Johnson City, 1951-58; writer, announcer Sta. WCHL & WUNC-TV, Chapel Hill, N.C., 1958-59; from instr. to radio network mgr. U. Tenn., 1959-70, from asst. to assoc. prof. communications, 1970-80; prof. broadcasting U. Tenn., Knoxville, 1980—, asst. dean Coll. Communications, 1981-93, acting dean, 1990-91; assoc. dean, 1993—; mem. cmty. adv. bd. WSJK-WKOP Pub. TV, 1995—. Author: Multiple Ownership in Television and Broadcasting, 1979, (textbook) Radio, TV, and Cable Programming, 1984, 94, Broadcast Advertising, 1979, 88, 91; contbr. articles to profl. jours. Mem. Soc. Profl. Journalists, Assn. Edn. in Journalism and Mass. Comms., Broadcast Edn. Assn. Republican. Presbyterian. Lodge: Optimist (So. Knoxville v.p. 1972—, pres., 1974, lt. gov. Tenn. dist. internat. chpt., 1976). Home: 1724 S Hills Dr Knoxville TN 37920-2937 Office: U Tenn 426 Communications Bldg Knoxville TN 37996

HOWARD, JOHN LORING, trust banker; b. Auburn, N.Y., Apr. 12, 1935; s. Chauncey Frisbie and Ruth Dorothea (Burrows) H.; m. Catherine Edith Swaffin, July 1, 1961; children: John Loring, Jr., Sarah Catherine. BS, Cornell U., 1957; postgrad., NYU, 1961-62; grad. with distinction, Southwestern Grad. Sch. Banking, 1970. V.p. Chase Manhattan Bank, New York, 1961-77; sr. v.p., div. mgr. RepublicBank Houston, 1978-82; sr. v.p., group mgr. RepublicBank Trust Co., Houston, 1983-87, NCNB Tex. Nat. Bank, Dallas, 1988-91; sr. v.p., group mgr. NationsBank of Tex., N.A., Dallas, 1992-95, v.p., 1996—. Elder Munn Avenue Presbyn. Ch., East Orange, N.J., 1963-64; chmn. troop com. Boy Scouts Am., New Providence, N.J., 1975-77, dist. chmn. Friends of Scouting, Houston, 1980-82, vice chmn. North Trail dist. com., Dallas, 1990-93, chmn., 1994-95; mem. fin. com. Spring Woods United Meth. Ch., Houston, 1981-84. 1st lt. USMC, 1957-60. Mem. Am. Soc. Corp. Secs. (sec. S.W. regional group 1984-85), Govt. Fin. Officers Assn. Republican.

HOWARD, LOUNITA COOK, journalist; b. Lebanon, Tenn., July 30, 1962; d. Gordon Lew and Sandra Marie (Davis) Cook; m. Bobby Le Howard, Feb. 19, 1983. BS, Middle Tenn. State U., 1985. Intern The Bus. Jour., Nashville, 1985; staff writer The Nashville Bus. Jour., 1985-86; staff writer The Lebanon Democrat, 1986-89, news editor, 1989—. Agy. coord. Wilson County United Way, 1990, mem. comms. com., 1991-92; mem. adv. bd. March of Dimes, Wilson County, 1991; mem. Leadership Wilson, 1995. Recipient Appreciation plaques Wilson County Edn. Assn., 1988, Enhanced 911 Wilson County, 1990; Sch. Bell award Tenn. Edn. Assn., 1988, 89, Cert. of Recognition, 1990, Cert of Appreciation, March of Dimes, 1991, Mng. Editors awards Tenn. Assoc. Press. Mem. Tenn. Press Assn. (1st pl. award 1989, 90), Soc. Profl. Journalists, Lebanon Bus. and Profl. Women's Club (2d v.p. 1993-94, 1st v.p. 1994-95, pres. 1995-96, Woman of Yr. 1994-95, Young Careerist 1990). Baptist. Office: The Lebanon Democrat 402 N Cumberland St Lebanon TN 37087-2306

HOWARD, PIERRE, state official; m. Nancy Elizabeth Barnes; children: Christopher, Caroline. Grad., U. Ga., 1965, JD, 1968. Former mem. Ga. Senate, Atlanta, former asst. floor leader, former chmn. human resources com.; lt. gov. State of Ga., Atlanta, 1991—. Mem. Phi Beta Kappa. Office: 1201 W Peachtree St Atlanta GA 30309-3424 also: State Capitol Office Lt Gov Rm 240 Atlanta GA 30334

HOWARD, RICHARD RALSTON, II, medical health advisor, researcher, financier; b. Winnfield, Kans., May 26, 1948; s. Richard Ralston and Ione (Mayer) H. BBA, Loyola U., New Orleans, 1970; MPH, Tulane U., 1977, MS, 1984, DrPH, 1988. Researcher Loyola U., 1973; educator Dominican Coll., New Orleans, 1977; educator Sch. Pub. Health Tulane U., New Orleans, 1978-82, researcher Sch. Medicine, 1979-88; med. health advisor Howard Med. Clinic, Slidell, La., 1982-91; founder The Inst. Econ. Tech. Rsch., New Orleans, 1993—. NIH grantee, 1979; VA grantee, 1984. Mem. Internat. Platform Assn., Am. Assn. Individual Investors, Beta Beta Beta. Home: 3531 Nashville Ave New Orleans LA 70125-4339

HOWARD, STANLEY LOUIS, investment banker; b. New Kensington, Pa., Oct. 18, 1948; s. Stanley Joseph and Anne Irene (Mentecki) Hoderowski; m. Kathryn Lynn Franz, July 31, 1971 (div. Dec. 1981). BS, MIT, 1970; MBA, Harvard U., 1972. Sr. account exec. Cyphernetics Corp. div. ADP Network Svcs., N.Y.C., 1972-75; mgr. fin. systems IU Internat., Phila., 1975-76; v.p. Citibank, N.A., N.Y.C., 1976-81, Lehman Bros. Kuhn Loeb, N.Y.C., 1981-83; exec. v.p. Dean Witter Reynolds, Inc., N.Y.C., 1983-88; sr. v.p., dir. fin. Deutsche Bank Govt. Securities, Inc., N.Y.C., 1988-91; CFO Paresco, Inc., Jersey City, 1991-95; pres. NeuroFax LLC, New Smyrna Beach, Fla., 1995—. U.S. Sec. of Labor fellow, 1970. Republican. Roman Catholic. Home: 60 W 9th St New York NY 10011-8908 Office: NeuroFax LLC 4448 Saxon Dr New Smyrna Beach FL 32169-4135

HOWARD, THAD ALAN, research analyst; b. Wilmington, N.C., Sept. 15, 1960; s. Julius F. and Ruby E. (Swart) H.; m. Elizabeth M. Howard, Sept. 10, 1994. BS, Campbell U., Buies Creek, N.C., 1982; MS, Appalachian State U., Boone, N.C., 1986. Rsch. assoc. Roche Biomed. Labs., Burlington, N.C., 1986-88; rsch. technologist Duke U. Med. Ctr., Durham, N.C., 1988-90, rsch. analyst, 1990—. Mem. Sierra Club (outings leader 1995). Office: Duke U Med Ctr Box 2916 139 MSRB Rsch Dr Durham NC 27710

HOWARD, THARON WAYNE, English literature educator; b. Kansas City, Mo., Mar. 8, 1961; s. Darold Wayne and Carmen Lawana (Duzan) H.; m. Wynona R. Phillips, May 31, 1980; children: Bryce J., Logan W. BA cum laude, U. Mo., Kansas City, 1985; MA, Purdue U., 1987, PhD, 1992. Grad. instr. Purdue U., West Lafayette, Ind., 1987-92; asst. prof. dept. English Clemson (S.C.) U., 1992-96, assoc. prof., 1996—; dir. NCR/Clemson Usability Testing Facility, 1993—. Mem. editorial bd. The Bull. of Assn. for Bus. Comm., 1992—; prodn. editor S.C. Rev., 1992—, The Upstart Crow: A Shakespeare Jour., 1992—; contbr. articles to profl. jours. Mem. MLA, Nat. Coun. Tchrs. English, Conf. on Coll. Composition and Comm., Soc. for Tech. Comm., Assn. for Bus. Comm., Rhetoric Soc. Am., Soc. for Critical Exch., Ind. Tchrs. of Writing. Home: 215 Mulberry Ave Clemson SC 29631-2322 Office: Clemson U Dept English Strode Tower Box 341503 Clemson SC 29634-1503

HOWARD-PEEBLES, PATRICIA N., clinical cytogeneticist; b. Lawton, Okla., Nov. 24, 1941; d. J. Marion and R. Leona (prestidge) Howard; m. Thomas M. Peebles, Aug. 16, 1975. BSEd, U. Ctrl. Okla., 1963; student, Randolph-Macon Coll. Women, 1964; PhD in Zoology (Genetics), U Tex. at Austin, 1969. Diplomate Am. Bd. Med. Genetics; cert. clin. cytogeneticist, med. geneticist. Sci. and history tchr. Piedmont (Okla.) Pub. Schs., 1963-64; biochem. technician biochemistry sect. biology divsn. Oak Ridge (Tenn.) Nat. Lab., 1964-66; instr. rsch. pediatrics dept. pediatrics, instr. cytotech. U. Okla. Health Scis. Ctr., Oklahoma City, 1971-72; asst. prof., dir. Cytogenetics Lab. U. So. Miss., Hattiesburg, 1973-77, assoc. prof., dir. Cytogenetics Lab., 1977-80; assoc. prof. dept. pub. health, staff Lab. Med. Genetics U. Ala., Birmingham, 1980-81; assoc. prof., dir. Cytogenetics Lab. dept. pathology U. Tex. Health Sci. Ctr., Dallas, 1981-85, prof., dir. Cytogenetics Lab., 1985-87; prof. dept. human genetics Med. Coll. Va., Richmond, 1987—; clin. cytogeneticist, dir. Postnatal Lab. Genetics & IVF Inst., Fairfax, Va., 1987—; Am. Cancer Soc. postdoctoral fellow dept. human genetics U. Mich. Med. Sch., Ann Arbor, 1969-70, dept. human genetics and devel. Coll. Physicians and Surgeons, Columbia U., N.Y.C., 1970-71; genetic cons. Ellisville (Miss.) State Sch., 1973-80; attending staff dept. pathology Parkland Meml. Hosp., Dallas County Hosp. Dist., 1981-87; mem. sci. adv. com. Fragile X Found., 1985—; mem. Internat. Standing Com. on Human Cytogenetic Nomenclature, 1991-96. Contbr. articles to profl. jours., chpts. to books; reviewer Am. Jour. Human Genetics, Am. Jour. Med. Genetics, Clin. Genetics, Human Genetics. Fellow Am. Coll. Med. Genetics (founding mem.); mem. AAAS, Am. Soc. Human Genetics, Assn. Genetic Technologists, Tex. Genetics Soc. (chmn. planning com. ann. meeting 1984), Delta Kappa Gamma, Sigma Xi. Baptist. Office: Genetics & IVF Inst 3020 Javier Rd Fairfax VA 22031-4627

HOWARDS, STUART S., physician, educator; b. Milw., Mar. 29, 1937; s. Harvey H. and Anne (Levin) H.; m. Carter N. Howards, Aug. 20, 1966; children: Penelope P., Hugh N. BA, Yale U., 1959; MD, Columbia U., 1963. Intern in surgery Peter Bent Brigham Hosp., Boston, 1963-64, resident in urology, 1968-71; resident in surgery Childrens Hosp., Boston, 1964-65; rsch. assoc. NIH, Bethesda, Md., 1965-68; asst. prof. urology and physiology U. Va., Charlotteville, 1971-74, assoc. prof., 1974-76, prof., 1976—, chief divsn. pediat. urology, 1986—; chmn. exam com. Am. Bd. Urology, 1985-91, pres., 1992-93. Editor: Infertility in the Male, 1991, 2d edit., 1990, Adult and Pediatric Urology, 1991, 3d edit., 1995; editor Jour. Urology, 1983—. Maj. USPHS, 1965-68. Recipient Career Investigation award NIH, 1973-78. Fellow Am. Acad. Pediats.; mem. Am. Urologic Assn. (Golden Cystoscope award 1981, Scott award 1990, Hugh Young award 1991), Clin. Soc. Genitourinary Surgeons, Am. Fertility Soc. (bd. dirs. 1994—), Soc. Andrology, Geniturinary Surgeons, Am. Assn. GU Surgeons (sec.-treas. 1992—). Home: 1150 W Leigh Dr Charlottesville VA 22901-7706 Office: U Va Hosp Jefferson Park Ave Charlottesville VA 22908

HOWARTH, ELIZABETH H., financial advisor; b. Staunton, Va., Dec. 18, 1944; d. Harry Nash and Sara Katherine (wilson) Hodges; m. B. Roberts Howarth, Aug. 26, 1967 (div. Jan. 1985); children: David, William, Sara; m. L. Ellis Michael, Oct. 29, 1993. BA, Randolph Macon Woman's Coll., Lynchburg, Va., 1967; MEd, James Madison U., Harrisonburg, Va., 1985; postgrad., U. South Fla., 1989-95. Med. technician Med. Coll. Va., Richmond, 1967-69; tchr. Albert H. Hill Jr. H.S., Richmond, 1969-70, St. Peter's Sch., Peekskill, N.Y., 1970-71, Storm King Sch., cornwall, N.Y., 1971-73; owner Wilson Jewelers, Harrisonburg, 1973-75; tchr. James Madison U., Harrisonburg, 1985-89, U. South Fla., Tampa, 1989-91; fin. advisor Raymond James & Assocs., Tampa, 1991—. Pres. adv. coun. Tampa Bay Rsch. Inst., 1995—; co-founder Woman's Cancer Resource Ctr., 1995—. Mem. Fla. Women's Alliance, Network Exec. Women, Randolph-Macon Woman's Coll. Alumnae Assn. (pres. 1995—), Athena Soc. Episcopalian. Office: Raymond James and Associates 100 S Ashley Dr Ste 1400 Tampa FL 33602-5309

HOWE, EVELYN FREEMAN, cultural organization administrator; b. Spartanburg, S.C., Jan. 11, 1929; d. D. Odell and Jane Tabitha (Bryson) Freeman; m. Jack Dean Howe, June 10, 1950; children: Andrew Walter, Angela Jane. BA, Limestone Coll., 1948; MA in Edn., Winthrop Coll., 1967. Social studies tchr. Whitmire (S.C.) High Sch., 1948-50; tchr. 2d grade Beaverdam Elem. Sch., Gaffney, S.C., 1950-51; social worker Portsmouth (Va.) Welfare Dept., 1952-54; caseworker Cherokee County Dept. Social Svcs., Gaffney, 1955-58; tchr. 6th grade Draytonville Elem. Sch., Gaffney, 1960-67; prin., librarian Corinth & Alma Elem. Schs., Gaffney, 1967-74; tchr. 6th grade Blacksburg (S.C.) Elem. Sch., 1974-81; tchr. 5th grade J. Paul Beam Elem. Sch., Gaffney, 1981-87; exec. dir. Cherokee County Literacy Assn., Gaffney, 1987—. Pres. Cherokee Hist. and Preservation Soc., Gaffney, 1987-88, 95—, v.p., 1988—; sec. Cherokee County Social and Health Orgn. Coun., 1987—, pres., 1992-93, subcom. chmn., mem. task force on reading improvement Cherokee County Sch. Dist., 1988; mem. Leadership Cherokee VIII, 1992-93. Recipient Svc. to Community award Limestone Coll., 1978, Svc. to Coll., 1989. Mem. Cherokee County Literacy Assn. (trainer 1986—, pres. Gaffney chpt. 1970-85), Cherokee County Reading Coun. (1st pres. Gaffney chpt. 1985-86), S.C. Edn. Assn. (bd. dirs. Columbia chpt. 1983-87), Limestone Coll. Alumni Assn. (sec. bd. Gaffney chpt. 1986-88), AAUW (pres. Gaffney br. 1960-62, 74-76, 94—, S.C. State Community Rep. 1990-92, chair by-laws com. 1992—), Altrusa Club Gaffney, Inc. (charter, v.p. 1993—), Delta Kappa Gamma (sec. Gaffney chpt. 1988-90, pres. 1990-92). Democrat. Presbyterian. Home: 219 Crestview Dr Gaffney SC 29340-2848 Office: Cherokee County Literacy 409 W Buford St Gaffney SC 29341-1701

HOWE, JOHN PRENTICE, III, health science center executive, physician; b. Jackson, Tenn., Mar. 7, 1943; s. John Prentice and Phyllis (MacDonald) H.; children: Lindsey Warren, Brooke Olmsted, John Prentice IV. BA, Amherst Coll., 1965; MD, Boston U., 1969. Diplomate Am. Bd. Internal Medicine, internal medicine and cardiovascular disease. Research assoc. cellular physiology Amherst Coll., 1963-64; research assoc. cardiovascular physiology Boston U. Sch. of Medicine, 1966-67, lectr. medicine, 1972-73; intern Boston City Hosp., 1969-70, asst. resident, 1970-71; research fellow in medicine Harvard U., 1971-73, Peter Bent Brigham Hosp., 1971-73; survey physician Framingham Cardiovascular Disease Study, Nat. Heart and Lung Inst., 1971; asst. clin. prof. medicine U. Hawaii, 1973-75; asst. prof. medicine U. Mass., 1975-77, assoc. prof., 1977-85, vice chmn. dept. medicine, 1975-78, asst. dean continuing edn. for physicians, 1976-78, assoc. dean profl. affairs and continuing edn., 1978-80, acad. dean, 1980-85, vice chancellor, 1980-85, acting chmn. dept. anatomy, 1982-85; pres., prof. medicine U. Tex. Health Scis. Ctr., San Antonio, 1985—; assoc. chief div. medicine U. Mass. Hosp., 1975-78, dir. patient care studies dept., 1975-80, chief of staff, 1978-80. Mem. editorial bd. Archives Internal Medicine, 1991—; contbr. numerous articles to profl. jours., chpts. to books. Trustee S.W. Found. for Biomed. Rsch., San Antonio Med. Found., S.W. Rsch. Inst. Maj. M.C, U.S. Army, 1973-75. Alfred P. Sloan scholar Amherst Coll., 1962-65; recipient Ruth Hunter Johnson award Boston U. Sch. of Medicine, 1969. Fellow ACP, Am. Coll. Cardiology, Am. Coll. Chest Physicians; mem. AMA (del. ho. of dels. 1995—, coun. on sci. affairs 1993—), Am. Heart Assn. (fellow coun. clin. cardiology), Tex. Med. Soc. (coun. med. edn. 1986—, ho. of dels. 1989—), Tex. Soc. Biomed. Rsch. (pres.), Bexar County Med. Soc. (exec. com. 1985—, pres. 1996), Alpha Omega Alpha, Omicron Kappa Epsilon.

HOWE, LYMAN HAROLD, III, chemist; b. Wilkes-Barre, Pa., Nov. 5, 1938; s. Lyman Harold and Esther Madeline (Smith) H.; B.S., Duke U., 1960; M.S., Emory U., 1961; Ph.D., U. Tenn., 1966; m. Mary Louise Reinhart, June 16, 1962; 1 dau., Jennifer. Rsch. assoc. Emory U., 1960-61; rsch. and teaching assoc. U. Tenn., 1962-66; rsch. chemist water mgmt. TVA, Chattanooga, 1966—. Fellow ASTM (water com. results advisor 1976—, Max Hecht award 1985, Award of Merit 1993); mem. Am. Chem. Soc., Nat. Mgmt. Assn., Am. Contact Bridge League (Ace of Clubs award, third place Chattanooga Club Master of Yr. award 1989, reviewer environ. sci. and tech. 1989), U.S. Chess Fedn. Presbyterian. Clubs: Torch (1st v.p. chpt. 1981, pres. 1982-83, 2d v.p. 1984-88), The Nost. Co-author publs. in field. Home: 1241 Mountain Brook Cir Signal Mountain TN 37377-2127 Office: 150-401 Chestnut St Chattanooga TN 37402-1011

HOWE, RICHARD DAVIS, academic administrator, professor, leadership in educational studies; b. Latham, Ill., May 6, 1939; s. Kenneth Elisha and Eva Theatrice (Davis) H.; m. Betty Carol Barker, Jan. 7, 1978; 1 child, Caroline Elizabeth. BS, Appalachian State U., 1961, MA, 1962; PhD, UCLA, 1972. Instr. Brevard (N.C.) Coll., 1962-64; prof., basketball coach Warren Wilson Coll., Swannanoa, N.C., 1964-67; teaching asst. UCLA, 1967-68; cons. Occidental Coll., L.A., 1968-69; asst. exec. dir., treas. League for Innovation in the Community Coll., L.A., 1969-73; mem. chancellor's staff Appalachian State U., Boone, N.C., 1973—; dir. faculty salary surveys

Coll. and Univ. Personnel Assn., Washington, 1973—. Contbr. numerous articles to profl. jours. Named Disting. Alumnus, Appalachian State U., 1988. Mem. Coll. and Univ. Pers. Assn. (v.p. coun. 1980-83, Achievement award 1981-82), Higher Edn. Pers. Assn. N.C. (pres. 1986-88), UCLA Doctoral Alumni Assn. (pres. 1972-73), Rotary (pres. Boone chpt. 1987-88, 94-95, gov. dist. 7670 1990-91, 96-97), Phi Kappa Phi, Phi Delta Kappa (pres. 1968-70). Episcopalian. Office: Appalachian State U 128 Administration Boone NC 28608

HOWELL, ALLEN WINDSOR, lawyer; b. Montgomery, Ala., Mar. 10, 1949; s. Elvin and Bennie Merle (Windsor) H.; m. Donna K. Graffander, Sept. 2, 1989; children: Christopher Darby, Joshua Darby. BA, Huntington Coll., 1971; JD, Jones Sch. Law, 1974. Bar: Ala. 1974, U.S. Supreme Ct. 1977, U.S. Ct. Appeals (fed. cir.) 1983, U.S. Ct. Appeals (11th cir.) 1981, U.S. Tax Ct. 1979, U.S. Claims Ct. 1982, U.S. Dist. Ct. (mid. dist.) Ala. 1975, U. Dist. Ct. (so. dist.) Ala. 1978. Archivist Hist. Rsch. Ctr. Air U., Maxwell AFB, Ala., 1972-75; pvt. practice Montgomery, 1975-82, 83—; adj. prof. Faulkner U., Montgomery, 1975—, law sch. 1983-85; asst. atty. gen., chief legal sect. Ala. Medicaid Agy., Montgomery, 1982-83. Author: Alabama Civic Practice Forms, 1986, 2d edit., 1992, Alabama Torts Case Finder, 1988, Alabama Personal Injury and Tort Law, 1996. Hon. lt. col., aide de camp Gov. Ala., 1974. Mem. ABA (contbr. editor profl. liability newsletter, litigation sect. 1990-92), Assn. Trial Lawyers Am., Montgomery County Bar Assn. (newsletter editorial com. 1984-85), Nat. Bd. Trial Adv. (cert. civil litigation 1981, 86, 91, examiner ethics, evidence and civil procedure). Mem. Ch. of Christ. Office: 608 S Hull St Montgomery AL 36104-5808

HOWELL, ARTHUR, lawyer; b. Atlanta, Aug. 24, 1918; s. Arthur and Katharine (Mitchell) H.; m. Caroline Sherman, June 14, 1941; children: Arthur, Caroline, Eleanor, Richard, Peter, James; m. Janet Kerr Franchot, Dec. 16, 1972. AB, Princeton U., 1939; JD, Harvard U., 1942; LLD (hon.), Oglethorpe U., 1972. Bar: Ga. 1942. Assoc. F.M., 1942-45; ptnr. Alston & Bird (and predecessor firms), 1945-89, of counsel, 1989—; bd. dirs., gen. counsel Atlantic Steel Co., 1960-93; pres., bd. dirs. Summit Industries, Inc.; bd. dirs. Enterprise Funds; chmn. bd. dirs. Crescent Banking Co.; past pres. Atlanta Legal Aid Soc.; emeritus mem. bd. dirs. Crescent Bank and Trust Co. Pres. Met. Atlanta Cmty. Svcs., 1956, dir., 1953—; pres. Cmty. Planning Coun., 1961-63; gen. chmn. United Appeal, 1955; spl. atty. gen. State Ga., 1948-55; spl. counsel Univ. Sys. Ga., State Sch. Bldg. Authorities, 1951-70; adv. com. Ga. Corp. Code, 1967—; chmn. Atlanta Adv. Com. Pks.; trustee, past chmn. Oglethorpe U.; trustee Princeton, 1964-68, Morehouse Coll., Atlanta Speech Sch., Westminister Schs., Atlanta, Episcopal H.S., Alexandria, Va.; past trustee Inst. Internat. Edn., mem. exec. com. 1969-72; elder, trustee, chmn. bd. trustees Presbyn. Ch., 1985-89. Named hon. alumnus Ga. Inst. Tech. Mem. ABA, Ga. Bar Assn., Atlanta Bar Assn., Am. Law Inst. (life), Lawyers Club of Atlanta (past pres.), Am. Judicature Soc., Soc. Colonial Wars, Capital City Club, Piedmont Driving Club, Commerce Club, Homosassa Fishing Club, Nassau Club, Princeton Club, Phi Beta Kappa. Home: 200 Larkspur Ln Highlands NC 28741 Office: Alston & Bird One Atlantic Ctr 1201 W Peachtree St NW Atlanta GA 30309-3400

HOWELL, BENITA JANKLE, anthropologist; b. Asheville, N.C., Jan. 26, 1944; d. Benno Jankle and Mariella (Burton) Jankle Taylor; m. Thomas Stevens Howell, Sept. 4, 1965. BA, Duke U., 1965; MS, U. Ill., 1967; PhD, U. Ky., 1978. Asst. prof. anthropology U. Tenn., Knoxville, 1980-86, assoc. prof. anthropology, 1987—; cons. cultural heritage, tourism, humanities coun. rsch. projects, Tenn., Va., S.C., Ky., 1982—; advisor cultural conservation conf. Am. Folklife Ctr., Washington, 1990; mem. adv. commn. Nat. Pks. and Conservation Assn., Washington, 1989-90. Author, editor: Cultural Heritage Conservation in the American South, 1990; contbg. author: Environmental Analysis: The NEPA Experience, 1993, Putting Folklore to Use, 1994, Conserving Culture: A New Discourse on Heritage, 1994. Fellow Am. Anthrop. Assn., Soc. for Applied Anthropology (exec. com. 1986-90, editor-in-chief Practicing Anthropology jour. 1986-90, sec. 1994—), So. Anthrop. Soc. (councillor), Phi Beta Kappa.

HOWELL, BRADLEY SUE, librarian; b. McKinney, Tex., July 15, 1933; d. Jessie Leonard and Carrie Pearl (Nickerson) LaFon; m. Richard Dunn Howell, May 18, 1957; children: Mark Richard, Celeste Ella, Jane Elizabeth. BS in Edn., So. Meth. U., 1955; MS in Library Sci., East Tex. State U., 1968. Tchr., J.B. Hood Jr. High Sch., Dallas, 1955-56, Mineral Wells Jr. High Sch. (Tex.), 1957-58; libr. Ascher Silberstein Sch., Dallas, 1963, San Jacinto Sch., Dallas, 1960-62, 65-81, Woodrow Wilson High Sch., Dallas, 1981—. Pres. Tex. United Meth. Hist. Soc., 1980-84; sec. South Cen. Jurisdiction, Archives and History of United Meth. Ch., 1980-88, v.p. local ch. sect. The United Meth. Hist. Soc., 1989-95, chmn., 1995—; pres. PTA, Woodrow Wilson High Sch., 1983-84; leader Camp Fire, Inc., 1970—. Recipient Wakan award Camp Fire, Inc. 1976, Hiiteni award, 1982, Sawnequas award, 1988; Terrific Tchr. award Texas PTA, 1984, Jim Collins Outstanding award, 1986, Honor award nat. Sch. Pub. Relation Assn., 1986, Dallas Positive Parents award, 1987, Golden Flame award, 1990. Mem. Dallas Assn. Sch. Librs. (pres. 1975-76), Tex. Assn. Sch. Librs., Tex. Libr. Assn. (chmn. archives and history roundtable 1990-92), Am. Libr. Svcs. To Children (Newbery com. 1980) Delta Kappa Gamma (state achievement award 1988, Golden Gift Leadership Mgmt. award 1985), Alpha Delta Pi, Phi Delta Kappa, Delta Psi Kappa, Pi Lambda Theta. Democrat. Home: 722 Ridgeway St Dallas TX 75214-4453 Office: Woodrow Wilson High Sch 100 S Glasgow Dr Dallas TX 75214-4518

HOWELL, BRUCE INMAN, academic administrator; b. Roanoke Rapids, N.C., Mar. 12, 1942; s. Leroy Inman and Pauline (Massey) H.; m. Mable Lea Smith, Aug. 22, 1965; children: Bruce Inman Jr., Virginia Lea. BS in English and History, East Carolina U., 1964, MA in History and Sch. Adminstrn., 1965; postgrad., N.C. State U., 1971, 84; grad. Continuing Edn. and Community Service Adminstrn. Program, Mich. State U., 1971; EdD in Higher Edn. and Cmty. Coll. Adminstrn., Duke U., 1976. Cert. grad. tchr., prin., supr., N.C., investment banker, stock exchange and brokerage office procedures. Instr., grad. asst. East Carolina U., Greenville, N.C., 1964-65; stockbroker Interstate Securities Corp., Charlotte, N.C., 1968-70; dean continuing edn. Lenoir C.C., Kinston, N.C., 1970-75; pres. Sampson Tech. Coll., Clinton, N.C., 1975-80, Wake Tech. C.C., Raleigh, N.C., 1980—; adj. prof. Dept. Adult and Community Coll. Edn., N.C. State U., 1982—, gen. adv. com., 1982—; mem. Wake County-Raleigh Pvt. Industry Coun., 1983—, Raleigh Econ. Devel. Roundtable, 1984-85, exec. com.; adv. N.C. govt. agys., Wake Co. Communities in Schs., 1990—; adv. Cen. Carolina Consortium, 1993—, pres., 1996—; mem. numerous ednl. commns. and task forces. Author: Debasement: A Problem of Imperial Rome, 1966, The Lenoir County Story, 1968; editorial bd. Community Coll. Review, N.C. State U., 1982—; contbr. articles to profl. jours. Mem. Lenoir County Schs. Vocat. Adv. com., 1972-75, Econ. Devel. Com., Fuguay-Varina; bd. dirs. Lenoir County Heart Fund, 1972, Lenoir County Fair Assn., 1970, Branch Banking & Trust Co., Cary, N.C., 1980—; mem. Wake County Interagy. Coord. Coun., 1981—; membership com. N.C. Lit. and Hist. Assn., 1978; mem. adminstrv. bd. Westminster United Meth. Ch., 1973-76; active First United Meth. Ch., Clinton, 1977-81, chmn. adminstrv. bd., White Plains, 1981—. Grad. fellow East Carolina U., 1964-65; Kellogg Community Svcs. fellow, Lenoir Community Coll., 1971; named one of Outstanding Young Men Am., 1975, 77, 78, Jacyee of Yr., 1967, Outstanding Old Jaycee of Yr., 1971; recipient Chief Exec. Officer award So. Region Assn. Community Colls., 1989. Mem. Am. Coun. on Edn., Nat. Coun. Cmty. Svcs. Continuing Edn., Nat. Coun. Resource Devel., So. Assn. Colls. and Schs. (mem. evaluation com. 1982—), N.C. Assn. Colls. and Univs. (mem. govtl. agys. liaison com. 1983—, pres. 1993), N.C. C.C. Adult Edn. Assn., N.C. Assn. Pub. C.C. Pres. (numerous com. assignments, pres. 1986-87), N.C. Employees Assn., Nat. Geneal. Soc. (N.C. chpt.), Am. Numismatic Assn., Greater Raleigh C. of C. (mem. adv. com. manpower resource devel. program 1980, leadership round table 1983—, higher edn. roundtable 1986—), Cary C. of C. (mem. econ. devel. com. 1983—, edn. task force com. 1987—), Fuquay-Varina C. of C. (bd. dirs. 1987-90), Execs. Club of Raleigh (pres. 1996—), Phi Delta Kappa, Kappa Delta Pi. Home: 1105 Queensferry Rd Cary NC 27511-6426 Office: Wake Tech Community Coll 9101 Fayetteville Rd Raleigh NC 27603-5655

HOWELL, CHARLES MAITLAND, dermatologist; b. Thomasville, N.C., Apr. 14, 1914; s. Cyrus Maitl and Lilly Mae (Ammons) H.; m. Betty Jane Myers, Feb. 12, 1949; children—Elizabeth Myers, Pamela Jane. B.S., Wake Forest U., Winston-Salem, N.C., 1935; M.D., U. Pa., 1937. Intern Charity Hosp., New Orleans, 1937-38; resident in medicine Burlington County Hosp., Mt. Holley, N.J., 1938-39; sch. physician Lawrenceville (N.J.) Sch., 1939-42; resident in pathology N.C. Baptist Hosp., Winston-Salem, 1947-48; resident in dermatology Columbia-Presbyn. Med. Ctr., N.Y.C., 1948-50; resident in allergy Roosevelt Hosp., N.Y.C., 1950-51; practice medicine specializing in dermatology Winston-Salem, 1951—; mem. staff N.C. Bapt., Forsyth Meml. hosps.; mem. faculty Bowman Gray Sch. Medicine, Wake Forest U., 1951-86, head. sect., 1984-86, prof. dermatology, 1967-84, prof. emeritus, 1984, head sect., 1961-86, acting head sect., 1984-86. Served as officer M.C. AUS, 1942-46. Fellow Am. Acad. Dermatology, Am. Acad. Allergy; mem. N. Am. Clin. Dermatol. Soc., N.Y. Acad. Scis. Democrat. Baptist. Clubs: Old Town (Winston-Salem); Bermuda Run Country (Clemmons, N.C.). Home: 1100 E Kent Rd Winston Salem NC 27104-1116 Office: 340 Pershing Ave Winston Salem NC 27103-2513

HOWELL, CLAUDE FLYNN, artist; b. Wilmington, N.C., Mar. 17, 1915; s. Claude Flynn and Jessie Campbell Nurney. Hon. degree, Wake Forest U., U. N.C. Exhbns. include St. John's Mus. Art, Wilmington, N.C., 1995, Fayetteville (N.C.) Mus. Fine Arts, 1995, Hickory (N.C.) Mus. Fine Arts, 1995, Greenville (N.C.) Mus. Fine Arts, 1995, N.C. Mus. Fine Arts, Raleigh, 1995; Claude Howell Plz. dedicated, Wilmington, N.C., 1996. Home: 44 Carolina Apts Wilmington NC 22222 Office: PO Box 214 Wilmington NC 28402

HOWELL, JAMES TENNYSON, allergist, immunologist, pediatrician; b. Memphis, Jan. 25, 1944. MD, U. Ark., 1970. Diplomate Am. Bd. Allergy & Immunology, Am. Bd. Pediatrics. Intern Tampa Gen. Hosp., 1970-71; resident in pediatrics Children's Med. Ctr., Dallas, 1973-76; fellow in allergy and immunology Tex., Galveston, 1976-78; with St. Edwards Mercy Med. Ctr., Ft. Smith, Ark. Mem. AMA, Am. Acad. Pediatrics. Office: Cooper Clinic 6801 Rogers Ave Fort Smith AR 72903

HOWELL, JENNIFER CHANDLER, human resources representative; b. Sylacauga, Ala., Nov. 25, 1956; d. James Coleman and Bonnie Jean (Haynes) Chandler; m. Jesse Clyde Howell, Dec. 26, 1976; children: James Clinton, Joanna Cristine, Jeffrey Charles. BA in Sociology, U. Tenn., Chattanooga, 1989, MS in Indsl./Organizational Psychology, 1991. Sales clk. Waldenbooks, Chattanooga, 1975-76; spl. sales clk. Army and Air Force Exchg. Svc., Bamberg, Fed. Republic of Germany, 1978-79, Ft. Devens, Mass., 1982; clk./typist Directorate Engring. and Housing, Bamberg, 1985-86; with adminstrv. svcs. staff Army Community Svc., U.S. Army, Bad Toelz, Fed. Republic of Germany, 1987-88; ofcl. checks clk. Pioneer Bank, Chattanooga, 1989-90; teaching asst. psychology dept. U. Tenn., 1990-91; tng. specialist Westinghouse Savannah River Co., Aiken, S.C., 1991-92, human resource rep. ednl. coord., compensation analyst, 1992—; cons. U. Tenn., Chattanooga, 1991—; adj. prof. Limestone Coll. Vol. blood bank ARC, Ft. Devens, 1981-83; vol. supr. fin. counselors Army Community Svc., U.S. Army, Ft. Devens, 1983; asst. leader Girl Scouts Am., Aiken, 1991—; vol. Aiken Sports Leagues, 1991—. Mem. ASTD, Soc. Indsl./Organizational Psychology (student), Nat. Soc. Human Resource Mgmt., U. Tenn. Chattanooga Soc. Human Resource Mgmt. (pres. 1990-91), Chattanooga Soc. Human Resource Mgmt. (student liaison 1990-91), U. Tenn. Chattanooga Indsl./Organizational Alumni Assn. (coord.), Nutcracker Guild, Golden Key, Aiken Strikers Soccer Assn. Republican. Baptist. Home: 718 S Boundary SE Aiken SC 29801 Office: Westinghouse Savannah River Co Centennial 3 Rm 117 Aiken SC 29801

HOWELL, LEO A., metals manufacturing executive; b. 1921. BS, U. Tenn., 1943. With Revere Copper & Brass Inc., 1949-58, Reynolds Metal Co., 1943-49, 58-63; v.p. H.K. Porter Co., 1963-66, Comml. Metals Co., Dallas, 1977—; with Howell Metal Co., 1966—. Office: Comml Metals Co PO Box 218 New Market New Market VA 22844*

HOWELL, LINDSEY RAIFORD, mathematics educator; b. Seven Springs, N.C., Oct. 15, 1952; d. Benjamin Braxton and Estelle (Grady) Raiford; m. James Calvin Howell, July 22, 1981; children: Heather Van Roekel Turner, Jeff Howell, Jennifer Howell. BS, Valdosta (Ga.) State Coll., 1974. Cert. math. educator, N.C. Math. tchr. Mt. Olive (N.C.) Jr. H.S., 1974-80, Spring Creek Jr. H.S., Seven Springs, N.C., 1980-92, So. Wayne H.S., Dudley, N.C., 1992—. Mem. Providence United Meth. Ch., 1994—, New Covenant Sunday Sch. Class, 1990—; chaplain Wayne County, N.C. Hwy. Patrol Aux., 1995-96, v.p., 1996—. Mem. N.C. Coun. Tchrs. Math., N.C. Assn. Educators, Alpha Delta Kappa (Gamma Gamma chpt. treas. 1988-92, v.p. 1993-94, pres. 1994-96, v.p. N.C. dist. 1996—). Methodist. Home: 402 Providence Church Rd Goldsboro NC 27530 Office: So Wayne HS 128 Southern Wayne Rd Dudley NC 28333

HOWELL, PAMELA ANN, federal agency professional; b. Pensacola, Fla., Mar. 12, 1957; d. Thomas Pugh and Edith Corinne (McGowan) H.; children: Corinne Elizabeth Howell Meadows. BS, Mississippi Coll., 1978. Benefit authorizer Social Security Adminstrn., Birmingham, Ala., 1979—. H.S. coach Tabernacle Christian Sch., Gardendale, Ala., 1993—. Mem. Am. Fedn. Govt. Employees (v.p.). Republican. Baptist. Home: 712 Cherrybrook Rd Kimberly AL 35091-9744

HOWELL, RALPH RODNEY, pediatrician, educator; b. Concord, N.C., June 10, 1931; s. Fred Lee and Grace Mary (Blackwelder) H.; m. Sarah Vosburg Esselstyn, Nov. 19, 1960 (dec.); children: Grace Meyer, Elizabeth Eriksson, John Esselstyn. BS, Davidson Coll., 1953; MD, Duke U., 1957. Intern Duke U., 1957-58, resident in pediatrics, 1958-59, research fellow in pediatrics and medicine, 1959-60; clin. assoc. and staff NIH, Bethesda, Md., 1960-64; assoc. prof. pediatrics Johns Hopkins U., Balt., 1964-72; pediatrician-in-chief Univ. Children's Hosp. at Hermann, Houston, 1972-87; chmn. med. bd. Univ. Children's Hosp. at Hermann, 1972-87; David Park prof. U. Tex. Med. Sch., Houston, 1972-89, chmn. dept. pediatrics, 1972-87; prof., chmn. dept. pediatrics U. Miami Sch. Medicine, 1989—; sec. med. staff Jackson Meml. Hosp., Miami, 1992-93, v.p. med. staff, 1993-96; cons. pediatrics M.D. Anderson Hosp. and Tumor Inst., 1972-89; mem. metabolism study sect. NIH, 1973-77, chmn. maternal and child health adv. com., 1983-86; mem. exec. com. Nat. Practitioner Data Bank; mem. nat. clin. adv. com. Nat. Found. March of Dimes, 1973-79; mem. nat. med. adv. bd., bd. dirs. Muscular Dystrophy Assn., chmn. sci. adv. bd.; vis. prof. Inst. Molecular Genetics, Baylor Coll. Medicine, Houston, 1988; chief pediatrics Childrens Hosp., U. Miami-Jackson Meml. Med. Ctr., 1989—. Author: (with G.H. Thomas) Selected Screening Tests for Genetic Metabolic Diseases, 1973, (with F.H. Morriss, L.K. Pickering) Role of Human Milk in Infant Nutrition, 1986; contbr. articles to profl. jours. Trustee Jackson Lab. Bar Harbor, Maine; dir. Caldwell B. Esselstyn Found., Claverack, N.Y., 1987-92, pres., 1992—; bd. dirs. Congl. Ch. Found., Coconut Grove, Fla. Served to sr. surgeon USPHS, 1960-64. Fellow Am. Acad. Pediatrics (com. on genetics); mem. AMA, Am. Pediatric Soc.,Soc. Pediatric Rsch., Houston Pediatric Soc. (pres. 1978-79), Tex. Med. Assn., Soc. Inborn Errors of Metabolism (pres. 1981), Miami Pediatric Soc., Fla. Med. Assn., Am. Coll. Med. Genetics (bd. dirs. 1991—, treas. 1995—), Pi Kappa Alpha, Banker's Club (Miami), Cosmos Club (Washington). Home: L'Hermitage Villa 66 2000 S Bayshore Dr Miami FL 33133 Office: U Miami Sch Medicine Dept Pediatrics D-820 PO Box 016820 Miami FL 33101-6820

HOWELL, THOMAS, history educator; b. Houston, Jan. 20, 1944; s. John Thomas and Hazel (Hall) H.; m. Donna Jo Walker, Aug. 14, 1971; children: Catherine Jewell, Judith Hazel. B.A., La. Coll., 1964; M.A., La. State U., 1966, Ph.D., 1971. Instr. La. State U., 1967-68; instr. La. Coll., Pineville, 1968-70, asst. prof., 1970-72, assoc. prof., 1972-77, prof., 1977, Crowell prof., 1984—, chmn. dept. history and polit. sci., 1975-95, chmn. div. social and behavioral scis., 1995—; lectr. La. Coun. for Humanities, 1983, 86, 87, 90—; project dir. La. Endowment for Humanities, 1989. Mem. La. Elections Integrity Commn., 1980-86, vice chmn., 1981; coord. La. Civitan Youth Citizenship Seminar, 1975-76; commr. Gulf Coast Athletic Conf., 1981—; mem. NAIA Nat. Eligibility Commn., 1983—, chmn., 1995—; mem. hearing com. disciplinary bd. La. Bar Assn. Mellon summer fellow, 1981; Fulbright lectr. U. Iceland, 1986-87. Mem. La. Hist. Assn., So. Hist. Assn., SW Assn. Pre-Law Advisers, Orgn. Am. Historians, So. Bapt. Hist. Assn., Alpha Chi, Omicron Delta Kappa. Baptist. Home: 216 Myrtle St Pineville LA 71360-5164 Office: La Coll Dept History Pineville LA 71359

HOWELL, WILLIAM ASHLEY, III, lawyer; b. Raleigh, N.C., Jan. 2, 1949; s. William Ashley II and Caroline Erskine Greenleaf; m. Esther Holland, Dec. 22, 1973. BS, Troy State U., 1972; postgrad. U. Alabama, Birmingham, 1974-75; JD, Birmingham Sch. Law, 1977. Bar: Ala. 1977, U.S. Dist. Ct. (no. dist.) Ala. 1977, U.S. Ct. Appeals (5th cir.) 1977, U.S. Supreme Ct. 1982, U.S. Ct. Appeals (11th cir.) 1983, U.S. Dist. Ct. (mid. dist.) Ala. 1987. Atty. pub. defender div. Legal Aid Soc. of Birmingham, 1977-78, civil divsn. Legal Aid Soc. Birmingham, 1978-81; dist. office atty. SBA, Birmingham, 1980-82, supervising atty. Ala. Dist., 1982—; spl. asst. U.S. Atty. (Middle Dist.), Ala., 1988—; part-time instr. legal and social environ. and human resources mgmt. Jefferson State C.C., Birmingham, 1993. Contbr. articles to profl. jours. Bd. dirs. Hoover Homeowners Assn., 1977-81, Southside Ministries, Inc., 1990-91, v.p., 1990-91; bd. dirs. SafeHouse of Shelby County, Inc., 1990-93, vice chmn., 1991-93; mem. outreach commn., Episc. Ch. of St. Francis of Assisi, Pelham, Ala., 1992, 95; del. State Conv., alternate del., 1993, 94; vol. reader Radio Reading Svc. Network for Blind, 1991-93; active Shelby County Econ. Devel. Coun., 1993-94. Recipient Am. Jurisprudence Criminal Procedure Book award; named Outstanding Spl. Asst. U.S. Atty. Mid. Dist. Ala., 1992. Mem. ABA (sect. corporation, banking and bus. law), Fed. Bar Assn. (sec. Birmingham chpt. 1980-81, del. nat. conv. 1993, 94, del. mid year meeting, 1994-95), Ala. Bar Assn. (com. on future of the profession 1978-81, 83-84, com. on quality of life 1992-93, sect. bankruptcy and corp. law, sect. bankruptcy and comml. law, sect. corp. counsel, sect. banking and bus. law), Birmingham Bar Assn., Birmingham Venture Club, Sigma Delta Kappa (v.p., Outstanding Sr. award 1977). Episcopalian. Office: US SBA 2121 8th Ave N Ste 200 Birmingham AL 35203-2398

HOWERTON, JACK THOMPSON, manufacturing engineer, consultant; b. Bethesda, Md., Sept. 13, 1949. Student, Trident Tech. Coll., 1967-68. Assemblies worker Lockheed, Charleston, 1968-70; methods specialist GE, Charleston, 1970-85; pres., owner Prodn. Svcs., Charleston, 1985-86; sr. systems analyst Grumman Data Systems, Charleston, 1986-87; mfg. cons. Ingersoll Engrs., Charleston, 1987-89; sr. sys. engr. Systems Engring. Assocs. Co., Charleston, 1989—; mem. adv. bd. Trident Tech. Coll., Charleston, 1988—; mem. Binary Cutter Location Internat. Com., Davenport, Iowa, 1988—. Mem. Soc. Mfg. Engrs. (sr., cert. mfg. engr., chmn. 1987-88), S.C. Soc. Engrs., Lowcountry Blues Preservation Soc. (prodn. mgr. 1989), Masons (32d degree, master 1988), Shriners. Home: 215 Columbia Dr Ladson SC 29456 Office: Systems Engring Assocs Co Trident Rsch Ctr 5300 International Blvd North Charleston SC 29418

HOWIE, JOHN ROBERT, lawyer; b. Paris, Tex., June 29, 1946; s. Robert H. and Sarah Francis (Caldwell) H.; m. Evelyn Eileen Yates, May 3, 1969; children: John Robert, Ashley Elizabeth, Lindsey Leigh. BBA, North Tex. State U., 1968; JD, So. Meth. U., 1976. Bar: Tex. 1976, U.S. Dist. Ct. (no. dist.) Tex. 1977, U.S. Ct. Appeals (5th, 9th, 10th and 11th cirs.), U.S. Supreme Ct. 1985, U.S. Dist. Ct. (so., ea., and we. dists.) Tex. 1987; cert. in personal injury trial law Tex. Bd. Legal Specialization, 1982. Law Offices of Windle Turley, Dallas, 1976-88, Misko & Howie, 1988-95, ptnr. Howie & Sweeney, LLP, 1995—; adj. prof. trial advocacy So. Meth. U. Sch. Law, 1988-89, 92—, mem. exec. com. Editor The Verdict, 1981-87. Lt. comdr. USN, 1968-73. Fellow So. Trial Lawyers Assn., Roscoe Pound Found. Civil Trial Adv.-Nat. Bd. Trial Adv. (cert. civil trial law), Internat. Acad. Trial Lawyers; mem. Tex. Trial Lawyers Assn. (bd. dirs. 1983—, chmn. product liability com. 1988-89), Dallas Trial Lawyers Assn. (sec.-treas. 1984, v.p. 1985, pres. 1986), Assn. Trial Lawyers Am. (vice chmn. aviation sect. 1984-85, chmn. 1986, Wiedemann Wysocki award 1990), Am. Bd. Trial Advocates (sec. Dallas chpt. 1988, pres. 1989), ABA (vice chmn. aviation law sect. 1986-91, chair 1992), State Bar Tex. (aviation law sect. coun. 1994—, personal injury trial specialist), Lawyer/Pilots Bar Assn., Internat. Soc. Air Safety Investigators (contbr. Million Dollar Argument series 1989), Pres.'s Coun. U. North Tex. Democrat. Presbyterian. Home: 6508 Turtle Creek Blvd Dallas TX 75205-1244 Office: Howie & Sweeney LLP 2911 Turtle Creek Blvd Ste 1400 Dallas TX 75219

HOWORTH, LUCY SOMERVILLE, lawyer; b. Greenville, Miss., July 1; d. Robert and Nellie (Nugent) Somerville; m. Joseph Marion Howorth, Feb. 16, 1928. A.B., Randolph-Macon Woman's Coll., 1916; postgrad., Columbia U., 1918; J.D. summa cum laude, U. Miss., 1922. Bar: Miss. 1922, U.S. Supreme Ct. 1934. Asst. in psychology Randolph-Macon Woman's Coll., 1916-17; gauge insp. Allied Bur. Air Prodn., N.Y.C., 1918; indsl. research nat. bd. YWCA, 1919-20; gen. practice law Howorth & Howorth, Cleveland, Greenville and Jackson, Miss., 1922-34; U.S. commr. So. Jud. Dist. Miss., 1927-31; assoc. mem. Bd. Vet. Appeals, Washington, 1934-43; legis. atty. VA, 1943-49; v.p., dir. VA Employees Credit Union, 1937-49; assoc. gen. counsel War Claims Commn., 1949-52, dep. gen. counsel, 1952-53, gen. counsel, 1953-54; ptnr. James Somerville & Assocs. (overseas trade and devel.), 1954-55; atty. Commn. on Govt. Security, 1956-57; pvt. practice law Cleveland, Miss., 1958—; mem. nat. bd. cons. Women's Archives, Radcliffe Coll.; mem. lay adv. com. study profl. nursing Carnegie Corp. N.Y., 1947-48; chmn. Miss. State Bd. Law Examiners, 1924-28; mem. Miss. State Legislature, 1932-36, chmn. com. pub. lands, 1932-36; treas. Com. for Econ. Survey Miss., 1928-30; mem. Research Commn. Miss., 1930-34. Editor: Fed. Bar Assn. News, 1944; assoc. editor: Fed. Bar Assn. Jour., 1943-44; editor: (with William M. Cash) My Dear Nellie-Civil War Letters (William L. Nugent), 1977; contbr. articles profl. jours. Keynote speaker White House Conf. on Women in Postwar Policy Making, 1944, at conf. on opening 81st Congress. Recipient Alumnai Achievment award Randolph-Macon Woman's Coll., 1981, Lifetime Achievmenet award Schlesinger Libr. of Radcliffe Coll., 1983; named for her outstanding lifetime achievments by Senate Concurrrent Resolution, adopted by Senate and Ho. of Reps., 1984; recipient Excellence medal Miss. U. for Women, 1989. Mem. AAUW (nat. dir., 2d v.p. 1951-55, mem. found. 1960-63), Nat. Fedn. Bus. and Profl. Women's Clubs (nat. dir.; rep. to internat. 1939, chmn. internat. conf. 1946), Nat. Assn. Women Lawyers, Miss. Library Assn. (life), Miss. Hist. Soc. (dir. 1982—, Merit award 1983), DAR, Daus. Am. Colonists, Am. Legion Aux. (past sec. Miss. dept.), Assembly Women's Orgns. for Nat. Security (chmn. 1951-52), Phi Beta Kappa, Pi Gamma Mu, Phi Alpha Delta, Alpha Omicron Pi (Wyman award 1985), Delta Kappa Gamma, Omicron Delta Kappa, Phi Kappa Phi (hon.). Democrat (del. nat. conv., 1932). Methodist. Club: Soroptimist (Washington). Address: 515 S Victoria Ave Cleveland MS 38732-3738

HOWSON, ROBERT E., construction company executive; b. 1931. BSCE, La. Tech. Univ., 1953; MSCE, Tulane Univ., 1961. Chief engr. offshore div. McDermott Inc., 1957-63, v.p. Cen. and S.Am., 1972-74, v.p. North Sea, 1974-80; sr. v.p. Ingram Contractors Inc., 1964-72; sr. v.p. and group exec. McDermott engring. McDermott Engring., 1980-81; pres., COO, McDermott Marine Constrn., New Orleans, 1981-86; pres., COO, McDermott Internat., Inc., New Orleans, 1987—, chmn. bd., CEO; also bd. dirs. Babcock & Wilcox & McDermott Internat. Inc. 1st lt. USMC, 1953-55. Office: McDermott Inc 1450 Poydras St Ste 1850 New Orleans LA 70112-6010

HOWZE, JAMES DEAN, art educator, artist; b. Lubbock, Tex., Apr. 8, 1930; s. James Hugh and Blanche Beatrice (Hanna) H.; m. Alva Jean Ethridge, Dec. 29, 1960; children: James Murray, Alison Jean, Jennifer Page. BA, Austin Coll., 1951; postgrad., Art Ctr. Sch., 1954-55; MS, U. Mich., 1958. Graphics design & illustration various advt. agys., Tex., Okla. & Mich., 1955-58; illustrator, graphics sect. The Artillery and Guided Missile Sch., Ft. Sill, Okla., 1956-57; instr., asst. prof., assoc. prof. Dept Archt. & Allied Arts Tex. Tech., 1958-68, prof. dept. art, 1968-92, prof. emeritus, 1992—; coord. art program Tex. Tech., 1964-68, coord. advt. art program, 1968-70, area rep. 2-dimensional studio art, 1979-80, dir. freshman core dept. art, 1981-87, assoc. chmn. dept. art, 1988-91; dir. Tex. Tech. Art Workshop, Taos, 1973-77. Co-author: Creating and Understanding Drawings, 1990, 95; represented in local, regional, nat. and internat. exhbns., most recently including Tex. Tech. Gallery, 1960—, N.Mex. Jr. Coll., Hobbs, 1984, Masters Gallery, San Diego State U., 1988, Amarillo (Tex.) Art Ctr., 1988, Miniature Art Soc. Fla., Tampa, 1988, Hayter Meml. Exhbn. Small Prints, Japan, Far East, 1989, Marymount Coll., N.Y.C., 1993, Holman Hall Gallery, Trenton (N.J.) State Coll., 1994, Nat. Drawing Assn., Nassau C.C., L.I., N.Y., 1994. 1st lt. U.S. Army, 1951-54. Recipient 1st Annual Disting. Faculty award Tex. Tech. Dept. Art Alumni Assn., 1991. Mem. NEA, Nat. Drawing Assn., Tex. Assn. Schs. Art, Dallas Soc. Visual Comm. (hon.). Presbyterian. Studio: 2503 45th St Lubbock TX 79413-3629

HOY, ERIC STUART, clinical microbiologist; b. Elmhurst, Ill., Feb. 27, 1948; s. Robert Peter and Grace Muriel (Conrad) H.; m. Carolyn Ruth Nelson, May 20, 1972; children: Karen Elizabeth, Robert Allen. BS, U. Ill., Chgo., 1974, MS in Microbiology, 1976, PhD in Pathology, 1987. Clin. microbiologist Condell Meml. Hosp., Libertyville, Ill., 1974-76, Consol. Med. Labs., Highland Pk., Ill., 1976-86; chief sci. officer The Rupp & Bowman Co., Irving, Tex., 1986—; cons. scientist Immuno Concepts, Inc., Sacramento, Calif., 1981—; clin. microbiology cons. No. Ill. Clin. Labs., McHenry, 1984-91; clin. asst. prof. U. Tex. Med. Ctr., Dallas, 1987—. With USN, 1968-74. Mem. N.Y. Acad. Scis., Am. Soc. for Microbiology, Ill. Soc. for Microbiology, The Honor Soc. Phi Kappa Phi. Republican. Home: 1117 Laon Ln De Soto TX 75115-7705 Office: The Rupp & Bowman Co 8710 W Royal Ln Irving TX 75063-2539

HOY, WILLIAM IVAN, minister, educator; b. Grottoes, Va., Aug. 21, 1915; s. William I. and Ileta (Root) H.; student Lees-McRae Coll., 1933-34; BA, Hampden-Sydney Coll., 1936; BD, Union Theol. Sem., 1942; STM, Bibl. Sem. N.Y., 1949; PhD, U. Edinburgh, 1952; m. Wilma J. Lambert, Apr. 29, 1945; children: Doris Lambert Hoy Bezanilla, Martha Virginia. Tchr. high sch., Va., 1936-39; interim pastor Asheboro (N.C.) Presbyn. Ch., 1948, 52-53; asst. prof. Bible, Guilford Coll., 1947-48; asst. prof. religion U. Miami, from 1953, prof., 1963-81, chmn. dept. religion, 1958-79, prof. religion emeritus, 1981—; cons. World Coun. Christian Edn., Lima, Peru, 1971. Moderator, Presbytery of Everglades, 1960-61, stated clk., 1968-73, 78-79; interim stated clk. Presbytery of Tropical Fla., 1991-93; moderator Synod of Fla., 1985-86; pres. Greater Miami Ministerial Assn., 1964, 80-82; mem. bd. Christian edn. Presbyn. Ch. U.S., 1969-73, mem. Gen. Assembly Mission Bd., 1978-88; bd. dirs. Met. Fellowship Chs., 1970—, v.p., 1972-73, exec. sec., 1974-76, mem. Task Force on World Hunger, 1978-81; trustee Davidson Coll., 1975-87, South Fla. Ctr. Theol. Studies, 1985-96; participant profl. internat. confs., Barcelona, Lausanne, Rome, Sydney, Goettingen, others, and three White House confs. for religious leaders. Served to comdr. USNR, ret. Decorated Purple Heart; awarded keys of Cities of Miami Beach (twice) and Coral Gables, 1987; named to Honorable Order of Ky. Colonels. Fellow Soc. Sci. Study Religion; mem. Internat. Assn. Historians Religion, Soc. Bibl. Lit., Am. Acad. Religion, Am. Soc. Ch. Hist., Studiorum Novi Testamenti Societas, Scottish Ch. History Soc., Religious Rsch. Assn., Internat. Conf. Sociology of Religion, Am. Oriental Soc., Internat. Sociol. Assn., Res. Officers Assn. (past nat. chaplain, nat. councilman 1965-66, pres. Fla. dept. 1965-66, v.p. for navy dept. Fla.), Seabee Vets. Am., Iron Arrow, Am. Legion, Rotary (pres. S. Miami club 1991-92, Paul Harris fellow (2)), Phi Kappa Phi, Omicron Delta Kappa (province dep., mem. gen. coun. 1971-76, Disting. Svc. Key 1976, Robert L. Morlan Faculty Sec. nat. award 1990), Lambda Chi Alpha Hall of Fame, 1996, Alpha Psi Omega, Theta Delta, Omega. Co-author: History of the Chaplains Corps, USN, Volume 6; also articles and book revs. in various publs. Home: 5881 SW 52nd Ter Miami FL 33155-6330 Office: PO Box 248348 Miami FL 33124-8348

HOYE, ROBERT EARL, adult education educator; b. Warwick, R.I., Jan. 12, 1931; s. S. Earl and Alice (Landry) H.; m. Patricia Buswell, Aug. 20, 1955; children: Robert Earl Jr., Joanne D., Peter M., Kathleen B. BA, Providence Coll., 1953; MS, St. John's U., N.Y.C., 1955; PhD, U. Wis., Madison, 1973. Instr. St. John's U., 1953-55; dir. guidance Middleboro (Mass.) Pub. Schs., 1955-56, Rutland (Vt.) Pub. Schs., 1956-57; dean Champlain (Vt.) Coll., 1957-58; supt. Frontier Regional Sch. Dist., Deerfield, Mass., 1958-60; New Eng. dir. Sci. Rsch. Assocs. subs. IBM, Chgo., 1960-65; nat. dir. Learning Systems div. Xerox Corp., N.Y.C., 1965-66; dir. Instrnl. Media Lab. U. Wis., Milw., 1966-73; asst. v.p. U. Louisville, 1974-81, prof. urban policy, coord. grad. program in health systems, 1981-95, prof. edn., 1992-95, prof. emeritus, 1995—; cons. to mgmt., Louisville, 1966—. Author: Index to Computer Based Learning, 1973; editor Edn. Jour., 1968-73; also articles. Recipient cert. of merit San Diego State U., 1983, Grad. Teaching Excellence award U. Louisville, 1984, gold medal Project Innovation, 1984. Fellow Am. Acad. Med. Adminstrs. (diplomate, chmn. editl. bd. 1986-94), Royal Soc. Health (Statesman in Healthcare Adminstrn. award 1992). Democrat. Roman Catholic. Home: 2238 Wynnewood Cir Louisville KY 40222-6342

HOYT, CLARK FREELAND, journalist, newspaper editor; b. Providence, Nov. 20, 1942; s. Charles Freeland and Maude Leslie (King) H.; m. Jane Ann Hauser, Sept. 30, 1967 (div. Jan. 1978); m. Linda Kauss, Aug. 22, 1988. A.B., Columbia U., 1964. Research asst. to U.S. Senator, Washington, 1964-66; reporter Lakeland (Fla.) Ledger, 1966-68; politics writer Detroit Free Press, 1968-70; Washington corr. Miami Herald, 1970-73; nat. corr. Knight Newspapers, Washington, 1973-75; news editor Washington bur. Knight Newspapers, 1975-77; bus. editor Detroit Free Press, 1977-79, conv. editor, 1979-80, asst. to exec. editor, 1980-81; mng. editor Wichita Eagle-Beacon, Kans., 1981-85; news editor Washington Bur., Knight-Ridder Newspapers, 1985-87, bur. chief, 1987-92, v.p. news, 1993—. Recipient Pulitzer prize nat. reporting, 1973. Clubs: Nat. Press (fin. sec., bd. govs. 1975), Gridiron. Home: 220 W Rivo Alto Dr Miami Beach FL 33139-1258 Office: One Herald Plz Miami FL 33132

HRNA, DANIEL JOSEPH, pharmacist, lawyer; b. Taylor, Tex., March 19, 1940; s. Stephan Peter and Anna Ludmilla (Baran) H.; BS, U. Houston, 1963, JD, 1970; m. Velma Isobel Lesson, Sept. 3, 1963 (dec. Jan. 1994); children: Anna Marie, Daniel Steven, Brian Keith. Bar: Tex. 1972. In mgmt., Gunning-Casteel Co., El Paso, Tex., 1963-65; dir. pharmacy svcs. Tex. Inst. Rehab. & Rsch., Houston, 1966-79; dir. pharmacy Alief Gen. Hosp., Belhaven Hosp., Houston, 1979-85, West Houston Med. Ctr., 1985-88; mem. faculty Baylor U. Coll. Medicine, 1977-79, Sharpstown Gen. Hosp., 1988-94; with Owen Healthcare, Inc. at Sharpstown Gen. Hosp., 1990-94; pvt. practice, 1994—. Mem. ABA, Am. Pharm. Assn., Tex. Pharmacy Assn., State Bar Tex., Tex. Soc. Hosp. Pharmacists, Am. Soc. Pharmacy Law, Am. Hosp. Assn., Harris County Pharm. Assn., Houston Bar Assn., Galveston-Houston Pharm. Hosp. Assn., Czech Heritage Soc. Tex. (legal adv., trustee), Profl. Photographers Guild Houston (hon.), Delta Theta Phi, Kappa Psi, Phi Delta Chi. Roman Catholic. Office: 11920 Beechnut St Houston TX 77072-4034

HRUSKA, FRANCIS JOHN, marine surveyor and consultant; b. Trnovec N/V, Czechoslovakia, Jan. 19, 1935, came to U.S., 1977; s. Ferdinand and Julia (Klepanec) H.; m. Ludmila Liptak, Apr. 19, 1958; children—Zuzana, Daniela, Martin. Grad. with honors, Nautical Sch. for Inland Waterways, Czechoslovakia, 1952, State Nautical Sch., Poland, 1955; student Walsey Hall Corr. Coll., Oxford, Eng., 1973-74. Cert. master mariner, 1961, marine pilot, 1969. Ships nautical officer Czechoslovak Ocean Shipping, Prague, 1955-62; exec. nautical engr. State Nautical Authority, Czechoslovakia, 1962-66; master C.S.P.D. Sea Branch, Czechoslovakia, 1966-68; marine pilot Ghana Rys. and Ports, 1968-72, Nat. Port Authority, Liberia, 1972-75; harbour master, chief marine officer, 1975-77; marine surveyor Nautech, Inc., Latham & Assocs., Master Marine Cons., Inc., New Orleans, 1978-82; pres. Plimsoll Marine Surveyors, Inc., Covington, La., 1983—; chmn. exam. bd. for pilots Nat. Port Authority, Monrovia, Liberia, 1975-77; nautical advisor Govt. of Liberia, 1975-77; cons. Comprehensive Study for Devel. of Port of Monrovia, 1975-77, Elbe-Oder-Danube Waterways System, Czechoslovakia, 1963-66. Contbr. articles to profl. jours. Office: Plimsoll Marine Surveyors Inc PO Box 8528 Mandeville LA 70470-8528

HSING, YU, economics educator; b. China, Mar. 12, 1947; came to U.S., 1973; s. Tsu-Yuan and Z.Z. (Dai) H.; m. Hsiu Shi Wang, Nov. 1, 1976; 1 child, Frances Wei. MS, U. Ore., 1975; MA in Econs., U. Tenn., 1980, PhD in Econs., 1983. Asst. prof. Southeastern La. U., Hammond, 1987-89, assoc. prof., 1989-94, prof., 1994—; head dept. economics/bus. rsch. Southeastern La. U., 1990—. Contbr. articles to profl. jours. Recipient awards for disting. paper Southwestern Econ. Assn., Dallas, 1990, Southwestern Soc. Economists, 1994. Mem. Am. Econ. Assn., Southern Econ. Assn., Mo. Valley Econ. Assn. Office: Southea La Univ Dept Econs Bus Rsch Hammond LA 70402

HSU, MING-YU, engineer, educator; b. Kweiyang, Kweichow, China, Dec. 4, 1925; s. Pei-Kung and Wan-Ju (Hsiao) H.; m. Chih-Ju Yao, Jan. 1, 1952; children: Chi-Hsing, Chi-Yun, Chi-En, Chi-Che, Chi-Cheng. BE, Nat. Kweichow U., 1948; Dipl.Engr., Delft Tech. U., The Netherlands, 1959. Registered profl. engr., Ill., Ga., Fla., S.C. Prof. Cheng-Kung U., Tainan, Taiwan, 1960-68; dir. Land Devel. Commn., Taipei, 1960-68; engring. cons. Ministry of Housing & Utilities, Sehba, Libya, 1968-71; sr. engr. Philipp Holzmann Ag., Hamburg, Fed. Republic of Germany, 1971-74, Weber, Griffith & Mellican, Galesburg, Ill., 1974-80; chief engr. Chatham Engring. Co., Savannah, Ga., 1980-82; sr. cons. Hussey, Gay, Bell & DeYoung, Inc., Savannah, 1982—; prof. Savannah Coll. of Art and Design, 1986—; designed and constructed numerous indsl. office, apt. and comml. bldgs., marine structures including docks, loading platforms, marinas, shipyards and water and waste water treatment structures. Contbr. articles on structural engring. to profl. jours. Mem. Nat. Soc. Profl. Engrs., ASCE. Home: 1115 Wilmington Island Rd Savannah GA 31410-4508 Office: Hussey Gay Bell & DeYoung 329 Commercial Dr Savannah GA 31406-3630

HSU, PATRICK KUO-HENG, languages educator, librarian; b. Hefei, Anhui, China, July 3, 1936; came to U.S., 1965; s. Hsiang-Chang and Yi-Yun (Tan) H.; m. You-Wei Gina Wang, Feb. 1, 1962; children: David Shing, Jim Chi. BA, Nat. Cheng-Chi U., Mucha, Taipei, Taiwan, 1960; MSLS, Western Mich. U., 1968. Asst. libr. Ripon (Wis.) Coll., 1968-77, assoc. libr., 1977-85, libr., 1985; assoc. prof., libr. dir. Tex. Luth. U., Seguin, 1985-91, prof., univ. libr., dir. info. svc., 1991—; dir. Univ. Students in Am. from Taiwan Consortium, Seguin, 1990-96. Translator, editor: A Selection of Modern One-Act-Plays, 1971; translator: Theory of Literature, 1976. Dir. Chinese Soc. San Antonio, 1989-95; mem. World Affairs Coun. San Antonio, 1993—, San Antonio Chinese Cult. Inst. (chmn. bd.), 1994-95; advisor Overseas Chinese Affairs Commn., Republic of China, 1994—. Fellow Internat. Ctr. Asian Studies; mem. ALA, MLA, Assn. Asian Studies, Chinese Lang. Tchrs. Assn., Tex. Libr. Assn., Seguin Lions. Office: Tex Luth Univ 1000 W Court St Seguin TX 78155-5978

HU, CHEN-SIEN, surgeon; b. Taiwan, Mar. 11, 1949; m. Li Ling; children: Jessica, Johnathan. MD, Taipei (Taiwan) Med. Sch., 1974; M in Pub. Health, Johns Hopkins U., 1977. Diplomate Am. Bd. Surgery, Am. Bd. Colon Rectal Surgery. Surgical resident Union Meml. Hosp., Balt., 1977-82; vascular fellow Tex. Heart Inst., Houston, 1982-83; colon-rectal resident U. Tex., Houston, 1983-84; chief surgery Columbia HCA Hosp., New Port Richey, Fla., 1993—. Fellow Am. Coll. Surgeons, Am. Soc. Colon Rectal Surgery; mem. Soc. Laprascopic Surgeons, Soc. Am. Gastrointestinal Endoscopic Surgeons. Office: 5719 High St New Port Richey FL 34652-4036

HUA, KIEN ANH, computer science educator; b. Mar. 17, 1958; s. Ngai Nam and Van Kien (Luu) H.; m. Chau Minh Tran, Jan. 1, 1983; children: Kathleen, Casey, Andrew. BS in Computer Sci., U. Ill., 1982, MSEE, 1984, PhD in Elec. Engring., 1987. Adv. engr. fellow group IBM Mid-Hudson Labs., Kingston, N.Y., 1987-90; assoc. prof. computer sci., dir. database systems lab. U. Ctrl. Fla., Orlando, 1990—; reviwer, cons., speaker and instr. in field. Referee jours.; contbr. numerous articles to profl. jours.; patentee in field. Mem. IEEE (Best paper award 1990, Best presenter award 1990). Office: U Ctrl Fla Dept Computer Sci Orlando FL 32816

HUANG, BINGRU, plant physiologist; b. Nanpi, People's Republic China, Nov. 12, 1963; s. Yan ming and Shang qi (Meng) H.; m. Ping Zhang, Mar. 6, 1988; children: Eddie Zhang, Lisa Zhang. BS, Hebei Agrl. U., 1984; MS, Shandong Agrl. U., 1987; PhD, Tex. Tech. U., 1991. Rsch. asst. Tex. Tech. U., Lubbock, 1988-91; rsch. assoc. UCLA, 1991-93, U. Ga., Griffin, 1993-96, Kans. State U., 1996—. Author: (with others) Plant Roots: The Hidden Half, 1995, Plant Resistance to Water Logging, 1996; contbr. articles to profl. jours. Mem. Am. Soc. of Crop Sci., Am. Soc. of Agronomy, Toastmaster Internat. (v.p. edn.). Office: Kansas St Univ 2021 Throckmorton Hall Manhattan KS 66506

HUANG, DENIS KUO YING, chemical engineer, consultant; b. Canton, China, May 14, 1925; came to U.S., 1948; s. Shui Fu and Wai Men Wong; married; 1 child, Lloyd K. BS in Math., St. John's U., 1944; BSChemE, U. Calif., Berkeley, 1950; MSChemE, U. Maine, Orono, 1951; DChemE, Poly. Inst. Bklyn., 1958. Head chemist Internat. Paper Co., Phila., 1958-62; sr. rsch. chemist Simoniz Co., Chgo., 1962-65; sr. rsch. engr. Westvaco Corp., Laurel, Md., 1965-78; process engring. cons. Fed. Paper Bd., Augusta, Ga., 1978-90; cons. Tech. Cons. Internat., Singer Island, Fla., 1990—; cons. UNDP to China, 1983, OAS, 1972, Argentina UNIDO, 1970; tech. expert to India. Patentee in field; contbr. articles to encyclopaedia, profl. jours. Mem. TAPPI, Sigma Xi, Phi Lambda Upsilon. Home: 426 SW Fairway Landing Port Saint Lucie FL 34986

HUANG, ENG-SHANG, virology educator, biomedical engineer; b. Chia-Yi, Taiwan, Republic of China, Mar. 17, 1940; came to U.S., 1968; s. Juong-Sun and King-fa (Ong) H.; m. Shu-Mei Huong, Dec. 26, 1965; children: David Y., Benjamin Y. BS, Nat. Taiwan U., Taipei, Taiwan, 1962, MS, 1964; PhD, U. N.C., 1971. Asst. prof. U. N.C., Chapel Hill, 1973-78, assoc. prof., 1978-86, prof., 1986—; virology program leader Cancer Rsch. Ctr., Chapel Hill, 1979-91; mem. virology study sect. DRG/NIH, Bethesda, Md., 1978-82; mem. AIDS basic rsch. rev. com. Nat. Inst. Allergy & Infectious Diseases/NIH, 1988-90; chmn. Internat. Sci. Promotion Com., U.S. chpt., 1988—. Contbr. articles to Molecular Biology of Human Cytomegalovirus, Devel. Abnormality Induced by Cytomegalovirus Infection, Interaction between Cytomegalovirus and Human Immunodeficiency Virus. Chmn. membership com. Soc. Chinese Bioscientists in Am., Washington, 1988-89. Lt. ROTC, 1964-65. NIH fellow, 1971-73, Rsch. Career Devel. award NIAID, NIH, 1978-83; grantee in field. Mem. AAAS, Am. Soc. Microbiology, N.Y. Acad. Sci., Am. Cancer Rsch. Democrat. Office: U NC Lineberger Cancer Ctr Chapel Hill NC 27599

HUANG, (MARGARET) JANICE FERNALD, mathematics educator; b. Boston, Mar. 10, 1942; d. Henry Grant and Margaret (Wyer) Fernald; m. Thomas Tao-Shing Huang, June 12, 1965; children: Margaret Lucile, Steven Henry. AB, Brown U., 1963; MA, U. Ill., 1965, PhD, 1992. Tchr. Washington Coll. Acad., Limestone, Tenn., 1974-79; asst. prof. math. Milligan (Tenn.) Coll., 1979-84, assoc. prof., 1984-93, prof., 1993-94; assoc. prof. math. East Tenn. State U., Johnson City, 1994—; math. coach Acad. Decathlon Team U. Sch., Johnson City, 1986-90; project coord. NSF Grant, 1986-89. Judge sci. fair East Tenn. State U., 1986, math. fair Ashley Acad., 1987, geometry fair Liberty Bell Middle Sch., 1988. Grantee: Eisenhower Tchr. Tng. grants, 1993, 94, 96. Mem. Math. Assn. Am., Nat. Coun. Tchrs. Math., Tenn. Math. Tchrs. Assn., Upper East Tenn. Coun. Math., Am. Math. Soc., Sigma Xi. Office: East Tenn State U Dept Math Box 70663 Johnson City TN 37614

HUANG, JUNG-CHANG, computer science educator; b. Taoyuan, Taiwan, Apr. 7, 1935; Came to U.S., 1961; Diploma elec. engring., Taipei (Taiwan) Inst. Tech., 1956; MS in Elec. Engring., Kans. State U., 1962; PhD in Elec. Engring., U. Pa., 1969. Telecom. engr. Chinese Govt. Radio Adminstrn., Taipei, 1958-60; planning engr. AT&T, Western Elec. Co., Allentown, Pa., 1962-66; teaching and rsch. fellow U. Pa., Phila., 1967-69; asst. prof. dept. computer sci. U. Houston, Tex., 1969-73; assoc. prof. dept. computer sci. U. Houston, 1973-80, prof. dept. computer sci., 1980—, chmn. dept. computer sci., 1992-96; vis. prof. U. Udine, Italy, 1990; referee NSF rsch. grant proposals; vice chmn., treas. 1975 Symposium on Computer Architecture; conf. chmn., program com. chmn. Seventh Tex. Conf. on Computing Systems; mem. program com. 1978 Workshop on Software Testing and Test Documentation, 8th Tex. Conf. on Computing Systems, Third Internat. Conf. on Distributed Computing Systems; vis. Computer Sci. Accreditation Commn., 1985-91; cons., spkr. and presenter in field. Referee: ACM Computing Surveys, Comm. of the ACM, IEEE Trans. on Computers, IEEE Trans. on Software Engring., IEEE Computer, IEEE Software, Internat. Jour. Computer Math., Data Processing Letters, Software Practice Experience, others; contbr. articles to profl. jours. 2d lt. Chinese Air Force, Taiwan, 1956-58. Recipient Teaching fellowship U. Pa., 1967, Rsch. fellowship U. Pa., 1968-69, U. Houston Faculty Rsch. Initiation grant, 1971, NASA-ASEE Faculty Rsch. fellowship, 1972, 73, NSF Internat. Travel grant, 1973, NSF Rsch. grants, 1977-80, 80-83, U. Houston grant for computer network, 1984, NSF Rsch. Equipment grant, 1984, NAVY-ASEE Sr. Summer Faculty fellowship, 1984, Rsch. grant Tex. Advanced Rsch. Program, 1988-91, Rsch. grant U. Houston Inst. Space Systems Ops., 1992, 94, others. Mem. IEEE, IEEE Computer Soc., Assn. for Computing Machinery, Phi Kappa Phi, Sigma Xi. Office: Dept Computer Sci Univ Houston Houston TX 77204-3475

HUANG, PHILIP P., physician; b. N.Y.C., Apr. 17, 1961; s. Yen Ti and Toshiko H.; m. Lori Argo, May 27, 1989; children: Carolyn, Michelle. BA, Rice U., 1982; MD, U. Tex., 1986; MPH, Harvard U., 1990. Intern, resident family practice Brackenridg Hosp., Austin, 1986-89; EIS officer Ctr. for Disease Control, Atlanta, 1990-92; chief bur. chronic disease Tex. Dept. Health, Austin, 1992—. Lt. commdr. USPHS, 1990-92. Office: Tex Dept Health 1100 W 49th St Austin TX 78756

HUANG, YAO-WEN, food science educator, researcher; b. Shang-Hung, Fukien, China, Jan. 12, 1947; came to U.S., 1976; s. Chia-Teh and Shu-Ying (Lee) H.; m. Ping-yuan Chiang, Jan. 4, 1974; children: William, Jane, Kevin. BS, Nat. Taiwan Ocean U., Keelung, Taiwan, Republic of China, 1968; MS, U. Ga., 1978, PhD, 1983. Assoc. instr. Nat. Taiwan Ocean U., 1969-73, instr., 1973-76; rsch. assoc. U. Ga., Brunswick, 1983-88; asst. prof. U. Ga., Athens, 1988-94, assoc. prof., 1994—; vis. rschr. Academia Sinica, Taipei, 1971-72; cons. prof. Shanghai Fishery U., 1994—. Bd. dirs. Orgn. for Chinese Ams., Atlanta, 1988-89. Mem. Inst. Food Technologists (Outstanding Grad. Prof. 1993), Am. Assn. Cereal Chemists (approved methods com. 1986-94), Internat. Assn. Milk, Food and Environ. Sanitarians (chair seafood quality and safety com.), Chinese Am. Food Soc. (pres. 1990-91, Disting. Svc. award 1990, Profl. Achievement award 1993), Lions (lion tamer Brunswick chpt. 1987-88, tail twister Athens chpt. 1988-89, 1st v.p. 1989-90, 92-93, 96-97, pres. 1990-91, 93-94, Melvin Jones fellow 1994), Gamma Sigma Delta (Disting. Tchg. award 1996). Office: U Ga Food Sci & Tech Dept Athens GA 30602

HUANG, YEE-WEI, strategic analyst, chemical engineering educator; b. Tao-Yuan, Taiwan, Jan. 4, 1959; came to U.S., 1982; s. Ming-Chung and Yeh-Chiao (Fan) H.; m. Yu-Hua Hsu, July 17, 1987; children: Rune-Wen, Yee-Wen. BSChemE, Nat. Taiwan U., 1980; MSChemE, Kans. State U., 1984, MS in Computing & Info. Sci., 1987, PhD in Chemical Engring., 1988. Rsch. asst. Dept. Chemical Engring. Kans. State U., Manhattan, 1982-88, teaching fellow, AI Lab. System adminstr., 1986-88; computer sci. cons. Health and Environ., Inc., Manhattan, 1987-88; rsch. assoc. Advanced Mfg. Inst., Kans. Tech. Entrepreneur Ctr. of Excellence, Manhattan, 1988—; v.p., dir. rsch. & devel. Odin Corp., Manhattan, 1988-92; founding ptnr. Olson Huang & Assocs., Manhattan, 1990-92; staff strategic analyst Motorola, Inc., Austin, 1992—, emerging computing ops. Asian Pacific program. mgr., 1994—, mem. tech. staff, 1995—; cons. Process Database, Manhattan, 1987—; adj. asst. prof. Kans. State U., Manhattan, 1988—; rsch. asst. Council for Econ. Planning & Devel., Taipei, Taiwan, 1980. Contbr. numerous articles to profl. jours.; presenter in field; patentee in field. Rsch. grantee Kans. State U., Motorola, Ctr. of Excellence, Kans. Dept. Transp., Okla. Ctr. Advancement Sci. and Tech., others. Mem. IEEE, Am. Assn. Artificial Intelligence, Am. Inst. Chem. Engring., Internat. Neural Network Soc., N.Y. Acad. Scis., Sigma Xi, Tau Beta Pi. Home: 9501 Scenic Bluff Dr Austin TX 78733-6026 Office: Motorola Inc 6501 W William Cannon Dr Austin TX 78735-8523

HUANG, YEN TI, civil engineer; b. Taipei, Taiwan, Feb. 4, 1927; came to U.S., 1957; s. Tan Kun Huang and Mu Lin; m. Toshiko Naomi Saito Imano, July 4, 1958; 1 child, Philip Po-Wen. BSc, Nat. Taiwan U., Taipei, 1950; MASc, U. Toronto, Can., 1957; PhD, Columbia U., 1961. Registered profl. engr., Tex., N.Mex., Ont., Taiwan. Mem. rsch. staff Sperry Rand Rsch. Ctr., Sudbury, Mass., 1961-63; project geophysicist Atlantic Refining Co., Dallas, 1963-65; sr. geophysicist Geotech (subs. Teledyne Co.), Garland, Tex., 1965-68; mem. tech. staff Collins Radio Co., Richardson, Tex., 1968-70; CEO, pres. Y.T. Huang & Assocs., Dallas, 1970—, San Tai Internat. Corp., Dallas, 1973—; adj. prof. U. Tex., Arlington. Founder of numerical transform theorem used in digital transform; patentee gyroscopic apparatus, modular inflatable dome structures, modular space framed earthquake resistant structures, modular roof structures, and semi-submerged, movable, modular offshore platform. Co-chair Tex. Asian Rep. Caucus, 1982. Econ. Coop. Am./Joint Commn. on Rural Reconstruction scholar Taiwan Dept. Edn., 1951-52. Mem. ASCE (com. tower found. design stds. 1989-96), Internat. Soc. Offshore and Polar Engrs. (session chmn. 1991-94), N.Y. Acad. Scis., Tech. Club Dallas (v.p. 1993-95, pres.-elect 1996), Rotary, Dallas Coun. on World Affairs. Unitarian. Office: Y T Huang & Assocs Inc Windy Forest Pl 9638 Greenville Ave Dallas TX 75243-4164

HUANG, YINGHUA, plant molecular biology researcher, educator; b. Jingmen, Hubei, China, Oct. 22, 1952; came to U.S., 1983; s. Xianyuan and Weiying (Lu) H.; m. Xiaoping Guo, Sept. 25, 1979; 1 child, Joanne. BS in Forestry and Horticulture, Huazhong Agrl. U., Wuhan, China, 1977; postgrad., Zhongshan U., Canton, China, 1981; PhD in Biol. Scis., Mich. Tech. U., 1991. Rsch. asst. Huazhong Agrl. U., 1975-77; rsch. assoc. Wuhan Inst. Botany/Chinese Acad. Scis., 1977-79, asst. rsch. scientist, 1979-81, dir. rsch. group, 1981-83; grad. rsch. asst. Mich. Tech. U., Houghton, 1986-91, mgr. Forest Biotechnology/Tissue Culture Lab., 1989-91; sr. rsch. specialist plant molecular genetics dept. forestry Okla. State U., Stillwater, 1991-93, rsch. asst. prof. plant molecular biology dept. forestry, 1993—; vis. rsch. scientist Pa. State U., University Park, 1983-86; presenter in field. Contbr. over 42 articles to sci. and profl. jours. Recipient John S. Song award World Congress Cell and Tissue Culture, 1991. Mem. AAAS, Am. Soc. Plant Physiologists, Am. Soc. Agronomy, Am. Soc. Hort. Scis., Crop Sci. Soc. Am., Genetics Soc. Am., Mcpl. Arborists and Urban Forsters Soc. (chmn. tree selection com. 1992—), Tussie Culture Assn., Internat. Soc. for Plant Molecular Biology, Sigma Xi, Xi Sigma Pi. Office: Okla State U 008C Ag Hall S Stillwater OK 74078-6013

HUBBARD, JULIA FAYE, accountant; b. Lebanon, Tenn., Apr. 27, 1948; d. Joe Pate Jr. and Rachel (Trice) H. BSBA, Tenn. Technol. U., 1970; postgrad. in Acctg., U. Tenn., 1974-77. CPA. Sec. Sch. Nursing Vanderbilt U., Nashville, 1970-71; bookkeeper Ingram Corp., Nashville, 1971-72; acct., bookkeeper White & Ensor CPA's, Birmingham, Ala., 1972-74, Internat. Div. Joe M. Rodgers Constrn. Co., Nashville, 1974-79; supr. Ryan, Connelly, Primm & Outhier CPA's, Nashville, 1979-83; prin. Taylor & Assocs. CPA's, Nashville, 1983-86; owner, mgr. Julia F. Hubbard, Acctg. & Cons., Nashville, 1986-93; CFO Contour Med. Tech. Inc., La Vergne, Tenn., 1993-94; prin. Grannis, Whisenant & Assocs., P.C., Lebanon, Tenn., 1994—; asst. to developer, project coord. R.B. Investments Co., Nashville, 1985; owner, designer Juliana Designs, Nashville, 1986—. Fellow Nat. Assn. Accts. (officer, bd. dirs. 1981-85), Tenn. Soc. CPAs (mem.-at-large). Republican. Methodist. Office: 148 Public Sq Lebanon TN 37087-2736

HUBBARD, WILLIAM JAMES, library director; b. Grand Rapids, Mich., July 17, 1941; s. Willard Wright and Sara (Rast) H.; m. Barbara Ockun, Sept. 8, 1962; children: William, Thomas, James, Gregory. Engr., supr. Rochester (N.Y.) Telephone Corp., 1963-71; contract libr. Xerox Corp., Webster, N.Y., 1971-72; libr. circulation SUNY, Fredonia, 1973-75; libr. user svcs. Va. Poly. Inst. and State U., Blacksburg, 1975-80; dir. libr. svcs. Va. State Libr., Richmond, 1980-88; univ. libr. Jacksonville (Ala.) State U., 1988—. Author: Stack Management, 1981; assoc. editor Ala. Librarian; contbr. articles to profl. jours. Mem. Am. Soc. Info. Sci., Southeastern Libr. Assn., Ala. Libr. Assn., Nat. Assn. of Scholars. Office: State U Univ Libr Jacksonville AL 36265

HUBBELL, BILLY JAMES, lawyer; b. Pine Bluff, Ark., May 21, 1949; s. Arley E. and Mary M. (Duke) H.; m. Judy C. Webb, Feb. 21, 1981; children: Jennifer Leigh, William Griffin. BE, U. Cen. Ark., 1971; JD, U. Ark, Little Rock, 1978. Bar: Ark. 1978, U.S. Dist. Ct. (ea. dist.) Ark. 1978, U.S. Ct. Appeals (8th cir.) 1987. Tchr. Grady (Ark.) High Sch., 1971-78; assoc. Smith and Smith, McGehee, Ark., 1978-79; ptnr. Smith, Hubbell and Drake, McGehee, 1979-86, Griffin, Rainwater & Draper, P.A., Crossett, Ark., 1987-90; dep. prosecuting atty. Ashley County, Ark., 1989-90; mcpl. judge Crossett, 1991—, pvt. practice, 1991—. Candidate Ark. Ho. of Reps., Lincoln County, 1984. Sgt. USAR, 1970-76. Mem. Ark. Bar Assn., S.E. Ark. Legal Inst. (chmn. 1984-85, Ashley County Bar Assn. (pres.). Democrat. Baptist. Office: PO Box 574 Crossett AR 71635-0574

HUBBELL, ELIZABETH WOLFE, English language educator; b. Chgo., Mar. 10, 1940; d. Richard Russell and Elizabeth (Laughlin) Wolfe; m. John T. Hubbell, July 13, 1963; children: John Andrew, Richard Randolph. BA, Wellesley Coll., 1962; MA in Tchg. Secondary English, U. N.H., 1988. Composition tutor Masconomet Regional Jr. Sr. H.S., Topsfield, Mass., 1985-87; intern English tchr. Masconomet Regional Jr. Sr. H.S., Topsfield, 1987-88; tchr. Hovnanian Armenian Sch., New Milford, N.J., 1989-91; dept. chair, instr. Cecils Coll., Asheville, N.C., 1988—. Sch. bd. mem. Contoocook Valley Region, Peterborough, N.H., 1977-83; exec. com. mem. N.H. Sch. Bds. Assn., Concord, 1982-83; sch. bd. chair Conval/Jaffrey-Rindge Region, Peterborough, 1983; singer Asheville Choral Soc.; choir mem. 1st Presbyn. Ch., Asheville. Named Tchr. of the Yr., N.C. Assn. Schs. and Colls., 1993. Presbyterian. Office: Cecils Coll PO Box 6407 1567 Patton Ave Asheville NC 28806

HUBBELL, KATHERINE JEAN, marketing consultant; b. Norfolk, Va., Mar. 5, 1951; d. Lester Earle and Katherine Jean (Bush) H.; m. Daryl Paul Domning, July 10, 1987. BA in English, BS in Math., Clemson U., 1974; MBA in Mktg., Va. Polytech. Inst. & State U., 1991. Info. systems engr. MITRE Corp., McLean, Va., 1975-79; mem. tech. staff MITRE Corp., Bedford, Mass., 1980-81; design engr. GE, Wilmington, Mass., 1979-80; budget assoc. nat. hdqs. ARC, Washington, 1982-92; mktg. cons. Dominion Group, Vienna, Va., 1993—; database mgr. Nat. Christian Life Cmtys. of U.S., 1993—. Recreation vol. ARC, Bethesda Naval Hosp., 1976-79; vol. Holy Cross Hospice, 1984-87; strategic planning com. Christian Life Cmtys. Mid-Atlantic Region, 1989-90; allocations com. United Way Nat. Captiol Area, 1989-91. Mem. Am. Mktg. Assn., Assn. Part-Time Profls., Soc. Competitive Intelligence Profls. Home: 9211 Wendell St Silver Spring MD 20901-3533 Office: The Dominion Group 8229 Boone Blvd Ste 710 Vienna VA 22182-2623

HUBER, CLAYTON LLOYD, marketing professional, engineer; b. Corpus Christi, Tex., May 4, 1955; s. James Lloyd and Lealla Jean (Snyder) H.; m. Verna Marlene May, Aug. 16, 1975; children: Konstanze Marlena, James Clayton, Katerina Nicole, Kassandra Kay. BS in Chem. Engring., W.Va. Inst. Tech., 1978. Registered profl. engr., W.Va.; cert. energy mgr. Project engr. Am. Cyanamid Co., Willow Island, W.Va., 1978-80; process engr. Mobay Chem. Corp., New Martinsville, W.Va., 1980-82; process design engr. Mobay Chem. Corp., Charleston, S.C., 1982-85; indsl. utilization specialist Hope Gas, Inc., Clarksburg, W.Va., 1985-88; mgr. mktg. tech. svc. Hope Gas, Inc., Parkersburg, W.Va., 1988-89; mgr. indsl. and tech. mktg. Hope Gas, Inc., Clarksburg, W.Va., 1989-95, mgr. residential, comml., tech. mktg., 1995—. Mem. W.Va. 4-H Club All Stars, Jacksons Mill, 1974—, Clarksburg Madrigal Singers; elder Ch. of Christ. Mem. NSPE, AIChE, Soc. Plastics Engrs., Assn. Energy Engrs., Am. Chem. Soc., Environ. Engrs. and Mgrs. Inst. of Assn. Energy Engrs. (charter), Nat. Coun. on Weights and Measures, W. Va. Natural Gas Vehicle Coalition (chair mktg. and devel. com.), W. Va. Environ. Inst., W. Va. Soc. Profl. Engrs. (pres. T. Moore Jackson chpt., state chmn. membership com., state bd. dirs.), Am. Assn. Cost Engrs. (bd. dirs.). Democrat. Home: 225 Paula Blvd Clarksburg WV 26301-3940 Office: Hope Gas Inc PO Box 2868 805 Bank One Ctr W Clarksburg WV 26301

HUBER, DONALD SIMON, physician; b. Clarendon, Pa., Apr. 18, 1929; s. Walter Casper and Mary Agnes (Earley) H.; m. Mary Hanks, Sept. 6, 1958; children: Donald Scott, Mark Walter, Mary Lisa. BA, Duke U., 1951, MD, 1954. Diplomate Am. Bd. Internal Medicine, Am. Bd. Allergy and Immunology. Intern Charity Hosp., New Orleans, 1954-55; resident internal medicine Tulane U. Hosp., New Orleans, 1955-56, 58-60; pvt. practice Huntsville, Ala., 1960—; clin. assoc. prof. medicine Sch. Primary Med. Care, Huntsville, 1985—. Lt. commdr. USN, 1956-58, USNR, 1958-60. Fellow Am. Coll. Allergists; mem. AMA, Am. Acad. Allergy and Immunology, Ala. Soc. Allergy and Immunology (pres. 1985), Huntsville Rotary Club (bd. dirs. 1978). Republican. Methodist. Home: 502 Eustis Ave SE Huntsville AL 35801-4112

HUBER, DOUGLAS CRAWFORD, pathologist; b. S. Charleston, W.Va., June 11, 1939; s. Abram Paul and Mary Ashley (Grow) H.; m. Deena Rae Freedman, Aug. 8, 1969; children: Adam Crawford, Laura Kristen; m. Angelika Madelon Pohl, June 3, 1961 (div. 1965); 1 child, Heidemarie Jutta. Student, Harvard U., 1958, 59; AB, Emory U., Atlanta, 1960; MD, Emory U. Sch. of Med., Atlanta, 1964. Assoc. pathologist Baldwin County Hosp., Milledgeville, Ga., 1971-72, Leary Lab., Boston, 1972-73; lab. dir. Homer D. Cobb Mem. Hosp., Phenix City, Ala., 1973-79; gen. practitioner Leonard Morse Hosp., Natick, Mass., 1979-80; lab. dir. Promina Douglas Hosp., Douglasville, Ga., 1980—; med. dir. Roche Biomedical Lab., Atlanta Div., Tucker, Ga., 1989-93; deputy state commr. Coll. Am. Pathologists Lab. Inspection Program, Skokie, Ill., 1976-79; v.p. Ala. Assn. Pathologists, Birmingham, 1979. Pres. Nam Vets of Ga., 1982-85; capt. with U.S Army, 1965-67. Fellow Coll. Am. Pathologists, Am. Soc. Clinical Pathologists.

HUBER, HERBERT EUGENE, human resource development consultant; b. Crestline, Ohio, Oct. 26, 1950; s. Harold J. and N. Beatrice (Rainy) H.; m. Elizabeth A. Gresmer, June 17, 1973; children: Kimberly L., Kelly R. BS, U.S. Air Force Acad., 1973; MPA, Auburn U., Montgomery, Ala., 1982. Commd. 2d lt. USAF, 1973, advanced through grades to maj., 1984; chief offensive systems br. 93d Bombardment Wing, Castle AFB, Calif., 1986-88; chief computer based tng. 436 Tng. Squadron, Dyess AFB, Calif., 1988-91, chief tng. and edn., 1991-93; ret. USAF, 1993; mgr. employee devel. Temple-Inland Forest Products Corp., Diboll, Tex., 1993—. Bd. dirs. Tex. State Tech. Coll. Found., Austin, 1993—. Mem. ASTD, Am. Mgmt. Assn., Internat. Soc. for Performance Improvement, Profl. Assn. of Diving Instrs. Presbyterian. Office: Temple Inland Forest Products Corp Employee Devel Ctr 213 N Temple Dr Diboll TX 75901

HUBER, JOHN MICHAEL, lumber executive; b. N.Y.C., Oct. 13, 1958; s. Edward F. and Mary Elizabeth (Fallon) H. BA with honors in Philosophy, Boston U., 1981. Lumber broker Mor-Wood, Inc., Morehead, Ky., 1981-84; chmn., CEO Acorn Industries, Inc., Morehead, 1984-95; v.p. Pallet Pallet, Inc.; CEO Diamond Forest Resources, Inc., Clearfield, Ky., 1986—; CFO Clearcreek Hardwoods, Grayson, Ky., 1988—; co-founder H.M.I. LLC. Active Rowan County Learning Found., Morehead, 1989—, Am. Heart Found., St. Jude's Children's Hosp., Sloan Kettering Cancer Inst.; bd. dirs. Rowan County Adult Basic Edn. and Literacy Adv. Bd. Named to the Hon. Order of Ky. Col's. Mem. Citizens Against Govt. Waste (sustaining mem., cert. appreciation 1988, 89, 90), Nat. Congl. Rep. Com. (cert. appreciation 1988, 89, 90), Nat. Wooden Pallet and Container Assn., Internat. Assn. Pallet Recyclers (bd. dirs. 1992-94, pres. 1994, past pres. 1995), Masons. Roman Catholic. Office: Diamond Forest Resources Inc 2 Acorn Ln Morehead KY 40351

HUBERT, SCOTT HAROLD, accountant, educator; b. Meridian, Miss., Jan. 16, 1949; s. Scott Francis and Edwina (Cunningham) H. BA in Psychology, Southern Meth. U., 1971; MEd in Edn. Psychology, U. N.C., 1975; EdS, Miss. State U., 1977, MPPA, 1978, MEd in Ednl. Adminstrn., 1990; postgrad., U. Miss. Tchr. spl. edn. Meridian & Newton County Pub. Schs., Meridian, Miss., 1974-79; cmty. devel. specialist City of Meridian, 1979-81; accountant Bookkeeping Svc. Co., Meridian, 1982—; instr. psychology & govt. East Ctrl. C.C., Decatur, Miss., 1982—. Active Meridian Little Theatre, 1976—; past bd. dirs. Meridian Exch. Club, Meridian Symphony Orch., Meridian Arts Coun., Meridian Mus. of Art, Lauderdale County Boys & Girls Club; vol. Miss. State Games. Recipient Outstanding Cmty. Svc. award Gov. of Miss., 1984, Citizenship award Keep Am. Beautiful Commn., Meridian. Mem. ASPA, Navy League of U.S., Order of Demolay (past chevalier & master counselor), Kappa Sigma. Democrat. Presbyterian. Home: 4609 Broadmoor Dr Apt 129 Meridian MS 39305

HUBERTY, CARL J, statistician/methodologist, educator; b. Lena, Wis., Nov. 14, 1934; s. Clement N. and Rosalie C. (Vander Peren) H.; children: Greg, Brian, Jeff, Kurt. BS, U. Wis., Stevens Point, 1956; MS, U. Wis., Madison, 1958; PhD, U. Iowa, 1969. Asst. prof. U. Wis., Oshkosh, 1965-66; prof. U. Ga., Athens, 1969—; cons. in field. Author: Applied Discriminant Analysis, 1994; contbr. articles to profl. jours. Mem. Am. Statis. Assn., Am. Ednl. Rsch. Assn. Home: 120 Plantation Dr Athens GA 30605-4020 Office: U Ga 325 Aderhold Hall Athens GA 30602-7143

HUBIG, STEPHAN MARIA, chemistry educator; b. Saarbrücken, Germany, Oct. 20, 1954; came to U.S., 1984; s. Karl Heinz and Elisabeth (Marschand) H.; m. Maria Isabella Diaz, Oct. 29, 1989; 1 child, Anna Renée. PhD in Chemistry, U. Tübingen, Germany, 1984. Postdoctoral rsch. assoc. U. Tex., Austin, 1984-86, rsch. scientist assoc., 1987-88, rsch. scientist, 1988-91; rsch. asst. prof. U. Houston, 1992—. Contbr. articles to profl. jours.; patentee chem. actinometer. Fellow Studienstiftung des Deutschen Volkes, Fed. Gov. of Germany, 1973-83. Mem. Am. Chem. Soc., Interam. Photochem. Soc., European Photochemistry Assn. Home: 2111 Brimberry Houston TX 77018 Office: U Houston Dept Chemistry Houston TX 77204-5641

HUCHTEMAN, RALPH DOUGLAS, lawyer; b. Garland, Tex., Oct. 8, 1946; s. Ray Edwin and Hazel Laverne (Clark) H.; m. Sherry Lynn Horner, Mar. 12, 1994; children: Lara Victoria, Brett Norman, Bryan Randolff. AA, Okla. Mil. Acad., 1966; BA in Polit. Sci., Okla. State U., 1969; JD, Okla. U., 1972. Bar: Okla. 1972, U.S. Dist. Ct. (we. dist.) Okla. 1972. Ptnr. Doak & Huchteman, Oklahoma City, 1972-73, Wolf & Wolf P.C. (formerly Wolf, Wolf, Huchteman & Graven), Norman, Okla., 1982-88; prin. Huchteman Law Offices, Norman, 1989—; assoc. mcpl. judge, Noble, Okla., 1990—; vis. asst. prof. Coll. Bus., Okla. U., 1972-73; temporary justice Okla. Ct. Appeals, Oklahoma City, 1982-83. State exec. sec. Student Lobby for Higher Edn., Stillwater, Okla., 1968-69. Served to 1st lt., U.S. Army, 1973. T.A. Shadid scholar Okla. U., 1969; recipient A.C. Hunt Practice Ct. award, Okla. U., 1972. Mem. Okla. Bar Assn., Ann. of Trial Lawyers of Am., Okla. Trial Lawyers Assn., Norman C. of C. Democrat. Office: Huchteman Law Offices 301 1/2 E Main St Norman OK 73069-1306

HUCK, LEWIS FRANCIS, lawyer, real estate consultant and developer; b. Bklyn., Mar. 19, 1912; s. Frank and Jessie (Green) H.; LLB, St. John's U., 1938, LLM, 1939; m. Frances M. Love, Jan. 7, 1950 (dec. 1985); children: Janet Ahearn, L. Frank, William G. (dec.), Robert L., James J.; m. Virginia I. Reid, Apr. 18, 1987. Bar: N.Y. 1939, Tex. 1939, Mass. 1939, U.S. Dist. Ct. (so. dist.) Tex. 1992. Practice law, 1939—; with trust dept. Guaranty Trust Co. N.Y., 1929-41; atty. Gen. Electric Co., Schenectady, 1945-47, chem. counsel, 1947-48, atomic energy counsel, 1948-51, gen. mgr., Richland, Wash., 1951-55; asst. to exec. v.p. Gen. Dynamics Corp., 1955-57; lawyer, real estate cons. and developer, 1957-68; v.p., dir., cons. real estate devel. Eastern Airlines, Inc., 1968-88; pres. Huck Enterprises Co. Inc., 1980—; bd. dirs. Sea-Air Shuttle Corp. Served maj. AUS, 1941-45. Democrat Home: 15084 Kimberley Ct Houston TX 77079-5125

HUCKABEE, MICHAEL DALE, governor; b. Hope, Ark., Aug. 24, 1955; m. Janet McCain, May 25, 1974; children: John Mark, David, Sarah. BA in Religion magna cum laude, Ouachita Bapt. U., Arkadelphia, Ark., 1976; postgrad., Southwestern Bapt. Theol. Sem., Ft. Worth, 1976-77. Ordained to ministry So. Bapt. Conv., 1974. Pastor Walnut Street Bapt. Ch., Arkadelphia, 1974-75, Immanuel Bapt. Ch., Pine Bluff, Ark., 1980-85; evangelist various Christian ministries; pastor Beech Street 1st Bapt. Ch., Texarkana, Ark., 1986—; Lt. Gov. State of Ark., 1993-96, governor, 1996—; founder, past pres. Am. Christian TV Sys., Pine Bluff; pres. Ark. Bapt. Conv., 1989—; mem. adv. bd. So. Bapts. for Life; numerous others. Weekly newspaper columnist Positive Alternatives. Former bd. govs. Ark. Boys State; former county coord. Unborn Child Amendment Com., Pine Bluff; former pres., bd. dirs. Jefferson County unit Am. Cancer Soc., pres., 1984-85; former participant, bd. dirs. Leadership Pine Bluff; bd. dirs. B.O.N.D., bus. orgn. for new downtown, Texarkana, Friendship Ctr., Texarkana; mem. allocations com., vol. United Way Texarkana; mem. citizen's adv. com. Texarkana Sch. Bd.; spkr. to numerous chs., schs. and bus. orgns.; mem. procedures rev. com. St. Michael Hosp., 1988-90; chmn. Texarkana Easter Seals Telethon, 1993-94; pres. Ark. Bapt. State Conv., 1989-91. Mem. Nat. Religious Broadcasters, Texarkana Ministerial Alliance (TV chmn.), Texarkana C. of C. Home: 2 Cambridge Dr Texarkana AR 75502-3002 Office: Office of the Gov State Capitol Rm 250 Little Rock AR 72201-1091

HUCKABY, EDWARD EARL, architect; b. Regansburg, Germany, Nov. 11, 1951; parents Am. citizens; s. Edward Vernon and Mary Lou (Hoffman) H.; children: Erin, Kristin, Courtney. B.Environ. Design, Tex. A&M U., 1973, MArch, 1974. Lic. architect, Tex. Intern architect Bernard Johnson, Inc., Houston, 1975-76; project architect Falick Klein Partnership, Inc., Houston, 1976-81, prin./owner/sr. project designer, 1985—; project architect Richard Fitzgerald & Ptnrs., Houston, 1981-84; prin. architect Turner/Huckaby Architects, Houston, 1984-85; spkr. seminars on health care design. Archtl. designs include Menil Collection Mus., Meml. N.W. Hosp. Recipient 1st place in comml. health care design Houston Chronicle, 1993, 94. Mem. AIA, Tex. Soc. Architects, Soc. for Care of Children's Health, Acad. for Arch. for Health. Republican. Episcopalian. Home: 4602 Nassau Dr Sugar Land TX 77479

HUCKINS, HAROLD AARON, chemical engineer; b. Cambridge, Mass., Nov. 28, 1924; s. Harold Aaron and Julia E. (Nugent) H.; m. Elizabeth L. Kearns, Nov. 15, 1952; children: Richard W., Robert M., Christopher N. Patricia A., Leslie K. BSChemE, Northeastern U., 1945; ASME, Lowell Inst., 1946; postgrad., Boston U., 1947-49, U. Pitts., 1950-52. Chem. process engr., asst. project mgr. Monsanto Chem. Co., Boston-Everett, Mass., 1945-49; sr. process engr., group leader Koppers Co. Chem. Div., Pitts., 1949-53; mgr. pilot plants, project mgr. Sci. Design Co., Inc., N.Y.C., 1953-66; v.p. tech. ops. Oxirane Chem. Co., Princeton, N.J., 1966-73; v.p. tech. assessment Halcon SD Group, N.Y.C., 1973-85; pres. Princeton Advanced Tech., Inc., 1985—; dir. Assn. Cons. Chemists and Chem. Engrs. div., N.Y.C., 1990-93, program chair, 1992-93; dir. Materials Tech. Inst., St. Louis, 1976-85. Co-author: The Chemical Plant, 1966; contbr. articles to profl. jours. Fellow AIChE (chair ctrl. Jersey sect. 1976-77, dir mgmt. divsn. 1981-82, dir. materials engring. and sci. divsn. 1992-93, chmn. chem. tech. materials com. 1983-84, chmn. John Fritz medal commn. 1989, chmn. entrepreneurial forum 1994—, Chem. Engring. Practice award 1994); mem. Am. Soc. Materials, Am. Chem. Soc., Am. Ceramic Soc. Nat. Assn. Corrosion Engrs. (conf. chmn. 1984), Comml. Devel. Assn., Mensa Internat., Country Club of Hilton Head Island, Port Royal Racquet Club. Office: Princeton Advanced Tech Inc 4 Bertram Pl Hilton Head Island SC 29928-3936

HUDACEK, GEORGE C., tax specialist; b. Wheeling, W.Va., Nov. 24, 1942; s. Prince Albert and Angela Teresa (Lisak) H.; m. Judith M. Marsh, May 9, 1944; 1 child, Jessica R. BS, W.Va. U., 1965; AS, W.Va. No. U., 1991. Loan officer Budget Fin. Co., San Francisco, 1965-67; trust, tax officer Wells Fargo Bank, San Francisco, 1968-70, Bank of Calif., San Francisco, 1971-84; tax cons. Putney and Barton, Walnut Creek, Calif., 1984-85; pres., CEO Pay Less Taxes, Wheeling, W.Va., 1985—; bd. dirs. Wheeling Cycle and Marine, Blakley and Buturla Engring., Caldwell, Idaho; pres. Black Diamond Investment Club, 1947-94; tax cons. Buckley, Inc., San Francisco, 1985-94. Comptr. no. W.Va. Coun. 4 Good Politics, 1991-94; fund raiser United Way, 1985-95; v.p. bd. advisors St. Ladislaus Ch., 1990-95. Named Hon. Adm. Cheery River Navy of W.Va., 1990. Mem. Soc. Enrolled Agts., Polish, Athletic, Polit. Club (rec. sec. 1992-95), Bikers Am. (treas. 1992-95), Kain Club, Ind. Order Loyal Am., Jet Ski Club (treas. 1992-95), W.Va. U. Alumni Assn. (social chmn. Wheeling chpt. 1985-95). Roman Catholic. Home and Office: 20 Schuberts Ln Wheeling WV 26003-4622

HUDDLE, RITA KEGLEY, medical, surgical and home health nurse, administrator; b. Wythe County, Va., Dec. 26, 1955; d. Kenneth Leo and Neva Mae (Gallimore) Kegley; m. Jeb Stuart Earhart Huddle, Jan. 1, 1982; 1 child, Lauren Nichole. AA, Wytheville Community Coll., 1977. Cert. med.-surg. nurse ANCC. Staff nurse med.-surg. unit Norfolk (Va.) Gen. Hosp., 1980; charge nurse surg. unit Wythe County Community Hosp., Wytheville, Va., 1977-80, staff nurse ICU and CCU, 1980-85, house supr., 1985-87, dir. med. svcs., 1987-90, home health case mgr., 1990-93, home health clin. supr., 1993—. Home: RR 5 Box 108 Wytheville VA 24382-9509 Office: Circle Home Care Wythe County Cmty Hosp 600 W Ridge Rd Wytheville VA 24382

HUDDLESTON, BILLY PETE, petroleum engineer; b. Iraan, Tex., Feb. 2, 1934; s. Acie Ray and Jewell Charity (Dukes) H.; m. Flora Mae Huddleston, Aug. 26, 1956; children: Peter Duke, William Paul, Lisa Lee Currie. BS in Petroleum Engring., Tex. A&M U., 1957. Registered profl. engr., Tex. Petroleum engr. Marathon Oil Co., various cities, 1957-65; ind. cons. Houston, 1966—; chmn. Huddleston & Co., Inc., Houston, 1967—, Peter Paul Petroleum Co., Houston, 1973—; vis. prof. Tex. A&M U., College Station, 1981—; bd. dirs. Am. Energy Fin. Corp., Houston, 1983-84, OXYCO, Houston, 1983-85; mem. petroleum adv. bd. SEC, Washington, 1979-81, Fin. Acctg. Standards, Stamford, Conn., 1981-82; mem. engring. adv. com. Tex. A&M U., 1990—. Contbr. articles to profl. jours. Chmn. YMCA, Houston, 1977-78, PTA, Houston, 1979-80; mem. fin. com. Chaplewood Meth. Ch., Houston, 1980-82. Named Disting. Engring. Alumnus Tex. A&M U., 1995. Mem. Soc. Petroleum Engrs., Soc. Petroleum Evaluation Engrs., Tau Beta Pi. Office: Huddleston & Co Inc 1111 Fannin Ste 1700 Houston TX 77002

HUDDLESTON, JOHN FRANKLIN, obstetrics and gynecology educator; b. Jacksonville, Fla., June 26, 1942; s. Paul Mc Kisson and Mary Rebecca (Robinson) H.; m. Kathryn Ann Welch, Dec. 30, 1982; children: Suzanne Marie, Edward Ryan, John Stuart, Mary Kathryn, Ryan Mc Kisson. BS, U. Fla., Gainesville, 1963; MD, Duke U., 1967. Diplomate Am. Bd. Ob-Gyn, Am. Bd. Maternal-Fetal Medicine. Dir. maternal-fetal medicine Sch. of Medicine, U. Ala., Birmingham, Ala., 1963-86; pvt. practice Jacksonville, Fla., 1986-89; prof., dir. maternal-fetal medicine Sch. of Medicine, Emory U., Atlanta, 1989-96, Coll. of Medicine, U. Fla. Sch. of Medicine, Jacksonville, 1997—. Contbr. to profl. jours., articles, and book chpts. Surgeon USPHS, 1969-71. Mem. Ctrl. Assn. Obstetricians and Gynecologists, Am. Gynecologic and Obstetrics Soc., Soc. Perinatal Obstetricians, South Atlantic Assn. Obstetricians and Gynecologists. Office: U Fla Health Scis Ctr Dept Ob/Gyn 655 W 8th St Jacksonville FL 32209

HUDDLESTON, JOSEPH RUSSELL, judge; b. Glasgow, Ky., Feb. 5, 1937; s. Paul Russell and Laura Frances (Martin) H.; m. Heidi Wood, Sept. 12, 1959; children: Johanna, Lisa, Kristina. Bar: Ky. 1962, U.S. Ct. Appeals (6th cir.) 1963, U.S. Supreme Ct. 1970. Ptnr. Huddleston Bros., Bowling Green, Ky., 1962-87; judge Warren Cir. Ct. Div. I, 1987-91, Ky. Ct. Appeals, 1991—; mem. Adv. Com. for Criminal Law Revision, 1969-71; mem. exec. com. Ky. Crime Commn., 1972-77. Mem. ABA, Ky. Bar Assn. (ho. of dels. 1971-80), Assn. Trial Lawyers Am. (state del. 1981-82), Ky. Acad. Trial Attys. (bd. govs. 1975-87, pres. 1978), Bowling Green Bar Assn. (pres. 1972), So. Ky. Estate Planning Council (pres. 1983), Bowling Green-Warren County C. of C. (bd. dirs. 1987-91), Jefferson Club (Louisville), Port Oliver Yact Club (Bowling Green), Phi Alpha Delta. Democrat. Episcopalian. Home: 644 Minnie Way Bowling Green KY 42101-9210 Office: 1945 Scottsville Rd Ste 101 Bowling Green KY 42104-5824

HUDDLESTON, MARILYN ANNE, international business financier, merchant banker, educator; b. Fayetteville, N.C., Jan. 28, 1953; d. Allen Paul and Julia Jewel (Hill) Miller; m. Roby Dwayne Huddleston, Sept. 13, 1946; children: Michelle, Christopher, Mathew Anthony, Danyel Paul, Michael David. D in Humanities Law (hon.), Central Tex. U., 1974; diploma Acad. of Coll. of Real Estate, 1977; postgrad. El Paso Community Coll; PhD in Humanities & Law, London Inst. Applied Sci. & Rsch. Owner, fin. cons. Cherokee Fin. Investments, Killeen, Tex., 1983-88; owner, broker All Am. Ins. Agy., Killeen, 1984-88; realtor, assoc. Exec. Fin., Austin, Tex., 1986-88; owner Geodesic Homes of Tex., Killeen, 1984-88; chmn., CFO Wall Street Internat., 1988-90, chmn. bd. dirs., 1988—; tchr. St. Joseph Catholic Sch., Killeen, 1991-92, tchr., adminstr., 1991-94; merchant banker Baytree Investors, Killeen, 1990—, chmn., CEO, CFO, 1995—; grant writer, adminstrv. asst. to pres. and CEO Advantage Adult Day Care & Health Svcs., Harker Heights, Tex., 1994-95, admin. support KISD Title I, 1995—. Author: Miracle Baby at Bracken Ridge Hospital, 1979; Financial Consulting Made Easy, 1983. Pres. Mil. Council of Catholic Women, Stuttgart, Fed. Republic Germany, 1980, Non-Commnd. Officers Wives, Stuttgart, 1980-82, Ciudad del Niño Orphanage Assn., Killeen, 1979—; instr. Christian Religion, Killeen, 1976-91, St. Joseph Cath. Sch., Killeen. Recipient Silver Poet award World of poetry Poets, 1989. Mem. Nat. Assn. Female Execs., Internat. Assn. Bus. and Fin. Cons. (hon.), Fort Hood Bd. Realtors, Nat. Assn. Realtors, Tex. Assn. Realtors Soc. Female Execs. (v.p. 1984-86), Internat. Soc. Financiers (cert.). Independent. Roman Catholic. Avocations: singing, writing, tennis, macrame.

HUDGENS, KIMBERLYN NAN, accounting specialist; b. Hartwell, Ga., June 18, 1964; d. Kenneth Howard and Nan (Skelton) H.; m. Douglas Howard Abrams, June 30, 1990. BS in Indsl. Engring., Auburn U., 1988; BA in Math., Ogelthorpe U., 1988; postgrad., Mercer U., 1993—. Registered engr. in tng. Field rep. Law Assocs., Inc., Atlanta, 1988-89; assoc. quality engr. ABB Power T&D Co., Athens, Ga., 1989-91; rep. mem. svcs. Atlanta Gas Light Co., 1992-95, acctg. specialist, 1995—. Democrat. Methodist. Home: 3310 Hart Way Snellville GA 30278-4686

HUDGINS, CATHERINE HARDING, business executive; b. Raleigh, N.C., June 25, 1913; d. William Thomas and Mary Alice (Timberlake) Harding; m. Robert Scott Hudgins IV, Aug. 20, 1938; children: Catherine Harding Adams, Deborah Ghiselin, Robert Scott V. BS, N.C. State U., 1929-33; grad. tchr. N.C. Sch. for Deaf, 1933-34. Tchr. N.C. Sch. for Deaf, Morganton, 1934-36, N.J. Sch. for Deaf, Trenton, 1937-39; sec. Dr. A.S. Oliver, Raleigh, 1937, Robert S. Hudgins Co., Charlotte, N.C., 1949—, v.p., treas., 1960—, also bd. dirs. Mem. Jr. Svc. League, Easton, Pa., 1939; project chmn. ladies aux. Profl. Engrs. N.C., 1954-55, pres., 1956-57; pres. Christian High Sch. PTA, 1963; program chmn. Charlotte Opera Assn., 1959-61, sec., 1961-63; sec. bd. Hezekiah Alexander House Restoration, 1949-52, Hezekiah Alexander House Aux., 1975—, treas., 1983-84, v.p., 1984-85, pres., 1985-89; sec. Hezekiah Alexander Found., 1986—; past chmn. home missions, annuities and relief Women of Presbyn. Ch., past pres. Sunday Sch. class; mem. Heritage Foun. Press. Club, 1995—, Empower Am., 1995—. Named Woman of Yr. Am. Biographical Soc., 1993. Mem. N.C. Hist. Assn., English Speaking Union, Internat. Platform Assn., Mint Mus. Drama Guild (pres. 1967-69), Internat. Biog. Ctr. Eng. (dep. dir. gen.), Heritage Found. (pres. club, 1994), Empower Am. (leadership coun. 1995), Daus. Am. Colonists (state chmn. nat. def. 1973-74, corr. sec. Virginia Dare chpt. 1978-79, 84-85, state insignia chmn. 1979-80), DAR (mem. nat. chmn.'s assn., rec. sec. nat. officers club 1990—, chpt. regent 1957-59, chpt. chaplain 1955-57 N.C. program chmn. 1961-63, state chmn. nat. def. 1973-76, state rec. sec. 1977-79, hon. state regent for life, chmn. N.C. Geneal. Register 1982, nat. vice chmn. S.E. region Am. Indians 1989—, rec. sec. Nat. Officers Club 1990-92, v.p. N.C. State Officer's Club 1991-92, pres. 1992-94), Children Am. Revolution (N.C. sr. pres. 1963-66, sr. nat. corr. sec., 1966-68, sr. nat. 1st v.p. 1968-70, sr. nat. pres. 1970-72, hon. sr. nat. pres. life 1972—, 2d v.p. Nat. Officers Club, 1st v.p. 1977-79, pres. 1979-81), Huguenot Soc. N.C., Carmel Country Club (Charlotte), Viewpoint 24 Club, (v.p. 1986, pres. 1987). Home: 1514 S Wendover Rd Charlotte NC 28211-1726 Office: Robert S Hudgins Co PO Box 17217 Charlotte NC 28270-0099

HUDGINS, DON FRANKLIN, city official; b. Gadsden, Ala., Feb. 28, 1940; s. Willie and Lorene (Smith) H.; children: Donald Scott, Elizabeth Ann, Jeffrey Kyle, Alyson Paige; m. Sandra Dale Smedley Miller, Jan. 1, 1984; 1 child, Jon Mark. Student, U. Ala., 1976, Gadsden State Coll., 1978, Valdosta State Coll., 1983, Emergency Mgmt. Inst., Emmitsburg, Md., 1988, 92. Cert. emergency mgr. State trooper Dept. Pub. Safety, Montgomery, Ala., 1960-67; installer We. Electric Corp., Gadsden, Ala., 1967-75; dir. Gadsden/Etowah County Emergency Mgmt. Agy., 1975—; chmn. Gadsden Emergency Planning Com., 1988—; mem. County Emergency Bd., Gadsden, 1976—. Bd. dirs. Etowah County Food Bank, Gadsden; mem. Gadsden Amateur Radio Club, Gadsden Civitan Club. 010Nat. Coordinating Coun. on Emergency Mgmt. (state rep. region IV), Ala. Emergency Mgmt. Coun. (v.p. 1987, pres. 1991). Democrat. Baptist. Home: 116 Larkhaven Dr Rainbow City AL 35906-3006 Office: Gadsden Emergency Mgmt 90 Broad St Gadsden AL 35901-3757

HUDGINS, LOUISE NAN, art educator; b. Ft. Worth; d. Joe Wallace and Lillian Frances (Taylor) H. BA, U. North Tex., 1960, postgrad., 1965. Cert. tchr. art, Tex. Fine arts supr. Dallas Ind. Sch. Dist., 1981-82; tchr. art Lida Hooe Elem. Sch., Dallas, 1966-81, Greiner Arts Acad., Dallas, 1982-86, Hotchkiss Montessori Acad., Dallas, 1986-94, Dealey Montessori Acad., Dallas, 1994—; state textbook com. Tex. Edn. Agy., Austin, 1981-82, com. mem., cons., 1984-85, workshop presenter U. Tex., 1989-91, Montessori Certification Program, Dallas, 1992-95, Pine Bluff, Ark., 1995; mem. com. Tex. Art Assessments Study, Richardson, 1993. Co-author: (tchr. textbook) Through Their Eyes, 1989; contbg. author: (student textbooks) Inside Art, 1992. Named Elem. Tchr. of Yr. Oak Cliff C. of C., Dallas, 1980. Mem. ASCD, Nat. Art Edn. Assn., Tex. Art Edn. Assn. (chair elem. divsn. 1983-84, rep. assembly 1987-89, Elem. Art Educator of Yr. 1988), Dallas Art Edn. Assn. (pres. 1988-89). Home: 1451 Winding Brook Cir Dallas TX 75208-2926

HUDICK, ANDREW MICHAEL, II, finance executive; b. Holly Springs, Miss., May 11, 1958; s. Joseph Frank and Marie Carmella (Peters) H. BSCE, U. Va., 1980; Cert. fin. planner, Coll. for Fin. Planning, 1982,

MS in Retirement Planning, 1991. Registered investment advisor, U.S., Va. Engr. Norfolk & Western Rwy., Roanoke, Va., 1980-81; prin., founder, head Fee-Only Fin. Planning, L.C., Roanoke, 1981—; adj. faculty Va. Polytech. and State U., 1994-96. Fin. planning columnist Blue Ridge Bus. Jour., 1989-94, Va. Skyline, 1986-89; contbr. articles to profl. jours. Bd. dirs. Assn. Retarded Citizens, Roanoke, 1985, Mental Health Assn. Roanoke, 1984-86, treas. 1986; chmn. speaker's bur. United Way Roanoke Valley, 1985-86. Recipient Disting. Svc. award Mental Health Assn., 1984, 86, Outstanding Svc. award United Way Roanoke Valley, 1986; named Outstanding Vol., Va. Skyline Girl Scout Coun., Salem, 1986, one of Top 60 Fin. Advisor, Worth Mag., 1994, one of Top 200 Fin. Advisors, Worth Mag., 1996. Mem. Inst. Cert. Fin. Planners (cert.), Nat. Assn. Personal Fin. Advisors (bd. dirs., v.p. 1993, treas. 1994, pres. 1995-96), Internat. Assn. Fin. Planning (pres. 1987-88), Internat. Bd. Stds. and Practices for Cert. Fin. Planners (bd. examiners 1989-93), Registry of Fin. Planning Practitioners, Toastmasters (treas. Roanoke chpt. 1984-85, pres. 1985, dist. 66 gov. 1986, advanced speaking cert.). Office: Fee-Only Financial Planning, L.C. 355 W Campbell Ave SW Roanoke VA 24016

HUDLICKY, MILOS, former chemistry educator; b. Prelouc, Czechoslovakia, May 12, 1919; came to U.S., 1968; s. Jaroslav and Marie H.; m. Alena Vyskocilova, July 2, 1946; children: Tomas, Eva. PhD, Tech. U., Prague, 1946. Rsch. chemist Rsch. Inst. of Rubber Tech., Zlin, Czechoslovakia, 1940-45; asst. prof. Inst. of Chemistry and Tech., Prague, 1945-48; postdoctoral fellow Ohio State U., Columbus, 1948; assoc. prof. Inst. Chem. Tech., Prague, 1949-58; rsch. chemist Rsch. Inst. Pharm. Biochemistry, Prague, 1958-68; assoc. to full prof. Va. Polytech. Inst., Blacksburg, Va., 1968-89, prof. emeritus, 1989. Contbr. articles to profl. jours., author books in field. Recipient Alan Clifford award Va. Polytech. Inst., 1989, Votocek medal Czech. Chem. Soc., 1992. Office: Va Polytech Inst Dept Chemistry Blacksburg VA 24601

HUDNUT-BEUMLER, JAMES DAVID, theology educator; b. Detroit, Feb. 21, 1958; s. Arthur Karl and Joyce Ann (Mills) Beumler; m. Heidi Allen Hudnut, July 18, 1987; children: Julia, Adam. BA, Coll. Wooster, 1980; MDiv, Union Theol. Sem., N.Y.C., 1983; MA, Princeton U., 1986, PhD, 1989. Adminstrv. dir., lectr. Woodrow Wilson Sch. Pub. and Internat. affairs Princeton (N.J.) U., 1988-91; program assoc. Lilly Endowment, Inc., Indpls., 1991-93; dean faculty, exec. v.p. Columbia Theol. Sem., Decatur, Ga., 1993—; mem. adv. bd. Faculty Grant Ctr. of Assn. Theol. Schs., Pitts., 1994—; trustee Griffith Theol. Found., Decatur, 1993—; dir. Nat. History of Am. Religion, Decatur, 1995—. Author: Looking for God in the Suburbs, 1994, (chpts.) The Churches' Public Role, 1991; contbr. articles to profl. jours. Mem. Phi Beta Kappa. Democrat. Presbyterian. Home: 700 Kirk Rd Decatur GA 30030 Office: Columbia Theol Sem 701 Columbia Dr Decatur GA 30031

HUDSON, ANN THOMPSON, women's health nurse; b. Richmond County, N.C., Sept. 15, 1957; d. Amos Woodrow and Evelyn Louise (Russell) Thompson; children: Edward Robin, Amy Michelle. ADN, Richmond Community Coll., Hamlet, N.C., 1981. Cert. in inpatient obstetrics, Neonatal Advanced Life Support; fetal monitor cert. Respiratory therapy technician Richmond Meml. Hosp., Rockingham, N.C., 1976-78, staff nurse, labor and delivery, 1978-90, head nurse labor and delivery, 1990—, RNC, office mgr., 1992—; instr. nursing asst. program Richmond Community Coll. Home: 211 Fairway Dr Rockingham NC 28379-9484

HUDSON, CHARLES DAUGHERTY, insurance executive; b. La Grange, Ga., Mar. 17, 1927; s. J.D. and Janie (Hill) H.; m. Ida Cason Callaway, May 1, 1955; children: Jane Alice Hudson Craig, Ellen Pinson Hudson Harris, Charles Daugherty, Ida Hudson Hughes. Student Auburn U., 1945-48; LLD, La Grange Coll.; LHD (hon.) Mercer U., 1987, Auburn U, 1992. Ptnr. Hudson Hardware Co., La Grange, 1950-57; ptnr. Hammond-Hudson Ins. Agy., La Grange, 1957-58, owner, 1958-78; pres. Hammond, Hudson & Holder Inc., 1978-94, chmn. bd., 1994—; bd. dirs., mem. exec. com. Citizens & So. Nat. Bank, La Grange, 1963-90; mem., bd. dirs. Citizens & So. Ga. Corp., The Citizens & So. Nat. Bank, Atlanta, 1990—; acting pres. La Grange Coll., 1979-80; v.p., bd. dirs. La Grange Industries, Inc., 1956—, Hudson Maddox Enterprises, 1965—; ptnr. PCH Properties, 1981—; bd. dirs. C&S Investment Advisors, Inc., Atlanta, C&S Ga. Corp.; chmn. bd. dirs. First Annuity Corp., LaGrange, Ga.; bd. dirs., chmn. trust com. NationsBank of Ga. Mem. exec. com. Camp Viola, La Grange, 1956—, chmn. bd. trustees, 1988—; mem. pres. adv. council Ga. State U.; v.p., trustee Callaway Found., Inc., 1965—, Fuller E. Callaway Found., 1957—; former chmn. La Grange chpt. United Fund; trustee, chmn. Florence Hand Home Charitable Trust, 1982—; mem. La Grange Bd. Edn., 1967-88, chmn., 1971-74, 81-83; mem. pres. adv. bd. Med. Coll. Ga., Augusta, 1989—; trustee Ga. Bapt. Found., 1990—; chmn. endowment com. Ga. Bapt. Conv., 1983-85; trustee Scottish Rite Children's Hosp., Atlanta, 1990—; chmn. bd. trustees La Grange Coll., 1970-95, chmn. exec. comm., 1995—; trustee, chmn. bd. Ga. Bapt. Hosp., Atlanta, 1973, 76-77; trustee West Ga. Med. Ctr., La Grange, 1950—, chmn., 1993—, treas., 1978-79; trustee, past pres. Troup County Hist. Soc., 1975—, mem. staff Ga. gov., 1959-62, 63-66, 71-74, Ala. gov., 1975; mem. Downtown La Grange Devel. Authority, 1976—; trustee Ga. Trust for Historic Preservation, 1981—, Callaway Ednl. Assn., 1968-80; mem. La Grange Bicentennial commn., 1975-76, George E. Sims Nursing Scholarship Fund; mem. bd. dirs., v.p. Ga. Dept. of Corrections, 1983—, sec., 1983-84, vice chmn., 1985-86, chmn., 1987-88; chmn. Hosp. Equipment Fin. Authority, 1985—; trustee West Ga. Youth Council, 1970—; bd. dirs. Auburn U. Found., 1987—, trustee, chmn. bd. Ga. Assoc. Chiefs of Police Fd., 1993—; leader Aetna Life & Casualty, 1980-81, 86-87; pres. adv. coun. Ga. State U.; mem. 21st century commn. Auburn U. Recipient Pres.'s award Colonial Life Ins. Co., 1966, 69-70, 75-80, Disting. Alumni award Ga. Mil. Acad-Woodward Acad., 1971, Disting. Service award Ga. Hosp. Assn., 1980, Respect Law award Optimists Assn., 1977, Pub. Service award Ga. Assn. of AIA, 1977, Leading Producer award Aetna Life and Casualty, 1979; Paul Harris fellow, 1984. Mem. Ga. Assn. Ind. Ins. Agts., Ga. Sch. Bd. Assn. (area dir.), SAR, Amicale de Groupe LaFayette (hon.), Chattahoochee Valley Art Assn., La Grange C. of C. (bd. dirs.), Newcomen Soc. N.Am., Ga. Hosp. Assn. (trustee 1980—), U. Ga. Gridiron Secret Soc., Sigma Alpha Epsilon, Beta Gamma Sigma. Clubs: Highland Country, Lafayette (LaGrange); Commerce (Atlanta); Aetna Life and Casualty Pres.'s. Lodges: Masons, Shriners, Elks, Rotary (pres. 1964-65). Home: 407 Country Club Rd Lagrange GA 30240 Office: Hammond Hudson & Holder Inc 206 W Haralson St Lagrange GA 30240

HUDSON, FRANK PARKER, retired company executive; b. Americus, Ga., Dec. 12, 1918; s. Percy Wilbur and Janie Inez (Martin) H.; m. Elizabeth Lee Podlich, June 3, 1945; children: Frank Parker, Stephen Edward, James Burnett. BSChemE, Ga. Inst. Tech., 1941. Ptnr. Spotswood Parker & Co., Atlanta, 1946-65; pres. Spotswood Parker & Co., 1965-87; chmn. bd., chief exec. officer SyncroFlo, Inc., Atlanta, 1974-87; gen. ptnr. Miami Circle Assocs., Ltd., Atlanta, 1984—; mgr. Causeway Properties, Atlanta, 1974—. Author: An 1800 Census for Lincoln County, Ga., 1977, A 1790 Census for Wilkes County, Ga., 1988, Wilkes County Georgia Tax Records 1785-1805, 1996; contbr. articles to profl. jours.; patentee in field. Trustee The R.J. Taylor, Jr. Found., Atlanta, 1987-89. Maj. U.S. Army, 1941-45. Mem Buckhead Club. Episcopalian. Home: 7 Ivy Chase NE Atlanta GA 30342-4550

HUDSON, JOHN LESTER, chemical engineering educator; b. Chgo., 1937; s. John Jones and Linda Madeline (Panozzo) H.; m. Janette Glenore Caton, June 29, 1963; children: Ann, Barbara, Sarah. BS, U. Ill., 1959; MS in Engring., Princeton U., 1960; PhD, Northwestern U., 1962. Registered profl. engr., Ill. Asst. prof. chm. engring. U. Ill.-Urbana, 1963-69, assoc. prof., 1969-75; prof., chmn. dept. chem. engring. U. Va., Charlottesville, 1975-85; mem. Ctr Advanced Studies U. Va., 1985-86, prof., 1986-88, Wills Johnson prof., 1988—; mgr. Ill. Div. Air Pollution Control, Springfield, 1974-75; cons. to various industires and govt. agys., 1966—. Contbr. articles to profl. jours. Recipient Humboldt award, 1989; NSF fellow, 1962, Fulbright fellow, 1961-63, 82-83. Mem. AIChE (Wilhelm award 1991), Am. Chem. Soc. Home: 1920 Thomson Rd Charlottesville VA 22903-2419 Office: U Va Dept Chem Engring Thornton Hall Charlottesville VA 22903-2442

HUDSON, LINDA, health care executive; b. Tuscaloosa, Ala., Feb. 12, 1950; d. Elvin and Clara (Duke) Hudson; m. Charles Garrett Kimbrough, May 26, 1984. BS in Edn., U. Ala., 1971; MS in Psychology, U. So. Miss., 1984. Lic. profl. counselor. Recreational therapist West Ala. Rehab. Ctr., Tuscaloosa, 1971-72; flight attendant Delta Air Lines, Miami and New Orleans, 1972-80; pvt. practice psychotherapist Hattiesburg (Miss.) and Atlanta, 1984—; program dir. Eating Disorders Adventist Health System/Wedst, Atlanta, 1985-88, regional dir./cons., 1986-87, exec. dir. mental health svcs., 1988-89; owner Hudson Cons. Assocs., 1989—, nat. cons., 1986—. Contbr. articles to profl. jours. Mem. Covington Jr. Svc. League, La., 1981-83; co-chmn. St. Tammany Rep. Polit. Action Com., 1980-81; coord. United Way of St. Tammany Parish, 1979-80. Mem. Women Healthcare Execs., Ga. Mental Health Counselors Assn., Nat. Coun. Sexual Addiction and Compulsivity (bd. dirs., v.p.). Democrat. Office: Ste 238 1090 Northchase Pkwy Marietta GA 30067-6402

HUDSON, MICHAEL CARL, biology educator; b. Washington, July 23, 1960; s. Michael Boyd and Elaine Ann (Coleman) H.; m. Yvette Maria Huet, July 14, 1984; 1 child, Lucas Raul Huet Hudson. BA in Biology, Boston U., 1982; PhD in Microbiology, U. Kansas, 1987. Instr. U. Kansas, Washington U.; assoc. prof. U. N.C., Charlotte; mem. Biology Dept. Adv. Com., 1991-93, biosafe com., 1991—, chair biology dept. curriculum com., 1992, univ. faculty patent com., 1995—, biology dept. grad. com., 1994—. reviewer: (sci. jour.) Infection and Immunity, Applied Environmental Microbiology Jour. Bacteriology, (chpts. for book) Microbiology 5th edit.; contbr. numerous articles to sci. jours. Recipient William Arnold Grad. Fellows award, 1987, Cora M. Downs award for Excellence in Rsch. and Teaching, 1985, 86, Nat. Rsch. Svc. award NIH, Nat. Inst. Dental Rsch. award; grantee NIH, N.C. Biotech. Ctr., Carolinas Med. Ctr., U. N.C. at Charlotte. mem. AAAS, Am. Soc. Microbiology, Sigma Xi. Office: U NC Dept Biology Charlotte NC 28223

HUDSON, PAUL J., physician; b. N.Y.C., Oct. 5, 1950; s. Edward Peter and Jean A. (Remer) H.; m. Clare D., Aug. 24, 1974; children: Elisabeth, John, Amy, Hannah. BA, U. Rochester, 1972; MD, Johns Hopkins U., 1976, MPH, 1977. Resident U. Rochester (N.Y.) Sch. Medicine, 1977-80; asst. prof. U. S.C. Sch. Med., Columbia, 1980-82; epidemiology intelligence officer Ctr. for Disease Control, Atlanta, 1983-85; med. epidemiologist Vt. State Health Dept., Burlington, 1985-86; med. cons. SIM, Addis Ababa, Ethiopa, 1986-91; emergency med. physician Chaplain Valley Physician Hosp., Plattsburgh, N.Y., 1992-95; med. officer Internat. Nepal Fellowship, Poklora, 1995—. Fellow ACP; mem. Christian Med. Dental Soc. Home: care INF Box 5, Pokhara Nepal Office: SIM PO Box 7900 Charlotte NC 28241

HUDSON, RALPH MAGEE, writer, artist; b. Fields, Ohio, Dec. 18, 1907; s. Claude Henry and Agnes May (Magee) H.; m. Alice Louise Dale, Feb. 22, 1929 (dec. Nov. 1985); m. Lillian Phillups, Dec. 20, 1986; children: Shirley Hudson Musgrave, Agnes Genevieve Hudson Patrick. BA, BS, Ohio State U., 1930, MA, 1931; EdD, U. Ala., 1965. Acting head, instr. art dept. Morehead (Ky.) State Coll., 1931-32, 33-36; head art dept. U. Ark., Fayetteville, 1936-46; prof., chmn. art dept. Miss. State Coll. for Women, Columbus, 1947-69, U. Ala., Huntsville, 1969-74, 74-79; vis. prof. art Inst. Allende, San Miguel de Allende, Mex., spring 1974; guest curator Black Artists/South Exhbn., Huntsville Mus. Art, 1979. Author: (exhbn. catalog) Black Artists/South, 1979, report on Afro-Am. project for NEH, 1974; paintings exhibited in mus. and galleries in 6 Southeastern states, 1940-90. Pres. Southeastern Coll. Art Conf., 1966, N.E. Miss. Assn. of Phi Beta Kappa, 1967, Miss. Art Assn., 1950. Mem. SAR, Huntsville Mus. of Art, Rotary Club (Paul Harris fellow 1971—), Phi Beta Kappa, Tau Sigma Delta, Kappa Pi, Phi Kappa Phi (internat. v.p. 1950—), Theta Chi. Episcopalian. Home: 2706 College Park Cir NW Huntsville AL 35805

HUDSON, ROBERT FRANKLIN, JR., lawyer; b. Miami, Fla., Sept. 20, 1946; s. Robert Franklin and Jane Ann (Reed) H.; m. Edith Mueller, June 19, 1971; children: Daniel Warren, Patrick Alexander. BSBA in Econs., U. Fla., 1968, JD, 1971; summer cert., U. London, 1970; LLM in Taxation, NYU, 1972. Bar: Fla. 1971, N.Y. 1975. Law clk. to judge Don N. Laramore U.S. Ct. Claims, Washington, 1972-73; assoc. Wender, Murase & White, N.Y.C., 1973-77; ptnr. Arky, Freed, Stearns et al, Miami, 1977-86, Baker & McKenzie, Miami, 1986—; mem. policy com., 1990-93, mem. client credit com., 1992—; mem. adv. bd. Tax Mgmt., Inc., Washington, 1986—, Fgn. Investment N.Am., London, 1990—; legal counsel to her majesty's Britanic Counsel, Miami. Author: Federal Taxation of Foreign Investment in U.S. Real Estate, 1986; contbr. articles to legal publs. Bd. dirs. Fla. Philharmonic, 1996—, Hudson Arts Ctr. Found., 1994—, Performing Arts Ctr. Found., 1994, Concert Assn. Fla., 1992—, exec. com., 1993—, vice chmn., 1994—. Mem. ABA, Fla. Bar Assn. (chmn. tax sect. 1989-90), Internat. Fiscal Assn. (v.p. S.E. region U.S. br. 1985-92, exec. coun. 1987—), Inter-Am. Bar Assn., Internat. Bar Assn., Internat. Tax Planning Assn., Coll. Tax Lawyers, World Trade Ctr. (bd. dirs. 1992-94), S.E./U.S. Japan Assn., Japan Soc. South Fla. (chmn. pub. affairs com. 1991—, bd. dirs. 1993—, treas. 1995-96, pres. 1996—), German-Am. Trade Coun., Swiss-Am. C. of C., Brit.-Fla. C. of C., Greater Miami C. of C. (bd. dirs. 1992-95, group v.p. 1992-93), Miami City Club, Rotary (bd. dirs. 1984-93). Democrat. Methodist. Office: Baker & McKenzie 701 Brickell Ave Ste 1600 Miami FL 33131-2852

HUDSON, SHIRLEY SPENCER, librarian; b. Terrell, Tex., July 18, 1944; d. George and Ernestine S. Lacy; divorced; 1 child, Christine Michelle. BS, Jarvis Christian Coll., Hawkins, Tex., 1967; MLS, E. Tex. State U., 1970. Cert. tchr., Tex. Tchr. Corsicana (Tex.) Ind. Sch. Dist., 1967-69; asst. libr. Jarvis Christian Coll., 1969-72, dir. libr. svcs., 1990—; asst. libr. Vernon (Tex.) Regl. Jr. Coll., 1972-75; dir. libr. svcs. Midland (Tex.) Coll., 1975-81; asst. libr., system analyst Southwestern Christian Coll., Terrell, Tex., 1981-90. Registrar Girl Scouts U.S., Terrell, 1988, adult coord., 1989, adult/vol. leader, 1990. Named to Outstanding Young Women of Am., 1967. Mem. ALA, NAFE, Tex. Libr. Assn., Delta Sigma Theta, Delta Kappa Gamma. Democrat. Baptist. Office: Jarvis Christian Coll PO Drawer G Hawkins TX 75765

HUDSON, W. GAIL, social worker; b. Waxahachie, Tex., Apr. 15, 1953; d. Billy M. and Sarah W. (Bowen) H.; m. Garry H. Gillan, Sept. 7, 1991; 1 child, Logan Thomas Gillan. BS, S.W. Tex. State U., 1975, MA, 1976; PhD, So. Ill. U., 1979; MSW, U. Tex., Arlington, 1989. Lic. master social worker, advanced clin. practitioner. Asst., assoc. prof. Millikin U., Decatur, Ill., 1978-87; dept. chair communications Millikin U., Decatur, 1984-87; adj. faculty U. Tex., Arlington, 1987-89; social work fellow M.D. Anderson Hosp., Houston, 1988; social work intern U. Houston Counseling, 1989; social worker U. Houston Counseling & Testing, 1989-92, dir. employee assistance program, 1992—; rep. AIDS Consortium of Tex., 1991; tng. cons. Caterpillar Tractor Co., Decatur, 1979-81; planning com. Nat. Conf. Against Sexual Assault, 1994; cons. Profl. Devel. Program, Decatur, 1979-81; adj. grad. faculty dept. counseling psychology U. Houston, 1991—. Cons. Houston Area Planning Commn. for Substance Abuse Program, 1990-91; treas. ERA Decatur, 1978-82; vol. Coalition Against Domestic Violence, Decatur, 1979-81. Cons. Houston Area Planning Commn. for Substance Abuse Program, 1990-91; prin. investigator/dir. prevention of substance abuse, U. Houston and Higher Edn. Consortium, Houston/Galveston, 1991-94. Grantee U.S. Dept. Edn. Mem. NASW, NOW, Am. Coll. Personnel Assn. (bd. dirs. 1991, 94), Am. Assn. Counseling and Devel.. Home: 1123 Burning Tree Rd Humble TX 77339-3933 Office: U Houston Counseling 4800 Calhoun Rd Houston TX 77004-2610

HUDSON, WALTER TIREE, artist; b. Lynchburg, Va., Apr. 10, 1943; s. Randolph Ward Hudson and Frances Anderson (Tyree) Hudson-Phillips; m. Patricia Fay Dearing, Aug. 23, 1963 (div. Sept. 1972); children: Walter Preston Tyree, William Alfred Dearing. Grad. h.s., Campbell County, Va. Reader Lynchburg Pub. Libr., 1976—. Exhibited at The Framery, 1985-95, Lynchburg (Va.) Pub. Libr., 1987—, Lynchburg Recreation Dept., 1988—, Daily Bread, 1989—, Adult Daycare Ctr.-Va. Bapt. Hosp., 1989-94, Ehrich's Optitions, 1992—, U. Tex., Houston, 1993, Lynchburg Fine Arts Ctr., Lynchburg PO, 1994, Lynchburg Voter Registration Office, 1995, Free Clinic of Va., 1995, Irby L. Hudson Collection, 1995, Lynchburg Social Svcs., 1987—, Lynchburg Pub. Housing Authority, 1986—, 101 Quinlan St., 1996, 504 Brevard St., 1996, 1818 Langhorne Sq., 1996. Active Court St. United Meth. Ch.; mem. Doggiewood Coalition, 1996. Mem. Lynchburg Stamp Club. Methodist and Mormon. Home: 3475 Fort Ave Apt 326 Lynchburg VA 24501-3834

HUDSON, WILLIAM MARK, insurance company executive, owner; b. Parkesburg, W.Va., Oct. 30, 1932; s. Morton Arden and Dorthy (Medealf) H.; m. Margie Webb, Oct. 3, 1953; children: William Mark II, Jay Lynn, Janet. Student, Fla. U., 1964-65, Fla. LaSalle U., 1971. Sgt. USMC, Albany, Ga., 1951-54; mgr. W.T. Grant Co., several cities, 1954-65; owner, agent Bill Hudson Ins. and State Farm Ins. Co., Orange Pk., Fla., 1965—; pres. BILMARJA, Inc., Orange Pk., 1987—. Chmn. Clay County (Fla.) Transp. Authority, 1988-90, 95-96; travel cons. Get a Way Travel, Orange Park, 1994—; elder St. Giles Presbyn. Ch., Orange Park, 1990—; treas. Clay County C. or C., 1987-88; mem. stewardship com. St. Augustine Presbyn. Ch., chmn. planned giving com., 1996. Mem. Rotary (Paul Harris fellow 1983, Morocco Patrol (capt. 1989-90), Shriners (pres. Motor Corp. 1974-75, pres. Patrol Assn. 1989-90, sec. southeastern Motor Corps 1972-74), Masons (vice chmn. 1996-97, pilgramage com. 1993-94, chmn. membership com. 1990-93), Order of Demolay, Knights Comdr. of Ct. of Honour, Legion of Honor (dean 1996-97). Republican. Presbyterian. Office: Bill Hudson Ins Co 793 Blanding Blvd Ste H Orange Park FL 32065-5720

HUDSON-YOUNG, JANE SMITHER, real estate investor; b. Altavista, Va., July 5, 1937; d. Victor Nelson and Elois Reynolds Smither; A.A.S. summa cum laude in Mgmt., Central Va. Community Coll., 1978; m. J. Lee Hudson, May 15, 1954; 1 child, Michael Edward; m. Gordon M. Young, July 9, 1989. Adminstrv. asst. Altavista (Va.) High Sch., 1954-55; with Lane Co., Inc., Altavista, 1956-89, exec. sec. to chmn. bd., 1976-81, exec. sec. to chmn. exec. com., 1981-84, spl. asst. for pub. rels. communications, 1984-86, acct. exec. nat. accts, 1986, asst. sales mgr. contract div., 1986-87, mktg. adminstr., 1988-89; realtor R. B. Carr & Co., Altavista, 1980-87, assoc. broker, 1985-87; mem. adv. bd. Am. Fed. Savs. and Loan, 1985-89; pres. Hudson-Young Investments, 1989—. Corr. Lynchburg (Va.) News., 1966-72. Mem. town coun. Town of Altavista, 1980-86; sec. Altavista Community Improvement Coun., 1981-82; mem. bd. deacons First Bapt. Ch., Altavista, 1980-83. Home and Office: 1100 Heritage Plantation Dr Pawleys Island SC 29585

HUDSPETH, HARRY LEE, federal judge; b. Dallas, Dec. 28, 1935; s. Harry Ellis and Hattilee (Dudney) H.; m. Vicki Kathryn Round, Nov. 27, 1971; children: Melinda, Mary Kathryn. BA, U. Tex., Austin, 1955, JD, 1958. Bar: Tex. 1958. Trial atty. Dept. Justice, Washington, 1959-62; asst. U.S. atty. Western Dist. Tex., El Paso, 1962-69; assoc. Peticolas, Luscombe & Stephens, El Paso, 1969-77; U.S. magistrate El Paso, 1977-79; judge U.S. Dist. Ct. (we. dist.) Tex., El Paso, 1979—; chief judge U.S. Dist. Ct. (we. dist) Tex., El Paso, 1992—. Bd. dirs. Sun Carnival Assn., 1976, Met. YMCA El Paso, 1980-88. Mem. ABA, El Paso Bar Assn., U. Tex. Exstudents Assn. (exec. coun. 1980-86), Chancellors, Order of Coif, Phi Beta Kappa. Democrat. Mem. Christian Ch. (Disciples of Christ). Office: US District Court 433 US Courthouse El Paso TX 79901

HUERTA, BALDEMAR See FENDER, FREDDY

HUEWITT, KENNETH RAY, auditor; b. Killeen, Tex., Feb. 12, 1962; s. Samuel Huewitt and Olenia Paden Stallings; m. Pamela Carol Elder, Feb. 6, 1988; children: Hunter Drake, Hailey Danielle. BBA in Acctg., S.W. Tex. State U., San Marcos, 1985. CPA, Tex., Va.; cert. govt. fin. mgr.; cert. fin. svcs. auditor. Auditor U.S. Dept. HUD, Washington, 1987-93; sr. audit specialist Resolution Trust Corp., Rosslyn, Va., 1993-95; audit specialist FDIC, Washington, 1995—. Recipient Spl. Achievement award U.S. Dept. HUD, 1992, award for patriotic svc. U.S. Dept. Treasury, 1993, Spl. Achievement award Resolution Trust Corp., 1994. Mem. AICPA, Tex. Soc. CPAs, Va. Soc. CPAs, Inst. Internal Auditors. Office: FDIC 801 17th St Washington DC 20434

HUEY, F. B., JR., minister, theology educator; b. Denton, Tex., Jan. 12, 1925; s. F.B. and Alma Gwendolyn (Chambers) H.; m. Nonna Lee Turner, Dec. 22, 1950; children: Mary Anne Huey Lisbona, Linda Kaye Huey Miller, William David. BBA, U. Tex., 1945; MDiv, Southwestern Bapt. Theol. Sem., 1958, PhD, 1961. Ordained to ministry So. Bapt. Conv., 1956. Pastor Bolivar Bapt. Ch., Sanger, Tex., 1956-59, Univ. Bapt. Ch., Denton, 1959-61; prof. Old Testament So. Brazil Bapt. Theol. Sem., Rio de Janeiro, 1961-65; prof. Old Testament Southwestern Bapt. Theol. Sem., Ft. Worth, 1965-95, chmn. D in Ministry program, 1978-79, assoc. dean for PhD program, 1984-90; ret., 1995; pastor Rush Creek Bapt. Ch., Arlington, 1989-93; guest prof. Bapt. Theol. Sem., Ruschlikon, Switzerland, 1971-72; guest prof. Canadian So. Bapt. Sem., Cochrane, Can., 1996. Author: Exodus: Bible Study Commentary, 1977, Chinese edit., 1983, Yesterday's Prophets for Todays' World, 1980, Chinese edit., 1991, Jeremiah: Bible Study Commentary, 1981, Chinese edit., 1982, Numbers: Bible Study Commentary, 1981, Chinese edit., 1988, Ezekiel-Daniel, 1983, (with others) Student's Dictionary for Biblical and Theological Studies, 1983, Helps for Beginning Hebrew Students, 1981, Jeremiah-Lamentations: New American Commentary, 1993; translator: (with others) New American Standard Bible, 1971, New International Version Bible, 1978, International Children's Version Bible, 1983; editor Southwestern Jour. Theology, 1975-78; contbr. articles to profl. jours. Mem. Soc. Bibl. Lit., Nat. Assn. Profs. Hebrew, Nat. Assn. Bapt. Profs. Religion, Delta Sigma Pi, Beta Gamma Sigma, Theta Xi. Home: 6128 Whitman Ave Fort Worth TX 76133-3547

HUEY, GEORGE IRVING, JR., computer senior systems consultant; b. Chula Vista, Calif., June 8, 1957; s. George I. Sr. and Grace C. (Beck) H. BSEE, Ctrl. Mo. State U., 1980. Computer programmer Bendix Corp., Kansas City, Mo., 1978-82; software cons. Info. Industries Inc., Kansas City, 1982-83; systems mgr. Aramco Svcs. Co., Houston, 1983-84; sr. system tech. specialist Saudi Aramco, Saudi Arabia, 1985-87, supr. comm. ops. data systems support unit, 1987-90; sr. sys. cons. Intergraph, Huntsville, Ala., 1991-95; prin. cons. Microsoft Corp., Redmond, Wash., 1995—; internat. cons. Intergraph, Huntsville, 1991-95. Author software applications. Mem. Nat. Athlete Strength Assn. (powerlifter, submaster 1991—, 3d pl. 1992 nat. regionals, 2d pl. 1993 nat. regionals), PADI Dive Club (dive master). Home: 5695 W Rochelle #201 Las Vegas NV 89103

HUEY, MARGIE LOU, medical, surgical and critical care nurse; b. Birmingham, Ala., Feb. 14, 1955; d. James Leonard and Violet Agnes (Morris) Clark; m. Charles M. Huey, Oct. 11, 1974. BSN, U. Ala., Birmingham, 1984. Cert. ACLS. Emergency staff nurse St. Mary's Hosp., Athens, Ga., med.-surg. charge nurse, ICU staff nurse, orthopedics and spl. surgery charge nurse; mem. D.A.T., mem. Ga. Hurricane Watch Team; vol. Ga. E.M.A.; instr. ACLS. Disaster nurse, instr. ARC.

HUFF, ARCHIE VERNON, JR., college administrator; b. Columbia, S.C., Feb. 17, 1937; s. Archie Vernon and Margaret Elise (Wannamaker) H.; m. Kate Marie Trivette, July 29, 1974; children: Vernon Edward, Mary Wannamaker. AB magna cum laude, Wofford Coll., 1959; BD, Yale U., 1962; MA, Duke U., 1968, PhD, 1970. Ordained to ministry United Meth. Ch., 1962. Assoc. pastor Washington St. United Meth. Ch., Columbia, S.C., 1962-65; asst. prof. history Furman U., Greenville, S.C., 1968-74, assoc. prof. history, 1974-81, prof. history, 1981—, v.p. acad. affairs, dean, 1995—. Author: Langdon Cheves of South Carolina, 1977, History of South Carolina in the Building of the Nation, 1991, Greenville: History of the City and County in the South Carolina Piedmont, 1995; editor: Writing South Carolina's History, 1992. Chair bd. trustees Spartanburg Meth. Coll., 1969-81, 86—; mem., chair S.C. Commn. on Archives and History, Columbia. Fulbright fellow U. Edinburgh, Scotland, 1959-60, Woodrow Wilson fellow Yale U., 1960-61. Mem. Rotary, Phi Beta Kappa, Phi Alpha Theta. Democrat. Home: 30 Glenrose Ave Greenville SC 29609 Office: Furman U 3300 Poinsett Hwy Greenville SC 29613

HUFF, CYNTHIA FAE, medical and orthopedic nurse; b. Albany, Ga., Jan. 3, 1950; d. Henry and Mary Catherine (Vannell) Piedmont; m. Michael Brian Shumaker, June 24, 1972 (div. 1979); 1 child, Brian Michael; m. Byron Lee Huff, Apr. 15, 1983. Diploma, Stuart Circle Hosp., Richmond, Va., 1970. RN, Va. Staff nurse St. Mary's Hosp., Richmond, 1970-71, asst. head nurse orthopedics, 1971, staff nurse emergency room, 1971-72, 73-74, head nurse orthopedics, 1972-73; office nurse Richmond, 1978-82; staff nurse Urology

Ctr., Richmond, 1983-84; owner Sesroh Farm-Registered Quarterhorses, Powhatan, Va., 1984-89; nurse-technician for veterinarian for large and small animals, Midlothian, VA., 1986-90; staff nurse Amelia (Va.) Nursing Ctr., 1993—; nurse technician Edda C. Eliasson, D.V.M., Amelia, 1995—; bd. dirs. Amelia Patrons for Animal Welfare. Mem. Nat. Assn. Physicians' Nurses, Am. Heart Assn. (CPR instr.). Republican. Methodist. Home: 3009 Moyer Rd Powhatan VA 23139-7220

HUFF, DENNIS LYLE, marketing professional; b. Chgo., Oct. 8, 1955; s. Barry Sanders Huff and Janada Jean (Patterson) Montgomery; 1 child, Alicia Jean; m. LouAnn Fae Gorder, Nov. 8, 1992. AS in Marine Tech., Coll. Oceaneering, 1984. Diver instr. Comml. Dive Ctr., Long Beach, Calif., 1984-87; owner Flight Shop, California City, 1987-90, Houston Export Co., 1990-92; exec. v.p. AMS, Inc., Oklahoma City, 1992—. With USMC, 1975-81. Home: 31882 Camino del Cielo Trabuco Canyon CA 92679 Office: AMS Inc 2601 NW Expressway St Ste 1210W Oklahoma City OK 73112-7208

HUFF, JEROME JOSEPH, JR., newspaper executive; b. Valdosta, Ga., Aug. 31, 1943; s. Jerome Joseph and Martha Gem (McElroy) H.; m. Linda Diane Smith, June 4, 1967; children: Brian, Jonathan, Michael. BA in Journalism, U. Ga., 1967. Sportswriter Athens (Ga.) Banner-Herald, 1965, sportswriter, reporter, copy editor, 1967-68, city editor, news editor, 1970-74; news editor Bulloch Herald and Times, Statesboro, Ga., 1966; publicity dir. Jackson Electric Membership Corp., Jefferson, Ga., 1968-70; exec. editor Amarillo (Tex.) Globe-News, 1974-82, asst. gen. mgr., 1983-86, gen. mgr., 1986-87; v.p., gen. mgr. Marietta (Ga.) Daily Jour. and Neighbor Newspapers, 1988-94; mng. editor Southwest Times Record, Fort Smith, Ark., 1995—. Chmn. adv. bd. Salvation Army, Amarillo, 1982, Marietta, 1993-94; pres. bd. Goodwill Industries, Amarillo, 1976-78. Mem. Am. Soc. Newspaper Editors, Soc. Profl. Journalists (pres. N.E. Ga. chpt. 1973), Rotary (pres. Amarillo club 1987, bd. dirs. Marietta club 1991-92). Home: 9800 Kingsley Pl Fort Smith AR 72908 Office: Southwest Times Record 920 Rogers Ave Fort Smith AR 72901

HUFF, JIMMY LAURENCE, nurse; b. La Junta, Colo., Feb. 16, 1950; s. Russell Loyal Huff and Pauline Ellen (Porter) Kibler; m. Julia Ann Belden, Jan. 20, 1973 (div. Aug. 1982); 1 child, Anessa. AA, North Platte Coll., 1970; student, Nebr. Western Coll., 1970-71; diploma, West Nebr. Gen. Hosp. Sch. Nursing, 1973; AAS, ITT Tech., Nashville, 1989; B in Applied Sci. Electronics Engring., ITT Tech., Indpls., 1990. Charge nurse, surgical/orthopedic unit West Nebr. Gen. Hosp., Scottsbluff, 1973-74, assoc. dir. nursing, 1974-76; assoc. charge nurse med. ward USAF Med. Ctr., Wright-Patterson AFB, Ohio, 1976-78; OIC spl. med. equipment, flight nurse 9th Aeromedical Evacuation Sqdn., Clark AB, Philippines, 1978-80, flight clin. coord., 1980-81; asst. charge nurse-multisvc. ward USAF Hosp., Blytheville AFB, Ark., 1981-82, charge nurse, outpatient svcs., 1982-84, OIC emergency svcs., 1984-86; night charge nurse orthopedic unit HCA Donelson Hosp., Inc., Nashville, 1986-89; staff nurse orthopedics St. Vincent Hosp., Indpls., 1989-90, staff devel. cons. orthopedics, 1990-91; clin. analyst Mgmt. Info. Systems Bapt. Hosp., Nashville, 1991—; clin. advisor sch. nursing, West Nebr. Gen. Hosp., 1973-76; cons. Lifeflight, Memphis, 1984-86. Maj. USAFR, mobilized Desert Shield/Storm, 1991. Mem. IEEE, Nat. Assn. Orthopedic Nurses, Air Force Assn., Am. Legion. Lutheran. Home: 120 Tomarand Rd Antioch TN 37013

HUFF, LULA ELEANOR LUNSFORD, controller, accounting educator; b. Columbus, Ga., July 5, 1949; d. Walter Theophilus and Sally Marie (Bryant) Lunsford; m. Charles Efferidge Huff Jr., June 11, 1972; 1 child, Tamara Nicole. BA, Howard U., 1971; MBA, Atlanta U., 1973. CPA, Ga. Acct. Ernst and Young, Columbus, 1973-76; internal auditor First Consol. Gov., Columbus, 1976-84; instr., chair dept. acctg., dir. pers. mgmt. Troy State U., Phenix City, Ala., 1979-89; sr. fin./cost analyst Pratt and Whitney, Columbus, 1984-89; controller Pratt and Whitney, Southington, Conn., 1989-92, Columbus, 1992-95; contr. for precision components internat. Pratt and Whitney Joint Venture, Columbus, 1995-96; tchr. Troy State U., Phenix City. Mem. fin. bd. Diocese of Savannah; mem. Liberty Theater Hist. Preservation Bd., Columbus Housing Authority Bd., Columbus Hist. Found. Bd., Columbus Literate Comty. Program Inc. Bd., Columbus Beyond 2000, 1989-90; active Concharty coun. Girl Scouts, Inc., Women of Achievement, 1995. Recipient Disting. Black Citizen award Sta. WOKS, 1978, Black Excellence award Nat. Assn. Negro Bus. and Profl. Women's Clubs, Inc., 1977, Outstanding Svc. award St. Benedict Cath. Ch., 1971-76, cert. of merit Congressman Jack Brinkley, 1976, Achievement award Links Inc., 1976, Outstanding Achievement and Svcs. award 1st African Bapt. Ch., 1975, Ga. Jaycees Outstanding Young Woman award, 1989, Leadership Columbus award C. of C., 1983-84, Women on the Move award Spencer Owlettes, 1992; named Outstanding Woman of Yr., Ledger Enquirer Newspaper, 1976, Profl. Woman of Yr., Iota Phi Lambda, 1977, Bus. Woman of Yr., 1979, Columbus Ga. Outstanding Young Woman, Jaycees, 1980, Columbus Young Woman, 1980. Mem. NAACP, Am. Mgmt. Assn., Ga. Soc. CPAs, Howard U. Alumnae Assn., Urban League, Push, Toastmasters Am., Links, Inc. (Achievement award 1976), Delta Sigma Theta (auditor 1991). Roman Catholic. Home: PO Box 1742 Columbus GA 31902

HUFF, MARGARET JOAN FARRIS, librarian; b. Danville, Ky., Oct. 23, 1925; d. Maurice Joseph and Irene Driscoll (Kennedy) Farris; m. Frank Rouse Huff, Nov. 7, 1948; children—Frank Rouse, Thomas Farris, Mary Anne Weathers. A.B., U. N.C., 1947; B.S. in Library Sci., 1948. Asst. librarian VA Hosp., Columbia, S.C., 1948-49; asst. librarian Calhoun County Pub. Library, St. Matthews, S.C., 1967-68; librarian Orangeburg-Calhoun Tech. Coll., Orangeburg, S.C., 1968-77, dean Learning Resource Ctr., 1977-88; del. S.C. Gov.'s Conf. Library, Info. Service, Columbia, 1979. Mem. ALA, Southeastern Library Assn., S.C. Library Assn. (sec. 1977), S.C. Tech. Edn. Assn. (bd. dirs. 1982-87, Educator of Yr.-Aminstr., Mgr. 1988), So. Assn. Colls. and Schs. (vis. com. mem.), Edisto Med. Auxiliary (pres. 1988). Democrat. Methodist. Home: 111 Dantzler St Saint Matthews SC 29135-1413

HUFF, PATSY STOLTZ, pharmacist, pharmacy educator; b. Asheboro, N.C., Oct. 15, 1950; d. Weldon Robert and Margaret (Betts) S.; m. Barry Dean Huff, June 21, 1970 (div. Sept. 1996); 1 child, Michael Weldon Huff. BS in Pharmacy, UNC, 1973, PharmD, 1994. Lic. pharmacist, N.C., Ga. Pharmacist mgr. Orange-Chatham Comprehensive Health, Carrboro, N.C., 1974-83; clin. instr. UNC, Chapell Hill, 1974-82, clin. asst. prof., 1982-94, ambulatory care pharmacist student health svcs., 1984-86, dir. pharmacy student health svcs., 1986—, clin. assoc. prof. Sch. Pharmacy, 1994—; pharmacist Duke-Watts Family Medicine, Durham, N.C., 1983-84; mem. pharmacy edn. com. Meniscus Ednl. Inst., Bala Cynwyd, Pa., 1994—; mem. purchasing com. N.C. Divsn. Purchase and Contract, Raleigh, 1988—. Contbr. articles to profl. jours., chpts. to books. Mem. Am. Coll. Health Assn. (chair pharmacy sect. 1991-95, Cert. Merit 1993), Am. Soc. Health-Sys. Pharmacists, Am. Pharm. Assn., N.C. Soc. Hosp. Pharmacists (Cont. Excellence award 1994). Methodist. Office: UNC CB # 7470 Chapel Hill NC 27599

HUFF, RUSSELL JOSEPH, public relations and publishing executive; b. Chgo., Feb. 24, 1936; s. Russell Winfield and Virgilist Marie (McMahon) H.; BA in Philosophy cum laude, U. Notre Dame, 1958; BS in Theology, Cath. U. Santiago (Chile), 1960; MA in Communication Arts, U. Notre Dame, 1968; ordained priest Roman Cath. Ch., 1962; m. Beverly Diane Staschke, 1968, 1 child, Michelle Lynn. Exec. editor Cath. Boy, and Miss, Notre Dame, Ind., 1963-68; mng. editor Nation's Schs., McGraw Hill, Chgo., 1968-70; v.p. pub. affairs Homart Devel. Co., Chgo., 1971-76; dir. public relations Sears, Roebuck Co. Internat. Ops., Chgo., 1976-82, dir. public affairs Sears Roebuck Found. Internat. Projects, 1981-82; sr. v.p., sales and mktg. dir. Mineca Internat., Inc., Chgo., 1982-84; v.p. pub. relations Lofino Poppa Devel. Corp., Sarasota, Fla., 1984-85; pres., co-owner R.J. Huff & Assocs., Inc., 1985—; real estate broker, 1985—. Recipient Outstanding Mag. award Cath. Press. Assn., 1965, 67; named for Best Cover, Nation's Schs., 1968; cert. Gemological Inst. Am., cert. jr. coll. tchr., Calif. Mem. Pub. Relations Soc. Am. (accredited 1976—), Chicagoland Mil. Collectors Soc. (dir. quar. expositions 1981-82), Am. Soc. Mil. Insignia Collectors, Orders and Medals Soc. Am., Nat. Fgn. Trade Council, Public Affairs Council, Conf. Bd., Internat. Bus. Council, Internat. Visitors Center Chgo., Partners of the Ams. (cert. for advancement Latin Am. relations 1980), São Paulo Partners (cert. for advancement Brazil-U.S. relations 1979, dir. Ill.), Chgo. Assn. of Commerce and Industry, U.S.-Spanish C. of C. of Middle West (dir.), War Memorabilia Collectors Soc. (exec. dir.). Roman Catholic. Author: Come Build My Church, 1966; On Wings of Adventure, 1967; Wings of WW II, 1985, Companion to Wings of World War II, 1987, Winging It, vols. I & II, 1992; editor, publisher (quarterly jour.) Wings and Things of the World, 1987-93, Wings and Things of the World for Sale, 1993-95; cons., editorial contbr. Aviation Treasures. Office: RJ Huff & Assocs Inc 4062 Kingston Ter Sarasota FL 34238-2632

HUFF, SHERRI LYNN, physical education educator; b. Owensboro, Ky., Sept. 29, 1963; d. John and Darleen Mae (Westphal) H. BS in Recreation, U. Ala., Birmingham, 1985; MA in Athletic Adminstrn., U. Ala., 1988, MA in Phys. Edn., 1990; EdS in Phys. Edn., U. Montevallo, 1994; cert. edn. adminstrn. K-12, Samford U., 1995. Cert. Rank AA tchr. phys. edn. K-12, rank 1 ednl. adminstr. grades K-12, Ala. Pre-sch. tchr. Jewish Comty. Ctr., Birmingham, Ala., 1985-88; phys. edn. tchr.'s aide, coach mid. sch. basketball Hewitt-Trussville Mid. Sch., Trussville, Ala., 1990-91; tchr. elem. phys. edn. K-5 Washington Elem. Sch., Birmingham, 1991-92; basketball coach Washington Mid. Sch., Birmingham, 1991-92; volleyball coach Tarrant (Ala.) H.S., 1993-94; basketball coach Tarrant Mid. Sch., 1992-95; tchr. elem. phys. edn. K-4 Tarrant Elem. Sch., 1992-96; golf coach Tarrant H.S., 1995-96, basketball coach, 1995-96; phys. edn. program specialist Birmingham City Schs., 1996—; summer activities instr. U. Ala., Birmingham, 1988-95; com. mem. bldg. leadership team Tarrant Elem. Sch., 1994-96; com. mem. sch. accreditation Fultondale (Ala.) Elem. Sch.-So. Assn. of Colls. and Schs., 1994. Coord. Jump Rope for Heart program Am. Heart Assn., Birmingham, 1992-96; coord. Jingle Bell Run for Arthritis Found., Birmingham, 1994-96. Named Faculty Mem. of Nat. Blue Ribbon Sch., U.S. Dept. Edn., 1994; inducted into Apollo H.S. Athletic Hall of Fame, 1996; Mervyn Goldstein Meml. scholar U. Ala., 1985-86; Adminstrn. Samford U. scholar, 1995—. Mem. ASCD, NEA, AAHPERD, Nat. Fedn. Interscholastic Coaches Assn., Ala. State Assn. for Health, Phys. Edn., Recreation and Dance (state bd. mem. dist. rep. 1993-95, v.p.-elect 1996—, presenter phys. edn. workshop 1993, coord. fall and spring conf. store), Ala. H.S. Athletic Dirs. and Coaches Assn., Magic City Phys. Educators and Coaches Assn. (pres. 1992-93). Republican. Presbyterian. Home: 153 Ashford Ln Alabaster AL 35007 Office: Rickwood Field Dept Ath Birmingham City Schs 1137 2nd Ave W Birmingham AL 35204-4502

HUFF, WILLIAM JENNINGS, lawyer, educator; b. Summerland, Miss., Mar. 3, 1919; s. William Yancey and Hattie Lenora (Robinson) H.; BS with honors, Miss. State U., 1956; MA (asst. fellow 1956-59), Rice U., 1957, PhD (Tex. Gulf Producing Co. fellow 1960), 1960; LLB, U. Miss., 1947, JD, 1968; m. Frances Ellen Rossman, Feb. 26, 1944; 1 son, John Rossman. Bar: Miss. 1947, Tenn. 1948. Closing atty. Commerce Title Guaranty Co., Memphis, 1947-49; atty., adviser FCC, Washington, 1953-54; asso. prof. geology U. So. Miss., Hattiesburg, 1960-65; asst. prof. natural scis. Mich. State U., East Lansing, 1966-68; assoc. prof. geology U. S. Ala., Mobile, 1968-82; ret., 1982; practice law, Pascagoula, Miss., 1982-90. Served with USAF, 1941-45, judge adv., 1949-52; lt. col. USAF ret. Decorated Air medal with ten oak leaf clusters. Mem. ABA, Miss. Bar, Tenn. Bar, Miss. Trial Lawyers Assn., Am. Trial Lawyers Assn., Am. Assn. Petroleum Geologists, Soc. Econ. Mineralogists and Paleontologists, Paleontol. Research Soc., N.Y. Acad. Sci., Sigma Xi, Phi Delta Phi, Sigma Gamma Epsilon. Lodges: Masons, Shriners. Contbr. articles to various publs. Home: 5917 Montfort Rd S Mobile AL 36608-3555

HUFFMAN, D. C., JR., pharmacy executive, association administrator. BS in Pharmacy, U. Ark., 1966; PhD in Pharmacy Administrn., U. Miss., 1971. Pharmacist Crank Drug Co., Inc., Little Rock, 1966-67; asst. prof., dir. divsn. pharmacy adminstrn. U. Tenn. Coll. Pharmacy, Memphis, 1970-73, assoc. prof., chmn. dept. pharmaceutics, 1973; exec. v.p. Am. Coll. Apothecaries, 1971—, prof., chmn. dept. pharmacy, 1974-89, vice chancellor adminstrn., 1984-89; exec. dir. NARD Mgmt. Inst., Alexandria, Va., 1989—, sr. v.p. practice and mgmt., 1992—; presenter numerous seminars. Contbr. articles to profl. jours. Archer Drug Co. scholar, 1966; recipient Lederle Faculty award, 1971; fellow NDEA, 1967-70, Am. Found. for Pharm. Edn., 1967-70. Fellow Am. Coll Apothecaries (exec. v.p.); mem. AAAS, Am. Assn. Colls. Pharmacy, Am. Pharm. Assn., Tenn. Pharm. Assn., Okla. Pharm. Assn. (hon.), Ark. Pharm. Assn. (hon. life), Am. Soc. Assn. Execs., Nat. Assn. Retail Druggists, Kappa Psi, Rho Chi. Office: American College of Apothecaries 5788 Stage Rd Ste 206 Bartlett TN 38134-4563

HUFFMAN, DALE L., food science educator; b. Churchville, Va., July 23, 1931; s. Elmer L. and Ina M. Huffman; m. Jo-Ann Johnson, Feb. 4, 1956; children—Sharon, Randy, Emily. Student Bridgewater Coll. (Va.), 1950-52; B.S., Cornell U., 1959; M.S., U. Fla., 1960, Ph.D., 1962. Research scientist Swift Research and Devel. Ctr., Chgo., 1962-63; asst. prof., assoc. prof., prof. meat sci. Auburn (Ala.) U., 1963-94, dir. Food Technology Inst., Auburn U., 1994—, prof. and dir. emeritus, 1995—; indsl. fellow Armour and Co., 1970-71. Served with USAF, 1952-56. Recipient award of Merit Ala. Cattleman's Assn.; Harry L. Rudnick educators award Nat. Assn. Meat Purveyors, 1984; sr. research award Ala. Agrl. Expt. Sta., 1984, Special Recognition award Auburn U. Agrl. Alumni Assn., 1991, Contributions to Ala. Agrl. award Ala. Agribusiness Coun., 1991, Svc. to Agrl. award Ala. Farmers Fedn., Agrl. Excellence award Nat. Agrl. Mktg. Assn, 1994; commendation for outstanding contbns. to Ala. agr. Ala. Legislature, 1984; named to Ala. Livestock Hall of Fame by Ala. Cattle and Livestock Industry, 1990, named One of Four Who Make a Difference in Agrl. Top Producer Mag., 1991, named Man of the Year in Svc. Agrl. Progressive Farmer Mag., 1992, named Southerner by Southern Living Mag., 1992. Mem. Meat Sci. Assn. (pres. 1982, Meat Processing award 1983, Signal Svc. award, 1988), Am. Soc. Animal Sci., Sigma Xi (pres.), Gamma Sigma Delta (pres.), Alpha Zeta. Contbr. numerous articles on meat sci. to profl. jours. Home: 219 Deer Run Rd Auburn AL 36830-4103

HUFFMAN, DAVID CURTIS, minister; b. Burlington, N.C., Mar. 28, 1950; s. Donald Tyson and Merle (Walker) H.; m. Elaine Janine Wolf, June 25, 1988; children: Katherine Elizabeth Wolf, Anna Elaine Huffman. BA, U. N.C., 1972; MDiv, Princeton Theol. Sem., 1976. Ordained to ministry Presbyn. Ch. (U.S.A.), 1976. Student asst. min. Franklin Lakes (N.J.) Presbyn. Ch., 1973-76; asst. min. Old South Ch., Boston, 1976-79, assoc. min., 1979-81; pastor Trinity Presbyn. Ch., Raleigh, N.C., 1981—; chmn. profl. devel. com. Orange Presbytery, Durham, N.C., 1982-84, chmn. peacemaking com., 1982-85, mem. com. on ministry, 1983-87; chmn. com. on ministry New Hope Presbytery, Rocky Mount, N.C., 1988-90, 93, examinations com., 1995—; pres. Presbyn. Urban Coun., Raleigh, 1988; commr. to gen. assembly Presbyn. Ch., U.S.A., 1995. Merrill fellow Harvard Div. Sch., 1986. Mem. Raleigh Ministerial Assn., Soc. Bibl. Lit., Phi Beta Kappa, Beta Theta Pi. Democrat. Home: 8705 Mansfield Dr Raleigh NC 27613-1337 Office: Trinity Presbyn Ch 3120 New Hope Rd Raleigh NC 27604-4948

HUFFMAN, GLENN, genealogist; b. Harrisonburg, Va., June 19, 1953; s. Rudolph Bernard and Phyllis (Wimer) H. BA in History, Bridgewater Coll., 1975. Office asst. Nat. Coun. on Crime and Delinquency, Washington, 1975-77; typist Libr. of Congress, Washington, 1978-80, searcher, filer, editor, 1980-88; enumerator U.S. Census Bur., Harrisonburg, 1989; cataloguer Harrisonburg-Rockingham Hist. Soc., Dayton, Va., 1989-90; genealogist Bridgewater, Va., 1990—. Co-author: Three Immigrant Wimer Brothers, 1982; author: Wampler, 1982, Immigrant Henry Wimer, 1995. Mem. Pendleton County (W.Va.) Hist. Soc., Harrisonburg-Rockingham Hist. Soc. Home: 312 N Main Bridgewater VA 22812

HUFFMAN, JOAN BREWER, history educator; b. Springfield, Ohio, Aug. 18, 1937; d. James Clarence and Berniece (Notter) Brewer; m. James Russell Huffman, Aug. 21, 1959; children: Jill Elizabeth, Jean Elaine. AB, Ohio U., 1959; MA, Ga. State U., 1968, PhD, 1980. Adj. prof. Wesleyan Coll., Macon, Ga., 1981-82; instr. history Macon Coll., 1968-72, asst. prof., 1972-81, assoc. prof., 1981-86, prof., 1986—; owner The Printed Page, Macon, Ga., 1993—; chmn. History adv. com. U. System Ga., 1986-87. Contbr. articles to profl. jours. Mem., bd. dirs. Oklahatche Pk., Perry, Ga., 1966-68, Macon Coll. Found., 1985-90, Ga. Endowment for Humanities, Atlanta, 1983-87. Katharine C. Bleckley scholar English-Speaking Union, 1977. Mem. N.Am. Conf. on Brit. Studies, Am. Hist. Assn., Southern Hist. Assn. (membership com. 1988-89), Ga. Assn. Historians (pres. 1982-83), Phi Beta Kappa, Phi Alpha Theta (award 1978). Home: 135 Covington Pl Macon GA 31210-4445

HUFFMAN, PATRICIA ELIZABETH, software engineer; b. San Juan, P.R., Oct. 15, 1948; d. Charles Martin and Ruby L. (Zimmerman) Huffman; m. Larry James Walters, Jan. 26, 1990. BS in Math. with distinction, U. Ariz., 1970. Ptnr., real estate broker Falcon Realty, Inc., Tucson, 1982-85; analyst SCP Constrn., Tucson, 1985-86; sr. med. utilization review analyst Blue Cross/Blue Shield of Ariz., Tucson, 1986-88; sr. program systems analyst PRC Inc., Alexandria, Va., 1984-94; programmer analyst III User Tech. Assocs., Inc., Arlington, Va., 1994—. Leader Girl Scouts Am., Phoenix, 1977-79. Mem. Chi Omega. Home: 6107 Gardenia Ct Alexandria VA 22310-1787 Office: User Tech Assocs Inc 4301 Fairfax Dr Ste 400 Arlington VA 22203-1627

HUFFMAN, ROBERT ALLEN, JR., lawyer; b. Tucson, Dec. 30, 1950; s. Robert Allen and Ruth Jane (Hicks) H.; m. Marjorie Kavanagh Rooney, Dec. 30, 1976; children: Katharine Kavanagh, Elizabeth Rooney, Robert Allen III, Simeon Ross. BBA, U. Okla., 1973, JD, 1976. Bar: Okla. 1977, U.S. Dist. Ct. (no. dist.) Okla. 1977, U.S. Ct. Appeals (10th cir.) 1978, U.S. Supreme Ct. 1982. Assoc. Huffman, Arrington, Kihle, Gaberino & Dunn, Tulsa, 1977-81, ptnr. 1981—. Mem. ABA, Tulsa County Bar Assn., Fed. Energy Bar Assn. Republican. Roman Catholic. Clubs: Southern Hills Country (Tulsa), Summit Club. Home: 4136 S Wheeling Ave Tulsa OK 74105-4232 Office: Huffman Arrington Kihle Gaberino & Dunn 1000 Oneok Plz Tulsa OK 74103

HUFFSTETLER, PALMER EUGENE, transportation executive, retired lawyer; b. Shelby, N.C., Dec. 21, 1937; s. Daniel S. and Ethel (Turner) H.; m. Mary Ann Beam, Aug. 9, 1958; children: Palmer Eugene, Ben Beam, Brian Tad. BA, Wake Forest U., 1959, JD, 1961. Bar: N.C. 1961. Practiced in Kings Mountain, N.C., 1961-62, Raleigh, N.C., 1962-64; with State Farm Ins. Co., Orlando, Fla., 1962; gen. legal counsel Carolina Freight Corp., Cherryville, N.C., 1964-93, sec., 1969-90, sr. v.p., 1969-89, also dir., 1971-94, exec. v.p., 1985-93, pres., 1993-95. Author, composer: Senior Man on Carolina Line, Fifty Years Ago. Chmn. Cherryville Zoning Bd. Adjustment, 1967-70; mem. N.C. Gasoline and Oil Insp. Bd., 1974-76; class chmn. Wake Forest Coll. Fund, 1971-79, decade chmn., 1981-82; mem. governing body, chmn. adminstrv. com. So. Piedmont Health Systems Agy., 1975-77; mem. Cherryville Econ. Devel. Commn., 1982-87, Cherryville Econ. Devel. Com., 1995—; pres. Cherryville Devel. Corp., 1986—; bd. dirs. C. Grier Beam Truck Mus., 1982—, pres. 1982-96; bd. dirs. Schiele Mus., Gastonia, N.C., 1985-88, Gaston Meml. Hosp., 1990-93, vice-chmn. bd.; mem. N.C. Gov.'s Hwy. Safety Commn., 1985-88; mem. v.p. Ctrl. and So. Rate Bur., 1984-89; trustee Brevard Coll., 1987-93. Mem. ABA, N.C. State Bar, N.C. Bar Assn., S.C. Motor Truck Assn. (dir. 1982-95), N.C. Trucking Assn. (dir. 1982-95), Am. Trucking Assn. (exec. com. 1993-95), N.C. Com. Bus. and Devel. Methodist (mem. adminstrv. bd. 1965-69, 71-72, chmn. adminstrv. bd. 1969-70, 79, trustee 1970-73). Home: 2141 Fairways Dr Cherryville NC 28021-2115

HUGE, DONALD SEHRT, physician; b. New Orleans, Sept. 18, 1930; s. August F. and Mae (Sehrt) H.; m. Martha Anderson, Dec. 21, 1956; children: Vaughan Clark, Charner Bolin. BA, So. Meth. U., 1953; MD, Baylor U., 1957. Diplomate Am. Bd. Quality Asuurance. Residency Hermann Hosp., Houston, 1960-63; internship M.D. Anderson Hosp., Houston, 1963-64; pvt. practice Houston, 1965-87; med. dir. Am. Med. Intern, Houston, 1987-89, Affiliated Healthcare, Houston, 1989-90; med. dir. Metlife, Houston, 1990-91, network dir., 1991-93; med. dir. New York Life/Sanus, Houston, 1993—; medical dir. HMO Tex., 1994—. Bd. dirs. Vis. Nurses Assn., Houston, 1990, Am. Bd. Quality Assurance, Fla., 1990. Lt. USN, 1958-60, PTO. Fellow Am. Coll. Med. Quality (pres. 1993-95, editorial com.), Nat. Assn. Managed Care Physicians Bd. Episcopalian. Home: 3216 W Alabama Ct Houston TX 77027-5915 Office: HMO Texas 11011 Richmond Rd # 900 Houston TX 77042

HUGE, HARRY, lawyer; b. Deshler, Nebr., Sept. 16, 1937; s. Arthur and Dorothy (Vor de Strasse) H.; m. Reba Kinne, July 2, 1960; 1 child, Theodore. AB, Nebr. Wesleyan U., 1959; JD, Georgetown U., 1963. Bar: Ill. 1963, D.C. 1965, S.C. 1985. Assoc. Chapman & Cutler, Chgo., 1963-65; assoc. Arnold & Porter, Washington, 1965-71, ptnr., 1971-76; sr. ptnr. Donovan, Leisure, Rogovin, Huge & Schiller, Washington, 1976-92, Shea and Gould Internat., Washington, 1992-94; ptnr. Powell Goldstein Frazer & Murphy, Washington, 1995—; bd. dirs. Huge Sales, Inc., Gatlinburg, Tenn., Hyatt Legal Plans Inc., Cleve., Mikell House Devel. Corp., Chaleston, S.C.; pres. Am. European Fund, Washington, 1989—; chmn., trustee United Mine Workers Health and Retirement Funds, 1973-78; chmn. bd. dirs. Hollings Cancer Ctr., Charleston, S.C. Contbr. articles to legal jours. Pres. Voter Edn. Project, Atlanta, 1974-78; mem. Pres.'s Gen. Adv. Com. Arms Control, 1977-81; trustee Nebr. Wesleyan U., 1978—; mem. task force local govt. Greater Washington Rsch. Ctr., 1981-82; spl. master Friends for All Children, Inc., U.S. Dist. Ct. D.C. With U.S. Army, 1960; officer USNG, 1960-65. Mem. ABA (co-chmn. legis. com. litigation sect. 1981), D.C. Bar Assn. (bd. profl. responsibility 1976-81). Home: 94 Rutledge Ave Charleston SC 29401 also: 1230 24th St NW Washington DC 20037 Office: Powell Goldstein Frazer & Murphy 1001 Pennsylvania Ave NW Washington DC 20004

HUGGARD, JOHN PARKER, lawyer; b. Midland, Tex., Dec. 7, 1945; s. Peter John and Dorothy (Sampson) H. BA, U. N.C., 1971, JD, 1975; MA, Duke U., 1989. Bar: N.C. 1975, U.S. Dist. Ct. (ea. dist.) N.C. 1975, U.S. Ct. Appeals (4th cir.) 1975, U.S. Tax Ct. 1976, U.S. Ct. Claims 1976, U.S. Ct. Customs 1977, U.S. Ct. Mil. Appeals 1977, U.S. Dist. Ct. D.C. 1979, U.S. Supreme Ct. 1979, U.S. Ct. Internat. Trade 1981, U.S. Ct. Customs and Patent Appeals 1982; cert. fin. planner. Sr. ptnr. Hensley & Overby, Raleigh, N.C., 1975-88, Hensley, Huggard, Obiol & Bousman, Raleigh, 1988—; alumni disting. prof. Law and Econs. N.C. State U., Raleigh, 1975—. Author: The Adminstration of Decedents' Estates in North Carolina, 1985, North Carolina Estate Settlement Guidebook, 1995; contbr. articles to profl. publs. With USMC, 1964-68, capt. USNR. Mem. ABA, Am. Bus. Law Assn., Assn. Trial Lawyers Am., N.C. Bar Assn., N.C. Acad. Trial Lawyers, N.C. Coll. Advocacy, Acad. Outstanding Tchrs., Wake County Bar Assn., Phi Beta Kappa. Democrat. Roman Catholic. Home: 8621 Kings Arms Way Raleigh NC 27615-2029 Office: Hensley Huggard Obiol & Bousman 124 St Marys St Raleigh NC 27605-1809

HUGGINS, CANNIE MAE COX HUNTER, retired elementary school educator; b. Belton, Tex., July 16, 1916; d. Jesse Daniel and Mary Alice (Hamilton) Cox; B.S., Mary Hardin Baylor Coll., 1940; M.S., San Marcos Tchrs. Coll., 1942; postgrad. U. Tex., 1946-47, Tex. Tech U., 1956-70, U. San Diego, 1975, St. Mary's U., 1976; m. William Dudley Hunter, June 5, 1938 (div. 1967); children—Darline, Bob Roy; m. 2d, Bertrand Huggins, Aug. 4, 1979 (dec. July 19, 1980). Tchr. pub. schs., Belton, 1935-38, Galveston, Tex., 1938-42; mem. staff testing dept. U. Ariz., 1942-43; reading cons. Phoenix Pub. Schs., 1943-45; tchr.-counselor pub. schs., Killeen, Tex., 1946-54; classroom tchr., Lubbock, Tex., 1954-74; tchr. first grade bilingual lang. devel. Posey Elementary Sch., Lubbock, Tex., 1974-96; pres. CM Corp. First aid chmn. ARC, Lubbock County, 1960-63, first aid instr., 1956—; area dir. March of Dimes, 1958-63; tchr. high sch. dept. First Bapt. Ch., Lubbock, 1960—; state advisor U.S. Congl. Adv. Bd., 1985—; mem. Lubbock Hospice Vol. Program. Recipient Outstanding Service award ARC, 1966; Bronze award CONTACT Lubbock. Cert. educator, Tex. Mem. Assn. Childhood Edn. Internat., NEA, Tex. Tchrs. Assn., Tex. Classroom Tchrs. Assn., Nat. PTA, Tex. Edn. Assn., Lubbock Educators Assn., Lubbock Classroom Tchrs. Assn., AAUW, Am. Bus. Women's Assn., S. Plains Writers Guild, YWCA, Lubbock, Killeen chambers commerce. Baptist. Club: University City (Lubbock). Home: 4626 30th St Lubbock TX 79410-2423

HUGGINS, RICHARD LEONARD, development director; b. Wheeling, W.Va.; s. Gerald and Josephine Huggins. BA, Davis and Elkins Coll., Elkins, W.Va., 1960; MDiv, Union Theol. Sem., Richmond, Va., 1963; postgrad., Princeton Sem., Pitts. Sem. Ordained to ministry Presbyn. Ch. Sr. pastor Presbyn. chs., Pa., N.J., 1963-76, Internat. Ch., Aruba, 1976; pastor First Presbyn. Ch., New Cumberland, W.Va., 1976-86; regional rep. for Fla. Presbyn. Ch. Found., Inc., 1986-89, regional mgr. for 13 states and P.R., 1989-91; pres., CEO HRT Assocs., 1991-92; cons. for funds devel., mktg.

and strategic planning Altamonte Springs, Fla., 1992-94; dir. Fla. Presbyn. Homes, Lakeland, 1994—; bd. chmn. Multicultural Ctr., Inc. Charter mem. Ctrl. Fla. Planned Giving Coun.; past pres. Duvall Home Found.; del. Pa. Constl. Conv., 1967-67; chmn. City Planning Commn. Named Disting. West Virginian, State of W.Va., 1980, God and Svc. medal Boy Scouts Am., 1984; named to Outstanding Young Men of Am., 1969. Mem. Am. Mgmt. Assn., Am. Planning Assn., Nat. Soc. Fund Raising Execs., Nat. Coun. for Non-Profit Bds., Health, Human Svcs. Bd. (exec. bd.), Alcohol, Drug and Mental Health (chmn. cmty. rels.), Rotary. Home: 1601 Archers Path Lakeland FL 33809-5063

HUGHES, ALFRED CLIFTON, bishop; b. Boston, Dec. 2, 1932; s. Alfred Clifton and Ellen Cecelia (Hennessey) H. A.B., St. John's Sem. Coll., 1954; S.T.L., Gregorian U., Rome, 1958, S.T.D., 1961. Ordained priest Roman Cath. Ch., 1957, ordained bishop, 1981. Asst. pastor St. Stephen's Parish, Framingham, Mass., 1958-59, Our Lady Help of Christians, Newton, Mass., 1961-62; lectr. St. John's Sem., Brighton, 1962-65, spiritual dir., 1965-81, rector, 1981-86; aux. bishop Archdiocese of Boston, 1981-93; regional bishop of Merrimack Region, 1986-90; vicar for adminstrn. Archdiocese of Boston, 1990-93; bishop of Baton Rouge, 1993—; chmn. NCCB Com. on Doctrine, 1991-94. Author: Preparing for Church Ministry, 1979; contbr. articles to profl. jours. Mellon and Davis Founds. grantee, 1976. Mem. Catholic Theol. Soc. Am. Office: Cath Life Ctr PO Box 2028 1800 S Acadian Thruway Baton Rouge LA 70821-2028

HUGHES, ANN NOLEN, psychotherapist; b. Ft. Meade, Md.; d. George M. and Georgie T. Nolen; m. Edwin L. Hughes, Oct. 21, 1961; 1 child, Andrew G. BS in Psychology, Rollins Coll., 1985, MA in Counseling, 1986; student in pub. speaking and human rels., Dale Carnegie Inst., 1981; student, Duke U., 1950-52. Lic. mental health counselor; nat. cert. counselor; nat. cert. gerontol. counselor. Supr. top secret control, audio/visual small parts supply U.S. Army, Continental U.S. and Tokyo; adminstrv. sec. Sys. Devel. Corp., Rand Corp., Santa Monica, Calif.; adminstrv. asst., editor, exec. sec., adminstrv. sec. Aerospace Corp., El Segundo, Calif.; staff therapist Circles of Care, Melbourne, Fla.; developer program for leading divorce support groups for Brevard Women's Ctr. Various leadership positions PTA, Pittsford, N.Y., Brookfield, Wis., 1968-81; mem. Brevard Cmty. Chorus; docent Space Coast Sci. Ctr., 1991-92. Mem. ACA, Assn. for Adult Devel. and Aging, Space Coast PC User's Group, Nat. Geneal. Soc., Geneal. Soc. South Brevard, Suntree Country Club, Brevard County Alumnae Assn. of Kappa Kappa Gamma, Kappa Kappa Gamma. Presbyterian. Office: PO Box 410162 Melbourne FL 32941-0162

HUGHES, ARTHUR HYDE, accountant; b. Lansing, Mich., May 15, 1952; s. Francis Aloysius and Alice Catherine (Hyde) H.; m. Ellen Marie Krempa, Feb. 13, 1982; children: Bradley Allan, Allison Marie. BS magna cum laude, Fla. State U., 1974; postgrad., U. Tex., Dallas, 1978. CPA, Tex. Treas. Excella Trading Corp., Ft. Worth, 1977-79; with ARCO, Dallas, 1975—; revenue analyst Gas Revenue Acctg., Dallas, 1975-82; sr. acct. Oil Revenue Acctg., Dallas, 1982-85; client rep. Revenue Projects Group, Dallas, 1985-87; supr. Gas Data Services, Dallas, 1987-88, Gas Systems Redevel., Dallas, 1988-89; production acctg. cons. ARCO, Dallas, 1989-90, sr. revenue compliance auditor, 1990-96; internat. acct. ARCO Algeria, 1996—; pvt. practice oil and gas acctg. Garland, 1996—; petroleum auditing and cons., 1996—; mem. Petroleum Data Exch. Steering Com., Denver, 1985-87, chmn. Gas Revenue Acctg., Data Exch. Com. (subs Petroleum Data Exch.) Dallas, 1986-87, spl. com. electronic data exch. of Coun. of Petroleum Acctg. Socs., Dallas, 1986—. Contbr. articles to profl. jours.; developer petroleum industry Gas Revenue Acctg. Data Exchange system with Gen. Elec., 1985. Alternate del. Tex. Rep. Conv., 1982; active Nat. Right to Life, Washington. Mem. AICPA, Tex. Soc. CPAs, Petroleum Acctg. Soc., NRA (life), Tex. Rifle Assn., Ducks Unltd., Toastmasters, Gun Owner, Am., Mensa, Intertel, Phi Eta Sigma, Phi Kappa Phi, Beta Gamma Sigma. Roman Catholic. Home and Office: 6405 Limerick Ln Garland TX 75044-3435

HUGHES, BARBARA ANN, dietitian, public health administrator, nutritionist; b. McMinn County, Tenn., July 22, 1938; d. Cecil Earl and Hannah Ruth (Moss) Farmer; BS cum laude in Home Econs. Carson Newman Coll., Jefferson City, Tenn., 1960; MS in Instl. Mgmt., Ohio State U., Columbus, 1963; MA (Adonarium Judson scholar), So. Bapt. Theol. Sem., 1968; MPH, U. N.C., Chapel Hill, 1972; postgrad. in nutrition U. Iowa, 1974, U. N.C., 1975-85, Case Western Res. U., 1979, Walden U.; PhD 1988; m. Carl Clifford Hughes, Oct. 13, 1962. Registered, lic. nutritionist, dietitian. Instr., clin. dietitian Riverside Meth. Hosp., Riverside Whitecross Sch. Nursing, Columbus, 1963-66; consulting dietitian Mount Holly Nursing Home, Ky. Dept. Mental Health, 1966-68, eastern region N.C. Bd. Health, Raleigh, 1968-73; dir. Nutrition and Dietary Services br., Div. Health Services, N.C. Dept. Human Resources, Raleigh, 1973-89, also dir. Women-Infants-Children Program; pres. B.A. Hughes and Assocs., 1990—; asst. to Rep. Karen Gottovi 14th Dist. N.C. Ho. of Reps., Gen. Assembly N.C., 1994; adj. instr. Case Western Res. U., Cleve., 1988-89; adj. asst. prof. dept. nutrition Sch. Public Health, U. N.C., Chapel Hill, 1975-89; mem. adv. bd. Hospitality Edn. program N.C. Dept. Community Colls., 1974-80, adv. com. Ret. Senior Vol. Program, Raleigh and Wake County, N.C., 1975-79, N.C. Network Coordinating Council for End-Stage Renal Disease, 1975, Nat. Adv. Council on Maternal, Infant, and Fetal Nutrition, Spl. Supplemental Food Program for Women, Infants, and Children, Dept. Agr., 1976-79, adv. com. Nutrition Edn. and Tng. program N.C. Dept. Pub. Instrn., 1978-80; mem.-at-large adv. leadership coun. N.C. Cooperative Ext. Svc., 1994—; advisor com. to Wake County N.C. Cooperative Ext. Svc., 1992—, chair. adv. coun., 1994-96; coord. undergrad. program in gen dietetics East Carolina U.; apptd. rep. Coll of Agrl. and Life Scis. N.C. State U. to Nat. Coun. for Agrl. Rsch. Extension and Tchg., 1996—; apptd. mem. Wake County Bd. Commrs. to New Wake County Human Svcs. Bd., 1996—; apptd. to adv. bd. Agromedicine Program East Carolina and N.C. State Univs., 1996—; adv. council N.C. Gov.'s Office Citizen Affairs; cons. dietitian Augusta Victoria Hosp. and Jerusalem (Israel) Crippled Childrens Center, 1968; witness U.S. congressional and Senate hearings in field. Active edn. programs Pullen Memorial Bapt. Church, Raleigh, deacon, 1976-80, 94—, area ministry capt., 1977-78, personnel com., 1978-80; bd. dirs. Community Outreach, 1989-92, futuring com., 1995—, coordinating coun. vice-chair, 1996—; dietitian/dir. food service archeol. expedition to Israel, 1968; bd. dirs. N.C. Literacy Assn. 1978-83, 93—, pres., 1981-83; v.p. Wake County Literacy Council, 1986-87; trustee Gardner-Webb Coll., Boiling Springs, N.C., 1979-82, chmn. curriculum com., 1981-82; chmn. Coalition Pub. Health Nutrition, 1983-85; del. various Democratic Convs., 1981-84, precinct sec.-treas., 1981-83, 1st vice chmn., 1983-85, 2nd vice chmn., 1993—, chair, 1985-87; chmn. adv. bd. dept. home econs. Carson-Newman Coll.; area coord. (N.C.) Pacific Intercultural Exch., 1990—; chair Wake County Affiliate food festival com., 1991-92, chair edn. and community program com., 1992—, Am. Heart Assn., bd. dirs., 1992-94; precinct coord. Ruth Cook for N.C. Senate, Dist. 14, 1994; chair chronic disease com. Wake County Bd. Health, 1995-96, chair nominating com., 1996; apptd. mem. First Wake County Human Svcs. Bd., 1996—; pres. State N.C. Coun. Social Legislation, 1993—; dir. N.C. Bds. of Health, 1994—; del. Altrusa Internat., Inc. to 4th World Conf. on Women, Beijing, China, 1995; nutrition staff writer Sr. Source, Raleigh Extra, Durham Morning Herald. Named Woman of Yr., Wake County, 1975, N.C. Outstanding Dietitian of Yr., 1976, N.C. Outstanding Dietitian, Southeastern Hosp. Conf. for Dietitians, 1978; recipient Disting. Alumna award Carson-Newman Coll., 1983, Eleanor Roosevelt Humanitarian award Altrusa Internat., 1995. Fellow N.C. Inst. Polit. Leadership; mem. AAUW (life, pres. Raleigh br. 1971-75, 91-93, pres. N.C. div. 1978-80, coordinator Wake Women Celebrate, 1995, coord. partners for heart disease and stroke prevention 1995, nat. bd. dirs. 1980-82, area rep. 1980-82, nat. edn. found. bd. dirs. 1987-91, ednl. equity roundtable 1992), Am. Dietetic Assn. (del. 1971-74, 87-89, pres. N.C. state assn. 1976-77, N.C. network legis. coordinator 1978-81, 92—, nat. nominating com. 1979-80, nat. chmn. council on practice 1982-83, nat. chair legislation and pub. policy com. 1985-87, nat. area coord. Ho. of Dels. 1989-92, Commn. Dietetic Registration assessment devel. com. for credential of FELLOW program 1994, 95, nat. mem. bylaws com. 1989-90, 91-92, chair resolutions com. 1990-91), APHA (exec. com. So. br. 1977-87, sec.-treas. 1979-80, 1st v.p. 1980-81, Catherine Cowell award 1994, chair award com. food and nutrition sect. 1995-96), So. Health Assn. (pres. 1982-83, chair nominating com. 1985-86, 91-92, awards com. 1992-93, Spl. Meritorious award 1989), Assn. State and Territorial Pub. Health Nutrition Dirs. (pres. 1977-79, dir. 1981-89, liaison to Assn. Faculties Grad. Program in Pub. Health Nutrition, chair legis. and pub. policy com. 1984-89, Commendation award 1989), N.C. Assn. Bds. of Health, N.C. Council Foods and Nutrition (dir. 1976-78, chmn. membership 1975, nominating com. 1979). N.C. Council Women's Orgns. (mem. at large, bd. dirs. 1989-92, leadership com. 1991—, chair nutrition subcom., Wellness in State Employees adv. bd. 1989-91), Am. Acad. Health Adminstrn., Soc. Nutrition Edn., Nutrition Today Soc., N.C. Acad. Public Health, Ohio State U. Alumni Assn. (life), U. N.C. Gen. Alumni Assn. (life), U. N.C. Public Health Alumni Assn. (life), Altrusa Internat. (pres. Raleigh club 1973-74, 93-96, dir. 1976-78, 90—, 1st vice gov. 1978-79, chmn. nomination com. 1980-82, gov. dist. Three, 1979-80, internat. vocat. services chmn. 1977-79, 1st v.p. 1985-87, pres.-elect 1987-89, pres. 1989-91), Altrusa Internat. Found. (1st v.p. 1985-87, chmn.-elect 1990-92, chmn. 1992—, bd. dirs. 1993—), Greater Raleigh C. of C. (mem. west area bus. coun., chair legis. com., rep. leadership Raleigh 10 1994—, bd. dirs. leadership Raleigh Alumni Assn.), Women's Forum N.C. (young leadership award com. 1989-90, 92—, newsletter editor bd. dirs. 1992—, adminstr. 1995—), Kappa Omicron Nu. Achievements include olympic torchbearer. Co-author: Diet and Kidney Disease, Assn. for N.C. Regional Med. Program, 1969; contbr. numerous papers, articles to symposia, periodicals in field, vol. areas. Home: 4208 Galax Dr Raleigh NC 27612-3714

HUGHES, BYRON WILLIAM, lawyer, oil exploration company executive; b. Clarksdale, Miss., Nov. 8, 1945; s. Byron B. and Francis C. (Turner) H.; m. Sarah Eileen Goodwin, June 23, 1973 (div.); children: Jennifer Eileen, Stephanie Ann. BA, U. Miss., 1968; JD, Jackson Sch. Law (now Miss. Coll. Law), 1971. Bar: Miss. 1971, U.S. Supreme Ct. 1975; cert. real estate appraiser. Atty., abstractor Miss. Hwy. Dept., 1971-76; atty., ind. landman Byron Hughes Oil Exploration Co., Jackson, Miss., 1976-92; prosecutor, child support enforcement atty., Miss. Dept. Human Svcs., 1992—; tchr. high sch.; real estate broker. Mem. ABA, Miss. Bar Assn., Hinds County Bar Assn., Bolivar County Bar Assn., Am. Judicature Soc., Am. Landmen Assn., Nat. Assn. Real Estate Appraisers, Miss. Child Support Assn., Miss. Landmen Assn., Ala. Landmen Assn., Black Warrior Basin Petroleum Landmen Assn., Am. Assn. Petroleum Landmen (cert. profl. landman 1991), Ole Miss. Alumni Assn., Miss. Coll. Alumni Assn., Miss. Art Assn., Miss. Child Support Assn., Sigma Delta Kappa. Methodist. Home: PO Box 1485 Jackson MS 39215-1485 Office: PO Box 1485 Jackson MS 39215-1485

HUGHES, DAVID HENRY, manufacturing company executive; b. Orlando, Fla., Dec. 20, 1942; s. Harry C. and Pauline B. Hughes; m. Rebecca Wilkins; 1 child, Kristin E.; m. Linda Cooper, Apr. 26, 1986; children: Patrick, Shelby. BS, U. Fla., 1965, JD, 1967. Mgmt. trainee Hughes Supply Inc., Orlando, 1968-72, pres., chief operating officer, 1972-74, pres., chief exec. officer, 1974-86, chmn., former pres., chief exec. officer, 1986—, also dir.; bd. dirs. Sun Banks Inc., Orlando, SunTrust Banks Inc., Atlanta. Bd. dirs. U. Cen. Fla. Rsch. Pk., Orlando, Orlando Regional Med. Ctr.; trustee U. Cen. Fla.; mem. bd. overseers Rollins Coll., Winter Park, Fla., Young Pres.'s Orgn. Mem. Fla. Bar Assn., Fla. Coun. of 100. Republican. Office: Hughes Supply Inc PO Box 2273 200 N Orange Ave Ste 200 Orlando FL 32801

HUGHES, DONNA JEAN, librarian; b. Alexandria, Va., Mar. 24, 1959; d. John William and Wilma Connie (Beavers) H. BS cum laude, Longwood Coll., Farmville, Va., 1981; MS in Libr. Sci., U. N.C., Chapel Hill, 1985. Lic. tchr., Va. Children's libr. Thomas Hackney Braswell Meml. Libr., Rocky Mount, N.C., 1983-88, Wake County Pub. Librs., Raleigh, N.C., 1988-90; children's svcs. and outreach svcs. libr. Handley Regional Libr., Winchester, Va., 1990—; storyteller Nat. Storytelling Assn., 1983—. Mem. youth svcs. adv. com. Libr. of Va., Richmond, 1991-96; music dir. Broadway (Va.) Bapt. Ch., 1990—, Sunday sch. dir., 1991—; co-founder singles ministry Sunset Ave. Bapt. Ch., Rocky Mount, 1984-90; singer Shenandoah Valley Chorus, 1990-95. Named Employee of the Yr., City of Winchester, 1992. Mem. ALA, Va. Libr. Assn. (Jefferson Cup award com. 1995-96), Children and Young Adult Roundtable (chair, mem. Jefferson Cup award com. 1995-96), Lord Fairfax Assn. of Educations of Young Children, Quota Internat. (com. chair, bd. dirs. 1994-96), New Mkt. Garden Club (com. chair 1992—), Phi Kappa Phi. Baptist. Office: Handley Regional Library 100 W Piccadilly St Winchester VA 22601

HUGHES, EDWIN LAWSON, retired management consultant; b. Pittsburg, Kans., Aug. 11, 1924; s. Edwin Byron and Vera (Lawson) H.; m. Ann Turner Nolen, Oct. 21, 1961; 1 child, Andrew George; children from previous marriage: John Lawson, James Prescott. BSEE, Mo. Sch. Mines, 1949; MSEE, U. Ill., 1950. Registered profl. engr. Fla. Group leader Systems Devel. Corp., Santa Monica, Calif., 1957-60; tech. dir. Gen. Motors, Oak Creek, Wis., 1960-71; v.p. engring. Xerox Corp., Webster, N.Y., 1971-81, Santec Corp., Amherst, N.H., 1981-82; chmn., pres., chief exec. officer Fla. Data Corp., Melbourne, 1982-83; pvt. practice cons. Melbourne, 1984-88; ret. Contbr. articles and papers to profl jours.; inventor computers, copiers; patentee in field. Com. mem. Boy Scouts Am., Pittsford, N.Y., 1974-76; mem. Brevard Cmty. Chorus. With U.S. Army, 1943-46, ETO. Mem. IEEE (sr.), NSPE, Fla. Engring. Soc., Space Coast PC User's Group (pres. 1991-95, sec. 1988-91, treas. 1995—), Suntree Country Club. Republican. Home and Office: 447 Pauma Valley Way Melbourne FL 32940-1918

HUGHES, ELAINE WOOD, literature educator; b. Graysville, Ala., Apr. 3, 1941; d. Floyd Romaine and Audrey Mildred (Gossett) Wood; m. Robert Basol Hughes, Jr., Sept. 12, 1959; children: Kevin Murff, Beth Elaine, Robert Basol III. BA with highest honors, U. Montevallo, Ala., 1969; PhD, U. Ala., 1979. Legal sec. Louis Fleisher & Marvin Cherner Attys., Birmingham, Ala., 1958-59, to atty., Opelika, Ala., 1959-60; sec. Auburn (Ala.) U., 1960-61; billing clk. Ampex Corp., Opelika, 1961-62; instr. English U. Montevallo, 1974-77, asst. prof., 1977-81, assoc. prof., 1981-89, prof., 1989—; lectr. Read Ala.!, 1989-90. Mem. Shelby County Bd. Edn., Columbiana, Ala., 1974-80, chair, 1977-80; bd. dirs. Tannehill State Park Commn., McCalla, Ala., 1990—, Brierfield (Ala.) Ironworks Park, 1980-90; active PTA, Athletic Boosters, Litter Task Force; campaign chair for Dem. Party candidates. NDEA fellow, 1971-74. Mem. South Atlantic MLA, Ala. Coll. English Tchrs. Assn., Ala. Coun. Tchrs. of English, Nat. Coun. Tchrs. of English, Ala. Assn. for Women Deans, Adminstrs. and Counselors (v.p. mem.), AAUW (br. pres. 1986-90, legis. liaison 1990), Omicron Delta Kappa, Delta Kappa Gamma, Sigma Tau Delta (internat. pres. 1994—, bd. dirs. 1984—). Methodist. Home: PO Box 300 Montevallo AL 35115-0300 Office: U Montevallo Sta # 6501 Montevallo AL 35115

HUGHES, GAYLE WOMACK, civil engineer, educator; b. Nashville, Apr. 18, 1944; d. Roy Hampton and Allyne (Jacobs) Womack; m. Jerry D. Hughes, Sept. 5, 1966; children: Lisa, Kathy, Emily. BCE, Vanderbilt U., 1966, MSCE, 1993. Registered profl. engr., Tenn. Road design engr. Tenn. Dept. Transp., Nashville, 1966-70; cons. civil engring. Nashville, 1970-77; prof. civil engring. tech. Nashville State Tech. Inst., 1977—. Mem. Nat. Soc. Profl. Engrs., Tenn. Soc. Profl. Engrs., Am. Soc. Engring. Edn., Am. Water Assn., Am. Soc. of Civil Engring., Am. Assn. of Univ. Profs., Tau Beta Pi, Chi Epsilon. Mem. Christian Ch. (Disciples of Christ). Home: 231 Derby Ln Franklin TN 37069 Office: Nashville State Tech Inst. 120 White Bridge Rd Nashville TN 37209-4515

HUGHES, GEORGE EDWARD, college president; b. Gettysburg, Pa., May 7, 1950; s. Edward Allen and Oneda Margaret (Collins) H.; m. Sarah Elizabeth Miles; children: Laurie Bay, Jennifer, Lauren. AB, Catawba Coll., 1972; MA, Middle Tenn. State U., 1973; PhD, So. Ill. U., 1977. Coordinator, mental health technol. Jackson (Tenn.) State Community Coll., 1973-74, psychology instr., 1974-75; adminstrv. asst. so. Ill. U., Carbondale, 1975-77; instr., div. chmn. Miss. County Community Coll., Blytheville, Ark., 1977-82; dean acad. and student affairs North Country Community Coll., Saranac Lake, N.Y., 1982-85; pres. Hazard (Ky.) Community Coll., 1985—; cons., instr. Jackson Area Council on Alcholo and Drug Dependency, 1974-75; co-founder, mng. exec. Stress Assocs., Hazard, 1982—; sportscaster, KLCN/KHLS Radio, Blytheville, 1982. Author: Stress and Burnout Workbook, 1982; contbr. numerous edn. articles to jours. Sec. Hazard C.C. Adv. Bd., 1985—; mem. Southwest Area Health Edn. Ctr., 1986—, Hazard Ind. Coll. Found., 1989—; bd. dirs. Commn. on Future Ky.'s C.C.'s, Lexington, 1989, Hazard Ind. Coll. Found., 1988—, East Ky. Corp., 1990—; bd. govs. Frontier Nursing Svc.; pres. Hazard-Perry County Indsl. Devel. Commn., 1991; mem. Pvt. Industry Coun., 1991; treas., mem. exec. com. Leadership Ky., 1991—; vice chairman Samaritan East Ctr., 1992—. Named Vol. of the Yr., Ky. Assn. C. of C, 1987, Outstanding Coll. Pres., U. Tex., 1989; recipient Leadership award Leadership Ky., 1988, Man of the Yr. award; fellow U. Ky. 1990—. Mem. Am. Assn. Community, Jr. and Tech. Colls., Nat. Coun. for Resource Devel., Hazard-Perry County C. of C. (pres. 1986-88), Leadership Ky. Alumni Assn. (v.p. 1989), Kiwanis (sec.-treas. Blytheville 1980-82, Kiwanian of Yr. award 1980), Lions. Democrat. Presbyterian. Home: 318 Lyttle Blvd Hazard KY 41701-1740

HUGHES, GEORGE FARANT, JR., retired safety engineer; b. Roanoke, Va., June 22, 1923; s. George Farant and Pattie (Shafer) H.; m. Frances Miriam Perdue, July 1, 1950. BS, Va. Mil. Inst., 1948. Registered profl. engr., Va., Calif.; cert. safety profl. With roadway maintenance dept. N. & W. Ry. Co., Roanoke, 1948, with Liberty Mut. Ins. Co., Roanoke, Balt., 1949-61, asst. div. mgr., Pitts., 1962-63; safety supr. Westinghouse Electric Corp., Balt., 1963-64; supr. safety and accident prevention, Buffalo, 1965-67; safety dir. U.S. Naval Weapons Sta., Yorktown, Va., 1967-73; head occupational safety U.S. Naval Safety Center, Norfolk, Va., 1973-83, dep. dir. shore safety programs, 1984-88, ret., 1988. Served with AUS, 1943-46, 50-52. Decorated Bronze Star with oak leaf cluster, Purple Heart. Mem. Am. Soc. Safety Engrs. (profl. mem.), Western N.Y. Safety Conf. (dir. 1966-67), Nat. Soc. Profl. Engr., Va. Safety Assn. (bd. dirs. 1979-88), Nat. Eagle Scout Assn., SAR, Assn. Presevation Va. Antiquities (bd. dirs. 1984-87), Vets. Safety. Home: 520 Randolph St Williamsburg VA 23185-3518

HUGHES, HARLEY ARNOLD, career officer, retired, corporation consultant; b. Adair, Okla., Oct. 5, 1935; s. Arnold and Bernita (Richardson) H.; m. Grace Flores, May 25, 1980 (div.); children: Debra Hughes Kube, Denise, Deana Hughes Amendolia. BS in Biology, Okla. State U., 1957; MBA, U. Colo., 1967; posgrad., Nat. War Coll., 1974. Mem. Air Force Assn., Univ. Club (Washington), Army Navy Club, Fairfax Hunt Club. Commd. 2d lt. USAF, 1957, advanced through grades to lt. gen., 1985, various positions from cockpit to command, 1957-82, dep. chief staff plans and ops., dir. strategic nuclear target planning, 1982-85, dep. chief staff plans and ops., 1985-88, ret., 1988; sr. v.p. BETAC Corp., 1988-91; pres., cons. H. One, Inc., Alexandria, Va., 1991—; bd. dirs. Command Tech. Inc., Warenton, Va. Mem. Univ. Club, Fairfax Hunt Club. Baptist. Home: 5208 Bedlington Ter Alexandria VA 22304-3551

HUGHES, J. DEBORAH, health care administrator; b. Pitts., Mar. 24, 1948; d. James Francis and Margaret Veronica (Wiullmier) H. Diploma, Columbia Sch. Nursing, Pitts., 1969; BSN, La Roche Coll., 1987; M of Pub. Mgmt., Carnegie-Mellon U., 1988. Cert. nursing adminstr., med. staff coord., profl. in healthcare quality. Staff nurse Forbes Health Sys., Pitts., 1969-78, head nurse recovery, 1978-79, supr. nursing, 1979-84, clin. asst. to med. dir., 1984-88, dir. med. staff svcs., 1988-90; quality tracking mgr. Humana Inc., Louisville, 1990-91; regional quality mgmt. dir. Galen Healthcare, Inc., Louisville, 1991-92; sr. cons. quality and resource mgmt. Metri Cor, Inc., Louisville, 1992-94; mgr. accreditation svcs. and performance improvement HCIA, 1994—. Mem. Am. Soc. for Quality Control, Nat. Assn. healthcare Quality, Ky. Assn. Quality Assurance Profls., Ky. Soc. Healthcare Risk Mgmt., Nat. Assn. Med. Staff Svcs., Internat. Soc., Quality Assurance, Sigma Theta Tau. Office: HCIA 462 S 4th Ave Ste 405 Louisville KY 40202-3469

HUGHES, JAMES BAKER, JR., retail executive, consultant; b. Englewood, Calif., Nov. 15, 1938; s. James Baker Hughes Sr. and Mary Alma (Nettleton) Gaston; m. Jeanette Ann Martin, July 20, 1968; children: Heather, Hollis Ann. BS, U. Houston, 1961. CPA, Tex. V.p. Deep River Armory, Inc., Houston, 1958-65, pres., 1965-88; sales mgr. Tex-Products Machinery & Supply, Houston, 1989-92, acct., 1992—; instr. continuing end. U. Houston, 1976-77; assoc. prodr. Chisos Film Prodns., Houston, 1969-70; cons. State of Mex. Police Dept., 1976-78, Smithsonian Instn., 1988; CFO French Prodn. Inc., Houston, Arena Power Co., Houston, Midwest Centrifuge Sys., Houston, Electro-Peten S.A., Guatemala City, Guatemala, La Rucia Aviation, Inc., Saxet Foods, LLC, Houston, Bald Eagle Mining Co., Expedite Oyster, Inc.; treas. Bald Eagle Mining Co. Author: Confederate Gunmakers, 1961, Mexican Military Arms, 1968; contbr. articles to profl. jours.; inventor range finding sight. Rep. campaign worker Harris County, Tex.; various pos. St. Martin's Episcopal Ch., Houston, 1954—; bd. dirs. Young Reps. Harris County, 1968; dir. fin. Inst. for Rsch. on Small Arms in Internat. Security, Alexandria, Va., 1993—; treas. Sean Ashley House, Houston, 1993—. Recipient Bronze Benefactor Medal Royal Life Saving Soc., 1978. Mem. Nat. Rifle Assn. (life), Houston Gun Collectors Assn. (life, pres. 1960-61), Inst. Internac. De Historia Mil. in Mexico City (hon.), Soc. du Vignoble LeGodet (bd. dirs. 1985—). Republican. Clubs: Meml. Drive Country (pres. 1978-79), Racquet (Houston). Office: PO Box 571716 Houston TX 77257-1716

HUGHES, JAMES G., pediatrics educator; b. Memphis, Sept. 11, 1910; s. Allen Hughes; m. Jane Barker, 1935; children: Allen H., Jane Hughes Coble, Sarah Hughes Smith, Anne Hughes Sayle. BA, Rhodes Coll., Memphis, 1932; MD, U. Tenn., Memphis, 1935. Diplomate Am. Bd. Pediatrics (bd. dirs. 1952-58, examiner 1949-80). Rotating intern City of Memphis Hosp., 1935-37, resident in pediatrics, 1938-39, pediatrician-in-chief, 1960-76; resident in pediatrics Children's Meml. Hosp., Chgo., 1937-38; instr. pediatric postgrad. edn. Okla. Med. Assn., 1940-42; assoc. prof. pediatrics U. Tenn. Coll. Medicine, 1946-52, prof., 1952-76, chmn. dept., 1960-76, prof. emeritus, 1976—; chief staff Le Bonheur Children's Hosp., Memphis, 1959-60, med. dir., 1972-76, now sr. cons. Ctr. for Children in Crisis; former mem. Com. for Cert. in Child Psychiatry; hon. prof. U. Guadalajara, Mex., U. San Carlos de Borromeo, Guatemala; cons. WHO, 1955; pediatric cons. Rockefeller Found., 1956; cons. Alliance for Progress program U.S. Dept. State, Brazil, 1963; pediatric cons. to surgeon gen. U.S. Army, 1954, 59, 72. Author: Lectures in Pediatrics, 1940, Pediatrics in General Practice, 1952, The American Academy of Pediatrics: The First Fifty Years, 1980; coauthor: Synopsis of Pediatrics, 1963, 6th edit., 1984, Spanish edit., 1966; also numerous articles. Sr. warden Calvary Episcopal Ch., Memphis, 1978—; trustee Inst. for Pediatric Svc., Johnson and Johnson Co., 1979—. Col. M.C., U.S. Army, 1942-45, MTO, brig. gen. Res. ret. Decorated Legion of Merit with oak leaf cluster; recipient Outstanding Med. Alumnus award U. Tenn., 1977, Disting. Alumnus award Rhodes Coll., 1987, James G. Hughes award Memphis-Shelby County Child Sexual Abuse Coun., 1988. Mem. AMA (Abraham Jacobi award 1975), Am. Acad. Pediatrics (pres. 1965-66, Pediatrician of Yr. award Tenn. chpt. 1990), Soc. for Pediatric Rsch., So. Soc. for Pediatric Rsch., Internat. Pediatric Assn., Assn. Med. Sch. Pediatric Dept. Chairmen, Tenn. Med. Assn., Tenn. Pediatric Soc., Memphis and Shelby County Med. Assn., Memphis and Mid-South Pediatric Soc., Alpha Omega Alpha, Phi Chi, Omicron Delta Kappa, Kappa Sigma; hon. mem. numerous fgn. pediatric socs. Office: Le Bonheur Ctr Children in Crisis 2400 Poplar Ave Ste 318 Memphis TN 38112-3211

HUGHES, LESLIE IVAN, librarian; b. Jackson, Miss., June 19, 1960; s. Charles Elmer and Eva Lois (Martin) H.; m. Liddia Marie Ramsey, May 21, 1988; 1 child, William Brandon. AA, Copiah-Lincoln Jr. Coll., Wesson, Miss., 1981; BS, Univ. So. Miss., 1984, MLS, 1987. Sch. libr. Fannie Mullins Elem., Brookhaven, Miss., 1984-86; libr. Clarke Coll., Newton, Miss., 1987-90; libr. dir. Kemper-Newton Regional Libr., Union, Miss., 1990-96; libr. Choctaw Ctrl. H.S., Philadelphia, Miss., 1996—. Minister of music, Emmanuel Bapt. Ch., Union, 1988—. Mem. Miss. Libr. Assn. Home: 90 Floyd Rowzee Rd Union MS 39365 Office: Choctaw Ctrl HS Rte 7 Box 72 Philadelphia MS 39350

HUGHES, LIN GEARING, lawyer; b. St. Louis, Jan. 26, 1947; d. James Laddie Jr. and Doris Irene (Agricola) Gearing; m. Mark R. Hughes, May 24, 1969 (div. May 1978); 1 child, Mark R. Jr. BA in English, Govt., Tarleton State U., 1969; MA in Polit. Sci., U. North Tex., 1976, PhD in Polit. Sci., 1981; JD, Tex. Tech. Sch. Law, 1987. Editor Stephenville (Tex.) Daily Empire, 1969; reporter Denton (Tex.) Record-Chronicle, 1969-70; teaching asst., teaching fellow U. North Tex., Denton, 1970-72; reporter Denton Record-Chronicle, 1972-73; teaching fellow U. North Tex., Denton, 1976-78; asst. prof. Tex. Tech. U., Lubbock, 1979-85; assoc. atty. McGinnis, Lochridge & Kilgore, L.L.P., Austin, Tex., 1987-93, ptnr., 1994—. Mem. contbr. Nature Conservancy, 1993—, All Saints Episcopal Ch., Austin, 1988—. Mem. ABA (litigation sect., antitrust sect.), Tex. Bar Assn. (contbg. editor antitrust and bus. litigation sect. 1993), Travis County Bar Assn. (coun. litigation sect. 1987—), Leadership Tex., Order of Coif, Order of

Barristers. Democrat. Office: McGinnis Lochridge & Kilgore LLP 919 Congress Ave Ste 1300 Austin TX 78701-2444

HUGHES, LINDA RENATE, lawyer, arbitrator, mediator; b. Hanau, Fed. Republic Germany, Oct. 25, 1947; came to U.S. 1950; d. J.A. and Ilga (Vankins) Eglite. BA magna cum laude, U. Minn., 1968; JD cum laude, Wayne State U., 1980. Bar: Mich. 1980, Ga. 1982, Fla. 1984; cert. mediator, magistrate judge. Human resource mgr. Browning Marine Co., St. Charles, Mich., 1973-76; law clk. to judge U.S. Dist. Ct. (ea. dist.) Mich., 1980-81; asst. county atty. Hillsborough County, Fla., 1985-89; ptnr. Alpert, Josey, & Hughes, P.A., Tampa, 1989-95; instr. Valdosta State Coll. (Ga.), 1981; adj. prof. U. Detroit Law Sch., 1982; researcher comparative labor policy, Leigh Creek, Australia, 1983. Editor-in-chief Advocate, Wayne State U. Law Sch., 1979-80, also law rev. With Community Mental Health Intervention, Saginaw, Mich., 1975-76, Ann Arbor, Mich., 1976-78, Clearwater Fla., 1984; dept. registrar Voter Registration, Pinellas County, Fla., 1983-84. Author: Employer's Price for Polygraph, 1986, Section 1983: Who is the Client: Employee or Government, 1988, Hypnosis of Civil Plaintiffs, 1991. Mem. ABA, AAUW (Saginaw chpt. sec. 1974-75), Am. Arbitration Assn. (panel of neutrals), Fed. Bar Assn., State Bar Mich., Ga. State Bar, Fla. State Bar Assn. (chair govt. lawyers sect. 1986-89, mem. mid-yr. com. 1988-89, spl. com. on governance 1988-91, past chair com. on profl. ethics 1989-95, mem. all bar conf. 1989-95), Hillsborough County Bar Assn. (jud. evaluation com. 1986-90), Fla. Women Lawyers Assn. (officer, bd. dirs.), Tampa Club. Home: 584 Luzon Ave Tampa FL 33606-3669

HUGHES, LISA LYNN, lay church worker; b. Pinehurst, N.C., Apr. 16, 1964; d. Rollow Hershel and Annie Ruth (McIntosh) H. BA in Psychology, U. N.C., 1994. Youth leader Brownson Meml. Presbyn. Ch., Southern Pines, N.C., 1987-92, 94—, elder, 1988-91, Sunday sch. tchr., 1988-89, dir. Christian growth, youth dir., 1991; youth advisor Coastal Carolina Presbytery, Presbyn. Ch. (U.S.A.), 1989-91; dir. Moore County Day Reporting Ctr., 1995—; exec. dir. Drug-Free Moore County, Inc., Carthage, N.C., 1990-95, bd. dirs., 1996—. Vol. Bethesda Link, 1990-95; mem. Moore County Youth Svcs. Commn., 1990-91, Jr. Svc. League, 1993—, Moore for Tomorrow Lifestyle Task Force, 1993—, Moore Interagy. Coun., 1993-94, chmn., 1994-95; mem. Moore County Criminal Justice Partnership Adv. Bd., 1994-95; mem. C. of C. Drug Awareness Task Force, 1990—. Home: 1440 E Hedgelawn Way Southern Pines NC 28387-7429

HUGHES, LYNN NETTLETON, federal judge; b. Houston, Sept. 9, 1941; m. Olive Allen. BA, U. Ala., 1963; JD, U. Tex., 1968; LLM, U. Va., 1992. Bar: Tex., 1966. Pvt. practice, Houston, 1966-79; judge Dist. Ct. Tex., Houston, 1979-85; U.S. dist. judge So. Dist. Tex., Houston, 1985—; adj. prof. South Tex. Coll. Law, 1973—, U. Tex., 1990-91; Tex. del. Nat. Conf. State Trial Judges, 1983-85; mem. com. on asbestos case mgmt. Nat. Dist. Ct., 1987-91; cons. Tex. Jud. Budget Bd., 1984; lectr. Tex. Coll. Judiciary, 1983; mem. task force on revision rules of civil procedure Supreme Ct. Tex., 1991-95; cons. on constn. Republic of Moldova, 1993, European Community, 1989, Ukraine, 1995, Romania, 1996. Mem. adv. bd. Houston Jour. Internat. Law, 1981—, chmn., 1989— mem. adv. dirs. Internat. Law Inst., U. Houston, 1995—. Trustee Rift Valley Rsch. Mission, 1978—; mem. St. Martins Episcopal Ch. Fellow Tex. Bar Found.; mem. ABA, Fed. Bar Assn. (bd. dirs. Houston chpt. 1986-89), Am. Law Inst., Maritime Law Assn., Houston Bar Assn., Tex. Bar Assn. (nominations com. jud. sect. 1983, court cost, delay and efficiency com. 1981-90, vice chmn. 1984-86, selection, compensation and tenure state judges com. 1981-85, vice chmn. 1982-83, liaison with law schs. com. 1987-92, plain lang. com. 1989—), Am. Judicature Soc., Am. Soc. Legal History, Am. Anthrop Assn., Houston Philos. Soc., Am. Inn of Ct. XV (pres. 1986-92), Phi Delta Phi. Office: US Court House 11122 515 Rusk Ave Houston TX 77002-2605

HUGHES, MICHAEL KENT, trade association executive; b. Columbus, Ga., Nov. 7, 1955; s. Arthur T. and Lydia J. Hughes; m. Linda J. Gurney, Oct. 4, 1980; children: Lauren, Lisa, Brian. BA in Polit. Sci. magna cum laude, Coll. of Charleston, 1977; JD, U. S.C., 1980; M Sports Adminstrn., Ohio U., 1990. Assoc. Ness, Motley, Loadholt and Richardson, Charleston, S.C., 1984-86, Rosen, Rosen and Hagood, Charleston, 1986-89; grad. asst. golf coach Ohio U., Athens, 1989-90; intern U.S. Golf Assn., Far Hills, N.J., 1990; exec. dir. Nat. Golf Course Owners Assn., Charleston, 1990—; mem. selection panel for lifetime achievement award in journalism PGA of Am.; rep. ABA; asst. to dean Law Sch. U. S.C.; mem. adv. bd. PGA Tour Hall of Fame. Bd. dirs. Nat. Golf Found.; mem. bd. Athletic Fundraising Assn. of Coll. of Charleston. With JAGC, USN, 1980-84. Recipient U.S. Golf Assn. Howard Creel Fellowship award, Ohio U. NFL Scholarship award. Mem. U.S. Golf Assn. (pub. golf com.), Met. Exch. Club Charleston (mem. bd.). Episcopalian. Office: Nat Golf Course Owners Assn 1461 Center Street Ext # B1 Mount Pleasant SC 29464-4649

HUGHES, MICHAEL RANDOLPH, evangelist; b. Newport News, Va.; s. Luke Jr. and Patsy Ruth (Jewell) H.; m. Carolyn Delight Williamson, Mar. 20, 1981; children: Amanda, Patsy. Diploma, Memphis Sch. Preaching, 1976; cert. in theology, Ala. Christian Sch. Religion, 1982, BA, 1984; MS, Troy State U., 1987; postgrad., So. Christian U., 1992—. Min. Newport News Ch. of Christ, 1977-80, 81-83, Ch. of Christ of Clyattville, Ga., 1980-81, 83-85, City Boulevard Ch. of Christ, Waycross, Ga., 1985-87, Hampton (Va.) Ch. of Christ, 1988-92; instr. Bible Ga. Christian Sch., Dasher, 1985-87; min. Green's Lake Road Ch. of Christ, East Ridge, Tenn., 1992—; dir., instr. Bible, Idlewild Christian Camp, Surry, Va., 1977-80; youth worker Ga. Christian Children's Home, Dasher, 1985-87; missionary Mil. Outreach, Germany, 1988-90, Chs. of Christ, India, Malaysia, Taiwan, 1992—. Author: Tax Record System, 1980; contbr. articles to relgious publs. Community organizer North End Huntington Heights Preservation Assn., Newport News, 1977-80; tax preparer VITA, Valdosta, Ga., 1986-87. Recipient award of merit Memphis Sch. Preaching, 1977. Mem. Givens Orgn., Memphis Sch. Preaching Alumni Assn. (bd. dirs. 1991-95). Home: PO Box 9510 Chattanooga TN 37412-0510 Office: Green's Lake Rd Ch of Christ 1209 Green's Lake Rd Chattanooga TN 37412-2319

HUGHES, PATRICIA NEWMAN, academic administrator; b. Vicksburg, Miss., Apr. 16, 1964; d. Horace Wilbur Sr. and Florence (Hearn) Newman; m. Tommy Wade Hughes, Dec. 29, 1990; 1 child, Newman Price; stepchildren: Amber Brooke, Kala Marie. BA, Miss. State U., 1986. Coord. prospect rsch. Office of Devel. Miss. State U., 1989-93, coord. prospect mgmt. Office of Devel., 1993—. Mem. Assn. Profl. Rschrs. for Advancement, Coun. Advancement and Support of Edn. Democrat. Baptist. Office: Miss State U PO Drawer 6149 200 Walker Rd Mississippi State MS 39762

HUGHES, PAUL ANTHONY, minister, musician, songwriter, author, publisher; b. Tulsa, Sept. 14, 1957; s. James Barrie and Naomi Ruth (Kinard) H. BS in Indsl. Distbn., Tex. A&M U., College Station, 1980; MDiv in Christian Edn., Assemblies of God Theol. Sem., Springfield, Mo., 1986; postgrad., Baylor U., 1987. Ordained to ministry Assemblies of God, 1989. Pastoral asst., adult tchr., asst. supt. Magnolia Hill Assembly of God, Livingston, Tex., 1988-90; tchr. Bible, musician, religious writer, songwriter, 1990—; asst. pastor First Assembly of God, Liberty, Tex., 1992-94; adult Bible tchr. Evangel Assembly of God, Houston, 1994-96. Editor, pub.: Insight on Religion, History and Society, 1995—; contbr. articles, book revs. Singles pastor Grace Assembly of God, Houston, 1996—. Mem. Soc. Bibl. Lit., Am. Acad. Religion, Soc. Pentecostal Studies. Home: 1111 Woods Dr Liberty TX 77575-3609

HUGHES, RAY HARRISON, minister, church official; b. Calhoun, Ga., Mar. 7, 1924; s. J.H. and Emma Hughes; m. Marian Euverla Tidwell; children—Janice, Ray H., Donald, Anita. A.A. Lee Coll., B.A., Tenn. Wesleyan Coll.; M.S., Ed.D., U. Tenn.; Litt. D., Lee Coll., Cleveland; EdD U. Tenn. Tenn. Ordained to ministry Ch. of God, 1950. Pastor, Fairfield Ch. of God (Ill.), 1945-46, North Chattanooga Ch. of God, 1948-52, Nat. Sunday Sch. and youth dir., 1952-56; organized churches in Spain, Md., Ill., Tenn., Ga.; pres. Lee Coll., Cleveland, Tenn., 1960-66, 82-84; pres. theol. seminary Ch. God Sch. Theology, 1984-86, 1st asst. gen. overseer, 1986-90; Md.-Del.-D.C. overseer Ch. of God, 1956-60, 3d asst. gen. overseer, 1992-94, 1st asst. gen. overseer, 1994—. Mem. exec. council 1956-60, 62-82, 86-90, 92—, exec. dir. gen. bd. edn., 1st asst. gen. overseer, 1970-72, gen. overseer, 1972-74, 78-82, Ga. overseer, 1974-76; speaker for convs., preaching missions, ministers retreats. Chmn. Pentecostal Fellowship of N.Am.; chmn. Pentecostal World Conf., 1990—. Mem. Nat. Assn. Evangelicals (pres.), Pi Delta Omicron, Phi Delta Kappa. Author: Planning for Sunday School Programs, 1960; Order of Future Events, 1962; What is Pentecost?, 1963; The Effect of Lee College on World Missions, 1963, The Transition of Church Related Junior Colleges To Senior Colleges, 1966; Church of God Distinctives, 1968; The Outpouring of the Spirit; Dynamics of Sunday School Growth, 1980; Pentecostal Preaching, 1981, Who is the Holy Ghost, 1992; editor the Pilot; contbr. in field. Address: Pentecostal World Conf PO Box 4815 Cleveland TN 37320-4815

HUGHES, ROBERT DAVIS, III, theological educator; b. Boston, Feb. 16, 1943; s. Robert Davis and Nancy (Wolfe) H.; m. Barbara Brunn, June 12, 1965; children: Robert David, Thomas Dunstan. BA, Yale U., 1966; MDiv, Episcopal Divinity Sch., 1969; MA, St. Michael's Coll., U. Toronto, Ont., Can., 1973, PhD, 1980. Ordained deacon Episcopal Ch., 1969, priest, 1970. Assoc. rector Good Shepherd Ch., Athens, Ohio, 1969-72; vicar Epiphany Ch., Nelsonville, Ohio, 1969-72; asst. curate St. Anne's Ch., Toronto, 1972-75; instr. Sch. of Theology, U. of the South, Sewanee, Tenn., 1977—, assoc. prof. systemic theology, 1984-92; prof. systematic theology U. of the South, Sewanee, Tenn., 1992—; bd. dirs. Anglican Ctr. Christian Family Life, Sewanee, 1981—; mem. Dept. Christian Edn. Ecumenical Commn. Alcohol and Drug Commn., Diocese Tenn., 1981-88. Contbr. articles to various publs. Soloist Toronto Chamber Soc., 1975-77; pres., soloist Sewanee Chorale, 1977—; vol. Community Chest, Boy Scouts Am., Sewanee, 1979-84; pres. Sewanee Chem. Dependency Assn., 1982. Episcopal Ch. Found. fellow, 1972—, Kent fellow Danforth Found., 1975-77; Sabbatical grantee Mercer and Conant funds., 1984, 91. Mem. AAUP (v.p. chpt. 1982-83, pres. 1985-87, v.p. state conf. 1990-94, pres. 1994-96), Conf. Anglican Theologians (sec.-treas. 1986-95, v.p. 1996—), E.Q.B. Club (bd. dirs. 1981-83), Crystal Lake Yacht Club (Frankfort, Mich.). Office: Sch of Theology 335 Tennessee Ave Sewanee TN 37383-0001

HUGHES, SANDRA K., nursing administrator; b. Cin., Nov. 19, 1949; d. Zedic E. and Audrey B. (Brown) Craycraft; m. Harold D. Hughes, Nov. 22, 1969; children: Becky Kay, Erik D., Thomas A. Diploma, Christ Hosp. Sch. Nursing, 1983; BSN, Coll. Mt. St. Joseph, 1990. Cert. gastroenterology, emergency nurse, pediatric nurse. Interim DON Children's Med. Ctr. of Dallas; GI clin. nurse coord. Children's Med. Ctr., Cin., surg. nurse coord., emergency med. systems coord., DON gastroenterology and children's liver transplant program; speaker in field, 1991-94. Bd. dirs. Juvenile Diabetes Found., Greater Cin.; mem. ARC Crisis Support Nurse Team. Mem. Emergency Nurses Assn. (publicity chmn., past sec. Greater Cin. chpt.), Buckeye State Nurses Orgn. (pres. 1989-90, past treas., sec., chpt. chmn.), Assn. of Pediatric Gastroenterology and Nutrition Nurses (profl. edn. com. 1991-92, bd.dirs. 1994-95, chmn. edn. com. 1994—), Soc. of Gastroenterology Nurses and Assocs., Inc. (rsch. com. 1993-95, chmn. pediat. spl. interest group newsletter 1995—), Soc. of Internat. Gastroenterol. Nurses and Endoscopy Assocs. Home: 800 E Ash Ln Apt 814 Euless TX 76039-4714

HUGHES, SELMA ELIZABETH, special education educator; b. Cardiff, Clamorgan, Gt. Britain, May 3, 1926; came to U.S., 1965; d. Digby Thomas and Vida (Evnon) Leyshon; m. Nathan Hughes, Dec. 4, 1954; children: Richard, Clare, Simon. BS in Econs., London U., 1945, B Comm., 1946; MEd, So. Meth. U., 1970; PhD in Spl. Edn., Tex. Woman's U., 1974. Asst. statistician Ministry of Food, London, 1947-50; statistician southwestern div. Nat. Coal Bd., Cardiff, U.K., 1950-54; tchr. lang. learning disability Preston Hollow Presbyn. Weekday Sch., Dallas, 1970-73; doctoral teaching fellow dept. spl. edn. Tex. Woman's U., Denton, 1973-74; instr. edn., coord. elem. student tchrs. Dallas alt. program So. Meth. U., 1975; asst. prof. spl. edn. East Tex. State U., Commerce, 1975-82, assoc. prof., sr. mem. grad. faculty, 1982-91, prof. psychology and spl. edn., 1991-93. Contbr. articles to profl. jours. Mem. ASCD, AAUP, World Fedn. Mental Health, Internat. Coun. Psychologists, Coun. Exceptional Children, Internat. Reading Assn., Nat. Coun. Tchrs. Math., Assn. Children and Adults with Learning Disabilities, Tex. Assn. Coll. Tchrs., Pi Lambda Theta. Office: East Tex State U 2600 Motley Dr Mesquite TX 75150-3840

HUGHES, SHELIA ELIZABETH ANN, newspaper editor, reporter; b. Bogalusa, La., Aug. 14, 1965; d. Woodrow Wilson and Earline Elizabeth Ann (Riley) H. BA in Communications, Loyola U., New Orleans, 1987. Perspective editor Bogalusa Daily News, 1988—; newsroom desk asst. Sta. WWL-TV, New Orleans, 1990-91. Contbr. poems to Red Beans and Rice lit. mag., 1986-87. Mem. La. Press Assn. (1st pl. div. award family news coverage 1988, 3d pl. div. award family news coverage 1989), Bogalusa Woman's Club, Alpha Sigma Nu. Democrat. Home: 55322 M Toney Rd Franklinton LA 70438-8120 Office: Bogalusa Daily News 525 Avenue V Bogalusa LA 70427-4413

HUGHES, STEVEN BRYAN, gas measurement company executive; b. Holdenville, Okla., Feb. 15, 1956; s. Harvey and Rosella Mae (Storts) H.; m. Ronda Lynn Coker, May 18, 1974; children: Stephen, Rachel, Caleb. Grad. high sch., Wetumka, Okla. Measurement technician Transok Pipeline Co., Wetumka, 1977-80; supr. gas measurement Transok Pipeline Co., Tulsa, 1980; owner, cons. Hughes Gas Measurement, Wetumka, 1980-93, pres., 1993—; ptnr. Data Resource Systems, Wetumka, 1991—; gas measurement cons. Illini Carrier, L.P., Granite City, Ill., 1990-92; contract measurement mgr. Oxley Petroleum, Tulsa, 1988—. Author, developer: (computer software) Wellhead Data Collection Program, 1991-94; editor, developer: (computer software) Total Flow/Chart Conversion Program, 1992-94. Teen Sunday sch. tchr. Pentecostal Holiness Ch., Wetumka, 1984-96, Sunday sch. supt., 1984-96, deacon bd. mem., 1990-96; cub master troop 483 Boy Scouts Am., Etumka, 1985-86. Recipient Leadership award Pentecostal Holiness Ch., Wetumka, 1985. Mem. Soc. Petroleum Engrs. (assoc.). Democrat. Home: RR 1 Box 51-a Wetumka OK 74883-9714 Office: Hughes Gas Measurement Inc Rt 1 Box 51-A Wetumka OK 74883

HUGHES, SUE MARGARET, retired librarian; b. Cleburne, Tex.; d. Chastain Wesley and Sue Willis (Payne) H. BBA, U. Tex., Austin, 1949; MLS, Tex. Woman's U., 1960, PhD, 1987. Sec.-treas. pvt. corps. Waco, Tex., 1949-59; asst. in public services Baylor U. Library, Waco, 1960-64; acquisitions librarian Baylor U. Library, 1964-79, acting univ. librarian, summer 1979, dir. Moody Library, 1980-89; interim univ. libr. Baylor U., Waco, 1989-91, spl. materials cons., 1991-92; ret., 1992. Mem. AAUP, ALA, Southwestern Library Assn., Tex. Library Assn., AAUW, Delta Kappa Gamma, Beta Phi Mu, Beta Gamma Sigma. Methodist. Club: Altrusa.

HUGHES, VESTER THOMAS, JR., lawyer; b. San Angelo, Tex., May 24, 1928; s. Vester Thomas and Mary Ellen (Tisdale) H. Student, Baylor U., 1945-46; B.A. with distinction, Rice U., 1949; LLB cum laude, Harvard U., 1952. Bar: Tex. 1952. Law clk. U.S. Supreme Ct., 1952; assoc. Robertson, Jackson, Payne, Lancaster & Walker, Dallas, 1955-58; ptnr. Jackson, Walker, Winstead, Cantwell & Miller, Dallas, 1958-76, Hughes, Luce, Hennessy, Smith & Castle, Dallas, 1976—, Hughes & Hill, Dallas, 1979-85, Hughes & Luce, Dallas, 1985—; bd. dirs. Exell Cattle Co., Amarillo, Tex., LX Cattle Co., Amarillo, Murphy Oil Corp., El Dorado, Ark., Austin Industries, Dallas ; adv. dir. First Nat. Bank Mertzon; tax counsel Communities Found. of Tex., Inc.; mem. adv. com. Tex. Supreme Ct., 1985—. Contbr. articles on fed. taxation to profl. jours. Bd. dirs. Juvenile Diabetes Found. Inc., Dallas, 1982—; trustee Dallas Bapt. Coll., 1967-77; v.p., trustee, exec. com. Tex. Scottish Rite Hosp. for Children, 1967—; bd. overseers vis. com. Harvard Law Sch., 1969-75. 1st lt. JAGC U.S. Army, 1952-55. Mem. ABA Assn. (coun. sect. taxation 1969-73), Dallas Bar Assn., Am. Law Inst. (coun. 1966—), Am. Coll. Tax Counsel, Southwestern Legal Found., Am. Coll. of Trust and Estate Counsel, Harvard Law Sch. Assn. (sec. 1984-86), Met. Club (Washington), Harvard Club (N.Y.C.), Masons, Order Ea. Star, Phi Beta Kappa, Sigma Xi. Democrat. Baptist. Office: Hughes & Luce 1717 Main St Ste 2800 Dallas TX 75201-7342

HUGHES, WAUNELL MCDONALD (MRS. DELBERT E. HUGHES), retired psychiatrist; b. Tyler, Tex., Feb. 6, 1928; d. Conrad Claiborne and Bernice Oletha (Smith) McDonald; B.A., U. Tex. at Austin, 1946; M.D., Baylor U., 1951; m. Delbert Eugene Hughes, Aug. 14, 1948; children—Lark, Mark, Lynn, Michael. Intern VA Hosp., Houston, 1951-52; resident Parkland Hosp., Dallas, 1964-67; practiced gen. medicine in Tyler, Tex., 1952-64; acting chief psychiatry service VA Hosp., Dallas, 1967-68, asst. chief, 1968-73, chief Mental Hygiene Clinic and Day Treatment Center, 1973-82, unit chief acute inpatient psychiatry Med. Center, 1982-88; clin. instr. psychiatry Southwestern Med. Sch., U. Tex. Health Sci. Center, Dallas, 1968-88; psychiat. cons. Dallas Family Guidance Clinics, 1990. Chmn. pre-sch. vision and hearing program Pilot Club, Tyler, 1960-64. Mem. Am. Med. Women's Assn. (pres. Dallas 1980-81), Am. Psychiat. Assn., Am. Group Psychotherapy Assn., (pres. Dallas chpt. 1984-86), North Tex. Soc. Psychiat. Physicians (co-chair Mental Health Mental Retardation pro bono clinic com. Dallas chpt. 1989-91, mem. patient advocacy com. 1992—), Dallas Area Women Psychiatrists (archivist 1985—), Alpha Epsilon Iota (pres. 1950-51). Home: 3428 University Blvd Dallas TX 75205-1834

HUGHES, WILLIAM ANTHONY, bishop; b. Youngstown, Ohio, Sept. 23, 1921; s. James Francis and Anna Marie (Philbin) H. Degree, St. Charles Sem., Balt., St. Mary's Sem., Cleve.; M.A. in Edn, Notre Dame U., 1956. Ordained priest Roman Catholic Ch., 1946; pastor chs. in Boardman and Massillon, Ohio, 1946-55; prin. Cardinal Mooney High Sch., Youngstown, 1956-65; supt. schs. Diocese of Youngstown, 1965-72, episcopal vicar of edn.., 1972-73, vicar gen., 1973-74; aux. bishop, 1974-79; bishop of Covington, Covington, Ky., 1979—; ret. bishop Covington, KY. Office: Cathedral of Assemption 1140 Madison Ave Covington KY 41011-3116

HUGHES, WILLIAM JOSEPH, management consultant; b. Kansas City, Mo., Oct. 11, 1953; s. Joseph Rowland and Ann (Hemingway) H.; m. Mary Alice Knight, Apr. 25, 1981; children: Charles, Allison, Kirstin. BSME, U. Va., 1975. Various positions Brown & Root, Inc., Houston, 1975-79; sr. cons. Arthur Andersen & Co., S.C., Houston, 1979-81, mgr., 1981-87; ptnr. Andersen Cons., Houston, 1987—. Editor, contbg. author: Natural Gas Trends, 1988. Mem. ASME, Houston Club. Episcopalian. Office: Andersen Cons 711 Louisiana St Ste 1200 Houston TX 77002-2716

HUGHES, WILLIAM L., health delivery system administrator; b. Richmond, Ky., July 23, 1952; s. Paul and Joann (Broaddus) H. BS, Ea. Ky. U., 1974, MS, 1976; MPH, Tulane U., 1985, MBA, 1985. Adminstrv. fellow Allegheny Health Svcs., Pitts., 1985; asst. v.p. Bristol Meml. Hosp., Bristol, Tenn., 1985-86; v.p. fin. and chief fin. officer The Hosp. of the Good Samaritan, L.A., 1986-92; v.p. fin., CFO U. Colo. Hosp., Denver, 1992-95; v.p., chief fin. officer M.D. Anderson Cancer Ctr. Outreach Corp., Houston, 1995—; bd. dirs. U. Colo. Perinatal Inst. Chmn. med. support com. Calif. Spl. Olympics, 1988-90. Capt. U.S. Army, 1976-81. Mem. Am. Hosp. Assn., Healthcare Fin. Mgmt. Assn., Am. Coll. Healthcare Execs., Rotary Club of Houston, Colo. Perinatal Found. (bd. dirs.), Med. Group Mgmt. Assn. Republican. Episcopalian. Office: MDACC Outreach Corp 7505 South Main Ste 500 Houston TX 77030

HUGHSTON, MILAN ROSS, librarian; b. Clarksville, Tex., May 5, 1954; s. Thomas Ross and Eugenia (Milan) H. BJ, U. Tex., 1976, MLS, 1977; diploma in Mus. Studies, U. Manchester, 1979. Libr. Amon Carter Mus., Fort Worth, 1979—. Presbyterian. Office: Amon Carter Museum 3501 Camp Bowie Blvd Fort Worth TX 76107-2631

HUITT, JIMMIE L., rancher, oil, gas, real estate investor; b. Gurdon, Ark., Aug. 21, 1923; s. John Wesley and Almedia (Hatten) H.; m. Janis C. Mann, Oct. 30, 1945; children—Jimmie L., Jr., Allan Jerome. B.S. in Chem. Engring., La. Tech. U., 1944; M.S. in Chem. Engring., U. Okla., 1948, Ph.D., 1951. Registered profl. engr., La. Research engr. Mobil Oil Corp., Dallas, 1951-56, Gulf Research Co., Pitts., 1956-67; ops. coordinator Kuwait Oil Co., London, 1967-71; gen. mgr. Gulf Oil-Zaire, Kinshasa, 1971-74; mng. dir. Gulf Oil-Nigeria, Lagos, 1974-76; sr. v.p., exec. v.p. Gulf Oil Exploration and Prodn. Co., Houston, 1976-81, pres., 1981-85; rancher Four Jays Ranch, Industry, Tex., 1986—. Contbr. articles to profl. jours.; patentee in field. Served to 1st lt. U.S. Army, 1944-47. Mem. Soc. Petroleum Engrs. (chmn. various coms. 1956—). Republican. Lodges: Masons, Shriners. Office: Four Jays Ranch PO Box 236 Industry TX 78944-0236

HULCE, DURWARD PHILIP, theatrical lighting designer; b. Baton Rouge, Apr. 30, 1948; s. Durward Clare and Kathryn Venita (Lee) H. BA, La. State U., 1974; cert. completion, Patrice Lumumba U., Moscow, 1975. Head stage electrician Miller Outdoor Theater, Houston, 1984-90; tour leader Ariel Birding Tours, 1986—; theatrical lighting designer Nightlights of Houston, 1988—; head stage electrician Houston Ballet, 1991—. Author: (newsletter) Uncommon Birds of the Upper Texas Coast, 1990—. Houston Audubon Soc. rep. to Friends Hermann Park, 1993—; bd. dirs. Tex. Ptnrs. in Flight, Houston, 1993—. Sgt. USAF, 1968-72. Mem. Am. Ornithol. Union, Cooper Ornithol. Soc., Wilson Ornithol. Soc., Orgn. for Tropical Studies, Internat. Coun. for Bird Preservation, Tex. Ornithol. Soc. (life), Houston Outdoor Nature Club (compiler xmas bird count 1987—). Home and Office: Ariel Birding Tours 339 W 23rd St Houston TX 77008-2030

HULL, EDWARD WHALEY SEABROOK, freelance writer, consultant; b. Washington, Mar. 10, 1923; s. Edward Seabrook III and Hortense Carver (Marshall) H.; m. Nellie Phinizy Fortson, June 25, 1944; children: Edward, John, Thomas, Nellie Phinizy Hull Price. Student, Union Coll., Schenectady, 1939-42; M Marine Affairs, U. R.I., 1970; PhD in Marine Sci., U. S.C., 1987. Chief copy boy Times-Herald, Washington, 1947; corr. Washington Bur., McGraw-Hill, 1948-51; editor Whaley-Eaton Fgn. Letter, Washington, 1951-53; bur. chief McGraw-Hill World News, London, 1954-56; assoc. editor Missiles & Rockets mag., Washington, 1956-58; ea. rep. Diversey Engring., Inc., Washington, 1958-60; editor, pres., dir. Nautilus Press, Inc., Washington, 1960-73; pres., dir. Intel, Inc., Washington, 1964-67; editor, pub. Geo-Marine Technology, 1964-67, Geo Marine Tech., Washington, 1964-67; cons. Washington, S.C., 1969-85; freelance writer, Yonges Island, S.C., 1987—; dir. S.C. Writers Workshop, Columbia and Charleston, 1991-92. Author: Rocket to the Moon, 1958, The Bountiful Sea, 1964; editor: Peenemunde to Canaveral (D.K. Kuzel), 1962; contbr. numerous articles on rocketry, space flight, oceanography, also others, to profl. publs. 1st lt. USMCR, 1942-45, PTO. Decorated Air medal; fellow Woodrow Wilson Internat. Ctr. for Scholars, 1970-71. Mem. Nature Conservancy, Appalachian Trail Conf., Wilson Ctr. Assocs. (assoc.), Nat. Press Club (Washington), Poetry Soc. of S.C. (exec. bd. 1994—, dir. 1994—). Democrat. Episcopalian. Home: 7717 White Point Rd Hollywood SC 29449-6223

HULL, JAMES ERNEST, religion and philosophy educator; b. Laurel, Miss., June 30, 1928; s. Tillette Reyphord and Gladys Evelyn (Reeves) H.; m. Jo Welch, July 7, 1956; children: Alan Walter, Timothy Olen, Richard James. AB, So. Meth. U., 1950, MDiv cum laude, 1952; PhD, U. Edinburgh (Scotland), 1959; postgrad., Yale U., 1968, U. Oxford, U. Cambridge, Eng. Ordained to ministry Meth. Ch., 1953. Preacher Ch. of Scotland and Meth. chs., Scotland, 1956; assoc. pastor St. Mary's Parish Kirk, Haddington, Scotland, 1957-58; minister Scarsdale (N.Y.) Congregational Ch., 1958-60; prof., chmn. dept. religion and philosophy Lambuth Coll., Jackson, Tenn., 1960-66; prof., chmn. dept. religion and philosophy Greensboro (N.C.) Coll., 1966—, Jefferson-Pilot prof. religion and philosophy, 1976—; arts cons. various denominations throughout the South, 1966—, various sems., 1966—, S.E. jurisdiction United Meth. Chrs., 1968-78; cons., tchr. chs., Miami, Fla., 1972-80; mem. World Theol. Conf., Oxford U., Eng., 1969, Piedmont Colls. Archaeol. Dig, Beersheba, Israel, 1973. Author: Beyond the Dream, Live Justuce-Love Peace, Symphony of Spirit and Stone, On the Way, 1976, Ecumenical Celebrations—Interfaith Resources, 1991; contbr. articles to profl. jours. Assoc. minister Grace United Methodist Ch., Greensboro, 1978-79; gen. coun.. U. Edinburgh, del., 1976—. Lt. USN, 1953-56. Recipient commendation 11th Workshop Christian-Jewish Rels., Charleston, S.C., 1989, 1st Nat. award for exemplary teaching Gen. Bd. Higher Edn. and Ministry, United Meth. Ch.; named one of 10 Most Outstanding Citizens, Greensboro News and Record, 1985; Lilly scholar Duke U., 1976; Bryan Found. grantee, 1991, 96. Mem. AAUP, N.C. Assn. Profs. of Religion, Piedmont Interfaith Coun. (co-founder), Civitan Club (chaplain). Home: 5409 Southwind Rd Greensboro NC 27455-1152 Office: Greensboro Coll PO Box 19734 Greensboro NC 27419-9734

HULL, JOHN DOSTER, retired insurance company executive; b. White Plains, N.Y., Oct. 24, 1924; s. Robert Franklin and Mary Catharine (Doster) H.; m. Joyce Elizabeth Holroyd, June 12, 1948 (div. Oct. 1966); children: Thomas Scott, Amy Louise Hull Campbell, James Burgess, Bonnie Jo Hull Hart; m. Alice Ida Moore, Dec. 11, 1970. BA, Hiram Coll., 1951; MSFS, Am. Coll., 1983; postgrad. in law, U. Md., 1949. CLU, Chartered fin. cons.

Personnel placement officer U.S. VA, Washington, 1951-55; adminstrv. asst. U.S. Navy Dept., Washington/Orlando, Fla., 1955-60; agt. Mut. Life of N.Y., Orlando, 1960-67; dist. mgr. Jefferson Standard Life, Orlando, 1967-69; assoc. mgr. Acacia Mut. Life, Orlando, 1969-71; account mgr. The Acacia Group, Orlando, 1971-94, ret., 1994; instr. Orange County Adult Edn. and Rollins Coll., Orlando and Winter Park, Fla., 1973-77; lectr. Stetson U., Rollins Coll. and U. Cen. Fla., Orlando, 1975-78. Mem. Alcohol, Drug Abuse and Mental Health Planning Coun., Dist. 7, 1985-91, chair forensics subcom.; bd. dirs. Safety Coun. fo Ctrl. Fla., 1985-93; mem. state com. Seminole County Dem. Party, 1988-91; treas. Unitarian Ch. Endowment Fund, 1988-94, others. Recipient scholarship Cen. Fla. CLU Soc., Orlando, 1978. Mem. Am. Soc. CLUs and Chartered Fin. Cons. (pres. 1976-77), South Orlando Sertoma (pres. 1966-68, 87, Outstanding Mem. 1969), Mental Health Assn. Fla. (v.p. 1982-83), Mental Health Assn. Ctrl. Fla. (pres. 1993-94), Mental Health Assn. Oragne County Pres. 1983-84), U. Club Winter Park (bd. dirs., chair philos. discussion group, v.p. 1996-97), DAV and EX-POWs in Romania, Nat. Assn. Life Underwriters (Nat. Quality award, Nat. Sales Achievement award), Million Dollar Round Table. Unitarian. Home: 546 Lake Ave Altamonte Springs FL 32701-3639

HULL, MARGARET RUTH, artist, educator, consultant; b. Dallas, Mar. 27, 1921; d. William Haynes and Ora Carroll (Adams) Leatherwood; m. LeRos Ennis Hull, Mar. 29, 1941; children: LeRos Ennis, Jr., James Daniel. BA, So. Meth. U., Dallas, 1952, postgrad., 1960-61; MA, North Tex. State U., 1957, postgrad. R.I. Sch. Design, 1982. Art instr. W.W. Bushman Sch., Dallas Ind. Sch. Dist., 1952-57, Benjamin Franklin Jr. High Sch., Dallas, 1957-58; art instr. Hillcrest High Sch., Dallas, 1958-61, dean, pupil personnel counselor, 1961-70; tchr. children's painting Dallas Mus. Fine Art, 1956-70; designer, coordinator visual art careers cluster Skyline High Sch., Dallas, 1970-71, Skyline Career Devel. Ctr., Dallas, 1971-76, Booker T. Washington Arts Magnet High Sch., Dallas, 1976-82; developer curriculum devel./writing art, 1971-82; artist, ednl. cons., 1982—; mus. reprodns. asst. Dallas Mus. Art, 1984-93. Group shows include Dallas Mus. Fine Arts, 1958, Arts Magnet Faculty Shows, 1978-82, Arts Magnet High Sch., Dallas Art Edn. Assn. Show, 1981, D'Art Membership Show, Dallas, 1982-83; represented in pvt. collections. Trustee Dallas Mus. Art, 1978-84. Mem. Tex. Designer/Craftsmen, Craft Guild Dallas, Fiber Artists Dallas, Dallas Art Edn. Assn., Tex. Art Edn. Assn., Nat. Art Edn. Assn., Dallas Counselors Assn. (pres. 1968), Delta Delta Delta.

HULL, STEPHEN SIMMONS, JR., medical educator; b. Jersey City, July 9, 1953; s. Stephen Simmons and Jean Helen (Holthausen) H.; m. Kathryn E. H. Reilly; children: Thomas, David, Kaitlyn. B in Biology, U. Mass., 1975; M in Bio-Med. Engring., Worcester Poly. Inst., 1979; D in Physiology and Biophysics, Mich. State U., 1983. Diplomate Am. Acad. Surg. Rsch. With dept. vet. sci. U. Mass., 1972-75; with Worcester Found. for Exptl. Biology, Shrewsburg, Mass., 1973-79; with dept. bio-med. engring., teaching asst. Worcester Poly. Inst., 1975-79; with dept. physiology, teaching asst. Mich. State U., 1979-83, 83-86; with Okla. Med. Rsch. Found., Oklahoma City, 1986-90; with dept. physiology U. Okla. Health Scis. Ctr., Oklahoma City, 1990—; lectr. Mich. State U., East Lansing, 1984-86, Okla. U. Health Sci. Ctr., 1986, U. Ctrl. Okla., 1989—; vis. teaching prof. med. physiology Universidad Autonoma De Guadalajara, Mex., Assn. Pan Am. States, 1986—; mem. various coms. Mich. State U. and Okla. U. Health Sci. Ctr.; presenter in field. Contbr. chpt. to book and articles to profl. jours; patentee in field. Named Summer Rsch. fellow Worcester Found. for Exptl. Biology, 1974-75, Rsch. fellow Am. Heart Assn. Mich., Mich. State U., 1984-86; recipient Bio-Med. Engring. Teaching/Rsch. fellowship Worcester Poly. Inst., 1976-79, NIH Nat. Rsch. Svc. award pre-doctoral fellowship Mich. State U., 1979-83, Grad. Office award Mich. State U., 1980, H. Lowell Stone Young Investigator award Okla. Affiliate Am. Heart Assn., 1987; grantee in field. Mem. AAAS, IEEE, Am. Physiol. Soc., Engring. in Medicine and Biology Soc., Okla. Acad. Sci., Soc. for Exptl. Biology and Medicine, Acad. Surg. Rsch., Am. Heart Assn. (coun. on basic sci.), Sigma Xi. Episcopalian. Office: Okla Univ Health Scis Ctr Dept Physiology PO Box 26901 Oklahoma City OK 73190-0901

HULL, THOMAS GRAY, federal judge; b. 1926; m. Joan Brandon; children: Leslie, Brandon, Amy. Student, Tusculum Coll.; JD, U. Tenn., 1951. Atty. Easterly and Hull, Greeneville, Tenn., 1951-63; mem. Tenn. Ho. of Reps., 1955-65; atty., prin. Thomas G. Hull, 1951-72; chief clk. Tenn. Ho. of Reps., 1969-70; judge 20th Jud. Cir., Greeneville, Morristown and Rogersville, Tenn., 1972-79; legal counsel to Tenn. Gov. Lamar Alexander, 1979-81; judge U.S. Dist. Ct. (ea. dist.) Tenn., 1983—. Served as cpl. U.S. Army, 1944-46. Mem. Tenn. Bar Assn. (chmn. East dist. com. 1969), Greenville Bar Assn. (pres. 1969-71), Tenn. Jud. Conf. (del. 1972-79, vice chmn. 1974-75, com. to draft uniform charges for trial judges). Republican. Office: Office of US Dist Judge 101 W Summer St Greeneville TN 37743-4944

HULL, WILLIAM EDWARD, theology educator; b. Birmingham, Ala., May 28, 1930; s. William Edward and Margaret (King) H.; m. Julia Wylodine Hester, July 26, 1952; children: David William, Susan Virginia. BA, Samford U., 1951; MDiv, So. Bapt. Theol. Sem., Louisville, 1954, PhD, 1960; postgrad., U. Gottingen, Germany, 1962-63, Harvard U., 1971. Ordained to ministry Bapt. Ch., 1950. Pastor Beulah Bapt. Ch., Wetumpka, Ala., 1950-51, Cedar Hill Bapt. Ch., Owenton, Ky., 1952-53, 1st Bapt. Ch., New Castle, Ky., 1953-58; from instr. to assoc. prof. So. Bapt. Theol. Sem., Louisville, 1954-67, prof., 1967-75, dean theology and provost, 1969-75; pastor 1st Bapt. Ch., Shreveport, La., 1975-87; provost Samford U., Birmingham, Ala., 1987-96, prof., 1996—. Author: Gospel of John, 1964, Broadman Bible Commentary, 1970, Beyond the Barriers, 1981, Love in Four Dimensions, 1982, The Christian Experience of Salvation, 1987, (with others): Professor in the Pulpit, 1963, The Truth That Makes Men Free, 1966, Salvation in Our Time, 1978, Set Apart for Service, 1980, Celebrating Christ's Presence Through the Spirit, 1981, The Twentieth Century Pulpit, Vol. II, 1981, Minister's Manual, 1983-87, Biblical Preaching: An Expositor's Treasury, 1983, Preaching in Today's World, 1984, Heralds to a New Age, 1985, Getting Ready for Sunday: A Practical Guide for Worship Planning, 1989, Best Sermons 2, 1989; contbr. articles to profl. publs. Mem. Futureshape Shreveport (La.) Commn., 1985-87. Recipient Denominational Svc. award Samford U., 1974, Liberty Bell award Shreveport Bar Assn., 1984, Brotherhood and Humanitarian award NCCJ, 1987. Mem. Nat. Assn. Bapt. Profs. Religion (pres. 1967-68), Am. Acad. Religion, Soc. Biblical Lit., The Club (Birmingham), Univ. Club (Shreveport), Vestavia Country Club (Birmingham), Rotary, Phi Kappa Phi, Phi Eta Sigma, Omicron Delta Kappa. Home: 435 Vesclub Way Birmingham AL 35216-1357

HULL, WILLIAM MARTIN, JR., ophthalmologist; b. Rock Hill, S.C., June 23, 1937; s. William Martin and Elizabeth (McDowell) H.; m. Anna Transou, Dec. 14, 1963; children: William Martin III, Alice Howard. BS, Davidson Coll., 1959; MD, Duke U., 1963. Diplomate Am. Bd. Ophthalmology. Intern in medicine Duke Hosp., Durham, N.C., 1963-64, resident in ophthalmology, 1964-67; practice medicine specializing in ophthalmology, Rock Hill, S.C., 1969—; pres. Rock Hill Eye Clinic; mem. staff Piedmont Med. Ctr., 1969—, chief of staff, 1980; bd. dirs. First Union of S.C., People First of Rock Hill. Chmn. S.C. Med PAC, 1975—; bd. dirs. Rock Hill ARC, 1976-80, Catawba Sch., Rock Hill, 1976-81; bd. dirs. S.C. Bd. Health and Environ. Control, 1994—, vice-chmn. Maj. M.C., U.S. Army, 1967-69, Vietnam. Fellow Am. Acad. Ophthalmology; mem. S.C. Med. Assn. (trustee 1978—, vice chmn. bd. trustees 1983-84), S.C. Ophthalmology Assn., (exec. com. 1976-81), York County Med. Soc. (v.p., then pres. 1976-80), Rock Hill C. of C. (bd. dirs. 1978-81), Rock Hill Country Club, Rock Hill Cotillian Club (pres. 1976-81). Episcopalian. Avocations: tennis, skiing, reading, traveling, golfing. Home: 550 Meadowbrook Ln Rock Hill SC 29730-3729 Office: Rock Hill Eye Clinic DEHEC Bd 1565 Ebenezer Rd Rock Hill SC 29732-1806

HULLS, JAMES ROBERT, emergency physician; b. Columbus, Ohio, Sept. 5, 1947; s. Charles Robert and Margaret Rose (Chichka) H.; m. Suzanne Lynn Evans, Dec. 18, 1971; children: Michelle, Kristin. BA, Ohio State U., 1969, MD, 1973. Diplomate Am. Bd. Emergency Medicine, Am. Bd. Forensic Examiners. Intern, resident U. South Fla., 1973-74; emergency physician Univ. Cmty. Hosps., Tampa, Fla., 1974—; asst. dir. emergency dept. Univ. Community Hosp., Tampa, 1993-96; med. advisor City of Tampa Fire Rescue, 1978-96. V.p. North Hillsborough Am. Heart Assn., 1996—. Fellow Am. Coll. Emergency Physicians; mem. AMA, Am. Coll. Forensic Examiners, Am. Heart Assn. (v.p. North Hillsborough chpt.), Hillsborough County Med. Assn. (editl. bd. 1993—). Methodist. Office: Univ Community Hosp 3100 E Fletcher Ave Tampa FL 33613-4613

HULT, KAREN MARIE, political science educator; b. Gary, Ind., Apr. 26, 1956; d. Robert Julius and Rita Ann (Mayer) H. BA, Creighton U., 1978; postgrad., Harvard U., 1979; PhD, U. Minn., 1984. Asst. prof. govt. Pomona Coll., Claremont, Calif., 1984-89, assoc. prof., 1990, dir. program in pub. policy analysis, 1988-90; assoc. prof. polit. sci. Va. Poly. Inst. and State U., Blacksburg, 1990—; analyst HHS, Washington, 1982; cons. Orange County Grand Jury. Author: Agency Merger and Bureaucratic Redesign, 1987, Governing Public Organizations, 1990, Governing the White House, 1995; contbr. articles to profl. jours. Mem. Am. Polit. Sci. Assn., Midwest Polit. Sci. Assn., So. Polit. Sci. Assn., Am. Soc. for Pub. Adminstrn., Policy Studies Orgn. (Lowi award 1990), LWV, AAUW (Palmer fellow 1987-88), NOW, NARAL, Presidency Rsch. Group (Neustadt award 1996). Office: Va Poly Inst and State U Dept Polit Sci Blacksburg VA 24061

HULTQUIST, KARL ALBERT, medical educator; b. Ann Arbor, Mich., Nov. 27, 1951; married; 2 children. BS, Ea. Mich. U., 1974; student, Wayne State U., 1975-76; grad. in respiratory therapy, U. Chgo., 1976. Cert. respiratory therapy technician; registered respiratory therapist; ACLS. Respiratory therapy technician No. Mich. Hosps., Inc., Petoskey, Mich., 1974-75; staff respiratory therapist St. John Hosp., Detroit, 1975-77, Munson Med. Ctr., Traverse City, Mich., 1977-78, Butterworth Hosp., Grand Rapids, Mich., 1978-79; neonatal pediatric clin. coord. Columbus-Cuneo-Cabrini Hosps., Chgo., 1979-80; staff respiratory therapist U. Mich., Ann Arbor, 1980-85, rsch. assoc., clin. coord., instr., 1985-92; instr. Washtenaw C.C., Ann Arbor, 1984-85; rsch. assoc., educator Miami (Fla.) Children's Hosp., 1992—; clin. adj. instr. Ferris State Coll., Big Rapids, Mich., 1978-79; lectr. in field. Contbr. numerous articles to profl. jours. Mem. Am. Soc. Artificial Internal Organs, Am. Assn. Respiratory Care (charter), Nat. Bd. Respiratory Care, Extracorporeal Life Support Prgn. (charter, exec. com. devices and techniques), Soc. Critical Care Medicine. Home: 8856 SW 156th Ter Miami FL 33157-2067 Office: Miami Children 3100 SW 62nd Ave Miami FL 33155-3009

HUMANN, PAUL HULDRICH, writer, photographer; b. Lincoln, Nebr., Nov. 11, 1937; s. H.C. and Glendora (Young) H. BA, Wichita State U., 1961; JD, Washburn U., 1964. Bar: Kans. 1964, U.S. Ct. Appeals (10th cir.) 1964. Atty. Jochems, Sargent & Blass, Wichita, Kans., 1964-71; writer, photographer Hollywood, Fla., 1972—; chmn. bd. dirs. New World Publs., Jacksonville, Fla., 1988—. Author, photographer: Cayman - Underwater Paradise, 1979, Cayman Seascapes, 1986, Galapagos - A Terrestrial & Marine Phenomenon, 1988, A Visit to Grand Cayman, 1988, Beautiful Isles Cayman, 1986, Karibik, 1989, Caraibes, 1989, Reef Fish Identification, 1989, 93, Reef Creature Identification, 1992, Reef Coral Identification, 1993, Galapagos Fish Identification, 1993, Coastal Fish Identification, California to Alaska, 1996; editor: Ocean Realm Mag., 1986-88; contbr. articles and photos to mags. including Nat. Geographic, Skin Diver, Scuba Times, Sportdiving, Sea Frontiers. Pres. Reef Environ. Ednl. Found., Key Largo, Fla., 1991—. Home: 4980 SW 61St Ave Davie FL 33314

HUMBERT, MELANIE LANN LILES, dietitian; b. Henderson, Ky., Dec. 16, 1957; d. Bobby Maurice and Sue Emma (Sauer) Liles; m. Vernon H. Humbert Jr., Jan. 26, 1985; children: Jaimie Lauren, Laurel Corinne. BS in Dietetics, U. Ky., 1975-79. Registered dietitian. Asst. foodsvc. dir. ARA Food Svcs., Lexington, Ky., 1979-83; reg. dietitian Unicare Health Systems, Evansville, Ind., 1983-85; dietitian, nutritionist Valley Health Systems, Huntington, W.Va., 1986-90; bd. dirs. Am. Heart Assn., Huntington, W.Va., 1988-90; chmn. Food Festival, Henderson, Ky., 1995-96; vol. Am. Diabetes Assn., Huntington, 1988-90. Mem. Jr. League, Evansville, Huntington, 1988-92. Mem. Am. Dietetic Assn., Ky. Dietetic Assn., Western Dist. Ky. Dietetic Assn. (awards and honors chmn. 1993-95, treas. 1995-97, Good Samaritan Soc. (fall festival chmn. 1992). Democrat. Roman Catholic. Home: 7674 Green River Rd Henderson KY 42420

HUMBLE, JOAN MARIE, elementary school educator; b. Plainwell, Mich., Mar. 13, 1937; d. John and Goldie Marie Gores; m. Gary W. Humble, Aug. 17, 1957; children: Gary, Anne Marie, Susan Joan, Michael John, Matthew James. BA, Coll. of Santa Fe, 1981; MEd, Lesley Coll., 1989. Tchr. St. Francis Sch., Santa Fe, 1981-82, St. Joseph Sch., El Paso, Tex., 1982-84, Ysleta Ind. Sch. Dist., El Paso, 1986-94, Canutillo (Tex.) Ind. Sch. Dist., 1994—; instr. El Paso C.C., 1989—. Named Tchr. of Yr., Dolphin Terrace Elem. Sch., El Paso, 1994. Mem. Tchrs. English As Second Lang. Roman Catholic.

HUMBLE, LINDA FAYE, librarian, educator; b. Clarksville, Tenn., June 24, 1964; d. Otto William Jr. and Ida Joan (Knight) Kilian; m. Louis Edward Humble Jr., Feb. 25, 1983 (div. Apr. 1989). BS, Austin Peay State U., 1993. Sales assoc. K-Mart, Clarksville, 1985-93; property mgr. Harris Realty, Clarksville, 1993; tchr. Draughons Jr. Coll., Clarksville, 1994-95, libr., 1993—. Democrat. Methodist. Home: 885 Cumberland Dr Clarksville TN 37040 Office: Draughons Jr Coll 1860 Wilma Rudolph Blvd Clarksville TN 37040

HUME, ELLEN HUNSBERGER, broadcast executive, media analyst, journalist; b. Chevy Chase, Md., Apr. 24, 1947; d. Warren Seabury and Ruth (Pedersen) H.; m. John Shattuck, Feb. 14, 1991; 1 child, Susannah; stepchildren: Jessica, Rebecca, Peter. BA, Harvard U., 1968; PhD (hon.), Daniel Webster Coll., 1990. Reporter Somerville (Mass.) Jour., 1968-69; feature writer Santa Barbara (Calif.) News Press, 1969-70; pub. service dir., copy writer KTMS Radio, Santa Barbara, 1970-72; edn. reporter Ypsilanti (Mich.) Press, 1972-73; bus. reporter Detroit Free Press, 1973-75; met. reporter L.A. Times, 1975-77; congl. reporter L.A. Times, Washington, 1977-83; White House corr., polit. writer Wall St. Jour., Washington, 1983-88; exec. dir. Shorenstein-Barone Ctr. on Press and Politics Harvard U., Cambridge, Mass., 1988-93; moderator The Editors TV program, Montreal, Que., 1990-93; adj. lectr. Kennedy Sch. Govt., 1991-93, Medill Sch. Journalism, 1993-94; commentator Washington Week in Rev. PBS-TV, 1973-88, CNN, 1993—; exec. dir. The Democracy Project, PBS, 1996—. Kennedy Inst. Politics fellow Harvard U., 1981, Annenberg Washington Program fellow, 1993-95. Mem. Coun. of Fgn. Rels., Fund for Free Expression, Nat. Press Club. Methodist. Office: Pub Broadcasting Svc 1320 Braddock Pl Alexandria VA 22314

HUME, EVELYN CALDWELL, accounting educator, financial consultant; b. Maryville, Tenn., Apr. 30, 1945; d. Richard H. and Mary Ruth (Maples) Caldwell; m. Clair N. Hume, Dec. 27, 1974; children: Angela Denise Cannon, Dianne Raines Watson. BA in Acctg., U. West Fla., 1983, MA in Acctg., 1984; PhD in Acctg., La. State U., 1988. Owner, CEO Mountain Homes, Inc., Atlanta, 1972-82; asst. prof. acctg. Ga. State U., Atlanta, 1988-93; assoc. prof. acctg. U. South Ala., Mobile, 1993—; dir. Gulf Coast Coun. Nat. Assn. Investors, Pensacola, Fla., 1995—; treas. Profiteers Investment Group, Orange Beach, Ala., 1994—. Contbr. articles to profl. jours. Troop leader Girl Scouts of Am., Atlanta, 1973-75, Jackson, Tenn., 1975-80. Named Bus. Educator of the Yr., Alpha Sigma Alpha, Atlanta, 1991; recipient doctoral rsch. award, Richard D. Irwin Found., Baton Rouge, 1988, Woman Entrepreneur award Women's Bus. Orgn., Atlanta, 1980. Mem. AAUW, Am. Acctg. Assn., Am. Taxation Assn., Nat. Tax Assn., Inst. Mgmt. Accts. Office: 33093 River Rd Orange Beach AL 36561-5721 Office: U South Alabama University Blvd Mobile AL 36688

HUMES, DAVID WALKER, accountant; b. Flint, Mich., Apr. 19, 1954; s. Daniel Baker and Mary Nell (Walker) H.; divorced; children: Baker Maxwell, Madison Campbell. BA, Centre Coll., 1976. CPA, Ky.; lic. real estate agt., lic. ins. agt., Ky.; cert. personal trainer/fitness counselor Aerobics and Fitness Assn. Am. CPA Coopers & Lybrand, Louisville, 1976-80; internal auditor Brown & Williamson Tobacco Co., Louisville, 1980-81; controller Ashford Stud, Versailles, Ky., 1981-83; treas. James Motor Co., Lexington, Ky., 1983-84; pvt. practice David W. Humes CPA PSC, Versailles, 1984—; bd. dirs., v.p., sec. Amber's Magic Pizza, Lexington, Ky.; pres. Number One Sun, Inc. dba Versailles Athletic Club, 1991—. Bd. dirs. BGT for Hist. Preservation, Lexington, 1987-92, v.p., 1989, pres., 1990-91; rep. for Midway to Archtl. Rev. Bd. of Woodford County, Versailles, 1988-90; chmn. BGT Revolving Fund, Lexington, 1988-89; campaign treas. Barrows for Ky. Ho. of Reps., Trapp for Urban County Govt. 10th Dist. Councilman, Trapp for Ky. Ho. of Reps.; mem. Midway City Coun., 1990-93; appointee Versailles-Woodford County Planning and Zoning Bd., Versailles-Woodford County Tech. Rev. Com., 1990-92. Mem. AICPA, Ky. Soc. CPAs, Woodford County Hist. Soc., Woodford County Fair Saddle Horse Show (advisor 1988-93), ISSAC Shelby Soc. of Centre Coll., Nat. Trust for Hist. Preservation, Lions Club Internat. Democrat. Roman Catholic. Home: 110 Maple St Versailles KY 40383 Office: PO Box 999 125 N Main St Versailles KY 40383-0999

HUMM, CHARLES ALLEN, sales and marketing professional; b. Jefferson City, Mo., Dec. 2, 1942; s. Leonard J. and Hazel T. (Schwartz) Humm; m. Elizabeth D. Houseman, May 31, 1943; children: Melani, Anita, Stephanie, Natalie, Brett. B of Journalism, U. Mo., 1964; MBA in Mktg., St. Louis U., 1973. CFP; registered investment advisor. Product mgr. Ralston Purina, St. Louis, 1973-77; v.p. account supr. Wells Rich Greene-Gardner Advt., N.Y.C. and St. Louis, 1965-73; mktg. mgr. Anheuser Busch, St. Louis, 1977-79; v.p. mktg. Norton Simon-Avis, Garden City, N.Y., 1979-82; sr. v.p. mktg. Merrill Lynch Credit Corp., Jacksonville, Fla., 1982-95, sr. v.p., group mgr. mortgage and credit svcs., 1995—. Contbr. articles to profl. jours. Mem. Keel Club United Fund, Jacksonville, 1993. Recipient Pub. Rels. Merit award L.A. Press Club, 1993, Golden Anvil PRSA, 1985. Mem. Securities Industry Inst., Mortgage Bankers Assn. Republican. Roman Catholic. Home: 2633 S Ponte Vedra Blvd Ponte Vedra Beach FL 32082-4525 Office: Merrill Lynch Credit Corp 4802 Deer Lake Dr E Jacksonville FL 32246-6484

HUMMEL, DANA D. MALLETT, librarian; BA in Art History, Smith Coll., 1957; MA in Libr. and Info. Sci., Denver U., 1968; postgrad. Def. Lang. Inst., 1961, Instituto Mexicano-Norteamericano de Relationes Culturales, 1962, John F. Kennedy Ctr. for Spl. Warfare, 1974, Nat. War Coll., 1976, No. Va. Bus. Sch., 1978, Cath. U. Am., 1981. Head libr., administrn., Howard AFB Libr., C.Z., 1969-70; asst. libr. Holmes Intermediate Sch., 1970-71; tchr. Spanish and substitute tchr. J.E.B. Stuart High Sch., 1972-77; sec. Office of exec. dir.-Africa The World Bank, 1978-79; personal sec. to rector Falls Ch. (Va.), 1979-81; mgr. Info. Svcs. Ctr., BDM Internat. subs. Ford Aerospace Co., McLean, Va., 1981-88. Mem. vestry Falls Ch. Episcopal Ch., 1982; del. Republican State Conv., 1981, 86; pres. Ravenwood Civic Assn., 1979-80, 80-81, 81-82; rep. Mason Dist., Fedn. Civic Assns.; mem. ann. plan rev. task force Mason Dist., 1981-82; gov. trustee Fairfax County Pub. Libr. Bd., 1982-88; chmn. bd. trustees Fairfax County. Named Outstanding Woman of Yr., Fairfax County Bd. Suprs. and Com. of Women, 1982. Mem. AAUP, ALA, Am. Soc. for Info. Sci., Spl. Libr. Assn., Va. Libr. Assn., D.C. Libr. Assn., Women in Def., Villa D'Este Assn. (bd. dirs. 1995—), Jr. League Sarasota, Fla. Home: 7355 Villa D Este Dr Sarasota FL 34238-5649

HUMMEL, KAY JEAN, physical therapist; b. Cleve., Apr. 24, 1943; d. Lloyd Elmer and Olive Agnes (Latou) Hetherington; m. Charles William Hummel (div. Feb. 1984); children: Patrick H., Robin E. BA, Miami U., Oxford, Ohio, 1965; cert. in phys. therapy, Columbia U., N.Y., 1966. Lic. phys. therapist, La.; cert. ofcl. Games Uniting Mind and Body. Staff phys. therapist St. Joseph's Hosp., Chgo., 1966-68, Wrightwood Extended Care Facility, Chgo., 1967-68, Suburban Hosp., Bethesda, Md., 1969, Holy Cross Hosp., Silver Spring, Md., 1969-70; asst. chief phys. therapist Community Gen. Hosp., Syracuse, N.Y., 1970-76; itinerant phys. therapist Caddo Parish Schs., Shreveport, La., 1976—; pvt. practice Shreveport, 1985—; bd. dirs. Games Uniting Mind & Body, Inc. Mem. U.S. Cerebral Palsy Athletic Assn. (regional classifier), Presbyn. Women's Club of Shreveport, Kappa Delta Alumni Assn. Office: Caddo Exceptional Sch 3202 William Ave Shreveport LA 71103-4246

HUMMELL, BURTON HOWARD, food distribution company executive; b. Chgo., Aug. 17, 1932; s. Arnold A. and Martha (Ellenstein) H.; m. Joan Claire Lapin, Aug. 23, 1953; children: Ross Bennett, Arthur Robert, Reed Evan. BBA, U. Miami, Coral Gables, Fla., 1953. V.p. ops. S.E. Rykoff & Co., L.A., 1963-75; pres. Internat. Foodservice Co., Carson, Calif., 1975-80; pres., CEO Robert Orr-Sysco Foodservices, Nashville, 1980—, chmn., ceo, 1996—; mem. Dirs. Coun. Sysco Corp. Bd. dirs. Arthritis Found., Nashville Symphony, Nashville Inst. of Arts, Heart Gala Bd.; sr. co-chair Nat. Conf.; Met. commr. for Nashville Conv. Ctr.; mem. corp. bd. Baptist Hosp., Julia Hereford Soc. Nat. Hotel/Motel Assn. scholarship established in his honor Cornell U., 1986. Mem. Foodsvc. Mktg. Assn. (pres. 1972-75), Les Amis d'Escoffier, Un Ete du Vin, Confrerie de la Chaine des Rotisseurs (bailli honoraire of Nashville chpt.), Nashville City Club, L'Ordre Mondail, Golf Club of Tenn., Rotary. Jewish. Home: 601 Lynnbrook Rd Nashville TN 37215-1025 Office: Robert Orr-Sysco Food Svcs 1 Hermitage Plz # 305137 Nashville TN 37209-1002

HUMPHREVILLE, JOHN DAVID, lawyer; b. Harrisburg, Pa., Feb. 4, 1953; s. Robert E. and Winifred (MacNulty) H.; m. Laurie Wettstone, Mar. 6, 1976; children: Caroline Elizabeth, John Evin. BS, Pa. State U., 1977; MA in Govt. Adminstrn., U. Pa., 1984; JD, Cath. U. Am., 1986. Bar: Fla. 1986, U.S. Dist. Ct. (mid. dist.) Fla. 1987, D.C. 1988. Dir. bur. real estate Pa. Dept. Gen. Svcs., Harrisburg, 1979-80; dep. adminstrv. asst. to gov. State of Pa., Harrisburg, 1980-83; assoc. Shackleford, Farrior, Stallings & Evans, P.A., Tampa, Fla., 1986-90; ptnr. Icard, Merrill, Cullis, Timm, Furren & Ginsburg, P.A., Tampa, 1990; asst. to atty. gen. U.S. Dept. Justice, Washington, 1990-91; ptnr. Quarles & Brady, Naples, Fla., 1991—; mem. Fed. Jud. Adv. Commn., 1989-91; spl. counsel Asst. Atty. Gen. environ. divsn. U.S. Dept. Justice, Washington, 1991. Office: Quarles & Brady 4501 Tamiami Trl N Ste 300 Naples FL 34103-3023

HUMPHREY, JOHN EDWARD, psychiatrist; b. Milledgeville, Ga., Nov. 7, 1949; s. John Edward Humphrey and Colleen June (Moore) Filley; divorced; children: Melissa Jordan, Zachary John; m. Karen M. BS in Applied Psychology, Ga. Inst. Tech., 1971; MD, Duke U., 1975; resident in psychiatry, U. Washington, Seattle, 1978. Diplomate Am. Bd. Psychiatry and Neurology. Med. dir. Valley Cities Mental Health Ctr., Auburn, Wash., 1978-79; intensive svcs. dir. Trend Mental Health Ctr., Hendersonville, N.C., 1979-80; outpatient clin dir. Mecklenburg County Mental Health, Charlotte, N.C., 1980-82; psychiatrist Eastover Psychol. & Psychiat. Group P.A., Charlotte, N.C., 1982—; cons. Bapt. Counseling Ctr., Charlotte, 1983—. Mem. Am. Psychiat. Assn., Mecklenburg County Med. Soc. Office: Eastover Psychol & Psychiat Group PA 3303 Latrobe Dr Charlotte NC 28211-4851

HUMPHREYS, CHARLES RAYMOND, JR., retired research chemist; b. Wilmington, N.C., Aug. 14, 1911; s. Charles Raymond and Lilian Miller (Kenly) H.; m. Mary Lillian Knotts, June 22, 1940; 1 child, Howard Joshua. BS in Chemistry, Duke U., 1934. Analytical chemist duPont Ctrl. Chem. Dept., Wilmington, 1934-38; rsch. chemist original nylon rsch. sect. duPont, Wilmington, 1939-43, supr. field rsch. textile fibers dept., 1943-48; asst. mgr. tech. svd. Ducilo, Buenos Aires, Argentina, 1948-50, mgr. tech. svc. and market analysis, 1951-53; asst. mgr. export sales, textile fibers duPont, Wilmington, 1954-56, sr. rsch. chemist textile rsch. end use devel., 1956-72. Author: The Devil's Left Ear, 1989, Panthers of the Coastal Plain, 1994; patentee in field. Lectr. to civic groups, Wilmington, N.C., 1973-96. Mem. Lower Cape Fear Bird Club, Hobby Greenhouse. Republican. Home: 1132 Princeton Dr Wilmington NC 28403

HUMPHREYS, HOMER ALEXANDER, former principal; b. nr. Waynesboro, Va., Feb. 7, 1902; s. Lewis Greenberry and Annie (Sampson) H.; B.A., Bridgewater Coll., 1928; M.A., U. Va., 1941, research fellow, 1943-44; m. Ruth Elizabeth Gilbert, Sept. 1, 1926; children—Faye (Mrs. Hezekiah Sadler), Joye (Mrs. James Malcolm Hart Harris, Jr.), Anne (Mrs. Richard Edward Talman), Homer Alexander, Jane (dec.), Kaye. Instr. Moyock (N.C.) High Sch., 1928-29; prin. Darlington Heights (Va.) High Sch., 1929-33, Green Bay (Va.) High Sch., 1934-44; supervising prin. West Point (Va.) High Sch., 1944-65; gen. supr. instrn. Williamsburg-James City County Schools, 1965-67; instr. Bridgewater Coll., summer 1944; dir. aviation edn. Mont. State U., Missoula, also Eastern Coll. Edn., Billings, Mont., summers 1954, 55, U. Va., Charlottesville, summers 1956-71; instr. Coll. William and Mary Extension, 1963-68. Coordinator, Civil Def., King William County and Town of West Point, 1950-61. Served from 2d lt. to lt. col. USAF, CAP, 1945—; dir. aviation edn. Va. Wing, Civil Air Patrol, 1956-65. Mem. NEA (past 2d zone v.p. dept. audio-visual instrn.), Va. High Sch. League (chmn.

1955-57), King William-King and Queen Edn. Assn. (pres. 1956-58), Phi Delta Kappa. Kiwanian (pres. West Point 1949, lt. gov. capital dist. div. four 1956). Author: A History of Education in Prince Edward County, Va., 1941; column Wings Over Va., 1956-62; also numerous articles, reports and surveys. Home: 110 Oxford Cir Williamsburg VA 23185-3226

HUMPHREYS, MARGARET ELLEN, historian, educator, physician; b. New Orleans, Dec. 6, 1955; d. Kelton Brooks and Mary Ellen (Donnelly) H. BA, U. Notre Dame, 1976; MA, Harvard U., 1977, PhD, 1983, MD, 1987. Diplomate Am. Bd. Internal Medicine. Lectr. Harvard U., Boston, 1990-92; asst. prof. Duke U., Durham, N.C., 1993—; physician Harvard Cmty. Health Plan, Quincy, Mass., 1990-93, Duke U., Durham, 1993—; mem. publs. com. Wood Inst., Phila., 1994—. Author: Yellow Fever and the South, 1992; contbr. articles to profl. jours. Mem. ACP, Am. Assn. for History of Medicine (coun. 1993), History of Sci. Soc., Soc. Gen. Internal Medicine, Phi Beta Kappa, Sigma Xi. Democrat. Episcopalian. Office: Duke Univ Dept History Box 90719 Durham NC 27708

HUMPHREYS-MUSSELMAN, CAROLYN EARL (LYN EARL), marriage and family counselor; b. Little Rock, Apr. 19, 1926; d. Robert David and Caro Lee (Reed) Earl; m. Patrick O'Keefe Humphreys, June 19, 1948 (dec. Feb. 1972); children: Laureen Humphreys Schmidt and Kathleen Humphreys Dean (twins); m. John E. Musselman, Oct. 21, 1978. AA, Chevy Chase Jr. Coll., 1945; BA, U. N.C., 1947; MS, Tex. Women's U., 1979. Lic. Tex. State Bd. Examiners Profl. Counselors, Tex. State Bd. Examiners Marriage and Family Therapists. Asst. counselor M.H.M.R., Abilene, Tex., 1979-80; counselor Pastoral Care & Counseling Ctr., Abilene, Tex., 1980-81, pvt. practice, Albany, Tex., 1981—; presenter in field, owner Foreman's Cottage Musselman Ranch bed and breakfast. Mem. Am. Counseling Assn., Am. Assn. Marriage & Family Therapy, Tex. Counseling Assn., Tex. Assn. Marriage & Family Therapy (Tex. state bd. of agy. on aging 1981-82), DAR (regent 1994—), Dallas Woman's Club, Albany Study Club (treas. 1990-92), Phi Beta Phi. Republican. Methodist. Home and Office: Jolyn Box 1477 Albany TX 76430

HUMPHRIES, FREDERICK S., university president; b. Apalachicola, Fla., Dec. 26, 1935; m. Antoinette Humphries; children: Frederick S., Robin Tanya, Laurence Anthony. B.S. magna cum laude, Fla. A&M U., 1957; Ph.D. in Phys. Chemistry (fellow), U. Pitts., 1964. Pvt. tutor sci. and math., 1959-64; asst. prof. chemistry U. Minn., Mpls., 1966-67; asso. prof. chemistry Fla. A&M U., 1964-67, prof. chemistry, 1964-67, dir. 13 coll. curriculum program, 1967-68; dir. summer confs. Inst. for Services to Edn., 1968-74, dir. interdisciplinary program, 1973-74, dir. two-univs. grad. program in sci., 1973-74, v.p., 1970-74; pres. Tenn. State U., Nashville, 1974-85, Fla. A&M U., Tallahassee, 1985—; cons. to various colls. and univs.; mem. bd. grad. advocates Meharry Med. Coll. 1976, co-chmn. Reston's Black Focus, 1973; bd. dirs. So. Growth, Nat. Merit Scholarship Corp. Bd.; bd. regents 5-Yr. Working Group for Agriculture, chmn. State Univ. System of Fla.; adv. coun. Panhandle Regional Ctr. Excellence in Math., Sci., Computers, Tech.-FAMU & U., West Fla.; Nat. Assn. Ednl. Opportunities sci. and tech. adv. com., vice chmn. bd. dirs.; mem. Nissan adv. com. HBCUs. Contbr. articles on higher edn. to profl. publs. Chmn. Fairfax county Anti-Poverty Commn., 1972-74, White House Sci. and Tech. Adv. Com., on Edn. Blacks in Fla.; bd. dirs. YMCA, 1975—, Walmart Corp., Brinker Internat., Barnett Bank Tallahassee; bd. ann. minority bus. Youth Ednl. Svc. Embarkment; commn. Future of South, 1986, com. tech. and innovation commn.; steering com. Apalachicola Bay Area Resource Planning and Mgmt.; subcom. Fed. Student Fin. Assistance-Office for the Advancement of Pub. Black Colls., chmn. adv. com. Recipient Disting. Svc. to Advancement of Edn. for Black Americans award Inst. for Svcs. to Edn., Disting. Edn. and Adminstr.; Meritorious award Fla. A&M U., Human Rels. award Met. Human Rels. Commn., Nashville, 1978, Thurgood Marshall Ednl. Achievement award Johnson Publ. Co., 1990; named an Outstanding Alumnus of Pitts. U., 1986. Mem. NIH (nat. adv. com. neurol. and communicative disorders and stroke coun.), AAUP, AAAS, NAACP, Am. Chem. Soc., Am. Assn. Higher Edn., Nat. Assn. State Univs. and Land-Grant Colls. (chmn.), Nat. Assn. Equal Opportunity Bd. Dirs. (chmn.), Assn. Minority Rsch. Univ., Alpha Kappa Mu (pres., award), Alpha Phi Alpha (Meritorious Svc. award). Office: Fla A&M U Office of President Tallahassee FL 32307

HUMPHRIES, JAMES DONALD, III, lawyer; b. Newark, Ohio, Sept. 27, 1944; s. Howald Garland and Marjorie Louise (Bailey) H.; m. Patricia Lawver, Apr. 8, 1972; children: James Donald IV, P. Laing. BS, Washington and Lee U., 1966, JD cum laude, 1969. Bar: Ga. 1970, Fla. 1987, D.C. 1988. Assoc. Kilpatrick & Cody, Atlanta, 1969-73; ptnr. Harland, Cashin, Chambers & Parker, Atlanta, 1973-75, Morton, Humphries & Payne, Atlanta, 1976-79, Varner, Stephens, Humphries & White, LLP, Atlanta, 1979—; bd. dirs. various cos. Mem. Lawyers Club Atlanta (pres. 1982-83), Atlanta Lawyers Found. (trustee 1984-88, chmn. 1986), Atlanta Legal Aid Soc. (pres., bd. dirs. 1987-94). Republican. Episcopalian. Clubs: Capital City, Old War Horse Lawyers Litigation. Home: 790 Kinloch NW Atlanta GA 30327-3628 Office: 3350 Cumberland Cir NW Ste 1700 Atlanta GA 30339-3332

HUMPHRIES, JOAN ROPES, psychologist, educator; b. Bklyn., Oct. 17, 1928; d. Lawrence Gardner and Adele Lydia (Zimmermann) Ropes; m. Charles C. Humphries, Apr. 4, 1957; children: Peggy Ann, Charlene Adele. BA, U. Miami, 1950; MS, Fla. State U., 1955; PhD, La. State U., 1963. Part-time instr. psychology dept. U. Miami, Coral Gables, Fla., 1964-66; prof. behavioral studies dept. Miami-Dade C.C., 1966—. Registered lobbyist State of Fla. Presenter in field. Prodr., prin. host (videos) Strategies in Global Modern Academia: Issues and Answers in Higher Education, 1993-94; prodr. and host (video) Strategies in Global Modern Academia: Issues and Answers in Higher Education, II, 1995. Mem. Biofeedback Delegation to the People's Republic of China and Hong Kong, 1995. Mem. AAUP (past v.p. and sec., pres. Miami-Dade C.C. chpt. 1986—, past v.p. Fla. conf., 1986-88, mem. exec. bd. Fla. conf. 1989-90, mem. Nat.), AAUW (life, former v.p. Tamiami branch 1983-88, Appreciation award 1977) Biofeedback Soc. of Am. (pres. 1989—), Biofeedback Assn. Fla. (pres. 1990—), Internat. Platform Assn. (gov. 1979—, Silver Bowl award 1993), APA, Am. Psychol. Soc. (charter), Fla. Psychol. Assn., Mexico Beach C. of C. (bus. 1991—), North Campus Speaker's Bur. (award for community lecture series), Physicians for Social Responsibility, Internat. Soc. for Study Subtle Energies and Energy Medicine (charter), Inst. Evaluation, Diagnosis and Treatment (past v.p. 1975-87, pres. 1987—, former bd. dirs.), Dade-Monroe Psychol. Assn., Assn. Applied Psychophysiology and Biofeedback, Noetic Scis., Colonial Dames 17th Century, N.Y. Acad. Scis. (life), Regines in Miami, Soc. Mayflower Descs. (elder William Brewster colony), Hereditary Order of Descendants of Colonial Govs., Phi Lambda (founder's plaque 1976, appreciation award 1987), Phi Lambda Pi. Democrat. Clubs: Country of Coral Gables (life), Jockey (life). Editorial staff, maj. author: The Application of Scientific Behaviorism to Humanistic Phenomena, 1975, rev. edit., 1979; researcher in biofeedback and human consciousness. Home: 1311 Alhambra Cir Coral Gables FL 33134-3521 Office: Miami Dade CC North Campus 11380 NW 27th Ave Miami FL 33167-3418

HUMPHRIES, LAURIE LEE, child and adolescent psychiatrist, researcher; b. Atlanta, Apr. 26, 1944; d. Olin Price and Laurie (Baggarly) L.; m. Asa Alan Humphries Jr., July 22, 1972; 1 child, Laura Catherine. BA, Emory U., 1966, MD, 1973. Diplomate Am. Bd. Psychiatry and Neurology. Resident in psychiatry Emory U. Sch. Medicine, Atlanta, 1973-75, fellow in child psychiatry, 1975-77, asst. prof., 1978-81; asst. prof. U. Ky., Lexington, 1981-87, assoc. prof., 1987-92, prof., 1992—. Recipient of Child-Adolescent Acad. award NIMH, 1989-94, Disting. Alumni award Westminster Schs., 1990. Fellow APA, Am. Acad. Child and Adolescent Psychiatry, Kappa Kappa Gamma (Nat. Alumni award, 1988). Office: U Ky Dept Psychiatry 820 N Limestone St Lexington KY 40505-3552

HUMWAY, RONALD JIMMIE, state agency administrator; b. Little Rock, Aug. 1, 1945; s. James Joseph and Rosalie (Ferguson) H.; m. Deborah Ann Northcutt, June 26, 1970; children: James Russell, Zachary Paul. AA, Southwestern Coll., Oklahoma City, 1967; BS in Econs., Oklahoma City U., 1969; BS in Acctg., U. Ark., Little Rock, 1978. CPA, Ark.; cert. fraud examiner. Field auditor Holiday Inns, Inc., Memphis, 1969-70; field auditor, supr. Ark. Div. Legis. Audit, Little Rock, 1970—; regional mgr. Ark. Div. Legis. Audit, Jonesboro, 1985—. Served with USAR, 1963-71. Mem. AICPA, Assn. Govt. Accts. (sec.-treas. Ctrl. ARk. chpt. 1976-77), SCV, Assn. Cert. Fraud Examiners. Baptist. Home: 2709 White Cir Jonesboro AR 72404-6961 Office: Ark Div Legis Audit 2920 Mcclellan Dr Ste 1110 Jonesboro AR 72404-7207

HUNG, MIEN-CHIE, cancer biologist; b. Taiwan, Sept. 4, 1950. BS in Chemistry, Nat. Taiwan U., 1973, MS in Biochemistry, 1977; MA, PhD, Brandeis U., 1983. Postdoctoral fellow Whitehead Inst. MIT, 1984-86; asst. prof. virology tumor biology dept. U. Tex. M.D. Anderson Cancer Ctr., Houston, 1986-91, assoc. prof., 1991-94, prof. virology, 1994—; dir. Breast Cancer Basic Research Prog. and Hubert L. and Olive Stringer Endowed Prof., 1996—; mem. spl. rev. com. for PO-1 Nat. Cancer Inst. L.A., 1990, grant rev. com. Israel Sci. Found., 1993-94, NIH Pathology B Study Sect., 1994—, nat. biochemistry study sect., 1994—; mem. adv. bd. Inst. fur Klinische Chemie und Laboratoriumsmedizin-Zentrallaboratorium, Germany, 1993-94, Nat. Taiwan U. Hosp., 1992-94; cons. R Gene Therapeutics Inc., 1994-96, Devel. Ctr. for Biotechnology, Taipei, Taiwan, 1994; guest prof. Xiaman U., Peoples Republic of China, 1991-93, Shanghai Med. U., 1994-96. Mem. editl. bd. Oncology Reports, 1994-96, Biomed. Jour., 1994-96; contbr. numerous articles to profl. jours. With Taiwanese Mil., 1973-75. Mem. Am. Assn. for Cancer Rsch., AAAS, Am. Soc. Microbiology, Metastasis Rsch. Sco., Soc. Chinese Bioscientists in Am. No., Am. Taiwanese Profs. Assn. Home: 5762 Birdwood Rd Houston TX 77096-2109 Office: U Tex MD Anderson Cancer Ctr BF 7-001 Box 79 Houston TX 77030

HUNGATE, JOSEPH IRVIN, III, computer scientist; b. San Antonio, Nov. 17, 1956; s. Joseph Irvin Jr. and Betty Lou (Hatzenbuehler) H.; m. Santa Michelle Haines, May 15, 1993; children: Brittany Nicole, Annabel Sue. BS in Computer Sci., U. S.C., 1979, MS in Computer Sci., 1981; postgrad., U. Va., 1982-83. Teaching asst. U. S.C., Columbia, 1979-81; sr. systems analyst GE, Charlottesville, Va., 1981-85; mgr. software devel. TRW, Fairfax, Va., 1985-88, prin. investigator, 1996—; mgr. field engring. TRW, London, 1988-93; supervisory computer scientist Nat. Inst. Stds. and Tech. U. S. Dept. Commerce, Gaithersburg, Md., 1993-96; mem. EIA Working Group RS-511, Detroit, 1983-85; recruitment coord. Affirmative Action, Fairfax, 1986-88; spl. liaison European Workshop on Open Sys., Brussels, 1993-96; chmn. Open Sys. Implementator's Workshop, Gaithersburg, 1993—. Mem. Va. Student Aid Found., Charlottesville, 1985—; vol. coord. blood svcs. ARC, Fairfax, 1985-88; vol. Arlington County (Va.) Dem. Com., 1985—; bd. dirs. Hungate Family Hist. Soc., Inc., Chevy Chase, Md., 1989—. Recipient commendation USN, London, 1990; scholar S.C. Ednl. Found., 1975. Mem. IEEE Computer Soc., Assn. for Computing Machinery, Am. Mgmt. Assn., Sigma Phi Epsilon. Methodist. Home: 967 N Rochester St Arlington VA 22205-1524 Office: TRW FPI/3121 One Federal Systems Park Fairfax VA 22033

HUNKER, FRED DOMINIC, internist, medical educator; b. Montgomery, Ala., Nov. 13, 1947; s. Joseph Frederick and Frances Cecelia (Armbruster) H.; m. Edith Margaret McCulloch, Sept. 25, 1976; children: Marie Elizabeth, Emily Kathleen, Jacob Dominic. BA in English, Creighton U., 1969; MD, U. Nebr., 1974. Diplomate Nat. Bd. Med. Examiners, Am. Bd. Internal Medicine (SEP com. 1992-96), subspeciality pulmonary medicine (mem. self-evaluation process com. for pulmonary disease 1992-96); lic. physician Ala. Intern U. Ala. Sch. Medicine, Birmingham, 1974-75, resident, chief resident and instr. medicine, 1975-77, 78-79, fellow in pulmonary medicine, 1977-78, clin. asst. prof., 1979-93, clin. assoc. prof., 1993—; founder Montgomery Pulmonary Cons., P.A., 1979; pres. med. staff St. Margaret's Hosp., 1986-88; chmn. coun. on animal and environ. health Ala. Bd. Pub. Health, 1983-86; regional adv. bd. Mutual Assurance Inc., Birmingham, 1990—; chmn. dept. medicine Bapt. Med. Ctr., 1982-84, chmn. ICU com. 1987-91, exec. com., 1982-84; exec. com. St. Margaret's Hosp./Humana Montgomery, 1988—, credentials com., 1985—. Contbr. articles to profl. jours. Bd. dirs. Am. Lung Assn. Ala., 1984—, exec. com. 1990—, v.p., 1996—, chmn. awards and grants com. 1984-96; Montgomery adv. bd. S.E. Health Plan, 1985-88; physician vol. Maceio, brazil, 1973; bd. dirs. Queen of Mercy Elem. Sch., 1986-91, Combined Montgomery Cath. Schs., 1992—; founding mem., bd. dirs. Endowment Found. for Queen of Mercy Sch.; chmn. Physician's divsn. United Way Campaign, 1987-88; charter mem., bd. dirs. Physicians and Dentists Charities, Montgomery, 1988-91, Leadership Montgomery Class X, 1993-94; mem. coalition for Tobacco Free Ala. Knight Comdr. of the Equestrian Order of the Holy Sepulchre, 1990—. Fellow Am. Coll. Chest Physicians; mem. AMA, ACP (assoc.), Am. Thoracic Soc. (coun. of chpt. reps., state rep. 1988-94, tng. and continuing med. edn. com. 1992-94), Ala. Thoracic Soc. (pres. 1986-87), Nat. Assn. Med. Dirs. of Respiratory Care, Am. Soc. Internal Medicine, Med. Assn. State of Ala. (controlled substances adv. com. 1992-93, coun. on med. edn. 1991-95), Med. Soc. Montgomery County (pres. 1988-89, bd. censors 1989-96), Montgomery C. of C., KC (3d degree), Capital City Club. Roman Catholic. Home: 1595 Gilmer Ave Montgomery AL 36104-5619 Office: Montgomery Pulmonary Cons 1440 Narrow Lane Pky Montgomery AL 36111-2654

HUNNICUTT, VICTORIA ANNE WILSON, school system administrator; b. Tyler, Tex., July 23, 1944; d. Leroy G. and N. Joseline (Bobo) Wilson; m. John Walter Hubble, July 29, 1967 (div. Oct. 1972); m. Buford D. Hunnicutt, Aug. 1, 1982. BA, Emory and Henry Coll., 1966; MEd, Mercer U., 1970; Ed specialist, U. Ga., 1993. Tchr. Spanish/English Marion (Va.) Sr. H.S., 1966-67; tchr. Spanish Ballard Hudson Middle Sch., Macon, 1967-68; reading specialist Robins AFB Sch. System, Warner Robins, Ga., 1973-74, Spanish tchr., 1968-70, classroom tchr., 1970-86, computer/sci. specialist, 1986-90, prin. Robins Elem. Sch., 1991, curriculum coord., 1990—; adj. prof. Tift Coll., Forsyth, Ga., 1985-88, Ft. Valley State Coll., 1993—. Treas. Bibb County Dem. Women, Macon, Ga., 1986-88, membership chair 1989-93. Mem. AAUW, ASCD, NSTA, NAFE, Nat. Coun. Tchrs. of English, Ga. Coun. of Internat. Reading Assn., Internat. Reading Assn., HOPE Coun., Ga. coun. of Internat. Reading Assn. (pres. 1994-95), Nat. Audubon Soc., Ocmulgee Audubon Soc. (edn. chair 1986-93, v.p. 1991-92), Air Force Assn. (treas. chpt. 296 1989-91, v.p. for aerospace edn. chpt. 296 1991-93, v.p. chpt. 296 1993-94, v.p. for aerospace edn. Ga. State AFA, 1992—, Tchr. of Yr. 1995, Jane Shirley McGee award 1990, Medal of Merit 1990). Democrat. Methodist. Office: Robins AFB Sch System 1050 Education Way Robins AFB GA 31098-1043

HUNSTEIN, CAROL, judge; b. Miami, Fla., Aug. 16, 1944. AA, Miami-Dade Jr. Coll., 1970; BS, Fla. Atlantic U., 1972; JD, Stetson U., 1976. Bar: Ga. 1976; U.S. Dist. Ct. 1978; U.S. Ct. Appeals 1978; U.S. Supreme Ct. 1989. Legal practice Atlanta, 1976-84; judge Superior Ct. of Ga. (Stone Mt. cir.), 1984-92; justice Supreme Ct. of Ga., Atlanta, 1992—; chair Ga. Commn. on Gender Bias in the Judicial System 1989—; pres.-elect Coun. of Superior Ct. Judges of Ga. 1990—. Recipient Clint Green Trial Advocacy award 1976, Women Who Made A Difference award Dekalb Women's Network 1986. Mem. Ga. Assn. of Women Lawyers, Nat. Assn. of Women Judges (dir. 1988-90), Bleckley Inn of Ct., State Bar Ga. Office: Supreme Ct Ga 244 Washington St Rm 572 Atlanta GA 30334

HUNT, CHRISTINE MARIE, gastroenterologist; b. Alexandria, Va., Nov. 11, 1956; d. Kenneth Francis and Cornelia Ann (Buckley) Hunt; m. Gregg Martin Stave, Sept. 12, 1987; 1 child, Elise Adriana. BS in Biochemistry, U. Mass., 1978; MD, Boston U., 1982. Diplomate Am. Bd. Internal Medicine with subspecialty in gastroenterology; lic. physician N.C. Intern Boston VA Med. Ctr., 1982-83, resident in internal medicine, 1983-85; fellow in gastroenterology Med. Coll. Va./McGuire VA Med. Ctr., 1985-87; instr. internal medicine/gastroenterology Med. Coll. Va., 1987-88; staff physician and rsch. assoc. McGuire VA Med. Ctr., 1987-88; asst. prof. internal medicine/gastroenterology Duke U. Sch. Medicine, Durham, N.C., 1988—; lectr. in field; seminar organizer. Ad hoc reviewer Gastroenterology; contbr. articles to profl. jours., chpts. to books. Mem. Am. Gastroenterol. Assn., Am. Assn. Study Liver Disease. Office: Duke Univ Sch Medicine Divsn of Gastroenterology PO Box 3064 Durham NC 27710

HUNT, DAVID FORD, lawyer; b. Ft. Worth, Apr. 7, 1931; s. John Greffrey and Bernice (Ford) H. BS, North Tex. State U., 1954; JD, Vanderbilt U., 1960. Bar: Tex. 1961. Law clk. to U.S. dist. judge No. Dist. Tex., 1960-62; pvt. practice, Dallas, 1962-94; ptnr. Jenkens & Gilchrist, P.C., Dallas, 1980-92, of counsel, 1993-94; atty. pvt. practice, Roanoke, Tex., 1995—; chmn. com. on admissions Dist. 6 Tex. State Bd. Law Examiners, 1978-87. Contbr. articles to legal jours. Co-chmn. pollwatchers com. Dallas County Republican Com., 1964; Sec. Bootstrap Ranch, 1972-74; pres. So. Methodist U. Lambda Chi Edn. Found., 1972-76. Served with AUS, 1954-56. Mem. Tex. Bar Assn., Dallas Bar Assn., Vanderbilt U. Law Sch. Alumni Assn. (pres. Dallas chpt. 1972-75), Lambda Chi (chancellor 1966-68). Home and Office: RR 3 Box 225D Roanoke TX 76262-9639

HUNT, JAMES BAXTER, JR., governor, lawyer; b. Guilford County, N.C., May 16, 1937; s. James Baxter and Elsie (Brame) H.; m. Carolyn Joyce Leonard, Aug. 20, 1958; children: Rebecca Hunt Hawley, James Baxter Hunt III, Rachel Hunt, Elizabeth Hunt. BS in Agrl. Edn., N.C. State U., 1959, MS in Agrl. Econs., 1962; JD, U. N.C., 1964. Bar: N.C. 1964. Econ. advisor H.M. Govt. of Nepal for Ford Found., 1964-66; ptnr. Kirby, Webb and Hunt, 1966-72; lt. gov. State of N.C., 1973-77, gov., 1977-85, 1993—; ptnr. Poyner and Spruill, Raleigh, N.C., 1985-93; originator, bd. dirs. Triangle East; chmn. N.C. State U. Emerging Issues Forum; bd. of visitors Wake Forest U. Author: Acreage Controls and Poundage Controls, Their Effects on Most Profitable Practices for Flue-Aired Tobacco, 1964, Rally Around the Precinct, 1968. Trustee Atlantic Christian Coll.; state pres. Young Dems., 1968; del. Dem. Nat. Conv., 1968; mem. Carnegie Forum on Edn. and Econ. Task Force on Teaching as a Profl., 1986; chmn. Nat. Bd. for Profl. Teaching Standards, 1987—, Nat. Commn. on Teaching and Am.'s Future, 1994. Recipient 1st ann. Harry S. Truman award Nat. Young Dems., 1975, James Bryant Conant award Edn. Commn. States, 1984, Nat. 4-H Outstanding Alumnus award, 1984, Soil Conservation Honors award, 1986, Child Health Advocate award Am. Acad. Pediatrics, 1994; named Outstanding Young Man of Yr., Wilson Jr. C. of C., 1969, Outstanding Govt. Ofcl. in Cmty. Edn., Nat. Assn. Cmty. Edn., 1977, Outstanding Govt. Leader in U.S. Conservation Achievement award Nat. Wildlife Fedn., 1983, State Grangeman of Yr., 1985. Mem. Nat. Govs. Assn. (chmn. task force on technol. innovation mem. exec. com., chmn. edn. com. of the states and nat. task force on edn. for econ. growth 1982-83, leadership team on controlling crime and violence 1994, mem. nat. edn. goals panel 1994). Presbyterian. Office: Office of the Governor 116 W Jones St Raleigh NC 27603-1300*

HUNT, JOHN EDWIN, insurance company executive, consultant; b. Ozark, Ala., Jan. 13, 1918; s. Tim Atticus and Ada (Arnold) H.; m. Winnifred Prichard; children: Jacqueline, John Edwin Jr., Geoffery, Scott, Richard; md. 2d Leona Snowden. Student, Columbus U., Washington, 1938-40, Pace U., 1940-41; diploma in banking, Am. Inst. Banking, 1942; diploma in ins., Travelers Ins. Co., 1944. Aide to regional adminstr., chief auditor Fed. Housing Adminstrn., Washington, 1938-40; with trust dept. Riggs Nat. Bank, Washington, 1940-42; asst. trust officer Fla. Nat. Bank, Jacksonville, 1942-44; asst. mgr. Travelers Ins. Co., Jacksonville, 1944-45, gen. agt. regional br., 1945-58; pres. John E. Hunt & Assocs., Tallahassee, 1972-84; chmn. bd. dirs. Hunt Ins. Group-Spl. Law Enforcement Agy. and Self-Ins. Fund Adminstrn., Tallahassee, 1984—; pres. John Hunt & Assocs., Miami, Fla., 1958-72; pres. Ins. Cons. and Analysts, Tallahassee, 1972—; bd. dirs. Renex Corp. Past chmn. pvt. industry coun. Pres. Reagan's Job Tng. Partnership Act; past mem. Gov's Adv. Coun. for Ins.; bd. dirs. Great Smoky Mountains Railway; founder Fla. Police Chiefs Edn. & Rsch. Found., Inc.; trustee, mem. pres.'s coun. Fla. So. Coll., Lakeland, 1986—. Mem. Fla. Assn. Surplus Lines, Fla. Assn. Ins. Agts., Com. of 99 (past pres., bd. dirs., law enforcement com. 1984-85), Greater Miami Mortgage Brokers Assn. (pres. 1964-65), Fla. Jr. C. of C. (nat. dir. state v.p. 1950-52), Fla. Police Chiefs Assn. (hon., life), Fla. Sheriffs Assn. (hon., life), Killearn Golf and Country Club, Fla. Econ. Club, Tiger Bay Club, Govs. Club, Masons, Shriners, Elks (life). Mem. Fla. Assn. Surplus Lines, Fla. Assn. Ins. Agts. Com. of 99 (past pres., bd. dirs., law enforcement com. 1984-85), Greater Miami Mortgage Brokers Assn. (pres. 1964-65), Fla. Jr. C. of C. (nat. dir., state v.p. 1950-52), Fla. Police Chiefs Assn. (hon., life), Fla. Sheriffs Assn. (hon., life), Killearn Golf and Country Club, Fla. Econ. Club, Tiger Bay Club, Govs. Club, Masons, Shriners, Elks (life). Democrat. Home: PO Box 14015 Tallahassee FL 32317-4015 Office: Hunt Ins Group Inc 2324 Centerville Rd Tallahassee FL 32308-4318

HUNT, J(ULIAN) COURTENAY, artist; b. Jacksonville, Fla., Sept. 17, 1917; s. Julian Schley and Ruth Rosalind (Loftin) H.; student Ringling Sch. Art, 1946-47, Farnsworth Sch. Art, 1948-52. Artist, 1950—; tchr. pvt. classes painting, 1950—; exhibited in one-man shows at Cummer Gallery of Art, Jacksonville, 1963—, Flair Gallery, Palm Beach, Fla., 1970-71; exhibited in group shows at Palm Beach Art Gallery, Soc. Four Arts, Palm Beach, 1968-69, Audubon Artists of Am., N.Y.C., Allied Artists Am., N.Y.C., 1952-56, Atlanta High Mus., 1950-54, St. Augustine (Fla.) Art Assn., 1970-73, Sarasota (Fla.) Art Assn., 1952-56, Fla. Artists Group Show at Norton Art Gallery of the Palm Beaches, 1975; portraits in permanent collections U. Fla., Gainesville, Jacksonville U., City Hall of Jacksonville, Duval County Circuit Ct., Jacksonville, Ind. Life Ins. Co., Jacksonville. Served with USAAF, 1942-46; ETO. Address: 2587 Windwood Ln Orange Park FL 32073-6126

HUNT, OLIVER RAYMOND, JR., thoracic and cardiovascular surgeon; b. Darlington, S.C., Apr. 23, 1923; s. Oliver Raymond Sr. and Annie Reid (Muldrow) H.; m. Eleanor Margaret Morgan, Dec. 16, 1944; children: David Morgan, Margaret Muldrow, Rebecca Elaine, Sarah Fredricka. AB, Berea Coll., 1947; MD, U. Louisville, 1951. Diplomate Am. Bd. Surgery, Am. Bd. Thoracic and Cardiac Surgery. Asst. in anatomy U. Louisville, 1950; intern Edward W. Sparrow Hosp., Lansing, Mich., 1951-52; fellow in surgery Mayo Found., Rochester, Minn., 1954-58, fellow in thoracic surgery, 1958-60; staff surgeon VA Hosp., Oteen, N.C., 1960-61; clin. assoc. SUNY, Buffalo, 1963-64, asst. prof. surgery, 1964-69, asst. dean, assoc. dean clin. affairs, 1965-67, 67-69; clin. asst., assoc. prof. surgery U. N.C., Chapel Hill, 1969-91; pvt. practice surgery Wilmington, N.C., 1969-91; CEO Regal Tomaoes Internat. Ltd., Nev., 1991—; v.p., bd. dirs. Jugoso Y Pulpas de San Gerado S.A., Costa Rica, 1989—; v.p. med. staff Cape Fear Hosp., Wilmington, 1978, 79, pres., 1980-81, chief of staff, 1972, exec. com., 1978-82; cons. med. edn. Nat. U., Asuncion, Paraguay, 1965-67. Contbr. numerous articles to profl. jours. Bd. dirs. New Hanover Bank, Wilmington, 1972-75, Planters Nat. Bank, Wilmington, 1976-87, Wilmington Devel. Corp., 1981-87, Wilmington Concert Assn., 1970-94; civil svc. commn. City of Wilmington, 1972-81. Lt. USNR, 1943-46. Named Rsch. scholar Dept. Chemistry U. Louisville, 1948-51; recipient Mosby prize for Scholarship, U. Louisville, 1948; named Hon. Prof., Nat. U. Asuncion, 1967. Mem. AMA, N.C. Med. Soc., New Hanover Med. Soc., Soc. Thoracic Surgery, N.Y. Acad. Sci., N.C. Lung Soc., Alpha Omega Alpha, Phi Kappa Phi.

HUNT, PAMELA STAFFORD, secondary school educator; b. Altus, Okla.; d. James P. Jr. and Edna Earle (Snyder) S.; m. W. Gaddis Hunt; children: Gregory Todd, Lari Anne. BS, Miss. State U., 1967, MEd, 1973. Cert. tchr., Miss. Tchr. Starkville (Miss.) Sch. Dist., 1972—; instr. Miss. State U., 1989—; co-dir. Youth Leadership Conf., 1990-91; mem. com. Miss. Textbook State Rating Com., Jackson, 1992-93, Miss. Curriculum Revision Com., Jackson, 1990-92; evaluator So. Accreditation for Colls. and Schs., Vicksburg, Miss., 1990-91; Miss. team leader Mid South Japan Schs. Project, 1992-93. Recipient Bettersworth award Miss. Edn. TV Authority, 1985, Nat. Disting. Tchr. award Nat. Coun. Geographic Edn., 1987. Mem. ASCD, Miss. Coun. Social Studies (v.p. 1989-90, pres. 1990-91), Miss. Profl. Educators, Starkville Profl. Educators, Starkville PTA, Nat. Coun. Social Studies, Delta Kappa Gamma (corr. sec. 1992-95), Phi Mu House Corp. (sec. 1993-95). Republican. Methodist. Home: 1106 E Lee Blvd Starkville MS 39759-9218 Office: Starkville High Sch Yellow Jacket Dr Starkville MS 39759

HUNT, RAY L., petroleum company executive; b. 1943; s. H.L. and Ruth (Ray) H.; m. Nancy Ann Hunt; 5 children. BBA, So. Meth. U., 1965. With Hunt Oil Co., Dallas, 1958—, chmn. bd., CEO, 1994—; chmn., pres., CEO Hunt Consolidated Inc., Dallas, 1994—. Mem. Nat. Petroleum Coun. (chmn.), Am. Petroleum Inst. (exec., pub. policy com.). Office: Hunt Consolidated Inc 1445 Ross Ave Dallas TX 75202-2785

HUNT, ROBERT GAYLE, government official; b. Greeley, Colo., Aug. 2, 1933; s. Ray and Myrtle Marie (Dunham) H.; m. Harriet Gertrude McNeel, June 10, 1955 (div. 1978); children—Leslie Lynn Hunt King, Linda Jean, Julia Gail Hunt Walsh, Gregg Bryan, Robert John. BA, U. No. Colo., 1955; MPA, Syracuse U., 1957; student Fed. Exec. Inst., Charlottesville, Va., 1973.

Various positions housing and cmty. devel. programs HUD, Washington, 1957-79, spl. asst. to dep. asst. sec. FHA, 1979-89, dir. mgmt. svcs. div., 1989—. Pres. Kings Park Civic Assn., Springfield, Va., 1966-67; elder Providence Presbyterian Ch., Fairfax, Va., 1968-71, 79-82, 1986-89; pres. Fairfax County Fedn. Citizens Assn., 1970-71; chmn. Citizens for Sch. Bonds, 1973; mem. Fairfax County Sch. Bd., 1973-77; pres. Social Ctr. for Psychiat. Rehab., Inc., Merrifield, Va., 1983-85; chmn. Fairfax Cmty. Ministry, 1983-85, treas., 1990-96; pres. Fairfax Com. of 100, 1986-88; bd. dirs. No. Va. Mental Health Assn., Annandale, 1988-94; Fairfax County Adv. Task Force on Cultural Facility, 1988-89; spokesperson Clean Water Coalition, 1970; mem. pres.'s cir. Psychiat. Rehab. Svcs., Inc., Fairfax, 1994—, mem. planned giving com., 1996—; mem. exec. com., bd. dirs. Comty. Ministry No. Va., Oakton, Va., 1996—. Named Outstanding Citizen, Kings Park Civic Assn., 1975; recipient citation Fairfax County Sch. Bd., 1973, Disting. Service award, 1977. Avocations: sailing, fishing. Home: 8910 Cromwell Dr Springfield VA 22151-1120 Office: US Dept Housing & Urban Devel 451 7th St SW Washington DC 20410-0001

HUNT, RODNEY DALE, chemist, researcher; b. Easley, S.C., Sept. 27, 1960; s. Oliver Larry and Shirley Jean (Campbell) H. BS, Clemson U., 1983; PhD, U. Va., 1987. Rsch. intern Hercules Rsch. Ctr., Wilmington, Del., 1983; rsch. and teaching asst. U. Va., Charlottesville, 1983-87, rsch. scientist, 1989-91, vis. rsch. scientist, 1992—; rschr. Battelle's Columbus (Ohio) Divsn., 1988-89; rsch. assoc. III Oak Ridge (Tenn.) Nat. Lab., 1991-93, program mgr./rsch. staff mem., 1993—. Coach Farragut (Tenn.) Little League, 1993—. Dept. of Energy grantee, 1991—; recipient award Dept. Energy, 1994. Mem. Am. Chem. Soc. (Outstanding Sr. award 1983), Mortar Bd., Sigma Xi, Sigma Phi Epsilon, Phi Kappa Phi. Office: Oak Ridge Nat Lab PO Box 2008 Oak Ridge TN 37831-6221

HUNT, T(HOMAS) W(EBB), retired religion educator; b. Mammoth Spring, Ark., Sept. 28, 1929; s. Thomas Hubert and Ethel Clara (Webb) H.; m. M. Laverne Hill, July 22, 1951; children: Melana Claire Hunt Monroe. MusB, Ouachita Bapt. U., 1950; MusM, N. Tex. State U., 1957, PhD, 1967. Mem. faculty Southwestern Bapt. Theol. Sem., Ft. Worth, 1963-87; life cons. for prayer Bapt. Sunday Sch. Bd., Nashville, 1987-94, ret., 1994; lectr. confs. in field. Author: The Doctrine of Prayer, 1986, Music in Missions, 1986, The Disciple's Prayer Life, 1988, The Mind of Christ, 1995, In God's Presence, 1995. Mem. Assn. Mins. and Coords. Discipleship. Home: 3915 Cypress Hill Dr Spring TX 77388-5798

HUNT, WANDA BURTON, finance executive; b. Salyersville, Ky., June 15, 1953; d. Seldon B. and Ula Maxine (Mullins) B.; m. William Gordon Hunt, Apr. 13, 1973; children: Shannon Kaye, William Ryan, Nathaniel Gordon. BS, U. Ky., 1981, MBA, 1985. Cert. mgmt. acct. Assembler GTE Sylvania, Wincester, Ky., 1972-76; acct. Wallace's Book Store, Lexington, Ky., 1982; city treas. City of Winchester, 1982-86; acctg. mgr. Lexington Clinic, Inc., 1989-90; contr., treas. Campton (Ky.) Electronic Mfg., 1990-93; fin., material mgr. Summit Polymers, Inc., Mt. Sterling, Ky., 1993—. Treas. Clark County Rep. Com., 1984-92, Winchester Youth Soccer League, 1984-86; bd. dirs. Clark County Band Boosters, Winchester. Mem. Inst. of Mgmt. Accts. Republican. Baptist. Office: Summit Polymers Inc 160 Clarence Dr Mount Sterling KY 40353-9072

HUNTER, DIANA ROMAINE, editor; b. Arlington Heights, Ill., Dec. 20, 1961; d. Joseph James and Romaine Anne (Hamous) Pappas; m. Steven Richard Gonzalez, Sept. 21, 1986; children: Anthony Michael, Brenden James. Grad. high sch., Dania, Fla. Copywriter, typesetter Supertype, Miami, 1984-87, Printing Factory, Miami, 1987-89; editl. dir. Women's Publ., Ft. Lauderdale, Fla., 1989—; cons. in field. Author: Economy for Women, 1992; editor: Ready...Set...Build, 1993, A Woman's Guide to Self Defense, 1993. Mem. Publishers Mktg. Assn. Office: Womens Publ Inc 13326 SW 28th St Ste 102 Fort Lauderdale FL 33330-1102

HUNTER, DOUGLAS LEE, elevator company executive; b. Greeley, Colo., May 3, 1948; s. Delmer Eural and Helen Converse (Haines) H.; m. Janet Lee Snook, May 26, 1970; children: Darin Douglas, Joel Christopher, Eric Andrew, Jennifer Lee. Student, Phillips U., Enid, Okla., 1966-70; BA cum laude, Sioux Falls Coll., 1979; postgrad., N.Am. Bapt. Sem., Sioux Falls, 1977-79. Elevator constructor Carter Elevator Co., Inc., Sioux Falls, S.D., 1971-72, rep., 1972-74, contr., 1974-78, sec.-treas., 1978-82, v.p., 1982-87, pres. 1987-93; ptnr. Lifters Ltd., Sioux Falls, S.D., 1984-90, CEO 1987-96; bd. dirs Home Fed. Savings Bank, HF Fin. Corp.; U.S. del. Forum Bus. in Vietnam, Ho Chi Minh City, 1993; guest lectr. Nat. Econs. U., Hanoi, Vietnam, 1995. Mem. gen. bd. Christian Ch., Indpls., 1984-88; mem. regional bd. Christian Ch. in the Upper Midwest, Des Moines, 1985-87; bd. dirs. Glory House, Sioux Falls, 1983-86; teaching leader Bible Study Fellowship, Sioux Falls, 1981-92; vice chmn. Greater Sioux Empire Billy Graham Crusade, 1986-87; mem. internat. bd. dirs. Fellowship of Cos. for Christ Internat., 1993—, v.p., 1994—; bd. dirs. Am. Mongolia Found., 1992—; active S.D. Trade Del. to Mongolia, 1993—. Trustee N.Am. Bapt. Sem., 1989—. Named Outstanding Young Religious Leader Sioux Falls Jaycees, 1974. Mem. S.D. Family Bus. Coun., Sen. Larry Pressler's Small Bus. Adv. Com., Nat. Assn. Elevator Contractors, Nat. Assn. Elevator Safety Authorities, Constrn. Specifications Inst., Christian Businessmen's Com. U.S., Sioux Falls C. of C. Republican. Lodge: Rotary. Avocations: golf, tennis, reading, music. Home: 695 Wyndham Place Cir Lawrenceville GA 30244-3629 Office: Fellowship Cos for Christ Internat 4201 N Peachtree Rd Atlanta GA 30341-1207

HUNTER, EDWIN FORD, JR., federal judge; b. Alexandria, La., Feb. 18, 1911; s. Edwin Ford and Amelia (French) H.; m. Shirley Kidd, Nov. 9, 1941; children—Edwin Kidd, Janin, Kelley. Student, La. State U., 1930-33; LL.B., George Washington U., 1938. Bar: La. bar 1938. Mem. firm Smith, Hunter, Risinger & Shuey, Shreveport, 1940-53; mem. La. Legislature, 1948-52; exec. counsel Gov. La., 1952-53; mem. La. State Mineral Bd., 1952; judge, now sr. judge U.S. Dist. Ct., Western Dist. La., 1953—, also mem. adv. com. on civil rules., 1971-76. Served as lt. USNR, 1942-45. Mem. Am. Bar Assn. (La. state chmn. jr. bar sect. 1945), Am. Legion (post comdr. 1945, judge adv. Dept. La. 1948), Sigma Chi. Roman Catholic. Home: 1000 Bayou Oak Ln Lake Charles LA 70605-2634 Office: US Dist Ct 611 Broad St Ste 243 Lake Charles LA 70601-4380

HUNTER, HAROLD RAY, city official; b. Athens, Tenn., Aug. 8, 1943; s. Thomas Elbert and Minnie Lou (Allowy) H.; m. Mary Ellen Wilcox, June 29, 1973; 1 child, Lisa Beth. Grad. high. sch., Athens. Cmty. devel. dir. City of Athens, 1965—; advisor Mayors Adv. Com., 1974-79, McMinn County Clean Cmty. Commn., 1988—, Athens Regional Planning Commn., 1967—; alt. mcpl. judge City of Athens, 1968—. With U.S. Army Res., 1960-68. Mem. Lions Club (1st v.p.). Baptist. Home: 600 Linden Circle Athens TN 37303 Office: City of Athens 815 N Jackson St Athens TN 37303-2652

HUNTER, HASSELL EUGENE, petroleum engineer, consultant; b. Haskell, Tex., May 18, 1923; s. Eugene Clark and Audrey Willis (Key) H.; m. Thelma Lucille Williams, Feb. 24, 1950 (dec. Sept. 1990); children: Karen Jane, Russell Eugene. BBA, Tex. A & I U., 1948; postgrad., Hardin-Simmons U., 1949, McMurry Coll., 1955, Tex. U., 1956. Registered profl. engr., D.C. Asst. mgr. F. M. Robertson Oil Co., Abilene, Tex., 1948-51; drilling engr. Rhodes Drilling Co., Abilene, 1951-64; chief drilling engr. U.S. Atomic Energy Commn., Las Vegas, Nev., 1964-73; sr. staff engr. Conoco, Inc., Houston, 1973-85; pres., chief engr. Hassell E. Hunter, Inc., Houston, 1985—; bd. dirs. Inst. Shaft Drilling Tech., Seattle; designated rep. U.S. Nat. Com. on Tunneling Tech., Washington, 1983-86. Contbr. articles to profl. jours. Recipient cert. merit U.S. Army Air Forces, Sioux Falls, S.D., 1943, cert. appreciation Atomic Energy Commn., Las Vegas, 1970, spl. achievement award, 1971. Mem. AIME (Soc. Petroleum Engrs.), Inst. Shaft Drilling Tech. (dir. 1980-90, program dir. 1980-86, Disting. Svc. award 1986). Home and Office: 7226 Tall Pines Dr Houston TX 77088-6604

HUNTER, LARRY LEE, electrical engineer; b. Versailles, Mo., Mar. 5, 1938; s. Donnan Kleber and Molly Opal (Roe) H.; m. Marcella Ann Avey, Feb. 1, 1959; children: Cynthia Lynn Hunter Chapman, Stuart Roe. BSEE, U. Mo., 1963; MBA, Fla. Inst. Tech., 1984. System test engr. McDonnell Aircraft Corp., St. Louis, 1963-65; design engr. Magnavox Co., Urbana, Ill., 1965-66, R&D engr., 1966-68; project engr. LTV Electrosystems, Garland, Tex., 1968-69, systems engr., 1969-70; program mgr. Dorsett Electronics, Tulsa, 1970-73; program mgr. Harris Corp., Melbourne, Fla., 1973-75, bus. area mgr., 1975-85; v.p. mktg., engring., program mgmt. Teledyne Lewisburg, Tenn., 1985-88; gen. mgr. Precision Cable div. AMP Inc., Greensboro, N.C., 1990-96; pres. L.H. Assocs., Columbia, Tenn., 1988-90; dir. global cable sys. bus. group AMP Inc., Greensboro, N.C., 1996-97; pres. L.H. Assocs., Greensboro, N.C., 1997—. Inventor thermometer; contbr. articles to profl. jours. Mem. IEEE, Eta Kappa Nu. Republican. Methodist. Home: 505 Willoughby Blvd Greensboro NC 27408-3133

HUNTER, MARY JANE, journalist; b. Atlanta, Oct. 31, 1919; d. Cecil Olney and Mary (Cheves) Burns; m. Joseph Lawton Hunter, Oct. 8, 1944; children: Mollie Hunter Hill, Ellen Hunter Wine. Journalist Freeport (Grand Bahamas) News, 1965-70; women's editor The Breeze, Cape Coral, Fla., 1970-74, asst. editor, 1974-76; journalist News-Press, Ft. Myers, Fla., 1976-79, asst. editorial pg. editor, 1979-92; mem. emeritus News Press Edtl. Bd., 1992-95; editorial writer, columnist, original editorial bd. USA Today, Washington, 1982-83, regional editor in Ft. Myers, 1983-90. Recipient Robert F. Kennedy Found. award (as editorial writer of News-Press team), 1990, Best of Gannett award, 1978, Gannett Outstanding Achievement award (dept.), 1985, several state awards, 1972-81. Mem. Nat. Conf. Editorial Writers. Home: 18 Woodmont Fort Myers FL 33907-7512

HUNTER, NANCY DONEHOO, education educator; b. Atlanta, July 11, 1956; d. Joseph Andrew and Sophia (Sellers) Donehoo; m. Charles James Hunter IV, Dec. 1, 1979; children: Katherine Elizabeth, Charles James V. BA, Asbury Coll., 1981; MA, Morehead (Ky.) State U., 1984; postgrad., U. Ky., 1989. Dir. Christian edn. 1st United Meth. Ch., Clewiston, Fla., 1981-82; assoc. prof. Maysville (Ky.) C.C., 1983—; mem. partnership coordination coun. Destination Graduation, Frankfort, Ky., 1989-91; tutor trainer Ky. Literacy Coun., Frankfort, 1990—. Author: Peer Tutor Trainer Manual, 1989. Bd. dirs. Community Literacy Coun., Mason County, Ky., 1988—; choir dir. Trinity Meth. Ch., Maysville, 1990—. Recipient Vol. Svc. award Mason County Schs., 1987, 91; grantee U.S. Dept. Edn., 1989-91. Mem. ASCD, Internat. Reading Assn., Nat. Assn. Devel. Educators, Coll. Reading and Learning Assn., Ky. Assn. Devel. Educators (treas. 1989-90, conf. dir. 1989—). Home: PO Box 203 Washington KY 41096-0203 Office: Maysville Community Coll US 68 Maysville KY 41056

HUNTER, RICHARD GRANT, JR., neurologist, executive; b. San Antonio, Aug. 22, 1938; s. Richard Grant Hunter Sr. and Elton (Hall) Samouce; m. Margaret Jenkins (div. Dec. 1984); m. Sandra K. Miesel-Conrad; children: Richard Grant III, Brandon Scott. BS, Ga. Inst. Tech., 1960; MBA, U. Pa., 1961; MD, U. Va., 1968. Diplomate Am. Coll. of Physicians, Am. Soc. Neuroimaging, Am. Bd. Internal Medicine, Am. Bd. of Psychiatry and Neurology. Systems analyst N.C. Nat. Bank, Charlotte, 1962-63; ops. rsch. analyst U.S. Geol. Survey, Washington, 1963-64; med. intern Grady Meml. Hosp., Atlanta, 1968-69; resident medicine Emory U. Hosps., Atlanta, 1969-71; resident psychiatry Emory U. Hosp., Atlanta, 1971-72, 89-91; resident neurology U. Va. Hosp., Charlottesville, 1972-75; neurologist U. Va. Hosp., Martha Jefferson Hosp., Charlottesville, 1975-83; chief of neurology Gwinett Med. Ctr., Atlanta, 1983-89; pres. Dixon Biotherapeutics Inc., Atlanta, 1985-86, neuropsychiatrist, behavioral neurologist, 1989—; pres. Charlottesville Neurology Inc., 1975—; bd. dirs., pres. Dixon Biotherapeutics Inc., Atlanta, Plantation at Lenox; bd. dirs. Charlottesville Neurology Inc. With U.S. Army, 1961-62. Fellow Am. Acad. Neurology, ACP; mem. AMA, Behavioral Neurology Soc., Med. Soc. Va., Med. Assn. Ga., Va. Neurol. Soc., Ga. Neurol. Soc., Am. Psychiat. Assn., Am. Neuropsychiat. Assn., Ga. Psychiat. Assn., Am. Soc. Neuroimaging, So. Clin. Neurology Soc., Transcultural Psychology, Farmington Country Club, Farmington Hunt Club, River Bend Gun Club, Milrock Gun Club, Alpha Omega Alpha, Med. Honor Soc ., Engring. Honor Soc. Episcopalian.

HUNTER, RICHARD SAMFORD, JR., lawyer; b. Montgomery, Ala., May 8, 1954; s. Richard Samford and Anne (Arendell) H.; m. Jane Messer, June 28, 1981; children: Richard Samford III, Benjamin Arendell. Student, Berklee Coll. of Music, 1974-75; BA, U. N.C., 1977; JD, Samford U., 1980. Bar: N.C. 1980, U.S. Dist. Ct. N.C. 1981. Assoc. Green & Mann, Raleigh, N.C., 1980-82, Smith, Debnam, Hibbert & Pahl, Raleigh, 1982-85; ptnr. Futrell, Hunter & Bingham, Raleigh, 1985—; program chmn. media law U. N.C., Chapel Hill, 1983-84; mem. faculty NCATL Nat. Inst. Trial Advocacy, 1987. Composer, performer (TV musical) The Tomorrow Show, 1975. Corp. fund raiser United Way, Wake County, N.C., 1984-85; mem. clergy's sermon evaluation com. Christ Episc. Ch., Raleigh; bd. dirs. Raleigh Chamber Music Guild, 1986-88; bd. dirs. Food Bank of N.C., 1990—. Mem. ABA, N.C. Bar Assn., Wake County Bar Assn. (bd. dirs. 1986-89, chmn. 1988-89), Assn. Trial Lawyers Am. (Stalwart fellow Roscoe Pound Found.), N.C. Acad. Trial Lawyers (program chmn., speaker various seminars, chmn. speakers bur. 1984-85, bd. govs. 1986—, v.p. pub. svc. and info. com. 1988-90, v.p. membership 1990-91, v.p. legis. 1991—, pres. 1993-94), Kiwanis, Sphinx, Phi Alpha Delta. Democrat. Home: 813 Graham St Raleigh NC 27605-1124 Office: Futrell Hunter & Bingham 207B Fayetteville Street Mall Raleigh NC 27601-1309

HUNTER, ROBERT CHARLES, food company executive; b. Furstenfeldbruk, Germany, Apr. 2, 1948; s. John Columbus and Ellen Gertrude (Genge) H.; m. Rebecca Ann Hendrick, Oct. 31, 1972; children: Amy Catherine, Emily Jane, Brandon Charles. BA, Coll. Artesia, 1969. V.p. C-B Truck Lines, Inc., El Paso, Tex., 1969-74; with distbn. mgmt. Frito Lay, Inc., Dallas, 1974-78; sr. dir. Franchise Svcs., Inc., Wichita, Kans., 1978-81; v.p. Franchise Svcs., Inc., Wichita, 1981-84; v.p. restaraunt franchising Pizza Hut, Inc., Wichita, 1984-86; pres. and CEO PepsiCo Food Systems, Dallas, 1986—. Active Dallas Easter Seals Soc. for Children, 1992-96, mem. adv. coun., 1992—; pres. Young Audiences Greater Dallas, 1989-91; founder, chmn. David J. Ewing Scholarship Fund, 1991—, Tex. Christian U. Parents Coun., 1991-96; mem. Tex. Christian U. New Frontier Bd., 1994—; North Tex. U. Hotel and Restaurant Adv. Bd., 1994—; bd. dirs. S.W. Family Inst., Dallas, 1989-92, Ctr. for Non-Profit Mgmt., 1992—, The Child Care Group, 1995—; chmn. fin. com. Northwood U. Arts Program Bd., 1993-94; mem. Dallas Assembly, 1994—. Mem. Young Pres. Orgn., U.S. C. of C. (bd. dirs. 1995—), Dallas Mus. Art Assocs., Dallas Theater Ctr., Northwood Club. Methodist. Home: 6605 Dartbrook Dr Dallas TX 75240-7919 Office: PepsiCo Food Systems 14841 Dallas Pky Dallas TX 75240

HUNTER, SUE PERSONS, former state official; b. Hico, Tex., Aug. 21, 1921; d. David Henry and Beulah (Boatwright) Persons m. Charles Force Hunter; children: Shelley Hunter Richardson, Kathy Hunter McCullough, Margaret Hunter Brown. BA, U. Tex., 1942. Air traffic controller CAA (now FAA), San Antonio and Houston, 1942-52; writer Bissonet Plaza News, 1969-72; coordinator Goals for La., 1971-74; adminstrv. dir. Jeff Publs. Inc., 1974; press sec. Jefferson Parish Dist. Atty., 1972-75, communications cons., 1975-78; adminstr. Child Support Enforcement Div., 1979-85; contbg. editor The Jeffersonian, 1975-76. Pres. United Ch. Women East Jefferson (La.), 1958-59, LWV Jefferson Parish, La., 1961-64, also bd. dirs., 1962-67, 93-96; mem. probation services com. Cmty. Svcs. Coun., Jefferson, 1966-73, v.p., 1970-72; mem. Library Devel. Com. La., 1967-71, Nat. Com. for Support of Pub. Schs., 1967-72; mem. Goals Found. Council Met. New Orleans, 1969-75, sec. 1970, 72; mem. Goals La. Task Force State and Local Govt., 1969-70; pres. MMM Investment Club, 1969-72; bd. dirs. New Orleans Area Health Planning Council, 1969-75, Friends of Westminster Tower, 1986, Coun. for Internat. Visitors, 1990—, pres. 1991-93, programmer, 1994—; bd. dirs. Jefferson Twenty Five, 1991—, v.p., 1995-96; mem. adv. coun. La. State Health Planning, 1971-76; title I adv. council La. State Dept. Edn., 1970-72; vice chmn. Jefferson Women's Polit. Caucus, 1977-78, chmn., 1979, treas., 1980; bd. dirs. New Orleans Area/Bayou-River Health Systems Agy., 1978-82, pres., 1980, 81; mem. Task force for La. Talent Bank of Women, 1980; exec. bd. La. Child Support Enforcement Assn., 1980-86, pres., 1982-84; bd. dirs., legis. chmn. Nat. Child Support Enforcement Assn., 1983-86; mem. Gov.'s Commn. on Child Support Enforcement, 1984-88; mem. La. Statewide Health Coordinating Coun., 1980-83, mgmt. com. edn. fund League of Women Voters La., 1988-89. Recipient Outstanding Citizens award Rotary Club, Metairie, La., 1962, River Ridge award, 1976. Mem. Am. Assn. Individual Investors (pres. New Orleans chpt. 1986-88), New Orleans Panhellenic (pres. 1956-57), Fgn. Rels. Assn. (bd. dirs. New Orleans chpt. 1992—, sec. 1996—), Les Pelicaneers (pres. 1988-90), Earn and Learn Investment Club (pres. 1992-94), Alpha Xi Delta. Presbyterian (elder). Home: 210 Stewart Ave New Orleans LA 70123-1457

HUNTER, WILEY LEIGH, middle school educator; b. Raleigh, N.C., Feb. 29, 1956; s. Wiley Knox and Betsy Lee (Morgan) H. BS, Atlantic Christian Coll., Wilson, N.C., 1978. In-sch. suspension aide East Millbrook Mid. Sch., Raleigh, 1979-80; in-sch. suspension tchr. Martin Mid. Sch., Raleigh, 1980-83, sci. tchr., 1983-86, health/phys. edn. tchr., 1986—; basketball ofcl. Mem. Nat. Assn. Sports Ofcls., Nat. Soccer Coaches Athletic Assn., Profl. Educators of N.C., N.C. Coaches Assn., N.C. Alliance Health, Phys. Edn., Recreation and Dance. Baptist. Home: 905 Hillsborough St B-3-B Raleigh NC 27603 Office: Martin Middle School 1701 Ridge Rd Raleigh NC 27607

HUNTLEY, WILLIAM THOMAS, III, insurance agent, consultant; b. Greensboro, N.C., Mar. 13, 1935; s. William Thomas Jr. and Lillian (Johnson) H.; m. Gladys Louise Bowden, Aug. 11, 1953; children: David C., William Thomas IV, Charlton A., Kimberly L. BA in Econs., Davidson (N.C.) Coll., 1958. Cert. CPCU. Field rep. Aetna Casualty & Surety Co., Atlanta, 1958-62; marine dept. mgr. Chubb & Son, Inc., Atlanta, Dallas, 1962-67; sr. v.p. Pritchard & Jerden, Inc., Atlanta, 1967-96; exec. v.p. Estate Adminstrn. Svcs., Inc., Atlanta, 1995—; mng. gen. ptnr. Huntley-Bradley Ltd. Partnership, Southern Pines, N.C., 1995—. Pres. Optimist Club, Atlanta, 1968-69; com. chair Atlanta C. of C., 1969, Peach Bowl, 1969-75. Mem. Coun. of Ins. Agts. and Brokers (pres. 1990-91), Atlanta Assn. Ind. Ins. Agts. (pres. 1979-80), Ind. Inst. Agts. Ga. (bd. dirs. 1979-81), Atlanta Athletic Club, Golf Club Amelia Island. Republican. Presbyterian. Home: 2030 Riverside Rd Roswell GA 30076-4026 Office: Estate Adminstrn Svcs 5303 Fairfield W Atlanta GA 30338

HUOT, RACHEL IRENE, biomedical educator, research scientist; b. Manchester, N.H., Oct. 16, 1950; d. Omer Joseph and Irene Alice (Girard) H. BA in Biology cum laude, Rivier Coll., 1972; MS in Biology, Cath. U. Am., 1976, PhD in Biology, 1980. Sr. technician Microbiol. Assocs., Bethesda, Md., 1974-77; chemist Uniformed Svcs. Univ. of Health Scis., Bethesda, 1977-79; biologist Nat. Cancer Inst., Bethesda, 1979-82; postdoctoral fellow S.W. Found. for Biomed. Rsch., San Antonio, 1982-85, asst. scientist, 1985-87, staff scientist, 1987-88; instr. U. Tex. Health Sci. Ctr., San Antonio, 1988-89; asst. prof., dir. basic urologic rsch. La. State U., New Orleans, 1990-96; judge sr. div. Alamo Regional Sci. Fair, San Antonio, 1989-90. Contbr. articles to profl. jours. Vol. ARC; active Stephen Ministry. NSF grantee, 1972-74; recipient NIH Rsch. Svc. award, 1983-86, Searle Young Investigator award, 1994. Mem. AAAS, LWV, AAUW, AMA, Am. Soc. for Microbiology, Am. Assn. Cancer Rsch., Am. Soc. Cell Biology, Fedn. Am. Scientists, Sci. Club (pres. 1971-72), Soc. for In Vitro Biology, N.Y. Acad. Scis., St. Vincent De Paul Soc., Sierra Club, Fedn. Am. Soc. Experiment Biology, Sigma Xi, Iota Sigma Pi, Delta Epsilon Sigma. Democrat. Roman Catholic. Home: 701 Merrick St Shreveport LA 71104

HUPALO, MEREDITH TOPLIFF, artist, illustrator; b. Tarpon Springs, Fla., Apr. 28, 1917; d. Walter and Maurine (Martin) Topliff; cert. in design Pratt Inst., 1938; m. Nicholas Hupalo, July 13, 1940 (dec. Sept. 1977); children: Walter Topliff, John Nicholas. One-woman shows: Tarpon Springs Public Libr., 1945, Valley Stream (N.Y.) Mus., 1962, Contemporary Arts, Inc., N.Y.C., 1966, Jet Clubs Internat., N.Y.C., Henry Waldinger Libr., Valley Stream, N.Y., 1977, East River Savs. Bank, Valley Stream, 1978; two-person show: Art League of Daytona Beach, 1986; represented in permanent collection Valley Stream Pub. Libr., Tarpon Springs (Fla.) Pub. Libr., Eastern Airlines Exec. Offices, N.Y.C.; tchr. printmaking Nassau County (N.Y.) Home Extension Svc.; art adviser Valley Stream Mus., 1962-64; illustrator Eastern Airlines, 1964-68; artist Shell Oil Co., 1968-70; designer Continental Can Co., N.Y.C., 1970-73; art tchr. Astor (Fla.) Community Ctr., 1980-82. Active Mt. Dora Ctr. for the Arts of Lake County, 1991. Recipient spl. award oil painting 34th Nat. Spring Exhbn. Nat. Art League L.I., 1964, gold medal in oil painting 35th Membership Show, 1965; 1st pl. fine art Fla. Silver Springs Arts & Crafts Festival, 1980; 1st place award Umatilla Fall Festival (Fla.), 1983 merit award, 1985; merit award Tampa Realistic Artists, 1984; Best in Show award Nat. League Am. Pen Women, 1984; 1st pl. Fla. Extension Homemakers Cultural Arts; Award of Distinction, Pioneer Art Settlement, 1987, Honorable Mention Pioneer Art Settlement, 1991, 1st Pl. award Ann. Lake County Juried Art Show Mt. Dora Ctr. for Arts, 1992, Best in Show and 1st in Graphics awards Umatilla Fall Festival, 1993. Mem. Fla. Watercolor Soc. (assoc., participating artist II), Nat. Art League L.I. (treas. 1959-60), Art League of Daytona Beach (Lillian Gittner Meml. award 1988, 64th membership show Grumbacher gold award 1996), Nat. League Am. Pen Women (Fla. br. 1987, v.p. 1991, Grumacher silver medal 1995), Mus. Arts and Scis., DeLand Mus., Astor Area C. of C. (dir. 1981-82). Methodist. Works include Paintings With Markers, 1972. Home: 55809 Dale Cir Astor FL 32102-2628

HUPFELD, STANLEY FRANCIS, health care executive; b. Balt., July 18, 1944; s. Stanley Francis and Dorothy (Heibler) H.; m. Suzanne Dunne, July 20, 1968; children: Matthew, Kelly, Kate. BA, U. Tex., Austin, 1966; MS, Trinity U., San Antonio, 1972. Asst. adminstr. Providence Meml. Hosp., El Paso, Tex., 1972-73; pres. St. Joseph's Hosp., El Paso, 1973-77; pres. All Saints Hosp., Ft. Worth, 1977-87; pres., CEO Intergris Health, Inc., Bapt. Med. Ctr. of Okla., 1987—; trustee Tex. Hosp. Assn., 1983-87; chmn. Dallas/Ft. Worth Hosp. Coun., 1980-81; mem. affiliate faculty dept. health care adminstrn. Trinity U., 1992—. Campaign chmn. Tarrant County United Way, Ft. Worth, 1986; dir. Interfirst Bank Univ., Ft. Worth, 1986; trustee VHA, 1987—, VHA of Okla., 1987—, Okla. City Art Mus., 1990; campaign chmn. United Way of Ctrl. Okla., 1989, pres., 1990; trustee Nat. Conf. of Christians and Jews, 1989—, ARC, Oklahoma City chpt., 1987-88, Leadership Oklahoma City, 1987-95; adv. bd. Okla. Centennial Sports, 1989-90, Governance Inst., 1995—; trustee Forward Okla., 1987-92; mem. Greater Oklahoma City Hosp. Coun., 1987—; trustee Ctrl. Okla. Ambulance Trust, 1988-89; mem. Okla. Acad. for State Goals, 1988, adv. com., 1989-90; mem. Young Pres.' Orgn., 1989—; trustee Okla. Philharmonic Orch., 1990-91; bd. dirs. Allied Arts, 1992-93; bd. cons. Kirkpatrick Ctr., 1990—; mem. Nat. Com. for Quality Health Care Tough Choices Com., 1991—. 1st lt. U.S. Army, 1968-70. Recipient Dean Duce award Trinity U. Health Care Alumni Assn., 1980-81. Fellow Am. Coll. Healthcare Execs.; mem. Oklahoma City C. of C. (trustee 1988—, vice chmn. 1988-92, chmn. elect 1993, chmn. 1994), Oklahoma State C. of C. and Industry (trustee 1990—, dir. 1990—), Okla. Hosp. Assn. (trustee 1989-92), Oklahoma City Rotary (dir. 1987-89). Home: 6715 Avondale Dr Oklahoma City OK 73116-6001 Office: Integris Health 3366 NW Expressway Ste 800 Oklahoma City OK 73112

HURD, ERIC RAY, rheumatologist, internist, educator; b. Columbus, Kans., July 5, 1936; s. Myron Alexander and Isobel (Moore) H.; m. Beverly Jean Button, June 14, 1962; children: Sherryl Lynn, Susan Rae, Brent Eric. BS, U. Tulsa, 1958; MD, U. Okla., 1962. Intern St. John's Hosp., Tulsa, 1962-63, resident in internal medicine, 1963-65; research fellow U. Tex., Dallas, 1965-67, instr. internal medicine, 1967-68, asst. prof., 1968-73, assoc. prof., 1973-80, prof., 1980—; cons. rheumatologist, attending physician Parkland, VA Hosps.; dir. John Peter Smith Hosp. Arthritis Clinic, Ft. Worth; chief rheumatology VA Hosp., 1982—, mem. immunology research merit rev. bd.; assoc. Baylor Arthritis Ctr., 1981—; mem. med. and sci. com. North Tex. Arthritis Found., bd. med. dirs., 1988—, chmn. profl. edn. com.; traveling guest lectr. Tex. Med. Assn., Belgium and Fed. Republic Germany, 1990. Contbr. articles to profl. jours. Served to maj. U.S. Army, 1963-74. Recipient Clin. Scholar award Arthritis Found., 1975-77; named Outstanding Cons. Faculty Mem. John Peter Smith Hosp., 1983-84, Outstanding Part-time Clin. Prof. John Peter Smith Hosp., 1989-90. Mem. ACP, Am. Assn. Immunologists, Am. Fedn. Clin. Research, Am. Rheumatism Assn. (cooperating clinics com. 1968-74, Founding Fellow 1986), Tex. Rheumatism Assn. (sec.-treas. 1976-79, 2d v.p. 1979-80), Tex. Med. Soc., Dallas County Med. Soc., Phi Eta Sigma. Democrat. Methodist. Office: Arthritis Ctrs of Tex 712 N Washington Ave Ste 200 Dallas TX 75246-1632

HURDLE, THOMAS GRAY, urologist; b. Roanoke, Va., Nov. 15, 1919; s. Grover Cleveland and Bronna (Garrison) H.; m. Eloise Spence, Mar. 14, 1945; children: Patricia Ann, Marilyn Sue, Edward Thomas. BS, Roanoke Coll., 1942; MD, Med. Coll. Va., 1945. Diplomate Am. B. Urology. Intern Doctor's Hosp., Washington, 1945-46; preceptorship urology Dr. A.A. Creecy, Newport News, Va., 1948-52; resident urology VA Med. Teaching Group Hosp., Memphis, 1952-53; chief resident urology VA Med. Teaching

Group Hosp., 1953-54; urologist VA Hosp., Fayetteville, N.C., 1954-55; attending physician, cons. urology Highsmith-Rainey Meml. Hosp., Fayetteville, 1954—; cons. Sampson County Meml. Hosp., Clinton, N.C., 1954—, Betsy Johnson Meml. Hosp., Dunn, N.C., 1956-65; attending physician, cons. Cape Fear Valley Hosp., Fayetteville, 1956—; sec. Cumberland County Med. Soc., Fayetteville, 1956-63. Contbr. article to Va. Med. Jour., 1950, Jour. Urology, 1955. Mem. Lions, Hampton, Va., 1950-52. With Med. Corp., U.S. Army, 1943-45, 46-48. Award named in his honor Cumberland County Med. Soc., 1992. Fellow ACS; mem. AMA, Am. Urol. Assn., Carolina Urol. Assn. (sec. 1985-87, pres.-elect 1987-88, pres. 1988-89), Cumberland County Med. Soc. (pres. 1965, chmn. awards com. 1964—), Am. Assn. Clin. Urologists, N.C. State Med. Soc. (life, 50 Yr. Club), So. Med. Assn. Republican. Methodist. Home: 234 Courtyard Ln Fayetteville NC 28303-4605 Office: Fayetteville Urology Assocs 1786 Metromedical Dr Fayetteville NC 28304-3861

HURLBURT, HARLEY ERNEST, oceanographer; b. Bennington, Vt., Apr. 12, 1943; s. Paul Rhodes and Evelyn Arlene (Lockhart) H. BS in Physics (scholar), Union Coll., Schenectady, 1965; MS, Fla. State U., 1971, PhD in Meteorology, 1974. NASA trainee Fla. State U., 1970-72; postdoctoral fellow advanced studies program Nat. Center Atmospheric Research, Boulder, Colo., 1974-75; staff scientist JAYCOR, Alexandria, Va., 1975-77; oceanographer Naval Oceanographic and Atmospheric Rsch. Lab. (merged with Naval Rsch. Lab., 1992), Stennis Space Center, Miss., 1977—, br. head, 1983-85; adj. faculty Marine Sci. U. So. Miss., Stennis Space Ctr., 1993—, Meteorology Fla. State U., Tallahassee, 1995—; mem. nat. adv. panels NASA satellite surface stress working group, 1981-84, minerals mgmt. service interagy. adv. group, 1982-89, world ocean circulation experiment working group on numerical modeling, 1984-96, USN space oceanography working group, 1986-89; co-chmn. working group on global prediction systems, ocean prediction workshop, 1986; internat. working group on acoustic monitoring of world ocean Sci. Com. Oceanic Rsch., 1991-96; internat. working group on modelling subarctic North Pacific circulation North Pacific Marine Sci. Orgn., 1994-95; project leader to develop the world's first eddy-resolving global ocean prediction model for the USN, 1987—. Contbr. numerous articles to profl. jours. V.p. Burgundy Citizens Assn., 1976-77. Weather officer USAF, 1965-69. Recipient Disting. Scientist medal 13th Internat. Colloquium, Liege, Belgium, 1981, Publ. award for best basic research paper Naval Ocean Research and Devel. Activity, 1980, 90; Office Naval Research grantee, 1975-77, 84—, Dept. Energy grantee, 1975-78, Tex. A&M U. grantee, 1976, Office of Naval Technology grantee, 1987-93, Space Warfare Systems grantee, 1989-94, Advanced Rsch. Projects Agy. grantee, 1993-95, Strategic Environ. Rsch. and Devel. Program grantee, 1994-95. Mem. Am. Meteorol. Soc., Am. Geophysical Union, Oceanography Soc., Phi Sigma Kappa, Sigma Xi (Kaminski Publ. award 1991), Sigma Tau, Chi Epsilon Pi. Methodist. Home: 507 Hermitage Ct Pearl River LA 70452-3903 Office: Naval Rsch Lab Code # 7320 Stennis Space Center MS 39529-5004

HURLBURT, SIDNEY HOLLADY, newspaper editor; b. Morrisville, Vt., May 22, 1940; s. Roderic Wright and Rhoda Maie (Hollady) H.; B.A. cum laude, Syracuse U., 1961; postgrad. (Fulbright scholar) Victoria U., Wellington, N.Z., 1962-63; m. Carol Joan Johnson, Mar. 7, 1964; children—Heather Fiona, Holly Siobhan. Writer, editor, mgr. AP, Atlanta, Providence, Concord, N.H., Boston and Washington, 1961-62, 63-67, regional editor, asst. news editor, Washington, 1967-70; adminstrv. asst. U.S. Sen. Charles Mathias Jr., Washington, 1970-72; minority staff dir. U.S. Senate Com. on D.C., 1972-73; news editor Gannett News Svc., Rochester, N.Y., 1973; mng. editor The Evening News, Newburgh, N.Y., 1973-74; mng. editor, exec. editor Burlington (Vt.) Free Press, 1975-80; exec. editor News-Jour. Papers, Wilmington, Del., 1980-84; editor/columns USA Today, Arlington, Va., 1984-95, editl. writer/editor, 1995—. Mem. Am. Soc. Newspaper Editors, Soc. Profl. Journalists, AP Mng. Editors Assn. (dir. 1978-84). Office: USA Today 1000 Wilson Blvd Arlington VA 22209-3901

HURLEY, ALFRED FRANCIS, university administrator, historian, retired career officer; b. Bklyn., Oct. 16, 1928; s. Patrick Francis and Margaret Teresa (Coakley) H.; m. Joanna Helen Leahy, Jan. 24, 1953; children: Alfred F., Thomas J., Mark P., Claire T., John K. B.A., St. John's U., 1950; M.A., Princeton U., 1958, Ph.D., 1961. Enlisted U.S. Air Force, 1950, commd. lt., 1952, advanced through grades to brig. gen., ret., 1980; v.p. adminstrv. affairs U. North Tex. (formerly North Tex. State U.), Denton, 1980-82, pres., 1982—; chancellor U. North Tex. and U. North Tex. Health Sci. Ctr., Ft. Worth, 1982—; mem. adv. com. USAF hist. program sect. USAF, Washington, 1982-86, chmn., 1984-86; mem. bd. visitors Air U., 1993—. Author: Billy Mitchell, Crusader for Air Power, 1964, (rev. edit.), 1975; co-editor: Air Power and Warfare, 1979. Decorated Legion of Merit (2); Guggenheim fellow, 1971-72, Eisenhower Inst., Smithsonian fellow, 1976-77; recipient Pres.'s medal St. John's U., 1990. Mem. Soc. for Mil. History (trustee 1973-78, 81-85), U.S. Commn. Mil. History (trustee 1978-80), Air Force Hist. Found. (trustee 1980—), Am. Assn. State Colls. and Univs. (coun. state reps. 1989-92), Am. Hist. Assn. (chmn. NASA fellowship com. 1993), Coalition Urban and Met. Univs. (co-chair 1993—), Coun. Pub. Univ. Prsidents and Chancellors (chmn. 1987-89), Alliance for Higher Edn. of North Tex. (trustee 1983-89, chmn. coun. of pres. 1989-90), North Tex. Commn. (chmn. 1995—). Roman Catholic. Home: 828 Skylark Dr Denton TX 76205-8012 Office: U North Tex Office Pres & Chancellor Denton TX 76203-3737

HURLEY, FRANK THOMAS, JR., realtor; b. Washington, Oct. 18, 1924; s. Frank Thomas and Lucille (Trent) H.; A.A., St. Petersburg Jr. Coll., 1948; B.A., U. Fla., 1950. Reporter St. Petersburg (Fla.) Evening Independent, 1948-53; editor Arcadia (Calif.) Tribune, 1956-57; reporter Los Angeles Herald Express, 1957; v.p. Frank T. Hurley Assos., Inc. realtors, 1958-64, pres., 1964—; sec., dir. Beau Monde, Inc., 1977-79. Elected St. Petersburg Beach Bd. Commrs., 1965-69; chmn. Pinellas County Traffic Safety Council, 1968-69; apptd. mem. Pinellas County Hist. Commn., 1993—; apptd. Pinellas County Sesquicentennial Coord. Com., 1995; pres. Pass-A-Grille Community Assn., 1963, Gulf Beach Bd. Realtors, 1969; mem. St. Petersburg Mus. Fine Arts, St. Petersburg Beach Aesthetic and Hist. Rev. Bd., chmn. 1994—; bd. govs. Palms of Pasadena Hosp., 1979-86. Served with USAAF, 1943-46. Mem. Fla. Assn. Realtors (dir., dist. v.p. 1971), St. Petersburg Suncoast Assn. Realtors (life, Ambassadors award, 1994), St. Petersburg Beach C. of C. (dir., pres. 1975-76, Citizen of Yr. award 1983), Fla. Hist. Soc., Am. Legion, Sigma Delta Chi, Sigma Tau Delta. Author: Surf, Sand and Post Card Sunsets, 1977. Home: 2808 Sunset Way Saint Petersburg FL 33706-4133 Office: 2506 Pass A Grille Way Saint Petersburg FL 33706-4160

HURLEY, JAMES DONALD, JR., computer consultant, lawyer; b. La Salle, Ill., June 11, 1935; s. James Donald and Emily Elizabeth (Reinhard) H.; BA, U. Ill., 1957, LLB, 1959; children: Katherine, Mary, James Donald III, Ellen. Bar: Ill. 1959, U.S. Cts. Appeals, U.S. Dist. Ct. (no. dist.) Ill., U.S. Tax Ct. Chief exec. officer Reilley, Inc., La Salle, 1986-92; past chmn. nat. MIS printing com. Postal Instant Press. Treas. Save Our Keys Com., 1996. Mem. Mensa, Cheeca Club. Home: 81648 Overseas Hwy PO Box 817 Islamorada FL 33036 Office: 81648 Overseas Hwy # 17 Islamorada FL 33036-3700

HURLEY, JEFFREY SCOTT, research chemist; b. Pitts., Feb. 19, 1963; s. William Stephen and Mary Agnes (Wholey) H. BS in Chemistry, Gannon U., Erie, Pa., 1985; MS in Chemistry, Ga. Inst. Tech., Atlanta, 1990, PhD in Chemistry, 1992. Sr. rsch. chemist Hoechst Celanese Corp., Charlotte, N.C., 1992—; cons., Atlanta, 1989-92. Author: Emerging Technologies in Hazardous Waste Management IV, 1994; contbr.: Phase Transfer Catalysis, 1994. Mem. Am. Chem. Soc. (organic, polymer material sci. and engring. and polymer divsn., Carolina Piedmont sect.). Office: Hoechst Celanese Corp 2300 Archdale Dr Charlotte NC 28210

HURLEY, JOHN STEVEN, electrical engineering educator, research scientist; b. Orlando, Fla., Jan. 10, 1955; s. Johnnie and Josie L. (Henderson) H. BS in Physics, Fla. State U., 1976, MS in Physics, 1980; PhD in Elec. Engring., Howard U., 1991. Instr. elec. engring. dept. Howard U., Washington, 1984-88; asst. prof. elec. engring. dept. U. S.C., Columbia, 1988-90; assoc. prof. math. dept. Hampton (Va.) U., 1990-93; assoc. prof. physics Ctrl. State U., Wilberforce, Ohio, 1993-94; cons. Ohio Bd. Regents, Columbus, 1993-94; rsch. scientist Wright Patterson AFB, Dayton, 1993-94; assoc. prof. engring. Clark Atlanta (Ga.) U., 1994—, dir. Avalon AI2 Beta Test Ctr.; cons. Systran Corp., Dayton, 1993-94, Ohio Bd. Regents, Columbus, 1993-94; adv. bd. mem. Office Naval Rsch., Washington, 1994; reviewer NASA Minority U. Rsch. and Edn. Divsn., Washington, 1994. Mentor Atlanta (Ga.) Middle Schs., 1994—. Fellow Am. Soc. Engring. Edn. (rsch. fellow); mem. IEEE, Sigma Xi, Tau Beta Pi. Baptist. Office: Clark Atlanta Univ 223 James P Brawley Dr Atlanta GA 30314

HURLEY, LAURENCE HAROLD, medicinal chemistry educator; b. Birmingham, U.K., Jan. 29, 1944; s. Harold Harcourt and Mary (Cottrell) H.; children: Bridget, Nicole. BPharm, U. Bath, U.K., 1967, DSc, 1996; PhD, Purdue U., 1970. Apprentice pharmacist Boots the Chemist, Birmingham, 1963-64; hosp. pharmacist Birmingham Gen. Hosp., 1967; postdoctoral fellow U. B.C., Vancouver, 1970-71; asst. prof. U. Md., Balt., 1971-73; from asst. to assoc. to full prof. U. Ky., Lexington, 1973-80; prof. U. Tex., Austin, 1981—, Henry Burlage prof., 1983-86, James Bauerle prof., 1986-88, George Hitchings prof. drug design, 1988-91, George Hitchings regents chmn. drug design, 1992—; cons. Upjohn Co., Kalamazoo, 1979—, Smith Kline French, Phila., 1984-87, Abbott Labs., 1992-94; mem. sci. adv. bd. Sun Pharm. Corp.; chmn. bioorganic and natural products study sect. NIH, 1986-88; dir. Chemistry Inst. Drug Devel., San Antonio. Sr. editor Jour. Medicinal Chemistry; contbr. numerous articles to profl. jours. Recipient George Hitchings award in innovative drug design, 1988, Volwiler Rsch. Achievement award, 1989, Rsch. Achievement award in medicinal chemistry Am. Pharm. Assn., 1992; named Outstanding Investigator Nat. Cancer Inst., 1989, 94. Fellow AAAS; mem. Am. Chem. Soc. (Medicinal Chemistry award 1994). Democrat. Home: 5915 Northwest Pl Austin TX 78731-3660 Office: U Tex Coll Pharmacy Austin TX 78712

HURLEY, WILLIAM JOSEPH, retired information systems executive; b. N.Y.C., June 14, 1939; s. William and Anna Rita (Hubschman) H.; m. Dorothy Ann Mellett, Sept. 23, 1961 (dec.); children: William, Terrianne, Barbara, Daniel; m. Marianne F. Jordan, Mar. 17, 1990. BBA, Pace U., 1968, MBA, 1973. Dir. info. system Gen. Foods Corp., White Plains, N.Y., 1973-79; dir. systems devel. Securities Industry Automation Corp., N.Y.C., 1979; dir. mgmt. info. systems Schering Plough Corp., Kenilworth, N.J., 1979-81, sr. dir. mgmt. info. systems, 1981-83, v.p. mgmt. info. service, 1983-88; v.p. world wide info. systems Technicon Corp., Tarrytown, N.Y., 1988-90; dir. info. systems Miles Inc., Tarrytown, 1990-95. Pres. New City (N.Y.) vol. Fire Engine Co. 1, 1979-81; commr. New City Fire Dist., 1983-94. Served with USMC, 1956-59. Mem. Soc. Info. Mgmt., Assn. Systems Mgmt. (v.p. 1981), Am. Legion. Republican. Roman Catholic. Home: Unit 504 3150 North A-1-A Fort Pierce FL 34949

HURN, PAULA CLARK, social services administrator; b. Montabello, Calif., Dec. 18, 1952; d. Charles E. and Mary Jo (Givens) Clark; m. A. Daniel Hurn, Mar. 4, 1989; adopted children: Marianah Alexis and Marcus Alexander (twins). BS, U. Montevallo, Ala., 1975. Aquatics and pre-sch. dir. YMCA of Birmingham (Ala.)-Shades Valley, 1977-83; br. mgr. YMCA of Greater Louisville, 1983-90, YNCA of Chattanooga-North River, 1990—. Mem. NAFE, Assn. Profl. Dirs., Hikson C. of C. (sec.), Kiwanis. Republican. Episcopalian. Office: North River YMCA 4138 Hixson Pike Chattanooga TN 37415-3112

HURST, ANNE SHIRLEY, reference librarian; b. Auburn, Ala., Aug. 18, 1948; d. Fred Wilson and Mary Gilchrist (Powell) Shirley; m. William Calhoun Hurst, Dec. 21, 1974; children: Sarah Lee Davidson, William Burlington. BA, Miss. Women's U., 1970; MS, La. State U., 1971. Catalog libr. U. Tenn., Martin, 1971-73; reference libr. La. State U., Baton Rouge, 1973-77, Athens (Ga.) Regional Libr., 1977-81, U. Ga., Athens, 1989—. Mem. ALA, Southeastern Libr. Assn., Ga. Libr. Assn. Presbyn. Home: 211 Great Oak Dr Athens GA 30605 Office: U Ga Main Libr Athens GA 30605

HURT, JOSEPH RICHARD, law educator; b. Laurel, Miss., Nov. 17, 1953; s. James Albert Sr. and Wanda (Perreault) H.; m. Jan Marie Jones, Aug. 13, 1977; children: Rosanna Marie, Jan Elizabeth, Margaret Delle. BA, Miss. Coll., 1975; MA, Baylor U., 1978, JD, 1979; LLM, Yale U., 1986. Bar: Miss. 1980. Asst. prof. Miss. Coll. Sch. Law, Jackson, 1980-83, assoc. prof., 1983-87, prof., 1987—, asst. dean, 1982-84, assoc. dean, 1984-88, 90-91, dean, 1991—; chair adv. com. rules Miss. Supreme Ct. Mem. ABA (legal edn. and admission to bar sect.), Miss. Bar Assn. (bd. dirs. young lawyers div. 1981-84, 87-90, co-chairperson minority involvement com.), Hinds County Bar Assn. (membership svcs. com., chair People's Law Sch. com.), Jackson Young Lawyers Assn. (mem. law-related edn. com.), Charles Clark Inn, Am. Inns of Ct. Baptist. Home: 310 Monterey Dr Clinton MS 39056-5736 Office: Miss Coll Sch Law 151 E Griffith St Jackson MS 39201-1302*

HURT, W. GLENN, obstetrics and gynecology educator; b. Richmond, Va., Sept. 6, 1938; s. Waverly Powell and Frances Eppes (Scott) H. BS, Hampden-Sydney (Va.) Coll., 1960; MD, Med. Coll. Va., Richmond, 1964. Diplomate Am. Bd. Ob/Gyn. Asst. prof. Med. Coll. Va., 1969-73, assoc. prof., 1973-78, prof. ob/gyn., 1978—. Editor: Postreproductive Gynecology, 1990, Urogynecologic Surgery, 1992. Lt. comdr. USNR, 1969-71. Fellow ACOG; mem. Am. Urogynecologic Soc. (past pres.), South Atlantic Assn. Obstetricians and Gynecologists (past pres.), Phi Beta Kappa, Alpha Omega Alpha. Office: Med Coll Va PO Box 980034 Richmond VA 23298-0034

HURWITZ, CHARLES EDWIN, manufacturing company executive; b. Kilgore, Tex., May 3, 1940; s. Hyman and Eva (Engler) H.; m. Barbara Raye Gollub, Feb. 24, 1963; children: Shawn Michael, David Alan. BA, U. Okla., Norman, 1962. Chmn. bd., pres. Investam. Group, Inc., Houston, 1965-67, Summitt Mgmt. & Research Corp., Houston, 1967-70; chmn. bd. Summit Ins. Co. of N.Y., Houston, 1970-75; with MCO Holdings, Inc. (and predecessor), Los Angeles, from 1978, chmn. bd., chief exec. officer, from 1980, dir., from 1978; chmn., pres., CEO Maxxam Inc., Houston, also dir. Jewish. Office: Maxxam Inc 5847 San Felipe St Houston TX 77057-3008

HURWITZ, JULIA LEA, immunologist; b. Schenectady, July 21, 1954; d. Henry Jr. and Alma (Rosenbaum) H.; m. Chris Coleclough, May 16, 1982; children: Jennifer Ann, Elizabeth Claire. BS, Cornell U., 1976; PhD, Johns Hopkins U., 1981. Postdoctoral fellow Wistar Inst., Phila., 1981-83, rsch. assoc., 1983-85; mem. Basel (Switzerland) Inst. Immunology, 1985-88; asst. mem. dept. immunology St. Jude Children's Rsch. Hosp., Memphis, 1988-93, assoc. mem., 1993—; asst. prof. dept. pathology U. Tenn., Memphis, 1991—; spkr. immunology seminars and meetings; grant reviewer NIH Study Sect., 1995. Assoc. editor Jour. Immunology, 1995—; contbr. articles to profl. jours., chpts. to books. Cancer Rsch. Inst. postdoctoral fellow; recipient New Investigators Rsch. award NIH, 1984-85; grantee Nat. Cancer Inst., 1992—, NIH, Nat. Inst. of Allergy and Infectious Diseases, 1993-95. Mem. Am. Assn. Immunology. Office: St Jude Childrens Rsch Hosp 332 N Lauderdale St Memphis TN 38105-2729

HURWITZ, RICHARD LOUIS, medical sciences educator; b. Albany, N.Y., Oct. 22, 1951; m. Mary Y. Hurwitz; children: Rebecca, Debra. BS cum laude, Rensselaer Polytechnic Inst., 1975; MD, Albany Med. Coll., 1975. Diplomate Am. Bd. Pediatrics, subspecialty of hematology-oncology. Chief resident Mpls. Children's Hosp., 1977; pediatric resident U. Minn., Mpls., 1975-78, postdoctoral fellow dept. pediatrics, 1978-80, rsch. fellow dept. biochemistry, 1979-80; sr. fellow pharmacology U. Wash., Seattle, 1980-84; asst. prof. dept. pediatrics Baylor Coll. Medicine, Houston, 1984-94, asst. prof. dept. cell biology, 1984-94, asst. prof. dept. ophthalmology, 1991-94, assoc. prof. dept pediatrics, 1995—, assoc. prof. cell biology, 1995—, assoc. prof. dept. ophthalmology, 1995—; adj. asst. prof. U. Houston, 1991—; investigator Pediatric Oncology Group, Nat. Cancer Inst., 1985—. Contbg. author: Principles and Practice of Pediatrics, 1989, 2d edit., 1994, Drug Formulary and Information, 1992; contbr. articles to profl. jours.; author abstracts. Recipient awards NIH, 1983-84, 85-86, 89-90, 86-96, Nat. Rsch. Svc. award, 1980-81, Clin. Oncology Career Devel. award Am. Cancer Soc., 1985-88; travel fellow Assn. for Rsch. in Vision and Ophthalmology, 1983, others. Fellow Leukemia Soc. Am.; mem. AMA, Am. Acad. Pediatrics, Am. Soc. Biochemistry and Molecular Biology, Assn. Rsch. in Vision and Ophthalmology, Harris County Med. Soc., Houston Pediatric Soc., Pediatric Oncology Group, Soc. for Pediatric Rsch, Tex. Med. Assn. Office: Baylor Coll Medicine 6621 Fannin St Houston TX 77030-2303

HUSBANDS, ANITA ROSETTE, desktop publisher; b. St. Louis, May 16, 1965; d. Enoch Joseph and Rose Dolores (Boiley) Cole; m. Noel Stephen Husbands, July 2, 1992; 1 child, Nehemiah. BS in Engring. Mgmt., U. Mo., Rolla, 1989; BS in Computer Sci., Lander U., Greenwood, S.C., 1992. Computer sys. analyst Monsanto Chem. Co., Greenwood, 1989-90; adj. faculty mem. Piedmont Tech. Coll., Greenwood, 1990-93; tech. support analyst Datastream Sys., Greenville, 1993-94; owner, desktop pub. Fox Graphics, Greenwood, 1994—. Author: (booklet) Resume Writing Tips, 1988. Counselor Club 44, St. Louis, 1978-84; exec. com. mem. Greenwood Rep. Party, 1995-96. Recipient Recognition award Outstanding Coll. Students of Am., 1988. Mem. ASCD, Piedmont Reading Coun., Nat. Coun. Tchrs. Math., Kappa Delta Pi. Roman Catholic. Office: Fox Graphics 718 B Montague Ave Greenwood SC 29649

HUSSAIN, MOINUDDIN SYED, geologist, reservoir engineer, consultant; b. Hyderabad, India, Dec. 28, 1931; s. Karimuddin Syed and Hafeeza Begum (Khan) H.; m. Aziza Moin Quadri, Aug. 20, 1942; children: Qutub, Ayesha, Arju. BS, Osmania U., Hyderabad, 1954; DIC, Imperial Coll., London, 1963; MS, London U., 1964. Registered profl. geologist, Calif. Asst. groundwater geologist Groundwater Devel. Orgn., Lahore, Pakistan, 1955-56; test geologist Std. Vacuum Oil Co. (ESSO), Karachi, Pakistan, 1956-62; superintending geologist Oil and Gas Devel. Corp., Karachi, Pakistan, 1962-69; mgr. exploration/projects Dawood Petroleum Ltd., Karachi, Pakistan, 1969-73; project geologist Hallenbeck McCoy and Assoc., Berkeley, Calif., 1973-75; sr. geologist Dow Chem. Co., USA, Houston, 1975-81; sr. internat. geologist Union Tex. Petroleum Corp., Houston, 1981-85; cons. Hycarbex, Inc., Houston, 1985—; mem. adv. bd. Hycarbex, Inc., Houston, 1985—; advisor Dawood Group of Industries, Karachi, 1969-73; del. to Pakistan, U.S. Dept. of Energy. Founding mem. Internat. Explorationist Group, Houston, 1984. Mem. Am. Assn. Petroleum Geologists (cert. geologist, alt. del. 1984, Cert. of Recognition award 1987), Bangladesh Geol. Soc. (life), Pak-Am. Petroleum Soc. (founder 1983), Houston Geol. Soc. (Svc. award 1985). Republican. Muslim. Office: Hycarbex Inc PO Box 218341 Houston TX 77218

HUSSEY, WARD MACLEAN, lawyer, former government official; b. Providence, Mar. 13, 1920; s. Charles Ward and Agnes (Shaw) H.; children—Thomas Ward, Carolyn Anne Hussey Bourdow, Wendy Ellen Hussey Addison. AB, Harvard U., 1940, LLB, 1946; MA, Columbia U., 1944. Bar: D.C. 1946. With Office of Legis. Counsel, U.S. Ho. of Reps., 79th to 100th Congresses, Washington, 1946-89, dep. legis. counsel, 1970-72, legis. counsel, 1972-89; adviser to fgn. govts. on tax reform, 1989—. Co-author: Basic World Tax Code, 1992, rev. edit., 1996. With USNR, 1942-46. Fellow Harvard Internat. Tax Program (sr.). Home: 312 Princeton Blvd Alexandria VA 22314-4719

HUSTON, EDWIN ALLEN, transportation company executive; b. Dayton, Ohio, June 27, 1938; s. Robert Hyde and Rosemary Barlow (Kuntz) H.; A.B., Amherst Coll., 1960; M.B.A., Harvard U., 1962; m. Jane Nicholas, May 28, 1966. Spl. asst mergers and acquisitions NCR Co., Dayton, 1962-66; controller NCR de Venezuela, Caracas, 1967-69; v.p., controller Fin. Internat. Cons., Ft. Lauderdale, Fla., 1969-73; asst. treas. Ryder System, Inc., Miami, Fla., 1973-74, exec. v.p. fin., 1979-87, now chief fin. officer, sr. exec. v.p. fin.; v.p. fin. Truckstops Am., Nashville, 1974-79; former chmn. Fed. Res. Bank Atlanta; bd. dirs. Unisys Corp.; past chmn., bd. dirs. Sta WPBT Pub. TV, Miami; pres., trustee, Ft. Lauderdale Art Museum. Served with Air N.G., 1963. Republican. Roman Catholic. Mem. Coral Ridge Country Club, Lauderdale Yacht Club. Office: Ryder System Inc 3600 NW 82nd Ave Miami FL 33166-6623

HUSTON, FRED JOHN, retired automotive engineer; b. Muskegon, Mich., June 12, 1929; s. Fred and Sadie (Borgman) Huston; m. Jacqueline Terry, Apr. 28, 1957; children: Sandra, William. BSME, Mich. Tech. U., 1952. Engr. trainee IHC (Navistar), Ft. Wayne, Ind., 1952, test engr., 1953; mech. engr. asst. Aberdeen (Md.) Proving Ground, 1953-55; test engr. IHC (Navistar), Ft. Wayne, 1956, project engr., 1956-82; supr., chassis engr. M.A.N. Truck & Bus Corp., Cleveland, N.C., 1983-86; design engr. Thomas Built Buses, Inc., High Point, N.C., 1987-88, supr. body design, 1988-89, supr. chassis design, 1989-91, sr. staff engr., 1992-94; ret., 1994. With U.S. Army, 1953-55. Mem. Soc. Automotive Engrs. Methodist. Home: 603 Westchester Dr High Point NC 27262-7426

HUSZAGH, FREDRICK WICKETT, lawyer, educator, information management company executive; b. Evanston, Ill., July 20, 1937; s. Rudolph LeRoy and Dorothea (Wickett) H.; m. Sandra McRae, Apr. 4, 1959; children: Floyd McRae, Fredrick Wickett II, Theodore Wickett II. B.A., Northwestern U., 1958; J.D., U. Chgo., 1962, LL.M., 1963, J.S.D., 1964. Bar: Ill. 1962, U.S. Dist. Ct. D.C. 1965, U.S. Supreme Ct. 1966. Market researcher Leo Burnett Co. Chgo., 1958-59; internat. atty. COMSAT, Washington, 1964-67; assoc. Debevoise & Liberman, Washington, 1967-68; asst. prof. law Am. U., Washington, 1968-71; program dir. NSF, Washington, 1971-73; assoc. prof. U. Mont., Missoula, 1973-76, U. Wis.-Madison, 1976-77; exec. dir. Dean Rusk Ctr., U. Ga., Athens, 1977-82; prof. U. Ga., 1982—; chmn. TWH Corp., Athens, 1982—; chmn. Profession Mgmt. Techs., Inc., Athens, 1993—; dir. TWH Scv. Corp.; cons. Pres. Johnson's Telecommunications Task Force, Washington, 1967-68; co-chmn. Nat. Gov.'s Internat. Trade Staff Commn., Washington, 1979- 81. Author: International Decision-Making Process, 1964; Comparative Facts on Canada, Mexico and U.S., 1979; also articles. Editor Rusk Ctr. Briefings, 1981-82. Mem. Econ. Policy Council, N.Y.C., 1981-89. NSF grantee, 1974-78. Republican. Presbyterian. Home: 151E Clayton St Athens GA 30603-1985 Office: U Ga Law Sch Athens GA 30602

HUSZAR, ARLENE CELIA, lawyer, mediator; b. N.Y.C., May 1, 1952; d. Charles and Dora (Toffoli) H.; m. Victor M. Yellen, May 6, 1978; 1 child: Mariette Huszar Yellen. BA, Fla. Atlantic U., 1973; JD, U. Fla., 1976. Bar: Fla. 1977, U.S. Dist. Ct. (mid. and no. dists.) Fla. 1978, U.S. Ct. Appeals (5th and 11th cirs.) 1978, D.C. 1979, U.S. Supreme Ct. 1982; cert. fed. and cir. ct. mediator. Pvt. practice Gainesville, Fla., 1977-80; mng. atty. Fla. Instl. Legal Svcs., Gainesville, 1980—. Author: (with others) Termination of Parental Rights, 1993, Adoption, 1992. Mem. City of Gainesville Citizens Adv. Com. for Cmty. Devel., 1976-79, Fla. Bar Com. on the Legal Needs of Children, 1984-85; mem. steering com. juvenile law sect. Nat. Legal Aid and Defender Assn., 1986-87; vice chmn. Alachua County Citizens Adv. Com., Dept. Criminal Justice Svcs., 1986-95; precinct committeewoman Alachua County Dem. Exec. Com., 1986—. Named one of Outstanding Young Women of Am., 1975. Mem. LWV, Assn. Trial Lawyers Am., Nat. Assn. Counsel for Children, Eighth Jud. Cir. Bar Assn. (bd. dirs. 1994—). Roman Catholic. Office: Fla Instl Legal Svcs 1110 NW 8th Ave Ste C Gainesville FL 32601-4969

HUTCHENS, RUBY R., executive secretary; b. Reidsville, N.C., June 6, 1961; d. Paul Hubert Sr. and Sally Mae (Stanley) Rickman; m. Thomas Penn Hutchens, June 1, 1957; 1 child, James Donald. AAS, Rockingham C.C., Wentworth, N.C., 1990. Sec. Antioch Bapt. Ch., Reidsville, 1993—. Author poems, songs, all occasion card verses. Home: 973 Ashley Loop Rd Reidsville NC 27320

HUTCHEON, WALLACE SCHOONMAKER, history educator; b. N.Y.C., June 27, 1933; s. Wallace Schoonmaker and Dorothy Mae (Tate) H.; m. Margaret Marie Crossen, Sept. 29, 1963; children: Dorothy Lee, Hillary Ann. BS in Agrl. Econs., Pa. State U., 1954; MA in History, George Washington U., 1969, MPhil in History, 1971, PhD in History, 1975. Commd. ensign U.S. Naval Res., 1955, advanced through grades to comdr., 1970; comm. officer Naval Air Sta., Key West, Fla., 1955-59; edn. officer in USS Kitty Hawk, 1962-64; air intelligence officer CVW-2, 1964-66; intelligence analyst, 1966-70, released to inactive duty, 1970, ret., 1976; lectr. George Mason U., Fairfax, Va., 1970; instr. St. Marys Coll., Md., 1971; asst. prof. history No. Va. C.C., Annandale, 1971-75, assoc. prof., 1975-80, prof., 1980—, head dept., 1974—, asst. chmn. div. social scis. and pub. services, 1979—; mgmt. tng. cons. Health Resources Adminstrn., HEW, Hyattsville, Md., 1978; cons. mil. evaluations program Am. Coun. Edn., Washington, 1980; cons. coll. hist. textbooks Houghton-Mifflin Co., Boston, Mass., 1992—; mem. adv. bd. Annual Editions, Dushkin Pub. Co.; pub. speaker Mariners Mus., D.C. Historians Luncheon, others. Author: Robert Fulton: Pioneer of Undersea Warfare, 1981. Contbr. to manuscripts collection U.S.

Navy History Divsn. Recipient Outstanding Contributions to Edn. award Alumni Fedn. No. Va. C.C., 1993, 95. Mem. U.S. Naval Inst., Orgn. Am. Historians, No. Va. Assn. History (bd. dirs. 1994, v.p. 1995), U.S. Capitol Hist. Soc., Delta Chi. Democrat. Episcopalian. Avocations: swimming, reading, music, theatre. Home: 4425 Village Dr Fairfax VA 22030-5642 Office: No Va CC 8333 Little River Tpke Annandale VA 22003-3743

HUTCHERSON, DONNA DEAN, music educator; b. Dallas, July 10, 1937; d. Lamar Shaffer and Lenora Fay (Newbern) Clark; m. George Henry Hutcherson, Jan. 31, 1959; children: Lamar, Michael, Mark Lee, Holly (dec.), Shela. B. Music Edn., Sam Houston State U., Huntsville, Tex., 1959; MA in Music, Stephen F. Austin State U., Nacogdoches, Tex., 1974; postgrad., Memphis State U., 1986-89. Cert. tchr. usic K-12, Orff levels 1, 2, 3 and master and computer literacy, Tex. Tchr. music 4th and 5th grades Carthage (Tex.) Ind. Sch. Dist., 1958-59; tchr. music grades 1-5 and h.s. choir Hallsville (Tex.) Ind. Sch. Dist., 1969-75, tchr. music K-4, 1975-78, tchr. music grades 3-4, 1978-86, tchr. music 4th grade, 1986—; contbr. Jour. of Music Edn. Delegation to Vietnam Citizen Ambassador Program, 1993. Contbr. articles to profl. jours. Mem. Music Educators Nat. Conf. (registered in music edn.), Tex. Music Educators Conf. (Tri-M chmn. 1993—), Tex. Music Educators Assn. (region IV chmn. 1975-93), Am. Orff Schulewerk Assn., Tri M Internat. Music Honor Soc. (local chpt. sponsor 1992—, hon. mem.). Methodist. Home: RR 2 Box 107-c Hallsville TX 75650-9630 Office: Hallsville Intermediate Sch PO Box 810 Hallsville TX 75650-0810

HUTCHERSON, KAREN FULGHUM, healthcare consultant; b. Winston-Salem, N.C., Oct. 1, 1951; d. John Fulghum and Viola Sprinkle Shaw; m. Victor J. Hutcherson, Dec. 18, 1970; children: Shannon Renae, Ashley Michelle. Diploma, N.C. Bapt. Hosp. Sch. Nursing, 1972; BSN, N.C. A&T State U., 1981; MBA, Wake Forest U., 1990. RN. Staff nurse N.C. Bapt. Hosp., Winston-Salem, 1972; oncology nurse clinician Cancer Ctr., Wake Forest U., Winston-Salem, 1972-81; oncology nurse educator Bowman Gray Sch. of Med., Wake Forest U., Winston-Salem, 1981-87, dir. nursing cancer ctr., 1982-87; asst. dir. clin. support svcs. Bowman Gray Sch. Medicine, Winston-Salem, 1987-96; cons. healthcare and orgnl. devel. Hayes Consulting and Tng. Group, Inc., Winston-Salem, 1996; dir. consulting svcs. Mgmt. Directions of N.C., Winston-Salem, 1996—; curriculum coord., primary inst. Cancer Ctr., 1980-87; mem. spkrs. bur. A.H. Robbins Pharms. Co., 1983-88; cons. S.E. Cancer Control Consortium, Winston-Salem, 1987-90. Author: Patient Education in Understanding Cancer: An Introductory Handbook, 1986; co-author: Understanding Cancer Treatment: A Guide for You and Your Family, 1988, Cancer Chemotherapy Guidelines, 5th edit., 1985. Chmn. western div. nursing com. N.C. Am. Cancer Soc., 1981-82, speakers' bur., 1982, bd. dirs. 1988-92.; mem. spl. rev. com. clin. community oncology program Nat. Cancer Inst., Bethesda, Md., 1987. Recipient Leadership award Babcock Grad. Sch. Mgmt., Wake Forest U., 1992. Mem. ANA, Am. Acad. Ambulatory Nursing Adminstrn., Med. Ctr. Nursing Assn., Piedmont Oncology Assn. (numerous coms.), Oncology Nursing Soc. (mem. com.), Nat. League for Nursing, Am. Orgn. Nursing Execs., Med. Group Mgmt. Assn., S.E. Cancer Control Consortium, N.C. Nurses Assn. (legis. com. 1989, vice chmn. commun. health coun., del. conv. 1987, 88, 89, 90, 91), Sigma Theta Tau. Home: 754 Lacock Ave Rural Hall NC 27045-9742 Office: Mgmt Directions of N C Ste 301 380 Knollwood St Ste M Winston Salem NC 27103

HUTCHESON, J. STERLING, allergist, immunologist, physician; b. Richmond, Va., Apr. 17, 1936; s. James P. and Daisy-Clarke (Lorentz) H.; m. Nancy Montgomery Sanders, May 20, 1961; children: Anne Farrar, Betsy Dulaney. Student, Roanoke Coll., Va., 1953-55; BA, U. Va., 1955-57; MD, The Johns Hopkins U., 1957-61. Diplomate Am. Bd. Allergy and Clin. Immunology. Intern in medicine U. Va., Charlottesville, Va., 1961-62; resident in medicine Med. Coll. Va., Richmond, Va., 1962-64; fellow in allergy and immunology U. Va., Charlottesville, Va., 1964-65; asst. prof. medicine Medical Coll. Va., 1967-68; dir. Med. Coll. Va., 1967-68; staff Nalle Clinic, Charlotte, 1968-89; pvt. practice Carolina Asthma and Allergy Ctr., 1990—; founder Allergy Clinic USAF Acad. Hosp., Colo., 1965-67; cons. Blue Cross/Blue Shield of N.C.; adj. asst. prof. pediats. U. N.C. Sch. Medicine, Carolinas Med. Ctr., Charlotte. Bd. trustees Charlotte County Day Sch., 1974-85; bd. dirs. Friends of Music Queens Coll., 1994—. Capt. USAF M.C. Fellow Am. Acad. Allergy and Immunology, Am. Coll. Allergy and Immunology; mem. Southeastern Allergy Assn., N.C. Soc. Allergy and Clin. Immunology (former pres.). Episcopalian. Home: 4200 Arbor Way Charlotte NC 28211-3812 Office: Carolina Asthma & Allergy Bldg 400 2711 Randolph Rd Charlotte NC 28207-2027

HUTCHINS, CYNTHIA BARNES, special education educator; b. Macon, Ga., Apr. 29, 1954; d. Robert O. and Emily Ann (Coody) Barnes; m. Joe Thrash Hutchins, June 15, 1975; children: Joey, Jason. BS in Edn., U. Ga., 1976, MEd, 1981; EdS, Brenau U., 1996. Cert. tchr., Ga. Tchr. Bethlehem (Ga.) Elem. Sch., 1976-78, Winder (Ga.) Elem. Sch., 1983-85, Auburn (Ga.) Elem. Sch., 1985-92; tchr., staffing coord. Bramlett Elem. Sch., Auburn, 1992—; mem. spl. edn. adv. com., mem. inclusion task force, mentor tchr., tchr. support specialist Barrow County, 1990—. Sunday sch. tchr. Midway Meth. Ch., Carl, Ga., 1975-80, 90-93; leader Boy Scouts Am., Barrow County, 1986-90; active PTO. Named Tchr. of Yr., Auburn Elem. Sch., 1986. Mem. ASCD, Coun. for Exceptional Children, Alpha Delta Kappa, Phi Delta Kappa. Home: 1165 Bankhead Hwy Winder GA 30680-3431

HUTCHINS, GEORGIA CAMERON, critical care nurse; b. Detroit, Jan. 21, 1957; d. Jessie Cameron and Letha A. (Minor) Taylor; m. Joseph Hutchins, Aug. 28, 1976; children: Justin C., Jason E., Jarron E. BS, Alcorn State U., 1990. CPR instr. Staff nurse ICU Jefferson-Davis Meml. Hosp., Natchez, Miss.; instr. dept. baccalaureate nursing Alcorn State U. Mem. NSNA, Eliza Pillars State RNs Assn. Home: 10 Upper Kingston Rd Natchez MS 39120-9704

HUTCHINS, KAREN LESLIE, psychotherapist; b. Denver, Sept. 9, 1943; d. Kimball Frederick and Bonnie Illa (Small) H.; divorced; 1 child, Alec Klinghoffer. BA, U. Denver, 1965; MA, George Washington U., 1972. Lic. profl. counselor clin. hypnotherapist; cert. clin. hypnotherapist; cert. chem. dependency specialist; registered sex offender treatment provider. Tchr. Washington D.C. Sch., 1966-70; asst. housing adminstr. George Washington U., Washington, 1970-72; counselor/instr. No. Va. C.C., Annandale, Va., 1972-77, Austin (Tex.) C.C., 1977-80; co-owner Hearts Day Care, Austin, 1980-81; supr./therapist MaryLee Resdl. Treatment, Austin, 1981-82; child protective svc. worker Dept. Human Resources, Austin, 1982-84; probation officer Adult Probation Travis County, Austin, 1984-90; lead therapist Cottonwood Treatment Ctrs., Bastrop, Tex., 1990-91; psychotherapist Austin, 1991—. Author conf. presentation: Beyond Survival, 1990-92, Why Me? vs. Spirtuality, 1993, Integrating the Wounded Soul, 1994, Ritually Abused Children, 1994, Recognizing PTSD Symptoms in Children, 1996. Vol. trainer Hotline, Austin, 1993—. Mem. ACA, Internat. Soc. Trauma and Stress Studies, Tex. Assn. Alcoholism and Drug Abuse Counselors. Democrat. Jewish. Office: Cicada Recovery Svcs 3004 S 1st St Austin TX 78704-6373

HUTCHINSON, DAVID ROBERT, IV, sales executive; b. Huntington, Ind., June 29, 1945; s. David Robert and Orpha Marie (McKee) H.; m. Lynn Dorothy Gooley, July 2, 1966; children: Holly Lynn, Heather Leah. Announcer WFFG Radio, Marathon, Fla., 1962-65, WSRF Radio, Ft. Lauderdale, Fla., 1965-69; salesman WSRF/WSHE Radio, Ft. Lauderdale, 1969-72; salesman WGMA Radio, Ft. Lauderdale, 1972-74, sales mgr., gen. mgr., 1974-77; sales mgr. WQYK Radio, Tampa-St. Petersburg, Fla., 1977—. Mem. Nat. Assn. Credit Mgrs. (dir. 1981-86). Republican. Presbyterian. Home: 2104 Flamingo Pl Safety Harbor FL 34695

HUTCHINSON, JULIUS STEVEN, financial services company executive; b. Greensboro, N.C., Oct. 10, 1952; s. Jimmie Wayne and Geneva (Chester) H.; m. Karen Barber, Apr. 2, 1982; children: Cassandra, Raymond, Jason, Bryant, Aaron, Andrew, Joshua. Student, Guilford Tech. Community Coll., 1981-86. Cert. fin. planner. Enlisted USMC, 1969, advanced through grades to sgt., 1976, resigned, 1978; mgr. Food Dimensions, Inc., San Francisco, 1978-81, Macke Co., Greensboro, 1981-83; v.p. Fin. Group, Greensboro, 1983-84; exec. v.p. Cornwallis Investment Corp., Greensboro, 1984-86; pres., chief exec. officer Delta Fin. Svcs. Corp., Greensboro, 1986—. Republican. Baptist. Office: Delta Adv Group Inc Ste 100 3300 Battleground Ave Greensboro NC 27410

HUTCHINSON, OLIN FULMER, JR., transportation executive, data processing consultant; b. Batesburg, S.C, Nov. 28, 1943; s. Olin Fulmer Sr. and Alma Marie (Rogers) H.; m. Mary Susan Edge, Mar. 18. 1972; children: Jason Fulmer, Crystal Marie. B in Commerce, U. Richmond, 1970; postgrad. in computers, Charlotte, N.C., 1975—. Corp. traffic mgr. Lea Industries, Inc., Richmond, Va., 1964-71; branch mgr. C&B Fork Lift, Inc., Lynchburg, Va., 1971-74; v.p. Fuller Transp., Inc., Columbia, S.C., 1977-78; traffic mgr. Seabrook Blanching, Sylvester, Ga., 1978-80; asst. mgr. transp. svcs. Belk Stores Svcs., Inc., Charlotte, 1980—; owner Computer Svcs., Charlotte, 1981—; speaker on hist. topics; owner, driver Hutchinson Racing Team, Richmond, 1969-72. Author various hist. books and poems; editor, compiler: My Dear Mother & Sisters (Alfred B. Mulligan), 1992. Active community affairs, Charlotte, 1980—. Mem. S.C. Hist. Soc., Dutch Fork Geneal. and Hist. Soc., Old Newberry Dist. Geneal. Soc., West Atando Bus. Assn. (v.p., treas. 1980—), SAR, SCV (1st lt. comdr. 1985-86), Mil. Order Stars and Bars, Ye Olde Mecklenburg Geneal. Soc., Sertoma (various offices). Home: 4706 Cheviot Rd Charlotte NC 28269-4559 Office: Belk Stores Svcs Inc 2301 Nevada Blvd Charlotte NC 28273-6421

HUTCHINSON, RICHARD GLENN, medical educator, researcher; b. La Grange, Ga., Aug. 18, 1933; s. Richard (dec.) and Margaret (Jordan) H.; m. Celeste Clanton, June 20, 1959; children: Richard G. Jr., Wendell C. BA, Emory U., 1955; MD, Med. Coll. Ga., 1959. Intern Bapt. Hosp., Nashville, 1959-60; resident in internal medicine Med. Coll. Ga. Hosps., 1960-63, Ga. Heart Assn. fellow in cardiology, 1963-64; faculty U. Miss. Med. Sch., Jackson, 1967—, prof. medicine, 1986—, dir. preventive cardiology program, attending physician univ. hosp.; mem. Nat. Speakers Bur., Internat. Med. Edn. Corp., 1974-84; program com. chmn. Southeastern Regional Hypertension Conf., Biloxi, Miss., 1983; ad hoc cons. and chmn. for numerous ad hoc coms. Nat. Heart, Lung and Blood Inst., 1980—, mem. steering com. and chmn. publs. com. atherosclerosis risk in communities study, mem. steering com. and editorial rev. com. nat. aspirin myocardial infarction study; presenter, lectr. and rschr. in field. Reviewer Archives of Internal Medicine, 1986-87, 91—; author: Coronary Prevention: A Clinical Guide, 1985; contbr. chpts. to books and articles to profl. jours. Mem. adminstrv. bd. Broadmeadow United Meth. Ch., Jackson. Capt. USAF, 1964-66. Recipient Acad. award in preventive cardiology Nat. Heart, Lung and Blood Inst., 1979, Bronze Disting. Svc. award Miss. Affiliate Am. Heart Assn., 1983, Silver Disting. Svc. award Miss. Affiliate Am. Heart Assn., 1989. Fellow ACP (Traveling scholarship award 1970), Am. Coll. Cardiology, Coll. Chest Physicians (steering com. sect. on hypertension 1983-87, abstract rev. annual session Chgo. 1983, Dallas 1984, San Francisco 1986), Am. Heart Assn. (fellow coun. on cardiovascular epidemiology), Miss. Heart Assn. (bd. dirs. 1981-91, exec. com. 1982-90, sec. 1985-86, v.p. 1986-87, pres.-elect 1987-88, pres. 1988-89), Sigma Xi, Eta Sigma Psi. Methodist. Office: Univ Miss Med Ctr 2500 N State St Jackson MS 39216-4500

HUTCHISON, HUMPHREY GRAY, retired compensation and benefits consulting company executive; b. Maryville, Tenn., Oct. 2, 1919; s. Gustavus Alexander and Elizabeth Sue (Callaway) H.; m. Betsy Ann Dana, Aug. 9, 1944; children: Humphrey Gray Jr., Frederick Dana, Rebecca H. Saunders. BS in Math., Harvard Coll., 1941. CLU, 1947. Sales rep. Penn Mut. Life Ins. Co., Maryville, 1941-42, 46-50; gen. agt. Penn Mut. Life Ins. Co., Raleigh, N.C., 1950-65; founder, chief exec. officer Hutchison & Assocs., Inc., Raleigh, 1950-95; mng. ptnr. Dana Bldg. Co., Raleigh, 1968—; mem. So. Pension Conf., Atlanta, 1978-91. Editor: (newsletter) Executive Slants on Employee Benefits, 1966-93. Trustee Tenn. Mil. Inst., Sweetwater, 1948-68; comdr. Am. Legion, Maryville, 1946-50; elder White Meml. Ch., Raleigh, 1961—; patron mem. N.C. Mus. of History Assocs., Raleigh, 1976—, Raleigh Little Theatre, 1950—; mem. Rep. Presdl. Task Force, Washington, 1989—. Maj. U.S. Army, 1942-46, Eng., France and Germany. Decorated Bronze Star. Mem. Am. Coll. Life Underwriters, Harvard Club (pres. Research Triangle N.C. chpt. 1994-96), Racquet Shores Tennis Club (sec., treas. 1980-95), Carolina Country Club, Lions (Marvin Jones Fellowship award 1994). Democrat. Presbyterian. Home: 1501 Pineview St Raleigh NC 27608-2119

HUTCHISON, KAY BAILEY, senator; b. Galveston, TX, July 22, 1943; d. Allan and Kathryn Bailey; m. Ray Hutchison. BA, U. Tex., 1992, LLB, 1967. Bar: Tex. 1967. TV news reporter Houston, 1969-71, pvt. practice law, 1969-74; press sec. to Anne Armstrong, 1971; vice chmn. Nat. Transp. Safety Bd., 1976-78; asst. prof. U. Tex., Dallas, 1978-79; sr. v.p., gen. counsel Republic of Tex. Corp., Dallas, 1979-81; of counsel Hutchison, Boyle, Brooks & Fisher, Dallas, 1981-91; mem. Tex. Ho. of Reps., 1972-76; elected treas. of Tex., 1990, U.S. senator from Tex., 1993—. Fellow Am. Bar Found., Tex. Bar Found.; mem. ABA, State Bar of Tex., Dallas Bar Assn., U. Tex. Law Alumni Assn. (pres. 1985-86). Republican.

HUTMAN, BURTON S., psychiatrist, educator; b. N.Y.C., Feb. 6, 1932; s. Herman W. and Regina Hutman; m. Jacqueline Kalchman, Mar. 5, 1961; children: Herbert, Cherie, Bernard, Michael. BA with honors in Psychology, Johns Hopkins U., 1954; MD, U. Pitts., 1960. Rotating intern Jewish Hosp., Cin., 1960-61; resident in psychiatry, teaching fellow U. Pitts. Med. Sch., 1961-64; pvt. practice, Washington, 1966-70, Miami, Fla., 1978-81, 84-85; asst. prof. U. Miami, 1970-78, clin. asst. prof., then clin assoc. prof., 1978—; assoc. dean, cons. for academics, lectr. Am. U. of Caribbean Med. Sch., Brit. W.I., 1981-84; staff psychiatrist Health Rehab. Svcs., Miami, 1985-86, 90-91; med. exec. dir. Fla. Landmark Ctr., 1986-90; dir. psychiat. svcs. Bayview Ctr. for Mental Health, North Miami, Fla., 1991-96; clin. asst. prof. psychiatry Nova Southeastern Osteo. Med. Sch., 1993—; attending psychiatrist, dir., developer of crisis stblzn. unit (first in state of Fla.), U. Miami-Jackson Med. Ctr., 1970-77; compensation examiner Miami VA Hosp., 1976-78; courtesy attending Mt. Sinai Med. Ctr., 1977—; staff psychiatrist Miami Jewish Hosp. and Home for Aged, 1979-81, Douglas Gardens Cmty. Mental Health Ctr., 1980-81; med. edn. dir. Golden Glades Med. Ctr., Miami, 1989. Bd. dirs. Hebrew Acad. Miami, Miami Beach, Fla., 1979-83; panelist Mental Health Assn., Miami; panelist on geriatrics for TV sta., Miami. Lt. comdr. USN, 1964-66. Fellow Am. Physicians Fellowship; mem. Am. Psychiat. Assn. (life), South Fla. Psychiat. Soc. (life), Am. Acad. Pain Mgmt. (life, diplomate, mem. editl. bd. 1985), Am. Assn. Physician Execs., Assn. Orthodox Jewish Scientists (nat. bd. dirs. 1970-71), Nepesh, Mesorah, Phi Sigma Delta, Phi Epsilon Pi, Phi Lambda Kappa. Address: PO Box 402367 Miami FL 33140-0367 Office: East Coast Med Mgmt 2020 NE 163rd St North Miami Beach FL 33162

HUTSON, HENRY CRITCHFIELD, academic administrator; b. Charleston, S.C., May 27, 1927; s. William Elliott and Katherine Curtis (Critchfield) H.; m. Harriet Lowndes Rhett Maybank; children: Mary Pope Maybank Hutson Waring, William Elliott II. BA in Polit. Sci., U. of the South, Sewanee, 1950; postgrad., U. S.C., 1951-52; M. in Ednl. Adminstrn., Western Carolina U., 1969. Stockbroker Johnson Lane Space/R.S. Dickson, Charleston, 1958-63; instr. Christ Sch., Arden, N.C., 1963-71, asst. headmaster, 1967-71; headmaster Sewanee (Tenn.) Acad., 1971-77; adminstrv. officer U. of the South, Sewanee, 1971-77; headmaster Christ Sch., 1977-87, East Cooper Sch., Mt. Pleasant, S.C., 1987-89; dir. spl. projects Coll. Charleston, 1989—, recording sec. bd. trustees, 1991—; Mem. bd. trustees U. of the South, 1980—, bd. advisors St. Andrews-Sewanee Sch., St. Andrews, Tenn., 1983—. Maj. USMC, 1945-46, 53-56, Korea. Mem. Phi Delta Kappa.

HUTSON, HERBERT DON, wholesale distribution executive; b. Cross Plains, Tex., Dec. 20, 1936; s. Herbert Henry and Mary Bertha (Witt) H.; m. Alice Ann Harper, Aug. 29, 1959; children: Bruce Randall, Brenda Irene, Lisa Michelle. BA, U. Tex., 1969. Oper. mgr. Graybar Electric, Austin, 1963-66; sr. underwriter Aetna Life & Casualty, Dallas, 1969-73; spl. agent, field mgr. Commercial Std. Ins. Co., San Antonio, 1973-75; owner, mgr. Villa Motel, San Antonio, 1973-85; owner Video Country, San Antonio, 1985-87; video wholesale distributor SAVE, San Antonio, 1987-96. Coauthor: (cookbook) Tomas' Tequila Book, 1992. Home: 270 E Skyview Dr San Antonio TX 78228 Office: SAVE 114 E Arrowhead Dr San Antonio TX 78228

HUTTENSTINE, MARIAN LOUISE, journalism educator; b. Bloomsburg, Pa., Jan. 26, 1940; d. Ralph Benjamin and Marian Louise (Engler) H. BS, Bloomsburg State U., 1961, MEd, 1966; postgrad., Rutgers U., 1962-63; PhD, U. N.C., 1985. High sch. English & journalism tchr., dept. chmn., 1961-66; asst. prof. Lock Haven (Pa.) U., 1966-73, assoc. prof. English, 1973-74; teaching asst., lectr. Sch. Journalism, U. N.C., Chapel Hill, 1974-76; cons., dir. Diener & Assocs., Research Triangle Park, N.C., 1975-86; asst. prof. journalism, Coll. Comm. U. Ala., Tuscaloosa, 1977-93; assoc. prof. comm. Coll. Comm. and Fine Arts Jacksonville State Univ., 1993-95; assoc. prof. Radford (Va.) U., 1995—. cons. various publs., Ala., 1977—. Contbr. papers to profl. lit. Adult leader, vol. worker Episc. Ch., 1994—. NDEA fellow, Newspaper Fund fellow Rutgers U., 1962-63. Mem. ACLU, NAFE, Assn. Edn. in Journalism and Mass Communication, Nat. Fedn. Press Women, Ala. Media Profls. (Communicator of Yr. 1994), Kappa Tau Alpha, Ala. SPJ Club. Home: 494 Fombys Ferry Rd Ohatchee AL 36271-5146 Office: Radford U Dept Media Studies Box 6932 Radford VA 24142

HUTTON, MICHAEL THOMAS, planetarium and observatory administrator; b. Levittown, N.Y., Feb. 4, 1951; s. James Joseph and Lorraine (Strolheim) H.; m. Marilyn Snofsky, Jan. 13, 1973 (div. Oct. 1983); m. Joanne Aguiar, Nov. 11, 1989. BS, SUNY, Plattsburgh, 1972; MEd, Clarion (Pa.) State U., 1976. Tchr. Mohanasen Mid. Sch., Albany, N.Y., 1973-74; dir. planetarium Clearfield (Pa.) High Sch., 1974-76, Astronaut Meml. Hall, Cocoa, Fla., 1977—; bus. mgr. Voyages, Jackson, Miss., 1990—; sec.-treas. C-360 Systems, Inc., Reno, 1987-93, pres., 1992-94; cons. Navarro Coll., Corsicana, Tex., 1993-94; host Internat. Planetariums, Salt Lake City, 1994. Contbr. articles to profl. jours.; sound engr. film Space Shuttle, An American Adventure, 1985; designer Astronaut Meml. Planetarium, 1993. Chmn. social devel. United Way, Cocoa, 1992-93; founder Space Coast Sci. Edn. Alliance, Cocoa, 1993; founding mem. Apollo Silver Anniversary Com., Cocoa Beach, Fla., 1993-94. Recipient Cir. of Excellence award Photonics Spectra, 1993, Exemplary Practices award Fla. Assn. C.C.'s, 1993; grantee Fla. Arts Coun., 1993; internat. study exch. fellow Rotary, 1986. Fellow Internat. Planetarium Soc. (coun. 1990—), Royal Astron. Soc.; mem. S.E. Planetarium Soc. (conf. chmn. 1979, 87), Rocky Mountain Planetarium Soc., Digistar Users Groups (conf. chmn. 1994). Office: Astronaut Meml Planetarium & Obs 1519 Clearlake Rd Cocoa FL 32922-6503

HUTZLER, LISA ANN, mental health nurse, adult clinical psychologist; b. Marietta, Ohio, Oct. 8, 1955; d. Donald Hayes and Winifred Maxine (Clark) Hutzler; m. Ernest Edwin Miller Jr., May 24, 1980; children: Nathan Andrew Miller, Daniel Seth Miller. BA in Psychology, Marietta Coll., 1977; AAS, Parkersburg Community Coll., W.Va., 1980; MA in Psychology, W. Va. Grad. Coll., 1995. RN, W.Va. RN adult psychiat. unit Cuyahoga Falls (Ohio) Gen. Hosp., 1982-83; staff nurse adult mental health St. Joseph's Hosp., Parkersburg, 1980-82, 85-91; personal care nurse Braley and Thompson, Vienna, W. Va., 1992-93. Vol. Boy Scouts Am./standard first aid instr., ARC. Mem. ANA, W.Va. Nurses Assn.

HUX, ROBERT C., company executive; b. 1946. BS in Bus. Mgmt., Tex. A&M U. CPA, Tex. Acct. Ernst & Ernst, 1967-76; various exec. positions, 1976-90; co-founder, pres., CEO, HEI Corp.; co-founder, chmn. Focal Corp.; founder, chmn. Forest Recycling, L.C.; chmn. bd. MCX Corp., Houston; owner, operator 14 Blockbuster Video Stores, Harris County, Tex.; also founder several other cos. Active Houston Livestock Show and Rodeo. Office: MCX Corp 1717 St James Pl Ste 600 Houston TX 77056

HUYETT, DEBRA KATHLEEN, elementary education educator; b. Massillon, Ohio, Oct. 10, 1955; d. William Wilbur and Vivian Delores (Anderson) H. BA, Stetson U., 1978. Cert. elem. and early childhood edn. tchr., Fla. Dir. assistance and long distance operator Gen. Telephone, Myrtle Beach, S.C., summer 1974-76; desk clk. Bon Villa Motel, Myrtle Beach, summer 1976-79; tchr. Lake Orienta Elem. Sch., Altamonte Springs, Fla., 1978-88, Bear Lake Elem. Sch., Apopka, Fla., 1988—; curriculum rep. Lake Orienta Elem. Sch., 1980-88, v.p. PTA, 1984-85; mem. Sch. Adv. Bd., 1995-97. Campaign vol. City Coun. Rep., Massillon, 1973; counselor Orange County Jail Ministry, Orlando, Fla., 1988-91. Named to Most Admired Men and Women of the Yr., 1995. Mem. Fla. Reading Conv. (chairperson Orlando chpt. 1983-84, chairperson for transp. and tours 1985-86), Seminole Edn. Assn. (faculty rep. Sanford, Fla. chpt. 1980-81), Seminde County Reading Coun., Delta Kappa Gamma. Republican. Baptist. Home: 893 Little Bend Rd Altamonte Springs FL 32714-7514

HWANG, TE-LONG, neurologist, educator; b. Hualien, Taiwan, Republic of China, Nov. 4, 1943; came to U.S., 1976; s. Tien-Fu and Tien (Liu) H.; m. Ai-Yu Chau, June 15, 1943; children: Tang-Hau Jimmy, Tang-Chieh George. MD, Nat. Def. Med. Ctr., Taipei, Taiwan, 1970. Intern New Brunswick (N.J.) Affiliated Hosps., 1976-77; pathology resident North Shore Univ. Hosp., Manhasset, N.Y., 1977-79; neurology resident U. Tex. Med. Sch., Houston, 1979-82; neuro-oncology fellow U. Tex. M.D. Anderson Cancer Ctr., Houston, 1983-85; attending neurologist VA Hosp., Topeka, Kans., 1986-88, Columbia, S.C., 1988—; assoc. prof. U. S.C. Sch. Medicine, Columbia, 1988-94, prof., 1994—. Mem. Am. Acad. Neurology, Am. Heart Assn. Stroke Coun. Home: 7 Birchbark Ct Columbia SC 29223-9002 Office: 3555 Harden Street Ext Columbia SC 29203-6815

HYATT, CATHY BEAVER, elementary school educator; b. Mooresville, N.C., Sept. 2, 1955; d. Jimmy Lee and Catherine Lucille (Fisher) Beaver; m. Franklin Murry Hyatt, June 6, 1976; children: Jennifer Nicole, Adam Alexander Lee. BS in Elem. Edn., ASU, 1976; MEd, Gardner-Webb, 1985; M in Adminstrn., U. N.C., 1995, M in Supervision, 1996. Cert. tchr., N.C.; cert. nat. bd. early childhood generalist. Tchr. Park View Elem., Mooresville, N.C., 1976-92, South Elem., Mooresville, 1992-95; instructional program coord. WR Odell Elem., Concord, N.C., 1995—; univ. supr. of student tchrs. U. N.C., 1992-94. Co-author: (handbook) Nocions, 1988. Deacon 1st Bapt. Ch., 1995—. Mem. ASCD, Profl. Educators of N.C., Kappa Kappa Iota. Baptist. Home: 7480 Beaver Ln Kannapolis NC 28081

HYDE, GORDON LEE, surgeon, educator; b. Alma, Mich., May 24, 1932; s. Frank Calvin and Laverne Hyde; m. Constance Ruth Hilton, June 18, 1955; children: Martha, Robert, Anne. BS, U. Mich., 1955, MD, 1957. Intern U. Mich. Med. Ctr., Ann Arbor, 1957-58, resident, 1958-62; pvt. practice Lexington, Ky., 1962-79; assoc. prof. dept. surgery U. Ky. Med. Ctr., Lexington, 1979-85, prof., 1985—; chief of surgery Ctrl. Bapt. Hosp., Lexington, 1970-72; adminstrv. fellow U. Ky. Coll. Medicine, Lexington, 1981-82; clin. instr. dept. surgery U. Mich. Med. Ctr., 1962, asst. clin. prof., 1963; assoc. clin. prof. U. Ky. Med. Ctr., 1973-79; vis. prof. U. Mich. Med. Ctr., 1971, 82, U. S.C., Columbia, 1982, 87, Rutgers U., New Brunswick, N.J., 1985, Charlotte (N.C.) Meml. Hosp., 1986, Maricopa County Hosp., Phoenix, 1986, Orlando (Fla.) Regional Med. Ctr., 1986, many others; cons. in field. Assoc. editor: Surgery, 1988-92, Vascular Forum, 1993; contbr. over 100 articles to profl. jours. Mem. alumni bd. U. Mich. Med. Ctr., 1983-88; bd. dirs. Shepherd's Halfway House for Men, 1986—; active Mayor's Ad Hoc Com. for Alcohol and Drug Problems, 1990—, Mayor's Task Force on Drunken Driving, 1982-83, Lexington-Fayette Urban County Coun. Task Force, 1990—; bd. dirs. Ky. War on Drugs Inc., 1983-84, HOPE Ctr., 1987—, Chrysalis Halfway House for Women, Lexington, 1982—; active Gov.'s Champions Against Drugs, 1987—. Recipient 1st ann. Gordon L. Hyde award U. Ky. Residency Program, 1981. Mem. Am. Assn. Clin. Anatomists, Am. Bd. Surgery, ACS (pres.-elect Ky. chpt. 1978, pres. 1979-80, bd. govs. on impaired physician 1990—), Am. Heart Assn., AMA, Am. Soc. Addiction Medicine (state pres. 1986), Ctrl. Surg. Assn., Fayette County Med. Soc. (sec. 1966, v.p. 1967), Frederick A. Coller Surg. Soc. (pres. 1986-87), Internat. Cardiovascular Soc., Internat. Soc. for Surgery, Ky. Med. Assn., Ky. Surg. Soc. (pres. 1986-87), Ky. Vascular Surgery Soc., Lexington Surg. Soc., many others. Home: 3311 Brookhill Cir Lexington KY 40502-3310 Office: U Ky Dept Surger Rm C-220 800 Rose St Lexington KY 40536-0084

HYDE, JAMES A., service executive; b. Oklahoma City, Nov. 16, 1945; s. Charles D. and Margret W. (Dray) Hyde; divorced; children: James A. Jr., Laurie. BBA in Acctg., U. Okla., 1969; JD, Oklahoma City U., 1972. CPA, Okla. Tax acct. Kerr McGee Corp., Oklahoma City, 1969-70; controller Bone & Joint Hosp., Oklahoma City, 1970-74, hosp. adminstr., 1974—; clinic adminstr. McBride Clinic, Inc., Oklahoma City, 1974—; bd. dirs. Park Ave. N.A., Oklahoma City, Okla. Hosp. Assn., MPSI, Dewey, Okla.; sec.-

treas. Bone and Joint Hosp. Bldg. Corp., Oshco, Inc.; sec., mng. ptnr. Merth Leasing Co. Chmn. Arthritis Bowl, 1980-81, Downtown Oklahoma City City Spring Arts Festival, 1979—, allocation com. United Way, 1986; Co-chmn. Oklahoma City Fall Arts Festival, 1983; pres., bd. dirs. Arthritis Found. 1981—; pres. Oklahoma City Area Hosp. Council, 1981-82; mem. Okla. Estate Planning Council, adv. and informational group Businessmen's Forum for Sen. Don Nichols, goals com. Oklahoma City C. of C. Mem. Am. Acad. Med. Adminstrs., Am. Soc. Hosp. Attys., Healthcare Fin. Mgmt. Assn., Am. Inst. CPA's, Okla. Soc. CPA's, Okla. State Bd. Pub. Accountancy, ABA, Okla. County Bar Assn., Okla. State Bar Assn., Young Pres. Orgns., Phi Gamma Delta, Phi Delta Phi. Democrat. Methodist. Clubs: Dinner, Golf and Country (Oklahoma City). *

HYDE, JAMES FRANKLIN, chemist, consultant; b. Solvay, N.Y., Mar. 11, 1903; s. Burton DeForest and Amelia (Bennett) H.; m. Hildegard Erna Lesche, June 25, 1928; children: Ann Hildegard, James F. Jr., Sylvia Hyde Schuster. AB, Syracuse U., 1923, MA, 1925; PhD, U. Ill., 1928. Postdoctoral fellow Harvard U., 1928-30; chemist Corning Glass Works, 1930-51; sr. scientist, chem. researcher Dow Corning Corp., 1951-75; indsl. chem. rsch. cons. Marco Island, Fla., 1975—; abstractor Glasstechnische Berichte Chem. Abstracts, Ceramic Abstracts. Contbr. articles to profl. jours. Recipient Mich. Patent Law Assn. award, 1963, Perkin medal Am. sect. Soc. Chem. Industry, 1971, Midgley award Detroit sect. Am. Chem. Soc., 1974, Fire of Genious award Saginaw Valley Patent Law Assn., 1982, Midland Matrix Festival award for exellent in sci., 1978; named Whitehead Meml. Lectr. engring. sect. NRC, 1971; elected to Plastics Hall of Fame, 1975. Mem. Am. Chem. Soc., Am. Inst. Chemists, AAAS, N.Y. Acad. Scis., Alpha Chi Sigma, Sigma Xi, Phi Beta Kappa. Home: 544 Yellowbird St Marco Island FL 34145-2846

HYDE, PEARL, medical/surgical and critical care nurse; b. Loup City, Nebr., Feb. 3, 1951; d. Charles T. and Esther (Gudenrath) Hyde; children: Michael, Michele, Mitchell, David, Crystal, Vancil. ADN, Pueblo (Colo.) Community Coll., 1990; BSN, Beth-El Coll. Nursing, 1992. Cert. EMT, unit coord.; lic. nurse. Oral hygienist Salida, Colo., dental asst.; unit coord. Heart of the Rockies Med. Ctr., Salida, gen. nurse. Capt. U.S. Army. Home: PO Box 74 Salida CO 81201

HYDE, WILLIAM FREDERICK, economics and forestry educator, researcher, consultant; b. Rochester, N.Y., Sept. 7, 1942; s. Frederick R. and Ruth (Stetson) H.; m. Dolores Tiongco, Dec. 30, 1989. BA, Am. U., Washington, 1969, MA, 1970; MS, U. Mich., 1975, PhD, 1977. Asst. prof. U. N.H., Durham, 1973; sr. rsch. assoc. Resources for the Future, Washington, 1973-78; assoc. dir. Pacific Northwest Forest Policy Project, Vancouver, Wash., 1978-79; assoc. prof. Duke U., Durham, 1979-88; pres. Natural Resources Mgmt.; br. chief Econ. Rsch. Svc., Washington, 1988-93; head forestry dept. Va. Tech., 1993-95. Editor: Forest Sci., 1992-95; assoc. editor Jour. Environ. Econs. Mgmt., 1991-94; assoc. editor Silva Fennica, 1994—. 1st lt. U.S. Army, 1964-68. Rockefeller Found. Environ. Quality fellow, 1969-73. Mem. Am. Econ. Assn., Soc. Am. Foresters, Assn. Pub. Policy Analysis and Mgmt., Assn. Environ. and Resource Economists, Soc. Risk Analysis, Am. Agrl. Econs. Assn., Sigma Xi, Phi Kappa Phi. Author: Timber Supply, Land Allocation & Economic Efficiency, 1980, Economic Evaluation of Investments in Forestry Research, 1983, Forestry Sector Intervention: The Impacts of Public Regulation on Social Welfare, 1987, The Economic Benefits of Forestry Research, 1992; contbr. articles to profl. jours., chpts. to books. Home: 202 Fincastle Dr Blacksburg VA 24060-5034

HYDEN, JOE BAILEY, lawyer; b. Dallas, Sept. 23, 1939; s. Bailey S. and Geneva (Coley) H.; m. Charlotte Todd, Oct. 23, 1984; 1 child, Todd Michael. BA, Baylor U., 1962; JD, So. Meth. U., 1968; MDiv, Southwestern Sem., Ft. Worth, 1970. Bar: Tex. 1968. Assoc. Touchstone, Bernays & Johnston, Dallas, 1969-72; ptnr. Green, Gilmore, Rothpletz & Hyden, Dallas, 1973-81, Guittard & Hyden, Dallas, 1982—. Mem. ABA (trial evidence com.), Dallas Bar Assn. (com. on continuing legal edn. 1972—, chmn. 1989). Republican. Baptist. Office: Guittard & Hyden Two Energy Sq 4849 Greenville Ave Ste 680 Dallas TX 75206-4124

HYLAND, BRIAN CHRISTOPHER, sales executive; b. Hollywood, Fla., Nov. 25, 1967; s. William lloyd and Patricia Ann Hyland; m. Georgia Sakell, Sept. 5, 1992. BS in Econ., George Mason U., Fairfax, Va., 1990; MBA, Boston U., 1996. Intern Arthur Andersen and Co., Washington, 1988-89; signals intelligence officer U.S. Marine Corps, Okinawa, Japan, 1991-93; co. exec. officer Jacksonville, N.C., 1994-95; co. comdr., 1995-96; mgr. consumer sales and svc. Ameritech, Milw., 1996—. Election ofcl., alt. election ofcl. U.S. Govt., Fairfax, Va., 1988-96. Capt. USMC, 1991-96. Recipient Navy Achievement medal Dept. Navy, Okinawa, Japan, 1993, Cert. of Achievement Dept. Navy, Rayong, Thailand, 1993, Dir.'s trophy Dept. Navy, Camp Lejeune, N.C., 1995. Mem. Boston U. Internat. Alumni Assn. Home: N26 W26452 Quail Hollow Rd Pewaukee WI 53072

HYLANDER, WALTER RAYMOND, JR., retired civil engineer; b. Memphis, July 22, 1924; s. Walter Raymond and Mary Howard (Douglass) H.; m. Marjorie Jean Gunter, Mar. 8, 1951; children: Walter Raymond, Joyce Elizabeth. BS, U.S. Mil. Acad., 1945; MS in Civil Engring., MIT, 1950. Registered profl. engr., N.Y., Miss. Commd. 2d lt., U.S. Army, 1945, advanced through grades to col., 1969, ret., 1973; tng. dir. Bechtel Power Corp., Grand Gulf, Miss., 1974-76; tng. and edn. mgr. Saudi-Arabian Bechtel Co., Jubail, 1976-77; tng. dir. St. Regis Paper Co., Montecello, Miss., 1978-79; chief civil engr. Bechtel Power Corp., Grand Gulf, 1979-86; chmn. Panel of Experts on Mine Warfare, NATO, London, 1962-65; sr. advisor on engr. tng., Vietnam, 1967-68; mem. U.S. Army Com. on Mil. History, West Point, N.Y., 1972-73; mem. U.S. ACDA, Washington, 1968-69. Contbr. articles to profl. jours. Fellow ASCE; mem. Soc. Am. Mil. Engrs., Nat. Assn. Model Railroaders, La. Miss. Christmas Tree Assn., Phi Kappa Phi. Methodist. Avocations: growing Christmas trees, model railroading, Civil War history. Home: Rosswood Plantation Lorman MS 39096

HYLE, CHARLES THOMAS, marketing specialist; b. Atlanta, Feb. 7, 1961; s. Howard Hopkins and Mary C. (McQuaid) H.; m. Sarah Jane Snyder. BS, BS cum laude, 1984. Acct. mgr. MSA, Atlanta, 1984-86, systems cons., 1986-88; mktg. svcs. mgr. worldwide UNISYS Corp., Atlanta, 1988-92; mktg. rep. Marcam Corp., 1992-96; product engr. SAP America, Inc., Atlanta, 1996—. Scoutmaster Boy Scouts Am. Mem. Am. Prodn. Inventory Control Soc. Office: SAP America Inc 6 Concourse Ste 1200 Atlanta GA 30328

HYMAN, ALBERT LEWIS, cardiologist; b. New Orleans, Nov. 10, 1923; s. David and Mary (Newstadt) H.; m. Neil Steiner, Mar. 27, 1964; 1 son, Albert Arthur. BS, La. State U., 1943; MD, 1945; postgrad., U. Cin., U. Paris, U. London, Eng. Diplomate: Am. Bd. Internal Medicine. Intern Charity Hosp., 1945-46, resident, 1947-49, sr. vis. physician, 1959-63; resident Cin. Gen. Hosp., 1946-47; instr. medicine La. State U., 1950-56, asst. prof. medicine, 1956-57; asst. prof. Tulane U., 1957-59, assoc. prof., 1959-63, assoc. prof. surgery, 1963-70, prof. research surgery in cardiology, 1970—, prof. clin. medicine Med. Sch., 1983—, adj. prof. pharmacology Med. Sch., 1974—; dir. Cardiac Catheterization Lab., 1957—; sr. vis. physician Touro Hosp., Touro Infirmary, Hotel Dieu; chief cardiology Sara Mayo Hosp.; cons. in cardiology USPHS, New Orleans Crippled Children's Hosp., St. Tammany Parish Hosp., Covington La. area VA, Hotel Dieu Hosp., Mercy Hosp., East Jefferson Gen. Hosp., St. Charles Gen. Hosp.; electrocardiographer Metairie Hosp., 1959-64, Sara Mayo Hosp., Touro Infirmary, St. Tammany Hosp.; cons. cardiovascular disease New Orleans VA Hosp.; cons. cardiology Baton Rouge Gen. Hosp.; Barlow lectr. in medicine U. So. Calif., 1977; mem. internat. sci. com. IV Internat. Symposium on Pulmonary Circulation, Charles U., Prague. Mem. editorial bd. Jour. Applied Physiology; contbr. over 250 articles to profl. jours. Recipient award for rsch. of the Hadassah, 1980, Vis. Scientist award Wellcome Found., Univ. Coll., London, 1991, Disting. Achievement award Am. Heart Assn., 1992, 93, Dickinson-Richards lectr., 1990. Fellow ACP, Am. Coll. Chest Physicians, Am. Coll. Cardiology, Am. Fedn. Clin. Rsch.; mem. AAUP, Am. Heart Assn. (fellow coun. on circulation, fellow coun. on clin. cardiology, mem. coun. on cardiopulmonary medicine, regional rep. coun. clin. cardiology, chmn. sci. com. cardiopulmonary coun. 1981, chmn. cardiopulmonary coun., rsch. com. bd. dirs., editl. bd. mem. Circulation Rsch., edit. bd. mem. Am. Jour. Physiology, Heart Disease and Stroke, Jour. Applied Physiology, Dickinson Richards Meml. Lectr. 1986, 92, Disting. Sci. Achievement award 1993), La. Heart Assn. (v.p. 1974, Albert L. Hyman Ann. Rsch. award, Wellcome Rsch. Found. Vis. Scientist award Univ. Coll. London 1992, Disting. Achievement award outstanding sci. contbns. to cardiopulmonary medicine), Am. Soc. Pharmacology and Exptl. Therapeutics, So. Soc. Clin. Investigation (chmn. membership com.), So. Med. Soc. (Seale-Harris award 1988), Am. Physiol. Soc., N.Am. Soc. Pacing and Electrophysiology, Orleans Surg. Soc. (hon.), New Orleans Surg. Soc. (hon.), N.Y. Acad. Scis., Nat. Am. Heart Assn. (vice-chmn. rsch. com.), Alpha Omega Alpha. Home: 5467 Marcia Ave New Orleans LA 70124-1052 Office: 3601 Prytania St New Orleans LA 70115-3610

HYMAN, EDWARD SIDNEY, physician, consultant; b. New Orleans, Jan. 22, 1925; s. David and Mary (Newstadt) H.; m. Jean Simons, Sept. 29, 1956; children: Judith, Sydney, Edward David, Anne. BS, La. State U., 1944; MD, Johns Hopkins U., 1946. Diplomate: Am. Bd. Internal Medicine. Intern Barnes Hosp., Washington U., St. Louis, 1946-47; fellow in medicine Stanford U., San Francisco, 1949-51, asst. resident in medicine, 1950-51, Peter Bent Brigham Hosp., Boston, 1951-53; teaching fellow in medicine Harvard U., Boston, 1952-53; practice medicine specializing in internal medicine, New Orleans, 1953—; dir. kidney unit Charity Hosp., New Orleans, 1953-55; investigator Touro Research Inst., New Orleans, 1959; dir. Hyman Corp.; mem. staff Sara Mayo Hosp., 1954-79, chief of staff, 1968-70, trustee, 1970-78; mem. staff Touro Infirmary, New Orleans, St. Charles Hosp.; panelist Pres.'s Commn. on Health Needs of Nation, 1952; cons. water quality New Orleans Sewerage and Water Bd., 1978; mem. research adv. com. Cancer Assn. New Orleans, 1976—, La. Bd. Regents, 1983. Contbr. articles to profl. jours. NIH grantee, 1960-81; Am. Heart Assn. grantee, 1962-65. Fellow ACP; mem. Am. Fedn. Clin. Rsch., Am. Soc. Artificial Internal Organs, Am. Physiol. Soc. Biophys. Soc. (chmn. local arrangements 1971, 77, 81, 87), Am. Soc. Microbiology, AAAS, Pvt. Drs. Am. (co-founder 1968, v.p. 1968—, Dist. Svc. award 1981), Orleans Parish Med. Soc. (gov. 1972-80), La. State Med. Soc. (ho. of dels. 1970-81). Jewish. Subspecialties: Internal medicine; Biophysics. Current work: Clincial internal medicine, biochemistry, biophysics, nephrology, artificial organs, water quality, government in medicine, cause of death in renal failure, significance of bacteria in urine. Isolated aldosterone, 1949; patentee sheet plastic oxygenator (artificial heart), oil detection device; inventor telephone transmission of electrocardiogram, early data transmission; inventor hydrogen platinum detection of heart shunts, Method for detection of bacteria in urine, Systemic Coccal Disease, Desert Storm Syndrome (following the Persian Gulf War) as a bacterial disease (SCD), Silicone Implant Disease as a bacterial disease, as a manifestation of Systemic Coccal Disease. Office: 3525 Prytania St Ste 200 New Orleans LA 70115-3549

HYMAN, HAROLD M., history educator, consultant; b. Bklyn., July 24, 1924; s. Abraham and Rebecca (Hermann) H.; m. Ferne Beverly Handelsman, Mar. 11, 1946; children: Lee Rosenthal, Ann Root, William Hyman. BA with honors, U. Calif. L.A., 1948; MA, Columbia U., 1950, PhD, 1952; LHD (hon.), Lincoln Coll., 1984. summer instr. Columbia U., 1953, U. Wash., 1960, Bklyn. Coll., 1962, U. Chgo., 1965; vis. asst. prof. UCLA, 1955-56; sr. Fulbright lectr. in Am. History and Law, grad. faculty polit. sci. U. Tokyo, 1973; faculty of law Keio U., 1973; adj. prof. legal history Bates Coll. Law U. Houston, 1977, of Am. legal history U. Tex. Law Sch., 1986; Meyer vis. disting. prof. legal history NYU Sch. Law, 1982-83; cons. and spkr. in field. Asst. prof. Earlham Coll., 1952-55; assoc. prof. Ariz. State U., 1956-57; prof. UCLA, 1957-63, U. Ill., 1963-68; William P. Hobby Prof. History Rice U., 1968—; summer instr. Columbia U., 1953, U. Wash., 1960, Bklyn. Coll., 1962, U. Chgo., 1965; vis. asst. prof. UCLA, 1955-56; grad. faculty pol. sci. U. Tokyo, 1973; faculty of law Keio U., 1973; adj. prof. legal history Bates Coll. law U. Houston, 1977, of Am. legal history U. Tex. Law Sch., 1986; Meyer vis. disting. prof. legal history NYU Sch. Law, 1982-83; cons. and speaker in field. Author: Era of the Oath: Northern Loyalty Tests During the Civil War and Reconstruction (Albert J. Beveridge award Am. Hist. Assn. 1981), 1954, To Try Men's Souls: Loyalty Tests in American History (Sidney Hillman Found. prize 1960), 1981, Stanton: The Life and Times of Lincoln's Secretary of War, 1962, Soldiers and Spruce: Origins of the Loyal Legion of Loggers and Lumbermen: The Army's Labor Union of World War I, 1963, A More Perfect Union: The Impact of the Civil War and Reconstruction on the Constitution, 1973, Union and Confidence: The 1860s, 1976, (with William Wiecek) Equal Justice Under Law: Constitutional History, 1833-1880, 1982, paperback, 1983, Quiet Past and Stormy Present? War Powers in American History, 1986, American Singularity: The 1787 Northwest Ordinence, the 1862 Homestead-Morrill Acts, and the 1944 GI Bill, 1986, Oleander Odyssey: The Kempners of Galveston, 1870-1980, (Coral H. Tullis Meml. prize Tex. A&M U. Press 1990, T. R. Fehrenbach Book award Tex. Hist. Comsn. 1990, Ottis Lock Endowment award E. Tex. Hist. Assn. 1991), 1990; editor (with Ferne B. Hyman) The Circuit Court Opinions of Salmon Portland Chase, 1972; contbr. numerous articles to profl. jours. Elected lay mem. Houston Bar Assn. Grievance Com., 1985-88; mem. numerous U. coms. The Constitution, Law, and Am. Life in the Nineteenth Century: A conf. named in his honor, Rice U. and NYU Sch. Law, 1989; named U.S. Presdl. appointee to permanent com. Oliver Wendell Holmes Trust, 1993-2001. Mem. Am. Hist. ssn. (numerous coms. and offices), Am. Soc. Legal History (pres. 1993-95), Orgn. Am. Historians (various coms. and offices), So. Hist. Assn. Office: Rice University Dept History-MS 42 6100 South Main Houston TX 77005-1892

HYMAN, ROGER DAVID, lawyer; b. Oak Ridge, Tenn., Apr. 23, 1957; s. Marshall Leonard and Vera Lorraine (McKinney) H.; 1 child, Cristina Alicia. BA, Vanderbilt U., 1979; JD, U. Tenn., 1984. Clk. Oak Ridge Nat. Lab., 1977-78, 81; air personality, news reporter Stas. WKDA, WKDF, Nashville, 1979; program dir. Sta. WBIR-FM, Knoxville, Tenn., 1979-80; assoc. atty. Hindman & Holt, Attys., Knoxville, Tenn., 1984-85; asst. atty. gen. State of Tenn., Knoxville, 1986-95; with Law Offices of Roger D. Hyman Powell, Tenn., 1995—. Bd. dirs. Knoxville Christian Sch., 1991-93. Democrat. Mem. Ch. of Christ. Home: 2713 Windemere Ln Powell TN 37849-3782 Office: 7315 Clinton Hwy Ste B PO Box 1304 Powell TN 37849

HYMAN-SPRUTE, BETTY HARPOLE, technical equipment consultant; b. Jasper, Tex., Nov. 20, 1938; d. Russell Charles and John Francis (Hilton) Harpole; m. Arthur Siegmar Hyman (dec.); children: Norma Sullivan, Eric, Jonathan, Lee Ann; m. Gerald J. Sprute. BA in Psychology, U. Tex., San Antonio, 1979. Spl. project coord. Tex. Stores, San Antonio, 1975-79; communications cons. Southwestern Bell Tel., Midland, Tex. and San Antonio, 1980-82; tech. cons. AT&T/Lucent Technologies, San Antonio, 1983-85, 88—, Intelliserve Corp., Dallas, 1987-88; cons. IMS Group, San Antonio, 1985-87. Mem. devel. com. San Antonio Spl. Olympics, San Antonio Conservation Soc., 1975-96, San Antonio World Affairs Coun., 1985-92, 1994—; bd. dirs S.Tex. Chidren's Habilitation Ctr., San Antonio, 1985-87; mem. Riverfront task force in Asheville. Mem. Am. Bus. Women's Assn. (program com. 1987-88), Tex. Tennis Assn. (ranked player 1976-90), Prime Time Tennis Club (v.p. 1985-86), Blue Ridge Dance Club (pres. 1993-94). Republican. Episcopalian. Home: 3459 River Way San Antonio TX 78230 Office: 107 W Nakoma St San Antonio TX 78216-2723

HYNAN, LINDA SUSAN, psychology educator; b. Ft. Sill, Okla., Nov. 20, 1953; d. Christy J. and Barbara Jean (Camp) Genzel; m. Edward F. Hynan, Feb. 3, 1973; 1 child, Patrick Shane. MS, U. Ill., 1982, PhD, 1993. Tchg. asst., rsch. asst. dept. psychology U. Ill., Urbana, 1980-91; rsch. asst. dept. psychology Del. State Coll., Dover, 1983—; asst. prof. dept. psychology, neurosci., inst. grad. stats. Baylor U., Waco, Tex., 1991—; cons. Infosphere Devel. Systems, Waco, Tex., 1986—; reviewer Allyn & Bacon/Simon & Schuster, Needham Heights, Mass., 1992, 95, Harcourt Brace Coll. Publs., 1994, Worth Pubs., Inc., 1995. Contbr. chpt. to book Cognitive Bias, 1990, articles to profl. jours.; spl. reviewer jour. Behavior Rsch. Methods Instruments and Computers. Fellow U. Ill., 1988-89. Mem. APA, Am. Ednl. Rsch. Assn., Am. Psychol. Soc., Am. Statis. Assn., McLennan County Psychol. Assn., Midwestern Psychol. Assn., Psychometric Soc., Soc. for Judgement and Decision-Making, Soc. for Applied Multivariate Rsch., Soc. for Math. Psychology, Southwestern Psychol. Assn., Ctrl. Tex. Women's Alliance, Thyroid Found. Am., Inst. Math. Statistics, Am. Radio Relay League, Am. Numismatic Assn., Phi Kappa Phi. Home: 1312 Western Ridge Dr Waco TX 76712-8709 Office: Baylor Univ Psychology and Neurosci PO Box 97334 Waco TX 76798-7334

HYND, GEORGE WILLIAM, neuropsychology educator; b. Portland, Oreg., Oct. 8, 1947; s. William Brown and Flavell Lorraine (Hayner) H.; m. Cynthia Rae Tullis, Aug. 23, 1969; children: April, Brian. BA, Pepperdine U., 1970, MA, 1971; MEd, U. Guam, Agana, 1975; EdD, U. No. Colo., 1976. Elem. tchr. L.A. Archdiocese, 1970-72; sch. psychologist Govt. of Guam, Agana, 1972-74; asst. prof. No. Ariz. U., Flagstaff, 1976-79; assoc. prof. neuropsychology U. Ga., Athens, 1979-83, prof., 1983—, rsch. prof., 1985—, sch. dir., 1990—. Author: Pediatric Neuropsychology, 1988, Neuropsychological Assessment in Clinical Child Psychology, 1988; editor Sch. Psychology Rev., 1981-83. Recipient Disting. Alumni award Pepperdine U., 1987, U. No. Colo., 1988. Fellow APA (Lightner-Witmer award 1982), Nat. Acad. Neuropsychology. Democrat. Office: U Ga Dept Psychol 570 Aderhold Athens GA 30602

HYNER, KAREN ELAINE, language educator, writer; b. Charlotte, N.C., Jan. 1, 1955; d. Harold Walker and Murline Marsh (Simpson) Wyatt; m. Dale Dee Hyner, Feb. 4, 1983 (dec. July 1991); children: Paige Denina, Catherine Nicole, Rivka Yael. BA in French cum laude, Wake Forest U., 1977; MA in French Lit., Rice U., Houston, 1980; postgrad., U. Dijon, France, 1976. Cert. tchr. French, Tex., N.C. Instr. English English Lang. Svc., Houston, 1977-78; instr. English Rice U., Houston, 1979, grad. teaching fellow in French, 1977-79; tech. translator-French Michelin Tire Co., Sandy Springs, S.C., 1979-81; acad. advisor Saudi Arabian Edn. Mission, Houston, 1981-82; tchr. French Kannapolis (N.C.) Mid. Sch., 1989-93, Stanly County Schs., Albemarle, N.C., 1993—; creator, dir. French program Kannapolis Mid. Sch., 1989-93. Author fiction and poetry. Cannon scholar, 1973. Mem. Fgn. Lang. Assn. N.C., Am. Assn. Tchrs. French. Home: 517 Hunter Ave Kannapolis NC 28083-4031

HYSLOP, NEWTON EVERETT, allergist, immunologist; b. Newton, Mass., 1935. MD, Harvard U., 1961. Diplomate Am. Bd. Allergy and Immunology, Am. Bd. Internal Medicine. Intern Mass. Gen. Hosp., Boston, 1961-62, resident in medicine, 1962-63, fellow in infectious disease, 1966-68; resident in medicine Peter Bent Brigham Hosp., Boston, 1965-66; with Tulane U. Med. Ctr., New Orleans; prof. medicine Tulane U. Mem. ACP, Am. Assn. Immunologists, Am. Soc. Microbiology, Infectious Disease Soc. Am. Office: Tulane U Med Ctr Dept Infectious Diseases 1430 Tulane Ave New Orleans LA 70112-2699

IACOBUCCI, GUILLERMO ARTURO, chemist; b. Buenos Aires, May 11, 1927; s. Guillermo Cesar and Blanca Nieves (Brana) I.; m. Constantina Maria Gullich, Mar. 28, 1952; children: Eduardo Ernesto, William George. MSc, U. Buenos Aires, 1949, PhD in Organic Chemistry, 1952. Came to U.S., 1962, naturalized, 1972. Research chemist E.R. Squibb Research Labs., Buenos Aires, 1952-57; research fellow in chemistry Harvard U., Cambridge, Mass., 1958-59, prof. phytochemistry U. Buenos Aires, 1960-61; sr. research chemist Squibb Inst. Med. Research, New Brunswick, N.J., 1962-66; head bio-organic chemistry labs. Coca-Cola Co., Atlanta, 1967-74, asst. dir. corp. research and devel., 1974-87, mgr. biochemistry and basic organic chemistry group, 1988-93, ret. 1993; adj. prof. chemistry Emory U., 1975—. John Simon Guggenheim Meml. Found. fellow, 1958. Fellow Am. Inst. Chemists; mem. AAAS, Assn. Harvard Chemists, Am. Chem. Soc., N.Y. Acad. Scis., Am. Soc. Pharmacognosy, Phytochemical Soc. N.Am., Smithsonian Instn., Planetary Soc., Sigma Xi. Achievements include structure/activity correlations and molecular design of sweeteners; use of enzymes in asymmetric organic synthesis; natural products chemistry; contbr. articles on organic chemistry to sci. jours. Patentee in field. Home: 160 N Mill Rd NW Atlanta GA 30328-1837 Office: Emory U Dept of Chemistry 1515 Pierce Dr Atlanta GA 30322

IANNICELLI, JOSEPH, chemical company executive, consultant; b. N.Y.C., Aug. 5, 1929; s. Peter and Catherine (Gugliotti) I.; m. Betty Peterson, June 28, 1978; children: Mark, Rex, Gina. SB, MIT, 1951, PhD, 1955. Rsch. chemist Textile Fibers, E.I. DuPont, Wilmington, Del., 1955-60; tech. dir. Clay Div. J.M. Huber, Macon, Ga., 1960-70; founder, chief exec. officer Aquafine Corp., Brunswick, Ga., 1970—, Aero-Instant Corp., Brunswick, Ga., 1988—; co-founder IMPEX Corp., Brunswick, Ga., 1988—; cons. Consol. Goldfields Australia, Sydney, 1976-78, Rio Tinto, Madrid, 1980-82, Hoganes, Malmo, Sweden, 1984. Author: Evaluation and Comparison of Crossfield and Solenoid Field Magnetic Filters, 1981; co-author: A Survey-Benneficiation of Industrial Minerals, 1980; contbr. over 30 articles to profl. jours. Pres. Ga. Tidewater Conservation Assn., Brunswick, 1991-92; bd. dirs. Jekyll Island (Ga.) Citizens Assn., 1992—, pres., 1993—; govt. appointment as mem. Jekyll Island (Ga.) Citizens Resource Coun., 1995—; foreman Glynn County Grand Jury, Brunswick, 1989. Recipient Rsch. grant NSF, 1980, 84, Elec. Power Rsch. Inst., 1980. Fellow Am. Inst. Chemists; mem. Tech. Assn. of Pulp and Paper Industry (chmn. pigments com. 1971-72). Home: 28 Saint Andrews Dr Jekyll Island GA 31527-0901 Office: Aquafine Corp 3963 Darien Hwy Brunswick GA 31525-2423

IAQUINTO, JOSEPH FRANCIS, electrical engineer; b. Phila., Nov. 9, 1946; s. Francis Edward Iaquinto and Maria Carmina (Mancini) Feldman; m. Jo-Carol Maniscalco, Nov. 21, 1977; children: Joseph Michael, Jonathan Franklin. BSEE, Drexel U., 1969; MSEE, Stanford U., 1971. Registered professional engineer, Pa., Va. Teaching asst. Stanford (Calif.) U., 1969-71; sr. project engr. GM Corp., 1971-75; regional system engring. mgr. Memorex Corp., King of Prussia, Pa., 1975-77; sr. prin. engr. Computer Sci. Corp., Falls Church, Va., 1977-80; dir. devel. Tesdata Systems Corp., Tyson's Corner, Va., 1980-82; staff engr. HRB-Singer Co., Lantham, Md., 1982-84; sr. staff engr. Lockheed Electronics Co., Vienna, Va., 1984-86; mem. tech. staff MRJ div. Perkin Elmer, Oakton, Va., 1986-89; system engr. Ford Motor Co., Dearborn, Mich., 1989-93; engring. mgr. A.C. Nielsen, Dunedin, Fla., 1993-94; mgr. sys. engring. E'On Corp., Reston, Va., 1994-95; mem. tech. staff Data Networks Corp., Reston, Va., 1995—. Author: Memorex 1380 Internal and Lesson Plan, 1977, Simulation of Microwave Propagation in the Atmosphere, 1987; co-author: (with H. Brandt) Control Engineering Application to Automobiles, 1973; author: (with others) Secure Internetwork Data Communications, 1979, Mission Planning System Specification, 1985; contbr. articles to tech. publs. Instr. ARC, Mich. and Pa., 1971-77; treas. Macomb County Young Reps., Sterling Heights, Mich., 1975; councilman Longacre PTA, Farmington, Mich., 1990-92. Recipient acad. scholarship Phila. Sch. System. Mem. IEEE, Nat. Soc.Profl. Engrs., Inst. Soc. Am. Roman Catholic.

IBACH, DOUGLAS THEODORE, minister; b. Pottstown, Pa., July 23, 1925; s. Hiram Christian and Esther (Fry) I.; BS in Edn., Temple U., 1950, postgrad. Sch. Theology, 1950-52; MDiv, Louisville Presbyn. Theol. Sem., 1954; m. Marion Elizabeth Torok, Sept. 2, 1950; children—Susan Kay, Marilyn Lee, Douglas Theodore, Grace Louise. Ordained to ministry Presbyn. Ch., 1953; pastor, Pewee Valley, Ky., 1952-55, West Nottingham Presbyn. Ch., Colora, Md., 1955-61, Irwin, Pa., 1961-67, Knox Presbyn. Ch., Falls Church, Va., 1967-72, United Christian Parish Reston (Va.), 1972-87; exec. dir. Camping Assn. of the Presbyteries of Northwestern Pa., Mercer, Pa., 1986-90; pastor Pulaski (Pa.) Presbyn. Ch., 1990-94; parish assoc. Presbyn. Parish of the Valleys, Middletown, Va., 1994—. Youth ministry cons. Nat. Capital Union Presbytery, 1967-86; ecumenical officer Nat. Capital Presbytery, chmn. stewardship com., 1986—; mem. ecumenical rels. com. Synod of Virginias, also mem. Interfaith Conf. of Metro Washington; bd. dirs. Reston Inter-Faith, Inc.; dir. Presbyn. Internat. Affairs Seminars. adv. bd. Christmas Internat. House; mem. ch. devel. and redevel. com., Christian edn. com. Lake Erie Presbytery, stated supply Pulaski (Pa.) Presbyterian Ch.; pres. New Wilmington Ministerium; exec. dir. Camping Assn. of Presbyteries of No. Pa., 1986-90; chair ecumenical task force Shenandoah Presbytery; bd. dirs. E.A.R.S., Beaver Castle Girl Scout Coun.; sec. Winchester-Frederick County Ministerium, 1995—. With USNR, 1943-44. Mem. Council Chs. Greater Washington (pres., chmn. instl. ministry commn.), Piedmont Synod U.P. Ch. (dir. youth, camping), Acad. Parish Clergy Assn. Presbyn. Christian Educators, Fairfax County Council Chs. (pres.), Com. 100 Fairfax County, Mercer Fun Club (bd. dirs.), Rotary (v.p., sec. Stephens City chpt. 1995—). Home: 110 Suffolk Circle Stephens City VA 22655 Office: Presbyn Parish of the Valley 7152 Middle Rd Middletown VA 22645

IBACH, MICHAEL BRETT, physician, educator; b. Phila., Feb. 21, 1963; s. John Raymond Ibach and Catherine Elizabeth (Henlin) Poole; Marcy Joan Vandoff, July 9, 1988; children: Caroline Rose, Banjamin John. BS in Biology, Tulane U., 1985; MD, U. South Fla., 1989. Intern Albert Einstein Med. Ctr., Phila., 1989-90, resident in internal medicine, 1990-92; fellow in gastroenterology La. State U. Med. Ctr., Shreveport, 1992-95, instr. medicine, 1994-95; staff gastroenterologist Overton Brooks VA Med. Ctr., Shreveport, 1994-95; gastroenterologist pvt. practice, Jackson, Tenn., 1995—. Contbr. articles to profl. jours. Mem. AMA, ACP, Am. Gastroenterological Assn., Am. Coll. Gastroenterology, Am. Soc. for Gastrointestinal Endoscopy. Office: 27 Med Ctr Dr Jackson TN 38301

IBAÑEZ, ALVARO, patent design company executive, artist; b. Bucaramanga, Santander, Colombia, Jan. 18, 1951; came to U.S., 1981; s. Epimenio and Maria Delia (Muñoz) I.; m. Marta Cecilia Arias, Dec. 30, 1971 (div. Dec. 1991); children: Carlos Humberto, Alvaro Antonio, Diana Saray. Fine arts, David Manzur Acad., Bogotá, Colombia, 1972; structural draftman, ACADITEC, Bogotá, Colombia, 1974. Elem. tchr. German Pena Sch., Bogotá, Colombia, 1971; with sales dept. Grolier Internat., Bogotá, Colombia, 1973-74; civil engring. draftsman Adminstrv. Dept. Cmty. Action, Bogotá, Colombia, 1974-76; gen. ins. mgr. Gilabert & CIA, Santa Marta, Colombia, 1976-77; farmer El Roble Ranch, Santa Marta, Colombia, 1976-77; sales mgr. Onix Ltda., Bucaramanga, Colombia, 1977-78; owner, mgr. Distrisiba Ltda., Bucaramanga, Colombia, 1977-80; sales mgr. Coramex Andina Ltda., Bogotá, Colombia, 1980-81; with Radian, Inc., Alexandria, Va., 1984—, Birch, Stewart, Kolasch & Birch, Falls Church, Va., 1985—, Diversified Technologies, Alexandria, Va., 1986—; pres., founder A-Ibañez Art Design, Inc., Falls Church, Va., 1985—; freelance Pub. Health Ctr., Bogotá, Colombia, 1971-74, Guillermo Victorino SA, Bogotá, 1973-74, Felix A. Clavijo Co., Bogotá, 1973-75, Metron Publicity, Bucaramanga, Colombia, 1977-80, Tulio Ramirez, 1980-81, Fabio Hernandez Salazar, Bogotá, 1980-81; with Lascaris Design Group Internat., Washington, 1984. One-man shows include Georgetown Streets, Washington, 1981, Sovran Bank CC, Springfield, Va., 1985; exhibited in group shows at David Manzur Acad., Bogotá, Colombia, 1974, Dicas Fine Arts Ctr., Bogotá, Colombia, 1979, Santander Indsl. U., Bucaramanga, Colombia, 1979, Arlington Ctr., Va., 1982, Falls Church Recreation Park, Va., 1982, Latin Am. Art League, Alexandria, Va., 1991, Desfile de las Americas, Washington, 1993, Martin Luther King Meml. Libr., Washington, 1994, 96, Art Mus. Ams.-Orgn. Am. States, Washington, 1994, Strathmore Hall Arts Ctr., North Bethesda, Md., 1994, AT&T, Oakton, Va., 1994, Washington, 1994, Cultural Mexican Inst., Washington, 1994, Montgomery County Exec. Office Bldg., Rockville, Md., 1994, Bell Atlantic, Arlington, Va., 1994, Silver Spring, Md., 1994, Torpedo Factory Art League, Alexandria, Va., 1994, Moscoso Gallery, Washington, 1995, Fla. Mus. Hispanic and Latin Am. Art, Miami, 1995, Montgomery County Exec. Office Bldg., Rockville, Md., 1995, NASA Hdqs., Washington, 1995, Pan Am. Health Orgn., Washington, 1995, SED Ctr., Washington, 1996. Sponsor World Vision, Tacoma, Wash., 1987—, Child Devel. Ctr., Falls Church, Va., 1989—, Crystal Cathedral, Glandale, Calif., 1992—. Recipient 1st prize drawing Prismacolor Contest, 1958. Mem. Worldwide Fine Art Promotions, Hispanic Museo Art, Art League, Torpedo Factory. Republican. Office: A Ibañez Art Design Inc 200 Park Ave Ste 304 Falls Church VA 22046

IBANEZ, JANE BOURQUARD, stress management consultant, lecturer; b. New Orleans, Oct. 11, 1947; d. Albert John and Josephine (Vachetta) Bourquard; m. Manuel Luis Ibanez, Oct. 16, 1970; children: Juana, Vincent, William, Marc. BS, U. New Orleans, 1970. Lab. researcher in organic chemistry U. New Orleans, 1967-68, genetics lab. instr., 1968-69, fitness instr., 1972-90, yoga and meditative instr., 1972-90, stress mgmt. instr., 1980-90; profl. lectr., stress mgmt. cons., 1972—; bd. examiners Tex. Supreme Ct., 1993—; guest lectr. U. New Orleans, Tex. A&M, Kingsville, ABWA Conv., South Tex. Banker's Assn., others. Author producer: (audiotapes) Childhood Stress, 1985, Yoga Workout, 1985, Jane's Way Mini Workout, 1986. Chmn. Tex. A&M U.-Kingsville Fund for Instnl. Advancement, Kingsville, 1989—, also presdl. asst.; pres. Am. Cancer Soc., Kingsville, 1992-94; mem. devel. bd. Spohn Kleberg Hosp., Kingsville, 1990—, trustee, vice chmn., 1991-93; chmn. devel. bd. Am. Heart Assn., Kingsville, 1990—; bd. dirs. Corpus Christi Women's Shelter, 1991-95; trustee South Tex. Ranching and Heritage Festival, 1992—. Mem. AAUW, Kingsville Garden Club, U. New Orleans Fitness Club (pres. 1975-89). Roman Catholic. Home: 905 N Armstrong Ave Kingsville TX 78363-3687 also: 2319 Prentiss Ave New Orleans LA 70122-5309

IBANEZ, MANUEL LUIS, university official, biological sciences educator; b. Worcester, Mass., Sept. 23, 1935; s. Ovidio Pedro and Esperanza Fe (Perez) I.; m. Jane Marie Bourquard, Oct. 16, 1970; children: Juana Lia Cristina, Vincent Ovidio, William Dayan, Marc Albert. B.S. cum laude, Wilmington Coll., 1957; M.S., Pa. State U., 1959, Ph.D., 1961. Asst. prof. Bucknell U., Lewisburg, Pa., 1961-62; postdoctoral fellow UCLA, 1962; sr. biochemist IICA de la OEA, Turrialba, Costa Rica, 1962-65; assoc. prof., chmn. dept. U. New Orleans, 1965-70, prof., 1977-90, assoc. dean grad. sch., 1978-82, assoc. vice chancellor acad. affairs, 1982-83, acting vice chancellor, 1983-85, vice chancellor acad. affairs, provost, 1985-89, prof. emeritus, 1990—; pres. Tex. A&M U., Kingsville, 1989—. Author: Basic Biology of Microorganisms, 1972; contbr. articles to profl. jours. Regent Smithsonian Inst., 1994—; mem. Alliance for Good Govt., New Orleans, 1980. NSF coop. fellow, 1958-61. Mem. Am. Assn. State Colls. and Univs., Kingsville C. of C. (pres. 1991), Rotary, KC, Sigma Xi. Democrat. Roman Catholic. Office: Tex A&M Univ-Kingsville Office of Pres PO Box 101 Kingsville TX 78364-0101

IBRAHIM, NUHAD KHALIL, oncologist; b. Lebanon, Jan. 10, 1954. BSc, Am. U. of Beirut, Lebanon, 1975; MB, ChB, Baghdad Med. Coll., Iraq, 1980. Diplomate Am. Bd. Internal Medicine. Surgical internship Am. U. Beirut Med. Ctr., Lebanon, 1980-81, resident in gen. surgery, 1981-83, fellow clinical hematology-oncology, 1983-86; attending med. oncologist Lebanses Cancer Ctr., Byblos, Lebanon, 1986-87; resident in internal medicine SUNY Health Sci. Ctr., Bklyn., 1988-90, St. Luke's-Roosevelt Hosp., N.Y.C., 1990-91; fellow in medical oncology U. Tex. M.D. Anderson Cancer Ctr., Houston, 1991-95, asst. prof. medicine, asst. internist, 1995—. Contbr. articles to profl. jours. Recipient ASCO Travel award, 1993; M.D. Anderson Cancer Ctr. Rsch. Grant award, 1993. Home: 3910 Abbeywood Pearland TX 77584 Office: 1515 Holcombe Blvd Houston TX 77030-4009

ICE, BILLIE OBERTA, retail executive; b. Grantsville, W.Va., July 17, 1962; d. Clovis Drexell and Sherron Lea (Fowler) I. BA, Glenville (W.Va.) State Coll., 1984. Asst. mgr. Hecks Discount Stores, Nitro, W.Va., 1985-87; softlines mgr. Hills Dept. Stores, Canton, Mass., 1991-92, gen. mgr., 1992—, hardlines mgr., 1991; gen. mgr. plan Hills Dept. Stores, 1991-92, gen. mgr., 1992-93; store mgr. Revco Drug Stores, Twinsburg, Ohio, 1993—. With U.S. Army, 1981-82. Mem. Nat. Assn. Female Execs., VFW Ladies Aux., Am. Legion. Democrat. Baptist. Home: PO Box 1401 Johnson City TN 37605 Office: Revco Drug Store 305 W Sullivan St Kingsport TN 37660-3621

ICKES, WILLIAM KEITH, audiology educator; b. Salt Lake City, Feb. 4, 1926; s. William Bunn and Lucile C. (Christenson) I.; m. Shirley Doris Hallman,. Aug. 27, 1946; children: William J., Bonnie Jean, Patricia Lynn, Joy Marie. BS, U. Utah, 1948, MS, 1949; PhD, So. Ill. U., 1960. Audiologist Detroit Hearing Ctr., 1950-52, Mich. Assn. for Better Hearing, Lansing, 1952-54; exec. dir. Des Moines Hearing and Speech Ctr., 1954-62; dir. speech and hearing clinic Tex. Tech U., Lubbock, 1962-68, chmn. dept. speech and theatre, 1968-76, prof. dept. comm. disorders, 1976-90, prof. emeritus, 1987—. Contbr. articles to profl. jours. With U.S. Army Air Corps., 1944-45. Recipient Meritous Svc. award Southwest Region Nat. Rehab. Assn. Fellow Am. Speech and Hearing Assn. (cert. of clin. competence-audiology); mem. Tex. Speech and Hearing Assn. (v.p. 1965-66, Honors of the Profession 1977), Tex. Rehab. Assn. (pres. 1982-83, President's Meritorious Svc. award 1980). Home: 4306 57th St Lubbock TX 79413

IDE, ARTHUR FREDERICK, author, publisher; b. Waverly, Iowa, Sept. 29, 1945; s. Herbert Frederick Ide and Ruby Lucile Borchardt Borlaug. BA, State Coll. of Iowa, 1967; MA, U. No. Iowa, 1968, Ariz. State U., 1972; PhD, Carnegie-Mellon U., 1974. Asst. prof. Iowa Lakes C.C., Estherville, 1968, Mauna Olu Coll., Paia, Maui, Hawaii, 1970-71; asst. prof. and area coord. European studies U. San Diego, 1974-77; asst. prof. Eastfield Coll., Dallas, 1977-82; pubr. and CEO Ide House, Inc., Mesquite, Tex., 1979-84. Author: Battered and Bruised: All the Women of the Old Testament, 1993, Moses: Making of Myth and Law, 1992, Noah and the Ark, 1992, Yahweh's Wife, 1991, Islam and Woman, 1986, God's Girls: Ordination of Women in the Early Christian and Gnostic Churches, 1985, Kay Bailey Hutchison: Lone Star Girl, 1993, From Stardom to Scandal: The Rise & Fall of Kay Bailey Hutchison, 1994, Guilty Until Proven Innocent: The Illusion: Texas Justice -- Dallas Style, 1991, Bush-Quayle: The Reagan Legacy, 1989, Heaven's Hustler: The Rise and Fall of Jimmy Swaggart, 1988, numerous others. Mem. ACLU, Am. Hist. Assn., Nat. Abortion Rights Action League, Tex. Abortion Rights Action League, People for the Am. Way. Democrat. Office: PO Box 140361 Irving TX 75014-0361

IDO, YOSHIMITSU, computer company program executive; b. Tokyo, Oct. 19, 1941; came to U.S., 1991; s. Yoshio and Teiko (Sasa) I.; m. Kazuko Nishino, Apr. 30, 1970; children: Yoko, Reiko. BE, U. Tokyo, 1965. Engr. NKK Steel Works, Tokyo, 1965-70, mgr. steel mill designer, 1970-78; mgr. tech. mgmt. rsch. Engring. Assoc. Japan, Tokyo, 1978-80; mgr. chemical plant NKK Steel Works, Tokyo, 1980-81; corp. planning, 1981-86, mem. electronics divsn., 1986-91; program dir. NKK, Dallas, 1991-94; processor devel. CONVEX Computer, Richardson, Tex., 1994-95; HP-Convex Tech. Ctr., Dallas, 1995—. Translator: Industrial Project Management, Basic Electronics for Scientist; mng. editor Handbook of Control and Measurement; contbr. articles to profl. jours. Me. IEEE, Project Mgmt. Inst., Assn. Computing Machinery, Inst. Physics. Office: Convex Computer Corp 3000 Waterview Pky Richardson TX 75080-1400

IDOL, JOHN LANE, JR., English language educator, writer, editor; b. Deep Gap, N.C., Oct. 28, 1932; s. John Lane and Annie Lulu (Watson) I.; m. Marjorie Anne South, Nov. 24, 1955. BS, Appalachian State U., 1958; MA, U. Ark., 1961, PhD, 1964. English tchr. Blowing Rock (N.C.) Union Sch., 1958-59; English tchr., writer Clemson (S.C.) U., 1965—; dir. grad. studies in English Clemson U., 1969-74; table leader Ednl. Testing Svc., Princeton, N.J., 1990—. Author: Thomas Wolfe Companion, 1987; co-author: Hawthorne and the Visual Arts, 1991; editor: The Hound of Darkness (Thomas Wolfe), 1986; co-editor: Mannerhouse (Thomas Wolfe), 1985, Nathaniel Hawthorne, The Contemporary Reviews, 1994, The Party at Jack's (Thomas Wolfe), 1995; contbr. articles and poems to lit. jours. Treas. Clemson Area Arts Coun. 1984-85; chmn. Adv. Com. on Accomodation Taxes, 1985-90; pres. Friends of Clemson Community Libr., 1989-90. With U.S. Air Force, 1951-55. Recipient Award of Merit, AAUP, S.C. chpt., 1986; NDEA fellow U. Ark., 1959; named Alumni Disting. Prof., Clemson U., 1993. Mem. MLA, Nathaniel Hawthorne Soc. (pres. 1984-86, editor Nathaniel Hawthorne rev. 1983-92), Herman Melville Soc., Thomas Wolfe Soc. (pres. 1981-83), Southeastern Name Soc. (pres. 1988-90), Philol. Assn. of the Carolinas (pres. 1984, Honored Tchr. 1986), Soc. for Study of So. Lit. (v.p. 1992-94), Mark Twain Circle, Phi Beta Kappa (Piedmont Area pres. 1981-83, 89-91), Phi Kappa Phi. Home: PO Box 413 Hillsborough NC 27278-0413

IEYOUB, RICHARD PHILLIP, state attorney general; b. Lake Charles, La., Aug. 11, 1944; s. Phillip Assad and Virginia Khoury I.; m. Sandra Claire Bates, Aug. 12, 1972; children: Amy Claire, Nicole Anne, Brennan Jude, Richard Philip Jr.; m. Caprice Brown. BA in history, McNeese State U., 1968; JD, La. State U., 1972. Bar: La. 1972, U.S. Supreme Ct. Spl. prosecutor to atty. gen. State of La., Baton Rouge, 1972-74; assoc. Camp, Carmouche, Lake Charles, 1974-76; mem. Stockwell, Sievert, Lake Charles, 1976-78, Baggett, McCall, Singleton, Ranier, Ieyoub, Lake Charles, from 1978; sole practice Lake Charles; dist. atty. Calcasieu Parish, 1985-92; atty. gen. State of La., 1992—; instr. criminal law McNeese State U.; chmn. La. Drug Policy Bd., New Orleans Met. Crime Task Force; mem. La. Commn. on Law Enforcement, President's Commn. on Model State Drug Laws, 1992—; mem. bd. dirs. La. State U. Alumni Assn. Bd. dirs. S.W. La. Health Counseling Svcs., Crime Stoppers of Lake Charles; mem. Parish coun. Immaculate Conception Cathedral Parish, Lake Charles; vice chmn. La. coord. coun. on the prevention of drug abuse and treatment of drug use; mem. La. commn. on law enforcement; apptd. by gov. to adv. bd. La. D.A.R.E.; chmn. New Orleans Metropolitan Crime Task Force, Gov's. Military Adv. Commn. Named Outstanding Pub. Ofcl. for Diocese Lake Charles, 1990; recipient Disting. Alumnus award McNeese State U., 1994. Mem. ABA (vice chmn. prosecution function com.), Assn. Trial Lawyers Am., Nat. Assn. Criminal Def. Lawyers, La. Bar Assn. (lectr. criminal law), Nat. Dist. Attys. Assn. (pres., bd. dirs. 1990-91), Nat. Assn. Attys. Gen. (exec. working group on prosecutorial rels.), La. Dist. Attys. Assn. (pres., bd. dirs. 1989-90), Nat. Coll. Dist. Attys. (bd. regents 1991), S.W. La. Bar Assn. (exec. com. 1979), So. Attys. Gen. Assn. (elected chmn.), Sierra Club. Democrat. Roman Catholic. Office: Justice Dept PO Box 94005 Baton Rouge LA 70804-9005*

IGLEHART, KENNETH ROBERT, newspaper editor; b. Dallas, Apr. 14, 1951; s. Robert H. and Jane (Whitcomb) I.; m. Norma Murray; children: Alex, Leigh. Student, Johns Hopkins U., 1969-72. Corr. Keene (N.H.) Sentinel, 1973-76, reporter, 1976-77; news dir. Franklin Pierce Coll., Rindge, N.H., 1973-74; reporter Jaffrey (N.H.) Ledger, 1974-75, Naples (Fla.) Daily News, 1977-79; assignment editor News Am., Balt., 1979-86; news dir. Johns Hopkins U., Balt., 1986-87; mng. editor Times Pub. Group, Towson, Md., 1987-88, Jour. Newspapers, Springfield, Va., 1988-95; exec. editor Jour. Newspapers, 1988-95; mng. editor Balt. Mag., 1995—. Recipient Best News Spot 2d Pl. award New Eng. Press Assn., 1977. Office: Balt Mag Jour Newspapers 16 S Calvert St Baltimore MD 21202

IGNATONIS, SANDRA CAROLE AUTRY, special education educator; b. Dixon Mills, Ala., June 6, 1942; d. Charles Franklin Autry; m. Algis Jerome Ignatonis, June 15, 1968; children: Audra Carole, David Jerome. BA, Samford U., 1964; cert. in Gifted Edn., Kennesaw State U., 1989. Cert. tchr., Ga. Tchr. Jefferson County Bd. Edn., Birmingham, Ala., 1964, Huntsville (Ala.) Bd. Edn., 1964-71, Epiphany Cath. Sch., Miami, Fla., 1981, Cobb County Bd. Edn., Marietta, Ga., 1982, Bartow County Bd. Edn., Cartersville, Ga., 1990-92, Sequoria Group, Inc., Roswell, Ga., 1996; mem. Sch. Self-Governance Com., Emerson, Ga., 1990-91, Soccer Adv. Bd., Marietta, 1985-89; judge, mem. Social Sci. Fair Competitions, Huntsville, 1964-71. Team mom Metro N. Youth Soccer Assn., Marietta, 1991-92; block parent Somerset Subdivision, Marietta, 1982-86; polit. chmn. Student Nat. Edn. Assn., Samford U., Birmingham, Ala., 1963-64. Recipient grant Samford U. Faculty, 1963. Mem. Ga. Supporters of Gifted, Profl. Assn. Ga. Educators. Republican. Roman Catholic.

IGO, JOHN, English language educator; b. San Antonio, May 29, 1927; s. John N. and Anna (Woller) I. BA in English, Trinity U., 1948, MA, 1952. Acquisitions libr., mem. English faculty Trinity U., San Antonio, 1952-53; mem. English faculty San Antonio Coll., 1953—. Author: God of Gardens, 1962, Alien, 1977, The Mitotes, 1989, The Third Temptation of St. John, 1993; (dramas) Claudius the Falconer, 1988, Oenone, 1993. V.p. Friends of Pub. Libr., San Antonio, 1976-86; mem. Mayor's Adv. Coun., San Antonio, 1984, Com. of 100, Tex., 1956; project mgr. theatre archive San Antonio Pub. Libr., 1976—. Recipient Nat. Lit. award Nat. Soc. Arts and Letters, 1954, S.W. Writers award S.W. Writers Conf., 1962, Nortex Writers award Poetry Soc. Tex., 1977, Playwrights Festival awrd Center Stage, 1978. Mem. Tex. Folklore Soc., Coll. Conf. Tchrs., Bexar Libr. Assn., S.W. Am. Lit. Soc., San Antonio Theatre Coun. (chmn. 1969-76), Alamo Theatre Arts Coun. (exec. v.p. 1990-93). Democrat. Roman Catholic. Home: 12505 Woller Rd San Antonio TX 78249-9506 Office: San Antonio Coll 1300 San Pedro Ave San Antonio TX 78212-4201

IGOE, TERENCE B., airport terminal executive; b. Phila., Nov. 9, 1941; s. Thomas B. and Elizabeth R. (Graham) I.; m. Patricia Diane Voss, Sept. 14, 1994; children: Michael, Suzanne. BS in Aviation Mgmt., Met. State Coll. Denver, 1974. Accredited airline exec. Adminstrv. asst. Stapleton Internat. Airport, Denver, 1975-80; airport mgr. Cheyenne (Wyo.) Airport Bd., 1980, Natrona County Internat. Airport, Casper, Wyo., 1980-84; exec. dir. Met. Knoxville Airport Authority, 1984—; bd. dirs. Airports Coun. Internat. N.Am.; examiner Am. Assn. Airport Execs., 1991-93. Bd. dirs. Jr. Achievement of East Tenn., Nat. Kidney Found. East Tenn. Capt. U.S. Army, 1966-71, Vietnam. Mem. Skal Club, Rotary. Home: 10550 Lakecove Way Knoxville TN 37422 Office: Knoxville Airport Authority PO Box 15600 Knoxville TN 37901-5600

IHNDRIS, RAYMOND WILL, chemist; b. Sterling, Ind., Apr. 1, 1920; s. Will and Vada Mae (Sutton) I.; m. Violet Elizabeth Parrish, Nov. 22, 1942; children: Raymond Lane, Robert Bruce. BS, Rollins Coll., Winter Park, Fla., 1955. Chemist USDA Bur. Entomology & Plant Quarantine, Orlando, Fla., 1946-55; pesticide chem. rschr. USDA Bus. Entomol. Rsch. divsn., Beltsville, Md., 1956-60; head cancer chemotherapy sci. rsch. sect. CCNSC-NIH, Bethesda, Md., 1960-74; with toxicology info. program Nat. Libr. Medicine-NIH, Bethesda, 1974-78; ret. CCNSC-NIH, Bethesda, Md., 1978. Staff sgt. USAF, 1941-45. Mem. Am. Chem. Soc., Am. Soc. Info. Scientists. Congregationalist. Home: 682 Granville Dr Winter Park FL 32789-1417

IKARD, FRANK NEVILLE, JR., lawyer; b. Wichita Falls, Tex., June 26, 1942; s. Frank Neville and Jean (Hunter) I.; children: Frank III, Jean, Charles. BA, U. Tex., 1965, JD, 1968. Bar: Tex. 1968; cert. Tex. Estate Planning and Probate Law Bd. of Legal Specialization. Assoc. then ptnr. Clark, Thomas, Winters, & Shapiro, Austin, Tex., 1968-84; mng. ptnr. Jenkens & Gilchrist, Austin, 1985-88; ptnr. Johnson & Gibbs, Austin, 1988-92, Ikard & Golden, Austin, 1992—. Pres. probate and trust law coun. Tex. Acad. Real Estate, Austin, 1988-89; bd. dirs. Paramount Theatre, Austin, 1988-89, pres. bd. dirs., 1991-92; mem. fiduciary litigation com. Am. Coll. Trust and Estate Coun., 1991-92. Fellow Am. Coll. Probate Counsel, Tex. Bar Found.; mem. State Bar Tex. (chmn., sec.-treas. legis. com. real estate, probate trust law sect. 1983-84, coun. chmn.), Travis County Bar Assn., Tarry House, Headliners, Austin Club. Home: 6820 Cypress Pt N Apt 7 Austin TX 78746-7149 Office: Ikard & Golden 823 Congress Ave # 910 Austin TX 78701-2429

IKOSSI-ANASTASIOU, KIKI, electrical and computer engineer; b. Nicosia, Cyprus, Dec. 23, 1954; came to U.S., 1978; d. George J. and Margarita K. (Vavlitis) Ikossi; m. Chris Anastasiou, Aug. 27, 1977; children: Georgia-Charithea, Michael-George. BSEE, Nat. Tech. U., Athens, Greece, 1977; MS, U. Cin., 1982, PhD, 1986. Rsch./tchg. asst. U. Cin., 1980-86; sr. rsch. scientist Universal Energy Sys., Dayton, Ohio, 1986-90; asst. prof. elec. and computer engring. La. State U., Baton Rouge, 1990-96, assoc. prof., 1996—; reviewer NSF, Washington, 1993—; summer faculty rsch. fellow Navy-Am. Soc. Engring. Edn., Naval Rsch. Lab., Washington, 1991, sr. summer faculty rsch. fellow, 1992—. Contbr. articles to profl. publs. Recipient 5 awards for contbns. Am. Soc. Engring. Edn./Navy, 1991-96; U. Cin. coun. rsch. fellow, 1982, 83, 79-85; rsch. grantee NSF U.S. Navy, La. Quality Support Edn., 1991—. Mem. IEEE (mem. tech. program com. for internat. microwave symposium, reviewer 1995—), AAAS, Am. Soc. Engring. Edn., Washington Acad. Sci., N.Y. Acad. Sci., Electrochem. Soc. Metall. Home: 2245 College Dr # 200 Baton Rouge LA 70808 Office: La State U Elec and Computer Engring South Campus Dr Baton Rouge LA 70803

ILDERTON, JANE WALLACE, small business owner; b. Gainesville, Ga., Mar. 10, 1936; d. William Lewis and Fay E. (Montgomery) Wallace; m. James Wilson Ilderton, June 12, 1954; children: James Wilson Jr., Mark Joseph, Andrew William. Grad. high sch., Gainesville. Owner, operator Designs by Jane, Charleston, S.C.; mfr., designer SGM Baby Bags Co., 1988—. Mem. Market Mchts. Assn., Charleston Trident C. of C., Smocking Arts Guild of Am., Longstreet Soc. (charter), United Daus. Confederacy (charter). Episcopalian. Office: Designs by Jane 188 Meeting St Charleston SC 29401-3155

ILIFF, VICKI WEBER, special education educator; b. Atlantic, Iowa, Feb. 5, 1953; d. Robert Gene and Virginia Mae Weber; m. George Robert Iliff, July 30, 1977; 1 child, Megan Laurel. BS in Spl. Edn., Ill. State U., 1974; MA in Ednl. Adminstrn., Sangamon State U., 1977. Cert. specific learning disabilities tchr., Fla., emotionally handicapped tchr., Fla., learning disabilities tchr., Ill., socially/emotionally handicapped tchr., Ill., educable mentally handicapped tchr., Ill., elem. tchr., Ill., administr., Ill. Coord. programs for students with behavior disorders LaSalle County Edn. Alliance for Spl. Edn., Streator, Ill., 1977-80; spl. edn. cons. Ottawa (Ill.) Elem. Schs., 1980-83; adj. faculty Warner So. Coll., Lake Wales, Fla., 1989-90; curriculum supr./learning disabilities specialist Vanguard Sch., Lake Wales, Fla., 1983-91; varying exceptionalities tchr. Shelley S. Boone Mid. Sch., Haines City, Fla., 1991-93; in-class model tchr. McLaughlin Md. Sch., Lake Wales, 1993-95; Cluster math tchr., chmn. math. dept. Roosevelt Acad., 1995—; spkr. numerous confs. and workshops; ednl. cons. UNICEF to a consortium of Caribbean nations; mem. adv. com. Fla. Diagnostic and Learning Resources System III, 1983-89; mem. steering com. Ill. Coun. for Children with Behavior Disorders, 1982; program chairperson Ill. Fedn. Coun. for Exceptional Children State Conv., 1981; trainer strategy intervention model, Fla. performance measurement sys., and clin. edn. model. Field editor Teaching Exceptional Children, 1988—. Methodist.

ILLADE, BORIS JULIUS, elementary school educator; b. Viveiro, Lugo, Spain, July 3, 1957; came to U.S., 1981; s. Jose Angel and Maria (Illade) Perez. BA Psychology, Fla. State U., 1983; cert. teaching, U. Tex., Austin, 1991. Cert. bilingual tchr., Tex. Tchr. Ft. Worth Ind. Sch. Dist., 1991-92, Dallas Ind. Sch. Dist., 1992—. Mem. Mensa. Home: Apt 206 7324 W Ohio Ave Lakewood CO 80226

IMBEAU, STEPHEN ALAN, allergist; b. Portland, Oreg., Nov. 25, 1947; s. David A. and Marjory Anne (Jacobsen) I.; m. Shirley Ruth Burke, Aug. 18, 1979; children: Stephanie Frances, Andrew Paul, Charles Burke. BA, U. Calif., Berkeley, 1969; Dr.med., U. Calif., San Francisco, 1973. Diplomate Am. Bd. Internal Medicine, Am. Bd. Allergy. Intern U. Wis., Madison, S.C., 1973-74; resident in internal medicine U. Wis., Madison, 1974-75, resident in allergy, 1976-78, resident in infectious diseases, 1978-79; pvt. practice Florence, S.C., 1980—; mem. S.C. budget and control bd. S.C. Data Oversight Coun., 1993—. Contbr. articles to profl. jours. Chmn. Florence Symphony Orch., 1985-91; bd. dirs. Big Bros., 1989-92, Am. Lung Assn., 1982-86, Florence County Progress, chmn. 1993-95. Fellow ACP; mem. AMA (S.C. alt. del. 1992—), Am. Acad. Allergists, S.C. Med. Soc. (trustee 1988-90, sec. bd. 1990-94, treas. 1995—, S.C. Ambassador of the Yr. 1995), Florence County Med. Soc. (pres. 1984-85), Florence County Devel. Authority, Lions (pres. 1987-88). Home: 950 Park Ave Florence SC 29501-5734 Office: 901 E Cheves St #440 Florence SC 29503

IMEL, JOHN MICHAEL, lawyer; b. Cushing, Okla., Aug. 4, 1932; s. Arthur Blaine and Hazel Monnet (Kelly) I.; m. Patricia Ann Carney, July 31, 1954; children: Blythe Michele, Kathryn Ann, Dixie Lynn, Sally Louise. BS, U. Okla., 1954, JD, 1959. Bar: Okla. 1959, U.S. Dist. Ct. (no. dist.) Okla. 1961, U.S. Ct. Appeals (10th cir.) 1961, U.S. Supreme Ct. 1962, U.S. Dist. Ct. (we. dist.) Okla. 1967, U.S. Dist. Ct. (ea. dist.) Okla. 1971. Asst. atty. County of Tulsa, 1959-60; mcpl. judge City of Tulsa, 1960-61; U.S. atty. U.S. Dept. Justice, Tulsa, 1961-67; ptnr. Moyers, Martin, Santee Imel & Tetrick, Tulsa, 1967—. Regent U. Okla., Norman, 1981-88; trustee Children's Med. Ctr., Tulsa, 1979-84. Capt. USNR, 1954-56. Fellow Am. Bar Found., Am. Coll. Trial Lawyers (state chmn. 1987-88); mem. Am. Inns of Ct. (program chmn. 1989-90, Exemplary Leadership award 1996), So. Hills Country Club (bd. govs. 1993—), Tulsa Club (pres. 1990), Rotary (pres. 1968-69). Democrat. Methodist. Home: 3920 E 58th Pl Tulsa OK 74135-7823 Office: Moyers Martin Santee Imel & Tetrick 320 S Boston Ave Ste 920 Tulsa OK 74103-3729

IMHOFF, ROBERT JAY, educational administrator; b. Lakeview, Mich., June 20, 1949; s. Carl A. and Freda B. (Bard) I.; m. Jacquelyn F. Mercer, Sept. 2, 1972; children: Kristin, Danika, Brandon, Keegan. BA, Spring Arbor Coll., 1972; MA, Mich. State U., 1975. Cert. tchr., Mich. Dean of student devel. John Wesley Coll., Owosso, Mich., 1975-79, Bartlesville (Okla.) Wesleyan Coll., 1979-83, Belhaven Coll., Wilmore, Ky., 1983-84, Biola U., La Mirada, Calif., 1984-85; v.p. Tri-State U., Angola, Ind., 1985-92, Belhaven Coll., Jackson, Miss., 1992—; pres. Brandon Aslans Soccer Club, 1993—. Mem. Nat. Assn. Student Pers. Adminstrs., Assn. Coll. Pers. Adminstrs., Assn. Christians in Student Devel., Kiwanis. Republican. Office: Belhaven Coll 1500 Peachtree St Jackson MS 39202-1754

IMRHAN, SHEIK NAZIR, industrial engineer, educator; b. Bagotsville, Demarara, Guyana, Jan. 4, 1950; came to U.S., 1979; s. Imran and Husna B. Imrhan; m. Victorine Lall, May 10, 1975; children: Sabine M., Savina N. BSc, U. Guyana, Turkeyen, 1973, diploma in edn., 1975; MS in Stats., MS in Indsl Engring., U. Ala., Tuscaloosa, 1981; PhD, Tex. Tech U, 1983. Registered profl. engr., Tex. Master high schs., Georgetown, Guyana, 1968-

75; shift mgr., chemist Guyana Sugar Corp., Wales, 1975-76; master Grand Turk Island High Sch., Turks and Caicos Islands, 1976-79; teaching asst. U. Ala., 1979-81, vis. asst. prof., 1984; rsch. asst. Tex. Tech U., Lubbock, 1981-83; asst. prof. La. Tech U., Ruston, 1984-87; assoc. prof. indsl. engring. U. Tex., Arlington, 1987—; conf. presenter; indsl. cons. in musculoskeletal injuries. Author: Help! My Computer is Killing Me: Preventing Aches and Pains in the Computer Workplace, 1996; editor Internat. Jour. Indsl. Ergonomics, Internat. Jour. Indsl. Engrs.; contbr. articles on ergonomics and human factors to profl. jours. and conf. procs. Mem. Inst. Indsl. Engrs., Human Factors Soc. Am., Ergonomics Soc., North Tex. Human Factors Soc. (bd. dirs.-elect 1989-90). Home: 5110 Trail Head Dr Arlington TX 76013-5321 Office: U Tex Box 19017 Arlington TX 76019

IMSEIS, MANUEL YUSUF, pediatrician, allergist, immunologist; b. Lydda, Palestine, 1939. MD, Am. U. Beirut, 1965. Diplomate Am. Bd. Allergy & Immunology, Am. Bd. Pediatrics. Intern Am. U. Hosps., Beirut, 1964-65; resident in pediatrics Tulane U.- Charity Hosp., New Orleans, 1973-75; fellow in pediat. & adult allergy and immunology La. State U.-Charity Hosp., New Orleans, 1975-77; with Meadowcrest Gen. Hosp., Gretne, La.; clin. asst. prof. medicine and pediats. La. State U.- Charity Med. Ctr. Mem. LAS, Am. Acad. Allergy and Immunology, Am. Coll. Allergy and Immunology, Am. Coll. Chest Physicians, Southern Med. Assn. Office: 812 Avenue F Ste 202 Marrero LA 70072-1940

INABINET, GEORGE WALKER, JR., retired state agency administrator; b. Cameron, S.C., Sept. 24, 1927; s. George Walker and Elizabeth (Wolfe) I.; m. Helen Ruth Davis, Sept. 27, 1947; children: Pamela Ruth, Jeffrey Walker. Cert. EE, S.C. Area Trade Sch., Columbia, 1949; Bus. Mgmt. degree, U. S.C., 1951; electronics engr. cert., Nat. Radio Inst., Washington, 1967. Asst. dir. S.C. Dept. Hwys., Columbia, 1951-53; adminstr. transp. S.C. Dept. Edn., Columbia, 1953—; ret. Chmn. Boy Scouts Am., Sandy Run, S.C., 1965-70; pres. Sandy Run Cmty. Club, 1966-70, S.C. Football Ofcls. Assn., Columbia, 1971-72; mem. White House Coun. on Youth, Washington, 1972-76; chmn. Calhoun County Tri-Centennial Commn., 1970; chmn. adminstrn. bd. Mt. Zion United Meth. Ch., Sandy Run, 1952-75; mem. Gov.'s Com. on Comm.; vice chmn., Calhoun County Planning Commn., Calhoun County Facilities Com.; pres. ch. coun. Sandy Run Luth. Ch. Mem. Assn. Pub. Safety Communications Officers (pres. 1979-81), Assn. Pub. Communications Officers (v.p. 1979-80, pres. 1980-81), S.C. Assn. Pupil Transp. (v.p. 1981-82, pres. 1982-83), Am. Legion. (chmn. state oratorical com. 1989—), Masons, Shriners. Home: Windy Hill Star Rte Box 194 Swansea SC 29160

INABINET, LAWRENCE ELLIOTT, retired pharmacist; b. Orangeburg, S.C., June 15, 1933; s. Boysie Benjamin and Alrona Minerva (Robinson) I.; m. Velma Vincent Ferguson (div.); children: Rhett Elliott, Bonny Susan Murphy. BS in Pharmacy, U. S.C., 1963. Registered pharmacist. Retail pharmacist chain and ind. drug stores, 1963-69; staff hosp. pharmacist S.C. State Hosp., Columbia, S.C., 1969-71; staff pharmacist Hawthorne Pharmacy, Columbia, S.C., 1971-72, Hemingway (S.C.) Pharmacy, 1990-93, Revco Drug Stores, Marion, S.C., 1993-95; pharmacy supr. S.C. Dept. Corrections, Columbia, 1972-79; retail pharmacist Ind. Drug Stores, 1979-84; hosp. pharmacist Baker Hosp., North Charleston, S.C., 1984-86; asst. dir. pharmacy Marion (S.C.) Meml. Hosp., 1986-90. Author: (text) Civilian-Military Time Converter; patentee medicating device for animals; contbr. poems to pubs. Deacon Bapt. ch. With USN, 1954-58. Mem. Am. Legion, Masons (past master, masonic knight templar), Kappa Psi. Home: 1-B Greenwood Park Marion SC 29571-9406

INCAPRERA, FRANK PHILIP, internist; b. New Orleans, Aug. 24, 1928; s. Charles and Mamie (Bellipanni) I.; BS, Loyola U. of South, 1946; MD, La. State U., 1950; m. Ruth Mary Duhon, Sept. 13, 1952; children: Charles, Cynthia, James, Christopher, Catherine. Diplomate Am. Bd. Internal Medicine. Intern, Charity Hosp., New Orleans, 1950-51, resident, 1951-52; resident VA Hosp., New Orleans, 1952-54; practice medicine specializing in internal medicine, New Orleans, 1957—; med. dir. Internal Medicine Group, New Orleans, 1973—; med. dir. Owens-Ill. Glass Co., New Orleans, 1961-85, Kaiser Aluminum Co., Chalmette, La., 1975-84, Tenneco Oil Co., Chalmette, 1978-84, Lutheran Nursing Home, 1990—; assoc. med. dir. Cigna Health Plan of La., 1991—; co-founder Med. Ctr. E. New Orleans, 1975; clin. assoc. prof. medicine Tulane U. Sch. Medicine, 1971-87, clin. prof. medicine, 1987—; clin. prof. medicine La. State U., 1994—; med. dir. Luth. Nursing Home, 1990—; adv. bd. Healthcare New Orleans, 1991—; mem. New Orleans Bd. Health, 1966-70. Bd. dirs. Meth. Hosp., 1971—, sec., 1992—, Lutheran Home New Orleans, 1976-80, Chateau de Notre Dame, 1977-82, New Orleans Opera Assn., 1975—; mem. New Orleans Human Relation Com., 1968-70; bd. dirs. Emergency Med. Svcs. Coun., 1977-86, pres., La. southeastern region, 1979-81; bd. dirs. New Orleans East Bus. Assn., 1980-95, v.p., 1981-83; bd. dirs. Luth. Towers, 1988-89, Peace Lake Towers, 1988-89, La. State U. Med. Ctr. Found. Bd., 1989-91; mem. pastoral care adv. com. So. Bapt. Hosp., 1982-83; mem. pres's. adv. bd. coun. Loyola U. of South, 1989—. Capt. USAF, 1955-57. Fellow ACP, Am. Geriatrics Soc.; mem. AMA, Am. Coll. Physician Execs., Am. Coll. Physicians (gov. 1995—, Laureate award 1993), La. Med. Soc. (v.p. 1975-76), Orleans Parish Med. Soc. (sec. 1972-74), New Orleans Acad. Internal Medicine (pres. 1969), La. Occupl. Medicine Assn. (pres. 1971-72), La. State Med. Soc. (v.p. 1975-76), La. Soc. Internal Medicine (exec. com. 1975—, pres. 1983-85), New Orleans East C. of C. (dir. 1979-85), La. State U. Med. Sch. Alumni Assn. (pres. 1989-90), Order of St. Louis, Blue Key, Delta Epsilon Sigma, Optimists Club (bd. dirs. 1964-69, New Orleans). Home: 2218 Lake Oaks Pky New Orleans LA 70122-4345 Office: 5640 Read Blvd New Orleans LA 70127-3140

INDERBITZIN, LAWRENCE BEN, psychiatry educator; b. Muskegon, Mich., Sept. 15, 1939; s. Milton Davis and Helen (Hill) I.; m. Ann Lucille Wagner, June 4, 1960; children: Sarah, Kurt. Student, Kalamazoo Coll., 1957-60; MD cum laude, U. Mich., 1964; postgrad., Balt.-D.C. Inst. Psychoanalysis, 1971-77. Diplomate Am. Bd. Psychiatry and Neurology; cert. psychoanalyst; lic. Maryland, Mich., Ga. Asst. resident psychiatry Albert Einstein Coll. Medicine, Bronx, N.Y., 1965-66, chief resident psychiatry, 1968-69; intern Meml. Hosp. Long Beach, Calif., 1964-65; rsch. psychiatrist Lab. Psychopharmacology NIMH, Washington, 1969-70; clin. asst. prof. to asst. prof. to assoc. prof. Georgetown U., Washington, 1970-83; cons. psychiatrist Community Mental Health Ctr., Washington, 1970-85; private practice Washington, 1970-85; cons. psychiatrist VA Hosp., Washington, 1971-85; asst. to assoc. to full prof. Sch. Medicine Emory U., Atlanta, 1985—; dir. outpatient rsch., site dir. residency training Grady Meml. Hosp., 1987-91; attending psychiatrist and psychoanalyst, training and supervising analyst Psychoanalytic Inst. Emory U., Atlanta, 1985—; dir., 1991-95; dir. clin. svcs. Grady Meml. Hosp, 1987—; supr. Emory Med. Care Found., 1988—; lectr. in field. Reviewer Jour. Am. Psychoanalytic Assn., 1986-91, editorial bd. 1991-93; editorial reader Psychoanalytic Quarterly, 1990, editorial bd., 1995; editorial bd. Internat. Jour. Psychoanalysis, 1993; contbr. numerous articles to profl. jours. Lt. Commdr. U.S.P.H.S., 1966-68. Recipient Commendation Excellent Svcs. D.C., 1984, 85. Fellow APA; mem. Am. Psychoanalytic Assn., Am. Coll. Psychiatrists, Internat. Psychoanalytic Assn., Ga. Psychiatric Assn., Atlanta Psychoanalytic Soc., Balt.-D.C. Soc. Psychoanalysis, Phi Kappa Phi, Alpha Omega Alpha. Home: 5119 Chastleton Dr Stone Mountain GA 30087-1443 Office: Emory U Psychoanalytic Inst Room 414 1701 Upper Gate Dr NE Rm 414 Atlanta GA 30307-1023 also: Grady MEMl Hosp Dept Psychiatry 80 Butler St SE Atlanta GA 30303-3031

INFANTE-OGBAC, DAISY INOCENTES, sales and real estate executive, marketing executive; b. Marbel, The Philippines, Aug. 3, 1946; came to U.S., 1968; d. Jesus and Josefina (Inocentes) I.; children: Desiree Josephine, Dante Fernancio, Darrell Enerico; m. Rosben Reyes Ogbac, Jan. 30, 1987. AA with highest honors, Notre Dame of Marbel, Philippines, 1963; AB in English magna cum laude, U. Santo Tomas, Manila, 1965, BS in Psychology, 1966; MA in Communications, Fairfield U., 1971. Columnist, writer Pinoy News mag., Chgo., 1975-76, Philippine News, Chgo., 1977-80; cons. EDP Cemco Systems, Inc., Oak Brook, Ill., 1980-81; pres. Daisener, Inc., Downers Grove, Ill., 1980-82; cons. EDP Robert J. Irmen Assocs., Hinsdale, Ill., 1981-82; pres. Data Info. Systems Corp., Downers Grove, Ill., 1982-84; broker, co. mgr. Gen. Devel. Corp., Chgo., 1984-86; columnist, writer Via Times, Chgo., 1984-86; owner, pres. Marbel Realty, Chgo., 1984-88; exec. v.p. Dior Enterprises, Inc., Chgo., 1986-88; real estate sales mgr. M.J. Cumber Co., Grand Cayman, Cayman Islands, 1988-89, Vet. Real Estate, Orlando, Fla., 1989-90; sales mgr. All Star Real Estate, Inc., Orlando, 1990-92; ruby network mktg. exec. Melaleuca, Inc., 1991—; pres. Dior Enterprises, Inc., Orlando, 1992—; bd. dirs. Network Mktg. Alliance, 1996—. Author: Poems of My Youth, 1982; (lyrics and music) My First Twenty Songs, 1981; featured contbr. poems; American Poetry Anthology, vol. VIII, no. 4, Best New Poets of 1987; inventor fryer-steamer. Sec. Movement for a Free Philippines, 1984. Mem. NAFE, Am. Soc. Profl. Exec. Women, Philippine C. of C. (sec. Chgo. chpt. 1985), Bayanihan Internat. Ladies Assn., Lions (twister Fil-Am. club 1978-79). Roman Catholic.

INFOSINO, IARA CIURRIA, management consultant; b. Campinas, Sao Paulo, Brazil, Aug. 24, 1952; came to the U.S., 1982; d. Humberto and Mafalda (Pavan) C.; m. Konstantinos Stavropoulos, Feb. 2, 1980 (div.); m. Charles J. Infosino, Feb. 24, 1995; 1 child, Melissa Rose. BS in Math., São Paulo State U., São José do Rio Preto, Brazil, 1974; MS in Applied Math., UNICAMP, Campinas, Brazil, 1982; PhD in Ops. Rsch., Stanford U., 1989. H.S. tchr. Colegio Santo Andre, São Jose'do Rio Preto, Brazil, 1973-74; tchg. asst. UNESP, São Jose'do Rio Preto, Brazil, 1974; asst. prof. Bus. Sch., São Jose'do Rio Preto, Brazil, 1973-75, UNICAMP, Campinas, Brasil, 1978-82; sr. cons. Bender Mgmt. Cons., Arlington, Va., 1989—. Mem. INFORMS Inst. Office: Bender Mgmt Cons 1755 Jefferson Davis Hwy Ste 904 Arlington VA 22202

INGEBRIGTSEN, CATHERINE WILLIAMS, rehabilitation consultant, health education specialist; b. Lake Charles, La., May 28, 1955; d. Thomas Humphrey and Jane Catherine (Caldwell) Williams; 1 child, Jennifer Catherine Bittle. BS, Old Dominion U., 1978, MS summa cum laude, 1983; diploma profl. nursing, Norfolk Gen. Hosp., 1978. Intensive care unit nurse DePaul Hosp., Norfolk, Va., 1979-80; cons. Internat. Rehab. Assn., Virginia Beach, Va., 1980-82; ptnr., pres., cons. OccuSystems, Norfolk, 1982-85; prin., pres. Cathy Bittle & Assocs., Norfolk, 1985—; health edn. cons. Peninsula Health Dept., Newport News, Va., 1985—, dir. grant writing program, 1985-86; educator Diabetes Inst., Virginia Beach, 1984-88; speaker in field. Com. mem. Tidewater Health Fair Task Force, Norfolk, 1983. LCDR Nurse Corps Res. Program USN, 1988—. Mem. Am. Assn. Counseling and Devel., Am. Assn. Phys. Health, Edn., Recreation and Dance, Old Dominion U. Grad. Student Assn. (pres. 1982-83), Phi Kappa Phi. Republican. Roman Catholic. Avocations: sailing, biking, skiing, running, rollerskating. Home: 3241 River Rd Green Cove Springs FL 32043 Office: Case Mgmt Enterprises Inc PO Box 2281 Orange Park FL 32067-2281

INGERSOLL, MARGARET LEE, school principal; b. Columbus, Ga., Aug. 2, 1950; d. Thad and Charlie (Josey) Lee; m. Rudolph Ingersoll; children: Brandi, Brandon. BS cum laude, Mercer U., 1972; MEd, Ga. State U., 1975, EdS, 1983, postgrad., 1983-86. Cert. tchr., Ga. Tchr. biology Muscogee County Sch. Dist., Columbus, 1972-74; tchr. hearing impaired pvt. sch. and Muscogee County Sch. Dist., Columbus, 1974-86; prin. 30th Ave Elem. Sch., Columbus, 1986-91, River Rd. Elem. Sch., Columbus, 1991—. Named to Outstanding Young Women of Am., 1983. Mem. ASCD, Nat. Assn. Elem. Prins., Ga. Assn. Elem. Prins. (Sch. Bell award 1990), Muscogee Elem. Prins. Assn. (sec. 1988-90, pres.-elect 1994-95, pres. 1995—), Phi Delta Kappa, Kappa Delta Pi. Baptist. Office: River Rd Elem Sch 516 Heath Dr Columbus GA 31904-4844

INGLETT, BETTY LEE, retired media services administrator; b. Augusta, Ga., Oct. 6, 1930; d. Wilfred Lee and Elizabeth Arelia (Crouch) I. BS in Edn., Ga. State Coll. for Women, 1953; MA in Library, Media and Edn. Adminstrn., Ga. So. U., 1980; EdD in Edn. Adminstrn., Nova U., 1988. Tchr. James L. Fleming Elem. Sch., Augusta, Ga., 1953-63, Murphey Jr. High Sch., Augusta, 1963-64, Sego Jr. High Sch., Augusta, 1964-68, Glenn Hills High Sch., Augusta, 1968-75; media specialist Nat. Hills Elem. Sch., Augusta, 1975-80; prin. Lake Forest Elem. Sch., Augusta, 1980-84, Joseph R. Lamar Elem. Sch., Augusta, 1984-86; dir. ednl. media services Richmond County Bd. Edn., Augusta, 1986—; owner, operator Betty Inglett Enterprises, Augusta. Contbr. articles to profl. jours. Bd. dirs. Am. Heart Fund, 1975-80, Am. Cancer Fund, 1986—; del. Dem. State Conv., 1982; council mem. PTA. (life), 1985. Named Administr. of Yr., 1988-89. Mem. Richmond County Edn. Assn. (sec. v.p. 1961-63, Adminstr. of Yr. 1989-90), AAUW (v.p. 1957-59), NEA, Ga. Assn. Edn., Ga. Assn. Ednl. Leaders, Ga. Library Media Dept., Ga. Library Assn., Ga. Assn. Instructional Tech., Ga. Assn. Curriculum Instructional Supr., Profl. Leadership Assn., Cen. Savannah River Area Library Assn., Alpha Delta Kappa, Phi Delta Pi, Phi Delta Kappa. Baptist.

INGRAM, GEORGE CONLEY, lawyer; b. Dublin, Ga., Sept. 27, 1930; s. George Conley and Nancy Averett (Whitehurst) I.; m. Sylvia Williams, July 26, 1952; children: Sylvia Lark, Nancy Randolph, George Conley. A.B., Emory U., 1949, LL.B., 1951. Bar: Ga. 1952. City atty. City of Smyrna, Ga., 1958-64, City of Kennesaw, Ga., 1964; judge Cobb County Juvenile Ct., 1960-64, Superior Ct., Cobb Jud. Cir., 1964-68; assoc. justice Supreme Ct. Ga., 1973-77; spl. asst. atty. gen. State of Ga., 1979-86; ptnr. Alston & Bird, Atlanta, 1977—; mem. State Commn. on Compensation, 1987—; staff, faculty Judge Advocate Gen. Sch. U.S. Army U. Va., 1952-54; southeast panel mem. Judicial Arbitration & Mediation Svcs., Inc.; endispute Alternative Dispute Resolution. Trustee The Carter Ctr., Inc., The Eleventh Cirs. Hist. Soc. Inc., Vasser Woolley Found. Inc.; mem. coun. Emory U. Law Sch. 1st lt. JAGC, USAR, 1952-54. Recipient Disting. Svc. award Kennesaw Mountain Jaycees, 1961, Ga. Jaycees, 1961, Emory Law Sch. Alumni Assn., 1985; Disting. Citizen award City of Marietta, Ga., 1973; Len Gilbert Leadership award Cobb County C. of C., 1985; Cobb County Citizen of Yr. award, 1990; hon. life mem. Ga. PTA. Fellow Am. Bar Assn. Found., Am. Coll. Trial Lawyers, Ga. Bar Found., Internat. Soc. Barristers, Am. Acad. Appellate Lawyers, Marietta-Cobb Mus. Art; mem. ABA, State Bar Ga. (Tradition of Excellence award 1987), Cobb and Atlanta Bar Assns., Lawyers Club of Atlanta, Old War Horse Lawyers Club, Am. Law Inst., Ga. C. of C. (bd. dirs.) Cobb County C. of C. (Pub. Svc. award, 1970) Order of Coif (hon.), Georgian Club (bd. mem.), World Trade Club (bd. mem.), Marietta Rotary Club, Piedmont Driving Club, Phi Delta Phi, Omicron Delta Kappa. Methodist. Home: 540 Hickory Dr Marietta GA 30064-3602

INGRAM, JUDITH MYRNA, university specialist; b. Atlanta, Aug. 29, 1942; d. Thaddius Slater and Georgia (Williams) Allen; m. Ronald Nathaniel Myrick, June 6, 1965 (div. May 1968); children: Monica Lynn Myrick, Jill Jeanine Myrick; m. Nathaniel Bruce Ingram, Dec. 23, 1993. BA, Spelman Coll., 1964; MFA, Fla. State U., 1979. Youth program dir. Young Women's Christian Assn., Atlanta, 1964-66, 68-69; drama specialist City of Atlanta Parks & Recreation, 1969-75; registration specialist Ga. State U., Atlanta, 1981-82, conf. coord., 1982-88, adminstrv. coord., 1988-91, program specialist, 1991, unit head pub. svc., 1991-92; program devel. specialist Ga. State U., 1992—. Author: (play) Weavers of Dreams of Spells of Blues n' Things, 1977. Bd. dirs. Neighborhood Arts Ctr., 1987-90; mem. campaign staff Ivan Allen for mayor, 1961; adv. com. In Celebration of Women; vol. opening and closing ceremonies 1996 Centennial Olympic Games; vol. Habitat for Humanity. Named Woman of Achievement Young Women's Christian Assn., 1991; Ga. Humanities Coun. grantee, 1990; Diuguid Found. fellow, 1977. Democrat. Methodist. Office: Ga State U Div Continuing Edn PO Box 4044 Atlanta GA 30302-4044

INGRAM, KENNETH FRANK, state supreme court justice; b. Ashland, Ala., July 7, 1929; s. Earnest Frank and Alta Mary (Allen) I.; m. Judith Louise Brown, Sept. 3, 1954; children: Jennifer Lynn Ingram Malone, Kenneth Frank Jr. BS, Auburn U., 1951; LLB, Jones Law Sch., 1963. Bar: Ala. 1963, U.S. Dist. Ct. (no. dist.) Ala. 1965, U.S. Dist. Ct. (mid. dist.) Ala. 1966. City councilman City of Ashland, Ala., 1956-58; mem. Ho. of Reps., Ala., 1958-66; presiding judge 18th Jud. Cir. Ct., Ala., 1968-87; judge Ala. Ct. Civil Appeals, Montgomery, 1987-89, presiding judge, 1989-91; assoc. justice Ala. Supreme Ct., Montgomery, 1991—; mem., chmn. Ala. Jud. Inquiry Commn., 1979-87. Contbr. articles on jud. ethics to profl. pubs. With USMC, 1952-54. Mem. ABA, Ala. Bar Assn., Masons. Democrat. Methodist. Home: 264 1st St N Ashland AL 36251 Office: Ala Supreme Ct 300 Dexter Ave Montgomery AL 36104-3741

INGRAM, MICHAEL ALEXANDER, operations and management consultant; b. Alexandria, St. Ann, Jamaica, Nov. 6, 1958; came to U.S., 1978; s. Esric Lionel and Carmen Eloise (Khouri) I. BS, U. Fla., 1983, M in Health Sci., 1986. Instr. II Eagle's Watch Cluster Facility, Daytona Beach, Fla., 1984; clin. case mgr. Corner Drug Store, Gainesville, Fla., 1986-88; protective investigator supr. Fla. Dept. Health and Rehabilitative Svcs., Kissimmee, 1988—. Recipient Merit award State of Fla., 1989. Mem. Nat. Rehab. Assn., Am. Assn. for Counseling and Devel., Am. Rehab. Counseling Assn., Phi Theta Kappa, Rho Chi Sigma. Democrat. Anglican. Home: 1056 Vista Palma Way Orlando FL 32825 Office: Fla Dept Children and Families & Rehabilitative Svcs 400 W Robinson St Ste S-837 Orlando FL 32801

INGRAM, OSMOND CARRAWAY, JR., minister; b. Birmingham, Ala., Sept. 5, 1952; s. Osmond Carraway and Frances Elizabeth (McReynolds) I.; m. Ann Lochamy, Dec. 21, 1973; children: Joshua Carraway, Jared Scott. BS, U. Ala., Birmingham, 1973; M in Religious Edn., Southwestern Sem., Ft. Worth, 1977. Ordained to ministry Bapt. Ch., 1978. Min. music and youth First Bapt. Ch., Elkhart, Tex., 1976-78; assoc. pastor youth and outreach Bethel Bapt. Ch., Houston, 1978-80; min. edn. and youth Vinesville Bapt. Ch., Birmingham, 1980-81; min. youth Calvary Bapt. Ch., Scottsboro, Ala., 1981-85, First Bapt. Ch., Minden, La., 1985-89; assoc. pastor youth Immanuel Bapt. Ch., Lexington, Ky., 1989-91; minister edn. and youth 1st Bapt. Ch., Elizabethton, Tenn., 1993—; mem. Pregnancy Aid Ctr., Minden, bd. dirs. 1986-89, sec. and treas., 1988-89. Author: Youth in Discovery, 1991-96; contbr. articles to profl. jours. Mem. La. Bapt. Youth Mins. Assn. (sec. and treas. 1987-88, v.p. 1988-89), Ky. Bapt. Religious Edn. Assn., Ky. Bapt. Youth Mins. Assn. Home: 111 E G St Elizabethton TN 37643-3217 Office: 1st Bapt Ch 212 E F St Elizabethton TN 37643-3212

INGRAM, SHIRLEY JEAN, social worker; b. Louisville, Oct. 22, 1946. BA in Social Sci., U. Hawaii, Pearl City, 1979; MSW, Fla. State U., 1982. Lic. clin. social worker, Fla.; bd. cert. diplomate social worker, qualified clin. social worker, Md.; cert. family mediator Fla. Supreme Ct., 1991. Case mgr. Geriatric Residential Treatment Ctr., Crestview, Fla., 1982-84; case mgmt. supr. Okaloosa Guidance Ctr., Fort Walton Beach, Fla., 1984-86; family counselor Harbor Oaks Hosp., Fort Walton Beach, 1986-87; pvt. practice Fort Walton Beach, 1987-95; social worker USAF Family Advocacy Office, Hurlburt Field, Fla., 1995—. Mem. Mental Health Assn. Okaloosa County (sec. bd. dirs. 1988—, mem. adv. bd. dirs. Area Agy. on Aging, chmn. adv. bd. dirs., Okaloosa County Area Agy. on Aging, pres.), NASW, Long Term Care Ombudsman Coun., AAUW, Sertoma. Home: 3 Palm Dr Shalimar FL 32579 Office: USAF Family Advocacy Office Hurlburt Field FL 32579

INGRAM-TINSLEY, DOROTHY CATHERINE, library automation specialist, horse stables owner; b. Albemarle, N.C., Feb. 28, 1960; d. Daniel Hoyett and Lillian Ruth I.; m. Richard Edward Tinsley, July 1, 1989. B, Appalachian State U., 1981; ML, Cath. U. Am., 1982; student, J. Sargent Reynolds, 1983-93, Stanly County C.C., 1994—. Notary Pub., N.C. Tech. svc. libr. Telesec, Inc., Kinsington, Md., 1981-83; dir. data maintenance Va. State Libr., Richmond, Va., 1983-85, head serials dept. serials and automation, 1985-88; libr. specialist Fed. Res. Bank of Richmond, 1988-93; owner, mgr. Albemarle Stables, 1994—, New Horizons Equine Edn. Ctr., 1995—; rep. Innovative Enhancements Com., Berkeley, Calif., 1993. Active Richmond (Va.) Jaycees, 1985-86. Mem. ALA, N.C. Libr. Assn., Spl. Librs. Assn., Stanly Horse Coun., N.C. Horse Coun., Am. Quarter Horse Assn. Avocations: hunting, camping, crafts, writing. Home: 32034 Valley Dr Albemarle NC 28001 Office: Albemarle Stables 32034 Valley Dr Albemarle NC 28001

INHABER, HERBERT, physicist; b. Montreal, Que., Can., Jan. 25, 1941; s. Samuel and Mollye (Blumenfeld) I.; m. Elizabeth Rose Bowen, Dec. 21, 1964 (div. 1981); m. Donna Ponce, 1996. BS, McGill U., 1962; MS, U. Ill., 1964; postgrad., U. Rochester, 1965-67; PhD, U. Okla., 1971. Sci. advisor Sci. Council Can., Ottawa, 1971-72; policy analyst Fed. Dept. Environment, Ottawa, 1972-77; vis. lectr. dept. history sci. and medicine Sch. Forestry and Environ., Yale U., New Haven, 1975; sci. advisor Atomic Energy Control Bd., Ottawa, 1977-80; lectr. physics dept. Carleton U., Ottawa, 1976-80; coordinator Office Risk Analysis, Oak Ridge (Tenn.) Nat. Lab., 1980-84; prin. Risk Concepts Inc., Oak Ridge, 1984-87, pres. A Word to the Wise, Washington, 1987-89; exec. scientist NUS Corp., Gaithersburg, Md., 1987-88; pres., chief scientist Light Fantastic, Inc., Rockville, Md., 1988-89; prin. Ecology and Environment Inc., Lancaster, N.Y., 1990-91; prin. scientist Westinghouse Savannah River Co., Aiken, S.C., 1992—. Author: Environmental Indices, 1976, Physics of the Environment, 1978, Energy Risk Assessment, 1982, What in the World, 1984, How Rich is Too Rich, 1992, (weekly column) Oak Ridger, 1981-86; contbr. articles to Chgo. Tribune, Christian Sci. Monitor, others. Pres. Oak Ridge Friends of the Library, 1983-84. Served with RCAF, 1957-61. Mem. Am. Nuclear Soc. (bd. dirs.), Soc. Risk Analysis (nat. membership chmn., nat. publicity chmn.), AAAS, Am. Phys. Soc., Can. Assn. Physicists, Air Pollution Control Assn., N.Y. Acad. Scis., Health Physics Soc., Washington Ind. Writers, Assn. Waste Mgmt. Profls., Mensa, Sigma Xi, Sigma Pi Sigma. Achievements include first to show quantitatively that renewable energy sources had higher risk per unit energy than nuclear, kink in lognormal distribution of income leading to definition of excess income; designed first national quantitative environmental index, first workable system for siting undesirable facilities; research in sub-field of geographic analysis in sociology of science. Home: 26 Timberidge Rd North Augusta SC 29841-9724 Office: Westinghouse Savannah River Co 730-4B Aiken SC 29802

INHOFE, JAMES M., U.S. senator; b. Des Moines, Nov. 17, 1934; m. Kay Kirkpatrik; children: Jim, Perry, Molly, Katy. BA, U. Tulsa, 1973. Pres. Quaker Life Ins. Co.; mem. Okla. Ho. Reps., 1966-69, Okla. State Senate, 1969-77; mayor City of Tulsa, 1978-84; mem. 1st Dist. Okla. Ho. of Reps., 1987-94; U.S. senator from Okla., 1995—, mem. armed svcs. com., intelligence com., mem. environment and pub. works com. Served with U.S. Army, 1955-56. Republican. Office: 453 Russell Senate Bldg Washington DC 20510-3601

INMAN, DANIEL JOHN, mechanical engineer, educator; b. Shawano, Wis., May 10, 1947; s. Glen and Wilma (Sidebotham) I.; m. Catherine Little, Sept. 18, 1982; children: Jennifer W., Angela W., Daniel J. BS, Grand Valley State, Allendale, Mich., 1970; MAT, Mich. State U., 1975, PhD, 1980. Instr. physics Grand Rapids (Mich.) Ednl. Park, 1970-76; technical staff Bell Labs., Whippany, N.J., 1978; rsch. asst. Mich. State U., East Lansing, 1976-79, 79-80, instr., 1978-79; prof. SUNY, Buffalo, 1980; chmn. U. Buffalo, 1989-92; Samuel Herrick prof. engring., sci., mechanics Va. Tech., 1992—; dir. Mech. Sys. Lab., Buffalo, 1984; adj. prof. Brown U., Providence, 1986; cons. Kistler Instrument Corp., Amherst, N.Y., 1985-90, Kodak, 1990—; bd. visitors Army Rsch. Office, 1995-97. Author: Vibration: Control Stability and Measurement, 1988, 90, Eng Vibration, 1994; assoc. editor SEM Jour. of Theoretical and Exptl. Modal Analysis, 1986, Mechanics of Structures and Machines, Jour. Intelligent Material Sys. and Structures, 1992—, Jour. Smart Materials and Structures, 1993—. Presdl. Young Investigator NSF, 1984-89. Fellow ASME (chair Buffalo sect. 1986-87, assoc. editor Vibration, Acoustics, Stress and Reliability in Design, 1984—, Jour. Applied Mechanics, tech. editor Jour. Vibration and Acoustics 1990—, Disting. Lectr. 1995—), AIAA (assoc.); mem. IEEE, Control Sys. Soc., Am. Acad. Mechanics, Soc. Indsl. and Applied Math., Am. Helicopter Soc., Soc. Engring. Sci. (bd. dirs.). Home: 3545 Deer Run Rd Blacksburg VA 24060-9091 Office: Va Tech Inst Dept Enring Sci and Mechs Blacksburg VA 24061-0219

INMAN, MARGARET E., elementary education educator; b. Danville, Ill.; d. Leland M. and Lois E. (Jenkins) I. BS, Olivet Nazarene U., 1972; postgrad., U. South Fla., Fla. State U. Cert. elem. phys. edn. tchr., phychology, ARC. Phys. edn. tchr., coach Evang. Sch., Ft. Myers, Fla.; phys. edn. instr. Ft. Myers; tchr. Bonita Elem. Sch., Bonita Springs, Fla. Scout leader Girls Scouts U.S. Named Coach of Yr. Soccer League Lee County, 1981. Mem. Fla. Athletic Assn., NEA, Am. Alliance for Health, Phys. Edn., Tchr.'s Assn. Lee County Schs., Fla. Recreation, Dance, and Phys. Edn. Assn., Ft. Myers Phys. Edn., State APHERD. Home: 316 Ohio Rd Lehigh Acres FL 33936-4948

INNES-BROWN, GEORGETTE MEYER, real estate and insurance broker; b. Wilmington, Del., Mar. 20, 1918; d. George and Flora Sue

(Saunders) Meyer; m. Andrew T. Innes, Jr., Nov. 26, 1947 (dec.); m. Roy Glen Brown, Jr., March 6, 1991. Grad. high sch.; cert. appraiser Villanova Coll, 1974; grad. in Real Estate Law, Theory, Conveyancing and Practice, Phila. Bd. Realtors Sch., 1945; grad. in Fire, Marine, Casualty Ins., North Phila. Realty Bd. Sch., 1946. Lic. Realtor, Pa.; ins. broker. Realtor, Phila., 1945—; ins. broker, Phila., 1946—, also appraiser; residential single family home builder, Bucks County, Pa., Princeton, N.J., 1955-61. Mem., speaker Juniata Park Civic Assn., Phila., 1984. Recipient Knights Legion award Italian-Am. Press, 1971. Mem. Phila. Women's Realty Assn. (pres. 1949-51; Woman of Yr. 1972-73; pres. bd. govs. 1949-85), Am. Bus. Women's Assn. (chpt. v.p. 1971, Businesswoman of Yr. 1971), North Phila. Realty Bd. (v.p. 1975, 76, pres. 1977, Gustav A. Wick award 1979), Delaware Council Realty Bds. (sec. 1974), Real Estate Multiple Listing Burs. (treas. 1972-76), Nat. Assn. Realtors (sec.-treas. and v.p. chpt. 1975-80), Phila. Bd. Realtors (v.p. residential div. 1975), Sigma Lambda Soc. (chpt. pres. 1948). Avocations: golf; dancing; gardening; cooking; embroidery. Home: 1162 Walnut Ter Boca Raton FL 33486-5565

INSCHO, EDWARD WILLIAM, physiology educator; b. Owego, N.Y., July 25, 1954. BA in Biology, Mercyhurst Coll., 1976; MS in Biology and Exptl. Medicine, St. Thomas Rsch. Inst., 1978; PhD in Physiology, U. Cin., 1987. Rsch. asst. Biology and Cancer Rsch. Lab. Mercyhurst Coll., Erie, Pa., 1972-76; grad. rsch. asst. dept. biology St. Thomas Rsch. Inst., Cin., 1976-78; lab. asst. dept. neurophysiology Inst. Devel. Rsch., Cin., 1978-80; grad. rsch. asst. dept. physiology and biophysics U. Cin. Coll. Medicine, 1980-87, lab. instr. dept. physiology, 1983-86, med. tutor dept. physiology, 1984-85; physiology lectr. U. Ala., Birmingham, 1988; rsch. instr. dept. physiology Tulane U. Sch. Medicine, New Orleans, 1989-91, rsch. asst. prof. dept. physiology, 1991-92, asst. prof. dept. physiology, 1992—. Reviewer Am. Jour. Physiology: Renal, Heart, Regulatory, Hyptersion, Jour. Clin. Investigation, Mineral and Electrolyte Metabolism, Jour. Hypertension; contbr. articles to profl. jours. Recipient Rsch. fellowship NIH, 1984-87, 87, 88, Univ. Rsch. Coun. Travel award U. Cin., 1984, 85, Eckstein Meml. Fund Travel award, U. Cin., 1984, Amgen Young Investigator award Nat. Kidney Found., 1992, 93. Mem. Am. Physiol. Soc. (travel award 1993), Am. Heart Assn. (coun. kidney and cardiovasc. disease, travel award 1989, Established Investigator award 1995—). Office: Tulane Univ Sch Medicine Dept Physiology SL # 39 1430 Tulane Ave New Orleans LA 70112-2699

INSCHO, JEAN ANDERSON, social worker; b. Camden, N.J., Oct. 31, 1936; d. George Myrick and Alfrida Elizabeth (Anderson) Hewitt; m. James Ronald Inscho, June 4, 1955 (div. Mar. 1982); children: James Ronald Jr., Cynthia Ann, Michael Merrick. BA, Fla. Atlantic U., 1971; MA in Coll. Teaching, Auburn U., 1974. Lic. bachelor social worker. Instr. So. Union State Jr. Coll., Wadley, Ala., 1973-75; social worker Jefferson County Dept. Human Resources, Birmingham, Ala., 1976-77, Shelby County Dept. Human Resources, Columbiana, Ala., 1977-78, Houston County Dept. Human Resources, Dothan, Ala., 1978—; adj. instr. Troy State U., Dothan, 1982—. Bd. dirs., v.p. Adolescent Resource Ctr., 1992-93, sec., 1993-95; mem. Alzheimer's Assn., Dothan Area Bot. Gardens. EPDA fellow Auburn U., 1973, 74. Mem. Ala. State Employees Assn. (v.p. Wiregrass chpt. 1987-91, bd. dirs. 1996—), Dist. 7 State Employees Assn. (polit. action com. rep., 1994-96), Ala. Master Gardeners (bd. dirs.), Wiregrass Master Gardeners (pres. 1994-95), Am. Daffodil Soc., Ala. Gerontol. Soc. Episcopalian. Office: Houston County Dept Human Resources 1605 Ross Clark Cir Dothan AL 36301-5438

INSKEEP, EMMETT KEITH, physiology educator, researcher; b. Petersburg, W.Va., Jan. 11, 1938; s. Emmett Van Meter and Junia Marie (Clower) I.; m. Ansusan Presby, Aug. 27, 1960; children: Todd Keith, Thomas Clower. AA, Potomac State Coll., 1957; BS, W.Va. U., 1959; MS, U. Wis., 1960, PhD, 1964. Fellow in genetics U. Wis., Madison, 1959-61, genetics instr., 1961-64; asst. prof. animal and vet. scis. W.Va. U., Morgantown, 1964-69, assoc. prof. animal and vet. scis., 1970-73, prof. animal and vet. scis., 1974—, chmn. reproductive physiology, 1965—. Mem. editorial bd. Animal Reprodn. Sci., 1992-95. Recipient rsch. award Nat. Assn. Animal Breeders, 1981, Am. Soc. of Animal Sci., 1987, merit award Gamma Sigma Delta. Mem. Soc. for the Study of Reprodn. (pres. 1992-93). Office: WVa U PO Box 6108 Morgantown WV 26506-6108

INVESTER, M. DOUGLAS, consumer products company executive. Chmn. of bd. Coca Cola Enterprises, Atlanta. Office: Coca Cola Enterprises PO Box 723040 Atlanta GA 31139-0040

INZANA, THOMAS JOSEPH, microbiologist, educator; b. Rochester, N.Y., Sept. 5, 1953; s. Anthony Edward and Josephine (Ninfo) I.; m. Karen Renee Dyer, Sept. 28, 1996; children: Christopher Thomas, Jason Aaron, Jeannine Marie. BS, U. Ga., 1975, MS, 1978; PhD, U. Rochester, 1982. Diplomate Am. Bd. Med. Microbiology. Postdoctoral fellow Baylor Coll. Medicine, Houston, 1982-84; asst. prof. Wash. State U., Pullman, 1984-87; asst. prof. microbiology Va. Poly. Inst. and State U., Blacksburg, 1987-91, assoc. prof. microbiology, 1991-96; prof., 1996—; grant reviewer USDA, Washington, 1985—; dir. Clin. Microbiology Lab. for Va. Md. Regional Coll. of Veterinary Medicine Teaching Hosp. Author: Diagnostic Procedures in Veterinary Bateriol and Mycology, 1990, Topley and Wilson's Microbiology and Microbial Infections, 9th edit., 1996; mem. editl. bd. Vet. Rsch. Comm., 1992—; reviewer Jour. Infectious Diseases, Jour. Clin. Microbiology, Infection Immunity, Am. Jour. Vet. Rsch., Immunol. Infectious Diseases; contbr. articles to profl. jours. Recipient Beecham award Va. Md. Regional Coll. Vet. Medicine, 1989; grantee USDA, 1984—, Ctr. Innovative Tech., 1987—, Nat. Pork Prodrs. Coun., 1990-91, various pharm. and diagnostic cos., 1987—. Mem. AAAS, Am. Soc. Microbiology (editorial bd. Cumitechs, 1992—),mem. sub-com. Nat. Com. Clin. Lab. standard, 1995—, Internat. Endotoxin Soc., Conf. Rsch. Workers in Animal Disease. Roman Catholic. Office: Va Poly Inst and State U Dept Biomed Scis/Pathobiol Blacksburg VA 24061-0342

IOPPOLO, FRANK S., JR., lawyer; b. Rockville Centre, N.Y., Nov. 13, 1966; s. Frank S. and Carmella L. (Marrone) I. BA, Wake Forest U., 1988; JD, Fordham U., 1991. Bar: Fla. 1991, U.S. Dist. Ct. (mid. dist.) Fla. 1991, D.C. 1992, N.Y. 1992, U.S. Dist. Ct. (so. dist.) Fla. 1992, U.S. Supreme Ct. 1995. Assoc. Baker & Hostetler, Orlando, Fla., 1991-96, Greenberg, Traurig, Hoffman, Lipoff, P.A., Orlando, 1996—. Bd. regents Leadership Fla., 1995-96; chmn. bd. Orlando Marine Insts., Inc., 1995; bd. dirs. Assoc. Marine Insts., Inc., 1995—; pres., chmn. bd. Bay Point of Bay Hill Property Owners Assn., Inc., Orlando, 1994-96; chmn. bid for bachelors fundraiser March of Dimes, Orlando, 1994-96. Mem. ABA, Fla. Bar Assn., Orange County Bar Assn., N.Y. State Bar Assn., D.C. Bar Assn., Wake Forest U. Alumni Assn. Ctrl. Fla. (pres. 1995-96). Office: Greenberg Traurig Hoffman Lipoff Rosen & Quentel PA 111 N Orange Ave Ste 2050 Orlando FL 32801

IRBY, B(ENJAMIN) FREEMAN, obstetrician, gynecologist; b. Birmingham, Ala., June 13, 1938; s. Benjamin Freeman and Frances (Stone) I.; m. Mary Elizabeth Sharp, Dec. 28, 1960; children: Robert, Anne, Joy. AA, Jacksonville (Fla.) U., 1959; degree, Emory U., 1960, MD, 1964. Diplomate Am. Bd. Obstetrics and Gynecology. Commd. 2d lt. U.S. Army, 1963, advanced through grades to maj., 1969; intern Fitzsimmons Gen. Hosp., Denver, 1964-65; resident in ob-gyn. Fitzsimmons Gen. Hosp., 1966-69; resident in gen. surgery Martin Army Hosp., Ft. Benning, Ga., 1965-66; chief prof. svc. U.S. Army, Ft. McPherson, Ga., 1969-72; resigned U.S. Army, 1972; pvt. practice Jacksonville, Fla., 1972—; chmn. dept. ob-gyn Meml. Med. Ctr., Jacksonville, 1985-91; med. staff officer Meml. Med. Ctr., 1991-96, med. staff pres., 1997—. Fellow Am. Coll. Obstetricians and Gynecologists; mem. AMA, Duval County Med. Soc., Fla. Med. Assn., Am. Fertility Soc., Jacksonville Ob-Gyn. Soc. (pres. 1988), Am. Soc. Law and Medicine, Am. Coll. Physician Execs. Office: N Fla Ob-Gyn Assocs Meml Divsn 3627 University Blvd S Ste 200 Jacksonville FL 32216-4256

IRBY, HOLT, lawyer; b. Dodge City, Kans., July 4, 1937; s. Jerry M. and Virgie (Lorean) I.; m. LaVerne Smith, May 27, 1956; children: Joseph, Kathy, Kay, Karon, James. BA, Tex. Tech U., 1959; JD, U. Tex., 1962. Bar: Tex. 1962, U.S. Dist. Ct. (no. dist.) Tex. 1963. Asst city atty. City of Lubbock (Tex.), 1962-63; assoc. Hugh Anderson, Lubbock, 1963-66; gen. counsel, sec. Mercantile Fin. Corp. (Tex.), Dallas, 1966-69; gen. counsel, v.p. Ward Food Restaurants, Inc., Dallas, 1969-71; pvt. practice, Garland, Tex., 1971—. Mem. lawyer referal com. State Bar Tex., 1977, 78. Mem. bd. deacons First Baptist Ch., Garland, 1974-84, chmn., 1976-77; bd. dirs. Garland Assistance Program, 1980, Dallas Life Found., 1980-90, Toler Children's Community, 1983-85; bd. dirs. Garland Civic Theatre, 1986—, pres., 1990-91,92-93, v.p. 1991-92; mem. Garland Drug Task Force, 1990; deacon South Garland Bapt. Ch. 1992—, chmn. 1993-94. Mem. Garland Bar Assn. (bd. dirs. 1986-96, sec. 1992-93, v.p. 1993-94, pres. 1995-96), Dallas Bar Assn., Tex. Bar Assn., Tex. Trial Lawyers Assn., Tex. Assn. Bank Counsel, Praetor Legal Frat. (named outstanding mem. 1962), Lubbock Jaycees (dir. 1963-65), Kiwanis (dir. 1973-74). Office: NationsBank Bldg 705 W Avenue B Ste 404 Garland TX 75040-6241

IRELAN, ROBERT WITHERS, metal products executive; b. Takoma Park, Md., Mar. 10, 1937; s. Charles Morris and Julia Mae (McKenzie) I.; m. Barbara Lucille Mitchell, Mar. 21, 1959; children: Robert Withers Jr., Jonathan M. BS, U. Md., 1960. Copy reader, copy editor Wall St. Jour., Washington, 1960-66; assoc. editor Nation's Bus. Mag., Washington, 1966-68; pub. rels. rep. Kaiser Industries Corp., Oakland, Calif., 1968-70; exec. asst. to chmn. Kaiser Affiliated Cos., Oakland, 1970-79; mgr. corp. rels. Kaiser Aluminum & Chem. Corp., Oakland, 1979-82; midwest regional v.p. pub. affairs Kaiser Aluminum & Chem. Corp., Ravenswood, W.Va., 1982-85; corp. v.p. pub. rels. Kaiser Aluminum & Chem. Corp., Oakland, 1985—, Maxxam, Inc., Houston, 1990—. Co-author, co-editor: Lessons of Leadership, 1967. Bd. dirs. Boys & Girls Clubs of Oakland, 1987—. Mem. Pub. Rels. Soc. Am. (pres. Oakland-East Bay chpt. 1990, Eddy 1987), U. Md. Alumni Assn., Crow Canyon Country Club, Sugar Creek Country Club. Democrat. Lutheran. Home: 24 Crestwood Cir Sugar Land TX 77478-3914 Office: Maxxam Inc PO Box 572887 5847 San Felipe St Houston TX 77057-3008

IRIBAR, MANUEL R., internist, health facility administrator; b. Guantanamo, Cuba, July 27, 1953; s. Jose Orlando and Ana Emilia (Coda) I. AA, Miami Dade Community Coll., 1973; MD, U. Autonoma de Guadalajara, Mexico City, 1977. Diplomate Nat. Bd. Med. Examiners. Intern U. Miami/Jackson Meml. Hosp., Miami, Fla., 1980-81; resident internal medicine U. Miami/Jackson Meml. Hosp., 1981-83; surg. asst. Coral Gables Hosp., Fla., 1978-79; emergency rm. physician Mexican Red Cross Emergency Rm., Ciudad Juarez, Mexico, 1979; surg. asst. South Shore Hosp., Miami Beach, Fla., 1979-80; med. dir., internist Internat. Med. Ctr. #1, Miami, 1983-84, Kings Point Med. Ctr., Delray Beach, Fla., 1984-87, Omni Med. Ctr., Miami, 1984—; exec. med. dir., owner E. Hollywood (Fla.) Med. Ctr.; mem. Quality Assurance Com Aventura Hosp. and Med. Ctr., Miami, Fla., 1993—, Credentials Com. Humana Health Care Plans, Miramar, Fla., 1994—. Mem. leadership council Cuban Am. Nat. Found., Miami, 1988—; trustee Miami Children's Hosp. Found., 1996—. Recipient Mejor Alumno award, U. Autonoma de Guadalajara, Mexico, 1974-77. Mem. AMA, Fla. Med. Assn., Dade County Med. Assn., Am. Geriatrics Soc., Am. Internal Medicine Soc., ACP, Am. Coll. Medicine, Am. Coll. Physician Execs., So. Med. Assn. Republican. Roman Catholic. Home: 8132 NW 164th Ter Hialeah FL 33016-6195

IRONS, ISIE IONA, retired nursing administrator; b. Rixford, Pa., Oct. 26, 1934; d. William Ellis and Catherine (Fitzgerald) Irons. Grad. RN, Buffalo Gen. Hosp., 1955; BSN, U. Buffalo, 1959; MPH, U. N.C., 1962. OPD clin. dir. Buffalo Gen. Hosp.; nursing supr. N.Y. Telephone, Buffalo; asst. staff mgr., nursing mgr. So. Bell, Atlanta, asst. staff mgr. Recipient Best Bedside Nursing award, 1955. Home: 6435 Windsor Trace Dr Norcross GA 30092-2376

IRONS, ROBERT EUGENE, music educator; b. Falls Church, Va., Jan. 2, 1964; s. Jimmy Aaron and Mary Elizabeth (Call) I. MusB in Music Edn., U. North Ala., 1993. Cert. tchr., Tenn., Ala. Band dir. Hardin County H.S., Savannah, Tenn., 1993—; band dir. Hardin County Mid. Sch., Savannah, 1993—, choral dir., 1993-94. Capt. USAR, 1990-91. Mem. Soc. for Preservation and Encouragement of Barbershop Quartet Singing in America, Music Edn. Nat. Conf., Percussive Arts Soc., Kappa Kappa Psi (alumni). Republican. Lutheran. Home: Rt 7 Box 371A Savannah TN 38372 Office: Hardin County HS 909 S Pickwick Rd Savannah TN 38372

IRONS, WILLIAM LEE, lawyer; b. Birmingham, Ala., June 9, 1941; s. George Vernon and Velma (Wright) I. BA, U.Va., 1963; JD, Samford U., 1966. Bar: Ala. 1966, U.S. Dist Ct. (no. dist.) Ala. 1966, U.S. Ct. Appeals (5th cir.) 1966. Dir. mil. justice Maxwell AFB, Ala., 1963-69; law clk. Speir, Robertson & Jackson, Birmingham, 1964-66; asst. judge adv. Whiteman AFB, Mo., 1966-67, Gunther AFB, 1967-68; ptnr. Speir, Robertson, Jackson & Irons, 1970-71, Speir & Irons, 1971-72, William L. Irons & Assocs., 1972—; U.S. trustee, 1964-86; instr. sr. officers Judge Adv. Gen.'s Sch. Air War coll., Air Univ., Maxwell AFB. Candidate Ala. Ho. Reps. 1966. Deacon, Sunday sch. supt. Mountain Brook Bapt. Ch. Served to capt. USAF Strategic Air Command. Decorated Commendation medal and citation USAF, Cong. medal of honor; named Outstanding Jr. Officer Vietnam War, USAF, 1969; DuPont Regional scholar U.Va., scholarship Freedom's Found. Mem. ABA, Birmingham Bar Assn., Assn. Trial Lawyers Am., Nat. Assn. Cert. Judge Advs., Fed. Bar Assn., Nat. Res. Officer Assn., Newcomen Soc., St. Andrews Soc., SAR (pres. Ala. chpt., writer numerous cover stories on Am. Revolution era, Taylor award 1990, U.S. Senate Commendation for Authorship of Colonial Navy 1992, senate commendation state of N.Y. for Chronicles of the Am. Revolutionary War 1995), Descendants of Washington's Army at Valley Forge (capt. of the guard, com. admiral state of Md. 1995), Nat. Lawyers Club, Sigma Delta Kappa. Democrat. Baptist. Home: 3855 Cove Dr Birmingham AL 35213-3801 Office: 1227 City Federal Bldg Birmingham AL 35203

IRVIN, THOMAS T., state commissioner of agriculture; b. Hall County, Ga., July 14, 1929; s. C.T. and Gladys Lee (Hogan) I.; m. Edna Bernice Frady, June 1, 1947; children: James, Johnny, David, Londa Irvin Wilson, Lisa Irvin Collier. Owner lumber bus. Clarkesville, Ga., 1944-67; exec. sec. to Gov. State of Ga., Atlanta, 1967-69, commr. agriculture, 1969—; pres. So. U.S. Trade Assn., New Orleans, 1982-83, 91-92, So. Assn. State Depts. Agriculture, Atlanta, 1972-73, Nat. Assn. State Depts. Agriculture, Washington, 1986-87. Contbr. articles to profl. jours. Chmn. bd. trustees Hazel Grove Elem. Sch., Habersham County, Ga., 1952-56; state rep. Ga. Gen. Assembly, 1956-67; mem., chmn. Habersham County Bd. Edn., 1956-76; dir. Ga. Sch. Bds. Assn., 1959-69, pres., 1968-69; mem. Stone Mountain Meml. Assn., 1969-78, chmn., 1969-74; chmn. bd. trustees Truett-McConnell Coll., 1990-96, chmn., 1996—; chmn. Ga. Devel. Authority; deacon Antioch Bapt. Ch.; mem. Ga. Finance and Investment Com., Ga. Bldg. Authority, Ga. Agrirama Authority, Ga. State Employees Benefit Coun., Ga. Pay-for-Performance Task Force. Recipient Disting. Svc. award Ga. Sch. Bds. Assn., 1976, Outstanding Svc. award Stone Mountain Meml. Assn., 1978, Nat. award for Agrl. Excellence, 1988, Workhorse of Yr. award Southeastern Poultry and Egg Assn., 1989, Richard B. Russell Pub. Svc. award Ga. Assn. Dem. County Chairmen, 1990, Environ. Friend Industry award Ga. Green Industry Assn., 1993, Disting. Svc. award U. Ga. Coll. Vet. Medicine, 1994, award of merit Ga. Med. Assn., 1992; named to Hall of Fame, Ga. Agrirama, 1990, Vidalia Onion Hall of Fame, 1990; named Dem. of Yr., Ga. Young Dems., 1990. Mem. AGHON Soc., Gridiron Soc., Alpha Gamma Rho, Alpha Zeta. Democrat. Baptist. Office: Ga Dept Agriculture Capitol Sq Atlanta GA 30334

IRVINE, WILLIAM BURRISS, management consultant; b. Wheeling, W.Va., July 20, 1925; s. Russell Drake and Elizabeth (Carney) I.; m. Allen Claywell; children: William, Mary, Edward. BA in Econs., Cornell U., 1949. V.p. Basil L. Smith System, Phila., 1949-66; pres. Pa. Graphic Arts, Inc., Phila., 1966-78, Classified Devel. Corp., Chapel Hill, N.C., 1978—; pres. Victor O'Neil Studios Div. Herff Jones, Inc., N.Y.C., 1972-75; trustee Cornell Delta Phi Edn. Found., N.Y., 1985—. Author: Treasury of College Humor, 1947. Mem. St. Elmo Club of Phila., St. Elmo Club of N.Y., Delta Phi (sec. 1960-62). Republican. Roman Catholic.

IRWIN, LINDA BELMORE, marketing consultant; b. Portland, Oreg., Apr. 29, 1950; d. Calvin C. and Dorothy B. (Belmore) Harper; m. Michael Hugh Irwin, June 24, 1989. Student Portland State U., 1968-72. With Hyatt Regency-New Orleans, 1975-78, catering Hyatt-Regency-Capitol Hill, Washington, 1978-80, dir. catering Hyatt-Anaheim, Calif., 1978-80; mgr. Dockside Yacht Sales, Annapolis, Md., 1981-85; dir. sales and mktg. Loew's Hotel, 1985-86; dir. mktg. Annapolis Marriot, 1986-88; ind. mktg. cons., Washington and Dallas, 1988—; ambassador State of Md., Annapolis, 1986-88; mktg. chair Tourism Council Annapolis and Anne Arundel County; curricula advisor Anne Arundel Community Coll.; mem. fund raising com. Ch. Circle Beautification Trust. Mem. Nat. Banquet Mgrs. Guild (founder Los Angeles chpt.), Nat. Assn. Female Execs. (area dir. 1985—), Annapolis C. of C. (ambassador 1985-88), Greater Washington Soc. of Assn. Execs., Anne Arundel Trade Council, Md. Tourism Council (adv. bd.), Internat. Platform Assn. Republican. Episcopalian. Avocations: sailing, travel, literature, calligraphy, ballet.

IRWIN, NED L., archivist, historian, writer; b. Jonesborough, Tenn., Jan. 15, 1955; s. Ned Cleveland and Mary Alice (Rogers) I.; m. Amy Green, Dec. 21, 1991; 1 child. BS, East Tenn. State U., 1977; MS in Libr. Sci., U. Tenn., 1987; postgrad., U. Oxford, Eng., 1989. Reporter, city editor Bristol (Va.) Herald-Courier, 1977-78; educator Washington County Bd. Edn., Jonesborough, 1978-84; asst. editor, pub. Pigeon Forge (Tenn.) Newspapers, Inc., 1984-86; practicum McClung Hist. Collection, Knoxville, Tenn., 1987; archivist spl. collections Chattanooga-Hamilton County Libr., 1988-94; archivist Archives of Appalachia, East Tenn. State U., Johnson City, Tenn., 1994—. Author: Guide to Manuscript Collections, 1990; contbr. articles to profl. jours. Fellow Acad. Cert. Archivists; mem. ALA, Tenn. Archivists (pres. 1996-97), Soc. Am. Archivists, Orgn. Am. Historians, So. Hist. Assn., East Tenn. Hist. Assn. Methodist. Home: 409 E Main St Jonesborough TN 37659-1425 Office: East Tenn State U Archives/Spl Collections Box 70665 Johnson City TN 37614-0665

IRWIN, RICHARD CRAIG, pediatrician; b. Oklahoma City, Aug. 29, 1953; s. Glen E. and Frances Jeanne (Satterlee) I. BS in Zoology, U. Okla., 1975, MD, 1979. Diplomate Am. Bd. Pediatrics., Nat. Bd. Med. Examiners. Intern then resident in pediatrics U. Okla. Coll. Medicine, Tulsa, 1979-82, fellow in devel. pediatrics, 1982-84; fellow in inpatient tng. John F. Kennedy Inst./Johns Hopkins Med. Instns., 1984; devel. pediatrician Tulsa Devel. Pediatrics and Ctr. for Family Psychology; clin. assoc. prof. U. Okla. Coll. Medicine; mem. staff Hillcrest Med. Ctr., Shadow Mountain Inst., Laureate Psychiat Clinic and Hosp.; mem. hon. staff St. Francis Hosp.; gov. apptd. mem. Okla. State Interagy. Coord. Coun. Early Childhood Intervention, 1987—; mem. spl. task force on needs of handicapped children and their families Okla. Commn. on Children and Youth, 1986—; devel. cons. Family Support Program, 1983—; numerous presentations, workshops in field. Author: (audiocassette) Attention Deficit Disorder-Ten Most Most Common Question, 1993. Trustee Town and Country Sch., 1989—. Recipient Fields of Svc. award for vol. svcs. Child Sexual Abuse Children's Protective Svcs. Coun. Greater Tulsa, 1983. Fellow Am. Acad. Pediatrics (children and devel. disabilities sect. 1991—), Soc. Devel. Pediatrics; mem. AMA, Okla. State Med. Assn., Tulsa County Med. Soc., Nat. Coun. Learning Disabilities, Nat. Learning Disabilities Assn., Okla. Assn. Learning Disabilities, Children with Attention Deficit Disorder (Green County adv. bd. 1989—, Ctrl. Okla. adv. bd. 1991—), Tulsa Cerebral Palsy Assn. (adv. bd. 1988—), Tulsa Parents of Down Syndrome Children (adv. bd. 1987—). Office: 4520 S Harvard Ave Ste 200 Tulsa OK 74135-2900

ISA, SALIMAN ALHAJI, electrical engineering educator; b. Okene, Kwara, Nigeria, Aug. 13, 1955; came to U.S., 1983; s. Isa Onusagba and Mariyamoh (Anawureyi) I. MSEE, Syracuse U., 1984, PhD, 1989. Elec. engr. Radio Oyo (NYSC), Ibadan, Nigeria, 1979-80, Aladja Steel Plant, Warri, Nigeria, 1980-82; grad. tchg. asst. Syracuse (N.Y.) U., 1985-89; assoc. prof. S.C. State U., Orangeburg, 1989—. Contbr. articles to profl. jours. Bd. dirs. Rev. Ravanel Scholarship Fund, Charleston, S.C., 1990—; pres. Nigerian Student Union, Syracuse U., 1986-89. Mem. IEEE, Material Rsch. Soc., Am. Vacuum Soc., Phi Beta Delta Honor Soc. Office: SC State Univ PO Box 7355 300 College St NE Orangeburg SC 29117-0001

ISAAC, WALTER LON, psychology educator; b. Seattle, May 31, 1956; s. Walter and Dorothy Jane (Emerson) I.; m. Susan Victoria Wells. BS, U. Ga., 1978; MA, U. Ky., 1983; postgrad., U. Ga., 1988-89; PhD, U. Ky., 1989. Advanced EMT Athens (Ga.) Gen. Hosp., 1977-79; teaching asst., rsch. asst. U. Ky., Lexington, 1979-87, instr. gifted student program, 1985, 87; instr. evening classes U. Ga., Athens, 1988, temp. asst. prof., 1989; asst. prof. psychology, mem. grad. faculty East Tenn. State U., Johnson City, 1989—; reviewer McGraw-Hill Pub. Co., Cambridge, Mass., 1990—. Contbg. author: Aging and Recovery of Function, 1984; contbr. articles to profl. jours. Bd. dirs. Upper East Tenn. Sci. Fair, Inc., 1992—; advisor to Gamma Beta Phi Honor Soc., 1994—. Mem. AAAS, Am. Psychol. Soc., Am. Assn. Lab. Animal Sci., Southeastern Psychol. Assn., Soc. for Neurosci., Sigma Xi (grantee 1987). Home: 905 Carroll Creek Rd Johnson City TN 37601-2401 Office: East Tenn State U Dept Psychology PO Box 70649 Johnson City TN 37614-0649

ISAACS, HAROLD, history educator; b. Newark, Dec. 19, 1936; s. Albert Lewis and Bertha (Wohl) I.; m. Doris Carol Mack, Apr. 25, 1974. BS in History, U. Ala., University, 1958, MA in History, 1960, PhD in History, 1968. Grad. tchg. fellow in history U. Ala., University, 1959-62; instr. in history Memphis State U., 1962-65; asst. prof. history Ga. Southwestern Coll., Americus, 1965-70, assoc. prof. history, 1970-79, prof. history, 1979—; bd. dirs. Ga. Consortium, Inc., 1979—. Author: Jimmy Carter's Peanut Brigade, 1977; founder, editor Jour. of Third World Studies, 1984—. Advisor Young Dems., Ga. Southwestern Coll., 1965-80. Recipient Tchr. of Yr. award Alpha Phi Alpha, 1982, Outstanding Svc. award Americus Early Bird Civitan Club, 1983, Outstanding Historian and Humanitarian award SABU, 1994, Presdl. Citation for Disting. Svc., 1995. Mem. Assn. Third World Studies, Inc. (founder, pres., exec. dir., 1983-91, treas. 1983—, Presdl. award 1992), Latin Am. Studies Assn., World History Orgn., Am. Hist. Assn., Nat. Coun. for Social Scis. Democrat. Jewish. Home: 1004 Hickory Dr Americus GA 31709-2122 Office: Ga Southwestern Coll Dept History and Polit Sci 800 Wheatley St Americus GA 31709-4635

ISAACSON, MARVIN GERALD, psychiatrist; b. Bklyn., July 23, 1918; s. Julius and Ida I.; student CCNY, 1937-40; M.D., Coll. Physicians and Surgeons, 1944; cert. psychiatry, neurology and neurosurgery Syracuse U., 1951; m. Illene Juanita Rosenberg, Mar. 25, 1970; children—Anita Louise, Dean Marco Freitag, Clark J. Freitag. Intern, Maimonides Hosp., Bklyn., 1943-45; resident Parkway Gen. Hosp. N.Y.C., 1945-49; supervising psychiatrist Willard State Hosp., 1949-52; practice medicine specializing in psychiatry, Miami, Miami Beach, Fla., 1954—; attending psychiatrist Jackson Meml. Hosp., Miami, 1955—; cons. St. Francis Hosp., Miami Beach, Fla., 1969-91, VA Hosp., 1955-59, Mt. Sinai Hosp., Miami Beach, 1955-59; exec. dir. P. L. Dodge Meml. Hosp., Miami, 1962-82; instr. U. Miami Med. Sch., 1955-72, asst. clin. prof., 1972-90, instr. Nursing Sch., 1975-89; cons. in psychiatry Dodge Hosp., Miami, 1982-85; cons., attending in psychiatry Harbor View Hosp., Miami. Pres., P. L. Dodge Found., 1962-90, bd. dirs. 1959-82; dir. Jewish Vocat. Service, 1964-80; bd. dirs. Dade County Council on Alcoholism, 1971-78, Humane Soc. of Dade County, 1974-90, v.p. 1986-91, pres., 1990; chmn. med.-psychiat. staff Broward County Mental Health Div., Fla., 1984-90; med. dir., 1990—; bd. dirs. Douglas Gardens Community Mental Health Center, 1981-82. Mem. Bass Mus., Miami Beach, 1985—, Miami Social Register, 1987—; mem. Com. of 100, 1988—; grand benefactor Greater Miami Opera Guild, 1990—, Miami Internat. Press Club, 1989—. With USAF, 1952-54. Recipient Cert. of Appreciation, Dade Community Coll., 1981. Mem. World Med. Assn., AMA, Am. Psychiat. Soc., Nat. Assn. Pvt. Psychiat. Hosps. (mem. legis. com. 1981), Fla. Assn. Pvt. Psychiat. Hosps. (pres. 1975), S. Fla. Psychiat. Soc. (chmn. ins. com. 1971-72), Fla. Med. Assn., Dade County Med. Assn., Williams Island Country Club, La Gorce Country Club. Democrat. Jewish. Office: Broward County Divsn Mental Health 100 SW 84th Ave Hollywood FL 33025-1419

ISBELL, GARNETT KNOWLTEN, II, retail executive; b. Navasota, Tex., Feb. 4, 1946; s. Garnett Knowlten Isbell and Mildred (Cabiness) Goldthwaite; m. Sue Ellen Kipling, Apr. 15, 1970 (div. 1982); 1 child, David Kipling; m. Mary E. Eaton, Mar. 5, 1984; children: Marc, Neves. BBA, Tex. Christian U., 1968. Parts mgr. C. Jim Stewart & Stevenson, Houston, 1969-72, ops. mgr., 1972-74, sales rep., 1974-75, div. mgr., 1976-86, v.p., div. mgr., 1986—. Mem. Young Exec. Material Handling Equipment Distbrs. Assn. (pres. 1985—), Hyster Dealer Coun., Houston Indsl. Truck Assn., Material Handling Distbrs. Assn., Houston C. of C., Houston Rotary, Forum Club, Lakeside Country Club (Houston), Kappa Sigma (pres. 1967). Republican. Office: 8787 East Fwy Houston TX 77029-1701

ISDALE, CHARLES EDWIN, chemical engineer; b. DeQuincy, La., Mar. 10, 1942; s. Vester Edwin and Katherine Gwendolyn (Wincey) I.; m. Lucille Brown, Aug. 26, 1962; children: Charles Edwin Jr., Jennifer Denise Hunt, Amberly Lauren. BSChemE, La. State U., 1965; MBA, So. Ill. U., 1978. Registered profl. engr., Ill., La. Chem. engr. Firestone Synthetic Rubber, Lake Charles, La., 1965-69, A.E. Staley Mfg. Co., Decatur, Ill., 1969-72; dir. engring. and maintenance VIOBIN Corp., Monticello, Ill., 1972-80; pres. Control Enterprises, Inc., Savoy, Ill., 1980-95; Control Enterprises, Inc., College Station, Tex., 1995—; cons. Nabisco Brands, East Hanover, N.J., 1984—, Clorox, Jackson, Miss., 1987—, Alpharma, Chicago Heights, Ill., 1987—, Chinook Group, Sombra, Ont., Can., 1987—. Active Covenant Family Ch., College Station. Mem. NSPE, AIChe (sect. chmn. 1972-73), Instrument Soc. of Am. (Man of Yr. 1986), Am. Oil Chemists Soc., Assn. of Am. Cereal Chemists. Home: 715 Canterbury Dr College Station TX 77845 Office: Control Enterprises Inc PO Box 10297 College Station TX 77842-0297

ISELIN, ELLIN, television producer; b. Detroit, Dec. 16, 1965; d. Fritz and Barbara I. BA, Hanover (Ind.) Coll., 1988; student, U. Salzburg, Austria, 1986-87; postgrad., Cornell U., 1989, U. Munich, Germany, 1990-91. Reporter WORX Radio, Madison, Ind., 1986-88; anchor/reporter WHCU Radio, Ithaca, N.Y., 1988-89; reporter NewsCenter 7, Ithaca, N.Y., 1989-90; intern Congress-Bundestag, Munich, 1990-91; promotion prodr. KOTV, Tulsa, 1991—; co-owner Sensuassinine Cards, Tulsa, 1993. Author novels and poetry; actress theater, film, commls. Big sister Big Bros. and Big Sisters of Green Country, Tulsa, 1992-93; community counselor AYUSA, Tulsa, 1992—. Nat. Presbyn. Ch. scholar, 1984-88, 1st Presbyn. Ch. Deacon's scholar, 1985. Mem. Alpha Delta Pi. Home: 200 Starcrest Dr Apt 50 Clearwater FL 34625-3802

ISENBERG, PAUL DAVID, financial executive; b. Chester, Pa., May 8, 1949; s. Paul Robinson and Katherine Mary (Rogers) I.; m. Shelly Sconyers, May 25, 1979; children: Kimberly Nicole, Sean Bradley. BSBA in Econs., U. Fla., 1975. Cert. fin. planner, Fla. Mgmt. trainee Chrysler Corp., Orlando, Fla., 1976-77; mgr. territory sales Keebler Corp., Fla., 1977-79; account exec. Merrill Lynch, Ft. Lauderdale, Fla., 1979-82; assoc. v.p. Prudential Bache Securities, Plantation, Fla., 1982—; pres. Isenberg Fin. Svcs., Plantation, 1989-92; exec. v.p., CFO, prin. Sterling Fin. Cons., Ft. Lauderdale; pres. P.D. Isenberg & Assocs., Inc.; instr. Broward C.C., Davie, Fla., 1986—. Mem. exec. com. Broward County Reg. Orgn., 1984-86; dist. voting marshall, Plantaton, 1980-88; vol. Big Bros. Am., Gainesville, Fla., 1975; bd. dirs. Fla. Ocean Scis. Inst., Ft. Lauderdale; mem. adv. bd. Flamingo Gardens. With USN, 1969-73, Vietnam. Mem. Inst. Cert. Fin. Planners, Internat. Assn. Fin. Planners (registered rep., lic. commodity broker and agt.), Assn. for Investment Mgmt. and Rsch., Fla. Goldcoast Cert. Fin. Planners Assn., Ft. Lauderdale Area Stockbrokers, Fin. Analysts Soc. South Fla., Toastmasters, Phi Delta Theta (bd. dirs., v.p. 1987-92). Home: 13940 Monticello St Fort Lauderdale FL 33325-1262

ISENSEE, SCOTT HARLAN, computer scientist; b. Longbranch, N.J., Dec. 31, 1957; s. Harlan G. and Kathleen A. (Cookson) I.; m. Dawn Radcliffe. BS in Psychology, N.D. State U., 1980; MS in Indsl. Psychology, Kans. State U., 1983; MS in Computer Sci., U. N.C., Charlotte, 1991. Cert. profl. ergonomist. Human factor scientist IBM, Austin, Tex., 1983—. Author: The Art of Rapid Prototyping. Home: 411 S Ridge Cir Georgetown TX 78628-8216 Office: IBM 11400 Burnet Rd Austin TX 78758-3406

ISGETT, DONNA CARMICHAEL, critical care nurse, administrator; b. Ga., July 12, 1963; d. William Eugene and Sara Lois (Brazier) Carmichael; m. Carroll Eugene Clark Jr.(div.); m. John Thomas Isgett. AD, Floyd Coll., 1984; BS, Ga. State U., 1989; MSN, Med. U. S.C., 1990. RN, Ga., S.C. Emergency nurse Redmond Pk. Hosp., Rome, Ga., 1984-86; charge nurse emergency Piedmont Hosp., Atlanta, 1986-89; flight nurse Med. U. S.C., Charleston, 1989-92; dept. dir. mobile ICU Roper Lifelink Emergency Transport Svc., Charleston, S.C., 1992—. Mem. ANA, AACN (CCRN), Nat. Flight Nurse Assn., Emergency Nurses Assn., Phi Kappa Phi. Home: 354 Jenny's Farm Ln Huger SC 29450-9690

ISHIHARA, OSAMU, electrical engineer, physicist, educator; b. Osaka, Japan, Nov. 15, 1948; came to U.S., 1974; s. Mamoru and Tomoe (Maeda) I.; m. Yohko Miyake, May 5, 1974; children: Reiko, Takeki, Yuko, Sachiko. BS, Yokohama (Japan) Nat. U., 1972, MS, 1974; PhD, U. Tenn., 1977. Postdoctoral fellow U. Saskatchewan, Saskatoon, Can., 1977-80, profl. rsch. assoc., 1980-84; assoc. prof. dept. elec. engring. Tex. Tech. U., Lubbock, 1985-87, assoc. prof. dept. elec. engring. and physics, 1987-89, prof. dept. elec. engring. and physics, 1989—; vis. prof. dept. energy engring. Yokohama (Japan) Nat. U., 1992; vis. prof. dept. elec. engring. and computer sci. Kumamoto (Japan) U., 1993; grad. advisor Dept. Elec. Engring., Tex. Tech. U., Lubbock, 1986-94, faculty advisor Eta Kappa Nu, 1987-94; faculty advisor Assn. Japanese Students, 1990—; bd. dirs. South Plains Regional Sci. and Engring. Fair, Lubbock, 1990—. Contbr. rsch. articles to profl. jours. Japan Soc. Promotion of Sci. fellow, 1974-77. Mem. IEEE Nuclear and Plasma Sci. Soc. (sr., exec. com.), Am. Phys. Soc. (Plasma Physics divsn.), Phys. Soc. Japan, Sigma Xi, Phi Kappa Phi, Phi Beta Delta. Office: Texas Tech Univ Dept Of Elec Engring Lubbock TX 79409

ISLAM, ANISUL MOHAMMED, economist; b. Dhaka, Bangladesh, May 2, 1952; came to U.S., 1986; s. M. Shah and Momena (Akhtar) Jamal; m. Shahida P. Islam, Aug. 14, 1986; children: Laboni, Tanzina. BA with honors, U. Dhaka, 1972, MA in Econs., 1973; MA in Econs., U. Waterloo, 1978; PhD in Econs., U. Alta., 1985. Asst. prof. U. Dhaka, 1975-77, U. Sask., Can., 1985-86, U. Ctrl. Ark., Conway, 1986-87, Sul Ross State U., Alpine, Tex., 1987-90; assoc. prof. U. Houston, 1990—; rsch. assoc. U. Dhaka, 1974-75, U. Alta., 1980-81. Co-author: Foreign Capital Savings and Growth, 1986, Exploration in Exnomics, 1989; editor Kathakali, 1992—, Balaca Newsletter, 1992—. Dir. literary programs Bangladesh-Am. Lit. Art and Cultural Assn., Houston, 1992—; gen. sec. Bangladesh Assn. Edmonton (Can.), 1982-84. Rsch. grantee U. Houston, 1991-92, 93-94, Prairie View (Tex.) A&M U., 1991-92, 92-93. Mem. Am. Econs. Assn., Am. Enterprise Forum, Southwestern Fedn. Adminstrv. Disciplines, MidSouth Econs. Assn., Missouri Valley Econ. Assn., Bangladesh Econs. Assn., Internat. Trade and Fin. Assn. Office: U Houston-Downtown 1 Main St Houston TX 77002-1001

ISOM, CHRISTINA MICHELLE, early childhood educator; b. Midland, Tex., May 20, 1971; d. John William and Linda Ann (Bandsma) I. BS, U. Tex., 1993; postgrad., U. North Tex., 1995—. Cert. early childhood, elem., reading, phys. edn. tchr. Tex. Kindergarten tchr. Wills Point (Tex.) Ind. Sch. Dist., 1994-96; pre-kindergarten tchr. Richardson Ind. Sch. Dist., 1996—. Mem. Kindergarten Tchrs. of Tex., Dallas Assn. for the Edn. of Young Children (scholarship 1996), Nat. Assn. for the Edn. of Young Children, Assn. of Tex. Profl. Educators, Ex-Students Assn. of the U. of Tex. Home: 8200 Southwestern Blvd # 1714 Dallas TX 75206

ISOM, SAM, engineering executive; b. Shelbyville, Tenn., Aug. 29, 1942; s. Wiley Samuel and Edna (Lokey) I.; m. Edna Neuhoff, Feb. 20, 1982; children: LeAnne Rich, Wiley Samuel III, Heather Gayle, Holly Anne. Chief estimator Constrn. div. U.S. Army C.E., Nashville, 1974-78; contract adminstr. U.S. Army C.E., 1978-79; chief contract adminstrn. br. U.S. Army C.E., Holcut, Miss., 1979-80; sr. contract adminstr. U.S. Army C.E., Nashville, 1980-86; asst. area engr. Waste Isolation Pilot Plant U.S. Army C.E., Carlsbad, N.Mex., 1986-87; WIPP closeout task force leader U.S. Army C.E., Albuquerque, 1987; resident engr. Holloman AFB Resident Office USACE, Alamogordo, N.Mex., 1987-88; chief contract adminstrn. br. U.S. Army C.E., Albuquerque, 1988-89; resident engr Cuchillo Dam Resident Office U.S. Army C.E., Truth or Consequences, N.Mex., 1989-91; pres. SICC Cons. Inc., Brentwood, Tenn., 1991—; guest lectr. U. N.Mex., 1988-91, Memphis State U., 1985-86. Contbr. articles to profl. jours. Recipient Key to City of Pineville, Ky., 1980. Mem. Am. Nuclear Soc., Naval Inst., KC, Elks. Home: 1118 Oman Dr Brentwood TN 37027-4119 Office: SICC Cons Inc PO Box 2548 Brentwood TN 37024-2548

ISOM, THERESA GILLESPIE, nursing administrator; b. Memphis, Mar. 3, 1953; d. Ernest Bernette and Emma Pearl (McClelland) Gillespie; m. Robert Earl Isom, June 6, 1987; 1 child, Antonio Harvey. ADN, Shelby State C.C., 1981; BS in Health Arts, Coll. St. Francis, 1990; MS in Adult Edn., U. Tenn., 1992; BSN, Union U., 1994. RN, Tenn. Staff nurse Meth. Hosp. Ctrl., Memphis, 1975-90, preceptor recovery rm., 1984-86; float charge nurse Trinity Nursing Agy., Memphis, 1983-91; clin. leader Meth. Ctrl., Memphis, 1989-90; nursing dir. Tenn. Tech. Ctr., Memphis, 1991—; mem. State Testing, Nashville, 1993—. Treas. Nat. Coalition 100 Black Women, Memphis, 1993—. Named Tchr. of Yr., 1992-93; Job Tng. Partnership Act grantee, 1993, 94. Mem. ANA, Tenn. Nurses Assn., Tenn. Orgn. Nurse Execs., Tenn. Hosp. Assn., Nat. Civil Rights Mus. Democrat. Baptist. Office: Tenn Tech Ctr Memphis 550 Alabama Ave Memphis TN 38105-3604

ISRAEL, SEYMOUR D., engineering company executive; b. 1933. With Pitts. Testing Lab., Ft. Pierce, Fla., 1955-64; pres. Universal Engring. Scis., Orlando, Fla., 1964—. Office: Universal Engring Scis 3532 Maggie Blvd Orlando FL 32811-6697

IUDICELLO, KATHLEEN ANN, English language educator; b. Washington, Sept. 26, 1968; d. Alphonse Iudicello and Maureen Ellen Doyle. BA, Ariz. State U., 1990, MA, 1992; postgrad., George Washington U., 1995—. Cert. English tchr. Ariz. C.C. Adj. faculty Estrella Mountain C.C. Ctr., 1993-94, full-time faculty, 1994-95; editor, writer, rschr. Five Star Publs., Chandler, Ariz., 1993—; part-time English instr. George Washington U., Washington, 1996; rsch. asst. Ctr. for Media and Pub. Affairs, Washington, 1996—. Co-editor Impositions, 1996—. Acad. fellow George Washington U., 1996—. Democrat. Home: 1679 32d St NW Washington DC 20007

IVER, ROBERT DREW, dentist; b. Miami, Fla., Feb. 6, 1947; s. William Henry and Jeanette (Minden) I.; m. Lisa Marie Stettner-Iver, May 5, 1974. Student, Ohio State U., 1965-66, U. Miami, 1966-68; DDS, Georgetown U., 1972. Pvt. practice dentistry Miami Beach, Fla., 1974—. Lt. USNR, 1968-81. Fellow ADA; mem. Fla. Dental Assn., East Coast Dist. Dental Soc., Acad. Gen. Dentistry, Miami Beach Dental Soc., Gold Coast Acad. Gen. Dentistry, Am. Radio Relay League, N.Am. Fishing Club, Dade Radio Club Miami, Everglades Amateur Radio Club. Office: 1205 Lincoln Rd Ste 203 Miami FL 33139-2365

IVES, MAURA CAREY, English language educator; b. Wheeling, W.Va., Oct. 15, 1960; d. Maurice Verdell and Geraldine Joyce Carey; m. Gary Wilson Ives, July 12, 1981. BA in English, Bethany Coll., 1982; MA in English, U. Va., 1984, PhD in English, 1990. Assoc. prof. Tex. A&M U., College Station, 1990—. Mem. MLA, So. Ctrl. MLA, Bibliog. Soc. Am. (fellowship 1987), Bibliog. Soc. U. Va. Office: English Dept Tex A&M Univ College Station TX 77843

IVEY, CHERYL LYNN, oncological nurse specialist; b. Omaha, Apr. 15, 1956; d. Robert Irwin and Patricia Marie (Barton) VandeBrake; m. John William Ivey, Jan. 6, 1979; children: Amanda, Matthew. ADN, Gulf Coast C.C., Panama City, Fla., 1982; BS, U. So. Miss., Long Beach, Miss., 1990; MSN, U. So. Ala., Mobile, 1992. Staff RN Brookwood Med. Ctr., Birmingham, 1982-83, Pvt. Duty Nursing, Picayne, Miss., 1983-84; staff RN Meml. Hosp. at Gulfport, Miss., 1984-89, inpatient oncology at Gulfport, 1989-90, radiation oncology at Gulfport, 1990-92, clin. nurse specialist oncology, 1992—; owner Oncology Solutions, Gulfport, Miss., 1992—; mem. Miss. Cancer Pain Initiative, Tupelo, Miss., 1993—; chairperson Nurses Edn. Subcommittee of Am. Cancer Soc., Jackson, Miss., 1993—. Contbr. chpts. to books, articles to profl. jours. Breast/prostate screening coord., Gulfport, Miss., 1990—; cancer survivor's day celebration coord., Gulfport, 1990—; govt. rels. corr. Oncology Nursing Soc., Gulfport, 1993—. Mem. ANA, Am. Assn. Clin. Nurse Specialists, Oncology Nursing Soc., Miss. Gulf Coast Oncology Nursing Soc. (nominated Oncology Nurse of Yr. 1993), Miss. Nurses Assn. (awards com., approver unit for So. Miss. 1996, mem. wellness task force 1996, v.p. dist. 5 1995, nominated Oncology Nurse of Yr. 1992-94), Advanced Practice Nurses Assn., Intravenous Nurses Assn., Sigma Theta Tau. Home: 11351 Oakleigh Blvd Gulfport MS 39503-3973 Office: Meml Hosp Gulfport 4500 13th St Gulfport MS 39501-2515

IVEY, JAN DENISE, health services administrator; b. Birmingham, Ala., Aug. 2, 1955; d. Eugene Bryant and Marjorie Jean (Young) I. BSN, U. Ala Sch. Nursing, 1977, MS in Nursing, 1982. Cardiovasc. clin. specialist Med. Coll. Va., 1982-88; nurse Med. Coll. Va., Richmond, 1989; critical care nurse Chippenham Med. Ctr., Richmond, Va., 1989-93; adminstrv. coord. Heart Ctr. U. Va. Health Scis. Ctr., Charlottesville, 1993-94, patient care svc. mgr. thoracic and cardiovasc. svcs., 1994-96; clin. svcs. mgr. U. Va. Health Schs. Ctr., Charlottesville, 1996—. Missionary Mission World Presby. Ch. Am. Recipient Doris B. Yingling Rsch. award. Mem. AACN, Sigma Theta Tau, Omicron Delta Kappa.

IVEY, MICHAEL WAYNE, mortgage banker; b. Albany, Ga., Nov. 27, 1964; s. Samuel Warlick and Barbara Ann (Norton) I. BBA, U. Ga., 1986. Cert. mortgage broker. Mortgage broker First So. Mortgage, Atlanta, 1986-87, Fed. Savs. Bank, Atlanta, 1987-88, Paragon Mortgage Corp., Atlanta, 1988-94; br. mgr., mortgage banker Globe Mortgage, Atlanta, 1994-95; br. mgr., regional v.p. First Mortgage Network, Atlanta, 1995—. Exec. coun. mem. Realtors Polit. Action Com., Cobb County, Atlanta, 1987—; mem. Leadership Cobb, 1996-97. Mem. Mortgage Broker Assn., Mortgage Bankers Assn., Cobb County Bd. Realtors (affiliate, young coun. exec. 1988-92, vice chmn. 1991-93), Cobb Insiders (pres. 1989-90, bd. dirs. 1988-92), Cobb C. of C. (Leadership Cobb Class 1996-97). Republican. Methodist. Home: 4682 Dudley Ln NW Atlanta GA 30327-3331 Office: First Mortgage Network 2100 Powers Ferry Rd NW Ste 430 Atlanta GA 30339-5014

IVEY, SHARON ELIZABETH THURMAN, sales executive; b. Henderson, Tex., Oct. 23, 1948; d. Mart B. and Nelwyn Joyce (Parker) Thurman; m. Terry Dwight Ivey, Nov. 3, 1973 (dec. 1985); 1 child, Erin Thurman. BA in History, Tex. Tech. U., 1970; MEd, Steven F. Austin U., 1977. Tchr. Houston Ind. Sch. Dist., 1975-80, 1985-91; with radio sales dept., announcer Sta. KGAS, Carthage, Tex., 1994—; v.p. Carthage Svc. League, 1991—. V.p., social chairperson Poe Sch. PTO, Houston, 1985-91; active Harris County Dems., Houston, 1975-91, Planned Parenthood, Houston, 1985—, Emily's List, Washington, 1990—; co-chair United Way Panola County, sec., 1993—; mem. adminstrv. bd. 1st United Meth. Ch., 1993—, family life coord., 1993-94. Named Woman of Yr. Beta Sigma Phi, 1995. Mem. Carthage C. of C. (bd. dirs. agrl. com. 1994—). Home: 313 Davis Carthage TX 75633

IVEY, WILLIAM JAMES, foundation executive, writer, producer; b. Detroit, Sept. 6, 1944; s. William James and Grace Christine (Hammes) I.; m. Saundra Keyes, June 19, 1969 (div. 1976); m. Patricia A. Hall, Mar. 5, 1977 (div. 1982). B.A. in History, U. Mich., 1966; M.A. in Folklore and Ethnomusicology, Ind. U., 1969. Dir. Country Music Found., 1971—; assoc. prof. music Bklyn. Coll., 1979-80; adj. prof. music Blair Sch. Vanderbilt U., 1983-84; chmn. folk music panel Nat. Endowment Arts, 1976-78, chmn. folk arts panel, 1985-86; bd. dirs. Nashville Songwriters Assn., 1974-75. Prin. writer 1987 Grammy Lifetime Achievement Awards, CBS-TV, 1988 Grammy Awards, CBS-TV; writer, producer In The Hank Williams Tradition, PBS-TV, 1990; co-producer Marlboro Music Festival, 1989-91; writer, producer Country Music Hall of Fame, CBS TV, 1992; contbr. articles to profl. jours., chpts. to books. Recipient Billboard Country Liner Notes of Year award, 1974; Grammy award nominations, 1975, 83, Best Album Notes; sr. research fellow Inst. Studies Am. Music, 1979-80. Mem. Writer's Guild Am., Nat. Acad. Rec. Arts and Scis. (trustee 1976-80, 88-89, 91-95, v.p. 1980-81, 83-84, nat. pres. 1981-83, nat. chmn. 1989-91), Am. Folklore Soc. (exec. bd. 1982-85), Soaring Soc. Am., Nashville Area C. of C. (chmn. conv. and visitors com. 1984-88), Nashville Tourism Commn., Nat. Acad. TV Arts and Scis. (bd. govs. Nashville chpt. 1984-88), Acad. TV Arts and Scis., Copyright Soc. of the South, Pres. Com. on the Arts and the Humanities. Office: Country Music Found 1 Music Cir N Nashville TN 37203-4310

IVIE, BRENDA KAREN, adult literacy educator; b. Oklahoma City, Dec. 26, 1952; d. James Robert and Ethel Belle (Ward) Fails; m. Tommy Joe Ivie, Oct. 25, 1975; children: Sheila Kay (dec.), Blaine Christopher. Cosmetology instr. Capitol Beauty Coll., Oklahoma City, 1978-81, Hollywood Beauty Sch., Norman, Okla., 1982-83; owner Miss B's Beauty Salon, Oklahoma City, 1984-87; adult literacy recruiter Southwestern C.C., Creston, Iowa, 1988-90; adult literacy coord. Little Dixie C.A.A., Broken Bow, Okla., 1991—; public speaker Adults Involved in Edn., Broken Bow, 1991—, adult literacy tutor, 1991—, TESOL instr., 1991—, pre-GED tutor, 1991—. Mem. Laubach Literacy Action, McCurtain Svc. Providers Assn. Baptist. Office: Adults Involved in Edn 1010 N. Campbell Broken Bow OK 74728

IVY, BERRYNELL BAKER, critical care nurse; b. Shreveport, La., June 24, 1954; d. Berry William and Zilphia Margaret (Nix) Baker; m. Kenneth James Ivy, Sr.,Apr. 17, 1988. ADN, Northwestern State U., 1981. RN, La., Tex.; cert. BLS, ACLS; cert. neurosci. RN; cert. CCRN. Charge nurse Doctors Hosp., Shreveport, La., 1982-85; staff nurse ICU Schumpert Med. Ctr., Shreveport, La., 1985-88; staff nurse ICU Bayshore Med. Ctr., Pasadena, Tex., 1988-89, asst. head nurse ICU, 1989-92; staff nurse/charge nurse ICU Bossier Med. Ctr., Bossier City, La., 1993—; co-chmn. profl. practice com. La. Organ Procurement Assn., Bossier City, 1988—. Mem. AACN, Nat. League Nurses, Am. Assn. Neurosci. Nurses. Home: PO Box 52 Haughton LA 71037-0052

IWANSKI, LAWRENCE MATTHEW, career officer; b. Owsego, N.Y., Sept. 27, 1966; s. Francis Lawrence and Linda Anne (Mullen) I. BS in Econs., U.S. Mil. Acad., 1988. Commd. 2d lt. U.S. Army, 1988, advanced through grades to capt.; flt. platoon leader U.S. Army, Ft. Bragg, N.C., 1989-90, air ops. officer, 1990-91, asst. ops. officer, 1991-92; maintenance platoon leader U.S. Army, Camp Eagle, Korea, 1993-94; prodn. control officer U.S. Army, Savannah, Ga., 1994-95, support ops. officer, 1995-96. Mem. St. Patrick's Day Parade Com., Savannah, 1996-97; mem. K.C., Savannah, 1993—. Mem. Army Aviation Assn. of Am. (Iron Mike chpt. treas. 1991-92), VFW, Am. Legion, First City Club Savannah, Assn. of the U.S. Army. Republican. Roman Catholic. Home: 162 Belle Grove Dr Richmond Hill GA 31324

IYER, R. RAVI, engineering consultant; b. Hyderabad, India, June 26, 1953; came to U.S., 1975; s. Krishnaswamy and Pattu (Sundaram Rajaqopalan; m. Hemalatha Ravi Viswanathan, Jan. 18, 1983; 1 child, Shruti. BTech, Osmania U., Hyderabad, India, 1975; MS, Okla. State U., 1976. Registered profl. engr., Tex.; cert. EMT, safety specialist, Tex. Process engr. Vineland (N.J.) Chem. Co., 1979-80; sr. project engr. Owens-Illinois, Internat., Vineland, 1980-87; supr. Blasland, Bouck & Lee, Edison, N.J., 1987-88, Sterling Chem. Co., Texas City, Tex., 1988-91; pres. SHRIE Quality, Houston, 1991—. Regional tech. editor: Chemical Processing, 1996; assoc. editor Tomes/Micromedex, 1996; book reviewer environ. Progress, 1990-91. Okla. State U. Tchg./Rsch. Assistantship, 1975-77; Nat. Merit scholar, 1970-75. Mem. AIChE, Am. Industrial Hygiene Assn., World Safety Orgn., Water Environment Fedn., Health Physics Soc., Air and Waste Mgmt. Assn. Hindu. Office: SHRIE Quality 16806 Soaring Forest Dr Houston TX 77059-4006

IZARD, MARY KATHRYN, reproductive biologist; b. Jackson, Miss., Mar. 15, 1952; d. William Henry and Kathryn Elizabeth (Klumb) I.; m. Lewis Hutchison Traver, Oct. 13, 1978 (div. July 1986). BS, Duke U., 1974; MS, N.C. State U., 1978, PhD, 1981. Rsch. tech. dept. micro- and immunobiology Duke U., Durham, N.C., 1974-76, colony mgr. Primate Ctr., 1982-88, asst. dir. R&D Primate Ctr., 1988-89; rsch. reproductive biologist Research Triangle Inst., Research Triangle Park, N.C., 1989-93; assoc. adj. prof. Duke U., Durham, 1987-95; head divsn. primate breeding and behavior LABS, Inc., Yemassee, S.C., 1995—; cons. Space Biosphere Ventures, Tucson, 1987-93. Editor: Creatures of the Dark, 1995; contbr. articles to sci. jours. Mem. AAAS, Internat. Primatol. Soc., Am. Soc. Primatologists. Democrat. Presbyterian. Office: Labs of Va PO Box 195 Yemassee SC 29902

IZLAR, ROBERT LEE, forester; b. Waycross, Ga., Dec. 5, 1949; s. Durham Wright and Marion Ethel (Odom) I.; m. Janice Elaine Bullard, Aug. 10, 1974; children: Olivia Frances Tate, Durham Joel Poinsett. BS in Forest Resources, U. Ga., 1971, M Forest Resources, 1972; MBA, Ga. So. U., 1977. Registered forester. Teaching fellow U. Ga., Athens, 1971-72; dist. mgr. Brunswick Pulp Land Co., Woodbine, Ga., 1974-78; div. forester Am. Pulpwood Assn., Jackson, Miss., 1978-84; exec. v.p. Miss. Forestry Assn., Jackson, 1984-87; exec. dir. Ga. Forestry Assn., Atlanta, 1987—; forest History cons. U. Miss. Ctr. for the study of Southern Culture; del. IX World Forestry Cong., Mexico City, 1986; cons. Finnish, Swedish govts., disting. vis. lectr., Yale U. Sch. of Forestry and environ. studies, long term Ecological rsch. team, asst. adj. prof. of Forest Policy. Contbr. articles to profl. jours., chpts. to books. 1st lt. U.S. Army, 1972-74, Korea; lt. col. Res., 1982—. Named Outstanding Young Alumnus, U. Ga., 1986; NSF fellow, 1972; recipient Aghon Award, 1996. Mem. Nat. Coun. Forestry Assn. Execs. (pres. 1991-92), Soc. Am. Foresters (Ga. divsn. pres. 1995), Royal Forestry Soc., Commonwealth Forestry Assn. (hon. sec. 1977—), U. Ga. Alumni Soc. (v.p. 1983, 93-96), Commerce Club, Gridiron Club, Scottish Rite, York Rite, Hospitaler Order St. John, Blue Key, Saepalo Island Nat. Estvarine, Rsch Adv. Com. Sigma Xi. Xi Sigma Pi, Gamma Sigma Delta, Alpha Zeta, Alpha Phi Omega, Alpha Mu Epsilon, Phi Kappa Phi. Episcopalian.

IZYUMOV, ALEXEI, political economy educator; b. Sofia, Bulgaria, Sept. 3, 1956; came to U.S., 1991; s. Igor and Lucia (Kopajeva) I.; m. Elena; children: Katya, Irina. MA in Polit. Economy, Moscow State U., 1979; PhD in Internat. Polit. Economy, Nat. Acad. Scis., Moscow, 1985. Rsch. fellow Nat. Acad. Scis., 1982-87, sr. rsch. fellow, 1987-91; vis. prof. Inst. European Studies, Vienna, Austria, 1991, U. British Columbia, Vancouver, 1991; vis. prof. econs. & polit. sci. U. Tulsa, 1992-94; vis. prof. econs. U. Louisville, 1994—; fellow Freedom Forum Media Ctr. Columbia U., N.Y.C., 1991-92. Mem. Am. Econ. Assn., Am. Polit. Sci. Assn., Russian Econ. Soc., Russian Fgn. Policy Assn. Office: U Louisville Dept Econs Louisville KY 40292

JABLON, ELAINE, education consultant; b. N.Y.C., Dec. 8, 1950; d. James and Frances (Augone) Georgallas; m. Steven Ira Jablon, June 23, 1976. AA in Early Childhood Edn., Marjorie Webster Jr. Coll., Washington, 1971; BEd in Elem. Edn., U. Miami, 1973, MEd in Learning Disabilities, 1974. Tchr. Broward County Pub. Schs., Ft. Lauderdale, Fla., 1974-76; tchr. Orange County Pub. Schs., Orlando, Fla., 1976-77, substitute tchr., 1977-82; substitute tchr. Osceola County (Fla.) Pub. Schs., 1977-82; cons. edn. cen. Fla., 1977—; counselor youth diversion program, Orlando, 1978-80. Vol. Jack Eckerd for Fla. Gov., Kissimmee, 1977-78; info. rep. Epilepsy Found. of Am., Osceola, 1980-87. Mem. Am. Assn. Univ. Women (chairwoman), Am. Bus. Women's Assn. (edn. chairwoman 1980-82), Fla. Network for Family and Parent Edn. (founding mem.), Assn. Early Childhood Edn. Internat., Assn. Supervision and Curriculum Devel., The Fla. Ctr. for Children and Youth, Council Exceptional Children -- Early Childhood Div. and Learning Disabilities Div., Fla. Fedn. Council for Learning Disabilities (writing com.), Fla. Assn. for Children and Adults with Learning Disabilities, U. Miami Alumni Assn. Cen. Fla., Kissimmee Bus. and Profl. Women's Club (pres. 1985-86.). Lodge: Sons of Italy of Orlando (trustee 1978-80), Sons of Italy of Osceola County (trustee 1988). Office: 808 Hastings Dr Kissimmee FL 34744-5804

JACEWICZ, MICHAEL, neurologist, educator; b. Creteil, France, Aug. 13, 1950; m. Bertha Ellen Means, Mar. 11, 1989; 1 child, Natalie Lauren. BA in English cum laude, Harvard U., 1973; MD, Case Western Res. U., 1978. Diplomate Am. Bd. Psychiatry and Neurology. Intern in neurology Univ. Hosp., Cleve., 1978-79; fellowship in neurology Cerebral Metabolism Lab. Cornell Med. Ctr., N.Y.C., 1979-80; resident in neurology N.Y. Hosp.-Cornell Med. Ctr., Meml. Sloan Kettering, N.Y.C., 1980-83; fellowship Cerebrovascular Disease Rsch. Ctr. N.Y. Hosp.-Cornell Med. Ctr., N.Y.C., 1984-88, asst. prof. neurology and neurosci. Cerebrovascular Disease Rsch. Ctr., 1988-92; asst. prof. dept. neurology U. Tenn. Coll. of Medicine, Memphis, 1992—, chief neurology svc. Regional Med. Ctr., 1992—, adj. asst. prof. dept. anatomy and neurobiology, 1992—; assoc. prof. dept. neurology U. Tenn. Coll. Medicine, Memphis, 1994—; bd. dirs. neurology residency tng. program U. Tenn., Memphis; dept. rep. to exec. com. U. Tenn. Faculty Orgn. of Coll. of Medicine, 1992—; neurology cons.; mem. grad. med. edn. com. Bapt. Meml. Hosp., 1993—. Asst. editor Neurology Alert, 1991-92; contbr. chpts. numerous books and publs.; contbr. articles to profl. jours. Recipient Elliott Hochstein Housestaff Teaching award Cornell U., 1982, NIH grant, 1986-89, 89-90, 91—, Miles Lab. grant, 1990-91, UTMG Rsch. grant, 1992-93. Mem. Am. Acad. Neurology, Soc. for Neurosci., Alpha Omega Alpha. Home: 9140 Anderton Springs Cv Memphis TN

38133-0900 Office: Univ Tenn Coll Medicine Dept Neurology 855 Monroe Ave Rm 421 Memphis TN 38103-4901

JACINTO, GEORGE ANTHONY, social worker, educator, consultant; b. Gilroy, Calif., Dec. 21, 1949; s. George Peter and Isabelle Agnes (Joseph) J. BS in Criminology-Corrections, Calif. State U.-Fresno, 1974; postgrad. Wash. Theol. Union, 1975, U. Wis., 1980, Boise State U., 1981; MEd in Guidance and Counseling-Gen. Personnel Services, Albertson Coll. of Idaho, 1982; MSW in Clin. Social Work, Fla. State U., 1990. Cert. rehab. counselor; lic. clin. social worker. Youth minister Ch. St. Michael, Olympia, Wash., 1976-77; dir. youth ministry St. James Congregation, Franklin, Wis., 1977-80; diocesan youth dir. Cath. Diocese of Boise, Idaho, 1980-83; intern. counselor drug and alcohol Salvation Army, Boise, 1982; dir. religious edn. St. Andrew Ch., Orlando, Fla., 1983-84; intern Orange County Dept. Soc. Svcs., Orlando, Fla., 1988; vocat. rehab. counselor DLES, State of Fla., Orlando, 1984-88, vocat. rehab. cons., 1988-89; social worker Fla. Hosp./Rebound, Orlando, 1989-91; vocat. program specialist Fla. Hosp. Med. Ctr., Orlando, 1991-92; mental health specialist Orange County Cmty. Corrections Dept., Orlando, 1992-96; adj. faculty Fla. State Univ. Sch. Social Work, Orlando, 1994-95, U. Ctrl. Fla., Orlando, 1994-96 clin. instr. Sch. Social Work, 1996—; part-time home health social worker Olsten Health Svcs., Winter Park, Fla., 1991-92—; fair hearings officer Orange County Dept. of Social Svcs., Orlando, 1991-92; part-time youth minister Good Shepherd Ch., Orlando, 1985-88; founder Am. Life Planning Assocs., Orlando, 1985—; social worker, career and life planning cons., youth programming cons. Active diversion program Union St. Ctr., Olympia, Wash.; campaign leader for children's toys Indo-China Refugee Relief, Milw.; mem. adv. community agys. concerned with youth issues; coord. community svc. program for young people, Franklin, Wis.; chair Dept. of Social Work Adv. Coun. U. Cen. Fla., 1991-92. Mem. NASW (chair Cen. Fla. unit 1990-92, bd. dirs. Fla. chpt. 1990-92, del. assembly, 1993, Nat. HIV task force Fla. Chpt. Liaison, central unit social worker of the year 1993, del. assembly 1996), World Future Soc., Nat. Rehabilitation Assn., Inst. Noetic Scis., New Age Network. Home: PO Box 533154 Orlando FL 32853-3154 Office: U Ctrl Fla Sch Social Work PO Box 163358 Orlando FL 32816-3358

JACK, JANIS GRAHAM, judge; b. 1946. RN, St. Thomas Sch. Nursing, 1969; BA, U. Balt., 1974; JD summa cum laude, South Tex. Coll., 1981. Pvt. practice Corpus Christi, Tex., 1981-94; judge U.S. Dist. Ct. (so. dist.) Tex., Corpus Christi, 1994—. Mem. ABA, Fed. Judges Assn., Fifth Cir. Dist. Judges Assn., Nat. Assn. Women Judges, Tex. Bar Found., State Bar Tex., Coll. State Bar Tex., Tex. Acad. Family Law Specialists, Corpus Christi Bar Assn., Corpus Christi Family Law Assn., Order of Lytae, Phi Alpha Delta. Office: US Dist Ct 521 Starr St Corpus Christi TX 78401-2349

JACKEL, SIMON SAMUEL, food products company executive, technical marketing and business consultant; b. N.Y.C., Nov. 11, 1917; s. Victor and Sadie (Ungar) J.; m. Betty Carlson, Jan. 22, 1954; children: Phyliss Marcia (dec.), Glenn Edward. AM, Columbia, 1947, PhD, 1950; BS, CCNY, 1938; postgrad. U. Ill., 1941-42. Head fermentation div. Fleischmann Lab., Stamford, Conn., 1944-59; v.p. R & D Vico Products Co., Chgo., 1959-61; dir. lab., R & D Quality Bakers of Am. div. Sunbeam Baked Foods, Greenwich, Conn., 1961-74, v.p., rsch. dir., 1974-84; dir. R & D, mem. operating com. Bakers R & D Svc., Greenwich, 1969-84; pres. Plymouth Tech. Svcs., 1951—; dir. hearing aid audiology Jewish Home and Hosp. for Aged, N.Y.C., 1951-76. Mem. sci. adv. com. Am. Inst. Baking, 1970-91, mem. sanitation edn. adv. com., 1978-81. Mem. industry adv. com. N.D. State U., 1971-85; chmn. Am. Bakers Assn. tech. liaison com. to U.S. Dept. Agr., 1975-87; chmn. investment com., bd. dirs. Clearwater Unitarian Universalist Ch. Found., 1994—. Recipient USAAF Exceptional Civilian Svc. award, 1943, Wisdom Hall of Fame award, 1978; USPHS rsch. grantee, 1947-50. Fellow AAAS, Am. Inst. Chemists, Am. Assn. Cereal Chemists (chmn. milling and baking div. 1973-74, chmn. N.Y. sect. 1973-74, Charles N. Frey award 1981, bakery columnist Cereal Foods World 1984-95, hon. fellow 1993); mem. Am. Chem. Soc. (50 yr. membership award 1995), Am. Soc. Bakery Engrs. (chmn. tech. info. svc. com. 1979-95), Am. Bakers Assn. (nutrition com. 1971-77, chmn. tech. liaison com. to U.S. Dept. Agr. 1975-87, food tech. regulatory affairs com. 1977-91; alt. gov. 1978-87, assoc. gov. 1988-95), Ind. Bakers Assn. (cons., food safety com. 1977-80, labeling com. 1978-84, tech. affairs com. 1978-84, co-chmn. labeling and good mfg. practices com. 1984-94), Inst. Food Technologists, N.Y. Acad. Sci., N.Y.C. Chemists Club, Sigma Xi, Phi Lambda Upsilon. Mem. Unitarian Universalist Ch. Tech. editor Bakery Prodn. and Mktg. Mag., 1968-85; contbr. articles to tech. jours. Patentee in field. Office: 684 Hidden Lake Dr Tarpon Springs FL 34689-2600

JACK-MOORE, PHYLLIS, work/family strategist, educational consultant; b. Charlotte, N.C., Aug. 23, 1934; d. William Thomas and Connie LaVerne (Childers) Harris; children: Michael Harris, Julie Dawn Jack Rodgers. BA, U. N.C., 1965, MEd, 1969; postgrad., North Tex. State U., 1982-83. Cert. tchr., N.C., Tex. Elem. tchr. Chapel Hill (N.C.) Pub. Schs., 1965-68; staff devel. coordinator Learning Inst. N.C., Durham, 1969-72; child devel. specialist Tex. Dept. Human Resources, Ft. Worth, 1975-77; child care tng. coordinator North Tex. State Univ., Denton, 1978-81; dir., owner Resources for Children, Inc., Ft. Worth, 1984-88; pvt. practice Ft. Worth, 1988—; instr. Tarrant County Jr. Coll., Ft. Worth, North Tex. State U., 1982—; frequent guest speaker; appearances on TV; coord. for tng. in establishment of pub. sch. kindergarten program in State of N.C., 1972-73; cons. for family support svcs. State Dept. Pub. Instrn., Raleigh. Contbg. author: Room to Grow; mem. editorial rev. bd. Child Care Quar., Austin, 1984—. Trustee Tarrant County Youth Collaboration, 1982-86; bd. dris. Tarrant County Med. Aus., 1983-84; adv. bd. Ft. Worth's A Better Childhood Com., 1990—; coord. Tex. State Parent Action, 1989—; gov.'s task force mem. Head Start Collaboration, 1991—. Recipient Brous Outstanding Advocate award, 1984, All State Good Hands award, 1996. Mem. Nat. Assn. for the Edn. of Young Children (gov. bd. nominee 1988—, nat. field rep. 1983—), Tex. Assn. for the Edn. of Young Children (state pres. 1982-83, Adminstr. of the Yr. award 1993), Ft. Worth Assn. for the Edn. of Young Children (pres. 1976-78), So. Assn. for Children Under Six (com. chair 1978-80, conf. co-chair 1987), Rotary, Phi Beta Kappa, Phi Delta Kappa. Methodist. Club: Ft. Worth Woman's (v.p. and auditor 1983-86). Lodge: Rotary.

JACKSON, ANDREW EDWIN, engineering educator, researcher; b. Tahoka, Tex., Sept. 4, 1950; s. James Ray and Hazel Naomi (Tull) J.; m. Sherion Janette Hudgins, May 30, 1970; children: Jonathan Andrew, Stacey Leann. BA in Math., U. Louisville, 1974; MBA, Embry-Riddle Aero. U., Orlando, Fla., 1989; PhD in Indsl. Engring. and Mgmt. Systems, U. Ctrl. Fla., Orlando, 1995. Commd. ensign USN, 1974, advanced through grades to lt. comdr., 1983; ret. U.S. Navy, 1988; project mgr. Coleman Rsch. Corp., Orlando, 1988-91; adj. instr. Embry-Riddle Aero. U., MacDill AFB, Fla., 1991-95; vis. instr. indsl. engring. and mgmt. systems U. Ctrl. Fla., Orlando, 1991-95; asst. prof. aeronautical technology Ariz. State U., Tempe, 1995—; airport approach lighting systems rschr. and cons., 1995—; aviation Human Factors Rschr., 1993—; benchmarking cons. NASA, Titusville, Fla., 1992-95, AT&T, Orlando, 1994, Orange County Sheriff's Office, Orlando, 1994. Contbr. articles to profl. jours. Recipient Humanitarian Svc. medal USN, 1979, Davis Productivity award U. Ctrl. Fla., 1993, Outstanding Pub. Sector Orgn. award U. Ctrl. Fla., 1993. Mem. IEEE, Inst. Indsl. Engrs., Am. Soc. Engring. Edn., Am. Soc. Quality Control, Nat. Space Soc., Ret. Officers Assn., Tau Beta Pi, Alpha Pi Mu. Republican. Methodist. Home: 6001 S Power Rd Bldg 324-9112 Mesa AZ 85206 Office: Ariz State U Coll Engrg Tech and Aero 6001 S Power Rd Bldg 425 Mesa AZ 85206-0999

JACKSON, BARBARA W., school system administrator; b. Eudora, Ark., Feb. 13, 1929; d. John Leonard Sr. and Elise (Thompson) Wall; children: John David, Cheryl Lynn Jackson Woodberry, Charles Robert. BS, Ark. State Tchrs. Coll., 1949; MEd, U. Ga., 1968, EdS, 1973, EdD, 1983. Cert. counseling and sch. psychologist, Ga. Psychologist Clarke County Sch. Dist., Athens, Ga., counselor elem.; counselor elem.-title III Franklin County Sch. Dist., Royston, Ga.; coord. chpt. I and testing Clarke County Sch. Dist., Athens. Contbr. articles to profl. jours. Mem. APA, ASCD, Nat. Assn. Sch. Psychologists, Ga. Assn. Sch. Psychologists, Ga. ASCD, Ga. Ednl. Rsch. Assn., Profl. Assn. Ga. Educators, Alpha Chi, Kappa Delta Pi, Phi Kappa Phi, Delta Kappa Gamma.

JACKSON, BLYDEN, English language educator; b. Paducah, Ky., Oct. 12, 1910; s. George Washington and Julia Estelle (Reid) J.; m. Roberta Bowles, Aug. 2, 1958. AB, Wilberforce U., 1930; AM, U. Mich., 1938, PhD (Rosenwald fellow 1947-49), 1952; LHD (hon.), U. Louisville, 1977; LittD (hon.), Wilberforce U., 1978, U.N.C.-Chapel Hill, 1985, U. Ky., 1990. Tchr. English, pub. schs. Louisville, 1934-45; asst., then assoc. prof. English Fisk U., 1945-54; prof. English, head dept. Southern U., 1954-62, dean Grad. Sch., 1962-69; prof. English U. N.C., 1969-81; assoc. dean U. N.C. (Grad. Sch.), 1973-76, spl. asst. to dean, 1976-81; disting. vis. prof. U. Miss., U. Del., Wayne State U.; spl. rsch. criticism Negro lit. Author: Black Poetry in America, 1974, The Waiting Years, 1976, A History of Afro-American Literature, Vol. 1, 1985; co-author: Black Poetry in America; adv. editor So. Lit. Jour.; contbr. articles to profl. jours. Established Blyden and Roberta Jackson Grad. fellowship in English, U. N.C., Chapel Hill., 1989. Mem. MLA (chmn. 20th century lit. div. 1976), Nat. Coun. Tchrs. English (Disting. lectr. 1970-71, chmn. coll. sect. 1971-73, trustee rsch. found. 1975-79), Coll. Lang. Assn. (v.p. 1954-56, pres. 1956-58, assoc. editor bull. and jour.), Speech Assn. Am., N.C. Tchrs. English, Alpha Phi Alpha. Home: 102 Laurel Hill Rd Chapel Hill NC 27514-4323

JACKSON, BOBBY CHARLES, consumer products company executive; b. Booneville, Miss., Aug. 3, 1957; s. Clarence and Hazel Mae Jackson; m. Melissa Faye Shinault, May 6, 1978; children: Chayance, Jermaine. Assoc. degree, N.E. C.C., 1978; BSGS in Gen. Health and Phys. Edn., Recreation, Delta State U., 1995. Cert. fire protection, bus. adminstrn., Miss.; cert. fitness coord. Phys. therapist tech. Bapt. Meml. Hosp., Booneville, Miss., 1980-84; coord. phys. fitness City of Corinth, Miss., 1984-85, fireman I, 1988—; tng. officer Corinth Fire Dept., 1995; mgr. trainee Dana Corp., Corinth, 1985-86; machinist A Delta Internat. Machinery Corp., Tupelo, Miss., 1986-87; resident owner Jackson Enterprises, Boonville, Miss., 1985-92. Mem. Am. Mgmt. Assn., Am. Running and Fitness Assn., Nat. Football Ofcls. Assn., Nat. Sporting Good Assn., Internat. Assn. Fire Fighters (v.p.), Miss. Fire Fighters Assn. Baptist. Home: RR 1 Box 546-a Booneville MS 38829-9801 Office: Tri Sports 102 S Main St Booneville MS 38829-3311

JACKSON, BRENDA S., nursing educator; b. Richmond, Va., Jan. 24, 1948; d. Jobe Vernon and Alma Louise (Sanderson) Smith; m. Charles H. Jackson, III, Aug. 28, 1976; children: Charles H. IV, Jobe Sanderson. BSN, Med. Coll. Va., Richmond, 1970; MSN, U. Tex. Health Sci. Ctr., San Antonio, 1976; PhD, U. Tex., Austin, 1984. Evening charge nurse SICU San Antonio Community Hosp.; care corps Santa Rosa Med. Ctr., San Antonio; asst. prof. U. Tex. Health Sci. Ctr., San Antonio; prof., dir. nursing programs U. of Incarnate Word, San Antonio. Contbr. articles to profl. jours. 1st lt. USAF, 1971-74. Named Mildred McIntyre Nurse Vol. of the Yr., Tex. affiliate of Am. Heart Assn., 1987. Mem. Am. Assn. Critical Care Nurses, Am. Nursing Assn., Tex. Nursing Assn., Nat. League Nursing, Tex. League for Nursing, Am. Heart Assn. (bd. dirs., pres.-elect affiliate), Sigma Theta Tau (chpt. past pres.), Phi Kappa Phi, Sigma Zeta, Alpha Sigma Chi. Home: 307 Zornia Dr San Antonio TX 78213-2115

JACKSON, C. GARY, otologist; b. Trenton, N.J., Mar. 26, 1947; s. Wilbur C. and Florence L. Jackson; m. Diane H. Jackson; children: Kimberly, Jennifer. BS in Biology cum laude, St. Joseph's U., Phila., 1969; MD, Temple U., 1973. Lic. physician, N.C., Tenn.; diplomate Am. Bd. Otolaryngology. Intern, resident surgery and otolaryngology U. N.C., Chapel Hill, 1973-77; fellow otology and neurotology The Otology Group P.C., Nashville, 1977-78, physician, 1978—; clin. prof. dept. surgery divsn. otolaryngology U. N.C. Sch. Medicine, Chapel Hill; clin. prof. dept. otolaryngology, head and neck surgery Vanderbilt U. Sch. Medicine, Nashville, clin. prof. hearing and speech scis.; v.p. The EAR Found., Nashville; vice chmn. CME subcom. Bapt. Hosp., 1990; mem. active staff Bapt. Hosp., Nashville; mem. vis. staff Vanderbilt U. Hosp., Nashville; mem. courtesy staff Met. Nashville Gen. Hosp.; provisional staff Centennial Med. Ctr., Nashville; presenter various orgns. and univs.; lectr. hosps., staffs, lay groups. Editor-in-chief Am. Jour. Otology; mem. editl. bd. Jour. Skull Base Surgery and Related Scis., Skull Base Surgery, Otolaryngology-Head and Neck Surgery; expert analyst Otolaryngology: The Jour. Club Jour.; author: (with M.E. Glasscock and A.F. Josey) Brain Stem Electric Response Audiometry, 1981, The ABR Handbook: Auditory Brainstem Response, 1987; Surgery of Skull Base Tumors, 1990; contbr. articles to profl. jours. Fellow ACS; mem. AMA, Am. Acad. Otolaryngology-Head and Neck Surgery (bd. govs., mem. nominating com. 1991, cert. of honor 1985), N.Am. Skull Base Soc. (publ. com. 1992, dir. at large 1994), Am. Otological Soc. (mem. coun. 1994, mem. program adv. com. 1992-94), Am. Neurotology Soc. (v.p. 1989, chmn. membership and credentials com. 1987-92), Tenn. Acad. Otolaryngology-Head and Neck Surgery (pres. 1988), Cochlear Implant Study Group, Internat. Skull Base Soc., Nashville Acad. Medicine, Nashville Surg. Soc., Internat. Coll. Surgeons in Otolaryngology (vice regent 1986-89), Nashville Acad. Otolaryngology-Head and Neck Surgery, Auditory-Verbal Internat., Inc., Nathan A. Womack Surg. Soc., Prosper Meniere Soc., Tenn. Med. Assn., Triological Soc., Upper Cumberland Med. Soc., Temple U. Med. Alumni Assn. Office: The Otology Group 300 20th Ave N Ste 502 Nashville TN 37203-2132

JACKSON, CHARLES BENJAMIN, minister; b. Columbia, S.C., July 16, 1952; s. Thomas and Ezella (Rumph) J.; m. Robin Lynn Hoefer, Apr. 21, 1953; children: Charles B. Jr., Candace Celeste. BS, Benedict Coll., 1974; MDiv, Morehouse Sch. of Religion, of Interdenominational Theol. Ctr., Atlanta, 1977; DD, Morris Coll., 1985. Ordained to ministry Bapt. Ch., 1965; cert. clin. counselor. Pastor Brookland Bapt. Ch., West Columbia, S.C., 1971—; gospel announcer WOIC Radio AM, Columbia, S.C., 1984—; pres. S.C. Bapt. Congress of Christian Edn., 1983-86; v.p. Gethsemane Bapt. Sunday Sch. Congress, 1975—; bd. dir. Edn. and Publ. Bd. Progressive Nat. Bapt. Conv. Recipient James H. Clark Meml. Preaching award, Protestant Fellowship, Fund for Theol. Edn., others. Mem. NAACP, Rotary, Kappa Alpha Psi. Democrat. Home: 6727 Valleybrook Rd Columbia SC 29206-1054

JACKSON, CHARLES EDWARD, technologist, educational consultant; b. Port Arthur, Tex., July 16, 1959; divorced; children: James V., Charles C. BA, U. Tex., 1983. Exec. dir. Verde Valley C. of C., Cottonwood, Ariz., 1985-87, Santa Maria (Calif.) C. of C., 1987-90; mgr. software Tellabs, Inc., Round Rock, Tex., 1990-91; rschr. S.W. Edn. Devel. Lab., Austin, Tex., 1991-92; engr. School Vision of Tex., Austin, 1992-93; dir. tech. Del Valley Ind. Sch. Dist., Austin, 1992-93; mgr. network svcs. Edn. Svc. Ctr. XIII, Austin, 1993—. Author: God on the Internet, 1996. Vol., AIDS Svcs. of Austin, Tex. Dem. Com., Met. Interactive Network; mem. City of Pflugerville (Tex.) Charter Commn. Mem. U.S. Distance Learning Assn., Soc. for Info. Mgmt., Internat. Soc. for Tech. in Edn., Fellowship of Reconciliation. Presbyterian. Office: Edn Svc Ctr XIII 5701 Springdale Austin TX 78723

JACKSON, CHARLES WAYNE, food products executive, former telecommunications industry executive; b. Louisville, June 3, 1930; s. Wayne O. and Geneva Drake J.; m. Sallie I. Lambert, June 21, 1954 (div. Feb. 1980); m. Elizabeth J. Soptic, June 1, 1980; children: Thomas, Carol E., Charles N. BEE, Ga. Inst. Tech., 1952. Student engr. AT&T, Cin., 1954-55; dist. plant engr. AT&T, Jacksonville, Fla., 1955-56; comml. rep to acctg. asst. AT&T, Atlanta, 1956-59; transmission systems engr. to plant design engr. AT&T, Kansas City, 1963-66; project mgr. to dir. major project Western Elec. Co., N.Y.C., 1966-69; engr. dir. TWX coord. to bus. relations dir. AT&T, N.Y.C., 1969-75; dir. pvt. lines rates Long Lines Co., Somerset, N.J., 1975; dir. pvt. lines rates to dir. planning Long Lines Co., Bedminster, N.J., 1975-81; dir. data prog. svcs. to dir. svc. devel. mktg. dept. AT&T, Bedminster, 1981-87; cons. pvt. practice Brandenburg, Ky., 1987-90; v.p. H&R Block Franchise, 1990-92; owner Squire Taber Apple Orchard, 1992—. 1st. lt. U.S. Army, 1952-54. Mem. Elks. Methodist. Home and Office: 604 Strawberry Pt Brandenburg KY 40108-9038

JACKSON, CYNTHIA WILLIFORD, special education educator; b. Mobile, Ala., Oct. 30, 1949; d. Gerald Dee and Mary Evelyn (Johnson) W.; m. Alan P. Jackson, Aug. 18, 1973; 1 child, Julie Lynette. BS in Elem. Edn., John Brown U., 1971; MS in Spl. Edn., U. Ctrl. Ark., 1972; postgrad., U. Ala., 1993—. Cert. tchr., Ala. Resource tchr. Decatur (Ark.) Elem. Sch., 1972-73, Montgomery (Ala.) County Sch. System, 1973-75, Birmingham (Ala.) City Schs., 1976-80; instr. Horizons Program-UAB, Birmingham, 1992-94; rsch. asst., adj. U. Ala., Tuscaloosa, 1995—; pvt. cons. Auburn (Ala.) City Schs., 1989-91; psychometrist, Montgomery, 1975-76. Author: (with others) Profile of Commitment, 1995; contbr. articles to profl. jours. Mem. Coun. for Exceptional Children, Kappa Delta Pi. Baptist. Home: 2521 Altadena Forest Cir Birmingham AL 35243 Office: U Ala Coll Edn Box 870231 Tuscaloosa AL 35487

JACKSON, DANIEL WYER, electrical engineer; b. Louisville, June 28, 1929; s. Dugald Caleb Jr. and Elisabeth Uhl (Wyer) J.; m. Doris C. Maier, Oct. 1, 1955; children: Daniel B., Barbara E., Gordon S. BSEE, Lehigh U., 1950. Registered profl. engr., Va. Test engr. GE Co., Lynn, Mass., and Schenectady, N.Y., 1950-51; test engr. gen. engring. lab. GE Co., Schenectady, 1953; sr. evaluation engr. industry control dept. GE Co., Schenectady and Salem, Va., 1954-62; product prodn. engr. industry control dept. GE Co., Salem, 1962-68, design engr., 1968, product engr., 1968-69, sr. product engr., 1969-81, sr. product engr. drive systems dept., 1981-91; freelance engr. Roanoke, Va., 1991—; bd. dirs. Southcon, Inc., L.A., 1991-95, conv. dir., 1994, chmn. bd., 1994-95. Adult leader Boy Scouts Am., Schenectady & Roanoke, 1954-80; officer of election Roanoke County, Va., 1962-87; deacon Covenant Presbyn. Ch., Roanoke, 1969-72, elder, 1974-76, 92-94, 97-99. 1st lt. U.S. Army, 1951-53, Korea. Recipient Silver Beaver award Blue Ridge coun. Boy Scouts Am., 1979. Mem. IEEE (life, sr., bd. dirs. 1990-91, region 3 dir. 1990-91, chmn. nat. engrs. week com. 1991-92, chmn. prof. activities coun. engrs. info. com. 1993, vice chmn. region 3 1988-89, chmn. Va. coun. 1985-86, chmn. Va. mountains sect. 1981-82, chmn. EAB profl. devel. com. 1994-97, chmn. EAB continuing edn. com. 1992-93, chmn. USAB awards and recognition com. 1994-96, outstanding svc. awards 1983, 86, 93, centennial medal 1984, meritorious svc. to ednl. activities bd. award 1991), NSPE (pres. Roanoke chpt. 1974-75), Va. Soc. Profl. Engrs. (outstanding svc. award 1976). Republican. Home: 5704 Castle Rock Rd Roanoke VA 24018-6106

JACKSON, DOROTHY FAYE GREENE, nursing educator; b. Marlin, Tex., Mar. 18, 1947; d. Shellie Tom and Ruby Lee (O'Neal) Greene; m. David Lee Jackson, Jr., Dec. 20, 1967; children: David Lee III, Danese. AAS, Odessa Coll., 1967; BSN, West Tex. State U., 1977; MSN, U. Tex., Galveston, 1980. RN, Tex. Staff nurse Med. Ctr. Hosp., Odessa, Tex., 1967-68, charge nurse CCU, 1968-72, mgr. quality assurance and infection control, 1979-80, dir. nursing, critical care and edn., 1980-81, bd. mgrs. Med. Ctr. Hosp., 1988-89; instr. nursing Odessa Coll., 1972-79, 81-93, dept. chair, 1993; asst. prof. Sch. Nursing Tex. Tech. U. Health Scis. Ctr., Odessa, 1993—; advanced practice nurse Sch. Medicine Family Practice Ctr. Tex. Tech. Health Scis. Ctr., Odessa, 1994—; mem. adv. bd. Head Start, Odessa, 1981—; cons. to long term care facilities, Odessa, 1991-93, clin. specialist in gerontological nursing, 1994—; v.p. Seabury Nursing Home, 1985—; presenter Nat. Conf. on Gerontol. Nursing Edn., Norfolk, Va., 1992. Contbr. articles to jours. in field. Bd. dirs. Odessa Cultural Coun., 1989-93, Midland-Odessa Symphony and Chorale, 1991-94. Mem. ANA, Jr. League Odessa, Phi Delta Kappa, Sigma Theta Tau, Alpha Kappa Alpha. Episcopalian. Home: 410 E 42nd St Odessa TX 79762-6856 Office: Tex Tech U Univ Health Scis Ctr 800 W 4th St Odessa TX 79763

JACKSON, EUGENE BERNARD, librarian; b. Frankfort, Ind., June 18, 1915; s. John Herman and Goldie Belle (Michael) J.; m. Ruth Lillian Whitlock, Aug. 6, 1941. BS with distinction, Purdue U., 1937; BS in Libr. Sci. with honors, U. Ill., 1938, MA, 1942; LHD (hon.), Purdue U., 1994. Asst. engring. library U. Ill., 1938-40; asst. charge newspaper div. U. Ill. Library, 1940-41; documents librarian U. Ala., 1941-42; with tech. dept. Detroit Pub. Library, 1942-46; chief reference library Wright Field, Ohio; chief library sect. Central Air Documents Office, Dayton, Ohio, 1946-49; chief research information sect. Research and Devel. Command, Q.M.C., Washington, 1949-50; chief div. aero. intelligence NACA, 1950-52, chief div. research information, 1952-56; head library dept. research labs. Gen. Motors Corp., Warren, Mich., 1956-65; chmn. corp. com. tech. lit. Gen. Motors Corp., 1959-65; dir. information retrieval and library services IBM Corp., Armonk, New York, 1965-71; library cons. in automation, Grad. Sch. Library Sci. U. Tex., Austin, 1971-72; prof. library sci. U. Tex., 1971-85, prof. emeritus, 1985—; mem. chancellors coun. The U. Tex. Sys., 1996—; v.p. Engring. Index, Inc., 1967-68, pres., 1968-73; also dir. Attendee Gordon Research Confs. on Sci. Information, N.H., 1964—; vis. summer lectr. U. Mich., 1965, U. Ill., 1968; mem. task force United Engring. Info. System, 1966; cons.; U.S. mem. documentation com., adv. group aero. research and devel. NATO, Paris, France, 1953-61, chmn., 1955-56, dep. chmn., chmn. elect., 1960-61; McBee lectr. Simmons Coll., Boston, 1956; ofcl. U.S. del. gen. assemblies Fedn. International de Documentation, Tokyo, 1967, The Hague, 1968, Buenos Aires, 1970, Budapest, 1972, chmn. U.S. nat. com., 1970-72. Author: (with Ruth L. Jackson) Industrial Information Systems, 1978; editor: Special Librarianship, a New Reader, 1980; contbr. articles to profl. jours., chpts. to books. Mem. tech. adv. com. Macomb County (Mich.) Planning Commn. Served with AUS, 1943-46. Mem. Spl. Libraries Assn. (pres. 1962-63), A.L.A., Am. Soc. Info. Scis., AIAA (sec. Mich. 1964-65), Assn. Records Mgrs. and Adminstrs. Protestant Episcopalian (vestryman, lic. lay reader). Home: 8512 Silver Ridge Dr Austin TX 78759-8143

JACKSON, EVELYN ARDETH, nurse; b. Great Falls, Mont., Feb. 11, 1929; d. Henry and Esther Lillian (Morris) Bergdorf; m. Elmer Donald Jackson, May 16, 1952; children—Donita Jo, Jenice Evelyn. Student Gonzaga U., 1947-48; RN, St. Luke's Sch. Nursing, Spokane, Wash., 1950; postgrad. St. Joseph's Coll., Roanoke, Va., 1983-85. Cert. case mgr. 1992. Staff nurse in doctors' offices, Spokane, 1950-55, Houston, 1956-68; 76-78; supr. M.D. Anderson Hosp. and Cancer Inst., Houston, 1968-76; nursing supr. Austin Steel Co., Houston, 1978-80; charge nurse Reed Rock Bit Co., Houston, 1980—; safety instr. Reed Tool Co. Instr. ARC, 1980—; active Cancer Soc.. Mem. Am. Heart Assn., Houston Occupl. Health Nurses Assn. (documentation com. 1980-81, telephone com. 1981-82, nomination com. 1982-83, dir. 1982—, pres. 1993, 94), Am. Occupl. Health Assn., Tex. Occupl. Health Assn. (dir. 1986—), Nat. Mgmt. Assn., Profl. and Bus. Women, Am. Security Coun., U.S. Senatorial Club (presdl. task force 1985, Washington). Republican. Methodist. Home: 6510 Cedar St Katy TX 77493 Office: Reed Rock Bit PO Box 2119 Houston TX 77252-2119

JACKSON, FRANCIS CHARLES, physician, surgeon; b. Rutherford, N.J., Sept. 2, 1917; s. Frank Emil and Margaret Charlotte (Kuhn) J.; m. Joan Gloria Mortenson, Sept. 1, 1949; children: Geoffrey P., Bradford M., Gregory C., Donna E. B.A., Yale U., 1939; M.D., U. Va., 1943. Diplomate Am. Bd. Surgery, Nat. Bd. Med. Examiners. Intern N.Y. Hosp.-Cornell Med. Center, 1944, asst. resident surgery, 1945, from asst. resident surgery to 1st asst. chief resident surgeon, 1947-49, chief resident surgeon, 1950; practice medicine specializing in gen. and vascular surgery Pitts., 1952-70; cons., chief surgeon Arabian Am. Oil Co., Dhahran, Saudi Arabia, 1951; asst. chief surg. service VA Center, Togus, Maine, 1952; chief surg. service, dir. Gen. Surg. Residency Program, VA Hosp., Pitts., 1952-70; dir. surg. service VA Central Office, Washington, 1970-72; spl. asst. to chief med. dir. for emergency and disaster med. services VA Central Office, 1972-73, dir. emergency and disaster med. services staff, 1973-75; mem. cons. staff Presbyn.-Univ. Hosp., Pitts., 1959-70; asst. in surgery Sch. Medicine Cornell U., 1946-49, asst. in anatomy, 1946, instr. surgery, 1950; asst. prof. surgery Sch. Medicine U. Pitts., 1953-60, assoc. prof. surgery, 1961-65, prof. surgery, 1965-70, sec. exec. com. dept. surgery, 1964-70, MEND coordinator, 1967-68; clin. prof. surgery Georgetown U. Sch. Medicine, George Washington U. Sch. Medicine, Washington, 1970-75; chmn. dept. surgery Sch. Medicine Tex. Tech U., Lubbock, 1975-80; prof. surgery Sch. Medicine Tex. Tech U., 1975—, assoc. dean clin. edn., 1980-82; med. dir. S. Plains Emergency Med. Services, 1978—; prof., chmn. emeritus dept. of surgery Tex. Tech. Med. Sch. Medicine, 1996; cons. Carnegie-Mellon Inst., 1969-71, Westinghouse Electric Corp. (Health Systems), AVCO Corp.; chmn. local com. VA Adj. Cancer Chemotherapy Study, 1957-70; chmn. exec. com. Operation Prep. Pitts. Annual Med.-CD Disaster Drill, 1958-60; mem. ad hoc com. disaster med. surveys, div. med., vice chmn. com. emergency med. services Nat. Acad. Scis.-NRC, 1964-74; mem. surg. drugs adv. com. FDA, 1971-75; mem. panel on physicians asst. CSC, 1971-73; cons. on emergency and disaster services USPHS, 1965-72; VA rep., alternate observer, nat. health resources adv. com. Office Preparedness, 1972-75; VA rep., mem. interdepartmental com. on emergency med. services HEW, 1974-75; mem. ad hoc com. on emergency med. services communications, interdepartmental adv. com. on radio communications Office Telecommunications Policy, 1973-75. Author: Role of Medicine in Emergency Preparedness, 1968; contbr. articles to surg.

jours.; creator surg. exhibits. Trustee Peddie Sch., 1972-74. Served as lt. (j.g.) USNR, 1945-46, to lt. comdr., M.C. 1953-55. Recipient Pfizer award of merit U.S. CD Council, Mpls., 1960, Key to City Louisville, 1964, Billings Gold Medal award AMA, 1966. Fellow A.C.S. (past chmn. residents program com. Southwestern Pa. chpt.; chmn. subcom. disaster, surgery and communications of trauma com., trauma com. 1966-78, exec. com. 1976-78, pres. Southwestern Pa. chpt. 1970, gov. 1970-74); mem. AMA (chmn. com. disaster med. care, Council Nat. Security 1958-67), Pa. Med Soc. (chmn. commn. on emergency med. services), Allegheny County Med. Soc., Soc. Biol. Research U. Pitts. Sch. Medicine, Pitts. Surg. Soc., Am. Assn. Surgery of Trauma, So. Surg. Assn., Assn. VA Surgeons (founding), Central Surg. Assn., Soc. Surgery Alimentary Tract, Assn. Mil. Surgeons U.S. (Stitt award 1968), Pitts. Acad. Medicine (Man of Year award 1969), D.C. Med. Soc., Am. Surg. Assn., Société Internat. de Chirurgie, Tex. Surg. Soc., Tex. Med. Assn. (chmn. surg. sect. program com. 1981-82, subcom. on accreditation of continuing med. edn. programs 1983-92, com. on continuing edn. 1959-92, cons.), Lubbock Surg. Soc., Lubbock-Crosby-Garza County Med. Soc., Alpha Omega Alpha. Lodge: Rotary. Office: Dept of Surgery Sch Medicine Tex Tech U Lubbock TX 79430

JACKSON, FRANK DONALD, university director; b. Luling, Tex., July 25, 1951; s. Robbie Sr. and Willie Louise (Smith) J.; m. Vanessa Williams, Sept. 5, 1978; children: Tracy S., Ayanna N. BA in Geography, Prairie View A&M U., 1973. Commd. ens. USN, 1995, advanced through grades to capt.; divsn. officer USS Long Beach USN, San Diego, 1973-76; CIC surface officer USS Coral Sea USN, Alameda, Calif., 1976-78; OIC naval beach group USN, Little Creek, Va., 1978-80; navigation instr. ROTC/Prairie View (Tex.) A&M U. USN, 1980-82, resigned, 1982; dir. Meml. Ctr. Prairie View A&M U., 1982-87, dir. aux. svcs., 1987-95, dir. student initiatives, 1995—. City councilman City of Prairie View, 1982-92; county commr. Waller County Commrs. Ct., Hempstead, Tex., 1993—; pres. Prairie View Vol. Fire Fighting Assn., 1986-95. City councilman City of Prairie View, 1982-92; county commr. Waller County Commrs. Ct., Hempstead, Tex., 1993—; pres. Prairie View Vol. Fire Fighting Assn., 1986—. Mem. Prairie Nat. Alumni Assn. (historian 1992—), Prairie Hall Grand Lodge of Tex. (sr. warden 1988—), Alpha Phi Alpha (historian 1994-95). Democrat. Baptist. Home: 321 Sycamore St PO Box 475 Prairie View TX 77446 Office: Prairie View A&M U 667 3d St Prairie View TX 77445

JACKSON, GAINES BRADFORD, environmental science educator; b. Minden, La., Sept. 1, 1943; s. Oscar Branche and Cleo Marie (Bradford) J.; m. Janie Yvonne Mee, Aug. 18, 1966 (div. Dec. 1974); children: Sherri Lynnette, Mitchell Bradford; m. Suk Ling Chow, Apr. 18, 1989; children: Bradford C., Harry C. BS, West Tex. State U., 1965; MS in Environ. Sci., U. Tex., 1972; DrPH, Columbia Pacific U., 1983. Environ. chemist Tex. State Dept. Health, Houston, 1968-70; rsch. statis. aide Environ. Health Inst., Houston, 1970-72; pres. Total Environ. Svcs. and Testing U. Tex. Sch. Pub. Health, Oklahoma City, 1972-73; rsch. biologist II Okla. State Dept. Health Water Quality Svc., Oklahoma City, 1973-77; engr., sci. instr. Rose State Coll., Midwest City, Okla., 1977—. Author: Easy to Make Laboratory Benchsheets for the Water Utility Technician Using Your Office Copier, 1989, Water Chemistry Manual for Water & Spentwater Personnel, 1990, 93, Compendium of Technical and Non-Technical Terms for the Water Utility Field, 1994; contbr. articles to profl. jours.; inventor water utility converter and water wheel. Mem. Water Pollution Control Fedn., Okla. Water Pollution Assn., Pollution Control Assn. Okla. (Outstanding Sec. Edn. and Pub. Rels. award 1988), Am. Chem. Soc., Okla. Assn. Community and Jr. Colls. Mem. Christian Ch. Home: 1260 Three Oaks Cir Midwest City OK 73130-5309 Office: Rose State Coll Engring Sci Div 6420 SE 15th St Oklahoma City OK 73110-2704

JACKSON, GERALDINE, entrepreneur; b. Barnesville, Ga., Oct. 30, 1934; d. Charles Brown and Christine (Maddox) J.; 1 child, Prentiss Andrew. Nurses aide Grady Hosp., Atlanta; mail handler U.S. Post Office, Cicero, Ill.; sec., tour guide Walgreens Lab., Chgo.; credit clk. Sterling Jewelers, Atlanta; owner, broker Gerris Automobile Leasing Svc., Atlanta. Mem. Nat. Law Enforcement Officer Meml. Fund; assoc. mem. presdl. task force Rep. Nat. Com.; active Sacred Heart League. Mem. AARP, DAV, NAACP, NAFE, Nat. Assn. Police Orgn. (assoc. mem. pres. task force), Internat. Assn. Chief Police, Ga. Sheriff's Assn., Nat. Right to Life. Democrat. Home and Office: 1890 Myrtle Dr SW Apt 422 Atlanta GA 30311-4954

JACKSON, GILCHRIST L., surgeon; b. Dayton, Ohio, Sept. 30, 1948; s. William Hughes Jr. and Margaret Langhorne (Alexander) J.; m. Katina Ballantyne, Nov. 28, 1970; children: Marina, Alex, Scott, George. BA, Vanderbilt U., 1970; MD, U. Louisville, 1974. Fellow U. Tex. M.D. Anderson Cancer Ctr., Houston, 1979-80, faculty, 1980-81; active staff Kelsey-Seybold Clinic, Houston, 1981—; active staff St. Luke's Episc. Hosp., Houston, 1981—, Meth. Hosp., Houston, 1981—, VA Hosp., Houston, 1981-83, Ben Taub Hosp., Houston, 1981—; courtesy staff Tex. Children's Hosp., Houston, 1981—; mem. dir. Crump Cancer Ctr., Houston, 1984-95, Kelsey-Seybold Cancer Program, 1994—; prin. investigator Tex. Cmty. Oncology Network, Nat. Surg. Adjuvant Breast and Bowel Project, 1986-95. Contbr. articles to profl. jours. Active student recruitment com. Vanderbilt U., 1991, Mus. Fine Arts, Houston, 1995, Mus. Natural Sci., Houston, 1995; bd. dirs. West Univ. Little League, Houston, 1990, 91. Mem. Am. Cancer Soc. (pres. 1987-89, v.p. 1985-87), Thyroid Soc. Am. Republican. Presbyterian. Office: Kelsey Seybold Clinic 6624 Fannin Ste 1700 Houston TX 77030

JACKSON, GLENN RICHARD, information services executive; b. Atlanta, Feb. 13, 1954; s. Richard Thomas and Elizabeth Jane (Hendrix) J.; m. Sally Reese Prescott, Mar. 19, 1983; children: William, Laura, Sara Alice. BS in Psychology, Ga. State U., 1976, MA in Philosophy, 1985. Analyst So. Bell Tel. & Tel., Atlanta, 1978-82, Emory U., Atlanta, 1982-84; asst. mgr. Fed. Res. Bank, Atlanta, 1984-88; dir. info. svc. Info. Am., Atlanta, 1988-91, Gerber Alley, Atlanta, 1991-93; owner Seamless Technologies, Atlanta, 1993—. Author (book): John Wesley - A Call to the Modern World, 1986; author software: Lawoffice, 1992. Mem. U.S. Strategic Inst., U.S. Naval Inst., Psi Chi. Republican. Presbyterian.

JACKSON, GREGORY ALLEN, minister; b. Kansas City, Mo., June 4, 1956; s. Lester Allen Jr. and Janet Lou (Door) J.; m. Paula Sue Epperson, June 11, 1977;. BA in Religion, William Jewell Coll., 1978; MRE, Midwestern Bapt. Theol. Sem., 1980, D in Ministry, 1992. Min. youth and edn. High Point Bapt. Ch., Kansas City, 1977-81; min. edn. and adminstrn. Cen. Bapt. Ch., North Little Rock, Ark., 1981-94; minister of Christian edn. 1st Bapt. Ch., Bolivar, Mo., 1994—; state spl. worker Children's Sunday Sch., Kansas, 1979-81, Adult and Gen. Officer Sunday Sch., Ark., 1981—; Sunday sch. growth cons. Mem. census com. North Little Rock, 1990. Homer and Augusta Jones scholar Midwestern Bapt. Theol. Sem., Kansas City, 1979, 80, 81. Mem. Nat. Assn. Ch. Bus. Adminstrs. (pres. Ark. chpt. 1990-91), Ark. Bapt. Religious Edn. Assn., So. Bapt. Religious Edn. Assn., Mo. Bapt. Religious Edn. Assn. Office: 1st Bapt Ch PO Box 358 Bolivar MO 65613

JACKSON, GUIDA MYRL, writer, magazine editor; b. Clarendon, Tex., Aug. 30; d. James Hurley and Ina (Benson) Miller; m. Prentice Lamar Jackson (div. Jan. 1986); children: Jeffrey Allen, William Andrew, James Tucker, Annabeth Jackson; m. William Hervey Laufer, Feb. 14, 1986. BA, Tex. Tech U.; MA, Calif. State U., Dominguez Hills, 1986; PhD, Greenwich U., Hilo, Hawaii, 1990. Tchr. secondary sch. English, Houston Ind. Sch. Dist., 1951-53, Ft. Worth Ind. Sch. Dist., 1953-54; pvt. tchr. music, freelance writer, Houston, 1956-71; editor newsletter Tex. Soc. Anesthesiologists, Austin, 1972-80; editor-in-chief Tex. Country mag., Houston, 1976-78; mng. editor Touchstone, lit. mag., Houston, 1976—; contbg. editor Houston Town and Country mag., 1975-76; lectr. English, U. Houston, 1986—, book editor Arte Publico, 1987-88; freelance writer, Houston, The Woodlands, Tex., 1978—; instr. Montgomery Coll., 1996—. Author: (novel) Passing Through, 1979, (play) The Lamentable Affair of the Vicar's Wife, 1989, (biog. reference) Women Who Ruled, 1990 (best reference lists award Libr. Jour. and Sch. Libr. Jour. 1990), (nonfiction) Virginia Diaspora, 1992, (lit. reference) Encyclopedia of Traditional Epic, 1994 (best reference list award ALA), (lit. reference) Traditional Epics: A Literary Companion, 1995, Encyclopedia of Literary Epics, 1996; editor: (anthologies) Heart to Hearth, 1989, African Women Write, 1990, (nonfiction) Legacy of the Texas Plains, 1994, Through the Cumberland Gap, 1995. Mem. Women in Comm., PEN Ctr. West, Houston Writers Guild, Woodlands Writers Guild, Dramatists Guild, Montgomery Arts Coun. Office: Touchstone Lit Jour PO Box 8308 Spring TX 77387-8308

JACKSON, HAROLD, journalist; b. Birmingham, AL, Aug. 14, 1953; s. Lewis and Janye (Wilson) J.; m. Denice Estell Pledger, Apr. 30, 1977; children: Annette Michelle, Dennis Jerome. Diploma, Ramsay High Sch., 1971; BS in Journalism/Political Sci., Baker U., 1975. Reporter Birmingham Post-Herald, Ala., 1975-80, UPI, Birmingham, Ala., 1980-83; state news editor UPI, 1983-85; asst. nat. editor Phila. Inquirer, 1985-86; asst. city editor Birmingham News, Ala., 1986-87; editorial writer Birmingham News, 1987-94; editorial page writer The Balt. Sun. Recipient Pulitzer Prize for editorial writing, 1991. Mem. Nat. Assn. Black Journalists (named journalist of the yr. 1991), Birmingham Assn. Black Journalist (pres. 1987-90), Soc. of Professional Journalists (named green eyeshade 1989). Presbyterian. Office: The Baltimore Sun 501 N Calvert st Baltimore MD 21278

JACKSON, HARPER SCALES, JR., healthcare executive; b. Ft. Smith, Ark., Feb. 23, 1951; s. Harper S. and Adele J.; m. Virginia Kay Stack, June 4, 1976; children: Laura Elizabeth, Kathrin Ann, Susan Virginia. BSBA, U. Ark., 1973; M in Health Adminstrn., Washington U., 1979. Mgr. Neiman-Marcus Co., Dallas, 1973-77; adminstrv. asst. to Michael E. DeBakey, M.D. Baylor Coll. of Medicine, Houston, 1979-81; asst. v.p. The Meth. Hosp., Houston, 1981-83, v.p., 1983-85, sr. v.p. support svcs., 1985-89, sr. v.p. patient svcs., 1989-93, sr. v.p. surgery svcs. and clin. support, 1993-95, sr. v.p. prof. and surg. svcs., 1995—; bd. dirs. LifeGift, mem. founding coun., mem. exec. com. 1994—, chmn. 1996—, sec. 1995—; bd. dirs. Vis. Nurse Assn., Houston, Washington U. Alumni Assn., bd. dirs., chmn.-elect, 1994-96, bylaws com., 1992—, chmn., 1996—; adj. faculty Washington U. Sch. Medicine, St. Louis, 1992—. Adminstrv. bd. First United Meth. Ch., Sugarland, Tex., 1988-91, facility assess com., 1995-96; chmn. healthcare campaign coun. United Way of Tex. Gulf Coast, Houston, 1988; adv. coun. Ft. Bend (Ind.) Sch. Dist. Sch.-Bus. Partnership; bd. trustees AORN Found., 1992-94, v.p., 1992-93, chmn. policy com., 1993-94; bd. dirs. Am. Heart Assn., East Ft. Bend divsn., 1990—, pres., 1993-94, chmn. nominating com., 1995, mem. quality improvement network #1 Healthcare Forum. Recipient Cert. of Appreciation, Am. Heart Assn., 1984. Fellow Am. Coll. Healthcare Execs. (mem. Houston chpt., chmn. mem. com. 1996—); mem. Am. Hosp. Assn., United Weslayan Hosp. Assn., Tex. Hosp. Assn. (ad hoc com. corp. values and ethics, leadership forum, del. to 1992 conv.), U. Ark. Alumni Assn., Drs. Club Houston, Sweetwater Country Club, Omicron Delta Kappa, Beta Gamma Sigma, Sigma Iota Epsilon, Phi Gamma Delta (life). Office: The Meth Hosp 6565 Fannin St Houston TX 77030-2704

JACKSON, JACQUELINE, assistant principal; b. Indpls., Aug. 14, 1950; d. Johnnie and Thelma (Smith) Rose; m. Anthony Joseph Jackson, Dec. 24, 1974 (Nov. 1995); children: Marcus Reginald, Jacqueline Christina. BA, Park Coll., Kansas City, Mo., 1972; MS, Nova U., 1984. Cert. elem. edn. tchr., Fla. Tchr. Omaha Pub. Sch., 1972-74, Capital Sch. Sys., Dover, Del., 1974-76, Dept. of Defense, Lakenheath, Eng., 1976-79; tchr. Dade County Pub. Sch., Miami, Fla., 1984-89, reading coord., 1989-91, asst. principal, 1991—. Mem. Internat. Reading Assn., Fla. Reading Assn., Dade Reading Coun. (hon., pres. 1984—), Alpha Delta Kappa, Dade Assn. Secondary Adminstrs. Home: 17700 SW 112 Ave Miami FL 33157 Office: 145500 SW 96th St Miami FL 33187

JACKSON, JANIS LYNN, biology educator; b. Houston, May 9, 1952; d. Harrell James and Patricia Ann (Vernon) Odom; m. James Arthur Jackson, May 18, 1974; 1 child, Megan Michelle. AA, San Jacinto Coll., 1972; BS, East Tex. State U., 1974, MS, 1976. Biology instr. McLennan C.C., Waco, Tex., 1975—; mem. chmn. instrn. subcom. McLennan C.C., Waco, 1980-81, chmn. faculty coun. rep., 1981-82, compensation com., 1990, co-chmn. instl. self study, 1990-91, profl. devel. com., 1992-93, mem. Tartan Scholars design com., 1995; judge paper presentations North Tex. Biol. Assn., Commerce, 1983, Tex. Acad. Sci., Nacodoches, 1990; vol. Assn. Locally Involved Vols. in Edn., Inc., Waco, 1979; rep. Gt. Tchrs. Workshop, Waco, 1989. Co-author: Basic Biological Concepts, 1983, rev. edit., 1984, 90, 95. Co-leader Camp Fire, Inc., Waco, 1993—; mem. Parents Assn.-St. Louis, Waco, 1991—. Recipient Nat. Inst. Staff and Orgn. Devel. Excellence award Internat. Conf. on Tchg. Excellence, 1991, 94. Mem. Tex. Jr. Coll. Tchrs. Assn., Instns. Master Plan Task Force (steering com. 1989). Republican. Presbyterian. Home: RR 5 Box 994 Waco TX 76705-9612 Office: McLennan C C 1400 College Dr Waco TX 76708

JACKSON, JEROME ALAN, biological scientist, educator, researcher; b. Ft. Benning, Ga., Feb. 4, 1943; s. Wayne Clark and Phyllis Mae (Monroe) J.; m. Nancy Ann Niemann, Aug. 7, 1965 (div. Mar. 1983); children: Jerome Alan, Paul Clark, Ann Christine, Peter Michael; m. Bette Jean Schardien, Mar. 12, 1984; children: Steven Brent, Matthew Clifford. BS, Iowa State U., 1965; PhD, U. Kans., 1970. Instr. biology West H.S., Bakersfield, Calif., 1965-66; asst. prof. dept. zoology Miss. State U., Mississippi State, 1970-74, assoc. prof., 1974-79, curator of birds, 1970—, curator of mammals, 1987—, prof. dept. biol. scis., 1979—; pres. Eco-Inventory Studies, Inc., Mississippi State, 1988—; co-host Ms. Outdoors, WCBI TV, Columbus, Miss., 1988—; scientist, expdn. to Cuba, Nat. Geographic Soc., 1988; short term tech. advisor in Indonesia, Acad. for Edn. Devel./U.S. Agy. Internat. Devel., 1994. Author/editor 12 books about birds or nature, including Vulture Biology and Management, 1993; contbr. over 200 articles to profl. jours. and over 100 articles to popular mags. Trustee N.Am. Loon Fund, 1986-89. Recipient Excellence in Sci. Teaching award Miss. Sci. Tchrs. Assn., 1992, Outstanding Cmty. Environ. award Southwire Co., 1993, Outstanding Contbn. to Sci. in Miss. award Miss. Acad. Scis., 1990; named Man of Yr., Inland Bird Banding Assn., 1976. Fellow AAAS, Am. Ornithologists Union, Explorers Club; mem. Wilson Ornithol. Soc. (pres. 1983-85, editor Wilson Bull. 1974-78), Assn. Field Ornithologists (editor jour.), Miss. Ornithol. Soc. (editor Miss. Kite 1976—, pres. 1971-72). Methodist. Office: Miss State U Dept Biol Scis Box GY Mississippi State MS 39762

JACKSON, JESSE LUTHER, III, pastor; b. Kinston, N.C., Jan. 15, 1947; s. Jesse Luther Jr. and Iris Elizabeth (Cauley) J.; m. Carol Ann Vest, Aug. 24, 1968; children: Jesse Luther IV, James Joshua. BS in Aerospace Engring., N.C. State U., 1968; MME, U. So. Calif., L.A., 1976; MDiv, Mid-Am. Bapt. Theol. Sem., Memphis, 1979. Ordained to ministry So. Bapt. Conv., 1979. Sr. sys. engr. Garrett AiResearch, Torrance, Calif., 1968-76; sem. asst. Bellevue Bapt. Ch., Memphis, 1976-79; sr. pastor Williston (Tenn.) Bapt. Ch., 1979-82, Marble City Bapt. Ch., Knoxville, Tenn., 1982-87, Westwood Hill Bapt. Ch., Virginia Beach, Va., 1987—; pres. Fayette County Pastors' Conf., Somerville, Tenn., 1981-82; tchr., trainer Evangelism Explosion Internat., Ft. Lauderdale, Fla., 1987—. Recipient Hudgin's award Tenn. Bapt. Conv., Brentwood, 1981, Eagle award So. Bapt. Sunday Sch. Bd., Nashville, 1985, Top Ten in Evangelism Bapt. Gen. Assn. Va., Richmond, 1988-93. Home: 1645 Lola Dr Virginia Beach VA 23464-8009 Office: Westwood Hill Bapt Ch 865 Woodstock Rd Virginia Beach VA 23464-2122

JACKSON, JIMMY LYNN, engineer, consulting spectroscopist; b. Claremore, Okla., Sept. 14, 1957; s. Michael R. and Frances L. (Harrison) J. Field svc. engr. Labtest Equipment Co., L.A., 1979-84, Spectro A.I., Inc., Fitchburg, Mass., 1984-94; pres. Jimmy Jackson Svcs., Inc., Shelby, Ala., 1994—. Mem. ASTM, ASM, A2LA, AFS. Office: Jimmy Jackson Svcs Inc PO Box 409 Shelby AL 35143

JACKSON, JOHN HOLLIS, JR., lawyer; b. Montgomery, Ala., Aug. 21, 1941; s. John Hollis and Erma (Edgeworth) J.; m. Rebecca Mullins, May 27, 1967; 1 child, John Hollis III. A.B., U. Ala., 1963, J.D., 1966. Bar: Ala. 1966, U.S. Dist. Ct. (no. dist.) Ala. 1969, U.S. Ct. Appeals (11th cir.) 1993. Sole practice, Clanton, Ala., 1967—; county atty. Chilton County Commn., Clanton, 1969—; mcpl. judge Clanton, 1971—, Jemison, Ala., 1984—; dir. First Nat. Bank, Clanton, 1974-83; mem. adv. bd. Colonial Bank, Clanton, 1983—. Bd. dirs. Chilton-Shelby Mental Health Bd., Calera, Ala., 1974-83, pres., 1974-79; mem. State Democratic Exec. Com., Birmingham, Ala., 1974—; del. Democratic Nat. Conv., N.Y.C., 1976; mem. County Democratic Exec. Com., Chilton County, 1982—. Served to 1st lt. U.S. Army, 1966-67. Mem. Ala. Young Lawyers Sect. (exec. com. 1969-70), Chilton County Bar Assn., (pres. 1969, 74), Ala. State Bar Assn. (bd. bar commrs. 1984-87, chmn. adv. com. to bd. bar examiners 1986-87, 93—, 19th cir. indigent def. commn. 1983—), Phi Alpha Delta. Democrat. Methodist. Lodge: Kiwanis. Home: Samaria Rd Clanton AL 35045 Office: PO Box 1818 500 2nd Ave S Clanton AL 35046-1818

JACKSON, JOHNNY W., minister; b. Shamrock, Tex., Aug. 4, 1933; s. John W. and Faye Leota (Gregory) J.; m. Nancy Jean Howdeshell, June 26, 1953; children: Danny Michael, Stephen Mark, Faye Luanne, Lauree Sue. BA, Abilene Christian U., 1974. Ordained to ministry Chs. of Christ, 1954. Min. Ch. of Christ, Pottsboro, Tex., 1954-55, Morton St. Ch. of Christ, Denison, Tex., 1955-58, Abrams Ch. of Christ, Richardson, Tex., 1958-64, Southside Ch. of Christ, Amarillo, Tex., 1964-66, Cen. Ch. of Christ, Houston, 1966-69, So. MacArthur Ch. of Christ, Irving, 1969-79, Eldridge Rd. Ch. of Christ, Sugar Land, 1979-82, Rolling Hills (Tex.) Ch. of Christ, DeSoto, 1982—; bd. dirs. Cedar Green Living Ctr., DeSoto. Contbr. articles to profl. jours. Mem. Rotary (sec. De Soto chpt. 1986-87). Home: 1408 Richards Cir De Soto TX 75115-2911 Office: Rolling Hills Ch of Christ 115 W Belt Line Rd De Soto TX 75115-4939

JACKSON, JONATHAN JENE, quality assurance professional; b. Wallace, Idaho, Jan. 21, 1937; s. Theodore C. Jackson and Verna Mae (Jackson) Teixeira; m. Gerri C. Regan, May 23, 1993; four children, from previous marriage. AA, Fresno (Calif.) City Coll., 1973; BS, Calif. State U., Fresno, 1979, MPA, 1981. Cert. quality auditor; cert. quality engr. Sys. engr. Lockheed Missile & Space Co., Sunnyvale, Calif., 1959-70; dep. sheriff, coroner Madera (Calif.) Sheriff's Office, 1971-82; quality control supr. Electronic Scales Internat., San Luis Obispo, Calif., 1984-85; quality assurance mgr. Applied Nav. Devices, San Luis Obispo, Calif., 1985-86; procurement quality assurance rep. Gen. Dynamics, Pomona, Calif., 1987-88; sr. field quality rep. Allied Signal Aerospace, Teterboro, N.J., 1988-89; quality assurance program/project advisor Rockwell Internat., Cape Canaveral, Fla., 1989-96; mem. product assurance staff IV United Space Alliance, Cape Canaveral, 1996—. Instr., trainer ARC, Madera, 1975-80, Am. Heart Assn., Madera, 1977-80. With USAF, 1955-58. Mem. Am. Soc. Quality Control (sr. mem., sect. chmn.-elect 1996—),Am. Inst. Parliamentarians (region VII gov. 1984-86), Toastmasters Internat. (dist. 33 gov. 1986-87, awards 1982, 85, 87), Am. Legion, Masons, Shriners, Elks. Home: PO Box 378 Orchard Park NY 14127-0378 Office: United Space Alliance 8600 Astronaut Blvd Cape Canaveral FL 32920-4306

JACKSON, JOSEPH ESSARD, religious organization administrator; b. Negril, Jamaica, May 22, 1951; came to the U.S., 1968; s. Redverse and Edna Artilla (Gordon) J.; m. Elaine Marie Jacintho, July 1, 1978; children: Joseph E. II, Jonathan N. BS, Westfield State Coll., 1975; MAR, Yale U. Divinity Sch., 1981; CAS, Harvard U., 1983; DMin, Wesley Theol. Sem., 1993. Ordained to ministry , 1983. Counselor urban edn. program Westfield (Mass.) State Coll., 1972-74, 80; teaching fellow Harvard U., 1982-83; math. tchr. Springfield (Mass.) Pub. Schs., 1983-84; v.p. external rels. Charge, Inc., Glen Ellyn, Ill., 1984; history tchr. Tech. High Sch., Springfield, 1984-86; adj. prof. Ch. of God Sch. Theology, Cleveland, Tenn., 1986-89; sr. pastor Harvest Temple Ch. of God, Forestville, Md., 1989-92; exec. dir. Black ministries Ch. of God Internat. Offices, 1992—; asst. prof. religion dept. Bible and Christian Ministries Lee Coll., Cleveland, 1986-89; assoc. min. Ch. of God, Hartford, Conn., 1980-86; keynote speaker many confs. and convs. Author: Reclaiming Our Heritage, 1993; contbr. articles to profl. jours. Active alumni com. Tech. High Sch., 1984-85, Blue Hills Child Care Ctr., Hartford, 1981-86, State Bd. Edn., So. New England, 1984-89, Music Bd., So. New England, 1979-84, State Youth and Christian Edn. Bd. Ch. of God, So. New England; mem. ministerial devel. bd. State of Tenn., 1987-89. Mem. NAACP (bd. dirs. 1984-85), Nat. Assn. Evangelicals (bd. adminstrs. 1993—, mem. exec. com. 1994—, treas. 1995—). Democrat. Office: Ch of God Internat Offices PO Box 2430 Cleveland TN 37320-2430

JACKSON, JUDITH ANN, elementary education educator; b. Picayune, Miss., June 22, 1944; d. Roy Austin and Oleta Maria (Atkinson) Calhoun; m. David Harris Jackson, Dec. 31, 1965 (dec. Oct. 1990); children: Stacy Ann, William Austin. AA, Pearl River Jr. Coll., 1964; BS, U. So. Miss., 1966. Cert. elem. tchr. Reading tchr. Purvis (Miss.) Elem., 1965-66; 1st grade tchr. Bertie Rouse Sch., Picayune, 1966-68; 4th grade tchr. Scott County Christian Sch., Harperville, Miss., 1971-72; presch. dir., tchr. Forest (Miss.) Bapt. Ch. Kindergarten, 1984-87; elem. tchr. Gulfview Elem., Hancock County, Miss., 1993—. Home: 905 Longo St Waveland MS 39576-3234

JACKSON, KAREN LEE, elementary school educator; b. Canoga Park, Calif., July 24, 1964; d. Ralph Albert and Marjorie Jane (Lunde) Schultz; m. Ronald Lee Jackson, Aug. 29, 1984; 1 child, Elizabeth Ann. AA, Temple (Tex.) Jr. Coll., 1984; BA, U. Tex., 1993. Cert. tchr., Tex. Tchr. Temple Ind. Sch. Dist., 1993—; tchr. trainer in reading success insvc. Tex. Edn. Agy., Killeen, 1994. Author: (poetry) Collage, 1983. Mem. Tex. Edn. Exes. Republican. Home: PO Box 1496 Temple TX 76503

JACKSON, LOLA HIRDLER, art educator; b. Faribault, Minn., Mar. 2, 1942; d. Earl Arthur and Marian Barbara (Pavek) Hirdler; children: Carilyn, Cherilyn, Marc. BS in Art Edn., Mankato State U., 1972, MA, 1975. Cert. tchr. Instr. art YWCA, Mankato, 1968-70; art instr. Mankato Area Vocat. Tech. Inst., 1971-72; pres., tchr., art dir. Jackson Studios, Mankato, 1969-78; art tchr. New Richland (Minn.) High Sch., Mankato (Minn.) State U., 1973-74; pres. Lola Ltd. Lt'ee Art Distbn., N.C., 1976—; tchr. art Lincoln Sch. Math. and Sci. Tech., Greensboro, N.C., 1988-90, chmn. dept., 1988, 89-90; tchr., chmn. art dept. Shallotte Mid. Sch., 1990—; instr. art Brunswick C.C., Supply, N.C., 1990—; staff artist The Reporter, 1970-73; pres., bd. dirs. Fine Arts Inc., Gallery 500, Mankato, 1972-75. Bd. mem. Mankato Area Found., 1976-83. Recipient award Busch Found. Minn. Arts Coun., Nat. Endowment Arts, 1974. Mem. Profl. Pictures Framers Assn., N.C. Assn. of Edn. Republican. Roman Catholic.

JACKSON, LADY LOYD APPLEBY, personnel executive; b. Toccoa, Ga., July 8, 1946; d. Samuel Cecil and Lillian Loyd (Collins) Appleby; m. Joseph Howard Torrence, July 27, 1968 (div. 1973); 1 dau., Katherine Loyd; m. Thomas Houston Jackson, May 3, 1974; children: Thomas Houston, Jr., John Andrew. B.A., Mary Baldwin Coll., 1968. Cert. profl. in human resources. Exec. trainee Sears, Roebuck & Co., Phila., 1968-69; tng. adminstr. Genesco, Inc., Nashville, 1969-72; adminstrv. asst. State Tenn. Dept. Human Svcs., Nashville, 1972-73, dir. office svcs., 1973-77, dir. personnel, 1977-80; dir. personnel ARC, Nashville, 1980-81; asst. dir. personnel Nashville Electric Svc., 1981-90; dir. Mayor's Office Econ. Devel., 1990—; sec.-treas. The Guide Co., Inc., 1984—. Vice chmn. bd. Mcpl. Auditorium Bd., Nashville, 1976-77; sec., treas. Tenn. Personnel Adv. Council, Nashville, 1978-79; mem. Outlook Nashville Personnel Com., Leadership Nashville, 1986-87; bd. dirs. United Methodist Neighborhood Ctrs., Nashville, 1984—, chmn. personnel com., 1985; bd. dirs. ARC Nashville chpt., 1988—, Am. Lung Assn. Tenn., 1988—; cons. Jr. Achievement, 1986. Recipient Laurel Soc. award Mary Baldwin Coll., 1968, Bess Maddox award, 1987; named Woman of Yr. Bus. and Profl. Women's Club, 1987. Mem. ARC (Nashville chpt.), Am. Heart Assoc. (bd. dirs. Nashville chpt. 1990—, chmn.-elect 1992—), Indsl. Personnel Assn. (chmn. operating com. 1982-83, sec. treas. v.p. 1984, pres. 1985), Am. Soc. Personnel Adminstrs. (program com. chmn. 1984, sec. 1986, v.p. 1987, pres. Nashville chpt. 1988), Internat. Assn. Quality Circles (co-founder, dir. Central Tenn. chpt. 1982-83, James House Williamson award 1989). Democrat. Mem. Woodmont Christian Ch. Office: Mayor's Office Econ Devel 214 2nd Ave N Ste One Nashville TN 37201-1647

JACKSON, LYNN ROBERTSON, lawyer; b. Montgomery, Ala., Nov. 20, 1947; d. Arthur Borders Jr. and Mozelle (Martin) Robertson; m. George Thomas Jackson, Aug. 16, 1969; children: Katherine, William Borders. BS, U. Ala., 1970; JD, Faulkner U., 1979. Bar: Ala. 1981, U.S. Dist. Ct. Ala. 1984. Ptnr. Jackson and Faulk, Clayton, 1981-83, Andrews and Jackson, Clayton, 1983-84; pvt. practice Clayton, 1984-92; ptnr. Jinks, Smithart & Jackson, Clayton, 1992—; chair mandatory legal edn. Ala. State Bar, 1990—; mem. permanent code com., bench and bar rels. com. Ala. State Bar. City atty. City of Clayton, 1984—; bd. trustees Town and County Libr., Clayton, 1990—; trustee Ala. Law Found., 1989—. Mem. ABA, Ala. State Bar Assn. (bar commr. 1985—), Assn. Trial Lawyers Am. Episcopalian.

Home: Licklog Farm Clayton AL 36016 Office: Jinks Smithart and Jackson Court Sq Clayton AL 36016

JACKSON, MAE BOGER, executive adminstrative assistant, secretary; b. Winston-Salem, N.C., May 19, 1963; d. Billy Charles and Leona (Heath) Key; m. John Talbert Jackson, June 13, 1987; 1 child, Thomas William. Student, U. N.C., Charlotte, 1981-83; BS, Johnson Bible Coll., 1986. Cert. profl. sec. Adminstrv. asst., exec. sec. The Shelton Cos., Winston-Salem, 1986-88; office automation specialist, personnel mgr. POPI Temp. Svcs., Winston-Salem, 1988-90; exec. asst. Inmar Enterprises, Inc., Winston-Salem, 1990-92, Chesapeake Display and Packaging co., Winston-Salem, 1992—. Mem. NAFE, Profls. Sec. Internat. (treas. 1990, v.p. 1991, pres.-elect 1992, pres. 1993-94, Winston-Salem Sec. of Yr. N.C. divsn. 1991, 96, Winston-Salem Outstanding mem. of Yr. award 1993), Assn. Info. Sys. Profls., Office Automation Soc. Internat. Mem. Christian Ch. (Ch. of Christ). Home: 310 Gatewood Dr Winston Salem NC 27104-2432 Office: Chesapeake Display & Packaging Co PO Box 12669 Winston Salem NC 27117-2669

JACKSON, MARSHA LOUISE, French language educator; b. Macon, Ga.. BA, Emory U., 1969; MA, Ga. State U., 1976. French tchr. Clarkston (Ga.) H.S., 1971-76, Tucker (Ga.) H.S., 1976-77, Berkmar H.S., Lilburn, Ga., 1979-82, Parkview H.S., Lilburn, 1987—. Mem. Am. Assn. of Tchrs. of French, Fgn. Lang. Assn. of Ga. Office: Parkview High Sch 998 Cole Dr Lilburn GA 30247

JACKSON, MAYNARD, securities executive; b. Dallas, 1938; s. Maynard Holbrook and Irene (Dobbs) J.; m. Valerie Richardson; 5 children. BA in Polit. Sci., Morehouse Coll., 1956; JD cum laude, N.C. Cen. U. Atty. NLRB, Atlanta; vice mayor City of Atlanta, 1969, mayor, 1973-82, 1990-94; mng. ptnr. Chapman and Cutler, Atlanta, 1982—; chmn. Jackson Securities Inc., Atlanta, 1994—. Mem. exec. com. Dem. Nat. Com., Dem. Party, Ga.; pres. Nat. Conf. Dem. Mayors, Nat. Black Caucus of Local Elected Ofcls.; chmn. U.S. Local Govt. Energy Policy Adv. Com., Urban Residential Fin. Authority, Atlanta, Downtown Devel. Authority, Atlanta, transp. com. Atlanta Regional Commn., Rebuild Am. Coalition U.S. Conf. Mayors; founding chmn. Com. of Arts, U.S. Conf. of Mayors, Atlanta Econ. Devel. Corp.; trustee Atlanta Coun. Internat. Corps.; founder Nat. Assn. Securities Profls. Mem. Phi Beta Kappa. Office: Jackson Securities Inc 100 Peachtree St, Ste 2250 Atlanta GA 30303-2825*

JACKSON, MICHAEL WAYNE, judge, lawyer; b. Selma, Ala., Nov. 18, 1963; s. Claude Jackson and Anne (Ford) Tucker. BS, Centre Coll., Danville, Ky., 1985; JD, Fla. State Law Sch., 1988. Bar: Fla. 1989, Ala. 1991, U.S. Dist. Ct. (so. dists.) Ala. 1994, U.S. Dist. Ct. (mid. dist.) Ala. 1995. Asst. dist. atty. Dist. Atty.'s Office, Marion, Ala., 1990-91, Selma, Ala., 1991-94; pvt. practice Selma, Ala., 1994—; judge Mcpl. Ct., Selma, Ala., 1995—. Vol. Atty. Op. Stand By, Tallahassee, Fla., 1994—; mem. state dem. exec. com., Ala., 1995—; mem. Ala. Dem. Conf., Ala. New South Coalition. Mem. Ala. State Bar Assn., Fla. State Bar Assn., Dallas County Bar Assn., Phi Alpha Delta. Home: 920 Lapsley St Selma AL 36701 Office: Selma Mcpl Courthouse PO Drawer L Selma AL 36702-0401

JACKSON, R. GRAHAM, architect; b. Sherman, Tex., July 1, 1913; s. Watt J. and Lilly Thompson (Graham) J.; m. Reba Martin, Jan. 6, 1940 (dec. Oct. 1967); m. Violet Stephen Lawrence, May 1, 1971. B.S. in Architecture, Rice U., 1935. With R. Graham Jackson, Architect, 1936-45; ptnr. Jackson & Dill, Architects, Houston, 1946-53, Wirtz, Calhoun, Tungate & Jackson, Architects, Houston, 1953-65, Calhoun, Tungate & Jackson, Architects, Houston, 1965-75, Calhoun, Tungate, Jackson & Dill, 1975-82, CTJ&D, 1983—; asst. prof. architecture U. Houston, part time 1947-51; vis. lectr., critic Rice U., 1963-67. Archtl. works include design Lyndon B. Johnson Spacecraft Center, NASA, Houston, Willford Hall Hosp, Lackland AFB, Tex., Ryon Engring. Bldg., Rice U, Houston, Hankammer Sch. Bus., Baylor U, communications bldg. Tex. Tech. U, Darnall Army Hosp, Ft. Hood, Tex., Burleson acad. quadrangle Baylor U, Waco, Tex., Bergstrom AFB Hosp, Austin, Tex., library and performing arts bldgs. Sam Houston State U, Huntsville, Tex., 2d Bapt. Ch, Houston, Vets. Hosp, Temple, Tex., Coll. Tech., U. Houston, master plan Buckner Children's Village, Beaumont, Tex., Westbury Bapt. Ch, Houston, Chem. and Petroleum Engring. Bldg. U. Tex., Austin, 2d Bapt. Ch., Houston. Mem. founding com. Houston Baptist U.; mem. Rice U. Fund Council, Houston Mus. Fine Arts, Friends of Bayou Bend, Houston Symphony Soc. Fellow Constrn. Specifications Inst. (pres. Houston chpt. 1958-59, region dir. 1961-64, chmn. conv. program com. 1965), AIA (treas. Houston chpt. 1950, pres. 1959, mem. nat. adminstrv. office practice com. 1951-53, 67-73, 78-81); mem. Am. Mgmt. Assn., Am. Arbitration Assn. (panel of arbiters), Rice U. Alumni, Rice U. Assos., Houston Baptist U. Alumni Assn. (hon.), Houston C. of C. (edn. com. 1950-53). Baptist (deacon). Clubs: Houston, Rice U. Faculty. Office: C T J & D Architects 6200 Savoy Dr Ste 630 Houston TX 77036-3315

JACKSON, RAYMOND A., federal judge; b. 1949. BA, Norfolk State U., 1970; JD, U. Va., 1973. Capt. U.S. Army JAGC, 1973-77; asst. U.S. atty. Ea. Dist. Va., Norfolk, 1977-93; judge U.S. Dist. Ct. (ea. dist.) Va., Norfolk, 1993—; mem. judicial conf. U.S. Ct. Appeals (4th cir.). Active Day Care and Child Devel. Ctr., Tidewater, 1980-86; bd. dirs. Peninsula Legal Aid Ctr., 1977. Col. USAR, 1977—. Mem. U.S. Dist. Judges Assn., Va. State Bar, Old Dominion Bar Assn., Norfolk-Portsmouth Bar Assn., South Hampton Rds. Bar Assn., Am. Inn Ct. (Hoffman-l'Anson chpt.). Office: 600 Granby St Norfolk VA 23510-1915

JACKSON, RAYMOND CARL, cytogeneticist; b. Medora, Ind., May 7, 1928; s. Thornton Comadore and Flossie Oliva (Booker) J.; m. T. June Snyder, Oct. 24, 1947; children: Jeffrey Wayne, Rebecca June. AB, Ind. U., 1952, AM, 1953; PhD, Purdue U., 1955. Instr. to asst. prof. U. N.Mex., Albuquerque, 1955-58; asst. prof. of Botany U. Kans., Lawrence, 1958-60, assoc. prof. of Botany, 1961-64, prof. of Botany, 1964-71, prof. and chmn. Botany, 1969-71; prof. and chmn. biol. scis. Tex. Tech U., Lubbock, 1971-78, Horn prof. of Biol. Scis., 1990—; chmn. interdepartmental PhD Program in Genetics, U. Kans., chmn. dept. Botany, U. Kans., 1969-71; speaker and presenter in field. Contbr. numerous articles to profl. jours. Staff sgt. USAF, 1946-49. Mem. Genetics Soc. Am., Genetics Soc. of Can., Soc. for the Study of Evolution, Botanical Soc. of Am. (BSA Merit award 1992), Am. Soc. Plant Taxonomists, Internat. Orgn. of Plant Biosystematists, Delta Phi Alpha, Sigma Xi, Phi Sigma. Republican. Home: 7922A Aberdeen Ave Lubbock TX 79424-2808 Office: Dept Biol Scis Tex Tech Univ Lubbock TX 79409

JACKSON, REED MCSWAIN, educational administrator; b. Albemarle, N.C., Apr. 10, 1950; d. Wade Hampton and Louise Reed (Floyd) McSwain; m. William Austin Jackson, July 24, 1984. BA, Coker Coll., 1972; MEd, Francis Marion Coll., 1978; cert. Prin.'s Exec. Program, U. N.C., 1995. Lic. sch. adminstrn., sch. supervision, mentor, reading tchr. 2d grade tchr. Darlington (S.C.) County Schs., 1972-76; 4th grade tchr. Marlboro County Schs., Bennettsville, S.C., 1976-78; chpt. I reading tchr. Halifax (N.C.) County Schs., 1980-90, asst. prin. S.E. Halifax High Sch., 1990-91, dir. testing and secondary edn., 1991-95; accountability/instrnl. specialist Nash-Rocky Mount Schs., N.C., 1995—; mem. steering com. Roanoke Valley Tech Prep Consortium, Weldon, N.C., 1991—, chairperson mktg. com., 1991—; cons. So. Assn. Colls. and Schs.; chair Local Option Testing Svcs. governing bd.-N.C. state com. Mem., officer Tar River Embroiderers Guild, Rocky Mount, N.C., 1983-90; mem. Adv. Coun. for Coop. Extension Agy., Halifax, N.C., 1992. Named Halifax County Tchr. of Yr., 1984-85, Eastman Mid. Sch. Tchr. of Yr. 1984. Fellow N.C. Ednl. Policy Fellowship Program; mem. ASCD, Nat. Assn. Secondary Sch. Principals (named Leader 1-2-3 Coach), Phi Delta Kappa. Home: 4052 Ketch Point Dr Rocky Mount NC 27803-1418 Office: Nash/Rocky Mount Schs 800 Fairview Rd Rocky Mount NC 27801

JACKSON, RICHARD BRINKLEY, metal company executive; b. Wilmington, N.C., July 3, 1929; s. Lloyd Franklin and Lelia (Jones) J.; m. Betty Hodnett, June 28, 1958; 1 child, Richard Alan. BS in Indsl. Rels., U. N.C., 1956. Div. personnel mgr. Dan River, Inc., Danville, Va., 1956-63; div. dir. personnel Reynolds Metals Co., Richmond, Va., 1963-77; v.p. personnel and labor rels. Reynolds Internat., Inc., Richmond, 1977-94, sr. v.p. adminstrn., 1995—. With USAF, 1947-52. Mem. Nat. Fgn. Trade Coun., Machinery and Allied Products Inst. (Human Resource Coun.), Brandermill Country Club (Midlothian). Home: 1236 Shirlton Rd Midlothian VA 23113-4540 Office: Reynolds Internat Inc 6601 W Broad St Richmond VA 23230-1701

JACKSON, ROBERT KEITH, manufacturing company executive; b. South Bend, Ind., Apr. 20, 1943; s. Orval Russell and Dorothy Alice (Gailey) J.; m. Cheryl Dee Bronkhorst, Nov. 6, 1965; children: Jennifer Lynn, Stephen Robert. BS, Western Mich. U., 1966; MBA, Vanderbilt U., 1987. Vocat. tchr. Warren (Mich.) Consol. Schs., 1967-68; mfg. engr. Eaton Corp., Kalamazoo, 1968-77, gen. supt., 1977; gen. supt. Eaton Corp., Kings Mountain, N.C., 1977-80; plant mgr. Eaton Ltd., Manchester, Eng., 1980-84, Eaton Corp., Shelbyville, Tenn., 1984-91; mgr. mfg. and quality assurance Truck Components Ops. Eaton Corp., Kalamazoo, 1991-93; plant mgr. Eaton Corp., Humboldt, Tenn., 1993—; mem. adv. coun. indsl. studies Mid. Tenn. State U., Murfreesboro, 1985-91, Sch. Bus., 1990-91; mem. machine tool tech. adv. com. Jackson (Tenn.) State C.C., 1994—; mem. devel. com. U. Tenn. at Martin, mem. mech. engring. adv. bd., 1995-96. Trustee Eaton Pub. Policy Assn., Cleve., 1985-89. Mem. Tenn. Assn. Bus. (bd. dirs. 1989-91), Rotary, Elks, KC. Republican. Roman Catholic. Home: 640 Dogwood Dr Monteagle TN 37356-2010 Office: Eaton Corp Axle-Brake Divsn 899 Eaton Dr Humboldt TN 38343-1567

JACKSON, ROBERT L., suncare, skincare products company executive; b. Elizabethtown, Ky., June 11, 1962; s. Harold L. and Mary E. (Miller) J.; m. Karen Renee Miller, Aug. 31, 1985; children: Nolan, Mariel. BS in Bus., Murray (Ky.) State U., 1985; cert. mergers and acquisitions, Am. Mgmt. Assn., Chgo., 1986. Acctg. asst. HT Mktg. Inc., Murray, 1981-83, credit mgr., 1983-84, treas., 1984-86, sec.-treas., chief fin. officer, 1986-88, exec. v.p., dir., 1988-91, pres., chief oper. officer, 1991—. Bd. commrs. Murray Calloway County Hosp., 1989-95; bd. dirs. Pad-Mur Radiation Therapy Ctr., Murray, 1990-95; mem. Mayors Task Force Strategic Planning, Murray, 1989-90, Murray Planning Commn., 1993-94; county chmn. Jones for Gov. Ky., Murray, 1990-91, apptd. by gov. to bd. dirs. West Ky. Corp., 1992-95; bd. dirs. Murray Calloway County YMCA, 1988-92, Habitat for Humanity, Murray, 1988-90, Murray-Calloway County Econ. Devel. Corp., 1994—; mem. Dem. Nat. Com., 1992-96, Ky. Dem. Ctrl. Exec. Com., 1992-96; super del. Dem. Nat. Conv.; appt. by gov. Econ. Devel. Ptnrship. Bd., 1995, Higher Edn. Nominating Bd., 1996. Named Citizen of Yr. Murray Calloway County C. of C. Mem. Murray Calloway County C. of C. (pres. 1994-95), Murray State U. Alumni Assn. (pres. 1996—, nat pres. 1996-97), Murray Country Club, Rotary Club, Pi Kappa Alpha (Man of Yr. 1984). Democrat. Methodist. Home: 1108 County Cork Dr Murray KY 42071-2711 Office: HT Mktg Inc PO Box 790 Murray KY 42071-0790

JACKSON, ROBERT LEE, real estate agent, broker; b. Alamogordo, N.Mex., Dec. 31, 1963; s. J.W. Jackson. AA, SUNY, Albany, 1985, BS in Psychology, 1993; BSBA in Adminstr. Mgmt., U. Ark., Fayetteville, 1986. Owner Borderman's Reef Apts., Albuquerque, 1986-94, Innovative Concepts, 1995—. Recipient 1st pl. award CNN/U.S.A. Today stock option contest, Atlanta, 1991. Mem. Exch. Club Am., Mercedes Club Am., Wall Street Club (charter mem.), Phi Kappa Tau (sec., co-founder 1983-86). Office: 2367 Green Acres Rd # 118 Fayetteville AR 72703-2839

JACKSON, ROBERT LEWIS, dermatologist; b. Marion, Ind., Sept. 3, 1952; s. Lewis Albert and Violet Agatha (Burden) J.; m. Deborah Jeneal Pittman, Sept. 1, 1979; children: Ryan Lewis, Ian Robert. BA in Zoology, Miami U., Oxford, Ohio, 1974; MD, Meharry Med. Coll., 1978. Diplomate Am. Bd. Dermatology. Intern Akron (Ohio) City Hosp., 1978-79; resident in dermatology UCLA King-Drew Med. Ctr., 1983-86; pvt. practice Memphis, 1987—; courtesy staff Eastwood Hosp., Memphis, 1987—, Bapt. Hosps., Memphis, 1987—; cons. staff St. Joseph Hosp., Memphis, 1987—, Meth. Hosps., Memphis, 1987—, St. Francis Hosp., Memphis, 1988—. Contbr. articles to profl. jours. With USPHS, 1979-83. Mem. Am. Acad. Dermatology, Am. Soc. Dermatol. Surgery, Tenn. Med. Assn., So. Med. Assn., Memphis Dermatology Soc., Memphis-Shelby County Med. Soc. Home: 8312 Scruggs Dr Germantown TN 38138-6133 Office: 3960 Knight Arnold Rd Ste 109 Memphis TN 38118-3001

JACKSON, RONALD PIPPIN, social services agency administrator; b. Atlanta, Aug. 7, 1950; s. Arthur Pippin and Hazel (Holt) J.; m. Elizabeth Joslin, Dec. 5, 1970; children: Arthur P. II, Franklin Clay. BA in Polit. Sci., David Lipscomb U., 1972. Program coord. Muscular Dystrophy Assn., Atlanta, 1977-78; assoc. minister Sandy Springs Ch. of Christ, Atlanta, 1978-82; pub. rels. cons. Jackson & Assocs., Atlanta, 1982-87; dir. devel. and pub. rels. Auditory Edn. Ctr., Atlanta, 1987-88; exec. dir. Ga. AGAPE, Inc., Smyrna, Ga., 1988-91, Ga. State Golf Found., 1991—; pres., exec. dir. Make A Wish Found. Metro Atlanta. Pres. Crabapple Mid. Sch. PTA, 1993-95; v.p. Roswell North Elem. Sch. PTA, 1987-88, 89-90, pres., 1992-93; pres. Atlanta 1000, 1982-88; bd. dirs., v.p. Atlanta Bible Camp, 1986-88; vol. baseball and soccer coach Roswell Recreation Dept., Atlanta; mem. Fulton County Bd. Edn., 1997—. Named one of Outstanding Young Men of Am., 1986. Mem. Pub. rels. Soc. Am., Nat. Soc. Fund Raising Execs., Kiwanis (pres. Atlanta-Perimeter Center chpt. 1988-89, Outstanding Officer 1989, disting. lt. gov. divsn. 14 Ga. dist. 1990-91). Mem. Ch. of Christ. Home: 1120 Wordsworth Dr Roswell GA 30075-2836 Office: Make A Wish Found Metro Atlanta 1905 Powers Ferry Rd Ste 205 Atlanta GA 30339

JACKSON, RUTH ROBERTSON, insurance company executive; b. Grady County, Okla., Apr. 17, 1939; d. Gordon James and Rose Viola (Ritter) Robertson; m. Mahlon Bruce Slocum, Dec. 30, 1957 (div. 1972); children: Laura Wynn Robertson, Jill Michele Hawkins; m. Gilbert Shepard Jackson, May 31, 1987. Student, Okla. Coll. for Women, 1957-58, Midwestern U., 1961, El Centro Community Coll., 1980. Legal sec. Wichita County Judge, Wichita Falls, Tex., 1960-62, Douglas E. Bergman Law Firm, Dallas, 1962-64; sec. claims Excalibur Ins. Co., Dallas, 1971-75; sr. sec. claims Excalibur Ins. Co., Carrollton, Tex., 1975-79, asst. sec., treas., 1979-84, pres., 1984-91; supr. compliance Excalibur Holdings, Inc., Carrollton, 1979-82, dir. compliance and analysis, 1982-84, dir. underwriting, 1984. Fin. sec., precept leader First Baptist Ch., Marlow, Okla., 1993—; sec. Rep. Women of Stephens County. Republican. Baptist. Home: 905 W Osage St Marlow OK 73055-3267

JACKSON, SANDRA LEE, health facility administrator; b. Tulsa, July 15, 1955; d. Marvin Cecil and Helen Lee (Wright) J. BSN, U. Tulsa, 1979. From staff nurse CCU to adminstrv. dir. clin. data svcs. Hillcrest Med. Ctr., Tulsa, 1979-90; v.p. patient svcs. Cancer Treatment Ctr., Tulsa, 1990-91, v.p. ops., 1991-95, pres./CEO, 1995—. Mem. NAFE, Am. Burn Assn., Rsch. Inst. Am. Coll. Osteopathic Health CAre Execs., Okla. Nursing Assn., Am. Coll. Healthcare Execs., Assn. of Cancer Execs. Home: PO Box 702317 Tulsa OK 74170-2317 Office: Cancer Treatment Ctr Tulsa 8181 S Lewis Ave Tulsa OK 74137-1222

JACKSON, STEPHANIE ANN, nurse; b. Thomasville, N.C., Jan. 2, 1960; d. Ellis Wade and Nancy (Myers) J. BSN, East Carolina U., 1982. Staff nurse Pitt County Meml. Hosp., Greenville, N.C., 1981-83, N.C. Bapt. Hosp., Winston-Salem, N.C., 1983-87, Duke U. Med. Ctr., Durham, N.C., 1987-91, Rex Hosp., Raleigh, N.C., 1991-94; nurse clinician Health Infusion, Morrisville, N.C., 1994; nurse clinician Coram Health Care (formerly Health Infusion), Morrisville, N.C., 1995, infusion care mgr. Goldsboro and Kinston brs., 1995—. Republican. Home: 4616 Bayspring Ln Raleigh NC 27613

JACKSON, STEPHEN ERIC, police official; b. Seymour, Ind., July 9, 1946; s. Ralph Marshall Jackson and Dolly Katherine (Britt) Tudor; m. Cheryl Jane Hallman, June 23, 1967 (div. 1985); children: Kirstina Leigh, Brandi Annette; m. Margaret Ann Skelton, Oct. 17, 1986 (div. 1989); m. Candy Sandler Clinard, Sept. 30, 1995. BA in Sociology, N. Tex. State U., 1976; grad., Tex. Law Enforcement Inst., 1991; MPA, U. North Tex., 1993. Lic. mediator, 1996. Police officer, sgt. Denton (Tex.) Police Dept., 1970-81; customer svc. mgr. Amerace Corp., Denton, 1981-83; chief of police U. North Tex., Denton, 1983—; v.p. Denton County Chiefs of Police, Denton, 1986—. Contbr. articles to profl. jours. Precinct chmn. Denton County Rep. Party, 1982-85; mem. Pub. Transp. Task Force, Denton, 1989; chmn. steering com. Leadership Denton, 1990-95, 97—), Leadership Denton Alumni Assn., 1991—; mem. parking com. Main St. Denton, Inter-Assn. Task Force on Alcohol and Other Substance Abuse Issues, 1995—, diversity tng. facilitator Nat. Coalition Bldg. Inst., 1990—. Mem. Internat. Assn. Campus Law Enforcement Adminstrs. (v.p. 1995-96, pres. elect 1996—), Tex.-N.Mex. Assn. Coll. and Univ. Police Depts. (Pres.'s award 1985, treas. 1993-96, Adminstr. of Yr. 1993), Internat. Assn. Chiefs of Police. Office: U North Tex Police Dept PO Box 13467 Denton TX 76203-6467

JACKSON, SUSANNE LEORA, creative placement firm executive; b. Rochester, N.Y., June 9, 1934; d. Daniel T. and Gertrude (Grantham) Sheriff; m. David K. Jackson, Mar. 12, 1954; children: Jonnie Sheehan, Jaynette Kettler. Student, Santa Fe Sch. Art, 1952-53, Midwestern U., 1953-55. Supr. ANR Prodn. Co., Houston, 1976-83; v.p. Robinhawk Drafting & Design, Houston, 1983-85; pres., CEO Houston Creative Connections, 1985-96—; advt. & mktg. dir. Geotech Assn., Houston, 1989-90; past pres. Am. Inst. Design & Drafting, 1984-86; CEO The Agy., 1996—, Full Svc. Advt. Agy., 1996—, Houston Tech. Connections, 1996—, Outsource and Tech. Placement, 1996—; bd. dirs. HyperDynamics. Design cons.: (mag.) Urbane, 1989-94. Mem. Mus. Fine Arts, Houston, 1988-95, Greater Houston Partnership, 1989-95; bd. dirs. Literacy Advance, 1993—. Mem. NAFE, Houston Advt. Fedn. (Silver and Merit awards 1989, Merit award 1990, Bronze award 1991, 2 Bronze awards 1992, 2 Gold and 4 Merit awards 1992, Gold and Bronze awards 1995), Greater Heights C. of C. (bd. dirs. 1994—, vice-chmn. 1996), Galleria C. of C., Rotary (treas. 1992, pres.-elect 1993, pres. 1994), U.S. C. of C. (Blue Chip Enterprise award 1993). Republican. Episcopalian. Office: Houston Creative Connection 701 N Post Oak Rd Ste 675 Houston TX 77024-3829

JACKSON, TERRENCE J., coal company executive; b. New Kensington, Pa., Oct. 8, 1948; s. Russell Thomas and Julia Ann (Popp) J.; m. Melissa Ann Bottner, Sept. 10, 1977; children: Todd, Drew, Brady, Cory, Lindsay. BA, Yale U., 1970; MBA, U. Pa., 1975. Sales rep. Consolidation Coal Co., Detroit, 1975-78, dist. sales mgr., 1978-80; dist. sales mgr. Consolidation Coal Co., Chgo., 1980-81; sales mgr. Phillips Coal Co., Richardson, Tex., 1981-84; gen. sales mgr. North Am. Coal, Cleve., 1984-87; v.p. mktg. & sales Anker Energy, Morgantown, W.Va., 1987-91; chmn., CEO Great Western Coal Inc., Houston, 1991—; also bd. dirs. Great Western Coal Inc., Coalgood, Ky.; bd. dirs. Great Western Resources Inc., Houston, Crockett Collieries Ky. Inc., Coalgood, Harlan Fuels Co., Coalgood. Bd. dirs. Houston YMCA Camping Svcs., 1993—; coach Ponderosa Cowboys, Houston, 1993—. Presbyterian. Office: Great Western Coal Inc 1111 Bagby St Ste 1700 Houston TX 77002-2546

JACKSON, THOMAS HAROLD, JR., public relations administrator; b. Atlanta, Dec. 15, 1951; s. Thomas Harold Jackson Sr. and Claire Dickey (Jones) Plymel; m. Sharon Aileen Broome, Nov. 22, 1975; children: Thomas Harold III, Stanley David. AA, Oxford Coll. Emory U., 1971; AB in History, U. Ga., 1973, postgrad., 1973-75; postgrad., Harvard U., 1994. Announcer WLAG AM-FM Radio, LaGrange, Ga., 1970-71; ops. mgr., announcer WGAU/WNGC Radio, Athens, Ga., 1971-74; corr. The Atlanta Constitution, 1974-80; broadcast editor pub. info. dept. U. Ga., Athens, 1974-75; gen. mgr. WLAG/WWCG Radio, LaGrange, 1975-77; news dir. WTRP Radio, LaGrange, 1977-80; reporter/bur. chief WXIA-TV, Atlanta, 1980-88; dir. pub. info. U. Ga., Athens, 1988—; stadium announcer U. Ga. Redcoat Band, Athens, 1974—; pres., bd. dirs. Ga. APBroadcasters, Atlanta, 1986-87, 77-80, 85-88. Del. United Meth. Gen. Conf., St. Louis, 1988, Louisville, 1992; chair Bishop's blue-ribbon study com.; chmn. adminstrv. bd. Athens 1st Meth. Ch., 1993-94, also vice-chmn., lay spkr., mem. fin. coms., staff-parish, stewardship and worship commns.; chmn. Troup Co. Dem. com., LaGrange, 1976-77; mem. U. Ga. Olympic planning com., 1993-96; mem. Athens 96 Olympics coord. com., 1993-96. Recipient reporting awards AP, 1976-82, (10), Pacemaker award AP, 1973, 76, 79, Sch. Bell award Ga. Assn. Educators, 1985; named Disting. Alumnus Oxford Coll. of Emory U., 1989. Mem. Soc. Profl. Journalists, Coun. Advancement and Support of Edn., Athens Area C. of C. (bd. dirs. 1995—, exec. com. 1995, univ./cmty. rels. com. 1993-94, chair 1994), Phi Kappa Phi, Phi Alpha Theta, Phi Mu Alpha Sinfonia. Home: 1021 Rossiter Ter Watkinsville GA 30677-5124 Office: U Ga Pub Info Alumni House Athens GA 30602

JACKSON, VAUGHN LYLE, artist, consultant; b. Raymond, Ohio, Jan. 7, 1920; s. Edwin Clarence and Minnie Myrtle (Spain) J.; m. R. Joan Strickland, June 30, 1956 (dec. Dec. 1993); children: Rena Gwen, Edwin Colt, Tobey Ann. AA, Am. U., 1964, BA, 1969. Staff artist The Columbus (Ohio) Citizen, 1938-43; advt. artist S. Kann Sons, Washington, 1946-47, Kal, Ehrlich & Merrick Advt., Inc., Washington, 1947-52; artist, illustrator, asst. art dir. Ops. Rsch. Office Johns Hopkins U., Chevy Chase, Md., 1952-63; publ. art dir. Rsch. Analysis Corp., McLean, Va., 1963-67, visual and graphics mgr., 1967-72; visual and graphics mgr. Gen. Rsch. Corp., McLean, 1972, tech. publs. dir., 1972-76; visual dir. Sys. Planning Corp., Arlington, Va., 1976-91; cons. Sys. Planning Corp., Arlington, 1991-93. Vol. Media Gen. Telethon, Cable and Fairfax (Va.) County Coun. of Arts, 1993. T5 and staff sgt. U.S. Army, 1943-45, ETO. Recipient Purchase award City of Fairfax, Va., Commn. on the Arts, 1995. Mem. Nat. Watercolor Soc., Fairfax Com. of 100, Ky. Watercolor Soc. (exhibiting mem.), Va. Watercolor Soc., Pa. Watercolor Soc., Midwest Watercolor Soc., Washington Watercolor Assn. (v.p. 1960, 1st Place award 1988), Phila. Water Color Club, The Art League, Arts Coun. Fairfax County, Fairfax Art League Inc. (bd. dirs. 1987-93, v.p. 1991, pres. 1992, Best in Show award 1988). Office: Ten Penny Studio PO Box 54 Fairfax Station VA 22039-0054

JACKSON, WILLIAM PAUL, JR., lawyer; b. Bexar, Ala., July 7, 1938; s. William Paul and Evelyn Mabel (Goggans) J.; m. Barbara Anne Seignious, Sept. 30, 1966; children: Jennifer Anne, Susan Barrett, William Paul III. BS in Physics, U. Ala., 1960, JD, 1963. Bar: Ala. 1963, D.C. 1969, Va. 1975. Law clk. to judge Ala. Ct. Appeals, Montgomery, 1965; assoc. Bishop and Carlton, Birmingham, Ala., 1965-68, Todd, Dillon and Sullivan, Washington, 1968-70; founding ptnr. Jackson & Jessup, Washington and Arlington, Va., 1970-76; pres., sr. atty. Jackson & Jessup, P.C., Washington and Arlington, Va., 1976—; advisor Oren Harris chair of transp. U. Ark., 1974-91. Comments editor U. Ala. Law Rev., 1962, leading articles editor, 1963; contbr. articles to legal jours. V.p. McLean Hunt Homeowners Assn., Va., 1974, pres., 1975-76; bd. dirs. McLean Citizens' Assn., 1976-78; pres. McLean Legal Action Fund, Inc., 1977-81; session mem. Lewinsville Presbyn. Ch., 1981-84; v.p. The Marjoribanks Family, 1994-96, pres., 1996—; active The Alexandria Chorale, 1985-94. 1st lt. Signal Corps, U.S. Army, 1963-65. Recipient Pub. Service awards Am. Radio Relay League, 1958; recipient merit award Armed Forces Communications and Electronics Assn., 1963; Sigma Delta Kappa scholar, 1963. Mem. ABA, Arlington Bar Assn., Fed. Bar Assn., Ala. State Bar, Va. State Bar, D.C. Bar, Va. Bar Assn., Bar Assn. D.C., Transp. Lawyers Assn. (chmn. legis. com. 1989-90), Assn. for Transp. Law, Logistics and Policy (nat. pres. 1991-92, chmn. nominating com. 1992-93, chmn. membership com. 1993—, chmn. D.C. chpt. 1989-90, com. govtl. rels. 1975-90, motor editor Assn. Highlights 1992—, Presdl. award 1994), Am. Judicature Soc., So. Transp. Logistics Assn. (exec. dir. 1970—), Ea. Indsl. Traffic League (exec. dir. 1978-88), Bench and Bar Honor Soc. (pres. 1963), Omicron Delta Kappa. Presbyterian (elder). Home: 1003 Spring Hill Rd Mc Lean VA 22102-1331 Office: Jackson & Jessup PC PO Box 1240 3426 N Washington Blvd Arlington VA 22210-0540

JACKSON LEE, SHEILA, congresswoman; b. Queens, N.Y., Jan. 12, 1950; m. Elwyn C. Lee; 2 children. BS, Yale U.; JD, U. Va. Sr. counsel select com. on assassinations U.S. Ho. of Reps., 1977; trial atty. Fulbright and Jaworski, 1978-80; sr. atty. United Energy Resources, Inc., 1980; assoc. judge Houston Mcpl. Ct., 1987-89; mem. Houston City Coun., 1990-94, 104th Congress from 18th Tex. dist., 1995—. Democrat. Office: US House Reps 1520 Longworth House Office Bldg Washington DC 20515

JACO, THOMAS WRIGHT, hazardous materials administrator; b. Columbia, S.C., Mar. 12, 1946; s. Doyle Daniel and Thelma (Costner) J.; m. Linda Mattox, Apr. 20, 1968; children: Joseph Daniel, Matthew Thomas. Degree, U. Ga., 1967, Clemson U., 1969. Paramedic Richland County EMS, Columbia, 1971-87; dep. dir. Richland County Hazardous Materials, Columbia, 1987—; cons. Crossed-Keys, Columbia, 1989-90. Mem. Local Emergency Planning Com., Columbia, 1989—, coord., 1990; mem. emergency svcs. ARC, Columbia, 1990. Mem. S.C. Law Enforcement Officers Assn., S.C. Emergency Preparedness Assn., DIVEX Superfund Mitigation Team, Richland County Regional Arson Task Force, DIVEX Mitigation Response Team, Internat. Assn. Bomb Technicians, Internat. Assn.

Arson Investigators, S.C. Fire Inspectors Assn. Episcopalian. Office: Richland County Hazardous Materials 1410 Laurens St Columbia SC 29204-1880

JACOB, BRUCE ROBERT, dean, academic administrator, law educator; b. Chgo., Mar. 26, 1935; s. Edward Carl and Elsie Berthe (Hartmann) J.; m. Ann Wear, Sept. 8, 1962; children—Bruce Ledley, Lee Ann, Brian Edward. B.A., Fla. State U., 1957; J.D., Stetson U., 1959; LL.M., Northwestern U., 1965; S.J.D., Harvard U., 1980; LLM in Taxation, U. Fla., 1995. Bar: Fla. 1959, Ill. 1965, Mass. 1970, Ohio 1972. Asst. atty. gen. State of Fla., 1960-62; assoc. Holland, Bevis & Smith, Bartow, Fla., 1962-64; asst. to assoc. prof. Emory U. Sch. Law, 1965-69; research assoc. Ctr. for Criminal Justice, Harvard Law Sch., 1969-70; staff atty. Community Legal Assistance Office, Cambridge, Mass., 1970-71; assoc. prof. Coll. Law, Ohio State U., 1971-73, prof., dir. clin. programs, 1973-78; dean, prof. Mercer U. Law Sch., Macon, Ga., 1978-81; v.p., dean, prof. Stetson U. Coll. Law, St. Petersburg, Fla., 1981-94, prof., 1994—. Contbr. articles to profl. jours. Mem. Fla. Bar, Sigma Chi. Democrat. Home: 1946 Coffee Pot Blvd NE Saint Petersburg FL 33704-4836 Office: Stetson U Coll Law 1401 61st St S Saint Petersburg FL 33707-3246

JACOB, KAREN HITE, music director; b. Wilkensburg, Pa., Feb. 14, 1947; d. Bernard Wayne and Ann (Teck) Hite; m. John Brent Jacob, Mar. 23, 1973; 1 child, R. Taylor. BM, U. N.C., Greensboro, 1969, MA in Tchg., 1970. Cert. tchr. N.C. Tchr. Ctrl. Piedmont C.C., Charlotte, N.C., 1970-82; music dir. St. John's Episcopal Ch., Charlotte, N.C., 1982-91; artistic dir. Carolina Pro Musica, Charlotte, 1977—; music dir. Caldwell Meml. Presbyn., Charlotte, 1991—. Performances in Poland and Peru, 1993, 96. Com. mem. Carolinas Organ Com., Charlotte, 1989—, Charlotte Sister Cities Com., Charlotte, 1991—; bd. dirs. N.C. Episcopal Diocese Liturgical Commn. USIA grantee to teach English and music in Russia, 1995. Mem. Am. Guild of Organists (bd. dirs. Charlotte chpt. 1981—), Southeastern Hist. Keyboard Soc. (newsletter editor). Office: PO Box 32022 Charlotte NC 28232

JACOB, ROBERT ALLEN, surgeon; b. Cleve., July 25, 1941; s. John B. and Elaine Irene (Puleo) J.; m. M. Elaine Sheppard, Aug. 23, 1980; children: Kristen Elizabeth, Alexandra Elaine. BA, Case Western Res. U., 1963; MSc, Ohio State U., 1966, MD, 1969. Diplomate Am. Bd. Orthopaedic Surgeons, Am. Acad. Pain Mgmt. Orthopaedic surgeon Bluegrass Orthop. Group PSC, Louisville, 1976—; pres. med. staff Sts. Mary & Elizabeth Hosp., Louisville, 1991—; med. dir. Ky. Pain Therapy Ctr. Contbr. articles to profl. jours. Local fundraising chmn. Orthop. Edn. and Rsch. Found., Sts. Mary & Elizabeth Hosp., 1990-91; bd. dirs. Kentuckiana Hemophilia Found., 1987-89, Hosp. Found., 1991-93. Maj. U.S. Army, 1974-76. Recipient Outstanding Svc. award Kentuckiana Hemophilia Found., 1986, Cert. of Recognition, 1987. Fellow Am. Acad. Orthopaedic Surgeons; mem. Ky. Med. Assn., Southern Med. Assn., Jefferson County Med. Assn., Louisville Orthopaedic Assn., Louisville Soc. Physicians and Surgeons (v.p. 1980, pres. 1984). Republican. Roman Catholic. Home: 7512 Chestnut Hill Dr Prospect KY 40059-9484 Office: Bluegrass Orthop Group 1900 Bluegrass Ave Ste 203 Louisville KY 40215-1144

JACOBS, ALAN, lawyer; b. Balt., Jan. 7, 1947; s. Jerome and Mildred (Carlin) J.; m. Paula Ference Kaiser, May 16, 1979; children: Mark, Michelle, Jeremy, Katherine. BS, U. Md., 1969; JD, U. Balt., 1975. Bar: Calif. 1977, D.C. 1978, Tex. 1993; CPA, Md., Calif. Staff SEC, Washington, 1972-76; mem. Zipser, Snyderman, et al., L.A., 1976-79; gen. counsel House of Fabrics, Inc., Van Nuys, Calif., 1979-80; v.p., sec., gen. counsel ICN Pharms., Inc., Costa Mesa, Calif., 1980-81; mem. Jones, Day, Reavis & Pogue, L.A., 1981-86, Dallas, 1986-91; exec. v.p., sec., gen. counsel D.R. Horton, Inc., Arlington, Tex., 1991-92, also bd. dirs.; mem. McGlinchey Stafford Lang, A Profl. LLC, Dallas, 1993—, pres.; adj. prof. Southwestern U. Sch. of Law, 1985-86. With USAR, 1969-75.

JACOBS, BETTY CARLA, library director; b. Jackson, Tenn., Aug. 16, 1951; d. J. G. and Betty Jo (Rogers) Wise; m. Jerry Lee Jacobs, Nov. 28, 1992; children: Jennifer, Angela, Rebecca. BA in Elem. Edn., Union U., 1973; M of Libr. and Info. Sci., U. Tenn., 1982; MA in Christian Edn., So. Bapt. Theol. Sem., 1986; EdD in Curriculum and Instrn., Memphis State U., 1992. Cert. tchr. K-12, Tenn. Tchr. 3d grade Dyer County Sch. Dist., Dyersburg, Tenn., 1974-75; tchr. Mission Sch. So. Bapt. Fgn. Mission Bd., Paraguay, 1975-77; tchr. 1st and 2d grade West Carroll Sch. Dist., Trezevant, Tenn., 1977-82; interlibr. loan libr. So. Bapt. Theol. Sem., Louisville, 1984-86; pub. and tech. svcs. libr. Union U., Jackson, Tenn., 1987-92, automation project dir., 1991-93, dir. libr., 1992-96; dir. libr. Franklin Coll., Franklin, Ind., 1996—; conf. and workshop leader Ky. Bapt. Woman's Missionary Union, Louisville, 1984-86; automation cons. Union U., 1989—. Prodr., editor (videos for local cable TV) Storytelling, 1985. Mem. ALA, So. Bapt. Libr. Assn. (sec. nominating com. 1990-94), Tenn. Libr. Assn. (staff devel., continuing edn. com. 1990—), Kappa Delta Pi. Southern Baptist. Home: 60 Pleasant Plains Rd Jackson TN 38305-9622 Office: Hamilton Libr Franklin Coll 501 E Monroe St Franklin IN 46131-2512

JACOBS, DAVID LEE, art educator; b. Cin., Dec. 28, 1945. BA, U. Cin., 1967; MA, U. Tex., 1969, PhD, 1978. Asst. prof. Wayne State U., Detroit, 1974-87; assoc. prof. U. Tex., Arlington, 1987-90; prof., chair dept. art U. Houston, 1990—. Editor Exposure, 1984-89; co-curator travelling exhbn. and book: Ralph Eugene Meatyard: An American Visionary, 1992. Nat. Endowment for the Arts Critic's grantee, 1985. Office: U Houston Dept Art Houston TX 77204-4893

JACOBS, DELORES HAMM, secondary education educator; b. Tuscaloosa, Ala., Mar. 1, 1947; d. Howard Murphy and Nellie Mae (Booth) Hamm; m. Paul Thomas Jacobs, June 1, 1966; 1 child, Michael Paul. BS in Secondary Edn., U. Ala., 1971; BS in Middle Sch. Edn., Samford U., 1991; MA in Secondary Edn., U. Ala., Birmingham, 1974. English and Title I reading tchr. Locust Fork (Ala.) H.S., 1971-85; speech instr. Pizitz Middle Sch., Vestavia Hills, Ala., 1985-86, tchr. English, instr., 1986—, curriculum coord. English dept.; student-tchr. sponsor U. Ala., Birmingham, Samford U., Birmingham. Contbr. poetry to various poetry publs. and editorials to Tuscaloosa News, Vestavia Hills edn. newsletters, Am. Poetic Soc. poetic vols. Bd. dirs. First Ch. of the Nazarene Pre-Sch. and Daycare Sch., Vestavia Hills, 1987-93, ch. organist, 1976—; sch. rep. United Way; rep. Heart Fund, Jefferson County, Ala., vol. Olympic Games, 1996. Mem. NEA, Ala. Edn. Assn., So. Assn. of Schs. (accreditation com., visitation team), Nat. Coun. Tchrs. English, Ala. Reading Assn., Vestavia Hills Garden Club, Chi Delta Phi. Republican. Office: Pizitz Middle School 2020 Pizitz Dr Vestavia Hills AL 35216

JACOBS, HARRY MILBURN, JR., advertising executive; b. New Bern, N.C., July 23, 1928; s. Harry Milburn and Nina (Gibbs) J.; m. Barbara Ann Mills; children—Kathryn, Christopher, Letitia. Student East Carolina U., 1947-49; B.F.A., Corcoran Sch. Art, 1952. Graphic artist The Hecht Co., Washington, 1952-53, art dir., 1952-53; art dir. Bradham & Co., Greensboro, N.C., 1953-54; sr. art dir. Bradham & Co., Greensboro, 1956-59; assoc. art dir. Cargill, Wilson & Acree, Richmond, Va., 1959-61, creative dir., Charlotte, N.C., 1961-68, creative dir., Richmond, 1969-74, pres., 1971-74; pres. Martin Agy., Richmond, Va., 1977-83, vice chmn., 1983-86, chmn. bd., 1986—, CEO, 1989, Chmn. emeritus, Served with U.S. Army, 1954-56. Scoutmaster, Boy Scouts Am., 1956-58, mem. exec. coun. Robert E. Lee Coun., 1987-89; bd. dirs. sch. comm. Va. Commonwealth U.; trustee Woodberry Forest Sch., St. Mary's Coll.; bd. visitors Sch. Journalism U. N.C., Chapel Hill, Va. Commonwealth U. Found.; bd. overseers Corcoran Sch. Art, Washington; bd. dirs. Meml. Guidance Clinic, Richmond Children's Mus., Marymount Park, Goodwill Industries, Richmond Sch. Ballet, Virginians in Support of Guard and Res., Downtown Presents; bd. dirs. exec. com. Richmond Renaissance. Recipient numerous advt. awards; named Advt. Man of Yr. Silver Medal, Am. Advt. Fedn., 1972; named to Top 100 Creative People, 1972, 75, 81, Best Men in Advt. McCalls Mag., 1992; elected to Va. Communications Hall of Fame, 1986, N.C. Advt. Hall of Fame, 1991; named One of Nations Top Advt. Leaders Wall St. Jour., 1989. Mem. Copy Club of N.Y., Art Dirs. Club of N.Y. Republican. Clubs: Bull & Bear, Commonwealth (Richmond), Capital. Home: 1431 Floyd Ave Richmond VA 23220-4663 Office: Martin Agy 500 N Allen Ave Richmond VA 23220-2904

JACOBS, JAMES A., insurance professional; b. Richmond, Va., Mar. 5, 1947; s. Alexander S. and Rosalie (Want) J.; m. J. Isabel Goldberg, Mar. 21, 1976; children: Stephen, Ellen. BS in Chemistry, U. Richmond, 1969. CLU; chartered fin. cons. Rep. Equitable Ins. Cos., Petersburg, Va., 1971-82, dist. mgr., 1982-89; dist. mgr. Equitable Ins. Cos., Richmond, Va., 1989-90; owner Jacobs Fin. Group, Chesterfield, Va., 1990—; speaker numerous assns. throughout the U.S. and Can. Contbr. articles to profl. jours. Pres. Petersburg Tri-Cities YMCA, 1982, Kiwanis Breakfast Club, Petersburg, 1982; bd. dirs. Chester (Va.) and YMCA Chester Recreation Assn.; coach basketball team boys, 1989, basketball team girls, 1991-93. Named Underwriter of Yr., State of Va., 1980. Mem. Va. Assn. Life Underwriters (pres. 1981), Million Dollar Round Table (life and qualifying mem., sales idea com. 1988-89, pub. svc. com. 1989-90, chmn. pub. rels. com. 1990-91, program devel. com. 1993-94, sales ideas com. 1994-95, chmn. MDRT sales idea com. 1995-96, featured MDRT poster campaign 1996, vice chair afternoon sessions annual meeting, 1997), Equitable Life CLUs Assn. (trustee 1994—, So. Region Honor Agt. 1993), Richmond CLU/ChFC (PACE chmn. 1993-95). Republican. Jewish. Office: Jacobs Fin Group PO Box 548 10105 Krause Rd Ste 100 Chesterfield VA 23832-6573

JACOBS, JAMES PAUL, retired insurance executive; b. Augusta, Ark., May 14, 1930; s. James Leonard and Ida Lee (Taylor) J.; m. Joan Gillum, Aug. 18, 1956; 2 children: LeAnn Mulligan, Caryl Lynn Watson. Student, Louis A. Allen Mgmt., 1970; Assoc. in mgmt., Ins. Inst. of Am., 1971. Underwriter trainee Ins. Co. of N. Am., Phila., 1954-55; underwriter Ins. Co. of N. Am., Richmond, Va., 1955-58, supervising underwriter, 1958-64, underwriting mgr., 1964-68; underwriting mgr. Ins. Co. of N. Am., Detroit, 1968-71; casualty mgr. Montgomery & Collins, Inc., L.A., 1971-73; ptnr. Tabb Brockenbrough & Ragland, Richmond, Va., 1973-1995, ret., 1995; mem. agts. adv. coun. Comml. Union Ins. Co., Boston, Gt. Am. Ins. Co. Cin., Cigna Cos. Phila., Pa. Mfrs. Assn. Ins. Co., Phila., ITT Hartford, Conn., Jonathan Trumbell Assocs., Md. Ins. Group Agts. Forum, U.S. Fidelity and Guaranty Co.; bd. dirs. "All Industry" Va. "I" Day Corp., Richmond; instr. U. Richmond, 1965-78. Author articles in profl. jours. Active in Colonial Williamsburg Assocs., Friends of Kennedy Ctr., Smithsonian Assocs.; bd. dirs. Daily Planet, Richmond (non-profit orgn. for aiding the homeless), pres., 1995—. Capt. USMC, 1951-54. Mem. CPCU (bd. dirs. 1979-82, regional v.p. 1981, chpt. officer 1976-79). Republican. Methodist. Home and Office: 1510 Westshire Ln Richmond VA 23233-3034

JACOBS, JOHN, IV, marketing professional; b. West Newton, Mass., Sept. 25, 1952; s. John Jacobs III and Mary Louise Molony. BSc, Colo. Sch. Mines, 1975. Head sci. dept. Forman Schs., Litchfield, Conn., 1978-79; geophysicist CGG Data Processing, Denver, 1980-81; project mgr. CGG Data Processing, Houston, 1981-82; mgr. remote computing svcs. CGG Data Processing, Denver, 1982-83; mgr. 3D workstation CGG Data Processing, Houston, 1983-84; mgr. geophysical workstation Sun E&P Co., Dallas, 1984-88; nat. tech. mgr. Sierra Geophysics, Houston, 1988-91; mktg. mgr. Halliburton Energy Svcs., Houston, 1991-94; product mgr. KaPRE Software Inc., Boulder, 1994-96; mgr. exploration database Anadarko Petroleum Corp., Houston, 1996—. Mem. Am. Mktg. Assn., Soc. Exploration Geophysicists, Geophysical Soc. Houston.

JACOBS, JOSEPH JAMES, lawyer, communications company executive; b. Toronto, Ont., Can., Mar. 18, 1925; came to U.S., 1925; s. Sidney and Hildred Veronica (Greenberg) J.; m. Carole Evelyn Bent, Jan. 22, 1946 (div. 1972); children—Carole Lynn Urgenson, Joseph James III; m. Edna Mae Meincke, Jan. 5, 1973. J.D., Tulane U., 1950. Bar: La. 1950, N.Y. 1951, U.S. Dist. Ct. (so. dist.) N.Y. 1953, U.S. Ct. Mil. Appeals 1953, U.S. Ct. Appeals (2d cir.) 1977, U.S. Ct. Appeals (D.C. cir.) 1980. Assoc. Proskauer, Rose, Goetz & Mendelsohn, N.Y.C., 1950-53; asst. gen. counsel, asst. to pres. Am. Broadcasting Co., N.Y.C., 1954-60; gen. atty. Metromedia, Inc., N.Y.C., 1960-61; dir. program and talent negotiations United Artists TV, Inc., 1961-66; atty. United Artists Corp., N.Y.C., 1966-69; v.p., counsel United Artists Broadcasting, Inc., N.Y.C., 1969-71; gen. atty. ITT World Communications Inc., N.Y.C., 1972-74; v.p., legal dir. ITT Communications Ops. and Info. Services Group (formerly U.S. Telephone & Telegraph Corp.), N.Y.C. and Secaucus, N.J., 1974-83, ITT Communications and Info. Services, Inc., Secaucus, 1983-87; v.p., gen. counsel U.S. Transmission Systems, Inc., Secaucus, 1984-87, ITT World Communications Inc., Secaucus, 1984-87; of counsel Seyfarth, Shaw, Fairweathr & Geraldson, N.Y.C., 1988-89; v.p., gen. counsel Graphic Scanning Corp., Englewood, N.J., 1989-91; v.p., gen. counsel Ram/BSE, L.P., Woodbridge, N.J., 1992; pvt. practice, Wainscott, N.Y., 1992-95. Bd. editors Tulane Law Rev., 1949, asst. editor-in-chief, 1950; cons. 1996—. Served with parachute inf. U.S. Army, 1943-46, ETO, PTO, to maj. USAFR ret. Mem. Assn. Bar City of N.Y., Fed. Bar Assn., Order of Coif. Republican. Jewish. Office: 6380 Sweet Maple Ln Boca Raton FL 33433

JACOBS, SISTER MARGARET MARY, nursing administrator; b. Cin., Jan. 11, 1945; d. John J. and Elizabeth M. (Brady) J. Diploma, St. Joseph Infirmary Sch., 1967; AB in Biology, Thomas Moore Coll., 1973; BSN, Coll. of Mt. St. Joseph, 1983; MA in Nursing Adminstrn., NYU, 1996. RN, Ohio, Ky.; cert. adult nurse practitioner. Nurse St. Joseph Hosp., Lexington, Ky., 1976-77, Our Lady of the Way Hosp., Martin, Ky., 1967-76, St. Francis/St. George Hosp., Cin., Holy Family Home, Melbourne; patient care coord. Hospice of Big Sandy, Paintsville, 1985-93; mem. speakers bur. on pain control Purdue Frederick Co. Compiled textbook on basic coronary care. Mem. ANA, Ky. Nurses Assn.

JACOBS, MARILYN ARLENE POTOKER, gifted education educator, consultant, author; b. N.Y.C., Oct. 22, 1940; m. David Jacobs, Dec. 10, 1960. BA in Psychology, Hunter Coll. CUNY, 1961, MS in Edn., 1963; cert. in gifted edn., U. South Fla., 1977. Cert. elem. edn., gifted and early childhood edn., Fla. Tchr. Yonkers (N.Y.) Pub. Schs., 1961-63; dir., tchr. Creative Corners Pre-Sch., Pomona, N.Y., 1971-74; tchr. of gifted, tchr. trainer Pinellas County Schs., Clearwater, Fla., 1975—; pvt. practice computer edn. cons., 1987—; freelance grant writer, 1988—. Contbr. articles to profl. jours. Recipient numerous county, state and nat. Econs. Edn. Curriculum awards, 1982—. Mem. NEA, ASCD, Coun. for Exceptional Children (Educator of the Yr. 1985), Assn. for Gifted, Fla. Assn. Computer Educators, Phi Delta Kappa, Phi Beta Kappa, Kappa Delta Pi, Psi Chi. Office: Eisenhower Elem Sch 2800 Drew St Clearwater FL 34619-3010

JACOBS, TIMOTHY ANDREW, epidemiologist, international health consultant; b. St. Petersburg, Fla., Nov. 5, 1944; s. W. Andrew and Virginia (Ott) J.; m. Carolyn Martin, Nov. 4, 1972; 1 child, Jenny Thuy Ha. BSN, U. Fla., 1970; MS, PNP, U. Utah, 1976; PhD, Internat. Inst. Advanced Studies, 1979; C.T.M., Liverpool (Eng.) Sch. Tropical Medicine, 1982; cert. hosp. epidemiology, U. Iowa, 1985; MPH, Yale U., 1991. Nat. design and media cons. Nat. Assn. Pediatric Nurse Assocs. and Practitioners, Cherry Hill, N.J., 1977-83; asst. prof., co-coord. community health nursing U. N.D., Grand Forks, 1980; vol. epidemiologist, pub. health specialist Vinh Children's Hosp., Vinh City, Vietnam, 1989; pediatric staff nurse I U. Fla. Pediatric Svc., Shands Teaching Hosp., Gainesville, 1970; instr. pediatric nursing U. Utah Coll. Nursing, Salt Lake City, 1976-77; pvt. cons. Internat. Cmty. Health and Epidemiology, New Haven, 1990-94; med. supr., health svcs. mgr. Brown & Root Logcap Med. Clinic, Port-au-Prince, Haiti, 1994-95; med. tech. proposal cons. UN, Rwanda, Angola, 1995; specialist Home Health Care, Tampa, Fla., 1996—; vol. pub. health scientist, cons. Hanoi (Vietnam) Sch. Pub. Health; cons. epidemiologist Vinh and Huong Son, Vietnam, 1993; internat. edn. cons. U. Am., New Orleans, 1994. Contbg. editor Episource, 1991, Resources in Epidemiology; contbr. articles to profl. jours.; contbr. to poetry jours. Capt. Nurse Corps, U.S. Army, 1968-73, Vietnam. Recipient Cert. of Achievement in HIV-AIDS Edn., AIDS Project, New Haven, Conn., 1994. Fellow Royal Soc. Tropical Medicine and Hygiene (London), Am. Biog. Inst.; mem. AMA, VFW, Am. Legion, Vietnam Vets. Am., Nat. Assn. Pediatric Nurse Assocs. and Practitioners (com. dir. graphics & logos mil. chpt., former chmn. nat. art and exhibits subcom., former mem. pub. rels. com., Cert. Recognition 1983), Am. Pub. Health Assn. (epidemiology sect., internat. healthsect.), Fla. Pub. Health Assn., Nat. Adolescent Health Promotion Network, Assn. Mil. Surgeons U.S., Ret. Army Nurse Corps Assn., Liverpool Tropical Sch. Assn. (Eng.), Assn. Yale Alumni in Pub. Health, Consortium for Internat. Nursing Edn., Rsch. & Practice, U.S.-Vietnam Friendship Assn., Doctorate Assn. N.Y. Educators, Fleet Marine Force Corpsman Assn. (former Conn. rep., charter mem.), U.S. Navy Corpsmen United Assn., Am. Assn. Navy Hosp. Corpsmen, U.S. Army (Vietnam) 24th Evacuation Hosp. Assn. (com. asv. reunion 1993), Vets. Vietnam Restoration Project, U.S. Com. Scientific Cooperation with Vietnam, N.Y. Acad. of Sci., Sigma Xi, Sigma Theta Tau (charter mem. Gamma Rho chpt.), Phi Kappa Phi. Home: 11333 Calgary Cir Tampa FL 33624-4804

JACOBSON, CHARLES ALLEN, aerospace company executive; b. Cresco, Iowa, June 2, 1925; s. Julius and Beulah Rosella (Peterson) J.; m. Marjorie Helen Minear, June 18, 1947; children: Janelle Paige, Charles Allen Jr., Robert Roger, Julian Kent, Joan Leigh. BS in Aerospace Engring., Iowa State U., 1952; postgrad., St. Louis U., 1956-57. Engr. McDonnell Aircraft Corp., St. Louis, 1952-59, group engr., 1959-64, project dynamics engr., 1964-68; dir. Houston ops. McDonnell Douglas Astronautics Co., 1968-84; v.p., gen. mgr. McDonnell Douglas Tech. Svcs. Co., Huntsville, Ala., 1984-85, McDonnell Douglas Space Systems Co., Houston, 1985-90; pres. GB Tech., Inc., Houston, 1990—; bd. dirs. M Bank, Clear Lake, Houston; mem. NASA Johnson Space Ctr. Team Excellence Forum; mem. devel. and adv. coun. U. Houston at Clear Lake, 1987-90; mem. Engring Found. adv. coun., U. Tex., Austin, 1989—; pres. Clear Lake Transp. Partnership, Houston, 1990—. Dir. Rotary Nat. Award for Space Achievement, Houston, 1984—; dir. Clear Lake Area Econ. Devel. Found., Houston, 1983-84, 86-89, Clear Lake Symphony, Houston, 1987-89; chmn. Bay Area YMCA, Houston, 1981-82; mem. hon. bd. March of Dimes Walk Am., Houston, 1980; vice chmn. fin. Boy Scouts Am. Baysmore dist., 1987-89; adv. dir. Clear Lake Coun. Tech. Socs., 1989—; vice chmn. aerospace Houston area US Savs. Bonds Campaign, 1988. Lt. cmmdr. USNR, 1943-67. Recipient NASA Pub. Svc. medal, 1981, Profl. Achievement Citation for Engring., Iowa State U., Ames, 1988; named Tech. Adminstr. of Yr., Clear Lake Coun. Tech. Socs., 1984; Rotary Internat. Paul Harris fellow, 1983. Fellow AIAA (assoc., Gemini Achievement award 1966); mem. Armed Forces Comms. and Electronics Assn. (bd. dirs. 1987-89), Nat. Contract Mgmt. Assn., Navy League, South Shore Harbor Country Club (bd. dirs. 1987-89), Space Ctr. Rotary (pres. 1982-83). Republican. Home: 2908 Doral Ct League City TX 77573-4412 Office: GB Tech Inc 2200 Space Park Dr Ste 400 Houston TX 77058-3680

JACOBSON, ERIC SHELDON, internist, infectious diseases physician; b. Phila., Dec. 30, 1941; married; 3 children. BS, Stanford U., 1963; MD, U. Wis., 1970, PhD in Physiol. Chemistry, 1973. Diplomate Am. Bd. Internal Medicine. Intern U. Colo. Med. Ctr., Denver, 1970-71; resident Providence Med. Ctr., Portland, Oreg., 1973-75; fellow Barnes Hosp. and Washington U., St. Louis, 1975-77; staff physician McGuire Vets. Affairs Med. Ctr., 1977—; asst. prof. medicine div. infectious diseases Med. Coll. Va., Richmond, 1977-84, assoc. prof. medicine div. infectious diseases, 1984-95; prof. medicine divsn. infectious diseases McGuire Vets. Affairs Med. Ctr., 1995—, coord. non-house staff svc., 1990—; chmn. infection control com. McGuire VA Med. Ctr., 1978-83, mem. pharmacy and therapeutics com., 1978-83, mem. R&D com., 1981—, mem. utilization rev. com., 1988-92; mem. pub. adv. bd. NIH Bacteriology and Mycology II Study Sect., NIH AIDS-Related Infections Study Sect., VA Dept. Infectious Disease Merit Rev. Bd. Contbr. articles to profl. jours. Recipient GM scholarship, 1959-63, Hon. Nat. Merit scholarship, 1959-63, NSF fellowship, 1963-664, Rsch. Hons. scholarship U. Wis. Med. Sch., 1963-70, Am. Cancer Soc. scholarship, 1965-70, NIH Rsch. Svc. fellowship, 1976-77, NIH Ind. Extramura Rsch. grant, 1979-82, 85-88; Vet. Affairs Merit Rev. Rsch. grantee, 1977-88, 90—. Mem. Am. Soc. Microbiology, Am. Fedn. Clin. Rsch., Infectious Diseases Soc. Am., Internat. Soc. for Human and Animal Mycology, Richmond Acad. Medicine. Home: 1006 W 43rd St Richmond VA 23225-4615 Office: McGuire VA Hosp Box 111-C 1201 Broad Rock Blvd Richmond VA 23249-0001

JACOBSON, GERALDINE MEERBOTT, radiation oncologist; b. Ft. Dix, N.J., July 11, 1950; d. Joseph Otto and Jeanne Adele (Bonnabeau) Meerbott; m. Marcus Jacobson, Mar. 25, 1975 (div. Jan. 1987); 1 child, Justin; m. Patrick R.M. Thomas, Mar. 2, 1996. BS with high honors, Mich. State U., 1972; postgrad., U. South Fla., 1975-76, U. Miami, 1976-77; MD, U. Utah, 1981. Diplomat Am. Bd. Radiology, Nat. Med. Examiners. Intern in pathology U. Utah Med. Sch., Salt Lake City, 1981-82; resident Radiation Therapy Ctr., LDS Hosp., Salt Lake City, 1982-85; vis. resident in radiation therapy Princess Margaret Hosp., Toronto, Can., 1984; instr. Divsn. Radiation Oncology, Dept. Radiology U. Utah Med. Ctr., Toronto, 1985-87; dir. radiation therapy RTOC, Brooksville, Fla., 1987-89; asst. prof., asst. dir. clin. rsch. dept. radiation therapy U. Tex. Med. Br., Galveston, 1989-90; radiation oncologist Lykes Ctr. for Radiation Therapy, Morton Plant Hosp., Clearwater, Fla., 1990-92; med. dir. Bayfront Cancer Care Ctr., St. Petersburg, Fla., 1992—; oncology com. Bayfront Med. Ctr., 1992—, radiation safet com., 1992—, rsch. and rev. com., 1994—; radiation therapy tech. adv. com. HCC, 1993—; mediation com. Pinellas County Med. Soc., 1990—; presenter in field. Contbr. articles to profl. jours. Bd. dirs. WMNF Community Radio, Tampa, Fla., 1993—. Clin. fellowship Am. Cancer Soc., 1984-85. Mem. AMA, Am. Soc. Therapeutic Radiology and Oncology, Radiol. Soc. N.Am., Am. Soc. Clin. Oncology, Am. Coll. Radiology, Am. Assn. Women Radiologists, Gyn Oncology Group, Radiation Therapy Oncology Group. Office: Bayfront Cancer Care Ctr 701 6th St S Saint Petersburg FL 33701-4814

JACOBSON, HELEN GUGENHEIM (MRS. DAVID JACOBSON), civic worker; b. San Antonio; d. Jac Elton and Rosetta (Dreyfus) Gugenheim; m. David Jacobson, Nov. 6, 1938; children: Liz Helenchild, Dottie J. Miller. BA, Hollins Coll. With news and spl. events staff NBC, N.Y.C., 1933-38. 1st v.p. San Antonio, Bexar County coun. Girl Scouts U.S.A., 1957-63; Tex. State rep. UNICEF, 1964-69; bd. dirs. U.S. com. UNICEF, 1970-80, hon. bd. dirs., 1980—; bd. dirs. Nat. Fedn. Temple Sisterhoods, 1973-77, Temple Beth-El Sisterhood, Youth Alternatives, Inc.; bd. dirs. Child Guidance Ctr., chmn. bd., 1960-63; bd. dirs. Sunshine Cottage Sch. for Deaf Children, chmn. bd., 1952-54; pres. Cmty Welfare Coun., 1968-70; pres. bd. trustees San Antonio Pub. Libr., 1957-61; trustee Nat. Coun. Crime and Delinquency, 1964-70, San Antonio Mus. Assn., 1964-73; bd. dirs. Cancer Therapy and Rsch. Found. South Tex., 1977—, sec., 1977-83; pres. S.W. region Tex. Coalition for Juvenile Justice, 1977-79; chmn. Mayor's Commn. on Status of Women, 1972-74; del. White House Conf. on Children, 1970; mem. Commn. on Social Action of Reform Judaism, 1973-77; chmn. Foster Grandparent project Bexar County Hosp. Dist., 1968-69; sec. Nat. Assembly for Social Policy and Devel., 1969-74; pres. women's com. Ecumenical Ctr. for Religion and Health, 1975-77; chmn. criminal justice planning com. Alamo Area Coun. of Govts., chmn., 1975-77, 1987-88; mem. Tex. Internat. Women's Yr. Coordinating Com., 1977; co-chmn. San Antonio chpt. NCCJ, 1980-84; chmn. United Negro Coll. Fund Campaign, 1983, 84; sec. nat. bd. Avance, Inc., 1991-93; trustee Target 90/Goals for San Antonio, 1986-90; hon. mem. bd. dirs. Witte Mus., 1994—. Recipient Headliner award for civic work San Antonio chpt. Women in Communications, 1958, Nat. Humanitarian award B'nai B'rith, 1975, City of Peace award, 1991; named Vol. Woman of Yr. Express-News, 1959, Spl. Svc. award Tex. Soc. Psychiat. Physicians, 1994; honoree San Antonio chpt. NCCJ, 1970, Nat. Jewish Hosp., 1978; inductee San Antonio Women's Hall of Fame, 1986, others. Mem. Nat. Coun. Jewish Women (Hannah G. Solomon award 1979), Internat. Women's Forum, San Antonio 100, Argyle Club. Home: 207 Beechwood Ln San Antonio TX 78216-7345

JACOBSON, JAMES LAMMA, JR., data processing company executive; b. Washington, May 19, 1946; s. James Lamma Jacobson Sr. and Hazel Virginia (Howard) Jacobson Tatelman; m. Dayle Barbara Jackson, Dec. 30, 1972; children: Julie, Christie, Jennie. BBA, Drexel U., 1969. Systems engr. IBM Corp., Arlington, Va., 1969-70, mktg. rep., 1970-74; mktg. instr. IBM Corp., Atlanta, 1975-76; mktg. mgr. IBM Corp., Akron, Ohio, 1977-79; founder, pres. Jacore Techs., Inc., Atlanta, 1979-84, chmn., 1985—; exec. cons. Mainline Info. Systems, Tallahassee, 1991-92; pres. Jacobson & Horne, Inc., Tallahassee, 1992—; chmn. JSS Enterprises, 1996—; chmn. JSS Enterprises, 1996—. Chmn. Vida Nueva of North Fla.; pres. Faith Chapel. Mem. Ch. of God. Home and Office: Jacobson & Horne Inc 116 Eastern Ave Augusta ME 04330-5840

JACOBSON, JERRY IRVING, biophysicist, theoretical physicist; b. Bklyn., Jan. 25, 1946; s. Saul Lane and Miriam (Cassin) J.; m. Debra Maria Delso, Aug. 18, 1975; children: Solomon, Jacqueline, Faith, Maria. BA,

Bklyn. Coll., 1963-66; DDS, DMD, Temple U., 1970; PhD, CUNY, 1983. Oral surgeon Tremont Med. Group, Bronx, N.Y., 1972-73, University Ave. Med. Group, Bronx, N.Y., 1973-77; pvt. practice Westchester and New City, N.Y., 1972-82; pres. Perspectivism Found., Jupiter, Fla., 1980—, Inst. Theoretical Physics & Advanced Studies for Biophys., Jupiter, 1985—, Alzheimers Rsch. Found., Jupiter, 1990—, Jacobson Resonance Inc., Jupiter, 1991—, Magneto Therapeutics Mfg., Inc., 1994—, Jacobson Resonance Machines Inc., 1995—; prof. rsch., dir. microgravity and electromagnetics Inst. Molecular Medicine, U. Calif., Irvine, 1996; CEO, pres. Pioneer Svcs. Internat., Ltd.; founding bd. dirs. dept. microgravity and bioelectromagnetics rsch. Inst. Molecular Medicine, Irvine, prof. rsch.; spkr. in field. Contbr. articles to profl. jours.; holder med. and plasma physics and dental patents in U.S. and 80 other countries. Served to capt. Army Dental Corps, 1970-72. Mem. Am. Phys. Soc., Bioelectromagnetics Soc., European Bioelectromagnetics Soc., Italian Assn. Biomed. Physics, Internat. Assn. Biologically Closed Electric Circuits (mem. internat. adv. bd.). Home and Office: 2006 Mainsail Cir Jupiter FL 33477-1418

JACOBSON, PETER LARS, neurologist, educator; b. Englewood, N.J., Feb. 17, 1951; s. George Pershing and Mona (Friedman) J.; m. Karen Joy Frenkel, June 11, 1972; children: Kersten Jenny, Lars Edward II. BA summa cum laude, Princeton U., 1973; MD, Washington U., 1977. Chief resident in neurology U. N.C. Hosp., Chapel Hill, 1980-81; fellow in electroencephalography Mayo Clinic, Rochester, Minn., 1981-82; pres. Pinehurst (N.C.) Neurology, P.A., 1982—; clin. prof. neurology U. N.C., Chapel Hill, 1982—, adj. prof. journalism, 1990—; chmn. dept. neurology Moore Regional Hosp., Pinehurst, 1985-87. Columnist The Pilot, 1989—. Trustee The O'Neal Sch., Southern Pines, N.C., 1992—. Recipient Lange Med. Book prize Washington U., 1976, Samson F. Wennerman award in surgery, 1977, Cert. of Appreciation, State of N.C., 1987; Mosby scholar, 1977. Fellow Am. Acad. Neurology, Am. EEG Soc.; mem. N.C. Neurol. Soc. (pres. 1990-91), Am. Med. Writers Assn., Alpha Omega Alpha, Phi Beta Kappa. Office: Carolina Headache & Pain Ctr PA PO Box 37 Pinehurst NC 28374

JACOBSON, ROBERT ARTHUR, management consulting executive; b. Chgo., Nov. 28, 1949; s. John George and Shirley Virginia (Clemensen) J. AS with honors, Chgo. City Coll., 1969; BS, N.Mex. Highlands U., 1972, MS, 1974. Cert. master productivity specialist. Staff mem. Integrated Control Systems, Inc., Punta Gorda, Fla., 1974-77, project dir., 1977-82, unit v.p., 1982-85, European chief of ops., 1985-86, N.Am. chief of ops., 1986-88, worldwide chief of ops., 1988—. Co-author: Colorado Region 9 Economic Inventory and Data Base, 1973. Fellow Western Interstate Commn. for Higher Edn., 1973. Mem. Assn. Productivity Specialists (chmn. bd. dirs. 1987—), Paducah (Ky., hon. citizen 1971), Sigma Alpha Epsilon. Home: 3750 N Lake Shore Dr Chicago IL 60613-4238 Office: Integrated Control Systems 900 W Marion Ave Punta Gorda FL 33950-5308

JACOBY, PETER FREDRICKSON, music educator; b. Laramie, Wyo., July 27, 1947; s. Glenn J. and Dorothy (Fredrickson) J.; m. Margaret E. Judd, Mar. 5, 1973 (div. 1983). BA in Music magna cum laude, U. Wyo., 1969; Diploma, U. Vienna Acad. Music, Austria, 1975. Opera coach Zurich Opera House, Switzerland, 1975-76; gen. ptnr. E.L. Price Assoc., San Francisco and Chgo., 1976-78; exec. dir. The Prelude Co., San Francisco, 1978-80; pres., chief exec. officer Bighorn Energy Co., Ft. Collins, Colo., 1980—; exec. v.p. Newcomb Securities Co., N.Y.C., 1981-84; sr. mgr. E.L. Price Bank, Galveston, Tex., 1983-87; pres., chief exec. officer Code A Check, Inc., Cheyenne, Wyo., 1988-89; prof., Moore Sch. Music U. Houston, 1989—. Bd. dirs. Van Ness Arts Ctr., San Francisco, 1978-79, Ft. Collins Art Inc., 1981-82. Sgt. U.S. Army, 1969-71. Republican. Episcopalian. Home: 938 Cortlandt Houston TX 77008 Office: U Houston Moores Sch Music Houston TX 77204-4893

JADLOW, JOSEPH MARTIN, economics educator; b. Nevada, Mo., Oct. 27, 1942; s. Joseph Martin and Polly Jene (Yancey) J.; m. Janice Lynn Wickstead; children: Joanna, Jennifer. BA, Cen. Mo. State, 1964, MA, 1965; PhD, U. Va., 1970. Asst. prof. Okla. State U., Stillwater, 1968-72, assoc. prof., 1972-76, prof. econs., 1976—, head dept. econs., 1993—; cons. numerous law firms. Contbr. articles to profl. jours. Mem. Am. Econ. Assn., So. Econ. Assn. (sec.-treas. 1977—), Lions (pres. 1991-92, bd. dirs. 1985-93). Republican. Methodist. Avocations: sports, jogging. Office: Coll Bus Adminstrn Okla State U Stillwater OK 74078

JAEGER, MARC JULIUS, physiology educator, researcher; b. Berne, Switzerland, Apr. 4, 1929; came to U.S., 1970; s. Francis K. and Jeanne (Perrin) J.; m. Frances Dick, Dec. 1960 (div. 1972); children: Dominic, Olivia; m. Ina Claire Burlingham-Forbes, June 23, 1973. BA, Gymnasium, Berne, 1948; MD, U. Berne, 1954. Diplomate Swiss Bd. Pulmonary Diseases. Resident U. Hosp. of Berne, 1954-63; asst. prof. U. Fribourg, Switzerland, 1963-69; assoc. prof. Coll. of Medicine U. Fla., Gainesville, 1970-76, prof. Coll. of Medicine, 1976—. Contbr. over 50 articles to profl. jours. Democrat. Home: 5915 SW 36 Way Gainesville FL 32608 Office: U Fla Coll of Medicine Gainesville FL 32610

JAEGER, RICHARD CHARLES, electrical engineer, educator, science center director; b. N.Y.C., Sept. 2, 1944; s. O. Fred and Mary Jane (Shatzer) J.; m. Joan Carol Hill, Dec. 28, 1964; children: Peter, Stephanie. BSEE with high honors, U. Fla., 1966, M in Engineering, 1966, PhDEE, 1969. Staff engr. IBM Corp., Boca Raton, Fla., 1969-72, adv. engr., 1972-74, 77-79; rsch. staff mem. IBM Corp., Yorktown Heights, N.Y., 1974-76; assoc. prof. Auburn (Ala.) U., 1979-82, prof. elec. engring. dept., 1982-90, alumni prof., 1983-88, disting. univ. prof., 1990—; dir. Ala. Microelectronics Ctr., Auburn, 1984—; mem. program com. Internat. Solid State Circuits Conf., San Francisco and N.Y.C., 1978-93, program vice chmn., 1992, program chmn., 1993; program co-chmn. Internat. VLSI Cirs. Symposium, Kyoto, Japan, 1988-89, conf. co-chmn., Honolulu, 1990; cons. IBM, InSouth, Digital Equipment corp., Control Data Corp. Author: Introduction to Microelectronic Fabrication, 1988, Microelectric Circuit Design, 1997; editor: IEEE Jour. Solid State Cirs., 1995—, Microelectronic Circuit Design, 1997; contbr. more than 175 tech. papers to profl. jours.; patentee in field. Grantee NSF, Semicondr. Rsch. Corp., Dept. Def., Ala. Rsch. Inst., 1979—. Fellow IEEE; mem. Solid State Cirs. Coun. IEEE (pres. 1990-91, v.p. 1988-89, sec. 1984-87), Computer Soc. IEEE (bd. govs. 1985-86, Outstanding Contbn. award 1984). Home: 711 Jennifer Dr Auburn AL 36830-7116 Office: Auburn U Ala Microelectronics Ctr 420 Broun Hall Auburn AL 36849-5201

JAENISCH, HOLGER MARCEL, physicist; b. Salt Lake City, Apr. 22, 1963; s. Klaus Peter Reinhardt and Sieglinde Erika (Freimann) J.; m. Theresa Lynn Snyder, May 24, 1985; children: Falco Alexander, Marcel Fabry, Marcus Antone. MS, Columbia Pacific U., 1989, PhD, 1990. Teaching asst. U. Utah Physics Dept., Salt Lake City, 1979-82; laser engr. Com Tel Inc., Salt Lake City, 1982-85; sr. engr. Odetics Inc., Anaheim, Calif., 1985-88; sr. optical engr. Talandic Rsch. Corp., Irwindale, Calif., 1988-89; sr. rsch. assoc. NASA MSFC, Huntsville, Ala., 1989-90, UAH Ctr. Applied Optics, Huntsville, Ala., 1990-91; sr. scientist Nichols Rsch. Corp., Huntsville, Ala., 1991-92; sr. scientist Tec-Masters Inc., Huntsville, 1992—, program mgr. of level 13 and theater high altitude area defense (THAAD) seeker modeling for (THAAD) ind. validation & verification, 1994—; assoc. prof. So. Calif. U., West Coast U., U. Ala., Huntsville; pres. Licht Strahl Engring., Madison, Ala., 1989—. Author: Genesis II: Chaos/Fractals, 1989, Laser Analogy Using Video Feedback, 1990; contbr. tech. papers to publs. Founder enterprise squadron U.S. CAP, Salt Lake City; bd. dirs. Huntsville Sr. Citizen Ctr., 1992. Recipient U.S. Army Medal for Excellence in Sci., Harvey Eckenrode award South Eastern Simulation Conf., 1992, 93, Best Paper award, 1994, 95. Mem. IEEE, SPIE, OSA, Astron. League, U.S. Parachute Assn. (instr., Profl. Assn. Diving Instrs. diver, dive master, Cross Country award), Masons, Shriners, Scottish Rite. Independent. Home: 135 Dexter Cir Madison AL 35758-9545 Office: Tec-Masters Inc 1500 Perimeter Pky NW Huntsville AL 35806-3520

JAFFE, JEFF HUGH, retired food products executive; b. Washington, Dec. 25, 1920; s. Henry A. Jaffe and Mildred (Loewenberg) Auslander; m. Natalie Rubin, Dec. 31, 1945; children: Bonita Jaffe Berens, Holly Anne. BS in Archtl. Engring., Va. Poly. Inst. and State U., 1943. Chmn. bd. dirs., pres. The Chunky Corp. (name changed to Ward Foods, Inc.), 1950-67; pres., chief exec. officer The Chunky Corp. (name changed to Ward Candy Inc.), 1967-69; pres., chief exec. officer Candy, Chocolate and Biscuit Group Ward Foods Inc., 1969-71, pres., chief operating officer, 1971-72; chmn. bd. dirs., chief exec. officer The Chunky Corp. (name changed to Ward Foods, Inc.), 1972-73; chmn. bd. dirs., pres. Schutter Candy Co., 1958-67, Klotz Confection Co., 1960-67; pres., chief exec. officer The Schrafft Candy Co., 1974-78; v.p. consumer products group Gulf and Western Industries, 1974-78; pres., chief exec. officer Bernan Foods, Inc., 1980-85, retired, 1985; past bd. dirs. Creative Output, Inc.; bd. dirs. Community Nat. Bank of S.I., N.Y., Ward Foods, Inc., Ward Candy Co., Oxford Energy Co. Bd. dirs. Young Pres.'s Orgn., Woodmere Acad., Village Hewlett Bay Park (past chmn. and pres.). Mem. Assn. Mfrs. of Confectionery and Chocolate, Candy Execs. Club, Property Owners Assn. (Sailfish Point, Fla., chmn. transition com., chmn. emeritus, CEO). Home: 6500 SE Harbor Cir Stuart FL 34996-1952

JAFFE, RICHARD PAUL, corporate executive, lawyer; b. New Haven, May 20, 1946; s. Samuel A. and Frances Diane (Molstein) J.; grad. The Choate Sch., 1963; B.A., Tufts U., 1968; M.B.A., Columbia U., 1971; J.D., Boston U., 1974; m. Jeanne Ellis, Aug. 18, 1968; children—Suzanne, Samuel Abraham. Bar: Mass. 1974, U.S. Dist. Ct. Mass., 1975, U.S. Tax Ct., 1975; assoc. law firm Arabian, Brankey, Chopelas and Eizman, Boston, 1975-78; ptnr., Arabian, Brankey, Jaffe & Kennedy, Boston, 1978-81; pres. The Jaffe Cos., Daytona Beach, Fla. and Boston, 1981—; instr. bus. adminstrn. Boston U., 1978-79. Mass. seminar leader The Problems of Drugs and Narcotics, 1967-70; guest speaker Govs' Conf. on Drug Dependency, Boston, 1968; del. N.H. Lakes Preservation Assn., 1978-80. Mem. ABA, Internat. Conf. Shopping Centers, Nat. Assn. Home Builders. Office: 1500 Beville Rd Daytona Beach FL 32114-5643

JAFFE, SANDRA MICHELLE, special education educator; b. El Paso, Tex., Oct. 6, 1966; d. Stanley Harris and Rhoda (Rosenfield) J. BS in Edn., U. Tex., 1990. Lic. cosmetologist, 1985; cert. generic spl. edn. K-12, regular edn. K-8, 3rd grade tchr. ESL, mediator for cts. With domestics dept. K-Mart, El Paso, 1980-85; waitress Carros, El Paso, summer 1986, Fed. Junction, Denver, 1986-87; cocktail waitress Meili Chinese Restaurant, El Paso, summer 1987; vol. Austin (Tex.) Ind. Sch. Dist., 1988-90, student tchr., substitute tchr., 1990; tchr. spl. edn. Garland (Tex.) Schs., 1990—; substitute tchr. Dallas Ind. Sch. Dist., 1990-91; tchr. spl. edn., mentally retarded/learning disabilities/emotionally disabled, Dallas, 1991-94; tchr., tutor Exemplary Ctr. for Instrn., Dallas, 1991-94. Tchr., trainer, vol. Spl. Olympics, 1993-94; vol. CHAMPS (Children Have and Model Positive Peer Skills), 1994, El Paso Pub. Schs., 1981-82. Recipient Student medals Spl. Olympics, 1993. Mem. NEA, Vocat. Indsl. Clubs Am., Tex. Edn. Assn., Texas Exes (life), Classroom Tchrs. Dallas, Coun. for Exceptional Children, Tex. State Tchrs. Assn. Democrat. Jewish. Home: 2021 Via Corona Carrollton TX 75006-4614 Office: 6929 Town North Dr Dallas TX 75231-8117

JAFFE, STEPHEN ABRAM, composer, music educator; b. Washington, Dec. 30, 1954; s. Howard W. and Elizabeth (Boudreau) J.; m. Mindy Oshrain, May 29, 1988; children: Anna Aliza, Elana Felice. AB, U. Pa., 1977, AM, 1978; postgrad., Conservatoire de Musique, Geneva. Teaching fellow U. Pa., Phila., N.C., 1977; composer, pianist, condr., 1978—; from lectr. to instr. Swarthmore (Pa.) Coll., 1979, 86; asst. prof. Duke U., Durham, N.C., 1981-88, assoc. prof., 1988—, dir. grad. studies, 1991-93, chmn., 1993-96; part-time assoc. Moravian Coll., Bethlehem, Pa., 1978; dir. Encounters with the Music of Our Time, Duke U., Durham, 1981—. Composer: (orch. work) Four Images, 1983, (chamber orch. work) Concerto "Singing Figures" for Oboe and Ensemble, 1994, (string quartet work) First Quartet, 1991, (vocal work) Pedal Point for Baritone and a Consort of Low Instruments, 1994, Songs of Turning (chorus and orchestra), 1996. Recipient Brandeis U. Creative Arts citation, 1989, Rome prize Am. Acad. in Rome, 1981, Kennedy Ctr. Friedham award J.F.K. Ctr. for Performing Arts, 1991, Am. Acad. Arts and Letters prize, 1993; Guggenheim Found. fellow, 1983. Mem. BMI (affiliate), Chamber Music Am. Address: PO Box 90665 Durham NC 27708-0665 Office: Duke U Dept Music 6695 College Station Durham NC 27707 also: Theodore Presser Co Bryn Mawr PA 19010

JAGANNATH, SUNDAR, physician, educator; b. Golden Rock, India, Nov. 11, 1951; came to U.S., 1977; s. Manjula Samy; 3 children. MD, Maharaja Sayajirao U., Baroda, India, 1974, Maharaja Sayajirao U., Baroda, India. Diplomate Am. Bd. Internal Medicine. Rotating intern Sri Sayaji Gen. Hosp., Baroda, 1975, resident in internal medicine, 1976; resident in internal medicine Bronx (N.Y.)-Lebanon Hosp. Ctr., 1977-79, Harper-Grace Hosp., Wayne State U., Detroit, 1979-80; fellow in med. oncology U. Tex.-M.D. Anderson Hosp. and Tumor Inst., Houston, 1980-82; asst. internist, clin. instr. U. Tex.-M.D. Anderson Cancer Ctr., Houston, 1982-84; asst. prof. clin. medicine U. Tex. SCC-M.D. Anderson Hosp. and Tumor Inst., Houston, 1984-87; asst. prof. medicine U. Tex.-M.D. Anderson Cancer Ctr., Houston, 1987-89, assoc. internist, 1988-89; assoc. prof. U. Ark for Med. Scis., Little Rock, 1989-93, assof. prof. pathology, 1990-93, chief bone marrow transplantation, 1989—, prof. medicine and pathology, 1993—. Contbr. or co-contbr. articles to med. jours. Fellow ACP; mem. Am. Soc. Clin. Oncology, Am. Soc. Hematology. Office: Univ Ark for Med Scis 4301 W Markham Slot # 508 Little Rock AR 72205

JAGGERS, STEVEN BRYAN, minister; b. Frankfort, Ind., Mar. 7, 1962; s. Winston Churchill and Karen Sue (Hitch) J. BA, Purde U., 1984; BA summa cum laude, Tenn. Bible Coll., Cookeville, 1988, MA summa cum laude, 1991. Youth minister Sycamore Ch. of Christ, Cookeville, 1985-87, Monterey Ch. of Christ, Cookeville, 1987-88; assoc./youth minister Livingston (Tenn.) Ch. of Christ, 1988-95; minister West Side Ch. of Christ, Yorktown, Ind., 1995—. Author/illustrator: (books) God, Are You Really Up There?, 1989, Tell Me About Jesus Church, 1990, What Must I Do To Be Saved?, 1990, Creation or Evolution: What's the Big Deal?, 1991, Does the Bible Really Have the Answer to Today's Questions, 1991, Who is Jesus, 1992, What Does My Friend's Church Believe?, 1992, Three in One: Father Son and Holy Spirit, 1993, Why Can't I Be Happy?, 1993, Which Way to Heaven?, 1994; author: Christian Science: From God or Man?, 1991, A Ready Reference Dictionary of Non-Christian Religions, 1988. Named to Outstanding Young Men of Am., 1985. Mem. Rotary. Home: 8400 W Ashford Ln Muncie IN 47304 Office: West Side Church of Christ PO Box 265 Yorktown IN 47396

JAGOE, KEVIN DEAN, musician; b. El Paso, Tex., June 9, 1959; s. John Henry Jagoe Jr. and Grace Colleen (Murphy) Klement. BA, Southwestern at Memphis, 1981; MM in Music Edn., U. Tex., 1983; grad. performance diploma, St. Louis Conservatory, 1987-89; postgrad., Tex. Tech. U., 1991—. Cert. tchr. Tex. Strings program dir., tchr. grades 6-12 Marshall (Tex.) Ind. Sch. Dist., 1983-85; orch. dir. grades 6-12 Victoria (Tex.) Ind. Sch. Dist., 1986-87; interim orch. dir. Ctrl. Visual and Performing Arts H.S., St. Louis Pub. Schs., 1989; instr. of music Maryville U., fall 1991. Viola performer, composer numerous orchs. Garden cons., designer 21st St. Garden, Heart of Lubbock, 1996, parliamentarian and newsletter editor South Overton Residential and Cmml. Assn., 1994—; garden coord. South Overton Cmty. Garden, 1995; adv. com. Tex. Tech. U., U. Ctr. for Food Svc., 1991—; garden rep. Lubbock Green, 1995; mem. Trinity Episcopal Ch., St. Louis, 1990—; precinct delegate Lubbock County Rep. Conventions, 1992, 96; vestry mem., jr. warden, lay reader Alter Guild Mem. at Ch. of the Holy Communion, St. Louis, 1987-90; stage technician Marhsall Jr. High PTA, 1985; usher U. of Tex. Performing Art Ctr. Scholarship St. Louis Conservatory of Music; Southwestern grant; Southwestern Scholar award. Mem. Am. Cmty Gardening Assn. (conv. scholarship 1995), Nat. Arbor Day Found., Nat. Audobon Soc., Nat. Cathedral Assn., Nat. Trust for Historic Preservation, Smithsonian Assn., Am. String Tchrs. Assn., Am. Viola Soc., Mid-West Internat. Band and Orch. Clinic, Tex. Composers Forum, Tex. Music Educators Assn., Tex. Orch. Dirs. Assn., Phi Kappa Lambda, Kappa Sigma. Episcopalian. Home: 1993 Crescent Dr Las Cruces NM 88005

JAHADI, MOHAMMAD REZA, surgeon; b. Khorramshahr, Iran, Dec. 31, 1936; Naturalization Houston, Tex., 1980.; m. Parichehr Cheri Golshan; children: Kambiz, Kamran, Catherine. MD, Pahlavi U., Shiraz, Iran, 1966. Diplomate Am. Bd. of Colon and Rectal Surgery. Intern Meml. Hosp., Worcester, Mass., 1968-69, resident gen. surgery, 1969-71; resident gen. surgery Henry Ford Hosp., Detroit, 1971-73; resident fellow in colon and rectal surgery Baylor U. Med. Ctr., Dallas, 1973-75; pvt. practice, 1975—; attending staff, dept. surgery St. Mary's Hosp., Galveston, Tex., 1975—, chmn. dept. surgery, 1985-87; pres.-elect med. staff St. Mary's Hosp., Galveston, 1994-95, pres., 1996; v.p. Galveston Physician Svcs. Assn., 1992—; bd. dirs. Gulf Coast Ind. Practice Assn.; clin. instr. dept. surgery U. Tex., 1975-96, clin. asst. prof. dept. family medicine, 1978-85. Assoc. editor Worcester Med. News, 1970-71. Mem. exec. bd. Boy Scouts of Am., 1982—, Am. Heart Assn., 1987-91, pres.-elect, 1988-89, pres., 1989-90, Galvston Crime Stoppers, 1989-92; community advisor Jr. League, Galveston, 1989—. Recipient cert. Merit Southwestern Surgical Congress, 1974, Am. Coll. Surgeons, 1973; named Galveston Man of the Yr. for Edn. and Medicine Galveston Daily News, 1992, Disting. Svc. award Galveston Jaycees, 1981; recipient Unsung Hero award Galveston Daily News, 1992; named Admiral Tex. Navy State Gov. Mark White, 1981; named in his honor Reza Jahadi's Day Galveston Mayor and City Council, 1981. Fellow Am. Soc. Colon and Rectal Surgeons (edn. com. award for best paper, 1975, Am. Soc. Gastro Intestinal Endoscopy, Mid-West Soc. Colon and Rectal Surgeons, Baylor Soc. Colon and Rectal Surgeons, Gulf Coast Soc. Colon and Rectal Surgeons, Tex. Soc. Colon and Rectal Surgeons (pres. elect 1992-93, pres. 1993-94); mem. AMA (recognition awards, 1978, 81, 87), Galveston County Med. Soc. (exec. bd. 1981—, chmn. pub. rels., 1981—, v.p. 1981, 87, 88, pres. elect 1989, pres. 1990, outstanding dedication and svc. award, 1975-93), Tex. Med. Assn. (alternate del. 1985-87, del. 1988—, chmn. ref. com. 1989, 91, vice councilor 1990—, sec. 1992-93, v.p. dist. 8, 1988, pres. elect. 1989, pres. dist. 8, 1990, outstanding contribution award, 1991), Southern Med. Assn., Roy D. McClure Surgical Soc., Galveston Island Rotary (bd. dirs. 1977-81, v.p. 1978-79, pres. elect., 1979-80, pres. 1980-81, dist. 591 chmn. study exchange 1981-83, coord. internat. exchange 1981-83, dist gov. rep. 1981-90, chmn. dist conf. 1988, most outstanding new U.S. citizen award, 1980, voc. svcs. award dist. 591, 1981, outstanding rotarian of the year, 1985, 87, outstanding rotarian of the year dist. 591, 1981, significant achievement award dist. 591, 1981, role of fame award dist. 591, 1981, royal worthen award, 1987-88, Vernon Sheffield award, 1989), Rotary Internat. (asst. sgt. at arms, 1982, Paul Harris fellowship, 1981, 88), Galveston C. of C. (exec. bd. 1981-85, v.p. 1982, 83), Galveston Sunday Coffee Club, Galveston Knight of Momus, Galveston Tandum Club. Home: 7718 Beluche Dr Galveston TX 77551-1522 Office: Ste 922 200 University Blvd Galveston TX 77550

JAHN, STEVE CURTIS, small business owner; b. Mpls., Sept. 14, 1940; s. Don C. and Mary Ann (Gormley) J.; m. Carol L. Krafty, Sept. 27, 1991. MS, U. Minn., 1975. Cert. Master Auto Technician-Automotive Svc. Inst. Am. Dist. svc. rep. Chrysler Corp., Detroit, 1966-69; dir. automotive svc. Target Stores/Dayton Hudson, Mpls., 1969-75; pres. CellStar Inc., Mpls., 1975-88; owner Vacation Car Care, Marco Island, Fla., 1988—; bd. dirs. AA, Marco Island, sec., 1988-91, treas., 1991—. Chmn. archtl. com. Timbershore Home Owners Assn., Mpls., 1979-81. With USMC, 1958-63. Republican. Lutheran. Home and Office: Vacation Car Care 1232 Fruitland Ave Marco Island FL 33937-2820

JAKUS, STEPHANIE, writer, composer, musician, instructor; b. Melrose Park, Ill., Nov. 8, 1926; d. Victor and Anna (Yutelis) Novicky; div.; children: Aldie, Larry. MusB in Piano, Chgo. Musical Coll., 1950; MusM in Music Composition, Am. Conservatory Music, 1961; studied piano with Ruth Wilkins Tyer, Howard Wells, Margery Giles, Mollie Margolies, studied theory and composition with Rosseter G. Cole, Leo Sowerby, studied musicology with Hans Rosenwald. Journalist Garfield News and Austinite, Chgo., 1946; piano accompanist Stone Camryn Sch. of Dance, Chgo., 1947-50, Charlene Rose Sch. Dance, River Forest, Ill., 1951-54; co-prodr., dir. Backyard Frolics, River Forest, 1959-61; piano tchr. River Forest, 1947-75; journalist Oak Leaves, Oak Park, Ill., 1968-70; free lance writer Cherry Circle Mag., Chgo., 1970-75; freelance writer various mags., 1975—; mem. adv. coun. St. Paul Fed. Music Contests, Chgo., 1977-79. Author: Alone...Woman in Maturity, 1978, The Sick Society Part 1 - The Medical Profession, The Courtship of Mary Todd (play); composer musical: In the Park; composer various art songs, pop songs, vocal and theatrical songs, chamber music, orchestral music, piano theory, piano concerto, piano solos, arrangements for young piano students, four players at 1 piano, 2 pianos. Cub reporter UNO Conf., San Francisco, 1945; vol. Dem. Senators Adlai Stevenson, Ted Leverenz, River Forest, 1974, Dem. Senator Alan Cranston, Forest Park, 1983; v.p., dir. MacDowell Artists Assn., Oak Park, 1952-60; leader Com. to Join Triton Coll., River Forest, 1970; sec., treas. Soc. Am. Musicians, Chgo., 1975-80. Named 1st Place winner in piano Chgo. Tribune Music Festival, 1946, 1st Place winner for play on A. Lincoln, Ill. Sesquicentennial, 1968. Ecumenical Ch. Home and Office: # 104 800 N Lemon St Sarasota FL 34236

JAMAIL, JOSEPH DAHR, JR., lawyer; b. Houston, Oct. 19, 1925; s. Joseph Dahr and Marie (Anton) J.; m. Lillie Mae Hage, Aug. 28, 1949; children: Joseph Dahr III, Randall Hage, Robert Lee. B.A., U. Tex., 1950, J.D., 1953. Bar: Tex. 1952. Pvt. practice Houston; asst. dist. atty. Harris County, Tex., 1954-55; prof. tort law U. Tex., 1981. Contbr. articles to profl. jours. Served to sgt. USMCR, 1943-46. Fellow Internat. Acad. Law and Sci., Internat. Soc. Barristers, Internat. Acad. Trial Lawyers, Am. Coll. Trial Lawyers, Inner Circle of Advocates; mem. Am., Houston bar assns., Houston Jr. Bar (dir. 1954-55, treas. 1955-56, v.p. 1956-57, pres. 1957-58), State Bar Tex. (chmn. grievance com. 1963, chmn. town hall task force 1973-74), Tex. Assn. Plaintiff Attys. (dir. 1961-63), Joseph D. Jamail, Chair University of Texas Law School, Assn. Trial Lawyers Am., Am. Judicature Soc., Am. Bd. Trial Advocates, Lawyer-Pilot Bar Assn., Delta Theta Phi. Home: 3682 Willowick Rd Houston TX 77019-1114 Office: Jamail & Kolius 500 Dallas St Ste 3434 Houston TX 77002-4710

JAMES, ARTHUR PETTUS, economist, educator; b. Anniston, Ala., Jan. 31, 1949; Arthur Paul and Margaret Leverne (Totherow) J.; m. Jill Ann BostickM Aug. 16, 1986 (div. 1994). BA in Economics, Birmingham-So. Coll., 1971; MA, U. Ala., 1974; PhD, U. Mo., 1989. Asst. prof. Coll. Bus. and Commerce, Livingston (Ala.) U., 1974-75; instr. dept. econs. Jacksonville (Ala.) State U., 1975-77; rsch. asst. dept. econs. U. Mo., Columbia, 1977-79, tchg. asst., 1979-81; asst. prof. dept. econs. U. North Ala., 1982-86; asst. lectr. dept. econs. Tex. A&M U., College Station, 1987-89, dir. undergrad. honor programs in econs., 1989—, lectr. dept. econs., 1990-94; rsch. assoc. Ctr. for Econ. and Mgmt. Rsch. U. South Fla., Tampa, 1994—; instr. extension divsn. U. Mo., Columbia, 1980; adj. asst. prof. Columbia (Mo. Coll., 1980-82; vis. asst. prof. dept. econs. Tex A&M U., 1986-87. Contbr. articles to profl. jours. Mem. Nat. Acad. Econs. and Fin. Experts, Can. Regional Sci. Assn., Mo. Acad. Sci., Western Econs. Assn., Western Regional Sci. Assn., Nat. Tax Assn./Tax Inst. Am., Midsouth Acad. Econs. and Finance, So. Econ. Assn., Southwestern Social Sci. Assn. Methodist. Office: Tex A&M U 3403 BSN USF CEMR 4202 E Fowler Ave Tampa FL 33620-9900

JAMES, BARBARA WOODWARD, small business owner, interior designer, antique appraiser, consultant; b. Owensboro, Ky., Feb. 14, 1936; d. J.T. and Thelma (Newman) Woodward; m. William E. James, Feb. 19, 1951 (div. June 1953); 1 child, Keith Douglas. Vice pres., Fla. Containers Inc., Sebring, 1978-81; v.p. Libra Ltd., 1980-88, Barda Svcs. Inc., Tampa, Fla., 1981-87; v.p., gen. mgr., owner BJ's Lounge of Tampa, Inc., 1981-86; founder, owner Flamingo Bar and Grill, Clearwater, Fla., 1986-89, BJ's Lounge, Tampa, 1989-94, The Clique, 1994—, Fanny's, Inc., Tampa, Fla., 1995—, The Oasis, Tampa, Fla., 1996—, Corsair Lounge, 1996—. Democrat. Roman Catholic.

JAMES, CEOLA, lawyer, judge; b. Vicksburg, Miss., Dec. 17, 1947; d. Willis Jr. and Alean Ross; divorced; children: Chantrice Aleana, Jamaal. B, Jackson State U., 1967; JD, Miss. Coll., 1977. Tchr. English and French Hunter High Sch., Drew, Miss., 1968-70; law clk. Miss. Bar Legal Svcs., Vicksburg, Miss., 1974-76; staff atty. Ctrl. Miss. Legal Svcs., Vicksburg, 1976-77; pvt. practice Vicksburg, 1977—; spl. master judge Chancery Ct., Vicksburg, 1992—. Author: (poetry) Nine Days of Moody Weather, 1992. Mem. Phi Delta Psi, Alpha Kappa Alpha. Democrat. Baptist. Home: PO Box 1465 Vicksburg MS 39181-1465 Office: Ceola James Atty at Law 1216 East Ave Vicksburg MS 39180-3932

JAMES, EARL EUGENE, JR., aerospace engineering executive; b. Oklahoma City, Feb. 8, 1923; s. Earl Eugene and Mary Frances (Godwin) J.; m. Barbara Jane Marshall, Dec. 15, 1945 (dec. Feb. 2, 1982); children: Earl

Eugene III, Jeffrey Allan; m. Vanita L. Nix, Apr. 23, 1983. Student Oklahoma City U., 1940-41; BS, U. Okla., 1945; postgrad. Tex. Christian U., 1954-57; MS, So. Meth. U., 1961. Asst. mgr. Rialto Theatre, 1939-42; with Consol. Vultee Aircraft Co., San Diego, 1946-49; with Convair, Ft. Worth, 1949-89, group engr., 1955-57, test group engr., supr. fluid dynamics lab., 1957-81, engring. chief Fluid Dynamics Lab., 1981-89. Asst. dist. commr. Boy Scouts Am., 1958-59; adviser Jr. Achievement, 1962-63; mem. sch. bd. Castleberry Ind. Sch. Dist. (Tex.), 1969-83; chmn. bd. N.W. br. YMCA, 1971. Served to lt. (j.g.) USNR, 1942-46; PTO. Author/editor over 1000 engring. reports. Fellow AIAA (assoc.); mem. Air Force Assn. (life), U.S. Naval Inst. (assoc.), Gen. Dynamics Mgmt. Assn., Nat. Mgmt. Assn., Okla. U. Alumni Assn. (life), Tex. Congress Parents and Tchrs. (hon. life), Pi Kappa Alpha, Alpha Chi Sigma, Tau Omega. Methodist. Democrat. Clubs: Squaw Creek Golf, Camera. Lodge: Elks.

JAMES, FOB, JR. (FORREST HOOD JAMES), governor; b. Lanett, Ala., Sept. 15, 1934; s. Forrest Hood Sr. and Rebecca (Ellington) J.; m. Bobbie Mae Mooney; children: Forrest Hood III, Timothy E., Patrick F. BSCE, Auburn U., 1955. Mem. Montreal Alouettes, Ont., Can., 1956-57; constrn. supt. Ala., 1958-62; founder, chmn. bd. Diversified Products Corp., 1962-78; gov. State of Ala., 1978-82, 96—. Active Cystic Fibrosis Found., Boy Scouts Am., Ala. Saftey Coun., Jr. Achievement, Future Farmers Am. Served as lt. U.S. Army, 1957-58. Mem. Young Pres.'s Orgn., Ala. Road Builders Assn. (hon. life), Am. Legion, Spade Honor Soc., Alpha Sigma Epsilon. Republican. Address: Governor's Mansion 1142 S Perry St Montgomery AL 36104-3734

JAMES, FRANCES CREWS, zoology educator; b. Phila., Sept. 29, 1930; divorced; children: Sigrid Bonner, Helen Olson, Avis James. AB in Zoology, Mount Holyoke Coll., 1952; MS in Zoology, Louisiana State U., 1956; PhD in Zoology, U. Ark., 1970. Summer rsch. asst. Am. Mus. Natural History, NYC, 1950; grad. teaching asst. Louisiana State U., 1952-54; part time instr., botany, zoology, and physical edn. U. Ark., 1960-70; rsch. assoc. U. Ark. Mus., 1971-73; asst. program dir. ecology NSF, Washington, 1973-76, assoc. program dir., 1976; assoc. prof. and curator of birds and mammals Fla. State U., 1977-84, prof. and curator of birds and mammals, 1984—; instr. summer faculty U. Minn., 1978-81; vis. prof. fall semester Cornell U., Ithaca, N.Y., 1988; rsch. assoc. spring semester Smithsonian Inst., 1989; adv. coun. Systematic and Environ. Biology, Smithsonian Fgn. Currency Program, 1983-87; mem. nongame wildlife adv. program Fla. Game and Fresh Water Fish Commn., 1985-86; bd. dirs. World Wildlife Fund/Conservation Found., Cornell Lab. Ornithology, Am. Inst. Biol. Scis.; ctrl. com. mem. Internat. Ornithol. Congress; com. mem. Nat. Rsch. Coun. Editorial Bd.: American Birds, 1978—, Ecology and Ecological Monographs, 1989—, Annual Review of Ecology and Systematics, 1986-90; assoc. editor 1991—; Current Ornithology, assoc. editor, 1982-87, American Midland Naturalist, 1978-84. Contbr. numerous articles to profl. jours. NSF grantee 1979, 80, 83, U.S. Fish and Wildlife Svc. grantee, 1980 (2), FSU Found. grantee, 1982, 91, Nat. Geographic Soc. grantee 1983 (2), 1984, 85, 86, 87, 88, Fla. Game and Fresh Water Fish Comm. grantee, 1986-87, Cayahoga Trust grantee, 1986—, Nat. Fish and Wildlife Found. grantee, 1990-92, R. G. Crews Fund grantee, 1990-91, Conservation and Rsch. Found grantee, 1991. Fellow AAAS, Sigma Xi, Soc. Systematic Zoology; mem. Am. Ornithologist Union (pres. 1984-86, fellow 1976, permanent mem. coun., 1984—, Eliot Coues award 1992), Wilson Ornithological Soc., Am. Inst. Biological Sciences, Cooper Ornithological Soc. Home: 2113 Gibbs Dr Tallahassee FL 32303-4765 Office: Florida State Univ Dept Biological Scienc Tallahassee FL 32306-2043

JAMES, HUGH NEAL, video, record, movie producer, director; b. Commerce, Ga., Oct. 10, 1952; s. Carl and Viola (Thomas) J.; m. Debra Lane Taylor, Aug. 19, 1984 (div.). Student, Gainesville Jr. Coll., 1972-73. Pres. Neal James Orgn., Inc., Athens, Ga., 1979—, Cottage Blue Music BMI, Nashville, 1986—, Prodns. Unlimited, Nashville, 1987—; v.p. Video Zine Enterprises Inc., Athens, 1987—; pres. 3d Coast Video Promotions, Nashville, Neal James Music BMI, Hidden Cove Music ASCAP, Millennium II Prodns., Neal James Prodns. Featured songwriter The Nashville Network, 1987; produced projects featuring George Jones, Willie Nelson, Hank Cochran, Dottie West, Merle Haggard, Vern Gosdin, Johnny Paycheck. Recipient 16 nominations for songwriting Country Music Assn., 1984, 85, 87, Producer of Yr. award, 1993. Mem. Am. Fedn. Musician, Music Video Assn., Nat. Entertainment Journalists Assn., Nat. Acad. Rec. Arts and Scis., Country Music Assn., Broadcast Music Inc.

JAMES, JEANNIE HENRIETTA, education educator; b. Greenville, S.C., Dec. 5, 1921; d. Portice J. and Essie Virginia (Ross) J.; B.S., Berea (Ky.) Coll., 1945; M.S., U. N.C., 1949; postgrad. Iowa State U., 1955-56; Ed.D., Pa. State U., 1965. Tchr. home econs. Stowe (Vt.) High Sch., 1945-48; asst. prof. to assoc. prof. home econs. Lincoln Meml. U., Harrogate, Tenn., 1949-59; asst. prof. to assoc. prof. home econs. Ill. State U., Normal, 1959-75; assoc. prof. early childhood edn. U. S.C., Columbia, 1975-79, Spartanburg Meth. Coll., 1980; mem. Ill. White House Conf. on Children and Youth, 1969-70. Mem. Nat., S.C. assns. for edn. young children, Soc. for Research and Child Devel., AAUP, World Orgn. for Edn. Children, S.C. Home Econs. Assn., So. Highlands Handicraft Guild, Am. Home Econs. Assn. (program chmn. sect. 1977-79), AAUW, Phi Kappa Delta, Zeta Tau Alpha. Contbr. articles to profl. jours. Home: Belmont Dr # 205 Fountain Inn SC 29644-9481

JAMES, KATHRYN KANAREK, electrical engineer; b. N.Y.C., July 16, 1949; d. Jesse Jay and Dora Dorothy (Sader) Kanarek; m. Hugh R. James, Aug. 1982 (div.). BS, MIT, 1969, MSEE, EE, 1971; postgrad., Va. Tech. Ctr. Pub. Adminstrn., 1992—. Computer analyst Computer Systems Engring., North Billerica, Mass., 1971-72; staff mem. MIT Lincoln Lab., Lexington, Mass., 1972-73, MITRE Corp., Bedford, Mass., 1973-76, Analytical Systems Engring. Corp., Burlington, Mass., 1976-77; elec. engr. Combined Arms Combat Devel. Activity U.S. Army, Ft. Leavenworth, Kans., 1978-86; rsch. staff Inst. Def. Analyses, Alexandria, Va., 1986-90; engr. TRW Corp., McLean, Va., 1990-91; sr. engr. Tech. Planning Inc., Rockville, Md., 1991-93; pres. directional thinking TRW Test and Evaluation Engring. Svcs., Arlington, Va., 1993—; sr. systems analyst Walcoff & Assocs., 1994; sr. engr. CTA Inc., Rockville, Md., 1995; prin. engr. RMS Techs., Washington, 1996—. Mem. Jr. Women's Symphony Alliance, Kansas City, 1980-86. Grad. fellow Nat. Sci. Found., 1969-71. Mem. IEEE, Armed Forces Communications and Electronics Assn., Am. Soc. Pub. Adminstrn., Nat. Coun. Jewish Women (life), Sigma Xi, Tau Beta Pi, Eta Kappa Nu, Pi Alpha Alpha. Jewish. Club: Toastmasters (pres. local chpt. 1976). Home: 3726 King Arthur Rd Annandale VA 22003-1322 Office: RMS Techs Inc 1755 Jefferson Davis Hwy 600 Maryland Ave SW # 305 E Washington DC 20024

JAMES, KAY LOUISE, management consultant, healthcare executive; b. Little Rock, Feb. 13, 1948; d. Charles Robert and Mary Virginia (Morgan) J. BA, Vanderbilt U., 1970; MBA, U. Chgo., 1986. Diplomate Am. Coll. Healthcare Execs.; CPA, Ill., Mo. Mgr. Wallace Community Mental Health Ctr., Nashville, 1973-78; sr. cons. Ernst & Whinney, Washington, 1978-79; sr. cons. Ernst & Whinney, Chgo., 1979-81, mgr., 1981-84; dir. Am. Hosp. Supply Corp., Evanston, Ill., 1984-85; mgr. Am. Hosp. Supply Fin. Corp., Evanston, 1985-86; sr. mgr. KPMG Peat Marwick, Kansas City, Mo., 1986-89, ptnr., 1989-92; ptnr. Katz, James & Assocs., Inc., Plymouth Meeting, Pa., 1992-93; pres. James Mgmt. Assocs., Inc., Nashville, 1994—; speaker healthcare topics various grad. programs and profl. assns.; mem. Women's Leadership Forum of Dem. Nat. Com. Reviewer The Coming Home Program, San Francisco, 1993. Mem. AICPA, Am. Hosp. Assn., Med. Group Mgmt. Assn., Healthcare Fin. Mgmt. Assn., The Healthcare Forum. Democrat. Office: James Mgmt Assocs 3200 W End Ave Ste 500 Nashville TN 37203-1322

JAMES, KEITH ALAN, lawyer; b. Wichita, Kans., Sept. 29, 1957; s. Anthony Ray James and Patricia Ann Jones; Elaine Penelope Johnson, Aug. 14, 1982. BA, Harvard U., 1979, JD, 1982. Bar: Pa. 1982, U.S. Dist. Ct. (ea. dist.) Pa. 1982, Fla. 1988. Atty. Girard Bank, Phila., 1982-84; assoc. Wolf, Block, Schorr & Solis-Cohen, Phila., 1984-87, West Palm Beach, Fla., 1987-88; assoc. Shapiro & Bregman, West Palm Beach, 1988-90, ptnr., 1990-91; ptnr. Greenberg, Traurig, Hoffman, Lipoff, Rosen & Quentel, P.A., West Palm Beach, 1991-96; founder, pvt. practice Keith A. James, P.A., West Palm Beach, 1996—. Bd. dirs. A Better Chance in Lower Merion, Ardmore, Pa., 1984-87; mem. Leadership Fla., 1988-90, bd. regents, 1989-90, 91-93, chmn., 1995-96; mem. Fla. Commn. Human Rels., 1992—, chmn., 1993-95; bd. dirs. Edn. Partnership Palm Beach County, Inc., 1988-91, Cmty. Found. Martin and Palm Beach Counties, 1994—, vice chair, 1996—; bd. trustees JFK Med. Ctr., 1994-95, Quantum Found., 1995—. Mem. Associated Marine Insts. (bd. trustees 1989—), Palm Beach Marine Inst. (bd. dirs. 1989—, chmn. 1994-95), Harvard Club of the Palm Beaches (pres. 1990), Fox Club. Democrat. Office: 1655 Palm Beach Lakes Blvd West Palm Beach FL 33401-2225

JAMES, L. ELDON, JR., development consultant; b. Hampton, Va., May 1, 1955; s. L. Eldon and Aurelia Quinby (Mitchell) J.; m. Mary Beth Carrigan (div.); m. Mary Austine Twigg, May 19, 1984; children: Martina M., Aurelia F., L. Eldon III. BS in Recreation Resource Mgmt., Va. Commonwealth U., 1977, MS in Urban and Regional Planning, 1979. Asst. to park engr. Colonial Nat. Hist. Park, Yorktown, Va., 1976; supr. parks City of Bristol, Va., 1977; transp. planning intern Wilbur Smith & Assocs., Richmond, Va., 1978; grad. teaching asst. Va. Commonwealth U., Richmond, 1978-79; grants adminstr. Va. Commn. of Outdoor Recreation, Richmond, 1979-84; recreation cons. Va. Divsn. of Parks and Recreation, Richmond, 1984; mgr./asst. dir. no. Va. 4-H ctr. Va. Coop. Ext. Svc., Front Royal, Va., 1984-85; dir. parks and recreation dept. King George County, King George, Va., 1985-87, dir. dept. planning and comty. svcs., 1987-89, county adminstr., 1989-94; pvt. cons. comml., indsl. and residential devel., 1994—. Bd. dirs. Rappahannock Security Ctr., Fredericksburg, Va., 1990-94, Found. of Va. Recreation and Parks Soc., Richmond, 1990—; chmn. bd. dirs. Potomac Gateway Welcome Ctr., King George, 1989—; adv. com. Germanna C.C. Ctr. for Bus. Studies, Locust Grove, Va., 1991—; mem. King George County Schs. Expansion Com., 1992-94; bd. dirs. Rappahannock Regional Criminal Justice Acad., 1990-94; mem. adv. com. Sml. Bus. Devel. Ctr., Mary Washington Coll., 1991, others. Mem. Va. Recreation and Parks Soc. (pres. 1988, Fellows award 1993, Presdl. award 1983, 87), Va. Local Govt. Mgmt. Assn., Nat. Assn. County Adminstrs., Internat. City/County Mgrs. Assn. (assoc.), Va. Assn. of Counties (Chesapeake Bay Act tech. adv. com.), King George County C. of C. (pres. 1995—), Optimist Club. Methodist. Home: PO Box 611 10436 Hudson Rd King George VA 22485-3149 Office: PO Box 470 10436 Hudson Rd King George VA 22485

JAMES, LINDA GREEN, education specialist administrator, researcher; b. Memphis, Nov. 21, 1947; d. Frank Allen and Mary Elizabeth (Hankins) Green; m. John Newton Osborne, Feb. 7, 1975 (div. June 1979); 1 child, Suzanne; m. Phillip Harold James, Oct. 17, 1980; 1 child, Sarah Elizabeth. BA, U. Tenn., Martin, 1970; MA, Calif. State U., Long Beach, 1975; EdD in Higher Edn., U. Memphis, 1995. Instr. Memphis State U., 1979-85, dir. Wordsmith, 1984-85; asst. prof. Jackson (Tenn.) State C.C., 1985-90; adminstrv. intern State Tech. Inst. Memphis, 1990-91; asst. dir. Mid South Quality Productivity Ctr., Memphis, 1991-92; dir. acad. devel. State Tech. Inst. Memphis, 1992-93; edn. specialist Nat. Inst. Stds. and Tech., Gaithersburg, Md., 1993-94; systems mgmt. specialist U. Tenn., Martin, 1994-95; dir. assessment State Tech. Inst. Memphis, 1995—; bd. dirs., v.p. Greater Memphis Area Award for Quality; mem. adv. com. Nat. Govs. Conf. Edn., 1994; cons. City of Memphis Dept. Planning, 1993; mem. editl. bd. CQI Newsletter, 1994—; mem. adv. coun. Total Quality Learning Sys. Am. Soc. Quality Control, 1995—; trainer Koalaty Kids, 1996. Facilitator Leadership Memphis Diversity Program, 1993; vol. Girl Scouts, N.W. Tenn., 1986-89. Recipient grant Bell-South, 1991-93, fellow Tenn. Collaborative Acad., 1990-91. Mem. Am. Assn. Higher Edn., Am. Soc. Quality Control (assoc., Memphis sect. co-chair quality forum 1992-93), Tenn Assn. Devel. Educators, Phi Delta Kappa. Home: 51 Perkins Extd Memphis TN 38117 Office: State Tech Inst Memphis 5983 Macon Cv Memphis TN 38134-7642

JAMES, LOUIS MEREDITH, personnel executive; b. St. Augustine, Fla., June 12, 1941; s. Claire Meredith and Katherine Louise (Colson) J.; m. Karen Lee Libby, Nov. 25, 1966 (div. Mar. 1974); children: Michelle Lee, Kevin Meredith; m. Antoinette Frances Guerrero, Dec. 23, 1978; 1 child, Aaron Teague. BA, U. Minn., 1964. Personnel mgr. Army & Air Force Exch. Svc., worldwide, 1967-77; salary and wage specialist DOD Wage Staff, Rosslin, Va., 1977-82; dep. chief DOD NAF Wage Divsn. Nat. Br., Alexandria, Va., 1982—. Commr. Transp. Safety Commn., Vienna, Va., 1986—, vice chair, 1992-93, chair, 1993-96. 1st lt. U.S. Army, 1964-67. Decorated Purple Heart. Mem. DAV (life), VFW (life), Vietnam Vets. Am. (life, local chpt. state coun. and nat. com. rep., bd. dirs., v.p., pres. 1987—), Lions (v.p., bd. dirs., chmn. membership com. Vienna chpt.). Republican. Presbyterian. Home: 106 Ross Dr SW Vienna VA 22180-6718 Office: Dept Def 1400 Key Blvd Rosslyn VA 22209-5144

JAMES, MICHAEL THAMES, information technology executive, consultant; b. Gulfport, Miss., Feb. 16, 1949; s. William Denning and Christell (Cruthirds) J.; m. Debra Lynn Bryant, May 21, 1983; children: William Bryant, Shelley Christine. BS, U.S. Naval Acad., 1971; MS, U. So. Calif., 1978. Commd. ensign USN, 1971, advanced through grades to lt., 1975, resigned, 1978; mktg. rep. IBM, South Bend, Ind., 1978-79; cons. Price Waterhouse, Houston, 1979-85; internal cons. Shell Oil, Houston, 1985-86; mgr. systems devel. & support Carolina Power & Light, Raleigh, 1986-91; v.p. Sprint Kansas City, 1991-93; ptnr. KPMG Peat Marwick, Dallas, 1994-96; prin. Scott, Madden & Assocs., Dallas, 1996—; guest lectr. N.C. State U., 1989-91. Mem. computer studies adv. bd. Meredith Coll., 1987-91; adv. bd. Kansas City Met. Spl. Olympics, 1993; mem. industry steering com. Sch. Bus., U. Kans., 1993-94. Mem. Inst. Mgmt. Cons. (sec.-treas. Houston chpt. 1984-85), U.S. Naval Acad. Alumni Assn. (sec.-treas. Triangle area chpt. 1987-91). Republican. Presbyterian. Home: 4525 Emerson Dr Plano TX 75093-7226

JAMES, NANCY CAPLAN, pharmacist, researcher; b. Detroit, May 22, 1959. BS in Pharmacy, U. Mich., 1982, PharmD, 1983. Lic. pharmacist, Mich., N.C. Am. Soc. Hosp. Pharmacists clin. pharmacy resident Health Scis. Ctr. U. Ill., Chgo., 1983-84; clin. drug rsch. fellow clin. pharmacokinetics/dynamics sect. U. N.C. and Burroughs Wellcome Co., Research Triangle Park, 1984-85; clin. trials specialist clin. pharmacokinetics/dynamics sect. Burroughs Wellcome Co., Research Triangle Park, 1985-86, clin. rsch. assoc., 1986-87, clin. rsch. scientist, 1987-88; clin. pharmacokineticist clin. pharmacokinetics dept. Glaxo Inc., Research Triangle Park, 1988-89, group leader bioequivalence, 1989-91, group leader clin. evaluations, 1991, assoc. dir. R & D project planning, 1991-92, head full devel. planning R & D project planning, 1992-94, dir. full devel. planning R & D project planning, 1994-95; internat. dir. anti-infective and antiviral planning Glaxo Wellcome Inc., 1995—; presenter in field. Author: (with others) Clinical Drug Trials and Tribulations, 1988, Antiepileptic Drug Interactions, 1989; contbr. articles to profl. jours. Recipient Outstanding Achievement in Pharmacy award, Merck, Julia E. Emmanuel award U. Mich., 1982, James B. Angell scholarship, 1981-82. Mem. Am. Assn. Pharm. Scientists, Am. Coll. Clin. Pharmacy, Drug Info. Assn., Project Mgmt. Inst., Rho Chi, Phi Lambda Upsilon. Home: 2944 Bally Bunion Way Raleigh NC 27613-5402 Office: Glaxo Wellcome Inc 5 Moore Dr Durham NC 27701-4613

JAMES, PETER ROBERT, computer programmer; b. Las Cruces, N.Mex., June 19, 1965; s. Robert Allen and Ruth (Lenius) J.; m. Linda K. Gray, Feb. 13, 1988 (div. Sept. 1993). BS in Computer Sci. Engring., Milw. Sch. Engring., 1987. Programmer IBM, Rochester, Minn., 1987-91; programmer IBM, Rsch. Triangle Park, N.C., 1991—. Inventor work station customization, download mechanism for 5494. Mem. Assn. for Computing Machinery, Triangle Troglodytes (editor 1993—), Sierra Club. Home: 5500-63A Fortunes Ridge Dr Durham NC 27713 Office: IBM PO Box 12195 Research Triangle Park NC 27709

JAMES, RANDY RAY, English language educator; b. Shreveport, La., Apr. 19, 1969; s. Ruth Ann James. BA, La. State Univ., 1991; MA, Ea. Kentucky Univ., 1992; student, U. Southwestern La., 1993—. Eng. composition instr. Ea. Ky. Univ., Richmond, 1992-93; adminstrv. asst. Scott County Devel. Ctr., Georgetown, Ky., 1993; tchg. asst. U. Southwestern La., Lafayette, 1995—, grad. asst. spl. svc. dept., 1996—. Bibliographer composition, rhetoric. Dir. musicians Univ. Southwestern La. Gospel Choir, Lafayette, 1993—; organist Gethsemane Ch. of God in Christ, Lafayette, 1993—, Emmanuel Ch. of God in Christ, Opelousas, La., 1996—. Delta Beta Rho scholar La. State Univ., 1989, Leola B. Bryant scholar Ch. of God in Christ, Shreveport, 1990. Mem. Rsch. Assn. Minority Profs., Nat. Black Grad. Student Orgn., Sigma Tau Delta. Home: USL Box 44707 Lafayette LA 70504

JAMES, TRACEY FAYE, screenwriter; b. Wilmington, Ohio, Feb. 4, 1963; d. James Whitney and Lydia Wanell (Wethington) J. Student, Art Instrn. Schs., 1980, Arlington Career Ctr., 1985. Freelance screenwriter San Antonio, 1981—; sports photographer No. Va. Sun, Arlington, Va., 1988. Author screenplays: Nights of Terror, 1987, Dark Lords, 1991, Diamond Run, 1996. Recipient award for patriotic svc. U.S. Treasury, 1981. Republican. Episcopalian.

JAMES, VERNON LESTER, pediatrician, educator; b. Liberty, N.C., Mar. 12, 1929; m. Dessie Oliver, July, 1976. BS in Zoology, U. N.C., 1951, MD, 1955. Diplomate Am. Bd. Pediatrics; lic. physician, N.C., Mass., Ohio, Kans., Tex. Rotating intern Ohio State U., Columbus, 1955-56, pediatric resident Children's Hosp., 1956-58; rsch. fellow dept. child health Harvard Med. Sch., Boston, 1964-65; tng. fellow Children's Hosp. Med. Ctr., Boston, 1964-65; rsch. fellow pediatrics Boston Lying-in Hosp., 1964-65; dir. ambulatory svcs. dept. pediatrics Coll. Medicine U. Ky., Lexington, 1966-69; dir. Cystic Fibrosis Clinic, Diagnostic and Treatment Ctr. U. Ky. Med. Ctr., Lexington, 1967-75; dir. ambulatory care svcs. Wesley Med. Ctr., Wichita, 1978-79, dir. Child Evaluation Ctr., pediatrician High-Risk Infant Follow-Up Clinic, 1977-79; chief of staff Santa Rosa Children's Hosp.; pvt. practice San Antonio, 1985-95; med. dir., pediatric devel. program Santa Rosa Children's Hosp., San Antonio, 1995—; asst. prof. dept. pediatrics U. Ky. Sch. Medicine, 1966-70, assocs. prof., 1970-75, prof., 1975-85; clin. prof. U. of Tex. Med. Sch., 1985—; mem. active staff Santa Rosa Children's Hosp., 1985—, Met. Hosp., 1985-91, Bapt. Med. Ctrs., 1985-93, Women's and Children's Hosp., 1985-93, Meth. Hosp., 1985—; instr. dept. family health care Children's Hosp. Harvard Med. Sch., Boston, 1964-65; asst. prof. dept. pediat. Sch. Medicine U. Ky., Lexington, 1965-71, assoc. prof., 1971-75; prof. dept. pediat. Sch. Medicine U. Kans., Wichita, 1975-79, clin. prof., 1979-85; mem. clin. staff and tchg. panel Wesley Med. Ctr., Wichita, 1975-85; chief pediatric sect. Wesley Med. Ctr., 1984; mem. exec. bd. Med. Soc. Sedgwick County, 1984; clin. prof. dept. pediat. U. Tex. Health Sci. Ctr., San Antonio, 1985—; med. cons., Children Habilitation Ctr., San Antonio; presenter in field. Contbr. articles to profl. jours. Mem. adv. bd. Brighton Sch. Developmentally Delayed Children; child advocate Sedgwick County Dist. Ct.; mem. health adv. com. Wichita Head Start; mem. Sedgwick County Zoological Soc.; mem. governing bd. Santa Rosa Children's Hosp.; mem. San Antonio Botanical Soc.; mem. St. Francis Episcopal Ch. Maj. USAF, 1956-62; col. USAFR, 1962-89, ret. Recipient Outstanding Contbn. award Nat. Coun. Prevention Child Abuse, 1977; grantee Bureau Edn. of Handicapped, 1976, 77, 78, March of Dimes U. Kans. Medicine Endowment Found. for Genetics Clinic, 1977, 78, Wesley Med. Endowment Found., 1984. Mem. AMA, Am. Acad. Pediatrics (Ann. Journalism award 1977), Tex. Acad. Pediatrics, Tex. Pediatric Soc., Tex. Med. Assn., Bexar County Med. Soc., San Antonio Pediatric Soc. (pres. 1991), Wichita State U. Intercollegiate Scholarship Assn., Wichita C. of C. Office: Santa Rosa Children's Hosp 519 W Houston St San Antonio TX 78207

JAMESON, VICTOR LOYD, retired magazine editor; b. Clayton, N.Mex., Sept. 4, 1924; s. Earl Percy and Juna Dorothy (Kephart) J.; m. Barbara Oswald, July 13, 1947 (div. Dec. 1982); children: Ronald Wallace, Michael Loyd; m. Frances Russell Furlow, Nov. 8, 1986. BA, East N.Mex. Univ., 1949. Tchr. Hobbs (N.Mex.) Mcpl. Schs., 1949-51; reporter, editor Hobbs Daily News-Sun, 1951-63; journalist, writer United Presbyn. Ch., N.Y.C., 1964-73, dir. info., 1973-83; editor, pub. Presbyn. Survey mag., Louisville, 1983-91, editor emeritus, 1992—. Co-author: Bull at a New Gate, 1964; editor: What Does God Require of Us Now, 1971, The Main Trail, 1974; author: Dear Hearts - Conversations with Presbyterians, 1994; contbr. articles to profl. jours. Served to sgt. OSS Army, 1943-46, ETO. Recipient E. H. Shaffer award N.Mex. Press Assn., 1955, Editorial Writing award Religious Pub. Rels. Coun., 1986, Disting. Author award Presbyn. Writers Guild, 1992. Mem. Assoc. Ch. Press, Presbyn. Writers Guild (v.p.). Democrat. Presbyterian. Home: 232 Raintree Dr Hendersonville NC 28791

JAMIESON, MICHAEL LAWRENCE, lawyer; b. Coral Gables, Fla., Mar. 2, 1940; s. Warren Thomas and Ruth Amelia (Gallman) J.; children: Ann Layton, Thomas Howard; m. Elizabeth Marie Peeples, Dec. 31, 1992. B.A. in English, U. Fla., 1961, J.D. with honors, 1964. Bar: Fla. 1964, U.S. Dist. Ct. (mid. dist.) Fla. 1964. Teaching asst. U. Fla., 1964; law clk. U.S. Ct. Appeals (5th cir.), 1964-65; assoc. Holland & Knight and predecessor firms, Tampa, Fla., 1965-69, ptnr., 1969—, chmn. bus. law dept., 1992—. Editor-in-chief U. Fla. Law Rev., 1963. Trustee Law Ctr. U. Fla., chmn. bd. dirs., 1986-88; bd. dirs., chmn. Bus. Com. for the Arts Inc., 1989-90; trustee Tampa Bay Performing Arts Ctr. Inc., 1989—, chmn. devel. coun., 1990-91; trustee Cmty. Found. Greater Tampa, 1990—; chmn. devel. com. Fla. C. of C. Found., 1992-95; mem. Tampa Leadership Conf., Golden Triangle Civic Assn. Recipient Gertrude Brick Law Rev. award, 1963. Fellow Am. Bar Found.; mem. ABA (mem. com on corp. laws, mem. com. on fed. regulation of securities), Am. Law Inst., Hillsborough County Bar Assn., Greater Tampa C. of C. (mem. bd. govs. 1988-91), Com. 100 (mem. policy bd. 1989-92), Univ. Club, Tampa Club (bd. dirs. 1985-89, pres. 1987-88), Order of Coif, Phi Kappa Phi.

JAMIESON, RUSSELL LADEAU, JR., insurance executive, consultant; b. Camden, N.J., Mar. 22, 1958; s. Russell L. Sr. and Virginia E. (Horray) J. Student, MICS Marine Fin. Sch., 1985-90; cert., Fla. Ins. Sch., 1986, 88. Lic. property and casualty ins. agt., life and health ins. agt., mortgage broker. Sales mgr. Deptford (N.J.) Honda, 1980-82, Brevard Cycle Sport, Melbourne, Fla., 1982-85; bus. mgr. Anchorage Yacht Basin, Melbourne, 1985-87, Hatteras of Lauderdale, Ft. Lauderdale, Fla., 1987-91; pres. Future Investments, Inc., Ft. Lauderdale, 1985—, Primerica Fin. Svcs., Melbourne, Fla., 1991—; mng. agt., v.p. Friendly Ins. Agy., Merritt Island, Fla., 1992-94; pres., owner, agt. Fla. Hiway Ins., Inc., Cocoa Beach, Fla., 1994—; pres. Puritan Budget Plan Premium Fin. Co., Atlanta, 1994—; notary pub. State of Fla., Ft. Lauderdale, 1987—; personal leadership Creative Mgmt. Concepts, Ft. Lauderdale, 1987-91; ins. agt. Hatteras of Lauderdale, 1987-91; specialist in Marine fin. and registry. Mem. Splty. Ins. Agts. Assn., Cocoa Beach C. of C. Office: Fla Hwy and Marine Ins 72 S Orlando Ave Cocoa Beach FL 32931-4721

JAMISON, CONNIE JOYCE, sociology educator; b. Nashville, Jan. 4, 1954; d. William Earl and Mary Helen (Fleming) J.; m. Tom Kaardal (div. Nov. 1988). BS in Sociology, Mid. Tenn. State U., 1985, MA in Sociology, 1988; postgrad., Tenn. State U., 1994—. Prevention coord. Alcohol and Drug Coun., Nashville, 1987-92; adj. prof. sociology Belmont U., Nashville, 1988-94, Trevecca Nazarene U., Nashville, 1993—; adj. prof. sociology Tenn. State U., Nashville, 1993—, grad. asst., 1995—. Mem. AAUW, Am. Sociol. Assn., Phi Gamma Mu, Phi Delta Kappa. Home: 2814 Hastings Rd Nashville TN 37214-3222

JAMISON, ROBERT EDWARD, mathematics educator; b. Tampa, Fla., Dec. 21, 1948; s. Robert Edward and Lucie Mae (Boyd) J.; children: Elizabeth, Margaret. BS in Math., Clemson U., 1970; MS in Math., U. Wash., 1973, PhD in Math., 1974. Asst. prof. La. State U., Baton Rouge, 1974-79; prof. math. Clemson (S.C.) U., 1979—; vis. asst. prof. U. Bonn, Fed. Republic Germany, 1975-76; Humboldt fellow U. Erlangen, Fed. Republic Germany, 1976-77, U. Frieburg, Fed. Republic Germany, 1984; vis. prof. U. Berne, Switzerland, 1986-87, Cornell U., Ithaca, N.Y., 1993-94; math. cons. Computer Corp. Am., Boston, 1992, Praxis Internat., Boston, 1993, 95, Cumulative Inquiry, Croton, N.Y., 1994-95. Contbr. numerous articles to profl. publs.; patentee in field. Candidate for City of Clemson City Coun., 1980. Grantee Alexander von Humboldt Found., 1976-77, 84, NSF, 1978-79, 80-82, 80-85, Office of Naval Rsch., 1988-89, Dwight Eisenhower Math. and Edn. Act, 1991, 92, 93, Pearce Ctr., 1992. Office: Clemson U Dept Math Scis Clemson SC 29634-1907

JANDA, PAUL L., historian, educator; b. Victoria, Tex., Mar. 17, 1959; s. Laddie F. and Bettie (Clarke) J. Student, Victoria Coll., 1977-78; BA, Sam Houston State U., 1980, MA, 1982; MPA, Southwest Tex. State U., 1991. Cert. tchr., Tex. Tchg. asst. Sam Houston State U., Huntsville, 1980-82; tchr. Head Start Program, Victoria, Tex., 1982-83; analyst U. Houston, Victoria, 1983-89; instr. history, polit. sci. Victoria Coll., 1993—. Mem.

SCV (adjutant, Honor award 1995), SAR (v.p. 1994—), Tex. Jr. Coll. Tchrs. Assn., Tex. State Hist. Assn., Save Tex. Cemeteries, Inc., Victoria Preservation, Inc. Roman Catholic. Home: 474 FM 622 Victoria TX 77905

JANDREAU, JAMES LAWRENCE, program manager; b. St. Francis, Maine, Sept. 8, 1943; s. Leon L. and Cora (O'Clair) J.; m. Leslie Kinney, June 2, 1965 (div. Dec. 1981); children: James L., Joel L.; m. Judy K. Ayres, May 23, 1986. BA in Math. and Acctg., U. Maine, Orono, 1965; MBA, George Washington U., 1972. Commd. 2d lt. U.S. Army, 1965, advanced through grades to col., 1992, ret.; with computer ops., plans and programs officer USA Continental Army Command, Ft. Monroe, Va., 1968-70; project/procurement mgr. USA Computer Sys. Support and Evaluation Command, Washington, 1971-73; commdr., pers. officer Regional Pers. Ctr., Darmstadt, Germany, 1974-75; pers. mgr. USA Mil. Pers. Ctr., Schwetzingen, Germany, 1975-78; pers. dir. Dep. Chief of Staff for Pers., Washington, 1978-81; project mgr. Asst. Sec. of the Army, Washington, 1981-83; adjutant gen. 1st Inf. Divsn., Ft. Riley, Kans., 1983-85; chief info. tech. divsn. Joint Chiefs of Staff, Washington, 1986-89; dir. info. sys. USA Pers. Info. Sys. Command, Alexandria, Va., 1989-92; dep. dir., project mgr. Ogden Govt. Svcs., Fairfax, Va., 1992-94; program mgr. Computer Data Sys., Inc., Rockville, Md., 1994-95; asst. v.p., bus. info. systems NISH, Vienna, Va., 1995—. Home: 8313 Graceway Dr Lorton VA 22079-1346 Office: NISH 2235 Cedar Ln Vienna VA 22182-5200

JANES, JOSEPH ANTHONY, JR., optometrist; b. El Paso, Tex., Nov. 1, 1951; s. Joseph Anthony and Mildred Caroline (Dechant) J.; m. Janet Elaine Johnson, Jan. 10, 1976; children: Kelly Marie, Michael Harrison, Stephen Christopher. BS in Optometry, U. Houston, 1974, OD, 1976. Optometrist Farah Mfg., El Paso, Tex., 1976-77, Bellaire (Tex.) Eye Assocs., 1977-80; lectr. U. Houston Coll. Optometry, 1978-80, asst. prof., 1980-84; pres., optometrist Bellaire Contact Lens. Assoc., Houston, 1982—; adj. asst. prof. U. Houston Coll. Optometry, 1984-90; adj. assoc. prof. U. Houston, 1991—; v.p., sec. Laser Eye Ctr L.L.C., 1996—; adv. bd. Vistakon Inc., Jacksonville, Fla., 1986; bd. dirs. Laser Eye Inst. Houston, 1996—. Contbr. articles to profl. jours. Fellow Am. Acad. Optometry, Nat. Acad. Eye Surgery; mem. Am. Optometric Assn., Tex. Optometric Assn., Harris County Optometric Assn., Nat. Acad. Eye Surgery, Sigma Nu Frat. (treas. alumni assn. 1981). Office: Bellaire Contact Lens Assoc 6699 Chimney Rock Rd Ste 200 Houston TX 77081-5339

JANICE, BARBARA, illustrator; b. Bklyn., Jan. 25, 1949; d. Irving and Blanche (Lass) Rothman; 1 child, Stacey-Alissa Mirsky. BS in Biology, L.I. U., 1971; studied with, Frank Netter, MD. Staff illustrator Courier-Life Pubs., Bklyn., 1975-78, The Village Voice, N.Y.C., 1978-80; art dir., dept. anatomy SUNY Health Sci. Ctr., Bklyn., 1989-91; freelance illustrator Walt Disney Prodns., N.Y.C., 1990-95, Orlando, Fla., 1990-95; art dir. EuroDisney, Paris, 1990-95; illustrator EuroDisney, Orlando, N.Y.C., 1991-94; art dir. for Donald Duck character EuroDisney, Ft. Lauderdale, Fla., 1994—; human rels. analyst Microsoft Corp., 1995—; dir. Barbara Janice Graphics, N.Y.C. and Fla., 1980—; guest spkr. Pratt Sch. Art and Design, Bklyn., 1991; art dir. for character Donald Duck, EuroDisney, Paris, 1992—. Illustrator: Current Operative Urology, 6th edit., 1989, A Historical Profile of the Children's Medical Center, 1990, 2d rev. edit., 1992, The Day the Alphabet Was Born, 1991; represented in permanent collections SUNY Health Sci. Ctr., EuroDisney, Paris, Tokyo Disneyland. Vol. artist Coalition for the Homeless, N.Y.C., 1985, 91, AIDS Coalition, Ft. Lauderdale, N.Y.C., 1992—. Recipient 1st place N.Y. Art Critics award, 1984, 2d place award, 1992. Mem. Assn. Med. Illustrators, Soc. Illustrators (1st place 34th ann. exhbn. 1991, 2d place 33d ann. exhbn. 1990), Graphic Artists Guild (profl. rep.). Jewish. Home: 3881 NW 122nd Ter Sunrise FL 33323-3360 Office: Microsoft 899 W Cypress Creek Rd Fort Lauderdale FL 33309-2072

JANJAN, NORA ANITA, radiation oncologist; b. July 3, 1953. BS in Biology with honors, U. Ariz., 1975, MD, 1979. Diplomate Am. Bd. Radiology; lic. physician, Wis., Ariz., Calif., Tex.; cert. radiation oncologist. Intern internal medicine Baylor Coll. Medicine, Houston, 1979-80, resident in internal medicine, 1980-81; resident in radiotherapy, 1981-84; faculty assoc. in radiotherapy U. Tex. M.D. Anderson Hosp. and Tumor Inst., Houston, 1984-86; asst. prof. dept. radiation oncology Med. Coll. Wis., Milw., 1986-91; assoc. prof. divsn. radiotherapy M.D. Anderson Cancer Ctr., Houston, 1991—; cons. radiotherapy U.S. HHS, 1992-93, U.S. Nuclear Regulatory Commn., 1994. Editor: (oncology sect.) Year Book of Pain, 1993, Pain Digest, 1994; mem. editorial rev. bd. Cancer jour., 1993. Mem. ACP, AMA, Am. Assn. Cancer Edn. (mem. program com. 1991-92), Am. Soc. Clin. Oncology (mem. cancer edn. com. 1993), Am. Pain Soc. (mem. com. on quality care standards for acute pain and cancer pain 1993), Am. Soc. Therapeutic Radiolgoy and Oncology (mem. task force on nuc. regulation 1993—, mem. appropriateness guidelines task force 1994), Am. Coll. Radiology, Am. Endocurietherapy Soc., Am. Radium Soc., Radiol. Soc. N.Am. (mem. program com. 1994—), Internat. Assn. Study Pain, Soc. Surg. Oncology. Office: Univ Tex MD Anderson Ctr Radiotherapy Divsn Box 97 1515 Holcombe Blvd Houston TX 77030-4009

JANKOWSKI, JOHN EDWARD, JR., foundation administrator; b. South Bend, Ind., June 2, 1955; s. John and Constance Gay (Maenhout) J.; m. Judy Renee Goldberg, June 25, 1978; children: Kathryn Felice, Jeffrey Ellis. Student, Ind. U., 1973-75; BSFS magna cum laude, Georgetown U., 1977; MA, Johns Hopkins U., 1982. Rsch. asst. Resources for the Future, Washington, 1978-82; asst. dir., strategic & policy analysis Distilled Spirits Coun., Washington, 1982-87; program dir. rsch. & devel. surveys Nat. Sci. Found., Arlington, Va., 1987—. Contbr. articles to profl. jours. Recipient Spl. Achievement awards, 1989, 91. Mem. Am. Econ. Assn., Soc. Gov. Econs., Phi Beta Kappa, Sigma Xi. Office: NSF 4201 Wilson Blvd Arlington VA 22230-0001

JANKUS, ALFRED PETER, international management and marketing consultant; b. N.Y.C., Apr. 16, 1923; s. Walter and Antanina (Raulinaitis) J. Student Army Specialized Tng. Program, NYU, 1943-44; M Internat. Mgmt., Am. Grad. Sch. Internat. Mgmt., Glendale, Ariz., 1947. Gen. mgr. for L.Am. Coca-Cola Co., 1947-51; pres. Internat. Mgmt. Assocs., 1952-63, Intermart Corp., Miami, 1955-56; export mgr. P. Ballantine & Sons, Newark, 1955; real estate broker and resort devel. and mktg. cons. for various developers, Fla., Bahamas, Mex., Caribbean, 1963-80; pres. Internat. Mgmt. & Mktg. Group, Royal Palm Beach, Fla., 1980—. Author: (with Neil M. Malloy) Venezuela—Land of Opportunity, 1956; author: Management Engineering and Consulting, 1961. Tech. sgt. AUS, 1942-46, ETO. Mem. Fla. Freelance Writers Assn., Am. Grad. Sch. Internat. Mgmt. Thunderbird Alumni Assn. (bd. dirs. 1985-86). Republican. Roman Catholic.

JANNEY, OLIVER JAMES, lawyer, plastics and chemical company executive; b. N.Y.C., Feb. 11, 1946; s. Walter Coggeshall and Helen Jennings (James) J.; m. Suzanne Elizabeth Lenz, June 21, 1969; children: Oliver Burr, Elizabeth Flower. BA cum laude, Yale Coll., 1967; JD, Harvard U., 1970. Bar: Mass. 1970, N.Y. 1971, Fla. 1991. With Walston & Co., Inc., N.Y.C., 1970-73, asst. v.p., 1971-73; assoc. Cleary, Gottlieb, Steen & Hamilton, N.Y.C., 1973-76; with RKO Gen., Inc., N.Y.C., 1976-90, asst. sec., 1977-85, asst. gen. atty., 1978-82, asst. gen. counsel, 1982-85, sec., gen. counsel, 1985-89; v.p., gen. counsel, sec. Uniroyal Tech. Corp., Sarasota, Fla., 1990—. Former pres. River Rd. Assn., Scarborough, N.Y.; vestryman St. Mary's Episcopal Ch., Scarborough, 1977-82, treas., 1978-82. Served to 1st lt. USAR, 1969-77. Mem. ABA, N.Y. State Bar Assn., Assn. Bar City N.Y., Sleepy Hollow Country Club (Scarborough), Longboat Key (Fla.) Club. Republican. Home: 3651 Bayou Cir Longboat Key FL 34228-3005 Office: Uniroyal Tech Corp 2 N Tamiami Trl Sarasota FL 34236-5574

JANSSENS, JOE LEE, controller; b. Alpine, Tex., Apr. 13, 1964; s. Charles Louis Janssens and Sue Ellen (Cheairs) Ticknor; m. Diana Bookout, Sept. 9, 1995; children: Ryan, Stephanie. BBA in Fin., Tex. A&M U., 1986. CPA, Tex.; cert. mgmt. acct. Staff auditor Price Waterhouse, Houston, 1988-89; consol. acct. Energy Ventures, Inc., Houston, 1989-92; sr. internat. acct. Ashland Exploration, Inc., Houston, 1992-95; controller Peak Svcs. USA Ltd., Texas City, Tex., 1996—. Mem. Tex. Soc. CPAs, Inst. Mgmt. Accts. Roman Catholic. Home: 8402 Roos Houston TX 77036 Office: Peak Svcs USA Ltd PO Box 1758 Texas City TX 77592

JAQUES, JAMES ALFRED, III, communications engineer; b. Akron, Ohio, July 6, 1940; s. James Alfred Jr. and Rosemary (McDonald) J.; m. Maryellen McCarthy, June 8, 1963; children: Jacquelyn Dawn, Jody Lynne, James Justin, Jill Danielle. BSEE cum laude, N.C. State U., 1968; MS cum laude, Naval Postgrad. Sch., 1975. Commd. ens. USN, 1961, advanced through grades to lt. comdr.; br. chief Def. Comm. Agy. USN, Alexandria, Va., 1979-83; ret. USN, 1983; asst. program mgr., chief engr. TRW, Inc., Fairfax, Va., 1983-92; chief engr. Applied Quality Comm., Chesapeake, Va., 1992-95; CEO Engring. Design Group, Chesapeake, Va., 1994—; system architect Can. Iris Program, Napean, Ont., 1990. Author, editor numerous papers in field. Pres. Lake Smith Civic League, Virginia Beach, Va., 1993-95; mem. exec. bd. Coun. Civic Orgns., 1996—. Mem. IEEE (student chmn. 1973-75), Armed Forces Comm. Electronics Assn. (local sec.-treas. 1984, standards com. 1991), Internet Engring. Working Group. Republican. Roman Catholic. Home: 1001 Five Forks Rd Virginia Beach VA 23455-4807 Office: Engring Design Group 825 Greenbrier Cir Ste 102 Chesapeake VA 23320

JAQUISH, MICHAEL PAUL, human resources administrator; b. Narrows, Va., Dec. 18, 1934; s. Charles Earl and Leona Emma (Jones) J.; m. Merna Ruth Swayne, June 18, 1955; children: Kathryn Lee Jaquish Engebretsen, Michael Allen. BS in Indsl. Tech., Engring., Tenn. Tech. U., 1958; postgrad., U. Utah, 1962-63. Cert. compensation profl. Tech. writer Raytheon Missile Systems, Bristol, Tenn., 1959-61; engr./analyst supr. Thiokol Chem. Corp., Brigham City, Utah, 1961-64; tech. editor ARO, Inc., Arnold Engr. Devel. Ctr., Tenn., 1964-72; human resources adminstr. Sverdup Inc., Tullahoma, Tenn., 1972-84; gen. mgr., personnel dir. Anderson Computers, Huntsville, Ala., 1984-85; mgmt. cons. Montgomery, Ala., 1985; human resource systems mgr., mgr. salary adminstrn. Crawford Long Hosp. Emory U., Atlanta, 1985—; v.p., bd. dirs. Convalescent Supplies, Athens, Tenn.; pres. Michael Jaquish and Assocs. Inc.; cons. in mgmt. and computer systems. Author: Personal Resume Preparation, 1968; contbr. articles and revs. to profl. jours. Tchr. adult Sunday sch., Tullahoma, Atlanta, 1964—. With U.S. Army, 1956-57. Recipient Dr. Nobel Guthrie award Memphis Amateur Radio Club, 1970, Outstanding Leadership award Middle Tenn. Amateur Radio Soc., 1985. Mem. Am. Compensation Assn., Assn. Human Resource Systems Profls. (pres. 1990-91, Mem. of Yr. 1989, 91), Am. Soc. for Pers. Adminstrn. (pres. 1981), Inst. Indsl. Engrs., Air Force Assn., Soc. Tech. Writers and Editors, Nat. Mgmt. Assn. Presbyterian.

JARALLAH, TAJUDDIN MUFARRIDUN OLUWATOYIN, food service executive, chef; b. Lagos, Nigeria; came to U.S., 1976; s. Ralph Omobolaji and Adebisi Juradat (Folami) Gaji; m. Frannie Mae Campbell (div. 1986); m. Frances Joella Moore, Nov. 14, 1986; children: Sinmi, Lola, Jaffar. Postgrad. in criminal sci. sociology, U. Colo., 1982. Chef apprentice Bagauda Lake Resort, France, Grand VéFour Restaurant, Paris; asst. mgr. Church's Fried Chicken, Chgo., 1977-80; exec. sous chef Café De France, Denver, 1980-84; asst. mgr. tng. Cracker Barrel Restaurant, Atlanta, 1985; exec. chef Pickett Ste. Hotel, Atlanta, 1985-88; exec. chef, owner The Catering Chef, Atlanta, 1988—; corp. chef, v.p. Imperial Fez Morrocan Restaurant, Atlanta and Vail, Colo., 1992-94; pres. Real Essence Mktg. and Pub. Rels., Inc.; restaurant cons. Jazz Cafe Internat., Buckhead, Ga., 1993, Bird Cage Cafe, Atlanta, 1993-94, Vassura Trattoria, Atlanta, 1994—, Flamingo Joe, Atlanta, 1994—. Author: West African Cookery, 1979, Christianity or Islam, 1993, What a True Muslim Believes, 1994; editor: Muslim Challenge, 1992, Religion Challenge, 1993, The Talking Toques, 1994, Les Toques Blanches, U.S. Chef's Jour., 1995—. Founder, chmn. African Muslim Orgn., Atlanta, 1992; chmn. Ammal Muslim Orgn., Atlanta, 1993—; project dir. Operation Chef and Child, 1993—. Islamic scholar Periodica Islamica, Kuala Lumpa, Malaysia, 1993. Mem. Am. Culinary Fedn. (bd. dirs. Atlanta chpt. 1993—, cert. exec. chef), Atlanta Chefs and Cook Assn. (chmn. election com. mem. 1993—), Les Toques Blanches USA (chmn. nat. history com. Atlanta chpt., chmn. pub. rels. com. Atlanta chpt. 1993-95), Les Toques Blanches Internat. (U.S. coord. Switzerland chpt. 1995—), Les Toques Blanches Korea (hon. mem., internat. coord. for internat. culinary exch. program 1995—), Nat. Ice Carving Assn., Nat. Restaurant Assn., Ga. Hospitality and Travel Assn. (sec. olympic task force com. 1993-94), Atlanta Metro Travel Assn. Home: 1113 Tamarack Trl Forest Park GA 30050-3115

JARAMILLO, JUAN CAMILO, marine biologist; b. Medellin, Colombia, June 25, 1963; arrived in U.S., 1988; s. Eduardo and Stella (Posada) J.; m. Christina Elena Roldan, Sept. 30, 1988. BS in marine biology, Univ. de Bogota, Bogota, Colombia, 1988; MA in marine affairs, Univ. Miami, 1995. Curator birds/reptiles Miami Seaquarium, Miami, 1989-91; rsch. asst. Univ. Miami, 1991-93, tech. specialist, 1993-95; rsch. staff Harbor Br. Oceanographic Inst., Ft. Pierce, Fla., 1995—; adj. faculty Miami Dade Cmty. Coll., Miami, 1992-93; computer graphics artist, 1994—. Office: Harbor Br Oceanographic Inst 5600 US & North Fort Pierce FL 34946

JARAMILLO, JUANA SEGARRA, dean; b. San Sebastian, P.R., Mar. 24, 1937; d. Joaquin M. and Carmen M. (Gerena) Segarra; m. Edgar J. Jaramillo, Apr. 13, 1957; children: Jeanette, Yila, Yvonne, Melissa, Edgar Jr. BA, Poly. Inst. P.R., San German, 1956; postgrad., U. Fla., 1956-57; MS, La. State U., 1963. Libr. dir. Inter-Am. U., Aguadilla (P.R.) Regional Coll., 1975-76, cons. libr. and accreditation, 1983—; libr. U.P.R.-Aguadilla Regional Coll., 1976-77, libr. dir., 1983-86, libr., 1986-89, chair steering com. for accreditation, mem. directive coun. honors program, 1989—, dir. instl. planning and rsch., 1989-90, libr. dir., 1990-94; acting assoc. acad. dean, 1994—, dean/dir., 1994—; libr. dir. EDP Coll. P.R., San Sebastian, 1979-83; acting assoc. acad. dean U. P.R., Aguadilla, 1994, dean, dir., 1994—; mem. steering com. nat. edn. program Am. Coun. Edn., P.R., 1982-86, adv. bd. Coun. Higher Edn., P.R., 1982—. Author: Manual bibliografico Electronica, 1987; co-author: El Desarrollo del Pensamiento Critico en Futuros Maestros, 1989; contbr. articles to profl. jours. Mem. Club Civico de Damas, Aguadilla, 1989—. With U.S. Army, 1963-66. Mem. ALA, Am. Assn. Higher Edn., Assn. Caribbean Univs., Rsch. and INstl. Librs., Sociedad de Bibliotecarios de P.R. (pres. continuing edn. 1984-90), Rotary-Anns (pres. 1974), Internat. Altrusan, Alpha Delta Kappa. Office: UPR Aguadilla PO Box 160 Ramey Aguadilla PR 00604

JARES, ANDREA LYNN, newspaper reporter; b. Houston, June 25, 1972; d. Richard Paul and Jerry Frances (Wise) J. BA in Journalism, Baylor U., 1994. Asst. night news editor The Lariat, Waco, Tex., 1992, night news editor, 1993, city editor, 1993, opinion page editor, 1994; copy editor Waco Tribune-Herald, 1994; police reporter Temple (Tex.) Daily Telegram, 1994-95, asst. lifestyles editor, 1995-96; Bay City bur. reporter Victoria (Tex.) Advocate, 1996—. Vol. Literacy Ctr., Waco, 1994, VA Hosp., Waco, 1990-92. David McHam Journalism scholar, 1994; named Outstanding Sr. Woman, Mortar Bd. Mem. Soc. Profl. Journalists, Humane Soc. U.S. Roman Catholic. Home: 2905 Ave L Bay City TX 77414 Office: Matagorda County Advocate/Victoria Advocate 1709 7th St Bay City TX 77414

JARIC, MARKO VUKOBRAT, physicist, educator, researcher; b. Beograd, Serbia, Yugoslavia, Mar. 17, 1952; came to U.S. 1974; s. Vojin and Mileva (Vukobrat) J.; m. Slavica Vukelic, May 30, 1975 (div. 1979); m. Gabriele Weber, Dec. 10, 1982 (div. 1987); m. Tamara Hunt, Nov. 13, 1987 (div. 1990); m. Marija Nikolic, July 11, 1995; 1 child, Voyin Pavle. Dipl., Beogradski U., 1974; PhD, CUNY, 1978. Rsch. assoc. U. Calif., Berkeley, 1978-80, Free U., West Berlin, 1980-82; vis. assoc. prof. Mont. State U., Bozeman, 1982-84; vis. scholar Harvard U., Cambridge, Mass., 1984-86; assoc. prof. Tex. A&M U., College Station, 1986-90, prof. physics, 1990—; adj. prof. Nikola Tesla U., Knin, Republic Serbian Krayina, 1993-95; adj. prof. physics dept. U. Calif., Santa Cruz, 1994—; vis. scientist Cornell U., Ithaca, N.Y., 1995-96; vis. mem. Inst. for Theoretical Physics, U. Calif., Santa Barbara, 1987-88; vis. assoc. prof. U. Calif., Santa Cruz, 1989-90; vis. scholar Inst. des Hautes Etudes Scientifiques, Bures-sur-Yvette, France, 1981, 83; rsch. fellow Einstein Ctr. for Theoretical Physics, Rehovot, Israel, 1982, 83; vis. fellow Nonlinear Sci. Inst., Santa Cruz, 1989-90; rsch. assoc. Inst. Physics, Zemun, Yugoslavia, 1990-95, Physics Dept. U. Calif., Santa Cruz, 1991-94. Editor book series: Aperidicity and Order, 1988—; editor proceedings, Quasicystals, 1990; contbr. articles to profl. jours. Recipient October Prize, City of Belgrade, 1974; Fulbright grantee, 1974-80; Miller Inst. fellow, 1978-80, Alexander von Humboldt fellow, 1981-82. Mem. Am. Phys. Soc., Biophys. Soc. Office: Tex A&M Univ Physics Dept College Station TX 77843-4242

JARIC, ROBERT RONALD, business executive; b. Youngstown, Ohio, May 22, 1942; s. Matthew Paul and Ann Louise (Skrtic) J.; m. Donna Ann Leonard, Sept. 27, 1977; 1 child, Amber Leigh. BS, Youngstown State U., 1964. Sales trainer Proctor & Gamble, Cleve., 1965-69; area sales mgr. Control-O-Fax Corp., Waterloo, Iowa, 1969-78; nat. sales mgr. Comshare Target Software, Atlanta, 1978-81; sales mgr. Digital Communications Assocs., Norcross, Ga., 1981-86, Rabbit Software, Malvern, Pa., 1986-88; dir. sales CBIS, Inc., Norcross, 1988-91; v.p. CBIS, Inc. Norcross, 1991-94; v.p. sales and mktg. Image Info., Inc., Roswell, Ga., 1994—; pub. spkr. in field. Contbr. articles to profl. pubs. Active Cobb County (Ga.) Rep. Party, 1988—. Sgt. U.S. Army, 1964-66. Mem. ALA, Am. Mgmt. Assn., Local Area Network Dealers Assn., S.E. Software Assn., Sales and Mktg. Execs. of Atlanta. Mem. Unitarian Ch. Home: 1091 Saint Louis Pl NE Atlanta GA 30306-4526 Office: Image Info Inc 105 Hembree Park Dr Ste A Roswell GA 30076-3867

JARNIGAN-WILLIAMS, ANGELA RENEE, elementary school educator; b. Savannah, Ga., Mar. 14, 1956; d. Walter Edwin and Marie Antoinette (Hardrick) Jarnigan; m. Walter Willis Williams, Apr. 2, 1985; children: Albert Clayton Smith II, Alisha Colette McKinnis. Student, S.C. State U., Orangeburg, 1974-77; BS, Armstrong State Coll., Savannah, 1989. Cert. tchr. elem. edn., Ga. Tchr. Young World, Greensboro, N.C., 1979-81, Parent and Child Day Care, Savannah, 1982-83; switchboard operator Hyatt Regency-Savannah, 1982, 83; para-profl. Chatham-Savannah Bd. Edn., 1984-88; tchr. 1st grade Windsor Forest Elem. Sch., Savannah, 1989—; camp tchr. Meml. Day Sch., Savannah, 1987; mentor Savannah-Chatham County Bd. Edn., 1994—. Mem. NEA, Ga. Assn. Educators, Chatham Assn. Educators. Roman Catholic. Home: 1705 Vassar St Savannah GA 31405-1739

JARRARD, MARILYN MAE, nursing consultant, nursing researcher; b. York, Nebr., July 13, 1939; d. Frederick Albert and Esther Marie (Kollmann) Elze; m. William John Jarrard (div.); children: Rebecca Ann, Melissa Linn. Diploma in nursing, Luth. Sch. Nursing, Sioux City, Iowa, 1959. RN, Iowa, Fla.; cert. nutritional support nurse. Staff nurse U. Iowa Hosps. and Clinics, Iowa City, 1959-60, 69-70, minimal care charge nurse, 1971-74, staff nurse medical oncology, 1974-75, hyperalimentation nurse, 1975-79; staff nurse VA Hosp., Iowa City, 1960-65; charge nurse Offutt Air Base Hosp., Omaha, 1965-66; hyperalimentation nurse clinician Northwestern Meml. Hosp., Chgo., 1979-81; nutritional support nurse, team coord. Leila Hosp. and Health Ctr., Battle Creek, Mich., 1981-87; clin. specialist wound care Smith & Nephew Perry, Massillon, Ohio, 1987-89; clin. specialist-I.V. Smith & Nephew Wound Mgmt. Divsn., Inc., Largo, Fla., 1989—; cons. and rschr. in field. Contbr. numerous articles to profl. jours. With USNG, 1976-79. Mem. Nat. Assn. Vascular Access Networks, Assn. for Profls. in Infection Control and Epidemiology, Inc., Soc. for Healthcare Epidemiology Am., Oncology Nursing, Am. Soc. Parenteral and Enteral Nutrition (nursing faculty 1977), Intravenous Nurses Soc. Home: 9209 Seminole Blvd Apt 130 Seminole FL 33772

JARRELL, DONALD RAY, medical technologist; b. Barberton, Ohio, Sept. 25, 1963; s. Paul Everett and Minnie Marie (Aldridge) J.; m. Sandra Leilani Hawkins, May 20, 1989. BS in Chemistry, Marshall U., 1985, MA, 1988. Shift ops. mgr. Lab. Corp. Am., Research Triangle Park, N.C., 1987—. Mem. Am. Chem. Soc. Democrat. Baptist. Home: 706 Huffman Mill Rd Apt 16A Burlington NC 27215-5147 Office: Lab Corp Am 1912 Alexander Dr 1904 Alexander Dr Research Triangle Park NC 27709

JARRELL, IRIS BONDS, elementary school educator, business executive; b. Winston-Salem, N.C., May 25, 1942; d. Ira and Annie Gertrude (Vandiver) Bonds; m. Tommy Dorsey Martin, Feb. 13, 1965; 1 child, Carlos Miguel; m. 2d, Clyde Rickey Jarrell, June 25, 1983; stepchildren—Tamara, Cris, Kimberly. Student U. N.C.-Greensboro, 1960-61, 68-69, 74-75, Salem Coll., 1976; B.S. in Edn., Winston-Salem State U., 1981; postgrad. Appalachian State U., 1983; M in Elem. Edn., Gardner-Webb Coll., 1992. Cert. tchr., N.C.Tchr. Rutledge Coll., Winston-Salem, 1982-84; owner, mgr. Rainbow's End Consignment Shop, Winston-Salem, 1983-85; tchr. elem. edn. Winston-Salem/Forsyth County Sch. System, 1985-96; dir. Knollwood Bapt. Pre-Sch., 1996—. Contbr. poetry to mags. Mem. Assn. of Couples for Marriage Enrichment, Winston-Salem, 1984-86, Forsyth-Stokes Mental Health Assn., 1985-86; mem. Planned Parenthood. Mem. Internat. Reading Assn., N.C. Assn. Adult Edn., Forsyth Assn. Classroom Tchrs., Nat. Assn. Female Execs., NOW, Greenpeace, World Wildlife Fund, KlanWatch. Democrat. Baptist. Avocations: singing, writing, sewing, gardening, reading. Home: 101 Cheswyck Ln Winston Salem NC 27104-2905

JARRELL, PATRICIA LYNN, photojournalist; b. South Charleston, W.Va., Jan. 21, 1952; d. Ronald Eugene and Barbara Anne (Hill) J.; m. Timothy James Shortt, Mar. 10, 1990. Photographer PCA Internat., Tampa, Fla., 1974-77, Linwood/Gittings, Houston, 1977-78; sr. photographer Gittings/Neiman Marcus, Dallas, 1978-80; studio photographer PCA Internat., Dallas and Orlando, 1980-85; photographer, mgr. Charlton Studios, Altamonte Springs, Fla., 1985; photographer Fla. Today/Gannett, Melbourne, Fla., 1985—; owner Pat Jarrell Photography, Melbourne, Fla., 1996—; mem. discussion panel covering tragedy Fla. Press Women, 1989. Works exhibited at So. Newspaper Pubs. Assn., 1989, Armory Art Ctr., West Palm Beach, Fla., 1994. Recipient Photojournalism/Spot News award Internat. Soc. Newspaper Design, 1986-87, award of excellence in photojournalism Soc. Newspaper Design, 1986-87, Best News Photography award Fla. Press Club, 1987, Clarion/News Photography award Women in Comms., 1988, 1st Pl./Spot News Fla. Soc. Newspaper Editors, 1988, 1st Pl. News Photography award Fla. Press Women, 1988, 1st Pl. Color Feature award Fla. Soc. Newspaper Editors, 1990. Mem. NOW, Nat. Press Photographers Assn. Democrat. Home: 1802 Crane Creek Blvd Melbourne FL 32940-6788 Office: Fla Today Newspaper Gannett Plaza PO Box 419000 Melbourne FL 32941-9000 also: Pat Jarrell Photography PO Box 410532 Melbourne FL 32941-0532

JARRELL, STEPHEN BROOKS, economics educator; b. Huntsville, Ala., Jan. 10, 1949; s. Lawson E. and Elizabeth E. (Absher) J.; m. Marcia Ellen Thompson, Jan. 3, 1981; children: Jennifer, Jason, Sara, Shane. BS in Math., U. Ala., Tuscaloosa, 1971; MS in Econs., Purdue U., 1972, PhD in Econs., 1978. Prof. econs. Western Ky. U., Bowling Green, 1975-88, U. Mont., Air Force Inst. Tech. MBA Program, Great Falls, 1980-81, Western Carolina U., Cullowhee, N.C., 1988—; interim head of dept. econs. and fin. Western Carolina U., 1994-95. Author: Basic Business Statistics, 1988, Basic Statistics, 1994; contbr. articles to profl. jours. Mem. Am. Econ. Assn., Am. Statis. Assn., Phi Beta Kappa, Omicron Delta Epsilon, Pi Mu Epsilon. Office: Western Carolina U Dept Econs Fin Inernat Bus Cullowhee NC 28723

JARRETT, HARRY WELLINGTON, III, biochemistry educator; b. Charleston, S.C., June 19, 1950; s. Harry Wellington II and Sally Modelle (Bookout) J.; m. Karen Jean Mears, May 27, 1977; children: Harry, Alexander, Patience. BS in Biology, U. S.C., 1972; PhD in Biochemistry and Nutrition, U. N.C., 1976. Postdoctoral fellow Mayo Clinic, Rochester, Minn., 1976-77, U. Calif., San Diego, 1977-80; asst. biochemist U. Ga., Athens, 1980-82; asst. prof. Purdue Sch. Sci., Indpls., 1982-88, assoc. prof., 1988-89; assoc. prof. biochemistry U. Tenn., Memphis, 1989-94, prof., 1994—; cons. Alltech Assoc./Applied Sci., Deerfield, Ill., 1986-90, Scott, Foresman and Co., Dallas, 1987, Harper Collins Pubs., N.Y.C., 1992, NIH, Bethesda, Md., 1993. Mem. editl. bd. Bio Techniques, 1991-96; patentee in field. Rsch. grantee NIH, Bethesda, 1989—, Muscular Dystrophy Assn., Tucson, Ariz., 1993-95. Mem. AAAS, Am. Soc. Biochemistry and Molecular Biology. Office: U Tenn Dept Biochemistry 858 Madison Ave Memphis TN 38103-3409

JARVIS, BILLY BRITT, lawyer; b. Amarillo, Tex., Jan. 9, 1943; s. Billy and Francis Olivia (Beck) J.; m. Linda Jean Holt, Feb. 26, 1965; children: William Britt, Anne Marie, Bonnie Lea. BS in Agrl. Econs., Tex. A&M U., 1965; JD, So. Meth. U., 1968. Bar: U.S. Dist. Ct. (no. dist.) Tex. 1972, U.S. Supreme Ct. 1975. Asst. county atty. Hutchinson County, Borger, Tex., 1968-69; pvt. practice law Spearman, Tex., 1971—; bd. dirs. 1st Nat. Bank Spearman. Contbr. articles to profl. jours. Leader Hansford County 4-H, 1976-91. Capt. U.S. Army, 1969-71, Vietnam. Decorated Bronze Star. Mem. Tex. Bar Assn., Panhandle Bar Assn., Tex. Conf. Bar Pres., Phi Delta

Phi, Masons, Shriners. Democrat. Office: 124 W Kenneth St Box 515 Spearman TX 79081

JARVIS, DAPHNE ELOISE, laboratory administrator; b. Lithia, Fla., Feb. 18, 1945; d. Grady Edwin and Vera Eloise (Smith) Smith; m. Hubert E. Jarvis, Aug. 1, 1964; 1 child, Jessica Ellen. BS, Blue Mountain Coll., 1966; MA, Spalding U., 1972. Cert. med. technologist with specialist in blood bank. Med. technologist St. Anthony's Hosp., Louisville, 1968-69, Clark County Meml. Hosp., Jeffersonville, Ind., 1969-73; asst. to edn. coord. ARC, Washington, 1973-75; dir. Grace Bapt. Ch. Sch., Bryans Rd., Md., 1978-83; sect. chief blood bank Physicians Meml. Hosp., LaPlata, Md., 1975-76, 83-84; supr. donor blood labs. Southwest Fla. Blood Bank, Tampa, 1984-87, dir., 1987-89; asst. dir. tech. svcs. Ark. Region ARC, Little Rock, 1989-93, dir. tech. svcs./hosp. svcs. Ark. Regional Blood Svcs., 1993-95; mfg. team leader Lifeblood-Midsouth Regional Blood Ctr., Memphis, 1995—; lectr. UAMS Sch. Med. Tech., Little Rock, 1989-95. Children's leader Ingram Blvd Bapt. Ch., West Memphis, Ark., 1995—. Mem. Am. Assn. Blood Banks, South Ctr. Assn. Blood Banks (membership com. 1989-95). Office: Lifeblood Midsouth Reg Blood Ctr 1040 Madison Ave Memphis TN 38104-2106

JARVIS, ELBERT, II (JAY JARVIS), employee benefits specialist; b. Washington, N.C., Sept. 20, 1944; s. Elbert J. Sr. and Laura F. (Lilley) J.; m. Anita Kleinfeld, Nov. 28, 1968 (div. Nov. 1983); 1 child, Elbert J. III; m. Audrey H. Liebross, July 28, 1991; 1 child, Benjamin Grover. A of Bus. Adminstrn., No. Va. C.C., 1972; BSBA, George Mason U., 1974. Sales mgr. Baumgarten Co., Washington, 1970-71; sales rep. Mass Mut., Washington, 1974-84; pres. The Pers. Dept., Inc., Annandale, Va., 1983—; founder No. Va. Group Health Alliance. Editor: (student handbook) Focal Point, 1973, Beth El Temple 1995-97, bd. dirs. Directory chair, 1990, 91, 92, 94. Scoutmaster, Webelos leader Boy Scouts Am., Clifton and Arlington, Va., 1970-71, 85-86; mem. county com., state del. Arlington Rep. Party, 1975-85; pres., sec. Arlington Jaycees, 1980-82; pres., bd. dirs. Lafayette Village Cmty. Assn., Annandale, Va., 1994-95, Beth El Hebrew Congregation, 1994—. With USCG, 1963-66. Mem. Am. Compensation Assn., Health Underwriters Assn. (sec. No. Va. chpt. 1996—), Washington chpt. Cert. Employee Benefit Specialists (assoc.), Arlington C. of C. (chmn. comms. com. 1983, bd. dirs. 1988-92, 92-94, chmn. sml. bus. coun. 1990, 92, chmn. expo com. 1991, chmn. awards and sml. bus week 1994, Disting. Svc. awards 1989), Soc. Employee Benefits Profls., Alexandria C. of C. (mem. advantage program com. 1993-96), Fairfax County C. of C. (vice chmn. sml. bus. awards 1993-94, mem. team captain 1996), Lafayette Village Comm. Assn. (pres.). Jewish. Home: 7828 Ashley Glen Rd Annandale VA 22003-1556 Office: The Pers Dept Inc Ste 720 7617 Little River Turnpike Annandale VA 22003

JARVIS, JAMES HOWARD, II, judge; b. Knoxville, Tenn., Feb 28, 1937; s. Howard F. and Eleanor B. J.; m. Martha Stapleton, June 1957 (div. Feb. 1962); children—James Howard III, Leslie; m. Pamela K. Duncan, Aug. 23, 1964 (div. Apr. 1991); children: Ann, Kathryn, Louise; m. Gail Stone, Sept. 4, 1992. BA, U. Tenn., 1958, JD, 1960. Bar: Tenn. 1961, U.S. Dist. Ct. (ea. dist.) Tenn. 1961, U.S. Ct. Appeals (6th cir.) 1965. Assoc. O'Neil, Jarvis, Parker & Williamson, Knoxville, Tenn., 1960-68, mem., 1968-70; mem. Meares, Dungan, Jarvis, Maryville, Tenn., 1970-72; judge Law and Equity Ct., Blount County, Tenn., 1972-77, 30th Jud. Cir. Ct., Blount County, 1977-84, U.S. Dist. Ct. (ea. dist.) Tenn., Knoxville, 1984-91, chief judge, 1991—. Past bd. dirs. Maryville (Tenn.) Coll.; past mem. and chmn. fin. com. St. Andrews Episc. Ch.; past bd. dirs. Detoxification Rehab. Inst. of Knoxville. Mem. ABA (com. ethics and profl. responsibility), Tenn. Bar Assn. (bd. govs. 1983-84), Am. Judicature Soc., Tenn. Trial Judges Assn. (past mem. exec. com.), Tenn. Jud. Conf. (pres. 1983-84), Blount County Bar Assn., Knoxville Bar Assn., Great Smoky Mountains Conservation Assn., Phi Delta Phi, Sigma Chi. Republican. Home: 6916 Stone Mill Rd Knoxville TN 37919-7431 Office: Howard H Baker Jr US Courthouse 800 Market St Knoxville TN 37902-2312

JARVIS, JOANN HELTON, counselor; b. Indpls., Nov. 15, 1962; d. Albert and Velda (Caldwell) Helton; m. Jesse Jarvis, Mar. 3, 1985. BA in Bus. Adminstrn., Lincoln Meml. U., 1986, BA in Elem. Edn., 1988, MA in Elem. Guidance, 1991. Rank I Std. Guidance, Ea. Ky. U., 1996. Coord. youth svc. ctr. Bell County Schs., Pineville, Ky., 1992-93; tchr. Bell County Schs., Pineville, 1992-93, guidance counselor, 1993—. Home: Rt 4 Box 85B Middlesboro KY 40965

JARVIS, JOHN CECIL, lawyer; b. Clarksburg, W.Va., May 11, 1949; s. James M. and Maud Lee (Duncan) J.; m. Rebecca Ann Ullom; children: Amy, Jennie, Brian. BS in Civil Engring., Lehigh U., 1971; JD, Vanderbilt U., 1975. Bar: W.Va. 1975. Ptnr. McNeer, Highland, McMunn and Varner L.C., Clarksburg, 1975—; chmn., bd. dirs. United Hosp. Ctr., Inc.; bd. dirs. One Valley Bank of Clarksburg. Democrat. Presbyterian. Office: McNeer Highland et al PO Box 2040 Clarksburg WV 26302-2040

JARVIS, ROBERT MARK, law educator; b. N.Y.C., Oct. 17, 1959; s. Rubin and Ute (Hacklander) J.; m. Judith Anne Mellman, Mar. 3, 1989. BA, Northwestern U., 1980; JD, U. Pa., 1983; LLM, NYU, 1986. Bar: N.Y. 1984, D.C. 1985, U.S. Dist. Ct. (ea. and so. dists.) N.Y. 1984, U.S. Ct. Mil. Appeals 1985, U.S. Ct. Internat. Trade 1987, U.S. Ct. Appeals (2d cir.) 1987, U.S. Supreme Ct. 1987, U.S. Ct. Appeals (11th cir.) 1989, U.S. Ct. Appeals (D.C. cir.) 1990, U.S. Claims Ct. 1990, Fla. 1990. Assoc. Haight Gardner Poor & Havens, N.Y.C., 1983-85, Baker & McKenzie, N.Y.C., 1985-87; asst. prof. law ctr. Nova Southeastern U., Ft. Lauderdale, Fla., 1987-90, assoc. prof., 1990-92, prof., 1992—; adj. instr. law Yeshiva U., N.Y.C., 1986-87; vis. asst. prof. Tulane U., New Orleans, 1988; adj. prof. law St. Thomas U., Miami, 1991—; lectr. BAR/BRI bar rev. courses, 1991-95; chmn. bd. dirs. Miami Maritime Arbitration Bd., 1993-94; vice chmn. bd. dirs. Miami Internat. Arbitration and Mediation Inst., 1993-94; mem. adv. bd. Carolina Acad. Press, 1996—. Co-author: AIDS: Cases and Materials, 1989, 2d edit., 1995, AIDS Law in a Nutshell, 1991, 2d edit., 1996; author: Careers in Admiralty and Maritime Law, 1993, An Admiralty Law Anthology, 1995; mem. editl. bd. Washington Lawyers, 1988-94, Jour. Maritime Law and Commerce, 1990-92, assoc. editor, 1993-95, editor, 1996—, Maritime Law Reporter, 1991—; mem. editl. adv. bd. Transnat. Lawyer, 1991—; mem. adv. bd. World Arbitration and Mediation Report, 1990—, U. San Francisco Maritime Law Jour., 1992-95; contbg. editor Preview U.S. Supreme Ct. Cases, 1990-95. Mem. ABA (vice chmn. admiralty law com. young lawyers divsn. 1992-93, chair 1993-94), Fla. Bar Assn. (admiralty law com. 1988-95, vice chmn. 1991-92, chmn. 1992-93, exec. coun. internat. law sect. 1992-96), Maritime Law Assn. U.S. (continuing legal edn. com. 1988—), Southeastern Admiralty Law Inst., Assn. Am. Law Schs. (chmn.-elect maritime law sect. 1991-93, chmn. 1993-94), Northwestern U. Club South Fla. (v.p. 1992-93, pres. 1993-95), Phi Beta Kappa, Phi Delta Phi (province pres. 1989-91, coun. 1991-93), Acacia. Democrat. Jewish. Office: Nova Southeastern U Law Ctr 3305 College Ave Fort Lauderdale FL 33314-7721

JARVIS, SUZANNE JONES, secondary school educator; b. Metter, Ga., Nov. 8, 1960; d. James M. and Martha Lou (Carden) Jones; m. James Franklin Jarvis, Jr., Apr. 25, 1987. AA, Mid. Ga. Coll., 1980; BS in Comm. Arts, Ga. So. Coll., 1982, MEd, 1983, EdS, 1990. Weekend editor Statesboro (Ga.) Herald, 1982-83; pub. rels. specialist Mid. Ga. Coll., Cochran, 1983-85; asst. to dean of grad. sch. Ga. So. Coll., Statesboro, 1985-88; English tchr. Swainsboro (Ga.) H.S., 1988-89; Coordinated Vocat. and Acad. Edn. coord./applied comm. tchr. Metter (Ga.) H.S., 1989—. Presenter in field. Adv. bd. dirs. Ga. Coop. Ext., Metter, 1994-95; bd. dirs. Child Abuse Coun., Metter, 1995-96. Recipient Disting. Alumni award Mid. Ga. Coll., 1984. Mem. Nat. Coun. Tchrs. English, Applied Comm. Consortium, Ga. Assn. Theater Educators, Kappa Delta Pi (pres. 1991-92). Methodist. Home: 449 S College St Metter GA 30439 Office: Metter HS 431 W Vertia St Metter GA 30439

JARVIS, WILLIAM ROBERT, epidemiologist, educator; b. Oakland, Calif., June 2, 1948; s. John James and Mattie Belle (Steele) J.; m. Janine M. Jason, July 4, 1982; children: Danielle Kristin, Ashley Alana. BS in Psychology with honors, U. Calif., Davis, 1970; MD, U. Tex., Houston, 1974. Intern U. Tex. Med. Ctr., Houston, 1974-75; resident in pediatrics Children's Hosp. Los Angeles, 1975-77; pediatric infectious disease fellow Toronto Hosp. for Sick Children, 1977-78; fellow pediatric infectious diseases, virology, public health Yale U. Sch. Med., 1978-80; commd. med. officer USPHS, 1980, advanced through grades to capt., 1990; asst. chief Nat. Nosocomial Infections Surveillance Systems Ctrs. for Disease Control, Atlanta, 1981-90, asst. chief epidemiology br., 1984-87, chief epidemiology br. hosp. infections program, 1987-91, chief investigations and prevention br. hosp. infections program, 1991—, acting dir. hosp. infections program, 1996; asst. prof. pediatric infectious disease and immunology Emory U., Atlanta, 1985-96, assoc. prof., 1996—; mem. Joint Commn. on Accreditation of Health Care Orgns. Infection Control Indicator Task Force. Contbr. articles to med. jours., chpts. to books. Mem. Infectious Disease Soc. Am., Am. Soc. Microbiology, Am. Fedn. for Clin. Research, Soc. Hosp. Epidemiologists (severity of illness working group 1987), Sigma Xi. Roman Catholic. Home: 827 W Ponce De Leon Ave Decatur GA 30030-2859 Office: Ctrs Disease Control Invest and Prevention Br Mailstop E-69, 1600 Clifton Rd Atlanta GA 30333

JASICA, ANDREA LYNN, mortgage banking executive; b. Orlando, Fla., Aug. 21, 1945; d. Walter S. and Florence E. (Pasek) J. AA in Pre Bus. Adminstrn. cum laude, Orlando Jr. Coll., 1965; BS with honors, Rollins Coll., 1976. Sec. Am. Mortgage Co. Fla. Inc., Orlando, 1965-68; closing specialist Charter Mortgage Co., Orlando, 1968-70, Gen. Guaranty Mortgage Co. Inc., Winter Park, Fla., 1971; sr. loan processor C.E. Brooks Mortgage Co. Inc., Orlando, 1971-79; v.p. mktg. Twin Homes Ltd., Orlando, 1980-83; asst. v.p., mgr. region Atlantic Mortgage and Investment Corp. subs. Atlantic Nat. Bank, Orlando, 1984-86; v.p. Commerce Nat. Mortgage Co., Winter Park, 1987-88; supr. Bur. of Census, U.S. Dept. Commerce, Orlando, 1990; investor, 1990—; real estate assoc. Atlantic-to-Gulf Realty Inc., 1972-73, Medel Inc., Maitland, Fla., 1973-74; instr. Mortgage Personnel Svcs. Inc. Contbr. articles to profl. jours. Home: 1011 E Harwood St Orlando FL 32803-5706

JASKOT, PAMELA E., librarian; b. Utica, N.Y., Aug. 21, 1954; d. George Harvey and Vera (Neff) Esper; m. Richard H. Jaskot, June 4, 1977; children: Russell, Ryan. BS in Edn., SUNY, Fredonia, 1976; MLS, N.C. Cen. U., 1985. Cert. tchr., libr., N.C. Comm. outreach coord. N.Y. Comm., Dunkirk, 1977-78; ednl. rsch. assoc. NTS Rsch. Co., Durham, 1981-83; tchr. N.Y. State Pub. Schs., 1976-77, 78-80; ref. asst. Durham County Libr., 1983-85, outreach libr., 1985-90, pub. rels. libr., 1990—; com. chmn. Durham Pub. Schs. Reading Adv. Com., 1995—. Coord. church program Holy Infant, Durham, 1992-95; crisis counselor Hassle House, Durham, 1980-82. Mem. ALA (grantee program humanities 1996), N.C. Libr. Assn. (conf. coord., pub. rels. 1990-91). Home: 1529 Sedwick Durham NC 27713

JASZCZAK, RONALD JACK, physicist, researcher, consultant; b. Chicago Heights, Ill., Aug. 23, 1942; s. Jacob and Julia (Gudowicz) J.; m. Nancy Jane Bober, Apr. 15, 1967; children: John, Monica. BS with highest honors, U. Fla., 1964, PhD, 1968. Staff physicist Oak Ridge Nat. 1969-71, AEC postdoctoral fellow, 1968-69; prin. rsch. scientist Searle Diagnostics, Inc., 1971-73, sr. prin. rsch. scientist, 1973, rsch. group leader, 1973-77, chief scientist, 1977-79; assoc. prof. radiology Duke U. Med. Ctr., Durham, N.C., 1979-89, prof., 1989—, assoc. prof. biomedical engring., 1986-91, prof., 1992—; rsch. prof. Inst. of Stats. and Decision Scis., 1992-93; founder, chmn. bd. dirs. Data Spectrum Corp., Chapel Hill, N.C.; investigator Nat. Cancer Inst. Grant, 1983—, Dept. Energy Grant, 1989—. Contbr. articles to profl. jours.; patentee in field. Fellow NASA, 1964-67, U. Fla., 1967-68; RCA scholar, 1963-64. Fellow IEEE; mem. Soc. Nuclear Medicine, Am. Phys. Soc., AAAS, Am. Assn. Physicists in Medicine, Soc. Photo-Optical Instrumentation Engrs., Sigma Xi, Phi Beta Kappa, Phi Kappa Phi, Tau Sigma, Sigma Pi Sigma. Home: 2307 Honeysuckle Rd Chapel Hill NC 27514-1716 Office: Duke U Med Ctr PO Box 3949 Durham NC 27710

JAUCH, LAWRENCE RANDALL, business educator, consultant; b. Chgo., Mar. 12, 1943; s. Harold Randall and Jeanne Carolyn (Double) J.; m. Cathy Ann Campanella, July 2, 1966; children: Lisa Marie Jauch Bradley, Jill Elizabeth Jauch. BS, So. Ill. U., 1965, MSEd, 1967; PhD, U. Mo., 1973. Asst. prof. mgmt. Kans. State U., 1973-76; prof. So. Ill. U., 1976-87; Biedenharn prof. Northeast La. U., 1987—. Co-author: Strategic Management, 1988, Organization Theory, 1982, The Managerial Experience, 1994; assoc. editor: Delta Bus. Rev., 1991—. Chmn. coord. com. Northeast Campus Ministries Coop Day Care Ctr., Monroe, 1991-96. Mem. Acad. of Mgmt. (newsletter editor 1995-97, procs. editor 1992-94), So. Mgmt. Assn. (bd. dirs. 1990-92), Southwest Acad. of Mgmt. (pres. 1992-93). Home: 310 Cheyenne Dr West Monroe LA 71292 Office: Northeast La U Admn 3-17 NLU Monroe LA 71209

JAUNAL, BRIDGET KENNEDY, energy and environmental company executive, consultant; b. Austin, Tex., Dec. 22, 1961; d. Temple Richard and Maureen Elizabeth (Charles) Kennedy; m. Garry William Jaunal, May 5, 1990. BS in Civil Engring., Tex. A&M U., 1984; MBA, Rice U., 1989. Registered profl. engr. Design engr. Walter P. Moore & Assocs., Inc., Houston, 1984-85; engr. Houston Lighting & Power, 1985-88; supervising engr. Cygna Energy Svcs., Houston, 1988-91; v.p., treas., CFO Caledonian Assocs., Inc., Rosenberg, Tex., 1991-92, pres., CEO, 1993—. Active Calvary Episcopal, Richmond, Tex., 1990—. Alice Pratt Brown scholar Rice U., 1987-89, Washington Campus scholar, 1988, Charles H. Hugg scholar Tex. A&M U., 1980-84; recipient Acad. Achievement award Tex. A&M U., 1980-84. Mem. ASCE (br. chmn. 1985), NSPE, Am. Nuclear Soc., Nat. Trust, Tex. Soc. Engrs., Constn. Specifications Inst., Tex. Hist. Found., Smithsonian Inst., Tex. A&M Century Club. Republican. Office: Caledonian Assocs Inc 1810 Avenue M Rosenberg TX 77471-3509

JAVID, NIKZAD SABET, dentist, prosthodontics educator; b. Kashan, Iran, May 24, 1934; s. Salam and Pika (Farhang) Javid-S.; m. Mahnaz Zolfaghari, Oct. 22, 1942; children: Nikrooz, Behrooz, Farnaz. DMD, U. Tehran, Iran, 1958; cert., U. Chgo., 1970; MSc, Ohio State U., 1971; MEd, U. Fla., 1981. Asst. prof. U. Tehran, 1959-69, prof., dean, 1975-79; asst. prof. Ohio State U., 1971-73, assoc. prof., 1973-74; assoc. prof. removable prosthodontics U. Fla., 1974-75, prof., 1982; pvt. practice dentistry specializing in prosthodontics, Gainsville, Fla., 1980—; cons. in field; guest lectr. numerous internat. meetings. Author books, including: Stress Breaker in Partial Denture, 1966, Cleft Palate Prosthetics, 1968, Complete Denture Construction, 1974, (with Sara Nawab) Essentials of Complete Denture Prosthodontics, 1988; contbr. numerous articles to profl. jours. Named Outstanding Clin. Instr. of Yr. Student Dental Council, Columbus, Ohio, 1973, Outstanding Tchr. of Yr. 1990, Excellent Clin. Prof., U. Fla., 1994, Most Outstanding Prof. of Yr., 1996. Fellow Internat. Coll. Dentists, Internat. Coll. Prosthodontics, Am. Coll. Prosthodontics, Am. Acad. Maxillofacial Prosthetics, Royal Soc. Health (Eng.); mem. Iranian Dental Assn. (dir. 1975-78), ADA, Internat. Assn. Dental Research (sec.-treas. Iran div. 1978). Lodge: Lions. Home: 3941 NW 67th Pl Gainesville FL 32653 Office: U Fla PO Box 100435 Gainesville FL 32610-0435

JAY, JAMES ALBERT, retired insurance company executive; b. Superior, Wis., Aug. 24, 1916; s. Clarence William and Louie (Davies) J.; student pub. schs., Mpls.; m. Margie Hoffpauir, Dec. 23, 1941; 1 son, James A. Franchise with The Stauffer System of Calif., 1946-49; Ala. dist. mgr. Guaranty Savs. Life Ins. Co., Montgomery, Ala., 1949-51, state mgr. La., 1951-95, dir., 1952-95, La. gen. agent, 1964-95; La. gen agt. Gen. United Life Ins. Co. of Des Moines (merged with Lincoln Liberty Life Ins. Co., Des Moines, with All Am. Life Ins. Co., Chgo. 1984), 1969-95. Com. chmn. Attakapas council Boy Scouts Am., Alexandria, La., 1955, council commr., 1961-62, commr. Manchac dist., 1967—. Served as cpl. USMC, 1942-45, PTO. Decorated Purple Heart. Mem. Nat., Baton Rouge life underwriters assns., Gen. Agts. and Mgrs. Conf., Internat. Platform Assn. Methodist. Elk. Home: 5919 Clematis Dr Baton Rouge LA 70808-8886

JAYASINGHE, MAHINDA DESILVA, cardiologist; b. Colombo, Sri Lanka, Apr. 21, 1937; came to U.S., 1972; s. Maulis Desilva and Aggresha (DeSilva) J.; m. Inda Kumari Pandita-Gunewardene, Nov. 8, 1973. MD, U. Ceylon, Sri Lanka, 1963; Diploma in Child Health, Royal Coll. Physicians, London, 1972. Diplomate Am. Bd. Pediatric Cardiology. Intern Gen. Hosp., Colombo, 1963-64; resident U. Louisville Affil. Hosp., 1972-76; med. officer Dept. of Health, Colombo, 1964-68; pvt. practice Baton Rouge, 1976—. Contbr. articles to profl. jours. Fellow Am. Coll. Cardiology, Am. Coll. Chest Physician, Am. Acad. Pediatrics. Home: 645 Castle Kirk Dr Baton Rouge LA 70808-6016 Office: 7777 Hennessy Blvd Ste 308 Baton Rouge LA 70808

JAYROE, WILLIAM GORDON, oilfield service company executive; b. Ft. Worth, Sept. 3, 1956; s. Stanley Gordon and Billie Jean (Broughton) J.; m. Margie Elizabeth Waters, Dec. 26, 1977 (div. 1989); children: William Chase, Christine Elizabeth; m. Sally Yvonne Small, Apr. 5, 1991; children: Hunter Gordon, Haley Alexandra. BS in Indsl. Distbn., Tex. A&M U., 1980. Dist. sales & serviceman, office mgr., svc. technician Hughes Tools Co., Brown-Hughes divsn., 1980-81, dist. salesman, 1981-83; dist. mgr. Hughes Tools Co., Brown-Hughes divsn., Corpus Christi & Laredo, Tex., 1983-84; S.W. regional mgr. Tex. and N.Mex., Brown & McMurry Products Hughes Tool Co., Hughes Prodn. Tools Divsn., 1984-86; regional sales mgr. Brown, Centrilift & McMurry Hughes Tool Co., Hughes Prodn. Equipment Divsn., 1986-87; regional ops. mgr. Baker Hughes Inc., Baker Svc. Tools Divsn. Brown Products, 1987; CEO Hunter Energy Inc., 1988-89; pres., owner Turbeco Inc., Houston, 1987—; pres., chief oper. officer Petrovalve U.S.A., 1994—. Mem. Petroleum Equipment Suppliers Assn., Soc. Petroleum Engrs., Am. Petroleum Inst. (chair spl. com.), Tex. A&M Former Students Assn. (gold mem. 1980-94), Greater Houston C. of C. Republican. Home: 15122 Carols Way Dr Houston TX 77070-1117

JAYSON, SHARON KAY, reporter; b. Dallas, Apr. 28, 1955; d. Robert and Louise Adele (Jacobs) J.; m. Kenneth Neil Herman, Jan. 7, 1978; children: Tracey Elise, Jeremy Jayson. BJ, U. Tex., 1976. Radio reporter WFAA Radio, Dallas, 1976-77; TV and radio anchor, reporter KGBT-TV/KELT-FM, Harlingen, Tex., 1978-79; TV anchor, producer, reporter KTBC-TV, Austin, Tex., 1979; TV producer, reporter KVUE-TV, Austin, 1980; capitol bur. chief radio Tex. State Network, Austin, 1981-87; dir. svc. Tex. Daily Newspaper Assn., Austin, 1987-90; reporter Austin Am.-Statesman, 1990—. Mem. Soc. Profl. Journalists (pres. 1991-92, Sunshine award 1992), Tex. Media (chair 1988-90), Nat. Coun. Jewish Women, Hadassah, Jewish Women Internat. (pres. 1985-87). Jewish. Home: 3900 Petra Path Austin TX 78731-1405 Office: Austin Am Statesman PO Box 670 Austin TX 78767-0670

JEANNETTE, JOAN MARIE, pediatrics nurse; b. Orlando, Fla., Sept. 16, 1961; d. Roy Benedict and Joan Theresa (Pleus) Laughlin; m. Ronald Clayton Jeannette, Apr. 25, 1987; 1 child, Patrick Laughlin. BSN, Vanderbilt U., 1983. Cert. pediatrics nurse, 1995. Staff nurse Vanderbilt Children's Hosp., Nashville, 1983-85, asst. nurse coord., 1985-87; office nurse Mid-South Pediat. Urology, Nashville, 1987-89; rehab. nurse pediats. Sea Pines Rehab., Palm Bay, Fla., 1989-90; nurse mgr. pediats. Polk Gen. Hosp., Bartow, Fla., 1990-93; nurse supr. Highlands Regional Med. Ctr., Sebring, Fla., 1993-94; head nurse pediatrics Highlands Regional Hosp., Sebring, Fla., 1994-95, dir. womens and children, 1995—. Recipient Polk County Outstanding Nursing award, 1992; grantee Jr. League of Lakeland, Fla., 1993.

JEANSONNE, ANGELA LYNNE, senior analyst; b. Honolulu, Oct. 3, 1961; d. Charles Preston and Beverly Jean (Ulstad) McKinney; m. William C. Jeansonne, June 11, 1988. BA, Am. U., 1984; MA, George Washington U., 1992. Legis. analyst Sch. Bd. Assn., Washington, 1983-84; edn. analyst Ind. Fed., Washington, 1984-86; analyst Xerox Corp., Arlington, Va., 1986-88; sr. analyst Student Loan Mktg. Assn., Washington, 1988-95. Recipient acad. scholars Am. Univ., Washington, 1982-84, Bryce Harlow scholarship, 1991. Mem. AAUW, Bus. and Profl. Women. Republican. Methodist. Address: PO Box 2787 Columbus MD 21045

JEANSONNE, JEROLD JAMES, technical communications manager; b. Jennings, La., Oct. 8, 1965; s. Vernon Joseph and Opal J. (Desselle) J. BA, La. State U., 1987; MA, N.E. La. U., 1989; PhD, Okla. State U., 1996. Internship Halliburton Svcs., Duncan, Okla., 1991; freelance tech. writer with Atlatl Comm. Inc., Perry, Okla., 1991-94; proposal writer for telecomm. mgmt. program Okla. State U., Stillwater, 1994—; documentation specialist DataStream Sys., Inc., Greenville, S.C., 1994-96, Tech. Comm. Mgr., 1996—; instr. N.E. La. State U., 1987, 89-90, Okla. State U., 1988-89; tech. writing inst. Okla. State U., Stillwater, 1991-94; judge STC Publs. contest. Contbr. articles to profl. publs. Vol. Big Bros./Big Sisters of Am., 1991-93. Recipient Della A. Whitaker Grad. scholarship Soc. for Tech. Comm., 1993. Mem. Sigma Tau Chi. Roman Catholic. Home: 331 Bethel Way Simpsonville SC 29681 Office: Datasys Inc 50 Datastream Plaza Greenville SC 29605

JEDZINIAK, LEE PETER, lawyer, educator, state insurance administrator; b. Springfield, Mass., June 1, 1956; s. Leo Stanley and Helena (Ludwin) J. BA in Polit. Sci., The Citadel, 1978; JD, U. S.C., 1981. Bar: S.C. 1981, U.S. Dist. Ct. S.C. 1982, U.S. Ct. Appeals (4th cir.) 1982, U.S. Ct. Appeals (11th and D.C. cirs.) 1983, U.S. Ct. Appeals (3d, 5th and 10th cirs.) 1984, U.S. Tax Ct. 1985, U.S. Ct. Appeals (9th cir.) 1985, U.S. Supreme Ct. 1985. Law clk. to presiding justice 15th Jud. Cir. Ct., Conway, S.C., 1981-83; atty. consumer advs. office State of S.C., Columbia, 1983-85, staff counsel dept. ins., 1985-88, gen. counsel dept. ins., 1988-95, dir. ins., 1995—; profl. lectr. MPA and MBA depts. Golden Gate U., 1984-90, St. Leo Coll., 1990-93, Troy State U., 1991—. Mem. S.C. Bar Assn., Citadel Alumni Assn. Roman Catholic. Office: SC Dept Ins 1612 Marion St Columbia SC 29201-2939

JEFFERIES, JOSEPH VINCENT, safety engineer; b. Edgewood, Ky., Apr. 27, 1967; s. Patrick Joseph and Mary Ann (DeVore) J.; m. Melissa G. Brown, May 16, 1992. BS, Murray State U., 1990, MS, 1992. Cert. safety profl. Contract safety engr. Occidental Chemical Corp., Muscle Shoals, Ala., 1992-93; safety assoc. Occidential Chemical Corp., Taft, La., 1993-94, safety engr., 1995-96; sr. safety engr., 1996—. Mem. Am. Soc. Safety Engrs. (v.p. River Parish sect. New Orleans chpt. 1994-95, pres. New Orleans chpt. 1995—). Office: Occidental Chemical Corp LA 3142 Hahnville LA 70057

JEFFERIES, WILLIAM MCKENDREE, internist, educator; b. Richmond, Va., Oct. 1, 1915; s. Richard Henry and Mary Adeline (Harris) J.; m. Jeanne Telfair Mercer, Dec. 28, 1946 (dec. Dec., 1991); children: Richard Mercer, Scott McKendree, Colin Tucker, Leslie McLaurin. BA summa cum laude, Hampden Sydney Coll., 1935; MD, U. Va., 1940. Diplomate Am. Bd. Internal Medicine. Instr. in Math., Physics, Chemistry McGuires Univ. Sch., Richmond, Va., 1936; resident Mass. Gen. Hosp., Boston, 1940-42; flight surgeon San Antonio Aviation Cadet Ctr., 1942; post surgeon India China Div. Air Transport Command, 1943-45, divsn. med. inspector, 1945; rsch. fellow Am. Cancer Soc. Com. on Growth NRC Harvard Med. Sch., Boston, 1946-49; from instr. to asst. prof. medicine Case Western Reserve Med. Sch., Cleve., 1949-92; clin. prof. medicine U. Va. Sch. of Medicine, Charlottesville, 1993—; mem. internship com. Univ. Hosps., Cleve., 1955-65; bd. dirs. Brush Found., 1966-67; mem. com. for human investigation Luth. Med. Ctr., Cleve., 1977-92; chmn. diabetes adv. com. Euclid Gen. Hosp., Cleve., 1979-82. Author: (med. books) Safe Uses of Cortisone, 1981, Safe Uses of Cortisol, 1996; contbr. articles to profl. jours., chpts. to books. Com. mem. Boy Scouts Am., Shaker Heights, Ohio, 1957-68; past chmn. coun. of deacons, bd. of ministry and fellowship Plymouth Ch. of Shaker Heights. Lt. col. med. corps U.S. Army (attached to air force) India Burma Theatre. Fellow ACP; mem. AAAS, SAR, AMA, N.Y. Acad. Scis., Albermarle County Med. Soc., Am. Thyroid Assn. (Van Meter award 1949), Clin. Immunology Soc., Endocrine Soc., Am. Fertility Soc., Am. Fedn. for Clin. Rsch., Ctrl. Soc. for Clin. Rsch., Friends of Nat. Libr. of Medicine, Am. Legion, Cheshire Cheese Club, Raven Soc., Phi Beta Kappa, Omicron Delta Kappa, Alpha Omega Alpha, Kappa Alpha, Phi Beta Pi.

JEFFERSON, SANDRA TRAYLOR, choreographer, ballet coach; b. Tarboro, N.C., Feb. 28, 1942; d. Charles Labon and Doris Vivian (Parker) Traylor; m. Milton Franklin Jefferson, July 2, 1960; children: Mark Franklin, Todd Christopher. Student, Parks Sch. Dance, Petersburg, Va., 1947-58, Sch. of the Richmond (Va.) Ballet, 1958-60; diploma, Julia Mildred Harper Sch. Dance, Richmond, 1960; studied with Robert David Brown, Sterling, Va., 1978-80. Soloist Ballet Impromptu, Richmond, 1958-60; freelance dance instr. Chantilly, Va., 1968-70; ballet coach Artistic Skating Club of Sterling, 1980; founder, dir. Ballet for Skaters, Manassas, Va., 1980-89; artistic dir., cons. in choreography No. Va. Artistic Skating Club, Manassas, 1986-89; artistic dir. Skating Club of Manassas, 1989; founder, dir. Ballet for Skaters, Seabrook, Md., 1989-94; choreographer, ballet coach Nat. Capitol Dance and Figure Club, Seabrook and Washington, 1989-94; founder, dir. Ballet for Figure Skaters, Sterling, Va., 1993-94; students include nat. medalists in the U.S. and Can. and mems. Can. World Team, U.S. Olympic Sports Festival Team; freelance choreographer, ballet coach, Sterling, 1993—. Developer: Brosano Technique Vocabulary of Movement, 1986, Free Form Ballet, 1993; co-developer (artistic skating technique) Brosano Technique, 1981. Social dir. Jaycee-ettes, Winchester, Va., 1963-67. Recipient Achievement award Jaycee-ettes, 1963, 64, 65, 66, 67, U.S. S.E. Soc. Roller Skating Tchrs. Am. award, 1988, World Decoration of Excellence award Am. Biog. Inst., 1989. Mem. Profl. Dance Tchrs. Assn. Methodist. Home and Office: 507 S Maple Ct Sterling VA 20164-2710

JEFFORDS, EDWARD ALAN, former state attorney general; b. Rector, Ark., Nov. 28, 1945; s. Roy Ezra and Sylvia Belle (Dickinson) J.; AA, Victor Valley Coll., 1967; student U. Wis. Mgmt. Inst., 1977; BS, USNY-Albany, 1983; JD, Baylor U. Sch. Law, 1985; postgrad. Harvard U., 1991; DHL (hon.) Harington Coll., 1976. Bar: Tex. 1985, U.S. Dist Ct. (we. dist.) Tex. 1985, U.S. Ct. Appeals (5th cir.) 1985, U.S. Dist. Ct. (so. dist.) Tex. 1986, U.S. Dist. Ct. (no. dist.) Tex. 1988, U.S. Supreme Ct. 1989; bd. cert. civil trial law, personal injury law, Tex. bd. legal specialization, 1990; cert. civil trial adv., Nat. Bd. Trial Advocacy, 1995. Editor, Auburn (Wash.) Globe-News, 1967-70; fine arts editor Tacoma News-Tribune, 1970-75; exec. dir. Ozark Inst., Eureka Springs, 1976-82; asst. atty. gen. State of Tex., Austin, 1985-92; exec. editor Baylor Law Rev., 1984-85; adj. prof. Nat. U. of Costa Rica, 1989-90; exec. dir. Pan Am. Ednl. Found., 1989—; trustee Regents Coll., USNY, 1990—; advocate Nat. Coll. Advocacy. With USAF, 1963-67. Mem. ABA, Travis County Bar Assn., Tex. Trial Lawyers Assn., Assn. Trial Lawyers Am., Am. Judicature Assn., Order of Barrister, State Bar Coll., State Pro Bono Coll., Univ. Club, Million Dollar Adv. Forum, Delta Theta Phi. Office: PO Box 2521 Austin TX 78768-2521

JEFFREY, SHIRLEY RUTHANN, publisher; b. Durant, Okla., Aug. 5, 1936; d. Hubert D. and Pauline (Blain) Carr; m. Dwight W. Jeffrey, Oct. 6, 1966; children: Robin Kimberly Reese, Paula Cherie Lyon, Michelle Jolie Jeffrey. AA, El Camino Coll., Gardena, Calif., 1962; BA, U. So. Calif., L.A., 1966. Cert. Ikebana tchr., Tokyo. Publisher Pelican Publs., Denton, Tex. Co-author: Gesneriad Judges Manual, 1989; author/editor: Internat. Cookbook, 1990, Episcias, 1990; contbr. articles to various jours. Hdqs. worker Rep. Ctrl. Com., Denton, 1988, coord. vols., 1993-94, mem. exec. com., precinct chmn., 1993—, polit. campaign mgr., 1995-96, 1st vice chmn., Denton County Rep. Party; bd. dirs. Am. Cancer Soc., Denton, 1975-77; referee U.S. Soccer Fedn., Denton, 1980-81. Mem. NAFE, Nat. Assn. Securities Dealers (registered rep.), U.S. SEC (registered investment advisor) Gesneriad Soc. Internat. (pres. 1987-90), North Tex. African Violet Judges Coun. (pres. 1975-76), First African Violet Soc. of New Orleans (pres. 1973-74), Nat. Assn. Parliamentarians, Tex. State Assn. Parliamentarians, Am. Gloxinia and Gesneriad Soc. (sr. judge), Am. Assn. Ret. Persons (chpt. bd. dirs. 1992—), others. Episcopalian. Home: 1918 Williamsburg Row Denton TX 76201-2227 Office: Pelican Publs PO Box 720 Denton TX 76202-0720

JEFFREYS, CHARLES WAYNE, advertising executive; b. Fort Worth, Feb. 18, 1945; s. Charles T. and Bessie V. (Chance) J.; m. Penny L. Howell, June 15, 1968; 1 child, William T. BBA, Tex. Christian U., 1967. Salesman Fort Worth Star-Telegram, 1967-68; asst. mgr. All Ch. Press, Fort Worth, 1968-70; v.p. Dally Advt., Dallas, 1970—. Scoutmaster Boy Scouts Am., Arlington, Tex.; past chmn. N.W. Christian Ch., Arlington. Mem. Advt. Club Fort Worth, Rotary (chair pub. rels. Arlington chpt. 1976—). Home: 2001 Candlewood Dr Arlington TX 76012-2207 Office: Dally Advt 3535 Travis St Dallas TX 75204-1448

JEFFREYS, MARGARET VILLAR (PEGGI JEFFREYS), oil company executive; b. Pensacola, Fla., Mar. 1, 1953; d. William Edward and Betty Sue (Cimiotti) Villar; m. E. Geoffrey Jeffreys, Feb. 28, 1975. Student, Pensacola Jr. Coll., 1971-72; numerous seminars. Sec., treas. Major Oil Co., Jackson, Miss., and Mobile, Ala., 1973-75, v.p., 1975-77; v.p. The Jeffreys Co., Inc., Mobile, 1977-91, pres., 1991—; sec.-treas. Koala Energy Co., LLC; adminstr. Miller, Hamilton, Snider & Odom, L.L.C. Attys., 1995-96; ind. cons., 1996—. Pres. Art Patrons League, Mobile, 1982-83, 1st v.p., 1981-82, treas., 1979-81, allied arts coun. rep., 1982-83; pres. Freedoms Found. at Valley Forge, Mobile, 1983-84, v.p. for awards, 1982-83, v.p. for edn., 1980-82; pres. midtown Mobile Assn., 1980-91; treas. Women of Trinity Episcopal Ch., Mobile, 1982-84, pres. 1989-90; dir. Wilmer Hall Children's Home, Mobile, 1990-93. Mem. Ala. Petroleum Landmen's Assn. (sec. 1983-84, bd. dirs. 1986-89), Am. Assn. Petroleum Landmen, Assn. Legal Adminstrs., Bienville Club (Mobile), Pt. Clear (Ala.) Tennis Club. Episcopalian. Home: 1001 Loma Alta Tower 100 Tower Dr Daphne AL 36526-7461 also: 4047 Mansion Dr NW Washington DC 20006 Office: The Jeffreys Co Inc PO Box 66227 106 5th St Daphne AL 36526

JEFFRIES, CAROL J(EAN), information systems educator; b. Denver, Oct. 5, 1957; d. John Deitz and Elta Frances J. B in Mus. Edn. magna cum laude, Baylor U., 1979; MBA in Info. Sys., U. Tex., Arlington, 1984, PhD in Bus. Adminstrn., 1990. Music educator Richardson (Tex.) Ind. Sch. Dist., 1979-82; grad. asst. U. Tex., Arlington, 1982-84, asst. instr., 1984-88; lectr. U. N.C., Charlotte, 1989-90, asst. prof., 1990-96; assoc. prof. Our Lady of the Lake U., San Antonio, 1996—; textbook reviewer Addison-Wesley Pub. Co., Reading, Mass., 1990, Susan Solomon Comm., Cupertino, Calif., 1991. Sys. analyst, cons. Catawba Indian Nation, Rock Hill, S.C., 1991-93, Family Ctr., Charlotte, N.C., 1994-95. Rsch. grantee Belk Coll Bus., 1992. Mem. AAUP, AAUW, Decision Scis. Inst., Assn. for Computing Machinery, Info. Resource Mgmt. Assn., Assn. for Info. Sys., Assn. for Info. Tech. Profls., Beta Gamma Sigma, Alpha Iota Delta, Gamma Beta Phi, Pi Kappa Lambda. Office: Our Lady of the Lake Univ Sch Bus and Pub Adminstrn 411 SW 24th St San Antonio TX 78207-4689

JEHLE, KATHRYN ELIZABETH, criminal justice educator, lawyer; b. Birmingham, Ala., July 28, 1964; d. Lawrence Thomas Jr. and Rebecca Louise (Hawsey) J. BS, Auburn U., 1989, MS, 1990; JE, Faulkner U., 1993. Cert. legal asst. technician, legal asst. adminstr. Law intern Atty. Gen.'s Office of Ala., Montgomery, 1989-90; law clk. Sasser & Littleton, Montgomery, 1991-93; instr. art Factory, Montgomery, 1994—; adj. instr. criminal justice Troy (Ala.) State U., 1994—. Mem. Victims of Crime and Leniency (V.O.C.A.L.), Montgomery, 1989-94. Mem. Auburn U. Alumni Assn. Republican. Roman Catholic. Home: # 1027 2600 Vaughn Lakes Dr Montgomery AL 36117

JELKS, MARY LARSON, retired pediatrician; b. Galva, Ill., 1929. MD, U. Nebr., 1955. Diplomate Am. Bd. Pediats., Am. Bd. Allergy and Immunology. Intern Johns Hopkins Hosp., Balt., 1955-56, resident, 1956-57, 58-60; resident Grace-New Haven Hosp., 1957; fellow U. Fla. Tchg. Hosp., 1960-61; clin. asst. prof. U. South Fla.; ret. Fellow Am. Acad. Allery and Immunology, Am. Acad. Pediats.; mem. AMA. Home: 1930 Clematis St Sarasota FL 34239-3813

JELSMA, DENNY GENE, water company executive; b. Pella, Iowa, Nov. 12, 1945; s. Irvin and Helen Lucille (Bruns) J.; m. (div. Apr. 1986); m. Martha McConnell, June 2, 1990. Student, A.I.B. Bus. Sch., 1965. Salesman Midwest Bus. Forms, Knoxville, Iowa, 1965-68; salesman, sales mgr. Lindsay Soft Water, Oskaloosa, Iowa, 1968-71; from mgr. to owner, pres. Lindsay Soft Water, Jacksonville, Fla., 1971-75; from. dist. sales trainer to regional mgr., field v.p. Culigan USA, Northbrook, Ill., 1975-1985; owner, pres. Culligan Water Conditioning, Inc., Kingsland, Ga., 1985-94. Author: The Jelsma Family History, 1994. A founding father Nat. Culligan Dealer Assn. Named Ky. Col. by Gov. Ky. Mem. Nat. Rifle Assn., Rotary, Masons (life), Shriners. Home: 2238 Winding Creek Ln Jacksonville FL 32246-4136 Office: The Jelsma Co 2238 Winding Creek Ln Jacksonville FL 32246-4136

JENAB, S. ABE, civil and water resources engineer; b. Isfahan, Persia, Mar. 26, 1936; came to U.S., 1959; s. Mohamad Taghi and Soghra (Beigom) J.; children: Jenia, Jima. MS, Utah State U., 1962, PhD, 1967. Registered profl. engr. Instr. Tehran U., 1962-64; from asst. prof. to assoc. prof. Utah State U., Logan, 1967-69; vis. prof. Utah Stae U., Logan, 1983-85; dir. water resources engring. dept. Agrl. Devel. Bank of Iran, Tehran, 1969-70; pres., mgr. Aabadin Engring. Inc., Tehran, 1973-83; assoc. prof. Tehran, Isfahan and Shiraz Univs., Iran, 1969-83; sr. engr. St. Johns River Water Mgmt. Dist., Palatka, Fla., 1985—; cons. Iranian Plan Orgn., Tehran, 1973-83; advisor, cons. Ministry of Water and Power, Tehran, 1975-83; cons. Hwy. Dept., Ogden, Utah, 1984-85, Iranian Plant Orgn., 1970-75; tech. cons. UN Devel. Program; numerous cons. positions. Contbr. more than 30 articles to profl. jours. Recipient Hon. medal Internat. Commn. on Irrigation, 1972; grantee U.S. Dept. Agr., 1967, Iranian Plan Orgn., 1970, others. Mem. ASCE, Am. Soc. Agrl. Engrs. Home: PO Box 1922 Palatka FL 32178-1922 Office: St Johns River Water Mgmt PO Box 1429 Palatka FL 32178-1429

JENKIN, DOUGLAS ALAN, computer consultant; b. Dovercourt, England, Sept. 14, 1932; came to U.S., 1973; s. William Douglas and Violet Foss (Harvey) J.; m. Rosemary Joan Finch, July 30, 1937 (dec.); children: Paul, Sally, Richard, Christopher. BA in Natural Sci., Oxford, England, 1956, MA, 1959. Chartered engr. Process engr., planner Esso Petroleum Co., Fawley, England, 1956-63; econs. engr. Altona Petrochem. Co., Altona, Victoria, Australia, 1963-65; systems analyst C-E-I-R Ltd., London, 1965-68; programmer C-E-I-R, Inc., Washington, 1968-69; mgr. math. program Scicon Ltd., London, 1969-73; lectr. computer sci. Birkbeck Coll., London, 1970-73; examiner computer sci. London U., 1970-73; mgr. North Am. Scicon Ltd., Houston, 1973-74; v.p. Bonner and Moore Assocs., Inc., Houston, 1974-91; staff analyst AspenTech. (formerly Setpoint Inc.), Houston, 1991—. Contbr. articles to profl. jours. Served as pilot officer RAF, 1951-53, England. Fellow British Computer Soc.; mem. Inst. for Ops. Rsch. and the Mgmt. Svc. Home: 213 Elkins Lk Huntsville TX 77340-7305 Office: AspenTech 14701 Saint Marys Ln Houston TX 77079-2905

JENKINS, ALAN DELOSS, urologic surgeon, educator; b. Carlsbad, N.Mex., Dec. 10, 1949; s. Robert Deloss and Alice Dorothy (Anderson) J.; m. Barbara Jean Sprowls, June 6, 1970; children: Katherine Hamilton, Peter Anders, Andrew Deloss, Matthew Persson. SB in Physics, MIT, 1971; MD, Boston U., 1975. Resident surgery U. Va., Charlottesville, 1975-77, resident urology, 1977-81, asst. prof. urology, 1984-90, assoc. prof., 1990—; rsch. fellow Mayo Clinic, Rochester, Minn., 1981-83; asst. prof. surgery U. Tex. Med. Sch., Houston, 1983-84; mem. exam com. AUA/ABU, Houston, 1988-92. Assoc. sect. editor Jour. Urology, 1985; asst. editor Jour. Endourology, 1987; co-author: Stone Surgery, 1991. Fellow ACS; mem. Am. Urol. Assn. Home: 250 Spring Ln Charlottesville VA 22903-7645 Office: U Va Sch Medicine Dept Urology Box 422 Charlottesville VA 22908

JENKINS, CLARA BARNES, psychology educator; b. Franklinton, N.C.; d. Walter and Stella (Griffin) Barnes; BS, Winston-Salem State U., 1939; MA, N.C. Ctl. U., 1947; EdD, U. Pitts., 1964; postgrad., N.Y.U., 1947-48, U. N.C.-Chapel Hill, 1963, N.C. Agrl. and Tech. State U., 1971; m. Hugh Jenkins, Dec. 24, 1949 (div. Feb. 1955). Tchr. pub. schs., Wendell, N.C., 1939-43, Wise, N.C., 1943-45; mem. faculty Fayetteville State U., 1945-53, Rust Coll., Holly Spring, Miss., 1953-58; asst. prof. Shaw U., 1958-64; prof. edn. and psychology St. Paul's Coll., Lawrenceville, Va., 1964-91 ; vis. prof. edn. Friendship Jr. Coll., Rock Hill, S.C., summer 1947, N.C. Agrl. and Tech. State U., 1966-83. Former mem. bd. dirs. Winston-Salem State U. Notary pub., N.C.; bd. dirs. annual giving fund U. Pitts.; United Negro Coll. Fund Faculty fellow, 1963-64; Am. Bapt. Conv. grantee, 1963-64. Mem. AAUP, Nat. Soc. for Study Edn., NEA, AAUW, Am. Hist. Assn., Va. Edn. Assn., Am. Acad. Polit. and Social Sci., AAAS, Internat. Platform Assn., Assn. Tchr. Educators, History Edn. Soc., Doctoral Assn. Educators, Am. Assn. Higher Edn., Am. Soc. Notaries, Acad. Polit. Sci., Am. Psychol. Assn., Soc. Research in Child Devel., Am. Soc. Notaries, Jean Piaget Soc., Philosophy of Edn. Soc., Soc. Profs. Edn., Am. Soc. Notaries, Leadership Coun., So. Poverty Law Ctr., Phi Eta Kappa, Zeta Phi Beta, Phi Delta Kappa, Kappa Delta Pi. Episcopalian. Home and Office: 920 Bridgers St Henderson NC 27536-3736

JENKINS, CLAUSTON LEVI, JR., college president; b. Durham, N.C., Mar. 4, 1938; s. Clauston Levi Sr. and Mary (Asbill) J.; m. Elizabeth H. Boney, Dec. 11, 1993. AB, U. N.C., 1960; MA, U. Va., 1963, PhD, 1966; JD, U. N.C., 1975. Tchr. English Broughton High Sch., Raleigh, N.C., 1961; asst. prof. U. Wis., Madison, 1966-68, asst. dir. acad. programs, 1968-70; coord. instnl. studies N.C. State U., Raleigh, 1970-73, univ. counsel, 1976-86; pres. St. Mary's Coll., Raleigh, 1986—. Mem. Raleigh C. of C. (bd. dirs.), Phi Beta Kappa, Phi Eta Sigma. Home: 1209 College Pl Raleigh NC 27605-1802 Office: St Marys Coll 900 Hillsborough St Raleigh NC 27603-1689

JENKINS, DANIEL EDWARDS, JR., physician, educator; b. Omaha, July 19, 1916; s. Daniel Edwards and Anne (Finley) J.; m. Dora Solis, Aug. 1, 1942; children—Daniel Edwards III, Mark Schering, Tessa Ann. Student, Hampden-Sydney Coll., 1934; B.A., U. Tex., 1936, M.D., 1940. Intern, then resident U. Mich. Hosp., 1940-44; asst. prof. medicine, chief med. tuberculosis unit U. Mich. Med. Sch., 1946-47; asst. prof. medicine Baylor Coll. Medicine, 1947-55, prof. internal medicine, 1956—, chief sect. pulmonary diseases, 1947-74, chief sect. environ. medicine, 1974-91; part-time pvt. practice, 1947-91; pvt. practice Respiratory Cons. of Houston, 1991-96; chief pulmonary disease service Harris County Hosp. Dist., 1947-74; cons. VA, 1949-75. Contbr. articles to profl. jours. Med. bd. dirs. Harris County Hosp. Dist., 1967-90. Recipient So. Conf. award So. Tb Conf., 1967. Fellow A.C.P., Am. Coll. Chest Physicians (pres. So. chpt. 1958); mem. AMA, Am. Thoracic Soc. (pres. 1958-59), Am. Fedn. Clin. Research, Am. Clin. and Climatol. Assn., Am. Lung Assn. (dir. 1958-75, pres. 1967-68, Hall of Fame 1980), Tex. Tb and Respiratory Disease Assn. (dir. 1949-82, pres. 1966-67, hon. dir. 1982—), Alpha Omega Alpha, Alpha Kappa Kappa. Home: 3550 Sun Valley Dr Houston TX 77025-4146

JENKINS, DOLORES CHRISTINA, librarian, consultant; b. Gainesville, Fla., July 7, 1946; d. Thomas Joseph and Maria Carmen (Busto) J. BA in History, Fla. Atantic U., 1969; MSLS, Fla. State U., 1970. Asst. dir. Cocoa (Fla.) Pub. Libr., 1970-72; journalism libr. U. Fla., Gainesville, 1973—; dir. U.S. newspaper program Fla./NEH/Libr. Congress, 1993—. Author: State Media Law Sourcebook, 1992; editor: First Amendment Issues and the Mass Media, 1991. With USN, 1970. Mem. Assn. for Edn. in Journalism and Mass Comm. (chmn. mass comm. bibliographers 1992-94, newsletter editor 1990—), Fla. News Libr., Fla. Defenders the Environ., Jane Austen Soc. N.Am. (regional coord. Fla. 1989-95). Office: Univ Fla Libraries 142 Library W Gainesville FL 32611-2048

JENKINS, EDWIN FRED, minister; b. Birmingham, Ala., Aug. 21, 1948; s. Warren Frederick and Johnnie Louise (Milstead) J.; m. Joan Evans, Dec. 21, 1969; children: Andrew Edwin, Matthew Russell, Amanda Elyese. Student, U. Ala., 1966-67; BA, Samford U., 1970; MDiv, Southwestern Bapt. Theol. Sem., 1973, DMin, 1976. Ordained to ministry So. Bapt. Conv., 1972. Pastor Lone Willow Bapt. Ch., Cleburne, Tex., 1972-73, First Bapt. Ch., Milford, Tex., 1973-75, Calvary Bapt. Ch., Rosenberg, Tex., 1975-79, First Bapt. Ch., Katy, Tex., 1979-84, Hilldale Bapt. Ch., Birmingham, Ala., 1984—; instr. religion Jefferson State Community Coll., Birmingham, 1987-90, Samford U. Ext., Birmingham, 1985-86. Fund raising chmn. Salvation Army, Rosenberg, 1976; trustee Bapt. Home for Sr. Citizens, Birmingham, 1987-89; mem. State Bd. of Mission, Ala. Bapt. Conv., 1990—, vice chmn., 1993-94, mem. exec. com., 1993—, chmn., 1995-96. Mem. Am. Assn. Christian Counselors, Birmingham Bapt. Assn. (vice moderator 1990-92, moderator, 1992-94, vice chmn. campus ministries 1986-87), Pastors for Life, Birmingham Bapt. Mins. Conf. (pres. 1989-90), Birmingham Brasilia Partnership (chmn. steering com. 1989-92), Richmond-Rosenberg C. of C., Rosenberg-Richmond Optimist Club (bd. dirs. 1977-78), Rotary (Katy, Tex.), Civitan Internat. Home: 534 24th Ave NW Birmingham AL 35215-2329 Office: Hilldale Bapt Ch 533 Sunhill Rd NW Birmingham AL 35215-2346

JENKINS, FRANCES OWENS, retail owner; b. Leonard, Tex., Nov. 12, 1924; d. R. Melrose and Maureen (Durrett) Owens; m. William O. Jenkins (div. 1961); children: Steven O., Tamara. Student theatre arts East Tex. State U., 1939-42, Ind. U., 1945-48, U. Tenn., 1954-56. Fashion model Rogers Modeling Agy., Boston, 1950-52, Rich's, Knoxville, Tenn., 1955-60; owner, instr. Arts Sch. of Self-Improvement and Modeling, Knoxville, 1959-69; owner, pres. Fran Jenkins Boutique, Knoxville, 1964-95, ret., 1995; cons. Miss Am. Pageant, Knoxville, 1958-66. Actress Carousel Theatre, Knoxville, 1955-58. Home: 8833 Cove Point Ln Knoxville TN 37922-6402

JENKINS, HELEN WILLIAMS, administrative dietitian; b. Marion, N.C., Aug. 1, 1921; d. John Andrew and Ethel W. (Bailey) Williams; m. Marshall D. Jenkins, Feb. 17, 1946; children: Barbara Ann, Ronald Lee. BS cum laude, Carson-Newman, Jefferson City, Tenn., 1944; MA, Emory U., 1974. Registered and Lic. dietitian. Mgr. food svc. Roane Anderson Co., Oak Ridge, Tenn., 1944-45; food svc. asst. dir. Emory U., Atlanta, 1945-55, food svc. dir., 1955-84, dir. dietetic internship, 1967-70, asst. prof. nutrition, 1970-90, food svc. liaison, 1984—; historian Nat. Assn. Coll. and Univ. Food Svc., 1990-91; adv. Vocat. Edn. Bd., Ga. 1965-73; publ. editor nat. Assn. Coll. & Univ. Food Svc., Chgo., 1965-68; pres. Ga. Dietetic Assn., Atlanta 1963-64, Southeastern Hosp. Dietitian Assn., Atlanta, 1959-60. Author: Systems Management in Dietetics, rev. 1988; contbr. articles to profl. jours. Mem. Nat. Assn. Coll. and Univ. Food Svc., Am. Dietetic Assn. (com. chmn. 1965-69), Ga. Nutrition Coun. (pres. 1968-69, nominating com. 1993-94), Dieticians in Coll. and Univ. Food Svc. (nominating com. chmn. 1989-90), Ga. Dietetic Assn. (teller 1994-95), Altrusa Internat. (Atlanta) (pres. 1961-62). Republican. Baptist. Home: 2331 N Decatur Rd Decatur GA 30033-5503 Office: Emory Univ PO Box YY Atlanta GA 30322-1001

JENKINS, HOWARD M., supermarket executive; b. 1951. MBA, Emory U. With Publix Supermarkets, Inc., Lakeland, Fla., 1966—, v.p. rsch., exec. v.p., 1976-90, chmn. bd. dirs., CEO, 1990—. Office: Publix Supermarkets Inc PO Box 407 Lakeland FL 33802-0407 also: 1936 George Jenkins Blvd Lakeland FL 33801*

JENKINS, JAMES SHERWOOD, JR., pharmacologist; b. Franklin, Tenn., July 25, 1941; s. Jim S. and Martha (Austin) J.; divorced; children: Gregory S., Leah E., Gerald B., Cheryl C., Jason J.; m. Tina M. Jenkins; children: Kenneth, Candice, Christina. BS, David Lipscomb U., 1962; Pharmacy degree, U. Tenn., 1965, PD, 1974; Cert. Geriatic Practice, U. Miss., 1987. Diplomate Am. Acad. Pain Mgmt.; lic. pharmacist, pharmacologist. Clin. practice, rsch., 1969—, pvt. rsch. in hypertension therapy and others, 1980—. Mem. editl. adv. bd. Am. Jour. Pain Mgmt.; contbr. articles to profl. jours. Holder over 40 world and U.S. aviation speed records. Fellow Am. Coll. Apothecaries; mem. Nat. Aeronautic Assn. (life), Phi Delta Chi. Office: Clin Pharmacology Cons PO Box 772 Goodlettsville TN 37070-0772

JENKINS, JOHNIE NORTON, research geneticist, research administrator; b. Barton, Ark., Nov. 3, 1934; married, 1959; 2 children. BSA, U. Ark., 1956; MS, Purdue U., 1958, PhD in Genetics, 1960. Rsch. assoc. in agronomy U. Ill., Urbana, 1960-61; rsch. geneticist Agrl. Rsch. Svc., USDA, 1961-80; dir. Crop Sci. Rsch. Lab. Agrl. Rsch. Svc., USDA, Mississippi State, Miss., 1980—; prof. crop sci. and mem. grad. faculty Miss. State U., 1964—. Recipient Mobay Cotton Rsch. Recognition award. Fellow AAAS, Am. Soc. Agronomy, Crop Sci. Soc. Am.; mem. Entomol. Soc. Am. Office: USDA-ARS Crop Sci Rsch Lab PO Box 5367 Mississippi State MS 39762

JENKINS, LINDA DIANE, accountant; b. Detroit, Jan. 8, 1960; d. Robert A. Martinez and Marillyn June (Owens) Scheere; m. George Edwin Jenkins, Oct. 21, 1978 (div. May 1992); children: Stephanie Marie, Mark Richard. Student, RETS Electronics Sch., Detroit, 1978; AA in Bus. Adminstrn. with honors, St. Petersburg Jr. Coll., Tarpon Springs, Fla., 1987; BS in Acctg., U. South Fla., 1991. CPA, Fla. Acct. Carl Lawson & Assocs., Inc., New Port Richey, Fla., 1986-88, Garcia & Ortis PA CPA's-GOC Inc., St. Petersburg, Fla., 1992; treas. New Life Foursquare Gospel Ch., Bayonet Point, Fla., 1988-90; fin. adminstr. M.P. Spychala & Assocs., Inc., Safety Harbor, Fla., 1988-91; project acct., network adminstr. Harbour Assocs. Constrn. Co., Tampa, Fla., 1992-94; pvt. practice acctg. Clearwater, Fla., 1994—. Fla. Soc. CPAs. Home: 1701 Marion St Clearwater FL 34616-6200 Office: Linda D Jenkins CPA 1701 Marion St Clearwater FL 34616-6200

JENKINS, LORETTA JEAN, retired educator; b. Wharton, Tex., Feb. 16, 1945; d. Jesse Leary and Gillis Marie (Rhoades) Jones; m. William Earl Jenkins, Aug. 19, 1967; children: Dana Gerber, Barrett Keith, Audrey Annette, David Wayne. AA, Ctrl. Coll., McPherson, Kans., 1965; BA, Greenville Coll., 1968. Cert. tchr., Tex. 5th grade tchr. Junction City (Ky.) schs., 1968-69; spl. edn. tchr. Boyle County (Ky.) schs., 1969-70; tchr. lang. and Tex. history Alto (Tex.) Ind. Sch. Dist., 1981-84; 4th grade tchr. Trinity Episcopal Sch., Marshall, Tex., 1985-87; 7th grade lang. tchr. Marshall Ind. Sch. Dist., 1988-90; part-time staff statement rm. Heritage Bank, Wharton, 1995—. Author: A Woman's Conversations with God, 1994; contbr. poetry to N.Y. Poetry Soc., 1985. Sunday sch. tchr. First United Meth. Ch., Alto, Summit United Meth. Ch., Marshall; tutor Hosts Program, Wharton, 1995-96. Named Mother of Yr., Marshall Mall, 1986. Home: 911 Meadow Ln Wharton TX 77488

JENKINS, MARGARET BUNTING, human resources executive; b. Warsaw, Va., Aug. 3, 1935; d. John and Irma (Cookman) Bunting; children: Sydney, Jr., Terry L. Student, Coll. William and Mary, 1952; AA in Bus. Adminstrn., Christopher Newport U., 1973; BA in Human Resource Devel., St. Leo Coll., 1979; M in Human Resources, George Washington U., 1982; PhD in Human Rsch. Mgmt., Columbia Pacific U., 1986. Rehab. counselor, tchr. York County Schs., Yorktown, Va.; mgr. Waterfront Constrn. Co., Seafood Corp., Seaford, Va., 1960-72; labor rels. specialist Naval Weapons Sta., Yorktown, 1974-77; staffing specialist NWS, Yorktown, 1977-78; position classification specialist supr. shipbldg. repair Naval Weapons Sta., Newport News, Va., 1978-81; supr. pers. mgmt. specialist SupSHIP, Newport News, 1981-90; pers. mgmt. specialist Naval Weapons Sta., Yorktown and Cheatham, Williamsburg, Va., 1990-95; bd. dirs. various health orgns.; owner Jenkins Consulting. Author: Organizational Impact on Human Behavior, 1996; (poetry) Heron Haven Reflections, 1996; poetry published in Mists of Enchantment, 1995, Treasured Poems of America, 1996, Poets of the 90's. Recipient Navy Meritorious Civilian Svc. award SUPSHIP, Newport News, 1990, 2 Navy commendations, others. Mem. Soc. for Human Resource Mgmt., Fedn. Women's Clubs, Sierra Club, Audubon Soc., Nature Conservancy, Classification and Compensation Soc. (pres. 1984), 4-Alumni Assn., Toastmasters Internat. (pres. 1985-87, various offices, award), Internat. Soc. of Poets (Disting. mem. 1996), Internat. Platform Assn. Methodist. Home and Office: PO Box 203 Seaford VA 23696-0203

JENKINS, MARIE HOOPER, manufacturing company executive, engineer; b. Alexandria, La., Apr. 22, 1929; d. Jesse Joseph and Katie B. Hooper; m. Charles Edward Jenkins, Jan. 28, 1950 (div. May 1990); children: Nancy Marie von Minden, Charles Edward Jr.. B.S. in Chem. Engring., U. Wash., 1956. Founder, prin. Decision Systems, Austin, Tex., 1975-76; chmn. bd., pres. NAPP Inc. and subsidiary LACE Engring., 1977—. Active Leadership Tex. program, Leadership Am., 1988, Tex. Found. for Women's Resources; bd. dirs. Com. Wild Basin Wilderness, 1993—. Mem. Am. Inst. Chem. Engrs. (chmn. Mojave Desert sect.), Calif. Soc. Profl. Engrs. (founding sec., treas. Desert Empire chpt.), Tex. Soc. Profl. Engrs., Nat. Soc. Profl. Engrs., Leadership Tex. Alumni Assn., Leadership Am. Alumnae Assn., Nat. Property Mgmt. Assn., Nat. Contract Mgmt. Assn., Greater Austin C. of C. (exec. com. North Cen. area coun.). Episcopalian. Home: 3710B Meredith St Austin TX 78703-2021 Office: NAPP Inc & LACE Engring 2104 Kramer Ln Austin TX 78758-4045

JENKINS, MARK GUERRY, cardiologist; b. Charleston, S.C., July 6, 1957; s. Oliver Hart and Lois (Metze) J.; m. Kathy Ann Moses, June 20, 1980; children: Anne Elizabeth, Andrew Guerry. BA, U. Va., 1979; MD, Med. U. S.C., 1983. Diplomate Am. Bd. Internal Medicine, Am. Bd. Cardiovascular Diseases, Am. Bd. Clin. Cardiac Electrophysiology. Resident in internal medicine U. Va., Charlottesville, 1983-86; fellow in cardiology U. N.C., Chapel Hill, 1986-89; cardiologist Cardiovascular Cons., P.C., Savannah, Ga., 1989—; dir. clin. cardiac electrophysiology Meml. Med. Ctr., 1989—, chief cardiology sect., 1993—. Contbr. articles to profl. jours. Fellow Am. Coll. Cardiology; mem. AMA, AHA (sec. 1st dist. med. soc. 1993—), Savannah Golf Club, Alpha Omega Alpha, Phi Beta Kappa. Office: Cardiovascular Cons PC 4750 Waters Ave Ste 302 Savannah GA 31404-6268

JENKINS, MARSHALL WHITFIELD, communications consultant, entrepreneur; b. Dayton, Ohio, Apr. 8, 1952; s. Bobbie Whitfield and Louise (Stafford) J.; m. Catherine Fogle. AA, Brevard C.C., Cocoa, Fla., 1972; BA, U. South Fla., 1975; MS, Fla. State U., 1978. Program analyst Planning Rsch. Corp., Cocoa Beach, Fla., 1978-81; assoc. engr. Martin Marietta Aerospace, Kennedy Space Ctr., Fla., 1982-83; project and product assurance engr. (mgmt. system analyst) Lockheed Space Ops. Co., Titusville, Fla.,

1983-91; founder, owner Quaylor Comm., Melbourne, Fla., 1991—. Vol. Spl. Olympics Dist. Competitions, Merritt Island, Fla., 1983. Mem. Am. Mgmt. Assn., Space Coast Seminole Boosters Inc. (pres. Melbourne, Fla. 1986-87, bd. dirs. 1987-88), Fla. State U. Seminole Boosters Inc. (Brevard County, Fla. area chmn. 1987-88), Fla. State U. Alumni Assn., Tau Kappa Epsilon. Republican. Methodist. Home: 4365 Windover Way Melbourne FL 32934-8518

JENKINS, PAMELA RUTH, medical researcher; b. Denver, Aug. 26, 1949; d. Richard Parks and Geneva (Shaver) Carr; m. Larry William Jenkins, May 25, 1974; children: Michael, Tyler, Ryan. BSN, U. No. Colo., 1971; MSN, Va. Commonwealth U., 1981; postgrad., N.C. State U., 1993—. Commd. U.S. Army, 1969, advanced through grades to lt. col., 1990; staff nurse U.S. Army, U.S. and Germany, 1971-74, head nurse, 1974-79; critical care nurse U.S. Army, Germany, 1981-83; quality assurance nurse U.S. Army, Ft. Bragg, N.C., 1983-86, infection control officer, 1986-90; chief HIV sect. U.S. Govt., Ft. Bragg, N.C., 1990-91; sr. rsch. assoc. Henry M. Jackson Found., Ft. Bragg, N.C., 1991—; cons. Environ. Resource Ctr., Fayetteville, N.C., 1990-92. Chairperson Cumberland County HIV Task Force, Fayetteville, 1991-93, Dogwood AIDS Consortium, Fayetteville, 1992-93. Decorated Legion of Merit. Mem. Internat. AIDS Soc. Episcopalian. Home: Henry M Jackson Found Preventive Medicine Svc WAMC Fayetteville NC 28303 Office: Henry M Jackson Found WAMC Preventive Medicine Svc Fort Bragg NC 28307

JENKINS, RICHARD LEE, manufacturing company executive; b. Lynchburg, Va., July 20, 1931; s. Robert Julian and Beulah Vivian (Crews) J.; m. Doris E. Rucker, Dec. 24, 1958; children: Terena M., Richard C. BA, Lynchburg Coll., 1957; MBA, U. Mass., 1970. Various fin. mgmt. positions Gen. Electric Co., Lynchburg, Schenectady, N.Y., and Pittsfield, Mass., 1957-72; controller, mgr. Mfg. Transformer div. Allis-Chalmers, Pitts., 1972-75; gen. mgr. Indsl. Pump div. Allis-Chalmers, Cin., 1975-79; sr. v.p. Lynchburg Foundry, 1979-81; gen. mgr. service div. Siemens-Allis, Inc., Atlanta, 1981-84; sr. v.p. adminstrn. and internat. ops., chief fin. officer Diversified Products Corp., Opelika, Ala., 1984—; treas., bd. dirs. Micah Corp. of Berkshire County, Pittsfield, 1968-72; bd. dirs. Va. Nat. Bank, Lynchburg, 1979-81. Auditor ARC, Pittsfield, 1966; bd. dirs., exec. on loan United Community Services, Pittsfield, 1972; campaign chmn. Piedmont Heart Assn., Lynchburg, 1980. Served with USN, 1950-54, Korea. Clubs: Cherokee Country (Atlanta), Saugahatchee Country (Opelika). Home: 2245 Springwood Dr Auburn AL 36830-7231 Office: Diversified Products Corp 309 Williamson Ave Opelika AL 36804-7313

JENKINS, ROBERT BERRYMAN, real estate developer; b. Evanston, Ill., Oct. 11, 1950; s. Clive Ridley and Genevieve (Brown) Crawford J.; m. Carol Lynn Lealey, Sept. 22, 1984; children: Paul Brown, Leighanne Kealey. BEE, Cornell U., 1972; postgrad., U. W. Fla., 1974. Cert. Profl. Solar Technology, 1984. Owner Fothergill's Outdoor Sportsman, Aspen, Colo., 1978-81; owner, engr. Sophisticated Solar, Aspen, 1983-85; owner/pres. Sandhill Devels., Gulf Breeze and Aspen, 1985—; pres. Roaring Fork Liquors, Inc., Glenwood Springs, Colo., 1992—. Grad. Leadership Santa Rosa County, Fla., 1988-89. Recipient U.S. Dept. Energy Nat. Award for Energy Innovation, 1987, Gov.'s Energy award Fla. Gov., 1987; named Man of Yr., Gulf Breeze, 1991. Mem. Internat. Coun. Shopping Ctrs., Trout Unltd. (life). Republican. Methodist. Office: Sandhill Devels 400 Gulf Breeze Pky Ste 305 Gulf Breeze FL 32561-4458

JENKINS, ROBERT LEE, information system specialist; b. Covington, Ky., Oct. 4, 1948; s. Robert Leland and Margaret Casson (Monroe) J.; m. Maritza Olivos, Dec. 27, 1980; children: Robert Efrain, Jessica Itzie, Alexander Lee, Michael Bryan. BSBA, Xavier U., Cin., 1981; MBA, U. Louisville, 1992. Data processing programmer Kiechler Mfg. Co., Cin., 1971-72; gen. mgr. Howard Johnson Co., Bowling Green, Ohio, 1972-77; with prodn. dept. Ford Motor Co., Sharonville, Ohio, 1977-82; sr. auditor Rankin, Rankin & Co., CPAs, Covington, 1983-86; prin. examiner Nat. Credit Union Adminstrn., Louisville, 1986-90; v.p., chief info. officer Ky. Telco Fed. Credit Union, Louisville, 1990-94; prin. ptnr. The Harrigan Group, Louisville, 1990—; mgr. network and telecomm. sys. Siemens Electromechanical Components, Inc., Princeton, Ind., 1995—. Commr. City of Meadowbrook Farm, Ky., 1989-91. With U.S. Army, 1968-70, Vietnam. Decorated Bronze Star, Purple Heart. Mem. Credit Union Execs. Soc., Ky.-Ind. PC User Group, Hon. Order Ky. Cols. (gov.'s staff), Louisville C. of C., DAV. Roman Catholic. Home: 8055 Woodland Dr Newburgh IN 47630 Office: Siemens Electromechanical Components Inc 200 S Richland Creek Dr Princeton IN 47671-0001

JENKINS, ROBERT SEVERANCE, concrete construction engineer, consultant; b. Clinton, Mass., May 17, 1936; s. Percy and Madeleine Hoyt (Child) J. BSCE, Worcester Poly. Inst., 1958. Registered profl. engr., Ga., Fla., Pa. Field engr. Raymond Concrete Pile Co., Phila., 1959-61; geotech. engr. Joseph S. Ward, Inc., Phila., 1961, Site Engrs. Inc., Moorestown, N.J., 1961-66; cons. Law Engring., Inc., Atlanta, 1966—. 1st lt. U.S. Army C.E., 1958-59. Fellow Am. Concrete Inst.; mem. ASTM. Home: 1096 Delaware Ave SE Atlanta GA 30316-2470 Office: Law Engring Inc 396 Plasters Ave NE Atlanta GA 30324-3951

JENKINS, RONALD VANCE, university administrator; b. Greenville, S.C., May 8, 1965; s. Francis Ronald Jenkin and Patricia Ann Bagwell Norwood. BA in Journalism, U. S.C., 1987; MA, Furman U., 1995. Account exec. Goudlock Advt., Greenville, S.C., 1987-89, Leslie Advt. Agy., Greenville, 1989-90; dir. comm. Furman U., Greenville, 1990—. Writer, music critic: The Greenville News, 1995—. Mem. Greenville Chorale, former mgr., soloist, 1991—; bd. dirs. pub. rels. com. Am. Heart Assn., Greenville, 1991—, Upstate Coun. on Family Violence (edn. chair 1995—; fund raising pub. rels. chmn. Vision 20/20 Campaign FBC Taylors, S.C., 1992-93, diaconate, 1995—; mem. Upstate Reps., 1993—; vol. United Way, Mental Health Assn., Greenville, 1996—; organist, music asst. Aldersgate United Meth. Ch., Greenville, 1996—. Recipient Addy award Advtg. Fedn. of Greenville, S.C., 1988, 95. Mem. Am. Guild of Organists, Pub. Rels. Soc. Am. (accredited in pub. rels.). Baptist. Home: 218 Devenger Rd Greer SC 29651 Office: Furman U 3300 Poinsett Hwy Greenville SC 29613

JENKINS, RONALD WAYNE, lawyer; b. Johnson City, Tenn., Aug. 14, 1950; s. James Herman and Peggy Sue (Hutchinson) J.; children: April Chalice, Kimberly Michelle, Robert Herman, Ronald Wayne II. BSEE, U. Tenn., 1972, JD, 1980. Bar: Tenn. 1980, U.S. Supreme Ct. 1986, U.S. Ct. Appeals (6th cir.) 1986, U.S. Dist. Ct. (ea. dist.) Tenn. 1986. Assoc. M. Lacy West, P.C., Kingsport, Tenn., 1980-83, Herndon, Coleman, Brading & McKee, Johnson City, 1984-86; ptnr. Herndon, Coleman, Brading & McKee, 1986—. Editor-in-chief tenn. Law Rev., 1979. Mem. ABA, Tenn. Bar Assn., Washington County Bar Assn., Nat. Aeronautic Assn., Aircraft Owners and Pilots Assn., Tau Beta Pi. Office: Herndon Coleman PO Box 1160 104 E Main St Johnson City TN 37605-1160

JENKINS, STEVEN MARVIN, controller; b. Salisbury, Md., Mar. 2, 1949; s. Marvin Clarence and Helen (Parker) J. BA, U. Fla., 1972; MA, Gordon-Conwell Theol. Sem., South Hamilton, Mass., 1977; cert. in info. systems, U. North Fla., 1983, MBA, 1992. CPA, Fla.; cert. info. systems auditor. Sales rep. McBee Systems, Jacksonville, Fla., 1978-81; staff acct. James G. Culpepper, CPA, P.A., Jacksonville, 1981-83; mgmt. acct. Canada Dry Bottling Co., Jacksonville, 1983-84; EDP auditor Fla. Nat. Bank, Jacksonville, 1984-86; sr. EDP auditor CSX Corp., Jacksonville, 1986-88; treas. CSX Comml. Svcs., Inc., Jacksonville, 1988-90, contr., 1990-93; with Blue Cross & Blue Shield Fla. Treas. Presbyn. Ch., Jacksonville, 1982-87, elder, 1986-87; treas. PC Users Group., Jacksonville, 1986-88. Mem. Nat. Assn. Accts. (Manuscript award 1982), Fla. Inst. CPAs (Ednl. Found. scholar 1983, life mem. Found.), EDP Auditors Assn., Beta Gamma Sigma. Republican. Office: Blue Cross/Blue Shield Fla 8928 Freedom Commerce Pky Jacksonville FL 32256-8264

JENKS-DAVIES, KATHRYN RYBURN, retired daycare provider, civic worker; b. Lynchburg, Va., Oct. 9, 1916; d. Charles Arthur and Jessie Katherine (Moorman) Ryburn; m. Thomas Edgar Jenks Jr., Sept. 9, 1941 (dec. June 1975); children: Thomas Edgar III, Jessika, Timothy; m. Robert E. Davies, Dec. 27, 1986. BS, State Tchr. Coll., 1938; postgrad., Mary Washington Coll., 1947-48, U. Va., 1957-58, William and Mary Coll., 1967-68, Va. Commonwealth U., 1969-70. Elem. tchr. various schs., Grundy, Va., 1939-41; phys. therapist U.S. Army, Ft. Bragg, N.C., 1942; operator motor pool U.S. Army, Ft. Still, Okla., 1943-44; occupational therapist U.S. Army, Augusta, Ga., 1944-45; instr. phys. edn. King George (Va.) High Sch., 1947-48; instr. phys. edn. Stafford (Va.) High Sch., 1949-50, substitute tchr., 1950-53; owner, dir. Kay's Kindergarten, Fredericksburg, Va., 1959-82. Featured in Fredericksburg Times mag., The Free Lance-Star and Richmond Newspapers. Counselor Girl Scouts U.S.A., Grundy, Va., 1939-41; life mem. Kenmore Assn., 1949—; mem. Hist. Fredericksburg Found., Inc., 1953—, Mental Health Bd., 1978-84; founder Ford Franklin Found., 1968-78; mem. Fredericksburg Clean Cmty. Commn., 1987—; rep. United Way, Fredericksburg; instr. art ceramics Cmty. Ctr. Fredericksburg, 1950-80; bd. dirs. Miss Fredericksburg Fair Pageant, 1965-88; participant cmty. parades; coord. Fredericksburg Agrl. Fair 18th Century Craft People and Artisans, 1988-93, also others; bd. dirs. Antique Farm Implements, Gas and Steam Engines, 1989-93; active State Fair of Va., 1981—, Am. Heritage Showcase endl. reenactment Pioneer Farmstead, 1981—. Recipient Virginia Ellison Vol. Svc. award Fredericksburg Clean Community Commn., 1976-87, Recognition of Svc. award, 1983-84, 1st, 2nd. and 3rd pl. trophies cmty. parades, awards radio Stas. WFLS and WFVA, 1949-89; honored by Kiwanians for travelogue for fund raiser, 1995—. Mem. AAUW (advt. chmn. travelogue 1971-89, Donor Honoree award 1983, bd. dirs. 1971-79), Lioness Club (bd. dir. 1968-87, Lioness Tamer 1984, Tongue Wagger 1985), Soroptimist Internat. Fredericksburg (life mem., sec. 1971-73, pres. 1973-75, bd. dirs. 1971-78, co-chmn. Soroptimist Travelogue 1991-93, First Class Pub. Recognition Trophy 1986, Women Helping Women award 1982, named 1 of 5 who have made a difference in cmty. 1994), Order of Eastern Star, Nat. League of Fredericksburg (bd. dir., Svc. Recognition Trophies 1963, 69, 80), Izaac Walton League (bd. dir. Dog Mart parade 1965-72). Republican. Episcopalian. Home: 8 Blair Rd Fredericksburg VA 22405-3025

JENNINGS, DENNIS RAYMOND, accountant; b. Coleman, Tex., Sept. 28, 1942; s. Raymond Earl and Montie Elizabeth (Moore) J.; m. El Wanda Key, Oct. 31, 1964; children: Jon Marc, Jamie Dennis, Amy Elizabeth. BBA cum laude, Tex. Tech U., 1970. CPA, Tex. Mgr. Peat, Marwick, Mitchell & Co., Dallas, 1970-76, Coopers & Lybrand, Tulsa, 1976-79; ptnr. Coopers & Lybrand, New Orleans, 1979-88, Dallas, 1988—; quality control team leader Coopers & Lybrand, 1981-85, nat. quality control coord. west region, 1988-89, Atlantic region, 1990-91, chmn. pers. com. SW region, 1983-84, mem. pers. com., 1985—, oil and gas com., 1985—; co-chmn. Nat. Energy Practice, 1994-96, internat. advisor, 1996. Author: Petroleum Accounting, Principles, Procedures & Issues, 4th edit., 1996; co-author: Petroleum Accounting Principles, Procedures, and Issues, 4th edit., 1996; contbg. author: (brochure) The Revised Petroleum Accounting Rules, 1980, Survey of Accounting Principles in Oil and Gas Industry, 1994; editor Devels. in Fin. Reporting, Petroleum Devel. and Fin. Mgmt. Jour., 1990—. Bd. dirs. U. New Orleans Oil and Gas Conf., 1985-88; mem. acctg. adv. council A.B. Freeman Sch. of Bus. Tulane U., New Orleans, 1986-88; mem. audit adv. com. New Orleans Parish Sch. Bd., 1980-83. Mem. AICPA, Tex. Soc. CPAs, La. Soc. CPAs (bd. dirs. New Orleans chpt., cert. of merit 1985, 87), New Orleans C. of C. (chmn. govtl. affairs com. 1984-88, west bank coun. edn. com. 1985-86, exec. com. 1987, Outstanding Svc. award 1985), Open, Inc. (bd. dirs., vice chmn., treas., chmn. fin. com.), Coun. Petroleum Accts. Soc. of Dallas (pres., exec. com., chmn. FASB-SEC reporting com., program chmn. N.Am. Petroleum Acctg. Conf., chmn. program chmn., bd. dirs.), Aurora Garden Club, Petroleum Club, Royal Oaks Country Club, Chaparral Club. Republican. Office: Coopers & Lybrand LLP 1999 Bryan St Ste 3000 Dallas TX 75201-6820

JENNINGS, EDWARD THEODORE, JR., public administration educator; b. New Orleans, June 6, 1946; s. Edward Theodore and Claire (Daley) J.; m. Kathleen Ann Broussard, Aug. 12, 1967; children: Alayne M., Bryan R., Kathryn A. BA in Polit. Sci., U. New Orleans, 1968, MA in Polit. Sci., 1972; PhD in Polit. Sci., Washington U., St. Louis, 1977. Asst. prof. dept. polit. sci. SUNY, Buffalo, 1977-80, dir. grad. program pub. policy/adminstrn. dept. polit. sci., 1979-80; asst. prof. dept. pub. adminstrn. U. Mo., Columbia, 1980-82, assoc. prof. dept. pub. adminstrn., 1982—, chair dept. pub. adminstrn., 1982-89, dir. grad. studies dept. pub. adminstrn., 1984-86, 88-89; assoc. prof. pub. adminstrn. Martin Sch. Pub. Adminstrn. U. Ky., Lexington, 1989—, dir. grad. studies, MPA program Martin Sch. Pub. Adminstrn., 1991-94, acting dir. Martin Sch. Pub. Adminstrn., 1994-95; mem. faculty senate, 1995-98; vis. asst. prof. dept. polit. sci. Tulane (La.) U., 1976-77; staff coord. citizens adv. com. Joint Interim Com. on Modernization & Improvement Mo. Gen. Assembly, 1974-75; interviewer La. Divsn. Employment Security, 1972; mem. faculty senate SUNY, Buffalo, 1979-80; mem. grad. sch. faculty senate U. Mo., 1982-89, chair social sci. sector, 1985-87, exec. com., 1985-87, faculty coun. com. on adminstrv. rev., 1987-88; cons. Mo. Divsn. Pers., 1981, Mo. Divsn. Community and Econ. Devel., 1982-85, Mo. Divsn. Budget and Planning, 1984, Mo. Divsn. Job Devel. and Tng., 1987-89, Mo. Youth 2000 Commn., 1988, Nat. Commn. for Employment Policy, 1991, 93; presenter, conductor workshops in field. Co-author, editor: From Nation to States: The Small Cities Community Development Block Grant Program, 1986, The Revitalization of the Public Service, 1987, Welfare System Reform, 1993; mem. editl. bd. Urban Affairs Quar., 1985-90, Am. Rev. PUb. Adminstrn., 1987—; contbr. articles to profl. publs. Grantee SUNY Rsch. Found., 1978, Mo. Divsn. Community and Econ. Devel., 1982, 83, 84, Mo. Divsn. Job Devel. and Tng., 1987, 88, Nat. Commn. for Employment Policy, 1991, 92, 93, 94; summer rsch. fellow U. Mo.-Columbia Rsch. Coun., 1981. Mem. ASPA (nat. coun. 1986-89, 93-97, vice-chair nat. conf. program com. 1991, chair nat. conf. program com. 1992, v.p. 1993-94, pres.-elect 1994-95, pres. 1995-96), Am. Polit. Sci. Assn. (presenter at ann. meeting 1975, 76-77, 78, 80, 93, 94), Midwest Polit. Sci. Assn. (presenter at ann. meeting 1978, 80), Policy Studies Orgn., Mo. Polit. Sci. Assn. (v.p. 1982-83, pres. 1983-84, presenter), Nat. Assn. Schs. of Pub. Affairs and Adminstrn. (prin. rep. 1982-89, 94-95, chair curriculum com. 1987-88, commn. peer rev. and accreditation). Home: 4525 Longbridge Ln Lexington KY 40515-6105 Office: U Ky Martin Sch Pub Adminstrn Lexington KY 40506-0027

JENNINGS, HENRY SMITH, III, cardiologist; b. Atlanta, May 16, 1951; s. Henry Smith Jr. and Elizabeth (Martin) J.; m. Polly Cooper; 1 child, Mary Bailey. BS summa cum laude, Davidson Coll., 1973; MD, Vanderbilt U., 1977. Diplomate Am. Bd. Internal Medicine, subspecialty cardiovascular diseases, Nat. Bd. Med. Examiners; lic. physician and surgeon, Tenn. Intern internal medicine Vanderbilt U. Affiliated Hosps., Nashville, 1977-78, resident internal medicine, 1978-80; fellow clin. cardiology divsn. cardiology dept. medicine Vanderbilt U., Nashville, 1980-82; clin. instr. medicine Vanderbilt U. Sch. Medicine, Nashville, 1982-89, asst. clin. prof. medicine, 1989—; med. dir. Cardiac Rehab. Ctr. St. Thomas Hosp., Nashville, 1984—; mem. active staff St. Thomas Hosp., Nashville; vis. staff Vanderbilt U. Med. Ctr., Nashville; mem. courtesy staff Centennial Med. Ctr., Nashville. Contbr. articles to profl. jours. Bd. dirs. Heart Inst., St. Thomas Hosp., Nashvile, 1992-94, Tenn. Heart Inst., 1989-91. Justin Potter med. scholar Vanderbilt U. Sch. Medicine, Nashville, 1973-77; recipient Physician's Recognition award AMA, 1985-88, 89-92, 92-95, 95—. Fellow ACP, Am. Coll. Cardiology, Am. Coll. Chest Physicians, Coun. Clin. Cardiology Am. Heart Assn., Soc. Cardiac Angiography and Interventions (cert. of proficiency in diagnostic cardiac catheterization and angioplasty 1989-92, 92-95, 96-99), Am. Soc. Cardiovascular Interventionists; mem. Internat. Soc. Heart Transplantation,Am. Heart Assn., So. Med. Assn., Tenn. Med. Assn., Nashville Acad. Medicine, Nashville Soc. Internal Medicine, Nashville Cardiovascular Soc. (bd. trustees 1992—). Methodist. Home: Northumberland 3 Castle Rising Nashville TN 37215-4126 Office: Page-Campbell Cardiology PC Ste 900 4230 Harding Rd Nashville TN 37205-2013

JENNINGS, ROSS GRANT, accounting educator; b. San Francisco, Jan. 18, 1952; s. Neilon Merle and Lorraine Marie (Petersen) J.; m. Karen Serig, Sept. 4, 1982; 1 child, Chandler Philip. BA, U. Calif., Davis, 1974; MBA, U. Calif., L.A., 1979; PhD, U. Calif., Berkeley, 1987. Budget analyst USN, Vallejo, Calif., 1974-77; instr. Rice U., Houston, 1980-81; asst. prof. U. Tex., Austin, 1987-93, assoc. prof., 1993—. Contbr. articles to profl. jours. Treas. Golden Gate Audubon Soc., Berkeley, 1983-86. Named GTE Emerging scholar Notre Dame U., 1987. Mem. Am. Acctg. Assn., Am. Fin. Assn., Am. Econ. Assn., Can. Acad. Acctg. Assn. Office: Univ Tex Cba 4M # 202 Austin TX 78712

JENNINGS, WAYLON, country musician; b. Littlefield, Tex., June 15, 1937; m. Jessi Colter; 4 children. Disc jockey Littlefield and Lubbock, Tex.; with Buddy Holly's Band, 1958-59; founder The Waylors. Perfomer nightclubs; rec. artist with RCA, 1965—, others; albums include Ol' Waylon, Black on Black, It's Only Rock and Roll, Waylon and Co., (with Johnny Cash) Heroes, 1986, Waylon Live, A Man Called Hoss, 1988, Full Circle, 1988, The Eagle, 1990, (with Willie Nelson) Waylon & Willie, Are You Sure Hank Done it This Way, 1992, WWII, Take It To the Limit, 1987, Clean Shirt, 1991, Too Dumb For New York, Too Ugly for L.A., 1992, Only Daddy That'll Walk the Line: The RCA Years, 1993, Waymore's Blues Part II, 1994; narrator: (TV series) The Dukes of Hazzard, from 1979, (mem. with Willie Nelson, Johnny Cash, Kris Kristofferson) The Highwayman, Highwayman 2, 1990; host TV series The Legends of Country Music: Waylon Jennings and Friends, 1995; rec. children's album Cowboys, Sisters, Rascals and Dirt, 1993. Named Male Vocalist of Yr. by Country Music Assn., 1975, Vocal Duo of Yr. Waylon Jennings/Willie Nelson, 1976; recipient Album of Yr. award for Wanted-The Outlaws by Country Music Assn., 1976, Single of Yr. award (with Willie Nelson) for Good Hearted Women, 1976.

JENRETTE, THOMAS SHEPARD, JR., music educator, choral director; b. Roanoke, Va., Feb. 1, 1946; s. Thomas Shepard and Virginia Catherine (Harris) J. BA, U. N.C., 1968, MusM, 1970; D of Mus. Arts, U. Mich., 1976. Choral dir. Cummings High Sch., Burlington, N.C., 1969-72; dir. cultural arts Burlington (N.C.) City Schs., 1972-73; dir. choral activities S.W. State U., Marshall, Minn., 1976-79, East Tenn. State U., Johnson City, 1979—; dir. music First Christian Ch., Johnson City, 1981-84, Covenant Presbyn. Ch., Johnson City, 1991—; guest condr. choral festival N.C. High Sch., Raleigh, 1987, Govs. Sch. for Arts, Murfreesboro, Tenn., 1987, Nat. Seminar of Intercollegiate Men's Choruses, Inc., 1992; guest condr. N.C. All-State Male Choir, 1997. Grantee East Tenn. State U., 1988, 90, 96. Mem. Am. Choral Dirs. Assn. (life, conductor 1986, 88, 94, so. div. convs., 89 nat. conv.), Tenn. Music Educators Assn. (conductor state convs. 1990, 91, 94, dir. White House, Christmas 1989, Canticum Novum Festival, Caracas, Venezuela, 1996), Internat. Fedn. Choral Music, Nat. Assn. Tchrs. Singing, The Coll. Music Soc. (life), Music Educators Nat. Conf. (condr. so. divsn. conv. 1997), Phi Mu Alpha (hon.), Omicron Delta Kappa, Pi Kappa Lambda. Home: 2734 E Oakland Ave # C-25 Johnson City TN 37601-1885

JENSEN, ANDREW ODEN, obstetrician, gynecologist; b. El Paso, Tex., Aug. 30, 1920; s. Andrew Rudolph and Annie Laura (Oden) J.; m. Patricia deMaret Steele, May 10, 1952; children: Elise Ann Jensen Murphy, Nancy Marie Jensen Jett, Andrew Oden Jr. BA, So. Meth. U., 1941; MD, U. Tenn., Memphis, 1949. Diplomate Am. Bd. Ob-Gyn. Intern Episcopal Hosp., Phila., 1949-50; resident Hermann Hosp., Houston, 1950-53; clin. instr. Baylor U. Coll. Medicine, Houston, 1951-53; chief ob-gyn Med. Arts Clinic, Brownwood, Tex., 1954-55; pvt. practice Denison, Tex., 1955-74, Temple, Tex., 1975-86; locum tenens Salt Lake City, 1986—; cons. in ob.-gyn. Lake Cumberland Dist. Health Dept., Somerset, Ky., 1974-75, Perrin AFB, Sherman, Tex., 1956-69; lectr., del. people-to-people program Nat. Congress Ob-Gyn in China, 1984. Bd. dirs. Brownwood Jr. C. of C., Denison C. of C., 1959-62. Fellow Am. Coll. Obstetricians and Gynecologists, Tex. Assn. Ob-Gyn; mem. AMA, Soc. Med. Soc., Grayson County Med. Soc. (pres. 1969-70), Cen. Assn. Obstetricians and Gynecologists, Am. Fertility Assn., West Tex. Ob-Gyn Soc., Rotary (pres. Denison 1966-67, Paul Harris fellow 1990). Democrat. Episcopalian. Home: 3330 Wimbledon Dr Cibolo TX 78108-2162

JENSEN, ANNETTE M., mental health nurse, administrator; b. Albert Lea, Minn., Jan. 16, 1952; d. Oliver H. and Ardis R. (Nelson) J. BSN, Winona (Minn.) State U., 1974; postgrad., Calif. Coll. Health Scis. Staff nurse in adolescent psychiatry C.B. Wilson Ctr., Faribault, Minn., 1974-76, 79-80, Abbott Northwestern Hosp., Mpls., 1981-82; charge nurse in child psychiatry Med. Coll. Ga., Augusta, 1983-87; adminstr. child psychiat. program Charter Hosp. of Augusta, 1987-91; staff educator/quality mgmt. in psychiatry Ga. Regional Hosp. at Augusta, 1990-92; team leader child psychiatry Charter Peachford Hosp., Atlanta, 1992—. Mem. Girl Scouts of Am. Mem. NAFE, AAUW, ANA, Ga. Nurses Assn., Assn. Child/Adolescent Psychiat. Nurses, Am. Camping Assn. Presbyterian. Home: 725 Josh Ln Lawrenceville GA 30245-3157

JENSEN, GARY FRANKLIN, sociology educator; b. Eugene, Oreg., Jan. 29, 1944; s. Ellroy Peter and Lois Eleanor (Hills) J.; m. Janet Loree Smith, Sept. 14, 1963 (dec. May 1981); children: Jennifer, Wendy; m. Sheila Carroll McCloskey, Jan. 2, 1982; children: Jason, Brian, Kevin. BS, Portland State U., 1966; MA, U. Wash., 1968, PhD, 1972. Asst. prof. U. N.C., Chapel Hill, 1970-73; Asst. prof. U. Ariz., Tucson, 1972-77, assoc. prof., 1977-83, prof., 1983-89, assoc. dean, 1987-88; prof., chmn. Vanderbilt U., Nashville, 1989—. Author: Delinquency: A Sociological View, 1980, Sociology of Delinquency: Current Issues, 1981, Readings in Juvenile Delinquency, 1982, Delinquency and Youth Crime, 1992; contbr. articles to profl. publs. Bd. dirs. Project Return, Nashville, 1989-92. Grantee NIMH, 1974-76, 75-77, 78-89, Social and Behavioral Sci. Rsch. Inst., 1986-87, U. Ariz., 1988-89, Vanderbilt U., 1990-91, 92-93, NSF, 1993-94; Tektronics Found. scholar, 1962-66; Woodrow Wilson fellow, 1967. Mem. Am. Sociol. Assn., Am. Soc. Criminology, So. Sociol. Soc., Alpha Kappa Delta. Democrat. Roman Catholic. Home: 2102 25th Ave S Nashville TN 37212-4200 Office: Vanderbilt U Dept Sociology Nashville TN 37235

JENSEN, HARLAN ELLSWORTH, veterinarian, educator; b. St. Ansgar, Iowa, Oct. 6, 1915; s. Bert and Mattie (Hansen) J.; m. Naomi Louise Geiger, June 7, 1941; children: Kendra Lee Jensen Belfi, Doris Eileen Jensen Futoma, Richard Harlan. D.V.M., Iowa State U., 1941; Ph.D., U. Mo., 1971. Diplomate: Charter diplomate Am. Coll. Vet. Ophthalmologists (v.p. 1970-72, pres. 1972-73). Vet. practice Galesburg, Ill., 1941-46; small animal internship New Brunswick, N.J., 1946-47; small animal practice Cleve., 1947-58, San Diego, 1958-62, Houston, 1962-67; faculty U. Mo., Columbia, 1967-80; chief ophthalmology U. Mo., 1967-80, prof. emeritus Vet. Sch., 1980—, assoc. prof. ophthalmology Med. Sch., 1972-80; cons. in vet. ophthalmology to pharm. firms; guest lectr., prof. ophthalmology U. Utrecht (Netherlands) Vet. Sch., 1973; tchr., lectr. various vet. meetings; condr. seminar World Congress Small Animal Medicine and Surgery, 1973, 77. Author: Stereoscopic Atlas of Clinical Ophthalmology of Domestic Animals, 1971, Stereoscopic Atlas of Ophthalmic Surgery of Domestic Animals, 1974; co-author: Stereoscopic Atlas of Soft Tissue Surgery of Small Animals, 1973, Clinical Dermatology of Small Animals, 1974; contbr. articles to profl. jours. Recipient Gaines award AVMA, 1973. Mem. Am. Vet. Radiology Soc. (pres. 1956-57), Am. Vet. Ophthalmology Soc. (pres. 1960-62), Farm House Frat., Rotary (pres. Pacific Beach, Calif. 1960-62, pres. Columbia 1977-78), Sigma Xi, Phi Kappa Phi, Phi Zeta, Gamma Sigma Delta. Mem. Bible Ch. Home: 82 Legend Rd Fort Worth TX 76132-1024

JENSEN, KAREN MARIE, librarian; b. N.Y.C., Oct. 28, 1955; d. Gunnar Janus and Leonora (Kirchner) J. BA, Beloit Coll., 1976; MLS, U. Wis., 1978. Libr. Newfound Harbor Marine Inst., Big Pine Key, Fla., 1979-80; libr. children's Monroe County Pub. Libr., Key West, Fla., 1980—; planning com. mem. Fla. Libr. Youth Program, 1994-96, Fla. Summer Libr. Program, 1988-90; mem. young adult adv. coun. State Libr. Fla., 1985. Sec. Southernmost Bocce League, Key West, 1990, Big Bros./Sisters Monroe County, Key West, 1986-87, pres., 1985-86. Mem. ALA, Fla. Libr. Assn. (Children's Caucus 1985-87, 90-92, chair 1991-92). Office: Monroe County Pub Libr 700 Fleming St Key West FL 33040-6828

JENSEN, TERESA ELAINE, financial planner; b. Honesdale, Pa., Aug. 11, 1948; d. James Bernard Jensen and LaVaughn Beatrice (Tomlinson) Nixon. Student, San Antonio Coll., 1966-67. Cert. fin. planner; registered investment advisor. V.p. Outdoor Sports Ctr., San Antonio, 1968-73; tchr. New Age Sch., San Antonio, 1973-76; organizer, negotiator Nat. Maritime Union, Galveston, Tex., 1973-76; agt., sales mgr. B&B Assocs., San Antonio, 1977-78; pvt. practice San Antonio, 1978-80; pres. Money Mgrs. Inc., San Antonio, 1981—; adj. instr. Coll. Fin. Planning, Denver, 1985—, St. Mary's U., San Antonio, 1985—; expert witness for legal community. Mem. Big Sister Alamo Area Big Bros. & Big Sisters, San Antonio, 1981, bd. dirs. 1985. Recipient Presdl. Citation C. of C., 1982. Mem. Inst. Cert. Fin. Planners (v.p. Cen. Tex. soc. 1986-87, pres. 1987-88, chmn. 1988-89, state chmn. 1991—), Internat. Assn. Fin. Planners, Internat. Bd. Standards and

Practices for Cert. Fin. Planners. Republican. Office: Money Mgrs Inc The Lincoln Center 7800 W Ih 10 Ste 636 San Antonio TX 78230-4750

JENSEN, W. LYNNE, nursing educator; b. Salt Lake City, July 23, 1957; d. Percy Leondo and Wilma Beth (Oswald) Neal; m. Gregory Leo Jensen, June 17, 1983; children: Michael Wayne, Laura Ann. ADN, Weber State U., 1985, BSN, 1995; postgrad., Tex. A&M U., 1996—. CPR instr., neonatal adv. life support instr., adv. cardiac life support instr., pediat. adv. life support instr., advanced life support for obstetric provider. Staff nurse McKay-Dee Hosp., Ogden, Utah, 1984-85; med.-surg. staff nurse Tooele Valley (Utah) Regional Med. Ctr., 1985-86, ICU staff nurse, 1986-90, edn. coord., 1989-90; DON Tooele Valley Home Health, 1990-91; staff nurse Fountain Valley (Calif.) Regional Med. Ctr., 1991-92; house supr., ICU staff nurse Bee County Regional Med. Ctr., Beeville, Tex., 1991-92; instr. LVN program Bee County Coll., 1992-93; edn. mgr., performance improvement coord. Bee County Regional Med. Ctr., 1993—; chairperson adv. bd. Diabetic Support Group, 1993—; mem. Home Health Edn., 1993—; coord. seminars and workshops for cmty. and health profls. Leader Cub Scouts, Beeville, 1994; various leadership pos. Ch. of Jesus Christ of Latter Day Saints, 1990—; mem. Board Cmty. Health Edn. Task Force, 1996—; mem. Bee County Health Edn. Cmty. Task Force; mem. adv. bds. Bee County Rural Initiatives, Nicotine Intervention, Srs. Bee Ware, CQ Com.; speaker at various civic and community events. Mem. ANA, AACN (mem. bd. dirs. 1994, rural health outreach rep. 1994), Coastal Bend Health Care Assn. (v.p. Corpus Christi area 1993-94). Home: 30 Encino Loma Beeville TX 78102 Office: Bee County Regional Med Ctr 1500 E Houston St Beeville TX 78102-5312

JENTZ, GAYLORD ADAIR, law educator; b. Beloit, Wis., Aug. 7, 1931; s. Merlyn Adair and Delva (Mullen) J.; m. JoAnn Mary Hornung, Aug. 6, 1955; children: Katherine Ann, Gary Adair, Loretta Ann, Rory Adair. BA, U. Wis., 1953, JD, 1957, MBA, 1958. Bar: Wis. 1957. Pvt. practice law Madison, 1957-58; from instr. to assoc. prof. bus. law U. Okla., 1958-65; vis. instr. to vis. prof. U. Wis. Law Sch., summers 1957-65; asso. prof. to prof. U. Tex., Austin, 1965-68, prof., 1968—, Herbert D. Kelleher prof. bus. law, 1982—, chmn. gen. bus. dept., 1968-74, 80-86. Author: (with others) Business Law Text and Cases, 1968, Business Law Text, 1978, Texas Uniform Commercial Code, 1967, rev. edit., 1975, West's Business Law: Alternate UCC Comprehensive Edition, 6th edit., 1996, Legal Environment of Business, 1989, Texas Family Law, 7th edit., 1995, West's Business Law: Text and Cases, 6th edit., 1995, Fundamentals of Business Law, 3d edit., 1996, Business Law Today, 3d edit., 1994, Business Law Today-Comprehensive Edition, 3d Edit., 1994, Business Law Today-The Essentials, 3d edit., 1994; dep. editor Social Sci. Quar., 1966-82, editl. bd., 1982-94; editor-in-chief Am. Bus. Law Jour., 1969-74, adv. editor, 1974—. Served with AUS, 1953-55. Recipient Outstanding Tchr. award U. Tex. Coll. Bus., 1967, Jack G. Taylor Tchg. Excellence award, 1971, 89, Joe D. Beasley Grad. Tchg. Excellence award, 1978, CBA Found. Adv. Coun. award, 1979, Grad. Bus. Coun. Outstanding Grad. Bus. Prof. award, 1980, James C. Scorboro Meml. award for outstanding leadership in banking edn. Colo. Grad. Sch. Banking, 1983, Utmost Outstanding Prof. award, 1989, CBA award for excellence in edn., 1994, Banking Leadership award Western States Sch. Banking, 1995. Mem. Southwestern Fedn. Adminstrv. Disciples (v.p. 1979-80, pres. 1980-81), Am. Arbitration Assn. (nat. panel 1966-96), Acad. Legal Studies in Bus. (pres. 1971-72, exec. com. 1989-94, Faculty award of excellence 1981), So. Bus. Law Assn. (pres. 1967), Tex. Assn. Coll. Tchrs. (pres. Austin chpt. 1967-68, exec. com. 1979-80, state pres. 1971-72), Wis. Bar Assn., Omicron Delta Kappa, Phi Kappa Phi (pres. 1983-84). Home: 4106 N Hills Dr Austin TX 78731-2826 Office: U Tex CBA 5.202 MSIS Dept Austin TX 78712

JERMAN, WILLIAM EDWARD, editor; b. Cleve., May 1, 1931; s. William J. and Elizabeth (Cockman) J.; m. W. Mollie (div.); children: Ben, Rebecca. AB, Providence Coll. Freelance copy-editor; bus. mgr. Cleve. Hearing & Speech Ctr.; editor Irish Univ. Press. Vol. driver ARC. Office: 550 1st Ave S Apt 806 Saint Petersburg FL 33701-4130

JERMYN, HELEN WILLIAMS, air force officer, environmental engineer; b. Kowloon, Hong Kong, Nov. 11, 1957; came to U.S., 1975; d. Thomas Armstrong and Yin Hing (Mak) Williams; m. Peter David Taffet, May 14, 1978 (dec. Dec. 1980); m. Richard Anthony Jermyn, Jr., Mar. 26, 1990. BS in Chem. Engring. and Material Sci., Syracuse U., 1979; MS in Chem. Engring., U. Rochester, 1983, MBA in Fin. and Econs., 1986. Lic. securities dealer; lic. ins. agt., N.Y. Devel. engr. Chrysler Corp., Highland Park, Mich., 1979-80; sr. devel. engr. Mobil Chem. Co., Macedon, N.Y., 1980-85; rsch. assoc. and teaching asst. U. Rochester, N.Y., 1987; commd. 2d lt. USAF, 1987, advanced through grades to capt., 1988; plant mgr. Med. Ctr., Keesler AFB, Miss., 1987-88; environ. R&D and devel. engr. Hdqrs. Air Force Engring. and Svcs. Ctr., Tyndall AFB, Fla., 1988-91; chief bioenviron. engring. Air Force 325 Med. Group, Tyndall AFB, Fla., 1991—; guest speaker in field. Patentee low temperature ashing of plastic media waste; contbr. articles to profl. jours. Judge sci. fair Bay County Sch. System, Panama City, Fla., 1989, 90, 91; worker Spl. Olympics, Biloxi, Miss., 1988; project leader Savs. Bond Campaign, Keesler AFB, 1988. Recipient Air Edn. and Tng. Command Bioenviron. Engr. of Yr. award, 1993. Mem. Am. Soc. Mil. Engrs., Am. Inst. Chem. Engrs., Air Force Assn., Am. Chem. Soc., Officers Club. Roman Catholic.

JERNIGAN, JOSEPH MICHAEL, public utilities administrator; b. Ocala, Fla., Feb. 23, 1949; s. Emory Joseph and Anne Ethel (Rivenbark) J.; m. Jane Renea Burkholder, Apr. 5, 1975; children: Aaron Gray, Ashley Ryan, Adam Michael. BA, Old Dominion U., 1973; M Interdisplinary Studies, Va. Commonwealth U., 1992, postgrad., 1992—. Project mgr. Svc. Steel Erectors, Inc., Chester, Va., 1973-81; pres. MJA, Inc. Constrn. Mgrs., Chester, 1981-87; project adminstr., mgr. H.C. Yu & Assocs. Engrs., Richmond, Va., 1987-88; project mgr. Univ. Richmond, Va., 1988-89, Roy Jorgenson Assocs., Ft. Lee, Va., 1990-91; adminstr. Richmond Dept. Pub. Works, 1991-95; sr. utility engr. Richmond Dept. Utilities, 1995—; mem. dept. TQM Devel. Team, Dept. Utilities, Richmond, 1995—; cons. for quality devel. JMJ Exec. Devel., Chester, Va., 1992—; mem. dist. selection com. Boy Scouts Am., Chesterfield, 1994; VA Divsn. adjutant, Sons of Conf. Vets., Petersburg, Va., 1980-81. Scoutmaster Boy Scouts Am., Chester, 1987—; coach/mgr. youth baseball Chesterfield Baseball Clubs, 1988—. With USNG, 1970-76. Recipient Commonwealth fellowship Va. Commonwealth U., Richmond, 1992. Mem. Alpha Tau Omega. Republican. Methodist.

JERNIGAN, VERLAND HENRY, retired newspaper writer; b. Hillsboro, Tenn., Mar. 4, 1911; s. Marion Marlin and Theora Addie (Gentry) J.; m. Verna Lee Thomas, Nov. 12, 1932; children: Virginia Sue Jernigan Bryan, Thomas Marlin. Lic. real estate agt., ins. and stock broker. Newspaper writer and printer Murfreesboro, Tenn. and Hopkinsville, Ky., 1930-42; freelance writer, 1942-76; freelance writer, photographer Southeastern Outdoor Press Assn., 1964-96; freelance writer, columnist Manchester (Tenn.) Newspaper, 1948-84; columnist The Independent, Manchester, 1990—. Author: History of TOWA 1942-90. Pres. Manchester Football Team, 1929, Manchester Golf Assn., 1970, Manchester Golf Course. Recipient Cartter Patton award Tenn. Conservation League, 1964, Tom Rollins award Southeastern Outdoor Press Assn., 1974; named to Ctrl. H.S. Hall of Fame. Mem. Southeastern Outdoor Press Assn. (life; pres. 1971-73), Tenn. Outdoor Writers Assn. (life; pres. 1967, 1st place black and white photo award 1988, 89, 2d place color photo award 1988), Tenn. Conservation League (life; pres. 1963), Outdoor Writers Assn. Am. (bd. dirs. 1979-81), Tenn. Hist. Soc., Masons, NRA (life). Methodist. Home: 616 Adams St Manchester TN 37355-2102

JEROME-EBEL, ANGELA MARIE, pediatrics nurse; b. Belleville, Ill., June 19, 1958; d. William Charles and Mary Margaret (Voellinger) J.; m. Cameron Ebel. BSN, So. Ill. U., 1980; MSN, Yale U., 1987. Pediatric staff/charge nurse Oliver C. Anderson Hosp., Maryville, Ill., 1980-81; camp nurse Camp Wekeela for Children, Canton, Maine, 1984; staff/charge nurse pediatric ICU Cardinal Glennon Children's Hosp., St. Louis, 1981-85, 86; staff nurse Quality Care, Bridgeport, Conn., 1986-87, Nurse Care, Inc./New Eng. Home Care, Milford, Conn., 1985-87; adj. clin. instr. Old Dominion U., Norfolk, Va., 1988—; coordinator Va. Medicaid Health Care, 1988-93; pulmonary clin. nurse specialist for ventilator dependent children, discharge planner Children's Hosp. of the King's Daus., Norfolk, Va., 1987-93; part time clin. nurse specialist, staff nurse home health Children's Hosp. King's Daus., 1993—, part-time clin. edn. specialist dept. edn., 1994—; ednl. cons. Passy-Muir, Inc.; clin. edn. specialist Dept. Edn., 1993—; cons. and lectr. in field. Contbr. chpt. to book. Home: 4176 Prindle Ct Apt 101 Chesapeake VA 23321-3654

JESPERSEN, SUSAN HOWELL, career counselor, educator; b. Plant City, Fla., Apr. 7, 1942; d. Graham Latting and Elizabeth (Chambers) Howell; m. Charles Zinck Jespersen, June 2, 1961 (div. Jan. 1975); children: Kristina Lynn, Kevin Ashley; m. Thomas S. Truxal II, Sept. 3, 1988. BA in Bus. Mgmt., U. So. Fla., 1981, postgrad., 1981-83; D in Bus. Adminstrn., Nova Southeastern U., 1996. Cert. instr. Office mgr., co-owner Floyd R. Slayton Assoc., Tampa, Fla., 1975-79; benefits adminstrv. aide Tampa Elec. Co., 1979-81, ind. contractor, 1982-83; corp. recruiter Fla. Steel Corp., Tampa, 1981-82; pers. mgr. mktg. Chloride Inc., Tampa, 1983-85; counselor, v.p. Drake Beam Morin Inc., Coral Gables, Fla., 1986-89; self-employed cons., counselor T & S Resources, Port St. Lucie, Fla., 1989-91; grant counselor, adj. instr. Indian River C.C., Ft. Pierce, Fla., 1991—; adj. instr. MBA program Nova Southeastern U., Ft. Lauderdale, 1996—. Mem. ASTD, ACA, Fla. Vocat. Equity Assn. (sec.-treas. 1993-95, pres.-elect. 1995-96, pres. 1996-98), Soc. Human Resource Mgmt., Fla. Assn. C.C.s, Phi Kappa Phi. Office: Indian River CC 3209 Virginia Ave Fort Pierce FL 34981-5541

JESSE, JAMES EDWARD, engineering executive; b. Omaha, Jan. 16, 1946; s. Albert and Elsa Martha J.; m. Joyce Lynn Rozela, July 11, 1971 (div. July 1981); children: Jill, Jennifer. BSEE, Ill. Inst. Tech., 1968. Elec. engr. Motorola, Chgo., 1968-71, Ft. Lauderdale, Fla., 1971-75; engring. group leader Motorola, Ft. Lauderdale, 1975-79, engring. sect. mgr., 1979-85; dir. engring. Audio Intelligence & Devices, Ft. Lauderdale, 1985-88, v.p., dir. engring., 1988-92; v.p., dir. engring. Westinghouse Aid, Ft. Lauderdale, 1992—; instr. Broward C.C., Ft. Lauderdale, 1979-82, Motorola, 1982; cons. Telectron, Ft. Lauderdale, 1979-80. Patentee in field. Mem. communications elec. career merit achievement planning com. Fla. STate Dept. Edn., Ft. Lauderdale, 1981. Mem. IEEE.

JESSEN, MICHAEL ERIK, surgeon, educator; b. Melita, Manitoba, Can., May 26, 1958; came to U.S., 1986; s. Paul Erik and M. Isabelle (Spafford) J. Student, U. Manitoba, Winnipeg, Can., 1975-77, MD, 1981. Diplomate Nat. Bd. Med. Examiners, Am. Bd. Surgery, Am. Bd. Thoracic Surgery; lic. Med. Coun. Can.; cert. gen. surgery specialsit, cardiovascular and thoracic surgery specialist Royal Coll. Surgeons Can. Intern U. Manitoba, 1981-82; resident in gen. surgery U. Man., 1982-86; rsch. fellow surgery Duke U. Med. Ctr., Durham, N.C., 1986-88, resident in thoracic surgery, 1988-90; asst. prof. thoracic and cardiovascular surgery U. Tex. Southwestern Med. Ctr., Dallas, 1991—; chief cardiothoracic surgery Dallas VA Med. Ctr.; presenter in field. Contbr. numerous articles and abstracts to publs. Isbister scholar, 1976, U. Manitoba Alumni scholar, 1976, Maxwell Rady scholar, 1977, Morton Stall scholar, 1977; faculty fellow U. Manitoba, Can. Heart Found. fellow, 1987; grantee Am. Heart Assn., 1987, 94, Tex. Advanced Tech. Program, 1991. Fellow ACS, Royal Coll. Physicians and Surgeons Can., Am. Coll. Cardiology; mem. AMA, Am. Heart Assn. (coun. cardiovascular surgery), Am. Soc. for Artificial Internal Organs, Soc. Thoracic Surgeons, Soc. Univ. Surgeons. Home: 900 Meadow Creek Dr Apt 2062 Irving TX 75038-3170 Office: U Tex Southwestern Med Ctr 5323 Harry Hines Blvd Dallas TX 75235-7200

JESSUP, JAN AMIS, arts volunteer, writer; b. Chgo., Aug. 10, 1927; d. Herman Harvey and Anita (Lincoln) Sinako; m. Everett Orme Amis, Dec. 20, 1970 (dec. Nov. 1981); m. Joe Lee Jessup, Apr. 16, 1989. BA, U. Minn., 1948; postgrad., Rutgers U., 1969-70. bd. dirs., exec. com. Broward Ctr. for Performing Arts Pacers, Fort Lauderdale, Fla., 1985-88, pres., 1987-88; speaker U. Internat. Bus., Beijing, 1985. Active various not-for-profit orgns. including Girl Scouts U.S., Boy Scouts Am., Presbyn. Ch., others; mem. Beautification Com., Lighthouse Point, Fla., 1978-89, sec., 1988-91; rep. to Fla. Art Orgns., 1987-88; bd. dirs. Archways, Ft. Lauderdale, 1987-91; trustee Miami City Ballet, 1991-94; mem. adv. bd. Guild of the Palm Beaches, 1994-95; mem. bd. govs. Fla. Philharm. Orch., 1981—, v.p. representing all affiliates, 1985-87, 92, 94-96, mem. exec. com., 1989-93, v.p. individual giving, 1991-92, bd. dirs., 1994—, chmn. affiliate com., 1994-95, v.p. vols., 1995-96, chmns. adv. coun., 1996—; bd. dirs. Fla. Grand Opera, 1993—; bd. dirs. Concert Assn. Fla., Inc., 1996-97; mem. bus. com. for arts Palm Beach Cultural Coun., 1993—, 96-97; advisor Friends of Philharmonic, 1996-97. Mem. Nat. Soc. Arts and Letters, Am. Symphony Orch. League (vice chmn. 1989-90, sec. vol. coun. 1986-87, v.p. 1987-88, pres. 1989-90, advisor 1990-91, assoc. Resource Devel. Inst. 1996—, league assoc. 1996-97), The Opus Soc. (bd. dirs., mem. exec. com. 1981—, chmn. 1981-85), Ft. Lauderdale Philharm. Soc. (bd. dirs. 1986—), Opera Soc. (sec. 1986-87, v.p. pub. rels. 1987-88), Gold Coast Jazz Soc. (bd. dirs. 1992—, v.p. 1994—), Royal Dames of Cancer Rsch. (bd. trustees 1995—), Concert Assn. Fla., Inc. (bd. dirs. 1996—), Boca Raton Resort and Club, Royal Palm Yacht Club, Royal Palm Country Club, Women's Club, Sea Grape Garden Club (past pres.). Republican. Home: 133 Coconut Palm Rd Boca Raton FL 33432-7975

JESSUP, JOE LEE, business educator, management consultant; b. Cordele, Ga., June 23, 1913; s. Horace Andrew and Elizabeth (Wilson) J.; m. Janet Amis, Apr. 16, 1989. B.S., U. Ala., 1936; M.B.A., Harvard U., 1941; LL.D., Chung-Ang U., Seoul, Korea, 1964. Sales rep. Proctor & Gamble, 1937-40; liaison officer bur. pub. rels. U.S. War Dept., 1941; spl. asst. and exec. asst. Far Ea. div. and office exports Bd. Econ. Warfare, 1942-43; exec. officer to chief of staff Svcs. of Supply-Europian Theatre, 1943-44; exec. officer, office deptl. adminstrn. Dept. State, 1946; exec. sec. adminstr.'s adv. coun. War Assets Adminstrn., 1946-48; v.p. sales Airken, Capitol & Service Co., 1948-52; assoc. prof. bus. adminstrn. George Washington U., 1952, prof., 1952-77, prof. emeritus, 1977—, asst. dean Sch. Govt., 1951-60; pres. Jessup and Co., Ft. Lauderdale, Fla., 1957—; bd. dirs. Giant Food, Inc., Washington (audit comm. 1974-75), 1971-75, Am. Equity Investors, Inc., 1986-87, Hunter Assn. Labs, Fairfax, Va., 1964-69 (exec. comm. 1966-69, exec. v.p. 1967, gen. mgr. 1969), coordinator air force resources mgmt. program, 1951-57; del. in edn. 10th Internat. Mgmt. Conf., Sao Paulo, Brazil, 1954, 11th Conf., Paris, 1957, 12th Conf., Sydney and Melbourne, Australia, 1960, 13th Conf., Rotterdam, Netherlands, 1966, 14th Conf., Tokyo, 1969, 15th Conf., Munich, Germany, 1972; mem. Md. Econ. Devel. Adv. Commn., 1973-75. Mem. Civil Svc. Commn., Arlington County, Va., 1952-54; mem. nat. adv. coun. Ctr. for Study of Presidency, 1974—; mem. bd. overseers Lynn U., Boca Raton, 1991—; mem. adv. bd. Youth Automotive Tng. Ctr., Hollywood, Fla., 1993—; mem. Atlanta regional panel for selection of White House fellow, 1990-95, mem. Miami regional panel, 1994-95; trustee Tng. Within Industry Found., Summit, N.J., 1954-58, Philharm Orch., Fla., 1986-91; mem. Chaine des Rotisseurs, 1987-92, 94—. Decorated Bronze Star; recipient cert. of appreciation Sec. of Air Force, 1957. Mem. Acad. Mgmt., Chaine des Rotisseurs, Harvard Club (N.Y.C.), Univ. Club (Washington), Tower Club (Ft. Lauderdale, Fla.), Royal Palm Yacht and Country Club. Home: 133 Coconut Palm Rd Boca Raton FL 33432-7975

JESSUP, STEVEN LEE, ceramics engineer; b. Balt., Nov. 29, 1954; s. Robert Eugene and Mary Jane (Smith) J. BS in Ceramic Engring., Va. Poly. Inst., 1976. Student mgr. Southwestern Co., Nashville, 1975-76; process engr. Reichhold Chems. Inc., Irwindale, Calif., 1977-80, Guardian Industries, Corsicana, Tex., 1980—. Precinct chmn. Navarro County Republican Party, Corsicana, 1990—; water safety instr. ARC, Ellicott City, Md., 1972; YMCA open water scuba diver, Mexia, Tex., 1992. Named one of Outstanding Young Men of Am., 1978. Home: 2825 W 5th Ave Corsicana TX 75110-3917

JESTER, CARROLL GLADSTONE, lawyer; b. Macon, Ga., May 5, 1957; s. Carroll Gladstone and Annie Jean (Bazemore) J.; m. Laura Ann Spencer, Aug. 17, 1985; children: Annie Catherine, Carroll Elizabeth. BA, U. Ga., 1979, JD, 1982. Bar: Ga. 1982, U.S. Dist. Ct. (no. dist.) Ga. 1982, U.S. Ct. Appeals (11th cir.) 1983, U.S. Dist. Ct. (mid. dist.) Ga. 1989, U.S. Dist. Ct. (so. dist.) Ga. 1991. Assoc. Rogers, Magruder, Hoyt, Sumner & Brinson, Rome, Ga., 1982-85, Swift, Currie, McGhee & Hiers, Atlanta, 1985-89; assoc. Goldner, Sommers, Scrudder & Bass, Atlanta, 1989-91, ptnr., 1991—. Contbg. friend Friends of Zoo Atlanta; angel The Alliance Theatre, Atlanta; mem. The Ga. Conservancy, Ga. Trust for Hist. Preservation, St. Luke's Presbyn. Ch. Mem. ABA (torts and ins. sect.), Atlanta Bar Assn., Ga. Def. Lawyers Assn., U. Ga. Bulldog Club, SAR, Honorable Order Ky. Cols. (col.), Sigma Chi (undergrad. treas. 1978, Best Pledge 1976), Phi Delta Phi, Phi Alpha Theta. Office: Goldner Sommers Scrudder & Bass 900 Circle 75 Pky Ste 850 Atlanta GA 30339

JETER, KATHERINE LESLIE BRASH, lawyer; b. Gulfport, Miss., July 24, 1921; d. Ralph Edward and Rosa Meta (Jacobs) Brash; m. Robert McLean Jeter, Jr., May 11, 1946. BA, Newcomb Coll. of Tulane U., 1943; JD, Tulane U., 1945. Bar: La. 1945, U.S. Dist. Ct. (we. dist.) La. 1948, U.S. Tax Ct. 1965, U.S. Supreme Ct. 1971, U.S. Dist. Ct. (ea. dist.) La. 1975, U.S. Ct. Appeals (5th cir.) 1981, U.S. Dist. Ct. (mid. dist.) La. 1982. Assoc. Montgomery, Fenner & Brown, New Orleans, 1945-46, Tucker, Martin, Holder, Jeter & Jackson, Shreveport, 1947-49; ptnr. Tucker, Jeter, Jackson and Hickman and predecessors, Shreveport, 1980—; judge pro tem 1st Jud. Dist. Ct., Caddo Parish, La., 1982-83; mem. adv. com. to joint legis. subcom. on mgmt. of the community; pres. YWCA of Shreveport, 1963; hon. consul of France; Shreveport, 1982-91; pres. Little Theatre of Shreveport, 1966-67; pres. Shreveport Art Guild, 1974-75; mem. task force crim justice La. Priorities for the Future, 1978; pres. LWV of Shreveport, 1950-51. Recipient Disting. Grad. award Tulane U., 1983. Mem. Am. Law Inst., La. State Law Inst. (mem. coun. 1980—, adv. com. La. Civil Code 1973-77, temp. ad hoc. com. 1976-77, sr. officer 1993—), Am. Law Inst., Pub. Affairs Rsch. Coun. (bd. trustees 1976-81, 91—, exec. com. 1981-84, area exec. committeeman Shreveport area 1982), ABA, La. Bar Assn., Shreveport Bar Assn. (pres. 1986), Nat. Assn. Women Lawyers, Shreveport Assn. for Women Attys., C. of C. Shreveport (bd. dirs. 1975-77), Order of Coif, Phi Beta Kappa. Contbr. articles on law to profl. jours. Home: 3959 Maryland Ave Shreveport LA 71106-1021 Office: 401 Edwards St Ste 905 Shreveport LA 71101-3146

JEW, HENRY, pharmacist; b. Hong Kong, June 10, 1950. BS in Pharmacy, U. Ga., 1974. Preceptor to externship program So. Sch. of Pharmacy, U. Ga., 1974-78; researcher Brompton's Mixture, 1977-78; pharmacist VA Med Ctr, Decatur, Ga., VNS Inc., Atlanta.

JEWELL, CHARLES LINWOOD, JR., information systems specialist, programmer; b. Washington, Sept. 27, 1962; s. Charles Linwood and Sheila Sue (Smith) J. BA in Mgmt. with honors, Nat.-Louis U., 1992. Lic. real estate agt., Va. Lead clk. office automation JAG USAF, Bolling AFB, D.C., 1983-85; network ops. specialist Fed. Bur. Prisons, Washington, 1985-86; computer programmer, analyst Def. Info. Systems Agy., Pentagon, D.C., 1986-91; sr. computer programmer, analyst Air Force Intelligence, Springfield, Va., 1991-92; chief comm.-computer sys. office Joint Svcs. Survival, Evasion, Resistance and Escape Agy., Ft. Belvoir, Va., 1992-95; computer programmer, analyst Def. Intelligence Agy., Def. Human Intelligence Svc., Arlington, Va., 1995—. Mem. IEEE Computer Soc., Novell Network Users Internat. Home: 5819H Rexford Dr Springfield VA 22152-1044 Office: Defense Intelligence Agy DHS Rm 1010H 3100 Clarendon Blvd Arlington VA 22201

JEWELL, GEORGE HIRAM, lawyer; b. Fort Worth, Jan. 9, 1922; s. George Hiram and Vera (Lee) J.; m. Betty Jefferis, July 21, 1944; children: Susan Jewell Cannon, Robert V., Nancy Jewell Wommack. B.A., U. Tex., 1942, LL.B., 1950. Bar: Tex. 1950. With Baker & Botts, Houston, 1950—, sr. ptnr., 1960-90, counsel, 1990—. Trustee Tex. Children's Hosp., Houston, 1977—, pres., 1982-83, chmn., 1984-86; bd. dirs. Schlumberger Found., N.Y.C., 1982—. Served to lt. USNR, 1943-46, 50-51. Fellow Am. Coll. Tax Counsel, Am. Bar Foun.; mem. ABA, Houston Country Club, Coronado Club (pres. 1976-77), Old Baldy Club (chmn. 1993—), Eldorado Country Club (pres. 1995-96), Order of Coif, Phi Beta Kappa, Phi Delta Phi. Home: 6051 Crab Orchard Rd Houston TX 77057-1447 Office: Baker & Botts 1 Shell Plz Houston TX 77002

JEWELL-KELLY, STARLA ANNE, educational administrator; b. Klamath Falls, Oreg., Sept. 8, 1940; d. John Trippett and Anna Marie (Morgan) Matthews; m. Joseph Power Jewell, June 18, 1960 (div. May 1985); children: Ronald Kevin, Errin Paul, Tara Elaine; m. Robert Clayton Kelly, Dec. 27, 1986. BS in Elem. Edn., So. Oreg. State Coll., 1962; MS in Curriculum & Instrn. Adminstrn., U. Oreg., 1978. Cert. tchr. grades k-12, cert. sch. adminstr. Elem. tchr. Josephine County Schs., Grants Pass, Oreg., 1962-66; jr. high tchr. Petersburg (Alaska) High Sch., 1966-70; dir. community edn. Umpqua C.C., Roseburg, Oreg., 1975-79; asst. dir. continuing edn. So. Oreg. State Coll., Ashland, 1979-80; dir. C.C. instr. Office of C.C., Salem, Oreg., 1980-83; dir. C.C. planning and adminstrn. Office of C.C., Salem, 1983-86, commr. for C.C., 1986-87; asst. state supt. schs. Oreg. Dept. Edn., Salem, 1987-89; exec. dir. Nat. Community Edn. Assn., Fairfax, Va., 1989—; dir. Coalition of Adult Edn. Orgns., Washington, 1989—, sec.-treas., 1993—; mem. Ednl. Leaders Consortium, Washington, 1989—; cons. The Prins. Ctr.-Harvard, Cambridge, Mass., 1990, State Bd. Edn., Guam, 1991. Author: (monthly column) Community Education Today, 1989-94. Campaign worker Non-Partisan-State Supts. Position, Salem, 1980-83, United Way, Alexandria, Va., 1992-94, Am. Cancer Soc., Fairfax, Va., 1994; com. chair United Way, Salem, 1987-89. Recipient fellowship U. Oreg., Eugene, 1976-78, Ednl. Policy fellowship Inst. for Ednl. Leadership, Washington, 1985. Mem. Am. Soc. Assn. Execs., Oreg. Community Edn. Assn. (C.S. Mott Meml. award 1982), Nat. Coalition for Parent Involvement in Edn. (treas. 1989-94), Nat. Community Edn. Assn. (chair awards 1983-85, Leadership award region IV 1990), Coun. for Instrl. Adminstrn. (sec. 1980-83). Episcopalian. Office: Nat Community Edn Assn 3929 Old Lee Hwy Ste 91 Fairfax VA 22030-2421

JEYAPRAKASH, AYYAMPERUMAL, biologist, researcher; b. Sholavandan, Tamil Nadu, India, Feb. 21, 1951; came to U.S., 1983; s. Ayyamperumal and Mookammal Jeyaprakash; m. Margret S. Packiam, Jan. 26, 1977; 1 child, Augustin. BSc, Madurai (India) U., 1972, MSc, 1974; PhD, Utkal (India) U., 1982. Postdoctoral scientist U. Mass., Amherst, 1983-86; postdoctoral rsch. geneticist U. Calif., Berkeley, 1986-89, asst. specialist, 1989-92; sr. biologist U. Fla., Gainesville, 1993—. Contbr. articles to profl. jours. Recipient Centenary medal U. Mass./Agrl. Experiment Sta., 1986. Mem. AAAS. Home: 1700 SW 16th Ct M-28 Gainesville FL 32608 Office: Univ of Florida Dept Entomology/Nematology Hull Rd Bldg 970 Gainesville FL 32611

JHAMB, INDAR MOHAN, physician; b. New Delhi, Oct. 10, 1952; came to U.S., 1978; s. Suraj Bhan and Kaushalya (Tandon) J.; married, 1978; 2 children. MBBS, U. Delhi, New Delhi, 1970, MD, 1974. Diplomate Am. Bd. Allergy and Immunology, Am. Bd. Pediatrics. Resident U. Delhi, 1975-78; resident U. Louisville, 1979-81, fellow, 1981-83; pvt. practice Bowling Green, Ky. Fellow Am. Coll. Allergy and Immunology, Am. Acad. Pediatrics; mem. Am. Assn. Cert. Allergists. Office: 1228 Ashley Cir Bowling Green KY 42104-5803

JHIN, MICHAEL KONTIEN, health care executive; b. Hong Kong, Jan. 26, 1950; came to U.S., 1958; s. Paul Y. and Monica J. BSME, Rensselaer Poly. Inst., 1971; MBA, Boston U., 1974. Adminstrv. asst. St. Vincent Hosp., Worcester, Mass., 1974-76; asst. dir. Thomas Jefferson U. Hosp., Phila., 1976-79, assoc. dir., 1979-84; exec. dir., CEO Temple U. Hosp., Phila., 1984-88; exec. v.p. Long Beach (Calif.) Meml. Health Sys., 1988-90; pres., CEO St. Luke's Episcopal Hosp., Houston, 1990—, St. Luke's Episcopal Health Sys., Houston, 1995—. Bd. dirs. Houston Hosp. Coun., 1991-96, chmn. bd., 1994-95, Jr. Achievement, 1991—. Fellow Am. Coll. Healthcare Execs.; mem. Rensselaer Alumni Assn. (v.p. 1994-96, pres.-elect 1995-96, pres. 1996—), Am. Hosp. Assn. (regional policy bd. 1992-95), Tex. Hosp. Assn., Young Pres.'s Orgn. Office: St Luke's Episcopal Hosp 6720 Bertner St Houston TX 77030-2604

JIANG, BAI-CHUAN, optical educator; b. Hongzhou, Zhejiang, China, June 21, 1944; came to the U.S., 1987; s. Gaoquan and Yueru (Zhao) J.; m. Wei-Fen, Feb. 4, 1970; 1 child, Alexander Xingzhi. BS, Fudan U., 1966; MS, Chinese Acad. Scis., Shanghai, 1982; PhD, Acad. Sinica, Shanghai, 1986. Optics engr. Shanghai Camera Factory, 1967-78; rsch. asst. Acad. Sinica, Shanghai, 1978-81; rsch. assoc. Chinese Acad. Scis., Shanghai, 1982-86; vis. scientist physiology dept. U. Toronto, Ont., 1986-87; post-doctoral fellow psychology dept. Pa. State U., University Park, 1987-88; post-doctoral fellow U. Houston (Tex.), Coll. Optometry, 1988-89, asst. prof., 1990—. Contbr. articles to profl. jours; patentee in field. Recipient Outstanding Young Scientist grant Chinese Acad. Scis., 1985-86, Rsch. fellowship Nat. Rsch. Coun. Can., 1988, Rsch. fellowship Med. Rsch. Coun. Can., 1989,

NIH grant, 1991—, Rsch. grant Bausch & Lomb InVision Inst., 1993. Fellow Am. Acad. Optometry; mem. AAAS, Assn. for Rsch. in Vision and Ophthalmology, Human Factor and Ergonomics Soc., Sigma Xi.

JIANG, HUBIN, entrepreneur, software engineer; b. Jiangsu, China, Mar. 26, 1961; came to U.S., 1987; s. Zhizhen Jiang and Xiangmei Hu. B of Engring., Nanjing (China) Inst. Tech., 1982; MSEE, U. Md., 1990, postgrad., 1992—. Faculty mem. dept. automatic control engring. Nanjing Inst. Tech., 1982-85; rschr. McMaster U., Can., 1985-87; rsch. assoc. dept. meteorology U. Md., College Park, 1987-89; R & D dir. Micronet Software Corp., College Park, 1988-90; knowledge engring. group leader U. Md., College Park, 1990; sr. computer sys. cons. Earth Satellite Corp., Chevy Chase, Md., 1990; sci. officer Vidar Sys. Corp., Herndon, Va., 1990-93; pres. Worldwares, Inc., McLean, Va., 1992-94; sr. sys. engr. Intrafed, Inc., Washington, 1993-94; pres., CEO Quatex, Inc., Herndon, 1994—. Inventor Md. image visualization and analysis system, system method for automatic recognition of document. Mem. IEEE, IEEE System, Man, and Cybernetics Soc., Pattern Recognition Soc. Office: Quatex Inc Ste 200 620 Herndon Parkway Herndon VA 22070

JIMENEZ, REYNALDO LUIS, foreign language educator; b. La Habana, Cuba, July 13, 1946; came to the U.S., 1962; s. Ricardo J. Jimenez; m. Carmen E. Jimenez, Aug. 27, 1968; children: Raquel, Rebeca. BA, U. Ill., 1969, MA, 1970, PhD, 1974. Cert. Spanish lang. oral proficiency tester ACTFL. Asst. prof. The Ohio State U., Columbus, 1974-79; assoc. prof. U. Fla., Gainesville, 1980—; chari Spanish AP test devel. Ednl. Testing Svc., Princeton, 1988-91, question leader AP reading; chief faculty cons. for Spanish AP Nat. Exam., 1996—; acting assoc. dir. Ctr. for L.Am. Studies, U. Fla., Gainesville. Author: Cabrera Infante and Tres Tristes Tigres, 1980. Mem. MLA, Am. Assn. Tchrs. Spanish and Portuguese. Home: 3310 NW 27th Ave Gainesville FL 32605

JIMMAR, D'ANN, elementary education educator, fashion merchandiser; b. Leighton, Ala., Dec. 10, 1942; d. Harry D. Qualls and Lillian Jimmar. BS in Elem. Edn., Ala. A&M U., 1965, MS in Urban Studies, 1973; PhD in Higher Edn., Iowa State U., 1986. Elem. tchr. Limestone County Bd. Edn., Athens, Ala., 1966-68, Huntsville (Ala.) City Bd. Edn., 1968-71; instr. dept. community planning and urban studies Ala. A&M U., Huntsville, 1973-78; rsch. asst. dept. sociology and anthropology Iowa State U., Ames, 1978-79, rsch. aide, 1980-81, 82-83; ednl. aide, substitute tchr. Ames Community Sch. Dist., 1983-86; coord. practicums Nova U., Ft. Lauderdale, Fla., 1986-87; tchr. Downtown Adult Edn. Ctr., Ft. Lauderdale, 1987-88, Apollo Mid. Sch., Hollywood, Fla., 1988-89, Greenview Elem. Sch., Columbia, S.C., 1989-91; dir. rsch. edn. NuWAE Ent., Houston, 1991-92; retail salesperson Foley's/May Co., 1992—. Sec.-treas. Ames Tenant Landlord Svcs., 1982-83, bd. dirs. 1982-, 83, 84-85, chmn., 1984-85. Recipient svc. award Local Govt. Study Commn., Huntsville, 1972, Ms. Alumni award Ala. A&M U., 1978. Mem. ASCD, Ala. A&M U. Alumni Assn. (chaplain 1977-78), Phi Delta Kappa, Delta Sigma Theta. Home: 8001 W Tidwell Rd Apt 416 Houston TX 77040-5536

JINRIGHT, NOAH FRANKLIN, vocational school educator; b. Banks, Ala., Dec. 5, 1936; s. William Carroll and Ila Marie (Garrett) J.; m. Sarah Ann (Graham) Nickolson, Nov. 21, 1959 (div. Sept. 1974); children: Charlene M., Lisa A., Michael D.; m. Frances Lenora Gaskins, June 11, 1978; children: Diana Carol, Jonathan Franklin. Cert. archtl. and mech. drafting, Columbus (Ga.) Tech., 1971, cert. plate and pipe welder, 1984, CNC, 1983. Operator scale Bibb Textiles, Columbus, 1954-56; operator press and share Columbus Iron Works, 1957-58; ins. agt. Interstate Life, Columbus, 1958-61; winder starter/generator Joe Hooten, Inc., Columbus, 1960; fireman City of Columbus, 1960-66; advt. rep. Jinright Enterprises, Columbus, 1966; ins. agt. Security Life of Ga., Columbus, 1966; operator share and press Pascoe Steel, Columbus, 1966-67; machinist Goldens' Foundry and Machine Works, Columbus, 1967; carpenter, roofer Muscogee County Sch. Dist., Columbus, 1968-72; pattern maker Pekor Iron Works, Columbus, 1972-78; instr. metals tech. Kendrick H.S., Columbus, 1978—. Exec. trainer Precision Metalforming Assn., 1996. Mem. Internat. Soc. Welding Educators (program adv. bd.), Am. Foundry Soc., Am. Welding Soc., Vocat. Indsl. Clubs Am. (advisor, cert. of appreciation region VIII 1996), Trade and Indsl. Educators Ga. Methodist. Home: 2040 Lee Rd 427 Phenix City AL 36867 also: PO Box 63 Columbus GA 31902-0063 Office: Kendrick HS 6015 Georgetown Dr Columbus GA 31907-4611

JIRRAN, RAYMOND JOSEPH, social studies educator; b. Cleve., Mar. 29, 1934; s. Raymond Wenceslaus and Elizabeth Katherine (Koryta) Jirkans; m. Bette Mae Kelly, June 13, 1964. AB, St. Joseph's Sem. Coll., Washington, 1959; BS in Edn., Kent State U., 1960, MA, 1961, PhD, 1972. Instr. St. Procopius Coll., Lisle, Ill., 1966-67; asst. prof. Ea. Ky. U., Richmond, 1967-69; asst. prof. history Thomas Nelson C.C., Hampton, Va., 1969-72, assoc. prof., 1972-73, prof., 1973—. Author: From Adam to Atom, 1968—. Sec. Newport News (Va.) Dem. Com., 1985-91. Mem. AAUP (Va. conf. pres.-elect 1996—), NAACP (life), Va. Social Sci. Assn. (pres. 1978-79), Nat. Assn. Parliamentarians, Assn. for Study Afro-Am. Life and History, Lions (pres. Northampton 1982-84, Lion of Yr. award 1988), John Henry Cardinal Newman Hon. Soc. Roman Catholic. Home: 1168 Willow Green Dr Newport News VA 23602-7158 Office: Coll Thomas Nelson Communit Hampton VA 23670

JIRSA, JAMES OTIS, civil engineering educator; b. Lincoln, Nebr., July 30, 1938; s. Otis Frank and Anna Marie (Skutchan) J.; m. Marion Ansley Coad, Aug. 7, 1941; children: David, Stephen. BS, U. Nebr., 1960; MS, U. Ill., 1962, PhD, 1963. Registered profl. engr., Tex. Asst. prof. civil engring. U. Nebr., Lincoln, 1964-65; asst. prof. then assoc. prof. Rice U., Houston, 1965-72; assoc. prof. then prof. U. Tex., Austin, 1972-82, Finch prof. engring., 1982-84, Ferguson prof. civil engring., 1984-88, dir. Ferguson Structural Engring. Lab., 1985-88, Janet S. Cockrell Centennial chair in engring., 1988—; research engr. Portland Cement Assocs., 1965; engr. H.J. Degenkolb Assocs., San Francisco, 1980. Contbr. articles to profl. jours. Fulbright scholar U. Paris, 1963-64; recipient Rsch. award Japanese Soc. for Promotion Sci., 1980, 94, J.A. Boase award Reinforced Concrete Rsch. Coun., 1993. Fellow Am. Concrete Inst. (TAC chmn. 1985-88, bd. dirs. 1987-90, Alfred Lindau award 1986, Wason medal 1977, Reese award 1977, 79, Bloem award 1990); mem. NAE, ASCE (com. chmn. 1972-81, Reese award 1970, 91, Huber Research prize 1978), Earthquake Engring. Research Inst., Structural Engring Assn. Tex., Internat. Assn. for Bridge and Structural Engrs., Nebr. Czech Orgn. (King Charles award 1983). Office: U Tex Dept Civil Engring 10100 Burnet Rd Austin TX 78712-1076

JOCHIM, MICHAEL EUGENE, food service executive; b. Evansville, Ind., Aug. 15, 1945; s. Leonard Nicholas and Marjorie Beatrice (Moore) J.; m. Judith Ann Bassemier, Aug. 21, 1965; children: Linda, John Michael, Stephanie, Alexis. Student, Christian Bros. Coll., Memphis, 1963-65; BS in Mktg., U. Evansville, 1977. Bank teller, loan officer Old Nat. Bank, Evansville, 1968-71; v.p. purchasing Evansville Food Distbrs., 1971-79; exec. pres. Pocahontas Foods USA, Richmond, Va., 1979—, pres., 1996—; bd. dirs. Ctrl. Va. Food Bank. Mem. Evansville Jaycees, 1971-77, bd. dirs., 1976-77; pres. Marion Day Sch. for Handicapped, Evansville, 1977-79; bd. dirs. Virginia Randolph Sch. for Handicapped, 1981-83, Ctrl. Food Bank, 1995—. With U.S. Army, 1966-68, Vietnam. Mem. VFW, KC, Nat. Frozen Food Assn. (food svc. counsel Hershey, Pa. chpt. 1986-95, bd. dirs. 1989-95). Republican. Roman Catholic. Office: Pocahontas Foods USA 7420 Ranco Rd Richmond VA 23228-3702

JOCZIK, MARK TAMETOMO, program director; b. Andrews AFB, Md., Jan. 11, 1967; s. Robert Louis and Kiyo (Hamamoto) Turkoly-Joczik. AA, Valley Forge Coll., 1987; BA in Polit. Sci., The Citadel, 1990. Account mgr. World Fin. Corp., Charleston, S.C., 1992-93; procurement officer Med. Univ. S.C., Charleston, 1993—. Sec. Charleston County Libr. Bd., 1995—; exec. com. mem. Charleston Young Rep., 1995—; mem. Big Bros. Adv. Bd., Charleston, 1995—. 1st lt. U.S. Army, 1990-92. Mem. Charleston Exch. Club, Am. Legion Post 112, Lowcountry Airborne Assn. (3d vice chair), Assn. Citadel Men. Roman Catholic. Home: 3 Rutledge Ave Charleston SC 29401 Office: Med Univ South Carolina 171 Ashley Ave Charleston SC 29425

JODOIN, JEFFREY CHARLES, software engineer; b. Rochester, N.Y., Mar. 29, 1969; s. Ronald E. and Martha E. (Buder) J. BS, Rochester Inst. Tech., 1992. Software engr. Asea Brown Boveri, Rochester, N.Y., 1989-91; software engr., project lead Millennium Computer Corp., Pittsford, N.Y., 1992-96; software engr., object developer LDDS World Com., Tulsa, 1996—. Mem. IEEE, IEEE Computer Software Soc.

JOE, GEORGE WASHINGTON, clinical researcher, quantitative methodologist; b. Augusta, Ga., Feb. 22, 1943. BS, U. Ga., 1965, EdD, 1969. Rsch. scientist Inst. of Behavioral Rsch./Tex. Christian U., Ft. Worth, 1969-70, asst. prof., 1970-74, assoc. prof., 1974-83; rsch. scientist Tex. Christian U., 1989—; rsch. scientist behavioral rsch. program Tex. A&M U., College Station, 1983-89. Author monographs in field; contbr. articles to profl. jours., chpts. to books. Mem. Am. Edn. Rsch. Assn., Phi Beta Kappa, Phi Kappa Phi, Sigma Xi. Office: Tex Christian U PO Box 298740 Fort Worth TX 76129 also: PO Box 9482 Fort Worth TX 76147-2482

JOFFE, DAVID JONATHON, lawyer; b. Manhatten, N.Y., Mar. 8, 1962; s. Seymour Joffe and Saretta Hoyt (Hill) Prescott; m. Hillary Ray Joffe, June 25, 1994; 1 child, Alexander Seymour. BA, Fla. State U., 1984; JD, U. Miami, Coral Gables, Fla., 1988. Bar: Fla. 1989, U.S. Dist. Ct. (so. dist.) Fla. 1989, U.S. Dist. Ct. (mid. dist.) Fla. 1989, U.S. Ct. Appeals (11th cir.) 1989. Legal intern Dade County Pub. Defenders, Miami, 1988-89; assoc. Randy S. Maultasch, Esquire, Miami, 1989-90; owner, ptnr. Ticket Attys., P.A., Coconut Grove, Fla., 1992—; pvt. practice Coconut Grove, 1990—; mem. C.J.A. Panel Atty. for So. Dist. of Fla. Dir., chmn. com. Dade County Young Dems., Miami, 1990. Mem. ABA, ATLA, Nat. Assn. Criminal Def. Lawyers, Assn. Fla. Trial Lawyers, Fla. Assn. Criminal Def. Attys. Democrat. Jewish. Office: 2900 Bridgeport Ave Ste 401 Coconut Grove FL 33133-3606

JOHANSEN, EIVIND HERBERT, special education services executive, former army officer; b. Charleston, S.C., Mar. 7, 1927; s. Andrew and Ruth Lee (Thames) J.; m. Dolores E. Klockmann, June 9, 1950; children: Chris Allen, Jane Elizabeth. B.S., Tex. A&M U., 1950; M.S., George Washington U., 1968; postgrad., Harvard U., 1955, Army Command and Gen. Staff Coll., 1963, Naval War Coll., 1967, Advanced Mgmt. Program, U. Pitts., 1971. Quartermaster officer U.S. Army, 1950-79, advanced through grades to lt. gen., 1977; strategic planner Office Joint Chiefs of Staff, 1968-69, group comdr., 1969-70; army dir. distbn., 1970-72, army dir. materiel, 1972-75; comdg. gen. Army Aviation Systems Command, St. Louis, 1975-77; army dep. chief staff for logistics Washington, 1977-79; ret., 1979; pres., CEO Nat. Industries for Severely Handicapped, Inc., 1979-92; mem. exec. council, chmn. mgmt. improvement com. Fed. Exec. Bd., St. Louis, 1975-77; bd. advs. Am. Def. Preparedness Assn., St. Louis, 1975-77, tech. and mgmt. adv. bd., Washington, 1977-79; chmn. Army Logistics Policy Council, 1977-79; bd. advs. Army Logistic Mgmt. Coll., 1978-79, Army Mgmt. Engring. Coll., 1978-79. Contbr. articles to profl. jours. Mem. President's Com. for Purchase from Blind and Other Severely Handicapped, Washington, 1973-74, chmn., 1975; mem. President's Com. on Employment of Handicapped; bd. dirs., chmn. ind. ops. com. Mo. Goodwill Industries, 1975-77; chmn. youth program Jr. Achievement, St. Louis, 1975-77; sponsor Air Explorer Post, Boy Scouts Am., 1975-77; bd. dirs. Q.M. Found., 1979-88, 92-93. Decorated DSM, Legion of Merit with two oak leaf clusters, Bronze Star, numerous others; recipient Tex. A&M Disting. Alumnus award, Disting. Svc. award Nat. Industries for Severely Handicapped, 1992, Disting. Career award Nat. Assn. Rehab. Facilities, 1992; named to Quartermaster Hall of Fame, U.S. Army, 1992. Mem. Assn. U.S. Army (bd. advisors St. Louis 1975-77), Am. Helicopter Soc., Army Aviation Assn. Am., Ret. Officers Assn., Nat. Rehab. Assn., Tex. A&M Alumni Assn. Washington (exec. bd. 1974, 78-79, pres. 1975, bd. dirs. 1993-95), George Washington U. Alumni Assn., U. Pitts. Alumni Assn., Harvard U. Alumni Assn., Toastmasters. Home: 6310 Windpatterns Trl Fairfax Station VA 22039-1207

JOHANSON, KNUT ARVID, JR., engineering executive; b. St. Augustine, Fla., Feb. 27, 1936; s. Knut Arvid and Constance Elinor (Harrison) J.; BS in Elec. Engring. Tex. A&I U., 1959; MS in Chem. Engring., U. Houston, 1978; m. Eleanor Marie Friesen, Nov. 28, 1956; children: Michael James, David Bryan, Phillip Arvid. Registered profl. engr., La., Tex., Calif. Instrumentation engr. maintenance dept. Union Carbide Corp., Texas City, Tex., 1959-67, sr. control sys. engr., Taft, La., 1967-72, control sys. commissioning engr. UNIFOS plant, Stenningsund, Sweden, 1971, group leader sys. engring. group, Port Lavaca, Tex., 1973-90; prin. control sys. engr. Union Carbide Corp., Houston, 1990—; control sys. mgr. EQUATE Joint Venture, 1994-96; instr. LaMarque Ind. Sch. Dist., 1964-66, Victoria Coll., 1977. Served with U.S. Army, 1960-62. Mem. Instrument Soc. Am. (v.p., exec. bd. 1975-77, 85-87). Baptist. Contbr. articles to profl. jours. Home: 2010 Dowling Dr Richmond TX 77469-5114 Office: Union Carbide 1 Sugar Creek Ctr Blvd Ste 400 Sugar Land TX 77478

JOHNS, CHRISTOPHER KALMAN, art educator; b. Racine, Wis., Dec. 2, 1952; s. Robert Arthur and Margaret Helen (Vasaas) J.; m. Mary Ellen Blackman, Aug. 23, 1973; 1 child, Eric Robert. Student, U. Wis., Milw., 1971-73; BFA, San Francisco Art Inst., 1975; MFA, Stanford U., 1977. Instr. Charles Wustum Mus., Racine, Wis., 1977-78; prof. La. State U., Baton Rouge, 1979—; resident fellow Vt. Studio Colony, Johnson, Vt., 1988. One-man show U. Ala., Huntsville, 1992; 2-man show Sylvia Schmidt Gallery, New Orleans, 1993; exhibited in group shows City Gallery, Raleigh, N.C., 1987, Jan Cicero Gallery, Chgo., 1990. Fellow La. Div. Arts, 1986, So. Arts Fedn., 1988. Home: 864 Albert Hart Dr Baton Rouge LA 70808-5807 Office: La State U Sch of Art 123 Design Baton Rouge LA 70803

JOHNS, ELIZABETH JANE HOBBS, educational administrator; b. Roanoke Rapids, N.C., July 18, 1941; d. Florence Eugene and Elizabeth Holt (Massey) Hobbs; m. Lewis Clarence Johns, Apr. 7, 1961; 1 child, Karen Anne Johns Cuccaro. AA with honors, Valencia Community Coll., 1984; BSBA with honors, Fla. So. Coll., 1988; MS in Mgmt., Fla. Inst. Tech., 1996. Med. receptionist Dr. Harold Knowles, Orlando, Fla., 1959-61; sec. Lockheed Martin, Orlando, 1961-77, edn. adminstr., 1977—, chair bd. credit union, 1987—; bd. dirs. Martin Marietta Fed. Credit Union; mem. diamond counsel Roy E. Crummer Grad. Sch. Bus., 1991—. Mem. community adv. bd. sch. continuing edn. Hamilton Holt Sch., continuing edn. council for women Valencia Community Coll., 1984—. Named one of Outstanding Women in Bus., 1985, one of Top Ten Employees, Martin Marietta Aerospace, Orlando, 1983, one of Top 100, 1978. Mem. Am. Bus. Women's Assn., Valencia Community Coll. Alumni Assn. (bd. dirs. 1984-93), Orlando C. of C. (post secondary edn. task force), Phi Theta Kappa. Republican. Methodist. Home: 3201 Holiday Ave Apopka FL 32703-6635 Office: Lockheed Martin Elec/Missil MP 147 5600 Sand Lake Rd Orlando FL 32819-8907

JOHNS, MICHAEL DOUGLAS, public policy analyst, consultant, writer, former government official; b. Allentown, Pa., Sept. 8, 1964; s. Glenn Franklyn and Nancy Louise (Hummel) J.; m. Nicole Denise Miles, Sept. 30, 1995. Student, Cambridge (Eng.) U., 1984; BBA in Econs., U. Miami, 1986. Editl. intern Nat. Journalism Ctr., Washington, 1983; Lyndon Baines Johnson intern Congressman Don Ritter, Washington, 1984; asst. editor Policy Rev. Mag., Washington, 1986-88; fgn. policy analyst The Heritage Found., Washington, 1988-91; spl. asst. to pres. Drew U., Madison, N.J., 1991-92; speechwriter to Pres. of U.S. The White House, Washington, 1992; speechwriter to U.S. Sec. Commerce U.S. Dept. Commerce, Washington, 1992-93; dir. rsch. Internat. Rep. Inst., Washington, 1993-94; mgr. corp. comm., sr. writer Eli Lilly and Co., Indpls., 1994-95; pub. policy analyst, cons., writer Fairfax, Va., 1995—; adj. fellow Alexis de Tocqueville Instn., Arlington, Va., 1994—; fgn. policy group advisor Dole for Pres., Inc., Washington, 1996—; authored speeches and ofcl. statements for former pres. George Bush, including July 4th nat. TV address to the nation, departure statement with Japanese Prime Minister, speeches to Office of Nat. Drug Control Policy, Nat. Inst. for Responsible Fatherhood and Family Devel., Am. Legion/Boys Nation, others; sr. advisor to devel. projects Internat. Rep. Inst., Kuwait, Turkey, other nations, 1993-94; directed and contributed to nat. and internat. mktg. and comms. strategies for cancer, cardiovascular, ctrl. nervous system, endocrine, and infectious disease pharm. products Eli Lilly and Co., 1994-95; guest polit. and pub. policy analyst for numerous TV and radio programs including MacNeil/Lehrer News Hour, C-SPAN, CNBC, PBS Nightly Bus. Report, Fox Morning News, Voice of Am., BBC, others; guest lectr. UN, Vassar Coll., U. N.C., Chapel Hill, others; U.S. adv. coun. Mozambique Inst., London; participant various seminars. Author: U.S. and Africa Statistical Handbook, 1990, 2d edit., 1991; contbg. author: Freedom in the World: The Annual Survey of Political Rights and Civil Liberties, 1993; contbg. editor USSR Monitor newsletter, The Heritage Found., 1989-91; peer reviewer The Harvard Internat. Jour. of Press/Politics Harvard U.; alumni bd. advisors Campus mag. Intercollegiate Studies Inst., Wilmington, Del.; contbr. numerous articles to profl. jours, periodicals and newspapers, including Wall St. Jour., Christian Sci. Monitor, Chgo. Tribune, others; author numerous acad. and pub. policy rsch. studies; reported from Africa, Asia, L.Am., Middle East, Persian Gulf and former Soviet Union for numerous publs. Key club mem. United Way; active Luth. Ch. of the Holy Spirit, Emmaus, Pa.; mem. The Coca-Cola Civic Action Network. Recipient Shell Oil Co.'s Century III Leadership award, 1981, Svc. award Kiwanis, 1982, cert. appreciation Spl. Olympics, 1983, award of appreciation Lao Vets Am., 1995, numerous citations in Congl. Record, U.S. Congress. Mem. Nat. Journalism Ctr. Alumni Coun., Iron Arrow Honor Soc. U. Miami, Assn. on Third World Affairs, Reagan Alumni Assn., Bush/Quayle Alumni Assn., Puente de Jovenes Profls. Cubanos, Pub. Rels. Soc. Am., Washington Ind. Writers, Lambda Chi Alpha (Hall of Fame 1996). Republican. Lutheran. Home: 4150 Zinnia Ln Fairfax VA 22030

JOHNSEN, ERIK FRITHJOF, transportation executive; b. New Orleans, Aug. 17, 1925; s. Niels Frithjof and Julia Anita (Winchester) J.; m. Dorothy Edna Lee, May 3, 1953 (dec. Jan. 1977); children: Karen Klara Johnsen Baldwin, Erik Lee, Anne Elisabet, R. Christian; m. Dolly Ann Souchon, Mar. 22, 1978. BS, U.S. Mcht. Marine Acad., 1945; BBA, Tulane U., 1948. V.p. Cen. Gulf Steamship Corp. (now Cen. Gulf Lines Inc.), New Orleans, 1952-66; pres. Cen. Gulf Lines Inc., New Orleans, 1966—, also bd. dirs.; pres. Internat. Shipholding Corp., New Orleans, 1979—, also bd. dirs.; bd. dirs. World Trade Ctr., 1st Commerce Corp., New Orleans; vice chmn., bd. dirs. Waterman Steamship Corp., New Orleans, 1989—; sr. U.S. dir. Baltic and Internat. Maritime Conf., Copenhagen, 1986—. Hon. consul Govt. of Norway, 1985—; bd. dirs. Bus. Coun. New Orleans, 1987—, Tulane U. Bd. Adminstrs., 1974—. With Mcht. Marine, 1942-46; lt. USN, 1950-52. Mem. World Trade Club of New Orleans (hon. life), Pickwick Club, New Orleans Country Club. Office: Ctrl Gulf Lines 650 Poydras St Ste 1700 New Orleans LA 70130-6101 also: Waterman Marine Corp 1 Whitehall St New York NY 10004-2109

JOHNSON, ALBERT WILLIAM, mortgage banker, real estate broker; b. Raleigh, N.C., June 25, 1919; s. Will Thomas and Evie (Barnes) J.; m. Margaret Hayes, Oct. 25, 1945; children: Albert William II, Brian Allen, Douglass Stevens. BS in Commerce, U. N.C., 1940; postgrad., Mich. State U., 1964. Cert. mortgage banker, real estate financier, real estate appraiser. Commd. cadet USAF, 1940-55, advanced through grades to col., ret., 1955; asst. judge advocate gen. Gen. Staff of Hdqrs. 14th Command USAF, Orlando, Fla.; war plans officer Gen. Staff Hdqrs. Tactical Air Command USAF, Langley Field, Va.; war plans officer Gen. Staff NATO Hdqrs., Paris; NATO war plans officer Sec. of Air Force Office Pentagon, Washington; co-founder, real estate broker, mortgage banker Dobson & Johnson, Nashville, 1955—, chmn., CEO; chmn., CEO Albert William Johnson Ins. Co., Inc., Met. Land Corp., Fed. Title and Securities Corp., Dobson & Johnson Capital Corp., Outdoor Resorts of Am.;dir. Fidelity Investment & Bond Corp.; past dir. N.Y. Stock Exch. listed real Estate Investment Trust. Life mem. bd. trustees Scarritt Coll. for Christian Workers, Nashville, chmn. exec., investment and bus. affairs coms.; life mem. bd. trustees Winchendon (Mass.) Sch. Boys; past dir. Mid. Tenn. Heart Assn.; patron Cheekwood Hort. Soc.; past dir. Internat. Com. on Fgn. Rels.; assoc. Grad. Sch. Bus., Vanderbilt U. Decorated Disting. Svc. Medal France, DFC with one oak leaf cluster, Air medal with six oak leaf clusters, Purple Heart, numerous others; recipient The Freedome Medal U.S. Civilian Decoration; Disting. fellow of mortgage banking, Mich. State U., 1964. Mem. Nat. Soc. Real Estate Fin. (past pres., chmn. bd. govs.), Mortgage Banking Assn. Am., Nat. Assn. Cert. Mortgage Bankers (past pres., chmn. bd.), Nashville Mortgage Bankers Assn. (bd. dirs., past pres.), Cert. Real Estate Appraisers Assn. (dir.), Mortgage Bankers Assn. Am. (vice chair ednl. com.), Tenn. Mortgage Bankers Assn. (past pres.), Nashville Bd. Realtors (past dir.), Nat. Assn. Real Estate Bds., Tenn. Bd. Realtors, Nashville Bd. Realtors, Nashville Home Builders Assn., Nashville Apt. Owners and Developers Assn., Nat. Soc. Real Estate Fin. (chmn. bd. govs. 1983-91, bd. govs. 1983-92), C. of C. of U.S., Nashville C. of C., Alumni Assn. U. N.C. (life), Nashville Rotary Club, Belle Meade Country Club, Cumberland Club, Univ. Club (life), N.Y. Athletic Club (life), The World trade Ctr. Windows of the World, Doubles Club, Everglades Club, Bath and Tennis Club, Palm Beach Yacht Club, Club Colette, Pres.'s Club. Phi Kappa Sigma. Presbyterian. Home: The Grove Apt 402 420 Elmington Ave Nashville TN 37205 Office: 2209 Crestmoor Rd Ste 220 Nashville TN 37215

JOHNSON, ALEX CLAUDIUS, English language educator; b. Freetown, Sierra Leone, Aug. 14, 1943; came to U.S., 1991; s. Eunice Angela (Thorpe) J.; m. Daphne Marvel Taylor; children: Marvin, Joyemi. BA in English Lang. and Lit. with honors, U. Durham, Eng., 1968; MA in English and Am. Lit., U. Kent, Canterbury, Eng., 1971; MPhil in Linguistics, U. Leeds, Eng., 1974; PhD in English, U. Ibadan, Nigeria, 1982. Tchr. various h.s., Freetown, Sierra Leone, 1968-69, 71-72; sr. lectr., lectr. English dept. Fourah Bay Coll., Sierra Leone, 1974-88, sr. lectr., acting head classics/philosophy dept., 1987-88, prof., head English dept., 1988-91; prof. English lang. and Creole studies U. Bayreuth, Germany, 1982-84; vis. prof. S.C. State U., Orangeburg, 1991-92, prof., 1992; acting vice prin. Fourah Bay Coll., 1989, 90, acting prin., summer 1990, dean faculty of arts, 1989-91; cons. UNESCO, 1985-89; external assessor U. Cape Coast, Ghana, 1988. Contbr. articles to internat. profl. jours., papers to internat. confs. and symposia. Chief examiner West Africa Examinations Coun., Accra, Ghana, 1978-91, Inst. Edn., U. Sierra Leone, 1980-91; chair Nat. Primary Curriculum Revision Com., 1981. Mem. AAUP, Coll. Lang. Assn., African Lit. Assn., West African Linguistic Soc. (sec., organizer 13th West African Langs. Congress, Freetown, 1978), West African MLA (exec. com. 1981-82). Episcopalian.

JOHNSON, ALFRED CARL, JR., former navy officer; b. Joliet, Ill., Oct. 2, 1930; s. Alfred Carl and Frances (Wright) J.; m. Beverly Jean Raisler, Dec. 27, 1953; children: Sheri Lynn, David Craig, Laura Lee. Student, U. Ill., 1948-51, Naval Post Grad. Sch., 1958-59, Naval War Coll., 1964-65; BS in Systems Analysis, George Washington U., 1968. Enlisted USN, 1952, advanced through grades to capt., 1974; served as head systems analysis Nat. Mil. Command System, Joint Chiefs of Staff, Washington, 1965-68; air ops. officer USS J.F. Kennedy CVA-67, Norfolk, Va., 1968-70; squadron comdr. Composite Squadron 5, Okinawa, Japan, 1970-71; ops. officer USS Midway CVA 41, San Francisco, 1971-73; dir. programming and budget Naval Aviation, Chief of Naval Ops., Washington, 1973-77; air wing comdr. Airwing 6, Pensacola, Fla., 1977-79; chief staff Naval Edn. Tng., Pensacola, 1979-84; ret., 1984—. Contbr. articles to jours. Scout leader Boy Scouts Am., 1961—. Decorated Legion of Merit with two gold stars, Bronze Star. Mem. Assn. Naval Aviation, Rotary (trustee, Paul Harris fellow), Psi Upsilon, Am. Security Coun. Home: 4984 Prieto Dr Pensacola FL 32506-5381

JOHNSON, ALONZO BISMARK, legal assistant, court administrator; b. Natchez, Miss., Aug. 1, 1958; s. Albert Zena and Bettie Dee (Brown) J. Student, Xavier U., 1976-78; MusB Edn., Alcorn State U., 1980. Piano instr. Houston's Sch. Music, New Orleans, 1977-78; dep. dist. ct. clk. Dallas County Dist. Clks. Office, 1981-84; probation officer I Dallas County Adult Probation Dept., 1984-89; regional civil rights compliance specialist Tex. Dept. Human Svcs., Arlington, 1989-90; min. of music Good Shepherd Bapt. Ch. Irving, Tex., 1989-94; court adminstr. IV-D Family Court of Dallas, 1992—; minister of music West Mt. Horeb Bapt. Ch., Dallas, 1994—. Guest pianist Sta. WYES-TV, New Orleans, 1977, Jackson (Miss.) Symphony Orch., 1979, 80; founder Youth Inspirational Interdenominational Choir, Fayette, Miss., 1978. Recipient Outstanding Music award Dallas Metroplex Temple of Elks #1305, 1984, 85; B-Sharp Music scholar Xavier U., 1977, Fine Arts scholar Alcorn State U. Mem. NAACP, Dallas Assn. Ct. Adminstrn., Heroines of Jericho, Mason, Phi Mu Alpha Sinfonia (charter mem. 1977, sec. 1977-78). Baptist. Home: 2007 Maryland Ave Dallas TX 75216-1929

JOHNSON, ANNE TRIPPE, secondary school educator; b. Milledgeville, Ga.; d. Walter Robert and Mary Sanders (Rudisill) Trippe; children: James

Lambert Johnson Jr., Anna Maria Johnson. BS in Edn., Ga. State U., 1967, MEd, 1971, EdS, 1991. Cert. spl. edn. tchr., related vocat. instr., Ga. Spl. edn. tchr. DeKalb County Schs., Ga., 1969-70, 71-72; spl. edn. tchr. Atlanta Pub. Schs., 1972-77; interrelated tchr. Murphy High Sch., Atlanta, 1981-89; related vocat. instr. Mays High Sch., Atlanta, 1989—; mem. John F. Kennedy Ctr. Adv. Coun., Atlanta, 1981— (chairperson 1983); mem. Bobby Dodd Ctr. Adv. Coun., Atlanta, 1982-85. V.p. Ponderosa Civic Assn., Atlanta, 1988, Huntington Homeowners Assn., 1992-95. Mamie Jo Jones scholar, 1990-91. Mem. Coun. for Exceptional Children, Ga. Vocat. Assn., Nat. Assn. Vocat. Edn. for Spl. Needs Persons, Atlanta Assn. Educators. Home: Unit S-3 3825 Lavista Rd Tucker GA 30084-5109 Office: Benjamin E Mays High Sch 3450 Benjamin E Mays Dr SW Atlanta GA 30331-1906

JOHNSON, ANTHONY O'LEARY (ANDY JOHNSON), meteorologist, consultant; b. Tampa, Fla., Apr. 19, 1957; s. Paul Bryan and Katie Hobbs (Nunez) J. BS in Meteorology, Fla. State U., 1979. Cert. cons. meteorologist. Courthouse runner Gregory, Cours, et. al., Tampa, 1977; water resources planner S.W. Fla. Water Mgmt. Dist., Brooksville, 1978; staff meteorologist Sta. WTVT-TV, Tampa, 1979-82, systems mgr., 1982-89, weather office mgr., 1989—; meterol. cons. Gulf Coast Weather Svc.-Weather Vision, Tampa, 1979—; software devel. mgr. TTI Techs. Inc., Tampa, 1989-92; site coord. Space Sci. and Engring. Ctr. U. Wis., Madison, 1989—. Active capital improvements com. Plantation Homeowners Assn., Tampa, 1991; judge Hillsborough Regional Sci. Fair, Tampa, 1990, 91, 92, 96; fundraiser Dunedin Youth Guild, 1992, Northside Mental Health Hosp. Aux., 1993, 94, Children's Home, Pinellas Aux., 1993, 94, 95; vol. Sch. Enrichment Vols. in Edn. (SERVE), 1992. Mem. AAAS, Am. Meteorol Soc. (Seal of Approval for TV weathercasting 1982—, v.p. West Fla. chpt. 1984-85, pres. 1989-92, 94—), Internat. Platform Assn., Phi Beta Kappa, Pi Mu Epsilon, Chi Epsilon Pi. Republican. Office: Sta WTVT-TV Weather Svc 3213 W Kennedy Blvd Tampa FL 33609-3006

JOHNSON, ARNOLD RAY, public relations executive; b. Baton Rouge, Sept. 15, 1954; came to U.S., 1954; s. Hillery and Sedonia (Celestine) J. BA, Xavier U., 1977. Chmn., CEO U.S.A. Pub. Rels., Baton Rouge, 1989—, Inter-Continental Transp., New Orleans, 1989—. Knights Peter Clare Cath. Orgn. Mem. Beta Rho Omega. Republican. Roman Catholic. Home: 2480 78th Ave Baton Rouge LA 70807 Office: Inter-Continental Transport Inc 1 Canal Pl Ste 2500 New Orleans LA 70114

JOHNSON, AUDREY JACKSON, minister; b. New Orleans, Oct. 7, 1936; d. Solomon Neal Jackson Sr. and Dorothy (Hudson) Jones; m. Felix Joseph Johnson Jr., Sept. 7, 1957; children: Felix Joseph III, Troy Tyrone, David Joel. BA in Psychology, So. U., 1959; BSN, Dillard U., 1963; MRE, New Orleans Bapt. Sem., 1976. Ordained to ministry Bapt. Ch., 1990; cert. vocat. edn., clin. pastoral edn., curriculum devel., La. Community ch. educator Sunday sch. New Orleans Bapt. Sem., 1974-76; dir. youth dept. Gloryland Mt. Gillion Bapt. Ch., New Orleans, 1975-78; dir. Christian edn. Beacon Lights Bapt. Ch., New Orleans, 1982-84; asst. to pastor Christian Unity Bapt. Ch., New Orleans, 1989—; nurse educator pediat. AIDS program Childrens Hosp., New Orleans, 1989-95; supr. cmty. bd. programs cmty. organizing Indsl. Area Found. Tng.; min. edn. Christian Unity, New Orleans, 1989—, women ministry, 1989; past nursing instr.; prodr. vedeo on HIV infection and women; presenter in field. Contbr. articles to profl. jours. Mem. NAACP, Nat. Coun. Negro Women, Assoc. of Clin. Pastoral Edn., Nurses Assn., Women for Women with AIDS, Nat. Urban Leage. Office: Christian Unity Bapt Ch 1700 Conti St New Orleans LA 70112-3606

JOHNSON, BARBARA ANNE UMBERGER, business owner, editor, publisher; b. Staunton, Va., Feb. 16, 1939; d. Gordon William and Billie Lois (Patton) Umberger; m. Gilbert Dixon Johnson, Jan. 23, 1960; children: Gilbert Scott, William Bryant. AAS, Indian Valley Colls., 1976; BA in Anthropology, George Washington U., 1978; MS in Counseling and Guidance, Nova U., 1981. Tech. editor Electronic Data Systems Corp., Alexandria, Va., 1978—, pub. affairs mgr.; product implementation mgr., account mgr. Policy Mgmt. Systems Corp., Columbia, S.C., 1984; postgrad. in gerontology Midlands Tech. Coll., Columbia, 1995—; columnist Mil. Families, 1979-80. Editor, pub. South Carolina Association of Naturalists: The First Ten Years, 1993; author news column Military Families, 1979-80. contbr. book revs. to profl. jours.; founder, pub. monthly newsletters Mechanics Lien Bull., Pub. Record Report, Capital Corner. Campaigner Rep. Party, Columbia; mem. environ. adv. bd. Cen. Midlands Regional Planning Coun.; mem. Solid Waste Mgmt. Task Force; mem. Leadership Columbia 1993-94; mem. Main Street Devel. Assocs., 1993-95; vol. Palmetto Sr. Care, 1995—. Cpl. USMC, 1957-60. Mem. NAFE, LWV, Soc. for Tech. Comms., Nat. Contract Mgrs. Assn., Media Women S.C., S.C. C. of C., Columbia C. of C. (chair enterprisers network, riverfront planning com., small bus. devel. bd.), Ret. Officers Wives Club (v.p., 1987-90), Sertoma (v.p. Richland club 1992, pres. Richland club 1993, chmn. bd. dirs. 1994). Methodist.

JOHNSON, BARBARA H., retired opera company manager; b. Eldon, Mo., Sept. 2, 1931; d. Theodore R. and Mathilda Kathryn (Haldiman) Herfurth; m. John Harold White Jr., June 8, 1952 (div. Sept. 1982); 1 child, John Harold III; m. Samuel Britton Johnson, Dec. 20, 1982. BS in Edn., Belhaven Coll., 1951; JD, Miss. Coll., 1972. Bar: Miss. Sec. Sky & Telescope Mag., Boston, 1952-54; elem. sch. tchr. Pemberton County Schs., Ft. Dix, N.J., 1954-56; pvt. practice law Jackson, Miss., 1974-78; exec. dir. Friends of the Arts in Miss., Jackson, 1984-87; gen. mgr. Miss. Opera, Jackson, 1969-78, 89-91, 92-94; ret., 1994. Chmn. Miss. Arts Festival, Jackson, 1974; pres. Miss. Opera, 1983, mem. exec. com., 1954-97; bd. dirs. O.P.E.R.A. Am., 1975-77; pres. Family Svc., Jackson, 1976; bd. dirs. Miss. Symphony, Jackson, 1983; mem. exec. com. Nat. Kidney Found. of Miss., 1983-87. Recipient Vol. Activies award Goodwill Inc., 1994. Mem. PEO, Miss. Women Lawyers Assn., Miss. State Bar Assn., Univ. Club, One O'Clock Luncheon Club. Home: 22 Eastbrooke Jackson MS 39216

JOHNSON, BARRY LEE, public health research administrator; b. Sanders, Ky., Oct. 24, 1938; s. Otto Lee and Sarah Josephine (Deatherage) J.; m. Billie Reed, Aug. 19, 1960; children—Lee, Clay, Scott, Reed, Sarah. B.S., U. Ky., 1960; M.S., Iowa State U., 1962, Ph.D., 1967. Elec. engr. USPHS, Cin., 1960-70; bioengr. EPA, Cin., 1970-71; bioengr. Nat. Inst. for Occupational Safety and Health, HHS, Cin., 1971-77, rsch. adminstr., 1978-86; asst. adminstr. Agy. for Toxic Substances and Disease Registry, 1986—; also asst. surgeon gen., 1990—. Editor: Behavioral Toxicology, 1974, Neurotoxicology, 1986; editor Neurotoxicology, 1979, Archives Environ. Health jour., 1980, Toxicology and Industrial Health, 1985, Prevention of Neurotoxic Illness, 1987, Advances in Neurobehavioral Toxicology, 1990, Jour. of Clean Tech. and Environ. Scis., 1991. Pres. S.E. Cin. Soccer Assn., 1978-80. Recipient Commendation medal USPHS, 1980, 84, Superior Performance medal USPHS, 1986, Meritorious Svc. award USPHS, 1988, Disting. Svc. medal Asst. Surgeon Gen., 1990; USPHS fellow 1962-65. Mem. Am. Pub. Health Assn., Am. Conf. Govt. Hygienists, Am. Assn. Clin. Toxicology, Internat. Conf. Occupational Health, Am. Coll. Toxicology, Soc. of Occupational and Environ. Health, Nat. Environ. Health Assn., Internat. Assn. for Exposure Analysis.

JOHNSON, BETH EXUM, lawyer; b. Beaumont, Tex., July 4, 1952; d. James Powers Jr. and Betty Jean (Clement) Exum; m. Walter William Johnson, Apr. 25, 1981; 1 child, Stratton William. BA in Psychology, Tulane U., 1974; JD, Loyola U., New Orleans, 1985; LLM in Energy and Environ., Tulane U., 1989. Bar: La. 1985, Tex. 1993, U.S. Dist. Ct. (ea. dist.) La. 1985, U.S. Dist. Ct. (we. and mid. dists.) 1989. Paralegal McCloskey, Dennery, Page & Hennesy, New Orleans, 1975-80; oil and gas abstractor of title Frawley, Wogan, Miller & Co., New Orleans, 1980-82; assoc. trust counsel, asst. v.p. and trust officer Hibernia Nat. Bank, New Orleans, 1985-95; legal cons. New Orleans, 1995-96; assoc. Gelpi and Assocs., PLC, New Orleans, 1996—; faculty La. succession practice Tulane U., New Orleans, 1990-94, environ. law practice, 1991-94; mem. fundraising com. and atty. honor roll New Orleans Pro Bono Project. Mem. New Orleans Estate Planning Coun. Mem. ABA, La. Bar Assn., New Orleans Bar Assn., Friends City Park, Premier Athletic club, Rivercenter Tennis Club, Cavalier King Charles Spaniel Club, Phi Alpha Delta, Kappa Alpha Theta. Home: 959 Harrison Ave New Orleans LA 70124-3837 Office: 203 Carondelet St Ste 907 New Orleans LA 70130

JOHNSON, BETTY ZSCHIEGNER, treasurer-secretary; b. Portage, Wis., June 20, 1933; d. Roy Lamar and Emma Minnie (Stoeckman) Zschiegner; m. Sidney Darrell; 1 child, Jeffrey Darrell Johnson. Student, Cen. Bible Coll., 1951-54. Organist First Assembly of God Ch., Memphis, 1954—, sec., bookkeeper, 1954-64; sec., treas. Delta Services, Inc., Memphis, 1968—; bookkeeper First Assembly of God Ch., Memphis, 1974-77; sec., treas. Quality Built Homes, Inc., Memphis, 1976—. Named Central Bible Coll. scholar, 1954. Mem. Home Builders Assn. Republican. Office: Delta Services Inc PO Box 38926 Memphis TN 38183-0926

JOHNSON, BEVERLY PHILLIPS, bank officer; b. Richmond, Va., May 14, 1963; d. Harold Thomas and Betty Lucille (Trammell) Phillips; m. Robert Mark Johnson, Nov. 29, 1985; children: Margaret Elizabeth, Laura Ellen. BS, Lee Coll., Cleveland, Tenn., 1985. Comptroller Frank White Co., Cleveland, Tenn., 1983-86; credit analyst 1st Am. Nat. Bank, Chattanooga, 1986-88; mortgage banker 1st Am. Nat. Bank, Cleveland, Tenn., 1988-89; comml. real estate banker 1st Am. Nat. Bank, Chattanooga, 1989-92; comml. lender, v.p. SunTrust Bank, Cleveland, Tenn., 1992—. Divsn. campaign chairperson United Way, Bradley County, Cleveland, 1987-90, 93, 96; treas. Cleveland Cmty. Concert Assn., 1989—, pres., 1995—; mem. Leadership Cleveland, 1991-92; bd. dirs. Am. Heart Assn., blockwalkers capt., 1993; bd. dirs. Cleveland Family YMCA, 1993—, treas., 1995—; bd. dirs. 1st United Meth. Child Devel. Ctr., 1992; trustee First United Meth. Ch. Mem. Main St. Cleveland (treas. 1995—), Rotary (pres. Cleveland 1995—), Cleveland Country Club (assoc.), Civitan (bd. dirs. Cleveland chpt. 1984-91, 93—, Chattanooga chpt. 1991-92), United Way Pillars Club, Lee Coll. Pres. Cir., Cleveland/Bradley C. of C. (econ. devel. coun. 1992—). Republican. United Methodist. Home: 1220 Bramblewood Trl NW Cleveland TN 37311-4107 Office: Suntrust Bank PO Box 1149 Cleveland TN 37364-1149

JOHNSON, BOREHAM BOYD, printing company executive, consultant, accountant; b. Clinton, N.C., Feb. 11, 1952; s. Alderman Boreham and Carolyn (Mills) J.; m. Barbara Hagan, Apr. 8. 1978; children: Cameron, David, Laura. BA in Econs., Hampden-Sydney (Va.) Coll., 1974; MBA, Va. Commonweatlh U., 1977. CPA, Va. Investment officer Sovran Bank (formerly F&M), Richmond, Va., 1974-77; asst. dir. Va. Energy Div., Richmond, 1977-79; v.p. Crestar Bank, Richmond and Roanoke, Va., 1979-87; pres. Jamont Press, Roanoke, 1987—, vice chmn. bd., 1994—; bd. dirs. Printing Industries of Va., Richmond; Va. del. to White House Conf. on Small Bus., Va. chmn. tech. com. Pres. Coun. Cmty. Svcs., Roanoke, 1988-89; maj. corp. chmn., pacesetter chmn. United Way of Roanoke Valley, 1986; bd. dirs. spl. events com. City of Roanoke, 1986-89; bd. dirs. Sci. Mus. Western Va., 1993—; vestry St. John's Episcopal Ch. Named Disting. Vol., United Way of Roanoke, 1986; recipient Young Men of Am. award Jr. C. of C., 1986. Mem. AICPAs, Commonwealth Club, Shenandoah Club, Roanoke Country Club, C. of C. (bd. dirs. small bus. coun. 1987-90), Masons, Scottish Rite. Home: 2924 Rosalind Ave SW Roanoke VA 24014-3220 Office: Jamont Press Inc 339 Luck Ave SW Roanoke VA 24016-5013

JOHNSON, BRUCE KING, internist; b. Harriman, Tenn., Oct. 24, 1918; s. Samuel King and Laura Monro (Jones) J.; m. Leila N. Wright Johnson, Apr. 3, 1942 (dec. Nov. 1957); m. Iris Dudley Thomas, May 14, 1959 (dec. Nov. 1991); m. Patricia Jean Miller, Aug. 13, 1994. BS, Birmingham So. Coll., 1940; MD, U. Tenn. Health Scis., Memphis, 1944. Diplomate Am. Bd. Internal Medicine; recert. Gen. practice medicine Flat Creek, Ala., 1945-49; resident N.C. Bapt. Hosp., Winston-Salem, N.C., 1949-51; sr. resident U. Ala. Hosp., Birmingham, 1951-52; pvt. practice internal medicine Birmingham, 1952-59; med. dir. Birmingham Med. Group, 1959-68; practice medicine Simon Williamson Clinib, 1968-87; physician advisor staff clin. quality mgmt. Bapt. Med. Ctr.-Princeton Unit, Birmingham, 1987—. Mem. adminstrv. bd. First Meth. Ch., Birmingham, 1965—. Recipient Physicians Recognition award AMA, 1972, 79, 84, 87, 91, 94. Fellow ACP (life); mem. Med. Assn. Ala. (50 yr. award 1995), Alpha Omega Alpha. Office: Simon Williamson Clinic PA 833 Princeton Ave SW Birmingham AL 35211-1311

JOHNSON, CARL FREDERICK, marriage and family therapist; b. July 18, 1947. BA in Psychology, Northwestern U., 1969; MA in Clin. Psychology, Ga. State U., 1975. Lic. marriage and family therapist, Ga. Grad. tchg. asst. Ga. State U., Atlanta, 1972-73; family therapist Bridge Family Ctr., Atlanta, 1973-80; pvt. practice The Family Workshop, Atlanta, 1979—; adj. instr. Dekalb C.C., Clarkston, Ga., 1981-82; appointee Ga. Composite Bd. Profl. Counselors, Social Workers and Marriage and Family Therapists, 1985-93. Contbr. articles to profl. jours. Fellow Am. Assn. for Marriage and Family Therapy (Divnsl. Contbn. award 1993); mem. Ga. Assn. for Marriage and Family Therapy (Outstanding Contbn. award 1983, 85, 93, Lifetime Achievement/Disting. Svc. award 1996, chair legis. affairs com. 1980-85, 93-95), Assn. Marital and Family Therapy Regulatory Bds. (founder, pres. 1987-91, coord. devel. nat. licensing exam in marital and family therapy 1989-92). Home: 751 N Parkwood Rd Decatur GA 30030-5023 Office: Family Workshop 752 Houston Mill Rd NE Atlanta GA 30329-4210

JOHNSON, CAROLYN E., medical/surgical nurse; b. Laurel County, Ky., July 4, 1956; d. Lowell Nelson and Dorlea (Taylor) Buchanan; m. Gary Blaine Johnson, Dec. 27, 1985; 1 child, Leah Beth. Cert., Pineville Sch. Practical Nursing, 1977; ADN, Lincoln Meml. U., Harrogate, Tenn., 1982. Lic. practical nurse, Ky. Staff nurse Cumberland Valley Dist. Health Dept., Barbourville, Ky., Knox County Gen. Hosp., Barbourville; staff nurse emergency room Bapt. Regional Med. Ctr., Corbin, Ky., supr. gastro-clin. lab.; community health nurse Whitley County Health Dept., Williamsburg, Ky. Home: 207 Northland Dr Corbin KY 40701-8714

JOHNSON, CAROLYN W. (CARRIE JOHNSON), historian, author; b. Milw., Apr. 29, 1941; d. James Cabell and Carol Sutherland (Wagner) J. BA magna cum laude, Smith Coll., 1964. Legis. asst. hon. Charles Mc C. Mathias Jr. U.S. Ho. Reps., Washington, 1965-68, U.S. Senate, Washington, 1969-71; minority staff dir. U.S. Senate Com. on the D.C., Washington, 1971-72; mem. editorial bd. The Washington (D.C.) Post, 1972-79; pvt. practice historian, writer Arlington, Va., 1980—. Contbr. articles to profl. jours. Chmn. Chesapeake and Ohio Canal Nat. Hist. Pk. Commn., Sharpsburg, Md., 1982-87; active Arlington (Va.) County Planning Commn., 1986—, chmn., 1991. Recipient Study fellowship Washington Post-Duke U., 1977, Ind. Study fellowship NEH, 1982-83. Mem. Orgn. Am. Historians, Arlingtonians for a Better County (bd. dirs. 1980—).

JOHNSON, CHARITY HONORÉ, publishing executive; b. Hollywood, Fla., June 1, 1954; d. Stanley Herbert Jr. and Bernice Laura (Notvest) J.; m. Joseph John Orsini, Mar. 4, 1989; 1 child, Joey-Lyn Orsini. BA, Goucher Coll., 1976; MA, Johns Hopkins U., 1982. Researcher, asst. Ralph Nader, Washington, 1972; mktg. trainee Md. Nat. Bank, Balt., 1975-76; supr., contract negotiator City of Balt., 1976-79, coord. sr. svcs., 1979-83; devel. mgr. Coconut Grove Playhouse, Miami, 1985-86; mng. editor Pickering Press, Miami, 1986-90; publ. Valiant Press, Miami, 1990—. Editor: (book) Florida Bank Monitor, 1973-77, (book) Maryland Bank Monitor, 1976-77, Trade Newsletter Forum, 1974; contbr. article to Aging and Work jour. Mem. vestry St. Stephens Ch., Coconut Grove, Fl., 1991-94, treas., 1994; asst. leader Girl Scouts Tropical Fla., Miami, 1989-96. Mem. Coconut Grove C. of C. (sec., bd. trustees 1986-88), Coconut Grove Woman's Club. Democrat. Episcopalian. Office: Valiant Press PO Box 330568 Miami FL 33133

JOHNSON, CHARLENE DENISE LOGAN, medical/surgical and pediatric nurse; b. Portsmouth, Ohio, Jan. 31, 1955; d. Paul Franklin and Rhoedna (Dawson) Logan; m. Edwin Christopher Johnson Sr., July 29, 1994. ADN, Morehead (Ky.) State U., 1986. RN, Ky. Staff nurse Our Lady of Bellefonte Hosp., Ashland, Ky., 1986-87; charge nurse St. Claire Med. Ctr., Morehead, 1988—. Home: RR 1 Box 103 Vanceburg KY 41179 Office: St Claire Med Ctr 222 Medical Cir Morehead KY 40351-1179

JOHNSON, CHARLES ANDREW, political scientist, educator; b. Elkins, Aug. 25, 1948; s. Forest Jay and Marie Margret (Vanscoy) J.; m. Barbara Jean Walkiewicz, Nov. 22, 1970; children: Carly J., J. Travis. BS, Towson State Coll., 1970; MA, U. Md., 1972; PhD, U. Ky., 1977. Asst. to pres. Towson State Coll., Balt., 1970; asst. prof. Tex. Tech. U., Lubbock, 1976-78; asst. prof., assoc. prof. Tex. A&M U., College Station, 1978-86, prof., 1986—, assoc. dean liberal arts, 1987-92, dept. head polit. sci., 1992—. Author: Judicial Politics, 1984; editor: American Courts, 1991; contbr. articles to profl. jours. Participant German Acad. Exch. Svc., 1995; expert witness U.S. Dist. Ct. (no. dist.) Tex., Lubbock, 1978, (Paris divsn.) Dallas, 1982. Grantee NSF, 1980-83, 87-89. Mem. Am. Polit. Sci. Assn. (sect. chair 1983-84, newsletter editor 1985-87), So. Polit. Sci. Assn. (exec. com. 1984-87). Office: Tex A&M Univ Dept Polit Sci 102 Bolton Hall College Station TX 77843

JOHNSON, CHARLES OWEN, retired lawyer; b. Monroe, La., Aug. 18, 1926; s. Clifford U. and Laura (Owen) J. BA, Tulane U., 1946, JD, 1969; LLB, Harvard U., 1948; LLM, Columbia U., 1955. Bar: La. 1949. Sole practice, Monroe, 1949-50; mem. law editorial staff West Pub. Co., St. Paul, 1953; atty. Office of Chief Counsel, IRS, Washington, 1955-79, chief Ct. Appeals br. Tax Ct. Div., 1968-79. Author: The Genealogy of Several Allied Families, 1961. Served with AUS, 1950-52. Mem. Fed. Bar Assn., La. Bar Assn., Nat. Lawyers Club, Nat. Gavel Soc. (past treas., past pres.), Soc. Colonial Wars (past dep. gov. D.C. soc., lt. gov., gov.), SAR, S.R. (past pres. D.C. Soc.), Soc. War of 1812 (past pres. D.C. soc.), S.C.V., Soc. Colonial New Eng. (past gov. gen. nat. soc.), Nat. Soc. Descendants Early Quakers (past nat. presiding clk.), Sons Union Vets., St. Andrew's Soc. Washington, Royal Soc. St. George, Sons and Daus.. of Pilgrims (past treas., 2nd deputy gov. gen.), Huguenot Soc. S.C., Huguenot Soc. La. (past pres.), Soc. Descs. Jersey Settlers, La. Colonials, Sons and Daus. of Province and Republic of West Fla., 1763-1810 (past gov.), Jamestowne Soc., Soc. Descs. Old Plymouth Colony, Order Ams. of Armorial Ancestry (past pres.), Soc. Descs. Colonial Clergy (past chancellor gen.), Hereditary Order Descs. Colonial Govs. (past gov. gen.), First Families of Ga. (past chancellor gen.), Order Founders and Patriots of Am. (past gov. D.C. and La. Soc.), Order First Families Miss. 1699-1817 (gov. gen. 1967-69), Mil. Order Stars and Bars (past judge adv. gen.), Soc. Cin., Hereditary Order First Families of Mass. (registrar gen.), Va. Geneal. Soc., Miss. Hist. Soc., Va. Hist. Soc., Order First Families of R.I. and Providence Plantations, 1636-1647 (past gov. gen.), Order of Descendants of Colonial Physicians and Chirurgiens (pres. gen.), Sons and Daughters of Colonial and Antebellum Bench and Bar, 1565-1861 (pres. gen.), Army and Navy Club of Washington, City Tavern Club of Georgetown, Harvard Club, Masons, KT, Shriners, Order Ea. Star, Phi Beta Kappa. Home: 2111 Jefferson Davis Hwy # 809 S Arlington VA 22202-3137

JOHNSON, CHARLES SIDNEY, JR., chemistry educator; b. Albany, Ga., Mar. 7, 1936; s. Charles Sidney and Mary Virginia (Reid) J.; m. Ellen Cook McFarland, Sept. 3, 1958; children—David Mason, Daniel Cook. B.S. in Chemistry, Ga. Inst. Tech., 1958; Ph.D. in Phys. Chemistry, Mass. Inst. Tech., 1961. Nat. Acad. Sci.-NRC postdoctoral fellow, instr. U. Ill., 1961-62; asst. prof. Yale, 1962-66, asso. prof., 1967; prof. chemistry U.N.C., 1967—, M. A. Smith prof., 1988—. Author: Problems and Solutions in Quantum Chemistry and Physics, 1974, rev. edit., 1986, Laser Light Scattering, 1994; editl. bd. Jour. Magnetic Resonance, 1971—; contbr. articles to profl. jours. NSF fellow, 1958-61; Yale Faculty fellow, 1966-67; Alfred P. Sloan fellow, 1966; J.S. Guggenheim Meml. fellow, 1972-73. Fellow AAAS, Am. Phys. Soc.; mem. Kappa Phi, Sigma Xi, Tau Beta Pi. Home: 902 Kings Mill Rd Chapel Hill NC 27514-4923

JOHNSON, CHARLIE JAMES, minister; b. Barnesville, Ga., Sept. 24, 1923; s. Emory Moses and Ruth B. (Traylor) J.; m. Mary Ellen Upton, June 7, 1957; children: Marcus Anthony, Michael A. (dec.). Student, Ft. Valley (Ga.) State Coll., 1940-42; BA, Morehouse Coll., 1956; BD, Morehouse Sch. Religion, 1960, MDiv, 1973; ThD summa cum laude, Trinity Theol. Sem., Newburgh, Ind., 1980, D Ministry summa cum laude, 1982. Ordained to ministry Bapt. Ch., 1949; joined United Presbyn. Ch. in U.S.A., 1961. Pastor New Hope Bapt. Ch., Dalton, Ga., 1951-61, Bethesda Presbyn. Ch., Johnson City, Tenn., St. James Ch., Kingsport, Tenn., Tabernacle Ch., Greeneville, Tenn., 1951-61, 1st United Presbyn. Ch., Athens, Tenn., St. Paul United Presbyn. Ch., Sweetwater, Tenn., 1966-82; ret. Presbytery of East Tenn., 1983; adj. prof. Cedine Bible Inst., Spring City, Tenn., 1983-85; treas. Athens Ministerial Assn., 1975-76. Weekly columnist Daily Post-Athenian, 1967—, Monroe County Adv., 1989—. Mem., counselor CONTACT McMinn-Meigs-Monroe Counties, Tenn., bd. dirs., 1989-90. Fellow Trinity Theol. Sem., 1986. Mem. Kiwanis (bd. dirs. Sweetwater club 1989-90). Home and Office: 179 Upton Rd Sweetwater TN 37874-9015

JOHNSON, CHERYL ELIZABETH, writer, publisher, educator; b. Grand Rapids, Mich., Aug. 3, 1952; d. Thomas Joseph and Lutricia Pat (Jones) Devine; m. Robert Dwayne Johnson, Jan. 19, 1972; children: Cherie Elizabeth, Marianne Roxie. AA, Alvin (Tex.) Community Coll., 1975; BS in Elem. Edn. summa cum laude, U. Houston, 1977. Elem. tchr. Pearland (Tex.) Ind. Sch. Dist., 1977-78, Santa Fe (Tex.) Ind. Sch. Dist., 1978-81, Alvin Ind. Sch. Dist., 1981-83; ind. writer, tchr. Alvin, 1983—; cons. Tex. Assessment Acad. Skills, Alvin, 1983—, Criterion-Referenced Assessment Program for Tex., U.S. Nat. Assessment Ednl. Progress, Norm-Referenced Vol. Assessment Program for Am.; founder Devine Ednl. Corp. Author: Kids Excel Standardized Test Help: Every Student a Success, Teens Excel, Grades K-12, 1991-94. Home and Office: PO Box 1115 Alvin TX 77512-1115

JOHNSON, CHRISTY LYNN RODEHEAVER, nurse; b. Macon, Ga., Nov. 11, 1956; d. Charles Stewart and Dorothy (Roper) Rodeheaver; m. Herbert Clay Johnson Jr., June 5, 1974. ADN, Gordon Coll., 1977; cert. RN 1st asst., Delaware Community Coll., 1989; BA in Health Care Bus., Stephens Coll., 1991; BSN, N.Y. State Regents Coll., 1994. RN first asst., Ga.; cert. nurse oper. rm. Staff nurse med./surg. unit HCA Coliseum Med. Ctrs., Macon, Ga., 1977-79, head nurse med./surg. unit, 1979-82, staff nurse oper. rm., 1982-89, RN 1st asst., 1989—. Mem. Assn. Oper. Rm. Nurses (chair nat. RN First Assts. splty. assembly 1995-96), Southeastern Surg. Nurses Assn., Ga. Nurses Assn., Nat. League for Nursing. Home: 1528 Rumble Rd Forsyth GA 31029-8945

JOHNSON, CLARENCE RAY, minister; b. Port Arthur, Tex., Jan. 31, 1943; s. Ervin Ray and Mina Frances (Cox) J.; m. Betty Olene Mears, Nov. 22, 1962; children: Gregory Clarence, Garemy Kevin, Darren Kendall, Sherry Lynn. Ordained to ministry Ch. of Christ, 1962. Min. Hwy. 29 Ch. of Christ, Liberty Hill, Tex., 1962-63, Jonestown Ch. of Christ, Leander, Tex., 1963-70, Springhill (La.) Ch. of Christ, 1970-75, La Porte (tex.) Ch. of Christ, 1975-84, Exton (Pa.) Ch. of Christ, 1984-91, Shiloh Ch. of Christ, Mexia, Tex., 1991—; tchr., counselor Sabinal (Tex.) Bible Camp, 1978-80. Author: (with others) Is It Lawful?, 1989, Psalms to Sing, 1995, series of tracts, 1983-94, series of bible study work books, 1995-96; news editor Gospel Guardian, 1971-73; contbr. articles to profl. jours. Trustee Liberty Hill Ind. Sch. Dist., 1968-70; panel mem. life issues seminar La. State U. Med. Coll., Shreveport, 1973. Republican. Home: 819 E Commerce St Mexia TX 76667-2960 Office: Shiloh Ch of Christ Highway 39 S Mexia TX 76667

JOHNSON, CLARENCE TRAYLOR, JR., circuit court judge; b. Trenton, Fla., Aug. 16, 1929; s. Clarence Traylor and Jessie Granade (Wilson) J.; m. Shirley Ann Traxler, Aug. 30, 1957; children: James Waring, Robert Dale, Douglas Earl, Jan Elizabeth. BSBA, U. Fla., 1955, JD, 1958. Ptnr. Cone, Wagner, Nugent, Johnson, McKeown & Dell, West Palm Beach, Fla., 1958-71; cir. ct. judge 18th Jud. Cir. of Fla., Brevard and Seminole Counties, 1971-92; chmn. Fla. Conf. of Cir. Judges, 1990-91; mem. Fla. Bench Bar Commn., State of Fla., 1990-92; faculty Fla. Jud. Coll., 1988-90; mem. Fla. Fed.-State Jud. Coun., 1989-91, Jud. Coun. Fla., 1989-91. Pres. Jr. C. of C., Cocoa, Fla., 1963-64; chmn. bd. Cen. Brevard YMCA, Cocoa, 1965-66; pres. YMCA, Brevard County, 1968-71, Rotary, Cocoa, 1965-66. With USAF, 1950-54. Recipient Disting. Svc. award Cocoa Jaycees, 1965, Jud. Achievement award Acad. Fla. Trial Lawyers, 1987. Mem. ABA, Brevard County Bar Assn. (pres. 1969-70), The Fla. Bar (bd. govs. 1970-71). Lutheran. Home: 600 Heron Dr Merritt Island FL 32952-4022

JOHNSON, CLIFFORD VINCENT, college administrator; b. New Orleans, Nov. 15, 1936; s. William James and Floy (Wade) J.; m. Margaret Klavins, Feb. 5, 1960; children: William, Stephen, Lisa, Mara. BA, Dillard U., 1957; MAT, Harvard U., 1970. Rsch. asst. U. Ill., Chgo., 1958-59, Childrens Hosp.-U. Chgo., 1959-61; biochemistry researcher Université de Paris, 1962-68; dir. spl. tutorial program Tufts U., Medford, Mass., 1969-70; sr. program assoc. Inst. for Svcs. to Edn., Washington, 1970-76, dir. curriculum and faculty devel., 1976-79; spl. asst. to the pres. Clark Coll.,

Atlanta, 1982-83; exec. dir. I've Known Rivers, Inc., New Orleans, 1983-84; v.p. for devel. Dillard U., New Orleans, 1985—; cons. Nat. Adv. Coun. on the Edn. of Blacks in Am., 1980, Media Assocs., Inc., Washington, 1979-81, Bronx (N.Y.) Community Coll., 1979-80, NEH, Washington, 1981-85. Contbg. author: Best Short Stories by Negro Writers, 1967; exec. producer (documentary film) New Orleans Concerto, 1978; prodn. supr. (documentary film) In Search of Improvisation, 1983. Bd. dirs. Arts Media Svcs., Inc., Washington, 1981-83, New Orleans Mus. Art, 1990-96; mem. adv. coun. New Orleans Jazz and Heritage Festival Found., 1990—; mem . cmty. adv. bd. WWOZ-FM; mem. La. State Police Commn., 1991-94. Recipient Creative Program award Nat. Univ. Extension Assn., 1973, Spl. Appreciation award S.C. State U., 1976; Martin Luther King Jr. fellow Harvard U., 1968. Mem Nat. Soc. Fund Raising Execs. (v.p. La. chpt. 1988-91, Outstanding Fund Raiser of Yr. award 1992, bd. dirs., found. bd. dirs. 1993). Home: 5511 St Roch Ave New Orleans LA 70122-5252

JOHNSON, CLIFTON HERMAN, historian, archivist, former research center director; b. Griffin, Ga., Sept. 13, 1921; s. John and Pearl (Parrish) J.; student U. Conn., 1943-44; BA, U. N.C., 1948, PhD, 1959; MA U. Chgo., 1949; postgrad. U. Wis., 1951; m. Rosemary Brunst, Aug. 2, 1960; children: Charles, Robert, Virginia. Tutor, LeMoyne Coll., Memphis, 1950-53, asst. prof., 1953-56, prof., 1960-61, 63-66; asst. prof. East Carolina Coll., 1958-59; asst. libr. and archivist Fisk U., 1961-63; exec. dir. Amistad Rsch. Ctr., New Orleans, 1966-92, emeritus, 1992. Bd. dirs. La. World Expn., 1980-82, Lillie Carroll Jackson Mus., 1978-89, Countee Cullen Found., 1981-87, Friends of Archives La., 1978-90, La. Folklife Commn., 1982-85, Ctr. for Black Music Rsch., 1986—, New Orleans Urban League, 1994—. With AUS, 1940-45. Recipient NEH fellow, 1994. Mem. So. Hist. Assn., Soc. Am. Archivists, Assn. for Study Negro Life and History, Orgn. Am. Historians, Nat. Assn. Human Rights Workers. Author: (with Carroll Barber) The American Negro: A Selected and Annotated Bibliography for High Schools and Junior Colleges, 1968, A Legacy of La Amistad: Some Twentieth Century Black Leaders, 1989; editor: God Struck Me Dead: Religious Conversions and Experiences and Autobiographies of Ex-Slaves, 1969.

JOHNSON, CONSTANCE ANN TRILLICH, minister, internet service provider, small business owner, librarian, lawyer, writer, researcher, lecturer; b. Chgo., Apr. 16, 1949; d. Lee and Ruth (Goodhue) Trillich; m. Robert Dale Neal, Dec. 25, 1972 (div. 1988); 1 child, Adam Danforth; m. Lewis W. Johnson Jr., Feb. 14, 1990. BA in French, U. Tenn., 1971, cert. Sorbonne, 1970; MLn, Emory U., 1979; JD, Mercer Law Sch., 1982; PhD magna cum laude Internat. Sem., 1995. Bar: Ga. 1982. Reservationist AAA, Tampa, Fla., 1971-72; libr. tech. asst. I, Mercer U., Macon, Ga., 1973-74, libr. tech. asst. II, 1974-78; teaching asst. Mercer Law Sch., Macon, 1981; asst. prof. Mercer Med. Sch., Macon, 1980-82; pvt. practice, Macon, 1982-86; min. Ch. Tzaddi, 1986-89; writer/researcher ADC Project, 1988-89; min. Alliance of Divine Love, 1988—; co-owner Christians on the Net, 1995—; of counsel Read Found., Evansville, Ind., 1989; mgr. Lifestream Assocs., 1989; freelance editor Page Design Co., 1989; assoc. AA Computer Care, Winter Park, Fla., 1989; founder House of the Lord, 1989—; rsch. asst. Ctr. Constl. Studies, Macon, 1983; instr. bus. Wesleyan Coll., Macon, 1982; owner Christian Computer Care, Winter Park, Fla., 1990—; web designer Christians On The Net, 1995—. Mem. Ch. of Religious Rsch. Inc., 1992—. Author: (book) Treasures From Heaven, 1995; editor (periodical) Ray of Sunshine, 1989; assoc. prof. libr. sci., Internat. Sem., Plymouth Fla., 1991. Bd. dirs. Unity Ch., Middle, Ga., 1987, Sec., 1987. Bd. dirs. Macon Council World Affairs, 1981-82, Light of Creative Awareness, Northville, Mich., 1989; mem. Friends Emory Libraries, Atlanta, 1980-87; mem. Friends Eckerd Coll. Library, St. Petersburg, Fla., 1980-87. Mem. ABA, Am. Soc. Law and Medicine, Am. Judicature Soc., DAR (Kaskaskia chpt.), Mercer U. Women's Club (treas. 1974, pres. 1986, bd. dirs. 1987), Am. Assn. U. Women, Friends of the Libr., Mid. Ga. Gem and Mineral Soc., Macon Mus. Arts and Scis., La Leche League (sec. 1985), Phi Alpha Delta. Republican. Office: Christian Computer Care 1416 Pelican Bay Trl Winter Park FL 32792-6131

JOHNSON, CORWIN WAGGONER, law educator; b. Hamlet, Ind., Oct. 5, 1917; s. Lonnie Edmund and Nora Lee (Drake) J.; m. July 24, 1942; m. Evelyn Banks; children: Kent Edmund, Kirk Allan. B.A., U. Iowa, 1939, J.D., 1941; postgrad. (Sterling fellow), Yale U. Law Sch., 1941, 46. Bar: Iowa 1941, Calif. 1946, Tex. 1957. Spl. agt. FBI, Dept. Justice, 1942-46; instr. in law U. Iowa, 1946-47; asst. prof. law U. Tex., Austin, 1947-49; asso. prof. U. Tex., 1949-54, prof., 1954—. Co-author: Cases and Materials on Property, 7th rev. edit., 1996, Principles of Property, 3d rev. edit., 1989; contbr. articles to law revs. Mem. Austin Planning Commn., 1954-56. Mem. ABA, Tex. Bar Assn., Am. Law Inst., Order of Coif, Phi Beta Kappa. Democrat. Methodist. Home: 3425 Monte Vista Dr Austin TX 78731-5722 Office: U Tex Law Sch 727 E 26th St Austin TX 78705-3224

JOHNSON, CRYSTAL DUANE, psychologist; b. Houston, Mar. 2, 1954; d. Alton Floyd and Duane (Mullican) J.; m. Donald Beecher Hart, Mar. 21, 1989. BA, U. Tex., 1983, MS, 1985. Lic. profl. counselor, psychol. assoc., marriage and family therapist; cert. chem. dependency specialist. Student devel. specialist U. Tex., Tyler, 1985-86, intake counselor, 1986-88; staff psychologist Sabine Valley Ctr., Longview, Tex., 1987-88, Mental Health/Mental Retardation Ctr. of East Tex., Tyler, 1988-89; pvt. practice psychologist Tyler, 1989—; counselor Juvenile and Adult Probation Depts., 1988—, ICF/MR Residential Homes, 1991—; spl. edn. counselor, 1990—; counselor Child Protective Svcs., 1991—. Mem. Smith County Humane Soc., Tyler, 1985—, Humane Soc. of the U.S., Washington, 1987—, Am. Soc. Prevention Cruelty to Animals, 1987—, Nat. Wildlife Fedn., 1986—, World Wildlife Fedn., 1986—. Mem. Am. Psychol. Assn., Tex. Psychol. Assn., East Tex. Psychol. Assn.

JOHNSON, DAVID, medical administrator. Dir. divsn. oncology Vanderbilt Clinic, Nashville. Office: Vanderbilt Clinic Divsn Med Oncology Nashville TN 37232-5536

JOHNSON, DEBORAH CROSLAND WRIGHT, mathematics educator; b. Winston-Salem, N.C., July 17, 1951; d. Clayton Edward and Elizabeth Elliott (Bradley) Crosland; married; children: Jacqueline, Stephanie. BS in Math. Edn. magna cum laude, Appalachian State U., 1973; MEd in Math., U. N.C., Greensboro, 1976, cert., 1984. Cert. tchr., N.C., academically gifted. Tchr. math. Mt. Tabor H.S., Winston-Salem, 1973-76, McDowell H.S., Marion, N.C., 1976-78, Ctrl. Cabarrus H.S., Concord, N.C., 1978-81, Walter M. Williams H.S., Burlington, N.C., 1981—; mem. sch. improvement team Walter M. Williams H.S., 1989-92. Active First Presbyn. Ch., Burlington, 1988—. Mem. NEA, N.C. Assn. Educators, Nat. Coun. Tchrs. Math., N.C. Coun. Tchrs. Math., N.C. Assn. Gifted and Talented, Alpha Delta Kappa (hon. tchrs. sorority). Democrat.

JOHNSON, DEIRDRE ANN, social worker; b. New Orleans, Oct. 9, 1956; d. Albert Lavern and Ann Margaret (Bilas) J. BA in Sociology, N.C. Ctrl. U., 1986, MA in Student Pers., 1989. Counselor Coord. Coun. for Sr. Citizens, Durham, N.C., 1983-84, Duke Eye Ctr., Durham, N.C., 1984-86; counselor Svcs. for the Blind, Durham, N.C., 1987-88, social worker III, 1992—; instr. Ind. Living Rehab. Minictr. Div. Svcs. for the Blind, Durham, N.C., 1989; mem. adv. com. Data Link, Durham, 1993—. Mem. Alpha Kappa Delta. Home: 3427 Lees Chapel Rd Cedar Grove NC 27231-9702 Office: Svcs for the Blind PO Box 810 220 E Main St Durham NC 27701-3606

JOHNSON, DENNIS BURL, secondary school educator; b. Houston, Feb. 17, 1949; s. Burl Stroud and Patsy Ruth J.; m. Margaret Ann Lovick, July 12, 1980. BA in Teaching, Sam Houston State U., 1977; MS, U. Houston, 1992. Cert. Nat. Exec. Inst., 1978, Marilyn Burns Inst., 1989. Corr. Exxon Co., U.S.A., Houston, 1970-75; dist. exec. Boy Scouts Am., Tyler, Texas, New Orleans, 1977-84; educator Alvin (Tex.) Ind. Sch. Dist., 1984—; mem. profl. dist. comm. com. Alvin Ind. Sch. Dist., 1985—, v.p., 1987, pres., 1988-89, ins. com., 1986—, homework com., 1987, campus comm. com., 1986—, sick leave com., 1988-89, chmn. dept. sci., 1996—; cons. Ptnrs. in Space "Mars Project", NASA. Contbr. column to monthly newsletter Eh Las Bas, 1980-84; photos exhibited in Henderson Daily News, 1977-80. Pres. Houston, Tyler, Tex., New Orleans and Galveston, Tex. councils Boy Scouts Am., 1959—; mem. bd. ethics & compliance City of Alvin. Recipient Cathedral award Archbishop of New Orleans, 1983, Plus One Club award Boy Scouts Am., 1978, Region Pres. award, 1978, Commissioned Exec. award, 1977. Mem. NEA, Tex. State Tchrs. Assn., Alvin Tchrs. Assn., Sci. Tchrs. Assn. of Tex., Pro Rodeo Hall of Fame Soc. Methodist. Lodges: Lions, Rotary. Office: Alvin Ind Sch Dist 1910 Rosharon Rd Alvin TX 77511-4061

JOHNSON, DENNIS RAY, utility supply executive; b. Ft. Worth, Tex., Aug. 26, 1946; s. Ray W. and Joe Ann (Yeargan) J.; m. L.S. Longley Davis, July 14, 1964 (div. Oct. 1976); children: Dennis R. Jr., Bradley Todd. Diploma, Brantley Draughon Coll., Ft. Worth, 1969; cert., Tarrant County Jr. Coll., Ft. Worth, 1970. Pres. Atlas Utility Supply Co., Ft. Worth, 1967—; bd. dirs. Bowie State Bank; dir. Colleyville Econ. Devel. Corp. Mem. Am. Water Works Assn., Water and Sewer Distbrs. Am., Tex. Water Utilities Assn., Masons. Lutheran. Office: Atlas Utility Supply Co 2301 Carson St Fort Worth TX 76117-5212

JOHNSON, DEWEY E(DWARD), JR., dentist; b. Charleston, S.C., Mar. 19, 1935; s. Dewey Edward and Mabel (Momeier) J.; A.B. in Geology, U. N.C., 1957, D.D.S., 1961. Pvt. practice dentistry, Charleston, 1964-92, assoc. to Stanley H. Karesh, Charleston, D.D.S., 1970-77, tech. market rschr., designer, Charleston, 1970-90, indsl. designer, various orgns., 1965, 75, 77, 88, 91, 92. Served to lt. USNR, 1961-63. Mem. Royal Soc. Health, Charleston C. of C. (cruise ship com. 1969), ADA, Charleston Dental Soc., Hibernian Soc., Charleston Museum, Internat. Platform Assn., Charleston Library Soc., S.C. Hist. Soc., Gibbes Art Gallery, Preservation Soc. of Charleston, Navy League of U.S., Phi Kappa Sigma, Sigma Gamma Epsilon, Psi Omega. Congregationalist. Club: Optimist. Achievements include various scientific and engineering designs; patent in dental matrix device.

JOHNSON, DIANNE JEAN, human resources executive; b. Harvey, Ill., Sept. 12, 1948; d. Virgil Albert and Jean (Armstrong) Johnson; m. Dennis Michael Buchanan, May 7, 1988 (div. Sept. 1992). BBA in Mktg., U. Tex., 1970. Mktg. rsch. asst. Belden Assocs., Dallas, 1970-72; personnel staff Meisel Photochrome Co., Dallas, 1972-75; personnel staff Geosource, Inc., Houston, 1975-77, corp. compensation specialist, 1977-78; personnel officer, compensation and benefits mgr. Capital Bank, Houston, 1978-79; compensation specialist Anderson Clayton & Co., Houston, 1979-81, dir. human resources Ranger Ins. subs., 1981-84, corp. compensation dir., 1984-87; v.p. human resources NBC Bank, Houston, 1987-89; asst. v.p., mgr. compensation Tex. Commerce Bancshares, Houston, 1989-90; human resources cons., 1990-91; sr. compensation specialist Enron Corp., Houston, 1991-92, sr. human resources rep., 1993-96, human resources mgr., 1996—; co-chair So. Gas Assn. Compensation Roundtable, 1992. Mem. assoc. vestry Saint John the Divine Ch., Houston, 1983; bd. dirs. Meadowbriar Home for Girls, Houston, 1978-79; bd. mem. Escape Family Resource Ctr., 1995; active Leadership Tex., 1996. Mem. Houston Compensation Assn. (bd. dir. 1983-87, pres. 1985-86, v.p. 1984-85), Houston Personnel Assn. (com. 1982-84), Am. Soc. Personnel Adminstrs., Am. Compensation Assn. (com. 1983, 85-87), River Oaks Breakfast Club (Houston, v.p. membership 1988).

JOHNSON, DONALD HARRY, investment company executive; b. Racine, Wis., Oct. 15, 1944; s. Arthur Harryand Bernice (Monson) J.; m. Mary Diane Schomer, Sept.30, 1967; children: Karn Denice, Brian Donald. BS in Indsl. Engring., Bradley U., Peoria, Ill., 1967; MBA, Canisius Coll., Buffalo, 1972. Prodn. mgr. Westinghouse Elec. Corp., Buffalo, 1967-73; v.p. N. Christensen Real Estate, Racine, Wis., 1973-83; pres. Barrington Investments, Pompano Beach, Fla., 1983—; bd. dirs. Clarion Software Corp. Mem. Nat. Assn. Realtors (cert. commercial investment mem.), Rotary (pres.-elect 1983). Republican. Lutheran. Office: Barrington Investments 150 E Sample Rd Ste 200 Pompano Beach FL 33064-3550

JOHNSON, DONALD WAYNE, lawyer; b. Memphis, Feb. 2, 1950; s. Hugh Don and Oline (Rowland) J.; m. Jan Marie Mullinax, May 12, 1972 (div. 1980); 1 child, Scott Fitzgerald; m. Cindy L. Walker, Dec. 10, 1988; children: Trevor Christian, Mallory Faith. Student Memphis State U., 1968, Lee Coll., 1968-72; JD, Woodrow Wilson Coll. of Law, 1975. Bar: Ga. 1975, U.S. Dist. Ct. (no. dist.) Ga. 1975, U.S. Ct. Appeals (5th cir.) 1976, U.S. Tax Ct. 1978, U.S. Ct. Claims 1978, U.S. Supreme Ct. 1979, U.S. Ct. Appeals (11th, 9th, Fed., D.C. cirs.) 1984. Ptnr. Barnes & Johnson, Dalton, Ga., 1975-77, Johnson & Fain, Dalton, 1977-80; pvt. practice, Dalton, 1975-85, Atlanta, 1985—. Bd. dirs. Pathway Christian Sch., Dalton, 1978-85, Jr. Achievement of Dalton, 1978-84, Dalton-Whitfield County Day Care Ctrs., Inc.; legal counsel Robertson for Pres. com., Ga., 1988; bd. chmn. Ga. Family Coun., 1990—; Rep. chmn. Clayton County, 1993-95; Rep. gen. counsel 3rd Congl. Dist., 1993-95, Clayton County Rep. Party, 1995—; city atty. City of Forest Park, Ga., 1996—. Mem. Ga. Trial Lawyers Assn. (bd. govs. 1984), Ga. Bar Assn., ATLA, Christian Legal Soc. Mem. Ch. of God. Office: 140 Kathi Ave Ste G PO Box 187 Fayetteville GA 30214-0187

JOHNSON, EDDIE BERNICE, congresswoman; b. Waco, Tex., Dec. 3, 1935; d. Lee Edward and Lillie Mae (White) J.; m. Lacy Kirk Johnson, July 5, 1956 (div. Oct. 1970); 1 child, Dawrence Kirk. Diploma in Nursing, St. Mary's Coll. of South Bend, 1955; BS in Nursing, Tex. Christian U., 1967; MPA, So. Meth. U., 1976; LLD (hon.), Bishop Coll., 1979, Jarvis Coll., 1979, Tex. Coll., 1989, Houston-Tillotson Coll., 1993, Paul Quinn Coll., 1993. Chief psychiat. nurse psychotherapist Vets. Hosp., Dallas, 1956-72; state rep. Tex. Ho. Reps. Dist. 33-0, Dallas, 1972-77; regional dir. HEW, Dallas, 1977-79; exec. asst. to adminstr. for primary health care policy HEW, Washington, 1979-81; v.p. Vis. Nurse Assn. of Tex., Dallas, 1981-87; mem. Tex. State Senate, dist. 23, 1986-93, 103rd Congress from 30th Tex. dist., Washington, D.C., 1993—, 105th Congress from 30th Tex. dist., 1996—; cons. div. urban affairs Zales Corp., Dallas, 1976-77; exec. asst. personnel div. Neiman-Marcus, Dallas, 1972-75; pres. Eddie Bernice Johnson & Associates, Inc., Metroplex News, Dallas-Ft. Worth Airport. Bd. dirs. ARC. Recipient Citizenship award Nat. Conf. Christians and Jews, 1985; named an Outstanding Alumnus St. Mary's Coll. of Nursing, 1986. Mem. Alpha Kappa Alpha. Office: US Ho of Reps 1123 Longworth HOB Washington DC 20515

JOHNSON, EDWARD JOE, JR., foreign language educator; b. Palatka, Fla., Jan. 17, 1965; s. Edward Joe Johnson and Shirley Ann (Kirk) Wilson. BA magna cum laude, The Citadel, 1987; MA, U. S.C., 1992; postgrad., U. Fla., 1993—. Tchg. asst. dept. fgn. langs. U. S.C., Columbia, 1987-88; English lectr. U. de Haute Alsace, Mulhouse, France, 1988-90; tchg. asst., temporary faculty dept. fgn. langs. U. S.C., Columbia, 1990-92; lectr. dept. langs. Clinch Valley Coll., Wise, Va., 1992-93; tchg. asst. dept. romance langs. U. Fla., Gainesville, 1994—; translator in field. Choi mem., soloist, cantor Holy Trinity Episcopal Choir, Gainesville, 1993—; canvasser, telephone staff Human Rights Coun., Gainesville, 1994-95. Star of the West scholar The Citadel, Charleston, 1983-87; U. Fla. Coll. of Liberal Arts and Scis. fellow, Gainesville, 1993-94. Mem. MLA, South Atlantic MLA, Am. Soc. for 18th Century Studies. Democrat. Office: Dept Romance Langs Univ Fla Gainesville FL 32611

JOHNSON, EDWARD MICHAEL, lawyer; b. Waco, Tex., July 12, 1944; s. Edward James and Anne Margaret (Stuchly) J.; m. Yvonne Margaret Hill, May 7, 1977; children: Hilary Yvonne, Megan Joy, Michael David. BA in Polit. Sci., S.W. Tex. State U., 1967; JD, St. Mary's U. 1970. Bar: Tex. 1971, U.S. Dist. Ct. (we. and so. dist.) Tex. 1972, U.S. Ct. Claims 1972, U.S. Supreme Ct. 1976. Asst. law libr. Bexar County Law LIbr., 1968-69; briefing clk. Judge Preston H. Dial, Jr., 1969-70; briefing atty. U.S. Dist. Judge John H. Wood Jr., San Antonio, Tex., 1971-72, asst. U.S. atty. Dept. Justice, San Antonio, 1972-76, sole practice, San Antonio, 1976-81; sr. atty. Wiley, Garwood, Hornbuckle, Higdon & Johnson, San Antonio, 1980-81; pres. McCabe Petroleum Corp., San Antonio, 1981; chmn. bd., CEO, gen. counsel Blue Chip Petroleum Corp., San Antonio, 1981-83; pres., gen. counsel Harvest Investments Corp., San Antonio, 1983-87, also dir.; gen. ptnr. Med. Mobility Ltd. IV, San Antonio, 1984-87; mgr. Med. Mobility Joint Venture, San Antonio, 1984-87; exec. cons. Advance Tax Representation, Inc., 1987-88; gen. ptnr. Harvest Venture Capital Ltd. I, San Antonio, 1986-87; pres., gen. counsel Blue Chip Securities Corp., San Antonio, 1984-87; reg. rep. First Investors Corp., 1988-89; sr. atty. Jorrie, Zucker Sr. & Assocs., Inc. Atty's at Law, 1989-90; pres., CEO Johnson, Curney, & Fields, P.C. , 1990—. Host (radio program) The Christian Lawyer, 1990-91, (TV program) God's Army, 1990-92, Altar Call leader One to One Ministries, 1993—; nat. spkr. Internat. Networking Assn., 1995—, bd. dirs., 1997—. Co-chmn. fund raising Am. Heart Assn., San Antonio, 1982-84; bd. dirs. Am. Cancer Soc., San Antonio, 1982-84; chmn. San Fernando Cathedral Endowment Fund, San Antonio, 1986; mem. Gideons Internat., San Antonio, 1982-86, mem. exec. bd. San Antonio Christian Schs., 1983-84, San Antonio Christian Legal Soc., 1991—, Fed. Bar Licensing Bd., 1976-78; bd. dirs. Tex. Bible Coll., 1984-87, Christian Businessmen's Com., San Antonio, 1981-88, Cornerstone Christian Schs., San Antonio, 1991-92, mem., speaker, pres. Med. Ctr. chpt., 1988-91, mem. Full Gospel Businessmen's Fellowship, 1981-92, pres. 1985-88, field rep., 1988-92; bd. dirs. Assn. Spirit Filled Fellowships, 1991-93; pres. God's Army Internat. Found., Inc., 1990-92; gen. counsel, bd. dirs. Four Winds Ministries, Inc., 1992-93; scoutmaster Alamo area coun. Boy Scouts Am., San Antonio, 1973-74; founder, chmn. Christian Businessmen's Focus on the Family, San Antonio, 1984-85. Recipient spl. commendation Dept. Transp. 1973, Dept. Air Force HQ, ATC, 1974, Dept. Treasury, 1974; named Outstanding Asst. U.S. Atty. Dept. Justice, 1974, 75, one of Outstanding Young Men Am., 1975, one of Outstanding Young Texans, 1976. Mem. Fed. Bar Assn. (pres. San Antonio chpt. 1975-76; v.p. 1973-74, sec. 1972-73, treas. 1971-72, named outstanding chpt. pres. 1976), Tex. Bar Assn., San Antonio Bar Assn. Republican. Office: 800 Spectrum Bldg 613 NW Loop 410 at San Pedro San Antonio TX 78216-5509

JOHNSON, ELBERT NEIL, JR., internist; b. Dunn, N.C., Sept. 24, 1925; s. Elbert Neil and Frances Livingston (Johnson) J.; m. Thelma Ruth Smith, June 18, 1949; 1 child, Elbert III. BS, Wake Forest Coll., 1945; MD, Bowman-Gray Sch. Medicine, Winston-Salem, N.C., 1947. Diplomate Am. Bd. Internal Medicine. Intern Detroit Receiving Hosp., 1948-50; health officer Forsyth County Health Dept., Winston-Salem, 1950-51; med. officer USAR, 1951-53; resident Univ. Hosp., Augusta, Ga., 1953-54, Roper Hosp., Charleston, S.C., 1954-55; pvt. practice internal medicine Florence, S.C., 1955-56; staff physician VA Hosp., Columbia, S.C., 1956-58; pvt. practice internal medicine Columbia, 1958-89; med. cons. disability determination div. S.C. Dept. Vocat. Rehab., Columbia, 1990—. Trustee Baptist Med. Ctr., Columbia, 1985-89. Mem. AMA, Am. Soc. Internal Medicine, So. Med. Assn., S.C. Med. Assn., Columbia Med. Soc. Republican. Baptist. Home: 4611 Pine Grove Ct Columbia SC 29206-4517 Office: Disability Determination Div SC Dept Vocat Rehab 3600 Forest Dr Columbia SC 29204-4033

JOHNSON, ELLEN, linguist, educator; b. Atlanta, Sept. 17, 1959; d. Charles Edward and Rebecca (Paschal) J.; 1 child, Thomas Johnson Frasure. BA in Fgn. Langs., Rhodes Coll., 1980; PhD in Linguistics, U. Ga., 1992. Rsch. coord. Linguistic Atlas Project, Athens, Ga., 1987-94; adj. prof. Piedmont Coll., Demorest, Ga., 1994-95; instr. Ga. State U., Atlanta, 1995; asst. prof. U. Memphis, 1995-96, Western Ky. U., Bowling Green, 1996—. Author: Lexical Change and Variation in the Southeastern United States 1930-90, 1996; editor: (with others) Handbook of the Linguistic Atlas of the Middle and South Atlantic States, 1994; co-editor spl. issue Jour. English Linguistics, 1990; contbr. articles to profl. publs. Am. fellow AAUW, 1990-91; sr. Fulbright scholar U. Chile, Santiago, 1993. Mem. Am. Dialect Soc., Southea. Conf. on Linguistics. Mem. Soc. of Friends. Office: Western Ky U Dept English Bowling Green KY 42101

JOHNSON, ELLEN RANDEL, real estate broker; b. Canton, Miss., May 9, 1916; d. Robert Colquhoun and Laura Arabella (Taylor) Randel; m. Floyd Everett Johnson Sr.; children: Dolly Mae Johnson Day, Floyd Everett Johnson Jr. Student, Blue Mountain Coll., 1934-35; course in real estate, Miss. Realtors Inst., 1976-77. Bookkeeper E. Constantin, Jr., Yazoo City, Miss., 1951-54, 56-59; draftsman Miss. State Hwy. Dept., Yazoo City, 1955; office mgr. Miss. Chem. Corp. Fed. Credit Union, Yazoo City, 1963-66; freelance journalist Yazoo Herald, 1970-74; broker, owner Ellen Johnson Realty, Yazoo, 1977; broker, assoc. Phyllis Waltman Realtors and Century 21 Beard & McMahan Realtors, Hattiesburg, Miss., 1978-79; broker, owner Ellen Johnson, Realtor, Hattiesburg, 1979-91. Author: The Dining Table for Candida Patients, 1988, Yesterday, Today, For Tomorrow: A Family History, Colquhoun/Calhoun and Their Ancestral Homelands, 1993; contbr. articles to profl. jours. Charter dir. Yazoo Arts Council, 1973-75; chmn. civic quiz Am. Bus. Women's Assn., Hattiesburg, 1987. Mem. Nat. Assn. Realtors (Omega Tau Rho medal 1984), Nat. Women's Council Realtors, Miss. Women's Council Realtors (gov. 1984, v.p. 1983-84, by-laws chmn. 1984, Realtor of Yr. 1984), Hattiesburg Women's Council Realtors (v.p. 1982-83, Realtor of Yr. 1984), Miss. Assn. Realtors (by-laws com.), Hattiesburg Bd. Realtors (bd. dirs., com. chmn. 1979, 81, 84, v.p. multiple listing service 1982-83, pres. 1983-84, treas. 1987, Realtor of Yr. 1984). Republican. Baptist. Clubs: Mozart (Yazoo City) (pres. 1969); Miss. Music (Jackson) (jr. festival chmn. 1973-75). Home and Office: 1302 Estelle Ave Hattiesburg MS 39402-2719

JOHNSON, EUGENE FRANKLIN, JR., emergency room physician, osteopath; b. Princeton, W.Va., Sept. 25, 1956; s. Eugene Franklin and Mona Ann (Reed) J.; m. Gail Dianne Tyree, June 11, 1988; 1 child, Stephen. AS in Biology, Concord Coll., Athens, W.Va., 1980; DO, W.Va. Sch. Osteo. Medicine, 1984. Cert. surg. technologist. Surg. technologist Princeton Communinity Hosp., 1975-82; black lung physician Tri-Dist. Clinic, Algoma, W.Va., 1986-87; emergency physician Summer County Hosp., Hinton, W.Va., 1987-90; regional med. dir. W.Va. Regional Med. Systems, Beckley, 1987—; emergency physician Beckley Hosp., 1990—, Plateau Med. Ctr., Oakhill, W.Va., 1991—; advanced cardiac life support instr. Am. Heart Assn., 1986—, basic trauma life support instr., 1987—; instr. paramedics W.Va. Emergency Med. Svc., Beckley, 1987—; chmn. So. W.Va. Critical Care Com., 1986—; local preacher Free Meth. Ch., Princeton, 1978—; leader Boy Scouts Am., Princeton, 1974. Mem. Am. Osteo. Assn., Am. Coll. Emergency Physicians. Democrat. Home: 15 Hillcrest Dr Princeton WV 24740-2033 Office: Beckley Hosp 1007 S Oakwood Ave Beckley WV 25801-5935

JOHNSON, FRANK MINIS, JR., federal judge; b. Winston County, Ala., Oct. 30, 1918; s. Frank M. and Alabama (Long) J.; m. Ruth Jenkins, Jan. 16, 1938; 1 son, James Curtis (dec.). Grad., Gulf Coast Mil. Acad., Gulfport, Miss., 1935, Massey Bus. Coll., Birmingham, 1937; LLB, U. Ala., 1943, LLD (hon.), 1977; also LLD (hon.), Notre Dame U., 1973; LLD (hon.), Princeton U., 1974, Boston U., 1979, Yale U., 1980; J.D. (hon.), St. Michael's Coll., 1975. Bar: Ala. 1943. Ptnr. Curtis, Maddox & Johnson, 1946-53; U.S. atty. No. Dist. Ala., 1953-55; U.S. dist. judge Middle Dist. Ala., 1955-79; U.S. judge Ct. Appeals for 5th Circuit, 1979-81, Ct. Appeals for 11th Cir., 1981—; mem. Temporary Emergency Ct. Appeals of U.S., 1972-82; mem. rev. com. Jud. Conf., 1969-78, jud. ethics com., 1978-85, spl. com. on habeas corpus, 1971-78, chmn. adv. com. on civil rules, 1985-86. Served from pvt. to capt. inf. AUS, 1943-46. Decorated Purple Heart with oak leaf cluster, Bronze Star, Combat Infantryman's medal; recipient Thurgood Marshall award, 1993, Presdl. medal of Freedom, 1995. Mem. Ala. Acad. Honor. Office: US Ct Appeals 11th Cir PO Box 35 Montgomery AL 36101-0035

JOHNSON, FRANK WILLIAM, marketing professional; b. Sumter, S.C., Sept. 20, 1948; s. John William and Dorothy (Ferrigan) J.; m. Sally Gattshall, Nov. 25, 1970; children: Lauren Elizabeth, Mark William. BA in Polit. Sci., The Citadel, 1970; MS in Ops. Mgmt., U. Ark., 1976. Sales rep. Union Carbide Corp., Dallas, 1976-78; product mgr. Union Carbide Corp., N.Y.C., 1979-82; sales mgr. Steelcase Inc., Dallas, 1982-83; dir. mktg. VECTA div. Steelcase Inc., Dallas, 1984-86; dir. sales and mktg. Lista Internat., Dallas, 1986-87, Kewaunee Sci. Corp., Lockhart, Tex., 1987-92; v.p. sales and mktg. McCoy, Inc., Houston, 1992-95; v.p. Contract Specifix, Richmond, VA, 1995-96; pres. Saxton, Inc., Davenport, Iowa, 1996—. Served to capt. USAF, 1970-76. Mem. Sales and Mktg. Club. Republican. Presbyterian. Lodge: Shriners. Home: 845 Normandy Dr Iowa City IA 52246 Office: Saxton Inc 320 Main St Davenport IA 52801

JOHNSON, FREDERICK DEAN, former food company executive; b. Shreve, Ohio, Feb. 27, 1911; s. Harry H. and Grace Marcella (Cammarn) J.; AB, Coll. Wooster (Ohio), 1935; m. Haulwen Elizabeth Richey, June 19, 1937; children: Frederick Dean II, Mary Haulwen, Grace Elizabeth. Dir. research The Bama Co. (now Bama Food Products, Grocery Products Divsn. Borden Inc.), Birmingham, Ala., 1961-65, dir. research, Houston, 1965-76, dir. product devel. and tech. adviser, 1976-78, cons., 1978-93; U.S. del. FAO/WHO Codex Alimentarius Commn. Processed Fruits and Vegetables, 1973, 74, 75. Bd. dirs. Afton Oaks Civic Club, 1967-70, 82-94, pres. 1995;

chmn. precinct 178 Harris County, Tex., 1981-94, 96—; ruling elder Presbyn. Ch., 1947—. Mem. Internat. Jelly and Preserve Assn. (chmn. quality control adv. com. 1969-73, chmn. standards com. 1973-76, citation and plaque 1974), Inst. Food Technologists (charter), Am. Chem. Soc. (past sec., chmn. Wooster sect.), AAAS. Home: 4546 Shetland Ln Houston TX 77027-5518

JOHNSON, FREDERICK ROSS, international management advisory company executive; b. Winnipeg, Man., Can., Dec. 13, 1931; s. Frederick Hamilton and Caroline (Green) J.; m. Laurie Ann Graumann; children: Bruce, Neil. BComm, U. Man., 1952; MBA, U. Toronto, Ont., Can., 1956; LLD (hon.), St. Francis Xavier U., Antigonish, 1978, Barry (Fla.) U., 1980. Tchr. U. Toronto, 1962-64; dir. mktg. CGE, Toronto, 1964-66; mgr. mdse. T. Eaton Co., 1966-67; exec. v.p. GSW Ltd., 1967-71; pres. Standard Brands Ltd., Toronto, 1971, pres., chief exec. officer, 1972; v.p. Standard Brands, Inc., N.Y.C., 1973, sr. v.p., dir., 1974, pres., 1975-81, chief exec. officer, 1976-81, chmn., 1977-81, chmn., chief operating officer, 1981; pres., chief operating officer Nabisco Brands, Inc. (formerly Standard Brands, Inc. and Nabisco, Inc.), Parsippany, N.J., 1984-85, vice chmn., 1985-86; pres., chief oper. officer R.J. Reynolds Industries Inc. (known as RJR Nabisco, Inc. as of 1986), Winston-Salem, N.C., 1985-87; chief exec. officer RJR Nabisco, Inc., Atlanta, 1987-89; chmn., chief exec. officer RJM Group, Inc., Atlanta, 1989—; chmn. Bionaire Inc., Montreal, Can., 1992—; chmn. bd. dirs. Bionaire, Inc., Montreal, Que., Can., 1992—; bd. dirs. Am. Express, N.Y.C., Power Corp., Montreal, Black & McDonald, Toronto, Archer Daniels Midland, Decatur, Ill., Nat. Svc. Ind., Atlanta. Chmn. bd. N.Y.C. chpt. Nat. Multiple Sclerosis Soc., 1978-86. Lt. Ordance Corps Royal Can. Army. Mem. Grocery Mfrs. Assn. (bd. dirs.), Young Pres. Orgn., Brook Club (N.Y.C.), Links Club (N.Y.C.), Blind Brook Club (N.Y.C.), Econ. Club (N.Y.C.), Conn. Golf Club (Easton), Atlanta Country Club, Castle Pines Club (Colo.), Deepdale Club (Manhasset, N.Y.), Jupiter Hills Club (Fla.), Loxahatchee Club (Fla.), Mt. Bruno Country Club, Phi Delta Theta. Office: RJM Group Inc 200 Galleria Pky NW Ste 970 Atlanta GA 30339-5945

JOHNSON, GAYLE HARRISON, artistic director; b. Richmond, Va., Mar. 6, 1954; d. Mason Winfield and Adele Elizabeth (Kratz) J.; m. James Frederick Weaver, June 12, 1987; 1 child, Michael Justin. BA, Oberlin Coll., 1978; MusB, Oberlin Conservatory, 1978. Adminstrv. asst. Early Music Guild, Seattle, 1979-81; dir. Capriole, Seattle, 1979-87; artistic dir. Capriole, Williamsburg, Va., 1987—, Colonial Williamsburg Baroque Music Festival, 1995—; asst. choir dir. Williamsburg Presbyn. Ch., 1988—; mem. ensemble-in-residence Coll. of William and Mary, 1989-93, Old Dominion U., 1994—; adj. faculty Seattle Pacific U., 1979-85; pvt. tchr., 1979—; harpsichordist Colonial Williamsburg, 1987-88. Asst. choir dir. Williamsburg Presbyn. Ch., 1988—, Williamsburg Early Music Guild,1988-89, No. Rehab. Housing Coop., 1983-85. Newberry Libr. fellow, Chgo., 1977. Mem. Early Music Am., Chamber Music Am. Office: Capriole PO Box 558 Williamsburg VA 23187-0558

JOHNSON, GENE ALLEN, retired municipal environmental administrator; b. Nashville, Nov. 6, 1936; s. Percy Allen and Elizabeth (Russell) J.; m. Melba Sue Wallace, Dec. 24, 1955 (div. 1965); 1 child, Gene A. Jr. (dec.); m. Mary Lynn Whittle, May 25, 1967; 1 child, Elizabeth L. B in Engring., Vanderbilt U., 1957. Diplomate Am. Acad. Environ. Engrs.; profl. engr., Tenn.; registered land surveyor. Sanitary engr. Tenn. Dept. Health, Nashville, 1957-61; cons. engr. Hickerson, Adams & Johnson, Nashville, 1961-63; wastewater treatment engr. dept. water and sewer services Met. Govt. Nashville, 1963-73, chief engr., 1973-80, asst. dir., 1980-88, assoc. dir., 1988-94, A/E contract adminstr. dept. fin., 1994-96, ret., 1996; pres. Consol. Engring. Techs., Waverly, Tenn., 1996—. Mem. Am. Waterworks Assn., Water Environ. Fedn. Baptist. Home and Office: Consol Engring Techs 19 Gregson Pl Waverly TN 37185-2925

JOHNSON, GEORGE ANDREW, veterinary medicine and food science educator; b. Bklyn.; s. Franklin R. and Katie P. J.; children: George Jr. and Stacie. MS, Cornell U., 1972; DVM, Tuskegee U., 1961. Acting assoc. dean Washington Tech. Inst., 1972-74; assoc. dir. D.C. Coop. Extension Svc., Washington, 1974-77; adv. coun. on vocat. edn. D.C. Pub. Sch., Washington, 1977-79; chairperson, prof. N.C. A&T State U., Greesboro, 1978—; dean Washington Tech. Inst., 1972-73, chairperson, prof., 1973-74. Mem. Phi Beta Sigma (pres. 1959-61), Gamma Sigma Delta (asst. sec., sec., v.p., pres. 1983-90). Office: NC A&T State U Animal Scis 1601 E Market St Greensboro NC 27401-3209

JOHNSON, GEORGE WILLIAM, university president; b. Jamestown, N.D., July 5, 1928; s. George Carl and Mathilde (Trautman) J.; m. Joanne Ferris, June 11, 1955; children: Robert Craig, William Garth. B.A., Jamestown Coll., 1950; M.A., Columbia U., 1953, Ph.D., 1960. Asst. chmn. dept. English Temple U., Phila., 1964-66; assoc. dean liberal arts Temple U., 1966-67, chmn. dept. English, 1967-68, dean liberal arts, 1968-78; pres. George Mason U., Fairfax, Va., 1978—. Contbr. articles to scholarly jours. Bd. dirs. Elizabethtown Coll., 1989—. Served in U.S. Army, 1950-52. Named Washingtonian of Yr., 1984. Mem. Am. Assn. State Colls. and Univs. (mem. com. state rels. 1981-85, Va. rep. 1985-89, mem. mission to Mex. 1979, mem. mission to China 1984), Am. Council Edn., Bus. Higher Edn., Va. C. of C. (bd. dirs. 1993—), Golden Key Nat. Honor Soc. Roman Catholic. Office: George Mason U Office of Pres Fairfax VA 22030-4444

JOHNSON, GERALD BERTRAM, newspaper librarian, writer; b. Middlesboro, Ky., Nov. 8, 1944; s. Bertram Errol and Frances Pauline (Johnson) J. BA in Geography, U. Fla., 1967; MLS, Fla. State U., 1973. Libr. Fla. Dept. Natural Resources Marine Rsch. Lab, St. Petersburg, Fla., 1974-77; newspaper libr. Naples (Fla.) Daily News, 1979—. Mem. Old Naples (Fla.) Assn., 1990—, Collier County Hist. Soc., Naples, Fla., 1991—. Mem. Spl. Libr. Assn., Fla. News Librs. Assn., Fla. Press Club. Democrat. Episcopalian. Home: 207 Broad Ave S Naples FL 33940-7028 Office: Naples Daily News 1075 Central Ave Naples FL 34102-6237

JOHNSON, GERVAIS COLLINS, JR., computer scientist; b. Edwards AFB, Calif., Mar. 22, 1957; s. Gervais Collins and Georgia Mable (Cunningham) J. ASN, Angelo State U., San Angelo, Tex., 1978; BS, San Diego State U., 1984; MS, Stanford U., 1986. Computer cons. Equitable Life Assurance Co., San Diego, 1980-83; programmer/analyst Nat. Steel Shipbuilding Co., San Diego, 1984-85; sr. programmer/analyst Fed. Elec. Corp. (ITT), Vandenburg AFB, Calif., 1985-87, Peter R. Johnson & Assocs., San Francisco, 1987-88; sr. cons. GE Cons. Co., San Francisco, 1988-89; sr. programmer/analyst Harper Group, San Francisco, 1989-92; cons. Knowledge Ware, Inc., Atlanta, 1992-93; dir. info. technology architecture John Alden Systems Co., Miami, Fla., 1993—; cons. Reliance Cons. Group, Atlanta, 1993—. Creator/author software: Common System Architecture, 1993. Mem. IEEE Computer Soc., No. Calif. EDI User Group (pres. 1989-91), Object Mgmt. Group, ANSI EDI Standards Group. Democrat. Office: John Alden Systems Co 7300 Corporate Center Dr Miami FL 33126-1232

JOHNSON, GIFFORD KENNETH, testing laboratory executive; b. Santa Barbara, Calif., June 30, 1918; s. Elvin Morgan and Rosalie Dorothy (Schlagel) J.; m. Betty Jane Crockett, June 10, 1944; children: Craig, Dane, Janet. Student, Santa Monica (Calif.) City Coll., 1938-39, UCLA, 1940, Harvard Bus. Sch., 1944. With N.Am. Aviation, Inc., 1935-41; chief indsl. engr. Consol. Vultee Aircraft Corp., 1941-48; prodn. mgr. to pres. Chance Vought Aircraft Corp., 1950-61; pres., chief operating officer Ling-Temco-Vought, Inc., 1961-64; pres. S.W. Center Advanced Studies, 1965-69; chmn., pres., chief exec. officer Am. Biomed. Corp., 1969-79; exec. v.p. Nat. Health Labs., 1978-81; chmn., chief exec. officer Woodson-Tenent Labs. Inc., Dallas, 1981—. Mem. devel. bd. U. Tex., Dallas; v.p., trustee Excellence in Edn. Found.; pres. C.C. Young Meml. Home; bd. dirs. Tex. A&M Research Found. Mem. Am. Clin. Lab. Assn. (dir.), Navy League (life). Methodist (treas.). Clubs: Northwood Country; Salesmanship (Dallas). Home: 10555 Pagewood Dr Dallas TX 75230-4255 Office: 10300 NC Expy Bldg 4 Ste 220 Dallas TX 75231

JOHNSON, GORDON GUSTAV, mathematician, educator; b. Chgo., June 23, 1936; s. Gustav Hjalmar and Selma Maria (Hultman) J.; m. Nancy Mae Shupe, June 29, 1957; children: Cathy Lynn, Kim Marie, Carl Gustav, David Hjalmar. BSME, Ill. Inst. Tech., 1958; PhD in Math., U. Tenn., 1964. Cons. AEC, Oak Ridge, Tenn., 1961-63; fellow Oak Ridge Inst. Nuclear Studies, 1963-64; asst. prof. U. Ga., Athens, 1964-69; assoc. prof. Va. Polytech. Inst. & State U., Blacksburg, 1969-71; assoc. prof. U. Houston, 1971-74, prof., 1974—; sr. rsch. assoc. Nat. Rsch. Coun., Houston, Washington, 1978-81; vis. prof. Emory U., Atlanta, 1983-84; researcher Ins. Def. Analyses, Princeton, 1990-92. Founder, editor Houston Jour. Math., 1976-94. Pres. Clear Creek Basin Authority, Houston, 1973-74. Mem. Am. Math. Soc., Math. Assn. Am., Swedish Math. Soc., Sigma Xi. Home: 2010 Fairwind Rd Houston TX 77062-4514 Office: U Houston 4800 Calhoun Rd Houston TX 77204-3476

JOHNSON, HARRY WATKINS, defense analyst; b. Richmond, Va., Dec. 16, 1945; s. Harry Watkins and Ellen Katherine (Arvin) J.; m. Judith Indie Isbell, Sept. 6, 1969; children: Katherine Elizabeth, Blair Lawrence. BS, Va. Poly. Inst. and State U., 1968; MEd, Boston U., 1974. Commd. 2d lt. U.S. Army, 1968, advanced through grades to lt. col., 1985; staff officer U.S. Army, Ft. Pickett, Va., 1970-74; petroleum officer U.S. Army, Germersheim, Germany, 1974-77; asst. prof. mil. sci. U. Pitts., 1977-80; readiness officer U.S. Army, Nurnberg, Germany, 1980-81, exec. officer 501 S&T Batallion, 1981-83; dept. G-4 1st Armored Divsn. U.S. Army, Ansbach, Germany, 1983-84; chief logistics initiatives U.S. Army Logistics Ctr., Ft. Lee, Va., 1984-88; chief logistics concepts Quartermaster sch. U.S. Army, Ft. Lee, Va., 1988-91; project mgr. Mil. Profl. Resources, Inc., Ft. Lee, 1991—; v.p. Highty Tighty Alumni Inc., Blacksburg, Va., 1992—. Asst. scoutmaster Boy Scouts Am., Chester, Va., 1990—. Decorated Legion of Merit, bronze Star medal. Mem. Nat. Sojourners Inc. (pres. 1989-90), Sons of Confed. Vets., Masons, Shriner. Presbyterian. Home: 11440 Marsden Rd Chester VA 23831 Office: Military Professional Resources Inc PO Box 5203 Fort Lee VA 23801

JOHNSON, HENRY EUGENE, III, middle school educator; b. Hopewell, Va., Feb. 17, 1951; s. Henry E. Johnson Jr. and Sali (Wilson) Stegall; m. Laraine M. Johnson, July 6, 1973 (div. 1983); children: Catherine Hirst, Lara Webster; m. Roseanne Verrengia, Apr. 3, 1993; children: Matthew Verrengia, Nicholas Verrengia. BA, Fla. Atlantic U., 1973, MEd, 1979, EdS, 1982, EdD, 1988. Cert. tchr., Fla. Tchr. Horizon Elem. Sch., Sunrise, Fla., 1973-75; tchr. math. Bair Mid. Sch., Sunrise, 1975-82, tchr. English, 1978; tchr. math. Deerfield Beach (Fla.) Mid. Sch., 1983—, chmn. dept., 1984—, insvc. coord., 1986—; supr. testing Fla. Atlantic U., Boca Raton, 1982—; ednl. cons., 1987—; chmn. curriculum coun. Broward County Schs., Ft. Lauderdale, Fla., 1988—; dir. exceptional student edn. Hernando County, Fla., 1991—; dir. Ocala Ctr. of Saint Leo Coll.; presenter in field. Contbr. articles to profl. jours. Mem. Assn. for Supervision and Curriculum Devel., Nat. Coun. Tchrs. Math., Fla. Coun. Tchrs. Math., Broward County Coun. Tchrs. Math. (bd. dirs. dist. 5, 1974-80, Math. Tchr. of Yr. award 1985), Phi Delta Kappa. Republican. Episcopalian. Home and Office: 9299 Picasso St Spring Hill FL 34608-6345

JOHNSON, JAMES DOUGLAS, insurance executive; b. Atlanta, Nov. 17, 1950; s. Charles Raymond and Louise (Bradford) J.; m. Debra Danforth, Oct. 10, 1972 (div. June 1974); m. Linda Sue Gow, Feb. 12, 1983; 1 child, James Douglas Jr. Student, Community Coll. of Air Force, 1975-76, Daytona Beach Commumity Coll., 1976, Brevard Community Coll., 1978. Asst. dept. mgr. Sears Roebuck & Co., Atlanta, 1968-70; mng. ptnr. Dempsey Blanton Aviation Ins., Melbourne, Fla., 1975-83; br. mgr. NationAir Ins. Agys., Atlanta, 1983-85, exec. v.p., mktg. mgr., 1985—; adj. faculty mem. Fla. Inst. Tech., Melbourne, 1978-82; guest lectr. Ga. State U., Atlanta, 1984-86. Contbr. articles to profl. publs. Mem. Atlanta Regional Commn. Gen. Aviation System Plan Update Adv. Panel. With USAF, 1970-77. Mem. Ga. Air Transp. Assn. (bd. dirs. 1989-91, pres. 1992—), Nat. Air Transp. Assn., Nat. Bus. Aircraft Assn., Peachtree DeKalb Airport Assn. (bd. dirs. 1991), Aviation Ins. Assn., Metro Atlanta Aero Club, Shriners (founding mem. local temple 1980), Masons. Republican. Methodist. Home: 960 Thornbush Ct Lawrenceville GA 30245-7454 Office: NationAir Ins Agys PO Box 80525 Atlanta GA 30366-0525

JOHNSON, JAMES HAROLD, lawyer; b. Galesburg, Ill., May 3, 1944; s. Harold Frank and Marjorie Isabel (Liby) J.; m. Judith Eileen Moore, June 5, 1966; children: Todd James, Tiffany Nicole. BA, Colo. Coll., 1966; JD, U. Tex., 1969. Bar: N.Y. 1970, Colo. 1971, Tex. 1975. Assoc. Winthrop, Stimson, Putnam & Roberts, N.Y.C., 1969-70, Sherman & Howard, Denver, 1970-72; corp. counsel Tex. Instruments, Inc., Dallas, 1972-85; v.p., gen. counsel, sec. Am. Healthcare Mgmt., Dallas, 1985-86, Ornda Healthcorp, Dallas, 1986-94; shareholder Jenkens & Gilchrist, P.C., Dallas, 1994—. Mem. ABA, Tenn. Bar Assn., Am. Soc. Corp. Secs., Am. Acad. Hosp. Attys., Tex. Bar Assn., Nat. Health Lawyers Assn. Republican. Methodist. Home: 4513 Tuscany Dr Plano TX 75093-7043 Office: Jenkens & Gilchrist 1445 Ross Ave Ste 3200 Dallas TX 75202-2770

JOHNSON, JAMES HARVEY, veterinary medical educator; b. Snyder, Tex., May 16, 1945; s. Alba Vern and Virginia Pearl (Yoder) J.; m. Jocille Hanover, Aug. 10, 1968 (dec. Apr. 7, 1984); m. Alice Margaret Wolf, Mar. 10, 1985. BS, Tex. A&M U., 1968, DVM, 1969. Pvt. practice vet. medicine Bryan, Tex., 1964-72; rschs. USDA/Agrl. Rsch. Svc., College Station, Tex., 1972-77; wildlife artist Bryan, 1977-90; clin. resident in zool. medicine Tex. A&M U., College Station, 1990-93, clin. asst. prof., 1993—; cons. and lectr. in field. Contbr. articles to profl. jours. Named Tex. State Artist of the Yr. 1982-83, Tex. Legis. Mem. Am. Vet. Med. Assn., Assn. Avian Veterinarians, Am. Assn. Zoo Veterinarians, Am. Fedn. Herpetoculturists, Am. Fedn. Aviculture, Nat. Wildlife Fedn., Houston Avian Veterinarians, Sierra Vet. Med. Assn., Tex. Vet. Med. Assn. (avian practice com. 1992), Assn. Amphibian and Reptilian Veterinarians, Soc. for Study of Amphibians and Reptiles, Gamma Sigma Delta. Methodist. Home: 7198 Jones Rd Bryan TX 77807-9780 Office: Texas A&M Univ Coll Veterinary Medicine College Station TX 77843-4475

JOHNSON, JAMES HODGE, retired engineering company executive; b. Brantley, Ala., May 22, 1932; s. James Hodge Sr. and Julia Grace (McSwean) J.; m. Carol June Farris; 1 child, Mark Farris. BSChemE, U. Ala., Tuscaloosa, 1959; postgrad., Columbia U., 1978. Process engr. to gen. supt. Union Camp Corp., Savannah, Ga., 1959-73; v.p., div. mgr. Branchemco, Inc., Jacksonville, Fla., 1973-75; mill mgr. Champion Internat. Corp., Canton, N.C., 1975-79; resident mgr. Boise Cascade Corp., Rumford, Maine, 1979-81, St. Regis Paper Co., Jacksonville, 1982-83; gen. mfg. mgr. Kraft div. St. Regis Paper Co., West Nyack, N.Y., 1983-84; v.p., div. gen. mgr. Manville Forest Products Co., West Monroe, La., 1984-85; cons. Birmingham, Ala., 1986; dir. project devel. Rust Internat. Corp., Birmingham, 1987-94; ret., 1994. Rep. precinct leader Ga., Savannah, 1962-65; trustee Ind. Presbyn. Day Sch., Savannah; bd. dirs. Pine Tree Coun. Boy Scouts Am., Maine, 1975-79. With U.S. Army, 1953-56. Disting. Engring. fellow U. Ala., Tuscaloosa, 1988. Mem. Paper Industry Mgmt. Assn. (various positions Dixie div. 1975-79, program chmn. conf. 1979), Tech. Assn. Pulp and Paper Industry, Kiwanis (pres. 1990), Inverness Country Club, Toastmasters (pres. 1960-68), Tau Beta Pi. Republican. Presbyterian. Home: 3152 Bradford Pl Birmingham AL 35242-4602

JOHNSON, JAMES WILSON, pastor; b. Benson, N.C., Apr. 11, 1942; s. Roy Allen and Edna Mavoreen (Allen) J.; m. Charlotte Marie Smith, Aug. 15, 1964; children: Donna Marie, Johnnie Allen. BA in History and Edn., Meth. Coll., Fayetteville, N.C., 1964; postgrad., East Carolina U., 1964, Southeastern Bapt. Sem., Wake Forest, N.C., 1964—. Lic. to ministry So. Bapt. Conv., 1964, ordained, 1987. Interim pastor 15 chs., N.C., 1964-86; pastor Albertson (N.C.) Bapt. Ch., 1986—; driver edn. specialist N.C. Divsn. Motor Vehicles, Raleigh, 1968—; dir. brotherhood Ea. Bapt. Assn., Warsaw, 1987-91, chmn. nominating com., 1988-90, vice moderator, 1989-91, moderator, 1991-93, mem. numerous coms., 1968—. Bd. dirs. Duplin County Assn. for Retarded Citizens, 1969-79, v.p., 1975-77, pres., 1977-79. Mem. N.C. State Employees Assn. Home and Office: Albertson Bapt Ch 519 Boney St Wallace NC 28466-1830

JOHNSON, JANE PENELOPE, freelance writer; b. Danville, Ky., July 1, 1940; d. Buford Lee Carr and Emma Irene (Coldiron) Sebastian; m. William Evan Johnson, July 15, 1958; children: William Evan Jr., Robert Anthony. Grad., Famous Writer's Sch. Fiction, Westport, Conn., 1967; grad. writer's div., Newspaper Inst. Am., N.Y.C., 1969; LittD (hon.), The London Inst. Applied Rsch., 1993. Freelance writer Lexington, Ky., 1969—. Contbr. poetry to Worldwide Poetry Anthologies; contbr. articles to mags. Patron Menninger. Ennobled by Prince John, The Duke of Avram, Tasmania, Australia; semifinalist N.Am. Poetry Open; recipient 2 Editor's Choice awards for poetry Nat. Libr. of Poetry, 1994. Mem. NAFE, Smithsonian Assocs., Peale Ctr. for Christian Living, Sweet Adelines, Internat. Soc. Poets (life, advisor), Internat. Platform Assn., Nat. Writer's Club. Democrat. Office: PO Box 8013 Gardenside Br Lexington KY 40504

JOHNSON, JANET DROKE, legal secretary; b. Bristol, Tenn., Feb. 26, 1961; d. Jimmie D. and Nancy Bell (Sluder) Droke; children: Leslie Ann, Laurie Elizabeth. AA, East Tenn. State U., 1980; student, Milligan Coll., Johnson City, Tenn., 1988-89. With Sullivan County Election Commn., Blountville, Tenn., 1978; legal sec. Boarman & Vaughn, Johnson City, 1980-84; legal asst. Bob McD. Green and Assocs., Johnson City, 1985-89; fed. judicial sec. to U.S. cir. judge U.S. ct. Appeals, 4th Cir., Abingdon, Va., 1989—; mem. adv. bd. Legal Assistant Program, Milligan Coll., Johnson City, 1988-89. Asst. ch. clk., newsletter editor Bluff City Bapt. Ch., 1994—. Mem. ABA (assoc.), Tenn. Paralegal Assn. (treas. 1989, pub. rels. dir. 1990—), Appalachian Paralegal Assn., Fed. Judicial Secs. Assn. Republican. Home: PO Box 727 Bluff City TN 37618-0727 Office: US Court of Appeals 4th Cir PO Box 868 Abingdon VA 24212-0868

JOHNSON, JAY D., publishing executive; b. Amarillo, Tex., Mar. 13, 1962; s. Roy Lee and Annette (Hartman) J.; m. Rita Freeman, May 23, 1987. BA, U. North Tex., 1989. Asst. editor Beckett Publs., Dallas, 1989, assoc. editor, 1990, sr. editor, 1991, tech. svcs. mgr., 1992, mng. editor, 1992-94, dir. tech. svcs., dir. lic. products, 1996—. Recipient Publ. of the Yr. award Sports Collectibles Assn., 1992, 93. Mem. Am. Soc. Mag. Editors, Dallas Press Club. Office: Beckett Publs 15850 Dallas Pky Dallas TX 75248

JOHNSON, JENNIE, chaplain, social worker; b. Houston, Sept. 18, 1952; d. James L.C. and Marilyn Mildred (Frazier) J.; children: Thomas, Soniva. BS in Social Work, Tex. Woman's U., 1976; postgrad., Bishop's Sch. of Theology, Denver, 1979-80, Samaritan Theol. Sem., L.A., 1982-84, Episcopal Theol. Sem., Austin, Tex., 1986-87. Cert. social worker, Tex. Comdr. 94th Ord. Det. USAR, Ft. Carson, Colo., 1978-80; evaluator 1st maneuver tng. command USAR, Denver, 1980-81; prodn. control planner Elmo Semiconducter, L.A., 1981-83; quality control planner TRW Def. and Space Guidance, L.A., 1983-84; dir. chpt. svcs. Greater Amarillo (Tex.) Red Cross, 1985-86; chaplain Austin State Hosp., 1987-88, Brackenridge Hosp., Austin, 1988-91, Hospice Austin, 1992-95; asst. dir. Centex Chpt. ARC, Austin, Tex., 1995-96; conveener Integrity Austin, 1989-90, 92-94, 96—; presenter conf. Nat. Episcopal AIDS Coalition, Cin., 1990, mem., 1990—. Founding bd. dirs. Out Youth Austin/YWCA, 1990-92; mem. Tex. AIDS Network, Austin, 1992—; foster parent Casey Family Program, Austin, 1992-94; diocesan del. St. Michael's Episcopal Ch., Austin, 1988—, jr. warden, 1993-95, mem. vestry, 1993—, mem. com. for spiritual devel. of diocese; mem.-at-large Women for Social Witness Network, Nat. Episcopal Ch., 1992—; mem. Episcopal Womens Caucus, 1992—, Nat. Hospice Orgn., 1993—, Tex. Hospice Orgn., 1992—, presenter state conf., 1995, Order of St. Luke the Physician, 1984—. 1st lt. U.S. Army, 1975-80. Democrat. Office: Robinson Creek Home Care 1000 Westbank Dr Ste 6B-201 Austin TX 78746

JOHNSON, JERRY DOUGLAS, biology educator; b. Salina, Kans., Sept. 1, 1947; s. Maynard Eugene and Norma Maude (Moss) J.; m. Kathryn Ann Johnson, May 12, 1973; children: George Walker, Brett Arthur. BS in Zoology, Fort Hays State U., 1972; MS in Biology, U. Tex., El Paso, 1975; PhD in Wildlife Sci., Tex. A&M U., 1984. Teaching asst. biology dept. U. Tex., El Paso, 1973-75; instr. biology El Paso C.C., 1975—; adj. asst. prof. U. Tex., El Paso, 1984—; Piper prof. El Paso Community Coll., 1989-90; councilor bd. scientists Chihuahuan Desert Rsch. Inst., Alpine, Tex., 1991—. Co-author: Middle American Herpetology, 1988; contbr. articles to profl. jours. Bd. dirs. Meml. Park Improvement Assn., 1987—, El Paso Coun. for Internat. Visitors, 1988—, Parks and Recreation Bd., El Paso, 1991-94. Grantee Soc. Sigma Xi, 1974, Theodore Roosevelt Found. Am. Mus. Natural History, 1979, Exline Corp., 1980, NSF, 1992-96, NIH, 1992—; recipient El Paso Natural Gas Faculty Achievement award, 1995-96, Tchg. Excellence award Nat. Inst. for Staff and Orgnl. Devel., 1995-96. Mem. NSF, Nat. Ctr. for Acad. Achievement, Nat. Inst. Gen. Med. Sci., Soc. for Study of Amphibians and Reptiles (elector 1980, assoc. editor Geog. Distbn. Herpetol. Rev. 1993—), Southwestern Assn. Naturalists (assoc. editor 1977-85, bd. govs. 1985-89), Tex. Herpetol. Soc. (v.p., pres. 1995-96), El Paso Herpetol. Soc. (pres. 1993—), Herpetologists League, others. Home: 3147 Wheeling Ave El Paso TX 79930-4321 Office: El Paso CC Biology Dept PO Box 20500 El Paso TX 79998-0500

JOHNSON, JETSIE WHITE, nurse, consultant; b. Newport News, Va., Apr. 7, 1944; d. Breavoid Milton and Jetsie (Johnson) White; m. Henry Johnson Jr., Feb. 24, 1963; children: Cheryl Johnson Holmes, Henry Breavoid, Daryl Jay, Shamala Michelle. AAS magna cum laude, Thomas Nelson Community Coll., Hampton, Va., 1974; BS, Hampton U., 1985, MSN, 1987. RN, Va.; cert. family nurse practitioner, psychiat. clin. nurse specialist. Staff nurse Hampton Gen. Hosp., 1974-77; nurse practitioner Alvin Bryant, M.D., Hampton, 1978-80, VA Med. Ctr., Hampton, 1980-81; staff nurse VA Med. Ctr., Richmond, Va., 1983-84; nurse practitioner Naval Regional Med. Ctr., Norfolk, Va., 1981-82; nurse supr. Commonwealth Health Care, Hampton, 1982—; staff nurse Med. Coll. of Va., Richmond, 1988; nurse practitioner Ea. State Hosp., Williamsburg, Va., 1984-91; preceptor Old Dominion U., Norfolk, 1981-82, Hampton U., 1988-89; hon. instr. nurse practitioner program Med. Coll. of Va., 1979-80; cons. Alvin Bryant, M.D., 1981-91; mem. adv. coun. Hampton U. Nursing Ctr., 1989-90; pres. Minority Cancer Task Force, Hampton, 1989-92; corr. sec. Dept. Mental Health/Mental Retardation and Substance Abuse Svcs. Nurse Practitioner Practice Group, 1989-91. Co-leader Girl Scouts U.S., Hampton, 1985-86; v.p. La Progressive Ten, Hampton, 1982; pres. Young Profls. of Tidewater, Hampton, 1980-81. Recipient Cert. of Appreciation, Minority Cancer Task Force, 1985; NIMH Tng. grantee Dept. HHS, 1985, 86. Mem. Va. Coun. Nurse Practitioners, Phi Theta Kappa, Sigma Theta Tau. Democrat. Home: 66 Santa Barbara Dr Hampton VA 23666-1638

JOHNSON, JIMMY, professional football coach; b. Port Arthur, Tex., July 16, 1943. BA, U. Ark., 1965. Asst. coach Louisiana Tech. U., LA, 1965, Wichita State U., KS, 1967, Iowa State U., IA, 1968-68, U. Oklahoma, Norman, OK, 1970-72, U. Arkansas, AR, 1973-76, U. Pittsburg, 1977-78; head coach Oklahoma State U., OK, 1979-83, U. Miami, Miami, FL, 1983-88, Dallas Cowboys, Dallas, TX, 1989-94; sports commentator, football analyst Fox Network, 1994-95; head coach Miami Dolphins, 1996—. Coach NCAA Divsn. I championship team, 1987, Super Bowl (XXVII, XXVIII) championship team, 1992-93; named Coach of Yr. Walter Camp Found., 1986-87, NFL Coach of Yr. Coll. & Pro Football Newsweekly, 1990, UPI, 1990, AP, 1990, Football Digest, 1991; recipient Seattle Gold Helmet award, 1986. Office: Miami Dolphins 7500 SW 30th St Davie FL 33314-1020*

JOHNSON, JOHN RANDALL, SR., religious organization administrator; b. Marion, Va., July 26, 1945; s. Marvin Roy and Ida Alice (Roe) J.; m. Margaret Mae Sullivan, Aug. 8, 1965; children: John Jr., Brian, Joanna. BS in Mgmt., Va. Poly. Inst. and State U., 1971; MS in Mgmt., So. Nazarene U., 1984. Sec., treas., Christian edn. dir. Stoneville (N.C.) Internat. Pentecostal Holiness Ch., 1970-75; Sunday Sch. tchr. Bloomfield Dr. Internat. Pentecostal Holiness Ch., Macon, Ga., 1975-77, deacon, 1975-77, assoc. pastor, 1977-78; pastor Warner Robins (Ga.) Internat. Pentecostal Holiness Ch., 1978-79; contr. Internat. Pentecostal Holiness Ch., Oklahoma City, 1979—, sec.-treas., bd. dirs. Ext. Loan Fund, 1993—; adj. prof. Southwestern Coll. Christian Ministries, Bethany, Okla., 1985-90. Elder N.W. Christian Ctr., Oklahoma City, 1990—. Mem. Am. Mgmt. Assn., Nat. Assn. Evangelicals (mem.-at-large affiliate Christian Stewardship Assn. 1981—), Inst. Mgmt. Accts. Republican. Office: Intl Pentecostal Holiness Church 7300 NW 39th Expy Bethany OK 73008-2340

JOHNSON, JOHN ROBERT, petroleum company executive; b. Omaha, Apr. 17, 1936; s. Robert William and Hazel Marguerite (White) J.; BS, Davidson Coll., 1958; m. Margaret Elizabeth Roberts, June 20, 1959; children: Robert Harle, Martha Elizabeth. With Johnson Oil Co. Inc., Morristown, Tenn., 1961—, pres., 1963—; dir. Lakeway Pubs., First Vantage Bank; appointed Tenn. Petroleum Underground Storage Tank Bd., 1991—. Magistrate, Hamblen County Ct., 1968-78, chmn., 1971-72; pres. Hamblen County United Fund, 1969; pres. Great Smoky Mountain Coun. Boy Scouts

Am., 1977-78, 86; mayor Morristown, 1977-87, 91-95; mem. Tenn. Adv. Commn. on Intergovtl. Rels., 1987-95. Lt. U.S. Army, 1958-61. Recipient Disting. Svc. award Morristown Jr. C. of C., 1966; named Tenn. Mayor of Yr., Tenn. Mcpl. League, 1983. Mem. Morristown C. of C. (pres. 1976), Tenn. Oil Marketers Assn., Rotary. Democrat. Episcopalian Home: 1525 Morningside Dr Morristown TN 37814-5448 Office: 1206 S Cumberland St Morristown TN 37813-2615

JOHNSON, JOHNNY, research psychologist, consultant; b. Clarksdale, Miss., Jan. 10, 1938; s. Eddie B. and Elizabeth (Ousley) J.; children: Tonya, Anita. Student, Coahoma Jr. Coll., 1957, Hunter Coll., 1964, N.Y.U., 1963; BS, Tenn. State U., 1970, MS, 1974; postgrad., Saybrook Inst., 1987-89. Instr. Dept. of the Navy, Millington, Tenn., 1976-80, edn. specialist, 1980-87, curriculum advisor, 1987-88; prof. human resources mgmt. Pepperdine U., L.A., 1975-77; prof. psychology Shelby State C.C., Memphis, Tenn., 1985—. Actor: (films) Elvis, 1989, Memphis, 1990, The Firm, 1993, A Family Thing, 1995; recording artist with releases in jazz, blues and Latino. With USN, 1957-63. Mem. APA (assoc.), Am. Psychol. Soc., Soc. Psychol. Study of Social Issues, Assn. Black Psychologists, Soc. Psychol. Study Gay and Lesbian Issues, Internat. Platform Assn. Home: 773 Margie Dr Memphis TN 38127-2727

JOHNSON, JOHNNY, police chief. Chief Birmingham (Ala.) Police Dept. Office: Office of the Police Chief 710 20th St N Birmingham AL 35203-2216

JOHNSON, JOSEPH BENJAMIN, university president; b. New Orleans, Sept. 16, 1934; s. Sidney Thomas and Lillie Mickens J.; m. Lula Young; children—Yolanda, Joseph, Juliet, Julie. B.S., Grambling State U., 1957; M.S., U. Colo., 1967, Ed.D., 1973; postgrad., Harvard U., 1975-76; PhD (hon.), Gandhigram Rural U., Tamilnadu, India; LLD (hon.), Western Mich. U. Tchr. George Washington Carver High Sch., Shreveport, La., 1960-61, Booker T. Washington High Sch., Shreveport, 1962-63; with U. Colo., Boulder, 1969-77, exec. asst. to pres., 1975-77; pres. Grambling (La.) State U., 1977-91, Talladega (Ala.) Coll., 1991—; adv. Office Ednl. Rsch. and Improvement, U.S. Dept. Edn. Mem. Task Force on Econ. Devel., State of La., Commn. Colls. and Schs. So. Assn.; trustee Gulf South Research Inst.; mem. Steering Com. for Historically Black Colls., Ednl. Testing Service; past chmn. bd. dirs. Nat. Assn. for Equal Opportunity in Higher Edn.; mem. adv. com. Office for Advancement of Public Negro Colls.; past chmn. acad. adv. com. Black Entertainment TV; mem. La. State Fair; mem. bd. advs. La. Ctr. for the Blind; bd. dirs. Who's Who in the South and Southwest. Served with U.S. Army, 1958-60, 61-62. Recipient Thurgood Marshall Edn. Achievement award, W.E.B. Dubois award Assn. Social and Behavioral Scientists Inc., Jewish Tree of Life award; named to La. Black History Hall of Fame, 1991. Mem. Am. Assn. Adminstrs. Higher Edn., Am. Assn. Univ. Adminstrs., La. Assn. Educators, Am. Council Edn., Am. Assn. State Colls. and Univs. (mem. humanities com., com. on acad. and student personnel, com. on sci. and tech.), Nat. Assn. State Univs. and Land-Grant Colls., Nat. Black Alliance Grad. Level Educators, La. Edn. Research Assn., NCAA (pres.'s commn.), U. Colo. at Boulder Alumni Assn. (bd. dirs.), Phi Delta Kappa, Kappa Alpha Psi, Kappa Delta Pi. Office: Talladega Coll 627 Battle St W Talladega AL 35160-2354

JOHNSON, JOSEPH CLAYTON, JR., lawyer; b. Vicksburg, Miss., Nov. 15, 1943; s. Joseph Clayton and Rose Butler (Levy) J.; m. Cherrian Frances Turpin, Oct. 24, 1970; children: Mary Clayton, Erik Cole. BS, La. State U., 1965, JD, 1969. Bar: La. 1969, U.S. Dist. Ct. (ea. dist.) La. 1969, U.S. Dist. Ct. (mid. dist.) La. 1969, U.S. Dist. Ct. (we. dist.) La. 1979, U.S. Ct. Appeals (5th cir.) 1982. Ptnr. Taylor, Porter, Brooks & Phillips, Baton Rouge, 1969—; mem. civil justice reform act com. U.S. Dist. Ct. (mid. dist.) La., 1995—, chmn. 1996—. Bd. Editors Oil and Gas Reporter. Pres. Baton Rouge area Am. Cancer Soc., 1987-88. Served with U.S. Army, 1969-75. Mem. ABA, La. Bar Assn. (mem. ho. of dels. 1979-92, council rep. mineral law sect. 1986-94, chmn. mineral law sect. 1992-93), La. State Law Inst. (mineral code com.), Baton Rouge Bar Assn., Dean Henry George McMahon Am. Inn of Ct. Republican. Methodist. Club: Kiwanis. Office: PO Box 2471 Baton Rouge LA 70821-2471

JOHNSON, JUDY SHERRILL, secondary school educator, educational consultant; b. McComb, Miss., Aug. 27, 1944; d. Samuel Benton and Eunice (Ikard) Sherrill; m. Bill Johnson, Dec. 27, 1985; stepchildren: Christie, Karen, Laurie, Leslie. BSC, U. Miss., 1966; postgrad. U. Fla., 1967, Fla. Atlantic U., 1971, 73, 76, U. Cen. Fla., 1984, Ark. State U., 1981. Lic. tchr. N.C., Tenn., Ala., Fla., Miss. Mem. faculty Santa Fe Jr. Coll., Gainesville, Fla., 1966-68, Broward County Bd. Pub. Instrn., Ft. Lauderdale, Fla., 1968-76; tchr. Huntsville City Sch., Ala., 1976-81; ednl. cons., sales rep. McGraw-Hill Book Co., N.Y.C., 1981-85; cons. Hillsborough County Bus. Edn. Tchrs., Tampa, Fla., 1982; mem. adv. bd. Pinellas County Indsl. Arts Dept., Clearwater, Fla., 1982-84; mem. adv. bd. bus. edn. Pinellas County, Clearwater, 1984-85, Hillsborough High Sch., Tampa, 1982-85, Gaither High Sch., Tampa, 1984-85, chmn. adv. bd. adult night sch., 1985; judge state FBLA contests Miss., 1977, Fla., 1982-85. Active Rep. Party of Fla., 1982-85; mem. Symphony Guild, Ft. Lauderdale; project advisor Huntsville Christian Women's Club, 1987-88; sec. United Meth. Women's Club First United Meth. Ch., 1988; v.p. Heritage Quilters Huntsville, 1987-88, pres., 1988-89; chair mini-retreat First United Meth. Ch., Huntsville, 1988-89, chmn. evangelism work area, 1992-93; mem. planning com. Tenn. Valley Women's Retreat, 1988-94; tchr., leader Precept Bible Study, Precept Ministeries, 1988-90, Community Bible Study, 1989-90, core leader, 90-91, co-dir. internat. teaching dirs conf., 1990; tchr. Disciple Bible Study, 1993, 94; vice chair FUMC Coun. on Ministries, 1993, chair, 1994; vol. Huntsville Land Trust, 1988-89. Named Runner-up Advisor of Yr. Fla. Future Bus. Leaders Am., 1974. Mem. Delta Pi Epsilon, Alpha Delta Kappa (treas. 1980-81, various coms.), Phi Mu Alumnae (pres. 1969-71, collegiate dir. State of Fla. 1968-69, state day coord. 1970), Beta Sigma Phi, Phi Beta Lambda Alumnae, du Midi Gen. Federated Women's Club (publicity chmn. 1989-90, bd. dirs. 1991-93), Women's Guild of Huntsville Mus. of Art, Garden Guild of Botanical Gardens of Huntsville (chmn. long range planning com. 1991-93, sec. 1992-93, v.p. 1993-95, pres. 1995-96). Avocations: cross stitch, sewing, fishing, gardening. Home: 1409 Governors Dr SE Huntsville AL 35801-1319

JOHNSON, KATHERINE ANNE, health research administrator, lawyer; b. Medford, Mass., Apr. 20, 1947; d. Lester and Eileen Anne (Henaghan) J. BS, La. State U., 1969; MSA, George Washington U., 1972; JD, Cath. U., 1985. Bar: Md. 1985. Pub. health adviser HHS, Washington, 1970-76; dir. plan implementation SE Colo. Health Systems Agy, Colorado Springs, 1976-78; sr. mng. assoc. CDP Assocs., Inc., Atlanta, 1978-87, dir. legal affairs, 1986-87; v.p. Cancer CarePoint Inc., Atlanta, 1987; sr. mgr. Salick Health Care, Inc., Bethesda, Md., 1987-89; pvt. practice atty. cons., Potomac, Md., 1989-90; assoc. dir. for adminstrn. San Antonio Cancer Inst., 1990-96; dir. planning and adminstrn. CTRC Rsch. Found., San Antonio, 1996—; speaker in field. Contbr. articles to profl. jours. Vol. Ct.-Apptd. Spl. Adv. for Abused Children. Mem. Md. Bar Assn., Nat. Health Lawyers Assn., Am. Acad. of Soc. Rsch. Adminstrs., Healthcare Attys., Leadership Tex. Class of 1996. Office: CTRC Rsch Found 8122 Datapoint Dr Ste 600 San Antonio TX 78229-3264

JOHNSON, KATHRYN WEISNER, librarian; b. Karnack, Tex., Nov. 29, 1938; d. James and Thelma (Thomas) Weisner; m. Clifton Johnny Johnson, Jr., Aug. 21, 1961; children: Clifton Johnny III, Carl James, Christopher Joseph, Craig Jerome, Curt Johans. BS, Prairie View A&M, 1961; MS in Libr. Sci., Atlanta U., 1967. Tchr., libr. Galena Park (Tex.) High Sch., 1961-62, Fouke Hawkins (Tex.) High Sch., 1963-65; libr. assoc. Jarvis Cristian Coll., Hawkins, 1965-67; cataloger serials J. B. Cade Libr. So. U., Baton Rouge, La., 1972-82, acquisitions libr., 1982-86, collections devel. libr., 1985-87, reference and collection devel. libr., 1986—. Mem. ALA, La. Libr. Assn., Mensa. Jehovah's Witness. Home: 3517 Lavey Ln Baker LA 70714-3761 Office: So U Southern Br # PO Baton Rouge LA 70813

JOHNSON, KENNETH PAUL, librarian, writer; b. Norfolk, Va., Nov. 18, 1953; s. William Frederick and Elizabeth (Rice) J. BA, Centenary Coll., 1975; MLS, U. Ala., Tuscaloosa, 1977. Reference libr. Chesapeake (Va.) Pub. Libr., 1977-78, br. libr., 1978-84; dir. W.C. Rawls Libr. & Mus., Courtland, Va., 1984-88, Meherrin Regional Libr., Lawrenceville, Va., 1988-89; asst. dir. Halifax County/South Boston (Va.) Regional Libr., 1990—. Author: In Search of the Masters, 1990, The Masters Revealed, 1993, Initiates of Theosophical Masters, 1995. Co-chmn. Festival of Arts, South Boston, 1993; bd. dirs. Parsons-Bruce Art Assn., South Boston, 1992-96, Southside Art Bank, Lawrenceville, Va., 1988-89. Mem. Assn. for Rsch. and Enlightenment, Va. Libr. Assn. Office: Halifax County South Regional Libr 509 Broad St South Boston VA 24592-3225

JOHNSON, LADY BIRD (MRS. LYNDON BAINES JOHNSON), widow of former President of U.S.; b. Karnack, Tex., Dec. 22, 1912; d. Thomas Jefferson Taylor; B.A., U. Tex., 1933, B.Journalism, 1934, D.Letters, 1964; LL.D., Tex. Woman's U., 1964; D.Letters, Middlebury Coll., 1967; L.H.D., Williams Coll., 1967, U. Ala., 1975; H.H.D., Southwestern U., 1967; m. Lyndon Baines Johnson (36th Pres. U.S.), Nov. 17, 1934 (died Jan. 22, 1973); children: Lynda Bird Johnson Robb, Luci Baines. Mgr. husband's congl. office, Washington, 1941-42; owner, operator radio-TV sta. KTBC, Austin, Tex., 1942-63, cattle ranches, Tex., 1943—. Hon. chmn. Nat. Head-start Program, 1963-68, Town Lake Beautification Project; also cotton and timberlands, Ala. Mem. Advisory council Nat. Parks, Historic Sites, Bldgs. and Monuments; bd. regents U. Tex., 1971-77, mem. internat. conf. steering com., 1969; trustee Jackson Hole Preserve, Am. Conservation Assn., Nat. Geog. Soc.; founder Nat. Wildflower Research Ctr., Austin, 1982. Recipient Togetherness award Marge Champion, 1958; Humanitarian award B'nai B'rith, 1961; Businesswoman's award Bus. and Profl. Women's Club, 1961; Theta Sigma Phi citation, 1962; Disting. Achievement award Washington Heart Assn., 1962; Industry citation Am. Women in Radio and Television, 1963; Humanitarian citation Vols. of Am., 1963; Peabody award for White House TV visit, 1966; Eleanor Roosevelt Golden Candlestick award Women's Nat. Press Club; Damon Woods Meml. award Indsl. Designers Soc. Am., 1972; Conservation Service award Dept. Interior, 1974; Disting. award Am. Legion, 1975; Woman of Year award Ladies Home Jour., 1975; Medal of Freedom, 1977; Nat. Achievement award Am. Hort. Soc., 1984. Life mem. U. Tex. Ex-Students Assn. Episcopalian. Author: A White House Diary, 1970. Address: LBJ Libr 2313 Red River St Austin TX 78705-5702*

JOHNSON, LELAND "LEE" HARRY, social services administrator; b. Moscow Twp., Wis., Jan. 30, 1947; s. Amos Sanford and Bethellen (Otto) J.; m. Laurel Landry; children: Najib, Zack, Jessica, Karine. B degree, Gettysburg Coll., 1969; M degree, Ind. U.-Purdue U., 1971. Supr. psychiat. social work Rock County Guidance Clinic, Beloit, Wis., 1971-73; acting adminstr. Rock County Guidance Clinic, Janesville, Wis., 1974; program dir., coord. Rock County Mental Health Svcs., 1974-75; program dir. Columbia County Home & Unified Bd., Portage, Wis., 1975; svcs. program dir. Columbia County Home & Unified Bd., Portage, Wyocena, Wis., 1975-77; dir. human svcs. Columbia County Health Svcs., Portage, 1977; exec. dir. Navajo County Guidance Clinic, Winslow, Ariz., 1977-78, Coconino Community Guidance Ctr. Inc., Flagstaff, Ariz., 1978-85; human svcs. dir Eau Claire (Wis.) County Human Svcs., 1985-89; from dep. dist. adminstr. to dist. adminstr. Fla. Dept. Health & Rehab. Svcs., Jacksonville, 1989—. Mem. NASW, Acad. Cert. Social Workers. Home: 219 Sequoia Saint Augustine FL 32086 Office: Dept Health & Rehab Svcs 5920 Arlington Expy Jacksonville FL 32211-7156

JOHNSON, LEONARD HJALMA, lawyer; b. Thomasville, Ga., May 22, 1957; s. Hjalma Eugene and Laura Nell (McLeod) J.; m. Nancy Louise Brock, Dec. 13, 1981; children: Brock Hjalma, Paige McLeod. BBA, U. Fla., 1978, JD, 1980. bd. dirs., vice chmn. Lake State Bank, Land O'Lakes, Fla., 1989—. Assoc. Dayton, Sumner, Luckie and McKnight, Dade City, 1981-83, Greenfelder and Mander, Dade City, 1983-84; pres. East Coast Bank Corp., Ormond Beach, Fla., 1982—; pvt. practice Dade City, 1984-89; ptnr. Schrader, Johnson, Auvil & Brock, P.A., Dade City, 1990—; vice chmn. Bank of Madison (Fla.) County, 1985-88, N. Fla. Bank Corp., Madison, 1985-88, Bank at Ormond By-the-Sea, 1985—; bd. dirs. Lake State Bank, Land O' Lakes, Fla. Bd. dirs. Downtown Dade City Main St. Inc., 1987—; trustee Dade City Hosp., 1994—, chmn., 1996; mem. Leadership Fla. Mem. ABA, Fla. Bar Assn., Pasco County Bar Assn. (sec. 1982-83), Young Pres. Orgn., Dade City C. of C., Fla. Blue Key. Republican. Methodist.

JOHNSON, LEONARD ROY, physiologist, educator; b. Chgo., Jan. 31, 1942; s. Leonard W. and Pearl A. Johnson; children: Melinda, Ashley, Matthew. BA, Wabash Coll., 1963; PhD, U. Mich., 1967; MD (hon.), U. Krakow, Poland, 1990. Instr. med. sch. UCLA, L.A., 1967-69; asst. prof. med. sch. U. Okla., Oklahoma City, 1969-71, assoc. prof., 1971-72; prof. med. sch. U. Tex., Houston, 1972-89; prof., chmn. U. Tenn. Coll. Medicine, Memphis, 1989—; chmn. physiology test com. Nat. Bd. Med. Examiners, Phila., 1989-91. Editor: Gastrointestinal Physiology, 4th edit., 1991, Physiology of the Gastrointestinal Tract, 3rd edit., 1994, Essential Medical Physiology, 1992. Recipient Merit award NIH, 1988; named R.D. McKenna Meml. Lect., Can. Assn. Gastroenterologists, 1996. Mem. Am. Physiol. Soc. (chmn. publs. 1993—, Horace W. Davenport Disting. lectr. 1995), Am. Gastroent. Assn., Polish Physiol. Soc. (hon.). Home: 7396 Twiller Cir Memphis TN 38133 Office: U Tenn Coll Medicine Dept Physiology 894 Union Ave Memphis TN 38103-3514

JOHNSON, LESLIE DIANE HORVATH, artist, graphic designer, small business owner; b. Trenton, N.J., Sept. 10, 1951; d. Lester Walter and M. Lee (Green) Horvath; m. Douglas James Johnson, Sep. 1, 1973. BA in Art Edn., Ohio State U., 1973. Graphic artist, tchr. various orgns., 1973-84; owner Southwind Studios, Forest, Va., 1981—; lectr. Liberty U., Forest Pub. Schs., Lynchburg Pub. Schs., Heritage Bapt. Ch., Lynchburg Art Club, others. Illus.: If I Had Long, Long Hair, 1986 (award 1987); artist pastel and acrylic paintings, 1985—. Recipient George Innes Jr. Meml. award for Best Pastel, The Salmagundi Club, N.Y.C., 1991. Mem. Nat. Assn. of Fine Artists, Pastel Soc. of Am. Home and Office: 204 Chelsea Dr Forest VA 24551

JOHNSON, LILLIAN BEATRICE, sociologist, educator, counselor; b. Wilmington, N.C., Nov. 8, 1922; d. James Archie and Mary Gaston (Atkins) J. AA, Peace Coll., 1940; BRE, Presbyterian Sch. Christian Edn., 1942; MS, N.C. State U., 1965, PhD, 1972. Dir. Christian edn. First Presbyn. Ch., Pensacola, Fla., 1945-47, Greenwood, S.C., 1947-48, Durham, N.C., 1948-51; club dir. Army Spl. Svcs., No. Command, Japan, 1951-53; teenage dir. YWCA, Washington, 1953-56, assoc. exec. Honolulu, 1956-59, exec. dir. Tulsa, 1959-62; instr. N.C. State U., 1962-72; asst. prof. Greensboro Coll., 1972-75; mem. faculty sociology dept. Livingston U., 1975-89, emerita prof., 1989—; pvt. practice family counselor, Fayetteville, N.C., 1989—. Ct. counselor, mediator Cumberland County Dispute Resolution Ctr. Mem. DAR (treas. Robert Rowan chpt.). Home: 325 N Cool Spring St Apt 202 Fayetteville NC 28301 Office: 155 Gillespie St Fayetteville NC 28301-5670

JOHNSON, LINDA KAYE, art educator; b. Port Lyautey, Morocco, Feb. 6, 1956; d. Arthur Joseph and Iona Belle (Marshall) J. BFA, Radford U., 1980; MS in Art Edn., Fla. State U., 1994. Art instr. dept. psychology Fla. State U., Tallahassee, summers 1985,86; art instr. Western Psychiat. Inst. and Clinic, Pitts., summers 1987-89, Blacksburg (Va.) Mid. Sch., 1981; jeweler Tallahassee, 1981-85; art instr. Fla. Pub. Schs., Fla., 1985—; participant Nat. Assessment of Edn. Progress, Fla. Team, 1994; chmn. Winter Festival Youth Art Show, Tallahassee, 1992, 93, 95; participating artist Very Spl. Arts Festival, Tallahassee, 1986-90; field test coord. Fla. Inst. for Art Edn.-CHAT, Tallahassee, 1992, 93; co-chair Arts for a Complete Edn. Coalition, 1993-96. Grantee Leon County Tchr.'s Assn., Tallahassee, 1992, Gadsden (Fla.) Edn. Found., 1986, 87. Mem. NEA, Profl. Art Instrs. Near Talla (pres. 1991-93), Fla. Art Educators Assn. (Fla. Mid. Sch. Art Educator of Yr. 1993), Nat. Art Educators Assn., Fla. Teaching Profession.

JOHNSON, LIZABETH LETTIE, insurance agent; b. Dallas, Aug. 24, 1957; d. Winfred Herschel Johnson and Mary Francis (Flowers) Goff; children: Brandi, Elissa. Student, Georgetown (Ky.) Coll., 1975-76, U. Ky., 1976-78. Staff analyst Met. Ins. Co., Lexington, 1979-81, ins. agt., 1981-82; sr. account agt. Allstate Ins. Co., Lexington, 1982—. Vol. Big Bros./Big Sisters, 1979-84, Life Adventure Camp, 1989-92; hotline counselor Lexington Rape Crisis Ctr., 1984-92, bd. dirs., 1988-91; vol. Christians in Comty. Svc., 1986-93; mem. Bluegrass Adoptive Parent Support Group, 1985-92. Fellow Life Underwriting Tng. Council; mem. NAACP, Nat. Assn. Life Underwriters, Progressive Execs. Democrat. Baptist. Office: Allstate Ins Co 694 New Circle Rd NE Rm 3 Lexington KY 40505-4513

JOHNSON, LONNIE, special education educator; b. Atoka, Okla., Feb. 28, 1934; s. Della (Wright) J.; m. Grace Malone, Dec. 26, 1962; children: Donna Renee, Lonnie Jr. BA in Polit. Sci., Northeastern U., Tahlequah, Okla., 1965; D Religion, Jackson Sem., North Little Roc, Ark., 1970; MA in Teaching, Oklahoma City U., 1983; LittD (hon.), Immaculate Conception Sem., Troy, N.Y., 1971. Cert. spl. edn. and polit. sci. tchr., Okla.; ordained to ministry A.M.E. Ch., 1958. Commr. City of Sapulpa, Okla., 1958-60; social worker Dept. Pub. Welfare, Tulsa, 1960-62; tchr. Kansas City (Mo.) Pub. Schs., 1962-65; counselor, dir. Neighborhood Youth Corp., Lawton, Okla., 1965-70; pres. Shorter Coll., North Little Rock, 1970-72; officer-in-charge USDA, Oklahoma City, 1972-78; pastor Allen Chapel A.M.E. Ch., Oklahoma City, 1978-81; tchr. spl. edn. Capital Hill High Sch., Oklahoma City, 1981—; cons. Govt. of Lesotho, Maseru, 1980—, A.M.E. Ch. in Haiti, 1981—. Founder World Hunger Orgn., 1978; cons. Walters for Gov., Oklahoma City, 1990. With USAF, 1955-56. Mem. Coun. for Exceptional Children, Am. Fedn. Tchrs., Alpha Phi Alpha (life). Democrat. Home: 6209 SE 57th St Oklahoma City OK 73135-5401

JOHNSON, MARGARET ANNE, sociologist; b. Ypsilanti, Mich., Oct. 23, 1964; d. John Daniel and Clarie Elaine (Campbell) J.; m. Murat Cil. BA in Sociology with honors, Tex. A&M U., 1987; MA in Sociology, U. Tex., 1990, PhD in Sociology, 1993. Teaching asst. in introductory sociology U. Tex., Austin, 1987-88, 91, teaching asst. liberal arts computer lab., 1988-89; rsch. asst., 1989-93; rsch. assoc. Population Studies Ctr. Urban Inst., 1990; lectr. social stats. and population problems U. Tex., Austin, 1993-94; asst. prof. sociology Okla. State U., Stillwater, 1994—. Contbr. articles to profl. publs. Bd. dirs. Payne County Habitat for Humanity. Dan Russell Sociology scholar, 1986; fellow Ctr. on Philanthropy, Ind., 1992-93. Mem. AAUW (v.p. membership Stillwater chpt.), Am. Sociol. Assn., Assn. Rsch. on Nonprofit Orgns. and Voluntary Action, Southwestern Social Sci. Assn., Sociologists for Women in Soc., Alpha Phi Omega. Office: Okla State U Dept Sociology 006CLB Stillwater OK 74078

JOHNSON, MARILYN, obstetrician, gynecologist; b. Houston, May 7, 1925; d. William Walton and Marilyn (Henderson) J.; B.A., Rice Inst., 1945; M.D., Baylor U., 1950. Intern, New Eng. Hosp. Women and Children, Boston, 1950-51; resident Meth. Hosp., Houston, 1951-53; resident in gynecology M.D. Anderson Tumor Inst., Houston, 1954, fellow, 1955; fellow in gynecol. pathology Harvard Med. Sch., 1952-53; practice medicine specializing in ob-gyn, Houston, 1954-81, Fredericksburg, Tex., 1981—; mem. staffs St. Joseph's, Meml., Meth., Park Plaza, Hill Country Meml. Rosewood, South Austin Community, Comfort (Tex.) Community hosps.; clin. instr. ob-gyn Coll. Medicine, Baylor U., 1954—, Postgrad. Sch. Medicine, U. Tex., 1954—; gynecologist De Pelchin Faith Home, Houston, 1954—, also Rice U., Richmond State Sch.; med. dirs. Birthright, Inc., Houston, 1973—; chief med. staff Hill Country Meml. Hosp., Fredericksburg, Tex., 1990-92; cons. Tex. bd. Blue Cross Blue Shield; pro-life public speaker. Bd. dirs. Right to Life, Houston, Found. for Life. Sandoz Labs. grantee, 1973, 75, Delbay Pharm. Co. grantee, 1977. Fellow Am. Coll. Obstetricians and Gynecologists; mem. AMA, Am. Soc. Colposcopic Pathologists, Tex. Med. Assn., Am. Med. Women's Assn., Internat. Infertility Assn., Harris County Med. Soc., Postgrad. med. Assembly S. Tex., Houston Ob-Gyn Soc., Tex. Folklore Soc. Republican. Baptist. Clubs: Zonta; Fredericksburg Rockhounds. Home: 205 S Orange St Fredericksburg TX 78624-3738 Office: 204 W Schubert St Fredericksburg TX 78624-3847

JOHNSON, MARK MATTHEW, museum administrator; b. Rochester, Minn., Dec. 10, 1950; s. Charles Michael Jr. and Jean Lee (Reid) J.; m. Amy Joy Schneider, Mar. 10, 1984. BA, U. Wis.-Whitewater, 1974; cert. Art Mus. Studies, U. Ill., 1976, MA, 1976. Teaching asst. art and design U. Ill., Urbana-Champaign, 1974-75; rsch. asst. Krannert Art Mus., Champaign, 1975; lectr. dept. mus. edn. Art Inst. Chgo., 1975-77; curator dept. art history and edn. Cleve. Mus. Art, 1977-81; asst. dir., keeper European collections Krannert Art Mus., 1981-85; dir. Muscarelle Mus. Art, Coll. William and Mary, Williamsburg, Va., 1985-94, lectr. dept. fine arts, 1985-94; dir. Montgomery (Ala.) Mus. Fine Arts, 1994—. Author: Idea to Image: Preparatory Studies from the Renaissance to Impressionism, 1980, Romeyn de Hooghe, 1989, Literacy Through Art, 1990, Nissan Engel: Nouvelles Dimensions, 1994, Hans Grohs: An Ecstatic Vision, 1996; organized, curated numerous exhbns., 1980—. Rsch. and travel grantee various mus. Mem. Assn. Art Mus. Dirs., Coll. Art Assn., Am. Assn. Mus. (accreditation com.), Internat. Coun. Mus. Office: Montgomery Mus Fine Arts PO Box 230819 One Museum Dr Montgomery AL 36123-0819

JOHNSON, MARSHALL HARDY, investment company executive; b. Raleigh, N.C., Sept. 7, 1923; s. William Thompson and Evie (Barnes) J.; m. Mary Lynn Lewis, June 24, 1947 (div. 1977); children: Marshall Hardy, Lynn Lewis Johnson-Titchener, Carter Johnson Overton; m. Beverly Ray Johnson, June 2, 1984. Student, U. N.C., 1942-43, 45-46; IBA, U. Pa., 1955-57. Reporter, analyst Dunn & Bradstreet, Raleigh, 1946-47; chmn., pres., CEO McDaniel Lewis & Co., Greensboro, N.C., 1947—; v.p. Scott & Stringfellow, Inc., Richmond, Va., 1993-96; mem. Midwest Stock Exch., Chgo., 1960-77; bd. dirs. First Citizen Bank & Trust, Greensboro, Mcpl. Coun., Raleigh; adv. dir. Friends Home, 1985-93. Contbr. articles to profl. jours. Dir. Young Dems., Greensboro, 1962-66, Jr. C. of C., Greensboro, 1964-70; deacon First Bapt. Ch., Greensboro. With USN, 1942-46. Fellow Fin. Fedn. Am.; mem. Am. Arbitration Assn. (nat. panel bd. 1963—), Nat. Assn. Securities Dealers (nat. panel arbitration 1985—), Securities Industries Assn. (Mid-Atlantic exec. com. 1986-93), Securities Dealers of Carolinas (pres. 1976), Magna Charta Baron, Odd Fellows, Kiwanis, Greensboro Country Club, City Club, Alpha Tau Omega. Home: 310 Kimberly Dr Greensboro NC 27408-5018 Office: McDaniel Lewis & Co 114 N Elm St Greensboro NC 27401-2241

JOHNSON, MARSON HARRY, criminologist; b. Lansing, Mich., Feb. 20, 1941; s. Harry Paul and Irene Vivian (Marquardt) J.; children: Marson Harry Jr., Caroline Jean, Sheryl Irene; m. Martha Kathleen Smith, May 1, 1994. BS, Mich. State U., 1969, MS, 1970, MA, 1973, PhD, 1980. V.p. Eaton Rapids (Mich.) Chem. Co., 1963; police officer Charlotte (Mich.) Police Dept., 1963-69; planning dir. Tri-County Regional Planning Commn., Lansing, Mich., 1969-72; asst. prof. W. Va. State Coll., Institute, 1972-74; dir. police svcs. Gaithersburg (Md.) Police Dept., 1974-77; instr. U. South Fla., Tampa, 1977-80; asst. prof. Pan Am. U., Edinburg, Tex., 1980-82; asst. dir. Fla. Inst. Law Enforcement, St. Petersburg, Fla., 1985-88; adminstr. U. South Fla., Lakeland, 1988—; pres. MHJ Criminal Justice Consultants, Tampa, 1982—; organizer delegation to Belarussia concerning criminal justice systems issues, 1993. Recipient Cert. of Appreciation, Internat. Assn. Chiefs Police, 1976-77, Miami Police Dept., 1988, CAUSE Vol. Search, 1984. Mem. Acad. Criminal Justice Scis., Am. Soc. Criminology, Police Mgmt. Assn., Fla. Council on Crime and Delinquency, Internat. Police Assn., Am. Legion, St. Patrick's day Assn., Charlotte Lodge, Saladin Temple. Home: 1655 Sailpoint Dr Bartow FL 33830-8409 Office: U South Fla 3433 Winter Lake Rd Lakeland FL 33803-9765

JOHNSON, MARY MURPHY, social services director, writer; b. N.Y.C., Mar. 5, 1940; d. Richard and Nora (Greene) Murphy; m. Noel James Johnson, Oct. 8, 1961; children: Valerie Johnson Powell, Donna Homan, Noreen Marie Pettitt, Richard. BA in English/History magna cum laude, Jacksonville State U., 1983, BS in Sociology magna cum laude, 1983, MA in History, 1984, B in Social Work magna cum laude, 1988. Cert. gerontology specialist. Asst. activities dir. Jacksonville (Ala.) Nursing Home, 1985-86; social services dir. Beckwood Manor, Anniston, Ala., 1987—; Cons. in field. Editor: Vladivostak Diary, 1987. Mem. AAU, Ala. Archaeol. Soc., Coosa Valley Archaeol. Soc. (sec. 1982-87), Soc. Ala. Archivists, Human Svcs. Coun., Vietnam Vets. Am., Soc. for Creative Anachronism (Reeve, Canton of the Peregrine), Phi Eta Sigma, Phi Alpha Theta, Sigma Tau Delta, Omicron Delta Kappa. Russian Orthodox.

JOHNSON, MIKE MCALLISTER, writer; b. Birmingham, Ala., Nov. 2, 1956; s. William Earl Jr. and Marilyn (McAllister) J. Grad. high sch., Brimingham. With Chariemagne Record Exch., Birmingham, Ala., 1987—. Author song lyrics and poems.

JOHNSON, MURRAY H., optometrist, researcher, consultant, lecturer; b. Montreal, Que., Can., Jan. 29, 1956; came to U.S., 1980; s. William and Leah (Bedzowski) J.; m. Linda Fluxman, Apr. 30, 1978; children: Warren Natan,

Tanya Yael, Arielle Carly. Diploma in Optometry, Witwatersrand Coll., Johannesburg, 1977; postgrad., U. Montreal, 1980; BS, U. Houston, 1981, OD, 1981, MSc in Physiol. Optics and Vision Sci., 1984; postgrad., U. Tex. Health Ctr., 1983. Lic. optometrist, Tex., therapeutic lic., Tex.; cert. ocular therapeutics for treatment and mgmt. ocular disease U. Houston. Clin. instr. U. Houston, 1981-85; researcher Inst. contact Lens Rsch., Houston, 1983-88; pvt. practice optometry specializing in contact lenses Eye & Contact Lens Assocs. North Tex., Dallas, 1985—; vis. asst. prof. U. Houston, 1984-85, adj. asst. prof., 1985-89; cons., clin. investigator Metro Optics, Inc., Dallas, 1989—; premktg. clin. evaluator, cons. and investigator to various contact lens and pharm. mfrs., 1989—; clin. investigator Paragon Optical, Mesa, Ariz., 1992; cons. Unilens Corp., Largo, Fla., 1989; bd. dirs. Equitable Bank-Dallas. Contbr. articles to profl. jours. Mem. clin. care com. Global Vision Inst., Global Vision Dallas, 1996—; mem. edn. com. Akiba Acad. Dallas, 1986-88, bd. dirs., 1986—, long range planning com., 1987-88, devel. com., 1993, v.p., treas., 1993-94, budget com., 1993—, scholarship com., 1994—; bd. dirs. Congregation Share Tefilla, Dallas, 1988-92; steering com. B'nai B'rith, 1986-88, treas., 1987-88; bd. dirs., assoc. bd. dirs. Equitable Bank, Dallas, 1994-96. Fellow U. Houston, 1981, grantee 1981, 82; Ezell Rsch. fellow Am. Optometric Found., 1983. Fellow Am. Acad. Optometry; mem. AAAS, Assn. Rsch. in Vision and Ophthalmology, Am. Pub. Health Assn. (vision care sect.), Am. Optometric Assn. (contact lens sect.), Tex. Optometric Assn., Dallas County Optometric Soc., Better Vision Inst., Am. Optometric Found. (Ezell fellows club), Sigma Xi. Jewish. Office: Eye & Contact Lens Assocs N Tex 18111 Preston Rd Ste 180 Dallas TX 75252-5470

JOHNSON, NAOMI BOWERS, nurse; b. Ft. Benning, Ga., Aug. 17, 1954; d. Bob and Henrietta Violet (Hoomalu) Bowers; m. James William Johnson, Dec. 7, 1973 (div.); children: Amelia, Melissa, Charity, James-William. ADN, Troy State U., Montgomery, Ala., 1974. Office supr., lab. supr., nursing coord. physician's office, Selma, Ala.; patients care coord. West. Ala. Home Health Agy., Selma; discharge planning/social svcs., SOBRA and clin. case mgmt. coord. Vaughan Regional Med. Ctr. Hosp., Selma; DON Dunn Nursing Home, Selma, Capitol Hill Health Care Ctr.

JOHNSON, NORMAN JAMES, physician, lawyer; b. Bklyn., Apr. 15, 1921; s. James Henry and Florence Gertrude (Crilley) J.; m. Bernadette Frances Lowe, Jan. 17, 1948; children: Michael Lowe, Christopher Day, Mark HUghes, David Hughes. AB magna cum laude, Fordham U., 1942; MD, SUNY, 1945; JD, U. Ga., 1979. Bar: Ga. 1981; cert. Am. Bd. Pediat., Am. Bd. Emergency Medicine. Intern Kings County Hosp., Bklyn., 1945-46; intern pediatrics The L.I. Coll. Hosp., Bklyn., 1948-49; resident cardiology Irvington House, Irvington-on-Hudson, N.Y., 1949-50; resident pediatrics Cin. Children's Hosp., 1950-51, chief resident pediatrics, 1951-52; assoc. prof. pediatrics U. Ark., Little Rock, 1952-56; chief pediats. Miners Meml. Hosp., Williamson, W.Va., 1956-59; asst. prof. pediatric medicine U. Tenn. Med. Sch., Memphis, 1959-61; from asst. chief to chief pediatrics Met. Hosp., Detroit, 1961-71; practice medicine specializing in pediats. Athens, Ga., 1972-77; clin. dir emergency medicine St. Mary's Hosp., Athens, 1976-86; with emergency medicine Hilton Head Hosp., Hilton Head Island, S.C., 1986-87; with Newton Gen. Hosp., Covington, Ga., 1987-95; instr. pediatrics U. Cin. , 1951-52, assoc. prof. pediatrics U. Ark., Little Rock, 1952-56, asst. prof. pediatrics U. Tenn., Memphis, 1959-61. Contbr. articles to profl. jours. Pres. PTA, Athens, 1975-76, Friends of Ga. Mus. of Art, Athens, U. Ga., 1985-86, 95-96. Capt. U.S. Army, 1946-48, PTO. Mem. ABA, AMA, Am. Acad. Pediatrics, Am. Coll. Emergency Physicians, Irish and Am. Pediat. Soc. Democrat. Roman Catholic. Home and Office: PO Box 305 Watkinsville GA 30677-0305

JOHNSON, OTTO BERNICE, JR., physician; b. Waynesboro, Ga., Mar. 12, 1939; s. Otto Bernice and Frances Elizabeth (Owens) J.; m. Susan Lillian D. Johnson, July 1, 1964; children: J. Daniel, R. Lee. BS, Emory U., 1961, MD, 1965. Diplomate Am. Bd. Internal Medicine, Am. Bd. Geriatrics. Intern U. Ala. Sch. Medicine, Birmingham, 1965-67, residency, 1969-71; MD Dublin (Ga.) Internal Medicine, 1971—; cjief of staff, Laurens Meml. Hosp., Dublin, Ga., 1974; pres. Laurens County Med. Soc., Dublin, Ga., 1974; CEO Dublin (Ga.) Internal Medicine, 1988-92; bd. trustees Laurens meml. Hos., Dublin, Ga., 1982-85, Fairview Park Hosp., 1982-85. Bd. trustees, adminstrv. bd., pres. Chancel choir First United Meth. Ch., 1988-92, 1993. Maj. U.S. Army, 1967-69, Vietnam. Recipient Combat Medics badge, Bronze Star, Purple Heart, Air Medal, U.S. Army, 1967-68. Mem. AMA, So. Med. Assn., Laurens County Med. Assn., Dublin Country Club. Office: Dublin Internal Medicine 104 Fairview Park Dr Dublin GA 31021-2500

JOHNSON, PAUL KIRK, JR., mental health nurse; b. Balt., July 27, 1951; s. Paul Kirk Sr. and Betty Lee (Duggan) J.; m. Janice Carolyn Long, Apr. 27, 1974; children: Paul K. III, Benjamin T. BSN, U. Md., 1979; MA in Health Svc. Mgmt., Webster U., 1987; MS Adult Psychiat. Mental Health Nursing, U. Ill., Chgo., 1989. Cert. clin. specialist in adult psychiat./mental health nursing, ANCC; advanced RN practitioner, Fla. Commd. ensign USN, 1979, advanced through grades to lt. comdr., 1989, navy hosp. corpsman, 1972-75; staff nurse Naval Hosp., San Diego, 1979-83; staff nurse, asst. family adv. Naval Hosp., Adak, Alaska, 1983-85; instr., psychiat. cons. Naval Hosp. Corps Sch., Great Lakes, Ill., 1985-88; clin. nurse specialist Naval Hosp., Jacksonville, Fla., 1989-92, USS Nassau Navy-Operation Desert Shield/Storm, 1990-91; ret. USN, 1992; asst. prof. Jacksonville (Fla.) U., 1992-94; clin. nurse specialist Bapt. Med. Ctr., Jacksonville, 1994-96; nurse practitioner Mental Health Ctr. Jacksonville, Inc., 1996—; adj. clin. instr. Jacksonville (Fla.) U., 1992. Contbr. chpt. to textbook. Decorated Navy Commendation medals USN, 1988, 92. Mem. Am. Coll. Counselors (clin. mem.), Sigma Theta Tau, Phi Kappa Phi. Home: 3836 Feather Oaks Dr E Jacksonville FL 32277-2293 Office: Mental Health Ctr of Jacksonville PO Box 9010 Jacksonville FL 32208

JOHNSON, PAUL MARSHALL, political science educator, consultant; b. Tulsa, Okla., Mar. 14, 1946; s. Charles Woodson and Frances Delane (Ebbs) J.; m. Armanda Margaret Sittig, Sept. 9, 1972; children: Charles Woodson II, Laura Elizabeth. BA in pol. sci. summa cum laude, Rice U., 1967; MA in pol. sci., Stanford U., 1968, PhD in pol. sci., 1978. Lecturer Yale U., 1976-78, asst. prof., 1978-81; asst. prof. Fla. State U., 1981-88; vis. asst. prof. U. Houston, Rice U., 1988-89; vis. lectr. U. Calif., Santa Cruz, 1989-90; asst. prof. Auburn U., Ala., 1991-92, assoc. prof., 1992—; Resident dir. Stanford U.-Universsytet Warszawski Exchange Program, Warsaw, Poland, 1973-74. Author: Redesigning the Communist Economy: The Politics of Economic Reform in Eastern Europe, 1989; co-author: Political Development and Political Change in Eastern Europe: A Comparative Study, 1976; co-editor: Rhythms in Politics and Economics, 1985; contbr. articles to profl. jours. With U. S. Army, 1969-71, Vietnam. Decorated Bronze Star medal, U.S. Army, 1971. Mem. Am. Political Sci. Assn., Am. Assn. Advancement of Slavic Studies, Internat Studies Assn. (governing coun. mem. 1982-84, nat. conv. program chmn. 1984). Office: Auburn U Dept Pol Sci 7080 Haley Ctr Auburn AL 36849

JOHNSON, PAUL VERNON, consulting civil engineer; b. Jackson, Mich., Aug. 13, 1950; s. Clifford and Donna Jean (Demorest) J.; m. Kathleen M. Tatti, Sept. 29, 1979; children: Paul J. T., Joseph P. T. BSCE, Mich. Tech. U., 1972. Registered profl. engr., Ga., Mich., Fla., La., Ark., Okla., Tex. Field engr. Pitometer Assocs., Chgo., 1973-81, dist. mgr., 1981-90, v.p., 1990—. Mem. Am. Water Works Assn. (contbr. papers), Ga. Water and Pollution Control Assn. Home: 860 Eagle Crossing Dr Lawrenceville GA 30244-5846

JOHNSON, PETER DEXTER, JR., mathematics educator; b. Elkin, N.C., May 4, 1945; s. Peter Dexter Sr. and Jessie (Jones) J.; m. Lesley Sanderson, Dec. 8, 1989 (div. Oct. 1995); stepson, Conor Christian; children: Chelsea Elspeth, Philip Sanderson. ScB in Applied Math., Brown U., 1967; PhD, U. Mich., 1973. Teaching fellow dept. math. U. Mich., Ann Arbor, 1968-73; asst. prof. dept. math. Emory U., Atlanta, 1973-74, Am. U. of Beirut, 1974-78; vis. assoc. prof. dept. math. U. Mich., Ann Arbor, 1978; assoc. prof. dept. math. Am. U., Beirut, 1979-80; assoc. prof. dept. math. Auburn (Ala.) U., 1982-88, prof. dept. math., 1988—; vis. asst. prof. Auburn U., 1978, 80-82; vis. asst. prof. dept. math. Kalamazoo Coll., 1979; vis. lectr. dept. math. U. Reading, Eng., 1983-85, 88-89. Co-author: Information Theory and Data Compression, 1996; editor: Geombinatorics; contbr. articles to profl. jours. Mem. steering com. Ams. for Justice in the Middle East, Beirut, 1977-78, 79-80; center fielder Faculty Softball Team, Beirut, 1977-78, 79-80; outfielder Hillel Softball Team, Auburn, 1985—, mgr., 1991-94. NDEA Title IV scholar, 1967-68; joint grantee Nat. Security Agy., 1987-89, NSF, 1994-97, ONR, 1995-97. Mem. Am. Math. Soc., Math. Assn. Am., Inst. Combinatorics and Its Applications, Sigma Xi (sec., treas. Beirut chpt. 1977-78). Home: 745 Sherwood Dr Auburn AL 36830-6045 Office: Auburn U Discrete Math 120 Math Annex Auburn AL 36849

JOHNSON, PETER FORBES, transportation executive, business owner; b. Salem, Mass., May 7, 1934; s. William Bennett and Sarah Loraine (Nee) J.; m. Mikell Kraus, Oct. 11, 1958; children: Krista, Todd, Karyn, Jennifer. BS, U.S. Mcht. Marine Acad., 1957. Deck officer Texaco, Port Arthur, Tex., 1958-63; from deck officer to master Reynolds Metals Co., Corpus Christi, Tex., 1963-65, port capt., 1965-68, operating mgr., 1968-71; internat. marine mgr. Gulf Miss. Marine Corp., New Orleans, 1971-72; cons. Peter F. Johnson & Assocs., New Orleans, 1972-73; exec. v.p. Pyramid Marine, Inc., New Orleans, 1973-76; pres., chief exec. officer, owner, chmn. bd. Pacific-Gulf Marine, Inc., New Orleans, 1976—; trustee Am. Maritime Officers, Dania, Fla., Seafarers Internat. Union, Camp Springs, Md., 1986—; bd. dirs. Nautilus Ocean Transport, Ltd., Islander Ship Holding, Inc., New Orleans. Lt. (j.g.) USNR, 1959-63. Mem. Coun. Am. Master Mariners, Soc. Naval Architects and Marine Engrs., Propeller Club U.S. (Maritime Man of Yr. 1986), U.S. Navy League, Southern Yacht Club, English Turn Country Club. Republican. Roman Catholic. Home: 3 Lakeway Ct New Orleans LA 70131 Office: Pacific Gulf Marine Inc PO Box 6479 New Orleans LA 70174-6479

JOHNSON, PHILIP LEWIS, retired research commission executive; b. Oneonta, N.Y., May 26, 1931; s. Robert A. and Hazel (Shaffer) J.; m. Judy Rodgers. BS in Agr., Purdue U., 1953, MS in Natural Resources, 1955; PhD in Plant Ecology, Duke U., 1961. Instr. botany U. Wyo., 1959-61; botanist U.S. Forest Svc., 1961-62; ecologist USA-CRREL, Hanover, N.H., 1962-67; assoc. prof. Sch. Forestry U. Ga., 1967-70, exec. dir. Environ. Ctr., 1979; divsn. dir. NSF, 1968-74; exec. dir. Oak Ridge Assoc. Univs., 1974-81; pres. John E. Gray Found., 1981-86; exec. dir. John E. Gray Instn., 1981-86, Arctic Rsch. Commn., Washington, Arlington, Va., 1988-94; asst. prof. biology Dartmouth Coll., 1963-67;. Contbr. more than 40 articles to profl. jours. With U.S. Army, 1955-57. James B. Duke fellow in botany Duke U., 1957-59. Fellow Arctic Inst. N.Am.; mem. AAAS, Ecol. Soc. Am., Brit. Ecol. Soc., N.Y. Acad. Scis., Sigma Xi. Home: 118 Maid Marion Pl Williamsburg VA 23185

JOHNSON, PHILIP WAYNE, lawyer; b. Greenwood, Ark., Oct. 24, 1944; s. John Luther and Flora (Joyce) J.; m. Carla Jean Newsom, Nov. 6, 1970; children—Betsy, Carl, Jeff, Laura, Philip. B.A., Tex. Tech U., 1965, J.D., 1975. Bar: Tex. 1975, U.S. Dist. Ct. (no. and we. dists.) Tex. 1976, U.S. Ct. Appeals (5th cir.) 1984, U.S. Supreme Ct. 1984; cert. in civil trial and personal injury trial law, Tex. Bd. Legal Specialization. Assoc. Crenshaw Dupree & Milam, Lubbock, Tex., 1975-80, ptnr., 1980—; mem. pattern jury charge and state judiciary rels com. State Bar Tex. Bd. dirs., pres. Lubbock County Legal Aid Soc., Tex., 1977-79; bd. dirs., chmn. Trinity Christian Schs., Lubbock, 1978-83, 85-89; bd. dirs., pres. S.W. Lighthouse for Blind, Lubbock, 1978-85 . Served to capt. USAF, 1965-72. Decorated Silver Star, D.F.C.; Cross of Gallantry (Vietnam). Fellow Am. Bar Found., Tex. Bar Found. (life); mem. ABA, Def. Rsch. Inst., Tex. Bar Assn., Tex. Assn. Def. Counsel (regional v.p. 1983-85, legislative v.p. 1992-93), Lubbock County Bar Assn. (pres. 1984-85), Phi Delta Phi. Home: 2301 60th St Lubbock TX 79412-3304 Office: Crenshaw Dupree & Milam 1500 Broadway St Lubbock TX 79401-3116

JOHNSON, RALPH RONALD, manufacturer's representative; b. Statesville, N.C., Feb. 17, 1936; s. Corbett Donald and Bertha (Mc Collum) J.; m. Jeffie Sue Chambers, Jan. 6, 1960 (div. June 1968); children: Jonathan Steven, Joel Starling III; m. June Love Washburn, Mar. 17, 1979; 1 child, Shanna Jonet. Salesman Am. Greetings Corp., Cleve., 1960-64, Esterbrook Pen Co., Cherry Hill, N.J., 1964-68, Champion Internat. Corp., Atlanta, 1968-71, Nat. Office Supply, Doraville, Ga., 1972-78, Sunbelt Mktg., N.A., Duluth, Ga., 1979—. Sgt. USMC, 1953-57, Korea. Republican. Baptist. Home: 1741 Mitzi Ct Duluth GA 30155 Office: Sunbelt Mktg NA 1741 Mitzi Ct Duluth GA 30155

JOHNSON, RAY MONROE, university medical administrator, physician; b. Chetopa, Kans., Apr. 28, 1940; s. Harold Jesse and Edith May (Sprangel) J.; m. Lynda Luise Hansen, Feb. 16, 1963; children: Jeffrey Michael, Kristina Luise Stuckey, Johanna Elizabeth. BA in Chemistry, Okla. State U., 1961; MD, U. Okla., 1965; student, Nat. War Coll., 1984-85. Diplomate Am. Bd Pediats. Commd. ensign USN, 1962, advanced through grades to capt., 1980; med. officer, flight surgeon USN, Cherry Point, N.C. and Rota, Spain, 1965-72; asst. chief pediats. Naval Hosp. USN, Charleston, S.C., 1974-77; chief pediats. Naval Hosp. USN, Pensacola, Fla., 1977-79; asst. chief pediats., dir. adolescent medicine Naval Hosp. USN, Portsmouth, Va., 1979-84; dep. program dir. Fleet Hosp., Naval Supply Command USN, Arlington, Va., 1985-87; ret. USN, 1987; med. dir. PRIMUS PHP Healthcare Corp., Alexandria, Va., 1987-89; med. dir. student health Am. U., Washington, 1989-90; med. dir. univ. health svcs. Stephen F. Austin State U., Nacogdoches, Tex., 1990-94; assoc. dir. for clin. svcs. Student Health Ctr. U. Tex., Austin, 1994—; cons. ambulatory care PHP Healthcare Corp., 1988-89; regional med. dir. Primary Medicine U.S., 1987-89; team physician NCAA athletes Am. U., 1989-90, varsity athletes Stephen F. Austin State U., 1990-94. Chmn. perinatal substance abuse task force Nacogdoches Cmty. Coalition, 1993-94; cons. Nacogdoches Health Jamboree, 1991-94. Fellow Am. Acad. Pediatrics; mem. Am. Coll. Sports Medicine, Soc. Adolescent Medicine, Deep East Tex. Rose Soc. (v.p., pres.), Nacogdoches Kiwanis Club. Lutheran. Office: Univ of Texas PO Box 7339 Austin TX 78713-7339

JOHNSON, RICHARD HAROLD, hospital foundation executive, fundraising consultant; b. Bridgeport, Conn., Feb. 28, 1942; s. Wilford George Johnson Jr. and Lorraine Rita (Hebert) Duplessis; m. Charmaine Mary Allard, Aug. 13, 1972 (dec. Oct. 1982); m. Gale Jeanne Griswold, May 12, 1984; stepchildren: April Ann Hines, Cristina Lynn Smith. BS, U. Bridgeport, 1969; postgrad., U. Mass., 1969; JD, U. Conn., 1975; cert. grad. Community Leadership Inst., Cape Cod C.C., 1992. Agt., mgr. Fidelity Union Life Ins. Co., various locations, 1969-73; atty. Brown & Nixon, Manchester, N.H., 1975-76; brokerage mgr. Travelers Ins. Co., Manchester, 1976-78; fin. planner Baldwin and Clarke, Bedford, N.H., 1978-79; assoc. dir. found. Morton Plant Hosp. Found., Clearwater, Fla., 1979-83; v.p., COO Boca Raton (Fla.) Community Hosp. Found., 1983-88; dir. planned giving Orlando (Fla.) Regional Healthcare Found., 1988-90; pres., CEO Cape Cod Hosp. Found., Hyannis, Mass., 1990-92; fund raising cons. Hyannis, Hyannis, 1992-93; pres. North Star Resources, Safety Harbor, Fla., 1993-94; exec. v.p. St. Anthony's Health Care Found., St. Petersburg, Fla., 1994-95; exec. dir. Indian River Hosp. Found., Vero Beach, Fla., 1995—; lectr. in field. Author: (Fla. Bar CLE course) Estate Planning & Probate..., 1990. Named Outstanding Young Man of Am., U.S. Jaycees, 1977. Mem. Hyannis C. of C., Boca Raton C. of C. (bd. dirs. 1986-88), Planned Giving Coun. Cape Cod (founder, pres. 1991-92), Planned Giving Coun. Cen. Fla. (co-founder, pres. 1990), Nat. Com. Planned Giving (del. nat. assembly 1990-92), Tampa Bay Area Planned Giving Coun. (bd. dirs. 1995), Planned Giving Coun. Indian River (founder, pres-elect 1995-96), Estate Planning Coun Pinellas County (bd. dirs. 1982-83), Boca Raton Estate Planning Coun. (co-founder, pres. 1987-88), Estate Planning Coun. Cape Cod, Nat. Soc. Fund Raising Execs. (cert., nat. bd. 1986, Outstanding Fund Raising Exec. award Palm Beach County chpt. 1986), Assn. Healthcare Philanthropy (accredited, conf. chair region IV 1987-88, lectr. conf. 1989, contbr. jour.), Rotary Club Boca Raton (Paul Harris fellow 1986, treas. 1986-88), Orlando Breakfast Rotary Club (bd. dirs. 1990), Vero Beach Rotary Club. Office: Indian River Hosp Found 1000 36th St Vero Beach FL 32960-4862

JOHNSON, RICHARD JAMES VAUGHAN, newspaper executive; b. San Luis, Potosi, Mex., Sept. 22, 1930; s. Clifton Whatford and Myrtle Louise (Hinman) J.; m. Belle Beraud Griggs, Aug. 6, 1955; children: Shelley Beraud, Mark Hinman. B.B.A., U. Tex., Austin, 1954. Asst. to exec. dir. Tex. Daily Newspaper Assn., 1955-56; with Houston Chronicle Pub. Co., 1956—, v.p. sales and mktg., 1971, exec. v.p., 1972, pres., 1973—, pub., 1987—, chmn. and pubr., 1990—; adv. dir. Tex. Commerce Bank-Houston, dir, Am. Gen. Corp., Mut. Ins. Co. Ltd. Bd. dirs. Tex. Med. Ctr., Greater Houston Partnership; chmn., CEO, and dir. Robert A. Welch Found.; bd. visitors M.D. Anderson Cancer Ctr., Meth. Hosp. With U.S. Army, 1952-54. Mem. Tex. Daily Newspaper Assn. (pres. 1978), Am. Newspaper Pubs. Assn. (past pres. and chmn.), River Oaks Club, Houston Club, Coronado Club. Unitarian. Office: Houston Chronicle Pub Co 801 Texas St Houston TX 77002-2906

JOHNSON, ROBERT HOYT, minister; b. Crawford, Ga., July 7, 1939; s. Sanford George and Sue Lene (Hardeman) J.; m. Dorothy Sparks, Oct. 20, 1962; children: Robert A., Gina Kay. Student, Johnson Bus. Coll., Athens, Ga., 1960-61; grad., Edn. Extension Ctr., 1990. Ordained to ministry So. Bapt. Conv., 1979. Deacon Johnson Dr. Bapt. Ch., Athens, 1971-78; pastor Freeman Creek Bapt. Ch., Farmington, Ga., 1978-86, Boldsprings Bapt. Ch., Monroe, Ga., 1987-92; interim min. Annie Mary Bapt. Ch., Monroe, Ga., 1993; dir. Royal Ambs., Sapeptu Bapt. Assn., Athens, 1972-77; with sales dept. Ivy-Coile Mfrs. Inc., Athens, 1978—; vice moderator Appalachee Bapt. Assn., Monroe, 1984, moderator, 1985-86, dean extension ctr., 1986—, dir. Sunday sch., 1989—. With USAR, 1958-64. Democrat. Home: 244 Doster Ave Monroe GA 30656-4705

JOHNSON, ROBERT LEE, JR., physician, educator, researcher; b. Dallas, Apr. 28, 1926; s. Robert L. and Doris (Miller) J.; m. Aileen Johnson, 1952; children: Stephen Lee, Robert Edward. BS, So. Meth. U., 1947; MD, Northwestern U., 1951. Intern Cook County Hosp., Chgo., 1951-52; resident in internal medicine Parkland Meml. Hosp., Phila., 1952-55; fellow nat. foun. infantile paralysis and clin. instr. U. Tex. Southwestern Med. Ctr., Dallas, 1955-56; fellow dept. physiol. and pharmacology Grad. Sch. Medicine U. Pa., Phila., 1956-57; asst. prof. U. Tex. Southwestern Med. Ctr., Dallas, 1959-65, assoc. prof., 1965-69, prof. medicine, 1969—; vis. staff Parkland Meml. Hosp., Dallas, 1957—, Zale Lipshy U. Hosp., Dallas, 1989—; cons. chest diseases VA Hosp., Dallas, 1966—; dir. chest medicine clinic Parkland Meml. Hosp., 1983—; mem. parent rev. com. Nat. Heart, Lung, and Blood Inst. for Spl. Ctrs. of Rsch. proposals, 1983-85; mem. Nat. Heart, Lung, and Blood Rsch. Rev. Com., 1985-89; mem. respiratory and applied physiology study sect. NIH, 1991-94. Assoc. editor: Jour. Clin. Investigation, 1972-77; mem. editl. bd. Jour. Applied Physiology, 1980-82, Circulation, 1996—; guest referee editor Jour. Applied Physiology, Am. Jour. Physiology, Chest, Circulation, Circulation Rsch., Am. Rev. Respiratory Disease, Am. Jour. Med. Sci., Jour. Clin. Investigation, Early Human Devel., Kidney Internat.; contbr. articles to profl. jours. With Naval ROTC, 1945-46; with USNR, 1944-46; maj. USAR, 1962. Mem. Am. Heart Assn. (cardiopulmonary coun. exec. com. mem. 1990-92, nominating com. cardiopulmonary coun. 1989—, chmn. 1990-92), Am. Thoracic Soc. (planning com. mem. 1987-90, com. proficiency standards 1985—, Scientific Accomplishment award 1996), Am. Coll. Chest Physicians, Am. Fedn. Clin. Rsch., Am. Physiol. Soc., Am. Soc. Clin. Investigation, Assn. Am. Physicians, Cen. Soc. Clin. Rsch., So. Soc. Clin. Rsch., Soc. Sigma Xi. Office: UT Southwestern Med Ctr 5323 Harry Hines Blvd Dallas TX 75235-7200

JOHNSON, ROBERT LEWIS, JR., retail company executive; b. Chgo., June 17, 1935; s. Robert Lewis Sr. and Gladys (Cherry) J.; m. Rose Harris; children—Rhonda, Rosalyn. B.A., Roosevelt U., 1958. Asst. mgr. Chgo. Housing Authority, 1960-65; v.p. concessions and contract sales Sears, Roebuck and Co., Chgo., 1965-91; chmn., chief exec. office Johnson Bryce Inc., Memphis, 1991—; dir. Rymer Corp., Chgo. Bd. dirs. Evanston Hosp., Ill., 1983-87, Suburban United Way, Chgo., 1987-91, Voices for Ill. Children, 1987-91, Rising Tide Found., Memphis C. of C.; chmn. Evanston Civil Service commn., 1981-88; trustee Roosevelt U., Chgo., 1986—, mem. alumni bd., 1984-88; mem. Sch. of Bus. Round Table Fla. A&M U., 1987—. Served with U.S. Army, 1958-60. Club: Druids. Home: 310 Barton Ave Evanston IL 60202-3302 Office: 4224 Premier Ave Memphis TN 38118-6103

JOHNSON, ROBERT WALTER, marine engineer, priest; b. Houston, Aug. 10, 1958; s. Bobby Joe and Ruth Ovella (Rotenberry) J. Student, S.W. Tex. State U., 1977-81. Chef Steak & Ale, Houston, 1973-75; pipe inspector Vetco Internat., Houston, 1976; electrician, jr. engr. various mcht. vessels, 1986-89, asst. engring. officer, 1989—; pres., CEO The Traveller, Unltd., Engring. & Environ. Cons., Webster, Tex., 1994—. Active Christian Coalition, Rep. Nat. Com.; mem. Citizens Com. for Right To Keep and Bear Arms. With USN, 1982-86. Mem. NRA (life), Am. Maritime Officers, Seafarers Internat. Union, 100 Club Houston. Mem. LDS Ch.

JOHNSON, ROGER WARREN, chemical engineer; b. Huntsville, Ala., Oct. 25, 1960; s. Frederic Allen and Joan (Bickum) J.; m. Margaret Jane Major, June 16, 1984. BChemE, Auburn U., 1984. Process engr. fibers divsn. E.I. DuPont de Nemours & Co., Waynesboro, Va., 1984-86; devel. engr. imaging systems E.I. DuPont de Nemours & Co., Brevard, N.C., 1986-87; R & D engr. Hercules Inc.-A&TP, Oxford, Ga., 1987-92; account mgr. Hercules Inc.-Absorbents and Textile Products, Oxford, Ga., 1992—. Mem. Nonwoven Fabrics Industry Assn. (INDA), Auburn Alumni Assn., Phi Kappa Phi. Home: 1410 Mclendon Ave NE Atlanta GA 30307-2129 Office: Hercules Inc PO Box 8 Oxford GA 30267

JOHNSON, RONDA JANICE, fundraising consultant; b. Muleshoe, Tex., Sept. 28, 1943; d. Randolph Revere and Betty Jo (Pool) J. BS in Edn., U. Tex., Austin, 1966; MBA, Houston Bapt. U., 1980. Cert. fund raising exec. Tchr. Galena Park Ind. Sch. Dist./Houston Ind. Sch. Dist., 1966-68; adminstrv. asst. Houston-Galveston Area Coun., 1968-69, Johns Hopkins U. Applied Physics Lab., Columbia, Md., 1969-73; dir. adminstrn. Edmondson Coll. Bus., Chattanooga, 1973-76; dir. Branell Women's Coll., Atlanta, 1976-78; dir. devel. U. Tex. Health Sci. Ctr., Houston, 1978-84, Houston Symphony Orch., 1984-85, Houston Child Guidance Ctr., 1985-87; pres. ctrl. divsn. Douglas M. Lawson Assocs., Inc., Houston, 1987-96; instr. Vol. Support Ctr., Houston, 1992, continuing edn. div. Rice U., Houston, 1992-95. Adv. bd. Houston Achievement Pl., 1992; bd. dirs. Escape Ctr., Houston, 1992-94. Named Woman of the Yr. by S.W. Houston News, 1994. Mem. Nat. Soc. Fundraising Execs. (bd. dirs. 1989-96, pres. 1994-95), Planned Giving Coun., Houstonian Network. Republican. Home: 5612 Saint Moritz St Bellaire TX 77401-2617 Office: Cargill Assocs 4701 Altamesa Blvd Fort Worth TX 76163-0339

JOHNSON, ROSEMARY WRUCKE, personnel management specialist; b. Leith, N.D., Sept. 21, 1924; d. Rudolph Aaron and Metta Tomina (Andersen) Wrucke; m. Robert Johnson Jr., Sept. 28, 1945 (div. 1964). Student, George Washington U., 1944-45, 47, Nat. Art Sch., Washington, 1943-45. Supr. Displaced Persons Commn., Frankfurt, Germany, 1950-52, FBI, Washington, 1952-81; cons. position mgmt. orgn. design Arlington, Va., 1981—. Mem. NAFE, Classification and Compensation Soc., Soc. FBI Alumni (membership chmn. 1985-91), Internat. Platform Assn. Lutheran. Home and Office: 2525 10th St N Apt 820 Arlington VA 22201-1968

JOHNSON, RUTH MARIE, educator; b. Grand Rapids, Mich., July 27, 1947; d. Foster S. and Esther M. Kochenderfer; m. Jeffery S. Johnson, Aug. 8, 1970; children: Emily Ruth, Jeffrey Scott II. BS, William Jennings Bryan Coll., 1969. Elem. tchr. Manatee County Sch. Bd., Bradenton, Fla., 1969-70; elem. tchr. reading recovery grade 1 Pasco Dist. Chpt. I-Basic Curriculum and Design Com., Land O'Lakes, Fla., 1970—. Named Tchr. of Yr., 1989. Mem. Am. Fedn. Tchrs., Fla. Edn. Assn., United Sch. Employees of Pasco, Alpha Delta Kappa. Home: PO Box 385 Zephyrhills FL 33539-0385

JOHNSON, SALLY A., nurse, educator; b. Rockford, Ill., Apr. 24, 1923; d. Herbert A. and Aileen (Peyton) Johnson; m. Bion D. Vickerman, 1994; children: Ann Elizabeth, Stacey Aileen; RN, Good Samaritan Hosp., 1945; student U. Ill., 1948-49; John Robert Powers model, 1946, Coranet model Miami, 1947; nurse obstetrics delivery Women's Hosp., N.Y.C., 1947-49, St. Francis Hosp., Evanston, Ill., 1953; charge, head nurse Broward Gen. Hosp., Ft. Lauderdale, Fla., 1968; night supr. Ashbrook Convalescent and Nursing Hosp., Scotch Plains, N.J., 1968—; owner Thomas A. Edison Brick Co., Sally Johnson Franz Enterprises. Council chmn. Betty Merit Tchrs. Scholarship, 1962; area nat. organizer Girl Scouts U.S.A., 1962-65; Westfield (N.J.) Round-Up and Health chmn., 1962-63; pres. Tamaques Sch., 1965, adviser Parent Tchr. Orgn., 1966, fgn. relationship chmn., 1967-68; exec. bd. chmn. Westfield High Sch. PTA Newsletter, 1968-70; chmn. Nat. Space Edn., Westfield, 1964; Westfield chmn. fgn. nurses Overlook Hosp., Summit, N.J., 1964-69. Recipient scholarship to Harvard U. Coll. Bus. Mem. Nat. Assn. Investors Corp., Am., Nat. Dist. Nurses Assns., NOW (N.J. coord. 1967-

68), Am. Contract Bridge League, Bridge Tchrs. Assn., Naples Investment Club (sec. 1995-96). Republican. Inventor holder for marking device. Home: 850 Tanbark Dr Apt 104 Naples FL 34108-8579

JOHNSON, SAMUEL (SAM JOHNSON), congressman; b. San Antonio, Tex., Oct. 11, 1930; m. Shirley L. Melton; children: James R., Gini Mulligan, Beverly Briney. BBA, So. Meth. U., 1951; M in Internat. Affairs, George Washington U.; grad., Armed Forces Staff Coll., Nat. War Coll. Joined USAF, 1950; fighter pilot USAF, Korea, Vietnam; prisoner of war USAF, 1966-73, former dir. Air Force Fighter Weapons Sch., former mem. Thunderbirds, wing commdr., air div. commdr., ret., 1979; founder home bldg. co., 1979; mem. Tex. Ho. of Reps., 1984-91, 102d-104th Congresses from 3d Tex. dist., Washington, D.C., 1991—; mem. ways and means subcom. Health, Oversight, and Social Security Coms.; mem. econ. and ednl. opportunities com., early childhood, youth and families subcom. Chmn. Republican Task Force on Am. Air Power. Decorated 2 Silver Stars, Disting. Flying Cross, 4 Air medals, 2 Purple Hearts. Office: 1030 Longworth HOB Washington DC 20515 also: 9400 N Central Expy Ste 610 Dallas TX 75231-5038 also: 1912 Ave K Ste 204 Plano TX 75074

JOHNSON, SAMUEL BRITTON, ophthalmologist, educator; b. Canyon, Tex., Apr. 25, 1926; s. Lee Livingston and Clementine (Smith) J.; m. Peggy Ruth Boswell, June 25, 1949 (div. May 8, 1980); children: Margaret Neal, Lee Sayers, Alice Boswell; m. Barbara Jean Herfurth, Dec. 20, 1982. BS, West Tex. A&M, 1946; MD, Tulane U., 1948. Diplomate Am. Bd. Ophthalmology. Intern Knoxville (Tenn.) Gen. Hosp., 1948-49; resident New Orleans Eye, Ear, Nose and Throat Hosp., 1949-50; chief resident New Orleans EENT Hosp., 1952-53; staff mem. ophthalmology Army Hosp., Ft. Sill, 1950-51, Navy, Quantico, Va., 1951-52; pvt. practice Jackson, Miss., 1953-55; prof., chmn. dept. ophthalmology med. sch. U. Miss., Jackson, 1955—; chief ophthalmology svc. Univ. Hosp., Jackson, 1955—; chmn. exec. com. State Comprehensive Plan Blind, Jackson, 1984-85, State Plan Svc. Blind, 1988-89; cons. in field. Author: (with others) Rhoades Textbook of Surgery, 1977, Textbook of Rehabilitation Counseling, 1993. Mem., pres., chmn. bd. dirs. Miss. Opera, Jackson, 1953-77, hon. bd. dirs. chmn. in perpituity, 1977—; mem. exec. com., trustee Miss. Sch. Blind, Deaf & Rehab.-Blind, 1979-89. Lt. USNR. Fellow ACS, Am. Acad. Ophthalmology, Law-Sci. Acad. Am.; mem. AMA, Miss. Eye, Ear, Nose and Throat Soc. (pres. 1969-70), La.-Miss. Ophthalmology and Otorhinolaryngology (pres. 1970), Ctrl. Med. Soc. of Miss. (pres. 1972-73), Miss. State Med. Soc., Signature/Royal Maid Blind Industries, Inc. (bd. dirs. 1985—). Office: U Miss Dept Ophthalmology 2500 N State St Jackson MS 39216-4500

JOHNSON, SHERRI DALE, educational consultant; b. Drumright, Okla., May 15, 1948; d. William Dale and Leota Mae (Mann) Roberts; m. James Earl Johnson, Aug. 5, 1972; children: Tara Nicole, Taylor Nichele. BS, Okla. State U., 1970; MS, North Tex. State U., 1980. Cert. secondary tchr., Tex., Okla. Tchr. English and speech Nathan Hale High Sch., Tulsa, 1970-76, Dallas Community Coll.-El Centro, 1976-77; tchr. speech and journalism Haggard Mid. Sch., Plano, Tex., 1976-78, Carpenter Mid. Sch., Plano, 1978-79, Clark High Sch., Plano, 1979-81; tng. cons. Dallas County Mental Health Assn., Dallas, 1984-87; dir. PhoneFriend, Plano, 1987—; ednl. cons. Plano Sch. Dist., 1987—. Author: Latchkey Survival Course: Handbook for Parents and Children, 1987. Tchr. suicide prevention Crisis Ctr. Collin County, Plano, 1989—, v.p. 1991, pres., 1992-93, exec. bd. dirs.; coord. STOP prog. Vines High Sch. PTO, Plano, 1988-89, pres., 1989—; cons. W.H.O. prog. Mental Health Assn., Dallas, 1987—; mem. speakers bur., chmn. childrens' youth com. Collin County Mental Health Assn., Plano, 1989—; mem. counselors' adv. com. Plano I.S.D., 1987—, Plano Community Police Acad., 1993—; com. mem. Keep Plano Beautiful Task Force, 1989—; chmn., founder Focus on Children, Child Abuse Prevention Coalition, 1989—. Recipient Vol. of Yr. in Edn. Div. award Collin County, 1990, J.C. Penny Golden Rule awrd, 1991. Mem. NEA, AAUW, Tex. Educators Assn., Internat. Platform Assn. Democrat. Home: 3420 Regent Dr Plano TX 75075-6239

JOHNSON, STACI SHARP, lawyer; b. Dallas, July 3, 1960; d. William Wheeler and Rublyin (Slaughter) S.; m. Byron Wade Johnson, Jan. 8, 1984; 1 child, Mollie Beatrice. BA in Dance, U. Tex., 1983, BA in Govt., 1983; JD, Tex. Tech. U., 1987. Bar: Tex. 1987, U.S. Dist. Ct. (ea. dist.) Tex. 1989, U.S. Dist. Ct. (no. dist.) Tex. 1990, U.S. Supreme Ct. 1991. Law clk. Dist. Atty.'s Office, Lubbock, Tex., 1987; rsch. asst. law libr. Tex. Tech. U., Lubbock, 1985-87; assoc. Henderson Bryant & Wolfe, Sherman, Tex., 1987-93, Law Offices of Richard E. Harrison, 1993-95; asst. atty. gen. Child Support divsn. Office of the Atty. Gen. of Tex., 1995—. Vol. Lubbock Crisis Ctr., 1985-87; mem. outreach com. Grace United Meth. Ch., Sherman, 1992; judge law and psychology Jan. term session Austin Coll., Sherman, Tex., 1992; Sunday sch. tchr. Stonebridge United Meth. Ch., 1995-96. Recipient Pro Bono Svc. award Legal Svcs. North Tex., 1991; named one of Outstanding Young Women of Am., 1987. Mem. Tex. Bar Assn., Tex. Young Lawyers Assn., Tex. Assn. Def. Counsel (co-author workers' compensation newsletter 1988), Grayson County Bar Assn. (mem. county law libr. com. 1989—, chair 1989-90, pres. 1990-91, sec. 1988-89, pres.-elect 1989-90, chair successful nomination of Judge R.C. Vaughan for Tex. Bar Found.'s Outstanding Jurist award 1990, chair minimum continuing legal edn. video presentations 1990-93, chair Law Day program 1992), Coll. of State Bar Tex., Phi Delta Phi. Methodist. Home: 707 Long Hill Ct Mc Kinney TX 75070-3230 Office: Office of the Atty Gen 201 S Jupiter Allen TX 75002

JOHNSON, STANLEY WEBSTER, college educator; b. Rocky Mount, N.C., Oct. 10, 1938; s. Charles Edward and Valaska (Graham) J. BS, Fayetteville (N.C.) State U., 1963; MS, Ind. U., 1966; PhD, U. N. Tex., 1982; postgrad., UCLA, 1968-69, Mt. St. Mary's Coll., L.A., 1974-76. Tchr. Balt. City Schs., 1963-64; asst. prof. history Grambling (La.) State U., 1966-72; tchr., ednl. therapist Cen. City Community Mental Health Ctr., L.A., 1973-74, Switzer Ctr. for Ednl. Therapy, Torrance, Calif., 1975-77; instr. L.A. S.W. Coll., 1976-77, Cooke County Coll., Gainesville, Tex., 1989—; tchr. Denton (Tex.) pub. schs., 1980—, L.A. Unified Sch. Dist., 1987-88; cons. in field. Active Dem. party, voter registration, 1984. Recipient Disting. Alumni award Nat. Assn. for Equal Opportunity in Higher Edn., 1985, Crown Zellerbach Found. award, 1968. Mem. NEA, NAACP, Tex. Tchrs. Assn., Alpha Kappa Mu. Home: 3345 Brooke St Denton TX 76207-7609

JOHNSON, STEPHEN SCOTT, journalist; b. Jacksonville, N.C., Oct. 3, 1959; s. Jimmy Lee and Barbara Jean (Smith) J. BS in Journalism, Ohio U., 1981; MMC in Journalism, U. S.C., 1995. Staff writer Greenville Piedmont, S.C., 1982, The Columbia Record, S.C., 1982-84; staff writer The State Newspaper, Columbia, S.C., 1984-88, asst. neighbors editor, 1988-89, asst. bus. editor, 1989-90, govt. editor, 1990-94, asst. news editor, 1994-96, editor CyberState, 1996—. Mem. Leadership S.C., 1996. Mem. Soc. Profl. Journalists (chmn. profl. devel. com. 1995-96, nat. bd. dirs. 1990-93), Investigative Reporters and Editors, Toastmasters. Office: The State Newspaper PO Box 1333 Columbia SC 29202

JOHNSON, TESLA FRANCIS, data processing executive, educator; b. Altoona, Fla., Sept. 2, 1934; s. Tesla Farris and Ruby Mae (Shockley) J.; m. Eleanor Mary Riggs, Oct. 17, 1975. BSEE, U. S.C., 1958; MS in Ops. Rsch., Fla. Inst. Tech., 1968; PhD in Adminstrv. Mgmt., Walden U., Mpls., 1990. Machinist apprentice Seaboard Airline Ry., 1952-54; asst. computer engr. So. Ry. System, Washington, 1958-61; sr. sci. programmer NCR, Dayton, Ohio, 1961-66; staff programmer IBM, East Fishkill, N.Y., 1966-72; mgr. Jay Turner Co., Grace, Idaho, 1973-74; programmer, analyst Ccybernetics & Systems, Inc., Jacksonville, Fla., 1974-77; systems analyst 1st Nat. Bank Md., Balt., 1977-78; sr. systems analyst GM, Detroit, 1978-80; tech. analyst Sunbank Data Corp., Orlando, Fla., 1980-81; mgr. data adminstrn. dept. Martin Marietta Corp., Orlando, 1981-92; tech. mgr. Computer Bus. Assocs., 1993—; adj. prof. bus. adminstrn. Valencia C.C., Orlando, 1989-94, Orlando Coll., 1990-92, Fla. Inst. Tech., Melbourne; mentor grad. sch. of computer resource mgmt. Webster U., 1993-94. Recipient cert. of appreciation NASA, 1969, Excalibur award. Mem. Acad. Internat. Bus., Tau Beta Pi, Sigma Phi Epsilon. Republican. Baptist. Home: 26203 Corkwood Ct Land O'Lakes FL 34639 Office: 1511 N Westshore Blvd Ste 260 Tampa FL 33607-4523

JOHNSON, THELMA JEAN, secondary and elementary education educator; b. San Augustine, Tex., Mar. 17, 1952; d. Willie F. and Iola V. (Polk) Harp; m. Ronald J. Johnson, Oct. 31, 1975; 1 child, Tiffany Michelle. BA, North Tex. State U., 1974; MA, Tex. So. U., 1989. Cert. elementary and secondary tchr., Tex. Tchr. Jesse H. Jones H.S., Houston, 1977-81, B.F. Terry H.S., Rosenberg, Tex., 1981-82, Jack Yates H.S., Houston, 1982-90, James Madison H.S., Houston, 1990-94, William S. Holland Middle Sch., Houston, 1994—. Youth dir. Our Mother of Mercy Catholic Ch., Houston, 1992—. Mem. NAACP, Soc. of Profl. Journalists, Journalism Edn. Assn., Nat. Scholastic Press Assn., Interscholastic League Press Conf. (Edith Fox King Disting. Educator in Tex. award 1996), Houston Assn. of Black Journalists. Democrat. Home: 12222 Crystalwood Houston TX 77013 Office: William S Holland Mid Sch 1600 Gellhorn Houston TX 77029

JOHNSON, THERESA PERUIT, librarian; b. Florence, Ala., Mar. 6, 1960; d. Richard Gordon and Rose Mary (Robertson) Preuit. BA, Judson Coll., Marion, ala., 1981; MLS, U. Ala., 1982. Online rsch. coord. U. Ala., Tuscaloosa, 1984-85, ref. libr., 1982-85; humanities ref. libr. Pace Libr., U. West Fla., Pensacola, 1985-88, 90-93, interlibr. loan coord., 1986-88, asst. to libr. dir., 1988-90, head circulation dept., 1993—. Editor Fla. chpt. ACRL Newsletter, 1988-95, The Southeastern Librarian, 1993—. Mem. ALA, Fla. Libr. Assn. (pubs. com. 1992—), Southeastern Libr. Assn. (editor 1992—), Beta Phi Mu. Office: University of West Florida Pace Library 11000 University Pkwy Pensacola FL 32514-5732

JOHNSON, THOMAS, economics educator; b. Hallitsville, Tex., Feb. 12, 1936; s. Lewis C. and Gladys (Gilmore) J.; m. Cleta Joy Anderson; children—David Eugene, Michael Joseph, Mark Alan. B.A., U. Tex., 1957; A.A., Navarro Jr. Coll., 1955; M.A., Tex. Christian U., 1962; M.E.S., N.C. State U., 1967, Ph.D., 1969. Engr., Convair, Ft. Worth, Tex., 1957-61, Ling-Temco Vought, Dallas, 1961-64; analyst Research Triangle Inst., Research Triangle Park, N.C., 1964-69; asst. prof. econs. and stats. So. Meth. U., Dallas, 1969-74, assoc. prof., 1974; prof. econs., stats. and biomath. N.C. State U., Raleigh, 1974—. Mem. Am. Soc. Quality Control, Am. Econ. Assn., Am. Statis. Assn., Am. Agrl. Econs. Assn., Phi Theta Kappa, Phi Kappa Phi, Pi Mu Epsilon. Republican. Baptist. Author: Toward Economic Understanding, 1976. Contbr. articles to profl. jours. Home: 325M Glen Echo Ln Cary NC 27511-9626 Office: NC State U Dept Agr & Resource Econ Box 8109 Raleigh NC 27695-8109

JOHNSON, VERNON EUGENE, history educator, educational administrator; b. Norfolk, Va., Oct. 25, 1930; s. Ellis Moses and Maude Louvenia (Wilkins) J.; m. Barbara Lucy Wynder, June 6, 1959; children: Kevin Bertram, Troy Eugene, Stacy Yvette. AB with distinction, Va. State Coll., 1951; MA, U. Pa., 1964; diploma with honors U.S. Army Command and Gen. Staff Coll., 1968; postgrad. Old Dominion U., 1977-78; advanced cert. in edn. Coll. William and Mary, 1979, EdD, 1982. Commd. 2d lt. U.S. Army, 1951, advanced through grades to lt. col., 1966, ret., 1979; adminstr., univ. collection mgr., adj. instr. Hampton (Va.) U., 1980-96; sr. prof. Tidewater Va. Ctr.; St. Leo Coll. of Fla., 1980—. Active Boys' Clubs. Decorated Legion of Merit with oak leaf cluster; recipient Brotherhood award, 1981, Jefferson Cup, 1982; named Man of Yr., 1981. Mem. Am. Assn. of Higher Edn., Am. Hist. Assn., Assn. for the Study Higher Edn., Nat. Hist. Assn., Assn. U.S. Army, Alpha Kappa Mu, Phi Alpha Theta, Omega Psi Phi (3d dist. rep.). Methodist. Club: Beau Brummell Civic and Social. Office: Hampton Univ Stone Bldg Hampton VA 23668

JOHNSON, VICKY K., beauty and computer consultant; b. Tillamock, Oreg., July 4, 1959; d. Wallace Raymond and Eleanore (Henke) J.; m. Thomas V. Johnson, Aug. 8, 1991. BS in Human Devel. and Performance, U. Oregon, 1987. Computer cons. Navarre, Fla., 1992—; beauty cons. Mary Kay, Navarre, 1995—. Mem. U.S. Officers Assn. (life). Home: 9421 Octavia Ln Navarre FL 32566

JOHNSON, WALKER P., museum administrator. Chmn. Mus. Arts and Sci., Macon, Ga. Office: Mus Arts and Sci 4182 Forsyth Rd Macon GA 31210-4806

JOHNSON, WALTER FRANK, JR., lawyer; b. Georgiana, Ala., Apr. 14, 1945; s. Walter F. and Marjorie Ellen (Carnathan) J.; m. Emily Waldrep, Nov. 23, 1969; children—Brian W., Stacey E. BS in Bus. Adminstrn., Auburn U., 1968; JD, Samford U., 1973. Bar: Ala. 1973, Ga. 1974. Assoc. Hatcher, Meyerson, Oxford and Irvin, Atlanta, 1973-74, Thompson and Redmond, Columbus, Ga., 1974-78; sole practice, Columbus, Ga., 1978—; asst. pub. defender, Columbus, 1978; acct. Union Camp Corp., 1968-70. Mem. ABA, Ala. State Bar, State Bar of Ga., Columbus Lawyers Club. Methodist. Home: 3235 Flint Dr Columbus GA 31907-2029 Office: 3006 University Ave PO Box 6507 Columbus GA 31907

JOHNSON, WANDA DALE JERNIGAN, property management executive; b. Selma, N.C., Apr. 30, 1955; d. Jesse James and Myrtle Irene Jernigan; m. Kenneth Bruce Johnson, June 10, 1974; 1 child, Donnie Leon. Degree in bus. adminstrn., ICS, Pa., 1989. Lic. real estate agt., N.C., S.C.; cert. color analyst; notary pub., N.C. Quality control insp. Sylvania, Smithfield, N.C., 1973-82; bookkeeper Automaster, Inc., Smithfield; adminstrv. asst. Adage, Inc., Raleigh, N.C.; tng. officer MDS & Assoc., Inc., Smithfield, 1989-95; exec. dir. Landmark Homes Realty Co., Smithfield, 1995—. Host area weekly TV program Just for Women. Active VFW; dir. sr. beauty pageants Johnston County Sr. Games, 1992, 93, 94, dir. cheerleading, 1993, 94; leader Pine Knoll Apts. chpt. 4-H, Smithfield, 1989, 90; active various Dem. events and campaigns, 1994, 95. Recipient Gov.'s award for Vol. Work, Gov. Hunt, N.C., 1994, various 4-H awards, awards for activities with sr. citizens. Baptist. Home: 163 Coats Rd Four Oaks NC 27524-8161

JOHNSON, WEYMAN THOMPSON, JR., lawyer; b. Atlanta, July 13, 1951; s. Weyman Thompson Sr. and Dixie LaNé (Peevy) J.; m. E. Allison Forkner, July 13, 1974; children: Chloe Forkner, Willa Rose. BA, Mercer U., 1973; JD, U. Ga., 1979. Bar: Ga. 1979, U.S. Dist. Ct. (no. dist.) Ga. 1979, U.S. Ct. Appeals (11th cir.) 1983, U.S. Supreme Ct. 1989. Reporter Columbus (Ga.) Ledger Newspaper, 1973-75; assoc. Fisher & Phillips, Atlanta, 1979-83, ptnr., 1984; assoc. Paul, Hastings, Janofsky & Walker, Atlanta, 1984-88, ptnr., 1988—. Author: Plant Closing Law, 1989. Bd. deacons First Bapt. Ch., Decatur, 1985—; chmn. Ga. chpt. Nat. Multiple Sclerosis Soc., Atlanta, 1990-94. Mem. ABA, Ga. Bar Assn., Atlanta Bar Assn. (chmn. labor sect. 1989-90, bd. dirs. 1991-92), Indsl. Rels. Rsch. Assn., Ga. Def. Lawyers Assn., Nat. M.S. Assn. (bd. dirs. 1995—), Eagles Landing Country Club. Home: 49 Sorrow Rd Stockbridge GA 30281-1841 Office: Paul Hastings Janofsky & Walker 600 Peachtree St NE 24th Fl Atlanta GA 30303-1808

JOHNSON, WILLIAM LAWRENCE, animal scientist, educator; b. Keene, N.H., Aug. 28, 1936; s. Stephen Guy and Elsie May (Prentice) J.; m. Nancy Lona Crane, June 6, 1958 (div. 1979); children: Warren E., Susan L., Steven L.; m. Thais DeAlmeida Bellomo, May 31, 1984 (div. 1995); children: Maya, Laisa. BS in Agriculture, U.N.H., 1958; MS, Cornell U., 1964, PhD, 1966. Asst. prof. animal sci. N.C. State U., Raleigh, 1966-74, assoc. prof. animal sci., 1974-80, prof. animal sci., 1980—; campus coord., mem. steering com. Ctr. for World Environ. and Sustainable Devel., Raleigh, 1991-94; rsch. advisor Nat. Inst. for Agrl. Rsch., Lima, Peru, 1988-91. Mem. editl. bd. Small Ruminant Rsch., 1987—; editor, co-editor 4 books; contbr. chpts. to books and over 50 articles to profl. jours. Grantee U. Calif., Davis, 1979-88. Mem. Am. Soc. Animal Sci., Internat. Goat Assn. Office: NC State U Dept Animal Sci Box 7621 Raleigh NC 27695-7621

JOHNSON, WILLIAM RAY, insurance company executive; b. West Union, Ohio, Feb. 12, 1930; s. A. Earl and Helen (Walker) J.; BS in Edn., Wilmington Coll., 1951; m. Anne Abrams, Mar. 27, 1954; children—Elizabeth Anne, William Randall. Tchr., theater dept. Miami U., Oxford, Ohio, 1951; divsn. mgr. Prudential Ins. Co. of Am., Waco, Tex., 1956-60; nat. tng. cons. Paul Revere Life Ins. Co., Dallas, 1960-65; health and accident ins. cons., Dallas, 1965-68; ptnr. Wiedemann & Johnson, Cos., Dallas, 1965-93; mem. exec. com. Cullen Frost Bank, Dallas, 1986-94, mem. trust com., 1986-94, chmn., 1991-94. Bd. dirs. Suicide Prevention of Dallas, 1973-81, pres., 1975-76; bd. dirs. Routh St. Ctr., 1975-78, Turtle Creek Manor, 1977-79, Sr. Citizens of Greater Dallas, Inc., 1977-81, Dallas Child Guidance Clinic, 1977-83; mem. Bishops Adv. Com. on Planning and Devel., Episcopal Diocese of Dallas, 1976-81; sr. warden St. Michael's Episcopal Ch., 1979-81; trustee Episcopal Theol. Sem. of SW, Austin, Tex., 1981-87, mem. exec. com., 1984-86; mem. bd. theol. edn. Episcopal Ch., N.Y.C., 1982-88; mem. exec. coun. Episcopal Diocese of Dallas, 1983-86, standing com., 1987-90; trustee St. Michael Sch., 1989-91, Greater Dallas Cmty. of Chs., 1986-89, mem. exec. com. 1987-88. Served to 1st lt. USAF, 1951-55. Mem. Multiple Sclerosis Soc. (bd. dirs. N. Texas Divsn. 1987-89), Anglican Sch. Theology (bd. trustees 1986-89). Club: Dallas Country. Office: 3500 Oak Lawn Ave # 300 Lb24 Dallas TX 75219-4349

JOHNSON, WILLIE SPOON, hospital administrator; b. Burlington, N.C., Apr. 14, 1943; d. William Luther and Ruth Viola (Baldwin) Spoon; m. Mark C. Johnson, Feb. 25, 1967; 1 child, Christy. Diploma in nursing, Watts Hosp. Sch. Nursing, Durham, N.C., 1964; BS, Pheiffer Coll., Misenheimer, N.C., 1971; MPH, U. N.C., 1983. RN, N.C., S.C., Calif.; cert. profl.in healthcare quality. Staff nurse med.-surg. Wesley Long Hosp., Greensboro, N.C., 1964-66; pub. health nurse Guilford County Health Dept., Greensboro, 1966-68; staff nurse ARC, L.A., 1967-68; pub. health nurse Health Dept., Sanford and Albemarle, N.C., 1968-72; dir. practical nurse edn. Sandhills C.C., Carthage, N.C., 1971-77; quality assurance/DRG coord. Humana Hosp. Greensboro, 1977-88; dir. quality mgmt. Women's Hosp. Greensboro, 1988—; mem. utilization rev. bd. Upjohn Health Care, Greensboro, 1980-92; cons. Quality Mgmt. Resources, Duluth, Ga., 1993—. Bd. mem. Health System Agy., 1976-77. Mem. Nat. Assn. Healthcare Quality (N.C. del. 1991, 93), Am. Soc. Healthcare Risk Mgmt., Healthcare Quality Certification Bd. (bd. mem. region III rep. 1993-96, sec.-treas. 1995-96), N.C. Assn. Healthcare Quality (bd. mem. 1989-94, co-chair edn. com. 1990-93). Lutheran. Home: 4532 Peeples Rd Oak Ridge NC 27310-9763 Office: Womens Hosp Greensboro 801 Green Valley Rd Greensboro NC 27408-7097

JOHNSON, WINSTON CONRAD, mathematics educator; b. Wellborn, Fla., Apr. 27, 1943; s. Charles Winston and Martha Gwendolyn (McLeran) J. BA, U. Fla., 1971, MEd, 1977, EdS, 1979. Cert. maths. tchr., Fla., Ga. Tchr. maths. Columbia High Sch., Lake City, Fla., 1971-76, Lake City (Fla.) Jr. High Sch., 1979-80, Hinesville (Ga.) Middle Sch., 1980-81; prof. maths. Cen. Fla. C.C., Ocala, 1981—. Sgt. USAF, 1966-70. Mem. Nat. Coun. Tchrs. of Maths., Math. Assn. Am., Fla. Devel. Ednl. Assn., Nat. Assn. for Devel. Edn., Fla. Coun. Tchrs. Maths. Democrat. Baptist. Home: PO Box 37 Wellborn FL 32094-0037 Office: Cen Fla C C 3001 SW College Rd Ocala FL 34474-4415

JOHNSON-COUSIN, DANIELLE, French literature educator; b. Geneva, Nov. 7, 1943; d. Edouard Henri and Suzanne Louise (Maurer) Cousin; m. Harry Morton Johnson, Jan. 25, 1970; 1 child, Eliza Suzanne. Cert. de Maturite cum laude Coll. of Geneva, 1962; BA, U. Alaska, 1966; MA, Purdue U., 1968; PhD, U. Ill., 1977; postgrad. Oxford U., summer 1968, Northwestern U., 1968-69, Maximilian U., Munich, 1970, Lozanov Workshop, Tenn. State U., 1985, Mellon Regional Seminar Lit. Crit., Vanderbilt U., 1987. Vis. lectr. U. Ill.-Urbana-Champaign, 1976-77; asst. prof. French Amherst Coll., 1979-82; asst. prof. French, Andrew W. Mellon fellow Vanderbilt U., Nashville, 1982-88; dir. Vanderbilt-in-France program, Aix-en-Pce, 1984-85; assoc. prof. French Fla. Internat. U., 1988—; cons. Princeton Ednl. Testing Svcs., 1993—. Contbr. articles to profl. jours. and papers to profl. meetings and conferences. U. Mass. Oxford scholar, 1968; U. Ill. summer fellow, 1971, fellow, 1972-73, Inst. Advanced Studies in Humanities vis. hon. fellow U. Edinburgh (Scotland), summer 1979; and numerous others. Mem. MLA, S. Atlantic MLA, Am. Assn. Univ. Women, Am. Assn. Tchrs. of French, Am. Soc. 18th-Century Studies, ACLA, Assoc. of Literary Scholars & Critics, Soc. des Etudes Staëliennes (Paris), Friends of George Sand, Assn. Mme de Charrière (Neuchâtel), Soc. Benjamin Constant (Lausanne), Soc. des Professeurs Francais et Francophones en Am., Soc. Diderot (Langres), Centre de Recherches Révolutionnaires Et Romantiques (Clermont-Ferrand), Soc. des Amis du C.R.R.R., Assn. J.J. Rousseau (Neuchâtel), Soc. Vaudoise d'Histoire et d'Archéologie (Lausanne), Fondation C.F. Ramuz (Lausanne), Internat. Soc. for Study of European Ideas, Internat. Parliament of Writers (Strasbourg), Internat. Dir. of 18th Century Studies, Oxford, Assn. Literary Scholars and Critics, Pi Delta Phi. Home: 9805 SW 115th Ct Miami FL 33176-2582 Office: Fla Internat U Dept Modern Langs Univ Park DM 493 C Miami FL 33199

JOHNSTON, CAROL ELIZABETH, English language educator; b. Norwood, Mass., Nov. 16, 1948; d. Charles James and Dorothy (Veator) Ingalls; m. Richard Johnston, Mar. 9, 1973 (div. 1993); 1 child, Catherine Faith. BA, Rollins Coll., 1970; MA, U. Fla., 1972; PhD, U. S.C., 1980. Tchr. English Colleton County Schs., Walterboro, S.C., 1972-73, Collier County Schs., Naples, Fla., 1973-75; asst. prof. Clemson (S.C.) U., 1980-88, assoc. prof., 1988-96, prof., 1996—. Author: Thomas Wolfe: A Descriptive Bibliography, 1987; Of Time and the Artist: Thomas Wolfe, His Novels, and the Critics; editor S.C. Rev., 1983—; cons. editor Thomas Wolfe Rev., 1992—; contbr. more than 20 articles to profl. jours. Grantee NEH, 1983-87. Recipient numerous NEA awards Nat. Endowment for Arts, 1983-87. Mem. MLA, So. Atlantic MLA, Philol. Assn. Carolinas, Thomas Wolfe Soc. (bd. dirs. 1988-96, Zelda Gitlin award 1989, Honors Prof. of Yr. 1989, Harriet Holman award for faculty excellence 1993, William B. Wisdom award 1995). Roman Catholic. Home: 102 Carriage Ln Pendleton SC 29670-9685 Office: Clemson U English Dept Clemson SC 29634

JOHNSTON, DANIEL, financial petroleum consultant; b. Billings, Mont., Aug. 28, 1950; s. Vincent Paul Johnston and Mary Jean (Hill) Sene; m. Jill Sue Gearhart, Feb. 19, 1977; children: Erik, Lane, Jill Danielle, Julianna, David. BSc in Geology, No. Ariz. U., 1977; MBA in Fin., U. Tex., 1987. Engr. Gearhart Industries, Ft. Worth, 1977-80, Gaffney Cline & Assoc., Dallas, 1980-83, Santa Fe Minerals, Dallas, 1983-84; prin. Daniel Johnston & Co., Inc., Dallas, 1985—; instr. Profl. Devel. Inst., U. North Tex., IBC Tech. Svcs. Ltd., Singapore; tchr. courses on oil co. fin. statement and analysis, econs. and risk analysis, and internat. petroleum fiscal systems to various profl. orgns. Tex., Okla., Jakarta, Sarawak, Kuala Lumpur. Author: Oil Company Financial Analysis in Nontechnical Language, 1992, International Petroleum Fiscal Systems and Production Sharing Contracts, 1994; (software) The Financial Analysts Tool Kit, 1991, Refinery Complexity Index, 1992, Worldwide Refinery Complexity Analysis, 1994, (with T.S. Schmidt) International Production Sharing Contract Cash Flow Model, 1992; contbr. articles to profl. publs.; mem. bd. cons. PETROMIN mag., Singapore, Petro Asian Bus. Report; mem. editorial adv. bd. World Energy Update, Oil & Gas Law and Taxation Rev.; guest editor spl. issue Petroleum Acctg. and Fin. Mgmt. Jour., 1994. Scoutmaster Boy Scouts Am., Ft. Worth, 1978-89. Mem. Am. Assn. Petroleum Geologists, Soc. Petroleum Engrs., Assn. Internat. Petroleum Negotiators. Mem. LDS Ch. Home: 1925 Edgewater Dr Plano TX 75075-8573 Office: Daniel Johnston & Co Inc 13355 Noel Rd Ste 500 Dallas TX 75240-6613

JOHNSTON, HARRY A., II, congressman; b. West Palm Beach, FL, Dec. 2, 1931; m. Mary Otley; children: Victoria, Rebecca. Ed., Va. Mil. Inst., 1953, U. Fla. Law Sch., 1958. Mem. Fla. Senate, former pres.; pvt. practice law, 1958-91; mem. 101st-104th Congresses from 14th (now 19th) Fla. dist., 1989-96; mem. fgn. affairs com., subcom. Africa, internat. ops., econ. policy, trade and environment, budget com. Mem. United Fund Palm Beach County, Norton Gallery, Girl Scouts U.S. With U.S. Army, 1953-55. Named Most Valuable Senator Fla. Press Corps, 1981. Mem. Palm Beach Bar Assn. (former pres.), Rotary (former pres. Greater West Palm Beach). Democrat. Presbyterian.

JOHNSTON, JAMES WESLEY, retired tobacco company executive; b. Chgo., Apr. 11, 1946; s. Ted and Irma (Hacker) J.; m. Beverly S. Cline, Nov. 10, 1967; children: Amanda E., Emily S. B.S. in Accountancy, U. Ill., 1967; M.B.A., Northwestern U., 1971. C.P.A., Ill. Fin. analyst Ford Motor Co., 1967-69; with N.W. Industries, 1969-79, dir. corp. devel., 1973-75, v.p. mktg., 1975-79; exec. v.p. Asia/Pacific R.J. Reynolds Tobacco Internat. Inc., 1979; pres., chief exec. officer Asia/Pacific R.J. Reynolds Tobacco Internat. Inc., Hong Kong, 1979-81; exec. v.p. R.J. Reynolds Tobacco Co., U.S., 1981-84; divsn. exec. consumer banking N.E. U.S. Citicorp, N.Y.C., 1984-89; chmn. CEO R.J. Reyolds Tobacco Co., Winston-Salem, N.C., 1989-95; chmn. R.J. Reynolds Tobacco Worldwide, Winston-Salem, N.C., 1993-96; vice chmn. RJR Nabisco, Inc., 1995-96, ret., 1996; bd. dirs. Wachovia Corp.,

Winston-Salem, Sealy Corp., Cleve. Treas., trustee, pres. Village of Bolingbrook, Ill., 1973-75; bd. dirs. Winston-Salem Bus. Inc., 1989—, N.C. Citizens for Bus. and Industry, Raleigh, 1989—; mem. mktg. com. Nat. Multiple Sclerosis Soc., N.Y.C., 1986—; active N.C. Bus. Coun. Mgmt. and Devel., Raleigh, 1989—; trustee Wake Forest U., Winston-Salem, 1991—; mem. bd. visitors Bowman Gray-Bapt. Hosp. Med. Ctr., Winston-Salem, 1991—. Mem. Greater Winston-Salem C. of C. (bd. dirs. 1989—), Old Town Club, Piedmont Club. Office: Ste 570 380 Knollwood Winston Salem NC 27103

JOHNSTON, JOHN BENNETT, JR., senator; b. Shreveport, La., June 10, 1932; m. Mary Gunn, 1956; children: Bennett, Hunter, Mary, Sally. Student, Washington and Lee U., U.S. Mil. Acad.; LL.B., La. State U., 1956. Bar: La. 1956. Mem. firm Johnston, Johnston & Thornton, 1959; mem. La. House Reps., 1964-68, La. Senate, 1968-72; U.S senator from La., 1972-96; chmn. Dem. senatorial campaign com., 1975-76; mem. appropriations com., ranking minority subcom. on energy and water devel., ranking minority com. on energy and natural resources, mem. budget com., mem. spl. com. on aging, mem. select com. on intelligence. Served to 1st lt. U.S. Army, 1956-59. Democrat. Office: US Senate 136 Hart Senate Bldg Washington DC 20510-1802

JOHNSTON, NEIL CHUNN, lawyer; b. Mobile, Ala., Feb. 23, 1953; s. Vivian Gaines and Sara Niel (Chunn) J.; m. Ashley Monroe Hocklander, Dec. 20, 1980; children: Katie, Neil Jr. BA, Southwestern at Memphis (name changed to Rhodes Coll.), 1975; JD, U. Ala., 1978. Atty. Hand, Arendall L.L.C., Mobile, Ala., 1978—; Com. mem. Ala. Law Inst. Com., Tuscaloosa, Ala., 1990; mem. Gov.'s Wetland Mitigation Task Force, 1994. Contbr. articles to profl. jours. Chmn. Project CATE, Mobile, 1987—; trustee The Nature Conservancy, Ala., 1990—; mem. Wetland Mitigation Banking Task Force, 1994-96. Recipient Ala. Gov.'s award-Water Conservationist, Ala. Wildlife Fedn., 1987. Mem. ABA, Ala. State Bar Assn. (chmn. environ. law sect. 1984-91, corp. banking, bus. law sect. 1984-91, corp. banking, bus. law sect. 1994-96), Mobile Bar Assn., Ala. Forestry assn., Ala. Law Inst. (mem. com. 1990), Rotary (pres. Mobile chpt. 1996—). Office: Hand Arendall LLC 3000 FNB Bldg Royal St Mobile AL 36602

JOHNSTON, SIDNEY PHILIP, historian; b. 1957; m. Ginger Charlotte Preston, 1983; children: Sidney Preston, Charlotte Virginia. BA in History, U. South Fla., 1982; MA in History, U. Fla., 1987. Coord., editor oral history program Fla. Mus. Natural History, 1984-86; jr. prin. Historic Property Assoc., Inc., St. Augustine, Fla., 1987—; chmn. DeLand (Fla.) Hist. Preservation Bd., 1993-95; lectr. in field. Editor: Pictorial History of West Volusia County, 1870-1960, 1993. Pres. Historic DeLand, Inc. Mem. West Volusia Hist. Soc. (dir.). Democrat. Methodist. Home: 535 N Clara Ave Deland FL 32720-3405

JOHNSTON, SUMMERFIELD K., JR., food products executive; b. 1954. V.p. Johnston Food Group, Inc., 1983-85; officer Cleveland (Tenn.) Coca-Cola, 1986-87; v.p., gen. mgr. Midwest Coca-Cola (subsid. Johnston Coca-Cola Bottling Co.), Mpls., from 1987, pres., regional ops., from 1987; vice chmn., CEO Coca-Cola Enterprises, Inc., Atlanta, GA. Office: Coca-Cola Enterprises PO Box 723040 Atlanta GA 33139-0040

JOHNSTON, W. MEDFORD, artist, educator; b. Atlanta, Mar. 2, 1941; s. William Posey and Sarah Lou (Medford) J.; m. Loraine Presley, Aug. 17, 1968. BA, Ga. State U., 1965; MFA, Fla. State U., 1967. Prof. painting Ga. State U., Atlanta, 1967—. Exhibited in group shows at New Orleans Mus. Fine Art, 1995—, Sandler/Hudson Gallery, 1996, 54th Ann Nat. Exhbn. of Contemporary Am. Painting, 1992, Cheekwood Nat. Contemporary Painting Exhbn., 1993. Recipient Regional fellowship So. Arts Fedn. and NEA, 1990. Office: Ga State Univ Sch of Art and Design University Plz Atlanta GA 30303

JOHNSTON, WESLEY JAMES, marketing educator, consultant; b. Jamaica, N.Y., June 30, 1945; s. James Albert and Bertha Harriett (Myers) J.; m. Myong Son Mun, Feb. 14, 1974; children: Natalie Anne, James Richard. BA in Econ., U. Pitts., 1967, MBA, 1975, PhD in Bus. Adminstrn., 1979; MA in Counseling Psychology, Ball State U., 1972. Grad. rsch. asst. U. Pitts., 1975-78; intern Cargill, Inc., Mpls., 1977; asst. prof. Ohio State U., Columbus, 1978-84, asoc. prof., 1984-86; asoc. prof. U. So. Calif., L.A., 1986-91; prof. Ga. State U., Atlanta, 1991—; vis. prof. Korea U., 1988, Dalian U. Tech., 1990, Helsinki (Finland) Sch. Econ. and Bus. Adminstrn., 1991, Ljubljana U., 1991, U. Western Sydney, Napean, 1995; cons., seminar leader to industry, univs. and profl. orgns.; reviewer Jour. Mktg., 1987—, Jour. Mktg. Rsch., 1982—; dir. Ctr. Bus. and Indsl. Mktg., Ga. State U., Atlanta, 1993—, doctoral program coord., dept. mktg., 1992-95. Author: Patterns in Industrial Buying Behavior, 1981, Purchasing in the 1990s: The Evolution of Procurement in Telecommunications, 1990; co-author: (with T. V. Bonoma and G. Zaltman) Industrial Buying Behavior, 1977, (with R. D. Blackwell and W. Wayne Talarzyk) Cases in Marketing Management and Strategy, 1985, (with C. L. Hinkle and E. F. Lanigan) Cases in Marketing Management: Issues for the 1990s, 1992; mem. editorial bd. Jour. Mktg., 1981-85, Jour. Personal Selling and Sales Mgmt., 1979-93, Jour. Indsl. and Bus. Mktg., 1983-93, editor 1993—, Jour. High Tech. Mktg., 1984-88; editor spl. issues Jour. Bus. Rsch.; contbr. numerous chpts. to books, articles to profl. jours., papers to profl. procs. Lt. col. USAF (Ret.), 1967-94. Ctr. for Creative Leadership summer fellow, 1977, Nat. Ctr. Export/Import Studies fellow, 1984-88, Am. Grad. Sch. Internat. Mgmt. Presdl. fellow, 1990; grantee Ohio State U., 1979-80, 82, 84-85, Housing and Urban Devel., Columbus Bd. Realtors, 1983-84, U. So. Calif., 1987-88; recipient Pa. State Senatorial scholarship, 1967. Mem. Am. Mktg. Assn. (Educators' Conf. discussant, session chair, reviewer 1979, 80, 82, 83, 84, 85, 86, 87, 88, 89, 90, 1st Place Dissertation award 1979, Mktg. Prof. of Yr., Ohio State U. chpt. 1986.), Assn. Consumer Rsch. (discussant, session chair, reviewer 1980, 81, 83, 84, 86, 87, 89, program com. 1989), Acad. Internat. Bus. (program com. 1982, 89), Beta Gamma Sigma. Home: 215 Camden Rd NE Atlanta GA 30309-1511 Office: Ga State Univ Dept of Mktg Atlanta GA 30303

JOHNSTONE, DEBORAH BLACKMON, lawyer; b. Birmingham, Ala., Jan. 26, 1953; d. T.C. Blackmon and Joan (Thompson) Ryals; m. David Johnstone, July 26, 1968 (div. 1976); children: Pamela, Robin. A.S., Jefferson Sch. Nursing, Birmingham, 1976; BA, Birmingham-So. Coll., 1982; JD, Birmingham Law Sch., 1986. Bar: Ala. 1986. Nurse Carraway Med. Ctr., Birmingham, 1976-86; assoc. Emond & Vines, Attys., Birmingham, 1986-88; atty., med.-legal cons. Am. Internat. Group, Bedford, Dallas, Ft. Worth, 1988—. Mem. ABA, ATLA, ACLU, AAAS, Ala. Trial Lawyers, Ala. State Bar, Tex. Bd. Nurse Examiners, Ala. Bd. Nursing, Consumers Union. Democrat. Roman Catholic. Office: 849 E Renfro St Burleson TX 76028-5019

JOHNSTONE, EDWARD HUGGINS, federal judge; b. 1922. J.D., U. Ky., 1949. Bar: Ky. 1949. Ptnr. firm Johnstone, Eldred & Paxton, Princeton, Ky., 1949-76; judge 56th Cir. Ct. Ky, 1976-77; judge U.S. Dist. Ct. (we. dist.) Ky., 1977—, chief judge, 1985-90; sr. judge, 1993. Mem. ABA, Ky. Bar Assn. Office: US Dist Ct 219 Fed Bldg 5th & Broadway Paducah KY 42001 Also: 262 US Courthouse 601 Broadway Louisville KY 40202

JOICE, NORA LEE, clinical dietitian; b. Kearney, Nebr., Mar. 5, 1948; d. Frank Rogers and Clarrisa Blanche (Drinnan) Jackson; m. David Wayne Joice, Dec. 21, 1973. BS, U. Ariz., 1971. Registered dietitian; lic. dietitian. Clin. dietitian St. Francis Hosp., Tulsa, 1972-76; pub. health nutritionist Tulsa City County Health Dept., 1976-81; clin. dietitian City of Faith Hosp., Marriott Corp., Tulsa, 1982-84, asst. chief dietitian, 1984-86, chief clin. dietitian, 1986-87, clin. nutrition specialist, 1987-89; cons. dietitian in long-term health facilities Marriott Corp., Tulsa, 1990-92; pvt. practice cons. dietitian Tulsa, 1992—; clin. dietitian Broken Arrow (Okla.) Med. Ctr., 1993-94; outpatient clin. dietitian St. John's Med. Ctr., Tulsa, Okla., 1995—. Mem. Okla. Dietetic Assn., Am. Dietetic Assn., Okla. Cons. Dietitians in Health Care Facilities, Dietitians in Gen. Clin. Practice. Democrat. Pentecostal. Home and Office: 2320 S Urbana Ave Tulsa OK 74114-3627

JOINER, ELIZABETH GARNER, French language educator; b. Atlanta, Feb. 15, 1939; d. Albert Ross and Bessie Mae (Sessions) Garner; m. Lawrence Don Joiner, June 8, 1964 (dec. July 1981); m. George Buford Norman, Aug. 8, 1996. BA, LaGrange Coll., 1959; MA, U. Ga., 1964; PhD, Ohio State U., 1974. Tchr. French and English Franklin County H.S., Carnesville, Ga., 1959-60, Winder (Ga.)-Barrow H.S., 1960-62; grad. tchg. asst. U. Ga., Athens, 1962-64, instr. French, 1964-65; instr. French Winthrop Coll., Rock Hill, S.C., 1965-68, asst. prof. French, 1968-74; asst. prof. French U. S.C., Columbia, 1974-77, assoc. prof. French, 1977-84, prof. French, 1984—. Author: (textbook) First-Year French, 1977, Departs, 1978, Horizons, 1984, Video-Verite, 1994, (monograph) The Older Foreign Language Learner, 1981; editor: Developing Communication Skills, 1978; contbr. chpts. to scholarly books including Developing Language Teachers for a Changing World, 1974—; contbr. articles to scholarly jours. Decorated Chevalier des Palmes Academiques, French Govt., 1991; NDEA fellow U.S. Govt., 1971-72. Mem. MLA, Am. Assn. Tchrs. of French, Am. Coun. on Tchg. of Fgn. Langs. (chair Birkmeier Award com. 1990-91), S.C. Fgn. Lang. Tchrs. Assn. (pres. 1977-78), Phi Kappa Phi, Phi Beta Kappa. Home: 9 Cassia Ct Columbia SC 29209-4226 Office: U S C Dept French and Classics Columbia SC 29208

JOINER, GEORGE HEWETT, historian, educator; b. Albany, Ga., June 9, 1941; s. George Hewett and Elnora (Brewer) J.; m. Martha Virginia Sasser, Feb. 2, 1973; children: Barbara Virginia, George Stubbs. BA, Emory U., 1963; MA, Northwestern U., 1966, PhD, 1971. Asst. prof. Ga. So. U., Statesboro, 1968-76, assoc. prof. history, 1976-84; dir. Bell Honors program Ga. So. Coll., Statesboro, 1981—, prof. history, 1984—; cons. numerous hons. programs in colls., 1984—. Contbr. articles to profl. jours. Recipient Ruffin Cup, Ga. So. U., 1989; Woodrow Wilson Found. fellow, 1963-64, Northwestern U. fellow, 1964-66. Mem. So. Regional Honors Coun. (pres. 1993-94, exec. com. 1992—, state coord. for Ga. 1991—, exec. sec.-treas. 1996—), Ga. Honors Coun. (pres. 1988-89), Western Conf. on Brit. Studies (pres. 1988-90, exec. com. 1982—), N.Am. Conf. on Brit. Studies (exec. com. 1988-90), Nat. Collegiate Honors Coun. (exec. com. 1994—). Office: Georgia Southern Univ Landrum Box 8036 Statesboro GA 30460

JOINER, LORELL HOWARD, real estate development and investment executive; b. Temple, Tex., Nov. 27, 1945; s. Burt Lawrence and Geneva Evelyn (Howard) J.; m. Cynthia Ann Morin, Mar. 30, 1968. BEcons., Trinity U., San Antonio, 1967; MArch, U. Tex., 1977. Registered architect, Tex. Exec. v.p. Tex. Diversified Properties, San Antonio, 1964-68; exec. v.p. Gen. Properties Devel., San Antonio, 1970-76, pres., chief exec. officer, 1976—; pres., chief exec. officer Gen. Properties Investment Inc., San Antonio, 1979—; bd. dirs. Internat. Modelbau GMBH, Geneva, 1986—. Author: Reliable Trackwork Construction, 1986; contbr. articles to profl. publs.; author script, narrator TV programs, Computer Show, 1987, Real Time Interface, 1987. Bd. dirs. San Antonio Community Theater, 1986-89, Tex. Transp. Mus., San Antonio, 1978—; vol. San Antonio Big Bros./Big Sisters, 1986—; mem. com. Muscular Dystrophy Assn. 1st lt. U.S. Army, 1968-70. Named Master Archtl. Model Builder, Nat. Model Bldg. Assn., 1980. Fellow Internat. Modelbau (bd. dirs. 1986—); mem. AIA (assoc., 1st place award for design 1980), Royal Automobile Club, Rolls Royce Owner's Club. Home: 7507 Shadylane Dr San Antonio TX 78209-2738 Office: Gen Properties Investment 18985 Marbach Ln San Antonio TX 78266-2132

JOINER, RONALD LUTHER, toxicologist; b. Ponchatoula, La., Mar. 19, 1945; s. Luther Lawrence and Rosalie Lillian (Lavigne) J.; m. Michelle Elizabeth Baham, Jan. 21, 1967; children: Randall Lee, Corey Alexander, Kyle McCahill. BS, Southeastern La. U., 1966; MS, La. State U., 1968; PhD, Miss. State U., 1971. Rsch. asst. La. State U., Baton Rouge, 1966-68; rsch. assoc. biochemist Miss. State U., State College, 1968-71; postdoctoral fellow Tex. A&M U., College Station, 1971-73; supr. toxicology Stauffer Chem. Co., Richmond, Calif., 1973-76; dir. COESH SRI Internat., Rosslyn, Va., 1976-80; v.p. health Battelle Meml. Inst., Columbus, Ohio, 1980-91; gen. mgr. TSI Redfield (Ark.) Labs., 1991-92; pres. Joiner Assocs., Inc., Sherwood, Ark., 1992-94; dir. health and environ. sci. Golder Assocs. Inc., Atlanta, 1994—; bd. dirs. N.C. State U./Battelle Meml. Inst., Raleigh, 1989-91; mem. instnl. rev. bd. Riverside Meth. Hosp., Columbus, 1990-91; mem. biotech. adv. bd. Nat. Ctr. for Toxicol. Rsch., Jefferson, Ark., 1991-94; presenter in field. Contbr. 0ver 60 articles to profl. jours., 2 chpts. to books. V.p. Homeowner's Assn., Springfield, Va., 1978-80, pres., Dublin, Ohio, 1986-91; campaign co-mgr. Shadid Election Group, Sherwood, Ark., 1993. Robert A. Welch Found. fellow, 1971-73. Mem. AAAS, Am. Chem. Soc., Soc. Toxicology, Soc. Risk Assessment (membership com. 1994—). Democrat. Roman Catholic. Home: 12210 Meadows Ln Alpharetta GA 30202 Office: Golder Assocs Inc 3730 Chamblee Tucker Rd Atlanta GA 30341

JOKL, ERNST F., physician; b. Breslau, Germany, Aug. 8, 1907; came to U.S., 1950, naturalized, 1958; s. Hans and Rose (Oelsner) J.; M.D., Breslau U., 1931; M.B., B.Ch., Witwatersrand U., Johannesburg, South Africa, 1936, PhD (hon), German Sport U., Cologne, 1991; m. Erica Lestmann, June 3, 1933; children: Marion Jokl Ball, Peter. Mem. faculty U. Ky. Coll. Medicine Lexington, prof. neurology and sport medicine, from 1952, Disting. prof., from 1964, prof. emeritus, from 1979; pres. research com. Internat. Council Sport and Phys. Edn., UNESCO; Prince Philip lectr. Ho. of Lords, Eng., 1983, 85. Decorated Grand Cross Merit (Fed. Republic Ger.); recipient Brit. Commonwealth Research medal Harveian Soc., 1950; research fellow Nat. Library Medicine, Bethesda, Md., 1977; hon. prof. univs. Berlin and Frankfurt-Main. Fellow Am. Coll. Cardiology; mem. AMA, Aerospace Med. Assn., Am. Coll. Sports Medicine (founder); hon. mem. Internat. Fedn. Sports Medicine. Club: Rotary. Author books, papers in field. Home: 340 Kingsway Dr Lexington KY 40502-1046

JOLIVET, DANIEL N., psychologist; b. Seattle, June 6, 1960; s. Vincent M. and Martha J. (Norris). BS in Math., U. Washington, 1982; BS in Psychology, 1983; MA in Clin. Psychology, Ga. State U., Atlanta, 1985; PhD in Clin. Psychology, 1992. Lic. Clin. Psychologist, Ga. Grad. teaching asst. Ga. State U., Atlanta, 1986-88; mental health asst. Laurel Heights Hosp., 1989; psychotherapist Charter Brook Counseling Ctr. of Cobb County, Marietta, Ga., 1989-90, Family Rels. Program, Griffin, Ga., 1990-91; psychodiagnostic testing cons. pvt. practice, Atlanta, 1988-92; counselor, cons. Personal Performance Cons., 1991-92; coord. of child and adolescent svcs. Henry County Counseling Ctr., Stockbridge, Ga., 1992-95; clin. dir. Quantum Behavioral Healthcare, Atlanta, 1995-96; clin. psychologist Open House, Inc., 1994—, Fairview Day Hosp., Jonesboro, Ga., 1996—; mem. Henry County Child Abuse Task Force, McDonough, Ga., 1992-95, chair, 1995; mem. Henry County Troubled Children Com., McDonough, Ga., 1992-95, Stockbridge (Ga.) Truancy Task Force, 1995, Prudential Healthcare Physician Adv. Subcom., Atlanta, 1995-96. Co-author: Human Love: A Bibliography, 1981; author: A Guide To Rorschach Interprestation, 1992. Mem. Democratic Nat. Com., 1994—, Sierra Club, 1994—, Habitat for Humanity, 1992—, Ga. Wildlife Fedn., 1992—, Atlanta. Mem. APA, Atlanta Group Psychotherapy Soc., Ga. Coun. on Child Abuse, Henry County Coun. on Child Abuse, South Metro Atlanta Therapist Assn. Democrat. Mem. United Ch. of Christ. Home: 103 King Hwy Decatur GA 30030 Office: Open House, Inc 11-A Lenox Pointe NE Atlanta GA 30324 Office: Fairview Day Hosp 102 W Mimosa Dr Jonesboro GA 30236

JOLLES, SCOTT ALAN, advertising executive; b. Wichita, Kans., Aug. 7, 1960; s. Stanley Elliott Rothenberg and Myra (Abelman) Jolles. AB in Journalism, U. Ga., 1983. Mfrs. rep. Superior Surgical Mfg. Co., Seminole, Fla., 1983-85; account exec. Petry Nat. TV, Atlanta, 1985-92, group sales mgr., 1992—. Mem. Am. Jewish Com. Mem. Atlanta Broadcast Advt. Club. Jewish. Office: Petry Nat TV 950 E Paces Ferry Rd NE Atlanta GA 30326-1119

JOLLIFF, ROBERT ALLEN, treasurer; b. Wooster, Ohio, Sept. 12, 1943; s. Samuel Martin and Ethel May (Eschliman) J.; m. Marcella Joanne Battig, Aug. 31, 1968; children: John Douglas, Laura Joanne. BS, Kent State U., 1965; MBA, U. Akron, 1974. Asst. cash mgr. B.F. Goodrich, Akron, Ohio, 1968-73; cash mgr. Aladdin Industries, Nashville, 1973-74; cash mgr. McDermott Inc., New Orleans, 1974-78, treas., 1978—; founder, owner Catlin Energy Corp., Cord Energy Resources Inc. Trustee Blood Ctr. SE La., New Orleans, 1986—. 1st lt. U.S. Army, 1966-68. Mem. Nat. Assn. Corp. Treas., Winchester Arms Collectors Assn., Masons. Republican. Methodist. Office: McDermott Inc PO Box 60035 New Orleans LA 70160-0035

JOLLY, ALLENE R., anesthesiology nurse; b. Memphis, Mar. 28, 1952; d. Allen Candler and Norma Rose (Goldman) Craven; m. David W. Jolly, July 10, 1970; children: Hope, David W., Brandi Nicole. AS, Itawamba Jr. Coll., Fulton, Miss., 1976; BS in Anesthesia, U. Miss., 1985. Cert. in anesthesiology. Staff nurse, neonatal ICU Gilmore Meml. Hosp., Amory, Miss.; ICU supr. Houston (Miss.) Community Hosp.; staff nurse anesthetist Aberdeen-Monroe County Hosp., Monroe, Miss., Clay County Med. Ctr., West Point, Miss.; chief nurse anesthetist Bapt. Meml. Hosp., Union County Anesthesia Svcs., New Albany, Miss. Mem. Am. Assn. Nurse Anesthetists. Home: 1169 County Road 101 New Albany MS 38652-9457

JOLLY, BRUCE OVERSTREET, retired newspaperman; b. Bay City, Tex., July 2, 1912; s. Irvin and Alice Gretchen (Overstreet) J.; m. Sarah Clark Tate Jeffress, Jan. 22, 1946; children—Bruce Overstreet, Jr., Edwin Jeffress. AB in English and Journalism, Franklin Coll., 1938. Reporter, Indpls. News, 1938-40, Post Tribune, Gary, Ind., 1940-42, 47-48; Washington corr. Daily News, Greensboro, N.C., 1949-65; with pub. relations dept. So. Ry., Washington, 1965-72. Author: The First Hundred Years, 1977; Keeping Up With Yesterday, 1985, A Century of Progress, 1990, Travels With Barbara, 1992; editor: The Brightness of His Presence, 1980. Bd. dirs. Sheltered Occupational Ctr. No. Va., Arlington, 1984-94; mem. planning commn. N.C. Tercentenary Celebration, 1962. With USAF, 1942-46, CBI. Recipient Cert. of Merit, State of N.C., 1963; alumni citation Franklin Coll., 1977. Mem. Nat. Press Club, Soc. of the South Pole (correspondent Antartic, 1963), Soc. Profl. Journalists, Arlington Knights of the Round Table (pres. 1982-83). Episcopalian. Avocations: golf, swimming, travel. Home: 8359 Alvord St Mc Lean VA 22102-1727

JOLLY, CHARLES NELSON, lawyer, pharmaceutical company executive; b. New Brunswick, N.J., Aug. 14, 1942; s. Nelson Frederick and Marie Mercedes (Montemayor) J.; m. Laurie Cherie Puryear, Feb. 5, 1992; children: T. Christopher, Susan Noel. BS, Holy Cross Coll., 1964; LLB, George Washington U., 1967. Bar: D.C. 1968, Tenn. 1984. Atty. Swift & Co., 1966-70; atty. Miles Labs., 1970-71, dir. legis. affairs, Washington, 1971-75, assoc. gen. counsel, Elkhart, Ind., 1975-77; bd. dirs., v.p., sec., gen. counsel Chattem Inc., Chattanooga, 1977-94; of counsel Chamblis & Bahner, Chattanooga, 1994—. Cand. U.S. Congress, 1994, 96. Mem. ABA, Tenn. Bar Assn., Chatanooga Bar Assn., D.C. Bar Assn., Non-Prescription Drug Mfrs. Assns. (past dir., vice chmn. exec. com.), Coun. Better Bus. Burs. of U.S. (dir.), Better Bus. Bur. of Chattanooga (past chmn., bd. dirs.), The Narrows Club (McConnelsburg, Pa.), Chattanooga Retriever Club (dir.).

JOLLY, WILLIAM THOMAS, foreign language educator; b. Helena, Ark., Apr. 8, 1929; s. Sidney Eugene and Eva (Jones) J. BA, Southwestern at Memphis, 1952; MA, U. Miss., 1958; PhD, Tulane U., 1968. Assoc. ancient langs., chmn. dept. Millsaps Coll., Jackson, Miss., 1959-65; assoc. prof. Greek and Latin Rhodes Coll., Memphis, 1965-75, prof., 1975-94, chmn. dept. fgn. langs., 1975-79, prof. emeritus, 1994—. With USN, 1953-55. Recipient Clarence Day award Day Found., 1991. Mem. Am. Philol. Assn/, Linquistic Soc. Am., Archaeol. Inst. Am., Classical Assn. Mid. West & South, Tenn. Classical Assn., Tenn. Philol. Assn., Am. Classical Legue. Democrat. Methodist. Home: 697 University St Memphis TN 38107-5138 Office: Rhodes Coll 2000 N Parkway Memphis TN 38112-1624

JONASON, PAULINE MARIE, retired art educator; b. N.Y.C., Jan. 26, 1928; d. Mario Gabriel and Concetta Virginia (Ruggio) Barbara; m. Charles Raymond Jonason, July 8, 1950; children: Raymond Charles (dec.), Ruthellen Harris, Randall Paul. BA in Edn., Queens Coll., 1948; postgrad., Columbia U., 1949; MA in Edn., CCNY, 1950; postgrad., Adelphi U., 1960. Opaquer Paramount Pictures Famous Studios, N.Y.C., 1944; teen-age program dir. Queens YWCA, Flushing, N.Y., 1948; art tchr. Hicksville (N.Y.) Jr. High Sch., 1949-52, Woodland Elem. Sch., Hicksville, 1955-61; art tchr. Hicksville Sr. High Sch., 1961-84, chmn. art dept., 1970-84, sr. class advisor, 1981-84, ret., 1984; artist Vero Beach, N.Y., 1984—. Lead actress in faculty plays, 1972, 74, 76; active Smithsonian Mus. Mem. NEA, AARP, Nat. Geog. Soc., Met. Mus. Art, Am. Mus. Natural History, Archaeol. Inst. Am., Ctr. for Arts, Planetary Soc., Am. Hibiscus Soc. (Indian River chpt.), Tri-County Tchrs. Retirement Coun., Ret. Hicksville Sch. Employees, Hicksville Classroom Tchrs. Assn., Earth Watch, Artists' Club. Home: 525 Banyan Rd Vero Beach FL 32963-1730

JONDAHL, TERRI ELISE, importing and distribution company executive; b. Ukiah, Calif., May 6, 1959; d. Thomas William and Rebecca (Stewart) J. AA in Bus. Adminstrn., Mendocino Coll., 1981; BA in Adminstrn. and Mgmt., Columbia Pacific U., 1993. Sec. to planning commn. County of Mendocino, Ukiah, Calif., 1977-80; office systems analyst County of Mendocino, Ukiah, 1980-83; micro systems analyst Computerland of Annapolis, Md., 1983-84; controller Continental Mfg. Inc., Nacogdoches, Tex., 1984-87; mktg. mgr. Continental Mfg. Inc., Nacogdoches, 1987-89, dir. sales and mktg., 1989-95, sec., treas., 1985-95; ptnr. CAB Inc., Norcross, Ga., 1995—; Mem. JSEC Com. Tex. Employment Commn., 1990-93. Co-author: National Federation of Business & Professional Women Local Organization Revitalization Plan, 1989. Mem. NAFE, Tex. Fedn. Bus. and Profl. Women (state pres. 1994-95), Nacogdoches Bus. and Profl. Women (pres. 1987-88), Ukiah Bus. and Profl. Women (pres. 1981-82), Nacogdoches County C. of C. (small bus. adv. com. 1990). Home: 1587 Martin Nash Rd Lilburn GA 30247 Office: CAB Inc 5964 G Peachtree Corners E Norcross GA 30071

JONDLE, MARNITA LEA, journalist, desktop publisher; b. Shenandoah, Iowa, Mar. 13, 1962; d. Virgil Wayne and Helen Margaret (Larabee) Hein; m. Brian Joseph Jondle, Dec. 29, 1984. BS in Journalism, N.W. Mo. State U., 1984; postgrad., Laramie County C.C., 1987. Registered massage therapist, 1996. Mng. editor Corydon (Iowa) Times-Rep., 1984; advt. coord. Wyo. Stockman-Farmer, Cheyenne, 1985; classified line advt. rep. Wyo. Tribune-Eagle, Cheyenne, 1986; edn., gen. assn. reporter Wyo. State Tribune, Cheyenne, 1986-87, news editor, edn. reporter, 1987-91; city editor Wyo. Tribune-Eagle, Cheyenne, 1991; pub. rels. coord. Laramie County Sch. Dist. # 1, Cheyenne, 1991-93; temporary agrl. editor/county reporter Medina Valley Times/Castroville (Tex.) & La Coste New Bull., 1993; mktg. svcs. adminstr. Colin Med. Instruments Corp., San Antonio, Tex., 1993—; editor, designer, co-owner Jondle Pub., Cheyenne and San Antonio, Tex., 1990—. Mentor Laramie County Sch. Dist. # 1, Cheyenne, 1993; edn. adv. bd. dirs. Head Start, Cheyenne, 1993. Mem. Am. Med. Writers Assn., Am. Mktg. Assn., Soc. Profl. Journalists, Associated Bodyworks & Massage Profls., Cheyenne C. of C. (tourism com. 1990, edn. com. 1990). Home: 2838 Bear Springs Dr San Antonio TX 78245-2570

JONER, BRUNO, aeronautical engineer; b. Oskarstrom, Sweden, Dec. 17, 1921; came to U.S., 1962, naturalized, 1967; s. Algot and Hanna (Erickson) J.; m. Ingrid Gustafsson, Oct. 3, 1953; children: Peter, Eva, David. BS in Aero. and Mech. Engring., Stockholm Inst. Tech., 1940. Tech. dir. Ostermans Aero AB, Stockholm, 1946-52; devel. engr. mgr. STAL Finspong, Sweden, 1952-57; mgr. aviation dept. Salen & Wicander, AB, Stockholm, 1957-62; project engr. Boeing Vertol Co., Phila., 1962-77, Boeing Marine Systems Co., Seattle, 1977-88, Boeing Huntsville (Ala.) Internat. Space Sta., 1988—. Author papers in field; co-author: Feasibility Study of Modern Airships. With Swedish Air Force, 1942-43. Assoc. fellow AIAA; mem. U.S. Naval Inst., Nat. Assn. Unmanned Vehicle Systems (charter). Home: 9414 Danese Ln SE Huntsville AL 35803-1304 Office: PO Box 240002 Huntsville AL 35824-6402

JONES, ALLISON BATES, oncology nurse; b. Montgomery, Ala., May 12, 1965; d. John Edwin and Mary (Bates) J. BSN, Auburn U., 1987; MSN, Troy State U., 1990. Staff nurse Bapt. Med. Ctr., Montgomery, 1989—; oncology educator, asst. prof. nursing Troy State U., Montgomery, 1990—. Mem. ANA, Oncology Nursing Soc., Sigma Theta Tau, Phi Eta Sigma. Office: Troy State U Sch Nursing 305 S Ripley St Montgomery AL 36104-4427

JONES, ALUN, artistic director. Degree in design, Monmouthshire Coll. Arts & Crafts; studied with Myra Silcox, Pontypool, Wales; student, Ballet Rambert Sch. Assoc. dir. Acad. Louisville Ballet, 1975-78; artistic dir. Louisville Ballet, 1978—; dancer Welsh Nat. Opera, London Festival Ballet, Zurich Opera House; assoc. artistic dir. Irish Nat. Ballet; founding mem., tech. dir. New London Ballet; guest tchr., choreographer Margo Marshall's City Ballet of Houston; tchr. Houston High Sch. Performing Arts, N.C. Sch.

Arts, Louisville Ballet, Va. Beach Civic Ballet, Huntsville (Ala.) Ballet; costume designer, scenery designer Houston Ballet, Tulsa Ballet Theatre, Louisville Ballet; choreographer London Festival Ballet, New London Ballet, Am. Ballet Theatre II, Tulsa Ballet Theatre, City Ballet of Houston, Austin Ballet, Honk Kong Ballet, Santa Barbara Festival Ballet, Mid-Columbia Regional Ballet. Chroreographer (ballets) The Merry Widow, The Trojan Women, The Lady of The Camellias, Cinderella, Romeo and Juliet. Office: Louisville Ballet 1300 Bardstown Rd Louisville KY 40204-1320

JONES, ANDREWNETTA, county government official; b. Memphis, Jan. 7, 1934. BA in Biology, Talladega Coll., 1955; cert. of med. tech., Meharry Med. Coll., 1957; postgrad., Memphis State U., 1980. Med. technologist E. H. Crump Hosp., Memphis, 1957-60, acting chief med. technologist, 1960; med. technologist LeBohneur Hosp., Memphis, 1967-68; supr. rsch. Mahalia Jackson's Chicken System, Inc., Memphis and Miami, Fla., 1968-69; mgr. quality control Mahalia Jackson's Food Products, Memphis and Miami, 1970-71; tech. cons. Whalum and Co., Memphis and Atlanta, 1972-73; br. exec. Sarah Brown Br. YMCA, Memphis, 1973-75; adminstr. Office Equal Opportunity Compliance Shelby County Govt., Memphis, 1976—. Bd. dirs. M.K. Gandhi Inst. for Nonviolence, Memphis Coun. for Internat. Visitors; mem. Gov.'s EEO Adv. Com.; trustee, mem. race rels. task force Goals for Memphis; permanent moderator legis. retreat Black Caucus of Tenn. Gen. Assembly; mem. adv. bd. Jobs for Tenn. Grads., Inc.; vol. med. technologist in community clinics Ibadan, Nigeria, 1962-64; mem. exec. YWCA, Lusaka, Zambia, 1965-67; leader Girl Guides Assn., Nigeria and Zambia. Mem. ASPA, Optimist Club, Alpha Kappa Alpha. Democrat. Office: Shelby County Govt Office Equal Opportunity 160 Mid-Am Mall Ste 969 Memphis TN 38103

JONES, ANNE ELIZABETH, motor license agent, insurance executive; b. Chgo., Nov. 26, 1945; d. George Edward and Betty Jane (Wise) Sybrant; m. Brenton Elvis Jones, Aug. 15, 1965 (div. June 1980); children: James Devon, Douglas Edward, Robert Derrick. Student, Ark. City Jr. Coll., Kans., 1962-64, Okla. State U., 1964-65. Credit mgr. Koppel's, Bartlesville, Okla., 1966-67; collector Am. Collection Agy., Bartlesville, 1967-72; office mgr. Paul Stumpff & Assocs., Bartlesville, 1972-82; owner A.J. Leasing, Inc., Tulsa, 1982—, Sooner Assocs., Inc., Tulsa, 1982—; motor lic. agt. Cen. Tag Agy., Tulsa, 1982—. Mem. Motor Lic. Agts. Assn. (exec. v.p. 1984-85, polit. liaison 1984, tchr. ins. and lic. law 1984, legis. chmn. 1986-87, exec. v.p., 1987—, liaison commn. sec. 1988-89, state sec. 1989-90), Ins. Women Tulsa (legis. chmn. 1984, pub. relations chmn. 1985, tchr. ins. classes 1979-85, cert. profl. ins. woman, bylaws chmn., 1987, chmn. pubs. 1989-90), Nat. Odometer Enforcement Assn., Midwest Taskforce on Odometer Enforcement, Soc. Cert. Ins. Counselors (apprentice faculty), Soc. of Cert. Ins. Svc. Reps. (seminar instr. 1989-92), Nat. Assn. Ins. Women (state orgn. chmn. 1985, Rookie of Yr. 1981, regional winner Lace Speak-Off 1985, 1st Runner-up Nat. Speak-Off 1985, Region vi chmn. pub. relations, 1986-87), Tulsa C. of C., Okla. Soc. Chartered Ins. Counselors (charter), Profl. Ins. Agts. Okla. (seminar instr. 1979-92), Ind. Ins. Agts. Okla. (seminar instr. 1979-83), Tulsa County Bar Assn. (fee arbitration bd. 1992-93), Toastmasters (Tulsa) (various offices, Area 1 Gov., 1987-88), Epsilon Sigma Alpha. Avocations: pub. speaking, motivational seminars, antique dealing, oil painting, photography. Office: Cen Tag Agy 2702 E 15th St Tulsa OK 74104-4738

JONES, BARBARA ARCHER, counselor, consultant; b. Lawrenceville, Va., Feb. 23, 1945; d. Wyatt and Marian (Blackwell) Archer; m. Wilbert Roosevelt Jones; children: Kyimberly, Brian. BA, Morgan State U., 1968; MEd, George Mason U., 1977; MA, George Washington U., 1983; cert. advanced grad. studies, Va. Tech. Inst., 1989, EdD, 1992. English tchr. Balt. Schs., 1968-70, Alexandria (Va.) City Schs., 1971-87; spl. edn. instr. No. Va. Community Coll., Annandale, fall 1981; asst. supr. Alexandria City Sch. Summer Youth Program, summer 1983; chairperson English and reading depts. Va. State Accreditation Vis. Com., Virginia Beach, winter 1987; secondary counselor Alexandria City Schs., 1987-88, elem. counselor, 1988—. Contbr. articles to profl. jours. Bd. dirs. spl. olympics com. Alexandria Dept. Human Svcs., 1986-93, Fairfax, Va., 1981-83. George Washington U. scholar, 1981; recipient Cert. of Appreciation, Vols. in Action, 1986, We Care of City of Alexandria, 1989. Mem. ACA, CEC, AAUW, Va. Counselors Assn., Va. Edn. Assn., Jack and Jill Am., Inc. (sec. Alexandria chpt. 1983-85, v.p. 1992-94, pres. 1994-96), Phi Delta Kappa, Alpha Kappa Alpha (sec. Arlington chpt. 1985-87, chpt. award 1990, Pan Hellenic Coun. award 1991).

JONES, BARBARA CHRISTINE, educator, linguist, creative arts designer; b. Augsburg, Swabia, Bavaria, Fed. Republic Germany, Nov. 14, 1942; came to U.S., 1964, naturalized, 1971; d. Martin Walter and Margarete Katharina (Roth-Rommel) Schulz von Hammer-Parstein; m. Robert Edward Dickey, 1967 (div. 1980); m. Raymond Lee Jones, 1981. Student U. Munich, 1961, Philomatique de Bordeaux, France, 1962; BA in German, French, Speech, Calif. State U., Chico, 1969, MA in Comparative Internat. Edn., 1974. Cert. secondary tchr., community coll. instr., Calif. Fgn. lang. tchr. Gridley Union High Sch., Calif., 1970-80, home econs., decorative arts instr., cons., 1970-80, English study skills instr., 1974-80, ESL coordinator, instr. Punjabi, Mex. Ams., 1970-72, curriculum com. chmn., 1970-80; program devel. adv. Program Devel. Ctr. Supt. Schs. Butte County, Oroville, Calif., 1975-77; opportunity tchr. Esperanza High Sch., Gridley, 1980-81, Liberty High Sch., Lodi, Calif., 1981-82, resource specialist coordinator, 1981-82; Title I coordinator Bear Creek Ranch Sch., Lodi, 1981-82, instr., counselor, 1981-82; substitute tchr. Elk Grove (Calif.) Unified, 1982-84; freelance decorative arts and textiles designer, 1982-85; internat. heritage and foods advisor AAUW, Chico, Calif., 1973-75; lectr. German, Schreiner Coll., Kerrville, Tex., 1993. Workshop dir. Creative Arts Ctr., Chico, 1972-73; workshop dir., advisor Bus. Profl. Women's Club of Gridley, 1972-74; v.p. Golden State Mobile Home League, Sacramento, 1980-82; mem. publicity Habitat for Humanity, Kerrville br., 1992-94. Designer weavings-wallhangings (1st place 10 categories, Silver Dollar Fair, Chico, 1970). Mem. AAUW (publicity dir. cultural activities Kerrville br. 1991-92), Am. Cancer Soc. (publicity 1992-95), United European Am. Club, Am. Assn. German Tchrs., U.S. Army Res. Non-Commd. Officer's Assn. (ednl. adv. 1984-86), German Texan Heritage Soc., Turtle Creek Social Ctr. (pioneer 1992—), Kerrville Garden Club (publicity 1993—), German Texan Heritage Soc., 1992—, Kappa Delta Pi. Avocations: fiber designs, swimming, travel, real estate. Home: 2894 Lower Turtle Creek Rd Kerrville TX 78028-9743

JONES, BETH WILEE, interior designer; b. Nashville, Oct. 14, 1961; d. Dickey Burrus amd Susie (Story) Wilee; m. Richard Lee Jones, Jr., Oct. 10, 1987. Degree in interior design, Nashville Sch. Interior Design, 1984. Cert. Nat. Coun. for Interior Design Qualification; cert. interior designer, Tenn. Sales clerk Wallpaper and Window Warehouse, Nashville, 1983-84, mgr., 1984-86; interior designer JoAnne Haynes & Assocs., Nashville, 1986-88, Moore's Interiors, Gallatin, Tenn., 1988-90; prin., interior designer Interior Collection, Hendersonville, Tenn., 1990—. Mem. Am. Soc. Interior Designers (chmn. cmty. svc., state sec. exec. bd. 1992-93, chmn. 1994-95, presdl. citation 1991). Mem. Ch. of Christ. Home and Office: The Interior Collection 129 Meadowvue Dr Hendersonville TN 37075-4296

JONES, BEVERLY WARD, state agency administrator. BA in Sociology, Rutgers U., 1969; MSW in Clin. Social Work, U. Md., 1976, post master's cert. in social work adminstrn., 1983. Lic. cert. social worker, Md. Office asst. dept. psychology Douglas Coll. Rutgers U., New Brunswick, N.J., 1965, 66; tchr.'s asst. Upward Bound Rutgers U., 1967; social work asst. II adoption dist. Balt. City Dept. Social Svcs., 1973-74, intake supr. Westwood Ctr., 1976-77, training specialist training and staff devel. divsn., 1977-78, case supr. child abuse-continuing svcs., 1978-79, dist. supr. child abuse-continuing svcs., 1979-84; program mgr. child protective svcs. Social Svcs. Adminstrn., Balt., 1984-87; sr. field cons. Child Welfare League Am., Washington, 1987-89; asst. dir. child welfare svcs. Anne Arundel County Dept. Social Svcs., Annapolis, Md., 1989-91; sr. assoc. Ctr. for Study of Social Policy, Washington, 1992; asst. dir. social work cmty. outreach svc. Sch. Social Work U. Md., Balt., 1992-93; dir. Divsn. Children and Family Svcs., Little Rock, 1993—; mem. adj. faculty, field instr. Sch. Social Work U. Md.; chairperson Ark. Child Welfare Oversight and Compliance Com. Mem. NASW, Am. Pub. Welfare Assn., Child Welfare League Am. (N.Am. kinship care policy and practice com., N.Am. commn. on chem. dependency and child welfare), Acad. Cert. Social Workers, Black Adminstrs. in Child Welfare, U. Md. Sch. Social Work Alumni Assn. (pres. bd. dirs.). Office: Human Svcs Dept PO Box 1437 Slot 636 Little Rock AR 72203*

JONES, BOB, fisheries association executive. Exec. dir. Southeastern Fisheries Assn. Address: 312 E Georgia St Tallahassee FL 32301

JONES, BOBBY EUGENE, state agency administrator, educator; b. Briceville, Tenn., Sept. 12, 1932; s. Lawrence John and Minnie (Chadwick) J.; m. Alta Roddy, Apr. 5, 1956 (dec. Sept. 17, 1966); 1 child, Bobby Eugene, Jr.; m. Retha Branam, Oct. 5, 1967 (div. Aug. 15, 1979); 1 child, William Thomas. LLD, U. Balt., 1958; BS, E. Tenn. State U., 1980; MS, U. Tenn., 1982, DEd, 1983. Cert. in accident reconstruction U.S. DOT. Gen. mgr. surg. equipment co., Tampa, Fla., 1959-65; gen. mgr., owner med. supply co., Knoxville, Tenn., 1966-79; team leader U.S. DOT, Knoxville, Tenn., 1980-83; exec. dir. Criminal Justice Adminstrn., Knoxville, Tenn., 1985—; mem. adv. bd. Tenn. Drug Abuse, Knoxville, 1995-96; cons. State Ct. Judges, Knoxville, 1991-96. Author: Self-Sustained Misdemeanor Probation, 1979. Dist. mgr. Anderson County Rep. Party, Clinton, Tenn., 1967-96; v.p. Neighborhood Watch, Briceville, Tenn., 1992-96. Served in USN, 1950-54, Korea. Mem. C. of C., Masons. Republican. Baptist. Office: Criminal Justice Adminstrn PO Box 9807 Knoxville TN 37940

JONES, BOBBYE FRANKS, state public works administrator; b. Tupelo, Miss., Dec. 26, 1931; d. William Tracy and Luna Virginia (Duvall) Franks; m. Ben David Jones, May 28, 1955; children: Rebecca Leigh Jones West, Traci Virginia Jones Clegg. BSc, U. Miss., 1953, MBA, 1955. Prof. Itawamba Jr. Coll., Fulton, Miss., 1953-55, 64-76, Perkinston (Miss.) Jr. Coll., 1955-56; tchr. Gulfport (Miss.) City Schs., 1957-60, Tupelo City Sch., 1961-62, Southeast Lauderdale Sch., Meridian, Miss., 1977-78; fiscal adminstr. Miss. Dept. Transp., Tupelo, 1983—. Sec./treas. PTA, Tupelo, 1961-62; pres. Fulton Civic Club, 1970; dir. Federated Women's Club, Jackson, Miss., 1967-73; troop leader, neighborhood chmn. Girl Scouts U.S., Fulton, 1966-73. Republican. Baptist. Home: 1406 Pinecrest Dr Tupelo MS 38801

JONES, BONNIE DAMSCHRODER, special education specialist; b. Cocoa, Fla., Dec. 20, 1945; d. Eugene Edward and Lu Jeanette (Hufford) Damschroder; m. Robert Kirk Jones, June 8, 1968; children: Kelly Anne, Jennifer Graham. BS in Edn., Capital U., Columbus, Ohio, 1967; MS in Edn., George Mason U., 1976; transition specialist cert., U. Hawaii, 1988; postgrad., Columbia U., 1991. Tchr. mental retardation Waterford (Conn.) Pub. Schs., 1967-68; tchr. mentally retarded Escambia County Schs., Pensacola, Fla., 1968-70; tchr. learning disabilities Fairfax County Schs., Fairfax, Va., 1975-78; curriculum specialist Newport News (Va.) Pub. Schs., 1978-80; program coord. Peninsula Area Coop. Ednl. Svcs. Day Treatment Regional Sch., Newport News, 1980-81; dist. transition coord. Hawaii Dept. Edn., Honolulu, 1984-88; program specialist Kans. Dept. Edn., Topeka, 1988-90; cons. in spl. edn. Kans. Bd. Edn., Topeka, 1990-91; rsch. asst. Columbia U. Tchrs. Coll., N.Y.C., 1991-92; tchr. learning disabilities Fairfax County Pub. Schs., Fairfax, Va., 1975-78, tchr., dept. chairperson, 1992—; adj. instr. George Mason U., Fairfax, 1976, Baruch Coll., 1992; supervising tchr. Hampton (Va.) Inst., 1981, U. Hawaii, Honolulu, 1988; mem. exceptional needs standards com. Nat. Bd. for Profl. Tchg. Standards, 1994—. Co-author: Identifying Handicapping Conditions, 1978, Career Awareness for Students with Handicaps, 1986, Implementing Transition Goals, 1992. Mem. Jr. League, Portland, Maine, Honolulu, and Topeka, 1983—; pres. USCG Officers' Wives Club, Portland, 1983, bd. dirs. Newport News, 1978-79, Honolulu, 1984-88, N.Y.C., 1991; co-chmn. carnival booth Punahou Sch., Honolulu, 1987, 88; treas. Red Hill Sch. PTA, Honolulu, 1985-87; bd. dirs. Internat. Divsn. Career Devel., 1989-94, treas., 1992-94; pres. Kans. Divsn. Career Devel., 1989-90. Recipient cert. of appreciation USCG, Boston, 1983, community svc. award, N.Y.C., 1991; Vocat. Educator of Yr. award Hawaii Vocat. Edn. Assn., 1987, Outstanding Contbn. to Transition award Kans. Div. on Career Devel., 1990. Mem. ASCD, NEA, Coun. for Exceptional Children (subcom. on knowledge and skills profl. standards com. 1990-94), Phi Delta Kappa. Home: 7726 Silver Sage Ct Springfield VA 22153-2126

JONES, BRENDA KAYE, public relations executive; b. Oklahoma City, Jan. 4, 1958; d. Bobby Lee and Betty Ruth (Hillburn) J. Student, Okla. Bapt. U., 1976-77; BA in Journalism, U. Okla., 1980. Polit. reporter, copy editor The Okla. Daily, Norman, 1978-80; field dir. of Coll. Reps. Rep. Nat. Com., Washington, 1979; office mgr. "Reagan for Pres. in 80" Fundraising Com., Washington, 1980; pers. rsch. asst. The White House and Office of Pres.-Elect, Washington, 1980-81; pub. liaison officer U.S. Info. Agy., Washington, 1982-85; office of presdl. pers. sr. writer The White House, Washington, 1985-88; sr. asst., prin. advisor to ambassador Am. Embassy, Bern, Switzerland, 1988-89; mktg. cons. The People's Pl., Washington, 1990-91; spl. asst. to chmn., dir. The Pres.'s Commn. on Mgmt. of A.I.D. Program, Washington, 1992—; dir. pub. rels Feed The Children, Oklahoma City, 1993-95; v.p. pub. rels. Ackerman McQueen Agy., Oklahoma City, 1995—. Vol. Don Nickles for U.S. Senate campaign and Ron Shotts for Gov., 1978; v.p. Okla. Coll. Reps., 1979-80, U. Okla. Washington Chpt., 1986-88. Selected as one of Outstanding Young Women in Am., 1979. Mem. Women in Comm. Inc., Pub. Rels. Soc. Am., Jr. League, Reagan Alumni Assn. Republican. Office: Ackerman McQueen 1601 NW Expressway Ste 1100 Oklahoma City OK 73118

JONES, BRERETON C., small business owner, former governor; b. Point Pleasant, W.Va., June 27, 1939; m. Elizabeth Lloyd; children: Lucy, Bret. BS, Univ. Va., 1961. Chmn. Gov's. Medicaid Task Force, 1985, former mem. gov's. coun. edn. reform; former mem. Ky. Bd. Agr.; former lt. gov. State of Ky., Frankfort, until 1991, gov., 1991-95; founder, pres. Ky. Health Care Access Found.; former coun. supr. Chandler Med. Ctr.; v.p. McDowell Cancer Rsch. Found. Bd.; owner Airdrie Stud Farm, Woodford County, Ky., 1972—; co-chair Appalachian Regional Commn.; chmn. So. State Energy Bd. Exec. Com. Mem. Prichard Com. Acad. Excellence, Ky. State U. Found.; trustee U. Ky.; bd. dirs. U. Ky. Equine Rsch. Found. Recipient Brotherhood award NCCJ, Cmty. Svc. award AMA, 1990, Nathan Davis award AMA, 1993. Mem. Nat. govs. Assn. (exec. com.), So. Govs. Assn., Dem. Govs. Assn. Office: Airdrie Stud Farm PO Box 487 Midway KY 40347*

JONES, CAROL ANN, psychology educator; b. Blytheville, Ark., June 26, 1950; d. Toler Bartow and Martha Ann (Sibley) Buchanan; m. Alan Keith Jones, Aug. 18, 1979 (divorced); 1 child, Martha Ann. BA in Edn., U. Miss., 1972, MEd, 1976, PhD, 1980. Psychologist U. Miss., Oxford, 1977-79; psychology intern Northeast Ark. Regional Mental Health Ctr., West Memphis, 1979-80; sch. psychologist Bryan (Tex.) Ind. Sch. Dist., 1980-81; prof. psychology Blinn Coll., Bryan, 1982-90; sch. psychologist Gulfport (Miss.) Pub. Schs., 1990-94; assoc. prof. psychology William Carey Coll. on the Coast, Gulfport, Miss., 1994—; coord. Harrison County Family Resource Consortium, 1992, Interagy. Coord. Coun., 1992; coord. Nat. Mental Health Assn. Cmty. Prevention Svcs. Program, 1992; adj. prof. psychology William Carey Coll., 1993-94. Mem. exec. com. Muscular Dystrophy Telethon, Bryan, 1989; mem. adv. bd. Parents as Tchrs., Bryan, 1992-94, Miss. Children's Rehab. Ctr., Gulf Coast Mental Health Ctr., 1991-94; bd. dirs. Mental Health Assn. of Harrison County, 1991-95, Miss. Forum on Children and Families, Parents as Tchrs., Gulfport; prevention program contact pilot program Nat. Mental Health Assn., mem. task force Interagency Coord. Coun. Mem. Brazos Valley Psychol. Assn., Jr. League BCS (chmn. rsch. and devel. 1989-90, bd. dirs. planning and cmty. coun. 1989-90), APA, Gulf Coast C. of C. (edn. com.), Rotary Internat., Phi Kappa Phi, Kappa Delta Pi, Phi Delta Kappa, Chi Omega (pres. 1985-89). Democrat. Methodist. Home: 9115 Cross Creek Cir Gulfport MS 39503-6116

JONES, CAROLYN ELLIS, publisher, retired employment agency and business service company executive; b. Marigold, Miss., Feb. 21, 1928; d. Joseph Lawrence and Willie Decelle (Forrest) Peeples; m. David Wright Ellis, May 30, 1945 (div. 1966); children—David, Lyn, Debbie, Dawn; m. Frank Willis Jones, Jan. 1, 1980. Student La. State U., 1949. Owner, mgr. Personnel and Bus. Service, Inc., Greenwood, Miss., 1962-88, now v.p.; owner Honor Pub. Co., Greenwood, 1988—. Author: The Lottie Moon Storybook, 1985; Editor: An Old Soldier's Career, 1974. Contbr. articles to religious and gen. interest publs. Mem. adv. bd. career edn. Greenwood Pub. Schs., 1975-76, mem. adv. bd. vocat.-tech. dept., 1975-88; conf. leader Miss. Bapt. Convention Singles Retreat, 1980; Mission Service Corps del. Home Mission Bd., So. Bapt. Conv., Hawaii, 1979. Mem. Greenwood C. of C. (edn. com. 1980—, guest speaker career day program local high sch.), Mothers Against Drunk Drivers, Altrusa Internat., Nat. Fedn. Ind. Bus., Miss Delta Rose Soc., Miss. Native Plant Soc., Gideon Aux. (pres. 1986-88). Avocations: writing, rose exhibitions, wildflowers. Office: Honor Pub 802 W President Ave Greenwood MS 38930-3326

JONES, CAROLYN EVANS, small business owner; b. Middleboro, Mass., Sept. 5, 1931; d. King Israel and Kleo Estelle (Hodges) Evans; m. John Homer Jones, Sept. 9, 1966 (dec. July 1986); 1 child, David Everett. BA in English, Tift Coll., 1952; M of Religious Edn., Carver Sch. Missions and Social Work (now So. Bapt. Theol. Sem.), 1958; BA in Art, Mercer U., 1982. Cert. secondary tchr., Ga. Tchr. McDuffie County Bd. Edn., Thomson, Ga., 1952-53, Colquitt County Bd. Edn., Norman Park, Ga., 1953-55; missionary Home Mission Bd. SBC, New Orleans and Macon, 1958-66; spl. edn. tchr. Bibb County Bd. Edn., Macon, 1968-70, 75-79; owner, operator Laney Co. Imprinted Specialties, Macon, 1986—. Contbr. numerous articles and poems to profl. jours. Bible tchr. YWCA, Macon, 1980-85; deacon 1st Bapt. Ch., Macon. Mem. Macon-Bibb County C. of C., Internat. Tng. in Comm., Alumnae Assn. Tift Coll. (exec. com.), Greater Macon Women Bus. Owners Club. Democrat. Office: Laney Co Imprinted Specialties 2451 Kingsley Dr Macon GA 31204-1718

JONES, CARTER HELM, fire department official; b. Manning, S.C., Aug. 15, 1946; s. Edloe Pendelton and Cooper Bell (Dickson) J.; m. Mary Jo McCarter, Sept. 28, 1975; children: Jonathan Carter, William Craig. AA, North Greenville Jr. Coll., 1966; BA, Presbyn. Coll., 1968; MEd, U. Ga., 1969. Rehab. counselor S.C. Dept. Vocat. Rehab., Sumter, 1969-73; tng. specialist Office of State Fire Marshal, Columbia, S.C., 1973-77; chief dept. Clarendon County Fire Dept., Manning, 1977—. Author (booklet) Arson-An Ignored American Tradition, 1986. Sunday sch. tchr. Clarendon Bapt. Ch., Alcolu, S.C., 1991—. Recipient Firefighter of Yr. award Ins. Women of Pee Dee, 1989, Firefighter of Yr. award Manning Fire Dept., 1989. Mem. Nat. Fire Protection Assn., Internat. Assn. Arson Investigators, Pee Dee Firefighters' Assn. (pres. 1981, Flanagan Fire Svc. award 1989), S.C. Firemen's Assn. (pres. 1966-80, Citizenship award 1983, S.C. Firefighter of Yr. award 1996). Office: Clarendon County Fire Dept PO Box 1330 Manning SC 29102

JONES, CHARLES EDWIN, chaplain, historian, bibliographer; b. Kansas City, Mo., June 1, 1932; s. Dess Dain and Dove (Barnwell) J.; m. Beverly Anne Lundy, May 30, 1956; 1 child, Karl Laurence. BA, Bethany-Peniel Coll., 1954; MALS, U. Mich., 1955; MS, U. Wis., 1960, PhD, 1968; postgrad., Episcopal Div. Sch., Cambridge, Mass., 1975-76. Ordained to ministry Reformed Episcopal Ch. as deacon, 1990. Libr. Park Coll., 1961-63; manuscript curator Mich. Hist. Coll. U. Mich., Ann Arbor, 1965-69; assoc. prof. history Houghton Coll., 1969-71; hist. cataloguer Rockefeller Libr. Brown U., 1971-76; chaplain-in-residence Quail Creek Nursing Ctr., Oklahoma City, 1989—. Author: Perfectionist Persuasion, 1974, Guide to the Study of the Holiness Movement, 1974, Guide to the Study of the Pentecostal Movement, 1983, Black Holiness, 1987, The Charismatic Movement, 1995; contbr. articles to scholarly jours. With U.S. Army, 1956-58. Mem. Am. Theol. Libr. Assn., Can. Ch. Hist. Soc. Democrat. Mem. Reformed Episcopal Ch. Home: 12300 Springwood Dr Oklahoma City OK 73120-1724

JONES, CHARLES ERIC, JR., lawyer; b. Phila., Dec. 21, 1957; s. Charles Eric and Janith (Van Orden) J.; m. Ronda Nolen, May 16, 1981; children: Charles Eric III, Courtney Elaine, Camille Elizabeth. BBA, U. Tex., 1980; JD, St. Mary's U., 1983. Bar: Tex. 1983, U.S. Dist. Ct. (no. dist.) Tex. 1985, U.S. Dist. Ct. (we. dist.) Okla. 1986, U.S. Dist. Ct. (we. and ea. dists.) Ark. 1987, U.S. Supreme Ct. 1988, U.S. Ct. Appeals (5th cir.) 1988, U.S. Dist. Ct. (ea. dist.) Tex. 1992. Briefing atty. Tex. Ct. Criminal Appeals, Austin, 1983-84; assoc. Nunn Griggs & Wetsel, Sweetwater, Tex., 1984; ptnr. Nunn, Griggs, Wetsel & Jones, Sweetwater, 1985-88, 1985-89; ptnr. Nunn, Griggs, Jones & Sheridan, Sweetwater, 1989-91, Jones & Edwards, L.L.P., Sweetwater, 1992-94, Jones, Edwards & Young, L.L.P., Sweetwater, 1995, Jones & Young, LLP, Sweetwater, Tex., 1995—; chmn. St. Mary's Legal Rsch. Bd., San Antonio, 1982-83; student instr. St. Mary's U., San Antonio, 1982-83, The Order of Barristers, 1983. Bd. dirs. Nolan County Hospice, Inc., Sweetwater, 1984-92, Nolan County Crimestoppers, Inc., Sweetwater, 1985-90, chmn., 1987-89; dir. adminstrv. bd. United Meth. Ch., Sweetwater, 1985-88; chmn. Nolan County United Way, 1985-87; co-chmn. City Coun. Libr. Bd., 1987—. Mem. ABA, Assn. Trial Lawyers Am., Tex. Bar Assn., Tex. Trial Lawyers Assn., Tex. State Bar Coll., Order of Barristers, Tex. Assn. Banking Counsel, Indp. Bankers Assn. Tex. Home: 804 Josephine St Sweetwater TX 79556-3312 Office: Jones & Young LLP PO Box 188 Sweetwater TX 79556-0188

JONES, CHARLES MARKS, JR., retired loan company executive; b. El Paso, Tex., Apr. 6, 1922; s. Charles Marks and Anna Patterson (Hiller) J.; m. Josephine Isabelle Elliott, Dec. 28, 1946; children: Nancy Hutcheson, Charles Marks III, Susan Hiller, Josephine Elliott, Lawson Elliott. BS, U. Ga., 1947. With Consol. Loan Co., Albany, Ga., 1946—; now pres., chief exec. officer Consol. Loan Co., Albany, until 1992; ret., 1992; bd. dirs. CNL Fin. Corp., Macon, Ga., 1st State Bank Corp., Albany. Pres. Albany Community Concert Assn., 1970-77, 86, Albany Little Theatre, 1973-76, Albany Mus. Art, 1975, Albany Area Arts Coun., 1978, Albany Symphony Orch. Assn., 1986; trustee U. of the South, Sewanee, Tenn.; bd. dirs. Albany Little Theatre, Albany Area Arts Coun., Albany Concert Assn. Lt. USNR, 1944-46, PTO. Mem. Albanfy Downtown Mchts. Assn. (bd. dirs.), Albany County C. of C. (past bd. dirs.), Kiwanis. Office: PO Box 46 430 W Tift Ave Albany GA 31702-0046

JONES, CHARLES WILLIAM, association executive; b. Montgomery, Ala., Mar. 20, 1936; s. Charles W. and Flaria (Duke) J.; children: Beth, Charles P. BS in Acctg., U. Ala., 1958. CPA, Ala. Ptnr. Aldridge Borden & Jones CPA, Montgomery, Ala., 1958-69; pres. Ring Around Products, Montgomery, 1969-77; assoc. gen. dir. Montgomery YMCA, 1978-94; exec. dir. Blue and Gray Assn., Montgomery, 1980—. Active Montgomery Bd. Edn., 1968-74. Mem. AICPA, Montgomery Lions Club (Lion of Yr. 1991), Montgomery Country Club. Office: Blue and Gray Assn 771 S Lawrence St Ste 106 Montgomery AL 36104-5005

JONES, CHARLOTTE, principal; b. Elk City, Okla., Dec. 21, 1949; d. S.G. and Mary Kathryn (Hartman) McLaury; m. Ray Loyd Jones, Apr. 3, 1969; children: Kathryn Denise, Ryan MacRay, Joshua Kyle. BS in Edn., U. Okla., 1976; MEd, Southwestern Okla. State U., 1991. Cert. tchr. math., counseling, social studies, lang. arts. Prin. Madison Elem. Sch., Okla. Pub. Schs., Norman. Mem. NEA, ASCD, ACA, Okla. Edn. Assn., Nat. Assn. Elem. Sch. Prins., Rotary, Phi Delta Kappa. Home: 4409 Oxford Way Norman OK 73072-3160

JONES, CHRISTOPHER JON, multimedia specialist; b. Ponca City, Okla., Mar. 14, 1969; s. Jon Phillip and Marilyn Marie (Watson) J.; m. Kelley Jean Turner, Dec. 30, 1989. BS in Edn., Baylor U., 1992, MS in Edn., 1993. Cert. secondary tchr., Okla., Tex. Grad. asst. Baylor U., Waco, Tex., 1992-93; multimedia curriculum specialist U. Cen. Okla., Edmond, 1993—. Mem. ASCD, Internat. Soc. Tech. in Edn., Assn. Ednl. Comm. and Tech. Office: U Cen Okla 100 University Dr Edmond OK 73034

JONES, CLYDE MICHAEL, hematologist; b. Birmingham, Ala., Dec. 4, 1947. AB, Birmingham So. Coll., 1970; MD, U. Ala., 1974. Lic. M.D., Tex., Md., Ala. Med. intern dept. medicine U. Ala. Hosps. and Clinics, Birmingham, 1974-75, jr. resident dept. medicine, 1975-76; fellow in medicine-hematology Johns Hopkins Hosp., Balt., 1976-78, fellow in med. oncology, 1978-79; med. officer lab. immunodiagnosis Nat. Cancer Inst., NIH, Bethesda, Md., 1979-82; faculty asst. medicine and oncology Johns Hopkins Hosp., Balt., 1979-82; asst. prof. internal medicine, hematology/oncology divsn. U. Tex. Med. Sch., Houston, 1982-89; assoc. prof. internal medicine, hematology/oncology divsn. U. Tex. Med. Sch. and M.D. Cancer Ctr., Houston, 1990—; assoc. dir. hematology/oncology U. Tex. Med. Sch., Houston, 1992—; assoc. prof. medicine M.D. Anderson Hosp., Houston, 1992—. Mem. editorial bd. Kidney Internat., 1984—, Cancer Rsch., 1986—, Jour. Immunology, 1988—; patentee in field; contbr. numerous articles to profl. jours. and chpts. to books. Ad hoc reviewer Merit Rev. Bd. for Hematology, U.S. VA, 1986-87; sci. rev. com. for Nat. Med. Student Rsch. Forum, 1986-88; mem. sci. rev. com. Arthritis Found. of Am., 1985-901 mem. ad hoc com. NIH Diabetes, Digestive and Kidney Diseases Spl. Grants Rev. Com., 1992-93. Recipient Student Rsch. award U. Ala. Sch. Medicine, 1972, NIH Nat. Rsch. Svc. award Johns Hopkins U., 1976-78, Bent Stethoscope award in Jr. Medicine Teaching, U. Tex. Med. Sch. at Houston, 1982-84; grantee NIH, 1985-88, 1990-94, 1992-94, AMGEN Labs., 1990—. Mem. AAAS, ACP, Internat. Soc. for Exptl. Hematology, Am. Fedn. for Clin. Rsch., Am. Soc. Hematology, Am. Assn. for Cancer Rsch., Am. Assn. Immunologists, Clin. Immunology Soc., Am. Soc. for Biochemistry and Molecular Biology, Tex. Med. Assn., Gulf Coast Hematology Soc. (pres.-elect 1990-91). Office: U Tex Health Sci Ctr 6431 Fannin Msb # 5016 Houston TX 77030

JONES, CONSTANCE IRENE, medical products executive; b. Mpls., July 12, 1943; d. Warren Merrill and Donna Jane (Stafford) Carlson; m. Dec. 10, 1965 (widowed July 11, 1980); 1 child, John. BA in Bus., U. Ctrl. Fla., 1984. Cert. Audioprosthologist, Fla. Regional sales mgr. Dental H., Orlando, Fla., 1985-88; hearing specialist Orange Hearing Ctr., Orlando, Fla., 1989-92; pres., hearing specialist Connie's Hearing Ctr., Orlando, 1993-94; pres., hearing specialist, chmn. Am.'s Choice Hearing, Orlando, 1995—. Committeewoman Rep. Precinct, Orange County, 1992. Mem. Internat. Hearing Soc., Fla. Hearing Aid Soc., Coun. Accreditation in Occpl. Hearing Conservation. Republican. Methodist. Home: 828 Ibsen Ave Orlando FL 32809 Office: Am's Choice Hearing Inc 5924 S Orange Ave Orlando FL 32809-4236

JONES, D. PAUL, JR., banker, lawyer; b. Birmingham, Ala., Sept. 26, 1942; s. D. Paul and Virginia Lee (Mount) J.; m. Charlene Dale Angelich, Aug. 1964; children: Holly, Allison, Paul, III. B.S., U. Ala., 1964, J.D., 1967; LL.M., N.Y. U., 1968. Bar: Ala. Mem. firm Balch, Bingham, Baker, Hawthorne, Williams & Ward, Birmingham, 1970-78, of counsel, 1978-86; exec. v.p., gen. counsel, dir. Compass Bancshares, Inc., Birmingham, 1978-84, vice chmn., 1984-89, pres., COO, 1989-91, chmn., CEO, 1991—; bd. dirs. Compass Bank, Golden Enterprises, Inc., Russell Lands Co., Fed. Res. Bank Atlanta, Bus. Coun. Ala.; exec. com. Pub. Affairs Rsch. Coun. Ala.; mem. Internat. Fin. Conf. Chmn. Ala. Bus. Charitable Trust Fund; mem. adv. bd. Better Bus. Bur. Birmingham; adv. bd. Salvation Army, Birmingham; bd. visitors Sch. Commerce and Bus. Adminstrn., U. Ala.; mem. pres.'s coun. U. Ala., Birmingham, pres.'s cabinet; mem. pres.'s coun. Ala. Inst. Deaf and Blind; ptnr. Econ. Devel. Partnership Ala.; grad. bd. trustees Leadership Birmingham; grad. Leadership Ala. Mem. ABA, Ala. Bar Assn. (chmn. sect. corp., banking and bus. law 1973-75, bd. bar examiners 1975-78), Birmingham Bar Assn., Am. Bankers Assn. (mem. govt. rels. coun. 1985-88), Ala. Bankers Assn. (pres. 1989-90, chmn. fin. com. 1990-91, exec. coun.), Retail Issues and Deposit Ins. Com., Bankers Round Table, Newcomen, Soc. Internat. Bus. Fellows, Birmingham C. of C., Birmingham C. of C. Found., Birmingham Bus. Leadership Group, Svc. Corps Ret. Execs. (adv. bd.), The Club, Old Overton, Country Club Birmingham, Willow Point Golf and Country Club (Alexander City), Rotary. Home: 3148 Guilford Rd Birmingham AL 35223-1217 Office: Compass Bancshares Inc PO Box 10566 Birmingham AL 35296 also: Compass Bancshares Inc 15 20th St S Birmingham AL 35233-2034

JONES, DALE P., oil service company executive; b. Gillham, Ark., Oct. 19, 1936; s. Ray Elgin and Alma Lee (Wheeler) J.; m. Anita Ruth Collier, Dec. 28, 1963; children: Lee Anna, Leisa. BS, U. Ark., 1958; postgrad., U. Okla., 1970. CPA, Ark., Tex. With Arthur Andersen & Co., 1958-59, 62-65; exec. Halliburton Co., various, 1965-93; vice chariman Halliburton Co., Dallas, 1989—. Chmn. bd., pres. Duncan Regional Hosp. Inc., 1977-80. Served to capt. USAF, 1959-62. Mem. AICPA, Am. Petroleum Inst., Tex. Soc. CPAs, Petroleum Club. Baptist. Office: Halliburton Co 3600 Lincoln Plz 500 N Akard St Dallas TX 75201-3320*

JONES, DAN LEWIS, psychologist; b. Halifax, Va., Oct. 8, 1951; s. Ernest Lewis and Mary Elizabeth (Francis) J.; m. Temple Kiger Jones, Aug. 17, 1974; children: Natalie Temple, Layla Michelle. BA, Appalachian State U., 1974; MA, West Ga. Coll., 1976; PhD, U. Kans., 1986. Lic. psychologist, N.C., Tenn., Calif., Va.; diplomate in counseling psychology Am. Bd. Profl. Psychology; cert. treatment of alcohol and other psychoactive substance use disorders, APA Coll. of Profl. Psychology. Instr. psychology N.C. Cen. U., Durham, 1976-79; counselor Adult Life Resource Ctr., U. Kans., Lawrence, 1979-84; psychology intern Counseling Ctr. U. Calif., Irvine, 1984-85; acting dir. adult life resource ctr. U. Kans., 1985-86; staff psychologist Counseling Ctr. Utah State U., Logan, 1986-88; psychologist Counseling Ctr. East Tenn. State U., Johnson City, 1988-89; sr. psychologist, dir. tng., asst. dir. Counseling and Psychol. Svcs., Appalachian State U., Boone, N.C., 1989—; part-time pvt. practice; cons. IRS, 1985, Bristol (Tenn.) Mental Health Ctr., 1989, N.C. Ct. Counseling Svcs., 1979. Author: (with others) Counseling Adults, 1985, editor; author (manual) The Stress management Workshop, 1985, (with others) AACD Stress Workshop Manual, 1985. Fellow Acad. of Counseling Psychology; mem. APA (chmn. spl. interest group on coll. counseling ctrs. divsn. 17), Am. Coll. Pers. Assn. (directorate commn. VII), Soc. of Psychotherapy Integration. Democrat. Home: 357 Fawn Boone NC 28607-9804

JONES, DANIEL RICHARD, English language educator, consultant; b. Jacksonville, Fla., May 26, 1952; s. Frank Jefferson and Gloria Loretta (Restivo) J.; m. Carol Ann Burns, Nov. 17, 1978; 1 child, Samuel Riley. BA with honors, Fla. State U., 1974, MA, 1976, PhD, 1979. Asst. prof. dept. humanities Embry-Riddle Aero. U., Daytona Beach, Fla., 1979-83; asst. prof. dept. English U. Ctrl. Fla., Orlando, 1984-87, assoc. prof., 1987—. Contbr. articles to profl. jours. Mem. Assn. Tchrs. Tech. Writing (exec. sec., treas. 1990—, Best Article award ATTW Jour., 1985), Soc. Tech. Comm. (numerous coms. Orlando chpt. 1984—), Coun. Programs in Tech. and Sci. Commn., Fla. Coll. English Assn., Nat. Coun. Tchrs. English. Democrat. Home: 427 Timberwood Trl Oviedo FL 32765-8369 Office: U Ctrl Fla Dept English 4000 Central Fla Blvd Orlando FL 32816

JONES, DARYL LAFAYETTE, state legislator, lawyer; b. May 31, 1955; m. Myoushi Carter; children: Derek, Durel, Michele. BS in Math. with honors, U.S. Air Force Academy, Colo., 1977; JD cum laude, U. Miami, Fla., 1987. Bar: Fla., 1988. Commd. 2nd lt. USAF, 1979; advanced through grades to maj. USAFR; flight leader, cope thunder mission comdr., F4 phantom II pilot USAF, Clark AFB, The Philippines, 1979-81; F4 phantom instr. pilot USAF, Homestead AFB, Fla., 1981-84; federal judicial clk. to Hon. Peter Fay 11 Cir. Ct. Appeals, Fla., 1987-88; A7 corsair pilot Puerto Rico Air Nat. Guard, Puerto Rico, 1988-89; asst. atty. with aviation divsn. Dade County Atty's Office, Fla., 1988-90; mem. Ho. Reps., Fla., 1990-92; assoc. Colson, Hicks, Eidson, Colson & Matthews, Fla., 1991-92, Fowler, White, Burnett, Hurley, Banick & Strickroot, PA, Fla., 1992—; mem. Fla. State Senate, Fla., 1992—. Contbr. to profl. jours. Lector Christ the King Ch.; bd. dir. Zoological Soc. Fla., ARC; mem. Homestead Fla Democratic Club; atty coach Dade County High Sch. Mock Trail, 1990. Maj. USAFR, 1989—. Recipient Iron Arrow award Miami Sch. Law, 1987, Politician of the Year award Zeta Phi Beta Sorority, Outstanding Freshman Rep. award Acad. Fla. Trial Lawyers, 1991, Coun. of the State Governments Svc. award Richmond Perrine Optimist Club, Freshman Legislator of the Year award Dade County Young Democrats, Politician of the Yr award Mu Gamma Zeta Chpt., Legislator of the Year award Midwives Assn. Fla., 1992, Execellence and Achievement award The Miami Agenda; named ZOB Price Waterhouse Government Up and Comer South Fla. Mag., Most Effective Freshman Rep. Miami Herald, 1991,. Mem. ABA, Dade County Bar Assn., Black Lawyer's Assn., The Flamingo Wing, Am. Legion. Office: 9300 S Dadeland Blvd Ste 401 Miami FL 33156-2719*

JONES, DAVID ALLAN, electronics engineer; b. Akron, Ohio, Oct. 16, 1942; s. Alva Jr. J. and Vera Henrietta (Seevers) Fuchs; m. Elizabeth Ann Cheek, Dec. 28, 1971; 1 child, Lindsey Ashok-Ray. BS in Math., U. Miss., 1965; MEE, Naval Postgrad. Sch., 1972. Commd. ensign USN, 1965, advanced through grades to comdr., 1979, ret., 1986; v.p. advanced programs Stanford Telecomm., Inc., Reston, Va., 1986—. Elder Presbyn. Ch., Annandale, Va., 1987-90. Decorated Commendation medal, Def. Meritorious Svc. medal, Navy Meritorious Svc. medal, Achievement medals. Mem. AIAA, Armed Forces Communications and Electronics Assn., IEEE.

JONES, DAVID ALLEN, health facility executive; b. Louisville, Aug. 7, 1931; s. Evan L. and Elsie F. (Thurman) J.; m. Betty L. Ashbury, July 24, 1954. BS, U. Louisville, 1954; JD, Yale U., 1960. Bar: Ky. 1960. Founder, chief exec. officer Humana Inc. (formerly Extendicare Inc.), Louisville, 1961—, also chmn., dir.; ptnr. Greenebaum, Doll and McDonald and predecessor, Louisville, 1965-69, of counsel, 1969-74; dir. Abbott Labs. Served as lt. (j.g.) USN, 1954-57. Mem. Louisville Area C. of C. Office: Humana Inc 500 W Main St Louisville KY 40202-2946*

JONES, DAVID ALWYN, geneticist, botany educator; b. Colliers Wood, Surrey, Eng., June 23, 1934; came to U.S., 1989; s. Trefor and Marion Edna Jones; m. Hazel Cordelia Lewis, Aug. 29, 1959; children: Catherine Susan, Edmund Meredith, Hugh Francis. BA, MA in Natural Scis., U. Cambridge, Eng., 1957; DPhil in Genetics, U. Oxford, Eng., 1963. Chartered biologist, UK. Lectr. in genetics U. Birmingham, Eng., 1961-73; prof. genetics U. Hull, Eng., 1973-89, head dept. plant biology and genetics, 1983-88; prof., chmn. dept. botany U. Fla., Gainesville, 1989—; chmn. membership com. Inst. of Biology, London, 1982-87. Co-author: Variation and Adaptation in Plant Species, 1971, Analysis of Populations, 1976, What is Genetics?, 1976, Zmiennosc i przystosowanie roslin, 1977; contbr. over 100 articles to profl. jours. Fellow Linnean Soc., Inst. Biology; mem. AAAS, Am. Soc. Naturalists, Bot. Soc. Am., Internat. Soc. Chem. Ecology (coun. 1983-84, 89-91, keynote spkr. ann. meeting 1984, pres. elect 1986-87, pres. 1987-88, past pres. 1988-89, co-editor Jour. Chem. Ecology 1994—), Brit. Assn. Advancement of Sci. (chmn. coord. com. for cytology and genetics 1974-87), Genetical Soc. Gt. Britain (convenor ann. meetings profs. of genetics 1983-88), Ecol. Genetics Group, Population Genetics Group, Soc. for Study of Evolution, Gamma Sigma Delta, Sigma Xi. Home: 7201 SW 97th Ln Gainesville FL 32608-6378 Office: U Fla Dept Botany 220 Bartram Hall Gainesville FL 32611-2009

JONES, DAVID BENTLEY, JR., auditor; b. Dallas, Nov. 16, 1968; s. David Bentley and Barbara Lee (Taylor) J. BBA in Acctg., U. Tex., 1991. CPA, Tex. Auditor Coopers & Lybrand LLP, Houston, 1991-94, Ernst & Young LLP, Houston, 1994—. Amb. Houston C. of C., 1993—. Mem. Tex. Investors (founder, pres. 1989-91). Republican. Home: 3525 Sage 1601 Houston TX 77056 Office: Ernst & Young LLP 1221 McKenney Houston TX 77010

JONES, DAVID CHARLES, international financial and management consultant; b. Cowes, Eng., Feb. 8, 1935; came to U.S., 1970; s. Charles Alfred and Alice Elizabeth (Rickman) J.; m. Gabrielle Clara Mabey, Sept. 28, 1957; children: Stephen Charles, Philip Simon (dec.), Catherine Claire. Cert. in acctg. and fin. mgmt., Chartered Inst. Pub. Fin. and Accountancy, London, 1961. Cert. acct., Eng. Clk. Brit. Rail, London, 1951-55, Isle of Wight (Eng.) County Coun., Newport, 1955-56; acct. Petworth (Eng.) Dist. Coun., 1956-59; chief acct. Kingswood (Eng.) Dist. Coun., 1959-61; sr. acct. Luton (Eng.) Borough Coun., 1961-63; tech. asst. Govt. of U.K., Entebbe, Uganda, 1963-68, Blantyre, Malawi, 1968-70; sr. fin. analyst World Bank, Washington, 1970-80, fin. adviser, 1980-87; cons. Internat. Fin. and Mgmt. Cons., Annandale, Va., 1987—, World Bank, Internat. Monetary Fund, 1987—; vis. lectr. Grad. Sch. Design, Harvard U., Cambridge, Mass., 1987—, rsch. fellow, 1994—, Grad. Sch., George Mason U., Fairfax, Va., 1990—; v.p. Internat. Devel. Tng. Inst., Washington, 1988—; sr. assoc. cons. Internat. Mgmt. Cons. Ltd., Eng.; expert testimony D.C. Com., U.S. Ho. of Reps. Author: Municipal Accounting for Developing Countries, 1984; contbr. articles to profl. jours. Cpl. R.A.F., 1953-55, Eng. Fellow Chartered Assn. of Cert. Accts.; mem. Chartered Inst. Pub. Fin. and Accountancy, Internat. Consortium on Govtl. Fin. Mgmt. (bd. dirs. 1980—). Episcopalian. Home: 4936 Andrea Ave Annandale VA 22003-4166

JONES, DAVID LANCE, nurse; b. Boaz, Ala., Apr. 19, 1967; s. K. David and Barbara (Harris) J. Diploma in practical nursing, Gadsden Tech. Inst., 1987; ADN, Northeast State Jr. Coll., 1990; BS in Mgmt., Internat. Coll., 1994. Cert. ACLS nurse, cert. trauma nurse, cert. in trauma nursing core course. Staff nurse emergency dept. Boaz-Albertville Med. Ctr., 1990-92; emergency rm.-staff nurse St. Thomas (V.I.) Hosp., Virgin Islands, 1992; asst. nurse mgr. progressive care unit St. Joseph Med. Ctr., Port Charlotte, Fla., 1992—; asst. nurse mgr. progressive care unit Bon Secours St. Joseph Hosp., Port Charlotte, 1993-94, adminstrv. rep., 1993-94, 94—; nurse mgr., emergency svc. Walker Meml. Med. Ctr., Wauchula, Fla., 1994; nurse mgr. med./surg./oncology Bon Secours St. Joseph Hosp., Port Charlotte, 1995—. Mem. ANA, Nat. League Nursing, Am. Assembly of Men in Nursing, Emergency Nurses Assn., Ala. Nurses Assn., Marshall County Nurses Soc. (chmn.-elect), Fla. Orgn. of Nurse Execs., Am. Assembly of Men in Nursing, ENA. Republican. Episcopalian. Home: 8316 Island Breeze Ln Tampa FL 33637-1050

JONES, DAVID RANDOLPH, retired air force officer, aerospace psychiatrist; b. Cooperstown, N.Y., Sept. 2, 1934; s. Thomas Thweatt and Mary Cuyler (Scanlon) J.; children by previos marriage: Michael, Charles, Sara, Aline. BS, Davidson (N.C.) Coll., 1954; MD, Duke U., 1958; M.P.H., Harvard U., 1962. Diplomate Am. Bd. Preventive Medicine, Am. Bd. Psychiatry and Neurology. Commd. 2d lt. U.S. Air Force, 1956, advanced through grades to col., 1972; gen. rotating intern USAF Hosp., Lackland AFB, Tex., 1958-59, resident in psychiatry Wilford Hall USAF Med. Ctr., 1975-78; resident in aerospace medicine Brooks AFB, Tex., 1962-64; chief Aeromed. Services, Torrejon AFB, Spain, 1967-71; dep. comdr. to comdr. USAF Hosp., Randolph AFB, Tex., 1971-75; chief neuropsychiatry br. Clin. Svcs. divsn. USAF Sch. Aerospace Medicine-Brooks AFB, Tex., 1978-86; mil. cons. USAF Surgeon Gen., 1982; clin. assoc. prof. psychiatry Uniformed Svcs. U. of Health Scis.-Bethesda, Md., 1980-86, clin. prof. 1986—; clin. asst. prof. psychiatry U. Tex. Health Scis. Center-San Antonio, 1979-87, clin. assoc. prof., 1987-92, clin. prof. 1992-95; cons. aerospace psychiatry Fed. Air Surgeon, 1994—. Decorated Legion of Merit with oak leaf clusters, Bronze Star Meritorious Svc., Air Medal with three oak leaf clusters, Commendation Medal with one oak leaf cluster; recipient Docere award USAF Sch. Aerospace Medicine, 1983. Fellow Am. Coll. Preventive Medicine, Aerospace Med. Assn., Am. Psychiat Assn. (Falk fellow 1976); mem. AMA, Tex. Med. Assn., Bexar County Med. Assn., Assn. USAF Flight Surgeons (pres. 1983), Assn. USAF Psychiatrists (sec.-treas. 1980), Aerospace Human Factors Assn. (pres. 1993-94). Presbyterian. Editor-in-chief Aviation Space Environ. Medicine, 1987-96; contbr. several med. articles to profl. publs., chpts. to books. Office: Aeropsych Assocs 4204 Gardendale # 203 San Antonio TX 78229-3132

JONES, DON CARLTON, insurance agent; b. Jacksonville, Tex., Aug. 6, 1943; s. Carlton P. and Sue (Galledge) J.; m. Pat Jones; children: Carlton, Vicki, Staci. BS, Sam Houston State U. Casualty underwriter Am. Gen. Ins. Co., San Antonio, 1967-69; spl. agt. Trinity Universal Ins. Co., Houston, 1969-73; sec., treas. Crockett (Tex.) Ins. Svc., 1973-82, pres., 1990—; pres. Hociston-Walken County Ins. Svc., Crockett, 1982—, Trinity (Tex.) Ins. Agy. Mem. Houston County Airport Commn., Crockett, 1985—; pres. Indsl. Devel. Authority, Crockett, 1986-90. Served with U.S. Army. Mem. Lions Club (past pres.), C. of C. (past pres.), Nat. C. of C., Ind. Ins. Agts. Tex., Cert. Ins. Counselors Tex., Soc. Cert. Ins. Counselors, Crockett C. of C. (pres. 1981—). Office: Crockett Ins Svc 206 S 5th St Crockett TX 75835-2029

JONES, DONNA GILBERT, social worker; b. Moline, Ill., Feb. 23, 1952; d. Kenneth Ray and Johnnie Faye (Adkins) Gilbert; m. David Lawrence Jones, Dec. 22, 1974 (div. Feb. 1995); children: Jonathan, Eric, Jessica. B in Social Work, U. Ala., 1974, MSW, 1978. Cert. social worker, Ala. State Bd. Social Work Examiners. Social worker Bryce Hosp., Tuscaloosa, 1975-78, Occupl. Rehab. Ctr., Birmingham, Ala., 1978-80; child protective svc. worker Shelby County Dept. Human Resources, Columbiana, Ala., 1983-86; coord. women's substance abuse Chilton-Shelby Mental Health Ctr., Calera, Ala., 1986-92; coord. children's day treatment, therapist, dir. Cahaba Valley Counseling, Birmingham, 1992—. Chairperson bd. dirs. Family Resources, Inc., Pelham, Ala., 1985-93; mem. Jefferson/Shelby Child Abuse Task Force, Birmingham, 1992—. Mem. Am. Acad. Experts in Traumatic Stress, Ala. Soc. Clin. Social Workers. Democrat. Office: Cahaba Valley Counseling 2232 Cahaba Valley Dr Birmingham AL 35242-2602

JONES, EDITH HOLLAN, judge; b. Phila., Apr. 7, 1949; BA, Cornell U., 1971; JD with honors, U. Tex., 1974. Bar: Tex. 1974, U.S. Supreme Ct. 1979, U.S. Ct. Appeals (5th and 11th cirs.), U.S. Dist. Ct. (so. and no. dists.) Tex. Assoc. Andrews & Kurth, Houston, 1974-82, ptnr., 1982-85; judge U.S. Ct. Appeals (5th cir.), Houston, 1985—. Gen. counsel Rep. Party of Tex., 1981-83. Mem. ABA, State Bar Tex. Presbyterian. Office: US Ct Appeals 12505 US Courthouse 12505 US Courthouse Houston TX 77002

JONES, EUINE FAY, architect, educator; b. Pine Bluff, Ark., Jan. 31, 1921; s. Euine Fay and Candie Louise (Alston) J.; m. Mary Elizabeth Knox, Jan. 6, 1943; children: Janis Fay, Jean Cameron. BArch, U. Ark., 1950; MArch, Rice U., 1951; DFA (hon.), Kans. State U., 1984; LHD (hon.), Drury Coll., 1985, Hendrix Coll., 1991; DHL (hon.), U. Ark., 1990. Asst. prof. architecture U. Okla., 1951-53; Frank Lloyd Wright Taliesin fellow, 1953; prof. architecture U. Ark., 1953—, chmn. dept., 1966-74, dean Sch. Architecture, 1974-76; pvt. practice architecture, 1953—; Rome Prize fellow in architecture and design, 1981; dean, u. prof. emeritus U. Ark., 1988. Served as lt., naval aviator USNR, 1942-45. Recipient nat. awards for archtl. design, Gold medal for distinction in archtl. design Tau Sigma Delta, 1984, Disting. Alumnus award U. Ark., 1982, Rice U., 1989; subject of book by Robert Ivy, Jr., AIA Press, 1992. Fellow AIA (Gold medal 1990); mem. Assn. Collegiate Schs. Architecture (Disting. Prof. award 1985), Soc. Archtl. Historians. Home: 1330 Hillcrest Ave Fayetteville AR 72703-1924

JONES, EVA JOYCE See BOWEN, EVA JOYCE

JONES, EVELENE MANNS, principal, minister; b. Henderson, Tex., Apr. 14, 1930; d. Joe Lee and Ethel Bell (Sanders) Manns; m. Walter L. Jones, Dec. 6, 1958; children: Jessie Alvin Watkins, Leaon Watkins. BS, North Tex. State U., 1964, MA, 1967, Mid-Mgmt. Cert., 1976; Diploma, So. Bible Inst., Dallas, 1982. Tchr. Ft. Worth (Tex.) Ind. Sch. Dist., 1964-70, program asst., 1970-82, asst. prin., 1982-88, prin., 1988—, assessor of Assessment Ctr., 1992-94. Contbr. articles to profl. jours. Chairperson edn. com. City of Ft. Worth, 1985-91; bd. dirs. Cultural Dist. Bd., Ft. Worth, 1989-92, Art Coun., Ft. Worth, 1989-92; pres. Nat. Women of Achievement, Ft. Worth, 1991-95, chaplain, 1989-91, 94-95; block capt. CHAOS Cmty. Orgn., Ft. Worth, 1968-90. Recipient Outstanding Contbn. award Delta Sigma Theta, 1989; named Tchr. of the Yr., Classroom Tchrs. Orgn. Ft. Worth, 1977, Disting. Svc. award, 1975, Cert. of Appreciation, A. Phillip Randolph Inst., Ft. Worth, 1992. Mem. NEA (life), Internat. Reading Assn., Black C. of C., NAACP (Civil Rights award 1978), Tex. Edn. Assn. (peer evaluator 1993-96), Tex. Elem. Prins. and Suprs. Assn., Ft. Worth Adminstrs. Democrat. Home: 1701 Flemming Dr Fort Worth TX 76112 Office: Fort Worth Ind Sch Dist 100 N University Fort Worth TX 76107

JONES, EVERETT RILEY, JR., oil company executive; b. Leitchfield, Ky., July 28, 1918; s. Everett Riley and Margie (Hatfield) J.; m. Lois Gibbins, July 15, 1950; children: Stacey Rae, Rande Leigh. Student, Spencerian C.C., 1936-37, U. Louisville, 1946-47. Lic. pub. acct., Ky. Sec. treas., dir. Lafitte Oil Corp., Louisville, 1947-49; ptnr. Fryer & Hanson Drilling Co., Dallas, 1950-58; pres., dir. Bengal Producing Co., Dallas, 1959—; dir. Dallas County Small Bus. Devel. Ctr., Inc. Trustee S.W. Engring. Found. Served to capt. USAAF, 1942-45. Decorated D.F.C., Air medal with 4 oak leaf clusters. Mem. Engrs. Club Dallas (past pres.) Dallas Petroleum Club (past pres.), Royal Air Force Club in London. Episcopalian. Home: 8002 Glen Albens Cir Dallas TX 75225-1822 Office: 8080 N Central Expy Dallas TX 75206-1806

JONES, FLORENCE M., music educator; b. West Columbia, Tex., Apr. 11, 1939; d. Isaiah and Lu Ethel (Baldridge) McNeil; m. Waldo D. Jones, May 29, 1965; children: Ricky, Wanda, Erna. BS, Prairie View A&M U., 1961, MEd, 1968; postgrad., Rice U., 1988, U. Houston, 1980. Cert. tchr. elem. edn., math. Tchr. English and typing Lincoln High Sch., Port Arthur, Tex., 1961-62; tchr. grades three and four Houston Ind. Sch. Dist., 1963-90, tchr. gifted and talented, 1990-94; tchr. piano Windsor Village Liberal Arts Acad., Houston, 1994—; dist. tchr. trainer Houston Ind. Sch. Dist., 1985-90; shared decision mem. Sch. decision Making Team, 1993-94; coord. gifted/talented program, Petersen Elem. Sch., Houston, 1990-94; participant piano Recital Hartzog Studio, 1985-88; film previewer Houston Media Ctr. Curriculum writer Modules to Improve Science Teaching, 1985; author sci. pop-up book, 1980, gifted/talented program, 1994; contbr. poems to lit. jours. Youth camp counselor numerous non-denominational ch. camps, U.S., 1961-89; active restoration of Statue of Liberty, Ellis Island Found., N.Y.C., 1983-85; lay minister Ch. of God, 1961-94. Recipient Letter of Recognition for Outstanding Progress in Edn., Pres. Bill Clinton, 1994, Congresswoman Sheilia Jackson Lee, Tex. Gov. George Bush, State Rep. Harold V. Sutton Jr., Houston Mayor Bob Lanier, Tex. Gov. Ann Richards; Gold Cup/Highest Music award Hartzog Music Studio, 1987, Diamond Key award Nat. Women of Achievement, 1995, Editors Choice award Nat. Library Poetry, 1995, others. Mem. NEA, Houston Assn. Childhood Edn. (v.p. 1985-88), Assn. for Childhood Edn. (bd. dirs. 1979-91), Houston Zool. Soc., World Wildlife Fund, Nat. Storytelling Assn., Tejas Storytelling Assn. (life), Soc. Children's Book Writers and Illustrators, Nat. Audubon Soc., Am. Mus. Natural History, Tex. Ret. Tchrs. Assn. (life), Internat. Soc. Poets (disting. life mem.), others. Democrat. Home: 3310 Dalmatian Dr Houston TX 77045-6520

JONES, F(RANCIS) WHITNEY, fund raising executive, consultant; b. Waterford, N.Y., May 10, 1944; s. Francis Whitney and Katherine (Draper) J.; m. Robyn Abrams, June 11, 1966 (div. 1984); children: Lindsay Draper, Christopher Austin; m. Suzanne Mewborn, Dec. 28, 1985; children: Alexander Whitney, Spencer Elliott. Student, U. Paris, 1964-65; AB, Hamilton Coll., 1966; PhD, U. N.C., 1971. Instr. English U. N.C., Chapel Hill, 1970-71; asst. prof. English St. Andrews Coll., Laurinburg, N.C., 1971-77; devel. dir. Old Salem, Inc., Winston-Salem, N.C., 1977-80; sr. cons. Ampersand, Inc., Winston-Salem, 1980-81; pres. Whitney Jones, Inc., Winston-Salem, 1981—; pres. Triad Fund-Raising Execs. Coun., Winston Salem, 1989-91. Active United Way cmty. program solving com., Winston-Salem, 1989-93, Arts Advocates of N.C., Raleigh, 1991—, Family Found. of N. Am., Milw., 1991—. Younger Humanists fellow Nat. Endowment for the Humanities, Washington, 1975. Mem. The Jargon Soc. (pres. 1977—), Green Hill Ctr. for N.C. Art (v.p. 1990), Nat. Soc. Fund Raising Execs. (pres. N.C. Triad chpt. 1991-95), Am. Assn. of Fund Raising Counsel. Democrat. Episcopalian. Home: 1221 Wilmar Place Ct Winston Salem NC 27104-1221 Office: Whitney Jones Inc 119 Brookstown Ave Winston Salem NC 27101-5245

JONES, FRANK GRIFFITH, lawyer; b. Houston, Sept. 11, 1941; s. A. Gordon and Grace (Griffith) J.; m. Deborah Ann Young, July 5, 1969; children: Russell G., Sarah G., Christopher Y. BS, Rice U., 1963; JD, U. Tex., 1966. Bar: Tex. 1966, U.S. Dist. Ct. (so., no. and ea. dists.) Tex., U.S. Ct. Appeals (5th and 8th cirs.); cert. civil trial specialist. Ptnr. Fulbright & Jaworski, Houston, 1966—; chmn. Fulbright & Jaworski Employment Commn., 1988-92. Mem. Fulbright and Jaworski policy com., exec. com., 1992-94; chmn. troop com. Boy Scouts Am., Houston, 1986-88; mem. Rice U. Fund Coun., Houston, 1987-93; pres. Baker Coll., Rice U., 1962-63; bd. dirs. Houston Symphony, Holly Hall. Lt. (j.g.) USNR, 1967-72. U. Tex. Law Sch. Keeton fellow, 1993—. Fellow Am. Coll. Trial Lawyers (ADR com. 1986—, chmn. 1992-94), Internat. Acad. Trial Lawyers; mem. ABA, Am. Bd. Trial Advs., Internat. Assn. Def. Counsel, Houston Bar Assn., Houston Young Lawyers Assn. (pres. 1972-73), Tex. Bar Assn., Tex. Bar Found., Houston Bar Found., Am. Bar Found., Houston Assn. Cert. Civil Trial and Appellate Specialists, Tex. Assn. Def. Counsel, Am. Counsel Assn., Def. Rsch. Inst., Tex. Assn. Cert. Civil Trial Specialists, Products Liability Adv. Coun., Houston City Club, Courthouse Club, Rotary, Phi Delta Phi (past pres.). Office: Fulbright & Jaworski 1301 Mckinney St Houston TX 77010

JONES, FRED T., museum administratorr. Pres. Greensboro (N.C.) Hist. Mus., Inc., 1996—. Office: Greensboro Hist Mus Inc 130 Summit Ave Greensboro NC 27401-3004

JONES, FREDERIC GORDON, family medicine educator; b. Coral Gables, Fla., Mar. 1, 1933; s. Gordon Bird and Annie Laurie (Bibb) J.; m. Lynn Peterson, Aug. 9, 1958; children: Ruth Llewellyn, F. Gordon Jr., Ashley Bibb. Student, Wofford Coll., Spartanburg, S.C., 1951-52; BS, U. Ga., 1954, MD, 1958. Bd. cert. in internal medicine and cardiovasc. disease; cert. in med. mgmt. Commd. 2d lt. USAF, 1958, advanced through grades to col., 1972, ret., 1978; chief cardiology Wilford Hall USAF Med. Ctr., 1972-76; chmn. Wright-Patterson Med. Ctr., 1976-78; prof. family medicine, asst. dean Med. U. S.C., 1978—; exec. v.p. med. affairs Anderson (S.C.) Area Med. Ctr., 1978—. Fellow ACP, Am. Coll. Cardiology, Am. Coll. Physician Execs., Am. Coll. Med. Quality; mem. Rotary (pres. 1991-92). Methodist. Home: 101 Victoria Cir Anderson SC 29621-4058 Office: Anderson Area Med Ctr 800 N Fant St Anderson SC 29621-5708

JONES, FREDERICK CLAUDIUS, English language and linguistics educator; b. Freetown, Sierra Leone, Apr. 9, 1943; m. Olivia Erica Metzger, July 17, 1982; children: Yvonne, Charlene, Lallie, Raymond. BA in English Lang. and Lit. magna cum laude, U. Durham, Eng., 1966; diploma in edn., U. Sierra Leone, 1967; MA in Linguistics and English, U. Leeds, Eng., 1972, PhD in Linguistics and Phonetics, 1983. Asst. prof. English lang. and lit. Milton Margai Advanced Tchrs. Coll., Freetown, 1970-75; supr. teaching practice U. Sierra Leone, 1973-84, asst. prof. English, dir. English dept. lang. lab., 1975-85; asst. prof. Inst. Linguistics, Tech. U. Berlin, 1985-90; assoc. prof. English St. Augustine's Coll., Raleigh, N.C., 1990—, dir. honors program, 1994—; part-time instr. U. Sierra Leone, 1972-75; part-time newsreader Sierra Leone Broadcasting Svc., 1969-85; examiner to chief examiner The Nat. Examinations Bd. at Standardized High Sch. Level; cons. YWCA, 1978. Editorial bd. publs. com. Ministry of Edn., Sierra Leone, 1978-85; contbr. articles to profl. jours.; editorial asst. A Krio-English Dictionary, 1980; co-producer, co-dir. (video): Insights into Writing Across the Curriculum, 1992. Mem. The West African Linguistic Soc., Australian Linguistic Soc., Societas Linguistica Europaea, The Linguistic Soc. Am., Soc. Pidgin and Creole Studies, Conf. on Coll. Composition and Comms., Nat. Coun. Tchrs. of English, Sigma Tau Delta. Methodist. Home: 1005 Mockingbird Dr Raleigh NC 27615-6125 Office: St Augustines Coll 1315 Oakwood Ave Raleigh NC 27610-2247

JONES, GASTON C(ARLISLE), adminstrative executive; b. Gulfport, Miss., May 31, 1918; s. Henry Hugh and Hilda (Gaston) J.; m. Carolyn Dupre Latta, Feb. 22, 1951. BSC, U. Miss., 1940; student, Northwestern u., 1941. CPA, Tex. With tax. dept. Arthur Andersen & Co., accts. and auditors, Houston, 1941-50; v.p., dir. F.A. Callery, Inc., Houston, 1950-66, pres., 1966-75; pres. C&J Services, Inc., Houston, 1975-84; v.p., bd. dirs. Callery Properties, Inc.; chmn. bd. Seminole Harvesting, Inc.; mng. partner Callery Judge Grove. Pres. Seminole Water Control Dist. Mem. Am. Inst. Accts., Phi Kappa Psi. Clubs: Beach Club, Palm Beach Polo and Country, Pundits. Office: Callery-Judge Grove LP 4001 Seminole Pratt Whitn Loxahatchee FL 33470

JONES, GLOWER WHITEHEAD, lawyer; b. Atlanta, May 4, 1936; s. Samuel L. and Alma (Powell) J.; m. Joanna Dayvault, Apr. 5, 1980; children: Mark, Jeff, Tom, Frank, Michael. Grad. Dartmouth Coll. 1958; JD, Emory U., 1963. Bar: Ga. 1962, U.S. Dist. Ct. Ga. 1963, U.S. Ct. Appeals (5th and 11th cirs.), U.S. Ct. Claims, U.S. Supreme Ct. Assoc. Smith, Swift, Currie, McGhee & Hancock, Atlanta, 1963-65; ptnr. Smith Currie & Hancock, Atlanta, 1967—. Author: Legal Aspects of Doing Business in North America and Canada, 1987, Alternative Clauses to Standard Construction Contracts, 1990, Construction Subcontracting: A Legal Guide for Industry Professionals, 1991, Wiley Construction Law Update, 1992, 93, 94, Construction Contractors: The Right To Stop Work, 1992, Remedies for International Sellers of Goods, 1993; mem. editorial bd. Ga. State Bar Jour.; contbr. articles to profl. jours. Mem. exec. bd. Met. Atlanta Boys' & Girls' Clubs, Inc., asst. sec., 1973-80, sec., 1980-83; bd. dirs. Samuel L. Jones Boys' & Girls' Club, Inc., So. Region Boys Clubs Am.; trustee, past pres. Atlanta Florence Crittendon Services, Inc.; bd. dirs. Carrie Steele Pitts Home; bd. dirs. Gate City Day Nursery Assn. Recipient Golden Boy award Met. Atlanta Boys' Club, 1971. Mem. ABA, Fed. Bar Assn., Internat. Bar Assn. (chmn. internat. sales com., chmn. UNCITRAL subcom.), Ga. Bar Assn., State Bar Ga., Atlanta Bar Assn. (former chmn. prepaid legal svcs. com., engr. lawyers rels. com.), Lawyers Club Atlanta, Am. Judicature Soc., Assn. Trial Attys. Am., Ga. Assn. Trial Lawyers, Dartmouth Coll. Alumni Club, Baylor Alumni Club, Emory U. Alumni Club, Atlanta Athletic Club, Ansley Park Golf Club, Dartmouth Club, World Trade Club, Phi Delta Theta. Home: 78 Peachtree Cir NE Atlanta GA 30309-3519 Office: Smith Currie & Hancock 2600 Harris Tower 233 Peachtree St NE Atlanta GA 30303

JONES, GRANT, former state senator; b. Abilene, Tex., Nov. 11, 1922; s. Morgan and Jessie (Wilder) J.; BBA, So. Methodist U., 1947; MBA, Wharton Sch., U. Pa., 1948; Doctorate (hon.), Abilene Christian U., 1981, McMurry U., 1983, Hardin Simmons U., 1985; m. Anne Smith, Aug. 21, 1948; children: Morgan Andrew, Janet Jones Pliego. Casualty underwriter Trezevant and Cochran, Dallas, 1950-54; ins. agt., Abilene, 1948-73; admitted to Tex. bar, 1974; pvt. practice law, mediator, also ind. ins. agt., 1954—; mem. Tex. Ho. of Reps. from 62d Dist., 1965-72, Tex. Senate from 24th Dist., 1973-89; chmn. S.W. Mediation, Inc., Abilene. Served as pilot USAAF, World War II. C.P.C.U. Mem. Nat. Assn. Ins. Agts. (dir. 1963), Tex. Assn. Ins. Agts. (past pres.). Democrat. Methodist. Home: 22 Glen Abbey St Abilene TX 79606-5022 Office: PO Box 5138 Abilene TX 79608-5138

JONES, HARTLEY M. (LEE), bank executive; b. Madison, Wis., Aug. 12, 1948; s. Robert Hartley and Jeannette (Carlmark) J.; m. Vicki Lee Schulkin, May 18, 1986; children: Matthew H., Daniel L. BA in Psychology, U. Wis., 1969; MBA in Fin., George Washington U., 1982. Fin. specialist U.S. DOT, Washington, 1976-82; fin. project mgr. Booz, Allen & Hamilton, Bethesda, Md., 1982-84; sr. fin. mgr. PRC Realty Systems, Inc., McLean, Va., 1984-91; program mgr. U.S. Dept. Treasury, Washington, 1991-95; v.p. Mellon Bank, Arlington, Va., 1995—. Bd. dirs. Arlington (Va.) Cmty. Residences, Inc., 1986—; mem. fiscal affairs adv. com. Arlington County, 1992—. Home and Office: 4219 N 25th St Arlington VA 22207

JONES, HELENE RASBERRY, nursing educator; b. Weleetka, Okla., Apr. 16, 1940; d. John Milburn and Florence Loretta (King) Rasberry; m. Thomas Graves Jones, June 29, 1974; children: Kimberly Anne, Kendall Lee. BSN, Okla. Bapt. U., 1962; MN, Emory U., 1970. RN, Okla., Miss. Instr. Bapt. Sch. Nursing, Oklahoma City, 1963-66; staff nurse Presbyn. Hosp., Oklahoma City, 1966-67; instr. William Rufus King State Tech. Inst., Selma, Ala., 1967-69; prof. Sch. Nursing U. Miss., Jackson, 1970-80, coord., asst. prof., 1986-90; asst. DON div. staff devel. Univ. Hosp., Jackson, 1990-95; dir. dept. of staff devel. Univ. Hosps. and Clinics, Jackson, 1995—; assoc. prof. U. Tulsa, 1981; asst. dir., coord. divsn. staff devel. Hillcrest Med. Ctr., 1983-86; cons. Miss. Regional Med. Program, Jackson, 1972; chair accreditation rev. com. Schs. Nursing and bd. trustees instns. higher learning, Jackson, 1979-80. Mem. coms. health check and awards, Jackson, 1986-90, Am. Heart Assn., 1986—, PTA, Jenks, Okla. and Jackson, 1970-84; Citizens Better Edn., Jackson, 1978-80. Lt. U.S. Army, 1961-63. Mem. ANA, Miss. Nurses Assn. (dist. #13 nurse educator II award 1993), Sigma Theta Tau. Republican. Baptist. Home: 65 Glenway Pl Brandon MS 39042-2530 Office: UMC Univ Hosp 2500 N State St Jackson MS 39216-4500

JONES, HERMAN OTTO, JR., corporate professional; b. Jacksonville, Fla., Dec. 1, 1933; s. Herman Otto Sr. and Esther (Powell) J.; m. Marjorie Seaver, June 4, 1955 (dec. June 1996); two children (dec.). BSA, U. Fla., 1956. V.p. Oak Crest Hatcheries, Inc., Jacksonville, 1956-71; exec. v.p. Oak Crest Enterprises, Inc., Jacksonville, 1958-71; dir. sales Diversified Imports, Inc., Lakewood, N.J., 1971-73, BEC Ltd., Winchester, Eng., 1973-78; sales rep. Paul Revere Ins. Co., Jacksonville, 1978-81; v.p. Anitox Corp., Buford, Ga., 1981-85; pres. Gateway Suppliers, Inc., Jacksonville, 1986—; v.p. Sales Agritek Bio Ingredients Corp., Montreal, Quebec, Can., 1993—. Contbr. articles to profl. jours. Vice chmn. bd. deacons Riverside Bapt. Ch., 1988-89, deacon, 1991-94, sec. of deacons, 1991-92, dir. Sunday Sch., 1992-93. Named Outstanding Mem., Fla. Poultry Fedn., 1965, Southeastern Poultry and Egg Assn., 1963, State Outstanding Young Farmer, Fla. Jaycees, 1968; recipient Disting. Service award, Jacksonville Jaycees, 1970. Mem. Greater Jacksonville Fair Assn., Rotary (bd. dirs. South Jacksonville 1989-91), Univ. Club, Masons (master), Shriners, Jesters, Order Ea. Star (past patron). Republican. Home: 411 S 1st St Jacksonville Beach FL 32210-5468

JONES, J. KENLEY, journalist; b. Greenville, S.C., Feb. 24, 1935; s. J. Clyde and Mildred Idel (Smith) J.; m. Margaret Jean McPherson, Dec. 11, 1965; children—Stephanie, Jason, Eleanor. Student, Furman U., 1953-55; B.S. in Speech, Northwestern U., 1957, M.S. in Journalism, 1963; postgrad., Columbia U., 1964-65. Reporter City News Bur. of Chgo., 1962; reporter, cameraman KRNT-TV, Des Moines, 1963-64, WSB-TV, Atlanta, 1965-69; fgn. corr. NBC News, Asia, 1969-72; corr. NBC News (Southeast Bur.), Atlanta, 1972—. Served with USNR, 1958-61. Recipient Overseas Press Club award for best television reporting from abroad, 1970. Mem. AFTRA, Nat. Acad. Television Arts and Scis. Presbyterian. Office: 100 Colony Sq Ste 1140 1175 Peachtree St Atlanta GA 30361

JONES, JACK EARL, plant breeding and genetics specialist, agronomist, researcher, consultant; b. Elbert County, Ga., July 30, 1925; s. William Amos and Katherine Ivey (McCall) J.; m. Georgia Henrietta Weathers, Mar. 11, 1928; 1 child, Lynda Dianne Jones Burdette. BS, U. Ga., 1948, MS, 1950; PhD, La. State U., 1961. Asst. prof. La. State U., Baton Rouge, 1950-61, assoc. prof., 1961-68, prof., 1968-90, prof. emeritus, 1990—; pvt. practice cons. Baton Rouge, 1993—. Plant breeder cotton cultivars, 1976—. Staff sgt. USAF, 1943-45. Recipient Cotton Genetics Rsch. award Joint Cotton Breeding Policy Commn., 1986. Mem. Crop Sci. Soc. Am., Am. Soc. Agronomy, Cotton Improvement Conf. (chmn. 1979, Cotton Genetics award 1986), La. Assn. Agronomist, Gamma Sigma Delta (Rsch. award 1979), Sigma Xi. Home: 246 Maxine Dr Baton Rouge LA 70808-6831 Office: La State Univ Dept Agronomy Sturgis Hall Baton Rouge LA 70803

JONES, JAMES BEVERLY, retired mechanical engineering educator, consultant; b. Kansas City, Mo., Aug. 21, 1923. BS, Va. Poly. Inst., 1944; MS, Purdue U., 1947, PhD in Mech. Engring., 1951. Asst. mech. engr. engr. bd. U.S. War Dept., Va., 1944-45; from asst. instr. to assoc. prof. mech. engring. Purdue U., 1945-57, prof., 1957-64; svc. engr. Babcock & Wilcox Co., 1948; devel. engr. Gen. Electric Co., 1951-52; sr. project engr. Allison divsn. Gen. Motors Corp., 1953; prof., head dept. mech. engring. Va. Poly. Inst. & State U., Blacksburg, 1964-83, cons., 1994—. NSF faculty fellow Swiss Fed. Inst. Tech., 1961-62. Mem. ASME (James Harry Potter Gold medal 1991), AIAA, Am. Soc. Engring. Edn., Sigma Xi. Home: 1503 Palmer Dr Blacksburg VA 24060-5634

JONES, JAMES OGDEN, geologist, educator; b. Punkin Center, Tex., July 25, 1935; s. Charles Armond and Onis Velva (Carter) J.; m. Marilyn Felty, Aug. 13, 1961; children: James II, Alan. BS, Midwestern State U., Wichita Falls, Tex., 1962; MS, Baylor U., 1966; PhD, U. Iowa, 1971. Welder Nat. Tank Co., Electra, Tex., 1953-57; geologist Shell Oil Co., Wichita Falls, Tex., 1958-60; grad. teaching asst. Baylor U., Waco, Tex., 1962-64, U. Iowa, Iowa City, 1964-68; geologist Texaco, Inc., Wichita Falls, 1966; geology prof. U. So. Miss., Hattiesburg, 1971; dept. head So. Ark. U., Magnolia, 1971-77; geology program chmn. U. Tex., San Antonio, 1978-82, geology prof., 1977—; commr. Ark. Oil and Gas Commn., 1975-76; researcher in field; lectr. in field. Editor: (book) Field Book for the Lower Cretacious Rocks of South Central Texas, 1996; contbr. articles to profl. jours. and field guides in sedimentology, stratigraphy and paleontology. With U.S. Army, 1968-70, lt. col. USAR. Nat. Teaching fellow, 1971-73. Fellow Geol. Soc. Am. (gen. chmn. ann. meeting. 1986, membership com. 1988-90, nominating com. 1995, mgmt. bd. so. ctrl. sect., vice chmn. 1995-96), North Am. Commn. on Stratigraphic Nomenclature, Tex. Acad. Sci. (chmn. geology sect. 1986-87, 94-95, vice chmn. 1985-86); mem. South Tex. Geol. Soc. (v.p. 1992-93, pres. 1994-95), Soc. Ind. Profl. Earth Sci. (cert., sec., treas. 1994, v.p. 1995), Soc. Sedimentary Geology (chmn. field trip com. ann. meeting 1989), Gulf Coast Sect. SEPM (v.p. 1995-96, pres.-elect 1997-98), Am. Assn. Petroleum Geologists (ho. of dels. 1995, field trip chmn. ann. meeting 1984), Nat. Assn. Geology Tchrs. (sec., treas. Tex. sect. 1992-94, v.p. 1994-96, pres. 1996-98), Internat. Assn. Sedimentologists, Am. Inst. Profl. Geologists (cert., sec.-treas. Tex. sect. 1996-98), Am. Geol. Inst. (GEOREF com. 1995-97), Res. Officers Assn., Am. Legion, Sigma Xi, Phi Sigma Kappa, Sigma Gamma Epsilon. Methodist. Home: 13226 Hunters Lark St San Antonio TX 78230-2018 Office: U Tex Dept Geology San Antonio TX 78249-0663

JONES, JAMES RICHARD, mechanical engineer; b. Danville, Ky., Jan. 9, 1947; s. James Elkin and Ophelia (Faulkner) J.; m. Patricia Ann Harlen, May 20, 1967 (div. 1979); children: Jerri Ann (dec.), James Patrick; m. Betty Lou Polk, May 26, 1985. AAS in Mfg. Tech., Lexington Tech. Inst., Ky., 1974. With IBM, Lexington, Ky., 1967-81; with IBM, Charlotte, N.C., 1981-86, procurement mfg. engr., 1986-87, assoc. engr., 1987-1992, sr. assoc. engr., 1992-93; document control adminstr. Accuride Inc., Charlotte, 1994-95; prodn. support Philip Morris USA, 1995-96, prodn. tech. II, 1996—; internal auditor, Internat. Standards Orgn. 9000; quality assurance auditor. Mem. Masons. Democrat. Mem. African Methodist Episcopal Zion Ch. Home: 7117 Ludwig Dr Charlotte NC 28215-1822

JONES, JAMES ROBERT, ambassador, former congressman, lawyer; b. Muskogee, Okla., May 5, 1939; m. Olivia Barclay, 1968; children—Geoffrey Gardner, Adam Winston. AB in Journalism and Govt., U. Okla., 1961; LLB, Georgetown U., 1964. Bar: Okla. 1964, D.C. 1964. Legis. asst. to Congressman Ed Edmondson, 1961-64; spl. asst. to Pres. Lyndon Johnson, 1965-69; mem. 93d-99th congresses from 1st Dist. Okla., 1973-87; chmn. budget com. 97th and 98th Congress; chmn. social security subcom. 99th Congress; ptnr. Dickstein, Shapiro & Morin, Washington, 1987-89; chmn. bd., chief exec. officer Am. Stock Exch., N.Y.C., 1989-93; U.S. amb. to Mexico, 1993—; bd. dirs. Overseas Devel. Corp., Am. Coun. Capital Formation; mem. adv. coun. on Social Security. Chmn. Am. Bus. Conf.; bd. dirs. ARC, Japan Soc. Served as capt. CIC AUS, 1964-65. Mem. Okla. Bar Assn., D.C. Bar Assn. Office: care US Embassy Mexico PO Box 3087 Laredo TX 78044

JONES, JAMES WILSON, physician, cell biologist; b. Muskogee, Okla., Oct. 13, 1941; s. James C. and Hildred L. Jones; m. Joan Wachna, Aug. 24, 1983; children: James A., Misty A., Cyndra L., Jena S. Student, U. Tulsa, 1959-62; MD, Tulane U., 1966, PhD, 1974, postgrad., 1981-82. Diplomate Am. Bd. Surgery, Am. Bd. Thoracic Surgery. Intern Phila. Gen. Hosp., 1966-67; resident in surgery Mayo Grad. Sch. Medicine, 1969-70; resident in gen. surgery Charity Hosp. La., 1971-73, 74-75, resident in thoracic surgery, 1973-74, 75-76, asst. clin. dir., co-dir. surg. intensive care unit, 1976-83; resident in thoracic surgery Ochsner Clinic, 1976; asst. prof. surgery sch. medicine Tulane U., New Orleans, 1976-83; chief surg. svc. VA Med. Ctr., Houston, 1983-85, 89—; assoc. prof. surgery and cell biology Baylor Coll. Medicine, Houston, 1983-85, 89—; surg. dir. Ritter Heart Inst., Toledo, 1985-89; mem. student affairs com. med. sch. Tulane U., 1977-82; mem. hosp. bylaws com. Tulane Med. Ctr., 1978-79, mem. transfusion com., 1980-81; mem. transfusion com. Charity Hosp. La., 1978-80, mem. tracheotomy audit, 1980-81; mem. clin. exec. bd. VA Med. Ctr., 1983-85, 89—, mem. various coms.; sr. cardiac surgeon King Faisal Hosp., Riyadh, Saudi Arabia, 1984; chmn. ICU-CCU com. St. Mary Hosp., Port Arthur, Tex., 1986-87, mem. med. ethics com., 1987; mem. trustee's cardiovascular com. Toledo Hosp., mem. critical care com.; mem. high sch. adv. com. health care professions Baylor Coll. Medicine, 1990-92, chmn. allied health com., 1992—; mem. Regional Cardiology Adv. Com., 1993—; mem. sub-com. indsl. rels. Annals Thoracic Surgery; cons., presenter in field. Author: Autotransfusion: Therapeutic Principles & Trends, 1993; mem. editorial bd. Internat. Rev. Anesthesiology, 1990—; contbr. articles to profl. jours.; patentee in field. Lt. comdr. M.C., USN, 1967-69. Recipient Fellowship Rsch. award Soc. Surg. Oncology, 1977, Ann. Svc. award, Mended Hearts; grantee NIH, 1963, 64, New Orleans Cancer Soc., 1965, Haemonetics Corp., 1988, Ortho Pharm., 1989, Berlex, 1990, Baxter-Edwards, 1991, 93, Sandoz Pharms., 1992; Rsch. fellow Am. Cancer Soc., 1975-76, 77-78; Hawthorne scholar, 1964-65, 65-66. Fellow ACS, Am. Coll. Cardiology, Am. Coll. Chest Physicians; mem. Am. Assn. Thoracic Surgery, Am. Heart Assn., Soc. Am. Inventors, Southeastern Surg. Congress, Southwestern Surg. Congress, So. Thoracic Surg. Assn., Internat. Cardiovascular Soc. (N.Am. chpt.), Michael E. DeBakey Internat. Surg. Soc., Soc. Thoracic Surgeons (mem. industry rels. com.), So. Surg. Assn., Tex. Surg. Assn., Houston Surg. Soc., Soc. Critical Care Medicine, Mayo Alumni Assn., Sigma Xi, Alpha Kappa Kappa, Alpha Omega Alpha. Office: VAMC Surg Svc 112 2002 Holcombe Blvd Houston TX 77030-4211

JONES, JANET HALL, child and adolescent psychiatrist; b. Whitesburg, Ky., Oct. 21, 1945; d. Hubert and Bessie Lee (Banks) Hall; m. John D. Jones Jr.; children: Callie Anne, Cara Rae. AB in Chemistry, U. Ky., 1967, MD, 1971. Diplomate Am. Bd. Psychiatry and Neurology, Am. Bd. Child Psychiatry; lic. psychiatrist Ky. Asst. prof. psychiatry U. Ky. Coll. Medicine, Lexington, 1975-79; staff psychiatrist Univ. Health Svc., Lexington, 1975-84; active staff Charter Ridge Hosp., Lexington, 1984-89; staff psychiatrist U. Ky. Health Svc., Lexington, 1989—. Bd. dirs., med. advisor Ky. Tourette's Syndrome, Lexington, 1988—; sec. Altrusa Internat., Inc. of Lexington, 1991-92, v.p., 1992-93, pres., 1993-94. Mem. Am. Psychiat. Assn., Am. Acad. Child Psychiatry, Ky. Psychiat. Assn., Ky. Acad. Child Psychiatry, Ky. Med. Assn., Ky. Pediat. Assn. Democrat. Presbyterian. Office: 4071 Tates Creek Rd Ste 308 Lexington KY 40517-3094 also: Univ Health Svc B163 Ky Clinic Lexington KY 40536

JONES, JEFFERY LYNN, software engineer; b. Aug. 5, 1960; s. Robert Meryl and Ione Dell (Eaves) J. Ptnr., co-owner Megabyn Assocs (previously JJ Enterprises), Oklahoma City, 1982—; v.p., co-owner Oklahoma Digital Techs., Inc., Oklahoma City, 1987—; ptnr. Nighthawk Bus. Ideas, Jones, Okla.; contract cons. Bank Tech Inc., Oklahoma City, 1985-86, Phillips Petroleum Corp., Bartlesville, Okla., 1986-87; cons. Union Oil Co. of Calif., Oklahoma City, 1989—. Co-author: (software) PetroTrak 2000 Lease/Production Petroleum Tracking System, 1991. Pres. Atari Computer Club, Oklahoma City, 1983-84. With USAF, 1978-80. Recipient Paul Harris award Rotary Internat., 1991. Home and Office: Nighthawk Bus Ideas 7833 NE 95th St Jones OK 73049-5801

JONES, JIM WAYNE, editor; b. Bowie, Tex., May 20, 1935; s. John Roy and Nancy Vera (Kilcreast) J.; m. Audrey Lee Johnson, June 5, 1987. BA, U. N. Tex., 1957; MA, Tex. Christian U., 1967. Reporter Ft. Worth Star-Telegram, 1957, metro editor, 1963-79, religion editor, 1979—. Mem. adv. bd. Robert Wood Johnson Found., 1993-95. Served with USAF Res. Fellow Rockefeller Found, 1982; recipient Tex. Bapt. Press award Bapt. Gen. Conv. Tex., Dallas, 1963. Mem. Ft. Worth Soc. Profl. Journalists (pres. 1980-81), Religion News Writers Assn. U.S. and Can. (pres. 1992-93). Home: 2020 Winter Sunday Way Arlington TX 76012 Office: Ft Worth Star-Telegram 400 W 7th St Fort Worth TX 76012

JONES, JOHN ARTHUR, lawyer; b. San Antonio, Fla., Oct. 9, 1921; s. Charles Garfield and Catherine Magdalene (Smith) J.; m. Margarette Lorraine Johnson, Nov. 17, 1949; children: Matthew, Lisa, Malcolm, Darby. JD with honors, U. Fla., 1949. Bar: Fla. 1949, U.S. Dist. Ct. (so. dist.) Fla. 1952, U.S. Ct. Appeals (11th cir.) 1982, U.S. Supreme Ct. 1978. Assoc., Holland & Knight and predecessors, Tampa, Fla., 1949-54; ptnr., 1954—; faculty Fla. Sch. of Banking, 1969-81. Served in U.S. Army, 1940-46; lt. col., USAR. Decorated Bronze Star. Fellow Am. Coll. Trust and Estate Counsel; mem. ABA, Fla. Bar Assn. (cert. wills, trusts and estates, chmn. real property probate and trust law sect. 1980-81), Hillsborough County (Fla.) Bar Assn., Internat. Acad. Estate and Trust Lawyers, Am. Coll. Real Estate Lawyers, Am. Bar Found., Masons, Shrine, Tampa Club, Univ. Club. Editor, contbr.: How To Live and Die With Florida Probate, 1972, Basic Practice Under Florida Probate Code, 1976, 94. Home: 5027 W San Miguel St Tampa FL 33629-5428 Office: Holland & Knight PO Box 1288 400 N Ashley Dr Ste 2300 Tampa FL 33602-4318

JONES, JOHN ELLIS, real estate broker; b. Odum, Ga., Oct. 28, 1941; s. Roland Warnell and Agnes Carridean (Brown) J.; m. Nellie Ann Dougherty, June 21, 1963; children: John Richard, Katherine Ann. BSBA, U. Fla., 1967. With FBI, Washington, D.C., 1959-64; mgr. Fed. Res. Bank, Jacksonville, Fla., 1967-69; asst. mgr. Blue Cross/Blue Shield of Fla., Jacksonville, 1969-72; mgr. Heavener Realty Co., Jacksonville, 1972-75; pres., owner John Jones Realty Inc., Jacksonville, 1975-77, ERA Mid. Ga., Macon, 1977-79, ERA-Jones Realty Co., Macon, 1979-81; assoc. broker McNair Realty Co., Macon, 1981-89, Sheridan Solomon Kernaghan Realtors, Macon, 1989-91; with Fickling and Co., Macon, Ga., 1991—; instr. real estate Macon Coll., 1980—, instr. real estate sales seminar, 1988—. Deacon San Jose Bapt. Ch., Jacksonville, 1975; Bible tchr. Vineville Bapt. Ch., Macon, 1979. Mem. Nat. Assn. Realtors (nominee Educator of Yr. 1996), Ga. Assn. Realtors (bd. dirs. 1994—), Macon Bd. Realtors (v.p. 1996, pres.-elect 1997—, bd. dirs. 1992—, sec. 1995), Ga. Realtors Inst., Realtors Nat. Mktg. Inst., Real Estate Educators Assn., Ga. Real Estate Educators Assn., Macon C. of C. (hon. life, bd. dirs. 1996—, amb. 1989, Ambs. award 1995), River North Country Club (bd. dirs. 1992-94), Cert. Residential Specialists (sec. Ga. chpt. 1995—, v.p. 1996-97, pres. 1997—). Republican. Home: 1117 Newport Rd Macon GA 31210-3310 Office: Fickling & Co 2960 Riverside Dr Macon GA 31204-1275

JONES, JOHN HARRIS, lawyer, banker; b. New Blaine, Ark., Apr. 9, 1922; s. Ira Burton and Byrd (Harris); m. Marjorie Crosby Hart, 1983. A.B., U. Central Ark., 1941; postgrad., George Washington U. Law Sch., 1941-42; LL.B., Yale, 1947. Bar: Ark. 1946, U.S. Supreme Ct. 1963. Communications clk. FBI, 1941-42; practice in Pine Bluff, 1947—; spl. judge Circuit Ct., 1950; chmn. bd. Pine Bluff Nat. Bank, 1964-77, pres., 1966-76; Mem. Ark. Bd. Law Examiners, 1953-59; Republican nominee for U.S. Senate, 1974; Rep. presdl. elector, 1980; v.p., dir. John Rust Found., 1953-60. Served to 1st lt. USAAF, 1943-45. Decorated Purple Heart, Air medal. Mem. Ark. Bar Assn., Jefferson County Bar Assn. (pres. 1959-60). Mem. Christian Ch. (elder 1963-65, trustee 1965-71, 78-84). Clubs: Eden Park (Pine bluff), Capital (Little Rock). Home: 4001 S Cherry St Pine Bluff AR 71603-7156 Office: National Bldg 104 Main St Pine Bluff AR 71601

JONES, JOHN LOU, arbitrator, retired railroad executive; b. Garnavillo, Iowa, July 22, 1929; s. Ira S. and Myrtle C. (Flagel) J.; m. Nancy H. Sikes, Feb. 2, 1953; children—Nanette, Robert, Eleanor, Stefani, Amanda, Jennifer, Eric. B.A., Luther Coll., 1950; M.S., MIT, 1954; A.M.P., Harvard U., 1974. Staff engr. Chrysler Corp., Detroit, 1957-59; dir. computer activities So. Ry. Co., Washington, 1963-64, asst. v.p.-data processing, Atlanta, 1964-69, v.p.-mgmt. info. services, 1969-82; exec. v.p.-adminstrn. Norfolk So. Corp., Va., 1982-87; bd. dirs. Norfolk & Western Ry., Roanoke, Va., So. Ry. Co., Atlanta; also bd. dirs. various ry. subs.; now arbitrator in massive dispute on intellectual property rights between IBM and Fujitsu Co.; bd. dirs. Visual Info. Techs. Corp., 1988-95. Bd. dirs. Va. Symphony, 1986-92, Urban League of Hampton Roads, 1985-87. Capt. USAF, 1951-57. Bd. dirs. Cultural Alliance of Greater Hampton Rds., 1984-87. Recipient Disting. Svc. award Luther Coll., 1976. Mem. Conf. on Data System Langs. (chmn. 1967-85), COBOL Devel. Com. (chmn. 1960-67), Am. Assn. R.R.s (data systems div.) (chmn. 1969-70), Am. Mgmt. Assn. (v.p. planning council 1970-72, Disting. Service award 1972), Better Bus. Bur. Norfolk (bd. dirs. 1983-87), Council Better Bus. Burs. (bd. dirs. 1984-90). Lutheran. Office: 909 Unicorn Trl Chesapeake VA 23320-7365

JONES, JOHN WARREN, associaton executive; b. Richmond, Va., May 3, 1952; s. Jeter King and Myrtle Newman J.; m. Melva Ann Reekes, June 23, 1974; children: Emily Diane, Benjamin Warren. BSc, Va. Commonwealth U., 1974. Exec. dir. Va. Sheriff's Assn., Richmond, 1977—; mem., chmn. grants subcom. Juvenile Justice and Delinquency Prevention Adv. Com., Richmond, Va., 1989-94. Contbr. Va. Sheriff Mag., 1980—. Mem. Va. Recreation Saltwater Fishing Bd., Newport News, Va., 1993—, chmn. 1995—. Mem. Nat. Sheriffs' Assn. (chmn. com. exec. dirs., pres. 1996-97. Office: Va Sheriffs' Assn Ste D 9507 Hull St Rd Richmond VA 23236

JONES, JOSEPH WAYNE, food and beverage company executive, entrepreneur; b. Wilmington, Del., Dec. 17, 1936; s. Joseph West Jones and Harriet (Bryan) Flink; m. Shirley Claire Sawyer, Sept. 5, 1959 (div. Sept. 1969); children: Summer, Jackson West, Jay Wayne; m. Patricia Lee Cossin, Dec. 26, 1970; 1 child, Jordan W. BS in Advt., U. Fla., 1958. Mgmt. trainee W.T. Grant & Co., Miami, Fla., 1958; with sales and mktg. The Coca-Cola Co., Atlanta, 1959-72; gen. mgr., v.p. The Coca-Cola (Japan) Co., Tokyo, 1972-77; sr. v.p., gen. mgr. Coca-Cola Europe & Africa, London, 1977-83; corp. v.p. The Coca-Cola Co., Atlanta, 1983-84; exec. v.p. The Stroh Brewery Co., Detroit, 1984-88; chmn. Mom's Best Cookies, Orlando, Fla., 1988-94; dir. mktg. snack foods Silverado Foods, Inc., Orlando, 1994-96; chmn., pres. Orlando Internat. Inst. for Advanced Edn., 1996—; chmn. code enforcement bd. City of Winter Park, 1991—. Contbg. author newspaper articles to Japan News, 1973-74. 988—, also past chmn.; Coord. day care ctr. United Appeal, Atlanta, 1961; founding mem. Internat. Triangle, London, 1981-83; contbr. Nat. Playing Fields Assn., London, 1982; bd. dirs. YMCA, Winter Park, 1988-94, also past chmn.; trustee, sec.-treas. Winter Park Meml. Hosp., 1991—; sec.-treas. Winter Park Health Found., 1994—; mem. mgmt. com., coun. ministries, stewardship chmn. 1st United Meth. Ch., Winter Park, 1991-97. With U.S. Army, 1958-59. Named Outstanding Trainee Cadet, U.S. Army Signal Corps, Ft. Gordon, S.C., 1958; recipient Aid to Children Worldwide award Variety Club Internat., London, 1981.

Mem. Assn. Nat. Advertisers (bd. dirs. 1987), Winter Park C. of C. (bd. dirs. 1994—), Grosse Pointe Club (Mich.), Renaissance Club (Detroit), Interlachen Country Club (membership devel. com. 1994—), Sigma Nu. Home: 751 Bonita Dr Winter Park FL 32789-2719 Office: The Virtual Univ 761 Pinetree Rd Winter Park FL 32789-1508

JONES, JULLIA ANN, nurse; b. Indpls., May 2, 1949; d. Quincy Lon and Shirley Ann (DeMoss) Brock; m. Arthur Eugene Jones, Apr. 6, 1967; children: Jeannette Marie Jones Burge, Tonya Lorrain. ADN, Skagit Valley Coll., 1982; student, SUNY, Albany, 1989—. LPN, Wash., Miss., Ind., Fla. Nurses aide, emergency med. technician Med. Pers. Pool, San Diego, 1976-79; LPN United Gen. Hosp., Sedro-Woolly, Wash., 1983, Meridian (Miss.) Regional Hosp., 1983-84, Norrell Healthcare and Am. Nursing Care, Indpls., 1984-93, Marion County Jail, Ocala, Fla., 1993—; med. instr., extern coord., med. coord. Pontiac Bus. Inst., Indpls., 1986—. Home: 16667 SW 35th St Ocala FL 34481-8747 Office: Marion County Jail Correctional Med Sys 700 NW 30th Ave Ocala FL 34475-5606

JONES, KATHRYN ANN, writer, artist; b. L.A., Oct. 12, 1956; d. Samuel Andrew and Wanda Faye (Smith) J.; m. Dan F. Malone, June 27, 1981. BA in English and Journalism, Trinity U., San Antonio, 1979. Staff writer Corpus Christi (Tex.) Caller-Times, 1979-81, Harts-Hanks Comm., Austin, Tex., 1981, Dallas Times Herald, 1984-86, Dallas Morning News, 1986-91; bur. chief MIS Week, Fairchild Pubs., Dallas, 1982-84; freelance writer Time, Life, D Mag., N.Y.C. and Dallas, 1991-93; contbg. writer N.Y. Times, 1993—. Co-author: How to Be Happily Employed in Dallas-Fort Worth, 1990, Fort Worth, 1990; exhibited in group shows Dallas Women's Caucus for Art, 1991, 94, 96. Recipient award of excellence Dallas Press Club, 1988. Mem. Assn. Women Journalists (bd. dirs. 1993), Dallas Women's Caucus for Art (bd. dirs. 1996), Southwestern Watercolor Soc. Home: 5140 Malinda Ln N Fort Worth TX 76112-3832

JONES, KENNETH, medical company executive. Dir. R&D Quest Med. Address: One Allentown Pkwy Allen TX 75002

JONES, KENNETH BRUCE, surgeon; b. Scottsville, Ky., Apr. 17, 1953; s. Kenneth C. and Betty (Miller) J.; m. Carol Jean Munger, June 28, 1980; children: Daniel, Christopher, Elizabeth. BS, U. Ky., 1974; MD, Vanderbilt U., Nashville, 1978. Diplomate Am. Bd. Surgery; cert. advanced trauma life saving. Surg. intern and resident U. Louisville Med. Sch., 1978-80; resident in surgery East Tenn. U. Med. Sch., Johnson City, 1980-82, chief resident, 1983; surgeon Claiborne Surg. Group, Tazewell, Tenn., 1983-84, N.E. Ark. Surg. Clinic, Jonesboro, Ark., 1984—; sec. med. staff Meth. Hosp., 1986-87, chief of surgery, 1988-90, vice chief of staff, 1989-91, chief of staff, 1992-94; chief of surgery St. Bernard's Regional Med. Ctr., 1996—; asst. clin. prof. surgery U. Ark. Area Health Edn. Ctr., Jonesboro, 1985—; cancer liaison of Am. Coll. Surgeons Commn. on Cancer to St. Bernard's, 1996—. Contbr. articles on surgery to profl. jours. Active sch. bd., 1993—; deacon So. Bapt. Ch. Justin Potter med. scholar, 1974-78. Mem. ACS (cancer liaison physician commn. on cancer), Am. Soc. Gen. Surgery, So. Med. Assn., Ark. Med. Assn., Soc. Am. Gastrointestinal Endoscopic Surgeons, Am. Soc. Bariatric Surgery, NRA, Ark. Wildlife Fedn., Ducks Unltd., Quail Unltd., Phi Beta Kappa. Baptist. Home: 2600 Nix Lake Dr Jonesboro AR 72401-8561 Office: NE Ark Surg Clinic 800 S Church St Ste 104 Jonesboro AR 72401-4176

JONES, LARRY LEROY, oil company executive; b. Sioux City, Iowa, May 29, 1935; s. Rae Leroy and Margaret Ellen (Acre) J.; m. Phyllis Joan Waggerby, June 18, 1956 (div. Apr. 1969); children: Scott Leroy, Curtis Mark, Wade Kordell, Andrea Lynn; m. Norma Jean Houser, Oct. 25, 1969; 1 child, Todd Bradley. BS, U. Nebr., 1958, MS in Geology, 1961. Geologist, geophysicist Std. Oil Co. Tex. (Chevron), Corpus Christi, Tex., 1958-65; exploration geologist Monsanto Co., Houston, 1965-68, Occidental Petroleum Corp., Houston, 1968-71; area geologist Belco Petroleum Corp., Houston, 1971-72; from exploration mgr. to pres. and COO Dixel Resources Inc., Houston, 1972-78; pres., CEO Spartan Petroleum Corp., Houston, 1978—. Contbr. articles to profl. jours.; spkr. in field. Elder Presbyn. Ch., Houston, 1984—; trustee U. Nebr. Found., Lincoln, 1975—; dir., chmn. adv. bd. dept. geology U. Nebr., 1984—. Capt. UAR, 1958-59. Named Hon. Consul Govt. Belize, 1988-89. Mem. Am. Assn. Petroleum Geologists (cert., del., dir. acad. liaison com.), Ind. Petroleum Assn. Am. (dir. exploration com.), Tex. Ind. Producers and Royalty Owners, Houston Geol. Soc., Houston Energy Fin. Group, Nottingham Club Houston (v.p. 1988-89), Govt. Belize (adv. for trade 1993—), Whitehall Club Houston (pres., dir. 1979—). Republican. Office: Spartan Petroleum Corp 14027 Memorial Dr # 266 Houston TX 77079-6826

JONES, LAWRENCE DAVID, insurance and medical consultant; b. Cloquet, Minn., Mar. 4, 1928; s. Ellsworth D. and Opal I. (Proctor) J.; divorced; children: David, Greta, Donald, Christopher, Laura, Sharon. B in Pharmacy, U. Utah, 1954; postgrad., U. N.D., 1960-62; MD, U. Minn., 1964. Bd. cert. ins. medicine. Owner, operator drug ctrs. Kemmerer (Wyo.), Big Piney, Trading Post and Sugar Bowl, 1955-60; intern St. Marys Hosp., Mpls., 1964-65; family practice physician Harlowton, Mont., 1965-69, Arcadia, Calif., 1969-74; med. dir. Teledyne Life Ins., L.A., 1974-79, Gt. Am. Life, L.A., 1977-79; sr. med. dir. Sentry Ins., A Mut. Co., Stevens Point, Wis., 1979-80; assoc. med. dir. First Colony Life Ins. Co., 1981-83; v.p., assoc. med. dir. First Colony Life Ins. Co., Lynchburg, Va., 1983-85; v.p., med. dir., 1985-90, ind. cons. in ins. medicine/underwriting, 1990—; mem. faculty Bd. Ins. Medicine Triennial Course, 1979, 82, 85, 88, 91; mem. adv. bd. Lab. Corp. Am., Cons. Physicians Network; mem. NIH coordinating com. Nat. Heart Attack Alert Program; chmn. NIH-Nat. Heart Alert Program Task Force on Managed Care; former mem. bd. dirs. Life and Health Ins. Rsch. Fund; former mem. adv. bd. Lifetime Corp. Am. Svc.Bur.-Meditest, others. Past chmn. utilization rev. com. Santa Teresita Hosp., Duarte, Calif.; past city health officer Harlowton; past county health officer Judith Basin County, Mont; past mem. bd. dirs. Health Sys. Agy., L.A., Deaconess Hosp. Sch. Nursing, Billings, Mont., past asst. scoutmaster, past. asst. dist. scout commr., past dist. scout commr., past scoutmaster. Sgt. U.S. Army, 1952-53, USAR, 1950-53. Mem. AMA, Med. Soc. Va., Calif. State Med. Assn., Am. Acad. Ins. Medicine (chmn. profl. and pub. rels. com.), Am. Coll. Cardiology (co-chmn. liaison com., others), Assn. Life Ins. Med. Dirs. Am. (past pres., past chmn. ethics com., past chmn. profl. and pub. rels. com., past chmn. mortality and morbidity com., others), So. Med. Assn. (chmn. sect. on cardiovascular disease 1994-95), Med. Soc. Va., others. Office: PO Box 388 Summit MS 39666-0388

JONES, LAWRENCE RYMAN, retired research chemist; b. Terre Haute, Ind., Jan. 8, 1921; s. Frank Arthur and Mary Naomi (Ryman) J.; m. Mary Jane Proctor, July 9, 1944; children: Trudi Beth, Lawrence R. II. BS, Ind. State U., 1946. Chemist Comml. Solvents Corp., Terre Haute, 1946-79; chemist, toxicologist St. Anthony Hosp., Terre Haute, 1957-60; mgr. Ryman Farm, Vigo County, Ind., 1957-86; pres. Rymark Labs., Terre Haute, 1970-80; rsch. scientist Internat. Mineral and Chem. Corp., Terre Haute, 1972-86, ret., 1986—. Patentee in field; contbr. over 200 articles to profl. jours. Elder Presbyn. Ch.; active Terre Haute City Coun., 1960-72, pres., 1968; pres. Sr. Citizens Wabash Valley, 1960-64; v.p. Sr. Citizen Housing Devel.; bd. govs. Task Force for Economy; past chmn. Am. chem. Soc., Wabash Valley; past bd. dirs. Am. Inst. Chemists, Exch. Club, Cmty. Theater, Swope Art Gallery; mem. County Zoning Commn.; ch. elder, Sunday sch. tchr. Youth Fellowship. Mem. Am. Chem. Soc. (former chmn. Wabash Valley sect.). Republican. Presbyterian. Home: 1219 E Alamito St Rockport TX 78382-2958

JONES, LEON HERBERT, JR. (HERB JONES), artist; b. Norfolk, Va., Mar. 25, 1923; s. Leon Herbert and Edna May (Curling) J.; student William and Mary Coll., 1942-44; m. Barbara Dean, Sept. 14, 1947; children: Robert Clair, Louis Herbert. Marine structural draftsman and designer Norfolk (Va.) Shipbuilding & Dry Dock Co., 1944-46; free-lance comml. artist, 1946-49; prin. Herb Jones Realty, Norfolk, 1949-58; owner, mgr. Herb Jones Art Studio, Norfolk, 1958—; one-man shows: Norfolk Mus., 1968, Potomac Gallery, Alexandria, Va., 1979, Salisbury Gallery, 1979, Walter C. Rawls Mus., Courtland, Va., 1967, Virginia Beach Maritime Mus., 1983 Village Gallery, Virginia Beach, Va., 1984, Va. Mus. Marine Scis., 1986-87, Olde Towne Gallery, 1987, Amoco Oil, 1989, Petersburg Area Art League (affiliate Va. Mus.), 1990, Surrey Borger Lions Club, Surrey, Eng., 1990, Sr. Showcase Creative Living Cen. Libr., Virginia Beach, Va., 1990, Norview Lions Club Sponsored Show for Handicapped, Norfolk, Va., 1991, Surrey (Eng.) Border Lions Club, 1990, Lions Internat., 1991, 93, Cypress Point Lions sponsored show to benefit handicapped, Va. Beach, 1993, Harborfest, 1995, 96; 45 year retrospective: Louis and Susan Jones Art Gallery, Norfolk, Va., 1994; group shows include: Chrysler Mus., Norfolk, 1973, 74, SUNY, Buffalo, 1966, Springfield (Mass.) Mus. Fine Arts, 1966, Mariners Mus., Newport News, Va., 1967-73, Va. Mus., Richmond, 1969, 71, Columbia (S.C.) Mus. Art, 1972, Winston-Salem (N.C.) Gallery Contemporary Art, 1970, 72, Norfolk Mus., 1963-69, Vladimir Arts, Winsbach, West Germany, 1978, 79, Chesapeake Bay Maritime Mus., Md., Mobile Mus. Traveling Show, 1983, Knoxville World's Fair in Fine Arts, 1982, Art Buyers Caravan, Atlanta, 1982, Colonial Wild Fowl Festival, Williamsburg, Va., 1983, Chesapeake Jubilee (Va., Excellence award) 1984, Peninsula Fine Arts Festival, Newport News, 1984, Currituck Wildlife Show, N.C., 1984, Medley of Arts, Hampton (Va.) Coliseum, 1984 (6 awards 1986-87), Easton Nat. Wildfowl and Art Exhibit, Easton, Md., 1984; Mid-Atlantic Art Exhibit, Virginia Beach, Va., 1985, Chincoteague Island Easter Festival, Va., 1985, (2 awards) 1989 (1st and 2d Pl. award), Harborfest Norfolk, Va., 1985-95, Mid-Atlantic Wildfowl Festival, 1986-93 (1st and 3d award), Hampton Wildlife Festival, 1986 (award 1989), Medley of the Arts, 1986, 87, Mid Atlantic Art Exhibits, 1986, 87, Hampton Fall Festival, (award) 1989, Sr. Showcase Creative Living Art Exhibit, Va. Beach, 1990, River Gallery, Chesapeake, Va., 1992, MidAtlantic Waterfowl Festival, Va. Beach, 1993; represented in permanent collections: Chrysler Mus., wardroom USS Skipjack, USS Iwo Jima, USS John F. Kennedy, USS Dwight D. Eisenhower, USS Seattle, USS Raleigh, USS Biddle, USS Whidby Island Commn., 1992, U. Va., Charlottesville, U.S. Treasury Dept., Library of Congress, Washington, Edenton Hist. Commn. (N.C.), USS Whidby Island, 1994, USS Hayler, 1995, also pvt. collections; commd. ltd. edit. print series Ducks Unltd., also Va. Beach Maritime Mus., Boy Scouts Am., Va. Mus. Marine Scis., Wavy TV affiliate of Lin Broadcasting Co., Judy Boone Real Estate, Official Harborfest Poster, 1993—, Harbor Fest Poster, 1993-95, Official Urbanna (Va.) Oyster Festival print, 1993, plaque Chesapeake Bay Bridge and Tunnel Commn., two spl. print edits. Letton Gooch Printers Inc. Recipient diploma di merito Universita delle Arti, 1981, Gold Centaur award 1983, three Awards of Excellence Printing Industries of the Virginias, 1987, 1st and 2d Pl. Awards of Excellence, 1989, Oscar d'Italia, Acad. Italia Calvatore, 1985, award Mid-Atlantic Waterfowl Festival, 1986, 1st and 3d Place awards, 1993, Great Citizen of Hampton Roads award Cox Cable TV, 1991, Best Art Print in Show award Printing Industries Va., 1995; named Cavalier of Arts, Acad. Bedriacense Calvatore, Italy, 1985, Hampton Roads Original, WTAR-AM Radio, 1990; selected as one of 100 leaders to judge "Best of Am.", U.S. News & World Report, 1990. Mem. Nat. Soc. Arts and Lit., Tidewater Artists Assn., Internat. Platform Assn., Virginia Beach Maritime Mus. (charter), Corr. Academie Europeene, Nat. Am. Film Inst., Lion's Internat. (hon., Melvin Jones fellow for dedicated humanitarian svcs. 1994). Methodist. Home and Office: 238 Beck St Norfolk VA 23503-4902

JONES, LESLIE FAYE, secondary mathematics education educator; b. Napoleonville, La., Oct. 5, 1970; d. Lloyd Alfred and Marion (Landry) J. BS, Nicholls State U., Thibodaux, La., 1991, MEd, 1992; PhD, La. State U., Baton Rouge, 1996. Tchr. St. James (La.) Parish Sch. Bd., 1992—. Mem. Am. Edn. Rsch. Assn., La. Assn. Educators, Phi Kappa Phi. Home: PO Box 176 Napoleonville LA 70390

JONES, LIONEL TROY, JR., electronic engineer; b. Brevard, N.C., July 4, 1938; s. Lionel Troy and Beatrice Virginia (Canup) J.; m. Helen June McMurrey, Dec. 3, 1965; 1 child, Michael Troy. BSEE, Va. Mil. Inst., 1961; postgrad., U. Houston, 1970-77. Engr. Schlumberger, Ltd., Houston, 1969-71, Ford-Aerospace, Houston, 1971-86, Eagle Engring., Houston, 1987, Geocontrol Sys., Houston, 1988, Allied Signal Tech. Svcs., Houston, 1989-96, Lockheed-Martin Corp., Houston, 1996—; cons. Horizon Engring., Houston, 1987. Officer, pilot USAF, 1962-69. Decorated Air Medal. Mem. IEEE, Internat. Soc. for Philos. Enquiry, Mensa. Home: 2706 Hazel St Pearland TX 77581

JONES, MALINDA THIESSEN, telecommunications company executive; b. Perryton, Tex., Jan. 23, 1947; d. Chester Francis Thiessen and Bobbye Pearson (Wallis) Schwalm; m. Hollis Bass Jones, Mar. 21, 1969 (div. 1972); 1 child, Reshad. B.A. in Psychology, U. Mo.-Kansas City, 1975. Rsch. asst. U. Kans. Med. Ctr., Kansas City, 1975-77; owner, mgr. Metro Shampoo Co., Kansas City, Mo., 1977-79; regional mgr. U.S. Telecom, Dallas, 1981-82, staff asst. to pres., Dallas, 1983-84, sr. planner, 1984-85; dir. mktg. Telinq Systems Inc., Richardson, Tex., 1985-86, dir. bus. devel. and corp. communications, 1986—; v.p. mktg. Dakota Group, Inc., 1989—; cons. in field. Editor conf. presentations, bus. plans. Vol. tchr. Sch. for Learning Disability, Operation Discovery, Kansas City, 1973-75; corp. liaison exec. assistance program Dallas C. of C./Dallas Ind. Sch. Dist., 1984; chmn. com. Therapeutic Riding Tex., Dallas, 1985. Recipient Outstanding Contbr. award Dallas Ind. Sch. Dist., 1984. Mem. NAFE, Nat. Mus. Assn. for Women in Arts, Assn. Women Entrepreneurs Dallas. Home: 1122 Overlake Dr Richardson TX 75080-6937 Office: Dakota Group Inc 1217 Digital Dr Richardson TX 75081-1970

JONES, MARGUERITE JACKSON, English language educator; b. Greenwood, Miss., Aug. 12, 1949; d. James and Mary G. (Reedy) Jackson; m. Algee Jones, Apr. 4, 1971; 1 child, Stephanie Nerissa. BS, Miss. Valley State U., 1969; MEd, Miss. State U., 1974; EdS, Ark. State U., 1983; postgrad. U. Ark., 1982. Tchr. English Henderson High Sch., Starkville, Miss., 1969-70, creative writing Miami (Fla.) Coral Park, 1970-71, English, head dept. Marion (Ark.) Sr. High Sch., 1971-78, East Ark. Community Coll., Forrest City, 1978-79; migrant edn. supr. Marion (Ark.) Sch. Dist., 1979-83; mem. faculty Draughons Coll., Memphis, 1978-83; assoc. prof. State Tech., 1984—; cons. writing projects; condr. workshops for ednl., bus., civic groups. Bd. dirs. Bountiful Blessings Christian Acad., Memphis; dir. Leadership Tng. Inst. for 4th Eccles. Jurisdiction, Tenn.; Christian edn. dir. Temple Deliverance-The Cathedral Bountiful Blessings, Memphis. Mem. ASCD, Nat. Coun. Tchrs. English, Ark. Assn. Profl. Educators, Memphis Assn. Young Children, Tenn. Assn. Young Children, Nat. Assn. Young Children, Phi Delta Kappa. Home: 1239 Meadowlark Ln Memphis TN 38116-7801 Office: State Tech Inst 5983 Macon Cove Memphis TN 38134-7642

JONES, MARK MITCHELL, plastic surgeon; b. Atlanta, Mar. 27, 1951; s. Curtis B. and Julia (Mitchell) J.; m. Regine M.F. Heckel, Jan. 10, 1980; children: Céline Julia Micheline, Cédric André Curtis. Student, Oxford (Ga.) Coll., 1971; BA in Chemistry, Emory U., 1973; DBA, U. Canterbury, Christchurch, New Zealand, 1975; BA, MA, Oxford (Eng.) U., 1977; MD, Med. Coll. Ga., 1979. Surg. intern Med. U. of S.C., Charleston, 1979-80; surg. resident Union Meml. Hosp., Balt., 1980-81; resident in otolaryngology Johns Hopkins Hosp., Balt., 1981-84, mem. staff, instr., 1984-85; resident in plastic surgery Stanford U. Med. Ctr., Palo Alto, Calif., 1985-86; chief resident in plastic surgery, 1987-88; assoc. Calif. Ear Inst., 1988-89; chief surgeon Atlanta Plastic Surgery Specialist, 1989—. Fulbright fellow in plastic surgery, Paris, 1986-87. Home: 985 Foxcroft Rd NW Atlanta GA 30327-2621 Office: Atlanta Plastic Surgery Specialist 2001 Peachtree Rd NE Ste 630 Atlanta GA 30309-1476

JONES, MARK PERRIN, III, special assistant to attorney general, editor; b. Searcy, Ark., Jan. 19, 1932; s. Mark Perrin Jones Jr. and Jamie Amanda (Baugh) Young; 1 child, Mark Perrin IV; m. Anna Lee McGill, July 28, 1970 (div. July 1993); children: Lana Lee Clark, Rodger Willis Duncan. BS in Journalism, U. Ark., 1953, MA in Govt., 1954. Editor The Daily Citizen, Searcy, 1954-83, editor emeritus, 1983—; adj. prof. U. Ctrl. Ark., Conway, 1984-89, Ark. State U., Beebe, 1985-87; candidate Lt. Gov., Ark., 1990; spl. asst. to atty. gen. Atty. Gen.'s Office, Little Rock, Ark., 1991—. V.p. Ark. Constl. Conv., Little Rock, 1969-70; mem. State Bd. Edn., Little Rock, 1959-68, State Bd. Higher Edn., Little Rock, 1986-92. Recipient Freedom of Info. award Ark. Press Assn., 1995; named one of Outstanding Young Men of Am., Ark. Jaycees, 1965. Mem. Nat. Assn. State Bds. of Edn. (life), Ark. Consistory, Shriners, Masons, Rotary (Paul Harris fellow 1982). Democrat. Presbyterian. Home: 2200 Andover Ct Apt 1304 Little Rock AR 72227-3963 Office: Atty Gens Office 323 Center St Little Rock AR 72201-2605

JONES, MARQUIS E., management sales executive, insurance executive; b. Charleston, Ark., Feb. 3, 1937; s. Marcus Paul and Vivian Hattie (Benefield) J.; m. Leslie A. Jeffries, Jan. 16, 1956 (div. Oct. 1983); children: Rebecca Jones Naylor, Cynthia Jones Williams, Marquis P., W. David; m. Diane E. Mckee, Dec. 23, 1983. BS in Music Edn., Memphis State U., 1959; MM in Clarinet Lit., Fla. State U., 1960. CLU, 1977, ChFC, 1994. Band dir. Young Harris (Ga.) Coll., 1960-62, Furman U., Greenville, S.C., 1962-64; sales rep. G. Leblanc Corp., Kenosha, Wis., 1964-70, Wallick Music Co., Pine Bluff, Ark., 1971; agt. N.Y. Life Ins. Co., Stuttgart, Ark., 1972-74; sales mgr. N.Y. Life Ins. Co., Little Rock and Tyler, Tex., 1974-80; gen. mgr. N.Y. Life Ins. Co., Beaumont, Tex., 1981, Monroe, La., 1982-89, New Orleans, 1989-94; cons. N.Y. Life Ins. Co., N.Y.C.; cons. Cambridge Agy. Systems, San Diego, 1994. Author: Advanced Studies for Clarinet, 1961, 13 Basic Studies for Clarinet, 1961, Fundamentals of Clarinet Playing, 1962; contbr. articles to profl. jours. Bd. dirs., tchr. Sunday Sch. Munholland Meth. Ch. Recipient Tannebaum Svc. to Humanity award Jaycees, 1972. Mem. Gen. Agts. and Mgrs. Assn. (Nat. Mgmt. award 1981-94), Soc. CLU/ChFC, U.S. Power Assn. (commdr. 1985), Mensa Soc. (local sec. 1983, 85), City Club (chmn. wine com. 1989-92, 96), Tower Club (chmn. wine com. 1987-89). Republican. Home: 7300 Lakeshore Dr Apt 28 New Orleans LA 70124-2464

JONES, MARY ANN, geriatrics nurse; b. Suffern, N.Y., July 15, 1943; d. Ralph and Hilva (Kelly) Osborne; m. Richard D. Jones, Aug. 31, 1985. AAS, Rockland C.C., Suffern, 1963; BS, St. Thomas Aquinas Coll., Sparkill, N.Y., 1983. Cert. dir. nursing adminstrn./long term care. Supr. to asst. DON Ramapo Manor Nursing Ctr., Suffern, 1964-87; coord. to DON Carnegie Gardens Nursing Ctr., Melbourne, Fla., 1987—. Mem. Nat. Assn. Dirs. Nursing Adminstrn. in Long Term Care, Fla. Assn. Dirs. Nursing Adminstrn. in Long Term Care (1st v.p. local chpt., cert. Dir. Nursing Adminstrn. in Long Term Care 1995), Gericulture Soc. Home: 426 Lackland St SW Palm Bay FL 32908-7111

JONES, MARY ELIZABETH, school counselor; b. Lake Charles, La.; d. Annie Walter and Thelma (Griffin) J. BS in Recreation, So. U., 1969; MA, 1977; Licensed profl. counselor. Program dir. YWCA, Baton Rouge, 1969-72; instr. So. U., Baton Rouge, 1972-74, career counselor, 1974-84; student personnel officer Baton Rouge Vocat. Tech. Inst., 1984-86; resource person Women's Skill Tng. Program, Baton Rouge, 1984-86; placement officer Jumonville Sr. Vocat. Tech. Sch., Baton Rouge, 1987-88; counselor, job developer, 1988—; cons. ind. contractor, 1988-90; substance abuse coord., La. State Penitentiary; advisor So. U. Tchrs. Job Fair, Baton Rouge, 1980—; resource person Women's Skill Tng. program, ednl. specialist Foster Care Pre-Vocat. project, 1988—. Bd. dirs. Battered Women's Program, Baton Rouge, 1985, also mem. exec. com., chmn. nominating com.; chmn. scholarship com. Scotlandville Area Adv., 1982. Recipient Community Services award Scotlandville Area Adv. Council, 1982. Mem. Nat. Family Opinion, Smithsonian Assn., Am. Assn. for Counseling and Devel., La. Sch. Counselors Assn., La. Vocation Assn., Am. Soc. For Tng. and Devel., 100 Black Women, Democrat. Roman Catholic. Avocations: traveling, reading, monogramming, hook rug weaving, interior design. Home: 1631 79th Ave Baton Rouge LA 70807-5431

JONES, MARY TRENT, endowment fund trustee; b. Durham, N.C., July 15, 1940; d. Josiah Charles Trent and Mary Duke (Biddle) Semans; m. James Parker Jones, June 27, 1964; children: James Trent, Benjamin Parker, Jonathan Edmund. AB, Duke U., 1963. Trustee The Duke Endowment, Charlotte, N.C., 1988—; chmn. Josiah Charles Trent Found., Durham, 1978-83; bd. dirs. Mary Duke Biddle Found., Durham, 1983—, Concert Artists Guild, N.Y.C., 1996—. Mem. Va. Perinatal Svcs. Adv. Bd., Richmond, 1986-91; sec. Va. Arts Commn., Richmond, 1989-92; trustee Va. Intermont Coll., Bristol, Va., 1986-91; mem. State Coun. Higher Edn. Va., Richmond, 1991-95; bd. trustees Va. Mus. of Fine Arts, Richmond, 1992—. Recipient outstanding alumni award Durham Acad., 1991. Mem. Va. Highlands Festival Bd. Episcopalian. Home: 107 Hillside Dr Abingdon VA 24210

JONES, MARYNEAL WILLIAMS, freelance writer; b. Florence, S.C., Aug. 12, 1934; d. Guilda Roy and Tessie Gertrude (Hudson) Williams; m. William Moore Jones, June 17, 1956; children: John Mark, Eric Louis. Student, U. S.C., 1954-55, Winthrop Coll., 1961-62. Editor-in-chief Chesterfield (S.C.) Advertiser, 1967-69, S.C. United Meth. Advocate, Columbia, S.C., 1979-88; dir. pub. rels. Chesterfield-Marlboro Tech. Coll., Cheraw, S.C., 1969-71; dir. news svc. Furman U., Greenville, S.C., 1971-78; freelance writer, Irmo, S.C., 1988—; pub. rels. cons. to numerous pub. and pvt. agys., S.C., 1971—. Author: L.D. Johnson: Prophet and Friend, 1983; contbr. numerous articles to regional and nat. periodicals. Bd. dirs. S.C. LWV, 1961-65, Tryon Little Theatre, Tryon Dance Guild, 1995—; del. S.C. Dem. Conv., 1992. Named Woman of Yr., Kershaw County, S.C., 1969, Gaston award Coll. News Assn. Carolinas, 1975, 18 writing awards United Meth. Assn. Communicators, 1979-88, Presdl. citation Claflin Coll., 1987, award S.C. Christian Action Coun., 1988.

JONES, MATTIE SAUNDERS, secondary school educator; b. High Point, N.C., Aug. 29, 1942; d. Newport Allen and Irene Edith (Balem) Saunders; m. David Louis Jones, Aug. 20, 1966; 1 child, David Louis Jr. BS, N.C. Cen. U., 1964; MST, Jackson State U., 1992; postgrad., Va. Commonwealth U., 1971, 77, 82-86, Va. State U., 1972-73, 77, U. Va., 1966, 77, Jackson State U. Cert. tchr., Miss. Tchr. pub. schs. Staunton, Va., 1964-68, Richmond, Va., 1969-88, Jackson, Miss., 1988-90; chmn. math. dept. Murrah High Sch.; contbr. to curriculum devel. for remedial math., computer programming; faculty sponsor Murrah High Sch. Mu Alpha Theta Nat. High Sch. Math. Honor Soc.; mem. tchr. edn. coun. Belhaven Coll., 1993—. Active St. Peter Bapt. Ch., Glen Allen, Va., 1980-88; mem. sr. usher bd., jr. matrons' aux. New Hop Bapt. Ch., Jackson, 1989—; bd. dirs. Glen Allen Youth Athletic Assn., 1977-81, treas., 1978-81; mem. parent com. Robert E. Lee coun. Boy Scouts Am., 1980-86, asst. chmn., then chmn., 1983-85; mem. Am. Contract Bridge League; mem. Ctrl. Miss. chpt. Nat. Coalition of 100 Black Women, 1992—. Mem. NEA, ASCD, AAUW, Nat. Coun. Tchrs. Math., Math. Assn. Am., Miss. Ednl. Computers Assn., Am. Bus. Women's Assn. (chmn. com. Virginia Randolph chpt. 1987-88), Miss. Coun. Tchrs. Math., Miss. Assn. Educators, N.C. Ctrl. U. Nat. Alumni Assn. (life), Order Ea. Star, Alpha Kappa Alpha (treas. Upsilon Omega chpt. 1987-88), Beta Delta Omega (rec. sec. 1991-92, treas. 1993—, treas. regional conf. 1995), Phi Delta Kappa, Pi Lambda Theta (rec. sec., pres. 1995-96). Home: 5950 Holbrook Dr Jackson MS 39206-2003

JONES, MICHAEL WAYNE, health services administrator; b. Amarillo, Tex., May 10, 1957; s. Robert Edgar and Ginger Louise (Smith) J. BSN, West Tex. State U., 1980; MBA, Wayland Bapt. U., 1987. CNAA; CEN, CCHP. Staff nurse, charge nurse N.W. Tex. Hosp., Amarillo, 1980—; prison health svc. adminstr. Tex. Tech. U. Health Sci. Ctr., Amarillo, 1989-95, dir. utilization mgmt., 1995—; alumnus advisor Kappa Alpha Order, West Tex. A&M U.; presenter Emerging Roles; Nursing in Correctional Instns.; Utilization Mgmt. in Correctional Health, Correctional Facility Nursing; guest lectr. to West Tex. A&M U. Sch. of Nursing. Bd. dirs. Leadership Amarillo; helping one student to suceed mentor Amarillo Ind. Sch. Dist.; bd. dirs. Golden Spread Boy Scouts Am.; loaned exec. United Way; mem. interfraternity adv. bd. West Tex. A&M U.; Institutional Ethics Comm.; N.W. Tex. Healthcare Sys. Mem. SAR, Sons of Confederate Vets., Emergency Nurses Assn., Panhandle Orgn. Nurse Execs. (pres.), Tex. Orgn. Nurses Execs. (state bd. dirs.), Am. Correctional Assoc., Am. Correctional Health Svcs. Assn. (bd. dirs), Tex. Panhandle Alumni (pres. Kappa Alpha Order), Leadership Amarillo Alumni, Sigma Theta Tau. Home: RR 1 Box 419 Amarillo TX 79121-9606 Office: Tex Tech U Health Scis 7120 I 40 W Ste 300 Bldg A Amarillo TX 79106-1708

JONES, MITCHELL MARK, medical researcher; b. Milan, Tenn., July 26, 1948; s. Mitchell M. and Mary Gwynn J.; m. Pansy Marie Dallahunty, April 18, 1975; children: Elizabeth Gwynn, Paul Austin. MS in physicians assistant, Duke U., 1974; BA, La. State U., 1975. Drug enforcement agent Bur. Narcotics and Dangerous Drugs, Thailand, 1973-74; nutritional rep. Ross Labs., Jackson, Miss., 1976-79; orthopedic cons. 3-M, Inc., Shreveport, La., 1979-81; physicians asst. Mallinckrodt, Inc., Colleyville, Tex., 1981—; bd. dirs. So. League, Tex., 1996—. Co-Author: (poetry collection) Ramblings, 1988. With U.S. Army, 1969-73, Vietnam. Decorated Silver Star, Bronze Star, Purple Heart. Mem. Ducks Unlimited, Celtic Heritage Assn., Kappa

Sigma. Protestant. Home and Office: 5817 Quality Hill Colleyville TX 76034

JONES, MONIAREE PARKER, occupational health nurse; b. Montgomery, Ala., Oct. 20, 1953; d. Jeffie Knod and Amanda Gertrude (Grier) Parker; m. C. Emile Jones, May 24, 1980; 1 child, William Andrew. Assoc. Nursing, Troy State U., 1974; BSN, U. Ala., 1980. Cert. occupational health nurse; cert. Red Cross instr. Nurse emergency rm. Elmore County Hosp., Wetumpka, Ala.; med. auditor State of Ala. Med. Svcs. Adminstrn., Montgomery; instr. women's tng. program State of La., Baton Rouge; occupational health nurse Georgia Gulf Corp., Plaquemine, La., 1984-91; dir. occupational health svcs. River West Med. Ctr., Plaquemine; occupational rehab. cons. Am. Internat. Health and Rehab. Svcs., Birmingham, Ala.; internal coord. CompSolution, Birmingham, Ala., 1992—; client svcs. mgr. Lake Shore Rehab. Ctr.; occupational health nurse State Farm Ins. Co., Birmingham. Mem. La. Assn. Occupational Health Nurses (pres. Baton Rouge chpt.), Ctrl. Ala. Occupational Nurses Assn. (pres.), Am. Assn. Occupational Health Nurses. Home: 1444 Oak Ridge Dr Birmingham AL 35242-3522 Office: State Farm Ins Co 100 State Farm Pkwy Birmingham AL 35209-7106

JONES, NANCY GALE, retired biology educator; b. Gaffney, S.C., Nov. 12, 1940; d. Louransey Dowell and Sarah Louise (Pettit) J. BA, Winthrop Coll., 1962; MA, Oberlin Coll., 1964; postgrad. Duke U. Marine Biology Lab., 1963, Marine Biol. Lab., Woods Hole, Mass., 1964, N.C. State U., 1965, Ohio State U., 1966, Ariz. State U., 1970. Lectr. biology Oberlin (Ohio) Coll., 1964-66; from instr. to asst. prof. zoology Ohio U., Zanesville, 1966-73; media specialist Muskingum Area Vocat. Sch., Zanesville, 1973-74; salesperson Village Bookstore, Worthington, Ohio, 1975. Vol. hortitherapist for mentally disabled adults Habilitation Svcs., Inc. Gaffney, S.C., 1977-80; vol. dir. emergency assistance to needy PEACHcenter Ministries, Gaffney, 1991-94; mem. planned giving adv. coun. Winthrop U. Recipient Winthrop U. Alumni Disting. Svc. award, 1996. Mem. Ohio Retired Tchrs. Assn., Sigma Xi (assoc.). Baptist. Home: 1643 W Rutledge Ave Gaffney SC 29341-1023

JONES, NEILL E., engineer, consultant; b. Shawnee, Okla., Aug. 3, 1941; s. Charles Neill and Roberta Sue (Lentz) J.; m. Rebecca Lou Dirting, Sept. 30, 1946; children: Amber Nicole, Allison Rene. BS in Engring, Physics minor Meteorology, U. Okla., 1964. Sr. planner Stearns Roger, Denver, Colo., 1973-86, DCSI, Englewood, Colo., 1986-87; sr. scheduler Lockwood Greene, Spartanburg, S.C., 1987-96; cons. pvt. practice, Spartanburg, S.C., 1987-96. Capt. U.S. Air Force, 1964-68, Phillipines. Baptist. Office: Lockwood Greene 1500 International Dr Spartanburg SC 29303

JONES, NICHOLAS CHARLES, writer, editor, broadcaster; b. Oxford, Md., Dec. 14, 1944; s. Jasper Lee and Isabelle Wanner (Willing) J. BS in Applied Math., Ga. Inst. Tech., 1966; postgrad. in Music Theory, Ga. State U., 1969-76. Tchr. Music and Math. Cobb County Schs., Mableton, Ga., 1974-75; broadcaster Sta. WGKA-FM, Atlanta, 1974—; host writer Atlanta Symphony Preview, 1976—; host-writer Opus Ga. Pub. TV, Atlanta, 1979-81; program annotator Atlanta Symphony Orch., Atlanta, 1981—, program editor, 1994—, supervising editor 50th anniversary exhbn., 1994-95; adminstr. Ga. Chamber Players, Atlanta, 1985—; bd. govs. Atlanta chpt. Nat. Acad. Recording Arts and Scis., 1988-91. Author: A Tribute to Robert Shaw, 1988, liner notes more than 20 compact discs, 1984—, concert notes, 1982—. Singer Atlanta Symphony Orch. Chorus, 1970—; vol., bd. dirs. Atlanta Botanical Gardens, Atlanta, 1979-81. Lt. USN, 1966-69. Recipient Sta. WSB-TV Vol. award, 1980. Home: 1500 Moore's Mill Rd NW Atlanta GA 30327-1436 Office: Atlanta Symphony Orch 1293 Peachtree St NE Atlanta GA 30309-3525

JONES, PEGGY W., postal official, poet; b. Marshall, Tex., Dec. 14, 1953; d. Herbert and Lottie Mae (Wilson) J. AAS in Pattern Design, El Centro Jr. Coll., 1981. Author: (poem) Tomorrow's Dream, 1996. Mem., vol. coord. Jr. Black Acad., Dallas, 1988-94; docent African Mus., Dallas, 1992-94. Mem. Afro Am. Postal League, First Class Toastmaster (v.p. 1986, v.p. edl., v.p., pres. 1986). Home: 6415 Rhapsody Ln Dallas TX 75241-2639 Office: Poet With A Vision PO Box 225583 Dallas TX 75222

JONES, PHILIP ARTHUR, real estate developer; b. Jonesboro, Ark., Jan. 29, 1968; s. Arthur Philip and Florence Therese (Shepherd) J. BS, Spring Hill Coll., 1990; MBA, Rosary Coll., River Forest, Ill., 1992. Exec. asst./liaison Office of the Governor, Little Rock, 1992-96; mng. ptnr. St. Louis Mgmt. Co., Jonesboro, 1996—; pres., mng. ptnr. So. Heritage Devel., Jonesboro, 1996—; founder Heritage Realty, Inc. Ctrl. Com. Dem. Party of Ark., Little Rock, 1993-94; exec. dir. Com. for Employer Support of the Guard and Res., Little Rock, 1996. Decorated Disting. Svc. medal Ark. N.G., Little Rock, 1996; named Hon. Dep. Sheriff Craighead County, Ark., 1990-96, Hon. Brigadier Gen. Gov., Adjutant Gen. State of Ark., 1996. Mem. Nat. Ctr. Housing Mgmt., Ark. Emergency Mgrs. Assn., Ark. Hist. Assn., Ark. Realtors Assn., Friends of Jonesboro Libr. (com. chair 1996), Greater Jonesboro C. of C., Ridgepointe Country Club. Roman Catholic. Home: 1017 S Culberhouse Jonesboro AR 72401 Office: 201 W Washington Jonesboro AR 72401

JONES, RANDOLPH SUTTON, archivist; b. Charleston, S.C., July 19, 1952; s. Shelton Jerome and Mary Claire (Pinckney) J.; m. Nancy Ellen Costello, Sept. 18, 1982. BA, Northwestern State U., Natchitoches, La., 1974; MA, N.E. La. U., 1982. Regional sales rep. Minute Man, East Flat Rock, N.C., 1978-80; archivist State of La., New Orleans, 1983-85; records sys. analyst State of Utah, Salt Lake City, 1985-88; records mgr. Orrick, Herrington & Sutcliffe, San Francisco, 1988-90; records mgr., archivist City of Oakland, Calif., 1990-93; archivist Vanderbilt U. Med. Ctr., Nashville, 1994—; automated sys. analyst U.S. Army, 1978-94; records mgmt. cons. Petaluma (Calif.) Mus., 1993-94. Contbr. articles to profl. jours. Adult leader Christian Youth Orgn., Franklin, Tenn., 1994-95. Maj. U.S. Army, 1974-78, USAR, 1974—. Mem. Soc. Am. Archivists, Assn. Records Mgrs. and Adminstrs. (v.p. San Francisco chpt. 1984—). Republican. Office: Vanderbilt University Medical Center Eskind Biomed Library Nashville TN 37232

JONES, REGI WILSON, data processing executive; b. Paris, Tenn., Sept. 4, 1960; s. Charles W. and Louise J. AS, Jackson State Community Hosp., Tenn., 1981; BS, U. Tenn., 1986; MS, Middle Tenn. State U., 1991. Med. tech. Vol. Gen. Hosp., Martin, Tenn., 1982-86; med. tech. So. Hills Hosp., Nashville, 1986-90, asst. supr. microbiology, 1990-91; systems installation coord. Info. Svcs. Hosp. Corp. Am., Nashville, 1991-96; network project mgr. for Gateway implementations Columbia Healthcare Corp., Nashville, 1996—; sys. interface cons. Columbia/HCA Info. Svcs., 1996—; lab cons., Nashville; med. adv. bd. MLO Mag., 1985-86. Asst. to dir. bands U. Tenn., martin, 1985-86, trumpet section leader, lead soloist. Named one of Outstanding Young Men in Am., 1989. Mem. AAAS, N.Y. Acad. Scis., NRA (Inst. for Legis. Action), Southea. Conf. Championship Club (charter), U. Tenn. Alumni Assn., Smithsonian Instn., Sigma Xi, Phi Mu Alpha. Home: 299 Belinda Pkwy Mount Juliet TN 37122 Office: Columbia/HCA Info Svcs 1 Park Plz Nashville TN 37202

JONES, REGINALD NASH, lawyer; b. Jarratt, Va., Feb. 11, 1943; s. Jesse Everett and Ruby Lee (Parson) J.; m. Anne Johnson Askew, Aug. 28, 1965; children: Charles Everett, Emily Reed. BA in Econs., U. Richmond, 1965, JD, 1968. Bar: Va. 1968. Assoc., ptnr. Willey, Jones & Waechter, Richmond, Va., 1970-79; prin. Press, Jones & Waechter, P.C., Richmond, 1979-93; pres. Press, Jones & Waechter, P.C., Richmond, 1986-93; ptnr. Williams, Mullen, Christian & Dobbins, Richmond, 1993—; mem. adv. bd. Fidelity Fed. Savs. Bank, 1987—; asst. staff judge adv. for So. Thailand, 1970; mem. Va. State Bar Coun., 1985-91. State youth coord., asst. campaign coord. Com. to Re-elect U.S. Sen. A. Willis Robertson, Richmond, 1966; citizen mem. Va. Bd. Medicine, 1986-91; trustee U. Richmond, 1982-86, mem. bd. assocs., mem. exec. com., 1986—; active River Rd. Bapt. Ch., Richmond, 1972—; bd. dirs. Jamestown-Yorktown Ednl. Trust, 1993—; mem. Pres.'s Coun. Va. Hist. Soc., 1996—. Recipient Disting. Svc. award U. Richmond Alumni, 1986. Fellow Va. Law Found. (bd. dirs. 1986-92, pres. 1989); mem. ABA (com. on credit union law 1981—), Richmond Bar Assn. (chmn. real estate sect. 1976-77, exec. com. 1976-78), Va. Bar Assn. (bar coun. 1985-91, chmn. legis. com. 1989-92), Henrico County Bar Assn. (founding pres. 1974-75), Hermitage County Club, Foundry Golf Club, Scabbard and Blade, Omicron Delta Kappa, Theta Chi, Phi Delta Phi. Home: 321 Clovelly Rd Richmond VA 23221-3701 Office: Williams Mullen Christian & Dobbins PO Box 1320 1021 E Cary St Richmond VA 23219-4000

JONES, RENEE KAUERAUF, health care administrator; b. Duncan, Okla., Nov. 3, 1949; d. Delbert Owen and Betty Jean (Marsh) Kauerauf; m. Dan Elkins Jones, Aug. 3, 1972. BS, Okla. State U., 1972, MS, 1975; PhD, Okla. U., 1989. Diplomate Am. Bd. Sleep Medicine. Statis. analyst Okla. State Dept. Mental Health, Okla. City, 1978-80, divisional chief, 1980-83, adminstr., 1983-84; assoc. dir. HCA Presbyn. Hosp., Okla. City, 1984—; adj. instr. Okla. U. Health Sci. Ctr., 1979—; assoc. staff scientist Okla. Ctr. for Alcohol and Drug-Related Studies, Okla. City, 1979—; cons. in field. Assoc. editor Alcohol Tech. Reports jour., 1979-84; contbr. articles to profl. jours. Mem. assoc. bd. Hist. Preservation, Inc., treas. 1994. Mem. APHA, Assn. Health Svcs. Rsch., Alcohol and Drug Problems Assn. N.Am., Am. Sleep Disorders Assn., N.Y. Acad. Scis., So. Sleep Soc. (sec.-treas. 1989-91), Phi Kappa Phi. Democrat. Methodist. Home: 401 NW 19th St Oklahoma City OK 73103-1911 Office: HCA Presbyn Hosp NE 13th at Lincoln Blvd Oklahoma City OK 73104

JONES, RICHARD WALLACE, interior designer; b. Canandaigua, N.Y., Dec. 6, 1929; s. William Wallace and Maybelle Louise (Smith) J.; m. Patricia Hardwick, June 24, 1957 (div. 1973). Student, Hobart Coll., 1946-47; tchr.'s cert., Longy Sch., Cambridge, Mass., 1952; postgrad., Yale U. Sch. Music, 1952-53. Owner, operator Richard W. Jones studios, Boston, Hartford, Conn., 1954-63; designer, mgr. House of Good Taste Pavilion, N.Y. World's Fair, 1963-66; design editor Redbook Mag., N.Y.C., 1967-72; sr. design editor Better Homes & Gardens mag., Des Moines, 1972-76; pres., dir. Circanow Interior Design Firm, Des Moines, N.Y.C., 1974-90; designer, mgr. D.H. Hershel Inc., Nantucket, Mass., 1978-81; ptnr., designer, buyer Portobello, Nantucket, 1981-83; dir. design Laura Ashley Inc., Ridgewood, N.J., 1989-90; interior designer Godfrey & Assocs., Naples, 1994—; curator Hammond Mus., Gloucester, Mass., 1950-60, Hill-Stead Mus., Farmington, Conn., 1962; del. Internat. Fedn. Interior Designers, Amsterdam, The Netherlands, 1975-76. Editor in chief Interiors mag., Residential Interiors, 1976-78. Mem. Pres.' Com. on Barrier Free Design, Washington, 1972-74. Recipient Dorothy Dawe award Sr. Design Editor, 1974. Fellow Am. Soc. Interior Designers (nat. pres. 1976. Disting. Svc. medal 1977); mem. Nat. Soc. Interior Designers (nat. pres. 1972-74), Nantucket C. of C. (bd. dirs. 1980-82, sign approval com. 1982-84). Presbyterian. Home: 292 14th Ave S Naples FL 34102 Office: Godfrey & Assocs 4380 Gulf Shore Blvd N Naples FL 34103-2663

JONES, RITA ANN, speech, theater educator; b. Tupelo, Miss., Sept. 9, 1947; d. Sammie Lee and Helen Juanita (Stone) J. AA, Itawamba Jr. Coll., 1967; BS, Miss. State U., 1969; MA, Miss. U. for Women, 1972. Tchr. Tremont (Miss.) High Sch., 1969-71, Winona (Miss.) Separate Sch. Dist., 1972-80, Holmes C.C., Goodman, Miss., 1980—. Dir. Little Theatre, Fulton, Miss., 1977-80, 84; pres. Bus. and Profl. Women, Winona, 1977-78; active local Meth. Ch. Mem. Tchr.'s Assn. Republican. Home: PO Box 236 Fulton MS 38843-0236 Office: Holmes CC Hill St Goodman MS 39079

JONES, ROBERT EUGENE, physician; b. Bauxite, Ark., Aug. 25, 1926; s. Curtis Whittemore and Rosina (Nelson) J.; m. Frances (Mickey) Harper, June 24, 1949; children: Eric R., Bryant, Gretchen M. Student, Tulane U., 1944-45; BS, U. Ark., Fayetteville, 1947; MD, U. Ark., Little Rock, 1951. Cert. correctional health profl. Intern St. Vincent Infirmary, Little Rock, 1951-52; pvt. practice physician Benton, 1953—; chief of staff Saline Meml. Hosp., Benton, Ark., 1965-66, 68-69; pres. Saline County Med. Soc., Benton, 1965-66, 68-69; med. dir. Ark. Region PHP Health, Pine Bluff, Ark., 1989-90; Benton, 1952—; med. dir. Mid Delta Health Systems. Inc., De Valls Bluff, Ark., 1994—; assoc. dept. community and family medicine U. Ark. for Med. Sci. With USN, 1944-45, 1st lt. Med. Corps, U.S. Army, 1953-55. Fellow Royal Soc. Health. Episcopalian. Home: 723 W Narroway St Benton AR 72015-3653 Office: Mid Delta Health Systems Market St De Valls Bluff AR 72041

JONES, ROBERT THADDUES, principal; b. Manhattan, N.Y., Jan. 11, 1938; s. Monte Jones and Adelle (Brown) Ousmane; m. Geneva Alafair Thomas, Nov. 24, 1957; 1 child, Terry David. BA, Claflin Coll., Orangeburg, S.C., 1961; postgrad., S.C. State U., 1962-67, U. S.C., 1967-68; MEd, LaVerne (Calif.) U., 1977. Cert. guidance, elem. and secondary supr., elem. and secondary prin., art. Art tchr., guidance counselor Bryson H.S., Fountain Inn, S.C., 1960-69; 1st and 5th grade tchr. Hayne Elem. Sch., Greenville, S.C., 1969-70; art tchr., biracial coord. Northwood Mid. Sch., Taylors, S.C., 1970-71; guidance counselor Berea Mid. Sch., Greenville, S.C., 1971-79, asst. prin., 1982-83; asst. prin. Woodmont H.S., Piedmont, S.C., 1979-82, N.W. Mid. Sch., Travelers Rest, S.C., 1983-84; prin. Cone Elem. Sch., Greenville, 1984-88, Alexander Elem. Sch., Greenville, 1988—. Asst. formulator model for S.C. schs. Guidance By Objectives, 1977. Vice chmn. Freetown Crime Watch Com., Greenville, 1986—; chmn. Parker Sewer & Fire Subdist., Greenville, 1988—; precinct pres. Tanglewood Dem. Precinct, Greenville, 1990; vice chmn. Greenville County Planning Commn., 1994; sec.-treas. N.W. Area Coun. Chamber, Greenville, 1994 (plaque 1994); v.p. for membership Blue Ridge Coun. Boy Scouts Am., Greenville, 1992; mem. Greenville Marchers Against Drugs, 1993-94 (plaque 1993). Recipient Silver Beaver award Boy Scouts Am., Greenville, 1988; named Ben E. Craig Outstanding Educator First Union Bank, Greenville, 1991, N.W. Area Bus. Edn. Partnership Prin. of Yr., Greenville, 1993. Mem. Palmetto State Law Enforcement Officers Assn. (sec. 1979-94, Plaque 1988), Masons, United Teaching Profession. Methodist. Home: 202 Hollywood Dr Greenville SC 29611-7320 Office: Alexander Elem Sch 1601 W Bramlett Rd Greenville SC 29611-4033

JONES, ROBIN RICHARD, pathology educator; b. Little Rock, Oct. 18, 1937; s. Jay and Marietta (Mayhan) J. BS, U. Ark., 1961, MD, 1962, MS, 1966, PhD, 1967. Diplomate Am. Bd. Pathology. Asst. prof. U. Ark., Little Rock, 1967-79, assoc. prof., 1979-89, prof., 1989—. Contbr. articles to profl. jours. Capt. USAR, 1963-73. Mem. AMA, Coll. Am. Pathologists. Office: U Ark Med Scis 4301 W Markham St Little Rock AR 72205-7101

JONES, ROGER LEE, pharmaceutical executive; b. Greer, S.C., Dec. 3, 1954; s. William Riley and Doris Juanita (Holcombe) J.; m. Teresa Kay Davis, May 18, 1974; children: Allyson Leigh, Roger Lee Jr., Erin Rebekah. BS, Carson-Newman Coll., 1977. Cert. med. rep., ordained min., Tenn.; lic. real estate broker. Prodn. control asst. Henrite Products, Morristown, Tenn., 1977-79, prodn. control. mgr., 1979-81; profl. med. rep. Syntex Labs., Inc., Morristown, 1982-86; dist. mgr. Syntex Labs., Inc., Milw., 1986-89; nat. accounts mgr. Syntex Labs., Inc., Greer, S.C., 1989—; cons. The Greer Group, Inc., 1990—. V.p. Greer H.S. Booster Club, 1990-93, pres., 1993—; pres. Tryon St. Elem. Sch. PTA, Greer, 1991; Sunday sch. tchr. Fairview Bapt. Ch., Greer, 1991; bd. dirs. Covenant Acad., Morristown, 1985-86. Mem. Visions of Excellence Ednl. Program for Better Schs., Eagle Club Carson-Newman Coll., Gamecock Club U. S.C., Lions (com. chmn. 1991—). Republican. Home: 302 Isaqueena Dr Greer SC 29651-8418 Office: Syntex Labs 3401 Hillview Ave Palo Alto CA 94304-1320

JONES, ROGER WALTON, English language educator, writer; b. Morristown, N.J., Nov. 22, 1953; s. Chastine Walton and Gloria (Gamble) J. BA in eng., Kenyon Coll., 1976; MA in eng., Southern Ill. U., 1979; PhD in eng., Tex. A&M U., 1989. Teaching asst. Southern Ill. U., Carbondale, 1978-79; adj. prof. Kean Coll., Newark, N.J., 1980; instr. Lamar U., Beaumont, Tex., 1981-83; teaching asst. Tex A&M U., College Station, 1984-89, lecturer, 1990; asst. prof. Howard Payne U., Brownwood, Tex., 1990-91; dir. acad. honors Ranger (Tex.) Coll., 1991—. Author: Larry McMurtry and the Victorian Novel, 1994; contbr. articles to profl. jours. Contbr., mem. Dem. Nat. Com., Washington. Recipient Merit Incentive award Lamar U., 1983. Mem. Modern Lang. Assn., S. Cen. Modern. Lang. Assn. Democrat. Episcopalian. Office: Ranger Coll College Cir Ranger TX 76470

JONES, ROSEMARIE FRIEDA, service executive; b. Heidelberg, Germany, May 15, 1950; came to U.S., 1952; d. Duane W. Blodgett and Imargard P. (Reinmuth) Boczanski; m. Curtis B. Jones, June 3, 1989; children: Spencer E. Jones, Steven T. Kratzer. BS in Bus. Edn., U. Nebr., 1972, MEd, 1980. Instr. Columbus (Ga.) Vo-Tech., 1975-76; adminstrv. asst. to commdr. 1st Inf. Divsn., Goeppingen, Germany, 1976-79; grad. asst. U. Nebr., Lincoln, 1979-80; instr. bus. occupations S.E. Community Coll., Lincoln, 1980-84; br. mgr. Imprimis Legal Staffing, Dallas, 1985—; adv. bd. Dallas County Community Coll., Brookhaven Coll., curriculum writer Eastfield Community Coll., Dallas; speaker in field; instr. bus. comms. Brookhaven Coll., Dallas. Recipient Victor Trophy Sales and Mktg. Execs. Dallas, 1991. Mem. Am. Mgmt. Soc., Assn. Information Systems Profls. (pres. 1984). Home: 1615 Auburn Dr Richardson TX 75081-3046 Office: Imprimis Legal Staffing 1717 Main St Ste 3390 Dallas TX 75201-7348

JONES, SARA WOODS, elementary education educator; b. Richmond, Va., Aug. 21, 1970; d. Ralph Leigh Woods and Joyce Ann (Redding) Woods-Jones; m. Keith Edward Jones, June 19, 1993. Assoc. in Edn., Gordon Coll., 1990; B in Edn., U. Ga., 1992; M of Ednl. Leadership, West Ga. Coll., 1995; EdS in Adminstrn. and Supervision, State U. of West Ga., 1996. Cert. PK-5. Tchr. Griffin (Ga.)-Spalding County Schs., 1992—, lead tchr. afterschool program, 1993—; chair Atkinson Elem. Leadership Team, Griffin, 1995, 96. Nat. Youth Gardening grantee Nat. Youth Gardening Assn., 1994. Mem. Profl. Assn. Ga. Edn. (bldg. rep. 1994—), Phi Delta Kappa. Roman Catholic. Home: 1516 Oakview Dr Griffin GA 30223

JONES, SHEILA MCLENDON, construction company executive; b. Bennettsville, S.C., July 11, 1965; d. Charlie Garrett and Ruby (Hatcher) McLendon; m. James Robert Jones, July 24, 1987; children: Robert Shane, Ashley Sunny. Student, Chesterfield/Marlboro Tech., 1981. Nurse asst. Marlboro Park Hosp., Bennettsville, S.C., 1983-84; inspectopr INA Bearing Co., Inc., Cheraw, S.C., 1985; with Big Apple Fashions, Cheraw, S.C., 1985; inspector ADS Co., Inc., Star, N.C., 1985-86; machine operator Legg's Hosery, Rockingham, N.C., 1986-87; masonry cons. Robert Jones Masonry, Morven, N.C., 1987—. Active Cmty. Choir of Morven, 1996—. Democrat. Baptist. Home and Office: PO Box 713 128 N Church St Morven NC 28119-8705

JONES, SONIA JOSEPHINE, advertising agency executive; b. Belize, Brit. Honduras, Nov. 9, 1945; came to U.S., 1962, naturalized, 1986; d. Frederick Francis and Elsie Adelia (Gomez) Alcoser; m. John Marvin Jones, Mar. 21, 1970; children: Christopher William Edward, Joshua Joseph Paul. Student, Lamar U., 1964-66. With Foley's Federated Dept. Store, Houston, 1965-67; media buyer Vance Advt., Houston, 1967-68; media buyer, planner O'Neill & Assocs., Houston, 1968-75; media supr. Ketchum Houston, 1975-76; v.p., media dir. Rives Smith Baldwin Carlberg/Y & R, Houston, 1976-86; sr. v.p. media dir. Black Gillock & Langberg, Houston, 1986-89; pres. JMM Group, Inc., Houston, 1989—; lectr. U. Houston, 1983—. Vol. Women in Yellow, Houston, 1966; mem. St. Thomas High Sch. Mothers Club, 1992—; translator vol. St. Cecilia Clinic, 1993—; mem. sch. bd. St. Cecilia Cath. Sch., St. Thomas High Sch. Women's Club, fundraising vol., 1992—. Mem. Houston Advt. Fedn. Republican. Office: JMM Group Inc 2500 City West Blvd Ste 300 Houston TX 77042

JONES, STEPHEN, lawyer; b. Lafayette, La., July 1, 1940; s. Leslie William and Gladys A. (Williams) J.; m. Virginia Hadden (div.); 1 child, John Chapman; m. Sherrel Alice Stephens, Dec. 27, 1973; children: Stephen Mark, Leslie Rachael, Edward St. Andrew. Student U. Tex. 1960-63; LLB, U. Okla. 1966. Sec. Rep. Minority Conf., Tex. Ho. of Reps., 1963; personal asst. to Richard M. Nixon, N.Y.C., 1964; adminstrv. asst. to Congressman Paul Findley, 1966-69; legal counsel to gov. of Okla., 1967; spl. asst. U.S. Senator Charles H. Percy and U.S. Rep. Donald Rumsfeld, 1968; mem. U.S. del. to North Atlantic Assembly, NATO, 1968; staff counsel censure task force Ho. of Reps. Impeachment Inquiry, 1974; spl. U.S. atty. No. Dist. Okla., 1979; spl. prosecutor, spl. asst. dist. atty. State of Okla., 1977; judge Okla. Ct. Appeals, 1982; civil jury instrn. com. Okla. Supreme Ct., 1979-81; adv. com. ct. rules Okla. Ct. Criminal Appeals, 1980; now mng. ptnr. Jones, Wyatt and Roberts, Enid, Okla.; adj. prof. U. Okla., 1973-76; instr. Phillips U., 1982—; counsel Phillips U., Japan; bd. dirs. Coun. on the Nat. Interest Found. Author: Oklahoma and Politics in State and Nation, 1907-62; co-author: France and China, The First Ten Years, 1964-1974, 1991; contbr. articles to various jours. Bd. dirs. /coun. on Nat. Interest Found.; acting chmn. Rep. State Com., Okla., 1982; Rep. nominee Okla. atty. gen., 1974, U.S. Senate, 1990; spl. counsel to Gov. Okla., 1995; mem. vestry, St. Matthews Episc. Ch., 1974, sr. warden 1983-84, 89-90. Mem. ABA, Okla. Bar Assn., Garfield County Bar Assn., Beacon Club, Petroleum Club (Oklahoma City), Oakwood Country Club (Enid). Office: PO Box 472 Enid OK 73702-0472

JONES, STEPHEN WITSELL, lawyer; b. Honolulu, Aug. 12, 1947; s. Allen Newton Jr. and Maude Estelle (Witsell) J.; m. Judy Kaye Mason, Aug. 13, 1977; children: MaryAnn, Adam, Kathleen. Student, Hendrix Coll., 1965-66; AB with high honors, U. Ill., 1969; JD with highest honors, U. Ark., Little Rock, 1978. Bar: Ark. 1978, U.S. Dist. Ct. (ea. and we. dists.) Ark. 1978, U.S. Ct. Appeals (7th and 8th cirs.) 1978, U.S. Supreme Ct. 1984. Rsch. statistician Ark. Dept. Parks and Tourism, Little Rock, 1971-72, dir. tourist info. ctr., 1972-74; affirmative action specialist Office of the Gov., Little Rock, 1974-75; dir. pers. Ark. Social Svcs. Div., Little Rock, 1975-77; mgmt. info. specialist Ark. Health Dept., Little Rock, 1977-78; assoc. House, Holmes & Jewell, Little Rock, 1978-84; ptnr. House, Wallace, Nelson & Jewell, Little Rock, 1984-86, Jack, Lyon & Jones, P.A., Little Rock, 1986—; adj. instr. div. lifelong edn. U. Ark., Little Rock, 1992—. Editor-in-chief U. Ark. Little Rock Law Rev., 1977; editor Ark. Employment Law Letter, 1995—; contbg. author: Employment Discrimination Law, 1983. Bd. dirs. United Cerebral Palsy of Ctrl. Ark., Little Rock, 1978—; chmn. Ark. Ice Hockey Assn., 1992—; mem. Leadership Greater Little Rock, 1990—. With U.S. Army, 1969-71. Recipient Svc. Recognition award United Cerebral Palsy of Ctrl. Ark., 1986, 95. Fellow Greater Little Rock C. of C.; mem. ABA (labor/litigation sect.), Ark. Bar Assn., Def. Rsch. Inst., Ark. Sch. Bds. Assn. Coun. Attys. Episcopalian. Home: 1724 S Arch St Little Rock AR 72206-1215 Office: Jack Lyon & Jones PA 3400 TCBY Tower 425 W Capitol Ave Little Rock AR 72201

JONES, SUEJETTE ALBRITTON, basic skills educator; b. Kinston, N.C., Mar. 27, 1923; d. Clyde A. and Carrie (Jackson) Albritton; m. William Edward Jones, Mar. 15, 1946 (dec.); 1 dau., Jocelyn Suejette. B.S. in Pub. Sch. Music, Va. State U., 1943; postgrad. U. Pa. Sch. Music, 1945, Winston-Salem State U., 1950-51, A&T State U., 1959-61, Shaw U., 1952, East Carolina U., 1970. Tchr. music, Greenville, N.C., 1943-45; clk. typist Navy Dept., Washington, 1945; interviewer N.C. Employment Security Commn., Kinston, 1946-47; tchr., choral dir. Bethel (N.C.) Union Sch., 1950-52; tchr. C.M. Eppes Sch., 1952-54, S. Greenville Sch., 1954-69, Eastern Elem. Sch., 1969-80; chorus accompanist, tchr. Wahl Coates Lab. Sch., East Carolina U., Greenville, 1980-85, ret., 1985; exec. dir. Partnership for Progress After Sch. Tutorial, 1992-93; instr. basic skills Pitt C.C., Greenville, 1993—. Former mem. Greenville Choral Soc., Tarboro Jubilee Singers. Mem. NEA, Opportunities Industrialization Ctrs. (bd. dirs. Pitts. 1992-93), N.C. Assn. Educators, So. Assn. Colls. and Schs. (vis. com. 1983-85), Delta Kappa Gamma, Alpha Kappa Alpha. Mem. Ch. of Christ. Lodge: Daus. of Isis. Composer: O Isis Dear, 1956.

JONES, SUSAN EMILY, English language educator; b. Lawrence, Mass., Dec. 23, 1943; d. Charles Albert and Elizabeth Empie (Wood) Wyman; m. Peter W. Jones, July 26, 1968 (div. Dec. 1986). BA in History, U. N.H., 1965; MA in English, Stetson U., 1990. Instr. humanities Ctrl. Fla. C.C., Ocala, 1994; instr. English Lake City (Fla.) C.C., 1994, Santa Fe C.C., Gainesville, Fla., 1995—. Bowers fellowship English Dept. U. Fla., 1994. Mem. MLA, Fla. Coll. English Edn. Asns., Philolog. Assn. Carolinas, Fla. Sun Cats Inc. (sec. v.p. 1992—). Roman Catholic.

JONES, SYLVIA, social worker; b. Greenville, S.C., Mar. 15, 1951; d. Odell and Evelyn (Brooks) J. BA, Shaw U., 1978. Lic. social worker, S.C. Econ. svcs. worker I Greenville County Dept. Social Svcs., 1979-87, spl. investigator, 1987-88, work support specialist, 1988-92, human svc. worker II, 1993—. Mem. city coun. City of Greer, S.C., 1990—, mayor pro-tempora, 1993-94; bd. dirs. Greer Hist. Mus.; mem. Alcohol and Drug Mgmt. Team, 1993—; mem. adv. bd. Greer Cmty. Reinvestment Corp., 1992—. Mem. Alpha Chi. Office: City of Greer 106 S Main St Greer SC 29650

JONES, TAYLOR BURNETT, cartoonist; b. Mineola, N.Y., Dec. 10, 1952; s. Scholten Burnett and Barbara Rose (Heisler) J.; m. Ellen Margaret Palm,

Dec. 30, 1986. BA, Cornell Coll., 1974. Intern Delta Dem.-Times, Greenville, Miss., 1974; cartoonist Charleston (W.Va.) Gazette, 1974-81; freelance cartoonist N.Y.C., 1982-89, Augusta, Ga., 1989—; syndicated caricaturist L.A. Times Syndicate, 1977—; contbg. polit. cartoonist El Nuevo Dia, San Juan, P.R., 1986—; contbg. cartoonist U.S. News and World Report, Washington, 1988-94. Author/illustrator: Add-verse to Presidents, 1982; illustrator: How to Talk Baseball, 1983, How to Talk Football, 1984, How to Talk Golf, 1985. Recipient Spl. award The Gong Show, 1977. Mem. Soc. Illustrators, Nat. Cartoonists Soc., Assn. Am. Editl. cartoonists.

JONES, THOMAS ALLEN, geologist, researcher; b. Delano, Calif., Dec. 28, 1942; s. Royal Newton and Marie Emily (Miller) J.; m. Toby Turner, Jan. 1, 1984. BS in Math., Colo. State U., 1964, MS in Statistics, 1967; MS in Geology, Northwestern U., 1968, PhD in Geology, 1969. Sr. rsch. geologist to rsch. advisor Exxon Prodn. Rsch. Co., Houston, 1969—. Co-author: Contouring Geological Surfaces with the Computer, 1986; co-editor: Computer Modeling of Geological Surfaces and Volumes, 1992; editor-in-chief Jour. Math. Geology, 1980-84; contbr. articles to profl. jours. Mem. Am. Statistical Assn., Internat. Assn. for Math. Geology (sec. gen. 1996—), Soc. Economic Paleontologists and Mineralogists, Math. Geologists of U.S. (sec. 1976-88), Phi Kappa Phi, Omicron Delta Kappa. Office: Exxon Prodn Rsch Co PO Box 2189 Houston TX 77252-2189

JONES, THOMAS WATSON, accountant, financial planner; b. Louisville, Ga., Aug. 9, 1951; s. A.P. Jr. and Kathryne (Arrington) J.; m. Victoria Norman, July 11, 1970; children: Kathryne E., Thomas Watson Jr. BBA in Acctg., Ga. So. U., 1973. CPA, Ga.; cert. fin. planner, pers. fin. specialist. Sr. acct. Spillane, Rhoads, Lebey and Sieg, Savannah, Ga., 1973-76; controller B.F. Diamond Constrn. Co. Inc., Savannah, Ga., 1976-77; pres. Jones, Polhill, Jones & Davis, CPA, Augusta, Ga., 1978—; treas. Indsl. Devel. Corp., Louisville, 1986—. Mem. AICPA, Inst. Cert. Fin. Planners, Ga. Soc. Cert. Pub. Accts. (estate planning com. 1995-96, chmn. tax forum com. 1993-95), Jefferson County C. of C. (bd. dirs. 1982-86). Presbyterian. Home: 3736 Pebble Beach Dr Martinez GA 30907 Office: Jones Polhill Jones & Davis CPAPC One Habersham Sq 3602 Wheeler Rd Augusta GA 30909

JONES, TOM EUGENE, mayoral assistant, public affairs officer; b. Forrest City, Ark., Apr. 5, 1948; s. Robert Nall Jones and Lee (Trail) Parnell; m. Carolyn Hays, July 2, 1970; children: Emily Morris, Adrienne Lee. BA, U. Memphis, 1970. Audio-visual specialist Memphis Bd. Edn., 1968-71; govt./ct. reporter Memphis Press-Scimitar, 1971-76; asst. to mayor, pub. affairs officer Shelby County Govt., Memphis, 1976—; teach. advisor Ptnrs. for Livable Places, Washington, 1987—; mem. com. on future and pres. coun. Rhodes Coll., 1989-91; mem. task force on image U. Memphis, 1992—; mem. steering com. Greater Memphis Partnership, 1994—; bd. dirs. Grant Info. Ctr., Germantown Arts Alliance, 1994—. Mem. exec. com. Memphis in May Festival, 1987—, Conv. and Visitors Bur., Memphis, 1987—; bd. dirs. Ctr. City Commn., Memphis, 1985—, nat. Civil Rights Mus., Memphis, 1988—; mem. race rels. com. Goals for Memphis, 1993-94; mem. riverfront revitalization commn. City of Memphis, 1994—; mem. light rail task force City of Memphis, 1994. Recipient Class of 1984 award Leadership Memphis, 1984, Vox award Pub. Rels. Soc., 1993. Mem. County Info. Officers (pres. 1981, bd. dirs. 1979-83), Nat. Assn. Counties (bd. dirs. 1982). Democrat. United Methodist. Home: 8103 Meadow Glen Dr Germantown TN 38138-6109 Office: Shelby County Pub Affairs 160 N Main St Ste 850 Memphis TN 38103-1876

JONES, VANCE HARPER, librarian, musician; b. Washington, N.C., Mar. 2, 1938; s. Henry Asbury and Elizabeth Lucille (Harper) J. MusB, U. Miami, 1961, MusM, 1963; M of Librarianship, Emory U., 1964; postgrad., U. N.C., 1971-74. Asst. ref. libr., art and music libr. Miami Beach (Fla.) Pub. Libr., 1964-66; asst. ref. libr. Valdosta (Ga.) State Coll., 1966-68; ref. libr. St. Augustine's Coll., Raleigh, N.C., 1968-69; music libr. U. Fla., Gainesville, 1969-71; libr. FCX, Inc., Raleigh, 1975; libr. Craven C.C., New Bern, N.C., 1976-81, dir. libr. svcs., 1981-90, dean libr. svcs., 1990—. Performed in concert nat. convention, Ypsilanti, Mich., 1995; editor Jour. New Bern Hist. Soc., 1988—; contbr. articles to profl. jours. Organist Bryan Meml. Meth. Ch., Miami, Fla., 1964-66, Moody Air Force Base, Valdosta, 1967, Christ Episcopal Ch., Valdosta, 1968, St. Timothy's Episcopal Ch., Raleigh, 1969, 72-76, Holy Trinity Episcopal Ch., Gainesville, 1970, Univ. United Meth. Ch., Gainesville, 1970-71, First Presbyn. Ch., New Bern, 1977—; co-chmn. beautification com. New Bern Area C. of C., 1988-90; mem. Swiss Bear Downtown Revitalization Corp., New Bern. Mem. N.C. Libr. Assn., N.C. C.C. Learning Resources Assn. (chmn. archive com. 1982-83), Am. Guild Organists, Organ Hist. Soc., Nat. Trust for Hist. Preservation, New Bern Preservation Found., New Bern Hist. Soc. (bd. dirs. 1989—, editor 1984—), Roanoke Island Hist. Assn., N.C. Preservation Found., U.S. Figure Skating Assn., Ice Skating Inst. Am., Skating Club N.C., N.C. Amateur Sports Club, Masons, Omicron Delta Kappa, Pi Kappa Lambda, Phi Mu Alpha, Sigma Alpha Epsilon. Home: PO Box 237 214 Tryon Palace Dr New Bern NC 28560 Office: Craven CC 800 College Ct New Bern NC 28562-4900

JONES, VAUGHN PAUL, healthcare administrator; b. Johnstown, Pa., Apr. 25, 1947; s. Gordon Kenneth and Luella Jane (Seesholtz) J.; m. Margaret Anne Boss, Oct. 20, 1973 (div. July 1985); m. Karen Tolbert, Nov. 22, 1985; 1 child, Stewart Conway. BS in Acctg., Ferris State U., 1971; MBA, Capital U., 1985; grad., Columbus (Ohio) Area Leadership Program, 1985-86. Cert. health care risk mgr., Fla. Auditor John W. Galbreath, Columbus, 1972-74; mgmt. analyst State of Ohio, Columbus, 1974-76; controller Functional Planning, Inc., Columbus, 1976-82; pres. North Area Mental Health Services, Inc., Columbus, 1982-87; assoc. exec. dir. Mental Health Svcs. of Orange County, Inc., Orlando, Fla., 1987-90; adminstrv. svcs. mgr. Progressive Cos. Fla. Div., Tampa, 1991-92; v.p. corp. svcs. Harbor Behavioral Health Care Inst., Inc., New Port Richey, Fla., 1992—; pres., CEO Gulf Coast Sys., Holiday, Fla., 1992—. Chmn. polit. letterwriting com. gubernatorial campaign, Columbus, 1985; vol. United Way Campaign. Recipient Senatorial citation State of Ohio, Columbus, 1985, House of Reps. citation State of Ohio, Columbus, 1986. Mem. Assn. MBA Execs., Rotary (v.p. Capital City West club 1981). Home: 3531 Woodmuse Ct Holiday FL 34691-2515 Office: The Harbor Behavioral Inc Health Care Inst 2739 US Highway 19 Holiday FL 34691

JONES, VIRGINIA MCCLURKIN, social worker; b. Anniston, Ala., Mar. 13, 1935; d. Louie Walter and Virginia Keith (Beaver) McClurkin; m. Charles Miller Jones Jr., Mar. 16, 1957; children: Charles Miller III, V. Grace. BA, Agnes Scott Coll., 1957; M.A., U. Tenn., 1965, MS in Social Work, 1979. Instr. English, U. Tenn., Knoxville, 1967-71; religious edn. dir. Oak Ridge Unitarian Ch., 1972-73, 76-78; co-owner, mgr. The Bookstore, 1973-76; instr. English, Roane State Community Coll., 1975-80; pvt. practice clin. social work, Oak Ridge, 1980—; cons. Mountain Community Health Ctr., Coalfield, Tenn., 1980-83, Valley Ridge Hospice, 1987-89. Mem. Nat. Assn. Social Workers, Oak Ridge Ministerial Assn., Knoxville Area Agnes Scott Alumnae (pres.), Univ. Club, Concord Yacht Club, Rotary. Democrat. Episcopalia. Contbr. articles to newspapers. Office: 1345 Oak Ridge Tpke # 358 Oak Ridge TN 37830-6408

JONES, VIVIAN M., secondary and elementary education educator; b. Etowah, Tenn., Oct. 19, 1941; d. James Washington and Bessie Mae (Miller) Givens; m. James H. Hines, Aug. 25, 1963; 1 child, Deanna Marie; m. Thomas B. Jones, Jr., Oct. 22, 1977. BS, Tenn. Tech., 1963, MA, 1974. Cert. elem./secondary edn. tchr., Tenn. Tchr. fifth grade McMinn County Bd. Edn., Athens, Tenn., 1966-67, tchr. reading and English, 1967-69, kindergarten tchr., 1969-88; tchr. English McMinn Cen. High, 1990—; state evaluator, career ladder Tenn. State Dept. of Edn., Nashville, 1988-90; tchr. English, adult edn., McMinn County Bd. Edn., Athens, 1973-88, homebound tchr., 1987—. Mem. Nat. Coun. Tchrs. of English, East Tenn. Tchrs. of English, NEA, Tenn. Edn. Assn., McMinn County Edn. Assn. (faculty rep. 1966—). Republican. Baptist. Office: McMinn Ctrl HS 145 County Road 461 Englewood TN 37329-5237

JONES, W. LANDIS, political science educator; b. Altoona, Pa., June 28, 1937; s. Charles H. and Naomi E. (Barefoot) Jones; m. Arnita A. Ament, Dec. 28, 1940; children: Gordon L., Jessica Bay,. BA, U. Pitts., 1958; MA, Emory U., 1959, PhD, 1964. Instr. Emory U., Atlanta, 1962-63; assoc. prof. Waynesburg (Pa.) Coll., 1964-67, U. Louisville, 1967-69; spl. asst. v.p. of U.S., Washington, 1969-70; prof. U. Louisville, 1970-76; dir. Pres. Commn. on White House Fellowships, Washington, 1977-81; vis. prof. U.S. Mil. Acad., West Point, N.Y., 1981-82; prof. U. Louisville, 1983—; commr. City of Robinswood, Ky.,1989—. Editor: (books) Pub. Papers of Gov. Wendell Ford, 1977, U.S. Religious Interest Groups, 1984. Chmn. Common Cause Ky., Louisville, 1985-91; dir. Louisville Com. on Fgn. Rels., 1986-90; candidate for Dem. Nomination to U.S. Ho. Reps., 3rd Congl. dist., Louisville, 1994. Named White House fellow Pres. of the U.S., Washington, 1969-70. Office: Univ Louisville Dept Polit Sci Louisville KY 40292

JONES, WALTER B., JR., congressman; b. Pitt County, N.C., Feb. 10, 1943; m. Joe Anne Jones; 1 child. BA in History, Atlantic Christian Coll., 1967. Rep. N.C. Ho. of Reps., 1983-92; mem. 104th Congress from 3d N.C. dist., 1995—. Republican. Office: US House Reps 214 Cannon House Office Bldg Washington DC 20515-3303

JONES, WALTER EDWARD, management consultant; b. Atlanta, Apr. 8, 1951; s. Walter B. and Jean S. (Sumner) J.; m. Luann Bailey, Sept. 21, 1974; children: Anna Christine, Abigail Louise. BBA in Econs., Oglethorpe U., 1977; MBA in Fin., Mercer U., 1983. With So. Bell Telephone, Atlanta, 1972-79, coord. mktg. and sales edn. and tng., 1979-82; divestiture transition staff AT&T, Atlanta, 1982-83; program dir. AT&T Ctr. for Exec. Edn., Columbus, Ga., 1983-85; sales, tech. and customer svc. mgr. AT&T, Nashville, 1985-86; pres. Exec. Edn. and Mgmt., Atlanta, 1987—; sr. ptnr. Corp. Learning and Devel., Riverside, Conn., The Sextant Group, Naples, Fla.; owner, v.p. Clock Svcs., Inc., Atlanta, 1977—. Mem. adv. bd. Ctr. Info. Comm. Scis. Ball State U., Muncie, Ind., 1986—, Fellow of Yr., 1987; chmn. sch. bd. Mt. Carmel Christian Sch., Atlanta, 1992—. Mem. Nat. Assn. Watch and Clock Collectors, U.S. Distance Learning Assn., Ga. Motortrucking Assn. (bd. dirs. 1981), Sales and Mktg. Execs. Office: Exec Edn and Mgmt Ste 100 1742 Mt Vernon Rd Atlanta GA 30338

JONES, WALTON LINTON, internist, former government official; b. McCaysville, Ga., Dec. 4, 1918; s. Walton Linton and Pearl Josephine (Gilliam) J.; m. Caroline Wells Schachte, June 5, 1943; children—Walton Linton III, Francis Stephen, Kathleen Caroline. B.S., Emory U., 1939, M.D., 1942. Diplomate Am. Bd. Preventive Medicine. Commd. lt. (j.g.) U.S. Navy, 1942, advanced through grades to capt., 1956; rotating intern U.S. Naval Hosp., Charleston, S.C., 1942-43, aerospace medicine, 1944; flight surgeon USMC Aircraft Squadrons, 1944-47; head aero. med. safety Navy Dept., 1947-53; sr. med. officer U.S.S. Randolph, 1953-55; dir. aero. med. ops. and equipment Bur. Medicine and Surgery, Navy Dept., 1955-64; dir. biotech. and human research div. NASA, 1964-66; ret. U.S. Navy, 1966; civilian dir. biotech and human research div. NASA, Washington, 1966-70, dep., dir. life scis., 1970-75, dir. occupational medicine, 1975-82, dir. occupational health, 1982-85; cons. aerospace medicine, 1985—; mem. exec. com. hearing and bioacoustics Nat. Acad. Scis., 1964-85, chmn., 1970, mem. exec. com. on vision, 1964-85; Kober lectr. Georgetown U., 1968. Leader, mem. com. Nat. Capital Area council Boy Scouts Am., Falls Church, Va., 1956-64. Decorated Legion of Merit; recipient Exceptional Service medal NASA, 1979, Outstanding Leadership medal NASA, 1985. Fellow Aerospace Medicine Assn. (Bauer award 1970, pres. 1980), AIAA (assoc., recipient John Jeffries award 1970), Royal Soc. Health; mem. Internat. Astronautics Acad., Assn. Mil. Surgeons (Founders award 1956), Internat. Acad. Aerospace Medicine.

JONES, WILLIAM ADRIAN, percussionist, education program administrator; b. Oakland City, Ind., Feb. 27, 1962; s. Rene Ardell Jones. BS in Music Mgmt., U. Evansville, 1985, BA in Spanish, 1986; MusB, U. Ky., 1990, MusM, 1993. Edn. program coord. Lexington (Ky.) Children's Mus., 1992-94; asst. counselor Calvary and Band Squadron The Culver Academies; asst. band dir. The Culver (Ind.) Academies, 1996; profl. performer with Owensboro Symphony Orch., 1981-83, Evansville (Ind.) Philharm. Orch., 1981-83, Encore Dinner Theatre, Evansville, 1986-87, Tales and Scales Performing Arts Troupe, Evansville, 1986-87, Evansville Symphonic Band, 1983-89, Lexington Philharm. Orch., 1992; pvt. instr. percussion Carl's Music Ctr., Lexington, 1992-95; coord. children's summer program Lexington C.C., 1994; percussion instr., arranger Princeton Cmty. High Sch., Princeton, 1996. Counselor Culver Summer Upper Camps, summer 1996. Recipient various scholarships, fellowships and awards. Mem. Ky. Alliance for Arts Edn. (bd. dirs., sec. 1994-95), Percussive Arts Soc., Mortar Bd., BSU Alumni and Friends Assn. (interim pres. 1995), Golden Key, Phi Beta Kappa, Omicron Delta Kappa, Pi Kappa Lambda, Sigma Delta Pi, Phi Mu alpha. Home: CEF #988 1300 Academy Rd Culver IN 46511-1291

JONES, WILLIAM HAWOOD, electrical engineer; b. Cooper, Tex., Jan. 20, 1927; s. Paul Adair and Demily (Delores) J.; m. Margaret Nadean Pittman, Oct. 20, 1947; children: Bonnie Jean, Margaret Angela. BSEE, Okla. U., 1951; MSEE, Syracuse U., 1962. Registered profl. engr., N.Y., Okla. Engr. GE, Syracuse, N.Y., 1952-65, Honeywell/Control Data, Oklahoma City, 1965-79; engr., mgr. Magnex Corp. subs. Exxon, San Jose, Calif., 1979-82; engr. Atasi Corp., San Jose, 1982-86; engr., mgr. Konica Tech. Inc., Sunnyvale, Calif., 1986—. Inventor, patentee in field. Mem. IEEE, Etta Kappa Nu. Office: Jones Consulting 6525 NW 115th St Oklahoma City OK 73162-2932

JONES, WILLIAM JOHN, music educator; b. Pontiac, Mich., Nov. 30, 1926; s. Percy Thomas and Evelyn Jessie (Bond) J.; m. Virginia Ann Lee, Aug. 8, 1953 (dec. Feb. 1986); children: Constance Ann, Evelyn Virginia, Glynis Lee, Cecilia Dorothy, Victoria Adeline. BA, Taylor U., 1947; BS in Edn., Wayne U., 1948, MA, 1949; PhD, Northwestern U., 1952. Tchr., Appalachian State Coll., Boone, N.C., 1954-61; instr., head dept. music Ferrum Jr. Coll., Va., 1961-63; prof., head dept. music Olivet Coll., Mich., 1963-65; prof., head dept. music U. South Ala., Mobile, 1965—; flutist Pontiac Symphony Orch., Mich., 1952-54, Battle Creek Symphony Orch., Mich., 1963-65, Mobile Symphony Orch., Ala., 1965-70. Nat. Endowment for Humanities grantee, 1978, 82. Mem. AAUP, Sonneck Soc., Coll. Music Soc., Am. Musicological Soc., Music Educators Nat. Assn., Phi Mu Alpha Sinfonia. Methodist. Avocations: stamps, languages. Home: 1100 Goldsboro Ct Mobile AL 36608-4206 Office: U South Ala Dept Music Mobile AL 36688

JONES, WILLIAM K., executive steel company; b. 1931. Sales rep to mgr. U.S. Steel Corp., Fairfield, Ala., 1953-72; gen.mgr. So. Metal Svc. Co., Gulfport, Miss., 1972-77; v.p. sales Hanna Steel Corp., Fairfield, Ala., 1977—. Office: Hanna Steel Corp 2812 Commerce Ave Fairfield AL 35064

JONES, WILLIAM KINZY, materials engineering educator; b. Miami, Fla., July 23, 1946; s. Harold Grover and Josephine (Kinzy) Jones; m. Sharon Mattingly, June 6, 1981; children: Kelli, Kinzy, Brent. BS, Fla. State U., 1967, MS, 1968; PhD, MIT, 1972. Mgr. engring. Cordis Corp., Miami, 1977-87; group head C.S. Draper Lab., Cambridge, Mass., 1972-77; dir. biomed. rsch. and innovation ctr. Fla. Internat. U., Miami, 1988; assoc. prof. engring. Fla. Internat. U., Miami, 1987-91; prof., assoc. dean for rsch. Fla. Internat. U., Miami, 1991—; adv. bd. Nat. Elec. Packaging and Product Conf., Des Plaines, Ill., 1988—; cons. in field. Contbr. articles to profl. jours.; patentee in field. Recipient rsch. award Fla. Internat. U., 1991. Mem. ASME, Internat. Soc. Hybrid Microelectronics (chmn. materials div. 1990, pres. 1992-93, Tech. Achievement award 1991, Fellow, 1992, Hughes award 1996). Republican. Home: 75550 Overseas Hwy # 534 Islamorada FL 33036-4005 Office: Fla Internat U University Park Campus Research Dept Miami FL 33199

JONES, WILLIAM REX, law educator; b. Murphysboro, Ill., Oct. 20, 1922; s. Cluade E. and Ivy P. (McCormick) J.; m. Miriam R. Lamy, Mar. 27, 1944; m. Gerri L. Haun, June 30, 1972; children: Michael Kimber, Jeanne Reeves, Patricia Combs, Sally Instone, Kevin. B.S., U. Louisville, 1950; J.D., U. Ky., 1968; LL.M., U. Mich., 1970. Bar: Ky. 1969, Fla. 1969, Ind. 1971, U.S. Supreme Ct. 1976. Exec. v.p. Paul Miller Ford, Inc., Lexington, Ky., 1951-64; pres. Bill's Seat Cover Ctr., Inc., Lexington, Ky., 1952-65, Bill Jones Real Estate, Inc., Lexington, Ky., 1965-70; asst. prof. law Ind. U., Indpls., 1970-73, assoc. prof., 1973-75, prof., 1975-80; dean Salmon P. Chase Coll. Law, No. Ky. U., Highland Heights, 1980-85, prof., 1980-93, prof. emeritus, 1993—; vis. prof. Shepard Broad Law Ctr., Nova Southeastern U., Ft. Lauderdale, Fla., 1994-95; mem. Ky. Pub. Advocacy Commn., 1982-93, chmn., 1986-93. Author: Kentucky Criminal Trial Practice, 2d edit., 1991, Kentucky Criminal Trial Practice Forms, 2d edit., 1993. Served as 1st sgt. U.S. Army, 1940-44. Cook fellow U. Mich., 1969-70; W.G. Hart fellow Queen Mary Coll. U. London, 1985. Mem. ABA, Nat. Legal Aid and Defenders Assn., Nat. Dist. Attys. Assn., Order of Coif. Office: No Ky U Nunn Hall University Dr Newport KY 41076

JONES, WILLIAM RICHARD, open systems product support representative; b. Morgantown, Ky., Sept. 27, 1952; s. James Edward Jones and Mahalia Jane (Kuykendall) Bratton; m. Marina del Pilar Lagario, Nov. 20, 1981. AA, Univ. State of N.Y., 1982, BS, 1984; student, U. Tenn., 1987-90. Cert. computer profl. Supr. radar work ctr. USS Midway (CV-41), Yokosuka, Japan, 1980-81; calibration technician Naval Oceanographic Facility, Ford Island, Hawaii, 1981-84; leading petty officer oe divsn. USS Cimarron (AO-177), Pearl Harbor, Hawaii, 1984-85; engring. assoc. Tenn. Valley Authority, Chattanooga, 1986-90, programmer analyst, 1990-92, systems programmer, 1992-95; open systems product support rep. BMC Software, Inc., Austin, Tex., 1995—. Recipient Ednl. & Rsch. Found. Essay Scholar Mensa, 1988, Grosswirth-Salny Essay Scholar, Magellan Web Page design award. Mem. Nat. Tech. Assn., Assn. for Computing Machinery, Black Data Processing Assocs., Am. Numis.Assn., Intertel, Tenn. State Numis. Soc., Am. Mensa Ltd., Am. Legion. Republican. Home: 11160 Jollyville Rd # 1503 Austin TX 78759 Office: BMC Software Inc R&D Divsn 10415 Morado Cir Bldg Austin TX 78759

JONES, WILLIAM RILEY, JR., real estate executive; b. Greenville, S.C., July 17, 1947; s. William Riley Sr. and Doris Juanita (Holcombe) J.; m. Mary Janice Rushton, Jan. 24, 1970; children: William R. III, Paula Michelle, Tara Brooke. Student, U. S.C., 1965-69, S.C. Sch. Real Estate, Columbia, 1982. Collection mgr. Mut. Fin., Columbia, 1969-70; asst. mgr. Gen. Electric Credit Corp., Columbia, 1970-71; inside salesman S.C.M. Glidden-Durkee, Columbia, 1971-72, credit mgr., 1972-75, auditor, 1975-77, salesman, 1977-79, br. mgr., 1979-82; salesman The Realty Group, Lexington, S.C., 1982-84; regional v.p. A.L. Williams & Assocs., Lexington, 1984-89; profl. med. rep. Syntex Labs., Inc., Palo Alto, Calif., 1989-94; agt. Jones Properties, Lexington, 1994—. Pres. Lexington Girls Softball League, 1994—. With U.S. Army, 1968-74. Fellow Columbia Bd. Realtors; mem. S.C. Dept. Ins., Pa. Dept. Ins., Nat. Assn. Real Estate Appraisers, Nat. Assn. Securities Dealers, S.C. High Sch. Football Ofcls. Assn., Am. Legion, Civitan Lodge (pres. Lexington chpt. 1987-88). Republican. Home: 500 Austin Mccartha Rd Gilbert SC 29054-9304

JONES, WINONA NIGELS, retired library media specialist; b. St. Petersburg, Fla., Feb. 24, 1928; d. Eugene Arthur and Bertha Lillian (Dixon) Nigels; m. Charles Albert Jones, Nov. 26, 1944; children: Charles Eugene, Sharon Ann Jones Allworth, Caroline Winona Jones Pandorf. AA, St. Petersburg Jr. Coll., 1965; BS, U. South Fla., 1967, MS, 1968; Advanced MS, Fla. State U., 1980. Libr. media specialist Dunedin (Fla.) Comprehensive H.S., 1967-76; libr. media specialist, chmn. dept. Fitzgerald Middle Sch., Largo, Fla., 1976-87; dir. Media Svcs. East Lake H.S., Tarpon Springs, Fla., 1987-93, ret., 1993. Active Palm Harbor and Pinellas County Hist. Soc.; del. White House Conf. for Libr. and Info. Svcs. Named Educator of Yr. Pinellas County Sch. Bd. and Suncoast C. of C., 1983, 88, Palm Harbor Woman of Yr. Palm Harbor Jr. Women's Club, 1989. Mem. ALA (coun. 1988-92), NEA, AAUW, ASCD, Fla. Assn. Media in Edn. (pres.), U. So. Fla. Alumni Assn., Assn. Ednl. Comm. and Tech. (divsn. sch. media specialist, coms.), Am. Assn. Sch. Librs. (com., pres.-elect 1989, pres. 1990-91, past pres., exec. bd. 1991-92), Southeastern Libr. Assn., Fla. Libr. Assn., Fla. State Libr. Sci. Alumni, U. South Fla. Libr. Sci. Alumni Assn. (pres. 1991-92, 92-93), Phi Theta Kappa, Phi Rho Pi, Beta Phi Mu, Kappa Delta Pi, Delta Kappa Gamma (parliamentarian 1989-90, legis. chmn. 1990, sec. 1994—), Inner Wheel Club, Pilot Club, Civic Club, Order of Eastern Star (Palm Harbor, past worthy matron). Democrat. Home: 911 Manning Rd Palm Harbor FL 34683-6344

JONES-GLAZE, BARBARA ANN, library media specialist; b. Dalton, Ga., Dec. 20, 1946; d. Jack and Beatrice (Walls) Jones; m. Steven Glaze, June 21, 1980; 1 child, Kipp-Cailean. BA in English, West Ga. Coll., 1968; BA in Music, U. Tenn., 1971; MEd, EdS, U. Ga., 1973; EdD, Vanderbilt U., 1991. Libr. media specialist Whitfield County Bd. Edn., Dalton, Ga., 1975, Westside Mid. Sch., Rocky Face, Ga., 1975—; pres. Phoebus Apollo, Inc., Dalton, Ga., 1985—. Author: Dewey Song, 1973. Mem. Am. fedn. Tchrs., Ga. Fedn. Tchrs. (state exec. sec., exec. coun., career ladder task force, legis. com., constl. com., sex edn. com. minority report com., legal affairs com. chair), Whitfield Fedn. Tchrs. (pres.), Kappa Delta Pi, Delta Theta Phi. Home: 912 W Lakeshore Dr Dalton GA 30720-5501

JONZ, JON GRAHAM, linguistics educator; b. El Paso, Tex., Sept. 20, 1944; s. Wallace Wray and Mary Jane (Graham) J.; m. Patricia Ann Schliesman, June 26, 1965; children: Jon Mathieu, Suzan DeVaan. BA, U. N.Mex., 1965, PhD, 1975; MA, U. Ariz., 1967. Instr. Coll. English Tutorial Program, Albuquerque, 1972-74; specialist in testing evaluation Commonwealth of Pa., New Holland, Pa., 1974-76; asst. prof. English dept. W.Va. State Coll., Institute, 1976-78; dir. comm. skills Tex. A&M U.-Commerce (formerly East Tex. State U.), 1978-83, assoc. prof. linguistics, 1983-89, prof. linguistics, 1989—. Co-author: Cloze and Coherence, 1994; editl. bd. S.W. Jour. of Linguistics, 1994—; contbr. articles to profl. jours. Bd. dirs., pres. Maloy Water Supply Corp., Commerce, 1989-95. Capt. USMC, 1967-70. Recipient Tchg. Excellence award Tex. Assn. of Coll. Tchrs., 1988-89. Mem. TESOL (Disting. Rsch. award 1991), Am. Assn. for Applied Linguistics, Linguistics Soc. Am., Linguistic Assn. of Can., U.S., Linguistic Assn. of the S.W. (pres. 1991-92), Phi Delta Kappa. Home: Rte 2 Box 74 Campbell TX 75422 Office: Tex A&M U-Commerce ET Station Commerce TX 75429

JORDAN, BELINDA LEE, nutritionist, dietitian; b. Arlington, Va., Oct. 4, 1960; d. Alfred Lowell and Eva Jean (Elwell) Barr; m. Thomas Robert Jordan, Jr., July 24, 1993; 1 child, Ian Patrick. BS in Family Resources cum laude, W.Va. U., 1983. Registered dietitian. Dietetic intern W.Va. U. Hosp., Morgantown, 1984-85; supr. Towers Foodservice , W.Va. U., Morgantown, 1982-84; nutritionist Monongalia County Health Dept. Women, Infants and Children program, Morgantown, 1985-95. Mem. Am. Dietetic Assn., W.Va. Dietetic Assn., Mountaineer Dietetic Assn., Phi Upsilon Omicron. Home: 1416 Mount Gordon Rd Salem VA 24153-1542

JORDAN, BETTY SUE, retired special education educator; b. Lafayette, Tenn., Sept. 4, 1920; d. Aubrey Lee and Geneva (Freeman) West; m. Bill Jordan, Oct. 22, 1950; 1 child, L. Nicha. Student, David Lipscomb Coll., 1939-41; BS, U. Tenn., 1943; registered dietitian Duke U. Hosp., 1945; MEd, Clemson U., 1973. Dietitian U. Ala., Tuscaloosa, 1945-46, Duke U., Durham, N.C., 1946-48, Stetson U., DeLand, Fla., 1948-50, Furman U., Greenville, S.C., 1950-52; elem. tchr. Greenville County Schs., S.C., 1952-66, tchr. orthopedically handicapped, 1966-85; with Shriners Hosp. for Crippled Children Sch.; pres. Robert Morris S.S. class U. Meth. Ch., 1992. Mem. NEA, Assn. Childhood Edn. (treas. 1980-85), United Daus. Confederacy (pres. Greenville chpt. 1978—), Greenville Woman's Club (exec. bd. 1991-94), Lake Forest Garden Club (pres. 1970-71, 77-79, 80-81, historian 1981-87, 1st v.p., 1991-92, Woman of Yr. awards 1991, 92, Rachel McKaughan Horticulture award 1992, 94, 95, Lois Russel Arrangement award 1993-95), Greater Greenville Rose Soc. (pres. 1983-84), Am. Rose Soc. (accredited rose judge 1986, rose arrangement judge, cons., Rosarian), Clarice Wilson Garden Club (pres. 1987-89, Woman of Yr. 1991, Award for Arrangements), Delta Kappa Gamma (pres. Tau chpt. 1976-78, state chmn. communications 1979-81, state chmn. rsch. 1983-85, leadership/mgmt. seminar Austin, Tex. 1989), Kappa Kappa Iota (state pres. 1972-73, conclave pres. 1983-85), Democrat. Methodist. Avocations: collecting antiques, growing roses, flower arranging. Home: 21 Lisa Dr Greenville SC 29615-1350

JORDAN, CHARLES MILTON, lawyer; b. Houston, Apr. 3, 1949; s. Milton Reginald and Jean (Burris) J.; m. Jeanette Lutz; children: Nicole Catherine, John Milton, Rebecca Louise Darnell. BBA, U. Tex., 1971, JD, 1975. Bar: Tex. 1975, U.S. Dist. Ct. (so. dist.) Tex. 1976, U.S. Supreme Ct. 1978, U.S. Ct. Appeals (5th cir.) 1979, U.S. Ct. Appeals (11th cir.) 1981, U.S. Dist. Ct. (no. dist.) Tex. 1982, U.S. Dist. Ct. (we. and ea. dists.) Tex. 1983. Assoc. Troutman, Earle & Hill, Austin, 1975-76, Simpson & Burwell, Texas City, 1976-78, Smith & Herz, Galveston, Tex., 1978-80; ptnr. Dibrell & Greer, Galveston, 1980-85, Barlow, Todd, Crews & Jordan P.C., Houston, 1986-88, Barlow, Todd, Jordan & Oliver, L.L.P., Houston, 1988—. Commr.

Commn. Texas City/Galveston Ports, 1984. Served to 1st lt. USAF, 1971-77. Recipient Outstanding Young Man Am. award, U.S. Jaycees, 1980. Mem. Tex. Bar Assn., Galveston County Bar Assn. (pres. 1981-82, bd. dirs. 1985-88), Tex. Young Lawyers Assn (bd. dirs. 1982-85, Outstanding Dir. award 1983-84), Galveston County Young Lawyers Assn. (pres. 1979-80, Outstanding Young Lawyer award 1981). Office: Barlow Todd Jordan & Oliver LLP 17225 El Camino Real Ste 400 Houston TX 77058-2768

JORDAN, DANIEL PORTER, JR., foundation administrator, history educator; b. Philadelphia, Miss., July 22, 1938; s. Daniel Porter and Mildred M. (Dobbs) J.; m. Lewellyn Lee Schmelzer, Dec. 18, 1961; children: Daniel P., Grace Dobbs, Katherine Lewellyn. BA, U. Miss., 1960, MA, 1962; PhD, U. Va., 1970. Various teaching positions overseas divsn. U. Md., 1962-65, . Richmond (Va.), 1968-69, U. Va., summers, 1970-72; prof. history VA Commonwealth U., Richmond, 1969-84, Ariz. State, 1995, dir. Stratford Hall Summer Sem., 1981-91; exec. dir. Thomas Jefferson Meml. Found. (Monticello), 1985—, pres., 1994—; scholar in residence U. Va., 1985—. Mem. adv. com. Papers of Thomas Jefferson (Princeton U.); contbr. articles on history to profl. jours. Mem. Sec. of Interior's adv. bd. Nat. Park System, 1984-88, chmn. 1987—; mem. Jeffersonian Restoration Adv. Bd. U. Va., 1985—; mem. rev. bd. Va. Hist. Landmarks Commn., 1981-92, vice chmn., 1984-89, chmn, 1989-92; mem. Nat. Parks and Conservation Bd., 1989-92, Ea. Nat. Bd., 1991—; pres. Richmond Civil War Roundtable, 1983. Served with inf. U.S. Army, 1962-65. Thomas Jefferson Found. fellow, 1965-68; recipient award of merit Am. Assn. for State and Local History, 1977, 88, Pub. Svc. award U.S. Dept. of Interior, Medal for Va. Svc. AIA, 1993. Mem. Am. Antiquarian Soc., Va. Hist. Soc. (bd. dirs. 1986-91), Mass. Hist. Soc., So. Hist. Assn. (life), Orgn. Am. Historians (life), Walpole Soc., Phi Beta Kappa (pres. Alpha of Va., 1995—), Omicron Delta Kappa, Sigma Chi. Methodist. Author: Political Leadership in Jefferson's Virginia, 1983; A Richmond Reader, 1733-1983, 1983, Tobacco Merchant: The Story of Universal Leaf Tobacco Company, 1995. Home and Office: Monticello Home of Thomas Jefferson PO Box 316 Charlottesville VA 22902-0316

JORDAN, DEANE LEROY, journalist, musician; b. Portland, Maine, Nov. 10, 1950; d. William Chappas and Mae Lydia (Putney) Jordan. BS summa cum laude, U. Maine, 1975; cert., USN Sch. Music, 1970; postgrad., U. Ctrl. Fla., 1978-80, Whitelands Coll., London, 1973. Cert. tchr., Fla., Maine. Pvt. practice as music tchr. Pownal, Maine, 1975-77; journalist Rockledge (Fla.) Reporter, 1980-83, Sanford (Fla.) Herald, 1983-87; pvt. practice as journalist Maitland, Fla., 1987—. Author: 1,001 Facts Somebody Screwed Up, 1993, More Facts Somebody Screwed Up, 1997. With U.S. Army, 1969-72. Mem. Am. Fedn. Musicians, Mensa, Mayflower Soc., Free Thinkers, Coun. for Dem. and Secular Humanism. Office: PO Box 1793 Maitland FL 32794

JORDAN, DON D., electric company executive; b. Corpus Christi, Tex., 1932; married. U. Tex., 1954; JD, So. Tex. Coll. Law, 1969. With Houston Lighting & Power Co. subs. Houston Industries, Inc., 1956—P02mgr. comml. sales, 1967-69, mgr. pers. rels., 1969-71, v.p., asst. to pres., 1969-71, 1971-73, group v.p., 1973-74, pres., 1974-82, chief exec. officer, also bd. dirs., 1977—, chmn., 1977—; also chmn., chief exec. officer Houston Industries, Inc.; bd. dirs. Tex. Commerce Bancshares, Tex. Med. Ctr., Tex. Heart Inst. Office: Houston Industries Inc 4400 Post Oak Pkwy Houston TX 77027

JORDAN, ERVIN LEON, JR., archivist, historian; b. Norfolk, Dec. 15, 1954; s. Ervin Leon and Carrie Elmora (Edwards) J.; m. Lorraine Frye, 1985. BA cum laude, Norfolk State Coll., 1977; MA, Old Dominion U., 1979. Cert. collegiate profl., Va. History tutor Spl. Svcs. Norfolk State Coll., 1975-76; counselor Camp E.W. Young, Cheasapeake, Va., 1977; rsch. asst. history dept. Old Dominion U., Norfolk, 1978; achives asst. tech. svcs. Old Dominion U. Archives, Norfolk, 1979-93, assoc. curator tech. svcs., 1993-96, curator tech. svcs., 1996—; from tech. svcs. asst. to tech. svcs. achivist U. Va. Libr., Charlottesville, 1979—; instr. U. Va., Charlottesville, 1981-85, asst. prof., 1985-96, assoc. prof., 1996—; archival cons., 1981—; grant reviewer NEH, Washington, 1987—; judge Nat. History Day, Charlottesville, 1988—; speaker, lectr., 1978—; adj. faculty lectr. African-Am. history Piedmont Va. C.C., 1993—; assoc. U.S. Civil War Ctr., La. State U. Author: 19th Virginia Infantry, 1987, Charlottesville and the University of Virginia In the Civil War, 1988, Black Confederates and Afro-Yankees in Civil War Virginia, 1995; contbr. poems and essays in pubs.; co-curator The African-Am. Experience, 1987; contbr. more than 25 articles to profl. jours. Mem. U. Va. Afro-Am. Faculty Staff Forum, Charlottesville, 1982-84, chmn. libr. faculty coun., 1993-94; mem. Cmty. Home Attention Adv. Bd., Charlottesville, 1983-86; mem. Somerset Pl. Found. Bd., Creswell, N.C., 1988—; mem. adv. com. on African-Am. Interpretation at Monticello Home of Thomas Jefferson; chmn. Task Force on Black History Month, Charlottesville, 1990. Recipient H.H. Clay Humane award Norfolk State Coll., 1977, Outstanding Alumnus award Phi Kappa Phi, Old Dominion U., 1994; grantee U. Va. Libr., 1987, 90; fellow Va. Ctr. for Humanities, 1990. Mem. NAACP, Va. Militaria Collectors, So. Hist. Assn., Assn. for Study Afro-Am. Life and History, Nat. Assn. for African-Am. Studies, Inc., Smithsonian Assocs., Soc. Am. Archivists, Mid-Atlantic Regional Archives Conf., Phi Alpha Theta. Episcopalian. Home: 811 Harris Rd Charlottesville VA 22902-6468 Office: U of Va Libr Charlottesville VA 22903-2498

JORDAN, GEORGE WASHINGTON, JR., engineering company executive; b. Chattanooga, Mar. 11, 1938; s. George W. and Omega (Davis) J.; m. Fredine Sims, July 20, 1968; 1 child, George W. III. BSEE, Tuskegee U., 1961; postgrad., Emory U. Mgmt. Inst., 1976; MS in Indsl. Mgmt., Ga. Inst. Tech., 1978. Design engr. Boeing Co., Seattle, 1961-64; test engr. Boeing Co., Huntsville, Ala., 1964-65; design engr. GE, Huntsville, 1965-66; mgr. Lockheed Corp., Marietta, Ga., 1966—; mem. flight simulation tech. com. AIAA, Washington 1984-88. Chmn. Atlanta Zoning Rev. Bd.; chmn. fin. com. Christian Fellowship Bapt. Ch., Atlanta. Mem. AIAA, Nat. Mgmt. Assn., Assn. MBA Execs., Am. Def. Preparedness Assn., Alpha Phi Alpha (life). Democrat. Home: 3609 Rolling Green Rdg SW Atlanta GA 30331-2325 Office: Lockheed 86 S Cobb Dr Marietta GA 30063-1000

JORDAN, HENRY HELLMUT, JR., management consultant; b. Heidelberg, Germany, May 31, 1921; came to U.S., 1934, naturalized, 1940; s. Henry H. and Johanna (Narath) J.; m. Hildegarde C. Dallmeyer, Mar. 11, 1942 (dec. 1987); children: Sandra, Michael, Patric, Henry Hellmut; m. Martha J. McClain Ghafary, Jan. 17, 1995. Student U. Cin., 1938-39. Commd. 2d lt. U.S. Army, 1942, advanced through grades to maj., 1956; staff officer Ordnance Corps; ret., 1961; mgr. prodn. and inventory control Sperry Corp., N.Y.C., 1961-66, dir. quality control and field svc. engring., 1967-68; mgmt. cons. Wright Assos. Inc., N.Y.C., 1969-70; pres. Henry Jordan & Assos., N.Y.C., 1970-74; mng. ptnr. Cons. Svcs., Inc., Atlanta, 1975-88; chmn. Ctr. for Inventory Mgmt., Sugar Hill, Ga., 1975—; chmn. bd. Crugers Svcs. Corp., Atlanta. Editorial bd. Jour. Prodn. and Inventory Mgmt.; editor: Production and Inventory Control Handbook, 1986, System Implementation Handbook, 1982, Cycle Counting for Record Accuracy, 1994. Mem. Sugar Hill United Meth. Ch. Mem. AIEE (sr. life), Inst. Mgmt. Cons. (cert.), Am. Prodn. & Inventory Control Soc. (chmn. curricula and cert. council; Presdl. award of Merit 1974, 89, hon. life 1989—), Am. Radio Relay League. Methodist. Club: Yacht Hilton Head. Home and Office: 900 Secret Cove Dr Sugar Hill GA 30518-5366

JORDAN, HENRY PRESTON, JR., manufacturering executive; b. Roanoke, Va., Sept. 3, 1926; s. Henry Preston and Emily Lucille (Luck) J.; m. June Farley Dyson, Sept. 4, 1948; children: Kathryn Jordan Streetman, Rebecca Jordan Lidard, June Preston. BS in Commerce, U. Va., 1950. Supt. comml. and indsl. constrn. Richardson Way and Elec. Corp., Roanoke, 1952-56; sales engr. H.C. Gundlach Co., Richmond, Va., 1958-64; pres. Jordan Metal Co., Richmond, 1964-76, Jordan Mech. Sales, Inc., Richmond, 1976—; chmn. lay adv. sheet metal dept. Richmond Tech. Ctr., 1974. Del. White House Conf. on Sm. Bus., 1986, 95; sec. Jr. Achievement, Roanoke, 1961-62, v.p., Richmond, 1971-73; pres. Beaumont Learning Ctr. Aux., 1979-81, Beaumont Correctional Ctr., 1995; nominating com. Richmond Bapt. Assn., 1993-94; moderator Derbyshire Bapt. Ch., 1982, chmn. bd. deacons, 1967; bd. dirs. Justice Fellowship of Va. Task Force, adv. coun. SBA Region III, Richmond, 1978-88, Cmty. Adv. Bd. State Penintentiary, Douglas S. Freeman H.S.; bus. adv. coun. Henrico County Police, lts. promotion bd., 1996; mem. Nat. Sm. Bus. Attitudes Rsch. Panel; organizing bd. Va. Youth Partnership Found., 1996. Recipient Achievement award Big Bros., Richmond, 1969; Douglas S. Freeman 12th Man award, 1971; Paul Harris fellow. Mem. ASHRAE (treas. Richmond chpt., pres. 1987-88, 2d pl. energy conservation award 1984, '85, 1st pl. 1987), Rotary (pres. West Richmond 1973-74, mem. dist. scholarship com.), Beta Theta Pi, Theta Tau, Lambda Pi. Republican. Home: 10107B Castile Ct Richmond VA 23233-6004 Office: PO Box 29785 Richmond VA 23242-0785

JORDAN, JOHN RICHARD, JR., lawyer; b. Winton, N.C., Jan. 16, 1921; s. John Richard Jordan and Ina Love (Mitchell) J.; m. Patricia Exum Weaver, June 19, 1949 (div.); children: Ellen Meares Jordan McCarren, John Richard, III.; m. Brenda Moore Harlow, June 27, 1982. B.A., U. N.C., 1942, J.D., 1948. Now sr. partner law firm Jordan, Price, Wall, Gray & Jones,, Raleigh,, N.C.; mem. staff Atty. Gen. N.C., 1948-51; mem. N.C. Senate (3 regular sessions, 1 spl. session), 1959, 61, 63. Contbr. articles and revs. to newspapers and mags.; editor: Why the Democratic Party, 1955. Candidate for lt. gov. N.C., 1964; mem. N.C. Bd. Higher Edn., 1964; mem. N.C. Commn. Higher Edn. Facilities, 1964—; chmn. N.C. Bd. Social Svcs., 1969-73; trustee U. N.C., 1969-73, bd. govs. U. N.C., 1973—, chmn. bd. govs., 1980-84; trustee Chowan Coll., 1979, 1981, 95—, trustee Ravenscroft Found., 1971-87, N.C. Supreme Ct. Hist. Soc., 1993—; mem. dirs. coun. Nat. Humanities Ctr, 1991; permanent chmn. N.C. Dem. Conv., 1974; chmn. bd. dirs. N.C. div. Am. Cancer soc., 1959, pres., 1960; mem. Gov.'s Cancer Commn., 1962-64; N.C. chmn. ARC, 1966, Nat. Soc. Crippled Children and Adults, 1963; pres. N.C. Arthritis Found., 1966-70; bd. dirs. N.C. Med. Found., pres. co-founders club of Found.; bd. dirs. Myesthenia Gravis Found. (Carolinas chpt, 1991—); bd. dirs. State Capitol Found.; pres. Friends of N.C. Archives, 1984-86; chmn. N.C. Council Econ. Edn., 1984-87; bd.dirs. N.C. Mus. History Assocs., 1983-86; pres. Henry Lee Soc., 1991-93; mem. Jud. Conf. U.S. Ct. Appeals; bd. dirs. N.C. Cmty. Found.; treas. N.C. Supreme Ct. Hist. Soc. Recipient award for scholarship and leadership Phi Delta Phi, 1948; Disting. Service award as Raleigh's Young Man of Yr., 1955; Disting. Service award N.C. Public Health Assn., 1964; Gold Medal award Am. Cancer Soc.; Disting. Alumni award Chowan Coll., 1983; inducted into N.C. Bar Hall of Fame, 1995. Mem. Wake County Bar Assn. (chmn. exec. com. 1955), N.C. Bar Assn., Am. Bar Assn., Am. Judicature Soc., N.C. Acad. Trial Lawyers, Internat. Bar Assn., English Speaking Union (dir.), Coral Bay Club, Pi Kappa Alpha, Phi Delta Phi. Baptist. Clubs: Carolina Country, Carolina, Sphinx, Capital City of Raleigh, Torch, Lions, Assembly of Raleigh. Home: 809 Westwood Dr Raleigh NC 27607-6644 Office: Jordan Price Wall Gray & Jones 200 Hillsborough Pl PO Box 2021 Raleigh NC 27602

JORDAN, JOHN WILLIAM, former oil company executive and chemist; b. Pitts., Apr. 25, 1912; s. Frank Craig and Harriet Sophia (Caywood) J.; m. Marian Emily Spies, June 1, 1936 (dec. Apr. 1978); children: Emily, Frank, John, Edward, Andrew; m. Norine Elizabeth Holt, Apr. 8, 1979. AB in Chemistry, Marietta Coll., 1934; PhD in Chemistry, Columbia U., 1938; ScD (hon.), Marietta Coll., 1959. Lab. asst. Marietta (Ohio) Coll., 1931-34; asst. food analysis and colloids Columbia U., N.Y.C., 1935-38; fellowship asst. Mellon Inst., Pitts., 1938-39, fellow, sr. fellow, 1941-51; plant chemist Pittsburgh-Corning Corp., Port Allegany, Pa., 1939-41; mgr. R&D Baroid div. Nat. Lead Co., Houston, 1951-55, tech. dir. Baroid div., 1955-76, cons. Baroid div., 1976-82; dir. Enenco, Inc., 1964-74; chem. cons. various indsl. cos., 1982-92. Author: The Eagle on U.S. Firearms, 1991; contbr. over 10 articles to profl. jours.; 12 patents. Named Pioneer Clay Sci. The Clay Minerals Soc., 1990. Mem. AAAS, Am. Chem. Soc., Phi Beta Kappa, Sigma Xi. Home: 1505 Butlercrest St Houston TX 77080-7613

JORDAN, KAREN LEIGH, newspaper travel editor; b. Freeport, Tex., Nov. 20, 1954; d. Matt Culum and Laura Louise (English) Arrington; m. William David Jordan, May 8, 1982; 1 child, Lauren Kathryn. BA in Journalism magna cum laude, Tex. A&M U., 1976. Intern Wall St. Jour., Dallas, summer 1976; asst. news editor Abilene (Tex.) Reporter-News, 1976-77; sports copy editor Dallas Morning News, 1977-79, asst. travel editor, 1979-81, travel editor, 1981—; judge journalism competition Univ. Interscholastic League, Tex., 1976. Contbg. writer (guidebook) Fodor's Tex., 1983—; writer (guidebook) Fodor's Dallas-Fort Worth, 1983—; copy editor Dallas-Ft. Worth Metroplex Football mag., 1978-80. Teaching asst. Garden Ridge Ch. of Christ, Lewisville, Tex., 1988—. Recipient state headline writing award AP Mng. Editors, 1977. Mem. Soc. Am. Travel Writers (writing, editing and photography awards 1981—), Phi Kappa Phi, Sigma Delta Chi, Alpha Lambda Delta. Office: Dallas Morning News Comm Ctr PO Box 655237 Dallas TX 75265-5237

JORDAN, LEWIS H., airline executive; b. Griffin, Ga.. BS in Aerospace Engring., Ga. Inst. Tech., 1967. Formerly asst. v.p. So. Airways; sr. v.p. ops. Flying Tiger Line, Inc., pres., chief oper. officer, resigned, 1986; exec. v.p., chief oper. officer Continental Airlines, Inc., Houston, 1986-91, pres, 1991-93; COO ValuJet Airlines, Inc., Atlanta, 1993—. Office: ValuJet Airlines Inc 1800 Phoenix Blvd Ste 126 Atlanta GA 30349-5555*

JORDAN, LINDA SUSAN DARNELL, elementary school educator; b. Greenville, Tex., Sept. 5, 1955; d. Charles Albert and Dorothy Nell (Everheart) Darnell; m. Mark Alan Jordan, Sept. 1, 1979; children: Sarah Tison, Michael Albert. BE, East Tex. State U., 1977. Cert. elem. edn. tchr. 1-8, secondary edn. tchr. 9-12. County ext. agt. Tex. A & M U., Wise County, Tex., 1977-81; tchr. Decatur (Tex.) Ind. Sch. Dist., 1981-87, 91—; tech. planning com. Decatur Ind. Sch. Dist., 1991-95, mem. campus improvement com., 1992-94. Sun. sch. educator First United Meth. Ch., Decatur, 1992-96, acolyte coord., 1990-91, 95—, Sun. sch. coord., 1989-90; mem. Decatur Jr. Woman's Club, 1977-79. Recipient Apple of the Month award Twin Lakes Hosp., 1992. Mem. Tex. Classroom Tchrs. Orgn. Home: RR 2 Box 478 Decatur TX 76234-9308 Office: Decatur Elem Sch 1300 Deer Park Rd Decatur TX 76234-4403

JORDAN, NEIL ROBERT, government telecommunications consultant; b. Montclair, N.J., Jan. 25, 1951; s. Robert Fredrick and Margaret Louise (Freehauf) J.; m. Elizabeth Anne Dodge, July 4, 1979 (div. Dec. 1982); 1 child, Jessica Anne; m. Susan Holman, Aug. 26, 1983; children: Clinton Robert, Kristen Alexandra. Student, U. Ariz., 1979-80, U. Md. Extension, 1978-79, 80-81. Automotive salesman GM, 1970-77; enlisted USN, 1973, radioman, telecommunications specialist, 1973-83, resigned, 1983; telecommunications mgr. Dept. of Def., U.S. Govt., 1985—; cons., CEO, Need To Know Cons., St. Marys, Ga., 1991—; speaker Mary Kay Cosmetics, Avon Cosmetics, Tupperware. Author: Auto Buying Power, 1991, Controlling Your Money, 1992, Your Time, Your Freedom, 1992, Positive Thinking, 1993, Free Publicity for Your Business, 1993, Your Business In-House Advertising Agency, 1993. Mem. Parent Tchrs. Assn. St. Marys, 1991. Mem. St. Marys C. of C. Republican. Methodist. Home: 306 Westgate Cir Saint Marys GA 31558-9514 Office: Need To Know Cons 325 Spur 40 # 142 Saint Marys GA 31558-1570

JORDAN, RANDALL WARREN, optometrist; b. Camilla, Ga., May 19, 1952; s. Billie Howard and Sara Ann (Richards) J.; m. Angela Marie Farmer, May 15, 1982; 1 child, Samantha Marie. BS in Biology, So. Coll. Optometry, 1987, OD, 1989. Supply and distbn. mgr. Phoebe Putney Meml. Hosp., Albany, Ga., 1981-85; ophthalmic technician Omni Eye Svcs., Memphis, 1987; optometrist Albany Retinal-Eye Ctr., Albany, 1989-90, Eyecare Assocs. Ga., Brunswick, 1990-91, Eye Med, Chamblee, 1992-95; optometrist Dougherty County Health Dept., Albany, 1989-90, Dept. Children's Med. Svcs., Albany, 1989-90, Lion's Club Vision Screening, Montezuma, Ga., 1989; mem. Emory Vision Correction Ctr. With U.S. Army, 1972-74. Mem. Am. Optometric Assn., Ga. Optometric Assn., Kiwanis, Beta Sigma Kappa, Omega Delta, Phi Theta Upsilon. Home: 895 1st NW Cairo GA 31728 Office: PO Box 268 Calvary GA 31729-0268

JORDAN, ROBERT ANDREW, accountant; b. Chillicothe, Ohio, Jan. 10, 1955; s. Robert Dulaney and Juanita (Clark) J.; m. Darlynne Marie Shrader, Oct. 8, 1977; children: Justin Andrew, Lindsey Dara, Jarrett Cole. AA in Bus. Adminstrn. with honors, Cerritos Coll., Norwalk, Calif., 1974; BA in Acctg. cum laude, David Lipscomb U., Nashville, 1976. CPA, Fla., Tenn. Supervising sr. acct. Peat, Marwick, Mitchell & Co., CPAs, Miami, Fla., 1976-81; audit supr. Blankenship, Summar & Assocs., CPAs, Nashville, 1981-82; audit mgr. Bishop, Bussell & Assocs., CPAs, Brentwood, Tenn., 1982-86; controller Cone Oil Co., Inc. & Cone Solvents, Inc., Nashville, 1986-89; acct., cons. R. Andrew Jordan, CPA, 1986—; sec., treas., bd. dirs. B&C Aviation Co., Inc., 1987-89; v.p. fin. Fetorgon Corp., Nashville, 1989-90; sec.-treas. Rustoff Products, Inc., 1990-94; treas., contr. FL Co., Inc., 1991-94. Mem. bus. adv. coun. David Lipscomb U., 1986-89; deacon fin. ministry Antioch Ch. of Christ, 1984-91; pres. Ogelsby Comty. Club, 1989, 90; asst. coach Brentwood Civitan Baseball, 1992. Mem. AICPA, Tenn. Soc. CPAs, Tenn. Hist. Soc. Home: 701 Edmondson Pike Brentwood TN 37027-8205

JORDAN, ROBERT LEON, federal judge; b. Woodlawn, Tenn., June 28, 1934; s. James Richard and Josephine (Broadbent) J.; m. Dorothy Rueter, Sept. 8, 1956; children: Robert, Margaret, Daniel. BS in Fin., U. Tenn., 1958, JD, 1960. Atty. Goodpasture, Carpenter, Dale & Woods, Nashville, 1960-61; mgr. Frontier Refining Co., Denver, 1961-64; atty. Green and Green, Johnson City, Tenn., 1964-66; trust officer 1st Peoples Bank, Johnson City, 1966-69; v.p., trust officer Comml. Nat. Bank, Pensacola, Fla., 1969-71; atty. Bryant, Price, Brandt & Jordan, Johnson City, 1971-80; chancellor 1st Jud. Dist., Johnson City, 1980-88; dist. judge U.S. Dist. Ct. (ea. dist.) Tenn., Knoxville, 1988—; mem. adv. com. U. Tenn. Law Alumni, 1978-80; sec. Tenn. Jud. Conf., 1987-88, mem. exec. com., 1988; del. Tenn. State-Fed. Judicial Coun., 1993—. Bd. dirs., v.p. Tri-Cities estate Planning Coun., Johnson City, 1969; bd. dirs. Washington County Tb Assn., Rocky Mount Hist. Assn., High Rock Camp, Johnson City, Jr. Achievement of Pensacola Inc.; bd. dirs., treas. N.W. Fla. Crippled Children's Assn., Pensacola. With U.S. Army, 1954-56. Named Boss of Yr. Legal Secs. Assn., Washington, Carter County, Tenn., 1982. Mem. Tenn. Bar Assn., Knoxville Bar Assn., Washington County Bar Assn. (pres.-elect 1980), Johnson City C. of C., Hamilton Burnett Am. Inn of Ct. (pres. 1993-94), Kiwanis (pres. Met. Johnson City Club 1969, Kiwanian of Yr. award 1986-87). Republican. Mem. Ch. of Christ. Office: US Dist Ct PO Box 2068 Knoxville TN 37901-2068

JORDAN, ROBERT W., lawyer; b. Wichita, Kans., Oct. 9, 1945. AB, Duke U., 1967; MA, U. Md., 1971; JD, U. Okla., 1974. Bar: Tex. 1974. Ptnr. Baker & Botts, LLP, Dallas; mem. Jessup Internat. Law Moot Ct. Team, 1973. Editor-in-chief Okla. Law Review, 1973-74. Lt. USNR. Fellow Tex. Bar Found., Dallas Bar Found.; mem. ABA, State Bar Tex., Dallas Bar Assn. (bd. dirs. 1991—, chair strategic planning com. 1992, co-chair civil bench bar conf. 1992, chair pres. task force vis. judges 1990, coun. antitrust and trade regulation sect. 1988—), Nat. Order Barristers, Phi Delta Phi. Office: Baker & Botts 2001 Ross Ave Dallas TX 75201-8001*

JORDAN, TIMOTHY EDWARD, secondary education educator; b. Knoxville, Iowa, Apr. 16, 1952; s. Richard and Elizabeth Edna (Miller) J. BS, Southwest Mo. State U., 1976, cert., 1982; MS in Edn., U. Tex. Pan Am., 1992. Cert. secondary tchr., Tex., Mo. Tech. dir. Springfield (Mo.) Civic Ballet, 1977-80; tchr. math. Chadwick (Mo.) Pub. Schs., 1981-82; tchr. math. and physics Marine Mil. Acad., Harlingen, Tex., 1983—, asst. dean acads., 1992-94; math. tchr. Weslaco (Tex.) H.S., 1994—. Mem. Nat. Coun. Tchrs. Math., Nat. Sci. Tchrs. Assn., Tex. Computer Edn. Assn. Home: 1607 Rio Hondo Rd Harlingen TX 78550-4007 Office: Weslaco HS Math Dept Weslaco TX

JORDAN, WILLIAM REYNIER VAN EVERA, SR., therapist, poet; b. Kansas City, Mo.; s. Russell Clinger and Lois Eleanor (Van Evera) J.; children: William, Michael, Paul. BS in Journalism cum laude, U. Fla., 1956; South Asia area specialist U. Pa., 1962; grad. Gen. Staff Coll., 1968; post-grad. U. West Fla, 1973-76; MA in Psychology, U. No. Colo., 1979; post-grad. U. So. Fla., 1986-87; PhD in Psychology, Calif. Coast U., 1989. Cpl. U.S. Army, 1947-48, with Mil. Intelligence Res., 1948-51, to 1st lt. inf., 1951-54 re-entered 1957, advanced through grades to lt. col., 1968; chief of plans and analysis psychol. ops. div. Mil. Assistance Command, Vietnam, 1970-71; group ops. officer, later spl. asst. to comdg. officer 902d Mil. Intelligence Group, Washington, 1971-72; ret., 1972; vol. psychotherapist Juvenile Detention, Pensacola, Fla., 1976-77; vol. psychotherapist Colorado Springs Social Svcs. Dept., Colo., 1977-78; psychotherapist Med. Clinic, Saint Petersburg, Fla., 1980-84, Epilepsy Found., Saint Petersburg, 1984-88; vol. VA Mental Health Clinic, Bay Pines, Fla., 1985—. Author: Darkness and Shadows, 1975; More Than Friends, 1978; Heat Lightning, 1984. Leader Rawalpindi coun. Boy Scouts Am., Pakistan, 1960-62, also troops at Ft. Bragg, N.C., Ft. Leavenworth, Kans., Ft. Holabird, Md., 1964-70; bd. dirs. YMCA, Dundalk, Md., 1969-71, Epilepsy Assn., Pensacola, Fla., 1975-77. Decorated Legion of Merit with oak leaf cluster; Cross of Gallantry with palm (Republic of Vietnam); named Vol. of Yr., Colorado Springs Social Svcs. Dept., 1978. Fellow Internat. Council Sex Edn. and Parenting; mem. Internat. Acad. Behavioral Medicine Counseling and Psychotherapy, Disabled Am. Veterans, Am. Psychol. Assn. (assoc.), Epilepsy Assn. Am. (pres.'s club), Am. Assn. Counseling and Devel. Democrat. Congregationalist. Avocation: photography. Address: 1051 79th Ave N Apt 111 Saint Petersburg FL 33702-1127

JORDEN, JAMES ROY, retired oil company engineering executive; b. Oklahoma City, Apr. 16, 1934; s. James Roy and Gordon (Peeler) J.; m. Shirley Ann Swan, Nov. 17, 1956; children: Philip Taylor, David Emerson. BS in Petroleum Engring., U. Tulsa, 1957. Engr. Shell Oil Co., various locations, 1957, 1960-81; petrophys. engr. advisor Shell Oil Co., Houston, 1981-85; mgr. petroleum engring. rsch. Shell Devel. Co., Houston, 1985-88, mgr. head office prodn., tech. tng., 1988-93; mgr. CPI tng. Shell Oil Co., Houston, 1993-95; retired, 1995; mem. industry adv. bd. petroleum engring. U. Tulsa, 1987-92, chmn., 1988; vis. com. petroleum engring. Colo. Sch. Mines, Golden, 1988-95. Co-author: Well Logging I, 1984, Well Logging II, 1986; co-inventor in field. 1st lt. USAF, 1957-60. Named to Hall of Fame, Petroleum Engring. Dept. U. Tulsa, 1985. Mem. Am. Inst. Mining, Metall. and Petroleum Engrs., Soc. Petroleum Engrs. (hon., pres. 1984, Disting. Svc. award 1988, DeGolyer Disting. Svc. medal 1991, bd. dirs. 1975-79, dir. svc. corps. 1984-90, life trustee found., treas. found. 1991-92, sr. v.p. found. 1993-95, pres. found. 1995—), Kappa Alpha. Republican. Presbyterian. Home: 10926 Piping Rock Ln Houston TX 77042-2728

JORGENSEN, ALFRED H., computer software and data communications executive; b. South Gate, Calif., May 1, 1934; s. Peter Hansen and Anna Christine (Nielsen) J.; AA, El Camino Coll., 1958; student UCLA, 1958-60; m. Carole Jean Scott, Sept. 3, 1959; children: Mark Alan, Lora Jean. Assoc. engr. Litton Industries, Beverly Hills, Calif., 1957-60; engr. Daystrom, Inc., 1960-64; with control systems divsn. Foxboro Co., Pitts., 1964-67, dist. and regional mgr., 1967-69; with Interactive Scis., Pitts., 1969-72, v.p., 1970-71; v.p. Computeria Inc., 1971, pres., 1971-72; v.p. Interactive Scis. Corp., Braintree, Mass., 1972-77, pres., 1977-80; exec. v.p. Nat. Data Corp., Atlanta, 1980-83; v.p. Cullinet Software Inc., 1983-85, v.p. Systems and Computer Tech., 1985-87; pres, chief operating officer Infosafe Corp., Atlanta, 1987-88; pres. Corp. Playmakers, 1988-96; dir. bus. alliances Sprint, 1990-95; gen. mgr. Applied Tech. Ctr., 1995—; bd. dirs. Process Corp., Pitts. Bd. dirs. Mass. Assn. Mental Health, 1977-79, v.p., 1978-79. Served with U.S. Army, 1954-56. Mem. Data Processing Mgmt. Assn., Assn. Iron and Steel Engrs., Instrument Soc. Am., IEEE, Cash Mgmt. Assn., Am. Mgmt. Assn., Nat. Platform Assn. Club: Pearson Yacht (commodore 1984). Home: 4491 Pineridge Cir Atlanta GA 30338-6540

JORGENSEN, JAMES H., pathologist, educator, microbiologist; b. Dallas, July 11, 1946; m. Jane Drummond, Feb. 18, 1978. BA, North Tex. State U., 1969, MS, 1970, PhD, 1973. cert. microbiologist. Rsch. assoc. Shriners Hosp. for Crippled Children, 1970-73; assoc. dir. Bexar County Hosp., 1973-75; instr. dept. pathology and dept. microbiology, Health Sci. Ctr. U. Tex., San Antonio, 1973-75, asst. prof., 1975-78, assoc. prof., 1978-84; cons. microbiologist Audie Murphy V.A. Hosp., San Antonio, 1973—; dir. clin. microbiology labs. Univ. Hosp., 1975—; prof. dept. pathology, dept. medicine, dept. microbiology, dept. clin. lab. scis., Health Sci. Ctr. Med. Ctr. Hosp., 1984—; mem. editorial bd. Antimicrobial Agts. and Chemotherapy, 1982-96, Jour. Clin. Microbiology, 1986-97, Clin. Infectious Diseases, 1995-96, Diagnostic Microbiology and Infectious Diseases, 1983-87, reviewer, 1992-93; reviewer of numerous sci. jours.; chairholder Nat. Com. for Clin. Lab. Standards, subcom. on antimicrobial susceptibility testing, 1990-96. Author: In Vitro Detection of Methicillin-Resistant Staphylococci, 1985, A Clinician's Dictionary of Bacteria and Fungi, 1986, Progress and Pitfalls in Staphylococcus Susceptibility Testing, 1987; editor Automation in Clinical Microbiology, 1987, Manual of Clinical Microbiology, 1995. Recipient Becton-Dickenson and Co. award in Clin. Microbiology, 1992; James W.

McLaughlin Pre-Doctoral fellow in Infection and Immunity, Med. Branch, U. Tex., 1971-73; Pre-Doctoral scholarship, North Tex. State U., 1969-70. Fellow Infectious Diseases Soc. of Am., Am. Acad. Microbiology; mem. Am. Soc. for Microbiology (Tex. branch chmn. clin. divsn. 1987-88), Southwestern Assn. of Clin. Microbiology, Tex. Infectious Diseases Soc. (pres. 1985-86), South Tex. Assn. of Microbiology Profls. (program dir. 1981-86, pres. 1989-90). Office: Univ of Texas Health Sciences Dept of Pathology 7703 Floyd Curl Dr San Antonio TX 78284-6200

JORGENSON, JAMES WALLACE, chromatographer, educator; b. Kenosha, Wis., Sept. 9, 1952. BS, No. Ill. U., 1974; PhD in Chemistry, Ind. U., 1979. From asst. to assoc. prof. U. N.C., Chapel Hill, 1979-87, prof. chemistry, 1987—. Mem. AAAS, Am. Chem. Soc. (Chromatography award 1993). Office: UNC Dept Chemistry Venable 045A Chapel Hill NC 27599-6045*

JOSEPH, GERALD WAYNE, director parks and recreation, consultant; b. Houston, Mar. 14, 1956; s. LeRoy and Ruby Lee (Allen) J.; m. Marjorie Lee Broussard; children: Justin D., Jared W. BS in Indsl. Arts, Tex. So. U., 1978, MS in Edn., 1983. Tchr. Houston Ind. Sch. Dist., 1978-89; chief clk. pct. 6 Harris County, Houston, 1989-90; social worker Gulf Coast Cmty. Svc., Houston; dir. parks and recreation City of Galena Park, Tex., 1991—. Mem. KC (youth dir 1993-95, mem. Coun. 803), Knights of Peter Claver (state fin. sec. 1992-94), Galena Park C. of C., Galena Park Rotary Club (treas. 1995-96), Galveston-Houston Holy Name Soc. (pres. 1996), Alpha Phi Alpha. Democrat. Roman Catholic. Office: City Galena Park PO Box 46 Galena Park TX 77547

JOSEPH, LURA ELLEN, librarian, geologist; b. Tulsa, Jan. 24, 1947; d. Don Roscoe and Ruth Elizabeth (Taplin) J. Student, St. Paul Bible Coll., 1965-67, Pan Am. Coll., 1967-68; BA in Anthropology, U. Okla., 1971, MS in Geology, 1981; MA in Psychology with honors, U. Cen. Okla., 1992; M of Libr. and Info. Studies, U. Okla., 1994. Cert. petroleum geologist. Exploration geologist Getty Oil Co., Oklahoma City, 1977-84; geologist Harper Oil Co., Oklahoma City, 1984-86, consulting geologist, 1986-88; sr. geologist Grace Petroleum, Oklahoma City, 1988-93, cons. geologist, 1993-95; phys. scis. libr. N.D. State Univ. Libr., Fargo, 1995—. Author: (with others) Hugo Reservoir I, 1971; contbr. articles to profl. jours. Active adv. coun. New Life Ranch, Inc., Colcord, Okla. Mem. Am. Assn. Petroleum Geologists, Geol. Soc. of Am., Spl. Libr. Assn., Geosci. Info. Soc., Sigma Gamma Epsilon, Psi Chi, Beta Phi Mu. Republican. Mem. Independent Evangelical Ch. Office: ND State U Libr PO Box 5599 Fargo ND 58105-5599

JOSEPH, MARY J., English educator; b. Palai, Kerala, India, Apr. 4, 1940; came to U.S., 1965; d. Ulahannan and Aleyamma (Vypana) Thoppil; m. Erat S. Joseph, Apr. 13, 1959; children: Bobby Z., Bina Joseph Mampilly. BA, U. Kerala, India, 1959, MA, 1961; PhD, La. State U., 1986. Instr. English U. Kerala, 1961-65, Marywood Coll., Scranton, Pa., 1968-73; instr. So. U., Baton Rouge, La., 1978-88, asst. prof., 1988-92, assoc. prof., 1992—. Author: Suicide in Henry James's Fiction, 1994; co-author: Sesquicentennial History of St. James Masonic Lodge, 1994; contbr. articles to profl. jours. Active St. Patrick Cath. Ch., Baton Rouge, 1979—, Kerala Assn. Greater New Orleans, 1986—; vol. Sisters of Charity, Baton Rouge, 1992-96. Mem. MLA, Coll. Lang. Assn. (award 1995), The Henry James Soc. Office: Southern Univ Dept English Baton Rouge LA 70813

JOSHI, BALAWANT SHANKAR, research scientist; b. Jamkhandi, Karnataka, India, Dec. 28, 1924; came to U.S., 1982; s. Shankar Baldixit and Parvati (Karandikar) J.; m. Prabha Garde, May 3, 1952; children: Usha, Sandhya. BS, Bombay U., 1945, BS in Tech., 1947, PhD in Tech., 1951; PhD, Cambridge (Eng.) U., 1955, ScD, 1984. Rsch. assoc. U. Chgo., 1955-57; sr. sci. officer Nat. Chem. Lab., Poona, India, 1958-61; sub-mgr. CIBA-GEIGY of India, Bombay, 1962-82; assoc. rsch. scientist U. Ga., Athens, 1982—. Editor: Recent Advances in the Chemistry of Natural and Synthetic Colouring Matters and Related Fields, 1982; patentee in field of oils and fats; contbr. over 200 articles to profl. jours. Fellow Indian Nat. Sci. Acad., Indian Acad. Sci., Maharashtra Acad. Sci.; mem. Sigma Xi. Home: 1520 S Lumpkin St Apt D2 Athens GA 30605-1373 Office: Univ Ga Chemistry Dept Athens GA 30602

JOSHI, VIJAY V., pathologist, educator; b. Poona, India, Mar. 10, 1936; came to U.S., 1965; m. Jayashree Nene. MBBS, Byramjee Jeejibhoy Med. Coll., India, 1959; MD, Grant Med. Coll., India, 1962; resident, Med. Coll. Va., 1965-68; PhD, U. Western Ontario, Canada, 1970. Diplomate Am. Bd. Pathology, Am. Bd. Anatomic Pathology, Am. Bd. Pediatric Pathology. Resident in pathology Grant Med. Coll., Bombay, Med. Coll. Va., Richmond, 1965-68; lectr. in pathology Grant Med. Coll., 1962-65; rsch. fellow U. Western Ont., Can., 1968-70; asst. prof. pathology Mont. (Can.) Children's Hosp., 1970-72; asst. prof. pathology and pediatrics Med. Coll. Va., 1972-74, assoc. prof., 1974-75; pediatric pathologist Postgrad. Inst. Med. Edn. and Rsch., Chandigarh, India, 1975-78; prof. pathology Govardhandas Sunderdas Med. Coll., Bombay, 1978-80; assoc. prof. pathology and pediatrics coterminus U. Medicine and Dentistry N.J., N.J. Med. Sch., Newark, 1981-86, prof. coterminus, 1986-88; prof. dept. pathology and lab. medicine, clin. prof. pediatrics E. Carolina U. Sch. Medicine, Greenville, 1988—; dir. pediatric pathology Children's Hosp. N.J., 1980-88, Pitt County Meml. Hosp., Greenville, 1988—; collaborator with pathology ctr., nat. Wilm-tumor study Children's Hosp. Denver, 1986; cons. to collaborative ctr. investigation of AIDS, Armed Forces, Instn. Pathology, Washington, 1986-87; cons. in pediatric pathology Beth Israel Med. Ctr., N.Y.C., 1992; U.S. coord. and participant joint CME program Med. Coun. India, Madras, 1988; mem. numerous nat. coms. Author: Common Problems in Pediatric Pathology, 1994, Handbook of Placental Pathology, 1994; editor: Pathology of AIDS and Other Manifestations of HIV Infection, 1990; contbr. numerous chpts. to books and articles to refereed jours., periodic reviewer prof. jours.; mem. editl. bd. Pediatric Pathology and Pediatric AIDS and HIV Infection: Fetus to Adolescent, 1990. Grantee AIDS Found., 1985, Pediatric Oncology Group, 1989, NIH, 1991. Mem. Am. Soc. Clin. Pathologists, Indian Assn. Pathologists and Microbiologists, Internat. Acad. Pathology (study group complications of perinatal care 1984—), Internat. Paediatric Pathology Assn. (coun.), Soc. Pediatric Pathology Assn. (coun.), Soc. Pediatric Pathology (chmn. mem. com. 1985-88, rsch. com. 1988-89, editl. bd. jour. 1987). Office: East Carolina U Sch Medicine Dept Pathology and Lab Medicine Brody Bldg Rm 1SO8 Greenville NC 27858

JOST, NORMA LILLIAN, secondary education educator, consultant; b. La Rochelle, France, Apr. 26, 1957; d. Ron Lowell and Norma Lorraine (Moechtar) Hofstad; m. Kenneth Jost Jr., Nov. 1, 1986; children: Daniel Logan, Michael Ryan. BSEE, U. Tex., Austin, 1984. Cert. in math., cert. tchr., Tex. Engring. tech. Motorola, Inc., Austin, 1978-83, elec. engr., 1983-89; math. educator Reagan H.S., Austin, 1990-96; pre-kindergarten to 12 math. specialist Austin Ind. Sch. Dist., 1996—; cons. U Tex. Coll. Bd., 1995—, Austin Ind. Sch. Dist., 1991—, Region XIII Svc. Ctr., Austin, 1992, 94. Recipient Presdl. Excellence in Math. Tchg. State award NSF, Tex., 1996-97. Mem. Nat. Coun. Tchrs. Math., Tex. State Tchrs. Math., Austin Area Coun. Tchrs. Math. (pres.-elect 1996—, sec. 1995-96).

JOST, WALTER PAUL, III, English language educator; b. St. Louis, Aug. 27, 1951; s. Walter Paul Jr. and Jeanne (Odell) J.; m. Marcella Frampton, June 4, 1977; children: Alexander, Alison. BA in English cum laude, St. Louis U., 1973; MA in English, U. Chgo., 1974, MA in Gen. Studies in Humanities, 1979, PhD Com. on Ideas and Methods, 1985. Asst. prof. rhetoric dept. U. Va., Charlottesville, 1983-89, assoc. prof., chmn. dept., 1989-95, assoc. prof. English dept., 1995—; mem. adv. bd. Rhetoric Soc. Quar., Renascence; spkr. in field. Author: Rhetorical Thought in John Henry Newman, 1989; contbr. articles to profl. jours. Rsch. grantee U. Va., summers 1987-88, 93, sr. fellow, 1994. Mem. MLA, Am. Soc. for History Rhetoric, Speech Comm. Assn., Amnesty Internat., Habitat for Humanity. Home: 149 Spring Mountain Rd Charlottesville VA 22902 Office: U Va Dept English 104 Bryan Hall Charlottesville VA 22901

JOVANOVIC, MILAN MIODRAG, electrical engineer, researcher; b. Belgrade, Yugoslavia, May 21, 1952; s. Kovacevic Petar and Nada Joseph (Ehrenreich) J.; m. Mirjana Dimitrije Kovacevic, Oct. 30, 1984; children: Maria, Maximilian. BSEE, U. Belgrade, 1976; MSEE, U. Novi Sad (Yugoslavia), 1981; PhD in Elec. Engring., Va. Tech., 1988. Lectr., researcher U. Novi Sad, 1976-83; researcher Va. Tech., Blacksburg, 1983-88, rsch. scientist, 1988-91, adj. prof., 1991—; dir. Delta Power Electronics Lab., Inc., Blacksburg, 1991—; cons. Signetics, Sunnyvale, Calif., 1987—, Singer Electronics, Wayne, N.J., 1988, Power Integrations, Mountain View, Calif., 1988-89, Internat. Power Devices, Inc., Brighton, Mass., 1990-91; adj. prof. Va. Tech., Blacksburg, 1991—. Author: (textbook) Basics of Electronics, 1983; contbr. papers to profl. jours.; inventor (3) high-frequency converters. Mem. IEEE Power Electronics Soc. (sr.), Sigma Xi, Phi Kappa Phi, Eta Kappa Nu. Home: 4008 Tall Oaks Dr Blacksburg VA 24060-8115 Office: Delta Power Electronics Lab Inc 1872 Pratt Dr Blacksburg VA 24060-6363

JOVE, RICHARD, molecular biologist; b. Barcelona, Cataluna, Spain, Feb. 5, 1955; came to U.S., 1960; s. Ricardo and Maria Rosa (Calmet) J.; m. Hua Yu, June 21, 1984. BA, SUNY, Buffalo, 1977, MS, 1978; M in Philosophy, Columbia U., 1981, PhD, 1984. Postdoctoral fellow Rockefeller U., N.Y.C., 1984-88; asst. prof. U. Mich., Ann Arbor, 1988-94, assoc. prof., 1994-95, dir. molecular oncology program Cancer Ctr., 1992-95; prof. U. So. Fla. Sch. of Med., Tampa, 1995—; dir. Molecular Oncology Program Moffitt Cancer Ctr. and Rsch. Inst., Tampa, 1995—. Recipient John S. Newberry prize Columbia U., 1984, Jr. Faculty Rsch. award Am. Cancer Soc., 1988-91; Damon Runyon-Walter Winchell Cancer Fund fellow, 1984-87. Mem. The Harvey Soc., Sigma Xi. Office: U So Fla Moffitt Cancer Ctr 12902 Magnolia Dr Tampa FL 33612-9416

JOWDY, JEFFREY WILLIAM, development executive; b. New Bern, N.C., Oct. 1, 1959; s. Albert Willoughby and Millicent (McKendry) J. BA in Journalism, U. Ga., 1983, postgrad. in speech communication, 1983-85; MA in Pers. Mgmt., Troy (Ala.) State U., 1987. Cert. fund raising exec. Employee relations mgr. Phoebe Putney Meml. Hosp., Albany, Ga., 1985-87; dir. South Ga. chpt. March of Dimes Birth Defects Found., Macon, Ga., 1987-90; devel. dir. Mount de Sales Acad., Macon, 1990-94; sr. mng. dir. Jerold Panas, Linzy & Ptnrs., 1994—; bd. dirs. Hamilton Holt Ednl. Loan Fund, mem. Nat. Ctr. for non-profit Bds., mem. alumni bd. Henry Grady Coll. Journalism, U. Ga. Alumni bd. dirs. Henry Grady Coll. Journalism, U. Ga.; mem. Ga. Coun. on Planned Giving, Nat. Ctr. for Nonprofit Bd. Mem. Nat. Soc. Fund Raising Execs., SAR (founder, pres. Ocmulgee chpt.), Macon C. of C., Macon Heritage Found., Mid. Ga. Cedars Club (v.p., chmn. pub. rels., bd. dirs.), Kiwanis (v.p., pres. Macon chpt., Kiwanian of Yr. award 1989), Phi Kappa Theta (sec. Delta Rho Found., founder, pres. Gamma Sigma Alumi chpt.). Republican. Lutheran. Home: 183 Desoto Pl Macon GA 31204-2811 Office: 500 N Michigan Ave Chicago IL 60611-3704

JOWERS, RONNIE LEE, university health sciences center executive; b. Columbia, S.C., July 4, 1951; s. Talbert Joseph and Mary Helen (Reed) J.; m. Kay Byars, July 6, 1974; children: C. Ryan, Ivey Amanda. BA, Furman U., 1973; MBA, Clemson U., 1984. Acct., mortgage banker First Piedmont Mortgage Co., Greenville, S.C., 1972-76; fin. mgr. Greenville Hosp. System, 1976-80; bus. mgr. Greenville Gen. Hosp., 1980-81; adminstr., med. edn. Greenville Hosp. System, 1981-87; adminstrv. dept. medicine Emory U., Atlanta, 1987-91, assoc. v.p. for health affairs, 1991—; exec. adminstr. Emory U. System Health Care, 1995—, sec. joint conf. com.; co-mgr. Emory Med. Care Found., Atlanta, 1989-90; chmn. adv. coun. S.C. Consortium of Community Teaching Hosps., Charleston, S.C., 1982-86; adj. asst. prof. Med. U.S.C.;. Transp. chmn. Beat Leukemia Celebrity Classic, 1988—; mem. nat. planning com. Sr. Adminstrn. of Acad. Health Ctr. meetings; Sunday sch. tchr. Smoke Rise Bapt. Ch., Stone Mountain, Ga., 1989-94, deacon, 1991, fin. com. chmn., 1996—; treas. Greenville Hosp. Sys. Credit Union, 1980-84, pres., 1985. Mem. Am. Coll. Healthcare Execs. (assoc.), Acad. Health Ctrs. Assn., Beta Gamma Sigma. Baptist. Home: 810 Eagle Cove Way Lawrenceville GA 30244-5843

JOYCE, EDWARD ROWEN, retired chemical engineer, educator; b. St. Augustine, Fla., Oct. 20, 1927; s. Edward Rowen and Annie Margaret (Cobb) J.; m. Leland Livingston White, Sept. 11, 1954; children: Leland Ann, Julia, Edward Rowen III, Theo, Adele. BS in Chem. Engring., U. Miss., 1950; M of Engring., U. Fla., 1969; MBA, U. North Fla., 1975. Registered profl. engr., Fla. Petroleum engr. Texaco, Harvey, La., 1953-55; project engr. Freeport Sulphur Co., New Orleans, 1955-59; chem. engr. SCM Corp., Jacksonville, Fla., 1959-81; profl. engr. Jacksonville Electric Authority, 1981-93, ret., 1993; adj. prof. U. North Fla., Jacksonville, 1977—, Jacksonville U., 1989—; newspaper columnist Fla. Times Union, Jacksonville, 1970-87. Co-author: Sulfate Turpentine Recovery, 1971; author booklet; patentee in field. Sci. fair judge Duval County Sch. System, Jacksonville, 1960-92; co-chmn. adv. com. U. North Fla., 1981-85; merit badge advisor Boy Scouts Am., Jacksonville, 1960—; advisor Jr. Achievement, Jacksonville, 1963; vestryman, lay Eucharistic minister, sr. warden local Episcopalian ch. Comdr. USN, 1950-53, Korea. Fellow Fla. Engring. Soc. (pres. Jacksonville chpt. 1983); mem. AICE (pres. Peninsular Fla. chpt. 1963-64), Phi Kappa Phi, Alpha Pi Mu, Gamma Sigma Epsilon. Democrat. Home: 5552 Riverton Rd Jacksonville FL 32277-1361

JOYCE, JAMES JOSEPH, cardiologist; b. Kansas City, Kans., May 7, 1952; s. Thomas Edward and Mary Jane (Keller) J.; m. Janice Marie Winter, Aug. 2, 1986. BS, Kans. State U., 1974, MS, 1975; DO, Kirksville Coll. Medicine, 1979; MD, Am. U., 1985. Diplomate Am. Bd. Internal Medicine, Am. Bd. Pediatrics. Intern Cmty. Hosp. South Broward, Hollywood, Fla., 1979-80; resident in internal medicine St. Luke's Hosp., Kansas City, Mo., 1980-81, St. Louis U. Hosps., 1981-83; resident in pediat. Kans. U. Med. Ctr., Kansas City, 1985-86; emergency medicine physician Seven Rivers Cmty. Hosp., Crystal River, Fla., 1987-88; pvt. practice St. Thomas, V.I., 1988-92; resident in pediat. Tulane U. Med. Ctr., New Orleans, 1992-94, fellow in pediat. cardiology, 1994—. Mem. AMA, ACP, Am. Coll. Cardiology, Am. Acad. Pediatrics. Roman Catholic. Home: PO Box 50667 New Orleans LA 70150-0667 Office: Tulane U Med Ctr New Orleans LA 70112

JOYCE, JOSEPH ANTHONY, nurse anesthetist; b. Danbury, N.C., Sept. 10, 1959; s. Billy Joe and Janet Irene (Martin) J.; m. Kathy Lynne Wyrick Wrenn, May 9, 1992. BS in Chemistry, U. N.C., Greensboro, 1981; AAS in Nursing, Forsyth Tech. Coll., 1983; diploma in anesthesia, Charleston (W.Va.) Area Med. Ctr., 1989. Staff nurse N.C. Bapt. Hosp., Winston-Salem, 1983-84, asst. head nurse burn ICU, 1984-85; staff nurse Stokes Reynolds Meml. Hosp., Danbury, N.C., 1987; staff nurse ICU Forsyth Meml. Hosp., Winston-Salem, 1986-87; staff nurse anesthetist Wesley Long Community Hosp., Greensboro, 1989—. Recipient fellowship AANA, 1996. Mem. Am. Assn. Nurse Anesthetists (cert. registered nurse anesthetist), Masons. Republican. Baptist. Office: Wesley Long Cmty Hosp 501 N Elam Ave Greensboro NC 27403-1118

JOYCE, LARRY WAYNE, physician; b. Richlands, Va., June 7, 1962; s. Estil Larry and Charlotte Pearline (Dye) J. AS summa cum laude, Southwest Va. C.C., 1982; BS in Biology & Chemistry cum laude, East Tenn. State U., 1984; DO, U. Health Scis., 1989. Med. lab. tech. Mattie Williams Hosp., Richlands, Va., 1978-86; instr. biology lab. Southwest Va. C.C., Richlands, 1984-85, instr. microbiology lab., 1987, instr. chemistry, 1986; resident East Tenn. U., Quillen Coll. Medicine, Johnson City, 1989-94; asst. prof. dept. pathology East Tenn. State U., Johnson City, Tenn., 1994—; staff pathologist VA Med. Ctr., Mountain Home, 1994—. Author: HIV Disease 1993, 94, 95, 96. HIV ednl. outreach Tri-Cities AIDS Project, Johnson City, 1990-92 (svc. awards 1990, 91); HIV educator Lambda Soc., Johnson City, 1990. Mem. Am. Assn. Med. Pers., Am. Soc. Clin. Pathologists, Coll. Am. Pathologists, Am. Osteopathic Assn., Am. Osteopathic Coll. Pathologists. Home: 2700 Indian Ridge Rd #35 Johnson City TN 37604-6476 Office: East Tenn State U Dept Pathology PO Box 70568 Johnson City TN 37614-0568

JOYCE, WALTER JOSEPH, retired electronics company executive; b. Pitts., Sept. 23, 1930; s. John Joseph and Olive Dorothy (Boyle) J.; BBA, Duquesne U., 1957; MBA, Columbia U., 1961; m. Dolores Marchessault, Dec. 2, 1961; children: Kevin, Jacqueline. CPA, Pa. Sr. acct. Coopers & Lybrand, Pitts., 1957-59; div. acct. Singer Co., N.Y.C., 1961-64; asst. factory contr. Singer Co., Bonnieres, France, 1964-65, contr., 1966-67; asst. contr. Singer Consumer Products, Paris, 1968-70; corp. contr. Conrac Corp., Stamford, Conn., 1973-83, v.p. indsl. group, 1984-87, also bd. dirs. Bd. dirs. Red Cross Youth, Conn., 1979. With AUS, 1953-55. Recipient Father/Son award Cub Scouts Am., 1972. Mem. Am. Mgmt. Assn., AICPA, Landmark Club, Columbia U. Alumni Bus. Club. Home: 6860 Gulfport Blvd S # 280 Saint Petersburg FL 33707-2108

JOYCE, WILLIAM ROBERT, textile machinery company executive; b. Springfield, Ohio, Mar. 18, 1936; s. Robert Emmet and Christel Beatrice (Beekman) J.; m. Betty Arlene Provonsha, Aug. 29, 1959; children—Jennifer Lynn, Janet Cathleen. BA in Bus., Calif. Western U., 1982; MBA, Calif. Coast U., 1984. Cert. mfg. engring. technician Soc. Mfg. Engrs., 1975. Mgr. engring. Heinicke Instruments, Hollywood, Fla., 1964-68; div. mgr. Jensen Corp., Pompano Beach, Fla., 1969-72; pres. Textiles Supply, Inc., Gerton, N.C., 1972-80; v.p., gen. mgr. Tex-Fab, Inc., Gerton, N.C., 1980-82; pres. Tex-nology Systems, Inc., Gerton, N.C., 1982-90; pres. Corrib Enterprises Ltd., Automation Cons., Fairview, N.C., 1981—; owner The Silver Hammer Jewelry Store Chain, N.C. Mem., co-founder Assoc. Woodland Owners N.C.; Upper Hickory Nut Gorge Vol. Fire Dept., Gerton. Served with USAF, 1958-64. Recipient innovative devel. award, 1985, award Optimist Club, 1953-54. Mem. NSPE, Profl. Engrs. N.C., Guild Master Craftsmen (internat. mem.) Nat. Rifle Assn., Soc. Mfg. Engrs., Am. Inst. Design and Drafting, Western Carolina Entrepeneurial Council, Handmade in Am. Craft Orgn. Republican. Baptist. Club: Gerton Community Civic. Patentee in field.

JOYNER, JO ANN, geriatrics nurse; b. Glenwood, Ga., Mar. 9, 1947; d. Roy and Lucille (Mercer) Powell; m. Henry Gene Lamb, Dec. 3, 1965 (div. 1984); children: Henry G. Lamb, Jr., Roy, Melinda, Jody; m. Robert Eugene Joyner, June 14, 1991. Diploma, Swainsboro Vocat./Tech., 1979; student, Ga. So. Coll., 1980. LPN, Ga. Staff nurse Meadows Meml. Hosp., Vidalia, Ga., 1980-82; staff nurse in ICU and critical care unit Toombs Alcohol and Drug Abuse Ctr., Vidalia, 1982-84; charge nurse Conners Nursing Home, Glenwood, Ga., 1984-85; supr. Bethany Nursing Ctr., Vidalia, 1990-92, charge nurse, 1985-92; nurse Claxton (Ga.) Nursing Home, Toombs Nursing and Intermediate Care Home, Lyons, Ga., 1992-93; staff nurse Laurens Convalescent Ctr., Dublin, Ga., 1994, 1994; staff nurse Meadow Brook Manor, 1994—, Dublin, 1994-95; relief house supervisor Dulinair Healthcare & Rehab. Ctr., Dublin, Ga., 1995-96; mem. ind. nursing registry, Claxton; nurse Meml. Med. Ctr., Savannah, Ga.; office nurse Montgomery County Correctional Inst., Mt. Vernon, Ga., Laurens Convalescent Ctr., 1994-95, Meadowbrook Manor, 1994—; 3-11 relief house supr., supr. medicare spl. unit, 1995-96. Democrat. Apostolic. Home: 315 Clover St Dublin GA 31021-7719

JOYNER, JOHN FRANKLIN, athletics educator, consultant; b. Fla., Dec. 27, 1946; s. Henry Dorsey and Irma Jean (Ibach) J.; m. Rosemarie Sullivan, June 17, 1978; children: Christine, Marilyn, Annette. B in Speech, Fla. State U., 1977. creative mktg. cons. to several large U.S. corps. Inventor: Sportwright, (team sports) Runball, Foothandball, Rangeball, 1990-93. Roman Catholic. Home: 1421 Ohio Ave Sebring FL 33872

JOYNER, WALTON KITCHIN, lawyer; b. Raleigh, N.C., Apr. 1, 1933; s. William Thomas and Sue (Kitchin) J.; m. Lucy Holmes Graves, Sept. 23, 1955; children: Sue Carson Clark, Walton K. Jr., James Y. II. AB in Polit. Sci., U. N.C., 1955, JD with honors, 1960. Bar: N.C.; lic. comml. pilot. Ptnr. Joyner & Howison, Raleigh, 1960-80, Hunton & Williams, Raleigh, 1980—; sec., treas. N.C. R.R. Co., Raleigh, 1966; bd. dirs. United Title Ins. Co., Raleigh; bd. mgrs. Wachovia Bank & Trust Co., N.C., 1969—; bd. govs. U.S. Power Squadrons, 1974-81. Assoc. editor U. N.C. Law Rev. Pres. Rehab. and Cerebral Palsy Ctr. Wake County, Raleigh, 1974; trustee St. Mary's Coll., 1990-91. Mem. ABA, N.C. Bar Assn. (treas. probate sect. 1983), Wake County Bar Assn. (chmn., bd. dirs. 1977), Law Alumni Assn. U. N.C. (bd. dirs.), Order of Coif, Phi Beta Kappa. Episcopalian. Club: Carolina Country (Raleigh) (pres. 1983-84). Home: 620 Marlowe Rd Raleigh NC 27609-7022 Office: Hunton & Williams 1 Hannover Sq PO Box 109 Fl 14 Raleigh NC 27602-0109

JOYNER, WILLIAM LAWRENCE, family physician, health center administrator; b. Phila., May 24, 1963; s. William Lawrence and Herliene (Pulley) J.; m. Deirdre Nicol Joyner, Feb. 13, 1996. BS, St. Joseph's U., Phila., 1981; MD, Jefferson Med. Coll., 1992. Diplomate Am. Bd. Med. Examiners. Resident dept. family medicine Duke U. Med. Ctr., Durham, N.C., 1992-95, chief resident, 1994-95; med. dir. New Hanover Cmty. Health Ctr., Wilmington, N.C., 1996—. Bd. dirs. N.C. Partnership for Children, Wilmington, 1996—. Named Resident of Yr., N.C. Acad. Family Physicians, 1994. Home: 1112 Harbour Dr Apt 105 Wilmington NC 28401 Office: New Hanover Cmty Health Ctr 408 N 111th St Wilmington NC 28401

JOYNER, WILLIAM LYMAN, physiology educator; b. Farmville, N.C., June 10, 1939; s. William L. Joyner and Hazel (Riley) Sandlin; m. Delorise Fowler, Sept. 12, 1964 (div. 1980); m. Christine Ann Eccleston, Dec. 23, 1982; children: William Jeffrey, Candace Darlene, Andrew William, Evan Cole. BS in Biology, Davidson Coll., 1965; MS in Parasitology, U. N.C., Chapel Hill, 1967, PhD in Physiology, 1971. Postdoctoral fellow Duke U. Med. Ctr., Durham, N.C., 1971-73; asst. prof. U. Nebr. Med. Ctr., Omaha, 1973-77, assoc. prof., 1977-83, prof. physiology and biophysics, 1983-89; prof., chair physiology James H. Quillen Coll. of Medicine E. Tenn State U., 1989—. vis. prof. numerous univs., 1969-83; lectr. in field; chmn. rsch. com. Am. Heart Assn., Nebr. affiliate, 1982; dir. Am. Heart Assn. Nebr. affiliate, 1981-84; editorial bd. jour. Microvascular Research, 1981—, Am. Jour. Physiology, 1985—; ad hoc reviewer numerous sci. jours.; NIH study sect., 1981-84, 1986—. Contbr. numerous articles to profl. jours. 1960-63, Korea. Recipient Pharmacia Travel award Microcirculatory Soc., 1975, Merit award U. Nebr. Coll. Medicine, 1983; NSF fellow; fellow Coun. on Circulation Am. Heart Assn.; vice chmn. Regional rsch. rev. and adv. com. Am. Heart Assn., 1982, chmn. 1984; Mid Am. honor lectr. U. Nebr. Med. Ctr. Mem. Am. Physiol. Soc., Circulation Group, AAAS, Internat. Soc. Lymphology (North Am. chpt.), Microcirculatory Soc. (program com. 1976, fin. com. 1977, fin. com. chmn. 1978-79, awards com. 1980-83, exec. coun. 1980-82, ad hoc com. soc. affiliations, 1983-84, pres. 1985). Democratic. Methodist. Avocations: hunting; fishing; wood working. Home: 159 Cecil Gray Rd Jonesborough TN 37659-6603 Office: East Tenn State U James H Quillen Coll Medicine PO Box 70576 Johnson City TN 37614

JOYNT, STEPHEN WALLACE, reporter, writer; b. Richmond, Oct. 11, 1961; s. Richard George and Joyce Laura (Wallace) J.; m. Nancy Kent Godwin Joynt, June 26, 1985. BA, U. Va., 1984; MA in Journalism, Columbia U., 1985. Reporter Birmingham (Ala.) Post-Herald, 1985-96; instr. Samford U., Birmingham, Ala., 1995-96; keynote spkr. Poynter Inst. Annual Writer's Conf., Albuquerque, 1996. Author: Jack's Law: The Rise and Fall of a Renegade Judge, 1996. Named News Writer of the Yr. Scripps Howard Newspapers, 1986, 93, 94; named to Scripps Howard Hall of Fame, 1994. Home: 2004 Springfield Loop W Birmingham AL 35242 Office: Birmingham Post-Herald PO Box 2553 Birmingham AL 35203

JUAREZ, ANTONIO, psychotherapist, consultant, counselor, educator; b. El Paso, Tex., Nov. 6, 1952; s. Juan Antonio and Amelia (Rivas) J. BS in Psychology, U.Tex.-El Paso, 1976, MA in Clin. Psychology, 1982; postgrad., N.Mex. State U., 1987—, Calif. Coast U., 1990—. Cert. counselor, clin. mental health counselor; lic. profl. counselor, Tex. Caseworker asst. El Paso Mental Health Ctr., 1978-79, caseworker III, 1982-83; clin. specialist S.W. Mental Health Ctr., Las Cruces, N.Mex., 1979-80; therapist, trainer S.W. Community House, El Paso, 1980-81; psychol. cons. El Paso Guidance Ctr., 1981-82, psychotherapist, 1983—, dir. N.E. svcs.; pvt. practice El Paso, 1987—; dir. Cross-Cultural Counseling Ctr., 1988—; instr. psychology El Paso C.C., 1988-90, counselor, cons.; cons. Citizens and Students Together, El Paso, 1983—, group facilitator Tai Chi Chuan Instr., Sun Valley Regional Hosp., El Paso, Tex., 1988; adj. prof. counseling Webster U., Ft. Bliss, Tex., 1995—. Mem. Latin Am. com. N.Mex. State U., 1985. Served with USAF, 1972-76. Fellow N.Mex. State U., 1981. Mem. U.S.-Mex. Border Health Assn., El Paso Psychol. Assn., Tex. Assn. for Counseling and Devel., Tex. Assn. for Children of Alcoholics, Am. Biographical Inst. Rsch. Assn., Golden Key Nat. Honor Soc. (N.Mex. state chpt.), Nat. Bd. For Cert. Counselors, Nat. Acad. For Clin. Mental Health Counselors, Ea. U.S.A. Martial Arts Assn. Democrat. Roman Catholic. Avocations: martial arts, playing stringed instruments. Home: PO Box 1493 Santa Teresa NM 88008-1493 Office: Cross-Cultural Counseling Ctr 2112 Trawood Dr # 3B El Paso TX 79935-3318

JUBRAN, RAJA JUBRAN, engineering and general contracting executive; b. Beirut, Dec. 3, 1957; came to U.S., 1977; s. Jubran Abdallah and Malak (El-Issa) J.; m. Michelle Mabry, Apr. 27, 1985; children: Omar, Nadim. BSCE, U. Tenn., 1981. Exec. v.p. Internat. Mktg. Co., Knoxville, Tenn., 1981-82; dir. network devel. Palestine Congress N.Am., Washington, 1983-85; pres., chief operating officer Denark-Smith Inc., Knoxville, 1985—. Recipient Key to City Knoxville, 1980, named Hon. Citizen Knoxville, Outstanding Young Men of Am., 1984. Fellow Am. Concrete Inst., Am. Soc. Engrs. Syrian Orthodox.

JUCHATZ, WAYNE WARREN, lawyer; b. N.Y.C., June 25, 1946; s. Warren Carl and Margaret E. (Trafford) J.; m. Linda K. Wilson, June 21, 1969; children: Bradley T., Scott W. BA, Franklin & Marshall Coll., 1968; JD, U. Va., 1974. Bar: N.Y. 1975, N.C. 1985. Assoc. Cadwalader, Wickersham & Taft, N.Y.C., 1974-77; asst. counsel R.J. Reynolds Industries Inc., Winston-Salem, N.C., 1977-79, assoc. counsel, 1979-80, sr. assoc. counsel, 1980-81; asst. gen. counsel R.J. Reynolds Tobacco Co., Winston-Salem, 1981-84, dep. gen. counsel, 1984-85, v.p., sec., gen. counsel, 1986-87, sr. v.p., sec., gen. counsel, 1987-93, exec. v.p., gen. counsel, 1993-95; exec. v.p., gen. counsel Textron Inc., Providence, 1995—. Served with U.S. Army, 1969-71. Office: Textron Inc 40 Westminster St Providence RI 02903-2596

JUDAH, FRANK MARVIN, school system administrator; b. Guymon, Okla., Sept. 13, 1941; s. Frank Morris and Margaret (Vaughan) J.; m. Rita Kay Paschal, Oct. 28, 1966; children: Frances Margaret (dec.), Frank Martin. BA, Tex. Tech. U., 1965; MA, Tex. A&M U., 1975, PhD, 1980. Cert. tchr., ednl. adminstr., Tex. Tchr. Reagan County Ind. Sch. Dist., Big Lake, Tex., 1967-73; adminstrv. asst. City of Sweetwater, Tex., 1974-76; dir. purchasing Killeen (Tex.) Ind. Sch. Dist., 1977-81; asst. supt. for adminstrn. Seguin (Tex.) Ind. Sch. Dist., 1981-85; asst. supt. for bus. DeSoto (Tex.) Ind. Sch. Dist., 1985—. Civil svc. commr. City of DeSoto, 1988-93. Mem. Tex. Assn. Sch. Bus. Ofcls. (vice chair cert. com. 1977-96), Assn. Sch. Bus. Ofcls. Internat., Rotary (pres., sec. DeSoto club 1986-89), Masons (treas. DeSoto lodge 1409 1987-90), Phi Delta Kappa. Home: PO Box 1346 De Soto TX 75123-1346 Office: DeSoto Ind Sch Dist 200 E Belt Line Rd De Soto TX 75115-5704

JUDAH, JANEEN SUE, petroleum engineer, lawyer; b. Houston, Sept. 29, 1959; d. Russell Jr. and Jacqueline Marie (Williams) J. BS, Texas A&M U., 1980, MS, 1983; MBA, U. Tex., 1987; JD, U. Houston, 1994. Bar: Tex., 1995; registered profl. engr., Tex., Okla., N.Mex., La. Instr. Tex. A&M U., College Station, 1982-83; engr. Bass Enterprises Prodn. Co., Midland, Tex., 1981-82; engr. Arco Oil & Gas Co., Midland, 1983-90, Houston, 1990-94; assoc. atty. McElroy & Sullivan, Austin, Tex., 1994-96; mgmt. cons. Arthur D. Little, Inc., Houston, 1996—; adjunct prof. UT-Austin, 1996—. Bd. dirs. March of Dimes, Midland, 1987-90, Midland Arts Assembly, 1989-90, Am. Heart Assn., Midland, 1989-90; chmn. allocations United Way, Midland, 1986-90. Mem. Soc. Petroeum Engrs. (chmn. 1989, bd. dirs. 1987-90, 92-96), Leadership Midla nd, Leadership Houston, Leadership Tex., Phi Mu (nat. collegiate fin. dir. 1988-90, nat. fin. dir. 1990-94, found. bd. trustees 1990-94). Republican. Baptist. Office: Arthur D Little Inc 1001 Fannin Ste 2050 Houston TX 77002

JUDD, BURKE HAYCOCK, geneticist; b. Kanab, Utah, Sept. 5, 1927; s. Zadok Ray and Elva (Haycock) J.; m. Barbara Ann Gaddy, Mar. 21, 1953; children: Sean Michael, Evan Patrick, Timothy Burke. BS, U. Utah, 1950, MS, 1951; PhD, Calif. Inst. Tech., 1954. Postdoctoral fellow Am. Cancer Soc. U. Tex., Austin, 1954-56; from instr. to prof. U. Tex., 1956-79, dir. Genetics Inst., 1977-79; geneticist Atomic Energy Commn., Germantown, Md., 1968-69; chief lab. genetics Nat. Inst. Environ. Health Sci., Research Triangle Park, N.C., 1979-95; vis. asst. prof. Stanford U., Palo Alto, Calif., 1960; Gosney vis. prof. Calif. Inst. Tech., Pasadena, 1975-76; adj. prof. U. N.C., Chapel Hill, 1979—, Duke U., Durham, 1980—; mem. panel genetic biology NSF, Washington, 1969-73, genetics study sect. NIH, Washington, 1974, 77, 79, 88, com. on germplasm resources NAS, Washington, 1976-77; chmn. human genome initiative rev. panel Dept. of Energy, Washington, 1988. Author: Introduction to Modern Genetics, 1980; editor: Molecular and Gen. Genetics, 1986-95; assoc. editor Genetics, 1973-78; contbr. articles to profl. jours. With U.S. Army, 1946-47. Fellow AAAS; mem. Am. Soc. Naturalists (sec. 1968-70), Genetic Soc. Am. (sec. 1974-76, v.p., pres. 1979-80). Home: 411 Clayton Rd Chapel Hill NC 27514-7613

JUDD, FRANK WAYNE, population ecologist, physiological ecologist; b. Wichita Falls, Tex., Aug. 23, 1939; married; 2 children. BS, Midwestern State U., 1965; MS, Tex. Tech U., 1968, PhD in Zoology, 1973. Teaching asst. biology Tex. Tech U., 1965-68, rsch. asst., instr., 1969-71; instr. dept. biology Pan Am U., 1968-69, from asst. prof. to prof., 1972-82; prof. biology Coastal Studies Lab., 1982; dir. Coastal Studies Lab. Pan Am U., 1984-94; adj. prof. dept. biol. scis. Tex. Tech U., 1983-89; vis. prof. dept. wildlife & fisheries sci., Tex. A&M U., 1989-91. Mem. Am. Soc. Ichthyologists & Herpetologists, Am. Soc. Mammalogists, Ecology Soc. Am., Herpetologists League. Office: University of Texas Pan American Dept Biology 1201 W University Dr Edinburg TX 78539-2909

JUDELL, HAROLD BENN, lawyer; b. Milw., Mar. 9, 1915; s. Philip Fox and Lena Florence (Krause) J.; m. Maria Violeta van Ronzelen, May 5, 1951 (div.); m. Celeste Seymour Grulich, June 24, 1986. BA, U. Wis., 1936, JD, 1938; LLB, Tulane U., 1950. Bar: Wis. 1938, La. 1950. Mem. firm Scheinfeld Collins Durant & Winter, Milw., 1938; spl. agent, adminstrv. asst. to dir. FBI, 1939-44; ptnr. Foley & Judell, L.L.P., New Orleans, 1950—; v.p., dir. Dauphine Orleans Hotel Corp., 1970—; mem. Tulane U. Bus. Sch. Coun.; Trustee, East Group Properties, 1981—, Sizeler Property Investors, Inc., Greater New Orleans YMCA, 1981—. Mem. ABA, La. Bar Assn., Nat. Assn. Bond Lawyers (bd. dirs., pres. 1984-85). Clubs: New Orleans Country, Lawn Tennis, Met. (N.Y.C.). Office: Foley & Judell 365 Canal St New Orleans LA 70130-1112

JUDGE, DOLORES BARBARA, real estate broker; b. Plymouth, Pa.; m. Richard James Judge; children: Susan, Nancy, Richard Jr. Student, North Harris County Coll., 1984-85, U. Tex., 1985, Houston Community Coll., 1988-89. Real estate agt. comml. real estate cos. in area, 1981-84; owner D-J Investment Properties, Conroe, Tex., 1984—; pres. Judge Real Estate, 1996—; pres., ptnr. J&M Mgmt. Co., 1996—; mem. first adv. bd. First Nat. Title Co., Conroe, 1989-90. Chmn. North Houston Econ. Devel. Showcase, 1990; bd. dirs. Montgomery County Crime Stoppers, Inc., 1993—. Mem. Comml. Real Estate Assn. Montgomery County (pres. 1986, 87, bd. dirs. 1988), Conroe C. of C. Office: D-J Investment Properties 180 Tara Park Conroe TX 77302

JUDGE, STEPHEN, advertising executive. Exec. v.p. Rapp Collins Worldewide, Trving, Tex.; also bd. dirs. Rapp Collins Worldwide, Trving, Tex.; now mng. dir. Rapp Collins Marcoa Inc., Trving, Tex. Office: Rapp Collins Worldwide 1440 Corporate Dr Irving TX 75038*

JUDICE, MARC WAYNE, lawyer; b. Lafayette, La., Oct. 22, 1946; s. Marc and Gladys B. Judice; m. Anne Keaty; children: Scott, Renee. BS, U. Southwestern La., 1969; MBA, U. Utah, 1974; JD, La. State U., 1977. Bar: La. 1977; CPA, La.; bd. cert. civil trial law, civil trial advocacy Nat. Bd. Trial Advocacy. Ptnr. Voorhies & Labbe, Lafayette, 1977-85, Juneau, Judice, Hill & Adley, Lafayette, 1985-93, Judice & Adley, Lafayette, 1993-94. Bd. dirs. Univ. Med. Ctr., Lafayette, 1991, Home Savs. Bank, Lafayette, 1996—; bd. trustees Women's & Childrens Hosp., Lafayette, 1992. Republican. Roman Catholic. Office: Judice Hill & Adley 926 Coolidge Blvd Lafayette LA 70503-2434

JUDY, ELAINE MARIE, secondary school educator; b. St. Petersburg, Fla., Jan. 24, 1970; d. Rodney Harmon and Mary Joanne (Adolphson) J. BS in Exercise and Sport Scis., U. Fla., 1993. Cert. health tchr., athletic trainer, Fla. Health tchr., athletic trainer DeLand (Fla.) H.S., 1994—; phys. edn. intern Gainesville (Fla.) H.S., 1993. Mem. Nat. Athletic Trainers Assn. Office: DeLand HS 800 N Hill Ave Deland FL 32724

JUHASZ, STEPHEN, editor, consultant; b. Budapest, Hungary, Dec. 26, 1913. Diploma in Mech. Engring., Tech. U., Budapest, 1936; Tekn Lic., Royal Inst. Tech., Stockholm, 1951. Spl. lectr. Royal Inst. Tech., Stockholm, 1949-51; mem. staff fuels rsch. lab. MIT, 1952-53; exec. editor Applied Mechanics Rev. Midwest Rsch. Inst., Kansas City, Mo.; exec. editor Applied Mechanics Rev. S.W. Rsch. Inst., San Antonio, 1953-59, former editor, former dir., cons. Contbr. articles to profl. jours.; patentee in field. Fellow ASME (Edwin F. Church medal 1992), AAAS; mem. AIAA, Balcones Heights Lions Club. Office: SW Rsch Inst 622 Culebra Rd PO Box 28510 San Antonio TX 78228*

JUHL, HAROLD ALEXANDER, military officer; b. Kearney, Nebr., June 24, 1950; s. Harold Ferdinand and Vivian Lea Louise (Simshauser) J.; m. Becky Sue Adams, July 30, 1971; children: Aaron A., Shane B. Student, Kearney State Coll., 1968-71, Pensacola (Fla.) Jr. Coll., 1977-79; BA, Colo. State U., 1985. Electronic technician GTE Corp., Chgo., 1971-73; enlisted USMC, 1973, advanced through grades to lt. col., 1990; helicopter pilot HML-267, Camp Pendleton, Calif., 1974-76; flight instr. USN VT-3, Milton, Fla., 1976-79; air officer 2d Bn. 4th Marines, Okinawa, Japan, 1979-80; KC-130 pilot, weapons-tactics instr. VMGR 252, Cherry Point, N.C., 1980-83, aviation safety officer, 1986-88; dir. of safety and standardization VMGR-252, 1988-89, Marine Aircraft Group 36, Okinawa, Japan, 1989-90; C-130 class desk officer Navair-Syscom, Washington, N.C., 1990-94; spl. ops. officer Marine Forces Atlantic, Camp LeJuene, N.C., 1994—; cons. Colo. State U. ROTC, Ft. Collins, 1984-85, Aerial Refueling Systems Adv. BGroup, Oxford, Eng., 1987—, KC-130 Aircraft Symposium, El Toro, Calif., 1987-94; presenter to NATO's Partnership for Peace Coordination Cell, Mons, Belgium, 1996; guest lectr. USN Acad., Annapolis, Md., 1983-84; mem. joint US-Japan Battle Studies Program, 1989-90; participant Warfighting Symposium, Okinawa, Japan, 1989, 90; exercise planner for Norway exercises, 1994, 95, 96. Cubmaster Boy Scouts Am., Quantico, Va., 1985-86; coach, referee Quantico Youth Soccer League, 1985; commr. Quantico Little League, 1986; coach Pop Warner Football, Newport, N.C., 1987, 88, 90; coach Ea. Carolina Soccer Assn., 1990-91. Recipient Shield of Service Boy Scouts Am., 1986. Mem. Marine Corps Assn., Marine Corps Aviation Assn., Golden Key, Experimental Aircraft Assn. (charter, bd. dirs. Beafort, N.C. chpt.). Club: Kearney Aero (pres. 1970-71). Home: 223 Star Hill Dr Swansboro NC 28584-8935

JULIAN, JIM LEE, lawyer; b. Osceola, Ark., Dec. 14, 1954; s. John Roland and Lucille Angela (Potts) J.; m. Patricia Lynn Roberts, Jan. 26, 1980; 1 child, Kathryn Elizabeth. BA, Ark. State U., 1976; JD, U. Ark., 1979. Bar: Ark. 1979, U.S. Dist. Ct. (ea. and we. dists.) Ark. 1979, U.S. Ct. Appeals (8th cir.). Assoc. Skillman & Durrett, West Memphis, Ark., 1979-82; staff atty. Ark. Power and Light Co., Little Rock, 1982-84; assoc. House, Wallace & Jewell, Little Rock, 1984-85, ptnr., 1986-89; ptnr. Chisenhall, Nestrud & Julian, Little Rock, 1989—. Pres. Crittenden County (Ark.) Young Dems., 1980-82; chmn. bd. dirs. Northside YMCA, 1992—. Mem. ABA, Ark. Bar Assn., Pulaski County Bar Assn., Ark. Assn. Def. Counsel, Major Sports Assn., North Hills Country Club. Methodist. Home: 3419 N Hills Blvd North Little Rock AR 72116-8501 Office: Chisenhall Nestrud & Julian 2840 First Commercial Bldg Little Rock AR 72201

JULIEN, DOROTHY COX, librarian; b. Bridgeton, N.J., July 27, 1943; d. James Pettit and Dorothy Edith (Adams) Cox; m. Denis Alan Julien, Dec. 28, 1968; children: Eric Alan, Holly Elizabeth. BA, Douglass Coll., 1965; MLS, U. R.I., 1966. Reference libr. R.I. Coll., Providence, 1966-68; br. libr. Lithonia (Ga.) Pub. Libr., 1979, Eastlake (Ohio) Pub. Libr., 1980-85, Medina County Dist. Libr., Medina, Ohio, 1985-86; sr. libr. Selby Pub. Libr., Sarasota, Fla., 1987—; mem. employee evaluation com. Sarasota County, Fla., 1991; conf. chairperson State Libr. Conf. Com., R.I., 1967-68. Mem. Fla. Libr. Assn., Bradenton Doll Collectors Club (pres. 1992-93). Republican. Home: 318 73rd St NW Bradenton FL 34209 Office: Selby Pub Libr 1001 Boulevard Of The Arts Sarasota FL 34236-4807

JUMELLE, ANTOINE JEAN MICHEL, surgeon; b. Haiti, Feb. 10, 1948; s. Eugene and Climene (Alisma) J.; m. Nahomi Ellen Pierre, Oct. 6, 1979; children: Patricia Eugenie, Antoine Daniel. M in Human Biology, U. Lille, 1975, MD, 1976. Diplomate Am. Bd. Surgery. Intern in surgery St. Francis Med. Ctr., Trenton, N.J., 1977-78, resident in gen. surgery, 1978-82; gen. surgeon Choctaw Nation Indian Hosp., Talihina, Okla., 1988—, coord. med. edn., 1989—. Author: Contribution a L'Etude de la Maladie D'Imerslund-Najman-Grasbeck, 1976 (Cum Maxima Laude award 1976). Mem. McAlester (Okla.) Pub. Schs. Mentoring Program, 1993—. Maj. lt. col., gen. surgeon U.S. Army, 1982-87. Recipient Area Dir.'s award Indian Health Svc., 1993, Exceptional Svc. award, 1994. Fellow ACS, Internat. Coll. Surgeons; mem. AMA, Okla. State Med. Assn. Roman Catholic. Home: 1825 S 13th St Mcalester OK 74501-7131

JUMONVILLE, NEIL TALBOT, history educator; b. Portland, Oreg., Oct. 7, 1952; s. Urie William and Annette Elizabeth (Ansley) J. BA in Econ. Thought, Reed Coll., 1977; MA in History, Columbia U., 1979; AM in History, Harvard U., 1983, PhD in History Am. Civilization, 1987. Editorial intern The Nation mag., N.Y.C., 1980-81; teaching fellow Harvard U., Cambridge, Mass., 1982-86, resident tutor history and lit. Dunster House, 1985-88, instr. history and lit., 1986-87, lectr. history and lit., 1987-90; asst. prof. dept. history Fla. State U., Tallahassee, 1990-93, assoc. prof. dept. history, 1993—; mem. steering com. History News Svc. Author: Critical Crossings: The New York Intellectuals in Postwar America, 1991; contbr. editorial page Tallahassee Sunday Dem., 1991—; contbr. articles, book revs. to profl. jours., newspapers. Richard T. Frost Meml. scholar Reed Coll., 1976, 77; grad. fellow Columbia U., 1978-79. Mem. NAACP, ACLU, Am. Hist. Assn., Orgn. Am. Historians, Oreg. Hist. Soc., Signet Soc., Harvard Club of Tallahassee (bd. dirs.), Phi Beta Kappa. Office: Fla State U Dept History Tallahassee FL 32306

JUNG, HILDA ZIIFLE, physicist; b. Gretna, La.; d. William Christian and Leonora Margaret (Giboney) Ziifle; m. Julius Robert Jung Jr., Nov. 2, 1968. BS, Tulane U., 1943. Engring. release clk. Higgins Aircraft Co., Michoud, La., 1943-44; rsch. physicist So. Regional Rsch. Ctr., USDA, New Orleans, 1944-79; retired, 1979. Contbr. articles to profl. jours.; patentee chem. process. Named Woman of Yr. New Orleans Fed. Exec. Bd., 1978. Mem. AAAS, AARP (program dir. Terrytown chpt. 1991-95, chmn. social com. 1989), Am. Chem. Soc. (sec. La. sect. 1977), Orgn. Profl. Employees Dept. Agrl. (life, pres. 1978, Profl. of Yr. 1979), Am. Legion Aux., Post 64 Chaplain, 1995, 96, Nat. Assn. Ret. Fed. Employees (life, 1st v.p., legis. chmn. 1980, pres. 1981, 92, pub. rels. officer 1984, 89-91, newsletter editor 1993, program chair 1995, program chmn. 1996), Sigma Xi. Lutheran.

JURGENSEN, MONSERRATE, clinical nurse, consultant; b. Guyanailla, P.R., Oct. 25, 1945; d. Francisco and Felicita (Feliciano) Muniz; m. Timothy J. Jurgensen, Dec. 1, 1978; children: Timothy J. Jr., Jeremy J. Diploma, Presbyn. Hosp. Sch. Nursing, San Juan, P.R., 1967; BSN, Barry U., 1990; postgrad., Webster U., 1992—. RN, Fla. Surg. unit and surg. ICU staff nurse U. Hosp., P.R., 1967-69; commd. 2d lt. USAF, 1969, advanced through grades to maj., 1986; pediat. unit staff nurse USAF Hosp., Sheppard AFB, Tex., 1969-70; orthopedic and psychiat. unit staff nurse USAF Hosp., Cam Ranh Bay, Vietnam, 1970-71; staff nurse obstetrics unit USAF Hosp., Torrejon AFB, Spain, 1971-74; obstetrics head nurse USAF Hosp., K.I. Sawyer AFB, Mich., 1974-78; staff nurse obstetrics unit, head nurse pediatric clinic USAF Hosp., Langley AFB, Va., 1978-81; med.-surg. nurse USAFR, Langley AFB, Va., 1984-86; staff nurse Primary Care Clinics USAFR, Norfolk, Va., 1985-86; staff nurse Cigna HMO, Miami, Fla., 1986-87; staff nurse long-term care unit VA Hosp., Miami, 1988-90, med.-surg. nurse psychiat. unit, 1990-91; quality control nurse, infection control Immunization Clinic, Duke Field, Fla., 1989-91; evening-night supr., mgr. med.-surg. unit same day surgery Army Hosp., Ft. Jackson, S.C., 1991-94; mgr. same day surgery med.-surg. unit Reynolds Army Cmty. Hosp., Ft. Sill, Okla., 1994—. Mem. Soc. Presbyn. Hosp. Sch. Nursing. Republican. Office: US Army Fort Sill Lawton OK 73503

JURICIC, DAVOR, mechanical engineering educator; b. Split, Croatia, Aug. 2, 1928; came to U.S., 1968; s. Mate and Slavka (Franceschi) J.; m. Milesa L. Harris, Mar. 10, 1984; 1 child, Ivanna Albertin. Dipl.Ing., U. Belgrade, Yugoslavia, 1952, DSc, 1964. Stress analyst Icarus Aircraft Industries, Zemun, Yugoslavia, 1953-58; rsch. engr. Inst. Aeronautics, Belgrade, 1958-63; asst. prof. U. Belgrade, 1963-65, assoc. prof., 1965-68; assoc. prof. S.D. State U., Brookings, 1968-73, prof., 1973-75; vis. prof. Stanford (Calif.) U., 1975-78; prof. mech. engring. U. Tex., Austin, 1978—. Contbr. numerous articles to profl. jours. Rsch. grantee various agencies, 1962—. Mem. ASME, Am. Soc. Engring. Edn. (Chester F. Carlson award 1993), Sigma Xi. Office: Univ of Texas Dept Mech Engring Austin TX 78712

JUST, CHESTER A., lawyer; b. Yonkers, N.Y., July 6, 1935; s. Stephen and Catherine (Urbanek) J.; m. Halina Dziuba, 1954 (div. 1972); children: Catherine, Judith, John, Mary, Nancy; m. Constance L. Kilyk, Jan. 13, 1978; children: Susan B., Alice B. BA, Rutgers U., 1957, JD, 1960. Bar: N.J., U.S. Supreme Ct. Pvt. practice Edison, N.J., 1961—; adminstrv. appeals supr. State of N.J. Labor Dept., Trenton, 1962-87; gen. counsel Fire Systems, Inc., Deerfield Beach, Fla., 1987-92, State of Fla., 1993-96. Author papers in field. Active various charitable, civic and religious orgns. Mem. various bar assns. Democrat. Roman Catholic. Home: 8501 Shadow Ct Coral Springs FL 33071-7480

JUSTEN, PETER ALLEN, financial services executive, entrepreneur; b. Elyria, Ohio, May 17, 1956; s. Kenneth Eugene Justen Sr. and Norene Virginia Scott. 1st v.p. Countrywide Funding, Pasadena, Calif., 1992-93; CEO Nat. Home Loan Ctr., Orlando, Fla., 1993-95, Pace Fin. Network, L.A., 1995—; Syndicated radio talk programs Am. Scene and Money Pro News, 1993-96; guest lectr. Entrepenurial programs for UCLA. Author: Clouds, 1996; contbr. articles to profl. jours. Bd. dirs. Native Mountain Wildlife Rescue, 1995-96. Recipient Coastal Clean Up award Calif. Coastal Commn., Malibu, 1995. Office: Pace Fin Network 700 13th St NW Ste 1160 Washington DC 20005

JUSTICE, DAVID CHRISTOPHER, baseball player; b. Cin., Apr. 14, 1966; m. Halle Berry, Jan. 1, 1993. Student, Thomas More Coll. With Atlanta Braves, 1985—. Named Rookie of Yr. Baseball Writers' Assn. Am., 1990, Sporting News, 1990; mem. Nat. League All-Star Team, 1993, 94; named to Sporting News Silver Slugger Team, 1993. Office: Atlanta Braves Atlanta-Fulton County Stadium PO Box 4064 Atlanta GA 30302-4064*

JUSTICE, EUNICE MCGHEE, missionary, evangelist; b. Fairchance, Pa., Feb. 13, 1922; d. Felix McGhee and Clara May Chavous; divorced; children: Rebecca L. Brothers, William Wood. Leader, youth dir. Avalon Zion Foursquare Ch., L.A., 1969-71; missionary, prayer warrior Pentecostal Faith Ch. for All Nations, N.Y.C., 1971-77, missionary, evangelist(ordained), 1979—; trainer missionaries, 1977—; prophetess, pres. Missionary Evang. Tng. Ctr., Inc., Tampa, Fla., AKA, Dorcas House Ministries, Tampa, 1986-93; producer Dorcas House childrens Workshop, Jones Intercable Pub. Access TV. Editor: Untitled, 1970; paintings exhibited Fla. and Ga., 1980—. Advocate for the poor, 1980—. Recipient Nat. Achievement award Nat. Assn. Negro Bus. and Profl. Womens Clubs, N.Y.C., 1956, Excellence in Gov. Publs. award Nat. Advt. Coun. Cols., Ohio, 1962. Mem. Browns Temple, Loveland Cogic. Home: 101 E Amelia Ave Tampa FL 33602-2235 Office: Dorcas House Ministries PO Box 664 Tampa FL 33601-0664

JUSTICE, WILLIAM WAYNE, federal judge; b. Athens, Tex., Feb. 25, 1920; s. William Davis and Jackie May (Hanson) J.; m. Sue Tom Ellen Rowan, Mar. 16, 1947; 1 dau., Ellen Rowan. LL.B., U. Tex., 1942. Bar: Tex. 1942. Ptnr. firm Justice & Justice, Athens, 1946-61; part-time city atty. Athens, 1948-50, 52-58; U.S. atty. U.S. Dist. Ct. (ea. dist.) Tex., Tyler, 1961-68, U.S. dist. judge, 1968—, chief judge, 1980-90. Subject of book William Wayne Justice, A Judicial Biography (Frank R. Kemerer), 1991. Vice pres. Young Democrats Tex., 1948; adv. council Dem. Nat. Com., 1954; alternate del. Dem. Nat. Conv., 1956, presdl. elector, 1960. Served to 1st lt. F.A. AUS, 1942-46, CBI. Recipient Nat. award Outstanding Fed. Judge Assn. Trial Lawyers Am., 1982, Outstanding Civil Libertarian award Tex. Civil Liberties Union, 1986. Episcopalian. Office: 211 W Ferguson St Ste 318 Tyler TX 75702-7222

JUSTIS, LEWIS CRAIG, manufacturing engineer; b. Greeneville, Tenn., Apr. 5, 1960; s. Danny Dean and Harretta Blanche (English) J.; m. Teresa Ann Teague, Aug. 27, 1983; 1 child, Leanne Nicole. BS in Indsl. Tech., Tenn. Tech. U., 1982. Mfg. engr. Kusan Mfg. Co., Franklin, Tenn., 1983-88; mgr. engr. Alladin Plastics Co., Surgoinsville, Tenn., 1988-89; mfg. engring. mgr. Moll Tool & Plastics Corp., Lavergne, Tenn., 1989-91; mfg. engr. Nissan Motor Mfg. Corp., Smyrna, Tenn., 1991—. Mem. Greystone Homeowner's Assn., Nolensville, Tenn., 1989—; career info./role model vol. Tenn. Tech. Alumni Career Resources Network, Cookeville, 1995—. Mem. Soc. Plastics Engrs. (treas. 1984-86, pres. 1992-93), BMW Car Club Am., Epsilon Pi Tau. Republican. Baptist. Home: 844 Stonebrook Blvd Nolensville TN 37135 Office: Nissan Motor Mfg Corp USA 983 Nissan Dr Smyrna TN 37167-4405

JUSTUS, CAROL FAITH, linguistics educator; b. Lodi, Ohio, Mar. 21, 1940; d. Ernest and Esther Mary (Cockrell) J.; m. Rahim Raman; div. 1976. BA in French, King Coll., 1960; MA in Linguistics, U. Minn., 1966; PhD in Linguistics, U. Tex., 1973. Assoc. prof., asst. prof., linguistics coord. SUNY, Oswego, 1973-77; asst. prof. U. Calif., Berkeley, 1977-82; rsch. assoc. U. Tex., Austin, 1982-84; tech. staff Microelectronics & Computer Tech. Corp., Austin, 1984-88; rsch. fellow U. Tex., 1988-89; assoc. prof. San Jose (Calif.) State U., 1989-94; rsch. fellow U. Tex., 1994—; adj. assoc. prof. Ctr. for Mid. Eastern Studies and Classics, 1995—. Review editor Diachronica, 1988-91; contbr. articles to profl. jours. NEH grantee, 1976. Mem. MLA (div. chair 1979, 81, 84, 87, del. 1991-93), Linguistic Soc. Am. (Inst. dir. 1976), Am. Oriental Soc., Societe de Linguistique de Paris. Home: 3517 Peregrine Falcon Austin TX 78746-7436

JUSTUS, JACK GLENN, farm organization executive, livestock farmer; b. Lead Hill, Ark., Oct. 29, 1931; s. Charles A. and Nancy C. (Mooneyham) J.; m. Freda Sue Anderson, Sept. 23, 1950; children: Michael, Thomas. AS, Ark. Poly. Coll., 1951; BS, U. Ark., 1953. County agt. coop. extension bur. USDA, Jonesboro, Melbourne and Piggott, Ark., 1954-60; dist. dir. field svcs. Ark. Farm Bur. Fedn., Little Rock, 1960-71, 1960-71, legis. dir., 1971-75, adminstrv. v.p., 1975-82, exec. v.p., 1982—; bd. dirs. Ark. Blue Cross/Blue Shield, Little Rock, 1st Comml. Banking Corp., Little Rock. Active Future Farmers Found., 4-H Club Found. Mem. Ark. C. of C. (bd. dirs. 1982—), Nat. Future Farmers Am. (hon. Am. farmer), Pleasant Valley Country Club. Mem. Ch. of Christ. Office: Ark Farm Bur Fedn PO Box 31 Little Rock AR 72203-0031

JUUL, LARRY CHRISTIAN, strategic planner; b. Omaha, Jan. 20, 1944; s. Herluf C. and Olga E. Juul; m. Karen E. Margensey, Mar. 20, 1982; children: Jennifer K., Stefanie E. BA, U. Nebr., 1966; MAPA, U. Va., 1990. Mgmt. analyst Defense Logistics Agy., Alexandria, Va.; program analyst Interstate Commerce Commn., Washington; logistics mgmt. specialist HQ Defense Logistics Agy, Alexandria. With U.S. Army, 1966-69, Korea. Mem. Coun. Logistics Mgmt., Am. Mktg. Assn., The Planning Forum, Am. Soc. Pub. Adminstrs., Fed. Mgrs. Assn. Office: HQ Def Logistics Agy Ste 2533 8725 John J Kingman Rd Fort Belvoir VA 22060-6221

JUVE, ARTHUR JAMES, aerospace electronics executive; b. Fargo, N.D., Dec. 16, 1951; s. Arthur James (dec.) and Osie Louise (Moore) J.; m. Ivy Dorothy Vorgert, June 3, 1972; children: Joshua, Nicholas. BS in Indsl. Tech. and Computer Sci., Moorhead (Minn.) State U., 1973; MS in Systems Mgmt., U. So. Calif., 1978; cert. electronic warfare,. Test dir. Gen. Dynamics, Ft. Worth, 1978-80, project mgr., 1980-81; project engr. Rediffusion Simulation, Inc., Arlington, Tex., 1981-83, proposal mgr., 1983-84; program mgr. Tracor Aerospace, Inc., Austin, Tex., 1984-89; purchasing mgr. CompuAdd Corp., Austin, 1989-93; ops. mgr. Tracor Aerospace, Inc., Austin, 1993—. USAF judge East Tex. Regional Sci. Fair, Kilgore, 1977; youth baseball commr. Walnut Creek Optimists, Austin, 1986, Delwood Optimists, Austin, 1987. Capt. USAF, 1973-78. Named one of Outstanding Young Men of Am., 1987, 89. Mem. Def. Electronics Assn., Air Force Assn. Republican. Lutheran. Home: 12010 Lincolnshire Dr Austin TX 78758-2212

KAALSTAD, OSCAR WILLIAM, management consultant; b. Lillestrom, Norway, Feb. 8, 1928; came to U.S., 1949; s. Oscar William and Solveig Elizabeth (Hansen) K.; m. Helen Joan Peterson, Nov. 29, 1952; children: Christina Marie, Oscar William. BSc, MIT, 1952. V.p. for Europe, W.R.

Grace & Co., N.Y.C., 1953-72; 0pres. Eutertic & Castolin Co., Lausanne, Switzerland, 1973-81, Arosa Corp., Winter Park, Fla., 1981-90; pres., chmn. bd. Swiss Am. Trading Corp., Orlando, Fla., 1985-90; pres. Euroconsult, Inc., Winter Springs, Fla., 1990—; bd. dirs. Manor House Properties, Inc., Winter Park, 1983-90; bd. dirs., mem. internat. adv. bd. Am. Internat. Group, N.Y.C., 1983-94. Patentee for drill bits. Hon. consul Norwegian Fgn. Svc., Lausanne, 1971-81; bd. dirs. Swiss Aid to Third World, Lausanne, 1976-81; chmn. Commonwealth-Am. Sch., Lausanne, 1974-78. With Norwegian Royal Engrs., 1946-47. Decorated knight 1st class Order of St. Olav (Norway), knight of St. John (Switzerland). Mem. Sons of Norway, MIT Club Orlando (bd. dirs. 1996—), Hagar Viking Club Orlando (pres. 1993-95). Evangelical. Home and Office: 700 Willow Run Ln Winter Springs FL 32708

KACZOR, WILLIAM STANLEY, journalist; b. Gary, Ind., July 17, 1946; s. Stanley W. and Rose H. (Potoniec) K.; m. Judith A Kallal, Dec. 28, 1968; 1 child, Anna Rose. BS in pol. sci., Eastern Ill. U., 1968; MS in journalism, Northwestern U., 1973. Sports editor Mattoon (Ill.) Journal-Gazette, 1966-67; night editor Coles County Daily Times, Charleston, Ill., 1967-68; reporter, editor Playground Daily News, Ft. Walton Beach, Fla., 1970-71; reporter Pensacola News Jour., Ft. Walton Beach, Fla., 1971-72, Pensacola (Fla.) News Jour., 1974-75, Gannett News Svc., Tallahassee, Fla., 1975-80, AP, Tallahassee, Fla., 1980-84; corr. AP, Pensacola, 1984—. With U.S. Air Force, 1969-73. Mem. Capital Press Club (pres. 1983). Home: 1253 Sanibel Ln Gulf Breeze FL 32561-2586 Office: AP PO Box 12710 Pensacola FL 32574-2710

KADER, JAC B., design engineer; b. N.Y.C., July 24, 1931; s. Hadj El Karoum and Dorothy (Bane) K.; m. Betty Isabella Baespflug, July 25, 1953; children: Thomas M., Kevin L., Curtis J., Julieann A., Alexander J., Christian L. Student, U. So. Calif., L.A., 1958, Purdue U., 1969. Automation engr. Hannibal Rsch., Inc., Santa Ana, Calif., 1958-62; design engr. Ford Aeroneutronics, Newport Beach, Calif., 1962-67; chief indsl. engr. Continental-Moss-Gordon, Montgomery, Ala., 1967-77; chief engr. Reese and Assoc. Engrs., Birmingham, Ala., 1977-80; sr. rsch. engr. Kader Robotics Corp., Birmingham, 1980-89; sr. engr. United Techs. Corp., Huntsville, Ala., 1989-94; mil. robotics cons., 1994—. Author: (guide) Mars Base Lava Tube Robotics, 1990, Robotics in Lunar Base Construction, 1991, Unattended Robotic Navigation, 1991, Robotic Satellite Servicing, 1992, PsychoKinectic Hyper Robotic Control, 1993, The Gene Chip, 1994, Embedded G-chips for Robotics on the Martian Surface, 1994, Battlefield Robotics, 1995; inventor automated mix pump vehicle, rendezvous and docking system, tripartite orbital guidance system. With U.S. Army, 1949-54, Korea. Fellow AAAS, AIAA (assoc.) (chmn. com. on stds. 1990-93); mem. Ala. Soc. Advancement Sci., N.Y. Acad. Scis. Republican. Mem. Christian Ch. Home: PO Box 94547 Birmingham AL 35220-4547

KADER, NANCY STOWE, nurse, consultant; b. Ogden, Utah, May 29, 1945; d. William Hessel and Mildred (Madsen) Stowe; m. Omar Kader, Jan. 25, 1967; children: Tarik, Gabriel, Aron, Jacob. BSN, Brigham Young U., 1967; postgrad., U. Md. RNICU Glendale (Calif.) Adventist Hosp., 1970-75; RN ICU Utah Valley Hosp., Provo, 1975-83; campaign coord. Matheson for Gov., Salt Lake City, 1976-85, Wilson for Senate, Salt Lake City, 1980; RN cons. MESA Corp., Reston, Va., 1984-85; mgr. cost containment Health Mgmt. Strategies, Washington, 1985-88; nurse cons. Birch & Davis, Washington, 1988-90; cons. Inst. Medicine NAS, Washington, 1990-92; cons. Pal-Tech Inc., Arlington, Va., 1992—; vice chmn. Utah State Bd. Nursing, Salt Lake City, 1977-83. Dem. county chmn., Utah, 1977-79; del. Dem. Nat. Conv., 1980; del. Va. State Dem. Conv., 1984-95; vice chmn. Gov.'s Commn. on Status of Women, Salt Lake City, 1975-78. Democrat. Home: 11401 Tanbark Dr Reston VA 22091-4121

KADHIM, ESTELLE BEVERLY, librarian, educator; b. Rock Island, Ill., June 16, 1933; d. George and Rose (Zaretsky) Buder; m. Abdul Wahhab Kadhim, June 12, 1955; children: Temma, Janon, Muna, Affifa, Dina. BA in Liberal Arts and Sci., U. Ill., 1955, MS in LS, 1959. Libr., dept. oceanography and meteorology Tex. A&M Coll., College Station, 1956-59; gifts and exch. libr. Kans. State U. Libr., Manhattan, 1960; asst. to dir. Kans. State Libr., Manhattan, 1960-61, head circulation dept., 1961-62; serials cataloger U. Calif.-San Diego, La Jolla, 1962-63; head, periodicals and documents Calif. State U., Fullerton, 1964-65; sch. libr. Am. Cmty. Ctr., Baghdad, Iraq, 1966-67; libr., head media ctr. Baghdad Internat. Sch., 1967-93; head children's dept. McAllen (Tex.) Meml. Libr., 1994—; tchr. Internat. Children's Ctr., 1968-69, Baghdad Internat. Sch., 1970-75. Mem. Tex. Libr. Assn. Office: McAllen Meml Libr 601 N Main St Mcallen TX 78501

KAGAN, CONSTANCE HENDERSON, psychotherapist, consultant; b. Houston, Sept. 16, 1940; d. Bessie Earle (Henderson) Davis; m. Morris Kagan, May 27, 1967. BA, Baylor U., 1962; MSSW, U. Tex. Austin, 1966; PhD, U. Okla., 1979. Lic. social worker, Va., Tex.; diplomate. Cons., 1966—, pvt. practice, 1969—; congl. fellow, 1981-82. Mem. NASW, Am. Philos. Assn. Home: 9804 Orchid Circle Great Falls VA 22066

KAGAN, JEFFREY ALLEN, telecommunications analyst, consultant, cilumni author, columnist; b. Albany, N.Y., Mar. 8, 1958; s. Joshua and Sharon Lee (Goodman) K.; m. Deborah Ann Hepinstall, Apr. 30, 1983; children: Jason Michael, Adam William, Jennifer Susanne. AAS in Advt., Russell Sage Coll., 1980. Owner, pres. freelance advt. agy., Albany, 1980-84; communications cons. Telecom USA/So. Net, Atlanta, 1984-85; major account mgr. ITT, Atlanta, 1985-87; pres., CEO Kagan Telecom Assocs., Atlanta, 1987—; columnistcommunication business success nnhhhh Atlanta Bus. Chronicle; columnist Communications Week, Success Mag.; media expert telecomm. Sta. WBS-AM Radio, Atlanta, 1991—, PBS "small Bus. Today"; high tech. adv. com. to U.S. Congressman Newt Gingrich. Contbr. numerous articles to profl. jours.; frequent pub. speaker. Office: Kagan Telecom Assocs PO Box 670562 Marietta GA 30066-0127

KAHANE, JOEL CARL, speech pathologist; b. Bklyn., Dec. 23, 1946; s. Harry and Ruth (Gold) K.; m. Joanne Kahane, Aug. 5, 1971; children: Michael Barry, Saar Joshua. BA Biology, Bklyn. Coll. of CUNY, 1969, MS Speech Pathology, 1972; PhD Biocommunication, U. Pitts., 1975. Cert. clin. competence in speech-lang. pathology. Tchg. asst. Bklyn. Coll., 1969-71; tchg. fellow U. Pitts., 1971-73; asst. prof. Memphis State U., 1974-80, assoc. prof., 1980-91; clin. assoc. prof. otolaryngology U. Tenn. Ctr. for Health Scis., Memphis, 1984—, clin. assoc. prof. rehab. scis., 1987—; prof. The Univ. Memphis, 1991—; cons. St. Jude Children's Rsch. Hosp., Memphis, 1989—; mem. scientific adv. bd. The Voice Found., Phila., 1993—. Editorial rev. bd. Jour. of Voice, 1990—, Am. Jour. of Speech-Lang. Pathology, 1991—; author: Atlas of Speech and Hearing Anatomy, Anatomy and Physiology of the Speech Mechanism; author exhibits in field. Bd. trustees Baron Hirsch Congregation, Memphis, 1984-90, Margolin Hebrew Acad./Yeshiva of the South, Memphis, 1986—. Recipient Disting. Alumnus award Bklyn. Coll., 1982. Fellow Am. Speech-Lang. and Hearing Assn. (Editor's award 1983, Sci. Exhibit awards 1973, 79); mem. Am. Cleft Palate Craniofacial Assn., Am. Assn. Phonetic Scis., Sigma Xi. Home: 5337 Laurie Ln Memphis TN 38120-2458 Office: Univ Memphis Sch of Audiology/Speech 807 Jefferson Ave Memphis TN 38105-5042

KAHLDEN, NANCY WARGO, director of studies; b. Morristown, N.J., Feb. 13, 1951; d. Frances Andrew and Winona Evelyn (Hill) Wargo; m. James Kennedy Kahlden, Dec. 22, 1971 (div. Feb. 1996); children: Jennifer Marie, Kristin Leigh. BS, U. Tex., 1973; MEd, Stephen F. Austin State U., Tex., 1976. Tchr. Austin Ind. Sch. Dist., 1973-74, Alief Ind. Sch. Dist., Tex., 1974-78; freelance alphabetic phonics therapist Houston, 1986-94; dir. studies Episcopal H.S., Bellaire, Tex., 1994—. Pres., v.p. PTO, St. Mark's Episcopal Day Sch., 1984-86, Houston; vol. St. Luke's United Meth. Ch., Houston, 1984-96; leader Girl Scouts Am., Houston, 1986-96. Mem. Assn. Supr. Curriculum Devel., Orton Dyslexia Soc. Home: 4130 Gramercy Houston TX 77025 Office: Episcopal High Sch 4650 Bissonnet Bellaire TX 77401

KAHLER, STEPHEN G., clinical biological geneticist, pediatrician; b. Evanston, Ill., Oct. 20, 1947. MD, Duke U., 1973. Diplomate Am. Bd. Med. Genetics, Biochem. Genetics, Am. Bd. Pediatrics. Intern U. Calif. San Diego Hosp., 1973-74, resident in pediat., 1974-76; fellow in genetics and metabolism U. N.C. Sch. Med., Chapel Hill, 1977-82; with Duke U. Med. Ctr., Durham, N.C.; assoc. clin. prof. pediat. Duke U. Mem. AMA, Am. Acad. Pediat., Am. Coll. Med. Genetics, Am. Soc. Human Genetics, Soc. Study Inborn Errors Metabolism, Soc. for Inherited Metabolic Disease. Office: Duke U Med Ctr PO Box 3528 Durham NC 27715-3528

KAHN, ALAN BRUCE, real estate development and construction executive; b. Columbia, S.C., Apr. 15, 1940; s. Irwin and Katie Kahn; m. Charlotte Segelbaum, Feb. 28, 1965: children: Kevin A., Monique B., Charles B. BA in History, Duke U., 1962; MBA in Fin., George Washington U., 1965. Pres. Kahn Devel Co., Columbia, 1968—; v.p. sec. M.B. Kahn Constrn. Co., Inc., Columbus, 1968—, chmn., 1990; mem. adv. bd. NCNB/SC, Columbia, 1970—, chmn., 1996. Bd. dirs. Columbia Area Mental Health Ctr., 1968-72, 74-78, chmn. 1971; sec. adv. bd. dirs. Providence Hosp., Columbia, 1973-80; bd. dirs. Columbia Jewish Community Ctr., Hist. Columbia Found., 1974-78, Salvation Army, 1983-85, Friends of Richland County Pub. Libr., 1981-84, Columbia Philharm. Orch., 1970-78, S.C. Arts Found., 1974-76; trustee Columbia Mus. Art and Sci., 1982-85; bd. dirs. Columbia Jewish Fedn., 1982—, treas. 1982-83, 88—, 2d v.p., 1984, chmn. endowment, 1985-89, pres.-elect, 1990, pres. 1993—; mem. partnership bd. U. S.C. Sch. Medicine, 1985—, v.p. 1992—. Recipient (with wife) Lyre award City of Columbia, 1978, Order of Palmetto Sate of S.C., 1988, State of Israel Bonds award, 1988, Disting. Svc. award Columbia Jewish Fedn. Mem. B'nai B'rith (Community Leadership award 1982). Office: Kahn Devel Co Highway 555 Flintlake Rd Columbia SC 29223

KAHN, ALAN HARVEY, therapist, administrator, consultant; b. Bklyn., Aug. 8, 1950; s. Murray and Dorothy Maxine (Nally) K. Student, Western Mich. U., 1968-69; BA in Psychology, Memphis State U., 1969-73, MEd in Rehab. Counseling, 1973-75, MS in Therapeutic Recreation Adminstrn., 1974-76. Cert. Rehab. Counsleor, Therapy Recreation Specialist. Instr. Northwest Jr. Coll., Senatobia, Miss., 1976-77; program coord. Muscular Dystrophy Assn., Memphis, 1977-78; dist. dir. Muscular Dystrophy Assn., Columbus, Ga., 1978-81; vocat. cons. Crawford Rehab. Svcs., Macon, Ga., 1982; recreation therapist VA, Waco, Tex., 1982-85; asst. chief recreation therapy Dept. Vetrans Affairs, Waco, 1985—. Author: (poetry) Many Voices, Many Lands, 1987, The Speed Bag Bible, 1995; contbr. articles to profl. publs. Bd. mem. City of Woodway (Tex.) Park Commn., 1990-93. Mem. Nat. Assn. Rehab. Profls. in Pvt. Sector, Tex. Assn. Rehab. Profls. in Pvt. Sector. Home: 432 Elmwood Rd Waco TX 76712-3830 Office: VA Med Ctr 4800 Memorial Dr Dept 11-K Waco TX 76711-1329

KAHN, CHARLES HOWARD, architect, educator; b. Birmingham, Ala., Feb. 10, 1926; s. Benjamin Arthur and Dorothy (Goldman) K.; m. Annette Lee, May 12, 1956; children: Kathryn Lauren, Sarah Elizabeth, Benjamin Arthur. A.B., U. N.C., 1946; B.C.E., N.C. State U., 1948; B. Arch., 1956; M.S., M.I.T., 1949; Fulbright grantee, Inst. di Urbanistico, Rome, 1957-58; postgrad., U. N.C., 1991. With Robert & Co. (architects and engr.), Atlanta, 1949-51, Frederick Snare Corp., N.Y.C., 1951-52, F. Carter Williams (AIA), Raleigh, N.C., 1952-54; propr. Charles Howard Kahn & Assocs. Architects and Engrs., Raleigh, N.C., 1954-68, Lawrence, Kans., 1968-91; prof. Sch. Architecture and Urban Design, U. Kans., Lawrence, 1968-91, prof. emeritus, 1991—; pvt. practice Charles H. Kahn, FAIA & Assoc., Chapel Hill, N.C., 1991—; vis. prof. Sch of Design, N.C. State U., 1992—. Works include Carter Stadium, N.C. State U., 1966, Minges Auditorium, E. Carolina Coll., 1967, Poliedro, Caracus, Venezuela, 1973; mem. editorial bd.: Jour. Archtl. and Planning Research. Bd. dirs. Cmty. Devel. Ctr., 1968-75; bd. dirs. Environ. R&D Found., 1968-91, v.p., 1975-87, pres. 1987-91; mem. Kans. Bldg. Commn., 1978-80. Recipient Hon. Alumnus and Disting. Alumnus awards U. Kans., 1989; Fulbright vis. rsch. scholar Gt. Brit., 1977-78. Fellow AIA; Mem. Assn. Collegiate Schs. of Architecture, Kans. Soc. Architects (pres. elect 1986, pres. 1987), Phi Beta Kappa, Phi Kappa Phi, Sigma Xi, Tau Beta Pi. Democrat. Jewish.

KAHN, DAVID MILLER, lawyer; b. Port Chester, N.Y., Apr. 21, 1925; m. Barbara Heller, May 9, 1952; children: William, James, Caroline. BA, U. Ky., 1947; LLB cum laude, N.Y. Law Sch., 1950. Bar: N.Y. 1951, U.S. Dist Ct. (ea. and so. dists.) N.Y. 1953, U.S. Supreme Ct. 1958. Sole practice, White Plains, N.Y., 1951-60; ptnr. Kahn & Rubin, White Plains, 1960-66, Kahn & Goldman, White Plains, 1967-80; sr. ptnr. Kahn & Landau, White Plains, N.Y. and Palm Beach Gardens, Fla., 1980-88, Kahn and Kahn, Fla. and N.Y., 1988—; lectr. N.Y. Law Sch., 1982—; spl. counsel Village Port Chester, N.Y., 1960-63; commr. of appraisal Westchester County Supreme Ct., 1973-77; counsel Chemplex Industries, Inc., BIS Communications Corp., Bilbar Realty Co. Chmn. Westchester County Citizens for Eisenhower, 1950-52; pres. Westchester County Young Republicans Clubs, 1958-60; Founder, chmn. bd. dirs. Port Chester-Rye Town Vol. Ambulance Corps., 1968-77; pres. Driftwood Corp., Amagansette, L.I., N.Y., 1984-91. Served with Counter Intelligence Corps. USAF, 1942-46. Recipient John Marshall Harlan fellow N.Y. Law Sch., 1990-93. Fellow Am. Acad. Matrimonial Lawyers (bd. govs. N.Y. chpt. 1976-79); mem. ABA, N.Y. State Bar Assn., Westchester County Bar Assn., White Plains Bar Assn., N.Y. Law Sch. Alumni Assn. (bd. dirs. 1970-80), Elmwood C. C. (legal counsel), Eastpointe Country Club. Home and Office: 6419 Eastpointe Pines St Palm Beach Gardens FL 33418 also: 175 Main St White Plains NY 10601-3105

KAHN, ELLIS IRVIN, lawyer; b. Charleston, S.C., Jan. 18, 1936; s. Robert and Estelle Harriet (Kaminski) K.; m. Janice Weinstein, Aug. 11, 1963; children: Justin Simon, David Israel, Cynthia Anne. AB in Polit. Sci., The Citadel, 1958; JD, U. S.C., 1961. Bar: S.C. 1961, U.S. Ct. Appeals (5th cir.) 1963, U.S. Ct. Appeals (4th cir.) 1964, U.S. Supreme Ct. 1970, D.C. 1978, U.S. Claims Ct. 1988; diplomate Nat. Bd. Trial Advocacy, Am. Bd. Profl. Liability Attys. (trustee 1989—). Law clk. U.S. Dist. Ct. S.C., 1964-66; prin. Kahn Law Firm, Charleston; adj. prof. med.-legal jurisprudence Med. U. S.C., 1978-87; mem. rules com. U.S. Dist. Ct., 1984-96. Chmn. campaign Charleston Jewish Fedn., 1986-87, pres., 1988-90, S.C. Organ Procurment Agy., 1987-94, chmn. bd. 1989-94, mem. nat. coun. Am. Israel Pub. Affairs Com., 1982-88, Hebrew Benevolent Soc., pres., 1994-96. Capt. USAF, 1961-64. Fellow Internat. Soc. Barristers; mem. S.C. Bar, ABA, Assn. Trial Lawyers Am. (state committeeman 1970-74, S.C. Trial Lawyers Assn. (pres. 1976-77), 4th Cir. Jud. Conf. (permanent mem.). Home: 316 Confederate Cir Charleston SC 29407-7431 Office: PO Box 898 Charleston SC 29402-0898

KAHN, GORDON BARRY, federal bankruptcy judge; b. Mobile, Ala., Dec. 3, 1931; s. Al and Molly (Prince) K.; 1 son, Andrew Fortier. BS, U. Ala., 1953, LLB, 1958; LLM, NYU, 1959; postgrad., U. London, 1957—. Bar: Ala. 1958. Practice in Mobile, 1959; mem. firm Lyons, Pipes & Cook, 1959-74; bankruptcy judge U.S. Dist. Ct. for So. Ala., 1974-96. Chmn. Mobile United Jewish Appeal, 1963-64; pres. Friends of Mobile Pub. Library, Jewish Community Center of Mobile, 1974; Trustee Mobile Pub. Library, 1973-74; bd. dirs. Salvation Army Mobile, 1973-74, B'nai B'rith Home for Aged, Memphis, 1973-74. Served to 1st lt. U.S. Army, 1953-55. Mem. Ala., Mobile County bar assns. Jewish. Lodge: Masons. Home: 2558 S Delwood Dr Mobile AL 36606-1726 Office: PO Box 361 Mobile AL 36601-0361

KAHN, HENRY SLATER, physician, epidemiologist, educator; b. Poughkeepsie, N.Y., May 6, 1943; s. Joseph and Selma (Schlachter) K.; m. Felicia Hance, 1967 (div. 1969); m. Mary Gillmor, Oct. 4, 1970; children: Jeremy Kahn, Daniel Gillmor. AB magna cum laude, Harvard U., 1964, MD, 1968. Diplomate Am. Bd. Internal Medicine. Resident in internal medicine Boston City Hosp., 1968-70; resident in pediatrics Lincoln Hosp., Bronx, N.Y., 1970-71; physician Mid-West Side Neighborhood Clinic, N.Y.C., 1971-72; epidemiologist U.S. CDC, Atlanta, 1972-74; physician DeKalb Grady Clinic, Atlanta, 1975—; asst. prof. Emory U. Sch. Medicine, Atlanta, 1974-78, assoc. prof., 1978—; vis. scientist U.S. CDC, 1986-89; clin. prof. Morehouse Sch. Medicine, Atlanta, 1990—. Chair Ga. chpt. Physicians for a Nat. Health Program, Atlanta, 1989—. Surgeon USPHS, 1972-74. Epidemiol. rsch. fellow Am. Cancer Soc., 1995—. Fellow ACP; mem. APHA, Soc. for Epidemiol. Rsch., Soc. Gen. Internal Medicine. Home: 947 Blue Ridge Ave NE Atlanta GA 30306-4416 Office: Emory U Dept Family and Preventive Medicine 69 Butler St Atlanta GA 30303-3219

KAHOA, LINDA LOU, public relations consultant; b. Springfield, Mo., July 3, 1943; d. Edward Leroy Sr. and Susannie (Bowen) Mills; m. George Michael Kahoa, July 15, 1978; children: Dennis Alan Gragert, Rebecca Susannie Settlemoir, Erin Kyle. Student, S.W. Mo. State U., 1961-63, 74-75, Oceanside Jr. Coll., Sayre Jr. Coll. Editor Jour. of Milking Shorthorn & Illawarra Breeds, Springfield, Mo., 1974-77; office mgr. Bob Wright Realty, Springfield, 1977-78; livestock sales mgr. Kahoa Cattle Svcs., 1979-84; pub. rels. cons. Kahoa Prodns., Cheyenne, Okla., 1980—; exec. sec.-treas. Okla. Shorthorn Assn., 1983-92; substitute tchr. 1910 One-Rm. Sch., Cheyenne, 1995—. Editor 100-Yr. History of Cheyenne and Roger Mills Country, Okla., 1995. Bd. dirs. Hist. Roger Mills Restoration and Preservation Com., Cheyenne, 1992—, Washita Battlefield Soc., Cheyenne, 1994—, Homebound Ministry; vol. Internat. Youth Exch. Svc.; past bd. dirs. Sagebrush Workshop for Mentally Retarded, Sayre, Okla., R. M. Co. Vets. Meml., Cheyenne, 1988; active Okla. Singing ChurchWomen, 1992—, sec. 1996-97, Red Hills Theatre Co., 1993—, GFWC Platonic Club, 1993—; docent Black Kettle Mus., Cheyenne, 1995—; bd. dirs. Roger Mills Arts & Humanities coun., 1994-96. Republican. Baptist. Office: Kahoa Prodns RR 1 Box 106 Cheyenne OK 73628-9759

KAIROFF, PETER DAVID, music educator, concert pianist; b. L.A., Oct. 30, 1955; s. Raquel Kairoff; m. Sarah Cathryn Felty, July 8, 1988; children: Daniel, Anna. BA, U. Calif., San Diego, 1978; MusM, U. So. Calif., L.A., 1980, DMA, 1985. Dir. piano accompanying U. Tex., Austin, 1985-86; asst. prof. music SUNY, Plattsburgh, 1986-88; assoc. prof. music Wake Forest U., Winston-Salem, N.C., 1988—; concert pianist solo recitals through U.S., Europe, and S.Am. Pianist CD recording: American Romantics, 1995. Fulbright grantee, 1984. Office: Wake Forest Univ Dept of Music Winston Salem NC 27109

KAISER, PHILIP MAYER, diplomat; b. Bklyn., July 12, 1913; s. Morris and Temma (Sloven) K.; m. Hannah Greeley, June 16, 1939; children: Robert Greeley, David Elmore, Charles Roger. A.B., U. Wis., 1935; B.A., M.A. (Rhodes scholar), Balliol Coll., Oxford (Eng.) U., 1939. Economist, bd. govs. Fed. Res. System, 1939-42; chief project ops. staff, also chief planning staff enemy br. Bd. Econ. Warfare and Fgn. Econ. Adminstrn., 1942-46; expert on internat. orgn. affairs State Dept., 1946; exec. asst. to asst. sec. labor in charge internat. labor affairs, 1946-47; dir. Office Internat. Labor Affairs, Dept. Labor, 1947-49, asst. sec. labor for internat. labor affairs, 1949-53; labor adviser to Com. for Free Europe, 1954; spl. asst. to Gov. W. Averell Harriman of N.Y., 1955-58; prof. internat. labor relations Sch. Internat. Service, Am. U., 1958-61; U.S. ambassador to Republic Senegal, Islamic Republic Mauritania, 1961-64; minister Am. Embassy, London, Eng., 1964-69; chmn. Ency. Brit. Internat. Ltd., London, 1969-75; dir. Guinness Mahon Holdings, Ltd., 1975-77; ambassador to People's Republic of Hungary, 1977-80, Austria, 1980-81; professorial lectr. Johns Hopkins Sch. Advanced Internat. Studies, 1983-85, Woodrow Wilson vis. fellow, 1984; sr. cons. SRI Internat., 1981—; Mem. interdept. com. to develop programs under Marshall Plan, 1947-48, interdept. com. to develop programs for Greek-Turkish aid and Point 4 Tech. Assistance, 1947-49, Internat. del. to Hungary's Parliamentary elections, 1990. Author: Journeying Far and Wide: A Political and Diplomatic Memoir, 1993. Bd. dirs. Am. Ditchey Found., Ptnrs. for Dem. Change, Soro Hungarian Found., Coun. Am. Ambs., Assn. Diplomatic Studies. Decorated knight comdr. Austrian Govt. Mem. Am. Assn. Rhodes Scholars, Coun. Fgn. Rels., Am. Acad. Diplomacy, Washington Inst. for Fgn. Affairs, Phi Beta Kappa. Home: 2101 Connecticut Ave NW Washington DC 20008-1728 Office: SRI Internat 1611 N Kent St Arlington VA 22209-2111

KAISER, ROBERT LEE, engineer; b. Louisville, June 28, 1935; s. Harlan K. and LaVerne (Peterson) K.; student U. Louisville, 1953-54, U. Ky., 1958-61; m. Margaret Siler; children: Robin Lee, Robert Lee. Draftsman, designer E.R. Ronald & Assos., Louisville, 1953-54, Thompson-Kissell Co., 1954-56; estimator, engr. George Pridemore & Son, Lexington, Ky., 1956-58; designer, engr., supr. Frankel & Curtis, Lexington, 1958-61; engr. Hugh Dillehay & Assos., 1961-65; owner, engr., operator K-Svc., Inc., 1965-74; project engr. Mason & Hanger, Silas Mason Co., Inc., 1974-77; v.p. Webb-Dillehay Design Group, 1977-81; pres. Kaiser-Taulbee Assos., Inc., Lexington, Louisville, Orlando, Fla.; past chmn., pres. and bd. dirs. Opportunity Workshop Lexington; vis. lectr. mech. engring. and Coll. Architecture, U. Ky. Mem., Ky. State Bd. of Registration for Engrs, and Land Surveyors, Ky. Task Force to Develop new Engring. and Surveying Laws; charter commn. merger Lexington-Fayette County govts.; mem. Ky. Airport Zoning Comsn., mem. Gov.'s Task Force on Ednl. Constrn. Criteria; trustee Humana Hosp., Lexington, Aviation Mus. Ky. Registered profl. engr., Fla., Ind., Ky., N.Mex., Ariz., Ill, Tenn., Ohio, Pa., N.C., W.Va. Mem. ASME, Nat., Ky. socs. profl. engrs., Lexington C. of C., ASHRAE (past pres. local chpt.), Assn. Energy Engrs. (past pres. local chpt., past v.p. region II), Rotary. Episcopalian. Home: 108 Sheldrake Ct Georgetown KY 40324-9213 Office: PO Box 480 Lexington KY 40585-0480

KAIVOLA, KAREN LENNEA, educator in English; b. Seattle, July 26, 1957; d. Robert L. Kaivola and Sonia J. (Easterly) Thomas. AB in English, Georgetown U., 1979; MA in English, U. Wash., Seattle, 1985, PhD in English, 1989. Tchg. asst. U. Wash., Seattle, 1984-89, instr. in English, advisor undergrads., 1989-91; dir. women and gender studies program Stetson U., Deland, Fla., 1995—; asst. prof. English Stetson U., Deland, 1991—, Neil Carlton chair in English, 1996—. Author: (book) All Contraries Confounded, 1991; also articles in profl. revs. Grantee: summer rsch. grant Stetson U., 1992, 93, 94. Mem. AAUW, MLA, Nat. Womens' Studies Assn., Virginia Woolf Soc. Office: Stetson U English Dept Box 8300 Deland FL 32720

KAK, SUBHASH CHANDRA, engineering educator, writer; b. Srinagar, Kashmir, India, Mar. 26, 1947; s. Ram Nath and Sarojini Chuni (Kaul) K.; m. Navnidhi Saklani Kak, Jan. 21, 1979; children: Abhinav Gautam, Arushi. BE, Kashmir U., 1967; PhD, Indian Inst. of Tech., 1970. Lectr. Indian Inst. of Tech., Delhi, 1971-74, asst. prof., 1974-79; assoc. prof. La. State U., Baton Rouge, 1979-83, prof., 1983—; vis. prof. Imperial Coll., London, 1975-76, Harvard U., Boston, 1996; cons. UN Devel. Program, Pune, India, 1989-90. Author: The Astronomical Code of the Rigueda, 1994, India At Century's End, 1994, In Search of the Cradle of Civilization, 1995; assoc. editor Vishva Vivek, 1992, Info. Scis., 1993, Jour. of Combinatorics, Info. and System Sci., 1995; inventor neural networks and methods for training them. Recipient Sci. Acad. medal Indian Nat. Sci. Acad., 1977, Kothari prize Kothari Scientific and Rsch. Inst., 1977; Tokten fellowship UN Devel. Program, 1986. Mem. AAAS. Office: La State U Dept Elec and Computing Engring Baton Rouge LA 70803

KALAS, FRANK JOSEPH, JR., financial consultant; b. Stafford Springs, Conn., Dec. 31, 1943; s. Frank Joseph and Margaret Mary (LaPanne) K.; m. Minh Tran, June 24, 1972; children: Jennifer Ann, Joanne Catherine. BBA, U. N.Mex., 1966; MS, U. Ark., London, Eng., 1974. Sr. auditor Knox & Scott, CPAs, Albuquerque, 1963-66; commd. officer USN, 1967, advanced through grades to capt., 1987; dir. fin. mgmt. office Naval Sea Systems Command, Washington, 1988-93; ret., 1993; mgr. material and prodn. svcs. Intermarine USA, Savannah, Ga., 1993-95; adj. prof. acctg. R.I. Coll., 1978-80, Far East divsn. U. Md., 1980-82. Author: Food Service Operations and Contracting, 1987. Decorated Meritorious Svc. medal, Legion of Merit. Mem. Am. Soc. Naval Engrs., Soc. Logistics Engrs. (pres. 1979-80), Profl. Picture Framer's Assn. (cert.), Am. Soc. Mil. Comptrs. (Outstanding Mem. award 1985), Nat. Amateur Press Assn., Inst. of Mgmt. Accts., Am. Prodn. and Inventory Control Soc. Roman Catholic. Office: Am Mgmt Systems Inc 1777 N Kent St Arlington VA 22209-2110

KALAS, J(OHN) ELLSWORTH, religious educator, minister; b. Sioux City, Iowa, Feb. 14, 1923; s. John Carl and Minnie (Barth) K.; m. Ruth Keshansky, Jan. 21, 1949 (div. June 1989); children: Taddy, David; m. Janet Stith, Sept. 4, 1994. BSc, U. Wis., 1951, postgrad., 1954-55; MDiv, Garrett Theol. Sem., 1954; postgrad., Harvard U., 1955-56; DD (hon.), Lawrence U., 1965, Asbury Theol. Sem., 1986. Min. Wesley Meth. Ch., Watertown, Wis., 1950-55; sr. min. First United Meth. Ch., Green Bay, Wis., 1956-62, Madison, Wis., 1962-72; sr. min. Ch. of the Saviour, Cleve., 1972-88; assoc. in evangelism World Meth. Coun., Lake Junaluska, N.C., 1988-93; Beeson min. in-residence Asbury Theol. Sem., Wilmore, Ky., 1993—; tng. lectr. Disciple Studies, Nashville, 1987—; lectr. Clergy Groups, 1988—. Author 15 books. Mem. Rotary Club (pres. 1984-85). Home: 3264 Blenheim Way Lexington KY 40503 Office: Asbury Theol Sem Wilmore KY 40390

KALAYILPARAMPIL, THOMAS ITTY, social worker; b. Kottayam, Kerala, India, Mar. 7, 1949; came to U.S., 1976; s. Itty K. and Mariamma

(Mathew) Itty; m. Achiamma thomas, May 8, 1975. BA, U. Kerala, 1970; MA in Humanities, U. Sagar, India, 1972. Accounts asst. Lana Pub. Co./ Stardust, Bombay, 1975-76; rsch. asst. U. Ill., Champaign-Urbana, 1976-80; data processing technician Dept. Human Svcs., Oklahoma City, 1980-82, social worker, 1982—. Editor the Marthoman newsletter, 1990-95. Joint sec. Okla. Malayalee Assn., Oklahoma City, 1995-96; youth dir. St. Thomas Orthodox Ch., 1990—, bldg. com. convener, 1990-94. Recipient Vol. award travellers' Aid Soc., Oklahoma City, 1992, achievement award State of Okla./Gov., 1995. Mem. Okla. Pub. Employee's Assn. (bd. dirs. 1992-96). Democrat. Office: Dept of Human Services 2409 N Kelly Ave Oklahoma City OK 73111

KALB, SARAH CUMMINS, principal; b. Covington, Ky., Sept. 26, 1957; d. Guerney T. and Elizabeth Ann (Appelman) Cummins; m. Robert H. ray, Dec. 16, 1978 (div. Sept. 1987); 1 child, Jonathan Hunter; m. George E. Kalb, Oct. 15, 1988; 1 child, Kathryn Elizabeth. BS, U. Ky., 1978; MS, Morehead (Ky.) State U., 1995. Cert. prin., Ky. Tchr. jr. h.s. Robertson County Bd. Edn., Mt. Olivet, Ky., 1979-80; spl. edn. tchr. Roberton County Bd. Edn., Mt. Olivet, Ky., 1980-86; spl. edn. tchr. Bracken County Bd. Edn., Brooksville, Ky., 1986-90, bus. edn. tchr., 1990-96; prin. St. Patrick schs., Maysville, Ky., 1996—; mem. Commn. on H.S. Grad. Requirements, State of Ky., 1996—; tech prep coord. Bracken County H.S., 1995—; sch. to work coord. Bracken County Schs., 1995—; cert. tchr. intern observer Ky. tchr. Internship Program, 1995—. Chairperson Ice Cream Social, St. James Cath. Ch., 1987, CCD instr., 1982-88, rosary leader, 1978—. Mem. Ky. Bus. Edn. Assn., Ky. Assn. Pep Orgn. Sponsors (10th region regional bd. dirs. 1982-88). Home: Rt 1 Box 280 Brooksville KY 41004

KALE, WALLACE WILFORD, JR., journalist, communicator, administrator; b. Charlotte, N.C., Sept. 2, 1944; s. Wallace Wilford and Martha G. (Irwin) K.; m. Louise Lambert Kale, Dec. 23, 1970 (div. 1988); 1 child, Anne-Evan Lambert; m. Kelly Hasty, May 22, 1993; 1 child, Walker Wilford. Student, Coll. William and Mary, 1962-67; BA in History, Park Coll., 1971. Asst. to dir. Minn. Pvt. Coll. Fund, Mpls., 1971; Williamsburg (Va.) bur. chief Richmond Times-Dispatch, 1971-92, sr. writer bus. news, 1992-93; chief pub. affairs divsn. Va. Marine Resources Commn., Newport News, 1994-95, sr. policy analyst, 1995—; journalist-in-resident numerous colls. and univs., 1980-92. Author: Hark Upon a Gale, 1985, Traditions, Myths and Memories, 1992; co-author: Davis Y. Paschall; A Study in Leadership, 199; editor: John A. Walker: His Success, His Vision and His Dreams, 1992. Mem. exec. com. Williamsburg-James City County Bicentennial Com., 1973-77; mem. Williamsburg rep. Regional Mental Health Bd., Newport News, 1974-76; bd. trustees Park Coll., 1988-89. 1st lt. U.S. Army, 1968-70. Recipient Journalism award Va. Farm Bur. Fedn., 1992, 93, Bronze Star; named Journalist of Yr., Va. AgriBus. Coun., 1993, Silver medal award for Alumni Publs. Coun. for the Advancement and Support of Edn., 1993. Mem. Soc. Profl. Journalists (bd. dirs. 1985-90), Soc. for Collegiate Journalists (nat. pres. 1979-81), Park Coll. Alumni Assn. (pres. 1988-89), Pulaski Club, Pub. Rels. Soc. Am., Richmond Soc. Profl. Journalists, Phi Alpha Theta, 1970—, Sigma Delta Chi Ednl. Found. (pres. 1984—). Presbyterian. Home: 427 Hempstead Rd Williamsburg VA 23188 Office: Va Marine Resources Commn 2600 Washington Ave Newport News VA 23607-4317

KALER, GERVIS WILTON, quality assurance professional; b. Mayfield, Ky., Sept. 2, 1952; s. Gervis Garland and Malinda Sue (Myatt) K. BS in Engring. Physics, Murray State U., 1981. Quality engr. Gen. Tire & Rubber Co., Marfield, 1981-84; corp. quality engr. Goshen (Ind.) Rubber Co., 1984-88; sr. quality engr. Schlegel Okla., Inc., Frederick, 1988-90; quality engr. G.F. Office Furniture, Ltd., Gallatin, Tex., 1990-92; quality mgr. metals The Troxel Co., Moscow, Tenn., 1992—. Mem. Am. Soc. Quality Control (cert., member statistics div. 1981—). Home: 375 Goldfinch Cv Collierville TN 38017-3100 Office: The Troxel Co Hwy 57 W Moscow TN 38057

KALISH, KATHERINE MCAULAY, lawyer, mediator; b. Pinehurst, N.C., Aug. 6, 1945; d. Hugh Page and Exie Katherine (Beasley) McAulay; m. David Marcus Kalish, Jr., June 18, 1967; children: David Marcus, Page McAulay. BA, Agnes Scott Coll., 1966; JD, Mercer U., 1979. Bar: Ga. 1979, U.S. Dist. Ct. (mid. dist.) Ga. 1979, U.S. Ct. Appeals (5th cir.) 1981, U.S. Ct. Appeals (11th cir.) 1982; cert. Ga. registered mediator Supreme Ct. of Ga. Office of Dispute Resolution. Elem. sch. tchr. Clayton County, Jonesboro, Ga., 1966-67; in office claims adjuster C.N.A., Atlanta, 1967-68; customer account auditor So. Ry., Atlanta, 1968-69; office mgr. David M. Kalish, DDS, Macon, Ga., 1971-73; asst. city atty. Macon, 1979-81; sole practice, Macon, 1981—. Judge pro hac Mcpl. Ct. City of Macon, Ga., 1981-82. Mem. Career Women's Network of Macon, Temple Beth Israel Sisterhood, Macon; bd. dirs. Ctr. for Continuing Edn. Women, Macon, 1981-90, Macon Fire and Police Pension Bd., 1983-91, Porter Found., 1985—, chair, 1990—, Mediators Mid. Ga. Mem. Macon Bar Assn., Ga. Bar Assn., ABA, YLS Coll. Placement and Forums Com., LWV. Home: 4800 N Mumford Rd Macon GA 31210-4039 Office: 3110 Ridge Ave Macon GA 31204-2312

KALISHMAN, REESA JOAN, accountant; b. Bronx, N.Y., Nov. 4, 1959; d. Samuel and Julia (Fluger) Deutch; m. Stuart Jay Kalishman, Sept. 5, 1981. AA with honors, Miami-Dade Community Coll., 1977; BBA, Fla. Internat. U., 1979. CPA, Fla. Staff acct. Holtz & Co., CPA's, Miami, Fla., 1979-80; semi sr. acct. Holtz & Co., CPAs, Ft. Lauderdale, Fla., 1980-81; staff acct. Oppenheim, Appel, Dixon CPAs, Miami, 1981; agt. IRS, Miami, 1981-86; group mgr., tax laws instr. IRS, Miami, Fla., 1986-87; group mgr. planning and spl. programs div. IRS, Ft. Lauderdale, Fla., 1987-89; group mgr., field exam., IRS, Ft. Lauderdale, 1989-92, 8300 compliance group mgr., 1992—; vol. income tax assistance provider IRS, Dade County, Fla., 1983; task force witness, participant Dept. Justice, Roanoke, Va., 1986, Miami, 1987. Campaign worker mayoral election North Miami Beach, Fla., 1978. Mem. Am. Inst. CPAs, Fla. Inst. CPAs, Phi Theta Kappa. Republican. Jewish.

KALISZEWSKI, CHARLES STANLEY, clergyman, international evangelist; b. Houston, July 18, 1950; s. Stanley Edward, Jr. and Charlene (Jackson) K.; m. Mary Suzanne Pierce, Jan. 8, 1972; children: Elizabeth Mary, Christopher Nathan, Catherine Renee. Student South Tex. Jr. Coll., 1969, Phillips U., 1970-71. Ordained to ministry Trinity Christian Ch., 1980, Jesus Hour Ministries, 1982, Full Gospel Evangelistic Assn., 1982. Internat. prophetic min., Houston, 1970—; pres., founder Jesus Hour radio programs, Nacogdoches, Tex., 1975-76, Jesus Hour Ministries, Houston, 1982—, Jesus Hour Ministerial Conv., 1982-94, World Ministry Fellowship, 1990, 91; ch. cons. Jesus Hour Ministries, Tex., 1970—, Argentina, 1996, Costa Rica, 1983-84, 86, 91-94, Mex., 1981, Guatemala, 1984, Spain, 1984-85, 87-96, Ghana, 1985, Portugal, 1989-90, 93-94, El Salvador, 1993, 96, Nicaragua, 1996, France, 1993-96, South Africa, 1994, Luxembourg, 1994-96, Portugal, 1993-95, Panama, 1996, Germany, 1995-96; founder Jesus Hour Ministerial Alliance, 1990, Internat. Sch. Prophecy, 1992, 94. Pub. The Prophetic Chronicles mag.; contbr. religious articles to jours. Avocations: writing, travel, flying. Office: Jesus Hour Ministries 8524 Hwy 6 N Ste 107 Houston TX 77095-2103

KALLMAN, KATHLEEN BARBARA, marketing and business development professional; b. Aurora, Ill., Mar. 23, 1952; d. Kenneth Wesley and Germaine Barbara (May) Eby. Legal sec. Sidley & Austin, Chgo., 1973-76, Winston & Strawn, Chgo., 1976-78; exec. sec. Beatrice Cos., Inc., Chgo., 1978-81, adminstrv. asst., 1981-83, asst. to chmn. bd. dirs., 1983-84, asst. v.p., 1984-85; pres., mng. dir. Stratxx Ltd., Charlotte, N.C., 1985—. Mem. Chgo. Coun. on Fgn. Rels., 1986—. Mem. Am. Soc. Profl. and Exec. Women, Nat. Assn. Women Bus. Owners, Charlotte Women Bus. Owners Assn., Charlotte Assn. Profl. Saleswomen. Office: Stratxx Ltd PO Box 470008 Charlotte NC 28247-0008

KALMAN, ANDREW, manufacturing company executive; b. Hungary, Aug. 14, 1919; came to U.S., 1922, naturalized, 1935; s. Louis and Julia (Bognar) K.; m. Violet Margaret Kish, June 11, 1949; children: Andrew Joseph, Richard Louis, Laurie Ann. With Detroit Engring. & Machine Co., 1947-66, exec. v.p., gen. mgr., 1952-66; exec. v.p. and dir. Indian Head, Inc., 1966-75, also dir.; dir. Acme Precision Products, 1959-80, Reef Energy Corp., 1980-84. Trustee emeritus Alma (Mich.) Coll.; bd. dirs. Am. Hungarian Found., New Brunswick, N.J. Home: 708 S Military St Dearborn MI 48124-2108 Office: 600 Woodbridge St Detroit MI 48226-4302

KALMAZ, ERROL EKREM, environmental scientist; b. Turkey, Jan. 2, 1940; came to U.S., 1962, naturalized, 1979; s. Memet and Ayse K.; student Queens Coll., 1962-63; BA in Chemistry, Okla. State U., 1969; MS in Environ. Sci. and Engring., U. Okla., 1972, PhD in Engring., 1974; m. Gulgun Durusoy, Oct. 3, 1974; children: Phyllis, Denise. Rsch. asst. Okla. Med. Rsch. Found., Oklahoma City, 1969-72, rsch. assoc., 1972-74; postdoctoral fellow, Duke U., Durham, N.C., 1974-76; asst. prof. dept. engrng. sci. and mechanics U. Tenn., Knoxville, 1976-79; sr. environ. sci. Henningson, Durham & Richardson, Inc., engring. cons., Santa Barbara, Calif., 1979-83; sr. rsch. sci. NASA Johnson Space Ctr., Houston, 1983-87, Walls Med. Found. U. Tex., Galveston, 1987-90; assoc. prof. U. South Fla. Coll. Pub. Health, Tampa, Fla., 1990-94, adj. assoc. prof. dept. civil engring., divsn. environ. engring.; v.p. Caltex Internat. Inc., Houston, 1994—; sr. rsch. assoc. NRC, Houston; cons. to industry, engrs. and govt. agys; bd. dirs. Advance Environ. Studies. Mem. AAAS, Am. Chem. Soc., Am. Coll. Toxicology, Inst. Environ. Scis. (tech. chmn. water quality impact), Internat. Soc. Ecol. Modeling, N.Y. Acad. Scis., Soc. for Computer Simulation, Am. Inst. Chemists, Sigma Xi. Contbr. articles to profl. jours., chpts. to books; patentee in field. Home: 7036 N Holiday Dr Galveston TX 77550-3028 Office: PO Box 580629 Houston TX 77258-0629

KALOSIS, JOHN JOSEPH, JR., physician, air force officer; b. Detroit, June 6, 1947; s. John Joseph and Terese Lucille (Peter) K.; m. Dana Garcia, May 17, 1980; children: Sandra, Gregory, Lisa, John III. BS, Mich. Tech. U., 1970; MBA, St. Mary's U., 1973; DO, N. Tex. U., 1977; MPH, U. Tex., 1981. Diplomate Am. Bd. Preventive Medicine, Am. Bd. Medical Mgmt., Nat. Osteopathic Med. Bd., Am. Bd. Family Practice. Commd. 2nd lt. USAF, 1970, advanced through grades to col., 1988; intern Wright-Patterson AFB, Fairborn, Ohio, 1977-78; resident aerospace medicine Brooks AFB, San Antonio, Tex., 1978-80; comdr. 655 Tactical Hosp., Yokota, Japan, 1980-84; med. inspector Air Force Inspector Gen., San Bernadino, Calif., 1984-86; chief flight surgeon Strategic Air Comd. Hqtrs., Offutt AFB, Nebr., 1986-87; comdr. 96th Strategic Hosp., Dyess AFB, Tex., 1987-89, 2nd Strategic Hosp., Barksdale AFB, La., 1989-91; postgrad. fellow USAF Family Practice, Omaha, Nebr., 1991-93; comdr. 6th med. group USAF Family Practice, MacDill AFB, Fla., 1994—; physician Group Family Practice, Port Charlotte, Fla., 1994—; examiner Am. Bd. Med. Mgmt., Tampa, Fla., 1989—. Bd. dirs. West Tex. Rehab. Ctr., Abilene, 1987-89, Hospice of Abilene, 1987-89. Fellow Am. Coll. Physician Execs. (ethics com.). Address: 7250 Riverside Dr Punta Gorda FL 33982-1568

KAMADA-COLE, MIKA M., allergist, immunologist, medical educator; b. Denver, Dec. 9, 1957; d. Tom Tsutomu and Nobuko Mary (Kumagai) K.; m. Joe Lyn Cole, Dec. 7, 1991. BA in Biology, U. Mo., 1980, BA in Chemistry, 1980, MD, 1982. Diplomate: Am. Bd. Allergy and Immunology, Am. Bd. Internal Medicine, Nat. Bd. Med. Examiners. Intern in medicine Barnes Hosp., St. Louis, 1982-83, jr. resident in medicine, 1983-84; rsch./clin. fellow in allergy and immunology Dept. of Rheumatology and Immunology Brigham and Women's Hosp., Boston, 1985-88; assoc. in medicine Washington U., 1982-85; rsch. fellow in medicine Harvard Med. Sch., 1985-88, instr. in pediatrics, 1988-90; instr. Southwestern Med. Sch., 1991-92, U. Tex. Health Sci., 1992—; staff Santa Rosa Healthcare, San Antonio, 1992—, Southwest Gen. Hosp., San Antonio, 1992—, Methodist Hosp., San Antonio, 1992—. Contbr. munerous articles to med. jours. Recipient Vice Chancellor for Student Affairs Honor, 1982, Honor Grad. award Am. Med. Women's Assn., Schering Rsch. award. Fellow Am. Coll. Allergy; mem. Am. Acad. Allergy and Immunology (mem. com. asthma mortality 1987—), Tex. Med. Assn., Bexar County Med. Soc. Home: 11 Inwood Terrace Dr San Antonio TX 78248-1657 Office: 205 E Evergreen St San Antonio TX 78212-4316

KAMEN, REBECCA ANN, sculptor, art educator; b. Phila., July 8, 1950; d. Isadore and Arden (Goldman) K. BS in Art Edn., Pa. State U., 1972; MS in Art Edn., U. Ill., 1973; MFA in Sculpture, R.I. Sch. of Design, 1978. lectr. in field; symposium panel Roanoke (Va.) Mus. Art, 1992, Nat. Sculpture Conf., Cin., 1987. One-woman shows include Arnold and Porter, Washington, 1985, Brody's Gallery, Washington, 1986, Leslie Cecil Gallery, N.Y.C., 1987, Winston Gallery, Washington, 1988, Mid. Tenn. State U., Mufreesboro, 1988, Jones Troyer Fitzpatrick Gallery, Washington, 1990, 92, Corland Jessup Gallery, Provincetown, Mass., 1993, McLean (Va.) Project for Arts, 1994; exhibited in group shows at Corcoran Gallery Art, Washington, 1980, 81, Miss. Mus. Art, Jackson, 1982, Artscape '83, '87, Balt., 1983, Pleiades Gallery, N.Y.C., 1983, School 33 Art Ctr., Balt., 1983, Balt. Mus. Fine Arts, 1984, Pub. Art Trust, Washington, 1984, 86, The Athenanium, 1985, Alexandria (Va.) Sculpture Festival, 1986, Gallery Z, N.Y.C., 1987, Little Rock Art Ctr., 1987, Cumberland Gallery, Nashville, 1989, Md. Art Place, Balt., 1989, Phila. Art Alliance, 1989, Danville (Va.) Mus. Fine Arts and History, 1989, Strathmore Hall Arts Ctr., Rockville, Md., 1989, Peninsula Fine Arts Ctr., Newport-News, Va., 1989, 92, (traveling) 93, Tartt Gallery, Washington, 1990, Acad. of Arts, Easton, Md., 1991, Roanoke (Va.) Mus. Arts, 1992, Sheffield City (Eng.) Poly., 1992, Bentley-Tomlinson Gallery, Scottsdale, Ariz., 1993, Elipse Art Ctr., Arlington, Va., 1994, Ctr. Creative Imaging, Camden, Maine, 1994; works published in (books) (Virginia Watson Jones) Contemporary American Woman Sculptors, 1986, (Jules and Nancy Heller) Encyclopedia of 20th Century North American Woman Artists, 1994, numerous newspapers and journals. Home: 2846 Summerfield Rd Falls Church VA 22042 Office: No Va CC 3001 N Beauregard St Alexandria VA 22311-5065

KAMERY, ROB HERLONG, economics educator, management consultant; b. Plainfield, N.J., Apr. 16, 1955; s. Lester Weidmann and Mary Ann (Padgett) K. BBA, U. Miss., 1976; MS, Winthrop Coll., Rockhill, S.C., 1978, U. Ark., 1981, 82. Fin. analyst Control Data Corp., Charlotte, N.C., 1978; tchr. Charlotte (N.C.)-Mecklenburg Schs., 1977-78; lectr. Memphis State U., 1978-79; instr. econs. Christian Bros. U., Memphis, 1979-83, asst. prof., 1987-94, assoc. prof., 1994—; vis. asst. prof. U. Ark., Fayetteville, 1982-83; cons. U.S. Army C.E., Memphis, 1988—. Contbr. articles to profl. jours., also monographs. Lt. USN, 1983-87, mem. Res. Mem. Soc. for Advancement Mgmt., Am. Econ. Assn., Missouri Valley Econ. Assn., Delta Sigma Pi (life), Pi Sigma Epsilon, Tau Kappa Epsilon (nat. advisor 1979). Republican. Office: Christian Bros U 650 E Parkway S Memphis TN 38104-5519

KAMINSKY, MANFRED STEPHAN, physicist; b. Koenigsberg, Germany, June 4, 1929; came to U.S., 1958; s. Stephan and Kaethe (Gieger) K.; m. Elisabeth Moellering, May 1, 1957; children: Cornelia B., Mark-Peter. First diploma in physics, U. Rostock, Germany, 1951; Ph.D. in Physics magna cum laude, U. Marburg, Germany, 1957. German Research Soc. fellow and grad. asst. in physics U. Rostock, 1950-52; lectr. Rostock Med. Tech. Sch., 1952; German Research Soc. fellow and research asst. Phys. Inst., U. Marburg, 1953-57, sr. asst., 1957-58; research asso. Argonne (Ill.) Nat. Lab., 1958-59, asst. physicist, 1959-62, assoc., 1962-70, sr. physicist, 1970-86, dir. Surface Sci. Center-CTR Program, 1974-80, dir. Tribology Program, 1984-86; sole propr. Surface Treatment Sci. Internat., Hinsdale, Ill., 1986—; cons. Office Tech. Assessment U.S. Congress, 1986, NRC com. on tribology, 1986-88; guest prof. Inst. Energy, U. Que., Montreal-Varennes, 1976-82; E.W. Mueller lectr. U. Wis., Milw., 1978; symposium chmn. Internat. Conf. Metall. Coatings, 1985-93. Author: Atomic and Ionic Impact Phenomena on Metal Surfaces, 1965; contbr. articles to profl. jours.; editor: Radiation Effects on Solid Surfaces, 1976; co-editor: Surface Effects on Controlled Fusion, 1974, Surface Effects in Controlled Fusion Devices, 1976, Dictionary of Terms for Vacuum Science and Technology, 1980. Bd. dirs. Com. 100, Hinsdale, 1970-75, 90-92, pres., 1973-74; pres. St. Vincent de Paul Soc., Hinsdale, 1972-73. Named Outstanding New Citizen of Year Citizenship Council Chgo., 1968; Japanese Soc. Promotion of Sci. fellow, 1982. Fellow Am. Phys. Soc.; mem. Am. Chem. Soc., Scientific Research Soc., Research Soc. Am., AASS, Union German Phys. Socs., Am. Vacuum Soc. (sr., trustee 1982-84, chmn. Midwest sect. 1967-68, co-founder Gt. Lakes chpt., dir. 1968-70, chmn. fusion tech. div. 1980-81, editorial bd. jour. 1978-83, hon. 1986), Internat. Union Vacuum Sci., Techs. and Applications (chmn. fusion div. 1984-86), Sigma Xi. Home: 906 S Park Ave Hinsdale IL 60521-4519 also: 300 Galen Dr Apt 506 Key Biscayne FL 33149 Office: Surface Treatment Sci Internat PO Box 175 Hinsdale IL 60522-0175

KAMM, DOROTHY LILA, art educator, artist, writer; b. Chgo., Apr. 6, 1957; d. Irving and Blanche (Topp) Kampf; m. Dean Steven Cohen, June 6, 1982; children: Erica Kamm-Cohen, Julia Kamm-Cohen. BFA, No. Ill. U., 1979; MFA, Sch. of Art Inst. of Chgo., 1984. Project dir. Michael Lopez Designs, Inc., Chgo., 1981-83; instr. dept. prof. arts MacCormac Jr. Coll., Chgo., 1981-84, profl. arts cons., 1986-87; mgr. merchandising design Robert Case & Assocs., Chgo., 1983; assoc., contbg. editor Visual Merchandising and Store Design, Cin., 1984-86; instr. Dayton (Ohio) Art Inst., 1985; columnist Dayton Daily News and Jour. Herald, 1985-87; artist, instr. Art Gallery at Smithfield, Stuart, Fla., 1988-94; instr. Martin County Coun. for the Arts, 1994—; judge art category Young Floridian Award, St. Lucie County, 1990—. Editor: Dorothy Kamm's Porcelain Collector's Companion, 1992—; contbr. articles to art jours. Mem. AAUW (founding mem., v.p. mem. 1987—, Poetry award 1988, 91), Questers (founding mem. 1996—), Internat. Porcelain Artists and Tchrs., Inc. (cert. artist and tchr., registered artist), Nat. League Am. Pen Women (founding mem., v.p. mem. 1989—, Honorable Mention in Nat. Letters Competition, Adult Non-Fiction Pub. Articles category 1994, Honorable Mention Dorothy Daniels Writing contest 1995, 3rd Pl. in Biennial Letters Competition/book manuscript Marjorie Davies Roller Non-Fiction award 1996), Art Assocs. of Martin County (Mert award 1993). Office: Porcelain Collectors Comp PO Box 7460 Port Saint Lucie FL 34985-7460

KAMO, YOSHINORI, sociology educator, writer; b. Ashikaga, Tochigi, Japan, June 20, 1958; arrived in U.S., 1983; s. Yutaka and Tamae (Iizuka) K.; m. Akiko Shimbo, March 21, 1982; children: Shota Jason, Kenta Sean. BA, Tokyo U., Japan, 1982; MA, U. Washington, Seattle, 1985; PhD, U. Washington, 1989. Rsch. asst. U. Washington, 1985-89; asst. prof. sociology La. State U., Baton Rouge, 1989-95, assoc. prof., 1995—; interpreter for Mr. and Mrs. Hattori in meeting with Pres. Clinton during Yoshi Hattori Shooting Trial, 1993. Author: A Japanese Boy Who Loved America: The Trial of Yoshi Hattori Shooting In Baton Rouge, 1993; editorial bd.: Rsch. On Aging, 1990—; contbr. to profl. jours. Mem. Am. Sociological Assn., So. Sociological Soc., Nat. Coun. Family Relations, Internat. Inst. Sociology. Home: 897 Baird Dr Baton Rouge LA 70808-5919 Office: La State U Dept Sociology Baton Rouge LA 70803

KAMP, ARTHUR JOSEPH, JR., lawyer; b. Rochester, N.Y., July 22, 1945; s. Arthur Joseph and Irene Catherine (Ehrstein) K.; m. Barbara Hays, Aug. 24, 1968. BA, SUNY, 1968, JD, 1970. Bar: N.Y. 1971, U.S. Dist. Ct. (we. dist.) N.Y. 1971, Va. 1973, U.S. Dist. Ct. (ea. dist.) Va. 1973. Atty. Neighborhood Legal Svcs., Buffalo, 1971; assoc. Diamonstein & Drucker, Newport News, Va., 1972-77; ptnr. Diamonstein, Drucker & Kamp, Newport News, 1977-84, Kamp & Kamp, Newport News, 1984-87, Kaufman & Canoles, 1987-96, David & Kamp, L.L.C., 1996—; v.p., Peninsula Legal Aid Ctr., Inc., 1978-92. Chmn. Newport News Planning Commn., 1994-95, commr., 1990—. Lt. USAF, 1971-72. Mem. ABA, Va. State Bar Assn., Newport News Bar Assn. (past bd. dirs., chmn. legal aid com.), Va. Bar Assn., Va. Peninsula C. of C. (bd. dirs., exec. com.). Democrat. Office: David & Kamp LLC 301 Hiden Blvd Ste 200 Newport News VA 23606

KAMP, GEORGE HAMIL, physician, radiology administrator; b. Little Rock, May 5, 1934; s. Henry W. and Georgia (Humberd) K.; m. Carol Bailey, Sept. 4, 1955 (div. 1984); m. Martha Ann Bauer, Nov. 16, 1984; children: Peter, Lisa Ramer, David, Marcus. BA with high honors, Hendrix Coll., 1956; MD with honors, U. Ark., 1960. Diplomate Am. Bd. Radiology. Resident in radiology U. Ark. Med. Ctr., Little Rock, 1961-63, chief radiology resident, 1963-64; physician U.S. Army Med. Corps, Ft. Dix, N.J., and South Vietnam, 1964-66; pvt. med. practice St. Francis Hosp., Tulsa, 1966—, chmn. radiology, 1990—, also bd. dirs.; bd. chancellors Am. Coll. Radiology, 1996—; mem. adv. com. Telemedicine of Fed. Communications Commn., 1996. Contbr. articles to profl. jours. Chmn. bd. dirs. Tulsa City-County Health Dept., 1981-91, mem. bd., 1978-91. Capt. U.S. Army, 1964-66, Vietnam. Fellow Am. Coll. Radiology (counselor for Okla. 1986-92, del. to AMA 1992—); mem. AMA (del. for Okla. 1988-91), Tulsa County Med. Soc. (pres. 1978), Okla. State Med. Assn. (pres. 1984-85, bd. dirs. 1982-88). Office: Saint Francis Hosp 6161 S Yale Ave Tulsa OK 74136-1902

KAMRAVA, MEHRAN, political scientist, educator; b. Karadj, Iran, Feb. 1, 1964; came to U.S., 1978; s. Hooshang and Efat (Randji) K. BA in Polit. Sci. and History, Calif. State U., Northridge, 1984; PhD in Social and Polit. Scis., U. Cambridge, Eng., 1989. Resident cons. Rand Corp., Santa Monica, Calif., 1987-88; rsch. dir. Inst. Internat. Studies, L.A., 1989-91; asst. prof. Rhodes Coll., Memphis, 1991-95, assoc. prof., 1995—. Author: Revolution in Iran: Roots of Turmoil, 1990, The Political History of Modern Iran: From Tribalism to Theocracy, 1992, Revolutionary Politics, 1992, Politics and Society in the Third World, 1993, Understanding Comparative Politics: A Framework for Analysis, 1996, Democrary in the Balance: Culture and Society in the Middle East, 1997; contbr. articles to profl. jours. and chpts. in books. J.S. Seidman Rsch. fellow Seieman Found., 1993-96. Home: 2730 Fletcher Crest Cove Cordova TN 38018 Office: Rhodes Coll 2000 N Parkway Memphis TN 38112-1624

KANAGY, STEVEN ALBERT, foundation administrator; b. Chgo., Sept. 26, 1956; s. John West and Hazel Elizibeth (Montgomery) K. Student, Kendall Coll., Evanston, Ill., 1974-76, W. Carey Coll., Hatiesburg, Miss., 1980, U. Southern Miss. Staff worker Longbeach Pub. Libr., Miss., 1978; mgr. Kanagy Art Found., Inc., Longbeach, Miss., 1982—; distbr. Amway Corp., Ada, Mich., 1984—; cmty. devel. explorer Harbour Dist., Gulfport, Miss., 1985-89, mng. ptnr., 1989—; mng. ptnr. Southeastern Restorations and Indsl. Trading, 1992—. Contbr. article to mag. Kendall Coll. scholar. Mem. Am. Mgmt. Assn., Nat. Trust for Hist. Preservation, Nat. Geographic Soc., Internat. Platform Assn., N.Am. Hunting Club. Republican. Roman Catholic. Home: PO Box 1014 Long Beach MS 39560

KANALY, STEVEN PATRICK, trust company executive; b. Oklahoma City, Aug. 9, 1953; s. E. Deane and Virginia Lee (Johnson) K.; m. Vicki Lynn Clemens, Feb. 9, 1989; children: Kamden Deane, Kourtney Louise. BBA in Fin. and Acctg., U. Tex., Austin, 1976. CFP, cert. trust and fin. advisor. With Fin. Synergies, Inc., Austin, Tex., 1974-76, The Kanaly Co., Houston, 1976-77; pres. Kanaly Trust Co., Houston, 1977—; adv. dir. Tanglewood Bank N.A., Houston, 1980-85; bd. dirs. Kanaly Trust Co.; speaker in field. Formerly chmn. adv. bd. Houston Symphony; formerly mem. exec. com. Muscular Dystrophy Assn. Am.; chpt. leader Am. Cancer Soc.; former team capt. United Way. Named One of America's Best Fin. Advisors, Worth mag., 1994. Mem. Inst. Cert. Trust Bankers, Inst. Cert. Fin. Planners, Nat. Assn. Personal Fin. Advisors, Houston Estate and Fin. Forum, Houston Bus. and Estate Planning Coun., Century Club of Coll. Bus. Adminstrn. and Grad. Sch. of Bus. at U. Tex. Austin, Houston Club, The Houstonian, Delta Tau Delta. Republican. Presbyterian. Office: Kanaly Trust Co Kanaly Trust Bldg 4550 Post Oak Place Dr Houston TX 77027-3106

KANE, RUTH ANNE, principal; b. Beaumont, Tex., Jan. 20, 1948; d. Lewis Barclay "Red" III and Lois Virginia (Metzke) Herring; m. Gabriel Christopher Kane, Apr. 27, 1974 (div. Sept. 24, 1980); children: David Kane, Elijah Kane. BS, U. Tex. at Austin, 1981; MEd, 1982, PhD, 1991. Cert. secondary English, Spanish, spl. edn., adminstrn. Tchr. Adventure Bound Sch., Charlottesville, Va., 1978-79, Austin State Sch., Tex., 1979-80, Clear Lake H.S., Houston, 1982-84, McCallum H.S., Austin, Tex., 1984-88; adminstrv. intern Fulmore Middle Sch., Austin, Tex., 1988; tchr. Travis H.S., Austin, Tex., 1988-89; asst. prin. Martin Jr. H.S., Austin, Tex., 1989-90, Reagan H.S., Austin, Tex., 1990-93; prin. Lanier H.S., Austin, Tex., 1993—; cons. Ednl. Svc. Ctr. Region XIII, Austin, Tex., 1989—; instr. ExCet Reviews, Austin, 1991—; test adminstr. Nat. Evaluation Sys., Mass., 1991-93. Co-author: Futurism in Education, 1988, Special Education ExCet Review Guide, 1993. Vol. AIDS Svcs. of Austin, Tex., 1993-94; mem. City of Austin Joint Truancy Task Force, Austin, 1993—, Leadership Austin, Tex., 1994-95. Recipient Career Advancement scholarship Bus. and Profl. Woman's Assn., 1980, Am. Bus. Women's Assn. scholarship Austin-Lake Travis chpt., Austin, Tex., 1980, 81, Jesse H. Jones scholarship Kappa Delta Pi Internat., 1990, Univ. fellowship U. Tex. at Austin, 1981. Mem. ASCD, Austin Assn. Secondary Sch. Adminstrs., Nat. Assn. Secondary Sch. Prin/ Tex/ Assn. Secondary Sch. Prin., Phi Delta Kappa, Delta Kappa Gamma. Home: 2704 Thrushwood Dr Austin TX 78757-6947 Office: Lanier H S 1201 Payton Gin Rd Austin TX 78758-6616

KANE, WILLIAM DUNCAN, JR., management educator; b. Boston, Jan. 17, 1936; m. Linda Overmyer, July 14, 1956; children: Duncan, Kristin, Lorin, Kevin, Robin, Jonathan. BA in History, La. Tech. U., 1970; MS in Systems Mgmt., U. So. Calif., 1973; PhD in Organizational Behavior, Cornell U., 1977. Commd. 2d lt. USAF, 1953, advanced through grades to sr. master sgt., 1970, ret., 1974—; faculty mem. Western Carolina U., Cullowhee, N.C., 1976—; chair faculty assembly U. N.C. System, Chapel Hill, 1993-94, 94-95. Dir. dist. 9B N.C. Wildlife Fedn., Raleigh, 1985—. Mem. Organizational Behavior Teaching Soc. (bd. dirs. 1979-82, asst. editor, 1988-94), Acad. Mgmt., AAUP (pres. N.C. conf. 1993-94), Phi Kappa Phi. Democrat. Roman Catholic. Home: PO Box 716 Cullowhee NC 28723 Office: Western Carolina U College Business Cullowhee NC 28723

KANELLIS, ANTHONY NICK, army officer, pilot; b. Kankakee, Ill., Dec. 17, 1960; s. Nick and Erna Kanellis. AA, Jefferson State U., 1983; BS in Finance, U. Ala., 1988; MA in Adminstrn., Ctrl. Mich. U., 1992. Commd. 2d lt. U.S. Army, 1980, advanced through grades to maj., 1989; pilot, ops. officer, manpower analyst U.S. Army, Atlanta, 1985-96; Res. coord., spl. ops. command Atlantic Command, Norfolk, Va., 1996—; loan adjustor South Trust Bank, Birmingham, 1983-85. Mem. Am. Soc. Mil. Comptrs., Res. Officers Assn., Jefferson State Alumni Assn. (pres. 1986-87). Home: PO Box 15488 Norfolk VA 23511

KANELLOS, NICOLÁS, foreign language and liberal studies educator, publisher; b. N.Y.C., Jan. 31, 1945; s. Constantino and Inés (de Choudens) K.; m. Cristelia Pérez, May 12, 1984; 1 child, Miguel José. BA, Fairleigh Dickinson U., 1966; MA, U. Tex., 1968, PhD, 1974; postgrad., U. Mex., Mexico City, 1964-65, U. Portugal, Lisbon, 1969-70. From asst. to assoc. prof. Ind. U. N.W., Gary, 1970-79; assoc. prof. U. Houston, 1979-85, prof., 1985—; founder, dir. Teatro Desengano del Pueblo, Gary, 1972-79; founder, pub. Arte Publico Press/U. Houston, 1979—; pub. The Americas Rev.; apptd. to Literature Policy Panel, Nat. Endowment for Arts, 1987; apptd. to Arts Adv. Com., Ednl. Testing Svc./The Coll. Bd., 1987; presenter papers in field assns., confs., univs., symposia U.S., Europe, Mex. Author: Mexican American Theatre: Legacy and Reality, Hispanic Bibliography, 1988, Biographical Dictionary of Hispanic Literature in the United States, 1989, The History of Hispanic Theatre in the United States up to World War II, 1990 (SW Con. Latin Am. Studies Book award 1991, Tex. Inst. Letters award 1991, San Antonio Conservation Soc. Book award, 1990), The Hispanic American Almanac: A Reference Work on Hispanics in the United States, 1993 (ALA award best reference work 1993); editor: Mexican American Theater, 1983, Las aventures de Don Chipote, Hispanic Theater in the United States, 1985 Short Fiction by U.S. Hispanic Authors, 1993; co-editor: Ginn Literature Series textbooks for h.s. English, Nuevos Pasos: Chicano and Puerto Rican Drama, 1979, 2d edit., 1989, Latino Short Fiction, 1980, Handbook of Hispanic Cultures in the United States 4 vols., 1993-94; mem. editorial bd. Latin Am. Theatre Rev., 1982—, Critica, 1983—, Confluencia, 1984—, Southwest Rev., 1990—, Latino Studies Jour., 1990—; contbr. numerous articles to profl. jours.; contbr. chpts to books; prodr. videos. Member Ind. Civil Rights Commn., Gary, 1974-75; mem. arts adv. com. N.Y. Coll. Bd., 1989—; lit. cons. NEA, Washington, 1985-90; pres. Bishop's Com. for the Spanish Speaking, Gary, 1974-76. Recipient Hispanic Heritage award Pres. Reagan, 1988, award Tex. Assn. Chicanos in Higher Edn., 1989, Commendation from Gov. Tex. for high standards of acad. excellence, 1989, Am. Book award pub., editor category, 1989; named 100 most Influentinal Hispanic in U.S. by Hispanic Bus. mag., 1989, 93; inducted Tex. Inst. Letters, 1984; NEH fellow, 1979, Eli Lilly Faculty Open fellow, 1976-77, Ford Found./Nat. Rsch. Coun. fellow, 1986-87, other awards, fellowships. Mem. Inst. Hispanic Culture of Houston, Hispanic Forum of Houston, Modern Lang. Assn. (N.Y.C. chpt.), Nat. Assn. Chicano Studies. Office: U Houston Arte Publico Press Houston TX 77204-2090*

KANG, BANN C., immunologist; b. Kyungnam, Korea, Mar. 4, 1939; d. Daeryong and Buni (Chung) K.; came to U.S., 1964, naturalized, 1976; A.B., Kyungpook Nat. U., 1959, M.D., 1963; m. U. Yun Ryo, Mar. 30, 1963. Intern, L.I. Jewish Hosp.-Queens Hosp. Center, Jamaica, N.Y., 1964-65, resident in medicine, 1965-67; teaching assoc. Kyungpook U. Hosp., Taegu, Korea, 1967-70; fellow in allergy and chest Creighton U., Omaha, 1970-71; fellow in allergy Henry Ford Hosp., Detroit, 1971-72; clin. instr. medicine U. Mich. Hosp., Ann Arbor, 1972-73; asst. prof. Chgo. Med. Sch., 1973-74; chief allergy-immunology Mt. Sinai Hosp., Chgo., 1975—; asst. prof. Rush Med. Sch., Chgo. 1975-84, assoc. prof., 1984-86; assoc. prof. U. Ky. Coll. Medicine, 1987-92, prof., 1992—; cons., 1976—, Nat. Heart, Lung, Blood Inst., 1979—; mem. Exptl. Transplantation Adv. Bd., Ill., 1985-86, Diagnostic and Therapeutic Tech. Assessment (AMA), 1987—, Gen. Clin. Rsch. Com. (NIH), 1989-93; adv. com. Ctr. for Biologics and Rsch., FDA, 1993-96; counselor Chgo. Med. Soc., 1984-86, mem. policy com., adv. com. to health dept. Chgo. and Cook County, 1984-86. Recipient NIH award U. Mich., 1972-73. Diplomate Am. Bd. Internal Medicine, Am. Bd. Allergy-Immunology. Fellow ACP, Am. Acad. Allergy; mem. Am. Fedn. Clin. Research, AMA, Inter-Asthma Assn. Contbr. over 50 articles to profl. jours. Home: 2716 Martinique Ln Lexington KY 40509-9509 Office: U Ky Coll Medicine K528 Albert B Chandler Med Ctr 800 Rose St Lexington KY 40536

KANG, MANJIT SINGH, geneticist, plant breeder; b. Punjab, India, Mar. 3, 1948; came to U.S., 1969, naturalized 1976; s. Gurdit Singh and Parminder Kaur (Brah) K.; m. Georgia Anna Crocker, Feb. 13, 1971. BS in Agr. with honors (India Council Agrl. Research scholar), Punjab Agrl. U., Ludhiana, India, 1968; MS, So. Ill. U., Edwardsville, 1971, MA in Botany, Carbondale, 1977; PhD, U. Mo., Columbia, 1977. Teaching asst. So. Ill. U., Edwardsville, 1969-71; research asst. plant and soil sci. So. Ill. U., Carbondale, 1971-72, preceptor plant and soil sci., 1972-74; grad. research asst. agronomy U. Mo., Columbia, 1974-77; research asso. Ctr. Biology of Natural Systems, Washington U., St. Louis, 1977; sr. plant breeder hybrid corn research sta. Cargill, Inc., St. Peter, Minn., 1977-78, research sta. mgr., 1979; research asso. agronomy U. Mo., 1980; asst. prof. genetics U. Fla. Everglades Rsch. and Edn. Ctr., Belle Glade, 1981-85; assoc. prof. agronomy La. State U., Baton Rouge, 1986-90, prof., 1990—. Author: Applied Quantitative Genetics, 1994; editor: Genotype-By-Environment Interaction, 1990, Genotype-By-Environment Interaction: New Perspectives, 1996. Contbr. articles to profl. jours. Mem. AAAS, Am. Soc. Agronomy, Am. Genetic Assn., Crop Sci. Soc. Am., Am. Soc. Sugar Cane Technologists, Internat. Soc. Plant Molecular Biology, Sigma Xi, Gamma Sigma Delta. Achievements include research on developing resistance to Aspergillus flavus and the carcinogen aflatoxin in maize grain. Home: 2477 Creekside Dr Baton Rouge LA 70810-6966 Office: La State U Dept Agronomy MB Sturgis Hall Baton Rouge LA 70803

KANG, SHIRLEY SEONG-YEON, meeting planner; b. Seoul, Korea, June 2, 1966; came to U.S., 1980; d. In Sung and Young Hee (Park) Cho; m. Hosul Kang, Sept. 12, 1992; 1 child, Carina. Hotel, restaurant & instit. mgmt., Va. Tech., 1989. Mgr. Vie de France Restaurant, McLean, Va., 1990-91; asst. conf. Crosspath Inc., Arlington, Va., 1991-92; coord. conf. JIL Sys., Inc., Arlington, 1992-94; planner meeting Cath. Charities USA, Alexandria, Va., 1994—. Mem. Am. Soc. Assn. Execs., Religious Conf. Mgmt. Assn., Korean-YMCA (adv. bd. 1990—). Office: Catholic Charities USA 1731 King St Ste 200 Alexandria VA 22314

KANGAS, DAVID MARTIN, army officer; b. Winchendon, Mass., June 12, 1957; s. Toivo Matti and Eleanor Amanda Kangas; m. Chong Suk Lee, Dec. 26, 1985; children: Alena, Esther. BS, Fitchburg (Mass.) State U., 1984; BSN, George Mason U., 1994; grad., Coll. Fin. Planning, Denver, 1990. RN, Wash. Commd. 2d lt. U.S. Army, 1984, advanced through grades to capt., 1990; platoon leader U.S. Army, Korea, 1984-86, comdr., 1986-87; comm. dir. U.S. Army, Fort Lewis, Wash., 1987-89; army recruiter U.S. Army, Red Bank, N.J., 1990-92; with U.S. Army, Fairfax, Va., 1992-94; med. and oncology staff nurse Madigan Army Med. Ctr., Tacoma, 1994—; registered nat. archives rschr. Author: Army Recruiting: The Untold Story, 1993; contbr. Garland's Ency. of the Korean War, 1994. Creator Hill 303 Meml. Project, Waegwan, South Korea, 1990. Named Cost Reduction Suggestor of the Yr., Ft. Sam Houston, 1995. Mem. Nursing Students Assn., Acad. Med.-Surg. Nursing. Home: 1674 S 60th St Tacoma WA 98408-2301

KANKANAHALLI, SRINIVAS, computer scientist, educator; b. Bangalore, India, May 7, 1960; came to U.S., 1985; s. Ramprasad Kanakapura and Sudha Ramprasad; m. Harini; 1 child, Sri Hari. BEng, Bangalore U., 1982; MTech, Indian Inst. Tech. Kanpur, 1985; PhD, N.Mex. State U., 1991. Rsch. engr. Indian Tel. Industries, Bangalore, 1982-83; UNIX sys. adminstr. U. S.C., Columbia, 1985; asst. prof. W.Va. U., Morgantown, 1990—; co-founder Cybermarche, Inc., Morgantown, 1994—. Mem. IEEE, Assn. Computing Machinery. Home: 3129 Sylvan Cir Morgantown WV 26505 Office: Dept Computer Sci Knapp Hall Morgantown WV 26505

KANNRY, SYBIL, retired psychotherapist, consultant, b. Tulsa, Okla., Oct. 1, 1931; d. Julius and Celia Bertha (Triger) Zeligson; children: Jeffrey Alan Shames, Erica Leslie Shames, Jonathan Adam Shames. Student U. Colo., 1949-51; BA, U. Okla., 1953; MSW, NYU, 1974. Diplomate in Clin. Social Work; cert. clin. social worker, N.Y., addiction counselor, employee assistance profl., alcoholism counselor, N.Y. Tchr. piano, Tulsa, 1956-61; psychiatric social worker Essex County Hosp., Cedar Grove, N.J., 1974-75, Rockland Psychiat. Ctr., Spring Valley, N.Y., 1975, adult team supr., 1975-78, adult team supr., Haverstraw, N.Y., 1978, clinic supr., Orangeburg, N.Y., 1978-83, clinic dir., Yonkers, N.Y., 1983-84; founder, dir. Indsl. Counseling Assocs., South Nyack, N.Y., 1982-84, Ctr. for Corp. and Cmty. Counseling, South Nyack, 1984-95; founder, pres. Tulsa Assn. for Childbirth Edn., 1957-59; adj. prof. psychology St. Thomas Aquinas Coll., Sparkill, N.Y., 1995. Fellow Soc. Clin. Social Work Psychotherapists; mem. Am. Assn. Marriage and Family Therapy (clin. mem.), Nat. Assn. Social Workers, Am. Orthopsychiat. Assn., Acad. Cert. Social Workers, Employee Assistance Profl. Assn., Soc. Clin. and Exptl. Hypnosis. Avocations: piano, tennis, travel. Home: 5860 Woodsway Dr Pfafftown NC 27040

KANTER, DONALD RICHARD, pharmaceutical and psychobiology researcher; b. Detroit, Jan. 22, 1951; s. Harry Richard and Dorothy May (Kelch) K.; m. Diane Lynn Fickert, July 9, 1971 (div. Sept. 1993); children: Sean Richard, Donald Mathew, Lauren Marie. B.A., Oakland U., Rochester, Mich., 1976; M.S., Eastern Mich. U., Ypsilanti, 1979; Ph.D., U. Cin., 1983. Instr. lectr. U. Cin., 1978-84; health scis. officer VA Med. Center, Cin., 1980-85; supr. med. affairs Genetic Systems, Seattle, 1985-88; dir. statistics, clin. rsch. Solvay Pharm.; cons. in field, Oakland U. grantee, 1976; NIMH grantee, 1984; VA merit grantee, 1984, Outstanding Contbn. Award, 1985. Mem. AAAS, Sigma Xi. Author: (with Karoly et al) Child Health Psychology, 1982; (with Daniel B. Berch) Sustained Attention in Human Performance, 1983; contbr. med. articles to profl. jours. Roman Catholic. Home and Office: 2034 Kinridge Trl Marietta GA 30062-1828 also: 901 Sawyer Rd Marietta GA 30062-2224

KANTER, L. ERICK, public relations executive; b. New Ulm, Tex., Dec. 15, 1942; s. Lawrence Kanter and Wilma A. Kellner; m. Mary Anne Meadows, Feb. 28, 1970. Staff reporter, Newsweek Mag., Houston, 1965-66, Newsweek Mag., Boston, 1970-71. Dir. media rels. U.S. Pay Bd. and Cost of Living Coun., Washington, 1971-74; dep. dir. pub. affairs NOAA, Washington, 1974-77; dir. pub. affairs White House Conf. on Econ. Devel., Washington, 1977-78, Presdl. Commn. on Coal Industry, Washington, 1978-80; cons. Energy Concepts, Inc., Washington, 1980-84; v.p. pub. info. and mktg. Investment Co. Inst., Washington, 1984-95; with Kanter & Assocs., Arlington, Va., 1995—. Co-author: Four Days, Forty Hours, 1970; editor: Final Report, White House Conference, 1978, Final Report, President's Commission on Coal, 1979. Lt. (j.g.) USN, 1967-69, Vietnam, the Pentagon. Mem. Nat. Press Club, Soc. Profl. Journalists. Office: Kanter & Assocs 3723 N Oakland St Arlington VA 22207

KANTIPONG, VARA P., allergist, immunologist, pediatrician; b. Chiang Mai, Thailand, 1944. MD, Chiengmai Hosp. U., 1968. Diplomate Am. Bd. Allergy and Immunology, Am. Bd. Pediatrics. Intern Jewish Hosp. U., Bklyn., 1970-71; resident in pediatrics St. Joseph Mercy Hosp., Pontiac, 1971-73, fellow in pediatric metabolism, 1973-75; fellow in allergy U. Tex. Health Sci. Ctr., San Antonio, 1980-82; staff mem. HCA Med Ctr., Plano, Tex. Mem. Am. Acad. Pediatrics, Am. Coll. Allergy and Immunology. Office: 3105 W 15th St Ste C Plano TX 75075-7700*

KANTNER, HELEN JOHNSON, church education administrator; b. Chgo., Oct. 22, 1936; d. Wilbert E. and Edna M. (Benson) Johnson; m. Robert O. Kantner, Aug. 22, 1959; children: Robert O. Jr., Sheryl Jackson. BA, Wheaton Coll., 1958; MS in Education, Youngstown State U., 1987. Asst. to prin. 1st Bapt. Day Sch., West Palm Beach, Fla., 1970-72; elem. tchr. Am. Heritage Schs., Ft. Lauderdale, Fla., 1973-76; social studies tchr. Champion High Sch., Warren, Ohio, 1977-88; edn. dir. Ocean Dr. Presbyn. Ch., North Myrtle Beach, S.C., 1988—. Vice pres. bd. dirs. Horry County (S.C.) Arts Coun.; bd. dirs. Christian Acad. of Myrtle Beach. Youngstown State U. scholar. Mem. NEA, Ohio Edn. Assn., Champion Classroom Tchrs. Home: 3610 Golf Ave Little River SC 29566-8024 Office: 410 6th Ave S North Myrtle Beach SC 29582-3306

KANTOR, DAVID SCOTT, insurance and tax consultant; b. Albermarle County, Apr. 21, 1959; s. Barry and Reatha Kantor; m. Sheryl Jean, Aug. 12, 1989; children: Zachary Taft, Alec Scott, Jake Tyler. Student, Va. Tech., Blacksburg, 1977-82. Pres. Kantor & Assocs. L.L.C., Virginia Beach, Va., 1988—. Mem. Gen. Agts. Mem. Assn., Norfolk Life Underwriters Assn., Nat. Life Underwriters Assn., Internat. Assn. for Fin. Planning, Million Dollar Round Table. Office: Kantor & Assocs LLC 208 Golden Oak Ct Ste 350 Virginia Beach VA 23452

KANTOR, ISAAC NORRIS, lawyer; b. Charleston, W.Va., Aug. 29, 1929; s. Israel and Rachel (Cohen) K.; m. Doris Sue Katz, June 17, 1956; children: Mark B., Cynthia Kantor Anderson, Beth Kantor Zachwieja. BA, Va. Mil. Inst., 1953; JD, W.Va. U., 1956. Bar: W.Va. 1956, U.S. Dist. Ct. (so. dist.) W.Va. 1956, U.S. Ct. Mil. Appeals 1957, U.S. Ct. Appeals (4th cir.) 1978, U.S. Dist. Ct. (no. dist.) W.Va. 1991. Ptnr Katz Katz and Kantor, Bluefield, W.Va., 1958-70, Katz Kantor Katz Perkins and Cameron, Bluefield, W.Va., 1970-82, Katz Kantor and Perkins, Bluefield, 1982—; town atty. Town of Bramwell, W.Va., 1970-75, Town of Petestown, W.Va., 1981-85; bd. dirs. Flat Top Nat. Bank, Bluefield, FCFT Inc., Bank Holding Co., Princeton, W.Va.; mem. vis. com. W.Va. U. Coll. Law, Morgantown, 1986-89. Parliamentarian W.Va. Dem. Exec. Com., 1964-68; co-chmn. W.Va. Gov.'s Jud. Selection Com., 1988—, mem. W.Va. Ethics Commn., 1995—; chmn. W.Va. div. Am. Cancer Soc., 1990-92, pres. New River Pkwy. Authority, 1996—. Capt. JAGC, USAF, 1956-58; mem. USAFR, 1953-61. Recipient Citizen of Yr. award Greater Bluefield Jaycees, 1980, Boss of Yr. award, 1992, St. George medal, Nat. Divsnl. award Am. Cancer Soc., 1993. Mem. W.Va. Trial Lawyers Assn. (pres. 1980-81), B'nai B'rith (pres. W.Va. coun. 1975-76). Jewish. Home: 231 Oakdell Ave Bluefield WV 24701-4840 Office: PO Box 727 Bluefield WV 24701-0727

KAO, RACE LI-CHAN, medical educator; b. Chungking, China, Dec. 1, 1943; came to U.S., 1967, naturalized, 1980; s. Yu-Ho and Tsing (Tsou) K.; m. Lidia Wei Liu, Aug. 18, 1969; children—Elizabeth, Grace. B.S., Nat. Taiwan U., 1965; M.S., U. Ill., 1971, Ph.D., 1972. Rsch. assoc. U. Ill., Urbana, 1972, Pa. State U., Hershey, 1972-75, asst. prof. physiology, 1976-77; asst. prof. surgery, physiology, biophysics U. Tex. Med. Br., Galveston, 1977-82, dir. cardiothoracic research, 1977-82; assoc. prof. surgery Washington U., St. Louis, 1982-83; dir. surg. rsch. Allegheny-Singer Rsch. Inst., Pitts., 1983-92; prof. surgery Med. Coll. Pa., Phila., 1988-92; prof., Carroll H. Long chair of excellence for surg. rsch. East Tenn. State U., Johnson City, 1992—; reviewer, cons. Nat. Heart, Blood and Lung Inst., NIH, 1984—. Contbr. numerous articles in field to profl. jours. Pres., U. Tex. Chinese Assn., 1980. Served with ROTC, Repub. of China, 1965-66. Nat. Taiwan U. Univ. scholar, 1962-65; grantee NIH, 1979—, Tex. Heart Assn., 1979-80, Upjohn Co., 1977-79, Pa. Heart Assn., 1986-89, Mo. Heart Assn., 1982-83. Mem. Coun. on Circulation, Coun. Basic Sci., Am. Heart Assn. Mem. Am. Physiol. Soc., Internat. Soc. Heart Rsch., Am. Soc. Artificial Internal Organs, Am. Inst. Biol. Sci., Nat. Soc. Med. Rsch., N.Y. Acad. Sci., AAAS, Nutrition Today Soc. Home: 4 Blackberry Ct Johnson City TN 37604-1466 Office: East Tenn State U Dept Surgery JH Quillen Coll Medicine Johnson City TN 37614-0575

KAO, TZU-MIN, physiatrist; b. Taiwan, 1939. MD, Kaohsiung Med. Coll., 1965. Diplomate Am. Bd. Physical Medicine and Rehab. Intern Christ Comm Hosp., Oak Lawn, 1967; resident in physical medicine and rehab. NYU Med. Ctr., 1968-70; fellow in physical medicine and rehab. U. Wash., Seattle, 1970-71; pvt. practice. Office: 4600 King St Ste 5J Alexandria VA 22302-1213*

KAPLAN, ANDREW JON, physician; b. N.Y.C., June 22, 1962; s. Michael Jay and Patricia (Fern) K.; m. Pamela Anne Shaw, June 7, 1987; children: Tamar Frances, Leah Rose. BA in Biochemistry, Washington U., St. Louis, 1983; MD, U. Tex. S.W., Dallas, 1987. Diplomate Am. Bd. Internal Medicine, Am. Bd. Cardiovascular Diseases; cert. Clin. Cardiac Electrophysiology Bd. Resident in internal medicine Duke U. Med. Ctr., Durham, N.C., 1987-90; fellow in cardiology sch. medicine Emory U., Atlanta, 1990-92, fellow in electrophysiology sch. medicine, 1992-93; chief resident in medicine, dir. electrophysiology Grady Meml. Hosp./Emory U., Atlanta, 1993-94. Contbr. articles to profl. jours. Mem. U.S. Holocaust Meml. Mus., Smithsonian Instn. Fellow S.W. Med. Found., 1985-87. Mem. AMA, ACP, Am. Coll. Cardiology (assoc.), Am. Coll. Chest Physicians, Am. Heart Assn., Am. Soc. Internal. Medicine, N.Am. Soc. Pacing and Electrophysiology, Med. Assn. Ga., Med. Assn. Atlanta, Phi Delta Epsilon. Democrat. Jewish. Home: 4302 N 56th Pl Phoenix AZ 85018

KAPLAN, CHARLES PAUL, real estate development association executive, educator, geographer, consultant; b. Chgo., Nov. 16, 1942; s. Charles Basil and Theresa (Shabatura) Fedun; m. Patricia Ann Barnett, Apr. 6, 1968 (div. July 1976); m. Carol Ann Willoughby, Sept. 1, 1979 (div. 1991); children: Nicholas Paul Fedun, Nathan Charles Willoughby; m. Leanne Roethemeyer, Feb. 16, 1995. BA, DePaul U., 1968; MA, U. Chgo., 1972, PhD, 1976. Cert. assn. exec. Product scheduling mgr. IBM, Chgo., 1960-68; rsch. assoc. U. Chgo., 1969-75, Mellon Found. fellow Ctr. for Urban Studies, 1970-75; prof. U. Houston, 1975-79; program mgr. U.S. Census Bur., Washington, 1979-81; dir. policy planning U.S. Synthetic Fuels Corp., Washington, 1981-84; exec. dir. Nat. Assn. Indsl. and Office Pks., San Antonio, 1984—; cons. Indsl. Rels. Ctr., U. Chgo., 1970-74, Internat. Survey Rsch. Corp., Chgo., 1974-87; mem. faculty Grad. Sch. Social and Policy Scis., U. Tex., San Antonio, 1987—, cons. to dean Sch. Engring., 1987—; pres. CPK & Assocs., 1979—. Co-author: Land Use, Urban Form and Environmental Quality, 1974, The Social Burdens of Environmental Pollution, 1977, Census '80, 1980; contbr. over 100 articles on urban and regional change to profl. publs. Bd. dirs., mem. exec. com. Target '90: Goals for San Antonio, 1985-90; mem. adv. bd. U. Tex. Sch. Architecture, 1988-94; chmn. Pub. Affairs Coun. San Antonio, 1985-90; chmn. Brooks AFB devel. Opportunities com. San Antonio City Coun., 1986-87, chmn. fin. and adminstrv. incentive to retain and rehabilitate landmark resources com., 1987-90. With USN, 1966-68. Mem. Concord Club. Mem. Ukrainian Cath. Ch. Home: 113 Sage Oaks Tr Boerne TX 78006

KAPLAN, DEBRA ARLENE, writer, photographer, media consultant; b. Torrington, Conn., June 17, 1952; d. Edward and Frieda (Schlesinger) K. A in Mass Comms., Becker Coll., Worcester, Mass., 1972. Staff writer Worcester Sales and News Recorder, 1972-73; entertainment writer Worcester Post, 1973-74; advt. sales WOTW AM/FM, Nashua, N.H., 1974-76; reporter Hartford Courant, Litchfield, Conn., 1976-78; staff writer, bus. editor, entertainment editor, City Hall reporter, Valley Wide reporter, polit. columnist Ansonia (Conn.) Evening Sentinel, 1978-88; promotions dir. Subway World Hdqrs., Milford, Conn., 1988-89; staff writer Sun Newspapers, Orlando, Fla., 1989-90; freelance writer Orlando, 1991-92; staff writer Apopka (Fla.) Chief, 1992-97; staff writer pub. rels. dept. Villages of Lady Lake (Fla.), 1997—. Mem. Fla. Hosp. Women's Adv. Coun., Apopka, 1994-96; mentor Orange County Compact, Orlando, 1989-90; vice chmn. programming Valley Arts Coun., Ansonia, 1986-88; bd. dirs. Valley chpt. Am. Heart Assn., 1985-88. Recipient Best Med. Series award Cmty. Health Ctrs. Am., 1992, 3d pl. sports story award Fla. Press Assn., 1995, Best Med. Series award Am. Cancer Soc., 1986. Jewish.

KAPLAN, EDWARD DAVID, lawyer; b. Newburgh, N.Y., Nov. 18, 1929; s. Sidney L. and Lucille C. (Toback) K.; m. Ursula L. Appel, Aug. 23, 1955; children—Karyn Joyce, Gayle Susan. B.A., Middlebury Coll., 1952; LL.B., Bklyn. Law Sch., 1957, J.S.D., 1957. Bar: N.Y. 1957, U.S. Dist. Ct. (so. dist.) N.Y. 1957, Tex. 1989. Sole practice, Newburgh, N.Y., 1957-68; ptnr. Finkelstein, Kaplan, Levine, Gittlesohn & Tetenbaum, Newburgh, 1968—; legal counsel N.Y. State Jaycees, 1964-65. Pres. Newburgh Area Indsl. Devel., 1975—; faculty Tex. Coll. Trial Advocacy, 1985—. Served with U.S. Army, 1952-54, Korea. Recipient Disting. Service award Newburgh Jaycees, 1965. Mem. Assn. Trial Lawyers Am., N.Y. State Trial Lawyers, N.Y. Bar Assn., Pa. Trial Lawyers, Tex. Trial Lawyers, Jaycees, Orange County Bar Assn. (pres. 1983-84). Jewish. Office: Fellow Roscoe Pound Foundation 12531 Elm Country Ln San Antonio TX 78230-2701

KAPLAN, EUGENE HERBERT, academic psychoanalyst; b. N.Y.C., Nov. 13, 1925; s. Samuel Wiener and Bertha Laura (Abramson) K.; m. Sarane Lenore Rosenberg, Aug. 17, 1952 (dec. May 1983); children: Saul James, Robert Edward, Aaron Val, Daniel John, Matthew William. BS in Chemistry, U. Mich., 1947; MD, NYU, 1951. Diplomate Am. Bd. Neurology and Psychiatry; cert. in psychoanalysis. Intern Presbyn. Hosp., Chgo., 1951-52; psychiat. resident Bellevue Hosp., N.Y.C., 1952-53, Hillside Hosp., Glen Oaks, N.Y., 1953-55; asst. clin. prof. Albert Einstein Coll. of Medicine, Bronx, 1964-70; clin. asst. prof. SUNY Downstate Med. Ctr., Bklyn., 1970-78; assoc. prof. clin. psychiat. SUNY, Stony Brook, 1973-83; clin. assoc. prof. Cornell U. Med. Coll., N.Y.C., 1983-85; prof. neuropsychiat. U. S.C. Sch. Medicine, Columbia, 1985—; affiliated staff psychoanalyst N.Y. Psychoanalytic Inst., 1960-68; sr. investigator Deaf Infant Nursery, Lexington Sch., Jackson Heights, 1975-79; asst. dir. U. N.C.-Duke U. Psychoanalytic, Chapel Hill, 1992—. Author: (with W.H. Wieder) Drugs Don't Take People, 1974; contbr. articles to profl. jours. With U.S. Army, 1943-46. Decorated Combat Inf. badge, Bronze Star, Purple Heart. Fellow Am. Psychiat. Assn. (life), Am. Soc. for Adolescent Psychiatry (life); mem. Am. Psychoanalytic Assn. (life, diplomate), Am. Psychosomatic Soc. (life). Jewish. Office: U SC Sch Medicine 3555 Harden Street Ext # 104A Columbia SC 29203-6815

KAPLAN, HYMAN M., internist; b. Atlanta, Feb. 16, 1942; s. Oscar and Rosalee (Clein) K.; m. Susan Miller, Aug. 21,1966; children: charles Ryan, Stacy Lynn. BA, Emory U., 1964; MD, Ga. Med. Coll., 1968. Diplomate Am. Bd. Internal Medicine, Am. Bd. Allergy and Immunology. Resident in internal medicine Ga. Med. Coll., Augusta, 1969-71; resident in allergy and immunology Walter Reed Army Hosp., Washington, 1971-73; practice medicine specializing in internal medicine and allergy and immunology Chattanooga, 1975—; clin. assoc. prof. medicine Chattanooga unit U. Tenn., 1976—. Served to maj. M.C., U.S. Army, 1971-75. Mem. Fellow ACP, Am. Acad. Allergy and Immunology; mem. AMA, Tenn. Med. Assn., Chattanooga Med. Assn. Office: 6624 Lee Hwy Chattanooga TN 37421-2421

KAPLAN, (NORMA) JEAN GAITHER, reading specialist, retired educator; b. Cumberland, Md., Dec. 14, 1927; d. Frank Preston and Elizabeth (Mcneil) Gaither; m. Robert Lewis Kaplan, Dec. 4, 1959; 1 child, Benjamin Leigh. AB in Edn., Madison Coll., Harrisonburg, Va., 1950; MA in Edn., U. Va., 1956; postgrad., U. Va., William and Mary, 1958-61; reading specialist degree, U. Va., 1976. Tchr. Frederick County Sch. System, Winchester, Va., 1950-51, Washington County Sch. System, Hagerstown, Md., 1951-55, Charlottesville (Va.) Sch. System, 1955-60, York County (Va.) Sch. System, 1962, Newport News Sch. System, Denbigh, Va., 1963, Internat. Sch. Bangkok, 1965-67; tutor Reston Reading Ctr., Fairfax County, Va., 1972-74; tutor homebound, substitute tchr. Fairfax County Sch. Systems, 1974-78; pvt. practice pvt. tutor McLean/Middleburg, Va., 1978-89; pres. Tutorial Svcs., Inc., McLean, 1985-87; sec. The Rumson Corp., Middleburg, 1981—. Mem. No. Va. Conservation Coun., Fairfax County, 1976-81; bd. dirs. Nat. Environ. Leadership Coun.; active Piedmont Environ. Coun. Mem. AAUW, LWV, Bangkok Am. Wives Assn., Tuesday Afternoon Club (pres. 1974-75, treas. 1995-96), Ayr Hill Garden Club, Soc. John Gaither Descs. Inc., Kappa Delta Pi, Alpha Sigma Tau. Home and Office: PO Box 1943 Middleburg VA 20118-1943

KAPLAN, JOCELYN RAE, financial planning firm executive; b. Lynbrook, N.Y., Apr. 23, 1952; d. Eugene S. and Adeline (Dembo) K. B.S., Northwestern U., 1975. Cert. fin. planner. Ins. agt. Fidelity Union Life Ins. Co., College Park, Md., 1976-77, Bankers Life Ins. Co., Rockville, Md., 1977-80; fin. planner Reutemann & Wagner, McLean, Va., 1980-82; fin. planning casewriter McLean Fin. Group, 1982-83; dir. fin. planning DeSanto Naftal Co., Vienna, Va., 1983-85; pres. Advisors Fin., Inc., Falls Church, Va., 1985—. Founding mem., treas. Congregation Bet Mishpachah, Washington, 1981, v.p., 1982, pres., 1983. Recipient Nat. Quality award Nat. Assn. Life Underwriters, 1978; Agt. of Yr. award Gen. Agt. and Mgrs. Assn., 1978. Mem. Internat. Assn. Fin. Planners, Inst. Cert. Fin. Planners, Registry of Fin. Planning Practitioners. Home: 1029 N Stuart St # 308 Arlington VA 22201 Office: Advisors Fin Inc 510 N Washington St # 300 Falls Church VA 22046-3537

KAPLAN, JUDITH HELENE, corporate professional; b. N.Y.C., July 20, 1938; d. Abraham and Ruth (Kiffel) Letich; m. Warren Kaplan, Dec. 31, 1958; children: Ronald Scott, Elissa Aynn. BA, Hunter Coll., 1955; postgrad., New Sch. for Social Rsch., 1955-56. Registered rep. Herzfeld & Stern, N.Y.C., 1963; agt. New York Life Ins. Co., N.Y.C., 1964-69; registered rep. Scheinman, Hochstin & Trotta, 1969-70; v.p. Alpha Capital Corp., N.Y.C., 1970-74; pres. Tipex, Inc., N.Y.C., 1966-84; v.p. Alpha Pub. Relations, N.Y.C., 1970-73; pres. Utopia Recreations Corp., 1971-73, Howard Beach Recreation Corp., 1972-73; chmn. bd. Alpha Exec. Planning Corp., 1970-72; field underwriter N.Y. Life Ins. Co., 1974-75; pres. Action Products Internat. Inc., 1978-87, chairperson, 1980—, Ronel Industries, Inc., 1982-84; pres. Orlando Orange, Inc., 1995; participant White House Conf. on Small Bus., 1979; founder Women's History Mus., Judith Kaplan & Warren Kaplan's Women's History Collection Cen. Fla. C.C., Ocala, 1991; advisor Kaplan Women's History Collection CFCC Found., Ocala, Fla. Author: Woman Suffrage, 1977; co-author: Space Patches-from Mercury to the Space Shuttle, 1986; contbg. editor: Stamp Show News, M & H Philatelic Report; creator, producer Women's History series of First Day Covers, 1976-81; contbr. articles to profl. jours. Active Wyo. adv. on woman suffrage; trustee Found. for Innovative Lifelong Edn. Inc., 1986-88; owner Orlando Orange, Inc. Profl. Baseball Team, 1995-96; bd. dirs. Ctrl. Fla. Regional Libr., 1996—. Named Outstanding Young Citizen Manhattan Jaycees, Small Bus. Person of Yr. State of Fla, 1986. Mem. NOW (ins. coord. nat. task force on taxes, v.p. N.Y. chpt., co-founder Ocala/Marion County chpt. 1982, bd. women's adv. coun. Ocala and Marion Counties 1986-88), Nat. Women's Polit. Caucus, Women Leaders Round Table, Nat. Assn. Life Underwriters, Assn. Stamp Dealers Am., Am. First Day Cover Soc. (life), Am. Philatelic Soc. (life), Bus. and Profl. Women, AAUW. Home: 2901 SW 41st St Apt 3508 Ocala FL 34474-7424 Office: 344 Cypress Rd Ocala FL 34472-3102

KAPLAN, KERRY JOSEPH, internist, cardiologist; b. Louisville, June 23, 1950; s. Robert and Barbara Helen (Rudin) K.; m. Leslie Diamond, Dec. 31, 1973 (div.); 1 child, Lauren Elyse; m. Debra Jill Levine, Sept. 1, 1985; children: Zachary Aron, Jori Lee, Alyson Bari. BS, Northwestern U., Evanston, Ill., 1972; MD, Northwestern U., Chgo., 1974. Diplomate Am. Bd. Internal Medicine, Am. Bd. Cardiovascular Disease, Am. Bd. Critical Care Medicine. Intern Northwestern U. Med. Sch., 1974-75, resident in internal medicine, 1975-77, fellow in cardiology, 1977-79; pvt. practice Clearwater, Fla., 1988—; attending physician, assoc. dir. med. intensive care area Northwestern U. Med. Sch., Chgo., 1979-88; pres. med. staff Mease Hosp., Dunedin, Fla., 1993; bd. dirs. Morton Plant Mease Hosp. Pres. Temple Ahavat Shalom, Palm Harbor, Fla., 1992-94. Fellow ACP, Am. Coll. Cardiology. Home: 1522 Silver Moon Ln Palm Harbor FL 34683-2108 Office: Coastal Cardiology Cons 34041 Us Highway 19 N Ste A Palm Harbor FL 34684-2648

KAPLAN, LAURA GARCIA, emergency and disaster preparedness consultant; b. Hollywood, Fla., Mar. 11, 1957; d. Thomas Tubens and Felicia (Acebal) Garcia; 1 child, Kristin. BSEE, U. Miami, 1979. Utilities exec. Fla. Power and Light Co., Miami, 1980-93, ops. mgr. Dade County, 1991-93; pres. L.G.K. Assocs., Inc., Ft. Lauderdale, Fla., 1993—. Author: Disaster Can Happen Anywhere in the World. . .Are You Prepared?, 1994, Emergency and Disaster Planning Manual, 1996. Counselor Soc. Abused Children, Kendall, Fla., 1985-86; instr. Jr. Achievement, Miami, 1986-87, Adult Illiteracy Program, 1987; bd. dirs. YWCA, 1988-92, Convenant House, 1995-96. Early admission scholar U. Miami, 1975; recipient Hurricane Andrew Hero award Dade County Rebuilding Program. Mem. Leadership Miami Assn., Greater Miami C. of C. Republican. Roman Catholic. Club: Hurricane. Office: LGK Assocs Inc 3100 SW 133rd Ter Davie FL 33330-4610

KAPLAN, LEE LANDA, lawyer; b. Houston, Jan. 26, 1952; s. Charles Irving and Ara Celine (Seligman) K.; m. Diana Morton Hudson, Feb. 6, 1982. AB, Princeton U., 1973; JD, U. Tex., 1976. Bar: Tex., U.S. Dist. Ct. (no., we., ea. and so. dists.) Tex., U.S. Ct. Appeals (5th, 11th and Fed. cirs.), U.S Supreme Ct. Law clk. to sr. cir. judge U.S. Ct. Appeals (5th cir.), Houston, 1976-77; assoc. Baker & Botts, L.L.P., Houston, 1977-84, ptnr., 1985-94; ptnr. Smyser Kaplan & Veselka, L.L.P., Houston, 1995—. Mem. Tex. Aerospace Commn., 1994—. Mem. ABA, State Bar Tex., Houston Bar Assn., Am. Intellectual Property Law Assn., Houston Intellectual Property Law Assn. Democrat. Jewish. Office: Smyser Kaplan & Veselka LLP Ste 2300 700 Louisiana St Houston TX 77002

KAPLAN, MARTIN P., allergist, immunologist, pediatrician; b. Bklyn., Oct. 28, 1928. MD, SUNY Downstate. Diplomate Am. Bd. Allergy & Immunology, Am. Bd. Pediatrics. Resident Jewish Hosp., Bklyn., 1954-55, SUNY Upstate Med. Ctr., Syracuse, 1957-58; fellow Children's Hosp., Washington, 1958-59; active staff mem. dept. medicine St. Joseph Hosp., Lexington, Ky., 1959—; clin. assoc. prof. pediatrics and medicine U. Ky. Coll. Medicine, 1989—. Mem. AAACI, ACAI, AMA, Ky. Med. Assn. Office: 2370 Nicholasville Rd Ste 102 Lexington KY 40503-3014

KAPLAN, PHILIP A., fitness professional; b. N.Y.C., Apr. 25, 1960; s. Harvey J. and Sally (Groman) K. Cert. personal fitness trainer Am. Coun. on Exercise. Nat. dir. svc. Scandinavian Health Spas, Akron, Ohio, 1986-88; pres. Personal Devel. Svcs., Fort Lauderdale, Fla., 1988—, Personal and Club Devel., Inc., Fort Lauderdale, 1990—; v.p. S.E. ops. Am. Leisure Corp., N.Y.C., 1992—; spkr. Internat. Health and Racquet Sportsclub Assn., Boston, 1991—, Club Industry, Fort Washington, Pa., 1993—. Author: Careers in Fitness, 1992, Mind and Muscle: Fitness for All of You, 1995, (book and audio cassette program) The Body You Love, 1996; pub. Health and Wealth Newsletter, 1992-96. Mem. Internat. Assn. Fitness Profls. Office: PA Kaplan and Assocs 1304 SW 160th Ave # 337 Fort Lauderdale FL 33326-1902

KAPLAN, TED ADAM, pediatrician, educator; b. Miami Beach, Nov. 30, 1961; s. Paul Richard and Loretta (Madell) K.; m. Lisa Nicole Sessoms, Sept. 29, 1988; children: Aaron Joseph, Isaac Abraham, Rivka Aviva. BA cum laude in Biochem. Scis., Harvard U., 1982; MD, U. Miami Sch. Medicine, 1986. Diplomate Am. Bd. Pediatrics. Intern in pediatrics U. Miami/Jackson Meml. Children's Hosp. Ctr., 1986-87, resident in pediatrics, 1987-89; rsch. asst. prof. dept. exercise sci. U. Miami, 1989—; dir. Children's Sports & Exercise Medicine Ctr., South Miami, 1989-94; attending physician Jackson Meml. Hosp. pediatric emergency room, 1989—, Dade County Schs. sports medicine program, 1987-95; founder, dir. pediatric exercise medicine svc. and exercise lab. U. Miami Sch. Medicine, 1989-95, asst. prof. clin. pediatrics, 1989-96, assoc. prof., 1996—; med. dir. Boggy Creek Gang Camp, 1995-96; clin. asst. prof. pediatrics U. Fla. Coll. Medicine, 1995-96; staff physician dept. pediatrics South Miami Hosp., 1989-95, Miami Children's Hosp., 1989-96, Sanford Pediatric Assocs., 1996—; team physician Coral Gables H.S., 1987-95, South Miami H.S., 1990-92, Miami Jackson H.S., 1987-90; apptd. mem. athletic adv. com. Dade County Sch. Bd., 1989-95; mem. Dade County Pub. Schs. Health Adv. Com., 1993-95; cons. Nuclear Regulatory Commn., 1990; organizer, dir. cystic fibrosis exercise program Doctor's Hosp., Coral Gables, 1990; lectr. in field. Asst. scoutmaster Troop 64 Boy Scouts Am., 1982-90. Fellow Am. Acad. Pediatrics (sect. on adolescent health 1990-92, sect. on sports medicine 1991—), Am. Coll. Sports Medicine (pediatric exercise com. 1993-97); mem. Am. Med. Soc. Sports Medicine (charter), Ctrl. Fla. Pediatric Soc., Fla. Pediatric Soc., Fla. Med. Assn., Dade County Med. Assn., N.Am. Soc. Pediatric Medicine. Jewish. Home: 102 Little Oak Ln Altamonte Springs FL 32714-6501 Office: Sanford Pediatric Assocs Hole in the Wall Gang Camp 209 San Carlos Ave Sanford FL 32721

KAPNICK, HARVEY EDWARD, JR., retired corporate executive; b. Palmyra, Mich., June 16, 1925; s. Harvey E. and Beatrice (Bancroft) K.; m. Jean Bradshaw, Apr. 5, 1947 (dec. 1962); m. Mary Redus Johnson, Aug. 5, 1963; children—David Johnson, Richard Bradshaw, Scott Bancroft. Student, James Miliken U., 1942-44; B.S., Cleary Coll., 1947, D.Sc. in Bus. Adminstrn. (hon.), 1971; MBA, U. Mich., 1948; D.H.L. (hon.), DePauw U., 1979. C.P.A., Ill. Mem. staff, mgr. Arthur Andersen & Co. (CPAs), Chgo., 1948-56, partner, 1956-62; mng. ptnr. Arthur Andersen & Co. (CPAs), Cleve., 1962-70; chmn., chief exec. Arthur Andersen & Co. (CPAs), 1970-79; dep. chmn. 1st Chgo. Corp., 1st Nat. Bank Chgo., 1979-80; pres. Kapnick Investment Co., 1980-84, 89—; chmn., pres., CEO Chgo. Pacific Corp., 1984-89; vice chmn. Gen. Dynamics, 1991-94, retired, 1994; past mem. Adv. Com. on Internat. Investment, TEch. and Devel., Adv. Com. for Trade Negotiations. Pres.'s Commn. on Pension Policy, Ill. Fiscal Commn., 1977; Adv. Com. Fed. Consol. Fin. Statements, 1976-78; life trustee Mus. Sci. and Industry, Northwestern U., Meninger Found., Orchestral Assn., Lyric Opera Chgo. 2d lt. USAAF, 1943-46. Clubs: Met. (Washington); Mid-America (gov. 1971-76, treas. 1974-76), Chgo., Univ., Indian Hill, Comml. (Chgo.), Naples Yacht, Hole-in-Wall, Port Royal. Home: 1500 Sheridan Rd Apt 1H Wilmette IL 60091 also: 4000 Rum Row Naples FL 34102 Office: 1300 Third St S Naples FL 34102-7239

KAPNICK, S. JASON, oncologist; b. Providence, Mar. 28, 1949; s. I.H. and Martha (Shaulson) K.; children: Senta, Isrel, Sesselja Edda. BLS summa cum laude, boston U., 1974; MD, Harvard Med. Sch., 1981. Surg. rsch. assoc. Harvard Med. Sch., Boston, 1976-77, assoc. in ob/gyn., lectr., 1981-85, instr. in gynecology, 1985-87; cons. in gynecologic oncology Dand Falber Cancer Inst., Boston, 1985-87; clin. fallow Am. Cancer Soc., Boston, 1985-87; dir. gynecol. oncology Good Samaritan Med. Ctr., West Palm Beach, Fla., 1989—; asst. cons. prof. gynecol. oncology Duke U. Med. Ctr., Durham, N.C., 1994—; reviewer of rsch. submissions Cancer med. jour., Bethesda, Md., 1995—; invited lectr. Good Samaritan Cancer Ctr., 1995, Palm Beach County Hosps., 1990—, Am. Cancer Soc., Bethesda, 1995. Contbr. articles on colon, breast, and female pelvic cancers to profl. jours. Vol., contbr. Ctr. for Family Svcs., West Palm Beach, 1992—; bd. dirs. Palm Beach Opera, 1992—. Mem. Harvard Club of Palm Beach. Office: Good Samaritan Med Ctr Dept Gynecol Oncology 1411 N Flagler Dr West Palm Beach FL 33401-3404

KAPPA, MARGARET MCCAFFREY, resort hotel consultant; b. Wabasha, Minn., May 14, 1921; d. Joseph Hugh and Verna Mae (Anderson) McCaffrey; B.S. in Hotel Mgmt., Cornell U., 1944; grad. Dale Carnegie course, 1978; cert. hospitality housekeeping exec.; m. Nicholas Francis Kappa, Sept. 15, 1956; children—Nicholas Joseph, Christopher Francis. Asst. exec. housekeeper Kahler Hotel, Rochester, Minn., 1944; exec. housekeeper St. Paul Hotel, 1944-47, Plaza Hotel, N.Y.C., 1947-51; exec. housekeeper, personnel dir. Athearn Hotel, Oshkosh, Wis., 1952-58; dir. housekeeping The Greenbrier, White Sulphur Springs, W.Va., 1958-84; cons., 1984—; tchr. housekeeping U.S. and fgn. countries; cons.; vis. lectr. Cornell U. Author: (with others) Managing Housekeeping Operations, 1989. Pres. St. Charles Borromeo Parish Assn., White Sulphur Springs, 1962, v.p., 1980, 82; tech. adv., host 2 ednl. videos Am. Hotel and Motel Assn., 1986; host Kappa on Kleaning for video Spectra Vision AHMA Ednl. Inst, 1994. Recipient diploma of honor Société Culinaire Philanthropique, 1961, Lamp of Knowledge award for promotion of professionalism Am. Hotel and Motel Assn., 1995. Mem. AARP, Cornell Soc. Hotelmen (pres. 1980-81, exec. com. 1981-82), Nat. Exec. Housekeepers Assn. (pres. N.Y. chpt. 1950), N.Y.U. Hotel and Restaurant Soc. (hon. life), Nat. Woman's Quota (charter mem. Greenbrier County), St. Charles Parish Assn., White Sulphur Springs Busy Bees, AARP, Senior Friends. Republican. Roman Catholic. Home and Office: 207 Azalea Trl White Sulphur Springs WV 24986-2001

KAPPATOS, KONSTANTINOS NICHOLAS, engineering executive; b. Ceffalonia, Greece; came to U.S., 1969; s. Nicholas Kappatos and Denise Kavadias; married, Dec. 4, 1988; children: Nicole, Christos. BSEE, Va. Poly. Inst. and State U., 1974; MSEE, George Washington U., 1977. Registered profl. engr. Va., Del. Sys. planning engr. Potomal Electric Power Co., Washington, 1974-77; elec. engr. Rural Electrification Adminstrn., Washington, 1974-77; sr. cons. Dalton Assocs. P.C., Fairfax, Va., 1982-84; v.p. engring. and ops. Old Dominion Elec. Coop., Glen Allen, Va., 1984—; mem. several coms. relating to electric utility coop. bus. Old Dominion/Va., Md. and Del. Assn./Nat. Rural Electric Coop. Assn., Richmond and Washington, 1984—. Registered lobbyist Va., Md. and Del. Assn., Richmond, 1984—. Officer Merchant Marines, Eng., 1961-67; officer Greek Royal Navy, 1967-69. Recipient Superior Achievement award USDA, 1990. Mem. NSPE. Home: 11516 Bridgetender Dr Richmond VA 23233 Office: Old Dominion Elec Coop 4201 Dominion Blvd Glen Allen VA 23060

KAPPELER, JANA SNAPP, publisher; b. Carlisle, Ky., Feb. 22, 1959; d. James Russell and Carolyn Jane (Delaney) Snapp; m. Victor Eugene Kappeler, Dec. 12, 1980; 1 child, Aaron Eugene. AS, Ea. Ky. U., 1979; BA, Eastern Ky. U., 1993; student, Cen. Mo. State U., 1990-91. Sr. patient account clk. Blue Grass Regional Mental Health Mental Retardation, Lexington, Ky., 1979-80; staff asst. dept. phys. therapy U. Ky., Lexington, 1980-82, adminstrv. asst. dept. mgmt., 1982-85; adminstrv. asst. dept. music Sam Houston State U., Huntsville, Tex., 1985-88; owner, pub. Alpha Enterprises, Richmond, Ky., 1989—. Reviewer Pub. Criminal Justice Jour., 1990—, Criminal Justice Newsletter, 1993—; pub., mng. editor Police Liability Rev., 1990—, Police Computer Rev., 1992-95; pub. Police Forum, 1991—, Police Futurist, 1993—, Jour. Offender Monitoring, 1994—. Mem. hospitality com. PTA Reese Sch., Warrensburg, Mo., 1990; historian PTA Ridgeview Sch., Warrensburg, 1991. Mem. Police Futurists Soc.

KAPTUROWSKI, EDWARD JAMES, electrical engineer; b. Shamokin, Pa., Aug. 14, 1951; m. Caroline Louise Kiehne, Sept. 6, 1981. BSEE, Pa. State U., 1973, MS in Computer Engring., 1988. Elec. engr. Uniform Tubes, Inc., Collegeville, Pa., 1973-78; project engr. Harris Corp., Champlain, N.Y., 1978-85; controls engr. ACS Inc., Malvern, Pa., 1988-89; sr. systems engr./architect Bell & Howell, Inc., Durham, N.C., 1989—. Mem. IEEE, IEEE Computer Soc., IEEE Info. Theory Soc. Home: 4801 Daysprings Ct Apex NC 27502 Office: Bell & Howell 3908 Patriot Dr Durham NC 27709

KARAU, JON OLIN, judge; b. Shelby, Mich., Sept. 15, 1918; s. Edward Karl and Pearl Margaret (Ackerman) K.; m. Luella Gay Nichols, Feb. 14, 1945 (dec. 1982); m. Lana Lee Lovelace, Jan. 15, 1983 (div. 1992); 1 child, Larry Jon; m. Louise Rogers, Sept. 17, 1995; 1 child, Bruce. BSIE, Can. Inst., Windsor, 1947; LLD, Detroit Coll. Law, 1956. Payroll auditor Fisher Body div., Flint, Mich., 1940-47; with Avery Corp., Detroit, 1947-49; supr. blueprint rm. Detroit Arsenal, 1949-59; specs. writer U.S. Govt.-Navy, Port Hueneme, 1959-63; specs. supr. U.S. Govt.-DSA, Detroit/Washington, 1963-68; sr. mgmt. officer USAF, Washington, 1968-73; stockbroker EGT-J.O. Karau Assocs., Sherman, Tex., 1973-78; mcpl. judge City of Pottsboro, Tex., 1978-90; ret.; cons. Grayson C.C., Denison, 1981; with Reiki Wellness Ctr., Denison, Tex. 1993—. Contbr. articles to profl. jours. Bd. dirs. ARC, Sherman, 1974-77, Campfire Denison; chmn. Grayson County Housing Authority, Sherman, 1986—. With U.S. Army, 1943-45, ETO; lt. col. USAR and Guards, 1947-85. Mem. Internat. Assn. Fin. Planning, Am. Inst. Mgmt., Am. Inst. Fin., Am. Inst. Indsl. Engrs., U.S. Def. Forces Assn., Tex. Mcpl. Cts. Assn., Tex. Judges Assn. (cons.), Mensa, Elks, Lions (regional chmn.), MAsons, Epsilon Delta Chi. Democrat. Home: RR 3 Box 528 H Pottsboro TX 75076-0907

KARCH, ROBERT E., real estate company executive; b. Bklyn., May 30, 1933; s. Charles H. and Etta R. (Becker) K.; AB, Syracuse U., 1953, MBA, 1958; student in Russian, Army Lang. Sch., Monterey, Calif., 1953-54; m. Brenda Schechter, Sept. 7, 1958; children: Barry S., Karen D., Brian D. With Nationwide Beauty & Barber Supply Co., Syracuse, N.Y., 1956-87, pres., 1966-74, chmn., 1974-87, also dir.; sales mgr. Helen of Troy Corp., El Paso, Tex., 1974-76, v.p. sales and mktg., 1976-79, also dir.; v.p., dir. Bormex Constrn. Inc., 1980-81; pres. The Prudential BKB, Realtors, 1994—; pres. Prudential BKB Realtors, Inc. (formerly BKB Properties, 1978—, Southwest Rental Svcs., 1992—; ptnr. BKB Ins. Agy., 1987-89; instr. investment real estate Acad. Real Estate, 1984-88. Pres. Syracuse Hebrew Day Sch., 1972-73. Served with U.S. Army, 1953-56. Lic. real estate broker, Tex., N.Mex., Colo.; lic. comml. pilot. Mem. Beauty and Barber Supply Inst., Direct Mail/Mktg. Assn., Aircraft Owners and Pilots Assn., Real Estate Securities and Syndication Inst., El Paso Real Estate Investment Club (pres. 1985), Jewish War Vets., El Paso Aviation Assn., El Paso Bd. Realtors (comml. investment div., mem. Exchangers Club, Top Vol. Producer award 1984, 85, 86, Best Real Estate Exchange award 1986), El Paso Apt. Assn., Coronado Country Club, Lancer's Club, Vista Hills Country Club. Author: Data Processing for Beauty/Barber Dealers, 1968. Pub. Real Estate Investor's Newsletter, 1982-87, Property Mgmt. Newsletter, 1985—. Home: 6016 Torrey Pines Dr El Paso TX 79912-2030 Office: Prudential BKB, Realtors 10622A Montwood Dr El Paso TX 79935-2704 also: 400 Shadow Mountain Dr El Paso TX 79912-4030 also: 5300 McNutt Rd PO Box 1748 Santa Teresa NM 88008-1748

KAREH, AHMAD RAGHEB, civil engineer; b. Damascus, Syria, Jan. 12, 1960; came to U.S., 1982; s. Ragheb and Fatima (Abou-Amin) K. BS summa cum laude in Civil Engring., La. Tech. U., 1984, MS in Engring., 1986. Registered profl. engr., Fla. Teaching asst. La. Tech. U., Ruston, 1984-87; staff engr. McManus Consulting Engrs., Monroe, La., 1987-88; project mgr. Alpha Engring. of Lee County, Inc., Ft. Myers, Fla., 1988-91; pres. Pokorny & Kareh, Inc., Ft. Myers, 1991—. Mem. Water Environment Fedn., 1986—. Mem. NSPE, ASCE, Am. Concrete Inst. (past pres., v.p., sec.-treas. Fla. Gulf chpt.), Fla. Engring. Soc., Kiwanis, Gamma Beta Phi, Phi Kappa Phi, Tau Beta Pi, Chi Epsilon, Pi Mu Epsilon, Sigma Tau Delta, Omicron Delta Epsilon. Home: 4232 Country Club Blvd Cape Coral FL 33904-5237 Office: Pokorny & Kareh Inc 1342 Colonial Blvd Ste 24 Fort Myers FL 33907-1004

KARFF, SAMUEL EGAL, rabbi; b. Phila., Sept. 19, 1931; s. Louis and Reba (Margalit) K.; m. Joan Mag, June 29, 1959; children: Rachel Karff Weissenstein, Amy Karff Halevy, Elizabeth Karff Kampf. AB magna cum laude, Harvard U., 1953; MAHL, DHL, Hebrew Union Coll., 1956. Rabbi Congregation Beth Israel, Hartford, Conn., 1958-60, Temple Beth El, Flint, Mich., 1960-62, Chgo. Sinai Congregation, 1962-74; sr. rabbi Congregation Beth Israel, Houston, 1975—; lectr. U. Chgo. Divinity Sch., 1968-75; vis. assoc. prof. U. Notre Dame, 1966-67; adj. prof. religious studies Rice U., Houston, 1976—. Author: Agada: The Language of Jewish Faith, 1970; editor Centennial Vol. Hebrew Union Coll.-Jewish Inst. of Religion, 1981-84; contbr. chpts. Judaism Religions of the World, 1982. Bd. dirs. United Way, Houston, 1991—, Inst. Religion, Houston, 1990—. Recipient Homiletics award HUC-JIR, Cin., 1956; John Harvard scholar Harvard U., 1951-52. Mem. Cen. Conf. Am. Rabbis (pres. 1989-91), Houston Philos. Soc., Phi Beta Kappa, Kiwanis. Office: Congregation Beth Israel 5600 N Braeswood Blvd Houston TX 77096-2901

KARGER, DELMAR WILLIAM, author, consultant, investor; b. Cape Girardeau, Mo., May 9, 1913; s. Ernest J. and Clara M. (Hellewege) K.; m. Paula E. Miller, July 5, 1935 (dec. Nov. 1958); children—Bonnie E., Karen R., Joyce P.; m. Edith Kennedy Loring, Jan. 11, 1962 (dec. Aug. 1969); m. Ruth Lounsberry Rivard, Oct. 31, 1970. Student, S.E. Mo. State Coll., 1931-32; B.S. in Elec. Engring, Valparaiso U., 1935; M.S. in Gen. Engring, U. Pitts., 1947. Registered profl. engr., Pa. Insp., surveyor C.E. U.S. Army, 1935; asst. chief electrician (E.E.) Internat. Harvester Co., 1935-39; acting chief elec. engr., 1939-40; asst. plant engr. Internat. Harvester Co., 1941-42; hdqrs. asst. chief mfg. engr., mfg. and repair divsn. Westinghouse Electric Corp., 1942-45, mgr. coop. edn. and all scholarship/fellowship programs, 1945-47; plant mgr. Pa. Electric Coil Corp., Pitts., 1947-49; mgr. orgn. systems and procedures Victor divsn. RCA, 1949-50; chief indsl. engr. RCA Service Corp., 1950-51; mgmt. cons. Booz, Allen & Hamilton, N.Y.C., 1951; chief plant and indsl. engr. Magnavox Co., 1951-58, mgr. new products govt. and indsl. products divsn., 1958-59; prof., head dept. mgmt. engring. Rensselaer Poly. Inst., Troy, N.Y., 1959-63, founding dean Sch. Mgmt., 1963-70, Ford Found. prof. mgmt., 1970-78; pres., dir. Randac Systems, Inc., Troy, 1961-63; dir. Golub Corp., Schenectady, 1963-68, Inst. for Resource Mgmt., Bethesda, Md., 1967-68; past dir. Fiber Glass Industries, Inc., Amsterdam, N.Y., Wellington Tech. Industries, Madison, Ga., Bunker Ramo Corp., Oak Brook, Ill., Scott & Fetzer Co., Lakewood, Ohio; dir. Info. Systems Inc., Arlington, Va.; ind. mgmt. cons. Author: (with F. Bayha) Engineered Work Measurement, 1957, 4th edit., 1986, The New Product, 1960, La Mesure Rationelle du Travail, 1962, (with R.G. Murdick) Managing Engineering and Research, 1969, 3d edit., 1980, (with A.B. Jack) Problems of Small Business in Developing and Exploiting New Products, 1963, (with R.G. Murdick) New Product Venture Management, 1972, (with R.G. Murdick) Long Range Planning and Corporate Strategy (manual and guide), 1977, 78, How to Choose a Career, 1978, (with W.C. Hancock) Advanced Work Measurement, 1982, Strategic Planning and Management: The Key to Corporate Success, 1991. Former mem. fin. com., bd. dirs. N.Y. div. Am. Cancer Soc. Recipient McKinsey prize for article on mgmt., 1967; Wiley prize as disting. faculty mem., 1978. Fellow AAAS, Am. Inst. Indsl. Engrs. (past nat. v.p., dir. inter-soc. affairs), Soc. Advancement Mgmt. (regional v.p.), Methods-Time Measurement Assn. Stds. and Rsch. (pres. 1958-60); mem. Acad. Mgmt. (past dir.), New Product Mgmt. and Devel. Assn. (v.p., dir.), DeFuniak Springs C. of C. (past dir.). Presbyterian. Home: 404 Circle Dr De Funiak Springs FL 32433-2565

KARIBO, JOHN MICHAEL, allergist, immunologist, pediatrician; b. Louisville, Ky., 1930. MD, U. Louisville. Diplomate Am. Bd. Allergy and Immunology, Am. Bd. Pediatrics. Intern St. Joseph Infirmary, 1963-64, resident, 1964-65; resident Children's Hosp., Louisville, 1965-66; fellow Cin., 1966-67. Office: 1261 Goss Ave Louisville KY 40217-1239*

KARLSON, KARL HENRIK, JR., pediatrician, educator; b. Plainfield, N.J., May 26, 1946; s. Karl Henrik and Jean Hall (Dundon) K.; m. Marilyn Katherine Naufftus, June 12, 1971; children: Mary Katherine, Karl William. BA with honors, Colgate U., 1968; MD, Tulane Med. Sch., 1972. Diplomate Am. Bd. Pediatrics, sub bd. in pulmonology. Pediatric resident Tulane Svc. Charity Hosp., New Orleans, 1972-74; pediatric pulmonology fellow Tulane Med. Sch., New Orleans, 1974-76; pediatric critical care fellow Mass. Gen. Hosp. and Harvard Med. Sch., Boston, 1976-77; asst. prof. pediatrics Tulane Med. Sch., New Orleans, 1977-78; asst. prof. pediatrics Med. Coll. Ga., Augusta, 1978-83, assoc. prof., 1983-87; assoc. prof. pediatrics U. Ark. Med. Scis., Little Rock, 1987-94, Eastern Va. Med. Sch., Norfolk, 1994—; dir. pediatric critical care Tulane Med. Sch., New Orleans, 1977-78; dir. cystic fibrosis ctr. Med. Coll. Ga., Augusta, 1978-87, Ark. Children's Hosp., Little Rock, 1987-94. Contbr. articles to profl. jours. Bd. dirs. Am. Lung Assn. Ga., Atlanta, 1980-86; med. advisor Ga. chpt. Cystic Fibrosis Found., Atlanta, 1979-87; bd. mem. Ga. Lung Assn., East Ctrl. br., Augusta, 1979-87. Fellow Am. Acad. Pediatrics, Am. Coll. Chest Physicians; mem. Am. Thoracic Soc.,Am. Sleep Disorders Soc., European Respiratory Soc. Office: Children's Hosp King's Daughters 601 Children's Ln Norfolk VA 23507

KARLSON, KEVIN WADE, trial, forensic, and clinical psychologist, consultant; b. Madison, S.D., Sept. 23, 1952; s. Howard Earl and Merna Eunice (Pearson) K. BS in Psychology, S.D. State U., 1974; MA in Clin. Psychology, Tex. Christian U., 1976; PhD in Clin. Psychology, U. Tex. Southwestern Med. Ctr., Dallas, 1983; JD, So. Meth. U., 1984. Lic. psychologist; cert. health svc. provider, Tex.; mem. Nat. Register Health Svc. Providers in Psychology. Counseling psychologist Tex. Christian U., Ft. Worth, 1975-77; psychology intern U. Tex. Southwestern Med. Ctr., 1978-80, Fed. Correctional Instr., Ft. Worth, 1980-81; psychol. assoc. Charles A. Kluge P.C., Dallas, 1981-84; pvt. practice forensic & clin. psychology Dallas, 1984-91; prin., trial cons. Trial Psychology Inst., Dallas, 1991-94; exec. devel. coach Leadership Devel. Ctr. Tex. Instruments, Dallas, 1994—; chair Tex. Psychology Polit. Action Com., 1989-91; adj. faculty U. Tex. Southwestern Med. Ctr. 1985—. Author: Loving Your Children Better, 1991; co-author: Child Care Screening System, 1993, Uniform Child Custody Evaluation System, 1993; contbg. author: Psychiatric and Psychological Evidence, 1987; contbr. chpt. to book. Pres. Children's Arts and Ideas Found., Dallas, 1989-90; bd. dirs. Sammons Ctr. for the Arts, Dallas.; mem. Dallas County Mental Health Assn., 1984—. Mem. APA, Tex. Psychol. Assn. (chair legis. com. 1986-91), Dallas Bar Assn. (grievance com.), Dallas Psychol. Assn. (chair ethics com. 1990-92), Brookhaven Country Club, Phi Alpha Delta. Republican.

KARNES, LUCIA ROONEY, psychologist; b. Moncton, N.B., Can., Mar. 9, 1921; d. Charles William and Jean Waring (Robson) Rooney; m. Thomas Campbell Karnes, June 7, 1946; children; Eleanore, Campbell, Timothy, Charles. BS, Ga. State Coll., 1942; MA, Emory U., 1946; PhD, U. N.C., 1967. Tchr. Decatur Girls High, Decatur, Ga., 1942-46; tchr. Summit Sch.,

Winston-Salem, N.C., 1947; prof. Salem Coll., Winston-Salem, 1949-54, 60-77; lang. therapist Bowman Grey Sch. Medicine, Winston-Salem, 1950-57, Orton Reading Ctr., Winston-Salem, 1957-72; dir. Ctr. for Spl. Edn., Salem Coll., Winston-Salem, 1972-77; pvt. practice psychology Winston-Salem, 1977—; dyslexic cons. Jefferson Acad., Winston-Salem, 1980—, Greenfield Sch., Wilson, 1986—, Wingate (N.C.) Coll., 1988—. Creator Using Computers in Psychology courses, 1972; author (video) Teaching Dyslexics, 1975. Founder, pres. state bd. LWV, Winston-Salem, 1953; pres. state bd. AAUW, Winston-Salem, 1950-54; bd. dirs. YWCA, Winston-Salem, 1950-54; v.p. bd. dirs. Arts Coun., Winston-Salem, 1954-60. Named Outstanding Reading Tchr., Reading Assn., Winston-Salem, 1982; fellow Orton-Gillingham Acad. Mem. APA, Orton Dyslexia Soc. (v.p. bd. dirs. 1960-77), N.C. Psychol. Assn., Assn. for Children with Learning Disabilities (v.p. bd. dirs. 1972—, Orton-Gillingham Acad. fellow), Sorosis Club, Delta Kappa Gamma. Democrat. Presbyterian. Home: 200 Lamplighter Cir Winston Salem NC 27104-3419

KARNS, BARRY WAYNE, lawyer; b. Baton Rouge, Aug. 28, 1946; s. William G. and Margery N. (Lanehart) K.; children: David Adam, Julie Shannon, Shelby Allison. BSBA, La. State U., 1968, JD, 1971. Bar: La. 1971; CPA, La. Asst. dir. La. State Bond Commn., 1973-78, dir., 1978-80; first asst. state treas. State of La., Baton Rouge, 1980-85; sr. v.p. Donaldson, Lufkin & Jenrette Securities Corp., Baton Rouge, 1985-88; atty. Brooks and McCollister Joint Venture, 1989-91, sr. atty. dept. ins., 1991-92. dep. gen. counsel, 1992—; treas. La Capitol Fed. Credit Union, 1979-86; lectr. Chmn., Dep. Sheriffs Supplemental Pay Bd., 1980-85; chmn. investment commn. La. Employees Retirement System, 1982-85; chmn. Kiwanis Found. Baton Rouge, Inc., 1980-84. La. State U. scholar, 1964-68. Mem. Phi Alpha Delta, Delta Sigma Pi. Democrat. Baptist. Office: PO Box 94214 Baton Rouge LA 70804-9214

KAROW, ARMAND MONFORT, medical facility executive; b. New Orleans, Nov. 11, 1941; s. Armand M. and Eunice Louise (Durham) K.; m. Ramona Evelyn McClelland, Sept. 5, 1964; children: Christopher A., Jonathan C. BA, Duke U., 1962; PhD, U. Miss. Med. Ctr., 1968. Lic. clin. lab. dir. Asst. prof. Med. Coll. Ga., Augusta, 1968-70, assoc. prof., 1970-75, prof., 1975—; pres., founder Xytex Corp., Augusta, 1975—; early scientific rsch. on tissue cryopreservation led to the establishment of Xytex Corp. in 1975 as one of the first clin. sperm banks; cons. on tissue preservation to U.S. Govt./NIH; cons. FDA. Editor: Organ Preservation for Transplantation, 1974, 2nd edit. 1981, Biophysics of Organ Cryopreservation, 1987; contbr. articles to profl. jours. Recipient Silver medal for Meritorious Svc. Am. Heart Assn., Ga. Affiliate, Atlanta, 1978, Disting. Faculty award Med. Coll. Ga., 1983; fellow NEH, Washington, 1980, sr. internat. fellow Fogarty Ctr., NIH, Washington, 1981. Fellow AAAS; mem. Am. Soc. Pharmacology and Exptl. Therapeutics, Am. Assn. Tissue Banks, Am. Soc. for Reproductive Medicine, Biotech. Industry Orgn. (bd. dirs. emerging cos. sect. 1993-94), European Soc. for Human Reproduction and Embryology, Soc. for Cryobiology (editl. bd. 1976—, bd. govs. 1977-80, 92—), Sigma Xi. Methodist. Office: Xytex Corp 1100 Emmett St Augusta GA 30904-5826

KARP, WARREN BILL, medical and dental educator, researcher; b. Bklyn., Feb. 12, 1944; m. Nancy Virginia Blanchard, Jan. 4, 1976; children: Heather Anna, Michael Aaron. BS in Chemistry, Pace U., 1965; PhD, Ohio State U., 1970; DMD, Med. Coll. Ga., 1977. Accredited by Coll. of Am. Pathologists. Grad. teaching asst. physiol. chemistry, 1966-68; grad. rsch. assoc. physiol. chemistry Ohio State U., 1968-70, postdoctoral rsch. assoc. pediatrics, 1970-71; with Med. Coll. Ga., Augusta, 1971—; prof. Sch. Grad. Studies Med. Coll. Ga., 1988—, prof. oral diagnosis and patient care svcs., 1988—, prof. oral biology, 1988—, prof. pediatrics, 1988—, prof. biochemistry and molecular biology, 1991—; dir. clin. perinatal lab. Med. Coll. Ga. Hosps. and Clinics, 1977—; dir. nutritional cons. svcs. Med. Coll. Ga. Dental Sch., 1987—; rsch. chmn. Ga. Nutrition Coun., 1989-90; lectr. and speaker in field. Author: Cadmium in the Environment: Part 2, Health Effects, 1981, Vitamin E in Neonatology, 1986; peer reviewer Pediatrics, 1984—, Jour. Pediatrics, 1985—; contbr. articles to profl. jours. Grantee EPA, 1971-75, Biomed. Rsch. Support, 1973, 80-81, Roche Labs., 1985-86, Am. Diabetes Assn., 1986, Am. Cyanamid Co., 1989-90, Dept. Pediatrics Rsch. Support, 1992-93. Mem. AAAS, Am. Chem. Soc., Am. Assn. Dental Rsch., Am. Heart Assn. (grantee 1981-82, nutrition com. 1988-91, health site com. 1990-91), N.Y. Acad. Scis., Ga. Inst. Human Nutrition, Ga. Perinatal Assn., Ga. Nutrition Coun. (rsch. chmn. 1989-90, nominating com. 1990-91), Internat. Assn. Dental Rsch., So. Soc. Pediatric Rsch., Sigma Xi (membership chmn. 1971-75, 78-80, awards com. 1979-80, treas. 1980-84, audtior 1985-86, pres. 1987-88). Home: 402 Hastings Pl Augusta GA 30907-9546 Office: Med Coll Ga Pediatrics Dept Bldg 114 Augusta GA 30912

KARPISCAK, JOHN, III, engineer, army officer; b. Teaneck, N.J., Nov. 11, 1957; s. John and Norma Lina (Alfano) K.; m. Linda Sue Anderson, June 11, 1983. AS, Mercer County Coll., 1977; BArch, Kans. State U., 1981; MBA, Rider Coll., 1983. Commd 2d lt. U.S. Army, 1983, advanced through grades to capt., 1986; platoon leader D Co. 52nd Battalion, Ft. Bliss, Tex., 1984, 43rd Engr. Co. 3rd Armored Cav., Ft. Bliss, Tex., 1984-85; exec. officer 43rd Engr. Co. 3rd Armored Cav., Ft. Bliss, 1985; architect Directorate Engring. and Housing., Ft. Bliss; battalion adj. 169th Engr. Battalion, Ft. Leonard Wood, Mo., 1987-88; commdr. Hdqrs. Co. 1st Engr. Brigade, Ft. Leonard Wood, 1988-89; space action officer U.S. Army Engr. Sch., Ft. Leonard Wood, 1989-91; bn. motor officer 802d Engr. Bn., Camp Humphreys, Republic of Korea, 1991-92; naval spl. ops. officer Naval Space Command, Dahlgren, Va., 1992-94; sr. engr. Allied Signal Tech. Svcs. Corp., Washington, 1994-95; scientist with U.S. Army Topographic Engring. Ctr., Alexandria, Va., 1995—. Fellow Explorer's Club; mem. AIAA, Brit. Interplanetary Soc., Armed Forces Comm. and Electronics Assn., Planetary Soc. Republican. Lutheran. Home: 1802 Genther Ln Fredericksburg VA 22401-5207 Office: US Army Topographic Engring Ctr Alexandria VA 22315

KARPISCAK, LINDA SUE, pediatrics nurse; b. Elizabeth, N.J., Mar. 10, 1958; d. Elof Folke and Margaret Florence (Cummings) Anderson; m. John Karpiscak III, June 11, 1983. BSN, Trenton State Coll., 1980. RN, Mo., Va., Tex.; cert. BCLS, NALS. Charge nurse postpartum/antepartum St. Elizabeth Hosp., Elizabeth, N.J., 1981-84; staff nurse pediatrics surg. unit Children's Hosp. Newark, 1980; staff nurse neonatal ICU, pediatrics ICU Providence Meml. Hosp., El Paso, Tex., 1984-85; staff nurse nursery Vista Hills Med. Ctr., El Paso, Tex., 1985-87; staff nurse mother-baby unit Alexandria (Va.) Hosp., 1987; home health nurse Mo. Home Care, Rolla, Mo., 1988-92; charge nurse nursery U.S. Army, Ft. Leonard Wood, Mo., 1989-92; staff nurse NICU Mary Washington Hosp., Fredericksburg, Va., 1992-94; supr. personal care aide Competent Health Care, Manassas, Va., 1995—, home health nurse, 1995—. Home: 1802 Genther Ln Fredericksburg VA 22401-5207

KARSCHAU-LOWENFISH, SONJA, breed association executive, publisher; b. Hamburg, Germany, June 2, 1941; came to U.S., 1966; children: Martin A. Lowenfish, Anders F. Lowenfish. Diploma, Sch. Econ., Hamburg, 1962, Cambridge (Eng.) U., 1964, Madrid (Spain) U., 1966; BA in Biology, SUNY, Purchase, 1981; MA in Urban Planning, Manhattanville Coll., 1976. Cert. arbitrator Am. Arbitration Assn. Cons. HRH Saka Aleshinloye Oba of Ilorin, Nigeria, 1980-85; founder, pres. Am. Warmblood Registry, Dobbs Ferry, N.Y.; founder Am. Holsteiner Horse Assn., 1977—. Pub. Warmblood News; mng. editor: Focus on Women, 1981. Mem. LWV. Lutheran. Office: Am Warmblood Registry PO Box 15167 Tallahassee FL 32317-5167

KARST-CAMPBELL, JUDY W. S., broadcast stations owner; b. Monroe, La., Feb. 15, 1941; d. Irving and Daisy Leila Ward-Steinman; m. Charles Edward Karst, Dec. 27, 1965 (div. 1980); children: Alexander Karst, Alicia Karst, Jacqueline Karst; m. Kenneth Wayne Campbell Sr., July 29, 1994. BA cum laude, La. Coll., Pineville, 1960; MA with honors, U. Hawaii, 1962; PhD with honors, Tulane U., 1971. Pres. Red River Homes, MBE, Inc., Alexandria, La., 1975-78; grad. fellow Chinese Inst. Columbia U., N.Y.C., 1962; grad. tchr. asst. in history U. Hawaii, Honolulu, 1960-62; vis. prof. history Chulalongkorn U., Bangkok, 1962-64; adj. prof. history La. State U., Alexandria, 1976-77; v.p., news dir. KDBS, Inc., Alexandria, 1976-84, pres., gen. mgr., 1984—. Writer, rschr., producer, voice for news spls. and documentaries. Bd. dirs. YWCA, Alexandria, 1990-92, La. Alliance for Mentally Ill., 1992—; bd. dirs. Easter Seals of La., sec., 1993; mem. coun. Arbitron Radio Adv. Coun., 1993—. Recipient Lifetime Broadcast Achievement award La. Assn. Broadcasters, 1996, Humanitarian award Country Radio Braodcasters, 1996, Mark Twain awards, others; named Woman of Yr., Bus. and Profl. Women, 1988. Democrat. Episcopalian. Home: 1106 Robin Ridge Ln Hiawassee GA 30546 Office: JWSC Enterprises LLC KDBS Inc 1106 Robin Ridge Ln Hiawassee GA 30546

KARULF, RICHARD E., surgeon, department chairman; b. Wichita, Kans., Sept. 30, 1955; s. Eugene J. and Marietta (Hancock) K.; married Deborah Kay Noel, April 22, 1978; 1 child, Erik A. BS in Physics, USAF Acad., Colo., 1977; MD, U. Minn., Mpls., 1983. Diplomate: Am. Bd. Surgery, Am. Bd. Colon and Rectal Surgery. Lt. col. USAF, 1977—. Fellow Am. Coll. Surgeons, Am. Soc. Colon and Rectal Surgeons, Tex. Soc. Colon & Rectal Surgeons (treas.); mem. Soc. Am. Gastrointestinal Endoscopic Surgeons, So. Med. Assn. (pres. colon and rectal sect.), Soc. Air Force Clin. Surgeon (treas.), Assn. for Acad. Surgery. Office: 59TH Medica Wing/PSSG 2200 Bergquist Dr, Ste 1 Lackland AFB TX 78236-5300*

KASHDIN, GLADYS SHAFRAN, painter, educator; b. Pitts., Dec. 15, 1921; d. Edward M. and Miriam P. Shafran; m. Manville E. Kashdin, Oct. 11, 1942 (dec.). BA magna cum laude, U. Miami, 1960; MA, Fla. State U., 1962, PhD, 1965. Photographer, N.Y.C. and Fla., 1938-60; tchr. art, Fla. and Ga., 1956-63; asst. prof. humanities U. South Fla., Tampa, 1965-70, assoc. prof., 1970-74, prof., 1974-87, prof. emerita, 1987—; works exhibited in 58 one-woman shows, 38 group exhbns.; maj. touring exhibits include: The Everglades, 1972-75, Aspects of the River, 1975-80, Processes of Time, 1981-91, Retrospective 1941-96, Tampa Mus. Art, 1996; represented in permanent collections: Taiwan, Peoples Republic of China, Columbus Mus. Arts, LeMoyne Art Found., Tampa Internat. Airport, Tampa Mus. Art, Kresge Art Mus., U. So. Fla., Tampa Mus. of Art, 1996—; lectr.; adv. bd. Hillsborough County Mus., 1975-83. Mem. U. S. Fla. Status of Women Com., 1971-76, chmn., 1975-76. Recipient Women Helping Women in Art award Soroptimist Internat., 1979, Citizens Hon. award Hillsborough Bd. County Commrs., 1984, Mortar Bd. award for teaching excellence, 1986. Mem. AAUW (1st v.p. Tampa br. 1971-72), Phi Kappa Phi (chpt.-pres. 1981-83, artist/scholar award 1987). Home: 441 Biltmore Ave Temple Terrace FL 33617

KASI, LEELA PESHKAR, pharmaceutical chemist; b. Bombay, July 15, 1939; came to U.S., 1971; d. Subbaraman and Lakshmi (Shastri) Peshkar; m. Kalli R. Kasi, June 10, 1971. BS, U. Bombay, India, 1958; PhD, U. Marburg, W. Germany, 1968. Jr. chemist Khandelwal Labs., Bombay, India, 1958-59; trainee Farbwerke Hoechst, Frankfurt, W. Germany, 1960; teaching asst. U. of Marburg, W. Germany, 1967-68; sr. chemist Boehringer-Knoll Ltd., Bombay, India, 1969-71; mgr. quality control Health Care Ind., Michigan City, Ind., 1972-77; mgr. quality control U. Tex.-M.D. Anderson Cancer Ctr., Houston, 1979-95, assoc. prof. nuclear medicine, faculty mem., 1990-95, dir. Exptl. Nuclear Medicine Lab., 1979-95; cons. Radiopharms. Devel., Houston, 1995—; mem. grad. faculty U. Tex., 1984-90. Asst. editor Jour. Nuclear Medicine, 1984-89. Mem. AAAS, Am. Assn. Cancer Rsch., Soc. of Nuclear Medicine. Home and Office: 4710 Mcdermed Dr Houston TX 77035-3706

KASKINEN, BARBARA KAY, author, composer, songwriter, musician, music educator; b. Manistee, Mich., June 26, 1952; d. Norman Ferdinand and Martha Agnes (Harju) Kaskinen; m. David H. Riesberg, Feb. 14, 1985 (div.). AA, Broward C.C., Coconut Creek, Fla., 1978; BA with honors, Fla. Atlantic U., 1981, MA, 1995; postgrad., Nova U., 1989. Instr. adult piano Atlantic H.S., Delray Beach, Fla., 1981-82; organist, combo dir. Affirmation Luth. Ch., Boca Raton, Fla., 1981-86; studio musician, composer/arranger Electric Rize Prodns., Margate, Fla., 1982-94; ind. instr. piano, electronic keyboard and guitar. Margate, 1979—; bass and keyboard player Electric Rize Band, Margate, 1982—; in-house composer and arranger Hansen House, Miami Beach, Fla., 1987-88; co-founder Oasis Coffee House, Boca Raton, 1990—; co-owner Electric Rize Pub., 1991—; grad. tchg. asst. Fla. Atlantic U., 1994-96, mem. adj. faculty, 1995—; asst. dir. T.O.P.S. Piano Camp, 1994—; mem. adj. faculty Broward C.C., 1996—, Broward Cmty. Coll., Coconut Creek, Fla., 1996—. Author: Barbara Riesberg's Adult Electronic Keyboard Course Book I, 1988, Books II and III, 1989. Reporter Coalition to Stop Food Irradiation, Broward, Fla., 1989. Mem. NOW, ASCAP, Fla. Atlantic U. Alumni Assn., Nat. Guild Piano Tchrs., Broward County Music Tchr.'s Assn. (treas.), Fla. State Music Tchr.'s Assn., Music Guild of Boca Raton. Home: 6601 NW 22nd St Pompano Beach FL 33063-2117

KASMIR, GAIL ALICE, insurance company official, accountant; b. N.Y.C., Aug. 19, 1958; d. Fred and Evelyn Silvie (Mailman) K. BSBA summa cum laude, U. Cen. Fla., 1979. CPA, Fla. Acct. Ernst and Young, Orlando, Fla., 1979-83; fin. mgr. Harcourt Brace Jovanovich (Harvest Life Ins. Co.), Orlando, Fla., 1983-85; sr. v.p., treas., sec., cons. to bd. dirs., mem. investment com. LifeCo Investment Group, Inc. and subs. Nat. Heritage Life Ins. Co., Maitland, Fla., 1985-89, exec. v.p., 1991-94; CFO Nat. Heritage Life Ins. Co. in Rehab., Orlando, Fla., 1994-95, Nat. Heritage Life Ins. Co., 1995—; bd. dirs., exec. v.p., sec.-treas., CFO Nat. Heritage Life Ins. Co., LifeCo Investment Group, Inc., LifeCo Mktg. Svcs. Vol. Am. Cancer Soc., 1987-94, Am. Soc. for Cancer Rsch., 1987—. Fellow Life Office Mgmt. Assn.; mem. AICPAs, Fla. Inst. CPAs, Ins. Acctg. and Systems Assn., Beta Alpha Psi, Beta Gamma Sigma. Republican. Jewish. Home: 1351 Richmond Rd Winter Park FL 32789-5060 Office: Nat Heritage Life Ins Co 950 S Winter Park Dr Casselberry FL 32707-5457

KASPERBAUER, ISABEL GILES, art educator; b. Huancayo, Peru, Jan. 26, 1940; came to the U.S., 1960; d. Andres Humberto and Sofia Catalina (Saez) Giles; m. Michael John Kasperbauer, June 3, 1962; children: Maria Isabel, John Michael, Paul Andrew, Sandra Anne. BS, Iowa State U., 1962; BA, U. Ky., 1980. Cert. tchr., Ky. Art and Spanish tchr. Newman Ctr. U. Ky., Lexington, 1975-77; art tchr. Living Arts and Sci. Ctr., Lexington, 1980-82; after sch. art tchr. So. Elem. Sch., Lexington, 1980-82; art and Spanish tchr. Lexington Sch., 1982-85, art tchr., 1985—; del. Internat. Woman's Yr. Conf., Houston, 1977; co-chair dept. fine arts Lexington Sch., 1993-96. V.p. Lexington Assn. for Parent Edn., 1967; treas. Lexington Talent Edn. Assn., 1971; co-pres. PTA James Lane Allen Sch., Lexington, 1978. Recipient Martha V. Shipman award Kappa Delta Pi, 1980. Mem. Ky. Art Edn. Assn. (sec. 1981-82, Art Educator of Yr. 1993), Am. Art Edn. Assn.

KASPUTYS, JOSEPH EDWARD, corporate executive, economist; b. Jamaica, N.Y., Aug. 12, 1936; s. Joseph John and Henrietta Viola (Derenthall) K.; m. Marilyn Patricia Kennedy, Oct. 29, 1953; children: Clare Victoria, Patricia Jeanne, Jacqueline Ann, Veronica Joy. BA magna cum laude, Bklyn. Coll., 1959; MBA with high distinction, Harvard U., 1967, DBA, 1972. Asst. to comptr. U.S. Dept. Def., Washington, 1967-70; dir. Office of Policy and Plans U.S. Maritime Adminstrn., Washington, 1972-73, asst. adminstr., 1973-75; asst. sec. U.S. Dept. Commerce, Washington, 1975-77; exec. v.p., COO Data Resources, Inc., Lexington, Mass., 1977-81, pres., CEO, 1981-84; exec. v.p. McGraw-Hill, Inc., N.Y.C., 1984-87; pres., COO Primark Corp. Inc., McLean, Va., 1987-88, chmn., CEO, 1988—; lectr. Am. U., Washington, 1967-68, Bentley Coll., Boston, 1971-72; assoc. prof., lectr. George Washington U., Washington, 1967-77; bd. dirs. Lifeline Systems, Inc., Boston. Bd. dirs. Hitachi Found., Washington, Coun. for Excellence in Govt., Washington; mem. Com. for Econ. Devel., Washington. Comdr. USN, 1956-76. Decorated Legion of Merit; Warren G. Harding Aerospace fellow, 1971. Mem. Nat. Econs. Club, Nat. Assn. Bus. Econs., Phi Beta Kappa. Republican. Roman Catholic. Clubs: Harvard Bus. Sch. (Boston); Capitol Hill (Washington). Home: 398 Simon Willard Rd Concord MA 01742-1624 Office: Primark Corp 1000 Winter St Waltham MA 02154-1248

KASS, EMILY, art museum administrator. Director Tampa (Fla.) Mus. of Art. Office: Tampa Mus Art 600 N Ashley Dr Tampa FL 33602-4305

KASSEWITZ, RUTH EILEEN BLOWER, retired hospital executive; b. Columbus, Ohio, May 15, 1928; d. E. Wallett and Helen (Daub) Blower; BS in Journalism-Mgmt., Ohio State U., Columbus, 1951; m. Jack Kassewitz, July 28, 1962 (dec.); 1 stepchild, Jack. Copywriter, Ohio Fuel Gas Co., Columbus, 1951-55, Merritt Owens Advt. Agy., Kansas City, Kans., 1955-56; account exec. Grant Advt., Inc., Miami, Fla., 1956-59; account supr. Venn/Cole & Assocs., Miami, 1959-67; dir. communications Ferendino/Grafton/Candela/Spillis Architects & Engrs., Miami, 1967-69; dir. communications Dade County Dept. Housing and Urban Devel., Miami, 1969-72; dir. communications Met. Dade County Govt., 1972-78; adminstr. pub. rels. U. Miami/Jackson Meml. Med. Ctr., 1978-90, ret., 1990. Pres., U. Miami Women's Guild, 1973-74; bd. dirs. Girls Scouts Tropical Fla., 1974-76, 81-83, Lung Assn. Dade-Monroe Counties, 1976-87, Met. YMCA, 1996—; mem. exec. com. Miami-Dade C.C. Found., 1984—; pres. Mental Health Assn. Dade County, 1982; mem. Miami Ecol. and Beautification Com., 1978—, also vice-chmn.; bd. govs. Barry U., Miami, 1981-83; trustee Nat. Humanities Faculty, 1981-83; trustee emeritus United Protestant Appeal, 1984-92; treas., past chmn. Health, Edn., Promotion Council, Inc.; adv. bd. Miami's for Me, 1987-88; mem. Coral Gables Cable TV Bd., 1983-86; ch. moderator Plymouth Congl. Ch., 1986-88 (trust. 1995—); community adv. bd. Jr. League Greater Miami, Inc., 1989-92; founding mem. Nat. Honor Roll Women in Pub. Rels., No. Ill. U., 1993. Recipient Disting. Service award Plymouth Congl. Ch., Miami, 1979; Ann Stover award, 1983, Golden Image award Fla. Pub. Rels.Assn, 1987; named Woman of Yr., Plymouth Congl. Ch., U. Miami Med. Sch., 1991. Fellow Public Relations Soc. Am. (pres. South Fla. chpt. 1969-70, nat. chmn. govt. sect. 1973-74, nat. dir., 1974-78; continuing edn. council 1981-83; Silver Anvil award 1973, Assembly del. 1970-73, 86-89, Paul M. Lund Pub. Svc. award 1993, Miami chpt. Lifetime Achievement award, 1995); mem. Women in Comm. (pres. Greater Miami chpt. 1962-63; Clarion award 1973, 75, Community Headliner 1985), Miami Internat. Press Club (bd. dirs. 1986-87, treas. 1992), Greater Miami C. of C. (gov. 1983-86), Rotary Club of Miami (bd. dirs., 1988—, pres. 1993-94). Home: 1136 Aduana Ave Miami FL 33146-3206

KASTEN, PAUL RUDOLPH, nuclear engineer, educator; b. Jackson, Mo., Dec. 10, 1923; s. Arthur John and Hattie L. (Krueger) K.; m. Eileen Alma Kiehne, Dec. 28, 1947; children: Susan (Mrs. Robert M. Goebbert), Kim Patrick, Jennifer. BSChemE, U. Mo., Rolla, 1944, M.S., 1947; Ph.D. in Chem. Engring., U. Minn., 1950. Staff mem. Oak Ridge Nat. Lab., 1950-88, dir. gas-cooled reactor and thorium utilization programs, 1970-78, dir. HTGR and GCFR programs, 1978-86, tech. dir. gas cooled reactor programs, 1986-88; cons., 1988—; guest dir. Inst. Reactor Devel., Nuclear Research Center, Jülich, Fed. Republic Germany, 1963-64; mem. faculty U. Tenn., Knoxville, 1953—, part-time prof. nuclear engring., 1965—. Fellow AAAS, Am. Nuclear Soc.; mem. Sigma Xi, Tau Beta Pi, Phi Lambda Upsilon. Lutheran. Office: 341 Louisiana Ave Oak Ridge TN 37830-8514 also: U Tenn Dept Nuclear Engring Knoxville TN 37996

KASTER, JAY, physical education educator; b. La Crosse, Wis., July 26, 1968; s. Sylvester Vernon and Barbara Ann (Dempsey) K.; m. Nicole Stover, July 23, 1994. BS, Ball State U., 1994. Adapted phys. edn. tchr. Wichita Falls (Tex.) Ind. Sch. Dist., 1994—. With U.S. Army, 1986-89. Mem. AAHPERD, Kappa Delta Pi, Phi Epsilon Kappa. Home: 4700 Taft Apt 344 Wichita Falls TX 76308 Office: Wichita Falls Ind Sch Dist 1104 Broad Wichita Falls TX 76308

KATCHEN, CAROLE LEE, writer, artist; b. Denver, Jan. 30, 1944; d. Samuel and Gertrude (Levin) K.; m. Philip Goldhammer, 1967 (div. 1970). BA, U. Colo., 1965. Freelance journalist, 1964—; corr. Life Mag., 1989-92; columnist Dance Action Mag., 1989-90 ; columnist, mem. editorial rev. bd. Colo. Woman Mag., 1976-80; cons. children's literature Volt Tech. Corp., 1971; presenter in field. Author: I was a Lonely Teenager, 1965, The Underground Light Bulb, 1969, Promoting and Selling your Art, 1978, Figure Drawing Workshop, 1985, Painting Face and Figures, 1986, Planning Your Paintings Step-by-Step, 1988 (Dutch edit. 1990), Your Friend, Annie, 1990, Creative Painting with Pastel, 1990, Watercolor, Oil, Acrylic, 1991, Dramatize Your Paintings with Tonal Values, 1993, Painting with Passion, 1994, Make Your Watercolors Look Professional, 1995, How to Get Started Selling Your Art, 1996; script writer, co-prodr. Screamplay, 1991; script writer (comml. audiotape) Let the Games Begin!, 1991, (video) Cafe Talk, 1986; contbg. editor Artist's Mag., 1985—, Today's Art & Graphics, 1980-81; editor, pub. Trip Mag., 1967-68; editor, copywriter Tempo Mag., 1964-65; one-woman shows include Denver Art Gallery, 1972, Denver Women's Press Club, 1974, Centro Colombo-Americano, Bogota, Colombia, 1974, Valhalla Gallery, Wichita, Kans., 1978, 1st Nat. Bank Denver, 1980, Cynthia Madden Gallery, Denver, 1981, Gerhard Wurzer Gallery, Houston, 1981, Gallery of S.W., Taos, N.Mex., 1981, Savageau's Gallery, Denver, 1984, Hooks-Epstein Gallery, Houston, 1985, Saks Galleries, Denver, 1993, Taylor's Contemporanea Art Gallery, Hot Springs, Ark., 1995; represented in permanent collections Mus. Outdoor Art, Englewood, Colo., Northwest Cmty. Hosp., Arlington Heights, Ill., AGIP, Houston, Petro Lewis Corp., Denver, Cherry Creek Nat. Bank, Denver, Rotan Mosle Corp., Denver, Denver Symphony Orch., Denver Women's Press Club, Penrose Cmty. Hosp., Colorado Springs. Recipient Outstanding Achievement in Art award West Valley Coll., 1970, Outstanding Working Woman award U.S. Dept. Labor and Colo. Coun. on Working Women, 1982, Spl. Recognition award Women in Design, 1988, Better Price Store award Okla. Art Workshops Ann. Exhibit, 1993, Holbein award Pastels USA Exhibit, 1994, Grumbacher gold medal Pastel Soc. N.Am., 1995, merit award Pastel Soc. Southwest, 1995; nominated Internat. Women of Yr., London, 1992-93. Mem. Pastel Soc. Am. (Kans. Pastel Soc. award 1990, Avelyn Goldsmith award 1993, Braida award 1996, master pastellist 1996), Internat. Assn. Pastel Socs. (mem. bd. dirs.). Office: 624 Prospect Ave Hot Springs National Park AR 71901

KATONA, ILDY MARGARET, allergist, immunologist, pediatrician; b. Hungary, 1947. MD, U. Budapest. Diplomate Am. Bd. Allergy and Immunology, Am. Bd. Pediatrics. Resident Semmelweis U., Budapest, 1971-74; resident Georgetown U., Washington, 1976-78, fellow, 1975-76, 78-80; prof. peds. & med. Uniform Svcs. U. Health Scis., 1993—. Home: 3630 N Peary St Arlington VA 22207-5329 also: USUHS Dept Peds 4301 Jones Bridge Rd Bethesda MD 20814-4712*

KATOOT, KAREN ROBBYN, critical care nurse; b. Olive Hill, Ky., June 16, 1960; d. Joe and Nina E. Porter; m. Mohammad W. Katoot, Nov. 21, 1981; children: Abdullah, Ibraheem. BSN, Ea. Ky. U., 1982; postgrad., St. Joseph's Coll., Maine, 1991—. RN, Fla., Tenn.; cert. advanced chemotherapy. Staff nurse ICU St. Thomas Hosp., Nashville, 1982-86; staff nurse II in bone marrow transplant unit Shands Hosp. at U. Fla., Gainesville, 1986-89; home health nurse Care One Nursing, 1989—. Named Most Outstanding BSN Nurse of 1982, Ea. Ky. U. Mem. AACN. Home: 1080 Laurian Park Dr Roswell GA 30075

KATRANA, DAVID JOHN, plastic and reconstructive surgeon; b. Moline, Ill., Oct. 16, 1945; s. Nicholas John and Marilyn Ann (Brown) K.; children: Nicole Elaine, Kimberly Ann. BA in Biology, Northwestern U., Evanston, Ill., 1967; DDS, Northwestern U., Chgo., 1971, MD, 1974. Diplomate Am. Bd. Plastic and Reconstructive Surgery. Resident oral surgery Northwestern U. Dental Sch., Chgo., 1971-72; intern surgery Northwestern U. McGraw Med. Ctr., Chgo., 1974-75, resident gen. surgery, 1975-77, resident plastic and reconstructive surgery, 1977-79; assoc. Houston Plastic Surgery Assocs., 1979-91; pvt. practice plastic surgery, 1991—; asst. clin. prof. plastic surgery Baylor Coll. Medicine, Houston, 1980—; dental cons. The Chgo. Bulls, 1977-79; instr. surgery, dental cons. Northwestern U. Med. Sch., Chgo., 1978-79; dir. burn unit Humana Hosp. Southmore, Pasadena, Tex., 1982-88; div. chief surgery Rosewood Hosp., Houston, 1984-86, pres. med. staff, 1988-89; plastic surg. cons. Houston Gamblers Profl. Football Team, 1984; mem. active staff Rosewood Med. Ctr.; mem. courtesy staff St. Luke's Episcopal Hosp., West Houston Med. Ctr., Meml. Hosp. at Memorial City, also others; lectr. various univs. and hosps. Contbr. articles to profl. jours. Bd. trustees Rosewood Med. Ctr., Houston, 1989—, chmn. bd., 1993-95; dir. Ctr. for WOund Care and Hyperbaric Medicine, Rosewood Med. Ctr., 1995—. Fellow ACS; mem. Undersea and Hyperbaric Med. Soc., Internat. Soc. Burn Injuries, Am. Burn Assn., Am. Soc. Plastic and Reconstructive Surgeons, Tex. Soc. Plastic Surgeons, Tex. Med. Assn., Harris County Med. Soc., Houston Soc. Plastic Surgeons. Home: Apt 32 5035 A Tangle Ln Houston TX 77056 Office: 9034 Westheimer Rd Ste 320 Houston TX 77063-3614

KATRITZKY, ALAN ROY, chemistry educator, consultant; b. London, Eng., Aug. 18, 1928; s. Frederick Charles and Emily Gertrude (Lane) K.; m. Agnes Juliane Dietlinde Kilian, Aug. 5, 1952; children: Margaret, Erika,

Rupert, Freda. B.A., Oxford U., 1951, B.Sc., 1952, M.A., 1954, D.Phil., 1954; Ph.D., Cambridge U., 1958, Sc.D., 1963; Sc.D. (hon.), U. Nac. Madrid, 1986, U. Poznan, Poland, 1990, U. Gdansk, Poland, 1994, U. East Anglia, U.K., 1995, Beijing Inst. Tech., 1995, U. Toulouse, France, 1996; Hon. Prof., Xian Modern U., 1995. ICI fellow U. Oxford, 1956-58; lectr. chemistry U. Cambridge, 1958-63; fellow Churchill Coll.; prof. chemistry U. East Anglia, 1963-80; dean U. East Anglia (Sch. Chem. Scis.), 1963-70, 76-80; Kenan prof. organic chemistry U. Fla., Gainesville, 1980—; dir. Fla. Inst. Het. Cpds., 1986—. Editor: Advances in Heterocyclic Chemistry, vols. 1-68, 1963—; regional editor: Tetrahedron, 1980—; chmn. editl. bd. Comprehensive Heterocyclic Chemistry, 1st edit., 9 vols., 1985, 2d edit., 10 vols., 1996, Comprehensive Organic Functional Group Transformations, 7 vols., 1995. Named Cavaliere Ufficiale. Fellow Royal Soc.; mem. Am., Brit., Japanese, Swiss, Italian (hon. mem.), Polish (hon. mem.) Chem. Socs., Internat. Soc. Het. Chem., Polish Acad. Sci. (fgn. mem.), Real Catalan Acad. Home: 1221 SW 21st Ave Gainesville FL 32601-8417 Office: U Fla Dept Chemistry Gainesville FL 32611

KATRITZKY, LINDE (AGNES JULIANE DIETLINDE), writer, researcher, educator; b. Ansbach, Germany, July 28, 1928; came to U.S., 1980; d. Friedrich Julius and Renate Sophie (Vocke) Kilian; m. Alan Roy Katritzky, Aug. 5, 1952; children: Margaret, Erika, Rupert, Freda. BA, U. Munich, Fed. Republic Germany, 1952; MA, U. Fla., 1984, PhD, 1988. Instr., adj. prof. dept. German and Slavic U. Fla., Gainesville, 1982—; vis. lectr. U. East Anglia, U.K., hon. chaplain, 1963-75. Author: Lichtenbergs Gedankensystem, 1995, Johnson and The Letters of Junius, 1996; contbr. articles on lit. and langs. to profl. jours. Guardian Fla. Guardian Ad Litem Program, Gainesville, 1980-84; prison vis. Mem. MLA, Am. Assn. Tchrs. of German, Am. Soc. Eighteenth Century Studies, Howe Soc. UF, Soc. German-Am. Studies, Oxford and Cambridge Club (assoc.), Phi Kappa Phi. Lutheran. Home: 1221 SW 21st Ave Gainesville FL 32601-8417 Office: U Fla Germanic/Slavic Lang & Lits Dept German and Slavic Studies Gainesville FL 32611

KATSINIS, CONSTANTINE, electrical engineering educator; b. Athens, Sept. 6, 1954. BS, Polytechnic U. of Athens, 1977; MS, U. R.I., 1979, PhD, 1982. Sr. rsch. assoc. Rsch. Ctr. for Nat. Def., Athens, 1983; rsch. asst. and rsch. assoc. I U. R.I., 1978-81, rsch. assoc. III, 1982; asst. prof. U. Ala., Huntsville, 1985-90, assoc. prof. elec. and computer engring., 1990—; vis. rsch. prof. dept. elec. engring. U. Denver, 1984-85; vis. rsch. engr. Standard Electrik Lorenz AG, Stuttgart, Germany, 1976; presenter confs. in field. Author chpts. books in field; contbr. articles to profl. jours. Grantee NSF, 1984-85, 1992, UAH 1987, Motorola, 1989, Silicon Compiler Systems Corp., 1990, Hewlett-Packard Lab., 1992, NASA, 1993, 1996, U.S. Army, 1996, others. Mem. IEEE (Outstanding Engring. Edn. award Huntsville, 1991, treas. Huntsville sect. 1989-91), IEEE Computer Soc., Eta Kappa Nu. Office: ECE Dept Univ Ala Huntsville AL 35899

KATZ, ELAINE MARCIA, nuclear engineering educator; b. Chgo., Oct. 31, 1942; d. Hymen and Esther (Schnidman) K. BSME, Purdue U., 1963; MS, U. Tenn., 1971, PhD, 1975. Registered profl. engr., Tenn. Mech. engr. Met. Sanitary Dist, Chgo., 1963-64, J.F. Pritchard & Co., Kansas City, Mo., 1964-66, Rust Engring. Co., Birmingham, Ala., 1966-68; sr. nuclear engr. Combustion Engring. Inc., Windsor, Conn., 1973-76; fgn. research assoc. French AEC, 1976-77; from asst. to assoc. prof. nuclear engring. U. Tenn., Knoxville, 1977—; summer faculty participant Oak Ridge Associated Univs., 1981. Summer faculty fellow NASA-ASEE Johnson Space Ctr., Houston, 1980, ASME congl. fellow as sci. advisor for Sen. Jim Sasser, Tenn., 1985, Lilly Found. fellow, 1978-79, ASME White House fellow in Office of Sci. and Tech. Policy, 1994; U. Tenn.-Knoxville Chancellor's Tchr. scholar, 1995—. Mem. ASME, Instrument Soc. Am., Am. Soc. Engring. Edn., Am. Nuclear Soc., Soc. Women Engrs. (student sect. faculty adv.). Home: 1964 Cherokee Bluff Dr Knoxville TN 37920-2221 Office: U Tenn Dept Nuclear Engring Knoxville TN 37996

KATZ, LOWELL DEAN, surgeon; b. Louisville, Ky., 1946. MD, U. Louisville, 1972. Diplomate Colon and Rectal Surgery. Intern U. Louisville Assoc. Hosp., 1972-73, resident in surgery, 1973-76; resident in colon and rectal surgery Greater Balt. Med. Ctr., 1976-78; staff mem. Jewish Hosp., Louisville; assoc. clin. prof. U. Louisville; group ptnr. Louisville Colon Rectal Assocs., Ky.; pvt. practice. Mem. Am. Coll. Surgeons, Am. Soc. Colon and Rectal Surgeons, Am. Soc. Gastro-Intestinal Endoscopy, Soc. Am. Gastrointestina Endoscopic Surgery. Office: Louisville ColoRectal Assocs 250 E Liberty St Ste 610 Louisville KY 40202-1536*

KATZ, M. MARVIN, lawyer; b. Laredo, Tex., May 12, 1935. BA, Tex. A&M Coll., 1954; LLB with honors, U. Tex., 1959. Bar: Rex. 1958, U.S. Dist. Ct. (so. dist.) Tex. 1959, U.S. Ct. Appeals (5th cir.) 1961, U.S. Supreme Ct. 1972. Ptnr. Mayer, Brown & Platt, Houston. Editor articles Tex. Law Rev., 1959. Chmn. City of Houston Planning Commn., 1980—. Mem. ABA, Houston Bar Assn., State Bar Tex., Am. Coll. Real Estate Lawyers, Tex. Coll. Real Estate Lawyers, Houston Real Estate Lawyers Coun., Phi Delta Phi, Order of Coif. Office: Mayer Brown & Platt 700 Louisiana St Ste 3600 Houston TX 77002-2730*

KATZ, WILLIAM DAVID, psychologist, psychoanalytic psychotherapist, educator, mental health consultant; b. N.Y.C., Sept. 14, 1915; s. Charles and Esther (Dann) K. AB, Bklyn. Coll., 1940; MA, NYU, 1942, PhD, 1953. Diplomate Am. Bd. Med. Psychotherapists (fellow) 1986, Am. Acad. Behavioral Medicine (fellow) 1986. Clin. intern and resident Hillside Hosp., 1950-53; pvt. practice as cons. psychologist and psychotherapist, N.Y., Fla., 1942—; staff psychotherapist Palms West Hosp., Fla., Wellington Regional Med. Ctr., Fla.; cons. psychologist Human Rels. Guidance Ctr., 1946-56; exec. dir. Civic Ctr. Clinic, Bklyn. Assn. Rehab. Offenders, Inc., 1951-55, Play Rsch. Inst., Inc., 1953-57; psychotherapist Group for Community Guidance Ctrs., 1955-57; psychotherapist Mental Health Inst., 1957-59, assoc. dir., 1957, exec. dir., 1958; clin. assoc. Psychol. Svc. Ctr., N.Y.C., 1968—; supr. psychotherapy Met. Ctr. Mental Health, N.Y.C., 1969—; asst. prof. psychology L.I. U., 1958-64, assoc. prof., 1964-70, prof., 1970-82, prof. emeritus, 1982—, asst. chmn. psychology dept., 1963-72, 74-76, acting chmn., 1966, 75; prof. U.S. Army Chaplain Ctr. and Sch., Fort Wadsworth, Fort Hamilton, 1970-77; psychotherapist Counseling & Psychotherapy Assocs., 1986-87. Assoc. editor Am. Imago, 1978-83, Am. Psychol. Assn., 1950—; contbr. articles to profl. jours. Recipient Cross of Honor, La Fundacion Internat., Eloy Alfaro, 1964. Fellow Am. Internat. Acad. (cert. and medallion 1957), Assn. Applied Psychoanalysis (exec. sec. 1963-67, 78-79, pres. 1968-69, 74-75; mem. AAAS, Am. Acad. Polit. and Social Scis., Interam. Soc. Psychology, Am. Acad. Psychotherapists, AAUP, Soc. Clin. and Exptl. Hypnosis, Coun. Psychoanalytic Psychotherapists, Am. Psychol. Assn., N.Y. State Psychol. Assn., N.Y. Soc. Clin. Psychologists, Bklyn. Psychol. Assn. (pres. 1971-72), N.Y. Acad. Scis., S.I. Mental Health Soc., Nat. Register Health Services Provider in Psychology, Bklyn. Assn. Mental Health, Pa., Richmond County Psychol. Assn. (pres. 1975), Palm Beach County Mental Health Assn., NYU Alumni Assn., KP Lodge (past chancellor), Shriners, Masons (past master), Psi Chi, Alpha Phi Omega, Tau Delta Phi. Home: 116 Village Walk Dr West Palm Beach FL 33411-2995

KATZENSTEIN, THEA, retail executive, jewelry designer; b. N.Y.C., Mar. 30, 1927; d. Carl E. and Lillian (Rosenblatt) Schustak; m. William Katzenstein, Sept. 10, 1950; children: Leo, Ranee. Student, Sarah Lawrence Coll., 1948-50; BS, Columbia U., 1962, MA, 1967. Pres. Gallery A., N.Y.C., 1967-71, Melita, N.Y.C., 1972-77, TK Studio, Miami Beach, Fla., 1977—; adj. prof. of jewelry Fla. Internat. U., 1989-90; enamelling instr. U. Miami, 1991. Author: Early Chinese Art and The Pacific Basin, 1967; painting, graphics and jewelry represented in numerous pvt. collections. Trustee Miami Metro Zoo, 1994—. Mem. Soc. N.Am. Goldsmiths, Enamel Guild South, Nat. Enamelist Guild, Fla. Soc. Goldsmiths (pres. S.E. chpt.), Fla. Craftsmen, Zonta (sec. Coral Gables chpt. 1989-90). Democrat. Jewish. Home: Apt 1501 9 Island Ave Miami Beach FL 33139-1360

KATZIN, DAVID SIMON, physician; b. Wilson, N.C., Aug. 3, 1933; s. George and Fannie (Baker) K.; m. Marian C. Baumgardner, June 28, 1967; children: Faye Elizabeth, Gregory Ari, Marc Eban. BS, U. Miami, 1955, MD, 1959. Diplomate Am. Bd. Internal Medicine. Resident in internal medicine Jackson Meml. Hosp., Miami, 1962-64; fellow in infectious diseases U. Miami Sch. Medicine, 1964-66; pvt. practice Miami and Estes Park, Colo., 1966-86; chief med. svc. Salisbury (N.C.) VA Med. Ctr., 1987—; asst. chief of staff Bapt. Hosp. Miami, 1976-78, chief of staff Estes Park Meml. Hosp., 1985-86. Bd. dirs. Hospice of Miami, 1976-81, Rowan County AIDS Task Force, Salisbury, 1991-93. Lt. USN, 1960-62. Home: 265 Larkspur Rd Salisbury NC 28146-8369 Office: Salisbury VA Med Ctr 1601 Brenner Ave Salisbury NC 28144-2515

KATZMAN, ANITA, author; b. N.Y.C., Feb. 6, 1920; d. Louis and Sylvia (Fox) Butensky; m. Nathan Katzman, Mar. 29, 1942 (dec. 1965); children: Mark, Drew, Bruce, Mindi. BA, N.Y. U., 1940. Author: My Name is Mary 1975. Founders Bd. Asolo Performing Arts Ctr., Sarasota Fla.; Bd. Dirs. Asolo Theater Festival Assn.; Devel. Bd. USF Gerontology Ctr., Tampa Fla., Sarasota-Manatee Jewish Found., Sarota Fla., Fla. Council Libraries. Recipient GTE Community Adv. Panel 1973, Community Acheivement award Women's Resource Ctr. Sarasota 1988, West Coast Woman Newspaper Sarasota 1989. Mem. The Author's Guild, The Author's League Am., Pan Pacific & Southeast Women's Assn., Lotos Club, Univ. Club Sarasota, Longboat Key Club. Democratic. Office: PO Box 56 Sarasota FL 34230-0056

KAUFFMAN, TERRY, broadcast and creative arts communication educator; b. San Francisco, Aug. 24, 1951; d. Raymond Roger and Patricia Virginia Kauffman. BA in Journalism summa cum laude, U. Calif., Berkeley, 1974; MA in Comm. summa cum laude, U. Tex., 1980; PhD, Union Inst., 1996. With Alta. Ednl. TV, 1970; sr. writer, prodr. and dir. Ampex Corp., Calif., 1980; news prodr., reporter, anchor ABC, Tex., 1974-75; mem. faculty dept. radio, TV and motion pictures U. N.C., Chapel Hill, 1985; mem. faculty dept. comm. N.C. State U., Raleigh, 1986—; mem. adj. faculty music, theatre and comm. dept. Meredith Coll., Raleigh, 1990—; mem. adv. bd., chmn. publicity Raleigh Conservatory Music; v.p. Wake Visual Arts Assn. and Gallery; tchr. art Meredith Coll., 1995—. Author: I'm Clueless, Confessions of a College Teacher, The Script as Blueprint, 1994; contbr. poetry to various publs.; composer, prodr., dir., composer for TV programs, including When the Wind Blows, The Rainbow, The Seasons of Change, PBS, Women Today, Profiles in Leadership; exhibited in art shows, San Francisco, Raleigh; prodr., dir., writer I'm One Person...Or Another, Thanksgiving (PBS), 1980—; writer, prodr. Consumer Hotline, PBS, Customs Operations at the Border; numerous others. Singer for chs. and retirement homes; past bd. dirs. Tex. Consumer Assn. Recipient Emmy nomination for documentary Otters from Oiled Waters, 1991. Mem. NATAS, Internat. TV Assn. (judge nat. contests), Nat. Broadcasting Soc. (8 1st place nat. awards 1973—, named Outstanding Mem., 1993-94, Profl. Mem. of Yr. 1994), Phi Kappa Phi. Home: 405 Furches St Raleigh NC 27607-4017

KAUFFMAN, THOMAS RICHARD, lawyer, consultant; b. Columbus, Ohio, June 3, 1959; s. James Runyan and Sarah Dillon (Dodd) K.; m. Victoria Doherty Heiden, Nov. 13, 1993. BA in Internat. Rels., Ohio State U., 1983; JD, U. Va., 1991. Bar: Va. 1991, U.S. Ct. Appeals (4th cir.) 1991, D.C. 1992. Imagery analyst CIA, Washington, 1985-88, summer assoc., 1989; summer assoc. Dyer, Ellis, Joseph & Mills, Washington, 1990, lawyer, 1991-94; cons. atty. Heiden Assocs., Inc., Washington, 1994—; pvt. practice law Fairfax, Va., 1995—; dir., sec. Potomac Riverside Farms, Inc., Martinsburg, W.Va., 1989—. Mem. editl. bd. Va. Jour. Internat. Law, 1989-90, sr. editl. bd., 1990-91; mng. editor (newspaper) Va. Law Weekly, 1988-91. Maj./squadron comdr. USAF Aux.-Civil Air Patrol, Ohio, Va., 1972—. Mem. ABA (sects. on internat. law and practice and law practice mgmt.), Va. Bar Assn. (sect. on law practice mgmt.), D.C. Bar Assn. (sects. on corp., fin. and securities law and internat. law), Arlington County Bar Assn., Fairfax County Bar Assn., Am. Mensa, Phi Delta Phi. Republican. Home: Apt 1133 1400 S Joyce St Arlington VA 22202 Office: 10625 Jones St Ste 201 Fairfax VA 22030

KAUFMAN, CHARLOTTE S., communications executive; b. Bridgeport, Conn., Mar. 8, 1918; d. Samuel N. and S. Elizabeth (Cohen) Schnee; m. William Kaufman, May 9, 1940. BA, U. Mich., 1938. Med. office assoc., 1941-63; dir. pub. rels. Parents and Friends of Retarded Children, Bridgeport, 1965-66; founder, exec. dir. Family Life Film Ctr. of Conn., Fairfield, Conn., 1967-74; exec. producer Topic '69/WNHC-TV, New Haven, Conn., 1969; project dir. pilot project with Social/Rehab. Svc. U.S. Dept. HEW, 1969-70; pub. rels. chmn. Friendship Fair of Aux./Bridgeport Regional Ctr. Retarded, 1979; founder CAT-TV, pub. access channel, Winston-Salem and Forsyth County, 1994; coord. five annual Film Day Workshops, Fairfield U., 1967-71; coord. coms. of jurors for Am. Film Festival, N.Y.C., 1968-74; chmn./mem. planning and adv. bd. Bridgeport Regional Ctr. for the Retarded; exec. bd. Bd. of Assocs., U. Bridgeport, others. Exec. producer: A Day in the Life of P.T. Barnum, 1971; author publs. in field. Vol. patient advocate for nursing homes, Southwestern Conn. Area Agy. on Aging, 1976-78; v.p. Oronoque Village Improvement Assn., 1986-88.

KAUFMAN, GLEN FRANK, art educator, artist; b. Fort Atkinson, Wis., Oct. 28, 1932; s. Eli J. and Elynor B. (Jensik) K. BS with honors, U. Wis., 1954; MFA, Cranbrook Acad. Art, 1959; cert., State Sch. Arts and Crafts, Copenhagen, 1960. Head fibers dept. Cranbrook Acad. Art, Bloomfield Hills, Mich., 1961-67; assoc. prof. art U. Ga., Athens, 1967-72, prof. art, 1972—, prof. in charge, fabric design, 1967—, grad. faculty, 1969—; staff designer Dorothy Liebes Design Studio, N.Y.C., 1960-61; designer Regal Rugs, Inc., North Vernon, Ind., 1966-82; vis. artist Sch. Textiles, Royal Coll. Art, London, 1976; juror The Albuquerque (N.Mex.) Mus., 1981, Midland (Mich.) Art Coun., 1985, Itami Craft Ctr., Osaka, Japan, 1991, others; panelist Visual Artists Fellowship/Crafts, Nat. Endowment for the Arts, Washington, 1992—; cons. in field; lectr. and workshop presenter in field. One-man shows include Gallery Maronie, Kyoto, Japan, 1984, Sembikiya Gallery, Tokyo, 1985, Arrowmont Sch. Arts and Crafts, Gatlinburg, Tenn., 1986, Fiberworks, Berkeley, Calif., 1987, Madison (Ga.)-Morgan Cultural Ctr., 1988, Fuji Gallery, Osaka, Japan, 1988, Wacoal Ginza Art Space, Tokyo, 1989, Allrich Gallery, San Francisco, 1990, Azabu Mus. of Arts and Crafts, Tokyo, 1991, Lamar Dodd Art Ctr., LaGrange (Ga.) Coll., 1992, Gallery Gallery, Japan, 1992, Wacoal Ginza Art Space, Tokyo, 1994, Gallery Nouveau, Pusan, Korea, 1994, Ba Tang Gol Arts Ctr., Seoul, korea, 1994, many others; exhibited in group shows at Columbia Mus. Art, S.C., 1980, No. Ill. U., DeKalb, 1981, Visual Arts Ctr. Alaska, Anchorage, 1982, Robert L. Kidd Gallery, Birmingham, 1983, Am. Craft Mus., N.Y., 1986, Denki Kaikan Gallery, Nagoya, Japan, 1987, Gayle Wilson Gallery, Southampton, N.Y., 1988, Sch. Visual Arts, N.Y., 1989, Itami Craft Ctr., Osaka, 1989 (Silver prize), Farrell Collection, Washington, 1991, Allrich Gallery, San Francisco, 1991, Nagoya Trade and Industry Ctr., 1991, New Visions Gallery Contemporary Art, Atlanta, 1992, Mus. Kyoto, 1992, Smithsonian Instn., Washington, 1992-93, Atlanta (Ga.) Fin. Ctr., 1993, The Nat. Mus. Modern Art, Kyoto, Japan, 1993, Art Inst. Chgo., Ill., 1993, Brenau U. Gallery, Gainesville, Ga., 1993, Mus. Kyoto, 1994, Asian Arts Ctr. Towson (Md.) State U., 1994, Am. Craft Museum, N.Y., 1995, Nogaya and Trade Industry Ctr., Japan, 1995, Gallery, Gallery, Kyota, Japan, 1995, Harbourfront Ctr., Toronto Can., 1995, Museé Marsil, Montreal, Can., 1995, The Brown/Grotta Gallery, Wilton, Conn., 1995, others; represented in permanent collections Am. Craft Mus., N.Y.C., Juraku Mus, Kyoto, Cleve. Mus. Art, Art Inst. Chgo., U. Wis., Madison, Itami City Craft Ctr., Hyogo Prefecture, Japan, Ithaca (N.Y.) Coll. Mus. Art, Long House Found., L.I., N.Y., Nat. Mus. Modern Art, Kyoto, Smithsonian Instn., Rockford Art Assn., Ill., S.C. Johnson Collection, U.S.A. Collection Contemporary Crafts, SUNY, Oneonta, Wichita Art Assn., Kans., pvt. collections; works illustrated in many books; contbr. articles to jours. Recipient Fulbright grant to Denmark, 1959-60, Grant for rsch. and travel to Europe, U. Ga., Dept. Art, 1973, Nat. Endowment for the Arts Craftsmen's Fellowship grant, 1976, Nat. Endowment for the Arts Svcs. to the Field grant, 1980-81, 81-82, Faculty Rsch. grant U. Ga. Athens Office of V.P. for Rsch., 1983-96, Nat. Endowment for the Arts Visual Artist's Fellowship grant, 1990, Ga. Coun. for the Arts Individual Artist grant, 1991, Sr. Faculty Rsch. grant U. Ga. Athens Rsch. Found., 1992, others. Fellow Am. Craft Coun.; mem. World Craft Coun., Surface Design Assn. (S.E. regional rep. 1977-80, pres. 1980-82, named hon. life mem. 1983), Phi Beta Delta. Office: Sch of Art Univ Ga Athens GA 30602

KAUFMAN, JAMES MARK, lawyer; b. Oklahoma City, Feb. 28, 1951; s. Milford James and Frances Aileen (Knight) K.; m. Katheryn Ann Kidd, Nov. 29, 1985; children: Nathan Jay, Kaitlin Ann, Jordan Paige. BBA, U. Okla., 1973, JD, 1976. Bar: Okla. Supreme Ct. 1976, U.S. Dist. Ct. (we. dist.) Okla. 1976, U.S. Ct. Appeals (10th cir.) 1977, U.S. Supreme Ct. 1983. Intern, assoc. Carson-Trattner, Oklahoma City, 1975-77; assoc. firm Cheek, Cheek & Cheek, Oklahoma City, 1977-81, McKinney, Stringer & Webster, Oklahoma City, 1981-84; mng. atty. Kaufman & Cheek, Oklahoma City, 1984-92; prin. Law Offices of James M. Kaufman, 1992-94; of counsel Fenton, Fenton, Smith, Reneau & Moon, 1994—. Mem. ABA (torts and ins. practice sects.), Okla. Bar Assn., Oklahoma County Bar Assn., Def. Research Inst., Sigma Chi. Democrat. Methodist. Office: 211 N Robinston Ste 800 Oklahoma City OK 73102-7106

KAUFMAN, JANICE HORNER, foreign language educator; b. Mattoon, Ill., Apr. 30, 1949; d. Daniel Ogden and Julia Betty (McDermid) Horner; m. Richard Boucher Kaufman, June 24, 1972; children: Julia Ogden, Richard Pearse. AB, Duke U., 1971; MA in Liberal Studies, Hollins Coll., 1979; postgrad., NYU, 1986; doctoral candidate in French, U. Va., Charlottesville, 1994—. Tchr. Roanoke (Va.) City Pub. Schs., 1971-72, North Cross Sch., Roanoke, Va., 1974-82; instr. in French Va. Poly. Inst. and State U., Blacksburg, 1984-86, 88, 90, 94, asst. dir fgn. lang. camps, 1984-85, administrv. dir., 1986; French, English interpreter, translator Coll. Architecture and Urban Studies, Blacksburg, 1988; instr. ESL U. Community Internat. Coun., Cranwell Internat. Ctr., Blacksburg, 1987-89; instr. French Hollins Coll., Roanoke, Va., 1989-90, Radford (Va.) U., 1989, 90; grad. teaching asst. U. Va., Charlottesville, 1992; student counselor Am. Inst. Fgn. Study, Greenwich, Conn., 1977; session leader Russell County Pub. Schs., Lebanon, Va., 1985, Va. Assn. Ind. Schs., Richmond, 1986; reader Mountain Interstate Fgn. Lgn. Conf., Radford U., 1990, East Carolina U., Greenville, N.C., 1991, Va. Poly. Inst. and State U., Blacksburg, 1992, Clemson (S.C.) U., 1993, Va. Fgn. Lang. Conf., Richmond, 1993, African Lit. Assn. Conf., Guadeloupe, 1993; asst. tchr. Am. Coun. for Internat. Studies "Toujours en France", 1995; faculty cons. advanced placement exam in French, Ednl. Testing Svc., Trenton State Coll., 1991, 92, 93, 94, 95. Mem. Jr. League of Roanoke Valley, Inc., 1975—, Jr. League of No. Va., 1995—; treas. Women of Christ Ch., 1984-86; Sunday sch. tchr. Christ Episc. Ch., Blackburg, 1987-89; co-coord. jr. high youth group St. Timothy's Episc. Ch., Herndon, Va., 1994-96, mem. Christian edn. com., 1995-96. Mem. MLA, Am. Assn. Tchrs. French, African Lit. Assn., South Atlantic MLA (presenter 1994), Jr. League of No. Va., Pi Delta Phi. Home: 900 Barker Hill Rd Herndon VA 20170-3014

KAUFMAN, LORETTA ANA, sculptor; b. N.Y.C., Feb. 17, 1946; d. Josip and Mildred Barbara (Klima) Racic; m. David Henry Kaufman, Mar. 11, 1970. AS, Palm Beach Jr. Coll., Lake Worth, Fla., 1967. Ceramist Ft. Lauderdale, Fla., 1975-76, Pretoria, South Africa, 1976-81; sculptor Piedmont, S.C., 1981—; instr. Greenville (S.C.) County Mus. of Art, 1988-89; artist in residence S.C. Arts Commn., Columbia, 1989-94, Shriner's Hosp. for Crippled Children, Greenville, 1990-91, Spartanburg County Sch. Dist., S.C., 1996; vis. artist U. S.C., Columbia, 1993; lectr. in field. Curator exhibitions, N.C., S.C., Va., 1991; author (catalog) Sculptors Exhibition, 1991. Recipient Purchase award NationsBank, London, 1989, 1st pl. Monarch Tile Ceramics Competition, 1988. Mem. Nat. Artists Equity Assn., Women's Caucus for Art, Tri State Sculptors Edn. Assn. Inc. (bd. dirs., S.C. state rep. 1988-95), Piedmont Craftsmen, Sierra Club, Environ. Def. Fund. Jewish. Home: 426 Lake El Jema Dr Piedmont SC 29673-9164

KAUFMAN, MARK DAVID, lawyer; b. St. Louis, Feb. 24, 1949; s. Rudolf Ernst and Edith (Greiderer) K.; m. Diane Brown Wolfes, June 11, 1983; 1 child, Mark David. BA, Northwestern U., 1971; JD, Duke U., 1974. Bar: Ga. 1974, U.S. Ct. Appeals (11th cir.) 1974, U.S. Dist. Ct. (no. dist.) Ga. 1974. Assoc. Sutherland, Asbill & Brennan, Atlanta, 1974-81, ptnr., 1981—. Contbr. articles to profl. jours. Mem. ABA, Ga. Bar Assn., Atlanta Bar Assn. (legal counsel 1979—, Exceptional Svc. award 1987, Pres.'s Disting. Svc. award 1979-80, Charles E. Watkins Jr. award 1989), Atlanta Bar Found. (legal counsel 1985—), Kiwanis, Order of Coif. Lutheran. Home: 3739 Cloudland Dr NW Atlanta GA 30327-2909

KAUFMAN, MYRON JAY, chemistry educator; b. N.Y.C., Mar. 24, 1937; s. Nathan and Matilda (Lowenstein) K.; m. June Lynn Tave, Aug. 4, 1961; children: Daniel, Aaron. BS, Rensselaer Poly. Inst., 1965; PhD, Harvard U., 1965. Asst. prof. Princeton (N.J.) U., 1965-72; assoc. prof. Emory U., Atlanta, 1972-76, prof., 1976—. Office: Chemistry Dept Emory Univ Atlanta GA 30322

KAUFMAN, STEPHEN LAWRENCE, radiologist, educator; b. Phila., Nov. 7, 1942; s. Abraham S. and Genevieve (Finestone) K. BA, U. Pa., 1963, MD, 1967. Resident in radiology, then fellow in cardiovascular radiology Johns Hopkins Med. Ctr., Balt., 1970-75, asst. prof. radiology, 1975-79, assoc. prof., 1980-88; prof. radiology, dir. cardiovascular and interventional radiology Emory U., Atlanta, 1988—. Author: Techniques in Interventional Radiology, 1982; editor: Biliary Radiology, 1992; contbr. articles to med. jours. Served as lt. comdr. USPHS, 1968-70. Fellow Soc. Cardiovascular and Interventional Radiology; mem. Radiol. Soc. N.Am., Am. Coll. Radiology, Am. Heart Assn., Ga. Radiol. Soc. Avocations: hiking, white-water rafting, golf, computers. Office: Emory U Hosp 1364 Clifton Rd NE Atlanta GA 30322-1059

KAUFMAN, WILLIAM, internist; b. Dec. 31, 1910; s. Leo and Marie Kaufman; m. Charlotte R. Schnee, May 9, 1940. BA, U. Pa., 1931; MA in Chemistry, U. Mich., 1932, PhD in Physiology, 1937, MD cum laude, 1938. Diplomate Am. Bd. Internal Medicine. Intern Barnes Hosp., Washington U. Sch. Medicine, St. Louis, 1938-39; asst. resident, then resident Mt. Sinai Hosp., N.Y.C., 1939-40; Emanuel Libman fellow Yale U. Sch. Medicine, New Haven, 1940-41, Dazian Found. fellow, clin. asst., 1940-42; pvt. practice Bridgeport, Conn., 1940-65; courtesy staff mem. Bridgeport Hosp., 1941-65; courtesy staff St. Vincent's Hosp., Bridgeport, 1941-65; assoc. med. dir. L.W. Frohlich and Co./Intercon Internat. Inc., N.Y.C., 1964-65, med. dir., 1965-67, dir. med. affairs, 1967-68; assoc. med. dir. Klemtner Casey, Inc., N.Y.C., 1969-70, dir. med. affairs, 1970-71; v.p., dir. med. affairs Klemtner Advt., Inc., N.Y.C., 1971, sr. v.p., dir. sci. and med. affairs, 1971-81; pres., chmn. program and pub. edn. coms. Acad. Psychosomatic Medicine, 1953-55; founder fellow, mem. governing coun. Collegium Internationale Allergologicum, 1955-62; chmn. psychosomatic sect. 3d Internat. Congress Allergology, 1958; D. C. Y. Moore Meml. lectr. Manchester (Conn.) Med. Soc., 1967; cons. Family Life Film Ctr. Conn. Inc., 1967-74; mem. screening jury med. edn. sect. Am. Film Festival, 1975. Author: The Common Form of Niacinamide Deficiency Disease (Aniacinamidosis), 1943, The Common Form of Joint Dysfunction: Its Incidence and Treatment, 1949; (drawings) Kaufman's Kritters, 1990; (play) People Like Us, A Bad Day for Spider; contbg. editor Internat. Archives Allergy and Applied Immunology, 1952-54, 67-69, Am. editor in chief, 1954-67; mem. bd. editorial collaborators Psychotherapeutica, Psychosomatica et Orthopaedagogica, 1955-62; contbg. editor Quar. Rev. Allergy and Applied Immunology, 1955; contbr. numerous articles to profl. and popular jours.; exhibited drawings and paintings at Housatonic Community Coll., New Canaan Art Show, others. Mem. adv. bd. Huxley Inst. So. Conn. for Biosocial Rsch., 1980-84. Recipient citation Internat. Assn. Gerontology, 1983, 1st Pl. award Faculty of Fine Arts, Housatonic Community Coll., 1983, Sci. and Math. medal Rensselaer Poly. Inst., 1928, Sternberg Meml. Gold medal, 1938. Hon. fellow Internat. Acad. Preventive Medicine (Tom Spies Meml. award and lectr. 1978); fellow AAAS, Am. Coll. Allergy, Asthma and Immunology (emeritus, chmn. pub. edn. com. 1951-55, chmn. com. on allergy of nervous system 1962, Award of Merit 1981), Am. Coll. Nutrition, ACP (life), Gerontol. Soc. Am. (mem. various sects.), N.Y. Acad. Medicine, Royal Soc. Medicine (London); mem. AMA (life), Am Psychosomatic Soc. (emeritus), Conn. State Med. Soc. (life), Fairfield County Med. Assn. (life), Nat. Assn. Sci. Writers, N.Y. Acad. Scis., Dramatists Guild, Sigma Xi, Alpha Omega Alpha, Phi Sigma, Phi Lambda Upsilon, Phi Kappa Phi. Home: 3180 Grady St Winston Salem NC 27104-4008

KAUFMAN-DERBES, LINDA RUTH, physician; b. Ann Arbor, Mich., Jan. 29, 1960; d. Bernard and Marion (Soffee) K. BA, U. Fla., 1984; MD, U. South Fla., 1990. Lab. asst. Dept. Botany U. Fla., Gainesville, 1982-83, rsch. asst. Dept. Pathology, 1983-84; rsch. asst. dept. psychiatry-child maltreatment div. U. N.C. Hosps., Chapel Hill, 1991-92; resident in psychiatry, 1990-94, fellow in child and adolescent psychiatry, 1993-95, chief fellow, 1994; mem. Residency Tng. Com. Task Force on Recruitment and Morale,

U. N.C. Hosps., Chapel Hill, 1990-91, mem. Residency Tng. Task Force for Child Psychiatry, 1991-92, mem. Continuous Quality Improvement Com., 1991-92, mem. Dept. Psychiatry Orientation Com., 1992-93. Author: Surviving a Car Accident, A Coloring Book for Parents and Children, 1991. Rep. U. Fla. Student Infirmary Adv. Bd., Gainesville, 1981; mem. Rape Awareness Group, Gainesville, 1982-84; vol. CPR instr., Gainesville, 1982-83. Mem. AMA, APA, NAFE, Am. Med. Women's Assn., N.C. Med. Soc., Am. Psychiat. Assn., Phi Beta Kappa, Phi Kappa Phi, Alpha Epsilon Delta, Alpha Lambda Delta, Phi Eta Sigma. Home: 1313 Mapunapuna Dr Diamondhead MS 39525 Office: Memorial Hosp 4500 13th St Gulfport MS 39502-1810

KAUFMANN, MARGARET C., psychiatrist, educator; b. Princeton, N.J., Sept. 21, 1952; d. Ralph James and Ruth Joan (Hackett) K.; m. William Raymond Lynch, May 29, 1976; children: Aaron James, Isaac Paul, Michael Joseph. BA, Grinnell Coll., 1975; MD, Southwestern Med. Sch., Dallas, 1979. Diplomate Am. Bd. Psychiatry and Neurology. Intern Timberlawn Hosp. and Baylor Hosp., Dallas, 1979-80; resident Timberlawn Psychiat. Hosp., Dallas, 1980-83; resident supr. Timberlawn Hosp. and Southwestern Med. Sch., 1983-91; pvt. practice Dallas, 1983—; attending physician Dallas County Hosp. Dist., Dallas, 1983—; mem. vis. med. staff Timberlawn Hosp., 1983—, supr. Affective Disorders Clinic, Southwestern Med. Sch., 1991, clin. assoc. prof., 1992-95. Editor North Tex. Soc. Psychiat. Physicians News, 1993-95; contbg. editor News for Women in Psychiatry, 1987-93. Active, com. mem. Dallas County Female Offender Project, 1993—; pres. Zero Tolerance for Violence, 1993—; pres., mem. bd. trustees St. John's Episcopal Sch., Dallas, 1984-90; den mother, mem. pack coordinating com. Boy Scouts Am., 1986-88; mem. bd. trustees Dallas Children's Theater, 1991—. Sol Ginsburg fellow Group for Advancement of Psychiatry, Cherry Hill, N.J., 1981. Fellow Am. Psychiat. Assn. (mem. com. 1980—); mem. AMA, Tex. Med. Assn., Dallas Med. Assn., Tex. Psychiat. Assn., Dallas Psychiat. Assn., Am. Med. Women's Assn., Dallas Area Women Psychiatrists (mem. steering com. 1980-90, editor newsletter 1984-90), Tex. Soc. Psychiat. Physicians (mem. exec. coun. 1985-91, chairperson com. on women 1985-91, assoc. editor newsletter 1984-92), Phi Beta Kappa (Grinnell Coll. chpt.). Office: 12890 Hillcrest Rd Ste 100 Dallas TX 75230-1504

KAUFMANN, ROBERT S., medical educator; b. Atlanta, Ga., Feb. 25, 1959; s. James A. and Jane K.; m. Pam Despinakis, Sept. 2, 1995. BS, U. Ga., Athens, 1981; MD, Morehouse Sch. Medicine, Atlanta, 1986. Diplomate Am. Bd. Internal Medicine. Clin. asst. prof. medicine Emory U. Sch. Medicine, Atlanta, 1993—. Vol. physician Mercy Mobile, Atlanta, 1990—. Mem. AMA, Med. Assn. Ga., Med. Assn. Atlanta, Am. Coll. Physicians, Am. Soc. Internal Medicine, So. Med. Assn., Atlanta Clin. Soc. Office: The Kaufmann Clinic 565 W Peachtree St NE Atlanta GA 30308

KAUGER, YVONNE, state supreme court justice; b. Cordell, Okla., Aug. 3, 1937; d. John and Alice (Bottom) K.; m. Ned Bastow, May 8, 1982; 1 child, Jonna Kauger Kirschner. BS magna cum laude, Southwestern State U., Weatherford, Okla., 1958; cert. med. technologist, St. Anthony's Hosp., 1959; J.D., Oklahoma City U., 1969, LLD (hon.), 1992. Med. technologist Med. Arts Lab., 1959-68; assoc. Rogers, Travis & Jordan, 1970-72; jud. asst. Okla. Supreme Ct., Oklahoma City, 1972-84, justice, 1984-94; vice chief justice Okla. Supreme Ct., 1994—; mem. appellate div. Ct. on Judiciary; mem. State Capitol Preservation Commn., 1983-84; mem. dean's adv. com. Oklahoma City U. Sch. Law; lectr. William O. Douglas Lecture Series Gonzaga U., 1990. Founder Gallery of Plains Indian, Colony, Okla., Red Earth (Down Towner award 1990), 1987; active Jud. Day, Girl's State, 1976-80; keynote speaker Girl's State Hall of Fame Banquet, 1984; bd. dirs. Lyric Theatre, Inc., 1966—, pres. bd. dirs., 1981; past mem. bd. dirs. Civic Music Soc., Okla. Theatre Ctr., Canterbury Choral Soc.; mem. First Lady of Okla.'s Artisans' Alliance Com. Named Panhellenic Woman of Yr., 1990, Woman of Yr. Red Lands Coun. Girl Scouts, 1990, Washita County Hall of Fame, 1992. Mem. ABA (law sch. accreditation com.), Okla. Bar Assn. (law schs. com. 1977—), Washita County Bar Assn., Washita County Hist. Soc. (life), St. Paul's Music Soc., Iota Tau Tau, Delta Zeta (Disting. Alumna award 1988, State Delta Zeta of Yr. 1987, Nat. Woman of Yr. 1988). Episcopalian.

KAUP, DAVID EARLE, law enforcement officer; b. Pitts., May 10, 1952; s. Paul Edwin and Patricia Elizabeth (Kaelin) K.; m. Pak Tu-Im, Nov. 24, 1979; children: Paul Marshall, Steven Lyle. BS in Criminal Justice Mgmt., Ctrl. Mo. State U., 1975; MS in Criminal Justice Mgmt., Sam Houston State U., 1988; MPA, U. Houston, 1994. Cert. master peace officer, Tex., profl. in criminal justice, U.S. Patrolman Clinton (Mo.) Police Dept., 1973-74, Lake Lotawana (Mo.) Police Dept., 1974-75; security guard Burns Internat. Security Service, Pitts., 1975-76; dep. Harris County Sheriff's Dept., Houston, 1980-81, detective, 1981-84, sgt., 1984—; instr. Calif. C.Cs., extension svc., 1977-79; security coord. Westminster Village Apts., Houston, 1981-84, com. chmn. Fairmont Park Crimewatch, LaPorte, Tex., 1987—; owner Keystone Rsch. & Cons. Svcs. Editor Union Star newspaper, 1993-95; editor/pub. The Texas Street Beat newspaper, 1995—. Trustee Shin Hae Won Orphanage, Pusan, Korea, 1978; bd. dirs. Fairmont Park East Homeowners Assn., 1990-92, pres., 1993-97; sec.-treas. Harris County Dep. Sheriff's Union, 1991. Mem. Harris County Dep. Sheriff's Assn., Citizens Adv. Coun., LaPorte Plant Mgmt. Assn., Masons. Mem. Harris County Dep. Sheriff's Assn., Masons. Home: 10911 Mesquite Dr La Porte TX 77571-4337 Office: Harris County Sheriff's Dept 1301 Franklin St Houston TX 77002-1925

KAVA, D. J., labor union administrator, artist, meteorologist; b. Springfield, Oreg., Mar. 9, 1946; s. Mathew Joseph and Faye Lorene (Smith) K.; m. Amy Ilene Leonhardht, Sept. 1969 (div. Jan. 1977). Student, Tex. Tech U., 1967, Moorhead State U., 1968-69, George Meaney Ctr. for Labor Studies, 1993. Civilian weather observer USN, Dallas, 1969-72; comm. technician Nat. Hurricane Ctr., Miami, Fla., 1972-73; meteorol. technician Nat. Weather Svc., Boothville, La., 1973, Waycross, Ga., 1974, Port Arthur, Tex., 1974-94; steward br. 2-38 Nat. Weather Svc. Employee's Orgn., Port Arthur, 1980—, chmn. health and safety, 1985—, vice chmn. so. region, 1986-89, chmn., 1989-94. Contbg. editor White Triangle News, 1977-88; exhibited in numerous group shows, 1984—. Bd. dirs. Art Studio, Inc., Beaumont, Tex., 1984-85, scribe tennants orgn., 1991—; curator Art at the Airport, Jefferson County Airport, Nederland, Tex., 1987—; mem. S.E. Tex. Arts Coun., 1986—. With USAF, 1964-68. Recipient President's award Nat. Weather Svc. Employees Orgn., 1993. Mem. AAAS, Nat. Weather Assn., Soc. Automotive Historians, 9 to 5. Home: 1755 Bandera Dr Beaumont TX 77706-2707 Office: 720 Franklin St Beaumont TX 77701-4424

KAVANAUGH, FRANK JAMES, film producer, educator; b. Chgo., Sept. 12, 1934; s. Kenneth James and Carol Mae (Wilkey) K.; m. Barbara Ann Barrett, Nov. 16, 1957; children: Franklin James Jr., Christopher Barrett, Kenneth Wilkey. BA, Lake Forest Coll., 1956; PhD, Union Inst., 1982. Producer, dir., exec. ABC-TV, Chgo., N.Y.C., 1956-67; pres. Ravens Hollow Ltd., Warrenton, Va., 1967-69; exec. producer Airlie Prodns., Warrenton, 1979-89; prof. comm., prof. med. and pub. affairs, comm. chair George Washington U., Washington, 1983-89; exec. dir. Airlie Found., 1979—; adj. prof. Union Inst. Grad. Sch., 1987—; pres. Kavanaugh Assocs., Inc., 1989—; v.p. Cooper Inst. for Advanced Studies in Medicine and Humanities, 1989—; pres. Internat. Acad. for Preventive Medicine. Asst. dir. TV Kukla, Fran & Ollie, 1958; producer film The Saving of the President, 1982 (Emmy award 1982); producer dir. films A Moveable Scene, 1968 (Emmy award nominee 1969), Flowers of Darkness, 1969 (Emmy award 1969), Bridge From No Place, 1970 (Emmy award 1970), The Possible Dream, 1970 (Emmy award 1970), More Than a Paycheck, 1978 (Emmy award nominee 1978), others; producer, dir., writer film Each Child Loved, 1972 (Emmy award 1972), others. Bd. dirs. Performing Arts Trust. Recipient Cup of Italy Italian Film Festival, Salerno, 1982, highest award Edinburgh Film Festival, Scotland, 1982, Blue Ribbon Am. Film Festival, N.Y.C., 1983, Gold medal Houston Internat. Film Festival, 1983. Mem. Nat. Acad. TV Arts and Scis. (life), C.I.N.E., Inc. (life), Dirs. Guild Am., Radio and TV Dirs. Guild, Mensa, Nat. Assn. TV Program Execs. (Iris award 1983), Broadcast Pioneers. Office: Kavanaugh Assocs Inc PO Box 713 Punta Gorda FL 33938-0713

KAW, AUTAR KRISHEN, mechanical engineer, educator; b. Srinagar, India, Feb. 15, 1960; came to U.S., 1982; s. Radha Krishen and Chuni Devi (Mattoo) K.; m. Sherrie Lynn Phillips, May 16, 1986; children: Candace Sandhya, Angelie Kristen. BE with honors, Birla Inst. Tech. & Sci., Pilani, India, 1981; MS, Clemson U., 1984, PhD, 1987. Student trainee Nat. Thermal Power Corp., New Delhi, India, 1980; maintenance engr. Escorts Tractors Ltd., Faridabad, India, 1981-82; grad. rsch. asst. Clemson (S.C.) U., 1982-83, prin. grad. asst., 1984-87; asst. prof. mech. engring. U. South Fla., Tampa, 1987-92, assoc. prof., 1992—, grad. student coord. mech. engring. dept., 1989-90, assoc. prof. mech. engring., 1992—. Contbr. articles to profl. publs. Recipient Ralph Teetor award 1991; named Outstanding Tchr., Coll. Engring., U. South Fla., 1990, Teaching Enhancement awardee, 1990, Tchg. Incentive Program award State of Fla., 1994. Mem. ASME (assoc., chpt. exec. com. 1989-90), Mech. Engring. Assn. India (pres. local chpt. 1982), Am. Soc. Engring. Edn. (recipient New Mechanics Educator award 1992), Soc. Engring. Sci., Am. Acad. Mechanics. Hindu. Office: U South Fla Mech Engring ENG 118 4202 E Fowler Ave Tampa FL 33620-9900

KAYE, ALAN LESLIE, library director; b. Bloomington, Ill., Aug. 31, 1952; s. Arthur E. and Annie L. (Tilley) K.; m. Shirley R. White, July 4, 1980; children: Wayne Alan, Travis Arthur. BA in Journalism, U. Ga., 1975; M in Librarianship, Emory U., 1979; MBA, Ga. So. U., 1987. Audio visual technician Ga. So. Libr., Statesboro, 1975-78, audio visual libr., dept. head, 1981-88; instrnl. svcs. libr. Clayton State Coll. Learning Resource Ctr., Morrow, Ga., 1979-81; asst. dir. patron svcs. Chestatee Regional Libr., Gainesville, Ga., 1988-92; dir. Roddenbery Meml. Libr., Cairo, Ga., 1992—. Mem. ALA, Southeastern Libr. Assn., Ga. Libr. Assn. (treas. 1993-95), Cairo Rotary club (pres. 1996—). Mem. Ch. of Christ. Office: Roddenbery Meml Libr 320 N Broad St Cairo GA 31728-2109

KAYE, CELIA ILENE, pediatrics educator; b. July 12, 1943; m. Tod B. Sloan. BS, Wayne State U., 1965, MS, 1968, MD, 1969, PhD, 1975. Diplomate Am. Bd. Pediatrics, Am. Bd. Med. Genetics; lic. physician, Mich., Ill., Tex. Resident in pediatrics Bronx (N.Y.) Mcpl. Hosp. Ctr., 1969-71, U. Ill. Hosp., Chgo., 1971-72; fellow in biochem. genetics Children's Meml. Hosp., Chgo., 1972-75; instr. pediatrics Northwestern U. Coll. Medicine, Chgo., 1974-75; from asst. prof. to assoc. prof. pediatrics U. Ill. Coll. Medicine, Chgo., 1975-89; chmn. divsn. genetics dept. pediatrics Cook County Hosp., Chgo., 1975-80, attending physician divsn. genetics, dept. pediatrics, 1980-89; dir. sect. genetics and genetics lab., divsn. pediatrics Luth. Gen. Hosp., Park Ridge, Ill., 1980-89, co-med. dir. Perinatal Ctr., 1986-89; dep. chmn. Santa Rosa Children's Hosp. Activities, co-dir. clin. cytogenics lab. U. Tex. Health Sci. Ctr., San Antonio, 1990—, prof. depts. pediatrics and cellular and structural biology, 1990—, chief sect. of metabolism, 1990—, vice chmn. dept. pediatrics, 1993—, co-dir. cytogenetics lab., 1990—; mem. quality assurance com. cytogenetics lab. dept. cellular and structural biology U. Tex. Health Sci. Ctr., 1991—, chair clin. faculty promotions com. dept. pediats., 1991—, chair com. for devel. plan for selection, evaluation and promotion of clin. faculty dept. pediats., 1990-91, med. perinatal mktg. com. dept. pediats., 1990-91, mem. residency adv. com. dept. pediats., 1990—, mem. faculty tenure and promotions com., 1995—, mem. search com., chmn. dept. pathology, 1995-96, mem. dual degree program com., 1995—, vice-chmn. bd. dirs. univ. physicians group, 1995—, mem. contract rev. com. 1995—; mem. clin. coord. com., 1990—, ad hoc clin. care com., 1990—, MSRDP adv. bd., 1991-93, search com. chmn. dept. medicine, 1992-93; chmn. program comm. sect. on genetics and birth defects Am. academy of pediat., 1995—; dir. sect. genetics, Ctr. Craniofacial Anomalies, U. Ill. Coll. Medicine, Chgo., 1975-85; mem. med. adv. bd. Santa Rosa Children's Hosp., 1990-91, mem. exec. com. sect. on genetics and birth defects, Am. Acad of pediat., 1995— dir. med. edn., 1991—, exec. com., 1992—, medicine policy com., 1992—, chair med. edn. com., 199—; assoc. med. dir. cytogenetics lab. Santa Rosa Med. Ctr., San Antonio, 1991—; vis. assoc. prof. pediats. Rush-Presbyn.-St. Luke's Med. Ctr., Chgo., 1979-89; mem. Genetics Task Force Ill., 1981-89, sec., 1981-83, pres., 1983-85; mem. genetics svc. com. Tex. Genetics Network, 1989—, chmn. steering com., 1992—; chmn. sci. adv. com. on birth defects Tex. Dept. Health, 1995—; del. Nat. Coun. Regional Genetics Networks, 1992—, mem. exec. com., 1993—; mem. Ill. Genetic and Metabolic Diseases Adv. Bd., 1984-89, chmn. lab. subcom., 1985-89; mem. sci. adv. com. Tex. Dept. Health, 1992—; mem. steering com. Children's Regional Health Care Network, San Antonio, 1992-93; mem. mgmt. com. Children's Regional Health Care Sys., San Antonio, 1993—; mem. instl. rev. bd. Cook County Hosp., Chgo., 1975-80, Luth. Gen. Health Care Sys., Park Ridge, Ill., 1988-89; chmn. pediat. edn. com. Luth. Gen. Hosp., Park Ridge, 1981-86, chmn. pediat. bioethics com., mem. faculty adv. com., 1986-89; mem. fac. com. tenure and promotion com., 1995, mem. serea com. chmn. dept. pathology, 1995-96, mem. cons. Med. Ctr. Hosp. Ward and Nursery, Bapt. Hosp. Sys., Santa Rosa Children's Hosp., Meth. Hosp., Humana Women's Hosp.; mem. by laws com. Santa Rosa Healthcare, San Antonio, 1995—. Mem. adv. bd. Am. Jour. Med. Genetics; reviewer Am. Jour. Human Genetics, Pediatric Dermatology; contbr. articles to profl. jours., chpts. to books. Mem. program planning com. March of Dimes Defects Found., Chgo., 1985-89, mem. health profl. adv. com., 1983-89, chmn., 1981-83; mem. health profl. adv. com. South Ctrl. Tex. chpt., 1989-90; bd. dirs., mem. exec. com. Harkness House for Children, Winnetka, Ill., 1988-89; mem. Ill. Spina Bifida Assn., 1983-89; mem. exec. bd. El Valor Corp. foricapped Children, Chgo., 1980-81; mem. med. adv. com. Tex. Sickle Cell Assn., 1990-91. Fellow Am. Coll. Med. Genetics (founding, edn. com. 1993—, moderator pub. health and delivery of svcs. sect. ann. meeting 1994); mem. AMA, Am. Soc. Human Genetics (info. and edn. com. 1990—), Am. Acad. Pediats. (genetics sect., judge sci. awards uniformed svcs. sect. 1992-93, chair program com. sect. on genetics and birth defects 1995—, mem. exec. com. sect. on genetics and birth defects 1995—), Soc. for Pediat. Rsch., Teratology Soc., Soc. for Inherited Metabolic Diseases, So. Soc. for Pediat. Rsch. (moderator genetics sect. ann. meeting 1993—), Tex. Med. Soc., Tex. Genetics Soc., Tex. Pediat. Soc., Bexar County Med. Soc., San Antonio Pediat. Soc. Office: U Tex Health Sci Ctr Genetics Dept 7703 Floyd Curl Dr San Antonio TX 78284-6200

KAYE, HOWARD, business executive. Pres. Polyhedron Labs., Inc., Houston. Office: Polyhedron Labs Inc 10626 Kinghurst Houston TX 77099

KAYE, JEFFERSON JAMES, orthopaedic surgeon; b. New Orleans, Sept. 5, 1947; s. Harry D.L. and Yvonne Lillian (Querie) K.; m. Joyce Carol Laroe, Aug. 6, 1972; children: Melanie Anne, Brian Randall. BA in Chemistry, Duke U., 1969; MD, Columbia Coll., 1973. Diplomate Am. Bd. Orthopaedic Surgery, qualifications in surgery of the hand, Nat. Bd. Med. Examiners; lic. physician, La. Rotating medicine/surgery intern Strong Meml. Hosp., U. Rochester, N.Y., 1973-74; orthopaedic surgery resident Ochsner Found. Hosp., New Orleans, 1974-77, chief orthopaedic resident, 1975; chief orthopaedic resident, chief hosp. resident E.A. Conway Meml. Hosp., 1976-77; microsurgery fellow dept. microsurgery U. Louisville, 1977, hand surgery fellow, 1977-78; pediatric orthopaedics rotation Kosair Hosp., U. Louisville, 1978; mem. staff dept. orthopaedics Ochsner Clinic and Ochsner Found. Hosp., New Orleans, 1979—, assoc. chmn. dept. orthopaedics, 1988—, chmn., 1994—; cons. staff Chabert Med. Ctr., Houma, 1979—; clin. instr. orthopaedic surgery Tulane Med. Sch., New Orleans, 1979-85, clin. asst. prof., 1985-90, clin. assoc. prof., 1990—, divsn. plastic surgery, 1994—; dir. orthopaedic edn. Alton Ochsner Med. Found., 1982-92, acting chmn. orthopaedic surgery, 1992-94, chmn., 1994—; examiner oral bd. exams. Am. Bd. Orthopaedic Surgery, 1986, 87, 89, 91, 92, 93, 95, 96; lectr. various seminars, confs., and meetings. Contbr. articles to profl. jours. A.B. Duke Meml. scholar, 1965-69. Mem. AMA, Am. Soc. Surgery of Hand (course planning com. 1985-87), Am. Acad. Orthopaedic Surgeons, Acad. Orthopaedic Soc., So. Med. Assn., La. State Med. Soc., La. Orthopaedic Assn., So. Orthopaedic Assn., Jefferson Parish Med. Soc. Office: Ochsner Clinic 1514 Jefferson Hwy New Orleans LA 70121-2429

KAYE, JEROME, accountant; b. N.Y.C., Jan. 10, 1923; s. Harry and Goldie (Harfen) K.; m. Harriet Phyllis Nagin, Mar. 16, 1946 (div. 1975); children: Billie Nora, Lenard Wayne, Bradley Steven. BA, Bklyn. Coll., 1943; MBA, CUNY, 1948. Acct. S.M. Kanarick & Co., N.Y.C., 1943-49; pvt. practice pub. acctg. Lynchburg, Va., 1949-65, 78-86; exec. v.p. Fed. Sweets & Biscuit Co., Clifton, N.J., 1965-70; pres. Universal Devel. Corp., Richmond, 1970-78; pvt. practice pub. acctg. Richmond, Va., 1978-86; v.p., dir. Womack, Burke and Co., Richmond, 1986-90; sr. assoc. Goodman & Co., Richmond, 1990-92; v.p., dir. LaLonde, Wooding & Kaye, Richmond, Va., 1992—; mem. Va. State Bd. for Accountancy, 1991—, chmn., 1994—. Pres. Agudath Sholom Congregation, 1953-54; active Lynchburg Jewish Community Coun., 1959-66; chmn., pres. com. employment of physically handicapped Lynchburg, 1955-56; treas., dir. Beth Ahabah Congregation, Richmond, 1982-85; pres., dir. Beth Sholom Home Va., Richmond, 1987-89; vice chmn. bd. govs. Beth Sholom Geriatric Svcs. Va., 1990-91. Mem. Va. State Bd. for Accountancy, Va. Soc. CPAs, N.Y. State Soc. CPAs. Home: 11814 Northglen Ln Richmond VA 23233-3431 Office: LaLonde Wooding & Kaye 1804 Staples Mill Rd Richmond VA 23230-3530

KAZEN, GEORGE PHILIP, federal judge; b. Laredo, Tex., Feb. 29, 1940; s. Emil James and Drusilla M. (Perkins) K.; m. Barbara Ann Sanders, Oct. 27, 1962; children: George Douglas, John Andrew, Elizabeth Ann, Gregory Stephen. BBA, U. Tex., 1960, JD with honors, 1961. Bar: Tex. 1961, U.S. Supreme Ct., U.S. Ct. Claims, U.S. Ct. Appeals (5th cir.), U.S. Dist. Ct. (so. dist.) Tex. Briefing atty. Tex. Sup. Ct., 1961-62; assoc. Mann, Freed, Kazen & Hansen, 1965-79; judge U.S. Dist. Ct. (so. dist.) Tex., Laredo, 1979—; founder, first pres. Laredo Legal Aid Soc., 1966-69; mem. Jud. Conf. Com. Crimina Law, 1990—, 5th Cir. Jud. Coun., 1991-94; adj. prof. law St. Mary's U. Sch. Law, 1990—. Pres. Laredo Civic Music Assn.; chmn. St. Augustine-Ursuline Consol. Sch. Bd.; bd. dirs. Boys' Clubs Laredo; trustee Laredo Jr. Coll., 1972-79; bd. dirs., v.p., pres. Econ. Opportunities Devel. Corp., 1968-70; past bd. dirs. D.D. Hachar Found. With USAF, 1962-65. Decorated Air Force Commendation medal; named Outstanding Young Lawyer, Larado Jaycees, 1970. Mem. ABA, Tex. Bar Found., Tex. Bar Assn., Tex. Criminal Def. Lawyers Assn., Tex. Assn. Bank Counsel, Tex. Assn. Def. Counsel, Laredo C. of C. (bd. dirs. 1975-76), 5th Cir. Dist. Judges Assn. (v.p. 1984-85, pres. 1986-88), U. Tex. Law Sch. Alumni Assn. (bd. dirs. 1976-77). Roman Catholic. Office: US Dist Ct PO Box 1060 Laredo TX 78042-1060*

KEAN, ORVILLE, academic administrator. Pres. U. V.I., St. Thomas. Office: Univ Virgin Islands Office of President 2 John Brewers Bay Saint Thomas VI 00802

KEANE, GUSTAVE ROBERT, architect, consultant; b. Vienna, Austria, Jan. 7, 1914; s. Robert Kien and Frances (Partl) K.; m. Constance van Lennep, Jan. 30, 1940; children—Robert van Lennep, John Francis. Archtl. engr., State U. Czechoslovakia, 1937. Designer Harvey Wiley Corbett, N.Y.C., 1940-43; with Eggers Partnership, N.Y.C., 1945-73; partner Eggers Partnership, 1963-73; archtl.-engring. cons., tech. adviser to attys. in def. of malpractice litigation against design professions; mgmt. cons. archtl. and engring. firms, 1973—; guest lectr. Bd. dirs. Bldg. Research Inst., Washington, Nat. Bd. Accreditation in Concrete Constrn. Prin. works include Am. Embassy, Ankara, Turkey, U.S. Naval Hosp, P.R., N.J. Coll. Medicine and Dentistry, Lafayette Hosp, N.Y. Times Printing Plant, BASF Corporate Hdqrs. N.J; Contbr. to books, jours. Past chmn. architects com. United Hosp. Fund. Fellow A.I.A., Am. Soc. Testing Materials; mem. Am. Assn. Hosp. Planning. Home and Office: 1012 Pelican Ct Bradenton FL 34209-8209

KEANINI, RUSSELL GUY, mechanical engineering educator, researcher; b. Denver, June 29, 1959; s. Russell Eldridge and Patricia Ann (Regan) K.; m. Yvette Michelle. BS, Colo. Sch. of Mines, Golden, 1983; MS, U. Colo., Denver, 1987; PhD, U. Calif., Berkeley, 1992. Bldg. specialist Nicor Exploration, Golden, 1984-85; structural designer Commerce City Supply, 1985-86; grad. rsch. asst. U. of Colo., Denver, 1985-87, U. of Calif., Berkeley, Calif., 1987-92; asst. prof. U. N.C., Charlotte, 1992—. Contbr. articles to profl. jours. Recipient Engring. Found. Rsch. Initiation award Engring. Found. and ASME, 1993-94, Alcoa Found. award, 1995, Jr. Faculty Enhancement award Oak Ridge Assoc. Univs., 1995; Colo. Sch. Mines scholar, 1982-83; NASA grad. rsch. fellow, 1988-89. Mem. AIAA, ASME, Am. Phys. Soc. Home: 409 Morris Dr Harrisburg NC 28075-9489 Office: U NC Charlotte Dept Mech Engring Charlotte NC 28223

KEAR, MARIA MARTHA RUSCITELLA, lawyer; b. Phila., May 9, 1954; d. Ulysses Thomas and Joan Marie (Hagner) Ruscitella; m. Daniel John Kear, May 31, 1988; children: Caitlin Joan, Daniel John II. BA, Elmira Coll., 1975; JD, Delaware Law Sch., Wilmington, 1978. Bar: Pa. 1979, Md. 1985, Va. 1991. Pvt. practice, Wayne, Pa., 1979-80, Paoli, Pa., 1982-83; corp. counsel C.D.M. Inc., Hatboro, Pa., 1980-82; gen. counsel Theriault's Inc., Annapolis, Md., 1983-85; corp. counsel Devel. Resources, Inc., Alexandria, Va., 1985-87; sr. atty., asst. corp. sec. People's Drug Stores, Inc., Alexandria, 1987-91; gen. counsel Jenco Group, 1991-92; ptnr. Fullerton & Kear, 1992-93; mng. ptnr. Kear & Gilbert, 1993—. Contbr. monthly newsletter The Dollmasters, 1983; contbr. The Law Forum, 1976—. Mem. Annapolis Law Ctr., 1983—; treas. Women's Law Ctr. Anne Arundel County. Mem. ABA, Pa. Bar Assn., Md. Bar Assn., Va. Bar Assn., Women's Bar Assn. Md., Internat. Conf. Shopping Ctrs., Delta Theta Phi. Republican. Roman Catholic. Home: 6801 Tepper Dr Clifton VA 20124-1639 Office: Kear & Gilbert 4085 Chain Bridge Rd Ste 300 Fairfax VA 22030-4106

KEARFOTT, JOSEPH CONRAD, lawyer; b. Martinsville, Va., Sept. 24, 1947; s. Clarence P. and Elizabeth (Kelly) K.; m. Mary Jo Veatch, Feb.10, 1969; children: Kelly, David. BA, Davidson Coll., 1969; JD, U. Va., 1972. Bar: Va. 1972, U.S. Dist. Ct. (ea. and we. dists.) Va. 1973, U.S. Ct. Appeals (4th cir.) 1973, U.S. Tax Ct. 1979, U.S. Ct. Appeals (1st cir.) 1981, U.S. Ct. Appeals (5th cir.) 1982. Law clk. to presiding judge U.S. Dist. Ct. (ea. dist.) Va., Richmond, 1972-73; assoc. Hunton & Williams, Richmond, 1973-80, ptnr., 1980—; lectr. NITA program, Washington and Lee U., 1982-83, Va. Com. on Continuing Legal Edn., 1984—; mem. 4th Cir. Jud. conf. Mem. Richmond Bd. Housing, 1977-85, Richmond Dem. Com., 1978-82; trustee Libr. Va. Found., 1994—, William Byrd Cmty. House, 1978-84, chmn., 1982-84; trustee United Way Svcs., Richmond, 1989-95, treas., 1993-95; trustee Libr. Va., 1989-94, vice chmn., 1990-91, chmn., 1991-92; trustee Trinity Episcopal Sch., 1986-94, treas., 1989-92, chmn., 1993-94. Mem. ABA, Va. Bar Assn. (Boyd Graves conf.), Def. Rsch. Inst., Richmond Bar Assn., Order of Coif, Bull and Bear Club. Home: 4436 Custis Rd Richmond VA 23225-1012 Office: Hunton & Williams East Tower Riverfront Pla 951 E Byrd St Richmond VA 23219-4040

KEARLEY, F. FURMAN, minister, religious educator, magazine editor; b. Montgomery, Ala., Nov. 7, 1932; s. John Ausban and Zelma Olene (Suggs) K.; m. Helen Joy Bowman, July 18, 1951; children: Janice Gail Kearley Mink, Amelia Lynn Kearley Johnson. BA, Ala. Christian Coll., (now Faulkner U.), 1954; MA, Harding U., 1956; MEd, Auburn U., 1960; MRE, ThM, Harding U., 1965; PhD, Hebrew Union Coll.-Jewish Inst. Religion, 1971; LLD (hon.), Lubbock Christian U., 1985. Min. of the Gospel. Evangelist Chs. of Christ, various cities, 1951—; chmn. Bible dept. Faulkner U., Montgomery, 1956-64; chmn., humanities div. Lubbock (Tex.) Christian Univ., 1970-75; dir., grad. studies in religion Abilene (Tex.) Christian Univ., 1975-85; dean Magnoila Bible Coll., 1993—; sec., treas. S.W. Region Evang. Theol. Soc., 1982-85; adv. bd. Gospel Svcs., Houston, 1985-95; pres.'s coun. Lubbock (Tex.) Christian Univ., 1986-94. Author: (book) God's Indwelling Spirit, 1974; editor: (book) Biblical Interpretation, 1986, (religious periodical) Gospel Advocate, 1985—; contbr. over 500 articles to jours. Recipient Alumnus of Yr. award Harding U., Searcy, Ark., 1985, Harding Grad. Sch. Religion, Memphis, 1986, Outstanding Christian Journalism award Freed-Hardeman U., 1994. Mem. Soc. Bib. Lit., Evang. Theol. Soc., Nat. Assn. Tchrs. and Profs. of Hebrew. Office: Gospel Advocate PO Box 726 Kosciusko MS 39090-0726

KEARNEY, ANNA ROSE, history educator; b. Mount Pleasant, Pa., Mar. 1, 1940; d. John Joseph and Marguerite Costello (Gettings) K. BA, St. Mary's Coll., Notre Dame, Ind., 1962; MA, U. Notre Dame, 1967, PhD, 1975; MS in Libr. Sci., Ind. U., 1983. Cert. tchr., Pa. Tchr. Hempfield Area Schs., Greensburg, Pa., 1962-66, Mishawaka (Ind.) Sch. Dist., 1967-68; teaching asst. U. Notre Dame, 1968-70, libr. clk., 1974-76, libr. assoc., 1976-86; divsn. chair gen. edn. Ind. Vo-Tech. Coll., South Bend, 1970-72; asst. to univ. libr. U. Louisville, 1986-89; assoc. prof. Am. history Jefferson C.C./U. Ky., Louisville, 1989—; faculty cons. Ednl. Testing Svc., San Antonio, 1993, 96. Contbr. articles to profl. jours. Judge Nat. History Day, Louisville and Indpls., 1990-94; exec. on loan United Way of St. Joseph County, South Bend, 1982; food coord. Ethnic Festival, South Bend, 1974; lector Our Lady of Lourdes Ch., Louisville, 1987—. Grantee U. Louisville, 1987, U. Notre Dame, 1988, Ky. Libr. Assn., 1988, NEH, 1990-92, 95. Mem. Assn. of Coll. and Rsch. Libs. (exec. com. for 5th nat. conf. 1987-89), Orgn. Am. Historians, So. Hist. Assn., Cath. Hist. Assn., Ky. Assn. Tchrs. History, Nat. Coun. of Women's Studies Assn., St. Mary's Coll. South Bend Alumnae Assn. (pres. 1984-85), Phi Alpha Theta. Democrat. Roman Catholic.

Home: 3316 Cawein Way Louisville KY 40220-1908 Office: Jefferson Cmty Coll/U Ky 109 E Broadway Louisville KY 40202-2005

KEARNEY, DOUGLAS CHARLES, lawyer, journalist; b. Gloucester, Mass., June 24, 1945; s. Charles Matthew Kearney and Jean (Tarr) Thomas. Student, Brown U., 1963-64; BA, Fla. State U., 1971, JD with high honors, 1973. Bar: Fla. 1974, Calif. 1976, U.S. Ct. Appeals (5th cir.) 1977, U.S. Dist. Ct. (mid. and so. dists.) Fla. 1978, U.S. Ct. Appeals (11th cir.) 1981, U.S. Supreme Ct. 1982, U.S. Dist. Ct. (no. dist.) Tex. 1985, Tex. 1986. Asst. pub. defender Office of Pub. Defender 2d Jud. Cir., Tallahassee, 1973-76; asst. atty. gen. Atty. Gen.'s Office State of Fla., Tallahassee, 1977-78, chief antitrust enforcement unit Atty. Gen.'s Office, 1978-79; prin. Law Offices of Douglas C. Kearney, Tallahassee, 1979-85; assoc. Brice & Mankoff, P.C., Dallas, 1985-87, mem., 1987-89; mem. Choate & Lilly, P.C., Dallas, 1989-92; prin. Kearney & Assocs., Dallas, 1992—. Pres. Legal Aid Found. of Tallahassee, Inc., 1984. With U.S. Army, 1965-68, Vietnam. Mem. Fla. Bar Assn., Tex. Bar Assn., Calif. Bar Assn. Episcopalian. Office: Kearney & Assocs 15105 Cypress Hills Dr Dallas TX 75248-4914

KEARNEY, SUSAN HOPE, writer; b. N.Y.C., Feb. 7, 1955; d. Herbert and Joan (Schreibersdorf) Gottlieb; m. Barry Lee Kearney, June 20, 1980; children, Tara, Logan. BBS, U. Mich. Author: Tara's Child, 1995, A Baby to Love, 1996. Coach Durant H.S., Fla., 1995. Named 3-time All-Am. Diver, NCAA, 1973-76. Mem. Romance Writers of Am. (spkr. nat. conv., Dallas 1996), Profl. Area Sisters, Inc., Tampa Area Romance Authors.

KEARNEY NUNNERY, ROSE, nursing administrator, educator, consultant; b. Glen Falls, N.Y., July 8, 1951; d. James J. and Helen F. (Oprandy) K.; m. Jimmie E. Nunnery. BS with honors, Keuka Coll., 1973; M of Nursing, U. Fla., 1976, PhD, 1987. Asst. prof. La. State U. Med. Ctr., New Orleans, 1976-87, U. of South Fla., Tampa, 1987-88; project coord. indigent health care U. Fla., Gainesville, 1984-85; dir. nursing programs SUNY, New Paltz, N.Y., 1988-94; project dir. MS in gerontol. nursing advanced nursing edn. grant U.S. Health Resources and Svcs. Adminstrn. Div. Nursing, 1992-94; head nursing dept. Tech. Coll. of the Lowcountry, Beaufort, S.C., 1995—. Bd. dirs. Ulster County unit Am. Cancer Soc., 1991-94, mem. nursing edn. com., 1990-92; bd. dirs. Mid-Hudson Consortium for Advancement Edn. for Health Profls., 1988-94, mem. nursing edn. com., 1988-92, mem. scholarship com., 1989-93, com. chmn., 1990-93, treas., 1992-94; mem. prof. devel. program SUNY, Albany, 1989-92; mem. adv. coun. Ulster C.C., 1989-94; mem. adv. regional planning group for early intervention svcs. United Cerebral Palsy Ulster County Inc., Children's Rehab. Ctr., 1989-91; mem. Ulster County adv. com. Office for Aging, 1991-94; state del. S.C. Conf. on Aging, 1995; bd. dirs. Beaufort County Coun. on Aging, 1995; mem. cmty. adv. bd. Hilton Head Hosp., 1996—, Hilton Head Med. Ctr. and Clinics, 1996—. Mem. ANA, S.C. Nurses Assn. (editl. bd. 1994—, chair 1996), Sigma Theta Tau. Roman Catholic. Home: 41 S Shore Ct Hilton Head Island SC 29928-7656

KEARNS, DARIEN LEE, marine officer; b. Berea, Ky., July 31, 1955; s. Ottis Lee and Norma Jean (Hornback) K.; m. Anita Kathryn Dennis, Dec. 10, 1977; children: Michael Douglas, Joshua Lee, Kathryn Elizabeth. BA in Comm., No. Ky. U., 1977. Commd. 2nd lt. USMC, 1977, advanced through grades to lt. col., 1995; battery officer/XO 2d Marine Divsn., Camp Lejeune, N.C., 1979-81; platoon comdr. nuclear ordnance platoon, commanding officer Ammo Co. USMC, Camp Lejeune, N.C., 1982-84; OIC detachment One, ammo co. officer USMC, Okinawa, Japan, 1984-85; battery comdr. 1st batallion, 10th MAR, 2d Marine divsn. USMC, Camp Lejeune, N.C., 1985-88; chief basic fire support br./instr. USMC, Ft. Sill, Okla., 1988-91; chief observer group Jerusalem/UN observer UN Truce Supervision Orgn., 1991-92; Marine aide to vice chief Naval Ops. OP NAV Staff, Pentagon, Washington, 1993-95; sect. head ground combat element PP&O, HQMC, Washington, 1995—. Contbr. articles to profl. jours. Decorated Merit Svc. medals, Joint Svc. Commendations medal, others. Mem. Masons (32 degree). Republican. Methodist. Home: 371 Qtrs Quantico VA 22134 Office: PP&O HQMC Attn POE 20 Washington DC 20380

KEARNS, JOHN WILLIAM (BILL KEARNS), electronics inventor and executive; b. Salem, W.Va., Oct. 30, 1935; s. John D. and Mary Agnes (Nutter) K.; m. Kathleen E. McIntyre, June 10, 1946; children: Mary A., John W. Jr., Chester Paul. BS, St. Mary Coll., Xavier, Kans., 1970; M., U. Mich., Lansing, 1978. Commd. 2d lt. U.S. Army, 1952; advanced through grades to lt. col. U. S. Army, 1973; ret. U.S. Army, various places, 1973; v.p. United Banking Group, W. Palm Beach, Fla., 1973-76; gen. agt. Mass. Mutual Life Ins. Co., Nashville, 1976-79; pres., owner Bill Kearns & Assocs. Inc., Brentwood, Tenn., 1979-88; pres., chief exec. officer Adcom, Paxton, Fla., 1988-91; owner Ed Smith's Antique Old Time Ice Cream Parlor & Fillin Sta., 1992—; bd. dirs. Sister Cities Internat., Washington. Contbr. articles to profl. jours.; inventor T Ball for children, elevator audio machine. Vice mayor City of Brentwood, 1983-85, commr. 1981-85; planning commr. 1981-83. Decorated Vietnamese Cross of Gallantry, Bronze Star, Air medal. Mem. Gideons Internat., Fla. C. of C., VFW, Rotary, Paxton Ruritan Club (pres. lt. gov., zone gov. dist. 27). Republican. Baptist. Home and Office: PO Box 5240 Paxton FL 32538-5240

KEARNS, RUTH MARY SCHILLER, bank executive; b. Sumter, S.C., July 1, 1946; d. John Hermann and Ruth (Robosson) Schiller; m. James Conrad Kearns, July 22, 1972. BA, U. So. Carolina, 1968, MBA, 1994. Sr. v.p., asst. corp. sec. Coastal Fed. Savs. Bank, Myrtle Beach, S.C., 1970—; v.p. Coastal Fin. Corp., Myrtle Beach, 1992—; bd. dirs. Myrtle Beach Area C. of C., 1984-86. Dir. Waccamaw Arts and Crafts Guild, Myrtle Beach, 1985-86; bd. dirs. Horry County United Way, 1987—; participant Leadership Grand Strand, 1982-83, Leadership S.C., 1983-84; mem. Horry County Higher Edn. Commn., 1987—, vice chmn., 1987-89; cmty. appearance bd. City of Myrtle Beach, 1996; mem. Sun Fun Festival Coun., 1983—; mem. Keep Am. Beautiful Com. Myrtle Beach, 1988—; mem. devel. coun. Coastal Carolina Coll., 1989-91. Named Woman of Yr. Gamma Pi Chpt. Beta Sigma Phi, Myrtle Beach, 1976, Alumna of Yr. award Coastal Carolina Coll., 1989. Mem. Coastal Advt. Fedn. (pres. 1984-85, Am. Advt. Fedn. Silver medal award 1988), S.C. Savs. & Loan League (young mgmt. divsn. 1988—), Toastmaster (treas. Myrtle Beach club 1985-87). Methodist. Home: 6101 Calhoun Rd Myrtle Beach SC 29577-2273 Office: Coastal Federal Savs Bank 2619 Oak St Myrtle Beach SC 29577-3129

KEATH, (MARTIN) TRAVIS, business valuation consultant; b. Laredo, Tex., June 5, 1966; s. Adrin Shaw and Saundra (Hunley) K.; m. Patricia Walker, Jan. 26, 1991; 1 child, Matthew Allan Walker. BBA, Tex. A&M U., 1988, MS, 1989. CPA, CFA. Cons. reorganization and litigation svcs. group Price Waterhouse, Dallas, 1989-91; mgr. valuation group Deloitte & Touche, LLP, Dallas, 1991-95; sr. assoc. Bus. Valuation Svcs., Inc., Dallas, 1995—. Mem. AICPA, Assn. for Corp. Growth, Assn. Investment Mgmt. and Rsch., Inst. CFAs, Am. Soc. Appraisers, Dallas Assn. Investment Analysts (sec./treas., bd. dirs., chmn. ethics and profl. conduct com., instr. CFA exam. rev. course), Phi Kappa Phi, Beta Gamma Sigma. Baptist. Home: 6203 Martel Ave Dallas TX 75214-3027 Office: Business Valuation Services 3030 LBJ Freeway Ste 1650 Dallas TX 75234

KEATING, FRANCIS ANTHONY, II, governor, lawyer; b. St. Louis, Feb. 10, 1944; s. Anthony Francis and Anne (Martin) K.; m. Catherine Dunn Heller, 1972; children: Carissa Herndon, Kelly Martin, Anthony Francis III. A.B., Georgetown U., 1966; J.D., U. Okla., 1969. Bar: Okla. 1969. Spl. agt. FBI, 1969-71; asst. dist. atty. Tulsa County, 1971-72; mem. Okla. Ho. of Reps., 1972-74, Okla. Senate, 1974-81; U.S. atty. No. Dist. Okla., 1981-84; asst. sec. U.S. Treasury Dept., Washington, 1985-88; assoc. atty. gen. Dept. Justice, 1988-89; gen. counsel, acting dep. sec. Dept. Housing and Urban Devel., Washington, 1989-93; atty. Richardson Stoops and Keating, Tulsa, 1993-95; gov. State of Okla., 1995—. Mem. Okla. Bar Assn. Office: Office Gov 212 State Capitol Bldg Oklahoma City OK 73105

KEATING, THOMAS PATRICK, health care administrator, educator; b. Cleve., Jan. 5, 1949; s. Thomas Wilbur and Margaret (Gahllagher) K.; m. Carolyn Elizabeth Kraft, Sept. 4, 1976; children: Jerrod Patrick, Kerri Ann. BS in Bus., Cleve. State U., 1971; MS in Bus., U. Toledo, 1973. Lic. nursing home adminstr.; cert. health care exec. Asst. dir. facilities U. Kans. Med. Ctr., Kansas City, 1977-80; dir. mgmt. svcs. Charleston (S.C.) County Park and Recreation Commn., 1980-84; adminstr. fin., support svcs. Med. U. of S.C., Charleston, 1984—, instr., 1987—, preceptor adminstrv. residency, master health svcs. adminstrn., 1990-93; adj. instr. Cen. Mich. U., Mt. Pleasant, 1979—, Rockhurst Coll., Kansas City, 1979-80, Kansas City (Kans.) Community Jr. Coll., 1978-80, Fayetteville (N.C.) Tech. Inst., 1974-75; accredited cons. SBA, Charleston, 1980-91; adj. prof. Webster U., St. Louis, 1981—, faculty U. Ala., New Coll., 1974; nursing home cons. Charleston County Mental Retardation Bd., Charleston, 1987-88. Contbr. articles to profl. jours. Vol. Driftwood Health Care Ctr., Charleston, 1981-83. Capt. U.S. Army, 1973-77, lt. col. USAR ret. Fellow Am. Coll. Health Care Execs.; mem. Sigma Phi Epsilon (com. chmn. 1970-71), Alpha Kappa Psi (com. chmn. 1972-73), KC. Roman Catholic. Club: Toastmasters (adminstrv. v.p. 1985-86). Home: 898 Farm Quarter Rd Mount Pleasant SC 29464-9518 Office: Med U SC 171 Ashley Ave Charleston SC 29425-0001

KEATON, FRANCES MARLENE, sales representative; b. Redfield, Ark., July 1, 1944; d. John Thomas and Pauline (Hilliard) Wells; m. Larry Ronald Keaton, Sept. 17, 1946. Cert. in acctg., Draughon's Sch. Bus., 1972. Lic. ins. agt. Acctg. supr. Home Ins. Co., Little Rock, 1962-70; auditor St. Paul Ins. Co., Little Rock, 1970-74; spl. agt. Continental Ins. Co., Little Rock, 1974—. Vol. Ark. Sch. for the Blind, Little Rock, 1968. Mem. Little Rock Field Club, Casualty Roundtable, Auditor's Assn., Ins. Women, Underwriters Roundtable, The Executive Female, Ind. Ins. Agts. Assn., Profl. Ins. Assn. Democrat. Methodist. Home and Office: 111 Red River Dr Sherwood AR 72120-5851

KEATON, LAWRENCE CLUER, safety engineer, consultant; b. Gainesville, Tex., Nov. 24, 1924; s. William Lenard and Lettie (Phipps) K.; m. Emalee Prichard, Feb. 22, 1947; children: Lawrel Larsen, L.C. Jr., T.E. BSME, U. Okla., 1945; MS in Safety Mgmt. (hon.), Western States U., 1989, PhD in Bus. Adminstrn. (hon.), 1989. Registered profl. engr., Tex.; cert. lightning protection inspector; diplomate Coun. of Engring. Specialty Bds. In various engring. positions Phillips Petroleum Co., Borger, Tex., 1946-65; project devel. engr. Phillips Petroleum Co., N.Y.C., 1964-65; mng. dir. Nordisk Philback AB, Malmo, Sweden, 1965-73; dir. carbon black ops. Europe and Africa Phillips Petroleum Co., 1973-74, world-wide dir. carbon black ops., 1974-76; mng. dir. Sevalco Ltd., Bristol, Eng., 1976-81; ind. cons., 1981-85; mng. ptnr. System Engring. and Labs. Northwest Tex., Amarillo, 1985—. 5 patents in petrochem. processes. Lt. (j.g.) USN, 1943-45, PTO. Mem. ASME, Am. Soc. Safety Engrs., Lightning Protection Inst., Nat. Assn. Corrosion Engrs., Nat. Acad. Forensic Engrs., Nat. Assn. Fire Investigators, Nat. Assn. Profl. Accident Reconstruction Specialists, Nat. Soc. Profl. Engrs., Soc. Am. Mil. Engrs., Tex. Soc. Profl. Engrs., Amarillo Rotary, Shriners, Masons, Amarillo Club, Am. Legion, Tenn. Squires. Methodist. Home: 1610 S Hughes St Amarillo TX 79102-2647 Office: System Engring and Labs NW Tex PO Box 1506 Amarillo TX 79105-1506

KEATON, MOLLIE M., elementary school educator; d. Lorenzo and Katie Mae (Thomas) K. BS, Kent State U., 1976; MA, Atlanta U., 1980, EdD, 1985. Counselor DeKalb County Bd. Edn., Decatur, Ga.; rsch. asst. Atlanta U.; tchr. Canton (Ohio) Bd. Edn. Mem. Assn. for Supervision and Curriculum Devel., Phi Delta Kappa. Home: 4076 Chapel Mill Bnd Decatur GA 30034-5335

KEATON, WILLIAM THOMAS, academic administrator, pastor; b. England, Ark., Aug. 29, 1921; m. Theresa Simpson, July 29, 1946; children: Sherrye Ann, William II, Bernard, Denise, Edwin, Karen, Renwick, Zelda, Aloysius. AA, Ark. Bapt. Coll., 1940-42; BA, U. Ark., 1948; MA, Columbia U., 1951. Supt. Howard County Sch. Dist. #38, Mineral Springs, Ark., 1951-56, East Side Sch. Dist., Menifee, Ark., 1956-61; prin. Quachita County High Sch., Bearden, Ark., 1961-68, Peake High Sch., Arkadelphia, Ark., 1968-70; coord. state programs Ark. Dept. Edn., Little Rock, 1970-85; pres. Ark. Baptist Coll., Little Rock, 1985—; vis. prof. Ala. State U., 1972; researcher Office of Edn., Washington, 1973; state insvc. coord. Region VI-AR, staff devel. specialist, Little Rock, 1970-85; staff assoc. adult edn. U. Tex., Austin, 1967-70, Lafayette, La., 1972; pastor Greater Mt. Zion Bapt. Ch., Ashdown, Ark., 1951-72, Greater Pleasant Hill Bapt. Ch., Arkadelphia, Ark., 1972-79, Canaan Missionary Bapt. Ch., Little Rock, 1979—; mem. pres. adv. bd. dirs. Historically Black Colls. and U., 1989. Mem. NCCJ, NEA (life), NAACP (life), Ark. Edn. Assn., Ark. Adult Edn. Assn. (pres. 1969-70), Union Dist. Assn. (dean 1980—), Nat. Assn. Pub. Continuing Edn., Nat. Assn. Equal Opportunity Higher Edn. (sec. 1988-93, bd. dirs. 1989), Masons, Alpha Phi Alpha, Phi Delta Kappa. Democrat. Baptist. Office: Ark Bapt Coll 1600 Bishop St Little Rock AR 72202-6067*

KEATS, PATRICIA HART, counselor, educator; b. Boise, Idaho, July 18, 1946; d. Robert James Hart and Joyce Elizabeth (Shroyer) Smith; m. Theodore Eliot Keats, Mar. 30, 1974; 1 child, Ian. AS, Piedmont Coll., 1982; BS, Mary Baldwin Coll., 1983; MEd, U. Va., 1986, EdD, 1992. Cert. Am. Bd. Radiologic Tech.; cert. Nat. Bd. Cert. Counselors; lic. profl. counselor, Va. Rsch. asst. U. Va., Charlottesville, 1982-83, 86-87; counselor Charlottesville, 1986—; mem. faculty, counselor Piedmont Community Coll., Charlottesville, 1987—; Honor lectr. Mary Baldwin Coll., 1988. Pres. Charlottesville Cmty. Children's Theatre, 1974-84, 78; mem. Charlottesville Light Opera Co., 1978—; supr. Albemarle County Fair, 1988—; exec. com. Jefferson Cmty. Theatre, 1991; bd. dirs. Epilepsy Assn. Va., 1993—. Mem. AACD, Am. Soc. Radiologic Tech., Psi Chi, Chi Sigma Iota. Home: 421 Key West Dr Charlottesville VA 22901-8423

KEATS, THEODORE ELIOT, physician, radiology educator; b. New Brunswick, N.J., June 26, 1924; m. Margaret E. McNamara, Aug. 27, 1949 (dec.); children—Matthew Mason, Ian Stuart B.; m. Patricia L. Hart, Mar. 30, 1974. B.S., Rutgers U., 1945; M.D., U. Pa., 1947. Diplomate: Am. Bd. Radiology (trustee). Intern U. Pa. Hosp., Phila., 1947-48; resident U. Mich. Hosp., Ann Arbor, 1948-51; instr. U. Calif. Sch. Medicine, San Francisco, 1953-54; asst. prof. U. Calif. Sch. Medicine, 1954-56; assoc. prof. U. Mo. Sch. Medicine, Columbia, 1956-59; prof. radiology U. Mo. Sch. Medicine, 1959-63; prof., chmn. dept. radiology U. Va. Sch. Medicine, Charlottesville, 1963-92; vis. prof. Karolinska Hosp., Stockholm, 1963-64; mem. adv. council Greenbrier Clinic. Author: Atlas of Roentgenographic Measurement, 6th edit., 1990, An Atlas of Normal Roentgen Variants That May Simulate Disease, 6th edit., 1995, Self-Assessment of Current Knowledge in Diagnostic Radiology, 2d edit., 1980, An Atlas of Normal Developmental Roentgen Anatomy, 1978, 2d edit., 1988, (with Thomas H. Smith) Radiology of Musculoskeletal Injury, 1990; editor-in-chief Current Problems in Diagnostic Radiology, 1981, Emergency Radiology, 1984, 2d edit., 1989, Applied Radiology, 1989; Am. editor Skeletal Radiology; editor Emergency Radiology, 1993—. Served with AUS, 1943-47; to capt., M.C. AUS, 1951-53. Fellow Am. Coll. Radiology (Gold medal 1995); mem. AMA, Am. Roentgen Ray Soc., Radiol. Soc. N.Am., Assn. Univ. Radiologists, Soc. Pediatric Radiology, So. Med. Assn., Internat. Skeletal Soc. (medal 1995), Soc. Emergency Radiology, Phi Beta Kappa, Sigma Xi, Alpha Omega Alpha. Home: 421 Key West Dr Charlottesville VA 22901-8423 Office: U Va Hosps Jefferson Park Ave Charlottesville VA 22911

KEATY, ROBERT BURKE, lawyer; b. Baton Rouge, July 7, 1949; s. Thomas St. Paul and Alicia (Armshaw) K.; m. Erin Kenny, July 6, 1973; children: Kellen Elizabeth, Kathryn Ellen, Robert Burke, Kaneil Erin, Rory Bridgette-Anne. BS, U. Southwestern La., 1971; JD, Tulane U., 1974. Bar: La. 1973, Tex. 1986. Law clk. to judge U.S. Dist. Ct. for Ea. Dist. La., New Orleans, 1974-76; ptnr. Keaty & Keaty, Lafayette, La., 1976—; mem. pres.'s com. Offshore Tng. and Survival Ctr., U. Southwestern La. Lafayette, 1988-89; co-chmn. United Giver Fund Jud. Legal, 1994, Bishops Charity Ball Legal Com., 1995. Member dean's adv. com. Tulane U. Law Sch., New Orleans, 1987; mem. dean's exec. adv. com. Coll. Bus. Adminstrn., U. Southwestern La., 1991. Sears scholar, 1971, Teagle scholar, 1973; recipient Most Outstanding Alumnus award U. S.W. La. Coll. Bus. Adminstrs., 1991. Fellow La. Bar Found. (lifetime charter mem.); mem. La. Bankers Assn., La. Trial Lawyers (gov. 1988, 92), Lafayette C. of C. (aviation com.), Mardi Gras Krewes, Gabriel, Townhouse, Kappa Sigma.

KECK, PHILIP WALTER, transportation executive; b. Wyandotte, Mich., Feb. 6, 1947; s. George and Genevieve (Baranowski) K.; m. Janice Dallas, Aug. 31, 1969; children: Derek James, Lisa Tiffany. BS, USAF Acad., 1969; MBA, U. Colo., 1982; postgrad., U. Tex., 1987—. Commd. 2d lt. USAF, 1969, advanced through grades to capt., 1972; instr. pilot USAF, Beale AFB, 1970-75, DaNang AFB, Vietnam, 1972; instr. USAF Acad. USAF, Colorado Springs, Colo., 1975-77; resigned USAF, 1977; pilot Braniff Internat. Airlines, Dallas, 1977-81; flight data supr. Denver Air Route Traffic Control Ctr., Longmont, Colo., 1981-82; account exec. Merrill Lynch, Denver, 1982-83; pilot Regent Air Corp., L.A., 1983-85; flight mgr., check airman Am. Airlines, Dallas, 1985—; fin. planner Merrill Lynch, Denver, 1982-83. Co-author (study guide) Windshear Microburst, 1987. Decorated D.F.C., Vietnam. Republican. Lutheran. Home: 786 Windemere Way Keller TX 76248-5210 Office: Am Airlines PO Box 619617 Dallas TX 75261-9617

KECKEL, PETER J., advertising executive; b. Berlin, Dec. 13, 1942; came to U.S., 1956; s. F. Paul and Frieda G. (Schmidt) K.; m. Katherine Alice Brown, Nov. 27, 1971. BS in Polit. Sci., U. Md., 1966, postgrad., 1966; grad., U.S. Infantry Sch., Ft. Benning, Ga., 1967; grad. advanced officers course, Adjutant Gens. Sch., Ft. Ben Harrison, Ind., 1971. Exec. dir. Med. Personnel Pool, Oklahoma City, 1973-74; regional dir. Medox div. Drake Internat., Oklahoma City, 1974-78; pres., owner Okla. Communities, Inc., Edmond, 1978—, Okla. Gold Jewelry, Inc., Edmond, 1982—; mktg. cons. to various orgns. and groups, 1978—. Bd. dirs. Edmond YMCA, 1980-81, Okla. Disaster Edn. Fund, 1995—. Served to capt. U.S. Army, 1966-73, Vietnam. Decorated Bronze Star; recipient Presdl. Vietnam Veterans Outstanding Community Achievement award Pres. Carter, 1979; received Key to the City of Garland, Tex. Mem. Am. Bus. Clubs (life; bd. dirs. 1979—, pres. 1985-86, chmn. bd. dirs. 1986-87, regional big hat chmn. 1986-87, 2d dist. gov. 1989-90, nat. big hat pres. 1991-92, mem. nat. new club bldg. com., Mr. Ambuc awards 1980-81, 83-84, 87-88, dist. 1987-88, Nat. Ambuc of Yr. 1988-89, top nat. mem. recruiter 1982—, top nat. fundraiser, excellence award 1982-83, #1 club pres. in country 1985-86, chartered New Ambucs chpt., 1988), U. Md. Alumni Assn. (life.), POW-MIA Orgn., Edmond C. of C. (life; officer, awards), Rep. Presdl. Task Force (life) and others. Republican. Lutheran. Club: Edmond Soccer (v.p., bd. dirs. 1977-79, coach, referee 1976-82). Home: 908 E 10th St Edmond OK 73034-5451 Office: Okla Communities Inc 222 E 10th St Plz Edmond OK 73034-4737

KEEBLER, LOIS MARIE, elementary school educator; b. Jasper, Ala., Nov. 24, 1955; d. Roosevelt T. and Marie (Smiley) K. Student, Cen. State U., Wilberforce, Ohio; cert., North Ala. Regional Hosps., 1981. Cert. tchr., Ala. Tchr. Mamani Vallied Children Devel. Ctr., Dayton, Ohio. Vol. pub. schs. Democrat. Baptist.

KEEFE, CAROLYN JOAN, tax accountant; b. Huntington Park, Oct. 11, 1926; d. Paul Dewey and Mary Jane (Parmater) K. AA, Pasadena (Calif.) City Coll., 1947; BA, U. So. Calif., 1950. Tax acct. Shell Oil Co., L.A., 1950-71; tax acct. Shell Oil Co., Houston, 1971-91, ret., 1991. Advisor Midwest Mus. of Am. Art, 1993—; vol. Houston Mus. of Fine Arts, 1991—; vol. docent Houston Mus. of Natural Sci., 1991—, Theatre Under the Stars, 1991—, Houston Pub. TV Channel 8, Houston, 1989—; donor 2 ann. coll. scholarships in memory of Paul Dewey and Mary Jane Keefe. Mem. LWV, Inst. Mgmt. Accts. (emeritus life mem.), Desk and Derrick Club (bd. dirs. 1994-95), Houston Alumni Club of Alpha Gamma Delta, USC Houston Alumni Club. Christian Scientist. Home: 1814 Auburn Trails Sugar Land TX 77479

KEEFE, JAMES WASHBURN, educational researcher, consultant; b. L.A., Oct. 23, 1931; s. James E. and Leah M. (Washburn) K.; m. Jean Showalter, Dec. 6, 1980. BA Maxima Cum Laude, St. Ambrose Coll., 1953; MusB, Mt. St. Mary's Coll., 1965, MA in Edn., 1966; EdD, U. So. Calif., L.A., 1973. Cert. tchr./adminstr., Calif. Dean of studies Pius X High Sch., Downey, Calif., 1962-67, prin., 1967-75; instr. U. So. Calif., 1972-75; lectr. Loyola Marymount U., L.A., 1975-77, adj. prof. edn., 1977-78; coord. rsch. Nat. Assn. Secondary Sch. Prins., Reston, Va., 1978-80, dir. rsch., 1980-95. Author: Instructional Leadership Handbook, 1984, 91, Learning Style Profile Handbook, 1989, The CASE-IMS School Improvement Process, 1991, Teaching for Thinking, 1992, Leadership in Middle Level Education, 1993, Redesigning Schools for the New Century, 1996, Instruction and the Learning Environment, 1996. Recipient Disting. Achievement award City of Downey, 1975, Award for Outstanding Ednl. Rsch. Calif. State U., Fullerton, 1992-93. Mem. ASCD, Am. Ednl. Rsch. Assn., Learning Environments Consortium, Nat. Assn. Secondary Sch. Prins., Nat. Cath. Ednl. Assn. (Disting. Svc. award 1981), Nat. Cath. Honor Soc. Office: JK Cons Ltd 1419 Belcastle Ct Reston VA 20194-1245

KEEGAN, MARY BARDEN, volunteer; b. Yonkers, N.Y., Nov. 18, 1921; d. James J. and Mary Agnes (Linehan) Barden; m. James Magner Keegan, June 12, 1948; children: James, Patrick, Colleen, Kathleen, Michael. BS in Edn., Columbia U., 1943, MA in Pers. Adminstrn., 1944. Mem. World Svc. Coun. YWCA of U.S.A, N.Y.C., 1962—; first pres., founder Women's Pub. Rels. Coun., St. Joseph's Hosp., Houston, 1963-66; bd. dirs., v.p. YWCA, Houston, 1965-71, Houston Area Urban League, 1981-86; Houston chair 1st Nat. Women's Conf., Houston, 1977; pres. U.S. del. Friendship Among Women, St. Paul, 1979—; co-chair Women in Devel. Adv. Com. Voluntary Fgn. Aid, Dept. State, Washington, 1983-93; founder, CEO, chmn. bd. End Hunger Network, Houston, 1985-95, chair emeritus 1995; bd. dirs. Citizens Network for Fgn. Affairs, Washington, 1987-94; U.S. dep. observer to Ireland Internat. Fund for Ireland, Washington, 1990-92; bd. dirs. St. Joseph Hosp. Found., Houston, 1984—, 1st v.p. exec. com., 1994, pres., 1995; bd. dirs., mem. exec. com., chmn. pub. affairs com. U. St. Thomas, Houston, 1994—; mem. adv. com. Houston Food Bank, St. Joseph Hosp. Benefit "For Our Children's Future", Fox TV; mem. internat. adv. com. Counterpart; trustee, advisor Care; gov. bd. St. Joseph Hosp. Recipient Brotherhood award NCCJ, 1981, Spl. Fundraiser award YWCA, Houston, 1981, Outstanding Woman award YWCA, 1986, Whitney M. Young Vol. Yr., Houston Area Urban League, 1987, U.S. Presdl. Hunger award Pres. U.S., 1987, Martin Luther King Jr. Life and Legacy award, 1989, Galleria C. of C. Commerce Cmty. Culture award, 1995; named Houston's Pioneer Houston Woman's Club, 1975. Mem. Fedn. Profl. Women, Houston Forum. Home: 121 N Post Oak Ln Apt 2304 Houston TX 77024-7717

KEELER, JAMES LEONARD, food products company executive; b. Richmond, Va., Jan. 31, 1935; s. Joseph McCauley and Nora Elizabeth (Thomas) K.; m. Joan Sandra Barnhart, Aug. 14, 1954; children: Mark Leonard, Tracy Ann, Steven James, Gregory Wayne. BS, Bridgewater Coll., 1957; JD, U. Va., 1983. Bar: Va. 1983; CPA, Va. Ptnr., acct. Hueston & Keeler, CPAs, Harrisonburg, Va., 1958-63; mng. ptnr., acct. Keeler, Phibbs & Co., CPAs, Harrisonburg, 1963-80; ptnr., atty. Wharton, Aldhizer & Weaver, Harrisonburg, 1983-88; chief exec. officer WLR Foods, Inc., Broadway, Va., 1988—, pres., 1990—. Vice chmn. Bridgewater (Va.) Coll., 1974-91, mem. exec. com., trsutee, 1974—; exec. adv. coun. James Madison U. Coll. Bus., Harrisonburg, 1989-95; bd. dirs. Valley of Va. Partnership for Edn., James Madison U., Rockingham Meml. Hosp., 1994—, Va. Econ. Devel. Partnership, 1995—; mem. Va. Bus. Coun., 1995—. Recipient disting. alumnus award Bridgewater Coll., 1990; named outstanding bus. person award Harrisonburg-Rockingham C. of C., 1995. Fellow Va. Soc. CPAs (pres. 1970-71, Outstanding Mem. 1977); mem. ABA, AICPA (governing coun. 1969-70, 74-75, 76-77), Va. Bar Assn., Va. C. of C. (bd. dirs. 1993—, vice chmn., exec. com. 1994—). Republican. Mem. Brethren Ch. Office: WLR Foods Inc PO Box 7000 Broadway VA 22815-7000

KEELEY, BRIAN E., hospital administrator; b. Cleve., Feb. 10, 1945. BA, Miami U., 1967; M Health Adminstrn., George Washington U., 1970. Asst. adminstrv. officer Naval Hosp., Newport, R.I., 1970-71; const. officer Naval Hosp., Groton, Conn., 1971-73; adm. res. Baptist Hosp. Miami, 1969-70, asst. adminstr., 1973-74, sr. asst. adminstr., 1974-79, adminstr., COO, 1979-86, pres., CEO, 1986-95; pres., CEO Baptist Health Syss., Miami, 1995. Mem. Fla. Hosp. Assn. Home: 7281 SW 47th Ct Miami FL 33143-6109 Office: Bapt Hosp Miami 8900 N Kendall Dr Miami FL 33176-2118

KEELEY, IRENE PATRICIA MURPHY, federal judge; b. 1944. BA, Coll. Notre Dame, 1965; MA, W.Va. U., 1977, JD, 1980. Bar: Va. Atty. Steptoe & Johnson, Clarksburg, W.Va., 1980-92; dist. judge U.S. Dist. Ct. (no. dist.), W. Va., 1992—; adj. prof. law coll. law W.Va. U., 1990-91; mem. bd. dirs. W.Va. U. Alumni Assn. Mem. vis. com. Coll. Law W.Va. U., 1987-91, 94—; mem. bd. advisors W.Va. U. Mem. ABA (judicial adminstrn. divsn. ct. tech. com.), Nat. Conf. Fed. trial Judges (exec. com.), W.Va. State Bar, W.Va. Bar Assn., Harrison County Bar Assn., Clarksburg Country Club, Oral Lake Fishing Club, Immaculate Conception Roman Cath. Ch.

Office: US Courthouse PO Box 2808 500 W Pike St Rm 202 Clarksburg WV 26302-2808*

KEELEY, MARK JAMES, nutritionist; b. Stillwater, Okla., Dec. 26, 1948; s. James Henry and Retha Labelle (Spradlin) K.; m. Elisabeth Ann Wentz, Aug. 15, 1970 (div. June 1986); 1 child, Blake Justin; m. Janice Marie Blecha, Sept. 12, 1987; stepchildren: Laura Christine Barnum, Kirk Joseph Barnum. BA, U. Kans., 1971; BS, U. Hawaii, 1978, MPH, 1979. Registered dietitian, lic. dietitian, Okla. Nutritionist USPHS, Nashville, Ark., 1979-81; pub. health nutritionist Okla. State Dept. Health, McAlester, 1981-83, Cherokee Nation Health Svcs., Tahlequah, Okla., 1984—; program dir. Women, Infants and Children Cherokee Nation Health Dept., Tahlequah, 1987—; contract nutritionist Devel. Disabilities Svcs., Tahlequah, 1992-94. Editor: (recipe booklets) Cookin' with Commodities, 1985, Commodity Classics, 1987; project coord. (video) A Diet You Can Live With, 1990. Asst. scoutmaster Boy Scouts Am., Tahlequah, 1991-94, 96—, scoutmaster, 1994-95; bd. dirs. Christian Action Relief and Edn., Tahlequah, 1992—, chmn., 1994—; chmn. bd. dirs. Cherokee County chpt., bd. dirs. Okla. affiliate Am. Diabetes Assn., 1994—. Sgt. USAF, 1972-76. Recipient Commandant's award Def. Lang. Inst., 1972, Cert. of Appreciation USDA, 1990, Excellence in Mgmt. award Cherokee Nation Donated Foods Program, 1992. Mem. Am. Dietetic Assn. (diabetes care and edn. practice group, renal dietitians practice group), Nat. Kidney Found. (coun. on renal nutrition), Am. Assn. Diabetes Educators, Gamma Sigma Delta. Roman Catholic. Home: 406 W Delaware St Tahlequah OK 74464-3612 Office: Cherokee Nation PO Box 948 Tahlequah OK 74465-0948

KEELING, ELIZABETH BURFOOT, health facility administrator; b. Wills Point, Tex., Jan. 23, 1959; d. Charles Andrews and Elizabeth Ligon (Wilson) Burfoot; m. Robert Walton Keeling, Aug. 31, 1985. ADN, La. Tech. U., 1983; BSN, N.E. La. U., 1985; MSN, U. Tex. Sch. Nursing, Arlington, 1991. RN, Tex., La. Staff nurse St. Francis Med. Ctr., Monroe, La., 1983-85; staff nurse Valley Bapt. Med. Ctr., Harlingen, Tex., 1985-86, nurse mgr., 1986-88, MIS coord., 1988-89; staff nurse Meth. Med. Ctr., Dallas, 1989-91, asst. dir. nursing, 1991-92, edn. dir., 1992-93, dir. women and children's svcs. and edn., 1993-94; asst. adminstr. patient care svcs. Med. Ctr. Mesquite, Tex., 1994-95; program dir. patient info. systems Meth. Med. Ctr., Dallas, 1996—. Mem. ANA, Tex. Nurses Assn., Tex. Orgn. Nurse Execs., Tex. Soc. Healthcare Educators (bd. dirs. 1992-94), Dallas Area Soc. Healthcare Educators (pres.-elect 1991-92, pres. 1992-94), Healthcare Info. Mgmt. Systems Soc., Sigma Theta Tau. Home: 649 S First St Hewitt TX 76643 Office: Meth Med Ctr PO Box 655999 Dallas TX 75265-5999

KEELING, LARRY DALE, journalist; b. Anderson County, Ky., May 5, 1947; s. Elmer Pascal and Ida Elizabeth (Gregory) K.; m. Cynthia Maria Taylor, Nov. 28, 1987. BA, U. Ky., 1969. Reporter Henry County Jour., Bassett, Va., 1972, Martinsville (Va.) Bull., 1972-74, Bradenton (Fla.) Herald, 1974-75, Lexington (Ky.) Herald, 1975-79; editorial writer Lexington (Ky.) Herald-Leader, 1979—. 1st lt. USAF, 1969-72, Taiwan. Finalist for Pulitzer prize, 1993; recipient Sigma Delta Chi award for editl. writing, 1993, Nat. Headliner award for editl. writing, 1994, Green Eyeshade award for editl. writing, 1995. Mem. Soc. Profl. Journalists (Bluegrass chpt.), Nat. Conf. Editorial Writers. Office: Lexington Herald-Leader 100 Midland Ave Lexington KY 40508-1943

KEELING, MARY ODELL, librarian; b. Norfolk, Va., Jan. 18, 1955; d. Earl Homer and Margaret Sinclair (Wright) Odell; m. Warren Frederick Keeling, Sept. 11, 1982; children: Pamela Sinclair, David Warren. BA, Va. Poly. Inst. and State U., 1977; MLS, Cath. U. Am., 1995. Libr. asst. Old Dominion U., Norfolk, 1978-83; archtl. rsch. libr. Colonial Williamsburg (Va.) Found., 1983-91, audiovisual svcs. libr., 1991-96, mem. archival mgmt. policy task force, 1988, mem. archtl. and archeol. drawings collection adv. group, 1988-91, mem. hist. negatives adv. group, 1989, mem. bldg. use and disposition com., 1989-90, mem. libr. mgmt. group, 1990-96, mem. audiovisual cataloging task force, 1992-93; libr. media ctr. specialist Newport News (Va.) Pub. Schs., 1996—. Contbr. articles to profl. jours. Mem. Newport News (Va.) Hist. Commn., 1993-94. Grantee Inst. for Mus. Svcs., 1990. Mem. Va. Ednl. Media Assn. Baptist. Office: BC Charles Sch 101 Youngs Rd Newport News VA 23602

KEENA, JANET LAYBOURN, artist; b. St. Joseph, Mo., Sept. 11, 1928; d. Allyn Lemuel and Elsie Anna (Parker) Laybourn. Student, Am. Acad. Art, Chgo., 1948-49, UCLA, 1963-64, U. Kans., 1972. One-woman shows include Albrecht Mus., St. Joseph, Mo., 1973, Jewish Cmty. Ctr., Kans. City, Mo., 1972, Ark. Art Ctr., Ft. Smith, 1974, Capricorn Gallery, Bethesda, Md., 1993, Plum Gallery, Md., 1990, Gallery Four, Alexandria, Va., 1992; exhibited in group shows at Nelson Gallery Art, Kansas City, Mo., 1973, Richmond (Va.) Mus., Ark. Art Ctr., Little Rock, 1982, Nat. Arts Club, N.Y.C., 1992, Cultural Alliance Greater Washington Artists, Capricorn Galleries, Bethesda, Md., Gallery 4, Alexandria, Va. and Europe, Md. Fedn. Art, Annapolis, 1982, Butler Mus., Youngstown, Ohio, 1992, Gallery Henoch, N.Y.C., 1992, South Bend (Ind.) Regional Mus., 1994; represented in permanent collections Am. Assn. Ret. Persons Hdqs., N.Y. Marriot Hotel, Arthur Andersen & Co., Oliver Carr Co., Fed. Res. Bank, also law firms, corps.; also pvt. collections. Mem. Nat. Arts Club. Home and Studio: 7501 Range Rd Alexandria VA 22306-2423

KEENAN, BARBARA MILANO, judge. Judge General Dist. Ct., Fairfax County, Va., 1980-82, U.S. Cir. Ct. (19th cir.), Fairfax County, Va., 1982-85, U.S. Ct. Appeals, Va., 1985-91; justice Supreme Ct. of Va., McLean, 1991—; assoc. justice Supreme Ct. Va., Richmond, 1991—. Office: Va Supreme Ct 100 N 9th St Richmond VA 23219*

KEENAN, MARY ELIZABETH, vocational education educator; b. Lancaster, Pa., Feb. 20, 1949; d. Robert Eugene Detwiler and Sarah Louella (Hostetter) Weigand; m. George Frederick Stephens, Oct. 19, 1974 (dec. 1995); m. Dale Wesley Keenan, June 10, 1996. Grad. in nursing, St. Joseph's Hosp., Lancaster, 1970; BS with Nursing Emphasis, Castleton (Vt.) State Coll., 1977, MA in Edn. with Adminstrn. Emphasis, 1982. RN, Pa., Vt.; lic. nursing home adminstr., Pa. Asst. dir. nurses Masonic Homes, Elizabethtown, Pa., 1970-74; shift supr. Springfield (Vt.) Convalescent Ctr., 1975-78; dir. nurses Hanson Court Convalescent Home, Springfield, 1978-79; instr. Community Coll. Vt., Springfield, 1979; exec. dir. Springfield Area Hospice, 1979-80; adminstr. Leader Nursing and Rehab. Ctrs., Manor Care Inc., Valley Forge, Pa., and Silver Spring, Md., 1981-84; mgmt. cons. Health Care Resources, Inc., Valley Forge, 1985; health care coord. Armstrong World Industries, Inc., Lancaster, Pa., 1985-87; corp. dir. personal care svcs. and staff devel. George M. Leader Family Corp., Hershey, Pa., 1988-91; sr. adminstr. Oak Leaf Manor, Inc., Millersville, Pa., 1991-92; health occupations coord. Monongalia County Tech. Edn. Ctr., Morgantown, W.Va., 1993-95; asst. prof. vocat. tech. edn. W.Va. U. Inst. Tech., Montgomery, 1995—; lectr. Pa. Health Care Assocs., Harrisburg, 1985, 89. Home: 518 Pleasantdale Rd Kingwood WV 26537-9701 Office: WVa Inst Tech 3415 Orndorff Hall Montgomery WV 25136

KEENE, GLADYS CRONFEL, allergist, immunologist, pediatrician; b. New Orleans, Sept. 22, 1939. MD, U. Tex., 1965. Diplomate Am. Bd. Allergy and Immunology, Am. Bd. Pediat. Intern R.B. Green Hosp., San Antonio, 1965-66; resident in pediat. U. Tex. Med. Br., Galveston, Tex., 1972-74; fellow in allergy and immunology U. Tex. Med. Br., Galveston, 1975; pvt. practice. Mem. Am. Acad. Pediat., Am. Acad. Allergy and Immunology, Am. Coll. Allergy and Immunology. Office: PO Box 2709 Laredo TX 78044-2709*

KEENE, MARY ELLEN, federal agency executive; b. Washington, July 30, 1955; d. William Charles and Doris Eva (Springer) Keene; m. Randy Duane Ferryman, Dec. 4, 1982. BS in Edn. with honors, George Mason U., 1977; MPA, Harvard U., 1992. With CIA, Washington, 1974—, imagery analyst specializing mil. assessments, 1979-84, mgr., sr. departmental requirements officer, 1984-86, first-line mgr., later middle mgr. planning/programming unit, 1986-87, first-line mgr. analytic unit, 1987-88, with Intelligence Cmty. Staff, Com. Imagery Requirements, 1988-90, middle mgr. customer svcs., 1990-93, middle mgr. analytic element, 1993—. Mem. Kappa Delta Pi.

KEENEN, HOWARD GREGORY, minister; b. Arkadelphia, Ark., Jan. 17, 1960; s. Marvin Dean and Shirlene (Finn) K.; m. Sami Tara Cathey, Sept. 21, 1984; children: Gregory Taylor-Dean, Jennifer Elizabeth, Chelsea Anne. Student, Okla. State U., 1979-80, Criswell Coll., 1985-87; diploma, Immanuel Bapt. Sem., 1988. Ordained to ministry Southern Bapt. Conv., 1982. Min. music First Bapt. Ch., Verdigris, Okla., 1979; assoc. pastor Trinity Bapt. Ch., Moore, Okla., 1980-85, Meadowbrook Bapt. Ch., Irving, Tex., 1985-87; assoc. pastor, min. music Morningside Bapt. Ch., Valdosta, Ga., 1987-88; sr. pastor 1st Bapt. Ch., Chelsea, Okla., 1988-91, Tuttle, Okla., 1991-96; sr. pastor Graceway Bapt. Ch., Oklahoma City, 1996—; pres. Pastors' Conf., Rogers Bapt. Assn., Claremore, Okla., 1991—; bd. dirs. Prayer Resources, Memphis; pres. Tuttle Ministerial Alliance, 1994-95. Republican. Office: Graceway Bapt Ch 1100 SW 104th St Oklahoma City OK 73139

KEENEY, STEVEN HARRIS, lawyer; b. Phila., Oct. 1, 1949; s. Arthur Hail and Virginia (Tripp) K.; m. Jean Ashburn, May 10, 1974 (div. Oct. 1986); 1 child, Christian Jeffrey; m. Wynn Everett, Oct. 15, 1988 (div. 1995). BA, Trinity Coll., Hartford, Conn., 1971; MA, Hartford Sem. Found., 1973; JD, U. Conn., 1980. Bar: Ky. 1980, U.S. Dist. Ct. (we. dist.) Ky. 1981, U.S. Dist. Ct. (ea. dist.) Ky. 1983. Staff reporter/edn. editor The Hartford Courant, 1971-74; asst. to supt. Hartford Pub. Schs., 1974-77; assoc. Igor Sikorsky & Assocs., Hartford, 1979-80, Brown, Todd & Heyburn, Louisville, 1980-82; ptnr. Barnett & Alagia, Louisville, 1982-88, Keeney & Willock, Louisville, 1988-90; prin. Amerilaw, Louisville, 1990-93; pres. LawTech Svcs. Co., Louisville, 1993—; mng. mem. Trautwein & Keeney PLLC, Louisville, 1993—. Co-author/editor: Death Benefit: A Lawyer Uncovers A 20 Year Pattern of Seduction, 1993, 94, Reader's Digest Today's Best Non-Fiction Vol. 24, 1994; contbr. articles to profl. jours. Bd. dirs. Hospice of Louisville, Inc., 1984-86; exec. dir. Juvenile Justice Pub. Edn. Project, West Hartford, Conn., 1978-80; pres. bd. dirs. Stage One: Louisville Children's Theatre, 1982-83; founding bd. dirs. Ky. Citizens for Arts, Frankfort, 1983; mem. Lebanon (Conn.) Bd. Edn., 1975-80; campaign mgr. Mazzoli 3d C.D. Ky., Jefferson County, 1982, 84; elder 2d Presbyn. Ch., Louisville, 1984-86. Recipient Disting. Contbn. award Nat. Com. for Prevention of Child Abuse, Ky. chpt., 1982, Disting. Svc. award Conn. Assn. Bds. of Edn., 1976, Profl. Achievement for Gen. Reporting Series award Soc. Profl. Journalists, Sigma Delta Chi, Conn. chpt. 1974. Mem. ABA (editl. com. The Tax Lawyer 1984-89), Assn. Trial Lawyers of Am., Ky. Acad. Trial Atty's., Ky. Bar Assn., Louisville Bar Assn., Million Dollar Advocates Forum, Oxmoor Golf and Steeplechase Club, Jefferson Club. Democrat. Presbyterian. Office: Trautwein and Keeney PLLC 1 Riverfront Plz Ste 510 Louisville KY 40202-2936

KEEPERS, CHARLES JOSEPH, building supply company executive; b. Wisconsin Rapids, Wis., Oct. 4, 1945; s. William Lincoln Keepers and Marie Ethel (Saunders) Suerth; m. Deborah Kay Fuller, Aug. 9, 1975; children: Kimberly, Eric, Christopher, Mandy. Asst. traffic mgr. Preway, Inc., Wisconsin Rapids, 1967-70, nat. product mgr., 1970-73; mfrs. rep. Keepers & Assocs., Houston, 1973-75; sales mgr. Gray-Walker Co., Houston, 1975-76, Houston Brick & Tile Co., 1976-92; pres. Builders Brick & Fireplace Co., Houston, 1992—. With U.S. Army, 1963-66. Mem. Greater Houston Builders Assn. Home: 8717 Fm 2920 Rd Spring TX 77379-2457 Office: Builders Brick & Fireplace 6730 John Ralston Rd Houston TX 77049-3308

KEEPLER, MANUEL, mathematics educator, researcher; b. Atlanta, Nov. 4, 1944; s. Gus Henry and Charssie (Prothro) K.; m. Dannie Lee Hornsby, June 17, 1966; 1 child, Adriane Kapayl Keepler. BS, Morehouse Coll., 1965; MA, Columbia U., 1967; PhD, U. N.Mex., Albuquerque, 1973. With U. N.Mex., 1967-70; asst. prof. math. Va. State Coll., Petersburg, 1970-71; assoc. prof., chairperson dept. math. Langston (Okla.) U., 1971-72; assoc. prof., chairperson dept. math. S.C. State Coll., Orangeburg, 1973-76, prof., 1976-90, chairperson dept. math., 1981-90; prof. math. N.C. Ctr. U., Durham, 1990—, chmn., 1996—; vis. prof. math. Cornell U., Ithaca, N.Y., 1989-90, summers 1990-95; mem. rev. panel Ednl. Testing Svc., Princeton, N.J., 1986; proposal evaluator NSF, Washington, 1987-89; mem. tech. adv. bd. S.C Rsch. Authority, Columbia, 1988-89; vis. prof. Dillard U., New Orleans, 1976. Author: Proof Techniques, 1988, (with others) Fundamentals of Mathematics, 1987; contbr. articles to profl. jours. Trustee S.C. State Coll., 1987-89, pres. faculty senate, 1987-89. Sloan Found. grantee, 1987, U.S. Dept. Edn. grantee, 1988, Xerox Corp. grantee, 1988. Mem. Am. Stats. Assn., S.C. Acad. Sci. (coun. 1984—, pres. 1988-89), Consortium for Computing in Small Colls. (com.)., N.C. Acad. Sci. (head Math. sec. 1996-98). Home: 850 Ellis Ave NE Orangeburg SC 29115-5065 Office: NC Ctrl U Dept Math and Computer Sci Durham NC 27706

KEETER, ROSEMARY EARLYN, home health and emergency room nurse; b. Lawrenceburg, Tenn., Nov. 16, 1964; d. Earl Edgar and Garnet Lanelle (Holloway) Blevins; m. Edward Keeter Jr., Oct. 10, 1990; children: Hannah Elizabeth, Adam Edward. ADN, Columbia State C.C., Tenn., 1986; diploma in critical care, U. Tenn., 1988; BSN magna cum laude, U. Ala., 1996. RN, Tenn., Ala.; cert. ACLS, BLS instr.; cert. PALS; cert. trauma nursing core course. Pediatric charge nurse Hillside Hosp., Pulaski, Tenn., 1986-88, charge nurse emergency dept., 1988-89; charge nurse emergency dept. Crockett Hosp., Lawrenceburg, 1989—; nursing supr. Cmty. Home Health, Lawrenceburg, 1996—. Mem. Emergency Nurses Assn. Home: 81 Crews Rd Lawrenceburg TN 38464-6134 Office: Crockett Hosp Highway 43 S Lawrenceburg TN 38464 also: Cmty Home Health 311 N Locust Ave Lawrenceburg TN 38464

KEETH, BETTY LOUISE, geriatrics nursing director; b. Hayward, Okla., Nov. 15, 1931; d. Harley Enoch and Violent Verona (Space) George; m. Melvin L. Gillham, May 4, 1951 (div. July 1979); children: Melvin L., Dennis Ray, Debra Lynne Gillham. ADN, Carl Albert Jr. Coll., 1984. LPN, Ark. DON MENA Manor, Mena, Ark., 1987-89, Living Ctrs. of Am., Oklahoma City, 1989-90, Westlake Sq. Ctr., Oklahoma City, 1990-91, Bethany Village, 1991-94, East Moore Nursing, Moore, Okla., 1994-95; dir. Ctrl. Okla. Christian Home, Oklahoma City, 1995—; cons. Precision Home Health, Oklahoma City. Registrar Lefiore County, Poteau, Okla., 1989; sec. Dem. Women, 1984-90. Home: 2908 Pinto Trl Edmond OK 73003-6667 Office: Ctrl Okla Christian Home 6312 N Portland Oklahoma City OK 73112

KEEVER, REBECCA REGAN, copy editor; b. Richmond, Va., July 4, 1955; d. William Whitfield and Peggy Elizabeth (Gibson) Regan; m. Joseph Jefferson Keever, Aug. 21, 1982; children: Virginia Grace, Andrew Whitfield Keever. BA, Mary Baldwin Coll., 1977; MS, Old Dominion U., 1991. Paralegal McGuire, Woods & Battle, Richmond, 1977-79, Kaufman & Canoles, Norfolk, Va., 1979-87; rsch. asst. Med. Coll. Hampton Roads, Norfolk, 1988-90; job analyst Canon Va., Inc., Newport News, 1990; pers. asst. Norshipco, Norfolk, 1990; administrv. analyst Dept. Social Svcs., Virginia Beach, Va., 1991-92; proofreader, copy editor of psychol. rsch. articles, books, 1994—. Editor newsletter Royster Meml. Presbyn. Ch., Norfolk, 1994—, elder, 1994—. Mem. Am. Soc. Tng. and Devel. (S.E. chpt.), Alliance Française, Phi Kappa Phi. Home: 409 Sinclair St Norfolk VA 23505-4359

KEGLEY, CHARLES WILLIAM, JR., political science educator, author; b. Evanston, Ill., Mar. 5, 1944; s. Charles William and Elizabeth Euphemia (Meck) K.; m. Ann Curry Taylor, Apr. 1, 1966 (div.); 1 child, Suzanne Taylor; m. 2d, Pamela Ann Holcomb, July 6, 1975 (div.); BA, Am. U., 1966; PhD, Syracuse U., 1971. Asst. prof. Sch. Fgn. Service, Georgetown U., 1971-72; prof., chmn. dept. govt. and internat. studies, 1981-85, dir. Byrnes Internat. Ctr., U. S.C., 1986-88, holder Pearce chair internat. studies, 1985—; vis. prof. U. Tex., 1976; Moses Back Peace Prof., Rutgers U., News Brunswick, N.J., 1989. Bd. Trustees Carnegie Coun. Ethics & Internat. Affairs, 1992—. Recipient Disting. Alumni award Am. U., 1984; R.M. Davis scholar, 1962-66; Maxwell fellow, 1968-69, 70-71; N.Y. State Regents fellow, 1969-70; Fulbright sr. scholar, 1978; Russell research awardee in humanities and social scis., 1982. Mem. Am. Polit. Sci. Assn., Am. Soc. Internat. Law, Am. Soc. Advancement Sci., Internat. Polit. Sci. Assn., Internat. Studies Assn. (assoc. dir. 1980-84, pres. 1993-94), Midwest Polit. Sci. Assn., Peace Sci. Soc., Peace Rsch. Soc., So. Polit. Sci. Assn., Pi Sigma Alpha, Omicron Delta Kappa, Delta Tau Kappa. Lutheran. Author: A General Empirical Typology of Foreign Policy Behavior, 1973; co-author, co-editor (with William Coplin): A Multi-Method Introduction to International Politics: Observation, Explanation and Prescription, 1971, Analyzing International Relations: A Multi-Method Introduction, 1975; co-author: (with Eugene R. Wittkopf) American Foreign Policy: Pattern and Process, 1979, 5th edit., 1996, World Politics: Trend and Transformation, 1981, 5th edit., 1995, (with Gregory A. Raymond) A Multipolar Peace? Great-Power Politics in the 21st Century, 1994; co-editor: (with Robert W. Gregg) After Vietnam: The Future of American Foreign Policy, 1971; (with Gregory A. Raymond, Robert M. Rood, Richard A. Skinner) International Events and the Comparative Analysis of Foreign Policy, 1975; (with Patrick J. McGowan) Challenges to America: U.S. Foreign Policy in the 1980's, 1979, (with Patrick McGowan) Threats, Weapons, and Foreign Policy, 1980, The Political Economy of Foreign Policy, 1981, Foreign Policy: USA/USSR, 1983; (with Eugene R. Wittkopf) Perspectives on American Foreign Policy, 1983, The Global Agenda: Issues and Perspectives, 1984, 4th edit., 1995; (with Patrick McGowan) Foreign Policy and the Modern World System, 1983; (with Eugene R. Wittkopf) The Nuclear Reader: Strategy, Weapons, War, 1985, 2d edit., 1989; (with Charles F. Hermann and James N. Rosenau) New Directions in the Study of Foreign Policy, 1987, (with Eugene R. Wittkopf) The Domestic Sources of American Foreign Policy, 1988, (with Gregory A. Raymond) When Trust Breaks Down: Alliance Norms and World Politics, 1990, (with Kenneth Schwab) After the Cold War: Questioning the Morality of Nuclear Deterrence, 1991, (with Eugene R. Wittkopf) The Future of American Foreign Policy, 1992; editor: The Long Postwar Peace: Contending Explanations and Projections, 1990, International Terrorism: Characteristics, Causes, Controls, 1990, Controversies in International Relations Theory: Realism and the Neoliberal Challenge, 1995; contbr. chpts. to books, articles to profl. jours. Home: 1829 Senate St Apt 17E Columbia SC 29201-3838 Office: U SC Dept Govt & Internat Studies Columbia SC 29208

KEHAYA, ERY W., tobacco holding company executive; b. 1923; married. With Standard Comml. Corp., Wilson, N.C., 1944—, pres., 1954—, now chmn. bd., chief exec. officer, also bd. dirs.; dir. Standard Commercial Corp. Office: Standard Comml Corp PO Box 450 Wilson NC 27894-0450*

KEHOE, JAMES W., federal judge; b. 1925. A.A., U. Fla., 1947, LL.B., 1950. Bar: Fla. Assoc. firm Worley, Kehoe & Willard, 1952-55; asst. county solicitor Dade County, Fla., 1955-57; assoc. firm Miltor R. Wasman, 1957-61; judge Civil Record Ct., Miami, 1961-63, 11th Jud. Cir. Ct., Fla., 1963-77, U.S. Ct. Appeals (3d cir.), 1977-79; judge U.S. Dist. Ct. (so. dist.) Fla., 1979—, sr. judge, 1993—. Mem. ABA, Fla. Bar Assn. Office: US Dist Ct 301 N Miami Ave, 8th FL Tower Miami FL 33128-7709*

KEHOE, WILLIAM JOSEPH, business educator; b. Cin., Feb. 19, 1941. AB, U. Cin., 1964; MBA, Xavier U., 1969; MA, Marshall U., 1973; D of Bus. Adminstrn., U. Ky., 1976. O'Dell prof. commerce U. Va., Charlottesville, 1975—, assoc. dean, 1982-92; pres. Albemarle County Police Found., 1993-95; bd. dirs. Fedn. Bus. Honor Socs. Chmn. Charlottesville Airport Authority, 1993, 96, vice chmn., 1992; pres. Jr. Achievement Ctrl. Va., 1985-87; vice chmn. Paramount Theatre and Cultural Ctr., 1990-92; mem. Albermarle County Indsl. Devel. Authority, 1986-94; chmn. Albemarle County Fiscal Resource Com., 1989-91; mem. Regional Econ. Adv. Coun., Commonwealth of Va., 1994—; chmn. Thomas Jefferson area United Way, 1994. Recipient Leaders' Leader award, 1988, Disting. Leadership award Nat. Assn. Community Leadership, 1989; Doctoral Consortium fellow. Mem. Am. Acad. Mgmt., Am. Mktg. Assn., Soc. for Bus. Ethics, Acad. Internat. Bus., Charlottesville C. of C. (chmn. 1990), Allied So. Bus. Assn. (pres. 1992), Beta Gamma Sigma (bd. dirs. 1990—). Home: PO Box 4454 Charlottesville VA 22905-4454

KEIL, JULIAN EUGENE, epidemiology educator and researcher; b. Charleston, S.C., Oct. 30, 1926; m. Barbara Willis; 3 children. BS, Clemson U., 1949, MS, 1968; DPH, U. N.C., 1975; cert. Epidemiology Summer Inst., U. Minn., 1974. Entomologist to head pesticide divsn. W.R. Grace & Co., Charleston, 1949-67; from instr. to asst. prof. divsn. preventive medicine Med. U. S.C., Charleston, 1968-77; chmn. dept. epidemiology and biostatistics Sch. Pub. Health U. S.C., Columbia, 1978-81, assoc. prof. dept. epidemiology and biostatistics, 1977-83; assoc. prof., then prof. epidemiology Med. U. S.C., Charleston, 1983-92, prof. emeritus, 1993—; presenter papers internat. convs. Contbr. chpts. to books, numerous articles to profl. jours. With U.S. Army, 1945-47. Nat. Inst. Environ. Health Scis. predoctoral fellow, 1973; grantee Nat. Heart, Lung & Blood Inst., 1991-93, Am. Heart Assn., 1985-87. Fellow Am. Coll. Cardiology, Am. Heart Assn. Coun. on Epidemiology; mem. Internat. Epidemiological Assn. Inc., S.C. Entomological Soc. (past pres.).

KEIM, ROBERT JOHN, otolaryngologist, educator; b. Geneva, Ill., July 20, 1934; s. Jacob A. and Adelaide Marie (Schrauth) K.; m. Arlene Caldwell, June 27, 1959; children: Alison Marie, Kimberly Anne. BA in Zoology, U. So. Calif., L.A., 1956; MD, U. So. Calif., 1961. Diplomate Am. Bd. Otolaryngology. Intern L.A. (Calif.) County Gen. Hosp., 1961-62, resident otolaryngology, 1962-63, 64-66; resident gen. surgery Santa Fe Coast Lines Hosp., L.A., 1963-64; chief otolaryngology USAF, Clark AFB, Philippines, 1966-68; sr. attending physician L.A. (Calif.) County-U. So. Calif. Med. Ctr., 1968-75, dir. outpatient svcs. dept. otolaryngology, 1968-75, chief neurotology dept. otolaryngology, 1969-75; asst. prof. otolaryngology U. So. Calif., L.A., 1968-75; assoc. prof. otolaryngology U. Okla., Oklahoma City, 1975-79, interim chmn. dept. otorhinolaryngology Coll. Medicine, 1978-79, assoc. clin. prof. dept. otolaryngology and maxillofacial surgery Coll of Medicine, 1979-80; dir. Hearing and Balance Ctr., Oklahoma City, 1980—; physician Huntington Meml. Hosp., Pasadena, Calif., 1972-75; cons. otology White Meml. Med. Ctr., L.A., 1972-75, St. Luke Hosp., Pasadena, 1974-75, Meml. Hosp. Glendale, Calif., 1974-75; cons. otolaryngology Glendale (Calif.) Adventist Hosp., 1972-75, Kaiser found. Hosp., L.A., 1973-75, Bone and Joint Hosp., Oklahoma City, 1981—, others; courtesy med. staff Bapt. Med. Ctr., Oklahoma City, 1986—, South Cmty. Hosp., Oklahoma City, 1986—; active staff Okla. Childrens Meml. Hosp., Okla. City, 1975-79, Bapt. Meml. Hosp., Memphis, Tenn., 1979-80; clin. staff otorhinolaryngology and dir. neurotology U. Okla., Okla. City, 1975-79; chief physician otorhinolaryngology VA Hosp., Okla. City, 1975-79; active staff otolaryngology dept. Presbyn. Hosp., Okla. City, 1980—, St. Anthony Hosp., Okla. City, 1980—, chmn. otolaryngology dept., 1982-86, 88; assoc. med. staff otolaryngology Mercy Health Ctr., Okla. City, 1984—; attending staff USAF Hosp. Tinker AFB, Okla., 1986—; exec. v.p. Am. Jour. Otology, Nashville, 1993-94, pres., 1994; presenter in field. Abstract editor: Am. Jour. Otolaryngology, 1978-83, mem. rev. bd., 1983—; editorial rev. bd.: Jour. Otolaryngology-Head and Neck Surgery, 1990—; contbr. articles to profl. jours. Res. officer USAF Med. Corps, 1962-66, capt., 1966-68. Decorated Commendation medal USAF, 1966; recipient Rsch. fellowships Lederle Labs., 1957-58, NSF, 1958-59, USAF Surgeon Gen.'s award Brooks Sch. Aerospace Medicine, San Antonio, 1967, John MacKenzie Brown award L.A. Soc. Otolaryngology, 1970; named Outstanding Alumnus U. So. Calif. Med. Sch., L.A., 1986. Fellow ACS (com. on assistance at surgery 1986), Am. Acad. Otolaryngology-Head and Neck Surgery (instr. 1976—, com. on sci. papers 1977-80, chmn. bd. govs. 1985, others), Am. Neurotology Soc. (audiology study com. 1975-79, exec. coun. 1977-88, exec. sec./treas. 1979-84, pres. 1985, others), Am. Laryngol., Rhinol. and Otol. Soc., Am. Otol. Soc.; mem. AMA, Okla. State Med. Assn., Okla. County Med. Soc. (alt. del. 1984, med. forum com. 1984).

KEISLER, JOSHUA ALLEN, career officer; b. Chgo., Sept. 6, 1972; s. Allen James and Cathleen Irean (O'Connell) K.; m. Kimberly Lynn Rickards, June 26, 1993; 1 child, Gentry Lynn. BA, U. Ga., 1994. Enlisted USMC, Macon, Ga., 1990; advanced through grades to 1st lt. USMC, Camp Pendleton, Calif., 1996—. Republican. Roman Catholic. Home: 404 Koelper St Oceanside CA 92054

KEISTLER, BETTY LOU, accountant, tax consultant; b. St. Louis, Jan. 2, 1935; d. John William and Gertrude Marie (Lewis) Chancellor; m. George E. Keistler, Aug. 3, 1957 (div. Mar. 1981); children: Kathryn M. Pyke, Deborah J. Birsinger. AS, St. Louis U., 1956; BBA, U. Mo., 1986. Asst. treas. A.G. Edwards & Sons, St. Louis, 1956-57; owner, mgr. B.L. Keistler & Assoc., St. Louis, 1969-82; contr. Family Resource Ctr., Inc., St. Louis, 1982-87; registered rep. Equitable Fin. Svcs., Mo., 1987-88; bus. mgr. Mo. Bapt. Coll., St. Louis, 1987-88, Barnes Hosp. Sch. of Nursing, St. Louis, 1989-91, U. South Fla., St. Petersburg, 1991—; cons. in field, 1982-91; cert. two star sales assoc. Youngevity, Inc., 1995, area assoc. trainer; registered rep. Equitable Fin. Svcs., 1987-88; adminstrv. and profl. coun. mem. U.

South Fla., 1994. Treas. Pky. Townhouses at Village Green, Chesterfield, Mo., 1985-87; exec. core United Way Greater St. Louis, 1984-91; mem. Gulfport Hist. Soc., 1996—; mem. Pasadena Bapt. Ch., Sunday sch. gen. sec., 1994-95, trustee. Scholar Phillip Morris Corp., St. Louis, 1982-84. Mem. Am. Bus. Womens Assn. (v.p. 1978-79, pres. Lewis & Clark chpt. 1979-80, treas. nat. conv. 1981, pres. ADITI chpt. 1988-90, Sand & Sea chpt. 1992—, Woman of Yr. 1979-80, 94-95), U. South Fla. Women's Club, Am. Soc. Women Accts., Ind. Accts. Mo. (sec. 1978-79, v.p. 1980-81, state sec. 1978-79), St. Louis Women's Commerce Assn., 1904 World's Fair Soc., Internat. Platform Assn., Gulfport Hist. Soc., Am. Biog. Inst. (hon. advisor, rsch. bd. advisors nat. divsn. 1991), NAFE, Gulfort Hist. Soc., Alpha Sigma Lambda (life, treas. 1985-87). Republican. Home: 6060 Shore Blvd S #103 Gulfport FL 33707

KEITH, BRIAN THOMAS, automobile executive; b. Houston, Aug. 2, 1951; s. Thomas Ross and Elsie Ann (Carden) K.; m. Anna Lee Rogers, Nov. 17, 1973; children: Kevin Patrick, Lindsay Rogers. BSBA, Samford U., 1973. Educator installation IBM, Birmingham, Ala., 1971-73; salesman Albeco-Ala. Bus. Equipment Co., Birmingham, 1973-74; pres., owner Walter S. White Auto Parts, Inc., Birmingham, 1974—; bd. dirs. Ala. Power Co. Vendor Rels. Bd., Birmingham; trustee Automotive Wholesalers Ins. Trust, Montgomery, 1985—, treas. investment com., 1992—. Pub. mag. Auto Svc. and Repair, 1988—; contbr. articles to publs. and mags. V.p. Park Bd. Patriot Baseball, Homewood, Ala., 1985-89; celebrity fundraiser Am. Cancer Soc., 1993; mem. canvass com. All Sts. Ch., Homewood, 1986-90, youth com., 1992—. Named Outstanding Young Men in Am., U.S. Jaycees, 1983; recipient Tech. Tng. award Arvvin Industries, 1983-88. Mem. Automotive Wholesalers Assn. Ala. (bd. dirs. 1985—, chmn. 1986-91, treas. 1992—, polit. action com. 1992—, exec. com. 1991—, Leadership award 1991), Automotive Svc. Industry Assn. (bd. dirs. 1992—, nat. polit. action com. 1993—, co-chmn. automotive com. 1994—), Birmingham C. of C., U.S. C. of C., Young Exec. Forum, Assn. Enterprises (pres. 1991-92), Jr. Achievement, Nat. Fedn. Ind. Bus. Episcopalian.

KEITH, CAMILLE TIGERT, airline marketing executive; b. Ft. Worth, Feb. 27, 1945; d. Marvin and Catherine Frances (Tuscany) K. Student, Tex. Tech U.; BA in Broadcasting and Journalism, Tex. Christian U., 1967. Pub. relations, publicity mgr. Sta. WFAA-TV, Dallas; media relations dir. Read-Poland Pub. Relations Co., Dallas; pub. relations dir. Southwest Airlines Co., Dallas, 1972-76, asst. v.p. pub. relations, 1976-78, v.p. pub. relations, 1978-84, v.p. spl. mktg., 1984—; chair Tex. Travel Summit, 1992, 93; mem. adv. bd. bus. leaders coun. City of Dallas Mktg. and Promotions. Com. Bd. dirs. Dallas Repertory Theatre, Communities in Schs., Vis. Nurses of Dallas, Vis. Nurses Tex., United Cerebral Palsy Dallas, Press Club, Dallas Found., Shared Housing, Project Independence for Older Ams., Jr. Achievement Dallas, exec. com., 1991-95; mem. adv. bd. sch. journalism com. Tex. Christian U.; mem. advt. com. Tex. Tech. U., Women's Ctr. of Dallas, adv. bd.; deacon, past chmn. dept. ch. growth Ctrl. Christian Ch., pres. women's fellowship, mem. adv. bd. nat. task force on comm.; sr. nat. v.p. Children Am. Revolution Women's Resource Ctr. YWCA, Dallas; bd. dirs. Dallas/Ft. Worth Area Tourism Coun., Dallas Heart Assn.; bd. advs. nat. Coun. on Aging; Gov.'s adv. bd. tourism, com. of 60 Tex. Dept. Commerce; v.p. pub. rels. Freedom Found., Dallas, 1989-94; pres. bus. womens group, Ctrl. Christian Ch., Christian Women's Fellowship; mem. adv. bd. Girl Scouts Am., Dallas, Sr. Citizens Greater Dallas, Ret. Sr. Vol. Program, Okla. Bus. and Leadership Coun., Okla. Dept. Aging, Tex. Dept. Aging; lay rep. nat. Eldercare Inst. on Elder Abuse and State Long Term Care Ombudsman Svc., SR. Tex. Newspaper, Dallas Ind. Sch. Dist., Tex. Dept. Health; active adminstrn. on aging project eldercare strategy task force Region VI Dept. Health and Human Svcs. Named Rising Star, Tex. Bus. Mag., 1984; named to Hall of Fame, Tex. Tech. Sch. Mass Comm.; recipient Women Helping Women Maura award Women's Ctr., Dallas, Nat. Heatlines award Women in Comms., 1994. Mem. Discover Tex. Assn. (bd. dirs.), Tex. Pub. Rels. Assn., Tex. Travel Industry Assn. (exec. com. 1990—, chair), Women in Comm., Inc. (Excellence in Comm. award), 500, Inc., Women Entrepreneurs of Tex. (adv. bd.), Tex. Children of the Am. Revolution (past nat. chaplain, regional v.p.), Tex. Women's Alliance, Exec. Women Dallas (bd. dirs. 1991-92, v.p. programs 1992-93, pres.-elect 1994-95, pres.), Greater Dallas C. of C. (bd. dirs. 1996—, pub. svc. com.), Children of the Am. Revolution (sr. nat. v.p. 1988-90, sr. nat. chaplain 1990-92, hon. v.p.), Press Club Dallas (pres. 1988-89), Dallas Advt. League (pres. 1980-81, Bill Kerrs Cmty. Svc. award), Leadership Tex. Alumni Assn., Exec. Women of Dallas (pres. 1994-95), Tex. Travel Industry Assn. (chair 1995-97). Office: Southwest Airlines Co PO Box 36611 Dallas TX 75235-1611

KEITH, CAROLYN AUSTIN, secondary school counselor; b. Mobile, Ala., July 15, 1949; d. Lloyd James Jr. and Aletia Delores (Taylor) Austin; m. Carlos Lamar Keith Sr., Aug. 14, 1971; children: Carlos Lamar Jr., Carolyn Bernadette Austin Keith. BA in English and History, Mercer U., 1971; cert. in gifted edn., Valdosta State Coll., 1979, MEd in Counseling, 1982, post-grad., 1987. Tchr. English Crisp County High Sch., Cordele, Ga., 1971-77; tchr. gifted Tift County Jr. High Sch., Tifton, Ga., 1977-81, Dooly County Sch. System, Vienna, Ga., 1981-82; counselor Worth County High Sch., Sylvester, Ga., 1982-86, Monroe Comprehensive High Sch., Albany, Ga., 1986-91, Dougherty Alternative Sch., Albany, 1991—; cons. Ga. State U., Atlanta, 1986-89, Dept. Family and Children Svcs., Albany, 1993, 94. Mem. West Point Parent's Club, U.S. Mil. Acad., 1992—, Dougherty County Commn. on Children/Youth, Albany, 1991-95; mem. adv. bd. Southwest Ga. Prevention Resource Ctr. Named Vol. of Yr., Dougherty County Coun. on Child Abuse, 1993, Student Assistance Program Counselor of Yr. for State of Ga., 1994. Mem. Am. Counseling Assn., Ga. Sch. Counselors Assn. (sec. 2d dist. 1985-91, Counselor of Yr. 1993), Am. Sch. Counselors Assn., Nat. Bd. Cert. Counselors, Ga. Lic. Profl. Counselors, South Ga. Regional Assn. Lic. Profl. Counselors. Democrat. Roman Catholic. Office: Dougherty County Altern Sch 600 S Madison St Albany GA 31701-3140

KEITH, LEROY, JR., former college president; b. Chattanooga, Feb. 14, 1939; s. Leroy Sr. and Lula (Martin) K.; m. Anita Halsey, Oct. 6, 1961; children: Lori, Susan, Kelli, Kimberly. BS, Morehouse Coll., 1961; MA, Ind. U., 1968, PhD, 1970; LLD (hon.), Bowdoin Coll., 1990, Dartmouth Coll., 1991. Tchr. Chattanooga Pub. Schs., 1961-66; adminstrv. asst. Bur. Ednl. Placement Ind. U., 1969-70; asst. prof. edn., asst. dean Dartmouth Coll., Hanover, N.H., 1970-72; assoc. v.p. U. Mass., 1973-75; chancellor Mass. Bd. Higher Edn., Boston, 1975-78; exec. v.p. U. D.C., 1978-82; v.p. for policy and planning U. Md. System, 1983-87; pres. Morehouse Coll., Atlanta, 1987-96; bd. dirs. Phoenix Mut. Life Ins. Co., Mut. Funds, 1976, William Jewett Tucker Found. Internship Program, 1970-71, Hartford Keystone Group, Boston, Blue Cross/Blue Shield Ga., Equifax, Inc., Md. Higher Bd. Edn. Supplemental Loan Authority, 1984-87, Atlanta Growth Fund Adv. Bd., 1991; mem. Ga. corp. bd. 1st Union Bank. Trustee St. Andrew's Episc. Sch., 1985-87, Morehouse Sch. Medicine, 1987, U. Ctr. Ga., 1987, The Westminster Schs., Atlanta, 1989-92, Northside Hosp., 1991, Atlanta Coun. Boy Scouts Am., Woodruff Arts Ctr., NAFEO, Atlanta Symphony, Baylor Sch., Sci/ Trek; mem. Pres. Bush's Adv. Bd. on Historically Black Colls. and Univs., 1992-93, Harry S. Truman Scholarship Found. Atlanta Regional Review Panel, 1991, adv. com. United Negro Coll. Fund, 1992, bd. dirs., 1991; bd. dirs. Nat. Assn. Independent Colls. and Univs., One to One Mentoring Partnership, Atlanta com. for Olympic Games, 1991, Inst. Internat. Edn., 1991, Atlanta Speech Sch., 1992-94, Pub. Edn. Found., 1992. Mem. Am. Inst. Mng. Diversity (bd. dirs. 1991), Am. Coun. on Edn. (coll. trends com. 1985-90), Jr. League Atlanta (community adv. bd., 1991), Rotary, Phi Beta Kappa.

KEITHLEY, BRADFORD GENE, lawyer; b. Macomb, Ill., Nov. 23, 1951; s. Sanderson Irish and Joan G. (Kenneday) K.; m. Ginger W. Wilhelmi, Mar. 26, 1994; children: Paul Michael, Rachel Austin Bernstein. BS, U. Tulsa, 1973; JD, U. Va., 1976. Bar: Va. 1976, Okla. 1978, D.C. 1979. Atty. Office of Gen. Counsel to Sec. USAF, Washington, 1976-78; ptnr. Hall, Estill, Hardwick, Gable, Collingsworth and Nelson, Tulsa, 1978-84; sr. v.p., gen. counsel Arkla, Inc. (name now NorAm Energy Corp.), Shreveport, La., 1984-90; ptnr. Jones, Day, Reavis and Pogue, Dallas, 1990—. Mem. ABA, Fed. Energy Bar Assn., Va. State Bar, Okla. Bar Assn., D.C. Bar Assn., Am. Gas Assn. (mem. legal sect.), Dallas Petroleum Club, Prestonwood Country Club. Home: 12652 Sunlight Dr Dallas TX 75230-1856 Office: Jones Day Reavis & Pogue 2300 Trammell Crow Ctr 2001 Ross Ave Dallas TX 75201-8001

KELAHER, JAMES PEIRCE, lawyer; b. Orlando, Fla., Oct. 28, 1951; s. Philip James and Neva Cecelia (Peirce) K. BA, U. Cen. Fla., 1973; JD, Fla. State U., 1981. Bar: Fla. 1981, U.S. Dist. Ct. (mid. dist.) Fla. 1982, U.S. Ct. Appeals (11th cir.) 1983, U.S. Supreme Ct.; cert. civil trial law. Assoc. Law Office of Nolan Carter, P.A., Orlando, 1981-83, Law Office of James Kelaher, P.A., Orlando, 1983-87; ptnr. Kelaher & Wieland, P.A., Orlando, 1987—. Contbr. articles to profl. jours. Eagle benefactor Rep. Party. Mem. ABA, ATLA (sustaining), Orange County Bar Assn., Acad. Fla. Trial Lawyers (sec. 1994-95, treas. 1995-96, pres.-elect 1996—, bd. dirs. coll. diplomates, membership exec. com. bd. trustees Fla. lawyers action group), Ctrl. Fla. Trial Lawyers Assn. (pres. 1992-94). Roman Catholic. Office: Kelaher & Wieland PA 390 N Orange Ave Ste 1500 Orlando FL 32801-1641

KELCE, WILLIAM REED, biochemist, toxicologist; b. Evansville, Ind., Nov. 7, 1958; s. William Merl Kelce and Constance Ann (Findley) Broeker; m. Chris Dennis, Aug. 7, 1981; children: Justin, Veronica. BA in Biology, Psychology, Washington U., St. Louis, 1981; MS in Physiology, Pharmacology, U. Mo., 1985, PhD in Physiology, Toxicology, 1989; post-grad. in Reproductive Toxicology, Johns Hopkins U., 1992. Grad. tchg. asst. dept. physiology U. Mo. Sch. Medicine, Columbia, 1986-87; rsch. asst. dept. biomed. scis. U. Mo. Coll. Vet. Medicine, Columbia, 1987-89; postdoctoral fellow dept. population dynamics div. reproductive biology Johns Hopkins U., 1989-92; prin. investigator U.S. EPA, Reproductive Toxicology, Research Triangle Park, N.C., 1992—. Contbr. articles to profl. jours. Recipient grant Johns Hopkins U., 1989-93, 90-93. Mem. Am. Chem. Soc., Soc. Toxicology (Young Investigator award 1st place 1991), Reproductive Toxicology Ctr., Soc. for Study of Reproduction (New Investigator award finalist 1989), Endocrine Soc., Am. Soc. Andrology. Republican. Home: 102 Portnoch Ct Cary NC 27511-6378 Office: US EPA Rsch Lab Reproductive Toxicology Nat Health & Environ Effect Durham NC 27711

KELEHEAR, CAROLE MARCHBANKS SPANN, administrative assistant; b. Morehead City, N.C., Oct. 2, 1945; d. William Blythe and Gladys Ophelia (Wilson) Marchbanks; m. Henry M. Spann, June 5, 1966 (div. 1978); children: Lisa Carole, Elaine Mabry; m. Zachariah Lockwood Kelehear, Sept. 15, 1985. Student Winthrop Coll., 1963-64; grad. Draughon's Bus. Coll., 1965; cert. in med. terminology Greenville Tech. Edn. Coll., 1972; grad. Millie Lewis Modeling Sch. Office mgr. S.C. Appalachian Adv. Commn., Greenville, 1965-68, Wood-Bergheer & Co., Newport Beach and Palm Springs, Calif., 1970-72; asst. to Dr. J. Ernest Lathem, Lathem & McCoy, P.A., Greenville, 1972-75, Gov. Robert E. McNair, McNair, Konduros, Corley, Singletary and Dibble Law Firm, Columbia, S.C., 1975-77; office mgr. Dr. James B. Knowles, Greenville, 1977-78; office mgr. Constangy, Brooks & Smith, Columbia, 1978-83; legal asst. to sr. ptnr. William L. Bethea Jr., Bethea, Jordan & Griffin, P.A., Hilton Head Island, S.C., 1983-88; adminstrv. asst./paralegal to Dr. Rajko D. Medenica, Hilton Head Island, 1988-95; adminstr. Dibble Law Offices, Columbia, S.C., 1995—; notary pub.; vol. Ladies aux. Greenville Gen. Hosp., 1966-72, South Coast Hosp., Laguna Beach, Calif., 1973, St. Francis Hosp, Greenville, 1974-76, Hilton Head Hosp., 1983-92. Mem. Hilton Head Hosp. Aux., Profl. Women's Assn. Hilton Head Island, Am. Bus. Women's Assn., Nat. Assn. Female Execs., Am. Soc. Notaries, Beta Sigma Phi. Home: PO Box 337 Lexington SC 29071-0337

KELEHER, MICHAEL CASSAT, cabinet maker; b. Asheville, N.C., June 8, 1955; s. Michael Francis and Barbara Nell (Cassat) K.; m. Jann Bridgett Wright, Sept. 9, 1978 (div. Oct. 1993); 1 child, Michael Francis. Student, N.C. State U., 1973-74; cert. in cabinet making, A-B Tech. Inst., Asheville, 1975. Owner Creative Woodcrafters, Inc., Asheville, 1976—; advisor bldg constrn. and cabinetry course A-B Tech. Coll., 1987—. Co-chmn. South Pack Sq. Adv. Com., Asheville, 1985-86; bd. dirs. 1st Presbyn. Ch. Child Care Ctr., 1992-95, chmn., 1995). Mem. N.C. Soc. Mayflower Descs., Ensign-Rhododendron Royal Brigade of Guards, Highlands Sports Car Club (v.p. 1991-92, pres. 1992-93). Republican. Office: Creative Woodcrafters Inc 17 Westside Dr Asheville NC 28806-2846

KELLAM, RICHARD B., judge; b. 1909. Bar: Va. bar 1934. Chief judge, sr. U.S. dist. judge U.S. Dist. Ct. for Va. Eastern Dist., Norfolk. Office: US District Court 344 US Courthouse 600 Granby St Norfolk VA 23510-1915

KELLAWAY, PETER, neurophysiologist, researcher; b. Johannesburg, Republic of South Africa, Oct. 20, 1920; s. Cecil John Rhodes and Doreen Elizabeth (Joubert) K.; m. Josephine Anne Barbieri, Apr. 1957; children: David, Judianne, Kevin, Christina, Jaime. BA, Occidental Coll., 1942, MA, 1943; PhD, McGill U., 1947; MD (hon.), U. Gothenberg, Sweden, 1977. Diplomate Am. Bd. Clin. Neurophysiology. Lectr. physiology McGill U., Montreal, Que., Can., 1946-47, asst. prof. physiology, 1947-48; assoc. prof. Baylor U. Coll. Medicine, Houston, 1948-61, prof., 1961-78, prof. neurology, 1978—, prof. div. neurosci., 1990—, dir. lab. clin. electrophysiology, 1948-65; dir. dept. clin. neurophysiology The Meth. Hosp., Houston, 1948-71, mem. attending staff, 1948—, chief, sr. attending physician Neurology Svc., 1971—; cons., neurophysiologist Hermann Hosp., Houston, 1949-73, dir. dept. electroencephalography, 1955-73; dir. electroencephalography lab. Ben Taub Gen. Hosp., Houston, 1965-79; mem. cons. staff, chief neurophysiology svc. Dept. Medicine Tex. Children's Hosp., Houston, 1972—; mem. cons. staff neurology St. Luke's Episc. Hosp., Houston, 1971-73, mem. cons. staff neurophysiology, chief neurophysiology svc., 1973—; dir. Blue Bird Circle Children's Clinic Neurol. Disorders The Meth. Hosp., 1949-60, dir. Blue Bird Circle Rsch. Labs., 1960-79, chmn. Instnl. Rev. Bd. Human Rsch., 1974-90, dir. Epilepsy Rsch. Ctr., 1975—; chmn. appointment and promotions com. Baylor U. Coll. Medicine, 1968-71, dir. Epilepsy Rsch. Ctr., 1975—, chief sect. neurophysiology Dept. Neurology, 1977—; cons., electrophysiologist VA Hosp., Houston, 1949—; cons. electroencephalography So. Pacific Hosp. Assn., Houston, 1949-57; cons., neurophysiologist M.D. Anderson Hosp. and Tumor Inst., Houston, 1953-62; mem. coun. adminstrs. Tex. Med. Ctr., Houston, 1954-60; cons. electroencephalography sect. NIH, 1961-62; hon. pres. Internat. Congress Clin. Neurophysiology, 1993. Author numerous books; editor Electroencephalography and Clin. Neurophysiology, 1968-71, cons. editor, 1972-75, hon. cons. editor, 1989; mem. editl. bd. Jour. Clin. Neurophysiology, 1995; contbr. over 180 articles to profl. jours. Recipient Sir William Osler medal Am. Assn. History of Medicine, 1946; grantee NIH, NASA; named Grass lectr. Am. Soc. EEG Technologists, 1989; Berger lectr., 1982, 92. Fellow Am. Acad. Pediat. (hon.), Am. Electroencephalographic Soc. (hon., coun. 1954, 64-66, treas. 1956-58, pres.-elect 1962-63, pres. 1963-64, Jasper award 1990); mem. APA, Am. Epilepsy Soc. (sec.-treas. 1955-58, pres.-elect 1959, pres. 1960, Lennox lectr. 1981, Disting. Clin. Investigator award 1989, Lennox award 1996), Am. Physiol. Soc., Am. Acad. Neurology, Am. Neurol. Assn., Can. Physiol. Soc., Internat. Fedn. Clin. Neurophysiology (hon. pres. internat. congress), Internat. League Against Epilepsy (Am. br.), So. Electroencephalographic Soc. (coun. 1953, v.p. 1954, pres. 1955), Ea. Assn. Electroencephalographic Soc., Ctrl. Encephalographic Soc., Houston Neurol. Soc. (v.p. 1957, pres. 1967, chmn. bd. trustees 1970-73), Soc. Neurosci., Child Neurology Soc., Epilepsy Assn. Houston/Gulf Coast (profl. adv. bd. 1985-92). Home: 627 E Friar Tuck Ln Houston TX 77024-5706 Office: Baylor Coll Medicine 1 Baylor Plz Houston TX 77030-3411

KELLEHER, DANIEL MICHAEL, trucking company executive; b. N.Y.C., July 8, 1943; s. Daniel Joseph and Margaret Mary (McDonald) K.; m. Linda Mary Euart, Aug. 30, 1969; children: David Ian, Julie Dennin. AB in Econs., Lafayette Coll., 1971; MS in Systems Analysis, Fla. Inst. Tech., 1979; MA in Nat. Security Affairs, U.S. Naval War Coll., 1985. Enlisted U.S. Army, 1966, advanced through grades to Brig. Gen., 1992, retired, 1993; exec. v.p. Trism Specialized Carriers, Marietta, Ga., 1993—. Pres. Thousand Oaks Homeowners Assn., Woodbridge, Va., 1975-77; pres. Mannheim (Germany) Sch. Bd., 1981-84; regional chmn. Boy Scouts Am., Ansbach, Germany, 1985-87. Recipient Bronze Star U.S. Army, Vietnam, 1969. Mem. Nat. Def. Transp. Assn. (pres. regimental chpt. 1990, 92), Assn. U.S. Army, Coun. Logistics Mgmt., Railway Indsl. Clearance Assn. Republican. Roman Catholic. Home: 3856 Harts Mill Ln NE Atlanta GA 30319-1814 Office: Trism Specialized Carriers Inc PO Box 6426 1425 Franklin Rd Marietta GA 30065

KELLEHER, HERBERT DAVID, airline executive, lawyer; b. Camden, N.J., Mar. 12, 1931; s. Harry and Ruth (Moore) K.; m. Joan Negley, Sept. 9, 1955; children: Julie, Michael, Ruth, David. BA cum laude, Wesleyan U., 1953; LLB cum laude, NYU, 1956. Bar: N.J. 1957, Tex. 1962. Clk. N.J. Supreme Ct., 1956-59; assoc. Lum, Biunno & Tompkins, Newark, 1959-61; ptnr. Matthews, Nowlin, Macfarlane & Barrett, San Antonio, 1961-69; sr. ptnr. Oppenheimer, Rosenberg, Kelleher & Wheatley, Inc., San Antonio, 1969-81; founder, gen. counsel, pres., chmn., dir. Southwest Airlines Co., Dallas, 1967—, now also chief exec. officer. Past chmn. adv. bus. coun. Bus. Sch. U. Tex.; past pres. bd. trustees St. Mary's Hall, San Antonio; past pres. Travelers Aid Soc., San Antonio. Named Chief Exec. Officer of Yr., The Fin. World, 1982, 90, Best Chief Exec. Regional Airline Industry Wall St. Transcript, 1982, Gold award, 1992, Bronze award, 1993, Great Entrepreneur 1992 Southwest CEO Coun.; named to Tex. Bus. Hall Fame, 1988; recipient Fin. Mgmt. award Air Transport World, 1982, Airline Industry Svc. award, 1988, Best Managed Airline, Airline Exec. award, 1990, Master Enterpreneur award Inc. Mag., 1991, Disting. Bus. Leadership award Coll. Bus. Adv. Coun. Univ. Tex., 1992, Bus. Statesman award Harvard Bus. Sch. Club Dallas, 1992, Pro Bono Publico award Dallas Advt. League, 1992, Stewardship of Tex. Values award Tex. Lyceum, 1992, Aircraft Operations Excellence award Am. Inst. Aeronautics and Astronautics, 1994; Olin scholar, Root Tilden scholar. Fellow Tex. Bar Found. (life); mem. ABA, San Antonio Bar Assn., Dallas Bar Assn., State Bar Tex. Home: 144 Thelma Dr San Antonio TX 78212-2516 Office: SW Airlines Co Box 36611 Love Field Dallas TX 75235-1611

KELLER, BEN ROBERT, JR., gynecologist; b. Big Spring, Tex., July 9, 1936; s. Ben Robert and Rowena Ward (Gibson) K.; children: Gwenyth Sue Keller Wood, Jennifer Lynn Keller Pleska, Amy Jo Keller Hightower, Ben R. III, Destry S.L. BA, U. Tex., 1959; MD, U. Tex., Dallas, 1961. Diplomate Am. Bd. Obstetrics and Gynecology. Intern Hermann Hosp., Houston, 1961-62, ob-gyn resident, 1962-65; pvt. practice Arlington, Tex., 1967-79, 87—, Glenwood Springs, Colo., 1979-87, Arlington, 1987—; clin. instr. U. Tex., Dallas, 1975-79; assoc. clin. prof. U. Colo., Denver, 1983-86; mem. active staff Arlington Meml. Hosp., 1989—; courtesy staff South Arlington Med. Ctr., 1990—. Bd. dirs. Planned Parenthood North Tex., 1990—; chmn. speakers bur. Am. Cancer Soc., Arlington, 1968-73; mem. Arlington Drug Abuse Com., 1969-72, Glenwood Springs (Colo.) Coun. on Drug Abuse, 1984-87; chmn. bd. elders 1st Christian Ch., Arlington, 1975-76; chmn. Texpac com. Tarrant County, Ft. Worth, 1972-75. Capt. M.C., USAF, 1965-67. Fellow Am. Coll. Ob-Gyn.; mem. Tex. Med. Assn. (del. 1972-79, treas. 1974-79), Tarrant County Med. Soc., Rotary Internat., Sunlight Ski Club (chmn. bd. dirs. 1985-86). Republican. Mem. Christian Ch. (Disciples of Christ). Office: 109 W Randol Mill Rd Ste 101 Arlington TX 76011-4608

KELLER, JOHN WARREN, lawyer; b. Niagara Falls, Aug. 6, 1954; s. Joseph and Edith Lillian (Kilvington) K.; m. Sandra D. Hubbard, Dec. 18, 1981; children: Sean, Christopher. BA, Rider U., 1976; JD, Coll. William and Mary, 1979. Bar: Ky. 1980, U.S. Dist. Ct. (ea. dist.) Ky. 1985, U.S. Ct. Appeals (6th cir.) 1988, U.S. Dist. Ct. (we. dist.) Ky. 1988. Staff atty. Appalachian Rsch. & Def. Fund Ky., Inc., Barbourville, 1979-82; assoc. F. Preston Farmer Law Offices, London, Ky., 1982-88; ptnr. Farmer, Keller & Kelley, London, 1988-91, Taylor, Keller & Dunaway, London, 1991—; mem. Fla. Adv. Com. on Arson Prevention, 1990—, Ky. Arson Task Force, 1994—; chair bd. dirs. Appalachian Rsch. & Def. Fund Ky., 1994—; founder, chmn. bd. dirs. Ky. Lawyers for Legal Svcs. to the Poor. Contbg. editor: ABA Annotations to Homeowner's Policy, 3rd edit., 1995. Bd. dirs. Christian Ch. in Ky., 1994—; del. Ky. Coun. Chs., 1994—; elder First Christian Ch., London, 1994—; pres. Access to Justice Found., 1996—. Recipient Access to Justice award Ky. Legal Svcs. Programs, 1995. Mem. ABA (vice chair property ins. law com. 1992—), Laurel County Bar Assn. (pres. 1992-93), Ky. Bar Assn. (mem. bd. govs. 1996—). Office: Taylor Keller & Dunaway 802 N Main St London KY 40741-1121

KELLERMANN, KENNETH IRWIN, astronomer; b. N.Y.C., July 1, 1937; s. Alexander Samuel and Rae (Goodstein) K.; m. Michele Kellermann; 1 child, Sarah. SB, MIT, 1959; PhD, Calif. Inst. Tech., 1963. Rsch. scientist CSIRO, Sydney, Australia, 1963-65; asst. scientist Nat. Radio Astronomy Obs., Green Bank, W.Va., 1965-67, assoc. scientist, 1967-69, scientist, 1978; asst. dir. Max Planck Inst. for Radio Astronomy, Bonn, Fed. Republic of Germany, 1978, dir., 1978-79, outside sci. mem., 1980—; sr. scientist Nat. Radio Astronomy Obs., Charlottesville, W.Va., 1980—; adj. prof. U. Ariz, Tucson, 1970-72; rsch. prof. U. Va., Charlottesville, 1985—. NSF fellow, Washington, 1965-66; recipient Rumford prize Am. Acad. Arts Scis., 1970, Warner prize Am. Astron. Soc., 1971, Gould prize NAS, 1973. Mem. NAS, Internat. Astron. Union (pres. com. 40 1982-85, pres. U.S. nat. com. 1990-92, Am. Astron. Soc., Internat. Radio Sci. Union, Am. Acad. Arts and Scis, Soviet Astron.Soc., Australian Astron. Soc. Office: Nat Radio Astron Obs Edgemont Rd Charlottesville VA 22903

KELLER-WOOD, MAUREEN, physiology researcher, educator; b. Poughkeepsie, N.Y, May 17, 1955; d. Charles and Anne Keller; m. Charles E. Wood, 1979. AB in Biochemistry, Vassar Coll., 1977; PhD in Endocrinology, U. Calif., San Francisco, 1982. Postdoctoral fellow dept. physiology U. Fla., Gainesville, 1983-85, asst. rsch. scientist dept physiology, 1985-88, asst. prof. dept. pharmacodynamics, 1988-93, assoc. prof. dept. pharmacodynamics, 1993—. Postdoctoral fellow NIH, 1984-85; grantee Am. Heart Assn., 1989—, NIH Rsch. grantee, 1988—; recipient NIH New Investigator award, 1985-88, Rsch. Career Devel. award, 1989-94. Mem. Am. Physiological Soc., Endocrine Soc. Office: U Fla Coll Pharmacy PO Box 100487 # U Gainesville FL 32608

KELLEY, BEVERLY CASHUL, principal; b. Buffalo, July 19, 1946; d. John and Mary (Fatta) Cashul; 1 child, Kristopher Gordon. BS, Fla. Atlantic U., 1968; MEd, U. West Fla., 1980; EdS, Nova U., 1985. Tchr. Eastpoint (Fla.) Elem. Sch., 1968-70; social studies tchr. Dixie County H.S., Cross City, Fla., 1972-74; reading tchr. Chapman Elem. Sch., Apalachicola, Fla., 1974-78; reading tchr. Apalachicola H.S., 1978-95, prin., 1995—. Mem. NEA, ASCD, Nat. Assn. Secondary Sch. Prins., FTP, GFWC, Fla. Fedn. Women's Clubs (historian 1996, state sewing chmn. 1986), Philaco Woman's Club (pres. 1982), Delta Kappa Gamma (chpt. pres. 1984-86), Apalachicola Bay C. of C. Democrat. Roman Catholic. Home: 50-26th St Apalachicola FL 32320 Office: Apalachicola High School 1 Shark Blvd Apalachicola FL 32320-1369

KELLEY, DEBRA STEPHENS, interior designer; b. Williamson, W.Va., Jan. 10, 1951; d. Wm. T. and Louise Marcum Stephens; m. Spain Camp Kelley, Sept. 1985; children: Lindsey, Ashton, Elizabeth, Brent. BS cum laude, W.Va. U., 1972. Interior designer Decorators Unltd., Hilton Head, S.S., 1983-86; pres. Kelley Designs, Inc., Hilton Head, S.C., 1986—. Prin. works include Island Med. Ctr., Relley's North, Port Royal Plaza, Primo's Orleans Plaza, Bravo, Park Plaza, Gaslight, Rick's Place, Reilleys at Ka'anapali, Hawaii, pvt. residences. Mem. Am. Soc. Interior Designers (allied, Carolinas chpt.), Internat. Soc. Interior Designers (assoc., bd. dirs. Carolina chpt.), Nat. Trust for Historic Preservation, C. of C. (exec. exch. com. 1992, 93). Presbyterian. Home: 3 Wagner Pl Hilton Head Island SC 29928-3909 Office: 30 New Orleans Rd Hilton Head Island SC 29928-4715

KELLEY, HENRY PAUL, university administrator, psychology educator; b. Cleburne, Tex., July 4, 1928; s. Henry Roul and Jane Frances (Wynn) K.; m. Lucerle DeCourcy Scott, Aug. 18, 1949; children: Roger Wynn, Scott Franklin, Gordon Henry. BA in Pure Math., U. Tex., 1949, MA in Ednl. Psychology, 1951; AM, PhD in Psychology, Princeton U., 1954. Cert. and lic. psychologist, Tex. Psychometric fellow Ednl. Testing Svc., Princeton, N.J., 1951-54; pers. mgmt. and evaluation psychologist pers. and tng. rsch. ctr. USAF, San Antonio, 1954; aviation exptl. psychologist U.S. Naval Sch. Aviation Medicine, Pensacola, Fla., 1955-57; coord. measurement svcs., testing and counseling ctr., from asst. to assoc. prof. ednl. psychology U. Tex. Austin, 1958-64, lectr., 1964-67, dir. measurement and evaluation ctr., prof. ednl. psychology, 1967—; regional dir. southwestern office Coll. Entrance Exam. Bd., Austin, 1964-67; regional coord. Project TALENT, Austin, 1959-61; mem. southwestern regional adv. com. Coll. Entrance Exam. Bd., Austin, 1968-73, vice-chmn. com. rsch. and devel., N.Y.C., 1970-73, chmn., 1973-76, mem. adv. panel econ. implications recognizing prior learning, 1979-80; vis. faculty mem. ann. inst. coll. entrance, acad. placement and student fin. assistance Coll. Entrance Exam. Bd. and U. N.C., Chapel Hill, 1975-94; tech. reviewer, panel mem. rsch. projects br., bur. edn. handicapped, office edn. HEW, Washington, 1977; asst. hearing officer minimum competency study Nat. Inst. Edn., 1980-81; mem. gen. faculty U. Tex. Austin, 1960-64, 67-80, sec., 1981—, mem. faculty senate, 1972-74, 81—, sec., 1975-79, adminstrv. adviser ednl. policy com., 1968—; reviewer comprehensive program fund improvement secondary edn. U.S. Dept. Edn., 1983; mem. rsch. adv. panel, manpower and pers. divsn. Air Force Human Resources Lab., Brooks AFB, San Antonio, 1984-86; mem. com. testing, coordinating bd. Tex. Coll. and Univ. Sys., Austin, 1985-86, mem. adv. com. basic skills testing, coordinating bd., 1987; mem. basic skills test rev. panel Tex. Edn. Agy., Austin, 1987; mem. Tex. acad. skills coun. Tex. Higher Edn. Coord. Bd., 1987-93, chmn. adv. com. tests and measurements Tex. acad. skills coun., 1987-93; mem. planning com. Ann. Tex. Testing Conf., 1987-94; cons. infield, spkr. in field. Author: (with Bruce Walker) Self-Audit of CLEP Policies and Procedures: A Guide to Policy Decisions for Colleges and Universities, 1981; contbr. articles to profl. jours. and publs. Lt. USNR. Recipient Edward S. Noyes award Coll. Bd., 1976, Advanced Placement Spl. Recognition award, 1985; recipient numerous grants in field. Fellow APA, Am. Psychol. Soc., Am. Assn. Applied and Preventive Psychology, Nat. Coun. Measurement Edn., Nat. Soc. Study Edn., Am. Assn. Higher Edn., Am. Evaluation Assn., Measurement Svcs. Assn., Psychometric Soc., Phi Beta Kappa, Phi Delta Kappa, Phi Eta Sigma, Phi Kappa Phi, Sigma Xi. Methodist. Home: 2522 Jarratt Ave Austin TX 78703-2433 Office: U Tex Austin PO Box 7246 Austin TX 78713-7246

KELLEY, JEFFREY WENDELL, lawyer; b. Urbana, Ill., June 8, 1949; s. Wendell J. and Evelyn V. (Kimpel) K.; m. Marsha Lynn Adams, Aug. 21, 1971; children: Julie M., Anna E., Adam J., Grant W. BA, Lipscomb Coll., 1971; postgrad., Vanderbilt U., 1971-72; JD, U. Ill., 1975. Bar: Ga. 1975, U.S. Dist. Ct. (mid. and no. dists.) Ga. 1975, U.S. Ct. Appeals (11th cir.) 1982. Assoc. Powell, Goldstein, Frazer & Murphy, Atlanta, 1975-82, ptnr. litigation dept., with bankruptcy splty., 1982—; speaker in field. Notes and comments editor U. Ill. Law Rev., 1974-75. Mem. ABA (litig. com.), Am. Bankruptcy Inst. (mem. com.), Ga. Bar Assn. (bench and bar com. 1988), Atlanta Bar Assn. (chmn. law day 1980), Lawyers Club Atlanta (rules and judiciary com. 1995). Republican. Mem. Ch. Christ. Office: Powell Goldstein Frazer & Murphy 191 Peachtree St NE, 16th Fl Atlanta GA 30303-1741*

KELLEY, LARRY DALE, retired army officer; b. Geary, Okla., Sept. 1, 1944; s. Cecil and Myrtle Irene (Burch) K.; m. Ellen Elizabeth Neeley; children: Sara M., Rebecca I., Lynette C., Stacey A. BS, Cameron U., 1974; M in Criminal Justice, Okla. City U., 1977; MBA, Ctrl. State U., 1980. Enlisted U.S. Army, 1964, advanced through grades to lt. col., 1990; ret., 1992; pers. officer/spl. forces officer, capt. U.S. Army, 1964-79; asst. sales mgr. Pacesetter Corp., Oklahoma City, 1980; acctg. mgr. Hertz Corp., Oklahoma City, 1981-84; systems mgr. U.S. Army, 1985-92; exec. dir. Sanctuary, Inc., 1994-95. V.p. student senate Cameron U., Lawton, 1973, pres. student senate, 1974; pres. chpt. 32 Spl Forces Assn., 1984, chpt. 95 Res. Officers Assn., 1988. Decorated Bronze Star, Combat Infantryman's badge, Sr. Parachutnts badge, Army Commendation medal, Presdl. Unit citation, Meritorious Unit citation, 4 Meritorious Svc. medals, 2 Army Achievement medals, Vietnam Parachutist badge, Vietnam Cross of Gallantry. Mem. VFW (life), DAV (life), Res. Officers Assn. (life), Ret. Officers Assn. (life), Spl. Forces Assn.

KELLEY, MARY ELIZABETH (LAGRONE), computer specialist; b. Temple, Tex., Feb. 12, 1947; d. Harry John and Mary Erma (Windham) LaGrone; m. Roy Earl Kelley, May 10, 1968; children: Roy John, James Lewis, Joanna Marylu. BS, U. Mary Hardin-Baylor, 1968. Cert. tchr., Tex. Math tchr. Killeen (Tex.) High Sch., 1977-78; clk. typist Readiness Region VIII, Aurora, Colo., 1979; statis. clk. Fitzsimons Army Med. Ctr., Aurora, 1980-81, mgmt. asst., 1981-83; clk. typist Corpus Christi (Tex.) Army Depot, 1984; mgmt. asst. Health Care Studies and Clin. Investigation Act, Fort Sam Houston, Tex., 1984-85; computer programmer/analyst Health Care Systems Support Act, Fort Sam Houston, 1985-88, computer systems analyst, 1988-92, computer specialist, 1992-94, data base adminstr., 1994-95, lotus notes sys. adminstr., 1995—; tchr. Fitzsimons Army Med. Ctr., 1978-79, cons., 1978-79. Author: (databases) Health Care Management System, 1988-94. Vol. Heidi Search Ctr., San Antonio, 1990, Friends of Safe House, Denver, 1980-83, Parents Encouraging Parents, Denver, 1979-83. Recipient achievement medal for civilian svc. Dept. Army, 1991. Mem. DAR, Daus. of Republic of Tex., United Daus. of Confederacy, Tex. Soc. of Mayflower Descs., Alpha Chi, Delta Psi Theta, Sigma Tau Delta. Roman Catholic.

KELLEY, MICHAEL G., critical care nurse, administrator; b. Enid, Okla., Mar. 1, 1949; s. Robert B. and Amanda F. (Reinhardt) K.; m. Bonnie Y. Kelley, June 25, 1979; children: Lorenda R., Julie F.; 1 stepchild, Charles M. Eaves. ADN, U. Nev., Las Vegas, 1972; BNS, U. Ky., 1980, MPA, 1986. BCLS. Staff nurse, operating room So. Nev. Meml. Hosp., Las Vegas, Cen. Bapt. Hosp., Lexington, Ky.; staff nurse, acting nurse mgr. operating room VA Med. Ctr., Lexington, nurse mgr. med. ICU; patient care mgr. PACU Cen. Bapt. Hosp., Lexington; staff nurse cardiac catheterization lab., operating rm. Ctrl. Bapt. Hosp. Contbr. articles to profl. jours. With U.S. Army, 1967-70. Mem. AACN, Assn. Oper. Rm. Nurses. Home: 106 Dogwood Ct Nicholasville KY 40356-2118

KELLEY, MICHAEL JAMES, medical services executive, author; b. Columbus, Ohio; m. Linda. BS, Fla. Atlantic U., 1976, MBA, 1980. Advisor to prime minister Turks and Caicos Islands, Brit. West Indies, 1978-79; chief adminstr. Ft. Lauderdale (Fla.) Eye Inst., 1980-87; v.p. Ambassador Real Estate Equities Corp., Tamarac, Fla., 1984-89, also bd. dirs.; v.p. Ambassador Fin. Group Inc., Tamarac, Fla., 1985-89; exec. dir. Retina Consultants Southwest Fla., Ft. Myers, 1990—; CEO Vision Rehab. Strategies, Ft. Myers, 1994—; CFO, bd.dirs. Lifevision, 1996—. Mem. Med. Group Mgmt. Assn. (AO pres. 1996—), Fla. Atlantic U. Alumni Assn. (bd. dirs. 1989-93), Visually Impaired Persons Inc. (adv. bd.). Office: Retina Cons 2668 Winkler Ave Fort Myers FL 33901-9336

KELLEY, ROBERT C., retired construction industry executive; b. 1932. Student, Westmar Coll. Pres. Varco Pruden, 1976-84; group v.p. United Dominion Industries, Inc., 1984-86, from sr. v.p. to COO, 1986-94; ret., 1994. Office: United Dominion Industries 2300 One 1st Union Ctr Charlotte NC 28202

KELLEY, SCOTT STREATER, orthopaedic surgeon; b. Des Moines, Jan. 18, 1957. BS, U. Iowa, 1979, MD, 1982. Intern SUNY, Syracuse, 1982-83; resident in orthopaedics SUNY, 1983-87; fellow in adult reconstruction Mayo Clinic, Rochester, Minn., 1987-88; staff orthopaedic surgeon Iowa Meth. Hosp., 1988-92; clin. asst. prof. U. Iowa, 1991-92; asst. prof. U. N.C., Chapel Hill, 1992—. Fellow ACS (assoc.), Am. Acad. Orthopaedic Surgeons; mem. AMA, Assn. for Arthritic Hip and Knee Surgery.

KELLEY, SYLVIA JOHNSON, financial services firm executive; b. Butte, Mont., Dec. 29, 1929; d. John O. and Hilja W. (Koski) J.; m. Dan H. Kelley, June 1, 1950 (div. Jan. 1973); children: David D., Bruce J., Sheila K. Miller, Mona K. Nance; m. Richard T. Marshall, June 10, 1979. CLU; ChFC; cert. fin. planner; registered fin. cons. Legal sec. various law firms, L.A., 1959-69; registered rep. Met. Life, N.Y.C., 1969-75, SMA Equities, Inc., Worcester, Mass., 1975-89, Multi-Fin. Securities Corp., Denver, Colo., 1989—; pres., chief exec. officer Advance Funding, Inc., El Paso, Tex., 1981—. Contbr. articles to profl. jours. Bd. dirs., chmn. bus. adv. com. Marina Del Rey C. of C., 1974-75; bd. dirs., pub. rels. chmn. Am. Heart Assn., El Paso, 1972-74; charter pres. El Paso Exec. Women's Coun., 1972-73; mem. fin. adv. com. El Paso C.C., 1992—; bd. dirs. El Paso Estate Planning Coun., 1993—. Mem. Am. Soc. CLUs and ChFC (past pres. El Paso chpt., bd. dirs. 1981-85), Registry of CFP Practitioners.

KELLGREN, GEORGE LARS, manufacturing company executive; b. Boras, Sweden, May 23, 1943; came to U.S., 1979; s. Lars Anders and Ann-Marie (Fröberg) Kjellgren; m. Rubi Caridad Godoy, Nov. 6, 1982; children: Adrian Anders, Derek Lars, Viveka Victoria. BS, Umea U., Sweden, 1967. Researcher, developer Husqvarna (Sweden) Arms Factory, Husqvarna, 1968; tech. officer Council for Sci. and Industrial Research, Pretoria, Republic of South Africa, 1969-74; mng. dir. Interdynamic Forsknings AB, Stockholm, 1975-79; tech. dir. Intratec U.S.A., Inc., Miami, 1979-83; pres. Grendel, Inc., Cocoa, Fla., 1983-95; CEO Kel-Tec CNC Industries, Inc., Cocoa, 1995—. Contbr. articles to profl. jours.; inventor firearms. Republican. Lutheran.

KELLING, DAVID HENRY, educational administrator, accountant; b. Pasadena, Tex., Oct. 6, 1953; s. Henry Adolf Walter and Bonnie Ruth (Cayton) K.; m. Rebecca Sue Harper, May 14, 1983 (div. Feb. 1987); m. Connie Gayle Turner, May 23, 1992. BBA in Acctg., Tex. A&M U., 1975. CPA, Tex.; cert. bank auditor. Acct. Lower Colo. River Authority, Austin, Tex., 1976-78; sr. auditor Tex. Commerce Bancshares, Austin, 1978-81; controller, v.p. First Victoria (Tex.) Nat. Bank, 1981-83; chief fin. officer, sr. v.p. Bay Bancshares, Inc., La Porte, Tex., 1983-87; prin. David H. Kelling, CPA, La Porte, 1983-90; acct. Tiller & Co., Baytown, Tex., 1987-90; sr. acct. div. acctg. and corp. svcs. Resolution Trust Corp., Houston, 1990-91; audit sr. BDO Seidman & Co., Houston, 1992-93; internal auditor Goose Creek Consol. Ind. Sch. Dist., Baytown, 1993—; Bd. dirs. Bay Banc Data Services, La Porte. Photographic works include 1988 Ray Miller's Spirit of Texas Calendar. Treas. Good Shepherd Luth. Ch., Leander, Tex., 1981-83; mem. New Wine Christian Ch. of Baytown, Tex., 1992—. Mem. AICPAs, Tex. Soc. CPAs, Nat. Assn. Accts, Bank Adminstrn. Inst., Soc. Chartered Bank Auditors, Tex. A&M U. Alumni Assn., Beta Alpha Psi (v.p. 1974-75, Outstanding chpt. mem. 1975, Recognition award 1975), Phi Kappa Phi, Optimist (v.p. Victoria chpt. 1980-81). Republican. Home: 3823 Youpon Dr La Porte TX 77571-4325 Office: Goose Creek Consol ISD 1415 Market Baytown TX 77522

KELLOGG, CHRISTINA ANNE, marine microbiologist; d. Dimitri Alexander and Mary J. Kellogg. BS, Georgetown U., 1991; postgrad., U. South Fla., 1991—. Mem. AAAS, Assn. for Women in Sci., Am. Soc. for Microbiology. Office: University of South Florida 140 7th Ave S Saint Petersburg FL 33701-5016

KELLOGG, JACK LORENZO, fundraising executive, lawyer; b. Frankfort, Ind., Mar. 7, 1933; s. Oscar and Lucille Estella (Cline) K.; m. Patricia A. Rossworn, Oct. 24, 1959 (div. 1976); children: John Rossworn, Patrick Dilworth, Peter Cline; m. Ann Marie Hill, Nov. 10, 1979. AB, Wabash Coll., Crawfordsville, Ind., 1955; JD, NYU, 1958. Bar: N.Y. 1959. Pvt. practice N.Y.C., 1959-80; pub. Princeton (N.J.) Community Phone Book, Inc., 1980-88; dir. planned giving Arthritis Found., Inc., Pompano Beach, Fla., 1988-89; dir. devel., mem. exec. com. Red Cloud Sch., Inc., Pine Ridge, S.D., 1990-95; v.p. Cath. Charities Archdiocese of Denver, 1996—. Mem. Nat. Soc. Fund Raising Execs. (bd. dirs. Fla. chpt. 1989), Wabash Coll. Alumni Assn. (alumni bd. 1971-73). Home: 4 Clarendon Ct Williamsburg VA 23188 also: 1177 Race St # 705 Denver CO 80206 Office: 200 Josephine St Denver CO 80206-4710

KELLOGG, MICHAEL STUBBS, computer specialist; b. Houston, Sept. 12, 1958; s. William Lawrence and Benita Marie Kellogg; m. Linda Annette Metcalf, Nov. 15, 1991; 1 child, William Edward. AA, Blinn Coll., 1978; postgrad., Stephen F. Austin State U., 1979. Sr. systems analyst Navacom Corp., Navasota, Tex., 1979-85; sales mgr. ComputerLand of Huntsville, Tex., 1985-88; sales and engring. profl. Trinity Industries, Navasota, 1988-90; technician supervisory control and data acquistion City of College Station, Tex., 1990—. Mem. choir St. Paul's Episcopal Ch., Navasota, past vestry mem. Mem. Brazos Valley Netware Users Group, Navasota Lions Club (pres. 1990, zone chmn. 1991, dist. 2-S5 cabinet 1991, Pres.'s Bronze award).

KELLUM, NORMAN BRYANT, JR., lawyer; b. Maysville, N.C., Aug. 12, 1937; s. Norman Bryant and Dollie Elizabeth (Mallard) K.; m. Ruth Taylor, Nov. 24, 1968; children: Ruth Elizabeth, Catherine Ann. BS, Wake Forest U., 1959, JD, 1965. Bar: N.C. 1965, U.S. Dist. Ct. (ea. dist.) N.C. 1965, U.S. Dist. Ct. (mid. dist.) N.C. 1991, U.S. Ct. Appeals (4th cir.) 1968, U.S. Supreme Ct. 1994. Salesman, mgr. The Southwestern Co., Nashville, summers 1962-68; research asst. N.C. Supreme Ct., Raleigh, N.C., 1965-66; atty. Norman Kellum Jr., New Bern, N.C., 1966-68; ptnr. Beaman & Kellum, New Bern, 1968-75; owner Beaman, Kellum, Hollows & Jones, P.A. and predecessor firms, New Bern, 1975-94; shareholder, pres. Kellum & Jones, New Bern, 1994—; bd. dirs. Triangle Bank, New Bern. Deacon, trustee First Bapt. Ch., New Bern. 1st lt. U.S. Army, 1960-62; trustee Meredith Coll., 1988-92, 94—, chmn., 1996; bd. visitors Wake Forest U. Sch. Law, 1992—. Mem. ATLA, N.C. State Bar, N.C. Acad. Trial Lawyers (bd. govs. 1983-87), N.C. Bar Assn., Ea. N.C. Inn Ct. (pres. 1995), Am. Bd. Trial Advs., New Bern Hist. Soc., Wake Forest U. Law Sch. (Alumni of Yr. award 1993). Office: Kellum & Jones PO Box 866 New Bern NC 28563-0866

KELLY, ANNE CATHERINE, retired city official; b. Buffalo, Mar. 6, 1916; d. John Patrick and Elizabeth Marie (Edwards) Donohue; m. Thomas Edward Kelly, Apr. 19, 1941 (dec. 1993); children: Maureen Anne Kelly, Michael Thomas, Edward John, Kevin Joseph, Theresa Elizabeth Callahan. Student SUNY-Buffalo. Tchr., St. Teresa Sch., Buffalo, 1956-64; clk. City of Buffalo, 1964, sec. to comptroller, 1967-70, coun. clk., 1970-76, sr. coun. clk., 1976-81. Com. woman N.Y. Democratic Com., 1970-87, mem. exec. bd., 1970-87; vice chmn. Erie County Dem. Com., 1985-87; past pres. Mercy League of Buffalo Mercy Hosp., Nash Ladies Guild, South Side Dem. Club; mem. Women for Downtown Buffalo. Roman Catholic. Clubs: Daus. of Erin, Nash Ladies. Lodge: KC (past pres. Nash guild). Home: 9 Haig Pl Apt 404 Dunedin FL 34698-8547

KELLY, CAROL WHITE, company executive; b. Shreveport, La., Dec. 23, 1946; d. Verlin Ralph and Mary Louise (Humphries) White; m. James Patrick Kelly, June 6, 1968; children: Mary Louise, Christopher John. BA, Centenary Coll. La., Shreveport, 1968. Corp. sec., treas. Kelly Law Firm P.C., Atlanta, 1986—. Mem. NAFE, Ga. Baptist Med. Guild (life), Atlanta Hist. Soc., Atlanta Ballet Guild (life), Internat. Platform Assn., High Mus. Art, Episcopal Ch. Women (sec.-treas. 1976-80), Chi Omega Alumnae Assn. (pres. 1979-80). Office: Kelly Law Firm PC Ste 1510 200 Galleria Pky NW Atlanta GA 30339-5946

KELLY, DAVID REID, pathologist; b. Morganton, N.C., Nov. 21, 1947; s. Everett Oree and Paris Dereama (Keever) K.; children: Marie Keever, David Reid Jr. AB, U. N.C., 1970; MD, U. Tenn. Ctr. Health Scis., 1974. Diplomate Am. Bd. Pathology, Clin. and Anatomic Pathology, Am. Bd. Pediatric Pathology. Intern, then resident U. Ala., Birmingham, 1974-78; Am. Cancer Soc. fellow dept. pathology and lab. medicine U. Minn., Mpls., 1978-79; pathologist-in-chief, med. dir. labs. Children's Hosp., Birmingham, 1979—; clin. prof. of pathology U. Ala.-Birmingham, 1985—; pathology cons. Pediatric Oncology Group, Chgo., 1979—. Author: Comprehensive Textbook of Oncology, 1986, Clinical Pediatric Oncology, 1991, Pediatric Neoplasia: Morphology and Biology, 1996; contbr. articles to Cancer, Pediat. Pathology, Am. Jour. Clin. Pathology, Med. and Pediat. Oncology, Kidney Internat. Leader Cub Scouts and Boy Scouts Am., Birmingham, 1988-94. Fellow Am. Soc. Clin. Pathologists, Coll. Am. Pathologists; mem. AMA (physician recognition award 1980, 91, 95), Soc. for Pediat. Pathology, Soc. Hematopathology, U.S. Acad. Pathology, Can. Acad. Pathology, Phi Alpha Theta, Phi Kappa Phi. Baptist. Office: Children's Hosp of Ala 1600 7th Ave S Birmingham AL 35233-1711

KELLY, EAMON MICHAEL, university president; b. N.Y.C., Apr. 25, 1936; s. Michael Joseph and Kathleen Elizabeth (O'Farrell) K.; m. Margaret Whalen, June 22, 1963; children: Martin (dec.), Paul, Andrew, Peter. BS, Fordham U., 1958; MS, Columbia U., 1960, PhD, 1965. Officer in charge Office of Social Devel., Ford Found., N.Y.C., 1969-74; officer in charge program related investments Ford Found., 1974-79; exec. v.p. Tulane U., New Orleans, 1979-81, pres., 1981—; dir. policy formulation div. Econ. Devel. Adminstrn., Dept. Commerce, Washington, 1968; spl. asst. to adminstr. SBA, Washington, 1968-69; spl. cons. to sec. Dept. Labor, 1977; bd. dirs. So. Edn. Found., La. Land and Exploration Co., Nat. Captioning Inst., Assn. Gov. Bds. Colls. and Univ., Econ. Devel. Commn. State of La.; mem. Humphrey Fellows Nat. Adv. Bd., Bus. Higher Edn. Forum, com. econ. devel. Gabelli Enterprises Inc., exec. com. Assn. Am. Univs.; pres. Commission NCAA, Found. for Biomed. Rsch., Nat. Sci. Bd., 1996; former chair Presidential Adv. Bd. Pres. city coun., councilman-at-large City of Englewood, N.J., 1974-77; bd. advocates Planned Parenthood of La. Mem. AAUP, La. Conf. Univs. and Colls., La. Assn. Ind. Colls. and Univs., Bus. Coun. New Orleans, City Club, Inc., Met. Area Com., New Orleans Ednl. Telecom. Consortium. Democrat. Roman Catholic. Home: 2 Audubon Pl New Orleans LA 70118-5526 Office: Tulane U Office of President New Orleans LA 70118

KELLY, EDWARD JOHN, V, counselor; b. Saratoga Springs, N.Y., July 10, 1936; s. Edward John IV and Blanch Marie (O'Connor) K.; children: Edward J. VI, Patrick J., Kevin J., Michael J., Kathleen M. Student, Union Coll., Schenectady, N.Y., 1954-56; MEd in Guidance and Counseling, Campbell U., Buies Creek, N.C., 1990; student, U. Dayton, 1967; BA in History, N.C. Wesleyan Coll., 1982. Commd. USAF, 1956, advanced through grades to lt. col., 1975; instr. navigation Strategic Air Command USAF, various locations, 1958-69; scheduler KC-135 USAF, Castle AFB, Calif., 1970-71, chief bomber ops., 1972-73; chief KC-135 planner USAF, Anderson AFB, Guam, 1973-84; 8AF chief of tng. Anderson AFB, Guam, 1974-75; dir. ops. and tng. USAF, Seymour Johnson AFB, N.C., 1977-78; ret. USAF, 1979; job developer, counselor Wayne C.C., Goldsboro, N.C., 1979-80, dir. coop. edn., job placement and apprenticeship, 1980—; chmn. County Workforce Devel. Coun., Goldsboro, 1980—; com. chmn. N.C. Internship Coun., 1985-93, N.C. trails com. chmn. 1989-92. Author: Canoeing the Neuse River, 1983, Your Move Into the World of Work, 1988. Chmn. task force Waynesborough State Pk., 1983-86, 90-94, 96—; scoutmaster Boy Scouts Am., Merced., Calif. and Guam, Goldsboro, 1971-86, coun. commr., Goldsboro, 1976-81, 84-88, dist. chmn., 1982-84; cand. Rep. Party, Wayne County, 1982, 84, 86. Recipient Silver Beaver award Boy Scouts Am., 1973. Mem. DAV, VFW, Coop. Edn. Assn., N.C. Coop. Edn. Assn. 9bd. dirs. 1985—, pres. 1994, Outstanding Profl. 1994), N.C. Placement Assn. (program co-chmn. 1990, Outstanding Profl. 1994), Neuse Trails Assn., Air Force Assn. (pres. 1980-82, 90-91, Merit medal 1989), County Pers. Assn. (pres. 1992). Home: 170 Quail Dr Dudley NC 28333-9518 Office: Wayne CC PO Box 8002 Goldsboro NC 27533-8002

KELLY, GERALD WAYNE, chemical coatings company executive; b. Charleston, W.Va., May 21, 1944; s. Wayne Woodside and Sarrah (Myers) K.; m. (div.); children: Scott Wayne, Lauren Melissa (dec.); m. Elizabeth Long, Nov. 18, 1983. BS, W.Va. U., 1966. From sales corr. to regional mgr. duPont Corp., various locations, 1966-83; bus. mgr. Decatur (Ala.) divsn. Whittaker Corp., 1983-85; v.p. Decatur divsn. Morton Internat., 1985-86, pres. Decatur divsn., 1986-93; v.p. Morton Indsl. Coatings, Morton Internat., Chgo., 1993—; pres./owner IRP Inc., Falkville, Ala., 1992—. Bd. dirs. Ind. Cystic Fibrosis Found., Indpls., 1971-73. Mem. Nat. Coil Coaters Assn., Nat. Paint and Coatings Assn., Beta Theta Pi. Republican. Methodist. Home: 14 Tartan Ridge Rd Burr Ridge IL 60521-8905 Office: Morton Internat 100 N Riverside Plz Chicago IL 60606 also: IRP Inc PO Box 670 Falkville AL 35622-0670

KELLY, JEFFREY JENNINGS, mechanical engineer; b. Columbia, S.C., July 28, 1947; s. Jesse Jennings and Mary Katherine (Hawkins) K.; m. Betty Jane Vickers, June 15, 1980 (div. May 1984). BS in Math., Va. Poly. Inst. and State U., 1970, PhD in Engring. Mechanics, 1981. Mathematician Naval Surface Weapons Ctr., Dahlgren, Va., 1970-76; grad. rsch. asst. Va. Poly. Inst. and State U., Blacksburg, 1977-79, rsch. assoc., 1979-81; mech. engr. David Taylor Rsch. Ctr., Bethesda, Md., 1981-82; asst. prof. Old Dominion U., Norfolk, Va., 1983-85; rsch. fellow U. Southampton, Eng., 1985-87; rsch. engr. Northrop Corp., L.A., 1987-90; staff engr. Lockheed Corp., Hampton, Va., 1990—; cons., Southampton, 1986, Hampton, 1991. Referee Jour. of Acoustical Soc. Am., 1981-82. NASA/Am. Soc. Engring. Edn. fellow NASA, Langley, Va., 1983-84. Mem. AIAA (sr.), N.Y. Acad. Scis., Inst. Noise Control Engring., Sigma Xi, Pi Mu Epsilon, Phi Kappa Phi. Home: 260 Marcella Rd Apt 1003 Hampton VA 23666-2591 Office: Lockheed Martin Engring & Scis NASA Langley Rsch Ctr MS303 Hampton VA 23681-0001

KELLY, JOHN LOVE, public relations executive; b. N.Y.C., Jan. 30, 1924; s. Joseph John McDermott and Mary Florence Keenan (Love) K.; m. Helen M. Griffin Hanrahan, June 28, 1952; children: Janet Ann, J. Scott. BS, St. Peter's Coll., 1951; postgrad. N.C. State U., 1966. Buyer exec. tng. program R.H. Macy's, N.Y.C., 1951-53; mktg. exec. Sanforized div. Cluett Peabody Co., N.Y.C., 1953-58; advt. account exec. Batton, Barton, Durstine & Osborn, N.Y.C., 1958-59; advt. mgr. Am. Cyanamid Co., N.Y.C., 1959-64; dir. advt. Fiber div. FMC Corp., N.Y.C., 1964-76; v.p., dir. pub. rels. and communications Avtex Fibers Inc., N.Y.C., 1976-85; cons. Brazilian Govt. Trade Bur., 1990-93, Lenzing Austria, 1993; pres. Kelhan Ltd., 1985-89. Cath. co-chmn. Peekskill area NCCJ, 1961-64, bd. dirs. Westchester County, 1969-79, nat. bd. dirs., 1966-69; trustee Mercy Coll., Dobbs Ferry, N.Y., 1965-69; trustee emeritus St. Peter's Coll.; councilman Town of Cortlandt (N.Y.), 1962-66, mem. Simon Wiesenthal Ctr., Am. Conf. for Irish Studies, Zoning Bd., 1971-74, mem. Bd. Ethics, 1975-79; mem. Cardinal's Com. of Laity, 1961-71; mem. Greater N.Y. Area coun. Boy Scouts Am., 1971-79. Mem. Pub. Rels. Soc. Am., Assn. Nat. Advertisers, Pub. Rels. Club N.Y., Am. Fiber Mfr. Assn. (chmn. pub. rels. com., edn. and pub. rels. subscoms.), Bd. Trade N.Y. (textile sect., v.p. 1954-60), Am. Israel Friendship League, Am. Irish Hist. Soc., Internat. Platform Assn., St. Peter's Coll. Alumni Assn. (bd. dirs. 1959-65), Hudson Valley Gaelic Soc., Interreligious Affairs Com. Diocese Venice, Fla., Knight Equestrian Order of the Holy Sepulchre of Jerusalem, Mission Valley Golf and Country Club (Laurel, Fla.), The Univ. Club N.Y.C. Democrat. Roman Catholic. Office: 9000 Midnight Pass Rd Sarasota FL 34242-2927

KELLY, JOHN PRICE, hospital administrator; b. Daingerfield, Tex., May 26, 1944; s. Allen Wilbur Price and Eunice G. (Carter) Kelly; divorced; children: Sheena D., Trieston R. BS in Indsl. Edn., Prairie View A&M U., 1966; MPH, U. Calif., Berkeley, 1971; M in Pub. Adminstrn. and Mgmt., U. Okla., 1978. Tchr., counselor Job Corp., Lincoln, Nebr., 1966-69; commd. ensign USN, 1969, advanced through grades to capt., 1988; COO med. planning USN, Phila., 1982-84; COO U.S. Naval Hosp., The Philippines, 1984-85; v.p. resources 18 hosps./dental facilities USN, Pacific Rim Countries, 1985-89; v.p. resources N.W. region USN, 1989-92, ret., 1992; v.p. materials mgmt. Dallas County Hosp. Dist., Dallas, 1992—; instr. George Washington U., Washington, 1978-80; minority devel. mgr. USN, 1982-92. Contbr. articles to profl. and naval publs. Decorated Navy Commendation medal (2). Mem. Am. Coll. Healthcare Execs., Masons (various offices), Shriners. Republican. Episcopalian. Home: 1421 Acapulco Dr Dallas TX 75232-3003 Office: Dallas County Hosp Dist 5201 Harry Hines Blvd Dallas TX 75235-7708

KELLY, KATHLEEN S(UE), communications educator; b. Duluth, Minn., Aug. 6, 1943; d. Russell J. and Idun N. Mehrman; m. George F. Kelly, Apr. 29, 1961; children: Jodie A., Jennifer L. AA, Moorpark (Calif.) Coll., 1971; BS in Journalism, U. Md., College Park, 1973, MA in Pub. Rels., 1979, PhD in Pub. Communication, 1989. Accredited pub. rels.; cert. fundraising exec. Dir. pub. info. Bowie (Md.) State U., 1974-77; asst. to dean, instr. Coll. Journalism U. Md., College Park, 1977-79, assoc. dir. devel., 1979-82; v.p. Mt. Vernon Coll., Washington, 1982-83; dir. devel. U. Md., College Park, 1983-85, assoc. dean, lectr. Coll. Journalism, 1985-88, asst. dean Coll. Bus. and Mgmt., 1988-90; prof. U. S.W. La., 1991—; cons. NASA, NIH, Mt. St. Marys Coll., 1986—; lectr. CASE, Pub. Rels. Soc. Am., 1987—. Author: Fund Raising and Public Relations: A Critical Analysis, 1991, Building Fund-Raising Theory, 1994. Named PRIDE Book award winner Speech Comm. Assn., 1991, article award winner 1994, John Grenzebach award winner for rsch. on philanthropy CASE and Am. Assn. Fund-Raising Coun., 1991, PRIG award winner for outstanding dissertation Internat. Comm. Assn., 1990, winner 1995 Pathfinder award Inst. for Pub. Rels. Rsch. and Edn. Fellow Pub. Rels. Soc. (chmn. ednl. and cultural orgn. sect. 1989, pres. Md. chpt. 1986-87, Pres.' Cup 1981, nat. bd. dirs. 1994-96); mem. Nat. Soc. Fund Raising Execs. (mem. rsch. coun.), Coun. Advancement and Support of Edn. (women's forum 1983), Phi Kappa Phi. Democrat. Home: 1033 Rue Bois De Chene Breaux Bridge LA 70517-6735 Office: U SW La Dept Comm PO Box 43650 Lafayette LA 70504-3650

KELLY, LINDA SUE, personnel specialist; b. Peoria, Ill., Aug. 13, 1951; d. Richard Paul and Helen Margaret (Roedell) Steubinger; m. Bruce Phillip Kelly, Mar. 17, 1972; children: Ryan Patrick, Lauren Elizabeth. BS in Interdisciplinary Studies, U. Houston, 1995. Pers. specialist Ft. Bend Ind. Sch. Dist., Sugar Land, Tex., 1986—. Mem. Am. Assn. Sch. Pers. Adminstrs., Gulf Coast Assn. Sch. Bus. Pers. Republican. Office: Fort Bend ISD 16431 Lexington Blvd Sugar Land TX 77478

KELLY, MARGARET ELIZABETH, financial analyst, planner; b. Ridley Park, Pa., Apr. 1, 1960; d. Albert Jeremiah Jr. and Margaret Mae (Claybyn) K. BS, Duke U., 1982; MBA, U. Tex., 1990. CPA, Tex. Staff auditor Deloitte Haskins & Sells, Houston, 1982-84, sr. auditor, 1984-85, sr. tax cons., 1985-88; sr. fin. analyst Pepsi-Cola, Pitts., 1990-91, supr. planning & analysis, 1991-92; bus. planner W.Va. market unit Pepsi-Cola, 1992-93, bus. planner Houston market unit, 1993-95; customer adminstrn. mgr. Landmark Graphics Corp., Houston, 1995; sr. assoc. Continental Airlines, Houston, 1996—. Mem. Pho Kappa Phi, Phi Eta Sigma. Home: 2125 Augusta Dr Apt 18 Houston TX 77057-3713 Office: Continental Airlines Inc Suite 1852 2929 Allen Pkwy Ste 1856 Houston TX 77019

KELLY, MARY JOAN, librarian; b. Baton Rouge, Nov. 25, 1947; d. Theodore McKowen Sr. and Patricia Marilyn (Faul) Wilkes; m. Karl Joseph Nix; 1 child, Patricia Lynn. BS, La. State U., 1970, MEd, 1973, EdD, 1980. Cert. English and social studies tchr., city/parish materials and/or media ctr. dir., La. Instr. conversation class La. State U., Baton Rouge; writer, prodr. The Video Co., Baton Rouge; freelance writer DBA-Creative Spl., Baton Rouge; tchr. East Baton Rouge Parish Sch. Bd., ret., 1991; prin. St. Isidore Mid. Sch., 1991-95; libr. Holy Family Sch., Port Allen, La., 1995—; presenter in field. Contbr. numerous articles to profl. jours.; sponsor yearbook and lit. mags. Mem. Non-Pub. Sch. Commn., La. Bd. Elem. and Secondary Edn., 1992—. Mem. NEA (mem. com.), ASCD, Citizens for Ednl. Freedom, NCEA, La. Mid. Sch. Assn., La. Prin. Assn., La. Assn. Educators (mem. com.), East Baton Rouge Parish Assn. Educators (v.p.), La. Assn. Classroom Tchrs. (mem. com.), East Baton Rouge Parish Assn. Classroom Tchrs. (pres.), Nat. Coun. Tchrs. English, Assn. Ednl. Comm. and Tech., La. Assn. Ednl. Comm. and Tech., Internat. Platform Assn., La. Libr. Assn., Capital Area Reading Coun., Gamma Beta Phi, Phi Lambda Pi, Phi Delta Kappa. Home: 4442 Arrowhead St Baton Rouge LA 70808-3905

KELLY, MARY QUELLA, lawyer; b. Appleton, Wis., Mar. 9, 1940. BA, Marquette U., 1962; MA, U. Tenn., 1964, PhD, 1969; JD, St. Mary's U., San Antonio, 1974. Bar: Tex. 1975. Former ptnr. Fulbright & Jaworski LLP, San Antonio; ptnr. Groce, Locke & Hebdor, San Antonio. Co-author: Texas Environmental Law Handbook, 1993. Mem. ABA, Nat. Assn. Bond Lawyers, State Bar Tex., Tex. Assn. Bank Counsel, Tex. Water Conservation Assn. (dir. 1990-93), San Antonio Bar Assn. (founder, chair environ. law sect. 1990-92), Phi Delta Phi, John M. Harlan Soc. Office: Hoops & Levy 300 Convent Ste 900 San Antonio TX 78205*

KELLY, ROBERT HART, physician, internist; b. Ft. Worth, May 7, 1955; s. Gordon Brooks and Joan Elizabeth (Perkins) K.; m. Paula Jean Ghormley, Jan. 8, 1977; children: James Patrick, Martha Claire, Gwendolyn Paige. BA, Amherst Coll., 1977; MD, U. Tex., 1981. Diplomate Am. Bd. Internal Medicine, Am. Bd. Geriat. Medicine. Intern and resident Okla. U., Oklahoma City, 1981-82, resident, 1982-84; pvt. practice Ft. Worth. Office: 929 College Ave Fort Worth TX 76104-3048

KELLY, ROBERT VINCENT, III, transportation executive; b. Sheboygan, Wis., May 22, 1962; s. Robert Vincent Jr. and Margaret Cecilia (Taylor) K. BSE, U. Mich., 1984; MBA, Case Western Res. U., 1986. Ops. analyst Burlington No. R.R., Chgo., 1986-87, mgr. ops. analysis, 1987-88; asst. market mgr. intermodal mktg. Burlington No. R.R., Ft. Worth, 1988, market mgr. intermodal mktg. no. region capacity mgmt., 1989-93, dir. fin. and operational econs., 1993-96; N.Am. rail contracting mgr. Sea-Land Svc., Dallas, 1996—. Vol. Habitat for Humanity, Adopt-a-Sch. tutor. Mem. Inst. Indsl. Engrs. (sr. mem.), Am. Mktg. Assn., Transp. Rsch. Forum, Inst. Ops. Rsch. and Mgmt. Sci. Home: 1700 Hilltop Ln Arlington TX 76013-3245 Office: Sea-Land Svc 4100 Alpha Rd Dallas TX 75244

KELLY, THADDEUS ELLIOTT, medical geneticist; b. N.Y.C., 1937. MD, Med. Coll. S.C.; PhD, Johns Hopkins U. Diplomate Am. Bd. Genetics (pres. 1993-94), Am. Bd. Pediatrics. Prof. pediatrics U. Va., Charlottesville, dir. med. genetics. Office: U Va Hosp Div Med Genetics PO Box 386 Charlottesville VA 22908-0386*

KELLY, THOMAS CAJETAN, archbishop; b. Rochester, NY, July 14, 1931; s. Thomas A. Kelly and Katherine Eleanor (Fisher) Conley. A.B., Providence Coll., 1953; S.T.L., Dominican House of Studies, Washington, 1959; D.Canon Law, U. St. Thomas, Rome, 1962; S.T.D. (hon.), Providence Coll, 1979; D.H.L. (hon.), Spalding Coll., 1983. Ordained priest Roman Cath. Ch., 1958. Sec. Dominican Province, N.Y.C., 1962-65; sec. Apostolic Del., Washington, 1965-71; assoc. gen. sec. Nat. Conf. Cath. Bishops-U.S. Cath. Conf., Washington, 1971-77; gen. sec. U.S. Cath. Bishops Conf. Washington, 1977-82, ordained Roman Cath. aux. bishop, 1977; archbishop Archdiocese of Louisville, 1982—; chmn. Cath. Conf. Ky., Louisville, 1982—. Chancellor Bellarmine Coll.; bd. dirs. St. Luke Inst. Recipient Veritas medal St. Catharine Coll., 1984. Mem. Canon Law Soc. Am., Nat. Cath. Edn. Assn. (chmn. bd. dirs. 1991-94). Home and Office: 212 E College St Louisville KY 40203-2334

KELLY, THOMAS JOSEPH, information systems specialist; b. Waterbury, Conn., Sept. 15, 1956; s. Thomas Joseph Jr. and Elsa Ann (Mrazik) K. Grad. high sch., Southington, Conn.; cert. in programming, Computer Processing Inst., East Hartford, Conn., 1978. Bus. systems analyst Choice-Vend, Inc., Windsor Locks, Conn., 1976-80; project leader Digital Equipment Corp., Maynard, Mass., 1976-80, 1980-82; project mgr. Farm Credit Banks of Springfield, Agawam, Mass., 1982-85; mgr. application devel. Berkshire Health Systems, Pittsfield, Mass., 1985-88, info. systems dir., 1988-91; info. systems cons. Comsys Tech. Svcs., Rockville, Md., 1991—; prin. Thomas Kelly Cons., Windsor Locks, 1980-85. Named Mr. Future Bus. Leader Am. Future Bus. Leaders Am., 1974, Pres. of Yr. Conn. Jr. Achievement, 1974. Mem. Assn. Computing Machinery, Digital Equipment Computer Users Soc. Republican. Home: 45268 Persimann Ln Sterling VA 20165 Office: Sybase Inc 6550 Rock Spring Dr Ste 800 Bethesda MD 20817

KELLY, TIMOTHY MICHAEL, newspaper editor; b. Ashland, Ky., Nov. 28, 1947; s. Robert John and Pauline Elizabeth (Henneman) K.; m. Carol Ann Knight, Aug. 2, 1969; children: Kimberly, Kevin. BA, U. Miami, Fla., 1970. Sports copy editor, writer The Courier-Jour., Louisville, 1970-71; exec. sports editor The Phila. Inquirer, 1971-75; dep. mng. editor Dallas Times Herald, 1975-81; mng. editor The Denver Post, 1981-84; exec. editor Dallas Times Herald, 1984; editor Daily News, Los Angeles, 1984-87; mng. editor The Orange County Register, Santa Ana, Calif., 1987-89; editor, sr. v.p. Lexington Herald-Leader, Lexington, Ky., 1989-96, pub., 1996—; juror Pulitzer Prize, 1987-88. Recipient Knight-Ridder Excellence award for Cmty. Svc., 1995. Mem. Am. Soc. Newspaper Editors, Sigma Delta Chi. Roman Catholic. Office: Lexington Herald Leader 100 Midland Ave Lexington KY 40508-1943

KELLY, VINCENT MICHAEL, JR., orthodontist; b. Tulsa, Mar. 15, 1933; s. Vincent Michael and Ivy Maria (Phelps) K.; m. Donna Deane Amis, June 1955 (div. 1972); children: Kevin Marie, Leslie Rene, Karen Elizabeth, Carolyn Michelle, Kathleen Ann; m. Aleatha Wilkinson Kelly. BA in Biology, U. Mo., Kansas City, 1954, DDS, 1957, Orthodontist, 1962, MS in Oral Histology, 1963. Diplomate Am. Bd. Orthodontics. Pvt. practice Tulsa, 1963—; asst. prof. orthodontics St. Louis U., 1972-76; assoc. prof. U. Okla., Oklahoma City, 1980-90; bd. dirs. State Bank NA, Tulsa, Nature Works Inc. Patentee in field. Organizer, bd. mem. Arvest Savs. and Loan, Tulsa, 1995. Capt. USAF, 1957-59. Mem. Tweed Found. Orthodontic Rsch. (instr. 1966-79), Am. Assn. Orthodontics, S.W. Soc. Orthodontics, Okla. Orthodontic Assn. (pres. 1976), Tulsa County Dental Soc., Coll. Europeen Orthodontie (hon. life mem.), Soc. Panamena de Orthodoncia Panama (hon. life), Soc. Colombiana de Orthodoncia Colombia (hon. life), Assn. Mex. Orthodoncia Med. (hon.), European Soc. Lingual Orthodontists (hon.), So. Hills Country Club, Arrowhead Yacht Club, Bailli (pres. Tulsa chpt.), Chaîne des Rôtisseurs. Republican. Roman Catholic. Home: 6517 Timberlane Rd Tulsa OK 74136-4520 Office: 4550 S Harvard Ave Tulsa OK 74135-2906 also: 333 W Blue Starr Dr Claremore OK 74017-5810

KELLY, WILLIAM FRANKLIN, JR., lawyer; b. Houston, Feb. 12, 1938; s. William Franklin and Sara (McAshan) K.; m. Ingrid Leach, Sept. 11, 1965; children: Kristin Adams, Sara McAshan. BA, Stanford U., 1960; LLB, U. Tex., 1963. Bar: Tex. 1965. Assoc. Vinson & Elkins, Houston, 1965-72, ptnr., 1972—. Served to 1st lt. U.S. Army, 1963-65. Fellow Houston Bar Found; mem. ABA, Tex. Bar Assn., Houston Bar Assn. Episcopalian. Club: Forest (Houston), The Houston. Home: 600 E Friar Tuck Ln Houston TX 77024-5707 Office: Vinson & Elkins LLP 2300 First City Tower 1001 Fannin Houston TX 77002

KELLY, WILLIAM JAMES, III, lawyer; b. St. Louis, July 26, 1967; s. William James Jr. and Lenore (Bastian) K.; m. Mary McNamara, Dec. 29, 1990; 1 child, Natalie Miles. BA, Tulane U., 1989; JD, St. Louis U., 1992. Bar: La. 1992, U.S. Dist. Ct. (ea., we. and mid. dists.) La. 1992, U.S. Ct. Appeals (5th cir.) 1994. Assoc. Adams and Reese, New Orleans, 1992—. Author articles in field. Mem. ABA (labor and employment planning bd. young lawyers divsn. 1994-96), FBA, La. State Bar Assn., Am. Judicature Soc., Serra Internat. (trustee 1994—), Sigma Chi (chpt. advisor 1994—), Alpha Sigma Nu. Roman Catholic. Office: Adams and Reese 4500 One Shell Sq New Orleans LA 70139-4501

KELTON, WILLIAM JACKSON, English language and social science educator; b. Christiana, Tenn., Aug. 10, 1932; s. William Bradshaw and Minnie (Jackson) K.; m. Martha Diane Rooker, Dec. 29, 1973. BS, Mid. Tenn. State U., 1954; MA, Peabody Coll., 1959; PhD, Vanderbilt U., 1971. Minister 1st Bapt. Ch., Wartrace, Tenn., 1954-59; tchr. Webb Sch., Bell Buckle, Tenn., 1954-56; instr. Mid. Tenn. State U., Murfreesboro, 1956-57, 66-68; prof. Cumberland U., Lebanon, Tenn., 1959-64; assoc. prof. Belmont Coll., Nashville, 1969-72, Nashville State Tech. Inst., 1981—; interim minister 1st Presbyn. Ch., Manchester, Tenn., 1961, Short Creek Bapt. Ch., Christiana, Tenn., 1965-75; owner Kelton Farms, Christiana, 1959-79; speaker at schs., chs., clubs and orgns., 1964—. Author: Studies of Swift and of Hawthorne, 1971, 72. Mgr. various state polit. campaigns, 1966, 70, 74; chaplain Valley Dist. Civitan Internat., Nashville, 1965, lt. gov., 1966. Mem. So. Speech Assn., Nat. Coun. Tchrs. of English, Masons. Democrat. Baptist. Home: 109 Boxwood Dr Franklin TN 37064-6914 Office: Nashville State Tech Inst 120 White Bridge Rd Nashville TN 37209-4515

KEMBLE, JAMES RICHARD, professional engineering services executive; b. Mishawaka, Ind., Sept. 28, 1935; s. Richard Ralph and Lucille Marie (Wickey) K.; m. Dorothy Faye Millican, Oct. 1960 (div. 1961); m. Anne Duval, Oct. 6, 1962; children: Dawn Marie, Joseph James, Lisa Marie, Theresa Marie. Student, Notre Dame U., 1953-54, Purdue U., 1954-59; B in Gen. Studies, U. Nebr., Omaha, 1969. Clk. stock rm. Powell Tool Supply, Inc., South Bend, Ind., 1952-54; truck driver South Bend Supply Co., 1959; commd. 2d lt. U.S. Army, 1959, advanced through grades to maj., 1967, ret., 1979; tech. writer VSE Corp., Alexandria, Va., 1979-80, sr. logistic engr., 1980-82, div. mgr. plans and programs, 1982-84, mgr. air launched missile group, 1984-86; asst. v.p., mgr. Systems Engrng. Group, Washington, 1986-94; v.p., mgr. air systems ops. divsn. Value Sys. Svcs., Arlington, 1994—. Decorated Bronze Star, Meritorious Svc. medal with 3 oak leaf clusters, Joint Svc. Commendation medal, Army Commendation medal with 1 oak leaf cluster. Mem. Am. Def. Preparedness Assn., KC. Roman Catholic. Home: 5300 Holmes Run Pky Alexandria VA 22304-2834 Office: VSE Corp 1725 Jefferson Davis Hwy Arlington VA 22202-4102

KEMMER, SUZANNE ELIZABETH, linguistics researcher, educator; b. Chgo., Nov. 7, 1959; d. Robert William and Marie Anne (Koegel) K.; m. Michael Barlow, Jan. 5, 1987. BA, Rice U., 1980; postgrad., U. Munich, 1980-81; MA in German, Stanford U., 1985, PhD in Linguistics, 1988. Tchr. English as fgn. lan. Stanford (Calif.) U., 1982-85, rsch. asst., 1985-88; asst. prof. U. Calif., San Diego, 1988-93; assoc. prof. Rice U., Houston, 1994—; co-founder, editor Athelstan Publs., La Jolla, Calif., 1987—; co-founder, pres. Cortica Press, La Jolla, 1991—. Author: The Middle Voice, 1993; co-editor: On Language, 1990, Studies in typology and Diachrony, 1990; contbr. articles and revs. to profl. jours. Mem. Linguistics Soc. Am., Internat. Soc. for Hist. Linguistics, Linguistics Assn. Great Britain, Internat. Cognitive Linguistics Assn., Phi Beta Kappa (scholar1983). Office: Rice University 6100 Main St Houston TX 77005

KEMP, BERNARD WALTER, JR., marketing executive; b. Washington, Mar. 9, 1950; s. Bernard Walter Sr. and Virginia Louise (Stephenson) K.; m. Angela Faye Reed, Oct. 13, 1990; 1 child, Gina. BA, Va. Union U., 1973; postgrad., Howard U., 1973-75. Adminstrv. asst. U.S. Dept. Transp., Washington, 1975-76; pres., owner Kemarr Assocs., Alexandria, Va., 1982—; CEO, owner Am./Internat. Commn. Network, Alexandria, 1996—; mem. Brain Trust-Capitol Hill, Washington, 1985-86; active corp. execs. SBA, Washington, 1985-86; lectr. in field. Editor newspaper column The Capital Spotlight, 1985-87. Mem. Nat. Steering Com., Washington, 1996; mem. choir Million Man March, Washington, 1995; mem. Dem. Senatorial Campaign Com., 1996—. With USN, 1976-82. Mem. Power Brokers, Calvin Coolidge Alumni Assn. Baptist. Home: 420 N Armistead St Alexandria VA 22312 Office: Kemarr Assocs PO Box 9282 Alexandria VA 22304

KEMP, BETTY RUTH, librarian; b. Tishomingo, Okla., May 5, 1930; d. Raymond Herrell and Mamie Melvina (Hughes) K.; BA in Libr. Sci., U. Okla., 1952; MS, Fla. State U., 1965. Extramural loan libr. U. Tex., Austin, 1952-55; libr. lit. and history dept. Dallas Pub. Libr., 1955-56, head Oaklawn Br., 1956-60, head Walnut Hill Br., 1960-64; dir. Cherokee Regional Libr., LaFayette, Ga., 1965-74; dir. Lee County Libr., hdqrs. Lee-Itawamba Libr. System, Tupelo, Miss., 1975-92; bd. libr. commrs. State of Miss., 1979-83, chmn., 1979-80. Chmn. Chickasaw Hist. Soc., 1994—; active Native Am. Chickasaw Nation, United Meth. Women. Mem. AAUW, ALA, Nat. Soc. Daus.Am. Colonists, Nat. Soc. U.S. Daus. of 1812, United Daus. of the Confedercy, Nat. Soc. Dames of Ct. of Honor, Am. Indian Cultural Soc. (Norman Okla.), First Families Twin Ters., Beta Phi Mu. Democrat. Home: 3313 Winchester Cir Norman OK 73072-2937 Office: Kemp Rsch & Cons Svc PO Box 720531 Norman OK 73070

KEMP, EDGAR RAY, JR., retail executive; b. Corsicana, Tex., Sept. 15, 1924; s. Edgar Ray and Earla Mae (Brennan) K.; m. Margaret Ellen Letzig, Sept. 17, 1949; children: William R., Daniel B., Ellen C., Michael E. B.B.A., U. Ark., 1948. C.P.A., Ark. Pvt. C.P.A. practice, 1948-58; treas. M. M. Cohn Co., 1958-63; vice chmn. Dillard Dept. Stores, Inc., Little Rock, 1963—, also vice chmn., chief adminstrv. officer.; v.p. bd. dirs. Dillard Travel Inc., Little Rock; Chmn. Little Rock br. Fed. Res. Bank of, St. Louis. Served with USAAF, 1943-45; Served with USAF, 1951-52. Mem. Am. Inst. Accts., Nat. Assn. Accts., Sigma Chi, Alpha Kappa Psi. Roman Catholic. Office: Dillard Dept Stores Inc PO Box 486 900 W Capitol Ave Little Rock AR 72201-3108 also: Dillard Travel Inc 1600 Cantrell Rd Little Rock AR 72201-1110*

KEMP, GINA CHRISTINE, social services provider; b. New Orleans, June 5, 1968; d. Donald Rue and July Carol (Sallee) K.; m. Patrick E. Hutto, May 15, 1994; 1 stepchild, Patrick B. BA in Psychology, So. Coll., Collegedale, Tenn., 1989; MA in Edn., U. Ga., 1991. Cert. nat. counselor; master addiction counselor; criminal justice specialist. Sociology tchr. So. Coll., 1989; counselor offender rehab., GED examiner IW Davis Detention Ctr., Jefferson, Ga., 1991; counselor offender rehab. drug specialist Alcovy Diversion Ctr., Monroe, Ga., 1991-96; v.p. H&M Sales, Loganville, Ga., 1994—; social svc. provider Rockdale Mental Health, Conyers, Ga., 1996—; boot camp officer Ga. Dept. Corrections. Mem. ACA, Internat. Assn. Addictions and Offender Counseling, Chi Sigma Iota, Psi Chi. Republican. Adventist. Home: 2823 Claude Brewer Rd Loganville GA 30249-4203 Office: Rockdale Mental Health 1429 Business Center Dr Conyers GA 30207

KEMP, JOHN RANDOLPH, journalist, author, academic administrator; b. New Orleans, Feb. 6, 1945; s. Frank LaGrange and Eileen Moira (O'Brien) K.; m. Elizabeth Ruth Earhart, June 15, 1968; 1 child, Virginia Elizabeth. BA, Loyola U., New Orleans, 1968; MA, U. So. Miss., 1973; postgrad., La. State U., 1975-77. Chief curator La. State Mus., New Orleans, 1972-78; journalist The Times-Picayune, New Orleans, 1978-83, contbg. art critic, 1984—; freelance writer Covington, La., 1983—; dir. univ. rels. Southeastern La. U., Hammond, 1983—; art critic Sta. WYES-TV, New Orleans, 1987—; co-founder New Orleans Writers Conf., 1989. Author: Martin Behrman of New Orleans: Memoirs of a City Boss, 1977, New Orleans: An Illustrated History, 1981, Lewis Hine: Photographs of Child Labor in the New South, 1986, Manchac Swamp: Louisiana's Undiscovered Wilderness, 1996; co-editor: Louisiana Images, 1880-1920: A Photographic Essay by George Francois Mugnier, 1975, Louisiana's Black Heritage, 1978; contbr. articles to numerous nat. and regional mags. and publs., 1983—, articles to ann. Fodor guidebooks, 1984—. Pres. Northlake Mus. and Nature Ctr., Covington, La., 1984-85; bd. dirs. Christ Episcopal Sch., Covington, 1986-89; mem. adv. bd. New Orleans Tennessee Williams Literary Festival, 1992—. Fellow Nat. Trust and Williamsburg Foundn.'s Summer Inst. for Hist. Adminstrn.; grantee NEH and Nat. Endowment for the Arts. Mem. Coun. Advancement and Support Edn. (bd. dirs. dist. IV 1989-90, 93-95, numerous awards 1984—), Am. Assn. State Colls. and Univs. (com. mem. Washington 1990—), La. Higher Edn. Pub. Rels. Assn. (pres. 1991-93), New Orleans Big Easy Entertainment (awards nominating com.). Home: 401 W 24th Ave Covington LA 70433-2513 Office: Southeastern La U PO Box 880 Hammond LA 70402-0880

KEMP, MAE WUNDER, real estate broker, consultant; b. Balt.; d. Edward J. and Helen (Robel) Wunder; m. George C. Segerman, May 17, 1941 (div. 1959); children: Barbara, George C.; m. Robert B. Kemp, July 23, 1960 (dec. 1989). BA, Notre Dame Coll., 1941. Pres. Realty Sales corp., Balt., 1958-60; records mgmt. cons. Boeing Co., Seattle, 1960-65; v.p., real estate broker Satellite Realty, Mercer Island, Wash., 1973-76; real estate broker Washington Properties Real Estate, Seattle, 1970-76; assoc. broker John L. Scott Real Estate, Seattle, 1976-92; tech. adviser of real estate North Seattle C.C., 1973-80. Mem. Seattle Women's Commn., 1973; precinct committeewoman Seattle Rep. Com., 1973; v.p. Freedoms Found., Valley Forge, Pa., 1974; past pres., pres. emeritus Hawthorne Hills Community Club, Inc., Seattle, 1974-90; chmn. Seattle's First Citizen Award. Recipient 5 State Regional Chmn. award, Woman of Yr., Omega Tau Rho medal Nat. Assn. Realtors, Seattle, Sales Assoc. of Yr. award Seattle Real Estate Bd., Outstanding Woman in Real Estate award Past Pres. Club, Woman of Day award Sta. KIXI, CBS. Mem. Wash. Assn. Realtors, Seattle-King County Bd. Realtors (bd. dirs.), Nat. Assn. Real Estate Brokers, Women's Assn. Hilton Head Island, Wash. Athletic Club, Country Club Hilton Head (mem. com., house com.), Navy League of U.S., Hilton Head Island Coun. Republican. Roman Catholic. Home: The Cypress 99 Bird Song Way D-401 Hilton Head Island SC 29926

KEMP, STEPHEN FRANK, pediatric endocrinologist, educator, composer; b. Newport, Oreg., Mar. 21, 1947; s. Frank Shirley and Charla Mae (Wait) K. BA, U. Oreg., 1969; PhD in Biochemistry, U. Chgo., 1974, MD, 1976. Diplomate Am. Bd. Pediatrics. Intern Stanford U., 1976-77, resident in pediatrics, 1977-78; postdoctoral fellow in pediatric endocrinology, 1978-80; asst. prof. pediatrics and chief pediatric endocrinology U. South Ala., Mobile, 1980-84; asst. prof. pediatrics U. Ark. for Med Sci., 1984-86, asst. prof. biochemistry, 1985—, assoc. prof. pediatrics, 1986-95, prof. pediatrics, 1995—, chief pediatric endocrinology, 1987—. Vice pres. Ala. affiliate Am. Diabetes Assn., 1982-84, pres., 1986-88, chmn. youth com. Ark. affiliate, mem. camp com; bd. dirs. Human Growth Found. Recipient NIH postdoctoral nat. research service award, 1978-80. Fellow Am. Coll. Endocrinology; mem. Med. Assn. State Ala., Am. Pediatric Soc., Am. Fedn. Clin. Research, Southern Soc. Pediatric Research, Endocrine Soc. Democrat. Episcopalian. Composer various choir, organ and orchestral works; contbr. articles to profl. jours. Home: 8 Victoria Cir Maumelle AR 72113-6423 Office: U Ark for Med Sci Dept Pediatrics 800 Marshall St Little Rock AR 72202-3591

KEMP, STEPHEN FREDERICK, physician; b. Richmond, Va., Dec. 30, 1960. BA, Duke U., 1983; BS, Va. Commonwealth U., 1986; MD, Med. Coll. Va., 1990. Diplomate Am. Bd. Allergy and Immunology, Am. Bd. Internal Medicine, Nat. Bd. Med. Examiners. Aide Fairfield Br. County of Henrico Pub. Libr., Richmond, Va., 1979; clk. emergency dept. Richmond Meml. Hosp., 1984-88; clk. hosp. learning resource ctr. Med. Coll. of Va. Hosps., 1987-88; resident physician dept. internal medicine U. Tenn. Coll. Medicine, Memphis, 1990-93; advanced subsplty. resident divsn. allergy immunology dept. internal medicine U. South Fla., Tampa, 1993-95, advanced subsplty. resident clin. lab. immunology divsn., 1995-96; asst. prof. medicine and pediats. divsn. divsn. allergy and immunology, depts. internal medicine and pediats. U. South Ala., Mobile, 1996—; physician participant Am. Acad. Immunology Health Policy Edn. Network, 1993—; fee-basis physician allergic and immunologic evaluations Vets. Compensation and Pension Clinic, James A. Haley Vet. Hosp., Tampa, 1994-96, fee-basis physician gen. med. evaluations, 1994-96; asst. collection and analysis of air pollen samples Hillsborough County, Fla., 1993-94, chief analyst collection and microscopic analysis of air pollen sample, 1994-96. Contbr. numerous articles to profl. jours. Mem. Christ United Meth. Ch., 1996—; physician vol. asthma and allergy sect. Judeo-Christian (Free) Health Clinic, Tampa, 1994-96, influenza vaccine adminstrn. for men's and women's basketball teams U. South Fla., Tampa, 1993; cardiac emergency med. tech. Henrico Vol. Rescue Squad, Richmond, 1982-88, Tuckahoe Vol. Rescue Squad, Richmond, 1988. Mem. AMA, ACP, AAAS, Am. Acad. Allergy, Asthma and Immunology (aerobiology com. 1995—, anaphylaxis com. 1995—, adverse reactions to foods com. 1995—, urticaria and angioedema com. 1995), Am. Coll. Allergy, Asthma and Immunology, Joint Coun. Allergy, Asthma and Immunology, Asthma and Allergy Found. Am., Ala. Soc. of Allergy and Immunology, Mobile Pediat. Soc., Omicron Delta Kappa (charter), Phi Kappa Phi, Phi Sigma. Office: USA Allergic Diseases Ctr 307 University Blvd N Mobile AL 36688-3053

KEMP, THOMAS JAY, librarian; b. Nashua, N.H.; s. Willard Henry and Eleanor Frances (Huse) K.; m. Vi Tuong Lam; children: Andrew Thomas, Sarah Eleanor. BA, Brigham Young U., 1973, MLS, 1974; cert. photographic preservation, Rochester Inst. Tech., 1979. Office supr., history div. Lee Library, Brigham Young U., Provo, Utah, 1971-74; local history and genealogy librarian Ferguson Library System, Stamford, Conn., 1974-86; grant reviewer NEH, Washington, 1978-84; ref. librarian Sacred Heart U., Fairfield, Conn., 1980-82; head librarian Weed Meml. Library, 1981-82, Turn of River Library, 1982-86; asst. dir. Pequot Library, Southport, Conn., 1986-89; libr. dir. Hist. Soc. Pa., Phila., 1989-91; dir. spl. collections dept. U. So. Fla. Libr., Tampa, Fla., 1991—; tchr. Office of Continuing Edn., Stamford, 1975-80; lectr. in field; called to testify U.S. Senate hearings on the new archivist of U.S., 1986; called as Bishop The Ch. of Jesus Christ of Latter-day Saints, Temple Terrace, Fla., 1993—; mem. U. So. Fla. Faculty Senate, 1992-96, sec., 1994-95; chair U. So. Fla. Libr. Coun., 1996-98. Author: Office of Patriarch to the Church in The Church of Jesus Christ of Latter-day Saints, 1981, Stamford, Connecticut 1872 City Directory, 1981, Connecticut Periodical Index, 1981-86, Genealogies in the Ferguson Library, 1982, Connecticut Researcher's Handbook, 1982, Connecticut Biography and Portrait Index, 1985-89, Genealogies in Connecticut Libraries and Historical Societies, 1985, Kemp Family of County Cavan, Ireland, 1985, Inexpensive Items for Building Your Genealogical Library, 1977, Home Study Courses of Interest to Genealogists and Local Historians, 1986, Kemp Bibliography, 1986, Kemp Family Records, 1986, Kemp Family Passport Records, 1986, Vital Records Handbook, 1988, Connecticut Divorces Granted by Resolve of the General Assemby of the State of Connecticut, 1988, Connecticut Changes of Name Granted by Resolve of the General Assembly of the State of Connecicut, 1988, Darien Connecticut, 1989 Vital Records: An Index to Birth, Engagement, Marriage and Death Announcements, 1990, Litchfield County, Connecticut Obituary Announcements 1989, 1990, New Canaan, Connecticut 1989 Vital Records: An Index to Birth, Engagement, Marriage and Death Announcements, 1990, International Vital Records Handbook, 1990, 94, Connecticut Historians and Genealogists 1890-1990, 1991, Genealogy Annual, 1995—; editor: Connecticut Ancestry, 1987-89, Richmond Family News Jour., 1971-76, Gradalis Review, 1973-74; local history and genealogy collection Thomas Jay Kemp Genealogy and Local History Collection Darien Libr., 1989; contbr. articles to profl. jours. Missionary to Colo.-N.Mex. Mission, Denver, 1968-70; bd. dirs. Pa. Ctr. for the Book, 1990-91. With USN, 1965-71. Recipient Hattie M. Knight award NYU, 1974, Merit award Conn. League Hist. Socs., 1983. Mem. Assn. for Bibliography of History, New Eng. Libr. Assn. (bibliography com. 1979-80), Conn. Libr. Assn. (hon. mention, Librarian of the Yr, 1987), Orgn. Am. Historians U.S. newspaper project, 1977), Am. Libr. Assn., (ref. svcs. div., chmn. history sect. 1989-90, chmn. nominations com., 1984, chmn. program com. 1983, pre-conf. planning com. 1981, genealogy com. 1978-82, local history com. 1986-91, 1996—), Coun. of Nat. Libr. Info. Assns. (chmn. 1989-90), New Eng. Archivists, N.H. Libr. Assn., N.Y. Geneal. and Biog. Soc., Geneal. Soc. Pa. (pubs. com. 1989—, acquisitions com. 1989—), Libr. Assn. (U.K.), Libr. Assn. of Ireland, Libr. Assn. China, Soc. Am. Archivists, Am. Soc. Indexers (pres. 1987-88), Assn. Profl. Genealogists (exec. v.p. 1988-90, trustee 1990-92), Middlesex Geneal. Soc. (Darien, Conn., bd. dirs. 1984-

89, trustee 1989—), Gen. Soc. Mayflower Descendants (bd. assts. Conn. 1983), SAR, Order of Founders and Patriots, Phi Alph Theta. Mem. LDS Ch. Office: U South Fla Libr Spl Collections 4202 E Fowler Ave Tampa FL 33620-9900

KEMP, THOMAS JOSEPH, electronics company administrator; b. Holy Cross, Iowa, Aug. 17, 1943; s. Joseph Peter and Margaret Gertrude (Wilgenbusch) K.; m. Ruth Anne Pfohl, Aug. 22, 1964; children: Geoffrey Joseph, Jennifer Anne, Julie Marie, Jack Thomas. BA in Bus. Acctg., Loras Coll., 1964; MS in Sys. Mgmt., St. Mary's U., San Antonio, 1978. Commd. 2d lt. USAF, 1964, advanced through grades to lt. col., 1980, pilot, mgr., 1964-85; ret., 1985; Instructional systems design mgr., dep. program mgr. United Airlines Svcs. Corp., Irving, Tex., 1985-87; divsn. mgr., project mgr. Flight Safety Svcs. Corp., Irving, 1987-90; program mgr. ElectroCom Automation, Arlington, Tex., 1990—. Congl. advisor Vets. and Budget Com., Ft. Worth, 1994—; pres. Tarrant County Vets. Coun., Ft. Worth, 1995-96. Mem. ASTD, VFW (life), Internat. Soc. for Performance Instrn., Air Force Assn. (life, state pres. Tex. 1995-97, Exceptional Svc. award 1990, 91, 94), Am. Legion, KC (dep. grand knight, Knight of Month and Family of Month awards). Republican. Roman Catholic. Home: 3608 Kimberly Ln Fort Worth TX 76133-2147 Office: ElectroCom Automation 2900 Avenue E Arlington TX 76011-5210

KEMPA, MARK ANDREW, accountant; b. Rochester, N.Y., Dec. 28, 1971; s. Stanley and Mary Dorothy (Szymanski) K.; m. Eve Davila, Dec. 15, 1995. BS in Acctg., Barry U., Miami, Fla., 1993; postgrad., Fla. Internat. U., 1996—. CPA, Ga., Fla. Asst. contr. Internat. Voyager Media, North Miami, Fla., 1993—. Mem. Delta Sigma Pi, Alumni Assn. Republican. Roman Catholic. Home: 13620 SW 109th Ave Miami FL 33176 Office: Internat Voyager Media 11900 Biscayne Blvd Ste 300 North Miami FL 33181-2726

KEMPER, ROBERT VAN, anthropologist, educator; b. San Diego, Nov. 21, 1945; s. Ivan L. and Roberta (King) K.; m. Sandra L. Kraft, Sept. 9, 1967; 1 child, John Kraft. BA, U. Calif., Riverside, 1966; MA, U. Calif., Berkeley, 1969, PhD, 1971. Postdoctoral fellow U. Calif., Berkeley, 1971-72; asst. prof. So. Meth. U., Dallas, 1972-77, assoc. prof., 1977-83, prof., 1983—, chmn., 1992-94; visiting rsch. scholar U. Iberoamericana, Mexico City, 1970, 79-80, Ctr. U.S.-Mex. Studies, LaJolla, Calif., 1983, U. Nat. Autónoma Mex., Mexico City, 1990-91, El Colegio de Michoacán, Zamora, Mex., 1991; sec. Inst. Study of Earth and Man, Dallas, 1989-92; Coun. Preservation Anthrop. Records; founding chair Commn. Anthropology Tourism, Internat. Union Anthrop. and Ethnol. Scis., 1993—. Author: Migration and Adaptation, 1977; co-author: History of Anthropology, 1977; co-editor: Anthropologists in Cities, 1974, Migration Across Frontiers, 1979, (series) Contemporary Urban Studies, 1990—; editor Socio Cultural Anthropology, Am. Anthropologist, 1985-90, Human Orgn., 1995—; mem. editl. bd. Ency. World Cultures, 1990—. Elder North Pk. Presbyn. Ch., Dallas, 1987-89, 95—; mem. Mcpl. Libr. Adv. Bd., Dallas, 1975-79. Fulbright fellow, 1979-80, 91-92, Wenner-Gren fellow, 1974-76, 79-83, Woodrow Wilson fellow, 1966-67. Fellow AAAS, Am. Anthrop. Assn. (bd. dirs. 1990-92), Soc. Applied Anthropology (chmn. Malinowski award com. 1979-80, bd. dirs. 1995—); mem. Latin Am. Studies Assn. (co-chmn. XI Internat. Congress 1983), Soc. Urban Anthropology (pres. 1988-90), Soc. Latin Am. Anthropology (pres. 1981-82), Phi Beta Kappa (pres. chpt. 1987-88). Home: 10617 Cromwell Dr Dallas TX 75229-5110 Office: So Meth Univ Dept Anthropology 3225 Daniel Ave Dallas TX 75275

KEMPNER, ISAAC HERBERT, III, sugar company executive; b. Houston, Aug. 28, 1932; s. Isaac Herbert and Mary (Carroll) K.; m. Helen Hill, July 1, 1967. Grad., Choate Sch., 1951; B.A., Stanford U., 1955, M.B.A., 1959. Asst. v.p. Tex. Nat. Bank, Houston, 1959-64; v.p., sec.-treas., mgr. raw sugar Imperial Holly Corp (formerly Imperial Sugar Co.), Sugarland, Tex., 1964-71, chmn. bd., 1971—; pres. Foster Farms Inc.; bd. dirs., chmn. Houston br. Dallas Fed. Res. Bank; trustee H. Kempner Trust Assn. Trustee Meth. Health Care Sys., Houston; trustee, treas. Contemporary Arts Mus., Houston. Mem. Coronado Club, Bayou Club, Camden Ale and Quail Club. Office: Imperial Holly Corp PO Box 9 1 Imperial Sq Sugar Land TX 77487

KENADY, DANIEL EDWARD, surgery educator; b. Washington, Feb. 20, 1947; m. Mary Elizabeth Hammond, Dec. 21, 1969; children: Daniel Edward Jr., Carrie Michele. BS in Distributed Scis., Am. U., 1968; MD, Georgetown U., 1972. Diplomate Am. Bd. Surgery, Nat. Bd. Med. Examiners. Intern Georgetown U. Hosp., Washington, 1972-73, resident in surgery, 1973-74, 76-78; clin. assoc. surgery br. Nat. Cancer Inst., HEW, USPHS, NIH, Bethesda, Md., 1974-76; resident in surgery Med. Coll. Wis. Affiliated Hosps., Milw., 1978-79; fellow in surg. oncology & head and neck surgery U. Tex. System Cancer Ctr.-M.D. Anderson Hosp.-Tumor Ctr., Houston, 1979-80; asst. prof. surgery U. Ky. Med. Ctr., Lexington, 1980-85, assoc. prof., 1985-92, prof., 1992—; asst. instr. surgery Med. Coll. Wis., 1978-79; staff physician VA Med. Ctr., Lexington, 1980—; spkr. to numerous hosps., healthcare orgns., med. assns., 1976—. Contbr. numerous articles and abstracts to med. jours. Bd. dirs., mem. prof. ednl. com. Fayette County chpt. Am. Cancer Soc., 1982—, mem. pub. edn. com., 1983-88, chmn. profl. edn. com., 1990—, bd. dirs. Ky. divsn. 1988—, v.p. 1991-92, pres. 1993-94, mem. exec. com., 1991—, chmn. Fayette County breast cancer detection awareness subcom., 1988-89, mem. pub. edn. com., 1990—, mem. fin. com., 1992-93, also other coms.; asst. scoutmaster troop 186 Boy Scouts Am., 1987-88, 91—, scoutmaster, 1989-91; bd. dirs. Ctrl. Ky. Blood Ctr., Inc., 1990-91, 94—. Grantee VA, NIH, others; jr. faculty clin. fellow Am. Cancer Soc., 1983-86. Fellow ACS (exec. com. Ky. chpt. 1988-92, pres. 1991-92); mem. Soc. Head and Neck Surgeons (coms. 1988—), Soc. Surg. Oncology, Am. Radium Soc. (rsch. award 1976), S.W. Oncology Group, Ky. Med. Assn., Fayette County Med. Soc. (exec. com. 1988-93, sec.-treas. 1990, pres. 1996—), Lexington Surg. Soc. (v.p. 1988, pres. 1989), Ky. Surg. Soc. (sec.-treas. 1988-91), Ctrl. Surg. Assn., Sigma Xi, Phi Kappa Phi. Office: U Ky 800 Rose St Lexington KY 40536-0084

KENAN, THOMAS STEPHEN, III, philanthropist; b. Durham, N.C., Apr. 19, 1937; s. Frank Hawkins Kenan and Harriet Gregg (DuBose) Gray. BA in Econ., U. N.C., 1959. Trustee Sarah G. Kenan Found., Durham, 1968-74, N.C. Mus. Art, Raleigh, 1972-91, Raudleigh Found. Trust, 1981-95, N.C. Sch. the Arts, Winston-Salem, 1983-91, Mary Duke Biddle Found., Durham, 1984-91, W.R. Kenan Charitable Trust, Chapel Hill, N.C., 1986-91, U. N.C. Arts and Sci. Found., Chapel Hill, 1989-91; exec. com. Flagler System, Inc., Palm Beach, Fla., 1968-91; dir. Kenan Transport Co., Chapel Hill, 1968-91; pres. Westfield Co., Durham, 1971-91. Founder Liberty Hall Restoration Commn., 1966, Duplin Outdoor Drama Soc., 1976; trustee The Duke Endowment. Mem. Hope Valley Country Club, Treyburn Golf and Country Club, Breakers Beach and Golf Club, Univ. Club, Landfall Golf and Tennis Club. Episcopalian. Office: William R Kenan Jr Charitable Trust Kenan Ctr Bowles Dr Chapel Hill NC 27515-3858

KENDALL, DAVID NELSON, chemist; b. Gardner, Mass., Oct. 20, 1916; s. Nelson Learned and Helen (Parker) K.; m. Ruth Bacon Spencer, June 13, 1942; children: Douglas S., Bertrand N., Katherine H. BA, Wesleyan U., Middletown, Conn., 1938, MA, 1939; PhD, Johns Hopkins U., 1943. Rsch. chemist Nat. Lead Co., titanium div., Sayreville, N.J., 1943-44; head IR spectroscopy lab. Am. Cyanamid Co., Bound Brook, N.J., 1944-53; founder, pres. Kendall Infared Labs., Plainfield, N.J., 1953-87; prin. spectroscopist David Kendall Assocs., Hilton Head, S.C., 1987-88. Editor: Applied Infrared Spectroscopy, 1966; contbr. articles to profl. jours., chpt. to book. Residential chmn. United Way, Plainfield, 1952. Fellow Am. Inst. Chemists; mem. Am. Chem. Soc., Assn. Cons. Chemists and Chem. Engrs. (pres. 1965, 66, councillor), Soc. Applied Spectroscopy (pres. 1950, 51, gold medal 1973), Coblentz Soc. (exec. com. 1948, 49), Phi Beta Kappa, Sigma Xi. Unitarian.

KENDALL, JOE, federal judge; b. Dallas, 1954; m. Veronica Kendall, 1975; children: Drew, Greg, Alan. BBA, So. Meth. U., 1977; JD, Baylor U., 1980. Bar: Tex. 1980, U.S. Ct. Appeals (5th cir.) 1980, U.S. Supreme Ct. 1980; cert. criminal law specialist. Police officer Dallas Police Dept., 1972-78; asst. dist. atty. Dallas County Dist. Attys. Office, 1980-82; pvt. practice Dallas, 1982-86; judge Tex. State Dist. Ct., Dallas, 1987-92, U.S. Dist. Ct. (no. dist.) Tex., Dallas, 1992—. Office: US Dist Ct 1100 Commerce St, 16 Fl Dallas TX 75242-1027*

KENDALL, JONATHAN PHILO, rabbi; b. Youngstown, Ohio, July 31, 1946; s. Milton and Ann (Philo) K.; children: Jessica, Rebecca. BA in Philosophy and Linguistics, Ohio State U., 1968; MA, U. Calif. Santa Barbara, 1986. Ordained rabbi, 1975. Asst. rabbi Temple Solael, West Hills, Calif., 1974-76; assoc. rabbi Temple Israel of Hollywood, L.A., 1976-79; rabbi Congregation B'nai Brith, Santa Barbara, Calif., 1979-89; sr. rabbi Temple Beth Am, Miami, Fla., 1989-95; rabbi Temple Beit Hayam, Stuart, Fla., 1995—; mem. nat. rabbinic cabinet United Jewish Appeal, 1983—, chair western region, 1985-89, bd. western region campaign cabinet, 1985-89, chair West Coast Gesher Missions, 1986, 87, 88; regional chair Rabbinic Network for Ethiopian Jews, 1986-89; bd. Santa Barbara Jewish Fedn., 1980-89; chair Jewish Community Rels. Coun. Santa Barbara, 1985-89; creator Jewish Family Svc., Santa Barbara, 1986; mem. bd. South Dade Fedn., 1990—; mem. Synagogue Fedn. Task Force, 1991—; lectr. religious studies dept. U. Calif., Santa Barbara, 1982-84, 87. Contbr. articles to profl. jours. Sec. Hospice of Santa Barbara, 1981-83; mem. bd. St. Vincent's Sch., 1981-89; founder Santa Barbara Interfaith Coun. Peace, 1983-89, Interfaith Coalition for Homeless, 1984-89, Transistion House, 1986; allocations chair United Way of Santa Barbara, 1986-89; chair Santa Barbara County Fed. Emergency Mgmt. Agy., 1987-89; mem. bd. Dade County Health and Rehab. Svcs., 1992, Task Force for Prevention Child Abuse and Neglect, 1992—, Dist. Juvenile Justice, 1992, Dade County Coalition on Aging, 1990—. Mem. Miami Bd. Rabbis, Ctrl. Conf. Am. Rabbis, Palm Beach Bd. Rabbis.

KENDALL, SUSAN GARDES, librarian; b. Hagerstown, Md., Aug. 24, 1948; d. George Austin and Jeanne Faust (Smith) Gardes; m. Steven Walter Kendall, May 25, 1974; children: Kimberly Ann, Kristen Jeanne. BA, William Woods Coll., Fulton, Mo., 1970; MA, Ohio State U., 1971; MLS, Simmons Coll., 1974. Reference libr. Simmons Coll., Boston, 1973-74, Harper Coll., Palatine, Ill., 1976-81, Marquette U., Milw., 1982; head adult svcs. Brookfield (Wis.) Pub. Libr., 1982-87, Batavia (Ill.) Pub. Libr., 1988-90; reference libr. Cobb County Pub. Libr., Marietta, Ga., 1990-93; br. mgr. Cobb County Pub. Libr., Marietta, 1993—; treas. Mgmt. Recruiters, Lithia Springs, Ga., 1990—; bd. dirs. Gardes Investments Ltd., Columbus, Ohio, 1972—. Contbr. articles to profl. jours. Vol. Olympic Games, Atlanta, 1996; leader Girl Scouts, 1982-94; instr. ESL, Marietta, 1996—; mem. Cobb Literacy Coalition, 1994—. Mem. S.E. Librs. Assn. (award com. 1993-95), Ga. Libr. Assn. (pub. librs. 1993-95, award com. 1996—). Methodist. Office: Cobb County Libr Sys 266 Roswell St Marietta GA 30060

KENDIG, EDWIN LAWRENCE, JR., physician, educator; b. Victoria, Va., Nov. 12, 1911; s. Edwin Lawrence and Mary McGuire (Yates) K.; m. Emily Virginia Parker, Mar. 22, 1941; children: Anne Randolph (Mrs. R.F. Young), Mary Emily Corbin (Mrs. T.T. Rankin). B.A. magna cum laude, Hampden-Sydney Coll., 1932, B.S. magna cum laude, 1933, D.Sc. hon., 1971; M.D., U. Va., 1936. House officer Med. Coll. Va. Hosp., Richmond, Bellevue Hosp., N.Y.C., Babies Hosp., Wilmington, N.C., Johns Hopkins Hosp., Balt., 1936-40; instr. pediatrics Johns Hopkins U., 1944; practice medicine specializing in pediatrics Richmond, 1940-94; dir. child chest clinic Med. Coll. Va., 1944-94, prof. pediatrics, 1958—; chief of staff St Mary's Hosp., Richmond, 1966-67; cons. on diseases of chest in children, 1944-94, William P. Buffum orator Brown U., 1978; Abraham Finkelstein Meml. lectr. U. Md., 1983; Derwin Cooper lectr. Duke U., 1984; Renato Ma Guerrero lectr. U. Santo Tomas, Manila, 1984; Bakwin Meml. lectr. NYU-Bellevue Hosp., 1986. Contbr. numerous articles on desease of chest in children to profl. publs.; editor: Disorders of Respiratory Tract in Children, 1967, 72, 77; co-editor: (with V. Chernick) Disorders of Respiratory Tract in Children, 4th edit., 1983, cons. editor to V. Chernick, 5th edit., pub. as Kendig's Disorders of the Respiratory Tract in Children, 1990; (with C.F. Ferguson) Pediatric Otolaryngology, 1972; contbg. editor: (books) Gellis and Kagan Current Pediatric Therapy, 13 edits., 1993, Burg, Ingelfinger, Wald Current Pediatric Therapy, 14th edit., Antimicrobial Therapy, Kagen, 3 edits., Practice of Pediatrics, Kelley, Practice of Pediatrics, Maurer, Allergic Deseases of Infancy, Childhood and Adolescence, Bierman and Pearlman, James, Sarcoidosis and Other Granulomatous Diseases, 1994; former mem. editl. bd. Pediat. Pulmonology; former mem. editl. adv. bd. Pediat. Annals; former mem. editl. bd. Pediat., Alumnews U. Va., 1988. Chmn. Richmond Bd. Health, 1961-63; bd. visitors U. Va., 1961-72; former mem. bd. dirs. Va. Hosp. Svc. Assn.; former ofcl. examiner Am. Bd. Pediatrics; mem. White House Conf. on Children and Youth, 1960; pres. alumni adv. com. U. Va. Sch. Medicine, Charlottesville, 1974-75; past bd. dirs. Maymont Found., Richmond; bd. dirs. Children's Hosp., Sheltering Arms Hosp.; former mem. adv. bd. Ctr. for Study of Mind and Human Interaction, U. Va. Sch. Medicine, 1988; mem. steering com. One Hundred Twenty Fifth Anniversary, Med. Coll. of VA Hosps., 1986; former bd. dirs. St. Mary's Health Care Found., 1990. Recipient resolution of recognition Va. Health Commr., 1978, Obici award Louise Obici Hosp., 1979, Bon Secours award St. Mary's Hosp., 1986, Keating award Hampden-Sydney Coll., 1989; named an Outstanding Alumnus Sch. Medicine U. Va., 1986; The Edwin Lawrence Kendig Jr. Disting Professorship in Pediatric Pulmonary medicine named in honor Med. Coll. Va. Commonwealth U. Mem. AMA (pediat. residency rev. com.), Am. Acad. Pediat. (past pres. Va. sect., chmn. sect. on diseases of chest, mem. exec. bd. 1971-78, nat. pres. 1978-79, Abraham Jacobi Meml. award with AMA, 1987, cons. com. on internat. child health), Am. Acad. Pediat. for Latin Am. (ofcl. adv. to exec. bd. 1988), Va. Bd. Medicine (former pres.), Richmond Acad. Medicine (pres. 1962, chmn. bd. trustees 1963), Va. Pediat. Soc. (past pres.), Am. Pediat. Soc., So. Med. Assn., So. Soc. Pediat. Rsch., Internat. Pediat. Assn. (cons., standing com., medal 1986), Med. Soc. Va. (editor Va. Med. Quarterly 1982, resolution of recognition), Soc. Cin., Raven, Phi Beta Kappa, Alpha Omega Alpha, Tau Kappa Alpha, Kappa Sigma, Omicron Delta Kappa. Episcopalian. Clubs: Commonwealth, Country of Va; Farmington (Charlottesville). Home: 5008 Cary Street Rd Richmond VA 23226-1643 Office: Va Med Quarterly 4205 Dover Rd Richmond VA 23221

KENDRICK, DANIEL FREDERICK, III, real estate executive; b. Waco, Tex., May 14, 1948; s. Edward Storey and Anna Wiman Kendrick. BA, U. Ga., 1970; MBA, Ga. State U., 1976; ThM, Columbia Seminary, 1992. Fin. analyst First Atlanta Bank, 1973-75; sr. fin. analyst Johnston Properties, Associated Capital, Atlanta, 1975-78; regional fin. officer Krupp Investors, Boston, 1978-83; sr. v.p. Murray Properties, Dallas, 1983-89; pvt. practice investor Atlanta, 1990—. Bd. dirs. Atlanta Interfaith AIDS Network, 1991—, Congretations for Affordable Housing, Atlanta, 1992—, Arthritis Found., 1989—, elder Presbyn. Health Edn. Welfare Assn., 1989—; elder Ctrl. Presbyn. Ch., 1993—.

KENDRICK, DARRYL D., lawyer; b. Eden, N.C., Sept. 27, 1956; s. Harold D. and June (Martin) K.; m. Patricia A. Cook, Sept. 18, 1981; children: Ashlyn Brianna, Kristyn Amanda, Caitlyn Samantha. BSBA, U. N.C., 1978; JD with honors, U. Fla., 1985. Bar: Fla. 1986, U.S. Dist. Ct. (mid. dist.) Fla. 1986. Claims adjuster Nationwide Ins. Co., Orlando and Gainesville, Fla., Houston, 1979-83; pvt. practice Jacksonville, 1987—; gen. counsel JAZZIZ mag., Gainesville, 1987—; founding mem. Donohoe & Kendrick, 1992. Mem. Acad. Fla. Trial Lawyers, Fla. Acad. Profl. Mediators, First Coast Trial Lawyers Assn., Fla. Assn. Collection Profls., Jacksonville Bar Assn. Democrat. Lutheran. Office: 1817 Atlantic Blvd Jacksonville FL 32207-3403

KENDRICK, LELAND RAY, physician; b. Picayune, Miss., July 26, 1952; s. William Issac and Della Mae (Jarrell) K.; m. Melinda Kay Thigpen, June 11, 1976; children: Jessica Raquel, Jennifer Kaliegh. AD, Pearl River Jr. Coll., Poplarville, Miss., 1972; BS in Pharmacy, U. Miss., Oxford, 1975; MD, U. Miss., Jackson, 1989. Pharmacist Slidell (La.) Meml. Hosp., 1976-85; resident in family medicine U. Miss. Med. Ctr., Jackson, 1989-92; pvt. practice medicine Waveland, Miss., 1992—. Mem. AMA, Am. Acad. Family Physicians, Miss. Med. Assn., Phi Theta Kappa, Alpha Omega Alpha, Phi Kappa Phi. Baptist. Home: 233 Marcus Dr Waveland MS 39576 Office: 1903 Waveland Ave Waveland MS

KENDRICK, MARK C., real estate executive; b. Augsburg, Germany, Dec. 30, 1957; (parents Am. citizens); s. Chester Delmon and Eva Anna (Mitterndorfer) K.; m. Sharon K. Greenland, 1993. AA in Law Enforcement, Fayetteville (N.C.) Community Coll., 1982; BA in Social Work, Methodist Coll., Fayetteville, 1983; M in Guidance, Campbell U., Ft. Bragg, 1986. Emergency response team Moore Meml. Hosp., Pinehurst, N.C., 1974-76; mgr. Fleishman's, Fayetteville, 1977-78; mgr. furnishings Nowells, Fayetteville, 1978-79; deputy Cumberland Co. Sheriff's Dept., Fayetteville, 1982-83; ptnr. Kendrick Real Estate, Fayetteville, 1983—, KD Graphics, Fayetteville, 1989—. Vol. N.C. Dept. of Corrections, 1981-82, intern, 1980; spl. dep. Cumberland County Sheriff's Dept., 1982—, dep. search and recovery team, 1991—; comptr. Cape Fear Fair Assn., 1985-88; v.p. Cumberland County Heart Assn., 1984-85; sub-sgt. Cumberland County Rescue Squad, 1979-82; adv. commn. Fayetteville Parks and Recreation, 1982-86; bd. dirs. Fayetteville Sr. Citizens Svc. Ctr., 1983-86, Fayetteville Parks and Recreation Five Yr. Study Commn., 1984-86, Cumberland Interfaith Hospitality Network, Inc., 1995—; pres. Cumberland County Smart Start, 1995—; Fayetteville City Councilman, 1986—; mem. Fayetteville Revitalization Commn., 1986-89, Fayetteville-Cumberland County Liaison Com., 1986-89, City-County Fire Liaison Com., 1986-89, City-County Fire Liaison Com., 1986-87, ARC Disaster Team, 1984-86, Young Dem. Club, N.C. Trnasp. Adv. Com., 1989—; chmn. City Streets-Sidewalks and Transp. Com., 1989—, City County Liaison, 1986-87; sec. Myrover-Reese Fellowship Homes, Inc., 1992—; exec. com. Fayetteville Hospitality House, 1992-96; chmn. N.C. Partnership for Children, 1995—, mem. state strategic planning com., 1996—; Sunday Sch. dir. Grace Bapt. Ch., 1996—. Named 1st 10th Degree Jaycee in Nation U.S. Jaycees, 1985, one of Five Outstanding Young Men in N.C. Farm Bur., 1985, Outstanding Young Person in Govt., 1986; recipient Disting. Svc. award, 1985, Charles Kulp Jr. Meml. award U.S. Jaycees, 1985, Thomas Jefferson award Sta. WTVD-TV, 1986. Mem. Fayetteville Jaycees (pres. 1984-85, treas. 1985-87), N.C. Jaycees (regional dir. 1985-86, awards chmn. 1986-87, Freedom Guard award 1984, Linn D. Garibaldi award 1985-86, Larry Bowers Meml. award 1986), Meth. Coll. Alumni Assn. (bd. dirs. 1985-95, v.p. 1993-95), KP, Toastmasters (N.C. state speaker 1984), Lions (v.p., Fayetteville host 1996—), Lambda Chi Alpha. Democrat. Baptist. Home: PO Box 40841 Fayetteville NC 28309-0841 Office: Kendrick Real Estate PO Box 40841 Fayetteville NC 28309-0841

KENDRICK, RICHARD LOFTON, university administrator, consultant; b. Washington, Nov. 19, 1944; s. Hilary Herbert and Blanche (Lofton) K.; m. Anne Ritchie, Mar. 5, 1966; children: Shawn Elizabeth, Christopher Robert. BS in Bus. and Mktg., Va. Poly. Inst., 1971; postgrad. U. Ky., 1978-80. Adminstr., U.S. Army Security Agy., Washington, 1965-69; with credit, sales and adminstrv. depts U.S. Plywood-Champion Internat., Pa., N.C. and Va., 1971-77; purchasing dir. James Madison U., Harrisonburg, Va., 1977-78, fin. officer, 1978-85; cons. Systems and Computer Tech. Corp., Malvern, Pa., 1986; dir. fin. svcs., Hillsborough C.C. System, Tampa, Fla., 1986-87, agt. Mass Mut. Life Ins., Harrisonburg, Va., 1987-88; asst. vice chancellor/treas. U. Ark., Fayetteville, 1988-92; dir. fin. svcs. Clinch Valley Coll. U. Va., Wise, Va., 1992—, affirmative action, equal oportunity officer treas., CVC Found., affirmative action-equal opportunity officer; credit cons. to plywood and lumber industry; cons. to higher edn.; home builder, designer World War II dioramas. Leader, treas. Boy Scouts Am., Harrisonburg, 1977-86; mem. Ashbury United Meth. Ch., 1975-77, Trinity United Meth. Ch., 1992—. Served with U.S. Army, 1965-69. Recipient New Idea award U.S. Plywood-Champion Internat., 1972; named Profl. Pub. Buyer, Nat. Inst. Govt. Purchasers, 1977. Mem. Am. Mktg. Assn., Nat. Assn. Accts., Nat. Assn. Coll. and Univ. Bus. Officers, Fin. Officers of State Colls. and Univs., So. Assn. Coll. and Univ. Bus. Officers, Internat. Platform Assn., Ark. Assn. of U. and Coll. Bus. Officers, Nat. Assn. Cash Mgrs. Methodist. Clubs: Exchange (Harrisonburg), Kiwanis. Home: PO Box 1018 Norton VA 24273-0893 Office: Clinch Valley Coll Fin Svcs Office College Ave Wise VA 24293

KENDRICK, ROBERT WARREN, university administrator; b. Houston, July 9, 1946; s. Alford Manuel and Alpha Mae (Carter) K.; m. Margaret Walker, June 9, 1973. BA, U. Houston, 1969, JD, 1977; mgmt. cert., Harvard U., 1989. Cert. security cons., law enforcement and security instr. Dist. exec. Boy Scouts Am., Monroe, La., 1974; corp. security coord. Foley's Dept. Stores, Houston, 1975-77, staff legal asst., 1978-81; exec. dir. Crimestoppers of Houston, Inc., 1982; coord. criminal justice ct. U. Houston-Downtown, 1983-85, assoc. dir. criminal justice ct., 1985-87, dir. criminal justice ct., 1987-89, exec. dir. divsn. continuing edn., dean's coun., 1989—, spl. asst., provost, 1996—; bd. mem. Am. Soc. Indsl. Security Found., Washington, 1988—, Internat. Found. Protection Officers, Cochrane, Can., 1988-89, U. Tex. Health Sci. Ctr. Community Adv. Bd., Houston, 1987-89. Editorial adv. bd. Security Jour., 1989—. Councilman, City of Bellaire, Tex., 1984-86, planning and zoning commr., 1982-84; bd. dirs. Learning Resource Network, 1993—; mem. regional criminal justice planning com. Houston-Galveston Area Coun. Govts., 1984—; founding bd. dirs. Crime Stoppers Houston, 1981; grand juror Harris County Grand Jury, Houston, 1989; mem. Mayor's Tex. City Action Plan Task Force, 1993; mem. Mayor's Imagine Houston Project, 1994—; criminal justice com. Leadership Houston, 1989—; chmn. profl. devel. Press Club of Houston, 1996. Capt. U.S. Army, 1971-73. Recipient Corp. Security award Security World Mag., 1977. Mem. Am. Soc. Indsl. Security (chpt. chmn. 1980, Security Svc. award 1994), Risk and Ins. Mgmt. Soc. (local bd. mem. 1979-81), Tex. Pub. Rels. Assn., Harris County Area Chiefs of Police, Buffalo Bayou Partnership (security com. advisor 1988—), Houston C. of C. (chmn. crime control com. 1988—), Leadership Houston (grad., bd. dirs. 1992—). Office: U Houston Downtown 1 Main St Houston TX 77002-1001

KENDRICKS, VIVIAN DAVIS, education educator; b. Thomasville, Ga., May 24, 1928; d. Aurelius Darius and Eula Mae (Davis) Davis; m. Henry A. Hunt, June 4, 1974 (div. 1975); m. James W. Kendricks, Dec. 28, 1978. B.S., Clark Coll., Atlanta, 1948; M.S., S.C. State Coll., Orangeburg, 1966; M.A., Fisk U., Nashville, 1970; Ph.D., Fla. State U., 1976. Chairperson sci. Ctr. High Sch., Way Cross, Ga., 1968-70; chairperson dept. home econs. Fort Valley Coll., Ga., 1973; vis. asst. prof. allied scis., Fla. A&M U., 1973-76; asst. prof. home econs. Fort Valley State Coll., Ga., 1979, assoc. prof. edn., 1979—; supr. student teaching, 1984; tchr. sci. Plant City High Sch., Fla., 1984-85; vis. sci. practitioner Hillsborough Community Coll., Tampa, Fla. Named Tchr. of Yr., Way Cross C. of C., 1969. Mem. AAUW (chair internat. women 1984-85), LWV, Toastmistress Internat., Clark Coll. Alumnae Assn. (nat. sec. 1976-79), Sigma Xi, Delta Sigma Theta, Phi Delta Kappa, Kappa Delta Epsilon (chpt. advisor, dir. S.E. regional chpt., 1994—), Democrat. Congregationalist. Avocations: bass guitar; piano; voice. Home: 1313 W State St Tampa FL 33606-1144 Office: Fort Valley State Coll 805 State College Dr Fort Valley GA 31030-3242

KENLEY, ELIZABETH SUE, commerce and transportation executive; b. Kansas City, Mo., Oct. 4, 1945; d. Ralph Raymond and Josephine Allen (Wells) Cummins. BS, Kans. U., 1968, MPA, 1972. Asst. city mgr. Winfield (Kans.), 1968-70; adminstrv. asst. Kansas City (Mo.) Police Dept., 1970; cons., 1973; with E.I. DuPont Co., Kingwood, Tex., 1974—, regional tech. buyer, 1977-79, cons., plant start up, 1979, regional tech. buyer, 1980-82; internat. project buyer Aramco, Houston, 1982-86, quality assurance liaison, supr. refinery no. area projects unit, 1986-89, owner, pres. Internat., Inc. , Houston, 1988—. Mem. Houston C. of C., Am. Mgmt. Assn. Home: 9632 Briar Forest Dr Houston TX 77063-1007 Office: 2230 Harbor St Houston TX 77020-7506

KENNA, JOHN THOMAS, priest; b. N.Y.C., July 19, 1919; s. John Joseph and Nadja Louise (Leahy) K. AB, St. Mary's Sem., Balt., 1943; MDiv, Holy Apostles Sem., Cromwell, Conn., 1987. Ordained priest Roman Cath. Ch., 1988. Assoc. pastor St. Patrick's Ch., Corpus Christi, Tex., 1988-93; chaplain Mt. Carmel Retirement Home, Corpus Christi, Tex., 1993—; dir. NCCJ, Kans. region, 1948-50, Ky. region, 1950-56; assoc. dir., Chgo. region, 1956-58; founding dir., Religious Activities Div., Nat. Safety Coun., 1958-60; instr. St. Basil's Coll., Stamford, Conn., 1945-47. Author: Safety in the 60's, 1959, Latinization of the U.S., 1983 (for 1983 Yearbook, Encyclopedia Britannica). Co-founder, bd. dirs. Nat. Cath. Conf. for Interracial Justice, Chgo., 1959-80; bd. dirs. Safer Found, Chgo., 1980-83; regional dir. Nat. Easter Seals Soc., 1966-68; dir. info. svcs., Pres. Kennedy's Com. on Youth Employment, 1961-63; dir. leadership devel., Nat. Coun. Cath. Men, Washington, 1960-61. With U.S. Merchant Marine, 1943-44. Mem. Corpus Christi Ministerial Alliance (pres. 1990-92). Democrat. Home and Office: Mt Carmel Retirement Home 4130 S Alameda St Corpus Christi TX 78411-1529

KENNEDY, BEVERLY (KLEBAN) B., financial consultant, radio talk show host; b. Pitts., Sept. 23, 1943; d. Jack and Ida (Davis) Kleban; m. Thomas E. Burris, Dec. 31, 1967 (div.); 1 child, Laura Danielle Burris; m. Ed

A. Kennedy, Jan 14, 1984; stepchildren: Kathleen, Patricia, Thomas. BS, Pa. State U., 1964; postgrad., Va. Commonwealth U., 1967. Founder, exec. dir. Broward Art Colony, Inc., Broward County, Fla., 1978-80; dir. sales Holiday Inn, Plantation, Fla., 1980-81; agent, registered rep. Equitable Life Assurance Soc., Ft. Lauderdale, Fla., 1982—; pres. Fin. Planning Svcs. Assn., Inc., Ft. Lauderdale, Fla., 1984-86; owner, fin. cons. Beverly B. Kennedy & Assocs., Ft. Lauderdale, Fla., 1982—; adv. bd. Transflorida Bank, 1983-88; bd. arbitration Nat. Assn. Securities Dealers, Inc., 1992-96. Talk show host Sta. WWNN, 1992-93. Bd. dirs. Community Appearance Bd., 1988-89, Riverwalk, Ft. Lauderdale, 1988-89; trustee Police and Fireman Fund of Fort Lauderdale, 1990-91; appointed by gov. to Fla. State Bd. Profl. Engrs., 1988-91; cons. Com. on Fin. for Nat. Coun. examiners for Engring and Surveying, 1990-91; Rep. nominee for U.S. Congress 20th dist. Fla., 1992, 94. Named Woman of the Year (Bus. for Profit), Women in Communications, Broward County, 1986, Bus. & Profl. Women, 1988-89, oustanding alumni, Pa. State Univ. Coll . Edn., 1988-89. Mem. Internat. Assn. Fin. Planning, Nat. Assn. Life Underwriters, East Broward Fed. Women's Rep. Club (pres. 1992-93).

KENNEDY, BONNIE RUTH, creative writer, instructor; b. San Angelo, Tex., Aug. 6, 1956; d. James Portis Ribble and Dorthy Lou Edwards; m. Danny Calaway Green, June 15, 1973 (div. 1982); children: Krista Kaye, Tucker Calaway; m. Alan Dwight Kennedy, Aug. 1, 1989; 1 child, Jamie Ruth. Student, Southwestern Oreg. C.C., North Bend, Oreg., 1978, 83, Inst. Children's Lit., Redding Ridge, Conn., 1988. Registered literary artist, Tex. Owner, instr. Painting With Words, San Angelo, Tex., 1988; artist-in-residence Marshall (Tex.) Ind. Sch. Dist., 1988-89; artist-in-residence Arts Coun., Silsbee, Tex., 1990, Longview, Tex., 1990-91, Denton, Tex., 1991-92; artist-in-residence Lakewood PTA, Dallas, 1992-93, Navarro Arts Coun., Corsicana, Tex., 1993, Acad. Excellence, San Angelo, 1993, Jr. League, Tyler, Tex., 1994, San Angelo Mus. Fine Arts/Children's Art Mus., 1994, 95, 96; instr. Tchr. Workshop/Lakewood Ind. Sch. Dist., 1993; co-founder Care-A-Lot, Hydro-Maintenance Co., 1995—. Creator: Painting With Words: The Creative Writing/Creative Thinking Workshop, 1987.

KENNEDY, CORNELIUS BRYANT, lawyer; b. Evanston, Ill., Apr. 13, 1921; s. Millard Bryant and Myrna Estelle (Anderson) K.; m. Anne Martha Reynolds, June 20, 1959; children: Anne Talbot, Lauren K. Mayle. A.B., Yale U., 1943; J.D., Harvard U., 1948. Bar: Ill. 1949, D.C. 1965. Assoc. Mayer Meyer Austrian & Platt, Chgo., 1949-54, 55-59; asst. to U.S. atty. Dept. Justice, Chgo., 1954-55; counsel to minority leader U.S. Senate, 1959-65; sr. ptnr. Kennedy & Webster, Washington, 1965-82; of counsel Armstrong, Teasdale, Schlafly & Davis, Washington, 1983-88; public mem. Adminstrv. Conf. U.S., 1972-82, sr. conf. fellow, 1982-90, chmn. rulemaking com., 1973-82. Contbr. articles to law jours. Fin. chmn. Lyric Opera Co., Chgo., 1954; chmn. young adults group Chgo. Coun. Fgn. Rels., 1958-59; pres. English Speaking Union Jrs., Chgo., 1957-59; trustee St. John's Child Devel. Ctr., Washington, 1965-67, 75-87, pres., 1983-85 ; exec. dir. Supreme Ct. Hist. Soc., 1984-87. 1st lt., AC U.S. Army, 1942-46. Fellow Am. Bar Found.; mem. Am. Law Inst., ABA (coun. sect. adminstrv. law 1967-70, chmn. sect. 1976-77), Fed. Bar Assn. (chmn. com. adminstrv. law 1963-64). Clubs: Legal Club Chgo., Explorers, N.Y. City, Capitol Hill, Chevy Chase (Md.), Sailing of Chesapeake (Annapolis, Md.), Adventurer's (Chgo.). Home: 7770 Old Georgetown Pike Mc Lean VA 22102

KENNEDY, ELIZABETH CAROL, psychologist, educator; b. Rochester, N.Y., May 5, 1948; d. Carl Elmore and Ruth Frances (Loebs) Riggs; m. James Barry Elvin, July 29, 1967 (div. Jan. 1989); 1 child, Krista Ann; m. William Jerald Kennedy, Aug. 12, 1989. AA, Broward C.C., Coconut Creek, Fla., 1986; BA, Fla. Atlantic U., 1989, MA, 1993, postgrad. Paraprofl. gifted edn. Havencroft Elem. Sch., Olathe, Kans., 1980-83; asst. recreational therapist South Fla. State Hosp., Pembroke Pines, 1987-88; asst. mental health therapist Ft. Lauderdale (Fla.) Hosp., 1986-89; instr. psychology Fla. Atlantic U., Boca Raton, 1990-96; asst. prof. Southeastern Okla. State U., Durant, 1996—; rsch. asst. Fla. Atlantic U., Boca Raton, 1993-96; therapist Boca Raton, 1994-96; statis. cons. South Fla., 1994-96. Co-author: (book chpt.) Conflict in Child and Adolescent Development, 1992; contbr. articles to profl. jours. Mem. APA, Am. Psychol. Soc., Soc. for Rsch. in Child Devel., Phi Kappa Phi (scholarship 1989), Psi Chi. Home: 5204 Creekwood Dr Durant OK 74701 Office: Southeastern Okla State U Dept Psychology/Counseling Durant OK 74701-0609

KENNEDY, J. JACK, JR., law clerk, lawyer, business investor; b. Abingdon, Va., June 11, 1956; s. J. Jack Sr. and Bobbie Lee (Porter) K.; m. Susan Maura Muir, June 30, 1979; children: J. Jack III, Jillian Susanne. BS, Clinch Valley Coll. of U. Va., 1978; cert. in internat. study, U. London, 1977; MA in Polit. Sci., East Tenn. State U., 1982; JD equivalent, Va. State Bar, 1982; BA in Orgnl. Mgmt., Va. Intermont Coll., 1994. Bar: Va. 1982, U.S. Dist. Ct. (we. dist.) Va. 1982, U.S. Ct. Appeals (4th cir.) 1982, U.S. Tax Ct. 1982, U.S. Ct. Claims 1982, Supreme Ct. Va. 1982, U.S Internat. Ct. Trade 1992. Mem. Va. Ho. of Dels., Richmond, 1988-91, Va. State Senate, Richmond, 1991-92; clk. Cir. Ct. for Wise County and City of Norton, Va., 1995—; bd. dirs. Black Diamond Savs. Bank, Turkey Gap Caol Co., Inc. State pres. Young Dems. Va., 1984-85; nat. sec. Young Dems. Am., 1985; chmn. City of Norton (Va.) Dem. Com., 1982-92, 9th congl. dist. Dem. Com., 1985-89; del. Dem. Nat. Conv., 1984, 88, 92; state chmn. Va. Assn. Local Dem. Chairs, 1986-87. Named Outstanding Young Dem. Va., 1985. Mem. ABA, Va. State Bar, Va. Bar Assn., Wise County Bar Assn., Va. Trial Lawyers Assn., Wise County C. of C., Va. Cir. Ct. Clks. Assn., Kiwanis, Internat. Banknote Soc., Phi Sigma Kappa. Baptist. Home and Office: 699 Fox Run Rd SE Norton VA 24273-2722 also: Court House 206 Main St PO Box 1248 Wise VA 24293

KENNEDY, JERRIE ANN PRESTON, public relations executive; b. Quanah, Tex.; children: Brandon, Cameron. Student, Sunset Sch. Preaching, Lubbock, Tex., 1975-78, Jo-Susan Modeling Sch., Nashville, 1984, Film Actors Lab., 1986. Co-prodr. Vincent Cirrincione & Assocs., N.Y., 1986; freelance internat. mktg. and public rels. exec. U.S., and Papua, New Guinea, 1988—; military del. NATO Allies for The French Liaison, Ft. Hood, Tex., 1992. Author screenplay, also fed. and comty. pub. spl. events prodn. Recipient 1st and 3d pl. awards Modeling Assn. Am., N.Y.C., 1985.

KENNEDY, JOAN CANFIELD, volunteer; b. Washington, Mar. 24, 1931; d. Austin Francis and Gertrude Rita (MacBride) Canfield; m. Keith Furnival Kennedy, Feb. 11, 1956; children: Joseph Keith, Austin Robert, Thomas Canfield, Richard Furnival. BA, Coll. New Rochelle, 1953. Trustee Ctr. Preventive Psychiatry, White Plains, N.Y., 1973-85, Catawba Lands Conservancy, 1992-95; bd. dirs. Scarsdale chpt. LWV, 1974-85, Charlotte-Mecklenburg (N.C.) chpt., 1985-89, pres. 1989-93, bd. dirs. N.C., 1993-96); bd. dirs. Coll. New Rochelle Alumnae Assn., 1977-81, 89-92; chmn. Coun. Human Rels., Scarsdale, N.Y., 1983-85; bd. dirs. New Neighbors League, 1986-87, Shalom Homes, 1987-88, Kids Voting N.C., 1993-97. Recipient Ursulas Laurus Citation, 1968, Angela Merici award, 1988; named New Neighbor of Yr. New Neighbors League, 1987. Mem. Niantic Bay Yacht Club, Larchmont (N.Y.) Yacht Club. Roman Catholic. Home: 1441 Carmel Rd Charlotte NC 28226-5011

KENNEDY, JOE DAVID, JR. (JOEY KENNEDY), editor; b. Dayton, TX, Mar. 28, 1956; s. Joe David Sr. and Patricia Ann (Harper) K.; m. Veronica Elaine Pike, Feb. 2, 1980. BA, U. Ala., Birmingham, 1988. Reporter gen. assignments Houma (La.) Daily Courier, 1974-76; dir. news, sports Sta. KJIN-AM/KCIL-FM, Houma, 1976-77; reporter gen. assignments Cullman (Ala.) Times, 1977-78; asst. sports editor Anniston (Ala.) Star, 1978-81; sports copy editor Birmingham News, 1981-83, asst. editor lifestyle, 1983-85, editor photography, 1985-86, Sunday editor, 1986-89, editor book revs., 1986-95, editorial writer, columnist, 1989—; book reviewer Sta. WVTM-TV, Birmingham, 1990-91. Mem. Houma-Terrebonne Bicentennial Commn., 1975-76; press sec. rep. gubernatorial candidate Guy Hunt, Ala., 1978; tutor literacy Birmingham Pub. Schs. Adult Learning Ctr., 1990-91; judge J.C. Penney Golden Rule Awards for Vols., 1992; lectr. Lee Coll. Springs Art Festival, Baytown, Tex., 1992; mem. adv. bd. Sch. Journalism, U. Miss., 1992—; bd. dirs. So. Mus. Flight, 1992-93; mem. Leadership Birmingham Class, 1994-95, AIDS Care Team, 1994—; bd. dirs. A Baby's Place, 1996—; mem. Ct. Appointed Spl. Advocates for Children, 1996—. Named Comm. Alumnus of Yr., U. Ala., Birmingham, 1991, One of the Top 20 Grads., U. Ala., Birmingham, 1994; recipient various awards L.A. Press Assn., 1974-77, Ala. Press Assn., 1981-83, Ala. Sportswriters Assn., 1978-81, Hector award Troy State U., 1991, 92, 94, 95, Pulitzer prize for edtl. writing, 1991; winner Nat. Edn. Writers Assn. 1994 Ed. press award, 1995. Mem. Christian Ch. Home: 1309 Ingram Ave Birmingham AL 35213-1503 Office: Birmingham News 2200 4th Ave N Birmingham AL 35202

KENNEDY, JOHN H., JR., former state official; b. May 1, 1954; m. Marnie; 2 children. BA, Okla. City U.; MA, Harvard U., 1988. Founder, chmn. Irish Realty; sec. of state State of Okla., 1991-94; bd. dirs. Omniplex Sci. Mus., Arts Pla., Ballet Okla., Cassady Sch. Alumni Assn., Okla. City U. Assn. Former state treas. Young Dems. Office: Irish Realty 1120 NW 63rd St Ste 380 Oklahoma City OK 73116*

KENNEDY, JOHN JOSEPH, JR., military officer; b. Phila., Aug. 12, 1956; s. John Joseph and Suzanne Marie (Gleason) K.; m. Lynn Ann Campbell, Sept. 2, 1978; children: James Patrick, Sean Douglas, Meghan Elizabeth. BS in Psychology, St. Joseph's U., Phila., 1978; MA in Polit. Sci., Marquette U., 1986; postgrad., Squadron Officers Sch., Air Command and Staff Coll., 1983, Air War Coll., 1996. Commd. 2d lt. USAF, 1978, advanced through grades to lt. col., 1994; ops. officer 71st Tactical Control Flight, MacDill AFB, Fla., 1978-81; standardization/evaluation contr. Detachment 2, 621st Tactical Control Squadron, Mangilsan, South Korea, 1981-82; chief ops. reports br. 507th Tactical Air Control Wing, Shaw AFB, S.C., 1982-83; air force advisor 128th Tactical Control Flight, Milw., 1983-86; chief range mgmt. br. 18th Tactical Fighter Wing, Kadena AFB, Okinawa, Japan, 1986-89; nat. def.. fellow U. Md., College Park, 1989-90; sr. drug policy analyst Office of Nat. Drug Control Policy, Washington, 1990-92; asst. ops. officer-mission 964th Airborne Warning and Control Squadron, Tinker AFB, Okla., 1993-94; dep. comdr. 963d Airborne Air Control Squadron, Tinker AFB, Okla., 1994-95; comdr. 5552d Ops. Support Squadron, Tinker AFB, 1995-97, 963rd Airborne Air Control Squadron, Tinker AFB, 1997—. Catechist St. Edward's Cath. Parish, Bowie, Md., 1991-92, Holy Family Cath. Parish, Maxwell AFB, Ala., 1992-93, St. John the Bapt. Cath. Parish, Edmond, Okla., 1996—, hospitality min., 1994—. Decorated Air Force Commendation medal Dept. of the Air Force, Milw., 1986, Meritorius Svc. medal Dept. of the Air Force, Kadena AFB, Okinawa, 1989, Def. Meritorious Svc. medal Sec. of Def., Washington, 1992, Aerial Achievement medal Dept. of the Air Force, 1995. Mem. Am. Polit. Sci. Assn., Air Force Assn., Aircraft Owners and Pilots Assn. Republican. Roman Catholic. Office: 963 AACS/CC Ste 201 7513 Sentry Blvd Tinker AFB OK 73145-9012

KENNEDY, KEITH CLYDE, mechanical engineer, entrepreneur, administrator; b. Lufkin, Tex., Feb. 3, 1966; s. Oscar and Bettie Ruth (Ingram) K.; m. Lisa C. Taylor, July 4, 1987; 1 child, Hunter Taylor. BS, Tex. A&M U., 1989; MBA, U. Dallas, 1996. Rschr. Tex. A&M U., College Station, 1988-89; divsn. field engr. Mobil Oil, Inc., Dallas, 1989-92; project engr., Cole McDonald Environ. Consultants, Inc., Dallas, 1993-94; project engr., mgr. Tex. Instruments, Dallas, 1994—; task force mem. U.S. Black Engrs. Orgn., Balt., 1992; pres. Taylor-Kennedy Found., 1992—. Chmn., coord. various cmty. projects, 1984-95; chmn. Adopt-a-Hwy., College Station, 1987-89; dep. voters' registrar Dallas County, Tex., Dallas, 1989-95; advisor Tex. A&M U. Minority Engring. Program, 1989-92; coord., adminstr. Adopt-a-Sch. program Mobil Pipe Line Co., Dallas, 1991-92; mem. Dallas Urban League, and numerous others. Recipient Cmty Vol. award, Lufkin Top Teens Am., Buck Weirus Spirit award TAMU, President's award Lufkin, Pres. Acad. Fitness award, Lufkin, A Philip Randolph State Leadership award, Austin, Southwestern Black Leadership Co. award, 1992, Adopt-A-Sch. Vol. award, 1992, others. Mem. ASME (assoc.), Soc. Petroleum Engrs. (assoc.), Nat. Soc. Black Engrs. (advisor 1989-92, comp. award 1991-92), Nat. Black MBA Assn. (life), Southwestern Black Leadership Orgn., Dallas Alliance Minority Engring., Tex. Alliance Minotiry Engring., Alpha Phi Alpha (life), Sigma Iota Epsilon. Home: 1809 Lacy Ln Mesquite TX 75181-1563

KENNEDY, KIMBERLY KAYE, history educator, bookkeeper; b. Naples, Fla., Nov. 2, 1961; d. George Eugene and Viola (Passmore) K. BA, Valdosta Coll., 1989, MA, 1990. Mgr. asst. Avon Products, Valdosta, 1983-88; bookkeeper Kennedy Rentals, Valdosta, 1983—; history educator Ga. Mil. Coll., Valdosta, 1993—; owner Kennedy Rentals, Valdosta, 1994—. Author: What Rainbow Means, 1976 (Internat. Order of Rainbow 1st pl. award 1986), (with others) Reflections, 1978. Recipient Grand Cross of Color Internat. Order of Rainbow, 1977. Mem. Order Ea. Star (worthy matron 1982-83). Democrat. Methodist. Home: 3647 Guest Rd Valdosta GA 31605-4833 Office: Ga Mil Coll 3010 Robinson Rd Moody AFB GA 31699-1518

KENNEDY, LEO RAYMOND, engineering executive; b. Cleve., Dec. 29, 1942; s. Leo Raymond and Jane (Brady) K.; m. Doris Elaine Jurgens, Feb. 18, 1967; children: James Raymond, Brian Robert, Kristin Lee. BS, U.S. Mil. Acad., 1965; EdM, U. Ill., 1972; MBA, L.I. U., Greenvale, N.Y., 1975; grad., Army War Coll., Carlisle, Pa., 1986. Commd. 2d. lt. U.S. Army, 1965, advanced through grades to col., 1987; adc U.S. Army, Korea, 1970; assoc. dir. admissions U.S. Mil. Acad., West Point, N.Y., 1972-75; dir. pers. mgmt. armored divsn. U.S. Army, Killeen, Tex., 1976-78; chief staff divsn. U.S. Army, Clay Kaserne, Germany, 1980-82; comdr. battalion U.S. Army, Colorado Springs, Colo., 1982-85, inspector gen. inf. divsn., 1985-86; dir. resource mgmt. Pentagon U.S. Army, Washington, 1986-92; pres., CEO Kennedy & Assocs., Fairfax, Va., 1993-96; sr. analyst Sci. Applications Internat. Corp., McLean, Va., 1996—; mem. acquisition budget com. Army program, Washington, 1987-92; guest spkr. fed. budgeting process, Washington, 1988-92. Decorated Legion of Merit, Bronze Star medal. Mem. Soc. Mil. Comptrs., Non-Commd. Officers Assn. (hon. life), N.Y. Acad. Scis., Kappa Delta Pi. Republican. Roman Catholic.

KENNEDY, (HENRY) MARK, judge; b. Greenville, Ala., May 5, 1952; s. D.M. and Marjorie W. Kennedy; m. Peggy W. Kennedy, Dec. 15, 1973; 1 child, Leigh Chancellor. BA, Auburn U., 1973; JD cum laude, Samford U., 1977. Bar: Ala. 1977. Clk. to presiding justice Ala. Ct. Criminal Appeals, 1977, staff atty., 1978; former judge Ala. Cir. Ct., 15th Jud. Cir.; now justice Ala. Supreme Ct., Montgomery. Mem. ABA, Ala. State Bar, Montgomery County Bar Assn., Ala. Assn. Dist. Judges. Democrat. Baptist. Office: US Supreme Ct Ala 300 Dexter Ave Montgomery AL 36104-3741*

KENNEDY, NANCY J., education educator; b. Mobile, Ala., May 18, 1953; d. Arvel L. and Rubie Irene (Pope) K. BS in English and Speech, U. Montevallo, 1974; MEd in Spl. Edn., U. South Ala., 1985. Cert. tchr. Ala. Advt. clk. Mobile Press Register, 1974-75; English tchr. Ind. Meth. Sch., Mobile, 1975-76; advt. coord. J.C. Penney Stores, Mobile, 1976-77; specific learning disabilities tchr. Mobile County H.S., Grand Bay, Ala., 1978-81; English/reading tchr. Palmer Pillans Mid. Sch., Mobile, 1981-82, Mae Eanes Mid. Sch., Mobile, 1982-84; English tchr. Theodore (Ala.) H.S., summers 1985-94; specific learning disabilities tchr. Azalea Mid. Sch., Mobile, 1984-95, Daphne (Ala.) Elem. Sch., 1995—; asst. residential coord. summer devel. session, Spring Hill Coll., Mobile, Ala., 1987-91; instr. for Upward Bound Program, Spring Hill Coll., 1991-93; presenter at Dist. VI mtg., Delta Kappa Gamma, 1996; chmn. multidisciplinary evaluation team, Daphne Elem. Sch., 1995—. Sunday sch. tchr. Springhill Bapt. Ch., Mobile, 1993—; chmn. Family Symphony, 1994-95; usher Saenger Theatre Vol., Mobile, 1993—; mem. steering com. Operation Thanksgiving, Mobile, 1988-93; mem. Symphony Com., Mobile, 1985—, Art Patrons League, Mobile, 1990—. Mem. Delta Kappa Gamma (leadership conf.), U. Montevallo Alumni Assn., U. South Alabama Alumni Assn. Baptist.

KENNEDY, NANCY LOUISE, retired draftsman; b. Mar. 14, 1925; d. William Richardson and Mary Enroughty (Youmans) Humphrey; m. William Dwyer Kennedy, Sept. 3, 1952 (dec. May 1953); 1 child, Kathleen Dwyer. Student, Gulf Park Coll., 1943; B of Interior Design, Washington U., 1948. Land draftsman Carter Oil Co., Ft. Smith, Ark., 1954-60, Sinclair Oil and Gas, Oklahoma City, 1960-69, Atlantic Richfield Oil and Gas Co., Tulsa, 1969-82. Mem. Altar guild Trinity Episcopal Ch., Tulsa. Mem. Kappa Alpha Theta. Republican. Home: 6362 S 80th East Ave Apt D Tulsa OK 74133-3825

KENNEDY, ROBERT, international affairs educator; b. Newark, Sept. 20, 1939; s. Cecil L. (stepfather) and Marie E. (Rega) Smith; m. Vevonna M. Clark, Nov. 4, 1966; children: Shaun C., Teague C. BS, USAF Acad., Colorado Springs, Colo., 1963; MA, Georgetown U., 1964, PhD, 1978. With USAF, 1963-71; fgn. affairs officer U.S. Arms Control and Disarmament Agy., Washington, 1974; sr. researcher strategic studies inst. U.S. Army War Coll., Carlisle, Pa., 1974-83; Dwight D. Eisenhower prof. nat. security studies U.S. Army War Coll., 1983-85; dep. comdt. NATO Def. Coll., Rome, 1985-88; prof. dept. nat. security studies U.S. Army War Coll., 1988-89; prof. sch. internat. affairs Ga. Inst. Tech., Atlanta, 1989—; dep. dir. Ctr. for Internat. Strategy, Tech. and Policy, Atlanta, 1990—; cons. Inst. for Pub. Policy Devel., Washington, 1977-78. Author, editor: The Defense of the West: Strategic and European Security Issues, 1984, U.S. Policy Towards the Soviet Union: A Long Term Western Prospective 1987-2000, 1988, Alternative Conventional Defense Postures for the European Theater, Vol. I, 1990, Vol. 2, 1992, Vol. 3, 1993; mem. editl. bd. Atlantic Community Quarterly, 1987-89, ORBIS, 1982-87; contbr. articles to profl. publs. Mem. adv. bd. Notre Dame Internat. Sch., Rome, 1986-88, Cumberland Valley High Sch., Mechanicsburg, Pa.; mem. exec. com., chmn. joint chiefs of staff Process for Accreditation of Joint Edn., Washington, 1991—; acad. assoc. Atlantic Coun. U.S., 1989—. With USAFR, 1971-86. Recipient Superior Civilian Svc. award, U.S. Army, 1989; named Oustanding Young Men of Am., U.S. Jaycees, 1972; Fulbright scholar, 1965-66; Georgetown U. fellow, 1974, Atlantic Coun. U.S. sr. fellow, 1983-84. Mem. Internat. Inst. for Strategic Studies, Internat. Studies Assn. (chmn. sect. on mil. studies 1985-87), Friedensforschung und Europaische Sicherheitspolitik. Home: 6975 Hunters Knls NE Atlanta GA 30328-1762 Office: Ga Inst Tech Sch Internat Affairs Atlanta GA 30332-0610

KENNEDY, ROBERT SAMUEL, experimental psychologist, consultant; b. Bronxville, N.Y., Jan. 10, 1936; s. Robert and Helen (Marshall) K.; m. Margaret Draper, Aug. 23, 1964 (div. Aug. 1976); children: Kathryn Jeannete, Robert Carpenter, Richard Marshall, Kristyne Elizabeth. BA in English and Philosophy, Iona Coll., 1957; MA in Experimental Psychology, Fordham U., 1959; PhD in Sensation and Perception, U. Rochester, 1972. Commd. ensign USN, 1959, advanced through grades to commdr., ret., 1981; rsch. psychologist divsn. psychology Naval Sch. Aviation Medicine, Pensacola, Fla., 1959-65; head diver evaluations divsn. Naval Med. Rsch. Inst., Pensacola, Fla., 1968-70; head br. human factors engring. Naval Missile Ctr., Point Mugu, Calif., 1972-76; head human factors divsn. Naval Air Devel. Ctr., Warminster, Pa., 1976; officer-in-charge dept. bioengring. scis. Naval Aerospace Med. Rsch. Lab. Detachment, New Orleans, 1976-79, head dept. human performance, 1977-79; head dept. human performance Naval Biomed. Lab., New Orleans, 1979-81; facility dir. Essex Corp., Columbia, Md., 1981—; v.p. Essex Corp., Orlando, Fla., 1987—; prof. U. Ctrl. Fla., Orlando, 1987—; lectr. grad. dept. Psychology Laverne Coll., Point Mugu, 1973-76, dept. Sys. Mgmt. U. So. Calif., 1975-76; cons. NASA/Johnson Space Ctr., Houston, 1995—, Sys. Tech., Inc., Univs. Space Rsch. Assn., Monterey Techs.,, Inc., Battelle, Am. Inst. Biol. Scis., Performance Metrics, Bolt, Beranek & Newman, NAS/Nat. Sci. Rsch. Coun., NASA/Ames Rsch. Ctr., U.S. Navy Med. R & D Command; expert witness in human factors Ala., Fla., Ga., Miss., N.Mex.; prin., assoc. investigator numerous projects; presenter numerous cons. Consulting editor, Aviation, Space, and Environmental Medicine, editorial adv. bd., 1991—, Behavior Research Methods, Instruments and Computers, Jour. Experimental Psychology: General, Perceptual and Motor Skills, Military Psychology, Ergonomics, Pediatrics, Perception and Psychophysics; co-author numerous tech. reports; contbr. chpts. to books, articles to profl. jours. Fellow APA (military divsn., pres. applied exptl. and engring. divsn. 1989-90), Am. Psychol. Soc., Aerospace Med. Assn. (Raymond F. Longacre awd., 1993); mem. AAAS, Am. Soc. Safety Engrs., Aerospace Human Factors Assn. (exec. com. 1991, individual differences tutorial group), Behavioral Toxicology Soc., Human Factors Soc. (forensics profl. group, visual performance tech. group, consulting editor), Soc. Neurosci., Behavioral Toxicology Soc., Illuminating Engring. Soc., Undersea Med. Soc. (individual differences tech. group), Barany Soc., N.Y. Acad. Scis., Psychonomic Soc., So. Soc. Philosophy and Psychology, SAFE Assn. Office: Essex Corp 1040 Woodcock Rd Ste 227 Orlando FL 32803-3510

KENNEDY, SUSAN ESTABROOK, historian, educator, dean; b. N.Y.C., June 8, 1942; d. Austin Lovell and Dorothy V. (Ogden) Estabrook; m. E. Craig Kennedy, Jr., Nov. 28, 1970. BA summa cum laude, Marymount Manhattan Coll., 1964; MA, Columbia U., 1965, PhD, 1971. Lectr. in history Hunter Coll., N.Y.C., 1966-67; from instr. to asst. prof. Temple U., Phila., 1967-73; from asst. prof. to assoc. prof. Va. Commonwealth U., Richmond, 1973-81, prof. history, 1981—, assoc. dean Coll. Humanities and Scis., 1993-96, interim dean Coll. Humanities and Scis., 1996—. Author: The Banking Crisis of 1933, 1973, If All We Did Was to Weep at Home, 1979, America's White Working Class Women, 1981; contbr. articles to profl. jours., chpts. to books. Named to Outstanding Young Women of Am., 1978; John Simon Guggenheim Meml. Found. fellow, 1978-79, Perrine fellow Hoover Presdl. Libr. Assn., 1982-83, 93-94; Danforth Assoc., 1980-86. Mem. Am. Hist. Assn. (life), Orgn. Am. Historians (life), Phi Kappa Phi (life, pres. Va. Commonwealth U. chpt. 1991-92). Home: 8200 Notre Dame Dr Richmond VA 23228 Office: Va Commonwealth Univ Coll Humanities & Sciences PO Box 842019 Richmond VA 23284

KENNEDY, THOMAS PATRICK, financial executive; b. N.Y.C., Oct. 13, 1932; s. Andrew Francis and Marie P. (Scullen) K.; m. Mary P. Drennan, Jan. 14, 1956 (dec.); children: Thomas Patrick, Kevin M. (dec.), Michael J., Mary P. Kennedy Handsman, Deborah A. Kennedy Carter. BS, St. Peter's Coll., 1958; postgrad., Seton Hall U., 1959. Accountant, Haskins & Sells, CPAs, N.Y.C., 1953-54, 55-57; staff Emerson Radio & TV, N.Y.C., 1957-58; various exec. positions CBS, N.Y.C., 1958-67; with Ford Found., N.Y.C., 1967; dir. fin. Pub. Broadcasting Lab., N.Y.C., 1967-69; with Children's TV Workshop (Sesame St.), N.Y.C., 1969-80, v.p. fin. and adminstrn., 1969-78, treas. 1969-78, sr. v.p., 1978-80; exec. dir. Ctr. Non-Broadcast TV, 1980-85; pres. Tomken Mgmt., Ltd., 1980—, chmn. bd., 1983—; chmn. bd., chief exec. officer Effie Techs. Inc., 1984—; v.p., corp. fin. Jersey Capital Mkts Group, Inc., 1987-88; chief exec. officer, chmn. bd. Corp. Strategies Group, Inc., 1988-89; v.p. Vantage Securities, Inc. (co-venture with Whitehall Fin. Group), 1991-94; cons. in field; bd. advisers Franciscan Communication Ctr.; bd. dirs., exec. dir. Ctr. for Non-Broadcast TV, 1980-85. With C.E., U.S. Army, 1954-55. Mem. Fin. Exec. Inst., Internat. Radio and TV Soc., Inst. Broadcast Fin. Mgmt., Nat. Assn. Accountants, Internat. Broadcast Inst., Internat. Inst. Communication, Internat. Assn. Fin. Execs., Am. Assn. Ind. Investors, Am. Legion. Roman Catholic.

KENNELLY, MICHAEL FRANCIS, school system administrator; b. Moyvane, Ireland, May 22, 1914; came to the U.S., 1930; s. Timothy and Mary Jane (Hanrahan) K. BA, Spring Hill Coll., 1937; BA in Edn., Nat. U., Dublin, 1948, MA with honors, MEd with honors, 1949. Prin. St. John's High Sch., Shreveport, La., 1949-53; rector, pres. Jesuit High Sch., Tampa, Fla., 1953-59, rector, v.p. cmty. rels., 1991—; founder, rector, pres. Strake Jesuit Coll. Prep., Houston, 1959-70; rector, pres. Loyola U., New Orleans, 1970-74; pastor Sacred Heart Ch., Tampa, 1980-90; pres., chmn. bd. dirs. W.W.L. Radio & TV, New Orleans, 1968-74. Named Honorary Citizen State of Tex., Austin, 1970, City of Baton Rouge, La., 1969; mem. speakers' adv. com. State of Tex., 1970; bd. advisors Hispanic Needs and Svcs., Inc., Tampa, 1991-94. Recipient Palmes Academiques Republique Francaise Ministiere de L'Education, 1975. Fellow Nat. Cath. Edn. Assn., Jesuit Assn. Colls. and Univs. Roman Catholic. Home and Office: 4701 N Himes Ave Tampa FL 33614

KENNER, MARY ELLEN, marketing and communications executive; b. Darlington, Wis., Jan. 7, 1941; d. Horace James and Adean Elizabeth (McDonald) Smith; BS, Marquette U., 1963, MBA, U. West Fla., 1988, cert. assn. exec., 1994; m. John Miller Kenner, Sept. 27, 1975. Fashion dir. spl. events Federated Store, Milw., 1962-63; mktg. ofcl. Ohio Bell and Wis. Telephone Cos., 1963-66; coll. mktg. instr. Milw. Inst. Tech., 1966-67; advt. positions AT&T and Wis. Telephone Co., 1967-78; advt. dir. No. States Power Co., Mpls., 1978-83; pres. Kenner Enterprises, 1983—; adj. prof. U. West Fla., 1988-89; dir. mktg. and communications Printing Industries Am., Alexandria, Va., 1989-91; dir. mktg. and pub. rels. Am. Production & Inventory Control Soc., 1992—; mem. steering com. 1st Conf. Consumerism. Recipient Clio award, 1974, Effie award, 1978, 79, 81. Mem. Am. Mktg. Assn., Am. Soc. Assn. Execs. (cert. assn. exec.), Direct Mktg. Assn Wash., Minn. Ctr. Arts, Milw. Advt. Club (dir. 1969-72, sec. 1973-76), U. West Fla.

and Marquette U. alumni assns., Belleek Collectors Club. Roman Catholic. Home: 2211 Marthas Rd Alexandria VA 22307-1827

KENNER, WILLIAM DAVIS, III, psychiatrist; b. Kingsport, Tenn., Oct. 3, 1943; s. Kenneth Bynum and Charlotte (Lineback) K.; m. Carole Freeman, May 23, 1970; children: William IV, Mary Clay, Michael. Student, Tulane U., 1961-63; BS, U. Tenn., 1965; MD, U. Tenn., Memphis, 1969. Lic. physician, Tenn., Md. Rotating med. intern Bapt. Meml. Hosp., Memphis, 1969-70; resident in adult psychiatry and fellow child psychiatry Inst. Psychiatry and Human Behavior, U. Md. Hosp., Balt., 1970-73; fellow in child psychiatry Vanderbilt U. Hosp., Nashville, 1975-76; pvt. practice adult and child psychiatry/psychoanalysis Nashville, 1977—; asst. prof. psychiatry Vanderbilt U. Med. Sch., Nashville, 1973-75, 76-77, assoc. clin. prof. psychiatry and child psychiatry, 1977—; dir. Vanderbilt Admission Unit of ctrl. State Hosp., 1973-75; lectr. in field; cons. Fed. Pub. Defender for Middle Dist. of Tenn., Fed. Atty. Gen. State of Tenn., Atty. Gen. State of Tenn., Bd. Profl. Responsibilities of Supreme Ct. Tenn., Dist. Atty. for Davidson County, Tenn., Helen Ross McNabb Cmty. Mental Health Ctr. Forensic Team, Boys Town Home of Md., others; hosp. staff Vanderbilt Child and Adolescent Psychiat. Hosp., Vanderbilt U. Hosp., Centennial Med. Ctr.; cons. staff Bapt. Hosp. Contbr. articles to profl. jours. Mem. quality assurance com. for adolescent unit Centennial Med. Ctr., chmn. ethics com., 1994—, mem. ad hoc com. to write guidelines for impaired physicians, impaired physicians com.; mem. Tenn. dept. Mental Health and Retardation Commn. to Establish Guidelines for Violent Patients, Commn. to Establish Voluntary Admission Procedure, forensic transfer com. Mem. Am. Psychiat. Assn., Nashville Acad. Medicine, Tenn. Acad. Child Psychiatry, Am. Assn. Adolescent Psychiatry, Am. Psychoanalytic Assn. (mem. study groups), Internat. Psychoanalytic Assn. Office: 113 30th Ave N Nashville TN 37203-1325

KENNON, PAMELA CANERDAY, secondary school educator; b. Opelika, Ala., Nov. 9, 1961; d. Thomas Donald and Norma (Fowler) Canerday; m. John Carlton Kennon, Jr., Jan. 12, 1985; children: Kate, Carly, Jake, Sam. Student, Chipola Jr. Coll., Marianna, Fla., 1980-81; BS in Edn. cum laude, U. Ga., 1984; MEd, Brenau U., 1994. Phys. edn. tchr. Greensboro (Ga.) Primary Sch., 1984-85; tchr. 2d grade Jefferson (Ga.) Elem. Sch., 1985-93; tchr. 4th grade Oconee County Intermediate Sch., Watkinsville, Ga., 1993—; softball coach Jefferson (Ga.) High Sch., 1988-92, Oconee County High Sch., 1993—. Named Tchr. of Yr., Tchr. of Month Jefferson Elem. Sch., 1988, 90. Mem. Golden Key Hon. Soc. Baptist. Home: 1640 S Barnett Shoals Rd Watkinsville GA 30677-2215 Office: Oconee County Intermediate Sch Watkinsville GA 30677

KENNY, LAWRENCE WAGNER, economist; b. Balt., June 29, 1950; s. William W. Kenny and Margaret G. Ziegfeld; m. Christine M. Nitz, Aug. 22, 1970. BA, Wesleyan U., 1972; MA, U. Chgo., 1975, PhD, 1977. Asst. prof. U. Fla., Gainesville, 1975-80; vis. scholar Nat. Bur. Econ. Rsch., Chgo., 1977-78; assoc. prof. U. Fla., Gainesville, 1980-90, prof., 1990—, chmn., 1991—. Author: Microeconomics with Business Applications, 1987; contbr. articles to profl. jours. Recipient White prize Wesleyan U., 1971, Wilde prize, Wesleyan, 1972, USPHS fellowship NIMH, 1972-75. Mem. Am. Econ. Assn., Western Econ. Assn., Pub. Choice Soc., So. Econ. Assn., Econometric Soc. Home: 2031 NW 57th Ter Gainesville FL 32605-3399 Office: Univ Fla Dept Economics Gainesville FL 32611

KENRICH, JOHN LEWIS, lawyer; b. Lima, Ohio, Oct. 17, 1929; s. Clarence E. and Rowena (Stroh) Katterheinrich; m. Betty Jane Roehll, May 26, 1951; children: John David, Mary Jane, Kathryn Ann, Thomas Roehll, Walter Clarence. BS, Miami U., Oxford, Ohio, 1951; LLB, U. Cin., 1953. Bar: Ohio 1953, Mass. 1969. Asst. counsel B.F. Goodrich Co., Akron, Ohio, 1956-65; asst. sec., counsel W.R. Grace & Co., Cin., 1965-68, v.p. Splty. Products Group divsn., 1970-71; corp. counsel, sec. Standex Internat. Corp., Andover, Mass., 1969-70; v.p., sec. Chemed Corp., Cin., 1971-82, sr. v.p., gen. counsel, 1982-86, exec. v.p., chief adminstrv. officer, 1986-91, ret., 1991. Trustee Better Bus. Bur., Cin., 1981-90; mem. bus. adv. coun. Miami U., 1986-88; mem. City Planning Commn., Akron, 1961-62; mem. bd. visitors Coll. Law U. Cin., 1988-92; mem. area coun. trustees Franciscan Sisters of Poor Found., Cin., 1989-93; bd. govs. Arthritis found. Southwestern Ohio chpt., 1992-95; mem. Com. on Reinvestment City of Cin., 1991-93. 1st lt. JAGC U.S. Army, 1954-56. Mem. Ohio Bar Assn., Am. Arbitration Assn., Beta Theta Pi, Omicron Delta Kappa, Delta Sigma Pi, Phi Eta Sigma. Republican. Presbyterian. Home and Office: 116 Wickersham Dr Savannah GA 31411-1376

KENT, BARTIS MILTON, physician; b. Terrell, Tex., June 23, 1925; s. Bartis William and Annie (Smalley) K.; student So. Meth. U., 1942-44; M.D., Baylor U., 1948; m. Ann L. Kiel, July 6, 1954; children—Susan Ruth, Martha Lucille, Bartis Michael. Intern, Jefferson Davis Hosp., Houston, 1948-49; resident pathology Mass. Meml. Hosps., Boston, 1951; resident in internal medicine Baylor U., 1953-56; indsl. physician Humble Oil Co., Houston, 1949-51; instr. dept. medicine U. Iowa, 1956-58; staff physician Iowa City VA Hosp., 1956-58; practice medicine specializing in internal medicine, Muskogee, Okla., 1958—; cons. Muskogee VA Hosp.; clin. asst. prof. medicine U. Okla. Sch. Medicine, 1975—. Chmn., Muskogee County chpt. Am. Nat. Red Cross, 1963-65. Served with USAF, 1951-53. Decorated Air medal. Diplomate Am. Bd. Internal Medicine. Mem. A.C.P., Indsl. Med. Assn., Soc. Nuclear Medicine, Am. Fedn. Clin. Research, Am. Heart Assn., Aerospace Medicine Assn., Am., Okla. socs. internal medicine, Muskogee C. of C. Methodist. Mason (Shriner). Home: 800 N 45th St Muskogee OK 74401-1505 Office: 211 S 36th St Muskogee OK 74401

KENT, DAVID L., genealogist, publisher; b. Nampa, Idaho, July 1, 1940; s. John Lloyd and Edith (Davis) K.; m. Carol Joy Miller, Dec. 19, 1974; children: Robert Lloyd, Susannah Mary, Zachary Miller, David Clark, Genevieve Carol. BA cum laude, Brigham Young U., 1966; postgrad., U. Utah, 1966-67. Cert. geneal. record specialist Bd. for Cert. Genealogists. Auditor IRS, Boise, Idaho, 1960-61; analyst Hughes Aircraft Co., Orchard, Idaho, 1961-62; editor Brigham Young U. Press, Provo, Utah, 1963-66; constable Salt Lake County, Salt Lake City, 1966-67; editor Ind. TV Authority, London, 1968-71; statistician World Bank, Washington, 1972-73; geneal. record specialist, Washington and Austin, Tex., 1973—; founder Erespin Press, Austin, 1980—; founder The Press at Humanities Rsch. Ctr., U. Tex., Austin, 1986—. Author: Barbados and America, 1980, Foreign Origins, 1981, Westchester County New York Supplement, 1993; contbr. articles to profl. jours. Counselor Am. Friends Sc. Com., Austin, 1982-84, home schooling orgns., 1976—. Mem. Nat. Geneal. Soc. (War of 1812 project 1979-80, cert. of appreciation 1978, 80), Am. Typecasting Fellowship, Amalgamated Printers' Assn. (archivist 1992—), Hakluyt Soc., Gen. Soc. Mayflower Descs. (life), Descs. Illegitimate Sons and Daus. Kings of Britain. Home: 6906 Colony Loop Dr Austin TX 78724

KENT, GARY WARNER, film director, writer; b. Walla Walla, Wash., June 7, 1933; s. Arthur Everett and Iola Pearl (Nixdorff) K.; m. Joyce Peacock, 1954; children: Greg, Colleen, Andy; m. Rosemary Gallegly, 1960; children: Chris, Alex, Mike; m. Shirley Willeford, July 3, 1977. Student, U. Wash., 1951-52, San Diego State U., 1952-53, Del Mar Coll., 1956. Broadcaster Sta. KSIX, Corpus Christi, Tex., 1955, Sta. KTHT, Houston, 1956; actor Alley and Playhouse Theatres, Houston, 1956-59; actor motion pictures, 1959-73; gen. ptnr. PMK Prodns., Dallas, 1973-80, Signature Prodns., Austin, Tex., 1982-85; v.p. Power Dance Corp., Austin, L.A., Tex., 1985—; produced stunts and spl. effects films Targets, Paramount, Phantom of the Paradise, 20th Century Fox, Hell's Angels on Wheels, Fanfare, Psychout, Am. Internat., Satan's Sadists, Dracula vs. Frankenstein, Lost, Independent Internat., Man Called Dagger, MGM, The Forest, Wide World Entertainment, Return of County Yorga, Vampire, Killers Three, Savage Seven, Dick Clark Prodns., The Shootings, Ride the Whirlwind, New Pacific Films, Flight of Balck Angel, 1991 Warbirds, 1991, Lethal Pursuit, Guns of Dragon, Colof of Night, 1994; for TV Daniel Boone, 20th Century TV, Man From U.N.C.L.E., MGM, New Adam Twelve, Warner Bros.; stunt cons. Mon Frere Prodns., 1995. Writer, dir.: Rainy Day Friends, 1987, The Pyramid, 1987, (HBO spl. movie) L.A. Bad, 1990; writer: Where's Bassett's Body?, 1992, Streetcorner Justus, 1994. Active Spl. Olympics, Austin, 1990. With USN, 1953-55. Recipient Best Spl. Stunt award in motion pictures Stuntman awards, Hollywood, Calif., 1987. Mem. SAG, AFTRA, Amnesty Internat., Greenpeace, Austin Film Soc., Austin Writer's League, Ind. Feature Project West. Democrat.

KENT, HARRY ROSS, construction executive, lay worker; b. Upland, Pa., Oct. 17, 1921; s. Bernard Cleveland and Edith Mary (Johnson) K.; m. Aurelia Naomi Canady, Jan. 15, 1945; children: Jennifer Gayle, Edith Marie. BS in Physics and Chemistry, Coll. William and Mary. Instr. physics Citadel, 1947-51; with Canady Constrn. Co., 1951-78, sec.-treas., 1960-74, pres., 1974-78; v.p. K.C. Stier & Co., Inc., 1974-78; v.p., sec. Stier Kent and Canady, Inc., 1978—; mem. exec. coun. World Meth. Coun., 1991-96. Mem. commn. on stewardship and fin., Asbury Meml. Meth. Ch., Charleston, 1949—, treas. 1951-58, 68—, lay mem. ann. conf. 1955-70, 80—, trustee, 1963-74, chmn. long-range planning com., 1957-70, tchr. ch. sch.; mem. bd. bldg. and ch. location Charleston Dist. United Meth. Ch., 1958—, pres. bd. missions and ch. extension, 1958—, dist. trustees, 1960—, chmn. bd. dist. trustees, 1984—, chmn. bd. missions, 1975—; mem. bd. lay activities S.C. ann. conf. United Meth. Ch., 1957-96, mem. coordinating coun., 1960-68, vice-chmn. continuing com. on merger, conf. lay leader, 1970-80, chmn. equitable salary commn., 1984-88, mem. coun. on fin. and adminstrn., 1988-96, vice chair 1992-95, chair 1995-96, del. Southea. jurisdiction conf., 1960, 64, 72, 76, 80, 84, 88, 92, 96, gen. conf. 1966, 68, 70, 72, 76, 80, 84, 88, 92, gen. conf. on ministries, 1980-88, chmn. Africa sect. of advance com., mem. gen. bd. discipleship, 1988-96; conf. pres. United Meth. Men, 1984-92; mem. exec. bd. Coastal Carolina coun. Boy Scouts Am., 1960—, chmn. Charleston dist. bd., 1967; various exec. positions St. Andrew's schs. PTA, 1963-68; bd. dirs. Piedmont Nursing Ctr., 1967-82, treas. 1970-82; vice chmn. civil engring. adv. bd. Trident Tech. Coll., Charleston, 1969-71, chmn. 1970-80; pres. Charleston Boys Coun., 1982-86, 91-94, v.p. 1987-91; mem. S.C. State Licensing Bd. for Contractors, 1980—, vice chair 1989-91, chair 1992—. Lt. cmmdr. USNR, WWII. Recipient God and Country award, Scouters award, Scoutmasters Key 60 Yr. Vet. award, Silver Beaver award Boy Scouts Am., God and Svc. award United Meth. Ch./Boy Scouts Am. Mem. ASTM, Associated Gen. Contractors, Am. Phys. Soc., Am. Assn. Physics, Tchrs., Charleston Trident C. of C. Home: 2935 Doncaster Dr Charleston SC 29414-6723

KENT, JACK THURSTON, retired mathematics educator; b. Sardis, Tenn., Sept. 26, 1908; s. John Franklin and Daisy Josephine (Craven) K.; m. Pauline Elizabeth Oates, May 27, 1936; children: Christine Elizabeth Johnson Ellis, David Harbet. AB, Lambuth Coll., 1930; MA, U. Ark., 1931; postgrad., Ohio State U., 1931-33, Yerkes Obs., U. Chgo., Williams Bay, Wis., 1949-52. Prof. of math. Lambuth Coll., Jackson, Tenn., 1930; grad. asst. U. Ark., Fayetteville, 1930-31, Ohio State U., Columbus, 1931-33; prof., head math. dept. Ft. Smith (Ark.) Jr. Coll., 1933-35, Ark. Tech. Coll., Russellville, 1935-36; from instr. to assoc. prof. Tex. A&M U., College Station, 1936-74; retired, 1974; vis. lectr. Tex. Acad. Sci./NSF, 1957-65; area dir. Am. Meteor Soc., Ark., Mo., Tex., 1930-45, Moon Watch Program, Bryan, Tex., 1957-61. Author: Unified Mathematics for High Schools; editor: Binary Stars; contbr. sci. papers in astronomy to profl. publs. Chmn. March of Dimes, Bryan, 1953; mem. Equalization Bd., College Station, 1951; scoutmaster to coun. Boy Scouts Am., Russellville, Ark., 1936, Bryan, 1952-65. Ford Found. grantee, 1949-52. Democrat. Methodist.

KENT, NANCY LEE, elementary school educator; b. Balt., Aug. 30, 1956; d. Lawrason Lee and Orpha Jeanne (Wolfe) K. BA in Elem. Edn., Coll. of William and Mary, 1978. Lic. tchr., Va. Tchr. York County Schs., Yorktown, Va., 1978-81, 83—; clk. typist, counselor Langley AFB, Hampton, Va., 1984, 86; co-owner Golden Blue-The Tour Co. Ltd.; summer counselor NASA Langley Rsch. Ctr., Hampton, 1978-81, 83, 85, 87, 88; Va. delegation leader People to People, U.K., 1994, to Australia/New Zealand, 1995. Deacon Denbigh Presbyn. Ch., 1987-90, sec., 1987-88, fin. co-chmn., 1989-90, mem., 1971—; bd. dirs. Tabb Elem. Sch. Parent Tchr. Student Orgn., 1984-94, Va. Peninsula chpt. Am. Heart Assn., 1987-90; mem. Va. Ind. Polit. Network; sec. City of Newport News Youth Svcs. Commn., 1992-94, vice chair, 1994-95; bd. dirs. Colonial Coast Girl Scout Coun., 1993-94; co-dir. Golden Blue, The Tour Co., Ltd. Mem. NEA, Nat. Sci. Tchrs. Assn., Nat. Coun. Math., Am. Bus. Women's Assn. (edn. chmn., Chpt. Woman of Yr. award 1988), Va. Edn. Assn., York Edn. Assn. (sec. 1991-92, v.p. 1992-94, pres. 1994-96), Jr. League Hampton Roads, Hampton Roads Jaycees (pres. 1988-89, chmn. bd. dirs. 1989-90), Va. Jaycees (life; regional bd. dirs. 1989-90, state chaplain 1990-91, mem. Found. 1990-94), Jr. Chamber Internat. (senator), Va. Reading Assn., Newport News Reading Coun. Home: 630 Saint Andrews Ln # 204 Newport News VA 23608

KENT, PHILIP, communications executive. Pres. Turner Home Entertainment Turner Broadcasting Sys., Atlanta. Office: Turner Broadcasting sys 1 CNN Ctr Box 105366 Atlanta GA 30348-5366

KENT, ROBERT B., artist, educator; b. Cleve., June 23, 1924; m. Celeste Zalk, Dec. 18, 1948; children: William, Kenneth, Brian. BA, Western Res. U., 1950, MA, 1951; postgrad, Columbia U., 1952-53; EdD, U. Calif., Berkeley, 1968. Cert. expressive therapist. Art instr. El Paso (Tex.) City Schs., 1953-54, Stockton (Calif.) Unified Schs., 1954-56, Tamalpais High Sch., Mill Valley, Calif., 1956-67; assoc. prof. U. Ga., Athens, 1967-93, emeritus, 1993—; lectr. Denmark, Sweden and Israel. Mem. editorial bd. Ill. State U. Publ.; contbr. articles to profl. jours. Mem. Am. Art Therapy Assn., Nat. Expressive Therapy Assn., World Assn. for Prevention Drug and Alcohol Abuse (internat. bd. govs.). Home: 332 Stonybrook Cir Athens GA 30605-6029

KENT, SAMUEL B., federal judge; b. 1949. BA, U. Tex., 1971, JD, 1975. Pvt. practice Royston, Rayzor, Vickery & Williams, Galveston, Tex., 1975-90; judge U.S. Dist. Ct. (so. dist.) Tex., Galveston, 1990—; adj. prof. bus. and ins. law Tex. A&M U., Galveston, 1981-86, proctor in admiralty, 1976—. Mem. Maritime Law Assn. Office: US Courthouse 601 Rosenberg St Ste 613 Galveston TX 77550-1738

KENWORTHY, JAMES LAWRENCE, lawyer, government affairs and international trade consultant; b. Kansas City, Mo., Sept. 24, 1937; s. George Lawrence Woods and Aurelia Esther (Miller) K.; m. Martha Higgins Swift, Apr. 27, 1968 (div. 1974); children: James Randolph, Nancy Wheeler; m. Linda Rose Adelmeyer, Apr. 28, 1979. BS, Rockhurst Coll., 1959; JD, Georgetown U., 1962. Bar: Mo. 1962, D.C. 1975, U.S. Ct. Internat. Trade 1983, U.S. Supreme Ct. 1976. Assoc. Sheridan, Baty, Markey, Sanders, Edwards & Carr, Kansas City, 1962-64; legis. asst. U.S. Sen. Edward V. Long, Washington, 1964-66; atty. Fgn. Claims Settlement Commn. of USA, Washington, 1966-67; asst. dir. tax.-legal Nat. Fgn. Trade Coun., N.Y.C., 1967-69; atty. Office Fgn. Direct Investment, U.S. Dept. Commerce, Washington, 1969-70; assoc. Kirkwood, Kaplan, Russin & Vecchi, Santo Domingo, Dominican Republic and Bogota, Columbia, 1970-74; sr. atty. Office of Gen. Counsel, U.S. Dept. Commerce, Washington, 1974-81; pvt. practice Kansas City, 1980-85; ind. cons. internat. trade and investment Washington, 1985-92; internat. trade/investment cons. Nathan Assocs., Inc., Arlington, Va., 1992—. Author: Laws, Regulations and Policies of the People's Republic of China on Foreign Trade and Investment; contbr. articles to profl. jours. Rep. nominee for U.S. Congress, 5th Dist. Mo., Kansas City, Jackson Co., Mo., 1984; candidate U.S. Congress, 5th Dist. Mo., 1982. Mem. ABA (sect. on internat. practice), Nat. Economists Club (v.p. membership 1988-89, v.p. external affairs 1990-91, pres. 1991-92, 92-93). Republican. Roman Catholic. Office: Nathan Assocs Inc 2101 Wilson Blvd # 1200 Arlington VA 22201

KENYON, TERRY FRAZIER, lawyer; b. Pensacola, Fla., Nov. 27, 1955; s. Thomas and Colleen (Moore) K.; m. Kitty Koos, May 13, 1978; children: Kelly, Carl. BBA in Acctg. summa cum laude, Baylor U., 1978, JD cum laude, 1980. Bar: Tex. 1980; CPA, Tex. Assoc. Naman, Howell, Smith, Lee & Muldrow, Waco, Tex., 1980-81; ptnr. Lynch, Chappell & Alsup, Austin, Tex., 1981-91; prin. Terry F. Kenyon, P.C., Austin, 1992-95, Kenyon & Sproull P.C., Austin, 1995—. Rsch. topics editor Baylor U. Law Rev., 1979-80. Bd. dirs. Austin chpt. Planned Parenthood, 1982-91; pres. Baylor Jaycees, Waco, 1976-77; chair Industry Roundtable Com., Greater Austin C. of C., 1994-95; grad. Leadership Austin, 1994-95 class. Mem. Tex. Bar Assn., Travis County Bar Assn., Tex. Soc. CPAs. Office: Kenyon & Sproull PC 711 San Antonio St Austin TX 78701

KEOHANE, NANNERL OVERHOLSER, university president, political scientist; b. Blytheville, Ark., Sept. 18, 1940; d. James Arthur and Grace (McSpadden) Overholser; m. Patrick Henry III, Sept. 16, 1962 (div. May 1969); 1 child, Stephan; m. Robert Owen Keohane, Dec. 18, 1970; children: Sarah, Jonathan, Nathaniel. BA, Wellesley Coll., 1961, Oxford U., Eng., 1963; PhD, Yale U., 1967. Faculty Swarthmore Coll., Pa., 1967-73, Stanford U., Calif., 1973-81; fellow Ctr. for Advanced Study in the Behavioral Scis. Stanford U., 1978-79, 87-88; pres., prof. polit. sci. Wellesley (Mass.) Coll., 1981-93, Duke U., Durham, N.C., 1993—; bd. dirs. IBM. Author: Philosophy and the State in France: The Renaissance to the Enlightenment, 1980; co-editor: Feminist Theory: A Critique of Ideology, 1982. Trustee Colonial Williamsburg Found., 1988—, Ctr. for Advanced Study Behavioral Scis., 1991—, Nat. Humanities Ctr., 1993—, Doris Duke Charitable Found., 1996—; mem. MIT Corp., 1992—. Marshall scholar, 1961-63; AAUW dissertation fellow; inducted, National Women's Hall of Fame, 1995. Fellow Am. Acad. Arts and Scis., Am. Philos. Soc.; mem. Coun. on Fgn. Rels., Saturday Club (Boston), Watauga Club (N.C.), Phi Beta Kappa. Democrat. Episcopalian. Office: Duke Univ Box 9001 207 Allen Bldg Durham NC 27708-0001*

KEOUGH, DONALD RAYMOND, investment company executive; b. Maurice, Iowa, Sept. 4, 1926; s. Leo H. and Veronica (Henkels) K.; m. Marilyn Mulhall, Sept. 10, 1949; children: Kathleen Anne, Mary Shayla, Michael Leo, Patrick John, Eileen Tracy, Clarke Robert. BS, Creighton U., 1949, LLD (hon.), 1982; LLD (hon.), U. Notre Dame, 1985, Emory U., 1993, Trinity U., Dublin, Ireland, 1993, Clarke U., 1994. With Butter-Nut Foods Co., Omaha, 1950-61; with Duncan Foods Co., Houston, 1961-67; v.p., dir. mktg. foods div. Coca-Cola Co., Atlanta, 1967-71, pres. div., 1971-73; exec. v.p. Coca-Cola USA, Atlanta, 1973-74; pres. Coca-Cola USA, 1974-76; exec. v.p. Coca-Cola Co., Atlanta, 1976-79, sr. exec. v.p., 1980-81, pres., COO, dir., 1981-93; chmn. bd. dirs. Coca-Cola Enterprises, 1986-93; advisor to bd. Coca-Cola Co., Atlanta, 1993—; bd. dirs. Nat. Svc. Industries, Inc., Washington Post Co., H.J. Heinz Co., Home Depot, McDonald's Corp.; chmn. bd. Allen & Co., Inc., Atlanta, 1993—, Excalibur Technologies, Inc., 1996—. Mem. president's coun. Creighton U.; trustee U. Notre Dame, Lovett Sch. With USNR, 1944-46. Mem. Capital City Club, Piedmont Driving Club, Commerce Club, Peachtree Golf Club. Office: 200 Galleria Pkwy NW Ste 970 Atlanta GA 30339-5945

KEPFERLE, ROY CLARK, geology educator, consultant; b. Greeley, Colo., Dec. 28, 1926; s. Joseph Royal and Dorothy Gladys (Ayers) K.; m. Rhua Ethel Slavens, Oct. 27, 1951; children: Mary Rose, Michael, Gregory, Anne, Mary Elizabeth, Christopher, Theresa. BA, U. Colo., 1950; MS, S.D. Sch. Mines, 1954; PhD, U. Cin., 1972. Geologist U.S. Geol. Survey, Washington, 1950-81; assoc. prof. Ea. Ky. U., Richmond, 1982-87, prof., 1988-93, prof. emeritus, 1994—; cons. Inst. Gas Tech., Chgo., 1983; tech. advisor Ea. Oil Shale Symposium, Lexington, Ky., 1984-92; pres. Geol. Soc. Ky., Lexington, 1991. Author: (with others) Sedimentation in Submarine Fans, Canyons, Trenches, 1978, (bull.) U.S. Geol. Survey, 1954-93, Geologic Quadrangle Maps, 1963-77; co-author: (guidebooks) Geology in Kentucky, 1964-90. Sgt. U.S. Army, 1945-46. Recipient Unit Citation U.S. Geological Survey, 1971, 78. Fellow AAAS, Geol. Soc. Am. (Penrose grant 1968); mem. Am. Assn. Petroleum Geologists (profl. grant 1983), Soc. Economic Paleontologists and Mineralogists. Home: 915 Egan Hills Dr Cincinnati OH 45229-1109 Office: Ea Ky Univ Roark # 103 Richmond KY 40475

KEPHART, SHERRIE ANN, photojournalist, graphic artist; b. Tecumseh, Mich., Apr. 10, 1949; d. Elroy Cecil and Dorothy Jean (Swift) Johnston; m. William Haley Wilson, Aug. 15, 1980 (div. July 1992); children: Samuel Hayes, Thomas Lewis; m. Samuel Emerson Kephart, Jr., Jan. 2, 1993; children: Amber Kathleen Zumbro, Richard, Carl. BA in Journalism, Baylor U., 1994; M in Journalism, U. North Tex., 1996. Sales rep. Corpus Christi (Tex.) Caller-Times, 1978-80; owner The Picture Frame, Taylor, Tex., 1980-84; frame shop mgr. Michael's, Temple, Tex., 1985; ad sales mgr. Belton (Tex.) Jour., 1986; photographer, ad sales Salado (Tex.) Village Voice, 1987; co-owner, editor Troy (Tex.) Country Sun, 1988-89; frame shop mgr. Perry Bros., Temple, 1992-94; grad. asst. U. North Tex., Denton, 1995-96; adj. prof. applied graphic design tech. Collin County C.C., 1996—. Student aid to Sander Levin, Dem. Party, Mich., 1968; publicity organizer Taylor Civic Theater, 1980-84; organizer Troy Funfest-Troy Merchants, 1988-90, March for Jesus, Denton, 1996; organizer, facilitator Artfest, Taylor Hist. Soc., 1982; club leader, educator Denaville 4-H, Troy, 1988-90; bd. dirs. Bell County Fair Assn., Belton, 1985-90. Recipient Best Spl. Sect. award Mich. Press Assn., 1977. Mem. Am. Educators of Journalism and Mass Comm., Soc. Profl. Journalists, Tex. Coun. on Domestic Violence, Formerly Battered Woman's Task Force, Profl. Picture Framers Assn., Christians in Photojournalism. Home: 822 N Wood St Denton TX 76201 Office: Collin County CC Spring Creek Campus 2800 SpringCreek Pkwy Plano TX 75074

KEPLINGER, DUANE, architectural executive; b. Topeka, Kans., Jan. 11, 1926; s. Earl Alexander and Gladys Sarah (Wood) K.; m. Gloama Dentler; children: Stephen Earl, Richard Lee, Gregory Neil. BS in Archtiecture, Kans. State U., 1950. Registered architect, Kans. Supervisory architect FHA, Topeka, Kans. and Washington, 1950-74; chief standards HUD, Washington, 1974-76; dep. dir. architecture and engring. div. HUD, 1976-78, dir. office architecture and engring., 1978-81; v.p. Avalon Assocs., Alexandria, Va., 1981-94, ret., 1994. Cartoonist Civic Assn. paper, Alexandria, 1968-72. Served as cpl. USMC, 1944-46, 50-51, PTO. Mem. Nat. Inst. Bldg. Scis., Tau Sigma Delta. Democrat. Presbyterian. Home: 6100 Waterman Dr Fredericksburg VA 22407-8365

KEPPLE, THOMAS RAY, JR., college administrator; b. Pitts., Mar. 19, 1948; s. Thomas Ray and Virginia Grace (Hudson) K.; m. Jane Donaldson, Aug. 22, 1971 (dec. 1977); m. Patricia Witcher, May 25, 1994. B.A., Westminster Coll., 1970; M.B.A., Syracuse U., 1973, Ed.D., 1984. Dir. tech. tng. Morse div. Borg-Warner Corp., Ithaca, N.Y., 1970-73; dir. adminstrv. services Rhodes Coll., Memphis, 1975-81, dean adminstrv. services, 1981-86, provost, 1986-89, v.p. Univ. South, Sewanee, Tenn., 1989—; bd. dirs. Met Life Resources Retirement Adv. Bd. Author: Incentive Early Retirement Programs for Faculty. Bd. dirs. Sewanee Housing Inc.; mem. City of Winchester Indsl. and Commercial Retention Com.; mem. exec. com. Vollintine Evergreen Community Assn., Memphis, 1976-85, pres., 1981; mem. Biomed. Research Zone Bd., 1986; sec., treas. Health and Ednl. Facilities Bd. of Franklin County; bd. dirs. Liberty Bowl Classic. Mem. Internat. Soc. Planning and Strategic Mgmt. (v.p. communications 1984-85, pres. 1985-87), Nat. Assn. Coll. and Univ. Bus. Officers, Am. Assn. Higher Edn., Memphis Acad. Forum (pres. 1985-86), Coll. and Univ. Personnel Assn., Assn. Physical Plant Adminstrs., Omicron Delta Kappa. Presbyterian. Clubs: Ecce Quam Bonum. Lodge: Rotary. Avocations: swimming; oil painting. Home: PO Box 860 Sewanee TN 37375-0860 Office: U of South Office of VP 735 University Ave Sewanee TN 37383-0001

KERBY, RAMONA ANNE, librarian; b. Dallas, Feb. 5, 1951; d. Raymond Richard and Bette Lee (Rudd) Nolen; m. Steve Alan Kerby, Nov. 27, 1973. BA in Elem. Edn./Spanish, Tex. Wesleyan U., 1973; MEd in Counseling Edn., Tex. Christian U., 1975; MLS, Tex. Woman's U., 1980, PhD, 1984. Elem. sch. libr. J.B. Little Elem. Sch., Arlington, Tex., 1978-93; coord. sch. libr. media program Western Md. Coll. Author: Investigating the Effectiveness of School Library Instruction, 1984, Friendly Bees, Ferocious, Bees, 1987, 38 Weeks Till Summer Vacation, 1989, Asthma, 1989, Cocroaches, 1989, Beverly Sills, America's Own Opera Star, 1989, Amelia Earhart, Courage in the Sky, 1990, Samuel Morse, 1991, Frederick Douglass, 1994, Yearbooks in Science 1950-59, 1995. Recipient Siddie Jo Johnson award State of Tex., 1990; NEH tchr.-scholar, 1993-94. Mem. ALA, Tex. Assn. Sch. Librs. (chair 1989-90), Tex. Libr. Assn., Soc. Children's Book Writers, Authors Guild, Assn. Libr. Info. Sci. Edn., Alpha Chi, Beta Phi Mu.

KERBY, ROBERT BROWNING, communications consultant; b. Waynesboro, Va., Oct. 21, 1938; s. Guy Albert and Josephine (Carpenter) K. BS in Bus. Adminstrn., Va. Poly. Inst., 1960; postgrad. U. Richmond, 1964, Va. Commonwealth U., 1965, U. Va., 1968. Rep. mfrs. Josten Co., Owatonna, Minn., 1960-67; gen. sales mgr. Sta. WANV, Waynesboro, 1967; tech. editor Gen. Electric Co., Waynesboro, 1967-72; v.p., CEO Fishburne Hudgins Ednl. Found., Inc., Waynesboro, 1972-86, 1986—; chmn. Target-2000 com., City of Waynesboro, 1988—; comm. cons. RF Comm. Cons., Waynesboro,

1986—; advisor Sovran Bank, Waynesboro, 1982-89. Designer, author: (catalogue) Fishburne Mil. School, 1981 (1st place award Printers Assn. Va.'s, 1982). Chair funding dir. Shenandoah Valley Art Ctr., Waynesboro; bd. dirs., chmn. Waynesboro Redevel. Housing Authority, 1970-72; pres. Alumni Assn. Offices, 1960-71; chmn. publicity Robinson for Congress, 1970; chmn. fund raising and adv. bd. Salvation Army, 1967-68; chmn. Target 2000 Com. City of Waynesboro, 1988, mem. library adv. bd., 1995; chmn. prof. adv. bd. Waynesboro First Aid Ctr; trustee Waynesboro Pub. Libr., 1995. Named Outstanding Vol. of Yr., City of Waynesboro, 1990. Mem. SAR, Quarter Century Wireless Assn., Am. Radio Relay League. Republican. Methodist. Office: RF Comm Cons PO Box 991 Waynesboro VA 22980-0723

KERLEY, JANICE JOHNSON, personnel executive; b. Coral Gables, Fla., Nov. 28, 1938; d. Howard Love and Lois Dean (Austin) Johnson; m. Bobby Joe Kerley, May 16, 1959; children: Janice Elisabeth Kerley Smothers, Meredith Ann Kerley Tucker. AA, Stephens Coll., 1958; B in Music Edn., U. Miami, Fla., 1960. Tchr. Dade County Pub. Schs., Miami, 1960-69; asst. to v.p. engr. Racal-Milgo, Inc., Miami, 1972-80; dir. sales and mktg. B. Joe Kerley, Realtor, Miami, 1980-83; dir. customer service, ops. mgr. Modern-Age Furniture Co., Miami, 1983-85; chief exec. officer Adia Pers. Svcs., Greensboro, Winston-Salem, N.C., 1985—; CEO Jan-Ker, Inc., dba ADIA Pers. Svcs., Greensboro, Winston-Salem and ADIA Tech. Ctr., Greensboro, N.C. Named Small Bus. Person of Greensboro, Greensboro C. of C., 1988, Remarkable Woman of Greensboro, Greensboro Coll. Honor Soc., 1991. Mem. Am. Bus. Women's Assn. (nat. bd. dirs. 1978-79, trustee nat. scholarship fund 1978-79, named one of top ten businesswomen, 1988). Office: Adi Tech Ctr 7031 Albert Pick Rd Ste 100 Greensboro NC 27409 also: 4500 Indiana Ave Ste 35 Winston Salem NC 27106 also: ADIA Tech Ctr Ste 202 7031 Albert Pick Rd Greensboro NC 27409

KERMAN, HERBERT DAVID, radiation oncologist; b. Chgo., July 24, 1917; s. A.B. and Sarah (Horberg) K.; m. Ruth Harriet Rice, Jan. 14, 1943; children: David D., Jeffrey A., Steven C., Michael G. AB in Zoology and Chemistry, Duke U., 1938, MD, 1942. Diplomate Am. Bd. Radiology. Asst. prof. radiology Sch. Medicine U. Louisville, 1949-51, assoc. prof. radiology, 1951-56; staff radiologist Oak Ridge (Tenn.) Inst. Nuclear Medicine, 1950-52; cons. radiologist Oak Ridge Hosp., 1950-56; dir. dept. radiology Halifax Med. Ctr., Daytona Beach, Fla., 1956-80, dir. regional onnology ctr., 1984-95, med. dir. health policy, 1984-96; prin. investigator CCOP, Daytona Beach, Fla., 1987—; clin. asst. prof. dept. family medicine U. South Fla., Tampa, 1988-93, clin. assoc. prof. radiology, Tampa, 1996; clin. prof. allied health scis. U. Ctrl. Fla., Orlando, 1975-95; med. advisor Hospice of Volusia, 1979-85; med. dir. Hospice of Volusia/Flagler, 1985-87; mem. Health Program Office Adv. Coun., DHRS, 1981-82; bd. dirs. Children's Crises Team, HMC Children's Med. Svcs., 1980. Contbr. articles to profl. jours. Trustee, past pres. Mus. Arts & Scis., Daytona Beach; mem. South Peninsula Zoning Bd., 1967-77. Lt. comdr. USN, 1943-46. Decorated Bronze Star. Fellow Am. Coll. Radiology (emeritus, mem. faculty practice mgmt. seminars 1977-80, com. on free standing facilities 1987-90, com. on radiotherapeutic practice 1982, cancer control com. 1984); mem. AMA, AAAS, Fla. Med. Assn. (com. on relative value studies 1982-91, chmn. 1990-91), Am. Soc. Cancer Edn. (sr. mem.), Am. Coll. Physician Execs., Am. Roentgen Ray Soc. (emeritus), Am. Soc. for Therapeutic Radiology and Oncology (bd. dirs. 1983-86, profl. practice com. 1980-88, pub. rels. com. 1986-88, co-chmn. com. on regionalization 1979-83), Am. Soc. Clin. Oncology (membership com. 1980), Am. Radium Soc. (sr. mem., program com. 1977, nominating com. Fla. chpt. 1987, pub. rels. com. 1988), Brit. Inst. Radiology, Fla. Radiol. Soc. (chmn. radiation oncology sect. 1976-77), Fla. Soc. Clin. Oncology (hon. life, bd. dirs. 1980-86), N.Y. Acad. Medicine, Radiation Rsch. Soc., Radiol. Soc. N.Am. (counselor Fla. 1968-73), Soc. Nuclear Medicine, So. Med. Assn., So. Radiol. Conf., Halifax River Yacht Club, Oceanside Country Club. Home: 2616 S Peninsula Dr Daytona Beach FL 32118-5631 Office: Halifax Med Ctr 303 N Clyde Morris Blvd Daytona Beach FL 32114-2709

KERMODE, JOHN COTTERILL, pharmacology educator, researcher; b. Changi, Singapore, June 10, 1949; arrived in U.S. 1983; s. Alfred Cotterill and Rose Price (Roberts) K. BA with honors, Cambridge (Eng.) U., 1970, MA, 1974; PhD, London U., 1983. Rsch. scientist U. Coll. Hosp. Med. Sch., London, 1970-74; rsch. biochemist U. Coll. Hosp., London, 1975-83; postdoctoral fellow U. Conn. Health Ctr., Farmington, Conn., 1983-87; postdoctoral assoc. U. Vt., Burlington, 1987-90; rsch. chemist McGuire VA Med. Ctr., Richmond, Va., 1990-93; rsch. asst. prof. Med. Coll. Va., Richmond, 1990-93; asst. prof., dept. pharmacology and toxicology U. Miss. Med. Ctr., Jackson, Miss., 1993—. Mem. editl. bd. Jour. Receptor & Signal Transduction Rsch., 1991—; contbr. articles to profl. jours. Recipient Earnest G. Spivey Meml. Rschr. award, 1994; Cambridge (Eng.) U. scholar, 1967; Am. Heart Assn. grantee, Va., 1991, Miss., 1994. Mem. Am. Soc. Pharmacology & Exptl. Therapeutics, Am. Heart Assn. (coun. basic sci.), N.Y. Acad. Scis. Home: 57 Redbud Ln Madison MS 39110-9615 Office: U Miss Med Ctr 2500 N State St Jackson MS 39216-4500

KERN, ANGELINE FRAZIER, educational administrator; b. Jackson, Tenn., Apr. 27, 1939; d. William Raymond and Sarah Louise (Harris) Frazier; divorced; children: Tiffany Louise, Kevin James. BA, Lambuth Coll., Jackson, 1961; MA, Memphis State U., 1962; postgrad., U. Tenn., 1963. Cert. assessor trainer, Nat. Assn. Secondary Sch. Prins. Tchr. phys. edn. Jackson City Schs., 1960-62; tchr. English, guidance counselor Georgian Hills Jr. High Sch., Memphis, 1962-65; guidance counselor Colonial Jr. High Sch., Memphis, 1965-70; adminstrv. asst. Kingsbury High Sch., Memphis, 1970-72; prin. Avon Elem. Sch., Memphis, 1972-77, Balmoral Elem. Sch., Memphis, 1977-93, Cordova Sch., 1993—. Mem. adv. bd. East Memphis YMCA, 1984-87; mem. Memphis City Beautiful Commn., 1985-89; pres. St. John's Creek Home and Garden Club, Memphis, 1968-70. Recipient Youth Svc. award YMCA, Memphis, 1983, Vol. Recognition award, 1986; finalist Rotary Club Prin. of Yr. award, 1989. Mem. NEA, Nat. Assn. Elem. Sch. Prins., Assn. for Sch. Curriculum Devel., Tenn. Assn. Elem. Sch. Prins. (fall conf. planning com. 1985), Memphis Pub. Sch. Prins. Assn. (auditing com. 1983-85), Memphis State U. Rebounders, Educators Bridge Club, Phi Delta Kappa, Delta Kappa Gamma (fin. chmn. Epsilon chpt. 1976-84, corr. sect. 1990-92). Republican. Roman Catholic. Office: Cordova Sch 900 N Sanga Rd Cordova TN 38018-6562

KERN, CONSTANCE ELIZABETH, retired real estate broker; b. Cleve., Dec. 18, 1937; d. Walter Anthony and Irene (Davies) Matthews; divorced; children: James, David, Douglas, Kathleen. Student, John Carroll U., 1957, Case Western Res. U., 1958; BA in Speech and English, Marietta (Ohio) Coll., 1959; postgrad., Sul Ross State U., Midland, Tex., 1967-68, Comml. Coll. Real Estate, Ft. Worth, 1984, 86. Cert. tchr., Ohio, Tex.; lic. real estate broker, Tex. Tchr. South Euclid and Lyndhurst (Ohio) Schs., 1959-60; sec. Pan Am. Petroleum, Midland, 1960-61; tchr. St. Ann's Sch., Midland, 1967-69; real estate agt. McAfee & Assocs., Arlington, Tex., 1985-86; real estate broker Constance Kern Real Estate, Arlington, 1986-94, property mgr., 1986-94; ret. Constance Kern Real Estate, 1994; oil operator, investor, Midland and Arlington, 1975-92. Vol. Pink Ladies Midland Meml. Hosp., 1970-73; troop leader Brownies Girl Scouts Am., Midland, 1971; vol. speech therapist Children's Service League Cerebral Palsy Ctr., Midland, 1975-76. Mem. Pi Kappa Delta. Republican. Roman Catholic.

KERN, EDNA RUTH, insurance executive; b. Rochester, N.Y., Dec. 31, 1945; d. Carl H. and Mildred B. (Fronk) McRorie; m. Charles E. Kern, Nov. 1, 1968 (div. July 1975); 1 child, Barbara Renee. BBA summa cum laude, Tex. Wesleyan Coll., 1978. CLU, ChFC. Pvt. detective Statewide Detective Agy., Orlando, Fla., 1968-78; agt. Pacific Mut. Ins., Ft. Worth, 1978-79, Conn. Mut. Ins., Ft. Worth, 1979-83; gen. agt. Gen. Am. Life Ins., Ft. Worth, 1983-85; ins. owner Kern & Assocs., Ft. Worth, 1985—; life underwriters tng. fellow Nat. Assn. Life Underwriters. Pres. All Sts. Hosp. Execs. Forum, Ft. Worth, 1986-87, Women's Health Forum, 1994-96; bd. dirs. YWCA 1984-85. Mem.Mem. Nat. Assn. Health Underwriters (registered, sec.-treas. 1990-91, Disting. Svc. award), Tex. Assn. Health Underwriters (state sec., bd. dirs. 1987-88, pres. 1988-90, Outstanding Texan of Yr. award, Hollis Roberson award), Ft. Worth Assn. Life Underwriters (bd. dirs. 1986-91, moderator 1984-86, chmn. health com. and edn. com. 1986-88), Tarrant County Assn. Health Underwriters (pres. 1986-87), Sales and Mktg. Execs. (bd. dirs. Ft. Worth chpt. 1985-87, v.p. 1986-87, sec. 1994-95, pres. 1995-96), Mensa. Republican. Office: Kern & Assocs PO Box 100356 Fort Worth TX 76185-0356

KERN, HOWARD PAUL, hospital administrator; b. N.Y.C., Jan. 23, 1957; married. BA, NYU, 1978; M Health Adminstrn., Va. Commonwealth U., 1981. Adm. res. Sentara Hosp., Norfolk, Va., 1980-81, adm. asst. med. staff, 1981-82, dir. amb. care svcs., 1982-83; asst. adminstr. Sentara Norfolk Gen. Hosp., 1983-86, sr. vp., 1986-90, adminstr., 1990-95; pres. Sentara Southside Hosps., Norfolk, 1995—. Home: 3200 Chapham Cross Virginia Beach VA 23452-6162 Office: Sentara Norfolk Gen Hosp 6015 Poplar Hall Dr Norfolk VA 23502*

KERNS, DAVID VINCENT, lawyer; b. Salt Lake City, Jan. 29, 1917; s. Clinton Bowen and Ella Mae (Young) K.; m. Dorothea Boyd, Sept. 5, 1942; children—David V., Clinton Boyd. B.Ph., Emory U., 1937; J.D., U. Fla., 1939. Bar: Fla. 1939, U.S. Dist. Ct. (mid. dist.) Fla. 1939, U.S. Dist. Ct. (so. dist.) Fla. 1978, U.S. Dist. Ct. (no. dist.) Fla., U.S. Ct. Appeals (11th cir.) 1981, U.S. Supreme Ct. 1988. Assoc. Sutton & Reeves, Tampa, Fla., 1939-41, Fowler & White, Tampa, 1945-47; ptnr. Moran & Kerns, Tampa, 1948-49; resident atty. Fla. Road Dept., 1949-53; research asst. Supreme Ct. Fla., 1953-58; dir. Fla. Legis. Reference Bur., 1958-68, Fla. Legis. Service Bur., 1968-71, Fla. Legis. Library Services, 1971-73; gen. counsel Fla. Dept. Adminstrn., 1973-82; mem. Fla. Career Service Commn., 1983-86; spl. master Fla. Senate, 1987-96; legal cons. chief inspector gen. Fla. Gov. Office, 1995—. Contbr. articles to profl. jours. Served with U.S. Army, 1941-45. Mem. Fla. Govt. Bar Assn. (pres. 1966, J. Ernest Webb Meml. award 1982), Fla. Bar (bd. govs. 1978-84), Tallahassee Bar Assn. (spl. dir. 1993-95). Democrat. Methodist. Home: 418 Vinnedge Ride Tallahassee FL 32303-5140

KERNS, STEPHEN RIMMER, insurance executive; b. South Charleston, W.Va., Oct. 22, 1952; s. Woodrow J. and Anna Marlene (Snyder) K.; m. Deborah Jean Huffman, Dec. 20, 1975; children: Matthew Stephen, Amber Marie. BBA, Marshall U., 1975. CLU; ChFC. Ins. agt. Fidelity Union Life Ins., Huntington, 1975; claim adjuster trainee USF&G Ins. Co., Charleston, 1976, claim adjuster, 1976-77; life spl. agt. trainee Fidelity and Guaranty Life Ins. subs. USF&G, Charleston, 1977-78; life spl. agt. Fidelity and Guaranty Life Ins. (formerly USF&G) Ins. Co., Charleston, 1978-82, life supt., 1982-84, life sales and mktg. rep., 1984-85, life sales and mktg. cons., 1985-91, life sales mgr., 1991-92; v.p. Clendenin (W.Va.) Ins. Agy., Inc., 1992—. Bd. dirs., sec. Elk Valley Christian Sch., Elkview, W.Va., 1987-89, bd. dirs., chmn., 1989-96; trustee Mt. Pleasant Bapt. Ch., 1993-94. Mem. Am. Soc. of CLU and ChFC (pres. Charleston chpt. 1988-89), Nat. Assn. of Life Underwriters (Charleston chpt.). Republican. Office: Clendenin Ins Agy Inc 12 Elk Ave W Clendenin WV 25045-9723

KERNS, WILMER LEE, social science researcher; b. Dayton, Va., May 17, 1932; s. Lee Doil and Madeline A. (Grim) K.; m. Marian Iris May, Mar. 21, 1957 (div. 1963); children: Mark Wayne, Susan Kaye Kerns Mitchell; m. Shirley Mitchell Walton, June 19, 1965; children: Robert Todd, Lynelle Madeline, Jacob Scott Walton. AB, Trevecca Nazarene Coll., 1957; AM, U. Mich., 1960; PhD, Ohio State U., 1971. Cert. tchr., counselor, Va. Math. tchr. Norfolk (Va.) Pub. Schs., 1957-59; counselor Washington-Lee High Sch., Arlington, Va., 1960-65; social worker Arlington (Va.) County Pub. Schs., 1965-67; civil rights specialist U.S. Office Edn., Washington, 1967-69; rsch. assoc. Ohio State U., Columbus, 1969-71; assoc. regional commr. Social and Rehab. Svc., Chgo., 1971-74; planning officer Social and Rehab. Svc., Washington, 1974-75, divsn. chief, 1975-77; sr. rsch. analyst Social Security Adminstrn., Washington, 1977—. Author: Shanholtzer History and Allied Family Roots, 1980, Historical Records of Old Frederick and Hampshire Counties, Va., 1992; Frederick County, Virginia: Settlement and First Families, 1730-1830, 1995; columnist The W.Va. Advocate, 1982-92 (Excellence in Journalism award 1992). Lay minister Truro Episcopal Ch., Fairfax, Va., 1988-91. With USN, 1950-53. Decorated Air medal; named Disting. West Virginian, Gov. of W.Va., 1989. Mem. Morgan County Hist. Soc., Winchester-Frederick County Hist. Assn. Republican. Home: 4715 38th Pl N Arlington VA 22207-2914 Office: Social Security Adminstrn 4301 Connecticut Ave NW Washington DC 20008-2304

KERR, ALVA RAE, writer, editor, association executive; b. Borger, Tex., July 29, 1926; d. Rene Lawerence and Georgia Margaret (Jones) McDonald; m. Gary Karp, Jan. 23, 1946 (dec. 1969); children: Pamela Karp Roper, Victoria, Richard; m. Glenn Enevold Kerr, Nov. 18, 1977. Student U. of Ams., Mex., 1970; BA, U. Houston, 1972; MA, George Washington U., 1975. Real estate broker Coldwell Banker Realtors, McLean, Va., 1975-83, writer, editor, D.C. area, 1984; writer, editor Nat. Capital chpt. Multiple Sclerosis Soc., Washington, 1984-86; editor, publ.: The Will to Win, 1996; corr. sec. UN World Com. Decade of Disabled Persons, Washington, 1985-86; writer, editor Retired Officers Assn. of Houston, 1990—; lectr. Nat. Security Agy., Fort Meade, Md., 1983, Somerset Civic Assn., Fairfax, Va., 1983, B'nai Brith, McLean, 1984, also others. Vol. spl. asst. on community program Nat. Orgn. on Disability, Washington, 1985-86; active Soc. for Performing Arts of Harris County, 1986-88. Recipient Commendátiere for Outstanding Newsletter, Ret. Officers Assn., 1990—. Mem. AAUW, Scriptwriters of Houston, Campanille Writer's Group, Assn. Adms.-Texas Navy, Phi Delta Gamma (pres. 1984-86). Avocations: writing, music. Home: 17006 Hillswind Cir Spring TX 77379-4505

KERR, CHARLOTTE BOWDEN, interior designer; b. Macon, Ga., Oct. 8, 1939; d. Charles Loyren and Urney Fields Bowden; m. W.H. Rivenbark, July 12, 1958 (div. 1979); children: W.H., Charles, Thomas; m. R. Douglas Kerr, Sept. 16, 1989. BS, U. Ala., Tuscaloosa, 1972, MS, 1977. Lic. interior designer, Fla., D.C.; cert. interior designer, Va. Sec., asst. grant writer U. Ala., 1971-74, grad. teaching asst., 1974-76; asst. mgr. Sherwin Williams, Tuscaloosa, 1976; interior designer Joanne James Interiors, St. Petersburg, Fla., 1977-81; pres. Markham-Sebring, Inc., Clearwater, Fla., 1982-89; dir. design Cado Internat., Inc., Oakton, Va., 1989-93; sr. interior designer Marriott Internat., 1993—; bd. dirs. Boley Manor, Inc., Suncoast RMH; cons. Marriott Corp. West Fla. editor Fla. Designers Quar.; prin. works include 1st Nat. Bank Clearwater, Clearwater Beach Hotel, Heritage Hotel, St. Petersburg, Habana Med. Ctr., Tampa, Fla., Ronald McDonald House, St. Petersburg, Poe Inst., Tampa, Salvation Army, Gulf Hotel, Bahrain, Saudi Arabia, Kanoo Hotel, Bahrain, Villa in Al Hada, Marriott Hotel, Riyadh, Saudi Arabia, Children's Villa at Rakkah Palace, Saudi Arabia, Hotel Meridien, Baghdad, Iraq, Marriott Hotels in Beirut, Buenos Aires, London, Paris, Moscow, Bermuda, London. Bd. dirs. Tuscaloosa (Fla.) Bicentennial Com., MMAX Arts, Crafts and Music Festival. Mem. Am. Soc. Interior Designers (North Fla. chpt., bd. dirs.), Fla. Mental Health Assn. (bd. dirs.), Pinellas Mental Health Assn. (bd. dirs.), Phi Epsilon Omicron. Home: 10333 Emerald Rock Dr Oakton VA 22124-2705

KERR, DONALD CRAIG, retired minister; b. Pitts., July 29, 1915; s. Hugh Thomson and Olive (Boggs) K.; m. Nora Minetta Lloyd, Sept. 12, 1942; children: Donald Jr., Elizabeth, Douglas. BA, Princeton U., 1937; MDiv, Princeton Theol. Sem., 1940; ThD, U. Toronto, Ont., Can., 1942. Ordained to ministry Presbyn. Ch. (U.S.A.), 1940. Min. East Kiskacoguillas Presbyn. Ch., Reedsville, Pa., 1942-47, 1st Presbyn. Ch., New Haven, 1947-48; min. Roland Pk. Presbyn. Ch., Balt., 1948-80, pastor emeritus, 1980; pastoral assoc. Presbyn. Ch., Sarasota, Fla., 1980-87; chaplain Plymouth Harbor, Sarasota, 1982-91; moderator Presbytery of Balt., 1960-61, mem. bd. pensions, exec. com., 1963-66. Author: How the Church Began, 1953, What the Bible Means, 1954, History of Religion in America, 1975; editor: Design for Christian Living, 1952. Recipient 50-yrs. in ministry plague Lake Joseph Community Ch., 1989, 50-yr. Ordination Recognition, 1992. Mem. St. Andrew's Soc. (trustee, chaplain 1980-91, cert. appreciation 1990), Ivy League Club (v.p. 1991, pres. 1992-93), Princeton Club (pres. 1988-90), Univ. Club Sarasota, Sarasota Yacht Club, Sara Bay Club, Gibson Island Club, Shriners, Masons (32 degrees). Home: Apt 330 5220 Manz Pl Sarasota FL 34232

KERR, JAMES WILSON, engineer; b. Balt., May 21, 1921; s. James W. and Laura Virginia (Wright) K.; m. Mary Thomas Montgomery, Feb. 25, 1945 (div., dec.); children: April Kerr Miller, Catherine Kerr Wood (dec.), Wilson, Andrew; m. June Walker, Dec. 27, 1977 (div.); m. Jance White Bain, Jan. 19, 1985. BS with honors, Davidson Coll., 1942; MS, NYU, 1948; postgrad. Freiburg U., 1957-60, Brookings Inst., 1970, 75, Fed. Exec. Inst., 1982; PhD, Kennedy Western U., 1989. Commd. 2d lt. U.S. Army, 1942, advanced through grades to lt. col., 1964; with inf., World War II, Korea; electronic staff, Ft. Bragg, N.C., 1948-51; weapons rsch., N.M., 1953-57; adviser French Army, 1957-60; staff electronics, Ft. Monroe, Va., 1960-62; rsch. mgr., div. dir. CD, Pentagon, 1962-64, as civilian, 1964-81, asst. assoc. dir. Fed. Emergency Mgmt. Agy. for Rsch., 1981-85; sr. staff Michael Rogers, Inc., Winter Park, Fla., 1986—; dir. Mt. St. Helen's Tech. Office, 1980; v.p. Latherow & Co., Arlington, Va., 1965-86. Advanced English instr. French Army, 1957-60; cons. Am. Nat. Red Cross Mus., 1968-85, Smithsonian Instn. Dept. Postal History, 1966-85, NSF, 1976-85. Vol. fireman N.Y. State, 1946-48, Fairfax County, Va., 1969—; fire commr. Fairfax County, 1975-81, chmn., 1977-81, Orange County, Fla., 1986—, pres., 1987-90, Pike County, Ala., 1994—; active Boy Scouts Am., in U.S., Asia and Europe, 1933—; chmn. library bd., Orangeburg, N.Y., 1946-48. Decorated Bronze Star with three oak leaf clusters, Purple Heart; recipient Silver Beaver award Boy Scouts Am., 1956, James E. West, 1994; Fulbright selectee, Japan, 1986; registered profl. engr., Calif. Fellow AAAS, Explorers Club; mem. NAS (various coms. 1962-87), Internat. Assn. Fire Chiefs (chmn. rsch. com. 1969-88, chief sci. adviser 1982-86), Fed. Fire Council, Nat. Fire Protection Assn. (chmn. hosp. disaster com. 1973-96), Presdl. Nat. Def. Exec., SAR (Fire Safety medal 1995), Black Forest Mardi Gras (Germany), Nat. Communications Club, Pentagon Officers Athletic Club, IEEE (sr.), Elks, Phi Beta Kappa, Gamma Sigma Epsilon, Delta Phi Alpha. Presbyn. (elder 1963—). Author: Korean-English Phrase Book, 1951; 19th Century Korea Postal Handbook, 1965, 2d edit., 1990. Editor Korean Philately mag., 1971-80, 85-95. Contbr. articles to profl. jours. Club: University (Fla.). Home: PO Box 927 Troy AL 36081-0927 Office: MR Inc 199 E Welbourne Ave Winter Park FL 32789-4337

KERR, RITA LEE, writer, storyteller; b. Okmulgee, Okla., Oct. 29, 1925; d. Walter H. Roberts and Maya M. (Smith) Wilson; m. Larry L. Kerr, Apr. 10, 1943; children: Kayita L. Kerr Stephens, Donald L. Kerr. BS, Trinity U., 1954. Cert. tchr. elem. edn., Tex. Tchr. San Antonio Ind. Sch. Dist., 1954-82; writer hist. books for children, 1982—, storyteller elem. schs., 1985—. Author: (hist. fiction) Girl of the Alamo, 1984, Juan Seguin, 1985 (Hist. award 1986), Immortal 32, 1985, Texas Rose, 1986, Texas First Lady, 1986, Texas Marvel, 1987, The Alamo Cat, 1988, Texas Footprints, 1988, Texas Rebel, 1989, Texas Cavalier, 1989, Tex's Tales, 1990, Ghost of Panna Maria, 1990, A Wee Bit of Texas, 1991, Christopher and Pony Boy, 1991, The Haunted House, 1992, Texas Forever, 1993, Texas Orphan, 1994. Active DAR (historian), P.E.O., Daus. of War of 1812, Daus. of Republic of Tex., San Antonio Geneal. Hist. Soc. Mem. Tex. Libr. Assn. Republican. Baptist. Home: 214 Shadywood Ln San Antonio TX 78216-7336

KERR, RUSSELL GREIG, chemistry educator; b. Edinburgh, Scotland, Nov. 17, 1959; came to the U.S., 1986; s. Melville Greig and Agnes Kerr (Bain) K.; m. Stacey Scott Beeh, Aug. 19, 1995; 1 child, Melissa Lim. BS, U. Calgary, 1982, PhD, 1986. Postdoctoral fellow Stanford (Calif.) U., 1986-91; asst. prof. Fla. Atlantic U., Boca Raton, 1991—. Contbr. articles to profl. jours. and chpts. to books. Grantee NIH, USDA, Petroleum Rsch. Fund. Mem. Am. Chem. Soc., AAAS, Am. Soc. Pharmacognosy, Coun. for Undergrad. Edn. Roman Catholic. Office: Fla Atlantic U Dept Chemistry 777 Glades Rd Boca Raton FL 33341-0991

KERR, WALTER BELNAP, retired missile instrumentation engineer, English language researcher, consultant; b. Salt Lake City, Oct. 14, 1926; s. Walter Affleck and Marion Adeline (Belnap) K.; m. Raida Nebeker, May 2, 1952 (dec. Mar. 1992); children: Valerie Jean Kerr Lemon, Grant Mercer, Janice Arlene Kerr Hahn, Marilyn, Ed, James, Patricia, Douglas; m. Lillian Grace Hamilton Ettinger, Oct. 1, 1992. BA in French, U. Utah, 1951, BSEE, 1955; MBA in Internat. Bus., U. So. Calif., 1972. Electrical engr. Hughes Aircraft Co., L.A., 1955-61, 67-69; missile instrumentation engr. Hercules Inc., Salt Lake City, 1961-66, 84-89, Rockwell Internat., Anaheim, Calif., 1969-70; investment broker Titan Capital Corp., L.A., Ogden, Utah, 1970-79; electrical engr. White Motor Corp., Ogden, 1979-84; tax examiner IRS, Ogden, 1990-91, ret., 1991; cons. Soc. for the Advancement of Good English, Pittsford, N.Y., 1985-86. Author: (book) Instrumentation Methods, 1963, (card) Pocket Guide to Good English, 1984; inventor. Juggler St. Benedict's Hosp., and various grade schs., h.s., univs., shopping ctrs. and chs., 1947—. With USN, 1945-46, 1st lt. U.S. Army, 1951-53. Mem. IEEE, The Planetary Soc., World Wildlife Fund, Soc. for the Preservation of English Lang. and Literature. Republican. LDS. Home: 306 Messer Rd Murphy NC 28906

KERSHAW, CAROL JEAN, psychologist; b. New Orleans, Apr. 11, 1947; d. Neal Howard and Gloria Jackson (Moss) Perkins; m. John William Wade, Aug. 20, 1983; stepchildren: Chris Wade, Stephen Wade, Tiffany Wade. BS in Secondary Edn., U. Tex., 1969; MS in Speech Communication, North Tex. State U., 1971, MEd in Counseling, 1976; EdD in Counseling, East Tex. State U., 1979. Lic. psychologist, Tex. Assoc. prof. DeVry Inst., Dallas, 1971-73; instr., counseling psychologist East Tex. State U., Commerce, 1976-78; counselor, instr. Tarrant County Jr. Coll., Hurst, Tex., 1971-74; dir. spl. svcs. Goodwill Industries, Dallas, 1974-76; marriage and family therapist, cons. mental health clinic Tex. Dept. Mental Health and Retardation, Greenville, 1977-79; asst. prof., dir. grad. program in marriage & family therapy Tex. Woman's U., Denton, 1980-83; coord. child devel. dept. Tex. Woman's U., Houston, 1983-88; pvt. practice Inst. for Family Psychology, Houston, 1986—; co-dir. Milton H. Erickson Inst. Houston, 1986—; bd. dirs. Milton H. Erickson Inst. Tex., Houston, 1986—; internat. presenter in field. Author: Therapeutic Metaphor in the Treatment of Childhood Asthma: A Systemic Approach, Ericksonian Monographs, Vol. 2, 1986, The Couple's Hypnotic Dance, 1992, The Healing Power of the Story, Ericksonian Monographs, Vol. 9, 1994, audio Mind/Body Healing and Hypnosis, 1996; co-author: Learning to Think for an Organ, Bridges of the Bodymind, 1980, Psychotherapeutic Techniques in School Psychology, 1984, Restoring the Mind: Using Therapeutic Narrative in Psychotherapy in Ericksonian Methods, 1994. Sec. Tex. Assn. for Marriage and Family Therapy, 1978-80. Recipient Visionary award, Meritorious Svc. award Tex. Assn. for Marriage & Family Therapy, 1980. Mem. Am. Psychol. Assn, Am. Assn. for Marriage and Family Therapy (clin., approved supr.), Soc. for Exptl. & Clin. Hypnosis, Am. Soc. for Clin. Hypnosis (cons., appointed to ethics com., 1996), Internat. Soc. for Clin. & Exptl. Hypnosis, Psi Chi. Democrat. Methodist. Office: Inst for Family Psychology 2012 Bissonnet St Houston TX 77005-1647

KERSHNER, WILLIAM ROBERT, theatre educator; b. Denver, May 15, 1952; s. Robert Earl and Lula Belle (Davis) K.; m. Nancy Yumiko Dodge, June 23, 1974; children: Geoffrey, Philip. BA, U. No. Colo., 1974; MA, U. So. Calif., 1976, PhD, 1981. Asst. prof. drama U. Mont., Missoula, 1981-87; asst. prof. Sweet Briar (Va.) Coll., 1987-92, assoc. prof., 1992—, chmn. dept. theatre arts, 1987—; bd. dirs. Renaissance Theatre Co., Lynchburg, 1990—; treas. Arts Coun. Cen. Va., Lynchburg, 1991, bd. dirs.; bd. dirs. Friends of Acad. of Music, Lynchburg. Dir. 25 plays, 1976—; contbr. articles to profl. jours. Mem. Am. Soc. Theatre Rsch., Assn. Theatre in Higher Edn., Va. Theatre Assn., S.E. Theatre Conf., Soc. Stage Dirs. and Choreographers (assoc.). Home: RR 6 Box 406 Amherst VA 24521-9578 Office: Sweet Briar Coll Dept Theatre Arts PO Box AO Sweet Briar VA 24595-0055

KERVEN, DAVID SCOTT, computer science educator, consultant; b. Jersey City, Jan. 3, 1967; s. Arnold Hilton and Sheila Gail (Cohen) K.; m. Jenny Helen Ehrlich, Dec. 17, 1995. BSEE, Johns Hopkins U., 1985-88; MS in Computer Sci., N.J. Inst. Tech., 1989; MS in Computer Engring., U. Southwestern La., 1990, PhD in Computer Sci., 1993; post grad., Ga. State U. School of Law, 1995—. Programmer biomed. engring. dept. Johns Hopkins U., Balt., 1987, programmer Homewood Computing Facilities, 1987-88; systems analyst acad. computing dept. N.J. Inst. Tech. Computing Svcs., 1988-89; cons. Exec. Systems, Inc., Lafayette, La., 1989-90; project leader NASA R & D hypermedia project U. Southwestern La., Lafayette, 1990-92, lectr. dept. computer sci., 1992-93; asst. prof. dept. computer and info. scis. Clark Atlanta U., 1993—; legal cons., Lafayette, 1991-92. Contbr. articles to sci. jours. Scholar Western Electric Fund, 1985-88, Hopkins scholar, 1985; grad. fellow U. Southwestern La., 1989-92, fellow Exec. Sys. Inc., 1990-92; summer faculty fellow NASA, 1994, 95. Mem. Assn. for Computing Machinery, IEEE Computer Soc., Nat. Science Tchrs. Assn., American Bar Assn., Atlanta Bar Assn., Upsilon Pi Epsilon, Zeta Beta Tau. Office: Clark Atlanta U Dept Computer Sci James P Brawley Dr at Fair Atlanta GA 30314

KERWIN, JOSEPH PETER, physician, former astronaut; b. Oak Park, Ill., Feb. 19, 1932; m. Shirley Ann Good; children: Sharon, Joanna, Kristina. B.A., Coll. Holy Cross, 1953; M.D., Northwestern U., 1957. Flight surgeon USN, 1959, aviator, 1962; astronaut, 1965; mem. Skylab 2 Crew, 1973; rep. Australia NASA, 1982-83; dir. Space-Life Sci., 1984-87; mgr. EVA systems Lockheed Missiles & Space Co., 1987—, mgr. Houston Manned Programs, 1990—. •

KERWIN, WALTER THOMAS, JR., career officer, consultant; b. West Chester, Pa., June 14, 1917; s. Walter Thomas and Mary Joseph (Farra) K.; m. Barbara Walker Connell, July 10, 1940 (dec. 1980); children: Bruce Richard, Ann Kerwin Walker; m. Marion Thompson McCutcheon, Oct. 27, 1984. BS, U.S. Mil. Acad., 1939; postgrad., Command and Gen. Staff Coll., 1948, Armed Forces Staff Coll., 1953, U.S. Army War Coll., 1957, Nat. War Coll., 1960; LLD (hon.), U. Akron, 1976; M in Mil. Art and Sci., Command and Gen Staff Coll., 1978. Commd. 2nd lt. U.S. Army, 1939, advanced through grades to gen., 1973; commdg. gen. 3d armored divsn. arty. U.S. Army, Hanau, Germany, 1961-63; chief nuclear activities SHAPE U.S. Army, Paris, 1963-65; commdg. gen. 3d armored divsn. U.S. Army, Frankfurt, Germany, 1965-66; asst. dep. chief staff ops. gen. staff U.S. Army, Washington, 1966-67; chief staff mil. asst. command U.S. Army, Saigon, Vietnam, 1967-68; commdg. gen. II field force Vietnam U.S. Army, Bien Hoa, 1968-69; dep. chief staff pers. gen. staff U.S. Army, Washington, 1969-72; commdg. gen. continental army command U.S. Army, Norfolk, Va., 1973; commdg. gen. forces command U.S. Army, Atlanta, 1973-74; vice chief staff U.S. Army, Washington, 1974-78; cons. Martin Marietta Corp., Bethesda, Md., 1978-94, Lockheed-Martin, 1994—; assoc. dir. Los Alamos (N.Mex.) Sci. Lab., 1953-56; bd. dirs. Gen. Employment Enterprises, Oakbrook, Ill.; mem. bd. mgrs. Army Emergency Relief, 1982—. Chmn. Army Air Force Mut. Aid Assn., Arlington, Va., 1982—; mem. strategy com. Army Hist. Found., 1995—. Recipient Disting. Svc. medal Commonwealth of Pa., 1975, numerous mil. awards and decorations; named to Henderson Hall of Fame, Westchester, Pa., 1991. Fellow Nat. Def. U. Capstone Program (emeritus); mem. Am. Def. Preparedness Assn. (comdr. Chief award 1984), West Point Soc. (Castle-Duty Hon. award 1993), U.S. field Arty. Assn. (pres.).

KESLER, RICHARD WILLIAM, pediatrician, educator; b. Pitts., Apr. 15, 1941. s. Howard Frank and Helen L. (Wiltfong) K. BA, Johns Hopkins U., 1963; MD, Duke U., 1967. Resident in pediats. Johns Hopkins U., Balt., 1970, chief resident in pediats., 1972-74; prof., vice chmn. dept. pediats. U. Va. Health Sci. Ctr., Charlottesville, 1974—. Office: U Va Sch Medicine Med Ctr Box 386 Charlottesville VA 22908-0001

KESSEN, GEORGE WILLIAM, employment agency manager; b. Ft. Wayne, Ind., Dec. 17, 1942; s. John Henry and Mildred Josephine (Winbaugh) K. AA, Internat. Jr. Coll., Ft. Wayne, 1976; postgrad., Ind. U., 1979. Cert. Profl. Personnel Cons. Pres., owner Kessen Recreation Ctr., Ft. Wayne, 1972-83; security officer/credit mgr. Peoples Trust Bank, Ft. Wayne, 1959-73; office mgr. Farm Bur. Ins., Ft. Wayne, 1973-82; employment cons. Lincoln Personnel, Inc., Ft. Wayne, 1982-83, Gen. Employment, Inc., Tampa, Fla., 1984-88; supr./cons. Gen. Employment, Inc., Tampa, 1988-91, agy. mgr., 1993-96; agy. mgr. Triad Pers., Inc., Tampa, 1996—; profl. personnel con. Gen. Employment, Inc., Triad Personnel, Inc., Chgo., 1996—. Author: (book) Measuring Your Success in Sales, 1996. Mem. ARC, Ft. Wayne and Tampa, 1976—. With U.S. Army, 1966-68. Mem. Bally's Internat. Roman Catholic. Office: Triad Pers Inc Ste 124 5201 W Kennedy Blvd Tampa FL 33609

KESSLER, JOHN PAUL, JR., financial planner; b. Bronxville, N.Y., Sept. 4, 1946; s. John Paul and Helen Claire (Hopper) K.; m. Michelle McCall Hunter, June 30, 1993. BBA in Fin., Tex. Tech. U., 1965-71. Cert. fin. planner, registered investment advisor. Life ins. agt. Met. Life Ins. Co., Lubbock, Tex., 1970-73; pension trust adminstr. Rep. Nat. Life, Dallas, 1973-78, Am. Founders Life, Austin, 1979-81; acct. for state appropriations Tex. State Comptr., Austin, 1981-84; fin. planner J. Paul Kessler & Assocs., Dallas, 1984-95, Kessler Fin. Group (formerly J. Paul Kessler & Assocs.), Dallas, 1995—; pension cons. Kessler Fin. Group, Dallas, 1984—. Mem. Am. Mgmt. Assn., Dallas Estate Planning Coun., Dallas Employee Benefit Assn., Inst. Cert. Fin. Planners, North Dallas Fin. Forum, Nat. Assn. Securities Dealers (registered rep.), Tex. Tech Ex-Student Assn., North Dallas C. of C., McKinney C. of C. Republican. Presbyterian.

KESSLER, KENDALL SEAY FERIOZI, artist; b. Washington, Nov. 4, 1954; d. Dan John and Anne Fletcher (Trotter) Feriozi; m. Clyde Thomas Kessler, June 25, 1977; 1 child, Alan. BA in Art Edn., Va. Polytech. Inst. & State U., 1976; MFA in Painting & Printmaking, Redford U., 1983. Tchr. art, Spanish Cherrydale Christian Sch., Arlington, Va., 1976-77; tchr. community arts sch. Radford (Va.) U., 1980-82, adminstr., 1982-83; tchr. art Fine Arts Ctr., Pulaski, Va., 1984; instr. art Radford U., 1985-87, 88-93, interim gallery dir., 1987-88; freelance profl. artist, tchr. Radford, 1993—. Illustrator (poetry books) Shooting Creek, 1982, Dancing at Big Vein, 1987, Preservations, 1989; book jacket illustrator: The Rosewood Casket by Sharon McCrumb, 1996; exhibited in group shows Agora Gallery, Soho, N.Y., 1994, 95. Officer PEO Sisterhood, Radford, 1992-94, mem., 1989—; mem. Lamplighters, Radford Pub. Libr., 1991—, Valley-Wide Newcomers, Radford, 1993—. Recipient Am. Artist award Soc. West Coast 4th Nat. Exehibit, Scramento, Calif, first place Oils, Paris (Tex.) Art Fair, 1991. Mem. Nat. Mus. Women in Arts, Internat. Platform Assn., Blacksburg Regional Art Assn., Lynwood Artists, Piedmont Arts Assn., Am. Artist award, Pastel soc. of the West Coast 4th Nat. Exhibit, juror, Daniel Greene, firts placeOils, Paris Art Fair, 1991. Home: PO Box 3612 Radford VA 24143-3612

KESSLER, KENNETH MICHAEL, cardiologist; b. Phila., May 6, 1945; s. Louis Harry and Jayne Catherine (Baker) K.; m. Rhonda Michelle Brotman, June 25, 1966; children: Kimberly, Danielle. Student, Temple U., 1962-64; MD, Temple U. Sch. Medicine, 1968. Diplomate Am. Bd. Internal Medicine and Cardiovascular Diseases. Med. intern Temple U. Hosp., 1968-69; clin. pharmacology fellow Temple U. Sch. Medicine, 1969-70; med. resident Temple U. Hosp., 1970-71, cardiology fellow, 1971-73; asst. prof. medicine Temple U., Phila., 1975-78; asst. prof. medicine U. Miami Sch. Medicine, 1978-83, assoc. prof. medicine, 1983-86, prof. medicine, 1986—; assoc. dir. div. cardiology U. Miami Sch. Medicine, 1990—; chief cardiology sect. VA Med. Ctr., Miami, 1985—. Contbr. more than 200 articles to profl. jours., chpts. to books, med. abstracts. Pres.'s. coun. Miami Children's Hosp. Maj. U.S. Army M.C., 1973-75. Recipient achievement award for pharmacology Upjohn Co., 1968, award in cardiovascular rsch. Am. Heart Assn. Southeast Pa. Affiliate, 1968. Fellow ACP, Am. Coll. Cardiology (editl. bd. 1988-92), Am. Heart Assn.; mem. Alpha Omega Alpha. Office: VA Med Ctr Sect Cardiology (111A) 1201 NW 16th St Miami FL 33125-1624

KESSLER, MARGARET MARIE, artist, writer; b. Auburn, Ind., Aug. 15, 1944; d. Kenneth Albert and Edna Marie (Cardinal) Jennings; m. Jere Wayne Kessler, June 10, 1962; children: Wade John, Paul David. Freelance artist, writer Richardson, Tex.; condr. art club demonstrations and workshops nationwide. Author, artist: Painting Better Landscapes, 1987; author, artist articles in The Artist's Mag. (oil painting featured on cover Feb. 1985), North Light Mag., Southwest Art Mag.; co-author: Everything You Ever Wanted to Know About Oil Painting, 1993. Recipient Best Traditional Painting award Hoosier Salon, Indpls., 1983, Best Show awards Artists and Craftsmen Associated, Dallas, 1981, 84, 85, 87, 92, Outstanding Tchr. award 1988, Best of Show award Regional Painting and Sculpture Show, Richardson, 1987, Hon. Mention Am. Artist's Profl. League, Salmagundi Club, N.Y.C., 1984, Gold medal Grumbacher Art awards, 1994, Silver, 1982, Bronze, 1983, Top 100 Arts for the Parks award, Jackson, Wyo., 1989. Mem. Artists and Craftsmen Associated (signature mem. 1983, pres. 1985-86). Home and Studio: 330 Ridgehaven Pl Richardson TX 75080-2569

KESTLE, WENDELL RUSSELL, cost and economic analyst, consultant; b. Casper, Wyo., July 23, 1935; s. Philip Clayton and Ruby Maxine (Clifton) K.; m. Anne Marie Joujon-Roche, Nov. 18, 1961; children: Martha Anne, Joan Marie, Wendell Russell Jr. BA in Econs., Calif. State U., Northridge, 1961. Cost engr. Rand Corp., Santa Monica, Calif., 1961-63; mem. ops. rsch. staff Lockheed Aircraft Co., Burbank, Calif., 1963-65; mem. tech. staff Hughes Aircraft Co., El Segundo, Calif., 1965-66; sr. rsch. staff assoc. Northrop Corp., Hawthorne, Calif., 1966-69; sr. scientist Booz-Allen Applied Rsch., Inglewood, Calif., 1969-70; mgr. TRW, Inc., Redondo Beach, Calif., 1970-71; pvt. practice Carson, Calif., 1971-72; project mgr. PRC, Inc., Huntsville, Ala., 1972—; cons. in field, Washington. Author, editor sci. documents. With USN, 1952-56, Korea. Recipient letter of commendation NASA, 1976, 80, 92, 95. Mem. AAAS, Am. Econ. Assn., Ops. Rsch. Soc. of Am., Nat. Space Soc., Planetary Soc., Bot. Garden Soc. of Huntsville, Historic Huntsville Soc., Friends of the Library, Am. Legion. Roman Catholic. Home and Office: 7904 Seville Dr SE Huntsville AL 35802-3124

KESTON, JOAN BALBOUL, government agency administrator; b. N.Y.C., Feb. 6, 1937; d. Sol and Adele (Gredinger) Balboul; (div. Mar. 1986); children: Lisa, Vicky, Sol. BA, N.Y.U., 1958; postgrad., Rutgers U., 1959; MPA, U. So. Calif., 1981, D in Pub. Adminstrn., 1991. Br. mgr. Social Security Adminstrn., Rockville, Md., 1978-86; exec. dir. Pub. Employees Roundtable, Washington, 1984-94, pres., 1994—; exec. asst. to dir. adminstrn. and mgmt. Office of Sec. of Def., Arlington, Va., 1994-96; sr. policy advisor Def. Info. Sch. Am. Forces Info. Svcs., Office of Sec. of Def., Ft. Meade, Md., 1996—. Editor: (books) Hagadah, 1972, Building Bridges with the Community, 1995, (newsletter) Unsung Heroes, 1986-94; co-author: (booklet) How to Celebrate Public Service Recognition Week, annually, 1986-94; contbr. articles to profl. publs. Recipient Office of Sec. of Defense Outstanding Performance award, 1991, PRes. Coun. Mgmt. Improvement Cert. Mgmt. Excellence, 1988. Mem. ASPA (nat. coun., Pres. award 1990), Federally Employed Women, Drs. Pub. Adminstrn. Assn. of U. So. Calif., Am. Consortium Pub. Arminstrn., Sr. Exec. Assn., World Affairs Coun., Inter Policy Inst. Jewish. Home: 330 Lynn Manor Dr Rockville MD 20850-4429

KETCHAND, ROBERT LEE, lawyer; b. Shreveport, La., Jan. 30, 1948; s. Woodrow Wilson and Attie Harriet (Chandler) K.; m. Alice Sue Adams, May 31, 1969; children: Peter Leland, Marjory Attie. BA, Baylor U., 1970; JD, Harvard U., 1973. Bar: Tex. 1973, Mass. 1973, D.C. 1981. Assoc., ptnr. Butler & Binior, Houston, 1976-85, Washington, 1981-82; shareholder Brodsky & Ketchand, Houston, 1985-88; ptnr. Webster & Sheffield, Houston, 1988-90; atty. pvt. practice, Houston, 1990-92; ptnr. Short & Ketchand, Houston, 1992—. Pres. Prisoner Svcs. Com. Houston, 1986; deacon South Houston Bapt. Ch., 1976—; gen. counsel, dir. Houston Met. Ministries, 1986-88; dir. Interfaith Ministries; gen. counsel Houston Bus. Roundtable, 1988—. Lt. USNR, 1973-76. Mem. ABA, Tex. Bar Assn., Houston Bar Assn. (chmn. dispute com. 1989-90). Home: 2707 Carolina Way Houston TX 77005 Office: Short & Ketchand 11 Greenway Plz Ste 1520 Houston TX 77046

KETCHUM, HARRY WILBUR, JR., software engineer; b. Selma, Ala., Apr. 6, 1937; s. Harry Wilbur and Sybil May (Leuty) K. BA in Math., Am. U., 1961; MS in Computer Sci., George Washington U., 1983, AS in Computer Sci., 1989. Program writer Am. Fin. & Mgmt. Corp., 1963-65, 69-72; program designer and implementer U. Md., 1965-66; program designer and writer Macke Vending Inc., 1966-67; software designer and writer George Washington U., Washington, 1968-69; cons. Sigmatics, 1972-73; computer systems specialist System Devel. Corp. (now UNISYS), 1973-84; sr. tech. assoc. OSDI Def. System, Inc., 1984-85; computer scientist Computer Scis. Corp., 1985-88; software engr. Andrulis Rsch. Corp., 1988-89, Statistica, Inc., Reston, Va., 1989-94; sr. software engr. Sci. Applications Internat. Corp., McLean, Va., 1994—; cons. Nat. Hdqs., SSS, Suitland, Md., 1972-73. Mem. Data Processing Mgmt. Assn., Assn. for Computing Machinery, Sigada Inst. Republican. Presbyterian. Home: 4877 Battery Ln # B Bethesda MD 20814-2724 Office: Sci Applications Internat 1710 Goodridge Dr Mc Lean VA 22102-3603

KETNER, KENNETH LAINE, philosopher, educator; b. Mountain Home, Okla., Mar. 24, 1939; s. Louis Elaine and Johnnie Lucille (Hannah) K.; m. Berti Gabriella Zehetmeier, Aug. 24, 1964; 1 child, Kenneth Laine Jr. B.A. in Philosophy, Okla. State U., 1961, M.A., 1967; M.A. in Folklore, UCLA, 1968; Ph.D. in Philosophy, U. Calif., Santa Barbara, 1972. Part-time instr. Okla. State U., 1964-67; teaching asst. U. Calif., Santa Barbara, 1969-70; mem. faculty Tex. Tech U., Lubbock, 1971—; prof. philosophy Tex. Tech U., 1977—, chmn. dept., 1979-81; founder, dir. Inst. Studies in Pragmaticism, 1972—; Charles Sanders Peirce prof. philosophy, 1981—; asst. prof. philosophy and folklore UCLA, summers, 1972, 74; co-organizer C.S. Peirce Bicentennial Internat. Congress, Amsterdam, Netherlands 1976; Peirce Sesquicentennial Internat. Congress, Harvard U., 1989. Author: A Critical Study of Stephen C. Pepper's Approach to Metaphysics, 1967, An Essay on the Nature of World Views, 1972, An Emendation of R.G. Collingwood's Doctrine of Absolute Presuppositions, 1973; editor, compiler: Charles Sanders Peirce: Contributions to the Nation, 4 parts, 1975, 78, 79, 87, Comprehensive Bibliography of Works of C.S. Peirce, 1977, rev. edit., 1986, Reasoning and the Logic of Things, 1993, A Thief of Peirce, 1995; founder, gen. editor Peirce Studies, 1979—, Philosophical Inquiries, 1989—, more. Capt. USAR, 1962-64. Grantee NSF; Grantee Nat. Endowment Humanities; Grantee Am. Council Learned Socs. Fellow Charles S. Peirce Soc. (pres. 1973); mem. Am. Philos. Assn., Rotary, Free Mason, Tau Kappa Epsilon. Democrat. Home: PO Box 65135 Lubbock TX 79464-5135 Office: Texas Tech Univ Library 304 A Lubbock TX 79409-0002

KETRON, CARRIE SUE, secondary school educator; b. Clifton, Tex.; d. Randolph Allen and Mary (Waggoner) Ogden; m. N.M. Ketron, Aug. 4, 1984; children: John, Robert. B of Applied Arts and Scis., U. North Tex., 1990, MEd, 1993. Tchr. Duncanville (Tex.) High Sch., 1982—. Named Tchr. of Yr. Tex. Vocat. Tech. Assn., 1990. Mem. Golden Key Honor Soc., Am. Vocat. Assn., Cosmetology Instructors' of Pub. Schs. (parliamentarian 1989-90), Vocat. Indsl. Clubs Am. (advisor 1986-93), Iota Lambda Sigma Sigma (pres. 1995-96), Phi Theta Kappa, Alpha Chi. Baptist. Home: 2 Lookout Cv Granbury TX 76048-4310

KEULEGAN, EMMA PAULINE, special education educator; b. Washington, Jan. 21, 1930; d. Garbis H. and Nellie Virginia (Moore) K. BA, Dumbarton Coll. of Holy Cross, 1954. Cert. tchr. elem. and spl. edn. Tchr. St. Dominic's Elem. Sch., Washington, 1954-56, Sacred Heart Acad., Washington, 1956-59, Our Lady of Victory, Washington, 1959-63, St. Francis Acad., Vicksburg, Miss., 1963-78; tchr. Culkin Acad., Vicksburg, 1978-91, substitute tchr. spl. edn., 1991—. Treas. PTA, Vicksburg, 1980. Mem. Internat. Reading Assn. (pres. Warren County chpt.), Colonial Dames 17th Century (state v.p. 1987-89, state pres. 1989, hon. state pres. 1991—), Daus. Am. Colonists (state pres. 1992-94, hon. state pres. 1994—, chaplain 1985-89), DAR (chpt. regent 1967-69, sec. 1994, chpt. chaplain 1996). Republican. Roman Catholic. Home: 215 Buena Vista Dr Vicksburg MS 39180-5612 Office: Cedars Elem School 235 Cedars School Cir Vicksburg MS 39180-2571

KEULING-STOUT, FRANCES EILEEN, literature and poetics educator; b. Bronx, N.Y., June 3, 1946; d. William Augustus and Frances Theresa (Hebron) Keuling; m. Henry Smith Stout, Mar. 3, 1984. BA, St. John's U., Bklyn., 1967; MA, NYU, 1972, MPhil, 1984, postgrad., 1978—. English tchr. Scanlan H.S., Bronx, 1968-75; univ. supr. secondary English Queens Coll., Flushing, N.Y., 1975; instr. English U. N.C., Charlotte, 1975-79; preceptor English composition NYU, N.Y.C., 1980-83; treas. & office adminstr. Keuling-Stout, P.C., Big Stone Gap, Va., 1988—; adj. instr. English Nassau C.C., L.I., N.Y., 1974-75. Author of poetry. Active Women's Pastoral Project, Com. for U.S. Bishops, Big Stone Gap, 1988-89; pres. Sacred Heart Parish Coun., Big Stone Gap, 1990-91; mem. steering com. Appalachian Sch. Law, Va., 1994-96, deans selection com., 1996—. Scholar English Speaking Union, Charlotte, summer 1978; Fellowship grantee for poetry Am. Poet, 1978. Mem. MLA (Am. Lit. sect.). Roman Catholic. Home: 17 Wyandotte Ave West Big Stone Gap VA 24219 Office: Keuling-Stout PC 123 Wood Ave East Big Stone Gap VA 24219

KEUNG, YI-KONG, oncologist, hematologist; b. Hong Kong, Jan. 27, 1961; came to U.S., 1989; m. Amy Keung, June 3, 1989; 2 children. MB, BS, U. Hong Kong, 1985. Intern, resident U. Med. Unit Hong Kong U., 1985-89; fellow in hematology/med. oncology U. So. Calif., L.A., 1989-92, fellow in bone marrow transplant, 1992-93; asst. prof. divsn. oncology/hematology Tex. Tech. U. Sch. Medicine, Lubbock, 1993—, dir. bone marrow transplant, 1994—; investigator Southwest Oncology Group, U.S., 1993, Nat. Cancer Inst., U.S., 1993. Mem. AMA, ACP, Am. Soc. Hematology. Office: Tex Tech Univ Health Scis 3601 Fourth St Lubbock TX 79430

KEVORKIAN, RICHARD, artist; b. Dearborn, Mich., Aug. 24, 1937; s. Kay and Stana (Bedeian) K.; m. Salpy Bouroujian; children: Anna, Raffi, Soseh and Ellina (twins), Serar. BFA, Richmond Profl. Inst., 1961; MFA in Painting, Calif. Coll. Arts and Crafts, 1962. Instr. drawing and painting Richard Bland Coll., Petersburg, Va., 1961-64; instr. dept. fine arts Va. Commonwealth U., Richmond, 1962-66, asst. prof. dept. painting and printmaking, 1967-69, assoc. prof., 1969-77, prof., 1967-93, prof. emeritus, 1993, chmn. dept., 1969-81. One-man exhbns. include Aaron Gallery, Washington, Marita Gilliam Gallery, Raleigh, N.C.; exhbns. include Birmingham Mus. Art, Ala., 1977, Greenville County Mus. Art, S.C., 1977, Southeastern Ctr. Contemporary Art, Winston-Salem, N.C., 1977, 78, Hunter Mus. Art, Chattanooga, 1978, Va. Mus. Fine Art, 1983, U. Tenn., Knoxville, 1983. Mem. selection bd. for visual arts Va. Ctr. for Creative Arts, Sweet Briar. Served with N.G., 1955-63. NEA individual sr. artists grantee, 1972, Va. Commonwealth U. Sch. Arts faculty creative research grantee, 1974, Nat. Endowment for Arts, Southeastern Ctr. Contemporary Arts grantee, 1976; Guggenheim fellow, 1978. Home: 7909 Rock Creek Rd Richmond VA 23229-6643

KEWALRAMANI, LAXMAN SUNDERDAS, surgeon, consultant; b. Jaipur, India, Mar. 10, 1943; came to U.S., 1970, U.S. citizen; s. Sunderdas K. and Sugnidevi Kewalramani; m. Dropadi Chellani, May 29, 1970; children: Anupama, Mukul. MB, BS, U. Rajasthn, Jaipur, 1965, M of Surgery, 1969. Diplomate Am. Bd. Phys. Medicine & Rehab., Am. Bd. Electrodiagnostic Medicine (fellow), Am. Acad. Pain Mgmt. (fellow). Fellow neurol. surgery U. Calif. Davis-Sacramento Med. Ctr., 1970-71, resident in phys. medicine and rehab., 1971-73; asst. prof. dept. phys. medicine and rehab. U. Calif., Davis, 1973-76; asst. prof. depts. phys. medicine and rehab. Baylor Coll. Medicine, Houston, 1976-79; assoc. prof. sect. rheumatology and rehab. dept. medicine sch. medicine La. State U., New Orleans, 1979-82; dir. rehab. rsch., coord. patient care La. Rehab. Inst. and Charity Hosp., New Orleans, 1979-82; pvt. practice in phys. medicine and rehab., orthopedic medicine, electrodiagnostic medicine and thermography, 1982—; med. dir. Health South Rehab. Ctr., Harahan, La., 1989-91; med. dir. rehab. unit Chalmette (La.) Med. Ctrs., 1991-92; med. dir. spine and orthopedic inst. Elmwood Med. Ctr., Jefferson, La., 1993—; cons. rehab. medicine svc. crippled children svcs. sect. VA Hosp., 1975-76; mem. quality assurance com. Charity Hosp. and La. Rehab. Inst., New Orleans, 1979-82; presenter in field. Reviewer manuscripts, cons. editorial bd. Archives Phys. Medicine and Rehab., 1977-80; contbr. 2 chpts. to books and 96 articles to profl. jours. Cons. Cluster Living and Shared Providers, 1978; trustee New Orleans Pharmacy Mus., 1993—. Fellow Am. Acad. Phys. Medicine and Rehab. (mem. assessment diagnostic and therapeutic modalities and devices, subcom. med. practice 1985-86); mem. Am. Spinal Injury Assn., Am. Assn. Physicians India (mem. ethics and grievance com. 1992—), Am. Assn. Electrodiagnostic Medicine, Am. Assn. Electromyography and Electrodiagnosis (mem., liaison rep. to profl. stds. com. 1984—), La. State Med. Soc., La. Phys. Medicine and Rehab. Soc., Orleans Parish Med. Soc., Internat. Med. Soc. Paraplegia. Republican. Hindu. Home: 3305 Saint Charles Ave New Orleans LA 70115-4533 Office: Elmwood Med Ctr 417 S Johnson St New Orleans LA 70112-2237 also: 417 S Johnson St New Orleans LA 70112-2237

KEWLEY, SHARON LYNN, systems analyst, consultant; b. Geneseo, Ill., Sept. 23, 1958; d. James Leslie and Geraldine (Myers) K. BBA with honors, U. Miami (Fla.), 1988. Gen. agent Varvaris & Assocs., Cedar Rapids, Iowa, 1981-84; programmer, analyst U. Miami, Coral Gables, Fla., 1984-88; systems analyst Metro Dade County, Miami, 1988-91, Nat. Coun. on Compensation Ins., Boca Raton, Fla., 1991-93; owner Boca Byte, Boca Raton, Fla., 1993—; owner Boca Byte, Boca Baton, Fla. Mem. NAFE, Kendall Jaycees, Nat. Gold Key Honor Soc., PADI Divemaster. Republican. Lutheran. Office: Boca Byte PO Box 7072 Boca Raton FL 33431-0072

KEY, JANICE DIXON, physician, medical educator; b. Hickory, N.C., Aug. 14, 1954; d. Charles Dennis and Mary Louise (Edgerton) Dixon; m. L. Lyndon Key Jr., May 27, 1973; children: Rebecca Louise, Emily Edgerton. BS, U. N.C., 1976, MD, 1980. Clin. instr. Harvard Med. Sch., Boston, 1984-85; clin. assoc. prof. Sch. of Medicine, U. N.C., Greensboro, N.C., 1985-91; asst. prof. Med. U. of S.C., Charleston, S.C., 1991—. Author: Ambulatory Pediatric Care, 1992; contbr. to profl. jours. com. mem. S.C. Adolescent Task Force, Charleston, 1993, S.C. Dept. Edn., Columbia, 1992, S.C. Sch. Health Advisory, Columbia, 1992; co-chairperson Sch. Health Com., Charleston, 1992—; community adv. bd. Jr. League, Charleston, 1994;. Recipient Faculty Rsch. award U. N.C., 1978. Fellow Am. Acad. Pediatrics; mem. Am. Soc. Human Genetics, Soc. Adolescent Medicine (chpt. pres. 1991—), Am. Med. Women's Assn., S.C. Med. Assn., S.C. Pediatric Med. Soc. (CME com. 1994—), Phi Beta Kappa, Phi Eta Sigma. Democrat. Presbyterian. Office: 171 Ashley Ave Charleston SC 29425-0001

KEY, KAREN LETISHA, pharmaceutical executive; b. Sanford, N.C., Jan. 17, 1957; d. Kermit Lee and Ruth (Whitaker) K. BS in Phys. Edn., Appalachian State U., 1978; MBA, U. N.C., 1993. Profl. sales rep. Burroughs Wellcome Co., Florence, S.C., 1982-84; field trainer Burroughs Wellcome Co., Kernersville, N.C., 1984-87; field mgmt. trainee then asst. product mgr. Cardiovasculars/Antivirals/Psychotropics, Research Triangle Park, N.C., 1987-90, dist. sales mgr. psychiatry, 1990-91, asst. to sr. v.p. prodn. and engring., 1991-92, mgr. mktg. tng. and devel., 1991-92, product mgr. neuromuscular blockers, 1993-94; product mgr. Zoverax/Valtrix, 1994—; project mgr. care mgmt. divsn. Glaxo Wellcome, Raleigh, N.C., 1995; dir. bus. ops. Glaxo Wellcome, Raleigh, 1996—. Choir mem. Lakewood Bapt. Ch., tchr. Sun. sch. Republican. Baptist. Office: 4011 West Chase Blvd Raleigh NC 27607

KEYES, BENJAMIN B., therapist; b. Alexandria, Va., Sept. 18, 1953; s. Jay F. and Harriet Edith (Champagne) K.; m. Natalie Ann Keyes, Nov. 1, 1989; children: Shawn David, Jasmin Victoria, Sara Danielle, Alyssa Marie, Amanda Beth. MA, U. South Fla., 1978; PhD, Internat. Coll., 1985; ThD., DMin., Zoe Coll., 1985; DD, Reeves Christian Coll., 1987. Lic. profl. counselor, Tex., mental health counselor, Fla., practitioner, cons.; nat. cert. mental health counselor. Psychologist Baker Correctional Instn., Olustee, Fla.; prof. grad. sch. Fla. Beacon Bible Coll., Largo; dir. Charis Inc., Clearwater, Fla.; dir. clin. programs partial hospitalization Rapha Inc., Pasadena, Tex.; clin. dir. Bridgework Ministry, Clearwater; pvt. practice counselor, cons.; evaluator accreditation Dept. Corrections, 1984; dir. Manors Hosp., Largo, Fla.; program dir. Medfield Hosp., Largo; CEO Daylight Partial Hospitalization Programs, St. Petersburg, Fla. Co-author: Family Training Manual, E Pluribus Unum From Many to One; author: Sexuality, Learning and Teaching Modality, Christian Counseling, Substance Abuse Manual, A Christian Approach to Inner Healing No More Turning Away, A Christian Approach to Treating Dissociative Identity Disorder; contbr. articles to profl. jours. Recipient Appreciation cert. ARC, 1980-84, Youth award Trinity United Meth. Ch., 1980-81. Mem. AACC, Am. Mental Health Counselors Assn., Am. Counseling Assn., Assn. Ambulatory Behavioral Healthcare, Am. Rehab. Counseling Assn., Assn. Religious and Value Issues Counseling, Christians Who Do Therapy Assn., Assn. Christian Therapists, Internat. Soc. Study of Dissociation (mem. Tampa Bay chpt.), Internat. Assn. Counselors and Therapists (bd. dirs.), Fla. Ambulatory Partial Hospitalization Assn., Network of Christian Counselors, Upper Pinellas Minsterial Assn. (treas., v.p.), Fla. Rehab. Assn. (past exec. bd.), Fla. Rehab. Counseling Assn. (past regional rep.), Psi Chi. Home: 6095 2d Ave S Saint Petersburg FL 33707

KEYES, DAVID ELLIOT, scientific computing educator, researcher; b. Bklyn., Dec. 4, 1956; s. Elliot Fuller and Edna (Corsini) K.; married; 2 children. BSME, Princeton U., 1978; MS in Applied Math., Harvard U., 1979, PhD in Applied Math., 1984. Rsch. assoc. Yale U., Dept. Computer Sci., New Haven, Conn., 1984-85; asst. prof. Yale U., Dept. Mechanical Engring., New Haven, 1986-90; assoc. prof. dept. mech. engring. Yale U., 1990-94; assoc. prof. dept. computer sci. Old Dominion U., 1993—; dir. Program in High Performance Computing and Comm., Va. Inst. for Computer Applications and Sci. Engring., Langley Rsch. Ctr., 1994—; vis. scientist Inst. Computer Applications in Sci. and Engring., Hampton, Va., 1990, sr. rsch. assoc., 1993—. Editor: Domain Decomposition Methods in Partial

Differential Equations, 1991, Domain-based Parallelism and Problem Decomposition Methods, 1995, Domain Decomposition Methods in Scientific and Engineering Computing, 1995, Parrallel Munerical Alogrithms, 1996; mem. editorial bd. Internat. Jour. for Supercomputer Applications, 1994—; contbr. articles to profl. jours. Named Presdl. Young Investigator, NSF, Washington, 1989. Mem. ASME, AIAA (coun. mem. 1991-93, chair 1992-93), Soc. Indsl. and Applied Math. (sec. 1991-93, vis. lectr. 1992—), Assn. for Computing Machinery, The Combustion Inst., Tau Beta Pi, Sigma Xi, Phi Beta Kappa. Office: ICASE NASA Langley Rsch Ctr MS 403 Hampton VA 23681-0001

KEYES, DAVID TAYLOR, telecommunications company administrator; b. Providence, Feb. 18, 1947; s. Leonard Taylor and Alice (Whitwam) K.; m. Martha Ann Bearden, Dec. 22, 1973; children: Joshua Ryan, Caroline Louise. BBA, Fla. Internat. U., 1977; MS in Mgmt. Sci., U. Miami, 1981. Cert. quality engr. Communications technician Network Ops. AT&T, Miami, Fla., 1973-81, sales supr. Nat. Accounts, 1981-84; staff supr. Network Engrng. AT&T, Atlanta, 1984-87; quality cons. Network Svc. div. AT&T, Conyers, Ga., 1987—. With USN, 1967-73, Vietnam. Mem. Am. Soc. Quality Control. Home: 4158 Azalea Ct Lithonia GA 30058-7257

KEYES, EMMALOU, nurse practitioner; b. Hutchinson, Kans., Nov. 13, 1931; d. Ferguson and Virginia Lucile (Copenhaver) Reynolds; m. Mark B. Cripe, Nov. 13, 1953 (div. 1962); m. William Robert Keyes, Mar. 24, 1967 (dec. Mar. 1989); children: Lee Edward, Jay Scott. BS in Nursing, Pan Am. U., 1984; MS in Nursing, Corpus Christi State U., 1988. Cert. family nurse practitioner. Pub. health nurse Hidalgo County Health Dept., Edinburg, Tex., 1952-77; family nurse practitioner Hidalgo County Health Care Corp., Edinburg, 1977-79; title XIX screener Tex. Dept. Health, Austin, 1979-80; sch. nurse Progreso (Tex.) Ind. Sch. Dist., 1980-82; clinic services dir. Planned Parenthood, McAllen, Tex., 1982—; bd. dirs., disaster nurse ARC, McAllen; instr. Pan Am. nursing dept. BSN program U. Tex. Mem. Am. Nurses Assn., Tex. Nurses Assn. (dist. pres., treas., bd. dirs.), Am. Pub. Health Assn., Nat. Assn. Nurses in Family Planning, Am. Heart Assn. Episcopalian. Home: 21 S 35th St Mcallen TX 78501-8233 Office: Planned Parenthood 1017 Pecan Blvd Mcallen TX 78501-4345

KEYES, JOYCE ANN HESTER, academic director, consultant, researcher; b. Oxford, N.C.; d. Melvin and Mary Elizabeth Hester; div. 1993; children: Rhonda, Barrett, Chastity. BS in Edn., Ind. U., 1972, MS in Spl. Edn., 1975; DEd in Adminstrn. and Supervision, Va. Poly. and State U., 1982. Cert. elem. tchr., N.C., supt., N.C., behaviorally and emotionally handicapped, N.C., reading, N.C., exceptional children program adminstr., N.C., prin., N.C., curriculum instructional specialist, N.C. Tchr. Hammond (Ind.) City Schs., 1972-73; faculty asst., grad. asst. Ind. U.-Purdue U., Indpls., 1974-76; instr. Ind. Pub. Schs., Indpls., 1976-77, Pensacola (Fla.) Jr. Coll., 1977; instr. spl. edn. Norfolk (Va.) Pub. Schs., 1978-79; spl. edn. resource Frederick (Md.) County Schs., 1979-83; grad., rsch. asst. Va. Poly. and State U., 1981-82; adminstr. edn., spl. educator Dept. Navy, 1984-87; lectr. U. N.C., Wilmington, 1987-88; ednl. cons. Ednl. Diagnostic-Prescriptive Ctr., Jacksonville, N.C., 1987-92; evaln. specialist evaln. and rsch. dept. Wake County Pub. Schs., Raleigh, 1993-94; dir. edn. dept. Shaw U., Raleigh, 1994—. Bd. dirs. Onslow County Arts Coun., Jacksonville, N.C., 1988-90. Mem. Am. Ednl. Rsch. Assn., Wake, Durham and Orange Counties' Higher Edn. Triangle Alliance, N.C. Assn. Tchr. Educators, Coun. Exceptional Children, Coun. Adminstrs. Spl. Education, Coun. Children with Behavioral Disorders, CEC Divsn. Learning Disabilities, Coun. Ednl. Diagnostic Svcs., Phi Delta Kappa, Delta Sigma Theta. Home: 8208 Old Deer Tr Raleigh NC 27615 Office: Shaw U 118 E South St Raleigh NC 27601

KEYES, SAMUEL WAYNE, JR., lawyer; b. Brookhaven, Miss., Feb. 13, 1953; married; 2 children. BS in Community and Regional Planning, U. So. Miss., 1976; JD, U. Miss., 1981. Bar: Miss. 1981. Planner Gulf Regional Planning Commn., Gulfport, Miss., 1975-76; dir. Jackson County Community Devel., Pascagoula, Miss., 1976-78; pvt. practice, lawyer Gulfport, Jackson, Miss., 1981-85; asst. atty. gen. State of Miss., 1985-93, dep. atty. gen., 1993-94; with firm Crosthwait Terney PLLC, Jackson, Miss., 1994—. Lt. col. Miss. Air N.G., 1977—. Decorated Bronze Star. Mem. Miss. Bar (bd. dirs. govt. law sect. 1991-93, sec., treas. 1994-95, vice chair 1995-96, chair 1996-97), Capital Optimist Club (pres. 1987-88, bd. dirs. 1991-92), Leadership Miss., Phi Delta Phi, Phi Kappa Phi, Pi Gamma Mu. Southern Baptist. Office: Crosthwait Terney PLLC PO Box 2398 Jackson MS 39225-2398

KEYSER-FANICK, CHRISTINE LYNN, banker, marketing professional; b. Ft. Dodge, Iowa, Nov. 16, 1956; d. Archie Harlan and LaVonne Janette (Larsen) Keyser. AA, Iowa Cen. Community Coll., Ft. Dodge, 1976; BA, U. No. Iowa, 1979; MA, Drake U., 1985; grad. with honors, Sch. Bank Mktg., Boulder, Colo., 1990. Educator Marshalltown (Iowa) Community Schs., 1979-84; v.p. LaGrave Klipfel Clarkson, Inc., Des Moines, 1985-87; pub. rels. and mktg. cons. Des Moines, 1987-88; asst. prof. Drake U., Des Moines, 1988; dir. mktg. 1st Interstate Bank, Des Moines, 1988-89; v.p. Am. Trust & Savings Bank, Dubuque, Iowa, 1989-94; sr. v.p. San Antonio Fed. Credit Union, 1994—; speaker leadership confs. various univs., 1985—; v.p. Women in Mgmt., 1991, pres.-elect, 1992-93, pres., 1993. Contbr. articles to Iowa Commerce Mag., 1988-93. Bd. dirs. Iowa Soc. to Prevent Blindness, Des Moines, 1987-91, Dubuque Main St. Ltd., 1990-93, v.p., 1993; bd. dirs. Dubuque Symphony Orch., 1990-93, Dubuque Coun. for Diversity, 1992-94; bd. dirs., bus. devel. chair Dubuque Main St., 1991-94; mem. pub. rels. com., devel. com. San Antonio area coun. Girls Scouts, U.S., 1994—; mem. pub. rels. com., memls. com. San Antonio chpt. Am. Heart Assn. Named New Bd. Mem. of Yr., Iowa Soc. to Prevent Blindness, 1988, Vol. of Yr., Iowa Main St., 1993; recipient Nat. Charlotte Danstrom Women of Achievement award, 1992. Mem. Pub. Rels. Soc. Am. (pres. Greater Dubuque chpt. 1993, v.p. 1991-92, San Antonio chpt. bd. dirs. 1995—, pres.-elect 1996, accredited), Bank Mktg. Assn. (adv. coun. 1989-93), ITS Inc. Mktg. Com. Advertisers of Dubuque (legis. chair 1990-93, bd. dirs. 1991-93), Dubuque Area C. of C. (membership adv. coun. 1993-94, media coord. Iowa Trade Symposium 1990, All Am. City com. 1994-95). Home: 7114 Valley Trails St San Antonio TX 78250-3477 Office: San Antonio Fd Credit Union PO Box 1356 San Antonio TX 78295-1356

KEYSERLING, HARRY L., pediatric infectious disease physician, researcher; b. Beaufort, S.C., Dec. 10, 1950; s. William King and Polly Leah (Jacobson) K. BA, Johns Hopkins U., 1973; MD, Georgetown U., 1977. Asst. prof. pediats. Emory U. Sch. Medicine, Atlanta, 1982-90, assoc. prof. pediats., 1990—; med. dir. microbiology/virology labs. Egleston Children's Hosp., Atlanta, 1989—. Nat. bd. dirs. Physicians for Social Responsibility, Atlanta, 1994—. Fellow Am. Acad. Pediats. (chmn. infectious disease com. Ga. chpt.); mem. Am. Soc. Microbiology, Pediat. Infectious Disease Soc., So. Soc. for Pediat. Rsch., Soc. for Healthcare Epidemiology Am. Office: Emory U Sch Medicine 2040 Ridgewood Dr NE Atlanta GA 30322

KEZAR, DENNIS DEAN, English language educator; b. Oxford, Eng., June 29, 1968; came to U.S., 1970; s. Dennis D. and Sandra (Knight) K. BA, U. of South, 1990; MA, U. Va., 1992, postgrad., 1992—. Tchr. Phillips Andover (Mass.) Acad., 1990-91, Choate Rosemary Acad., Wallingford, Conn., 1992-93; instr. Renaissance drama U. Va., Charlottesivlle, 1992—; instr. U. of South, Sewanee, Tenn., 1995; lectr. Sewanee Summer Seminar, 1995. Contbr. articles to profl. jours. DuPont fellow U. Va., 1992-96, dissertation fellow, 1996-97. Mem. Renaissance Assn. Am., Internat. Shakespeare Assn., South Ea. Lang. Assn. Episcopalian. Home: 1212 Wertland St Charlottesville VA 22903 Office: U Va Dept English Bryan Hall Charlottesville VA 22903

KHALEELUDDIN, MANSOOR, broadcast executive. BBA in Mktg., U. Okla., 1989, MBA in Mktg., 1991. Mktg. cons. The Music Gallery, Ltd., Oklahoma City, 1989-90; promotions dir., music dir., asst. program dir. Sta. KRXO-FM Radio, Oklahoma City, 1990—. Presdl. scholar U. Okla. Home: 3020 Weymouth Way Norman OK 73071-7270 Office: 820 SW 4th St Moore OK 73160

KHALIL, A. ARIF, cardiologist; b. Baghdad, Jan. 16, 1964; s. Mohammed Ali and Latifa (Kaftan) K. MD, Royal Coll. Surgeons, Dublin, Ireland, 1988. Lic. physician, Ireland, Eng., Calif., Tex. Intern Internat. Missionary Tng. Hosp., Dragheda, Ireland, 1988-89; resident in internal medicine Baylor Affiliated Hosps., Houston, 1989-92, cardiology fellow, 1992-96; pvt. practice gen. and internat. cardiology South Tex. Med. Clinics, Wharton, Tex., 1996—. Mem. AMA, Am. Coll. Cardiology. Office: South Texas Medical Clinics 2100 Regional Medical Dr Wharton TX 77488

KHAN, KHALID SAIFULLAH, engineering executive; b. Calcutta, India, Sept. 19, 1949; arrived in Can., 1974; s. Tahir Ali and Fatima (Bibi) K.; m. Jamila Bibi, Apr. 20, 1982; children: M. Tariq, Kamron. BEE, Osmania U., 1973; MEE, Concordia U., Montreal, Can., 1978. Asst. exec. engr. Teleglobe Can., Montreal, 1978-80; R&D engr. GTE Internat., Waltham, Mass., 1980-82; sr. engr. Aydin Corp., San Jose, Calif., 1982-84; project engrng. mgr. FMC Corp., Dallas, 1984-86; tech. mktg. mgr. Dalsat Inc., Plano, Tex., 1986-89; system engr. Andrew Corp., Richardson, Tex., 1989-90; mgr. SATCOM engrng. MCI Telecomm., Richardson, 1990-96; dir. Lockheed Martin Missiles and Space, Sunnyvale, Calif., 1996—; tchr. U. Dallas, Tex., 1988-91; seminar presenter in field. Contbr. articles to profl. jours. Mem. IEEE, Order of Engr. of Que., Can. Home: 3708 Glover Dr Plano TX 75074 Office: Lockheed Martin Missiles and Space 1322 Crossman Ave Sunnyvale CA 94089-1113

KHAN, MASRUR ALI, nuclear and chemical engineer, physicist; b. Faridpur, Bangladesh, Sept. 24, 1949; arrived in U.S. 1971; s. Yakub Ali Khan and Mahbuba (Karim) Begum; m. Cynthia Louise Reilly, Aug. 8, 1975; children: Tarik, Alia. BS in Physics, U. Dhaka, 1971; BSChemE, U. Wis., 1974, BS in Nuclear Engring., 1976. Group leader for environ. group Commonwealth Edison Co.; with H.B. Robinson Plant; project mgr. Carolina Power and Light Co.; cons. Brunswick Steam Electric Plant, 1981-94, Pub. Svc. Electric and Gas Co., 1989-90, Pa. Power and Light Co., 1990-92; pres. Khan Consulting Svcs., Cary, N.C.; with ConEd, 1995—; mgmt. cons., ind. reviewer N.Y. Power Authority's DBDs, 6 ConEd nuc. cites; cons. Pa. Power and Light Co. Contbr. articles to profl. jours. Mem. ASME, AIChE, Am. Mgmt. Assn., Project Mgmt. Inst., Assn. for Info. and Image Mgmt., Assn. Computing Machinery, Am. Nuclear Soc. Home: 217 Brendan Choice Cary NC 27511-5508

KHAN, MOHAMMAD SHAMIM, civil engineer; b. Gorakphur, India, Feb. 1, 1957; came to U.S., 1991; s. Mohammad Ismail and Nagina Ismail Khan; m. Shabina Farhat Ali, Apr. 4, 1987; 1 child, Mariam Shamim. BSCE, Aligarh Muslim U., Uttar Pardesh, India, 1980; MSCE, U. Petroleum and Minerals, Dhahran, Saudi Arabia, 1985; PhD in Civil Engring., Okla. State U., 1992. Registered profl. engr., D.C., Md. Asst. engr. Uttar Pardesh State Bridge Corp., 1982-83; rsch. asst. dept. civil engring. U. Petroleum and Minerals, 1983-85, rsch. engr. Rsch. Inst., 1985-90; rsch. assoc. Okla. State U., Stillwater, 1991-92; dir. rsch. and mktg. Concorr, Inc., Herndon, Va., 1993-95; dept. mgr. Profl. Svc. Industries, Inc., Fairfax, Va., 1995—. Contbr. articles to profl. jours. Recipient Okla. State U. Grad. Rsch. award, 1992; Nat. Merit scholar Uttar Pardesh Edn. Bd., 1973. Mem. ASCE, Am. Concrete Inst., Nat. Assn. Corrosion Engrs. (Mars Fontana fellow 1991), Phi Kappa Phi, Tau Beta Pi, Chi Epsilon. Islam. Home: 9451 Lee Hwy #403 Fairfax VA 22031 Office: Profl Svc Industries Inc 2930 Eskridge Rd Fairfax VA 22031

KHAN-DAWOOD, FIRYAL SULTANA, obstetrics/gynecology educator; b. Addis Ababa, Ethiopa, Dec. 24, 1948; came to U.S., 1977; d. Furqan Hassan and Mariam Sultana (Naqvi) Khan; m. Mohamed Yusoff, July 14, 1978; children: Fatimah, Fauzia, Firdaus, Hassan. BSc in Med. Biochemistry, U. Surrey (Eng.), 1969; MSc in Steroid Endocrinology, U. Leeds (Eng.), 1970; PhD in Biochemistry, U. London (Eng.), 1977. Rsch. assoc. Cornell U. Med. Sch., N.Y.C., 1977-79; rsch. assoc. U. Ill., Chgo., 1979-80, instr., 1980-83, asst. prof. Ob-gyn., 1983-89, assoc. prof. Ob-gyn., 1989-90; assoc. prof. Ob-gyn. U. Tex., Houston, 1990—. Contbr. 80 articles to profl. jours. Syntex scholar U. Leeds, 1969-70; NIH grantee, 1989. Mem. AAAS, Biochem. Soc., Assn. Clin. Biochemists, Soc. Endocrinology, Endocrine Soc., Soc. for Study of Reproduction, Soc. for Gynecol. Investigation, Am. Fertility Soc., Soc. for the Study of Fertility, Am. Ligand Assay Soc., Assn. for Women in Sci., Women in Endocrinology, Assn. of Women Faculty and Faculty Wives, Sigma Xi. Muslim. Office: U Tex Med Sch 6431 Fannin St Houston TX 77030-1501

KHARIF, WALI RASHASH, history educator; b. Madison, Fla., Dec. 23, 1950; s. Ernest Frank Everett and Julia Mae (Brown) Rains; m. Dorthy Jean Whitlock, Apr. 13, 1974 (div. Aug. 1976); m. Shakura Diane Davis, Aug. 3, 1977; children: Muhammad, Sharia, Raushan, Khalil. BA in History and Govt., Fla. State U., 1972, MA in History, 1973, PhD in History, 1983. Rsch. asst. Inst. for Social Rsch. Fla. State U., Tallahassee, 1973, security guard I, 1973-74; dist. enforcement coord. Fla. Dept. Environ. Regulation, Tallahassee, 1974-84; temp. instr. divsn. bus. and social scis. South Ga. Coll., 1984-86; rsch. assoc., tutor Kharif & Assocs. Ednl. Svcs., Tallahassee, 1986; case processor divsn. of inspections Fla. Dept. Agr., 1986-88; assoc. prof. history dept. Tenn. Tech. U., Cookeville, 1988—; part-time instr. history dept. Fla. State U., 1975; mem. search com. Tenn. Tech. U., 1989-90, 90-91, 92-93, student affairs com., 1989—, advisor Black Students Orgn., 1989—; mem. Tenn. Conf. Historians; adv. bd. dirs. So. Conf. Afro-Am. Studies, Inc., 1992-95; lectr. and presenter in field. Contbg. author: A Tennessee Unionist: Andrew Johnson and Reconstruction of the South, 1989; contbr. book revs., articles to pub. jours. Coord. United Way Campaign, Tenn. Tech. U., 1991, 92; exec. bd. dirs. Lazarus House Hospice, Cookeville, 1990—, 2d v.p., 1992-94, pres., 1994-95; active Fla. Hist. Soc. Recipient Outstanding Achievement award Tallahassee chpt. Assn. for Study of Afro-Am. Life and History, 1974, Cert. Appreciation, Tenn. Tech. Upward Bound Program, 1991, 92, Sponsor of Yr. award Black Student Orgn., Tenn. Tech. U., 1990; William Randolph Hearst Senate youth scholar Hearst Found., 1968-70; faculty rsch. grantee Tenn. Tech. U., 1990-91, 91-92, 93-94; grad. fellow Fla. State U., 1972-74. Mem. AAUP (pres. Tenn. Tech. U. chpt. 1992-94), Assn. Social and Behavioral Scientists, Inc., Cookeville chpt. Toastmasters Internat., Tenn. History Club (sponsor), Chi Lambda chpt. Omega Psi Phi (advisor), Phi Alpha Theta. Democrat. Muslim. Office: Tenn Tech U Dept History PO Box 5064 Cookeville TN 38505

KHAWAJA, MABEL MASUDA, English language educator; b. Jhelum, Pakistan, Aug. 23, 1944; came to U.S., 1969; d. Ronald Peter and Dorothy (Martin) Deane; m. Azizur Rehman Khawaja; children: Atif N., Samina K. MA in History, Panjab U., Lahore, Pakistan, 1965; cert. of advanced studies, Grenoble (France) U., 1968; MA in English, Western Ill. U., 1972; PhD in English, W.Va. U., 1979. Asst. editor Bible Concordance World Coun. Chs., Lahore, 1965-66; high sch. tchr. Convent of Jesus and Mary, Murree, Pakistan, 1967-68; grad. asst. Western Ill. U., Macomb, 1969-71; instr. W.Va. U., Morgantown, 1972-76, fellow, 1977-79, asst. prof. English dept., 1979; asst. to editor Better Times Weekly, Morgantown, 1976; French translator Dept. Def., Ft. Monroe, Hampton, Va., 1980-82; translator, coord., editor Dept. Def., Ft. Monroe, Hampton, 1982-90; assoc. prof. English Hampton (Va.) U., 1990—; cons. Campus Internat. Ministry, Wesley Found., Fairmont, W.Va., 1971-72; vis. assoc. prof. English W.Va. U., 1979. Cons.: The Humanistic Tradition, 1993; contbr. essay, revs., poems, articles to profl. publs. Tchr. Adopt-A-Sch. program U.S. Army Tng. and Doctrine, Hampton, 1988-89; leader Girl Scouts U.S.A., Hampton, 1989-90; capt., block worker Am. Heart Assn., Hampton, 1991-94. Recipient Golden Poet award World of Poetry, 1992, Editor's Choice award Nat. Libr. Poetry, 1993, 94, 95, Outstanding Poet award, 1994, Cert. of Poetic Achievement, Amherst Soc., 1991, Lit. Merit awards Creative Arts and Scis. Enterprises, 1992, 93, Hon. Mention award Iliad Press, 1993; grantee NEH, 1995. Mem. MLA (participant and contributor conv. program 1993, 95, 96 and publ.), Nat. Coun. Tchrs. of English (mem. com. on tech. comm. 1993-96), Internat. Soc. Poets (life, Merit award 1993), Am. Poets Soc. Democrat. Episcopalian. Office: Hampton U Dept English Hampton VA 23668

KHAYAT, ROBERT C., chancellor; b. Moss Point, Miss., Apr. 18, 1938; m. Margaret D. Khayat; children: Margaret D. Khayat Bratt, Robert C. Jr. BAE, U. Miss., 1961, JD, 1966; LLM, Yale U., 1981. With Wash. Redskins, 1960-64; pvt. practice in law, mcpl. judge City of Moss Point, Pascagoula, Miss., 1967-69; mcpl. judge City of Oxford, Miss.; pvt. practice in law Oxford, 1975-77; mem. faculty Sch. Law U. Miss., University, 1969—, vice-chancellor for univ. affairs, 1984-89, prof. law, interim dir. athletics, 1994, chancellor, 1995—; pres. NCAA Found., 1989-92. Contbr. articles to law jours. Chmn. United Fund Oxford-Lafayette County First Dr., 1971, Law Ctr. Dedication Com., 1978-79; chmn. courthouse restoration com. Lafayette County Courthouse, 1977; pres. M-Club Alumni chpt. U. Miss. Alumni Assn., 1970-71, Oxford-Lafayette County C. of C., 1973-74, Fellowship of Christian Athletes adult chpt., 1983; bd. trustees United So. Bank; tchr. young adult Sunday sch. Oxford-University United Meth. Ch. Recipient Nat. Football Found. Disting. Am. award, 1987, 89; featured in Springboard to Success sect. of 1987-88 The NFL and You; Sterling fellow Yale U., 1981; Miss. Law Jour. Endowed scholar, 1994. Mem. ABA, ATLA, Miss. State Bar, Miss. Bar Found. (trustee 1988-89), Lamar Order, Omicron Delta Kappa, Phi Delta Phi, Phi Kappa Phi. Office: U Miss Chancellor's Office 109 Lyceum University MS 38677

KHIM, JAY WOOK, high technology systems integration executive; b. Taegu, Korea, Oct. 22, 1940; came to U.S., 1965; s. Joon Mook and Soon E. (Lee) K. BS in Agrl. Econs., Kyung Pook U., Korea, 1963, MA in Agrl. Econs., 1966; postgrad. PhD program in Econs., U. Md., 1965-69; LLD (hon.), Randolph-Macon Coll., 1988; PhD (hon.), Kyungpook Nat. U., Republic of Korea, 1990. Mem. rsch. staff Brookings Instn., Washington, 1967-69; sr. economist NAB, Dept. of Labor, Washington, 1969-72; sr. assoc. Planning Rsch. Corp., Washington, 1972-74; chmn., CEO JWK Internat. Corp., Washington, 1974—, Internat. Trade and Investment Corp., Washington, 1977—. Author, editor more than 100 research reports, articles for fed. govt. in fields of health, energy, def., transp., housing and internat. affairs. Bd. dirs. George Mason Inst., George Mason U., Fairfax, Va., 1983—; mem. World Presidents Orgn., 1992—, chmn. Washington Met. chpt., 1994; bd. govs. U. Md. Alumni Assn.; bd. trustees Fairfax Hosp. Assn., 1986—; candidate for U.S. Congress from 11th Va. dist., 1992; chmn. fin. com. Rep. Party, Va.; commr. Small and Minority Bus. Commn., Fairfax County, 1992. Fulbright scholar, 1965, 66; recipient Sam Ill Found. award Korea, 1962, 63. Mem. Young Pres.'s Orgn., Pres. Club of Am. Mgmt. Assn., Nat. Security Assn., Am. Def. Preparedness Assn., Am. Econ. Assn., Fairfax C. of C. (bd. dirs. 1984-87), World Pres.'s Orgn. (chmn. Washington Met. chtp. 1994-95), City Club, Tower Club, Robert Trent Jones Club, Tournament of Players Club, Internat. Club (D.C.), River Bend Country Club, Fairbanks Golf and Country Club (San Diego). Office: JWK Internat Corp 7617 Little River Tpke Ste 1000 Annandale VA 22003-2603 also: 10900 Tara Rd Potomac MD 20854-1342

KHOURY, RIAD PHILIP, corporation executive, financial consultant; b. Beirut, May 27, 1935; came to U.S., 1979; s. Philip Mitri and Efrocine (Moujaes) K.; m. Samira Saade, Apr. 24, 1964; children: Philip, Marc, Serge. Graduate studies in fin. and mgmt. Ind. fin. cons. Baghdad, Iraq, 1955-58; ind. fin. investment adviser Jeddah, Saudi Arabia, 1959-61; mgr. Eastern Comml. Bank, Beirut, 1962-65; chief exec. officer United Bank of Lebanon and Pakistan, Beirut, 1965-70; vice chmn., chief exec. officer ADCOM Bank, Beirut, 1971-74; pres. Khoury Assocs. Internat., Annandale, Va., 1980—; banking and fin. cons. Lebanese Ministry Fin., Beirut, 1978-79. Recipient Officier Scientifique De L'ordre Du Merite award Le Merite, Paris, 1964, Cravate D'Honneur award Groupment Philantropique, Brussels, 1965. Home and Office: 6320 Wendy Ann Ct Fairfax VA 22039-1619

KHUSHF, GEORGE PETER, bioethicist; b. Flushing, N.Y., July 13, 1961; s. Mikhail Georges and Rosa Marie (Acksteiner) K.; m. Cheryl Renee Elam, May 31, 1986; children: Abigail Christine, Michael Joseph. BS summa cum laude, Tex. A&M Univ., 1983; MA, Rice Univ., 1990, PhD with distinction, 1993. Grad. teaching fellow Rice Univ., Houston, 1986-88; grad. fellow The Univ. Tubingen, Tubingen, Germany, 1988-89; rsch. assoc. Ctr. for Ethics, Medicine & Pub. Issues, Houston, 1989-93; mng. editor The Journal of Medicine & Phil., Houston, 1993-95; humanities dir. Ctr. for Bioethics, Univ. S.C., Columbia, 1995—; asst. prof. phil. Univ. S.C., Columbia, 1995—. Asst. editor: Jour. Medicine & Phil., 1995—, Christian Bioethics, 1995—; editor: Centerpiece: Newsletter of the USC Ctr. for Bioethics, 1995—; contbr. articles to profl. jours. Mem. ethics com. S.C. Medical Assn. Rockwell vis. scholar U. Houston, 1995. Mem. Am. Phil. Assn., Soc. Health & Human Values, Am. Acad. Religion, Hegel Soc. Am., N.A. Kant Soc., Phi Kappa Phi, Tau Beta Phi, Phi Eta Sigma. Office: Univ S C Dept Phil & Ctr for Bioethics Columbia SC 29208

KHWAJA, WAQAS AHMAD, English language educator, writer; b. Lahore, Punjab, Pakistan, Oct. 14, 1952; came to the U.S., 1994; s. Sultan Ahmad and Irshad Sultan (Begum) K.; m. Maryam W. Khurshid, Nov. 2, 1978; children: Fatima W., Omer W., Maham W., Murtaza W. BA, Govt. Coll., Lahore, 1971; LLB, Punjab U., Lahore, 1975, MA in English, 1979; MA, PhD in English, Emory U., 1995. Pvt. practice lawyer Lahore, 1983-93; vis. asst. prof.. Agnes Scott Coll., Decatur, Ga., 1995-96, 96—; tchr. instr, vis. faculty mem. dept. English Emory U., 1995, 96; spl. corr. Pakistan and Gulf Economist, Lahore, 1983-84; vis. prof. Quaid-e-Azam Law Coll., Lahore, 1988-91, Punjab Law Coll., Lahore, 1988-92; vis. faculty Lahore Coll. for Arts and Scis., 1989-90, Punjab U., Lahore, 1990-91, Directorate of Tng., Income Tax, Lahore, 1992-93. Author: (poems) Six Geese From A Tomb At Medum, 1987, Mornings in the Wilderness, 1988, Writers and Landscapes, 1991, Mariam's Lament and Other Poems, 1992, The Aesthetics of Civilized Life, 1995; editor, translator Short Stories From Pakistan, 1992. Grad. fellow Rotary Internat., Emory U., 1979-80; Internat. Writing fellow U. Iowa, 1988. Mem. MLA. Muslim. Office: Agnes Scott Coll Dept English Buttrick 220 141 East College Ave Decatur GA 30030

KIBILOSKI, FLOYD TERRY, business and computer consultant, editor, educator; b. Coldwater, Mich., Dec. 24, 1946; s. Floyd Benedict and Lucille Henrietta (Cholaj) K.; m. Peggy J. Foreman, Apr. 20, 1974; children: Sean, Angie. BBA in Acctg., Western Mich. U., 1978; MA in Computer Resource Mgmt., Webster U., 1989. CPA; cert. data processor; cert. Microsoft trainer. Enlisted USAF, 1966, advanced through grades to capt., ret., 1990, acct., 1966-70, computer technician, 1970-77, acct., computer cons. Bristol Leisenring and Co., 1977-80; computer cons. USAF, U.K., 1980-85, St. Louis, 1985-90; owner, editor Louisville (Ky.) Computer Times, 1990—; adj. prof. McKendree Coll., Lebanon, Ill., 1985-90, City Colls. of Chgo., 1982-84, Embry-Riddle Aero. U., 1983-84, U. Md., 1984; chair computer sci. dept. Sullivan Coll., Louisville, 1993—, adj. prof., 1990—, motivational lectr., speaker. Author: Computer in the Audit, 1980, (human system seminar) Get the Most from Yourself, 1993. Co-founder Passioinist Ctr., Louisville. Mem. Air Force Assn. Republican. Roman Catholic. Home and Office: 3135 Sunfield Cir Louisville KY 40241-6527

KIDD, CLAREN MARIE, librarian; b. Geary, Okla., Mar. 14, 1944; d. Clarence Lloyd and Meta Marie (Zobisch) Base; m. Robert Lee Kidd, III. BA, U. Okla., 1966, MA, 1967; MLS, U. Pitts., 1972. Tchr. 7th grade geography Norman (Okla.) Pub. Schs., 1967-68; tchr. high sch. earth sci., geography Rantoul (Ill.) Twp. High Sch., 1968-71; interlibr. loan libr. U. Okla., Norman, 1972-73, geology libr., 1973—; senator U. Okla. Faculty Senate, Norman, 1990-93. Compiler: Union List of Geological Field Trip Guidebooks of Excursions of Australia, 1988, Union List of Geological Field Trip Guidebooks of North America, 1989. Named to U. Okla. Assocs. Disting. lectureship, 1988. Mem. Geosci. Info. Soc. (pres. 1985, internat. issues 1993—, guidebooks com. 1974—), Am. Geol. Inst. (mem. soc. coun. 1987-89). Office: U Okla 100 E Boyd St #R220 Norman OK 73019-0628

KIDD, DARLENE JOYCE, social services administrator, nurse; b. Clintonville, Wis., Feb. 3, 1935; d. Clarence Louis Julius and Elvira Norman (Horn) Krueger; m. Donny Ramon Kidd, Apr. 29, 1955 (dec. Mar. 1968); children: Andrew Louis, Kevin Hugh, Donny Ramon, Jr., Patrick Ozwald Michael. BBA, U. Okla., 1974; grad. student, Cen. State U., Milw., 1990. RN, Okla. Staff nurse Presby. Hosp. (Wesley Hosp.), Oklahoma City, 1955-56; emergency room supr. Stillwater (Okla.) Mcpl. Hosp., 1956-58; charge nurse Mercy Hosp., Dubuque, Iowa, 1958, Benton Harbor, Mich., 1959-61; charge nurse Winnebago (Wis.) State Hosp., 1963-65; adminstrv. staff, nurse Camp Classen, YMCA, Davis, Okla., 1968-72; billing mgr. Univ. Hosp. and Clinics, Oklahoma City, Okla., 1975-79; team leader Hillcrest Osteo. Hosp., Oklahoma City, 1979-80; dir. Health Care Profls., Oklahoma City, 1980-81; exec. dir. Big Bros./Big Sisters of Greater Oklahoma City, Inc., 1981-89, also bd. dirs., past. treas., past v.p.; dir. quality assurance Ctrl. Home Care, 1990-93; dir. quality assurance and billing Integrity Home Health Care, 1993—, dir. nurses, 1994—. Bd. dirs. Neighborhood Devel. and Conservation Ctr., Oklahoma City, 1982; pres. Oklahoma City chpt. Gold Star Wives Am., 1984-85, regional pres. 1988-89; active Big Bros./Big Sisters, 1981-89. Kerr Found. fellow, 1982. Mem. U. Okla. Alumni Assn. (life). Democrat.

Lutheran. Clubs: Women for Women (v.p. 1981-82), Soccer Bus. Tips (Oklahoma City) (pres. 1983).

KIDD, HILLERY GENE, educational publisher; b. Cin., May 8, 1945; s. Herbert Kidd and Amber L. (Smith) Reed; m. Sylvia Jean Smith, Dec. 21, 1971 (div. Nov. 1980); 1 child, Shane Thomas. Student, Austin Peay State Coll., 1963-64. Owner KIDD Contrs., Cin., 1969-72; ptnr., v.p. So. Cemetaries Svcs., Inc., Fayetteville, N.C., 1972-73; state sales dir. Life Safety Inc., Clearwater, Fla., 1975; sales mgr. Jodean Water Conditioning, Lutz, Fla., 1973-78; owner Advanced Water Sys., Largo, Fla., 1978-83; regional v.p., securities broker A.L. Williams Corp., Largo, 1983-86; rep. Uniway of Mid-East Tenn., Knoxville, 1986-92; pres., CEO H.G. KIDD Corp., Boulder City, Nev., 1993—. Author: (textbooks) Human Growth and Development, 1992, Introductory Psychology, 1993, Introductory Sociology, 1993; editor: General Biology: Microbiology, Human Anatomy and Physiology, 1993, English Composition with Essay, American Literature, 1993—, Commonalities in Nursing Care—A, 1993, Commonalities in Nursing Care—B, 1993—, Differences in Nursing Care—A, 1993—, Differences in Nursing Care—B, 1993—, Differences in Nursing Care—C, 1993—, Occupational Strategies in Nursing, 1993—. Lt. col. mil. affairs Tenn. Def. Force, 1989-94. 1st lt. Spl. Forces U.S. Army, 1965-68. Mem. Order of DeMolay (counselor 1961-62, life mem.). Republican. Office: PO Box 60067 Boulder City NV 89006

KIDD, JAMES MARION, III, allergist, immunologist, educator; b. Baton Rouge, Dec. 15, 1950; s. James Marion Jr. and Germaine Elizabeth (Hunt) K.; m. Carolyn Ann Kelley, Apr. 29, 1981; children: Mackenzie Elizabeth, Katherine Anne. MD, La. State U., 1976. Diplomate Am. Bd. Internal Medicine, Am. Bd. Allergy and Immunology; lic. physician, La., Fla., Wis. Resident physician La. State U. Sch. Medicine, New Orleans, 1977-79; rsch. fellow Med. Coll. Wis., Milw., 1980-82; pvt. practice in allergy and immunology Allergy, Asthma, and Immunology Clinic, Baton Rouge, 1982—; clin. asst., prof. medicine La. Sch. Medicine, New Orleans, 1982—; clin. asst., prof. community medicine and pub. health Tulane U. Sch. Medicine, New Orleans, 1992—. Fellow Am. Coll. Physicians, Am. Acad. Pediat., Am. Acad. Allergy and Immunology, Am. Coll. Chest Physicians; mem. La. Allergy Soc. (pres. 1989-90, exec. sec.-treas. 1992-96), Baton Rouge Allergy Soc. (pres. 1990—), Rotary (Paul Harris fellow). Office: James M Kidd III MD 8017 Picardy Ave Baton Rouge LA 70809-3538

KIDD, THORNTON LENOIR, JR., allergist; b. San Antonio, Aug. 3, 1932; s. Thornton Lenoir and Lillian Beatrice (Watts) K.; 1 dau., Sharlyn Gail; m. Betty Louise., San Antonio Coll., 1950-51, Trinity U., 1951-52; student U. Tex., 1952-53, MD, 1957. Diplomate Am. Bd. Pediatrics, Am. Bd. Allergy and Immunology, Am. Bd. Allergy. Intern, Brackenridge Hosp., Austin, Tex., 1957-58; resident U. Tex. Med. Br.-Galveston, 1958-60, fellow in allergy, 1960-61 practice medicine specializing in allergy, Austin, 1963-64, Pasadena, Tex., 1964—; mem. staffs Bayshore Hosp., Southmore Hosp. Bd. regents Am. Coll. of Allergy; clin. instr. dept. family practice Health Sci. Dept. U. Tex., Houston; con. El Buen Samaritano, Aquismon, Mex. Served to lt. comdr. USPHS, 1961-63. Mem. Am. Coll. Allergists, Am. Assn. Cert. Allergists, Am. Coll. Chest Physicians, AMA, So. Med. Assn., Houston Allergy Soc. (pres. 1984-86), Asthma and Allergy Found. Am., Internat. Corr. Soc. Allergy, Tex. Med. Assn., Am. Assn. Clin. Immunology and Allergy, Am. Acad. Allergy. Republican. Baptist.

KIDD, VALLEE MELVINA, charitable foundation manager; b. Zora, Mo., Jan. 5, 1918; d. Alva Joseph and Pauline Louise (Nolte) Lefever; m. Vernon Noble Kidd, Nov. 5, 1937 (dec. Dec. 1970); children: Elaine Louise Green, Vernon N. Jr., Margaret Ruth Keener. Exec. asst. Grimes Gasoline Co. and related ops., Tulsa, 1977-86; mng. trustee Otha H. Grimes Found., Tulsa, 1986—. Pres. Gilcrease Mus. Service Orgn. (Gillies), Tulsa, 1973-74; bd. dirs. Thomas Gilcrease Mus. Assn., Tulsa, 1976-81. Mem. Tuesday Book Club (pres. 1974-75). Republican. Presbyterian. Office: Otha H Grimes Found PO Box 3183 Tulsa OK 74101-3183

KIDDA, MICHAEL LAMONT, JR., psychologist, educator; b. Jackson, Miss., May 24, 1945; s. Michael Lamont and Annie Laurie (McKeithen) K.; m. Ellen Gordon, Aug. 23, 1977; children: Patrick Gordon, John McKeithen. BA in English, Centenary Coll., Shreveport, La., 1969; MDiv, U. South, Sewanee, Tenn., 1972; MS in Social Psychology, U. Ga., 1984, PhD in Social Psychology, 1987. Youth cons. Cathedral of St. Philip, Atlanta, 1974-76; counselor All Saints' Sch., Vicksburg, Miss., 1977-79; coord. of assessment J.C. Smith U., Charlotte, N.C., 1989-94, assoc. prof. psychology, 1985—, dept. head, 1987-89; coord. Grad. Student Conf./Personality and Social Psychology, Athens, 1981; bd. trustees N.E. Ga. Area, Cmty. Resource Coun., Athens, 1980-83, v.p., 1982, tech. adminstrn., 1984; data analysis cons., Athens, 1980-85; presenter in field. Contbr. articles to profl. jours. and to On-line and CD-Rom data bases; author newsletter ETS Higher Edn. Assessment, 1993. Adv. bd. Washington Hghts. Project, Nat. Children's Def. Fund, Charlotte, 1994; chair evaluation com. Fighting Back Against Drugs, Charlotte, 1992-94; com. mem. cub scouts pack 19 Boy Scouts Am., Huntersville, N.C., 1994—. Recipient Nat. Retention Excellence award Noel-Levitz Ctrs., J.C. Smith U., 1993, Cross of Nails award St. Michael's Cathedral, Coventry, Eng.; Retention and Performance grantee Pew Charitable Trusts, 1994, Equipment grantee AT&T Found., 1991, grantee: Am. Psychol. Assn., 1996, United Negro Coll. Fund, 1996, other grants; Inst. Non-Traditional Ministries rsch. fellow. Mem. Am. Assn. for Higher Edn., Am. Statis. Assn., Am. Psychol. Soc., Soc. Southeastern Social Psychologists, Internat. Platform Assn., Sigma Xi, Sigma Tau Delta, Psi Chi. Home: PO Box 674 Huntersville NC 28078-0674 Office: Johnson C Smith Univ 100 Beatties Ford Rd Charlotte NC 28216-5302

KIDDOO, RICHARD CLYDE, retired oil company executive; b. Wilmington, Del., Aug. 31, 1927; s. William Richard and Nellie Louise (Bounds) K.; m. Catherine Schumann, June 25, 1950; children: Jean L., William R., Scott F., David B. BSChemE, U. Del., 1948. With Esso Standard Oil and Esso Internat. Inc., Md., N.J., N.Y., 1948-66; internat. sales mgr. Esso Europe Inc., London, 1966-67; mng. dir., chief exec. officer Esso Pappas Indsl. Co., Athens, Greece, 1967-71; pres. Esso Africa Inc., London, 1971-72; v.p. Esso Europe Inc., London, 1973-81; v.p. mktg. Exxon Co., U.S.A., Houston, 1981-83; pres. Exxon Coal Internat., Coral Gables, Fla., 1983-86, ret.; vice chmn. mktg. com. Am. Petroleum, Washington, 1983. With USMC, 1945-46. Decorated Cross of King George I of Greece; recipient medal of distinction U. Del. Mem. AICE, Am. Petroleum Inst., Gibson Island Club, Circumnavigators Club. Home: Broadwater Way Gibson Island MD 21056

KIEFER, ROY WILLIAM, aerospace company executive; b. N.Y.C., June 19, 1946; s. Harry and Ruth (Pfeiffer) K.; m. Beverly Karen Lange, Apr. 17, 1987; children: Christine, Kelly, Ryan. BA, Ohio Wesleyan U., 1968; MBA, Duke U., 1978; diploma, Indsl. Coll. Armed Forced, 1986. Commd. ensign USN, 1969, advanced through grades to comdr., 1983; dir. logistics F/A-18 and F-14 programs Aviation Supply Office, Phila., 1978-82; dir. planning Navy Stock Fund Naval Supply Systems Command, Washington, 1982-85; dep. program mgr. A-6 EA-6 programs Naval Air Sys. Command, Washington, 1986-89; mgr. tech. requirements Navy advanced programs Lockheed, Mariett, GA, 1989-95; dir. Navy TACAIR programs Lockheed Martin, Washington, 1995—; sec. Sealar Corp., Washington, 1990-95. Mem. alumni bd. visitors Fuqua Sch. Duke U. Decorated 2 Meritorious Svc. medals, 3 Navy Commendation medals, 3 Navy Achievement medals. Mem. Mil. Order Carabao, Retired Officers Assn., Duke Club Washington, Army Navy Club Washington.

KIEFER, WALTER SCOTT, geophysicist, educator; b. Perth Amboy, N.J., June 28, 1962; s. Walter George and Elizabeth (Muldoon) K. BS in Physics and Astronomy, Tex. Christian U., 1984; MS in Planetary Sci., Calif. Inst. Tech., 1986, PhD in Planetary Sci. and Geophysics, 1990. Rsch. assoc. Nat. Rsch. Coun., Greenbelt, Md., 1990-93; rsch. scientist Lunar and Planetary Inst., Houston, 1993—. Author: (slide set and booklet) The Red Planet: A Survey of Mars, 1995; contbr. articles to profl. jours. Mem. Stephen Dwornik Prize Com. Lunar and Planetary Sci. Conf., Houston, 1993-95. Fellow NSF, 1984-87. Mem. Am. Geophys. Union, Phi Beta Kappa, Sigma Xi. Office: Lunar and Planetary Inst 3600 Bay Area Blvd Houston TX 77058

KIEHL, ERMALYNN MARIA, perinatal nurse; b. Pa., Dec. 26, 1946; d. Harry K. and Ermalynn M. (Steele) Beitsch; m. Larry R. Kiehl, Dec. 27, 1964; children: Barbara, Larry Jr., Daneene. Diploma, Ind. Hosp. Sch. Nursing, 1974; BSN, Ind. U. Pa., 1979; MSN, U. Fla., 1985, PhD, 1994. Nursing instr. Ind. Hosp. Sch. Nursing, Indiana, Pa.; pub. health nurse Pa. Dept. Health, Indiana; head nurse, dir. perinatal svcs. Fla. Hosp. Med. Ctr., Orlando, 1981-93; asst. prof. U. Ctrl. Fla., Orlando, 1994—. Mem. ANA, Nat. Coun. Family Rels., So. Nursing Rsch. Soc., Assn. Women's Health, Obstetric, and Neonatal Nurses (past ednl. coord. Fla. chpt.), Nat. Perinatal Assn., Healthy Mothers/Healthy Baby Coalition, Sigma Theta Tau (past pres.), Theta Epsilon. Home: 1721 Crown Point Woods Cir Ocoee FL 34761-3720

KIELBORN, TERRIE LEIGH, secondary education educator; b. Miami, Fla., Sept. 25, 1955; d. Gerald and Dolores Eloise (Adams) Carter; m. Gerald Albert Kielborn, Mar. 31, 1979; children: Carl Gerald, Katie Leigh, Sarah Beth. BA in Edn., Fla. Atlantic U., 1977; MA with honors, U. South Fla., 1986; postgrad., U. Fla. Cert. elem. tchr., mid. sch. social studies, Fla. 6th grade tchr. Belleview Mid. Sch., Ocala, Fla. Contbr. articles to profl. jours. Chair bd. dirs. environ. edn. com. Marion County Audubon Soc., 1991, pres., 1992-93; mem. mid. sch. sci. curriculum com. Marion County, 1994-96; chairperson sch. adv. coun. 1993-95. Named Tchr. of Yr., 1979, 92, 94; Phi Theta Kappa scholar, 1975, Minigrants, 1990-96, Profl. Enhancement Program grantee, 1989-96, PTO grantee, Dreams grantee, 1995, Tech. grantee, 1993-95, Marion County Soil and Conservation grantee, Fla. Growers and Nurseryman grantee; recipient NEWEST award, 1991, Sci. Grasp award , 1991, Sci. Grasp award Upjohn, 1992, Golden Apple award Marion County, 1992, Fla. Explorer's! Workshop award, 1995; nominated for presdl. award for excellence in sci., 1991, 94, 95, 96; Ag in the Classroom Best Idea award, 1996, Delta Exn. Outstanding Science Activity award, 1993; field rsch. on exotic grass of a state park, 1996. Mem. NSTA (presenter nat. conf. 1992, 95, 96, S.E. regional conf. 1993, local leader 1994), Nat. Assn. Earth Sci. Tchrs., Fla. Assn. Earth Sci. Tchrs., Fla. Coun. Tchrs. Math. (regional bd. dirs. 1992-94, presenter state conf. 1992, 93), Fla. Assn. Sci. Tchrs. (presenter state conf. 1996, regional dir. Region III 1995—), League Environ. Educators Fla., Marion Edn. Assn.-Fla. Tchrs. Profession (rep. 1986-87), Fla. Native Plant Soc. (co-v.p. Big Scrub 1992), Tchrs. Math. Edn. Marion County, Nat. Mid. Level Sci. Tchrs. Assn., Tchrs. Involved in Maths. Edn., Alpha Delta Kappa (sgt.-at-arms 1990-91, v.p. 1992-94), Phi Kappa Phi. Office: 10500 SE 36th Ave Belleview FL 34420-2866

KIELY, DAN RAY, lawyer, banking and real estate development executive, consultant; b. Ft. Sill, Okla., Jan. 2, 1944; s. William Robert and Leona Maxine (Ross) K.; BA in Psychology, U. Colo., 1966, JD, Stanford U., 1969; children: Jefferson Ray, Matthew Ray. Bar: Colo 1969, D.C. 1970, Va. 1973. Assoc. firm Holme, Roberts and Owen, Denver, 1969-70; pres. DeRand Equity Group, Arlington, Va., 1973-89; pres., chmn. bd. Bankwest Corp. and related banks, Denver.; pres., dir. United Gibralter Corp. Del., Inc., Unocam, Inc., 1987—; ptnr. Starlin & Kiely, P.C., 1989-94; trustee DeRand Real Estate Investment Trust, 1974—; chmn. Pace Holdings, Inc., Washington, 1988-93, Washington Capital Corp., 1989—, Surry Internat., Ltd., 1995—; speaker, lectr. in field. Deacon, McLean (Va.) Bapt. Ch., 1977-80. Served as officer, USAR, 1969-73. Decorated Legion of Merit; cert. property mgr. Mem. ABA, Nat. Bd. Realtors, Inst. Real Estate Mgmt., Nat. Assn. Rev. Appraisers, Internat. Coun. Shopping Ctrs., Nat. Assn. Real Estate Investment Trusts, D.C. Bar Assn., Va. Bar Assn., Colo. Indsl. Bankers Assn. (bd. dirs. 1985-87), The Internat. Inst (cert. valuer). Home: 67 Norwich C West Palm Beach FL 33417

KIENEL, FREDERICK EDWARD, financial executive; b. Marietta, Ga., July 29, 1938; s. Frederick Bernard and Louise (Gantt) K.; m. Norma Breazeale, July 24, 1965; children: Frederick Dowell, Meredith Paige, Jennifer Anne. BS in Indsl. Mgmt., Ga. Inst. Tech., 1962; postgrad., U. Richmond, 1966-69, Dean Witter Wharton Sch., 1985-87. Prodn. control engr. Allied Chem. Corp., Hopewell, Va., 1965-67; staff indsl. engr. Reynolds Metals Co., Richmond, 1967-68; acct. exec. Merrill Lynch, Richmond, 1968-73, instnl. acct. exec., 1973-78; sr. v.p., mgr. Dean Witter Reynolds, Inc., Richmond, 1978—; sr. mgmt. adv. mem. Dean Witter Reynolds, Inc., N.Y.C., 1981-82. Trustee Trinity Episcopal Sch., Richmond, 1987; mil. aide de camp to gov. State Va., 1982-86. 1st lt. USMC, 1962-65, lt. col. Res., 1965-82. Mem. NYSE (arbitration com. 1985—), Nat. Assn. Securities Dealers (arbitration com. 1985—), Richmond C. of C., Va. C. of C., Va. Securities Industry Assn. (pres. 1992—), Va. Coun. Econ. Edn. (chmn. bd. dirs., mem. exec. com.), Ga. Tech. Alumni Assn. (pres. 1977-78), Bull and Bear Club. Republican. Roman Catholic. Office: Dean Witter Reynolds Inc 600 E Main St Ste 350 Richmond VA 23219

KIENER, JOHN LESLIE, judge; b. Ft. Madison, Iowa, June 21, 1940; s. Cyril Joseph and Lucille Olive (Golden) K.; m. Carol Lynn Winston, June 4, 1966; children—Susan, Gretchen. BA cum laude, Loras Coll., 1962; JD, Drake U., 1965. Bar: Iowa 1965, Tenn. 1972, U.S. Supreme Ct. 1974. Practice, Decorah, Iowa, 1965-68; asst. atty. gen. State of Iowa, 1968-72; ptnr. firm Cantor & Kiener, 1972-80; city judge Johnson City (Tenn.), 1975-80; gen. sessions judge, Johnson City, 1980—; continuing edn. tchr., bus. law East Tenn. State U., 1975—. Mem. ABA, Tenn. Bar Assn., Washington County Bar Assn. Republican. Lodges: Rotary, Elks. Avocations: stamp collecting, genealogy. Contbr. articles to profl. jours. Home: 2403 Camelot Cir Johnson City TN 37604-2938 Office: Gen Sessions Ct Downtown Ctr Courthouse 101 E Market St Johnson City TN 37604-5724

KIERNAN, WILLIAM JOSEPH, JR., lawyer, real estate investor; b. Salem, Mass., Mar. 19, 1932; s. William Joseph and Jane Catherine (Harrington) K.; m. Nancy Stipurko, Nov. 11, 1953; children—Cecilia, William, Claudia, Matthew. B.S. cum laude, Coll. Holy Cross, 1953; J.D. magna cum laude, Harvard U., 1959. Bar: Wis. 1959, Fla. 1981, U.S. Ct. Mil. Appeals 1967, U.S. Supreme Ct. 1967. Assoc. Foley & Lardner, Milw., 1959-66, ptnr., 1966—, chief govtl. fin. team, 1979—, exec. com., 1983-92, ptnr., 1987-92; lectr. law Marquette U. Sch. Law, Milw., 1963-70; mem. faculty Cannon Fin. Sch., 1990-95. Contbr. articles to profl. jours. Mem. adv. bd. Salvation Army. Served to comdr. USNR, 1953-76. Mem. ABA, Wis. Bar Assn., Fla. Bar Assn., Milw. Bar Assn., Miami Estate Planning Inst. (adv. com.), League Wis. Municipalities, Nat. Inst. Mcpl. Law Officers, Mcpl. Fin. Officers Assn., Nat. Bond Counsel, Navy League. Roman Catholic. Clubs: Univ., Harvard of Wis. (exec. com.), Tampa. Office: Foley & Lardner 100 N Tampa St Ste 2700 Tampa FL 33602-5810

KIESNOWSKI, BRIAN, surgeon; b. San Jose, July 11, 1960; s. Thomas Joseph and Norma Kiesnowski; m. Meredith Diane Harper, July 22, 1995. BS, BA, U. Calif., Berkeley, 1984; MPH, U. Calif., 1988; MT, UCLA, 1985; MD, Rush Med. Coll., Chgo., 1992. Med. technologist UCLA Hosp., 1984-86, Merritt Hosp., Oakland, Calif., 1986-87, Alta Bates Hosp., Berkeley, 1986-88; instr. microbiology, infectious disease U. Calif., Berkeley, 1986-88; resident in surgery Cedars-Sinai Hosp., L.A., 1992-93, Virginia-Mason Hosp., Seattle, 1993-94, Pitt County Meml. Hosp., Greenville, N.C., 1994—. Calif. Dept. Health scholar, 1986-88. Mem. AMA, ACS, Am. Soc. Microbiologists, Am. Homebrewers Assn., Am. Soc. Clin. Pathologists.

KIEWRA, GUSTAVE PAUL, psychologist, educator; b. Garden City Park, N.Y., July 25, 1943; s. Gustave Francis and Alice (Kozyrski) K.; m. Donna Elaine Womack, Nov. 29, 1969; children: Amy Marie, Christopher Paul, Jessica Lauren. BA, Franklin Coll., 1967; MA, Ball State U., 1968, EdD, 1972. Instr. psychology Fla. Jr. Coll., Jacksonville, 1968-70; counselor, asst. prof. counselor edn. Western Ky. U., Bowling Green, 1972-76; prof. psychology Piedmont Va. C.C., Charlottesville, 1976—; mem. psychology peer group planning com. Va. C.C. Sys., 1996; mem. bldg. com. Piedmont Va. C.C., 1993-96, planning coun., 1996—. Bd. dirs. Western Albemarle Rescue Squad, Crozet, Va., 1987, 88, Am. Lung Assn., Charlottesville, 1986-88; coord. Neighborhood Watch, Crozet, 1985-96; mem. sch. improvement com. Crozet Elem. Sch., 1990-91; mem. Piedmont (Va.) Cmty. Coll. Planning Coun., 1995-96. Recipient svc. award Piedmont Va. C.C., 1981, 86, 91. Mem. APA, Va. Psychol. Assn., Am. Assn. Marriage and Family Counselors, Va. C.C. Assn. (rep. faculty affairs com. 1990-92), Faculty Profl. Assn., Internat. Platform Assn., Lions (pres. Crozet, Va. 1989-92, Key award 1991, Advancement Key award 1991, Master Key award 1992, 100% Pres. award 1990-92, Dist. Gov. Membership Growth award 1990-92, Va. Multiple Dist. 24 Achievement award 1990-92, Pres. Svc. Appreciation award 1992, Achievement award medal 1992, Melvin Jones fellow Internat. Found.), Phi Delta Kappa, Phi Theta Kappa (hon., faculty advisor 1980-88), Phi Delta Theta. Home: 1440 Birchwood Dr Crozet VA 22932-9441 Office: Piedmont Va CC 501 College Dr Charlottesville VA 22902-7589

KIGER, JOSEPH CHARLES, history educator; b. Kenton County, Ky., Aug. 19, 1920; s. Carl C. and Genevieve (Hoelscher) K.; m. Jean Myrick Moore, Mar. 27, 1947; children: Carl A., John J. A.B., Birmingham-So. Coll., 1943; M.A., U. Ala., 1947; Ph.D., Vanderbilt U., 1950. Teaching fellow Vanderbilt U., 1948-50; instr. history U. Ala., summer 1950, Washington U., St. Louis, 1950-51; dir. research select com. to investigate founds. U.S. Ho. of Reps., 1952; staff asso. Am. Council Edn., Washington, 1953-55; asst. dir. So. Fellowships Fund, Chapel Hill, N.C., 1955-58; asso. prof. history U. Ala., 1958-61; prof. history U. Miss., 1961—, chmn. dept. history, 1969-74, emeritus, 1990—, dir. program on founds. and Comparable orgs., 1993—; cons. non-profit orgns., also govt., 1954—. Author: Operating Principles of the Larger Foundations, 1954, (with others) Sponsored Research Policy of Colleges and Universities, 1954, American Learned Societies, 1963, (with others) A History of Mississippi, 1973; editor: Research Institutions and Learned Societies, 1982, International Encyclopedia of Foundations, 1990, Internat. Encyclopaedia of Learned Societies and Academies, 1993; co-editor: Foundations, 1984, Historiographic Review of Foundation Literature, Motivations and Perceptions, 1987. Served to capt. USMCR, 1942-46. Guggenheim fellow, 1960; grantee Russell Sage Found., 1953; grantee Rockefeller Found., 1961; grantee Am. Philos. Soc., 1964; grantee Am. Council of Learned Socs., Nat. Acad. Scis., 1980. Mem. Am. Hist. Assn., So. Hist. Assn. (life). Home: Country Club Rd Oxford MS 38655 Office: U Miss 107 Isom Hall University MS 38677

KIGER, RONALD LEE, price analyst; b. Pasadena, Calif., Dec. 30, 1940; s. Wallace Lee and Ilo Marie (Smith) K.; m. Carole Ann Bates, Apr. 10, 1965 (div. Dec. 1978); children: Darren Lee, Lorene Elizabeth. Student, U. Calif., Berkeley, 1958-62; BBA, Armstrong Coll., 1964. Auditor GAO, San Francisco, 1964-66; sr. auditor Def. Contract Audit Agy., San Francisco, 1966-84; material price analyst Lockheed Missiles and Space Co., Sunnyvale, Calif., 1984-91, Lockheed Aeronautical Systems Co., Marietta, Ga., 1991—. State dir. U.S. Jaycees, Castro Valley, Calif., 1968, pres., 1969, dist. lt. gov., Alameda County, Calif., 1970, state credentials chmn., Calif., 1970. Mem. Assn. Govt. Accts. (sec. 1968, spl. activities dir. 1982-83, pres. 1983-84, newsletter editor 1984-85, nat. chpt. recognition com. 1985-87, regional v.p. western region, 1988-89, nat. awards com. 1989-91, nat. nominating com. 1990). Democrat. Mem. Christian Ch. Home: 4523 Savage Dr Marietta GA 30066-1425

KIHLE, DONALD ARTHUR, lawyer; b. Noonan, N.D., Apr. 4, 1934; s. J. Arthur and Linnie W. (Ljunngren) K.; m. Judith Anne, Aug. 18, 1964; children—Kevin, Kirsten, Kathryn, Kurte. B.S. in Indsl. Engring., U. N.D., 1957; J.D., U. Okla., 1967. Bar: Okla. 1967, U.S. Dist. Cts. (we. and no. dists.) Okla. 1967, U.S. Ct. Appeals (10th cir.) 1967, U.S. Supreme Ct. 1971. Asso., Huffman, Arrington, Scheurich & Kincaid, Tulsa, 1967-71, ptnr., 1971-78; shareholder, dir., officer Arrington Kihle Gaberino & Dunn, Tulsa, 1978—, pres., 1994—. Dist. chmn. Boy Scouts Am., 1983-85, cubmaster, 1986-88, coun. coms., 1988—, campiree chmn., 1990; mem. Statewide Law Day Com., 1982-86, chmn., 1983-85; trustee Brandon Hall Sch., Atlanta, 1991—, chmn., 1995. Lt. U.S. Army, 1957-59. Recipient Silver Beaver award Boy Scouts Am. Mem. ABA, Okla. Bar Assn. (chmn. constnl. bicentennial com. 1986-89), Constitution 200 (exec. com. 1986-89), Tulsa County Bar Assn., Order of Arrow (vigil), Sigma Tau, Phi Delta Phi, Order of Coif, Sigma Chi (Tulsa alumni pres. 1995). Republican. Clubs: Tulsa (bd. govs. 1987-94, pres. 1992), Southern Hills County (Tulsa), Q Club Tulsa (scribe 1991—). Home: 4717 S Lewis Ct Tulsa OK 74105-5135 Office: 1000 ONEOK Plz 100 W 5th St Tulsa OK 74103-4240

KIKO, PHILIP GEORGE, lawyer; b. Massillon, Ohio, July 16, 1951; s. Willard LeRoy and Stella Jane (Schroeder) K.; m. Colleen Duffy; children: Jamie Lynn, Sarah Elizabeth, Philip George Jr., Michael Ryan. BA, Mount Union Coll., 1973; JD, George Mason Sch. Law, 1977. Bar: Va. 1977, D.C 1978, U.S. Ct. Appeals (D.C. cir.) 1978. Assoc. legal counsel, broadcast asst. Nat. Rep. Congl. Com., Washington, 1973-79; exec. asst., legis. counsel Congressman Sensenbrenner, Washington, 1979-83; assoc. counsel judiciary com. U.S. Ho. Reps., Washington, 1983-86; acting dir. policy and enforcement Office for Civil Rights U.S. Dept. Edn., Washington, 1986-87; officer, bd. dirs. Kiko Heating & Air Conditioning, Canton, Ohio, 1973-89; legis. counsel Dept. Interior, Washington, 1987-89, dir. budget and program resource mgmt., 1989-92, dep. dir. office hearings and appeals, 1992-94; assoc. adminstr. procurement and purchasing U.S. Ho. of Reps., Washington, 1995—; v.p. bd. dirs. Law Offices of Colleen Duffy Kiko P.C., 1996—; bd. dirs., sec. Pers. Dept., Arlington, Va. Mem. Arlington Rep. Com., 1978-93, 95—, Fair Housing Bd., Arlington, 1980; v.p. Arlington Hts. Citizen Assn., 1991-96; pres. St. Charles Sch. PTO, 1994—. Recipient Exceptional Svc. award Sec. Interior, 1988, Presidl. Meritorious Svc. award, 1992. Mem. Va. State Bar Assn., D.C. Bar Assn. Roman Catholic. Home: 3500 Arlington Blvd Arlington VA 22204-1721 Office: US House of Representatives care Chief Adminstrv Officer H-112 Capital Bldg Washington DC 20515

KILBORNE, GEORGE BRIGGS, investment company executive; b. N.Y.C., Oct. 7, 1930; s. Robert Stewart and Barbara Briggs K.; BA, Yale U., 1952; m. Lucie Wheeler Peck, Nov. 12, 1960 (div. 1978); children: George Briggs, Kim McNeil, Sarah Skinner. V.p. William Skinner & Sons, N.Y.C., 1955-60; pres. Bus. Rsch. Co., Birmingham, Mich., 1961-74, Creative Capital of Mich., Inc., 1962-70; ptnr. Comac Co., 1968-70; chmn., pres. First Citizen Bank, Troy, Mich., 1970-74; engaged in real estate investing and cons., Palm Beach, Fla., 1975-79; mng. dir. corp. acquisitions Bessemer Securities Corp., N.Y.C., 1980-84; pres. Bay St. Corp., Palm Beach, 1984—; pres. Pon Capital Corp., Braintree, Mass., 1987-89; chmn. State Bank of Mich., Coopersville, 1966-68, Muskegon Bank & Trust, Mich., 1967-68, Bank of Lansing, Mich., 1968-69; vice-chmn. Indsl. State Bank, Kalamazoo, 1964-66, Creative Capital Corp., N.Y.C., 1968-70; dir. Watts Industries, Inc., North Andover, Mass., 1981-84, Roller Bearing Corp. of Am., West Trenton, N.J., 1987-92, Diversified Comms., Portland, Maine, 1982-92, Sencorp Sys., Inc., Hyannis, Mass., 1989-92. Bd. dirs. Oakland unit Am. Cancer Soc., Mich., 1973-74; mem. Rep. Com., Dist. 13, Palm Beach County, Fla., 1976-80; mem. Palm Beach County Exec. Com., 1976-80; bd. dirs. Palm Beach Rep. Club, 1977-80. Served to lt. (j.g.) USN, 1973-55. Recipient Disting. Svc. award First Citizen Bank, Troy, 1974, Midwest Assn. Small Bus. Investment Cos., 1970. Mem. Nat. Assn. Small Bus. Investment Cos. (gov. 1967-70, mem. exec. com. 1967, pres. Midwest assn. 1970), New Eng. Venture Capital Assn. Clubs: Yale of the Palm Beaches (pres. 1979-80), Bath and Tennis (Palm Beach, Fla.), Wianno (Mass.), Yacht, Everglades (Palm Beach), Univ. (N.Y.C.), River (N.Y.C.).

KILBORNE, WILLIAM SKINNER, English language educator, playwright, lyricist, writer; b. Cambridge, Mass., Oct. 18, 1936; s. William Skinner and Elizabeth (Briggs) K.; m. Irene McDonald, July 1, 1961; children: William III, Frances McDonald. BA in History, Yale U., 1958; MA in English, NYU, 1965. Headmaster Woodstock (Vt.) Country Sch., 1968-71; chair dept. English, dir. studies Ft. Worth (Tex.) Country Day Sch., 1971-89; instr. English Tarrant County Jr. Coll., Hurst, Tex., 1989—. Co-author, lyricist (mus. plays) Head Over Heels, 1983, SHS Pinapore, 1983, (children's mus. play) Little Red Riding Hood, 1978; co-author (drama) A Week From Thursday, 1994. Pres. Ft. Worth chpt. Internat. Soc. Torch Clubs. With U.S. Army, 1959-60. Democrat. Home and Office: 2200 Huntington Ln Fort Worth TX 76110-1744

KILBOURNE, LEWIS BUCKNER, food service company executive; b. New Orleans, Jan. 25, 1947; s. Lewis Perkins K.; m. Mary A. Kilbourne, Mar. 23, 1968 (div. May 1983); children: Jessica Helen, Jocelynn Anne, Robert Thomas; m. Deanna Burditt, Aug. 24, 1985; children: Alexander Scott, Katherine Emily. BA, La. State U., 1972; MA, U. Pa., 1975, PhD, 1977. Banking officer 1st City Nat. Bank, Houston, 1977-80; treas., v.p. Nat. Convenience Stores, Houston, 1980-84; v.p., chief fin. officer Church's Fried Chicken, San Antonio, 1984-86; CFO, sr. v.p. Brock Hotel Corp. and Showbiz Pizza, Dallas, 1986-88; CFO, exec. v.p. Al Copeland Enterprises, New Orleans, 1988-91; also bd. dirs.; fin. mgmt. cons. Kilbourne & Assocs., Houston, 1991-94; sr. v.p., CFO, treas. Sonic Corp., Oklahoma City, 1994—;

bd. dirs. Showbiz Pizza Time, Inc., Irving, Tex., Leadership Oklahoma City. Bd. dirs. Okla. ARC, 1994—, La. div. U.S. Olympic Com., New Orleans, 1990-92, San Antonio coun. Jr. Achievement, 1984-86, Tex. coun. Boy Scouts Am., San Antonio, 1984-86. With USAF, 1966-70. Mem. Fin. Execs. Inst. Nat. Restaurant Assn., Internat. Franchise Assn., Nat. Corp. Cash Mgmt. Assn. (charter), Fin. Mgmt. Assn., Food Svc. and Lodging Inst., New Orleans C. of C. (bd. dirs. 1989-90), Am. Red Cross Okla. (bd. dirs.), Rotary Club. Methodist. Home: 3408 Hickory Stick Rd Oklahoma City OK 73120-5515 Office: Sonic Corp 101 Park Ave Oklahoma City OK 73102-7204

KILBY, JACK ST. CLAIR, electrical engineer; b. Jefferson City, Mo., Nov. 8, 1923; s. Hubert St. Clair and Vina (Freitag) K.; m. Barbara Annegers, June 27, 1948; children: Ann, Janet Lee. BEE, U. Ill., 1947; MS, U. Wis., 1950; DEng (hon.), U. Miami, 1982; DSc (hon.), U. Wis., 1990; DEng (hon.), Rochester Inst. Tech., 1986; DSc (hon.), U. Ill., 1988; DSc, Rensselaer Poly. Inst., 1990; DSc (hon.), Yale U., 1995. Program mgr. Globe-Union, Inc., Milw., 1948-58; asst. v.p. Tex. Instruments, Inc., Dallas, 1958-70; self-employed inventor Dallas, 1970—; disting. prof. elec. engring. Tex. A&M U., 1978-85; inventor monolithic integrated circuit, others; cons. to govt. and industry. Served with AUS, 1943-45. Recipient Nat. Medal of Sci., 1969, 90, Ballentine medal Franklin Inst., 1967, Alumni Achievement award U. Ill., 1974, Holley medal ASME, 1982, 89; inducted into Nat. Inventors Hall of Fame, U.S. Patent Office, 1981. Fellow IEEE (Sarnoff medal 1966, Brunetti award 1978, Medal of honor 1986); mem. NAE (Zworykin medal 1975, co-recipient Charles Stark Draper prize 1989, Kyoto prize for tech. achievement 1993). Home: 7723 Midbury Dr Dallas TX 75230-3211 Office: Ste 155 6600 Lyndon B Johnson Fwy Dallas TX 75240-6531

KILE, DARRYL ANDREW, professional baseball player; b. Garden Grove, Calif., Dec. 2, 1968. Student, Chaffey Jr. Coll. With Houston Astros, 1987—; mem. Nat. League All-Star Team, 1993. Office: Houston Astros PO Box 288 Houston TX 77001-0288*

KILE, MIKE, protective services official; b. Savannah, Ga., Dec. 3, 1946; s. John Wallace and Verna Lee (Parker) K.; m. Helen Bazemore; children: Julie, Janie, Alyson. Grad., Screven H.S. Police chief Sardis (Ga.) Police Dept., 1969; dep. sheriff Screven County Sheriff Dept., Sylvania, Ga., 1970-74, chief dep. sheriff, 1974-83, sheriff, 1993—; police chief Hiltonia (Ga.) Police Dept., 1984-92. Pres. Screven County Jaycees, 1974-75, 80-84, sec. treas., 1976-79; pres. Screven County Exchange Club, 1989-92, sec., treas., 1993-94; chmn. Empty Stocking Fund, 1975-95, Muscular Dystrophy Assoc., 1970-95, Arthritis Found., 1988-92; mem. Hiltonia Vol. Fire Dept., 1985—; officer Screven County H.S. Booster Club, 1990. Recipient Law Enforcement Officer of the Year, 1975. Mem. Screen County C. of C., Ga. Sheriff's Assn., Ga. Peace Officers Assn., Santa's Pockets, Nat. Sheriff Assn., Rotary, Optimist Club of Screven County. Home: 121 Johnson Dr Sylvania GA 30467 Office: Screven County Sheriff's Office 339 Rocky Ford Rd Sylvania GA 30467

KILGORE, DONALD GIBSON, JR., pathologist; b. Dallas, Nov. 21, 1927; s. Donald Gibson and Gladys (Watson) K.; m. Jean Upchurch Augur, Aug. 23, 1952; children: Michael Augur, Stephen Bassett, Phillip Arthur, Geoffrey Scott, Sharon Louise. Student, So. Meth. U., 1943-45; MD, Southwestern Med. Coll., U. Tex., 1949. Diplomate Am. Bd. Pathology, Am. Bd. Dermatopathology, Am. Bd. Blood Banking. Notary Pub. Intern Parkland Meml. Hosp., Dallas, 1949-50; resident in pathology Charity Hosp. La., New Orleans, 1950-54, asst. pathologist, 1952-54; pathologist Greenville (S.C.) Hosp. System, 1956—, dir. labs., 1985—; dir. labs. Greenville Meml. Hosp., 1972—; cons. pathologist St. Francis Hosp., Shriners Hosp., Greenville, Easley Baptist. Hosp.; vis. lectr. Clemson U., 1963—; asst. prof. pathology Med. U. S.C., 1968—; pres. Pathology Assocs. of Greenville, 1983—. Recipient Disting. Svc. award S.C. Hosp. Assn., 1976. Fellow Coll. Am. Pathologists (life, assemblyman S.C. 1968-71), Am. Soc. Clin. Pathologists (councilor S.C. 1959-62), Am. Soc. Dermatopathology; mem. Am. Assn. Blood Banks (life, adv. coun. 1962-67, insp. committeeman Southeast dist. 1965—), AMA (ho. of dels. 1978-94), So. Med. Assn., S.C. Med. Assn., (exec. coun. 1969-76, 1978-94, pres. 1974-75; A.H. Robins award for Outstanding Cmty. Svc. 1985), Am. Soc. Cytology, Am. Coll. Nuc. Medicine, Nat. Assn. Med. Examiners, S.C. Inst. Med. Edn. and Rsch. (pres. 1974-80), S.C. Soc. Pathologists (pres. 1969-72), Richard III Soc. (co-chmn. Am. 1966-75), Am. Numis. Soc. (life), Soc. Ancient Numismatics (life), Am. Numis. Assn. (life), Blue Ridge Numis. Assn. (life), Royal Numis. Soc. (life), S.C. Numis. Assn. (life), Mensa (life), S.C. Congress Parents and Tchrs. (life), Greenville County Dental Soc. (hon. life), Greater Greenville C. of C., Greenville County Hist. Soc. (life), Hist. Greenville Found. (exec. com. 1994—), Preservation Soc. of Charleston (life), S.C. Hist. Soc. (life), Tex. State Hist. Assn. (life), Thomas Wolfe Soc. (life), Medieval Acad. of Am. (life), Archeol. Inst. Am. (life), Brookgreen Gardens Found. (life), Friends of Tewkesbury Abbey (life), Canterbury Cathedral Trust in Am. (life), Assn. Friends of Lincoln Cathedral (life), U.S. Power Squadron, Confrerie des Chevaliers du Tastevin (chevalier Atlanta chpt.), Soc. Med. Friends of Wine, Wine Acad. Am. (life), Soc. Wine Educators, Les Amis du Vin (life), Confrerie de la Chaine des Rotisseurs (bailli and conseiller de L'Ordre Mondial Greenville chpt.), Epicurean Assn. of Am. (selection com.), Clan MacDuff Soc. Am. (exec. coun. 1980—), St. Andrews Soc. Upper S.C. (bd. govs. 1991-93), So. Meth. U. Alumni Assn. (life), Highland Park H.S. Alumni Assn. (life), Phi Eta Sigma, Phi Chi. Democrat. Presbyterian (ruling elder 1969—). Clubs: Commerce (life), Poinsett (life), Torch (pres. 1964-65), Greenville Country (life), Thirty-Nine (pres. 1981-82), Chandon. Lodge: Rotary (Paul Harris fellow 1988). Home: 129 Rockingham Rd Greenville SC 29607-3620 Office: 8 Memorial Medical Ct Greenville SC 29605-4485

KILGORE, JANICE KAY, musician, educator; b. Dallas, July 6, 1955; d. Jean Kendall and Dorothy Helen (King) K. Student, Oral Roberts U., 1973-76; AA, Mountain View Coll., 1979; MusB, U. North Tex., 1983, M in Mus. Edn., 1990, doctoral studies in music performance. Cert. music tchr., Tex. Tchr. aide ESL Dallas Pub. Schs., 1979, substitute tchr., 1979-83, class piano tchr., 1983-84, choir dir./class piano instr., 1988-90, orch. tchr., 1992—; owner TNET Telecomm. Network Engring. Technologies LLC, 1995—; asst. dir. Jazz Singers, Oral Roberts U., Tulsa, 1975-76; music dir., vocalist, keyboardist, booking agent, violist Janal, High Soc., Dallas Woodwind Ensemble Imperial String Quartet, Imperial Brass Ensemble, 1978—; music instr. Project Upward Bound, Denton, Tex., 1981; tech. Waxahachie (Tex.) Ind. Sch. Dist., 1990-92, choir dir., coord. dept. voice, orch. tchr., 1992-96; class keyboard instr. Baldwin Family Music, Dallas, 1987-89; music instr. North Lake Coll., Irving, Tex., 1990—; creator, dir. numerous outdoor concerts; owners Southwest Music Enterprises. Author: British English to American English Dictionary, 1994; composer (symphonic poem) Scottish Suite, 1977, (choral work) The Wisemen, 1990; contbr. articles to mags. dir. Urbandale Christian Ch., Dallas, 1977-79, Centenary United Meth. Ch., Dallas, 1984-85, First United Meth. Ch., Midlothian, Tex., 1985-87, St. Luke United Meth. Ch., Dallas, 1989-90, First United Meth. Ch., Waxahachie, 1990-93, Trinity United Meth. Ch., Duncanville, Tex., 1993-94, Tyler St. United Meth. Ch., Dallas. Recipient Missionary Svc. award United Meth. Women, 1986. Mem. Tex. Music Educators Assn. (presenter 1994), Tex. Choral Dir. Assn., Tex. Orch. Dirs. Assn., Dallas Music Educators Assn., Denton B. Soc., Wichita Falls Symphony Orchestra, Kappa Delta Pi, Pi Kappa Lambda. Republican. Home: 317 Oak Meadow Ln Cedar Hill TX 75104-3283

KILGORE, JOE EVERETT, JR., army officer; b. Chattanooga, Dec. 11, 1954; s. Joe Everett and Jewell Yvonne (Nunley) K.; m. Mary Nijhuis, Aug. 21, 1982. BA in Biology, U. Tenn., Chattanooga, 1976; MS in Systems Mgmt., U. So. Calif., 1980; MA in Internat. Rels., Salve Regina Coll., Newport, R.I., 1990; MS in Nat. Security, U.S. Naval War Coll., Newport, 1990. Cert. diving officer and civilian diving instr. Commd. 2d lt. U.S. Army, 1976, advanced through grades to lt. col., 1987; platoon leader 101st Airborne Div., Ft. Campbell, Ky., 1976-79; detachment comdr. 1st bn. 7th Spl. Forces Group, Ft. Bragg, N.C., 1980-83, co. comdr. hdqs., 1983-84; plans and ops. officer U.S. Army Western Command, Ft. Shafter, Hawaii, 1985-89; comdr. A Co., 2d bn. 1st Spl. Forces Group, Ft. Lewis, Wash., 1990-91, exec. officer 2d bn., 1991-92; commander 1st bn. 7th SFGA U.S. Army, 1995—; exec. officer 1st Spl. Forces Group, 1992; inspector gen. USSOCOM, 1993; dir. tng. Down Under Divers, Waipahu, Hawaii, 1985-89; instr. scuba diving Aquidneck Island Divers, Salve Regina Coll., 1989-90. Contbr. articles to mil. and diving publs. Advisor Explorer Post 5101, Boy Scouts Am., Chattanooga, 1972-76; dir. Explorer Olymics, U. Tenn., 1975; instr. oxygen first aid Divers Alert Network, Chapel Hill, N.C., 1991; instr., disaster vol. ARC; spkr. jr. ROTC program, Oahu, Hawaii, 1985-89. Mem. NRA (life), Nat. Assn. Underwater Instrs. (life, instr.), Spl. Forces Assn. (life, membership com. 1991-92), Assn. U.S. Army, Res. Officers Assn., Am. Legon, N.Am. Fishing Club (life charter), Beta Beta Beta. Methodist. Home: 1612 Hennessy Pl Fayetteville NC 28303

KILGOUR, FREDERICK GRIDLEY, librarian, educator; b. Springfield, Mass., Jan. 6, 1914; s. Edward Francis and Lillian Bess (Piper) K.; m. Eleanor Margaret Beach, Sept. 3, 1940; children: Christopher Beach, Martha, Alison, Meredith. AB, Harvard U., 1935; student, Columbia Sch. Library Service, summers 1939-41; LLD (hon.), Marietta Coll., 1980, Coll. of Wooster, 1981; DHL (hon.), Ohio State U., 1980, Denison U., 1983, U. Mo., Kansas City, 1989. Staff Harvard Coll. Library, 1935-42, OSS, 1942-45; dep. dir. office of intelligence collection and dissemination U.S. Dept. State, 1946-48; librarian Yale Med. Library, 1948-65; asso. librarian for research and devel. Yale U. Library, 1965-67; mng. editor Yale Jour. Biology and Medicine, 1949-65; lectr. in history of sci. Yale U., 1950-59, lectr. history of tech., 1961-67; fellow Davenport Coll., 1950-67; pres., exec. dir. Online Computer Library Ctr., OCLC, Inc., 1967-80, vice chmn. bd. trustees Online Computer Library Ctr., 1981-83; founder trustee Online Computer Libr. Ctr., 1984—; Disting. rsch. prof. U. N.C., Chapel Hill, 1990—. Author: Library of the Medical Institution of Yale College and Its Catalogue of 1865, 1960, The Library and Information Science CumIndex, 1975; co-author: Engineering in History, 1956, 90; author: Collected Papers, 2 vols., 1984; editor: Book of Bodily Exercises, 1960, Jour. Library Automation, 1968-71; contbr. to scholarly jours. Served as lt. (j.g.) USNR, 1943-45, overseas duty. Decorated Legion of Merit; recipient Margaret Mann citation in cataloging and classification, 1974, Melvil Dewey medal, 1978; Acad./Research Librarian of Year, 1979; Library Info. Tech. award, 1979, numerous others. Mem. ALA, Am. Soc. Info. Sci. (Merit award 1979), Soc. for History of Tech. Club: Cosmos (Washington). Home: 207 Carolina Meadows Villa Chapel Hill NC 27514-8500

KILKELLY, BRIAN HOLTEN, lighting company executive; b. East Orange, N.J., June 20, 1943; s. Daniel Joeseph and Mary Lorretta (Brown) K.; m. Judith Louise Kroger, May 21, 1966; children: Christopher, James. BS in Mktg., Fairleigh Dickinson U., 1968; MBA, Ga. State U., 1986. Sales rep. Thomas Lighting Div., Northern, N.J., 1965-68; mktg. svcs. Globe Inc., Hazelton, Pa., 1968-70; manpower devel./product mgr. Lithonia Lighting Div., Conyers, Ga., 1970-75; nat. market devel./southeastern mgr. Cooper Lighting Div., Atlanta, 1975-88; prin. Kilkelly Mgmt. Cons. Group, Conyers, 1988-89; partner Landmark Commercial & Investment Real Estate Inc., Conyers, 1988-95; CEO Peachtree Lighting Inc., Covington, Ga., 1988—; Bd. dirs. Tech Able Handicapped Tech. Access.; guest lectr. bus. sch. Ga. State U. Contbr. articles to profl. jours. Active Kiwanis Internat. Conyers, 1988—, The Planning Forum, Vision 2020 Region Bd.; vol. Olympics, Atlanta, 1996. With USNR, 1961-67. Mem. Nat. Assn. Realtors (Ga. chpt., comml. coun., strategic planning com.), Nat. Fire Protection Assn. (joint 101/70 com.), Illuminating Engring. Soc. (chmn. tech. com. 1975—), Japan Am. Soc., Ga. Assn. Real Estate Exchangers, KC (grand knight, 1st degree team, chmn. com., Cert. of Merit 1990), EMBA Alumni Assn. (steering com., fund raising). Republican. Roman Catholic. Home: 2377 Country Club Dr SE Conyers GA 30208-5101

KILLAM, JILL MINERVINI, oil and gas company executive; b. Pitts., Sept. 6, 1954; d. Virginio Lucien and Helen Elizabeth (Safgren) Minervini; m. Clayton Henry Killam, June 4, 1973. AAS with high honors, Eastfield Jr. Coll., Mesquite, Tex., 1974; BBA with high honors, U. Tex., Arlington, 1985. CPA, Tex. Asst. to treas. CKB & Assocs., Dallas, 1985-89, v.p., chief acctg. officer, 1989-92; v.p., CFO Box Energy Corp. (formerly OKC Ltd. Partnership), Dallas, 1992-96. Mem. AICPA (Elijah Watt Sells award 1985), Tex. State Bd. Pub. Accts. (lic., Spl. award for Outstanding Achievement 1986), Tex. Soc. CPAs (state and Dallas chpt.), Petroleum Accts. Soc. Dallas, Inst. Mgmt. Accts. Republican. Roman Catholic. Office: Box Energy Corp 8201 Preston Rd Ste 600 Dallas TX 75225-6211

KILLEBREW, FLAVIUS CHARLES, biology educator, academic administrator; b. Canadian, Tex., Apr. 2, 1949; s. Wilbur N. and Nellie M. (Davidson) K.; m. Kathy C. Bartley, Dec. 23, 1981; 1 child, Arian. BS in Biology, West Tex. State Univ., 1971; MS in Biology, West Tex. State U., 1972; PhD in Zoology, U. Ark., 1976. Grad. asst. U. Ark., Fayetteville, 1972-76, mus. asst., 1974-76; asst. prof. biology West Tex. A&M U., Canyon, 1976-81; assoc. prof. West Tex. State U., Canyon, 1981-88, prof., 1988—, grad. dir., 1988-91, grad. dean, 1991-94; dir. regional div. Tex. Engring. Experiment Sta., Canyon, 1991—; provost, v.p. for acad. affairs, 1994—; adj. prof. Tex. A&M U., College Station, 1990—. Sponsor T-Anchor 4-H, Canyon, 1985-90, WT Speakers Bur., Canyon, 1986—. Grantee U.S. Army Corps Engrs, 1978, Killgore Rsch. Ctr., 1989-91. Mem. Herpetologists League, Soc. for Study of Amphibians, Am. Soc. Ichthyologists, Assn. Tex. Grad. Schs. (pres. 1993), Masons, Tri Bet, Alpha Chi. Methodist. Office: West Tex A&M U WT Box 727 Canyon TX 79016

KILLGALLON, CHRISTINE BEHRENS, healthcare administrator; b. Portsmouth, Ohio, June 29, 1958; d. Carl William Behrens and Karin Rita (Roeder) Behrens-Ellis; m. William Casley Killgallon, June 21, 1989. AS in Sci., Brunswick Coll., 1979, AS in Nursing, 1981; BA in Econs., George Mason U., 1987; M in Healthcare Adminstrn., Xavier U., 1989. CCRN. Staff nurse Bath County Community Hosp., Hot Springs, Va., 1981-82; critical care nurse U. Va. Med. Ctr., Charlottesville, Va., 1982-85; med. paralegal Donahue, Ehrmantraut, Montedonico, Washington, 1986; adminstrv. intern U. Va. Med. Ctr., Charlottesville, 1987; adminstrv. resident Alleghany Regional Hosp., Lowmoor, Va., 1989-95; exec.v.p. Odin Co., 1995—; bd. dirs. Odin Co.; v.p. comms. Odin Sys. Internat. Mem. aux. Safe Harbor, St. Simons, Ga., 1991; active Med. Assistance Program, Brunswick, 1990, Rep. Women's Orgn., St. Simons, 1990; mem. found. bd. S.E. Ga. Regional Med. Ctr. mem. AACCN, Am. Hosp. Assn., Am. Coll. Healthcare Execs., Golden Isles Investment Club St. Simons (pres. 1994), Omicron Delta Epsilon Theta. Presbyterian. Home: 1335 Hilltop Rd Charlottesville VA 22903-1224

KILLGORE, LE, journalist, political columnist; b. Poughkeepsie, N.Y., Mar. 16, 1926; m. James A. Killgore, July 24, 1948; children: Lynne, Robert, Andrew. BA in Romance Langs., Skidmore Coll., 1948; postgrad., Auburn U., 1961-62. Classroom tchr. music Stare Baldwin Sch., Dallas, 1949-50, The Little Sch., Dallas, 1950-51; substitute tchr. DOD Sch., Clark AB, Philippines, 1964-65, Dayton Ohio Schs., 1966-67, Jeb Stuart High Sch., Fairfax County, Va., 1967-68; staff writer Standard-Times, San Angelo, Tex., 1972-79, sr. staff writer, 1979-83, political affairs editor, 1983-92; polit. cons. San Angelo, Tex., 1992—; co-host radio/TV pub. affairs show. Staff writer, editor Officers Wives Club mags., Clark AB, Philippines, 1964, McClellan AFB, Calif., 1966, Panama Canal Zone, 1969-71. Recipient Overall Excellence in News Gathering award Headliners Club, 1973, Outstanding Continuous Coverage of Edn. award Tex. State Tchrs. Assn., 1977, Excellence in Health-related Reporting Tex. Med. Assn., 1977. Mem. Soc. Profl. Journalists (pres. San Angelo chpt. 1984, bd. dirs. 1986, 87, 89).

KILLHOUR, WILLIAM GHERKY, paper company executive; b. Phila., June 2, 1925; s. William Brelsford and Jean (Gherky) K.; AB in Econs., U. Pa., 1947; m. Josephine Quarrier Greenwood, July 12, 1947; children: Daphne S. (Mrs. John David Polys), William Brelsford II, Jean Gherky (Mrs. David Akers), Gilson Engel. Salesman, Quaker City Paper Co., York, Pa., 1947-50; co-founder W.B. Killhour & Sons, Inc., Phila., 1950, salesman, treas., mgr. printing paper div., 1950-61, pres., 1961-84; v.p. sales Killhour Comml. Paper Co., 1984—; mem. Paper Distbn. Coun. of U.S., 1977-81; past mem. mcht. adv. com. Sorg Paper Co., Scott Paper Co., Howard Paper Mills, Kimberly Clark. Pres., Stafford Sch. PTA, 1959; advisor Savannah Coll. of Arts and Designs; head coach, founder Hilton Head H.S. crew, 1989-94; mem. Land Bank Commn., Town of Hilton Head Island, 1994—; mem. U.S. Rowing Masters Com., rep. S.E. U.S.A. Region, 1994—. Served from ensign to lt. (j.g.) USNR, 1944-46; PTO. Mem. U.S. Rowing Assn. (cert., past chmn. Master's com., coach 1991) Paper Trade Assn. Phila. (pres. 1966), Nat. Paper Trade Assn. (regional dir. 1974—, mem. indsl. paper com. 1972-73, nat. treas. 1977-78, nat. v.p. 1978-80, pres. 1980-81), Susquehanna Litho Club (pres. 1970), Jr. Execs. Club Graphic Arts of Phila. (dir. 1955-60), St. Andrews Soc. Phila., York Club Printing House Craftsmen, Fearing Family Orgn., Mayflower Soc., Merion Cricket Club, Palmetto Rowing Club (founder, pres., head coach Hilton Head, S.C.), Philadelphia Racquet Club (chmn. squash racquets com. 1972-82), Country of York, Undine Barge Club, Spanish Wells Golf Club (Hilton Head, S.C.), Masons, S.C. Yacht Club (Hilton Head). Nat. age group champion double sculls, 1982, 85, 91, nat. single sculls champion, 1985, world single sculls champion, 1990, Can. Henley single sculls champion, 1985, world 8-oar crew champion, Toronto, 1985, world 4-oar crew champion, 1985, 87, 90-95, world double sculls bronze, 1985, world double sculls champion, 1990-92, nat. 8-oar crew age group champion, 1986, 88, 89-90, 92-93, nat. 4-oar crew age group champion, 1987-91, Nat. Quad champion, 1991, World Quad, 1993-94, world 8 champion 1985, 87-90, 92-93, 95, single scull winner Head of Chattahoochie Regatta, Atlanta 88, and numerous others.

KILLIAN, JANICE KAY NELSON, music educator, researcher; b. Mitchell, S.D., Jan. 31, 1946; d. Selmer J. and V. Nadine (Barriger) Nelson; m. Larry H. Killian II, June 18, 1981; children: Larry H. III, Michael R. Student, Augustana Coll., Sioux Falls, S.D., 1964-66; BME, U. Kans., 1968; MA, U. Conn., 1973; PhD, U. Tex., 1980. Cert. tchr., Tex., Minn., Conn., Kans. Music tchr. East Hartford (Conn.) Sch. Dist., 1969-74; choral dir. Edina (Minn.) Sch. Dist., 1974-77; asst. instr. U. Tex., Austin, 1977-80; asst. prof. SUNY, Buffalo, 1980-83; choral dir. Austin (Tex.) Sch. Dist., 1983-85, Carrollton-Farmer's Br. Sch. Dist., Carrollton, Tex., 1985-90; assoc. prof. Tex. Woman's U., Denton, 1990—; adj. prof. U. Tex., Austin, 1983-84; cons. Hal Leonard Pub. Corp., Milw., 1994—. Author: (textbook series) Essential Elements for Grades 7-12 Choir, 1996; contbr. articles to profl. jours. Recipient Mary Mason Lyons award Tex. Woman's U., 1995, PTA Lifetime award Carrollton PTA, 1989, Supt.'s award Carrollton Pub. Schs., 1988, East Hartford Pub. Schs., 1973. Mem. Am. Choral Dirs. assn. (collegiate advisor 1980—), Nat. Assn. for Music Therapy, Tex. Music Edn. Assn., Tex. Music Edn. Conf., Music Educators Nat. Conf. (state collegiate chair), Rotary. Office: Texas Womans University Dept Performing Arts Denton TX 76204

KILLIAN, LEWIS MARTIN, sociology educator; b. Darien, Ga., Feb. 15, 1919; s. Lewis Martin and Edith (Robinson) K.; m. Katharine Newbold Goold, Apr. 11, 1942; children: Katharine Newbold, Lewis Martin, John Calhoun. A.B., U. Ga., 1940, M.A., 1941; Ph.D., U. Chgo., 1949. Asst. prof. sociology U. Okla., 1949-52; asso. prof. sociology Fla. State U., 1952-57, prof., 1957-68, chmn. dept. sociology, 1966-68; prof., head dept. sociology U. Conn., 1968-69; prof. U. Mass., Amherst, 1969-84; prof. emeritus U. Mass., 1984—; vis. prof. UCLA, 1965-66, U. Hawaii, 1972; vis. lectr. Thames Poly., London, 1980-81; adj. prof. U. W. Fla., 1986—; Disting. vis. prof. U. Del., 1986. Author: (with Ralph H. Turner) Collective Behavior, 1957, 3d rev. edit., 1987, (with Charles M. Grigg) Racial Crisis in America, 1963, The Impossible Revolution, 1968, White Southerners, 1970, rev. edit., 1985, The Impossible Revolution: Phase II, 1974, Black and White: Reflections of a White Southern Sociologist, 1994. Cons. com. disaster studies NRC, 1952-57, cons. to atty. gen. of Fla., 1954-55; chmn. human rights advocacy com., dist. 1, State of Fla., 1991-93; mem. Fla. Statewide Human Rights Advocacy Com., 1994—. Col. USAR, ret. Guggenheim fellow, 1975-76. Mem. Am. Sociol. Assn. (mem. coun. 1975-79), So. Sociol. Soc. (pres. 1989-90), Phi Beta Kappa, Omicron Delta Kappa, Kappa Alpha, Phi Kappa Phi. Home: 8820 Burning Tree Rd Pensacola FL 32514-5605

KILLINGSWORTH, MAXINE ARMATHA, special education educator; b. Ft. Worth, Apr. 29, 1935; d. Marshall Raphael and Jewel Catherine (Robertson) Reliford; m. Prince B. Oliver Jr., June 16, 1963 (div.); m. Lee Killingsworth Jr., Sept. 4, 1975; 1 child, Saladin Charles. BS, Bethune-Cookman Coll., 1957; teaching cert., N. Tex. State U., 1957; MEd, Prairie View U., 1960; postgrad., Tex. Christian U., 1971-75. Cert. elem. tchr., spl. edn1. tchr., Tex., Wis. Classroom tchr. Ft. Worth Ind. Sch. Dist., 1958-63, 64-90, 1996—; classroom tchr. Milw. Pub. Schs., 1964; pvt. piano tchr., Ft. Worth, 1966-76. Organist, pianist Mt. Hermon Missionary Bapt. Ch., Ft. Worth, 1986—, , dir. of music, 1985—, dir. Bapt. tng. union, 1976—; chmn. Black Arts Festival, 1961; campaign sec. John Hill for Gov., Ft. Worth. Ft. Worth Ind. Sch. Dist. grantee, 1986; recipient Music Ministry Svc. award Mt. Zion Bapt. Ch., 1980, Svc. award Mt. Hermon Bapt. Ch., 1986, Campfire Girls, Inc., 1960. Mem. Ft. Worth Classroom Tchr. Assn. (Tchr. of Yr. 1961, faculty rep. 1958-62), NEA, Tex. State Tchr. Assn., Coun. for Exceptional Children, Bethune-Cookman Alumni Assn., Delta Sigma Theta (pres. Ft. Worth alumnae chpt. 1961-65, Leadership award 1984). Democrat. Home: 2612 Glen Gardens Ave Fort Worth TX 76119-2721

KILLORIN, EDWARD WYLLY, lawyer, tree farmer; b. Savannah, Ga., Oct. 16, 1928; s. Joseph Ignatius and Myrtle (Bell) K.; m. Virginia Melson Ware, June 15, 1957; children: Robert Ware, Edward Wylly, Joseph Rigdon. BS, Spring Hill Coll., Mobile, 1952; LLB magna cum laude, U. Ga., 1957. Bar: Ga. 1956. Pvt. practice in Atlanta, 1957—; ptnr. firm Gambrell, Russell, Killorin & Forbes, 1964-78; sr. ptnr. firm Killorin & Killorin, 1978—; lectr. Inst. Continuing Legal Edn. Ga., 1967—. Adj. prof. law Ga. State U., 1984-87. Chmn., Gov.'s Adv. Com. on Coordination State and Local Govt., 1973, Gov.'s Legal Adv. Council for Workmen's Compensation, 1974-76; bd. regents Spring Hill Coll., 1975-82, trustee, 1981-91. Served with AUS, 1946-47, 52-54. Recipient Disting. Alumnus award Spring Hill Coll., 1972. Mem. ABA, Internat., Ga. (chmn. jud. compensation com. 1976-77, chmn. legis. com. 1977-78), Atlanta (editor Atlanta Lawyer 1967-70, exec. com. 1971-74, chmn. legislation com. 1978-80) bar assns., Am. Judicature Soc., Lawyers Club Atlanta, Atlanta Legal Aid Soc. (adv. com. 1966-70, dir. 1971-74), Nat. Legal Aid and Defender Assn., Internat. Assn. Ins. Counsel (chmn. environ. law com. 1976-78), Atlanta Lawyers Found., Ga. Bar Found. (life), Ga. Def. Lawyers Assn. (dir. 1972-80), Ga. C. of C. (chmn. govtl. dept. 1970-75, chmn. workmen's compensation com. 1979—, Disting. Svc. award 1970-75), Def. Research Inst. (Ga. chmn. 1970-71), Spring Hill Coll. Alumni Assn. (nat. pres. 1972-74), U. Ga. Law Sch. Assn. (nat. pres. 1986-87, Disting. Svc. Scroll 1989), Ga. Forestry Assn. (life, bd. dirs. 1969—, pres. 1977-79, chmn. bd. 1979-81), Am. Forestry Assn., Demosthenian Lit. Soc. (pres. 1957), Sphinx, Blue Key, Gridiron, Phi Beta Kappa, Phi Beta Kappa Assos., Phi Kappa Phi, Phi Delta Phi, Phi Omega. Clubs: Capital City, Peachtree Golf, Commerce, Buckhead (Atlanta); Oglethorpe (Savannah), Highland Country Club (LaGrange). Roman Catholic. Contbr. articles to legal jours. Home: 436 Blackland Rd NW Atlanta GA 30342-4005 Office: Killorin & Killorin 11 Piedmont Ctr NE Atlanta GA 30305-1738

KILLORIN, ROBERT WARE, lawyer; b. Atlanta, Nov. 12, 1959; s. Edward W. and Virgina (Ware) K. AB cum laude, Duke U., 1980; JD, U. Ga., 1983. Bar: Ga. 1984, U.S. Dist. Ct. (no. dist.) Ga. 1984, U.S. Ct. Appeals (11th cir.) 1984. Ptnr. Killorin & Killorin, Atlanta, 1984—. Mem. ABA, Atlanta Bar Assn., Ga. Def. Lawyers Assn., State Bar Ga. (chair SCOPE com. 1986, young lawyers sect. legis. affairs com. 1989-91, instr. mock trial program 1989—), Ga. C. of C. (govtl. affairs com.), Internat. Assn. Def. Counsel, Nat. Assn. Underwater Instrs., Nat. Speliological Soc., U. Ga. Pres.'s Club. Home: 5587 Benton Woods Dr NE Atlanta GA 30342-1308 Office: Killorin & Killorin 11 Piedmont Ctr NE Ste 825 Atlanta GA 30305-1738

KILMARTIN, JOSEPH FRANCIS, JR., business executive, consultant; b. New Haven, Mar. 11, 1924; s. Joseph Francis and Lauretta M. (Collins) K.; student St. Thomas Sem., 1944; BA, Holy Cross Coll., 1947; m. Gloria M. Schaffer, June 26, 1954; children: Joanne, Diane. Prodn. mgr. A.C. Gilbert Co., New Haven, 1947-49; profl. performer Broadway show Small Wonder, also TV shows Your Hit Parade, Philco Playhouse, Armstrong Circle Theatre, 1949-50; producer NBC-TV, N.Y.C., 1950-53; v.p. sales Cellomatic Corp., N.Y.C., 1953-59; sr. v.p. Transfilm Inc., N.Y.C., 1959-62, MPO Videotronics, N.Y.C., 1962-66; pres. Bus. Programs Inc., Larchmont, N.Y., 1966-75, Greenwich, Conn., 1975—; pres. Kilarnold Corp.; lectr. in field, cons. Mexican Dept. Agrarian Affairs and Colonization, 1974—. Active fund-raising Cmty. Chest, 1947-49, ARC, 1947-49, Boy Scouts Am., 1958-66, United Fund, 1970-73; mem. Congl. Adv. Bd., Presdl. Task Force, Atlantic Coun., Conn. Venture Group, Mil. Affairs Coun., Fayetteville, N.C., Harnett County Strategic Planning Commn.; bd. dirs. Lee County Arts Coun.; pres. Highland Trace Land Devel. Co.; mem. exec. com., chmn.

Lee County Rep. Party Coun.; chmn. Carolina Trace Cmty. Action Com. Recipient medal of excellence Mexican Agrarian Affairs and Colonization Dept., 1976; Golden Medallion award in bus. communication Miami Internat. Film Festival, 1978. Mem. Am. Mgmt. Assn., TV Execs. Soc., Pres.'s Assn. Republican. Clubs: Larchmont (N.Y.) Yacht Club, Westchester Country Club, Univ. Club (N.Y.C.), Carolina Trace Country Club, Lambs. Home: 241 Lakeview Dr Sanford NC 27330-8397

KILPATRICK, BILLIE KAY, rehabilitation nurse; b. Holdenville, Okla., Dec. 23, 1942; d. William Earl and Hettie Elnora (McCarn) Davis; m. V. Bruce Kilpatrick; 1 child, Kimberly Kay Kilpatrick Branstetter. RN, U. Nebr., 1974. CRRN, RN, CCM, Nebr., Okla. Staff nurse operating room, recovery room, emergency room Douglas County Hosp., Omaha, 1974-75; pub. health nurse Omaha Pub. Schs. and Mental Retardation Ctr., 1975-77; charge nurse med.-surg. unit, critical care unit Audrain Med. Ctr., Mexico, Mo., 1981-82; dir. nursing Ozark (Mo.) Care Ctr., 1982-83; nursing supr., discharge planner, hosp. liaison Allied Nurse Care, Inc., Oklahoma City, 1984-86; dir. med. case mgmt., cert. rehab. nurse cons., v.p. Rehab. Svcs. Assocs., Inc., Oklahoma City, 1986—, also bd. dirs.; speaker in field. Mem. ANA, Assn. Rehab. Nurses, Okla. Assn. Rehab. Nurses (pres. 1987-89), Okla. Nurses Assn., Nat. Head Injury Found., Okla. Head Injury Found., Nat. Assn. Rehab. Profls. in Pvt. Sector, Okla. Assn. Rehab. Profls. in Pvt. Sector. Republican. Lutheran. Office: PO Box 720802 Oklahoma City OK 73172-0802

KILPATRICK, CHARLES OTIS, newspaper editor, publisher; b. Fairview, Okla., June 16, 1922; s. John E. and Myrtle (Arant) K.; m. Margie Ada Partin, June 3, 1944; children: Kent Fairles, Millicent Kye, Mark Kevin. B.A., Stephen F. Austin State Coll., 1942. With daily newspapers Nacogdoches, Tex., 1940-42; with Daily Sentinel, Nacogdoches, 1946-48, Courier-Times, Tyler, Tex., 1948-49; regional editor Tyler Morning Telegraph, 1949, mng. editor, 1949-50; mem. staff Evening News, San Antonio, 1950-51; Sunday Editor San Antonio Express, 1951-54; asst. mng. editor Evening News, 1954-55, mng. editor, 1955-56; asst. exec. editor San Antonio Express and San Antonio News, 1957-58, exec. editor, 1958, v.p., 1971; pub. San Antonio Express, 1971-72; editor, pub. San Antonio Express and News, 1972-91, ret., 1991; corp. dir. features Harte-Hanks Newspapers, San Antonio, 1972-73; pres. Tex. Film Features, Inc., 1980-91; cons. Hearst Corp., 1993—. Bd. dirs. Incarnate Ward Coll., 1974-82, Mex.-Am. Cultural Inst., 1982-90, San Antonio Symphony, pres., 1984-86; bd. dirs. United Way, Goodwill Rehab. Services, San Antonio Indsl. Found.; pres. Goodwill Rehab Service, 1984-85; trustee S.W. Research Center. Lt. col. USMCR, 1942-62. Pulitzer prize journalism juror, 1963, 64, 67, 71, 75; named Tex. Newspaper Leader of Yr. Tex. Daily Newspaper Assn., 1984. Mem. Am. Newspaper Pubs. Assn., So. Newspaper Pub. Assn., Am. Soc. Newspaper Editors, Tex. A.P. Mng. Editors Assn. (pres. 1963), Tex. Daily Newspaper Assn. (pres. 1983), San Antonio C. of C. (dir.), Argyle Club, Conopus Club. Episcopalian. Office: Express-News Corp Ave E & 3d St San Antonio TX 78205

KILPATRICK, CLIFTON WAYNE, book dealer; b. Pontiac, Mich., Nov. 16, 1949; s. Martin Laverne and Shirley Irene (Powell) Ball. Grad. high sch., Ortonville, Mich. With Royal Castle (restaurant), Miami, Fla., 1969-71, Yankee Clipper (restaurant), Ft. Lauderdale, Fla., 1971-73, Creightons (restaurant), Ft. Lauderdale, Fla., 1973-75; book collector Trivia King, Ft. Lauderdale, Fla., 1975-93. Author: Trivia Professor, 1980. Democrat. Methodist. Home and Office: 903 NE 30th Dr Oakland Park FL 33334-2654

KILPATRICK, JAMES JACKSON, JR., columnist, author; b. Oklahoma City, Nov. 1, 1920; s. James Jackson and Alma Mia (Hawley) K.; m. Marie Louise Pietri, Sept. 21, 1942; children: Michael Sean, Christopher Hawley, Kevin Pietri. BJ, U. Mo., 1941. Reporter Richmond (Va.) News Leader, 1941-49, chief editorial writer, 1949-51, editor, 1951-67; writer nat. syndicated column, TV commentator. Author: The Sovereign States, 1957, The Smut Peddlers, 1960, The Southern Case for School Segregation, 1962, The Foxes' Union, 1977, (with Eugene J. McCarthy) A Political Bestiary, 1978, (with William Bake) The American South: Four Seasons of the Land, 1980, The American South: Towns and Cities, 1982, The Writer's Art, 1984, The Ear is Human, 1985, A Bestiary of Bridge, 1986, Fine Print - Reflections on the Writing Art, 1993; editor: We the States, 1964; co-editor: The Lasting South, 1957. Vice chmn. Va. Com. on Constl. Govt., 1962-68; chmn. Va. Magna Carta Com., 1965; trustee Thomas Jefferson Ctr. for Protection of Free Expression, 1990—, Supreme Ct. Hist. Soc., 1987—. Recipient medal of honor for distinguished service in journalism U. Mo., 1953; ann. award for editorial writing Sigma Delta Chi, 1954; William Allen White award U. Kans., 1979; Carr Van Anda award Ohio U., 1987; named to Okla. Hall of Fame, 1978. Fellow Soc. Profl. Journalists; mem. Nat. Conf. Editorial Writers (chmn. 1955-56), Black-Eyed Pea Soc. Am. (No. 1 Pea pro tem 1965—), Gridiron Club, Charleston Yacht Club. Whig. Episcopalian.

KIM, BRUCE CHANGSHIK, research engineer; b. Seoul, Republic of Korea, Nov. 13, 1958; came to U.S., 1971; s. David Emanuelle and Kil Ja (Lim) K.; m. Moon Young Park, May 17, 1987; children: Janet Caroline, Julie Sarah. BSEE, U. Calif., Irvine, 1981; MSEE, U. Ariz., 1985; postgrad., Ga. Inst. Tech., 1991-96. Mem. tech. staff Hughes Aircraft Co., Tucson, 1981-84; design engr. Signal Allied, Tucson, 1984-87; rsch. engr. Ga. Inst. Tech., Atlanta, 1988-91; rsch. cons. in computer networks. Author: Network Control and Management, 1991. Mem. IEEE, Korean Scientists and Engrs. Home: 2187 Surrey Ct Marietta GA 30067-6667 Office: Ga Inst Tech Sch Elec and Computer Engring Atlanta GA 30332

KIM, CHANGWOOK, computer science educator; b. Taegu, Korea, Jan. 18, 1953; came to U.S., 1980; s. Jeonghan and Yungeum (Park) K.; m. Hae Reung Park, Aug. 14, 1980; children: Andrew Eugene, David Yuson. BS, Seoul Nat. U., 1975; MS, Pa. State U., 1982; PhD, Northwestern U., 1986. Systems programmer Korea Telecommunications Co., Seoul, 1978-80; teaching asst. Northwestern U., Evanston, Ill., 1984-85, U. Tex., Richardson, 1985-86; asst. prof. U. Okla., Norman, 1986-92, assoc. prof., 1992—. Contbr. articles to profl. jours. Lt. Korean Navy, 1975-78. Mem. IEEE, European Assn. Theoretical Computer Sci., Assn. Computing Machinery. Office: U Okla Sch Computer Sci Norman OK 73019

KIM, CHONG SOONG, aerosol technology and environmental health researcher, engineer; b. Inchon, Korea, Dec. 1, 1945; came to U.S., 1971; m. Insook Park, June 10, 1972; children: Jeffrey Hosuk, Audrey Wonkyung, Monica Sookyung. BSME, Seoul Nat. U., 1968; MSME, U. Wis., 1973; PhD, U. Minn., 1978. Rsch. engr. Atomic Energy Rsch. Inst., Seoul, 1970-71; aerosol specialist Mt. Sinai Med. Ctr., Miami Beach, Fla., 1978-80; dir. Aerosol Rsch. Lab. Mt. Sinai Med. Ctr., Miami Beach, 1980-90; sr. rsch. scientist EPA, Nat. Health and Environ. Effects Rsch. Lab., Research Triangle Park, N.C., 1990—; adj. asst. prof. U. Miami (Fla.) Sch. Medicine, 1983-86, adj. assoc. prof., 1987-90, U. N.C. Sch. Medicine, Chapel Hill, 1990—; invited speaker U.S.-Fed. Republic Germany Environ. Workshop, 1987, Internat. Conf. for Aerosols in Medicine, 1988, Korean Internat. Workshop in Sci. and Engring., 1989, Respiratory Drug Delivery Symposium, 1990, Internat. Symposium on Clean Room Tech. and Contaminations Control, 1990, FDA Sci. Adv. Bd. Mtg., 1993, Assn. Official Analytic Chemists Internat. Symposium, Fine Particle Soc. annual meeting, 1994; ad hoc referee NIH, 1988, 91, VA, 1989, NSF, 1990. Mem. editorial bd. Jour. Aerosol Medicine, 1988—; contbr. articles to profl. jours.; inventor aerosol rebreathing system. Mem. ASME, Am. Assn. Aerosol Rsch., European Aerosol Assn., Internat. Soc. Aerosols in Medicine, Am. Thoracic Soc. Presbyterian. Home: 109 Brighton Ct Chapel Hill NC 27516-9005 Office: US EPA Nat Health & Environ Effects Rsch Lab Durham NC 27711

KIM, E. EDMUND, radiology educator; b. Seoul, Korea, Oct. 3, 1942; came to U.S., 1970; s. Myung-Soo and Hyo-Sun (Lee) K.; m. Bo-Ok Yang, Dec. 12, 1970; children: Patrick, Sharon, Matthew. MD, Seoul Nat. U., 1966, MS, 1968. Diplomate Am. Bd. Radiology, Am. Bd. Nuclear Medicine, Am. Bd. Diagnostic Radiology, Korean Bd. Preventive Medicine. Intern Greater Balt. Med. Ctr./Johns Hopkins Med. Instns., 1970-71; resident West Pa. Hosp./U. Pitts., 1971-74; asst. prof. radiation medicine U. Ky., Lexington, 1976-79, assoc. prof. radiation medicine, 1979-81; assoc. prof. radiology U. Tex., Houston, 1981-83, prof. radiology, 1983—, chief experiment nuclear medicine, 1987—. Grantee GE, 1989-91, FDA, 1992-94. Fellow Am. Coll. Nuclear Medicine (pres. 1994-95), Am. Coll. Radiology; mem. Soc. Nuclear Medicine, Radiol. Soc. N.Am., Soc. Magnetic Resonance. Republican. Presbyterian. Home: 7 Magnolia Bend Dr Houston TX 77024 Office: U Tex MD Anderson Cancer Ctr 1515 Holcombe Blvd Houston TX 77030

KIM, EARNEST JAE-HYUN, import and export company executive; b. Seoul, Korea, Dec. 9, 1938; s. Chang-Nyun and Gui-Nim (Yun) K.; m. Jung-Ki Eun, Mar. 25, 1967; children: Yoo-Kyoung, Ja-Hong, Young-Joo, Do-Hyung. Degree, Hanyang U., 1961; postgrad., Sung Kyun Kwan U., 1975. Reporter Daily Econ. News, Seoul, 1966-74; exec. dir. STAF Corp., Seoul, 1975-82; dir. Korea Fedn. Handicrafts Coops., Seoul, 1979-82; pres. Buenos Amigos, Inc., Laredo, Tex., 1982-95, Buenos Hermanos L.L., 1992—, Nueva Moda Mundo, Mexico City, Mex., 1990—, Buenos Amigos de Mex. S.A., 1994—, Amiguitas S.A. de C.V., Mexico City, 1995—. Inventor, patentee Method of Casting, Method of Jewelry Making. Recipient Spl. Congl. Recogniton, Congressman Albert Bustamante, 1988, Cert. of Excellence, Senator Judith Zaffirini, 1983, Cert. of Appreciation, Mayor of Laredo, 1988, Cert. of Appreciation, Am. Legion, 1988. Mem. Laredo C. of C., Lions (v.p. Laredo evening club 1991—, pres. award 1989), Laredo Country club. Buddhist. Home: 413 Chevy Chase Dr Laredo TX 78041-2702 Office: Nueva Moda Mundo SA de CV, Argentina 47 #4 Colonial Centro, Mexico City 06090, Mexico

KIM, JOHN CHAN KYU, electrical engineer; b. Tokyo, June 15, 1935; came to U.S., 1958; s. Ke Jun and Young Sok Kim; m. Tong-Rahn Chu, Sept. 11, 1965; children: Janet M., William H., Douglas S. Student, Seoul Nat. U., 1954-57; BSEE, Tri-State U., 1959; MSEE, Mich. State U., 1960, PhD in Elec. Engring., 1962. Instr. Tri-State U., Angola, Ind., 1961-62; sr. rsch. engr. Systems Rsch. Labs., Inc., Dayton, Ohio, 1962-64, Honeywell, Inc., Mpls., 1964-65; sr. staff engr. E-System Inc., Falls Church, Va., 1965-69; mgr. advanced comm. systems TRW, Inc., McLean, Va., 1969-95; tech. fellow TRW, Inc., Fairfax, Va., 1996—; nat. judge Math Counts, Alexandria, Va., 1996—. Author: Naval Shipboard Communications Systems, 1994. Bd. dirs. Vol. Ctr. of Fairfax (Va.) County, 1992—; scoutmaster Boy Scouts Am., McLean, 1983-84. Mem. IEEE, Armed Forces Comms. and Electronics Assn., Nat. Security Industry Assn. Methodist. Home: 8006 Snowpine Way Mc Lean VA 22102-2420 Office: TRW Inc 7600 Colshire Dr Mc Lean VA 22102-7600

KIM, PYUNG-SOO, martial arts educator; b. Seoul, Korea, Dec. 4, 1939; came to U.S., 1968; s. Chong Won Jun and Duk In (Lee) Kim; m. Sonnya Park Kim; children: Sean Kim, Tasha Kim. B.Russian Lang. and Lit., Han Kuk U. Fgn. Studies, Seoul, 1963. 1st degree Black Belt, 1953. Founder Kong Soo Do Club, Joong Ang H.S., Seoul, 1954, Kwon Bop Martial Arts Club, Han Kuk U. Fgn. Studies, Seoul, 1957-63; tchr. Spl. Police Detachment Korean Pres., 1958; tchr. hand-to-hand combat tng. Republic of Korea Army, 8th Divsn., 1961-63; founder Korean Tae Kwon/Karate Acad., Seoul, 1963; chief instr. Kang Duk Won Martial Arts Assn., Seoul, 1964, 8th U.S. Army and HQ I Corps, 1964-67; founder Kim Soo Coll. Tae Kwon-Karate, Houston, 1968, ChaYon-Ryu, Houston, 1970—; pres. Byung in Martial Arts Friendship Assn., Houston, 1994—; lectr. in field; faculty martial arts various univs. including Rice U.; Tae Kwon Do coord. U.S. Olympic Festival '86, Houston; flight choreographer Houston Grand Opera, 1986; advisor World Martial Arts Coun., 1990. Editor, corr. Black Belt Mag., 1964-67; author: Palgue 1,2,3, 1973, Palgue 4,5,6, 1974, Palgue 7 & 8: Black Belt Requirements, 1976, History of ChaYon-Ryu, 1990. Recipient citation for contbn. to elevating Korean nat. image in world Korean Govt., 1970; named Best Karate Instr. in Houston, Houston Press, 1990; commendation U.S. Pres. Bill Clinton, 1993; promoted to 10th Degree Black Belt. Mem. World Tae Kwon Do Fedn. (founder). Office: ChaYon-Ryu Internat Martial Arts Assn 1740 Jacquelyn Houston TX 77055

KIM, THOMAS KUNHYUK, college administrator; b. Shanghai, Peoples Republic of China, Feb. 18, 1929; came to U.S., 1948, naturalized, 1960; s. Hong Suh and Chong (Kim) K.; m. Martha Alice Zoellers, June 4, 1958; children—Lawrence Thomas, Catherine Ann. B.A., Berea Coll., 1952; M.B.A., Ind. U., 1954; Ph.D., Tulane U., 1961; L.H.D., Southwestern U., 1973; LHD, Berea Coll., 1993. Asst. prof. econs. U. Akron, O., 1961-62; asso. prof. Baker U., Baldwin, Kans., 1962-65; prof. Tex. Tech. U., Lubbock, 1965-70; pres. McMurry U., Abilene, Tex., 1970-93, chancellor, 1993-94; vis. prof. econs. and economist-in-residence Abilene Christian U., 1994—. Author: Introductory Mathematics for Economic Analysis, 1971. Mem. Phi Kappa Phi, Omicron Delta Epsilon. Methodist (del. gen. conf. 1972). Office: 1 City Ctr 241 Pine St Ste 8LD Abilene TX 79601

KIM, YOUNG KIL, aerospace engineer; b. Pusan, Korea, June 18, 1956; came to U.S., 1984; naturalized, 1988; s. Tae Hyun and Myong Ok (Shin) K.; m. Susan Katherine Hong, July 16, 1981; children: Steven Charles, Christina Kay. BS, Seoul Nat. U., Rep. of Korea, 1979; MS, Ga. Inst. Tech., 1985, PhD in Aerospace Engring., 1991. Rsch. engr. Korean Inst. Aero. Tech. Korean Air Lines, Seoul, 1978-84; vis. rsch. engr. Agy. for Def. Devel., Daedog, Republic of Korea, 1981-82; rsch. assoc. Univs. Space Rsch. Assn., Huntsville, Ala., 1991-93; rsch. engr. U. Ala. Rsch. Inst., Huntsville, 1993-96; sr. rsch. engr. U. Ala. in Huntsville Rsch. Inst., 1996—. Mem. AIAA, Korean-Am. Scientists and Engrs. Assn. Roman Catholic. Home: 9010 Cannstatt Dr Huntsville AL 35802 Office: U Ala in Huntsville Rsch Inst Huntsville AL 35899

KIMBALL, CURTIS ROLLIN, investment advisor, appraiser; b. Grand Rapids, Mich., Dec. 21, 1950; s. Rollin Hibbard and Jane Ann (Walterman) K.; m. Marilyn M. Quaderer; 1 child, Neil Curtis. BA, Duke U., 1972; MBA, Emory U., 1984. Comml. lending and trust portfolio mgr. Wachovia Bank and Trust Co., N.A., Winston-Salem, N.C., 1972-81; v.p., trust mgr. bus. owner services group Citizens and So. Nat. Bank, Atlanta, 1981-88; prin., nat. dir. Willamette Mgmt. Assocs., Inc., Portland, Oreg., 1988—, mng. prin. Atlanta office, 1995—. Chair activities coun. Portland Art Mus., 1993-94. Fellow Inst. Chartered Fin. Analysts; mem. Am. Soc. Appraisers (sr., pres. Atlanta chpt. 1985-86, treas. Portland chpt. 1993-94); mem. Nat. Assn. Bus. Econs. (pres. Portland chpt. 1992-93), Family Firm Inst., Indian Hills Country Club. Republican. Episcopalian. Avocations: running; fencing; tennis. Office: Willamette Mgmt Assocs Inc 1355 Peachtree St NE Ste 1470 Atlanta GA 30309

KIMBELL, RICHARD LEE, professional computer consultant; b. Magnolia, Ark., Dec. 25, 1949; s. Aubrey Lee and Ruth (Young) K. BBA in Mgmt., Computer Info. Systems, So. Ark. U., 1987. Computer cons., owner Happy Hackers, Magnolia, 1988—; job placement specialist Ark. Rehab. Svcs., El Dorado, 1989—; ptnr. K&L Assocs., Chidester, Ark., 1993—. Co-author: Confidential Personal Organizational Handbook, 1992; author (computer program) Confidential Personal Organization System, 1993. Mem. NRA, Washington, 1983—, NRA Inst., Washington, 1991—, We the People, 1992—. Recipient Outstanding Achievement in Mgmt. award So. Ark. U., 1988. Mem. Nat. Rehab. Assn., Ark. Rehab. Assn. Baptist. Home: Route 1 1904 N Washington Magnolia AR 71753

KIMBERLING, CHARLES RONALD, academic administrator; b. Cleve., Sept. 24, 1950; s. Foster Leroy Kimberling and Mary Ellouise (Courtright) Ford; m. Diana Ruth King, Mar. 20, 1992; 1 child, Keith Ronald. BA summa cum laude, Calif. State U., Northridge, 1972, MA in Mass Comm., 1977; AM in Am. Studies, U. So. Calif., 1974, AM in English, 1977, PhD in English, 1981; HHD (hon.), Paul Quinn Coll., Waco, Tex., 1984; LLD (hon.), Cin. Met. Coll., 1985; HLD (hon.), Edward Waters Coll., 1986; DCL (hon.), St. Augustine's Coll., 1987; HLD (hon.), West Coast U., 1987. Editor, news reporter City News Svc., L.A., 1972-74; asst. prof. journalism Calif. State U., Northridge, 1975-80; exec. sec. U.S. Dept. Edn., Washington, 1981-82, dep. asst. sec. for higher edn. programs, 1982-85, asst. sec. for postsecondary edn., 1985-88; exec. dir. Ronald Reagan Predl. Found., 1988-90; exec. v.p. United Edn. and Software, L.A., 1989-91; sr. v.p. Phillips Colls., Inc., Gulfport, Miss., 1991-96; chancellor Fla. Met. U., Tampa, 1996—; commr. U.S.-Japan Friendship Commn., Washington, 1985-88; trustee West Coast U., 1988—, Coll. Oceaneering, Wilmington, Calif., 1993—. Author: Kenneth Burke's Dramatism and the Popular Arts, 1982; contbr. chpt. to: Academy in Crisis, 1995. Del. White House Conf. on Youth, Estes Park, Colo., 1971; vol. Reagan-Bush Presdl. Campaign, Calif., 1980; edn. advisor Bush Presdl. Campaigns, 1988, 92. Recipient Disting. Alumnus citation bd. trustees Ventura County C.C., 1983, Norka Image award, The Norka Corp., Simi Valley, Calif., 1989; Raubenheimer fellow U. So. Calif., 1974. Mem. Calif. Scholarship Fedn., Calif. State U.-Northridge Alumni Assn. (Disting. Alumnus award 1987, Disting. Journalism Alumnus 1987), U. So. Calif. Alumni Assn., Phi Kappa Phi, Kappa Tau Alpha. Republican.

KIMBLE, GLADYS AUGUSTA LEE, nurse, civic worker; b. Niagara Falls, Can., June 28, 1906; d. William and Florence Augusta Baker (Buckton) Lee; naturalized citizen of the U.S.; RN, Christ Hosp., Jersey City, 1929; BS, Columbia U. Tchrs. Coll., 1938, MA, 1948; m. George Edmond Kimble, Jan. 5, 1952. Nurse, Willard Parker Hosp., N.Y.C., 1931; asst. and supervisory relief nurse Margaret Hague Maternity Hosp., Jersey City, 1931-37; staff nurse, relief supr. Manhattan Eye, Ear and Throat Hosp., N.Y.C., 1937-38; sr. staff, asst. nurse supr. Vis. Nurse Svc., N.Y.C., 1938-41; sr. pub. health nurse USPHS, Little Rock, 1941-43; pub. health supr. Providence (R.I.) Dist. Nursing Assn., 1943-46; edn. dir. Jersey City Pub. Health Nursing Svc., 1946-49, also instr. Seton Hall U., South Orange, N.J., 1947-49; pub. health nurse cons. U.S. Inst. Inter-Am. Affairs, Brazil, 1949-51; dir. pub. health dept. Englewood (N.J.) Hosp., 1951-53; nurse coord. exch. visitor nurse program Overlook Hosp., Summit, N.J., 1964-71. Recipient Appreciation award for svc. rendered Providence Hosp., 1944; Woman of Yr. award Essex County Bus. and Profl. Women, 1968. Fellow Am. Pub. Health Assn. (life), mem. Sarasota (Fla.) Geneal. Soc. (charter), Daus. of the Nile, (charter, Sarasota), Ladies Oriental Shrine of N.Am. (SAR-I Ct 79), NYLA Temple 152., Royal Order of Jesterettes, Eillim Ives #18, Sarasota. Episcopalian. Home: 4540 Bee Ridge Rd Apt 12 Sarasota FL 34233-2524

KIMBLER, LARRY BERNARD, real estate executive, accountant; b. Lucasville, Ohio, Sept. 6, 1938; s. Benjamin F. and Elizabeth L. (Kerr) K.; m. Susanna Hayes, June 20, 1964; children: Beth Ann, Carolyn Sue. BBA, U. Cin., 1964. CPA, Ohio; lic. real estate broker, Conn., Tex., N.Y. Acct. Peat, Marwick, Mitchell & Co., Cin., 1964-68; mgr. acctg. and taxes Andrew Jergens & Co., Cin., 1968-70; exec. v.p. Am. Lakes & Land Co., Houston, 1970-74; from group controller real estate and minerals to gen. mgr. land utilization Internat. Paper Co., 1974-81; pres. Internat. Paper Realty Co., N.Y.C., 1977-81; v.p. corp. real estate GTE, Stamford, Conn., also pres. GTE Realty Corp., 1981-89; prin. Kimbler Assocs., Inc., Stamford, 1989-91; exec. v.p. office pres. Staubach Alliance Svcs., Inc., Dallas, 1991—, also bd. dirs.; bd. dirs., mem. exec. com. Stamford Econ. Assistance Corp.; past pres. Westchester So. Conn. chpt., NACORE; trustee, treas. Low-Heywood Thomas Sch., Stamford; lectr., speaker in field; mem. adv. bd. Homer Hoyt Inst.; officer, bd. dirs. Indsl. Devel. Rsch. Coun.; editl. adv. bd. Bldg. Econs. Contbr. articles to profl. jours. With AUS, 1956-59. Mem. Am. Inst. Corp. Asset Mgmt. (bd. govs.), Nat. Assn. Corp. Real Estate Execs. (master corp. real estate designation, chpt. pres.), Am. Inst. CPA's, Indsl. Devel. Research Council (bd. dir., Officer Disting. Service award 1983, 87, Master Profl. Designation), Am. Found. for Blind (chmn. bd. dirs. SW Region). Presbyterian. Republican. Home: 5403 Bent Trl Dallas TX 75248-2034 Office: Ste 1100 6750 Lyndon B Johnson Fwy Dallas TX 75240-6522

KIMBRELL, DEBORAH ANN, geneticist, educator; b. San Angelo, Tex., July 22, 1950; d. Billy Lee and Dorothy (Babish) K.; m. S. Ingemar C. Olsson, June 15, 1991. BA in Biology and Psychology with honors, Mills Coll., 1972; PhD in Genetics, U. Calif., Berkeley, 1985. Rsch. technician dept. respiration physiology Max Planck Inst. Exptl. Medicine, Göttingen, Germany, 1973-74; NIH predoctoral trainee dept. genetics U. Calif., Berkeley, 1979-85; Am. Cancer Soc. postdoctoral fellow dept. genetics U. Cambridge, Eng., 1985-88; Swedish MRC vis. scientist fellow dept. microbiology U. Stockholm, 1988-90; asst. prof. dept. biology and Inst. Molecular Biology U. Houston, 1991—. Contbr. articles to profl. jours. Pres. Rsch. and Scholarship Fund grantee U. Houston, 1991, 92-93; grantee Houston Coastal Ctr., 1992-94, Am. Cancer Soc., 1993—. Mem. AAAS, Genetics Soc. Am. Office: U Houston Dept Biology Houston TX 77204

KIMBROUGH, ROBERT COOKE, III, infectious diseases physician; b. Washington, Nov. 26, 1941; s. Robert Cooke Jr. and Victoria Walton (Fitz Gerald) K.; m. Susan Jane Brackney (div.); children: Susan Fitz Gerald Kimbrough Gilson, Robert Cooke IV; m. Susan Kay Utterback, Apr. 11, 1974; children: John Williams, Bradley Warren. BS, U. Kans., 1963; MD, U. Kans., 1969. Diplomate Am. Bd. Internal Medicine. Intern, resident Baylor Coll. Medicine, Houston, 1969-73; chief resident St. Luke's Episcopal Hosp., Houston, 1972; fellow in infectious disease Baylor Coll. Medicine, 1972-74, U. Oreg. Med. Sch., Portland, 1974-75; instr. infectious diseases U. Oreg. Health Scis. Ctr., Portland, 1975-79; from asst. prof. to assoc. prof. infectious diseases Oreg. Health Scis. U., Portland, 1979-89; pvt. practice The Ferrell-Duncan Clinic, Inc., Springfield, Mo., 1989-93; prof. infectious diseases Tex. Tech. U. Health Scis. Ctr., Lubbock, 1993—. Reviewer Archives Internal Medicine, Jour. Infectious Diseases, Clin. Infectious Diseases, Annals Internal Medicine. Fellow ACP (chmn. assoc. com. 1984, 85, v.p. Oreg. chpt. 1986, pres. 1987-89, Howard P. Lewis tchg. award 1988), Infectious Diseases Soc. Am.; mem. AMA, Am. Fedn. Clin. Rsch., Am. Soc. Microbiology, Am. Assn. History of Medicine, Am. Osler Soc., Oreg. Med. Assn. (chmn. nominating com. 1985, chmn. pharmacy liaison com. 1986-89, trustee 1987-89, profl. cons. com. 1987-89), Multnomah County Med. Soc. (chmn. strategic planning com. 1985, sec. 1986, v.p. 1987, pres.-elect 1988), Tex. Med. Assn., Lubbock Med. Soc., Garza Med. Soc., Crosby County Med. Soc.,. Home: 3109 80th St Lubbock TX 79423 Office: TTUHSC Dept Medicine 3601 4th St Lubbock TX 79430

KIMBROUGH, WILLIAM ADAMS, JR., lawyer; b. Selma, Ala., July 21, 1935; s. William Adams and Elizabeth (Bradford) K.; m. Kay Lindsey, Dec. 28, 1958; children: Mary Elizabeth, William Adams. B.A. (Union Carbide scholar), U. of South, 1957; LL.B., U. Ala., 1961. Corr. Nat. Carbon Co., Chgo., 1957-58; mem. firm Lindsey & Christopher, Butler, Ala., 1961; asst. U.S. atty., 1962-65; gen. atty. Gulf, Mobile & Ohio R.R. Co., Mobile, Ala., 1965-70; mem. firm Stockman, Bedsole & Kimbrough, Mobile, 1970-76, Adams, Adams & Kimbrough, Grove Hill, Ala., 1976-77; U.S. atty. So. Dist. Ala., Mobile, 1977-81; mem. Turner, Onderdonk, Kimbrough & Howell, P.A., Chatom and Mobile, 1981—. Mem. Ala. State Dem. Exec. Com., 1966-70, Mobile County Dem. Exec. Com., 1991—. Served with U.S. Army, 1958, 61-62. mem. ABA, Am. Judicature Soc., Ala. Bar Assn., Mobile County Bar Assn. (v.p.), Am. Coll. Trial Lawyers, Nat. Assn. Former U.S. Attys., Nat. Assn. Criminal Def. Attys., Ala. Trial Lawyers Assn., Bienville Club, Country Club of Mobile, Omicron Delta Kappa. Methodist. Office: 1359 Dauphin St Mobile AL 36604-2140

KIMERER, NEIL BANARD, SR., psychiatrist, educator; b. Wauseon, Ohio, Jan. 13, 1918; s. William and Ruby (Upp) K.; m. Ellen Jane Scott, May 22, 1943; children: Susan Leigh, Neil Banard, Brian Scott, Sandra Lynn. B.S., U. Toledo, 1941; M.D., U. Chgo., 1944; postgrad. (fellow), Menninger Sch., 1947-50. Diplomate Am. Bd. Psychiatry and Neurology. Intern Emanuel Hosp., Portland, Oreg., 1944; resident psychiatry Winter VA Hosp., Topeka, 1947-50; asst. physician Central State Hosp., Norman, Okla., 1950; cons. Central State Hosp., 1955—; chief out-patient psychiat. clinic U. Okla. Sch. Medicine, Oklahoma City, 1951-53; instr. dept. psychiatry, neurology and behavioral scis. U. Okla. Sch. Medicine, 1953-61, assoc. prof., 1961-69, clin. prof., 1969-85, clin. prof. emeritus, 1985—; practice medicine specializing in psychiatry Oklahoma City, 1953—; med. dir. Oklahoma City Mental Health Clinic, 1953-68; chmn. dept. psychiatry Bapt. Med. Ctr. Okla., 1979-83. Author: To Get and Beget, 1971, Independence Means Swim or Sink, 1995; contbr. articles in field to profl. jours. Mem. exec. com. Okla. Family Life Assn., 1958-60; bd. dirs. Oklahoma City Jr. Symphony Soc., 1959. Served as pfc ASTP, 1943-44; to capt. M.C. AUS, 1945-47. Fellow Am. Psychiat. Assn. (life); mem. AMA (life), Okla. Med. Assn., Oklahoma County Med. Soc., Oklahoma City Clin. Soc., AAAS, Alpha Kappa Kappa (pres. Nu chpt. 1943). Lodge: Rotary. Home: 2800 NW 25th St Oklahoma City OK 73107-2228 Office: 2600 Northwest Expy Oklahoma City OK 73112

KIMMEL, A. JUNE MILLER, council executive; b. Detroit, May 27, 1931; d. Charles Kenneth and Alonda Sara (Donovan) Miller; m. Donald Loraine Kimmel Jr., June 16, 1960 (div. May 1983); children: Stephen Garrett, Charity Allen, Christopher Donald, Benjamin Haines. Grad., George Sch., 1949; student, Goucher Coll., 1949-51; BA, U. Pa., 1953. Prodn. editor Holiday Mag., Phila., 1953; rsch. assoc. Towers, Perrin, Forster & Crosby, Phila., 1954; admissions officer, dean's office Temple U. Med. Sch., Phila., 1958-60; reading cons. Mooresville (N.C.) City Schs., 1976-78; region dir.

N.C. Coun. for Women, Charlotte, 1984—; mem. Domestic Violence Adv. Bd., Charlotte, 1986—, chair, 1995—. Author: (newsletter) Women's Issues, 1986—. Precinct chair Dem. Party, Davidson, N.C., 1973, 74, 75; chair Charlotte (N.C.) Solid Waste Adv. Com., 1978-80; mem. Mecklenburg Solid Waste and Hazardous Bd., Charlotte, 1980-84. Named Woman of the Yr., Coll. of Arts and Scis., U. N.C., Charlotte, 1990; recipient Women of Courage award Charlotte (N.C.)/Mecklenburg Women's Commn., 1992. Mem. AAUW, R.I. LWV (state bd. 1966), Barrington LWV (pres. 1967-69, Tribute 1969), Charlotte/Mecklenburg LWV (bd. mem. 1974-79, 94—)), N.C. LWV (bd. mem. 1980-93), Women's Agenda, N.C. Women's Polit. Caucus (pres. 1994, 95), SE Women's Studies Assn. Mem. Soc. of Friends. Home: PO Box 595 750 Dogwood Ln Davidson NC 28036 Office: NC Coun for Women 500 W Trade St Ste 360 Charlotte NC 28202-1153

KIMMEL, CHARITY ALLEN, small business owner, writer; b. Balt., Jan. 5, 1961; d. Donald Lorraine and Alonda June (Miller) K.; m. Jeff Wilson, Oct. 7, 1995. BA, Queens Coll. Bus. Adminstrn., 1984. With Charlotte (N.C.) Meml. Hosp., 1980-81, Old World Deli, Lake Wylie, S.C., 1984-85, Fortune Media/Charlotte Mag., 1985, ABM, Pineville, N.C., 1985-86, HESCO, Pineville, N.C., 1986, Internat. Bearings Co., Charlotte, 1986-87, The Herald, Rock Hill, S.C., 1987-88, Lake Wylie Mag., 1987-88; sales exec. HFH USA Corp., Charlotte, 1988-94; owner FWBC, Charlotte, 1994—. Author: The Man With The Golden Mask, 1994; newspaper writer. Democrat. Mem. Soc. of Friends.

KIMMEL, MAREK, biomathematician, educator; b. Gliwice, Poland, Sept. 17, 1953; came to U.S., 1982; s. Zbigniew and Janina (Rybicka) K.; m. Barbara Stankiewicz, June 27, 1981; children: Jan, Katarzyna. MS, Silesian Tech. U., Gliwice, 1977, PhD, 1980. Asst. prof. Silesian Tech. U., 1977-82, Sloan-Kettering Inst., N.Y.C., 1982-90; assoc. prof. dept. stats. Rice U., Houston, 1990-94, prof., 1994—; cons. rsch. div. IBM, Yorktown Heights, N.Y., 1989—. Co-editor: Mathematical Population Dynamics, 1991,95; contbr. articles to profl. jours., including Jour. Theoretical Biology, Biometrics, Genetics. Grantee Nat. Cancer Inst., 1985, NSF, 1989. Mem. Am. Statis. Assn., Inst. Math. Statistics, Am. Math. Soc., Cell Kinetics Soc. Roman Catholic. Office: Rice U Dept Stats PO Box 1892 Houston TX 77251-1892

KIMMEL, PAUL ROBERT, financial and systems director; b. Balt., Sept. 7, 1947; s. Walter William and Lisette Marie Elizabeth (Hasenzahl) K.; m. Cynthia Ann Bowers, Nov. 17, 1984; children: Elliott Paul, Charlotte Lisette Marie. BS in Engring. summa cum laude, Case Inst. Tech., 1969; MBA, Harvard Sch. Bus. Adminstrn., 1975. CPA. Mfg. mgr. Procter & Gamble Co., Cin., 1969-73; sr. acct. Arthur Andersen & Co., Boston, 1975-78; dir. mfg. and control Brilliant Seafood Co., Boston, 1978-79; sr. analyst Am. Cyanamid Co., Wayne, N.J., 1979-81; plant controller Shulton Inc., Mays Landing, N.J., 1981-83; mgr. acctg. and systems Am. Cyanamid Co. Med. Internat. Div., Wayne, N.J., 1983-85; dir. corp. acctg. Hartz Mountain Corp., Harrison, N.J., 1985-86; v.p. Citibank/Citicorp, N.Y.C., 1986-89; controller Airwick Industries, Wayne, N.J., 1989-90; dir. acctg. devel. Reckitt & Colman Inc., Wayne, N.J., 1990-94; v.p., CFO Eurostar Perfumes, Inc., Pleasanton, Tex., 1994-95; v.p., CIO Tristar Corp., San Antonio, Tex., 1995—. Mem. AICPA, Fin. Execs. Inst., Inst. Mgmt. Acctg., Confrerie de la Chaine des Rotisseurs. Republican. Lutheran. Home: 1647 Thrush Ct Cir San Antonio TX 78248-1756 Office: Tristar Corp 12500 San Pedro Ave Ste 500 San Antonio TX 78216

KIMMEL, TROY MAX, JR., meteorologist; b. Kilgore, Tex., Aug. 2, 1957; s. Troy Max and Diane King (Lipscomb) K. BS in Geography, Tex. A&M U., 1983. News editor, weathercaster Sta. KCNY, San Marcos, Tex., 1975-77, Sta. WKCU-AM-FM, Corinth, Miss., 1977-78; weathercaster Sta. KBTX-TV, Bryan, Tex., 1979-84; meteorologist Sta. KVUE-TV, Austin, Tex., 1984-89; chief meteorologist, 1989-93; chief meterologist Lower Colo. River Authority, Austin, 1993-94; chief meteorologist Sta. KTBC-TV, Austin, 1994—; lectr. dept. geography U. Tex., Austin, 1988—; mgr. KimCo Meteorol. Svcs., Austin, 1981—; faculty advisor Kappa Sigma, U. Tex., 1991—; mem. housing corp. Pi Kappa Alpha, Southwestern U., 1989-92. Bd. dirs. Brazos Valley chpt. March of Dimes, Bryan, Tex., 1981-84, Ctrl. Tex. chpt., 1984-86, Capital Area United Cerebral Palsy, 1988-90, 93—; co-host, host Muscular Dystrophy Telethon, Sta. KBTX-TV, Bryan, 1982-83, Sta. KVUE-TV, Austin, 1987; co-host United Cerebral Palsy Telethon, Sta. KVUE-TV, 1986-87, Children's Miracle Network Telethon, 1988-89, 91, 92, 93; mem. cmty. adv. coun. AIDS Svcs. Austin. Recipient Outstanding Achievement awards UPI, 1983, 85, Best TV Weathercast in Tex. award UPI, 1984-87, Best Weathercast in Austin, Austin Chronicle, 1990, 91, 95, Best Weathercast in Tex. award AP, 1990, 92, 2d pl., 1991. Mem. Am. Meteorol. Soc. (TV and radio seals of approval, sec.-treas. Cen. Tex. chpt. 1985-86, v.p. 1986-87, pres. 1987-90, nat. bd. on women and minorities 1991-94, nat. bd. Broadcast Meteorology 1992-94), Nat. Weather Assn. (TV Seal of Approval, Broadcaster of Yr. 1988), Tex. Alliance for Geog. Edn. Methodist. Home: 6512 Sans Souci Cv Austin TX 78759-5163 Office: KTBC-TV Channel 7 10th and Brazos 119 E 10th St Austin TX 78701

KIMMONS, KENT ALLEN, logistics engineer; b. Ocala, Fla., Apr. 12, 1965; s. Jesse Mercer Jr. and Alice (Grant) K. BS in Bus. Adminstrn., U. Fla., 1987. Sales assoc. Am. Panel Corp., Ocala, 1988; sr. logistics engr. United Space Alliance, Cape Canaveral, Fla., 1989—. Author: (software) Crystal Ball, 1995. Deacon of Fin. Faith Presbyn. Ch., Merritt Island, Fla., 1993-94. Mem. Soc. of Logistics Engrs. Office: United Space Alliance 8600 Astronaut Blvd Cape Canaveral FL 32926

KIMWELI, DAVID MUTUA, psychologist; b. Machakos, Kenya, Jan. 17, 1955; came to U.S., 1984; s. Samson Kimweli and Alice (Waiu) Mutunge.; m. Joyce Kimweli, Apr. 18, 1981; children: David, Faith Sally. BA, Johnson Bible Coll., Tenn., 1985; MA, W. Ga. U., 1989; student, U. Ky., 1994—. Headmaster Maiani Secondary Sch., Yoani, Machakos, Kenya, 1977-79; acct. Ministry of Water Devel., Embu, Eastern Province, Kenya, 1979-83; pres. Reach and Touch, Inc., Carrollton, Ga., 1984—; dir. World Missions, Atlanta, 1990, Reach Kenya, Douglasville, Ga., 1992. Author: Spiritual Fullment, 1988. Recipient Athletic Championship Machakos Dist, Nunguni Macha Kos, 1974; named Best Sunday Sch. Tchr., A.I.C. Ch., Mukaa, 1975. Mem. Am. Psychol. Assn., Ky. State Bd. of Psychologists. Republican. Office: 1713 Jennifer Rd Lexington KY 40505-3055

KIN, LESLIE SCHULTZ, legislative assistant; b. Waukegan, Ill., Mar. 26, 1970; d. Norman Alexander and Kathleen Marie (Cunningham) Schultz; m. Stephen John Kin, Aug. 7, 1992. BA, Ohio U., 1992; postgrad., U. South Fla., 1993—. Legis. asst. Fla. Legis., Tampa, 1994—. Co-editor Grassroots Newspaper, 1993-94. Field rep. Rep. Party of Fla., Tampa, 1994; intern Pinellas County, Clearwater, Fla., 1994, City of Clearwater, 1994; asst. to chairperson Hillsborough County Rep. Party, Tampa, 1993-94; precinct del. Athens County (Ohio) Rep. Party, 1990-92; sec., mem. Tampa Bay Young Reps., 1993—; event staff Hillsborough Lincoln Day Dinner, Tampa, 1993; pres. Ohio U. Coll. Reps., Athens, 1990-91. Mem. Am. Soc. Pub. Adminstrn., Sigma Kappa (sec., v.p. membership), Pi Alpha Alpha, Phi Alpha Delta.

KINARD, FREDRICK WILLIAM, retired college dean; b. Leesville, S.C., Oct. 14, 1906; s. Jacob William and Annie Elizabeth (Schroder) K.; m. Lina Barr, Sept. 12, 1929 (dec. 1976); children: Anne Kinard Davenport, Fredrick William; m. Betty Murray, Apr. 20, 1981. BS, Clemson (S.C.) U., 1927; MS, U. Va., 1932, PhD, 1933; MD, U. Tenn., 1945. Asst. in chemistry Med. Coll. S.C., Charleston, 1927-30; instr. physiology to prof. physiology Med. Coll. S.C., 1933-53, dean Sch. Grad. Studies, 1965-77, emeritus, 1977—; instr. biochemistry U. Va., Charlottesville, 1930-33; faculty Southeastern Sch. Alcohol Studies, Athens, Ga. Contbr. articles to profl. jours. Named Outstanding Non-Alumnus, Med. U. S.C., 1987, Newberry Coll., 1988. Mem. Charleston Yacht Club, Charleston Rifle Club, Elks, Sigma Xi, Phi Kappa Phi, Alpha Omega Alpha, Rho Chi. Lutheran. Home: 2 Johnson Rd Charleston SC 29407-7515

KINASEWITZ, GARY THEODORE, medical educator; b. N.Y.C., Aug. 17, 1946; m. Kathlee Anne O'Sullivan, Aug. 16, 1969; children: Amanda, Judith, Gregory. BS, Boston Coll., 1968, MEd, 1969; MD, Wayne State U., 1973. Diplomate Am. Bd. Internal Medicine. Rsch. assoc. U. Pa., Phila., 1978-79, asst. prof. medicine, 1979-80; asst. prof. medicine La. State U. Med. Ctr., Shreveport, 1980-83, assoc. prof. medicine and physiology, 1983-88; coord., cardiovascular rsch. N.W. La. Biomed. Rsch. Ctr., Shreveport, 1987-88; prof. medicine and physiology La. State U. Med. Ctr., Shreveport, 1988; prof. medicine and physiology Okla. U. Health Scis. Ctr., Oklahoma City, 1988—, chief pulmonary and crit. care medicine, 1988—; mem. cardiovascular biology Okla. Med. Rsch. Found., Oklahoma City, 1994—; mem. rsch. adv. com. N.W. La. Biomed. Rsch. Found., 1985-88; univ. rep. Am. Fedn. Clin. Rsch., 1984-87. Author: (book) Pulmonary Function Testing: Principles and Practice, 1984. Bd. dirs. Am. Heart Assn., La., 1983-87, Am. Lung Assn., Okla., 1991—. Recipient Albert Hyman award Am. Heart Assn., La., 1981. Fellow Am. Coll. Chest Physicians (pathophysiology adv. com. 1983-86), Am. Coll. Physicians; mem. Am. Thoracic Soc. (coun. of chpt. reps. 1992-95), So. Soc. for Clin. Investigation, Cen. Soc. Clin. Rsch., Am. Physiol. Soc., Alpha Omega Alpha. Office: Univ Okla Health Scis Ctr Rm 3SP 400 920 Stanton Young Oklahoma City OK 73104

KINCADE, DORIS HELSING, apparel marketing educator; b. Roanoke, Va., Nov. 15, 1951; d. Carl Edward and Katherine Elizabeth (May) Helsing; m. William James Kincade, June 10, 1972. BS, East Carolina U., 1973, MS in Home Econs., 1974; PhD, U. N.C., Greensboro, 1988. Lectr. Peace Coll., Raleigh, N.C., 1974-78, dept. coord., 1978-86; market analyst HKH Partners, Research Triangle Park, N.C., 1982--; asst. statistician Cone Mills Corp., Greensboro, N.C., 1987-88; lectr. U. N.C., Greensboro, 1988-89; asst. prof. Auburn U., Ala., 1989-92; asst. prof. Va. Poly. Inst. and State U., Blacksburg, Va., 1992-96, assoc. prof., 1996—; cons. Triangle L & C, Rsch. Triangle Pk., 1986-93, S.E. Region Ala. Apparel Mfrs., 1990-92; mem. New Century Coun., 1993-95; rsch. reviewer Internat. Textile and Apparel Assn., Am. Collegiate Retailing Assn.; guest lectr. East Carolina U., 1983. Contbr. articles to profl. and trade jours. Recipient grants Rayon/Acetate Coun. N.Y., 1989, Russell Corp., 1990, Vanity Fair Corp., 1992, J.C. Penney Retail Rsch., 1992, Vol. Inter-Industry Coun. Stds., 1993, Va. Tech. Found., 1995; fellow Textile Clothing Tech. Corp., Nat. Apparel Rsch. Ctr. Mem. Am. Collegiate Retailing Assn., Acad. Mktg. Sci., Am. Soc. for Quality Control, Assn. Family and Consumer Scis., Internat. Textile and Apparel Assn. (reviewer Clothing and Textile Rsch. Jour. 1993-95, mem. editl. rev. bd. 1995—), Textile Apparel Linkage Coun., Phi Kappa Phi, Phi Upsilon Omicron, Kappa Omicron Nu. Office: 109 Wallace Hall Va Poly Inst and State U Blacksburg VA 24061

KINCAID, CAROLYN WADE, special education educator; b. Cynthiana, Ky., Aug. 22, 1948; d. Joseph Daniel and Norma Vivian Martin; m. Wilburn R. Kincaid, June 5, 1966; children: Wil, Jennie, Richard. BA in Sociology and History, Ea. Ky. U., 1985, MA in Spl. Edn., 1991. Cert. secondary tchr., tchr. of exceptional children. Rank I spl. edn. tchr. Pulaski County Bd. Edn., Somerset, Ky., 1987—. Info. giver Spl. Olympics, Somerset, 1987-94. Mem. NEA, Ky. Edn. Assn., Pulaski County Edn. Assn., Kappa Delta Pi. Home: 210 Linwood Dr Somerset KY 42501-1121

KINCAID, ELSIE ELIZABETH, educational therapist; b. Vernon, Tex., Nov. 29, 1929; d. Richard Oscar Paul and Bertha Rosanna (Quast) Schuetze; m. Richard Warren Kincaid, June 1, 1949; children: Carol Jean, Richard Warren, Sandra Elizabeth, Robert Rendall. AA, Del Mar Coll., 1949; BS magna cum laude, Tex. Agrl. and Industry U., 1976; MS, Corpus Christi (Tex.) State U., 1978; PhD, Columbia Pacific U., 1985. Dir., diagnostician, edn. therapist Corpus Christi Acad. Devel. Services, 1979-80; dir., diagnostician, ednl. therapist Corpus Christi Acad. Devel. Svcs., Corpus Christi, 1980-86; diagnotician, ednl. therapist Acad. Devel. Svcs., Corpus Christi, 1987; ednl. therapist Clinic for Learning Disabilities, Dallas, 1989; pvt. practice McKinney and Dallas, Tex., 1990-92, Plano, Tex., 1992—; spl. edn. substitute tchr. Corpus Christi Ind. Sch. Dist., 1986-88. Author: Reasoning Process As Early Intervention for Reading Disability, 1985, The Preschool Diagnostic Development Screening Test, 1987. V.p. Symphony Guild Corpus Christi, 1973; bd. dirs. Ada Wilson Hosp. for Children, Corpus Christi, 1986-89, Samaritan Counseling Ctr. of Coastal Bend, 1987-89 (v.p. 1988), Holy Family Sch., McKinney, 1990-92; mem. adv. bd. "Any Baby Can" Project, Corpus Christi, 1988-89; mem. High Risk Infant Task Force, Art Mus. So. Tex. and Corpus Christi, 1988-89; vol. Collin County Community Food Pantry, 1990-91. Mem. Jennete Hammer Guild (pres. 1984-85), CPA Wives (pres. 1970), Mental Health Assn. Collin County, Estate Garden Club (pres. 1981), Daus. of King (v.p. 1986-88), Plano Rep. Womens Club, Plano Chamber Orch. Encore, Kappa Delta Pi (Xi Omicron chpt.), Beta Sigma Phi (Xi Chi Pi chpt.), Heard Natural Sci. Mus. and Wildlife Sanctuary of McKinney Guild. Republican. Episcopalian. Home and Office: 1820 Azurite Trl Plano TX 75075-2106

KINCAID, EUGENE D., III, lawyer; b. Uvalde, Tex., Mar. 7, 1941; s. Eugene D. and Lochie M. (Mundine) K. BA, Baylor U., 1962; JD, U. Tex.-Austin, 1966. Bar: Tex. 1966. Briefing atty. Tex. Ct. Criminal Appeals, 1967-68; asst. city atty. San Antonio, 1969; atty. Tex. Water Rights Commn., Austin, 1970-71; sole practice, Uvalde, 1971-89. chmn. EDK Ranches Inc., AVK Ranch Co. Inc.; pres. Kincaid Internat., 1989-90, Llano Rio Ranch Ltd., Montelenoso Min. Ltd., Loma Escondida Land LL Co. Chmn. Uvalde Housing Authority, 1972-80; mem. Uvalde Arts Council. Mem. State Bar of Tex., Border Dist. Bar Assn., Uvalde County Bar Assn. (pres. 1972), Magna Charta Barons, McNay Art Inst., Uvalde Country Club, Pi Sigma Alpha, Sigma Delta Pi. Republican. Anglican. Office: 243 N Getty PO Box 1769 Uvalde TX 78802-1769

KINCAID, TINA, entertainer, producer; b. Lenoir, N.C., Dec. 24, 1959; d. Joseph George and Betty Gail (Prestwood) K.; m. Stephen Kim Cretella, June 11, 1988 (div. May 1994). Student, Am. Theater Arts, 1979-81. Entertainer, 1979—; TV producer, actor Video Record Albums of Am., Pasadena, Calif., 1980-83; v.p. sales, mktg. prodns. Amity Sales Inc., Hudson, N.C., 1980—; co-founder, producer, singer T'NT Entertainments, Inc., Pasadena, 1981-83; founder, pres. ProductVision, Inc., L.A., 1984-86; co-founder, v.p. prodns. Kincaid Enterprises, Morganton, N.C., 1988-89; founder, owner VAT Pub., Hudson, 1989—; cons. Mary Kay Cosmetics, Hudson, 1989—; co-founder, v.p., performer Rappin' Grandmas, Inc!, Hickory, N.C., 1991—; founder, owner Gingerbread Treasures, Hudson, 1992—; owner Charmingly Yours, Hudson, 1995—; entertainer, singer The Troy Cory China Goodwill Concert Tour, 1991. Actor, author TV spl. Catching Christmas, 1981; singer, author album Isn't A Shame, 1990, The Real Country, 1990; co-songwriter album/CD: Dancing Across the Finish Line, 1995; author, editor: The Wedding Book, 1990, Recipes for Love, 1991. Mem. SAG. Republican. Mem. Christian Ch. Home: 4491 Magnolia Ln Hudson NC 28638-8708

KINCANNON, GLEE TALBOT, dietitian; b. Santa Monica, Calif., July 31, 1934; d. Emmett Linden and Harriet Ena (Patterson) T.; m. Don F. Kincannon, Aug. 25, 1957; children: David Lee, Laura Diane. BS in Home Econs., Pacific Union Coll., 1956; MS in Food Nutrition and Adminstrn., Okla. State U., 1965, EdD in Home Econs. Edn., 1978. Asst. dietitian univ. food svc. Okla. State U., 1957-60, instr. food, nutrition and instn. adminstrn. dept., 1968-78; dietitian Rolla (Mo.) Pub. Sch. System, 1965-66; cons. nutritionist Nutrition Counseling Svc., Stillwater, Okla., 1978—; bus. mgr. Environ. Engring. Cons., Inc., Stillwater, 1985—. Contbr. articles to profl. jours. Mem. AAUW (sec. 1975-77), Am. Bus. Women's Assn. (v.p. 1984, rec. sec. 1985, Woman of Yr. 1986), Okla. Cons. Nutritionists (treas. 1983-87), Okla. Dietetic Assn. (career guidance com., nominating com. 1975, 78, exec. bd. 1973-78, reporter 1973-78), Am. Dietetic Assn. (bd. editors Jour. 1986-91, chmn. cons. nutritionists-pvt. practice 1985, state coord. 1978-87), Stillwater Country Club (bd. dirs. 1986-89, sec. bd. dirs. 1986-87, pres. 1988-89). Office: Nutrition Counseling Svc 311 S Duck St Stillwater OK 74074-3219

KINCHEN, THOMAS ALEXANDER, college president; b. Thomasville, Ga., Dec. 28, 1946; s. George H. and Annie L. (Castleberry) K.; m. Ruth Ann Hunter, Aug. 27, 1967; children: Alex, Lisa Ann. AB summa cum laude, Ga. So. Coll., 1969; MEd, U. Ga., 1975; MDiv, New Orleans Bapt. Theol. Sem., 1979, EdD, 1982. Pastor several chs., 1972-76; v.p. New Orleans Bapt. Theol. Sem., 1982-86; exec. dir., treas. W.Va. Conv. So. Bapt., Scott Depot, 1986-90; pres. Fla. Bapt. Theol. Coll., Graceville, 1990—. Editor Laos: All the People of God, 1984; contbr. articles to profl. jours. Bd. dirs. Area Devel. Coun., Graceville, 1991; mem. edn. commn. So. Bapt. Conv., 1992—; pres. bd. dirs. Jackson County Devel. Coun. Mem. So. Bapt. Adult Edn. Assn. (v.p. 1994—), Graceville C. of C. (pres. 1993), Kiwanis, Phi Kappa Phi, Alpha Psi Omega. Office: Fla Bapt Theol Coll 5400 College Dr Graceville FL 32440-1831

KIND, MIMI P., art educator; b. Kingsport, Tenn., Nov. 27, 1954; d. Ralph Stokley and June E. (Ramsey) Price; m. William Rigby Kind III, June 19, 1976; children: Kathryn Camille, Mimi Cameron. BS, East Tenn. State U., 1976, MA, 1980. Cert. tchg., ednl. adminstrn. Advt. profl. Montgomery Ward, Kingsport, 1976; tchr. art Bristol (Tenn.) City Schs., 1976—, coach cheerleading, 1994—; mem. Scholastic Arts Adv. Bd., Kingsport, 1984-85; evaluator So. Assn. Colls. and Schs., Gray, Tenn., 1991, Bluff City, Tenn., 1992. Mem. NEA, Tenn. Edn. Assn., East Tenn. Edn. Assn., Bristol Tenn. Edn. Assn. Democrat. Baptist. Home: 509 Vance Dr Bristol TN 37620 Office: Bristol Tenn City Schs Tenn H S 1112 Edgemont Ave Bristol TN 37620

KINDALL, SUSAN CAROL, music educator; b. Greenville, S.C., Feb. 26, 1967; d. Keith Lavern and Ella Joyce (Clayton) K. BMus, Bob Jones U., 1988, MMus, 1990; D of Musical Arts, U. Okla., 1994. Faculty mem. Bob Jones U., Greenville, 1988-90; music faculty mem. U. Okla., Norman, 1990-94; music instr. Ouachita Bapt. U., Arkadelphia, Ark., 1994-96; coord. Ouachita Bapt. U., 1995; Am. music festival and piano competition coord., Richard Cumming Concert and lectr. series U. Okla., 1993. Mem. Music Tchrs. Nat. Assn., Ark. State Music Tchrs. Assn., S.C. Music Tchrs. Assn., Greenville Music Tchrs. Club, Arkadelphia Philharm. Club. Home: 2 Capewood Ct Greenville SC 29609 Office: Ouachita Bapt Univ 610 Ouachita Arkadelphia AR 71998

KINDER, RICHARD DAN, natural gas pipeline, oil and gas company executive; b. Cape Girardeau, Mo., Oct. 19, 1944; s. Luke Frazelle and Edna (Corbin) K.; m. Anne Lamkin; 1 child, Kara. BA, U. Mo., 1966, JD, 1968. Sole practice, Cape Girardeau, Mo., 1972-80; sr. atty. Continental Resources/Fla. Gas Cos., Winter Park, 1981-82, v.p., gen. counsel, 1982-84; sr. v.p., gen. counsel Houston Natural Gas Corp., 1985, HNG/InterNorth Inc., Houston, 1985-86; exec. v.p. law and corp. devel. Enron Corp., Houston, 1986-87, exec. v.p., chief of staff, 1987-88, vice chmn. bd., 1988-89, pres., COO, 1989—. Bd. dirs. Soc. Performing Arts, Houston, 1986—, Mus. Fine Arts, Houston, 1987—. Served to capt. U.S. Army, 1968-72. Mem. ABA, Mo. Bar Assn., Houston Bar Assn. Methodist. Clubs: Houston Racquet; Petroleum. Office: Enron Corp PO Box 1188 Houston TX 77251-1188*

KINDIG, EVERETT WILLIAM, history educator; b. Kansas City, Kans., Oct. 5, 1936; s. Everett Kenneth and Zella Muriel (Mueller) K.; m. Judith Ann Iler, Nov. 5, 1966; children: Everett William Jr., Aimee Elizabeth. BA, Stanford U., 1958, MA, 1963, PhD, 1975. Teaching asst. Stanford U., Palo Alto, Calif., 1959-61, grad. asst., 1964-65; instr. San Jose (Calif.) State U., 1967-70; acting asst. prof. Santa Clara (Calif.) U., 1970-71; instr. Midwestern State U., Wichita Falls, Tex., 1971-72, asst. prof., 1972-84, assoc. prof. dept. history, 1984—; mem. faculty libr. com. Midwestern State U., 1973-92, chmn., 1975-81, mem. rank and tenure com., 1992-95, also archivist. Contbr. articles and book revs. to profl. jours. Election judge Wichita County, Tex., 1984-91; lay reader Epsic. Ch., Diocese of Ft. Worth, Good Shepherd, Wichita Falls, 1980-93; dir. Epsic. Elem. Sch., Wichita Falls, 1980-84; pres. Quail Creek Homeowners Assn., Wichita Falls, 1987-93; cubmaster N.W. Tex. coun. Boy Scouts Am., 1984-85; chmn. Midwestern State U. com. Constrn. Bicentennial, 1987-93. Rsch. grantee Hardin Found., Wichita Falls, 1977, Midwestern State U., Wichita Falls, 1977, 88. Mem. Soc. Historians of Early Am. Republic, Mo. Hist. Soc., Stanford Alumni Assn., Phi Alpha Theta (faculty advisor Midwestern State U., 1972—), Coll. Republicans (faculty advisor Midwestern State U. 1980—). Republican. Methodist. Home: 4115 Seabury Dr Wichita Falls TX 76308-3107 Office: Midwestern State U 3410 Taft Blvd Wichita Falls TX 76308-2095

KINDRED, GEORGE CHARLES, lithography executive; b. Bklyn., Nov. 20, 1898; s. Robert C. and Caroline (Hoag) K.; spl. courses, Columbia and N.Y. U.; m. Dorothy Estabrook, Mar. 10, 1928; children—George Estabrook, John MacGregor. Buyer, W. R. Grace and Co., 1919-23; western sales mgr. Snyder and Black, 1923-28; pres. Kindred, MacLean and Co., 1928-59; pres. Underhill, Inv., Inc., 1959—. Served in U.S. Army World War I, USCG Aux., World War II. Fellow Graphic Arts Tech. Found.; mem. A.I.M., St. Andrews Soc., Point Purchase Advt. Inst. (founder, past pres.), Lithographers Nat. Assn. (past treas., dir.), Met. Lithographers Assn. (past pres.), Lithographic Tech. Found. (past treas., dir.), English-Speaking Union, Am. Legion, U.S. Power Squadrons. Episcopalian (vestryman). Clubs: Lotos (N.Y.C.); Fox Meadow Tennis; Saugatuck Harbor Yacht (Westport, Conn.); Sanderling (Siesta Key, Fla.). Home: 4822 Ocean Blvd Siesta Key Sarasota FL 34242

KING, ALLEN B., company executive. Pres. Universal Corp. Office: Universal Leaf Tobacco Co Inc Hamilton St at Broad PO Box 25099 Richmond VA 23260-5099*

KING, ALMA JEAN, former health and physical education educator; b. Hamilton, Ohio, Feb. 28, 1939; d. William Lawrence and Esther Mary (Smith) K. BS in Edn., Miami U., Oxford, Ohio, 1961; MEd, Bowling Green State U., 1963; postgrad., Fla. Atlantic U., 1969, '92, Nova U., Ft. Lauderdale, Fla., 1979. Cert. elem. and secondry tchr., Ohio, all levels incl. coll., Fla. Tchr. health, physical edn. Rogers Middle Sch., Broward County Bd. Pub. Instrn., 1963-64; assoc. prof. health, phys edn., recreation, dance Broward C.C., Fort Lauderdale, Fla., 1964-94; ret., 1994; dir. Intramurals and Extramurals Boward C.C., Fort Lauderdale, Fla., 1964-67, chair person Women's Affairs, 1978, health and safety com., 1975, faculty evaluation com. 1980-85, mem. faculty ins. benefits com. 1993-94. Sponsor Broward County Fire Fighters, Police; active mem. Police Benevolent Assn.; Historical Soc. Grantee Broward C.C. Staff Devel. Fund, 1988. Mem. AAHPERD, NEA, Fla. Edn. Assn., Fla. Assn for Health, Physical Edn., Recreation and Dance, Am. Assn. for Advancement of Health Edn., United Faculty of Fla., Fla. Assn. of C.C., Order of the Eastern Star (past Worthy Matron), Order of Shrine. Home: 4310 Buchanan St Hollywood FL 33021

KING, AMANDA ARNETTE, elementary school educator; b. Conway, S.C., Feb. 6, 1951; d. James Hilton and Maisie (Dunn) Arnette; m. Roachel Dent King III, Dec. 31, 1972; children: Roachel Dent IV, Amanda Catherine. AB, Coker Coll., 1973. Tchr. Darlington (S.C.) County Sch. Dist., 1972-75, 78-81, James F. Byrnes Acad., Florence, S.C., 1981-88, Darlington County Sch. Dist., 1988—. Mem. Society Hill (S.C.) Rescue Squad, Woodmen of World, Palmetto Project; bd. dirs. Darlington County Libr. Sys. Recipient Golden Apple award, 1993-94, Tchr. of the Yr. award James F. Byrnes Acad., 1988, Rosenwald/St. David's Elem. Sch., 1990, 93. Mem. S.C. Coun. Tchrs. Math., Internat. Reading Assn., Palmetto State Tchrs. Assn. (mem. com.), Coker Coll. Alumni Assn. (2d v.p. 1988—, Outstanding Alumni com. 1989-90, 93—). Baptist. Home: PO Box 58 Society Hill SC 29593-0058

KING, ANNIE ROBERTS, elementary and secondary education educator; b. Dublin, N.C., Dec. 7, 1933; d. Starslie Dewey adn Addie Mae (Dowless) Roberts; m. Charles Thomas King, Sept. 23, 1950 (div. Aug. 1994); children: Charles Thomas Jr., Clarence Donald, Jerry Lynn, Tammie Ann, David Jerome, William Eric. Grader Sachs Peanut Co., Dublin, 1960-62; head cashier Pope's Variety Store, Elizabethtown, N.C., 1976-79; mgr. King's Jewelry Store, Elizabethtown, N.C., 1980-82; substitute tchr. Bladen County Schs., 1990—. Ch. clk. Bethel Bapt. Ch., Dublin, 1971-77, WMU pres., 1978-80, sunday sch. tchr., mem. choir. Baptist.

KING, ARNOLD KIMSEY, JR., retired clergyman, nursing home executive, statistician; b. Durham, N.C., May 7, 1931; s. Arnold Kimsey and Edna May (Coates) K.; m. Marjorie Jean Fisher, June 22, 1952; children: Leslie Diane, Carole Jean, Arnold Kimsey III, Julia Paige. BA, U. N.C., 1955; M in Divinity, Duke U., 1959; DD, Am. Bible Inst., 1971. Ordained deacon Meth. Ch., 1956, elder, 1959; lic. nursing home adminstr., N.C. Enlisted USAF, 1951, served as staff sgt., various assignments in psychol. training, bus. adminstrn., mgmt.; min., organizer Aldersgate Methodist Ch., Chapel Hill, N.C., 1955-61; assoc. pastor Edenton St. Meth. Ch., Raleigh, N.C., 1961-64; pastor Ahoskie (N.C.) United Meth. Ch., 1964-70, Woodland (N.C.) United Meth. Ch., 1970-74; sec. N.C. Annual Conf., United Meth.

Ch., Raleigh, 1972-74; asst. adminstr. Meth. Retirement Homes Inc., Durham, 1974-75, adminstr., Durham, 1975-88; statistician N.C. Ann. Conf. of United Meth. Ch., 1988-94, ret., 1995; bd. dirs. Equity Homes Inc., Equity Retirement Housing, Marriott Vacation Resorts, Marriott's Swallowtail at Sea Pines; vis. prof. Meth. studies Southeastern Bapt. Theol. Sem., Wake Forest, N.C. Mem. N.C. Commn. on Health Svcs. Mem. Young Democrats Club, N.C. Gov.'s Com. on Aging, United Fund, Am. Cancer Soc.; councilman Town of Woodland, 1972-74; trustee, mem. exec. com. Goodwill Industries, Durham, 1974-78; theol. adv. to UN Internat. Yr. of Handicapped. Named Tar Heel of Week, Raleigh (N.C.) News and Observer, 1969. Mem. N.C. Bd. Examiners of Nursing Home Adminstrs., N.C. Hist. Assn. (past pres. United Meth. Conf.), Paralyzed Vets. Am., Disabled Am. Vets, N.C. Conf. Bd. Evangelism (past pres., v.p.), Optimists, Masons, Lambda Chi Alpha. Contbr. to USAF manuals; contbr. articles to profl. jours.; contbr. N.C. Christian Advocate Weekly, 1973-94; lectr. to profl. confs. Home: 5315 Yardley Ter Durham NC 27707-9740

KING, BARBARA JEAN, nurse; b. Cape Girardeau, Mo., June 28, 1941; d. Otto Samuel and Goldie Elizabeth (Clover) Fowler; student Weatherford Jr. Coll., 1965; RN, John Peter Smith Hosp. Sch. Profl. Nursing, 1969. Cert. advanced cardiac life support; m. Charles Basil King, Jr., Sept. 4, 1972; children—Otto Samuel, Christopher Lee. Head nurse pediatrics and isolation County Hosp., also intensive care and coronary care units Small Gen. Hosp., Ft. Worth, 1969-72; dir. nursing service Jarvis Heights Nursing Center, Ft. Worth, 1976-77; dir. nursing services Ft. Worth Rehab. Farm, 1978-80; staff nurse, asst. supr. shift Decatur Community Hosp. (Tex.), 1983-85; staff nurse and supr. Burdgeport Hosp., Tex., 1986—; clin. supr., patient care coord. Hospice of Tejas; instr. vocat. nursing Cooke County Coll., Gainesville, Tex., 1981; clin. care supr. home health dept. Faith Community Hosp., 1992, assoc. dir. 1993—; patient care coord. Family Svcs. Home Health Svcs., Inc., 1994, adminstrn, for choice, 1995; cons. convalescent centers and hosps. Chmn. child care com. Women of Moose, 1977—; ch. organist Bethel Baptist Ch., assoc. pianist, 1996. Served with M.C., USN, 1962-65. Mem. Dirs. Nursing Homes Assn. Tarrant County (v.p.). Democrat. Home: Route 1 RR 1 Box 198 Alvord TX 76225-9735

KING, BARBARA SUE, librarian; b. Okarche, Okla., July 16, 1955; d. Jack C. and Wilma (Smith) Boling; m. Glen M. King, Dec. 31, 1977 (div. June 1992). Assoc., El Reno Jr. Coll., 1975; BS in Libr. Sci., Southwestern Okla. State U., 1977; MLS, U. Okla., 1979. Pub. svcs. libr. Met. Libr. Sys., Oklahoma City, 1979-81, br. head Capital Hill br., 1980-81; reference libr. Oklahoma City C.C., 1981-87, coord. tech. svcs. and collection devel., 1987-89, dir. libr. svcs., 1989—. Mem. Assn. Libr. and Learning Ctr. Dirs. (pres. 1994-95), Okla. Coun. Acad. Libr. Dirs. Office: Oklahoma City CC 7777 S May Ave Oklahoma City OK 73159-4419

KING, BEVERLY ANN, publishing executive; b. Doylestown, Pa., Sept. 11, 1949; d. Harry and Hazel (Swain) K. Grad. high sch., Kintnersville, Pa., 1967. Founder, owner, editor, pub., contbr. Country Heritage, Clarksville, Ark., 1974-92, pub., contbr., 1992—. Performer, prodr. (albums) A Dobro Dozen, 1971, Drifting With the Dobro, 1972, Leave a Lot of Happy Tracks, 1974, An Instrumental Tribute to Brother Oswald, 1977, Backroads to Yesterday, 1982, Marty Robbins Scrapbook, 1984, Jewels of a King, 1986, Those Memories, 1987, Dobro Dreamland, 1986, Oswald's Golden Anniversary Album, 1988, also cassette albums, instructional videos; author, pub.: Country & Blue Grass Dobro, 1974, 36 Songs for Dobro, 1974, Dobroists' Scrapbook, 1976, 3d edit, 1995.

KING, CARL B., tool company executive; b. 1942; married. B.A., U. Tex., 1965, LL.B., 1966; M.B.A., Wharton Sch. Bus., U. Pa., 1968. Counsel corp. planning Exxon Corp., 1968-74; counsel Cameron Iron Works, Inc., Houston, 1974-75, v.p. corp. services, 1975-81, sr. v.p., sec., 1981-83, v.p., gen. mgr. oil tool div., 1984-89; former v.p., gen. mgr. oil tool div. Cooper Industries, Houston, from 1989; now v.p., gen. counsel Panhandle Eastern Corp., Houston. Office: Panhandle Eastern Corp 5400 Westheimer Ct Houston TX 77056-5310

KING, CARL EDWARD, employee screening executive; b. Pine Bluff, Ark., June 19, 1940; s. Carl B. King and Claudia Marie (Fulbright) Ingham; m. Jonna Sue DeWeese, Mar., 1964 (div. Nov. 1974); 1 child, Grant Edward; m. Paula Honor Finnell, Mar. 6, 1975. LLB, La Salle Extension U., 1971; BS in Criminal Justice, U. Nebr., Omaha, 1978; M in Bus. Mgmt., Cen. Mich. U., 1979. Enlisted USMC, 1957, commd. 2d lt., 1969, advanced through grades to maj., 1981; ops. officer, co. commdr. Mil. Police Co., Okinawa, Japan, 1973-74; asst. provost marshal USMC, Barstow, Calif., 1975; provost marshal USMC, Beaufort, S.C., 1975-77, Kaneohe Bay, Hawaii, 1978-81; ret. USMC, 1981; salesman Smith Protective Services, Houston, 1981-82, mgr. investigations div., sales mgr., 1982-83, v.p. mktg., 1983-84; co-founder, CEO Team Bldg. Systems, Houston, 1984—; pres., CEO, founder WNCK, Inc., Houston, 1992—; founder Insights-Corp. Selection Systems, Inc., Houston, 1992—; CEO Insights-Corp. Selection Systems, WNCK, Inc. Mem. loss prevention adv. bd. U. Houston, 1986—. Decorated Bronze Star, Purple Heart with oak leaf cluster. Mem. FBI Nat. Acad., Internat. Assn. Chiefs of Police, Am. Soc. Indsl. Security, Nat. Order Battlefield Commns., Marine Mustang Assn. Republican. Methodist. Home: 16 Diamond Oak Ct The Woodlands TX 77381-2820 Office: Insights Corp Selections Sys 600 Kenrick Dr Ste A2 Houston TX 77060-3631

KING, CAROLYN DINEEN, federal judge; b. Syracuse, N.Y., Jan. 30, 1938; d. Robert E. and Carolyn E. (Bareham) Dineen; children: James Randall, Philip Randall, Stephen Randall; m. John L. King, Jan. 1, 1988. A.B. summa cum laude, Smith Coll., 1959; LL.B., Yale U., 1962. Bar: D.C. 1962, Tex. 1963. Assoc. Fulbright & Jaworski, Houston, 1962-72; ptnr. Childs, Fortenbach, Beck & Guyton, Houston, 1972-78, Sullivan, Bailey, King, Randall & Sabon, Houston, 1978-79; circuit judge U.S. Ct. Appeals (5th cir.), Houston, 1979—; mem. coun. Am. Law Inst., 1991—. Trustee, mem. exec. com., treas. Houston Ballet Found., 1967-70; trustee, mem. exec. com., chmn. bd. trustees U. St. Thomas, 1988—; mem. Houston dist. adv. coun. SBA, 1972-76; mem. Dallas regional panel Pres.'s Commn. White House Fellowships, 1972-76, mem. commn., 1977; bd. dirs. Houston chpt. Am. Heart Assn., 1978-79; nat. trustee Palmer Drug Abuse Program, 1978-79; trustee, sec., treas., chmn. audit com., fin. com., mem. mgmt. com. United Way Tex. Gulf Coast, 1979-85. Mem. ABA, Fed. Bar Assn., State Bar Tex., Houston Bar Assn. Roman Catholic. Office: US Ct Appeals 11020 US Courthouse 515 Rusk St Houston TX 77002*

KING, CHARLES BENJAMIN, minister; b. Gasburg, Va., Oct. 20, 1942; s. James Skelton and Frances (Walton) K.; m. Patsy Mitchell, Sept. 11, 1965; children: James A., Katherine A. BA, Randolph-Macon Coll., 1964; MDiv, Duke U., 1967; cert. clin. pastoral edn., Med. Coll. Va., 1969. Ordained to ministry Meth. Ch. as deacon, 1965, as elder, 1969. Student pastor Bethel United Meth., Hanover, Va., 1963-64; youth dir. Noland Meml. United Meth. Ch., Newport News, Va., 1964; student minister 1st United Meth. Ch., Graham, N.C., 1965-67; minister St. Peter's United Meth. Ch., Montpelier, Va, 1967-70; minister of evangelism Trinity United Meth. Ch., Richmond, Va., 1970-72; minister Courtland (Va.) United Meth. Ch., 1972-76; sr. minister Westover Hills United Meth. Ch., Richmond, 1976-80, Christ United Meth. Ch., Norfolk, Va., 1980-84; assoc. dir. leadership devel. Va. United Meth. Conf., Richmond, 1984-89, dir. evangelism, 1989-94; supt. Farmville dist., 1994—. Author: Jesus the Christ, 1978; co-author: Revealing Christ: Sharing the Faith. Recipient Lifetime Membership award United Meth. Women, 1976, Growth Plus award Bd. of Discipleship, 1990.

KING, CHARLES MARK, dentist, educator; b. Ft. Benning, Ga., Mar. 15, 1952; s. Charles Ray and Marilyn Anita (Alexander) K.; children: Kelley Michelle, Kevin Marcus, Mark Alexander. BS, U. Ala., 1973, MS, 1977, DMD, 1981, postgrad. Birmingham Sch. Law, 1989—. cert. Pain Management Practitioner, 1992. Lab. technician Med. Lab. Assn., Birmingham, Ala., 1973-74; rsch. asst. dept. surgery Univ. Hosp., Birmingham, 1974-76, dept. anesthesiology, 1976-78; gen. practice dentistry, Birmingham, 1981—; clin. instr. U. Ala. Sch. Dentistry, Birmingham, 1982-89; mem. bd. advisors Dist. Dental Assts. Soc., 1984-90. Contbr. articles to profl. jours. Lt. col. Ala. Army NG. Named Best Clin. Instr., Student Body U. Ala. Sch. Dentistry 1985. Mem. Acad. Pain Management, Acad. Gen. Dentistry, Assn. Mil. Surgeons U.S., Nat. Assn. Doctors, Scottish Rite, Shriners, Masons, Delta Sigma Delta. Republican. Baptist. Avocations: archery, martial arts, hunting, water sports, flying. Masons, Shriners. Office: 5620 Chalkville Rd Birmingham AL 35235-2149

KING, CYNTHIA BREGMAN, writer; b. N.Y.C., Aug. 27, 1925; d. Adolph and Elsie (Oschrin) Bregman; m. Jonathan King July 26, 1944; children: Gordon Barkley, Austin Arthur (dec.), Nathaniel Bregman. Student, Bryn Mawr Coll., 1943-44, U. Chgo., 1944-46, N.Y.U., 1964-67. Assoc. editor Hillman Periodicals, N.Y.C., 1946-50; mng. editor Fawcett Publs., N.Y.C., 1950-55; creative writing tchr. The Awty Sch., Houston, 1974-75; book reviewer, N.Y. Times Book Rev., 1976-83, Detroit News, 1980-88; dir. short story symposium Friends of Detroit Pub. Libr. and Detroit Women Writers, 1985; creative writing residencies Mich. Coun. of the Arts, Detroit, 1976-86. Author: In the Morning of Time, 1970, The Year of Mr. Nobody, 1978, Beggars and Choosers, 1980, Sailing Home, 1982; editor Fripp Island Audubon Club Natural History Publs., 1990-92;. Mem. Pritchards Island adv. bd. U. S.C., Beaufort; pres. Fripp Island (S.C.) Audubon Club, 1991-92; asst. to chmn. Beaufort County Dem. Party, 1989-91. Creative Artist's grant Mich. Coun. for the Arts., 1985-86. Mem. The Authors Guild, Poets and Writers, Inc., Detroit Women Writers, Inc. (pres. 1979-81).

KING, DAVID STEVEN, quality control executive; b. Easton, Pa., May 16, 1960; s. Carl Stanley and Verna Marilyn (Frey) K. BS in Stats., Va. Poly. Inst. and State U., 1982. Cert. statistician, quality engr., reliability engr., quality auditor, ISO 900 lead assessor, quality assurance profl. Quality and product design engr. SIECOR Corp., Hickory, N.C., 1982-86; quality supr. Alcatel Cable Systems, Fordyce, Ark., 1987-89; quality assurance mgr. Aeroquip Corp., Heber Springs, Ark., 1989-90; quality control mgr. Progress Lighting, Cowpens, S.C., 1990-92; quality mgr. Dana Corp., Greenville, S.C., 1993-95; quality engr. Std. Products, Spartanburg, S.C., 1995—. Mem. Am. Soc. for Quality Control, Am. Stats. Assn., ASTM. Home: 11 Vale St Spartanburg SC 29301-5543

KING, DAVID THOMPSON, JR., geology educator; b. Birmingham, Ala., Oct. 4, 1951. BS, N.E. La. U., 1972; MS, U. Houston, 1976; PhD, U. Mo., 1980. Assoc. prof. Auburn (Ala.) U., 1980—; rsch. lunar soils of Apollo 15 and 17 NASA, 1973-76. Discoverer most complete tyrannosaurid dinosaur fossil in S.E. U.S., 1982; contbr. articles to profl. jours. Named Outstanding Prof., Auburn Alumni Assn., 1989. Office: Auburn Univ Dept Geology Auburn AL 36849-5305

KING, DEXTER SCOTT, foundation administrator; b. Atlanta, Jan. 30, 1961. Pres. Visionary Devel. Corp., Atlanta; dir. office spl. events and entertainment Martin Luther King, Jr. Ctr. Nonviolent Social Change, Inc. (The King Ctr.), Atlanta, chmn., pres., CEO, also bd. dirs., 1984—; spkr. in field. Exec. prodr. (record and video project) King Holiday. Named one of 50 Most Beautiful People, People Mag., 1995. Office: King Ctr Nonviolent Social Change 449 Auburn Ave NE Atlanta GA 30312-1590

KING, DON, boxing promoter; b. Cleve., Aug. 20, 1931; s. Clarence and Hattie K.; m. Henrietta King; children: Deborah, Carl, Eric. Boxing promoter, 1972—; owner Don King Prodns., Inc., Fla., 1974—; promoter various fighters including Muhammad Ali, Sugar Ray Leonard, Mike Tyson, Ken Norton, Joe Frazier, Larry Holmes, Roberto Duran, George Foreman. Office: care Don King Prodns Inc 871 W Oakland Park Blvd Fort Lauderdale FL 33311-1731

KING, FRANCES, education educator; b. Dallas, Nov. 14, 1929; d. Grover W. and Clara (Blailock) Beckham; m. Erwin C. King, Jr., Jan. 27, 1951; children: Carol, Melody. BA, Austin Coll., 1951; Writer's Cert., Children's Inst. of Lit., Redding Ridge, Conn., 1987. Cert. tchr. of mentally retarded, early childhood, learning disabilities, Tex. Tchr., fourth grade O'Brien (Tex.) Consolidated Ind. Sch. Dist., 1958-62; tchr., first grade, early childhood/spl. edn. tchr. Knox City (Tex.) Consolidated Ind. Sch. dist., 1961-71; spl. edn. tchr. mid. sch. Knox City-O'Brien Consolidated Ind. Sch. Dist., 1971-76, 76-89; spl. edn./adult edn. tchr. Knox City-O'Brien and Sweetwater Dist., Knox City, 1989-95; subs. tchr. Knox City-O'Brien Dist., 1995—; spl. edn. spelling coach Knox City H.S. Co-author: Guide Program for Special Education. Named Tchr. of the Yr. in Spl. Edn., Region IVX. Mem. Tex. State Tchrs. Assn. (local pres.), ATPE (local pres.).

KING, JACK HOWELL, transportation engineering executive; b. Jackson, Tenn., Mar. 1, 1952; s. Thomas Thaddeus and Lula Janette (Upchurch) K.; m. Nancy Lynne Herring, Apr. 1, 1989; 1 child, Melissa Lynne. BCE, U. Tenn., 1975, MCE, 1976. Registered profl. engr., Tenn., Fla. City traffic engr. City Cleve., Tenn., 1976-78; v.p. Cen. Distbrs., Inc., Jackson, Tenn., 1977-91; traffic studies engr. City of Tampa, Fla., 1978-79, asst. traffic engr., 1979-81, city traffic engr., 1981-84; dept. head hwy. design Watson and Co., Tampa, 1984-85; dept. head transp. engr. Greenhorne and O'Mara, Inc., Tampa, 1985-89; dist. roadway design engr. Fla. Dept. Transp., Tampa, 1990-93, dist. project mgmt. adminstr., 1993—. Mem. Inst. Transp. Engrs. (chmn. awards com. Fla. sect. 1988-90, dir. 1982-84). Methodist. Home: 4615 W Lowell Ave Tampa FL 33629-7628 Office: Fla Dept Transp 11201 N McKinley Dr Tampa FL 33612

KING, JAMES A., executive; b. 1939. BS, La. State U., 1961. Various mgmt. and exec. positions Gulf Oil Corp., 1961-85; v.p. refining, supply and transp. Crown Ctrl. Petroleum Corp., 1985-92; exec. v.p. transp. Coastal Corp., 1992—. Office: Coastal Eagle Point Oil Co 9 E Greenway Plz Houston TX 77046

KING, JAMES ANDREW, protective services educator and administrator; b. Corinth, Miss., Apr. 26, 1948; s. Doyal Andrew and Martha Lee (Ridings) K.; m. Hannelore Martha Wanner, Feb. 5, 1970; 1 child, Karl Joseph. B Pub. Adminstrn., Nat. U., San Diego, 1982, M Forensic Sci., 1983; PhD in Criminology, U. Ky., 1986. Cert. criminologist, protection specialist. Commd. U.S. Army, 1966, criminal investigator, instr., 1966-76, ret., 1976; commd. USN, 1977, criminal investigator, instr., 1977-91, ret., 1991; prof. criminal justice Nat. U., 1983-88; protective svc. specialist NATO, 1989-91; exec. dir. Internat. Bodyguard Assn., Brighton, Tenn., 1991—; cons. various nat. and internat. orgns., 1989—. Author: Providing Protective Services, 1989. Decorated Bronze Star (2), Purple Heart (2), Air medal, Cross Gallantry, Govt. Vietnam; named Ky. Col., Gov. State Ky., 1976, Knight Chevalier, Police Hall Fame, 1994, Legion Honor award, 1994. Mem. Nat. Tactical Officers Assn., Lambda Alpha Epsilon. Office: Internat Bodyguard Assn 458 W Kenwood Brighton TN 38011-6294

KING, JAMES LAWRENCE, federal judge; b. Miami, Fla., Dec. 20, 1927; s. James Lawrence and Viola (Clodfelter) K.; m. Mary Frances Kapa, June 1, 1961; children—Lawrence Daniel, Kathryn Ann, Karen Ann, Mary Virginia. BA in Edn., U. Fla., 1949, JD, 1953; LHD (hon.), St. Thomas U., 1992. Bar: Fla. 1953. Assoc. Sibley & Davis, Miami, Fla., 1953-57; ptnr. Sibley Giblin King & Levenson, Miami, 1957-64; judge 11th Jud. Cir. Dade County, Miami, 1964-70; temp. assoc. justice Supreme Ct. Fla., 1965; temp. assoc. judge Fla. Ct. Appeals (2d, 3d and 4th cirs.), 1965-68; judge U.S. Dist. Ct. (so. dist.) Fla., Miami, 1970—, chief judge, 1984-91, sr. judge, 1991—; temp. judge U.S. Ct. Appeals 5th cir., 1977-78; mem. Jud. Conf. U.S., 1984-87, mem. adv. commn. jud. activities, 1973-76, mem. joint commn. code jud. conduct, 1974-76, mem. commn. to consider stds. for admission to practice in fed. cts., 1976-79, chmn. implementation com. for admission attys. to fed. practice, 1979-85, mem. com. bankruptcy legis., 1977-78; mem. Jud. Coun. 11th Cir., 1989—; pres. 5th cir. U.S. Dist. Judges Assn., 1977-78; chief judge U.S. Dist. Ct. C.Z., 1977-78; long range planning commn. Fed. Judiciary, 1991-95. Mem. state exec. council U. Fla., 1956-59; mem. Bd. Control Fla. Governing State Univs. and Colls., 1964. Served to 1st lt. USAF, 1953-55. Recipient Outstanding Alumnus award U. Fla. Law Rev., 1980. Mem. Fla. Bar Assn. (pres. jr. bar 1963-64, bd. govs. 1958-63, Merit award young lawyer sect. 1967), ABA, Am. Law Inst., Inst. Jud. Adminstrn., Fla. Blue Key, Pi Kappa Tau, Phi Delta Phi. Democrat. Home: 11950 SW 67th Ct Miami FL 33156-4756 Office: James King Fed Justice Bldg 99 NE 4th St Ste 1127 Miami FL 33132-7799*

KING, JENNIE LOUISE, research director; b. Ft. Hood, Tex., Nov. 27, 1962; d. Homer Lee and Jennie Louise (Smith) Walker; m. Philip Jerome King, Apr. 23, 1994. BA in Speech Comms., Columbus Coll., 1984; postgrad., Mercer U., 1987-90. Intern Senator Mack Mattingly, Washington, 1984, Congressman Richard Ray, Washington, 1984; rsch. asst. The Robinson Humphrey Co., Inc., Atlanta, 1985-89; mktg. asst. Norrell Corp., Atlanta, 1989-90; rsch. assoc. The Carter Ctr., Inc., Atlanta, 1990-93, dir. rsch., 1993-94; dir. rsch. Boys & Girls Clubs Am., Atlanta, 1994—. Vol. Richard Ray for Congress Campaign Com., 1984, The Atlanta Project, 1992, Sta. WPBA-TV, Channel 30, 1996—; mem. adv. bd. Ga. Addiction Pregnancy and Parenting Family Enrichment Ctr., 1994—. Mem. NARAS (assoc.), Nat. Soc. Fundraising Execs., Atlanta Songwriters Assn. (v.p. 1992-93, 95—, bd. dirs. 1991-93, 95—, publicity chair, 1991-93, fundraising chair 1995—), Broadcast Music Inc., Nat. Acad. Songwriters, Am. Prospect Rsch. Assn. (pres. Ga. chpt. 1993-94), Columbus Coll. Alumni Assn. Methodist. Office: Boys & Girls Clubs Am 1230 W Peachtree St NW Atlanta GA 30309-3404

KING, JOHN ETHELBERT, JR., education educator, former academic administrator; b. Oklahoma City, July 29, 1913; s. John Ethelbert and Iosa (Koontz) K.; m. Glennie Beanland, Dec. 25, 1936; children: Wynetka Ann King Reynolds, Rebecca Ferriss King Wright. BA, N. Tex. State U., 1932; MS, U. Ark., 1937; PhD, Cornell U., 1941; LLD (hon.), Coll. of Ozarks, 1965; LHD (hon.), No. Mich. U., 1966, U. S.C., 1989. Latin tchr., coach Frisco (Tex.) Pub. High Sch., 1933-35; missionary to Native Ams. Presbyn. Ch. U.S.A., Okla., Ariz., 1938-43; asst. prof. N.Y. State Coll. Agr., Cornell U., Ithaca, 1945-47; acad. dean, provost, prof. U. Minn., Duluth, 1947-53; pres., prof. Emporia (Kans.) U., 1953-66; prof., pres. U. Wyo., Laramie, 1966-67; prof., chmn. dept. So. Ill. U., Carbondale, 1967-83; Disting. vis. prof., interim dean U. S.C., Columbia, 1984-90; ednl. adviser Civilian Conservation Corps, U.S. Forest Svc., Ozone, Ark., 1935-37; mentor Assn. Governing Bds. Univs. and Coll., Washington, 1977-90. Editor: Work and the College Student, 1967, Money, Marbles and Chalk, 1978. Life trustee U. Ozarks, Clarksville, Ark., 1965—. Officer USN, 1943-45, PTO. Recipient Disting. Alumnus award N. Tex. U., Denton, 1965, U. Ark., Fayetteville, 1983. Mem. NEA (life), Am. Assn. Colls. Tchr. Edn. (pres. 1966-67), Rotary, Blue Key, Omicron Delta Kappa, Lambda Chi Alpha, Sphinx Club, Phi Delta Kappa. Democrat. Office: U SC Coll Edn Columbia SC 29208

KING, JOSEPH WILLET, child psychiatrist; b. Springfield, Mo., Aug. 26, 1934; m. Doris Ann Toby; children: Pamela Renee, Timothy Wells, Michael Brian, Bradley Christopher. BA, So. Meth. U., 1956; MD, U. Tex. Southwestern, 1962. Diplomate Am. Bd. Psychiatry and Neurology; ordained deacon Episcopal Ch., 1996. Intern Baylor U. Med. Ctr., Dallas, 1962-63; resident in gen. psychiatry Timberlawn Psychiat. Hosp., 1963-64, Lisbon VA Hosp., 1965; fellow in child psychiatry U. Tex. Southwestern Med. Sch., 1965-67, Hillside Hosp., Glen Oaks, N.Y., 1967; staff child psychiatrist, dir. child and adolescent svcs. Timberlawn Psychiat. Ctr., Inc., Dallas, 1967-78; assoc. attending child psychiatrist dept. psychiatry Baylor U. Med. Ctr., Dallas, 1967-78; active attending child psychiatrist Children's Med. Ctr., Dallas, 1967-78; attending staff Dallas County Hosp. Dist./Parkland Meml. Hosp., 1967-78; cons. child psychiatry Girls Day Care Rehab. Ctr. Dallas County, Dallas, 1970-73; cons. child psychiatry and adminstrn. Meridell Achievement Ctr., Austin, Tex., 1971-73; dir. adolescent svcs. Portsmouth (Va.) Psychiat. Ctr., 1978-79; active attending child psychiatrist Maryview Hosp., Portsmouth, 1978-80; med. dir., chief exec. officer Psychiat. Inst. Richmond, Va., 1980-86; chief exec. officer, psychiatrist-in-chief Shadow Mountain Inst., Tulsa, 1987-90; v.p. Century Healthcare, Tulsa, 1987-90; assoc. clin. prof. Med. Coll. Va., Va. Commonwealth U., 1980-90, Med. Sch. U. Okla., Tulsa, 1987—. Contbr. articles to profl. jours. Fellow Am. Psychiat. Assn. (Okla. dist. br.), Am. Soc. Adolescent Psychiatry (nat. pres. 1975-76), Am. Orthopsychiat. Assn., Am. Coll. Psychiatrists; mem. AMA, Tex. Med. Assn. (various coms.), Dallas County Med. Soc. (various coms.), Am. Acad. Child and Adolescent Psychiatry (ins. com. 1981-86, pres. Okla. coun. 1991-92, state del. to nat. coun.), Tex. Soc. Child Psychiatry (past officer), Nat. Assn. Pvt. Psychiat. Hosps. (chmn. adolescent care com. 1971-81, multiple com./task force functions, pres. ind. for profit sect. 1991-92, trustee 1992-95), Okla. Med. Soc., Tulsa County Med. Soc., Tulsa Psychiat. Assn. (bd. dirs.), Alumni Assn. U. Tex. Southwestern Med. Sch. (pres. 1991-94). Office: 7146 S Braden Ave Tulsa OK 74136-6371

KING, KENNETH VERNON, JR., pharmacist; b. Lexington, Miss., Dec. 17, 1950; s. Kenneth Vernon Sr. and Louise (Jordan) K.; m. Janis Marie Guynes, June 12, 1976; children: Kenneth V. King III, Nanette Marie King, Jason Guynes King. AA, Holmes Jr. Coll., 1971; BS in Pharmacy, U. Miss., 1973; cert. sterile compounding dossage units, Profl. Compounding Ctrs. Am., Houston, 1993. Registered pharmacist, Miss., Pa.; cert. in sterile aseptic compounding medicinal units. Pharmacist Barretts Drug Store, Greenwood, Miss., 1973-74; registered pharmacist Eckerd Drugs, Greenwood, 1974-76, 77-88, Medi-Save Drugs Ellis Isle, Jackson, Miss., 1976; registered pharmacist Eckerd Drugs, Pearl, Miss., 1988-90, Jackson, 1990-92; compounding pharmacist Marty's Discount Drugs, Flowood, Miss., 1992-96, co-owner, 1996—; cons. Sta-Home Hospice care of Miss., Grace House of Jackson, 1992—, Hospice Care Found., Vicksburg, Miss., 1993-94; cons. Whispering Pines Hospice (inpatient), 1992—, Hospice of Ctrl. Miss. (outpatient), 1993—; owner, contractor, rschr., cons. Profl. Pharm. Svcs. in Miss., Jackson; owner Pharmakan Inc., Pharmakeus Inc.; presenter regional seminars Profl. Compounding Ctrs. of Am., Birmingham, Ala., 1993, 94, Charlotte, N.C., 1994, Symposium on Man and His Environment, Am. Acad. Environ. Medicine, 1995; clin. pharmacy instr. U. Miss. Sch. Pharmacy, Oxford, 1985-92, 95—; tchr. environ. illness VA Hosp.; hospice pharmacist, cons., 1992—; mem. Profl. Compounding Corp. Am., Houston, P2C2 Profl. Care, Inc., Houston; co-writer compounding criteria Miss. State Bd. Pharmacy, Pharmacy Practice Act, 1993, co-investigator prescribing protocols, 1994; participant AIDS Update '96 for Delta Region (Miss., Ark. and La.), Jackson, 1996; opening spkr. PCCA Nat. Conv. on Hospice Practice, 1996; presenter seminars on alternative dosing to joint convention of Miss. Hospice Orgns. and La. Hospice Orgns., 1996. Advisor Leflore County 4-H, Greenwood, 1974-76; aux. patrolman Greenwood Police Dept., 1982-86; drug identification specialist Greenwood Aux. Police Dept., 1984-85; pres., founder Human Ecology Action League Miss., Inc., 1988—, bd. dirs. 1991—, advt. coord., Atlanta, 1989%, sec., 1984—; coord. Environ. Assocs. Jack Eckerd, Inc., 1990-92; mem. Rainbow Whole Food Coop., 1989—; coord. regional support svcs. HEAL Inc., 1989—. Mem. Environ. Coalition of Miss. (co-founder), Environ. Assocs. of Jack Eckerd Inc. (coord.), Miss. Soc. Cons. Pharmacists. Mem. Word of Life Ch. Office: Profl Pharm Svcs 1050 B2 N Flowood Dr Jackson MS 39208

KING, K(IMBERLY) N(ELSON), computer science educator; b. Columbus, Ohio, Apr. 28, 1953; s. Paul Ellsworth and Marcelia Jeannette (Huston) K.; m. Cynthia Ann Stormes, Sept. 5, 1981 (div. Nov. 1991); m. Susan Ann Cole, Aug. 9, 1996. BS with highest honors, Case Western Res. U., 1975; MS, Yale U., 1976; PhD, U. Calif., Berkeley, 1980. Asst. prof. info. and computer sci. Ga. Inst. Tech., Atlanta, 1980-86, rsch. scientist, 1986-87; assoc. prof. math. and computer sci. Ga. State U., Atlanta, 1987—; cons. Norfolk So. Rwy., 1991. Author: Modula-2: A Complete Guide, 1988, C Programming: A Modern Approach, 1996; columnist Jour. Pascal, Ada, and Modula-2, 1989-90; contbr. articles to profl. jours. Vol. Ga. Radio Reading Svc., Atlanta, 1989—. Grad. fellow NSF, 1975-78; NSF grantee, 1981-84. Mem. AAUP, IEEE Computer Soc., Assn. for Computing Machinery, Tau Beta Pi. Home: 2661 Havermill Way NE Atlanta GA 30345-1427 Office: Ga State U Dept Math & Computer Sci Atlanta GA 30303

KING, LAURISTON RACKLIFFE, science research administrator, marine educator; b. Hartford, Conn., Mar. 24, 1943; s. Carl Clinton and Dawn Ardele (Dunphy) K.; m. Geraldine Bartley, June 12, 1965; children—Christopher Garrett, Paul Gregory, Brendan Carl. B.A., Tufts U., 1965; M.A., U. Conn., 1967, Ph.D., 1971. Inter-agy. liaison officer NSF, Washington, 1972-76; program mgr. marine sci. affairs, 1976-78; dep. dir. sea-grant coll. program Tex. A&M U., College Station, 1978-87, dep. dir. Office U. Research Services, 1987-93; assoc. vis. prof. Dept. Pol. Sci. Tex. A&M U., 1993-94; sr. rsch. sci. Sea Grant Coll. program, 1994—; cons. White House Office of Sci. and Tech. Policy, Washington, 1979-82. Author: Washington Lobbyists for Higher Education, 1975. Contbr. articles to profl. jours. Recipient Dissertation Research award NSF, 1968, postdoctoral fellowship award Woods Hole Oceanographic Instn., Mass., 1971-72; research grantee Tex. A&M Sea Grant Coll. Program, College Station, 1985. Mem. AAAS, Am. Polit. Sci. Assn., So. Polit. Sci. Assn. (best conv. paper award 1983), Marine Affairs and Policy Assn. (mem. ocean governance study group). Democrat. Methodist. Avocations: jogging; reading; gardening. Office: Tex A&M Univ Sea Grant Coll Program College Station TX 77843

KING, MARIAN EMMA, health and physical education educator; b. Miami, Fla., Aug. 6, 1949; d. Daniel Huffman and Emma (Smith) K. BS, Fla. State U., 1971; MS, Ga. State U., 1977, EdS, 1983; EdD, Nova Sotheastern U., 1996. Cert. health and phys. edn. tchr., Ga. Tchr. Atlanta City Schs./Howard High Sch., 1971-76, Atlanta City Schs./Washington High Sch., 1976-77, Atlanta City Schs./Northside High Sch., 1977-91, North Atlanta High Sch., 1991—; cons. Measurement Inc. Sponsor Easter Seal Shoot-Out, Atlanta, 1980-86, Am. Cancer Soc. Gt. Am. Smoke-Out, Atlanta, 1987-96, March of Dimes Walk Am., Atlanta, 1987-95, Diabetes Walk-A-Thon, Atlanta, 1990-96; worksite wellness coord. UNICEF Bike-A-Thon, 1989—, sponsor, 1990-91; first aid instr. and vol. ARC. Named Region 6AAA Coach of Yr., 1984, 85, Atlanta Area III Tchr. of Yr., 1989, Ga. Phys. Educator of Yr., 1990, Drug Free Schs., 1992-96, N. Atlanta Tchr. of Yr., 1996-97; grantee NAPPS, 1990-94. Mem. AAHPERD (chmn. so. dist. secondary phys. edn. coun. 1992-93, Ga. del. 1993, So. Dist. Secondary Phys. Edn. Tchr. of Yr. award 1990), Nat. Assn. Health Educators, Nat. Assn. for Sport and Phys. Edn., Nat. Assn. for Girls and Women in Sports, Assn. Advancement Health Edn., Ga. Assn. for Health, Phys. Edn., Recreation and Dance (comm. appointee 1993-94), Kappa Delta Pi. Home: 4085 White Oak Ln SW Lilburn GA 30247-2248 Office: North Atlanta High Sch 2875 Northside Dr NW Atlanta GA 30305-2807

KING, MARY SMOTHERS, association executive; b. Memphis, Oct. 28, 1937; d. Dwight Dewitt and Lillian Helen (Flowers) Smothers; m. Charles Stirling King, Jan. 18, 1963 (dec. 1982); children: Lillian Lee, Frances Elizabeth, Mary Nell. Student, McNeese U., Lake Charles, La., 1966-67, MusB, 1965; MA, Corpus Christi State U., Tex., 1985. Flight attendant Am. Air Lines, Buffalo, 1962; paralegal Pvt. Law Practice, Lake Charles, La., 1967-78; gen. mgr. Lake Charles Symphony, La., 1978-81; asst. controller White River Drilling Co., Corpus Christi, Tex.; exec. asst. Zoom, Inc. Prodn. Co., Corpus Christi, Tex., 1982-84; exec. dir. Camp Fire Council of Corpus Christi, Tex., 1984-85, USO of S. Tex., Inc., Corpus Christi, 1985-91; gen. mgr. PSYTEP Corp., 1991-92; master's level counselor Quinco Mental Health Ctr., Savannah, Tenn., 1992—; bd. dirs. Lake Charles Symphony, La., 1975-78, Heart Assn., Lake Charles, La., 1974, Bethune Day Care Ctr., Corpus Christi Tex., 1987—. Composer, Performer: Work for Organ & Voice, Psalm 97 1965; soloist multiple symphonies Operas Little Theatre, Tenn., La., Ark., Tex., 1956-73. Sec. Jr. League Lake Charles La., 1971-73; campaign mgr. Pol. Race for Dist. Judge Calcasieu & Cameron Parishes, La. 1978-79.La. 1978-79. Recipient Commander's award for Pub. Service, U.S. Army, 1989. Mem. Jr. League Corpus Christi, Nat. Assn. Female Execs., Young Men's Bus. Aux. Club Lake Charles (Pres. 1966-67), Lake Charles Club (Pres. 1970-71), Kiwanis Lions Club, Am. Bus. Women's Clubs, Rotary Corpus Christi, Rotary Savannah. Republican. Baptist. Home: 2407 Holt Dr Savannah TN 38372-1345

KING, OLIN B., electronics systems company executive; b. Sandersville, Ga., 1934; married. BS, N. Ga. Coll., 1953. With RCA Corp., 1956-57, Army Ballistic Missile Agy., 1957-60, Marshall Space Flight Ctr., 1960-61; pres. SCI Systems, Inc., Huntsville, Ala., 1966-81, chmn. bd., past pres., past dir., past CEO. Served to capt. U.S. Army, 1954-56. Office: SCI Systems Inc PO Box 1000 Huntsville AL 35807-4001*

KING, RALPH EDWIN, JR., health care educator; b. Vicksburg, Miss., Sept. 20, 1936; s. Ralph Edwin Sr. and Julia Wilma (Tucker) K. BA, Millsaps Coll., 1958; MDiv, Boston U., 1961, M of Theology, 1963; postgrad., Harvard Div. Sch., 1966. Ordained min. United Meth. Ch. Min. Belt (Mont.) Valley Meth. Ch., 1961, St. Andrew Meth. Ch., Worcester, Mass., 1962; chaplain, dean of students Tougaloo (Miss.) Coll., 1963-67; civil rights work and prison Coun. of Federated Orgns. and other orgns., 1960-69; sch. integration coord. Delta Ministry of Nat. Coun. of Chs., Jackson, Miss., 1967-70; nonviolence devel. rschr. Gandhi Peace Found., New Delhi, India, 1971; dir. Missippians for Creative Pub. Edn., Jackson, 1972-74; assoc. prof. Sch. of Health Related Professions, U. Miss. Med. Ctr., Jackson, 1974—; adj. prof. sociology and religion Millsaps Coll. Jackson, Miss., 1974—; cons. civil rights history Miss. Dept. of Archives and History, Jackson, 1980—; adv. bd. for religion Ctr. for the Study of So. Culture, Oxford, Miss., 1983—; cons. on elections Miss. AFL-CIO, Jackson, 1982-86. Author: (with others) To Redeem a Nation, 1993, Mississippi Writers/Nonfiction, 1988, America's Original Sin: Sojourner's Study Guide on White Racism, 1988, (preface) Jackson, Mississippi: Chronicle of Struggle and Schism, 1987. State chair, nat. bd. ACLU, N.Y., 1982-80; candidate, lt. gov., congress Miss. Freedom Dem. Party, Jackson, 1960's; nat. com. conv. del. Dem. Party, Atlantic City, Chgo., Miami, Washington, 1964-72. Merrill fellow Harvard U. Divinity Sch., 1966; civil rights rsch. grant Field Found., 1968-70, Miss. Humanites Coun., 1983-94. Mem. So. Sociol. Soc., Fellowship of Reconciliation, Nat. Right to Life Com., Alpha Eta. Democrat. United Methodist. Home: 4504 Meadowridge Dr Jackson MS 39206 Office: Sch of Health Related Professions 2500 N State St Jackson MS 39216-4500

KING, REGINA ANN, lawyer; b. Detroit, Sept. 15, 1942; m. William G. Tucker, Sept. 19, 1987. BA, U. Mich., 1965; MA, Mich. State U., 1970; JD, Cooley Law Sch., 1976. Bar: Mich. Juv. probation officer Macomb Co. Juv. Ct., Mt. Clemens, Mich., 1965-67; program analyst Mich. Dept. Social Svcs., Lansing, Mich., 1969-70, asst. dep. dir., legal liason, 1970-74; asst. atty. gen. Mich. Dept. of Atty. Gen., Lansing, 1976-87; pres., CEO Ad Astra, Ltd., Lapeer, Mich., 1989-92, Taylor-Gough Corp., Singer Island, Fla., 1992—; atty. Regina and King J.D., Lapeer, 1987; ex officio mem. Mich. Women's Commn., Lansing, 1971-73. Office: Regina Ann King JD 103 US Hwy 1 Ste SF-172 Jupiter FL 33477

KING, ROBERT AUGUSTIN, engineering executive; b. Marion, Ind., Sept. 3, 1910; s. Roy Melvin and Estella Bernice (Sheron) K.; m. Johanna A. Akkerman, July 19, 1975; children: Robert Alexander, Sharon Johanna, Estella Regina; children by previous marriage: Hugh Melbourne, Mary Elizabeth. BSChemE, U. Okla., 1935. Chief chemist Phillips Petroleum Co., Borger, Tex., 1935-43; sr. process engr. E. B. Badger & Sons, N.Y.C. and London, 1944-53; dist. mgr. Stone & Webster, N.Y.C., 1954-56; mng. dir. Badger Co., The Hague, Netherlands, 1957-64; pres. King-Wilkinson, Inc., Houston, 1965-84; also dir. King-Wilkinson, Inc.; pres. Robert A. King Inc., 1985—. Mem. Am. Inst. Chem. Engrs., Am. Chem. Soc., Inst. Petroleum (London). Democrat. Episcopalian. Clubs: Petroleum, Braeburn Country (Houston); Chemists (N.Y.C.). Home: 4 Tree Frog Dr Houston TX 77074-6617 Office: 8300 Bissonnet St Ste 260 Houston TX 77074-3903

KING, ROBERT BENNETT, technical marketing specialist; b. Pontiac, Mich., Sept. 19, 1928; s. Robert Bennett and Bessie (Korst) K.; m. Christina Horbach; children: Ira, Christian. BS, U.S. Mil. Acad., 1952; MS, Ohio State U., 1963. Commd. 2d lt. USAF, 1952, advanced through grades to col., 1972; pilot, ops. officer USAF, various including Vietnam, 1952-72; geodesy specialist Def. Mapping Agy. USAF, Washington, 1972-76; chief of dept. geodesy and surveys Def. Mapping Agy. USAF, 1976-77; def. attache USAF, Ankara, Turkey, 1978-81; ret. USAF, 1982; rsch. scientist DBA Systems, Fairfax, Va., 1982-86; sr. mgr. tech. mktg. Intergraph Corp., Reston, Va., 1987-93; ret., 1993; dep. dir. Topographic Ctr., Def. Mapping Agy., Washington, 1982. Mem. Def. Mapping and Charting Alumni Assn. (pres. 1988). Republican. Home: PO Box 1909 Middleburg VA 22117-1909

KING, ROBERT WALLACE, JR., nephrologist; b. Oklahoma City, Aug. 27, 1946; s. Robert W. and Evelyn Lou (Lowry) K.; m. Jeanne Ann Freeman, Mar. 24, 1979; 1 child, Emily Margaret; m. Suzanne Gilbert, June 29, 1968 (div. 1978); children: Anna Christina, Betsy Lowry. Student, Brown U., 1964-66; MD, U. Okla., 1971. Intern St. Anthony Hosp., 1971; med. resident Med. Coll. Va., Richmond, 1972-74; nephrology fellow Med. Coll. Va., 1974-75, U. Okla., Oklahoma City, 1975-76; pvt. practice nephrology Oklahoma City, 1976—; asst. clin. prof. U. Okla., 1982—; med. dir. dialysis transplant St. Anthony Hosp., Oklahoma City, 1982—, chmn. dept. medicine, 1986-88, dir. continuing edn., 1982-90; med. dir. United Health Care Mgmt. of Okla., 1994—. Author: Floating Fauna, 1993; contbr. articles to profl. jours. Pres. Crown Heights Neighborhood Assn., Oklahoma City, 1985, Okla. Organ Sharing Network, 1989; bd. dirs. Southeastern Organ Procurement Found., Richmond, 1984-92; dir. United Network for Organ Sharing, 1982-87. Named Outstanding Staff Mem., St. Anthony Hosp., 1977. Fellow ACP; mem. Okla. Med. Assn. (coun. on med. edn. 1986-91), Okla. Soc. Internal Medicine (program dir. 1980), Okla. Transplant Soc. (pres. 1989, 94), Rotary (dir. 1985-86). Home: 1425 NW 37th St Oklahoma City OK 73118-2802 Office: 1111 N Lee Ave Ste 400 Oklahoma City OK 73103-2620

KING, ROBERTA See CINCA, SILVIA

KING, SHARON A., elementary school educator; b. Owensboro, Ky., May 17, 1947; d. Charles Franklin and Catherine (Brown) Whitaker; m. Ronald Holton King, Oct. 8, 1966; children: Christopher, Tom, Cindy. BA, No. Ky. U., 1989, MEd, 1992. Cert. tchr. K-6, Ky.; cert. RANK I adminstrn. Head cashier/bookkeeper Liberty Loan Co., Cin., 1965-66; tchr. grade 4 Dayton (Ky.) Ind. Schs., 1990-92, 93—; tchr. grades 2-3 Bracken County Schs., Brooksville, Ky., 1992-93; tchr. grade 5-6 Lincoln Elem. Sch., Dayton; supr. intern program Ky. Intern Program/Lincoln Elem. Sch., Dayton, 1994—; assoc. Region 4 Svc. Ctr., 1996. Mem. ASCD, AAUW, NEA, Ky. Edn. Assn., Dayton Edn. Assn., Ky. Assn. Supervision and Curriculum Devel., Kappa Delta Pi (historian), Phi Delta Kappa. Republican. Home: RR 1 Box 319 Brooksville KY 41004-9756

KING, STEPHEN EMMETT, educational administrator; b. Hopkinsville, Ky., June 1, 1942; s. Emmett Southall and Ruth Virginia (Burchfield) K.; m. Linda Johnston, Nov. 11, 1967. MusB, West Ky. U., 1964; MS, Radford U., 1975; EdD, Va. Poly. Inst. and State U., 1991. Dir. bands Coeburn (Va.) High Sch., 1964-68, William Byrd High Sch., Vinton, Va., 1968-86; supr. fine arts Roanoke County Schs., Roanoke, Va., 1986—. Contbr. articles to profl. jours. Active Roanoke Symphony Soc. Bd., 1994—. Mem. ASCD, NEA, Music Educators Nat. Conf., Va. Edn. Assn., Va. Band and Orch. Dirs. Assn. (sec. 1984-86, pres.-elect 1986-88, pres. 1988-90), Am. Sch. Band Dirs. Assn. (state chmn. 1986-88), Va. Alliance for Arts Edn. (bd. dirs. 1991-96, sec. 1993-96), Va. Music Edn. Assn. (exec. bd. dirs., pres.-elect 1990-92, pres. 1992-94, v.p. 1994-96), Phi Delta Kappa, Phi Beta Mu, Phi Mu Alpha Sinfonia. Home: 5250 Keffer Rd Catawba VA 24070-2122 Office: Roanoke County Schs 5937 Cove Rd NW Roanoke VA 24019-2403

KING, STEVE MASON, judge, lawyer; b. Graham, Tex., Dec. 17, 1951; s. Beverly W. and Chloe (Stalcup) K.; m. Julia Ellen Milford, Mar. 30, 1974; children: Cassandra, Mason. BA cum laude, U. Tex., 1974; JD, Baylor U., 1976. Bar: Tex. 1977, U.S. Dist. Ct. (no. dist.) Tex. 1978, U.S. Ct. Appeals (5th cir.) 1981, U.S. Supreme Ct. 1981, U.S. Tax Ct. 1984, U.S. Dist. Ct. (ea. dist.) Tex. 1989. Assoc. Byrom, Butcher & Moore, Ft. Worth, 1977-78, Garrett & Stahala, Ft. Worth, 1978-83; ptnr. Garrett, Stahala & King, Ft. Worth, 1983-86, Epstein, Becker, Borsody & Green, Ft. Worth, 1986-87; pvt. practice Ft. Worth, 1987-94; judge Tarrant County Probate Ct. # 1, Ft. Worth, 1994—; with Nat. Coll. of Probate Judges; faculty Tex. Coll. of Probate Judges; mem. Tex. Guardianship Manual Revision Com. Note contbr.: The Handbook of Tex., 3rd edit. Trustee Buckner Bapt. Benevolences, Dallas, 1981—; parliamentarian Bapt. Gen. Conv. Tex., 1988-90; cert. mediator Dispute Resolution Svc. of Tarrant County. Fellow Tex. Bar Found.; mem. State Bar Tex., Tarrant County Bar Assn., Tarrant County Probate Bar Assn. (bd. dirs., pres. 1993-94), Ft. Worth Outdoor Sports Club (chmn. 1992-93), Magna Carta Barons (Somerset chpt.), Ft. Worth Club, Phi Delta Phi. Office: Tarrant County Courthouse Fort Worth TX 76196

KINGERY, TERRY HALL, sales professional; b. Franklin, Va., Sept. 7, 1956; s. Charles Fisher and Naomi Ruth (Hall) K. Student, U. Richmond, 1974-76; BSBA in Mktg., East Carolina U., 1980. Asst. mgr. front office Sea Pines Plantation, Hilton Head, S.C., 1981-85; asst. mgr. Omni Hotel at CNN Ctr., Atlanta, 1985-87, sales mgr., 1987-89; regional sales mgr. Sandestin Beach Hilton, Atlanta, 1989—. Contbr. articles to profl. newsletters. Mem. Atlanta Civil War Roundtable. Mem. Meeting Planners Internat., Ga. Hospitality Sales and Mktg. Assn. (pres. 1989-90), Buckhead Bus. Assn. (v.p. 1993-96), Skal Club (bd. dirs. 1993—), Rotary (Atlanta pub. rels. com.), Sigma Alpha Epsilon. Baptist. Home: 465 Springs End Ln Marietta GA 30068-3076 Office: Sandestin Beach Hilton Ste 1780 3340 Peachtree Rd NE Atlanta GA 30326-1078

KINGSTON, GEORGE WILLIS, retired naval officer, small business owner; b. Omaha, Feb. 26, 1916; s. George Clarence and Minnie Ella (Smead) K.; m. Gertrude Margaret Stoffel, Feb. 14, 1941 (dec. 1947); 1 child, Frank Martin; m. Marion Regina MacLachlan Devlieg, Aug. 21, 1947. Student, U. Nebr., 1947-49, U. Md., Washington, 1960-61, George Washington U., 1960; grad., U.S. Naval War Coll, Newport, R.I., 1961. Enlisted man USN, 1934, advanced through grades to comdr., 1958; ret., 1966; product devel. engr. Timber Engring. Co., Washington, 1968-81; owner, mgr. Custom Designs & Plans, Gulf Shores, Ala., 1966—, Foley, Ala., 1981—; cons. Svc. Corps Ret. Execs., Foley, 1982-96. Inventor structural wood fasteners. Past mem. bd. dirs. Nat. Safety Coun., Chgo.; chief bldg. advisor ARC, 1969-81, lectr. on disasters and first aid, 1969-85, chmn. Gulf Coast terr, 1985-87, dist. chmn., 1985; bd. dirs. Baldwin Heritage Mus., Elberta, Ala., 1982-94, Lillian (Ala.) Cmty. Club, 1986-88, Care House, Bay Minette, Ala., 1990—; mem. exec. com. Baldwin County Rep. Party, 1984—, parliamentarian, 1984—. Mem. Assn. Am. Red Cross Retirees (v.p. 1994—), VFW (post comdr. 1984-85), NRA (life, lectr. 1988), South Baldwin C. of C. (amb. 1984—), People to People Internat. (amb. 1987—), Nat. Assn. Fleet Tug Sailors (chmn. bd. dirs. 1990—), Optimists (pres. Foley 1991-92, parliamentarian Ala.-Miss. dist. 1992-96, lt. gov. 1992-93, 94-95). Roman Catholic. Home and Office: 1611 Woodbridge Cir E Foley AL 36535-2267

KINGSTON, JACK, congressman; b. Bryan, Tex., 1955; m. Libby Kingston; children: Betsy, John, Ann, Jim. BA in Economics, U. Ga. Salesman, v.p. Palmer & Cay Carswell Ins. Co., 1979-92; mem. Ga. State Ho. Reps., 1985-93, 103d Congress from 1st Ga. Dist., 1993—; mem. Ways and Means Com., 1985-93, Appropriations Com., Congl. Rural Caucus Exec. Bd., 1993—. Vol. Hospice, United Way; mem. NRA, Ducks Unlimited, Atlantic Coast Conservation Assn., Isle of Hope Community Assn. Recipient Guardian of Small Bus. award Nat. Fed. of Ind. Bus., 1992. Mem. Am. Legislative Exchange Coun., Soc. Chartered Property and Casualty Underwriters, Solomon's Lodge F&AM, Rotary (Paul Harris fellow). Republican. Episcopal. Office: US Ho Reps 1507 Longworth HOB Washington DC 20515*

KINNAIRD, SUSAN MARIE, special education educator; b. Grosse Pointe, Mich., May 3, 1954; d. William Burl and Ida Mae (Diehl) Cunningham; m. Henry Wayne Kinnaird Jr., Nov. 30, 1985. BA in Edn., Wayne State U., 1978; MA in Ednl. Adminstrn., U. Houston at Clear Lake, 1990. Cert. elem. tchr., spl. edn. tchr., spl. edn. supr., instrnl. supr., Tex. Parent trainer Dept. Mental Health, Warren, Mich., 1977-78; spl. edn. tchr. Houston Ind. Sch. Dist., 1978-95, spl. edn. coord., 1995—. Asst. coach Spl. Olympics, Houston, 1982, 84, 88-91; bell choir mem. Cen. Presbyn. Ch., Houston, 1979—. Grantee Houston Bus. Com. for Ednl. Excellence 1991, 92. Mem. Coun. for Exceptional Children (chpt. 100 newsletter editor 1990-92, sec. 1992-93, pres.-elect 1993-94, pres. 1994-95). Roman Catholic. Home: 8787 Hammerly Blvd Apt 1011 Houston TX 77080-6610 Office: Houston Ind Sch Dist SW Dist Office 5827 Chimney Rock Houston TX 77081

KINNEBREW, JAMES MELVIN, biblical theologian, educator, entrepreneur; b. Jackson, Miss., July 31, 1953; s. James M. and Iris Christabel (Langford) K.; m. Sandra Lee Carver, Dec. 24, 1974; children: James Michael, Joshua Andrew, Jason Lee. AA, Ctrl. Fla. C.C., 1973; BS, Liberty U., 1980; MDiv, Liberty Bapt. Sem., 1983; ThD, Mid.-Am. Bapt. Sem., 1988. Cert. tchr. Evang. Tchrs. Tng. Assn. Chaplain Eastwood Hosp., Memphis, 1982-83; pastor New Providence Bapt. Ch., Leachville, Ark., 1983-84, Providence Bapt. Ch., Kennett, Mo., 1984-85, 1st Bapt. Ch., Holcomb, Mo., 1985-87; asst. prof. theology Luther Rice Sem., Atlanta, 1988-93, assoc. prof. theology, 1993—, dean of faculty, 1993—; founder Christian Family Enterprises, Conyers, Ga., 1996—; rsch. cons. Atlanta Christian Apologetics Project, Atlanta, 1992—; lectr. in field. Mid-Am. Bapt. Theol. Sem. Tchg. fellow, Memphis, 1984-87. Mem. Evang. Theol. Soc. Office: Luther Rice Seminary 3038 Evans Mill Rd Lithonia GA 30038-2418

KINNEY, ABBOTT FORD, radio broadcasting executive; b. L.A., Nov. 11, 1909; s. Gilbert Earle and Mabel (Ford) K.; student Ark. Coll., 1923, 26, 27; m. Dorothy Lucille Jeffers, Sept. 19, 1943 (dec. Jan. 1986); children—Colleen, Joyce, Rosemary. Editor Dermott News, 1934-39; partner Delta Drug Co., 1940-49; pres., gen. mgr. S.E. Ark. Broadcasters, Inc., Dermott and McGehee, 1951—; corr. Comml. Appeal, Memphis, Ark. Gazette, Little Rock, 1935-53; research early aeros. Inst. Aero. Scis., 1941, castor bean prodn., 1941-42. Mem. Ark. Geol. and Conservation Commn., 1959-63; chmn. Ark. Planning Commn.; mem. Mississippi River Pkwy. Commn., Park Commn. Past pres., mem. exec. bd. DeSoto Area council Boy Scouts Am.; chmn. County Library Bd.; mem. past pres. Hosp. Adv. Bd.; mem. bd. McGehee-Dermott Indsl. Devel. Corp., Chicot Fair Assn., Christian Rural Overseas Program. Recipient Silver Beaver award Boy Scouts Am.; honored with Abbott Kinney Day by civic orgns. and schs. S.E. Ark., 1955; named one of Ark.'s 10 Outstanding Community Leaders, 1969. Mem. AIM, Nat. Assn. Radio and TV Broadcasters, Ark. Broadcasters Assn., Ark., S.E. Ark. chambers commerce, Internat. Broadcasters Soc. (editorial adv. bd.), Ark. Hist. Assn., Am. Numis. Assn. Club: Rotary. Office: SE Ark Broadcasters Inc Dermott AR 71638

KINNEY, CAROL STEWART, dietitian; b. Omaha, Apr. 14, 1938; d. George Franklin Stewart and Grace Sledge; m. Robert Bruce Kinney, Jan. 29, 1961; children: Rodney Michael, David Scott, Linda Grace. BS in Nutrition with hons., U. Calif., Berkeley, 1961; MS in Nutrition, U. Minn., 1963. Cert. diabetes educator; registered dietitian; lic. dietitian/nutritionist, Fla. Cons. to various nursing homes Tucson, Ariz., 1977-83; asst. in extension dept. Nutrition and Food Sci. U. Ariz., Tucson, 1983-84; cons. dietitian for med. personnel pool Home Health Care, Tucson, 1982-84; freelance copy editor Avi Pub. Co., Prentice-Hall, Benjamin Cummings, 1984-87; cook, garde manger dept. Lowes Ventana Canyon Resort, Tucson, 1986-87; sr. pub. health nutritionist Pinellas County Pub. Health Unit, St. Petersburg, Fla., 1988-91; nutrition educator Joslin Ctr. for Diabetes/Morton Plant Hosp., Clearwater, Fla., 1991—; instr. PEL program, Eckerd Coll., 1989-90; assoc. faculty instr. Pima C.C., Tucson, 1978-80; founder Cons. Dietitians in Health Care Facilities, 1985. Contbr. articles to profl. newsletters, books and publs. Active SHARE, St. Petersburg, 1991. Recipient award of Merit Ariz. Dietetic Assn., Tucson, 1980. Mem. Am. Assn. Diabetes Educators, Fla. West Coast Assn. Diabetes Educators (pres. 1993-95), Am. Dietetic Assn., Fla. Dietetic Assn., Pinellas Dist. of Fla. Dietetic Assn. (cmty. nutrition co-chair 1990-91, hunger com. chair 1988-89), Soc. Nutrition Edn. Home: 456 22nd Ave SE Saint Petersburg FL 33705-3304 Office: Joslin Ctr for Diabetes Morton Plant Mease Health C 323 Jeffords St Clearwater FL 34616-3825

KINNEY, JOHN PATRICK, dermatologist; b. St. Louis, July 18, 1942; s. John A. and Ruth K.; m. Janet Bekins Kinney, Sept. 5, 1970; children: Quintin D., Tracy L. BS, U. Tex., 1963; MD, U. Tex., Dallas, 1967. Intern Palo Alto/Stanford U. Hosp., 1967-68; rsch. officer NIH, Bethesda, Md., 1968-70; resident in dermatology NYU Skin and Cancer Hosp., N.Y.C., 1970-73, instr., asst. prof., 1973-74; dermatologist Palm Beach Med. Group, West Palm Beach, Fla., 1974—; chief dermatology divsn. St. Mary's Hosp., West Palm Beach, 1980-88; chief dermatology Good Samaritan Hosp., West Palm Beach, 1989-91; mem. Melanoma Task Force, West Palm Beach, 1996. Fellow Am. Acad. Dermatology, Am. Acad. Dermatologic Surgery; mem. Palm Beach County Dermatology Soc. (chpt. pres. 1979-80, sec. 1977-79). Office: Palm Beach Medical Group 4601 Congress Ave Ste 204 West Palm Beach FL 33407-3228

KINNEY, WILLIAM LEE, minister, religious writer; b. Akron, Ohio, Jan. 12, 1955; s. William Austin and Violette Myrtle (Smith) K.; m. Marguerite Elizabeth Ross, May 9, 1976; children: Daniel Lee, Elizabeth Anne. AB in Religion, Drew U., 1988; MDiv, Princeton Theol. Sem., 1991; postgrad., Drew U., 1987-88. Dir. youth ministries First Presbyn. Ch., New Vernon, N.J., 1983-84; asst. pastor-intern Meml. Ch., Dover, N.J., 1985-87; sem. intern Livingston (N.J.) Presbyn. Ch., 1988-89; cons. for evangelism and young adult ministries St. Mark United Meth. Ch., Hamilton Square, N.J., 1989-90; editor Testament Mag. Princeton Theol. Sem., Princeton, 1989-91; assoc. pastor 1st Presbyn. Ch., Hilton Head, S.C., 1991-95; sr. pastor First Presbyn. Ch., Pine Bluff, Ark., 1995—; editor, curriculum writer The Mason Early Edn. Found., Princeton, 1990-91; elder, commr. Presbyn. Ch. USA, New Vernon, 1982-86; trustee The Madison Day Care Ctr., 1985-88; ethics cons., Ethics Consulting Inc., Morristown, N.J., 1986-87; researcher and adminstrv. asst. Citizens' Com. on Biomedical Ethics, Summit, N.J., 1986-87. Author: Human Rights and Islam, 1994, When Nobody's There, 1994; editor-at-large: The Presbyterian Outlook; contbr. articles to profl. jours. Mem. N.J. Young Reps., Rockaway, 1973; pres. The Munger Chapel Soc. and Social Club, Princeton, 1988—; vice chmn., trustee Hilton Head Coll. Ctr., 1993-95; bd. dirs. Planned Parenthood, 1994-95, Am. Heart Assn., Hilton Head Island, 1994-95, Lyon Coll., Batesville, Ark. Recipient Cert. of Merit Am. Song Festival, 1979, ThD (hon.) Munger Chapel Soc. and Social Club, 1991. Mem. Am. Assn. Christian Counselors (assoc.), Am. Acad. Religion, The Presbyn. Writers Guild, The Nat. Writers Club, Santa Clara U. Ctr. for Applied Ethics. Office: 1st Presbyn Ch 540 William Hilton Pky Hilton Head Island SC 29928-3603

KINSER, DIANNE LEE, typography service executive; b. Wichita Falls, Tex., Jan. 28, 1944; d. Wayne Dee and Sara Ruth (Foster) Schall; m. Ralph E. Kinser, Dec. 30, 1964 (div. Nov. 1972); 1 child, Wayne. Student, U. Minn., 1961-62; AA in Edn., Palm Beach Jr. Coll., 1966; student, Fla. Atlantic U., 1967-70. Asst. advt. mgr. Stevenson's, Mpls., 1961-63; advt. mgr. Belk's, West Palm Beach, Fla., 1963-67; advt. asst. Palm Beach Newspapers, West Palm Beach, 1967-70; prodn. mgr. Artype, West Palm Beach, 1972-75; pres. The Type House, Inc., West Palm Beach, 1975—; instr. Palm Beach C.C., Lake Worth, Fla., 1985—, Northwood U., West Palm Beach, 1994—; mem. Career Counseling Network; mem. steering com. bd. advisors Fla. Atlantic U., Fla. Internat. U., Small Bus. Devel. Ctr., Internat. Trade Ctr.; instr., bd. advisors and instr. City West Palm Beach Small Bus. Devel. Edn. Program and Program Design Group. Featured guest (TV show) Good Morning, America. Del. White House Conf. on Small Bus., 1986, 95, Fla. Gov.'s Confs. on Small Bus.; mem. selection com. county airport concessions, mem. county small bus. leadership commn. Palm Beach County; mem. M/WBE adv. coun. Sch. Bd. Palm Beach County; mem. Palm Beach M/WBE Adv. Com.; bd. dirs. Boys & Girls Club Palm Beach County; pres. Boys & Girls Clubs West Palm Beach, 1994-96; chair cmty. steering com. Planned Parenthood; mem. continuing edn. adv. bd. Palm Beach. C.C.; mem. adv. bd. Bus. in Palm Beach. Named Adv. Yr. women in Bus., Fla. SBA, 1989; recipient Bus. Excellence award Nat. Assn. Women Bus. Owners, 1991. Mem. Am. Advt. Fedn., Greater Palm Beach C. of C., (small bus. and govt. coms.), Nat. Assn. Women Bus. Owners (local pres. 1986-87, nat. dir. 1987-88), Advt. Club of the Palm Beaches, Palm Beach County Women in Bus. (leadership coun.), Palm Beach County Small Bus. Leadership Commn. Home: PO Box 6463 Lake Worth FL 33466-6463 Office: The Type House PO Box 6463 Lake Worth FL 33466-6463

KINSER, KATHERINE ANNE, lawyer; b. Russellville, Ark., Apr. 25, 1954; d. Thomas Kinser and Nancy (Seminatore) Barber; m. Frank W. Sullivan III, Aug. 19, 1988. BA, U. Ark., Little Rock, 1979; JD, So. Meth. U., 1984. Bar: Tex. 1984, U.S. Supreme Ct. 1990; cert. family law specialist, Tex. Assoc. Michael F. Pezzulli, P.C., Dallas, 1984-86; pvt. practice, Dallas, 1986; ptnr. McCurley, Webb, Kinser, McCurley & Nelson, L.L.P., Dallas, 1986—; speaker in field. Contbr. articles to legal publs. Fellow Am. Acad. Matrimonial Lawyers; mem. ABA, State Bar Tex. (family law coun.), Tex. Acad. Family Law Specialists, Tarrant County Family Law Bar Assn., Dallas Bar Assn. (family law sect., sec. 1988-89, v.p. 1990-91, pres. 1991-92, mock trial com. 1987—), Phi Alpha Delta. Office: 1202 Elm St Ste 4620 Dallas TX 75202-3907

KINSEY, JOHN PAUL, consultant; b. Odessa, Texas, Mar. 27, 1943; s. Hershal Harry and Julia Blackford (Jette) K.; children: Melissa B., John Daniel. Student, So. Methodist U., Del Mar Jr. Coll. Dist. mgr. Micom Inc., Dallas, 1984-88; reg. dist. mgr. Intermec, Dallas, 1988-92; pres. Mossman Guitars Inc., Sulphur Springs, Texas, 1992—. Staff sgt. Army Res., 1964-92. Office: Mossman Guitars Inc 1813 Main St Sulpher Springs TX 75482

KINSEY, JULIA CATHERINE, medical records coding specialist; b. Midland, Tex., Jan. 12, 1957; d. Hershel H. and Julia Blackford (Jette) K.; m.

Bryce Douglas Welch, Apr. 3, 1993. Student Plan II honors Program, U. Tex., 1975-77. Cert. coding specialist. Instr. English conversation Lang. House, Inc., Takamatsu, Japan, 1978; med. transcriptionist Brackenridge Hosp., Austin, Tex., 1979-82, St. David's Hosp., Austin, 1982-84; coding technician St. David's Health Care Sys., Austin, 1984-94, Health Info. Assocs. LLC, Richardson, Tex., 1995—. Mem. Am. Assn. Med. Transcription (organizer, 1st pres. local chpt. 1983-84), Am. Health Info. Mgmt. Assn., Soc. Clin. Coding, Tex. Health Info. Mgmt. Assn., Am. Acad. Procedural Coders, Am. Hosp. Assn., Soto Zen. Soto Zen. Office: Austin Coding Coop PO Box 4540 Lago Vista TX 78645

KINSMAN, FRANK ELLWOOD, engineering executive; b. Westfield, Pa., Oct. 2, 1932; s. Ellwood L. and Josephine I. (Champney) K. m. Ednamae J. Reuter, June 12, 1954; children: Patricia Scott, Beverly Armstrong, Cheryl Beezley, Lora Moriconi. BSEE, John Brown U., 1958. Cert. energy mgr. Tech. staff Cornell Aero. Lab., Buffalo, 1958-61; sr. engr. Tex. Instruments, Dallas, 1961-79; v.p. Bywaters & Assocs., Cons. Engrs., Dallas, 1980-86; pres. Kinsman & Assocs., Cons. Engrs., Dallas, 1986—; ops. rsch. Cornell Aero. Lab., Buffalo, 1958-61; energy resources mgr. Tex. Instruments, Dallas, 1974-79; energy sys. analysis and design Bywaters & Assocs., also Kinsman & Assocs., Dallas, 1980—; mem. engring. adv. bd. John Brown U., Siloam Springs, Ark., 1970-72, 94—; vis. lectr. So. Meth. U., Dallas, 1984-85; energy cons. to univs., schs., hosps. and fed. and state agencies, 1987—. Contbr. articles to profl. jours. Bd. chmn. Grace Bible Ch., Dallas, 1990. With USN, 1950-53. Selected Alumnus of the Yr., John Brown U., 1994. Mem. ASHRAE, NSPE, Assn. of Energy Engrs. (sr.), Tex. Soc. Profl. Engrs.

KINSOLVING, SYLVIA CROCKETT, musician, educator; b. Berkeley, Calif., Sept. 30, 1931; d. Harold Waldo and Louise (Effinger) Crockett; m. Charles Lester Kinsolving, Dec. 18, 1953; children: Laura Louise, Thomas Philip, Kathleen Susan. AA in Voice, Piano magna cum laude, No. Va. Community Coll., 1983; BA, U. Calif., Berkeley, 1953. Solo vocalist various chs. Va., 1982—; pvt. tchr. piano Vienna, Va., 1983—; singer, soloist Unity Ch., Oakton, Va., 1980—, St. Andrew's Anglican Ch., Alexandria, Va., 1985—; active numerous local musical prodns., 1959—. Tour leader Vienna Newcomers, 1980. Mem. PEO, U. Calif. Alumni Club, Fairfax West Music Fellowship (sec. 1990—), Phi Theta Kappa, Pi Beta Phi. Democrat. Episcopalian. Home: 1517 Beulah Rd Vienna VA 22182-1417

KINTNER, TREVA CARPENTER, retired education educator; b. Topeka, Ind., Apr. 27, 1920; d. Adrian and Elizabeth (Burns) Carpenter; m. Loren D. Kintner, Aug. 25, 1946; children: Susan, David. BS, Manchester Coll., North Manchester, Ind., 1944; MS, U. Mo., 1952. Tchr. pub. schs. Milford, Ind., 1944-45, Wakarusa, Ind., 1945-46, Pickerington, Ohio, 1947-48; instr. U. Mo., Columbia, 1952-54; asst. prof. foods U. Mo., 1968-86; ret.; prof. Prince of Songkaa U. Pattani, Thailand, 1986. Contbr. articles to profl. jours. Bd. dirs. Citrus coun. Girl Scouts U.S., 1995—. U. Mo. scholar, 1981. Mem. AAUW (pres. 1987-89), Kissimmee Women's Club (pres. 1991, 92), Kissimmee Garden Club, Ret. Tchrs. Assn. (pres. 1989-91), Sigma Xi, Gamma Sigma Delta (award of merit 1986), Phi Upsilon Omicron (nat. coun. 1989-92, ednl. found. 1996-98), Delta Kappa Gamma. Address: 2775 Orchid Ln Kissimmee FL 34744-3015

KINZEY, OUIDA BLACKERBY, retired mathematics educator, photographer, photojournalist; b. Leeds, Ala., Feb. 6, 1922; d. George W. and Kate (Spruiell) Blackerby; m. William Thomas Kinzey, Feb. 6, 1943. AB, Birmingham So. Coll., 1942, EdM, 1959; advanced profl. diploma, U. Ala., 1964. Tchr. math. Phillips High Sch., Birmingham, Ala., 1942-44, Humes High Sch., Memphis, 1944-45; chmn. math. dept. Woodlawn High Sch., Birmingham, 1945-69; assoc. prof. math. Birmingham So. Coll., 1969-84, prof. emeritus, 1984—, dir. vis. profs. program, 1971-75, mem. alumni leadership bd., Gala adv. bd.; vis. math. prof. Samford U., 1989, 90, 91, 92, 93; cons., lectr., speaker and workshop dir. throughout S.E. region. Author: (audio-visual text) Creative Teaching Mathematically, 1973, (video) The World of Mathematics, 1990, (video) A Mathematical Adventure, 1991; author, photographer: (photographic essays) Back Roads of Alabama, Alabama's Covered Bridges, Coal Mining in Alabama, A Place to Worship, The Art of Awareness, Highlights of St. Clair County, A Tour of Blount County; photographs exhibited one man shows including Birmingham So. Coll., 1984, Samford U., 1985, Med. Ctr. East, 1986, Univ. Hosp., 1989, U. Ala., Birmingham, 1989, Birmingham Mus. of Art, 1989, Baptist Med. Ctr., Princeton, 1991, 92, Art Gallery Birmingham Pub. Libr., 1991, Mervyn Sterne Libr., 1991, 93, 94, 95, Jefferson County Ct. House Gallery, 1992, 93, Vincent's Gallery, 1992, St. Vincents Hosp., 1992, Children's Hands On Mus., Tuscaloosa, Ala., 1992, 93, 94, Ala. State Coun. on the Arts, Montgomery, Ala., 1993, Gadsden Cultural Ctr., Gadsden, Ala., 1994, Corp. Hdqs. Atrium, Ala. Power Co., 1995, Art Gallery, Brookwood Med. Ctr., 1995; Permanent Exhibition: Marguerite Jones Harbert Bldg., Birmingham Southern Coll., Ala. Grantee NSF, 1959, 61, 64, 71, Kellogg Found., 1978, Mellon Found., 1980, 81, 84, Title III, 1982; recipient Grand Nat. award NEA/Kodak, 1984, Cert. of Lifetime Personal Achievement Birmingham So. Coll., 1990, Disting. Alumni award Birmingham-So. Coll. Nat. Alumni Assn., 1992; named an Outstanding Educator of Am., 1972. Mem. AAUW, Ala. Assn. Coll. Tchrs. Math., Ala. Acad. Sci., United Daus. Confederacy, Nat. Coun. Tchrs. Math., Math. Assn. Am., Am. Math Soc. (joint policy bd. math. pub. info. resources com.), Ala. Edn. Assn., Ala. Poetry Soc. Ala. Writers' Conclave, Nat. League Am. PEN Women, Patrons Art Coun. East, Nat. League Arts and Letters, Phi Beta Kappa, Kappa Delta Pi, Delta Kappa Gamma, Kappa Delta Epsilon, Kappa Mu Epsilon, Theta Sigma Lambda, Delta Phi Alpha, Alpha Lambda Delta. Speech Arts Club (pres., v.p., sec., treas.). Republican. Methodist. Avocations: photography, collecting rocks, Indian artifacts and antiques. Home: 1413 Swallow Ln Birmingham AL 35213-1613

KIPNISS MACDONALD, BETTY ANN, artist, educator; b. Bklyn., Aug. 2, 1936; d. Samuel Simon and Stella Anita (Blackton) Kipniss; m. Gordon James MacDonald; divorced; children: Gordon, Maureen, Michael, Bruce. BA, Adelphi U., 1958; MA, Columbia U., 1960. Instr. Montshire Mus., Hanover, N.H., 1979-84, Lebanon (N.H.) Coll., 1984, Smithsonian Instn., Washington, 1985-95; pres., bd. dirs. Washington Printmakers Gallery. Exhbns. include Nat. Mus. Women in the Arts, Washington, 1994, 95; in permanent collections at Community for Creative Nonviolence, Washington, 1989, Mus. of Modern Art, Buenos Aires, 1988, Am. Cultural Ctr., New Delhi, India, 1992, Pa. State U., 1992; featured in William and Mary Review, 1992, 93, 94, 95, 96. Grantee Giorgio Cini Found., 1962, NEA, 1981; recipient 1st prize printmakers Washington Women's Art Ctr., 1986, Past Pres.'s award Mus. Fine Arts, Springfield, Mass., 1982, de Cordova Mus., Soc. Am. Graphic Artists N.Y., Merit award Currier Gallery of Art, 1987. Mem. L.A. Printmaking Soc. Home: 7222 Vistas Ln Mc Lean VA 22101-5076

KIRBY, DIANA CHERNE, nurse, retired military officer; b. Guttenberg, Iowa, Jan. 22, 1951; d. Albert Edward and Bernadette Lucretia (Berns) Cherne; BS in Nursing, U. Iowa, 1973; MS in Edn., U. So. Calif., 1977; MS in Nursing, U. Md., 1987; lic. pilot; m. Fred W. Kirby, Nov. 24, 1981. Mem. nursing staff Mercy Med. Ctr., Dubuque, Iowa, 1973-74; commd. 1st lt. Nurse Corps, U.S. Army, 1974, advanced through grades to lt. col., 1991; service in W. Ger.; community health nurse William Beaumont Army Med. Center, 1978-80, Ft. Leonard Wood, Mo., 1980-82, Ft. Meade, Md., 1987; chief community nursing Dewitt Army Community Hosp., Ft. Belvoir, Va., 1987-92, Korea, 1992-93; community health nurse Walter Reed Army Med. Ctr., Washington, 1993-95; pub. health nurse Fairfax County (Va.) Health Dept., 1995—; cons. community health nursing. Mem. APHA, Am. Nurses Assn., Va. Nurses Assn., Nat. Trust for Hist. Preservation, Am. Philatelic Soc., Sigma Theta Tau. Roman Catholic. Address: 6833 Silver Ann Dr Lorton VA 22079-1311

KIRBY, JACKIE, business owner; b. Mineral Springs, Ark., Oct. 9, 1947; s. Daniel Kirby and Mazell (Brown) Jones; m. Geraldine Griffin, Dec. 5, 1968; 1 child, Jacquelyn Renee. BS, So. Ill. U., 1983; MBA, Webster U., 1989. Steward Hdqrs. & Tng. Sta., Quantico, Va., 1969-72; advance to sgt., 1972; NCOIC shipping & receiving Marine Air Group-12, Iwakuni, Japan, 1973-74; NCOIC material control Marine Air Group-14, Eltoro, Calif., 1975-77; NCOIC recruiting sub-sta. Marine Recruiting Sub-Sta., Lufkin, Tex., 1977-80; NCOIC squadron support sect. Marine Air Group-11, Cherry Point, N.C., 1980-83; fiscal chief Marine Air Group-15, Iwakuni, 1983-84; NCOIC supply response sect. Marine Air Group-16, Tustin, Calif., 1984-86; logistics chief Marine Air Base-16, Tustin, Calif., 1986-87; materials mgr. Sta. Tng. Dept., Eltoro, 1987-88; store owner Kwik-Stop Mini Mart, Pine Bluff, Ark., 1988—; entrepreneur, 1988—. Alderman City Coun., Pine Bluff, 1991—, mem. pub. health and welfare com., mem. pub. works com., mem. traffic com.; commr. Pine Bluff Aviation Com., 1989-91; chmn. ACORN, Pine Bluff, 1988—; mem. Downtown Devel. Promotion Com., Pine Bluff, 1989—; pres. Interested Citizens for Voters Registration. Mem. Ret. Mil. Assn. (sgt. of arms 1988—), NAACP, Phi Beta Lambda (pres. 1990—). Methodist. Home: 5908 Bullock PO Box 2384 Pine Bluff AR 71613 Office: Kwik Stop Mini Mart 1102 W 2nd Ave Pine Bluff AR 71601-3902

KIRBY, JAMES EDMUND, JR., theology educator; b. Wheeler, Tex., June 24, 1933; s. James Edmund and Mamie (Helton) K.; m. Patty Ray Boothe, July 22, 1955; children: David Edmund, Patrick Boothe. B.A. cum laude, McMurry Coll., 1954; B.D., Perkins Sch. Theology, 1957, S.T.M., 1959; Ph.D., Drew U., 1963; postgrad., Cambridge (Eng.) U., 1957-58. Ordained to ministry United Meth. Ch., 1959; pastor First Meth. Ch., Roby, Tex., 1958-59, Milford (Pa.) Meth. Ch., 1960-61; asst. prof. Bible, McMurry Coll., Abilene, Tex., 1959-60; asst. prof. religion Sweet Briar Coll., Va., 1963-67; prof. religion, head dept. religion Okla. State U., Stillwater, 1967-70; head Sch. Humanistic Studies, 1970-76; dean, Prof. Ch. History Sch. Theology, Drew U., Madison, N.J., 1976-81; dean Perkins Sch. Theology So. Meth. U., Dallas, 1981-94, pres. ad interim, 1994-95, prof. ch. history, 1995—; teaching asst. Drew Theol. Sem., Madison, N.J., 1960-61; cons. bd. missions United Meth. Ch., South Africa, 1968. Contbr. articles to profl. jours.; bd. dirs. Wesley Works Editorial Project. John M. Moore fellow, 1957-58; Dempster fellow, 1962. Mem. Am. Acad. Religion, Soc. Values in Higher Edn., Am. Soc. Ch. History, Assn. United Meth. Theol. Schs., Alpha Chi, Omicron Delta Kappa. Home: 9235 Windy Crest Dr Dallas TX 75243-6222 Office: So Meth U Selecman Hall Perkins Sch Theology Dallas TX 75275

KIRBY, JOHN ROBERT, city engineer; b. St. Albans, W.Va., Mar. 16, 1961; s. James Edward and Collyn Elizabeth (Wolfe) K.; m. Cynthia Lynn Lowe, Dec. 30, 1988; children: Erica, Chad, Heather, Riley, Sean. BS, W.Va. Inst. Tech., 1984. Profl. engr. Fla. Naval architect Norfolk Naval Shipyard, Portsmouth, Va., 1980; student hydrologist U.S. Geol. Survey, Charleston, W.Va., 1981-84; project engr. A.R. Miller Engring., Orlando, 1984-88; asst. county engr. Osceola County, Kissimmee, Fla., 1988-92; city engr. City of Winter Garden, Fla., 1992—; adv. bd. Westside Vo-Tech. Drafting, Winter Garden, 1992—. Coach, bd. dirs. Winter Garden Little League, 1992—. Mem. Rotary Internat. Office: City of Winter Garden PO Box 770278 Winter Garden FL 34777

KIRBY, LE GRAND CARNEY, III, lawyer, accountant; b. Dallas, Feb. 25, 1941; s. Le Grand C. and Michie V. (Moore) K.; m. Jane Marie Daniel, June 14, 1958; children: Le Grand C. IV, Kimberli K., Kristina K. BBA, So. Meth. U., 1963, LLB, 1965. Bar: Tex. 1965; CPA, Tex. From staff acct. to ptnr. Arthur Young & Co., Dallas, 1965-80; ptnr., dir. litigation support Arthur Young & Co. (name now Ernst & Young), Dallas, 1983—; dep. chief acct. SEC, Washington, 1980-83; adv. counsel Fin. Reporting Inst., L.A., 1982—. Mem. ABA (acctg. and law com. 1983—), State Bar Tex. (securities com.), Am. Inst. CPA's, Tex. Soc. CPA's, Nat. Assn. Corp. Dirs. (pres. Dallas chpt. 1985-89), D.C. CPA's. Office: Ernst & Young LLP 2121 San Jacinto St Ste 500 Dallas TX 75201-6714

KIRBY, MARY WEEKS, elementary education educator, reading specialist; b. Cheverly, Md., Nov. 23, 1947; d. Isaac Ralph and Dorothea (Huppert) Weeks; m. William Charlie Kirby, Feb. 14, 1976; children: Joie, Fatimah, Tariq. B in Music Edn., James Madison U., 1969; MEd, Va. Commonwealth U., 1976; cert. Writers' Digest Sch., 1988. Cert. tchr. of music, reading and elem., Va. Music instr. Charles City County Schs., Providence Forge, Va., 1969-70, Hanover Learning Ctr., Va., 1970-72; sales cons. Boykins's Music Shop, Richmond, Va., 1972-74; elem. tchr. New Kent Pub. Schs., Va., 1974—, writing cons., 1980—; owner/operator Wacky Timepieces; presenter ednl. and reading workshops, 1980-82, 95. Sponsor Young Authors' Workshop, New Kent, 1985—; co-chmn., presenter Parents Anonymous of Va., 1984-88; trustee Islamic Ctr. of Va., 1985-88, sec., 1981-85, prin. Islamic Sch., 1995—; active Boy Scouts Am., Girl Scouts U.S., U.S. Naval Sea Cadet Corps. Mem. NEA, New Kent Edn. Assn. (officer 1977-81, 90-92, 94-95), Va. Edn. Assn., Internat. Reading Assn., Va. State Reading Assn., Richmond Area Reading Council (sec. 1982-83, bd. dirs. 1992—), Sigma Alpha Iota (life). Avocations: needlework, reading, swimming. Home: 1309 Bull Run Dr Richmond VA 23231-5103 Office: New Kent Pub Schs New Kent VA 23124

KIRBY, PRISCILLA CROSBY, dietitian; b. Dallas, Mar. 7, 1955; d. Frank Miller and Maydene (Cook) Crosby; m. Robert Darden Kirby, Sept. 27, 1980; children: Sarah Elizabeth, Bethany Jane; foster children: Zack, Shaina. BS, Purdue U., 1977. Registered dietitian. Dietetic intern Mass. Gen. Hosp., Boston, 1977-78; clin. registered dietitian Logansport (Ind.) Meml. Hosp., 1979-82, S.E. Ala. Med. Ctr., Dothan, 1990-91; cons. health care facilities Kirby & Assocs., Winamac, Ind., 1984-87, Abbeville, Ala., 1987—; community projects chair Western Ind. Dietetic Assn., Lafayette, 1979-80; nutrition dir. Campe Seale Harris, Ala., 1989—, bd. dirs., 1992—. Reporter Appris Study Guild, Abbeville, 1989-90, pres.-elect, 1990-91, pres., 1991-92; dir. mission friends 1st Bapt. Ch., 1989-91. Mem. Am. Dietetic Assn., So. Ala. Dietetic Assn. (pres. 1990-92), Dietitians Health Care Facilities (cons.), Henry County Health Coun., Am. Heart Assn., Ala. Dietetic Assn. (bd. dirs. 1990—, pres. bd. dirs. 1994—). Republican.

KIRBY, SARAH ANN VAN DEVENTER, aerospace engineer; b. Champaign, Ill., Mar. 10, 1961; d. David Bruce Kirby and Florence May Van Deventer. BS in Aerospace Engring., U. Mich., 1983; MEd, U. Houston, Clear Lake, 1989. Space systems ops. engr. NASA/JSC-MOD, Houston, 1983—. Contbr. articles to profl. jours. Bd. dirs. Hidden Cove Homeowners Assn., Friendswood, Tex., 1991—. Mem. AIAA (sr.). Home: 45 Hideaway Dr Friendswood TX 77546-4868 Office: NASA JSC Mail Code DF83 Houston TX 77058

KIRCHOFF, BRUCE KENNETH, plant scientist, educator; b. Detroit, Nov. 26, 1952; s. Kenneth Peter and Ruth Gertrude Kirchoff; m. Andrea Joice Shapiro, July 3, 1983. B Gen. Studies, U. Mich., 1975, MS, 1977; PhD, Duke U., 1981. Vis. asst. prof. botany La. State U., Baton Rouge, 1981-82; postdoctoral fellow Hebrew U. of Jerusalem, 1982-84; rsch. assoc. Fairchild Tropical Garden, Miami, Fla., 1984-86; asst. prof. biology U. N.C., Greensboro, 1986-91, assoc. prof. biology, 1991—. Contbr. articles to profl. publs.; author abstracts in field; co-author: Principles of Biology: Molecules to Organisms, 1992, Principles of Biology: Genes to Populations, 1992. Chmn. bd. dirs. emerson Waldorf Sch., Chapel Hill, N.C., 1990-91. Grantee NSF, 1983, 88, 89, 90, U. N.C.-Greensboro, 1988, 91, 93, 94, 95, 96. Mem. Am. Soc. Plant Physiologists, Bot. Soc. Am. (grantee 1987), Willi Henning Soc., Sigma Xi. Office: U NC Dept Biology Greensboro NC 27412

KIRGIS, FREDERIC LEE, JR., law educator; b. Washington, Dec. 29, 1934; s. Frederic Lee Sr. and Kathryn Alice (Burrows) K.; m. Carol Ruth Stroud, Feb. 1, 1957; children—Julianne, Paul Frederic. B.A., Yale U., 1957; J.D., U. Calif.-Berkeley, 1960. Bar: Colo. 1961, D.C. 1964, Va. 1983. Atty. Covington & Burling, Washington, 1964-67; from asst. prof. to prof. law U. Colo., Boulder, 1967-73; prof. law UCLA, 1973-78; prof. law Washington & Lee U., Lexington, Va., 1978—, dir. Frances Lewis Law Ctr., 1978-83, dean law sch., 1983-88. Author: International Organizations in their Legal Setting, 1977, 2d edit. 1993, Prior Consultation in International Law, 1983; contbr. articles to profl. jours. Pres. Maury River Soccer Club, Lexington, 1978-85. Served to capt. USAF, 1961-64. Recipient Deak award 1974; research fellow NATO, Brussels, 1978. Mem. Am. Soc. Internat. Law (v.p. 1985-87, sec. 1994—), Am. Law Inst., Internat. Law Assn. (Am. br.), Am. Jour. Internat. Law (bd. editors 1984-96), State Bar Va., Order of Coif. Democrat. Presbyterian. Home: 502 Jackson Ave Lexington VA 24450-1918 Office: Washington and Lee Univ Dept Law Lexington VA 24450

KIRK, DENNIS DEAN, lawyer; b. Pittsburg, Kans., Dec. 13, 1950; s. Homer Standley and Maida Corena (Rouse) K. AA, Hutchinson Community Jr. Coll., 1970. BS with distinction, No. Ariz. U., 1972; JD, Washburn U., 1975. Bar: Kans. 1975, U.S. Dist. Ct. Kans. 1975, D.C. 1977, U.S. Ct. Appeals (D.C. cir.) 1978, U.S. Supreme Ct. 1979, U.S. Ct. Appeals (5th cir.) 1981, U.S. Dist. Ct. Md. 1984, U.S. Tax Ct. 1984, U.S. Claims Ct. 1984, U.S. Ct. Appeals (fed. cir.) 1984, U.S. Ct. Mil. Appeals 1984, Va. 1990, U.S. Ct. Appeals (4th cir.) 1990. Trial atty. ICC, Washington, 1975-77; assoc. Goff, Sims, Cloud, & Stroud, Washington, 1977-82; pvt. practice law, Washington, 1982-90; ptnr. Slocum, Boddie, Murry & Kirk, Falls Church, Va., 1990-93; pvt. practice Dennis Dean Kirk, Esq., 1993—; pres., Law Facilities, Inc., Washington, 1982—. Vol. parole and probation officer Shawnee County, Kans., 1973-74; mem. Citizens' Adv. Task Force Group, Md. Nat. Park and Planning Commn., 1978-80; mem. citizens' task force on gen. plan amendments study Fairfax County Council, Va., 1981-82; mem. Seven Corners Task Force, Fairfax County, 1981-82, chmn. transp. and housing subcoms.; pres. Seven Springs Tenants' Assn., College Park, Md., 1976-80, Ravenwood Park Citizens' Assn., 1981-82; dir. Greenwood Homes, Inc., Fairfax County Dept. Housing and Community Devel., 1983—; mem. Gala Com. Spotlight the Kennedy Ctr., Pres.' Adv. Com. on the Arts, 1986-87; founding chmn., charter mem. Mason Dist. Jaycees, 1984-86; sec., gen. counsel, bd. dirs. U.S. Assocs. for the Cultural Triangle in Sri Lanka, 1983-90; commr. Consumer Protection Commn., Fairfax County, 1982—, vice chmn., 1996; mem. towing adv. bd. Fairfax County, 1993—; mem. Mason Dist. Rep. Com., 1981-91; Ravenwood precinct chmn. Rep. Orgn., Falls Church, Va., 1982-90; active Fairfax County Young Reps., Fairfax County Rep. Com., 1982—; bd. dirs. PTA Bailey's Elem. Magnet Sch., 1995—, v.p. 1996-97. Named to Honorable Order Ky. Cols. Mem. ABA, NRA (life), Assn. Trial Lawyers Am., Specialized Carriers and Rigging Assn., Am. Fed. Musicians (life), Masons (life), 1990, 96, Master of Lodge, D.C. Grand Lodge Masons, Grand Sword Bearer 1992), Shriners (life), Tall Cedars (life), Scottish Rite (life), Moose, Royal Arch (life), Phi Kappa Phi, Phi Alpha Delta (life, nat. capital area alumni chpt. justice 1984-86, 1994-96). Methodist. Avocation: music. Home: 6315 Anneliese Dr Falls Church VA 22044-1620 Office: 5201 Leesburg Pike Ste 1108 Falls Church VA 22041-3203

KIRK, JOHN ROBERT, JR., lawyer; b. Stuart, Va., June 21, 1935; s. John Robert and Mary Elise (Mustaine) K.; children: Karen Louise, Laura Elise, Rebecca Elizabeth. student Rice Inst., 1953-56; BSChemE, U. Tex., 1959; JD, U. Houston, 1966. Bar: Tex. 1966, U.S. Patent Office and Trademan 1967, U.S. Supreme Ct. 1973, U.S. Dist. Ct. (so. dist.) Tex. 1974, U.S. Ct. Claims 1975, U.S. Dist. Ct. (no. dist.) Tex. 1977, U.S. Ct. Appeals (5th cir.) 1980, U.S. Ct. Appeals (11th cir.) 1981, U.S. Ct. Appeals (fed. cir.) 1983. Patent atty. Jefferson Chem. Co., Houston, 1966-69, mgr. patent div., 1969-72; mem. Pravel, Gambrell, Hewitt, Kirk & Kimball, P.C., Houston, 1972-84, ptnr., 1973-84; ptnr. Baker & Kirk, P.C., 1984-87, Baker, Kirk & Bissex, P.C., 1987-90, Kirk & Lindsay, P.C., 1990-93, Jenkens & Gilchrist, 1993—; dir. Nat. Inventors Hall of Fame Found., Inc., 1979-82, 87—, treas., 1983-84, v.p., 1984-86, pres., 1986-87; adv. bd. U. Houston Intellectual Property Law Program, 1991—, Gulf Coast Regional Small Bus. Devel. Ctr., 1994—, Tex. Mfg. Assistance Ctr., Inc., 1995—. Served to lt. USMCR, 1958-60. Fellow Tex. Bar Found., Houston Bar Found, Coll. State Bar Tex., State Bar of Tex. (chmn. intellectual property law sect. 1977-78); mem. ABA (intellectual property law sect. coun. 1990-94, vice chmn. 1994-95, chmn. elect 1995-96, chmn., 1996—, com. chair 1982-90), Am. Intellectual Property Law Assn., Nat. Counsel Intellectual Property Law Assns. (vice chmn. 1986-87, chmn. 1987-88), commr of Patents Edn. Roundtable (commr. 1987-95), Houston Intellectual Property Law Assn. (pres.-elect 1989-90, pres. 1990-91, bd. govs. 1986-92), Houston Bar Assn., Licensing Execs. Soc., Nat. Inventive Thinking Assn. (adv. dir. 1990—), Inwood Forest Golf Club. Republican. Baptist. Office: 1100 Louisiana St Ste 1800 Houston TX 77002-5214

KIRK, LISA GAIL, association official; b. Mohawk, N.Y., May 28, 1965; d. Bruce H. and Grace M. (Garrett) K. BS, U. Del., 1987. Mgr. retail svcs. Sterns Office Furniture, Capital Heights, Va., 1987-91; contract mgr. Nat. Industries for Blind, Alexandria, Va., 1991; mgr. exec. career svcs. Club Mgrs. Assn. Am., Alexandria, 1991—. Author: Executive Career Services Kit, 1995. Mem. Am. Soc. Assn. Execs. Office: Club Mgrs Assn Am 1733 King St Alexandria VA 22314-2720

KIRK, RALPH GARY, anatomy educator; b. Erick, Okla., Dec. 21, 1936; s. P. Ralph and Ruby A. Kirk; m. Brigitte A. Kern, Feb. 14, 1966; 1 child, Benjamin. BA, Coll. of Wooster, Ohio, 1959; PhD, Yale U., 1966. Rsch. molecular biophysicist Am. Cyanamid, Stanford, Conn., 1966-68; rsch. assoc. Duke U., Durham, N.C., 1968-70, asst. prof., 1970-75; rsch. assoc. prof. U. Chgo., 1975-77; sr. rsch. assoc. Yale U., New Haven, Conn., 1977-83; prof. anatomy W.Va. U., Morgantown, W.Va., 1985—. Contbr. numerous articles to profl. jours. NIH fellow, 1959-66, 68-70; grantee NIH, 1970-83, NSF, 1970—. Mem. N.C. Soc. for Electron Microscopy and Microbeam Analysis, Microbeam Analysis Soc. Home: 237 Wagner Rd Morgantown WV 26505-7504 Office: WVa U Med Ctr Dept Anatomy Morgantown WV 26505

KIRK, ROBERT L., aerospace and transportation company executive; b. Charleston, W.Va., Jan. 4, 1929; s. William Edward and Lillian (Dunnigan) K.; three children. BS in Engring., Purdue U., 1952, PhD in Engring. V.p. ITT, N.Y.C., 1967-77; pres., CEO LTV Aerospace and Def. Co., Dallas, 1977-86; chmn., CEO Allied Signal Aerospace Co., 1986-89, CSX Transp. Inc., Jacksonville, Fla., 1989-92; chmn., dir. Brit. Aerospace Holdings, Inc., Arlington, Va., 1992—; dir. Harsco Corp., Reflectone, Inc., United Def., Brit. Aerospace plc. Trustee Ctr. for Strategic and Internat. Studies; bd. dirs. USAF Acad. Found.; fomer chmn., exec. coalition Nat. Initiative for Tech. and Disabled. Officer USN, 1952-55. Recipient Disting. Pub. Svc. award HHS. Fellow AIAA; mem. Aerospace Industries Assn. (chmn. bd. govs. 1986), Assn. Am. R.R. Dirs. Office: British Aerospace Holdings 1101 Wilson Blvd Arlington VA 22209

KIRK, ROBLEY GORDON, mechanical engineering educator; b. Coeburn, Va., Feb. 14, 1944; s. Robley Neal and Leona Margie (Robinette) K.; m. Janie Louise Isaacs, June 26, 1965; children: Timothy Alan, Andrea Denise. BSME, U. Va., 1967, MSME, 1969, PhD in Mech. Engring., 1972. Registered profl. engr., Va. Instr. U. Va., Charlottesville, Va., 1970-71; research engr. U. Va., Charlottesville, 1971-72; sr. engr. Pratt & Whitney Aircraft, East Hartford, Conn., 1972-75; devel. engring. Ingersoll-Rand Turbo Div., Phillipsburg, N.J., 1975-78; supr., rotor dynamics Ingersoll-Rand Turbo Div., Phillipsburg, 1978-85; assoc. prof. Va. Poly. Inst. and State U., Blacksburg, 1985-91, prof., 1991—; cons. Dresser-Rand, Olean, N.Y., 1987-96, Ingersoll-Dresser Pump Co., Phillipsburg, N.J., 1989-96, No. Rsch., Woburn, Mass., 1994-95. Patentee in field. Leader, Webelos, Boy Scouts Am., Blacksburg, Va., 1986. Named Young Engr. of Yr., NSPE, 1979, Equipment grantee, 1987; Walter Hudson award, ASLE, 1978. Mem. ASME, Soc. Tribology and Lubrication Engrs., Am. Soc. Lubrication Engrs., Sigma Xi, Tau Beta Pi. Republican. Presbyterian. Office: Va Poly Inst & State U Randolph Hall Blacksburg VA 24061

KIRKLAND, J. PAUL, bank executive; b. 1940. Grad., Auburn U. With Newport News (Va.) Shipbuilding and Drydock Co., 1961—; dir. Newport News Shipbuilding Employee Credit Union, 1978-84, past pres., now chmn. bd. dirs., 1984—. Office: Newport News Shpblg Emp Cr Un 3711 Huntington Ave Newport News VA 23607-2710

KIRKLAND, REBECCA TRENT, pediatric endocrinologist; b. Durham, N.C., Dec. 27, 1942; d. Josiah Charles Trent and Mary Duke (Biddle) Trent-Semans; m. John Lindsey Kirkland III, June 24, 1965. BA, Duke U., 1964, MD, 1968. Intern Baylor Coll. Medicine, 1968-69, resident in pediatrics, 1969-70, fellow in pediatric endocrinology, 1971-73, asst. prof. dept. pediatrics, 1975-81, assoc. prof., 1981-88, prof., 1988—; registrar Guy's Hosp., Hosp. for Sick Children, London, 1970; with U. Pa. Sch. Medicine, 1973-74, fellow, 1974-75; asst. physician divsn. endocrinology Children's Hosp. Phila., 1973-75; mem. staff Tex. Children's Hosp., 1975—, Harris County Hosp. Dist., 1975—; head ambulatory svcs. Tex. Children's Hosp., 1984—, dir. jr. league outpatient dept., 1984—. Contbr. articles and revs. to profl. jours. Active Leadership Tex., Leadership Houston; bd. dirs. AVANCE, Inc., 1992, YWCA, 1992; trustee Mus. Med. Sci., 1984-88; pres. Joseah C. Trent Meml. Found., Inc., 1983—, v.p., 1977-83; bd. dirs. Am. Leadership Forum, 1991, mem. selection com., 1989, 90, sec. bd. dirs. Houston/Gulf Coast chpt., 1989, 90, pres.-elect, 1991, pres., 1991-93; pres. Greater Houston Women's Found., 1994-96. NIH fellow, 1971-73; recipient Alumnae award Baldwin Sch., 1983, Disting. Alumni award Durham Acad., 1984, Goodheart Humanitarian award B'nai B'rith, 1986, Disting. Svc. award Duke U. Med. Alumni Assn., 1992, Recognition award Ctr. for Interaction: Man, Sci. and Culture, 1993, One Voice for Children award Tex. Network for Medically

Fragile and Chronically-Ill Children, 1993; named one of five Outstanding Women of Yr. Channel 13, Houston, 1984, Woman on the move Houston Post, 1989. Fellow Am. Acad. Pediatrics; mem. Endocrine Soc., Am. Fedn. For Clin. Rsch., So. Soc. for Pediatric Rsch., Lawson-Wilkins Pediatric Endocrine Soc., Houston Pediatric Soc., Tex. Pediatric Soc., Tex. Med. Assn., Soc. for Pediatric Rsch., Pediatric Endocrinology Soc. Tex., Ambulatory Pediatric Assn., Am. Pediatric Soc., Am. Acad. Pediatrics (pediatric endocrine sect.) 1990), Tex. Diabetes and Endocrine Assn. Office: Baylor Coll Medicine 1 Baylor Plz Houston TX 77030-3411

KIRKLAND, RUSSELL KERMIT, principal; b. Broxton, Ga., Apr. 20, 1942; s. Russell and Frankie (Harper) K.; m. Jama Ruth Lee, Jan. 28, 1958; children: Sarah Tamica, Russell Rashim. BS, U. Ga., 1965, MEd, 1970; edn. specialist deg., Ga. State U., 1977. Math. tchr. Forest Park (Ga.) Sr. High Sch., 1969-71; counselor W.A. Fountain Jr. High Sch., Forest Park, 1971-73, asst. prin., 1973-87, prin., 1987-89; prin. J.E. Edmonds Elem. Sch., 1989—. Capt. U.S. Army, 1965-68. Mem. NEA, Nat. Assn. Secondary Sch. Prins., Nat. Assn. Elem. Sch. Prins., Ga. Assn. Elem. Sch. Prins., Profl. Assn. Ga. Educators, Ga. Parents and Tchrs. Assn. (hon. life mem.), Ga. Assn. Middle Sch. Prins., Clayton County Dept. Elem. Sch. Prins., Ga. Assn. Ednl. Leaders, Kiwanis. Democrat. Baptist. Home: 6065 Prestige Valley Rd Morrow GA 30260-1454 Office: J E Edmonds Elem Sch 4495 Simpson Rd Forest Park GA 30050-1540

KIRKLEY, D. CHRISTINE (D. CHRISTINE KIRKLEY), non-profit organization administrator; b. Horton, Ala., Aug. 28, 1932; d. Vester Boyd and Josephine Prumrytle (Parrish) K.; m. Jack Stanley I, July 4, 1952; 1 child, Jack Stanley II. Student, U. Ala., 1951-52, Samford U., 1963-65, Cathedral Coll., 1982. Svr. rep. South Ctrl. Bell, Birmingham, Ala., 1984—; dir. Helpline Christian Outreach Ministries Inc, Birmingham, 1991—. Area mgr. Operating Blessing, Birmingham, 1989—; mem. Christian Helplines Internat., 1990—, sec. exec. com., 1994—. Mem. Telephone Pioneers Am. (fund raiser 1976-78, pres. 1979, cmty. edn. coord. 1982-83, drug abuse chairperson 1982-83), Internat. Platform Assn., Kiwanis. Mem. Assemby of God Ch. Office: Helpline Christian Outreach Ministries Inc 8 Roebuck Dr Birmingham AL 35215-8046

KIRKPATRICK, ELEANOR BLAKE, civic worker; b. Mangum, Okla., Mar. 10, 1909; d. Mack Barkley and Kathryn (Talbott) Blake; m. John Elson Kirkpatrick, June 20, 1932; 1 child, Joan Elson. B.A. in French, Smith Coll., 1931; D.Humanities (hon.), Oklahoma City U., 1968. 1st v.p. Kirkpatrick Found., Oklahoma City, Kirkpatrick Family Fund. Named to Okla. Hall of Fame, Okla. Heritage Assn., Oklahoma City, 1975, Woman of Yr., Redlands Coun. Girl Scouts, 1991; recipient Outstanding Woman Okla. Soroptimist Club, 1966, Evergreen Disting. Service award Nat. Assn. Mature People, Okla., 1982, Bd. Trustees award Omniplex Sic. Mus., Oklahoma City, 1984, Wall of Fame award Oklahoma City Pub. Sch. Found., 1990, Humanitarian award Nat. Conf. Christians and Jews, 1990, Humanitarian award Nat. Arthritis Found., Okla. chpt., 1993, Ptnrs. award World Neighbors, 1991, Pathmaker award Oklahoma County Hist. Soc., 1992, Outstanding Philanthropist award Civic Music Assn. Co-founder, hon. pres. Alliance Française, Oklahoma City; bd. dirs. Okla. City Art Mus.; mem. Oklahoma City Univ. Socs. Avocations: backgammon. Office: Kirkpatrick Oil Co PO Box 268822 Oklahoma City OK 73126-8822

KIRKPATRICK, PETER STEVEN, foreign language educator; b. Charles Town, W.Va., Sept. 13, 1964; s. Thomas McGuffin and Mary Ann (Neofotis) K.; m. Françoise Rondot, June 16, 1990. BA in French, Polit. Sci., U. Richmond, 1986; MA in French Lit., U. Va., 1988, PhD French Civilization, 1992. Fgn. corres. L'Humanité, Paris, 1988—; asst. prof. French Va. Commonwealth U., Richmond, 1992—; founder, dir. Va. Commonwealth U. French Film Festival, 1993—. Contbr. articles to profl. jours. Fulbright scholar, 1989-90. Mem. ACLU, MLA, AAUP, Assn. for French Cultural Studies (dept. comm. 1995), Am. Assn. for Tchrs. French, Semiotic Soc. Am. Roman Catholic. Office: Va Commonwealth Univ 820 W Franklin St Richmond VA 23284

KIRKPATRICK, SAMUEL ALEXANDER, university president, social and policy sciences educator. BS in Polit. Sci., Shippensburg U., 1964; MA in Polit. Sci., Pa. State U., 1966, PhD in Polit. Sci., 1968. Prof. polit. sci. U. Okla., dir. Bur. Govt. Rsch., 1969-77, dir. Scholar-Leadership Enrichment Program, 1975-77; prof. polit. sci., head dept. Tex. A&M U., 1977-84; prof. polit. sci., dean Coll. Liberal Arts and Scis. Ariz. State U., 1984-90; univ. pres., prof. social and policy scis. U. Tex., San Antonio, 1990—. Editor Am. Politics Quar., 1977-81; mem. editorial bd. Social Sci. Quar., 1969-75, Am. Jour. Polit. Sci., 1973-76, Polit. Behavior, 1984-85. Bd. dirs. Tex. Innovation Info. Network System, 1990—, San Antonio Med. Found., 1990—; bd. govs. S.W. Found. for Biomed. Rsch., 1990—; trustee S.W. Rsch. Inst., 1990—, World Affairs Coun. of San Antonio, 1990—, Tex. Rsch. Tech. Found., San Antonio World Trade Assn. Recipient Disting. Alumnus award Shippensburg U., 1987, Achievement in Affirmative Action award Ariz. State U., 1988; NSF fellow. Mem. Southwestern Social Sci. Assn. (pres. 1981-82), Southwestern Polit. Sci. Assn. (pres. 1975-76, exec. coun. 1980-82), Inter-Univ. Consortium for Polit. and Social Rsch. (chair exec. coun. 1982-85), Greater San Antonio C. of C. (bd. dirs. 1990—). Office: U Tex at San Antonio Office of Pres San Antonio TX 78249-0601*

KIRKSEY, LAURA ELIZABETH, medical, surgical nurse; b. San Antonio, May 11, 1943; d. Robert Taylor and Laura Hulda (Fischer) Autry; m. Frank Lynn Hays, May 27, 1961 (div. Oct. 1968); children: Frank Lynn, Michael Devin, Michele Dyanne; m. Franklin James Kirksey, Sept. 1, 1969; 1 child, James Che. AD in Edn., Garland County C.C., 1985, ADN, 1991; BSN, Henderstate State U., 1995; postgrad., U. Ark. RN, Ark. Claims clk. H. L. Davis Ins. Co., San Antonio, 1966-69; policy typist U.S.A.A. Ins. Co., San Antonio, 1969; key punch operator 1st Nat. Bank, St. Louis, 1972, Sigma Chem. Corp., St. Louis, 1972-74; data entry operator Hager Hinge Corp., St. Louis, 1974-78; office mgr. Chiropractic Ctr., Hot Springs, Ark., 1991-92; staff nurse Bapt. Meml. Hosp., Little Rock, 1991-92, St. Joseph Hosp., Hot Springs, Ark., 1992—; assoc. clin. instr. Henderson State U., 1995. Pres. South Hot Springs Lioness, 1985, sec., 1986. Mem. Student Nurses Assn. Home: 1605 Central Ave Hot Springs National Park AR 71901-6117 Office: St Joseph Hosp 300 Werner St Hot Springs National Park AR 71913-6406

KIRKSEY, TERRIE LYNN, multi-purpose senior center administrator, social work consultant; b. Shaw, Miss., Nov. 18, 1958; d. Clarence Clayton and Mary Juanice (King) K. B of Social Work, Delta State U., 1980; MSW, U. Tenn. Ctr. for Health Scis., 1985. Asst. dir. recreational therapy Rosewood Manor, Memphis, 1980, dir. social services, 1981-83; dir. social services Memphis Health Care Ctr., 1980-81, St. Peter Villa, Memphis, 1983-84; asst. dir. Josephine K. Lewis Ctr. for Sr. Citizens, Memphis, 1984-89, dir., 1989—; social work cons. Bapt. Home Plus Home Health Agy., Memphis, 1986-91, Hillhaven Raleigh, Memphis, 1989-90. Bd. dirs. Ret. Sr. Vol. Program, 1985-89, sec., 1986-87; bd. dirs. Alzheimer's Day Care Inc., sec., 1987—, pres.-elect, co-carers, 1990; bd. dirs. Memphis/Shelby County Coun. on Aging, 1989—. Mem. Phi Theta Kappa. Democrat. Office: Josephine K Lewis Ctr for Sr Citizens 1188 N Parkway Memphis TN 38105-2531

KIRSCH, THOMAS GERHARD WERNER, biochemist; b. Mannheim, Germany, Sept. 16, 1955; came to U.S., 1989; s. Edwin Georg Adam and Gerda Maria (Nagel) K. Student, U. Kaiserslautern, Germany, 1976-80; diploma in chemistry, Philipps U., Marburg, Germany, 1985, D of Natural Scis., 1988; postgrad., Oklahoma City C.C., 1996—. Tchg. asst. biochemistry Philipps U., Marburg, 1985-88; postdoctoral fellow Mich. State U., East Lansing, 1989-90; rsch. assoc. U. Okla., Norman, 1991-96, instr. cell biology, 1992-93. Contbr. articles to profl. jours. Mem. AAAS, Am. Soc. Plant Physiologists, Am. Soc. Cell Biology.

KIRSCHNER, KERRY GROOM, television personality, public policy foundation director; b. Cin., Dec. 4, 1946; s. William Kilian and Mary Alice (Groom) K.; m. Jane Ann Staudt, May 10, 1969 (div. Sept. 1993); children: Sean, Kent, Kelly, Katherine. BS, Georgetown U., 1968. Mgr. adminstrn. Smith Kline & French/Branson, Phila., 1968-70; mgr. consumer internat. market rsch. Schering/Plough, Kenilworth, N.J., 1970-71; dir. internat. ops. Mitchum/Revlon, Tuckahoe, N.Y., 1971-73; v.p. internat. ops. Frances Denney, N.Y.C., 1973-76; pres. Blue Heron Fruit Shippers, Sarasota, Fla., 1976-85; mayor City of Sarasota, 1985-91; dir. devel. Mote Marine Lab., Sarasota, 1991-94; talk show host Channel 4 TV, Sarasota, 1991—; exec. dir. The Argus Found., Sarasota, 1994—; bd. dirs. World Conf. of Mayors, Sr. Friendship Ctrs., Inc., Selby Gardens Found.; mem. urban and econ. devel. com. U.S. Conf. of Mayors, arts and cultural com., chmn. tourism and arts com.; mem. policy com. EPA Nat. Estuary Program. Bd. dirs. Sarasota Conv. and Vis. Bur., 1991—, Downtown Assn., Sarasota, 1993—, Sarasota Sister Cities Assn., 1993; mem., past chmn. Sarasota Redevel. Authority, Metro. Planning Orgn., Sarasota Tourist Devel. Coun.; mem. GTE Cmty. Adv. Bd.; co-chmn. State of Fla. Reps. for Clinton, 1992; mem. S.W. Fla. Commn. on Tourism, 1992; chmn. Fla. Transp. Disadvantage Commn., 1990; bd. dirs. S.W. Fla. Juvenile Justice Coun., Drug Free Communities, Kids Voting. Recipient Perfect 10 award Gulfshore Life, 1988; named Best City/County Ofcl. S.W. Fla., Gulfshore Life, 1989. Mem. Nat. Assn. Fund Raising Execs., Fla. Gift Fruit Shippers Assn. (fin. com.). Republican. Roman Catholic. Office: The Argus Found PO Box 49361 Sarasota FL 34230-6361

KIRSNER, KENNETH MARK, nurse anesthetist educator; b. Cin.. BSN, U. Miami, 1979, JD, 1990; MS, SUNY, Buffalo, 1985. Cert. RN anesthetist. Nurse anesthetist Mercy Hosp., Miami, Fla., 1984-85, U. Miami/Jackson Meml. Med. Ctr., 1985-90; trial atty. Nat. Labor Rels. Bd., Washington, 1990-91; asst. prof. nurse anesthesia U. Kans., Kansas City, 1991-92; dir. grad. program in nurse anesthesia Baylor Coll. Medicine, Houston, 1992—. Symposium editor U. Miami Law Rev., 1989-90. Mem. Fla. Bar Assn., Am. Assn. Nurse Anesthetists (assoc. editor jour. 1995—, mem. practice com. 1994-95), Internat. Anesthesia Rsch. Soc., Am. Assn. Nurse Attys., Tex. Bd. Nurse Examiners (advanced practice adv. com. 1994—). Office: Baylor Coll Medicine Dept Anesthesiology 6550 Fannin Ste 1003 Houston TX 77030

KIRTLEY, JANE ELIZABETH, professional society administrator, lawyer; b. Indpls., Nov. 7, 1953; d. William Raymond and Faye Marie (Price) K.; m. Stephen Jon Cribari, May 8, 1985. BJ, Northwestern U., 1975, MS in Journalism, 1976; JD, Vanderbilt U., 1979. Bar: N.Y. 1980, U.S. Dist. Ct. (we. dist.) N.Y. 1980, D.C. 1982, U.S. Dist. Ct. D.C. 1982, U.S. Ct. Appeals (4th cir.) 1982, U.S. Ct. Claims 1982, U.S. Ct. Appeals (D.C. cir.) 1985, U.S. Supreme Ct. 1985, Va. 1995. Assoc. Nixon, Hargrave, Devans & Doyle, Rochester, N.Y., 1979-81, Washington, 1981-84; exec. dir. Reporters Com. for Freedom of Press, Washington, 1985—; adj. faculty Am. U. Sch. Communication, 1988—. Exec. articles editor Vanderbilt U. Jour. Internat. Law, 1978-79; editor: The News Media and the Law, 1985—, The First Amendment Handbook, 1987, 4th edit., 1995, Agents of Discovery, 1991, 93, 95; columnist NEPA Bull., 1988—, Virginia's Press, 1991—, Am. Journalism Rev., 1995—; mem. editorial bd. Govt. Info. Quar., Comm. Law and Policy, Comm. Law and Policy. Bd. dirs. 1st Amendment Congress, Denver, Student Press Law Ctr., Arlington, Va.; mem. steering com. Libel Def. Resource Ctr., N.Y.C.; adv. bd. Pa. Ctr. for the 1st Amendment, University Park, Freedom Forum 1st Amendment Ctr., Nashville. Mem. ABA, N.Y. State Bar Assn., D.C. Bar Assn., Va. State Bar Assn., Sigma Delta Chi. Home: 724 Franklin St Alexandria VA 22314-4104 Office: Reporters Com Freedom of Press 1101 Wilson Blvd Ste 1910 Arlington VA 22209-2248

KIRTLEY, MICHELLE DIANE, training and development company executive; b. Alexandria, Va., Feb. 22, 1969; d. E. Lynn and Anne M. (McFarland) K. BA, Auburn U., 1991, MA, 1994; postgrad., La. State U., 1994—. Sr. assoc. Spectra-A Mgmt., New Orleans, 1993—; Prof., Tulane U. Contbr. articles to profl. jours. Mem. ASTD, Speech Comm. Assn., Internat. Listening Assn. (James I. Brown award 1996). Home: 5523 Laurel St New Orleans LA 70115 Office: PO Box 13591 New Orleans LA 70185

KISAK, PAUL FRANCIS, engineering company executive; b. Pitts., July 15, 1956; s. Paul F. and Catherine M. (Svaranowic) K. BSE in Nuclear Engring., Engring. Physics and Engring. Sci., U. Mich., 1982; MBA, Ea. Mich. U., 1984; postgrad., U. Va., 1986—. Lic. realtor, contractor. Intelligence officer, engr. CIA, Langley, Va., 1983-86; engr., diplomat U.S. Dept. of State, Washington, 1986-87; engr., program mgr. Space Applications Corp., Vienna, Va., 1987-88; founder, pres. KKI, Inc., Middletown, Va., 1986—; sr. scientist, program mgr. Info. Tech. & Application Corp., Reston, 1987-89; cons. devel. PFK Enterprises, Washington, 1986—; mem. working group Strategic Def. Initiative, 1986—. Holder software copyrights and trademarks. Caseworker U.S. Sen. John Glenn, Columbus, Ohio, 1979; del. Loudoun County Rep. Nat. Party, 1988—. Ea. Mich. U. scholar, Ohio State U. scholar; AlpheCCA Presdl. Sports awards, U.S. Dept. State Tribute of Appreciation. Mem. AIAA, ASME, Am. Phys. Soc., Am. Math. Soc., Am. Nuclear Soc., Am. Astronautical Soc., Am. Mgmt. Soc., Assn. MBA Execs., Bioengring. Soc., Mensa, Intertel, Texnikoi, Beta Gamma Sigma, Pi Mu Epsilon.

KISER, ANITA HOPE, project team leader, technical writer; b. Charlotte, N.C., June 24, 1955; d. Robert Phillip Sr. and Mary Faith (Hansil) K. AA, Ctrl. Piedmont C.C., 1976; BA, Queens Coll., 1982; MS in Info. Sci., U. N.C., 1988; MBA, Meredith Coll., 1996. Coord. sch. media Cabarrus County Schs., Concord, N.C., 1982-87; writer, project team leader IBM, Research Triangle Park, N.C., 1989—; computer cons. N.C. Dept. Pub. Instruction, Raleigh, 1985-88. Author: Using Appleworks in the School Media Center, 1988. Mem. NAFE, NOW. Home: 3520 Donna Rd Raleigh NC 27604-4270

KISER, GLENN AUGUSTUS, retired pediatrician, philanthropist, investor; b. Bessemer City, N.C., July 13, 1917; s. Augustus B. and May (Carpenter) K.; m. Katherine Parham, June 13, 1941 (dec. 1972); m. Muriel Coykendall, Feb. 4, 1973. BS, Duke U., 1941, MD, 1941. Diplomate Nat. Bd. Med. Examiners. Resident physician Duke Hosp., Durham, N.C., 1946-48; resident Johns Hopkins U., Balt., 1946; pvt. practice Salisbury, N.C., 1947-55; ret. Salisbury, 1955—; founder stockholder Food Lion, Inc.; med. cons. State of N.C., Raleigh, 1961-64, 75-76, New River Mental Health Ctr., Boone, N.C., 1976-77; chief pediatric dept. Rowan Meml. Hosp., Salisbury, 1947-55, chief of staff, 1951-52. Bd. advisors Chowan Coll., Murfreesboro, N.C., 1977-78; trustee Rowan Regional Med. Ctr. Found., Salisbury. With USPHS, 1941-46, surgeon, 1991-96. Recipient Exemplary Life Svc. award Catawba Coll., 1995. Mem. Pinnacle Club Duke Med. Ctr. (charter), Duke Med. Ctr. Alumni Assn. (coun. 1988), Duke U. Founders Soc., Lions (dep. dist. gov. N.C. chpt. 1959, pres. Milford Hills chpt. 1959, zone chmn. 1959, dep. dist. gov. 1960, internat. amb. 1961), Salisbury Country Club. Republican. Presbyterian. Home: 728 Klumac Rd Apt 138C Salisbury NC 28144-5716

KISER, JACKSON L., federal judge; b. Welch, W.Va., June 24, 1929; m. Carole Gorman; children: Jackson, William, John Michael, Elizabeth Carol. B.A., Concord Coll., 1951; J.D., Washington and Lee U., 1952. Bar: Va. Asst. U.S. atty. Western Dist. Va., 1958-61; assoc., then ptnr. R.R. Young, Young, Kiser, Haskins, Mann, Gregory & Young P.C., Martinsville, Va., 1961-82; judge U.S. Dist. Ct. (we. dist.) Va., 1982-93, chief judge, 1993—. Mem. Martinsville City Sch. Bd., 1971-77. With JAGC U.S. Army, 1952-55, capt. Res., 1955-61. Mem. Am. Coll. Trial Lawyers (state com.), Va. Bar Assn. (exec. com.), Va. State Bar, Va. Trial Lawyers Assn., 4th Cir. Jud. Conf. (permanent), Martinsville-Henry County Bar Assn., Order of Coif. Office: US Dist Ct PO Box 3326 700 Main St Danville VA 24543-3326*

KISER, MOSE, III, small business owner; b. Raleigh, N.C., Nov. 14, 1956; s. Mose Jr. and Joyce Ann (Carpenter) K.; m. Jean Louise Charles, May 15, 1982; children: Taylor Forbes, Margaret Stewart. BA in Psychology, N.C. State U., 1980. Sales trainee Odell Sentry Hardware, Greensboro, N.C., 1980, Wrangler Menswear, Greensboro, 1981-82; sales rep. Wrangler Menswear, Knoxville, Tenn., 1982-84; pres., owner, operator AuraTech, Inc., Greensboro, 1986—; bd. dirs. Greensboro Ice Sports. Adult dir. Greensboro Ice Sports, Inc., 1990; mem. Greensboro Sports Coun., 1990, also bd. dirs. Mem. HemoCue Assn. Regional Distbrs., Health Industry Distbrs. Assn., N.C. State U. Athletic Aid Assn., Greensboro Sports Coun., N.C. State U. Alumni Assn., Greesboro Country Club. Republican. Methodist. Home: 3106 Solara Trce Greensboro NC 27410-9053 Office: AuraTech Inc 7349-A W Friendly Ave Greensboro NC 27410

KISHIMOTO, YUJI, architect, educator; b. Tokyo, Nov. 6, 1938; s. Hideo and Miyo (Anesaki) K.; m. Toshiko Mitsumori, Oct. 22, 1970; 1 child, Kyo. BArch, Waseda U., 1963; MArch, Harvard U., 1965; EdM, U. Mass., 1976. Registered architect. Designer Vincent G. Kling Assocs., Phila., 1966-67; design critic Boston Archtl. Ctr., 1966-69; instr. R.I. Sch. of Design, Providence, 1966-70; ptnr. Design Collaboratives, Boston, 1967-71; instr. Deerfield (Mass.) Acad., 1971-76; asst. prof. U. Hawaii, Honolulu, 1976-78; assoc. prof. Va. Poly. Inst. and State U., Blacksburg, 1978-80; assoc. prof. Clemson (S.C.) U., 1980-87, prof., 1987—; coord. internat. program Coll. Architecture, 1994—; with Kishimoto and Assocs., Clemson, 1988—; urban design cons. Boston Redevel. Authority, 1966-67; design cons. Commonwealth Architects, Boston, 1966-68, Hawaii Group Architects, Honolulu, 1978; S.C. Amb. for Econ. Devel., 1989; co-coord. Clemson U./Hiroshima U. Exch. Program, 1991—; mem. Greenville City Chamber Sci. and Tech. Com., 1991-96. Oil and acrylic paintings exhbtd. George Walter Vincent Smith Art Mus., Springfield, Mass., 1974 (Springfield Art League award), one-man show Hilson Gallery Deerfield (Mass.) Acad., 1972 and 3-man show, 1971; contbr. articles to profl. jours. V.p. Clemson Area Internat. Friendship, Clemson, 1985-89; spl. asst. to pres. Clemson U. for U.S.-Japan rels., 1996—. Harvard U. fellow, 1964; travel grantee Asia Found., 1964, Deerfield Acad., 1972, 74; rsch. grantee Va. Poly. Inst. and State U., 1979, Clemson U., 1981, Clemson U. Provost, 1982; Clemson U. Innovation Fund grantee, 1989; named S.C. Ambassador for Econ. Devel., 1989. Mem. AIA, Assn. Collegiate Schs. Architecture N.Am. (chmn. ASCA-Japan com. 1992—, Japan liaison com.), Archtl. Inst. Japan, S.C. AIA, Japan Inst. Architects, Japan-Am. Assn. Western S.C. (pres. 1988-90, v.p. 1990—), Western S.C. Torch Club (sec. and pres.-elect 1993-94, pres. 1994-95), Sertoma (v.p. Clemson Club 1986-87). Home: 101 Hickory Ridge Ct Central SC 29630-9450 Office: Clemson Coll Arch Lee Hall Clemson U Clemson SC 29634-0503

KISHORE, ANAND, physician; b. Hyderabad, India, Nov. 16, 1951; s. Tilak and Susila Kishore; m. Lakshmi Kishore; children: Sandeep, Sanjay. MB BS, Osmania Med. Coll., Hyderabad, India. Resident Coney Island Hosp., N.Y.C., 1979-82, Montefiore Hosp., Pitts., 1982-84; asst. prof. medicine U. Ark. Med. Ctr., Little Rock, 1984-89, assoc. prof., 1989-90; dir. Gastrointestinal Lab. Radford (Va.) Hosp., 1990—. Fellow Am. Coll. Gastroenterology; mem. ACP, Am. Gastroenterology Assn. Home: 6 8th St Radford VA 24141-2422 Office: Community Med Ctr 701 Randolph St Ste 110 Radford VA 24141-3047

KISS, MARY CATHERINE CLEMENT, writer; b. Johnson City, Tenn., July 28, 1928; d. Hugh Wilfred and Ruby Pearl (Sammons) Clement; m. Alvin Ferencz Josef Kiss, Feb. 27, 1954; children: Tony, Stephen, Mary Margaret. Student, St. Mary-of-the-Woods Coll., Terre Haute, Ind., 1946-47; BA in Journalism, U. Mich., 1950. Staff writer Kingsport (Tenn.) Times News, 1950-90; video co-producer, script writer, cons. Get The Picture, Kingsport, 1990—; owner Mary Kiss Media Svcs., Kingsport, 1990—; staff writer The Independent, Bluff City, Tenn., 1994-95; freelance writer, 1996—. Recipient 1st Pl. award Best Local Feature Tenn. Press. Assn., 1970, 1st Pl. award Pub. Svc. Features, 1978. Mem. Investigative Reporters and Editors. Home and Office: Mary Kiss Media Svcs 100 Edmond Cir Kingsport TN 37663-2612

KISSEIH, LIBBY MALLOY, minister; b. Lumberton, N.C., Oct. 7, 1958; s. James Malloy and Edith McKoy; m. George Narh Kisseih, Jan. 8, 1980 (div. 20, 1994); 1 child, Jessica Naki. BA, Bennett Coll., 1980; MS, Howard U., 1983. Cons. Nat. Rsch. Coun., Washington, 1987-88; nat. rsch. asst. Nat. Del. Study, Washington, 1988-89; exec. dir. Nat. Congress Black Faculty Members, Washington, 1989; instr. polit. sci. dept. Howard U., Washington, 1992-93; instr. I Have a Dream Found., Washington, 1993; adj. instr. Richmond C.C., Hamlet, N.C., 1994-95; tutor Robeson C.C., Lumberton, N.C., 1995; owner Grant Writing Support Svcs., Fairmont, N.C., 1996—; pastor St. Matthew A.M.E. Ch., Wilmington, N.C., 1996—; intern U.S. Congress, Washington, 1987. Contbr. articles to profl. jours. Coord. cmty. outreach Southeastern Family Violence Ctr., Lumberton, N.C., 1986-87; conf. coord. One-Third of a Nation task force, Washington, 1989-90; mem., treas Microenterprise Program, 1995—. Recipient Nat. Oratorial award Nat. Women's Club, 1974, Nat. Black Polit. Sci. award Nat. Black Polit. Sci. Soc., 1989. Democrat. Mem. A.M.E. Ch. Home: Rte 1 Box 676 Fairmont NC 28340 Office: Grant Writing Support Svcs PO Box 785 Fairmount NC 28340

KISSELBURGH, ROBERT MCKIRDY, lawyer; b. Arlington, Calif., Aug. 20, 1959; s. David Austin and Marvis Sue (Norton) K.; m. Julianne Jackson, Oct. 13, 1984; children: Christopher, Ashley, Cody. BS in Criminal Justice and Sociology, Northwestern Okla. State U., 1985; JD, So. Meth. U., 1990. Bar: Tex. 1990, U.S. Dist. Ct. (no. dist.) Tex. 1991, U.S. Dist. Ct. (ea. dist.) Tex. 1995. Ptnr. McGuire & Levy, Irving, Tex., 1990—. Leader Boy Scouts Am., Garland, Tex., 1993—; vestry mem. Holy Trinity by the Lake Episcopal Ch., Rockwall, Tex. With USAF, 1979-87. Mem. ATLA, Tex. Trial Lawyers Assn., Dallas Bar Assn., Irving Bar Assn. Office: McGuire & Levy 1333 Corporate Dr # 350 Irving TX 75038-2509

KISSLING, FRED RALPH, JR., publishing executive, insurance agency executive; b. Nashville, Feb. 10, 1930; s. Fred Ralph and Sarah Elizabeth (FitzGerald) K.; m. Mary Jane Gallaher; children: Sarah FitzGerald, Jayne Kirkpatrick. BA, Vanderbilt U., 1952, MA, 1958. Spl. agt. Northwestern Mut. Life Ins. Co., Nashville, 1953-58, gen. agt., Lexington, Ky., 1962-80; gen. agt. New Eng. Mut. Life Ins. Co., 1981-87; mgr. life dept. Bennett & Edwards, Kingsport, Tenn., 1958-62; pres. Employee Benefit Cons., Inc., Lexington, 1961—; owner Lexington House, Inc., 1966—, Kennington Assocs., 1967—; prin. Kissling Orgn. 1987—, pub. Leader's mag., 1967—, editor, 1981—; owner, editor Fin. and Estate Planners Quar., 1993—; owner and pub. Life and Health Ins. Sales Mag., 1993—, editor 1996—. Author: Sell and Grow Rich, 1966; editor: Questionnaire in Pension Planning, 1970, Questionnaire in Estate Planning, 1971. Adv. bd. Salvation Army, Lexington, 1971—, chmn., 1988-91; gen. chmn. United Way of Blue Grass, 1975, bd. dirs., 1975-78, 80-83; trustee, chmn. bd. Lexington Children's Theatre, 1979-81, pres., 1981-83. Mem. Am. Soc. CLU's (chpt. pres. 1969-70, 80-81, regional v.p. 1971-73), Ky. Gen. Agts. and Mgrs. Assn. (pres. 1965-66), Million Dollar Round Table (life mem., v.p., program chmn. 1976), Assn. for Advanced Underwriting (bd. dirs. 1976-84, pres. 1982-83), Am. Soc. Pension Actuaries (bd. dirs. 1971-78, pres. 1974), Nat. Assn. of Estate Planning Councils (bd. dirs. 1986-92, pres. 1989-90), Am. Philatelic Soc., Sigma Chi, Lexington Club, Iroquois Hunt Club, Lafayette Club, Spindletop Hall, Masons, Shriners. Office: 98 Dennis Dr Lexington KY 40503-2915

KISSLO, JOSEPH ANDREW, cardiology, educator; b. Plymouth, Pa., Aug. 10, 1941; m. Katherine B. Kisslo, Aug. 17, 1983; 1 stepchild, Anthony Filly; children: Joseph Andrew III, Constance Marie, Michelle Ann. BS, U. Notre Dame, 1963; MD, Hahnemann U., 1967. Diplomate Nat. Bd. Med. Examiners; lic. to practice medicine, N.C., Conn., Pa., Va. Intern internal medicine Hahnemann U. Hosp., Phila., 1967-68; asst. resident in internal medicine Yale U.-New Haven Hosp., 1970-71; postdoctoral fellow in pediatric cardiology Yale U., New Haven, 1971-72; postdoctoral fellow in adult cardiology Duke U. Med. Ctr., Durham, N.C., 1972-74; assoc. in medicine cardiac catheterization lab. Duke U. Med. Ctr., Durham, 1974-75, asst. prof. medicine cardiac catheterization lab., 1975-77, assoc. prof. medicine, asst. prof. radiology, dir. cardiac diagnostic unit, 1977-83, assoc. prof. medicine, asst. prof. radiology, 1983-87, prof. medicine, asst. prof. radiology, 1987—; Inge Edler lectr. U. Lund, Sweden, 1991; vis. prof. or lectr. numerous socs. and univs. including Asean Fedn. Cardiology, Athens U., Greece, Brit. Med. Ultrasound Soc., Cairo U., European Soc. Cardiology, Finnish Soc. Cardiology, Georgetown U., Washington, Hamburg (Germany) U., Harvard U., Heart Assn. Thailand, Japanese Coll. Cardiology, Loyola U., Chgo., Med. Coll. S.C., Charleston, Mex. Mil. Med. Sch., Norwegian Soc. Cardiology, Royal Postgrad. Med. Sch., London, Thomas Jefferson U., Phila. Mem. editorial bd. Circulation, 1976-80, Clinics in Diagnostic Ultrasound, 1977—, Med. Ultrasound, 1977-83, Am. Heart Jour., 1980—, Am. Rev. Diagnostics, 1982-84, Echocardiology, 1984—, Am. Jour. Cardiac Imaging, 1986—, Cardiovascular Dynamics, 1986—, Jour. Am. Soc. Ethocardiology, 1987-91. Lt. commdr. USN, 1968-70. Recipient Silver medal for edn. Brit. Med. Soc., 1981. Fellow Am. Coll. Cardiology (chmn. allied health profls. com. 1983-87, echocardiology com. 1985—, N.C. affiliate), Am. Inst. Ultrasound in Medicine (bd. govs. 1983-86), N.C. Affiliate Am. Coll. Cardiology); mem. Am. Fedn. Clin. Rsch. (sr. mem.), Am. Registry of Diagnostic Med. Sonographers (bd. dirs. 1980-81), Am. Soc. Echocardiography (bd. dirs. 1976—, com. on two-dimensional standards 1977-84, com. physician tng. 1977-84, chmn. com. technician tng. 1979-89, exec. com. 1981—, v.p. 1981—, pres. 1983-85, chmn. legis. and regulatory com. 1984—, coun. intraoperative echocardiography 1993—), numerous others, Alpha Omega Alpha. Office: Duke U Med Ctr PO Box 3818 Durham NC 27702-3818

KISVARSANYI, EVA BOGNAR, retired geologist; b. Budapest, Hungary, Dec. 18, 1935; came to U.S., 1957; d. Kalman and Ilona (Simon) Bognar; m. Geza Kisvarsanyi, July 3, 1956; 1 child, Erika G. Student, Eotvos Lorand U., Budapest, 1954-56; BS in Geology, U. Mo., Rolla, 1958, MS, 1960. Geologist Mo. Geol. Survey, Rolla, 1959-68; from rsch. geologist to sect. chief Mo. Dept. Natural Resources/Geol. Survey Program, Rolla, 1968-90; asst. dir. MODNR/Geol. Survey Program, Rolla, 1990-93; cons. Sarasota, Fla., 1993—. Editor geological guidebooks, 1976—; contbr. articles to profl. jours. Fellow Geol. Soc. Am. (mem. rep. 1985-93), Soc. Econ. Geologists (rsch. com. 1989-92); mem Sigma Xi (pres. Rolla chpt. 1990-91).

KITCES, EDWARD NATHAN, dermatologist, physician; b. Ottawa, Ont., Can., Sept. 10, 1949; came to U.S., 1955; s. Samuel and Susan (Pearson) K.; m. Eileen Cantor, Sept. 12, 1982; children: James Ashley, Suzanne Katherine, Matthew Taylor, Hana Elizabeth. BS, George Washington U., 1971; MD, Med. Coll. Va., 1975, PhD, 1977. Diplomate Am. Bd. Dermatology. Lab. instr. biology George Washington U., Washington, 1969-71; instr. microbiology Med. Coll. Va., Richmond, 1975-77; resident in internal medicine Pitt County Meml. Hosp., Greenville, N.C., 1978-79; resident in dermatology Med. Coll. Va., 1979-81, instr. dermatology, 1981-85, asst. prof. dermatology, 1985-89; acting chief div. dermatology McGuire VA Hosp., Richmond, 1988-89; chmn. dept. dermatology McGuire Clinic, Richmond, 1990—; clin. adv. bd. Medicis Pharms., 1993—; clin. faculty Med. Coll. Va., 1989—; adv. bd. Va. Lupus Found., Richmond, 1993—; mem. Va. Dermatol. Malpractive Review Panel, 1988. Co-author: Oncogenesis and Herpes Viruses, 1977; contbr. articles to profl. jours. Recipient Inst. Med. Scientist scholarship Ins. Med. Scientist Scholarship Fund, 1974-77; Bd. Trustees scholar George Washington U., 1970-71. Fellow Am. Acad. Dermatology; mem. Am. Soc. Dermatologic Surgery, Richmond Dermatol. Soc. (presiding sec. 1992-94), Chaîne des Rotisseurs (Chevalier 1993—). Jewish. Office: McGuire Medical Group 7702 E Parham Rd Richmond VA 23294-4301

KITCHEN, BRENT A., airport executive; b. Topeka, Sept. 2, 1945. Student, Kans. State U.; BS in Aviation Mgmt., Embry-Riddle Aero. U., 1973. Airport mgr. City of Manhattan, Kans., 1973-78; asst. airport dir. Cedar Rapids, Iowa, 1978-81, Des Moines, 1981-86; dep. dir. airport facilities Tulsa Airport Authority, 1986-88, airport dir., 1988—. Served U.S. Army, Viet Nam. Office: Tulsa Internat Airport Authority PO Box 581838 Tulsa OK 74158-1838

KITCHEN, KRISTIN WILSON, journalist, social worker; b. Greenville, SC, May 1, 1957; d. Ray G. and Oranda (Amundrud) W.; m. John Thomas Kitchen, Jan. 5, 1980 (div. Nov. 18, 1991); 1 child, Jeremy. BS Bus. Adminstrn., U. Memphis, 1978, postgrad. in journalism, 1991-94; MS in Social Work, U. Tenn., 1996. Acctg. info. mgr. Middle Tenn. State U., Murfreesboro, Tenn., 1983-85; accts. receivable clk. S.G. Industries, Memphis, 1988-89, Stahl Internat., Memphis, 1990-91; social worker, mental health specialist S.E. Mental Health Ctr. Editor: newsletter; contbr. articles to newspapers, newsletters. Recipient: Mark of Excellence award Soc. Profl. Journalists, 1993, 94.

KITCHENS, FREDERICK LYNTON, JR., insurance company executive; b. Detroit, Sept. 30, 1940; s. Frederick Lynton and Madeline Dorothy (Jacobs) K.; m. Carol Ann Crane, Dec. 22, 1961; children: Frederick Lynton, Anne LeBaron, Susan Elizabeth. BA, Mich. State U., 1962. CPCU. Mgr. underwriting Royal Ins. Co., N.Y.C., 1968-70; asst. to pres. Grow, Keller, Englebert & Freese, Detroit, 1970-71; v.p. Dobson McOmber, Inc., Ann Arbor, Mich., 1971-73; exec. v.p. Hylant MacLean, Inc., Toledo, 1973-83; chmn., chief exec. officer Cherokee Ins. Co., Nashville, 1983-84; chmn. Coastal Plains Ins., Jacksonville, Fla., 1984—; instr. Coll. Ins., N.Y.C., 1969-70. Trustee Jacksonville Country Day Sch., 1985-90, Hope Haven Children's Clinic, 1988-91; dir. Jacksonville Commodores League; mem. Fla. Aviation Adv. Coun., 1990—, Leadership Jacksonville, 1991. Capt. U.S. Army, 1962-67, Vietnam. Decorated Bronze Star; recipient Commendation medal NATO, 1965. Mem. Jacksonville C. of C. (community devel. bd. 1986), Lloyd's of London (underwriting mem.), L.A. Yacht Club (commodore 1989—), Fla. Yacht Club Internat. (pres. North Fla. chpt. 1990-92), Rotary. Republican. Presbyterian. Office: Coastal Plains Ins PO Box 52897 Jacksonville FL 32201-2897

KITCHENS, LARRY EDWIN, university administrator; b. San Angelo, Tex., Dec. 7, 1940; s. Otis Paul and Hazel May (Hodgin) K.; m. Carolyn Kay Young, June 7, 1963; children: Kathy, David, Mark. BS in Social Sci. and Phys. Edn., Tex. Wesleyan Coll., 1963; MEd in Secondary Sch. Adminstrn., Tex. Christian U., 1969; postgrad., East Tex. State U., 1973-76. Tchr. history, golf coach, bldg. coordinator audio-visual services Ft. Worth Ind. Sch. Dist., 1963-67; dir. instructional media, instr. Tex. Wesleyan Coll., Ft. Worth, 1967-77; dean ednl. resources, chmn. various coms. Richland Coll., Dallas, 1977-86, acting v.p. student devel., 1986-87; dir. instrnl. svcs. Tex. Christian U., Ft. Worth, 1987—; Mem. sch.-industry coop. com. Tex. State Tech. Inst., 1977-79; mem. campus speaker's bur. Richland Coll. Chmn. citizens adv. bd. Hurst-Euless-Bedford Ind. Sch. Dist., Hurst, Tex., 1982-83; vice chmn. parks and recreation bd. Hurst Parks, 1982—. Named one of Outstanding Young Men in Am., 1970, 71. Mem. Assn. Ednl. Communications and Tech. (bd. dirs. 1976-79, div., pres. 1989-90, pres.-elect 1991-92, pres. 1992-93, William A. Fulton award for outstanding leadership), Tex. Assn. Ednl. Tech. (past v.p., bd. dirs., pres. 1976-77), Tex. Ednl. TV Assn. (chmn. various com.), Tex. Libr. Assn., Nat. Soc. for Supervision and Curriculum Devel. Democrat. Methodist. Lodge: Optimists. Home: 624 Post Oak Dr Hurst TX 76053-6520 Office: Tex Christian U PO Box 32892 Fort Worth TX 76129

KITCHENS, RONALD BLAKE, information technologies manager; b. Rockledge, Fla., July 3, 1965; s. Jimmy B. and JoAnn (Osteen) K. BS in Computer Sci., Fla. Inst. Tech., 1987, M Computer Sci., 1993; MBA, U. Ctrl. Fla., 1990. Simulation analyst ECC, Orlando, Fla., 1987-88; sr. systems engr. Automation Intelligence, Orlando, 1988-92; sr. project engr. RTC, Orlando, 1992-93; mgr. info. techs. Harcourt Brace & Co., Orlando, 1993—; cons. Caterpillar, Peoria, Ill., 1989-90, Zimmer (Bristol Myers), Warsaw, Ind., 1988-91, Martin Marietta, Orlando, 1989-92, AT&T, Orlando, 1992-93. Fellow Assn. Computing Machinery; mem. IEEE, Mensa, ISPE. Office: Harcourt Brace & Co 6277 Sea Harbor Dr Orlando FL 32821-8098

KITCHENS, WILLIAM CHARLIE, accountant; b. Jacksonville, Fla., Oct. 21, 1945; s. William Othar and Mazie Alice (Dugger) K. BBA, Ga. Coll., Milledgeville, 1981, postgrad., 1981. Cert. enrolled agt., accredited tax advisor. Income tax practitioner H&R Block, Macon, Ga., 1976-86; cost acct., dept. head West Point Pepperell, Milledgeville, 1981-82; asst. fin. examiner Ga. Dept. of Banking and Fin., Dublin, 1980; tax acct. Ga. Farm Bur. Fedn., Macon, 1982—. Served as staff sgt. USAF, 1965-68. Mem. Nat. Assn. Enrolled Agts., Ga. Assn. Enrolled Agts., Nat. Soc. Pub. Accts., Nat. Assn. Income Tax Practitioners. Republican. Baptist. Home: 544 Orange St # 1 Macon GA 31201-2014 Address: PO Box 7885 Macon GA 31209-7885 Office: Ga Farm Bur Fedn PO Box 7068 Macon GA 31298-4299

KITCHIN, CHRISTOPHER H., computer scientist, consultant; b. Lakewood, N.J., Dec. 20, 1947; s. Henry M. and Elsie B. (Knipe) K.; m. Boonchu Maitong Verner, Dec. 31, 1970 (div. May 1980); m. Martha J. Council, Dec. 1, 1990. BS in Bus., Limestone Coll., Spartanburg, S.C., 1989; M.Computer Sci., Kennedy-Western U., 1993. Instr. U.S. Govt., Ft. Gordon, Ga., 1985—; CEO, cons. H & J Enterprises, Blythe, Ga., 1995—. Author: Becoming Computer Literate, 1996. With U.S. Army, 1966-70, 71-78. Home: PO Box 153 Blythe GA 30805-0153 Office: H & J Enterprises 3608 Hwy 88 Blythe GA 30805

KITCHIN, KATE PARKS, retired guidance counselor and secondary English language educator; b. Scotland Neck, N.C., Apr. 16, 1911; d. John Arrington and Norma (Cloman) K. AB, U. N.C., Chapel Hill, 1931; MA, Columbia U., N.Y., 1943. Tchr. Woodland (N.C.)-Olney High School, 1931-36; tchr. English, counselor Rocky Mt. High School, 1936-79; guidance asst. summer sch. Appalachian State Tchrs. Coll., Boone, N.C., 1955, co-guidance dir., 1956, guidance dir., 1960; co-chmn. Report of So. States Work Conf. on Guidance in Pub. Schs., Daytona, S.C., 1956, N.C. Dept. Pub. Instruction. Author: Guidance-Services, 1960; contbr. articles to profl. jours. Pres. N.C. Dean's Assn., 1942-44; exec. sec. N.C. Student Coun. Congress, 1952-56; clk. Vestry Ch. of the Good Shepherd, Rocky Mt., 1979-93. Recipient DAR medal of honor, 1988; named Rocky Mt. Tchr. of the Yr., 1978, Rocky Mt. Woman of Yr., 1950, 65. Mem. Am. Assn. Ret. Persons (NRTA div.), N.C. Assn. Educators, Nash-Edgecombe Ret. Sch. Pers., Rocky Mt. Jr. Guild, Delta Kappa Gamma (pres. N.C. 1950-53). Democrat. Episcopalian.

KITNER, JON DAVID, art educator; b. El Paso, Tex., Oct. 26, 1946; s. Harold C. and Joyce M. (LaPaz) K.; m. Debra S. Johnsen, June 12, 1976; 1 child, Jason R. Student, Cleve. Inst. Art, 1964-65; BFA, Kent State U., 1969, MA, 1971. Instr. Stark Campus, Kent State U., Canton, Ohio, 1970-73, Broward Community Coll., Ft. Lauderdale, Fla., 1973-76; instr. Miami (Fla.)-Dade Cmty. Coll., 1973-76; assoc. prof. fin art Miami (Fla.)-Dade Community Coll., 1976-91, prof., 1991—, chmn. dept., 1988-94, mem. honors faculty, 1981-86, dir. art gallery, 1985-86; ofcl. evaluator Fla. Internat. U., Fla. Endowment for Humanities, Miami, 1987. One-man shows include Meeting Point Gallery, Miami, 1981, Green Gallery, Miami, 1984, Wakefield Galleries, Yorkshire, Eng., 1989; exhibited in group shows Mus. Art, Ft. Lauderdale, Fla., 1984 (award of Merit), Barbara Scott Gallery, 1993; monthly columnist Miami-Herald, 1988-89. Recipient U.S. Disting. Tchr. award U.S. Dept. Edn., 1986, Outstanding Faculty award Miami-Dade C.C., 1988, Nat. Tchg. Excellence award U. Tex. Nat. Inst. for Staff Devel., 1989, Arthur Hertz Endowed Tchg. Chair for Fine Arts and Humanities, 1994-97, Nat. Inst. for Staff and Orgnl. Devel. award for ednl. excellence 2d superior leadership U. Tex., 1995; Fulbright scholar, 1988-89. Mem. Fulbright Alumni Assn., Ctr. for Fine Arts. Office: Miami-Dade CC North Campus Dept Art & Philosophy 11380 NW 27th Ave Miami FL 33167-3418

KITTLE, ROBERT EARL, educational administrator; b. Flemington, W.Va., Jan. 10, 1935; s. Bertsel and Ruth (Ball) K.; B.A. in Elem. Edn., Alderson-Broaddus Coll., 1957; M.A. in Adminstrn., Marshall U., 1966, suprs. cert., 1973; suprs. endorsement, 1977; m. Marianna Arthur; children—Marian, Matthew. Prin. Taylor County Schs., 1957-62; tchr. Kanawha County Schs., Charleston, W.Va., 1962-65, prin., 1965-69, dir. elem. schs., 1969-72, dir. planning and accountability, 1972-73, asst. supt. dept. instrnl. programs Div. Curriculum and Instrn., 1972-78, supt. schs., 1979-84; supt. schs. Randolph County Schs., 1984-85, Harrison County Schs., 1985—. Bd. dirs. Region VII., United Hosp. Ctr., RESA VII; mem. exec. com. W.Va. Rural Devel. Coun.; v.p. W.Va. joint commn. vocat.-technical-occupl. edn., 1989—. Recipient W.Va. Superintendent of the Year, Am. Assn. of School Administrators, 1992, Leader of Learning award W.Va. Dept. Edn., 1992. Mem. W. Va. Sch. Health Com., W. Va. Fund Com. Mem. Am. Assn. Sch. Adminstrs., W.Va. Assn. Sch. Adminstrs. (pres.), North Central Assn., Phi Delta Kappa, Baptist. Clubs: Rotary, Masons, Shriners, The Century Club. Office: Harrison County Schs 408 Water St Clarksburg WV 26301-4649

KITTRELL, JOHN CABEEN, JR., artist, writer; b. Hamburg, Ark.; s. John Cabeen and Patsy Wells (Hankins) K.; m. Elaine Campbell, Dec. 19, 1969; children: Kathryn, Melanie, Heather, Thomas, Lynda, David. AA, Kemper Mil. Sch., Boonville, Mo., 1943; student So. Meth. U., 1943, Miami U., Oxford, Ohio, 1944; BBA, BA, U. Ala., 1969. Vice pres., ptnr. Kittrell Lumber Industries, Tyler, Tex., 1946-56; developer, builder Kittrell Heights, Snyder, Tex., 1956-58; owner, prin. Kittrell Pub. Relations Cons., Tyler, 1958-64, Huntsville, Ala., 1964-72; pub. affairs officer HHS, Washington, 1972-86; now portrait painter. One-man shows include Chilton Gallery, Mobile, Ala., 1991, 92, Wolff Gallery, Fairhope, Ala., 1993, 94; other exhbns. include Fine Arts Mus. of South, Mobile, Ea. Shore Mus. of Art, Fairhope, Corcoran Mus., Washington, Nat. Portrait Sem., Atlanta; author: Family Origins and Favorite Recipes, 1971; contbr. articles to numerous mags. and newspapers; artist. Mem. Order of Crown in Am., Rotary, Phi Delta Theta. Episcopalian. Avocations: jazz pianist, antique and art collector, horticulture, philately. Home: PO Box 644 Montrose AL 36559-0644

KITTS, ELBERT WALKER, minister; b. Knoxville, Tenn., Apr. 12, 1939; s. Robert Theodore and Grace Arminda (Van DeGriff) K.; m. Ellen Abner, May 11, 1956; children: David, Donna, Timothy, Ronald, Daniel, Paul, Jonathan, Angela. Ordained to ministry Bapt. Ch., 1965. Evangelist Tex. Valley Bapt. Ch., Knoxville, 1961-65; pastor Centerview Bapt. Ch., Knoxville, 1965-68, Valley Grove Bapt. Ch., Maynardville, Tenn., 1968-70, Emory Valley Bapt. Ch., Knoxville, 1970-74, Pleasant Hill Bapt. Ch., Powell, Tenn., 1974-84, Grace Missionary Bapt. Ch., Knoxville, 1985—; pres. Ednl. and Inspiritional Internat. Travel; founder, dir. TV and radio ministry Old Time Bapt. Hour, Knoxville, 1976-90; exec. dir. Bapts. United in Missions, Knoxville, 1982-89; founder, bd. dirs. Proclaiming Jesus to the World, St. Christopher and Nevis, 1982-90. Editor, pub. Bapts. United in Missions News Jour., 1982-90. Mem. bd. advisors Nat. Home Health, Inc., Knoxville, 1983; chmn. Midland Assn. for Endowment Carson Newman Coll., Jefferson City, 1983-86, Midland Assn. Tenn. Bapt. Children's Home Endowment, 1990-91. Republican. Office: PO Box 5873 Knoxville TN 37928-0873

KITZES, WILLIAM FREDRIC, lawyer, safety analyst, consultant; b. Bklyn., Nov. 24, 1950; s. David Louis and Rhoda Rachel (Feldman) K; m. Sandra Shimasaki, Apr. 7, 1979: children: Justin, Dana. BA, U. Wis., 1972; JD, Am. U., 1975. Bar: D.C. 1977. Legal advisor on product recalls U.S. Consumer Products Safety Commn., Washington, 1975-77, program mgr., 1977-80, regulatory counsel, 1980-81; v.p., gen. mgr. Inst. for Safety Analysis, Rockville, Md., 1981-83; prin. Consumer Safety Assocs., Potomac, Md., 1983—; cons. Toro Co., Bloomington, Minn., 1987—, Vendo Co., Fresno, Calif., 1987—, Nat. Assn. Attys. Gens., Washington, 1987—. Counsel Friends of Charlie Gilchrist, Montgomery County, Md., 1983; chmn. Fla. Consumers Coun., 1995—. Recipient silver medal for meritorious svc. U.S. Consumer Products Safety Commn., 1976. Mem. Am. Soc. Safety Engrs., Human Factors Soc., System Safety Soc. Home and Office: Consumer Safety Assocs 4501 NW 25th Way Boca Raton FL 33434-2506

KIYONAGA, JOHN CADY, lawyer; b. Atsugi, Japan, Dec. 27, 1953; s. Joseph Yoshio and Bina Mary (Cady) K.; m. Susan Marie Fraser, Dec. 5, 1980 (div. Oct. 1990); children: Joseph Yoshio, Anastasia. BA, Georgetown U., 1976; JD, MS in Journalism, Columbia U., N.Y.C., 1980. Bar: N.Y. 1981, D.C. 1990, Va. 1990. Assoc. Brown & Wood, N.Y.C., 1980-83; ins. officer Overseas Pvt. Investment Corp., Washington, 1984; ptnr. Kiyonaga & Kiyonaga, Alexandria, Va., 1990—. Contbr. articles and editl. writings to profl. publs. With U.S. Army, 1985-89. Mem. Hispanic Bar Assn. No. Va., Alexandria Bar Assn., Columbia Country Club, Army and Navy Club. Roman Catholic. Office: Kiyonaga & Kiyonaga 225 Reinekers Ln # 770 Alexandria VA 22314

KJELLSTRAND, WILLIAM SANDER, newspaper editor; b. Cin., Sept. 14, 1941; s. Arthur Gustav and Marie Dorothy (Haffey) K.; m. Leslie Louise Ruggles, June 18, 1966; children: Katherine Janet, Sarah Marie, Elizabeth Kent. BA, Ohio State U., 1963; MA, U. Tex., 1991, postgrad., 1991—. Reporter Cleve. Press, 1966-69, copyeditor, 1969-74, asst. news editor, 1975-76, news editor, 1976-82; news editor Austin (Tex.) Am. Statesman, 1982—. Editor, pub.: Fairview Park in Historical Review, 1976. Vestryman Episc. Ch. of Resurrection, Austin, 1988-90; del. Diocese of Tex. Coun., 1988-94; bd. dirs., v.p. Lakewood (Ohio) Hist. Soc. Mem. Speech Comm. Assn., Assn. for Edn. in Journalism of Mass Comm., Phi Kappa Phi. Home: 7205 Carlwood Dr Austin TX 78759-4603 Office: Austin Am Statesman PO Box 670 Austin TX 78767-0670

KJOS, OTTO DENNIS, construction industry executive; b. Seattle, Aug. 8, 1946; s. Harlen Otto and Walburga (Kraft) K.; m. Hazel Edith Hussey, June 28, 1969; children: Ian Brooke, Clayton Alexander. BSEE, San Diego State U., 1970. Cost engr. Fluor Corp., Irvine, Calif., 1970-85; gen. mgr., engr. Fluor Engrs., Inc., Irvine, Calif., 1985; v.p., gen. mgr. Fluor Daniel, Irvine, Calif., 1986-88, Phila., 1988-90; v.p. Fluor Daniel, Houston, 1990—. Engring. adv. bd. Calif. Poly. U., San Luis Obispo, 1987-88; bd. dirs. Jr. Achievement, Orange County, Calif., 1988, Calif. Engring. Found., 1988; bd. dirs. campaign chair United Way of Burlington County, N.J., 1989. Mem. Project Mgmt. Inst., Am. Assn. Cost Engrs., Sweetwater Country Club. Republican. Office: Fluor Daniel 1 Fluor Daniel Dr Sugar Land TX 77487

KLABOSH, CHARLES JOSEPH, aerospace research and development executive; b. Manchester, Conn., Mar. 11, 1920; s. Kasimeraz and Veronica (Christana) Klebosas; m. Lois Thaney Heiser, Oct. 6, 1958. BS in Aero. Engring., U. Mich., 1953; postgrad., U. Houston, 1962-68, U. North Fla., 1983-86. Sales engr. Pratt and Whitney Aircraft, East Hartford, Conn., 1941-43, 48-52; mgr., flight test USAF, Dayton, Ohio, 1953-55; sr. design engr., nuclear power plants Gen. Electric, Co., Evendale, Ohio, 1955-59, 61; sr. devel. engr., gasturbine power plants Am. Airlines, Inc., Tulsa, 1960; advanced space programs engr. NASA, Houston, 1961-67, mgr., lunar ops., 1967-72, space shuttle systems devel. engr., 1973-74; owner, exec. Charles Klabosh, Co., Jacksonville, Fla., 1974—. Inventor space shuttle remote manipulator system, 1974. With USAF, 1943-47. Mem. AIAA, AAAS, IEEE, N.Y. Acad. Sci., Soc. for Indsl. and Applied Math. Home: 4320 Gadsden Ct Jacksonville FL 32207-6218 Office: Charles Klabosh Co 6015 Morrow St E Ste 218 Jacksonville FL 32217-2126

KLAMON, LAWRENCE PAINE, lawyer; b. St. Louis, Mar. 17, 1937; s. Joseph Martin and Rose (Schimel) K.; m. Jo Ann Karen Beatty, Nov. 1957 (div. Feb. 1974); children: Stephen Robert, Karen Jean, Lawrence Paine; m. Frances Ann Estes, Mar. 1980. A.B., Washington U., St. Louis, 1958; J.D., Yale U., 1961. Bar: N.Y. 1964, Ga. 1992. Confidential asst. Office Sec. Def., Washington, 1961-62; spl. asst. to gen. counsel Office Sec. Def., 1962-63; asso. Cravath, Swaine & Moore, N.Y.C., 1963-67; v.p., gen. counsel Fuqua Industries, Inc., Atlanta, 1967-73; sr. v.p. fin. and adminstrn. Fuqua Industries, Inc., 1971-81, pres., 1981-89, chief exec. officer, 1989-91; chmn., 1991; sr. counsel Alston & Bird, Atlanta, 1991-95; pres., CEO Fuqua Enterprises, Inc., Atlanta, 1995—; chmn. Gov.'s Internat. Adv. Coun., 1992-95. Mem. bd. editors Yale Law Jour., 1959-61. Mem. ABA, Assn. Bar City N.Y., Atlanta Bar Assn., State Bar Ga., Atlanta C. of C. (bd. dirs.), Order of Coif, Phi Beta Kappa, Omicron Delta Kappa. Home: 2665 Dellwood Dr NW Atlanta GA 30305-3519 Office: Fuqua Enterprises Inc One Atlantic Ctr 1201 W Peachtree St NW Atlanta GA 30309-3400

KLANN, RICHARD, theology and religious studies educator; b. June 13, 1915; s. Paul and Wanda (Henry) K.; m. Martha Irene Christenson, Aug. 10, 1946; 1 child, Andrea Irene. BD, Concordia Sem., St. Louis, 1938; MA, Washington U., 1939; PhD, Columbia U., 1951; DD, Concordia Theol. Sem., Fort Wayne, Ind., 1986. Pastor Luth. Ch.-Missouri Synod, Tenn., Mo., 1940-42; chaplain U.S. Army S.W. Pacific Theater, Japan, 1942-46; pastor to students Greater N.Y.C., 1946-60; Atlantic dist. coord. theol. studies programs N.Y., 1961-63; prof. Concordia Sem., St. Louis, 1963-85, prof. emeritus, 1985—. Founding editor Concordia Jour., 1975; convention essayist for ch. convs.; contbr. numerous articles to profl. ch. publs. Named Outstanding Educator, Outstanding Educators of Am., 1975, Outstanding Prof., Students of Concordia Sem., 1985. Lutheran. Home and Office: 34245 Parkview Ave Eustis FL 32736-7230

KLAUDER, JOHN RIDER, physics educator; b. Reading, Pa., Jan. 24, 1932; s. David Streeper and Jean (Rider) K.; m. Robertha Howell, Sept. 11, 1953 (div. 1980); children: Karol Jean, Katherine Jane, Kim Ann, John Christopher; m. Agnes Nadasdi, July 26, 1980; 1 child, Jennifer Ann. BS, U. Calif., Berkeley, 1953; MS, Stevens Inst. Tech., 1956; PhD, Princeton U., 1959. Mem. tech. staff, then dept. head AT&T Bell Labs., Murray Hill, N.J., 1953-88; prof. depts. math. and physics U. Fla., Gainesville, 1988—; cons. Los Alamos (N.Mex.) Nat. Lab., 1978-89. Co-author: Fundamentals of Quantum Optics, 1968, Coherent States, 1985; editor Jour. Math. Phys., 1979-86. Fellow AAAS, Am. Phys. Soc.; mem. Internat. Assn. Math. and Physics (pres. 1988-91), Internat. Union Pure and Applied Physics (assoc. sec. gen. 1984-90). Office: U Fla Dept Physics/Math Gainesville FL 32611

KLAUS, KENNETH SHELDON, choral conductor, vocalist, music educator; b. Baton Rouge, La., Oct. 1, 1952; s. Kenneth Blanchard and Marian Ida (Fyler) K.; m. Phebe Darlene Arceneaux, Aug. 16, 1975; children: Christopher Fyler, Michael Calvin, Rachel Elizabeth. MusB, La. State U., 1974, MusM, 1976, PhD, 1983. Bass soloist St. James Episcopal Ch., Baton Rouge, summer 1972; dir. music Blackwater United Meth. Ch., Baker, La., 1972-79; interim dir. music Goodwood Bapt. Ch., Baton Rouge, summer 1980; dir. music First United Meth. Ch., Brookhaven, Miss., 1981-84, Houma, La., 1985—; violist Baton Rouge Symphony Orch., 1971-79; dir. choral music Copiah-Lincoln C.C., Wesson, Miss., 1979-84; dir. choral activities, assoc. prof. music Nicholls State U., Thibodaux, La., 1984—; vocal soloist New Orleans Opera, Miss. Opera, Baton Rouge Symphony, Concert Choir New Orleans, Chorale Acadienne, Jefferson Performing Arts Soc., La. Sinfonietta, also others; choral music clinician various high schs. and jr. high schs. in La. and Miss., ch. music workshops; adjudicator dist. and regional choral festivals in La. and Miss., solo/ensemble festivals in La. and Miss.; condr. various choirs. Author: Chamber Music for Solo Voice and Instruments, 1960-89, 1994; author book, CD, music and CD revs. The Choral Jour., 1985—. Bd. dirs. Thibodaux Playhouse, Inc., 1987-89, Nicholls State U. United Meth. Campus Ministry. Mem. Fellowship United Meths. in Music and Worship Arts (rep. La. conf. Acadiana dist.), Nat. Assn. Tchrs. Singing (Miss. artist award 1980), Am. Choral Dirs. Assn. (La. student activities chmn. 1985-93, chmn. La. vocal jazz and show choir 1993—), Music Educators Nat. Conf., La. Music Educators Assn., Music Tchrs. Nat. Assn. (nat. cert. voice tchr.), La. Music Tchrs. Assn., Phi Kappa Phi, Phi Mu Alpha Sinfonia, Pi Kappa Lambda. Home: 419 Cedar Tree Dr Thibodaux LA 70301-5728 Office: Nicholls State U Dept Music Thibodaux LA 70310

KLAUSMEYER, DAVID MICHAEL, scientific instruments manufacturing company executive; b. Indpls., Aug. 29, 1934; s. David M. and V. Jane (Donnellan) K.; m. Julie Ann Johnson, Oct. 29, 1955; children: Kathleen M., Kevin M., Gregory J. BSS, Georgetown U., 1955. Asst. to pres. White Cons. Ind., Cleve., 1957; auditor Ernst & Ernst, Cleve., 1957-59; pres. Photopipe, Inc., Cleve., 1960-63; v.p. McGregor & Werner Internat., Inc., Washington, 1964-70; internat. cons. Stratford of Tex., Houston, 1971-72; pres. FLR Corp., Houston, 1972-74, Southwest Cons., Houston, 1981-86, Imaging Products, Houston, 1987-90; pres. Nanodyanmics, Inc., Houston, 1988—, also bd. dirs.; pres. Corp. Devel., Houston, 1974-81; ptnr. Klausmeyer & Assoc., Houston, 1970—; dir. U.S. investment banking G.H. Securities, Grand Cayman Island, 1995—, dir. Pharm. Labs. Inc., Arlington, Tex., Applied Voice Technologies, Inc., Houston; bd. dirs. S.W. Venture Reification, Houston, TWK Techs., Charlotte, N.C., Lifestream Techs., Inc., Sands Point, Idaho; Applied Voice Recognition, Inc., Houston. With USCG, 1955-57. Republican. Roman Catholic. Home: 288 Litchfield Ln Houston TX 77024-6035 Office: Nanodynamics Inc 10878 Westheimer Rd # 178 Houston TX 77042-3202

KLAUSSNER, HANS, manufacturing executive. Pres. Hukla-Werke GmbH, Gengenberg, Germany, 1965—; chmn. Klaussner Investment Corp., Asheboro, N.C., 1979—, Klaussner Furniture Industries, Asheboro, N.C., 1979—, Klaussner Corp., Asheboro, N.C., 1979—, Prestige Fabricators, Inc., Asheboro, 1980—. Office: Klaussner Corp/Klaussner Furniture Industries 405 Lewallen St Asheboro NC 27203*

KLAW, BARBARA ANNE, language educator; b. Chgo., Mar. 22, 1957. BA cum laude in French, No. Ill. U., 1979; postgrad., Northwestern U., 1982-83; MA in French lit., U. Pa., 1985, PhD in French, 1990. Teaching asst. Northwestern U., Evanston, Ill., 1982-83; teaching asst. U. Pa., Phila., 1983-84, 84-85, 1986-87; lectr. Université de Dijon, Dijon, France, 1985-86, U. Pa., Phila, 1987-88; teaching asst. Penn-in-Tours program Faculté des Lettres, Tours, France, summer 1988; asst. prof. French No. Ky. U., Highland Heights, 1990—; faculty advisor Internat. Student Union, No. Ky. U., 1991-95; participant com. for modification of tng. program for new tchg. assts. Northwestern U., spring 1983. Numerous presentations in French and on French subjects; contbr. articles to profl. jours. No. Ky. U. summer fellow, 1991, 94. Mem. MLA, So. Atlantic MLA, Midwest MLA, Simone de Beauvoir Soc., Alliance Française de Cin., Am. Assn. Tchrs. French, Ky. Coun. Tchg. Fgn. Langs., Am. Coun. Tchg. Fgn. Langs., Women in French (treas. 1992—). Office: Lit and Lang No Ky U Highland Heights KY 41009-1500

KLEBER, BROOKS EDWARD, military historian; b. Trenton, N.J., Apr. 15, 1919; s. Brooks Charles and Eleanor Bennett (Stoddard) K.; m. Mae Emaline Stacey, Mar. 23, 1946. PhB, Dickinson Coll., 1940; MA, U. Pa., 1948, PhD, 1957. Asst. chief historian U.S. Army Chem. Corps, Army Chem. Ctr., Md., 1950-63; chief historian U.S. Continental Army Command, Ft. Monroe, Va., 1963-73, U.S. Tng. and Doctrine Command, Ft. Monroe, Va., 1973-80; dep. chief historian U.S. Ctr. Mil. History, Washington, 1980-84, asst. chief mil. history, 1984-87; ret.; cons. Time-Life WWII Series, Prisoners of War vol., 1981. Co-author: Chemicals in Combat in the U.S. Army in World War II, 1966; contbr. Dictionary of American Military Biography, 1984, The D-Day Encyclopedia, 1994. Capt. U.S. Army Inf., 1941-46, ETO (prisoner of war, Germany). Decorated Bronze Star, Combat Inf. badge, Meritorious Svc. medal; recipient two Dept. Army awards for civilian svc., 1983, 87, and one for exceptional civilian svc., 1993; named to Inf. OCS Hall of Fame, Ft. Benning, Ga., 1982. Fellow U.S. Army Mil. Inst.; mem. Soc. Mil. History (bd. trustees), Va. Res. Officers Assn. (pres. 1966-67). Home: 440 Summer Dr Newport News VA 23606

KLECK, GARY DAVID, criminologist, educator; b. Elmhurst, Ill., Mar. 2, 1951; s. William Gordon and Joyce (Edwards) K.; m. Diane Gomez, June 20, 1981; children: Matthew, Tessa. AB, U. Ill., 1973, AM, 1975, PhD, 1979. Teaching/research asst. U. Ill., Urbana, 1975-78; from instr. to assoc. prof. Sch. Criminology and Criminal Justice, Fla. State U., Tallahassee, 1978-91, prof., 1991—. Author: Point Blank: Guns and Violence in America. Contbr. articles to profl. jours. U. Ill. Found. fellow in sociology, 1974; recipient Michael Hindelang award, 1993. Mem. Am. Soc. Criminology. Democrat. Home: 489 Teenie Ct Tallahassee FL 32312-1044 Office: Sch Criminology/ Criminal Justice Florida State Univ Tallahassee FL 32306-2025

KLEER, NORMA VESTA, critical care nurse; b. London, Apr. 23, 1933; d. Harold N. and Julia Bonanova (Ball-Dale) Wragg; divorced; children: Valerie Mainguy, David. Diploma, Torbay (South Devon, Eng.) Hosp., 1954, St. Francis Hosp., Trenton, N.J., 1964. Critical care nursing mgr. Bayfront Med. Ctr., St. Petersburg, Fla.; dir. nursing PRN Inc., St. Petersburg, Am. Healthcare Mgmt., St. Petersburg; nursing coord. Care Plus Inc. Hi-Tech. Home Infusion Co., Fla.; case mgr., DON Bayada Nurses Home Care Specialists, St. Petersburg, Fla.; dir. nurses Nurses PRN, Tampa Bay, Fla.; pioneer in devel. of EMS Sys., Pinellas Co. Mem. Fla. Emergency Nurses Assn. (founder, 1st pres.).

KLEIN, BERNARD J., management specialist; b. 1945. Employee State of Calif., L.A., 1968-72, City of L.A., 1969-79, Atlantic Richfield, L.A., 1979-84; pres. Klein & Assocs. Inc., New Orleans, La., 1984-89, Klein Ainswrth & Co., Inc., New Orleans, 1989—; mng. ptnr. Astoria Gertna Belle Partnr, Metaire, La., 1992—. Office: Astoria Gretna Belle Partnr 1110 Veterans Blvd Ste 105A Metairie LA 70005

KLEIN, CHRISTOPHER CARNAHAN, economist; b. Anniston, Ala., July 5, 1953; s. Wallace Carnahan and Frances Luvona (Meaders) K.; m. Vicki Lynn Brown, May 7, 1983; children: Hannah Marie Brown, Colin Christopher Brown. BA in Econs., U. Ala., 1976; PhD in Econs., U. N.C., 1980. Economist FTC, Washington, 1980-86; economist Tenn. Pub. Svc. Commn., Nashville, 1986-94, rsch. dir., 1993-94, dir. utility rate div., 1994-96; chief utility rate divsn. Tenn. Regulatory Authority, Nashville, 1996—; mem. adj. faculty Mid. Tenn. State U., Murfreesboro, 1990—; mem. Fed.-State Joint Bd. Staff, 1994-96; mem. rsch. adv. com. Nat. Regulatory Rsch. Inst., Columbus, Ohio, 1990-95, chmn., 1993-95; mem. staff subcom. on gas Nat. Assn. Regulatory Utility Commrs., 1990-94. Contbr. articles to profl. jurs. Recipient cert. of commendation FTC, 1985. Mem. Nat. Assn. Bus. Economists, Am. Econ. Assn., So. Econ. Assn., Indsl. Orgn. Soc., Mid-South Acad. Econs. and Fin., Alpha Pi Mu. Office: Tenn Regulatory Authority 460 James Robertson Pkwy Nashville TN 37219-9021

KLEIN, DAVID STEPHEN, anesthesiologist; b. Washington, May 11, 1954; s. Milton T. and Lillian (Sachar) K.; m. Peggy Wilds, Nov. 6, 1982; 1 child, Bethany Ann. BS in Chemistry and Psychology cum laude, U. Md., 1976, MD, 1980; postdoctoral, Duke U., 1980-83. Diplomate Am. Bd. Anesthesiology, Am. Acad. Pain Mgmt.; cert. ACLS, ATLS, ACLS instr., combat anesthesia. Intern in surgery sch. medicine U. N.C., Chapel Hill, 1980-81; resident in anesthesiology sch. medicine Duke U., Durham, N.C., 1981-83; analytical chemist office pesticide programs U.S. EPA, Washington, 1976; staff anesthesiologist Shenandoah Valley Pain Clinic, King's Daus. Hosp., Staunton, Va., 1983-89, Rockingham Meml. Hosp., Harrisburg, Va., 1990—; mem. teaching faculty Portsmouth Naval Hosp., 1989-90, dept anesthesiology Nat. Naval Med. Ctr., 1990; clin. asst. prof. dept. anesthesiology Ohio State U., 1990; vis. lectr. U. Va., 1987, Bowman Grat Sch. Medicine, 1988, Portsmouth Naval Hosp., 1989, Ohio State U., 1989, 91, Nat. Naval Med. Ctr., 1990, 91, Washington Navy Yard, 1991; participant Wyeth-Ayers Labs. Vis. Prof. Program. Syntex Labs. Speakers Bur., Marion Labs. Speakers Program, Hoffman-LaRoche Speakers Program, Upjohn Speakers Bur., Glaxo Pharms.; bd. dirs. Valley Home Health, Inc., Staunton, Voice Ptnrs. Roanoke, DAKLE, Inc., Voice Ptrns. Va., CFO; mem. naval war coll.Policy and Strategy Cirriculum Air Commd. and Staff Coll., 1991; med. malpractice cons. Supreme Ct. Va., 1988—; presenter in field. Mem. editorial rev. bd. Can. Anesthetists' Jour., 1983-84, Mil. Medicine, 1986—; mem. editorial bd. Am. Jour. Pain, 1991; guest reviewer Hosp. Formulary, 1986—; contbr. over 35 articles and monographs to sci. jours. Commdr. med. corps USNR. Fellow Am. Coll. Pain Medicine, Am. Coll. Anesthesiologists; mem. AMA (guest reviewer jour. 1988—), Am. Soc. Anesthesiologists, Am. Soc. Regional Anesthesiology, Assn. Mil. Surgeons U.S., U.S. Naval Inst., Internat. Anesthesiology Rsch. Soc., Va. Soc. Anesthesiologists, Med. Soc. Va., Augusta County Med. Soc. (sec. 1984, pres. 1989), Rockingham County Med. Soc., Res. Officer Assn. (life), Naval Res. Assn. (life), Navy League (life), Alpha Chi Sigma, Phi Delta Epsilon, Omnicron Delta Kappa, Psi Chi, Phi Kappa Phi. Office: Shenandoah Valley Pain Clinic 109 Mactanly Pl Staunton VA 24401-2372

KLEIN, GAIL BETH MARANTZ, freelance writer, dog breeder; b. Bklyn., Dec. 1, 1946; d. Herbert and Florence (Dresner) Marantz; m. Harvey Leon Klein, Mar. 17, 1979. AB cum laude, U. Miami, Coral Gables, Fla., 1968, MEd, 1969, MBA, 1977. Cert. residential contractor, Fla. Asst. dir. student activities Miami-Dade Community Coll., 1969-79, instr. photography for mentally retarded adults, 1974, acting dir. student activities, 1976, acting advisor student publs., 1978-79, asst. prof. bus. adminstrn., 1979; dog breeder Vizcaya Shepherds, Palm Beach Gardens, Fla., 1979—; trainer Dog Obedience and Conformation Show Handling, West Palm Beach, 1980—; owner, CEO Word Master Profl. Comm.; freelance writer WordMaster Profl. Comms.; mgr. proposal devel., specialist Profl. Food-Svc. Mgmt., Inc.; cons., speaker in field; appeared on various radio talk shows. Editor (booklet) 1978 Consumers Guide to Banking, 1978, (newsletter) Newsletter of German Shepherd Dog Club Ft. Lauderdale, Inc., 1980-83, Sunshine State Shepherd, 1988-89; contbr. articles to newspapers and mags. Chair spl. events com. Third Century U.S.A., Dade County, Fla., 1976; mem. adv. com., mktg. cons. YWCA of Greater Miami, 1976-79; mem. comty. rels. com. Greater Miami Jewish Fedn., 1976-79; mem. Met. Miami Art Ctr., 1977-79; vice chair, chair appeals bd. Palm Beach County Animal Care and Control, 1989—, mem. pet overpopulation com., 1991-93; co-developer, co-adminstr. OFA Verifications for German Shepherd Dogs, 1985—; pub. info. coord. Am. Kennel Club, Palm Beach County, 1991-94. Recipient Job Training Partnership Act Employee of Yr. award State of Fla., 1994. Mem. Assn. Proposal Mgmt. Profls., Nat. Assn. Dog Obedience Instrs., Conformation Judges Assn. Fla., Inc., Palm Beach Users Group, Am. Sewing Guild, German Shepherd Dog Club Am., Inc. (hip dysplasia/orthopedic com. 1987-89), German Shepherd Dog Club of Can., Inc., German Shepherd Dog Club of Greater Miami (bd. dirs. 1981-82, 89-94, rec. sec. 1977-78, corr. sec. 1978-80, life), Jupiter-Tequesta Dog Club, Inc. (pres. 1984-85, bd. dirs., various other offices, Gaines Sportsmanship award 1993), Obedience Tng. Club Palm Beach County, Inc. (AKC Cmty. Achievement Merit award 1994), Wolf Song of Alaska (grant/proposal writer), Hadassah (life), Alpha Lambda Delta, Epsilon Tau Lambda, Phi Kappa Phi, Mortar Board. Republican. Jewish. Home: 12956 Mallard Creek Dr Palm Beach Gardens FL 33418

KLEIN, HARVEY ALLEN, clinical psychologist; b. Bronx, N.Y., Feb. 15, 1947; s. Sidney and Beatrice (Rauch) K.; m. Marilyn Penn; children: Michael, Jason, Jeffrey. BA, SUNY-Stony Brook, 1968; MS, St. John's U., 1970; PhD, U. Ga., 1972. Diplomate Am. Bd. Profl. Psychology. Psychologist I, Norristown State Hosp., Pa., 1972-73; asst. chief psychology svc. Bklyn. VA Outpatient Clinic, 1976-82, chief Day Treatment Ctr., 1975-82; pvt. practice psychology, S.I., N.Y., 1975-82, 85—; pvt. practice psychology, West Palm Beach, Fla., 1983—; cons. psychologist Parent Child Study Ctr., West Palm Beach, 1983—; cons. psychologist Western Palm Beach County Mental Health Clinic, Inc., 1987—, Nat Kahn Ctr. for children and family svcs., 1987—; psychologist Child and Family Therapy Assocs., Palm Beach Gardens, Fla., 1987-88; co-instr. course on attention deficit hyperactivity disorder devel. & treatment; cons. psychologist Glenheigh Hosp., 1988; vis. lectr. West Palm Beach Community Coll., Lake Worth, Fla., 1988—. Mem. APA, Children's Attention Deficit Disorders, Attention Deficit Disorders (adv. bd.), Fla. Psychol. Assn., Fla. Mental Health Assn., Assn. Clin. and Exptl. Neuropsychology (bd. dirs.), Phi Delta Kappa, Psi Chi. Home: 13133 Doubletree Cir West Palm Beach FL 33414-4038 Office: 1300 Corporate Center Way West Palm Beach FL 33414-8599

KLEIN, HARVEY LEON, engineering executive; b. Newark, Oct. 27, 1947; s. Arthur and Rosel (Lazarus) K.; m. Gail Beth Marantz, Mar. 17, 1979. BSME, Newark Coll. Engring., 1969. Cert. residential contr., Fla. Design engr. Pratt & Whitney, West Palm Beach, Fla., 1969-81, customer requirements engr., 1981-83, sr. design engr., 1983-86, mgr. conceptual design, 1986-93; mgr. tech. transfer and tng. program Pvt. Industry Coun., Inc., West Palm Beach, 1994; mgr. mech. engring. United Engrs., Inc., West Palm Beach, 1994—; lectr. in field. Contbr. articles to profl. jours.; patentee in field. Bd. dirs. Palm Beach Computer User Group, West Palm Beach, 1990-96. Newark Coll. Engring. scholar, 1966. Mem. ASME, Jupiter-Tequestra Dog Club (bd. dirs. 1974-96, Gaines Award for sportsmanship 1993, Pres.'s award 1991, 92, 94), German Shepherd Dog Club of Miami (pres., bd. dirs., life mem.), German Shepherd Dog Club of Am., German Shepherd Dog Club of Can., Fla. Assn. Kennel Clubs (v.p., del. 1989-95), Conformation Judges Assn. Fla., Pi tau Sigma, Tau Beta Pi. Home: 12956 Mallard Creek Dr Palm Beach Gardens FL 33418 Office: United Engineers Inc PO Box 109600 Beeline Hwy West Palm Beach FL 33410-9600

KLEIN, IRMA MOLLIGAN, career development educator, consultant; b. New Orleans, Jan. 5, 1936; d. Harry Joseph and Gesina Frances (Bauer) Molligan; m. John Vincent Chelena (dec. 1963); 1 child, Joseph William; m. Chris George Klein, Aug. 14, 1965. BS in Bus. Augustine Coll., postgrad. Mktg. Inst., Chgo., Loyola U., Chgo., Realtors Inst., Baton Rouge. Mgr. Stan Weber & Assocs., Metairie, La., 1971-75; tng. dir., 1975-81; cons. Coldwell Banker Comml. Co., New Orleans, 1981; dir. career devel. Coldwell Banker Residential Co., New Orleans, 1982-85; pres. Irma Klein Career Devel., Inc., Les Quarante Ecolieres, 1994-95; pres. Klein Enterprises, Inc., 1994—; instr. U. New Orleans, Bonnabel H.S., Realtors Inst., La. Real Estate Commn. Author: Career Development, 1982; Training Manual, 1978, Obtaining Listings, 1986, Participative Marketing, 1986, Marketing & Servicing Listings, 1987, Designing Training Curriculum, 1987, Participative Management. Active Friends of Longue Vue Gardens, La. Hist. Assn. Meml. Hall Found. Mem. La. Realtors Assn. (bd. dirs. 1973-74, grad. Realtors Inst. 1976), Jefferson Bd. Realtors (v.p. 1984), Edn. and Resources (cert., pres. La. chpt.), Rsch. Club of New Orleans (pres. 1984-85), Realtors Nat. Mktg. Inst. (amb. Tex. and La. 1985—, Outstanding Achievement award 1985, cert. broker 1980, residential specialist 1977), Nat. Assn. Realtors (nat. conv. speaker 1986), CRB (pres. La. chpt. 1982-83, chmn. edn.), CRS (pres. La. chpt. 1988-90), Forty Scholars Soc., Am. Dental Assts. Assn., Les Quarante Ecolieres. Republican. Roman Catholic. Clubs: Antique Study Group, Confederate Lit. (New Orleans) (pres.), Rsch. (New Orleans), Metairie Woman's. Avocation: antiques.

KLEIN, JERRY LEE, religion educator, minister; b. Walters, Okla., Oct. 25, 1947; s. Rudolf Anton and Mable Eula (Elliott) K.; m. Jane Ellen Keeth, Apr. 20, 1969; children: Jerry, Jr., John. AA, Cameron U., 1967; BA, Okla. Christian Univ. of Sci. and Arts, 1969; MA, Harding U., 1974; postgrad., N.Y. Inst., 1988-91. Instr. in Bible Henderson State Coll., Arkadelphia, Ark., 1970-71; pulpit minister Ch. of Christ, Comanche, Okla., 1971-75; instr. in Greek Prairie Hill Sch. of Bible, Comanche, 1974-75; pulpit minister Main St. Ch. of Christ, Lockney, Tex., 1975-82; prof. of religion Amarillo (Tex.) Coll., 1982-95, instr. part-time, 1995—; dir. Amarillo Bible Chair, 1982-94; min. Lawndale Ch. of Christ, Amarillo, Tex., 1995—; bible tchr. Caprock H.S., Amarillo, 1995—; edn. dir. Mountain Terrace Ch. of Christ, Memphis, Tenn., 1969-70, San Jacinto Ch. of Christ, Amarillo, 1984-89; campus coun. Amarillo Coll., 1982-94, chaplain, 1990-91; steering com. Amazing Grace Campaign, Amarillo, 1990. Author: Leadership in Christ, 1976, Leadership in Christ II, 1996, True Worship, 1995, (children's songs) Bible Teachers Mailbox, 1988; contbr. articles to religious jours. Dir. vols. Ark. Children's Colony, Arkadelphia, 1970-71; bd. dirs. VICA, Tascosa H.S., 1983-94; city chmn. Heart Fund and Kidney Found., Comanche, 1974-75; cubmaster Boy Scouts Am., Lockney, 1978-82; coach Little League Baseball, Lockney, 1978-82; mem. child welfare bd., Floyd County, Tex., 1980-82. Recipient spl. citation Ark. Children's Colony, 1971, certs. appreciation Tex. Dept. Health, 1982, Tex. Dept. Human Resources, 1983; named Favorite Prof. Bapt. Student Union, Amarillo Coll., 1989, 93. Mem. Soc. Bibl. Lit., Am. Acad. of Religion, Bibl. Archaeol. Soc., Lions (pres. Comanche chpt. 1974-75), Rotary, Kappa Chi (sponsor 1982-95). Republican. Home: 5614 Purdue St Amarillo TX 79109-5823 Office: Lawndale Ch of Christ 34th and Manhattan Amarillo TX 79120-0516

KLEIN, JOHN SHARPLESS, retired mathematics educator; b. Ossining, N.Y., Sept. 9, 1922; s. Edwin Benedict and Katharine Truman (Sharpless) K.; m. Nancy Deighton Wilkins, Aug. 24, 1963; children: Jeffrey, Carolyn Ann. BS, Haverford Coll., 1943; MS, MIT, 1949; PhD, U. Mich., 1959. Assoc. prof. Wilson Coll., Chambersburg, Pa., 1959-63, Monmouth Coll., West Long Branch, N.J., 1963-64; prof. math. Hobart & William Smith Colls., Geneva, N.Y, 1964-88. With USNR, 1943-45. Home: Apt 29A 1500 Bishop Estates Rd Jacksonville FL 32259

KLEIN, LINDA ANN, lawyer; b. N.Y.C., Nov. 7, 1959; d. Gerald Ira Klein and Sandra Florence (Kimmel) Fishman; m. Michael S. Neuren, Sept. 23, 1985. BA cum laude, Union Coll., 1980; JD, Washington & Lee U., 1983. Bar: Ga. 1983, D.C. 1984, U.S. Dist. Ct. (no. and mid. dist.) Ga. 1985, U.S. Ct. Appeals (11th cir.) 1986. Assoc. Nall & Miller, Atlanta, 1983-86, Martin, Cavan & Andersen, Atlanta, 1986-90; ptnr. Martin, Cavan & Andersen, 1990-93, Gambrell & Stolz, 1993—; instr. Nat. Ctr. Paralegal Tng., Atlanta, 1986. Mem. ABA (editor Trial Techniques newsletter 1989, vice-chmn. trial techniques com. 1989-90, chair elect 1990-91, chair 1991-92, vice chair Fidelity and Surety com. 1994—, mem. tort and ins. practice sect.), The State Bar of Ga. (mem. adv. com. legis. vice chair profl. liability com., chair study com. on rules of practice 1987—, evidence study com. 1989-90, atty.'s role in post conviction com. 1989—, bd. govs. 1989—, mem. exec. com. 1992—, sec. 1994-96, pres.-elect 1996—), Atlanta Bar Assn. (bd. dirs. Atlanta Coun. on Young Lawyers 1986-89, chair commn. on uniform rules of ct. 1986), Coun. of Superior Cts. Judges (ex-officio uniform rules com.), Internat. Bar Assn., Phi Alpha Delta, Pi Sigma Alpha.

KLEIN, MICHAEL EUGENE, art history educator; b. Phila., July 30, 1940; s. Daniel and Beatrice (Katz) K. BA, Rutgers Coll., 1962; MA, Columbia U., 1965, PhD, 1971. Lectr. Douglass Coll., New Brunswick, N.J., fall 1969; asst. prof. SUNY, Brockport, 1971-73, U. S.C., Columbia, 1973-77; asst. prof. art history Western Ky. U., Bowling Green, 1977-81, assoc. prof., 1981—; vis. curator Hirshhorn Mus. and Sculpture Garden, Smithsonian Instn., summer 1975. Contbr. articles to profl. jours., papers to confs. in field. Summer rsch. grantee U. S.C., summer 1975, Faculty rsch. grantee Western Ky. U., summer 1979, summer 1980; summer stipend NEH, Eng., 1980, Stanford U., 1979. Mem. Coll. Art Assn. Office: Dept Art Western Ky U Bowling Green KY 42101

KLEIN, MILTON MARTIN, history educator; b. N.Y.C., Aug. 15, 1917; s. Edward and Margaret (Greenfield) K.; m. Margaret Gordon, Aug. 25, 1963; children: Edward Gordon, Peter Gordon. B.S.S., CCNY, 1937, M.S. in Edn., 1939; Ph.D., Columbia U., 1954. Historian, USAAF, 1944-47; tchr. N.Y.C. pub. schs., 1947-57; vis. prof. Columbia U., summers 1959, 60, lectr. history, 1954-58; prof. history, chmn. dept. L.I. U., 1958-62, dean Coll. Liberal Arts and Sci., 1962-66; dean grad. studies and research SUNY-Fredonia, 1966-69; prof. history U. Tenn., 1969-84, alumni disting. service prof., 1977-84, Lindsay Young prof., 1980-84, prof. emeritus, 1984—, univ. historian, 1988—; Walter E. Meyer vis. prof. N.Y. U. Law Sch., 1976-77; chmn. Columbia U. Faculty Seminar on Early Am. History and Culture, 1971-72. Author: Social Studies for the Academically Talented Student, 1960, The Politics of Diversity: Essays in the History of Colonial New York, 1974, New York in the American Revolution: A Bibliography, 1974, The American Whig: William Livingston of New York, 1990, 93, Vol. Moments: Vignettes of the History the University of Tennesse, 1794-1994, 1994; also numerous articles; editor: Independent Reflector (William Livingston), 1963, A History of the American Colonies, 13 vols., 1973-86, New York-The Centennial Years, 1676-1976, 1976, Courts and Law in Early New York, 1978, The Twilight of British Rule in Revolutionary America: The New York Letter Book of General James Robertson, 1983; mem. editl. bd. Am. Jour. Legal History, 1970-76, N.Y. History, 1973—, Soundings, 1985—, U. Tenn. Press, 1972-75, Presidl. Studies Quar., 1992-96; adv. editor: Eighteenth-Century Studies, 1975-83, 93-95; adv. bd. America: History and Life, 1982—. Served to lt. col. USAF Res. Recipient Outstanding Teaching award U. Tenn. Alumni, 1974, Kerr History prize N.Y. State Hist. Assn., 1975, 92, Articles prize Am. Soc. 18th Century Studies, 1976; Fulbright lectr. U. Canterbury, Christchurch, N.Z., 1962; Ford Found. traveling fellow, 1955-56, Lilly Found.-Clements Libr. fellow, 1961; Am. Philos. Soc. grantee, 1973. Mem. Am. Hist. Assn., Orgn. Am. Historians, Am. Soc. 18th Century Studies (articles prize 1976), Southeastern Am. Soc. 18th Century Studies (dir. 1978-81, v.p. 1982-84, pres. 1984-85), AAUP (nat. council 1978-80), Am. Soc. Legal History (chmn. membership com. 1969-74, dir. 1971-76, 84-86, sec. 1975-77, v.p. 1978-80, pres. 1980-82), Am. Antiquarian Soc., Mass. Hist. Soc., Phi Beta Kappa, Sigma Alpha Mu, Phi Alpha Theta, Phi Kappa Phi, Omicron Delta Kappa, Golden Key. Home: 7103 Rotherwood Dr Knoxville TN 37919-7413

KLEIN, PETER WILLIAM, lawyer, corporate officer, investment company executive; b. Lorain, Ohio, Sept. 22, 1955; s. Warren Martin Klein and Barbara (Lesser) Pomeroy; m. Jennifer Lynn Ungers, Aug. 3, 1984. Student, U. Sussex, 1975-76; BA, Albion Coll., 1976; JD, Cleve. Marshall Coll. Law, 1981; LLM, NYU, 1982. Bar: Ohio 1981, Ill. 1984. Assoc. Guren, Merritt, Feibel, Sogg & Cohen, Cleve., 1982-84, Siegan, Barbakoff, Gomberg & Gordon, Ltd., Chgo., 1984-86; sr. v.p., mng. dir., gen. counsel Trivest Inc., Miami, Fla., 1986—. Mem. ABA (taxation sect., corp. sect., banking and bus. law). Home: 3618 Palmetto Ave Miami FL 33133-6221 Office: Trivest Inc 2665 S Bayshore Dr Ste 800 Miami FL 33133-5448

KLEIN, ROBERTA PHYLLIS, writer, editor, consultant; b. Columbus, Ohio, Dec. 26, 1934; m. Joseph Klein, Jan. 25, 1953; children: Kenneth, Wendy, Ronald, Karyn, Valerie. Attended U. Pitts., 1952-53, U. Miami, 1975-76. Exec. editor Fla. Designers Quar., Miami, 1978-83; editor-in-chief On Design mag., 1983-84; dir. Sunshine State Bank, South Miami, Fla., 1978-85; design writer Sunshine Mag., Ft. Lauderdale News/Sun Sentinel; former contbg. editor So. Accents Mag.; contbg. writer Restaurant Bus. Mag., 1987-91, stringer Money Mag., 1988; editor Fla. Real Estate Mag.; editor, writer Fla. Architecture Mag.; lectr. Purdue U., Ill., Inst. Bus. Designers, Am. Soc. Interior Designers. Contbr. to Fla. Design Mag., Architecture Mag., So. Fla. Bus., Jour., Archtl. Digest. Recipient Editl. awards Am. Soc. Interior Designers, Miami/Ft. Lauderdale, 1978, Inst. Bus. Designers, Fla. chpt., Miami, 1979, Interior Design Guild, Miami, 1981; Editl./Pictorial award AIA, Miami/Ft. Lauderdale chpt., 1980, Addy awards, 1977, Fla. Editl. award, 1989. Democrat. Jewish. Avocations: tennis, fishing, cooking, concerts, theatre. Office: 1111 Kane Concourse Ste 401 Bay Harbor Islands FL 33154

KLEIN, SALLY ROUNTREE, college educator; b. Savannah, Aug. 31, 1953; d. Edward Donald and Ann (Small) R.; m. Thomas Edward Klein, July 4, 1990; 1 stepchild, Karen. BS magna cum laude, East Tenn. State U., 1979; MS, Armstrong State Coll., 1985; EdS, Ga. So. U., 1989. Cert. in early childhood edn., middle sch. edn., edn. leadership, pharmacology. Pharmacology technician Lakeshore Mental Health Ctr., Knoxville, Tenn., 1973-76; tchr. sci. Savannah-Chatham Pub. Sch., 1980-86; asst. prin. Savannah-Chatham Pub. Schs., 1986-92; curriculum specialist Savannah-Chatham Pub. Sch., 1992-95; instr. Savannah Tech. Inst., 1995—. Author: The Oldest Tree in the Forest, 1992; editor: Tenacity in Adversity, 1993; editor, writer: Introduction to Continuous Quality Improvement, 1994. Active Savannah chpt. Am. Mensa, Ltd., 1984—, gifted children's coord., 1985-88. Named Chatham County Tchr. of Yr., 1983, Ga. Mid. Sch. Sci. Tchr. of Yr., 1985. Office: Savannah Tech Inst Savannah GA 31405

KLEIN, SCOTT RICHARD, acting and directing educator; b. Aberdeen, S.D., June 2, 1959; s. Richard Lewis and Jalois Mae (Janish) K.; m. Alecia Atwell, 1994. BA, Gustavus Adolphus Coll., 1981; MFA, Mankato State U., 1983. Actor, tchr. Ark. Arts Ctr., Little Rock, 1983-84; assoc. dir. Permian Playhouse, Odessa, Tex., 1984-89; instr. acting/directing, coach Cameron U., Lawton, Okla., 1989-92, asst. prof., 1992—, chmn., 1994—. Dir. plays including Echoes, 1983, Vanities,1985, A.B.C., 1986, Wiley and the Hairy Man, 1988, Night of January 16th, 1988, The Foreigner, 1989, The Barber of Seville, 1991, The Lion in Winter, 1992, Seascape, 1993; appeared in plays The Glass Menagerie, 1989, Anything Goes, 1989, A Funny Thing Happened, 1989, Charley's Aunt, 1986, The Crucible, 1991, Christopher Columbus: The Gypsy's Fortune, 1992; comml. for Kent Kwik, 1987 (Addy award). Rep., United Way, Lawton, 1989—; pres. S.W. Okla. Opera Guild, 1995—, bd. dirs. 1994—. Recipient Best Dir. award Kaleidoscope Co., 1988, Alpha Psi Omega, 1990, Outstanding Rsch. Performance, C.U. Sch. Fine Arts, 1994. Mem. Tex. Non-Profit Theatres (cons. 1984—, adjudicator 1995), Assn. Theatre in Higher Edn., S.W. Theatre Assn., Okla. Cmty. Theatre Assn., S.W. Okla. Opera Guild, 1994— (pres. 1995-96), Arts for All, Inc., Phi Kappa Phi. Home: 717 NW 36th St Lawton OK 73505 Office: Cameron Univ 2800 W Gore Blvd Lawton OK 73505-6320

KLEINBERG, HOWARD J., newspaper columnist; b. N.Y.C., Oct. 23, 1932; s. Benjamin and Ruth (Wile) K.; m. Natalie Bernstein, Feb. 22, 1953; children: Linda Kleinberg Landy, Eliot, Eileen Kleinberg Newmark, David. Student pub. schs. Mem. staff Miami (Fla.) News, 1950-65, 66-88, mng. editor, 1968-76, editor, 1976-88; nat. columnist Cox Newspapers, Miami, 1988—; history columnist Miami Herald, 1989—; pub. relations exec. Hank Meyer Assocs., Miami, 1965-66. Author: Miami, The Way We Were, 1985, The Great Florida Hurricane and Disaster, 1993, Miami Beach, A History, 1994. Mem. Orange Bowl Com. Served with AUS, 1953-55, Korea. Recipient 1st pl. award Fla. Edn. Assn., 1985, Miami Urban League Black Awareness award, 1975, 1st pl. awards for column writing, Cox Newspapers, 1987, 88.

KLEINFELD, DENIS A., lawyer; b. Chgo., Feb. 10, 1946; s. J. Laurence and Helen Kleinfeld; m. June Kleinfeld; children: Harrison, Jaclene. BS Accountancy, U. Ill., 1967; JD, Loyola U., Chgo., 1970. CPA; Bar: Ill., 1970, Fla., 1983. Atty. IRS, Chgo., 1970-74, Denis Kleinfeld & Assocs., Chgo., 1974-83, Kleinfeld & Assocs., Miami, Fla., 1983—; exec. com. Offshore Inst., Isle of Man, 1993-96; chmn. Soc. Trust and Estate, Inc., Miami, 1994-96; bd. dirs. Estate Planning Coun. of Greater Miami. Co-author: Practical International Tax Planning, 1995, Estate Planning for Florida Resident, 1994; author: Asset Protection Report, 1996; contbr. articles to profl. jours. Mem. Internat. Tax Planning Assn., Internat. Fiscal Assn., Soc. Trust and Estate Practitioners, Fla. Bar Assn., Ill. Bar Assn., Am. Assn. Attys.-CPAs, Fla. Soc. CPAs. Office: Kleinfeld & Giacosa LLP Ste 1940 One SE 3d Ave Miami FL 33131

KLEINKORT, JOSEPH ALEXIUS, physical therapist, consultant; b. Bronxville, N.Y., Jan. 28, 1946; s. Joseph P. and Marie C. (Richter) K.; m. Kathleen J. Kleinkort, Oct. 3, 1953; children: Pat, Mike, Kelly, Kristin, Kevin. BS in Phys. Therapy, St. Louis U., 1968; MA in Psychology, Ball State U., 1977; PhD (hon.), Medicina Alternativa, Copenhagen, 1983. Registered safety dir. World Safety Orgn. Dir. phys. therapy Phys. Therapy, Inc., Ft. Lauderdale, Fla., 1970-72; commd. officer USAF, 1972; dir. phys. therapy USAF Hosp.-Barksdale, Bossier City, La., 1972-74, USAF Hosp.-Torrejone, Madrid, 1974-78; asst. dir. Wilford Hall Med. Ctr., San Antonio, 1980-83; res. at rank of maj. USAF, 1983; pres. Chronic Pain Assn., Inc., San Antonio, 1983-88; exec. dir. Ft. Worth Back Inst., 1988-90; pres. Joseph A. Kleinkort, P.C., Roanoke, Tex., 1983—; exec. v.p. Worksteps Internat., 1996, sr. v.p., 1995—; cons. Dynatronics Corp., Salt Lake City, 1985—; bd. dirs. Magnetherapy, Inc., Seraph Found. Author: (book) Therapeutic Medical Devices, 1983, Thermal Agents Rehabilitation ; 1985, laser Application Technology, 1986. Precinct judge, San Antonio, 1988; bd. dirs.

Arlington Philharm. Symphony, 1993-94. Recipient Alumni Merit award St. Louis U., 1983; named Outstanding Phys. Therapist of Tex., Tex. Phys. Therapy Bd., 1985. Fellow Am. Coll. Orthopedics (membership sec. 1988-90), mem. Internat. soc. Lasers in Medicine and Sci., Am. Assn. Phys. Medicine and Rehab., Am. Phys. Therapy Assn., Tex. Phys. Therapy Assn. Home and Office: 303 Inverness Dr Roanoke TX 76262-8724

KLEINLEIN, KATHY LYNN, training and development executive; b. S.I., N.Y., May 2, 1950; d. Thomas and Helen Mary (O'Reilly) Perricone; m. Kenneth Robert Kleinlein, Oct. 30, 1983. BA, Wagner Coll., 1971, MA, 1974; MBA, Rutgers U., 1984. Cert. secondary tchr., N.Y., N.J., Fla. Tchr. English, N.Y.C. Bd. Edn., S.I., 1971-74, Matawan (N.J.) Bd. Edn., 1974-79; instr. English, Middlesex County Coll., Edison, N.J., 1978-81; med. sales rep. Pfizer/Roerig, Bklyn., 1979-81, mgr. tng. ops., N.Y.C., 1981-87; dir. sales tng. Winthrop Pharms. div. Sterling Drug, N.Y.C., 1987-88; dir. tng. Reuters Info. Systems, N.Y.C., 1988—; pres., dir. tng., Women in Transition, career counseling firm; pres. Kleinlein Cons.; pers. mgmt. officer U.S. Army Res., N.J., 1981-86; cons. Concepts & Producers, N.Y.C., 1981-85. Trainer United Way, 1982-83, mem. polit. action com., 1982—; mem. Rep. Presdl. Task Force, Washington, 1983—; mem. Sarasota Library Adv. Bd.; sec. Intracoastal Civic Assn.; elected com. mem. Epiphany Parish Coun.; exec. bd. Selby Found. Edn. Capt. U.S. Army, 1974-78. First woman in N.Y. N.G., 1974; first woman instr. Empire State Mil. Acad., Peekskill, N.Y., 1976. Mem. Rep. Women's Club, Alpha Omicron Pi. Republican. Roman Catholic. Home: 1840 Hudson St Englewood FL 34223-6433 Office: Kleinlein Cons 1840 Hudson St Englewood FL 34223-6433

KLEINMAN, GARY E., obstetrician, maternal-fetal specialist, educator; b. Jerusalem, Israel, Feb. 20, 1951; came to U.S., 1952; s. Henry and Dora (Wainshal) K.; m. Sherry Richman, Dec. 8, 1979; 1 child, Harold Solomon. BS in Biology, SUNY, Stony Brook, 1973; MD, Creighton U., 1977. Diplomate, Am. Bd. Ob-Gyn. Resident in ob-gyn. Georgetown U., Washington, 1977-81; maternal-fetal medicine fellow UCLA, 1981-83; perinatologist Kaiser Permanente Med. Ctr., San Francisco, 1983-85; dir. perinatology Fla. Coll. Med., Pensacola, 1985-90; instr. dept Ob-Gyn, pediatrics UCLA, 1990-91; fellow med genetics Harbor-UCLA Med Ctr., Torrance, 1990-91; acad. faculty asst. prof. UCLA, 1991-93; asst. adj. prof. dept. ob-gyn., UCLA, 1982-83; asst. clin. prof. dept. ob-gyn. and reproductive scis., U. Calif., San Francisco, 1984-85. Contbr. articles to profl. jours., chpt. on diabetes in pregnancy to med. book. Fellow Am. Coll. Ob-Gyn., Am. Coll. Med. Genetics, Am. Insts. of Ultrasound in Med., ; mem. Soc. Perinatal Obstetricians, Am. Soc. of Human Genetics, Fla. Obstetric and Gyn. Soc.,. Jewish. Office: U Fla Coll Med 5045 Carpenter Creek Rd Pensacola FL 03250

KLEINMAN, SUE, artist; b. N.Y.C., Nov. 12; d. Adolph and Sabina (Teitelbaum) Augustine; m. Samuel J. Kleinman (dec. Dec. 1985). BFA, Pratt Inst.; postgrad., Caton Rose Inst. Art, New Sch. Social Rsch.; pvt. studies with prominent artists, N.Y.C. docent Mus. of Art, Ft. Lauderdale, Fla., 1973—; lectr. in field. Exhibited oils Crown Gallery, N.Y.C., 1962, Ctr. Art Gallery, N.Y.C., 1969-72, Lord & Taylor Gallery, N.Y.C., 1973; one-woman shows include Pompano (Fla.) Pub. Libr., 1993, Contextual Gallery, Ft. Lauderdale, 1980; represented in permanent collections at Fairleigh Dickinson Coll., Rutherford, N.J., Maimonides Hosp., Bklyn., Brown U., Providence. Guide docent program Broward Art Guild, 1974; pres. Bklyn. Hebrew Home and Hosp. for Aged, 1963-65; mem. nat. planning com. Nat. Multiple Sclerosis Soc., 1971-74; v.p. spl. events Brandeis U. NWC, 1974—, v.p. nat. com.; bd. dirs. Am. Cancer Soc., Met. Geriatric Ctr., United Jewish Appeal, chmn. Queens divsn., 1960-63; exec. com. Pompano Rep. Com.; v.p. B'nai B'rith; founder Women's Am. ORT, 1980. Recipient Bronze medal Village Art Ctr., 1958, Hon. Mention award Rockport Art Assn., 1960, Silver medal Trade Bank N.Y. Mem. Artists Equity Assn., Nat. Women's Art Assn., Kew Forest Art Assn. (chmn. membership com. 1954-58, treas. 1958-60), PAN (del.).

KLEINMANN, RICHARD ECKERT, endocrinologist; b. Cleve., Dec. 1, 1947; s. Mortimer Valentine and Joan (Gerdy) K.; m. Linda Roseva Brown, May 1, 1976; children: Rebecca Linda, Joan Frances. BA magna cum laude, U. Pa., 1969, MD, 1973. Diplomate Am. Bd. Internal Medicine, Am. Bd. Endocrinology. Intern SUNY, Upstate Med. Ctr., Syracuse, 1973-74, resident, 1974-76; fellow in endocrinology U. Mass. Med. Sch., 1978-80; instr. in medicine Boston U. Sch. Medicine, 1976-78; instr. in medicine to asst. prof. medicine U. Mass. Med. Sch., 1978-81; asst. prof. of medicine to assoc. prof. medicine W.Va. U. Sch. of Medicine, 1981-88; clin. asst. prof. to clin. assoc. prof. medicine U. N.C. Sch. Medicine, 1988—; chief endorcine sect. Charlotte Meml. Hosp., 1992-95; co-dir. Nalle Clinic Diabetes Ctr., 1988—; physician dept. of endocrinology Nalle Clinic, Charlotte; med. staff Charleston Area Med. Ctr., 1981-88, Carolinas Med. Ctr., Charlotte, N.C., 1988—, Presbyn. Hosp., Charlotte, 1988—; cons. staff Mercy Hosp., Charlotte, 1988—; bd. dirs. Diabetes Svcs. Divsn. of Charlotte Community Health Svcs.; lectr. in field. Manuscript reviewer Jour. of Clin. Endocrinology and Metabolism; contbr. numerous articles to profl. jours. Fellow ACP, Am. Coll. Endocrinology; mem. Am. Diabetes Assn. The Endocrine Soc., N.C. Med. Soc., Am. Assn. Clin. Endocrinologists, Phi Beta Kappa. Office: Nalle Clinic 1918 Randolph Rd Charlotte NC 28207-2134

KLEINSORGE, WILLIAM PETER, metallurgical engineer; b. San Francisco, Feb. 10, 1941; s. William P. Kleinsorge; m. Kathryn Deane Vincent, Nov. 14, 1966; children—Elizabeth Louise, Victoria Anne. B.S. in Metall. Engring., U. Nev.-Reno, 1964. Registered profl. engr., S.C., Calif. Welding engr. Mare Island Naval Shipyard, Vallejo, Calif., 1965-69, Charleston-Naval Shipyard, 1969-70; supervisory welding engr. U.S. Naval Ship Repair Facility, Republic of the Philippines, Subic Bay, 1970-72; head welding engr. Charleston Naval Shipyard, 72-79; metall. engr. U.S. Nuclear Regulatory Commn., Atlanta, 1979—; cons. in field. Served with U.S. Army N.G., 1965-72. Mem. Am. Soc. Metals, Am. Welding Soc., Am. Soc. Mil., Engrs. Lodge: Mason.

KLEMM, WILLIAM ROBERT, scientist, educator; b. South Bend, Ind., July 24, 1934; s. Lincoln W. and Helen (DeLong) K.; m. Doris Isabell Mewha, Aug. 27, 1957; children: Mark, Laura. DVM, Auburn (Ala.) U., 1958; PhD, Notre Dame (Ind.) U., 1963. Assoc. prof. dept. physiology and pharmacology Iowa State U., Ames, 1963-66; interim head, prof. dept. biology Tex. A&M U., College Station, 1966-80, prof. dept. vet. anatomy and pub. health, 1980—; mobilization augmentee Human Systems Div. USAF, San Antonio, 1981-89. Author: Animal Electroencephalography, 1969, Science, The Brain & Our Future, 1969; editor: Discovery Processes in Modern Biology, 1977, Brainstem Mechanisms of Behavior, 1990, Understanding Neuroscience, 1995. Capt. USAF, 1958-60, Col. Res. ret. Mem. Soc. for Neurosic., Forum Enterprises, Inc. (pres.), Sigma Xi (pres. Tex. A&M U. chpt. 1990-91). Republican. Presbyterian. Office: Tex A&M U Dept Vet Anatomy/Pub Health College Station TX 77843

KLEPPER, ROBERT KENNETH, writer, journalist; b. Springfield, Mo., Nov. 11, 1966; s. Kenneth Herbert and Altha Ann (Shumate) K. Reference asst. Pensacola (Fla.) Pub. Libr., 1983-84; office worker Pensacola Tax Collector Office, 1984-85; purchasing agt. asst. Gen. Oceanics, Miami, 1992-93; historian, writer various publs., 1993-96; reviewer books and videos relating to silent era The Silents Majority Internet Website, 1996—; dist. historian FBLA, 1983-84, pres., 1984-85; mem. Pensacola State Exec. Coun. Author: Silent Films on Video, 1996, contbr. articles to jours., 1995-96. Vol. receptionist Escambia AIDS Svcs., Pensacola, 1994-95; mem. Silent Film Soc., Atlanta, 1994-95; sec. ACLU N.W. Fla, 1988; vol. worker Lois Benson for Congress, Pensacola, 1995. Named Outstanding Dist. Pres., Fla. state chpt. FBLA, 1985. Mem. W. Fla. Literary Fedn., Friends of Marion Davies Fan Club, The Silents Majority Classic Film Fan Club. Home: 1500 North 65th Avenue #3 Pensacola FL 32506-3917

KLEWANS, SAMUEL N., lawyer; b. Lock Haven, Pa., Mar. 2, 1941; s. Morris and Ruth N. K.; children: Richard Bennett, Ruth Elise, Paul Henry, Meg Ilene. A.B., U. Pa., 1963; J.D., Am. U., 1966. Bar: Va. 1966, U.S. Dist. Ct. (ea. dist.) Va. 1966, U.S. Dist. Ct. D.C. 1967, U.S. Ct. Appeals D.C. 1967, U.S. Ct. Appeals (4th cir.) 1967, U.S. Supreme Ct. 1971. Law clk., U.S. Dist. Ct. Ea. Dist. Va. 1966-67; ptnr. Fried, Fried & Klewans, Springfield, Va., 1970-86; prin. Klewans & Assocs., 1986-91, Grad, Logan & Klewans, 1991—; lectr. No. Va. Inst. Continuing Med. Edn., No. Va. Ctr. Quality and Health Edn. Served to 1st lt. JAGC-USAR, 1966-72. Mem. Fairfax County Bar Assn. (ethics and grievance com. 1971-72, mem. 75-76, courts com. 1975-76; jud. selection com. 1979-82, chmn. 1981-82), Va. State Bar (mem. disciplinary bd. 1976-84, vice chmn. 1982-83, chmn. 1983-84, lectr. continuing legal edn.), Practice Resource Group (lectr.), Professionalism Faculty. Office: 112 N Columbus St Alexandria VA 22314-3013

KLEY, JOHN ARTHUR, banker; b. Jericho, N.Y., Oct. 24, 1921; s. John and Annie (Upton) K.; m. Florence Elizabeth Cannon, Sept. 1, 1945 (dec. Apr. 1983); 1 dau., Martha Anne; m. Edna C. Dornhoefer, June 1984 (div. June 1987); m. Lorelei W. Lasecki. Apr. 1989. Grad., Stonier Grad. Sch. Banking, Rutgers U., 1952; B.P.S., Pace U., 1974. With Washington Irving Trust Co. (and successor County Trust Co.), White Plains, N.Y., 1937-76; asst. treas., asst. v.p., v.p. Washington Irving Trust Co. (and successor County Trust Co.), 1947-57, exec. v.p., 1957-60, pres., 1960-72, chmn. bd., 1972-76; v.p. Bank N.Y. Co., 1968-74, vice chmn., 1974-77; dir. Bank of N.Y., 1973-77. Past chmn. bd. trustees, trustee emeritus Westchester Community Coll.; past pres., chmn. Westchester Community Coll. Found.; past pres. Legal Aid Soc. West County; past chmn. bd. regents Stonier Grad. Sch. Banking, Rutgers U. Served from pvt. to maj. USAAF, 1942-46; lt. col. Res. Recipient Leffingwell medal, 1960. Mem. ABA (com. on mechanization of check handling, chmn. tech. com. 1954-64, N.Y. State Bankers Assn. (pres. 1969-70, The Pelican Bay Club (Naples, Fla.), Imperial Golf Club (Naples), Whippoorwill Club (Armonk, N.Y.). Episcopalian. Home: Apt 303 7515 Pelican Bay Blvd Naples FL 34108-6519

KLICH, MAREN ALICE, mycologist; b. Chgo., Apr. 12, 1952; d. Roger Harry and Dorothy Bessie Klich; m. Edward Joseph Mullaney, Apr. 29, 1989; 1 child, Gwen. BA in Biology and Psychology, St. Olaf Coll., 1974; MS in Botany, Iowa State U., 1978, PhD in Botany, 1980. Rsch. microbiologist So. Regional Rsch. Ctr. USDA-Agr. Rsch Svc., New Orleans, 80—; vis. scientist Commonwealth Sci. and Indsl. Rsch. Orgn., Australia, 1987. Author: A Laboratory Guide to the Common Aspergillus Species and Their Teleomorphs, 1988, Aspergillus: Biology and Industrial Applications, 1992; contbr. articles to profl. jours., chpts. to books. Mem. Mycol. Soc. Am., Am. Phytopathological Soc., Am. Soc. for Microbiology, Sigma Xi (chpt. sec. 1994). Lutheran. Office: USDA-Agr Rsch Svc So Regional Rsch Ctr 1100 Robert E Lee Blvd New Orleans LA 70124-4305

KLIESCH, WILLIAM FRANK, physician; b. Franklinton, La., Nov. 4, 1928; s. Edward Granville and Elsie Jeni (Sylvest) K.; m. May Virginia Reid, Dec. 17, 1955; children: Thomas Karl, William August, John Francis. BS, La. State U., 1949, MD, 1953. Intern Valley Forge Hosp., Phoenixville, Pa., 1953-54; intern in med. rsch. Charity Hosp., New Orleans, 1956-57; resident, fellow in internal medicine Ochsner Found. Hosp., New Orleans, 1957-59; pvt. practice New Orleans, 1959-69, Jackson, Miss., 1969—; dir. spinal injury svc. Miss. Meth. Rehab. Ctr., Jackson, 1980—. Capt. U.S Air Force, 1953-56. Fellow Am. Coll. Emergency Physicians; mem. Am. Spinal Injury Assn., Internat. Paraplegia Soc. Episcopalian. Home: 8892 Gary Rd Jackson MS 39212-9732 Office: Miss State Hosp Whitfield MS 39193

KLIEWER, KENNETH LEE, computational scientist, research administrator; b. Mountain Lake, Minn., Dec. 31, 1935; s. Henry Gerhard and Susan (Epp) K.; m. Kathleen Kay Zimmermann, Aug. 30, 1959; children—Steven Anthony, Lisa Jo, Christopher Lee. B.S. in Elec. Engring., U. Minn., 1957, M.S.E.E., 1959; Ph.D. in Physics, U. Ill., 1964. Asst. prof., assoc. prof., prof. dept. physics Iowa State U., Ames, 1963-81; assoc. physicist, physicist, sr. physicist Ames Lab.-Dept. Energy, 1963-81, program dir. solid state physics, 1974-78, assoc. dir. sci. and tech., 1978-81; assoc. lab. dir. for phys. research Argonne (Ill.) Nat. Lab., 1981-86, dir. advanced photon source design project, 1983-86; dean Sch. Sci. Purdue U., West Lafayette, Ind., 1986-91; asst. v.p. for rsch., 1991-92; dir. ctr. computational scis. Oak Ridge (Tenn.) Nat. Lab., 1992—; guest prof. U. Hamburg and Deutsches Electronen Synchrotron (DESY), Fed. Republic Germany, 1972-73, Free U. Berlin, 1974, Fritz Haber Inst., Berlin, 1975; vis. scientist Rockwell Internat. Sci. Ctr., Thousand Oaks, Calif., 1976; temporary program officer Dept. Energy, Washington, 1979-80; cons. Lester B. Knight & Assocs., Phys. Optics Corp., Argonne Nat. Lab.; mem. fusion policy adv. com. Dept. Energy, 1990-91. Editor: (with others) Non-Traditional Approaches to the Study of the Solid-Electrolyte Interface, 1980; contbr. articles to profl. jours. Illini fellow U. Ill., 1959-61; U.S. Steel Found. fellow, 1961-63. Fellow Am. Phys. Soc. (exec. com. div. condensed matter physics 1980-82), AAAS, Sigma Xi, Eta Kappa Nu, Tau Beta Pi. Home: 165 Whippoorwill Dr Oak Ridge TN 37830-8646

KLIMACK, WILLIAM KLAEVE, army officer; b. N.Y.C., Jan. 3, 1957; s. Emil William and Viola Valentine (Hall) K. BSChemE, Lehigh U., 1979; MS in Applied Math., Johns Hopkins U., 1990; M Mil. Arts and Sci., U.S. Army Command-Staff Coll., 1991; postgrad., USAF Inst. Tech., Wright-Patterson AFB, Ohio, 1996—. Commd. 2d lt. U.S. Army, 1979, advanced through grades to lt. col., 1995; platoon leader 2d Bn., 58th Infantry, Ft. Hood, Tex., 1979-81; exec. officer HHC, 2d Brigade, 2d. Infantry Div., Republic of Korea, 1981-82; ops. officer XVIII Airborne Corps, Ft. Bragg, N.C., 1983-84; co. comdr. Co. A, 1st Bn., 325 Airborne Infantry, Ft. Bragg, 1984-86; ops. rsch. analyst Army Materiel Systems Analysis Network, Aberdeen Proving Ground, Md., 1986-90; ops. officer 4th Bn., 17th Infantry, Ft. Ord, Calif., 1991-92; aide-de-camp to Lt. Gen. Ebbesen 2d Army, Atlanta, 1992-93; dep. chief, ops. asst. chief of staff 101st Airborne Divsn. (Air Assault), Ft. Campbell, Ky., 1993-94; chief ops. divsn., asst. chief of staff G3 101st Airborne Divsn. (Air Assault), Ft. Campbell, Ky., 1994; exec. officer 1st Brigade, 101st Airborne Divsn. (Air Assault), Ft. Campbell, 1994-95; chief staff US Forces, Haiti, 1995-96; mem. UN Mission in Haiti, 1995-96. Assoc. editor NSS News mag., 1987—. Fellow Explorers Club, Royal Geog. Soc.; mem. AIChE, NSPE, Am. Chem. Soc., Nat. Speleological Soc. (dir. Mt. Rainier Steam Caves study project, vol. Nat. Park Svc., membership com. 1984—), Internat. Glaciospeleological Survey, British Cave Rsch. Assn., Army-Navy Club. Lutheran. Home: 6303 Ashley Meadows Ct Dayton OH 45424-4862 Office: AFIT/ENS 29 P St Wright Patterson AFB OH 45433

KLIMCZUK, STEPHEN JOHN, business executive, foundation director; b. North Hollywood, Calif., Jan. 14, 1963; s. Leon and Wanda (Kotowicz) K.; m. Iris C.B. Massion, Sept. 6, 1991; children: Caroline, Julia. BA in Econs., UCLA, 1983; MBA, Harvard U., 1987. Assoc. cons. Bain & Co., Palo Alto, Calif., 1983-84; fin. analyst John Nuveen & Co. Inc., San Francisco, 1984-85; assoc. Goldman, Sachs & Co., N.Y.C., 1987-88; mgr. Nat. Review Inc., N.Y.C., 1988-89; dir., mem. bd. World Economic Forum, Geneva, 1989-95; dep. dir. global bus. policy coun. A.T. Kearney, Inc., Alexandria, Va., 1996—; mng. dir. World Link Publs. S.A., Geneva, 1991-92. Recipient Cavaliere, S.M.O. Constantiniano di San Giorgio, 1987; named officer Most Venerable Order of St. John, 1994; invested Knight of Malta, 1996. Fellow Royal Soc. Arts (London), Salzburg Seminar; mem. New Atlantic Initiative (founder), Harvard Club of N.Y.C. Roman Catholic. Home: 9801 Georgetown Pike Great Falls VA 22066 Office: 225 Reinekers Ln Alexandria VA 22314

KLINE, ALLEN HABER, pediatrician; b. Houston, May 2, 1931; s. Harry J. and Adrienne H. (Fibush) K.; m. Maude Rose Brown, June 14, 1953; children: Allen Jr., Glenn. Student, U. Tex., 1951; MD, Baylor U., 1955. Pediatric intern Johns Hopkins Hosp., Balt., 1955-56, pediatric resident, 1956-57; staff pediatrician U.S. Naval Hosp., Jacksonville, Fla., 1957-59; chief resident in pediatrics Tex. Children's Hosp., Houston, 1959-60; pvt. practice Houston, 1960—; clin. assoc. prof. pediatrics Coll. Medicine, Baylor U., 1960—. Contbr. articles to profl. jours. Lt. USN, 1957-59. Recipient 2d prize essay contest Am. Coll. Chest Physicians, 1955. Fellow Am. Acad. Pediatrics; mem. Tex. Pediatric Soc., Ambulatory Pediatric Assn., So. Med. Assn., Acad. Sports Medicine. Home: 517 Flintdale Rd Houston TX 77024-5105 Office: 3838 Hillcroft St Houston TX 77057-7707

KLINE, ALLEN HABER, JR., lawyer; b. Houston, June 17, 1954; s. Allen H. Sr. and Maude Rose (Brown) K.; m. Barbara Ann Byrd, July 24, 1982; children: Allison Ashley, Allen III. BA, U. Denver, 1976; JD, U. Miami, 1979. Bar: Tex. 1980, U.S. Dist. Ct. (so. dist.) Tex. 1980, U.S. Ct. Appeals (5th cir.) 1980, U.S. Ct. Appeals (11th cir.) 1983, U.S. Supreme Ct. 1985; bd. cert. personal injury trial law Tex. Bd. Legal Specialization. Sole practice Houston, 1980—. Mem. Houston Bar Assn., Coll. of the State Bar of Tex. Club: City Wide (Houston) (life). Office: Ste 2120 440 Louisiana St Ste 2120 Houston TX 77002-1636

KLINE, CHARLES C., lawyer; b. York, Pa., Jan. 12, 1946; s. Charles Henry and Julia (Jacob) K.; m. Laura Gray, June 8, 1968; children: Charles Reid, Johanna Gray. BBA in Finance, U. Miami, 1968, JD cum laude, 1971. Bar: Fla. 1971, Maine 1974, U.S. Dist. Ct. (so., mid. and no. dists.) Fla. 1974, U.S. Ct. Appeals (11th cir.) 1974, U.S. Supreme Ct. 1974, U.S. Ct. Claims 1974. From ptnr. to mng. ptnr. Mershon, Sawyer, Johnston, Dunwoody & Cole, Miami, Fla., 1971-88; exec. ptnr. White & Case, Miami, 1988—. Editor-in chief U. Miami Law Rev., 1971; contbr. articles to law revs. With USMCR, 1969-71, USCGR, 1971-75; Bd. dirs. U.S. Sailing Assn., 1989. Mem. Phi Kappa Phi, Omicron Delta Kappa. Republican. Congregationalist. Office: White & Case 1st Financial CtR 200 S Biscayne Blvd Miami FL 33131-2351*

KLINE, DAVID ADAM, lawyer, educator, writer; b. Keota, Okla., Sept. 27, 1923; s. David Adam and Lucy Leila (Wood) K.; m. Ruthela Deal, Aug. 25, 1947; children: Steven, Timothy, Ruthanna. Student Oklahoma City U., 1945-47; JD, Okla. U., 1950. Bar: Okla. 1949. Law clk., spl. master U.S. Dist. Ct., Okla., 1952-61; 1st asst. U.S. atty. Western Dist. Okla., 1961-69; judge Western Dist. Okla., U.S. Bankruptcy Ct., Oklahoma City, 1969-82; sr. shareholder Kline & Kline, Oklahoma City, 1983—; mem. arbitration panel program U.S. Dist. Ct. (we. dist.) Okla., 1985— mem. faculty Fed. Jud. Ctr., Washington, Nat. Seminar Bankruptcy Judges, 1971-86; adj. prof. law Oklahoma City U., 1980-84; cons. Norton Bankruptcy Law and Practice, 1986, Callaghan & Co. Bd. editors Okla. Law Rev.; Digest editor Am. Bankruptcy Law jour., 1974-77; contbg. author Digest Cowans Bankruptcy Law and Practice, 1983, interim and 1986 edit.; contbg. co-writer Briefcase, 1988—, A Little Book (A New Thing in the Earth), 1993, A Little Book II (The Blood of the Lion), 1995. Office: Kline & Kline 720 NE 63rd St Oklahoma City OK 73105-6438

KLINE, DENNY LEE, hazardous devices and explosives consultant; b. Boston, Jan. 31, 1939; s. Francis Marion and Sylvia Lee (Denny) K.; m. Sadie Mae Thompson, June 14, 1963; 1 child, Hank Von. Student, Vanderbilt U., 1957-58, Mid. Ga. Coll., 1959-61; BS, Ga. So. Coll., 1963; M. Forensic Sci., George WashingtonU., 1981. Cert. explosives and hazardous devices specialist. Tchr., coach football Harlem (Ga.) High Sch., 1963-65; tchr., coach Butler High Sch., Augusta, Ga., 1966-69; spl. agt., supr. FBI, Newark, 1970-76; supr.-examiner lab. explosives unit FBI, Washington, 1976-88; faculty instr. forensic sci. tng. and rsch. unit FBI Acad., Quantico, Va., 1988-90; pres., chief exec. officer ETA Consultants, Inc., Stafford, Va., 1990—; cons. Nuclear Diagnostic Sys., Inc., Lorton, Va., 1991-93; cons., v.p. Gen. Nucleonics, Tucson, 1994; course dir. anti-terrist assistance U.S. Dept. State, Baton, Rouge, 1990—; mem. exch. faculty Police Staff Coll., Bramshill, Eng., 1989; bomb technician FBI Hazardous Devices sch., Huntsville, Ala., 1976—; spl. investigator background investigation contract svcs. program FBI, 1995—. Contbr. articles to profl. jours. Mem. Internat. Assn. Bomb Technicians and Investigators, Am. Soc. for Indsl. Security, Internat. Assn. Chiefs of Police, Assn. Former Spl. Agts. of the FBI. Episcopalian. Office: ETA Cons Inc 1335 Aquia Dr Stafford VA 22554-2037

KLINE, GEORGE WILLIAM, II, television producer; b. San Antonio, July 5, 1949; s. Robert Walter and Adelaide McCall (Carter) K.; m. Kristin Scheffey, Mar. 5, 1977; children: Amanda Dupree, George William III, Luke Carter. BA, Austin Coll., 1971. Road mgr. Kris Kristofferson, N.Y.C., 1971-73; producer Sta. KERA-TV (PBS affiliate), Dallas, 1973-75; ind. producer Strongbow Prodns., L.A., 1975-77; producer Bill Stokes Assocs., Dallas, 1977-78; exec. producer Tannebring Rose Assocs., Dallas, 1978-82; pres. Geo. Kline Co., Inc., Dallas, 1982—; bd. dirs. U.S.A. Film Festival, Dallas, 1986-89; bd. dirs., v.p. Motion Picture Producers Tex., 1988—. Chmn. bd. Addison (Tex.) Airport, 1986; bd. dirs. St. Michael Sch., Dallas, 1990—; vestryman St. Michael and All Angels Ch., 1992—. Recipient award Comm. Arts mag., 1982; gold award Internat. Film and TV Festival, N.Y., 1983, 87-88, silver award, 1987; award Art Dirs. Club N.Y., 1983; gold award for best 30 second comml. Dallas Advt. League, 1986, 3 gold Addys, 2 silver Addys, 1987, silver Addy, gold Addy, 1992; Matrix award Women in Comm., 1987, Best of Show award 10th Dist. Addys., 1988, Mobius award, Chgo., 1991, gold award Houston Internat. Film Festival. Mem. Motion Picture Prodns. Tex. (v.p.), Assn. Ind. Comml. Prodns., Highland Pk. League, Egypt Exploration Soc. (London), Am. Rsch. Ctr. in Egypt, Balboa de Mazatlan S.A., Dallas Press Club, River Crest Country Club (Ft. Worth), Steeplechase Club (Ft. Worth), Dallas Country Club. Episcopalian. Office: George Kline Co Inc 3009 Maple Ave Dallas TX 75201-1244

KLINE, MARK WENDEL, pediatric medicine educator; b. Corpus Christi, Tex., Jan. 31, 1957; s. William Marshall and Elsie Marie (Ford) K.; m. Nancy Jean Edmunds, Nov. 11, 1989. BA, Trinity U., 1978; MD, Baylor Coll. Medicine, 1981. Diplomate Am. Bd. Pediatrics, Pediatric Infectious Diseases. Intern and resident in pediatrics Baylor Coll. Medicine, Houston, 1981-85, postdoctoral fellow infectious diseases, 1985-87; asst. prof. pediatrics St. Louis (Mo.) U. Sch. Medicine, 1987-89; asst. prof. pediatrics Baylor Coll. Medicine, Houston, 1990-92, assoc. prof. pediatrics, 1993—; co-prin. investigator Pediatric AIDS Clin. Trials Unit, Baylor Coll. Medicine, Tex. Children's Hosp., Houston, 1992—, assoc. dir. Gen. Clin. Rsch. Ctr., Baylor Coll. Medicine, Tex. Children's Hosp., Houston, 1992—. Contbr. chpts. to books and articles to profl. jours. Named One of Five Outstanding Young Texans, Tex. Jr. C. of C., 1993. Fellow Am. Acad. Pediatrics; mem. Am. Soc. for Microbiology, Infectious Disease Soc. Am., Soc. for Pediatric Rsch. Office: Tex Childrens Hosp 6621 Fannin St Houston TX 77030-2303

KLINE, PRISCILLA MACKENZIE, nursing educator; b. Elgin, Ill., Sept. 25, 1944; d. Gordon Innes and Esther May (Brooks) Mackenzie; m. Ellis Lee Kline, June 12, 1965; children: Heather, Heidi. BSN, U. Ill., 1965, MSN, 1969; EdD, Clemson (S.C.) U., 1987. RN, S.C. Project dir. Alzheimer's Community Edn. Project; pvt. practice Clemson; psychiat. nurse transitional care program Elgin State Hosp., 1967-68; lectr. psychiat. nursing Sacramento State Coll., 1968-69; in-svc. coord. Woodland (Calif.) Meml. Hosp., 1969-71; asst. prof. psychiat. nursing Edinboro (Pa.) State Coll., 1974-78; assoc. prof. Clemson U. Coll. Nursing, 1988—, assoc. dean, 1988-93, acting head dept. profl. svcs., 1991-93; nurse psychotherapist Clemson U. Coll. Nursing. Contbr. numerous articles to profl. jours. Vol. nurse Hospice of Anderson, S.C.; leader Girl Scouts U.S., 1976-89; mem. Alzheimer's adv. com. S.C. Commn. on Aging, 1987—, chair, 1989—. Recipient merit award AAUP, 1984, Centennial Outstanding Grad. award Clemson U. Coll. Edn., 1989, Award of Excellence S.C. League for Nursing, 1996. Mem. ANA (Pres.'s award S.C. chpt. 1993), Nat. League Nursing, S.C. League Nursing (Excellence award 1996), So. Nursing Rsch. Soc., S.C. Gerontol. Soc., Sigma Theta Tau (internat. treas. 1991-93, 93-95, Excellence in Nursing award 1993), Sigma Theta Tau Found. (chair, bd. dirs. 1994-95, treas. 1995—, 75th Anniversary Disting. Lectr. 1995—). Home: 203 N Elm St Pendleton SC 29670-1731 Office: Clemson U Coll Nursing Clemson SC 29634

KLINE, RONALD STEVEN, colon and rectal surgeon; b. Columbus, Miss., Dec. 8, 1947; s. Frank Edward Jr. and Gladys Muriel (Yarbrough) K.; m. Brenda Gayle Hartley, May 22, 1971; children: Brittany Denise, Grant Steven, Allison Blair. Student, U. Tex., Arlington, 1966-67, 68-69, U. Houston, 1967-68; MD, U. Tex., Galveston, 1973. Diplomate Am. Bd. Colon and Rectal Surgery. Intern in surgery Baylor U. Med. Ctr., Dallas, 1973-74, resident in gen. surgery, 1974-78, resident in colon-rectal surgery, 1978-79; pvt. practice, Arlington, 1979—; chmn. dept. surgery South Arlington Med. Ctr., 1990-91, vice chief of staff, 1991—, chief of staff, 1993—. Fellow ACS, Am. Soc. Colon and Rectal Surgeons; mem. AMA, So. Med. Assn., Tex. Med. Assn., Tex. Soc. Colon and Rectal Surgeons. Republican. Mem. Christian Ch. (Disciples of Christ). Office: 1000 N Davis Dr Ste F Arlington TX 76012-3202*

KLINE, TIMOTHY DEAL, lawyer; b. Oklahoma City, July 16, 1949; s. David Adam and Ruthela (Deal) K.; m. Alyssa Lipp Krysler, Aug. 29, 1985. BA, U. Okla., 1971, JD, 1976. Bar: Okla. 1976, U.S. Dist. Ct. (we. dist.) Okla. 1977, U.S. Ct. Appeals (10th cir.) 1977; cert. in bus. bankruptcy law and consumer bankruptcy Am. Bankruptcy Bd. of Certification. Law clk. to presiding justice U.S. Dist. Ct. (we. dist.) Okla., Oklahoma City, 1976-80; assoc. Linn, Helms, Kirk & Burkett, Oklahoma City, 1980-83; ptnr.

Kline & Kline, Oklahoma City, 1983—; adj. prof. law Oklahoma City U., 1980-84, 90. Mem. Am. Coll. Bankruptcy, Phi Delta Phi. Democrat. Office: Kline & Kline 720 NE 63rd St Oklahoma City OK 73105-6438

KLINGBIEL, PAUL HERMAN, information science consultant; b. Watertown, Wis., Nov. 3, 1919; s. Herman Carl and Elsa Helen (Zilisch) K.; Ph.B., U. Chgo., 1948, B.S., 1950; M.A., Am. U., 1966; m. Mildred Louise Wells, Nov. 30, 1968; stepchildren—Alice J. Blessley, Jo Ann Grayson. Abstractor, Armed Services Tech. Info. Agy., Dept. Def., Washington, 1953-58, editor Tech. Abstract Bull., 1958-60, dir. Office of Lexicography, 1960-66; phys. sci. adminstr., linguistics research Def. Documentation Center, 1966-79; sr. cons. Aspen Systems Corp., 1979-81; systems analyst PRC Data Services Co., Linthicum Heights, Md., 1981-82; lectr. Am. U., Washington, 1966-69; cons. div. med. scis. Nat. Acad. Scis., 1969-70. Served with AUS, 1943-46. Recipient Meritorious Civilian Service award, 1974, Disting. Career award, 1979. Fellow AAAS; mem. Assn. Computational Linguistics. Lutheran. Contbr. articles to profl. jours. Research in field of computational linguistics. Home: 1099 McMullen Booth Rd Clearwater FL 34619-3452

KLINGERMAN, ROBERT HARVEY, manufacturing company executive; b. Freeland, Pa., Nov. 10, 1939; s. Thomas Van and Emma Yeager (Hoffman) K.; m. Eleanor Jean Deemer, Aug. 31, 1963; children: Jeffrey Allen, Timothy Scott. BS in Chem. Engring., Lehigh U., 1961. Sr. applications engr. Elliott Co. div. Carrier Corp., Jeannette, Pa., 1961-66; project mgr. Stokes div. Pennwalt Corp., Phila., 1966-70, Cragmet Corp., Rancocas, N.J., 1970-74; v.p. engring. Cheston Co. (now Consarc Corp.), Rancocas, 1974-78; dir. ops. Inducto Heat, Madison Heights, Mich., 1978-82; pres. W.J. Savage Co., Knoxville, Tenn., 1982—, also bd. dirs.; bd. dirs. Metl-Saw, Inc., Benecia, Calif. Patentee in field. Mem. Abrasive Engring. Soc., Am. Soc. Metals, Nat. Machine Tool Bldrs., Soc. Mfg. Engrs. Republican. Methodist. Home: 700 Chateaugay Rd Knoxville TN 37923-2014 also: WJ Savage Co 1 Hopkins St Knoxville TN 37921

KLINGMAN, JOHN PHILIP, architect, educator; b. Phila., July 31, 1947; s. John Philip and Ethel Iva (Serfas) K. BSCE, Tufts U., 1969; postgrad., Stanford U., 1969-70; MArch, U. Oreg., 1983. Registered architect, La. Constrn. coord., project mgr. Payette Assocs., Inc., Boston, 1972-81; project architect LaBouisse & Waggonner Inc. Architects, New Orleans, 1986-89; cons. architect Waggonner & Ball, Inc. Architects, New Orleans, 1990—; asst. prof. Sch. Architecture Tulane U., New Orleans, 1983-90, assoc. prof., 1990—, assoc. dean, 1991-93; mem. archtl. rev. com. Historic Dists. Landmarks Commn., 1995—. Co-editor: Talk About Architecture: A Century of Architectural Education at Tulane, 1993. Home: 1309 Harmony St New Orleans LA 70115-3424 Office: Sch Architecture Tulane U New Orleans LA 70118

KLINK, ROBERT MICHAEL, consulting engineer, management consultant, financial consultant, property developer; b. Hamilton, Ind., Sept. 5, 1939; s. Robert Eli and Marie Ann (Parada) K.; m. Jessie Joyce Plummer, Sept. 10, 1960 (dec. Feb. 1966); children: Kevin Mark, Kent Michael, Kelly Martin, Kris Montgomery. Student, Tri State Coll., Angola, Ind., 1957; degree in Hwy. Engring., Purdue U., 1959; degree in Grad. Sch. Mgmt., Harvard U., 1976. Hwy. engr. Ind. State Hwy. Commn., Ft. Wayne, 1959-65; staff engr. Cities Svc. Oil Co., Inc., South Bend, Ind., 1965-66; client svcs. mgr., asst. to v.p. Clyde E. Williams & Assocs., South Bend, 1966-72; pres. Alpha Devel. Corp., South Bend, 1970-72; sr. v.p., CFO Snell Environ. Group, Inc., Lansing, Mich., 1972-77; pres. Klink Devel. Co., Dayton, Ohio, 1972-91; pres., chmn. Solar GeoThermo Energy Systems, Inc., Dayton, 1982—; pres., mng. ptnr. Klink Enterprises Co., Dayton, 1977—; pres., chmn. bd. Design Enterprise, Ltd., Dayton, 1977-91; chmn., pres. Cons. Info. Agy., Chattanooga, 1991—; bd. dirs. Pono Kai Resort, Kapaa, Kauai, Hawaii, Imperial Hawaii, Honolulu; cons. World Bank/USAID, Dacca, Bangladesh, Country of Brazil, Rio de Janeiro; cons. engr., mgmt. cons., project developer, cons. to govtl. agys. and Fortune 500 cos.; speaker in field. Patentee Solar and Geo Thermo Energy System; co-author: Water Handling Handbook, 1977. Trustee Centerville (Ohio) Community Ch., 1982-88, Okemos (Mich.) Community Ch., 1972-77; mem. The Presdl. Roundtable, Washington, 1989—, Rep. Senatorial Inner Circle, Washington, 1985—, Nat. Rep. Congrl. Com., 1986—. Recipient Outstanding Citizen award Am. Legion, Butler, Ind., 1953, Resolution of Appreciation Centerville City Coun., 1978, Resolution of Appreciation Greene County, 1989; named Hon. Citizen of Tenn., Nashville, 1989. Mem. Am. Water Works Assn. (life), Nat. Water Pollution Control Fedn., Profl. Svcs. Mgmt. Assn. (com. chair), Soc. for Mktg. Profl. Svcs. (com. chair), Ind. Hoosier Assocs., Ohio Early Birds. Christian and Missionary Alliance.

KLISZ, CYNTHIA ANN, state agency executive; b. Ind., July 30, 1967. BS, James Madison U., Harrisonburg, Va., 1989; MPA, Va. Commonwealth U., 1996. Policy intern Office of Gov., Richmond, 1988, fellow, summer 1989, dep. dir. constituent affairs, 1992-94; legis. asst. Mezzullo & McCandlish Law Firm, Richmond, 1989-92; legis. coord. Dept. Gen. Svcs., Richmond, 1994; exec. asst. to dir. Va. Medicaid, Richmond, 1994—. Founder 400 for Va., Richmond, 1993; bd. dirs. Jamestown Island Soc., Richmond, 1994—. Mem. Am. Soc. for Pub. Adminstrn. (mem. coun. 1995—). Home: 3316 Patterson Ave Richmond VA 23221-2308 Office: Dept Medical Assistance Services 600 E Broad St #1300 Richmond VA 23221

KLOESS, LAWRENCE HERMAN, JR., lawyer; b. Mamaroneck, N.Y., Jan. 30, 1927; s. Lawrence H. and Harriette Adelia (Holly) K.; m. Eugenia Ann Underwood, Nov. 10, 1931; children: Lawrence H. III, Price Mentzel, Branch Donelson, David Holly. AB, U. Ala., 1954, JD, 1956; grad., Air Command and Staff Coll., 1974, Air War Coll., 1976. Bar: Ala. 1956, U.S. Dist. Ct. (no. dist.) Ala. 1956, U.S. Ct. Appeals (5th cir.) 1957, U.S. Ct. Mil. Appeals 1971, U.S. Supreme Ct. 1971, U.S. Ct. Appeals (11th cir.) 1981. Sole practice, Birmingham, Ala., 1956-60; corp. counsel Bankers Fire and Marine Ins. Co., sole practice, Birmingham, 1962-66; dist. counsel for Ala. Office of Dist. Counsel U.S. Dept. Vets. Affairs, Montgomery, 1966-95. Vice chmn. Salvation Army adv. bd., 1981, mem. bd., 1978-81; mem. nat. conf. bar pres.'s ABA, 1981—; mem. adminstrn. bd. Frazer Meml. United Meth. Ch., 1987-90, 92—. Col. Judge Adv. Gen. USAFR, 1954-86, ret. Bd. dirs. Air Force Judge Advocate Gen. Sch. Found., 1996—. Decorated Legion of Merit, Meritorious Svc. medal with oak leaf cluster, Commendation medal; named Outstanding Judge Advocate USAFR, 1977 and 1979. Mem. ABA (nat. conf. bar. presidents 1981—), Ala. State Bar Assn. (chmn. editl. adv. bd. Ala. Lawyer, 1975-79, editorial bd. 1970-82, character and fitness com., chmn. law day com. 1973, chmn. citizen edn. com. 1974, CLE adv. com. 1983), Ala. Law Found. (trustee), Montgomery County Bar Assn. (chmn. law day com. 1972, chmn. state bar liaison com. 1975, chmn. bd. dirs. 1977, bd. dirs. 1979, chmn. and editor Montgomery County Bar Jour., ABA Merit award 1979-80, v.p. 1980, pres. 1981), Fed. Bar Assn. (pres. Montgomery Fed. Bar Assn. 1973), Citizens Conf. on Ala. Ct. (exec. com., sponsor of new jud. article to state constn. 1973), Citizens Conf. on Criminal and Juvenile Justice (mem. staff 1974), Farrah Law Soc., Res. Officers Assn. of U.S. (chpt. pres. 1978, state pres. 1982), Air Force Ret. Judge Advocates Assn., Sigma Delta Kappa (pres. U. Ala. chpt.), Theta Chi (Outstanding Alumni award 1976). Republican. Clubs: Montgomery Capital Rotary Club (pres. 1979, Paul Harris fellow), Montgomery Rotary Club (v.p. 1996), Maxwell-Gunter Officers (Montgomery), Blue Gray Cols. Assn., Mystic Soc. (Krewe of phantom host), Hon. Order Ky. Cols., Svc. Corps of Ret. Execs. Assn., Ala. Soc. for Cripple Children and Adults (bd. mem.). Contbr. articles on law to profl. jours. Home: 2601 F Scott Ct Montgomery AL 36106-2695 Office: 115 N Goldthwaite St Montgomery AL 36104-3407

KLOPFENSTEIN, REX CARTER, electrical engineer; b. Pittsfield, Mass., Mar. 3, 1938; s. Glenn A. and Jasimine V. (Carter) K.; m. Linda Gilgore, Oct. 6, 1962; children: Mark W., Eric G. BSEE, U. Conn., 1959; MEE, Syracuse U., 1963. Engr. GE, Syracuse, N.Y., 1959-63; lab. mgr. Melpar Div. E Systems, Falls Church, Va., 1963-70; mgr. hardware engring. Logicon Inc., Fairfax, Va., 1977-78; software and test mgr. Acuity Systems Inc., Reston, Va., 1978-81; engring. mgr. AMF Electronic Rsch. Lab., Sterling, Va., 1981-82; mem. tech. staff The MITRE Corp., McLean, Va., 1970-77, lead engr., 1982-96; lead engr. Mitretek Systems, Inc., McLean, Va., 1996—; sec. tech. com. X3K5 Am. Nat. Standards Inst., Washington, 1992-94. Contbg. author: Microcomputer Design and Application, 1977; contbr. articles to profl. jours. Mem. IEEE (No. Va. sect. sec. 1991-92, vice chmn., treas. 1992-93, chmn. 1993-94, nat. area coun. vice chmn. 1994-95, chmn. 1995-96), Assn. for Computing Machinery, Chi Phi. Republican. Home: 4224 Worcester Dr Fairfax VA 22032-1140 Office: Mitretek Systems Inc 7525 Colshire Dr Mc Lean VA 22102-7500

KLOTZ, DAVID WAYNE, executive, civil engineer; b. Victoria, Tex., Sept. 20, 1952; s. Bill W. and Dorothy (Brubaker) K.; m. Karen Wilson, July 20, 1974; children: Katheryne, David, Bradley, Valerie. BS in Civil Engring. with honors, Tex. A&M U., 1974; MS in Civil Engring., U. Houston, 1976. Registered profl. engr., Tex., La. Civil engr. Turner Collie & Braden, Houston, 1974-79; project mgr. Rady & Assocs., Ft. Worth, 1979-82, Dannenbaum Engring., Houston, 1982-85; pres., chief exec. officer Klotz Assocs., Inc., Houston, 1985—, Epilepsy Assn. Greater Houston, 1992—. Mem. Harris County Flood Control Task Force, Houston, 1987—, chmn., 1993-94; chmn. Clear Creek Parks Steering Com., Houston, 1987-91; adult tchr., deacon, fin. com. Tallowood Bapt. Ch.; umpire Bear Creek Little League, 1987-92; coach Katy Basketball, 1992-93; bd. dirs., mem. exec. com. Astros golf tourney chair Epilepsy Assn. Greater Houston, 1992—; mem. U. Houston Civil Engring. Adv. Com., 1996—. Mem. ASCE (employment conditions com. 1989-92, sec. 1991-92, vice chair 1992-93, chair 1993-94, corr. mem. com. engring. mgmt./orgnl. level 1988-92, state dir. Tex. sect. 1988-90, pres. 1990-91, pres. Houston br. 1987-88, Houston br. Award of Honor 1993, dir. Ft. Worth br. 1981-82, Hawley fellow 1976, Daniel Mead prize 1975, Tex. sect. Honor award 1994), Cons. Engrs. Coun. Tex. (chmn. membership com. 1989-90, state legis. com. 1993—, treas. 1995—, bd. dirs. 1993—, New Prin. of Yr. award 1987), Greater Houston Builders Assn. (cmty. devel. coun. 1983-89), Assn. Cons. Mcpl. Engrs. (v.p. 1992-93, pres. 1994-95, govt. steering com. 1996—), Am. Water Works Assn., Houston C. of C., "C" Club. Republican. Office: Klotz Assocs Inc 1155 Dairy Ashford St Ste 705 Houston TX 77079-3015

KLUTZ, ANTHONY ALOYSIUS, JR., health, safety and environmental manager; b. Wilkes-Barre, Pa., Dec. 2, 1954; s. Anthony A. Klutz and Matilda (Konopka) Weigand; m. LetaMarie A. Rydzewski, July 15, 1978; children: Athena Marie, Anthony A. III. BS, Kings Coll., Wilkes-Barre, 1976; MS, Rensselaer Poly. Inst., 1978; MBA, Clemson U., 1988. Material devel. engr. Sangamo Capacitor-Schlumberger, Pickens, S.C., 1978-87, product devel. engr., 1986-87; mgr. process engring. Sangamo Weston-Schlumberger, West Union, S.C., 1987-90; safety and environ. mgr. Schlumberger Industries, West Union, 1990-94, health, safety and environ. mgr. Electricity N.Am., 1994—. Vice chmn. Oconee County Local Emergency Planning Com., Walhalla, S.C., 1988—; mem. coun. Holy Cross Parish, Pickens, 1986-87. Mem. Am. Vacuum Soc., Electro Chem. Soc., Am. Soc. Materials, S.C. C. of C. (tech. com.), Mgmt. Club (pres. 1985, 92, v.p. 1991), KC (Knight of Mo. award Pickens 1988). Home: 398 Chinquapin Rd Easley SC 29640-7053 Office: Sangamo Weston-Schlumberger Hwy 11 West Union SC 29696-9610

KLUTZOW, FRIEDRICH WILHELM, neuropathologist; b. Bandoeng, Preanger, Indonesia, Aug. 6, 1923; came to U.S., 1953; s. Rudolph F.W. and Pauline (Van Thiel) K.; m. Apr. 2, 1954; children: Judith A., Michael J. MD, U. Utrecht, Netherlands, 1951. Diplomate Am. Bd. Neuropathology and Anatomic Pathology. Chief of staff Community Meml. Hosp., Oconto Falls, Wis., 1965-68; pathology resident U. Wis., Madison, 1968-72; neuropathologist VA Hosp., Mpls., 1972-75; dir. pathology dept. VA Hosp., Brockton, Mass., 1975-83, Wichita, Kans., 1983-87; chief of staff VA Hosp., Bath, N.Y., 1987-90; neuropathologist VA Hosp., Bay Pines, Fla., 1991—; clin. assoc. prof. pathology U. Rochester (N.Y.) Sch. Medicine, U. South Fla., Tampa. Prin. author: Neuropathology Manual: The Practical Approach, 1996; contbr. articles to profl. jours. Col. USAR, 1979-85. Paul Harris fellow Rotary Internat., Bath, 1990; recipient Outstanding Career award Dept. Vet. Affairs, Bath, 1990. Fellow Coll. Am. Pathologists; mem. Am. Assn. Neuropathologists. Republican. Home: PO Box 7846 Sarasota FL 34278-7846

KLYM, KENDALL, journalist; b. Hartford, Conn., Feb. 9, 1964; s. Nicholas and Lillian (Ostrowski) K. BA magna cum laude, Baylor U., 1994. Classical ballet dancer Kansas City (Mo.) Ballet, 1984-86; soloist ballet dancer Chgo. City Ballet, 1986-87; classical ballet dancer Dallas Ballet, 1987-88; pantomime dancer Tivoli Pantomine Theatre, Copenhagen, Denmark, 1988; prin. dancer State Ballet of Mo., Kansas City, 1988-89; ballet dancer Louisville Ballet, 1990-91; editl. intern Seeds Mag., Waco, Tex., 1992; assoc. editor Adventure West Mag., Incline Village, Nev., 1993; editor The Baylor Corral, Waco, 1993-94; city coun. reporter, feature writer Neighbors publ. of The Fresno (Calif.) Bee; staff reporter Carmel (Calif.) Pine Cone/Monterey Times; pub. rels. cons. Seeds Mag., Waco; freelance writer Presbyn. Today mag. Editor: The Asian Cultural Review, 1993, The Baylor Corral, 1993-94; freelance dance reviewer The Fresno Bee, Presbyterians Today mag.; contbr. articles to profl. jours. Group organizer Highland Presbyn. Ch., Louisville, 1990-92, Ctrl. Presbyn. Ch., Waco, 1992-94, fellowship group 1992-94; participant Habitat for Humanity, Waco, 1992. Recipient Fresno-Madera Area Agy. on Aging award for media coverage of sr. issues, 1995. Mem. Alpha Chi. Home: 440 Pine St Monterey CA 93940 Office: Carmel Pine Cone PO Box G-1 Carmel CA 93921

KMIEC, EDWARD URBAN, bishop; b. Trenton, N.J., June 4, 1936. Ed. s. John Kmiec and Thecla (Czupta) St. Charles Coll., Catonsville, Md., 1956; St. Mary's Sem., Balt., 1958; S.T.L. Gregorian U., Rome. 1962, Ordained priest Roman Cath. Ch., Dec. 20, 1961; ordained titular bishop of Simidicca and aux. bishop of Trenton, 1982-92; bishop of Nashville, 1992—. Address: The Catholic Center 2400 21st Ave S Nashville TN 37212-5302

KNAPP, CANDACE LOUISE, sculptor; b. Benton Harbor, Mich., Feb. 28, 1948; d. Claire Warren and Frances Mary (Collins) K.; m. Björn Andrén, Mar. 3, 1988. BFA, Cleve. Inst. Art, 1971; MFA, U. Ill., 1974. Sculptures exhibited in numerous galleries and colls. including Northwood Inst. Collection, West Palm Beach, Fla.; represented in permanent collections at Malone & Hyde, Memphis, Mobil Oil Co., Stockholm, HageGården Music Ctr., Edane, Sweden, others; included in book Contemporary American Women Sculptures; numerous commns. including St. Vincent de Paul Cath. Ch., Arlington, Tex., Padre Pio Found., Cromwell, Conn., Temple Emanuel, Dallas, West Haven, Conn., Tampa (Fla.) Gen. Hosp., Pub. Art Commn. City of St. Petersburg, Fla. Helen Greene Perry traveling scholar, 1971. Mem. Assn. Fla. Liturgical Artists (co-founder).

KNAPP, CHARLES BOYNTON, economist, educator, academic administrator; b. Ames, Iowa, Aug. 13, 1946; s. Albert B. and Anne Marie (Taff) K.; m. Lynne Vickers, Aug. 25, 1967; 1 dau., Amanda. B.S., Iowa State U., 1968; M.A., Ph.D., U. Wis., 1972. Asst. prof. econs., research assoc. Ctr. for Study of Human Resources, U. Tex., Austin, 1972-76; spl. asst. to Sec. of Labor Dept. Labor, Washington, 1977-79, dep. asst. sec. labor, 1979-81; assoc. prof. pub. policy George Washington U., 1981-82; assoc. prof. econs. Tulane U., New Orleans, 1982-87, sr. v.p., 1982-85, exec. v.p., 1985-87; pres., prof. econs. U. Ga., Athens, 1987—; bd. dirs. AFLAC Inc. Contbr. articles to profl. jours. Office: U Ga Lustrat House Athens GA 30602

KNAPP, DENNIS RAYMOND, federal judge; b. Buffalo, W.Va., May 13, 1912; s. Amon Lee and Ora Alice (Forbes) K.; m. Helen Ewers Jordan, June 1, 1935; children: Mary F., Margaret Ann, Dennis Raymond. AB, W.Va. Inst. Tech., 1932, LLD, 1972; AM, W.Va. U., 1934, LLB, 1940. Bar: W.Va. 1940. High sch. tchr. Putnam County, W.Va., 1932-35; supt. schs., 1935-37; practiced in Nitro, 1940-56; judge Ct. of Common Pleas, Kanawha County, W.Va., 1957-70; U.S. dist. judge for So. Dist. W.Va., Charleston, 1970—; Vice pres., dir. Bank of Nitro, 1949-70; v.p. Hygeia, Inc., 1968-70. Bd. dirs. Goodwill Industries, Inc., 1968-70; adv. bd. Marshall U., Huntington, W.Va. With AUS, 1944-46. Named Alumnus of Year W.Va. Inst. Tech., 1967. Mem. Am., W.Va. bar assns., W.Va. Jud. Assn., W.Va. Tech. Coll. Alumni Assn. (pres. 1968). Republican. Methodist. Home: PO Box 312 Nitro WV 25143-0312 Office: US Courthouse PO Box 2546 Charleston WV 25329-2546

KNAPP, FRED WILLIAM, entomologist, educator; b. Princeton, Ill., Oct. 14, 1928. BS, U. Ill.; MS in Entomology, Kans. State U., PhD in Entomology. Asst. prof. entomology U. Ky., Lexington, 1961-69, assoc. prof., 1969-71, prof., 1971—; asst. dir. Ky. Agr. Experimental Sta., 1993. Contbr. over 160 articles to profl. jours. Recipient Coopers Animal Health award, fellow Entomological Soc. Am., 1994, Disting. Svc. award Agriculture Kans. State U. Mem. Entomological Soc. Am. (pres. 1993—, hon. membership com., gov. bd. 1992-94, chair operational com. manual 1992-94). Office: U Kentucky Dept Entomology 500 S Limestone St Lexington KY 40508-3217

KNAPP, JANIS ANN, elementary school educator; b. Coffeyville, Kans., Nov. 15, 1949; d. Harry Clarence and Dorothy (Lehr) Herman; m. Stephen Foxall Knapp, Feb. 12, 1972; children: Marysa Monica, Stephen Weslee, Alexandria Annastasia, Janna Jacqualan. BE, U. Kans., 1971; MEd, Pittsburg State U., 1983, EdS, 1986. Cert. elem. tchr., Fla. Tchr. Overland Park (Kans.) Elem. Sch., 1971-72, Alamo Heights (Tex.) Jr. High Sch., 1972-73, Hoover Elem. Sch., Bartlesville, Okla., 1974, 79-80, Limestone Elem. Sch., Bartlesville, 1975-76, Whittier Elem. Sch., Coffeyville, 1980-83, Edgewood Elem. Sch., Coffeyville, 1983-85, J.C. Mitchell Community Sch., Boca Raton, Fla., 1985-88; math. specialist Palm Beach County Schs., Riviera Beach, Fla., 1988-90; tchr. Meadow Park Elem. Sch., Palm Beach, Fla., 1990-91, Conniston Mid. Sch., Palm Beach, 1991-93, Pine Grove Elem. Sch., Delray Beach, Fla., 1993—. Vol. high sch. debate judge, Delray Beach, Fla., 1990; Heart Fund vol., Ft. Lauderdale, 1985-91; assoc. mem. Rep. Club, Boca Raton, 1990-91. Mem. AAUW, Nat. Coun. Tchrs. of Math., Nat. Coun. Supts. Math., South Fla. Ctr. for Exec. Educators, Fla. Coun. Tchrs. Math., Fla. Assn. Math. Suprs., Fla. ASCD, Palm Beach County Classroom Tchrs. Assn., Phi Delta Kappa, Alpha Phi (pres. alumni assn.). Roman Catholic. Home: 18755 Cape Sable Dr Boca Raton FL 33498-6377 Office: Pine Grove Elem Sch 400 SW 10th St Delray Beach FL 33444-2214

KNAPP, JOHN CHARLES, public relations executive; s. Charles Julian and Grace (Taylor) K.; m. Kelly Lee Teske; children: Amanda Kelly, Tracy Grace, Charles John, Mary Margaret. BA in Comms., Ga. State U.; MA in Ethics, Columbia Theol. Sem., 1994; postgrad., U. Wales. Cert. pub. rels. Press sec. U.S. Congress; founder, editor The Atlanta Downtown News; founder, pres. Knapp, Inc.; mem. comms. adv. coun. Pres. Carter's Atlanta Project; co-chair crisis mgmt. Atlanta Com. for Olympic Games; bd. dirs. YES Atlanta, Ga. Coop. Svcs. Blind Inc.; founder So. Inst. for Bus. and Profl. Ethics; comms. chmn., bd. govs. Ga. Found. for Ind. Colls.; trustee Ga. State U. Found.; bd. dirs., v.p. Ga. State U. Alumni Assn.; past pres. Ga. State U. Young Alumni Coun.; pres. Ga. State U. Comms. Alumni Club. Mem. Pub. Rels. Soc. Am (treas., nat. assembly del. Ga. chpt.), Atlanta Press Club (past dir.), Ga. Econ. Developers Assn., Ga. Press Assn. Office: Knapp Inc 50 Hurt Plz SE Fl 10 Atlanta GA 30303-2914

KNECHT, JULIA ANN, firefighter, paramedic; b. Bayshore, N.Y., July 3, 1959; d. Thomas Francis and Patricia Adele (Lamberta) K. Student, Suffolk County Community Coll., Selden, N.Y., 1978-79, Daytona (Fla.) Community Coll., 1981-83, Seminole County Community Coll., Sanford, Fla., 1984—. Paramedic Flagler County Ambulance Service, Bunnell, Fla., 1983-84, Herndon Ambulance Service, Orlando, Fla., 1984; firefighter, paramedic Seminole County Fire Dept., Sanford, Fla., 1984—; reserve paramedic Daytona Beach Fire Dept., 1983-85; paramedic part time Rural Metro Ambulance Service, Orlando, 1986-91; vol. Osteen (Fla.) Fire Dept., 1986-92. Firefighter, paramedic Osteen (Fla.) Vol. Fire Dept., 1986—. Mem. Internat. Assn. Fire Fighters, Profl. Firefighters Fla. Republican. Presbyterian. Home: 2499 S Tipton Dr Deltona FL 32738-8741

KNEE, RUTH IRELAN (MRS. JUNIOR K. KNEE), social worker, health care consultant; b. Sapulpa, Okla., Mar. 21, 1920; d. Oren M. and Daisy (Daubin) Irelan; m. Junior K. Knee, May 29, 1943 (dec. Oct. 21, 1981). BA, U. Okla., 1941, cert. social work, 1942; MASSA, U. Chgo., 1945. Psychiat. social worker, asst. supr. Ill. Psychiat. Inst., U. Ill. at Chgo., 1943-44; psychiat. social worker USPHS Employee Health Unit, Washington, 1944-46, chief psychiat. social worker, 1946-49; psychiat. social work assoc. Army Med. Ctr., Walter Reed Army Hosp., Washington, 1949-54; psychiat. social work cons. HEW, Region III, Washington, 1955-56; with NIMH, Chevy Chase, Md., 1956-72; chief mental health care adminstrn. br. USPHS, 1967-72, assoc. dep. adminstr. Health Svcs. and Mental Health Adminstrn., 1972-73, dep. dir. Office of Nursing Home Affairs, 1973-74; long-term mental health care cons.; mem. com. on mental health and illness of elderly HEW, 1976-77; mem. panel on legal and ethical issues Pres.'s Commn. on Mental Health, 1977-78; liaison mem. Nat. Adv. Mental Health Coun., 1977-81. Mem. editorial bd. Health and Social Work, 1979-81. Bd. dirs. Hillhaven Found., 1975-86, governing bd. Cathedral Coll. of the Laity, Washington Nat. Cathedral, 1988-94. Fellow Am. Pub. Health Assn. (sec. mental health sect. 1968-70, chmn. 1971-72), Am. Orthopsychiat. Assn. (life), Gerontol. Soc. Am., Am. Assn. Psychiat. Social Workers (pres. 1951-53); mem. Nat. Conf. Social Welfare (nat. bd. 1968-71, 2d v.p. 1973-74), Inst. Medicine/Nat. Acad. Sci. (com. study future of pub. health 1986-87), Coun. on Social Work Edn., Nat. Assn. Social Workers (sec. 1955-56, nat. dir. 1956-57, 84-86, chmn. competence study com., practice and knowledge com. 1963-71), Acad. Cert. Social Workers (social work pioneer 1993), Am. Pub. Welfare Assn., DAR, U. Okla. Assocs., Woman's Nat. Dem. Club (mem. gov. bd. 1992-95, ednl. found. bd. 1992-96), Cosmos Club (Washington), Phi Beta Kappa (assoc. 1985—), Psi Chi. Address: 8809 Arlington Blvd Fairfax VA 22031-2705

KNEIPPER, RICHARD KEITH, lawyer; b. Kenosha, Wis., June 18, 1943; s. Richard F. and Esther E. (Beaster) K.; m. Sherry Hayes, Dec. 16, 1977; children: Ryan Hayes, Lindsey Merrill. BS, Washington and Lee U., 1965; JD, Cornell U., 1968. Bar: Tex. 1982, U.S. Dist. Ct. (so. dist.) N.Y. 1968, U.S. Ct. Appeals (2d cir.) 1971. Atty. Chadbourne & Parke, N.Y.C., 1968-81, Jones, Day, Reavis & Pogue, Dallas, 1981—; adv. com. Nat. Mus. Am., Smithsonian, Nat. Arts Edn. Initiative, Nat. Mus. Am. Art, Smithsonian Instn. Contbr. numerous articles to profl. jours. Bd. trustees, The Dallas Parks Found.; mem. profl adv. group Save Outdoor Sculpture!; chmn. Dallas Adopt-A-Monument; bd. dirs., mem. new bus. task force, mem. internat task force Health Industry Coun. Dallas-Ft. Worth Region. Mem. ABA, N.Y. Bar Assn., Tex. Bar Assn., Tex. Sculpture Assn., Assn. Bar City of N.Y. Episcopal. Office: Jones Day Reavis & Pogue 2300 Trammell Crow Ctr 2001 Ross Ave Dallas TX 75201-8001

KNESTRICK, JANICE LEE, art educator; b. Ft. Belvoir, Va., Sept. 5, 1953; d. Bernard Paul and Mary (Ryan) Yurchik; m. Joseph Collins Knestrick, July 5, 1980; children: Mary Bridgette, Brittany Megan. BS in Art Edn., Radford (Va.) U., 1975; postgrad., U. Va., 1980, George Mason U., 1980. Tchr., fine arts chmn. Manassas Park (Va.) High Sch., 1976-91; tchr., art dept. chmn. Brentsville Dist. Mid.-Sr. High Sch., Nokesville, Va., 1991-92; mem. vis. self-study com. Powhatan County High Sch., 1982; developer art program for elem. children Fairfax County Park Authority, Providence Recreation Ctr., 1982-83. Recipient Grants Wash. Post, 1989, Prince William County Pub. Schs. Edn. Found., 1991, Agnes Meyer Most Outstanding Tchr. award Wash. Post, 1990,. Mem. NEA, Va. Art Edn. Assn. (No. Va. Oustanding Art Tchr. of Yr. 1991), Manassas Park Edn. Assn., Prince William Edn. Assn. Home: 3473 Country Walk Dr Port Orange FL 32119-3156 Office: Volusia County Schs South Daytona Elem Sch Elizabeth Ave Daytona Beach FL 32119

KNIFFEN, DONALD AVERY, astrophysicist, educator, researcher; b. Kalamazoo, Apr. 27, 1933; s. Frerick Bowerman and Eva Virginia (Arp) K.; m. Janis Kay Nesom, June 14, 1952; children: Karyol Kniffen Poole, Donald Avery Jr., Kimberly Kniffen Giesbrecht. BS magna cum laude, La. State U., 1959; AM, Washington U., St. Louis, 1960; PhD, Cath. U. Am., 1967. Astrophysicist Goddard Space Flight Ctr., NASA, Greenbelt, Md., 1960-91; lectr. physics U. Md., College Park, 1978-87; project scientist Compton Gamma Ray Observatory, 1979-91; William W. Elliott prof., chmn. dept. physics and astronomy Hampden-Sydney Coll., Va., 1991—. Awarded Medal for Outstanding Leadership NASA, 1992, recipient Laurel Award, Space/Missiles, Aviation Week & Space Tech., 1991. Contbr. articles to profl. jours. Served with USN, 1952-56. Fellow Royal Astron. Soc.; mem. AAUP, Am. Phys. Soc., Am. Astron. Soc., Internat. Astron. Union, Sigma Xi. Democrat. Avocations: travel; reading, gardening. Home: PO Box 862 Hampden Sydney VA 23943 Office: Hampden-Sydney Coll Dept Physics Hampden Sydney VA 23943

KNIGHT, AUBREY KEVIN, vocational education educator; b. Oxford, Miss., May 2, 1947; s. Kenneth and Katherine (Bishop) K.; m. Bonnie Faye Cagle, Jan. 9, 1970; children: Aubrey Kenneth, Allen Keith. Grad., NRI Sch. Electronics, Washington, 1980; student, Itawamba C.C., Tupelo, Miss., 1987, Miss. State U., Starkville, 1988, 89, Northwest C.C., Oxford, Miss., 1988-89, 93-94. Owner and technician Yocona Electronics, Oxford, 1979-87;

electronics instr. Oxford-Lafayette Bus. and Indsl. Complex, 1987—; 1988, 89, 93. Mem. Miss. Assn. Electronics Instrs. (pres. 1990-92), Miss. Trade and Tech. Assn. (2d v.p. 1991-92, 1st v.p. 1992-93, pres. 1993-94), Miss Vocat. Indsl. Clubs of Am. (pres., Miss. bd. dirs. 1994-95). Baptist. Office: Oxford-Lafayette Bus & Indsl Complex 1904 Highway 7 S Oxford MS 38655-5361

KNIGHT, DAN PHILLIP, marketing executive; b. Rentz, Ga., Aug. 14, 1941; s. Daniel Prentice and Tommie Lou (Mullis) K.; m. Doris Kathleen McCleskey, July 20, 1963; children: Dana, Kirsten, Delana, Kiesha. BJ, U. Ga., 1963; JD, Atlanta Law Sch., 1967. Sales analyst Ford Motor Co., East Point, Ga., 1963-66; pub. rels., program dir. Ga. Heart Assn., Atlanta, 1966-68; pub. rels. dir., editor Ga. Mcpl. Assn., Atlanta, 1968-69; dir. advt., pub. rels. John H. Harland Co., Atlanta, 1969-72; dir. pub. rels. Burger King Corp., Miami, Fla., 1972-73; account exec. Grey Advt., N.Y.C., 1973-76; v.p. Pringle, Dixon, Pringle, Atlanta, 1976-79; dir. field ops. Habersham Plantation Corp., Toccoa, Ga., 1979-83; pres. Knight & Assocs., Baldwin, Ga., 1983—; com. chmn. Atlanta Advt. Club, 1969-72. Editor Urban Ga. mag., 1968-69. Sec. Alpharetta (Ga.) Planning Commn., 1970-72; com. chmn. MIA Crusade Project 4th of July parade, Atlanta, 1970. Recipient Outstanding Com. Chmn. award MIA Crusade Project, 1970; named one of Outstanding Young Men in Am., U.S. C. of C., 1971. Mem. Am. Mktg. Assn. (profl.), Alpharetta Jaycees (v.p. 1968-69, officer 1967-71, outstanding pub. speaker award 1970, disting. svc. award 1971). Republican. Baptist.

KNIGHT, DELOS LAVERN, JR., public relations executive; b. Bogalusa, La., July 3, 1931; s. Delos L. and Ruth (Vinyard) K., Sr.; m. Margaret Frances Rucker, Apr. 10, 1955; children: Delos L. III, Anne, Kevin T., Timothy O. BA in Journalism, La. State U., 1952. With Sta. WIKC, Bogalusa, La., 1955-59; pub. rels. rep. Crown Zellerbach Corp., Bogalusa, 1959-64, regional mgr. pub. relations, 1964-69, regional mgr. pub. affairs, Baton Rouge, La., 1969-79, dir. internal communications, San Francisco, 1979-82, dir. corp. communications, 1982-85, v.p. pub. affairs, 1985-86, pub. affairs cons. 1987-89; regional dir. Am. Forest and Paper Assn., 1989-95; pub. rels. cons., 1995—. Served to capt. U.S. Army, 1952-54. Mem. Pub. Rels. Soc. Am., Sigma Delta Chi. Republican. Presbyterian. Club: Press (Atlanta). Home: 505 Breakwater Ter Stone Mountain GA 30087-5307

KNIGHT, DIANE, special education educator; b. De Ridder, La., Dec. 2, 1955. BS, McNeese State U., 1976; MEd, Northwestern State U., Natchitoches, La., 1980, EdD, 1986. Cert. tchr., La., Ga. Tchr. English Vernon Parish Sch. Bd., Leesville, La., 1976-77; tchr. spl. edn. Natchitoches Parish Sch. Bd., La., 1978-80; ednl. diagnostician Natchitoches Parish Sch. Bd., 1985-88; tchr. spl. edn. Sabine Parish Sch. Bd., Many, La., 1983-85; dir. pupil appraisal Red River Parish Sch. Bd., Coushatta, La., 1988-89; asst. prof. Ga. Southwestern Coll., Americus, 1989-90, U. Southwestern La., Lafayette, 1990-95; assoc. prof. U. Ga., Athens, 1995-96; ednl. diagnostician Spl. Sch. Dist. # 1, 1996—; ednl. cons. and evaluator, Lafayette, 1990-95, Athens, Ga., 1995-96, Baton Rouge, 1996—; presenter in field. Contbr. articles to profl. jours. Mem. La. Assn. Evaluators, Coun. for Exceptional Children (learning disabilities divsn., tchr. edn. divsn.), Rotary, Phi Delta Kappa. Republican. Baptist. Home: 9771 Jefferson Hwy Apt # 154 Baton Rouge LA 70809 Office: ARDC-Hunt Correctional Ctr Spl Sch Dist # 1 PO Box 174 Saint Gabriel LA 70776

KNIGHT, GARY CHARLES, mechanical engineer; b. Bartlesville, Okla., Nov. 15, 1950; s. Charles Robert and Elizabeth India (Brown) K.; m. Lisa Jo Martin, Sept. 12, 1981; children: Amanda Joann, Gary Michael. BSME, U. Tulsa, 1981. Registered profl. engr., Okla.; commd. inspector Nat. Bd. Boiler and Pressure Vessel Inspectors. Results engr. I Pub. Svc. Co. Okla., Tulsa, 1981-83, results engr. II, 1983-87, results engr. III, 1987-89, maintenance supr., 1989-90, maintenance supt., 1990-92, asst. sta. mgr., 1992, sta. mgr., 1992—. With U.S. Army, 1970-73, Vietnam. Mem. ASME, NSPE, Okla. Soc. Profl. Engrs. Republican. Home: 6848 E 59th St Tulsa OK 74145-8212 Office: Pub Svc Co Okla PO Box 220 Oologah OK 74053-0220

KNIGHT, JAMES EUGENE, state agency administrator; b. Lancaster, S.C., Feb. 10, 1948; s. Thurlow and Myrtle Geneva (Mackey) K.; m. Sandra Elin Stenstrom, Jan. 13, 1979; children: Cameron Stenstrom Knight, Jordan Evan Knight. BA in Journalism, U. S.C., 1974, M in Mass Comm., 1981. Instr. journalism U. S.C., Lancaster, 1972-74; news dir. Sta. WLCM, Lancaster, 1972-74; dir. pub. rels. Safe Fed. Credit Union, Sumter, S.C., 1974-75; mgr. Sta. WLCM/WPAJ-FM, Lancaster, 1975-79; dir. pub. info. S.C. Dept. Labor, Columbia, 1980-89, exec. asst. to commr. labor, 1989-94; exec. asst. to dir. S.C. Dept. Labor, Licensing and Regulation, Columbia, 1994—; bd. dirs. Safe Fed. Credit Union chmn. bd., 1988-90. Sgt. USAF, 1968-72. Mem. Kappa Tau Alpha. Home: 618 Old Friars Rd Columbia SC 29210-3723 Office: SC Dept Labor Licensing & Regulation 3600 Forest Dr Columbia SC 29204-4033

KNIGHT, KENNETH VINCENT, leisure company executive, entrepreneurventure capitalists; b. Jersey City, N.J., Mar. 30, 1944; s. Julian (Konopacki) and Ellen (Gordon) Knight; m. Karen Keenan, June 1, 1968 (div. June 1978); 1 child, Karisa M.; m. Maria H. Herrera, June 17, 1983; children: Alexander, Maria B., Christina M. Student, Northwestern Coll., Iowa, 1962-65; BS in Mgmt., N.Y. Inst. Tech., 1966; MBA, Nova Southeastern U., 1976; grad., Officer Candidate Sch., FARNG, 1968. Commd. 2d lt. U.S Army, advanced through grades to 1st lt., 1970; mgr., customer/corp. rels. Cavanaugh Corp., Miami, Fla., 1966-68; asst. dir. corp. svcs. Burger King Corp., Miami, 1968-70; asst. to sr. v.p. investor rels. Deltona Corp., Miami, 1970-74; dir. corp./investor rels. Gen. Devel. Corp., GDV Corp., Miami and N.Y.C., 1974-78; v.p. resort affiliations, bd. dirs. Interval International, Miami, 1978-79, sr. v.p. mktg., 1979-82, exec. v.p., chief ops., 1983-84; pres., chief ops. Interval Internat. & Worldex, Miami, 1984-87, pres., 1987-89, vice chmn., 1989-92; founder, gen. ptnr. Leisure Fund, Ltd., Miami, 1992—; founder, chmn., CEO Leisurecorp Internat., Leisure Fund Assoc., L.P., Nev., 1995—; pres. MKH Mgmt., Inc., Miami, 1995—; bd. dirs., co-founder Worldex Corp., Miami, 1982-92, Worldex Travel Ctrs., 1983-92, Knight Family Holdings, Miami, 1988—, Leaguestar Pl., London, 1988-92, Nova Southeastern U. South Fla. Alumni; co-founder Worldex Corp., Denver and L.A., Worldex Europe Ltd., London, Intercambico Internationales de Vacienes, SA, Mexico City, 1985-92, Leisurecorp Internat., 1992—; mem. bd. advisors Ecotourism Natureshare Assn., Stowe, Vt., 1990, Brentwood Equities, 1994—, Voice Track Corp., 1996—, Century Found., grad. sch. bus. Nova Southeastern U., 1978—, bd. govs., 1992—, trustee, 1994—, spkrs. forum, 1995—, Dave Thomas's Ambs. Enterprise Program, Nova Southeastern U., 1995—; mem. Fla. Venture Forum, Fla. Internat. U., 1995—, Small Bus. Devel. Ctr., U. Ctrl. Fla., 1996—. Founder: (mags.) The Leisure Society, Dreamweavers; exec. pub.: (newspaper) Timesharing Times, 1980, (mag.) Timeshare Traveler, 1984-90, Directory Resorts, 1980-90; mem. editorial bd.: Vacation Industry Rev., 1985— (most traveled exec. 1984, speaker worldwide); author: Best Use for Resort Condominiums, 1972. Soccar asst. St. Thomas Episcopal Ch., 1965—; Cub scout den leader Boy Scouts Am., 1996—. 1st lt. USAR, 1966-93, ret. Recipient Achievers award Fla. Trend mag., 1983, 88, Inc. 500 award Inc. mag., 1984, The Capital award Nat. Leadership Coun., 1991, Nova U. Alumni award, 1992; named Fla.'s Best Internat. Co., Prestige Internat. mag., 1985, Alumni of Yr., Nova Southeastern U., 1993. Mem. Assn. Governing Bds. of Univs. and Colls., NSU South Fla. Alumni Assn. (bd. dirs. 1996—), Timesharing Inst. (bd. dirs. 1978-85), Pvt. Trust (trustee). Roman Catholic. Office: Leisurecorp Internat World Trade Ctr 80 SW 8th St Miami FL 33130-3003

KNIGHT, LILA CUCKSEE, executive secretary, poet; b. Chattanooga, Apr. 11, 1931; d. William Henry and Anna Leona (Bonine) Cucksee; children: David, Jonathan, Paul, Joel Knight, Sheryl Knight Carlock. Diploma in Sectl. Sci., Edmondson Jr. Coll., 1983; diploma Life Underwriters Tng. Coun., Chattanooga, 1986; life ins. lic. Modern Woodmen Sch., 1983. Pre-need sales woman Lakewood Memory Gardens, Rossville, Ga., 1983, Tenn./Ga. Meml. Park, Rossville, 1983; dist. rep. Modern Woodmen of Am., Rossville, 1983-84; ins. agt. United Ins. Co. of Am., Chattanooga, 1984-86; area sales mgr. World Book/Child Craft, Chattanooga, 1986; sr. clk., Gwinnett Mental Health/Mental Retardation/Substance Abuse Ctr., Lawrenceville, Ga., 1986-89; spl. edn. sch. bus driver Gwinnett County Sch. Sys., 1990—. Author of numerous poems; inventor in field. Mem. Lakeview Home-Sch. Orgn., Fort Oglethorpe, Ga., 1955-86. Mem. AARP, NAFE, Internat. Soc. Poetry, Boys Town, Lakeside Resort, Inc., Sr. Friends Club. Republican. Baptist. Avocations: poetry, hiking, swimming, singing. Home: PO Box 1734 Lawrenceville GA 30246-1734

KNIGHT, MARSHA DIANNE, special education educator; b. Kansas City, Mo., Dec. 13, 1954; d. William Eugene and Leona Belle (Kelton) Cox; m. Paul Ervin Knight, Mar. 24, 1928; children: Megan Dianne, Adam Christopher. AS in Secretarial Sci., Chattanooga State U., 1975; BS in Spl. Edn., U. Tenn., 1993, MEd, 1995. Sec. to pres. So. Combustion and Controls, Chattanooga, 1975-78; engring. asst. U.S. Stove Co., Chattanooga, 1979-86; grad. asst. U. Tenn., Chattanooga, 1993-94; tchr. spl. edn. Ridgeland H.S., Rossville, Calif., 1994—. Scholar U. Tenn., 1992. Mem. NEA, CEC, Kappa Delta Pi. Office: Ridgeland H S 2878 Happy Valley Rd Rossville GA 30741

KNIGHT, SAMUEL, JR., citrus and cattle company executive; b. 1943. With S.N. Knight & Sons, Inc., Belle Glade, Fla., 1964—, now pres. Office: S N Knight & Sons Inc 205 SW 1st St Belle Glade FL 33430-3469*

KNIGHT, SANDRA BLOOMSTER, emergency and critical care nurse; b. Ft. Pierce, Fla., Oct. 6, 1951; d. Otto Robert and Lorene Naomi (Herron) Bloomster; m. Keith Mathias Knight Sr., Mar. 19, 1977; 1 child, Keith Mathias. ASN, Miami Dade Coll., 1971; student, Fla. Internat. U., 1975-76, U. South Fla., 1976—; BS in Health Arts, Coll. of St. Francis. RN, Fla.; CEN, cert. PALS, ACLS, TNCC. Charge nurse emergency dept. Palmetto Gen., Hialeah, Fla., 1971-73, 74-76; staff nurse NICU Jackson Meml. Hosp., Miami, 1973; staff nurse emergency dept. South Miami Hosp., 1973-74; charge nurse emergency dept. Shands Teaching Hosp., Gainesville, Fla., 1976-78, Ft. Myers (Fla.) Community Hosp., 1978-80; mgr. The Family MedCenter, Ft. Myers, 1983-91; trauma cons. Lee Meml. Hosp., Ft. Myers, 1991-93, trauma nurse coord., 1993-94; emergency dept. clin. educator Naples (Fla.) Cmty. Hosp., 1995—; instr. pediat. advanced life support, Fla., 1989—, instr. emergency nurse pediats. course, instr. course in advanced trauma nursing; instr. Trauma Nurse Core Course, 1987—, instr. trainer, 1988—, nat. faculty, 1993—; co-chmn. Fla. State Trauma Com., 1988—. Reviewer ENA TNCC Manual, 4th edit.; mem. editl. bd., tech. advisor (nursing video series) Emergency Case Review. Mem. Am. Trauma Soc., Emergency Nurses Assn. (past sec. S.W. Fla. chpt. 1988, nat. TNCC faculty 1993—, pediat. com. 1993—).

KNIGHT, THOMAS JEFFERSON, JR., computer consultant, trainer; b. San Antonio, Oct. 21, 1955; s. Thomas Jefferson and Martha Lena (Craig) K.; m. Lois Ann Simmons, July 13, 1985 (div. Jan. 1993); 1 child, Thomas Jefferson III. BS, Baylor U., 1978; M Pub. Adminstrn., Golden Gate U., 1988. Commd. 2d lt. USAF, 1978, advanced thru grades to capt., 1988; chief of adminstrn. USAF 780th Radar Squadron, Fortuna AFB, N.D., 1978-79; squadron sect. comdr. USAF 325th Component Repair Squadron, Tyndall AFB, Fla., 1979-82; protocol officer USAF HQ Tactical Air Command, Langley AFB, Va., 1982-85; exec. officer USAF 487th Tactical Missile Wing, Comiso AS, Italy, 1985-86, USAF 57th Fighter Weapons Wing, Nellis AFB, Nev., 1986-90; resigned USAF, 1990; cons. Waco, Tex., 1990; software support and tng. mgr. Entré Computer Ctr., Waco, 1990—. Local commr. Panama City (Fla.) Boy Scouts Am., 1979-80. Mem. Air Force Assn. Presbyterian.

KNIPLING, EDWARD FRED, retired research entomologist, agricultural administrator; b. Port Lavaca, Tex., Mar. 20, 1909; s. Henry John and Hulda Lena (Rasch) K.; m. Phoebe Rebecca Hall; children: Edwina, Anita, Edward B., Gary D., Ronald R. B.S., Tex. A&M U., 1930; M.S., Iowa State U., 1932, Ph.D., 1947; D.Sc. (hon.), Catawba Coll., 1962, N.D. State U., 1970, Clemson U., 1972. With USDA, various locations, 1931-73; dir. entomology research div. USDA, Beltsville, Md., 1953-73. Author: Principles of Insect Population Suppression, 1979, Principles of Insect Parasitism Analysis from New Perspectives, 1992; contbr. more than 200 articles to profl. jours. Recipient Nat. Medal Sci., 1966, Rockefeller Pub. Svcs. award, 1966, Pres.'s award for Disting. Fed. Civilian Svc., 1971, World Food prize World Food Prize Found., 1992, Sci. and Tech. Found. Japan prize, 1995; named to Agrl. Rsch. Svc. Sci. Hall of Fame. Fellow Entomol. Soc. Am. (pres. 1952); mem. NAS, Am. Acad. Arts and Scis. Club: Cosmos. Home: 2623 Military Rd Arlington VA 22207-5117

KNIPPENBERG, JOSEPH MICHAEL, political science educator; b. San Francisco, May 9, 1957; s. Josephus Jacobus Maria and Ingeborg Katherina (Buttenhauser) K.; m. Charlotte Lee Boggus, Dec. 19, 1992; 1 child, William, Robert, Joseph. BA, Mich. State U., 1977; MA in Polit. Sci., U. Toronto, Ont., Can., 1978, PhD in Polit. Sci., 1986. Asst. prof. politics Oglethorpe U., Atlanta, 1985-92, assoc. prof., 1992—; chmn. divsn. history, politics and internat. studies, 1992—; vis. scholar Boston Coll., Chestnut Hill, Mass., 1988-89; vis. assoc. prof. polit. sci. Emory U., Atlanta, 1994; mem. Nat. History Stds. Rev. Panel, Ga. Dept. Edn., 1995-96. Co-editor Poets, Princes and Private Citizens: Literary Alternatives to Post-Modern Politics, 1996; contbr. articles to profl. jours. Recipient Faculty Appreciation award Omicron Delta Kappa, Oglethorpe U., 1991, Svc. award Alpha Phi Omega, Oglethorpe U., 1995, Donald C. Agnew Disting. Svc. award Oglethorpe Student Assn., 1995, Award for Teaching Excellence and Leadership Vulcan Materials Co., 1996; fellow John M. Olin Found., 1988-89, Salvatori fellow in acad. leadership Heritage Found., 1992-94; Rsch. grantee Earhart Found., 1991. Mem. Am. Polit. Sci. Assn., So. Polit. Sci. Assn., Midwestern Polit. Sci. Assn., Nat. Assn. Scholars, Assn. Scholars in Ga. (treas. 1990-94, trustee 1990—, pres. 1994—). Home: 1763 Remington Rd Atlanta GA 30341-1439 Office: Oglethorpe U 4484 Peachtree Rd NE Atlanta GA 30319-2737

KNISELY, DEBRA SUE, secondary education educator; b. Ravenna, Ohio, Dec. 7, 1952; d. Gordon Lewis and Wanda Eileen (Williams) K. BS, Kent State U., 1975; MS, U. Akron, 1982. Tchr. English Lake H.S., Uniontown, Ohio, 1976-80, Union Sch., Port-au Prince, Haiti, 1983-86; tchr. English, instr. drama, yearbook Drew Middle Sch., Miami, Fla., 1987-90; tchr. English, instr. tourism, yearbook Norland Sr. H.S., Miami, 1990—; grad. asst. U. Akron, Ohio, 1980-82; GED instr. Miami Lakes Tech. Sch., 1987-90. Union steward Port-au Prince Tchrs., 1984-86, United Tchrs. Dade, Miami, 1995—. Rockefeller Found. grantee, 1991. Mem. Nat. Coun. Tchrs. English, Pi Lambda Theta, Beta Lambda. Home: 10505 NW 10th St Pembroke Pines FL 33026 Office: Norland Sr High 1050 NW 195th St Miami FL 33169-3040

KNISKERN, JOSEPH WARREN, lawyer; b. Coral Gables, Fla., July 7, 1951; s. Kenneth Felix and Elise (Scofield) K. BSBA, U. Fla., 1973, JD cum laude, 1976. Bar: Fla. 1976; cert. real estate atty., Fla.; family mediator, Fla.; registered real estate salesperson, Fla. Assoc. Smathers & Thompson, Miami, Fla., 1976-83, ptnr., 1983-87; ptnr. Kelley Drye & Warren, Miami, 1987-93; pvt. practice Coral Gables, Fla., 1993—; authorized agt. Attys. Title Ins. Fund, Lawyers Title Ins. Corp. Author: When the Vow Breaks: A Survival and Recovery Guide for Christians Facing Divorce, 1993, Courting Disaster: What Runaway Litigation is Costing You and What Can Be Done to Stop the Fallout, 1995. Trustee Miami-Gables Ch. of Christ, 1979-86. Mem. ABA, Fla. Bar, Dade County Bar Assn., Christian Legal Soc., Cmty. Assns. Inst., Inst. for Christian Conciliation, Am. Assn. Christian Counselors. Republican. Office: 1550 Madruga Ave Ste 332 Coral Gables FL 33146-3039

KNOBEL, ROLAND JEFFERSON, health adminstration educator; b. N.Y.C., Feb. 23, 1923; m. Mary Jo Kishler Knobel, Feb. 23, 1946; children: Cathy, Bradley. BA, Miami U., 1946; MA in Econs., George Washington U., 1966; PhD, U. Mich., 1970. Commd. ensign USN, 1945, advanced through grades to comdr., ret., 1966; prof. Ga. State U., Atlanta, 1970-85; prof. emeritus, 1986; prof. Emory U., Atlanta, 1975—. Contbr. articles to profl. jours. Mem. Hemlock (bd. trustees 1991-95), Meml. Soc. Ga. (pres. 1993—). Home: 2637 Cosmos Dr Atlanta GA 30345

KNOLLE, MARY ANNE ERICSON, psychotherapist, business communications consultant; b. Kilgore, Tex., Jan. 7, 1941; d. Evert Eric and Frances Leone (Scott) Ericson; children by previous marriage: Clay Claflin, Sunny Claflin; m. John W. Knolle, Mar. 14, 1980; children: Sara Anne, Evelyn. BA, North Tex. U., 1962; MA in Communication, U. Tex., 1968; postgrad., UCLA, 1964-66; MA in Psychology, Houston Bapt. U., 1989. Editor co. publs. Gt. S.W. Life Ins. Co., 1962; prof. U. Balt., 1968, Miami (Fla.) Dade Coll., 1968, Savannah (Ga.) State Coll., 1969, U. Houston, 1972-76; dir. pub. relations Alvin (Tex.) Coll., 1970-72; founder, pres. Panorama Programs, Houston, 1972-76; coordinator mgmt. devel. tng. Brown & Root, Inc., Houston, 1970-79; div. founder, mgr. mgmt. and orgnl. devel. systems Diversified Human Resources Group, Inc., Houston, 1979—; founder, pres. Panorama Mgmt. Inst., Houston, 1979—, Panorama Cons., 1980—; pres., therapist Stepfamily Support Ctr., Inc., Houston, 1989—; cons. moot ct. U. Tex. Law Sch., 1965—. Judge regional speech contest Houston Jaycees; instr. Houston Community Coll., Alvin Community Coll., U. Balt., Savannah St. Coll. Recipient Blockbuster award United Way, 1979. Mem. Am. Soc. Tng. and Devel., Med. Psychol. & Legal Soc. (organizing founder 1992—), Houston C. of C. (chmn. edn. com.), Houston Indoor Tennis Club, Alpha Delta Pi (past pres. alumnae). Presbyterian. Office: Ste 300 4126 Twelve Oakes Towers Houston TX 77027

KNOTT, WILEY EUGENE, electronic engineer; b. Muncie, Ind., Mar. 18, 1938; s. Joseph Wiley and Mildred Viola (Haxton) K.; 1 child, Brian Evan. BSEE, Tri-State U., 1963; postgrad. Union Coll., 1970-73, Ga. Coll., 1987. Assoc. aircraft engr. Lockheed-Ga. Co., Marietta, 1963-65; tech. publs. engr. GE, Pittsfield Mass., 1965-77, sr. publs. engr., 1977-79, group leader, 1967-79; specialist engr. Boeing Mil. Airplane Co., Wichita, Kans., 1979-81, sr. specialist engr., 1981-84, 89-90, logistics mgr., 1984-85, customer support mgr., 1985-89; base mgr. Castle AFB, 1990-91; facilities plant ops. and maintenance engr. Everett (Wash.) div. Boeing Comml. Airplane Group, 1991-92, lead engr. 1992-93, prin. engr., 1993-95; part-time bus. cons., 1972—. Active Jr. Achievement, 1978-79, Am. Security Coun., 1975-90, Nat. Rep. Senatorial Com., 1979-86 , Nat. Rep. Congl. Com., 1979-87, Rep. Nat. Com., 1979-87 , Rep. Presdl. Task Force, 1981-86, Joint Presdl./Congl. Steering Com., 1982-86, Rep. Polit. Action Com., 1979-86, Mus. of Aviation, 1987-95; state advisor U.S. Congl. Adv. Bd., 1981-86; adviser Jr. Achievement, 1978-79. With AUS, 1956-59. Mem. Am. Def. Preparedness Assn. (life), Am. Mgmt. Assn., Soc. Logistics Engrs., U.S. Golf Assn. (assoc.), Fraternal Order Police (assoc.), Am. Fedn. Police (assoc.), Am. Assn. Retired Persons, Air Force Assn. (life), Assn. Old Crows, Boeing Mgmt. Club, Nat. Audubon Soc. Methodist.

KNOTTS, GLENN R(ICHARD), foundation administrator; b. East Chicago, Ind., May 16, 1934; s. V. Raymond and Opal Ione (Alexander) K. B.S., Purdue U., 1956, M.S., 1960, Ph.D., 1968; M.S., Ind. U., 1964; Dr. Med. Sci. (hon.), Union Coll., 1975; Sc.D. (hon.), Ricker Coll., 1975. Mem. profl. staff Bapt. Meml. Hosp., San Antonio, 1957-60; instr. chemistry San Antonio Coll., 1958-60; adminstrv. asst. AMA, Chgo., 1960-61, research assoc., 1961-62, dir. advt. eval., div. sci. activities, 1963-69; exec. dir. Am. Sch. Health Assn., Kent, Ohio, 1969-72; vis. disting. prof. health sci. Kent State U., 1969-72, prof., mem. grad. faculty dept. allied health scis., 1972-75, coordinator grad. studies and research, 1975; editor-in-chief, prof. med. journalism U. Tex. M.D. Anderson Cancer Ctr., Houston, 1975-85, head dept. med. info. and publs., 1975-79, dir. div. ednl. resources, 1979-85; dir. devel. U. Tex. Health Sci. Ctr. at Houston, 1985-88; prof. U. Tex. Grad. Sch. Biomed. Scis., 1983—; adj. prof. dept. journalism Coll. Communications U. Tex.-Austin, 1984—; exec. dir. Hermann Eye Fund, Houston, 1989—; vis. prof. health edn. Madison Coll., Va., summer 1965, Union Coll., Ky., summers 1965, 66, 69; vis. prof. health edn. Utah State U., summer 1965; vis. lectr. Ind. U., 1965-66; vis. lectr. pharmacology Purdue U., 1968-69; vis. prof. Pahlavi U. Med. Sch., Iran, summer 1970; adj. prof. allied health scis. Kent State U., 1975—; prof. dept. biomed. communications U. Tex. Sch. Allied Health Scis., Houston, 1976—; prof. dept. behavioral scis. U. Tex. Sch. Pub. Health, 1977—; cons. health scis. communications, 1969—; pres. Health Scis. Inst., 1973—; mem. exec. com. Internat. Union Sch. and Univ. Health and Medicine, Paris, 1969-72. Co-author various texts and filmstrips on health sci.; contbr. numerous articles to profl. jours.; cons. editor: Clin. Pediatrics, 1971—; contbg. editor: Annals of Allergy, 1972—; exec. editor: Cancer Bull., 1976-85; mem. numerous editorial bds. Bd. dirs. Med. Arts Pub. Found., Houston, 1977-80, Art League of Houston, 1986-88, Delia Stewart Dance Co., Houston, 1988-90; mem. adv. bd. World Meetings Inc., 1971-80, bd. trustees Mus. Art Am. West, 1987-89; trustee Houston Mus. Natural Sci., 1987-89. Served with U.S. Army, 1956-58. Recipient Gold medal French-Am. Allergy Soc., 1973. Fellow Am. Pub. Health Assn., Am. Sch. Health Assn. (mem. exec. com. 1968-72, editor Jour. Sch. Health 1975-76, Disting. Service award 1973), Am. Inst. Chemists, Royal Soc. Health; mem. Internat. Union Health Edn., AAHPER, Am. Acad. Pharm. Scis., Am. Med. Writers Assn., Am. Pharm. Assn., AAUP, Am. Chem. Soc., AAAS, AMA, Purdue U. Alumni Assn., Ind. U. Alumni Assn., Union Coll. Alumni Assn., Ricker Coll. Alumni Assn., Sigma Xi, Rho Chi, Sigma Delta Chi, Eta Sigma Gamma, Phi Delta Kappa, Kappa Psi. Republican. Presbyterian. Clubs: Marines Meml. (San Francisco); Univ. Faculty; Doctors (Houston), Pelican (Galveston, Tex.). Lodge: Rotary. Home: PO Box 20787 Houston TX 77225-0787 Office: Hermann Eye Fund 6411 Fannin St Houston TX 77030-1501

KNOTTS, ROBERT LEE, insurance executive; b. Thornton, W.Va., Jan. 14, 1942; s. James Bailey and Lena Louise (Jacobs) K.; m. Dottie Lue Watts, Aug. 20, 1967; children: Brice Alan, Lance Eric, Chandra Marie. ChFC, CLU. Sales, truck driver Wholesale Grocery, Grafton, W.Va., 1960-67; lineman, crew leader Monongahela Power Co., Grafton, 1967-78; agt., registered rep. N.Y. Life Ins., N.Y. Life Ins. & Annuity Corp., Charleston, W.Va., 1978—, NYLIFE Securities Corp., Charleston, 1978—; sec. bd. dirs. Grafton Homes, Inc. V.P. Taylor County Econ. Devel. Authority, Grafton, 1985-87; pres. Taylor Devel. Group, Inc., Grafton, 1987—. With USMC, 1960-64. Treas. Taylor County Dem. Exec. Com. Mem. Nat. Assn. Life Underwriters, Fairmont Assn. Life Underwriters, North Cen. W.Va. Chartered Fin. Cons., N. Cen. W.Va. Estate Planning Coun., Grafton Rotary (pres. 1979-81, 95-96, pres. edn. endowment 1991-96). Methodist. Office: NY Life Ins Co PO Box 599 Grafton WV 26354-0599

KNOWLES, CAROLYN SUE EDWARDS, secondary education educator; b. May 14, 1947; d. Lewis and Willie Inez (Ford) Edwards; m. William Limbret Knowles, Aug. 1, 1970; children: Cory Limbret, Heather Shantay. BS, Alcorn State U., 1968; MA, Fisk U., 1974. Tchr. Hunter High Sch., Drew, Miss., 1968-70, North Scott Sch., Forest, Miss., 1970-71, Morton (Miss.) Attendance Ctr., 1971-87, Forest Mcpl. Sch., 1987—; chmn. sci. dept. Forest Mcpl. Sch. Dist., 1992-94. Sec. East Ctrl. Health System Agy., Newton, Miss., 1978-80, Scott County Dem. Exec. Com., Forest, 1972—; chmn. East Ctrl. Cmty. Action Agy., Forest, 1988-92; active VFW Women Aux., Forest, Scott County Colored Women Federated Club, Forest, 1992; leader Girl Scouts U.S., svc. unit co-chmn. Scott County; youth dir. Concord Bapt. Ch.; asst. youth dir. 3d New Hope Dist.; vol. leader 4-H Club, coord. Capitol regional vol., 1993-94. NSF grantee, 1971-74; named Star Tchr. MS Econ. Coun. by Star Student Darryl Harvey Morton Attendance Ctr. Mem. NEA (pres. Scott/Forest Assn. Educators 1968), Miss. Assn. Educators (bd. dirs. 1993—), Miss. Sci. Tchr. Assn., Nat. Sci. Tchrs. Assn., Zeta Phi Beta. Home: 430 George St Forest MS 39074-3412 Office: Hawkins Mid Sch 803 E Oak St Forest MS 39074-4601

KNOWLES, JAMES BARRON, rehabilitative medicine physician; b. Jackson, Ga., Mar. 7, 1936; s. James ammons and Allie PEarl (Jimmerson) K.; m. Donna Marie Nasby, June 1, 1968; children: Kari Noel, Bryan Vincent, Gana Marie, Kelly Elizabeth. Diploma, Emory at Oxford, 1954-56; premed., Emory U., 1956-57; MD, Med. Coll. Ga., 1961; postgrad., U. Minn., 1966-70. Diplomate Am. Bd. Physical Medicine. Physiatrist Physical Medicne Group, Mpls., 1971, Sister Kenny Inst., Mpls., 1972; med. dir. Roger C. PEace Inst., Greenville, S.C., 1972-75; pvt. practice phys. medicine Greenville, 1976-77; physiatrist Nev. Indsl. Commn., Las Vegas, 1977-81; physician specialist Roosevelt Warm Springs (Ga.) Inst., 1981—, physician, 1985-86. Dir. ch. tng. First Bapt. Ch., Warm Springs, 1984-85, chair long range planning, 1984-85, deacon, 1987; dir. ch. tng. Merritt Bapt. Assn., Manchester, Ga., 1985—. Served to capt. USN, 1962-64. Fellow Am. Acad. Physical Medicine and Rehab.; mem. AMA, Meriwether County Med. Soc. (sec. 1985—), Am. Congress of Rehab. Medicne, So. Soc. Physical Medicne, Ga. Soc. Physical Medicine,. Republican. Office: PO Box 1000 Warm Springs GA 31830

KNOWLES, ROBERT GORDON, JR., editor; b. Augusta, Ga., Dec. 18, 1943; s. Robert Gordon and Kathleen (Keiter) K.; m. Penelope Bowen, Dec. 28, 1965 (div. Mar. 1973); children: Irene Fawn, Gordon Bowen; m. Jann Sailors, Oct. 11, 1975; 1 child, Ben Sailors. BA, Ga. State Coll., 1965;

postgrad. in internat. law, Morgan State Coll., 1970; M in Comm., Ga. State U., 1996. Accredited in pub. rels. Pub. Rels. Soc. Am., 1977. Pub. relations dir. Ga. Safety Council, Inc., Atlanta, 1973-74; info. specialist Ga. Dept. of Edn., Atlanta, 1974-75; regional rep. Ins. Info. Inst., Atlanta, 1975-76; asst. mgr. Ins. Info. Inst., Washington, 1976; regional mgr. Ins. Info. Inst., Atlanta, 1977-78; dir. pub. rels. LOMA, Inc., Atlanta, 1978-82; account exec. Carl Byoir & Assocs., Atlanta, 1982-84, sr. account exec., 1984-85, account supr., 1985-86; prin. Robert G. Knowles Assocs., Atlanta, 1986—; So. editor Nat. Underwriter Co., Atlanta, 1986-95; assoc. editor Nat. Underwriter Co., 1986-95; chmn. Pegasus Group Internat., Inc., Atlanta, 1986—; univ. instr. in field, 1986-88. Dir. Ga. Vets. Leadership Program, Atlanta, 1983—. Lt. col. gen. staff hdqs. Ga. State Def. Force, 1990-94, 95—; capt. USAR, 1961-71, Vietnam. Mem. Am. Legion (jr. vice comdr. post 134, 1989-90, comdr. 1991-92), Assn. Nat. Def. Exec. Res. (bd. dirs. 1986-87), Soc. Profl. Journalists, Atlanta Press Clubv, Ga. State U. Alumni Assn., Old Guard of Gate City Guard. Democrat. Methodist. Home: 1523 Colony East Cir Stone Mountain GA 30083-5408 Office: Pegasus Group Internat Inc PO Box 831824 Stone Mountain GA 30083

KNOWLES, STEPHEN HOWARD, space scientist; b. N.Y.C., Feb. 28, 1940; s. Howard Nesmith and Emily Aurelia (Kent) K.; m. Joan Elizabeth Brame, June 5, 1965; children: Jennifer, Katherine. BA, Amherst Coll., 1961; PhD, Yale U., 1968. Space scientist Naval Rsch. Lab., Washington, 1961-86; tech. dir. Naval Space Surveillance Ctr., Dahlgren, Va., 1986-93; tech. advisor Naval Space Command, Dahlgren, 1993—; vis. scientist Commonwealth Sci. and Indsl. Rsch. Orgn. Radiophysics Div., Sydney, Australia, 1974-76. Contbr. 75 articles to profl. jours. Mem. AIAA, Internat. Astron. Union, Am. Geophysical Union, Sigma Xi. Episcopalian. Home: 12107 Harbor Dr Lakeridge VA 22192-2201 Office: Naval Space Command Dahlgren VA 22448

KNOWLES-SMITH, JAIME ANN, elementary school educator; b. Sacramento, Calif., May 5, 1958; d. James Allen Sr. and Diana Mary (Brown) K.; 1 child, T. Shofner Smith, III. BA, U. South Ala., 1980; BS, William Cary Coll., 1985, MEd, 1990; postgrad., U. So. Miss., 1996—. Cert. tech. prep Tex., Miss. Dist. mgr. retail stores, Miss., Tex, 1978-83; exec. asst. QED (Quest Engring.), Humble, Tex., 1985-92; tchr. New Caney (Tex.) Ind. Sch. Dist., 1985-87; tchr., adv. Channelview (Tex.) Ind. Sch. Dist., 1987-92; dist. coord., tchr. Cleveland (Tex.) Ind. Sch. Dist., 1992-94; tchr. Harrison Ctrl. H.S., adv. Harrison County Schs., Gulfport, Miss., 1994—. Contbr. articles to mag., poem to book; asst. editor: Products Liability Book, 1989-90; publ.: Author Learning mag. Recipient Golden Apple award Houston Chronicle, 1992, Hon. Mention Gene Taylor's Office Tchr. of Yr., 1996. Fellow Tex. Assn. Suprs. Curriculum Devel.; mem. ASCD (fellow Tex. Pathways, Tchr. of Yr. 1993, 96), Nat. Tchrs. English, Assn. Journalistic Educators, Miss. ASCD. Republican. Home: 17581 Knowles Kove Saucier MS 39574 Office: Harrison County Schs 15600 School Rd Gulfport MS 39503

KNOX, BETTY EMMETT, educational administrator; b. Gastonia, N.C., Feb. 9, 1934; d. James Wilson and Laura Marie (Fowler) Emmett; m. John Jackson Knox, Jr., Aug. 12, 1956 (dec. Apr. 1988); 1 child, Joy Lynne. AA, Gardner-Webb Coll., 1954; BS cum laude, Appalachian State U., 1956, MA, 1958; EdS in Counseling, N.C. State U., 1977, EdD, 1979. Nat. cert. counselor. Tchr. N.C. and Fla. schs., 1956-59; counselor N.C. schs., 1960-66, 67-74, 75-76; asst. dir. admissions U. N.C., Charlotte, 1966-67; pres. Counseling and Ednl. Cons. Svcs., Raleigh, N.C., 1977—; dir. devel., rsch. and planning, pers., publ. rels. Randolph Community Coll., Asheboro, N.C., 1983-85; exec. dir. N.C. Community Colls. Found., Inc., Raleigh, 1985-89; exec. dir. coll. advancement Cape Fear Community Coll., Wilmington, N.C., 1992-94; trustee Gardner-Webb U., Boiling Springs, N.C., 1985-88, 91-94. Contbr. articles to profl. jours. Bd. dirs. Counseling and Human Devel. Found., Alexandria, 1978-79, dir. emeritus, 1979—; bd. dirs., treas. Found. for Ednl. and Econ. Devel., Raleigh, 1990-91; bd. dirs. Forty For the Future, Raleigh, 1992-94. Mem. AAUW, Am. Counseling Assn. (pres. 1978-79), Am. Sch. Counselor Assn. (pres. 1974-75, Excellence in Rsch. award 1985), Nat. Coun. Resource Devel., N.C. Sch. Counselor Assn. (pres. 1970-71), N.C. Counseling Assn. (pres. 1974-75), Barrett Leadership award 1982, R. Anderson scholar 1970), N.C. Coun. Officers for Resource Devel. (Crump Meml. scholar 1985), N.C. Assn. Instnl. Rsch., Execs Club Raleigh, Phi Theta Kappa (hon., Mary B. Dowless award 1994), Delta Kappa Gamma. Baptist. Home: 5100 Sandlewood Dr Raleigh NC 27609-4425

KNOX, BOONE A., bank executive; b. 1929. Pres. Allied Bank of Ga., Thomson, 1977—, now chmn. bd. dirs. Office: Allied Bank of GA 204 Main St Thomson GA 30824-1957*

KNOX, CHARLES HENRY, real estate executive; b. Little Rock, July 31, 1950; s. William H. and Oza Bell (Elliott) K.; m. Karen G. Minton, July 7, 1972; children: Brook W., Andrea K., Wade H. Student, Henderson State U., 1968-71; grad., Realtors Inst., 1983. Cert. residential specialist. Ptnr. Knox Constrn. Co., Lonoke, Ark., 1972-81; pres. Knox Realty Co., Inc., Lonoke, 1974—; bd. dirs. Lonoke County Residential Housing Bd., Cabot, Ark., 1986—. Bd. dirs. Cemetery Assn., Lonoke, 1978—, Lonoke Community Ctr., 1978—, Lonoke Swimming Pool Assn., 1978—; pres. Lonoke C. of C., 1981-82. Recipient Leadership award Lonoke C. of C., 1981-82. Mem. Lonoke-Prairie County Bd. Realtors (pres. 1985-86, 90-91, 91-92, v.p. 1989), Lonoke County Bd. Realtors (past officer), Ark. Realtors Assn. (congl. coord. 1987—), U.S. Jaycees (bd. dirs. Presdl. award 1973-74, Disting. Svc. award 1976). Mem. Ch. of Christ. Home: PO Box 306 Lonoke AR 72086-0306 Office: Knox Realty Co Inc 119 E 2d PO Box 83 Lonoke AR 72086-0083

KNOX, GLENDA JANE, retired health and safety specialist, educator; b. Abernathy, Tex., Mar. 8, 1939; d. Raymond Arnold and Viola Jane (Melton) Boykin; m. William Gene Bright, Mar. 2, 1954 (dec. July 1974); children: Rocky Dwain, Jeannie Ann, Mary Jane, Tommy Lynn; m. Arthur Richard Knox, May 1, 1978; step-sons: Ricky Lynn Stinson, Tony Ray Knox; foster son, Roy David Haney. Grad., Comml. Coll., Baton Rouge, 1985; student, Odessa Coll., 1986-89. Cert. water safety instrn. trainer, health and safety specialist, infant, presch. and parent swimming instr. specialist. Sales clk. Flying B Western Wear, Odessa, Tex., 1975-76; mgr. Redondo Western Wear, Odessa, Tex., 1976-78, Andy's Western Wear, Odessa, Tex., 1978-79; owner Classy Original's Western Wear, Odessa, Tex., 1979-81; water safety instr. Odessa Family YMCA, 1979-82; water safety instr. Odessa Coll., 1981-83, water safety coord., 1983-96, health and safety instr., 1987-96, aquatics coord. continuing edn., 1983-92; ret., 1996; instr. Arthritis Found. YMCA Aquatics Program, Odessa, 1990—, Aquatic Exercise Assn., Odessa, 1987—; instr. specialist ARC Adapted Aquatics, Midland, Tex., 1986—; lifeguard instr. trainer ARC, Odessa, 1979—, CPR instr. trainer, 1981—, 1st aid instr. trainer, 1981—, canoeing instr., 1988-91; water safety specialist Boy Scouts and Girl Scouts Am., Odessa, 1980—; 1st aid instr. Medic First Aid, Odessa, 1990—. Author, editor, artist: Water Aerobics, 1986; author, editor: Food Safety Svc., 1992; designer logo and pin West Tex. Ter. Am. Red Cross, 1988. Vol. Salvation Army, Odessa, 1979-83; mem. exec. bd. ARC, Odessa, 1992, nat. awards chmn., 1992-95, health and safety chmn. region III, terr. 3, 1987-95. Recipient Outstanding Vol. Svc. award Commodore Longfellow Soc., 1994, 95, ARC, 1994, others. Mem. NAFE, Commodore Longfellow Soc. (Outstanding Svc. award 1990, 94), Smithsonian Inst., Nat. Trust for Hist. Preservation, Northshore Animal League (Benefactor award 1988, 89). Baptist. Home: 10177 W 26th St Odessa TX 79763-6333

KNOX, HAVOLYN CROCKER, financial consultant; b. Charlotte, N.C., Oct. 20, 1937; d. Earl Reid and Etta Lorain (Wylie) Crocker; m. Charles Eugene Knox, July 20, 1963 (div. 1981); children: Charles Eugene Jr., Sandra Leigh. Cert. Stenography, U. N.C., Greensboro, 1956. ChFC, CLU. Exec. sec. Stellings-Gossett Theatres, Inc., Charlotte, 1956-57; legal sec. McDougle, Ervin, Horack & Snepp, Charlotte, 1957, Pierce, Wardlow, Knox & Caudle, Charlotte, 1957-63; adminstrv. asst. Charlotte-Mecklenburg Planning Commn., 1980; exec. asst. Conn. Mut. Life Ins. Co., Charlotte, 1981-86; assoc. The Hinrichs Fin. Group, Charlotte, 1986-91, Lyn Knox & Assocs., Charlotte, 1991—. Ops. dir. Eddie Knox for Mayor campaign, Charlotte; campaign mgr. Herb Spaugh for City Coun., Charlotte, 1981, 83, 85; registration chmn. Kemper Open Golf Tournament, Charlotte, 1976-79; pres. The Legal Aux., Charlotte, 1972-73; bd. dirs. Oratorio Singers of Charlotte, 1986-93. Recipient William Danforth Found. award, 1955. Mem. Am. Soc. CLU and ChFC (bd. dirs. Charlotte chpt. 1994-95), Nat. Assn. Life Underwriters, Charlotte Assn. Life Underwriters, Charlotte Estate Planning Coun., Charlotte Civitan Club. Republican. Presbyterian. Home: 2331 Carmel Rd Charlotte NC 28226-6322 Office: Lyn Knox & Assocs PO Box 4115 Charlotte NC 28226-0099

KNOX, JAMES LLOYD, bishop; b. Tampa, Fla., Jan. 16, 1929; s. Carlos Stephen and Jessie (Hardee) K.; m. Edith Laney Strawn, June 2, 1951; children: Richard Michael, Carol Anne. AB, Fla. So. Coll., 1951; BD, Emory U., 1954; Cert., Presbyn. Lang. Sch., San Jose, Costa Rica, 1959. On trial Fla. Conf., 1952; ordained deacon, 1953; full connection, elder, 1954. Pastor United Meth. Ch., Williamson, Ga., 1952-54, St. John's Meth. Ch., Tampa, Fla., 1954-58, Santiago de la Vegas Meth. Ch., Cuba, 1959-60; chaplain Wesley Sch., Cuba, 1959-60; pastor First Ch., Lomas de Zamora, Buenos Aires, Argentina, 1961-64; assoc. pastor First Meth. Ch., West Palm Beach, Fla., 1964; coord. Fla. Meth. Spanish Ministry, 1965-73; pastor Hyde Park United Meth. Ch., Tampa, 1973-77, 1st United Meth. Ch., St. Petersburg, Fla., 1983-84; supt. DeLand (Fla.) dist. United Meth. Ch., 1977-80, supt. Miami (Fla.) dist., 1980-83; elected to episcopacy 1st United Meth. Ch., 1984; bishop Birmingham (Ala.) area United Meth. Ch., Birmingham, Ala., 1984-92; bishop Atlanta area United Meth. Ch., Atlanta, 1992—; mem. gen. bd. Meth. Ch. in Argentina, 1963-64; mem. gen. bd. global ministries United Meth. Ch. Editor: Land of Decision, 1961-64; contbr. articles to Together, World Outlook, others. Supt. Buenos Airea South Dist., 1963-64; news corr. Argentina Bd. Missions; trustee Ward Coll., Barker Coll., Buenos Aires, 1961-64, Emory U., Wesleyan Coll., LaGrange Coll., Reinhardt Coll., Paine Coll., Young Harris Coll., Gammon Theol. Sem., Clark Atlanta U.; bd. councilors Carter Ctr. Home: 2339 Fair Oaks Rd Decatur GA 30033-1207 Office: United Meth Ctr 208 159 Ralph Mcgill Blvd NE Atlanta GA 30308-3353

KNOX, KENNETH JOE, development consultant; b. Indpls., May 8, 1938; s. Edward E. and Nellie M. (Purcell) K.; m. Dorothy A. Lester, June 8, 1962; children: Kathy L., Thomas A., Rebecca A., Amy J. BA, U. Indpls., 1960; MA, Ind. U., 1969. Cert. real estate broker; cert. CFRE by Nat. Soc. of Fund Raising Execs.; grad. exec. leadership Inst. on Philanthropy. Exec. dir. Boys' Club Assn., Indpls., 1965-73; br. mgr. Ga. Fed. Bank, Atlanta, 1973-74; assoc. dir. Neighborhood Reinvestment Corp., Washington, 1974-81; cons. Neighborhood Housing Svcs. Am., Oakland, Calif., 1982-92; pres., broker First Metro Realty, Lilburn, Ga., 1985-91; dir. resource devel. Neighborhood Reinvestment Corp., Tucker, Ga., 1992—. Contbr. articles to Boys' Clubs Am. Jour., 1973. Dir. various United Fund Agys., 1970-73; active Ind. Gov's. Youth Council, 1971-72. Mem. Nat. Soc. of Fund Raising Execs., Neighborhood Funders Group, Gwinnett Bd. Realtors. Home: 1697 Edinburgh Dr Tucker GA 30084 Office: Neighborhood Reinvestment Corp 2185 Northlake Pky Tucker GA 30084-4111

KNOX, RICHARD DOUGLAS, JR., healthcare executive; b. Bethesda, Md., Mar. 22, 1950; s. Richard D. Sr. and Margaret L. (Liming) K. BS, Va. Commonwealth U., 1973. CPA, Va. From staff mem. to sr. mgr. KPMG Peat Marwick, Richmond, Va., 1973-81, sr. mgr., 1981-86; v.p., CIO Children's Hosp. of King's Daus., Norfolk, Va., 1986-88, sr. v.p. fin., CFO, 1988—; treas. Internat. Ctr. for Children's Health, Norfolk, 1992—; bd. dirs. Ctr. for Pediatric Rsch., Norfolk, 1993—; sec.-treas. Network for Child and Adolescent Health, Norfolk, 1993—; treas. Children's Health Network, Norfolk, 1994—; sec. Pediatric Faculty Assocs., Norfolk, 1994—; treas. Barry Robinson Ctr., Norfolk, 1994—; mem. bus. adv. Norfolk State U., 1993—; bd. dirs. The Planning Coun., Norfolk, 1995—; bd. dirs. Vol. Hampton Roads, Norfolk, 1995—. Mem. AICPA, Healthcare Fin. Mgmt. Assn. Epsicopalian. Home: 509 55th St Virginia Beach VA 23451 Office: Childrens Hosp of Kings Daus 601 Childrens Ln Norfolk VA 23507-1910

KNOX, ROBERT BURNS, religious organization administrator; b. Concord, N.H., Feb. 26, 1917; s. Ralph Burns Knox and Ruby Aileen (Gillette) Dixon; m. Barbara Macauley Lovejoy, July 4, 1941; children: Robert B. Jr., Karen Lovejoy Knox Campbell. BA, U. N.H., 1941; MA, George Washington U., 1956; Ministry Program, U. of the South, 1981. Lic. lay min. Episcopal Ch. Cadet USAF, 1940, Col., 1970; chief of order dept. RCA Distbn. Corp., San Antonio, 1972-76, 77-79; ch. adminstr. St. George Episcopal Ch., San Antonio, 1979—; bd. dirs., treas. Order of St. Luke the Physician, Sch. Pastoral Care. Mem. interparish com. for Evangelism, San Antonio, 1987-89, compensation com. for Episcopal Diocese West Tex., 1990-93, armed forces com.. 1993-96. Recipient Legion of Merit with oak leaf cluster, others. Episcopalian. Home: 10614 Mt Ida San Antonio TX 78213-1738 Office: Saint George Episcopal Ch 6904 West Ave San Antonio TX 78213-1820

KNUCKLES, JOSEPH LEWIS, biology educator. BS in Biology and Chemistry, N.C. Ctrl. U., 1948, MS in Biology, 1950; PhD Parasitology/Biol. Scis., U. Conn., 1959; Cert. in Radiation Biology, St. Augustine Coll., Raleigh, N.C., 1964. Asst. prof. and dean of men Bishop Coll., Marshall, Tex., 1950-51, chmn. dept. sci., 1951-52; instr. biology and math. Fayetteville (N.C.) State U., 1956-59, prof. and biology coord., 1959-67, asst. football coach, 1956-70, prof. and chair dept. biol. and phys. scis., 1967-78, dir. coop. programs, 1970, dir. summer sch., 1971, dir. Consortium for Promotion Acad. Excellence in Biology, 1972-74, dir. sci. improvement and exptl. biology program, 1974-76; invited mem. People to People Pub. Health Del. to Peoples' Republic of China, summer 1988, Epidemiology Del., 1994, Parasitology Del. to Biejing, China and Mongolia, 1995. Contbr. articles to profl. jours. Capt. USPHS res. Named Outstanding Tchr., Fayetteville State U., 1974; recipient Man of Yr. award Coll. Heights Credit Union, 1979, Outstanding Svc. to Fayetteville State U. and the Cmty. award, 1985, Cert. of Appreciation for notable contbns. to United Bank, 1985, Outstanding and Dedicated Svc. to Fayetteville State U. award, 1985; Joseph L. Knuckles Meritorious Rsch. award named in his honor; recipient Chancellor's award for Meritorious Contbns., 1990, Chancellor's cert. of merit for Meritorious Contbns. to Fayetteville State U. and Outstanding Svc. to the Region and State, 1994, others. Mem. Sigma Xi, Beta Kappa Chi.

KNULL, WILLIAM H., III, lawyer; b. Coronado, Calif., Apr. 14, 1948. BA magna cum laude, Yale U., 1970; JD, U.Va., 1977. Bar: N.Y. 1978, Tex. 1987, U.S. Dist. Ct. (so., no., we. and ea. dists.) Tex., U.S. Dist. Ct. (so., ea. and no. dists.) N.Y., U.S. Ct. Appeals (2d and 5th cirs.). Editor notes Va. Law Rev., 1976-77. Lt. USN, 1970-74. Mem. ABA (litigation sect.), State Bar Tex., Houston Bar Assn., Order of Coif. Office: Mayer Brown & Platt 700 Louisiana St, Ste 3600 Houston TX 77002*

KNUSSMANN, WILLARD THEODORE, mechanical engineer; b. St. Louis, Aug. 3, 1942; s. Willard Ralph and Dorothy Lorretta (Mattes) K.; div.; children: Amy, Kristen, Jill. BSME, U. Mo., Rolla, 1965; MS in Engring. Mgmt., U. Mo., 1972; MBA, So. Ill. U., 1977; doctoral studies, St. Louis U., 1980-81. Registered profl. engr., Mo., Fla., Tex., Calif. Constrn. engr. Monsanto Co., St. Louis, 1969-71; mech. design engr. Monsanto Co., St. Peters, Mo., 1969; mgr. of engring. Monsanto Co., River, Conn., 1971; resident constrn. engr. Anheuser Busch Cos., St. Louis, 1971-79, sr. resident constrn. engr., 1979-83, engring. constrn. mgr., 1983—; expert witness on constrn. claims, bldg. codes; instr. East Idaho Tech. Coll., 1990-91; cons. in field. Lt. (j.g.) USN, 1965-69, Vietnam. Mem. ASME. Lutheran.

KNUTESON, KNUT JEFFERY, computer engineer; b. Spanish Fork, Utah, Nov. 1, 1949; s. Harold and Donna Fay (Gardner) K.; m. Kirsti Krogvik, Aug. 25, 1971 (div. Oct. 1988); children: Kathrine, Knut-Sigurd, Joshua, Kristian, Harold, Marie Elizabeth; m. Eva Luna, June 30, 1989; children: Luisa Eustacia, Yolanda Celestia, Rosa Elena, Linda Liliana, Joseph Henry; m. Ana Maria Teran, Feb. 5, 1994. Student, Brigham Young U., 1967-72; A in Electronics Tech., Utah Tech. Coll., 1979. Electronics monitor Amund Clausen A/S, Porsgrunn, Norway, 1972-73; electronics technician, libr. Orem (Utah) City Pub. Libr., 1977-79; electronics test and lab. technician Gen. Products div. IBM Corp., Tucson, 1979-82; computer systems technician and asst. programmer OmniSoft Corp., Salt Lake City, 1982-83; computer systems technician and cons. World Industries Cons., Inc., Tacoma, 1983-84; engr.-in-charge customer engring. KET Svc., Inc., Tooele, Utah and Minnetonka, Minn., 1984-88, Que Internat., Colonia LeBaron, Galeana, Chihuahua, Mex., 1988—; owner Profl. Communications, Galeana, Chihuahua, Mexico, 1993—; bd. dirs. OmniSoft, A.M.S.; cons. engr. Collier's Pub., 1980—; researcher, compiler, author of Mormon genetic materials. Author religious booklets; compiler indices to Mormon scholarly books. Mem. Brotherhood Liberty and Peace, Mex., 1988-95, chmn. fine arts com., 1989-94, sec. gen. coun., mem., 1990-93; sr. advisor Coll. Reps. Nat. Com., 1987—; active neighborhood crime watch Pima County Sheriff's Dept., Tucson, 1980-82; vol. fireman Corona de Tucson Fire Dept., 1980-83; dir. Manos De Auyda, U.S. and Mex., 1989-94; mem., supr. Comision Nacional de Emergencia, Galeana, Chihuahua, Mex., 1992-93; supr. Delegacion Galeana Federacion Nacional de Radiocomunicaciones de Mexico, 1992-94. Recipient Disting. Leadership award Am. Biog. Inst., 1988, Cert. of Appreciation 2d Amendment Found., 1985-87. Mem. Second Amendment Found. (nat. bd. advisors 1986—), Citizen's Com. for the Right to Keep and Bear Arms (nat. adv. coun. 1987—, Citizen of Yr. award 1982-87). Libertarian. Mormon. Home: 5013 Chromite #A-5 El Paso TX 79932 Office: F14 Bass Ctr 6001 Gateway West #300 El Paso TX 79925

KOACH, STEPHEN FRANCIS, distribution executive, retired army officer; b. N.Y.C., June 19, 1950; s. Harry Francis and Anna Nell (Burakowski) K.; m. Marie Annette Helms, Feb. 14, 1975; children: Sharon, Heather, Kristin. BS, St. John's U., 1972; MBA, Embry-Riddle Aero. U., 1988. Cert. master army aviator, comml. helicopter pilot. Asst. buyer J.W. Mays Inc., Bklyn., 1972-73; commd. 2d lt. U.S. Army, 1972, advanced through grades to maj., 1984; rifle platoon leader C Co. 2nd Bn. 503rd ABN Inf., Ft. Campbell, Ky., 1973-74; exec. officer HHC 2nd Bn. 503rd ABN Inf., Ft. Campbell, 1974; platoon comdr., ops. officer 1st Squadron, 17th Air Cavalry, Ft. Bragg, N.C., 1975-79; attack platoon comdr., exec. officer, ops. officer 501st AVN Bn., Katterbach, Fed. Republic Germany, 1979-82; brigade S-3, company comdr. Aviation Training Brigade, Ft. Rucker, Ala., 1982-86; sr. Army force planner ROK/US Combined Forces Command, Seoul, Republic of Korea, 1986-87; dir. plans, training, mobilization and security Ft. Monroe, Va., 1986-89; team chief hdqrs. U.S. Army Aviation Tech. Assistance Fielding Team, King Khalid Mil. City, Saudi Arabia, 1989-90; instr. Enterprise (Ala.) Jr. Coll., 1991-93; chief evaluation div. U.S. Army Aviation Ctr., Directorate of Evaluation and Standardization, Ft. Rucker, Ala., 1990-93; ret. U.S. Army, 1993; traffic mgr. Collins Sign Co., Inc., Dothan, Ala., 1993—. Mem. Hampton (Va.) Cup Regatta Com., Phoebus Celebration Com., Hampton, 1987-89, USS Newport News (Va.) Commissioning Com., 1988-89. Decorated Defense Meritorious Service medal. Mem. KC, Am. Legion, Army Aviation Assn. Am. Republican. Roman Catholic. Home: 107 Lake Oliver Dr Enterprise AL 36330-1436 Office: Collins Sign Co Inc PO Box 1253 Dothan AL 36302-1253

KOBDISH, GEORGE CHARLES, lawyer; b. Casper, Wyo., June 30, 1950; s. Richard Matthew and Jo Earl (Uttz) K.; m. Mary Ellen Griffith, Jan. 24, 1969; children: George Charles, Jr., Kelly Rebecca, Kimberlee Nelle. BBA with honors, U. Tex., 1971, JD, 1974. Bar: Tex. 1974, U.S. Dist. Ct. (no. dist.) Tex. 1975. Asst. atty. gen. State of Tex., Austin, 1974-76; assoc. McCall, Parkhurst & Horton L.L.P., Dallas, 1976-80, ptnr., 1981—. Bd. dirs. North Dallas Shared Ministries. Mem. Nat. Assn. Bond Lawyers, Tex. Bar Assn., Dallas Bar Assn., Royal Oaks Country Club, Tower Club, Dallas Friday Group, Serra Club of Dallas. Home: 9206 Arbor Branch Dr Dallas TX 75243-6308 Office: McCall Parkhurst & Horton LLP 717 N Harwood St Ste 900 Dallas TX 75201-6514

KOBETZ, RICHARD WILLIAM, criminologist, consultant; b. Chgo., Oct. 23, 1933; s. Nestor Joseph and Mary (Zurek) K.; m. Eleanore Marian Sever, Oct. 8, 1960; children: Kevin, Kimberly and Candice (twins). AA, Chgo. City Jr. Coll., 1959; student, Ill. Tchrs. Coll., 1964-66; MS in Pub. Adminstrn., Ill. Inst. Tech., 1968; D of Pub. Adminstrn., Nova U., 1978. Cert. personal protection specialist. Police officer Winnetka (Ill.) Police Dept., 1954-55; from police officer to sgt. to lt. Chgo. Police Dept., 1955-68; asst. dir. Internat. Assn. Chiefs of Police, Washington, 1968-79; exec. dir., trainer, cons. Exec. Protection Inst., Berryville, Va., 1979—; dir., trainer, cons. North Mountain Pines Tng. Ctr., Winchester, Va., 1979—; security cons. numerous U.S. corps., 1979—; active various security and enforcement agys., 1979—. Author: The Police Role and Juvenile Delinquency, 1971, Juvenile Justice Administration, 1973, Target Terrorism: Providing Protective Services, 1979, Providing Executive Protection, 1990, Vol. II, 1994; contbr. articles to profl. jours., chpts. to books. Acad. Security Educators and Trainers fellow, 1987. Mem. Acad. Security Educators and Trainers (pres., v.p. 1982—), Internat. Assn. Chiefs of Police (Achievement award 1979), Am. Soc. Indsl. Security, Am. Soc. Criminology, Am. Soc. for Pub. Adminstrn. Republican. Roman Catholic. Club: Nine Lives Assocs. (Berryville) (exec. sec. 1978—). Home and Office: Arcadia Manor RR 2 Box 3645 Berryville VA 22611-9568

KOBS, ALFRED W., engineer; b. Houston, Sept. 8, 1919; s. Arthur G. and Emma Louise (Bogs) K.; m. A. Pidd Miller, Sept. 22, 1950; 1 child, Pidd. AA, Lon Morris, Jacksonville, Tex., 1940; BSChemE, U. Tex., 1943; MSIE, U. Houston, 1958. Registered profl. engr., Tex. Engr. Eastern State Refinery, Houston, 1943-44, Union Carbide, Texas City, Tex., 1946-50, 52-62; ind. engr. Houston, 1962—. Precinct chmn. Dem. Party, Houston, 1994-96. Served with USN engrs., 1944-46, 50-52, lt. USNR. Mem. AIChE, Tex. Soc. Profl. Engrs., ISA, Masons. Methodist. Home: 7619 Windswept Ln Houston TX 77063-6223 Office: Kobs Engring 6400 Westpark Dr Houston TX 77057-7215

KOBY, WILLIAM A., company executive, lawyer; b. 1946. BA, U. Tex., JD. Bar: Tex. Co-founder, pres. The Applerock Group, L.C. ; pres. MCX Corp., Houston; lawyer HEI Corp.; gen. ptnr. Focal Mgmt. Co., L.P. Office: MCX Corp 1717 Saint James Pl Ste 600 Houston TX 77056

KOCH, DOTT CLARKE, writer; b. Ahoskie, N.C., Oct. 8, 1924; d. David Arthur and Agnes Leona (Jones) Clarke; m. William Julian Koch, Nov. 28, 1948; children: Patricia Koch Margolis, Jean Koch Hamilton, Deb Koch Plylar, David Frederick Koch. BA, Meredith Coll., 1947; MA, U. N.C., 1972. Author: (juv., beginning-to-read books) I Play at the Beach, 1954, Gone is My Goose, 1956, When the Cows Got Out, 1958, Up the Big Mountain, 1960, Let It Rain, 1962, Monkeys Are Funny That Way, 1964; (adult novel under pen name of Mary Mitchell Douglas) Flying With the Eagles, 1994; (movie scripts) Sweet Deception, 1996, Take That, Mr. Smugglesdorf!, 1996, The Underground, 1996, (audio novel) Sweet Deception, 1996. Home: 10610 NW 22nd St Pembroke Pines FL 33026-2312

KOCH, JAMES VERCH, academic administrator, economist; b. Springfield, Ill., Oct. 7, 1942; s. Elmer O. and Wilma L. K.; m. Donna L. Stickling, Aug. 20, 1967; children: Elizabeth, Mark. BA, Ill. State U., 1964; PhD, Northwestern U., 1968. Research economist Harris Trust Bank, Chgo., 1966; from asst. prof. to prof. econs. Ill. State U., 1967-78, chmn. dept., 1972-78; dean Faculty Arts and Scis., R.I. Coll., Providence, 1978-80; prof. econs., provost, v.p. acad. affairs Ball State U., Muncie, Ind., 1980-86; pres. U. Mont., Missoula, 1986-90, Old Dominion U., Norfolk, Va., 1990—. Author: Industrial Organization and Prices, 2d edit, 1980, Microeconomic Theory and Applications, 1976, The Economics of Affirmative Action, 1976, Introduction to Mathematical Economics, 1979. Mem. Am. Econ. Assn., Econometric Soc., Am. Assn. Higher Edn., AAUP. Lutheran. Home: 5000 Edgewater Dr Norfolk VA 23508-1720 Office: Old Dominion U Office of President Norfolk VA 23529

KOCH, NICOLE ANN, reporter; b. Topeka, Nov. 23, 1975; d. Edward Eugene and Mari Elizabeth (Mace) K. Student, U. Okla., 1995. Reporter Examiner Enterprise, Bartlesville, Okla., 1993-94; reporter (police) The Okla. Daily, Norman, 1994-96; copy editor The Okla. Daily, 1995; reporter, copy editor The Bismarck (N.D.) Tribune, 1995, The Tulsa (Okla.) World, 1996—; mem. adv. bd. Univ. Coll., Norman, 1995-96; mem. President's Leadership Class, Norman, 1994-95. Recipient State Journalist award Journalism Edn. Assn., Bartlesville, 1994, Director's award AP, Oklahoma City, 1995. Mem. Soc. of Profl. Journalists (pres. 1995-96). Republican. Roman Catholic. Home: 1931 Limestone Ct Bartlesville OK 74006 Office: The Okla Daily 860 Van Vleet Oval Norman OK 73019

KOCHERSBERGER, ROBERT CHARLES, JR., journalism educator; b. Buffalo, Apr. 25, 1950; s. Robert Charles and Marjorie M. (Owens) K.; m. Janet Couper Watrous, May 14, 1977; children: Charles, Anne. BA, St. Bonaventure U., 1972; MS, Syracuse U., 1979; PhD, U. Tenn., 1986. Journalist The Evening Press, Binghamton, N.Y., 1972-79; asst. prof. SUNY Coll., Cortland, 1979-86; assoc. prof. N.C. State U., Raleigh, 1986—; acad. specialist in Slovenia and Egypt, USIA, Washington, 1991-94; Fulbright prof. in Yugoslavia, 1991. Author: More than a Muckraker: Ida Tarbell's Lifetime in Journalism, 1994. Democrat. Episcopalian. Home: 415 S Boylan Ave Raleigh NC 27603-1909 Office: NC State U English Dept Raleigh NC 27695-8105

KOCHI, JAY KAZUO, chemist, educator; b. Los Angeles, May 17, 1927; s. Tsuruzo and Shizuko (Moriya) K.; m. Marion Kiyono, Mar. 1, 1959; children—Sims, Ariel, Julia. Student, Cornell U., 1945; B.S., UCLA, 1949; Ph.D., Iowa State U., 1952. Faculty Harvard U., 1952-55; NIH fellow Cambridge U., Eng., 1956; mem. faculty Iowa State U., 1956; with Shell Devel. Co., 1957-61; mem. faculty dept. chemistry Case Western Res. U., Cleve., 1962-69; prof. Case Western Res. U., 1966-69; prof. chemistry Ind. U., Bloomington, 1969-74; Earl Blough prof. chemistry Ind. U., 1974-84; Robert A. Welch Disting. prof. chemistry U. Houston, 1984—; cons. chemist, 1964—. Mem. Am. Chem. Soc., Chem. Soc. (London), Nat. Acad. Scis., Sigma Xi. Home: 4372 Faculty Ln Houston TX 77004-6601

KOCK, ROBERT MARSHALL, investment banker; b. Middletown, N.J., Aug. 31, 1942; s. Winston Edward and Kathleen (Redmond) K.; m. Sherry Tranum, Feb. 3, 1968; children: Cristobel Kathleen, Kimberly Tranum, Caroline Redmond, Robert Marshall Jr. Student, U. Bristol, England, 1962, U. Mich., 1961, U. Colo., 1959-60. Mgr. Pan Am. Airways, N.Y.C., 1964-68, Goldman Sachs & Co., N.Y.C., 1968-71; v.p. Goldman Sachs & Co., London, 1971-80; managing dir. Smith Barney Harris Upham Internat., Paris, London, 1980-87; pres., C.E.O. RMK Internat. Securities Inc., Hilton Head, S.C., 1990-92; ptnr. Little & Co., London, 1990-91; bd. dirs. Recovery Ctr. of Hilton Head, 1991-96; with Morgan Keegan & Co., Inc., Atlanta, 1993—; cons., Club of Rome, 1974; lectr., The City U., London, 1977. Contbr. articles to profl. jours. Vestry St. Luke's Episc. Ch., Hilton Head Island, S.C., 1990-93, sr. warden, 1991. Mem. Assn. Internat. Bond Dealers (market practice com. 1975-76), The Bond Club London (chmn. 1983-84), Annabel's London, Hurlingham Club London. Republican.

KOCUREK, PATRICIA TERRAZAS, elementary education educator; b. Brownsville, Tex., Mar. 9, 1935; d. Alberto and Bertha (Cortazar) Terrazas; m. Louis J. Kocurek Jr., Aug. 17, 1957; children: Louis J. III, Alberto T., Kristopher M., John R., Patricia A. Student, St. Mary's Coll., Notre Dame, Ind.; BA, Incarnate Word Coll., San Antonio, 1957; MA, Trinity U., 1976. Cert. bilingual tchr. Tchr. 5th grade Harlandale Ind. Sch. Dist., San Antonio; del. NEA, Lome Togo, Melbourne, Australia, San Jose, Costa Rica; chairperson site base decision making coun. Harlandale Ind. Sch. Dist. Active San Antonio Symphony League; founding mem. Tranchesi Meml. Svc. Corp.; past chair Wolf Trail Kids Kamp, Harry Jersig Speech and Hearing Ctr.; meml. chair Sunshine Cottage; precinct chair Bexar County Dems.; past mem. exec. com. Ella Austin Community Ctr.; past mem. exec. com., 1st v.p. Early Learning Inst.; former group leader Little Rock Scripture Soc.; past Christian child devel. dir. Our Lady of Grace Ch. Mem. NEA (bd. dirs. Dist. XX), Tex. State Tchrs. Assn. (bd. dirs. legis. contact, pres. region 7, bd. dirs., chairperson site based decision making com. Harlandale ISI), Harlandale Tchrs. Assn. (past pres., v.p., treas.), World Orgn. Teaching Profession, St. Monica's Guild, Alumnae of Sacred Heart, Equestrian Order of Holy Sepulchre. Democrat. Roman Catholic. Home: 108 Thelma Dr San Antonio TX 78212-2516

KOEHLER, RONALD GENE, art educator, sculptor; b. Cape Girardeau, Mo., Sept. 30, 1950; s. Melbourne Frederick and Bernice Marcelene (Seyer) K.; m. Mary Catherine Salley, Oct. 5, 1984; children: Michael Asbury, Adam Daniel, Sarah Reed. BS, S.E. Mo. State U., 1972, MA in Teaching, 1975; MFA, Memphis State U., 1980. Art instr. Athena R-8 Elem. Sch., DeSoto, Mo., 1972-73, Notre Dame High Sch., Cape Girardeau, 1973-76, St. Teresa Elem. Sch., Campbell, Mo., 1977-78; grad. asst. instr. Memphis State U., 1978-80; instr. art Delta State U., Cleve., Miss., 1980-82; staff asst. Arrowmont Sch. Art, Gatlinburg, Tenn., 1982-84; asst. prof. art Delta State U., Cleve., 1984-90, assoc. prof. art, 1990-93, prof. art, 1993—; workshop presenter Arrowmont Sch. Art, Gatlinburg, 1988-97, conf. presenter, 1993; juror Meridian (Miss.) Arts Coun., 1994; spkr., panelist Govs. Conf. on Arts, Jackson, Miss., 1987. Sculpture featured in Sculpture: Technique-Form-Content, 1989, rev. edit., 1995. Recipient Purchase award Del Mar Coll., 1988, Purchase award Cottonlandia Mus., 1989, Crosstie Arts Festival, 1994; hon. mention for excellence in fine woodworking Durham (Can.) Wood Show, 1992, Juror's award of merit Reding Mus. Art, 1993, Visual Arts fellowship Miss. Arts Commn., 1991; featured artist in Fine Woodworking mag., 1987, Woodwork mag., 1993. Mem. Am. Crafts Coun., Internat. Sculpture Ctr., Craftsmens Guild Miss., K.C. (Tootsie Roll drive chmn. 1988-93, youth free throw basketball 1988-92, Miss. blood drive chmn. 1984-96). Roman Catholic. Home: 400 S Bolivar Ave Cleveland MS 38732-3745 Office: Delta State Univ PO Box D 2 Cleveland MS 38732-0002

KOEHLER, SHARON KAY, hospice nurse; b. Marion, Ohio, Apr. 3, 1947; d. Richard Allen and Harriet Helen (Osmun) Sherman; m. Frederick J. Koehler, Sr., May 5, 1973; children: Kenneth Richard, Frederick John Jr. Grad., Lima Meml. Hosp. Sch. Nursing, 1968. RN, Fla., S.C. Charge nurse pediatrics Munroe Meml. Hosp., Ocala, Fla., 1969-71; office nurse Dr. James Casey, pediatrician, Ocala, 1971-73; phlebotomist Cen. Fla. Blood Bank, Orlando, 1973-74; pub. health nurse Richland/Lexington County Health Dept., Columbia, S.C., 1974-79; office nurse Dr. Bruce Marshall, surgeon, Clinton, S.C., 1981-83; sch. nurse Sebring (Fla.) Christian Sch., 1984-87; staff nurse Avon Park (Fla.) Cluster, 1987-88, Highlands County Home Health Agy., Sebring, Fla., 1988-90, Good Shepherd Hospice of Mid Fla., Sebring, 1990—; vol. speaker's bur. Good Shepherd Hospice, Sebring, 1987-90; organizer Hospice Svcs. Highlands County, Sebring, 1987-90. Bd. trustees Good Shepherd Hospice, Winter Haven, Fla., 1988-90; mem. Highlands County Sch. Health Adv. Com., 1984-87; sch. vol. Sun n Lake Elem. Sch., 1986-91, sch. adv. com., 1987-94, Sebring Mid. Sch., Sebring H.S.; mem. Sebring H.S. Band Parents, 1993—, Soccer Boosters, 1994—, Improvement Team, 1994-95; Sunday sch. tchr. Covenant Presbyn. Ch., 1983-92, Grace Bible Ch., 1995-96, mem. adult choir, 1983-92, mem. Christian edn. com., 1985-91, Christian edn. dir., 1984-86; v.p. Women in Ch., 1984-86; organizer Fall Festival as alternative to Trick or Treat. Mem. Hospice Nurses Assn. Presbyterian. Home: 3709 Dauphine St Sebring FL 33872-2816 Office: Good Shepherd Hospice Mid Fla Inc PO Box 1884 Sebring FL 33871-1884

KOEHN, GEORGE WALDEMAR, bank executive; b. Buffalo, 1943. Student, U. Miami, 1965, Rutgers U., 1973. Pres., CEO, chmn. SunTrust Bank of Ctrl Fla. NA. Office: SunTrust Bank of Ctrl Fla NA 200 S Orange Ave Orlando FL 32801-0215

KOELB, CHRISTINA HOLDING, elementary education educator; b. Cambridge, Mass., May 2, 1969; d. Clayton Talmadge Koelb Jr. and Barbara Brown (Dublin) Van Cleve. BA, U. Va., 1991; MEd, U. N.C., 1993. Cert. tchr. class G-elem. edn., reading, lang. arts, N.C. Chpt. 1 reading tchr. HOH Elem. Sch., Durham, N.C., 1993; tchr. French immersion 2d grade Fayetteville St. Elem. Sch., Durham, 1993-94; tchr. 3d grade Allen Jay Elem. Sch., High Point, N.C., 1994—. Tchr. Initiative grantee Durham Pub. Edn. Network, 1994. Mem. Internat. Reading Assn., Fgn. Lang. Assn. N.C., Can. Assn. Immersion Tchrs., Phi Delta Kappa, Phi Sigma Iota. Episcopalian. Office: Allen Jay Elem Sch 1311 E Springfield High Point NC 27263

KOELKER, GAIL, family nurse practitioner; b. Wichita, Feb. 5, 1956; d. John Howard and Jean (McWilliams) K. BSN summa cum laude, Ariz. State U., 1986; MS in Nursing, U. Tex., Arlington, 1993. RN Tex.; cert. family nurse practitioner. Staff nurse El Dorado Hosp. & Med. Ctr., Tucson, 1986-88; traveling nurse Travcorp, Inc., Walden, Mass., 1988-90; nurse home health Health Corp., Inc., Dallas, 1990-94; family nurse practitioner Good Sheperd Med. Ctr., Longview, Tex., 1994—; facilitator chronic pain/chronic disease support group Hughes Springs, Tex., 1995—; clin. preceptor nurse practitioner program U. Tex. Sch. Nursing, Arlington, 1993—; lectr. in field. Mem. Am. Acad. Nurse Practitioners, Am. Coll. Nurse Practitioners, Tex. Nurse Practitioners, Sigma Theta Tau, Phi Kappa Phi. Home: RR 1 Box 344 Avinger TX 75630-9641 Office: Good Shepherd Med Clinic Hwy 11 E PO Box 1440 Hughes Springs TX 75656

KOELLN, KENNETH, economics educator; b. Yonkers, N.Y., Oct. 30, 1942; s. Albert J. and Carita I. (Sykes) K.; m. Gretchel Geister, Jan. 7, 1972. BS in Literature, Clarkson U., 1965; MBA in Mgt. Sci., San Diego State, 1976; MA in Economics, Va. Tech, 1986; PhD in Economics, U. Fla., 1991. Marine officer USMC, Washington, 1965-86; rsch/tchg. asst. U. Fla., Gainesville, Fla., 1986-91; asst. prof. U. North Tex., Denton, Tex., 1991—. Contbr. articles to profl. jours. and various meetings. Recipient Lanzillotti Doctoral Dissertataion fellow U. Fla., 1990-91; grantee Tex. Higher Ed. Coord. Bd., 1994-95, AARP Andrus Found., 1991-92, 1993-94, Tex. Inst. for Rsch. and Edn. in Aging, 1993, UNT Rsch Initiation, 1991-93. Mem. Am. Econs. Assn., Mo. Valley Econs. Assn. Home: 3818 W University Dr Denton TX 76207 Office: Univ of North Texas Economics Dept PO Box 13408 Denton TX 76203-3408

KOEN, BILLY VAUGHN, mechanical engineering educator; b. Graham, Tex., May 2, 1938; s. Ottis Vaughn and Margaret (Branch) K.; m. Deanne Rollins, June 3, 1967; children: Kent, Douglas. B.A. in Chemistry, U. Tex., 1961, B.S. in Chem. Engring., 1961; S.M. in Nuclear Engring., MIT, 1962, Sc.D. in Nuclear Engring., 1968; Diplome d'ingenieur en Genie Atomique, L'institut National des Scis. et Techniques Nucleaires, France, 1963. Asst. prof. mech. engring. U. Tex., Austin, 1968-71, assoc. prof., 1971-80, Minnie S. Piper prof., 1980, prof., 1981—; dir. Bur. Engring. Teaching U. Tex.-Austin, 1973-76; prof. Ecole Centrale, Paris, 1983; undergrad advisor mech. engring., 1988-92; vis. prof. Tokyo Inst. Tech., 1994 (summer); cons., lectr. in field. Author: Definition of the Engineering Method, 1985; contbr. articles to profl. jours. Bd. dirs. Oak Ridge Associated Univs., 1975-76. Recipient Standard Oil Ind. award, 1970, W. Leighton Collins Distinguished and Unusual Service awd., Am. Soc. for Engineering Education, 1992. Fellow Am. Soc. Engring. Edn. (v.p. 1987-93, Chester Carlson award 1980, Ben Dasher best paper award 1985, 86, Helen Plants award 1986, William Elgin Wickenden best paper award 1986, Olmsted award, dir. 1982-84, W. Leighton Collins award 1992, Centennial medallion 1993); mem. Am. Nuclear Soc., Tex. Soc. Profl. Engrs., N.Y. Acad. Sci., Association des Ingenieurs en Genie Atomique, Rotary Club (Austin; Internat. fellow 1962), Phi Beta Kappa, Sigma Xi (disting. lectr. 1981-83), Tau Beta Pi. Quaker. Office: U Tex Dept Mech Engring Etc 5160 Austin TX 78712

KOENIG, HAROLD PAUL, management consultant, ecologist, author; b. Mason City, Iowa, Apr. 22, 1926; s. Reuben Harold and Dorothea (Paule) K.; m. Barbara Anne Rucker, June 29, 1974; 1 child, Kimberley Anne. Student Navy V-12 officer tng., Ohio Wesleyan U., 1944-45; BS, Iowa State U., 1947; MS, Ill. Inst. Tech., 1956. Registered profl. engr., Iowa, Minn., Ill., Ind., Fla.; ordained to ministry Bapt. Ch., 1994. Chief engr. Grain Processing Corp., Muscatine, Iowa, 1948-50; engr. mgr. Standard Oil Co. Ind., Whiting, Ind., 1953-56; with Booz, Allen & Hamilton, Chgo. and Genoa, Italy, 1956-64; v.p. Dresser Industries, Inc., Dallas, 1964-67; founder, chmn., pres., chief exec. officer, bd. dirs. Ecol. Sci. Corp., Miami and Lugano, Switzerland, 1967-73, Tele-Optics, Inc., West Palm Beach, Fla., 1986-90; chmn., pres., chief exec. officer, bd. dirs. Unionam., Inc. subs. Windham Power Lifts, Elba, Ala., 1974-76; dir. gen. Matisa, S.A., Lausanne, Switzerland, 1977-78, Canron Pipe & Hydraulics, Montreal, Que., Can., 1978-80; chief operating officer, bd. dirs. Tel-Tech Devices, Inc., Ft. Lauderdale, Fla., 1984-86; chmn. H.P. Koenig Mgmt. Cons., Miami, 1980-84, Jupiter, Satellite Beach, Fla., 1990—; cert. trainer Evang. Explosion Internat., Ft. Lauderdale, 1981—, cert. Evang. Explosion lectr., West Palm Beach, 1991—; advisor Citizens Democracy Corps, Russia, 1996. Author: Winning Against Satan-Applying Military Principles to Spiritual Warfare, 1991; also articles, lectures. Witness on environ. and ecol. matters U.S. Congress, Washington, 1969-71; mem. Citizens Democracy Corps, Khabarovsk, Sakhalin Island, Russia, 1996; mem. Pres.'s Com. on Environ. Quality, 1969-72; deacon Bapt. Ch., missionary to Kenya. Lt. comdr. USNR, 1944-46, 51-53, PTO. Recipient Meritorious Svc. award Govt. of Italy, 1962. Mem. Phi Gamma Delta (Golden Owl award), Gideon. Republican. Home and Office: 341 Lanternback Island Dr Indian Harbour Beach FL 32937-4708

KOEPKE, WULF, retired humanities educator; b. Luebeck, Germany, Sept. 24, 1928; came to U.S. 1965; s. Otto and Emma (Jahnke) K.; m. Monique Lehmann-Lukas, June 8, 1953; children: Niels, Detlev, Rebekka, Jens. Student, U. Hamburg, Germany, 1949, U. Freiburg, Germany, 1949-51; PhD, U. Freiburg, Germany, 1955; student, U. Paris, 1951-52. Lectr. U. Singapore, 1955-59; head divsn. Goethe Inst., Munich, Germany, 1959-65; assoc. prof. U. Ill., Chgo., 1965-68, Rice U., Houston, 1968-71; assoc. prof. Tex. A&M U., College Station, 1971-73, prof., 1973-92, disting. prof. humanities, 1992—. Author: Erfolglosigkeit, 1977, Lion Feuchtwanger, 1983, J.G. Herder, 1987, Understanding Max Frisch, 1990. Recipient Jean Peal medal Jean Paul Soc., Bayreuth, 1960. Mem. MLA, German Studies Assn. (pres. 1982-84), Am. Soc. Eighteenth Century Studies, Internat. Herder Soc. (pres. 1985-90). Home: 50 Winton St Roslindale MA 02131-4806

KOEPPE, PATSY PODUSKA, internist, educator; b. Memphis, Nov. 18, 1932; d. Ben F. and Lily Mae (Reid) Poduska; m. Douglas F. Koeppe Sr., Sept. 8, 1967; 1 child, Douglas F. Jr. BA, Tex. Woman's U., 1954; MD, U. Tenn., 1957. Intern Roanoke (Va.) Meml. Hosp., 1960-61; resident in internal medicine VA Teaching Group Hosp., Memphis, 1961-62, Lahey Clinic, Boston, 1962-63; fellow in endocrinology and metabolism U. Tex. Med. Br., Galveston, 1963-65; pvt. practice Kingsville, Tex., 1972-73; dir. Women's Health Care Ctr., College Park, Md., 1974-77; instr. internal medicine and endocrinology U. Tex., Galveston, 1965-69; asst. prof. endocrinology Med. Br., U. Tex., Galveston, 1969-72, asst. prof. internal medicine, 1969-72, 78-87; assoc. prof. U. Tex., Galveston, 1987-93, prof., 1994—; mem. grad. faculty biomed. sci. Med. Br., U. Tex., Galveston, 1983—, acting dir. div. geriatrics, 1991-92. Mem. Am. Geriatric Soc., Tex. Med. Assn., Tex. Med. Found., Galveston County Med. Soc. Presbyterian. Home: 323 Brookdale Dr League City TX 77573-1668 Office: Univ Tex Med Br 30325 Jennie Sealy Hosp D60 Galveston TX 77555-0460

KOEPPEN, KEVIN MICHAEL, counseling consultant; b. Manchester, N.H., May 24, 1952; s. Kenneth Ronald and Dorothy Ann (Goonan) K.; m. Virginia Ellen Beville, June 20, 1981; children: Matthew, Elizabeth. BS in Edn., Northwestern State U., Natchitoches, La., 1974, MEd, 1975; MA in Counseling, La. Tech. U., 1990. Nat. cert. counselor. Engr., supr. Owens-Ill., Shreveport, La., 1978-80; engr. Munsingwear, Winnfield, La., 1980-81; engr., supr. Crown Zellerbach/Manville, Joyce, La., 1981-89; counselor, instr. La. Tech. U., Ruston, 1989-90; counselor, cons. Resource Cons. Inc., Ft. Polk, La., 1991—; adj. prof. Upper Iowa U., Ft. Polk, 1994—. Asst. coord. job fair Army Career Alumni program, Ft. Polk, 1992—. With U.S. Army, 1975-77. Mem. Am. Counseling Assn., Nat. Employment Counselors Assn., Iota Lambda Sigma, Jr. Achievement (v.p. 1970). Republican. Home: RR 3 Box 19860 Winnfield LA 71483-9803

KOEPSEL, WELLINGTON WESLEY, electrical engineering educator; b. McQueeney, Tex., Dec. 5, 1921; s. Wesley Wellington and Hulda (Nagel) K.; m. Dorothy Helen Adams, June 25, 1950; children: Kirsten Marta, Gretchen Lisa, Wellington Lief. BS in Elec. Engring., U. Tex., 1944, MS, 1951; PhD, Okla. State U., 1960. Engr. City Pub. Service Bd., San Antonio, 1946-47; research sci. Mil. Physics Research Lab., U. Tex., 1948-51; research engr. North Am. Aviation, Downey, Calif., 1951; asst. prof. So. Methodist U., 1951-59; assoc. prof. U. N.Mex., Albuquerque, 1960-63, Duke U., 1963-64; prof., head dept. elec. engring. Kans. State U., Manhattan, 1964-76; prof. elec. engring. Kans. State U., 1976-84, prof. emeritus, 1984—; pres., owner, chief engr. Mutronic Systems, Austin, Tex. Contbr. articles profl. jours. Served from ensign to lt. (j.g.) USNR, 1944-46. Mem. IEEE, Sigma Xi, Eta Kappa Nu. Address: PO Box 26806 Austin TX 78755-0806

KOERBEL, PAMELA JEAN, corporation administrator; b. San Jose, Calif., Nov. 26, 1947; d. Carl John and Anna Margaret (Morris) Hoffman; m. Leigh F. Koerbel, Sept. 9, 1972; children: Michael, Mark, Sarah, Rebekah. BS in Elem. Edn., Wagner Coll., 1972; diploma in bibl. studies, Washington Bible Coll., 1985; postgrad., Prince George C.C., 1987-89, Trinity Theol. Sem., 1992—. Mgr. VIP Yarns, Rochester, N.Y., 1975-79; freelance writer, 1982—; dir., co-founder Post Abortion Ministries (P.A.M.), Landover Hills, Md., 1989—; keynote speaker various women's confs. and retreats, ch. svcs., coll. and high sch. groups, pro-life rallies; tchr. post-abortion counselor tng. workshops. Author: Abortion's Second Victim, 1986, 2d edit., 1991, Does Anyone Else Feel Like I Do? and Other Questions Women Ask Following an Abortion, 1990, Mommy, 2d edit., 1996, What's Abortion?, 1993, You Want ME to Speak About Abortion?, 1992, (with Leigh F. Koerbel) PARA-TEAM Reference Manual, 1991, expanded and revised, 1996, PARA-TEAM Discipleship Program, 1992; compiler, editor: If I Knew Then...A Collection of Post-abortion Poems, 1991, also brochures and periodicals; contbr. articles to profl. jours. Office: Post Abortion Ministries (P A M) PO Box 281463 Memphis TN 38168-1463

KOERBER, MARILYNN ELEANOR, gerontology nursing educator, consultant, nurse; b. Covington, Ky., Feb. 1, 1942; d. Harold Clyde and Vivian Eleanor (Conrad) Hilge; m. James Paul Koerber, May 29, 1971. Diploma, Christ Hosp. Sch. Nursing, Cin., 1964; BSN, U. Ky., 1967; MPH, U. Mich., 1970. RN, Ohio, S.C.; cert. gerontologist. Staff nurse premature and newborn nursery Cin. Gen. Hosp., 1964-65; staff nurse, hosp. discharge planner Vis. Nurse Assn., Cin., 1967-69; asst. dir. Vis. Nurse Assn., Atlanta, 1976-78; instr. Coll. Nursing, U. Ky., Lexington, 1970-71; supr. Montgomery County Health Dept., Rockville, Md., 1971-74; asst. prof. Coll. Nursing, U. S.C., Columbia, 1979-86, instr., 1987-89; alzheimer's project coord. S.C. Commn. on Aging, Columbia, 1988-90; dir. edn. and tng. Luth. Homes S.C., White Rock, 1988-91; grad. asst. U. S.C. Sch. of Pub. Health, 1991-94; trainer for homemakers home health aides S.C. Divsn. on Aging, 1991—; coord. to train homemakers home aides nursing assts. State Pilot Program, DSS and Divsn. on Aging, 1993—; mem. utilization rev. bd. Palmetto Health Dist., Lexington, 1984—; test item writer, nurse aide cert. Psychol. Corp., San Antonio, 1989, 91, 92; bd. examiners Nursing Home Adminstrn. and Community Residential Care Facility Adminstr., chmn. of edn. com., Columbia, S.C., 1990-93; presenter gerontol. workshops and residential care facilities adminstrn. Contbg. editor: (handbook) Promoting Caregiver Groups, 1984; reviewer gerontology textbooks, 1983-91; contbr. tng. video and manuals on Alzheimers, 1988 (hon. mention Retirement Rsch. Found. 1989). Del. S.C. Gov. White House Conf. on Aging, Columbia, 1981; chmn. ann. mtg. S.C. Fedn. for Older Ams., Columbia, 1989-91. USPHS trainee, 1965-67, Adm. on Aging trainee, 1969-70. Mem. ANA (recert. gerontol. nurse 1988, 92, community health nurse 1989, 93), S.C. Nurses Assn., Am. Pub. Health Assn., So. Gerontol. Soc., Gerontol. Soc. Am., S.C. Gerontol. Soc. (treas. 1989-91, Rosamond R. Boyd award 1986, Pres. award Mid State Alzheimers Chpt., 1993), Soc. for Pub. Health Edn., Am. Soc. on Aging, Alzheimers Assn. (bd. dirs. Columbia chpt. 1988-93, sec. 1992, chmn. nominating com. 1991-92; bd. dirs. S.C. combined health appeal 1991-93), Nat. Coun. on Aging, Nat. Gerontol. Nursing Assn. Democrat. Unitarian Universalist.

KOETH, LEONARD ALFRED, counselor, educator; b. Euclid, Ohio, Mar. 10, 1937; s. Leonard J. and Abbeline (Poutz) K.; m. Texie Ann Larson (dec. 1981); 1 child, Jimmy; m. Georgia Ownbey, Oct. 16, 1987. BS, Fla. State U., 1959, MBA, 1965; EdD, Nova Southeastern U., 1975. Buyer Higbee Co., Cleve., 1961-62, Wanamaker Co., Phila., 1962-65; prof. bus. Miami (Fla.)-Dade C.C., 1966-70, asst. to dean, asst. dean, then assoc. dean, 1970-77, asst. dir. adminstrn., 1977-80, adviser, counselor, 1980-96, prof. emeritus, 1996—; project dir., Career Horizons, Miami, 1975-76, State Plan for Vocat. Edn., Miami, 1980-81; cons., Action Life Planning Systems, Miami, 1975-81. Author: Career Model, 1975, Keys to Excellence Career planning for the 21st Century, 1995. Mem. Ptnrs. in Edn. Comdr. USCG, 1960-61. Mem. Nat. Coun. Student Devel., Am. Assn. Counseling (regional rep.), Nat. Career Devel. Assn., Nat. Employment Coun. Assn., Am. Mktg. Assn., Internat. Platform Assn., Assn. for Psychol. Type, Ret. Officers Assn., Res. Officers Assn., Fla. Assn. C.C.'s, Fla. Vocat. Assn., Am. Legion, Theta Chi. Democrat. Roman Catholic.

KOFFLER, WARREN WILLIAM, lawyer; b. N.Y.C., July 21, 1938; s. Jack and Rose (Conovich) K.; m. Barbara Rose Holz, June 11, 1959; m. Jayne Audri Goetzel, May 15, 1970; children: Kevin, Kenneth, Caroline. B.S., Boston U., 1959; J.D., U. Calif.-Berkeley, 1962; LLD, NYU, 1972. Bar: D.C. 1962, N.Y. 1963, U.S. Dist. Ct. D.C. 1963, Fla. 1980, Va. 1981, Pa. 1982. Atty. FAA, Washington, 1964; pvt. practice law, Washington, 1964, 78—, Hollywood, Palm Beach, and Miami, Fla., 1978—; atty. Fed. Home Loan Bank Bd., Washington, 1964-66; ptnr. Koffler & Spivack, Washington, 1967-77. Mem. ABA, Inter-Am. Bar Assn., Fed. Bar Assn., D.C. Bar Assn., Fla. Bar Assn., Va. Bar Assn., Assn. Trial Lawyers Am., Brit. Inst. Internat. and Comparative Law, Univ. Club (Washington), Bankers Club (Miami). Office: PO Box 31209 Palm Beach Gardens FL 33420 also: 1730 K St NW Washington DC 20006-3868

KOFINK, WAYNE ALAN, minister; b. Chgo., Apr. 21, 1949; s. Lawrence Howard and Catherine Elizabeth (Szlavik) K. MusB, Roosevelt U., 1971; MDiv, Luth. Sch. Theology, Chgo., 1976; BA in Philosophy, Fla. Internat. U., 1981, MS Adult Edn., 1985, EdD, 1991; postgrad., Westminster Choir Coll., 1982, St. Thomas U., 1984-85. Ordained to ministry Evang. Luth. Ch. in Am., 1977. Choir dir. Ascension Luth. Ch., Chgo., 1971-73; pastor Messiah Evang. Luth. Ch., Miami, Fla., 1977—; lectr. religious studies Fla. Internat. U., Miami, 1986—; interim pastor St. Thomas Luth. Ch., Miami, 1993; sec., v.p. Luth. Campus Ministry of Dade County, Miami, 1979-85; mem. Fla. Synod Worship Consultation, Tampa, 1988—; trustee Guardian Shepherd Luth. Sch., Coral Gables, Fla., 1990—; adj. South Fla. Ctr. for Theol. Studies, Miami, 1995—; chair Dade-Monroe conf. ELCA, Miami, 1996—. Editor (newsletter) Doxology, 1986-87; contbr. articles to profl. jours. Mem. adv. com. Miami-Coral Pk. Adult Edn. Ctr., 1988-93. Mem. Am. Acad. Religion, Soc. Bibl. Lit., Liturgical Conf., Hymn Soc. Am. Home: 3561 SW 117th Ave Apt 305 Miami FL 33175-1773 Office: Messiah Evang Luth Ch 9850 Coral Way Miami FL 33165-7514

KOGAN, GERALD, state supreme court justice; b. Bklyn., May 23, 1933; s. Morris and Yetta (Weinstein) K.; m. Irene Vulgan, Nov. 17, 1955; children: Robert, Debra, Karen. BBA, JD, U. Miami, Coral Gables, Fla., 1955. Bar: Fla. 1955. Sole practice Miami, Fla., 1955-60, 67-80; asst. state's atty. Dade County, Fla., 1960-67, chief prosecutor homicide and capital crimes sect., 1960-67; judge criminal div. Fla. 11th Jud. Cir. Ct., Miami, 1980-87, adminstrv. judge criminal div., 1984-87; justice Supreme Ct. Fla., Tallahassee, 1987—; adj. prof. law Nova U. Law Sch., U. Miami Sch. Law, Fla. State U. Sch. Law; mem. faculty Am. Acad. Jud. Edn. Served with CIC, AUS, 1955-57. Mem. ABA, Fla. Bar, Dade County Bar Assn. Office: Supreme Ct Fla 500 S Duval St Tallahassee FL 32399-1925*

KOGER, DAVID GORDON, satellite image analyst, photogeology consultant; b. Topeka, Apr. 27, 1951; s. John Marshall Sr. and Thurza Mae (Ellis) K.; m. Carol Ann Finkelston, Nov. 26, 1980; children: Matthew Benjamin, Kyle Joseph, Alexander James, Chase Andrew. BS, Kans. State U., 1975. Agent contract surety dept. Hussey Agency Inc., Topeka, 1976-79; analyst remote sensing/image analysis, tech. support and customer tgn. Interpretation Systems Inc., Overland Park, Kans., 1979-83; rsch. assoc. geology and environ. sci. depts. Tex. Christian U., Ft. Worth, 1983-86; cons. Koger Remote Sensing and Image Analysis, Ft. Worth, 1983—; image analyst Shroud of Turin Rsch. Project, Chgo., 1982, Mt. Ararat Rsch. Found. for Noah's Ark, Houston, 1985; enhanced video search for Titanic, Tex., 1983; organizer World Conf. Remote Sensing for Acid Rain, Germany, 1984; vice chmn. Geosat Com. Inc., Okla.; instr. tng. seminars Remote Sensing and Photogeology; frequent guest speaker in field. Assoc. editor Earth Observation Mag., 1992; contbr. to profl. jours. Mentor Big Brothers, Topeka, 1976-81. Cpl. USMC, 1969-71. Mem. Assn. Petroleum Geochem. Exploration (sec.), Geol. Remote Sensing Group, Ft. Worth Geol. Soc., Dallas Geol. Soc., Masons (32 degree), Shriners. Republican. Presbyterian. Office: Koger Remote Sensing 3204 Waits Ave Ste 2000 Fort Worth TX 76109-2332

KOGER, LINWOOD GRAVES, III, surgeon, educator; b. Balt., Feb. 21, 1951; s. Linwood Jr. and Margaret Koger; m. Iantha Angela Hill, June 4, 1987; children: Brian, Kelsey. Diploma, Balt. Poly. Inst., 1969; BS in Chemistry, Howard U., 1974, MD, 1978. Diplomate Am. Bd. Surgery, Nat. Bd. Med. Examiners. Intern in categorical surgery Howard U. Hosp., Washington, 1978-79; resident, chief resident gen. surgery Howard U. Hosp. and affiliated hosps., Washington, 1978-83; clinic physician PMAI, Inc., Hyattsville, Md., 1983; mem. assoc. staff Anne Arundel Gen. Hosp., Annapolis, Md., 1983-84; pvt. practice Annapolis, 1983-84, Balt., 1984-85; mem. assoc. staff North Charles Gen. Hosp., Bon Secours Hosp., Balt., 1985; plant infirmary physician Martin-Marietta Aerospace, Balt., 1985; asst. chief of surgery Meharry Svc. Alvin C. York VA Med. Ctr., Murfreesboro, Tenn., 1985-89; asst. prof. surgery Meharry Med. Coll., Nashville, 1986-89; mem.

courtesy staff S.W. Hosp. and Med. Ctr., Atlanta, 1989-90; courtesy staff South Fulton Hosp., East Point, Ga., 1990-91; mem. attending staff S.W. Community Hosp., Atlanta, 1990—; mem. active staff Ga. Bapt. Hosp., Atlanta, 1990—, South Fulton Hosp., East Point, 1991—, West Paces Ferry Hosp., Atlanta, 1992—; provisional active staff. Piedmont Hosp., Atlanta, 1991—; mem. provisional staff Northside Hosp., Atlanta, 1993—, Dekalb Med. Ctr., Decatur, Ga., 1993—; mem. courtesy staff Crawford Long Hosp., Atlanta, 1991—; active mem. Dunwoody Med. Ctr. (formerly Shallowford Hosp.), Dunwoody, Ga., 1993—; asst. prof. surgery Morehouse Sch. Medicine, Atlanta, 1989-95; presenter Howard U., 1973, Arundel Gen. Hosp., 1984, Alvin C. York VA Med. Ctr., 1986, 87, Meharry Med. Coll., 1987, Nat. Med. Assn., Orlando, Fla., 1989, S.W. Hosp., 1991, VA Med. Ctr., 1992, AMA, San Antonio, 1993. Contbr. articles to profl. jours. Fellow Am. Coll. Surgeons (mem. Ga. chpt.), Southeastern Surg. Congress, Internat. Coll. Surgeons, Internat. Fedn. Colls. Surgery (assoc.); mem. Soc. Am. Gastrointestinal Endoscopic Surgeons, Atlanta Med. Assn. (presenter 1990), Assn. Surg. Edn. (curriculum com., computer com.), Assn. VA Adminstrn. Surgeons, Assn. Acad. Surgeons, Soc. Surg. Infections, Soc. Laparoendoscopic Surgeons. Office: Ste 104 4470 N Shallowford Rd Dunwoody GA 30338

KOGUT, CARL ANDREW, economics educator; b. Woodbridge, N.J., Apr. 26, 1958; s. Michael P. and Margaret M. (Grimek) K. BA in Econs., U. Dallas, 1980; PhD in Econs., Tex. A&M U., 1984. Rsch. assoc. Tex. A&M U., College Station, 1984-85; asst. prof. econs. U. South Fla., Tampa, 1985-91; asst. prof. econs. Northeast La. U., Monroe, 1992-95, assoc. prof. econ., 1995—. Contbr. articles to profl. jours. Mem. Am. Econ. Assn., So. Econ. Assn., Econ. Sci. Assn. Republican. Roman Catholic. Home: 211 Roy Sullivan Rd West Monroe LA 71291-8204 Office: Northeast La U Dept Econs Fin Monroe LA 71209

KOH, CHRISTA M., technical translator, realtor, physical therapist; b. Berlin, Germany, Apr. 18, 1941; came to U.S., 1965; d. Hans Wolfgang and Maria Theresia Heinrich; m. Kwan S. Koh, July 1, 1972; children: Kimberly Kristen, Alexis Korene, Karsten Kwan. Cert., Phys. Therapy Sch., Berlin, 1961; lic. in phys. therapy, Chgo., 1969. Lic. realtor, Fla.; lic. phys. therapist, Ill., Germany. Intern in phys. therapy Evang. Hosp., Saarbruecken, Germany, 1962-63; staff phys. therapist Walton Hosp., Liverpool, Eng., 1963-64, St. Joseph Hosp., Guelph, Ont., Can., 1964-65, Schwab Rehab. Hosp., Chgo., 1965-68, Kostner Manor Nursing Home, Chgo., 1968-69; dir. phys. therapy St. Elizabeth's Hosp., Chgo., 1969-81, Bethesda Hosp., Chgo., 1981-85; realtor Century 21, Country Hills, Pitts., 1986-88; systems analyst Columbia Healthcare Corp., Ft. Myers, Fla., 1991-92; realtor Coldwell Banker McFadden & Sprowls, 1993-95, Guaranteed Real Estate Svcs., Inc., 1995—; technical translator Fischer Internat. Systems Corp., Naples, Fla., 1994—. Symphony usher, vol. S.W. Fla. Symphony Soc., 1993—; mem. Ft. Myers Women's Network, 1993-94, Chicagoland Phys. Therapy Dirs. Forum, 1975-85; vol. usher Barbara M. Mann Hall, 1994—. Mem. Am. Phys. Therapy Assn. (Fla. chpt.).

KOHL, HAROLD, missionary, educator; b. Linden, N.J., Dec. 13, 1923; s. Herman and Martha (Sperber) K.; m. Beatrice Minniebelle Wells, Mar. 21, 1946; children: Loren, Loretta, Lyndon. BA, Monmouth Coll., 1962; MA in Edn., NYU, 1968, postgrad., 1974; ThD in English Bible, Internat. Bible Inst., 1980. Ordained to ministry Assemblies of God Ch., 1948. Pastor, evangelist Assemblies of God Ch., W.Va., Md., 1944-50; pres. youth ministries Potomac Dist. Coun. Assemblies of God Ch., 1947-48; fgn. missionary Assemblies of God Ch., Colombo, Sri Lanka, 1950-56; pastor Assemblies of God Chs., N.J., 1956-61; missionary, tchr., educator Assemblies of God Ch., Far East, Pacific, Europe, 1961-94; ednl. cons. Assemblies of God Ch., Far East, Pacific, 1980-83; assoc. pastor Hayfield (Va.) Assembly of God, 1995—; pres. Bethel Bible Coll., Manila, 1963-68; pres., founder Far East Advanced Sch. Theology (now Asia Pacific Theol. Sem., Baguio City, The Philippines), Manila, 1964-73; adj. prof. Baguio City, 1991—; dean coll. divns. Internat. Corr. Inst. (now named ICI U.), Brussels, 1973-78, Belgium, 1983-88, Rhode St. Genese, Belgium, 1988—, mem. external faculty, Brussels/Irving, Tex., 1988-94. Mem. Soc. Pentecostal Studies, Religious Edn. Assn., Phi Delta Kappa, Phi Theta Kappa. Republican. Home: 429 Superior Ave Winchester VA 22601-4253

KOHL, KATHLEEN ALLISON BARNHART, lawyer; b. Ft. Leavenworth, Kans., Jan. 11, 1955; d. Robert William and Margaret Ann (Snowden) Barnhart. BS, Memphis State U., 1978; JD, Loyola U., New Orleans, 1982. Bar: La. 1982, U.S. Dist. Ct. (ea. dist.) La. 1982, U.S. Dist. Ct. (no. dist.) Tex. 1985, U.S. Ct. Appeals (5th cir.) 1986, U.S. Ct. Appeals (11th cir.) 1988, U.S. Supreme Ct. 1994. Assoc. Garrity & Webb, Harahan, La., 1982; revenue officer IRS, Dallas, 1984; sr. trial atty. EEOC, Dallas, 1984-86; sr. criminal enforcement counsel U.S. EPA, Dallas, 1986-91, chief water enforcement sect., office regional counsel, 1991-92; dep. dir. criminal enforcement counsel divsn. U.S. EPA, Washington, 1992-93, dir. criminal enforcement counsel divsn., 1993-94; sr. criminal enforcement counsel U.S. EPA, Dallas, 1994—; spl. asst. U.S. atty. (spl. assignment from U.S. EPA), U.S. Atty.'s Office, Montgomery, Ala., 1988-89; vis. instr. Fed. Law Enforcement Tng. Ctr., Glynco, Ga., 1987—; adj. prof. environ. crimes seminar Cornell U. Law Sch., spring 1993. Vol. instr. New Orleans Police Acad., 1981. Mem. La. Bar Assn. Office: EPA 1445 Ross Ave 6CID Dallas TX 75202

KOHLHASE, JANET ELLEN, economics educator; b. Buffalo, Apr. 4, 1953; d. William Lawrence and Margaret Hulda (Heick) K.; m. Steven G. Craig, Aug. 21, 1982. B.A., U. Ill., 1975; M.A., U. Pa., 1977, Ph.D., 1980. Asst. prof. Mich. State U., East Lansing, 1980-82; vis. asst. prof. U. Houston, 1982-83, asst. prof. dept. econs., 1983-89, assoc. prof., 1990—. Contbr. articles to publs. in field. Recipient Bronze Plaque award U. Ill., 1975. Mem. Am. Econs Assn., N.Am. Regional Sci. Assn. (mem. coun. 1990-93), Econometric Soc., Regional Sci. Assn. (treas. 1980-88, mem. internat. coun. 1993—), Nat. Tax Assn., Nat. Tax Inst. Office: U Houston Dept Econs Houston TX 77204-5882

KOHN, MICHAEL CHARLES, theoretical biochemistry professional; b. Bklyn., July 29, 1941; s. Mordecai and Rose (Teich) K.; m. Lynn Breeden Mitchell, Oct. 23, 1970. BS, MIT, 1964; PhD, U. S.C., 1970. NRC fellow Naval Underseas Ctr., Pasadena, Calif., 1971-73; rsch. prof. U. Pa., Phila., 1974-84, Duke U., Durham, N.C., 1984-91; expert Nat. Inst. Environ. Health Scis., NIH, Research Triangle Park, N.C., 1991—. Author: Practical Numerical Methods: Algorithms and Programs, 1987, 89; guest editor Bull. of Math. Biology, 1986, Jour. of Theoretical Biology, 1991; contbr. numerous articles to profl. jours. Grantee NIH, U. Pa., 1974-84, Duke U., 1984-91; fellowship Nat. Rsch. Coun., 1971-73. Mem. AAAS, Soc. for Math. Biology, Soc. for Computer Simulation, Sigma Xi. Office: NIEHS PO Box 12233 Durham NC 27709-2233

KOHR, ROBERT LEON, safety engineer. BS in Geology, Va. Poly. Inst. and State U., 1976. Registered profl. engr., Mass.; cert. safety profl., protection profl. Sr. loss control rep. Aetna Life and Casualty, Richmond, Va., 1977-79; safety supt. Blake Constrn. Co., Inc., Washington, 1979-80; regional dir. loss prevention Marriott Corp., Washington, 1980-90; prin. Kohr and Assoc., Mt. Airy, Md., 1990-91; sr. cons. occupational health and safety unit Arthur D. Little, Arlington, Va., 1991-96; prin. Kohr & Assocs., Herndon, Va., 1996—; cons. nat. tech. svc. program EPA Safety, Health Environ. Mgmt. Div., Dept. Enerty Nuclear Waste Superfund. Author: Accident Prevention for Hotels, Motels, and Restaurants, 1991; contbr. articles to profl. jours. Mem. ASTM (com. sec. pedestrian footwear-surface interaction, ceramic tile, com. mem. polishes, consumer products), Am. Soc. Indsl. Security (standing com. mem. lodging security), Am. Soc. Safety Engrs., Nat. Safety Coun., Nat. Fire Protection Assn., Bldg. Ofcls. and Code Adminstrn. Internat., Am. Hotel and Motel Assn. Address: 2627 Meadow Hall Dr Herndon VA 22071

KOINER, MICHELLE ELIZABETH, elementary school educator; b. Knoxville, Tenn., Jan. 1, 1969; d. Michael Raleigh and Darlene (Blanchard) K. BS in Art Edn., Radford U., 1994. Cert. art tchr., Va. Processor Stewart Title and Escrow, Fairfax, Va., 1990-92; art tchr. Rose Hill Elem. Sch., Alexandria, Va., 1994—, Fairfax County Pub. Schs., Springfield, Va., 1994—. Freelance photographer for mag. Am. Entertainment, 1994; contbr. photographs to book: The Best of College Photography, 1994 (Finalist). Mem. Nat. Art Edn. Assn. Democrat.

KOITA, SAIDA YAHYA, psychoanalyst, educator; b. Bombay, Jan. 5, 1945; d. A. and M. Kalvert; m. Yahya Koita; children: Zain, Selma. Student, Sophia Coll., Bombay; MD, Grant Med. Coll., Bombay, 1969; postgrad., Inst. Psychoanalysis, 1977-85. Diplomate Am. Bd. Psychiatry and Neurology; lic. psychoanalyst, Fla. Resident in ob-gyn. Grant Med. Coll., Bombay, 1969-71; intern in pediats. Jackson Meml. Hosp., Miami, Fla., 1974, resident in psychiatry, 1974-77, chief resident in psychiatry, 1976-77; clin. instr. psychiatry U. Miami Sch. Medicine, 1977-79, asst. prof. psychiatry, 1979-88, assoc. prof. psychiatry, 1988—; pvt. practice, 1977—; assoc. teaching analyst Balt. Inst. Psychoanalysis, 1988—; teaching analyst Fla. Psychoanalytic Inst. Mem. Am. Psychoanalytic Assn., Am. Psychiat. Assn., So. Med. Assn., Fla. Psychoanalytic Soc., South Fla. Psychiat. Soc. (patient rep. ethics com. 1987—, liaison to residents in psychiatry 1978-82, v.p. 1988-89, treas., panelist, moderator local symposiums). Office: 420 S Dixie Hwy Ste 4H Coral Gables FL 33146-2222

KOKESSCH, ALLEN J., entertainment industry executive; b. 1951. BA in Sociology, Bus., S.W. State U., Marshall, Minn., 1973. Various staff positions RAM Corp., Marshall, Minn., 1973-76; staff Dodge County Devel. Activity Ctr., Dodge Ctr., Minn., 1976-83; gen. mgr. Jackpot Junction Casino, Morton, Minn., 1984-92; exec. v.p. Casino Magic Corp., Bay Saint Louis, Miss., 1992—. Office: Casino Magic Corp 711 Casino Magic Dr Bay Saint Louis MS 39520-1808

KOKKINAKIS, DEMETRIUS MICHAEL, biochemist, researcher; b. Heraklion, Crete, Greece, Mar. 6, 1950; came to U.S., 1973; s. Michael-Byron and Kyriaki (Zeakis) K.; m. Jannie Tong, June 10, 1985; children: Michael Ross, Alexius Manuel. BS in Chemistry, Athens (Greece) Natl. U., 1973; MS, Pa. State U., 1975; PhD, W.Va. U., 1977. Welch fellow Tex. Tech U. Med. Sch., Lubbock, 1978-80; fellow Northwestern U. Med. Sch., Chgo., 1980-85, rsch. assoc., 1985-87, asst. prof., 1987-93; assoc. prof. U. Tex. Southwestern Med. Ctr., Dallas, 1993—; reviewer Merit Rev. Bd., Washington, 1988—, NIH, Bethesda, Md., 1990—. Author: (with others) Experimental Pancreatic Carcinogenesis, 1987; also articles. Chair Northwestern U. IACUC, 1989-93. Grantee Nat. Cancer Inst., 1987, Am. Cancer Soc., 1991. Mem. ACS, AAAS, Am. Assn. Cancer Rsch., N.Y. Acad. Sci. Republican. Home: 9677 Fallbrook Dr Dallas TX 75243-6151 Office: Univ Tex Southwestern Med Ctr 5323 Harry Hines Blvd Dallas TX 75235-7200

KOLASA, KATHRYN MARIANNE, food and nutrition educator, consultant; b. Detroit, July 26, 1949; d. Marion J. and Blanche Ann (Gasiorowski) K.; m. Patrick Noud Kelly, Jan. 3, 1983. BS, Mich. State U., 1970; PhD, U. Tenn., 1974. Test kitchen home economist Kellogg Co., 1971; instr. dept. food sci. and food systems adminstrn. U. Tenn.-Knoxville, 1973-74; asst. prof. dept. food sci. and human nutrition Mich. State U., East Lansing, 1974-76, assoc. prof., 1976-82; prof., chmn. food, nutrition and instn. mgmt. Sch. Home Econs., East Carolina U., Greenville, N.C., 1982-86, prof., head nutrition edn. and svcs. sect. Dept. Family Medicine, Sch. Medicine, 1986—, sect. head resident edn., 1995—; mem. subcom. food and nutrition bd. NAS on Uses of the RDA, 1981-83; cons. food and nutrition; vice chmn. edn. subcom. Am. Heart Assn. Consumer Nutrition, 1992-93. Recipient grants in nutrition and food service and med. nutrition edn., 1974—; Kellogg nat. fellow, 1985-88. Mem. Soc. Nutrition Edn. (pres. 1984, Career Achievement award 1995), Am. Instn. Nutrition, Inst. Food Technologists, Am. Dietetic Assn., Soc. Tchrs. Family Medicine. Roman Catholic. Author: (with Ann Bass and Lou Wakefield) Community Nutrition and Individual Food Behavior, 1978, (interactive video disc, with Ann Jobe) Cardiovascular Health: Focus on Nutrition, Fitness and Smoking Cessation, CD-ROM: Images of Cancer Prevention, The Nutrition-Cancer Link.

KOLB, HAROLD HUTCHINSON, JR., English language educator; b. Boston, Jan. 16, 1933. BA in English with honors, Amherst Coll., 1955; MA in Am. Studies, U. Mich., 1960; PhD in British and Am. Lit., Ind. U., 1968. Instr. English Valparaiso U., 1960-62; teaching assoc. Ind. U., 1962-65; from asst. prof. to prof. English U. Va., Charlottesville, 1967—; dir. Ctr. for Liberal Arts U. Va., Charlottesville, 1984—; project dir. NEH, 1972-76, 85-90, 90—; dir. Canadian Judicial Writing Program, 1981-84; guest prof. Am. studies U. Bonn, 1982. Author: The Illusion of Life-American Realism as a Literary Form, 1969, A Field Guide to the Study of American Literature, 1976, A Writer's Guide: The Essential Points, 1980, A Handbook for Research in American Literature and American Studies, 1994; contbr. articles to scholarly publs. Naval aviator, 1955-59. Recipient Armstrong prize in English, Amherst Coll., 1952, James A. Work prize U. Ind., 1965, Guggenheim fellowship, 1970-71, Faculty Leadership award Am. Assn. Higher Edn., Carnegie Found. for Advancement of Teaching and Change mag., 1986, Citation for Leadership in Rejuvenation of Secondary and Elem. Edn., Va. Bd. Edn., 1987, Phillip E. Frandson award for Innovation and Creative Programming, Nat. U. Continuing Edn. Assn., 1988, Outstanding Faculty award Va. Coun. Higher Edn., 1988. Mem. MLA (chmn. del. assembly steering com. 1984-85). Office: U Va English Dept Bryan Hall Charlottesville VA 22903

KOLBER, DANIEL HACKNER, lawyer; b. Miami, Fla., Mar. 27, 1953; s. Stanley and Marcia (Hackner) K.; m. Lesley Renee Houseman, Aug. 13, 1978; children: Lee, Sarah, Mark. BA in Polit. Sci. magna cum laude, Boston U., 1975; JD, U. Va., 1978; LLM, NYU, 1981. Bar: Va., 1978, Fla., 1978, N.Y., 1979, U.S. Dist. Ct. (ea. dist.) N.Y. 1979, U.S. Dist. Ct. (so. dist.) Fla. 1979, U.S. Ct. Appeals (4th cir.) 1979, Ga., 1985, U.S. Dist. Ct. (mid. dist.) Ga. 1985, U.S. Dist. Ct. (so. dist.) Ga. 1986. Assoc. Weil, Gotshal & Manges, N.Y.C., 1978-81; assoc. gen. counsel Kenai Corp., N.Y.C., 1981-84; exec. v.p. Air Atlanta, Inc., Atlanta, 1984-87; pres. Jackson Securities Corp., Atlanta, 1987—; arbitrator, Am. Arbitration Assn., N.Y.C., 1981—; registered prin., SEC, Washington, 1980—; mem. Securities Investor Protection Corp. Co-author, editor: Starting and Organizing a Business: A Legal and Tax Guide, 1980, 3d rev. ed., 1984; author legal articles on venture capital. Mem. Pres.' Adv. Council on Small Bus., 1985—. Mem. ABA (chmn. subcom. small bus. 1980-83, editor Corp. Notes mag., 1980-82, Gold Key award 1978), N.Y. State Bar Assn., Fla. Bar Assn., Ga. Bar Assn., Va. Bar Assn., Nat. Assn. Securities Dealers, Inc. Office: Jackson & Kolber 100 Peachtree St NW Ste 2250 Atlanta GA 30303-1906

KOLCHINSKY, ALEXANDER, geneticist educator; b. Moscow, May 10, 1952; came to U.S., 1991; s. Mark L. and Natalia A. (Eisenstein) K.; m. Irene E. Vinokurova, May 21, 1971; children: Daniel, Artemy. PhD of Biology, USSR Acad. Scis., 1978. Rsch. fellow, rsch. scientist Inst. Molecular Biology, Moscow, 1974-87; sr. rsch. scientist Inst. Gen. Genetics, Moscow, 1987-91; asst. rsch. prof. U. Tenn., Knoxville, 1991-94, U. Ill., Chgo., 1994—. Author: (textbook) Molecular Biology, 1988; contbr. articles to profl. jours. Mem. Internat. Soc. Plant Molecular Biology. Jewish. Office: Univ of Illinois at Chicago Dept Neurosurgery M/C 799 Chicago IL 60612

KOLESAR, EDWARD STEVEN, JR., electrical engineering educator; b. Canton, Ohio, June 24, 1950; s. Edward Steven Sr. and Margaret Jean (Skolosh) K.; m. Elinor Kropac, Oct. 2, 1976; children: Lauren Marie, Elizabeth Anne, Gregory Edward. BSEE, U. Akron, 1973; MBA, Midwestern U., 1976; MSEE, Air Force Inst. Tech., 1978; PhD, U. Tex., 1985. Registered profl. engr., Tex. Co-op engrng. student Hoover Co., North Canton, Ohio, 1970-72; elec. engr. Electronics Systems Div., Hanscom AFB, Mass., 1973-77; biomed. engr. Sch. Aerospace Medicine, San Antonio, 1979-82; prof. elec. engring. Air Force Inst. Tech., Dayton, Ohio, 1985-93; commd. 2d lt. USAF, 1973, advanced through grades to lt. col., 1989, ret., 1993; W.A. Moncrief prof. engring. Tex. Christian U., Ft. Worth, 1993—; cons. engr. sci. adv. bd. USAF, Washington, 1981, Johns Hopkins U., Balt., 1983, Ardex Inc., Austin, 1985, EG&G Mound Applied Tech. Lab., Miamisburg, Ohio, Ohio Aerospace Inst., Cleve., 1990-93, Edison Materials Tech. Ctr., Kettering, Ohio, 1991-93, Mission Rsch. Corp., Albuquerque, 1993—, SRI Internat., Menlo Park, Calif., 1993—, Technispan LLC, Lutherville, Md., 1995—, Lockheed Martin Corp., Fort Worth, 1996—. Patentee gas contamination detection device, electronic nerve agt. detector sensor for detecting chemicals, method for ion detection using differential resistance measurement of an ion exch. membrane, halogen detection with a solid state sensor, back-contact, vertical-junction solar cell, gaseous component identification with a polymeric film sensor, hybrid wafer scale integration. Judge Sci. Clubs Am., San Antonio, 1979-82, Dayton, 1985-93, Honors Sem. Program of Met. Dayton, 1988-93. Named one of Outstanding Young Men in Am., 1982; recipient R&D award USAF, 1987, Outstanding Engr. and Scientists award Engring. and Sci. Found., 1990, Walter E. Peterson Best Paper award for AutoTestCon 1992 Symposium. Mem. IEEE (sr., Harrell Rappaport Best Paper award NAECON symposium 1990-94), Am. Soc. Engring. Edn., Air Force Assn. (col. Charles A. Stone award 1989), Air Force Inst., Tech. Assn. Grads., Sigma Xi, Eta Kappa Nu, Tau Beta Pi, Omicron Delta Kappa. Republican. Roman Catholic. Home: 4801 River View Dr Fort Worth TX 76132-1147

KOLIN, PHILIP CHARLES, English language educator; b. Chgo., Nov. 21, 1945; children: Eric H., Kristin J. BS, Chgo. State U., 1966; MA, U. Chgo., 1967; PhD, Northwestern U., 1973. Instr. Ill. univs., 1967-70; asst. prof. English Milton (Wis.) Coll., 1973-74, U. So. Miss., Hattiesburg, 1974-78; vis. faculty mem. Inst. Tech. Comm., Gulf Park, Miss., 1981; assoc. prof. English U. So. Miss., Hattiesburg, 1978-83, prof. English, 1983—, Charles W. Moorman disting. prof. humanities, 1991-93. Author: Successful Writing at Work, 1982, 4th edit., 1994, Shakespeare in the South, 1983, Models for Technical Writing, 1985, Shakespeare and Southern Writers, 1985, American Playwrights Since 1945, 1989, Feminist Criticism of Shakespeare's Plays: An Annotated Bibliography and A Commentary, 1991, Roses for Sharron: Poems, 1993, Critical Essays on Titus Andronicus, 1995, Speaking on Stage: Interviews with Contemporary American Playwrights, 1996; co-editor Studies in Am. Drama, 1945-94, Miss. Folklore Register, 1976-88; contbr. articles to profl. jours. Recipient Book of Yr. award Am. Jour. of Nursing, 1980; U. So. Miss. Rsch. grantee; named Charles W. Moorman Disting. Prof. in the Humanities, 1991—. Mem. Miss. Philol. Soc., South Atlantic MLA, South Ctrl. MLA. Roman Catholic. Office: Dept English U So Miss So Sta Box 8395 Hattiesburg MS 39406-8395

KOLKER, ALIZA, sociology educator; b. Tel-Aviv, Feb. 1, 1948; came to U.S., 1961; d. Samuel Z. and Zahava (Bookspan) Kolker; m. Kenneth Leon Heitner, Aug. 28, 1978; children: Ariel Ron, Ethan Sam. BA, Barnard Coll., 1969; PhD, Columbia U., 1975. Prof. sociology George Mason U., Fairfax, Va., 1975—. Co-author: The Social Bases of Politics, 1987, Prenatal Testing, 1994; editor: Aging, 1982. Office: George Mason Univ Dept Sociology Fairfax VA 22030

KOLKER, SONDRA G., fund raising/special events executive; b. N.Y.C., Nov. 30, 1943; d. Morris Henry and Alice (Cohen) Budow; m. Justin William Kolker, Aug. 23, 1963 (div.); children: Lawrence Paul, David Brett. Student, Hofstra U. Dir. N.Y.C. Office N.Y. State Dem. Com., 1977-79; v.p., exec. dir. Fund for Higher Edn., N.Y.C., 1980-88; pres. Sondra Kolker & Assocs., Halesite, N.Y., 1988-96, Miami, Fla., 1996—; spl. cons. Internat. Devel. Svcs. subs NMP of Am., Inc., 1989-90; dist. rep. Congressman Robert J. Mrazek, 1990-93. Speechwriter for numerous speakers at corp. banquets, 1980-88. Bd. dirs. Huntington (N.Y.) Townwide Fund, 1978-96; active Huntington Hosp. Aux., 1965-96, Great Gatsby Soc. for Multiple Sclerosis, 1988-96, Marble Hills Civic Assn., Halesite, 1958-96; committeewoman Huntington Dem. Com., 1974-82; fundraiser/dist. rep. Congressman Robert J. Mrazek, L.I., N.Y., 1991-93. Recipient Meritorious Svc. award Huntington Twp. C. of C., 1974, 76, 77, 78, Bicentennial Citation Town of Huntington, 1977. Mem. NAFE, MOMA, Met. Mus. Art, Nat. Mus. Women in the Arts, L.I. Crafts Guild, Huntington Twp. C. of C., Women's Econ. Round Table, Huntington Bus. and Profl. Women. Jewish. Home and Office: Sondra Kolker & Assoc 9385 SW 77th Ave #3033 Miami FL 33156

KOLLANDER, MEL, social scientist, statistician; b. N.Y.C., Dec. 10, 1939; s. Max and Gisella (Balin) K.; m. Barbara Frankfort, Jan. 28, 1962 (div. 1984); children: Steven B., Sondra L. BS, NYU, 1962; MA, New Sch. for Social Rsch., 1964, postgrad., 1967. Statistician AT&T, N.Y.C., 1964-68; economist, statistician Mitre Corp., McLean, Va., 1968-71; sr. statistician Social Security Adminstrn., Balt., 1971-77; mgr., sr. statistician Westat, Inc., Rockville, Md., 1977-79; prin. survey statistician U.S. EPA, Washington, 1979-94, mgr. small community info. and data program, 1992-94; dir. Washington office Inst. Survey Rsch. Temple U., Washington, 1995—; advisor Govt. of Kuwait, 1991-92, WHO, Geneva, 1987-92; lectr. WHO, USDA Grad. Sch., 1990-92. Chief editor, author: Survey Management Handbook, 1985; chief editor: Guidance on Survey Design for Human Exposure, 1993, (booklet) An Introductory Guide to Human Exposure Assessment Locations (Heals) Studies, Survey Methods and Statistical Sampling, 1992; contbr. chpt. to book. Mem. Citizen Taskforce on Property Assessment, Montgomery County, Md., 1978. Mem. ASTM (stats. methods sect., indoor air subcom. 1988-91), Internat. Statis. Inst. (elected mem.), Am. Statis. Assn., Internat. Assn. Survey Statisticians. Home: 4521 Saucon Valley Ct Alexandria VA 22312-3163

KOLLMEYER, KENNETH ROBERT, surgeon; b. Berwyn, Ill., Feb. 1, 1947. BS in Biology-Chemistry, Randolph-Macon Coll., 1969; PhD in Physiology, U. Cin., 1973; MD cum laude, U. Colo., 1977. Diplomate Am. Bd. Surgery, Am. Bd. Gen. Vascular Surgery. Rsch. asst. Cardiac Rsch. Lab., Sch. Medicine U. So. Calif., L.A., 1967; head lab divsn. thoracic and cardiovascular surgery Med. Ctr. Va., Richmond, 1968-69; NIH rsch. fellow dept. clin. physiology Nat. Asthma Ctr., Denver, 1973-74; intern in surgery Parkland Meml. Hosp., Dallas, 1977-78, resident in surgery, 1978-80, chief resident in surgery, 1980-81; fellow in vascular surgery, instr. dept. surgery U. Tex. Southwestern Med. Sch., Dallas, 1981-82, clin. asst. prof. surgery, 1982—; dir. S.W. Vascular Lab., Dallas, 1982—; attending vascular surgeon Meth. Med. Ctr., Dallas, 1982—; mem. staff Charlton Meth. Hosp., St. Paul Med. Ctr., Parkland Meml. Hosp., Med. City Hosp.; teaching asst. dept. physiology U. Cin. Coll. Medicine, 1972-73; chmn. Doctors Care PA, Dallas; presenter in field. Contbr. articles to profl. publs. Fellow ACS; mem. AMA, Tex. Med. Assn., Tex. Surg. Soc., Dallas County Med. Soc., Dallas Soc. Gen. Surgeons, Soc. for Non-Invasive Vascular Tech., Nat. Hon. Biol. Soc., Parkland Surg. Soc., Alpha Omega Alpha. Office: SW Vascular and Surg Group Meth Med Ctr Pavilion II 221 W Colorado Blvd Ste 625 Dallas TX 75208-2345

KOLODZIEJ, ERIC WILLIAM, chemist; b. East Chicago, Ind., Aug. 16, 1960; s. Alex Stanley and Helen Marie (Napiwocki) K.; m. Beth Lynn Bierwagen, Aug. 4, 1984 (div. May 1989); m. Mary Collette Goodsell, Feb. 23, 1991; 1 child, Kyle William. BS in Chemistry, Valparaiso (Ind.) U., 1982; PhD in Analytical/Medicinal Chemistry, Purdue U., 1986. Sr. rsch. chemist Monsanto Corp. Rsch., St. Louis, 1986-89, sr. rsch. specialist, 1989-91; tech. specialist/group leader Monsanto Chem., Alvin, Tex., 1991-92; lab. supt. Arco Chem. Co., Channelview, Tex., 1992-93; quality assurance mgr. Arco Chem. Co., Pasadena, Tex., 1993—; adj. prof. chemistry Lindenwood Coll., St. Charles, Mo., 1986-91, San Jacinto Coll., Houston, 1991—; advisor steering com. Tex. State Tech. Coll., Harlingen, 1992—; mem. steering com. dept. chemistry Valparaiso U., 1994—. Contbr. articles to profl. jours. David Ross Rsch. fellow, 1986. Mem. ASTM, Am. Chem. Soc., Am. Soc. Mass Spectrometry, Am. Soc. Quality Control, Gulf Coast Lab Mgrs. Assn. (co-chmn. 1996—), Pi Kappa Alpha. Republican. Lutheran. Office: Arco Chemical Company-Bayport 10801 Choate Rd Pasadena TX 77507

KOLOEN, JOHN SEIVER, editor; b. Kenosha, Wis.; s. Irving Anton and Ellen Ann (Uhrin) K.; m. Laura Elizabeth McNeil Burns, May 31, 1991. BA in English, U. Wis., Kenosha, 1974. Reporter, photographer Zion-Benton (Ill.) News, 1975-78; editor Round Rock (Tex.) Leader Newspaper, 1978-86; gen. mgr. Lake Travis View Newspaper, Austin, Tex., 1986-88; pub. Austin Health & Fitness Mag., 1988-93, Micropendium Mag., Round Rock, Tex., 1984-93; editor Tex. Dept. Health, Austin, 1993—. Publicity chmn. Am. Cancer Soc., Round Rock, 1980-82; bd. dirs. Round Rock Tennis Assn., 1983-92. Mem. Soc. Profl. Journalists, Nat. Assn. Govt. Communicators. Home: 502 Windsor Rd Round Rock TX 78664-7639

KOLOMBATOVIC, VADJA VADIM, management consulting company executive; b. Belgrade, Serbia, Yugoslavia, Jan. 20, 1924; came to U.S., 1944; s. George Steven and Antigona (Kefala) K.; m. Virginia Doris Carter, 1946; children: Vadja Vadim Jr., Mimi Carter. BS, U. Ill., 1948; cert. in personnel mgmt., U. Richmond, Va., 1949. Office mgr. State Farm Ins. Co., Richmond, 1948-49; spl. agt. FBI, N.Y.C. and San Francisco, 1949-66; asst. legal attache FBI, Paris, 1966-69; legal attache FBI, Madrid, Spain, Paris,

1969-75; chief liaison sect. FBI, Washington, 1975-76; v.p. for internat. affairs Intertel, Washington, 1976-83, sr. v.p., 1983-85; exec. v.p. Intertel, Rockville, Md., 1985-89, pres., 1989-92, pres., CEO, 1993—, also bd. dirs.; v.p. Chalk's Internat., Miami, Fla., 1976-91. Served to lt. U.S. Army, M.I., 1946-47. Mem. Am. Legion, Soc. Former Spl. Agts., Assn. Former Intelligence Officers, Assn. Former Legats, REs. Officers Assn., Masons (32 deg.), Shriners (Fairfax, Va.), McLean C. of C. Republican. Home: 1171 Dolley Madison Blvd Mc Lean VA 22101-3019 Office: Intertel 6867 Elm St Mc Lean VA 22101-3846

KOLSUN, BRUCE ALAN, special education educator; b. Pitts., Apr. 9, 1952; m. Cynthia Phillips, May 26, 1979; children: Stacey Elizabeth, Phillips Bruce. AA, Allegheny Community Coll., 1973; BA in Psychology, W.Va. U., 1975; MA in Spl. Edn., Duquesne U., 1978; Ednl. Specialist degree, W.Va. Grad. Coll., 1996. Cert. W. Va. specific learning disabilities, mentally impaired and behavior disorder K-12, edn. administrn. K-12. Tchr. specific learning disabilities/mentally impaired Randolph County Sch., Elkins, W.Va., 1978-79; dir. edn. W.Va. Dept. Correction, Huttonsville, 1979-85; specific learning disabilities/mentally imparied tchr. Tygart Valley H.S., 1988095; prin. Homestead Elem. Sch., Dailey, W.Va., 1995—; instr. adult basic edn. Randolph County Schs., 1987-88, learning disabilities diagnostician, 1985-88, acting supr. spl. edn., 1987-88; instr. psychology Alderson-Broaddus Coll., Philippi, W.Va., 1985; clin. supr. for learning disabilities W.Va. U., Morgantown, 1986-87; dir. Braille project W.Va. Corrections and Dept. Edn., Huttonsville, 1982-83; tchr. specific learning disabilities Upshur County Schs., Buckhannon, W.Va., 1979-81; edn. cons. W.Va. Dept. Corrections, 1986. Chmn. Randolph County Rep. Exec. Com., Elkins, 1991; vice chmn. State of W.Va. Young Reps.; co-dir. W.Va. Young Reps. Alumni; elected to Elkins City Coun., 1993—, chmn. pers. com., mem. pub. safety and bldg. coms. Mem. W.Va. Univ. Alumni Assn., Duquesne Univ. Alumni Assn. Home: 220 Sylvester Dr Elkins WV 26241-3044 Office: Homestead Elem Sch PO Box 158 Dailey WV 26259

KOLTS, BYRON EDWARD, gastroenterologist; b. Provo, Utah, Aug. 12, 1939; married; 2 children. BA, U. Wash., 1960; MD, U. Rochester, 1964. Diplomate Am. Bd. Internal Medicine, subspecialty bd. gastroenterology, Am. Bd. Med. Examiners; lic. physician, Vt., Fla. Rotating intern Mary Hitchcock Meml. Hosp., Hanover, N.H., 1964-65; resident internal medicine Dartmouth Affiliated Hosps., 1965-66; resident internal medicine U. Vt., Burlington, 1966-67, chief resident, 1967-68, instr. medicine, 1968-70; postdoctoral clin. and rsch. fellow divsn. gastroenterology U. Fla., Gainesville, 1970-72, asst. prof. medicine divsn. gastroenterology, 1972-77, assoc. prof., 1977-83, dir. divsn. gastroenterology and nutrition, 1983-94; assoc. prof. medicine U. Fla. Health Sci. Ctr., Jacksonville, 1983-94, prof. medicine, 1994—; lectr., speaker various profl. confs. and meetings; honors and awards judge Am. Hemerocallis Soc., 1979-82. Contbr. articles to profl. jours., chpts. to books. Vol. coach Boys Club Alachua County, 1976-81. Capt. USAF, 1968-70. Grantee NIH, 1976-79, U. Fla., 1980, Roche Labs., 1983, 84-85, Ross Labs., 1984-87, Serono Labs., 1984-85, Smith, Kline and French Labs., 1985-887, Searle Labs., 1986-87, Marion Labs., 1987-88, Glaxo, Inc., 1987-91, Syntex Lab., 1987-89. Fellow ACP; mem. AMA (physician's recognition award 1983, 86, 89), Soc. Gastroenterology for State of Chihuahua, Mexico, Am. Gastroenterol. Assn., Am. Soc. Enteral and Parenteral Nutrition, Community Med. Svcs. Assn., Am. Fedn. Clin. Rsch., So. Med. Assn., Fla. Gastroenterol. Assn. (treas. 1988, sec. 1989, pres. 1991), Fla. Med. Assn., Fla. Soc. Internal Medicine, Duval County Med. Soc. (quality assurance com. 1986-89), Alpha Epsilon Delta. Office: U Fla Health Sci Ctr Gastroenterology Div 653 W 8th St Jacksonville FL 32209-6511

KOMERATH, NARAYANAN MENON, aerospace engineer; b. Thrissur, Kerala, India, June 3, 1956; m. Padma Komerath. B Tech. in Aeronautical Engring., Indian Inst. Tech., Madras, 1978; MS in Aerospace Engring., Ga. Inst. Tech., 1979, PhD in Aerospace Engring., 1982. Postdoctoral fellow aerospace engring. Ga. Inst. Tech., Atlanta, 1982-83, rsch. engr., 1983-85, asst. prof., 1985-90, assoc. prof., 1990-94, prof. aerospace engring., 1994—; engring. cons. Lockheed-Ga. Co., Marietta, 1985-88, Southwire Co., Carrollton, Ga., 1992-93; chmn. SCV, Inc., Alpharetta, Ga., 1994—; dir. John J. Harper Wind Tunnel, Ga. Inst. Tech., Atlanta, 1990—. Contbr. articles to profl. jours. Fellow AIAA (assoc., nat. tech. com. on aerodynamic measurement 1995—); mem. Am. Helicopter Soc. (nat. tech. com. on aerodynamics 1994-96), Am. Soc. Engring. Edn., Soc. Exptl. Mechs., Amnesty Internat., Sigma Xi. Office: Ga Inst Tech Sch Aerospace Engring Atlanta GA 30332-0150

KONDRACKI, EDWARD JOHN, lawyer; b. Elizabeth, N.J., Sept. 27, 1932; s. John and Catherine Chudio (Saas) K.; m. Barbara Terese Caruso; children: Carol Ann, Maryanne, Christopher. BSEE, N.J. Inst. Tech., 1959; JD with honors, George Washington U., 1963. Bar: Va. 1964, D.C. 1964, U.S. Dist. Ct. D.C. 1964, U.S. Dist. Ct. (ea. dist.) Va. 1964, U.S. Ct. Claims 1976, U.S. Ct. Customs and Patent Appeals 1976, U.S. Ct. Appeals (Fed. cir.) 1983. Patent atty. Gen. Electric Co., Washington, 1959-63; dir. Kerkam, Stowell Kondracki & Clarke, P.C. and predecessor Cameron, Kerkam & Sutton, Arlington, Va., 1963-65, ptnr., 1965—; dir. Patmark Paralegal Svcs., 1975-90. Served with USN, 1951-55. Mem. ABA, Am. Intellectual Property Law Assn., Internat. Assn. Protection Indsl. Property, Va. Bar Assn., U.S. Trademark Assn., Washington Patent Lawyers Club, D.C. Bar Assn. (chmn. com. internat. affairs 1973), Gt. Falls Hist. Soc., Marmota Farm Assn., KC, Tau Beta Pi, Eta Kappa Nu, Omicron Delta Kappa. Author: Trademarks-Servicemarks, Use, Usage and Protection, 1981; Proper Use of Trademarks and Service Marks, 1982; Common Pitfalls Encountered in Patenting Inventions, 1983; Copyright Protection of Computer Software. Office: 5203 Leesburg Pike Falls Church VA 22041-3401

KONIKIEWICZ, LEONARD WIESLAW, biomedical communications educator; b. Lvow, Poland, July 24, 1928; came to U.S., 1959; s. Lubin Adolph and Melania (Rogozinska) K.; m. Antonina Kazimiera Grodowska; 1 child, Annette Melany. BS in Liberal Arts, SUNY, 1981; PhD in Natural Sci., Universitatis Polonorum, London, 1985. Registered biomedical photographer, illustrator. Med. photographer Cornell U., N.Y.C., 1960-67; dir. visual communications Poly. Med. Ctr., Harrisburg, Pa., 1967-85; dir., clinics asst. prof. biomed. communications James H. Quillen Coll. of Medicine, East Tenn. State U., Johnson City, Tenn., 1985—; export cons. in U.S.-Eastern Europe; cons. NASA Plant Space Biology Lab. Author: Bioelectrography, 1984, Career of Joanna Kurtz, 1995; contbr. articles to profl. jours. and books; patentee in field. Vol. interpreter ARC, Harrisburg, 1979-85; mem. refugee com. Polish Cultural Assn., Harrisburg, 1982, v.p. 1978-79; vol. organist Our Lady Cath. Ch., Harrisburg, 1970-85; rschr. Cystic-Fibrosis, Cancer, Harrisburg, 1975-85; v.p. Polish Cultural Assn., 1978-79. Decorated Medal of Home Army; recipient 2d prize Pa. Arts Coun., 1972, best cover award Lab World, 1975, best med. picture award Med. World News, 1977; rsch. grantee Pa. March of Dimes, 1976-78, Pa. Cystic Fibrosis Found., 1978-81, Betatron Corp., 1983-84. Mem. Biol. Photog. Assn., Assn. Biomed. Communications Dirs., Internat. Asns. Polish Combat Vets. Home: 2023 Sundale Rd Johnson City TN 37604-3027 Office: East Tenn State U James H Quillen Coll Med PO Box 70583 Johnson City TN 37614

KONSELMAN, DOUGLAS DEREK, lawyer; b. Tampa, Fla., Oct. 3, 1958; s. Derek Konselman and Linda (Horton) Fisher. BA in Biology, U. South Fla., 1981; JD, Loyola U., New Orleans, 1984; LLM, Georgetown U., 1996. Bar: Fla., 1984, N.J. 1985, N.Y. 1985, D.C. 1985, U.S. Supreme Ct. 1986. Ptnr. Konselman & Co., Washington, 1991-96; mng. ptnr. Konselman & Ptnrs., N.Y.C., 1996—; mem. Practicing Law Inst., N.Y.C., 1985—, Tax Policy Task Force, 1995—. Contbr. articles to law jours. Bd. dirs. Boca Raton (Fla.) Mus. Art, 1987, Market Square West, 1995-96. Mem. Am. Corp. Counsel Assn., Am. Soc. Internat. Law, Fgn. Law Soc., Soc. for Internat. Devel., Asia Soc., Mensa. Republican. Presbyterian. Office: 801 Penn Ave NW Ste 1003 Washington DC 20004

KONSLER, GWEN KLINE, oncology and pediatrics nurse; b. Ithaca, N.Y., July 11, 1959; d. Donald E. and Katherine (Schillroth) Kline; m. Thomas Konsler, Jr., Apr. 9, 1983. BSN, U.N.C., 1981. Staff nurse pediatrics U. N.C. Hosps., Chapel Hill, 1981-84, edn. clinician, 1984-87, pediatric oncology nurse, 1986—; nursing coord. Camp Carefree; chmn. rsch. subcom. N.C. Cancer Pain Initiative, 1991-94. Mem. Assn. Pediatric Oncology Nurses, Oncology Nursing Soc., Sigma Theta Tau. Home: 3623 Hawk Ridge Rd Chapel Hill NC 27516-8851

KONSTANTINOV, TZVETAN KRUMOV, musician, concert pianist; came to U.S., 1979; s. Krum Christov and Maria Apostolov (Veselkov) K.; m. Lee-Ann Larson, Mar. 7, 1980. MusM, Bulgarian State Conservatoire, Sofia, Bulgaria, 1974; postgrad., Hochschule Fur Musik, Vienna, Austria, 1979. Prof. Bulgarian State Conservatoire, Sofia, Bulgaria, 1974-77, Levine Sch. Music, Washington, 1984-89, George Washington U., Washington, 1989—; bd. dirs. Arlington Met. Chorus. Am. debut at Meany Hall, Seattle, 1980; performer TV documentary including Music To Promote Democracy, 1990, Spotlight, 1988, Capital Concerts, 1989. Bd. dirs. Arlington Met. Choir, Washington. Recipient Diploma for Highest Achievements Fifth All-Bulgarian Competition, 1969, Laureate Second Nat. Competition, 1970. Mem. AAUP, Am. Liszt Soc., Am. Assn. for Promoting Bulgarian Culture, Am. Beethoven Soc. Home: PO Box 554 Mc Lean VA 22101-0554 Office: George Washington U Dept Of Music Washington DC 20052

KOON, WILEY EMMETT, JR., librarian; b. Winter Haven, Fla., June 1, 1963; s. Wiley Emmett and Clovis O'Deal (Word) K. BA, U. South Fla., 1988, MA, 1989. Bibliographic rschr. Tampa (Fla.) Hillsborough County Pub. Libr. System, 1987-89; chief libr. U. of South Fla., Ednl. Leadership Libr., Tampa, 1989-91; dir. libr. svc. Nat. Ednl. Ctr., Tampa (Fla.) Tech. Inst., 1989-91, 92—; rsch. analyst Crystals Internat., Plant City, Fla., 1991-92; legal rschr. Pritchard Info., Bethesda, Md., 1991-92, Practical Bus. Concepts, Plant City, 1992—; cons. Nat. Edn. Ctr., Tampa (Fla.) Tech. Inst., 1991-92. Speaker Nat. Archives Awareness Week, Plant City, 1992. Recipient Johnny Key Thompson scholarship U. South Fla., Tampa, 1988. Mem. SAR, Fla. Libr. Assn. (chair online searchers caucus 1992-93), Tampa Bay Libr. Consortium (bd. dirs. 1990-92, electronic resources com. 1994—), Suncoast Info. Specialists (bd. dirs. 1990-92), U. South Fla. Alumni Assn. Democrat. Presbyterian. Office: Nat Edn Tampa Tech 2410 E Busch Blvd Tampa FL 33612-8410

KOONCE, ELLIS EVERETT, insurance agent; b. Birmingham, Ala., Dec. 3, 1929; s. Ellis Everett and Gladys Iola (Drake) K.; m. Mary Dona Matthews, Dec. 9; children: Ellis Everett II, Mark Evans, Dona Lee. Grad. high sch., Tunica, Miss. Mem. exec. com. Ind. Ins. Agts. of Miss., Jackson, 1980-82, v.p., 1982-83, pres., 1983-84, chmn. fin. com., 1985-87, mem. fin. com., 1987-94; v.p. Woolfolk Co., Tunica, Miss., 1969-74; pres. Koonce and Erwin Ins. Agy., Tunica, 1974-85, Rimmer-Child-Koonce, Cleveland, Miss., 1985—. Bd. alderman Town of Tunica, 1969-73, mayor, city judge, 1973-81, city clk., 1985-89; sheriff Tunica County, 1990. Cpl. USAF, 1948-49; chief Tunica Vol. Fire Dept., 1959-61. Mem. Tunica Lions Club (pres. 1961-62), Masons (sec. 1952-62). Methodist. Home: PO Box 1257 Tunica MS 38676-1257

KOONS, DARELL J., artist, art educator; b. Albion, Mich., Dec. 18, 1924; s. John Jr. and Viola (Foss) K.; m. Joyce L. Sherwood, Dec. 26, 1952; children: Sandra L., John H., Sheryl L., Susan L., Mark A. BA in Art Edn., Bob Jones U., 1951; MA in Art Edn., Western Mich. U., 1955. Tchr. art Homer (Mich.) Community Schs., 1951-55; prof. art Bob Jones U., Greenville, S.C., 1955—. One-man shows include U. S.C., Wake Forest U., Mint Mus., Charlotte, N.C., Columbus (Ga.) Mus., Washington County Mus. Art, Hagerstown, Md., Jesse Besser Mus., Alpena, Mich., and others; exhibited in over 100 groups shows including Mead Paper Exhbn., Atlanta, Hunter Annuals, Chattanooga, S.E. Annuals, Atlanta, Soc. Four Arts, Palm Beach, Cushing Gallery, Dallas, Isaac Delgado Mus., New Orleans, Chico (Calif.) State Coll., Springfield (Mass.) Mus., Art in Embassies Program, 1989-90, represented in numerous pvt. collections. Recipient Alumnus of Yr. award Homer Community Sch., 1989. Home: 6 Yancey Dr Greenville SC 29615-1235

KOONS, ELEANOR (PEGGY KOONS), clinical social worker; b. Sarasota, Fla., July 26, 1927; d. James Lee and Odessa (Dobbs) Swafford; m. Nelson A. Koons, Dec. 27, 1945. BA in Human Resources, Eckerd Coll., 1986; MSW, U. So. Fla., 1988. Lic. clin. social worker. Indsl. nurse Electro-Mech. Rsch. Co., Sarasota, Fla., 1963-65; office mgr. Koons Constrn. Co., Sarasota, 1970-80; day treatment counselor Manatee Community Mental Health Ctr., Bradenton, Fla., 1980-81, day treatment counselor geriat. residential treatment sys., 1981-82, community liaison, counselor, 1982-83; office mgr. Koons Constrn. Co., 1983-88; hospice intern Hospice S.W. Fla., 1987-88, sr. social svc. counselor, 1988-92; pvt. practice Sarasota, 1992—; presenter Nat. Hospice Assn. Conf., Detroit, Fla. Hospice Symposium, Ocala, Fla. Assn. Pediatric Tumor Programs, State Conf., Clearwater, others. Mem. spl. adv. bd. Storytelling World; contbr. articles to Bereavement Mag. Recipient Retired Social Worker of Yr. award Tampa Bay (Fla.) Unit; Grad. record fellow U. So. Fla. Mem. NASW (co-chairperson 1993-94), ACA. Home: Rt 67 Box 219 Cullowhee NC 28723

KOONTZ, ALFRED JOSEPH, JR., financial and operating management executive, consultant; b. Balt., Mar. 6, 1942; s. Alfred J. and Mary Agnes (Valis) K.; m. Kay Francis Frank, Aug. 4, 1962; children—Debbie Kay, Denise Marie, Stacey Lynn, Alfred Joseph, III. BSBA, Pa. State U., 1964. CPA, Md. Mgr. Price Waterhouse & Co., Balt., 1964-73; sr. mgr. Price Waterhouse & Co., N.Y.C., 1973-74, Morristown, N.J., 1974-75; v.p. fin Piper Aircraft Corp., Lock Haven, Pa., 1975-80; sr. v.p. fin. Piper Aircraft Corp., 1980-85, sr. v.p. fin., treas., 1985-86; exec. v.p., chief operating officer Piper Aircraft Corp., Vero Beach, Fla., 1987-88; pres., dir. Piper Acceptance Corp., Lakeland, Fla., 1985-88; sr. v.p. fin. and adminstrn., treas., bd. dirs. Todd Shipyards Corp., Seattle, 1988-91; exec. v.p., CFO Pay'N Pak Stores Inc., Bellevue, Wash., 1992-93; pres. Alfred J. Koontz & Assoc., Vero Beach, 1993—; co-owner, CFO Pub. Telecomm. Providers, Inc., Vero Beach, 1993—. Mem. AICPA, Md. Assn. CPAs, Inst. Mgmt. Accts. Home: 1790 Sand Dollar Way Vero Beach FL 32963 Office: PO Box 4434 Vero Beach FL 32964

KOONTZ, LAWRENCE L., JR., judge; b. Roanoke, Jan. 25, 1940. BS, Va. Polytech. U., 1962. Asst. commonwealth's atty. Roanoke, 1967-68; judge Va. Juvenile & Domestic Rels. Dist. Ct., 1968-76, Va. Cir. Ct. (23rd cir.), 1976-85, Ct. Appeals of Va., 1985-95, Supreme Ct. of Va., 1995—. Mem. ABA, Va. State Bar Assn., Roanoke Bar Assn., Roanoke Valley Mental Health Assn. (pres.). Office: PO Box 687 Salem VA 24153-0687

KOOP, TOBEY KENT, research consultant, educational psychologist; b. Victoria, Tex., Jan. 3, 1955; s. Francis Dietrich and Jewel Virginia (Williams) K. BA, U. Houston, 1978; PhD, U. Tex., 1985. Rsch. cons. Austin, 1985—; owner statis. and psychometric software PsychStat, Austin, 1991—. Author: (chpt.) Facet Theory Approaches to Social Research, 1985; author (software and manual) PsychStat MAX 2.1, 1991, PsychStat MAX 2.2, 1993. Mem. U. Tex. Ex-students Assn., Phi Kappa Phi. Office: PsychStat 2605 Goldfinch Dr Cedar Park TX 78613-5113

KOOPMANN, RETA COLLENE, sales executive; b. Oklahoma City, Feb. 27, 1944; d. Henry William and Hazel (Rollins) Singleton; children: Rebecca Dawn, Christiana Collene. BS, Calif. Coast U., 1987, postgrad. in bus. adminstrn., 1987—. Front end mgr. Kroger Co., Cleve., 1969-72; with acctg. dept. Johns Manville, Denison, Tex., 1972-74; bakery/deli merchandiser Kroger Co., Columbia, S.C., 1974-83; v.p. bakery, deli ops. Kash n' Karry div. Lucky's Inc., Tampa, Fla., 1983-88, Kash n' Karry Food Stores Inc., Tampa, 1988-90; LBO, corp. dir. bakery/deli/sea food ops. United Supermarkets, Inc., Lubbock, Tex., 1990-91; mgr. regional supermarket accounts Tenneco-Packaging, Deerfield, Ill., 1991—. Author tng. manuals, 1984, 86, 87. Bd. trustees Jim Borck Ednl. Found., Inc., 1988—, pres. elect, 1993, chairperson of bd., 1994, 95, 96, chair com. for deli skills tng. program; vol. Spl. Olympics, Tampa, 1986, 87, 88; bd. govs. Am. Biog. Inst. Rsch. Assn., 1989—. Mem. NAFE, Internat. Deli/Bakery Assn. (exec. bd. 1986-89), Internat. Platform Assn., Retail Bakers Assn. (bd. dirs. 1989—, chmn. deli com., deli dir.), Eagles. Republican. Methodist. Home: 3010 Ridge Run Dr Hiram GA 30141-3337 Office: Packaging Corp Am 3010 Ridge Run Dr Hiram GA 30141-3337

KOOS, LEONARD ROBERT, French educator; b. Patterson, Calif., Aug. 9, 1958; s. Ralph Frederick and Ruth Catherine (Giaya) K. BA, UCLA, 1981; MA, Yale U&., 1983, MPhil, 1985, PhD, 1990. Rsch. asst. Yale U., New Haven, 1983, acting instr., 1985-88; vis. asst. prof. Emroy U., Atlanta, 1988-89; asst. prof. Reed Coll., Portland, Oreg., 1989-92; asst. prof. French Mary Washington Coll., Fredericksburg, Va., 1992—; vis. adj. prof. Monterey (Calif.) Inst. Internat. Studies, 1988, 90, 92. Contbr. articles to profl. jours.; editl. bd. Yale French Studies, 1984-85. Recipient Bourse d'études, French Govt., Paris, 1985-86; NEH Summer stipend, 1995; Yale U. Grad. fellow, 1983-85; Mary Washington Coll. Faculty Devel. grantee, 1996. Mem. MLA, Soc. for Lit. and Sci., South Ctrl. MLA. Democrat. Office: Mary Washington College 1301 College Ave Fredericksburg VA 22401

KOOSTRA, MARGARET ELIZABETH, library director; b. Columbus, Miss., Feb. 3, 1941; d. Gillman Egan Sr. and Lucy Maury (Swoope) Ellis; m. Richard Koostra, June 26, 1970 (div. Sept. 1985); children: Annie Laurie, Ashley Ellis. BS, Miss. State U., 1962, MA, 1963; MEd, Miss. U. for Women, 1975; M of Libr. Sci., U. Ala., 1990. Tchr. English and History West Lowndes Elem. Sch., Columbus, Miss., 1963-64, Caledonia (Miss.) Middle Sch., 1964-65; tchr. History and Govt. S.D. Lee Sr. H.S., Columbus, 1965-66; tchr. of history Miss. U. for Women, 1967-70; headmaster East Lowndes Acad., Steens, Miss., 1975-78, tchr. History and English, 1979-80; dir. Noxubee County Libr., Macon, Miss., 1981—. Active Dancing Rabbit Treaty Site adv. com., 1994—. Named Noxubee County Woman of the Yr., C. of C., 1988. Mem. DAR (Dancing Rabbit chpt. regent 1990-92), Miss. Libr. Assn., United Daughters of the Confederacy (state chmn. 1993-96), Miss. Soc. DAR (state chmn. 1995-98), Noxubee County Hist. Soc. Home: 306 N Wayne St Macon MS 39341 Office: Noxubee County Libr 103 E King St Macon MS 39341-2831

KOOTI, JOHN G., economist, educator; b. Hoveyzeh, Iran, May 23, 1951; came to U.S., 1975; s. Abaid and Zahdeiah (Salemi) K.; m. Lisa Gilbert, May 9, 1980; children: Ali Jon, Cameron Lee. BS, Jundi Shapour, Iran, 1974; MS, Mich. State U., 1980, PhD, 1980. Asst. prof., assoc. prof. econs. and bus. Albany (Ga.) State Coll., 1981-92, prof. econs. and bus., 1992—; adj. prof. econs. Andrew Coll., Cuthbert, Ga., 1989-91. Contbr. articles to profl. jours. Mem. Internat. Fedn. for Bus. Edn., Am. Econ. Assn., Nat. Assn. Forensic Economists, Ga. Assn. Econs. and Fin. Educators, Albany Dougherty C. of C. Office: Sch of Bus Albany State Coll Albany GA 31705

KOPATICH, WILLIAM EDWARD, computer company executive; b. Hampton, Va., June 16, 1946; s. John J. and Louise (Morgan) K.; m. Lynn McMillen, Feb. 14, 1977. Student, UCLA, 1964-66; BS in Indsl. Engring. and Ops. Rsch., U. Calif., Berkeley, 1968. Indsl. engr. Collins Radio Co., Newport Beach, Calif., 1968-70, Memorex Corp., Santa Clara, Calif., 1970-73; mgr. facilities planning, engr. Amdahl Corp., Sunnyvale, Calif., 1973-79; mgr. corp. svcs. Verbatim Corp., Sunnyvale, 1979-82; plant mgr. Verbatim Corp., Charlotte, N.C., 1982-87, dir. joint ventures, 1987-90, v.p. corp. planning and bus. devel., 1990-95; v.p. optical storage products Verbatim Corp., Charlotte, 1995—; bd. dirs. ITA, N.Y.C., v.p., 1994—; bd. dirs., treas. QIC, Santa Barbara, Calif., 1993-95. Bd. dirs., treas. Charlotte Urban League, 1983-89. Mem. Optical Storage Tech. Assn. (bd. dirs., treas. 1993-95, chmn. bd. dirs. 1995—). Office: Verbatim Corp 1200 W Wt Harris Blvd Charlotte NC 28262-8552

KOPCZICK, RON JAMES, communications director, editor; b. Morris, Ill., May 10, 1959; s. John Lee Kopczick and Eleanor Naomi (Kates) Rouse. BA in Ministerial Studies, Southeastern Coll., 1981. Assoc. editor PTL TV Network, Charlotte, N.C., 1981-82; editor PTL TV Network, Charlotte, 1982-88; dir. news/info. Nat. Religious Broadcasters, Parsippany, N.J., 1988-89; dir. comms. Nat. Religious Broadcasters, Manassas, Va., 1989—. Editor Heritage Herald, 1982-88, Religious Broadcasting, 1989—; exec. editor ann. Directory of Religious Media, 1989—. Recipient Blue Ribbon awards No. Ill. Scholastic Press Assn., DeKalb, 1976, 77, First Class awards Collegiate Press Assn., 1978, 80, Third Pl. Publs. award Internat. Assn. Bus. Communicators, N.C.-Piedmont, 1983, awards Evang. Press Assn., 1992, 93. Mem. Evang. Press Assn. Republican. Office: Nat Religious Broadcasters 7839 Ashton Ave Manassas VA 20109-2883

KOPELMAN, LORETTA MARY, philosophy educator; b. N.Y.C., Sept. 5, 1938; d. Frank Morris and Gertrude May (Veitch) K.; m. Arthur Edward Kopelman; children: Elizabeth, William. BA in Philosophy, Syracuse U., 1960, MA in Philosophy, 1962; PhD in Philosophy, U. Rochester, 1966. Asst. lectr. U. Rochester, N.Y., 1965-66, assoc. lectr., 1971-73, instr., 1974-76, asst. prof., 1976-78; lectr. U. Tenn., Nashville, 1967-68, New Haven Coll., 1968-69, U. Md., 1971; assoc. prof. med. humanities, dir. East Carolina U., Greenville, N.C., 1978-85, prof. med. humanities, 1985—, founding chair med. humanities dept., 1984—; founding mem. ethics com., med. staff Pitt County Meml. Hosp., 1986—; co-chair ad hoc human growth hormone rev. com. NIH, 1992; cons. in filed. Author: (with others) The Rights of Children and Retarded Persons, 1978, Ethics and Mental Retardation, 1984, Ethics and Critical Care Medicine, 1985, Children and Health Care: Moral and Social Issues, 1989; mem. editl. bd. Jour. Medicine and Philosophy, 1982-86, Clinical Med. Ethics, 1986—; referee book Random House; contbr. articles to profl. jours. Vis. prof. ethics Pitts. Children's Hosp., 1987; mem. ednl. com. Concern for Dying, 1988—; mem. external task force Joint Commn. on Accreditation of Healthcare Orgns., 1993. Fellow faculty Syracuse U., 1960-61, facutly U. Rochester, 1962-65, NEH, 1974-76; grantee NEH, 1983-84, U. Rochester, 1976-78, N.Y. State Dept. Mental Hygiene, 1976, N.C. Humanities Com., 1980-87, AMA Edn. and Rsch. Found., 1982-84, Arthur Davis Vining Found., 1982-84, Ross Labs., 1986-87, GTE, 1992-93. Fellow Assn. for the Advancement Philosophy and Psychiatry; mem. AAUP, Am. Philos. Assn. (con. 1982-85), Soc. for Health and Human Values (chair program dirs. 1990-91, editor essays and letters 1984-86), Mind Assn., Aristotelian Soc., Assn. Faculty in Med. Humanities, Hastings Ctr., Kennedy Inst. Ethics, European Soc. for Philosophy Medicine and Health Care, Soc. Law and Medicine, Phi Beta Kappa, Phi Kappa Phi, Theta Beta Phi. Democrat. Mem. Soc. of Friends. Home: 411 Queen Annes Rd Greenville NC 27858-6306 Office: East Carolina U Dept Med Humanities Brody Med Scis Bldg Greenville NC 27858

KOPF, JANET CAROLYN See CARMONY, JANET CAROLYN

KOPP, GEORGE PHILIP, JR., minister; b. Cin., July 17, 1927; s. George Philip and Ann Elizabeth (Suffield) K.; m. Janet Marie Thompson Schultz, Oct. 13, 1956. BA, Heidelberg Coll., 1950; BD, Eden Sem., 1955, MDiv, 1969. Ordained to ministry United Ch. of Christ, 1955. Pastor St. John's Ch., Middlebrook, Va., 1955-60, 83-85, ret.; commd. ensign USN, 1954, advanced through grades to lt. comdr., 1976, served as chaplain; ret., 1976, ret., 1976; dir. Ctr. Atlantic Conf. United Ch. Christ, 1983-88. With USN, 1945-51, USNR, 1952. Home and Office: 308 Valley View Dr Staunton VA 24401-2101

KOPPENHOEFER, ROBERT MACK, chemist; b. Cin., Sept. 4, 1909; s. Robert Emil and Emma (Mack) K.; m. Dorothy Fisgus, July 24, 1937; children: Kenneth Robert, Karen Castelloes. BAChemE, Cin. U., 1933, M in Chemistry, 1934, PhD in Biochemistry, 1936; cert. in mgmt., Mellon U., 1954, 62. Grad. sch. faculty U. Cin., 1936-39; leather chemist Socony-Vacuum Oil Co., Bklyn., 1939-46; rsch. chemist Mobil Oil-tech. div., Bklyn., 1946-49, supr., 1949-53; asst. mgr. Mobil Oil-tech. lab., N.Y.C., 1953-56; v.p. Mobil Chem., Metuchen, N.J., 1956-65; mgr. tech. lab. Mobil Oil Co., N.Y.C., 1965-74. Contbr. articles to profl. jours. Army leather devel. for war dept. NSF, Tanners Lab. U. Cin., 1943. Mem. Am. Chem. Soc., Am. Leather Chem. Assn. (pres. 1948-50, Alsop award, 1947), Petroleum Industry (25 yr. club). Republican. Home: 590110 Village Pl Longwood FL 32779-6038

KOPPERNAES, CHRISTIAN, electrical engineer; b. Halifax, N.S., Can., Jan. 15, 1961; came to U.S., 1986; s. Johan Devold and Barbara Joan (Longley) K.; m. Robin E. Dooley, Oct. 8, 1988; children: Leif, Finn. BSc in Physics, Dalhousie U., Halifax, N.S., 1983; BSEE, Tech. U. N.S., Halifax, 1986. Registered profl. engr., N.S. Rsch. engr. Am. Composite Tech., Boston, 1986-91; tech. dir. Coastal Engineered Products, Varnville, S.C., 1991-94, Omega Pultrusions, Varnville, 1994, Koppernaes Engring. Ltd., Beaufort, S.C., 1994—. Co-patentee method for degassing pultrusions, method for making a pultruded panel. Mem. IEEE, Assn. Profl. Engrs. N.S. Home: 2423 Pigeon Point Rd Beaufort SC 29902-4043

KORB, ELIZABETH GRACE, nurse midwife; b. Wilmington, N.C., Mar. 1, 1951; d. Carl Wilhelm Bissenger Korb and Betty Jane Stroup; m. Joel Vincent LeFebvre, May 19, 1973 (div. June 1976); m. James Clinton Queen, June 22, 1984; 1 child, James Michael Andrew Queen. BSN, U. N.C., Greensboro, 1973; MSN, U. Utah, 1980. Cert. nurse midwife. Staff nurse, instr. New Hanover Meml. Hosp., Wilmington, N.C., 1973-76; staff nurse Meml. Mission Hosp., Asheville, N.C., 1976-78, LDS Hosp., Salt Lake City, 1978-79; practising nurse midwife Dr. Michael Watson, Bamberg, S.C., 1980, Fletcher (N.C.) Ob-Gyn. Assocs., 1981-83, Nurse-Midwifery Assocs., Fletcher, 1983-85, Asheville (N.C.) Women's Med. Ctr., 1985-86, 88; practising nurse midwife, clin. coord. Regional Perinatal Assocs., Asheville, 1986-88; perinatal clin. coord., practicing nurse midwife Mountain Area Health Edn. Ctr., Asheville, 1988—; clin. preceptor Cmty.-Based Nurse-Midwifery Edn. Program, 1993—, East Carolina U. Nurse-Midwifery Edn. Program, 1993—; mem. mgmt. team Mountain Area Perinatal Substance Abuse Program, 1993—; bd. dirs. Mary Benson House, Asheville; mem. adv. panel Emory U., Nurse Midwifery in Pub. Sector, Atlanta, 1988—. Named to Outstanding Young Women of Am., 1982; recipient Profl. award March of Dimes, Asheville, 1993. Mem. ANA, Nat. Perinatal Assn., N.C. Perinatal Assn. (bd. dirs. 1988-93), N.C. Nurses Assn., Am. Coll. Nurse Midwives (N.C. del. legis. conf. 1993, 94, nominating com. 1981-82), Internat. Childbirth Edn. Assn., Phi Kappa phi, Sigma Theta Tau. Democrat. Lutheran. Office: Mountain Area Health Edn Ctr Ob-Gyn 60 Livingston St Ste 100 Asheville NC 28801

KORDSMEIER, WILLIAM FRANK, economics educator; b. Little Rock, Ark., Aug. 10, 1948; s. Leo Henry and Dorothy Ellen (Kenney) K.; m. Mary Kathryn Webb, Aug. 1, 1970 (div. 1987); children: Matthew Henry, Micah Lohr. BA in Econs., ;U. Dallas, 1970; MA, U. Ark., 1976; PhD, Tex. A&M U., 1986. Instr. Hendrix Coll., Conway, Ark., 1980-86; assoc. prof. U. Ctrl. Ark., Conway, 1986—; cons. Migrant Head Start, Conway, 1991-95, Cmty. Action Program, Conway, 1991—, Acxiom Corp., Conway, 1993-94, Schueck Steel, North Little Rock, 1987-88. Contbr. articles to profl. jours. Cons. Faulkner County Coalition for Drug-Free Youth, Conway, 1993-94; vol. St. Joseph's Bazaar, Conway, 1986-95. Mem. So. Econs. Assn., Midwest Econs. Assn. Roman Catholic. Office: U Ctrl Ark 201 Donaghey Ave Conway AR 72035

KORGAONKAR, PRADEEP KASHINATH, marketing educator; b. Bombay, India; came to U.S., 1974; s. Kashinath S. and Gulab (Rege) K.; m. Ronnie Silverblatt, Dec. 21, 1980; children: Brian Ross, Kevin Scott. BS, Bombay U., 1973; MBA, Clark U., 1976; PhD, Ga. State U., 1980. Asst. prof. Wayne State U., Detroit, 1980-83; asst. prof. Fla. Atlantic U., Boca Raton, 1983-85, assoc. prof., 1985-89, prof. mktg., 1989—, chmn. dept. mktg., 1987-93; cons. Boca Bank, Boca Raton, Med-Check, Inc., West Palm Beach, Fla., Bank Atlantic, Ft. Lauderdale, Fla., Fisher Theater, Detroit, Herman Miller, Atlanta; rsch. analyst market rsch. dept. Atlanta World Hdqs. Coca Cola; active numerous coms. Fla. Atlantic U., Boca Raton. Reviewer Jour. Bus. Rsch., Jour. Svcs. Mktg., Jour. Acad. Mktg. Sci., Jour. Retailing; contbr. articles to profl. jours. Recipient Levi Strauss Scholastic scholarship Ga. State U., 1978, Best Paper award So. Mktg. Assn., 1983; grantee (3) Direct Mktg. Policy Ctr. U. Cin. Mem. Am. MKtg. Assn., Acad. Mktg. Sci. (Best Paper award 1982).

KORHONEN, MARILYN RICE, educational grant writer; b. San Francisco, Aug. 7, 1963; d. James F. Rice and Cheryle J. (Menges) Langhorne; m. Lloyd J. Korhonen, Feb. 14, 1991; stepchildren: Mark, Paul, Jennifer Korhonen Kleinschmidt. BA, U. Okla., 1985, MBA, 1988, EdD, 1994. Continuing edn. program specialist U. Okla., Norman, 1986-87, asst. to vice provost, 1988-91; asst. to dean Tex. A&M U., College Station, 1991-93; mng. ptnr., owner The Write Tech. Group, Marquez, Tex., 1994—; grant reviewer U.S. Dept. Edn., U.S. Dept. Commerce, U.S. Dept. Health and Human Svcs., Washington, 1990—. Vol. grant writer Dalhart (Tex.) Cmty. Theatre, 1995; vol. Habitat for Humanity, College Station, 1992-94. Mem. NAFE, AAUW, Am. Assn. Adult and Continuing Edn., Tex. Coun. for Social Studies, Tex. Assn. Supervision and Curriculum Devel., Norman C. of C. Office: The Write Tech Group Rt 2 Box 344 C Marquez TX 77865

KORMILEV, NICHOLAS ALEXANDER, retired entomologist; b. Yalta, Crimea, Russia, Jan. 29, 1901; came to U.S., 1957; s. Alexander Nicholas and Catherine (Sakulin) K.; widower; 1 child, Alexander Nicholas. Diploma in engring. agronomy, State U., Zabreb, Yugoslavia, 1926. Prof. Agrl. Sch., Tetovo, Yugoslavia, 1931-32; adj. Directory of Agr., Skoplje, Yugoslavia, 1932-33, superior adj., 1933-40, councellor, 1940-41; sec. Ministry of Agr., Beograd, Yugoslavia, 1941-43; rsch. entomologist Nat. Mus. of Natural History, Buenos Aires, 1948-52, Inst. de Ciencias Naturales, San Miguel, Argentina, 1952-56; rsch. assoc. in entomology Bishop Mus., Honolulu, 1968-95. Author: Phymatidae Argentinas (Hemipteras), 1951, Revision of Phymatinae (Hemiptera), 1962, Mezirinae of Southeast Asia and Southern Pacific, 1971; (with Froeschner) Flat Bugs of the World, 1987, Phymatidae or Ambush Bugs of the World, 1989; contbr. 230 articles to profl. jours. With Yugoslavia Mil., 1939-40. Decorated Knight Cross of St. Sava, King of Yugoslavia, 1940. Home: 2930 54th St S Saint Petersburg FL 33707-5530

KORN, MICHAEL JEFFREY, lawyer; b. Jersey City, Dec. 22, 1954; s. Howard Leonard and Joyce Ellen (Blumenkranz) K.; m. Pamela Ann Van-Zandt, May 29, 1983; children: David Harold, Suzanne Faye. BA, U. Va., 1976; JD, U. Fla., 1979. Bar: Fla. 1980, U.S. Dist. Ct. (no. and mid. dists.) Fla., U.S. Ct. Appeals (5th and 11th cirs.). Jud. law clk. Fla. 1st Dist Ct. Appeal, Tallahassee, 1980-81; assoc. Boyer, Tanzler & Boyer, Jacksonville, Fla., 1981-84; pvt. practice Jacksonville, 1984-87; ptnr. Christian, Prom, Korn & Zehmer, P.A., Jacksonville, 1987-92, Prom, Korn & Zehmer, P.A., Jacksonville, 1992-95, Korn, Zehmer & Gellatly, P.A., Jacksonville, 1995—; mem. Fla. Appellate Ct. Rules Com., 1990—. Bd. dirs. North Fla. coun. Camp Fire, 1983-86, Jacksonville Jewish Fedn., 1985—, Youth Leadership Jacksonville, 1989-93, Jacksonville Cmty. Coun., 1989-94, pres., 1995; Mandarin Comty. Club, Jacksonville, 1988-91. Recipient Young Leadership award Jacksonville Jewish Fedn., 1992. Mem. Fla. Bar (litigation sect.), Jacksonville Bar Assn. (fee arbitration cir. 1987-90), Acad. Fla. Trial Lawyers (amicus com.). Democrat. Jewish. Office: Korn Zehmer & Gellatly PA 6620 Southpoint Dr S Ste 200 Jacksonville FL 32216-0940

KORNBLEET, LYNDA MAE, insulation, fireproofing and acoustical contractor; b. Kansas City, Kans., June 15, 1951; d. Seymore Gerald Kornbleet and Jacqueline F. (Hurst) Kornbleet Malka. BA, U. St. Thomas, Houston, 1979. Lic. real estate salesperson. Temporary counselor Lyman's Personnel, Houston, 1974-75; real estate salesperson Coldwell Banker, Houston, 1975-77; sales, office mgr. Acme Insulation, Dallas, also Houston, 1977-79; owner, pres. Payless Insulation, Houston, 1979—; contractor City of Houston, 1985—. Disadvantaged Bus. Cert. State of Tex., 1989—; vender Houston Bus. Coun. Named Contractor of the Yr., Sears Home Improvement, 1988; active Houston Ind. Sch. Dist., 1989—. Awarded and completed acoustical treatment of Astrodome for Rep. Nat. Conv. 1992; recipient award Internat. Cellulose 1,000,000 sq. ft., 1995-96. Mem. Houston Air Conditioning Coun. (bd. dirs. 1982-83), Cellulose Insulation Contractors (chmn. Houston 1981-82), Houston Bus. Coun., 1987—, Insulation Contractors Assn. Greater Houston (pres. 1991—). Democrat. Jewish. Avocations: bridge, golf. Office: Payless Insulation 207 Reinerman St Houston TX 77007-7228

KORNDORFFER, WILLIAM EARL, forensic pathologist; b. Natchez, Miss., Feb. 5, 1930; s. William Earl and Caroline Elizabeth (Lapthorn) K.; m. Betty Blair Hughes, June 18, 1954; children: William III, James Blair, Robert Craig, Brenda Lea. BS, U. Miss., 1952; MD, Harvard U., 1956. Diplomate Am. Bd. Pathology. Dir. labs Griffin-Spalding Co. Hosp., Griffin, Ga., 1963-65; co-dir. of labs Galveston Co. Meml. Hosp., Tex. City, Tex., 1965-68; dir. labs Rimmer Med. Labs., Dickinson, Tex., 1968-74, Danforth Meml. Hosp., Tex. City, 1968-74, Alvin (Tex.) Gulfcoast Hosp., 1968-74, Alvin (Tex.) Meml. Hosp., 1968-74, Angleton (Tex.) Danbury Hosp., 1968-74; chief med. exam Med. Examiner's Office, Tex. City, 1972—; asst. prof. pathology U. Tex. Med. Branch, Galveston, 1978—. Capt. USAF, 1958-60. Mem. AMA, Coll. Am. Pathologists, Am. Soc. Clin. Pathologists, Nat. Assn. Med. Examiners, Am. Acad. Forensic Scis., Soc. Nuclear Medicine, Elks, Moose. Roman Catholic. Home: 5000 Hwy 3 Dickinson TX 77539-6830 Office: Med Examiners Office 6607 Highway 1764 Texas City TX 77591

KORNGUT, IRWIN STEVEN, physician; b. Bklyn., Feb. 24, 1950; s. Lawrence J. and Rose (Fisher) K.; m. Debra Ann Schonfeld, Jan. 6, 1978; children: Kevin, Bryan, Alex. BA, Dartmouth Coll., 1972; MD, Duke U., 1976. Diplomate Am. Bd. Internal Medicine, Nat. Bd. Med. Examiners. Intern U. Tex. Southwestern Med. Sch., Dallas, 1976-77, resident, 1977-79; pvt. practice internal medicine Dallas. Mem. AMA, Tex. Med. Assn., Dallas County Med. Soc. Address: 8220 Walnut Hill Ln Ste 110 Dallas TX 75231-4406

KORNYLAK, HAROLD JOHN, osteopathic physician; b. Jersey City, Feb. 16, 1950; s. Andrew Thomas and Lucille Bertha (Reilly) K.; children: Laura, Michael. BS in Physics with honors, Stevens Inst. Tech., 1971; MA, Maharishi Internat. U., 1977; MS, Maharishi European Rsch. U., 1977; DO, U. New Eng., 1983. Mem. indsl. R & D staff Kornylak Corp., Hamilton, Ohio, 1971-73, mgr. data processing, 1974-79; researcher Maharishi European Rsch. U., Weggis, Switzerland, 1973-74; intern Mich. Osteo. Med. Ctr., Detroit, 1983-84; staff physician Indian Health Svc., USPHS, San Carlos, Ariz., 1984-87, St. Louis Orthopedic Sports Medicine Clinic, 1987-88; pvt. practice Virginia Beach, Va., 1989—; cons. in systems analysis; instr. Atlantic U., Virginia Beach, 1989—, Harold J. Reilly Sch. Massotherapy, Virginia Beach, 1989—. Mem. Am. Osteo. Assn., Am. Acad. Osteopathy, Am. Acad. Med. Acupuncture, Cranial Acad., Va. Osteo. Med. Assn. Home and Office: 1432 E Bay Shore Dr Virginia Beach VA 23451-3760

KOROTKIN, AUDREY RHONA, communications executive; b. Phila., Aug. 8, 1957; d. Arthur Lewis and Carol Ruth (Ruffner) K.; m. Don C. Clippinger, Oct. 21, 1989. BA in Russian Area Studies magna cum laude, U. Md., 1979; grad. rabbinic aide program, Union Am. Hebrew Congregations. Prodn. asst. NBC Nightly News, Washington, 1978-79; news anchorwoman Sta. WCBM Radio, Balt., 1978-79; news, sports, anchor reporter Sta. WBAL Radio, Balt., 1979-86; exec. dir. Triple Crown Prodns., Inc., Louisville, 1986-89; pres. Korotkin Assocs. Inc., Ft. Thomas, Ky., 1989—; student rabbi Hebrew Union Coll., Cin., 1994—. Contbg. editor Racing Action mag., 1989-94; contbg. writer The Backstretch mag., Thoroughbred Times, 1989-95. Mem. Cmty. Rels. Coun. Jewish Cmty. Fedn. of Louisville. Mem. Nat. Turf Writers Assn., Md. Racing Writers Assn., Nat. Steeplechase Assn., Phi Kappa Phi. Democrat. Jewish. Home and Office: 20 Klainecrest Ave Fort Thomas KY 41075-1930

KORPMAN, MICHAEL DAVID, family practice physician; b. New Brunswick, N.J., June 2, 1955; s. Ralf and Vera Korpman. BA, Andrews U., 1976; MD, Loma Linda U., 1979, MPH, 1982. Resident in family practice Fla. Hosp., Orlando, 1980-82; pathology fellow Sch. Medicine Loma Linda (Calif.) U., 1983-84; chair family practice dept. Cigna Health Care, Altamonte Springs, Fla., 1987—. Author: Passport to Health, 1995; inventor adhesive development. Mem. AMA, Am. Acad. Family Practice. Office: Cigna Healthcare of Florida 360 Douglas Ave Altamonte Springs FL 32780

KORSAH, KOFI, nuclear engineer; b. Saltpond, Ghana, Jan. 20, 1950; came to U.S., 1977; s. Isaac Francis and Ekua (Taakoa) K.; m. Hanna Howard-Turkson, Dec. 18, 1976; children: Ato, Kweku. BS, U. of Sci. and Tech., Ghana, 1973; M in Nuclear Engring., U. Mo., 1980, PhD, 1983. Asst. prof. elect. engring., nuclear physics U. Maine, Orono, 1982-84; asst. prof. U. Ghana, Accra, 1985-88, Tenn. Wesleyan Coll., Athens, 1988-90; rsch. staff mem. Oak Ridge (Tenn.) Nat. Lab., 1990—. Contbr. articles to IEEE Trans. in Nuclear Sci., Nuclear Instrn. and Methods, Am. Chem. Soc. jour., Trans. of Am. Nuclear Soc., Nuclear Engring. and Design. Mem. IEEE (sr.). Baptist. Home: 6520 Ellesmere Dr Knoxville TN 37921-3812 Office: Oak Ridge Nat Lab PO Box 2008 Oak Ridge TN 37831-2008

KORTH, CHARLOTTE BROOKS, furniture and interior design firm executive; b. Milw.; d. Lewis C. and Marguerite Peil Brooks; m. Robert Lee Williams, Jr., Oct. 25, 1944 (dec.); children: Patricia Williams, Melissa Williams O'Rourke, Brooks Williams; m. Fred Korth, Aug. 23, 1980. Student, U. Wis., 1941. Owner Charlotte's Inc., El Paso, Tex., 1951—, chmn., CEO, 1979—; pres. Paso del Norte Design, Inc., El Paso, 1978-81, 83—; mem. adv. com. for interior design program El Paso C.C., 1981—; mem. adv. bd. Southwest Design Inst., 1982—; ptnr. Wilko Partnership, 1981—; mem. adv. bd. Mountain Bell Telephone Co., 1976-79; mem. Sch. Architecture Found. Adv. Coun. U. Tex. Austin, 1985-91. Charter mem. Com. of 200, 1982—, Nat. Mus. Women in the Arts, 1985—; mem. Renaissance 400, El Paso, El Paso Women's Symphony Guild, El Paso Mus. Art. Recipient of Silver plaque Gifts and Decorative Accessories Mag., 1978; named Woman of Yr. by El Paso Am. Bus. Women's Assn., 1978, Outstanding Woman of Yr. by Women's Polit. Caucus, 1979. Mem. Am. Soc. Interior Designers (bd. dirs. Tex. chpt. 1977-82), El Paso Women's C. of C. (hon.), El Paso C. of C. (dir. 1976-82), Coronado Country Club (El Paso), Internat. Club (El Paso), Santa Teresa Country Club (N.Mex.). Avocations: travel, antiques, collectibles. Home: 6041 Torrey Pines Dr El Paso TX 79912-2029 also: Apt 101 4200 Massachusetts Ave NW Washington DC 20016-4753 Office: Charlotte's Inc 5411 N Mesa St El Paso TX 79912-5438

KORTSCHAK, SEPP AUGUST, cosmetics company executive; b. Weyer, Austria, Aug. 9, 1933; came to U.S., 1968; s. Josef Eduard and Hildegard Maria (Maierhofer) K.; m. Margaretha Adelheid Goetzfried, May 9, 1964; children: Brigitta H., Michael P. M in Pharmacy, U. Innsbruck, Austria, 1957; PhD in Organic Chemistry, U. Graz, Austria, 1965. Tchg. asst. U. Graz, 1958-65; dept. head Biochemie GmbH, Kundl, Austria, 1965-68; dir. rsch. and mfg. Internat. Multifoods (formerly Osborn Labs.), LeSueur, Minn., 1968-72; tech. dir. Fuller Labs., Eden Prairie, Minn., 1972-76; quality control mgr., tech. dir. Parke-Davis (subs. Warner-Lambert), Detroit, 1976-80; cons. med. rels. Mary Kay Cosmetics, Inc., Dallas, 1980-85, v.p. product quality and regulatory affairs, 1985-94, v.p. product safety and quality feedback, 1994—. Bd. dirs. Shakopee (Minn.) Parochial Sch., 1973-75. Mem. Am. Acad. Dermatology (affiliate), Am. Pharm. Assn. (assoc.), Soc. Cosmetic Chemists, Am. Chem. Soc., Am. Soc. for Quality Control, N.Y. Acad. Scis. Republican. Roman Catholic. Home: 9106 Cochran Heights Dr Dallas TX 75220-5034 Office: Mary Kay Cosmetics Inc 1330 Regal Row Dallas TX 75247-3616

KORUDA, MARK JOSEPH, surgeon, educator, nutrition educator; b. Jersey City, N.J., June 24, 1955; m. Barbara O'Brien, 1979. BS in Chemistry, Boston Coll., 1977; MD cum laude, Yale U., 1981. With Hosp. of U. Pa., Phila., 1981-88, U. Pa., Phila. VA Med. Ctr., 1984-86; asst. instr. surgery U. Pa. Sch. Medicine, Phila., 1982-87, instr. surgery, 1987-88; asst. prof. surgery Sch. Medicine U. N.C., Chapel Hill, 1988-93, asst. prof. nutrition, 1990-94, chief gastrointestinal sect. surgery, 1991—, assoc. prof. surgery Sch. Medicine, 1993—, assoc. prof. nutrition dept. nutrition, 1993—. Recipient Glaxo Pharmacotherapy Rsch. award Am. Coll. Clin. Pharmacy, 1990. Mem. ACP, Am. Soc. Parenteral and Enteral Nutrition, Assn. for Acad. Surgery (Mid-Atlantic chpt., Harry M. Vars Rsch. award 1986, Stanley Dudtick Rsch. Scholar award 1989), N.C. Med. Soc., Surg. Infection Soc., Phi Beta Kappa. Home: 136 Carolina Forest Ct Chapel Hill NC 27516-9033 Office: School of Medicine Univ North Carolina Chapel Hill NC 27599-7210

KOSAR, BERNIE JOSEPH, JR., professional football player; b. Boardman, Ohio, Nov. 25, 1963. BS in Finance and Econs., U. Miami, 1985. With Cleve. Browns, 1985-93, Dallas Cowboys, 1993-94, Miami Dolphins, 1994—; player NFL Pro Bowl, 1987. Office: Miami Dolphins 7500 SW 30th St Davie FL 33314*

KOSARIN, JONATHAN HENRY, lawyer; b. Bklyn., Aug. 13, 1951; s. Lester and Norma (Higger) K.; m. Gayle C. Skarupa, Nov. 27, 1982. BA in History magna cum laude, Syracuse U., 1973; JD, Bklyn. Law Sch., 1976; LLM in Govt. Contract Law, George Washington U., 1984; postgrad., U.S. Army Command and Gen. Staff Coll., 1990. Bar: N.Y. 1977, D.C. 1978, U.S. Supreme Ct. 1980, U.S. Ct. Claims 1981, U.S. Ct. Appeals (Fed. cir.) 1982. Commd. 2d lt. U.S. Army, 1973, advanced through grades to lt. col., 1991; prosecutor trial counsel U.S. Army, Ft. McClellan, Ala., 1977-78; adminstrv. law officer U.S. Army, Ft. McClellan, 1978-79, instr. law, 1979-80; trial atty. contract appeals div. U.S. Army, Washington, 1980-84; contracts atty. U.S. Army Hdqrs., Heidelberg, Fed. Rep. Germany, 1985-87; assoc. gen. counsel, dir. procurement law Fed Home Loan Bank Bd., Washington, 1987-89; assoc. counsel USN, Washington, 1989-94, dep. counsel, 1994—; adj. asst. prof. contract law JAG Sch., Charlottesville, Va., 1988-93, adj. assoc. prof., 1993-95, adj. prof., vice chmn., 1995—; adj. faculty contract law U. Va., 1989—. Vol. info. specialist Smithsonian Instn. Washington, 1993—. Mem. ABA, ATLA, D.C. Bar Assn., Titanic Hist. Soc., No. Va. Football Ofcls. Assn., Phi Alpha Delta, Phi Beta Kappa, Phi Kappa Phi. Democrat. Office: USN Office of Gen Counsel Arlington VA 22244

KOSCHNY, THERESA MARY, environmental biologist; b. Washington, Feb. 28, 1954; d. William Simon and Bertha Margaret (Clarkin) K. BS, George Mason U., Fairfax, Va., 1977, MS, 1982. Sales clk. Montgomery Ward Co., Falls Church, Va., 1977; clk. of investigation FBI, Washington, 1977-83; environ. biologist I-95 Compost Facility, Lorton, Va., 1983-85, Lower Potomac Pollution Control Plant, Lorton, Va., 1985—; mem. stream survey Water Control Bd. of Va., 1983. Reviewer wastewater manual Water Pollution Control Fedn. Treatment Plant Manual, 1990, 91. Mem. Am. Inst. Biol. Sci., Ecol. Soc. Am., No. Va. Sci. Ctr., Washington Ind. Writers. Home: 5704 Robinwood Ln Falls Church VA 22041-2606 Office: Lower Potomac Pollution Plt PO Box 268 Lorton VA 22199-0268

KOSSAETH, TAMMY GALE, intensive care nurse; b. San Antonio, Feb. 18, 1969; d. Kenneth Roland and Hermina Marie (Hilzfelder) K. BSN, U. Tex., San Antonio, 1991. RN, Tex.; cert. BLS instr.; cert. ACLS; cert. cardiac rehab. Staff nurse surg. ICU Audie L. Murphy VA Hosp., San Antonio, 1991—. Altar server St. Antony Claret, San Antonio, 1980—. Mem. ANA, Women's Internat. Bowling Congress (local league pres. and league sec. 1994-95, 95-96, 96—). Roman Catholic. Home: 12379 W Fm 471 # 3 San Antonio TX 78253-4808

KOSTAS, EVANS, manufacturing executive; b. Chgo., Jan. 13, 1935; s. James Christopher and Christina (Tavoulare) K.; m. Janet Leah Fontana, Sept. 15, 1962; children: Lauren, Ellen, James, Karen, John, Andrew. BS in Engring., Ill. Inst. Tech., 1970; MBA, U. Chgo., 1974. With Rockwell Internat., Chgo., 1953-75; sr. engring. exec. Rockwell Internat., Pitts., 1975-79; v.p. tech. Nordson Corp., Amhest, Ohio, 1979-84; chief exec. officer, pres. Pubs. Equipment Corp., Dallas, 1984—, chmn. bd. dirs.; CEO King Press Corp., Joplin, Mo.; bd. dirs. King Press, Joplin, KBA Motter Corp., York, Pa. Inventor in field. Former mem. vis. com. Case Inst. Tech., Cleve., 1981, bd. overseers Case Western Res. U., Cleve., 1982. Sgt. U.S. ARmy, 1956-58. Mem. Am. Mgmt. Assn., C.E.O. Coun. (adv. bd.). Greek Orthodox. Home: 5821 Wavertree Ln Plano TX 75093-4514 Office: Pub Equipment Corp 16660 Dallas Pky Dallas TX 75248-2618

KOSTIUK, MICHAEL MARION, JR., artist; b. Paris, Tex., Dec. 9, 1944; s. Michael Marion and Barbara Jane (Biard) K.; m. Eleanor Carton Dougherty, Oct. 14, 1972 (div. 1984); 1 son, Damian; m. Junko Baba, July 20, 1990. Student, U. Tex., 1963-66, Md. Inst. Art, 1969, Visual Studies Workshop, 1973. Pvt. comml. photographer, cinematographer and newsreel photographer, N.Y., Md., Tex., 1969-72; gallery dir., Dallas, 1973-74; project dir. Bookworks, 1982; artist in residence Yellow Springs Inst., Chester Springs, Pa., 1986, Ctr. Performing Arts Pa. State U., 1986; instr. photography and digital imaging Austin (Tex.) C.C., 1993—. One man shows include Franklin Furnace Archive, N.Y.C., 1978, Tex. Tech. U. Gallery, Lubbock, 1978, Phila. Art Alliance, Phila., 1982, Tony Zwicker Contemporary Artist Bookworks, N.Y.C., 1983; group shows include Nat. Library, Madrid, Spain, 1982, Caroline Corre Gallery, Paris, France, 1982-83, Cleve. Inst. Art., 1984, Mus. Gallery U. Calif., Davis, 1985, U. Chgo. Library, 1986; represented in permanent collections Dallas Mus. Fine Arts, U. Tex. Humanities Research Ctr., Austin, Mus. Fine Arts, Boston, New Orleans Mus. Art, San Antonio Mus. Assn. Whitte Mus., Jean Brown Archive, Tyringham, Mass., Amon Carter Mus., Fort Worth, Polaroid Collection, Europa and Cambridge, Mass., Author: (with others) Darkroom Dynamics: A Guide to Creative Darkroom Techniques, 1979. Served to sgt. AUS, 1966-69. Fellow Pa. Coun. Arts, 1986. Home: 4207 Avenue G Austin TX 78751-3815

KOSTRZEWA, RICHARD MICHAEL, pharmacology educator; b. Trenton, N.J., July 22, 1943; s. John Walter and Wladyslosa (Wnuk) K.; m. Florence Agnes Palmer, Sept. 4, 1965; children: Theresa, Richard, Joseph, Maria, Krystyna, Thomas, John Palmer, Francis, Roseanna, Monica. BS, Phila. Coll. Pharmacy and Sci., 1965, MS, 1967; PhD, U. Pa., 1971. Rsch. pharmacologist VA Hosp., New Orleans, 1971-75; asst. prof. pharmacology Tulane Med. Ctr.-New Orleans, 1972-76; asst. prof. physiology La. State U. Med. Center-New Orleans, 1975-78; assoc. prof., then prof. pharmacology East Tenn. State U. Med. Sch.-Johnson City, 1978—. Mem. exec. com. Appalachian March of Dimes, Johnson City, Tenn., 1980-88. Recipient Research award East Tenn. State U. Found., 1981. Mem. Am. Soc. Pharmacology, Soc. Neurosci., Internat. Brain Rsch. Orgn. Roman Catholic. Author: Pharmacology, 1995; mem. editorial adv. bd.: Peptides, 1980—; contbr. sci. articles to profl. publs. Achievements include NIMH project on tardive dyskinesia, Scottish Rite project on schizophrenia. Office: East Tenn State Univ PO Box 70577 Johnson City TN 37614

KOSUB, JAMES ALBERT, lawyer; b. San Antonio, Jan. 8, 1948; s. Ernest Pete and Lonie (Doege) K.; divorced; 1 child, James Jr.; m. Jane Stevens Cain, Aug. 11, 1979; children: Kathryn, Nicholas (dec.). Student, East Carolina U., 1970, San Antonio Coll., 1971-72; BS, SW Tex. State U., 1974; JD, St. Mary's U., San Antonio, 1977. Bar: Tex. 1978, U.S. Dist. Ct. (we. dist.) Tex. 1980, U.S. Ct. Appeals (5th cir.) 1981, U.S. Dist. Ct. (so. dist.) 1986, U.S. Supreme Ct. 1988, U.S. Dist. Ct. (no. and ea. dists.) Tex. 1990. Ptnr. Kosub & Langlois, San Antonio, 1978-79, Kosub, Langlois & Van Cleave, San Antonio, 1979-83; mng. ptnr. Kosub & Langlois, San Antonio, 1983-86; sr. ptnr. James A. Kosub, San Antonio, 1986-94; pvt. practice Eldorado, Tex., 1994—. Bd. dirs. Judson Ind. Sch. Bd. Trustees, Converse, Tex., 1975-81, Bexar County Fedn. Sch. Bds., San Antonio, 1977-80. Sgt. USMC, 1966-70. Fellow Tex. Bar Found., San Antonio Bar Found.; mem. ABA (EEOC liaison com. San Antonio chpt. 1987-93), San Antonio Bar Assn. (bd. dirs. 1990-92, sec. 1992-93), Fed. Bar Assn. 5th Cir. Bar Assn., Coll. of State Bar of Tex., State Bar of Tex. (coun. labor and employment sect. 1993—). Episcopalian. Office: James A Kosub 4 W Gillis Eldorado TX 76936-0460

KOSUDA, KATHLEEN L., library director. BA, SUNY, Albany, 1971, MLS, 1972; M Liberal Arts, U. South Fla., 1993. Libr. dir. St. Leo (Fla.) Coll., 1983—. Mem. AAUW (bd. dirs. Pasco County chpt.), Assn. Coll. and Rsch. Librs., S.E. Libr. Assn., Fla. Libr. Assn. Office: Saint Leo Coll 33701 State Rd 52 Saint Leo FL 33574

KOSZTARAB, MICHAEL, entomologist, researcher; b. Bucharest, Romania, July 7, 1927; came to U.S., 1957; s. Michael and Berta (Albert) K.; m. Matilda Pinter, Oct. 21, 1953; 1 child, Eva K. J.D.; BS, Hungarian U. Agr. Sci., Budapest, 1951; PhD, Ohio State U., 1962; hon. dr. U. Horticulture and Food Scis., Budapest, 1993. Extension asst. Hungarian State Bur. Plant Protection Budapest, 1947-50; asst. prof. Hungarian U. Agrl. Scis., Budapest, 1951-56; cons. entomologist Insect Control and Rsch., Inc., Balt., 1957-58, asst. dir. rsch., 1959-60; assoc. prof. Va. Poly. Inst. and State U., Blacksburg, Va., 1962-68, prof. entomology, 1968-92, dir. Ctr. for Systematics Collections, 1987-91; founding dir. Mus. Natural History, 1990—; chmn. planning com. Nat. Biol. Survey, 1984-86. Recipient W. E. Wine Faculty Achievement award, 1967, award Assn. Systematics Collections, Washington, 1994. Fellow Va. Acad. Sci.; mem. Hungarian Entomol. Soc. (hon.), Entomol. Soc. Am. (hon.), Entomol. Soc. Washington, Hungarian Acad. Sci. (corr.). Author: Scale Insects of Northeastern North America, 1996; co-author: Scale Insects of Hungary, 1978, Scale Insects of Central Europe, 1988; co-editor: Systematics of The North American Insects and Arachnids: Status and Needs; contbr. articles to profl. jours. Home: 614 Woodland Dr Blacksburg VA 24060-3235 Office: Va Poly Inst and State U Dept Entomology Blacksburg VA 24061

KOTEEN, JACK, management consultant, writer; b. N.Y., Aug. 22, 1919; s. Meyer and Eva (Gitlin) K.; m. Gloria Rogoff, Oct. 9, 1949; children: Glenn Michael, Douglas Evan. BA, NYU, 1940, attended John Hopkins Sch. for Advanced Internat. Studies. Mgmt. analyst Exec. Office of Pres. Fed. Govt. Agy., 1941-42; dir. devel. adminstrn., chief African tech. assist. in pub. and bus. adminstrn. in agy. for internat. devel. U.S. Dept. State, 1955-74; v.p. Assocs. for Mgmt. and Evaluation, 1975-79; ind. cons., 1980-90; dir. Strategic Mgmt. Ctr., 1991—; instr. U. Md., Am. U., USDA. Author: (book) Strategic Management in Public and Non-profit Organizations, 1989,

91, 2d edit., 1997. Chair bd. dirs. Internat. Program for Human Resources Devel., Bethesda, Md., 1981-85. 1st Lt. Army Air Corps, 1942-45. Named Hon. Paramount Chief Mpelle People, N. Liberia, 1960; recipient Superior Honor award U.S. Dept. of State, 1974. Home: 66 Northwoods Cir Boynton Beach FL 33436-7417

KOTTKE, BRUCE A., internist; b. Blue Earth, Minn., Jan. 22, 1929; s. Alvin R. and Alice (Vogel) K.; m. Ruth L. Schlenker, 1955; (div. 1974); children: John, Timothy; m. Ivette A. Irrizary, Mar. 22, 1974; children: August, Louis. BS summa cum laude, Hamline U., 1951; MD, U. Minn., 1954; PhD, Mayo Grad. Sch. Medicine, 1960. Diplomate Am. Bd. Internal Medicine. Dir. cardiovascular rsch. Mayo Clinic, Rochester, Minn., 1970-75; prof. of medicine Mayo Grad. Sch. of Medicine, Rochester, 1981-92; cons. Mayo Clinic, Rochester, 1981-92. Contbr. over 150 articles to profl. jours. Lt. U.S. Navy, 1955-57. Fellow Am. Coll. Cardiology (Disting. Investigator award Fla. chpt. 1993), Arterialsclerosis Coun. of Am. Heart Assn. Office: Watson Clinic 1600 Lakeland Hills Blvd Lakeland FL 33805-3019

KOTZ, NATHAN KALLISON (NICK KOTZ), news correspondent; b. San Antonio, Sept. 16, 1932; s. Jacob and Tybe (Kallison) K.; m. Mary Lynn Booth, Aug. 7, 1960; 1 child, Jack Mitchell. A.B. magna cum laude in Internat. Relations, Dartmouth Coll., 1955; student, London Sch. Econs., 1955-56. Reporter, Des Moines Register, 1958-64, Washington corr., 1964-70; also for other Cowles Publs. (newspapers); nat. corr. Washington Post, 1970-73; adj. prof. Sch. Communication, Am. U., Washington, 1978-86; sr. journalist in residence Duke U., 1983; corr. PBS Frontline, 1992; farmer, Broad Run, Va., 1980—. Free-lance writer, 1973; author: Let Them Eat Promises: The Politics of Hunger in America, 1969, Wild Blue Yonder: Money, Politics, and the B-1 Bomber, 1988; co-author: The Unions, 1971, A Passion for Equality: George Wiley and the Movement, 1977. Bd. dirs. Iowa Bds. Internat. Edn., 1962-64, Suburban Md. Fair Housing, 1966-72, Black Student Fund, 1976-86—, Penn-Faulkner, 1986—; bd. dirs. Fund for Investigative Journalism, 1977-86, chmn., 1978-82. Served to 1st lt. USMCR, 1956-58. Recipient Pulitzer prize for nat. reporting, 1968; Raymond Clapper Meml. award, 1966, 68; 2d pl., 1973; Disting. Service award Sigma Delta Chi, 1966; Robert F. Kennedy Journalism award, 1968; Spl. Merit award Am. U., 1981, award for pub. service Nat. Mag., 1985; Adj. Faculty award Am. U., 1985; Olive Brach award NYU Ctr. for War, Peace and News Media, 1989. Mem. Nat. Press Club, Cosmos Club, Phi Beta Kappa. Office: 1211 Conn Ave NW # 308 Washington DC 20036

KOUDELKA, GEORGE JOHN, music educator; b. Hallettsville, Tex., Feb. 27, 1945; s. John William and Hilda Barbara (Stavinoha) K. B MusEdn., Southwest Tex. State U., 1968; MEd, Prairie View A&M U., 1972. Cert. tchr. music and band, Tex. Instr. in percussion and music Southwest Tex. State U., San Marcos, 1967-69; dir. bands and music Flatonia (Tex.) Ind. Sch. Dist., 1969-82, Moulton (Tex.) Ind. Sch. Dist., 1982—. Contbg. author: A Passion for Polka, 1992, church cookbook, 1985, others. Pres. PTA, Flatonia, 1972-73. Mem. Tex. Music Edn. Assn., Music Edn. Nat. Conf., Woodmen of the World, KC (Grand Knight 1971-73), Sons of Hermann Ins. Soc. Home: PO Box 165 Flatonia TX 78941 Office: Moulton Ind Sch Dist PO Drawer C Moulton TX 77975

KOUSPARIS, DIMITRIOS, oil consulting company executive; b. Greece, May 16, 1949; came to U.S., 1973; s. John and Vicky Kousparis; m. Helen Pritzos, Dec. 26, 1976; children: Vicky, Johnny, Andy. BS, U. Athens, Greece, 1973; MS, U. Okla., 1975; PhD, U. Tulsa, 1979. Cons. Rsch. Ctr. Amoco Prodn. Co., Tulsa, 1976-78; interpreter geophysicist Conoco Inc., Houston, 1979-80, dir. exploratory wells, 1987-89, area geophysicist, 1989-90, economist, 1990-93; interpreter geophysicist Conoco, London, 1980-84; chief geophysicist Conoco, The Netherlands, 1984-87; founder, pres. Strategic Petroleum Investment Cons. Enterprise Inc., Katy, Tex., 1993—; dir. Greek lang. sch. Nea Vassileiada, 1992-95. Founder, pres. Nea Vassileiada, Hellenic ednl. and religious orgn., Houston, 1992, 93, 94, 95, 96; co-founder St. Basil the Great Greek Orthodox Ch., Houston, pres., 1993, 94. Mem. Soc. Exploration Geophysicists, Am. Assn. Petroleum Geologists.

KOUSSEFF, BORIS GEORGIEV, geneticist, pediatrician; b. Berlin, Mar. 15, 1935; came to U.S., 1970; s. George Vladimirov and Theodora (Friedrichs) K. MD, Higher Inst. Medicine, Sofia, Bulgaria, 1959. Diplomate Am. Bd. Pediatrics, Am. Bd. Clin. Genetics. Pediatrician Mcpl. Hosp., Ichtiman, Bulgaria, 1962-65, Children's Hosp., Bankja, Bulgaria, 1965-68; registrar in neonatology Royal Maternity Hosp., Glasgow, 1968-69; registrar in pediatrics County Hosp., York, Eng., 1970; resident in pediatrics U. Iowa, Iowa City, 1970-71, Albert Einstein Med. Ctr., Phila., 1971-72; fellow in genetics Mt. Sinai Hosp., N.Y.C., 1972-74; dir. Ctr. for Developmentally Disabled Children Queens Hosp., Jamaica, N.Y., 1974-77; dir. genetics So. Ill. U., Springfield, 1978-81, U. South Fla., Tampa, 1981—. Contbr. numerous articles to sci. and profl. jours. Fellow Am. Acad. Pediatrics; mem. AMA, Am. Pediatric Soc., Am. Soc. Human Genetics, Birth Defect and Glin. Genetics. Office: U South Fla Regional Genetics 10770 N 46th St Ste C-900 Tampa FL 33617-3442

KOUTNIK, CHUCK JOHN, librarian; b. Cleve., Mar. 8, 1951; s. Robert William and Dorothy Jane (Rupright) K.; m. Kim Frances Piner, Aug. 8, 1991. B of Religious Studies, Cleve. State U., 1974; MLS, Kent State U., 1984. Reference libr. Carrier Libr./James Madison U., Harrisonburg, Va., 1985; head tech. svcs. and automation Staunton (Va.) Pub. Libr., 1984-87; cataloger Radford (Va.) U., 1987-89; head tech. svcs. Iredell County Libr., Statesville, N.C., 1989-91; dir. Cen. Va. Regional Libr., Farmville, Va., 1991-95; cons. W.Va. Libr. Commn., Charleston, 1995-96; dir. Appotomax Regional Libr. System, Hoewell, Va., 1996—; presenter in field. Mem. ALA, W.Va. Libr. Assn., Rural Libr. Assn., Va. Libr. Assn. Office: Appotomax Regional Libr System 2545 E Cawson St Hopewell VA 23860

KOVACHEVICH, ELIZABETH ANNE, federal judge; b. Canton, Ill., Dec. 14, 1936; d. Dan and Emilie (Kuchan) Kovachevich. AA, St. Petersburg Jr. Coll., 1956; BBA in Fin. magna cum laude, U. Miami, 1958; JD, Stetson U., 1961. Bar: Fla. 1961, U.S. Dist. Ct. (mid. and so. dists.) Fla. 1961, U.S. Ct. Appeals (5th cir.) 1961, U.S. Supreme Ct. 1968. Research and adminstrv. aide Pinellas County Legis. Del., Fla., 1961; assoc. DiVito & Speer, St. Petersburg, Fla., 1961-62; house counsel Rieck & Fleece Builders Supplies, Inc., St. Petersburg, 1962; pvt. practice law St. Petersburg, 1962-73; judge 6th Jud. Cir., Pinellas and Pasco Counties, Fla., 1973-82, U.S. Dist. Ct. (mid. dist.) Fla., St. Petersburg, 1982—; chmn. St. Petersburg Profl. Legal Project-Days in Court, 1967; chmn. Supreme Ct. Bicentennial Com. 6th Jud. Circuit, 1975-76. prodr., coord. TV prodn. A Race to Judgement. Bd. regents State of Fla., 1970-72; legal advisor, bd. dirs. Young Women's Residence Inc., 1968; mem. Fla. Gov.'s Commn. on Status of Women, 1968-71; mem. Pres.'s Commn. on White House Fellowships, 1973-77; mem. def. adv. com. on Women in Service, Dept. Def., 1973-76; Fla. conf. publicity chmn. 18th Nat. Republican Women's Conf., Atlanta, 1971; lifetime mem. Children's Hosp. Guild, YWCA of St. Petersburg; charter mem. Golden Notes, St. Petersburg Symphony; hon. mem. bd. of overseers Stetson U. Coll. of Law, 1986. Recipient Disting. Alumni award Stetson U., 1970, Woman of Yr. award Fla. Fedn. Bus. and Profl. Women, 1981, ann. Ben C. Willard Meml. award, Stetson Lawyers Assn., 1983, St. Petersburg Panhellenic Appreciation award, 1964, Mrs. Charles Ulrick Bay award, St. Petersburg Rotary award, St. Petersburg Quarterback Club award, Pinellas United Fund award in recognition of concern and meritorious effort, 1968, Woman of Yr. award Beta Sigma Phi, 1970, Am. Legion Aux. Unit 14 Pres. award cmty. svc., 1970, Dedication to Christian Ideals award and Man of Yr. award KC Dists. 20-21, 1972. Mem. ABA, Fla. Bar Assn., Pinellas County Trial Lawyers, Assn. Trial Lawyers Am., Am. Judicature Soc., St. Petersburg Bar Assn. (chmn. bench and bar com., sec. 1969). Office: US Dist Ct 611 N Florida Ave Tampa FL 33602-4500*

KOVALCHUK, LISBETH (LEE) SUZANNE, association administrator; b. Youngstown, Ohio, May 5, 1952; d. George Edward and Suzanne Louise (Kacvinsky) Turocy; m. Sergius Feodor Kovalchuk, Oct. 26, 1975 (separated). BS in Edn., Youngstown State U., 1974; MA, U. Houston, Clear Lake, Tex., 1980. Tchr., dist. lead tchr. art Portsmouth (Va.) Pub. Schs., 1974-76; tchr., dept. head Pasadena (Tex.)) Ind. Sch. Dist., 1976-83; edn. mgr. Assoc. Credit Burs., Washington, 1984-91; mgr. cert. and acad. affairs Internat. Facility Mgmt. Assn., Houston, 1991—; adj. instr. Houston C.C. Sys., 1980-85; mem. adv. bd. Nat. Coun. on Qualifications for Lighting Professions, Bethesda, Md., 1995—. Mem. ASTD, Am. Soc. Assn. Execs. Office: Internat Facility Mgmt Assn 1 E Greenway Plz Ste 1100 Houston TX 77046

KOVALCIK, PAUL JEROME, surgeon; b. Buffalo, Apr. 16, 1943; s. Jerome G. and Dorothy I. (Kalinowski) K.; m. Janet I. Howe, Jan. 13, 1968; children: Julia, Peter, John, Matthew, Andrew. BA, CUNY, Flushing, 1965; MD, Georgetown U., 1969. Diplomate Nat. Bd. Med. Examiners, Am. Bd. Surgery, Am. Bd. Colon and Rectal Surgery; ATLS instr. Commd. ensign USN, 1969, advanced through grades to capt., 1984, ret. Med. Corps, 1989; intern medicine and surgery Naval Hosp., Boston, 1969-70, resident gen. surgery, 1970-73; resident gen. surgery Naval Regional Med. Ctr., Portsmouth, Va., 1973-74; fellow colon and rectal surgery Lahey Clinic, Boston, 1974-75; assoc. prof. surgery Ea. Va. Med. Sch., 1980—, Uniformed Svcs. U. Health Scis., 1986—; head dept. gen. surgery Naval Hosp. Portsmouth, 1985-87; cons. Naval Hosp. Portsmouth; chmn. CME com. Portsmouth Gen. Hosp.; chmn. ethics com. Maryview Hosp., Portsmouth; chmn. surg. endoscopy com. Chesapeake (Va.) Gen. Hosp.; assoc. examiner Am. Bd. Colon and Rectal Surgery; vis. prof. Greenville (S.C.) Hosp. System, 1984, U. S.C., Columbia, 1984, W.Va. U. Med. Ctr., Charleston, 1986, East Carolina U., Greenville, 1991, 93; lectr. Georgetown U., Washington, 1985, U.S. Naval Hosp., Guantanamo Bay, Cuba, 1986, U.S. Naval Hosp., Roosevelt Roads, P.R., 1987, U.O.A. Mid-Atlantic Regional Conf., 1987, Acute Combat Symposium Tidewater chpt. AMSUS, Norfolk, 1987, Trauma Symposium Naval Hosp., Roosevelt Roads, 1988, Thomas Jefferson U. Med. Sch., 1988, 90, Acute Combat Trauma Symposium, Norfolk, 1988, Piedmont Soc. Colon and Rectal Surgeons, Williamsburg, Va., 1990, Sardestin, Fla., 1992, Kiawah Island, S.C., 1993, Joseph F. Mulach Med. Lectr. Series St. Clair Hosp., Pitts., 1991, Student Cancer Conf. Ea. Va. Med. Sch., Norfolk, 1994; Thordur Thordarson Meml. lectr., Reykjavik, Iceland, 1987. Contbr. numerous articles to med. jours. Fellow Am. Coll. Surgeons, Am. Soc. Colon and Rectal Surgery; mem. AMA, Am. Soc. Colon and Rectal Surgeons (chmn. self-assessment com. 1988-92, recert. com., mem.-at-large to exec. coun. 1992—), Soc. Am. Gastrointestinal Endoscopic Surgeons (founder), Va. Surg. Soc., Lahey Clin. Alumni Assn. Republican. Roman Catholic. Home: 4762 River Shore Rd Portsmouth VA 23703-1518 Office: 3101 American Legion Rd Ste 15 Chesapeake VA 23321-5652 also: 927 Battlefield Blvd N Ste 200 Chesapeake VA 23320-4853

KOVAR, DAN RADA, pharmacist; b. Uniontown, Pa., Oct. 5, 1934; s. Daniel Rada and Annamabel (Craig) K.; m. Sandra Lynn Kregar, Aug. 10, 1963; children: Jennifer Lynn Kovar Blandford, Catherine Elizabeth Kovar. BS in Pharmacy, U. Pitts., 1958. Registered pharmacist, Pa., Ky. Pharmacist, mgr. Thrift Drug Co., Ashland, Ky., 1959-76, pharmacist, 1978-79; pharmacist, owner Laynes Pharmacy, Ashland, 1976-94; staff pharmacist Rite Aid, 1994—. Vol. faculty, bd. dirs. U. Ky. Coll. of Pharmacy Alumni Assn.; re-organizational pres. Greater Ashland Area Acad. of Pharmacy 1967; adminstrv. bd. Christ United Meth. Ch., Sunday sch. tchr.; advisor Ashland Area Hospice, Pathways Mental Health. Named Ky. Col. Mem. Nat. Assn. Retail Druggists, Nat. Assn. Bds. Pharmacy, Am. Coll. Apothecaries, Christian Pharmacists Fellowship Internat. (founding pres. Ky. chpt. 1988-93), Ky. Pharmacists Assn. (Bowl of Hygeia award 1988, vice speaker ho. of dels. 1992, speaker ho. of dels. 1993-94, bd. dirs. 1994—), Ky. Pharmacists Svc. Assn. (divsn. operation group). Office: Laynes Pharmacy 1913 Weymouth Dr Ashland KY 41101-3849

KOWALSKI, PAUL RANDOLPH, minister; b. Anderson, S.C., June 20, 1934; s. Paul William and Margaret Katharine (Mitchell) K.; m. Mary Frances Bagwell, Aug. 2, 1958; children: Kelly Bagwell, Robin Marie. BS, Clemson U., 1956; MDiv, Columbia Theol. Sem., 1960; DD (hon.), Presbyn. Coll., 1976. Ordained to ministry Presbyn. Ch. (U.S.A.), 1960. Min. Pendleton (S.C.) Presbyn. Ch., 1960-62, Abbeville (S.C.) Presbyn. Ch., 1962-67; sr. min. Reid Meml. Presbyn. Ch., Augusta, Ga., 1967-74, First Presbyn. Ch., Greenville, S.C., 1974—; trustee Outreach Found., Presbyn. Ch. (USA), Charlotte, N.C., 1980—, vice chmn., 1990—, chmn., 1993-94; mem. coun. Synod of South Atlantic, 1985—. Editl. writer Greenville Piedmont, 1985—. Bd. dirs. Columbia Theol. Sem., Decatur, Ga., 1976-85, Rabun Gap (Ga.) Nacoochee Sch., 1973-81, YMCA, Greenville, Chs. Uniting in Global Mission, 1992—; bd. visitors Presbyn. Coll., 1983-85. Named Young Man of Yr. Abbeville Jaycees, 1965; recipient Disting. Grad. award Clemson U., 1988. Mem. Rotary (pres. Augusta club 1970-71, Greenville club 1987-88, Paul Harris fellow 1988). Office: First Presbyn Ch 200 W Washington St Greenville SC 29601-2639

KOYM, ZALA COX, elementary education educator; b. San Antonio, July 21, 1948; d. Bruce Meador and Ruby Esther (Jordan) Cox; m. Charles Raymond Koym, July 5, 1969; children: Carol Ann, Cathy Lynn, Suzie Kay. BS in Edn., SW Tex. State U., 1970. Cert. supervision of tchr. effective practices. Elem. tchr. Schertz-Cibolo Ind. Sch. Dist., Schertz, Tex., 1970-71; substitute tchr. Alamogordo (N.Mex.) Pub. Schs., 1973-75; tchr. 5th grade Round Rock (Tex.) Ind. Sch. Dist., 1983-90, asst. prin., 1988-91, tchr. 2d grade, 1990-96, mentor tchr., 1993-96; 3rd, 4th grade multiage tchr. Fort Sam Houston Elem., San Antonio, Tex., 1996—; textbook advisor State of Tex., 1989; chairperson/coord. 5th grade level Round Rock Ind. Sch. Dist., 1986-90, 2d grade level chairperson, 1990-93; sci. lab. coord. Robertson Elem., Old Town Elem, 1983-89; presenter Sci. Workshop Round Rock Ind. Sch. Dist., 1993, 94; Fort Sam Houston Dist. Improvement Coun., 1996-97. Mem. PTA, 1981—, v.p. programs, 1994-95, site-based decision making campus rep., 1993-95; dir. vacation Bible sch. FUMC, 1984-86, 86-87, mem. scholarship com., 1992-94; neighborhood capt. March of Dimes, 1990, Am. Heart Assn., 1994, 95; mem. Campus Student Assistance Program Team, 1990-96, Old Town Bldg Leadership TEam, 1991-92. Mem. ASCD, Assn. Tex. Profl. Educators, Phi Delta Kappa (sec. 1991-93, assoc. historian 1994-95, v.p. programs 1995-96). Home: 8316 Traciney Blvd San Antonio TX 78255 Office: Fort Sam Houston Elem 3370 Nursery Rd San Antonio TX 78234

KOZACHEK, JANET LYNNE, artist, educator; b. Princeton, N.J., July 27, 1957; d. Walter and Agnes Robb (Davies) Kozachek; m. Nathaniel Owen Wallace, May 26, 1979. BA, Douglass Coll., New Brunswick, N.J., 1980; Cert. Grad. Study, Beijing (China) Ctrl. Art Acad, 1983-85; MFA, Parsons Sch. Design, N.Y.C., 1990. Tchr. English Hebei U., Baoding, China, 1981-82, Jilin U., Changchun, China, 1982-83; lectr. art European divsn. U. Md., 1986-87; arts-in-edn. artist S.C. State Arts Commn., 1993—; adj. prof. art Mercer County C.C., Trenton, N.J., 1990-91; guest lectr. Penland Sch. Art, N.C., 1985, Bluefield (W.Va.) State Coll., 1991, Kutztown (Pa.) U., 1991. Organizer six-artist show Gibbes Mus. Art, 1995; artist retrospective I.P. Stanback Mus., 1993; solo exhbns. include Gallerie de Vierde Dimensie, Plasmolen, Netherlands, 1989, Johnson and Johnson World Hdqrs., 1993, I.P. Stanback Mus., 1993, Goin Gallery, Charleston, S.C., 1994, Greenville (N.C.) Mus. Art, 1997; exhibited in group shows at Alexandria (La.) Mus. Art, 1992, Picolo Spoleto Exhbn., Charleston, 1993, Armory Art Ctr., West Palm Beach, Fla., 1993, Gibbes Mus. Art, Charleston, 1995, Summer Olympic Games, Stone Mountain, Ga., 1996, numerous others; work in numerous pvt. collections and I.P. Stanback Mus. Permanent Collection; featured in publs. Helena Rubinstein scholar, 1989-90; Orangeburg Arts Ctr. Small Grants awardee, 1993, 95. Democrat. Home: 639 Wilson St NE Orangeburg SC 29115

KOZERA, GREGORY ALLEN, oil and gas company executive, engineer; b. Pitts., Mar. 21, 1951; s. John F. and Eleanor M. (Cherok) K.; m. Lynnda K. Sweet, June 14, 1975; children: Corey, Dannielle, Gregory II. BS in Agrl. Engring., W.Va. U., 1973. Registered profl. engr., Mich., Ohio, W.Va. Engr.-in-tng. Halliburton Svcs., Albion, Mich., 1973-74, field engr., 1974-76, dist. engr., 1976-78; customer contact Halliburton Svcs., Columbus, Ohio, 1978-79; asst. dist. mgr. Halliburton Svcs., Wooster, Ohio, 1979-84; dist. mgr. Halliburton Svcs., Elkview, W.Va., 1984-93; spl. asst. Halliburton Svcs., Pitts., 1993; account rep., project mgr. Halliburton Svcs., Charleston, W.Va., 1993—. Coach Kanawha Valley Soccer League, Charleston, W.Va., 1984-94; cubmaster Boy Scouts Am., Pinch, W.Va., 1989-91, troop committeeman, 1990—, leader explorer advisor, Charleston, 1993—; youth group leader Our Lady of Hills Ch., Pinch, 1985—, parish coun. chmn., 1991—; pres. Elk River Soccer Club, Elkview, 1987-91; vol. cons. Jr. Achievement, 1992—, asst. Socccer Coach, Charleston Catholic H.S., 1996. Recipient Sportsmanship Regatta Tournament award Kanawha Valley Soccer League, 1988, Contbn. award Elk River Soccer Club, 1993. Mem. NSPE, Soc. Petroleum Engrs. (chmn. Ohio sect. 1978, gen. chmn. East regional meeting Charleston 1994), Am. Geol. Soc., Am. Soc. Agr. Engrs. (Student Honor award 1973). Roman Catholic. Home: 200 Willow St Elkview WV 25071-9422 Office: Halliburton Svcs PO Box 418 Elkview WV 25071-0418

KOZUCH, JULIANNA BERNADETTE, librarian, educator; b. Wallis, Tex., Feb. 16, 1921; d. Felix Joseph and Agnes Mary (Vrana) K. BA in English, Our Lady of the Lake U., San Antonio, 1951; MEd, Our Lady of the Lake U., 1961, MLS, 1972. Joined Sisters of Divine Providence order, Roman Cath. Ch., 1936; cert. tchr., Tex., Okla., La. Tchr. Sts. Cyril & Methodius, Granger, Tex., 1940-41, St. John's Sch., Fayetteville, Tex., 1941-42, 55-56, St. Ferdinand's Sch., San Fernando, Calif., 1942-43, Immaculate Conception, Houston, 1943-52, St. Joseph Meml., Enid, Okla., 1952-55, St. Mary's Sch., Natchitoches, La., 1956-57, St. Francis Sch., Iota, La., 1957-58, St. Joseph's Sch., Abilene, Tex., 1958-59, St. Genevieve, Lafayette, La., 1959-61, St. Peter and Paul Sch., New Braunfels, Tex., 1961-63, St. Pius, Pasadena, Tex., 1963-65, St. Anne's, Houston, 1965-70, Meml. High, Lafayette, La., 1972-73; tchr., libr. St. Mary's, San Antonio, Tex., 1970-72, St. Augustine, Laredo, Tex., 1973-77; with bookstore Our Lady of Lake U., San Antonio, 1977-78, ref. libr., 1978-85; head libr. Worden Sch., San Antonio, 1985—; mem. ethnic affairs Tex. Cath. Conf., 1978—, treas., 1982—; speaker Tex. Inst. Texan Cultures, 1983; translator for Czechoslovakia refugees, 1981—, Dr. Denton Belk; interviewed on Channel 36 TV, 1982, Channel 12, 1979, 82. Mem. math. textbook com. Galveston (Tex.) Houston Diocese, 1968-70; rep. religious women Bishop's Coun., Corpus Christi (Tex.) Diocese, 1976-77; docent Luth. Youth Conf., Inst. Texan Cultures, 1983. Recipient Disting. Svc. award Bayanihan Dance Troupe, 1977, Margil award Tex. Cath. Conf. on Cmty. Ethnic Affairs, 1985, Papal medal, 1987. Mem. AAUP (sec. 1979-82), Nat. Coun. Math. Tchrs., Nat. Cath. Libr. Assn. (treas. Houston chpt. 1968-70, treas. San Antonio chpt. 1970-72, Community Leader of Am. award 1969), Tex. Libr. Assn., Bexar County Libr. Assn. (membership com. 1970-72), Teenage Libr. Assn. (bd. dirs Houston chpt. 1968-70), Southwestern Libr. Assn., Our Lady of the Lake U. Assn. (sec. San Antonio chpt. 1980-82, historian 1982—), Our Lady of the Lake Sisters Orgn. (social com. 1978-79), Czech-Am. Cultural and Edn. Found. (bd. dirs. 1982—, Svc. award 1987). Democrat. Roman Catholic. Home: 602 SW 24th St San Antonio TX 78207-4620 Office: Our Lady of the Lake U 411 SW 24th St San Antonio TX 78207-4689

KRAATZ, KAREN LUCILLE, office manager; b. Detroit, June 29; d. Rolland Michael and Lucille Mary Ciagala; m. Gary L. Kraatz, Oct. 29, 1968; children: Gary L. Jr., Michael L., Brian L., Bruce L., Joseph L. Student pub. schs., Detroit. Asst. br. mgr., officer First Fla. Bank, N.A., Brooksville, Fla., 1983-91; office mgr. Brewer Meml. Funeral Home, Spring Hill, Fla., 1991—. Author: Great Poems of Our Time, 1991, In A Different Light, 1991, Listen With Your Heart, 1992, All My Tomorrows, 1992; author song; newspaper columnist Hernando Today, 1996—. Dir. Brooksville Raid Festival Inc., 1985; aux. dep. Hernando County Sheriff's Dept., Brooksville, 1987; v.p. Rep. Woman's Club, Brooksville, 1990; sec., bd. dirs. State of Fla. HRS/Health and Human Svcs. Bd. Dist. 13, 1993-97; dir., treas. Hernando County Child Abuse Prevention Bd., 1990-93; mem. West Hernando Little League, 1992-94; bd. dirs. Health Com. for Children and Youth, 1992-93. Mem. Friends of Libr. Republican. Roman Catholic. Office: Brewer Meml Funeral Home 280 Mariner Blvd Spring Hill FL 34609-5691

KRACKE, ROBERT RUSSELL, lawyer; b. Decatur, Ga., Feb. 27, 1938; s. Roy Rachford and Virginia Carolyn (Minter) K.; m. Barbara Anne Pilgrim, Dec. 18, 1965; children: Shannon Ruth, Robert Russell, Rebecca Anne, Susan Lynn. Student Birmingham So. Coll.; BA, Samford U., 1962; JD, Cumberland Sch. Law, 1965 . Bar: Ala. 1965, U.S. Tax Ct. 1971, U.S. Supreme Ct. 1971; individual practice law Birmingham, Ala., 1965—; pres. Kracke, Thompson & Ellis, 1980—. Deacon Ind. Presbyn. Ch., Birmingham, 1973-76, pres. adult choir, 1968—, Housing Agy. Retarded Citizens; pres. Ala. chpt. Nat. Voluntary Health Agys.; mem. exec. com. legal counsel Birmingham Opera Theatre, 1983-95; bd. dirs. Ala. Assn. Retarded Citizens, Jefferson County Assn. Retarded Citizens, 1983-91, pres.-elect, 1994-96, pres. 1996—; bd. dirs., founding pres. Birmingham chpt. Juvenile Diabetes Found. Served with USNR, 1955-61. Mem. Birmingham (exec. com., chmn. law libr., law day 1976), Ala. Bar Assn., ABA (award merit law day 1976), Am. Judicature Soc., Ala. Hist. Assn., So. Hist. Assn., The Club, Phi Alpha Delta (pres. chpt. 1964-65), Sigma Alpha Epsilon. Lodge: Rotary (pres. Shades Valley club 1988-89, Paul Harris fellow, sec. dist. 686 1990-91, dist. coord. comm., bd. dir., sec. ednl. found.). Editor, Birmingham Bar Bull., 1974—; bd. editors Ala. Lawyer, 1980-86; contbr. articles to profl. publs. Home: 4410 Briar Glen Dr Birmingham AL 35243-1743 Office: Kracke Thompson & Ellis Lakeview Sch Bldg 808 29th St S Birmingham AL 35205-1004

KRAEHE, ENNO EDWARD, history educator; b. St. Louis, Dec. 9, 1921; s. Enno and Amelia Roth (Henckler) K.; m. Mary Alice Eggleston, May 25, 1946; children: Laurence Adams, Claudia. BA, U. Mo., 1943, MA, 1944; PhD, U. Minn., 1948. Instr. history U. Del., 1946-48; asst. prof. history U. Ky., 1948-50, asso. prof., 1950-63, prof., 1963-64; prof. U. N.C., 1964-68; prof. U. Va., 1968-71, Commonwealth prof., 1971-77, William W. Corcoran prof., 1977-91, William W. Corcoran prof. emeritus, 1991—; vis. prof. U. Mo., 1946, U. Va., 1955, U. Tex., 1955, U. Minn., 1963; U.S. Dept. State Specialist in, Germany, 1953; mem. regional selection com. Woodrow Wilson fellowship Found., 1959-60; mem. Sr. Fulbright-Hayes History Screening Com., 1970-73. Author: Metternich's German Policy Volume I: The Contest with Napoleon 1799-1814, 1963; author: Volume II: The Congress of Vienna, 1814-1815, 1983; editor: The Metternich Controversy, 1971; mem. editl. bd. Ctrl. European History, 1967-72, Austrian History Yearbook, 1969-74; contbr. entries and articles to encys. and hist. jours., U.S. and Europe. Active Charlottesville Com. on Fgn. Rels.; mem. Nat. Coordinating Com. for Promotion of History, mem. policy bd., 1985-88; mem. Met. Opera Guild, Friends of Ky. Ctr. Recipient Best Book award Phi Alpha Theta; Fulbright scholar Austria, 1952-53; Guggenheim fellow, 1960-61, Am. Coun. Learned Socs. fellow, 1969, 73, resident fellow Rockefeller Ctr. in Bellagio, 1983; grantee NEH, 1973, 80, 83, NEH Libr. Preservation Screening Com., 1988. Mem. Am. Hist. Assn., Conf. Group for Ctrl. European History (mem. exec. bd. 1966-68), German Studies Assn. (mem. exec. coun. 1985—), So. Hist. Assn. (chmn. European sect. 1974, 75, Disting. Svc. award European sect.), Colonnade Club, Blue Ridge Swimming Club, Phi Beta Kappa. Episcopalian. Home: 130 Bennington Rd Charlottesville VA 22901-2653

KRAFT, FREDERICK GLENN, pharmacist; b. Martins Ferry, Ohio, May 20, 1953; s. Glenn R. and Myra Eileen (Lengacher) K.; m. Sue Ann Roth, July 2, 1977; 1 child, Laura Sue. BS in Pharmacy, U. Cin., 1976. Lic. pharmacist, Ohio, W.Va., Fla., Pa. Pharmacist Health Guard, Bellaire, Ohio, 1976-92, Revco D.S. Inc., Moundsville, W.Va., 1992—; cons. managed care pharmacy Kaiser HMO, White Plains, N.Y., 1989; participant Rorer Bus. Inst., J.L. Kellog Grad. Sch. Mgmt., Northwestern U., Evanston, Ill., 1990. Asst. Odyssey of the Mind, Bridgeport (Ohio) Schs., 1988, 89, 90; softball coach Bridgeport Jr. Sports Assn., 1986, 87; poison prevention program Bridgeport Pub. Schs., 1976—; mem., chmn. budget com. First Ch. of God, Bridgeport, 1989, 90, 91. Mem. Am. Pharm. Assn., Acad. Managed Care Pharmacy, Ohio Pharmacist Assn., Ohio-Marshall County Pharmacy Assn. (past pres. 1979-80, Pharmacist of Yr. 1992-93). Republican. Mem. Ch. of God. Home: 69609 Sunset Hts Bridgeport OH 43912-1656 Office: Revco # 0450 317 Lafayette Ave Moundsville WV 26041-1002

KRAFT, OTTO FRITZ, investment adviser, artist; b. Elizabeth, N.J., Mar. 13, 1929; s. Otto Kraft and Elizabeth C. (Vadder) Kerken; m. Patricia C. McCabe, Dec. 27, 1952 (div. July 1970); children: Roger, Mitchell, Gregory; m. Jacquelyn Hebert, Sept. 15, 1970 (div. Feb. 6, 1980; children: Jaime Irene, Otto F. II; m. Shirley Meyers Lund, Oct. 24, 1984. BS, Rutgers U., 1953, postgrad., 1953-54; cert. fin. planner, Coll. for Fin. Planning, Denver, 1994. Cert. fund specialist, v.p., gen. mgr. The Torit Corp., St. Paul, 1965-72; nat. sales mgr. Ulmer Pharm. Co., Mpls., 1963-65; dist. mgr. J. B. Roerig & Co. divsn. Pfizer, Mpla., 1958-63; v.p., gen. mgr. McKesson Co. divsn. Narco, Sylvania, Ohio, 1972-73; CEO, v.p. F&F Koenig Kramer divsn. Dentsply Internat., Cin., 1973-76; group v.p. Dentsply Internat., Haileah, Fla., 1976-79; cons. O. F. Kraft Mgmt., Mpls., 1980-81; v.p. New Hermes Inc., N.Y.C., 1981-83; pres. O. F. Kraft Mgmt. Assoc., Inc., Elizabeth and Edison, N.J., 1983-88; sole prop. O. F. Kraft Fin. Svcs., Tequesta, Fla., 1987—. One man exhbns. include Rue Third Gallery, N.Y.C., Capp Towers Gallery, Mpls., Old Log Theatre Gallery, Excelsion, Minn., Temple of Aaron Fine Arts

Gallery, St. Paul, Albert Lea Arts Ctr., Cinderella City Art Gallery, Denver; permanent collection St. Jude Cath. Ch. Treas. Heritage Oaks Homeowners Assn., 1995; mem. Rep. Club, Stuart, Fla., 1992-94, Health Facilities Authority, Martin County, Fla., 1994. Mem. Internat. Assn. Fin. Planning (pres. 1995), Inst. Cert. Fin. Planners, Am. Legion, Bonnette Hunting and Fishing Club. Home: 18528 SE Heritage Dr Tequesta FL 33469-1447 Office: O F Kraft Fin Svcs 18528 SE Heritage Dr Tequesta FL 33469-1447

KRAKAUER, THOMAS HENRY, museum director; b. Buffalo, Sept. 6, 1942; m. Janet MacColl, Dec. 20, 1968; 1 child, Alan Henry. AB, U. Rochester, 1964; MS, U. Miami, 1966; PhD, U. Fla., 1970. Asst. prof. biology Hollins Coll., Hollins College, Va., 1970-74; natural sci. chmn. Sci. Muc. Va., Richmond, 1974; sr. resident assoc. biology Hollins Coll., 1976-85; exec. dir. Sci. Mus. Assn. of Roanoke (Va.) Valley, 1976-85, N.C. Mus. Life and Sci., Durham, 1985—; adj. asst. prof. Va. Poly. Inst. and State U., Blacksburg, 1973. Bd. dirs. Assn. Sci.-Tech. Ctrs., Triangle Land Conservancy; bd. dirs., pres. Grassroots Sci. Mus. Named Conservation Educator of Yr. Va. Wildlife Fedn., 1978, 95. Mem. Assn. Sci.-Tech. Ctrs. (v.p. 1987, 95), Va. Assn. Mus. (past pres.), Am. Assn. Mus. Home: 128 White Horse Run Bahama NC 27503-8980 Office: NC Mus Life and Sci PO Box 15190 Durham NC 27704-0190

KRAKER, DEBORAH SCHOVANEC, special education educator; b. Enid, Okla., May 28, 1960; d. Charles Raymond and Marcella Ruth (Mack) Schovanec; m. Kevin Mark Kraker, July 10, 1987. BS, U. Ctrl. Okla., 1982; postgrad., Okla. State U., Stillwater, 1995—. Cert. tchr. spl. edn., learning disability/mentally handicapped. Customer svc. mgr. Skaggs, Oklahoma City, 1982-92; tchr. spl. edn. Edmond (Okla.) Pub. Schs., 1993—; tchr. Francis Tuttle Vocat. Tech. Ctr., Oklahoma City, 1993, 94, 95, mem. adv. bd., 1993-96. Mem. adv. bd. Francis Tuttle Vocat. Tech. Ctr., 1993—. Mem. NEA, Okla. Edn. Assn. (del. nat. assembly 1996), Edmond Assn. Classroom Tchrs., Coun. for Exceptional Children, Assn. Classroom Mems. (exec. bd.), Learning Disabilities Assn. Republican. Roman Catholic. Home: 2721 Berkshire Way Oklahoma City OK 73120-2704

KRAKOWER, TERRI JAN, biochemist, researcher; b. Houston, Mar. 9; d. Sidney and Delores K. BS in Biochemistry and Biophysics, U. Houston, 1979; postgrad., U. Calif., Davis, 1980; PhD in Chemistry, U. Tex., 1990. Grad. student asst. State of Calif. Air Resources Bd., Sacramento, 1981, 82; environ. quality specialist State of Tex. Air Control, Austin, summer 1984; predoctoral fellow tchg. and rsch. asst. U. Tex., Austin, 1987-90; staff fellow Boston Biomed Rsch. Inst., Boston, 1990-92; postdoctoral rsch. fellow Harvard Med. Sch., Boston, 1990-91; rsch. assoc. Baylor Coll. of Medicine, Houston, 1993-94; postdoctoral fellow dept. biochemistry U. Tex. Health Sci Ctr., San Antonio, 1994-96; major contbr. to Calif. document leading to first regulation of air emissions from hazardous waste disposal in U.S., State of Calif. Air Resources Bd., Sacramento, 1982; organic and biochem. lab. instr. U. Tex., Austin, 1986. Vol. Mus. of Sci., Boston, 1992. Recipient scholarship U. Calif, Davis, 1980; grantee: Tex. Pub. Edn. grants, U. Tex., 1986-89; named predoctoral rsch. fellow Nat. Inst. Alcohol and Alcohol Abuse, through Inst. for Neurosci., U. Tex., Austin, 1988-89. Mem. AAAS, Am. Chem. Soc., Am. Soc. Biochemistry and Molecular Biology. Home: 101 Westcott Houston TX 77007 Office: U Tex Health Sci Ctr Dept Biochemistry 7703 Floyd Curl Dr San Antonio TX 78284

KRAL, NANCY BOLIN, political science educator; b. St. Louis, Oct. 4, 1958; d. Alpha E. Jr. and Shirley Judith (Wiseman) Bolin; m. Kenneth Joseph Kral, June 12, 1982; 1 child, Kelly Ann. BS, U. Tex., 1979; MA, U. Houston, 1989. Tchr. govt. Round Rock Ind. Sch. Dist., Austin, Tex., 1980-84, Spring Ind. Sch. Dist., Houston, 1984-85, Klein Ind. Sch. Dist., Houston, 1985-88; instr. polit. sci. Houston Community Coll., 1987-88; prof. polit. sci., program coord. North Harris Montgomery Coll. Dist., Tomball, Tex., 1988—; asst. to chancellor North Harris Montgomery Coll. dist., Tomball, Tex., 1993; edn. chair Tomball Regional Arts Coun., 1991-93, bd. dirs.; bd. dirs. Tri-Magna Industries, Waco; del. U.S. Inst. of Peace Seminar, Washington, 1996. Co-author: Texas Government, 1995. Bd. dirs. Champion Forest Civic Assn., Houston, 1986-88, North Area chpt. Houston Symphony League, 1989—, Performing Arts Coun. North Houston, 1994-96; chair Tomball Coll. Law Day; pres. Northampton Homeowners Assn., 1985-86; del. Tex. Rep. Conv., Ft. worth, 1990, Dallas, 1992; faculty advisor Coll. Reps., Tomball Coll.; panelist Nat. Inst. Staff and Orgnl. Devel. Conf., 1992; mem. March of Dimes Guild; charter mem. Houston Holocaust Mus.; legis. chair N.W. Rep. Women, 1988-90, campaign chair, 1990-92. Taft fellow Abilene Christian U., 1988. Mem. NOW, AAUW, Am. Assn. Women in C.C., Tex. Jr. Coll. Tchrs. Assn. (chair govt. sect. 1991-92, legis. com. 1992—, sec. 1994, 95), Tex. Women's Polit. Caucus, Soc. Prevention Cruelty to Animals, Midwest Polit. Sci. Assn., Ctr. for Study of Presidency, U. Houston Alumni Assn., U. Tex. Austin Ex-Students' Assn., LWV, Alpha Xi Delta North Houston Alumnae (pres. 1990-92). Presbyterian. Home: 9319 Appin Falls Dr Spring TX 77379-6554 Office: North Harris Montgomery Coll Dist 30555 Tomball Pky Tomball TX 77375-4096

KRAMAN, STEVE SETH, physician, educator; b. Chgo., Aug. 30, 1944; s. Julius and Ruth (Glassner) K.; m. Lillian Virginia Casanova, May 29, 1972 (div. Apr. 1991); children: Theresa, Pilar, Laura. BS, U. P.R., 1968, MD, 1973. Asst. prof. U. Ky., Lexington, 1978-84, assoc. prof., 1984-90, prof., 1990—; chief of staff VA Med. Ctr., Lexington, 1986—. Contbr. articles to profl. jours. Mem. Am. Coll. Chest Physicians. Office: VA Med Ctr 2250 Leestown Rd Lexington KY 40511-1052

KRAMER, DENNY B., English language educator; b. Austin, Tex., Oct. 9, 1969; s. Dennis Lee and Margaret Helen (Anderson) K.; m. Deanne Michelle Seay, Nov. 11, 1995. BA in English, Baylor U., 1993, MA in Am. Studies, 1996. Cert. tchr., Tex. Customer svc. rep. Sam's Club (Wal-Mart), Waco, Tex., 1989-93; tchr. China Spring (Tex.) Ind. Sch. Dist., 1993-95; rsch. and editing asst. Inst. for Oral History at Baylor U., Waco, Tex., 1995-96; instr. English dept. Baylor U., 1996—; judge Heart of Tex. Regional History Fair, Waco, 1996. Pres. Lorena Ex-Students Assn., Lorena Ind. Sch. Dist., 1995-96, v.p. 1994-95; sch. bd. candidate Lorena Ind. Sch. Dist., 1993. Fellow Baylor Inst. for Oral History, 1995—; Waco Rotary Club scholarship, 1991, Young Scholar's symposium, Baylor U., 1995. Mem. MLA, Popular Culture/Am. Culture Assn., Am. Studies Assn., Smithsonian Inst. Democrat. Baptist. Home: 212 West Billington Waco TX 76706

KRAMER, ROY FOSTER, school superintendent; b. Maryville, Tenn., Oct. 30, 1929; m. Sara Jo Emerl; children: Steve, Sara Gray Cassell, Jane House. Bachelors degree, Maryville Coll., 1953; Masters degree, U. Mich., 1954. Asst. football coach Battle Creek (Mich.) H.S., 1954-55; head football coach Hudson H.S., Mich., 1956, Dowagiac H.S., Mich., 1957, Benton Harbor H.S., Mich., 1958-59, East Lansing (Mich.) H.S., 1960-64; asst. football coach Ctrl. Mich. U., 1965-66, head football coach, 1967-77; athletic dir. Vanderbilt U., 1978-90; commr. Southeastern Conf., 1990—; mem. investment com. NCAA, 1983-86, select com. to study intercollegiate athletics, 1984-86, com. for nat. drug testing policy, 1984-89, men's com. on coms., 1985-88, men's basketball com., 1987-92, spl. adv. com. to review distribution of revenue, 1989-93, basketball T.V. negotiating com., 1989-93, com. on infractions, 1988—; chmn. men's com. on coms. NCAA, 1987-88, men's basketball com., 1992; mem. exec. com. NACDA, 1993—. 1st lt. U.S. Army, 3 yrs. Recipient Disting. Alumnus award Maryville Coll., 1982, Contribution to Football award Mid. Tenn. chpt. Nat. Football Found. and Hall of Fame, 1982; named to Tenn. Sports Hall of Fame, 1989. Office: Southeastern Conf 2201 Civic Center Blvd Birmingham AL 35203-1103*

KRAMER, THOMAS ANDREW MOSS, psychiatry educator; b. Orange, N.J., June 3, 1957; m. Jane H. Feldman, Sept. 8, 1990. BA in Visual-Environ. Studies cum laude, Harvard Coll., 1978; MD, N.Y.U. Sch. Medicine, N.Y.C., 1983. Diplomate Am. Bd. Psychiatry and Neurology (examiner adult psychiatry orals 1992—), Psychiatry and Spl. Qualification in Addiction Psychiatry, Nat. Bd. Med. Examiners. Resident in psychiatry Payne Whitney Psychiat. Clinic, N.Y. Hosp.-Cornell U. Med. Coll., 1983-87; asst. attending psychiatrist Presbyn. Hosp., N.Y.C., 1987-89; attending psychiatrist Mt. Sinai Hosp., N.Y.C., 1989-91; asst. prof., dir. residency tng. and edn. dept. psychiatry Mt. Sinai Sch. Medicine, N.Y.C., 1989-91, adj. asst. prof., 1991—; asst. prof. U. Ark. for Med. Scis., Little Rock, 1991—, dir. psychiat. outpatient svcs., 1991-96; dir. dual diagnosis inpatient program Ark. Divsn. Mental Health, 1996—, staff psychiatrist Rsch. and Tng. Inst., 1996—; instr. clin. psychiatry Columbia U. Coll. Physicians and Surgeons, N.Y.C., 1987-89, asst. dir. postgrad. edn. Columbia U. and N.Y. State Psychiat. Inst., 1987-89; attending psychiatrist Univ. Hosp. Ark., Little Rock, 1991—, Bapt. Med. Ctr., Little Rock, 1991—, St. Vincent's Infirmary, Little Rock, 1991—; reviewer Acad. Medicine, 1992—; presenter in field. Assoc. editor Mt. Sinai Jour. Medicine, 1989-91; contbr. articles and abstracts to med. jours. Named Tchr. of Yr. dept. psychiatry Mt. Sinai Sch. Medicine, 1991; recipient Emile Eckart award for excellence in resident edn. U. Ark. for Med. Scis., 1991, Robert Shannon Award for greatest contbn. to student edn., 1993, 94, 95. Mem. Am. Psychiat. Assn. (com. on residency tng. and program com. N.Y. County dist. br. 1988-91, com. on info. systems 1995—), Am. Assn. Dirs. Psychiat. Residency Tng. (chmn. task force on electronic comm. 1989—, co-chmn. info. com., mem. exec. com. 1990—), Assn. for Acad. Psychiatry, Ark. Psychiat. Soc. (editor newsletter 1992-93, pres. 1994-95), Ark. Med. Assn., Pulaski County Med. Soc. Home: 6 Vantage Pt Little Rock AR 72207-1617 Office: Ark State Hosp Hendrix Hall 4313 W Markham Little Rock AR 72205

KRAMISH, MARC ERIC, lawyer; b. Far Rockaway, N.Y., Mar. 11, 1958; s. Daniel Aaron and Rhoda Lucile (Jacobs) K.; m. Kathryn Henry; children: Chelsea, David. BA, U. Fla., 1980; JD, Nova U., 1983. Bar: Fla. 1983. Pvt. practice Ft. Lauderdale, Fla. Asst. to Gov. Bob Graham, Tallahassee, Fla., 1980; del. Citizens Amb. Program. Mem. ABA, Fla. Bar Assn. (trial lawyers sect.), Assn. Trial Lawyers Am., Civil Justice Found., Acad. Fla. Trial Lawyers, Ft. Lauderdale (Fla.) Knights Rugby Football Club (player 1981-83), Am. Motorcyclist Assn. (mem. motorcycle injury litigation group). Home: 5301 NW 67th Ave Fort Lauderdale FL 33319-7223 Office: 2404 NE 9th St Fort Lauderdale FL 33304-3524

KRAMM, DEBORAH ANN, data processing executive; b. Pasadena, June 24, 1949; d. Donald F. and Mary (Roach) Coonan; m. Kenneth R. Kramm, Dec. 20, 1969; children: Deidre Lyn, Jonathan Russel. BA, U. Calif.-Irvine, 1971; MS, Mich. Tech. U., 1981. Math. asst. NASA-Jet Propulsion Lab., Pasadena, 1967-70; library asst. U. Calif. Irvine Libr., 1967-71; rsch. assoc. animal behavior lab. Mich. Tech. U. , Houghton, 1971-80; programmer/analyst Shell Oil Co., Houston, 1981-85, corp. auditor EDP, 1985-87, team leader systems analyst, 1987-88, group leader SLA, 1988-90, supr. resource planning and adminstrn., 1990-91, adminstrv. coord. product devel. ctr.-design ctr., 1991-93, bus. analyst sr. systems analyst, 1993-96, engagement mgr., 1996—; chmn. bd. MMARK, Houston, 1983-85. Contbr. articles to profl. jours.; Designer (program application software) Shell Point-of-Sale Terminal, 1982-85. Treas. KFHS Orch., 1986-88; co-leader Boy Scouts Am., Houston, 1981-83. AAUW scholar, 1980, Calif. State scholar, 1967-71. Mem. NAFE, AAUW (pres. br. 1975-81). Club: Shell Data Processors, Houston Bus. Forum (pres. bd. dirs.). Home: 5814 Pinewilde Dr Houston TX 77066-2324 Office: Shell Oil Info Ctr 1500 Old Spanish Trl Houston TX 77054-1818

KRANE, N. KEVIN, physician; b. Geneva, Switzerland, Dec. 13, 1952; m. Janet Krane; children: Spencer, Abby, Stewart. BS with high honors, Mich. State U., 1972; MD, Tulane U., 1977. Intern U. Mass. Med. Ctr., Worcester, 1977-78; resident Henry Ford Hosp., Detroit, 1978-80, chief resident, 1980-81, fellow in nephrology and hypertension, 1982-84; chief clin. nephrology Tulane U., New Orleans, 1990—, vice dean acad. affairs, 1994—, med. dir. dialysis, 1984-94, prof. medicine, 1995—; bd. dirs. ESRD Network 13, 1991—. Contbr. articles to Am. Jour. Kidney Diseases. Trustee Nat. Kidney Found. of La., 1991—, chmn. med. adv. bd., 1991—; trustee Congregation Gates of Prayer, Metairie, La., 1992-96. Recipient teaching awards. Fellow ACP; mem. Am. Soc. Nephrology, Internat. Soc. Nephrology, Am. Soc. Transplant Physicians. Home: 4528 Chateau Dr Metairie LA 70002-1510 Office: Tulane U Sch Medicine 1430 Tulane Ave New Orleans LA 70112-2699

KRANTZ, KENNETH ALLAN, military officer, judge; b. Brawley, Calif., Sept. 4, 1952; s. Bertil Allan and Nell Rowe (Morris) K.; m. Josephine Lucille Ursini, Nov. 30, 1985; children: Rebecca Lynn, Sarah Elizabeth. BA, Coll. Wooster, 1974; JD, Coll. William and Mary, 1977; LLM, George Washington U., 1984. Bar: Va. 1977, U.S. Ct. Mil. Appeals 1980, U.S. Army Ct. Mil. Rev. 1993. Commd. ensign USN, 1975, advanced through grades to comdr., 1991; def. counsel USN, Norfolk, Va., 1977-79, prosecutor, 1979-81; aircraft carrier legal officer USN, San Diego, 1981-83; mil. judge USN, Washington, 1984-87; staff atty. USN, Washington and Norfolk, 1987-93; mil. judge USN, Norfolk, 1993—. Mem. choir Va. Opera, 1990—. Mem. ABA, FBA, U.S. Naval Inst. (life), Naval War Coll. Found., Va. State Bar. Office: Navy-Marine Corps Trial Jud 9620 Maryland Ave Norfolk VA 23511-2909

KRAPIN, LEE COLEMAN, neurologist; b. N.Y.C., Apr. 22, 1947; s. Louis and Helen (Coleman) K.; m. Pamela Appelbaum, Sept. 5, 1993; 1 child, Ariella Limor. BA, Queens Coll., 1967; MD, Albert Einstein Coll. Medicine, 1971. Intern N.Y. VA Hosp., 1971-72; resident in neurology Albert Einstein Med. Ctr., 1972-74, resident in surgery and neurosurgery, 1974-75; Commd. ensign USN, 1975, advanced through grades to comdr.; neurologist Naval Hosp., Charleston, S.C., 1990—; clin. asst. prof. neurology Med. U. S.C., Charleston, 1990-94; neurologist Naval Hosp., Yokosuka, Japan, 1994-95, 95-96; chmn. bioethics com. Naval Hosp., 1993—. Jewish lay leader Naval Base, Charleston, 1990—. Mem. AMA, S.C. Med. Assn., Charleston Med. Soc. Democrat.

KRATE, NAT, artist; b. N.Y.C., Aug. 26, 1918; s. Samuel and Ida (Tuchschneider) K.; m. Helen Levy Krate, May 26, 1923; children: Iris Ann, David, Risa. Attended, WPA Art Sch., N.Y.C., 1934-35, Pratt Inst., N.Y.C., 1935-36, Art Students League, 1936-38, 46-47, Syracuse U., 1943-44. Art dir. Erland Advtg. Agy., N.Y.C., 1946-48; creative dir. Krate/Basch Advtg. Agy., N.Y.C., 1948-61; owner & dir. Nat Krate Co. Inc., N.Y.C. and Pittsfield, Mass., 1961-80; mem. adv. bd. Sarasota (Fla.) Art Assn., 1989-91, Longboat Key (Fla.) Art Ctr., 1986-88. Solo exhbns. include Becket Art Gallery, Mass., 1978, Welles Gallery, Lenox, Mass., 1981, Ana Sklar Gallery, Bal Harbor, Fla., 1985, Foster Harmon Galleries Am. Art, Sarasota, Fla., 1986, 89, 92, 94, Arvida Gallery, Longboat Key, 1986, Longboat Key Art Ctr., Fla., 1989, Donn Roll Galleries, Sarasota, 1994, 96; group exhbns. include Fla. Figure Show, Brevard Mus., Melbourne, Fla., 1993, 43d Ann All Fla. Boca Raton Mus., Fla., 1994, Fla. Artist Group, Mus. Arts & Science, Daytona Beach, Fla., 1994, 4th Biennial Exhbn., Huntsville Mus., Ala., 1994, Mobile Mus. of Art, Ala., 1996. Co-founder, mem. bd. dirs. Public Interest Com., Longboat Key, 1985-95; adv. cons. various candidates for public office, 1986-95. Staff sgt. U.S. Army, 1941-45. Mem. Rotary Internat. Home: 4737 Sweet Meadow Cir Sarasota FL 34238

KRATHEN, DAVID HOWARD, lawyer; b. Phila., Nov. 17, 1946; s. Morris S. and Lillian E. K.; m. Francine Ellen, Oct. 21, 1973; children: Richard, Stefanie, Michael. BBA, U. Miami, Fla., 1969, JD, 1972. Bar: Fla. 1972, D.C. 1972, N.Y. 1984, Colo. 1989, U.S. Supreme Ct. 1976. Atty. advisor ICC, Washington, 1972-73; asst. pub. defender 17th Jud. Cir., Ft. Lauderdale, Fla., 1973-74; ptnr. Glass, Krathen, Rastatter, Stark & Tarlowe, Ft. Lauderdale, 1974-78, Krathen & Sperry, P.A., Ft. Lauderdale, 1978-84, David H. Krathen, P.A., 1984-93, 1996—, Krathen & Roselli, P.A., 1993-96; pvt. practice Law Offices of David Krathen, 1996—; mem. Fla. Bar Grievance Com. 17 C, 1982-85, 1988-91, vice chmn., 1985, 89-90, chmn. 1990-91; mem. Jud. Adminstrn., Selection and Tenure Com., 1982-85, 4th Dist. Ct. of Appeal Jud. Nominating Commn., 1983-87, chmn. 1986-87; mem. jud. nominating commn. 17th Jud. Cir., 1991-95, chmn., 1994-95; apptd. by Fla. Gov. to State Ethics Commn., 1995—. Mem. Acad. Fla. Trial Lawyers (diplomate), Broward County Bar Assn. (bd. dirs. 1988-89), Broward County Trial Lawyers Assn. (bd. dirs. 1983-84, sec. 1984-85, v.p. 1985-86, pres. 1987-88), Assn. Trial Lawyers Am., Fla. Bar (bd. cert. civil trial lawyer 1984—), Nat. Bd. Trial Advocacy (bd. cert. civil trial advocate 1986—), Am. Bd. Trial Advocacy (advocate 1989—, sec. Ft. Lauderdale chpt. 1991-92, pres.-elect 1993-95, pres. 1995-96). Office: 888 E Las Olas Blvd Ste 200 Fort Lauderdale FL 33301-2239

KRATT, MARY NORTON, writer; b. Beckley, W.Va., June 7, 1936; d. William Randolph and Martha Hunter (Hood) Norton; m. Emil F. Kratt, Aug. 29, 1959; children: E. William, Laura Catherine, Mary Hunter. BA, Agnes Scott Coll., Decatur, Ga., 1958; MA, U. N.C., 1992. Ednl. cons. Charlotte (N.C.) Landmarks Commn., 1988, 90, Charlotte Pub. Libr., 1986; adj. instr. U. N.C., Charlotte, 1993—. Author: Marney, 1980, Spirit Going Barefoot (poetry), 1982, Southern Is..., 1985, 14th edit. 1992), Legacy: The Myers Park Story, 1986, The Imaginative Spirit: Literary History of Charlotte and Mecklenburg County, 1988, My Dear Miss Eva, 1990, A Little Charlotte Scrapbook, 1990, A Bird in the House, 1991, Charlotte: Spirit of the New South, 1992, The Only Thing I Fear is A Cow and A Drunken Man, 1991, On The Steep Side, 1993; poetry, articles pub. numerous lit. mags.; editorial bd. N.C. Lit. Rev. Bd. dirs. Mus. of New South, Charlotte, 1990-92. Recipient Oscar Arnold Young award for best original book of poems North Carolinian, 1983, ACE award for excellence in comm. Women in Comm., 1984, Spl. Merit award, 1990, Peace prize, History Book award N.C. Soc. Historians, 1987, Hist. Preservation award for vol. svc. Charlotte Landmarks Commn., 1990, Fortner award St. Andrews Coll., 1994, MacDowell Colony Artist Residency award N.C. Arts Coun., 1996. Mem. N.C. Writers Network (past bd. dirs.), N.C. Writers Conf. (chmn. 1991), Phi Kappa Phi. Home and Office: 7001 Sardis Rd Charlotte NC 28270-6057

KRATZ, DENNIS MERLE, language educator, college dean; b. Balt., June 22, 1941; s. Elmer Henry and Rhea (Reiff) K.; m. Abby Robinson, Aug. 30, 1964; 1 child, Matthew E. BA, Dartmouth Coll., 1963; MA, Harvard U., 1964, PhD, 1970. Asst. prof. Ohio State U., Columbus, 1972-78; assoc. prof. U. Tex. - Dallas, Richardson, 1978-85, prof., 1985—, dean undergrad. studies, 1994—. Author: Mocking Epic, 1980, Waltharius and Ruodlieb, 1984, Romances of Alexander, 1991; co-author: (with A. Kratz) Effective Listening Skills, 1995. Mem. Am. Lit. Translators Assn. (pres. 1987-89). Home: 1113 Mill Springs Richardson TX 75080 Office: U Tex Dallas Box 688 Richardson TX 75080

KRAUS, JEAN ELIZABETH GRAU, insurance agent; b. New Orleans, June 8, 1932; d. Adolph Eugene and Katherine Caroline (O'Nion) Grau; divorced; children: Steven, Marilyn, Laurence, Lorraine. BEd, Loyola U. of New Orleans, 1953, MS, 1972. Cert. tchr., La. Tchr. French and English Notre Dame Acad., Washington, 1954-55; tchr. French Orleans Parish Pub. Sch. Dist., New Orleans, 1953-54, 72-86; pvt. ins. agt., New Orleans, 1980—; tchr. gifted students Plaquemines Parish Pub. Schs., 1987-89; tchr. French East Baton Rouge, La., 1989-90, St. Charles Parish, La., 1990-91; registered rep. Jackson Nat. Fin. Svcs., New Orleans, 1993—. Author numerous poems, contbr. poetry to Scimitar and Song, Yearbook Modern Poetry, Reflections of Light Anthology, newspapers, mags. Pres. Aurora-Hyman-Kabel Civic Orgn., New Orleans, 1982—, del. Pres.' Council of Civic Orgns., 1984—; adv. bd. Algiers Community Network, 1985—; active Algiers Priorities Conv., 1986—, Non-Pack Police Support Group, West Bank Action Com. Mem. AAUW (past pres. Crescent City chpt.), Codofil, France-Amerique, Am. Assn. Tchrs. French, La. Edn. Assn., L'Athenee Louisinais, Internat. Platform Assn. Kappa Kappa Iota, Delta Epsilon Sigma, Kappa Delta Pi. Republican. Roman Catholic. Home and Office: 1601 Kabel Dr New Orleans LA 70131-3633

KRAUSE, LOIS RUTH BREUR, chemistry educator; b. Paterson, N.J., Mar. 26, 1946; d. George L. and Ruth Margaret (Farquhar) Breur; m. Bruce N. Pritchard, 1968 (div. May 1982); children: John Douglas, Tiffany Anne,; m. Robert H. Krause, June 16, 1990. Student, Keuka Coll., 1964-65; BS in Chemistry cum laude, Fairleigh Dickinson U., 1980, MAT summa cum laude, 1994; postgrad., Stevens Inst. Tech.; PhD, Clemson U., 1996. With dept. R & D UniRoyal, Wayne, N.J., 1966-68, Jersey State Chem. Co., North Haledon, 1968-69, Inmont, Clifton, N.J., 1969; from chemist to sr. analyst Lever Bros., Edgewater, N.J., 1976-80; process engr. Bell Telephone Labs., Murray Hill, N.J., 1980-84, RCA, Somerville, N.J., 1984-86; sr. engr. electron beam lithography ops. Gain Electronics Corp., Somerville, 1986-88; ind. tech. cons. Pritchard Assocs., Budd Lake, N.J., 1988-92; tchr. of math. and scis. Mt. Olive Bd. Edn. (temporary assignments), 1990-92; tchr. chemistry Morris Hills Regional Dist., 1992-93; instr. chemistry, vis. asst. prof. edn. Clemson U., 1994-95; instr. chem. labs., 1994-96, vis. asst. prof. edn., 1995-96, vis. asst. prof. chemistry, 1996—; presenter workshops and profl. papers for profl. confs. Patentee package design. Troop leader, trainer, cons. Bergen County council Girl Scouts U.S., 1969-80, troop leader Morris Area council, 1980-83, head com. Mt. Olive twp., 1980-81; den leader, den leader coach, trainer Boy Scouts Am., 1973-76. Peter Sammartino scholar, 1994. Fellow Am. Inst. Chemists; mem. IEEE (sr., Components, Hybrids and Mfg. Tech. Soc. semicondr. tech. subcom. electronic components conf. program com. 1981-86), NRA (life mem., endowment mem.), AAAS, ASCD, APA, Am. Soc. Quality Control, Soc. Women Engrs., Am. Chem. Soc., Assn. Women in Sci., N.Y. Acad. Scis., Nat. Sci. Tchrs. Assn., Nat. Woodlot Owners Assn., Arbor Day Found., Mensa, Marine Corps League Aux., Phi Omega Epsilon, Phi Delta Kappa (editor Clemson Kappan), Alpha Epsilon Lambda. Republican. Episcopalian. Home: 303 Cherokee Hills Dr Pickens SC 29671-8619 Office: Clemson U 265 Hunter Labs Clemson SC 29634

KRAUSER, JANICE, special education educator; b. Chgo., Apr. 30, 1951; d. John Francis and June (Fogle) K. BS, U. Tenn., 1973; MEd, Fla. Atlantic U., 1979. Tchr. John Sevier Elem. Sch., Knoxville, Tenn., 1973-76; substitute tchr. Broward County Schs., Ft. Lauderdale, Fla., 1976-78; tchr. Broward Estates Elem. Sch., Ft. Lauderdale, 1978-79, Attucks Mid. Sch., Hollywood, Fla., 1979-81; tchr., spl. edn. specialist South Broward High Sch., Hollywood, 1981-92; spl. edn. specialist New River Middle Sch., Ft. Lauderdale, 1992—; selected mem. Fla. Spkrs. Bur.; state-wide design team mem. of inclusion materials for sch.-based adminstrs. Co-author: (curriculum) Fundamental Math I and II, Consumer Math, Applied English I, II, and III, Fundamental English I, II, III. Zone chmn. U.S.Water Polo, Indpls., 1984-92; treas. Fla. Water Polo, 1982—; dist. del. U.S. Masters Swimming, 1987-95; mem. internat. congress Internat. Swimming Hall of Fame, Ft. Lauderdale, 1994—, (bd. dirs. 1989-93). Named Swimming Coach of Yr. Hollywood Sun-Tattle, 1984-85, Head Water Polo Coach U.S. Olympic Festival, 1986, 90. Mem. ASCD, Coun. Exceptional Children, Fla. Atlantic U. Alumni Assn., Pine Crest Alumni Assn. (bd. dirs. 1993—, sec. 1995—), Broward Libr. Found., Phi Delta Kappa. Home: 1610 NE 43d St Fort Lauderdale FL 33334

KRAUSS, WILLIAM EDWARD, engineering executive; b. Cleve., May 12, 1928; s. Jacob and Helen (Fuchs) K.; m. Barbara Allen Marlin, Aug. 3, 1957; children: Vicki, Ellen, Lori Anne. BME, Ohio State U., 1950, MS, 1953; PhD, U. Fla., 1970. Profl. engr., Fla., Ohio; cert. energy mgr., demand side mgr. Engring. mgr. Martin Marietta Corp., Orlando, Fla., 1959-74; chief engr. Mechtron Internat. Corp., Orlando, 1974-77; sr. staff mem. Brunswick Corp., Deland, Fla., 1976-77; mgr. product devel. Midland Ross, Toledo, 1977-79; v.p. engring. Cleaver Brooks, Milw., 1979-82; dir. Gas Rsch. Inst., Chgo., 1982-87, exec. scientist, 1987-92; v.p., prin. Krauss & Assocs., Inc., Goodlettsville, 1992—. Contbr. articles to profl. pubs. Mem. ASHRAE, ASME, NSPE (sr. mem.), Assn. Energy Engrs., Sigma Xi, Phi Beta Phi, Tau Beta Pi. Avocations: gardening, home renovation. Home: 515 Hanover Ct Goodlettsville TN 37072-2153 Office: PO Box 845 Goodlettsville TN 37070-0845

KRAVITCH, PHYLLIS A., federal judge; b. Savannah, Ga., Aug. 23, 1920; d. Aaron and Ella (Wiseman) K. B.A., Goucher Coll., 1941; LL.B., U. Pa., 1943; LL.D. (hon.), Goucher Coll., 1981. Bar: Ga. 1943, U.S. Dist. Ct. 1944, U.S. Supreme Ct. 1948, U.S. Ct. Appeals (5th cir.) 1962. Practice law Savannah, 1944-76; judge Superior Ct., Eastern Jud. Circuit of Ga., 1977-79, U.S. Ct. Appeals (5th cir.), Atlanta, 1979-81, U.S. Ct. Appeals (11th cir.), 1981—; mem. Jud. Conf. Standing Com. on Rules, 1994—. Trustee Inst. Continuing Legal Edn. in Ga., 1979-82; mem. Bd. Edn., Chatham County, Ga., 1949-55; mem. coun. Law Sch., Emory U., Atlanta, 1986—; mem. vis. com. Law Sch., U. Chgo., 1990-93; mem. regional rev. panel Truman Scholarship Found., 1992—; bd. vis. Law Sch., Ga. State U., 1994—. Recipient Hannah G. Solomon award Nat. Coun. Jewish Women, 1978, James Wilson award U. Pa. Law Alumni Soc., 1992. Fellow Am. Bar Found.; mem. ABA (Margaret Brent award 1991), Savannah Bar Assn. (pres. 1976), State Bar Ga., Am. Judicature Soc., Am. Law Inst, U. Pa. Law Soc. Office: US Ct Appeals 11th Cir 56 Forsyth St NW # 202 Atlanta GA 30303-2205

KRAVITZ, RUBIN, chemist; b. Framingham, Mass., Mar. 22, 1928; s. Abe and Lillian (Cohen) K. m. Geraldine Pudaim, Aug. 20, 1950 (dec.); children: Richard Alan, Steven Jay, Stuart Paul; m. Annabelle S. Durieux, July 16,

1978; 1 child, Michelle Pearl. BS, Northeastern U., 1952, D in Pharm, 1982. Analytical chemist FDA, HEW, Boston, 1956-61; analytical chemist Alcohol and Tobacco div. U.S. Treasury Dept., Boston, 1961-65; supr. phys. testing lab. plastic div. Am. Hoechst Corp., Leominster, Mass., 1967-78; rsch. chemist plastic div. Am. Hoechst Corp., Leominster, 1978-83; sr. devel. engr. EPS, 1983-85; pres. Nat. Plastics Mus. Inc., 1981-85; dir., pres. T.H.E. Hypnosis Ctr., Virginia Beach, Va., 1986-89; staff pharmacist MacDonald Army Hosp., Ft. Eustis, Va., 1987-89; chief pharmacist U.S. Army Health Clin., Fort Monroe, Va.; pres., chief exec. officer Cadet Labs., Virginia Beach, 1984—; chief pharmacist U.S. Army Health Clinic, Ft. Monroe, 1989—; del. Va. Pharm. Assn., 1988; mem. Mid-Atlantic Cholesterol Coun. Cubmaster Boy Scouts Am., Worcester, Mass., 1967-68; trustee, founding pres. Nat. Plastics Ctr. and Mus., 1985—. With USAAF, 1946-48. Mem. Assn. Mil. Surgeons U.S., Soc. Plastic Engrs. (newsletter editor 1969-71, treas. Pioneer Valley sect. 1972-73, v.p. 1973-74, chmn. tech. com. 1973, pres. Pioneer Valley sect. 1975-76, chmn. sect. museum 1979-85, achievement award 1981), ASTM (chmn. compression molding 1969-70, vice chmn. publicity and papers com. D-20 on plastics 1972-76, chmn. subcom. specimen preparation, chmn. sect. plastic furniture, chmn. specimen preparation 1976, chmn. task group Kravitz impact test method 1976, chmn. D 20.12 Olefin Plastics com., mem. exec. com. 1982-85), Assn. Analytical Chemists, Assn. to Advance Ethical Hypnosis, Am. Soc. Rsch. and Clin. Hypnosis, K.P. (chancellor comdr. 1963-64).

KRAWCZYK, MELINDA SUE, geriatrics nurse; b. Covington, Ky., Mar. 16, 1956; d. Robert William and Carol Wray (Bagby) Chapman; m. Edward John Krawczyk, May 4, 1976 (div. Aug. 1983); children: Kristen Lea, Justin Edward; m. Harold Marshall Rudolph White, July 23, 1987 (div. Aug. 1990). LPN, William Booth Meml. Hosp. Sch., Covington, 1975; ADN, No. Ky. U., 1988, BSN, 1991. RN, Ohio, Ky.; cert. gerontol. nurse ANCC. LPN oper. rm. tech. USN, 1975-79; LPN oncology staff nurse in charge of Laminar Flow Rm. Highland Park (Ill.) Hosp., 1980-81; LPN staff nurse Bapt. Convelescent Ctr., Newport, Ky., 1983-88; RN skilled charge nurse Summit/Hilltops Nursing Homes, Cin., 1988-89; RN skilled unit mgr. Woodspoint Geriatric Care Ctr., Florence, Ky., 1989-90; RN inservice/edn. coord. Woodspoint Geriatric Care Ctr., Florence, 1990-96, infection control nurse, 1992—; mem. numerous coms. Woodspoint Geriatric Care Ctr. including safety com. 1994—, health care review coord. 1993—, Medicare/Medicaid Rev. 1995—, quality assurance com. mem. 1992—, quality assurance com. chmn. 1995—; instr. intravenous insertion for LPN, Morehead (Ky.) State U., 1991—; cons., participant Scribner Advt. for Healthcare, Cin., 1991—. Instr. cmty. first aid and safety ARC, Cin., 1981—; instr. nonviolent crisis intervention Nat. Crisis Prevention, Cin., 1994—; assoc. mem. YMCA, 1993—. Served with USN, 1975-79, USNR, 1980-93; 1st lt. Nurse Corps, USAFR, 1993—. Honored for excellence in nursing practice 14th Annual Ky. Nurse Day Recognition Banquet, 1995. Mem. ANA, Res. Officers Assn. (life), Aerospace Med. Assn., Aerospace Nursing Sect., Assn. Mil. Surgeons U.S., Women in Mil. Svcs. for Am. (charter mem.), Nat. Gerontol. Nursing Assn., OKI Gerontol. Nursing Assn., Ky. Nurses Assn. Democrat. Baptist. Home: 15890 Pfanstiel Rd De Mossville KY 41033-9654 Office: Woodspoint Geriatric Care 7300 Woodspoint Dr Florence KY 41042-1567

KREBS, ELIZABETH LOUISE, photojournalist, editor; b. Ann Arbor, Mich., May 2, 1968; d. William Hoyt Krebs and Susan (Bartholomew) Hall. BA, Mich. State U., 1990; postgrad., U. Mo., 1993. Photo stringer Ingham County News Assn., East Lansing, Mich., 1990, Associated Press, Lansing, Mich., 1990; photojournalist, editor Lizardpix, Columbia, Mo., 1991-93; picture editor Detroit Free Press, 1992; mng. editor Weekend Mag., Columbia, 1994; picture editor Balt. Sun, 1994-96, St. Petersburg (Fla.) Times, 1996—. Mem. Nat. Press Photographers Assn., Soc. Profl. Journalists (chpt. sec. 1989-90), Kappa Alpha Mu.

KREBS, ROBERT PRESTON, lawyer; b. Pascagoula, Miss., July 20, 1948; s. Edmund Ory and Dorothy Nell (Davis) K.; m. Cynthia Schaub, Aug. 7, 1971. BA, St. Joseph Sem. Coll., St. Benedict, La., 1970; JD, U. Miss., 1974. Bar: Miss. 1974. Asst. dist. atty. Jackson County, Pascagoula, 1976-77; pvt. practice Pascagoula, 1975-77; assoc. John G. Corlew Law Office, Pascagoula, 1977-80; ptnr. Corlew, Krebs & Hammond, P.A., Pascagoula, 1980-84; pres. Krebs & Williams, P.A., Pascagoula, 1984—. Pres. J.C. Hist. Soc., Pascagoula, 1986-87, United Christian Outreach-Our Daily Bread, Pascagoula, 1986-87; chmn. J.C. Dem. Exec. Com., Pascagoula, 1976-83. Mem. ABA, Miss. State Bar Assn., Jackson County Bar Assn., Miss. Bar Found., Inc. Am. Judicature Soc., Jackson County Young Lawyers Assn. (pres. 1976-77), St. Joseph Sem. Coll. Alumni Assn. (pres. 1995-97). Roman Catholic. Home: 903 Ford Ave Pascagoula MS 39567-4924 Office: Robert P Krebs PA 3003 Magnolia St PO Box 1959 Pascagoula MS 39568-1959

KRECH, ALAN STARR, educational administrator; b. Hackensack, N.J., May 23, 1938; s. Edward M. and Virginia Debaun (Pardee) K.; m. Louise Adele Harrington, Dec. 30, 1961; children: Ruth K., Alan S. Jr., William M. BA in English, Cornell U., 1960, MA in Edn., 1963. Asst. prof., asst. dean faculty Corning (N.Y.) C.C., 1963-70; from planning officer to assoc. commr. S.C. Commn. Higher Edn., Columbia, 1970-96, dir. planning assessment and comms., 1996—; dir. S.C. Coun. Vocat. and Tech. Edn., Columbia, 1993-96; bd. dirs. S.C. Higher Edn. Assessment Network, Rock Hill; pres. So. Assn. C.C. Rsch., 1981-82; so. regional rep. The Coll. Bd., N.Y.C., 1981-83; cons. Ky. Coun. Higher Edn., Lexington, 1991-92. Contbr. articles to profl. jours. Active Westminister Presbyn. Ch., Columbia. Lt. (jg.) USN, 1960-62. Mem. Am. Assn. Higher Edn. Home: 501 Shadowbrook Dr Columbia SC 29210 Office: SC Commn Higher Edn 1333 Main St Ste 200 Columbia SC 29201

KREFTING, CAROL LEE, banker; b. Portland, Oreg., July 26, 1948; d. Richard L. and Irene (Vincent) Noland; m. Charles C. Krefting, Sept. 27, 1968; children: Richard C., Michael J. Student, U. Wash., 1967-68, Stonier Grad. Sch. of Banking Rutgers U., 1982-83. Non-profl. Riggs Nat. Bank, Washington, 1975, from asst. cashier to v.p., 1976-83; v.p. 1st Am. Bank of Va., McLean, 1983-87, 1st Am. Metro Corp., Silver Spring, Md., 1987; sr. v.p. 1st Am. Metro Corp., McLean, Va., 1987-93, Nations Bank Svcs. Co., Charlotte, N.C., 1993—; vice chair Bank Capital Markets Ops. Seminar, 1990; chair Am. Bankers Assn. Securities Ops. Seminar, 1991. Contbg. author: Bank Investments, 1982. Mem. NAFE, Fin. Markets Assn. Office: Nations Bank Svcs Co 200 N College St Charlotte NC 28202

KREISLE, JAMES EDWIN, physician internal medicine; b. Hempstead, N.Y., July 11, 1918; s. Matthew Ferdinand and Margaret Hanna Kreisle; m. Natalie Lenora Attwill, Oct. 5, 1946; children: James E., Helen Kreisle Holzen, Margaret Kreisle Clark, William H. BA, Univ. Tex., 1939; MD, Harvard Univ., 1942. Diplomate Am. Bd. Internal Medicine. Intern Mass. Gen. Hosp., Boston, 1942-43, resident, 1946-47; fellow Mayo Clinic, Rochester, Minn., 1947-49; pvt. practice Family Ptnr., Austin, Tex., 1949-75, Austin (Tex.) Diagnostic Clinic, 1975-91; retired, 1991—. Author: Letters from the ETO, 1990, I Love This Land, 1991, Forty Years After, 1992; contbr. articles to profl. jours. Active Econ. Opportunities Com., Austin, 1950, Healthcare Planning Com., Austin. Capt. U.S. Army, 1943-46, ETO. Decorated Bronze Star medal U.S. Army; recipient Laureate award Am. Coll. Physicains, 1988, Goldheaded Cane Physician award Travis County Medical Soc., 1990. Fellow Am. Coll. Physicians; mem. AMA, Retired Physicians Forum, Travis County Med. Soc., Tex. Medical Assn. (editorial com. 1949—), Tex. Club Internists (pres. 1972)., Phi Beta Kappa, Alpha Omega Alpha. Presbyterian. Home: 2509 Schulle Ave Austin TX 78703-1532

KREITZ, HELEN MARIE, retired elementary education educator; b. Taylor, Tex., Aug. 22, 1929; d. Joseph Jr. and Mary Lena (Miller) K. BA, U. Mary Hardin-Baylor, 1950; MEd, U. Tex., 1959. Cert. tchr., Tex. Bookkeeper Singer Sewing Machine Co., Taylor, 1950-51; advt. salesperson Taylor Times, 1951-52; tchr. Temple (Tex.) Ind. Sch. Dist., 1952-88. Lector, eucharastic min. St. Mary's Cath. Ch., Temple, 1974—. Mem. Tex. Ret. Tchrs. (life, treas. Temple chpt. 1991—), Tex. State Tchrs. Assn. (life, treas. Temple chpt. 1954-55), Tex. Classroom Tchrs. Assn. (life, pres. Temple chpt. 1967-69), U. Tex. Execs. (life), Pi Lambda Theta. Roman Catholic. Home: PO Box 3446 Temple TX 76505-3446

KREIZINGER, LOREEN I., lawyer, nurse; b. Syracuse, N.Y., Apr. 16, 1959; d. David F. and Blanche L. (Heaney) Mosher; m. Kenneth R. Kreizinger, Aug. 30, 1985; 1 child, Katelyn Rose. Grad. in nursing, Crouse-Irving Meml. Hosp., Syracuse, 1981; BS in Bus. with honors, Nova U., 1987, JD, 1990. Bar: Fla. 1990; RN, N.Y., Fla. Nurse ICU and infants neonatal unit, Syracuse, Ft. Lauderdale, Fla., 1979-86; med. malpractice cons. Krupnick, Campbell et al, Ft.Lauderdale, 1986-90, assoc., 1990-92, of counsel, 1992—; pvt. practice, Ft.Lauderdale, 1992—; instr. adult intensive care Crouse-Irving Meml. Hosp., 1981-82; adj. prof. Nova U., Ft. Lauderdale, 1994—; seminar instr. legal aspects of nursing Fla. Bd. Nursing, 1990-92; guest spkr. TV talk show Med. Malpractice, 1991. Sec., bd. dirs. Shepherd Care Ministries, Hollywood, Fla., 1993, 94; mem. choir 1st Bapt. Ch. Ft. Lauderdale, 1994—. Mem. ABA (law and medicine com. 1990—), FBA, ATLA (spl. L-Trytophen com. 1991-94), Fla. Bar Assn., Fla. Assn. Women Lawyers, Fla. Acad. Trial Lawyers, Broward County Women Lawyers Assn., Broward County Trial Lawyers Assn., Phi Alpha Delta. Republican. Office: 515 E Las Olas Blvd Ste 1150 Fort Lauderdale FL 33301-2268

KRENKE, FREDERICK WILLIAM, electrical engineer; b. Port Huron, Mich., Aug. 27, 1946; s. William Frederick and Marian Mable (Schaffer) K.; m. Constance Caye Aylesworth, Nov. 3, 1967 (div. 1979); children: Timothy, Kimberlee; m. Bonnie Jean Feakes, Sept. 7, 1979; children: Kalla, Ashley, Nicole. BSEE, U. Mich., 1973. Elec. constrn. engr. Bechtel Power Corp., various locations, 1973-84; elec. engr. Farley Nuclear Generating Sta. Delcon, Dothan, Ala., 1975-76, Jelco, Inc., Castledale, Utah, 1976-77, Ebasco Svcs. Inc., Cohasset, Minn., 1978-79, Matsco, Reform, Mo., 1982; start-up engr. Bechtel Power Corp.-Ariz. Pub. Svcs., Palo Verde, 1982-83; elec. engr. nuclear generating sta. Ill. Power Co., Clinton, 1984-85; lead elec. and instrument and control engr. Fla. Power and Light Co., Miami, 1985-87; start-up engr. Limerick Generating Sta. Gen. Physics Corp., Pottstown, Pa., 1987-89; elec. design engr. nuclear unit Rust Utility Svcs., Russellville, Ark., 1989-94; plant engr. Superior Graphite Co., Russellville, 1995—. With USN, 1968-69. Home: 251 Alaskan Trl Russellville AR 72801-8306

KREPEL, THOMAS LEON, dean; b. Crete, Nebr., May 5, 1951; s. Anton W. and Phyllis M. (Head) K.; m. Carol K. Ninegar, June 10, 1979; children: Patrick L., Philip A. BS, U. Nebr., 1972, MEd, 1979, PhD, 1983. Tchr. Bellevue (Nebr.) Pub. Schs., 1973-77; mem. legis. staff Nebr. Legislature, Lincoln, 1977-83; asst. prof. ednl. adminstrn. U. New Orleans, 1983-86; asst. to chancellor U. Nebr., Lincoln, 1986-90; assoc. prof. ednl. adminstrn. St. Cloud (Minn.) State U., 1990-92; dean univ. outreach Tex. A&M U., Corpus Christi, 1992—. Contbr. articles to profl. jours. Del. Dem. Conv., Stearns County, Minn., 1992, Lancaster County, Nebr., 1988; bd. dirs. Star City Holiday Parade, Lincoln, 1987-90. Fellow Inst. on Statis. Analysis for Edn. Policy/Am. Ednl. Rsch. Assn., Leadership Lincoln; mem. Nat. Coun. Profls. Ednl. Adminstrn. (com. chair, exec. bd. 1990—), Phi Delta Kappa. Office: Tex A&M U Corpus Christi 6300 Ocean Dr Corpus Christi TX 78412-5503

KRESS, ALBERT OTTO, JR., polymer chemist; b. Cullman, Ala., June 15, 1950; s. Albert Otto and Odell Pearl (Norris) K.; m. Ruth Jeanette Beach, Dec. 30, 1972 (div. Aug. 1978); children: Adrian Konrad, Katyna Ileana; m. Roby Lynn Rice, Apr. 14, 1984; 1 child, Ashley Alan Rice Kress. BS, U. Montevallo, 1972; PhD, U. Ala., 1979. Rsch. scientist Hercules Chem. Corp., Wilmington, N.C., 1979-83; rsch. assoc. Clemson (S.C.) U., 1983-84; assoc. prof. U. Montevallo, Ala., 1984-86; rsch. assoc. U. So. Miss., Hattiesburg, 1986-88; sr. scientist Schering-Plough HealthCare Products Corp., Memphis, 1988—. Contbr. articles to Jour. Organic Chemistry, Dissertation Abstracts Internat. B., Jour. Chem. Soc., Jour. Applied Polymer Sci. Recipient Dean's scholarship U. Ala., 1975. Mem. AAAS, Soc. Plastics Industry, Soc. Plastics Engrs., Am. Chem. Soc., Moose. Republican. Lutheran. Home: 9596 Pigeon Roost Rd Olive Branch MS 38654-2611 Office: Schering-Plough HealthCare Products Corp 3030 Jackson Ave Memphis TN 38112-2020

KRESS, MARY ELIZABETH, newspaper editor; b. Richmond, Va., Oct. 25, 1951; d. Samuel Kemp and Mary Elizabeth (King) Moody; m. Dean Herbert Kress, Jan. 20, 1973 (div. Feb. 1981); m. Ronald Lee Littlepage, Dec. 10, 1982: children: Ronald Kemp, Bramley Elizabeth. BS, Va. Commonwealth U., 1973. Editor M/G Fin. Weekly, Richmond, 1973-74, Richmond News-Leader, 1974-75, Petersburg (Va.) Progress-Index, 1975-77; editor The Fla. Times-Union, Jacksonville, 1977—, now mng. editor; guiest speaker Gannet Ctr. for Media Studies, N.Y.C., 1987. Active Riverside-Avondale Preservation, Inc., Jacksonville, 1987—; dir. Fla. Ballet at Jacksonville, 1980-81. Recipient Twin award YMCA, 1989. Mem. Investigative Reporters and Editors, Am. Soc. Bus. Writers and Editors, Ponte Vedra (Fla.) Inn Club. Home: 3331 Fitch St Jacksonville FL 32205-7824 Office: The Fla Times-Union 1 Riverside Ave Jacksonville FL 32202-4904*

KRESSLEY, KONRAD MARTIN, political science educator; b. Germany, May 2, 1941; came to U.S., 1950; BA in History, Western Md. Coll., 1963; MA in Internat. Rels., Boston U., 1970; MA in Govt. and Politics, U. Md., 1972; PhD in Polit. Sci., U. New Orleans, 1975; MPA, Harvard U., 1981. Dir. pub. adminstrn. program, asst. dir. urban studies Xavier U., New Orleans, 1975-77; dir. pub. adminstrn. program Catawba Coll., Salisburg, N.C., 1977-80; prof., dir. pub. adminstrn. program U. South Ala., Mobile, 1981—. Co-author: Louisiana Mayor's Handbook; contbr. articles to profl. jours. Lt. col. USAR, 1963-68. Mem. Ala. Polit. Sci. Assn. (pres. 1993-94), Atlantic Coun. of U.S. (instl. rep. 1986—), Harvard Club (pres. Mobile chpt. 1991-93). Home: 5559 Vanderbilt Ct Mobile AL 36608-3026 Office: U South Ala Dept Polit Sci Mobile AL 36688

KRETH, TIMOTHY KERWIN, cardiologist; b. N.Y.C., July 23, 1954; s. Kay McBride and Jeanne (West) K.; m. Joanie Wilson, Dec. 5, 1980; children: Matthew Adam, Phillip Andrew. BA cum laude, U. Dallas, 1976; MD, U. Ark., Little Rock, 1980. Diplomate Am. Bd. Internal Medicine, Am. Bd. Cardiology, Am. Bd. Med. Specialties. Intern Bapt. Meml. Hosp., Memphis, 1980-81, resident in internal medicine, 1981-83; fellow in cardiology U. Tenn., Memphis, 1983-85; staff cardiologist Cardiology Cons. of Memphis, 1985-90; pres., mng. ptnr. The Sutherland Clinic, Memphis, 1990—; chmn. emergency cardiac care com. Memphis chpt. Am. Heart Assn., 1986-88, pres., 1990; med. team mgr. Fed. Emergency Mgmt. Agy., Memphis, 1994-95. Co-chmn. Memphis Heart Gala, 1995. Recipient John Runyan MD, MACP Teaching award U. Tenn. Sch. Medicine, 1993. Fellow Am. Coll. Cardiology (chmn. pvt. sector rels. com. 1995). Office: The Sutherland Clinic 6005 Park Ave Ste 1003B Memphis TN 38119-5225

KRETZSCHMAR, CLAUDIA SUZANNE, physician; b. Ft. Leonardwood, Mo., Nov. 8, 1954; d. Edward Manuel and Jackline Marie (Myers) Miller; m. William Addison Kretzschmar Jr., May 30, 1976; children: Brendan Anthony, Russell Timothy. BS with high honors, U. Mich., 1976; MD, U. Chgo., 1981. Diplomate Am. Bd. Internal Medicine. Intern in internal medicine Michael Reese Hosp., 1981; resident in internal medicine Mt. Sinai Hosp., Milw., 1982; fellow in gastroenterology U. Wis., Madison, 1984-86; active staff Athens Regional Med. Ctr. and St. Mary's Hosp., 1987—; chmn. medicine dept. St. Mary's Hosp., Athens, Ga., 1988. Mem. Am. Gastroent. Assn., Athens Symphony Orch. Office: 700 Oglethorpe Ave Athens GA 30606

KRICK, PATRICK JOSEPH, transportation consultant, economist; b. Omaha, Dec. 24, 1953; s. Mathias Paul and Eileen Kathleen (McMinamen) K.; m. Kathleen Mary Dineen, Nov. 4, 1977; children: Dineen Marie, Mathias Paul. BS, U. Nebr., Omaha, 1976, MS, 1977. Rsch. analyst Mut. of Omaha, 1977-79; assoc. planner Omaha-Council Bluffs Met. Area Planning Agy., 1979-80; sr. econ. analyst Union Pacific R.R., Omaha, 1980-84; mgr. econ. analysis Burlington No. R.R., Ft. Worth, 1984-86, asst. dir. forecasts, budgets, 1986-87, sr. economist, 1987-90, dir. mktg., bus. analysis, 1990, dir. bus. planning, 1990—, asst. v.p. corporate analysis and devel., 1994-95; cons. Ft. Worth Sch. Dist., 1990. Contbr. articles to profl. jours. Del. Tex. Dem. State Conv., Austin, 1986; chmn. adv. com. Cable TV, Omaha, 1982-83. Nat. Consumer Affairs Internship scholar Am. Coun. Consumer Affairs-Couns. Consumer Orgns., 1977. Mem. Am. Econ. Assn., Nat. Assn. Bus. Economists, Planning Forum, Transp. Rsch. Forum. Roman Catholic. Office: The Kingsley Group 1901 Central Dr Ste 333 Bedford TX 76021

KRIDLER, JAMIE BRANAM, children's advocate, social psychologist; b. Newport, Tenn., Jan. 23, 1955; d. Floyd A. and Mary Leslie (Carlisle) Branam; m. Thomas Lee Kridler, Mar. 19, 1989; children: Brittani Audra, Houston Scott, Clark Eaton, Sabrina Morrow. BS, U. Tenn., 1976, MS, 1977; PhD, Ohio State U., 1985; cert. retailing, profl. modeling, Bauder Fashion Coll., Atlanta, 1973. Fashion coord. Bill's Wear House, Newport, Tenn., 1969-77; buyer Shane's Boutique, Gatlinburg, Tenn., 1977-78; instr. Miami U., Oxford, Ohio, 1978-81; asst. prof. U. Tenn., Knoxville, 1985-89; mktg. dir. Profitt's Dept. Stores, Alcoa, Tenn., 1989-90; mktg. cons. Kridler & Kridler Mktg., Newport, Tenn., 1990-93; children's advocate Safe Space, Newport, Tenn., 1993-95; adj. faculty U. Tenn., Knoxville, 1990—, Walters State Coll., Morristown, Tenn., 1990—, Carson Newman Coll., Jefferson City, Tenn., 1993—; founding mem. Cmty. House Coop., 1995—; mem. Nation Funding Collaborative on Violence Protection; participant Children's Defense Fund, Washington, 1992—; founding mem. Cmty. House Co-op. Costume designer Newport Theatre Guild: Guys and Dolls, Carousel, Fiddler on the Roof, Music Man, Crimes of the Heart, Rumors, Come Back to the Five and Dime, Jimmy Dean, Oliver, The Odd Couple, 1991—, The Sunshine Boys, 1991—, Miami U. Dance Theatre, Ice Show. Bd. dirs. Safe Space, 1991-92; v.p. Newport Theatre Guild, 1991-92, pres. 1992—. Named Outstanding Tchr., Miami U., Oxford, 1981, Outstanding Educator, U. Tenn., Knoxville, 1989; recipient numerous grants from univ. and non-profit orgns. Mem. NAACP, Lioness Club, Kappa Omicorn Nu. Democrat. Episcopalian. Home: 112 Woodlawn Ave Newport TN 37821-3031

KRIEG, REBECCA JANE, editor; b. Bloomington, Ill., Oct. 7, 1953; d. Russell Edward and Betty Ilena (Clesson) Krieg. BA summa cum laude in Christian Edn., Lincoln Christian Coll., 1977; BS in Math. with high distinction, U. Ky, 1993. Trainer self-help skills for retarded Lincoln Devel Ctr. (Ill.) 1975-76; women's editor Lincoln Courier, 1977-84; campus ministry intern Christian Student Fellowship, U. Ky., Lexington, 1984, undergrad. rsch. asst., 1991-93; copy editor Lexington Herald-Leader, Ky., 1985-91; freelance editor, 1993—. Vol. rep. Cen. Ill. chpt. Cystic Fibrosis Found., 1982-84; a founder Logan County Com. Against Domestic Violence and Sexual Assault, 1983, v.p., bd. dirs., 1983-84; vol. Rape Info. and Counseling Service, Springfield, Ill., 1982-83. Mem. Golden Key, Delta Epsilon Chi. Avocations: piano, singing, reading, gardening, birdwatching.

KRIEGER, PAUL EDWARD, lawyer; b. Fairmont, W.Va., Mar. 30, 1942; s. Paul Julius Krieger and Martha Frances (Graham) Ralph; m. Elizabeth N. Krieger, July 2, 1965; children: Andrew, Thomas. BS in Mining Engring., U. Pitts., 1964; postgrad. Pa. State U., 1964-65; LLB, U. Md., 1968; LLM, George Washington U., 1971. Bar: Md. 1968, D.C. 1973, Tex. 1979, U.S. Patent and Trademark Office, 1970. Faculty research asst. U. Md., 1967-70; assoc. Brumbaugh, Graves, Donohue & Raymond, N.Y.C., 1970-71; ptnr. Lane, Aitken, Dunner & Ziems, Washington, 1971-78; sr. pat. atty. Dresser Industries Inc., Dallas, 1978-79; ptnr. Pravel, Hewitt, Kimball & Krieger, Houston, 1979—; adj. prof. U. Houston Law Ctr., 1985—. Mem. ABA, Am. Bar Found., Am. Pat. Law Assn., Tex. Bar Found., Tex. Bar Assn., Houston Bar Found., Houston Pat. Law Assn., U.S. Trademark Assn., Lic. Exec. Soc. Home: 11 Sandalwood Dr Houston TX 77024-7122 Office: 1177 West Loop S Fl 10 Houston TX 77027

KRIEGER, ROBERT LEE, JR., human resource management consultant, educator, writer, travel planner; b. Louisville, Nov. 13, 1946; s. Robert Lee and June Elise (Waters) K. BBA, U. Memphis, 1968, MBA, 1969. Adminstrv. asst. to mayor City of Memphis, 1969-72; dir. devel. programs U. Memphis, 1972-74; cons. pvt. practice, Memphis, 1974-76; exec. v.p. Randall Howard & Assocs., Memphis, 1976-95, pres. KR Internat. Inc., 1995—; mem. faculty U. Memphis Coll. Bus., 1984—; worldwide travel cons. and meeting planner, 1962—; keynote spkr. numerous profl. groups. Trustee, life mem. Republican Presdl. Task Force, Washington, 1980—; mem. Rep. Nat. Adv. Com., Washington, 1972—, Rep. Regional Steering Com.; mem. U.S. Olympic Soc., Boulder, Colo., 1968—. Recipient U.S. Treasury award U.S. Dept. Treasury, 1971; Nat. Presdl. medal of Merit, Rep. Presdl. Task Force, 1984; Rep. Legion of Merit; Pres.'s award Memphis Cotton Carnival Assn., 1968-85. Mem. Data Processing Mgmt. Assn., Am. Mgmt. Assn., Am. Film Guild, Met. Opera Guild, U.S. Navy League, Nat. Wildlife Fedn., Alpha Delta Sigma, Sigma Delta Chi. Episcopalian. Clubs: Mensa, U. Memphis State Alumni. Avocations: writing, bowling, movies and photography, travel, public speaking. Home: 2948 Dalebrook St Memphis TN 38127-8316

KRIEGLER, ARNOLD MATTHEW, management consultant; b. Omaha, July 29, 1932; s. Matthew and Mildred Elsie (Svoboda) K.; m. Joan Virginia Godsey Kriegler, Nov. 24, 1954; children: Kurt, Karen. BSc in Bus. and Engring. Adminstrn., U. Nebr., Omaha, 1955; postgrad., U. Iowa, 1957-58. Chief draftsman Ballantye Electronics, Omaha, 1948-55; various mgmt. positions Collins Radio div. Rockwell Internat., Cedar Rapids, Iowa, 1957-76; dir. mfg. electronics ops. Rockwell Internat., Dallas, 1976-78, dir. prodn. ops. Collins Transmission Systems div., 1978-88; mgmt. cons. AMK Assocs., Plano, 1988—; mem. com. on computer aided mfg. NAS, Washington, 1978-81; mem. engring. scis. curriculum adv. com. U. Tex., Dallas, 1988—. 1st lt. USAF, 1955-57. Recipient Exec. of Yr. United Way, Cedar Rapids, 1973. Mem. Nat. Mgmt. Assn. (instr. 1977—, chpt. dir. 1978-79, Silver Knight Mgmt. 1989), Inst. Indsl. Engrs. (chpt. pres. 1973-74), Theta Chi (chpt. pres. 1954-55). Republican. Presbyterian. Home and Office: 3605 Seltzer Dr Plano TX 75023-5809

KRIMM, MARTIN CHRISTIAN, electrical engineer, educator; b. Shively, Ky., Dec. 15, 1921; s. Martin C. Sr. and E. Verlee (Boling) K.; m. Helenora Magdalyn Schenk, Feb. 11, 1946; children: Marsha Lee, Sharon Cecilia, David Leslie, Timothy Wilson. MSEE, U. Ky., 1962. Contractor Louisville, 1945-50, 56; design engr., cons. Am. Standard Rsch., Louisville, 1954-56; asst. prof. elec. engring. U. Ky., Lexington, 1957-90, VPA prof. emeritus, 1991—; areas of interest include electric power engring. and machines, electrobiology and psychobiocybernetics; profl. witness. Contbr. numerous broad-based articles for engring. edn. to profl. jours. With USN, 1942-45. Mem. AAUP, People's Med. Soc., HALT, Tau Beta Pi, Eta Kappa Nu. Home: 268 Camp Nelson Lancaster KY 40444

KRIMMER, LINDA K., business educator, accountant; b. Cassville, Mo., Oct. 26, 1945; d. Bert Neal and Katheryn Elaine (Hefley) Lawson; m. Richard J. Krimmer, Dec. 27, 1969 (div. Sept. 1991); children: Kathryn E. Bohannan, Richard J. II. AB in Bus., Crowder Coll., Neosho, Mo., 1966; BS in Edn., S.W. Mo. State Coll., Springfield, 1968. Divsn. mgr. Sears, Roebuck & Co., Springfield, 1968-69; owner, operator Sears Catalog Mcht., Seneca, Kans., 1976-82; bus. educator Sabetha (Kans.) Pub. Schs., 1979-84, Manhattan (Kans.) Pub. Schs., 1985-87, Prince William Schs., Woodbridge, Va., 1987—; acct. Nichols, Bergere & Zauzie, P.C., Woodbridge, 1992—. Bd. dirs. Lake Ridge Park and Recreation, Woodridge, 1996; mem. Occoquan Dem. Com., Woodbridge, 1993; recreational dir. Seneca (Kans.) Recreation, 1982-84. Mem. NEA, Va. Edn. Assn., Prince William Edn. Assn. (bd. dirs. 1987—), Va. Bus. Educators, Bus. and Profl. Women. Baptist. Home: 12142 Pineneedle Ct Woodbridge VA 22192 Office: Woodbridge Sr HS 3001 Old Bridge Rd Woodbridge VA 22192

KRIN, CHARLES STEVEN, osteopath; b. Omaha, May 8, 1956; s. James Charles and Malbe Darlene (Johnston) Krin; m. Theresa Ann Gaffney; children: Meggan Jennifer, Lisa Kathryn; m. DeAnna DeLane Jones; children: Joshua Dean, Christopher Steven, Jacob Matthew. Student, Thornton C.C., 1973-74; BS in Biology, Ill. State U., 1979; D in Osteopathic Medicine, U. Health Scis., 1987; postgrad., U. Nebr., 1987. Diplomate Am. Bd. Osteo. Examiners, Am. Bd. Family Practice; ACLS, pediat. advanced life support provider, Am. Heart Assn. Resident in family practice E.A. Conway Meml. Hosp., Monroe, La., 1987-90; family practice physician, staff physician emergency rm. Richardson Meml. Med. Ctr., Rayville, La., 1993—; family practice preceptor E.A. Conway Meml. Hosp. Family Practice Ctr., 1993—; physician reviewer Tenn. Peer Rev. Orgn., Memphis, 1992-93, Thompson La Fleu Clinic Quality Improvement. Contbr. articles to profl. jours. With US Army, 1979-83, capt. Med. Corps. Mo. Army Nat. Guard, 1983-87, capt. Med. Corps. US Army Res. ret. Fellow Am. Acad. Family Practice; mem. Am. Osteo. Assn., Am. Acad. Family Practice, Ark. Disaster Med. Assistance Team, Undersea and Hyperbaric Med. Soc., So. Med. Assn., Am. Coll. Osteo. Family Physicians, NRA (life). Office: Northeast La Health Ctr 1012 Louisa St Rayville LA 71269-2922

KRISHNA, J. HARI, hydrologist, engineer; b. Madras, India, May 13, 1948; came to U.S., 1968; s. J. Raghotham Reddy and J. Sarojini Devi; m. Laxmi Krishna, Mar. 26, 1972. BS, Osmania U., Hyderabad, India, 1967; MS, Kans. State U., 1971; PhD, Utah State U., 1979. Registered profl. engr.; cert. profl. hydrologist Am. Inst. Hydrology. Scientist, agrl. engr. ICRISAT, Hyderabad, 1972-81; internat. cons. FAO/UN, Bangkok, Thailand, 1981-82; asst. prof. Utah Water Rsch. Lab., Logan, 1982-84; rsch. scientist Tex. A&M Blackland Rsch. Ctr., Temple, 1984-88; dir./assoc. prof. V.I. Water Resources Rsch. Inst., St. Thomas, 1988-93; sr. hydrologist TNRCC, Austin, Tex., 1993—. Contbr. articles to profl. jours. Mem. Am. Rainwater Catchment Sys. Assn. (pres. 1994—, dir.-at-large 1989—), Phi Kappa Phi, Tau Beta Pi. Home: 12405 Uttimer Ln Austin TX 78753 Office: TNRCC MC-131 PO Box 13087 Austin TX 78711-3087

KRISHNA, N(EPALLI) RAMA, biochemist; b. Masulipatam, Andhra, India, Nov. 20, 1945; came to U.S., 1971; PhD, Indian Inst. Tech., Kanpur, 1972. Postdoctoral fellow Ga. Inst. Tech., Atlanta, 1972-73, U. Alta., Edmonton, Can., 1974-76; assoc. scientist Cancer Ctr. U. Ala., Birmingham, 1976-79, asst. prof. dept. biochemistry, 1979-85, assoc. prof., 1985-92, prof., 1992—, dir. nuclear magnetic resonance core facility, 1984—; cons. Ortho Pharm. Corp., Raritan, N.J., 1979-83. Contbr. articles to profl. jours. Recipient Leukemia Soc. Am. Scholar award, 1982-87. Office: Univ Ala Dept Biochemistry NMR Core Facility CHSB-B31 933 19th St S Birmingham AL 35205-3703

KRIZ, GEORGE JAMES, agricultural research administrator, educator; b. Brainard, Nebr., Sept. 20, 1936; s. George Jacob and Rose Agnes Kriz; m. Patricia Elizabeth Kelly (div. Feb. 1989); children: Rosalie Sue, Richard Patrick, Thomas George; m. Rhoda Mae Whitacre, June 23, 1989. BS in Agrl. Engring., Iowa State U., 1960, MS in Agrl. Engring., 1962; PhD, U. Calif., Davis, 1965. Lectr. U. Calif., Davis, 1965; asst. prof. agrl. engring. N.C. State U., Raleigh, 1965-68, assoc. prof., 1968-72, prof., 1972—, assoc. dept. head, 1969-73, asst. rsch. dir., 1973-81, assoc. rsch. dir., 1981—. Fellow Am. Soc. Agrl. Engring. (bd. dirs. 1983-85, found. trustee 1986-94, pres. 1995-96, presdl. citation 1988, 91); mem. Coun. Agrl. Scis. and Tech., Agrl. Rsch. Inst. (bd. dirs. 1993-96). Office: NC State U Box 7643 100 Patterson Hall Raleigh NC 27695-7643

KROGMANN, JOAN L., horse trainer, writer; b. Queens, N.Y., Oct. 12, 1936; d. Milton Irving and Hazel Darling (Diefenbacher) Andres; divorced; 1 child, Kimberley. Studied with Vladimer Littauer, Luis de La Vellette, George Brush, Frank Collins, others, 1958-75. Lic. real estate agent, N.Y. Owner Little Plains Stable and Little Plains Breeding Farm, L.I., N.Y., 1957-94; lic. real estate agent Century 21, N.Y., 1984-88; freelance writer N.Y., 1980-94; owner La Petite Cheval Farm, Loxahatchee, Fla., 1994—; organizer, creator L.I. High Score Awards, 1959-94; tchr. phys. edn., L.I., 1980-90; organizer L.I. Mini Circuit, 1984-90, Showcase Series, 1992 Galaxy Champions. Contbr. articles to various publs. Tchr., advisor Girl Scouts U.S., L.I., 1970-94, Boy Scouts Am., L.I., 1970-94; mem. bd. advisors Bd. Coop. Edn. Spl., L.I., 1979-94; pk. steward Town of Huntington, L.I., 1988-94, mem. conservation bd., 1988-94; active intensive care program Suffolk County Handicapped, L.I., 1993-94. Named Trainer of Yr., L.I. Mini Circuit, 1989-90, Pleasure Horse Champion, Nassau Suffolk Horsemans, 1991, 92, 93, 94, Trainer of Yr., North Shore Horse Shows, 1994. Mem. Am. Horse Show Assn. (show mgr.), Nat. Hunter Jumper Assn., Palm Beach Horse Industry Coun. (bd. dirs.), Palm Beach County Horseman's Assn. (bd. dirs.). Home: 13678 14th Pl Loxahatchee FL 33470-4905

KROGSTAD, DONALD JOHN, infectious diseases physician, educator; b. N.Y.C., Feb. 18, 1943; s. John C. and L. Ruth (Thompson) K.; m. Frances Stewart Marsh, June 19, 1965; children: Kirk Scott and Arric Paul (twins). AB, Bowdoin Coll., 1965; MD, Harvard U., 1969. Cert. in internal medicine, infectious diseases Am. Bd. Internal Medicine. Intern in medicine Mass. Gen. Hosp., Boston, 1969-70, asst. resident, 1970-71; epidemic intelligence svc. officer Ctrs. for Disease Control, Atlanta, 1971-73; Peace Corps vol. physician Llongue (Malawi) Gen. Hosp. and Nat. Med. Assts. Tng. Sch., 1973-75; jr. resident in medicine Mass. Gen. Hosp., Boston, 1975-76, rsch. fellow in infectious diseases, 1976-78; asst. prof. medicine and pathology Sch. Medicine Washington U., St. Louis, 1978-83, assoc. prof. Sch. Medicine, 1983-92; Henderson prof., chair dept. tropical medicine Tulane U. Sch. Pub. Health and Tropical Medicine, New Orleans, 1992—; mem. recombinant DNA adv. com. NIH, Bethesda, Md., 1990-94, mem. tropical medicine parasitology study sect., 1994-98; mem. adv. bd. Edna McConnell Clark Found., 1992-95. Mem. editl. bd. Antimicrobial Agts. Chemother., 1986-95; contbr. articles to profl. jours. Grantee Tropical Medicine Rsch. Ctr., NIH, 1996-2001, New Intiative in Malaria Rsch. grantee Burroughs-Wellcome Fund, 1996-97. Mem. Am. Soc. Tropical Med. Hygiene (chmn. sci. program com. 1984-89, pres. 1992). Office: Tulane U Dept Tropical Medicine 1501 Canal St New Orleans LA 70112

KROLL, LYNNE FRANCINE, artist; b. San Mateo, Calif., Dec. 18, 1943; d. Nathan and Dorothy (Smith) Cole; m. Jeffrey Joseph Kroll, June 9, 1963; children: Beth, Lisa, Andrew. AAS, Bklyn. C.C., 1963. Recipient Moses Worthman Meml. award Allied Artists Am., 1994, Dick Blick Materials award Audubon Artists ann. Exhibit, 1996, Curators Excellence award Ariz. Aqueous 11th Ann. Watermedia Exhibit., Judges Recognition award Mus. of New Art, 1996, Materials and Travel award Ky. Watercolor Soc., 1996, 5th Pl. Pitts. Watercolor Soc., 1996. Mem. Nat. Soc. Painters Casein & Acrylic, Nat. Assn. Women Artists (Distinction award 1995), Womens Caucus for Arts, Fla. Artist Group, Soc. Layerists Multi-Media, Fla. Watercolor Soc. (Strathmore Excellence award 1994), Tex. Watercolor Soc., Goldcoast Watercolor Soc. (Grumbacher Gold medallion 1994, Sax Arts & Crafts award 1994), Artist Orgn., Profl. Artist Guild. Home: 3971 NW 101 Dr Coral Springs FL 33065

KRONSNOBLE, JEFFREY MICHAEL, art educator; b. Milw., Feb. 9, 1939; s. Erwin Joseph and Ethel Irene (Johnson) K.; m. Mary Lu Bieke, Sept. 1, 1962 (div. Feb. 1973); children: Kristin Mary, John Matthew II, Sarah Jane; m. Jeanne Mingledorff, Mar. 18, 1978. BS in Art, U. Wis., Milw., 1961; MFA, U. Mich., 1963. Prof. U. South Fla., Tampa, 1963—. One-man shows include Milw. Jewish Ctr., 1963, Tampa Art Inst., 1964, U. South Fla., Tampa, 1964, 66, 69, 71, St. Petersburg Pub. Libr., 1965, New Orleans Mus. of Art, 1967, Edison Jr. Coll., Ft. Myers, Fla., 1969, St. Armands Gallery, Sarasota, Fla., 1969, 72, Orlando (Fla.) Mus. Art, 1970, Brevard Jr. Coll., Cocoa, Fla., 1970, Contemporary Gallery, St. Petersburg, 1970, Polk County Mus., Lakeland, Fla., 1971, Jacksonville (Fla.) Art Mus., 1971, Trend House Gallery, Tampa, 1971, 74, Ctrl. Fla. C.C., Ocala, 1974, U. South Fla., Tampa, 1974, 75, 76, U. Fla., Gainesville, 1975, Galleries Internat., Winter Park, Fla., 1978, Hodgell Hartman Gallery, Sarasota, 1979, ACA Galleries, N.Y., 1981, 84, 86, Deicas Art Gallery, La Jolla, Calif., 1982, Brevard C.C., Melbourne, Fla., 1983, Corbino Galleries, Sarasota, 1986, Eitharong Gallery, Orlando, 1988, Barbara Gilman Gallery, Miami, 1989, Miami-Dade C.C., 1989, Polk Mus. Art, Melbourne, Hollywood, Ft. Myers, 1990, Clayton Galleries, Tampa, 1992, 93, 96; exhibited in group shows at Art Souces, Inc., Jacksonville, 1980, Butler Inst. Am. Art, Youngstown, Ohio, 1980, 86, 87, Fla. Internat. U., Tamiami, 1980, Nat. Acad. Design, N.Y., 1980, 81, Tampa Mus., 1981, 85, Valencia C.C., Orlando, 1981, Mus. Fine Arts, St. Petersburg, 1982, Jacksonville Art Mus., 1982, 86, Wolfson Gallery, Miami, 1982, 85, Art Billboards, Jacksonville, 1983, ACA Galleries, 1983, North Miami Mus. and Art Ctr., Miami, 1983, Clearwater (Fla.) Performing Arts Ctr., 1983, Foster Harmon Galleries Am. Art, Sarasota, 1984, Polk Pub. Mus., Lakeland, Fla., 1984, 85, 87, 92, Barbara Gillman Gallery, 1984, U. South Fla., 1984, Fairfield (Conn.) U., 1985, Tampa Mus. Art-West, 1986, Fla. Gulfcoast Art Ctr., Belleair, 1986, Fed. Res. Bd., Washington, 1987, Wayne State U., Detroit, 1989, Fla. State U., 1990, Hanson Gallery, N.Y.C., 1991, Brevard Mus. and Art Ctr., 1992; represented in over 150 pvt. collections. Recipient Michael Gorman scholarship Cranbrook Acad. Art, 1961, Merit award in Drawing, Winter Park Art Festival, 1970, photography award, 1970, 1st prize Festival 13, Ea. U.S. Drawing Competition, Cummer Gallery of Art, 1970, Purchase prize Nat. Print and Drawing Exhbn., No. Ill. U. South Fla., 1968, Best in Show award Ocala Art Show, 1971, 1st prize Graphics award Gasparilla Festival Art Show, 1972, Festival of State Art Exhbn., 1972, Merit award Gasparilla Festival Art Show, Tampa, 1973, Winter Haven Painting Ann., Fla., 1975, Thomas B. Clarke prize Nat. Acad. Design, N.Y., 1980, William A. Paton prize, 1981, others; Rsch. Coun. grantee U. South Fla., 1971, 75; fellow Rackham Sch. Grad. Studies, 1961, Artist's fellow Fine Arts Coun. Fla., 1978, 81, 87. Home: 908 S Dakota Ave Tampa FL 33606-3004 Office: U South Fla Dept Art Tampa FL 33620

KROTOSKI, WOJCIECH ANTONI, research physician, educator; b. Riga, Latvia, June 20, 1937; came to U.S., 1949; naturalized U.S. citizen, 1955.; s. Ludwik Jozef and Leokadia Jozefina (Pawlowska) K.; m. Danuta Mary Gwozdziowski (annulled); 1 child, Aleksandra Krystyna; m. Judith Ann Goins, Aug. 2, 1985; 1 stepchild, John Alfred Bell IV. BA, UCLA, 1960, PhD, MD, 1968; MPH, U. Calif., Berkeley, 1974. Diplomate Calif. State Bd. Med. Examiners. Commd. med. officer USPHS, 1969, advanced through grades to med. dir., 1984; staff assoc. unit human malaria NIH, Atlanta, 1969-70, med. officer in charge unit human malaria, 1970-71; rsch. assoc. unit primate malaria NIH, Chamblee, Ga., 1971-72; clin. fellow tropical medicine Sch. Medicine U. Calif., San Francisco, 1972-74; resident internal and preventive medicine USPHS Hosp., San Francisco, 1972-74; asst. chief medicine, asst. chief clin. rsch. USPHS Hosp., New Orleans, 1975-78, chief tropical infectious disease rsch. program, 1975-81, chief clin. rsch., 1978-81; clin. assoc. prof. dept. tropical medicine Sch. Pub. Health and Tropical Medicine Tulane U., 1975-86; clin. assoc. prof. dept. tropical medicine and med. parasitology Sch. Medicine La. State U., New Orleans, 1978-84, clin. assoc. prof. infectious diseases Sch. Medicine, 1978—, assoc. mem. faculty Sch. Grad. Studies Med. Ctr., 1980—, clin. assoc. prof. internat. and tropical medicine Sch. Medicine, clin. assoc. prof. med. parasitology, 1984—; rsch. physician Gillis W. Long Hansen's Disease Ctr. La. State U., Baton Rouge, 1993-95; dir. Nat. Ambulatory Hansen's Disease Program, Bureau Health Care Delivery and Assistance USPHS, 1990-91; physician microbiologist, immunologist Nat. Hansen's Disease Ctr., Carville, La., 1981-83, dep. chief lab. rsch. br., 1983-85; rsch. physician lab. rsch. br. GWL Hansen's Disease Ctr., Carville, 1985-90, acting chief pathology rsch. dept. lab. rsch. br., 1992-93; ret. USPHS, 1995; adj. prof. tropical medicine Sch. Vet. Medicine La. State U., Baton Rouge, 1987-94, adj. prof. pathology, 1993—; mem. Marshall Islands health survey team Brookhaven (N.Y.) Nat. Lab., 1977-82, ctrl. clin. investigations com. Bureau Med. Svcs. USPHS, 1978-81; peer rev. panelist cholera rsch. devel. program Bd. Regents, State of La., 1980-81; cons. leprosy vaccine immunology leprosy sci. working group World Health Orgn., Geneva, Switzerland, 1982, 85; mem. Hansen's disease rsch. adv. com. bur. health care delivery and assistance USPHS, 1983-89; rsch. affiliate Delta Regional Primate Rsch. Ctr., Tulane U., Covington, La., 1984-87; participant New Orleans Infectious Disease Conf., 1984—; presenter in field. Contbr. numerous articles to med. and sci. jours. Recipient Cert. Merit, State of La. Bd. Regents Rsch. and Devel. Program, 1980; nominee Nobel Prize in physiology and medicine, 1989. Fellow Royal Soc. Tropical Medicine and Hygiene; mem. Am. Soc. Tropical Medicine and Hygiene (sci. program com. 1978-79), USPHS Profl. Assn. (sci. program chmn. 1989), Assn. Mil. Surgeons U.S., La.-Miss. Infectious Diseases Soc., La. Soc. Electron Microscopy, Internat. Leprosy Assn., Nat. Right-to-Life, Baton Rouge Right-to-Life, Southeastern Soc. Parasitologists. Roman Catholic. Office: La State U Veterinary Pathology Dept Baton Rouge LA 70803

KROTSENG, MARSHA VAN DYKE, higher education administrator; b. Indiana, Pa., May 10, 1955; d. Chester James and Helen Louise (Gibson) Van Dyke; m. Morgan Lee Krotseng, June 24, 1978. BA in Spanish, Coll. of William and Mary, 1977, MEd in Ednl. Adminstrn., 1981, EdD in Higher Edn., 1987. Spanish, journalism tchr. Lancaster County Pub. Schs., Irvington, Va., 1977-79; office mgr., computer programmer SEMCO, Inc., Newport News, Va., 1979-80; Spanish, German tchr. Newport News Pub. Schs., 1980-82; rsch. asst. Coll. of William and Mary, Williamsburg, Va., 1982-87; Gov.'s fellow Office of Sec. of Edn. Commonwealth of Va., Richmond, 1984; instnl. rsch. assoc., asst. prof. higher edn. U. Miss., Oxford, 1987-89; asst. dir., planning and inst. rsch. U. Hartford, West Hartford, Conn., 1989-91; dir. rsch. and info. systems State Coll. and Univ. Systems, Charleston, W.Va., 1991—; proposal review panel mem. Assn. for Study of Higher Edn.-Ednl. Resource Info. Ctr. Higher Edn. Report Series, 1992—. Author: (chpt.) Politics and Policy in the Age of Education, 1990; co-editor: Developing Executive Information Systems in Higher Education, 1993; mem. editl. adv. bd. Ednl. Studies, 1990-93; assoc. editor Review of Higher Edn., 1991-94. Unit coord. United Way Fund Drive, Hartford, 1989, 90; choir mem., soloist First Presbyn. Ch., Charleston, 1992—; mem. Charleston Women's Forum, 1994—; mem. Leadership W.Va., 1995. Recipient Outstanding Doctoral Rsch. award Va. Poly. Inst., 1988; named one of Outstanding Young Women of Am., 1985, 86, Outstanding West Virginian, Gov. of W.V.a, 1994, Leadership W.Va., 1995. Mem. Assn. for Study of Higher Edn. (bd. dirs. 1987-90, site selection com. chair 1990-93), Am. Assn. for Higher Edn., Am. Ednl. Rsch. Assn. (program co-chair divan. J 1988-89), Assn. for Instnl. Rsch. (publs. bd. 1990-92, exec. com., forum chair 1992-94), Nat. Postsecondary Edn. Coop. Coun. on Postsecondary Edn. Stats., Phi Beta Kappa, Kappa Delta Pi (Nat. Essay award 1987). Office: State Coll and Univ Sys Ctrl Office 1018 Kanawha Blvd E Charleston WV 25301-2827

KROUSE, HELENE JUNE, nursing educator; b. Bklyn., Mar. 24, 1955; d. Sidney and Gertrude (Silver) Kempner; m. John H. Krouse, May 6, 1979; children: Beth Melissa, Daniel Jacob. BS cum laude, SUNY, Bklyn., 1976; MS, U. Rochester, 1979; PhD, Boston Coll., 1984. Staff nurse Downstate Med. Ctr., Bklyn., 1976-77; instr. in nursing Hunter Coll.-Bellevue Sch. Nursing, N.Y.C., 1979-80; asst. prof., coord. med.-surg. nursing Emmanuel Coll., Boston, 1980-84; asst. prof. nursing Boston Coll., Chestnut Hill, Mass., 1984-89; adult nurse practitioner Mass. Eye and Ear Infirmary, Boston; adminstr., nurse practitioner Fla. Ear, Nose & Throat Specialists, Ormond Beach, 1989-94; assoc. prof. U. N. Fla., Jacksonville, 1995—, acting chairperson dept. nursing, 1996-97; faculty fellow Boston Coll., 1988, rsch. fellow, 1987. Contbr. articles to profl. publs. Grantee U. Rochester Alumni Seed Found., 1978-79, Emmanuel Coll., 1981-83. Mem. Oncology Nurse Soc., Am. Cancer Soc. (svc. and rehab. com. South Essex chpt., vol. phone bank), So. Nursing Rsch. Soc., Soc. Otorhinolaryngology and Head-Neck Nurses, Inc., Sigma Theta Tau (Clin. Rsch. award 1986-87, chair nominating com., eligibility com. Alpha Chi chpt.).

KROVETZ, L. JEROME, pediatric cardiologist; b. Rochester, N.Y., Feb. 28, 1929; s. Joseph Meir and Ida (Kiner) K.; children: Tina, David, Peter, Howard. BA, Cornell U., 1950; MD, SUNY, Syracuse, 1954; PhD, U. Minn., 1963. Diplomate Am. Bd. Pediatrics. Intern SUNY, 1954-55; resident U. Minn., 1957-59; Instr., rsch. fellow U. Minn., Mpls., 1959-61; asst. prof. U. Fla., Gainesville, 1961-64, assoc. prof., 1964-67; assoc. prof. Johns Hopkins U., Balt., 1967-74; prof. U. Va., Charlottesville, 1974-79; practice medicine specializing in pediatric cardiology Hollywood, Fla., 1979—; dir. cardiovascular labs. U. Fla., 1961-67; dir. pediatric cardiovsacular labs. Johns Hopkins U., 1967-74, dir. Specialized Ctr. Rsch., 1971-74. Co-author: Handbook of Pediatric Cardiology, 2d edit., 1979; contbr. articles to profl. publs. NIH fellow, 1959-65; recipient Rsch. Career Devel. award NIH, 1965-73. Fellow Am. Acad. Pediatrics; mem. Am. Heart Assn., Sociedad Mexicana de Cardiologia (hon.), Soc. Pediatric Rsch. (emeritus). Democrat. Jewish. Office: 4340 Sheridan St Ste 201 Hollywood FL 33021-3512

KRUCKENBERG, DINA KIRSTEN, elementary educator; b. Del Rio, Tex., Jan. 29, 1970; d. Roy Dean and Marsha Lynn (Cox) K. BA in Humanities, Trinity U., 1992, MA in Teaching, 1993. Cert. tchr., Tex. 1st grade tchr. Stewart Elem. Sch., San Antonio, 1993-95; 1st and 2d grade tchr. Ogden Elem., San Antonio, 1995—; instrnl. leadership team Stewart Elem. Sch., 1994-95, Ogden Elem. Sch., 1996—, acad. coord. tchr., 1996—. Children's program dir. Alamo Heights Presbyn. Ch., San Antonio, 1989—; cmty. activist Metro Alliance, San Antonio, 1994-95. Mem. Tex. State Sci. Tchrs. Assn., Assn. Tex. Profl. Educators, Kappa Delta Pi. Presbyterian. Office: Ogden Elem Sch 2215 Leal San Antonio TX 78207

KRUEGER, ARTUR W. G., international business consultant; b. Neuendorf, Ger., Jan. 16, 1940; came to U.S., 1975; s. Werner Georg and Charlotte (Klein) K.; Betriebswirt grad., Wirtschafts-Akademie, Bremen, Ger., 1968; MS in Bus. Policy, Columbia U., 1978. Mktg. exec., gen. mgr., Rosenthal A.G. Subsidaries in Spain, Scandinavia and U.S., 1970-79; pres. Am. European Cons. Co. Inc., Houston, 1980—; lectr. in field. Mem. Am. Mgmt. Assn., Space Found., Columbia Bus. Assocs., Internat. Bus. Council, Marine Tech. Soc., Instrument Soc. Am., Houston World Trade Assn., Norwegian-Am. C. of C., U.S. C. of C., German Am. C. of C., Swiss Am. C. of C., French Am. C. of C. Office: Am European Cons Co Inc PO Box 19686 Houston TX 77224-9686

KRUEGER, CHRISTINE MARIE, vocational studies educator; b. Gary, Ind., May 11, 1957; d. Arthur John and Edna Eloise (Klepser) K. BS in Edn., Murray State U., 1979, MA in Reading, 1988. Learning disabilities tchr. McNabb Elem., Paducah, Ky., 1980, St. Mary Elem., Paducah, 1980-87, Paducah Mid. Sch., 1987-94; vocat. edn. tchr. Paducah Middle Sch., 1994—; chairperson Positive Environ. Project, Paducah, 1988-93; area dir. Ky. Spl. Olympics, Frankfort, Ky., 1984—. Pres. Plays Rely on People Support/Market House Theatre, Paducah, 1985-87; clk. ch. session First Presbyn. Ch., Paducah, 1988; coach Ky. Spl. Olympics Internat., Paducah, 1987, 91, world games coach, 1995. Named Ambassador of Good Will, State Ky., Frankfort, 1987, Outstanding Vol., Western Ky. Mental Health, Paducah, 1989, Paducah Mid. Tchr. of Yr., Ky. Dept. Edn. and Paducah Ind. Schs., Frankfort, 1990; recipient Extra Mile award Paducah Area C. of C., 1989. Mem. Ky. Edn. Assn., Paducah Edn. Assn. (spl. edn. rep. 1991-92, instr. for crisis prevention/intervention inst. 1993—, chmn. insvc. com. 1994—).

KRUG, JOHN CARLETON (TONY KRUG), college administrator, library consultant; b. Evansville, Ind., Nov. 27, 1951; s. John Elmer and Mary Ellen (Moore) K.; m. Anna Marie Waters, July 3, 1983. B.A., Ind. State U., 1972, M.L.S., 1973; Ph.D., So. Ill. U.-Carbondale, 1985. Lic. minister Baptist Ch. Exec. dir. Olney (Ill.) Carnegie Pub. Libr., 1973-74; assoc. dean Wabash Valley Coll., Mt. Carmel, Ill., 1974-84; mem. Com. for U.S. Depository State Plan, Springfield, Ill., 1982-84; dir. librs. Maryville Coll., St. Louis, 1984-88; dir. libr. Bethany (W.Va.) Coll., 1988—; sec. pro-tem Ill. Basin Coal Mining Manpower Council, Mt. Carmel, 1974-79; mem. governing bd. exec. com. Higher Edn. Ctr. Cable TV, 1986-88. Author: Libraries Using/Planning for Microcomputers, 1986; also computer programs. Vice pres. bd. dirs. Wabash Area Vocat. Enterprises, Mt. Carmel, 1979-81; mem. bd. edn. Wabash Community Unit, Mt. Carmel, 1980-83; mem. exec. com. Community Edn. and Arts Assn., Carbondale, 1983-84; mem. visual arts adv. com. Ill. Arts Council, Chgo., 1982-84; pastor Hopewell United Meth. Ch., Bridgeport, Ill., 1976-77; lic. minister Terre Haute 1st Bapt. Ch. (Ind.), 1972—; elder Gateway Christian Ch., 1986-88; bd. dirs. Fair Haven Christian Sch., 1986-88. Conf. speaker Kans. State U., 1982. Mem. ALA, W.Va. Libr. Assn., Nat. Assn. for Preservation and Perpetuation of Storytelling, Pitts. Regional Libr. Ctr. Mem. Christian Ch. Home: PO Box 208 Bethany WV 26032-0208 Office: Bethany Coll T W Phillips Meml Libr Bethany WV 26032

KRUKONES, MICHAEL GEORGE, political science educator; b. Chgo., Nov. 3, 1944; s. George Henry and Bernice Barbara (Rozenski) K. B.S., Loyola U., Chgo., 1966; M.A., U. Minn., 1969; Ph.D., Miami U., Oxford, Ohio, 1979. Instr. U. Wis.-River Falls, 1969-72; research assoc. Computer Horizons, Chgo., 1973; teaching fellow Miami U., 1973-76; asst. prof. Ball State U., Muncie, Ind., 1976-79; assoc. prof. polit. sci. Bellarmine Coll., Louisville, 1979-85, prof., 1985—. Author: Promises and Performance: Presidential Campaigns as Policy Predictors, 1984. Contbr. articles to profl. jours. Bd. dirs. Highlands Ct. Inc., Louisville, 1983—. Mem. Am. Polit. Sci. Assn., Midwest Polit. Sci. Assn., Acad. Polit. Sci., Am. Acad. Polit. and Social Sci., Ctr. Study of Presidency. Democrat. Roman Catholic. Avocations: classical music, theater, reading. Office: Bellarmine Coll Dept Polit Sci Newburg Rd Louisville KY 40205

KRUPA, PATRICIA ANN, nurse, consultant; b. Floral Park, N.Y., Nov. 3, 1937; d. James Joseph and Jessie M. (Steinmann) Hynes; m. John W. Krupa, Nov. 5, 1960; children: John W. III, James J., Daniel C. Diploma, St. Johns Episc. Sch. Nursing, Bklyn., 1959; student, Nassau Community Coll., Garden City, N.Y.; BS in Community Mental Health, N.Y. Inst. Tech., Greenvale, 1992. Lic. nurse, N.Y., S.C. Rehab. nurse Jordan Rehab., Carle Place, N.Y., 1981-85; family counselor Plainview (N.Y.) Alcohol Rehab., 1989-90; discharge planner Winthrop U. Hosp., Mineola, N.Y., 1987-91; with Community Long Term Care, Mt. Pleasant, S.C., 1991—; mem. adv. bd. Berkley County Adult Protective Svcs.; co-chmn. Low Country Aids Svcs. Mem. N.Y. State Hospice Assn., St. John's Episcopal Hosp. Sch. Nursing Alumnae, Psi Chi. Home: 2049 Country Manor Dr Mount Pleasant SC 29464-7409 Office: Cmty Long Term Care 751 Johnnie Dodds Blvd # A Mount Pleasant SC 29464-3026

KRUSCHWITZ, ROBERT BRUCE, philosophy educator; b. Louisville, July 2, 1953; s. Verlin Corres and Ruth Elizabeth (Bostick) K.; m. Vicki Barron, Jan. 7, 1978. BA, Georgetown Coll., 1975; PhD, U. Tex., 1979. Prof. philosophy Georgetown (Ky.) Coll., 1979—; younger scholars award dir. NEH, 1995. Editor: The Virtues, 1987. Ethics com. Scott County Hosp., Georgetown, 1993—; vol. Habitat for Humanity, Scott County, 1990—; moderator Faith Baptist Ch., Georgetown, 1986—, deacon, 1983-85, pastor search com., 1985, 95, administrative com., 1984—. Grantee Ky. Humanities Coun., 1988. Mem. Soc. Christian Philosophers, Soc. Study Contemporary Visual Arts, Baptist Assn. Philosophy Tchrs. (sec.-treas. 1988—), Ky. Philosophical Assn. (pres. 1986-87), Ky. Philological Assn. Office: Georgetown Coll 400 E College St Georgetown KY 40324-1628

KRYSTEK, DENNIS JOHN, liberal arts educator; b. Chgo., Feb. 26, 1951; s. Daniel J. and Julia M. Krystek; m. Patricia G. Krystek. AA, Cypress (Calif.) Coll., 1975; BA, Calif. State U., Long Beach, 1977; JD, Loyola U., New Orleans, 1981; PhD, U. New Orleans, 1990. Bargaining unit chmn. United Auto Workers Union, L.A., 1970-78; pvt. practice law New Orleans, 1981-85; asst. prof. polit. sci. U. So. Miss., Long Beach, 1988—, dir. Gulf Park Poll, 1990—; polit. cons. Krystek & Assocs., Long Beach, 1992—; legal cons. City of Gretna, La., 1987; corp. dir. United Auto Workers Local 923 Credit Union, L.A., 1975-78; lectr. in field. Book reviewer coll. textbooks, 1988—; contbr. articles to profl. jours. Polit. envoy State of Miss. Havana, Cuba, 1994. Tchg./rsch. asst. U. New Orleans, 1985-88; Nat. Ctr. for State Cts. rsch. grantee, 1986; Loyola U.-New Orleans scholar, 1978-81. Mem. Am. soc. Pub. Adminstrn. (Miss. chpt. dir. 1995-96), La. State Bar Assn., Gulf Coast C. of C. (leadership seminar presenter 1996), Pi Sigma Alpha. Roman Catholic. Home: 15046 Pawnee Pl Kiln MS 39556 Office: University of Southern Mississippi 730 E Beach Blvd Long Beach MS 39560-6259

KRZYZEWSKI, MIKE, university athletic coach. Head coach U.S. Mil. Acad., West Point, N.Y., 1975-80, Duke U. Blue Devils, Durham, N.C., 1980—. Named Nat. Coach of Yr., 4 times. Office: Duke Univ Cameron Indoor Stadium Durham NC 27708-0556

KUBACAK, LAWRENCE DON, energy efficient design and construction company executive; b. Temple, Tex., Mar. 13, 1959; s. August Lawrence and Rita Jean (Kubacak); m. Janet Lee Fuchs (div.); 1 child, Tiffanie Brooke; m. Jeanne Lynn Hobson, June 24, 1984; children: Kristopher Larson, Matthew James, Courtney Jean, Jonathan Whitney, Makenzie Gayle. B of Environmental Design, Tex. A&M U., 1981. Pres. Four Seasons Landscape Co., College Station, Tex., 1982-85; v.p. Nantucket, Ltd., College Station, 1985-89; pres. Kubacak, Inc. Construction, College Station, 1989—, Brazos Valley's Premier Painting Co., 1996—; mem. adv. bd. First Fed. Savs. Bank, Bryan, 1992—. Bd. dirs. College Station Conf. Ctr., 1990-92; mem. adv. bd. Salvation Army, Bryan/College Station, 1994—, chmn. bldg. com. Mem. Nat. Assn. Home Builders (bd. dirs. 1991—, chmn. scholarship and edn. 1991-92, cert. of merit 1991-93, nat. dir. 1994-95, sec.-treas. 1995-96, v.p. 1996—), Tex. A&M U. Former Students Assn., Lions (bd. dirs. College Station club 1992—, Melvin Jones fellow 1994). Republican. Home: PO Box 10475 College Station TX 77842-0475 Office: Kubacak Inc Construction PO Box 10475 College Station TX 77842-0475

KUBE, HAROLD DEMING, retired financial executive; b. Buffalo, Wyo., June 16, 1910; s. Carl Christen and Inez (Mather) K.; m. Shirley Smith; children: Robert Ford, Thomas Smith. BS, U. Nebr., 1932; MBA, Harvard U., 1934. Owner Beef Cattle Farm, Warrenton, Va., 1950—; co-owner Resources Devel. Assocs., 1965-80; dir. emeritus Jefferson Savs. and Loan Assn., Warrenton, 1980—, Greater Washington Investors, Inc., 1987—; bd. dirs. A & K Land and Cattle Corp., Warrenton. Co-author: Manufacturing Distribution in U.S., 1938. With USN, 1944-46. Mem. Am. Econ. Assn. Episcopalian. Home and Office: 6470 Beverleys Mill Rd Broad Run VA 20137-2101

KUBIAK, DANIEL J., state legislator; b. Reagan, Tex., Mar. 19, 1938; s. John and Connie Kubiak; children: Kelly Dan, Alyssa Lea, Kody Earl. AA, Blinn Coll., Brenham, Tex., 1959; BBA, U. Tex., 1962, PhD, 1974; MEd, Midwestern U., 1968. Tchr., coach Vernon (Tex.) Pub. Schs., 1962-63,

Cypress-Fairbanks Pub. Schs., Houston, 1963-68; state rep. dist. 27 and 36 State of Tex., 1969-83, state rep. dist. 13, 1991—; pres., CEO Kubiak and Assocs., 1990—. Author: Ten Tall Texans, 1967, Monument to a Black Man, 1972; contbr. articles to profl. jours. Sr. adv. com. Alcohol Fuels of Tex., 1984; bd. dirs. Rockdale Christian Svcs., 1989-90; adv. bd. Tex. Dept. Agriculture, 1989-90, farmers adv. coun., 1984; mem. devel. coun. A&M Coll. Edn., 1993. Recipient Personalities of the South award, 1969, Disting. Svc. award Tex. Legis., 1970, Cert. of Appreciation, Calvert Tex. Chamber, 1971, Spl. award Tex. Indsl. Vocat. Assn., 1976, Cert. of Appreciation, Taylor Optimist Club, 1978, Spl. award Tex. Chiropractic Assn., 1979-82, Disting Svc. award Tex. Farmers Union, 1981, Milam County Businessman of Yr. award, 1984, Friend of Extension Home Econs. award, 1992, Outstanding Leadership award Ind. Cattleman's Assn., 1993, Legislator of Yr. award Tex. Pub. Employees Assn., 1993, Common Cause Star of Tex. Pub. Svc. Award, 1993, Wildlife Conservation award Tex. Sportsman's Assn., 1994, Legislator of Yr. award Tex. 4-H, 1994; named Man of Yr., Agriculture-Tex. County Agts. Assn., 1981; John T. Burton scholar, 1963; and others. Mem. Am. Traders Internat. (pres. 1989-90), Tex. Assn. Health Occupations (student adv. com. 1976-77), Tex. Air Nat. Guard (hon. life), Ctrl. Tex. Pvt. Industry Coun., Univ. Coop. Soc., Inc. (bd. dirs. 1961-62, 79), Midwestern U. Alumni Assn. (Disting. Alumni award 1982), C/T Cattlemen's Market Assn. (bd. dirs. 1985), Rockdale Community Action Assn. (pres. 1988-90),. Home: 223 Ackerman St Rockdale TX 76567-2901

KUBIC, FRANK, author, industrial engineer; b. N.Y.C., Feb. 16, 1926; s. Thomas and Anna (Dzur) K.; m. Anne Bovee McGowan, Feb. 7, 1959; children: Leslie Anne, Thomas Steven, Peter Francis, Elizabeth Bovee, Christopher Bovee, David Andrew. BSBA, Tri-State U., Angola, Ind., 1953; MBA, Siena Coll., Loudonville, N.Y., 1960. Engr. IBM, Kingston, N.Y., 1956-61; tng. office med. methods Washington Hosp. Ctr., 1961-65; dir. quality control and engring. U.S. Dept. of State, Washington, 1965-88. Author and epigramist For Nuggets of Wisdom-Books, 1990—. Served with USN, 1943-46, PTO. Known internationaly as "The Father of The Machine Readable Passport". Address: Nuggets of Wisdom Books PO Box 8 Rippon WV 25441-0008

KUCERA, LOUIS STEPHEN, virology educator; b. New Prague, Minn., June 23, 1935; s. Stanley Thomas and Helen Henrietta (Janda) K.; m. JoAnn Dorothy Martinson, Aug. 22, 1959; children: Gregory, Gary, Stephen, Scott. BS, St. John's U., 1957; MS, Creighton U., 1959; PhD, U. Mo., 1964. Postdoctorate Mayo Clinic, Rochester, Minn., 1964-66; postdoctorate St. Jude Children's Hosp., Memphis, 1966-68, asst. mem., 1968-70; asst. prof. microbiology Bowman Gray Sch. Medicine, Winston Salem, N.C., 1970-74, assoc. prof., 1974-80, prof., 1980—; rsch. cons. NIH, Bethesda, Md., 1980—, N.C. Assn. for Biomed. Rsch., Research Triangle Park, 1985—. Author: Fundamentals of Medical Virology, 1974, 2d edit., 1985. With U.S. Army, 1959-60. Rsch. grantee NIH, 1973—. Mem. Am. Soc. for Microbiology, Am. Soc. for Virology, Internat. Soc. Antiviral Rsch., Internat. Soc. for AIDS Rsch. Roman Catholic. Office: Bowman Gray Sch Medicine Medical Center Blvd Winston Salem NC 27157

KUDRAVETZ, DAVID WALLER, lawyer; b. Sumter, S.C., Feb. 2, 1948; s. George and Barbara (Waller) K.; m. Eleanor McCrea Snyder, June 21, 1969; 1 child, Julia McCrea. BS, U. Va., 1971, JD, 1974. Bar: Va. 1974, U.S. Tax Ct. 1974; CPA, Va. Assoc. Robert M. Musselman, Charlottesville, Va., 1974; ptnr. Carwile & Kudravetz, Charlottesville, Va., 1975-78, McClure, Callaghan & McCallum, Charlottesville, Va., 1979-81, McCallum & Kudravetz, P.C., Charlottesville, Va., 1982—; instr. fed. income taxation U. of Va. Sch. Continuing Edn., 1975-79. Mem. AICPA, Va. State Bar Assn., Charlottesville-Albemarle Bar Assn., Am. Assn. Atty.-CPAs, Va. Soc. CPAs. Home: PO Box 162 Earlysville VA 22936-0162 Office: McCallum & Kudravetz PC 250 E High St PO Box 224 Charlottesville VA 22902

KUEBLER, DAVID WAYNE, insurance company executive; b. New Orleans, Apr. 18, 1947; s. Royce Matthew and Rosemary (West) K.; children: Kendra Leigh, Krystal Lynn, Kira Louise. B. in Bus. Mgmt., Loyola U., New Orleans, 1969. Lic. ins. broker, investment mgr., CLU. Asst. mgr. Winn-Dixie, Inc., New Orleans, 1962-69; account exec. Travelers Ins. Co., St. Louis, 1969-74; sr. account exec. Gen. Am. Life., St. Louis, 1974-76; dist. mgr. Guardian Life Ins., New Orleans, 1976-81; pres. Profl. Planners, Inc., Kenner, La., 1981—; asst. chief of staff civil mil. ops. 377 Taacom, New Orleans, 1987. Coach girls athletics, Metairie, La., 1987. Col. USAR. Mem. Internat. Assn. Fin. Planners, Nat. Assn. Life Underwriters, New Orleans Assn. Life Underwriters, Million Dollar Round Table, Met Plus Group Millionaires. Democrat. Roman Catholic. Home: 29 Chateau Haut-brion Dr Kenner LA 70065-2062 Office: Profl Planners Inc PO Box 640877 Kenner LA 70064-0877

KUEHN, RONALD L., JR., natural resources company executive; b. Bklyn., Apr. 6, 1935; m. Allison Spencer, June 7, 1986; children: Kathleen, Kelly, Erin, Coleen, Shannon, Caroline, Ronald L. III. B.S., Fordham U., 1957, LL.B., 1964. Bar: N.Y. 1964. Assoc. Hughes, Hubbard & Reed, N.Y.C., 1964-68; exec. v.p., gen. counsel Allied Artists Pictures, N.Y.C., 1968-70; v.p., gen. counsel, sec. So. Natural Resources, Inc., Birmingham, Ala., 1970-79, exec. v.p., 1979-81; pres., chief operating officer Sonat Inc., 1982-83, pres., 1982—, chief exec. officer, 1983—, chmn., 1986—, also bd. dirs.; bd. dirs. Transocean Offshore, Inc., Sonat Exploration Co., So. Natural Gas Co., Union Carbide Corp., AmSouth Bancorp., Protective Life Corp., Praxair Inc.; trustee Tuskegee U., So. Rsch. Inst. Trustee Boys Club Am., Birmingham-So. Coll.; bd. dirs. area council Boy Scouts Am.; mem. pres.'s council U. Ala.-Birmingham. 1st lt. U.S. Army, 1958-59. Mem. ABA, N.Y. State Bar Assn., Assn. of Bar of City of N.Y., Fed. Energy Bar Assn., Newcomen Soc. of U.S., Bretton Woods Com., Gas Rsch. Inst. (bd. dirs.), Interstate Natural Gas Assn. (bd. dirs.), Nat. Petroleum Coun. Roman Catholic. Office: Sonat Inc 1900 5th Ave N Birmingham AL 35203-2610

KUEHN, THOMAS, history educator; b. Chgo., Apr. 10, 1950; s. Clifford Henry and Vivian (Mamczarz) K.; m. Linda Wood Berri, Sept. 2, 1972 (div. Nov. 1987); 1 child, Allison Berri. BA, Carleton Coll., 1972; MA, U. Chgo., 1973, PhD, 1977. Asst. prof. Reed Coll., Portland, Oreg., 1977-81; asst. prof. history Clemson (S.C.) U., 1981-84, assoc. prof., 1984-91, prof., 1991—. Author: Emancipation in Late Medieval Florence, 1982, Law, Family, and Women, 1991; co-editor: Western Societies, 2 vols., 1993; also articles. Summer fellow NEH, 1978, 89. Mem. Am. Hist. Assn., Renaissance Soc., Medieval Acad., Soc. for Italian Hist. Studies (counselor 1984—), 16th Century Studies. Office: Clemson U Dept History Hardin Hall Clemson SC 29634

KUEHNEL, JEAN, humanities educator; b. Milw., Oct. 5, 1964; d. Reno Walter and Rebecca (Pederson) K. BA magna cum laude, Lakeland Coll., 1987; MFA, Wichita State U., 1990. Writing lab. asst. Wichita (Kans.) State U., 1989, grad. teaching asst., 1987-90, lecturer, 1989; instr. Tri-County Tech. Coll., S.C., 1990-91, Clemson U., S.C., 1990-93; asst. prof. Clemson U., 1993—; grant writing, mktg. project devel., Clemson U., 1992—, reporter WKTS Radio Station, Sheboygan Wis., 1987; workshop leader various colls. Editor: The Green Laker, Ripon Wis., 1987, co-editor: The Mirror, Lakeland Coll., 1986-87; author short stories and poems. Chair. mkgt., mem. state coun., Visions for Youth Project, Clemson, S.C., 1992—. Recipient Teaching award Creative Writing Wichita State U., 1990, Gold Pen award Lakeland Coll., 1987. Home: 285 Seneca Springs Ldg Seneca SC 29678-5427 Office: 612 Strode Towers Clemson SC 29634

KUEHNERT, HAROLD ADOLPH, retired petroleum geologist; b. St. Louis, July 13, 1922; s. Theodore Julius Christian and Anna Marie (Lautner) K.; m. Elizabeth Jane Pirtle, Apr. 8, 1945 (dec. 1991); children: John Harold, James Charles, Thomas Alan; m. Mary-Kay Mummert, May 21, 1994. BS in Geology, Northwestern U., 1948. Cert. profl. geologist. Geologist Phillips Petroleum Co., Evansville, Ind., 1948-52, Salt Lake City, 1952-54; geologist Phillips Petroleum Co., Denver, 1954-61, divsn. devel. geologist, 1961-62; divsn. geologist Phillips Petroleum Co., Wichita Falls, Tex., 1962-63; divsn. exploration geologist Phillips Petroleum Co., Oklahoma City, 1963-65, region exploration dir. midcontinent region, 1965-69; exploration mgr. Rocky Mountain divsn. Phillips Petroleum Co., Denver, 1969-73; dir. exploration projects sect. Phillips Petroleum Co., Bartlesville, Okla., 1973-85. Flotilla staff officer USCG Aux., Decatur, Ala., 1995, 96. 2d lt. pilot USAAF, 1943-45. Mem. Am. Assn. Petroleum Geologists, Am. Inst. Profl. Geologists (charter), Ala. Geol. Soc. Home: 1541 Blackhall Ln SE Decatur AL 35601

KUERLEY-SCHAFFER, DAWN R., medical/surgical nurse; b. Bay City, Mich., June 8, 1959; d. Edward J. and Leaella Mae (Jacob) Kuerley; m. Michael B. Schaffer, May 30, 1986; 1 child, Randi Lea. Lic. practical nurse, Bay Practical Nurse Ctr., 1980; ADNB, Alpena Community Coll., 1986. RN. Mich., La., 1994. Practical nurse Tawas St. Joseph Hosp., Tawas City, Mich., staff nurse; RN, clinic head nurse Neurosurgery Tulane U. Med. Ctr., New Orleans. Clark Sawyer meml. scholar. Mem. Assn. Operating Room Nurses (cert. operating room nurse), Alpena Cmty. Coll. ADN Alumni Assn. (past pres.).

KUFELDT, JAMES, retail grocery store executive; b. 1938; married. BA, Anderson Coll., 1960. Store mgr. Winn-Dixie Stores Inc., Jacksonville, Fla., 1961-71, produce merchandising, then retail ops. supt., 1971-79, v.p., 1979-83, sr. v.p., 1983—, now pres., dir. Office: Winn-Dixie Stores Inc PO Box B Jacksonville FL 32203-0297*

KUHAIDA, ANDREW JEROME, JR., environmental manager; b. Wheeling, W.Va., Sept. 29, 1942; s. Andrew Jerome Sr. and Wilma Pauline (Liller); m. Delores Newman, June 1967; children: Steven A., Carrie A., Kevin J. BS in Geography, East Tenn. State U., 1967, MA in Geography, 1971; PhD in Geography/Geology, U. Denver, 1980. Registered profl. geologist. Group leader energy div. Oak Ridge (Tenn.) Nat. Lab., 1976-78; cons. Denver, 1979-80; sr. geographer sci. div. Henningson, Durham & Richardson, Knoxville, Tenn., 1980-81; from environ. sci. FUSRAP project to sr. scientist Bechtel Nat., Inc., Oak Ridge, 1981-88; project mgr. hazardous waste remedial action program Martin Marietta Energy Systems, Oak Ridge, 1988-90; from tech. coord. to mgr. tech. integration, policy and planning, environ. restoration program Lockheed Martin Energy Sys., 1990—. Bd. dirs., v.p. Woodland Neighborhood Assn., 1988-91; mem. Tenn. Mcpl. League, Transp. Policy Com., 1992, 93, Environ. Resources Policy Com., 1994, 95, Nat. League of Cities Energy, Environ. and Natural Resources Steering Com., 1994, 95; coach Oak Ridge Boxing Assn., 1981-84, bd. dirs., 1982-84, 88; coach Oak Ridge Boys Club, 1981-85, 89, Oak Ridge Baseball Assn., 1986-87; mem. environ. quality adv. bd. City of Oak Ridge, 1988, chmn., 1989-92, coun. mem., 1991-95, fin. audit com., 1991—, local oversight com., 1991—, city mgr. evaluation com., 1991-92, chmn. bd. and commn. attendance policy com., 1992—, city employee compensation policy com., 1992—. Named outstanding alumni U. Denver Geography Dept., 1989, 94. Mem. Geol. Soc. Am., Sigma Xi, Bechtel Employees Club of Oak Ridge (v.p. 1986, pres. 1987). Home: 107 Pembroke Rd Oak Ridge TN 37830-7516

KUHLER, RENALDO GILLET, museum official, scientific illustrator; b. Teaneck, N.J., Nov. 21, 1931; s. Otto August and Simonne L. (Gillet) K.; BA, U. Colo., 1961. Curator of history, illustrator exhibit and miniature diorama preparator Eastern Wash. State Hist. Soc. Mus., Spokane, 1962-67; mus. illustrator N.C. State Mus. Natural History, Raleigh, 1969—; designer, executor of art work for sci. illustrations, awards, brochures, pamphlets and periodicals Dept. Agr. and Mus., N.C., 1972-74; designer 36 illustrations for Handbook of Reptiles and Amphibians of Florida, Part 1 (Ray E. Ashton), 1981; contbr. many illustrations, Atlas of Freshwater Fishes of North America (David Lee), Endangered Threatened and Rare Fauna of N.C. (Ross, Rohde and Lindquist), Distribution Survey of N.C. Mammals (Lee, Funderburg and Clark); Endangered Threatened and Rare Fauna of N.C., part 1, (Mary K. Clark), Potential Effect of Oil Spills on Seabirds, etc. (Lee and Socci), Poisonous Snakes of N.C. (William M. Palmer), Reptiles of North Carolina (William M. Palmer and Alvin Braswell); gen. illustrator: American Firearms and the Changing Frontier (Waldo E. Rosebush); also contbr. to jours. and bulls.; calligrapher; creator wood handicrafts; violin maker, 1949. Mem. Nat. Trust Historic Preservation. Democrat. Avocations: experimenting with laminated paper and models of ships and trains, carburator fittings for smoking pipes, hiking. Office: NC State Mus Natural Scis 102 N Salisbury Raleigh NC 27611-7647

KUHN, ANNE NAOMI WICKER (MRS. HAROLD B. KUHN), foreign language educator; b. Lynchburg, Va.; d. George Barnett and Annie (Hicks) Wicker; m. Harold B. Kuhn. Diploma Malone Coll., 1933, Trinity Coll. Music, London, 1937; AB, John Fletcher Coll., 1939; MA, Boston U., 1942, postgrad., 1965-70; postgrad. (fellow) Harvard U., 1942-44, 66-68; hon. grad. Asbury Coll., 1978. Instr., Emmanuel Bible Coll., Birkenhead, Eng., 1936-37; asst. in history John Fletcher Coll., University Park, Iowa, 1938-39; librarian Harvard U., 1939-44; tchr. adult edn. program U.S. Armed Forces, Fuerstenfeldbruck Air Base, Germany, 1951-52; prof. Union Bibl. Sem., Yeotmal, India, 1957-58; lectr. Armenian Bible Inst., Beirut, Lebanon, 1958; prof. German, Asbury Coll., Wilmore, Ky., 1962—, co-dir. coll. study tour to East Germany and West Germany, 1976, 77, 78, co-dir. acad. tours, 1979, 80; dir. acad. tour, Russia, 1981, 85, Scandanavia, 1982, Indonesia, Singapore, 1983, Hong Kong and Thailand, 1983, 85, East Germany, West Germany, France and Austria, 1983, Russia and Finland, 1984, 85, 89, China, 1979, 84, 85, 89, Estonia, Latvia, 1985, 89, Poland, 1989, 91, 92, Portugal, Spain, France, Ireland, Scotland, Norway, England, 1987, The Balkans, Hungary, Czech Republic, Slovak Republic, Bulgaria, Romania and Turkey, 1992, alumni academic tour Malta, Sicily, Greece, Macedonia, 1995; tchr. Seoul Theol. Sem., fall 1978. Author: (pamphlet) The Impact of the Transition to Modern Education Upon Religious Education, 1950; The Influence of Paul Gerhardt upon Wesleyan Hymnody, 1960, Light to Dispel Fear, 1987; transl. German ch. records, poems, letters; contbr. articles to profl. jours. Del. Youth for Christ World Conf., 1948, 50, London Yearly Meeting of Friends, Edinburgh, Scotland, 1948, World Council Chs., Amsterdam, 1948, World Friends Conf., Oxford, Eng., 1952, World Methodist Conf., Oslo, Norway, 1961, Deutscher Kirchentag, Dortmund, Germany, 1963, German Lang. Congress, Bonn, W. Ger., 1974, Internat. Conf. Religion, Amsterdam, Netherlands, Poland, West Berlin, Fed. Republic Germany, 1986, Internat. Missionary Conf., Eng., 1987, Congress on the Bible II, Washington, 1987; participant Internat. Congress World Evangelization, Lausanne, Switzerland, 1974; del., speaker Internat. Conf. on Holocaust and Genocide, Oxford and London, 1988; speaker Founders Week Malone Coll., Ohio, 1989, Nat. Quaker Conf., Denver; mem. acad. tour Poland, 1988; vol. of various special assignments in Ctrl. and Eastern Europe. Recipient German Consular award, Boston, 1965, Thomas Mann award Boston U., 1967; named Ky. Col., 1978. Fellow Goethe-Institut for Germanisten, Munich, 1966-68, 70-71. Mem. AAUW, Am. Assn. Tchrs. German, NEA, Ky. Ednl. Assn., Lincoln Lit. Soc., Protestant Women of Chapel, Harvard Univ. Faculty Club (Cambridge, Mass.), Harvard Univ. Club Eastern and Ctrl. Ky. (Lexington), United Daughters of the Confederacy, Delta Phi Alpha (award 1963, 65). Mem. Soc. of Friends. Home: 406 Kenyon Ave Wilmore KY 40390-1033

KUHN, BOWIE K., lawyer, former professional baseball commissioner, consultant; b. Takoma Park, Md., Oct. 28, 1926; m. Luisa Hegeler; four children. B.A., Princeton, 1947; LL.B., U. Va., 1950. Bar: N.Y. 1951, U.S. Supreme Ct. 1972. With firm Willkie, Farr & Gallagher, N.Y.C.; legal counsel several baseball clients, 1950-69, rep. Maj. League club owners in negotiations with Maj. League Players Assn., 1968, commr. pro tempore of baseball, 1969, commr., 1969-84; of counsel Willkie, Farr & Gallagher, 1984-87; former ptnr. Myerson & Kuhn, N.Y.C., 1988-89; pres. The Kent Group Inc., Ponte Vedra Beach, Fla., 1990—, Sports Franchises, Inc., Milford, Conn., 1992—. Author: Hardball: The Education of a Baseball Commissioner, 1987. Office: The Kent Group Inc 136 Teal Point Ln Ponte Vedra Beach FL 32082-1935

KUHN, JAMES E., judge; b. Hammond, La., Oct. 31, 1946; s. Eton Percy and Mildred Louise (McDaniel) K.; m. Cheryl Aucoin, Dec. 27, 1969; children: James M., Jennifer L. BA, Southeastern La. U., 1968; JD, Loyola U. of South, 1973. Bar: La. 1973, Colo., U.S. Supreme Ct. 1978. Asst. dist. atty. 21st Jud. Dist. La., 1979-90; judge 21st Jud. Dist. Ct., Livinston, St. Helena, Tangipahoa, 1990-95; judge Ct. Appeals (1st cir.) Baton Rouge, 1995—; instr. history, govt. and criminal justice Southeastern La. U., Hammond, 1991—; lectr. in field. Founder For Our Youth; bd. dirs. La. Coun. Child Abuse, elected sec.-treas. Cong. of Ct. Appeal Judges for State of La. Mem. ABA, La. State Bar Assn. (Professionalism and Quality of Life com.), 21st Jud. Bar Assn., Livingston Parish Bar Assn., La. Supreme Ct. Appellate Cts. Performance Standards Commn. (judges tng. com.), Delta Theta Phi. Home: 8178 Hermitage Dr Denham Springs LA 70726-6224

KUHN, JOHN MARK, computer company executive, educator; b. Arlington, Va., Nov. 27, 1955; s. Thomas Edward and Mary Ella (Walker) K.; m. Linda Gayle Landry, Sept. 11, 1979; children: Jennifer Leigh, John Mathew. AS, Southeastern La. U., 1980, BA, 1981. V.p. Odessa (Tex.) Data Co., Inc., 1981—, N.A. Ednl. Systems Corp., Odessa, 1983—; instr. Odessa Coll., 1983—; commr. Grandfalls Housing Authority, 1983-86; mayor City of Grandfalls, 1986-92. Chmn. congregation bd. Grandfalls Union Ch., 1985-95; alderman City of Grandfalls City Coun., 1985-86, 94—; bd. dirs. Permian Basin Pvt. Industry Coun., 1992—, pres., 1995—; vol. fireman Grandfalls Vol. Fire Dept., 1986—, emergency med. technician, 1987—. Lodge: Optimists (bd. dirs. Odessa chpt. 1984-86). Home: PO Box 413 Grandfalls TX 79742-0413 Office: Odessa Data Co Inc 10200 W Us Highway 80 Midland TX 79706-2611

KUKLA, JON (KEITH), historian, museum director; b. Hustisford, Wis., Oct. 20, 1948; s. James George and Marion Ruth (Woelm) K.; m. Jeanette Margita Vos, May 30, 1970 (div. Dec. 1991); children: Amy Marie, Jennifer Anne; m. Kathryn Fay Prechter, Oct. 30, 1993; 1 child, Elizabeth Ross. AB in History with honors, Carthage Coll., 1970, MA in History, U. Toronto, Ont., Can., 1971, PhD in History, 1980. Rsch. asst. State Archivist of Va., 1973-74; editor Va. Cavalcade mag. Va. State Libr., 1974-76; dir. publs. Va. State Libr. and Archives, 1976-90; curator collections Hist. New Orleans Collection, 1990-92, dir., 1992—; tchr. U. Richmond, Va. Commonwealth U., U. New Orleans; vis. instr. history Carthage Coll., 1973; hist. advisor Spkr. of Ho. of Dels., and Gen. Assembly's Joint Subcom. on 200th Anniversary of Capitol of Va., 1984-90; hist. advisor Citizens Adv. Coun. Interpreting and Furnishing Exec. Mansion Va., 1985-90; mus. cons. Yorktown Victory Ctr., Jamestown-Yorktown Found., 1989-93, co-dir. summer inst. Bill of Rights secondary and mid.-sch. tchrs., 1992; exhbn. evaluator La. State Mus., 1991; exhbn. curator Over Here! The New Orleans Home Front in World War II, 1992; mem. prize jury 3d ann. mus. prize Am. Assn. Mus., 1992; mem. vis. com. visual arts dept. Loyola U., 1993—, chair curriculum subcom., 1994; mem. Jamestown Rediscovery Adv. Com., 1993—; spkr. in field. Author: Speakers and Clerks of the Virginia House of Burgesses, 1643-1776, 1981, Political Institutions in Virginia, 1619-1660, 1989, (with Elizabeth R. Herbener) The General Assembly of Virginia, 11 January 1978-27 April 1989: A Register of Members, 1990; editor, contbr.: The Bill of Rights: A Lively Heritage, 1987; editor: (with John T. Kneebone) A Key to Survey Reports and Microfilm of the Virginia Colonial Records Project, 2 vols., 1990; prodr. (documentary) The Long Weekend, 1993; mem. adv. coun. Biographical Dictionary of Early Pennsylvania Legislators, 1984-90; mem. editorial adv. bd. Va. Mag. History and Biography, 1982-84; The Papers of Sir William Berkeley, 1989—; contbr. chpts. to books and articles to profl. jours. Mem. state rev. bd. Va. Hist. Landmarks Commn., 1979-86, vice-chair, 1980-83, 87, chair, 1983-86; mem. gov.'s planning com. bicentennial of U.S. Constn. U. Va. Inst. Govt., 1982-85; mem. selection com. Va. Ctr. Humanities, 1986-87; mem. steering com. La. Ctr. Book, 1993—; bd. dirs. Va. Co. Found., 1989-92, mem. exec. com., 1989-90. Travel-to-Collections grantee NEH, 1984; fellow U. Toronto, 1970-71. Mem. Am. Hist. Assn. (mem. program com. 1987, Michael Kraus rsch. grantee 1991-92), Nat. Trust Hist. Preservation, Va. Hist. Soc., La. Hist. Soc. (chair by-laws com. 1993, chair Kemper Williams prize com. 1994—), La. Assn. Mus. (mem. coun. 1991-93), So. Hist. Assn. (mem. program com. 1985, mem. membership com. 1992), Assn. Documentary Editing (dir. publs. 1979-80, mem. coun. 1979-80, mem. publs. com. 1981-83, mem. edn. com. 1986-87). Lutheran. Office: Hist New Orleans Collection 533 Royal St New Orleans LA 70130-2113

KUKURA, RITA ANNE, elementary school educator; b. Tulsa, July 18, 1947; d. James Albert and Carmen Alberta (Parsons) Hayden; m. Joel Richard Graft, Oct. 28, 1967 (dec. Apr. 1969); m. Raymond Richard Kukura, Dec. 18, 1971 (div. 1981); children: Tiffany Carmen Noel, Austin Raymond. BS, Kent. State U., 1971; MS, Okla. State U., 1991. Cert. early childhood, nursery, elem. tchr., Okla., spl. edn. tchr. for emotionally disturbed. Tchr. kindergarten Southlyn Elem. Sch., Lyndhurst, Ohio, 1971-73; elem. tchr. Wakefield Acad., Tulsa, 1981-83, tchr. kindergarten, 1983-87; reg. early intervention coord. Okla. Dept. Edn., Tulsa, 1990-92; tchr. devel. delayed children, coord. integrated program Child Devel. Inst. Children's Med. Ctr., Tulsa, 1992-93; tchr. elem. sch. Prue (Okla.) Schs., 1993-95, Tulsa Pub. Schs., 1995—; manuscript reviewer for profl. orgns., 1989-91; mem. human rights com. Ind. Opportunities of Okla., 1995—; del. Okla. Edn. Assembly, 1995; grant reviewer for spl. grants State Dept. Edn., 1996; presenter and lectr. in field. Den leader Cub Scouts Am., Tulsa, 1984-88; com. mem. Boy Scouts Am., Tulsa, 1984-88; vol. officer worker Met. Tulsa Citizen Crime Commn., 1986; adv. com. Latchkey Project, Tulsa County, 1985; ad hoc task force on day care Interagy. Coord. Coun., 1989-91; nat. rep. Tourette Syndrome Assn. to Nat. Broadcasting Assn. AERho, 1990-93; mem. resource com. Ronald McDonald House, 1990-92, vol. Tulsa area, 1991—, STARBASE, 1993—, Drug Edn. for Youth, 1994; mem. adv. bd. Tulsa Regional Coordinating Coun. for Svcs. to Children and Youth and Families, 1991-92; planning com. symposium Magic Coun. Girl Scouts Am.; lt. sr. mem. Tulsa Composite Squadron CAP, 1992-94; active Human Rights Com. for Ind. Opportunities, 1995—; presenter numerous confs. Recipient Den Leader Tng. award Boy Scouts Am., 1988. Mem. AAUW (bd. dirs. Tulsa county chpt. 1991-93, mem. nomination com.), Fedn. Families for Children's Mental Health, Assn. for Care of Children's Health, Nat. Assn. Early Childhood Tchr. Educators, Nat. Tourette Syndrome Assn. (state pres. 1987-92, state dir. 1992-93, hon. mem. bd. dirs. 1993, area coord., fundraiser 1988-90), Gold Star Wives Am., Kappa Delta Pi, Omicron Nu, Alpha Epsilon Rho (hon. mem. S.W. region). Roman Catholic. Office: Anderson Elem Sch 1921 E 29th Pl N Tulsa OK 74110

KULESHA, KEVIN JOHN, investment banker; b. Englewood, N.J., May 15, 1956; s. Kasmier J. and Florence L. (Anguissola) K.; BSBA, Georgetown U., 1976; MSIA, Carnegie Mellon U., 1979. Field dir. Bradley for Senate Com., Bethesda, Md., 1975-76; commodity trader, Chgo., 1977; assoc. Morgan Stanley & Co., N.Y.C., 1979-83; v.p. Lazard Frères & Co., N.Y.C., 1983-86; Furman Selz Mager Dietz & Birney, 1986-87; v.p. Merrill Lynch Capital Markets, N.Y.C., 1987-88, dir., 1989-91; mng. dir. The Sandstone Group, Miami, Fla., 1991—. Mem. Jumby Bay Club.

KULHAVY, JOSEPH BANNISTER, lawyer, educator; b. Racine, Wisc., Apr. 28, 1964; s. Joseph Alderman and Willa Murdoch (Bannister) K. BA (hon.), So. Meth. U., 1986; JD, U. Tex., 1990. Bar: Tex. 1990. Instr. U. Tex., Austin, 1990—; private practice attorney Austin, 1991-95; instr. So. Careers Inst., Austin, 1995—; note editor Am. Jour. of Criminal Law, Austin, 1988-90. Contbr. articles to profl. jours. Coordinator Guanajuato Exchange Program, Austin, 1989; donor Daryl Slusher Campaign, Austin, 1996. Mem. Phi Beta Kappa, Omicron Delta Epsilon, State Bar of Tex. Democrat. Home: 516 E 40th St # 205 Austin TX 78751 Office: Southern Careers Inst 2301 S Congress Ste 27 Austin TX 78704

KULICH, ROMAN THEODORE, healthcare administrator; b. Benton Harbor, Mich., Mar. 1, 1953; s. Roman and Helen (Gadumski) K.; m. Janet Kay Zuhl, Sept. 14, 1974; children: Andrew Joseph, Stephanie Ann. BBA magna cum laude, Mich. State U., 1974. CPA, Mich. Sr. auditor Ernst & Ernst, Detroit, 1975-77; controller Sinai Hosp. of Detroit, 1977-81, dir. finance, 1981-84; dir. finance Health Alliance Plan, Detroit, 1984-86, v.p. adminstrn. and finance, 1986-91, group v.p., chief operating officer, 1991-95; pres., CEO Healthcare Okla., Okla. Health Alliance, 1995, Select Care, Troy, Mich., 1996—; bd. dirs. Onika Ins. Co. Tiscornia Found. Scholarship winner, St. Joseph, Mich., 1971. Fellow Health Care Fin. Mgmt. Assn. (pres. East Mich. chpt. 1990-91); mem. AICPA, Mich. Assn. CPAs, Greater Detroit C. of C. (bd. dirs.), Detroit Urban League (bd. dirs.), Am. Soc. Employers (bd. dirs.). Home: 2834 Pheasant Ring Dr Rochester Hills MI 48309 Office: Healthcare Okla Ste 1500 2401 W Big Beaver Rd Troy MI 48084

KULINSKI, STEPHEN EDWARD, interior designer; b. Balt., Aug. 20, 1955; s. Paul Dominic and Christine (Armstrong) K.; m. Fredricka Strumpf, Aug. 6, 1983. B in Design, U. Fla., 1977; MBA, U. North Fla., 1983. Sr. designer Reynolds, Smith & Hills, Jacksonville, Fla., 1977-80, project mgr., 1980-83; project dir. Gresham, Smith & Ptnrs., Nashville, 1983-84, dir. interior architecture, 1984—, assoc., 1985-88, sr. assoc., 1988—; dir. comml. architecture, 1990, prin., 1994—. Mem. bd. visitors U. Tenn., Knoxville, bd. dirs. 1994—, mem. bd. visitors U. Fla., Gainsville, mem. Nashville Young Leaders Coun., Bldg. Owners and Mgrs. Assn., Nat. Assn. Indsl. and Office Parks, Nashville C. of C., Rotary. Republican. Home: 6743 Pennywell Dr Nashville TN 37205-3055 Office: Gresham Smith and Ptnrs 3310 W End Ave Nashville TN 37203

KULKARNI, ARUN DIGAMBAR, computer science educator; b. Poona, India, Dec. 14, 1947; came to U.S., 1984; s. Digambar D. and Sumati D. Kulkarni; m. Vasanti Arun Kulkarni, Oct. 15, 1978; children: Himani, Prathit, Shradha. BE, Poona U., 1969; MTech, India Inst. Tech., Bombay, 1971, PhD in Elec. Engring., 1978. Devel. engr. Sarabhai Electronics Rsch. Ctr., Ahmedabad, India, 1971-73; scientist Nat. Remote Sensing Agy., Hyderabad, India, 1976-84; postdoctoral researcher Va. Poly. Inst. and State U., Blacksburg, 1984-85; asst. prof. computer sci. U. Tex., Tyler, 1986-91, assoc. prof. computer sci., 1991—; vis. faculty U. So. Miss., Hattiesburg, 1985-86. Author: Neural Networks for Image Understanding, 1994; contbr. chpts. to books, articles to profl. jours. Fulbright fellow, 1984. Mem. Assn. for Computing Machinery, Internat. Soc. Neural Networks. Home: 817 W Rieck Rd Tyler TX 75703-3528 Office: U Tex 3900 University Blvd Tyler TX 75799-0001

KULOK, WILLIAM ALLAN, entrepreneur, venture capitalist; b. Mt. Vernon, N.Y., July 24, 1940; s. Sidney Alexander and Bertha (Lembeck) K.; m. Susan B. Glick, June 26, 1965; children: Jonathan, Brian, Stephanie. BS in Econs., U. Pa., 1962. CPA, N.Y. Acct. David Kulok Co., N.Y.C., 1962-67; asst. to pres. Syndicate Mags., N.Y.C., 1967-70; founder Kulok Capital Inc., N.Y.C., 1970, pres., 1970—; chmn. of bd. Cmty. Production Inc.,; bd. dir. Listcomp Corp., Mail Mgmt. Corp., Mag. Devel. Fund, Lazard Spl. Equities Fund, ASA Internat. Ltd., N.Y. Import/Export Ctr., Inc., Ctr. for Exec. Edn., Arts & Events, Inc.; lectr. Wharton Sch., U. Chgo., NYU. Pres. N.Y. Soc. Ethical Culture, 1978-80; vice chmn. bd. Ethical Culture Schs., 1979, chmn., 1982-86. Mem. Am. Inst. CPAs, Rockaway River Country Club, Sleepy Hollow Country Club, Loxahatchee Club, Tryall Golf and Beach Club (Jamaica, W.I.). Home: 116 Echo Dr Jupiter FL 33458-7716

KULP, EILEEN BODNAR, social worker; b. Glens Falls, N.Y., Sept. 25, 1941; d. Joseph and Bertha (Choquette) Bodnar; m. Randolph Heath Kulp, June 5, 1961; children: Kimberly, Randolph Heath II, Kevin Joseph. B in Sociology, Hampton U., 1978; MSW, Norfolk State U., 1981. Lic. clin. social worker, Va.; diplomate in clin. social work Nat. Bd. Examiners; cert. addictions specialist. Social worker II adult chem. dependency Peninsula Hosp., Hampton, 1981-82, leader treatment team adolescent chem. dependency unit, 1982-84, sr. clinician adult chem. dependency unit, 1984-86, program coord. adult chem. dependency unit, 1986-88, dir. adult treatment programs, 1988-92; pvt. practice Newport News, Va., 1986-93; dir. new founds drug and alcohol programs Riverside Regional Med. Ctr., Newport News, 1994—; dir. New Founds., Newport News; mem. addictions profls. team People Exch. Program, Norway, Sweden, Germany, 1989—; dir. intensive outpatient treatment programs Chesseh & Assocs., 1993-94. Bd. dirs Hampton Count PTA's, pres., 1979-80; bd. dirs. Hampton City Schs. Bd. Edn., 1981-85, Safe Haven Home for Abused Children, 1993—, Commonwealth Va. Citizens Adv. Bd. Youth and Family Svcs., Dept. Corrections, 1989—; chmn. adv. bd. Hampton Juvenile and Domestic Rels. Ct., bd. dirs., 1984—. Mem. Va. Coun. Social Welfare (pres. Tidewater chpt. 1987-88), Nat. Assn. Social Workers, Va. Assn. Alcoholism and Drug Abuse Counselors, Am. Coun. Alcoholism, Hampton Mental Health Bd. (pres. 1988-89), Va. Soc. Clin. Social Workers, Va. Coun. PTA's (life), Acad. Cert. Social Workers (cert.), Alpha Kappa Mu. Roman Catholic. Home: 26 Sarfan Dr Hampton VA 23664-1760

KULSTAD, MARK ALAN, philosophy educator; b. Mpls., Jan. 8, 1947; s. Lauritz Steen and Phyllis Regina (Vanderschaegen) K.; m. Marcia Judith Citron, May 10, 1984. BA in Philosophy, Macalester Coll., 1969; PhD in Philosophy, U. Mich., 1975. Asst. prof. philosophy Rice U., Houston, 1975-81, assoc. prof., 1981-96, chmn. dept., 1988-92, prof., 1996—. Author: Leibniz on Apperception, Consciousness, and Reflection, 1991; editor: Essays on the Philosophy of Leibniz, 1977, (with J.A. Cover) Central Themes in Early Modern Philosophy, 1990; mem. editorial bd. History Philosophy Quar., 1985—. Woodrow Wilson fellow, 1969-70; rsch. fellow Alexander von Humboldt Found., 1979-80. Mem. Leibniz Soc. N.Am. (pres. 1981-83, editor newsletter 1981—, bd. dirs. 1990—), Am. Philos. Assn., G.-W.-Leibniz Gesellschaft, S.W. Philos. Soc., Phi Beta Kappa.

KUMAR, KRISHNA, physics educator; b. Meerut, India, July 14, 1936; came to U.S., 1956, naturalized, 1966; s. Rangi and Susheila (Devi) Lal; m. Katharine Johnson, May 1, 1960; children: Jai Robert, Raj David. BSc in Physics, Chemistry and Math., Agra U., 1953, MSc in Physics, 1955; MS in Physics, Carnegie Mellon U., 1959, PhD in Physics, Carnegie Mellon U., 1964. Research assoc. Mich. State U., 1963-66, MIT, 1966-67, rsch. fellow Niels Bohr Inst., Copenhagen, 1967-69; physicist Oak Ridge Nat. Lab., 1969-71; assoc. prof. Vanderbilt U., Nashville, 1971-77; fgn. collaborator AEC of France, Paris, 1977-79; Nordita prof. U. Bergen, Norway, 1979-80; prof. physics Tenn. Tech. U., Cookeville, 1980-83, univ. prof. physics, 1983—; lectr. in field; cons. various rsch. labs. Author: Nuclear Models and the Search for Unity in Nuclear Physics, 1984, Superheavey Elements, 1989; contbr. articles to profl. jours, books. Sec. India Assn., Pitts., 1958-59. Faculty advisor, assoc. mem. Triangle Fraternity, 1990—; deacon Presbyn. Ch., 1991-93; faculty Adv. Indian Assn. of Cookeville, 1994-95. Recipient gold medal Agra U., 1955; NSF rsch. grantee, 1972-75. Mem. Indian Phys. Soc., Am. Phys. Soc., Tenn. Acad. Scis., Internat. Community Hospitality Assn. (pres. 1992-94), Planetary Soc., Rotary (Paul Harris fellow, bd. dirs. internat. coms. 1991-92), Sierra Club, Phai Kappa Phai, Sigma Pi Sigma, Sigma Xi (bd. dirs., 1992-93, charter mem. chpt. installation, 1994). Democrat. Home: 718 W 12th St Cookeville TN 38501-7788 Office: Tenn Tech U Cookeville TN 38505

KUMBHAKAR, SUBAL CHANDRA, economics educator; b. Kumardihi, India, Apr. 2, 1954; came to U.S., 1981; s. Ramgati and Champa Kumbhakar; 1 child, Raaka G. BA in Econs., Calcutta (India) U., 1974, MA in Econs., 1977; MA in Econs., U. So. Calif., 1983, PhD in Econs., 1986. Asst. prof. dept. econs. U. Burdwan, India, 1977-81; teaching asst. dept. econs. U. So. Calif., L.A., 1981-83, instr., 1983-85, lectr., 1985; asst. prof. dept. econs. U. Tex., Austin, 1986-91, assoc. prof., 1991—; cons. The Rand Corp., Santa Monica, Calif., summers 1983-86; guest prof. U. Gothenburg, Sweden, 1990, 91, 93, 94, 95, 96. Contbr. articles to profl. jours; mem. adv. bd. Tech. Forecasting and Social Change: An Internat. Jour., 1991—; referee Jour. Econometrics, Jour. Am. Statis. Assn., Internat. Econ. Rev., Econ. Revs., Jour. Productivity Analysis, Jour. Bus. and Econ. Stats., Rev. Econs. and Stats., Scandinavian Jour. Econs., Oxford Econ. Papers, Jour. Comparative Econs., Jour. Applied Econometrics, Am. Jour. of Agrl. Econs. Grantee Univ. Rsch. Inst., 1991, KPMG Peat Marwick Found., 1992. Mem. Am. Econ. Assn., Econometric Soc. Home: 10407 Charette Cv Austin TX 78759-6172 Office: U Tex Dept Econs Austin TX 78712

KUMI-DIAKA, JAMES, college educator, researcher; b. Adukrom, Ghana, Sept. 23, 1946; m. Emelia Kumi-Diaka, Jan. 1, 1980; m. Emelia Kukuele Abosey; children: Yaw, Asieduwa, Kwabena, Asarebea. BS, U. Guelph, 1969; DVM, A.B. Univ., Zaria, 1974, MS, 1976, PhD, 1981. Asoc. prof. A.B. Univ., 1980-87; rsch. assoc. U. Guelph, 1987-90; assoc. prof. U. Wis., Madison, 1990-94; cons. Itervet. Can., Guelph, 1994. Contbr. articles to profl. jours. Mem. AAAS, Soc. for Theriogenology. Office: F Atlantic Univ 2912 College Ave Davie FL 33314-7714

KUMISKI, JOHN A., writer, photographer fly fishing guide and teacher; b. Cambridge, Mass., Sept. 2, 1952; s. John J. and Pauline A. K.; m. Susan Surprise, June 15, 1980; children: Maxx, Alex. BS, U. Mass., 1980. Cert. tchr., Fla. Science tchr. Am. Sch. Bahia, Brazil, 1980-84, Lake Howell H.S., Winter Park, Fla., 1985-87, Tuskawilla Mid. Sch., Oveido, Fla., 1987-96; owner, pres. Argonaut Publ. Co., Maitland, Fla., 1992—. Author: Fishing the Everglades, 1993, Saltwater Fly Fishing, 1994, Flyrodding Florida Salt, 1995; contbr. articles to popular publs. Served in U.S. Army, 1972-74. Mem. Backcountry Flyfishing Assn. (pres. 1990-91, 92-93), Fedn. Fly Fishers (coun. dir. 1993—). Office: Argonaut Publ Co PO Box 940153 Maitland FL 32794-0153

KUNCE, AVON ESTES, vocational rehabilitation counselor; b. Sarasota, Fla., Apr. 20, 1927; d. William Breckinridge and Avon Mary (Zahlten) Estes; m. Henry Warren Kunce, May 26, 1948; children: Catherine Avon Hilton, Nancy Lynn Evers, Christopher Warren, Cynthia Tyree Kent, James Breckinridge. BEd in Secondary Edn., U. Miami, 1972; MS in Mgmt., Fla. Internat. U., 1977. Social worker State of Fla. Health & Rehab. Svcs., Miami, 1972-76; social and rehab. svcs. supr. State Disabled Adult Abuse Investigation Unit Adult Congregate Living Lic., Miami, 1976-82; med. disability specialist State of Fla. Health & Rehab. Svcs., Miami, 1982-89; sr. vocat. rehab. counselor State of Fla. Dept. of Labor, Miami, 1989—. Pres. LWV, Rockhill, Mo., 1955, mem., Miami, 1965-69; mem. South Dade Dem. Women's Club, Miami, 1967-69. Mem. ASPA, Nat. Assn. Disability Examiners, Nat. Rehab. Assn., Phi Lambda Pi, Gamma Theta Upsilon, Epsilon Tau Lambda, Pi Alpha Alpha. Democrat. Quaker. Home: 5025 SW 74th Ter Miami FL 33143-6003 Office: State of Fla Vocat Rehabilitation 5040 NW 7th St Ste 330 Miami FL 33126-3422

KUNKEL, HARRIOTT ORREN, life science educator; b. Olney, Tex., July 3, 1922; s. Hugo O. and Mathilde A. (Schulz) K.; m. Beverly Virginia Davies, Dec. 18, 1960; children: Virginia Anne, Sheryl E. (Kunkel) Stolte. BS, Tex. A&M U., 1943, MS, 1948; PhD, Cornell U., 1950. Instr. Biochemistry U. Wis., Madison, 1950-51; asst. prof. to prof. Animal Sci & Biochemistry Tex. A&M U., College Station, 1951-62; assoc. dir. Tex. Arg. Experimental Station, College Station, 1962-67, dir., 1967-72; dean of agr. Tex. A&M U., College Station, 1967-88, prof. Life Scis., 1988—, dean emeritus, 1992—; edn. cons. USDA, Washington, 1988-93. Contbr. articles to profl. jours. Recipient Faculty Disting. Achievment award, Former students Tex. A&M U., 1956, 1987, VIP Citation FFA, Washington. Fellow AAAS, Am. Soc. Animal Sci.; mem. Agr., Food, and Human Value Soc. (Councilor, 1987-91). Lutheran. Office: Tex A&M U Dept Animal Sci College Station TX 77843-2471

KUNKLE, DANIELLE LYNN, staffing industry administrator, journalist; b. Phillipsburg, N.J., Oct. 13, 1973; d. George Edwin and Sharon Marie (Roland) K. BA in English and Journalism, Tex. Christian U., 1995. Editl. asst. Tex. Christian U., Ft. Worth, 1993-95; recruiter Remedy Staffing, Ft. Worth, 1995, sales supr., 1995-96; mgr. Remedy Staffing, North Richland Hills, Tex., 1996—; resume cons., Ft. Worth, 1995—. Asst. troop leader Cir. T Girl Scouts, Ft. Worth, 1995-96; patron Kimbell Art Mus., Ft. Worth, 1996. Mem. NRA, Soc. Profl. Journalists (Outstanding Grad. award 1995), Tex. Christian U. Mortar Bd., Golden Key Nat. Honor Soc., Phi Beta Kappa. Home: Apt #1410 5700 N Beach Fort Worth TX 76137 Office: Remedy Staffing 5424 Rufe Snow # 302 North Richland Hills TX 76180

KUNTZ, HAL GOGGAN, petroleum exploration company executive; b. San Antonio, Dec. 29, 1937; s. Peter A. and Jean M. (Goggan) K.; m. Vesta McClain, Oct. 7, 1983; children: Hal Goggan, Peter, Michael B., Vesta. BS in Engring., Princeton U., 1960; MBA, Oklahoma City U., 1972. Line, staff positions Mobil Oil Corp., Dallas, Oklahoma City, New Orleans, 1963-74; co-founder, pres. CLK Corp., New Orleans, Houston, 1974—, IPEX Co., New Orleans, 1975—; pres. Gulf Coast Exploration Co., New Orleans, 1979—, pres. CLK Investments I, II, III and IV, 1979—, CLK Producing, CLK Oil and Gas Co., CLK Exploration Co., 1980—; bd. dirs. North Houston Bank. Mem. Mus. Fine Arts, Houston, 1978—; mem. condrs. circle Houston Symphony, 1980; governing bd. Houston Opera. Served with AUS, 1960-63. Mem. Am. Mgmt. Assn., Nat. Small Bus. Assn., Inter-Am. Soc., Soc. Exploration Geophysics, Am. Assn. Petroleum Geologists, Aircraft Owners and Pilots Assn., Houston C. of C., River Oaks C. of C. Republican. Roman Catholic. Clubs: Petroleum of Houston, University of Houston; Argyle, Order of Alamo (San Antonio), Brae-Burn Country, The Coronado, Princeton of N.Y., River Oaks Country. Avocations: golf, skiing, birdshooting, flying. Office: CLK Co 1001 Fannin St Ste 1400 Houston TX 77002-6708

KUNZ, SIDNEY, entomologist; b. Fredericksburg, Tex., Dec. 24, 1935. BS, Tex. A&M U., 1958, MS, 1962; PhD in Entomology, Okla. State U., 1967. Survey entomologist Okla. State U., 1961-64, ext. entomologist, 1964-67; rsch. entomologist agr. rsch. svc. USDA, Kerrville, Tex., 1967-69; rsch. entomologist USDA, College Station, 1969-77; rsch. leader, rsch. entomologist sci. and edn. USDA, 1977-86; lab. dir. U.S. Livestock Insects Lab., Kerrville, 1986—; entomology cons. food & agr. orgn. UN Devel. Prog., Mauritius, 1973-74, USAID, Tanzania, IAEA, Somalia, 1982. Recipient CIBA-GEIGY/Entomol. Soc. Am. award CIBA-GEIGY Corp., 1991, Coopers award for Outstanding Accomplishments Vet. Entomology, Mallinckrodt Vet. Inc., 1995. Mem. Entomol. Soc. Am., Sigma Xi. Office: US Livestock Insects Lab 2700 Fredericksburg Rd Kerrville TX 78028-9184

KUNZE, DOLORES JOHANNA, veterinarian; b. Waltham, Mass., Mar. 29, 1950; d. John Herman and Dorothy (Angiulo) K.; m. Morrow Bradford Thompson, Mar. 20, 1976 (div. 1985). BS in Agriculture, U. Ga., 1972, DVM, 1976; MS, Mich. State U., 1980. Lic. veterinarian, N.C., S.C. Resident large animal dept. Coll. Vet. Medicine, Mich. State U., Lansing, 1977-80, asst. prof. vet. medicine, 1980-81; asst. prof. vet. medicine N.C. State U., Raleigh, 1981-84; staff veterinarian Aiken (S.C.) Animal Hosp., 1985-87, East Side Vet. Clinic, Spartanburg, S.C., 1987-88; pvt. practice Boiling Springs Animal Clinic, P.A., Inman, S.C., 1988—; bd. dirs. Spartanburg Vet. Emergency Clinic, sec., 1990-91, pres., 1994-96. Contbr. articles to profl. publs., 2 chpts. to books. Mem. AVMA, S.C. Vet. Med. Assn., Phi Zeta (Zeta chpt.). Presbyterian. Home: PO Box 16014 Spartanburg SC 29316-6014 Office: Boiling Springs Animal Clin 4370 Highway 9 Inman SC 29349-8582

KUREPA, ALEXANDRA, mathematician; b. Zagreb, Yugoslavia, Dec. 31, 1956; came to U.S., 1985; d. Svetozar and Zora (Lopac) K.; m. Rodney Anthony Waschka II, June 24, 1988; children: Andre Kurepa Waschka, Lana Kurepa Waschka. BS, U. Zagreb, 1978, MS, 1982; PhD, U. North Tex., 1987. Assoc. prof. math. U. Zagreb, 1987-88, Tex. Christian U., Ft. Worth, 1988-93, N.C. A&T State U., Greensboro, 1993-96, 1996—. Author: Matematica 2, 1989; contbr. articles to profl. jours. Rsch. grantee UNESCO, 1988, 89, U.D. Dept. Edn., 1995, 96. Mem. Am. Math. Soc., Math. Assn. Am., Assn. for Women in Math. Office: NC A&T State U Dept Math Greensboro NC 27411

KURIE, ANDREW EDMUNDS, mining geologist; b. Dallas, May 30, 1932; s. Charles Winfred and Katherine Doyle (Edmunds) K.; B.S. in Geology, Sul Ross State Coll., Alpine, Tex., 1954; M.A. in Geology, U. Tex. at Austin, 1956; m. Judith Ann Hankins, Feb. 14, 1970; children—Andrea, Mary Kay, Michael, Thomas, Teresa. Petroleum geologist Pure Oil Co., Fort Worth, 1956-63; geologist Utah State Dept. Hwys., Salt Lake City, 1964-67; mining geologist LaDomincia S.A. de C.V., Marathon, Tex., 1968-85, exploration supt., 1972-76, mgr. mines and exploration, 1977-85; cons. mining geologist, 1985-86; counselor Minas La Jabonera S.A. de C.V., Marathon, Tex., 1987—. Cert. profl. geologist. Fellow AAAS; mem. Geol. Soc. Am., Am. Assn. Petroleum Geologists, Am. Inst. Profl. Geologists, Explorers Club. Editor: West Tex. Geol. Soc. Membership Directory, 1962; contbr. articles to profl. jours. Home: Hwy 2627 Heath Crossing Marathon TX 79842-0386 Office: PO Box 386 Marathon TX 79842

KURTH, RONALD JAMES, university president, retired naval officer; b. Madison, Wis., July 1, 1931; s. Peter James and Celia (Kuehn) K.; m. Esther Charlene Schaefer, Dec. 21, 1954; children: Steven, Audrey, John, Douglas. BS, U.S. Naval Acad., 1954; MPA, Harvard U., 1961, PhD, 1970. Commd. ensign U.S. Navy, 1954, advanced through grades to rear adm., 1981; U.S. naval attache Moscow, 1975-77; comdg. officer NAS, Memphis at Millington, Tenn., 1977-79; mil. fellow Council Fgn. Relations, N.Y.C., 1979-80; exec. asst. to dep. chief naval ops. Dept. Navy, Washington, 1980-81, dir. Pol-Mil Policy and Current Plans, 1981-83, dir. Long Range Planning Group, 1983-84; U.S. def. attache Moscow, 1985-87; pres. U.S. Naval War Coll., Newport, R.I., 1987-90, Murray (Ky.) State U., 1990-94; dean acad. affairs Air War Coll., Maxwell AFB, Ala., 1994—; teaching fellow Harvard U., Cambridge, Mass., 1969-70. Author: The Politics of Technological Innovation in the Navy, 1970. Mem. nat. adv. bd. Boy Scouts Am. Decorated Def. D.S.M., Navy D.S.M., Legion of Merit with 2 gold stars, Meritorious Svc. medal with gold star. Mem. Am. Acad. Polit. Sci., U.S. Naval Inst. (life), Naval War Coll. Found. (life), U.S. Naval Acad. Alumni, Harvard U. Alumni, Rotary. Episcopalian. Office: Air War Coll 325 Chennault Cir Montgomery AL 36112-6427

KURTZBERG, JOANNE, pediatrics educator; b. N.Y.C., Nov. 18, 1950; d. Lawrence Kurtzberg; m. Henry S. Friedman; children: Joshua, Sara. BA, Sarah Lawrence Coll., 1972; MD, NYU, 1976. Intern in pediats. Dartmouth Med. Ctr., Hanover, N.H., 1976-77; resident in pediats. Upstate Med. Ctr., Syracuse, N.Y., 1977-79, clin. rsch. fellow in pediat. hematology/oncology, 1979-80; mem. faculty Duke Comprehensive Cancer Ctr., Durham, N.C., 1983—; sr. rsch. fellow in pediat. hematology/oncology Duke U. Med. Ctr., Durham, 1980-83, asst. prof., assoc. prof. pediat., 1983-88, prof., 1994—, dir. pediatric bone marrow lab., 1989—, dir. pediat. bone marrow transplant program, 1989—, mem. grad. faculty Grad. Sch. pathology dept., 1993—, assoc. prof. pathology, 1991—. Recipient R. Wayne Rundles award for excellence in cancer rsch., 1993, Basil O'Connor Starter Scholar Rsch. award, 1985-87. Fellow Leukemia Soc. Am. (spl. fellow, scholar 1986-89); mem. Internat. Soc. for Hematotherapy and Graft Engring., Am. Soc. for Blood & Marros & Transplantation, Am. Soc. Pediat. Hematology/Oncology, Am. Soc. Hematology, Soc. for Pediat. Rsch., Pediat. Oncology Group, Alpha Omega Alpha. Home: 1808 Faison Rd Durham NC 27705 Office: Duke U Med Ctr PO Box 3350 Durham NC 27710-3350

KURTZMAN, NEIL A., medical educator; b. Bklyn., June 18, 1936; s. Louis S. and Roselie (Yegla) K.; m. Sandra Sabatini, Feb. 14, 1976; children from previous marriage: Jonathan, Laura. BA with honors, Williams Coll., 1957; MD, N.Y. Med. Coll., 1961. Intern Robert Packer Hosp., Sayre, Pa., 1961-62; resident Ohio State U. Hosp., Columbus, 1962-63; asst. chief med. services Nobel Army Hosp., Ft. McClellan, Ala., 1963-64; med. resident William Beaumont Gen. Hosp., El Paso, Tex., 1964-65, chief med. resident, 1965-66; fellow in nephrology U. Tex. Southwestern Med. Sch., Dallas, 1966-68; chief renal div. Brooke Army Med. Ctr., Ft. Sam Houston, Tex., 1969-72; prof., chief nephrology sect. U. Ill. Coll. Medicine, Chgo., 1972-84; Arnett prof., chmn. dept. internal medicine, chief nephrology div. Tex. Tech U. Health Scis. Ctr., Lubbock, 1985—, chief of staff univ. med. ctr., 1990-92; mem. gen. medicine B study sect. Nat. Inst. Arthritis, Metabolic and Digestive Diseases, Bethesda, Md., 1978-83; mem. merit rev. bd. VA, Washington, 1979-82, chmn., 1981-82; mem. sci. adv. bd. Nat. Kidney Found., N.Y.C., 1981-92, chmn., 1988-90, v.p., 1990-92, pres., 1992-94; prin. investigator regulation urinary acidification NIH, Bethesda, 1978—. Author: Handbook of Urinalysis and Urinary Sediment, 1974, Pathophysiology of the Kidney, 1977; also more than 270 sci. papers, more than 600 sci. presentations; editor-in-chief Seminars in Nephrology, 1981—; assoc. editor Am. Jour. Nephrology; mem. editorial bd. 7 sci. jours.; referee 16 sci. jours. Faculty advisor Alpha Omega Alpha, U. Ill., 1977-84, Tex. Tech U. Health Sci. Ctr., 1985—. Served to lt. col. U.S. Army, 1963-72. Decorated U.S. Army Meritorious Svc. award; recipient Pres.'s award Nat. Kidney Found., 1990, Outstanding Acad. Achievement award N.Y. Med. Coll., 1992, So. Soc. for Clin. Investigation's Founder's award, 1996. Mem. Am. Physiol. Soc., Am. Soc. Clin. Investigation, Assn. Am. Physicians, Cen. Soc. Clin. Research, So. Soc. Clin. Investigation, Alpha Omega Alpha. Office: Tex Tech U Health Scis Ctr Sch of Medicine Lubbock TX 79430

KURZENBERGER, DICK, health services executive; b. Ind., Nov. 26, 1949; children: Jon Ross, Blake Mead. BBA, Ft. Lauderdale U., 1970; MBA, U. Palm Beach, 1971. Asst. dir. St. Mary's Hosp., West Palm Beach, Fla., 1972-75; adminstr. The Hauser Clinic, Houston, 1975-79, Post Oak Psychiatry, Houston, 1979-86; asst. adminstr. Green Oaks Hosp., Dallas, 1986-88; div. adminstr. St. Joseph Hosp., Houston, 1988-90; exec. dir., chief exec. officer Greenwood Group, Houston, 1990-92; div. mgr. Kelsey Seybold Clinic, Houston, 1992—; pres., bd. dirs. Mental Health Assn. of Houston and Harris County, 1989-90; chmn. psychiat. sect. Greater Houston Hosp., 1988-90; del. dir. State Mental Health Bd., Austin, 1987-92. V.p. MHA Houston, 1982-86, Dallas, 1987; del. Mental Health Needs Coun., Houston, 1989-90. Recipient Vol. of Yr. award United Way, 1986, MM award M.M. Anderson, 1978, John Z. Rasco award, 1993, BBH Adminstr. of Yr. award, 1994. Mem. Tex. Hosp. Assn., Med. Group Mgmt. Assn. Home: 8803 Ashridge Park Dr Spring TX 77379 Office: Kelsey Seybold Clinic 5757 Woodway Dr Houston TX 77057-1506

KUSE, JAMES RUSSELL, chemical company executive; b. Lincoln, Nebr., Aug. 20, 1930; s. Walter Herman and Gladys Katherine (Graham) K.; m. Shirley Rae Ernst, Sept. 27, 1953; children: Lynn Kuse Ehret, Carol Kuse Ehlen, Michael. B.S.Ch.E., Oreg. State U., 1955. Indsl. chems. salesman Ga.-Pacific Corp., Atlanta, 1967-68, mgr. splty. chem. div., 1968-70, mgr. chem. sales, 1970-74, mgr. comml. chems., 1974-76, v.p. chem. div., 1976-78, sr. v.p. chem. div., 1978-84; chmn. Ga. Gulf Corp., 1985—. Bd. dirs. Clark Coll., Atlanta, 1983. Served to cpl. U.S. Army, 1953-55. Mem. Am. Inst. Chem. Engrs., Am. Chem. Soc. Republican. Lutheran. Club: Capital City (Atlanta). Office: Georgia Gulf Corp 400 Perimeter Center Ter NE Atlanta GA 30346-1227

KUSHNER, GILBERT, anthropology educator; b. N.Y.C., July 7, 1933; s. Abraham and Sarah (Lipschitz) K.; m. Lorraine Etta Segall, Aug. 17, 1958; children: Andrew S., David B. BA in Sociology/Psychology, CCNY, 1954; MA in Anthropology, U. Ariz., 1958; postgrad., U. N.C., 1958-61; PhD, U. Ariz., 1968. Instr. in sociology and anthropology U. Houston, 1962-66; asst. to assoc. prof. anthropology SUNY, Brockport, 1968-70; from assoc. prof. to prof. U. South Fla., Tampa, 1970-74, assoc. dean, Coll. Social and Behavioral Scis., 1971-78, chair, dept. anthropology, 1971-85, track leader, dept. anthropology, 1986-89, prof. anthropology, 1974—. Author: Immigrants from India in Israel: Planned Change in an Administered Community, 1973, (with others) What Accounts for Sociocultural Change? A Propositional Inventory, 1962; co-editor: (with T.E. Downing) Human Rights and Anthropology, 1988, 91, (with G.P. Castile) Persistent Peoples: Cultural Enclaves in Perspective, 1981, (with others) Training Programs for New Opportunities in Applied Anthropology, 1974; contbr. chpts., articles, revs. to profl. jours. including Anthropology and Humanism Quarterly, Practicing Anthropology, Human Orgn. Fellow Royal Anthrop. Inst., Soc. for Applied Anthropology, Am. Anthrop. Assn.; mem. Am. Ethnological Soc., So. Anthrop. Soc., Assn. Social Scientific Study of Jewry, Israel Anthrop. Assn., Anthrop. Soc. Washington, Washington Assn. Profl. Anthrops., Soc. Urban Anthropology, Soc. for Humanistic Anthropology, Nat. Assn. for Practice of Anthropology, Suncoast Orgn. Practicing Anthropologists. Office: U S Fla Dept Anthropology Tampa FL 33620

KUSHNER, MICHAEL JAMES, neurologist, consultant; b. Hackensack, N.J., July 18, 1951; s. Samuel and Ruth Ellen (Paul) K.; m. Sarah Joan Warden, Aug. 14, 1976; 1 child, Hunter Paul. BA in Physics, Yale U., 1973; MD, NYU, 1977. Diplomate Am. Bd. Psychiatry, Am. Bd. Med. Examiners. Intern Parkland Meml. Hosp., U. Tex., Dallas, 1977-78; resident in neurology Neurol. Inst., Columbia-Presbyn. Med. Ctr., N.Y.C., 1978-81; rsch. assoc. U. Pa., Phila., 1981-83, asst. prof. neurology, 1983-90; attending physician Hosp. of U. Pa., Phila., 1983-90; with Wilson (N.C.) Neurology Ctr., 1992—; dir. SPECT facility Hosp. of U. Pa., 1986-90, asst. dir. neurovascular lab., 1987-90; mem. sensory disorders and lang. study sect. NIH, Bethesda, Md., 1988-90; cons. Dupont Med. Products Div., Billerica, Mass., 1987—; staff neurologist Wilson (N.C.) Neurology Ctr. Contbr. numerous articles to profl. jours. Interviewer alumni schs. com. Yale U., Phila., 1984—. Fellow Am. Acad. Neurology, Am. Heart Assn. (stroke coun.); mem. AMA, Internat. Soc. for Blood Flow and Metabolism, N.C. Neurol. Soc. (pres. 1995—), Yale of N.Y.C., Yale of Cen. N.C., Yale of N.C. Republican. Episcopalian. Home: 1110 Salem St NW Wilson NC 27893-2137 Office: Wilson Neurology Ctr PO Box 3148 Wilson NC 27895-3148

KUSSROW, NANCY ESTHER, educational association administrator. BA, Valparaiso U.; MA, U. N.C. Exec. dir. Nat. Assn. prins. of Schs. for Girls; ret., 1996. Office: 4050 Little River Rd Hendersonville NC 28739-8317

KUSY, ROBERT PETER, biomedical engineering and orthodontics educator; b. Worcester, Mass., Oct. 19, 1947; s. Stanley J. and Mary B. (Rutkiewicz) K.; m. Gisela Bauer, June 27, 1969; children: Kimberly, Kevin. BSME, Worcester (Mass.) Poly. Inst., 1969; MSMetE, Drexel U., 1971, PhD in Materials Sci., 1973. Rubber rsch. technician Vellumoid

Gasket Corp. divsn. Fed.-Mogul Corp., Worcester, 1966-69; rsch. asst. dept. metall. engring. Drexel U., Phila., 1969-72; rsch. assoc. Dental Rsch. Ctr., U. N.C., Chapel Hill, 1972-74, asst. prof. oral biology dept. orthodontics, Dental Rsch., 1974-79, assoc. prof. orthodontics dept. orthodontics, Dental Rsch., 1979-89, assoc. prof. biomed. engring. Sch. Medicine, 1985-89; prof. orthodontics, prof. biomed. engring. Schs. Dentistry and Medicine, U. N.C., Chapel Hill, 1989—, adj. prof. curriculum applied scis., 1990—; mem. adminstrv. bd. Grad. Sch. U. N.C., Chapel Hill, 1989-95; cons. Internat. Nickel, Structure-Probe, DuPont, Kodak, CTL Tech., Rising Star, Smiling Faces, Epolin, Dental Rsch. Corp., Tracor Aerospace, Enron Chem., Unitek, 3M, Ormco Corp., Flexmedics Corp., Lancer Orthodontics, Aristech, Orthodontic Ptnrs., Hutchinson Tech., Wyeth-Ayerst Rsch., Composite Products, A-Company, Ortho Organizers, U. N.C., Tom's of Maine, Implant Scis.; reviewer small projects grants NIH, 1985—, project site visitor, 1986—; mem. bd. sci. adv. com. Epolin Corp., 1986-89. Mem. rev. staff Am. Jour. Orthodontics, 1982—, Polymer, 1985—, Jour. Applied Polymer Sci., 1985—, Dental Materials, 1986—, Jour. Polymer Sci., 1987—, Jour. Biomed. Materials Rsch.-Applied Biomaterials, 1989—; mem. adv. bd. Jour. Materials Sci., Materials in Medicine; contbr. over 165 articles to profl. jours. Pres. Hills of the Haw Home Owners' Assn., 1986-88; mem. pastoral coun. Newman Ctr., 1986-87; organizer Sr. Basketball Club, Chapel Hill Cmty. Ctr., 1985-88; coach Children's Basketball League, Chapel Hill, Carrboro, 1981-82, 83-86; mem. ch. choir, 1987-89, 92—. Capt. U.S. Army, 1969-77. Recipient Focused Giving award Johnson & Johnson Co., 1993-96, B.F. Dewel Hon. Rsch. award Am. Assn. Orthodontists Found., 1995, Orthodontics Tchg. award Orthodontics dept. U. N.C.-Chapel Hill, 1996. Mem. N.Am. Thermal Analysis Soc., Am. Soc. Materials, Am. Chem. Soc. (divsn. polymer chemistry divsn. phys. chemistry), Internat. Assn. Dental Rsch., Am. Assn. Dental Rsch., Internat. Metallographic Soc., Soc. Biomaterials, Soc. Plastics Engrs. Roman Catholic. Office: U NC Bldg 210H Rm 313 CB # 7455 Chapel Hill NC 27599

KUTCHINS, MICHAEL JOSEPH, airport executive; b. Chgo., IL, Dec. 1, 1941; s. Jack M. and Bernice L. K.; children: Bradley Charles, Scott Freeman. B.S., U. Ill., 1962. Accredited airport exec. Reporter Sta. WICD-TV, Danville, Ill., 1962-63, Sta. WSOY AM-FM, Decatur, Ill., 1963-65; bus. editor, reporter Sta. WSOC AM-FM-TV, Charlotte, N.C., 1965-67; adminstrv. asst. to mgr. Douglas Mcpl. Airport, Charlotte, 1968-71; asst. dir. aviation San Antonio Internat. Airport, 1971-81, dir. aviation, 1981—. Mem. Am. Assn. Airport Execs. (pres. 1985-86, pres. South Cen. chpt. 1976). Home: 13426 Vista Del Rey San Antonio TX 78216-2233 Office: San Antonio Internat Airpt 9800 Airport Blvd San Antonio TX 78216-4837

KUTKA, NICHOLAS, nuclear medicine physician; b. Czechoslovakia, Dec. 17, 1926; s. Vladimir and Agatha (Flenko) K.; m. Anna Cizmar, Aug. 14, 1965; children: Andrew, Gregory. MD, Comenius U., Bratislava, Czechoslovakia, 1951; PhD, Slovak Acad. Scis., Bratislava, 1962. Diplomate internal medicine Postgrad. Edn. of Physicians, 1955, nuclear medicine Am. Bd. Nuclear Medicine, 1973. Asst. prof. inst. physiology Comenius U., Bratislava, 1951; intern, resident in internal medicine Mil. Hosp., Bratislava, 1952-55; chief dept. inst. endocrinology Slovak Acad. Scis., Bratislava, 1956-69; tech. asst. Internat. Atomic Engry Agy., Bogota, Colombia, 1969-70; resident in nuclear medicine Duke U., 1971-73; assoc. prof. radiology Baylor Coll. Medicine, Houston, 1973-95, 1995—; dir. nuclear medicine Ben Taub Gen. Hosp., Houston, 1978-81; chief nuclear medicine service VA Med. Ctr., Houston, 1982—; mem. med. staff univ. affiliated hosps. Houston, faculty Sch. Nuclear Medicine Tech.; fellow Internat. Atomic Energy Agy., Rome, 1962-63. Contbr. numerous articles to profl. jours; mem. editorial bd. Endocrinologia Experimentalis. Served with Health Service Czechoslovak Army, 1952-54. Recipient prize in nuclear medicine J.E. Purkyne, 1965. Mem. Harris County Med. Soc., Tex. Med. Assn., Soc. Nuclear Medicine, Am. Coll. Nuclear Physicians, Clin. Ligand Assay Soc. Office: VA Med Ctr 115 Nuclear Medicine Svc Houston TX 77030

KUTNICKI, BENJAMIN, family physician; b. Gutesloh, Germany, July 30, 1946; came to U.S., 1949; s. Solomon Joseph and Valeria (Siegleman) K.; m. Ruth Rotkel, May 9, 1974 (div. 1979); m. Mary Faith Hershey, Jan. 3, 1983; 1 child, Saul Davis. BS, U. Ky., 1969, MD, 1974. Assoc. Riverbourne Medical Ctr., Carrollton, Ky., 1977-78; ptnr. Riverbourne Medical Ctr., 1978-82; family physician pvt. practice, Warsaw, Ky., 1982—; asst. clin. prof. Dept. Family Practice U. Louisville, Ky., 1979—; mem. advisor Home Health Agy. Carroll County Hosp., Carrollton, 1986, Carroll County Bd. Health; chmn. Quality Assurance Utilization Rev. Com. Carroll County Hosp., 1980—, Continuing Edn. Com., 1980—; mem. dir. Carroll County Hosp., 1989—, Trimble Nursing Ctr., Bedford, Ky., 1986—, Valley Haven Rest Home, Sanders Ky., Swiss Villa Living Ctr., Vevay, Ind., 1995—. Fellow Am. Acad. Family Physicians; mem. TriCounty Medical Soc., Gallitin County Medical Soc., Jefferson County Medical Soc., Ky. Acad. Family Physicians, Ky. Med. Assn. Democrat. Jewish. Office: Box 128 302 W Main St Warsaw KY 41095-0128

KUVZINSKE, RICHARD, company executive. Sr. v.p. comml. ops. Mason & Hanger-Silas Mason Co. Address: 2355 Harrodsburg Rd Lexington KY 40504-3363

KUYKENDALL, JOHN WELLS, academic administrator, educator; b. Charlotte, N.C., May 8, 1938; s. James Bell and Emily Jones (Frazer) K.; m. Nancy Adams Moore, July 15, 1961; children—Timothy Moore, James Frazer. BA cum laude, Davidson Coll., 1959; BD cum laude, Union Sem., Richmond, Va., 1964; STM, Yale U., 1965; MA, Princeton U., 1972, Ph.D., 1975. Ordained to ministry Presbyterian Ch., 1965. Campus minister Presbyn. Ch., Auburn, Ala., 1965-70; mem. faculty Auburn U., 1973-84; pres. Davidson (N.C.) Coll., 1984—. Author: (with others) Presbyterians: Their History and Beliefs, 1978, Southern Enterprize: The Work of Evangelical Societies in the Antebellum South, 1982; contbr. articles to profl. jours. Recipient Algernon Sydney Sullivan award Auburn U., 1982. Mem. Am. Soc. Ch. History, Phi Beta Kappa, Omicron Delta Kappa, Phi Kappa Phi. Democrat. Office: Davidson Coll PO Box 1689 Davidson NC 28036-1689

KUZEL, ANTON JOHN, physician; b. Chgo., July 29, 1955; s. Anton John and Vivian Rose Kuzel; m. Linda Susan Molosky, May 24, 1986; children: Kristina, Kathryn. BS, U. Ill., 1977, MD, 1981, M in Health Professions Edn., 1985. Diplomate Am. Bd. Family Practice. Resident MacNeal Family Practice, Berwyn, Ill., 1981-84; asst. prof. Fairfax (Va.) Family Practice, 1984-90; assoc. prof. Dept. Family Practice Med. Coll. Va. Va. Commonwealth U., Richmond, 1990—. Author: Primary Care Research, 1990, Doing Qualitative Research, 1992; contbr. articles to profl. jours. Fellow Faculty Devel. Nat. Inst. on Alcoholism and Alcohol Abuse, 1988; recipient Grad. Edn. in Family Practice Health Resources and Svcs. Adminstrn., 1992, 96. Fellow Am. Acad. Family Physicians; mem. Soc. Tchrs. Family Medicine, N.Am. Primary Care Rsch. Group, Va. Acad. Family Physicians. Roman Catholic. Office: Medical College of Virginia Box 980251 Richmond VA 23298

KVASNOK, JOSEPH DOUGLAS, quality assurance professional; b. Cleve., June 21, 1958; s. Joseph Douglas and Dorothy May (Krosnosky) K.; m. Susanne Gabriele Sprengel, Oct. 16, 1982; children: Geoffrey Ryan, Kristina Loren, Jonathan Darren. Student, Brevard C.C., Melbourne, Fla., 1980-82, Cuyahoga C.C., Cleve., 1983; BS in Physics, Cleve. State U., 1988. Engring. technician Westinghouse Electric Corp., Cleve., 1977-87, quality engr., 1987-92; quality engr. Invacare Corp., Elyria, Ohio, 1993; quality mgr. Targ-It-Tronics, Inc., West Melbourne, Fla., 1993-96, M.C. Assembly & Test, Inc., Melbourne, 1996—. Sgt. USAF, 1978-82. Mem. Am. Soc. for Quality Control (cert. quality auditor), Phi Theta Kappa. Home: 2513 Kingsmill Ave Melbourne FL 32934-7581 Office: MC Assembly & Test Inc 751 North Dr Melbourne FL 32934-9289

KWIECINSKI, CHESTER M., artist; b. Youngstown, Ohio, July 7, 1924. MFA, Kans. City Art Inst., 1951. Cert. art tchr., Ohio. Graphic arts tchr. Warren (Ohio) City Schs., 1954-67; prof. art Coll. Artesia, N.Mex., 1967-71; art tchr. Artesia Art Acad., 1971-73; art mus. dir. Abilene (Tex.) Fine Arts Mus., 1973-80; freelance artist, restorer Abilene, 1980-88, freelance artist, 1988—. Fund raiser YMCA, El Paso, Tex., 1971-72. Served in U.S. Army, 1943-46. Recipient Best of Show Kendall Art Ctr., San Angelo, 1991, 1st place in watercolors Big Country Art Assn., Abilene, 1992. Home: 4010 Potomac Ave Abilene TX 79605-3810

KYKER, CHRISTINE WHITE (CHRIS KYKER), human services administrator; b. Temple, Tex., Mar. 30, 1925; d. Labon Edmondson and Grace Mae (Wrye) White; m. Rex Paxton Kyker, Sept. 1, 1946; children: Jerilyn Kyker Pfeifer, Robert Paxton Kyker, Melinda Lea Kyker Fullerton, Jan Christi Kyker Bryan, Richard Morris Kyker. BA, Abilene Christian U., 1946, MS, 1959, MA, 1960. Lic. master social worker. Instr. Abilene (Tex.) Christian U., 1946-50, 1954-63; guest lectr. Hardin-Simmons U., Abilene, 1965-72; exec. dir. Abilene Assn. for Mental Health, 1963-74; dir. West Cen. Tex. Coun. of Govts., Area Agy. on Aging, Abilene, 1974-79; exec. dir. Tex. Dept. on Aging, Austin, 1979-84; program specialist family and children svcs. Tex. Dept. Human Svcs., 1984-86; pres., CEO Disability Resources, Inc., 1986-92; with Chris Kyker and Assocs., Cons., Abilene, 1992—; Tex. coord. White House Conf. on Aging, 1981; pres. Nat. Mental Health Assn., Staff Coun., 1974, Tex. Mental Health Assn. Staff Council, 1973, Tex. Assn. of Area Agy. Aging Dirs., 1976; lectr. in field. Mem. bd. visitors Abilene Christian U., 1986—; rep. Tex. Silver-Haired Legislation, 1992-94. Recipient Alumni award Abilene Christian U., 1980. Mem. Ch. of Christ. Address: PO Box 5996 Abilene TX 79608-5996

KYLE, JOHN EMERY, mission executive; b. San Diego, July 7, 1926; s. John E. and Agnes (McDaniel) K.; m. Lois Ellen Rowland, June 8, 1947; children: Arlette Marie, Jayson Duane, Marcus Justin, Darlene Patricia. BS in Agriculture, Oreg. State U., 1950; BDiv, Columbia Theol. Sem., 1961, MDiv, 1971. Ordained to ministry Presbyn. Ch. in U.S., 1961. Sr. buyer Easwest Produce Co.-Safeway Stores Inc., San Francisco, 1951-57; pastor Presbyn. Ch. in U.S., Hazard, Ky., 1961-63; adminstr. Wycliffe Bible Translators, Manila, Philippines, 1964-73; coord. Mission to the World, Presbyn. Ch. in Am., Decatur, Ga., 1974-77;, 1988-94; coord. Wycliffe Bible Translators, Washington, 1977-79; missions dir. Intervarsity Christian Fellowship, Madison, Wis., 1979-88; exec. dir. Mission to the World Presbyn. Ch. in Am., Atlanta, 1988—; sr. v.p. Evang. Fellowship of Mission Agencies, Norcross, Ga., 1994—; trustee Columbia Bible Coll. and Sem., 1982-86, Concerts of Prayer Internat., Mpls., 1988—, Overseas Missionary Fellowship, Robesonia, Pa., 1982-86, A.D. 2000 Movement, San Jose, 1989—, Co mission, 1992—. Author: Now This Generation, 1990; editor: The Unfinished Task, 1982, Finishing the Task, 1987, Urban Missions, 1988. Midshipman USNR, 1944-45. Recipient Presdl. Merit medal Pres. of Philippines. Mem. Evang. Fgn. Missions Assn. (trustee 1989-94), Nat. Assn. Evang., Assn. Ch. Missions Com., World Evang. Fellowship, Concerts of Prayer Internat. Home: 5747 Brooklyn Ln Norcross GA 30093-4117 Office: Evang Fellowship Mission Ag 5747 Brooklyn Ln Norcross GA 30093-4117*

KYNERD, MARYBETH, sales executive; b. Meridian, Miss., May 14, 1962; d. Johnson Rudolph Jr. and Mary Frances (Davis) Kynerd. Student, Meridian Jr. Coll., 1980-82; BS in Dietetics, U. So. Miss., 1985. Sec. Meridian Jr. Coll., 1980; pub. broadcast comms. operator McRae's Dept. Store, Meridian, 1982, cashier, 1985, sales clk., 1986; pharms. sales rep. Merck & Co., Inc., Tupelo, Miss., 1986-87, Jackson, Miss., 1987-92; sr. hosp. rep. Merck & Co., Inc., Little Rock, 1992, urologic health sci. assoc., 1993-94, sr. profl. rep., 1995, S.E. region recruiting coord., 1996—. Named to Outstanding Young Women of Am., 1991. Mem. NAFE, Am. Dietetic Assn., U. So. Miss. Alumni Assn., Delta Gamma. Republican. Methodist. Home: 7500 Roswell Rd Apt 63 Dunwoody GA 30350

LABAND, DAVID NEIL, economics educator; b. Newport News, Va., July 31, 1956; s. Kenneth Albert and Cynthia Ann (Slater) L.; m. Anne Cullen McGeady, Feb. 18, 1983; children: Kimberley Anne, Shelley Elizabeth. BA in Econs. with honors, Va. Polytech. Inst. & State U., 1978, MA in Econs., 1980, PhD in Econs., 1981. Asst. prof., vis. fellow Va. Polytech. Inst. & State U., Blacksburg, 1981-82; asst. prof. Econs. U. Md., Balt., 1982-86; assoc. prof. Econs. Clemson (S.C.) U., 1986-92; prof. econs., chair dept. econs. and fin. Salisbury (Md.) State U., 1992-94; prof. econs., head dept. econs. Auburn (Ala.) U., 1994—. Author: Foreign Ownership of U.S. Farmlands: An Economic Perspective of Regulation, 1984, The Roots of Success: Why Children Follow in Their Parents' Career Footsteps, 1985, Blue Laws: The History, Economics and Politics of Sunday Closing Laws, 1987, Patterns of Corporate Philanthropy, 1988, Sex Discrimination in the Legal Profession, 1995; contbr. articles to profl. jours. Rep. County Coun. of PTAs, Wicomico County, Md., 1992-94. Office: Auburn U Dept Econs Rm 203 415 W Magnolia Ave Auburn AL 36832-4613

LABARDI, JILLIAN GAY, financial planner, insurance agent; b. Terre Haute, Ind., Feb. 24, 1945; d. Frank Moses and Joan (Forster) Pierson; m. Jack Alexander Labardi, June 24, 1968. Student, Am. Coll., Paris, 1963; Student, U. Madrid, 1964, Am. U., Washington, 1965, U. Florence, Italy, 1966, Cen. Piedmont Community Coll., Charlotte, N.C., 1984-86; student, Am. Coll., Bryn Mawr, Pa., 1982-89. Chartered fin. cons., CLU. Interpreter Desesco Internat.-Export Co., Florence, Italy, 1966-67; tri-lingual sec. U.S. Topographical Team, Livorno, Italy, 1967-68; mgr. internat. sales Whitin Internat., Charlotte, 1968-81; internat. sales cons. Concord (N.C.) Warehousing, 1981-82; agt., fin. planner Prin. Fin. Group, Charlotte, 1982—; ind. intrepreter-translator, Charlotte, 1968—; instr. Italian, Cen. Piedmont Community Coll., 1970-80. Vol. Internat. House, Charlotte, 1986—. Mem. Internat. Assn. Fin. Planning, Am Soc. CLUs, Am. Soc. Chartered Fin. Cons., Nat. Assn. LIfe Underwriters (Nat. Quality award 1984, 86-94, Nat. Sales Achievement award 1986-94), Women Bus. Owners (charter, treas. 1986—), Million Dollar Round Table, Chamber Prospectors Club, Charlotte Sales and Mktg. Club, Christopher Columbus Carolinas (founder, pres., bd. dirs.). Democrat. Roman Catholic. Home: 221 Scottridge Dr Charlotte NC 28217-4045 Office: Prin Fin Group 1 Morrocroft Ctr 6805 Morrison Blvd Ste 350 Charlotte NC 28211

LABAY, EUGENE BENEDICT, lawyer; b. El Campo, Tex., July 20, 1938; s. Ben F. and Cecelia M. (Orsak) L.; m. Katherine Sue Ermis, Dec. 29, 1962; children: Michael, Joan, John, Paul, David, Patrick, Steven. BBA, St. Mary's U., San Antonio, 1960, JD, 1965. Bar: Tex. 1965, U.S. Dist. Ct. (we. dist.) Tex. 1968, U.S. Dist. Ct. (no. dist.) Tex. 1973, U.S. Ct. Appeals (5th cir.) 1968, U.S. Ct. Appeals (11th cir.) 1981, U.S. Supreme Ct. 1980, U.S. Dist. Ct. (ea. dist.) Tex. 1986. Briefing atty. Supreme Ct. Tex., Austin, 1965-66; assoc. Cox & Smith Inc., San Antonio, 1966-71, ptnr., 1972-83, v.p., 1972-94; pvt. practice, 1994—. Served to 1st lt. U.S. Army, 1960-62. Mem. ABA, State Bar Tex. (chmn. sect. internat. law 1979-80), San Antonio Bar Assn., Fed. Bar Assn., Inter-Am. Bar Assn., Am. Judicature Soc., Catholic Lawyers Guild San Antonio, Phi Delta Phi, Roman Catholic. Clubs: Serna (San Antonio); KC (council grand knight 1982-83). Contbr. articles to legal jours. Home: 31720 Post Oak Trl Boerne TX 78015-4133 Office: 1140 Milam Bldg 115 E Travis St San Antonio TX 78205-1611

LABBE, PATRICK CHARLES, legal nursing consultant; b. Providence; s. Roland Herve and Lucille Rose (Chartier) L.; m. Linda Collette, May 8, 1979 (div. 1981); m. Pauline Rosemarie Allard Labbe, Mar. 15, 1985; children: David Richard, Christopher Micheal, Alicia Rose, Kathryn Tahirih. A in Health Sci. Nursing, Florence Darlington Tech. Coll., 1990; BS in Liberal Studies, Regents Coll., 1993; BSN, City Univ. L.A., 1993, MSN, 1994. RN, S.C.; cert. legal nursing cons., BLS. Staff nurse McLeod Regional Med. Ctr., Florence, S.C., 1990-91, 94-96; inservice coord. Correctional Med. Sys., Bennettsville, S.C., 1991-93; home health nurse Florence (S.C.) Vis. Nurses, 1993-94; staff nurse Florence Nursing Svc., 1991—; legal nurse cons. First Vision Profl. Svcs., Dillon, S.C., 1993—; health occupations instr. Dillon County Area Tech. Ctr., 1996—. Author: Inside the Radical Poet, 1981, Disease Prevention and Health Promotion in a Correctional Setting, 1994. Fellow Grand Coll. of Rites; mem. Am. Soc. Quality Control, Am. Assn. Legal Nurse Cons., N.G. Assn., Nat. League for Nursing, Assn. N.G. Nurses, Res. Officers Assn., The Philalethes, Internat. Assn. of Forensic Nurses, Masons (Lodge Blue #142), Scottish Rite Rsch. Soc., Pee Dee Scottish Rite Club, York Rite Bodes of S.C., Knights of Pytiyias. Mem. LDS Ch. Office: Dillon Am Tech Ctr Main St Dillon SC 29536

LABITZKE, DALE RUSSELL, chemical processing engineer; b. St. Louis, Mo., Dec. 3, 1945; s. Ralph Edgar and Thelma Lois Labitzke; m. Norine Bardill, July 1, 1994. BSChemE, Washington U., St. Louis, 1967. Registered profl. engr. Fla. Process engr. Olin Corp., East Alton, Ill., 1967-68; project engr. Olin Corp., St. Marks, Fla., 1969-71, sr. project engr., 1977; sr. project engr. Olin Corp., Tehran, Iran, 1978; sr. process engr. Olin Corp., St. Marks, Fla., 1979-81; assoc. project engr. Olin Corp., Jacksonville, Fla., 1982; project mgr. Olin Corp., Belgrade, Yugoslavia, 1983-85; process engring. mgr. Olin Corp., St. Marks, Fla., 1986-92, tech. mgr., 1993—; prin. Dale R. Labitzke and Assocs., Tallahassee, Fla., 1992—. Author: Ball Powder Theory and Practice, 1982. With U.S. Navy, 1971-76. Mem. Am. Def. Preparedness Assn., Fla. Engring. Soc. (bd. mem., rep.), AIChE, Nat. Soc. Profl. Engrs. Home: 1529 Chowkeebin Nene Tallahassee FL 32301-4705 Office: Olin Corp PO Box 222 Saint Marks FL 32355-0222

LABODA, GERALD, oral and maxillofacial surgeon; b. Phila., Aug. 15, 1936; s. Lewis and Rose (Waldman) L.; m. Sheila Lois Plasky, Aug. 2, 1956; children: Amy, Michèle, Alane, Bruce. Student, Temple U., 1954-56, DDS, 1960; postgrad., U. Pa., 1960-61. Diplomate Am. Bd. Oral and Maxillofacial Surgery. Resident physician in oral and maxillofacial surgery Jefferson U. Hosp., Phila., 1961-63; pvt. practice oral and maxillofacial surgery S.W. Fla. Oral Surgery Assocs., Ft. Myers, 1965—; sr. dir. Barnett Bank of Lee County, Ft. Myers; chmn. bd. trustees S.W. Fla. Regional Med. Ctr., Ft. Myers, 1989-94, sec. bd. trustees, 1974—; med. dir. S.W. Fla. divsn. Columbia/HCA Healthcare Corp., 1994—. Contbr. articles to profl. jours. Pres. YMCA of Lee County, 1976; pres. Found. for Lee County Pub. Schs., Ft. Myers, 1991; vice chmn. Downtown Redevel. Agy., Ft. Myers, 1985-93, chmn., 1993—; bd. dirs. United Way of Lee County, 1981. Fellow Am. Assn. Oral and Maxillofacial Surgeons (trustee Dist. III 1984-87, v.p. 1987-88, pres. 1989-90); mem. Fla. Soc. Oral and Maxillofacial Surgeons (pres. 1980-81), Fla. Dental Soc. of Anesthesiology (pres. 1978-79), S.W. Fla. Dental Soc. (pres. 1974), Oral and Maxillofacial Surgery Found. (bd. dirs. 1993—). Republican. Jewish. Office: SW Fla Oral Surg Assocs Summerlin Med Park 5285 Summerlin Rd Fort Myers FL 33919-7602

LABOR, GAYLE JOHNSON, English language educator; b. Chgo., July 22, 1949; d. Arthur Wilbur and Gene Adele (Gehrung) Johnson; m. Earle Gene Labor, May 25, 1996. BA in English cum laude, Centenary Coll., 1971; MA in Am. Studies, Bowling Green (Ohio) State U., 1972. Lectr. in English Centenary Coll., Shreveport, La., 1973-75; instr. English Bossier Parish Community Coll., Bossier City, La., 1975—. Mem. Humane Soc. of the U.S., 1984—, Shreveport Regional Arts Coun., 1985—. Mem. MLA, Coll. English Assn., North La. Hist. Assn. (Max Bradbury award 1994), Am. Studies Assn., Cambridge Club. Democrat. Presbyterian. Home: 2505 Melrose Ave Bossier City LA 71111-5931 Office: Bossier Parish Coll 2719 Airline Dr Bossier City LA 71111-5801

LABOUSIER, SUSAN EVELYN, choreographer, dancer; b. Boston, Mar. 25, 1954; d. Harry E. and Evelyn M. (Durant) Neeves; m. Richard L. Labousier, June 16, 1973; children: Michelle Lee, Wendy Ann. Student, MIT, Boston Conservatory, Boston Sch. Ballet, Brookline (Mass.) Ballet, Natick (Mass.) Sch. Ballet and Theatre Arts, Le Ctr. De Danse, Newton, Mass.; studies with Mme. Tatiana Ouroussoff and Pamela E. Feri; student in psychology and theatercraft, MIT, 1970-71; student, Boston Sch. Ballet, 1968-70, Natick Sch. Ballet, 1973, Le Centre de Dance, 1973-79, Edison Coll., Punta Gorda, Fla., 1995—. Cert. to teach, Dance Masters of Am., 1979, cert. for studies in prevention of dance injuries, Boston Children's Hosp., Div. Sports Medicine, 1979. Owner, dir. Susan Neeves Dance Studio, Roxbury, Mass, 1968-70, Fidelis Way Dance Workshop, Brighton, Mass., 1970-73; founder Franklin (Mass.) Dance Workshop, 1977—, Fla. Dance Workshop, 1991—. Dir./choreographer numerous Showtime prodns., 1968-92, A Family Affair, Brighton, Mass., 1970, Christmas Prodn., Franklin, 1984; choreographer The Unsinkable Molly Brown, Roxbury, Mass., 1968, The Drunkard, Franklin, 1979, My Fair Lady, South Boston, 1971, Franklin, 1987, Peter Pan, Summer Arts Sch., Pt. Charlotte, Fla., 1992, Oliver, Pt. Charlotte, 1992; choreographer, co-prodr. My Fair Lady, Pt. Charlotte, 1996. Choreographer Summerthing, Boston, 1968; dir./choreographer benefit prodn. Arthritis Found., 1983; founder, operator Susan Neeves Dance Studio, Mission Ch., Boston, 1968-70, Fidelis Way Dance Workshop, Brighton, Mass., 1970-73; model, dancer Mayor's Youth Activity Commn. Fashion Show, Boston, 1972; bd. dirs. Dance Masters Am., 1986-87; founder The Franklin Dance Co. Inc. as a charitable performing troupe, 1979—; active Franklin Arts Coun., 1986-87; founder, dir. Dance Badge Edn. Program, Girl Scouts Am., 1991—. Recipient Outstanding Citizenship award DAR, 1972, Brotherhood award Jewish War Vets. Am., 1972; recipient Award for Outstanding Performance at Boston City Hall, Mayor Kevin White, 1972. Mem. ASCAP, Charlotte County Arts & Humanities Coun., Charlotte County C. of C. Home and Office: 3357 Vassar St Port Charlotte FL 33980

LABYS, WALTER CARL, economics educator; b. Latrobe, Pa., July 25, 1937; s. Walter Henry and Mary Helen (Markiewicz) L.; m. Jane Elizabeth Reardon, Aug. 26, 1967; children: Walter Paul, Charlotte Alexandria. BSEE, Carnegie Mellon U., 1959; MBA, Duquesne U., 1962; MA, Harvard U., 1965; PhD, U. Nottingham, England, 1968. Sr. economist UN Conf. on Trade and Devel., Geneva, 1969-71; vis. prof. Grad. Inst. of Internat. Studies, Geneva, 1971-75; vis. scholar MIT, Cambridge, Mass., 1981-82; prof. of resource econs. W.Va. U., Morgantown, 1975—; cons. World Bank, Washington, 1987-90, UN, Geneva, Vienna, 1975-90. Author: Dynamic Commodity Models: Specification, Estimation, and Simulation, 1973, Market Structure, Bargaining Power and Resource Price Formation, 1980, Commodity Markets and Models: An Internat. Bibliography, 1987; co-author: Speculation, Hedging and Commodity Price Forecasts, 1970, Commodity Models for Forecasting and Policy Analysis, 1984, Le Viu, Unaivariate Test for Time Series Models; editor: Quantitative Models of Commodity Markets, 1975; co-editor: Commodity Markets and Latin Am. Devel.: A Modeling Approach, 1980, Quantitative Methods for Economic Analysis over Space and Time, Politiques Economiq et Matieres Premieres. Named UN fellow U. Helsinki, 1988-90; Claude Worthing Benedum Disting. scholar W.Va. U., 1990, Gunnar Myrdal Disting. scholar UN Economic Commn. for Europe, Geneva, 1991. Mem. Harvard Club of Western Pa., W.Va. U. Club (pres. 1986-87), Mountain Wine Tasting Soc. (pres. 1978-81), Phi Delta Phi (hon.). Home: 221 Grand St Morgantown WV 26505-7508 Office: WVa U Nat Resource Econ Program Morgantown WV 26506-6108

LACASSE, JAMES PHILLIP, lawyer; b. Delta, Colo., Oct. 21, 1948; s. Kyndall and Elizabeth Ann (Harrington) L.; m. Lynda Diane Manly, June 17, 1978; 1 child, Laura Elizabeth. BS in Acctg. with distinction, Ariz. State U., 1970; JD, Coll. of William and Mary, 1973. Bar: Va. 1973. Tax staff Arthur Andersen & Co., Washington, 1973-75; corp. tax coordinator Continental Telecom Inc., Atlanta, 1975-78; internat. tax mgr. R.J. Reynolds Co., Winston-Salem, N.C., 1978-83, western hemisphere treas., 1983-84; sr. tax counsel Sea-Land Corp., Iselin, N.J., 1984-86; dir. taxes Am. Pres. Cos., Ltd., Oakland, Calif., 1986-95; dir. fin. N.Am. Am. Pres. Cos., Ltd., Memphis. Mem. Downtown Crisis Ctr. Winston-Salem, 1983, bd. pilot commrs. Bays of San Francisco, San Pablo and Suisun; chairperson social ministry com. St. John's Lutheran Ch., Summit, N.J., 1986; deacon Piedmont Community Ch. Named one of Outstanding Young Men of Am. U.S. Jaycees, 1983. Mem. ABA, Va. Bar Assn., Tax Execs. Inst. Home: 1438 LeFleur Pl Memphis TN 38120 Office: Am Pres Cos Ltd 6060 Primacy Pkwy Memphis TN 38119-5745

LACEY, PEELER GRAYSON, diagnostic radiologist; b. Kosciusko, Miss., June 16, 1954; s. Dick Grayson and Beatrice (Peeler) L.; m. Holley Anne Westbrook, July 8, 1978; children: Peeler Grayson Jr., Lauren Elizabeth. BA in Chemistry, Emory U., 1975; MD, U. Miss., 1979. Diplomate Am. Bd. Radiology. Intern U. Miss Med. Ctr., Jackson, 1979-80, resident in diagnostic radiology, 1980-83; diagnostic radiologist South Cen. Regional Med. Ctr., Laurel, Miss., 1983—, Jasper Gen. Hosp., Bay Springs, Miss., 1983—; v.p. Radiology Assocs., Laurel, 1983—. Asst. scoutmaster Troop 32; exec. bd. mem. Pine Burr Area Coun. Boy Scouts Am., chmn. Nat. Eagle Scout Assn.; life mem. Nat. Eagle Scout Assn. Pine Burr Area Coun.; Sun. sch. tchr., deacon. First Bapt. Ch., Laurel. Named one of Outstanding Young Men of Am., 1987. Mem. AMA, NRA (life), Radiol. Soc. N.Am., So. Radiology Soc., Am. Coll. Radiology, Am. Heart Assn., Miss. State Med. Assn., Miss. Radiol. Soc., South Miss. Med. Soc. (past pres.), South Cen. Regional Med. Ctr. (pres. 1994), Roentgen Ray Soc., Cum Laude Soc., Safari Club Internat., Sigma Chi (life loyal Sig.). Home: 2432 Ridgewood Dr Laurel MS 39440-2147 Office: Radiology Assocs 235 S 12th Ave # 2427 Laurel MS 39440-4324

LACHENAUER, ROBERT ALVIN, retired school superintendent; b. Newark, Apr. 1, 1929; s. Alvin Frederick and Helen Louise (Bowers) L.; m. Patricia McConnell, June 14, 1952; children: Jane, Nancy, Robert. AB, Montclair State U., 1951, MA, 1956; EdS, Seton Hall U., 1983. Diplomate in sch. adminstrn., 1988; cert. sch. adminstr., N.J., sch. bus. adminstr., N.J., tchr., N.J., supr., N.J., secondary sch. prin., N.J. Tchr. Bd. Edn., Union, N.J., 1951-52, 54-57, asst. bd. sec., 1957-61; dep. supt. New Providence (N.J.) Sch. Dist., 1961-76, supt., 1976-91, vice pres. Rigorous Ednl. Assistance Deserving Youth Found., 1991-93; treas. sch. monies Morris-Union Jointure Commn., 1987-93; pres. Union County Sch. Bus. Ofcls., 1967-68, Title IV State Adv. Council, Trenton, N.J., 1976-78, Morris-Union Consortium, N.J., 1981-83, Union County Supts. Roundtable, 1983-84; adv. bd. Summit Trust Co., 1971-86. Elder treas. Presbyn. Ch., New Providence, 1958-62; treas. New Providence Hist. Soc., 1966-76; pres. United Way, New Providence, 1978; property mgr. Providence Presbyn. Ch., Hilton Head Island, 1993, elder, 1995. Served as seaman USN, 1952-54. Named Disting. Scholar of the Acad. Nat. Acad. for Sch. Execs., 1990. Mem. N.J. Assn. Sch. Adminstrs. (exec. bd. 1986-91), N.J. Assn. Sch. Bus Officials (pres. 1974-75), Assn. Sch. Bus Officials U.S. (professionalization com. 1974, membership chmn. 1976), N.J. Assn. Ednl. Secs. (adv. bd. 1976—, Outstanding Adminstr. of Yr. 1987). Lodge: Rotary (pres. 1980-81). Home: Sea Pines Plantation 84 Governors Rd Hilton Head Island SC 29928-3032

LACHMAN, ROY, research psychologist; b. Bklyn., Nov. 26, 1927; s. Morris and Lilly (Ladina) L.; m. Janet L. Miner, Sept. 1, 1971; 1 child, Dana Clare. BS in Psychology cum laude, CUNY, 1955; PhD in Exptl. Psychology, NYU, 1960. Lectr. NYU Sch. Engring., 1958-59; asst. prof. U. Hawaii, Hilo, 1959-60; dir. med. psychology Johns Hopkins Med. Sch., 1960-61; asst. prof. Hollins Coll., Roanoke, Va., 1961-63; assoc. prof. to prof. SUNY, Buffalo, 1963-71, grad. program dir. cognitive studies, 1965-70; prof. U. Kans., Lawrence, 1971-74; prof. psychology U. Houston, 1974—, dir. grad. studies psychology dept., 1974-77, dir. cognitive psychology grad. program, 1976-79; grant reviewer NAS, NIMH, NSF, NRC Can. Author: (with others) Cognitive Psychology and Information Processing, 1979; editor: (with others) Information Technology and Psychology: Prospects for the Future, 1982; contbr. articles to profl. jours., chpts. to books; manuscript cons. Behavioral and Brain Scis., Can. Jour. Psychology, Jours. Exptl. Psychology, Jour. Learning and Memory, Internat. Jour. Man-Machine Studies, New Ideas in Psychology, Psychol. Bull., Psychol. Rev., Psychonomic Jours. NSF, NIMH, NIA grantee, 1959—. Mem. APA, Am. Psychol. Soc., Am. Assn. Artificial Intelligence, Soc. for Computers in Psycohlogy, Psychonomic Soc. Home: 5511 Newcastle St Bellaire TX 77401-2711 Office: U Houston Dept Psychology Houston TX 77204

LACKEY, ROBERT DEAN, oil company executive, consultant; b. Great Bend, Kans., Nov. 28, 1950; s. Jack Vernon and Doshia Maudine (Bowman) L.; m. Betty Lou Lilly, Apr. 28, 1967; children: Judy Carol Lackey Harris, Jim Dean Lackey. Grad. high sch., Yale, Okla. Stockman Brownlee Grocery, Cushing, Okla., 1968-70; agronomist Okla. State U., Stillwater, 1970-74; machinist Cesna Aircraft, Wichita, 1974-75; foreman Traco Oilfield Constrn., Cushing, Okla., 1975-79; downhole pump technician Fluor Corp., Cushing, Okla., 1979-83; store mgr. Your Oilfield Supply, Cushing, Okla., 1983-85; blast foreman Cushing Rail Car, 1985-89; br. mgr. Arrow Pump & Supply Inc., Stroud, Okla., 1989—. Democrat. Baptist. Home: RR 1 Box 287 Yale OK 74085-9762 Office: Arrow Pump & Supply 202 N 6th Ave Stroud OK 74079-4016

LACKEY, S. ALLEN, petroleum company executive, corporate lawyer. BBA, U. Miss., 1963, JD, 1968. Bar: Miss. 1968. CEO, pres., legal gen. counsel Shell Oil Co., Houston. Office: Shell Oil Co 910 Louisiana St Houston TX 77002

LACKNER, RUDY PAUL, cardiothoracic surgeon; b. Queens, N.Y., July 25, 1958; s. Rudolph and Dorothy (Peplinski) L.; m. Carol Ann Cudone, May 15, 1990; children: Rudi, Pearl, Timothy. BS summa cum laude, Manhattan Coll., 1980; MD, N.Y. Med. Coll., 1985. Diplomate Am. Bd. Thoracic Surgery, Am. Bd. Gen. Surgery. Resident in gen. surgery L.I. Jewish Med. Ctr., New Hyde Park, N.Y., 1985-90; rsch. fellow in cardiothoracic surgery U. Chgo., 1990-91, resident in cardiothoracic surgery, 1991-93; fellow in thoracic transplant U. N.C., Chapel Hill, 1993-94; asst. prof. surgery, dir. lung transplant program U. Nebr., Omaha, 1994—. Recipient 1st prize ACS, 1989. Mem. Am. Coll. Chest Physicians, Am. Thoracic Soc., Assn. for Acad. Surgery, Internat. Soc. Heart and Lung Transplant, Epsilon Sigma Pi, Beta Beta Beta. Office: U Nebr Div Cardiothoracic Surgery 600 S 42nd St Omaha NE 68105-1002

LACKO, J. MICHELLE, physical education, health and science educator; b. San Diego, Nov. 2, 1968; d. John Michael and Betty Joyce (Chaplain) L. BS, Ea. N.Mex. U., 1991. Cert. tchr., leader level coach and sport sci., N.Mex. Supr. recreation Aztec (N.Mex.) Boys' and Girls' Club, 1988; receptionist Uniforce, Farmington, N.Mex., 1989; courtesy clk. Smiths, Farmington, 1989; instr. recreation City of Farmington Recreation Dept., 1990; groundskeeper Ea. N.Mex. U., Portales, 1991; substitute tchr. Portales Sch. Dist., 1991-92, Canyon (Tex.) Ind. Sch. Dist., 1992-93; phys. edn. tchr., coach Amarillo (Tex.) Ind. Sch. Dist., 1993—. Contbr. poems to profl. publs. Mem. ASCD.

LACOMB-WILLIAMS, LINDA LOU, community health nurse; b. Galion, Ohio, Oct. 1, 1948; d. Horace Allen and Roberta May (Black) Braden; m. Robert Earl LaComb, Feb. 1, 1970 (div. Aug. 1984); children: Robin Marie, Patrick Alan; m. Robert Allen Williams, Aug. 30, 1991; children Erin, Megan. BSN, Capital U., 1970. RN, Fla., Ohio. Staff nurse St. Anne's Hosp., Columbus, Ohio, 1970; pub. health nurse Hillsborough County Dept. Health, Tampa, Fla., 1970-80, community health nurse supr., 1980-87; sr. community health nurse Polk County Dept. Health, Lakeland, Fla., 1987-88; sr. RN supr. Children's Med. Svcs., Tampa, 1988-91, Lakeland, 1991—. 1st lt. flight nurse res. USAF, 1971-75. Recipient Boss of Yr. award Stawberry Chpt. of Am. Bus. Women's Assn., 1985. Mem. ANA, ARC, Fla. Nurses Assn. (grievance rep. state employees profl. bargaining unit 1976-87, pres. 1984-87, 1st v.p. 1989-91, Undine Sams award 1987, Nurse of Yr. award Dist. Four 1987), Sigma Theta Tau (Delta Beta chpt.). Republican. Presbyterian. Home: 502 Shamrock Rd Brandon FL 33511-5548 Office: Children's Med Svcs 1417 Lakeland Hills Blvd Lakeland FL 33805-3200

LACY, CLAUD H. SANDBERG, astronomer; b. Shawnee, Okla., June 5, 1947; s. Lester Claud and Leola Chrstine (Hinton) L.; m. Patricia Kathryn McCoy, Apr. 1, 1971 (div. 1984); m. Patricia Alison Sandberg, Dec. 19, 1988; children: Adrian R., Kathryn Mia Rose. MS in Physics, U. Okla., Norman, 1971; PhD in Astronomy, U. Tex., 1978. Vis. asst. prof. Tex. A&M U., College Station, Tex., 1978-80; asst. prof. astronomy U. Ark., Fayetteville, 1980-86, assoc. prof. astronomy, 1986—. Author: Astronomy Laboratory Exercises, 1981; contbr. articles to Astron. Jour. With U.S. Army, 1971-73. NSF grantee, 1981-84. Mem. Am. Astron. Soc., Internat. Astron. Union. Office: U Ark Dept Physics Fayetteville AR 72701

LACY, ELIZABETH BERMINGHAM, state supreme court justice; b. 1945. BA cum laude, St. Mary's Coll., Notre Dame, Ind., 1966; JD, U. Tex., 1969; LLM, U. Va., 1992. Bar: Tex. 1969, Va. 1977. Staff atty. Tex. Legis. Coun., Austin, 1969-72; atty. Office of Atty. Gen., State of Tex., Austin, 1973-76; legis. aide Va. Del. Carrington Williams, Richmond, 1976-77; dep. atty. gen. jud. affairs div. Va. Office Atty. Gen., Richmond, 1982-85; mem. Va. State Corp. Commn., Richmond, 1985-89; justice Supreme Ct. Va., Richmond, 1989—. Office: Va Supreme Ct PO Box 1315 100 N 9th St Richmond VA 23210

LACY, JOHN FORD, lawyer; b. Dallas, Sept. 11, 1944; s. John Alexander and Glenda Arcenia (Ford) L.; m. Cece Smith, Apr. 22, 1978. BA, Baylor U., 1965; JD, Harvard U., 1968. Bar: Tex. 1968. Assoc. atty. Akin, Gump, Strauss, Hauer & Feld L.L.P., Dallas, 1968-72, ptnr., 1973-82; pres. Ford Lacy PC (affiliated with Akin, Gump et al.), Dallas, 1982—; chmn. Normandy Capital Co., Dallas, 1978—. Contbr. articles to profl. jours. Cofounder, co-chmn. pres. rsch. coun. U. Tex. Southwestern Med. Ctr., Dallas, 1985-91; dir., Vis. Nurse Assn. Tex., 1994-96. With U.S. Army, 1968-74. Rsch. fellow Southwestern Legal Found., Dallas. Mem. ABA, Dallas Bar Assn., State Bar Tex. (coun. bus. law sect. 1992-95). Home: 3710 Shenandoah St Dallas TX 75205-2121 Office: Akin Gump Strauss et al Ste 4100 1700 Pacific Ave Dallas TX 75201-4618

LACZKO, BRIAN JOHN, theater director; b. Cleve., Aug. 7, 1952; s. Joseph John and Avonelle Dorothy (Toth) L.; m. Jill Maree Aude, Aug. 12, 1978; children: Brian John, Stefanie Dale. BA, Denison U., 1974; MA, W.Va. U., 1978. Prodn. mgr. Advent Theatre, Nashville, 1978-79; prodn. mgr. Tenn. Performing Arts Ctr., Nashville, 1980-81, dir. ops., 1981-82, asst. mng. dir., 1982-86; gen. mgr. Starwood Amphitheatre, Nashville, 1986-87; mng. dir. Tenn. Repertory Theatre, Nashville, 1987—; adjudicator Tenn. Arts Commn., Nashville, 1991—, chair adv. panel, 1992—, Met. Nashville Arts Commn., 1991—; mem. profl. cos. panel Opera-Musical Theatre Program NEA. Scenic and lighting dir. over 50 theater prodns. Mem. Am. Arts Alliance, Internat. Theatre Inst. of U.S., Theatre Communications Group, Nat. Alliance Musical Theatre Producers, Alliance Performing Arts Presenters, Tenn. Theatre Assn., Tennesseans for Arts, Nashville C. of C. Office: Tenn Repertory Theatre 427 Chestnut St Nashville TN 37203-4826

LADD, MARCIA LEE, medical equipment and supplies company executive; b. Bryn Mawr, Pa., July 22, 1950; d. Edward Wingate and Virginia Lee (McGinnes) Mullinix; children: Joshua Wingate, McGinnes Lee. BA, U. Pa., 1972; MEd, U. Va., 1973; MA, Emory U., 1979. Rsch. assoc. N.C. Tng. and Standards Coun., Raleigh, 1973-75; dir. counseling svc. N.C. State Youth Svcs. Agy., Raleigh, 1975-76; acad. dean Duke U., Durham, N.C., 1976-77; prin. Ladd & Assocs. Mgmt. Cons., Chapel Hill, N.C., 1979-88; v.p. adminstrn. CompuChem Corp., Research Triangle Park, N.C., 1988-91; v.p. mktg. Prentke Romich Co., Wooster, Ohio, 1991-94; v.p. ops. Exec. Staffing Svcs., Inc., Cary, N.C., 1994; pres., CEO, owner Triangle Aftercare, Durham, N.C., 1994—. Bd. dirs. Wayne County Arts Coun., Wooster, 1992, Stoneridge/Sedgefield Swim/Racquet Club, Chapel Hill, N.C., 1985-88, Oakwood Hist. Soc., Raleigh, 1981-84; mem. bd. visitors Carolina Friends Sch., Durham, 1986-89; Stephen min. Univ. Presbyn. Ch., Chapel Hill, 1994—, youth group leader, 1995—. Decorated Order of Long Leaf Pine Gov. of N.C., 1976. Presbyterian. Office: Triangle Aftercare 249 W Hwy 54 Durham NC 27713

LADDAGA, LAWRENCE ALEXANDER, lawyer; b. New Hyde Park, N.Y., Aug. 12, 1957; s. Carmine Michael and Adeline (Lauricella) L.; m. Beth Jane Goodlove, Nov. 12, 1983; children: Amanda May, Rachel. BA cum laude, U. S.C., 1978, JD, 1981. Bar: S.C. 1981, U.S. Dist. Ct. S.C. 1981, U.S. Ct. Appeals (4th cir.) 1981, U.S. Tax Ct. 1982, U.S. Supreme Ct. 1989. Assoc. Wise & Cole, P.A., Charleston, S.C., 1981-83; founding shareholder, sr. ptnr. Laddaga, Crout & Drachman, Charleston, 1983—. Bd. dirs., 1st v.p. Charleston chpt. Am. Cancer Soc., 1987-88. Mem. Healthcare Fin. Mgmt. Assn. (advanced mem., bd. dirs. 1991-94, sec., v.p. 1991-95, cert. mgr. patient accts., cert. managed care profl., pres. elect), S.C. Bar Assn. (chairperson health care law com. 1995-96), Charleston County Bar Assn., Nat. Health Lawyers Assn., S.C. Hosp. Assn., Order Ky. Cols., Kiwanis, Elks, Masons, Phi Beta Kappa. Home: 1391 Madison Ct Mount Pleasant SC 29464 Office: PO Box 939 145 King St Ste 317 Charleston SC 29401-2230

LADIN, EUGENE, communications company executive; b. N.Y.C., Oct. 26, 1927; s. Nat and Mae (Cohen) L.; m. Millicent Dolly Frankel, June 27, 1948; children: Leslie Hope, Stephanie Joy. B.B.A., Pace U., 1956; M.B.A., Air Force Inst. Tech., 1959; postgrad., George Washington U., 1966-69. Cost engr. Rand Corp., Santa Monica, Calif., 1960-62; mgr. cost and econ. analysis Northrop Corp., Hawthorne, Calif., 1962-66; dir. financial planning Communications Satellite Corp., Washington, 1966-70; treas., chief fin. and adminstrv. officer Landis & Gyr, Inc., Elmsford, N.Y., 1970-76; v.p., treas., comptroller P.R. Telephone Co., San Juan, 1976-77; v.p. fin. Comtech Telecommunications Corp., Smithtown, N.Y., 1977—; acting pres. Comtech Antenna Corp., St. Cloud, Fla., 1978-80; chmn., chief exec. officer Telephone Interconnect Enterprises/Sunshine Telephone Co., Balt., Md. and Orlando, Fla., 1980-82; pres. Ladin and Assocs., Cons. and Commodity Traders, Maitland, Fla., 1982-84; pres., chief fin. officer Braintech Inc., South Plainfield, N.J., 1984; sr. v.p. fin., chief fin. officer Teltec Savs. Communications Co., Miami, Fla., 1984-88; chief fin. officer Hurwitz Group Inc., North Miami Beach, Fla., 1988-91; cons. pvt. practice, 1991—; assoc. prof. acctg. So. Ill. U., East St. Louis, 1960; asso. prof. bus. U. Md., 1969-70; adj. prof. George Washington U., 1969-70; vis. prof. acctg. Pace U., 1970; cons. E. Ladin, Pembroke Pines, Fla., 1991—. Served to capt. USAF, 1951-60. Decorated Air Force Commendation medal; recipient Air Force Outstanding Unit award. Mem. Nat. Assn. Accts., Fin. Exec. Inst. Democrat. Jewish. Club: Flamingo Country Club. Home and Office: 13355 SW 16th Ct Apt 401E Hollywood FL 33027-2429

LADNER, ANN-MARIE CALVO, special education educator; b. Hartford, Conn., Feb. 6, 1949; d. Vincent J. and Mary S. (Santangelo) Calvo; m. R. Martin Ladner, June 19, 1971; children: Mary-Lorraine Amy Cox, R. Vincent, Michelle A. AS, Belleville Area Coll., 1983; BS in Speech and Theater, So. Ill. U., Edwardsville, 1985, MS in Edn., 1986; EdS, Auburn U. Montgomery, 1993. Cert. specific learning disabilities, Ala., psychometrist, Ala., sch. adminstr., Ala. Tchr. merchandising Skadron Coll. Bus., San Bernardino, Calif., 1981-82; tchr. English as second lang. Turkish-Am. Assn., Ankara, Turkey, 1986; tchr. speech and computers Ozel Atilim Lisesi, Ankara, 1987-88; tchr. English and reading St. Jude H.S., Selma, Ala., 1989-90; tchr. spl. edn. Selma Sch. Dist., 1990-92, Montgomery (Ala.) County Schs., 1992-93, 95—, Dept. Youth Svcs., Jemison, Ala., 1993-95. Libr. bd. dirs. City of Millbrook, Ala., 1992-94; bd. dirs. Turkish-Am. Assn., Ankara, 1987-88, Millbrook YMCA, 1993—; judge, coach Nat. Forensics League, Belleville, Ill., 1985. Named Competent Toastmaster, Toastmasters Internat., 1985; mini-grantee Montgomery Area Ccmty. Found., 1992. Mem. NEA, ASCD, Coun. Exceptional Children, Nat. Coun. Tchrs. Math., Ala. Edn. Assn., Mensa, Kappa Delta Pi. Home: 200 River Oaks Dr Apt 1D Wetumpka AL 36092 Office: Project Upward Madison Park Alt Sch Montgomery AL 36110

LA DUC, JOHN, manufacturing executive; b. 1943. BS, Purdue U., 1965; MBA, Stanford U., 1967. Econ. analyst Conoco Inc., N.Y.C., 1967-69; with Kaiser Aluminum Corp., 1969—, treas., 1987-89, v.p., CFO, 1989—. Office: Kaiser Aluminum Corp 5847 San Felipe St Houston TX 77057*

LADWIG, PATTI HEIDLER, lawyer; b. Harleysville, Pa., Aug. 28, 1958; d. L. Donald and Joan E. (Wright) Heidler; m. Manfred Friedrich Ladwig, July 30, 1983; 1 child, Brittney Nichole. BA in Psychology, U. Miami, 1980, JD, 1988. Bar: Fla. 1988, U.S. Dist. Ct. (so. dist.) Fla. 1988. Assoc. atty. Taplin, Howard & Shaw, West Palm Beach, Fla., 1988-92; ptnr. Shaw, St. James, & Ladwig, West Palm Beach, Fla., 1992, St. James & Ladwig, P.A., West Palm Beach, Fla., 1992-93; pvt. practice Patti Heidler Ladwig, P.A., West Palm Beach, 1993—; bd. dirs. Cmty. Assns. Inst., West Palm Beach, First Wellington, Inc.; mem. condominium and planned devel. com., real property, probate and trust law sect. Fla. Bar. Pres., bd. dirs. Treasure Coast Communities Assn., West Palm Beach, 1990—, Pine Lake Condominium Assn. Inc., Pembroke Pines, Fla., 1986-88; mem. community appearance com. ACME Improvement Dist., Wellington, Fla., 1990—, Condominium Owners Fla., 1991—, Fedn. Mobile Home Owners Fla., 1990—; del. Fla. Legis. Action Com., 1989-91. Mem. Fla. Bar Assn. (bus. law sect., mem. condominium and planned devel. com. real property, probate and trust law sect.). Lutheran. Office: Ste 640 1645 Palm Beach Lakes Blvd West Palm Beach FL 33401-2217

LAEMMRICH, GREGORY A., airline pilot; b. Milw., Aug. 16, 1950; s. Alexander John and Mary Theresa (Pakosta) L. BS in Aero. Sci. magna cum laude, Embry-Riddle Aero. U., 1984; AS in Aviation Tech., Ala. Aviation Tech. Coll., Ozark, 1992. Cert. airline transport pilot, FAA. Commd. 2d lt. U.S. Army, 1985, advanced through grades to maj., 1996; attack helicopter platoon leader U.S. Army, Mainz, West Germany, 1987-89; mil. instr. pilot, mil. flight comdr. U.S. Army, Ft. Rucker, Ala., 1989-93; ret. U.S. Army, 1993; airline capt. Express Airlines I, Memphis, 1993-96; DC-9 first officer Midwest Express Airlines, Milwaukee, 1996—; airplane owner/operator Instrn./Charter Ops., Enterprise, Ala., 1991-92; pilot Ga. N.G., Winder, 1995-96. Dancer Daytona Civic Ballet, Daytona Beach, Fla., 1981-83. Recipient various awards. Mem. Airline Pilots Assn. Roman Catholic. Home: 3334 W Rushkin St Milwaukee WI 53215

LAERM, JOSHUA, museum director, zoologist; b. Waynesboro, Pa., Sept. 27, 1942; s. Rolf and Idella Virginia (Benchoff) L.; m. Joanne Marie Zahner, June 13, 1981. B.A. in Philosophy, Pa., State U., 1965; M.S. in Zoology, U. Ill., 1972, Ph.D. in Zoology, 1976. Oceanographer U.S. Naval Oceanographic Office, Washington, 1966-69; predoctoral fellow Smithsonian Instn., Washington, 1972-73; dir. Mus. Natural History; prof. zoology U. Ga., Athens, 1976—. Contbr. articles to sci. jours. Recipient contracts and grants NSF, contracts and grants Sigma Xi, contracts and grants Theodore Roosevelt Fund, contracts and grants Ga. Dept. Natural Resources. Mem. AAAS, Am. Soc. Mammalogists, Am. Soc. Zoologists, Biol. Soc. Washington, Soc. Study of Evolution, Soc. Vertebrate Paleontology. Home: RR 2 Hull GA 30646-9802 Office: Mus Natural History U Ga Athens GA 30602

LAFFITTE, HECTOR MANUEL, federal judge; b. Ponce, P.R., Apr. 13, 1934; s. Miguel and Gilda (Colomer) L.; m. Nydia M. Rossy, June 13, 1958; children: Yasmin, Hector W., Bernice M., Walter M., Giselle M. BA, Interamerican U., 1955; LLB, U. P.R., 1958; LLM, Georgetown U., 1960. Bar: U.S. Dist. Ct. P.R. 1959, U.S. Ct. Appeals (1st cir.) 1959, Supreme Ct. P.R. 1959, U.S. Mil. Appeals 1960, U.S. Supreme Ct. 1976. Assoc. Hartzell, Fernandez & Novas, 1959-64; pvt. practice law, 1965-66; ptnr. Nachman, Feldstein, Laffitte & Smith, 1966-69, Laffitte & Dominguez, 1970-83; judge U.S. Dist. Ct. P.R., 1983—. Mem. ABA, Inst. Jud. Adminstrn. Office: US Dist Ct CH-142 Fed Bldg 150 Carlos Chardon Ave Hato Rey San Juan PR 00918-1757*

LAFLEUR, STEPHEN ALAN, electrical engineer, information technologist, systems intergration consultant; b. Shreveport, La., Sept. 18, 1953; s. Warren and Irene (Langill) LaF.; m. Marilyn Schroeder, May 19, 1979 (div. Nov. 1988); children: Genevieve, David; m. Dianne Elaine Witte, Feb. 16, 1990; children: Forrest, Hannah, Cameron. BSEE, La. State U., 1975. Registered profl. engr. Engr. Conoco, Houston, 1975-76; project engr. Arabian Am. Oil Co., Houston, 1976-79; exec. asst. then ops. supt. Arabian Am. Oil Co., Dhahran, Saudi Arabia, 1979-82, engring. supr., 1982-83; ops. mgr. Arabian Am. Oil Co., Yanbu, Saudi Arabia, 1983-84; staff engr. Kerr McGee Corp., Oklahoma City, 1984-85, tech. supr., 1985-87, systems devel. mgr., 1987-88, sr. cons. engr., 1988-93, mgr. emerging techs., 1993-95; pres. System Perspective, Ville Platte, La., 1995—. Patentee in field. With fundraising Young Reps., Houston, 1979. Summer Sci. scholar NSF, Baton Rouge, 1970, Top 100 scholar La. sTate U. Alumni, Baton Rouge, 1971. Mem. IEEE, Sigma Pi (alumni), Eta Kappa Nu, Tau Beta Pi (scholarship chmn. 1993). Roman Catholic. Office: 1401 W Lincoln Rd Ville Platte LA 70586-2020

LAFONT, LYDIA ANN, nurse manager; b. New Orleans, Mar. 13, 1955; d. Darwin Michael and Geraldine Marie (Terrebonne) L. Diploma, Charity Hosp. Sch. Nursing, 1977. RN, La. Staff nurse Charity Hosp., New Orleans, 1977-81, 97th Gen. Hosp., Frankfurt, Germany, 1981-85, Charity Hosp., New Orleans, 1985-87; staff nurse South La. Med. Ctr., Houma, 1987-90, RN mgr., 1990—. Sponsor Christian Children's Fund, Richmond, Va., 1990—. Mem. Charity Hosp. Sch. Nursing Alumni Assn. Republican. Roman Catholic.

LAFORGE, MARY CECILE, marketing educator; b. Mobile, Ala., Dec. 31, 1945; d. Siegfried Cecil and Nona Francis (Cardwell) Brutkiewicz; m. Robert Lawrence LaForge, June 10, 1972; children: Ryan Christopher, Scott Lawrence. BBA, Samford U., 1965, MBA, 1968; PhD in Mktg., U. Ga., 1980. Asst. mktg. research mgr. Progressive Farmer/So. Living Mags., Birmingham, Ala., 1965-67; asst. prof. mktg. James Madison U., Harrisonburg, Va., 1977-81; assoc. prof. mktg. Clemson U. (S.C.), 1981—. Fellow Acad. Mktg. Sci.; mem. Am. Mktg. Assn., So. Mktg. Assn., Assn. Consumer Research, Beta Gamma Sigma. Baptist. Home: 108 Knight Cir Clemson SC 29631-2114 Office: Clemson U Dept Mktg Sirrine Hall Clemson SC 29634-1325

LA FORGE, RAYMOND BERNARD, JR., marketing and sales consultant; b. Jersey City, Mar. 22, 1933; s. Raymond Bernard and Irene Veronica (Koeffler) LaF.; BS in Bus. Adminstrn., Monmouth Coll., West Long Branch, N.J., 1959; m. Sheridan J. Willie, Mar. 2, 1968; children: Raymond Bernard III, Ashley Alexandra. From sales to sales mgr. West Side Fgn. Cars, Asbury Park, N.J., 1957-59; with Dun & Bradstreet, Inc., 1960-86, fin. analyst, N.Y.C., 1960-64, with salesman credit svc., 1964-67, with salesman mktg. services, 1967-86, mgr. South Fla. mktg. svc. divsn., 1972-86; mem. pres.'s adv. coun. Duns Mktg. Svcs., 1979; dir. mktg. svcs. and new bus. devel. Strategic Mktg. Svcs., Hollywood, Fla., 1987-90; v.p., direct mktg., info. bus. and mktg. cons. Willow Haynes Pub.; pres. Planned Promotions, Inc., 1991—, pres. Surray Internat., 1996—; mktg. cons. U.P. Sunray Internat. Co., 1994. Republican. Country Club of Coral Gables, Racquet Club, Biltmore Club, Shriner, Jester, Mason, Rotary (past pres.).

LAFRAMBOISE, JOAN CAROL, middle school educator; b. Bklyn., June 23, 1934; d. Anthony Peter and Nellie Eva (Zaleski) Ruggles; m. Albert George Laframboise, Aug. 5, 1961; children: Laura J., Brian A. BS in Edn., Springfield (Mass.) Coll., 1956. Cert. tchr. social sci., and mid. sch.; cert. tchr. support specialist. Tchr. Meml. Jr. H.S., Wilbraham, Mass., 1956-61, Midland Park (N.J.) Jr./Sr. H.S., 1961-63, Luke Garrett Middle Sch., Austell, Ga., 1983-93; tchr. lang. arts Pine Mountain Middle Sch., Kennesaw, Ga., 1993—. Coun. pres. Knights of Lithuania, Westfield, Mass., 1973-75, Holyoke, Mass., 1975-76, New Eng. dist. pres., 1976-77; mem. Wistariahurst Mus. Assocs., Holyoke, 1975-77. Jr. League mini-grantee, 1991. Mem. ASCD, NEA, Ga. Assn. Educators, Cobb County Assn. Educators, Nat. Coun. Tchrs. English, Nat. Coun. Social Studies. Home: 2891 Dara Dr Marietta GA 30066-4009

LAFVING, BRIAN DOUGLAS, lawyer; b. Michigan City, Ind., Mar. 31, 1953; s. Allen Herschel and Barbara Joan (Rachow) L.; m. Diane Leigh Pierce, Aug. 16, 1975; children: Bridgette, Brandon, Brittany. BA, BFA, So. Meth. U., 1974, JD, 1977. Bar: Tex. 1977, U.S. Ct. Dist. (no. dist.) Tex., 1977. Assoc. Stalcup, Johnson, Meyers & Miller, Dallas, 1977-79, Baker, Glast, Riddle, Tuttle & Elliott, Dallas, 1979-80; ptnr. Glast & Miller, Dallas, 1980-83, Jones, Day, Reavis & Pogue, Dallas, 1983—. Mem. ABA, Tex. Bar Assn. Republican. Methodist. Office: Jones Day Reavis & Pogue 2300 Trammell Crow Ctr 2001 Ross Ave Dallas TX 75201-2911*

LAGERQUIST, MARION STEWART, art dealer, investor; b. Macon, Ga., Nov. 5, 1921; s. Fredrick Wilson and Irene Watson Lagerquist; m. Evelyn Joiner; children: Laura Jane, Emily Kay. Student, Emory U., 1939-43, Ill. Tech. Inst. Cert. underwriter Soc. Property and Casualty Underwriters. Ins. agt. Lagerquist and Co., Albany, Ga., 1940-47; exec. W.A. Alexander Co., Chgo., 1947-49; pres. Lagerquist and Co., Atlanta, 1949-67; exec. v.p. Kennesan Life, Atlanta, 1967; pres. Banker Fire & Marine, Atlanta, 1964-67, Planned Investment Corp., Atlanta, 1967-74; sec.-treas. Lagerquist Gallery, Atlanta, 1974—. With USAF, 1941-45. Mem. Nat. Assn. Mut. General Agts. (pres. 1962-63), Ga. Soc. CPCU (pres. 1959-60), Jaycees (Northside Atlanta pres. 1959). Democrat. Episcopalian. Home: 3235 Paces Ferry Pl Atlanta GA 30305

LAGIN, NEIL, property management executive, landscape designer; b. Bronx, N.Y., Jan. 10, 1942; s. Barney and Helen (Goldberg) L.; m. Pamela Christine Lagin; children: Jenny Janette, Laurence Connor. Buyer Alexanders, N.Y.C., 1961-69; sales mgr. Halldon, Ltd., N.Y.C., 1969-79; mgr., ptnr. in concession Michele Craig, Westbury, N.Y., 1979-85; ptnr. ALW Trading, "9", N.Y.C., 1985-87; owner, operator Accent Foliage, Delray Beach, Fla., 1987-89; pres. Neil Lagin Property Mgmt., Neil's Landscape Svc., Boca Raton, Fla., 1988—. Author poetry; exhibitor photography shows, Ward Nasse Gallery-Salon, 1975-79, Timothy Blackburn Gallery, 1978, Washington Art Show and others. Notary pub., Fla., 1990; mem. nursery adv. bd. Habilitation Ctr. for the Handicapped, Boca Raton, 1991—; mem. overall adv. com. Palm Beach County Ext., 1993—, sec., chair program rev. com.; bd. dirs. Greater Palm Beach Area Alzheimers Assn., 1993; mem. Environ. Resource Landscape Team; mem. Boca Raton Postal Customer Adv. Coun., 1994-96; memb. bd. dirs. Pheasant Walk Homeowners Assoc., 1996—. Named Fla. Master Gardener, Inst. Food and Agrl. Scis., U. Fla., 1989, Best Landscaper in Boca Raton, South Fla. Newspaper Network, 1991, Best Local Vol. in Boca Raton, 1994, Outstanding MAster Gardener, State of Fla., 1995. Mem. Internat. Palm Soc. (Palm Beach chpt.), Rare Fruit Coun. Internat. (Palm Beach chpt.), Boca Raton C. of C. (grad.

leadership program 1991), Boca Raton Postal Customer Adv. Coun. Home and Office: 17730 Maplewood Dr Boca Raton FL 33487-2171

LAGNEAUX, BOB, transportation company executive; b. 1947. With W.O. Johnson, CPA's, Lafayette, La., 1970-74, Hebert Constn. Co., Lafayette, 1974-80, Superior Hydraulics Inc., Broussard, La., 1980-82, Ace Transp. Inc., Lafayette, 1982—; with Dynasty Transp. Inc., Broussard, v.p. adminstrn. Office: Dynasty Transp Inc 3721 Hwy 90 E Broussard LA 70518

LAGRECA, JOHN S., transportation executive; b. Omaha, July 19, 1941; s. Angelo and Sarah (Fanciullo) LaG.; m. Mary H. Cusick, Aug. 12, 1967; children: Andrea, Andrew. BA, Creighton U., 1963, MBA, 1972. Cert. compensation profl., sr. profl. in human resources. Underwriter, market rsch. Mutual of Omaha, Omaha, 1970-74; compensation mgr. Fairmont Foods, Houston, 1974-78; compensation, benefits mgr. Anderson Clayton Foods, Dallas, 1978-80; dir. compensation, benefits Diamond Shamrock Corp., Dallas, 1980-88; dir. human resources, benefits EPIC Health Care Group, Dallas, 1988-94; dir. compensation and benefits Greyhound Lines Inc., Dallas, 1994—; cons. U. Dallas Human Resource Advisor Coun., 1990—. Scoutmaster, asst. scoutmaster, unit commr. Boy Scouts Am., Richardson, Tex., 1984—. Capt. U.S. Army, 1963-70. Mem. Am. Compensation Assn., Dallas Human Resource Mgmt. Assn. (v.p. 1991-93, 96—. Republican.

LAGRONE, JOHN MARTIN, computer scientist, educator; b. Temple, Tex., Jan. 20, 1954; s. Harry John and Mary Erma (Windham) LaG.; m. Elayne Clark Lewis, Mar. 9, 1976; 1 child, John Richard. BS, Mary Hardin-Baylor Coll., 1975. Cert. math. and history tchr., computer literacy, Tex. Edn. Agy. Tchr. math. Killeen (Tex.) Ind. Sch. Dist., 1975-78, 80-92; sales mgr. DRDR, Inc., Killeen, 1978-80; instrl. technologist Killeen Ind. Sch. Dist., 1992—. Author: Tools Palette Help, 1992; editor, author: The Town Crier, 1991. Charter mem. PTA, Palo Alto Mid. Sch., Killeen, 1995—, parlimentarian, 1996—. Named Educator of Month Rotary Club, 1990. Mem. SAR Tex. Soc. (Heart of Tex. chpt., chaplain, sec. 1989-96, Disting. Svc. award 1991), ABC/KISD Bowling League (pres.). Republican. Home: 2701 Chameleon Dr Killeen TX 76542 Office: Palo Alto Mid Sch 2301 W Elms Rd Killeen TX 76542

LAGRONE, LAVENIA WHIDDON, chemist, real estate broker; b. Conroe, Tex., Feb. 27, 1940; d. James Lewis and Cora Lee (DeLuish) Whiddon; A.A., Kilgore Coll., 1960; B.S., North Tex. State U., 1962; grad. med. tech. Baylor U. Med. Center, 1962; m. Doyle W. LaGrone, June 26, 1959 (div. Sept. 1965); 1 child, Russell Randal. Sr. technologist in spl. chemistry Baylor U. Med. Center, Dallas, 1962-63; research chemist, supr. labs., cardiovascular surgery Southwestern Med. Sch., Dallas, 1964-69, Upstate Med. Center, SUNY, Syracuse, 1969-70; research assoc., supr. lab., dept. surgery U. Tex. Med. Br., Galveston, 1970-74, research assoc., supr. labs., pediatric nephrology, 1974—, mem. chem. safety com., 1984-87; real estate broker DeLanney & Assocs., realtors, 1979-83; owner La Grone & Assocs., Realtors, 1983—. Chmn. student activities PTA Galveston, Tex., 1976-77. Recipient Top Real Estate Sales award, Top Real Estate Producer award, DeLanney & Assocs., 1979, also named Broker's Excellence award and Top Real Estate Commn. award, 1980, also Million Dollar Producer 1980-91. Mem. Am. Soc. Clin. Pathologists (registered med. technologist), Nat. Assn. Realtors, Tex. Assn. Realtors, Galveston Bd. Realtors, Multiple Listing Service (budget com., MLS com.), Phi Theta Kappa. Club: Bus. and Profl. Women's (pub. relations officer 1985-86, chmn. Young Careerist Award 1987, chmn. Woman of Yr. Award 1989, scholarship com. 1988). Contbr. articles to chemistry and med. jours. Home: 142 San Fernando Dr Galveston TX 77550-5712 Office: U Tex Med Br 301 University Blvd Galveston TX 77550-2708

LAHA, ROBERT RANDALL, JR., minister; b. Elizabethtown, Ky., June 19, 1951; s. Robert Randall and Mary Elmina (Bates) L.; m. Sally Ann Schield, Nov. 4, 1972; children: Robert III, Jennifer Ann, Benjamin Ryan. BS, Milligan Coll., 1972; DMin, Union Theol. Sem., 1980, ThM, 1981; PhD candidate, Grad. Theol. Found. and Oxford U. Ordained to ministry Presbyn. Ch., 1982. Assoc. pastor First Presbyn. Ch., Johnson City, Tenn., 1972-76; chaplain Richmond (Va.) Meml. Hosp., 1978-79; assoc. pastor First Presbyn. Ch., Richmond, 1980-89; pastor Campbell Meml. Presbyn. Ch., Weems, Va., 1989-91; sr. pastor Tuckahoe Presbyn. Ch., Richmond, Va., 1991—; instr. Union Theol. Sem., Richmond, 1983—; exec. coun. Presbytery of the James, Richmond, 1987-89, chair com. on ministry, 1987-88, mem. task force on urban ministry, 1985-89, mem. ch. devel., 1989—; mem. Gen. Assembly Coun. Presbyn. Ch. U.S.A.; chair Nominating Com.; corr. mem. Presbyn. Pub. Corp.; chair Faith and Life Com. Pres. Richmond First Club, 1987-88, bd. dirs. 1985-87; bd. dirs. Richmond Hill, 1985-87; scoutmaster Boy Scouts of Am., Johnson City, Tenn., 1972-76, commr., instr. Mem. Am. Assn. Pastoral Counselors. Democrat. Home: 9501 Oldhouse Dr Richmond VA 23233-3735

LAHART, F. VERN, publishing executive; b. Balt., Apr. 21, 1928; s. Stanley Thomas and Margaret (Byrne) L.; m. Eileen Patricia Ryan, Oct. 9, 1954; children: Christopher, Nancy, Daniel, Michael. BA, Loyola U., 1950, JD, 1951; M of Patent Law, John Marshall Law Sch., 1958. Ptnr. Brown, Jackson, Boettcher & Dienner, Chgo., 1954-74; pres., chief exec. officer RCL Enterprises, Inc., Allen, Tex., 1974—. Recipient Hall of Fame award Loyola U., 1974, Thomas Moore award Loyola Law Sch., 1978. Mem. Chgo. Bar Assn. (bd. dirs. 1972-74), Patent Law Assn. of Chgo. (sec. 1971-73), Ill. Bar Assn., Sierra Club (bd. dirs. 1985), Pvt. Industry Coun. of Collin County (vice chmn. 1990-93), Rotary (pres. 1984). Home: PO Box 3000 Allen TX 75002-1301 Office: RCL Enterprises Inc 200 E Bethany Dr Allen TX 75002-3804

LAIN, DAVID CORNELIUS, health scientist, researcher; b. Savannah, Ga., May 17, 1955; s. Marion Cornelius and Sandra (Weatherly) L.; m. Brenda Kay Gastin, May 24, 1980; children: Candace, Heather. BS, Columbia Pacific U., 1985, MS, 1985, PhD, 1987; JD, Newport U., 1996. Diplomate Am. Bd. Forensic Examiners, Am. Bd. Forensic Medicine; lic. respiratory care practitioner. Instr. dept. continuing edn. Ga. So. U., Statesboro, 1983; rsch. devel. coord. Meml. Med. Ctr. Inc., Savannah, Ga., 1983-87; rsch. coord., asst. prof. dept. allied health sci. Med. Coll. Ga., Augusta, 1987—; clin. mgr. Ohmeda Respiratory Care, Columba, Md., 1990-91, Healthdyne, Marietta, Ga., 1991—; bd. dirs. Ga. Soc. Cardiopulmonary Tech., Atlanta, 1987; mem. Respiratory Therapy Adv. Com., Augusta, 1987-90; cons. Aero-Med. Internat., 1987; rsch. affiliate Siemen Elem., Schaumburg, Ill., 1986; manuscript reviewer Am. Assn. Respiration Therapy, Dallas, 1988, Am. Col. Chest Disease, 1990. Contbr. articles to profl. jours. Recipient Appreciation award Am. Heart Assn., 1985, Outstanding Achievement award Calif. Coll. Health Sci., 1986. Mem. AAAS, So. Med. Assn., N.Y. Acad. Sci., Am. Assn. Respiratory Care, Nat. Bd. Respiratory Care (registered respiratory therapist). Democrat. Home: 2048 Honeydew Ln Kennesaw GA 30152 Office: Healthdyne 1255 Kennestone Cir Marietta GA 30066

LAINE, KATIE MYERS, communications consultant; b. Bluffton, Ohio, Oct. 2, 1947; d. George Emerson and Elanore (Keeney) Myers; m. Donald Edward Laine (div. Feb. 1990); 1 child, Brett Edward. BS in Edn., S.W. Tex. State U., 1970. Dir. vols. Austin (Tex.) Ctr. for Attitudinal Healing, 1983-86; talk show host Austin Cablevision, 1986-89; community rels. officer Laguna Gloria Art Mus., Austin, 1989-90; spl. events mgr. Ann Richards for Gov. Campaign, Austin, 1990—. Profl. TV talk show host Katie Laine and Friends. Mem. Mayor's Adv. Coun., Austin, 1989—, Austin Women's Polit. Caucus, 1989—, Emily's List, 1989—; vol. Mayor Lee Cooke Campaign, 1988, Ann Richards Campaign for Gov., 1989; tchr. Divorce Recovery Clinic. Mem. NOW, Women in Communications, Nat. Assn. for Corp. Speaker Activities, Paramount Producers. Home: 8703 United Kingdom Dr Austin TX 78748-6400 Office: Katie Laine Comms 8703 United Kingdom Austin TX 78748

LAING, MALCOLM BRIAN, geologist, consultant; b. Toronto, Ont., Can., Apr. 4, 1955; s. Alexander Duncan and Joan (Dawson) L.; m. Vicki Lynne; children: Megan Jené, Brian Duncan. BS in Geology, Tex. Christian U., 1978. Geologist Electro-Seise, Inc., Ft. Worth, 1978-79, Exploration Logging Co., Houston, 1979-80, Thomas-Powell Royalty Co., Ft. Worth, 1980-82, Lentex Petroleum Inc., Abilene, Tex., 1982-84; cons., 1984-90, Tex. Dept. Health, 1990-92, Tex. Water Commn., 1992-93, Tex. Natural Resource Conservation Commn., 1993—. Co-author: FW-190D Walk Around. Dir. Caprock chpt.; bd. dirs. Tex. Air Mus., 1995—. Mem. Am. Assn. Petroleum Geologists, Soc. Petroleum Engrs., Panhandle Squadron CAF (past leader), Phantom Squadron (past leader), West Tex. Wing CAF (past fin. officer, past CAF check pilot, past ops. officer). Republican. Baptist. Office: 4630 50th St Ste 600 Lubbock TX 79414-3509

LAING, RICHARD HARLOW, artist, educator; b. Apr. 19, 1932; s. Harlow Emerson and Leela (Linder) L.; m. Penelope Gamble; children: Scott, Lindsey; children from previous marriage: Lee Ann Laing Yates, Sharon Laing Klingele. BS in Art and Art Edn., Ea. Mich. U., 1954; MA in Fine Arts-Printmaking/Sculpture, Wayne State U., 1960; DEd in Art Edn. and Art, Pa. State U., 1976. Cert. tchr. art, cert. life tchr., Mich., N.C. Instr. design shop Coll. Architecture and Design U. Mich., Ann Arbor, 1954-55; instr. studio art and humanities Edsel Ford Sr. H.S., Dearborn, Mich., 1955-60; tchr. art-drawing and painting Interlochen (Mich.) Music and Arts Acad., summer 1957; asst. prof. art U. North Tex., 1960-68; grad. asst., then spl. grad. intern Pa. State U., 1967-69; prof., head art dept. Ball State U., Muncie, Ind., 1968-71; prof., chairperson art dept. Edinboro U. Pa., 1972-79; dean Sch. Art East Carolina U., N.C., 1979-83, prof., 1979—; coord. art edn., devel. specialist in cultural affairs Regional Devel. Inst., East Carolina U., 1983—; mem. continuing edn. task force, active several coms. East Carolina U.; presenter/lectr. profl. and ednl. instns., including U.S. SBA, 1981, Nat. Coun. Art Adminstrs., Chgo., 1973, Trans-Pan Art Assn., El Paso, Tex., 1966; cons. numerous orgns., including Tourism Dept. State of N.C., Jr. Coll. Albany, Toledu Mus. Art Sch., Calif. State U., Chico, L.A. and Fullerton, So. Ill. U.; participant/univ. rep. ednl. insts.; juror visual art exhbns., Mich., Tex., Ind., Pa., N.C. Exhibited in group shows at Mich. Watercolor Soc., 1957, 59, (1st cash prize 1957), AIA, Rice U., 1967, Ea. Ind. Art Exhbn., 1971, 72 (1st cash prizes), N.C. Mus. Art, 1980, 81, East Carolina U. Mus., 1979-88; one-man show at Dreyer Galleries, Houston, 1963; prin. commissioned works include stainless steel wall relief State Coll., Pa., 1966, bronze fountain sculptures Denton, Tex., 1967, AIA, Terre Haute, Ind., 1968, stained glass design and constrn. Elizabeth's Restaurant, Meadville, Pa., 1976; dir., prodr. sound slide shows, videos, 1985-88; graphic design art dir. brochures, placemats, mag. advts. Chmn. bd. dirs. N.C. Aero. Mus., Inc., 1984—, Playwrights Fund N.C., 1987; advisor to bd. dirs. Greenville Mus. Art, 1979, mem. acquisition com., 1987; mem. planning bd. Erie (Pa.) Summer Arts Festival, 1972, Erie Art Ctr., 1972; mem. coun. Boro of Venango, Pa., 1973, pres. coun., 1974-76, mem. zoning bd., 1973; advisor cmty. art-related projects and events; active N.C. Hist. Sites Commn.; deacon First Christian Ch., Greenville, 1981. With USNR, 1951-59. Recipient Pitt-Greenville Art Coun. Svc. award, 1981; NEA vis. artist grantee/dir., 1982, exhbn. grantee/dir. State Arts Coun., 1983. Mem. AAUP, Nat. Coun. Art Adminstrs. (chmn. rsch. com. 1974-76), Nat. Assn. Schs. of Art and Design (moderator programs on tech. and edn. of the art student 1983, site visitor various univs./colls. for MFA and BFA approval), Nat. Art Edn. Assn. (session moderator 1968, moderator student sect. 1969, mem. profl. materials com. 1969, 71, 73, recorder 1961), Coll. Art Assn., N.C. Art Edn. Assn. (Dist. Art Educator 1992), Muncie Art Assn. (bd. dirs. 1969-72), Rotary (bd. dirs. Greenville chpt. 1981-83, spkr. 1981—), N.C. Playwrights Assn. (pres. 1985). Democrat. Home: 204 Pineview Dr Greenville NC 27834-6434

LAIR, JUDITH ANNE TREVVETT, social services administrator, counselor; b. Richmond, Va., Mar. 26, 1942; d. William Thomas and Thelma A. (Dyson) Trevvett; m. Robert E. Lair, Jr., Sept. 15, 1962; children: Marlene, Karen, Gregory. Student, Mary Washington Coll., 1960-62, U. N.C., 1974-75; BA in Psychology, U. N.C., Asheville, 1977; MA in Edn., Western Carolina U., 1980; EdS, George Washington U., 1992. Cert. counselor; registered practicing counselor, N.C. Probation/parole officer N.C. Dept. Correction, Asheville, 1981-82; vocat. evaluator Sheltered Workshop, Columbus, N.C., 1982; mgr. N.C. Welcome Ctr., Columbus, 1982-85; asst. mgr. Eckerd's Drugs, Monroe, N.C., 1985-86; mgr. J.E's Dress Shop, Monroe, 1986; child support enforcement agent div. social services N.C. Dept. Human Resources, Charlotte, N.C., 1986-87; counselor, office mgr. Nat. Ctr. Treatment of Phobias, Anxiety and Depression, Washington, 1989-91, Ft. Balvoir Counseling Ctr., 1991-92; grad. asst. in counseling George Washington U., 1992; supr. Child Support Enforcement, Charlotte, 1993—; bereavement cons. Hospice of Polk County, Tryon, N.C., 1986-87. Mem. Thermal Belt Bus. and Profl. Women (Woman of the Yr. 1981, 84, Employee of the Yr. 1985), Psi Chi. Republican. Methodist. Home: 1009 Brantham Ct Charlotte NC 28211-2400

LAIRD, DORIS ANNE MARLEY, humanities educator, musician; b. Charlotte, N.C., Jan. 15, 1931; d. Eugene Harris and Coleen (Bethea) Marley; m. William Everette Laird Jr., Mar. 13, 1964; children: William Everette III, Andrew Marley, Glen Howard. MusB, Converse Coll., Spartanburg, S.C., 1951; opera cert. New Eng. Conservatory, Boston, 1956; MusM, Boston U., 1956; PhD, Fla. State U., 1980. Leading soprano roles S.C. Opera Co., Columbia, 1951-53, Plymouth Rock Ctr. of Music and Art, Duxbury, Mass., 1953-56; soprano Pro Musica, Boston, 1956, New Eng. Opera Co., Boston, 1956; instr. Stratford Coll., Danville, Va., 1956-58, Sch. Music Fla. State U., Tallahassee, 1958-60, dept. humanities, 1960-68; asst. prof. Fla. A&M U., Tallahassee, 1979-89, assoc. prof., 1990—; vis. scholar Cornell U., 1988. Author: Colin Morris: Modern Missionary, 1980; contbr. articles to profl. jours. Soprano Washington St. Meth. Ch., Columbia, S.C., 1951-53, Copley Meth. Ch., Boston, 1953-56, Trinity United Meth. Ch., Tallahassee, 1983—; mem. Saint Andrews Soc., Tallahassee, 1986—; judge Brain Bowl, Tallahassee, 1981-84. Recipient NEH award, 1988; Phi Sigma Tau scholar, 1960. Mem. AAUP, AAUW, Nat. Art Educators Assn., Tallahassee Music Tchrs. Assn., Tallahassee Music Guild, Am. Guild of Organists, DAR (mus. rep. 1984-85), Colonial Dames of 17th Century (music dir. 1984-85). Democrat. Club: University Wy Women's. Avocations: traveling, dancing. Home: 1125 Mercer Dr Tallahassee FL 32312-2833 Office: Fla A&M U Dept Humanities Room 405 Tucker Hall Tallahassee FL 32307

LAIRD, HUGH EDWARD, II, pharmacologist, toxicologist; b. Phoenix, Mar. 30, 1939; s. Clyde Wesley and Juanita (Gregg) L.; m. Marilyn Jo Long, June 11, 1961; children: Michael Edward, Deborah Gayle. BS in Pharmacy, U. Ariz., 1962, PhD in Pharmacology/Toxicology, 1974. Registered pharmacist, Ariz., Calif. Pharmacist, mgr. Laird Pharmacies, Tempe, 1962-68; prof. pharmacology/toxicology U. Ariz., Tucson, 1974-95; prof. pharmacology, chair dept. pharm. scis., Sch. Pharmacy Tex. Tech. U., Amarillo, 1995—; cons. Ariz. Poison Control Ctr., Tucson, 1974-80, Legal Profession, Tucson, 1989-94. Co-editor: Neurotransmitters and Epilepsy, 1987; contbr. numerous articles to profl. jours. Pres. Glenn Heights Neighborhood Assn., Tucson, 1991-94; chair Arcadia-Alamo Area Plan-City of Tucson, 1992. Grantee NIH, 1978-81, 92—, Ariz. Disease Control Commn., 1987-92. Mem. Am. Soc. Pharmacology and Experimental Therapeutics, Soc. for Neurosci., Soc. for Experimental Biology and Medicine, Am. Assn. for Cancer Rsch., Soc. In Vitro Biology. Office: Tex Tech U Health Sci Ctr Sch Pharmacy 1300 S Coulter Amarillo TX 79106

LAIRD, KIMBERLY JEANNE, medical librarian, educator; b. Grand Rapids, Mich., Dec. 23, 1961; d. Robert Bruce and Carolyn (DuMond) L. BA, Bethel Coll. and Sem., St. Paul, 1984; M in Info. Libr. Studies, U. Mich., 1987. Libr. radiation oncology U. Mich. Hosps., Ann Arbor, 1987; asst. info. svcs. libr. Libr. Health Scis., U. Ill., Chgo., 1988-91, asst. cataloging libr., 1991-92, asst. prof., 1988-92; tech. svcs. libr., asst. prof. med. libr. James H. Quillen Coll. Medicine, East Tenn. State U., Johnson City, 1992—. Mem. Med. Libr. Assn., Acad. Health Info. Profls. (sr.). Office: Medical Libr James H Quillen Coll of Med PO Box 70693 Johnson City TN 37614-0693

LAIRD, WILLIAM DAVID, manufacturing executive; b. Port Arthur, Tex., Sept. 5, 1944; s. Wade Raiford and Willie Mae (Zampini) L.; m. Mollie Annette Moore, Feb. 15, 1964; children: Melanie, Jennifer, Marcie. Sales Gulf Coast Machine, Beaumont, Tex., 1964-69; dist. sales mgr. Rucker Shaffer, Houston, 1969-75; v.p., ptnr. Control Flow Co., Inc., Houston, 1975—; pres., ptnr. Laird Exploration Co., Cypress, Tex., 1991—. Sgt. USMC, 1963-70. Home: 12722 Ravensway Dr Cypress TX 77429-2637

LAIZURE, STEVEN CASEY, pharmacy educator; b. Bethesda, Md., Mar. 22, 1958; s. Dallas Morgan and Louise (Kennedy) L.; m. Kathy Mae Laughter, Aug. 9, 1980; children: Sidney Morgan, Steven Parker. Pharm.D., U. N.C., 1983; postgrad., U. Fla., 1983-85, 86-87. Rsch. assoc. dept. pharmacy practice U. Fla., Gainesville, 1985-86; asst. prof. U. Tenn., 1987-93, assoc. prof., 1993—; mem. various coms. in field. Author abstracts, book chpts. in field; contbr. articles to profl. jours. Grantee Meth. Hosps. Found., 1989-91, 93, Am. Coll. Clin. Pharmacy, 1989-90, Am. Assn. Colls. Pharmacy, 1989-90, Nat. Found. Infectious Diseases, 1989-90, Am. Soc. Hosp. Pharmacists Rsch. and Edn. Found., 1991-92, NIH, 1995—, others; recipient Searle Fellowship Mentor award 1993. Mem. Am. Assn. Colls. of Pharmacy (Young Investigator award 1989), Am. Coll. Clin. Pharmacy. Office: U Tenn Dept Clin Pharmacy 26 S Dunlap St Memphis TN 38103-4909

LAKE, CHARLES DONALD, computer science educator, administrator; b. Mt. Clemme, Mich., June 26, 1962; s. Charles Delbert and Judith Ruth L. BS, U. S. Ala., 1984, MBA, 1988, postgrad., 1988—. Asst. to mgmt. Diamond Head Corp., Bay St. Louis, Miss., 1977-83; acct. Ark Oils, Inc., Daphne, Ala., 1983-84, Sta. WABB-FM, Inc., Mobile, Ala., 1985-86; owner John's Jubilee, Inc., Fairhope, Ala., 1985—; instr. computer sci. Faulkner State Jr. Coll., Bay Minette, Ala., 1986—, chmn. computer sci., bus. mgmt. and hospitality divsn., 1996—; cons. Pardyne Systems, Inc., Fairhope, 1988—; v.p. Faulkner State faculty senate, 1993—, chmn. adminstrv. process self-study, 1993-95. Reviewer books in field. Pres. Baldwin County Young Reps., Ala., 1993-95; bd. dirs. Baldwin County Solid Waste Com., 1991-93. Recipient Technologist of Yr. award Ala. Coun. for Tech. in Edn., 1995; recognized for Outstanding Achievement, Ala. Reunion, Gov. Guy Hunt, Montgomery, 1989. Mem. ACM (com. chair 1989—), Ea. Shore C. of C. (bd. dirs. 1989-90, Dedicated Svc. award 1989), Ea. Star, Faulkner Edn. Assn. (pres. 1993—), Scottish Rite, Greeno Lodge, Alpha Kappa Psi. Home: 2 Hammond Cir Bay Minette AL 36507-2657 Office: Dept Bus Computer Sci and Hospitality Faulkner State Coll Bay Minette AL 36507

LAKE, DAVID ALAN, investments lawyer; b. El Campo, Tex., Jan. 15, 1938; s. Cortus L. and Ottis W. (Noland) L.; m. Shirley L. Hill, Dec. 20, 1966; children: Joel, Jonathan, Jeffrey Kyle, Kristi. BA, Baylor U., 1960; BD, Southwestern Seminary, 1963; JD, So. Methodist U., 1966. Bar: Tex. 1966. Lawyer Nickerson & Lake, Pittsburg, Tex., 1966-68; pvt. practice Tyler, Tex., 1967—; gen. ptnr. Colonial Manor, Tyler, 1968-90, Golden Manor, Pittsburg, 1968-82; pres. Gardendale, Inc., Jacksonville, Tex., 1973-93, Am. Health Svcs., Inc., Tyler, 1977—, N.E. Tex. Contracting Co., Tyler, 1982—; sec., bd. dirs. Sunset Care Ctr., Jacksonville, 1973-79; bd. dirs. Cypress Bank, Fed. Savs. Bank, Pittsburg. Bd. dirs. Way of Life, Inc., Tyler, 1972-75, Smith County Heart Assn., Tyler, 1974-75; bd. dirs., chmn. Smith County Red Cross, Tyler, 1972-77; bd. dirs., Sunday sch. tchr. 1st Bapt. Ch., Tyler, 1972—; trustee East Tex. Bapt. U., Marshall, 1993—. Mem. Tex. and Smith County Bar Assn., Jacksonville Jaycees (bd. dirs. 1965-66), Petroleum Club, Emerald Bay club, Lee Booster Club (pres. 1977-78), Rotary Internat. (Paul Harris fellow 1990—, bd. dirs. South Tyler chpt. 1971-74, pres. 1978-79). Home: 815 Pinedale Pl Tyler TX 75701-9645 Office: 5620 Old Bullard Rd Ste 128 Tyler TX 75703-4358

LAKE, I. BEVERLY, JR., state supreme court justice. BS cum laude, Wake Forest U., 1925; LLB, Harvard U., 1929; LLM, Columbia U., 1940, SJD, 1947. Bar: N.C. 1928, U.S. Supreme Ct. 1954, U.S. Dist. Ct. (ea., mid. and we. dists.) N.C., U.S. Ct. Appeals (4th cir.). Pvt. practice Raleigh, 1929-32, 55-65, 78-86; dist. rationing atty. U.S. Office Price Adminstrn., 1943-45; staff atty. U.S. Nat. Prodn. Authority, 1951; asst. atty. gen. N.C., 1950-55, supreme ct. justice, 1965-78; prof. law Wake Forest U., 1932-51, Campbell U., 1978; vis. prof. law Duke U., 1945-46, U. Fla., 1947. Mem. ABA, N.C. State Bar, Wake County Bar Assn., N.C. Bar Assn. Democrat. Office: NC Supreme Ct PO Box 1841 Raleigh NC 27602-1841*

LAKE, NANCY JEAN, nursing educator, operating room nurse; b. Sandborn, Ind., May 13, 1942; d. Thomas Malone and Vivian Pearl (Meek) Wills; divorced; children: Brian, Deanna, Patrick. AS, Cleve. State Community Coll., 1972. RN, Ky., Ind., N.Y., Ark. Staff nurse geriatric unit Regional Hosp., Ft. Smith, Ark., 1973-74; pub. health staff nurse Ft. Smith, Ark., 1974; staff nurse Bradley County Hosp., Cleveland, Tenn., 1972-73; staff nurse recovery room and oper. room St. Anthony Hosp., Terre Haute Regional Hosp., Terre Haute, Ind., 1974-76; staff nurse oper. room, emergency room, med.-surg. fl. Washington County Hosp., Salem, Ind., 1976-77; oper. room. staff nurse Floyd County Hosp., New Albany, Ind., 1977-78; staff nurse oper. room Good Samaritan Hosp., Vincennes,, Ind., 1978-82; staff nurse oper. room and thoriac cardio vascular coord. Winthrope Univ. Hosp., Mineola, N.Y., 1982-86; staff nurse oper. room Humana Hosp., Audubon, 1986-92; staff nurse oper. rm. Jewish Hosp. Healthcare Ctr., 1990—. Home: 2912 Livingston Ave Louisville KY 40299-3112

LAKE, SIMEON TIMOTHY, III, federal judge; b. Chgo., July 4, 1944; s. Simeon T. Jr. and Helen (Hupka) L.; m. Carol Illig, Dec. 30, 1970; children: Simeon Timothy IV, Justin Carl. BA, Tex. A&M, 1966; JD, U. Tex., 1969. Bar: Tex. 1969, U.S. Dist. Ct. (so. dist.) Tex. 1969, U.S. Ct. Appeals (5th cir.) 1969, U.S. Supreme Ct. 1976, U.S. Ct. Appeals (3d cir.) 1981, U.S. Dist. Ct. (no. dist.) Tex. 1983. From assoc. to ptnr. Fulbright & Jaworski, Houston, 1969-70, 72-88; judge U.S. Dist. Ct. (so. dist.) Tex., Houston, 1988—. Past editor Houston Lawyer. Served to capt. U.S. Army., 1970-71. Fellow Tex. Bar Assn., Houston Bar Assn., State Bar Tex., Am. Law Inst. Office: US Dist Ct 9535 US Courthouse 515 Rusk Ave, RM 9535 Houston TX 77002*

LAKE, WESLEY WAYNE, JR., internist, allergist, educator; b. New Orleans, Oct. 11, 1937; s. Wesley Wayne and Mary McGehee (Snowden) L.; m. Abby F. Arnold, Aug. 1959 (div. 1974 children: Courtenay B., Corinne A., Jane S. AB in Chemistry, Princeton U., 1959; MD, Tulane U., 1963. Diplomate Am. Bd. Internal Medicine, Am. Bd. Allergy and Immunology. Intern Charity Hosp. of La., New Orleans, 1963-64, resident internal medicine, 1966-69; NIH fellow allergy and immunology La. State U. Med. Ctr., 1969-70; instr. dept. medicine Tulane U., New Orleans, 1967-69; fellow dept. medicine La. State U., New Orleans, 1969-70, instr. dept. medicine, 1970-73, asst. clin. prof. medicine, 1973-77; chief allergy clinic La. State U. Svc. Charity Hosp. La., New Orleans, 1970-77; assoc. clin. prof. medicine Tulane U., New Orleans, 1978—; temp. staff positions various hosps., 1963-70, including Baton Rouge Gen. Hosp., Our Lady of the Lake Hosp., Glenwood Hosp., St. Francis Hosp., Monroe, La., Lallie Kemp Charity Hosp., Independence, La., Huey P. Long Hosp., Pineville, La.; gen. med. officer outpatient clinic Hunter AFB, Savannah, Ga., 1964-65, gen. med. officer internal medicine svc., 1965-66; cons. physician Seventh Ward Gen. Hosp., Hammond, La., 1971-77, Slidell (La.) Meml. Hosp., 1971-89, St. Tammany Parish Hosp., Covington, La., 1977-85; cons. physician East Jefferson Hosp., Metairie, La., 1971-77, staff physician, 1990—; asst. vis. physician Charity Hosp. New Orleans, 1970-75, staff physician, 1975-77, vis. phys. Tulane divsn., 1979—; assoc. physician So. Bapt. Hosp., New Orleans, 1970-75, staff physician, 1975—, chmn. dept. medicine, chmn. internal medicine com., 1982-84, chmn. pharmacy and therapeutics, 1980-82, mem. investigative rev. com., 1984-85, mem. internat. medicine quality assurance com., 1989-94; staff physician Kenner (La.) Regional Med. Ctr. (formerly St. Jude Med. Ctr.), 1985—, chmn. quality assurance com., 1987-89. Author: (with others) Infiltrative Hypersensitivity Chest Diseases, 1975; contbr. articles to profl. jours. including Jour. Immunology, Internat. Archives Allergy and Applied Immunology, Jour. Allergy and Clin. Immunology; also chpts. in books concerning chest diseases. Fellow ACP, Am. Coll. Allergy, Sigma Xi; mem. New Orleans Acad. Internal Medicine, Musser-Burch Soc., S.E. Allergy Soc., La. Allergy Soc. (sec. 1975-76, v.p. 1976-77, pres. 1977-78). Republican. Episcopalian. Home: 1308 Bordeaux St New Orleans LA 70115 Office: 4224 Houma Blvd Ste 250 Metairie LA 70006

LAKER, JOSEPH ALPHONSE, history educator; b. Indpls., Mar. 17, 1941; s. Alphonse Joseph and Anna Catherine (Riegel) L. B.A. in History, Marian Coll., 1963; M.A. in History, Ind. U., 1967, Ph.D., 1975. Instr. St. Olaf Coll., Northfield, Minn., 1967-70, Ind. U., Bloomington, 1970-71, 72-74; asst. prof. Wheeling Coll., W. Va., 1974-81, assoc. prof. history, 1981—. Mem. Assn. Asian Students, Econ. History Assn., W. Va. Hist. Soc. Democrat. Roman Catholic. Avocations: tennis; golf; reading mystery stories. Office: Wheeling Coll 316 Washington Ave Wheeling WV 26003-6243

LAKIN, JAMES DENNIS, allergist, immunologist, director; b. Harvey, Ill., Oct. 4, 1945; s. Ora Austin and Annie Pitranella (Johnson) L.; m. Sally A. Stuteville, July 22, 1972; children: Margaret K., Matthew A. PhD, Northwestern U., 1968, MD, 1969; MBA in Med. Group Mgmt., U. St. Thomas, 1996. Diplomate Am. Bd. Internal Medicine, Am. Bd. Allergy and Immunology. Dir. allergy rsch. Naval Med. Rsch. Inst., Bethesda, Md., 1974-76; clin. prof. U. Okla., Oklahoma City, 1976-89; dir. lab., chmn. allergy and immunology dept. Oxboro Clinics, Bloomington, Minn., 1989—; dir. Fairview Allergy and Asthma Svcs., Bloomington, 1995—; bd. dirs. Okla. Med. Rsch. Found., Oklahoma City, 1980-89; regional cons. Diver Alert Network, Duke U., Chapel Hill, N.C., 1987—; cert. diving med. officer NOAA, 1988. Co-author: Allergic Diseases, 1971, 3d edit., 1986; contbr. articles, revs. to profl. publs. Councilperson Our Lord's Luth. Ch., Oklahoma City, 1978-88, Faith Luth. Ch., Lakeville, Minn., 1990-91. Lt. comdr. USN, 1970-76. Fellow ACP, Am. Acad. allergy and Immunology, Am. Coll. Chest Physicians; mem. Am. Assn. Immunologists, Med. Group Mgmt. Assn., Am. Coll. Physician Execs. Office: Oxboro Clinic 600 W 98th St Bloomington MN 55420-4773

LAKSHMIVARAHAN, SIVARAMAKRISHNAN, computer science educator; b. Karaikurichi, Tamil Nadu, India, June 12, 1944; came to U.S., 1975; s. Sankaran Sivaramakrishna and Subbulakshmi (Narayanan) Iyer; m. Shantha Sitaram Varahan, Feb. 5, 1973; children: Subha, Bharathram. BSc in Physics with distinction, U. Madras, India, 1964; BE in Elec. Tech. with distinction, Indian Inst. Sci., Bangalore, 1967, ME in Applied Electronics, 1969, PhD in Learning Algorithms, 1973. Rsch. asst. dept. elec. engring. Indian Inst. Sci., Bangalore, 1969-73; project asst. Sch. Automation Indian Inst. Tech., Bangalore, 1973; lectr., asst. prof. dept. computer sci. Indian Inst. Tech., Madras, 1973-75; vis. asst. prof. div. applied math. Brown U., Providence, 1975-76; asst. prof. dept. engring. and applied sci. Yale U., New Haven, 1976-78; assoc. prof. Sch. Elec. Engring. and Computer Sci., U. Okla., Norman, 1978-84, prof., 1984-92, prof. Sch. Computer Sci., 1992—, Hallibuurton disting. lectr. Coll. Engring., 1984-86, Assocs. disting. lectr., 1986-87, George Lynn Cross rsch. prof., 1995; vis. prof. U. Bonn, 1980, 82, U. Laval, Quebec City, Can., 1982, AMOCO Prodn. Rsch. Ctr., Tulsa, summer 1983, Nat. Inst. Standards and Tech., Gaithersburg, Md., summer 1985, Tech. Inst. for Higher Studies Monterrey, Mex., 1988, 90, 93, Nat. Tsing-Huo U., Hinshu, Taiwan, 1992, Indian Inst. Sch., Bangalore, 1993; cons. AMOCO Prodn. Rsch. Ctr., Nat. Inst. Standards and Tech.; colloquium speaker in field. Author: Lectures on Automata Theory, 1974, Learning Algorithms: Theory and Application, 1982, (with S.K. Dhall) Analysis and Design of Parallel Algorithms, 1990, Parallel Prefix Computations, 1994; editor: Procs. of Workshop on Parallel Processing using Heterogeneous Element Processor, 1985, spl. issue Info. Scis.-Internat. Jour., 1987; contbr. numerous articles to sci. jours., chpts. to books. Recipient Regents award for rsch. and creative activities U. Okla., 1982, Regents award for superior teaching, 1992; grantee NSF, 1981-83, 85, 86-87, 89-93, U. Okla. Office Rsch. Adminstrn., 1981, AMOCO, summers 1983-86, 1985-85, 87-88, U. Okla. Energy Resource Inst., 1984-86, Denelcor, Inc., 1985, Okla. Gov.'s Coun. on Sci. and Tech., 1986, More Okla. Sci. and Tech. Fellow IEEE (citation for contbns. to learning algorithms, parallel computing and their applications 1993), IEEE Computer Soc. (vice chmn. Oklahoma City chpt. 1982-83, chmn. 1983-85), Assn. for Computing Machinery (editl. bd. Applied Computing Rev. 1993—, nat. lectr. selection com. 1992-93, nat. lectr. 1989-92, faculty advisor student chpt. U. Okla. 1987-89, citation for contbns. to learning and parallel algorithms). Office: U Okla Sch Computer Sci Norman OK 73019

LALE, CISSY STEWART (LLOYD LALE), freelance writer; b. Port Arthur, Tex., Jan. 15, 1924; d. Lloyd M. and May (Cowart) Stewart; m. Max Sims Lale, Oct. 9, 1983. BJ, U. Tex., 1945. Reporter Record-News, Wichita Falls, Tex., 1945, News-Messenger, Marshall, Tex., 1945-47; editor Times-Rev., Cleburne, Tex., 1947-49; women's editor, columnist Star-Telegram, Ft. Worth, 1949-87; freelance writer, Ft. Worth mag., Ft. Worth, 1987—. Bd. dirs. Trinity Terr. Retirement Community, 1991-94; active Jewel Charity Ball. Cissy Stewart Day proclaimed by Ft. Worth City Coun., 1987, portrayed in outdoor mural City of Ft. Worth, 1987. Mem. Women in Comm., Inc. (nat. pres. 1968-71), Tex. State Hist. Assn. (pres. 1996-97), East Tex. Hist. Assn. (pres. 1994), Tex. Heritage, Inc. (bd. dirs. Ft. Worth chpt. 1990), Womans Club Ft. Worth, Ft. Worth Garden Club (v.p. 1995-96). Episcopalian. Home: # 101 3900 White Settlement Rd Fort Worth TX 76107-7822

LAM, CHUN HUNG, finance educator, consultant; b. Kowloon, Hong Kong, Oct. 6, 1947; came to U.S., 1966; s. Wing Cheong and Choi Chu (Chan) L.; m. Wai-Fung Edith Kong, June 14, 1975; children: Jon, Jay, Rick. BS in Edn., Duke U., 1971, MBA, 1974, PhD, 1977; MS in Edn., Princeton U., 1972. Bus. analyst Corning Internat., Corning, N.Y., 1974; instr. Duke U., Durham, N.C., 1976-77; asst. prof. Sch. Bus. Tulane U., New Orleans, 1977-81; assoc. prof. Cox Sch. Bus. So. Meth. U., Dallas, 1981—; chmn. Dept. Fin. Cox Sch. Bus. So. Meth. U., 1988-91; bd. dirs. Pacific Southwest Bank, Corpus Christi, Tex., 1990—, North Tex. Mesbic, Inc., Dallas, 1990-93, 1st Internat. Bank, Dallas, 1992—; mem. adv. bd. Trinity Christian Acad., Addison, Tex., 1992—; faculty senate exec. com. So. Meth. U., 1996—. Author: Microcomputer Application in Banking, 1986; contbr. articles to profl. jours. Recipient Howard Wissner Teaching award Tulane U., 1981, James B. Duke fellowship, 1976. Mem. Fin. Mgmt. Assn., Fin. Assn., Phi Beta Kappa, Tau Beta Pi. Office: Cox Sch Bus So Meth U Dallas TX 75275

LAM, PAULINE POHA, library director; b. Hong Kong, Oct. 21, 1950; came to U.S., 1971; d. Cheung and Kam-Chun (Mo) Li; m. Frank Sung-Lun Lam, Nov. 28, 1973; children: Candace See-Win Lam, Megan See-Kay Lam. BA, U. B.C., 1977; MLS, U. Tex., 1980; cert. City Mgmt. Acad., Austin C.C., 1994. Libr. dir. City of Cedar Park (Tex.); bd. dirs. Cedar Park Pub. Libr. Found., 1994—. Mem. Work Force Literacy Com. Literacy Coun. of Williamson County, 1995; bd. dirs. ARC of Ctrl. Tex., Austin, 1995—. Mem. ALA, Tex. Libr. Assn., Tex. Mcpl. League Libr. Dir. Assn. Office: Cedar Park Pub Libr 550 Discovery Blvd Cedar Park TX 78613-2200

LAM, SIMON SHIN-SING, computer science educator; b. Macao, July 31, 1947; came to U.S., 1966; s. Chak Han and Kit Ying (Tang) L.; m. Amy Leung, Mar. 29, 1971; 1 child, Eric. B.S.E.E. with distinction, Wash. State U., 1969; M.S. in Engring., UCLA, 1970, Ph.D., 1974. Research engr. ARPA Network Measurement Ctr., UCLA, Los Angeles, 1971-74; research staff mem. IBM Watson Research Ctr, Yorktown Heights, N.Y., 1974-77; asst. prof. U. Tex.-Austin, Austin, 1977-79, assoc. prof., 1979-83, prof. computer sci., 1983—; David S. Bruton Centennial prof. U. Tex., Austin, 1985-88, anonymous prof., 1988—; chmn. dept. computer sci. U. Tex.-Austin, Austin, 1992-94. Editor-in-chief IEEE/ACM Transactions on Networking, 1995—; editor: Principles of Communication and Networking Protocols; contbr. articles to profl. jours. NSF grantee, 1978—; Chancellor's Teaching fellow UCLA, 1969-73. Fellow IEEE (Leonard G. Abraham prize 1975); mem. Assn. for Computing Machinery (program chmn. symposium 1983). Office: Univ Tex Dept of Computer Sci Austin TX 78712

LAM, TUKIEN MICHAEL, internist; b. Saigon, Vietnam, Jan. 2, 1967; came to U.S., 1985; s. Pok Wo and Kwok Ying (Tang) L. BME, B Biology, MIT, 1989; MD, U. Chgo., 1993. Diplomate Nat. Bd. Med. Examiners. Resident in internal medicine U. Tex. Southwestern Med. Ctr., Dallas, 1993-96. Mem. AMA, ACP, Tex. Med. Assn.

LAMALIE, ROBERT EUGENE, retired executive search company executive; b. Fremont, Ohio, June 3, 1931; s. Glennis and Mildred M. (Hetrick) L.; m. Dorothy M. Zilles, June 20, 1953; children: Deborah, Dawn, Elaine. BA, Capital U., Columbus, Ohio, 1954; postgrad., Case Western Res. U. Asst. dir. recruiting Xerox Corp., 1959-62; mgr. orgn. planning and profl. recruiting Glidden Co., 1962-65; search cons. Booz, Allen & Hamilton, Inc., Cleve., 1965-67; pres., chief exec. officer Lamalie Assocs., Inc., Tampa, Fla., 1967-84, chmn. bd. dirs., chief exec. officer, 1984-87, chmn. bd. dirs., 1987-88; pres. Robert Lamalie, Inc., Marco Island, Fla., 1988-90, ret., 1990. Served with U.S. Army, 1954-56, Korea.

LAMAR, CHARLES WILBUR, III, lawyer; b. New Orleans, June 2, 1948; s. Charles Wilbur and Josephine (Pugh) L.; children: Allison Joy, Courtney Josephine, Madison Charles. BA, Harvard U., 1971; MA, Tufts U., Medford, Mass., 1972; JD, Boston U., 1975. Bar: La. 1976. Law clk. U.S. Dist. Ct., New Orleans, 1975-76; assoc. Breazeale, Sachse & Wilson, Baton Rouge, 1976-80; pvt. practice Baton Rouge, 1980-82; gen. counsel, sec. The Lamar Corp., Baton Rouge, 1982—, also bd. dirs.; bd. dirs. Woodlawn Land Co., Inc., Baton Rouge. Bd. dirs. La. Arts and Scis. Ctr., Baton Rouge, 1984-89, Baton Rouge Symphony Assn., 1989—. Mem. City Club. Home: 4559 Highland Rd Baton Rouge LA 70808-6541 Office: The Lamar Corp 5551 Corporate Blvd Baton Rouge LA 70808-2567*

LAMAR, JAMES LEWIS, JR., chemical engineer; b. Antlers, Okla., June 13, 1959; s. James Lewis and Priscilla (Henderson) L.; m. Carol Horton, May 16, 1982; children: Joy Loree, Amanda Beth. AS, Bee County Coll., 1979; BSChemE, Tex. A&I U., 1982. Cert. quality engr., 1991, cert. quality auditor, 1992, RAB quality systems lead auditor, 1993. Prodn. engr. Union Carbide Corp., South Charleston, W.Va., 1982-86; diagnostic engr. Union Carbide Chems. & Plastics, South Charleston, W.Va., 1986-90; sr. quality engr. Union Carbide Chems. & Plastics, League City, Tex., 1990-94; quality engr. UCC, Texas City, 1994—; instr. Tex. Dept. Commerce, Houston, 1992. Author/programmer software, 1989, 91, 92. Mem. Pine Dr. Babt. Sch. Bd., Dickinson, Tex., 1992. Named Jaycees Outstanding Young Men Am., 1983. Mem. Am. Soc. Quality Control (sr.), Cowboys for Christ. Republican. Office: Union Carbide Bldg 2-UP PO Box 471 Texas City TX 77592-0471

LA MARRE, MILDRED HOLTZ, business executive; b. Phila., May 10, 1917; d. Philip and Dora H.; student George Washington U., 1939-40; B.A., U. Md., 1966; m. Jack Understein, Dec. 25, 1938 (dec.); children: Robert, Norma Lisa, Norman, Gary; m. 2d, John La Marre, Feb. 14, 1981 (dec.). With Jack Understein Co., Washington, 1960-71; exec. asst. Muskie for Pres., Washington, 1971-72; researcher Carnegie Endowment Internat. Peace, Washington, 1973-76; personal asst., adminstrv. asst. to Under Sec. Lucy Wilson Benson, U.S. Dept. of State, 1977-78; exec. asst. Mike Barnes for Congress, 1978; pres. Internat. Personal Shopping Service, Ltd., N.Y.C., 1980-84; exec. asst. John La Marre Appraisers, 1982—; actress, print model, 1987—. Bd. dirs. Hebrew Home Greater Washington, 1970-83, Internat. Sickle Cell Anemia Research Inst., Washington, 1976-83, Asolo Theatre Guild, 1993—, pres. 1995-96; bd. dirs. Asolo Performing Arts Ctr., 1995-96. Democrat. Address: 1255 N Gulfstream Ave Sarasota FL 34236-8920

LAMB, IRENE HENDRICKS, medical researcher; b. Ky., May 9, 1940; d. Daily P. and Bertha (Hendricks) Lamb; m. Edward B. Meadows. Diploma in nursing, Ky. Bapt. Hosp., Louisville; student, Berea (Ky.) Coll., Calif. State U., L.A. RN, Ky. Charge nurse, head nurse acute medicine, med. ICU, surgical ICU, emergency room various med. ctrs., 1963-67; staff nurse rsch. CCU U. So. Calif./L.A. County Med. Ctr., 1968; nurse coord. clin. rsch. ctr. U. So. Calif./Los Angeles County Med. Ctr., L.A., 1969-74; sr. rsch. nurse cardiology Stanford (Calif.) U. Sch. Medicine, 1974-85, rsch. coord. pvt. clin., 1988; dir. clin. rsch. San Diego Cardiac Ctr., 1989-92; sr. cmty. health nurse Madison County Health Dept., Berea, 1993—; clin. rsch. cons., 1988—. Co-contbr. numerous articles to med. jours.; contbr. articles to nursing jours., chpts. to med. books. Mem. Am. Heart Assn. (cardiovasc. nursing sect.). Home: 107 Lorraine Ct Berea KY 40403-1317

LAMB, PATRICIA CLARE, poet; b. Houston, Nov. 14, 1935; d. Hugh Reginald and Margaret (McKeon) L. BA, U. St. Thomas, Houston, 1957; postgrad., U. Houston, 1959-65. Author: Why Horatio, 1985, Dwelling, 1988, All Men By Nature, 1993; contbr. numerous articles to profl. jours. Mem. Acad. Am. Poets. Democrat. Roman Catholic. Home: 3614 Montrose Blvd #405 Houston TX 77006

LAMB, PATRICK JOHN, research associate accountant; b. Charleston, W.Va., Oct. 22, 1938; s. Charles Bernard and Grace Frances (Jackson) L.; m. Kathleen Campbell, May 5, 1962; children: Christine M., Mary K., Charles P., Michael J., Karen P. BSBA, W.Va. State Coll., 1962; MBA, W.Va. Coll. Grad. Studies, 1984. Auditor W.Va. Tax Dept., Charleston, 1961-63; acct. The Diamond, Charleston, 1963-66, W.Va. Water Co., Charleston, 1966-69; sr. rsch. assoc., acct. W.Va. Rsch. League, Charleston, 1969—. Author: The Economic Impact of the Arts in West Virginia. Mem. W.Va. Pub. Accts. Assn., KC (grand knight 1986-88, 94-96, Cath. layman 1981, dist. dep. 1988-93, state warden 1993-95, state advocate 1995-96, state treas. 1996—). Republican. Roman Catholic. Home: 1403 Jackson St Charleston WV 25301-1909

LAMB, RONALD JAMES, dentist; b. Tulsa, Oct. 10, 1947; s. Jim Chester and Ruth Maxine (Kelly) L.; m. Pamela Jayne Compton, Oct. 15, 1976; children: Ronald James, Brittina Nichole, Robert Jeffrey. BS, Oral Roberts U., 1969; DMD, U. Louisville, 1974. Lic. dentist, Okla. Gen. practice dentistry Broken Arrow, Okla., 1974—; founder, pres. Ron Lamb Missions, Inc., Broken Arrow, 1976—; mem. adj. faculty Oral Roberts U., Tulsa, 1979-80; pres. India Practical Missions, Inc., Tulsa, 1985—; v.p. Health Teams Internat., Tulsa, 1986; 5-state regional dental del. Christian Med. Soc.; bd. dirs. Healthcare Ministries, Springfield, Mo. Author: Portable Mission Dentistry, 1995. Named to Tulsa Tribune Roll of Honor, 1980; recipient Tulsa award for Mankind, Sertoma, 1983. Mem. ADA (Svc. award 1983, Meritorious Internat. Svc. award 1993, 94), Christian Dental Soc. (pres.), Assembly of God Med. Assn. (sec., treas. 1995—), Christian Med. Dental Soc. (mem. dental adv. com. 1995—), World Dental Relief (pres., founder 1996—), Okla. Dental Assn., Tulsa County Dental Assn. Republican. Lodge: Gideons (pres. 1982-83). Office: 609 N Main St PO Box 747 Broken Arrow OK 74013-0747

LAMB, STACIE THOMPSON, elementary school educator; b. Abilene, Tex., Nov. 9, 1965; d. George Lyman and Shirley Elizabeth (Burton) T.; m. Dennis A. Lamb; children: Lane, Logann. BS in Edn., Lubbock Christian Coll., 1986; postgrad., Tex. Tech U. Elem. Edn. grades 1-6, Tex. 1st grade tchr. Lubbock (Tex.) I.S.D. Brown Elem., 1986-87; 3rd grade tchr., chairperson Morton (Tex.) I.S.D., 1987-89; 5th grade lang. arts tchr. Whiteface (Tex.) C.I.S.D., 1990—. Mem. ASCD, Classroom Tchrs. Assn. (sec. 1988-89, elem. rep. 1991-92). Home: 2104 Tech Dr Levelland TX 79336-7035 Office: PO Box 117 Whiteface TX 79379-0117

LAMB, SYDNEY MACDONALD, linguistics and cognitive science educator; b. Denver, May 4, 1929; s. Sydney Bishop and Jean Louisa (MacDonald) L.; m. Sharon Reese Rowell, June 17, 1956 (div. 1971); children: Christina, Sarah, Nancy; m. Susan Ellen Jones, May 15, 1977. BA, Yale U., 1951; PhD, U. Calif., Berkeley, 1958. From asst. to assoc. prof. linguistics U. Calif., Berkeley, 1958-64; from assoc. to prof. Yale U., New Haven, 1964-77; mng. ptnr. Semionics Assocs., Houston, 1977-93; prof. Rice U., Houston, 1980—; fellow Ctr. for Advanced Study in Behavioral Scis., Stanford, Calif., 1973-74. Author: Outline of Stratificational Grammar, 1966, (with others) Sprung from Some Common Source, 1991; inventor associative computer memory, 1977, 80, 4 patents; contbr. articles to profl. jours. NSF grantee, 1959-64, 66-70; Am. Council of Learned Soc. grantee, 1973-74. Mem. Linguistic Soc. Am. (exec. com. 1966-68), Linguistics Assn. of Can. and U.S. (pres. 1983-84, chmn. bd. dirs. 1995—), Houston Philos. Soc. (treas. 1985-86, v.p. 1991-92, pres. 1992-93). Office: Rice U Dept of Linguistics Houston TX 77251

LAMBERT, CAROL ANN, audiologist; b. Easton, Pa., June 15, 1947; d. Harry and Clara (Miller) L.; BA, U. Tulsa, 1972, MA, 1977; 1 child, Eugene Read. Lic. audiologist. Audiologist, Tulsa Otolaryngology, Inc., and U. Tulsa, 1977-78; speech reading instr. Tulsa Speech and Hearing Assn., 1977-78; audiologist Ear, Nose and Throat Consultants, Inc., Tulsa, 1978-83; audiologist U. Tulsa, 1983-89; pvt. practice audiology, Tulsa, 1987—; cons. audiologist Springer Clinic, 1979-80; cons. Okla. State Dept. Health, Tulsa Scottish Rite Clinic for Childhood Lang. Disorders, 1979-91; cons. audiologist Broken Arrow Med. Ctr., 1988—, Kaiser Rehab. Ctr., 1991-93, Okla. Early Intervention Program, 1991-93; adj. asst. prof. U. Tulsa, 1981-82; bd. advisors coll. nursing and applied health scis., U. Tulsa, 1991-92. Sustaining mem. Jr. League of Tulsa; mem. Philbrook Art Ctr.; bd. dirs. Children With Attention Deficit Disorder, 1991-93. Mem. NAFE, Nat. Assn. Women Bus. Owners, Am. Speech to Speech and Hearing Assn. (cert. in audiology), Acad. Rehabilitative Audiologist, Okla. Speech and Hearing Assn. (past sec.), Okla. Acad. of Audiology (mem. exec. com.), Tulsa Assn. Speech Pathologists and Audiologists (past pres., bd. dirs. 1988), Tulsa Speech and Hearing Assn. (past dir.). Home and Office: 1145 S Utica Ave # 302 Tulsa OK 74104-4013

LAMBERT, CLARISSA SAVELL, education educator; b. Mobile, Ala., May 27, 1959; d. David Vaughn and Elizabeth Louise (Sheppard) Savell; m. Terry Eugene Lambert, Mar. 26, 1983. BS cum laude, U. South Ala., 1981; MA with honors, Mobile Coll., 1988; student, U. So. Miss. Cert. tchr., adminstrn., Ala. Tchr. 5th grade Mt. Vernon Elem. Sch., 1981-83; tchr. 6th-8th grades Scarborough Middle Sch., Ala., 1983-91; tchr. Clark Math. and Sci. Sch., Chickasaw, Ala., 1991—. Mem. ASCD, NEA, Nat. Coun. Tchrs. Math., Ala. Edn. Assn., Mobile Edn. Assn., Alpha Lambda Delta, Lambda Sigma, Omicron Delta Kappa, Tau Beta Sigma, Kappa Delta Pi, Kappa Delta Epsilon, Alpha Delta Kappa. Home: 6259 Christopher Dr N Mobile AL 36609-2741

LAMBERT, DEBORAH KETCHUM, public relations executive; b. Greenwich, Conn., Jan. 22, 1942; d. Alton Harrington and Robyna (Neilson) Ketchum; m. Harvey R. Lambert, Nov. 23, 1963 (div. 1985); children: Harvey Richard Jr., Eric Harrington. BS, Columbia U., 1965. Researcher, writer The Nowland Orgn., Greenwich, Conn., 1964-67; model Country Fashions, Greenwich, Conn., 1964-67; freelance writer to various newspapers and mags., 1977-82; press sec. Va. Del. Gwen Cody, Annandale, Va., 1981-82; assoc. editor Campus Report, Washington, 1985—; adminstrv. asst. Accuracy in Media, Inc., Washington, 1983-84, dir. pub. affairs, 1985—; TV producer weekly program The Other Side of the Story, 1994—; bd. dirs. Accuracy in Academia, Washington; film script cons. The Seductive Illusion, 1988-89. Columnist: The Eye, The Washington Inquirer, 1984—, Squeaky Chalk, Campus Report, 1985—; contbr. articles to various mags.; producer: The Other Side of the Story, 1993—. Co-founder, mem. Va. Rep. Forum, McLean, 1983—; mem. Rep. Women's Fed. Forum. Mem. Am. Bell Assn., Pub. Rels. Soc. Am., DAR., World Media Assn., Am. Platform Assn. Republican. Presbyterian. Home: 1945 Lorraine Ave Mc Lean VA 22101-5331 Office: Accuracy in Media Inc 4455 Connecticut Ave NW Washington DC 20008-2328

LAMBERT, DOROTHY ELIZABETH, psychologist; b. Omaha, Dec. 13, 1942; d. Richard Parvin and Elizabeth Carter (Paddock) Jernigan; m. Edward Warren Lambert, Apr. 17, 1993. BA, U. Tenn., 1979, MS, 1982, PhD, 1989. Cert. psychologist, Tenn. Real estate broker Knoxville, Tenn., 1973-75; sec. State of Tenn., Knoxville, 1975-79; parole officer Tenn. Bd. of Paroles, Knoxville, 1979-93; tchr. (part-time) Knoxville Bus. Coll., 1982-83; psychology intern Meharry Med. Coll., Nashville, 1993-94; psychol. examiner Clover Bottom Devel. Ctr., Nashville, 1994-95; psychologist Prison Health Svcs., Nashville, 1995—; psychologist, part-time Nashville, 1996. Newsletter editor Nashville Area Psychol. Assn. Mem. Am. Psychol. Assn. (poster presenter Toronto 1993), Tenn. Psychol. Assn., Nashville Area Psychol. Assn., Am. Correctional Assn., Phi Beta Kappa. Home: PO Box 23404 Nashville TN 37202

LAMBERT, E. WARREN, psychologist; b. Memphis, May 15, 1945; s. Edward Joseph and Louise (Kiefer) L.; m. Dorothy E. Lambert. BA, U. Tex., Arlington, 1967; MA, Ind. U., 1970, PhD, 1973. Fellow med. psychology U. Calif. Med. Ctr., San Francisco, 1971; clin. psychologist Psychiatric Assn. Ctrl. N.Y., Syracuse, 1972-77; rsch. assoc. Vanderbilt U., Nashville, 1992—; adj. prof. U. Tenn., Knoxville, 1980-95. Contbr. articles to profl. jours. Mem. APA, Nashville Area Psychol. Assn.

LAMBERT, EDYTHE RUTHERFORD, retired language educator, civic volunteer; b. Candler, N.C., Oct. 6, 1921; d. John William and Addie Bell (Holcombe) Rutherford; m. Robert Stansbury Lambert, Mar. 7, 1946; children: Margaret Anne, Dorothy Lee (dec.). BA, U. N.C., Greensboro, 1942; MA, Clemson U., 1970. Tchr. French Linden (N.C.) High Sch., 1942-43; lab. tech. Am. Enka (N.C.) Corp., 1943-44; reporter Asheville (N.C.) Citizen-Times Co., 1944-46; with pub. relations dept. Shorter Coll., Rome, Ga., 1955; instr. Clemson (S.C.) U., 1966-68. Docent hist. house mus. Pendleton Hist. Found., 1974—; pres. Clemson Area Arts Council, 1978-79, Pickens County Friends of the Arts, S.C., 1981-82, Clemson Council Human Relations, 1987; bd. dirs. Clemson Child Devel. Ctr., 1976—. Recipient Algernon Sydney Sullivan award for community svcs. Clemson U., 1990, Human Rights award Baha'is of Pickens County, 1991. Mem. AAUW (pres. 1985—, Named Gift Recipient 1979, 86, fellow 1964, editor The Palmetto Leaf, 1984-86), Phi Kappa Phi. Democrat. Methodist. Club: Clemson U. Woman's (v.p. membership 1984-85).

LAMBERT, ETHEL GIBSON CLARK, secondary school educator; b. Atlanta, Apr. 18, 1943; d. Robert Harold and Ethel (Gibson) Clark; m. Hugh Felder Lambert, June 27, 1964 (div. Nov. 3, 1988); children: Courtney, Elizabeth, Hugh Lambert Jr. BA, Oglethorpe U., Atlanta, 1965; MEd, Kennesaw State Coll., Marietta, Ga., 1992; postgrad., State U. West Ga., Carrollton, 1995—. Lic. tchr. T-5, Ga. Tchr. Clayton County Bd. Edn., Jonesboro, Ga., 1965-66, Fulton County Bd. Edn., Atlanta, 1966-67; tchr. pre-sch. weekday program First Bapt. Ch., Gainesville, Ga., 1984-88; tchr. remedial edn. program Riverdale High Sch./Clayton County Bd. Edn., 1990—. Author: The Impact of Geography on the Campaigns of the Civil War Fought in Georgia, 1993, The Utilization of Georgia Historical Sites as Teaching Methodology in MIddle Grades Education, 1993, (juvenile) Obnoxious Bill, 1993, Research on Academic Motivation of Elementary, Middle and Secondary School Students in America, 1993, Reading Strategies that Address the Reluctant Reader in America's Public Middle and High Schools, 1995. Den leader Cub Scouts Am., Gainesville, 1980-83; mem. Christian Businessmen's Prayer Breakfast, Atlanta, 1990-95, 96. Mem. Profl. Assn. Ga. Educators, Order Ea. Star, College Park Women's Club, College Park Hist. Soc. Baptist. Home: 1881 Myrtle Dr SW Apt 711 Atlanta GA 30311-4919 Office: Riverdale High Sch 160 Roberts Dr Riverdale GA 30274

LAMBERT, JOSEPH EARL, state supreme court justice; b. Berea, Ky., May 23, 1948; s. James Wheeler and Ruth (Hilton) L.; m. Debra Hembree, June 25, 1983; children: Joseph Patrick, John Ryan. BS in Bus. and Econs., Georgetown Coll., 1970; JD, U. Louisville, 1974; completed sr. appellate judges seminar, NYU Sch. Law, 1987. Bar: Ky. 1974. Staff Sen. John Sherman Cooper U.S. Senate, Washington, 1970-71; law clk. to judge U.S. Dist. Ct., Louisville, 1974-75; ptnr. Lambert & Lambert, Mt. Vernon, Ky., 1975-87; justice Supreme Ct. Ky., Frankfort, 1987—. Mem. Bd. Regents Eastern Ky. U., Richmond, 1988-92. Recipient Disting. Alumni award U. Louisville Sch. Law, 1988. Mem. Ky. Bar Assn. Republican. Baptist. Office: Supreme Ct Ky 205 E Main St Mount Vernon KY 40456-2211*

LAMBERT, OLIVIA SUE, commercial artist, writer; b. Philippi, W.Va., July 10, 1939; d. Curtis Truman and Olive Virginia (Cox) L. BA in History, Alderson Broaddus Coll., 1961. Interim pub. rels. officer Alderson Broaddus Coll., Philippi, 1965; clk. Barbour County Ct. House, Philippi, 1966; free lance artist, writer Philippi, 1965—. Artist: (book jackets) History of Barbour County, 1965, History of Calhoun County, 1982; illustrator: (book) Wappatomaka, 1971; cartographer: Blue-Gray Reunion Map, 1993. Mem. Rep. Nat. Com., Philippi Sesquecentennial Com., Blue-Gray Reunion Com., Nature Conservancy. Mem. AAUW, Coll. Club, W.Va. Filmmakers Guild, W.Va. Writers Inc., Barbour County Writers Workshop, Order Eastern Star. Methodist. Home and Office: 4 Woodsboro Dr Rte 3 Philippi WV 26416

LAMBERT, VICKIE ANN, dean; b. Hastings, Nebr., Oct. 28, 1943; d. Victor E. and Edna M. (Hein) Wagner; m. Clinton E. Lambert, Jr., June 30, 1974; 1 child, Alexandra. Diploma, Mary Lanning Sch. Nursing, 1964; BSN, U. Iowa, 1966; MSN, Case Western Res. U., 1973; DNSc, U. Calif., San Francisco, 1981. RN, Ga. Acting chair dept. nursing adminstrn. Med. Coll. Ga., Augusta, 1982-84, coord. doctoral program nursing, 1984-85; coord. doctoral program nursing George Mason U., Fairfax, Va., 1986-88; assoc. dean Case Western Res. U., Cleve., 1989-90; dean Sch. Nursing Med. Coll. Ga., Augusta, 1990—. Contbr. articles to profl. jours. Fellow Am. Acad. Nursing; mem. ANA, Sigma Theta Tau, Sigma Xi. Home: 1421 Waters Edge Dr Augusta GA 30801

LAMBERT, WILLIE LEE BELL, mobile equipment company owner, educator; b. Texas City, Tex., Oct. 23, 1929; d. William Henry and Una Oda (Stafford) Bell; m. Eddie Roy Lambert, July 2, 1949; (dec. Mar. 1980); children: Sondra Kay Lambert Bradford, Eddie Lee. Degree in bus., Met. Bus. Coll., 1950; AAS, Coll. of Mainland, 1971; BS, Sam Houston U., 1976. Cert. hand and foot reflexologist, Hatha Yoga instr. Sec. Judges Reddell & Hopkins, Texas City, 1945-47, Charles Martin Petroleum, Texas City, 1948-50; acct. Goodyear Co., La Marque, Tex., 1968-70; serials libr. Coll. of the

Mainland, Texas City, 1970-77, instr., 1971—; exec. dir., office mgr. Mobile Air Conditioning, La Marque, 1977-80; owner Kivert, Inc., La Marque, 1982—; ptnr., exec. dir. A/C Mobile Equipment Corp., La Marque, 1988—; owner Star Bell Ranch, 1985—. Vol. Union Carbide Chems., Texas City, 1970—, Carbide Retiree Corp., Inc., Texas City, 1980—, Hospice, Galveston, Tex., 1985—, various polit. campaigns, Texas City, 1951-62; v.p. Coalition on Aging Galveston County, Tex. City, 1990—; vol. Baylor Coll. Medicine, Houston, 1990—; mem. adv. coun. bd. Galveston County Sr. Citizens, Galveston, 1990—; mem. planning bd. Heart Fund and Cancer Fund, Texas City, 1953-62, Santa Fe (Tex.) St. Citizens, 1990—; benefactor mem. Mainland Mus., Texas City, Tex., 1994—; sec. YMCA, 1947-55; sec. Ladies VFW, 1950-59; leader Girl Scouts Am., 1958-65; v.p. PTA, 1957-60; counselor Bapt. Ch. Camp, 1960-64; v.p. Santa Fe Booster Club, 1963-67; mem. Internat. Platform Assn., 1995—. Named Mother of Yr. Texas City/La Marque C. of C., 1990, Vol. of Yr. Heights Elem. Sch., Texas City Sch. Dist., 1959, Unsung Hero award Tex. City, 1995, 96, Most Glamorous Grandmother, 1985, Tex. Women's Hall of Fame, 1984. Mem. Internat. Platform Assn. Republican. Baptist. Home: 3422 K1/2 PO Box 1253 Santa Fe TX 77510

LAMBING, STEVEN JAY, aerospace engineer; b. Glen Cove, N.Y., Dec. 12, 1957; s. John Joseph and Marguerite Florence (Steyert) L. BS in Aerospace/Mech. Engring., U. Pitts., 1980; MS in Computer Sci., U. Ala., Huntsville, 1985. Aerospace engr. NASA Marshall Space Flight Ctr., Huntsville, 1980—. Mem. Nat. Arbor Day Found., Humane Soc. U.S. Office: NASA Marshall Space Flight Ctr EJ44 Huntsville AL 35812

LAMBIRD, MONA SALYER, lawyer; b. Oklahoma City, July 19, 1938; d. B.M. Jr. and Pauline A. Salyer; m. Perry A. Lambird, July 30, 1960; children: Allison Lambird Watson, Jennifer Salyer, Elizabeth Gard, Susannah Johnson. BA, Wellesley Coll., 1960; LLB, U. Md., 1963. Bar: Okla. 1968, Md. Ct. Appeals 1963, U.S. Supreme Ct. 1967. Atty. civil div. Dept. Justice, Washington, 1963-65; sole practice law Balt. and Oklahoma City, 1965-71; mem. firm Andrews Davis Legg Bixler Milsten & Price, Inc. and predecessor firm, Oklahoma City, 1971—; minority mem. Okla. Election Bd., 1984—, vice chmn., 1990-94; mem. profl. responsibility tribunal Okla. Supreme Ct., 1984-90; Master of Bench, sec.-treas. Luther Bohanan Am. Inn of Ct., Oklahoma City, 1986—, pres., 1994—. Editor: Briefcase, Oklahoma County Bar Assn., 1976. Profl. liaison com. City Oklahoma City, 1974-80; mem. Hist. Preservation of Oklahoma City, Inc., 1970—; del. Oklahoma County and Okla. State Republican Party Conv., 1971—; Okla. City Orch. League Inc., legal advisor, 1973—, bd. dirs., 1973—; incorporator, bd. dirs. R.S.V.P. of Oklahoma County, pres., 1982-83; bd. dirs. Congregate Housing for Elderly, 1978—, Vis. Nurses Assn., 1983-86, Oklahoma County Friends of Library, 1980-91, The Support Ctrs., Inc., 1989—. Mem. Okla. Women's Hall of Fame, 1995. Mem. ABA, Okla. Bar Assn. (pres. labor and employment law sect., bd. govs. 1992-94, pres. 1996), Oklahoma County Bar Assn. (bd. dirs. 1986—, pres. 1990), Oklahoma County Bar Found. (pres. 1988), Jr. League Oklahoma City (bd. dirs. 1973-76, legal advisor), Oklahoma County and State Med. Assn. Aux. (bd. dirs.), Seven Sisters Colls. Club (pres. 1972-76), Women's Econ. Club (steering com. 1981-86). Methodist. Home: 419 NW 14th St Oklahoma City OK 73103-3510 Office: 500 W Main St Oklahoma City OK 73102-2220

LAMBRO, DONALD JOSEPH, columnist; b. Wellesley, Mass., July 24, 1940; s. Pascal and Mary (Lapery) L.; m. Jacquelyn Mae Killmon, Oct. 6, 1968; 1 son, Jason Phillip. B.S., Boston U., 1963. Reporter, Boston Traveler, 1963; freelance writer Washington, 1965-67; statehouse reporter UPI, Hartford, Conn., 1968-70; reporter UPI, Washington, 1970-80; columnist United Feature Syndicate, Washington, 1981—; commentator AP Radio Network, 1982-83, Nat. Pub. Radio, 1984-85; writer, host TV documentary Star Spangled Spenders, 1982; host, co-writer PBS TV documentary Inside the Republican Revolution, 1995; nat. editor Washington Times, 1987-88; chief polit. corr. Washington Times, 1988—. Author: The Federal Rathole, 1975; The Conscience of a Young Conservative, 1976; Fat City: How Washington Wastes Your Taxes, 1980; Washington-City of Scandals, 1984; Land of Opportunity, 1986. Recipient Warren Brookes award for Excellence in Journalism, 1995. Albanian Orthodox.

LAMELL, ROBERT CHARLES, architect, artist; b. Oradea, Romania, Nov. 21, 1913; came to the U.S., 1950; s. Joseph and Elisabeth (Kiss) L.; m. Mary Agnes Pachta-Rayhofen, May 26, 1948; children: Arpad, Guido, Anthony. Arcthl. degree, Hindenburg Poly., Oldenburg, Germany, 1935; diploma, Poly. U., Budapest, 1942; postgrad., La. Tech. U., 1983. Registered architect, Okla. Architect Bucharest, Budapest, 1938-44; archtl. engr. British Royal Engrs. in Austria, 1945-50; architect W. Deitrick & J. C. Knight, Raleigh, N.C., 1950-55; v.p., architect C. L. Monnot Jr. and Assocs., Oklahoma City, 1955-88; freelance architect and artist Oklahoma City, 1988—; cons., lectr. in field. Exhibited in several one-man shows. Mem. Rep. Party, Alliance Francaise of Oklahoma City. Various art awards. Mem. AIA (emeritus), Knickerbocker Artists USA (signature), Nat. Watercolor Soc. Roman Catholic. Home and Office: 2640 W Wilshire Blvd Oklahoma City OK 73116-4013

LAMICA, GEORGE EDWARD, SR., writer, importor; b. Watertown, N.Y., Feb. 22, 1930; s. James Alfred and Madeline Catherine (Glossl) L.; m. Louise Holden, Feb. 22, 1951 (div. Feb. 1969); children: George Edward, Mary Catherine. AA, Wilmington Coll., 1954; BSBA, U. S.C., 1955. Mgmt. trainer Belks, Wilmington, N.C., 1951-79, Columbia, S.C., West Palm Beach, Fla.; ptnr. Martha's Flower Shoppe, Wilmington, 1979-86; owner Lamica Flowers Internat., Wilmington, 1986-88, Lamica Ltd. Internat., Wilmington, 1988-91; dir. New Hanover Workshop, Wilmington; cons. Liberty Furniture Co., Wilmington, Carribean Imports, Wilmington; mem. exec. com. New Hanover Spl. Olympics, Wilmington, 1984. Author: (book and screenplay) Day the Earth Cracked, 1992, The Odyssey of Herman, 1994, (book) Bride to Be Guide, 1993. Pres. Optimist Club, Wilmington, 1978—. With USMC, 1947-52, Korea. Mem. So. Writers Assn., Cape Fear Writers Assn. Home and Office: Lamica Ltd 2207 Shirley Rd Wilmington NC 28405

LAMID, SOFJAN, physician, educator; b. Pangkalan, West Sumatra, Indonesia, June 30, 1929; came to the U.S., 1969; naturalized, 1981.; s. Datuk Besar and Zamrud (Muhamad) L.; m. Burlini Tamin, Feb. 4, 1962; children: Dicky Sofwandi, Rudy Sofriza. MD, U. Indonesia, Jakarta, 1960; MSc in Pharmacology, U. Calif., San Francisco, U.S.A., 1962. Diplomate Am. Bd. Physical Medicine and Rehab. Chmn. dept. pharmacology U. Indonesia, Jakarta, Indonesia, 1960-68; residency in internal medicine, fellow in clin. pharmacology Southwestern Med. Sch., U. Tex., 1969-70; fellow in clin. pharmacology George Washington U., Washington, 1970-72; residency in anesthesiology Washington Hosp. Ctr., 1972-73; staff physician, clin. pharmacology Wood VA Med. Ctr., Milw., 1973-77, staff physican, spinal cord injury svc., 1977-84, acting chief, spinal cord injury svc., 1983-84; asst. adj. prof. pharmacology Med. Coll. Wis., Milw., 1975-77, asst. prof. physical medicine and rehab., 1978-84; residency in physical medicine and rehab. Medical Coll. Wis., Milw., 1978-91; assoc. prof. medicine and rehab. LSU Med. Ctr., New Orleans, 1984-87; assoc. dir. La. Rehab. Inst., New Orleans, 1984-87; pvt. practice New Orleans, 1987—; mem. staff Hotel Dieu Hosp., New Orleans, Jo Ellen Smith Med. Ctr., New Orleans, F. Edward Hebert Hosp., New Orleans; vis. prof. pharmacology U. Tex., Dallas, 1969-70; pres. QRS Lamid Enterprises, Inc. Mem. editorial bd. The Jour. Am. Paraplegia Soc., 1982—; manuscript reviewer Archives of Physical Medicine and Rehab., 1980—. Grantee Travenol Labs., 1984; grantee (with Richard Crout) Vitamin Drug Co., 1969-70, (with Raymond Jenkins) Beecham Massengil Pharmacology, 1970-72. Fellow Am. Acad. Physical Medicine and Rehab.; mem. Am. Soc. Clin. Pharmacology and Therapeutics, Am. Paraplegia Soc., Am. Congress Rehab. Medicine (program com. 1982-84, rehab. practice com. 1983—), Assn. Academic Psysiatrists, Dutch New Am. Club. Home: 3837 Sue Ker Dr Harvey LA 70058-1604

LAMIKANRA, OLUSOLA, food scientist; b. Ibadan, Oshun, Nigeria, Nov. 1, 1953; came to U.S., 1982; s. Joshua C. Adepoju and Elizabeth Oyeyemi (Omole) L.; m. Verian Dorothy Court Thomas, Oct. 9. 1982; children: Opeyemi, Adebola, Olufemi. BS, U. Lagos, Nigeria, 1978; PhD of Food Sci., U. Leeds, Eng., 1982. Sci. tchr. St. Finbars High Sch., Lagos, Nigeria, 1972-74; chemist Coca-Cola Bottling Co., Lagos, 1976-78; lectr. Kwara State Coll. Tech., Ilorin, Nigeria, 1978-79; instr., procter Dept. Food Sci. Univ. Leeds, Eng., 1980-82; rsch. assoc. Fla. A&M U./Fla. State U., Tallahassee, 1983; asst. prof. Divsn. Agrl. Scis. Fla. A&M U., Tallahassee, 1983-85, asst. prof. Ctr. Viticultural Scis., 1985-88, assoc. prof. Ctr. Viticultural Scis., 1988—, dir. Ctr. Viticultural Scis., 1992-93; adj. faculty Tallahassee C.C., 1982—; hon. prof. N.W. Agr. U., People's Republic of China. Contbr. articles to profl. jours. Com. mem. Space Life Scis. Tng. Program; mem. Fla. State Viticulture Adv. Coun.; male chorus mem. Bethel AME Ch., 1990—. Grantee Fla. Dept. Agr. Com., 1992-93, 91, USDA, 1991-94, Nat. Pesticide Control Lab., 1989. Mem. AAAS, Internat. Soc. Hypertension in Black People, Am. Chem. Soc., Am. Dietetic Assn. (assoc.), Am. Soc. Enology and Viticulture, Inst. Food Technologists (profl.), Fla. State Horticultural Soc., Fla. Grape Growers Assn. (bd. dirs. 1985-91). Home: 9018 Bob O Link Ct Tallahassee FL 32312-4011 Office: Viticulture Sci Ctr Fla A&M Univ Tallahassee FL 32307

LAMKIN, JANE EAGAR, elementary school educator; b. Chattanooga, Sept. 13, 1937; d. Henry Harrison Jr. and Jen (Henry) Eagar; m. Robert Howard Mills, June 18, 1960 (div. Sept. 1964); 1 child, Jennifer Mills Davis; m. William Pierce Lamkin, Mar. 17, 1973. BA in English, U. Ga., 1959; MA in Early Childhood Edn., Ga. State U., 1971, postgrad., 1976, 77, 83, 91; postgrad., Oglethorpe U., 1984. Jr. exec. trainee Bonwit Teller, N.Y.C., 1959-60; youth social worker Econ. Opportunity Atlanta, 1964-67; tchr. The Galloway Sch., Atlanta, 1969-80; tchr. pre-first The Lovett Sch., Atlanta, 1980-86, tchr. 1st grade, 1986—; presenter numerous seminars. Author: (program) We Meet the Artist, 1991. Active St. Dunstan's Ch., Atlanta, 1979—, High Mus. Art, Atlanta, 1988—. Named one of Outstanding Young Women of Am., 1965. Mem. So. Lit. Book Group, Ga. Ind. Sch. Assn. (presenter 1987, 90). Episcopalian. Home: 4201 Ridgehurst Dr Smyrna GA 30080-3114 Office: 4075 Paces Ferry Rd NW Atlanta GA 30327-3009

LAMM, HARRIET A., mathematics educator; b. Beeville, Tex., Dec. 4, 1948; d. James R. and Dorothy D. (Kendall) L. BA, Tex. Christian U., 1971; BS in Edn., S.W. Tex. State U., 1973, MEd, 1976; PhD, Tex. A&M U., 1993. Cert. secondary tchr., Tex. Instr. math. South San Antonio Ind. Sch. Dist., San Antonio, 1973-74; teaching asst. in math. S.W. Tex. State U., San Marcos, 1974-76; tchr. math. Seguin (Tex.) Ind. Sch. Dist., 1976-78, George West (Tex.) Ind. Sch. Dist., 1978-83, Lingleville (Tex.) Ind. Sch. Dist., 1983, Northside Ind. Sch. Dist., San Antonio, 1984-87, Beeville (Tex.) Ind. Sch. Dist., 1987-88; teaching asst. Tex. A&M U., College Station, 1991-92; instr. math. Bee County Coll., Beeville, 1988-91, 1992—; instr. math. Tarleton State U., Stephenville, Tex., 1983. Mem. Nat. Coun. Tchrs. Math., Tex. Coun. Tchrs. Math., Sch. Sci. and Math. Assn., Math. Assn. Am., Assn. Tex. Profl. Educators, Rsch. Coun. for Diagnostic and Prescriptive Math.

LAMON, KATHY LYNN, nursing administrator; b. Moultrie, Ga., July 24, 1961; d. James Daniel and Sammie Ruth (Fletcher) Miles; m. Thomas Eldred Lamon, Aug. 23, 1980. BSN, Valdosta State U., 1983. RN, Fla. Surg. staff nurse Putnam Cmty. Hosp., Palatka, Fla., 1983-84, surg. charge nurse, 1984-86, surg. asst. nurse mgr., 1986-87, nurse mgr. progressive care unit, 1987-90; sr. cmty. health nurse Putnam County Pub. Health Dept., Palatka, 1990; DON Palatka Health Care Ctr., 1991-94; asst. regional nurse North Fla. region Nat. Healthcare, Ocala, 1994—. Author: Pockety Buddy for Nurses PCH, 1991. Youth group leader Palatka Bapt. Temple, 1992-95. Recipient Dr. Frist Humanitarian award Hosp. Corp. of Am., 1988, Recipient of the Nat. Healthcare Patient Care award, 1994. others; named Outstanding Young Med. Profl., Jaycees, 1988. Mem. Nat. Assn. DON, Intravenous Nurses Soc., N.E. Fla. DON. Republican. Office: Nat Healthcare 3400 SW 27th Ave Ocala FL 34474-4404

LAMONICA, P(AUL) RAYMOND, lawyer, academic administrator, educator; b. Baton Rouge, June 10, 1944; s. Leonard and Olivia (Frank) L.; m. Dianne Davis, Aug. 23, 1971; children: Drew, Neal, Leigh. BA, La. State U., 1965, MA, 1966, JD, 1970. Bar, La. 1970. Law clk. to chief judge U.S. Dist. Ct. (we. dist.) La., 1970-71; assoc. Hebert, Moss & Graphia, Baton Rouge, 1971; judge pro tem 19th Jud. Dist. Ct., East Baton Rouge Parish, 1979; prof. La. State U. Law Sch., Baton Rouge, 1973-86; exec. counsel to La. Gov., 1983-84; U.S. atty. for mid. dist. La., 1986-94; vice chancellor, prof. law La. State U., Baton Rouge, 1994—; counsel La. Ho. of Reps., 1976-79, 80-83. Fellow Am. Bar Found.; mem. ABA, La. Bar Assn. (bd. govs. 1979). Republican. Roman Catholic. Office: La State U 210 LSU Law Ctr Baton Rouge LA 70803

LAMONT, ALICE, accountant, consultant; b. Houston, July 19; d. Harold and Bessie Bliss (Knight) L. BS, Mont. State U.; MBA in Taxation, Golden Gate U., 1983; CPA. Tchr. London Central High Sch., 1971-80; acct. Signetics, Sunnyvale, Calif., 1980-82; propr. Alice Lamont Ltd., 1985—. Mem. Atlanta Hist. Soc., High Mus. Art, Atlanta Botanical Garden, Brit. Amer. Bus. Group (mem. com., 1993—), Friend of Atlanta Opera, Atlanta Opera Guild, St. Philips Planned Giving Com. Fellow Ga. Soc. CPAs (chmn. Acctg. Inst. 1995—); mem. AAUW (life mem., audit chmn. 1993-95, mem. scholarship com. 1994—), Atlanta Tax Study Assn., Inst. Internal Auditors, English Speaking Union, Women Bus. Owners, Buckhead Bus. Assn., Atlanta Woman's Club (co-chair ways and means com. 1985-86, asst. treas. 1986-88, treas. 1990, 92-94), Women's Commerce Club (mem. adv. bd. 1994—).

LAMOREAUX, PHILIP ELMER, geologist, hydrogeologist, consultant; b. Chardon, Ohio, May 12, 1920; s. Elmer I. and Gladys (Rhodes) L.; m. Ura Mae Munro, Nov. 11, 1943; children: Philip E Jr., James W., Karen L. BA, Denison U., 1943, PhD (hon.), 1972; MS, U. Ala., 1949. Registered profl. geologist, Ga., N.C., S.C., Tenn., Ind., Ariz., Ark., Fla., Ky., Wyo., Pa. Geologist U.S. Geol. Survey, Tuscaloosa, Ala., 1943-45, dist. geologist Groundwater Office, 1945-57, div. hydrologist Water Resources Programs, 1957-59; chief Ground Water Br. U.S. Geol. Survey, Washington, 1959-61; state geologist, oil and gas supr. Ala. Geol. Survey, Tuscaloosa, 1961-76; pres. P.E. LaMoreaux & Assocs. Inc., Tuscaloosa, 1976-87, chmn. bd., 1987-90, sr. hydrologist, 1990—; lectr. Am. Geol. Inst. Coll. Program, 1969-71, Am. Geophys. Union Coll. Program, 1961—, NSF, Ala. Acad. Sci. H.S. Program, 1961—, No. Engring. and Testing, Salt Lake City, 1985, Ga. State U., Fla. State U., Vanderbilt U., Denison U., Auburn U., U. of Montpellier, France, U. Christ Church, New Zealand, University of Praetoria, Republic of South Africa; hydrogeology cons. to 30 fgn. countries. Editor in chief Jour. Environ. Geology, 1982—; editor in chief: Annotated Bibliography Carbonate Rocks, vols. 1-5; contbr. articles to profl. jours. Mem. Nat. Drinking Water Adv. Coun. EPA, 1984-88, mem. Tech. Rev. Group Oak Ridge Nat. Lab., 1984-88; trustee Denison U. Recipient Comdrs. medal C.E., 1990. Mem. NAE, ASTM, AIME, NAS (nat. rsch. coun. geotech. bd. 1990-92, water sci. and tech. bd. 1990—, bd. earth scis. and resources 1992—, earth resources com. 1995—), AAAS, Ala. Acad. Sci., Ala. Geol. Soc., Am. Assn. Petroleum Geologists (acad. liaison com., Ho. of Dels. 1970-72, com. preservation samples and cores, chmn. divsn. geosci. hydrogeology com.), Am. Geol. Inst. (chmn. com. on publs. 1968-70, pres. 1971-72, Ian Campbell award 1990, chmn. environ. geosci. adv. com. 1994—, William B. Heroy award 1995, bd. trustees), Am. Geophys. Union, Am. Inst. Hydrology, Am. Inst. Profl. Geologists (chmn. com. on rels. with govtl. agencies 1967-70, bd. dirs. 1969-70), Assn. Am. State Geologists (statistician 1966-69, chmn. liaison com. fed. agencies 1968-70, pres.), Geol. Soc. Am. (1st chmn. hydrogeology group 1963, chmn. O.E. Meinzer award com. 1965, cons. membership S.E. sect. 1967-68, chmn. nominating com., bd. dirs., bd. trustees, publs. com.), Geol. Soc. London, Internat. Assn. Hydrogeologists (pres. 1977-80, v.p. 1973-77, com. on water rsch. 1978-80, Karst Commn. 1961—, chmn. hydrology hazardous waste commn. 1983-91, mem. com. thermal and mineral waters 1994—, adv. to pres. 1995—), Internat. Water Resources Assn., Interstate Oil Compact Commn. (vice chmn. 1963, chmn. rsch. com.), Miss. Geol. Soc., Nat. Assn. Geology Tchrs., Nat. Rivers and Harbors Congress, Nat. Speleological Soc., Nat. Water Resources Assn., Nat. Water Well Assn., Soc. Econ. Geologists, Soc. Econ. Paleontologists and Mineralogists, Soil Conservation Soc. Am., Southeastern Geol. Soc., Ala. C. of C. (Pres.'s adv. com., Rep. of Energy 1980), Geol. Soc. Am. (chmn.); numerous others. Republican. Presbyterian. Office: P E LaMoreaux & Assocs Inc 2610 University Blvd Tuscaloosa AL 35401-1508

LAMOUREUX, GLORIA KATHLEEN, nurse, air force officer; b. Billings, Mont., Nov. 2, 1947; d. Laurits Bungaard and Florence Esther (Nielsen) Nielsen; m. Kenneth Earl Lamoureux, Aug. 31, 1973 (div. Feb. 1979). BS, U. Wyo., 1970; MS, U. Md., 1984. Staff nurse, ob-gyn DePaul Hosp., Cheyenne, Wyo., 1970; enrolled USAF, 1970, advanced through grades to col.; staff nurse ob-gyn dept. 57th Tactical Hosp., Nellis AFB, Nev., 1970-71, USAF Hosp., Clark AB, Republic Philippines, 1971-73; charge nurse ob-gyn dept. USAF Regional Hosp., Sheppard AFB, Tex., 1973-75; staff nurse ob-gyn dept. USAF Regional Hosp., MacDill AFB, Fla., 1976-79; charge nurse ob-gyn dept. USAF Med. Ctr., Andrews AFB, Md., 1979-80, MCH coord., 1980-82; chief nurse USAF Clinic, Eielson AFB, Alaska, 1984-86, Air Force Systems Command Hosp., Edwards AFB, Calif., 1986-90; comdr. 7275th Air Base Group Clinic, Italy, 1990-92, 42d Med. Group, Loring AFB, Maine, 1992-94; 347th Med. Group, Moody AFB, Ga., 1994-96; chief nursing svcs. divsn. Hdqrs. Air Edn. and Tng. Command, Randolph AFB, Tex., 1996—. Mem. Assn. Women's Health, Obstetric, and Neonatal Nurses (sec.-treas. armed forces dist. 1986-88, vice-chmn. armed forces dist. 1989-91), Air Force Assn., Assn. Mil. Surgeons U.S., Bus. and Profl. Women's Assn. (pub. rels. chair Prince George's County chpt. 1981-82), Assn. Healthcare Execs., Sigma Theta Tau. Republican. Lutheran. Home: 13515 Thessaly Universal City TX 78148

LAMOUREUX, WILLIAM ALBERT, poet; b. Montreal, Que., Can., Aug. 15, 1938; s. William C. and Beatrice (Benoit) L.; BA, Tufts U., 1964; postgrad. Boston U., 1964-65, U. Hawaii, 1974; came to U.S., 1938, naturalized, 1953. Partner, Lamoureux Funeral Home, Gardner, Mass., 1949-76; founder, propr. Librairie Francaise, Santurce, P.R., 1970-73; broker-salesman J.M. Urner Inc., Realtors, Honolulu, 1974-76; broker-salesman Portner & Portner, Inc., Realtors, Hollywood, Fla., 1978-82; right-of-way agent Fla. Dept. Transp., 1978-80; works include: (poetry) La lumiere se retire du bord de la terrasse..., 1960; Comme je traversais le pays des licornes, 1961; Un oranger, supreme emeraude, 1962. Republican. Roman Catholic. Home and Office: 5734 SE Horseshoe Point Rd Stuart FL 34997-2415

LAMPE, HENRY OSCAR, stockbroker; b. Bremen, Germany, Apr. 8, 1927 (parents U.S. citizens); s. Henry D. and Dorothea C. (Gatje) L.; m. Virginia Harvey, July 18, 1953 (dec. 1984); m. Margaret Sanger Marston, Mar. 4, 1989. BS with honors, Am. U., 1952. Investigator pub. safety Office Mil. Govt., Berlin, 1947-49; methods examiner Bur. Consular Affairs, Dept. State, 1952-53; investigator USIA, Office of Security, 1953-55; budget examiner Resources and Civil Works div. Bur. Budget, Washington, 1955-58; v.p., br. mgr. Birely & Co., Washington and Arlington, Va., 1959-66; v.p. Thomson McKinnon Securities Inc., Arlington, 1967-89; v.p. Prudential-Securities, Inc., Vienna, Va., 1989-94; dir., treas. Med.-Tech, Inc.; cons., lectr. in field. Co-author: Faculty Handbook, George Mason U., 1985. Mem. Joint George Mason U./Arlington County Adv. Bd., 1995—, Arlington Sister City Assn., 1993—, past chmn. Arlington Com. of 100, 1963—; mem. Va. Legislature, 1970-72, mem. bd., Arlington Sister City Comm., 1993; trustee Arlington Hosp. Assn., 1976-86, chmn. 1982-85; trustee Arlington Hosp. Found., 1986-89, sec., treas., 1988-89, Arlington Hosp. Adv. Bd., 1991-96; mem. bd. visitors George Mason U., 1980-88; vice chmn. Home Health Svcs. Co. Va., 1984-86; campaign chmn. Arlington Va. United Way, 1981; trustee United Way Metro D.C., 1982-90; mem. Va. Adv. Bd. on Aging, 1971-78; mem. White House Conf. on Aging, 1971, Arlington County Manpower Commn., 1974-76, No. Va. Regional Planning Commn., 1967-69; vice chmn. Va. Met. Areas Transp. Study Commn., 1970-74. With USN, 1945-46. Recipient merit citation U.S. Office Mil. Govt., Berlin, 1949, Lifetime Achievement award Am. U., 1987; named Arlington County Man of Yr., 1985. Mem. Arlington C. of C. (bd. dirs. 1985-92, exec. com. 1986-92, pres. 1990), Arlington Bus. Roundtable, Bond Club of Washington. Rep., Lions (Arlington). Lutheran. Avocation: gardening. Home: 2459 N Wakefield Ct Arlington VA 22207-3555

LAMPE, MARGARET SANGER, community activist; b. Tucson, Nov. 19, 1941; d. Stuart and Barbara (Peabody) Sanger; m. Donn Richard Marston, Mar. 21, 1961 (dec. 1988); children: Peggy Marston Van Cleave, Nancy Marston Stevenson, Michael Peabody Marston (dec.); m. Henry Oscar Lampe, Mar. 4, 1989. Student, U. Ariz., 1959-61, George Washington U., 1961-62. Office adminstr. L.T. Delyannis & Assocs., Arlington, Va., 1978-81, Bean, Kinney, Korman, Arlington, Va., 1985-91. pres., v.p., mem. PTA, Arlington, 1970-79; mem. task force delinquency prevention, Richmond, Va., 1976-78; mem., com. chair Va. Congress PTA, Richmond, 1975-79; mem., vice chair Va. Bd. Edn., Richmond, 1979-87; chmn. task force Nat. Inst. Edn., Washington, 1983; mem. Nat. Commn. Excellence in Edn., Washington, 1981-83; vice chair govt. affairs Nat. Assn. State Bds. Edn., Washington, 1984-85; bd. visitors Va. Poly. Inst. and State U., Blacksburg, 1988-92; mem. Arlington County Sch. Bd., 1995-96; v.p. Planned Parenthood Met. Washington, 1978-79; mem. women's com. Nat. Symphony, 1978-80. Recipient Outstanding Citizen award Arlington County Schs., 1978, 84, Outstanding Svc. Plaque Pres. Reagan, 1984, Outstanding Woman in Press Va. Press Corp., 1986-87, Cmty. Voice & Vision award Cable TV, 1996. Mem. Jr. League No. Va. (chair), No. Va. Assistance League, Women's Econ. Roundtable, Rock Spring Garden Club, Commonwealth Cir., Neighbors' Club. Home: 2459 N Wakefield Ct Arlington VA 22207

LAMPERT, MICHAEL ALLEN, lawyer; b. Phila., May 6, 1958; s. Arnold Leonard and Marilyn (Sternberg) L.; m. Angela Gallicchio, Dec. 6, 1987; 1 child, David Max. AB in Econs. cum laude, U. Miami, Coral Gables, Fla., 1979, postgrad., 1980; JD, Duke U., 1983; LLM in Taxation, NYU, 1984. Bar: Fla. 1983, D.C. 1984, Pa. 1984, U.S. Tax Ct. 1984, U.S. Ct. of Appeals for the Armed Forces 1995. Assoc. Cohen, Scherer, Cohn & Silverman, P.A., North Palm Beach, Fla., 1984-88; instr. div. continuing edn. Fla. Atlantic U., Boca Raton, 1988—; prin. Jacobson & Lampert, P.A., Boca Raton, 1988-91; pvt. practice West Palm Beach, 1991—. Mem. editl. bd. Southeastern Tax Alert, 1993—. Instr., trainer, chpt. vice-chair, emergency svcs. chair ARC, Palm Beach County, Fla.; bd. dirs. Jewish Fedn. Palm Beach County, 1989-91; bd. dirs. Jewish Family and Children's Svc. Palm Beach County, 1988—, treas., 1991-94; mem. nat. planned giving com. Weismann Inst., Israel. Recipient Safety award ARC, 1989, Cert. of Merit, Am. Radio Relay League, West Palm Beach Club, 1988, Cert. of Appreciation for Leadership, ARC Disaster Svcs., Palm Beach County, 1989, Disaster Svc. award, 1994, Human Resources award, 1993, Tax Law award Legal Aid Soc. of Palm Beach County and Palm Beach County Bar Assn., 1993. Mem. Palm Beach Tax Inst. (pres., bd. dirs.), Fla. Bar (exec. coun., tax sect.), Palm Beach County Bar Assn. (chair bus. and corp. continuing legal edn. com. 1989-90, chair legal assistance com. 1988-91, Tax Law award 1993), Legal Aid Soc. of Palm Beach County, Inc. Office: Ste 900 1655 Palm Beach Lakes Blvd West Palm Beach FL 33401-2211

LAMPERT, WAYNE MORRIS, corporate financier; b. N.Y.C., Feb. 4, 1941; s. William B. and Fagel (Lefrak) L.; m. Sara Joyce Kirsch, Sept. 11, 1966 (div. 1978); children: Marcie Lynn, Warren Harris. BA, Syracuse U., 1962; LLD, Fordham U., 1965; MArch, U. Houston, 1992. Bar: N.Y. 1966, Fla. 1976, Tex. 1987, U.S. Customs Ct., U.S. Supreme Ct. Mgmt. intern Gen. Svcs. Adminstrn., Washington, 1965-66; atty. Legal Aid Soc., N.Y.C., 1966-67; asst. dist. atty. Kings County Dist. Atty.'s Office, Bklyn., 1967-69; pvt. practice Queens, N.Y., 1969-71, Miami, Fla., 1976-86; law sec. N.Y. State Ct. Claims, N.Y.C., 1971-73; chmn. bd. dirs. Texam Exploration Co., Inc., Houston, 1986-88; owner Vision Travel, Inc., Coral Gables, Fla., 1977—; tchr. law Charron Williams Coll., Miami, 1976-78. Bd. dirs. LeFrak Found., Queens, 1962-70, Youth Ednl. Coun., Ft. Lauderdale, Fla., 1965—; campaign mgr. Morris Kirsch for Bklyn. Borough Pres., 1973. Fellow Met. Mus. Art; mem. Lawrence Yacht Club (treas. 1972-73), Neptune Flamingo Yacht Club (chaplain 1977-78, commdr. St. Thomas U.S. power squadron 1994-96), Kappa Phi Kappa, Phi Alpha Delta, Tau Sigma Delta. Republican. Office: 2222 Ponce De Leon Blvd Coral Gables FL 33134

LAMPTON, ROBERT DONALD, JR., chemical engineer, consultant; b. Newark, Ohio, Mar. 10, 1956; s. Robert Donald and Vera Nell (Smith) L.; m. Nancy Jane Cole, May 14, 1977; children: Robert Matthew, Amanda Kathryn, Michelle Erin. BS in Chem. Engring., Tex. A&M U., 1978; MBA in Mgmt., U. Houston, Clear Lake, Tex., 1984. Project leader Dow Chem. Co., Freeport, Tex., 1978-89; rsch. mgr. Internat. Paint Powder Coatings, Inc., Houston, 1989-93; cons. RDL Consulting, Friendswood, Tex., 1993—; cons. on epoxy coatings and coating processes USN, Port Hueneme, Calif., 1993—. Mem. ASTM (sec. com. epoxy coating task groups 1989—), Nat. Assn. Corrosion Engrs., Concrete Reinforcing Steel Inst. (sec. epoxy coating tech. com., sec. epoxy coating adv. com. 1989—), Beta Gamma Sigma (charter mem.). Home and Office: 1402 Silverleaf Dr Friendswood TX 77546-4876

LAMY, M(ARY) REBECCA, land developer, former government official; b. Ft. Bragg, N.C., Nov. 21, 1929; d. Charles Joseph and Sarah Esther (Koonce) L.; B.A., U. N.C., Greensboro, 1952. Procurement analyst Air Force MIPR Mgmt. Office, Washington, 1958-60, procurement and fiscal officer, 1960-68; budget analyst Naval Air Systems Command, Washington, 1968-69, indsl. specialist, 1969-71; indsl. specialist A.D.T.C., Eglin AFB, Fla., 1971-74, Def. Logistics Agy., Alexandria, Va., 1974-81; logistics mgmt. specialist Strategic Systems Project Office, Dept. Navy, Washington, 1981-82; procurement analyst Hdqrs. Dept. Army, Washington, 1982-85. Mem. Onslow Mus. Found. Bd. (emeritus), Onslow Meml. Hosp. Aux., 1985-91. Recipient Outstanding Performance awards U.S. Air Force, 1956, 65, 72, 73; Quality award Def. Logistics Agy., 1979, Outstanding Performance award, 1978, 79, Exceptional Service award, 1983, 84, 85; Comdr.'s award Hdqrs. Dept. Army, 1985; others. Mem. U. N.C. at Greensboro. Alumni Assn.

LANCASTER, CAROLYN HOHN, secondary school educator; b. Harrison/Allegheny County, Pa., July 24, 1952; d. Carl Maurice Sr. and Doris Myrtle (Gilday) Hohn; m. Walter T. Johnson, Sept. 4, 1971 (dec. Oct. 1979); 1 child, David Alan Johnson; m. Ronald Lee Lancaster, Mar. 31, 1988. AAS, Cape Fear Tech. Inst., Wilmington, N.C., 1986; BS, U. Ctrl. Fla., Orlando, 1981; MS, N.C. A&T State U., Greensboro, 1993. Cert. technology, electronics tchr., N.C. Computer technician Nat. Data Processing GE, Wilmington, 1986-88; electronics technician Applied Tech. Assn., New Bern, N.C., 1988-89; computer tchr. Onslow County Schs., Jacksonville, N.C., 1989-90; indsl. arts tchr. Person County Schs., Roxboro, N.C., 1992-93; technology tchr. Alamance County Schs., Graham, N.C., 1993—; technology advisor Technology Student Assn., Graham, N.C., 1993—; chairperson Raleigh Regional Program Area Leadership Coun. for Tech., 1996-97; vice chair Raleigh region Program Area Leadership Coun. for Tech., 1995-96. Mem. Jaycees, Orlando, 1980. With USCG Res., 1985-88. Recipient Tandy Tchr. Award cert. 1995-96; Profl. Devel. scholar N.C. Technology Educators Assn., 1993. Mem. NEA, N.C. Edn. Assn., Am. Vocat. Assn., Internat. Tech. Educators Assn., N.C. Tech. Educators Assn., Nat. Assn. Underwater Instrs. Methodist. Home: 114 Florence St Graham NC 27253-4002 Office: Graham HS 903 Trollinger Rd Graham NC 27253-1945

LANCASTER, CARROLL TOWNES, JR., business executive; b. Waco, Tex., Mar. 14, 1929; s. Carroll T. and Beatrice (Hollaman) L.; student U. Tex., 1948-51, 52-53; m. Catherine Virginia Frommel, May 29, 1954; children—Loren Thomas, Barbara, Beverly, John Tracy. Sales coordinator Union Tank div. Butler Mfg. Co., Houston, 1954-56, sales rep., New Orleans, 1956-57, br. mgr., 1957-60; asst. to exec. v.p. Maloney-Crawford Mfg. Co., Tulsa, 1960-62; mktg. cons., sr. asso. Market/Product Facts, Tulsa, 1962-63; market devel. asst. Norriseal Controls div. Dover Corp., Houston, 1963-66; area dir. Arthritis Found., Houston, 1966-69, dir. S.W. div., 1969-70; exec. dir. United Cerebral Palsy Tex. Gulf Coast, 1971-74; exec. dir. Leukemia Soc. Am., Gulf Coast, 1974-76, Lancaster & Assos., 1976—. Christian edn. tchr., 1966-70, supr., 1971, asst. youth football coach, Bellaire, 1967-68, 70-71; mem. Houston-Galveston Area Health Commn. Study Group, 1972-76, co-chmn., 1976; dir., essayist Tex. Low Vision Council, 1976-79, sec.-treas., 1978-81, pres., 1981-85; pres. Bellaire Civic Action Club, 1987-88; del. Houston Interfaith Sponsoring Com., 1979-81; bd. dirs. Council Chs. Greater Houston, 1966-68, v.p., 1968. Served with USNR, 1946-48, 51-52. Recipient award for securing free blood for indigent Harris County Hosp. Dist., 1968. Mem. Am. Mktg. Assn., Huguenot Soc., Military Order of Stars and Bars, San Marcos Acad. Ex-students Assn. (pres. 1982-84), SAR, Delta Sigma Phi. Episcopalian (vestryman 1975-78). Home: 4901 Holly St Bellaire TX 77401-5714 Office: PO Box 745 Bellaire TX 77402-0745

LANCASTER, H(AROLD) MARTIN, former congressman, former advisor to the President; b. Patetown Community, N.C., Mar. 24, 1943; s. Harold Wright and Eva (Pate) L.; m. Alice Matheny; children: Ashley Elizabeth, Mary Martin. AB, U. N.C., 1965, JD, 1967. Asst. staff judge adv. 12th Naval Dist., San Francisco, 1968; staff judge adv. USN, USS Hancock, 1968-70; ptnr. Baddour, Lancaster, Parker, Hine & Keller P.A., Goldsboro, N.C., 1970-86; rep. N.C. Gen. Assembly, Raleigh, 1978-86; mem. 100th-103rd Congresses from 3d N.C. dist., Washington, D.C., 1987-94; mem. armed svcs. com., readiness subcom., mil. pers. subcom.; chmn. morale, welfare and recreation panel; small bus. com. Mcht. Marine and Fisheries com.; chmn. judiciary com. N.C. Ho. of Reps., 1983-86; chmn. hwy. safety com., 1981-83; chmn. congrl. study group on German, 1994, North Atlantic Assembly, 1989-94; former mem. numerous other coms. Chmn. N.C. Arts Coun., 1977-81, Goldsboro Wayne Bicentennial Commn., 1975-76; pres. Community Arts Coun., 1973-74, Wayne Community Concert Assn., 1972-73; chmn. bd. trustees Wayne County Pub. Libr., 1979-80; chmn. Wayne chpt. ARC, 1978-79; mem. adv. bd. Z. Smith Reynolds Found.; deacon First Presbyn. Ch., 1972-75, elder, 1980-86. Recipient Disting. Svc. award Goldsboro Jaycees, 1977, N.C. Crime and Justice award Gov.'s Crime Commn., 1984, Spl. award Gov.'s Adv. Coun. for Persons with Disabilities, 1985, Valand award Mental Health Assn. N.C., 1985, Outstanding Legislators awards Neuse River Coun. Govts., N.C. Assn. Sch. Counselors, Nat. Security Leadership award, 1987, 89, 90, 91, 92, Sound Dollar award, 1988, 89, 90, Spirit of Enterprise award U.S. C. of C., 1989, 92, 93, Doer of Deeds award House Leadership, 1989, Pub. Health Svc. award N.C. Primary Care Assn., 1991, Charles Dick Medal of Merit, U.S. Nat. Guard Assn., 1992, Tad Davis Meml. award, U.S. Mil. Sports Assn., 1992; named N.C. and U.S. Alumnus of Yr., 4-H, 1987. Mem. ABA, Assn. Trial Lawyers Am., N.C. Bar Assn. (bd. govs.), Eighth Jud. Dist. Bar Assn., N.C. Acad. Trial Lawyers (Outstanding Legislator award), Wayne County Hist. Soc. Lodges: Masons, Shriners, Elks. Office: 4638 Main State Washington DC 20451

LANCASTER, JANE CLEO, historian, writer; b. Hamilton, Miss., Nov. 7, 1940; d. John Grover and Cleo (Crosby) Fairchild; m. Hollie Harwell Jr., Apr. 2, 1960; children: Phillip Anthony, Fonda Kay. BS, Miss. State U., 1966, PhD, 1986; MA, Miss. U. for Women, 1969. Tchr. dept. head Amory (Miss.) High Sch., 1969-73; fellow, teaching asst. Miss. State U., 1981-86; pvt. practice Hamilton, 1986—. Author: Removal Aftershock: The Seminoles' Struggles to Survive in the West, 1836-1866, 1994; contbr. articles to profl. jours. Chmn. bicentennial wagon train Town of Hamilton, 1975, Heritage chmn., 1975, Libr. Week chmn., 1975, cmty. pianist, 1962-85; former historian Agri-Belles, Hamilton. Miss. State U. fellow, 1981-84, 85-86. Mem. Nat. Mus. The Am. Indian, Orgn. Am. Historians, So. Hist. Assn., Okla. Hist. Soc., Monroe County Hist. Soc. (dir. 1970s), Phi Alpha Theta. Baptist. Home and Office: 40191 Highway 373 Hamilton MS 39746-8710

LANCASTER, KENDELL RENÉ QUESENBERRY, floral designer, business manager, administrator; b. Radford, Va., Oct. 24, 1956; d. William Clarence and Evelyn Allene (Young) Quesenberry; m. Ted Allen Carter, Sept. 20, 1974 (div. Dec. 1979); 1 child, Jesika Allene; m. Michael Bernard Lancaster, Nov. 29, 1985; stepchildren: Michael J., John David, Melanie A., Matthew O. AAS in Mktg., New River C.C., 1994; postgrad., Bluefield Coll. Designer, trainee Sun City (Fla.) Florist, 1975; designer Pulaski (Va.) Flower Shop, 1976-77; owner, designer Blue Ridge Flowers & Gifts, Pulaski, 1981; designer The Village Flower Shop, Radford, Va., 1982-84; instr., designer New River Community Coll., Dublin, Va., 1984-85; owner, designer The White Horse, Max Meadows, Va., 1985-92; designer Dublin Flower Shop, 1987-88, The Wicker Basket, Wytheville, Va., 1988-90, Flowers by Mary, Max Meadows, Va., 1988-90; designer, buyer The Draper (Va.) Mercantile, 1989—; office mgr. Rowland Express (Va.) Inc., 1994—; instr. designer New River C.C., 1994—; guest speaker Christian Women's Club, Wytheville, 1989, Rural Retreat (Va.) Lit. Club, 1990, Profl. Bus. Women's Club, Pulaski, 1981; judge Chautauqua Festival, Wytheville, 1989; designer Fine Arts Showcase of Home, Pulaski, Va., 1990; youth group leader, vol. notetaker New River C.C., 1992—; guest designer Teleflora Design Show, 1992. Baptist. Home: PO Box 392 Max Meadows VA 24360-0392

LANCASTER, TINA, real estate executive, small business owner, rancher; b. Austin, Tex., July 21, 1939; d. Ernest Thomas and Dorothy A. (Loya) Prado; children from a previous marriage: Christina M., Joseph P., M. Kathleen. Student, U. Notre Dame, St. Mary's Coll., South Bend, Ind., 1958-62, U. Pa., Austin Sch. of Bus./Real Estate, 1982-86. Cert. realtor, Tex. Owner, pres. Diversified Properties, Austin, 1972—; owner, publisher Austin Home & Gardens, 1978-84, San Antonio Homes & Gardens, 1978-84, The Catholic Journal, Austin, 1978-84; owner, pres. Diversified Prodns., Austin, 1978—; owner Escondido Internat. Bazaar, Austin, 1984—, Escondido Ranch, Austin, 1984—; owner, dir. Women's Health & Fitness Ctr., Austin, 1986-93, Diversified, USA, water purification and desalianation R & D; Diversified Cos., Diversified Worldwide; freelance hist. writer. Bd. dirs. Mayor's Alternative Sources of Income Com., Austin, 1982, Bowie High Sch., Austin, 1989-90. Named Most Successful Woman, Mexican-Am. Profl. Women's Assn., 1981. Mem. U.S. Bd. of Realtors, Tex. Bd. of Realtors, Austin Bd. of Realtors, Headliner's Club, Austin Club. Home: 2900 Frate Barker Rd Austin TX 78748-3522

LANCASTER, TYSON DALE, pharmacist; b. Ft. Lauderdale, Fla., Jan. 15, 1969; s. Tyrone Dale and Barbara Ray (Maseda) L. AA, Palm Beach (Fla.) C.C., 1989; BA in Chemistry, BS in Microbiology, Fla. Atlantic U., 1993; postgrad., Nova Southeastern U., 1996—. Dockloader UPS, Deerfield Beach, Fla., 1990-91; analytical chemist, quality control mgr., heavy metals waste mgr. Proto-Circuits, Ft. Lauderdale, Fla., 1993-94; pharm. lab asst. Southeastern U., N. Miami Beach, Fla., 1995; pharmacy intern Walgreens, Plantation, Fla., 1995—. Tech. writer Signs and Symptoms Nova Southeastern U., 1993-96; editor: (chpt.) The Script, 1994. Mem. Phi Delta Chi (office leadership com. 1994-95). Republican. Roman Catholic. Home: 4267 NW 34th Way Lauderdale Lakes FL 33309

LANCLOS, RITCHIE PAUL, petroleum engineer; b. Opelousas, La., Sept. 20, 1964; s. Curley Joseph and Velma Marie (Folks) L.; m. Courtney Thereśe Brennan, Mar. 26, 1994. BS in Petroleum Engring., U. Southwestern La., 1987; MS in Petroleum Engring. cum laude, Tex. A&M U., 1990. Registered profl. engr., La. Petroleum engr. exploration and prodn. Mobil Oil Corp., New Orleans, 1987-89, Conoco, Inc., New Orleans, 1990-93; petroleum engr. property acquisitions WRT Energy Corp., The Woodlands, Tex., 1994; petroleum engr. reservoir engring. Petrobras Am., Inc., Houston, 1995—; petroleum cons. The Scotia Group, Inc., Houston 1994—. Bd. dirs. Big Bros./Big Sisters, New Orleans, 1991-94, Boys/Girls Club, Lafayette, La., 1992-94, Vol. Instrs. Teaching Adults (VITA), Lafayette, 1991-94; loaned exec. United Way, New Orleans, 1993-94. Scholar Am. Petroleum Inst., Lafayette, 1985-86, scholar Texaco Rsch. Ctr., Texaco Inc., College Station, Tex., 1989-90; fellow Petroleum Engring., 1989-90. Mem. Soc. Petroleum Engrs., Tex. A&M U. Petroleum Engring. Alumni (v.p. 1994-95, thesis adv. com.). Republican. Roman Catholic. Home: 37 Fallshire Dr The Woodlands TX 77381

LAND, AMY N., home health nurse, hospice nurse, nursing administrator; b. McComb, Miss., Dec. 23, 1953; d. William M. and Nancy (Westbrook) Powell; m. Stephen E. Land, Dec. 31, 1988; children: Amanda, Andrea, William, Kyle. ADN, Southwest Miss. Community Coll., 1980; student, Miss. Coll. Staff nurse Southwest Regional Med. Ctr., McComb, 1979-82, Jeff Davis Meml. Hosp., Natchez, Miss., 1982-86; nursing supr. Home Care, Inc., Natchez, 1986-88; recert. nurse South Miss. Home Health, Inc., Jackson, 1988-91; staff nurse Hospice of Wilkes County, N.C., 1991-92; staff nurse, dir. nursing Hosp. Resource Home Health, 1993-94; staff nurse Lincoln County Home Health, 1995—. Mem. N.C. Nurses Assn., Miss. Nurses Assn., Western N.C. Pub. Health Assn. Home: 869 Hillard Ln Lincolnton NC 28092-8036

LAND, KENNETH CARL, sociology educator, demographer, statistician, consultant; b. Llano, Tex., Aug. 19, 1942; s. Otto Carl and Tillie (Lindemann) L.; m. Jacqueline Yvette Apere, Mar. 22, 1969; 1 child, Kristoffer Carl. B.A., Tex. Luth. Coll., 1964; M.A., U. Tex., 1966, Ph.D., 1969. Staff assoc. Russell Sage Found., N.Y.C, 1969-73; lectr. Columbia U., N.Y.C., 1970-73; assoc. prof. U. Ill.-Urbana, 1973-76, prof., 1976-81; prof. sociology U. Tex.-Austin, 1981-86; prof., chmn. dept. sociology Duke U., Durham, N.C., 1986—, John Franklin Crowell prof. sociology, 1990—. Editor: Social Indicator Models, 1975; Social Accounting Systems, 1981; Multidimensional Mathematical Demography, 1982; Forecasting in the Social and Natural Sciences, 1987; contbr. articles to profl. jours. Fellow Am. Statis. Assn., Am. Assn. for the Advancement of Sci.; mem. Sociol. Research Assn., Am. Sociol. Assn., Population Assn. Am., Am. Soc. Criminology. Lutheran. Office: Duke U Dept Sociology Durham NC 27708-0088

LAND, REBEKAH RUTH, marriage and family therapist; b. Columbus, Ga., Feb. 5, 1946; d. Roland Irving and Thelma Rebekah (Gibbins) Van Hooser; m. Richard Dale Land, Sr., May 29, 1971; children: Jennifer Rebekah, Richard Dale Jr., Rachel Elisabeth. AB, Samford U., 1967; M in Religious Edn., New Orleans Bapt. Theol. Sem., 1970; MSW, Tulane U., 1971; PhD, Tex. Woman's U., 1988. Cert. profl. counselor; cert. marital and family therapist; diplomate Am. Bd. Sexology. Sch. social worker Chattanooga Pub. Schs., 1967-68; edn. and youth dir. Trinity Bapt. Ch., New Orleans, 1968-69; caseworker Youth Study Ctr., New Orleans, 1972; adj. prof. Criswell Coll., Dallas, 1976-89; counselor First Bapt. Ch., Dallas, 1982-85; psychotherapist Minirth-Meier Clinic, Richardson, Tex., 1985-87; asst. dir. counseling Dallas Theol. Sem., 1987-89; pvt. practice Nashville, 1989—; coord. Trilogy Program Parthenon Pavilion Psychiat Hosp., Nashville, 1990-94. Mem. ACA, Am. Assn. Marriage and Family Therapy (clin.), Am. Assn. Sex Educators (cert. sex therapist), Counselors and Therapists, Assn. for Religious Values in Counseling. Republican. Baptist. Office: Parkview Towers 210 25th Ave N Ste 1010 Nashville TN 37203-1611

LAND, RICHARD DALE, minister, religious organization administrator; b. Houston, Nov. 6, 1946; s. Leggette Sloan and Marilee (Welch) L.; m. Rebekah Ruth Van Hooser, May 29, 1971; children: Jennifer, Richard Jr., Rachel. BA, Princeton U., 1969; ThM, New Orleans Bapt. Theol. Sem., 1972; D.Phil., U. Oxford, Eng., 1980. Ordained to ministry So. Bapt. Conv., 1969. Pastor S. Oxford Bapt. Ch., Oxford, Eng., 1972-75; prof. theology and ch. history Criswell Coll., Dallas, 1975-76, acad. dean, 1976-80, v.p. for acad. affairs, 1980-88; exec. dir. Christian Life Commn. So. Bapt. Conv., Nashville, 1988—; mem. exec. com. Nat. Coalition against Pornography, Cin., 1989—; bd. dirs. Bapt. Joint Com. Pub. Affairs, Washington, 1987-90, Nat. Pro-Life Religious Coun., Washington. Cons. editor Criswell Study Bible, 1979. Mem. Gov.'s Task Force on Welfare Reform, Austin, Tex., 1988, Pres.'s Campaign for a Drug-Free Soc., Washington, 1991—; bd. drs. Nat. Law Ctr., Arlington, Va., 1991—. Mem. Nat. Assn. Evangs. (Wheaton, Ill., bd. dirs. 1991—), Conf. on Faith and History, Evang. Theol. Soc., So. Bapt. Hist. Soc., Rotary. Office: Christian Life Commn 901 Commerce St Ste 550 Nashville TN 37203-3629

LAND, STEVEN JACK, minister, theology educator; b. Jasper, Ala., Sept. 23, 1946; s. Dewey Jackson and Mary Lovinia (Anderson) L.; m. Peggy Goude, Dec. 25, 1969; children: Alanna, Laura, Jonathan. BA, Birmingham So. Coll., 1968; MDiv, Emory U., 1972, PhD in Theology, 1991. Ordained to ministry Ch. of God (Cleveland, Tenn.). Pastor Midtown Mission Ch. of God, Atlanta, 1976-91; prof. pentecostal theology Ch. of God Sch. Theology, Cleve., 1979-91, acad. dean, 1991—; founder, dir. Atlanta's Mission Possible, Inc., 1970-81, pres., 1970-91; dean Pentecostal Inst., Inc., Atlanta, 1989-91; v.p. Evang. Ctr., Atlanta, 1990-91. Author: Do-Tell, 1974, Pentecostal Spirituality, 1991; author, editor: Church of God Heritage Papers, 1989; editor Internat. Jour. Pentecostal Theology, 1992—; contbr. numerous articles to profl. jours., book chpts. Legis. aide Ga. Ho. of Reps., Atlanta, 1971; bd. dirs., mem. moral concerns com. Christian Coun. of Met. Atlanta, 1975-79; trustee Mission Acres Children's Home, Monroe, Ga., 1979-91. Mem. Am. Acad. Religion, Soc. for Pentecostal Studies, Evangelicals for Social Action, Internat. Roman Cath. Pentecostal Dialog. Home: 2016 Woodchase Way NE Cleveland TN 37311-1461 Office: Ch of God Sch Theology 900 Walker St NE Cleveland TN 37311-5234

LANDAU, JACOB CHARLES, journalist; b. Englewood, N.J., Apr. 10, 1934; s. Jacob and Florence (Binaghi) L.; children: Nicholas Jacob, Ariel Elizabeth. AB, Harvard U., 1956; JD, NYU, 1961; LLD (hon.), Colby Coll., Waterville, Maine, 1978. News reporter Bergen Evening Record, Hackensack, N.J., 1957-60, AP, N.Y.C., 1960-63, Washington Post, 1963-66; dir. pub. info. U.S. Dept. Justice, Washington, 1968-69; supreme ct. reporter Newhouse Newspapers, Washington, 1966-68, 70-78; exec. dir. Reporters Com. for Freedom of the Press, Washington, 1970-85; syndicated law columnist Newhouse Newspapers-N.Y. Times Feature Svc., Washington, 1978-92; editor News USA, Arlington, Va., 1990-91; founder Student Press Law Ctr., Washington, 1975, bd. dirs., 1975-80; bd. dirs. Reporters Com. for Freedom of the Press, Washington, 1970-96, Joint Media Coalition, Washington, 1975-83, First Amendment Congress, Washington, 1978-85, Com. to Protect Journalists, N.Y.C., 1980-85; advisor Investigative Reporters and Editors, Indpls., 1975-76; project dir. Reporter and the Law, joint project of ABA and Am. Newspaper Pubs. Assn., Chgo., 1975-76; cons. ABA Fair Trial-Free Press Com., 1976-77. Founder/editor The Press Censorship Newsletter, 1973-78, The News Media and the Law, 1978-85, How to Use the Federal Freedom of Information Act (6 edits.), 1979-84, The Student Press Law Ctr. Newsletter, 1975-78; editor News Media Law and Legislative Update, 1980-85; contbr. articles to profl. jours. Recipient Elijah Parrish Lovejoy Freedom of the Press award Colby Coll., 1978, John Peter Zenger First Amendment award U. Ariz., 1979, Playboy First Amendment award Playboy Found., 1984, U. So. Calif. Journalism Sch. 25th Anniversary First Amendment award, 1985, First Amendment award Nat. Assn. Coll. Publs. Advisors, 1978, Nat. Reporting Bronze medal Soc. Profl. Journalists, 1967; Pulitzer Prize nominee, 1963; Nieman fellow Harvard U., 1968. Fellow Soc. Profl. Journalists (Nat. First Amendment award 1976); mem. ABA (Silver Gavel award for legal reporting 1968), D.C. Bar Assn., N.Y. Bar Assn., Harvard Club Washington, Nat. Press Club. Home and Office: 3800 Powell Ln # 511 Falls Church VA 22041

LANDAU, MICHAEL B., law educator, musician; b. Wilkes-Barre, Pa., July 3, 1953; s. Jack Landau and Florence (Rabitz) Simon. BA, Pa. State U., 1975; JD, U. Pa., 1988. Pres., founder Balloon-A-Grams of N.Y., N.Y.C., 1981-86, N.Y. Singing Telegrams, N.Y.C., 1981-86; assoc. Cravath, Swaine and Moore, N.Y.C., 1988-90, Skadden, Arps, N.Y.C., 1990-92; assoc. prof. Coll. Law Ga. State U., Atlanta, 1992—; vis. prof. law Dickinson Sch. Law; free-lance musician, Pa., N.Y., 1971—; guest lectr. Johannes Kepler U., Linz, Austria, summer 1994, 95, 96. Contbr. articles to law jours. on copyright, art, patent, entertainment law. Mem. ABA, N.Y. State Bar Assn., Internat. Bar Assn., Vol. Lawyers for Arts, Am. Fedn. Musicians, Am. Intellectual Property Law Assn., Copyright Soc. U.S. Am., Phi Kappa Phi, Omicron Delta Epsilon. Democrat. Office: Ga State U Coll Law University Pla Atlanta GA 30303

LANDERS, JAMES MICHAEL (JIM LANDERS), international editor; b. San Francisco, Calif., Feb. 11, 1951; s. William Edward and Loretta Mae (Fouts) L.; m. Susan Ann Moran, Dec. 26, 1981; children: Amy Foster, Noelle Christine, Jessica Elizabeth. BA in English with honors, Va. Poly. Inst. and State U., 1974. Staff writer The Washington Post, 1971-74; freelance journalist Belfast, Northern Ireland, 1974; staff writer The Richmond (Va.) Mercury, 1975, The Trenton (N.J.) Times, 1975-77; features editor Arab News, Jeddah, Saudi Arabia, 1978-79; sr. editor Saudi Bus. & Arab Econ. Report, Jeddah, 1979-80; Washington corr. The Dallas Morning News, Washington, 1981-88; internat. editor The Dallas Morning News, Dallas, 1988-94, internat. affairs corr. Washington bur., 1994—. U.S. del. French-Am. Found., Taormina Young Leaders Conf., 1989. Named Outstanding Washington corr. Nat. Press Club, 1985, Finalist Pulitzer prize for Explanatory Journalism, N.Y.C., 1990; recipient World Hunger Media award World Hunger Yr., N.Y.C., 1990, Pulitzer prize for Internat. Reporting, 1994. Mem. Coun. Fgn. Rels., Am. Coun. on Germany, Dallas Com. Fgn. Rels. Roman Catholic. Home: 5208 Knoughton Way Centreville VA 22020-3336 Office: The Dallas Morning News 1012 National Press Bldg Washington DC 20045

LANDERS, LINDA ANN, public relations and fundraising executive; b. Boston, July 1, 1964; d. Howard and Martha (McWeeney) Landers; m. Peter Lehmann Sutphen, Aug. 10, 1991. BA, Smith Coll., 1986. Reporter The Daily Californian, Berkeley, 1986-87; feature reporter, freelance Today's Woman, Cedar Rapids, Iowa, 1992-93, The Press Citizen, Iowa City, Iowa, 1992-93; journalist South Fla. Newspaper Network, Deerfield Beach, Fla., 1993—; coord. Project Safe Pl., Broward/Palm Beach region Lippman Family Ctrs. of Lutheran Min. of Fla., Ft. Lauderdale, 1995—; pub. rels. fundraising Joy of Motion Dance Ctr., Washington, 1989-90. Bd. dirs. The Primary Movers, Washington, 1989-90; mem. Palm Beach County Cultural Coun., Palm Beach, Fla., 1993-94, The Morikami Mus., Delray Beach, Fla., 1993-94, Fla. Artisians Craftsmen, St. Petersburg, Fla., 1993-94, The Nature Conservancy, 1994, Broward County Juvenile Diversion Coalition, The Mentor Connection. Named to Nat. Women's Hall of Fame. Mem: Soc. Profl. Journalists, Fla. Freelance Writers Assn.

LANDERS, SUSAN MAE, psychotherapist, professional counselor; b. Houston; d. James Edward and Frances Pauline (Braunagel) L. BS in Advt., U. Tex.; MS in Psychol. Counseling, U. Houston, Clearlake, 1994; cert. in sales, Dale Carnegie Inst. Lic. profl. counselor. Mktg. rep. K.C. Products, Houston, 1981-83; account exec. Williamson County Express, Austin, Tex., 1984; advt. cons. Stas. KMMM/KOKE, Austin, 1985; key account sales rep. GranTree Furniture Rental, Austin, 1986-89; individual habilitation counselor Ctr. for the Retarded Inc., Houston, 1990; case mgr. Mental Health and Mental Retardation Authority Harris County, Houston, 1991-92; primary therapist Riceland Psychiat. Hosp., 1994—. Mem. ACA, Am. Mental Health Counselors Assn., Tex. Counseling Assn., Tex. Mental Health Counselors Assn., Houston LPC Assn., Houston Group Psychotherapy Soc. Home: 4615 N Braeswood Blvd # 311D Houston TX 77096-2841 Office: Riceland Psychiat Hosp 4910 Airport Rosenberg TX 77471

LANDINI, ELIZABETH LEIGH, journalist; b. Lexington, Ky., July 20, 1971; d. Thomas Edward and Martha Ann (Lackey) L. BA, Murray (Ky.) State U., 1993. Writer Murray State News Bur., 1989-91; assoc./news editor The Murray State News, 1991-93; intern U.S. Rep. Carroll Hubbard, Washington, summer 1992; edn. reporter The Paducah (Ky.) Sun, 1993-95, features editor, 1995—. Class mem. Leadership Paducah, 1995-96; vol. Leadership Paducah Alumni, 1996—; adv. bd. Purchase Area Youth Salur Program, March of Dimes Mission Possible campaign, 1995; vol. in schs. Recipient Sch. Bell award Ky. Edn. Assn., 1995. Mem. Murray State U. Alumni Assn. (chpt. sec. 1994—), Woman's Club of Paducah Open Gate Garden Club. Office: The Paducah Sun 408 Kentucky Ave Paducah KY 42003-1550

LANDIS, HOMER WARREN, minister; b. New Hope, Va., Jan. 23, 1924; s. Henry Daniel and Elsie (Garber) L.; m. Wanda Francis Eavey, June 6, 1947; children: Katherine Elizabeth, Nancy Anne. BA, James Madison U., 1950; MDiv, Emory U., 1953; D of Ministry, Boston U., 1983. Ordained to ministry United Meth. Ch. as deacon, 1952, as elder, 1954; cert. clin. pastoral counselor. Pastor United Meth. Ch., Monterey, Va., 1952-54, Kilmarnock, Va., 1954-55; chaplain USAF, 1955-59; pastor United Meth. Ch., Newsoms, Va., 1959-61, Chuckatuck, Va., 1961-66; pastor Jolliff United Meth. Ch., Portsmouth, Va., 1966-69, United Meth. Ch., Marshall, Va., 1969-74, Phoebus United Meth. Ch., Hampton, Va., 1974-82; chaplain Dept. Vets. Affairs Med. Ctr., Hampton, Va., 1982—; pres. Va. United Meth. Chaplains Fellowshio, Hampton, 1989-95; work area leader Peninsula Dist. United Meth. Ch., Counsel on Ministries, 1975-80. Author: A Descriptive Evaluative Study of Ministry in Hospice, 1983. Dir. Am. Ex-prisoner of War chpt., Hampton, 1990-91. Chaplain col., USAFR, 1943-83, ret. Decorated Purple Heart, Bronze Star, Silver Star, Prisoner of War medal, Meritorious Svc. medal, Air Force Commendation medal; Croix DeGuerre (France). Mem. Inter-Faith Ministerial Assn., Nat. Mil. Chaplains Assn., Nat. Assn. Va Chaplains, Assn. Pastoral Counselors, Lions, Mil. Order of Purple Heart. Home: 3 Hatteras Lndg Hampton VA 23669-1515

LANDOLT, ARLO UDELL, astronomer, educator; b. Highland, Ill., Sept. 29, 1935; s. Arlo Melvin and Vesta (Kraus) L.; m. Eunice Jean Casper, June 8, 1966; 1 child, Jennifer; stepchildren: Lynda, Barbara, Vicky, Debra. B.A., Miami U., Oxford, Ohio, 1955; M.A., Ind. U., 1960, Ph.D., 1963. Mem. 1st wintering-over party Internat. Geophys. Year, Amundson-Scott South Pole Sta., Antarctica, 1957; asst. prof. physics and astronomy La. State U., 1962-65, asso. prof., 1965-68, prof., 1968—, dir. La. State U. Obs., 1970-88, acting chmn. dept. physics and astronomy, summers 1972-73, pres. faculty senate, 1979-80; program dir. astronomy sect. NSF, 1975-76; mem. governing bd. Am. Inst. of Physics, 1985-91, 95—; guest investigator Kitt Peak Nat. Obs., Tucson, Cerro Tololo Inter-Am. Obs.,Las Campanas Observatory, La Serena, Chile, Dyer Obs., Vanderbilt U., Goethe Link Obs., Ind. U. Rsch. grantee NSF, 1964, 66, 69, 71, 73, 75, 92-96, NASA, 1965, 92, Rsch. Corp., 1964, Air Force Office Sci., 1977-87, Space Telescope Sci. Inst., 1985-90, 92.

Fellow AAAS (sec. Sect. D 1970-78); mem. AAUP, Am. Astron. Soc. (sec. 1980-89, 95—), Internat. Astron. Union (sec. U.S. nat. com. 1980-89, 96—), Royal Astron. Soc. (Eng.), Astron. Soc. Pacific, Am. Polar Soc., Am. Philatelic Soc., Sigma Xi, Pi Mu Epsilon. Office: La State U Dept Physics And Astro Baton Rouge LA 70803-4001

LANDRAM, CHRISTINA LOUELLA, librarian; b. Paragould, Ark., Dec. 10, 1922; d. James Ralph and Bertie Louella (Jordan) Oliver; m. Robert Ellis Landram, Aug. 7, 1948; 1 child, Mark Owen. BA, Tex. Woman's U., 1945, B.L.S., 1946, M.L.S., 1951. Preliminary cataloger Library of Congress, Washington, 1946-48; cataloger U.S. Info. Ctr., Tokyo, Japan, 1948-50, U.S. Dept. Agr., Washington, 1953-54; librarian Yokota AFB, Yokota, Japan, 1954-55; librarian St. Mary's Hosp., West Palm Beach, Fla., 1957-59; librarian Jacksonville (Ark.) High Sch., 1959-61; coord. Shelby County Libraries, Memphis, 1961-63; head catalog dept. Ga. State U. Library, 1963-86, librarian, assoc. prof. emeritus, 1986—. Contbr. articles to library jours. Mem. Ga. Library Assn. (chmn. resources and tech. services sect. 1969-71), Metro-Atlanta Library Assn. (pres. 1967-68), ALA (chmn. cataloging norms 1979-80, nominating com. 1977-78), Southeastern Library Assn. (mem. govtl. rels. com. 1975-78, intellectual freedom com. 1984-86, mem. Rothrock awards com. 1987-90). Presbyterian. Home: 1478 Leafmore Rdg Decatur GA 30033-2110

LANDRENEAU, BETTY C., nursing educator, medical/surgical nurse; b. Pine Prairie, La., Oct. 10, 1940; d. Samuel R. and Agnes M. (McGhee) Cole; m. Hugh B. Landreneau, Oct. 26, 1984. BSN, U. Southwestern La., 1962; MS, U. Minn., 1982. RN, La., Mo., Tex.; lic. clin. specialist med.-surg. nurse, La. Staff nurse Lafayette (La.) Gen. Med. Ctr.; head nurse skilled care unit St. Anne's Home, St. Louis; nursing supr. Nat. Hansen's Disease Ctr., Carville, La.; instr. U. Southwestern La., Lafayette; staff nurse Univ. Med. Ctr., Lafayette. Mem. ACA, ANA (cert. med./surg. clin. specialist), La. Nurses Assn., Sigma Theta Tau (Delta Eta chpt).

LANDRENEAU, RODNEY EDMUND, JR., physician; b. Mamou, La., Jan. 17, 1929; s. Rodney Edmund and Blanche (Savoy) L.; M.D., La. State U., 1951; m. Colleen Fraser, June 4, 1952; children—Rodney Jerome, Michael Douglas, Denise Margaret, Melany Patricia, Fraser Edmund, Edythe Blanche. Intern, Charity Hosp., New Orleans, 1951-52, resident, 1952-54, 56-58; practice medicine specializing in surgery, Eunice, La., 1958—; pres., dir. Eunice Med. Center, Inc., 1960—; mem. staff Moosa Meml. Hosp., Eunice, 1958—, chief med. staff; vis. staff Opelousas Gen. Hosp., 1958—; assoc. faculty La. State U.-Eunice, chmn. community adv. com., v.p., chmn. La. State U.-Eunice Found., 1992-94; cons., staff Lafayette (La.) Charity Hosp.; cons. staff surgery Savoy Meml. Hosp., Mamou; pres. Eunice Med. Center, Inc.; mem. La. State Hosp. Bd., 1972—. Mem. Evangeline council Boy Scouts Am.; bd. dirs. Moosa Meml. Hosp., Eunice, 1986—, bd. govs., 1985-91, vice chmn. bd. dirs. Served with M.C., AUS, 1954-56. Recipient Physician's Recognition award AMA, 1978-85. Diplomate Am. Bd. Surgery. Fellow Internat. Coll. Surgeons (regional dir.), ACS (local chmn. com. trauma, instr.), Southeastern Surg. Congress, Pan Pacific Surg. Congress; mem. Am. Bd. Abdominal Surgeons, Am. Geriatrics Soc., St. Edmunds Athletic Assn., St. Landry Hist. Soc. (v.p. chpt.), St. Landry Parish Med. Soc. (pres. 1969-71, 85-87), Am. Legion, SCV, SAR, Alpha Omega Alpha. Democrat. Roman Catholic. Club: St. Edmund's High Sch. Scholastic Booster (pres. 1986—). Home: 1113 Williams Ave Eunice LA 70535-4939

LANDRUM, BEVERLY HOLLOWELL, nurse; b. Goldsboro, N.C., Jan. 28, 1960; d. Joseph Bryant and Doris Helen (Barnett) Hollowell; m. William Timothy Landrum; children: Amber, Justin, Caitlyn. ADN with honors, Florence-Darlington Tech., 1989; BSN summa cum laude, Med. U. S.C., 1995. RN, S.C.; cert. BLS, ACLS, NALS. Charge nurse Carolinas Hosp. System, Florence, S.C., 1989—. Neighborhood campaign organizer March of Dimes, Am. Heart Assn., Atlantic Beach, Fla. and Florence, 1982—; active Assn. Parents and Tchrs., Florence, 1993—. Mem. ANA, S.C. Nurses Assn., Sigma Theta Tau.

LANDRUM, THOMAS STEEL, university administrator; b. Macon, Ga., May 18, 1950; s. Jack Marion and Mary Elizabeth (Steel) L.; m. Susan Brown, Dec. 26, 1976; 1 child, Temperance Elizabeth. BA in History, U. Ga., 1972, MA in Journalism, 1987. Info. officer Lander Coll., Greenwood, S.C., 1973-76; info. officer U. Ga., Athens, 1976-79, asst. dir. pub. rels., 1979-85, dir. pub. rels., 1985-87, asst. to v.p. devel., 1987-91, asst. to pres., 1991—. Mem. Leadership Athens, 1985; past mem. N.E. Ga. bd. Boy Scouts Am. Mem. Nat. Assn. Presdl. Assts. in Higher Edn., Phi Kappa Phi, Blue Key. Democrat. Methodist. Office: U Ga Lustrat House Athens GA 30602

LANDRY, DEBBY ANN, computer programmer; b. Tacoma, July 27, 1963; d. Israel Joseph and Joyce Ann (Franzella) L.; 1 child, Jessica Elizabeth. BS, S.E. La. U., 1987; postgrad., U. So. Miss., 1994. Computer programmer Lockheed Engrng. and Scis., Bay St. Louis, Miss., 1988-92; programmer/analyst I Sverdrup Techs., Inc., 1992-94; computer assoc. sr. Lockheed Engrng. & Scis., Stennis Space Center, Miss., 1994—. Mem. Beta Sigma Phi. Democrat. Roman Catholic. Home: 1107 Rose Meadow Loop Slidell LA 70460-5105 Office: Lockheed Engrng & Scis Co Bldg 2105 Bay Saint Louis MS 39529

LANDRY, RONALD JUDE, lawyer, state senator; b. Lutcher, La., May 30, 1943; s. Ambroise Harry and Althae (Clement) L.; BA La. State U., JD; m. Mary Ellen Hebert, Aug. 14, 1965, (div.); children: Christopher Benton, Lauryn Elizabeth. Bar: La.; sole practice law, LaPlace, La., 1969—; mem. La. Senate, 1976—. Mem. St. John Assn. Retarded Citizens, La. Assn. Deaf, River Road Hist. Soc. Lodges: Kiwanis (River Region), Lions. Democrat. Roman Catholic. Address: PO Box 189 La Place LA 70069-0189

LANDRY, SARA GRIFFIN, social worker; b. Thomaston, Ga., Sept. 17, 1920; d. John Carl and Mary Thelma (Abercrombie) Griffin; m. Thomas Leonard Perkins, Dec. 22, 1939 (dec. Jan. 27, 1945); 1 child, Thomas Leonard Perkins Jr.; m. George Kimball Landry, Dec. 19, 1949 (dec. Aug. 30, 1971). AB in Social Work magna cum laude, Wesleyan Coll., 1980; MS in Family Counseling, Mercer U., 1981. Receptionist Social Security Adminstrn., Macon, Ga., 1945-50, clerical, 1960-65, svc. rep., 1965-78; dir., organizer Bibb County Foster Grandparent Program, Macon, Ga., 1981-84; coord. rsch. project Med. Ctr. of Cen. Ga., Macon, Ga., 1986-87; social worker, bd. dirs. Bibb County Sr. Citizens Inc., Macon, Ga., 1984—; sec. bd. dirs. Bibb County Sr. Citizens, Inc., Macon, Ga., 1989-90, pres. bd. dirs., 1990-91; bd. dirs. grant chmn. Family Counseling Ctr., Macon, 1986-92, 94—. Contbr. articles, poems and various short stories to profl. jours. Bd. dirs., v.p., com. chmn. Am. Cancer Soc., Macon, 1956—, hon. life mem., 1993—; sec., com. chmn. Dem. Women Bibb County, 1979—; mem., sec. Civic Woman's Club, Macon, 1955-61; mem. Coun. Cath. Women, St. Joseph's Parish, pres., 1956-58; mem., bd. dirs. Savannah Diocesan Coun. Cath. Women, 1957-59; bd. dirs. Macon Little Theatre, 1994-96. Recipient Disting. Alumnae award for cmty. svc. Wesleyan Coll., 1996, Svc. to Mankind award Sertoma Club of Macon, 1995; named Vol. of Yr., Bibb County Sr. Citizens, Inc., 1988, Am. Cancer Soc., 1987-88, Cherry Blossom Sr. Queen for Cmty. Svc., 1986; Fundraiser honoree Am. Cancer Soc., 1991; Sara Landry Day proclaimed in her honor Mayor of Macon, 1991. Mem. LWV, AAUW (pres. 1991-93), Wesleyan Coll. Alumnae Assn. (Sara Griffin Perkins Landry scholarship established for non-traditional age students 1994, Disting. Alumnae award for cmty. svc. 1996), Nat. Honor Soc., Macon Little Theatre. Democrat. Roman Catholic. Home: 3807 Drury Dr Macon GA 31204-1313

LANDSCHULZ, WILLIAM HARRAS, endocrinologist; b. Dubuque, Iowa, Apr. 22, 1960; s. William R. and Marja A. (Salmenpohja) L.; m. Katherine Tallman, Sept. 13, 1985. AB, MS, U. Chgo., 1982; postgrad., U. Helsinki, Finland, 1982-83, Columbia U., 1983-85; MD, PhD, Johns Hopkins U., 1991. Diplomate Am. Bd. Internal Medicine. Med. scientist scholar L&HI Med. Rsch. Fund, Washington, 1985-91; med. intern/resident Johns Hopkins Hosp., Balt., 1991-93; fellow in endocrinology Parkland Meml. Hosp., Dallas, 1993—; prin. investigator U. Tex.-Southwestern Med. Ctr., Dallas, 1993—. Co-author: Principles of Internal Medicine Companion Handbook, 1994. Recipient Wilson S. Stone Meml. award M.D. Anderson Cancer Rsch. Ctr., Houston, 1991, Michael A. Shanoff award Johns Hopkins U., 1989, Dr. Alfred Steiner award Coll. Physicians and Surgeons, N.Y.C., 1985. Mem. AAAS (Newcomb Cleveland prize 1990), AMA, ASIM, AACE, Endocrine Soc., Alpha Omega Alpha. Office: University of Texas Southwestern Med Ctr MC8591 5323 Harry Hines Blvd Dallas TX 75235-8591

LANDURETH, LEWIS JAMES (JIM LANDURETH), communications executive; b. Houston, Apr. 17, 1943; s. Lewis James and Iola Ruth (Hill) L.; m. Libbie Elaine Schobel, May 21, 1971 (div. 1996); 1 child, James Bradley. BS U. Houston, 1966; MS U. So. Calif., 1970. Instr. sci. Houston Sch. Dist., 1966-69; coord. instructional systems Meml. Hosp. Systems and Houston Bapt. U., 1969-77; coordinator audio visual services Meml. Care Systems, Houston, 1977-87; mng. ptnr. Landmark Comm., Houston, 1987—; assoc. D. Peterson and Assocs., 1987-88; dir. instl. media services Houston Ind. Sch. Dist., 1988—; cons. various hosps., Region IV Ednl. Svc. Ctr., 1967-69, Helene Fuld Health Trust, N.Y.C., 1971-86; producer various video tapes on healthcare, 1969—. Mem. parenting as prevention com. Tex. Commn. on Alcohol & Substance Abuse; bd. dirs. Houston Access Cable, treas., 1991, pres. 1994—; mgr. ednl. access cable channel, 1994, media literacy workshops, 1994; coord. Houston Tchrs. Assn. Citizenship Com., 1968-69; mem. ch. coun. St. Martin's Luth Ch., 1994-97, coun. sec., 1996. Recipient Award of Excellence Internat. Assn. Bus. Communicators, 1985. Mem. Internat. TV Assn. (treas. Houston chpt. 1978-86, chmn. nat. employee comm. 1986-88, Silver Seagull award of Merit 1984, Silver Excaliber award Pub. Rels. Soc. Am., 1994), Am. Society Tng. Devel. (editor 1977-78, chmn. awards com. 1978), Assn. Ednl. Tech. (pres. Houston chpt. 1974), Assn. Ednl. Comm. & Tech., Tex. Assn. for Ednl. Tech., Nat. Assn. of Regional Media Ctrs. Lutheran. Avocations: coaching youth sports, religious education. Home: 10914 Plainfield Houston TX 77031 Office: Houston Ind Sch Dist 3830 Richmond Ave Houston TX 77027-5864

LANDY, DAVID, anthropologist, educator; b. Savannah, Ga., June 4, 1917; s. Charles Edwin and Matilda (Rabinowitz) L.; m. Louise Fleming, Mar. 18, 1949 (dec. 1988); children: Laura Louise, Lisa Ann, Jonathan Fleming; m. Margaret Randall Holt Parish, Jan. 1, 1991. AA, Armstrong State Coll., 1948; BA in psychology, sociology, U. N.C., 1949, MA in anthropology, 1950; PhD in anthropology, Harvard U., 1956. Lectr., sch. social work Boston (Mass.) U., 1953-56; prin. investigator Harvard U., Boston, 1955-60, rsch. assoc. med. sch., 1955-60; prof. and assoc. prof. pub. health U. Pitts., 1960-70, prof. and chair anthropology, 1963-70; prof. and chair anthropology U. Mass., Boston, 1970-75, prof. emeritus, 1985—; adj. prof. anthropology U. N.C., Wilmington, 1992—. Author: Tropical Childhood, 1959, 1965; co-author: Halfway House, 1969, editor, co-author: Culture, Disease Healing, 1977; assoc. editor: Ethnology, 1963-70, Behavioral Science, 1965-70; contbr. articles to profl. jours. Treas. 1st Parish Ch., Scituate, Mass., 1987-90; trustee Unitarian Universalist Fellowship, Wilmington, 1991-93; pres. Soc. Med. Anthropology, Washington, 1980-82, mem. exec. com., 1978-80, 91-93. With U.S. Army, 1944-46, ETO. Recipient numerous grants. Fellow Am. Anthrop. Assn.; mem. Soc. Med. Anthropology, Soc. for Ethnohistory, So. Anthrop. Soc., Am. Assn. for the History of Medicine, Soc. for the Social History of Medicine, Assn. N.C. Anthropologists, Am. Ethnol. Soc., Soc. Psychol. Anthropology. Home: 218 Bretonshire Rd Wilmington NC 28405-4004

LANDY, LISA ANNE, lawyer; b. Miami, Fla., Apr. 20, 1963; d. Burton Aaron and Eleonora Maria (Simmel) L. BA, Brown U., 1985; JD cum laude, U. Miami, 1988. Bar: Fla. 1988, U.S. Dist. Ct. (so. dist.) Fla. 1988. Atty. Paul, Landy, Beiley & Harper, P.A., Miami, Fla., 1988-94, Steel Hector & Davis, Miami, Fla., 1994—. Bd. dirs. Miami City Ballet, 1992—, pres., 1996; bd. dirs. Women in Internat. Trade, Miami, 1992—, pres., 1994. Mem. ABA, Inter-Am. Bar Assn. (sec. young lawyers divsn. 1992).

LANDY, LOIS CLOUSE, principal, counselor; b. Pitts., June 12, 1947; d. Raymond Walter and Loretta (Smith) Clouse; m. Robert Charles Landy, Dec. 20, 1969; 1 child, Robert Raymond. BS, Pa. State U., 1969; MEd, Trenton State Coll., 1974; Edn. Specialist, Ga. So. Coll., 1980. Cert. adminstrn. and supervision sch. counselor, elem. tchr., Ga., Fla., N.J. Tchr. Penn Hills Sch. System, Pa., 1969-70, Chatham County Pub. Sch., Savannah, Ga., 1970-72, Camden City Sch., N.J., 1972-75; counselor, tchr. Volusia County Schs., Daytona Beach, Fla., 1975-77; tchr. J.G. Smith Elem., Savannah, 1977-78; counselor Penn Ave and Whitney Schs., Savannah, 1978-81, Hesse Elem. Sch., Savannah, 1981-86, asst. prin. White Bluff Elem. Sch., Savannah, 1986-88, May Howard Elem., Savannah, 1988-92; prin. Islands Elem. Sch., Savannah, 1992-95, Dorset Shoals Elem., Douglasville, Ga., 1995—. Author: Child Support (through small group counseling), 1982. Vol. counselor Rape Crisis Ctr., Savannah, 1978-81. Named Tchr. of Yr., Enterprise Elem. Sch. 1977-78, Outstanding Individual of Yr. Council for Exceptional Children, 1986. One of Outstanding Young Women Am., 1981. Mem. Ga. Sch. Counselors Assn. (2nd v.p. 1983-85, Counselor of Yr. 1979-80, Profl. Writer of Yr. 1980-81), Chatham County Counselors Assn. (chmn. 1979-80), Leadership Georgia, Alpha Delta Kappa (pres. 1982-84), Delta Kappa Gamma (pres. 1990-92), Phi Delta Kappa. Avocations: running, swimming. Home: 421 Walnut Grove Rd Peachtree City GA 30269 Office: Dorsett Shoals Elem 2866 Dorsett Shoals Rd Douglasville GA 30135

LANE, CASON WESLEY, writer, editor, media specialist; b. New Orleans, July 31, 1970; s. Spurgeon Wesley and Alice Angelyn (Forester) L. BS in Journalism, Tex. Christian U., Ft. Worth, 1992. Fine arts editor, reporter The Examiner-Enterprise, Bartlesville, Okla., 1992-93; comm. mgr. R.J. Reynolds Tobacco Co., New Orleans, 1993-94; asst. editor The Leader Newspapers, Houston, 1994-96; writer, editor, media specialist Houston C.C. Sys., 1996—. Mem. editl. bd. Movin' On, Houston, 1996—; writer The Public News, 1995. Vol. Milam House-Houston AIDS Found., Houston, 1996—; bd. dirs. Bartlesville Civic Ballet, 1992; project chmn. Bartlesville Jaycees, 1992. Scripps Howard Journalism scholar Tex. Christian U., 1991. Mem. Soc. Profl. Journalists, Nat. Coun. on Mktg. and Pub. Rels., Nat. Scrabble Assn. (1st place award Tex. 1996), Gulf Coast Pub. Rels. Consortium.

LANE, DANIEL MCNEEL, pediatric hematologist, lipidologist; b. Ft. Sam Houston, Tex., Jan. 25, 1936; s. Samuel Hartman and Mary Maverick (McNeel) L.; m. Carolyn Ann Spruiell, Nov. 28, 1958; children: Linda Ann, Daniel M. Jr., Maury S., Oleta K. MD, U. Tex.-Dallas, 1961; MS, U. Tenn., 1967; PhD, U. Okla., 1973. Asst. prof., head pediatric hematology/oncology U. Okla. Med. Ctr., Oklahoma City, 1966-72; rsch. fellow Okla. Med. Rsch. Found., Oklahoma City, 1969-72, adj. assoc. mem., 1986-92, adj. mem., 1993—; assoc. prof., head pediatric hematology/oncology Tulane Med. Sch., New Orleans, 1972-73; head hematology/oncology Oklahoma City Clinic, 1973-79; pvt. practice, 1979—; head Okla. Lipid Consultation Group, 1993-95; dir. clin. investigation Presbyn. Meml. Hosp., Oklahoma City, 1975-77; med. monitor HELP System project B. Braun Am., 1988-93, B. Braun Melsungen AG, FRG, cons.; assoc. prof. Tex. Tech. U. Health Scis. Ctr., Odessa, 1996—; chmn., bd. dirs. Poplar Pike Realtors, Inc., Memphis, 1973-85; cons. Programa de Prevenciondel Infarto en Argentina, La Plata. Fin. chmn. Dunlap for Congress, 1976; head Physicians for Gov. Nigh, 1978; Dem. candidate for Congress, 5th Dist., 1982. USPHS fellow, 1964-66; spl. rsch. fellow Nat. Heart Lung and Blood Inst., 1969-72. Mem. AMA, Am. Soc. Clin. Oncology, Am. Soc. Hematology, Am. Oil Chemists Soc., Am. Coll. Nutrition. Democrat. Episcopalian. Research on infant lipid nutrition, lipoprotein plasma pheresis, clin. hematology; pediatrics. Home: 5525 N Independence Ave Oklahoma City OK 73112 Office: Dept Pediat-Tex Tech U 800 W 4th St Odessa TX 79763

LANE, JAMES GARLAND, JR., diversified industry executive; b. Roxobel, N.C., Jan. 15, 1934; s. James Garl and Josie (Wembrow) L.; m. Janet Benthall Miller, Oct. 8, 1954; children—Bernice, Frances, Garland, Amy. B.S., U. N.C., 1959. Mem. audit staff S.D. Leidesdorf & Co., Greenville, S.C., 1959-65; v.p. finance Computer Servicenters, Inc., Greenville, 1965-68; exec. v.p., dir. Synalloy Corp., Spartanburg, S.C., 1968-73; pres. dir. Hewitt, Coleman & Assocs. subs. Continental Group, Inc., Greenville, 1973-86; chmn. bd., chief exec. officer Synalloy Corp., Spartanburg, 1986—; bd. dirs. Sunbelt Cos., Inc. Served with USMCR, 1953-56. Home: 120 Pentland Ct Greer SC 29651-9137

LANE, JAMES HAMILTON, quality assurance executive; b. Wilmington, Del., May 3, 1945; s. James Arthur and Helen (Connor) L.; m. Janet Mallot, Feb. 24, 1974 (div. May 1976); m. Catherine Garbutt Curtright, Apr. 20, 1988. BBA in Mgmt., Ga. State U., 1994. Quality assurance adminstr. Commn. National Energy Atomica-Nuclear, Rep. of China, 1974-76; quality assurance supr. Atomic Energy of Can. Ltd.-Nuclear, Argentina, 1978-80; quality assurance engr. Elec. Supply Commn. of South Africa-Nuclear, Rep. South Africa, 1981-85; sr. quality assurance specialist Gilbert/Commonwealth, Inc., Reading, Pa., 1980; quality program mgr. Gilbert/Commonwealth, Inc., Aiken, S.C., 1980-94; cons. quality assurance mgmt. Westinghouse/Dept. Energy, Aiken, 1988—, TVA Office Nuclear Power, Chattanooga, 1986-88, S.C. Electric and Gas, Columbia, 1985-86; quality assurance/quality control cons. Ebasco Svcs., Inc., N.Y.C., 1968-80. Named Tenn. State Doubles Champion, 1968. Mem. ASME, Am. Nuclear Soc., Am. Soc. for Quality Control, Am. Welding Soc., Am. Soc. Nondestructive Examination, Aircraft Owners and Pilots Assn., Golden Key Nat. Honor Soc., Phi Kappa Phi, Beta Gamma Sigma. Episcopalian. Home: 759 Piedmont Way NE Atlanta GA 30324-5121 Office: Gilbert Commonwealth Inc PO Box 1498 Reading PA 19603-1498

LANE, JERRY ROSS, alcohol and drug abuse service counselor; b. Pampa, Tex., June 3, 1944; s. Wilbur Howard and Christina Lavina (Hendrix) L.; m. Mary Lou Jetton, July 9, 1966; children: Jeffrey Ross, Tamara Noel. BS, McMurry U., 1968; MS in Counseling Psychology, Emmanuel Bapt. U., 1988, D in Counseling Psychology, 1991. Cert. and registered hypnotherapist, CHE. Tchr. Fannin Elem., Abilene, Tex., 1968-70, Tierra Blanca Elem., Hereford, Tex., 1970-72; acctg. and sales staff Lane and Co., Inc., Panhandle, Tex., 1972-74; min. music and edn. Memphis (Tex.) United Meth. Ch., 1974-75, First United Meth. Ch., McAllen, Tex., 1975-79; chaplain cancer treatment ctr. McAllen (Tex.) Br. M.D. Anderson Hosp., 1977-79; owner, counselor Snelling and Snelling Employment, Pampa, 1979-83; tchr. Travis Elem., Pampa, 1983-89; student asst. program coord. Pampa (Tex.) Ind. Sch. Dist., 1989-92; counselor, dir. drug/alcohol program Clarendon Coll. Pampa (Tex.) Ctr., 1992—; trainer Developing Capable People, Provo, Utah, 1990—; trainer family cmty. leadership Tex. Extension Svc., Amarillo, Tex., 1990—; parenting cons. Region XVI Edn. Svc. Ctr., Amarillo, 1991—, adv. bd. drug/alcohol, 1992—; cons. Cal Farley's Family Living Ctr., Borger, Tex., 1992—. Bd. dirs. Pampa (Tex.) Fine Arts, 1980-83, Pampa United Way, 1996; chmn. bd. Salvation Army, Pampa, 1982; bd. pres. Civic Ballet, Pampa, 1984; choir mem., bd. dirs. First United Meth. Ch.; vol. grief counselor Hospice of Panhandle. Named Family of Yr., Mormon Ch., Pampa, 1981, Top Gun, Tex. Tech. Dads and Moms Assn., Lubbock, Tex., 1990; grantee Tex. Coun. Assn. Drug/Alcohol, Pampa (Tex.) Ind. Sch. Dist., 1989-93. Mem. Am. Assn. Christian Counselor, Nat. Christian Counselor Assn., Tex. Christian Counselors Assn., Panhandle Christian Counselors Assn., Tex. Jr. Coll. Tchrs. Assn., Pampa C. of C. Home: 2007 Williston St Pampa TX 79065-3632 Office: Clarendon Coll Pampa Ctr 900 N Frost St Pampa TX 79065-5456

LANE, LAWRENCE JUBIN, retired electrical engineer, consultant; b. Morganton, N.C., Feb. 19, 1927; s. Lawrence and Sarah Virginia (Jubin) L.; m. Gladys Verna Lee Hock, Dec. 25, 1947 (dec. 1975); children: Priscilla Gayle Lane Purks, Richard Jubin; m. 2d Helen Elizabeth Sollazzo, Dec. 19, 1975. B.E.E., N.C. State Coll., 1950; M.S.E.E., U. Va., 1972. Lic. profl. engr., Va. Engr. GE, Schenectady, N.Y., 1950-54; class supr. GE, Phila., 1954-55; devel. engr. GE, Waynesboro, Va., 1955-63, sr. devel. engr., 1963-78; sr. systems design engr. GE, Roanoke, Va., 1978-83, cons. engr., 1983-95; ret., 1995. Patentee in field. Pres. Stuarts Draft PTA, Va., 1960, 61. Served as petty officer USN, 1944-46, 50-51. Recipient Managerial award Gen. Electric Co., 1965. Fellow IEEE (chpt. chmn. 1982-83); mem. Eta Kappa Nu, Tau Beta Pi, Phi Eta Sigma, Phi Kappa Phi. Methodist. Home: 4868 Warrior Dr Salem VA 24153-5816

LANE, LINDA LEE, landscape company executive; b. Baton Rouge, Dec. 25, 1952; d. Frank Jr. and Katie (Mae) L. Bus. mgmt., So. U., 1973, postgrad., 1979-82. Tchr. substitute Fayette County Sch. Sys., Fairburn, Ga., East Baton Rouge Parish Sch. Bd. Author: (poetry) Can't Keep it to Myself; songwriter. Mem. Internat. Soc. Poets, Phi Alpha Delta. Democrat. Baptist. Home: PO Box 960681 Riverdale GA 30296-0681

LANE, MARGARET BEYNON TAYLOR, librarian; b. St. Louis, Feb. 6, 1919; d. Archer and Alice (Jones) Taylor; B.A., La. State U., 1939, J.D., 1942; B.S. in Library Sci., Columbia U., 1941; m. Horace C. Lane, Jan. 6, 1945; children—Margaret Elizabeth, Thomas Archer. Reference and circulation asst. Columbia Law Library, N.Y.C., 1942-44; law librarian, asst. prof. U. Conn. Sch. Law, Hartford, 1944-46; law librarian La. State U. Law Sch., Baton Rouge, 1946-48; recorder documents La. Sec. of State's Office, Baton Rouge, 1949-75; law librarian Lane Fertitta, Lane Janney & Thomas, 1976—. Author: State Publications and Depository Libraries, 1981, Selecting And Organizing State Government Publications, 1987. Mem. depository library council to Pub. Printer, 1972-77; mem. plan devel. com. La. Fed. Depository Library, 1982-83. Treas. Delta Iota House Bd. of Kappa Kappa Gamma, 1965-68; mem. La. Adv. Coun. State Documents Depository Program, 1991—. Inducted into La. State U. Law Ctr. Hall of Fame, 1987. Mem. ALA (interdivisional com. public documents 1967-74, chmn. 1967-70; govt. documents round table, state and local documents task force 1972—, coordinator 1980-82; James Bennett Childs award 1981, anniv. honor roll 1996), La. Library Assn. (Essae M. Culver Disting. Service award 1976; chmn. documents com. 1982-83, Lucy B. Foote award subject specialist sect. 1986, Named in her honor Margaret T. Lane Award 1994), La., Baton Rouge Bar Assns., Mortar Bd., Phi Delta Delta, Kappa Kappa Gamma. Club: Baton Rouge Library. Home: 7545 Richards Dr Baton Rouge LA 70809-1547 Office: PO Box 3335 Baton Rouge LA 70821-3335

LANE, MARK ROBERT, journalist; b. Long Beach, Calif., Jan. 7, 1956; s. John R. and Catherine June (Boyce) L.; m. Ana Maria Pernia, Oct. 2, 1982; children: Rachel I., Nathaniel J. BA in History, Boston U., 1976, MA in History, 1979. Reporter The News-Jour., Daytona Beach, Fla., 1980-86; editl. writer The News-Jour., Daytona Beach, 1986—, assoc. editor, 1992—. Office: The News-Journal 901 6th St Daytona Beach FL 32117-3352

LANE, MARY FRANCES, health, physical education curriculum specialist; b. Lakeland, Fla., Jan. 25, 1955; d. Steve Joseph and Dorothy Jean (Giamaresi) Forgach; m. Charles Edwin Lane Jr., June 23, 1984. AA, U. South Fla., 1975; BS magna cum laude, U. Fla., 1977, MA in Phys. Edn., 1978. Cert. tchr., Fla. Phys. edn. tchr. Pinellas Cen./Walsingham Sch., Pinellas County, Fla., 1978-80, Wekiva Elem. Sch., Seminole County, Fla., 1983-84, Spring Lake Elem. Sch., Seminole County, 1984-87; adapted phys. edn. tchr. Walsingham Elem. Sch., Pinellas County, 1980-83; motor devel. specialist Seminole County Schs., Sanford, Fla., 1987—; lectr. ednl. and healthcare orgns.; cons. summer inst., Fla. Dept. Edn., Tallahassee, 1985, 90; tng. chair Spl. Olympcis, Sanford, 1987—; mem. Fla. Hosp. Neonatal/Pediatrics Med. Ethics Com.; adv. coun. Very Spl. Arts Festival; adj. faculty U. Cen. Fla. Author curriculum materials; contbr. articles to profl. jours. Mem. Morton F. Plant Hosp. Found., Clearwater, Fla., 1980-83. Grantee, Found. for Advancement of Community Through Schs., Seminole County, 1989, grantee Internat. Spl. Olympics, 1989. Mem. Coun. Exceptional Children, Fla. Assn. Health, Phys. Edn., Recreation and Dance (bd. dirs., treas. 1979-82, chair 1985-88), Phi Kappa Phi. Republican. Roman Catholic. Office: Seminole County Schs Ednl Support Ctr 400 E Lake Mary Blvd Sanford FL 32773-7125

LANE, NEAL FRANCIS, university provost, physics researcher, federal administrator; b. Oklahoma City, Aug. 22, 1938; s. Walter Patrick and Harietta (Hattie) Charlotta (Hollander) L.; m. Joni Sue Williams, June 11, 1960; children: Christy Lynn Lane Saydjari, John Patrick. BS, U. Okla., 1960, MS, 1962, PhD, 1964, DHL (hon.), 1995; DSc (hon.), U. Ala., 1994; ScD (hon.), Mich. State U., 1995; DHL (hon.), Marymount U., Arlington, Va., 1995; DSc (hon.), Ohio State U., 1996. NSF postdoctoral fellow, 1964-65; asst. prof. physics Rice U., Houston, 1966-69, assoc. prof., 1969-72, prof. space physics and astronomy, 1972-84, chmn. dept. physics, 1977-82; dir. divsn. physics NSF, Washington, 1979-80; chancellor U. Colo., Colorado Springs, 1984-86; provost Rice U., 1986-93; dir. NSF, Washington, 1993—; non-resident fellow Joint Inst. for Lab. Astrophysics U. Colo., Boulder, 1984-93, vis. fellow, 1965-66, 75-76; mem. commn. on phys. sci., math. and applications NRC, 1989-93; bd. overseers Superconducting Super Collider (SSC) Univs. Rsch. Assn., 1985-93; disting. Karcher lectr. U. Okla., Norman, 1983; disting. vis. scientist U. Ky., Lexington, 1980; mem. adv.

com. math. and phys. sci. NSF, 1992-93. Co-author: Quantum States of Atoms, Molecules and Solids, Understanding more Quantum Physics; contbr. articles to profl. jours. Active Cath. Commn. Intellectual and Cultural Affairs, 1991. Recipient George Brown prize for superior teaching Rice U., 1973-74, 76-77, Brown Coll. Teaching award Rice U., 1972-73; Alfred P. Sloan Found. fellow, 1967-71. Fellow Am. Phys. Soc. (councilor-at-large 1981-84, chmn. panel on pub. affairs 1983, exec. com. 1981-83, chmn. divsn. electron and atomic physics 1977-78), AAAS, Am. Acad. Arts and Scis.; mem. Am. Inst. Physics (gov. bd. 1984-87), Am. Assn. Physics Tchrs., Phi Beta Kappa, Sigma Xi (pres. elect 1992, pres. 1993). Roman Catholic. Office: NSF Office of Dir 4201 Wilson Blvd Arlington VA 22203-1803

LANE, PATRICIA S., nursing home administrator, media specialist; b. Louisville, July 3, 1932; d. Ransom Grady and Jessie Marie (Lee) Snowden; m. Fred Arlo Lane, Jan. 30, 1953; children: Pat, Freda, Cameron. BA, Stetson U., 1953, MA, 1975. Tchr. City High Sch., Chattanooga, 1953; sec. to dean So. Bapt. Theol. Sem., Louisville, 1954; tchr. Waggener Jr. High Sch., Louisville, 1955-56; church sec. Arlington Bapt. Ch., Jacksonville, Fla., 1957; librarian Lumberton (N.C.) High Sch., 1965; media specialist Mainland Sr. High Sch., Daytona Beach, Fla., 1966-72, DeLand High Sch., 1973-81; adminstr. DeLand Convalescent Ctr., 1982-90, Fairview Manor Ltd., Daytona Beach, FL, 1990-96; sec., treas. Coordinated Care, Inc., Deland, Fla., 1996—; chmn. Missions Devel. Coun., 1991-92. Sunday sch. sec. 1st Bapt. Ch., DeLand, Fla., 1989-93, mem. pers. com., 1987-90. Mem. Fla. Health Care Adminstrs. Assn. (sec. local dist. 1986-87). Democrat. Baptist. Home: 231 W Minnesota Ave Deland FL 32720-3477 Office: Coordinated Care Inc 403 S Amelia Ave Deland FL 32724-5917

LANE, SUSAN NANCY, structural engineer; b. Dayton, Ohio, Aug. 20, 1960; d. Richard Evenson and Nancy (Schmidt) L. BSCE, Pa. State U., 1982, MSCE, 1984. Registered profl. engr., Va. Asst. engr. Parsons Brinckerhoff-FG, Inc., Trenton, N.J., 1984-85; structural engr. Boyle Engring. Corp., Landover, Md., 1985; engr. I Parsons Brinckerhoff Quade & Douglas, Inc., Herndon, Va., 1985-88; rsch. structural engr. U.S. Dept. Transp., Fed. Hwy. Adminstrn., McLean, Va., 1988—; technician Ocean County (N.J.) Engring. Dept., Toms River, summers 1978-81; mem. prestressing steel com. Precast/Prestressed Concrete Inst., 1989—, R&D com., 1990—, bridge com., 1992—. Contbr. articles to Pub. Rds., PCI (Precast/Prestressed Concrete Inst.) Jour. Mem. ASCE (mem. reinforced concrete rsch. coun.), Am. Concrete Inst. (mem. prestressed concrete com. 1992—). Office: Fed Hwy Adminstrn 6300 Georgetown Pike Mc Lean VA 22101-2200

LANE, TOM CORNELIUS, lawyer; b. Borger, Tex., Dec. 3, 1948; s. Aubrey G. and Barbara Ellen (Cook) L.; m. Nanette Marie Betts, Jan. 25, 1969; children: Trevor C., Tom Cornelius Jr. BBA in Mktg., Tex. A&M U., 1971; JD, U. Tulsa, 1988. Bar: Okla. 1988, U.S. Dist. Ct. (no. dist.) Okla. 1988, U.S. Dist. Ct. (ea. dist.) Okla. 1995. Sales mgr. Sears, North Platte, Nebr., 1972-76, Motorola C&E, Laredo, Tex., 1976-79; gen. mgr. Autophone of Laredo, Inc., 1979-81; owner Laredo Comms., Inc., 1981-85; from clk. to atty. W.C. "Bill" Sellers, Inc., Sapulpa, Okla., 1987-95; prin. Tom C. Lane, Sr. & Assocs., Sapulpa, 1995—; atty. Ea. Okla. Legal Aid, Tulsa, 1990—. City commr. City Counsel, Sapulpa, 1992; fin. chmn. Boy Scouts Am., Sapulpa, 1993. With USN, 1985-92. Recipient Silver Key award ABA, Tulsa, 1988, Appreciation award Fraternal Order of Police, Sapulpa, 1992. Mem. Am. Trial Lawyers Assn. (membership com. 1993-94), Okla. Trial Lawyers Assn. (membership com.), Lions Club Internat., Masons. Democrat. Baptist. Office: Tom C. Lane Sr & Assocs PO Box 384 Sapulpa OK 74067

LANE, VICKI See MANOCCHIO, VIVIENNE CINDA

LANE, WALTER RONALD, JR., advertising executive, educator; b. Wilmington, N.C., Sept. 2, 1940; s. Walter Ronald and Dorothy (Holmes) L.; m. Judy Carol Smith, Nov. 14, 1963 (dec. Oct. 1992); 1 child, Sheri Lynn Lane Bevil. AB, U. Ga., 1963, MA, 1964. Promotion mgr. Ln. Labs./Mentho-Mulsion Co., Wilmington, 1961-62; advt. copywriter LSP Advt., Wilmington, 1962; account exec. Am. Lithograph/Case-Hoyt, Atlanta, 1964-67; copywriter Rhodes Advt., Atlanta, 1967; creative dir. SLRS Comms., Athens, Ga., 1967-73, pres., 1973—; prof. U. Ga., Athens, 1973—; mktg. cons. Ga. Inst. Comty. and Area Devel., 1975-81; coord. Am. Assn. Advt. Agys. Inst. Advanced Advt. Studies, Atlanta, 1981-86; advt. mgr. Jour. Advt., 1987-90; mem. accrediting coun. Accrediting Bd. Journalism Colls., 1993—; judge Addy Awards, Peabody Screening Com. Co-author: Advertising Media Problem Solving, 1968, A Perspective for Advertising/Marketing in Emerging European Countries, 1990, Kleppner's Advertising Procedure, 10th edit., 1988, 11th edit., 1990, 12th edit., 1993, 13th edit., 1996; prodr. TV videos; contbr. articles to profl. jours. Grantee Newspaper Advt. Pubs. Assn., 1990, Warning Labels design grantee Am. Cancer Soc./Ga. Med. Coll., 1990. Mem. Am. Advt. Fedn. (bd. dirs., mem. coun. govs. 1992-93, chmn. acad. divsn. 1992-93, mem. acad. divsn. exec. com. 1993-96, Hileman Outstanding Educator award 1987, Outstanding Svc. award 1986), Am. Advt. Found. (bd. dirs. 1992-95), Am. Mktg. Assn., Am. Acad. Advt., Atlanta Advt. Club, Greater Augusta Advt. Club. Presbyterian. Home: 193 Bent Tree Dr Athens GA 30606-1945 Office: SLRS Comms Inc PO Box 5488 Athens GA 30604-5488

LANE, WILLIAM ARTHUR, lawyer; b. Nashville, Sept. 16, 1958; s. Thomas Jennings Lane and Nancy Eleanor (Shirley) Boyd; m. Brenda Diane Kinamon, Dec. 5, 1981; children: Charles Thomas, John Ross. BS, Mid. Tenn. State U., 1980; JD, Nashville U., 1984. Bar: Tenn. 1986, U.S. Dist. Ct. (mid. dist.) Tenn. 1986, U.S. Ct. Appeals (6th cir.) 1986, U.S. Supreme Ct. 1990. Pvt. practice law Smyrna, Tenn., 1987-94, Murfreesboro, Tenn., 1994—; atty. Travelers Ins. Co., Nashville, 1990-91, U.S.F.&G Ins. Co., Nashville, 1991-92, Willis-Corroon Adminstrv. Svcs. Corp., 1992-94. Mem. Tenn. Bar Assn., Nashville Bar Assn., Assn. Trial Lawyers Am., Masons, Shriners, Sigma Delta Kappa. Baptist. Office: 3236 Dilton Mankin Rd Murfreesboro TN 37127-6641

LANEY, HOWARD ELIMUEL, clergyman; b. Maiden, N.C., Sept. 8, 1925; s. Charlie Ivy and Lottie Mae (Huffman) L.; m. Margie Ree Abernathy, May 29, 1943; children: Carolyn (Mrs. Joe Wells), Ricky Allen, Debra Lynn. Student, Gardner-Webb Coll., 1949-51, Furman U., Lenoir-Rhyne Coll., 1955-56, Sch. Pastoral Care, Winston Salem, N.C., 1958. Ordained to ministry Bapt. Ch., 1949. Pastor Faith Bapt. Ch., Lincolnton, N.C., 1951-56, Liberty Grove, Roaring River Chs., North Wilkesboro, N.C., 1956-60, Starnes Cove Bapt. Ch., Asheville, N.C., 1960-67, Providence (N.C.) Bapt. Ch., 1967-69, Anderson Grove Bapt. Ch., Albemarle, N.C., 1969-77, Fairplains Bapt. Ch., North Wilkesboro, 1977-88; supply pastor Ctr. Bapt. Ch., North Wilkesboro, 1988-89; pastor Boiling Springs Bapt. Ch., Purlear, N.C., 1989—; chaplain Chevrolet Co., Asheville; coroner North Wilkesboro, 1990—. Mem. adv. bd. Campbell Coll., Buies Creek, N.C., 1981—; bd. dirs. Deafness Ctr, North Wilkesboro, 1956—, Rest Home, Crime Stoppers, Mulberry Fairplains Fire Dept., 1967— (Fireman of Yr. 1984), First Responders, 1986—. Mem. Stone Mountain Bapt. Assn. (moderator 1979), Wilkes Ministerial Assn. (treas. 1989—). Home: 236 Mulberry Pine St North Wilkesboro NC 28659-8270

LANEY, JAMES THOMAS, ambassador, educator; b. Wilson, Ark., Dec. 24, 1927; s. Thomas Mann and Mary (Hughey) L.; m. Berta Joan Radford, Dec. 20, 1949; children: Berta Joan Vaughn, James T., Arthur Radford, Mary Ruth Laney Reilly, Susan Elizabeth Castle. BA, Yale U., 1950, BD, 1954, PhD, 1966; DD (hon.), Fla. So. Coll., 1977; LHD (hon.), Rhodes Coll., 1979; HHD (hon.), Mercer U., 1980; LLD (hon.), DePauw U., 1985; DD (hon.), Wofford Coll., 1986; LHD (hon.), Millsaps Coll., 1988, Austin Coll., 1990, W.Va. Wesleyan Coll., 1990, Yale U., 1993; DD (hon.), Emory U., 1994; LLD (hon.), U. St. Andrews, Scotland, 1994, Alaska Pacific U., 1994. Chaplain Choate Sch., Wallingford, Conn., 1953-55; ordained to ministry Meth. Ch., 1955; asst. lectr. Yale Div. Sch., 1954-55; pastor St. Paul Meth. Ch., Cin., 1955-58; sec. student Christian movement, prof. Yonsei U., Seoul, Korea, 1959-64; asst. prof. Christian ethics Vanderbilt U. Div. Sch., 1966-69; dean Candler Sch. Theology, Emory U., 1969-77, pres. univ., 1977-93; U.S. amb. to Republic of Korea, 1993—; vis. prof. Harvard Div. Sch., 1974. Author: The Education of the Heart, 1994; (with J.M. Gustafson) On Being Responsible, 1968; author essays. Pres. Nashville Community Rels. Coun., 1968-69; mem. Yale Coun. Com., 1972-77; bd. dirs. Fund Theol. Edn.; chmn. United Bd. Christian Higher Edn. in Asia, 1990-93; bd. dirs. Atlanta Symphony, 1979-91; chmn. bd. overseers com. to visit Harvard Div. Sch., 1980-85; mem. Yale U. Coun. Exec. Com., 1990-93; mem. Carnegie Endowment Nat. Commn. on Am. & the New World; mem. adv. com. Atlanta Project; chmn. so. dist. Rhodes Scholarship Com., 1980-90; bd. dirs. Atlantic Coun., 1987-93. With AUS, 1946-48. Selected for Leadership Atlanta, 1970-71; recipient Disting. Alumnus award Yale U. Div. Sch., 1979, 93, Kellogg award for leadership in higher edn., 1983, Wilbur Cross medal Yale Grad. Sch., 1996; D.C. Macintosh fellow Yale U., 1965-66. Mem. Am. Soc. Christian Ethics, Soc. for Values Higher Edn. (pres. 1987-91), Coun. on Fgn. Rels., Atlanta C. of C., Commerce Club, Phi Beta Kappa, Omicron Delta Kappa.

LANEY, VICKIE MOORE, nursing administrator; b. Vale, N.C., June 22, 1957; d. R.V. and Beatrice Marguerite (Weaver) Moore; m. Michael Wayne Laney, Dec. 26, 1976: children: Michael Andrew, Daniel Mitchell. AAS, Catawba Valley Coll., 1986. RN, N.C., S.C. Staff nurse in cardiac catheterization and critical care Catawba Meml. Hosp., Hickory, N.C., 1986-93; nursing supr. Lincoln County Hosp., Lincolnton, N.C., 1993-94; with Indsl. Health of N.C., Hickory, 1994; staff nurse Cardiac Cath Lab Catawba Meml. Hosp., Hickory, N.C., 1994—; instr. nursing asst. tng. Catawba Valley C.C., Hickory, 1989-94; IV nurse cons. Med. IV Home Health, Hickory, 1992-93. Pianist Jacobs Fork Bapt. Ch. Nursing scholar Catawba Valley Coll., 1984-86. Republican. Baptist. Home: 2820 Ledford Rd Vale NC 28168-8946 Office: Cardiac Cath Lab Catawba Meml Hosp 810 Fairgrove Ch Rd Hickory NC 28601

LANFORD, ROBERT ELDON, microbiologist, educator; b. Ft. Worth, Tex., Apr. 18, 1951; s. William Ernest and Rae (Morse) L.; m. Deborah F. Hanna, June 3, 1972. BS, U. Tex., Arlington, 1974; PhD, Baylor Coll., Houston, 1979. Asst. prof. virology/epidemiology Baylor Coll. Medicine, Houston, 1982-84; asst. scientist dept. virology and immunology S.W. Found. for Biomed. Rsch., San Antonio, 1984-85, assoc. scientist, 1986-89, scientist dept. viology and immunology, 1990—; adj. asst. prof. Dept. Microbiology, U. Tex. Health Sci. Ctr., San Antonio, 1984-85, adj. assoc. prof., 1986-91, adj. prof., 1991—. Contbr. numerous articles to profl. jours. Mem. Am. Soc. Microbiology, Am. Soc. Virology, Am. Soc. for Cell Biology. Office: SW Found for Bio Rsch Virology/Immunology 7620 NW Loop 410 San Antonio TX 78227-5301

LANG, DARICE MOUQUIN, technical writer; b. Glen Cove, N.Y., Aug. 9, 1956; d. Eugene Louis and Theresa Anne (Booy) Mouquin; m. William D. Lang, June 25, 1983. BS in Elec. Computer Engring., Clarkson U., 1978. Tech. writer Tex. Instruments, Dallas, 1979—. Mem. Soc. Tech. Comm., Spl. Interest Group for Tech. Comm. Office: Tex Instruments Inc M/S 8475 6550 Chase Oaks Blvd Plano TX 75023-2308

LANG, GAYDELLE MARIE, principal; b. New Orleans, July 17, 1951; d. Mary (Davis) L. BA, Dillard U., 1973; MA, Pepperdine U., 1975; EdD, U. Houston, 1995. Tchr. spl. edn. 3d and 4th grade Grace Elem. Sch., L.A., 1973-75; tchr. gifted/talented 4th grade Parent Elem. Sch., Inglewood, Calif., 1979-81, Houston Ind. Sch. Dist., 1979-81; team leader 5th grade Ridgemont Elem., Houston, 1981-83; sci. tchr. Sugar Land (Tex.) Mid. Sch., 1983-90; asst. prin. McAuliffe Mid. Sch., Houston, 1990-93; field svc. rep. Region IV Edn. Svc. Ctr., Houston, 1993-95; prin. Douglass Elem. Sch./Houston Ind. Sch. Dist., 1995—; mem. adv. bd. Wharton C.C.; spkr. on edn. Parent-Child Comm., 1993. Coun. mem. Sugar Land City Coun.; mem. Sugar Land Exch. Club, Ft. Bend Dem. Party, Sugar Land, Missouri City (Tex.) chpt. NAACP. Mem. ASCD, Nat. Alliance Black Sch. Educators, Tex. Assn. Secondary Sch. Prins., Phi Delta Kappa (historian). Home: 15627 Brookwood Lake Sugar Land TX 77478 Office: Douglass Elem Sch/Houston Ind Sch Dist 3000 Trulley St Houston TX 77004

LANG, JEAN MCKINNEY, editor, business educator; b. Cherokee, Iowa, Nov. 6, 1921; d. Roy Clarence and Verna Harvey (Smith) McKinney; BS, Iowa State U., 1945; MA, Ohio State U., 1969; postgrad. U. South Fla., 1972; m. Thomas E. Greef; 1 dau., Barbara Jean Wilcox; step-children: Mary McDonald, Daniel A. Greef. Merchandiser, jewelry buyer Rike-Kumler Co., Dayton, Ohio, 1952-59, Met. Co., Dayton, 1959-64; tchr. DeVilbiss High Sch., Toledo, 1966-67; chmn. dept. retailing Webber Coll., Babson Park, Fla., 1967-72; assoc. editor Wet Set Illustrated, 1972-75; sr. editor Pleasure Boating, Largo, Fla., 1975-84; tchr. bus. adminstrn. St. Petersburg (Fla.) Jr. Coll., 1974-88; adj. prof. bus. adminstrn., 1988—, securities arbitrator, 1992—; editor Suncoast Woman, 1986-88. Mem. U.S. Senatorial Bus. Adv. Bd.; mem. Nat. Boating Safety Adv. Council, 1979-81; Recipient recognition Nat. Retail Mchts. Assn., 1971, certs. of appreciation U.S. Power Squadron, 1976, Webber Coll., 1972. Mem. AAWU, Fla. Women's Alliance, Greater Tampa C. of C., Tampa Aux. Power Squadron, USCG Aux., Sales and Mktg. Execs. of Tampa (pres.'s award 1973), Fla. Freelance Writers Assn., Am. Mktg. Assn., Gulf Coast Symphony, Internat. Platform Assn., The Fashion Group, Fla. Coun. Yacht Clubs, Toledo Yacht Club (hon.), Tampa Yacht and Country Club, Chi Omega. Republican. Presbyterian. First woman to cruise solo from Fla. to Lake Erie in single-engine inboard, 1969, to be accepted into Fla. Council Yacht Clubs; yachting accomplishments published in The Ensign, Lakeland Boating, Yachting, Boote mags. Office: PO Box 402 Largo FL 33779-0402

LANG, JOHN CALVIN, physical chemist; b. Montclair, N.J., May 6, 1942; s. J. Calvin and Dorothy L. (Davenport) L.; m. Elizabeth Anne Houghton, June 25, 1966; 1 child, Phebe. BA, Wesleyan U., Middletown, Conn., 1964; MS, Cornell U., 1968, PhD, 1972. Rsch. chemist Procter & Gamble, Cin., 1975-84; rsch. assoc. ARCO Oil & Gas Co., Plano, Tex., 1984-86; prin. scientist, mgr. Alcon Labs., Inc., Ft. Worth, 1986-91, asst. tech. dir. drug delivery, 1992-95, assoc. tech. dir. drug delivery techs., 1996—; cons. Ctr. for Surface Sci. and Engring., U. Fla., Gainesville, 1987—; adj. assoc. prof. chemistry U. Tex., Arlington, 1986—. Contbr. articles to Jour. Chem. Physics, Jour. Pharm. Sci., Physica, others. Mem. Am. Chem. Soc. (chmn.-elect Dallas/Ft. Worth chpt. 1991, chmn. 1992), Am. Phys. Soc., Am. Assn. Pharm. Scientists, Controlled Release Soc. Home: 2106 Riverforest Dr Arlington TX 76017-1637 Office: Alcon Labs Inc R2-45 PO Box 6600 Fort Worth TX 76115-0600

LANG, LILLIAN OWEN, accountant; b. Yorkville, Tenn., Oct. 8, 1915; d. Hugh Preston and Susan (Davis) Owen; 1 child, John Sanford Lang. Student U. Tenn. Extension, 1956-62, Memphis State U., 1963-64, Memphis Acad. Arts, 1965-66. CPA, Tenn. Shipping clk. Buckeye Cellulose Corp., 1943-46; x-ray technician Memphis and Shelby County Health Dept., 1948-56; acctg. clk. Purex Corp., 1957-59; bookkeeper Electrolock, Inc., 1959-62; sec.-treas. Allied Bruce Terminix Cos., Inc., Mobile, Ala., 1962-80, v.p., 1980-86, also dir.; pvt. practice acctg., Memphis, 1986—; former dir. dir. affiliated corps. Leasing of Mobile, Inc., Terminix Services of Tupelo (Miss.). Mem. DAR, Tenn. Soc. CPAs (Memphis chpt.), Am. Soc. Women Accts. (pres. Mobile chpt. 1977-78, dir. S.E. area 1979-81). Mem. Disciples of Christ. Home and Office: 1960 N Parkway Apt 601 Memphis TN 38112-5053

LANG, MICHAEL JOHN, neonatologist; b. Mason City, Iowa, Nov. 9, 1956; s. Jack W. and Shirley A. (Durben) L.; m. Barbara J. Walls, June 3, 1978; 3 children. BSChemE, U. Nebr., 1978, MD, 1982. Resident in pediatrics U. Nebr., Omaha, 1985; fellow in neonatology The Children's Hosp., Kansas City, Mo., 1988; staff neonatologist William Beaumont Hosp., Royal Oak, Mich., 1988-92; asst. dir. neonatology St. Francis Hosp., Tulsa, 1992—. Contbr. articles to profl. jours. Fellow Am. Acad. Pediatrics. Office: Eastern Okla Perinatal Ctr Saint Francis Hosp 6161 S Yale Ave Tulsa OK 74136-1902

LANG, THOMAS FREDERICK, lawyer; b. Elyria, Ohio, Jan. 12, 1944; s. Carl Frederick and Martha (Hagedorn) L.; m. Marilyn March, June 1, 1968; children: Thomas F. Jr., Sarah, Anne. BS, U. Pa., 1966, MBA, 1968; JD, Fla. State U., 1974. Bar: Fla., U.S. Dist. Ct. (mid. dist.) Fla., U.S. Ct. Appeals (5th and 11th cir.), U.S. Supreme Ct. Assoc. Maguire, Voorhis & Wells, Orlando, Fla., 1975-77; ptnr. Jones & Bishop, Orlando, 1978-79, Swann & Haddock, Orlando, 1979-88, Bryant, Miller, Olive, Lang & Krupenbacher, Orlando, 1988, Parker, Johnson, Owen, Lang & Kruppenbacher, Orlando, 1989, Honigman Miller Schwartz & Cohn, Orlando, 1990-94; instr. U. Cen. Fla.-Allied Legal Svcs., 1978; gen. counsel Orlando Lions Profl. Soccer, 1988—; mediator Mcpl. Securities Rules Bd.; commr. Fla. Pub. Rels. Commn., 1977-79. Pres. U. Ctrl. Fla. Boosters, 1989-90; chmn. Orange County Civic Facilities Authority, 1990—; mem. secondary sch. com. U. Pa.; sr. warden Cathedral Ch. St. Luke, 1982-83; bd. dirs. Red Cross Ctrl. Fla.; mem. Weekends of Greater Orlando; treas. Ct. of Array, Diocese of Ctrl. Fla. With USN, 1968-72. Mem. Nat. Assn. Bond Lawyers, Greater Orlando C. of C. (dir.), Fla. Citrus Sports Assn., Downtown Orlando Athletic Club, Orlando Touchdown Club. Episcopalian. Office: Allen Lang Morrison et al 340 N Orange Ave Orlando FL 32801-1611

LANG, VICKI SCOTT, primary school educator; b. Phila., June 30, 1951; d. Daniel Scotty and Verna (Laret) L. BA, Elon Coll., 1972; Masters, Old Dominion U., 1984. Kindergarten tchr. Moyock N.C. Elem. Sch., 1974—. Recipient Tchr. of the Year award, Moyock Elem. Sch., 1981, Govs. award, RaleighN.C., 1990. Mem. NCAE, NCA of Young Educators. Home: 2217 Maple St Virginia Beach VA 23451-1307

LANGBAUM, ROBERT WOODROW, English language educator, author; b. N.Y.C., Feb. 23, 1924; s. Murray and Nettie (Moskowitz) L.; m. Francesca Levi Vidale, Nov. 5, 1950; 1 child, Donata Emily. A.B., Cornell U., 1947; M.A., Columbia U., 1949, Ph.D., 1954. Instr. English Cornell U., 1950-55, asst. prof., 1955-60; assoc. prof. U. Va., Charlottesville, 1960-63; prof. English U. Va., 1963-67, James Branch Cabell prof. English and Am. lit., 1967—; vis. prof. Columbia U., summer 1960, 65-66, Harvard U., summer 1965; mem. supervising com. English Inst., 1970-71, chmn., 1972; mem. Christian Gauss Book Award Com., 1984-86; U.S. Info. Svc. lectr. Japan, Taiwan, Hong Kong, 1988. Author: The Poetry of Experience: The Dramatic Monologue in Modern Literary Tradition, 1957, The Gayety of Vision: A Study of Isak Dinesen's Art, 1964, The Modern Spirit: Essays on the Continuity of Nineteenth and Twentieth Century Literature, 1970, The Mysteries of Identity: A Theme in Modern Literature, 1977, The Word From Below: Essays on Modern Literature and Culture, 1987, Thomas Hardy in Our Time, 1995; editor: The Tempest (Shakespeare), 1964; anthology The Victorian Age: Essays in History and in Social and Literary Criticism, 1967; mem. editl. bd. Victorian Poetry, 1963—, New Lit. History, 1969—, Bull. Rsch. in Humanities, 1977—, Studies in English Lit., 1978—, So. Humanities Rev., 1979—, Studies in Browning and His Circle, 1987—, Victorian Lit. and Culture, 1991—, Symbiosis, 1995—. Served to 1st lt. M.I. AUS, 1942-46. Ford Found. fellow Center for Advanced Study, Stanford, Calif., 1961-62; Guggenheim fellow, 1969-70; sr. fellow Nat. Endowment for Humanities, 1972-73; Am. Council Learned Socs. grantee, 1961, 75-76; fellow Clare Hall, Cambridge U., Eng., 1978; U. Va. Ctr. Advanced Study fellow, 1982; resident scholar Bellagio Study and Conf. Ctr. Rockefeller Found., Italy, June 1987. Mem. MLA (del. assembly 1979-81), AAUP, PEN, Assn. Lit. Scholars and Critics, Phi Beta Kappa. Home: 223 Montvue Dr Charlottesville VA 22901-2022

LANGBORT, POLLY, retired advertising executive; b. N.Y.C.; d. Julius and Nettie (Berman) L. BA, Adelphi U. Sec. Young & Rubicam, Inc., N.Y.C., media buyer, media planner, 1960-65, planning supr., 1965-70, v.p. group supr., 1970-75, v.p. dir. planning devel., 1975-80, sr. v.p., dir. planning, 1980-85, sr. v.p. direct mktg. and media services Wunderman, Worldwide div., 1985-86, exec. v.p. dir. mktg. & media services Wunderman, Worldwide div., 1986-90; assoc. pub. Lear's Mag., N.Y.C., 1990-91; ret., 1991. Author: DMA Factbook, 1986; contbr. articles to profl. jours. Spl. gifts chairperson Am. Cancer Soc., N.Y.C., 1985-90. Jewish. Home: 7614 La Corniche Cir Boca Raton FL 33433

LANGDALE, EMORY LAWRENCE, physician; b. Walterboro, S.C., Oct. 14, 1919; s. Clint May and Lillian Blanch (Reddish) L.; m. Maggie Lee Herndon (dec. 1971); children: Fred Emory, Betty Marlene, Thomas Wayne, Emory Lawrence, Jr.; m. Annie Newell Smith, Feb. 17, 1973. BS, Coll. Charleston, 1949; MD, Med. U. S.C., 1953. Diplomate Am. Acad. Physical Medicine and Rehab. Resident VA Hosp., Richmond, Va., 1963-66; chief rehab. medicine VA Med. Ctr., Hampton, Va., 1966-69; asst. prof. physical medicine and rehab. Med. Coll. Va., Richmond, 1969-74; med. officer Charleston (S.C.) Regional Naval Hosp., 1974-76; chief rehab. medicine VA Med. Ctr., Augusta, Ga., 1974-81; assoc. prof. Med. U. S.C., 1981-85; med. dir. Rehab. Svc. Colleton Rsch. Hosp., Walterboro, S.C., 1987-91; private practice No. Charleston, 1989—. With Coast Guard, 1942-45, ATO, PTO. Fellow Am. Acad. Physical Medicine and Rehab.; mem. AMA (physician's recognition award 1980), Med. Soc. Va., S.C. Med. Assn., So. Soc. Physical Medicine and Rehab., Charleston County Med. Soc. Republican. Baptist. Home: 1064 Stonehenge Dr Charleston SC 29406-2417 Office: 1250 Remount Rd Charleston SC 29406-3419

LANGDON, VICKI N., public information coordinator; b. Sherman, Tex., Apr. 22, 1960; d. Sue N. (Campbell) L. BS in Journalism with acad. distinction, East Tex. State U., 1982. Asst. news dir. Sta. KSEO/KLBC Radio, Durant, Okla., 1982-83, news dir., 1983; entertainment editor, staff writer The Denison (Tex.) Herald, 1983-93; coord. pub. info. Denison (Tex.) Ind. Sch. Dist., 1993—. Publicist (documentary) Mother Maybelle's Carter Scratch, 1989-90; photographer (cover videocassette tape) Johnny Cash Live in London, 1985, (souvenir concert program) Johnny Cash, 1985, (cookbook) Mother Maybelle's Cookbook, 1989, (feature story) Country Music People mag., 1991, (album cover) Helen Carter Clinch Mountain Memories, 1993, (album cover) Anita Carter Yesterday, 1995. Recipient award Tex. State Teachers Assn., Tex. Classroom Teachers Assn., Am. Cancer Soc. Tex. Div., Galveston County Press Club, Texoma Music Assn. Mem. Tex. Sch. Pub. Rels. Assn., Carter Family Fan Club (area rep.), John and June Cash Fan Club (Tex. co-rep.), Alpha Chi. Office: Denison Ind Sch Dist 1201 S Rusk Ave Denison TX 75020-6340

LANGE, DAVID L., law educator; b. Charleston, Ill., Dec. 7, 1938; s. Charles W.S. and Mary Helen Lange; m. Teresa Tetrick, July 30, 1972; children—David, Adam, Daniel, Jennifer, William. BS, U. Ill., Urbana, 1960, JD, 1964. Bar: Ill. 1964, N.C. 1989. Pvt. practice Chgo., 1964-71; gen. counsel media task force Nat. Commn. on Violence, Washington, 1968-69; gen. ptnr. Mediamix Prodns., 1970-71; assoc. prof. law Duke U., Durham, N.C., 1971-74; prof. law Duke U., 1974—; of counsel Parker, Poe, Adams & Bernstein, Charlotte, N.C., 1987-94; cons. in intellectual property Govt. of Vietnam, 1994—; dir. Internat. Ctr. for Intellectual Property and Telecom., 1996—. Office: Duke U Sch Law Durham NC 27708

LANGE, NIELS ERIK KREBS, biotechnology company executive; b. Soenderborg, Denmark, July 20, 1948; s. Erik Krebs and Estrid (Jensen) L. MSc in Engring., Denmarks Tech. U., Copenhagen, 1973. Cert. chem. engr. Rsch. scientist Denmarks Tech. U., 1974-75; rsch. chemist Novo Nordisk A/S, Bagsvaerd, Denmark, 1976-86, mgr. product devel. and process rsch., 1986-93, mgr. enzyme product devel., 1993-95; staff scientist Novo Nordisk Biochemicals, Inc., Franklinton, N.C., 1995—. Contbr. articles to profl. jours. Mem. AAAS, Am. Assn. Textile Chemists and Colorists (sr.), IEA Bioenergy Network. Home: 7212 Stonecliff Dr #5 Raleigh NC 27615 Office: Novo Nordisk Biochemicals Inc State Rd 1003 PO Box 576 Franklinton NC 27525

LANGENBURG, SCOTT EDWARD, surgeon; b. Bay City, Mich., Mar. 20, 1965; m. Lisa Maureen Forner, June 15, 1991; children: Christopher Scott, Zachary Edward. AB, U. Mich., 1987, MD, 1990. Diplomate Nat. Bd. Med. Examiners. Resident in surgery U. Va., Charlottesville, 1990-92, rsch. fellow in surgery, instr. surg. techniques, 1992-94; fellow in pediat. surgery Children's Hosp. Mich., 1997—. Author: (book chpt.) Reduced Size Lung Transplantation, 1993, Essentials of Surgery, 1994; contbr. articles to profl. jours. Mem. Am. Coll. Surgeons, Va. Med. Soc., Albemarle County Med. Soc., Am. Med. Student Assn., Christian Med./Dental Soc. Home: 221 Monte Vista Ave Charlottesville VA 22903 Office: U Va Box 181 Charlottesville VA 22903

LANGENHEIM, ROGER ALLEN, lawyer; b. Seward, Nebr., Feb. 21, 1935; s. Elmer L. and Esther L. (Gerkensmeyer) L.; BS, U. Nebr., 1957, LLB, 1960; m. Susan C. McMichael, Aug. 31, 1963; children: Ann Elizabeth, Mark Allen, Sara Ann. Admitted to Nebr. bar, 1960, Mo. bar, 1960; asso. firm Stinson, Mag, Thomson, McEvers & Fizzell, Kansas City, Mo., 1960-66; v.p., gen. counsel Black, Sivalls & Bryson, Inc., Kansas City, Mo., 1966-70; internat. atty. Dresser Industries, Inc., Dallas, 1970-71; group counsel Petroleum & Mineral Group, Houston, 1971-75; v.p., gen. counsel Oilfield Products Group, Houston, 1975-80; v.p., gen. counsel Magcobar Group,

Houston, 1980-85; assoc. gen. counsel Dresser Industries Inc., Houston, 1985-87, sr. assoc. gen. counsel, 1987-94, staff v.p., assoc. gen. coun., 1994—. Mem. ABA, Nebr. Bar Assn., Mo. Bar Assn., Order of Coif. Republican. Roman Catholic. Clubs: Houston Petroleum, Elks. Editor U. Neb. Law Rev., 1958-59. Home: 6408 Wickerwood Dr Dallas TX 75248-2901 Office: 2001 Ross Ave Dallas TX 75201-8001

LANGER, DALE ROBERT, electrical engineer; b. Kenosha, Wis., Dec. 21, 1947; s. Robert M. and Lucile A. (Brandt) L.; m. Sharon L. Bascombe, June 14, 1969; children: Michael J., Michelle M., Marissa K. BSEE, U. Wis., 1975. Electrical design engr. Tex. Instruments, Dallas, 1975-80; prin. engr. Zenith Data Systems, St. Joseph, Mich., 1980-83; mgr. comm. Exide Electronics, Raleigh, N.C., 1983—. Pres. locl br. Aid Assn. for Lutheran, Raleigh, 1995, Dallas, 1980. Mem. IEEE, Assn. for Computing Machinery. Home: 8913 Lindenshire Rd Raleigh NC 27615 Office: Exide Electronics 3201 Spring Forest Rd Raleigh NC 27604

LANGER, RALPH ERNEST, journalist; b. Benton Harbor, Mich., July 30, 1937; s. Ralph L. and Mary (Skuda) L.; m. Katherine B. McGuire, June 25, 1960; children: Terri B., Tammi L. Student, Central Mich. U., 1955-57; B.A. in Journalism, U. Mich., 1957-59. Telegraph editor, reporter Grand Haven (Mich.) Daily Tribune, 1959-60; mng. editor Port Angeles (Wash.) Evening News, 1962-66; copy desk Detroit Free Press, 1966-68; asst. mng. editor Dayton Jour. Herald, 1968, mng. editor, 1968-75; editor Everett (Wash.) Herald, 1975-81; mng. editor Dallas Morning News, 1981-83, exec. editor, 1983-86, v.p., 1986-91, sr. v.p., exec. editor, 1991—. Pres. Freedom of Info. Found. Tex., 1985-89, Nat. Freedom of Info. Coalition, 1992-93, Coun. of Presidents, 1991-92.. 1st lt. U.S. Army, 1960-62. Mem. Am. Soc. Newspaper Editors, Press Club Dallas (pres. 1985-86), A.P. Mng. Editors Assn. (bd. dirs. 1980—, sec. 1989, v.p. 1990, pres. 1990-91), Coun. of Pres.'s (founding pres. 1992-93), AP Mng. Editors Assn. Found. (pres. 1991-92), Scabbard and Blade, Alpha Phi Gamma, Sigma Phi Epsilon. Office: Dallas Morning News Comm Ctr PO Box 655237 Dallas TX 75261

LANGFIELD, RAYMOND LEE, real estate developer; b. Houtzdale, Pa., Jan. 31, 1921; s. Arthur H. and Sadie L. (Morris) L.; m. Helen Deborah Elion, Oct. 15, 1952; 1 child, Joanna Langfield Rose. BS in Indsl. Engring., Pa. State U., 1942. Registered profl. engr., Conn. Chief mgmt. engr. CIT Fin. Corp., N.Y.C., 1947-50; v.p. Mosler Safe Co., N.Y.C., 1950-60; pres. Spicer Fuel Co., Groton, Conn., 1960-86, United Fuel Corp., Groton, Conn., 1962-86, Spicer Gas Co., Groton, Conn., 1982-86, Conn. Hotel Corp., New London, Conn., 1986-94. Mem. Conn. Energy Adv. Bd., Hartford, 1985-87; pres. Grade Arts Ctr., New London, 1985-87. Lt. comdr. USNR, 1941-47. Mem. Southeast Conn. C. of C. (bd. dirs., chmn. bd. 1978-80), Ind. Conn. Petroleum Assn. (chmn. bd. 1973-74, Oil Man of Yr., 1975), New Eng. Fuel Inst. (bd. dirs. 1972-84), Navy League Conn. (bd. dirs. 1985-87). Jewish. Home: 23362 Torre Cir Boca Raton FL 33433-7026 Office: Conn Hotel Corp 35 Governor Winthrop Blvd New London CT 06320-6615

LANGFORD, JACK DANIEL, elementary school educator; b. Cookeville, Tenn., Jan. 15, 1960; s. Sam Harley and Mary Delma (Carr) L.; m. Marilyn Patricia Poteet. BS in Secondary Edn., Tenn. Tech. U., 1983, MA in Ednl. Adminstrn. and Supervision, 1987, MA, 1993. Lic. tchr., 17 tchg. endorsements. Bus. tchr. Dekalb County H.S., Smithville, Tenn., 1984; social studies tchr. White County Mid. Sch., Sparta, Tenn., 1985-92; 1st-6th grade title I tchr. Findlay Elem. Sch., Sparta, Tenn., 1992—; chmn. Findlay Improvement Team, Sparta, 1993—. Vice-pres. White County Natural Resource Conservation Svc.; mem. Nat. Arbor Day Found. Recipient Career Ladder II State of Tenn., 1995. Mem. ASCD, NEA, Tenn. Edn. Assn., Internat. Reading Assn., Nat. Geog. Soc., White County Edn. Assn., Tenn. Cattlemen's Assn., White-Van Buren Cattlemen's Assn., White County Farm Bur., Nat. Arbor soc., Phi Delta Kappa. Home: 1404 L Hudgens Rd Sparta TN 38583

LANGFORD, THOMAS ANDERSON, theology educator, academic administrator; b. Winston-Salem, N.C., Feb. 22, 1929; s. Thomas Anderson and Louie Mae (Hughes) L.; m. Ann Marie Daniel, Dec. 27, 1951; children: Thomas A. III, James Howard, Timothy Daniel, Stephen Hughes. AB, Davidson Coll., 1951, DD, 1975; BD, Duke U., 1954, PhD, 1958. Ordained to ministry Meth. Ch., 1952; from instr. to prof. religion Duke U., Durham, N.C., 1956—, prof. systematic theology, 1971—, William Kellon Quick Disting. prof. theology and Meth. studies, chmn. dept. religion, 1965-71, dean Div. Sch., 1971-81, vice provost for acad. affairs, 1984—, interim provost, 1990, provost, 1991-94, trustee Duke endowment, 1992—; vis. prof. U. N.C., 1962. Author: In Search of Foundations: English Theology 1900-1920, 1969, Introduction to Western Philosophy: Pre-Socratics to Mill, 1970; Editor: (with G.L. Abernathy) Philosophy of Religion, 1962, 2d edit., 1968, History of Philosophy, 1965, (with W.H. Poteat) Intellect and Hope, Essays in the Thought of Michael Polanyi, 1968, Christian Wholeness, 1979, The Harvest of the Spirit, 1981, Practical Divinity: Theology in the Wesleyan Tradition, 1983; Contbr. articles to profl. jours. World Meth. Council rep. in theol. discussions with Roman Catholic Ch. and Luth. World Fedn., 1975—, Reformed World Alliance, 1987; del. Gen. Conf. United Meth. Ch., 1976, 80, 84, 88; Southeastern Jurisdictional Conf., 1972, 76, 80, 84, 88; chmn. Duke self-study coordinating com. So. Assn. Colls. and Univs., 1975-76; trustee Bennett Coll., Greensboro; exec. com. World Meth. Council, 1976-81. Gurney Harris Kearns fellow, 1956-57; Dempster fellow, 1957; Am. Council Learned Socs. fellow, 1965-66; Soc. Religion in Higher Edn. fellow, 1969; named outstanding tchr. Duke, 1965; recipient E. Harris Harbison award Danforth Found., 1965-66. Mem. Am. Theol. Soc., Phi Beta Kappa. Office: Duke U Divinity Sch Box 90967 Durham NC 27708

LANGHAM, EDWARD LEE, secondary education educator; b. Calera, Okla., Oct. 9, 1949; s. Wiley Lee and Mable Elizabeth (Snider) L.; m. Nancy Sue Belsher, Nov. 16, 1968; 1 child, Joseph Lee. BS in Secondary Edn., U. North Tex., 1972; MS in Secondary Edn., Sul Ross State U., 1993, MS in Sch. Adminstrn., 1995. Cert. in mid-mgmt., superintendency, Tex. Automobile sales Toyota Dealer, Odessa, Tex., 1976-88; tchr. Ector County Ind. Sch. Dist., Odessa, 1972-76, 1988—. Mem. ASCD, Tex. State Tchrs. Assn. (v.p. 1994-95), Odessa Breakfast Optimists (dir., pres., v.p.). Home: 4709 Winchester Odessa TX 79762 Office: Ector County ISD Box 3912 Odessa TX 79760

LANGHAM, MAX RAYMOND, economist, educator; b. Tamalco, Ill., Feb. 28, 1930; s. Samuel Alvin and Helen Agnes (Wise) L.; m. Anna Lu Meyer, Sept. 3, 1954; children: Max R. Jr., Lu Ann, James W., Sanuel A. II. BS, U. Ill., 1952, MS, 1958, PhD, 1961. Asst. prof. La. State U., Baton Rouge, 1960-62; asst. prof., assoc. prof. U. Fla., Gainesville, 1962-70, prof., 1970-95, prof. emeritus, 1995—; vis. prof. U. Minn., St. Paul, 1968-69; rsch. officer Agr. Devel. Coun., Inc., Singapore, 1976, 77; econ. policy advisor Univ. Ctr., Dschang, Cameroon, 1989-91. Co-editor: Agriculture Sector Analysis in Asia, 1982, Agriculture Policy Analysis in Sub-Saharan Africa, 1992, Am. Jour. Agrl. Econs., 1972-74; contbr. articles to profl. jours. With USAF, 1952-56. Democrat. Presbyterian. Home: 106 SW 38th St Gainesville FL 32607-2729 Office: U Fla PO Box 110240 Gainesville FL 32611-0240

LANGLEY, PATRICIA ANN, lobbyist; b. Butler, Pa., Feb. 13, 1938; d. F.J. and Ella (Serafine) Piccola; m. Harold D. Langley, June 12, 1965; children: Erika, David. BA, U. Pitts., 1961; postgrad., Georgetown U., 1967, Cath. U. Am., 1985, George Mason U., 1990—. Legis. staff U.S. Congress, Washington, 1961-63; dir. social studies Am. Polit. Sci. Assn., Washington, 1963-65; legis. specialist U.S. Congress, Washington, 1965-67, caseworker, 1967-68; polit. staff Dem. Study Group U.S. Congress, Washington, 1969; Washington rep. Family Services Am., 1975-82, dir. Washington hdqrs., 1989-92, v.p. for govt. rels., 1992; pres. Policy Directions, Arlington, Va., 1992—; vis. lectr. George Mason U., Fairfax, Va., 1994; vis. lectr. in sociology George Mason U., Fairfax, Va., 1994; bd. dirs. Coalition for Children and Youth, Washington, 1977-78; chmn. steering com. for the Coalition on White House Conf. on Families, 1979-80, Ad Hoc Coalition on A.F.D.C., 1981-82; co-founder Ptnrs. in Change Group, 1996. Mem. Donaldson Run Civic Assn., Arlington, Va., 1980—; bd. mem. Va. Chamber Orch.; vol. guide Hillwood Mus., Washington. Recipient Service Recognition U.S. Dept. Health and Human Services, 1980. Mem. Am. Soc. Assn. Execs., Women in Govt. Rels., Nat. Coun. Femily Rels., North Va. Assn. Female Execs., Arnova, Groves Conf. Roman Catholic. Home and Office: 2515 N Utah St Arlington VA 22207-4031

LANGLEY, RICKY LEE, occupational medicine physician; b. Fountain, N.C., Aug. 31, 1957; s. Ernest Lee and Janie Ruth (Fulford) L.; m. Sandra Jane Ward, June 7, 1980; children: Patrick, Nicholas, Megan. BS magna cum laude, N.C. State U., 1979; MD, Bowman Grey Sch. Medicine, 1983; MPH, U. N.C., 1988. Diplomate Am. Bd. Internal Medicine, Am. Bd. Preventive Medicine. Intern East Carolina Sch. Medicine, Greenville, N.C., 1983-84, resident, 1984-86; asst. prof. dept. preventive medicine and health policy East Carolina U., Greenville, N.C., 1989-91, adj. asst. prof. dept. family medicine, 1989-91, adj. asst. prof. dept. environ. health, 1989—, asst. prof. dept. internal medicine, 1991; fellow Sch. Medicine Duke U., Durham, N.C., 1986-88, asst. cons. prof. in occupational medicine, 1989-90, asst. clin. prof. dept. community and family medicine, 1991-96; pvt. practice occupational medicine Health and Hygiene, Inc., Greensboro, N.C., 1988-89; pvt. practice internal and occupational medicine Mebane Med. Ctr., 1996—; adj. asst. prof. dept. biol. and agrl. engring. N.C. State U., 1995—; cons. in field; mem. planning com. on agrl. safety N.C. State Fair, 1991; mem. Task Force on Agri-Bus. for Gov.'s Commn. on Reduction of infant Mortality, 1992; mem. N.C. State Task Force on Blood-Borne Pathogens, N.C. Occupl. Health and Safety Adminstrn. 1991-92; presenter in field; mem. Nat. Park Producers Coun. Task Force on Worker Health and Safety, 1995; occupl. medicine residency program evaluator for NIOSH, 1992—, mem. spl. emphasis panel, 1996—; mem. agrl. safety and health coun. N.C. Dept. Labor, 1996—. Guest editor N.C. Med. Jour., 1992, 93, 95; contbr. articles to profl. jours. Vol. Greenville Cmty. Shelter, 1990, Health Hotline, WITN, 1990, 91, State Employee Wellness Day 1989, Adopt-A-Hwy. Project, 1989; Doctor of the Day, N.C. State Legislature, 1991; doctor on call blood dr. ARC, Greensboro, 1989; vol. Freemont Peoples Clinic, 1993; pub. affairs officer Coast Guard Aux., 1996—, flotilla 18-11, 1995—; hunting safety educator, N.C., 1996—. Lloyd T. Weeks scholar, 1978, Benjamin Elloit Ibie and Benjamin Elliot Ibie Jr. Meml. scholar, 1976. Fellow ACP, Am. Coll. Occupl. and Environ. Medicine, Am. Coll. Preventive Medicine; mem. AMA, N.C. Med. Soc. (environ. health subcom. 1991—), Am. Occupl. Med. Assn. (mem. med. ctr. occupl. health com. 1990—), Carolinas Occupl. Med. Assn. (sec.-treas. 1991-92, pres-elect 1992-93, pres. 1993-94, del. 1995—), Am. Coll. Occupation and Environ. Medicine (del. 1995-96), Am. Biol., Safety Assn., Am. Conf. Govt. Indsl. Hygienists, Am. Indsl. Hygiene Assn., Tarheel Archaeology Soc. (program chair 1996), Sigma Xi, Phi Kappa Phi, Phi Eta Sigma, Gamma Sigma Delta, Alpha Epsilon Delta. Home: 1506 Miles Chapel Rd Mebane NC 27302-9008 Office: Duke U PO Box 2914 Durham NC 27715-2914

LANGSTON, CAMILLE ANNE, rhetoric educator; b. Texarkana, Tex., May 8, 1969; d. Harvey Daniel and Lulu Rose (Martin) L.; m. Douglas Byron Keathley, June 25, 1994. BA, Baylor U., 1991; MA, St. Mary's U., San Antonio, 1994; postgrad., Tex. Woman's U., 1994—. Graphic designer Presbyn. Mo-Ranch, Hunt, Tex., 1991-92; grad. asst. St. Mary's U., San Antonio, 1992-94; ednl. skills specialist St. Philip's Coll., San Antonio, 1992-94, English adj., 1994; grad. tchg. fellow Tex. Woman's U., Denton, 1994—, writing ctr. coord., 1994—; Beta test cons. LeCroy Ctr., Dallas, 1995-96; student rep. Tex. Woman's U. Grad. Coun., Denton, 1996—; featured tchr. Daedalus Group, Austin, Tex., 1996; Tex. acad. skills program test assessor Nat. Evaluation Sys., Austin, 1996; presenter in field. Univ. scholar Tex. Woman's U., Denton, 1995, Autrey Nell Wiley scholar Tex. Woman's U. English Dept., Denton, 1996. Mem. MLA, South Ctrl. MLA, Nat. Coun. Tchrs. English, Alliance of Computers and Writing, South Ctrl. Women's Studies Assn., Computers and Writing Tchg. Assts., Phi Kappa Phi. Presbyterian. Home: 1911 Colorado Blvd Apt D Denton TX 76205 Office: Tex Womans Univ Denton TX 76204

LANGUM, DAVID JOHN, law educator, historian; b. Oakland, Calif., Oct. 24, 1940; s. John Kenneth and Virginia Anne (deMattos) L.; children: Virginia Eileen, John David. AB, Dartmouth Coll., 1962; JD, Stanford U., 1965; MA in History, San Jose State U., 1976; LLM in Legal History, U. Mich., 1981, SJD in Legal History, 1985. Bar: Calif. 1966, Mich. 1981, U.S. Supreme Ct. 1972. Research clk. Calif. Ct. Appeals, San Francisco, 1965-66; assoc. Dunne, Phelps & Mills, San Francisco, 1966-68; ptnr. Christenson, Hedemark, Langum & O'Keefe, San Jose, Calif., 1968-78; adj. prof. Lincoln U. Sch. Law, 1968-78; prof. law Detroit Coll. Law, 1978-83; prof. Old Coll. Sch. Law, Reno, Nev., 1983-85, dean, 1983-84; prof Cumberland Sch. Law Samford U., Birmingham, 1985—. Author: Law in the West, 1985, Law and Community on the Mexican California Frontier, 1987 (Hurst prize 1988), (with Harlan Hague) Thomas O. Larkin: A Life of Patriotism and Profit in Old California, 1990 (Carolina Bancroft prize, 1991), Crossing Over the Line: Legislating Morality and the Mann Act, 1994; contbr. articles on law and history to profl. jours. Mem. House of Flag, pro bono litigation, San Francisco, 1973-76; past pres. Victorian Preservation Assn., Santa Clara County, Calif. Mem. Am. Soc. for Legal History (bd. dirs.), Am. Hist. Assn., Orgn. Am. Historians, Western History Assn. (Bolton award 1978). Office: Samford U Cumberland Sch Law 800 Lakeshore Dr Birmingham AL 35229-0001

LANIER, ANITA SUZANNE, musician, piano educator; b. Talladega, Ala., May 21, 1946; d. Luther Dwight and Elva (Hornsby) L. BS in Music Edn., Jacksonville (Ala.) State U., 1969. Elem. music tchr. Talladega City Schs., 1969-81; librarian, elem. music tchr. Talladega Acad., 1981-84; tchr. piano and organ Talladega, 1981—. Organist Trinity United Meth. Ch., Talladega, 1981—. Recipient Commemorative Honor medallion, 1990, World Decoration of Excellence medallion, 1990; named Woman of the Yr., 1990, Rsch. Adv. of Yr., 1990, ABI, 1990. Mem. NAFE, AAUW, Am. Pianists Assn., Pilot Club (sec. 1977-78), World Inst. Achievement, Women's Inner Circle Achievement, Internat. Platform Assn., Delta Omicron. Home: 601 North St E Talladega AL 35160-2525

LANIER, DAVID EMORY, religion educator; b. Rome, Ga., Aug. 19, 1950; s. Oscar Emory and Bettie Jane (Trammell) L.; m. Sarah Haskew Simms, Dec. 23, 1978; 1 child, Jonathan Emory. BA, North Ga. Coll., 1972; MA, U. N.C., 1976; MDiv, Southwestern Bapt. Theol. Sem., Ft. Worth, 1984, PhD, 1988. Lang. arts tchr. Pamlico Comm. Sch., Washington, N.C., 1976-77; tchr. English and German Winston-Salem (N.C.)/Forsythe County Schs., 1977-81; prof. English and New Testament Criswell Coll., Dallas, 1989-92; assoc. prof. New Testament Southeastern Bapt. Theol. Sem., Wake Forest, N.C., 1992—. Editor: Faith and Mission jour., 1992—; book rev. editor Criswell Theol. Rev., 1989-91. Recipient Asa D. Hammock scholarship North Ga. Coll., 1968-72, Rotary scholarship Gainesville, Ga., 1972-73, Opal Cox scholarship Southwestern Bapt. Theol. Sem., Ft. Worth, 1983. Mem. Evangel. Theol. Soc., Majority Text Soc. Republican. Baptist. Home: 1016 Jumper Dr Wake Forest NC 27587 Office: Southeastern Bapt Theol Sem PO Box 1889te St Wake Forest NC 27588

LANIER, JAMES NEWTON, marketing executive; b. Faison, N.C., July 2, 1939; s. Cyrus and Lucy (Caroline) L.; m. Joanne Flowers, Mar. 3, 1962; 1 child, Melissa Ann. BS, Wake Forest U., 1961; MBA, Fla. State U., 1972; Cert. for Mil. Studies, Nat. War Coll., 1980; postgrad., U. Pitts., 1980. Tchr. Ouplin County Schs., Warsaw, N.C., 1961-62; ins. agt. and securities rep. United Svcs. Planning Assn. and Ind. Rsch. Agy. for Life Ins, Fairfax, Va., 1983-88; regional v.p. United Svcs. Planning Assn. and Ind. Rsch. Agy. for Life Ins, Ft. Worth, Tex., 1988-89, sr. v.p., dir. mktg., 1990-91, pres., dir., 1992—. Col. U.S. Army, 1962-83. Decorated Legion of Merit (2), Bronze Star medal, Joint Svc. Commendation medal; Wake Forest U. scholar, 1957. Mem. Nat. Assn. of Uniformed Svcs. (dir. 1986-90). Republican. Presbyterian. Home: 3500 Bellaire Park Ct Fort Worth TX 76109-2639 Office: USPA&IRA 4100 S Hulen St Fort Worth TX 76109-4953

LANIER, RANDALL CLARK, internist, chest physician; b. Savannah, Ga., Feb. 17, 1957; s. Clark Cavin and Pauline (Warren) L.; m. Kathy Martin, Dec. 24, 1984; children: Martin, Amanda, Callie. BS in Chemistry, Armstrong State U., 1979; BS in Pharmacy, U. Ga., 1981; MD, Med. Coll. Ga., 1985. Resident Richland Meml. Hosp., Columbia, S.C., 1985-88; fellow Darns VA Hosp., Columbia, S.C., 1988-90; physician Affinity Health Group, Tifton, Ga., 1990—; med. dir. Hospice of Tifton Area, 1995—. Fellow Am. Coll. Chest Physicians; mem. Tifton County Med. Soc. (pres. 1995), Rho Chi. Office: Affinity Health Group 712 E 18th St Tifton GA 31794-3649

LANIER, ROGER ALAN, regional dean; b. Claremore, Okla., Nov. 13, 1950; s. Burt and Velma Mae (Hogue) L.; m. Jere Rhea Ensey Hancheck, May 26, 1973 (div. Jan. 1992); children: Stacie Rhea, Robert Brett, Thomas Blake; m. Vickie Diane Silvers, June 11, 1993; 1 child, William Barrett Huffman Lanier. BA, Okla. City U., 1973; MS, U. Okla., 1974, PhD, 1977. Asst. dean for acad. affairs U. Tex. Med. Br., Galveston, 1977-80; assoc. dean for acad. affairs U. of Tex. Southwestern Med. Ctr., Dallas, 1980-85; assoc. dean for student affairs John Hopkins U., Balt., 1985-90; pres. Lanier & Assocs., Guthrie, Okla., 1990-93; regional dean Tex. Tech. U. Health Sci. Ctr., Amarillo, 1993—. Author: (with others) The Aged Patient, 1983; editl. bd. Jour. of Allied Health, Chgo., 1980-87; contbr. articles to profl. jours. Bd. dirs. Big Bros./Big Sisters, Amarillo, 1995; bd. trustees Tex. Panhandle Mental Health Authority, Amarillo, 1995. Recipient Cert. of Appreciation for Disting. Svc. Am. Soc. of Allied Health Professions, 1983, Outstanding Young Leader in Allied Health, 1984; named J. Warren Perry Disting. Author Jour. of Allied Health, 1988. Mem. Amarillo West Rotary Club. Home: 7201 Gainsborough Amarillo TX 79106 Office: Tex Tech U Health Sci Ctr 1300 Wallace Blvd Amarillo TX 79106

LANIER-GESELL, MARY CATHERINE (KITTY LANIER), public relations, advertising and marketing executive; b. Clarksburg, W.Va., Sept. 15, 1934; d. William Howard and Minnie Grace (Ferguson) Childs; m. Ellis Traub Jr., Aug., 1957 (div. May 1967); children: Douglas, David, Daniel, Donald; m. Gene R. LaNier, Sept. 17, 1968 (div. Sept. 1993); m. Henry O. Gesell, DDS, Aug. 9, 1995. AA in Social Sci. with honors, Miami Dade C.C., 1975; BA in Liberal Studies, Fla. Internat. U., 1977; postgrad., Fla. Atlantic U., 1981, U. Ctrl. Fla., 1988. Lic. ins. agt., Fla. Flight attendant Eastern Airlines, Inc., N.Y.C., 1955-57; pers. rep., recruiter Eastern Airlines, Inc., Miami Internat. Airport, 1965-78; free-lance pub. rels. profl., 1978-79; first adminstr. Flagler County Palm Coast branch Daytona Beach (Fla.) C.C., 1979-82; legis. aide Senator Edgar M. Dunn Jr., Daytona Beach, 1982-83; pres., ECO, p.r. cons. LaNier Assocs., Inc., 1983-92, mktg. cons., 1992—; v.p. Marcat, Inc., part-time 1971-77; amb. Eastern Airlines, Continental Airlines, Eastern Airlines Silverliners; sales rep. Gulfstream Airlines; mktg. cons., 1996. Past chpt. leader The Compassiate Friends; past mem. Flagler County Coordinating Coun., Flagler County Resource Coun.; past chmn. pub. rels. com. Volusia County Coun. on Aging, bd. dirs.; committeewoman Daytona Beach Dem. Com., 1982-86; past mem. Famous Beach chpt. Sweet Adelines. Mem. Ormond Beach C. of C. (past bd. dirs.), Grosse Pointe Garden Club, Grosse Pointe New Friends, Fla. Internat. U. Alumni Assn. (charter), Phi Theta Kappa. Home: 724 Shoreham Rd Grosse Pointe MI 48236

LANING, RICHARD BOYER, naval officer, writer, retired; b. Washington, Jan. 1, 1918; s. Richard Henry and Marguerite (Boyer) L., m. Ruth Richmond, Sept. 5, 1942; children: Christine, Lucille. BSEE, U.S. Naval Acad., 1940; MS in Biophysics & Nuclear Physics, U. Calif., Berkeley, 1950; postgrad., U.S. Nat. War Coll., 1960. Officer USS Yorktown, 1940-41, USS Hornet Doolittle Raid, Tokyo, Battle of Midway, 1941-42; exec. officer USS Salmon Pacific Fleet, 1942-44; nuclear weapons planner OPNAV, Washington, 1953-54; commdg. officer 5 subs. including commg. 2d nuclear sub. USS Seawolf, 1956; first Polaris tender USS Proteus USN, Scotland, 1960-62; asst. chief of staff Submarines Pacific USN, Pearl Harbor, Hawaii, 1962-63; ret. USN, 1963; corp. planner, mgr. biotech. programs United Aircraft Corp., Hartford, Conn., 1963-73; life ins. underwriter Equitable of Iowa, Orlando, Fla., 1973-77; writer Orlando, Fla., 1977—; cons. in field. Contbr. articles to profl. jours. Mem. U.S. Naval Inst., Naval Acad. Alumni, Fleet Res. Assn., Navy League, Adm. Nimitz Fedn., U. Calif. Alumni, Futurist Soc., Greater Orlando C. of C., Nat. Space Soc., Navy Submarine League, Univ. Club Winter Park, Mil. Order of World Wars, Retired Officers Assn. Home and Office: 5955 Turnbull Dr Orlando FL 32822-1740

LANKFORD, GEORGE EMERSON, III, social sciences educator; b. Birmingham, Ala., Aug. 18, 1938; s. George E. Jr. and E. Elaine (Jordan) L. BA in Journalism, La. State U., 1960; BD in Theology, Princeton Theol. Sem., 1963; PhD in Folklore, Ind. U., 1975. Asst. to Presbyn. campus pastor Princeton U., 1961-63; asst. pastor Gentilly Presbyn. Ch., New Orleans, 1963-66; campus minister Presbyn., U.S., Mobile, 1966-71; from instr. to asst. prof. theology Spring Hill Coll., Mobile, 1966-71; asst. prof. folklore Lyon Coll. (formerly Ark. Coll.), 1976-81, assoc. prof., 1981-86, prof., 1986-92, Pauline M. and Brooks Bradley prof. Social Scis., 1992—; dir. core curriculum Lyon Coll. (formerly Ark Coll.), 1978-82, dir. Microcomputer Learning Ctr. Project, 1981-84, dir. humanities program, 1985-88, dir. arts and humanities program, 1988-89; lectr. in field. Author: A Documentary Study of Native American Life in the Lower Tombigbee Valley, 1983, Native American Legends, 1987; assoc. editor Mid-Am. Folklore, 1979-86, editor, 1986—; bd. editors Ark. Hist. Quar., 1993-96; contbr. articles and book revs. to profl. jours. Mem. Gov.'s Com. on Ozark Folk Ctr., 1976-81; active Ark. Arts Coun., 1977-81, folk arts adv. com., 1982-86, folk arts apprenticeship panel, 1983-87; mem. grants rev. panel Ark. Mus. Svcs., 1979-81; mem. Meadowcreek Curriculum Com., 1981-85; bd. dirs. Ark. Endowment for Humanities, 1984-90; v.p. Batesville Cmty. Theatre, 1988-89, bd. dirs., 1989-91; mem. Ozark Folk Cultural Ctr. Commn., State of Ark., 1992—; trustee 1st Presbyn. Ch., Batesville, 1993—; trustee Old Ind. Regional Mus., 1993—. Rockefeller Theol fellow Princeton Theol. Sem., 1960, Andrew W. Mellon Faculty fellow U. Kans., 1986, NEH Summer Seminar fellow Ind. U., 1983, U. Mo., 1987, U. Ky., 1991; NEH Summer Inst. fellow U. Ga., 1989, U. Wis., 1994; grantee Rockefeller Found., 1976-79, NEH, 1977-80, Title III Student Microcomputer Learning Project, Ark. Coll., 1981-84, Gifted and Talented Sch., Ark. Coll., 1988; named Coun. Advancement and Support Edn. Ark. Prof. of Yr., 1991; recipient Faculty of Yr. award Kappa Sigma, Ark. Coll., 1990, Sears-Roebuck Found. award, 1989. Mem. Am. Folklore Soc., Mid-Am. Folklore Soc., Mo. Folklore Soc., Kans. Folklore Soc., Soc. Am. Archaeology, Southeastern Archeol. Conf., Ark. Archeol. Soc. (bd. advisors 1979-83), Ark. Hist. Assn. (bd. trustees, Best Community History award 1991), Independence County Hist. Soc. (pres. 1988-90), Jackson County Hist. Soc., Batesville Hist. Preservation Soc., Ark. Preservation Assn., World Future Soc., Zero Population Growth, Omicron Delta Kappa, Tau Kappa Alpha, Alpha Psi Omega. Democrat. Home: 1175 Dogwood Dr Batesville AR 72501-7506 Office: Lyon College Batesville AR 72501

LANPHER, LUCILLE MARLENE, auditor; b. Oceanside, N.Y., Sept. 30, 1946; d. George Edward and Arline Lucille (Stewart) Tucker; m. Charles Andrew Kyme, Sept. 23, 1967 (div. Sept. 19, 1988); children: Kimberly Ann, Heather Arline, Matthew Charles; m. James Francis Lanpher, Nov. 24, 1989. AS in Acctg. summa cum laude, Nassau C.C., 1973; BS in Acctg. summa cum laude, L.I. U., 1979. Pvt. practice acct. North Babylon, N.Y., 1980-84; tax auditor N.Y. Dept. Taxation and Fin., Hempstead, 1985-91, Fla. Dept. Revenue, West Palm Beach, 1992—. Mem., leader Girl Scouts U.S., North Babylon, 1978-85; pres. PTA Grace Episcopal Day Sch., Massapequa, N.Y., 1983; mem. vestry Ch. of Good Shepherd, Tequesta, Fla., 1993-96, jr. warden, 1994; precinct rep. Dem. Exec. Com. Palm Beach County, Fla.; mem. women's leadership forum Dem. Nat. Com. Mem. Sierra Club, Democratic Club. Office: Fla Dept Revenue 2468 Metrocentre Blvd West Palm Beach FL 33407-3105

LANSKA, DOUGLAS JOHN, neurologist; b. Milw., Aug. 8, 1959; s. Orville Emmanuel Lanska and Margaret Mary (Daly) Kenehan; m. Mary Jo Brook, June 26, 1982; children: Joseph, John. BS, U. Wis., 1980, MS, MD, 1984. Nat. Bd. Med. Examiners; Diplomate Am. Bd. Neurology, Am. Bd. Psychiatry. Intern in internal medicine U. Hosps., Cleve., 1984-85; resident in neurology U. Hosps. Cleve., 1985-88, instr. neurology, 1988-89; computer operator C.S.I. Corp., Butler, Wis., 1977-78, computer programmer, 1978, data processing mgr., 1979-82, cons. computer programmer, 1982-84; computer programmer Med. Coll. Wis., Milw., 1982, rsch. asst., 1982-83; assoc. Sanders-Brown Ctr. on Aging, Lexington, Ky., 1989—; asst. prof. U. Ky. Med. Ctr., Lexington, 1989-93, assoc. prof., 1993—; cons. Ky. Med. Rev. Bd., Frankfort, 1989—, Commonwealth Ky. Ctr. for Excellence in Stroke, Lexington, 1989-91, Internal Medicine Ctr. to Advance Rsch. and Edn., Washington, 1991—, AMA, Chgo., 1991—, Health Care Financing Adminstrn., Balt., 1991—, Agy. for Health Care Policy and Rsch., Rockville, Md., 1992—, Am. Bd. Psychiatry and Neurology, Deerfield, Ill., 1992—; staff neurologist VA Med. Ctr., Lexington, 1989—, Fed. Med. Ctr., Lexington, 1995—. Contbr. articles to profl. jours. Mem., participant Ky. Physicians Care Program/Life, 1989—. Recipient Rsch. Svc. award Nat. Inst. on Aging, 1989, Career Investigator Devel. award, Nat. Inst. Neurol.

Disease, Stroke, 1991. Mem. Am. Acad. Neurology, Am. Neurol. Assn., Math. Assn. Am., Soc. for Epidemiologic Rsch., World Fedn. Neuroloy, Internat. Soc. for History of Neurology, Ky. Geriatrics Soc., Phi Beta Kappa, Alpha Omega Alpha. Roman Catholic.

LANTIGUA, JOSE SALVADOR, computer engineer, consultant; b. Havana, Cuba, Mar. 18, 1953; came to U.S., 1960; s. Jose Gregorio and Hilda Simona (Barrial) L.; m. Pansy Reen Fuller, Mar. 5, 1977; children: Joseph Gabriel, Christina Simone. AA, Miami-Dade C.C., 1973; BA, Northwestern State U. La., 1978, BS, 1979; MA, Pepperdine U., 1980; M Computer Engring., Fla. Atlantic U., 1989. Engr. NASA, Houston, 1973-75; mgr. automation Blue Cross-Blue Shield, Jacksonville, Fla., 1981-83; regional engring. mgr. Victor Techs., Jacksonville, 1983-84; dir. sys. integration Abacus Data, Inc., Jacksonville, 1984-85; cons. engr. IBM, Jacksonville, 1985-93; mng. dir. Furash & Co., Washington, 1993-94; pres. Epi-Tech Corp., Alexandria, Va., 1994-96; v.p. ISS Corp., Stamford, Conn., 1996—. Author: Knowledge Rules from Dircted Graphs, 1989; contbr. articles to various publs. Advisor Jr. Achievement, Jacksonville, 1987. Maj. U.S. Army, 1975-80, mem. USAR, 1980—. Mem. IEEE, Am. Assn. for Artificial Intelligence, Assn. for Computing Machinery, Mensa, Phi Theta Gamma. Republican. Roman Catholic. Office: ISS Corp 100 First Stamford Pl Stamford CT 06902

LANZIDELLE, GEORGE ARTHUR, practical nurse; b. Phila., Jan. 21, 1958; s. Arthur Edward Lanzidelle and Jacqeline Ruth (Smith) Greenleaf; m. Rebeca Galindo-Castellares, Feb. 3, 1994. BA in Asian Studies, U. Okla., 1988; postgrad. LPN, Olka. Mental health aide Griffin Meml. Hosp., Norman, Okla., 1980-93; LPN Fed. Dept. Vets. Affairs, Oklahoma City, 1993, Okla. State Dept. Vets. Affairs, Norman, 1994—; EMT, Norman, 1982-86; tchr. 1st aid ARC, Norman, 1980-92, mem. disaster team, 1980-95. State del. Rep. Party, Norman, 1990-92; candidate for Norman City Coun., 1990-92; grad. Def. Lang. Inst., 1976; del. to student conf. nat. affairs Tex. A&M U., 1989. With USN, 1975-79. Black belt in Aikodo, Fugakukai Internat. Aikido Assn., 1992, 1st degree brown belt in jyodo, 1993. Roman Catholic. Home: 1513 Lakecrest Dr Norman OK 73071 Office: Oklahoma Dept Vets Affairs 1776 E Robinson ST Norman OK 73071

LAPIDUS, MORRIS, retired architect, interior designer; b. Odessa, Russia, Nov. 25, 1902; came to U.S., 1903, naturalized, 1914; s. Leon and Eva (Sherman) L.; m. Beatrice Perlman, Feb. 22, 1929 (dec. 1992); children: Richard L., Alan H. Student, NYU, 1921-23; B. Arch., Columbia, 1927. With Warren & Wetmore, N.Y.C., 1926-28, Arthur Weisner, N.Y.C., 1928-30; asso. architect Ross-Frankel, Inc., N.Y.C., 1930-42; prin. Morris Lapidus Assos., 1942-86; keynote speaker Conv. Preserving the Recent Past, U.S. Dept. Interiors, 1995. Author: Architecture-A Profession and a Business, 1967, Architecture of Joy, 1979, Man's Three Million Odyssey, 1988, A Pyramid in Brooklyn, 1989, Morris Lapidus: The Architect of the American Dream, 1992 (English and German edits. by Martina Duttmann); architect-designer: Fontainebleau Hotel, Miami Beach, Fla., 1954, Eden Roc Hotel, 1955, Lincoln Rd. Mall, Americana Hotel, Bal Harbor, Fla., 1956, Sheraton Motor Inn, N.Y.C., 1962, Internat. Inn, Washington, 1964, Fairfield Towers, Bklyn., 1966, Summit Hotel, N.Y.C., 1966, Paradise Island Hotel, Nassau, 1967, Paradise Island Casino, Nassau, 1968, Out-Patient and Rehab. Center, continuing care wing Mt. Sinai Hosp, Miami Beach, Fla., 1967, Research Bldg, 1981, congregation Beth Tfiloh, Pikesville, Md., 1967, Internat. Hdqrs. of Jr. Chamber Internat., Coral Gables, Fla., 1968, Americana Hotel, N.Y.C., 1968, Cadman Plaza Urban Redevel., Bklyn., 1969, Miami Internat. Airport, 1969-74, Penn-Wortman Housing Project, Bklyn., 1971, Bedford-Stuyvesant Swimming Pool and Park, Bklyn., 1970, El Conquistador Hotel, P.R., 1969, Trelawney Beach Hotel, Jamaica, W.I., 1973, Greater Miami Jewish Fedn. Hdgrs, 1970, Hertz Skycenter Hotel, Jacksonville, Fla., 1971, Aventura, Miami, 1971, U. Miami (Fla.) Concert Hall, 1972, Griffin Sq. Office Bldg, Dallas, 1972, U. Miami Law Library, 1975, Citizens Fed. Bank Bldg, Miami, 1975, Miami Beach Theater of Performing Arts, 1976, Ogun State Hotel, Nigeria, 1977, Exhbn. Designers, Forum Design, Linz, Austria, 1980; others; assoc. architect: Keys Community Coll, Key West, Fla., 1977, Churchill Hotel London, Grandview Apt. Complex, 1980, La Union Ins. Bldg., Guayaquil, Ecuador, 1983, Daniel Tower Hotel, Herzlea, Israel, 1983, Colony Performing Arts Ctr., 1983, Jabita Hotel, Nigeria, 1984; lectr. store, hotel design; one-man exhibit 40 Yrs. Art and Architecture, Lowe Gallery, Miami U., 1967, Fedn. Arts and Archtl. League N.Y., 1970, Weiner Galleries, 1972, Exhibit 55 Yrs. Architecture, Rotterdam, The Netherlands, 1992; exhibited at Bass Mus. of Art, 1994, Columbia U., 1995; monograph pub. in Basil's Switzerland, 1992. Mem. Miami Beach Devel. Commn., 1966-67. Winner nat. competition S.W. Urban Renewal Program in Wash., internat. competition for trade ctr. on The Portal Site in Washington; recipinet Justin P. Allman award Wallcovering Wholesaler's Assn., 1963; Outstanding Specifications award Gypsum Drywall Contractors Internat., 1968; cert. merit N.Y. Soc. Architects, 1971;, NYU Alumni Achievement award, 1955. Mem. Miami Beach C. of C. (gov.), Kiwanis. Home: 3 Island Ave Miami FL 33139-1363

LAPP, DERRICK EDWARD, army officer; b. Ballston Spa, N.Y., July 13, 1970; s. Gerald Patrick and Leona C. (Theilemann) L.; m. Andrea Tyminski, Nov. 30, 1996. BA in History with honors, Va. Mil. Inst., 1992. Commd. 2d lt. U.S. Army, 1992, advanced through grades to capt., 1996; exec. officer 10th Transp. Co., Ft. Jackson, S.C., 1994; prin. staff officer Tng. Ctr. Command, Ft. Jackson, 1995—. Decorated Army Achievement medal. Mem. Assn. U.S. Army (v.p. adminstrn. 1994-96). Republican. Episcopalian. Home: 1125 Paces Run Ct Columbia SC 29223 Office: Hdqrs Tng Ctr Command 3330 Magruder Ave Columbia SC 29207

LARGENT, MILDRED M., community health nurse; b. Liberty, Mo., Feb. 20, 1928; d. Eddie and Cleda May (Lynch) Lomelino; m. Wilbur Eugene Largent, Aug. 31, 1947; children: George William, Carolyn Marie Largent Dickinson. BS, Dallas County Jr. Coll., 1968; BS in Health Care Adminstrn., East Tex. State U., 1976. Cert. family nurse practitioner. Staff nurse, intensive cardiac care unit Doctors Hosp., Dallas; staff nurse STD clinic City of Dallas Health Dept., supr. health status monitoring; nurse, adult health program Dallas Health and Human Svcs.; adj. prof. U. Tex., Arlington. Recipient Svc. award Dallas Urban League. Mem. ANA, ARC, Tex. Nurses Assn., Tex. Pub. Health Assn., Am. Heart Assn., Coun. Primary Nurse Practitioners. Home: 2271 Springhill St Dallas TX 75228-4102

LARION, FLORIN-GEORGE, mechanical engineer; b. Cluj-Napoca, Romania, Mar. 12, 1955; came to U.S., 1988; s. George Michael and Aurelia Ana (Farkas) L.; m. Ioana Maria Vigu, Jan. 26, 1985; children: Laura and Sebastian (twins). B of Adminstrn., U. Cluj-Napoca, 1985; M. of Mech. Engring., Polytech. Inst., 1980. Jr. project engr. Republica Corp., Bucharest, Romania, 1980-81; project engr. Carbochi, Co., Cluj-Napoca, Romania, 1981-83; sr. project engr. Truck Repairs Co., Cluj-Napoca, Romania, 1983-88; design engr. Ft. lock Corp., Chgo., 1988-90; project engr. Danaher Corp., Gastonia, N.C., 1990—. Inventor in field. Home: 2433 Montrose Dr Gastonia NC 28054-2726 Office: Danaher Corp 1228 Isley Rd Gastonia NC 28052-8106

LARKAM, BEVERLEY MCCOSHAM, clinical social worker, family therapist; b. Vancouver, Can., Mar. 3, 1928; came to U.S., 1951; d. William Howard and Marjorie Isobel (Jerome) McCosham; children: Elizabeth, Charles, Daphne, Peter, John. Assoc. Royal Conservatory of Mus. of Toronto, U. Toronto, 1948; BA, U. B.C., 1949, BSW, 1950, MSW, 1951. Diplomatein Clin. Social Works, Lic. bd. cert. master social worker, advanced clin. practitioner, marriage and family therapist, chem. dependency counselor, clin. soc. work, Tex. Psychiat. social worker Brackenridge Hosp., 1952-54; chmn. dept. sr. high sch. Univ. Presbyn. Ch., Austin, Tex., 1952-55, mem. Christian edn. com., 1961-67, mem. community orgn. to establish classes for mentally retarded children, 1966-68, bd. dirs. developing and organizing nursery sch., 1967-70; social worker Counseling-Psychol. Svcs. Ctr. U. Tex., 1971-72; psychiat. social worker, chief supr. adult mental health, children's mental health Human Devel. Ctr.-South, Austin, 1972-79; pvt. practice marriage and family therapy, sex therapy and individual and group psychotherapy, Austin, 1975—; field supr. Sch. Social Work U. Tex.; cons. in field. Mem. City of Austin Commn. for Women, 1978—, chmn., 1982-84, emeritus, 1985—; organizer Austin Assn. for Marriage and Family Therapy, 1980-82; bd. dirs. Nat. Assn. Commns. for Women, 1985-87. Mem. Am. Assn. Marriage and Family Therapy (approved supr.), Am. Group Psychotherapy Assn. (cert. group psychotherapist), Southwestern Group Psychotherapy Soc. (sr. faculty), Am. Assn. Sex Educators, Counselors and Therapists (cert. sex therapist, supr.), Acad. Cert. Social Workers, Nat. Assn. Social Workers, Register Clin. Social Workers, Tex. Soc. for Clin. Social Work (bd. dirs. 1990—, pres. elect, 1996-97), PEO Sisterhood. Presbyterian. Home and Office: 2102 Raleigh Ave Austin TX 78703-2128 also: 207 E 9th St Georgetown TX 78626-5908

LARKAM, PETER HOWARD, electric utility executive, entrepreneur; b. Austin, Tex., Jan. 27, 1962; s. Charles Wilbur and Beverley Jane (McCosham) L.; m. Sandra Kay Freund, Dec. 27, 1991; children: William Charles, Matthew Alexander. BSChemE, U. Tex., 1986; BA in Mgmt. Engring., Claremont McKenna Coll., 1987; MBA, U. Tex., 1995. Registered profl. engr., Tex. Mgr. customer engring. svcs. Lower Colo. River Authority, Austin, Tex., 1986—; distributor Success Motivation Inst., Austin, 1990—; owner Achievement Concepts Engring. Scis., Austin, 1990—; dealer Achievement Rsch. and Verification Systems, Inc., Albuquerque, 1992—. Alumnus Leadership Austin, 1990-91, John Ben Shepperd Pub. Leadership Forum, Austin, 1989; steering com. Austin Adopt-a-Sch. Employers Support Parenting, Austin, 1991; co-chair edn. com. Teen Leadership Austin, 1995—; Austin Symphony Orch. Vol. Ushers, 1973—. Named Outstanding Young Men of Am., 1987-90, Outstanding Vol., Lower Colo. River Authority, 1989. Mem. NSPE, Internat. Platform Assn., Jaycees (pres. Austin chpt. 1989-90), Toastmasters (pres. West Austin II chpt. 1992, mentor Lake Austin chpt. 1993—), Project Mgmt. Inst. Home: PO Box 50062 Austin TX 78763-0062

LARKIN, DONALD W., clinical psychologist; b. Kingsport, Tenn., June 23, 1947; s. Clarence K. and Frankie E. (Fields) L.; m. Sharon Sue Marsh, Oct. 21, 1966 (div. Mar. 1989); 1 child, Doni Suzanne. BS in Psychology and Math., East Tenn. State U., 1980; MS in Clin. Psychology, Nova U., Ft. Lauderdale, Fla., 1982, PhD, 1987. Lic. clin. psychologist, Tenn. Psychology intern Miami VA, 1983-84; electrician, computer technician Tenn. Eastman Co., Kingsport, 1965-80; therapist Clin. Psychology Inst., Ft. Lauderdale, 1984-86; instr. Nova U., 1982-86; clin. psychologist Johnson City (Tenn.) Med. Ctr. Optifast Program, 1989-90; assoc. staff psychologist Woodridge Psychiat. Hosp., Johnson, 1987-93; clin. psychologist Fairview Assocs., Johnson, 1987—, clin. dir., 1989-93; clin. dir. Woodridge Psychiat. Hosp., Johnson City, 1993—; clin. asst. prof. Quillen Coll. Medicine, Johnson City, 1988—; adj. faculty East Tenn. State U., Johnson City, 1987—. Mem. Hawkins County Bd. Edn., Rogersville, Tenn., 1978-80. Mem. Am. Psychol. Assn., Tenn. Psychol. Assn., Inter-Mountain Psychol. Assn., Psi Chi, Kappa Mu Epsilon. Office: Woodridge Hosp 403 N State Of Franklin Rd Johnson City TN 37604-6034

LARKIN, MOSCELYNE, retired artistic director, dancer; b. Miami, Okla., Jan. 14, 1925; d. Reuben Frances and Eva (Matlogova) L.; m. Roman Jasinski, Dec. 24, 1943 (dec. 1991); 1 child, Roman. Studied with Serge Grigorieff, Lubov Tchernicheva, Mikhail Mordkin, Anatole Vilzak, Vincenzo Celli; hon. doctorate of Fine Arts, U. of Tulsa, 1991. With Ballet Russe, 1941-47, Ballet Russe de Monte Carlo, 1948-52; prima ballerina Radio City Music Hall, N.Y.C., 1951-52; with Alexandra's Danilova's Great Moments of Ballet touring co., 1952-54; established Tulsa Sch. Ballet, from 1956; artistic dir. Tulsa Civic Ballet, 1956-76, Tulsa Ballet Theater, 1976-91; artistic dir. emerita Tulsa Civic Ballet, 1991—. Dance performances include Mikhail Forkine's Paganini and Les Sylphides; Leonid Massine's Le Beau Danube, Symphonie Fantastique, Les Presages; George Balanchine's Concerto Barocco, Night Shadow, Cotillion; Agnes De Mille's Rodeo; David Lichine's Graduation Ball; Michael Maule's The Carib Peddler. Recipient Dance Mag. award, 1988, Gov. Arts award, 1988, Rogers State Coll. Lynn Riggs award, 1989, award of Am.,1992; named to Tulsa Press Clubb Headliner award, Okla. Hall of Fame, 1979, Tulsa Hall of Fame, 1988, Okla. Womens Hall of Fame, 1993, and numerous others. Mem. Southwestern Regional Ballet Assn. (exec. v.p. 1963-76), Nat. Assn. Regional Ballet. Home: 5414 S Gillette Ave Tulsa OK 74105-6434 Office: Tulsa Ballet Theatre 4512 S Peoria Ave Tulsa OK 74105-4563

LARKS, JACK, forensic engineer, consultant; b. Chgo., Nov. 16, 1926; s. Israel David and Freida Rebecca (Morgenstern) L.; m. Norma Jean Colwell, Dec. 24, 1957; children: Terri Lynn, Kevin Jon. BSCE, MIT, 1952, MSCE, 1953; MEd, U. Houston, 1980. Registered profl. engr. Commd. 2d lt. U.S. Army, 1944, advanced through grades to lt. col., 1974, retired, 1975; supr. facilities STL/TRW, Cape Canaveral, Fla., 1957-66; assoc. prof. U. Houston, 1971-81; sr. design engr. Gulf Interstate Engring., Houston, 1981; supr. profl. devel. Hydril Co., Houston, 1982-83; constrn. mgr. Eastern Indemity Co. of Md., Houston, 1983-84; engring. designer Houston-Decco, Houston, 1985; safety cons. Larks Engring./Cons., Houston, 1985—; mem. Ansi Z359 Com., Houston, N.Y.C., 1988—. Contbr. articles to profl. jours. Fellow Nat. Acad. Forensic Engrs.; mem. Nat. Safety Engrs., World Safety Orgn. (bd. dirs. Tex. chpt. 1988-91, cert. safety exec.), Human Factors 2nd Ergonomics Soc., Scaffold Industry Assn., Am. Concrete Inst., Nat. Fire Protection Soc., Am. Welding Soc., Vets. of Safety, ASTM (various coms.), ANSI (fall protection coms.). Office: Larks Engring/Cons 4762 Kingfisher Dr Houston TX 77035-4920

LA ROCCA, RENATO V., oncologist, researcher; b. Cin., June 16, 1957; m. Margaret Carolyn Cauthron, Sept. 5, 1987; children: Alessandra, Marcello, Victoria, Chae. MS, Liceo Sci. Statale, Turin, Italy, 1976; postgrad., U. Padua, Italy, 1976-80; MD, Cornell U., 1982. Diplomate Nat. Bd. Med. Examiners, Am. Bd. Internal Medicine, Am. Bd. Oncology. Resident in internal medicine N.Y. Hosp.-Cornell Med. Ctr., N.Y.C., 1982-85; med. oncology fellow medicine br. Nat. Cancer Inst., Bethesda, Md., 1985-88, sr. investigator medicine br., 1988-90; pvt. practice Kentuckiana Med. Oncology Assocs., PSC, Louisville, 1990—; clin. assoc. prof. medicine U. Louisville Sch. Medicine and U. Ky. Coll. Medicine; cons. Jansen Rsch. Found.; rschr. med. br. Nat. Cancer Inst., NIH, Bethesda; mem. steering com. Ky. Cancer Pain Initiative; chmn. cancer com. Jewish Hosp., Louisville. Author: (chpts. in books) Molecular and Cellular Biology of Prostate Cancer, Molecular Foundations Oncology; contbr. articles to profl. jours.; patentee in field. Recipient USPHS Commendation medal, 1990, Leadership award Am. Cancer Soc., 1995. Fellow ACP; mem. Am. Soc. Clin. Oncology, Am. Assn. Cancer Rsch., Am. Cancer Soc. (v.p. Ky. divsn.), Am. Coll. Physician Inventors, Am. Pain Soc., Jefferson County Med. Soc., Ky. Oncology Soc., Ky. Med. Assn., Ind. Med. Assn., Alpha Omega Alpha. Office: Kentuckiana Med Oncology Assn 250 E Liberty St Ste 802 Louisville KY 40202-1537

LAROCHE, CHRISTIAN SIMONS, museum director; b. Jacksonville, Fla., Jan. 6, 1922; d. George Washington and Marion Grace (Guest) Simons; m. James Nagle LaRoche, Apr. 29, 1951; children: George Simons, Frederic Francis. AB, Western Coll., Oxford, Ohio, 1944; MFA, Ind. U., 1950. Instr. Western Coll., 1944-46; instr. pvt. pottery studio Montgomery, Ala., 1959-62; dir. Heritage Mus., Valparaiso, Fla., 1972—; bd. dirs. Fla. Hist. Soc., 1975-76; mem. exec. com. Fla. Hist. Confederate, 1980-83. Vol. Jacksonville Art Mus., 1946-50. Recipient Citizen of Week award Bayou Times, 1983, Citizen of Week award Twin Cities (Fla.) C. of C., 1993, Community Recognition award Woodmen of World, 1994. Mem. AAUW (pres. Montgomery 1962-64, pres. Ft. Walton Beach, Fla. 1967-69, pres. Niceville, Fla. 1985-87, 88-89, dir. programs 1993—), DAR (Community Svc. award 1994). Republican. Episcopalian. Home: 428 Marion Dr Niceville FL 32578-1749 Office: Heritage Mus 115 Westview Ave Valparaiso FL 32580-1387

LAROCQUE, PAUL ROBERT, journalist, educator, retired, consultant; b. Worcester, Mass., Mar. 28, 1931; s. Alfred E. and Delia P. (St. George) LaR.; m. Barbara L. Shippee, Feb. 14, 1954 (div. June 1975); children: Belinda, Paul R. Jr., James M., Carol A., Mark A.; m. Paula Annette Goodhew, June 27, 1975. BA in Journalism, Mich. State U., 1961; MA in Journalism, North Tex. State U., 1983. Reporter/copy editor Lansing (Mich.) State Jour., 1958-61; reporter/state editor Milw. Jour., 1961-69; exec. editor Times, San Mateo, Calif., 1969-71; asst. mng. editor/mng. editor Enquirer and News, Battle Creek, Mich., 1971-76; editor Eagle, Bryan-College Station, Tex., 1976-78; editl. page editor Star-Telegram, Ft. Worth, 1978-82; journalism instr. Grayson County Coll., Dennison, Tex., 1982; asst. prof. journalism So. Meth. U., Dallas, 1983-90; student publs. dir. Tex. Christian U., Ft. Worth, 1990-94; ret., 1994; writing coach/intern coord. World-Herald, Omaha, summers 1990—; writing cons., 1990—; lectr. in field. Book reviewer Ft. Worth Star Telegram and Dallas Morning News; contbr. articles to profl. jours., newspapers and mags. Pres. Windemere Homeowners Assn., Arlington, Tex., 1984-88. Cpl. USMC, 1954-56. Recipient 1st place editl. writing award Tex. AP Mng. Editors, 1980, fellowship Poynfer Inst. for Media Studies, 1987, grant Ethics and Excellence in Journalism Found., 1987, grant M.G. O'Neil Found., 1994, Tex. Christian U. Ethics in Journalism Award, 1995. Mem. Freedom of Info. Found. Tex. (dir.), Soc. Profl. Journalists (nat. dir. 1989-91), AP Mng. Editors (nat. dir. 1977-78), Nat. Conf. Editl. Writers. Home and Office: 2110 Winter Sunday Way Arlington TX 76012

LAROUSSI, MOUNIR, electrical engineer; b. Sfax, Tunisia, Aug. 9, 1955; came to U.S., 1981; s. Habib and Manana (Jeloul) L.; m. Nicole Christine Mache, Aug. 28, 1986; children: Alexander Habib, Alyssa Jehan. BS in Elec. Engring., Tech. Faculty Sfax, 1979; MS in Elec. Engring., Nat. Sch. Radio and Elec., Bordeaux, France, 1981; PhD in Elec. and Computer Engring., U. Tenn., 1988. Grad. teaching asst. dept. elec. and computer engring. U. Tenn., Knoxville, 1983-85, rsch. asst. plasma sci. lab., 1984-88; asst. prof. Nat. Sch. Engring., Sfax, 1988-89; assoc. prof. Faculty Scis., Sfax, 1989-90; rsch. assoc. Plasma Sci. Lab. U. Tenn., Knoxville, 1990—. Asst. editor Physics Essays; contbr. articles to profl. jours. Recipient award Air Force Office Sci. Rsch., Washington, 1991. Mem. IEEE (Cir. and Systems Soc., Nuclear and Plasma Scis. Soc., Antennas and Propagation Soc.), Sigma Xi (rsch. award 1987). Office: U Tenn Dept Elec Engring Knoxville TN 37996

LARREY, INGE HARRIETTE, jazz and blues freelance photographer; b. Freiburg, Germany, Jan. 21, 1934; came to U.S., 1983; d. Friedrich W. and Claerle I. (Mueller) Luger; m. Toni Halter, Aug. 5, 1967 (div. 1977); m. Louis A. Larrey, June 13, 1981. Student, N.Y. Inst. Photography, Saudi Arabia, 1983. Au Pair, Finland, 1952; Various assignments Federal Republic of Germany in Turkey, Spain, Belgium, England, 1956-82; audit student in journalism, photography U. Houston, 1984; substitute employee with consulate gen. Federal Republic of Germany, Houston, 1985; visitors' Relations German real estate company, Houston, 1985—; internat. network mktg. Interior Design Nutritionals, 1995—. Works shown in more than a dozen exhbns., 1986-91; photographs in pvt. collections, in various publs., on cassette, record covers. Vol. Houston FotoFest, Women's Caucus for Art. Mem. Nat. Mus. of Women in the Arts (charter), Am. Image News Svc., Cultural Arts Coun. of Houston, Friends of Photography, Houston Ctr. for Photography, Jazz Heritage Soc. Tex., Milt Larkin Jazz Soc. (founding). Office: Sueba USA Corp 1800 West Loop S Ste 1323 Houston TX 77027-3211

LARRIEU, DUANE PAUL, translator, educator; b. New Orleans, Oct. 14, 1940; s. Lloyd P. and Edith Mae (Brown) L.; m. Kay Frances Smith, Aug. 19, 1967; children: Theodore, Christopher. AA, St. Joseph's Coll., Covington, La., 1960; BA, Notre Dame U., 1963; PhB, Sant'Anselmo U., Rome, 1964. Secondary tchr. New Orleans Pub. Schs., 1964, Holy Cross High Sch., New Orleans, 1965-66; instr. Tulane U., New Orleans, 1967-68; fgn. svc. officer U.S. Dept. State, Washington, 1968-81; intelligence officer U.S. CIA, Washington, 1981-92; translator Berlitz, Washington, 1981—, LTRS, Inc., Fairfax, Va., 1981—; substitute tchr. Manassas (Va.) City Pub. Schs., 1992—, Prince William County (Va.) Sch., 1992—; translator U.S. Joint Publs., Washington, 1993—. Author: Lingala-English Dictionary, 1979; contbr. numerous articles to profl. jours. NDEA classical fellow, 1966-68. Mem. Am. Translators Assn. (accredited translator, accreditation chair Nat. chpt. 1985). Roman Catholic. Home: 8230 Macbeth St Manassas VA 22110-3668

LARRY, R. HEATH, lawyer; b. Huntingdon, Pa., Feb. 24, 1914; s. Ralph E. and Mabel (Heath) L.; m. Eleanor Ketler, Sept. 10, 1938; children: David Heath, Dennis Ketler, Thomas Richard. A.B., Grove City Coll., 1934, LL.D., 1964; J.D., U. Pitts., 1937. Bar: Pa. 1937, D.C. 1937. Pvt. practice, 1937-38; atty. Nat. Tube Co., 1938-44, sec., dir., 1944-48; gen. atty. U.S. Steel Corp., Pitts., 1948-52; asst. gen. solicitor U.S. Steel Corp., 1952-58, adminstrv. v.p. labor relations, 1958-66, exec. v.p., asst. to chmn., 1966-69, vice chmn. bd., 1969-77; pres. N.A.M., 1977-80; of counsel Reed Smith Shaw & McClay, Washington, 1980—; dir. emeritus Textron, Inc. Bd. visitors U. Pitts. Sch. Law; trustee Grove City Coll.; former trustee Conf. Bd. Mem. Am. Iron and Steel Inst. Presbyn. Clubs: Met. (Washington); Economic (N.Y.C.); Gulf Stream Golf, Delray Beach Yacht, Gulf Stream Bath and Tennis, Little; Bermuda Run Country Club. Home: 4333 N Ocean Blvd Apt A53 Delray Beach FL 33483 also (summer): Bermuda Vlg # 3107 Advance NC 27006-9477

LARSEN, CLARK SPENCER, anthropology educator; b. Omaha, Apr. 10, 1952; s. Leon Reuben and Patricia Ann (Loper) L.; m. Christine E. Najjar, May 16, 1987. BA, Kans. State U., Manhattan, 1974; MA, U. Mich., 1975, PhD, 1980. Asst. prof. anthropology U. Mass., Dartmouth, 1979-83; asst. prof. anthropology No. Ill. U., DeKalb, 1983-85, assoc. prof. anthropology, 1985-87, chmn., assoc. prof. anthropology, 1987-89; assoc. prof. biol. anthropology Purdue U., West Lafayette, Ind., 1989-91; prof. biol. anthropology Purdue U., West Lafayette, 1991-93; assoc. prof. biol. anthropology U. N.C., Chapel Hill, 1993-95, prof. biol. anthropology, 1995—; rsch. assoc. Am. Mus. Natural History, N.Y.C., 1980—. Author: (monograph) Anthropology of St. Catherines 3, 1982, (book) Human Origins, 1985, 2d edit., 1991, Bioarchaeology: Interpreting Behavior from the Human Skeleton; editor: Antiquity and Origin of Native North Americans, 1985, (monograph) Archaeology of Mission Santa Catalina 2, 1990. NSF grantee, 1984-87, 87-89, 93-96, L.S.B. Leakey Found. grantee, 1990. Mem. AAAS, Am. Assn. of Phys. Anthropologists, Am. Anthropol. Assn., Soc. for Am. Archaeology, Paleopathology Assn., Sigma Xi. Office: U NC Rsch Labs of Anthropology Chapel Hill NC 27599-3120

LARSEN, ELIZABETH ANNE, sociologist; b. Annandale, Va., May 8, 1968; d. Felix Seymour and Jewell Ward (Pepper) Williams; m. Erik Allan Larsen, Aug. 10, 1991. BA in Econs., U. Va., 1990; MA in Sociology, George Mason U., 1996. Benefits and payroll coord. Barnes, Morris, Pardoe & Foster, Washington, 1992-96; instr. Chatham Coll., Pitts., 1996—. Mem. Am. Sociol. Assn., Alpha Kappa Delta. Home: 138 Breading Ave Pittsburgh PA 15202

LARSEN, ERIC, golf course design company executive. BS in Landscape Horticulture, N.C. State U. Registered landscape architect. Landscape architect various companies; v.p., sr. golf course architect Palmer Course Design Co., Ponte Verda, Fla., 1983—. Mem. Am. Soc. Golf Course Architects, Urban Land Inst. Office: Palmer Course Design Co. 572 Ponte Vedra Box 1639 Ponte Vedra Beach FL 32004

LARSEN, ERIC LYLE, data processing executive, author, consultant; b. Boston, Sept. 28, 1954; s. Ralph Irving and Betty Lois (Garner) L.; m. Jamie Beryl Strauss, Apr. 5, 1980; children: Caroline Jamie, Eric Ralph. BS in Engring., N.C. State U., 1978, cert. in writing, editing, 1979, postgrad., 1978-81. Staff writer The Technician, Raleigh, N.C., 1976-78; jr. tech. writer systems communications div. IBM Corp., Raleigh, 1978-79, assoc. info. developer communications products div., 1979-82, sr. assoc. info. developer, 1982-85; staff planner entry systems div. IBM Corp., Austin, Tex., 1985-86; v.p. J.S. Larsen Cons., Raleigh, 1984—; instr. info. sys. group IBM, Raleigh, 1986-87, market devel. rep. S.W. mktg. divsn., 1987-88, adv. devel. rep. cons., 1988-90 adv. mktg. rep., 1990-93; sr. client rep. IBM Govt. Sys., 1993—; ptnr. Premier Builders, 1989—. Author: Synchronous Data Link Control, 1979, Systems Network Architecture, 1981, Network Packet Switching Interface, 1983. Deacon, Sunday sch. tchr., dir. Christian edn., elder North Ridge Alliance Ch., Raleigh, 1974—. Mem. Rotary (Raleigh chpt. 1988—, sgt.-at-arms 1996-97), Friends of the Gallery N.C. State U. (bd. advisors, founding friend visual arts ctr. 1992), Capital City Club. Republican. Home: 14017 Bingham Dr Raleigh NC 27614-9010 Office: IBM Govt Sys 3200 Beechleaf Ct Raleigh NC 27604

LARSEN, ERIK, art history educator; b. Vienna, Austria, Oct. 10, 1911; came to U.S., 1947, naturalized, 1953; s. Richard and Adrienne (Schapringer de Csepreg) L.; m. Lucy Roman, Oct. 4, 1932 (dec. 1981); children: Sigurd-Yves, Annik-Eve., Erik-Claude (dec.); m. Anna Gallup Moses, May 8, 1982 (div. Sept. 1986); m. Katharina Ehling, Oct. 21, 1989. Candidate, Institut Superieur d'Histoire de l'Art et d'Archéologie, Brussels, 1931; Licentiate,

Louvain (Belgium) U., 1941; Docteur en Archéologie et Histoire de l'Art, 1959; D. honoris causa, Janus Pannonius U., Pécs, Hungary, 1992. Dir., editor-in-chief on semi-ofcl. cultural mission for Belgian Govt. Pictura, art. mag., Brussels, Rio de Janeiro, Brazil, 1946-47; research prof. art Manhattanville Coll. of Sacred Heart, 1947-55; instr. CCNY, 1948-55; lectr, then vis. prof. Georgetown U., 1955-58, assoc. prof. fine arts, 1958-63, prof., 1963-67, head dept. fine arts, 1960-67; prof. history of art U. Kans., 1967-80, prof. emeritus, 1980—; dir. Center for Flemish Art and Culture, 1970-80; cons. old masters' paintings, guest-prof. U. Salzburg, Austria, 1988. Author: books, the most recent being La Vie, Les Ouvrages et Les Eleves de Van Dyck, 1975, Calvinistic Economy and 17th Century Dutch Art, 1979, Anton van Dyck, 1980, Rembrandt, Peintre de Paysages: Une Vision Nouvelle, 1983, Japanese edit., 1992; Seventeenth Century Flemish Painting, 1985, The Paintings of Anthony van Dyck, 2 vols., 1988, Jan Vermeer. Catalogo completo, 1996; contbr. numerous articles, revs. to profl. publs., newspapers. Mem. Kans. Cultural Arts Commn., 1971-73; mem. Kans. Cultural Arts Adv. Council, 1973-79. Served with Belgian Underground, 1942-45. Decorated knight's cross Order Leopold, knight's cross Order of Crown, officer Order Leopold (Belgium); officer Order of Rio Branco (Brazil); recipient prix Thorlet, laureate Inst. France, Académie des sciences morales et politiques, 1962; Internat. Hon. Citizen, New Orleans, 1989; named hon. Ky. col., 1977. Fellow Soc. Antiquaries of Scotland; mem. Appraisers Assn. Am., Association des Diplomés en Histoire de l'Art et Archéologie de L'Université Catholique de Louvain, Académie d'Aix-en Provence (France) (corr.), Académie de Mâcon (France) (asso.), Académie d'Alsace (France) (titular), Comité Cultural Argentino (hon.), Schweizerisches Institut fuer Kunstwissenschaft (Zurich, Switzerland), Academia di Belle Arti Pietro Vanucci (Perugia, Italy) (hon.), Royal Soc. Arts (London) (Benjamin Franklin fellow); correspondent-academician Real Academia de Bellas Artes de San Telmo (Malága, Spain), Real Academia de Bellas Artes de San Jorge (Barcelona, Spain), Accademia Tiberina (Rome), Académie Royale D'Archéologie de Belgique (fgn. assoc.). Home: 511 S Washington St Beverly Hills FL 34465-4312

LARSEN, ETHEL PAULSON, retired secondary school educator; b. Superior, Wis., Jan. 24, 1918; d. Ole Peter Paulson and Petra Marie (Boardsen) Gilbertson; m. James Eugene Larsen, June 13, 1943; children: Robert, Karen Larsen DePalermo, Deborah Larsen Farmer, Candice Larsen Herrera. AA, Kendall Coll., 1940; student, U. Wis., 1940-44; BS, SW Tex. U., 1960; postgrad., U. Tex., 1961-67. Tchr. Lakefield (Minn.) Pub. Schs., 1944-46; credit mgr. Sagebiel's Automotive Parts, Seguin, Tex., 1948-49; supervisory clk. supply Edward Gary AFB, San Marcos, Tex., 1951-56; property/acctg. chief Gary Army Air Field, San Marcos, 1956-59; tchr. Seguin High Sch., 1960-80; substitute tchr. Seguin Pub. Schs., 1981-83; reporter, photographer Seguin Citizen newspaper, 1981; now ret.; developer speech-journalism curriculum, Minn. State Bd. Edn., 1945; pres. AAUW, Seguin, 1965-66, Seguin Classroom Tchrs., 1971-72; del. to Tex. State Tchrs. Assn., Austin, 1970. Founding mem. York Creek Flood Prevention Dist. for Hays, Comal and Guadalupe counties, 1953-54; Voice of Democracy chair VFW Aux., Geronimo, Tex., 1970-78; writer radio scripts for improved farm-city rels., 1956; vol. tax aide, Seguin, 1987-90; Circle leader 1st United Meth. Ch., Seguin, 1989—; mem. T.B. Bd. Guadalupe County, 1954-57. Mem. Nat. Writers Club, Seguin Garden Club, Seguin-Guadalupe County Ret. Tchrs. (pres. 1990—), Nat. Coun. State Garden Clubs, Inc. (life), Tex. Garden Clubs, Inc. (life), Tex. State Garden Clubs (life, Tex. dist. VII), Tex. Agrl. Ext. Svc. (master gardener), Order Ea. Star, Oakwood Art Group, Delta Kappa Gamma (Theta Kappa chpt. pres. 1978-80). Home: 1619 Driftwood St Seguin TX 78155-5211

LARSEN, JAMES BOUTON, biological scientist, educator; b. Detroit, July 28, 1941; s. Edward Arthur and Elizabeth (Bouton) L.; m. Anne Struhsaker; children: Nathan Frederick, Susan Larsen Boerwinkle. BS in Biology, Kalamazoo (Mich.) Coll., 1963; MS in Marine Biology, U. Miami, Coral Gables, 1966, PhD in Marine Biology, 1968. Grad. rsch. teaching asst. Inst. Marine Scis. U. Miami, 1963-67; postdoctoral fellow dept. biochemistry Colo. State U., Ft. Collins, 1967-68; asst. prof. dept. biology Hamline U., St. Paul, Minn., 1968-73; asst. prof. dept. biology U. So. Miss., Hattiesburg, 1973-76, assoc. prof. dept. biol. scis., 1976-93, prof., 1993—; investigator marine biol. lab. Woods Hole, Mass., 1982; vis. assoc. prof. dept. physiology and biophysics sch. medicine U. Miami, Coral Gables, 1982; assoc. rsch. prof. sch. pharmacy U. Conn., Storrs, 1987. Author: (with others) Physiological Effects of Carbon Monoxide, 1993, Carbon Monoxide and Human Lethality: Fire and Non-fire Studies, 1993, Low COHb Analysis in Fire Victims, 1986, Laboratory Manual for Human Physiology, 1984; author numerous papers, abstracts and jour. articles in field; presenter in field. Grantee U. So. Miss., Pub. Health Svc. NIH, NSF, The Soc. of the Plastics Industry, Product Safety Corp. Mem. AAAS, Am. Soc. Zoologists, Internat. Soc. Toxinology, Miss. Acad. Scis., Sigma Xi (pres. USM chpt. 1992-93). Office: U So Miss PO Box 9236 Hattiesburg MS 39406-9236

LARSEN, ROBERT WESLEY, artist, educator; b. Aurora, Ill., Nov. 22, 1923; s. Leonard Oliver and Emmy Julia (Youngberg) L.; m. Suzanne May Kesteloo, Oct. 1952; children: Julia, Robert, Caitlin. Student, Kans. City Inst. Art & Design, 1946-47, Detroit Sch. Soc. Arts/Crafts, 1947-50, Ringling Sch. Art, Sarasota, Fla., 1950-52. Tchr. Longboat Key Art Ctr., Fla., 1958, Manatee Art League, Bradenton, Fla., 1961-62, Prew Sch. Tutoring, Sarasota, 1963, Island Easel, Siesta Key, 1965, Ringling Sch. Art, Sarasota, 1966—; freelance muralist for Holiday Inn and Morrison Cafeteria, Inc., 1960-68. One-man shows include Sarasota Art Assn., 1953, Art Barn, Salt Lake City, 1956, Longboat Key Art Ctr., 1956, Tampa Art Inst., 1957, Manatee Art League, Bradenton, Fla., 1955, 62, Gladstone Gallery, Woodstock, N.Y., 1963, Parnassus Sq. Gallery, Woodstock, 1964, St. Armands Art Gallery, Sarasota, 1960-62, 65, Columbia (S.C.) Mus. of Art, 1967, Columbus Mus. of Arts and Crafts, 1968, Hilton Leech Gallery, Sarasota, 1973, Trend House Gallery, Tampa, 1974, Hodgell Hartman Gallery, Sarasota, 1976, 78, 80, Polk Pub. Mus., Lakeland, Fla., 1979, Edison C.C., Ft. Myers, Fla., 1979, Joan Hodgell Gallery, Sarasota, 1982, 86, Corbino Galleries, Sarasota, Fla., 1990, 94. Recipient Spl. Mention in Oils award 10th S.E. Exhbn., Atlanta, 1955, 12th S.E. Exhbn., 1957, State Fair, 1962, Spl. award Soc. of Four Arts, 1967, Hon. Mention 15th Ann. Maj. Fla. Artists Show, 1978. Home: 1395 40th St Sarasota FL 34234-4611

LARSON, BENNETT CHARLES, solid state physicist, researcher; b. Buffalo, N.D., Oct. 9, 1941; s. Floyd Everet and Gladys May (Hogen) L.; m. Piola Anne Taliaferro, June 6, 1969; children—Christopher Charles, Andrea Kay. B.A. in Physics, Concordia Coll., Moorhead, Minn., 1963; M.S. in Physics, U. N.D., 1965; Ph.D. in Physics, U. Mo., 1970. Rsch. physicist, group leader x-ray diffraction, sect. head thin films and microstructures solid state div. Oak Ridge Nat. Lab., Tenn., 1969—. Contbr. numerous articles to profl. jours. Recipient Sidhu award Pitts. Diffraction Soc., 1974. Fellow Am. Phys. Soc.; mem. Am. Crystallographic Assn. (Bertram E. Warren Diffraction Physics award 1985), Materials Research Soc. Office: Oak Ridge Nat Lab Solid State Dv Oak Ridge TN 37831

LARSON, D(AVID) MILES, music minister, vocal soloist, concert artist; b. Amarillo, Tex., Aug. 24, 1948; s. John Markin Sr. and Mildred Ellen (Reynolds) L.; m. Sharon Engstrom, Dec. 11, 1971; children: John M., Amy K. BA, U. So. Miss., 1984; MusM, U. Tenn., Chattanooga, 1985. Dir. music 1st Presbyn. Ch., Gulfport, Miss., 1975-79; min. mus. Lookout Mountain (Tenn.) Presbyn. Ch., 1979-85, 1st Presbyn. Ch., Concord, N.C., 1985-87, Clairmont Presbyn. Ch., Decatur, Ga., 1987—; choral clinician. Soloist Chattanooga Symphony, 1983-84, Atlanta Symphony, 1989-90, Atlanta Opera, 1989-92; soloist in concert, oratorio. With USAF, 1971-75. Mem. Nat. Assn. Tchrs. Singing, Am. Choral Dirs. Assn., Presbyn. Assn. Musicians. Office: Clairmont Presbyn Ch 1994 Clairmont Rd Decatur GA 30033-3410

LARSON, GREGORY PAUL, army officer; b. Ridgewood, N.J., Sept. 6, 1964; s. Charles Fred Jr. and Joan Ruth (Grupe) L. BS in Internat. Affairs, U.S. Mil. Acad., 1987. Commd. 2d lt. U.S. Army, 1987, advanced through grades to capt., 1992; detachment comdr. 3d Spl. Forces Group, Ft. Bragg, N.C., 1994—. Decorated Army Commendation medal (4). Mem. Assn. U.S. Army, Army Navy Country Club. Republican. Methodist. Home: 1010 Wood Creek Dr # 8 Fayetteville NC 28314-1114

LARSON, JANICE TALLEY, computer science educator; b. Houston, Sept. 29, 1948; d. Hiram Peak Talley and Jennie Edna (Forbes) Donahoo; m. Harold Vernon Larson, Apr. 8, 1977; children: Randall Neil, Christopher Lee. AA in Computer Sci., San Jacinto Coll., 1981; BA in Computer Info. Systems, U. Houston, Clear Lake, 1984, MA in Computer Info. Systems, 1988; postgrad. in instructional tech., U. Houston, 1994—. Programmer Control Applications, Houston, 1985-86, Tex. Eastern Pipeline, Houston, 1988-90; instr. computer sci. San Jacinto Coll., Houston, 1990-94; sponsor Computer Sci. Club, Houston, 1992-94. Mem. IEEE, U. Houston Alumni Assn., Phi Delta Kappa, Kappa Delta Pi.

LARSON, JUDY L., curator; b. Glendale, Calif., Mar. 9, 1952; d. John Arthur and Lorraine V. Larson. BA, UCLA, 1974, MA, 1978; postgrad., Emory U. Acting asst. curator Los Angeles County Mus. Art, L.A., 1978; sr. cataloguer Am. Antiquarian Soc., Worcester, Mass., 1978-85; curator High Mus. Art, Atlanta, 1985—. Author: (catalogue) Am. Illustration 1890-1925, 1986; co-author: (catalogue) Am. Paintings at High Mus. Art, 1994; editor: Graphic Arts and the South, 1993. Office: High Mus Art 1280 Peachtree St Atlanta GA 30309

LARSON, LARRY, librarian; b. El Dorado, Ark., July 18, 1940; s. Willie Lee and Myrtle Elizabeth (McMaster) L.; m. Dorothy Ann Bing, Apr 23, 1966; 1 child, Larisa Ann. BS, Ouachita Baptist U., 1962; MLS, George Peabody Coll., 1967. Asst. librarian, media specialist Hall High Sch., Little Rock, 1962-65; asst. librarian, circulation Ark. Tech. U., Russellville, 1965-67; asst librarian reference Hendrix Coll., Conway, Ark., 1967-73; head librarian U. Ark., Monticello, 1973-75; librarian, dir. N. Ark. Regional Library, Harrison, 1975-85, Ft. Smith (Ark.) Pub. Library, 1985—. Bd. dirs. Ft. Smith Hist. Soc., 1986-90; treas. bd. dirs. Pub. Awareness Com., Ft. Smith, Ark., 1986—. Mem. ALA, Ark. Libr. Assn. (vice chair membership com. 1968, Disting. Svc. award 1985, chair pub. libr. divsn., 1993), Ark. Libr. Devel. Dist. (chair 1985-87), Ark. Adminstrs. Pub. Librs. (chair 1988-89, del. Ark. govs.' conf. on librs. 1990), Noon Exchange Club. Democrat. Baptist. Home: 3114 S Enid St Fort Smith AR 72903-4445 Office: Ft Smith Pub Libr 61 S 8th St Fort Smith AR 72901-2415

LARSON, LORELL VINCENT, aviation consultant; b. Mpls., Oct. 24, 1918; s. Carl Adolph and Josephine (Olstad) L. BS in Aerodyn. Engring., U. Minn., 1940. Chief analysis and integration CAM-87 Engring. Aero Systems Div., Dayton, Ohio, 1958-61; chief analysis and integration Aero. Systems div. F-111 Engring., Dayton, 1961-63; sr. analyst Ltd. War Office, Dayton, 1963-69; chief engr. Pave Tack Program Aero Systems Div., Dayton, Ohio, 1969-75; aviation cons. Destin, Fla., 1975—; chmn., mem. Delivery Accuracy Group Joint Tech. Coordinating Group for Munitions Effectiveness, Washington, 1964-67. Mem. Am. Def. Preparedness Assn., USN Inst. (assoc.). Home: 86 Country Club Dr Destin FL 32541

LARSON, RICHARD SMITH, pathologist, researcher; b. Ithaca, N.Y., Aug. 27, 1962; s. Richard Ingwald and Judith Ann (Larsen) L.; m. Blaire Martin, June 4, 1989. AB in Chemistry summa cum laude, U. N.C., 1984; MD, Harvard U., 1990, PhD, 1990. Cert. anatomic and clin. pathologist Am. Bd. Pathology. Pathologist, resident Barnes Hosp., St. Louis, 1990-93; hematopathology fellow Vanderbilt U., Nashville, 1993-96; asst. prof., dir. clin. hematology lab. U. N.Mex., 1996—. Contbr. articles to profl. jours. including Jour. Biol. Chemistry, Procs. NAS, European Molecular Biology Orgn. Jour., Jour. Exptl. Medicine, Jour. Virology, Jour. Cell Biology, Advances in Immunology, Leukocyte Adhesion Molecules, Procs. Cold Spring Harbor Symposia on Quant. Biology, Leukocyte Typing IV, Cell Regulation, Immunol. Revs., Cardiac Pathology, Diagnostic Molecular Pathology, Am. Jour. Clin. Pathology, Blood, Pediatric Nephrology, Human Path. Cancer Rsch. Recipient Nat. Rsch. Sci. award, 1986-90, 92-93. Mem. Am. Soc. Clin. Pathologists, Coll. Am. Pathologists (chmn. future tech. com.), Am. Soc. Hematology, Assn. Molecular Pathologists, Phi Beta Kappa.

LARY, BANNING KENT, video producer, publisher; b. Chgo., Aug. 27, 1949; s. Banning Gray and Katherine Lee (Tedrow) L.; m. Janice Ann, Dec. 22, 1974 (div. Aug. 1977); 1 child, Venus Ayn Katherine; m. Valerie Maria Dalli, Dec. 28, 1987; children: Alexandra Lee, Kristin Gray. BJ, U. Tex., 1970. Mng. editor Beach & Town, Miami, Fla., 1976-77; gen. contractor Larydome Inc., Miami, 1977-80; exec. dir. Legal Devel. Resources, Austin, 1989—; pres. Promedion, Inc., Austin, 1990—; dir., 1985—; freelance writer, 1970—; creative troubleshooter, writer, editor various orgns.; video pub., 1987—. Author: Twist of Faith, 1996; writer, prodr., dir. Robbery! The Aftermath, 1988, Ten Commandments of Avoiding Legal Malpractice, 1989, Ten. Procedures for Avoiding Medical Malpractice, 1990, The Belli Tapes: Winning at Trial, 1991, Childproof: Home Safety Checklist, 1991; video prodr. Bad Paper, 1987, Extortion Set, 1988; prodr. The Sexual Harassment Prevention Kit, 1992 and many others; prodr. numerous TV commls.; contrb. articles to mags.; author: Twist of Faith, 1996; editor: How to Win Your Case in Court, 1996; pub. Do What You Want to Do, 1996; inventor roller washer II, golf swing muscle articulator. Mem. bd. Alpha Nu House Corp., Austin. Recipient Gold award for video prodn., 1987, silver award, 1988, 91, Prize Stories Anthology award, 1989, O'Henry awards, Best of Austin award Internat. Assn. Bus. Communicators, 1986, 93, Disting. Achievement award Am. Soc. Ind. Security-Video, 1987, 1st pl. U.S.A. Hometown Video Festival, 1991, award of excellence ACTV, 1992, Bronze award Charleston Internat. Film Festival, 1993, Bronze award Worldfest, 1995. Mem. Am. Acad. Poets, Tex. Writers League, Austin Writers League, Amnesty Internat., Sigma Chi. Office: Am Visionary Artists PO Box 3551 Austin TX 78764-3551

LASER, CHARLES, JR., oil company executive; b. Redford Twp., Mich., July 8, 1933; s. J.C. and Gertrude L. Student Mich. Tech. U., 1952-54, Cent. Mich. U., 1959-60; DD (hin.) Palm Beach Theol. Sem. Coll., 1991; m. Glenda Johnson, Sept. 27, 1972; 1 child, Susan Faye. With Retail Credit Co., 1958-60; exec. dir. Saginaw County Rep. Com., 1960-65; exec. dir. Rep. Com. D.C., 1967; fin. dir. San Joaquin Rep. Party, Stockton, Calif., 1968; owner Laser Advt., Bay City, Mich., 1969-75; exec. v.p. Vindell Petroleum, Inc., Midland, Mich., 1972-75, Geo Spectra Corp., Ann Arbor, Mich., 1977-86; pres. Laser Exploration Inc., Deerfield Beach, Fla. Chmn. Genesee County Rep. Com., 1981-82, mem. Broward County Rep. Exec. Com., 1987-88, indsl. bond screening com. Deerfield Beach, 1992; chmn. U.S. Senator Connie Mack Palm Beach County Round Table; bd. dirs. Palm Beach County Libr. Found., Shepherd Care Ministries, Hollywood, Fla., 1991—; adv. com. Tall Pines coun. Boy Scouts Am., mem. adv. bd. Gulf Stream Coun., 1980; mem. gov. prevention adv. com. Juvenile Justice Deliquency, Fla., 1988—; mem. adv. bd. Humanitarian Soc., 1989—; co-chmn. Fla. Symphonic Pops Orch., 1996-97. With U.S. Army, 1954-58. Mem. Deerfield Beach C. of C. (v.p.), World Trade Coun. (Palm Beach, Fla. chpt.), Detroit Econ. Club, Bankers Club (Boca Raton), Humanitarian Soc. (adv. bd.), Rep. Men's Club (past pres., v.p. Boca Raton chpt.), Gold Coast Venture Capital Club (Delray Beach chpt.), Palm Beach Roundtable (bd. dirs., treas., sec. 1994-96), Hillsboro Cove Condominium Assn. (pres. 1994), Rotary, Elks. Home: PO Box 8604 1523 E Hillsboro St Apt 131 Deerfield Beach FL 33441

LASH, ANDRÉ DUANE, minister of music; b. Coffeyville, Kans., May 18, 1947; s. Eugene Louis and Mildred Pauline (Benham) L.; m. Sheryl Diane Beaty. B in Music Edn., Pittsburg (Kans.) State U., 1969; MusM, Southwestern Baptist Seminary, Ft. Worth, Tex., 1974; MusD, Eastman Sch. Music, 1987. Instr. keyboard and music theory Brewton-Parker Coll., Mt. Vernon, Ga., 1974-79; organist, music assoc. Nall Ave. Bapt. Ch., Prairie Village, Kans., 1980; asst. prof. organ Okla. Bapt. U., Shawnee, 1980-86; organist, mus. assoc. St. John's Bapt. Ch., Charlotte, N.C., 1986-91, minister of music, 1991—; Spkr. in field. Am. editl. advisor Complete Organ Works of J.S. Bach, Mayhew edit., 1993. With U.S. Army, 1969-72. Fellow Am. Guild Organists (exam coord. Okla. City 1981-85, dean Charlotte chpt., 1989-91, dist. convenor N.C. 1993—), mem. Music Tchrs. Nat. Assn., So. Baptist Ch. Music Conf., S.E. Hist. Keyboard Soc. Democrat. Office: St John's Bapt Ch 300 Hawthorne Ln Charlotte NC 28204

LASKIN, DANIEL M., oral and maxillofacial surgeon, educator; b. Ellenville, N.Y., Sept. 3, 1924; s. Nathan and Flora (Kaplan) L.; m. Eve Pauline Mohel, Aug. 25, 1945; children: Jeffrey, Gary, Marla. Student, NYU, 1941-42; BS, Ind. U., 1947; MS, U. Ill., 1951. Diplomate Am. Bd. Oral and Maxillofacial Surgery. Mem. faculty U. Ill., Chgo., 1949-84, prof. dept. oral and maxillofacial surgery, 1960-84, head dept., 1973-84, clin. prof. surgery, 1961-84, dir. temporomandibular joint and facial pain research center, 1963-84; prof., chmn. dept. oral and maxillofacial surgery Med. Coll. Va., Richmond, 1984—; dir. temporomandibular joint and facial pain rsch. ctr. MCV, Richmond, 1984—; head dept. dentistry MCV Hosp., Richmond, 1986—; former attending oral surgeon Edgewater, Swedish Covenant, Ill. Masonic, Skokie Valley Community hosps., all Chgo.; former chmn. dept. oral surgery Cook County Hosp., Chgo.; cons. oral surgery to Surgeon Gen. Navy, 1977—; dental products panel FDA, 1988-92, cons., 1993—; Francis J. Reichmann Lectr., 1971, Cordwainer lectr., London, 1980. Author: Oral and Maxillofacial Surgery, Vol. I, 1980, Vol. II, 1985; contbr. articles to profl. jours.; editor-in-chief: Jour. Oral and Maxillofacial Surgery, 1972—; mem. editorial bd. Internat. Jour. Oral and Maxillofacial Surgery, 1978-88, Topics in Pain Mgmt., Densat, Internat. Jour. Oral and Maxillofacial Implants, Quintessence Internat., Revista Latino America Cirugia Traumatologia Maxilofacial, Virginia Dental Jour., Jour. Dental Rsch.; mem. internat. editorial bd. Headache Quar. Nat. hon. chmn. peer campaign A.A.O.M.S. Edn. and Rsch. Found., 1990. Recipient Disting. Alumni Svc. award Ind. U., 1975, William J. Gies editl. award hon. mention, 1975-77, 80, 88, 90, 91, 93, 95, 1st prize, 1978-79, 84, 87, 89, 92, 95, Simon P. Hullihen Meml. award, 1976, Arnold K. Maislen Meml. award, 1977, Thomas P. Hinman medallion, 1980, W. Harry Archer Achievement award for rsch., 1981, Heidbrink award, 1983, Disting. Alumnus award Ind. U. Sch. Dentistry, 1984, Rene Lefort medal, 1985, Semmelweis medallion Semmelweis Med. U., 1985, Golden Scroll award Internat. Coll. Dentists, 1986, Internat. award Friends Sch. Dental Medicine, U. Conn. Health Ctr., Donald B. Osborn award, 1991, Achievement medal Alpha Omega, 1992, Norton M. Ross Excellence in Clin. Rsch. award, 1993, Va. Commonwealth U. Faculty award of excellence, 1994; named Zendium Lectr., 1989, Edward C. Hinds Lectr., 1990, Disting. Practitioner Nat. Acads. Practice, 1992, Hon. Diplomate, Am. Soc. Osseointegration, 1992; fellow in gen. anesthesia Am. Dental Soc. Anesthesiology, fellow in dental surgery Royal Coll. Surgeons Eng., Glasgow Royal Coll. Physicians (hon.). Fellow AAAS, Am. Coll. Dentists, Internat. Coll. Dentists, Am. Acad. Implant Prosthodontists (academia), Acad. Internat. Dental Studies (hon.), Internat. Assn. Oral and Maxillofacial Surgeons (hon., exec. com. 1980—, pres. 1983-86, sec. gen. 1989-95, exec. dir. 1995—); mem. Ill. Splty. Bd. Oral Surgery, ADA (adv. com. advanced edn. in oral surgery 1968-75, cons. Coun. on Dental Edn. 1968-82, mem. Commn. on Accreditation 1975-76), Am. Assn. Oral and Maxillofacial Surgeons (editor Forum 1965-96, AAOMS Today 1996—, disting. svc. award 1972, pres. 1976-77, rsch. recognition award 1978, William J. Gies award 1979, dedication 73d ann. meeting and sci. sessions 1991), Internat. Assn. Dental Rsch., Am. Dental Soc. Anesthesiology (pres. 1976-78), Am. Soc. Exptl. Pathology, Am. Assn. Dental Editors, Royal Soc. Medicine, Brazilian Coll. Oral and Maxillofacial Surgery and Traumatology (hon.), Chilean Soc. Oral and Maxillofacial Surgery (hon.), Hellenic Assn. Oral Surgery (hon.), Sadi Fontaine Acad. (hon.), Internat. Congress Oral Implantologists (hon.), Soc. Maxillofacial and Oral Surgeons South Africa (hon., assoc. life), Am. Dental Bd. Anesthesiology (pres. 1983-92), Nat. Chronic Pain Outreach Assn. (adv. bd.), Japanese Soc. for Temporomandibular Joint (hon.), Am. Soc. Laser in Dentistry (hon. life), Internat. Study Group for the Advancement of TMJ Arthroscopy (hon.), William F. Harrigan Soc., Odontographic Soc., Can. Assn. Oral and Maxillofacial Surgeons (hon.), Sigma Xi, Omicron Kappa Upsilon. Office: Med Coll Va Dept Oral/Maxillofac Surg PO Box 980566 Richmond VA 23298-0566

LASLEY, CHARLES HADEN, surgeon, consultant; b. Lewisburg, Ky., Dec. 16, 1921; s. Marion Grinter and Helen May (Murray) L.; m. Mary Brown, June 14, 1946 (div. 1966); children: Mary Ann, Charles H., Jr., Robert Murray, David Marion; m. Janet Elizabeth Evans, Jan. 28, 1967; children: Tiffany Jean, Phillip Evans. BS in chemistry, biology, U. Fla., 1939-43; MD, Harvard Med. Sch., 1944-47. Diplomate Am. Bd. Thoracic Surgery, Am. Bd. Surgery. Intern in surgery Grady Hosp., Atlanta, 1947-48; asst. resident in surgery Grady Hosp., 1948-49; resident in surgery Gorgas Hosp., Ancon, Canal Zone, 1950; sr., chief resident surgery Gorgas Hosp., 1951, staff surgeon, chief gen. surgery, 1952-53; asst. chief orthopedic surgery USAH Ft. Carson, Colorado Springs, Colo., 1953-54; resident in cardiac surgery City of Hope Med. Ctr., L.A., 1954-55; resident in thoracic, cardiovascular surgery VAH Oteen, Asheville, N.C., 1955-56; pvt. practice thoracic, cardiovascular surgery Morton Plant Hosp., Clearwater, Fla., 1956-79; chief of surgery Morton Plant Hosp., 1971-72, chief thoracic, cardiovascular surgery, 1977-78; med. dir. Longevity Clin., Clearwater, 1977-78; med. cons. Wellness Ctr. Morton Plant Hosp., 1996—. Author: Veritas, 1996. Jazz drummer Red Suspenders Jazz Band, 1991—. With US Army, 1949-54. Mem. Am. Assn. for Thoracic Surgery, Am. Coll. of Sports Medicine, Soc. of Thoracic Surgeons, So. Thoracic Surgery Assn., Fla. Soc. of Thoracic and Cardiovascular Surgeons (president 1972), Suncoast Dixieland Jazz Society. Republican. Mem. First Christian Ch. Home: Unit 4 Pelican Pl 672 Poinsettia Rd Belleair FL 34616

LASON, SANDRA WOOLMAN, linguistics, ESL, and gifted educator; b. Chgo., July 30, 1934; d. Irwin Robert and Annette (Hassman) Woolman; m. Marvin Mitchell Lason, Feb. 8, 1959 (dec. 1972); children: Caryn Anne, Joel Steven, Scott David. BS with highest distinction, Northwestern U., 1956; MA, Northeastern Ill. U., 1976; postgrad., U. Okla., 1982—. Cert. K-12 tchr. Tchr. Sch. Dist. 69, Skokie, Ill., tchr., dir. gifted students, 1972-76; tchr., adminstr. MONACEP, Morton Grove, Ill.; freelance writer-editor; curriculum writer-editor The Economy Co., Oklahoma City; instr., assoc. dir. freshman English dept. U. Okla., Norman; prof., ESL coord. Oklahoma City Community Coll., 1983-95, ret.; ptnr. Communication Consultants; adj. prof. ESL Austin Coll., Sherman, Tex.; judge Okla. Olympics Mind, Mensokie Essay Contest; chmn. com. for ESL Okla. State Regents; mem. state legis. com. for internat. devel.; speaker presentations on writing, ESL and educating the gifted. Author: (with others) Gifted Galaxy: Oklahoma State Gifted Guide; writer, editor: K-8 Language Arts Series: Expressways; editor books and articles; contbr. articles to profl. jours. Officer Karen Brown chpt. Bobs Roberts Hosp., Chgo., Children's Meml. Hosp., Chgo.; bd. dirs. Okla. Hillel Found., Women's Resource Ctr., Norman; officer Kenton PTA. Mem. Tchrs. English as Second Lang., Okla. Tchrs. English as Second Lang., Mensa (gifted child coord. Ill. chpt.), Pi Lambda Theta, Alpha Epsilon Phi (officer alumnae chpt.). Home: 2103 Melrose Dr Norman OK 73069-5236

LA SORSA, WILLIAM GEORGE, lawyer, educator; b. Lancaster, Pa, Apr. 30, 1945; s. Francis Peter and Madge Marion (Hanson) L.; m. Linda Kay Chappell, Dec. 8, 1973. BA, Marquette U., 1967; JD, U. Tulsa, 1973. Bar: Okla. 1974, U.S. Dist. Ct. (no. dist.) Okla. 1976, U.S. Ct. Appeals (10th cir.) 1976, U.S. Supreme Ct. 1977, U.S. Ct. Mil. Appeals 1985. Asst. dist. atty. Tulsa County Dist. Atty.'s Office, Tulsa, 1974-80; assoc. Howard & Rapp, Tulsa, 1980-81, Gene C. Howard & Assocs., Tulsa, 1981-82; ptnr. Howard, La Sorsa & Widdows, Tulsa, 1982-85, La Sorsa & Weber, Tulsa, 1985-87, La Sorsa, Weber & Miles, P.C., Tulsa, 1987-93; shareholder Corbitt, La Sorsa, Rineer & Zacharias, P.C., 1993-96, Jones, Givens, Gotcher & Bogan, P.C., Tulsa, 1996—; adj. prof. Tulsa Jr. Coll., 1978-83, Langston U., 1983-84. Capt. U.S. Army, 1969-72, Vietnam; lt. col. Res. ret. Fellow Okla. Bar Found., Tulsa County Bar Found. (charter); mem. ABA (litigation, family law and office mgmt. sects.), Okla. Bar Assn. (family law sect., exec. com., bd. govs. 1994—), ATLA, Okla. Trial Lawyers Assn., Tulsa County Bar Assn. (chmn. fee arbitration com. 1992-93), Am. Inns. of Ct. (master, Hudson-Hall-Wheaton chpt.), Lions Club Internat. (pres. Brookside chpt. 1986-87), Porsche Club Am. (pres. War Bonnet region 1981-82). Republican. Roman Catholic. Office: Jones Givens Gotcher & Bogan PC 15 E 5th St Tulsa OK 74103-4309

LASOWSKI, ANNE-MARIE FRANCOISE, federal agency executive; b. Coronodo, Calif., July 20, 1964; d. Donald Thomas and Janine Josette (Cotta) L. BA, Wheaton Coll., Norton, Mass., 1986; MA, M.Govt. Adminstrn., U. Pa., 1988. Intern Office of Sen. Edward Kennedy, Washington, 1983, U.S. Labor and Human Resources Com., Washington, 1983, Common Cause, Washington, 1984, Congresswoman Pat Schroeder, Washington, 1985; profl. analyst (Kellogg fellow) Nat. Gov.'s Assn., Washington, 1987; asst. to exec. dir. Fellowship Commn., Phila., 1987; sr. evaluator U.S. Gen. Acctg. Office, Phila., 1988—. Mem. Am. Soc. Pub. Adminstrs., Acad. Polit. Sci., Assn. Govt. Accts. (cert. govt. fin. mgr.). Office: U S Gen Acctg Office 441 G St NW Washington DC 20548-0001

LASSETER, JANICE MILNER, English language educator; b. Gadsden, Ala., May 15, 1940; d. T.J. and Gwendolyn (Wagnon) Milner; m. James

Dewayne Lasseter, May 31, 1958; children: Mark, Ginger, Alan, Danny. Student, Samford U., 1963-65; BA, U. Ala., Huntsville, 1980, MA, 1982; PhD, U. Ala., Tuscaloosa, 1988. Instr. U. Ala., Huntsville, 1980-82, Tuscaloosa, 1984-87; assoc. prof., chair dept. English Samford U., Birmingham, Ala., 1987—; chair task force status women Samford U., 1990-92. Active Birmingham Women's Consortium, 1991—. Mem. MLA, AAUW (bd. dirs. 1991—), Am. Lit. Assn., Nat. Women's Polit. Caucus, Ala. Women's Polit. Caucus, Nathaniel Hawthorne Soc., Phi Kappa Phi. Democratic. Office: Samford U Birmingham AL 35229

LASSITER, DOROTHY TATE, library director; b. New Brunswick, N.J., Nov. 3, 1922; d. Nelson Thomas and Dorothy Octavia (Clements) T.; m. Cleveland Frissell Lassiter, Dec. 16, 1945; children: Mark Frissell, Keith Alan, Brian Eugene. BA in Sociology cum laude, Va. Union U., 1944; MS in Libr. Svc., Columbia U., 1960. Cert. libr., media specialist, N.Y.; cert. libr. dir., media specialist, Ga. Proof clk. Chase Manhattan Bank, N.Y.C., 1956-57; br. libr. Queensborough Pub. Libr., Jamaica, N.Y., 1958-65; head children's dept. White Plains (N.Y.) Pub. Libr., 1965-68; libr. Greenburgh Sch. Dist. 7, Harstdale, N.Y., 1968-69; ref. libr. Mamaroneck (N.Y.) Free Libr., 1969-71; adult svcs. libr. Ossining (N.Y.) Pub. Libr., 1972-73; libr. media specialist Mt. Vernon (N.Y.) High Sch., 1973-79; ref. libr. Pace U., White Plains, N.Y., 1979-80; libr. Atlanta-Fulton County Pub. Libr., 1981-82; libr. dir. Greenforest Bapt. Ch. Libr., Decatur, Ga., 1982—; libr. Portfolio Ctr., Atlanta, 1982-83; instr. Spelman Coll., Atlanta, 1984-85; substitute tchr. DeKalb County Bd. Edn., Decatur, 1984-88; libr. media specialist Greenforest Christian Academic Ctr., Decatur, 1989—. 1st Headstart libr. Designated storyteller 1965 N.Y. World's Fair. N.Y. Libr. Assn. scholar, 1950. Mem. ALA, NAACP (membership chmn.), Westchester Black Women's Polit. Caucus, UN Assn., Ch. and Synagogue Libr. Assn., Va. Union U. Alumni Assn. (Met. Atlanta chpt., regional v.p.), Alpha Kappa Alpha. Democrat. Baptist. Home: 4215 Abilene Ct Decatur GA 30034-6025 Office: Greenforest Bapt Ch Libr 3250 Rainbow Dr Decatur GA 30034-1713

LASSITER, JAMES MORRIS, JR., real estate investment executive; b. Norfolk, Va., July 8, 1941; s. James Morris Sr. and Louise (Gompf) L.; m. Patricia Edwards, Jan. 21, 1961 (div. May 1978); m. Mary Stahl, Sept. 11, 1985; children: Cynthia Louise, James Morris III. Student, Va. Mil. Inst., 1959-60, Old Dominion U., 1960-62. Agt. Prudential Ins. Co., Norfolk, Va., 1962-67; asst. dir. agys. Richmond (Va.) Life Ins. Co., 1967-68; mgr. United Mortgagee, Norfolk and Houston, 1968-71; account exec. Houston Land Investment, 1971-74; ptnr. So. Gen. Land Co., Houston, 1974—, Olex Energy Co., Houston, 1987—; v.p., ptnr. So. Gen. Fin. Assocs., 1989—; prin. So. Gen. Property Mgmt. Co., 1990—. Life mem. internat. com. Houston Livestock Show and Rodeo, 1971—. Mem. U.S. C. of C., Houston C. of C., Fort Bend C. of C., Norfolk Jr. C. of C. (bd. dirs. 1964-68), Heights C. of C., Center City Rotary Club (pres.). Methodist. Lodges: Masons, Shriners. Office: So Gen Land Co 770 S Post Oak Ln Houston TX 77056-1913

LASSLO, ANDREW, medicinal chemist, educator; b. Mukacevo, Czechoslovakia, Aug. 24, 1922; came to U.S., 1946, naturalized, 1951; s. Vojtech Laszlo and Terezie (Herskovicova) L.; m. Wilma Ellen Reynolds, July 9, 1955; 1 child, Millicent Andrea. MS, U. Ill., 1948, PhD, 1952, MLS, 1961. Rsch. chemist organic chems. div. Monsanto Chem. Co., St. Louis, 1952-54; asst. prof. pharmacology, divsn. basic health scis. Emory U., 1954-60; prof. and chmn. dept. med. chemistry Coll. Pharmacy, U. Tenn. Health Sci. Ctr., 1960-90, Alumni Disting. Svc. prof. and chmn., dept. medicinal chemistry, 1989-90, professor emeritus, 1990—; cons. Geschickter Fund for Med. Research Inc., 1961-62; rsch. contractor U.S. Army Med. R & D Command, 1964-67; dir. postgrad. tng. program sci. librarians USPHS, 1966-72; chmn. edn. com. Drug Info. Assn., 1966-68, bd. dirs., 1968-69; dir. postgrad. tng. program organic medicinal chemistry for chemists FDA, 1971; exec. com. adv. council S.E. Regional Med. Library Program, Nat. Library of Medicine, 1969-71; chmn. regional med. library programs com. Med. Library Assn., 1971-72; mem. pres.'s faculty adv. council U. Tenn. System, 1970-72; chmn. energy authority U. Tenn. Center for Health Scis., 1975-77, chmn. council departmental chmn., 1977, 81; chmn. Internat. Symposium on Contemporary Trends in Tng. Pharmacologists, Helsinki, 1975. Producer, moderator (TV and radio series) Health Care Perspective, 1976-78; editor: Surface Chemistry and Dental Integuments, 1973, Blood Platelet Function and Medicinal Chemistry, 1984; contbr. numerous articles in sci. and profl. jours.; mem. editorial bd. Jour. Medicinal and Pharm. Chemistry, 1961, U. Tenn. Press, 1974-77; composer (work for piano) Synthesis in C Minor, 1968; patentee in field. Trustee 1st Bohemian Meth. Ch., Chgo., 1951-52, mem. bd. stewards, 1950-52; mem. ofcl. bd. Grace Meth. Ch., Atlanta, 1955-60; mem. adminstrv. bd. Christ United Meth. Ch., Memphis, 1964-72, 73-75, 77-79, 81-83, 88-90, chmn. commn. on edn., 1965-67, chmn. bd. Day Sch., 1967-68. 1st lt. USAR, 1953-57, capt., 1957-62. Recipient Research prize U. Ill. Med. Ctr. chpt. Sigma Xi, 1949, Honor Scroll Tenn. Inst. Chemists, 1976, Americanism medal DAR, 1976; U. Ill. fellow, 1950-51; Geschickter Fund Med. Research grantee, 1959-65, USPHS Research and Tng. grantee, 1958-64, 66-72, 82-89, NSF research grantee, 1964-66, Pfeiffer Research Found. grantee, 1981-87. Fellow AAAS, Am. Assn. Pharm. Scientists, Am. Inst. Chemists (nat. councilor for Tenn. 1969-70), Acad. Pharm. Rsch. and Sci.; mem. ALA (life), Am. Chem. Soc. (sr.), Am. Pharm. Assn., Am. Soc. Pharmacology and Exptl. Therapeutics (chmn. subcom. pre and postdoctoral tng. 1974-78, exec. com. ednl. and profl. affairs 1974-78), Sigma Xi (pres. elect U. Tenn. Ctr. for Health Sci. chpt. 1975-76, pres. 1976-77, Excellence in Rsch. award 1989), Beta Phi Mu, Phi Lambda Sigma, Rho Chi. Methodist. Home and Office: 5479 Timmons Ave Memphis TN 38119-6932

LASSUS, JOSEPH PATRICK, parish official; b. New Orleans, July 17, 1955; s. Donald A. and Virginia A. (Collins) L.; m. Barbara Lee Anconetani, May 22, 1977 (div. Aug. 1985); 1 child, Barbara Marie; m. Naomi Ann Comeaux, Sept. 7, 1991. BA with honors, Tulane U., 1977; M of Urban & Regional Planning, U. New Orleans, 1984. Assoc. planner St. Bernard Parish Planning Com., Chalmette, La., 1984-91; asst. dir. Jefferson Parish, Harahan, La., 1991-92; dir. dept. planning and zoning St. Charles Parish, Hahnville, La., 1992—; cons. Preservation Consultants & Investments Co., Inc., New Orleans, 1982-85. Mem. Am. Inst. Cert. Planners, Am. Planning Assn., Pelican Regiment, Econ. Devel. Coun., Tulane U. Alumni Assn., U. New Orleans Alumni Assn. Roman Catholic. Office: Saint Charles Parish Dept Planning 15045 River Rd Hahnville LA 70057-2104

LAST, SONDRA CAROLE, public relations consultant, writer, teacher; b. Bklyn., Nov. 6, 1932; d. Irving B. and Lynn (Freedman) L.; m. S. Rosenberg, July 15, 1951 (div. 1958);m. R. Pritts, Apr. 14, 1961 (div. 1965); 1 child, Mikel Eve Renner. BS, UCLA, 1955, BA, 1956; MA, U. So. Calif., 1958, U. Fla., 1982. Dir. adminstrn. Escuela las Nereidas, Santurce, P.R., 1960-65; del. to Conf. on Poverty, Unemployment and Edn. UN, San Juan, P.R., 1965; acad. cons. Irwin W. Katz, Inc., Miami Beach, Fla., 1966-74; polit. and social commentator Sta. LOVE-AM, Miami, Fla., 1974-75; legis. aide, adminstrv. asst. Fla. Senator Gwen Margolis, Miami, 1974-85; coord. Conf. Former U.S. Secs. of State, Miami, 1985; legis. aide, adminstrv. asst. Fla. Rep. Irma Rochlin, Miami, 1986; exec. dir. Greater Biscayne Blvd. C. of C., Miami, Fla., 1988, Miami Commn. on Status of Women, 1989; owner, pres. Last Enterprises, Inc., Grand Island, Nebr., 1989-90, The Last Word, Ink., Grand Island, Nebr., 1989-90; adviser on normalization Peoples Republic China, Beijing, 1978, coord. trade show participation at Caribbean Conf., 1987; bd. dirs. The Phoenix Plan, Inc., Lyons Comm., Inc.; ptnr. LDW, Inc., Pub. Rels. and Advt.; cons. to small bus.; presentor writing workshop Grand Island Ctrl. Cmty. Coll., Omaha S.E. Cmty. Coll., Miami-Dade Cmty. Coll., Western N.E. Cmty. Coll. Scriptwriter The Loretta Young Show, Peter Gunn, Elmer Gantry, other TV prodns.; contbr. numerous articles to various nat. and regional publs.; author: Live and Work in South Florida, 1987, The Menopause Manual. Lobbyist Fla. Freelance Writers and Transition, Inc. Recipient Outstanding Achievement award Nat. Coun. Jewish Women, 1974, Trail Blazer award Federally Employed Women, 1975, Susan B. Anthony award Dade County NOW, 1976, Pub. Svc. award Federally Employed Women, 1978; Sondra C. Last Day proclaimed by City of North Miami Beach, Fla., 1979; named Community Leader North Miami Beach Commn. on Status of Women, 1979. Mem. Fla. Motion Picture/TV Assn., Internat. Women Writer's Guild, Fla. Freelance Writer's Assn., Screen Writers Guild Calif., Women in Communication, Adult and Continuing Edn. Assn. Nebr. Democrat. Home and Office: 928 Dixon Nursery Rd Brewton AL 36426-9501

LAST, SUSAN WALKER, curriculum developer; b. Waterbury, Conn., Sept. 26, 1962; d. Harold Alfred and Mary (Alferie) Hull; m. Michael Allen Walker, Feb. 11, 1984 (div. July 1988); 1 child, Cassandra Mary; m. Robert Lee Last, Sept. 26, 1992. BS, Ind. U., 1983. Ctr. dir. Sylvan Learning Corp., Arlington, Tex., 1984-88, franchise cons., 1988-89, dist. mgr., 1989-90; coord. of program devel. Sylvan Learning Systems, Arlington, 1991—; trainer, cons. Charles R. Hobbs Corp., Salt Lake City, 1989—; cons. Highpointe, Arlington, 1988—. Author: (curriculum) Study Skills Program, 1990, Study Power Video, 1991, Basic Math Program (K-8), 1994, Adult Reading Program, 1993, ESL program, 1995. Mem., speaker Parents Without Ptnrs., Arlington, 1991. Mem. ASCD, Children and Adults with Attention Deficient Disorder, Nat. Coun. Tchrs. of Math., Nat. Coun. Tchrs. of English. Home: 3902 Wrentham Dr Arlington TX 76016-2746 Office: Sylvan Learning Systems 4101 W Green Oaks Blvd Ste 327 Arlington TX 76016-4463

LASTER-SPROUSE, CHARLINE HIGGINS, health care facility administrator, educator, family therapist; b. San Angelo, Tex., Jan. 13, 1942; d. Charles Cleophus and Eunice Maxine (Frey) Higgins; m. Marvin Earl Sprouse Jr., July 29, 1988; children: Marvin Earl III, Amber Leigh, Lisa Kauai, Carleen Danielle McGuffy, John Paul, Alicia Denise Slaton, Angela Desiree Cooke, Robin C.D. De La Garza. Student, West Tex. U., 1964-65, 80-81, Columbus (Ga.) Coll., 1978-79, U. Tex. Med. Br., 1981-82; MA, U. Houston, 1988; postgrad., Trinity U., 1996—. Internat. lic. drug and alcohol counselor; lic. profl. counselor, Tex.; cert. hypnobehavioral therapist, neurolinguistic programmer practitioner. Mgr., hostess and waitress Spencecliff Restaurants, Honolulu, 1965-67; office mgr. Polly Grigg Designs, 1966-68; psychiat. occupational therapist, technician N.W. Tex. Psychiat. Pavilion, Amarillo, 1968-74; career placement specialist Snelling & Snelling, Amarillo, 1971-72; psycho-social dysfunction specialist U.S. Army Med. Corps, Ft. Benning, Ga., 1974-78; dispatcher League City (Tex.) Police and Fire Depts., 1981-82; chiropractic trainer, office mgr. Clear Lake, Tex., 1981-82; property mgr. Houston, 1984-88; J.T.P.A. addictions counselor, life skills tchr. Ed White Youth Ctr., Seabrook, Tex., 1987-88; family addictions therapist, educator, dir. family restoration Chemical Dependency Ctr., Las Cruces, N.Mex., 1990-94; rehab. dir. The Profl. Assessment Outpatient Treatment Ctr., Las Cruces, 1991—; case analyst II TYC Bootcamp Sheffield (Tex.) Youth Leadership Acad., 1991-96; primary svc. worker supr. chem. dependency treatment program Gainesville (Tex.) State Sch., 1996—; co-owner Bootcamp Cons., 1995-96; presenter N.Mex. Gov.'s Conf., Las Cruces, 1990, Western N.Mex. U., Silver City, 1991; facilitator MVH Community Edn., Las Cruces, 1990-91; addictions counselor, developer family edn. program St. Mary's Hosp., Galveston, 1987-90. Co-author: Human Phallacies, 1988, Streatcare Named Codependency, 1989, Connecting-A Guide to Great Relationship, 1990, Love at the Drive-Through Window, 1991, Political Correctness Exposed-The Pirahna in Your Bathtub, 1995, Championship Group Workbook. Provider Support Group Families of Desert Storm Troops, Las Cruces, 1990-91, His Holy Name Cath. Apostolic Ch., Las Cruces, 1990-91. Mem. ACA, NAFE, NRA, Soc. Ams. for Recovery, Concerned Women for Am., Nat. Assn. Alcohol and Drug Abuse Counselors, Vietnam Vets Am. (pres. Las Cruces chpt.), Vietnam Vets War on Drugs (v.p.), Tex. Assn. for Counseling and Devel., Tex. Assn. Alcoholism and Drug Abuse Counselors, N.Mex. Alcohol and Drug Abuse Counselors, N.Mex. Counseling Assn., El Paso Profl. Growth Assocs., Christian Counselors of Tex., Am. Assn. Christian Counselors, Trinity Coll. and Sem. Alumni, Trinity Ctr. Conflict, Am. Correctional Assn., Am. Ctr. for Law and Justice, Independent Order of Foresters. Office: 12840 Hillcrest Ste H-100 Dallas TX 75230 also: 15889 Preston Rd Ste 1035 Dallas TX 75248 also: 3417 N Midland Dr Ste 1908 Midland TX 79707

LATHAN, SAMUEL ROBERT, JR., internist, educator; b. Charlotte, N.C., Apr. 28, 1938; s. Samuel Robert Sr. and Callie Mims (Purvis) L.; m. Mary Amelia Hudson, Mar. 19, 1966; children: Caroline, Stewart, Robert. BS, Davidson (N.C.) Coll., 1959; MD, Johns Hopkins U., 1963. Diplomate Am. Bd. Internal Medicine. Physician Lowance Clinic, Atlanta, 1969-73, Colony Med. Group, Atlanta, 1973-80; prin. S. Robert Lathan, M.D. P.C., Atlanta, 1980—; pres. bd. dirs. Colony Med. Group, Atlanta, 1976-80; clin. instr., assoc. instr., then clin. asst. prof. medicine Emory U. Sch. Medicine, Atlanta, 1969—; mem. staff Piedmont Hosp., Atlanta, 1970—. Editor Atlanta Medicine, 1975-79; contbr. articles to profl. jours. Vol. Hippie Clinic, Atlanta, 1969-72; mem. speakers bur. MACAD, Atlanta, 1970-74; chmn. physicians group United Way, Atlanta, 1974; v.p., speaker Atlanta Coalition Against Tobacco, 1984—. Capt. USAF, 1967-69. Recipient WS Beaver award Sta. WSB Radio, 1985, 88. Fellow ACP, Am. Coll. Chest Physicians; mem. Med. Assn. Atlanta (bd. trustees 1971), Atlanta Clin. Soc. (v.p. 1977), Am. Heart Assn., Ga. Thoracic Soc., Am. Soc. Internal Medicine, Med. Assn. of Ga., Am. Med. Joggers Assn., Capital City Club, Piedmont Driving Club. Episcopalian. Home: 1175 Brookhaven Dr NE Atlanta GA 30319-3010 Office: 1938 Peachtree Rd NE Atlanta GA 30309-1258

LATHROP, GERTRUDE ADAMS, chemist, consultant; b. Norwich, Conn., Apr. 28, 1921; d. Williams Barrows and Lena (Adams) L. B.S., U. Conn., 1944; M.A., Tex. Woman's U., 1953, Ph.D., 1955. Devel. chemist on textiles/Alexander Smith & Sons Carpet Co. Yonkers, N.Y., 1944-52; research assoc. textiles Tex. Woman's U., 1952-56; chief chemist Glasgo Finishing Plant div. United Mchts. & Mfrs., Inc., Conn., 1956-57; chief chemist Old Fort Finishing Plant div. United Mchts. & Mfrs., Inc., N.C., 1957-63; research chemist United Mchts. Research Ctr., Langley, S.C., 1963-64; lab. mgr. automotive div. Collins & Aikman Corp., Albemarle, N.C., 1964-78; chief chemist, lab. mgr. Old Fort Finishing Plant div. United Mchts., 1979-82. Treas. 1st Congl. Ch., Asheville, N.C., 1985-87, bd. deacons, 1990-93; tax-aide counselor to elderly IRS, 1984—, Am. Assn. Ret. Person, Widowed Person Svcs., Asheville-Buncombe County, Inc., 1990-91, pres. Widowed Persons Svcs., 1992—; active RSVP Land of Sky, 1989-92; pub. rels. com. Swannanoa Valley, N.C., Am. Assn. Ret. Persons, 1984-92, v.p., 1992, treas., 1993-94. Recipient Nat. Cmty. Svc. award Am. Assn. Ret. Persons, 1989, 96, Widowed Person's Outstanding Individual Achievement award, 1994, Disting. Alumni award U. Conn. Sch. Family Studies, 1980-81, Woman of Yr. award, 1979, Bus. and Profl. Women's Club, Albemarle, Woman of Yr. award Bus. and Profl. Women's Club Asheville, 1980. Mem. ASTM (chmn. transp. fabrics on flammability com. 1973-75), Am. Chem. Soc. (emeritus), Am. Assn. Textile Chemists and Colorists (emeritus, sec., rsch. chmn., treas., vice chmn. 1962-64, chmn. edn. com. Piedmont sect. 1977-78), Bus. and Profl. Women's Club (chpt. pres. 1974-76), Iota Sigma Pi (emeritus mem.-at-large). Home and Office: PO Box 1166 Black Mountain NC 28711-1166

LATHROP-SKALOS, MARIA C., medical social worker; b. New Orleans, Dec. 17, 1966; d. Donald Dana and Wilma Anita (Wilson) L. BA in Psychology, Loyola U., New Orleans, 1987; MSW, Tulane U., 1989, ACSW, 1992, BCSW, 1993. Clin. assoc. Jo Ellen Smith Psychiat. Hosp., New Orleans, 1987-89; psychiat. social worker intern VA, New Orleans, 1988-89; psychiat. social worker St. Louis State Hosp., 1990; med. social worker Capitol Home Health, La Place, La., 1990—; contract clin. social worker Mercy & Bapt. Homecare, River Region Home Health, Dchsner Home Health; staff builder Apple Home Home Health, Maxima Home Health, R & R Home Health, Louise Davis Devel. Ctr. Mem. NASW, Am. Bus. Women Assn., La. Soc. Clin. Social Work. Episcopalian. Office: Mercy & Bapt Hosp 301 N Jefferson Davis Pky New Orleans LA 70119-5311

LATIMER, BILLIE LUAN, elementary education educator; b. Paducah, Tex., Dec. 2, 1936; d. Bascum and Mary (Freeman) Branscum; div.; 1 child, Brent. B of Gen. Studies, Tex. Christian U., 1987. Tchr. Hurst-Euless-Bedford (Tex.) Ind. Sch. Dist., 1985—; tchr. summer gifted program Hardin Simmons Univ., Abilene, Tex., 1989—. Mem. Assn. Tex. Profl. Educators, Gifted and Talented Assn., Reading Assn. Tex., Tex. Assn. Supervision Curriculum Devel.

LATIMER, PAUL JERRY, non-destructive testing engineer; b. Springfield, Tenn., July 21, 1943; s. Paul Daniel and Juanita Inez (Richey) L.; m. Sylvia Susan Cole, June 6, 1966; children: Zachary Nathaniel, Matthew Jason. BS in Physics with honors, U. Tenn., 1966, MS in Physics, 1979, PhD in Physics, 1983. Devel. engr. Oak Ridge (Tenn.) Nat. Lab., 1980-81; faculty rsch. assoc. Ohio State U., Columbus, 1981; rsch. asst. U. Tenn., Knoxville, 1981-83; sr. rsch. engr. Babcock and Wilcox, Lynchburg, Va., 1983—. Contbr. articles to profl. jours.; patentee in field. Co-leader cub pack Lynchburg Area coun. Boy Scouts Am., 1983-84; vol. United Way, 1994; mem. Pacer Club for United Way Support, 1993-96. Mem. Am. Soc. Nondestructive Testing (cert. Level III untrasonic methods), Sigma Pi Sigma. Home: 303 Juniper Dr Lynchburg VA 24502-5661 Office: Babcock and Wilcox Lynchburg Rsch Ctr Lynchburg VA 24506

LATIMER, W. H. (BILL LATIMER), agricultural company executive; b. 1938. With Adkins Feed Mill, Union City, Tenn., 1960-61, ptnr., 1961-67; pres. Warterfield Grain Co. (Inc.), Union City, 1968—, Quality Seeds Inc., Union City, 1970—, Farmers Grain & Fertilizer Co. Inc., Union City, 1970—, K T Distbrs. Inc., Union City, 1973—; v.p. Farmers Gin Co. Inc., Clinton, Ky. Office: Farmers Gin Co Inc Depot Extd Clinton KY 42031

LATIOLAIS, MINNIE FITZGERALD, nurse, hospital administrator; b. Vivian, La., Dec. 26, 1921; d. Thomas Ambrose and Mildred Surita (Nagle) Fitzgerald; m. Joseph C. Latiolais Jr., July 19, 1947; children: Felisa, Diana, Sylvia, Mary, Amelia, Joseph Clifton III. RN, New Orleans, 1943. Asst. night supr. Touro Infirmary, New Orleans, 1943; orthopedic surg. nurse Ochsner Clinic, New Orleans, 1943-47; asst. dir. nursing, Ochsner Found. Hosp., 1947; supr. Lafayette (La.) Gen. Hosp., 1960-64; adminstrv. asst., supr. oper. rm. Abbeville (La.) Gen. Hosp., 1964-68; gen. mgr., neurol. surg. nurse J. Robert Rivet, neurol. surgeon, Lafayette, 1968-78; hosp. cons. assoc. B.J. Landry & Assocs., hosps. cons., Lafayette, 1979-90; dir. nursing Acadia St. Landry Hosp., Church Point, 1981-82; supr. supplies, processing and distbn. Univ. Med. Ctr., Lafayette, 1982-90; bd. dirs. SW La. Rehab. Assn., 1975-89, pres., 1979-80; mem. Mid-La. Health Systems Agy., 1977-82, project rev. chmn., 1978-80; vice chmn. Acadica Regional Clearing House, 1984-86; mem. crafts and practical nurse com. Lafayette Regional Vocat.-Tech. Inst., 1980-84, chmn. 1983-84. Roman Catholic.

LATOUR, TERRY STEPHEN, archivist, librarian; b. Brackenridge, Pa., Sept. 5, 1955; s. Armand Louis and Dorothy B. (Gumpp) L.; m. Leslie Lynn Baldwin, May 30, 1980; 1 child, Stephanie Lynn. BA in Am. History, Allegheny Coll., 1978; MA in Am. History, Case Western Reserve U., 1980, MS in Libr. Sci., 1980; PhD in Libr. Sci., Fla. State U., 1995. Libr. asst. Case Western Reserve U., Cleve., 1979; rsch. intern Nat. Hist. Pub. and Records Commn., Washington, 1979; asst. archivist U. Akron, Ohio, 1980; curator spl. collections U. Southern Miss., Hattiesburg, 1980-86, dir. spl. collections, 1986-91, univ. archivist, 1991-95; dir. librs. Delta State U., 1995—; grant reviewer Nat. Hist. Pub. and Records Commn., Washington, 1983—, NEH, 1984—; project adv. Miss. Survey African/Am. Records, Jackson, Miss., 1990-92; preservation cons. Marion City Hist. Soc., Columbia, Mis., 1993-95; adv. bd. Miss. Health Scis. Info. Network, 1996—. News editor The Primary Source, 1987-95; contbr. to profl. jours. Vol. Miss. Blood Svcs., 1982-88, 96—, United Blood Svcs., 1988-95; asst. scoutmaster Boy Scouts Am., Hattiesburg, 1988-95; bd. dirs., editor Hattiesburg Hist. Soc., 1987-95. Andrew W. Mellon Rsch. fellow Bentley Historical Libr., 1984; named Archival Admin. mentor Nat Hist. Pub. & Records Commn., 1986-87; Access grantee NEH, 1990-93. Mem. ALA (sect. com. 1988-90), Soc. Am. Archivists (steering com. 1980-84, 86-89), Am. Hist. Assn., Orgn. Am. Historians, Miss. Libr. Assn. (pres. ACRL chpt. 1990), Soc. Miss. Archivists (pres. 1986-87), Exch. Club. Home: 606 Douglas Ave Cleveland MS 38732 Office: WB Roberts Libr Delta State U Cleveland MS 38733

LATTA, LOREN LEE, orthopaedic research educator; b. Owosso, Mich., Jan. 10, 1944; s. Edward and Wilma Louise (Throm) L.; m. Joan Sue Tallman, Nov. 4, 1966; children: Jason, Kristen, Bradford. BS in Mech. Engring., Mich. State U., 1966; MS in Biomed. Engring., U. Miami, 1978, PhD in Mech. Engring., 1979. Registered profl. engr., Fla. Field engr. Goss divsn. MGD Corp., Chgo., 1965-67; purchasing agt., chief engr. Pope Brace Co., Kankakee, Ill., 1967-69; sr. rsch. engr. Dow Chem., Rocky Flats, Colo., 1969-71; dir. new product devel. Pope Brace divsn. Parke-Davis, Kankakee, 1971-72; staff engr., dir. rsch. dept. orthopaedics and rehab. U. Miami, Fla., 1972-85; dir. orthop. biomech. lab. dept. orthops. Mt. Sinai Med. Ctr., Miami Beach, Fla., 1985—; assoc. prof. dept. biomed. engring. U. Miami, Coral Gables, Fla., 1988—; prof., dir. rsch. dept. orthops. and rehab. U. Miami, Fla., 1985—; mem. patent and copyright com. U. Miami, 1988—. Co-author: Functional Bracing of Fractures, 1992; mem. editl. bd. Jour. Orthop. Trauma, 1989—, Internat. Jour. Orthop. Trauma, 1990—; contbr. chpts. to books, articles to profl. jours. Recipient Orthop. Rsch. award Kappa Delta Soc., Chgo., 1976. Mem. ASTM (chmn. task/subcom. 1986-90, award for excellence 1992), Am. Acad. Orthop. Surgeons (mem. biomed. engrng. com. 1985-93), Orthop. Rsch. Soc., Internat. Soc. Fracture Repair (founding mem.), Assn. Rational Treatment of Fractures (founding mem. internat. spine study group), Orthop. Trauma Assn. (mem. rsch. com. 1991-93), Rehab. Engring. Soc. N.Am. Republican. Home: 10150 NW 10th St Plantation FL 33322-6526 Office: Univ Miami Sch Medicine 1150 Campo Sano Ave Coral Gables FL 33146-1174

LATTAL, KENNON ANDY, psychology educator; b. Selma, Ala., Jan. 7, 1943; s. Anton and Ella Gene (Agee) L.; m. Alice Darnell Hammer, Apr. 16, 1965; children: Kennon Matthew, Anna Rachel, Laura Ashley. BS, U. Ala., Tuscaloosa, 1964, PhD, 1969. Postdoctoral fellow U. Calif.-San Diego, LaJolla, 1971-72; asst. prof. W.Va. U., Morgantown, 1972-75, assoc. prof., 1975-79, prof., 1979-95, Centennial prof. psychology, 1995—. Co-editor: Experimental Analysis of Behavior, 1991; contbr. over 65 articles to profl. jours.; assoc. editor Jour. Exptl. Analysis of Behavior, 1982-86. Bd. trustees Cambridge (Mass.) Ctr. for Behavioral Studies, 1993—. Capt. U.S. Army, 1969-71. Benedum Disting. scholar W.Va. U., 1989. Fellow APA (pres. divsn. 25 1994, Outstanding Tchr. award 1987), Am. Psychol. Soc.; mem. Assn. Behavior Analysis (pres. 1994), Animal Behavior Soc. Home: 848 Vandalia Rd Morgantown WV 26505-6248 Office: W Va U Dept Psychology Morgantown WV 26506-6040

LATUS, TIMOTHY DEXTER, psychic consultant; b. Carlsbad, N.Mex., Nov. 15, 1946; m. Yolanda Torro, Dec. 14, 1981; children: Pluto, Patricia, Sally, Pablo. Student in Mass Comm., N.Mex. State U., 1964-68; student, U. of Metaphysics, 1986—; postgrad., The Esoteric Inst., 1986—; comm. learning instr., Summit U. La., 1996. Ordained Christian metaphysical minister. V.p. Soundville Records, Houston, 1969-72, Illuminati Video Prodn., Houston, 1972-75; pres. Haarick House Pub., St. Louis, 1975-79, Dallas, 1979-81; pres. Acad. Psychic Arts & Scis., N.Y.C., 1981, Albuquerque, 1982-85, Dallas, 1985—; pres. Life Stage Publ. Corp., 1989—, Insighters, USA, 1994—; gov. Ch. Creative Spirituality, Dallas, 1986—; minister, Universal Light of Cross Ch., Show Low, Ariz., 1984—. Author: Your Guardian Angel, 1987, Reach for Your Best Self, 1990, Star View Forecast, 1994, Instant StarSights Spiritual Astrology Advisory, 1996; co-author, editor: Future Pathway Report, 1990, BYOP, 1991; author, editor: The Timothy Letter, 1990—; editor: Profile: Your 21st Century Child, 1987, Mover and Shaker Video Rev. Mag., N.Y.C., 1980; producer: Instant Insights, 12 Tape Series on Metaphysical Subjects. Active Animal Legal Def. Fund. Named Outstanding Innovator Retail Week Mag., 1979, Expert to address Worldwide Videogramme Expn., Cannes, France, 1972. Mem. ACLU, The Reincarnationists, N.Mex. Psychic Soc. (gov. emeritus 1995—), Am. Counselors Soc., Spiritual Adv. Coun., Free to Live, People for Am. Way, Human Rights Legal Def. Fund, Nat. Speakers Assn., Sigma Delta Chi. Democrat. Office: #363 100 Turtle Creek Village Dallas TX 75219-4610

LAUBENTHAL, SANDERS ANNE, writer, editor; b. Mobile, Ala., Dec. 25, 1943; d. Wilbert Joseph and Mabel Eloise (Sanders) L. BA summa cum laude, Spring Hill Coll., 1965; MA in English, U. Ala., 1967, PhD in English, 1970. Asst. prof. English Troy (Ala.) State U., 1969-72; commd. 2d lt. USAF, 1973, advanced through grades to maj.; edn. and tng. officer Air U., Maxwell AFB, Ala., 1974-76; dep. chief of history 13th Air Force, Clark AB, The Philippines, 1976-77; asst. to assoc. prof. humanities Air Force Inst. of Tech., Wright-Patterson AFB, Ohio, 1977-80; chief rsch. mgmt. 544th Strategic Intelligence Wing, Offutt AFB, Nebr., 1981-84; asst. dean for rsch. Def. Intelligence Coll., Bolling AFB, D.C., 1984-86; chief intellegence prodn. mgmt. divsn. Pacific Air Forces, Hickam AFB, Hawaii, 1987-90; officer for scheduled def. intelligence prodn. Def. Intelligence Agy., Bolling AFB, 1990-93; editor A' Bhratach, 1994—. Author: Excalibur, 1973; editor A'Bhratach, 1994—. Mem. Legion of Honor of the Chapel of the Four Chaplains, Gaelic Soc. of Am, Clan Donald (newsletter editor, Award for Excellence 1994), Air

Force Assn., others. Roman Catholic. Home: 4652 E Pinewood Dr Mobile AL 36618 Office: Laubenthal Rsch & Pub 6915 Villa Del Rey Ct Springfield VA 22150

LAUBSCHER, ROBERT JAMES, consumer products company executive; b. Tucson, Mar. 20, 1961; s. James Albert and Geri Lee (Bird) L.; m. Deborah Elaine Fuggles, Apr. 14, 1984; children: Stephanie Claire, Samuel Robert, Jonathan Daniel. BA in Econs., Calif. State U., Northridge, 1985; AS in Fire Tech., Oxnard Coll., 1986; cert. in ind. tax prep., Coll. for Fin. Planning, Denver, 1989. Acctg. mgr. Morning Star Labs., Inc., Moorpark, Calif., 1985-89; acctg. and credit mgr. Am. Tombow, Inc., Westlake Village, Calif., 1989-92; v.p. ops. Am. Tombow, Inc., Norcross, Ga., 1992—; owner Gold Coast Acctg. Svcs., Camarillo, Calif., 1989-92. With USMCR, 1981-87. Mem. Am. Inst. Profl. Bookkeepers, Bus. Products Credit Assn., Nat. Eagle Scout Assn. Republican. Mem. Full Gospel Ch. Home: 6704 Vic Ar Rd Atlanta GA 30360-1317

LAUDER, ROBERT SCOTT, health education administrator; b. Hanover, N.H., June 29, 1965; m. Lisa Francis Lauder. Diploma, Bridgeport (Conn.) Hosp. Sch. Nursing, 1991. RN, Va.; cert. AHA CPR instr., trainer; 1st Aid instr. Nat. Safety Coun. Neuro ICU Bridgeport (Conn.) Hosp., 1991, cardiovascular nurse, 1991-92; pediatric critical care nurse Children's Hosp. of Kings Daughters, Norfolk, Va., 1992-95; health edn. coord. Riverside Rehab. Inst., Newport News, Va., 1995—; sr. instr. CPR and first aid Novamod, Bridgeport, 1988-91; pres. Initial Response Tng. Ctr., Smithfield, Va., 1992—; BLS task force, affiliate faculty Am. Heart Assn.; internat. faculty emergency cardiac care Operation Smile, Norfolk, 1994—. Home and Office: 104 Buckingham Way Smithfield VA 23430-6055

LAUER, SUSAN PARKER, primary school educator; b. Boston, Mar. 31, 1965; d. Lee Merkel and Dorothy Joan (Montgomery) P.; m. Carl Nyden Lauer, Feb. 16, 1992; 1 child, Elizabeth Lee. AB in Govt., Coll. of William and Mary, 1987; MEd in Early Childhood, U. N.C., 1989. Cert. kindergarten tchr., Va., N.C. Tchr. hearing impaired Fairfax (Va.) County Pub. Schs., 1990; tchr. kindergarten Rappahannock County Sch. Bd., Sperryville, Va., 1990-93; presch. tchr. Fredericksburg United Meth. Ch., 1994—. Author poem. Delta Delta Delta fellow, 1987-88. Mem. Warrenton (Va.) Fauquier Jaycees. Episcopalian. Home: 204 Barrows Ct Fredericksburg VA 22406-6447

LAUGHLIN, CHRISTINE NELSON, manufacturing company executive; b. Erie, Pa., Aug. 10, 1942; d. John Aaron and Frances Louise (Bauschard) Nelson; m. John William Andrews, Sept. 1, 1960 (div. 1971); children: Lynne Andrews Bargar, Denise; m. Robert W.H. Laughlin, Dec. 24, 1983. Student, U. Md., 1963-64, Allegheny Coll., 1974-75. Cert. in prodn. and inventory mgmt. Master scheduling supr. Joy Mfg. Co., Franklin, Pa., 1977-82; materials mgr. Gerber Garment Tech., Tolland, Conn., 1984-86; chief master scheduler Thermos Co., Norwich, Conn., 1986-87; mfg. systems mgr. Rogers Corp., Manchester, Conn., 1987-88; mgr. prodn. planning Gerber Garment Tech., Tolland, Conn., 1988-90; materials mgr. KCR Tech., East Hartford, Conn., 1990-91; ops. mgr. Polyplastex Internat., Clearwater, Fla., 1992-95; distbn. ops. analyst Tech Data Corp., Clearwater, Fla., 1995—. Vol. Erie Playhouse, 1970-72, Conn. Pub. Broadcasting, Hartford, 1985-86; cellist Allegheny Civic Symphony, Meadville, Pa., 1975-80, reader Recording for the Blind, Austin, Tex., 1982-83; former mem. managerial women's adv. bd. Behrend Coll. Mem. Am. Prodn. and Inventory Control Soc., Feather Sound Country Club. Republican. Presbyterian.

LAUGHLIN, LOUIS GENE, economic analyst, consultant; b. Santa Barbara, Calif., Sept. 20, 1937; s. Eston A. and Cornelia Helen (Snively) L.; student Pomona Coll., 1955-58; BA, U. Calif., Santa Barbara, 1960; postgrad. Claremont Grad. Sch., 1966-70, 85-86, Sch. Bank Mktg., U. Colo., 1974-75, Grad. Sch. Mgmt., U. Calif.-Irvine, 1983. Mgr., Wheeldex-L.A. Co., 1961-62; v.p. Warner/Walker Assocs., Inc., L.A., 1962; cons. Spectra-Sound Corp., L.A., 1964-65; rep. A.C. Nielsen Co., Chgo., 1962-64; rsch. analyst Security Pacific Nat. Bank, L.A., 1964-67, asst. rsch. mgr., 1967-68, asst. v.p., 1968-72, v.p., mgr. market info. and rsch. div., 1972-76, v.p. rsch. adminstrn., pub. affairs/rsch. dept., 1976-82, v.p. govt. rels. dept., 1982-85; dir. R & D Applied Mgmt. Systems, South Pasadena, Calif., 1986; pres. L.G. Laughlin & Assoc., Houston, 1987—; prin. Courtyard Holdings, Houston, 1988—; pres. CEO, Mastodon Capital Corp., Houston, 1988-89, 94—; corp. sec. Kestco Co. Inc., Laguna Beach, Calif.; mem. Nat. Conf. on Fin. Svcs., 1982-84, mem. policy coun., 1983-84; mem. policy coun. Nat. Conf. on Competition in Banking, 1978-79, 81. Sec. econs. Town Hall of Calif., 1966. Mem. Am. Econs. Assn., Western Econ. Assn., Nat. Assn. Bus. Economists, L.A. C. of C. (food and agr. adv. com. 1981).

LAUGHLIN, WILLIAM EUGENE, electric power industry executive; b. Sheffield, Ala., May 4, 1936; s. Rawlie Wayne and Nina Louise (Campbell) L.; m. Donna Lynn Blackburn, Jan. 3, 1958; children: Kevin McGregor, Christopher Scott, Laura Shannon, Alison Paige. BS, Auburn U., 1961. Registered profl. and electrical engr., Ala., Tenn., Miss. Elec. engr. Dept. Power, Water and Gas, City of Sheffield, 1961-66; chief engr., asst. mgr. Electric Plant Bd., Bowling Green, Ky., 1966-76; systems mgr. Bowling Green Mcpl. Utilities, 1975-77; gen. mgr. Fayetteville (Tenn.) Electric Systems, 1977-81, Talquin Electric Coop. Inc., Quincy, Fla., 1981—; bd. dirs., v.p. Seminole Electric Coop., Inc., Tampa, Fla.; pres. Fla. Rural Electric Coop. Assn., Tallahassee. Pres. Boys Club, Bowling Green, 1972; v.p. Bowling Green C. of C., 1975, Fayetteville C. of C., 1979; dist. chmn. Boy Scouts Am., Bowling Green, 1972, Fayetteville, 1978; pres. Fayetteville United Way, 1980. Mem. Nat. Rural Elec. Coop. Assn. (mem. regional com., nat. water task force 1995), Am. Water Works Assn., Rotary (bd. dirs. 1986-87, pres. Quincy club 1996—), Fayetteville 1978-79), Kiwanis (dir. Bowling Green club 1973-74). Democrat. Mem. Ch. of Christ. Home: 2110 Ellicott Dr Tallahassee FL 32312-3118 Office: Talquin Electric Coop Inc PO Box 1679 Quincy FL 32353-1679

LAUNIUS, BEATRICE KAY, critical care nurse, educator; b. Chisledon, Wiltshire, Eng., Dec. 14, 1954; came to the U.S., 1956; d. Wendell Arthur and Susie (Wright) L. Diploma, Charity Hosp. Sch. Nursing, New Orleans, 1975; BS in Biology, La. State U., Shreveport, 1990; BSN, Northwestern State U., 1996. RN, La.; CCRN, ANCC; cert. ACLS instr., pediatric advanced life support instr. Staff nurse surg. ICU Charity Hosp., New Orleans, 1976; staff nurse emergency room Schumpert Med. Ctr., Shreveport, 1975-76, 77-82, asst. head nurse surg. ICU, 1982-83, staff nurse surg. ICU, 1983-87; staff nurse surg. ICU La. State U. Med. Ctr., 1987-88, asst. supr. surg. ICU, 1988-90, supr. surg. ICU, 1990-92, critical care edn. coord., 1992—; spkr. in field. Mem. AACN (chpt. pres. N.W. La. 1994-96, spl. interest cons. for edn. region 12 1995-97, Reporter fellow 1993, group of 100 1996-97, advance directives task force 1996—), Soc. for Crit. Care Medicine, Soc. Trauma Nursing, So. Nurses Rsch. Soc., Sigma Theta Tau Internat. (outstanding nontraditional undergrad. student Beta Chi chpt. 1996). Office: La State U Med Ctr 1501 Kings Hwy Shreveport LA 71130-4228

LAU-PATTERSON, MAYIN, psychotherapist; b. N.Y.C., May 13, 1940; d. Justin S. and Susan (Lee) Lau; m. Oscar H. L. Bing, Dec. 26, 1962 (div. Dec. 1974); children: David C., Michael H.; m. Michael Morrow Patterson, Nov. 8, 1989. BA, Goucher Coll., 1962; MA, George Washington U., 1966; postgrad., Boston Coll., 1977. Lic. psychologist, Mass.; lic. profl. counselor, Tex.; diplomate in managed mental health care; chem. dependency specialist, marriage and family therapist, criminal justice specialist; compulsive gambling counselor, hypnotherapist, Tex.; cert. criminal justice specialist. Psychologist children's unit Met. State Hosp., Waltham, Mass., 1966-67, clin. psychologist, 1967-68, prin. psychologist, 1968-70, chief psychologist, 1970-76; chief psychologist South Cove Community Health Ctr., Boston, 1976-78; pvt. practice Newton, Mass., 1974-78, Gateway Counseling, Framington, Mass., 1975-78, Alamo Mental Health, San Antonio, 1978-92, The Patterson Relationship and Counseling Ctr., San Antonio, 1992—; clin. instr. psychology Dept. Psychiatry Harvard U. Med. Sch., Cambridge, MAss., 1974-76; instr. Tufts New Eng. Med. Ctr. Hosp., Boston, 1975-78; presenter Am. Acad. Child Psychiatry, 1973, 74. Contbr. articles to profl. jours. Office: Ste 200 3510 N St Marys St Ste 200 San Antonio TX 78212-3164

LAURA, ROBERT ANTHONY, coastal engineer, consultant; b. Syracuse, NY, June 4, 1955; s. John Emil and Rosemary (Ross) L.; m. Susan Ann Sieve, Dec. 30, 1978; children: Carolyn Ruth, Alyson Anne, Katy Marie. BS in Engring. Sci., SUNY, Buffalo, 1977; MS in Ocean Engring., U. Miami, Fla., 1980. Registered profl. engr., Fla. Sr. assoc. Post, Buckley, Schuh & Jernigan, Inc., Miami, Fla., 1979-88; sr. engr. Law Environ. Inc., Ft. Lauderdale, Fla., 1988-92; sr. civil engr. South Fla. Water Mgmt. Dist., West Palm Beach, Fla., 1992—. Contbr. articles to Jour. of Hydraulic Engring. and proceedings of sci. meetings. Recipient fellowship from Conoco to U. Miami, 1979. Mem. ASCE (control mem. coastal engring. tech. com. 1988—), Am. Water Resources Assn., Am. Shore and Beach Preservation Assn. Democrat. Roman Catholic. Home: 1081 Northumberland Ct Wellington FL 33414-8916 Office: South Fla Water Mgmt Dist PO Box 24680 West Palm Beach FL 33416-4680

LAURENT, J(ERRY) SUZANNA, technical communications specialist; b. Oklahoma City, Okla., Dec. 28, 1942; d. Harry Austin and M. LaVerne (Barker) Minick; m. Leroy E. Laurent, July 2, 1960; children: Steven, Sandra, David, Debra. AS in Tech. Writing, Okla. State U., 1986. With Technically Write, Mustang, Okla., 1960-75, acctg. adminstr., 1976-80, retail bus. mgr., 1981-87, owner, CEO, 1989-95; sr. tech. comms. specialist Applied Intelligence Group, Edmond, Okla., 1995—. Named Top Ten Bus. Woman of ABWA in the Nation 1997. Mem. Soc. Tech. Comm. (Superscript editor 1985, feature editor 1986, v.p., 1985, student chpt. pres. 1986, program coord. Okla. chpt. 1992-93, sec. 1993-94, v.p. 1994-95, state pres. 1995-96, other honors), Am. Bus. Women's Assn. (Dist. III v.p. 1988-89, conf. gen. chair 1992, editor Smoke Signals 1993-95, chmn. bd. dirs. Help Us Grow Spiritually 1993-95, Bull. award 1977, 81, 83, 84, 93, 95, Woman of Yr. 1977, 96, One of Top Ten Women of Yr. 1997, Bus. Assoc. of Yr. 1983-84). Democrat. Baptist. Home: 347 W Forest Dr Mustang OK 73064-3430

LAURIE, ROBIN GARRETT, lawyer; b. Mobile, Ala., June 10, 1956; s. George and Margaret Eloise (Garrett) L.; m. Deborah Dockery; children: Elizabeth Anne, Robin Garrett. AA, Marion (Ala.) Mil. Inst., 1976; BS in Bus., U. Ala., Tuscaloosa, 1978; JD, U.Ala., Tuscaloosa, 1988. Bar: Ala. 1988, U.S. Dist. Ct. (no., mid. and so. dists.) Ala. 1988, U.S. Ct. Appeals (11th cir.) 1988. Lawyer, ptnr. Balch & Bingham, Montgomery, Ala., 1988—. Lead articles editor Ala. Law Rev., 1986-88. Recipient Outstanding Svc. award Ala. Law Rev., 1988. Mem. ABA, Ala. State Bar, Montgomery County Bar Assn., Montgomery Rotary Club, Order of the Coif. Methodist. Office: Balch & Bingham 2 Dexter Ave Montgomery AL 36104

LAUTERBACH, EDWARD CHARLES, psychiatric educator; b. Chgo., Mar. 21, 1955; s. Edward G. and Virginia C. (Pochelski) L. AB cum laude, Augustana Coll., Rock Island, Ill., 1977; MD, Wake Forest U., 1982. Lic. psychiatrist, Mo., Pa., N.J., N.C,. Ga.; diplomate Nat. Bd. Med. Examiners, Am. Bd. Psychiatry and Neurology. Intern Washington U. Sch. Medicine/Barnes Hosp., St. Louis, 1982-83, resident in psychiatry, 1983-86; clin. asst. Washington U. Sch. Medicine/Barnes Hosp., 1982-86, U. Medicine and Dentistry of N.J., New Brunswick, 1986-87, Mercer U. Sch. Medicine, Macon, Ga., 1988; chief div. adult and geriatric psychiatry, dept. psychiatry and behavioral scis. Mercer U. Sch. Medicine, Macon, 1988—, coord. grand rounds dept. psychiatry and behavioral scis., 1989—; coord. grand rounds dept. psychiatry and behavioral scis. Mercer U. Sch. Medicine, Macon, N.C., 1989—; asst prof. psychiatry Mercer U. Sch. Medicine, Macon, 1988-92, assoc. prof., 1992-96, prof., 1996—, prof. internal medicine, 1996—; pvt. practice Charlotte, N.C., 1987-88; chair free comm. IVth World Congress Biol. Psychiatry, Phila., 1985; mem. neurology staff Lyons VA Hosp., 1986; active staff privileges in neurology Mercy Hosp., Charlotte, 1987, cons., 1987; active privileges in psychiatry Med. Ctr. Ctrl. Ga., 1994—, Coliseum Psychiat. Hosp., 1994—, dir. med. staff continuing edn., 1994-96. Editorial reviewer Neuropsychiatry, Neuropsychology, and Behavioral Neurology, 1990—, Jour. Neuropsychiatry and Clin. Neuroscis., Biological Psychiatry, Movement Disorders, others; contbr. articles to profl. jours. Rock Sleyster scholar Wake Forest U., 1981. Mem. AMA (panelist DATTA coun. of sci. affairs 1990—), Am. Acad. Neurology, Am. Psychiat. Assn. (course dir. 1990-92, 94-95, symposium chairwoman 1995-96), Am. Neuropsychiat. Assn. (rsch. com.), Ga. Psychiat. Physicians Assn. (state com. on continuing med. edn.), Bibb County Med. Soc., N.C. Psychiat. Assn., Mecklenburg County Med. Soc., Med. Assn. Ga., Movement Disorder Soc., Charlotte Psychiat. Soc.

LAUTIER, YVES LAURENT, physician; b. Tlemcen, Algeria, May 1, 1941; came to U.S., 1970; s. Etienne Georges and Georgette Adelaide (Herrmann) L.; m. Eloise Walne Dabney, July 19, 1969; children: Claire Dabney, Erik Laurent. MD, U. Montpellier, France, 1969. Diplomate Am. Bd. Psychiatry and Neurology. Intern Medical Coll. Va., Richmond, 1970-71, jr. asst. resident, 1971-72, asst. resident, 1972-73, sr. asst. resident, 1973-74; pvt. practice psychiatry McLean, Va., 1974-83, Pensacola, Fla., 1983—; medical dir. Bapt. Hosp., Pensacola, Fla., 1983—; chief psychiatry svc., 1987—. Mem. AMA, Am. Psychiat. Assn. Episcopalian. Home: 2942 Coral Strip Pky Gulf Breeze FL 32561-2635 Office: 4400 Bayou Blvd Ste 51 Pensacola FL 32503-1909

LAVALLEY, JUDY TUCKER, cardiology critical care nurse; b. Birmingham, Ala., Oct. 6, 1954; d. James Melvin and Clytee (Whitman) Tucker; divorced. Lic. practical nurse, Itawamba Jr. Coll., Tupelo, Miss., 1974, ADN, 1982; BSN, Miss. U. for Women, Tupelo, Miss., 1994. RN, Miss.; cert. in ACLS. Physician's asst. in cardiology Internal Medicine Assocs. Ltd., Tupelo; critical care nurse North Miss. Med. Ctr., Tupelo, staff nurse cardiac catheterization lab., noninvasive cardiol supr. Mem. AACN, Am. Acad. Med. Adminstrs., Miss. Nursing Assn., Sigma Theta Tau.

LAVATELLI, LEO SILVIO, retired physicist, educator; b. Mackinac Island, Mich., Aug. 15, 1917; s. Silvio E. and Zella (Cunningham) L.; m. Anna Craig Henderson, June 14, 1941 (dec. Sept. 1966); children: Nancy Jack, Mark Leo; m. Celia Burns, Jan. 23, 1967 (dec. May 1976); 1 stepchild, Faith Stendler (dec.); m. Barbara Gow, Nov. 22, 1976 (div. Jan. 1979; dec. Mar. 1995); stepchildren: Ann Deemer, Lindsay Deemer; m. Olwen Thomas, Mar. 4, 1982; stepchildren: Alice Ann Williamson (Mrs. Michael W. Cone), Caroline Hill Williamson, Thomas Holman Williamson, Hugh Stuart Williamson. BS, Calif. Inst. Tech., 1939; MA, Princeton U., 1943, Harvard U., 1949; PhD, Harvard U., 1951. Instr. physics, chemistry, algebra, calculus, symbolic logic Deep Springs (Calif.) Jr. Coll., 1939-41; instr. Princeton (N.J.) U., 1941; rsch. asst. Manhattan Dist. Office Sci. R&D, Nat. Def. Rsch. Coun., Princeton, 1942-43; jr. staff mem. Los Alamos (N.Mex.) Nat. Lab. (formerly Manhattan Dist. Site Y), 1943-46; rsch. asst. Harvard U., Cambridge, Mass., 1946-50; asst. prof. physics, staff mem. Control Systems Lab. U. Ill., Urbana, 1950-55, assoc. prof., 1955-58, prof., 1958-79, prof. emeritus, 1979—; mem. measuring groups and witness for Trinity, the Alamogordo Atomic Bomb Test, 1945; mem. design team orbit plotting/control circuit logic FM new cyclotron project Harvard U., 1946; observer air/ground exercises U.S. Dept. Def., Waco, Tex., 1952; observer joint air exercises NATO, Fed. Republic Germany, 1955; mem. project quick-fix Control Sys. Lab., 1953; cons. Ill. group Phys. Sci. Study Com., 1956-57, Sci. Teaching Ctr., MIT, 1966, Teheran Rsch. unit U. Ill., 1970; participant info. theory in biology conf. U. Ill., 1952. Producer silent film cassettes on orbit graphing U. Ill., 1964; co-interviewee video tape Logical Thinking in Children and Science Education, Nat. Japanese TV, Tokyo, 1970; phys. sci. cons. The Macmillan Science Series, 1970 edit., The Macmillan Co., N.Y.C., 1967-70; contbr. articles and revs. to profl. publs. Co-moderator discussion Fedn. Atomic Scientists, 1945, 1947. Recipient U. Ill. Undergrad Teaching award U. St. Andrews, Scotland, summer 1965; John Simon Guggenheim Meml. fellow U. Bologna, Italy, 1957. Fellow Am. Phys. Soc.; mem. Harvard Faculty Club (non-resident). Home: 10181 Seven Paths Rd Spring Hope NC 27882-9543

LAVDAS, LEONIDAS G., meteorologist, religion educator; b. Phila., Oct. 22, 1947; s. George L. and Jean E. (Barnett) L. BS in Meteorology, NYU, 1969; MS in Meteorology, Fla. State U., 1971. Rsch. meteorologist USDA-Forest Svc., Juliette, Ga., 1972—; chmn. parish edn. dept. Faith Luth. Ch., Warner-Robins, Ga., 1986-90, mem. ch. coun., 1987-90, adult Sun. sch. tchr., 1986—. Author, actor: Pontius Pilate Solioquy, 1990, others; actor Macon Area Community Theater, 1977-79, Warner Robins Little Theater, 1985. Mem. AAAS, Am. Meteorol. Soc., Air and Waste Mgmt. Assn., Nat. Weather Assn., U.S. Chess Fedn., Religious Book Club. Home: 215 Sun Valley Dr Warner Robins GA 31093-1058

LAVELLE, BRIAN FRANCIS DAVID, lawyer; b. Cleve., Aug. 16, 1941; s. Gerald John and Mary Josephine (O'Callagahan) L.; m. Sara Hill, Sept. 10, 1966; children: S. Elizabeth, B. Francis D., Catherine H. BA, U. Va., 1963; JD, Vanderbilt U., 1966; LLM in Taxation, N.Y.U., 1969. Bar: N.C. 1966, Ohio 1968. Assoc. VanWinkle Buck, Wall, Starnes & Davis, Asheville, N.C., 1968-74, ptnr., 1974—; lectr. continuing edn. N.C. Bar Found., Wake Forest U. Estate Planning Inst., Hartford Tax Inst., Duke U. Estate Planning Inst. Contbr. articles on law to profl. jours. Trustee Carolina Day Sch., 1981-92, sec., 1982-85; vice-chmn. Buncombe County Indsl. Facilities and Pollution Control Authority, 1976-82; bd. dirs. Geodetic Internat., Inc. U.S. div., Western N.C. Community Found., 1986— (sec. 1987-90); mem. Asheville Tax Study Group, 1981—, chmn., 1984; bd. advs. U.N.C. Annual Tax Inst., 1981—. Capt. JAG USAF, 1966-67. Mem. ABA, N.C. Bar Assn. (bd. govs. 1979-82, councillor tax sect. 1979-83, councillor estate planning law sect. 1982-85), Am. Coll. Trust and Estate Counsel (state chmn. 1982-85, regent 1984-90, lectr. continuing edn.), N.C. State Bar (splty. exam. com. on estate planning and probate law 1984-90, chmn. 1990-91, cert. 1987). Episcopalian (clk. vestry All Souls Ch.). Clubs: Biltmore Forest Country. Lodge: Rotary (Asheville). Home: 45 Brookside Rd Asheville NC 28803-3015 Office: 11 N Market St PO Box 7376 Asheville NC 28802

LAVEN, DAVID LAWRENCE, nuclear and radiologic pharmacist, consultant; b. Detroit, Jan. 31, 1953; s. Harold Sanford and Ada Rae (Blumenthal) L.; m. Maxine Frances Miller, May 14, 1977; children: Ryan Stuart, Cameron Alexander. BA in History, Biology, Albion Coll., 1975; BS in Pharmacy, U. N.Mex., 1981. Rsch. technologist, biodistbn. specialist U. N.Mex. Coll. Pharmacy, Albuquerque, 1978-81; asst. mgr. Syncor, Inc. (formerly Pharmatopes), Miami, Fla., 1981-84; instr. nuclear pharmacy U. Miami, 1982-85; pres., owner Gammascan Cons., Montgomery, Ala., 1982—; staff pharmacist Hollywood (Fla.) Med. Ctr., 1983-84; asst. mgr. Nuclear Pharmacy, Inc., Sunrise, Fla., 1984-85; dir. nuc. pharmacy program VA Med. Ctr., Bay Pines, 1985-96; mem. adv. panel on radiopharms. U.S. Pharmacopeial Conv. Inc., Rockville, Md., 1985—; cons. nuclear pharmacy Nat. Assn. Bds. Pharmacy, Chgo., 1987—; adj. asst. clin. prof. U. Fla. Coll. Pharmacy, Gainesville, 1986—, Nova-Southeastern U. Coll. Pharmacy, North Miami Beach, Fla., 1990—, Mercer U. Coll. Pharmacy, 1995—; edn. cons. Nuclear Tech. Rev. Series Rev., Inc., 1988—; mem. splty. coun. on nuclear pharmacy Bd. Pharm. Specialties, 1988-91; mem. Ala. Coun. Assn. Execs., 1996—, Nat. Coun. State Pharmacy Assn. Execs., 1996—. Co-author: Pharmacologic Alterations in the Biorouting/Performance of Select Radiopharmaceuticals Used in Cardiac Imaging, 1990, Pharmacologic Alterations with Biorouting/Performance of Radiopharmaceuticals Used in Nuclear Medicine Abscess, Liver/Spleen, and Tumor/Inflammation Imaging Procedures, 1992, Pharmacologic Alterations in the Biorouting of Radiopharmaceuticals Used in Nuclear Medicine Adrenal, Cerebral, Hepatobiliary, Pulmonary, and Renal Scintigraphic Studies, 1993, International Handbook of Drug-Radiopharmaceutical Interactions and Incompatibilities, 1994; Pharmacologic Alterations in the Biorouting/Performance of Radiopharmaceuticals Used in Cistrnography, Ferrokinetic Studies, Gastrointestinal Imaging, Schillings Testing, Thrombus Localization, Thyroid Uptake/Imaging, and Other Nuclear Medicine Procedures, 1994; editor, co-pub. Clini-Scan Monthly, 1982-84; co-guest editor Jour. Pharmacy Practice, Radiologic Pharmacy I, 1989, II, 1989, III, 1994, mem. editorial bd., 1991—; guest editor Fla. Jour. Hosp. Pharmacy, 1990, cons. editor, 1986-96; guest author In-Svc. Rev. in Nuclear Medicine, 1990—; mem. editorial bd. New Perspectives in Cancer Diagnosis and Management, 1992—; nat. field editor ASHP Signal Newsletter, 1985-87; contbr. chpt. to book. Mem. Henry Morgan chpt. B'nai B'rith, Southfield, Mich., 1975-77. Fellow Am. Soc. Hosp. Pharmacists (chmn. specialized practice group on radiologic pharmacy 1993-95, edn. program assoc. 1988-95, practice adv. panel 1992-93, mem. continuing edn. 1995—), Acad. Pharmacy Practice and Mgmt. (del. 1986—, edn. cons. 1987—, nuc. pharmacy sec. ednl. affairs com. 1983—, profl. and scientific affairs com. 1988—, regulatory affairs com. 1984—, Practitioner Merit award 1990, Presentation award 1990, 91, 94, Poster award 1990, 91, 94); mem. Am. Pharm. Assn. (chmn.-elect 1988-89, chmn. sect. on specialized pharm. svcs. 1989-90, chmn.-elect 1992-93, chmn. section on nuc. pharmacy 1993-94, edn. adv. com. 1988-89, 92-94, mem. nuc. pharmacy sect., mem. ednl. affairs com. 1983—, mem. profl. and sci. affairs com. 1988—, mem. regulatory affairs com. 1984—), Am. Assn. Colls. Pharmacy (mem. task force on residency programs and support 1990-91, mem. task force on assessment of experimental function 1994-95), Nat. Coun. State Pharmacy Assn. Execs., Ala. Coun. Assn. Execs., Am. Soc. Pharmacy Law, Fla. Pharmacy Assn. (chmn. ednl. affairs coun. 1989-90, chmn. nuclear pharmacy section 1987-89, 91-93, chmn. acad. pharmacy practice 1988-90, 93-95, chmn. orgnl. affairs coun. 1992-93, del. 1988—, edn. cons. 1987—, exec. com. 1989—, pres. com. 1989-90, 94-95, budget and fin. com. 1989-90, 94-95, mem. conv. planning com. 1989-93, 95, mem. exec. com. 1989-96, region XII rep. 1989-96, mem. task force on mission of pharmacy in Fla. 1989-92, 95, editor numerous proceedings for nuclear pharmacy lecture series 1993-96, Number 1 Club 1990, Disting. Young Pharmacist award 1990, Acad. Pharmacy Practice Practitioner Merit award 1992, Sidney Simkowitz Pharmacy Involvement award 1992, Disting. Svc. award 1993, Unit Assn. Newsletter awards 1994, 95 (2), 96), Acad. Pharmacy Practice (chmn. 1988-90, 93-95, chmn. nuclear pharmacy sect. 1987-89, 91-93, Poster Presentation 1st Pl. award 1995), Fla. Soc. Hosp. Pharmacists, Fla. Nuclear Medicine Technologists (mem. exec. coun. 1992—, editor Proceedings 22nd ann. meeting 1993, 24th ann. meeting 1995, 25th ann. meeting 1996), Internat. Pharm. Fedn. (scientific poster award 1992, vice chmn. nuclear pharmacy subsection, 1994-95, edn. con. Pharmacy World Congress 1992, 93, 95, 96, editor Radioimmunopharm.: Current and Future Considerations), Soc. Nuclear Medicine (mem. S.E. chpt., mem. govt. affairs com. 1985-86, program com. 1988-89, edn. cons. 1989—, chair pharmacy liaison com. 1995—, mem. Brewster Bill task force 1995, mem. NRC com. 1995—), Pinellas Pharmacist Soc. (mem. exec. com. 1989—, pres.-elect 1991-92, pres. 1992-93, newsletter editor, 1992-96, Pharmacist of Yr. award 1992, Pres' award 1993, FPA Unit Assn. Recognition award 1993, 95, PPS Merit award 1994, Practice Merit award 1994, Lifetime Merit award 1996), Pasco-Hernando Pharmacy Assn. (treas. 1990-93, mem. exec. com. 1990-94, Pharmacist of Yr. 1995), Hillsborough County Pharmacy Assn. (mem. exec. com. 1991—, sec. 1991-92, pres.-elect 1993-94, pres. 1994-95, 95-96, newsletter editor, 1994-96, Pres. award 1994-95, 95-96. Pharmacist of Yr. 1994), Polk County Pharmacy Assn., Internat. Pharmacy Fedn. (Sci. Poster award Sect. Hosp. Pharmacists 1992, editor proceedings spl. session Pharmacy World Congress 1993, vice chmn. nuclear pharmacy group 1994—), Ala. Pharmacy Assn. (exec. dir. 1996—), Kappa Psi, Psi Chi, Phi Alpha Theta, Beta Beta Beta. Home: 1542 Laurelwood Lane Montgomery AL 36117 Office: Ala Pharmacy Assn 1211 Carmichael Way Montgomery AL 36106-3672

LAVENANT, RENE PAUL, JR., lawyer; b. Highland Park, Ill., Feb. 6, 1925; s. Rene Paul and Marie C. (Nack) L.; m. Marjorie Ann Witter; children: Hilary, Mark, Amelie. B.S., Northwestern U., 1945; LL.B., Stanford U., 1949. Bar: Calif. 1949, N.Y. 1962, Tex. 1978. Successively atty., sr. atty., regional gen. counsel Mobil Oil Corp. and affiliates, Los Angeles, 1949-73, Casper, Wyo., 1949-73, Billings, Mont., 1949-73, N.Y.C., 1949-73, Paris and London, 1949-73; ptnr. in charge London office Fulbright & Jaworski LLP, Houston, 1973-78; sr. ptnr. Fulbright & Jaworski, Houston, 1978—. Mem. ABA, Houston Bar Assn. Home: Lafayette Pl Houston TX 77036 Office: Fulbright & Jaworski 1301 Mckinney St Houston TX 77010

LAVENDER, KENNETH, rare book librarian, educator; b. L.A., Apr. 3, 1940; s. Ernest Atwood and Gwendolyn Ruth (Jones) L. BA, U. Calif., Santa Barbara, 1961; MA, U. Calif., Berkeley, 1964; MS in LS, U. Ill., 1973; PhD in English, U. Calif., Santa Barbara, 1972. Asst. prof. English S.D. State U., 1972-74; asst. prof. librarianship U. S.C., 1974-77; humanities libr., acting dir. collection devel. U. Houston, Victoria, 1978-81; univ. bibliographer U. North Tex., Denton, 1981-89, curator rare book and Texana collections, 1989—; cons., workshop facilitator; presenter in field. Author monographs, articles, columns. V.p. Light Opera Co., Denton, 1993—. NEH/AMIGOS grantee, 1992, Summerlee Found. grantee, 1994. Mem. ALA, Assn. Coll. and Rsch. Librs. (edn. com. rare books and manuscripts sect. 1990-92), Assn. Libr. and Info. Sci. Edn., Alliance for Higher Edn. of North Tex. (preservation com. 1981—, chair 1987-89), Beta Phi Mu. Office: U North Tex Librs PO Box 5188 Denton TX 76203-0188

LAVENDER, ROBERT EUGENE, state supreme court justice; b. Muskogee, Okla., July 19, 1926; s. Harold James and Vergene Irene (Martin) L.;

m. Maxine Knight, Dec. 22, 1945; children—Linda (Mrs. Dean Courter), Robert K., Debra (Mrs. Thomas Merrill), William J. LL.B., U. Tulsa, 1953; grad., Appellate Judges Seminar, 1967, Nat. Coll. State Trial Judges, 1970. Bar: Okla. bar 1953. With Mass. Bonding & Ins. Co., Tulsa, 1951-53, U.S. Fidelity & Guaranty Co., Tulsa, 1953-54; asst. city atty. Tulsa, 1954-55, practice, 1955-60; practice Claremore, Okla., 1960-65; justice Okla. Supreme Ct., 1965—, chief justice, 1979-80; guest lectr. Okla. U., Oklahoma City U., Tulsa U. law schs. Republican committeeman, Rogers County, 1961-62. Served with USNR, 1944-46. Recipient Disting. Alumnus award U. Tulsa, 1993. Mem. ABA, Okla. Bar Assn., Rogers County Bar Assn., Am. Judicature Soc., Okla. Jud. Conf., Phi Alpha Delta (hon.). Methodist (adminstrv. bd.). Club: Mason (32 deg.). Home: 2910 Kerry Ln Oklahoma City OK 73120-2507 Office: US Supreme Ct Okla Rm 1 State Capitol Oklahoma City OK 73105

LAVENDER, T. J. (JODY), critical care nurse, administrator; b. Pine Bluff, Ark., Feb. 23, 1947; d. Charles Alpha and Josephine Lenad (Simpson) Weser; children: John Paul Gereaux, Lawrence Robert Lavender III. Diploma, Pines Vocat. Sch., Pine Bluff, 1973; ASN, AA, St. Petersburg Jr. Coll., Clearwater, Fla., 1981. Cert. critical care nurse, ACLS, BLS instr. Emergency room pool nurse Columbia Hosp., New Port Richey, Fla.; staff nurse emergency rm. Helen Ellis Meml. Hosp.; flight nurse, mktg. rep. Care Flight Air Ambulance, Clearwater; DON Nurses Inc., Tampa, Fla.; patient care coord. Paragon Home Care, Bayonet Point, Fla.; DON Rescare Supportive Svcs., 1991; staff nurse in emergency rm. Spring Hill (Fla.) Regional Hosp., 1991-93; flight nurse World Access Transport Svcs., Miami, 1993—, AAA Air Ambulance, Miami; lifeguard Air Ambulance, Gulf Breeze, Fla.; emergency rm. pool nurse Helen Ellis Meml. Hosp., Tarpon Springs, Fla., 1993—, North Bay Med. Ctr., New Port Richey, Fla., 1993—, Columbia New Port Richey, Fla.

LAVID, JEAN STERN, school director; b. Roanoke, Va., Jan. 4, 1943; d. Ernest George and Marianne (Stamm) Stern; m. Aug. 26, 1968 (div. 1989); children: Nathan, Eric, Craig, Brian, Laura. BA, Coll. William and Mary, 1965; MA, Wichita State U., 1986, specialist degree, 1989. Cert. permanent tchr. German, N.Y.; cert. supt., bldg. adminstr., Kans., Colo., N.Y., Va., N.H., Ohio, Ariz., Pa., Ky. Rural community devel. vol. Peace Corps, Turkey, 1965-67; tchr. German, Spanish and English Kenmore (N.Y.)-Tonawanda Sch. Dist., 1967-70; tchr. German Grand Island (N.Y.) Sch. Dist., 1978-82, coord. adult edn., prin., 1982; grad. rsch. asst. Wichita (Kans.) State U., 1984-86, instr. German, 1985; asst. prin. Unified Sch. Dist. 259, Wichita, 1986-88; supt., high sch. prin. Unified Sch. Dist. 314, Brewster, Kans., 1988-91; supt. Unified Sch. Dist. 271, Stockton, Kans., 1991-93; dir. edn. Computer Learning Ctr., Alexandria, Va., 1993; sr. dir. distbr. Nat. Safety Assocs., Lorton, Va., 1993-96; dir. KinderCare Learning Ctr., Alexandria, 1994; dir. edn. Gesher Jewish Day Sch. of No. Va., Fairfax, 1994; dir. Kinder Care Learning Ctr., Vienna, Va., 1994-95, Children's World Learning Ctr., Lake Ridge, Va., 1995—; mem. sch. community adv. coms., N.Y., Kans., 1975-86; chmn. Com. To Revise Fgn. Lang. Curriculum, Grand Island, 1981-83; judge Kans. Fgn. Lang. Competition, 1987. Contbr. numerous articles on ednl. leadership to profl. jours. Pres. Grand Island Food Coop., 1978-83, Waterford Food Coop., Wichita, 1983-88. mem. Am. Assn. Sch. Adminstrs., Assn. for Supervision and Curriculum Devel., Nat. Assn Secondary and Elem. Sch. Prins., Am. Assn. Tchrs. German, Kans. Assn. Sch. Adminstrs., Kans. Unitied Sch. Adminstrs., AAUW (active local, regional and state levels 1973—), Phi Kappa Phi, Phi Delta Kappa, Nat. Supts. Acad. Home: 9734 Hagel Cir Lorton VA 22079-4314 Office: Children's World Learning Ctrs 12781 Harbor Dr Woodbridge VA 22192

LAVIN, PATRICK JAMES, neurologist; b. Dublin, Ireland, May 21, 1946. Grad., Univ. Coll. Dublin, 1970, MB BCh, 1970. Diplomate Am. Bd. Neurology and Psychiatry. Intern St. Vincent's Hosp., Dublin, 1970-71, resident in medicine, 1971-73; gen. practice N.S., Can., 1973; registrar in gen. medicine Leicester Gen. Hosp., 1974-75; registrar in neurology St. James U. Hosp. and Chapel Allerton Hosp., Leeds, Eng., 1976-78; rsch. fellow, hon. sr. registrar Charing Cross Hosp., London, 1978; internist James Connolly Meml. Hosp., Dublin, 1979, Our Lady's Hosp., Navan, Ireland, 1979; registrar in neurology Adelaide Hosp. and St. Vincent's Hosp., Dublin, 1980; chief resident in neurology Case Western Res. U., Cleve., 1980-81, fellow in neuro-ophthalmology, 1981-83, mem. faculty medicine, 1982-83, instr. dept. neurology, 1982-83; asst. prof. dept. neurology, appointee dept. ophthalmology Vanderbilt U., Nashville, 1983-89, assoc. prof. dept. neurology, 1989—; dir. Ocular Motility Lab., Vanderbilt U.; cons. neuro-ophthalmologist VA Med. Ctr. Contbr. articles to profl. publs., chpts. to books; reviewer Archives of Neurology, Neurology, So. Med. Jour., N.Y. State Jour. Medicine. Mem. Royal Coll. Physicians of Ireland, Am. Acad. Neurology, Assn. for Rsch. in Vision and Ophthalmology, Nahsville Acad. Ophthalmology, Tenn. Acad. Ophthalmology, Clin. Eye Movement Soc., N.Am. Neuro-Ophthalmology Soc., S.E. Neuro-ophthalmology Soc. Office: Vanderbilt U Dept Neurology 2100 Pierce Ave Ste 351 Nashville TN 37212-3156

LAVINE, RICHARD IRA, legislative analyst; b. Worcester, Mass., Nov. 25, 1947; s. Hyman and Dorothy Anne (Poplin) L.; m. Catherine Marie Sims, Jan. 18, 1979; children: Max Sims, Abby Sims. BA magna cum laude, Harvard Coll., 1969; postgrad., Harvard Law Sch., 1971-72; JD cum laude, U. Pa. Law Sch., 1975. Bar: Pa. 1975, Tex. 1980; CFA. Jud. clk. Hon. Paul A. Chalfin, Ct. of Common Pleas, Phila., 1975-76; staff atty. Defender Assn. of Phila., Pa., 1977-79; sr. rschr. House Rsch. Orgn., Austin, 1984-94; fin. analyst Ctr. for Pub. Policy Priorities, Austin, 1994—. Author spl. legis. reports, 1984-94. Founder, bd. dirs. Live Oak Fund for Change, Austin, 1980-92; bd. dirs. Travis County Ctrl. Appraisal Dist., 1996—. Mem. Assn. for Investment Mgmt. and Rsch. Home: 803 Avondale Rd Austin TX 78704-2516 Office: Ctr Pub. Policy Priorities 900 Lydia St Austin TX 78702-2625

LAVIOLETTE, BRUCE EDWARD, maintenance administrator; b. Dover, N.H., Oct. 19, 1949; s. Henry Joseph and Lucinda Ann (de Rochmont) L.; m. Maryellen Kirkland, Oct. 11, 1981; children: Michelle, Amy. Degree in Elec. Engring., U. N.H., 1967-69; student marine engring, Maine Maritime Acad., 1971-72; BS in Sociology, SUNY, Albany, 1986, BS in Bus., 1987; MS in Mgmt., Golden Gate U., 1987; PhD in Ops. Engring. and Mgmt., Union Inst., 1993. Lic. master electrician, Maine. Lab. leader GE, Somersworth, N.H., 1969-74; nuclear electrician supr. Portsmouth (N.H.) Naval Shipyard, 1974-77; supr. elec. constrn. U.S. Naval Base, Guantanamo Bay, Cuba, 1977-78, elec. estimator and designer, 1978-82; mgr. indsl. facilities Shore Intermediate Maintenance Activity, Guantanamo Bay, Cuba, 1982-88; mgr. maintenance and repair Naval Aviation Depot, Cherry Point, N.C., 1988-90, head tools and property mgmt. br., 1990-91, br. head tools and indsl. planning, 1991-92, head prodn., planning and scheduling, 1993-95; head prodn. Naval Aviation Depot, Cherry Point, 1995—; intern to Dr. Edwards Deming. Inventor ionization rsch.; contbr. articles to profl. jours. Dir. fins. Our Lady of Peace Ch., Berwick, Maine, 1970-75, dir. edn., 1972-77; chmn. York County Dem. Com., 1971-75, Berwick Zoning Bd., 1976; mem. Mayor's Com. for Persons with Disabilities; chief game warden U.S. Naval Base, 1977-87; grad. sr. exec. mgmt. devel. program Naval Aviation Exec. Inst.; active Meals on Wheels, Homes for Humanity. Recipient Meritorious Civilian Svc. award U.S. Navy Dept., 1987. Mem. Internat. Assn. Elec. Insps., Fedn. Mgrs. Assn., Soc. Am. Mil. Engrs., New Bern. C. of C., Profl. Assn., Diving Instrs. (master scuba trainer), New Bern Hist. Soc., Internat. Assn. Eagle Scouts, Cousteau Soc., East Carolina U. Ednl. Found., Federally Employed Women, Aircraft Owners and Pilots Assn., Masons. Home: 423 Boros Rd New Bern NC 28560-8424 Office: Naval Aviation Depot C # 552 Cherry Point NC 28533

LAW, THOMAS HART, lawyer; b. Austin, Tex., July 6, 1918; s. Robert Adger and Elizabeth (Manigault) L.; m. Terese Tarlton, June 11, 1943 (div. Apr. 1956); m. Jo Ann Nelson, Dec. 17, 1960; children: Thomas Hart Jr., Debra Ann. AB, U. Tex., 1939, JD, 1942. Bar: Tex. 1942, U.S. Supreme Ct. 1950. Assoc. White, Taylor & Chandler, Austin, 1942; assoc. Thompson, Walker, Smith & Shannon, Ft. Worth, 1946-50; ptnr. Tilley, Hyder & Law, Ft. Worth, 1950-67, Stone, Tilley, Parker, Snakard, Law & Brown, Ft. Worth, 1967-71; pres. Law, Snakard, Brown & Gambill, P.C., Ft. Worth, 1971-84; of counsel Law, Snakard & Gambill, P.C., Ft. Worth, 1984—; bd. dirs., gen. counsel Gearhart Industries, Inc., Ft. Worth, 1960-88; gen. counsel Tarrant County Jr. Coll. Dist. Chmn. Leadership Ft. Worth, 1974-90; bd. regents U. Tex. System, 1975-81, vice chmn., 1979-81. Served to lt. USNR, 1942-46. Recipient Nat. Humanitarian award Nat. Jewish Hosp./Nat. Asthma Ctr., 1983; named Outstanding Young Man, City of Ft. Worth, 1950, Outstanding Alumnus, Coll. of Humanities, U. Tex., 1977, Outstanding Citizen, City of Ft. Worth, 1984, Bus. Exec. of Yr., City of Ft. Worth, 1987, Blackstone award for contbns. field of law Ft. Worth Bar Assn., 1990. Fellow Am. Bar Found., Tex. Bar Found., Am. Coll. Probate Counsel; mem. Ft. Worth C. of C. (pres. 1972), Mortar Bd., Phi Beta Kappa, Omicron Delta Kappa, Pi Sigma Alpha, Delta Sigma Rho, Phi Eta Sigma, Delta Tau Delta. Democrat. Presbyterian. Clubs: Ft. Worth (bd. govs. 1984-90), Century II (bd. govs. to 1985), River Crest Country, Exchange (pres. 1972), Steeplechase. Lodge: Rotary (local club pres. 1960). Home: 6741 Brants Ln Fort Worth TX 76116-7201 Office: Law Snakard & Gambill 3200 Bank One Tower 500 Throckmorton St Fort Worth TX 76102-3708

LAWBAUGH, EMANUEL SYLVESTER, IV, lawyer, educator; b. St. Marys, Mo., Mar. 31, 1935; s. Emanuel Sylvester III and Halita Joan (Bartlett) L.; m. Verna Catherine Tucker, Dec. 29, 1956 (dec.); children: Kathleen Ann, Steven Richard, James William, Christine Marie; m. Sonja Ann Semiginowski, Dec. 27, 1977; stepson: Jeffery Daniel Brophy. BS, Regis Coll., 1957; MEd, U. Mo., 1962; EdD, U. Miss., 1972; JD, U. Ark., 1983. Bar: Nebr. 1984, S.D. 1984, Okla. 1990. Commd. capt. USMC, 1963, advanced through grades to lt. col., 1974; plans officer Marine Corps Edn. Ctr., Quantico, Va., 1976-78; comdg. officer Marine Wing Communication Squadron, Okinawa, Japan, 1978-80; marine corps dir. Def. Elec. Analysis Ctr., Annapolis, Md., 1980-81; ret. USMC, 1981; dean admissions & fin. aid Yankton (S.D.) Coll., 1984; pvt. practice law Yankton, 1984-85; dir. devel. Buena Vista Coll., Storm Lake, Iowa, 1985-90; pvt. practice Westville, Okla., 1990—; prof. orgnl. behavior U. Va., Quantico, Va., 1976, mgmt. Pepperdine U., Malibu, Calif., 1977-78. Author: Survey of Marine Corps Education; contbr. articles to profl. jours. Trustee Buena Vista Work Activity Ctr., Storm Lake, 1986-90, Flaming Rainbow U., 1991-92; mem. bd. Quantico Dept. Schs., 1973-76. Decorated Purple Heart, Bronze Star, Vietnam Honor medal, Def. Meritorious Svc. medal; recipient svc. award ARC, 1975, 76. Mem. ABA, Nebr. Bar Assn., S.D. Bar Assn., Okla. Bar Assn., Marine Corps Assn. (fitness award 1980), Order of Arch, Kiwanis (pres. Fayetteville Sequoyah 1993—). Republican. Roman Catholic. Home: 2916 N Old Wire Rd Fayetteville AR 72703-4432 Office: Westville Utility Bldg Westville OK 74965

LAWLER, JAMES PATRICK, manufacturing executive; b. Syracuse, N.Y., Mar. 15, 1954; s. James Francis and Anna Victoria (Kudlacik) L.; m. Deborah Leigh Topping, Aug. 12, 1978; children: Leigh Anna, Jonathan Patrick. BS in Resources Mgmt., SUNY, Syracuse, 1975; MBA, East Carolina U., 1979. Tech. forester Weyerhaeuser Co., New Bern, N.C., 1976-78; dist. officer devel. Govt. of Botwana, Ghanzi, 1979-82; staff asst., MIS systems supr, TQM coord., finishing and shipping supt. Union Camp Corp., Franklin, Va., 1982-88, internal svcs. mgr., lead facilitator, 1990-95; mgr. orgnl. devel. Union Camp Corp., Franklin, 1995—; ops. mgr. pers. health care Blue Cross & Blue Shield, Roanoke, Va., 1989. Area coord. Va. Spl. Olympics, Surry, Va., 1990-95; chair Campaign for Human Devel., Richmond, 1988-89. Named Vol. of Yr., Va. Spl. Olympics, 1993, Tree Farm Inspector of Yr., N.C. Tree Farm Com., 1976. Mem. Toastmasters Internat. (sgt.-at-arms 1993-94, CTM award 1993, ATM award 1994). Roman Catholic. Home: 813 Cold Branch Dr Columbia SC 29223

LAWLESS, WILLIAM FRERE, mathematics and psychology educator; b. Logan, Utah, Aug. 24, 1942; s. William Clarence and Ruby Lee (Daigle) L.; m. Susan Virginia Baker Johnson, Dec. 27, 1965 (div. Oct. 1990); children: William Frere Jr., Desiree Simonne; m. Teresa Castelao, Feb. 12, 1993. MS in Mech. Engring., La. State U., 1977; MS in Psychology, Augusta Coll., 1987; PhD in Social Psychology, Va. Tech., 1992. Registered profl. engr., La. Nuclear waste mgmt. engr. Savannah River Site Dept. Energy, Aiken, S.C., 1977-83; asst. prof. math. Paine Coll., Augusta, Ga., 1983-88, 91-93, mem. faculty, assoc. prof. depts. math. and psychology, 1993—; mem. psychology faculty Augusta Coll., 1985-88; grad. rsch. and teaching asst. dept. psychology Va. Tech., Blacksburg, 1988-91; mem. nat. adv. coun. Hanford Edn. Action League, Spokane, Wash., 1989-91; mem. Citizen's Adv. Bd. Dept. Energy, Savannah River Site, Augusta, 1994—. Interviewed in documentary film Building Bombs: The Legacy, 1985-90. Lt. col. USMC, 1961-66, Res., 1966-81. Recipient letter of commendation Dept. Energy, 1977-93, Paine Coll. Tchg. Excellence and Campus Leadership award First Union Bank Ga., 1994; named Exemplary Tchr. United Meth. Ch., 1993; grantee NEH, 1991, NEC Info. Industry, 1991, Dept. Energy, 1992, RDL Labs., 1992, MasPar Computer Corp., Howard U., 1993—, Govt. Accountability Project, 1993, Am. Soc. Engring. Edn., 1994, 95, NIH, 1996. Mem. AAAS, APA, Am. Inst. Physicists (computers in physics sect.), Ga. Acad. Sci., Am. Psychol. Soc., Soc. Southeastern Social Psychologists, Soc. for Social Study of Sci., Phi Kappa Phi, Pi Tau Sigma, Tau Beta Pi, Psi Chi. Office: Paine Coll 1235 15th St Augusta GA 30901-3182

LAWRENCE, ALMA JEAN KELLEY, research nurse; b. Jackson, Miss., Jan. 15, 1958; d. Mary Lea (Kelley) Russell; m. David Lee Lawrence, Oct. 11, 1986; children: Javaria K., David Lee. Student, Jackson State U., 1979; BSN, Miss. Coll. Sch. Nursing, 1982. RN, Miss., Tex., Okla. Staff nurse Neonatal Intensive Care Unit, Parkland Meml. Hosp., 1983-85, Neonatal ICU/HIV Clinic, Parkland Meml. Hosp., 1989-90; pub. health nurse City of Dallas Pub. Health Clinics, 1985-88; infection control/employee health nurse Tri-City Hosp., 1988-89; sr. rsch. nurse, study coord. divsn. gen. internal medicine U. Tex. Southwestern Med. Ctr., Dallas, 1990-94; regional clin. assoc. Wyeth-Ayerst Rsch., Dallas, 1994—. Contbr. articles to profl. jours. Home: 4365 Fawnhollow Dr Dallas TX 75244-7426 Office: Wyeth-Ayerst Rsch 4365 Fawnhollow Dr Dallas TX 75244

LAWRENCE, CHRISTOPHER, engineering executive. Pres. Lawrence Engring., Inc., Jacksonville, Fla. Office: Lawrence Engring Inc 2000 Corporate Square Blvd Jacksonville FL 32216-1969

LAWRENCE, DAVID, JR., newspaper editor, publisher; b. N.Y.C., Mar. 5, 1942; s. David Sr. and Nancy Wemple (Bissell) L.; m. Roberta Phyllis Fleischman, Dec. 21, 1963; children: David III, Jennifer Beth, Amanda Katherine, John Benjamin, Dana Victoria. BS, U. Fla., 1963; postgrad. advanced mgmt. program, Harvard U., 1983; LHD (hon.), Siena Heights Coll., Adrian, Mich., 1985; HHD (hon.), Lawrence Inst. Tech., Detroit, 1986; LHD (hon.), No. Mich. U., 1987; LD (hon.), Barry U., 1991, Fla. Meml. U., 1992, Northwood U., 1993; U. Fla., 1993. Reporter, news editor St. Petersburg (Fla.) Times, 1963-67; news editor Style/Washington Post, 1967-69; mng. editor Palm Beach (Fla.) Post, 1969-71, Phila. Daily News, 1971-75; exec. editor Charlotte (N.C.) Observer, 1975-76, editor, 1976-78; exec. editor Detroit Free Press, 1978-85, pub., chmn., 1985-89; pub., chmn. The Miami Herald, 1989—. Bd. dirs. U. Fla. Found., PBS, Fla. Coun. of 100; chmn. United Way of Dade County; chmn. Miami Art Mus. Named Disting. Alumnus, U. Fla., 1982; recipient Nat. Human Rights award Am. Jewish Com., 1986, First Amendment Freedoms award Anti-Defamation League, 1988, Ida Wells Nat. award for advancement of minorities Nat. Assn. Black Journalists and Nat. Conf. of Edit. Writers, 1988, John S. Knight Gold medal Knight-Ridder, 1988, Silver Medallion award NCCJ, 1992, Disting. Svc. award Nat. Assn. Schs. Journalism and Mass Comm., 1992, Scripps Howard First Amendment award, 1993, Nat. Assn. of Minority Media Execs. lifetime achievement award. Mem. Am. Soc. Newspaper Editors (pres. 1991-92), Inter Am. Press Assn. (pres. 1995-96). Office: The Miami Herald 1 Herald Plz Miami FL 33132-1609

LAWRENCE, JAMES HUCKABEE, commercial realtor; b. Durham, N.C., Feb. 3, 1953; s. Henry Newman and Margaret (Huckabee) L.; m. Beth Hutt, June 28, 1975; children: Elizabeth, James, John. Student, Gulf Coast Community Coll., Panama City, Fla., 1971-72, Harvard Bus. Sch., 1980, Am. Mgmt. Assn., Washington, 1982. Pub. rels. profl. and sales rep. Sinclair Distbr., Panama City, 1965-69; v.p. new accounts and loans Lawrence Oil Co., Fina, Panama City, 1970-75; pres., credit factor Sports Emporium, Panama City, 1976-79; pres., gen. mgr. Lawrence & Sons Oil Co. Inc., Panama City, 1981-83; adminstr. Sun South Sch. Real Estate, Panama City, 1984-85; comml. realtor John Davidson Realty/REM Inc., Panama City, 1985—; exec. v.p., sec. Diamondhead Towers, Inc., Panama City Beach, Fla., 1990—; owner Realty Svcs. Inc. of the South, Panama City, Fla., 1993—; ptnr. Assoc. Mortgage Ventures aka AMV Inc., 1994—; bd. dirs. DHT Inc., DHT Condo Assn., Panama City Beach. State lobbyist Nat. Gasohol Commn., Tallahassee, 1977-81; mem. nat. adv. bd. Am. Security Coun., Washington, 1981-82; charter mem. Franklin Mint Assn., 1968—; asst. scoutmaster Boy Scouts Am., 1994—. With U.S. Army, 1972-78, Panama Canal. Named Aide de Camp, Ala. Gov., 1989, Ky. Col., 1989, Col. Govs.'s Staff, Tenn., 1990. Mem. Nat. Assn. Realtors, Fla. C. of C., U.S. C. of C. (state dir. 1980), Fla. Jaycees (bd. dirs. 1980-81), U.S. Jaycees (Goodwill Amb. 1974—), Am. Entrepreneurs Assn. Democrat. Episcopalian. Office: Realty Svcs of South Suite D 801 Jenks Ave Ste D Panama City FL 32401-2569

LAWRENCE, JOYCE WAGNER, health facility administrator, educator; b. N.Y.C., Apr. 3, 1942; d. Edward William and Bertha Beatrice (Merz) Wagner; m. William Robert Lawrence, Feb. 9, 1969; 1 child, Rebecca Suzanne. Diploma, Washington Hosp. Ctr., 1963; BS, St. Joseph's Coll., Windham, Maine, 1990. Cert. health care mgr., Va. Supr. Profl. Support Svcs., Virginia Beach, Va.; supr., asst. dir. nursing Med. Staff Svcs., Virginia Beach; supr. Health Care Resources, Inc., Norfolk, Va.; corp. dir., instr., coord. med./cna programs Tidewater Tech, Virginia Beach, Va.; instr. nurse aide program LTH, Norfolk. Lt. (j.g.) USNR, 1968-70. Recipient South Hampton Rds. Women-In-Transition award YWCA, 1991. Mem. Oncology Nurses Assn. (chmn., sec. local chpt.), Hampton Roads Home Health Assn. (chmn. com.), Southeastern Va. Am. Soc. Tng. and Devel., ABWA. Home: 1617 Ashton Dr Virginia Beach VA 23464-7717

LAWRENCE, KATHY, medical, surgical, and radiology nurse; b. Searcy, Ark., Dec. 9, 1949; d. S.V. and Pearl (Bolden) Smith; children: Ryan, Damon. ADN, Odessa (Tex.) Coll., 1977; BSN, U. Tex., Galveston, 1992, MSN, 1996. Cert. med. asst., diabetes educator, med.-surg. nurse. Head nurse, acting supr. Med. Ctr. Hosp., Odessa, 1978-80; asst. head nurse Meml. Gen. Hosp., Elkins, W.Va., 1980-81; staff nurse United Hosp. Ctr., Clarksburg, W.Va., 1981-83; field supr. Upjohn/Healthcare Svcs., Midland, Tex., 1983-85; primary nurse, physician's office Naidu Clinic, Odessa, 1985-88; nursing supr. U. Tex. Med. Br., Galveston, 1988-95, case mgr. outcomes evaluation and nursing rsch., 1995—. Mem. ANA, Tex. Nurses Assn., Am. Assn. Diabetes Educators, Am. Assn. Med. Assts. (sec. local chpt.), Am. Assn. Intravenous Therapists, Am. Radiol. Nurses Assn., Am. Assn. Neurosci. Nurses, Am. Med-Surg. Nurses, Case Mgmt. Soc. Am., Intravenous Nurses Soc., Alpha Nu Chi, Sigma Theta Tau. Home: 6315 Central City Blvd Apt 820 Galveston TX 77551-3809

LAWRENCE, KEN, columnist; b. Chgo., Nov. 11, 1942; s. Lawrence Edward and Mary Ewing (Glickauf) Burg; m. Patricia Rose Bridges, Feb. 6, 1964 (div. Sept. 1980); children: Vernon H. Davis, Max E.; m. Elizabeth Ann Sharpe, 1984 (div. Feb. 1993); m. Kathleen Wunderly, Feb. 24, 1995. Student, Shimer Coll., 1959-61, Roosevelt U., 1962-63, 68. Freelance film technician Chgo. and Gary, Ind., 1959-71; corr. Southern Conf. Ednl. Fund, Jackson, Miss., 1971-75; editor Greenwood Press & Univ. Press of Miss., Jackson, 1976; columnist Covert Action Info. Bull., Washington, 1979—, Stamp Collector, Albany, Oreg., 1982-86, Linn's Stamp News, Sidney, Ohio, 1987—, Am. Philatelist, State College, Pa., 1991—; dir. Am. Friends Svc. Com., Jackson, 1977-79, Anti-Repression Resource Team, Jackson, 1979-93. Author: Linn's Plate Number Coil Handbook, 1990, (booklet) The New State Repression, 1980; editor: Mississippi Slave Narratives, 5 vols., 1976, The Philatelic Communicator, 1989-94; contbr. (book) Dirty Work 2-The CIA in Africa, 1979. Trainer United Meth. Voluntary Svc., N.Y.C., 1980-83; organizer Nat. Anti-Klan Network, Atlanta, 1980-85; bd. dirs. South African Mil. Refugee Aid Fund, N.Y.C., 1977-85. Recipient Rosebud, MORE Journalism Rev., 1975, Cert. of Merit, Miss. Hist. Soc., 1976. Mem. Am. Philatelic Soc. (dir.-at-large 1991-93, sec. 1993-95, v.p. 1995—, Rsch. medal 1988), Am. Philatelic Congress, Jackson Philatelic Soc. (v.p. 1990-91, pres. 1992-93), Bur. Issues Assn. (gov. 1989—), The Manuscript Soc. Office: PO Box 8040 State College PA 16803-8040

LAWRENCE, PHENIS JOSEPH, commercial artist; b. Brookville, Ind., Aug. 11, 1926; s. Phenis Woodson Lawrence and Rose (Miller) Lawrence Pattie.; m. Lillian Warnock, Aug. 25, 1956; children: Melody Rose, Timothy Lee, Beverly Vida, Robert Phenis, David Warnock. BAA, U. Fla., 1950. Staff artist Bacon, Hartman & Volbrecht, Inc., St. Augustine, Fla., 1950; art dir. Bacon, Hartman & Volbrecht, Inc., Jacksonville, Fla., 1961-62; silk screen artist RICH's Dept. Store, Atlanta, 1950-51; staff artist Quick & Sacrey, Louisville, Ky., 1951; illustrator, supr. Tng. Facilities NATTC, NAS, Jacksonville, 1951-56; art dir. Miller Press, Inc., Jacksonville, 1956-60; owner, designer P.J. Lawrence Artist, Jacksonville, 1960—; art & prodn. mgr. Prudential Ins. Co., Jacksonville, 1984; freelance artist, Jacksonville, 1960—; corresponding rep. Nat. Soc. Art Dirs, N.Y.C., 1962-66. Art dir., designer, artist, prodn. mgr. numerous comml. works including (slide) Speak up for Value, 1963 (First Place award Advt. Fedn Am., 1964), (logo) Coffee Delite, 1963, (Merit award plaque Art Dirs. Club Jacksonville, 1964), (letterhead) Antique Bottle Collector's Club of Jacksonville, 1973. Chmn. Jr. C. of C. Jacksonville, 1958-60 (Del. Nat. Conv., 1960, cert. of Merit, 1958, Man of Month award, 1960). With USN, 1944-46. Mem. Sigma Phi Epsilon Alumni Assn. (treas. 1966-79), KC (3d and 4th deg.), NRA. Democrat. Roman Catholic. Home: 2014 Woodmere Cir Jacksonville FL 32210-3319 Office: PO Box 2141 Jacksonville FL 32203-2141

LAWRENCE, RAY VANCE, chemist; b. Vance, Ala., July 6, 1910; s. William Monroe and Frances (Ray) L.; m. Barbara New, June 22, 1935; children: Robert Craig, Richard Vance. BS, U. Ala., Tuscaloosa, 1931; MS, U. Tenn., Knoxville, 1933. Instr. chemistry Marion (Ala.) Mil. Inst., 1932-33; chemist TVA, Muscle Shoals, Ala., 1933-38, Naval Stores Sta., Olustee, Fla., 1938-41, Naval Stores Rsch. Div., Washington, 1941-43; head rosin rsch. So. Regional Rsch. Lab., New Orleans, 1943-50; head rosin rsch. Naval Stores Rsch. Lab., Olustee, 1950-58, dir., 1958-73; cons. Naval Stores, Lake City, Fla., 1973—; lectr. terpene chemistry U. Fla., Gainesville, 1953-57; lectr. Nanjing (China) Forestry U., 1979. Columnist, assoc. editor Naval Stores Rev., 1977-90; contbr. articles to profl. jours.; patentee in field. Mem Am. Chem. Soc. (chmn. Fla. sect. 1965, Fla. award 1971), Am. Oil Chemists Soc. Presbyterian. Home and Office: 5900 Wilson Blvd Apt 453 Arlington VA 22205-1550

LAWRENCE, RONALD EUGENE, healthcare company executive; b. Knoxville, Mar. 29, 1942; s. Harley Clyde and Owa Mae (Wood) L.; m. Carolyn B. Adams, Feb. 7, 1993; children: Thomas Michael, Elizabeth Marie, Richard Douglas. BS, U. Tenn., 1964; MBA, The Citadel, 1977. Distbn. analyst Continental Grain Co., St. Louis, 1964-66; plant distbn. mgr. Champion Internat., Courtland, Ala., 1970-72; ops. planning mgr. S.C. State Ports Authority, Charleston, 1972-77; corp. distbn. mgr. Giant Portland Cement Co., Inc., Columbia, S.C., 1977-80; pres. Lawrence Health Care, Inc., Knoxville, 1981—, Farragut Health Care Ctr., Inc., Knoxville, 1984—. Capt. USAF, 1966-70. Mem. Am. Coll. Health Care Adminstrs., Tenn. Health Care Assn. (bd. dirs. 1991), Knoxville C. of C. Office: Lawrence Health Care Inc 10703 Dutchtown Rd Knoxville TN 37932-3208

LAWRIMORE, EUGENE SALMON NAPIER, lawyer; b. Conway, S.C., May 26, 1947; s. Earl Wilson Lawrimore and Mildred Napier (Salmon) McDonald Schofield; m. Katrina van Buskirk Douglass Paris, June 5, 1976; children: Peyton Harrison Napier, Hunter laMastus Powell. BS in Bus. Adminstrn., U. S.C., 1969, JD, 1976. Bar: S.C. 1976, U.S. Dist. Ct. S.C. 1979, U.S. Supreme Ct. 1980. Legis. asst. Sen. Strom Thurmond, Washington, 1976-77; sole practice Georgetown, S.C., 1977-91; ptnr. Adams, Quackenbush, Herring & Stuart, P.A., Georgetown, 1991-93; gen. counsel Timberland Properties, Inc., Myrtle Beach, S.C., 1993—; instr. Horry-Georgetown Tech. Coll., 1977-79. Author: Doctrine of Unseaworthiness in the Fourth Circuit, 1976. Mem. exec. com. S.C. Reps., 1980, State Appeals Bd. Selective Svc. System, 1983—, S.C. State Devel. Bd., 1987-92; mem. exec. com., vice chmn. S.C. State Def. Base Devel. Commn., 1991-94; bd. dirs. Georgetown County Hist. Commn., 1985-88, chmn. 1986-88. Mem. ABA (regional coord. Can. law com. 1993-95), S.C. Bar Assn., Georgetown County Bar Assn. (sec. 1982-83, v.p. 1993-94, pres. 1993-94). Episcopalian. Home: 225 Broad St Georgetown SC 29440-3603 Office: 2594 Thunderbolt Ave Myrtle Beach SC 29577

LAWS, CHARLES GEORGE, mathematics educator, quality engineer; b. Clarksville, Tenn., May 31, 1943; m. Beverly A. Caroll, Aug. 31, 1986; Michele Ann, Rebecca Lynn. BA, Austin Peay State U., 1965; MA, U.

Tenn., 1969. Instr. Tenn. Tech. U., Cookeville, 1968-69; assoc. prof. Cleveland (Tenn.) Community Coll., 1969—; vis. lectr. in statis. U. Tenn., Knoxville, 1981-82; cons., trainer statis. process control John Manville Corp., Etowah, Tenn., 1987-88; instr. CQE/CQT Rev., Davidson/Textron Corp., Athens, Tenn., 1995; instr. introductory stats. and process improvement Duracell Corp., Cleveland, Tenn., 1996; adj. prof. Lee Coll., Cleveland, 1996. Tchr. Sunday sch. class Prospect Ch. of God, Cleveland, 1990—. Mem. Am. Soc. for Quality Control, Nat. Coun. Tchrs. of Maths. Office: Cleveland State Cmty Coll PO Box 3705 Cleveland TN 37320-3705

LAWS, GORDON DERBY, lawyer; b. Dallas, Feb. 1, 1949; s. Wilford Derby and Ruby (Whiteleather) L.; m. Barbara Ruth Hill, May 9, 1974; children: Gordon Derby Jr., Stephen Richard, Ruthanne. BA in Econs., Brigham Young U., 1973, JD, 1976. Bar: Utah 1976, Tex. 1986, U.S. Supreme Ct. 1981, U.S. Ct. Appeals (5th cir.) 1982, U.S. Dist. Ct. (we. dist.) Tex. 1987, U.S. Dist. Ct. (so. dist.) Tex. 1991. Trial atty. U.S. Justice Dept., Washington, 1976-81; asst. U.S. atty. Western Dist. Tex., San Antonio, 1981-87, asst. chief, civil divsn., U.S. atty., 1985-87; assoc. Gary, Thomasson, Hall & Marks, Corpus Christi, Tex., 1987-89; ptnr./mem. Gary, Thomasson, Hall & Marks, 1989—; mem. exec. com. Gary, Thomasson, Hall & Marks,1994—. Bishop Ch. of Jesus Christ of Latter Day Saints, Corpus Christi, 1990-95. Home: 4158 Eagle Dr Corpus Christi TX 78413 Office: Gary Thomasson Hall & Marks 210 Carancahua Ste 500 PO Box 2888 Corpus Christi TX 78403-2888

LAWSON, BEN F., lawyer, international legal consultant; b. Marietta, Okla., Feb. 7, 1939; s. Woodrow W. and Lennie L. (McKay) L.; children: Nicole, Benjamin C. BBA, U. Houston, 1965, JD, 1967. Bar: Tex. 1967. Atty. Monsanto/Burmah Oil, Houston, 1967-72; mgr. internat. acquisitions Oxy (formerly Cities Svc. Co.), Houston, 1972-78; gen. atty. Damson Oil Corp., Houston, 1978-81; gen. counsel, v.p. Newmont Oil Co., Houston, 1981-86; pvt. practice internat. law Houston, 1986—; cons. internat., 1987—. Contbr. numerous articles to profl. jours. Staff sgt. USAF, 1959-65. Fellow Houston Bar Found.; mem. ABA, Am. Corp. Counsel Assn. (chmn. oil and gas com. 1986-87). Republican. Address: 3027 Bernadette Ln Houston TX 77043-1302

LAWSON, BETH ANN REID, strategic planner; b. N.Y.C., Jan. 9, 1954; d. Raymond Theodore and Jean Elizabeth (Frinks) Reid; m. Michael Berry Lawson, Jan. 29, 1983; children: Rayna, Sydney. BA, Va. Tech., 1976; MPA, Golden Gate U., 1983. From systems analyst I to support ops. asst. City of Virginia Beach, Va., 1977-93; water conservation coord. City of Virginia Beach, 1993-94; owner Strategic Planning and Teamwork, Virginia Beach, 1993—; U.S. Army Corps. Engring. Va. Beach Cmty. Devel. Corp.; cons. Va. Beach Cmty. Devel. Corp., 1996, Lifesaving Mus. Va., 1994, Virginia Beach C.A.R.E. Com., 1995, Virginia Beach Rescue Squad, 1992—, Virginia Beach Mcpl. Employees Fed. Credit Union, 1992—, Virginia Beach Resort Area Adv. Commn., 1993, Virginia Beach Conv. and Visitors Devel. Bur., 1991-93. Sunday sch. tchr. Wycliffe Presbyn. Ch., Virginia Beach. Mem. Virginia Beach Rotary Club (Outstanding Employee 1993), Va. Tech. Alumni Assn. (pres. 1982-83). Home: 701 Earl Of Warwick Ct Virginia Beach VA 23454-2910 Office: Strategic Planning and Teamwork 701 Earl Of Warwick Ct Virginia Beach VA 23454-2910

LAWSON, BILLIE KATHERINE, elementary school educator; b. Cleveland, Tenn., Jan. 15, 1943; d. William Taylor and Katherine Beatrice (Kelley) L. BS in Elem. Edn., Lee Coll., 1970; postgrad., Exeter (Eng.) U., 1975; MEd, U. Tenn., 1975; postgrad., Trevecca Nazarene Coll., Nashville, 1989. Cert. elem. tchr., Tenn. Tchr. Prospect Sch., Cleveland, 1970-76, Trewhitt Elem. Sch., Cleveland, 1976—; mem. Gov.'s Coun. Gore del. 3rd Congl. Dist. Conv., Tenn., 1988. Recipient 4-H Leader award, 1985. Mem. NEA (local rep. to nat. conv.), Nat. Coun. Tchrs. of Math., Tenn. Edn. Assn. (local rep. to state conv.), Bradley County Edn. Assn. (treas., sch. rep., mem. coms.), U. Tenn. Alumni Assn., Lee Coll. Alumni Assn. Democrat. Baptist. Home: 198 Charles Cir SE Cleveland TN 37323-8814 Office: Trewhitt Elem Sch 610 Kile Lake Rd SE Cleveland TN 37323-8446

LAWSON, BONNIE HULSEY, psychotherapist; b. Dunnellon, Fla., July 7, 1932; d. Guy Wilton and Katrina (Lanier) Hulsey; 1 child, Christopher Paul. BS, Wake Forest U., Winston-Salem, 1954; MA, Stetson U., Deland, Fla., 1970; PhD, U. Ga., 1980. Asst. prof. Brunswick (Ga.) Coll., 1970-73; assoc. prof. Cen. Fla. U., Orlando, 1974-75; head human rels. sect. U. Ga., Athens, 1980—. Author TV prog.: Controlling Stress, 1981, Premenstrual Syndrome, 1985, HyperCard prog. Working with Adult Learners, 1989, Patient Relations Certificate Program, 1991. Bd. dirs., Hospice of Athens, 1986-88. Home: 441 Oak Tree Sq Athens GA 30606-2222 Office: U Ga Ctr Continuing Edn Athens GA 30602

LAWSON, CAROLE JEAN, religious educator, author, poet; b. San Antonio, June 18, 1944; d. Albert Joseph and Pearl Nettie (Garner) Fuller; m. James Ray Lawson, Sept. 7, 1962; children: Regina Anne (Lawson) Kacho, Clinton Ray. Founder Love Makes the World Go Around in Peace, Ft. Worth, Tex., 1988—; founder, dir. Healing Thru Love Seminars, Ft. Worth, Tex., 1988—; founder Sunshine 'n Rainbows Stress Overcomers, Ft. Worth, 1985-87; founder, head Omni-Vision Pub. and Prodns., Ft. Worth, 1990-93. Pub. editor Omni Vision newsletter, 1985-93; author: To God Be the Glory, poetry collection, 1988-90, My Rocky Mountain High, 1989, The Reflection of God's Smile, 1991. Sec. Lightly Speaking Forum, Ft. Worth, 1987-89; supporter of publicity Campaign for the Earth, 1990-91; founder, pres. Universal World Investments, Omni Vision Ministries, 1993—. Named Honorary Mayan Centurian. Mem. Internat. Platform Assn. Home and Office: 1112 Edney St Fort Worth TX 76115-4317

LAWSON, FRANCES GORDON, child guidance specialist; b. Lexington, Ky., Oct. 20, 1949; d. George Frank and Novella (Thomas) G.; m. Frank Darryl Lawson (div. Sept. 1974); children: Alisa Lynnette, Darlene Lawson-Barber. BA, Ea. Ky. U., 1971, MA, 1979, Rank I cert., 1987. Cert. tchr., counselor, Ky. Tchr. Mary Todd Elem Sch., Fayette County Pub. Schs., Lexington, 1971-82, child guidance specialist Johnson Elem. Sch.,, 1982-92, child guidance specialist Booker T. Washington Elem., 1992—; dir. social svc. Madeline McDowell Breckridge Camp Found. Inc., Lexington, 1987—. Mem. Ky. Sch. Counselors Assn., Fayette County Guidance Assn., Phi Delta Kappa, Delta Sigma Theta. Democrat. Baptist. Home: 3909 Kilgary Cir Lexington KY 40515-5207 Office: Booker T Washington Elem 798 Georgetown St Lexington KY 40508-1023

LAWSON, FRED RAULSTON, banker; b. Sevierville, Tenn., Mar. 26, 1936; s. Arville Raulston and Ila Mary (Lowe) L.; m. Sharon Sheets, Jan. 1, 1982; children: Terry Lee Lawson Akins, Laura Ann Lawson Rathbone, Kristi Watson Newvine. Student, U. Tenn., 1953-59, La. State U. Sch. Banking of South, 1965-68, Harvard Inst. Fin. Mgmt., 1968. From br. mgr. to exec. v.p. Blount Nat. Bank, Maryville, Tenn., 1958-68, pres., 1968-86, also bd. dirs.; pres. Tenn. Nat. Bancshares, Inc., Maryville, 1971-86, Bank of East Tenn., Knoxville, 1986-92; pres., CEO BankFirst, Knoxville, 1993—; mem. Ft. Sanders Alliance Investment Mgrs. Rev. Subcom.; bd. dirs. Fortress Corp., BancInsure. Mem. Blount County Indsl. Devel. bd., 1969—; chancellors assoc. U. Tenn., Knoxville, 1971-78; trustee Carson-Newman Coll., Jefferson City, 1984-94, Harrison-Chilhowee Bapt. Acad., Seymour, Tenn., 1972-85, Pellissippi State Found., 1989-96; adv. bd. U. Tenn. Med. Rsch. Ctr. and Hosp.; bd. regents Mid-South Sch. banking, Memphis, 1982-90; bd. dirs. Thompson Cancer Survival Ctr., Knoxville, 1987—, The Downtown Orgn., Tenn. Resource Valley, East Tenn. Hist. Soc., Maryville Coll., 1995—. Recipient Tenn. Indsl. Devel. Vol. award, 1977. Mem. Assn. Bank Holding Cos. (bd. dirs. 1978-82), Tenn. Bankers Assn. (chmn. state legis. com. 1980, banking practice com. 1983, bd. dirs. 1990—, pres. 1994-95). Republican. Baptist. Home: 2101 Cochran Rd Maryville TN 37803-2812

LAWSON, KAROL ANN, art museum curator; b. Davenport, Iowa, Nov. 10, 1958; d. Kenneth Leslie and Alice Jean (Peard) L. AB magna cum laude, Sweet Briar Coll., 1981; MA in Art History, U. Va., 1983, PhD in Art History, 1988. Program officer Arts Am. USIA, 1983; instr. in art history St. Mary's Coll. Md., 1986; curatorial assoc. and rsch. asst. Nat. Mus. Am. Art/Smithsonian Instn., Washington, 1987-91; curator of art The Columbus (Ga.) Mus., 1991-92, dir. of collections, 1992—; lectr. in field. Author articles on American landscape images, cartography and portraits. Va. Steele Scott Found. fellow The Huntington Libr. and Art Collections, 1992, Jeannette D. Black Meml. fellow, John Carter Brown Libr., Brown U., 1987, grad. fellow Va. Mus. of Fine Arts, 1984-85; recipient predoctoral fellowship Nat. Mus. Am. Art, Smithsonian Instn., 1985-86. Mem. Coll. Art Assn., Am. Soc. Eighteenth-Century Studies, Assn. Historians of Am. Art, Am. Assn. Mus., Am. Studies Assn., Southeastern Mus. Conf. Office: The Columbus Mus 1251 Wynnton Rd Columbus GA 31906-2810

LAWSON, MARY CAROLYN, elementary education educator; b. Ironton, Ohio, Nov. 23, 1941; d. LeRoy Davis Lawson and Elizabeth Alice (Fields) Fleck; children: Adam Wade Roach, Seth Joseph Roach, Paul Edwin Roach (dec.), Margaret Lawson Johnson. BA, U. South Fla., 1965, MA, 1988; student, East Carolina U., 1969-70, East Carolina U., 1982, UNC-Chapel Hill, 1970. Tchr. Washington County Schs., Plymouth, N.C., 1967-71; tchr. Hillsborough County Schs., Tampa, Fla., 1982-83, 1986—; sec. S.W. Fla. Coalition for Social Studies, 1990-95. Author various poems, monographs; painter, photographer. Altar guild St. John's Episcopal Ch., Tampa, 1995-96; convener Internat. Order of St. Luke the Phys., Tampa, 1996. Mem. Internat. Reading Assn., Hillsborough County Reading Assn., Phi Delta Kappa. Democrat. Episcopalian. Home: USF 30907 Tampa FL 33620 Office: Hillsborough Cty Schs 901 E Kennedy Blvd Tampa FL 33602-3507

LAWSON, MELANIE KAY, management administrator, early childhood consultant; b. Fort Valley, Ga., Feb. 8, 1955; d. William C. and Mamie Nell (Brown) Chapman; m. Robert Scott Lawson, Dec. 18, 1975; children: Robert Scott Jr., Joshua Cody, Ashley Jeanell. AA, Cisco Jr. Coll., 1984; BE in Elem./Spl. Edn., Hardin-Simmons U., 1988, MEd in Reading, 1990; MEd in Sch. Adminstrn., Abilene Christian U., 1992; MEd in Higher Edn., Tex. Tech. U., 1996. Cert. reading specialist, supr., mid-mgmt. tchr. Speech pathology asst. Head Start/Abilene Ind. Sch. Dist., Abilene, Tex., 1983-84; assoc. tchr. Head Start/AISD, Abilene, Tex., 1984-88, cert. tchr., 1988-90; English as second lang. tchr. AISD-Curriculum div., Abilene, Tex., 1990-92; kindergarten tchr. AISD-Long Elem. Sch., Abilene, Tex., 1992-93; asst. dir. Child Devel. Ctr., Dyess AFB, Tex., 1993-94; tng. mgr. 7 SVS Squadron, Dyess AFB, Tex., 1994—. Mem. Youth Task Force, Abilene City Govt., 1994-95, Higher Edn. Working Group, Tex. Head Start Collaboration Project; coord. Taylor County Work and Family Planning Series Conf., Tex. Workforce Commn., 1996-97. Recipient Key City Reading award Reading Coun., 1988. Mem. AAUW, Internat. Reading Assn., Nat. Assn. Edn. of Young Children (Membership Affiliate grant 1994, academy mentor 1995—, validator 1993—), Tex. Assn. Edn. of Young Children (at-large, Tex. Affiliate grant, 1993, 94, exec. bd., chair accreditation, Pres.'s Trust Fund Scholarship 1996), Big Country Assn. for Edn. of Young children (membership chair 1988-90, pres. 1992-94, state repl 1992-94), Tex. Assn. for Gifted/Talented (grant 1991), Coun. Early Childhood Profl. Recognition (rep. 1993—), Golden Key Honor Soc., Kappa Delta Phi, Phi Delta Kappa. Baptist. Home: 1702 Yorktown Dr Abilene TX 79603-4216 Office: 7 SVS Squadron 309 Fifth St Dyess AFB TX 79607

LAWSON, NANCY KATHERINE, medical/surgical nurse; b. Greenville, Miss., May 16, 1961; d. Carl Frederick and Nancy Long (Ruscoe) L. AA, U. Cen. Fla., 1984; BSN, U. South Fla., 1991, postgrad., 1991—. Staff nurse Tampa Gen. Hosp., Davis Islands, Fla.; home health nurse Home Health Care, 1992—. 2d lt. USAF, 1984.

LAWSON, SUSAN COLEMAN, lawyer; b. Covington, Ky., Dec. 4, 1949; d. John Clifford and Louise Carter Coleman; m. William Henry Lawson, June 6, 1980; 1 child, Philip. BA, U. Ky., 1971, JD, 1979. Bar: Ky. 1979. Ptnr. Lawson & Lawson, P.S.C., Harlan, 1995—; atty. Stoll, Keenon & Park, Lexington, Ky., 1979-80; atty., Harbert Constrn. Co., Middlesboro, Ky., 1980-81; ptnr. Buttermore, Turner, Lawson & Boggs, P.S.C., Harlan, Ky., 1981-94. Elder 1st Presbyn. Ch., Pineville, Ky., 1986—. Mem. ABA, Ky. Bar Assn., Harlan County Bar Assn. (pres. 1983), Order of Coif. Democrat. Home: 511 W Kentucky Ave Pineville KY 40977-1307 Office: PO Box 837 103 N 1st St Harlan KY 40831

LAWSON, WILLARD FRANCIS, JR., paper company owner, sales executive; b. Greensboro, N.C., Apr. 28, 1947; s. Willard Francis Sr. and Frances (Lee) L.; m. Katherine Elizabeth Whitlock, Aug. 3, 1947; children: Kevin, Katherine. BSBA, E. Carolina U., 1970; postgrad., N.C. State U., 1973, Fashion Inst. Tech., N.Y.C., 1976-77. Various positions Mt. Hope Finishing Co., Inc., Butner, N.C., 1970-75; with sales Mt. Hope Finishing Co. N.Y., N.Y.C., 1975-79; regional sales mgr. Orchard Corp. Am., St. Louis, 1979-82; product mgr. Häfele, High Point, N.C., 1982-86; pres., owner Lawson Paper Co., Inc., Statesville, N.C., 1986—; chmn., bd. dirs. Young Life. Adminstrv. bd. chmn. New Salem United Meth. Ch., Statesville, 1989—; officer Iredell County (N.C.) Youth Athletic Assn., 1986-89; chmn. bd. dirs. Young Life. Mem. Color Mktg. Group, Plywood Paneling Coun. (assoc.), Laminating Materials Assn. Republican. Office: Lawson Paper Co Inc 233 Nottingham Cir Statesville NC 28677-8201

LAWSON, WILLIAM DAVID, III, retired cotton company executive; b. Jackson, Miss., Oct. 30, 1924; s. William David Jr. and Elizabeth Vaiden (Barksdale) L.; m. Elizabeth Coppridge Smith, June 9, 1948; children: Margaret Monroe, William David IV, Susan Barksdale, Thomas Nelson. BS, Davidson Coll., 1948; MBA, U. Pa., 1949. Trainee T.J. White and Co., Memphis, 1949-52; v.p. W.D. Lawson and Co., Gastonia, N.C., 1952-70, pres., 1971-81; pres. Lawson, Lewis & Peat, Gastonia, 1981-85, Lawson Cotton Co., Gastonia, 1985-95; v.p. Hohenberg Bros. Co. div. Cargill Inc., Memphis, 1988-95; ret., 1995; hon. dir. 1st Union Nat. Bank, Gastonia. Bd. dirs. Sister Cities Com., Gastonia; elder Presbyn. Ch. 1st lt. infantry, U.S. Army, WWII. Named Cotton Man of Year Cotton Digest, 1969, 76. Mem. Nat. Cotton Coun. (advisor; pres. 1975-76), Am. Cotton Shippers Assn. (pres. 1968-69), Atlantic Cotton Assn. (pres. 1957-58), Cotton Coun. Internat. (pres. 1972-73), Am. Cotton Exporters Assn. (pres. 1979-80), Newcomen Soc., Gaston County C. of C. (pres. 1972-73), Am. Legion, Gaston Country Club, Gastonia City Club, Rotary (pres. 1964-65, dist. gov. 1995-96), Kappa Sigma. Clubs: Gaston Country, Gastonia City. Home: 1341 Covenant Dr Gastonia NC 28054-3816

LAWSON DONADIO, CAROLINA ANNA, foreign language educator, translator; b. Naples, Italy, Mar. 11, 1920; d. Joseph and Concetta (Bartolomeo) Donadio; m. Allan Leroy Lawson, Sept. 15, 1945; 1 child, John. Laurea in European langs., lit., instns., Western Group Instituto Universitario Orientale, Naples, Italy, 1946; PhD in French and Italian, Tulane U., 1971. Lectr. overseas div. U. Md., Leghorn, Italy, 1952; tchr. Warren Easton High Sch., New Orleans, 1958-61; teaching asst. Tulane U., New Orleans, 1961-64; instr. Tex. Christian U., Ft. Worth, 1964-65; lectr. Downtown ctr., U.Chgo., 1967-73, U. Akron, Ohio, 1975-76; pvt. practice lectr., translator, ind. scholar, freelance writer Moncks Corner, S.C., 1985—; vis. prof. Kent (Ohio) State U., 1977-84. Author: (textbook) Nuove Letture di Cultura Italiana, 1975; fgn. lang. editl. reviewer Ency. Brit. Chgo., 1971; rev. editor: Italian Culture, 1981-84; contbr. many articles and revs. in lit. criticism, art history, textbooks of fables, fairy tales and biographies to profl. and fgn. lang. publs. Recipient cert. of proficiency in Japanese lang. and culture Tokyo Coll., 1958. Mem. MLA, Am. Assn. Tchrs. of Italian, Am. Assn. Italian Studies, Am. Assn. Tchrs of French, Nat. Italian-Am. Found. Republican. Roman Catholic.

LAWSON-JOWETT, M. JULIET, lawyer; b. Mobile, Ala., May 26, 1959; d. William Max Lawson and Perina Juliet (Barich) Franc; m. Adam Geoffrey Jowett; 1 child, Caitlin Victoria Jowett. BA, U. Miss., 1981, JD, 1987. Bar: Miss. 1988, U.S. Dist. Ct. (no. and so. dists.) Miss. 1988. Tchr. Ocean Springs (Miss.) Sch. System, 1981-85; atty. Ronald W. Lewis & Assocs., Oxford, Miss., 1988-89; ptnr. occupl. hearing loss and hand-arm vibration syndrome Scruggs, Millette, Lawson, Bozeman & Dent, P.A., Pascagoula, Miss., 1989—; cons. Occupational Hearing Loss, P.A., 1989—. Contbr. articles to profl. jours. Mem. Walter Anderson Players, Ocean Springs, 1973-96. Mem. ABA, ATLA (chmn. occupational hearing loss litigation group 1990-94), Miss. Trial Lawyers Assn. (editor 1990-92), Magnolia Bar Assn. Democrat. Roman Catholic. Office: Scruggs Millette Lawson Bozeman & Dent PA 610 Delmas Ave Pascagoula MS 39567-4227

LAWTON, JOSEPH BENJAMIN, IV, commercial and residential interior designer; b. Orlando, Fla., Feb. 18, 1941; s. Joseph Benjamin III and Madalyne Beryl (Schimpf) L.; m. Karen Marie Murphy, Sept. 12, 1964; children: Kevin Michael, William Joseph. BBS, U. Miami, 1963. Pre-press/salesman Lawton Printers, Inc., Orlando, 1953-60; salesman Burdine's, Miami, Fla., 1962-63, exec. trainee, 1963-64, assoc. buyer, 1964-68, buyer, 1968-71, home fashion dir., 1971-75, home furnishings fashion dir., 1975-82; pres. Kartell USA, Inc., Greenville, S.C., 1982-88, JKL Design, Greenville, S.C., 1988—; mem. S.C. Arts Commn., 1991=-94, State Art Acquisitions Com., 1993-94, Design ARts Com.; mem. Met. Arts Coun. Designed Fla. Retrospective, 1976, East Meets West, Indonesia, 1980, Ireland Mist and Magic, 1982, AIA-Am. Soc. Interior Designers, Dallas, 1986, Columbia Mus. Kartell Retrospective, 1987, Contemporary Furniture Show, Javits, N.Y., 1987, Internat. Home Furnishings Show, High Point, N.C., 1983-88, Tahoe South, Rose Marie's Cafe, Bijou and Crescent City Grille Restaurants, Mercedes/Jaguar Showroom, Greenville. Pres. Plantation (Fla.) Police Athletic League, 1978-80; chmn. founder's night Peace Ctr. Performing Arts, Greenville, 1991; bd. dirs. Greenville Symphony Orch., 1989-93, design chmn. ball, 1989-91, chmn. design and lighting Pops Orch., 1991-93, Upstate Visual Arts Bd., 1994—. With U.S. Army, 1963-69. Recipient Citizen of Yr. award City of Plantation, 1980, Entree packaging award Housewares, 1985, Addy point-of-purchase award Am. Advt. Fedn., 1985, Addy Consumer Mag. award, 1985. Mem. S.C. Crafts Assn. (treas. 1987-92, bd. dirs. Yr. Am. Craft, state chmn. 1990—), Guild Greenville Symphony (hon. life), West Edn. Assn. (bd. dirs. 1986-90), Rotary. Republican. Roman Catholic. Home and Office: 4 Faversham Cir Greenville SC 29607-3648

LAXMINARAYANA, DAMA, geneticist, researcher; b. Hyderabad, India, Apr. 20, 1953; came to U.S., 1990; m. Dara Jayalakshmi; children: Dama Bhargavi, Dama Sriharsha. BSc, Osmania U., Hyderabad, 1974, MSc, 1976, PhD, 1982. Jr. sci. asst. dept. genetics Osmania U., 1977-78, lectr. dept. zoology, 1985-90; jr. rsch. fellow Indian Dept. Atomic Energy, 1978-81, postdoctoral fellow, 1982-85, rsch. assoc., 1983-85; postdoctoral fellow dept. medicine Case Western Res. U. Sch. Medicine, Cleve., 1990-91; rsch. assoc. dept. internal medicine Bowman Gray Sch. Medicine, Wake Forest U., Winston-Salem, N.C., 1991-94, rsch. instr., 1994—; conf. presenter in field. Contbr. articles to sci. jours., chpts. to books. Recipient internat. award Tata Meml. Trust, 1985; grantee Univ. Grants Commn. india, 1988-90, Lupus Found. Am., 1993-95, 96—. Mem. AAAS, Environ. Mutagen Soc. India, India Soc. Cell Biology, Soc. Geneticists and Cytologists India, N.Y. Acad. Scis. Home: 230 Melrose St Apt D Winston Salem NC 27103-1950 Office: Bowman Gray Sch Medicine Dept Internal Medicine Medical Center Blvd Winston Salem NC 27157

LAXSON, RUTH KNIGHT, artist; b. Roanoke, Ala, July 16, 1924; d. Edward Wilts and Ruby Melinda (Dunson) Knight; m. C.R. King, Nov. 29, 1942 (div. Aug. 1946); 1 child, Claude Roland King Jr.; m. Robert Earl Laxson, Jan. 31, 1953. Student, Atlanta Coll. Art, 1965-70. resident fellow Hambridge Ctr., 1995. One-women shows include Emory U., Atlanta, 1984, Nexus Contemporary Art Ctr., Atlanta, 1986, Book Exhibit Press, Atlanta, 1987, Lullwater Estates Salon, Atlanta, 1990, Atlanta Coll. Art, 1991, Pagination Exhibit Press 63 Plus, Atlanta, 1992, Letter Works and Sculpture/Arts Festival of Atlanta, 1995, Bookworks/U. Iowa, 1996; exhibited in group shows Tula Found. Gallery, Atlanta, 1991, San Antonio Art Inst., 1991, Rolling Stone Press, Atlanta, 1992, City Gallery at Chastain, Atlanta, 1993, Zeitgenossische Handpressendrucke, Hamburg, Germany, 1993, Atlanta Coll. Art, 1994, Banff Ctr., Alta., Can., 1994, Rolling Stone Press, 1996, Art Papers mag., 1996; represented in permanent collections High Mus., Atlanta, Ga. Coun. Arts, Atlanta, Getty Ctr. Mus., Malibu, Calif., Mus. Modern Art, N.Y.C., N.Y.C. Pub. Libr., Yale U., Stanford U., UCLA, U. Alta., Edmonton, Victoria and Albert Mus., London; author: illustrator: Playfulness Works, 1982, (Ho Go)2=It, 1986, Measure-Cut-Stitch, 1987, About Change About, 1989, Some Things Are Sacred, 1991, Imaging, 1991, Wheeling, 1992, Measureup. Grantee Lubo Found., 1990, Ga. Coun. for the Arts-Acquisitions, 1989-90, Dekalb Coun. for the Arts, 1986, NEA, 1980; Installation grantee Arts Festival of Atlanta, 1995. Mem. High Mus. Art (charter), Nexus Contemporary Arts Ctr. (adv. bd. mem. 1980-94), Ctr. for Puppetry Arts. Home: 2298 Drew Valley Rd NE Atlanta GA 30319-3968 Office: Press 63 Plus PO Box 190731 Atlanta GA 31119-0731

LAY, KENNETH LEE, diversified energy company executive; b. Tyrone, Mo., Apr. 15, 1942; s. Omer and Ruth E. (Reese) L.; m. Linda Ann Phillips, July 10, 1982; children: Robyn Anne, Mark Kenneth, Todd David, Elizabeth Ayers, Robert Ray. BA, U. Mo., 1964, MA, 1965; PhD, U. Houston, 1970. Corp. economist Exxon Corp., Houston, 1965-68; asst. prof. and lectr. in econs. George Washington U., 1969-73; tech. asst. to commr. FERC, 1971-72; dep. undersec. for energy Dept. Interior, 1972-74; v.p. Fla. Gas Co. (now Continental Resources Co.), Winter Park, Fla., 1974-76, pres., 1976-79; exec. v.p. The Continental Group, 1979-81; pres., chief operating officer, dir. Transco Energy Co., Houston, 1981-84; chmn., chief exec officer Houston Natural Gas Corp., 1984-85; pres., chief exec. officer, chief operating officer, dir. HNG/InterNorth (now Enron Corp.), Omaha, 1985—, also chmn. bd. dirs., Houston; asst. prof. George Washington U.; bd. dirs. Eli Lilly & Co., Trust Co. West, Compaq Computer Corp.; past chmn. Greater Houston Partnership; mem. President's Coun. on Sustainable Devel. Former chmn. bd. regents U. Houston; bd. trustees The H. John Heinz III Ctr. for Sci., Econs. & the Environment, The Bus. Coun., Am. Enterprise Inst.; Houston Host Com. for 1992 Rep. Nat. Conv.; co-chmn. 1990 Houston Econ. Summit Host. Com. Decorated Navy Commendation award; N.A.M. fellow; State Farm fellow; Guggenheim fellow. Mem. Nat. Petroleum Coun., River Oaks Country Club, Phi Beta Kappa. Republican. Methodist. Office: Enron Corp PO Box 1188 Houston TX 77251-1188

LAY, NORVIE LEE, law educator; b. Cardwell, Ky., Apr. 17, 1940; s. Arlie H. and Opha (Burns) L.; 1 dau., Lea Anne. B.S., U. Ky., 1960; J.D., U. Louisville, 1963; LL.M. (Cook fellow), U. Mich., 1964, S.J.D., 1967. Bar: Ky. 1963. Asst. prof. law U. Louisville, 1964-67, assoc. prof., 1967-70, prof., 1970—; asst. dean U. Louisville (Sch. Law), 1971-73, assoc. dean, 1973-84, acting dean, 1981-82; vis. prof. Southwestern U. Sch. Law, summer 1983, N.Y. Law Sch., 1983-84, Coll. of Law U. Iowa, summer 1989. Author: Tax and Estate Planning for Community Property and the Migrant Client, 1970; contbr. articles to profl. jours. Trustee St. Joseph's Infirmary, 1974-78, S.W. Jefferson Community Hosp., 1979-80, Suburban Hosp., 1981-84, Humana-Audubon Hosp., 1985-88, U. Louisville Law Sch. Alumni Found., from 1982-85; bd. dirs. Louisville Ballet, from 1982-88, Louisville Theatrical Assn., 1985-88, Louisville Art Gallery, 1984-87, Watertower Art Assn., 1986-89, Chamber Mus. Soc. of Louisville, 1985-88, Louisville Chorus, 1985-88, Ky. Contemporary Theatre, 1984, Ky. Country Day Sch., 1985-88, Ky. Arts Coun., 1991—; mem. Nat. Conf. Commrs. Uniform State Laws. Recipient Scholarship Key Delta Theta Phi, 1963, Outstanding Graduating Sr. award Omicron Delta Kappa, 1963. Fellow Am. Coll. of Trust and Estate Counsel (acad.), Am. Coll. Tax Counsel; mem. ABA, Ky. Bar Assn., Louisville Bar Assn., Am. Judicature Soc. Republican. Baptist. Office: U Louisville Sch Law Belknap Campus Louisville KY 40292

LAY, WILLIAM MAXWELL, JR., business educator, economics researcher; b. Chattanooga, Aug. 16, 1948; s. William Maxwell Sr. and Oma Garnett (Lowry) L.; m. Velda-Rae Luise Neal, June 1971; children: Robert Briarstone, Jonathan Maxwell. BA, Bob Jones U., 1971; ThM, Dallas Theol. Sem., 1975; MBA, Amber U., 1983; DA, Mid. Tenn. State U., 1993. Ops. officer InterFirst Bank, Dallas NA, 1980-85; cash mgmt. officer Bank of Va., Richmond, 1985-87; asso. prof. bus., head dept. bus., chair div. social sci. Bryan Coll., Dayton, Tenn., 1988—; v.p. publs. Tenn. Econs. Assn., 1996—. Editor: The Jour. of the Tennessee Econs. Assn., 1995, mng. 1996—; editor, pub.: Bryan Bus. Newsletter, 1994—; contbr. articles to profl. jours. Mem. Am. Econ. Assn., Phi Kappa Phi, Omicron Delta Epsilon, Beta Gamma Sigma. Republican. Office: Bryan Coll PO Box 7678 Dayton TN 37321-7000

LAYFIELD, LESTER JAMES, pathologist, educator. BS magna cum laude, U. Calif., Irvine, 1974; MD, UCLA, 1979. Diplomate in anatomic and clin. pathology Am. Bd. Pathology; diplomate Nat. Bd. Med. Examiners; lic. physician, Calif., N.C. Intern U. Wash., Seattle, 1979-80; resident UCLA, 1980-83, chief resident, 1983-84, adj. asst. prof. pathology, 1983-84, asst. prof. dept. pathology, 1984-89, assoc. prof., 1989-90; assoc. prof. dept. pathology U. Iowa Hosps. and Clinics, Iowa City, 1990-92; assoc. prof. dept. pathology Duke U. Med. Ctr., Durham, N.C., 1992—, dir. image analysis lab., 1992—, chief surg. pathology, 1993—; pathologist Childrens Cancer Study Group UCLA, 1984-90, dir. fine needle aspiration svc., 1984-

90; co-dir. cytology U. Iowa Hosps. and Clinics, Iowa City, 1990-92; lectr. cytopathology at local, regional and nat. workshops. Contbr. articles to profl. jours., chpts. to books. Am. Cancer Soc. jr. fellow, 1982. Mem. Am. Soc. Clin. Pathologists, Arthur Purdy Stout Soc., Phi Beta Kappa. Office: Duke U Med Ctr Dept Pathology Durham NC

LAYMAN, DAVID MICHAEL, lawyer; b. Pensacola, Fla., July 28, 1955; s. James Hugh and Winifred (Smith) L. BA with high honors, U. Fla., 1977, JD with honors, 1979. Bar: Fla. 1980. Assoc. Gunster, Yoakley, Criser & Stewart, West Palm Beach, Fla., 1980-83; assoc. Wolf, Block, Schorr & Solis-Cohen, West Palm Beach, 1983-87, ptnr., 1987-88; shareholder Shapiro and Bregman P.A., 1988-91, Greenberg, Traurig, Hoffman, Lipoff, Rosen & Quentel, P.A., West Palm Beach, Fla., 1991-93, Prom, Korn & Zehmer, P.A., Jacksonville, Fla., 1993-94, Mahoney Adams & Criser, P.A., Jacksonville, Fla., 1994-96, Greenberg, Traurig, Hoffman, Lipoff, Rosen & Quentel P.A., West Palm Beach, Fla., 1996—; mem. Attys. Title Ins. Fund. Contbg. editor U. Fla. Law Rev.; contbr. articles to profl. jours. Del. Statewide Rep. Caucus, Orlando, Fla., 1986; mem. Blue Ribbon Zoning Rev. Com., West Palm Beach, 1986; bd. dirs., pres. Palm Beach County Planning Congress, 1984-89; trustee South Fla. Sci. Mus., 1994-96; bd. dirs., sec., v.p. Ronald McDonald House, Jacksonville, 1994-96, Cultural Coun. of Greater Jacksonville. Named one of Outstanding Young Men in Am., 1980. Mem. ABA, Fla. Bar Assn. (bd. govs. young lawyers divsn. 1989-91), Palm Beach County Bar Assn. (pres. young lawyers sect. 1987-88), Fla. Blue Key, Palm Beach County Gator Club (pres., bd. dirs.), Omicron Delta Kappa, Sigma Chi, Phi Kappa Phi. Episcopalian. Office: 777 S Flagler Dr Ste 310E West Palm Beach FL 33401-6162

LAYNE, JOHN FRANCIS, accountant; b. Milw., Mar. 25, 1928; s. Lawrence E. and Blanche E. (Tetzlaff) L. A.A., Valencia Jr. Coll., 1971; B.S. in Bus. Adminstrn., U. Cen. Fla., 1972; m. Esther A. Ornberg, Mar. 10, 1951; children: Loretta E., John W., Mark L. Enlisted USAF, 1948, advanced through grades to chief warrant officer-4, 1964; test contr., systems devel. Air Proving Ground Ctr., Eglin AFB, 1962-65; standardization/evaluation contr. USAF, Far East, Okinawa and Vietnam, 1966-70; ret., 1970; acct. Electric Specialty, Orlando, Fla., 1971-74, controller, 1975-77; fin. field rep. Tupperware div. Dart, Orlando, 1978-90, credit analyst, 1991—. V.p. Cen. Fla. Assn. Sq. Dancers, 1977-78, pres., 1978-79, Couple of Yr. award, 1984, ; chmn. 1978 Fla. Sq. Dance Conv.; active Fla. Fedn. Sq. Dancers, 1978-82, pres., 1982-83; asst. bus. chmn. 46th Nat. Sq. Dance Conv. Decorated Bronze Star, Medal of Honor Republic of Vietnam; recipient Excellence award Far East coun. Boy Scouts Am., 1968, Am. Sq. Dance Soc., 1983. Mem. Nat. Soc. Pub. Accts., Nat. Assn. Enrolled Agts. (emeritus). Home: 1230 Walnut Grove Way Rockledge FL 32955-4630

LAYNE, MARGARET EDITH, environmental services administrator; b. Lynchburg, Va., Nov. 21, 1957; d. Charles S. and Mary Jane (Gannaway) L.; m. Bruce R. Locke, Aug. 15, 1981. BE in Environ. and Water Resources, Vanderbilt U., 1980; MS in Water Resources Engring., U. N.C., 1984. Registered profl. engr., N.C., Fla., Ga. Environ. engr. Bechtel Group, Inc., San Francisco, 1980-81, Houston, 1981-82; environ. engr. Hazen and Sawyer, Raleigh, N.C., 1984-86; environ. engr. Rsch. Triangle Inst., Research Triangle Park, N.C., 1986-88, rsch. environ. engr., 1988-89; sr. engr. ABB Environ. Svcs., Inc., Tallahassee, 1989-90, project mgr., 1990-91, sr. project mgr., 1991-95, ops. mgr., 1995—. Mem. NSPE, ASCE, Soc. Women Engrs. (bd. dirs. 1990—). Home: 4108 Zermatt Dr Tallahassee FL 32303-2252 Office: ABB Environ Svcs Inc 2590 Executive Center Cir Tallahassee FL 32301

LAYSON, WILLIAM MCINTYRE, research consulting company executive; b. Lexington, Ky., Sept. 24, 1934; s. Zed Clark and Louise (McIntyre) L.; m. Robin Dale Fort, July 28, 1982. B.S., MIT, 1956, Ph.D., 1961; postgrad., U. Sydney, Australia, 1957-58. Research scientist European Ctr. Nuclear Research, Geneva, 1960-62; research scientist U. Calif.-Berkeley, 1962-64; mem. tech. staff Pan Am World Airways, Patrick AFB, Fla., 1964-67; research scientist Gen. Research Corp., Rosslyn, Va., 1967-70; dir. Sci. Applications Internat. Corp., McLean, Va., 1970—, sr. v.p., chmn. incentives com., 1975-93; coord. def. nuclear programs, 1975—, chmn. ethics com., 1994—; pres. Langley Sch., 1995—; dir. Langley Sch., 1992—; pres. Layson's Buffalo Trace Farms, 1976—. Fulbright scholar U. Sydney, Australia, 1957-58. Mem. Am. Def. Preparedness Assn. Democrat. Presbyterian (elder). Home: 8301 Summerwood Dr Mc Lean VA 22102-2213 Office: Sci Applications Internat Corp 1710 Goodridge Dr Mc Lean VA 22102-3701

LAYTON, CHRISTOPHER JAMES, legislative liaison; b. New Castle, Pa., Dec. 31, 1969; s. James Charles and Carole Roswell (Lynch) L.; m. Rebecca Lynn Nations. BA in History, Coll. of William and Mary, 1992; MPA, Va. Commonwealth U., 1995. Inquiry supr. Va. Innovations Group, Richmond, 1994; legis. intern Va. Assn. of Counties, Richmond, 1994-95; legis. liaison City of Suffolk, Va., 1995—. Bd. dirs. Western Tidewater CSB, Suffolk, 1995—, Tidewater Regional Group Home, Chesapeake, 1996—, Children's Resources Hampton Roads, Chesapeake, 1996—. Mem. Am. Soc. Pub. Adminstrn., Internat. City Mgrs. Assn. Home: 5 Lavelle Ct Williamsburg VA 23185 Office: City of Suffolk 441 Market St Suffolk VA 23434

LAYTON, GARLAND MASON, lawyer; b. Boydton, Va., Aug. 20, 1925. LLB, Smith-Deal-Massey Coll. Law, 1952; LLD, Coll. of William and Mary, 1962. Bar: Va. 1951, U.S. Dist. Ct. (ea. dist.) Va. 1961, U.S. Supreme Ct. 1968. Sole practice Virginia Beach, Va., 1952—; of house counsel Layton & Layton Enterprises, Inc. Served with USMC, 1940-45, PTO. Mem. ABA, Fed. Bar Assn., Nat. Lawyers Club, Va. Beach Bar Assn. Democrat. Methodist. Office: 4809 Baybridge Ln PO Box 5211 Virginia Beach VA 23455

LAYTON, ROBERT GLENN, radiologist; b. Bklyn., Oct. 14, 1946; s. Irving and Charlotte (Bell) L.; m. Judith Helene Bohrer, May 31, 1969; children—Andrew, Julia. B.S., Union Coll., 1968; M.D., Boston U., 1972. Diplomate Am. Bd. Radiology. Resident in radiology, Boston City Hosp., 1972-75; jr. attending radiologist L.I. Jewish Hosp., Hillside, N.Y., 1975-76; staff radiologist Cedars Med. Ctr., Miami, Fla., 1978—; radiologist Highland Park Gen. Hosp., Miami, 1978-84; clin. asst. prof. U. Miami Sch. Med., 1985—. Pres., Michael-Ann Russell Jewish Community Ctr., Miami, 1980-82; bd. dirs. Jewish Community Ctrs. S. Fla., 1982-86; trustee Temple Sinai of North Dade, North Miami Beach, 1982—, v.p., 1985-92, pres., 1992-94. Served to maj. USAF, 1976-78. Mem. AMA, Am. Coll. Radiology, Am. Inst. Ultrasound in Medicine, Miami Radiol. Soc., Begg Soc., Alpha Omega Alpha. Jewish. Avocations: contemporary art, tennis, skiing. Office: Cedars Med Ctr Dept Radiology 1400 NW 12th Ave Miami FL 33136-1003

LAYTON, WILLIAM G., medical center administrator; b. Balt., Aug. 1, 1943; s. William H. and Jean Marie (Diener) L.; m. Suszanna E. Layton, Jan. 1, 1980; 1 child, Chrysanna E. Paramedic, Cen. Fla. Community Coll., Ocala, 1980. Lic. EMT. Paramedic Munroe Regional Med. Ctr., Ocala, 1980, supr. ambulance svc., 1981, mgr. ambulance svc., 1984, dir. ambulance svc., 1989—; v.p. Fla. Regional 6 C.I.S.D.; founder, dir., treas. N. Cen. Fla. Trauma Agy., 1990-92. Vice chmn. Marion County Emergency Mgmt. Coun., 1992—; mem. Withlacoochee Regional Local Emergency Planning Com., Dist. 5, 1990—. Recipient Brian G. McKay award for outstanding contbns. to Emergency Med. Svc. in North Cen. Fla., 1987. Mem. Coun. on Rural Emergency Med. Svc. (past pres., sec.), Emergency Med. Svc. Providers Assn. Fla. (dist. rep.), Am. Trauma Soc. (founding dir., sec. Fla. div.), Fla. Assn. County Emergency Med. Svcs. (bd. dirs. 1994-95), Ocala Civic Theater (bd. dirs. 1995—). Home: 8434 SW 69th Court Rd Ocala FL 34476-8157

LAZAR, RANDE HARRIS, otolaryngologist; b. N.Y.C., Feb. 27, 1951; s. Irving and Dorothy (Tartasky) L.; m. Linda Zishuk, Aug. 11, 1974; 1 child, Lauren K. BA, Bklyn. Coll., 1973; MD, U. Autonoma de Guadalajara, Mexico, 1978; postgrad., N.Y. Med. Coll., 1978-79. Diplomate Am. Bd. Otolaryngology-Head and Neck Surgery; lic. physician, N.Y., Ohio, Tenn. Gen. surgery resident Cornell-North Shore Community Hosp., Manhasset, N.Y., 1979-80; gen. surgery resident Cleve. Clinic Found., 1980-81, otolaryngology-head and neck surgery resident, 1980-84, chief resident dept. otolaryngology & communicative disorder, 1983-84; physician Otolaryngology Cons. Memphis, 1984—; fellow pathology head and neck dept. otolaryngologic pathology Armed Forces Inst. Pathology, Washington, 1983; pediatric otolaryngology fellow Le Bonheur Children's Med. Ctr., Memphis, 1984-85, dir. pediatric otolaryngology fellowship tng., 1989—, chief surgery, 1989, chief staff East Surgery Ctr.; chmn. dept. otolaryngology head and neck surgery Meth. Health Systems, 1990-91; courtesy staff Bapt. Meml. Hosp., Bapt. Meml. Hosp.-East, Eastwood Med. Ctr., Meth. Hosp., Germantown, Tenn.; chief dept. otolaryngology Les Passees Rehab. Ctr., 1988—. Contbr. articles to profl. jours. Bd. dirs. Bklyn. Tech. Found. Recipient award of honor Am. Acad. Otolaryngology-Head and Neck Surgery, 1991. Fellow Internat. Coll. Surgeons; mem. AMA, Am. Acad. Otolaryngology-Head and Neck Surgery, Am. Acad. Facial Plastic and Reconstructive Surgery, Am. Acad. Otolaryngic Allergy, Centurions Deafness Rsch. Found., Am. Auditory Soc., Nat. Hearing Assn., Soc. Ear, Nose Throat Advances in Children, Am. Soc. Laser Medicine and Surgery, So. Med. Assn., N.Y. Acad. Scis., Tenn. Med. Soc., Tenn. Acad. Otolaryngology-Head and Neck Surgery, Memphis and Shelby County Med. Soc., Memphis/Mid South Soc. Pediatrics. Office: Otolaryngology Cons Memphis 777 Washington Ave Ste 240P Memphis TN 38105-4566

LAZENBY, HENRY F., writer, consultant; b. Charleston, Aug. 21, 1950; s. Louis Wayne Sr. L. and Edith Violet Johnson; m. Lois Storms, June 22, 1974. BA, Columbia Internat. U., 1974; MDiv, Covenant Theol. Sem., 1978, ThM, 1979; PhD, Aberdeen U., 1982. Prof. religion and society Oxford Grad. Sch., Dayton, Tenn., 1984-92; dean Am. Ctr. for Religion/Soc. Studies, Oxford, Eng., 1989-93. Author: Orthodoxy-The Struggle for Faith, 1990, A Picnic in Eden, 1994; contbr. article to theol. jours. Served in U.S. Army, 1969-70, Vietnam. Recipient Diplomate award Oxford Soc. Scholars, 1989. Mem. Am. Acad. Religion. Home: 3414 Hill Dr Duluth GA 30136

LE, CAN, mechanical engineer, inventor, author; b. Tam Quan, Vietnam, Dec. 14, 1949; arrived in Guam, 1975; s. Trac and Phung Thi (Nguyen) L. AD, Eastfield Coll., Mesquite, Tex., 1988. Helper dept. mech. engring. U. Tex., Arlington, 1978; ind. designer and programmer Dallas, 1980—. Holder copyrights for multiplication and divsn. integrations, The Accurate PI, program P.V.T. Process, Labor Expansion; program inventor Condodrafters, others. 1st lt. Vietnamese Army, 1969-75. Roman Catholic. Home: 2824 San Diego Dr Dallas TX 75228-1646

LE, THUY XUAN, financial control systems developer, consultant; b. Hanoi, Vietnam, Apr. 25, 1927; came to U.S., 1975; s. Chinh Xuan Le and Ty Thi Tran; m. Thin Thi Dang, Sept. 9, 1957; children: Phuong-Tram, Phuong-Thoa, Tung, Thach. Agrégé Internat. Acctg. Systems, 1970. Adminstrv. specialist U.S. AID, Saigon, Vietnam, 1958-67; acct., cons. Commonwealth Svcs. Inc., Saigon, 1967-70; dir. Biemet, Saigon, 1970-71; gen. mgr. UICC, Saigon, 1971-75; coll. and univ. prof. Saigon, 1971-75; acct., contr. pvt. enterprises Washington, 1975-79; systems acct. D.C. Govt., Washington, 1980-81; dir., fin. control systems MRI, Falls Church, Va., 1981-85; pres. Prajna Instl., Alexandria, Va., 1985—; writer, cons. educator in field, 1957—. Author: Kim-Van-Kieu I, English Translation and Commentaries, 1963, Principles of Advanced Bookkeeping and Accounting, 1971, How to Establish a Uniform Chart of Accounts for Business Enterprises, 1971, How to Establish a Powerful General Ledger System for a Government, 1981; also textbooks in field; translator (poems) Kim-Van-Kieu, 1992 (award of excellence Libr. of Congress 1992), The Super Revelation, 1993, The Prajnaparamita Sutra, 1993, The Soul of Poetry Inside Kim-Van-Kieu, 1995, Dawnlight, 1996. Sec. gen. Puginier Alumni, Saigon, 1971-74; comptr. Assn. Vietnamese Scientists, Saigon, 1972-75. Mem. Internat. Platform Assn. Prajnaparamita yogi. Home and Office: 3701 Fort Worth Ave Alexandria VA 22304-1706

LE, TON DA, horticulturist, researcher; b. Hanoi, Vietnam, Apr. 10, 1935; U.S. citizen; s. Liem Da and Sam Thi; m. Norma Olivia Benitez, Apr. 9, 1981; children: Patricia D., Natalie D., Minh Dang. BSA, U. Fla., 1963, MSA in Fruit Crops, 1965, PhD in Hort. Sci., 1975. Dir.-mgr. Dalat Hort. Expt. Sta., Vietnam, 1965-68; specialist Ministry of Agr., Saigon, Vietnam, 1969-71, Ministry of Edn., Saigon, 1971-72; horticulturist Div. Tropical Rsch., United Brands, La Lima, Honduras, 1976-82; dir. rsch. Frutos Tropicales, S.A., Dominican Republic, 1982-84; horticulturist Chiquita Brands Internat., 1984-86; dir. applied rsch. Chiquita Brands Internat., Fla., 1986-92; dir. agrl. extension and quality assurance Latin Am. ops. Del Monte Fresh Produce Co., San Jose, Costa Rica, 1993-94; dir. tech. svcs. Del Monte Fresh Produce Co., Nogales, Ariz., 1994—. Contbr. articles to profl. jours. Ford Found. fellow, 1975, U.S. AID scholar, 1960-65, 72-75. Mem. Am. Soc. for Hort. Sci., Internat. Soc. for Hort. Sci., Fla. State Hort. Soc., Sigma Xi, Gamma Sigma Delta, Alpha Zeta. Republican. Office: Del Monte Fresh Produce NA 19 Kipper St Rio Rico AZ 85648-6236

LEACH, DOUGLAS EDWARD, history educator, writer; b. Providence, May 27, 1920; s. Arthur Edward and Saidee Waterman (Raybold) L.; m. Brenda Mason, June 24, 1950; children: Carol Lea-Mord, Bradford Raybold. BA, Brown U., 1942; MA, Harvard U., 1947, PhD, 1952. Instr., asst. prof. history Bates Coll., Lewiston, Maine, 1950-56; asst. prof. history Vanderbilt U., Nashville, 1956-59, assoc. prof. history, 1959-64, prof. history, 1964-86. Author: Flintlock and Tomahawk, 1958, Arms for Empire, 1973, Roots of Conflict, 1986, Now Hear This, 1987. Lt. USN, 1942-46. Recipient Fulbright lectureship U. Liverpool, Eng., 1959-60, Fulbright lectureship U. Auckland, New Zealand, 1967, Rsch. fellowship NEH, 1975-76, Harvie Branscomb Disting. professorship Vanderbilt U., 1981-82. Mem. AAUP, Am. Hist. Assn., Orgn. Am. Historians, So. Hist. Assn., Mass. Hist. Soc., Colonial Soc. Mass. Methodist. Office: Vanderbilt Univ Dept History Nashville TN 37235

LEACH, JAMES GLOVER, lawyer; b. Panama City, Fla., Jan. 26, 1948; s. Milledge Glover and Thelma Louise (Hamilton) L.; m. Judith A. Leach, Feb. 26, 1972 (div. 1987); children: Allison, Arica. AS, Gulf Coast Coll., 1968; BA, Duke U., 1970; MBA, Ga. State U., 1974, MI, 1976; JD, Drake U., 1989. Bar: Iowa 1990; CPCU 1977, CLU 1978. Bank officer Bank South, Atlanta, 1972-75; asst. v.p. Johnson & Higgins, Atlanta, 1975-78; pres. Nat. Gen. Ins. Co., St. Louis, 1978-85, AOPA Svc. Corp., St. Louis, 1985-87, Kirke-Van Orsdel Specialty, Des Moines, 1987-89, Gallagher Specialty, St. Louis, 1990-92; prin., dir., counsel Pauli & Co. Inc., St. Louis, 1992-93; gen. counsel Am. Safety Ins., Atlanta, 1993—; cons. McDonnell Douglas, St. Louis, 1987; dir. Gateway Ins. Co., St. Louis, 1992; corp. assembly Blue Cross/Blue Shield, St. Louis, 1991-92. Contbr. articles to profl. jours. 1st lt. USAF, 1970-72, Korea. Home: 2931 Torreya Way Marietta GA 30067 Office: Am Safety Ins Group Ste 200 1845 The Exchange NW Atlanta GA 30339-2022

LEACH, LUANN MARIE, elementary school educator, beauty consultant; b. Grand Rapids, Mich., Oct. 27, 1963; d. Robert Allen and Rose Clare (Williams) L. BS, Western Ky. U., 1989. Gymnastics instr. Pensacola (Fla.) Jr. Coll., 1989-90; elem. phys. edn. tchr. Ferry Pass and Beulah Elem. Sch., Pensacola, Fla., 1989-90, Myrtle Grove and Beulah Elem. Sch., Pensacola, Fla., 1990-92, Myrtle Grove and McArthur Elem. Sch., Pensacola, Fla., 1992-93, Myrtle Grove and Lipscomb Elem. Sch., Pensacola, Fla., 1993-95; gymnastics instr. Dmitri Bilozertchev Gymnastics Tng., Pensacola, Fla., 1995; elem. phys. edn. tchr. Lipscomb and N.B. Cook Magnet Sch. for the Performing Arts, Pensacola, Fla., 1995-96; soccer tchr. Lipscomb's After the Bell Program, Pensacola, Fla., 1996; elem. phys. edn. tchr. Oakcrest and Warrington Elem. Sch., Pensacola, Fla., 1996—; presenter in field. Vol. gymnastics tchr. Ferry Pass, Beulah, Myrtle Grove Elem. Schs., Pensacola, 1989-91; vol. coach Fit to Achieve Teams: Beulah and Myrtle Grove Elem. Schs., Pensacola, 1990-92; vol. tennis coach, coord. 10 teams Pensacola Jr. Tennis Assn., Pensacola, 1993-96; vol. coach Jogging Club for Myrtle Grove and Lipscomb Elem. Schs., Pensacola, 1994-95; Vacation Bible Sch. and Sunday sch. tchr. First Bapt. Ch., Pensacola, Fla., 1996—. Recipient Outstanding Tennis Coach award Pensacola Jr. Tennis Assn., 1993, cert. of achievement for the Model Phys. Fitness Sch. Program Fla. Govs. Coun. on Phys. Fitness and Sports, 1995. Mem. ASCD, Fla. Assn. for Health, Phys. Edn., Recreation, Dance and Driver Edn., Escambia County Phys. Edn. Assn. (sec. 1992). Republican. Home: 3421 Riverside Dr Pensacola FL 32514

LEADER, PAMELA SUSAN, controller; b. Springfield, Mass., Nov. 17, 1957; d. Charles Robert Jr. and Jane (Moody) L. BBA, So. Meth. U., 1984. Security courier Underwood Neuhaus, Dallas, 1976-77; adminstrv. asst. Bee Zee, Inc., Dallas, 1978-80; treas. Moody Oil Co., Inc., Dallas, 1980-91; pres. Moody Oil Co. Inc., Dallas, 1991—; fin. analyst Wyly Family Interests, Dallas, 1984-85; cons., reasercher Future Computing, Dallas, 1985-86; corp. contr. The Hayman Co., Dallas, 1986-91, H.C.I. Gen. Contractors, Inc., Dallas, 1989—; bd. dirs. Moody Oil Co., Inc., Dallas, Great Spaces, Inc., Dallas, H.C.I. Gen. Contractors, Inc., Dallas. Asst. program dir. budget internat. programs So. Meth. U., Dallas, 1984-88. Mem. U.S. Ski Assn., So. Meth. U. Alumni Assn., Energy Club of Dallas, Tanglewood Country Club. Home: 2904 Fondren Dr Dallas TX 75205-1914

LEAHY, LAWRENCE MARSHALL, health care administrator, marketing consultant; b. Astoria, N.Y., Oct. 15, 1949; s. Thomas Joseph and Fannie Marie (Jones) L.; m. Mary Joan Spratt, June 10, 1978; children: Larry, Erin. BS, U. Tenn., 1972; MA, Ball State, 1979; M in Health Care Adminstrn., Baylor U., 1984. Med. platoon leader 8th Med. Bn., Mannheim, Germany, 1972-74, co. comdr., 1974-76; health care adminstr. Walter Reed Army Med. Ctr., Washington, 1976-80; comptroller Dept. of the Army, Washington, 1980-82; info. mgr. Darnall Community Hosp., Killeen, Tex., 1984-86; asst. prof. Acad. Health Scis., San Antonio, 1986-90; exec. officer Seoul (Korea) Community Hosp., 1990-91; fin. analyst Health Svc. Command, San Antonio, 1991-92; exec. dir. Hospice South Tex., 1992-93; adminstr. Hospice New Braunfels, Tex., 1993-94; dir. program integrity Ruth Cons. and Assocs., Victoria, Tex., 1994—; Cons. Tex. A&M U., College Station, 1985; assoc. faculty U. Tex., San Antonio, 1987-88; adj. faculty Trinity U., San Antonio, 1989; asst. prof. Baylor U., Waco, Tex., 1989-90. Author: (with others) Health Planning A Primer, 1990. Explorer adv. Boy Scouts of Am., Washington, 1976-79, Killeen, 1984-85; handicapped scouting com. mem. Nat. Capital Area Com. on Handicapped Scouting, Bethesda, Md., 1978-82; bd. mem. Blue Bonnet Home, Yoakum, Tex., 1989-90. Lt. Col. U.S. Army, 1972-92. Names Outstanding Explorer Adv. Boy Scouts of Am., Bethesda, 1979. Mem. Am. Coll. Healthcare Execs (diplomate, treas. S. Tex. chpt. 1988-90), Coun. Hospice Profls., Tex. Assn. for Home Care (nominating com. 1996—). Republican. Roman Catholic. Home: RR 2 Box 155B Yoakum TX 77995-9535

LEAHY, ROBERT DAVID, communications executive; b. Arlington, Va., Feb. 17, 1952; s. Robert David Joseph and Margaret Ellen (Kennedy) L.; m. Eliabeth Ann McCahey, 1986. BA in Polit. Sci. cum laude, Loyola U., New Orleans, 1974; MA in Internat. Rels., Johns Hopkins U., 1976; postgrad., MIT, 1976-77, NYU, 1984, Brandeis U., 1978. Mem. overseas liaison com. Am. Coun. on Edn., Washington, 1974-76; staff mem. U.S. Dept. Labor, Washington, 1978-79; staff writer Congl. Quar. Inc., Washington, 1979-80; rsch. dir. Ernest Wittenberg Assocs. Inc., Washington, 1980-81; v.p. The Hannaford Co., Inc. (formerly Deaver & Hannaford, Inc.), Washington, 1981-84, Padilla and Speer, Inc., N.Y.C., 1984-85; dir. pub. and media rels. Internat. Telecommunications Satellite Orgn., Washington, 1985-87; v.p. corp. communications Andal Corp., N.Y.C., 1987-89; dir. media communications Internat. Paper, Purchase, N.Y., 1989-93; v.p. corp. rels. Bowater Inc., Greenville, S.C., 1993—. Nat. Investor Rels. Inst., Internat. Assn. Bus. Communicators, Pub. Rels. Soc. Am., Nat. Press Club, Nat. Assn. Mfrs., Conf. Bd., Am. Forest and Paper Assn., World Affairs Coun., Am. Polit. Sci. Assn., Am. Soc. Internat. Law, Ctr. Study of Presidency, Univ. Club (Washington), Georgetown Club (Washington). Republican. Episcopalian. Home: 307 Block House Rd Greenville SC 29615-6003 Office: Bowater Inc 55 E Camperdown Way Greenville SC 29601-3511

LEAHY, ROBERT MAURICE, education educator; b. N.Y.C., June 16, 1947; s. Maurice William and Lillian (Blaise) L. BS in Chemistry, Cortland (N.Y.) Coll., 1969; MEd in Counseling, U. Vt., 1974; PhD in Philosophy of Edn., Cornell U., 1986. Tchr. gen. sci. Nesaquake Jr. High Sch., Smithtown, N.Y., 1969-71; tchr. chemistry Maple Hill High Sch., Castleton-on-Hudson, N.Y., 1971-72; grad. asst. U. Vt., Burlington, 1972-74; grad. asst., rsch. asst. Cornell U., Ithaca, N.Y., 1975-77; instr. philosophy U. Tampa, Fla., 1979-85, Cortland Coll., 1985-86; instr. founds. of edn. Wayne State U., Detroit, 1986-89; assoc. prof. edn., chair dept. edn. Stetson U., De Land, Fla., 1989—; presenter in field. Author: (with Byrnes and Thompson) Comparative Anatomy Study Guide, 1988, also articles. Mem. AACD, Am. Ednl. Studies Assn., Am. Ednl. Rsch. Assn., Fla. Assn. for Tchr. Educators, John Dewey Soc., Philosophy of Edn. Soc., Phi Delta Kappa. Home: 416 N San Souci Ave Deland FL 32720-3435 Office: Divsn Edn PO Box 8419 Deland FL 32720

LEAKE, PRESTON HILDEBRAND, tobacco research executive; b. Proffit, Va., Aug. 8, 1929; s. Perry Hansford and Lydia Viola (Cox) L.; m. Elizabeth Ann Kelly, Dec. 5, 1954; children: Luther Hildebrand, Lawrence Albert. BS, U. Va., 1950; MA, Duke U., 1953, PhD, 1954. Rsch. supr. Allied Chem. Corp., Hopewell, Va., 1954-60; asst. rsch. dir. Albemarle Paper Mfg. Co., Richmond, Va., 1960-65; asst. to mng. dir. The Am. Tobacco Co., Hopewell, 1965-68, asst. mng. dir., 1968-70, asst. R & D dir., 1970-87, dir. R & D, 1987-88, v.p. rsch., 1988-91, ret., 1991; adj. prof. organic chemistry Va. Commonwealth U., 1963-64; tobacco industry rep. to Coun. for Tobacco Rsch., 1977-88; chmn. bd. dirs. Tobacco Inst. Testing Lab., 1977-88; adv. bd. chem. abstracts Va. Jr. Acad. Sci., 1986-88, mem. planning com., 1991-95; mem. Congl. Study Com., 1984-88; expert witness patent suit Toronto, 1993-95. Patentee amino acid synthesis and tobacco cigarette filter; contbr. articles to profl. jours. Chmn. Providence Jr. High Sch. PTA, Midlothian, Va., 1968-70, Clover Hill High Sch. PTA, 1971-72; chmn. bd. trustees Chesterfield County (Va.) Pub. Librs., 1974-77; mem. County Sch. Adv. Com., Chesterfield, 1969-70; judge chemistry sect. Jr. Acad. Sci., 1991-92; mem. Hopewell Community and Indsl. Panel for Environ. Improvement, 1992—. Recipient Army Chem. Corp fellowship, 1950-52, Allied Chem. fellowship, 1952-54. Mem. Am. Chem. Soc. (treas. 1966, sec. 1967, vice chmn. 1968, chmn. 1970, mem. People to People Goodwill Tour to England, Norway, USSR, Czechoslovakia, East and West Germany 1971, Disting. Svc. award 1976), Am. Inst. Chemists (chmn. 1962), Va. Acad. Sci., Computer Users Group (pres. Richmond chpt. 1984-86), James River Catfish Club (keeper of keys 1978-80), Rotary (sec. Hopewell 1992), Sigma Xi, Phi Lambda Upsilon. Home: 401 Delton Ave Hopewell VA 23860-1815

LEAKE, ROBERT EDWARD, JR., lawyer; b. Lake Charles, La., Dec. 2, 1927. LLB, La. State U., 1948. Bar: La. bar 1948, U.S. Supreme Ct. bar 1959. Practice in New Orleans, 1948—; ptnr. Leake & Andersson, 1987—. Fellow Am. Coll. Trial Lawyers; mem. ABA (ho. of dels. 1977-82), Internat. Assn. Def. Counsel (pres. 1978-79), Def. Rsch. Inst. (dir. 1977-79), La. Bar Assn. (gov. 1973-75), New Orleans Bar Assn. (pres. 1985), Fed. Ins. and Corp. Counsel. Office: Leake & Andersson 1100 Poydras St Ste 1700 New Orleans LA 70163-1701

LEAKE, WOODROW WILSON, professional society administrator; b. Rome, Ga., May 17, 1944; s. Woodrow Wilson and Mary Cleo (Brock) Sedberry; m. Patricia Lowe Wafer, Jan. 24, 1985; stepchildren: Jennifer Lowe, Lisa Sherman. BA, Emory U., 1966; PhD in Communications, U. Fla., 1973. Cert. assn. exec. Asst. prof. Valdosta (Ga.) State Coll., 1973-75; prof., dept. chair U. Vt., Burlington, 1975-78; dir. human resources and mktg. Bromberg and Co., Birmingham, Ala., 1978-80; exec. v.p., COO Rutherfords, Inc., Gainesville, Fla., 1980-82; founder, pres. Leake Enterprises and Wilson & Lowe, Gainesville, 1982-90; dep. exec. dir. Am. Soc. for Engring. Edn., Washington, 1990-94; exec. dir. Inst. Indsl. Engrs., Norcross, Ga., 1994—. Contbr. articles to profl. jours. Cons., vol. local, state and nat. polit. campaigns, 1960-88. Mem. Am. Soc. for Engring. Edn., Am. Soc. Assn. Execs., Coun. Engring. and Sci. Soc. Execs., Speech Communication Assn., Inst. Indsl. Engrs. Office: Inst Indsl Engrs 25 Technology Park/Atlanta Norcross GA 30092

LEAL, BARBARA JEAN PETERS, fundraising executive; b. Hartford, Ala., Oct. 24, 1948; d. Clarence Lee and Syble (Simmons) Peters; m. Michael Wayne Foster, 1966 (div.); children: Michaelle, Jonathan; m. Ramon Leal, 1991. AA, Enterprise State Jr. Coll., 1970; BA, U. South Fla., 1974; MA, Trinity U., San Antonio, 1975; postgrad. Universidad Nacional Autonoma de Mexico, 1982. Cert. fund raising exec. Instr., San Antonio Coll., 1975; planner Econ. Opportunities Devel. Corp., San Antonio, 1976, Alamo Area Council Govts., San Antonio, 1977-82; dir. planned giving Oblate Missions, San Antonio, 1982—; spkr. in field. Author: Paratransit Provider Handbook, 1978; contbg. author: Human Responses to Aging, 1976; Transportation for Elderly Handicapped Programs and Problems, 1978; contbr. articles to profl. publs. Named one of Outstanding Young Women of Am., 1985. Founding mem. Nat. Soc. Fund Raising Execs. (past pres. San Antonio chpt.), Am. Coun. on Gift Annuities, Coun. Advancement and Support Edn., San Antonio Planned Giving Coun. Democrat. Roman Catholic. Office: Oblate Missions PO Box 96 San Antonio TX 78291-0096

LEAPLEY, PATRICIA MURRAY, dietitian; b. Lowell, Mass.; d. Henry J. and Ruth (Slipp) Murray; m. Robert A. Leapley; children: Robert Jr., Deborah, John. BS in Nutrition and Edn., Framingham State Coll., 1959; MS in Allied Health Services, U. North Fla., 1986. Registered dietitian, Washington, cert. diabetes educator; lic. dietitian, Fla. Chief nutrition clinic Walter Reed Army Med. Ctr., Washington, 1976-79; coordinator diabetes program U. South Fla., Tampa, 1979-80; dir. nutrition BLD Nutrition Mgmt. Systems, Clearwater, Fla., 1980-84, Health Care Assocs., Rockville, Md., 1984; clin. nutrition specialist Riverside Hosp., Jacksonville, Fla., 1985-87; dir. nutrition services The Drs. Clinic, Jacksonville, 1987-88; diabetes and lipid nutrition specialist Dept. Vets. Affairs Lake City (Fla.) Med. Ctr. Author (book and slides): Food Facts for Diabetes and Weight Control, 1979; contbr. numerous articles to profl. jours. Served as capt. U.S. Army, 1959-64. Recipient Alumni Achievement award Framingham State Coll., 1979; first dietitian to develop diet for treatment of Phenylketonuria in children, Walter Reed Med. Amry Med. Ctr., 1960. Mem. Am. Assn. Diabetes Educators (bd. dirs. 1980-83, program chair VA/AADE diabetic educators group 1994-95), Am. Dietetic Assn. (exec. bd. 1972-79), Am. Diabetes Assn. (Jacksonville bd. dirs. 1985-93, Washington bd. dirs. 1973-79, coun. on epidemiology sec. 1982-89, chairperson Dept. Vet. Affairs 1993-95), Dept. Vet. Affairs/Am. Assn. Diabetes Educators. Home: PO Box 23398 Jacksonville FL 32241-3398

LEASON, JACK WALTER, investment advisor; b. Phila., Mar. 2, 1921; s. Israel and Sophia (Goodman) L.; m. Ruth Lederberg, Aug. 11, 1957 (div. 1978); children: Jonathan Oren, David Geoffrey. BS in Econs., U. Pa., 1942. Chartered fin. analyst. Analyst, acct. U.S. SEC, Phila., 1943-47; analyst Salomon Bros., N.Y.C., 1948; mgr. rsch. Shields & Co., N.Y.C., 1949-53; dir. instnl. rsch. Montgomery, Scott & Co., N.Y.C., 1953-58; dir. investment rsch. Gregory & Sons, N.Y.C., 1958-65; v.p. instnl. rsch. E.F. Hutton & Co., Inc., N.Y.C., 1965-74; investment adviser J.W. & Co., Ventnor, N.J., 1974-80; now investment advisor, fin. cons. Author: The Russian Economic Threat, 1961 (Vigilant Patriot award Freedoms Found.); contbr. articles to profl. publs. Mem. N.Y. Soc. Security Analysts, Inst. Chartered Fin. Analysts. Home and Office: 4309 Travis St Dallas TX 75205

LEASOR, JANE, religion and philosophy educator, musician; b. Portsmouth, Ohio, Aug. 10, 1922; d. Paul Raymond Leasor and Rana Kathryn (Bayer) Leasor-McDonald. BA, Wheaton Coll., 1944; MRE, N.Y. Theol. Sem., 1952; PhD, NYU, 1969. Asst. prof. Belhaven Coll., Jackson, Miss., 1952-54; dept. chmn. Beirut Coll. for Women, 1954-59; asst. to pres. Wheaton (Ill.) Coll., 1961-63; dean of women N.Y. Theol. Sem., N.Y.C., 1963-67; counselor CUNY, Bklyn., 1967-74; assoc. prof. Beirut U. Coll., 1978-80; tchr. internat. sch., Les Cayes, Haiti, 1984-85; pvt. tutor, 1985—; tchr. Fayette County (W.Va.) Schs., 1993—. Author religious text for use in Syria and Lebanon, 1960; editor books by V.R. Edman, 1961-63, Time and Life mags. Mem. Am. Assn. Counselors, Am. Guild Organists. Episcopalian. Home and Office: 606 Driftwood Dr Charleston WV 25306

LEATHER, VICTORIA POTTS, college librarian; b. Chattanooga, June 12, 1947; d. James Elmer Potts and Ruby Lea (Bettis) Potts Wilmoth; m. Jack Edward Leather; children: Stephen, Sean. BA cum laude, U. Chattanooga, 1968; MSLS, U. Tenn., 1978. Libr. asst. East New Orleans Regional Libr., 1969-71; libr. Erlanger Nursing Sch., Chattanooga, 1971-75; chief libr. Erlanger Hosp., Chattanooga, 1975-77; dir. Eastgate Br. Libr., Chattanooga, 1977-81; dir. libr. svcs. Chattanooga State Tech. Community Coll., 1981-95, dean libr. svcs., 1996—. Mem. Allied Arts, Hunter Mus., High Mus. Art. Mem. ALA, Southeastern Libr. Assn., Tenn. Libr. Assn. (chair legislation com.), Chattanooga Area Libr. Assn. (pres. 1978-79), Tenn. Bd. Regents Media Consortium (chair 1994-95), Phi Delta Kappa. Episcopalian.

LEAVELL, LANDRUM PINSON, II, seminary administrator, clergyman, educator, retired; b. Ripley, Tenn., Nov. 26, 1926; s. Leonard O. and Annie Glenn (Elias) L.; m. Jo Ann Paris, July 28, 1953; children: Landrum Pinson III, Ann Paris, Roland Q. II, David E. A.B., Mercer U., 1948; B.D., New Orleans Bapt. Theol. Sem., 1951, Th.D., 1954, D.D. Miss. Coll., 1981, Campbell U., 1989. Pastor Union Bapt. Ch., Magnolia, Miss., Crosby Bapt. Ch. (Miss.), First Bapt. Ch., Charleston, Miss., First Bapt. Ch., Gulfport, Miss., First Bapt. Ch., Wichita Falls, Tex., 1963-75; pres. New Orleans Bapt. Theol. Sem., 1975-95; pastor emeritus First Bapt. Ch., Wichita Falls, Tex., 1995. Mem. Bapt. Joint Com. Pub. Affairs, 1986-91; bd. dirs. Bapt. Cmty. Ministries, New Orleans, 1985-95, ret., 1995. Recipient George Washington Honor medal Freedoms Found., Valley Forge, Pa., 1968. Mem. New Orleans C. of C., Rotary (past pres. Paul Harris fellow). Author: Angels, Angels, Angels, 1973; Sermons for Celebrating, 1978; Twelve Who Followed Jesus, 1975; The Devil and His Domain, 1973; For Prodigals and Other Sinners, 1973; God's Spirit in You, 1974; The Harvest of the Spirit, 1976; John's Letters: Light for Living, 1970; Evangelism: Christ's Imperative Commission, 1979; The Doctrine of the Holy Spirit, 1983, Parting Shots, 1995. Home: 2100 Santa Fe Wichita Falls TX 76309

LEAVELL, MICHAEL RAY, computer programmer, analyst; b. Port St. Joe, Fla., Sept. 28, 1955; s. Ray Carl and Willodean (Griggs) L. AS in Electronics Tech., Gulf Coast Jr. Coll., Panama City, Fla., 1975; BS in Systems Sci., U. West Fla., 1979. Engr. Sta. WDTB-TV (now WMBB-TV), Panama City, 1976; radio announcer Sta. WJOE, Port St. Joe, 1979; computer programmer III, Fla. Dept. Labor, Tallahassee, 1979-80, computer programmer, analyst II, 1980-96, systems project analyst, 1996—. Office: Fla Dept Labor 244 Howard Bldg Tallahassee FL 32399

LEAVELL, WILLIAM A., publisher, editor; b. Montgomery, Ala., Apr. 12, 1923; William A. and Myrtle I. (Watson) L.; m. Patty J. Shobe, June 24, 1927; William A. III, Melissa I. BA, U. Ala., 1945; MA, George Washington U., 1947, PhD, 1949. Owner Leavell & Assoc., Belleair, Fla., 1950-62; columnist "Keep Off The Grass" syndicated column, 1963-73; editor, pub. Washington Report, Editor Release Svcs. (Washington Report), St. Petersburg, Fla., 1974—; regular guest on several radio and TV stas. Author: (novel) As Honest As Times Permit, 1974. Adminstrv. asst. Congressman Arthur Winstead Washington 1947-49. With USAF 1944-45. Home: 3610-38th Ave S # 88 Saint Petersburg FL 33711 Office: Editors Release Svcs PO Box 10309 Saint Petersburg FL 33733-0309

LEAVITT, GLENN SHEFFIELD, retired rehabilitation administrator; b. Boston, Sept. 23, 1935; s. J. Preston and Amy (Morris) L.; m. Eva Wilhelmine Ballé, Apr. 6, 1957; 1 child, Clifford Preston. BA in German and Russian, Pa. State U., 1961, MA in German and Comparative Lit., 1963; MA in Blind Rehab., Western Mich. U., 1971. Cert. rehab. tchr. of adult blind. Asst. prof. German and Russian, Albion (Mich.) Coll., 1963-70; rehab. tchr. Mich. Commn. for Blind Rehab. Ctr., Kalamazoo, 1972-76, edn. dir., 1976-80; program mgr., ctr. dir. Mich. Commn. for Blind Urban-Rural Ctr. for Ind. Living, Lansing, 1980-92; ret., 1992; guest lectr. Mich. State U., Lansing, 1983-87; fed. grant reviewer Rehab. Svcs. Adminstrn., Washington, 1986-92; mem. adv. bd. Cristo Rey Ctr., Lansing, 1983-87. Author: Oral-Aural Communications—A Teacher's Manual, 1974, The Language of My Soul—Anatomy of a Dyslexic Mind, 1994;; contbr. numerous articles to profl. jours. Vol. Meals on Wheels Program; mem. fund raising com. Mich. Dyslexia Inst.; bd. dirs. Erickson Learning Found. Mem. Orton Dyslexia Soc. (bd. dirs. Mich. br. 1990-92). Home: 26 Foxberry Dr Arden NC 28704-9400

LEAVITT, MARY JANICE DEIMEL, special education educator, civic worker; b. Washington, Aug. 21, 1924; d. Henry L. and Ruth (Grady) Deimel; BA, Am. U., Washington, 1946; postgrad. U. Md., 1963-65, U. Va., 1965-67, 72-73, 78-79, George Washington U., 1966-67; tchr.'s cert. spl. edn., 1968; m. Robert Walker Leavitt, Mar. 30, 1945; children: Michael Deimel, Robert Walker, Caroline Ann Leavitt Snyder. Tchr., Rothery Sch., Arlington, Va., 1947; dir. Sunnyside, Children's House, Washington, 1949; asst. dir. Coop. Sch. for Handicapped Children, Arlington, 1962, dir., Arlington, Springfield, Va., 1963-66; tchr. mentally retarded children Fairfax (Va.) County Pub. Schs., 1966-68; asst. dir. Burgundy Farm Country Day Sch., Alexandria, Va., 1968-69; tchr., substitute tchr. specific learning problem children Accotink Acad., Springfield, Va., 1970-80; substitute tchr. learning disabilities Children's Achievement Ctr., McLean, Va., 1973-82, Psychiat. Inst., Washington and Rockville, Md., 1976-82, Home-Bound and Substitute Program, Fairfax, Va., 1978-84; asst. info. specialist Ednl. Rsch. Svc., Inc., Rosslyn, Va., 1974-76; docent Sully Plantation, Fairfax County (Va.) Park Authority, 1981-87, 88-94, Childrens Learning Ctrs., vol. Honor Roll, 1987, Walney-Collections Fairfax County (Va.) Park Authority, 1989—; sec. Widowed Persons Svc., 1983-85, mem., 1985—. Mem. edn. subcom. Va. Commn. Children and Youth, 1973-74; den mother Nat. Capital Area Cub Scouts, Boy Scouts Am., 1962; troop fund raising chmn. Nat. Capitol coun. Girl Scouts U.S.A., 1968-69; capt. amblyopia team No. Va. chpt. Delta Gamma Alumnae, 1969; vol. Prevention of Blindness, 1980—; fund raiser Martha Movement, 1977-78; mem. St. John's Mus. Art, Wilmington, N.C., 1989—, Corcoran Gallery Art, Washington, 1989-90, 94—, Brunswick County Literacy Coun., N.C., 1989—; sunday sch. tchr. St. Andrews Episc. Ch., Burke, Va., 1995—, mem. search com., 1996. Recipient award Nat. Assn. for Retarded Citizens, 1975, Sully Recognition gift, 1989, Ten Yr. recognition pin Honor Roll, 1990. Mem. AAUW (co-chmn. met. area mass media com. D.C. chpt. 1973-75, v.p. Alexandria br. 1974-76, fellowship co-chmn., historian Springfield-Annandale br. 1979-80, 89-94, 94-95, name grantee ednl. found. 1980, cultural co-chmn. 1983-84), Assn. Part-Time Profls. (co-chmn. Va. local groups, job devel. and membership asst. 1981), Older Women's League, Nat. Mus. of Women in the Arts (charter mem.), Delta Gamma (treas. No. Va. alumnae chpt. 1973-75, pres. 1977-79, found. chmn. 1979-81, Katie Hale award 1989, treas. House Corp. Am. U. Beta Epsilon chpt. 1994—). Club: Mil. Dist. of Washington Officer's Clubs (Ft. McNair, Ft. Myer). Episcopalian. Home: 7129 Rolling Forest Ave Springfield VA 22152-3622

LEAVITT, MAURA LYNN, elementary education educator; b. Buffalo, N.Y., Mar. 7, 1946; d. Joseph Richard and Hermina (Wagner) Takats; m. Henry Clark Leavitt, Jan. 22, 1984. BA, Elmira Coll., 1968; MA, George Wash. U., 1977. Elem. tchr. Candor (N.Y.) Cen. Schs., 1968-72; ednl. dir., coord. Prelude Drug Rehab. Program, Arlington, Va., 1972-76; ednl. coord., tchr. Arlington County Jail - GED program, 1974-77, Argus House - Juv. Detention Home, Arlington, 1977; founder, dir. Ednl. Diagnostic Svcs., Arlington, 1978-81; adminstrv. asst. Caldwell, Prothro & Wilson, Arlington, 1981-84; tchr., elem. Flint Hill Prep. Sch., Oakton, Va., 1984-87; tchr., secondary history/govt. Clay/Langston Alt. Schs., Arlington, 1977-81; tchr., elem. Drew Model Sch./Alt. Sch., Arlington, 1987-91; tchr. Glebe Elem., Arlington, 1991—, curriculum devel. law related edn., 1992-94; notary pub., Arlington, 1981-88. Bd. dirs., v.p. No. Va. Hot Line, Arlington, 1984-86. Mem. Nat. Assn. Children with Learning Disabilities, Va. Assn. Children with Learning Disabilities, Arlington Assn. Children with Learning Disabilities, Greater Wash. Reading Coun., Va. State Reading Assn., Va. Coun. for Social Studies (bd. dirs. 1994-96), Nat. Coun. for Social Studies.

LEAVY, REBECCA SHREWSBURY, librarian; b. Valdosta, Ga., Mar. 4, 1946; d. Ralph Damon and Aline Wade (Lanier) Shrewsbury; m. Tyrel G. Moore, Aug. 19, 1967; 1 child, Brian Lanier Moore; m. Marvin D. Leavy, June 2, 1984. BA, Western Ky. U., 1967, MS in Libr. Sci., 1979. Cert. sch. libr. media specialist K-12, rank I tchr. Elem. sch. libr. Warren County Schs., Bowling Green, Ky., 1967-68; tchr. jr. h.s. Ohio County Schs., Hartford, Ky., 1968-69; libr. media specialist h.s. Hillsborough County Schs., Tampa, Fla., 1969-72; tchr. jr. h.s. Knoxville (Tenn.) City Schs., 1973, libr. jr. h.s., 1973-77; lab. sch. libr. media specialist Western Ky. U., Bowling Green, 1979-81, supr. Ednl. Resources Ctr., 1981-95; h.s. libr. media specialist Ohio County Schs., Hartford, Ky., 1995—. Bd. dirs. Big Brothers/Big Sisters, Bowling Green, 1982-85. Mem. ALA, Ky. Libr. Assn. (past sec. spl. librs. sect., acad. librs. sect., technology roundtable), Ky. Sch. Media Assn., Am. Quilters Soc., Phi Delta Kappa (v.p. membership 1989-92). Home: 1516 Singletree Ln Bowling Green KY 42103-1423 Office: Ohio County H S 1400 S Main St Hartford KY 42347-1853

LEBBY, GLORIA C., history educator; b. Orangeburg, S.C., July 12, 1956; d. Clarence Vivian and Eddie (Mitchell) L. BA, St. Augustine's Coll., 1976; MEd, S.C. State Coll., 1978; EdS, U. So. Miss., 1981; EdD, Nova Southeastern U., 1994. Cert. tchr., S.C., N.C., Miss., La. Instr. history Denmark (S.C.) Tech. Coll., 1993—; vis. instr. history S.C. State Coll., Orangeburg, 1991—. Cert. lay speaker U. Meth. Ch., Orangeburg, S.C., 1986-93. Named Outstanding Young Woman of Am., 1982, 84. Mem. AAUW (life), ASCD, S.C. Hist. Assn., Bamberg County Mental Health Assn., Nat. Coun. for Social Studies, U. So. Miss. Alumni Assn. (life), Order of Ea. Star, Order Golden Cir., Nat. Geographic Soc., Am. Legion Aux., Delta Sigma Theta (Denmark alumnae chpt. Dedicated Svc. award 1984, 90), Phi Alpha Theta. Methodist. Office: Denmark Tech Coll Dept History Denmark SC 29042

LEBLANC, EARLINE HART, special education educator; b. Beaumont, Tex., Mar. 15, 1923; d. Robert Monroe and Jewel Katherine (Jones) Hart; m. Joseph Paul LeBlanc, Jr., Nov. 14, 1941; children: Paula Louise, Madeline Kay, Darlene. BS in Elem. Edn., Lamar U., 1972, MEd in Spl. Edn., 1976. Registered profl. ednl. diagnostician. Tchr. spl. edn. Vidor (Tex.) Ind. Sch. Dist., 1972-78, edn. diagnostician, 1978-81, spl. edn. supr., 1981-91; retired, 1991; chmn. dept. spl. edn. Vidor Elem. Sch., 1974-78; bd. dirs. Personalized Ednl. Assts. Inc., Beaumont, 1979-83; early childhood coord. Vidor Ind. Sch. Dist., 1981—; curriculum coun. Region V Edn. Svc. Ctr., Beaumont, 1981—; ednl. diagnostician Harris County Dept. Edn., 1991-92, Huffman Ind. Sch. Dist., 1992-94. Vol. tchr. St. Pius X Cath. Ch., Beaumont, 1969-70; initiator Drug Edn./Awareness Program, Vidor, 1984-85. Mem. Tex. Coun. Adminstrs. Spl. Education, Tex. Ednl. Diagnosticians Assn., Tex. Tchrs. Assn. (life), Sabine Neches Ednl. Diagnosticians, Coun. Exceptional Children (v.p. local chpt.), Alpha Delta Kappa (Tex. Alpha Upsilon chpt.). Roman Catholic. Home: 6020 Marcus Dr Beaumont TX 77708-3715 Office: Spl Edn 6020 Marcus Dr Beaumont TX 77708-3715

LEBLANC, JAMES LEO, business executive, consultant; b. Ottawa, Ont., Can., May 12, 1955; came to U.S., 1993.; s. Leo Joseph and Ann (Curry) L.; m. Ruth Heather Faulkner, June 8, 1991. BA, Carleton U., 1982, MA in Internat. Affairs, 1984; MPA, Harvard U., 1994. Exec. asst. Amb. for Arms Control, Ottawa, Ont., Can., 1984-89; chief of staff Min. of Sci. and Technol., Ottawa, 1989-92, Min. of Foreign Affairs, Ottawa, 1992-93; pres. J. LeBlanc Internat. LLC, Alexandria, Va., 1994—; ptnr. Prospectus Assoc. Inc., Can., 1994—; prin. U.S. Tech. Internat. LLC, Washington, 1995—; bd. dirs., v.p. Can.-Am. Bus. Coun., Washington, 1995—; advisor Can. Advanced Tech. Assn., Can., 1994—. Bd. dirs. president's adv. coun., Carleton U., 1995—, Carlton U. (U.S.) Found., Washington, 1996—. Mem. Am. League of Lobbyists, Industry Adv. Coun., Harvard Club of Washington. Home: 5808 Woodlawn Green Ct Ste A Alexandria VA 22309 Office: J LeBlanc Internat LLC South Bldg 601 Pennsylvania Ave NW Ste 900 Washington DC 20004

LE BLANC, STACY ANN, animal science facility administrator; b. Lafayette, La., Oct. 7, 1963; d. William Eugene and Joyce Ann (Segrest) Le B. BS, Tex. A&M U., 1985, MS, 1988; MBA, U. Houston, Clear Lake, Tex., 1995. Cert. lab. animal technologist. Vet. tech. Friendswood (Tex.) Animal Clinic, 1980-88; from sr. vet. tech. to asst. to head animal resources br. Baylor Coll. Medicine, Houston, 1989-95; animal facility ops. mgr. M.D. Anderson Cancer Ctr., Houston, 1995—; badged committeeman Houston Livestock Show and Rodeo, 1993—. Patentee in field. Vol. Ronald McDonald Children's Charities, 1994, Houston A&M Club, 1992—, USO, Houston, 1992-95, Bay Area Aggies, Houston, 1994-95. Mem. Am. Assn. Lab. Animal Sci., 1989— (found. bd. dirs. 1996-98, found. capital endowment fundraising campaign 1996-2000, newsletter editor Tex. br. 1989—, pres.'s award 1993, publ. award 1994, recognition award 1995), Lab. Animal Mgmt. Assn. (awards vice-chair 1996, awards chair 1997), Am. Mgmt. Assn., Alpha Zeta. Republican. Roman Catholic. Office: MD Anderson Cancer Ctr 1515 Holcombe Blvd Box 063 Houston TX 77030

LEBOEUF, GIBSON GEORGE, government executive, engineer; b. San Juan, P.R., Dec. 19, 1945; s. Gibson John and Olga (Nasar) LeB.; m. Rose Teresa Morales, Oct. 11, 1969; children: Andrea Teresa, Gibson Carlos. BS in Mech. Engring., U. Detroit, 1969; postgrad., Am. U., 1974, Harvard U., 1985. Cert. in engring. mgmt. Ballistic missile submarine design engr. Puget Sound Naval Shipyard, Bremerton, Wash., 1972-73; ballistic missile submarine sr. engr. Naval Sea Systems Command, Washington, 1973-77, attack submarine sr. engr., 1977-80; advance ship design engr. Strategic Systems Program, Arlington, 1980-82, ship chief engr., 1982-88, ship br. head, 1988-91, nav. head, 1992; legislative fellow U.S. Senate, Washington, 1991-92; Navy chair Def. Systems Mgmt. Coll., Ft. Belvoir, Va., 1992—. Author manuals. Recipient numerous awards. Mem. Am. Soc. Engrs., Sr. Exec. Svc., Navy Hispanic Coun. (asst. sec.), Nat. Assn. Hispanic Fed. Execs., Harvard Bus. Club (Washington). Roman Catholic. Office: Dept DefSystems Mgmt Coll Navy Chair 9820 Belvoir Rd Fort Belvoir VA 22060-5565

LEBOW, JEFFREY ALBERT, manufacturing engineer; b. Evanston, Ill., Jan. 17, 1958; s. Jerry P. and Natalie (Shapiro) L.; m. Laurel Mary Lavin, May 29, 1988; children: Jeffrey Adam, Elizabeth Ward, Jeremy Philip II. BS in Indsl. Engring., U. Mich., 1980, MS in Indsl. Engring., 1981. Registered profl. engr., Ga.; cert. sys. integrator. Project engr. Weyerhaeuser Co., Tacoma, 1981-83; applications engr. Robot Systems, Inc., Norcross, Ga., 1983-85; project engr. Hayes Microcomputer Products, Inc., Norcross, 1985-86; project engring. group leader Mitsubishi Consumer Electronics Am. Inc., Braselton, Ga., 1986-94; mgr. tech. linkages office Econ. Devel. Inst. Ga. Tech., Atlanta, 1994—; mem. course faculty Logistics Inst.; speaker Uniform Code Coun., Dayton, Ohio, 1992; adv. bd. Leaders in Logistics. Designer (material handling system) Cabinet Conveyor, 1987-92. Pres. B'nai B'rith-Achim Lodge, Atlanta, 1986, bd. dirs., 1985-87. Named Most Valuable Mem. B'nai B'rith, 1987, Outstanding Young Mfg. Engr. Yr. Soc. Mfg. Engrs., 1992; recipient Productivity Achievement award for Mfg. Excellence, Modern Materials Handling mag., 1992. Mem. Inst. Indsl. Engrs. (sr., bd. dirs. Atlanta chpt. 1986-87, course faculty materials handling mgmt. course 1992), Robotics Internat. of SME (sr.), Electronic Industries Assn. (EIA retail bar code std. com. 1991-94), Tech. Transfer Soc., U. Mich. Alumni Assn. (life), Mensa, Michigamma, Vulvcans, Tau Beta Pi (life). Home: 3110 Brandy Sta NW Atlanta GA 30339-4406 Office: Ga Tech Econ Devel Inst 223 O'Keefe Bldg Atlanta GA 30332-0640

LEBOW, LAUREL MARY LAVIN, real estate developer, real estate asset manager; b. Newport, R.I., Feb. 5, 1956; d. Charles Vincent and Barbara (Hofheins) Lavin; m. Jeffrey A. Lebow, May 29, 1988. BS, Emory U., 1977. Gen. mgr. Source Enterprises, New Orleans, 1980-81; exec. Johnstown Am. Co., Atlanta, 1981-86; dir. asset mgmt. Club Properties, Inc., Atlanta, 1986-90; v.p. Mgmt. Solutions, Inc., Atlanta, 1990-92, CPA Realty, Inc., Atlanta, 1992—. Mem. Inst. Real Estate Mgmt., MENSA, Jr. League of Atlanta. Republican. Episcopalian. Office: CPA Realty Inc 2951 Flowers Rd S Ste 220 Atlanta GA 30341-5533

LECKIE, SHIRLEY ANNE, historian, educator; b. Claremont, N.H., June 15, 1937; d. Edward James Howard and Hazel Enola (Ralston) Casillo; m. William H. BA in History, U. Mo., Kansas City, 1967, MA in History, 1969; PhD in history, U. Toledo, 1981. Grad. asst. Univ. Toledo, Ohio, 1969-72; adviser Univ Toledo, 1972-73; dir. adult liberal studies Univ. Toledo, 1973-80; asst. dean, cont. edn. Univ. Toledo, Jackson, Miss., 1980-81; assoc. dean, continued edn. Millsaps Coll., Jackson, Miss., 1981-82; dir. continued edn. Univ. N. C., Ashville, 1983-85; asst. prof. history U. Ctrl. Fla., Orland, 1985-88; assoc. prof. history U. Ctrl. Fla., Orlando, 1988-95, prof. history, 1995—; co-chmn. adv. council, Ctr. Women, Toledo, 1977-78. Co-author: Unlikely Warriors, 1984; editor: Colonel's Lady on the Western Frontier, 1989, Elizabeth Bacon Custer and the Making of a Myth, 1993. Mem. Alumnae Leadership Asheville, 1984-85; rec. sec. Orlando Met. Women's Polit. Caucus, 1989. Mem. Orgn. Am. History, So. Hist. Assn., Western Hist. Assn. Democrat. Office: Univ Cen Fla University Ave Orlando FL 32817

LECLAIR, BETTY JO COGDILL, special education and early childhood educator; b. Oklahoma City, Sept. 25, 1934; d. Mark Loffett and Elma Elizabeth (Wade) Cogdill; m. Charles E. LeClair, Feb. 23, 1957 (div. 1988); children: Rebecca, Joan, Charles III, Laura, Jill. BA, Okla. Bapt. U., 1957; postgrad., Cen. State U., Edmond, Okla., 1970-71, U. S.C., 1974-95; MEd, Columbia (S.C.) Coll., 1988. Cert. elem., spl. edn. tchr., S.C. Spl. edn. tchr. Children's Opportunity Ctr., Ft. Worth, 1960-62; lang. missionary with Indians So. Bapt. Home Mission Bd., Oklahoma City, 1964-67; spl. edn. tchr. Child Study Ctr., Ft. Worth, 1968-69, Midlands Ctr., Columbia, S.C., 1970, Mill Creek Elem. Sch., Richland Dist. #1, Columbia, 1970-71; spl. edn. and resource tchr. Ft. Jackson (S.C.) Elem. Schs., 1971-93, 1st grade tchr., 1993—; former parent advisor for children ages birth-36 months S.C. Sch. for the Deaf and Blind; former mem. Coun. for Exceptional Children, hospitality chmn. chpt. 165, 1988-89, sec., 1989-90, historian, 1990-91. Active North Trenholm Bapt. Ch., Columbia; vol. Help Line of Columbia, 1993—. Mem. Coun. for Exceptional Children (hospitality chmn. chpt. 165, 1988-89, sec. 1989-90, historian 1990-91). Home: 1919 Stanley St Columbia SC 29204-4332 Office: Pierce Terr Elem Sch 5715 Adams Ct Columbia SC 29206-5379

LECLERE, DAVID ANTHONY, lawyer; b. New Orleans, Sept. 5, 1954; s. Paul Richard and Rosalee (Cefalu) LeC.; m. Karen Menzie; children: David II, Michael Joshua, Jacob Gunter. BA, La. State U., 1978, JD, 1979. Bar: La. 1979, U.S. Dist. Ct. (mid. dist.) La. 1979, U.S. Dist. Ct. (ea. dist.) 1982, U.S. Dist. Ct. (we. dist.) La. 1983, U.S. Ct. Appeals (5th cir.) 1984. Assoc. Perrault & Uter, Baton Rouge, 1979-81, jr. ptnr., 1981-83; ptnr. Perrault, Uter & LeClere, Baton Rouge, 1983-87, Schwab & LeClere, Baton Rouge, 1987-90; of counsel Powers, Vaughn & Clegg, Baton Rouge, 1990-91; ptnr. Duplechain & LeClere, Baton Rouge, 1991-93; pvt. practice David A. LeClere, A Profl. Law Corp., Baton Rouge, 1993—; asst. bar examiner. Assoc. chmn. East Baton Rouge Parish Notary Pub. Exam Com., 1982, chmn. dispute resolution com.; asst. State Bar Examiner; prof. paralegal studies La. State U. Mem. ABA, La. State Bar Assn., Comml. Law League of Am., Baton Rouge Bar Assn. Republican. Roman Catholic. Office: 8338 Summa Ave Ste 302 Baton Rouge LA 70809-3669

LECUYER, ROBERT RAYMOND, aviation maintenance administrator; b. Syracuse, N.Y., Dec. 13, 1965; s. Raymond Jeremy and Karen Penelope (Van Ornam) P.; m. Wendy Elizabeth Barrows, Jan. 13, 1990; children: Christopher, Andrew, Robbyn. AS, City Univ., Bellevue, Wash., 1990; BS, So. Ill. U., 1993; MS, U. Ark., 1996. From aviation ordnance tech. to aviation maintenance admin. U.S. Navy, Memphis, 1984—; mem. tech. adv. bd. State Tech. Inst., Memphis, 1994—; enlisted air warfare tng. coord. USN, 1994-95. Mem. Profl. Photographer's Soc. N.Y., Navy Memphis Ofcls. Assn., Am. Legion, Alpha Beta Gamma. Republican. Baptist. Home: 5823 Port Haven Dr Millington TN 38053 Office: Naval Support Activity 7300 3d Ave Millington TN 38054

LEDBETTER, CAL R., political scientist, educator; b. Little Rock, Apr. 29, 1929; s. Cal R. and Virginia M. (Campbell) L.; m. Brownie Williams, July 26, 1953; children: Grainger, Jeffrey (dec.), Snow. BA, Princeton U., 1951; JD, U. Ark., 1954; PhD, Northwestern U., 1960. Assoc. Mehaffy, Smith & Williams, Little Rock, 1954; chair polit. sci. dept. U. Ark., Little Rock, 1961-78, dean Coll. Liberal Arts, 1978-88, prof. polit. sci., 1988—; mem. Ark. Ho. of Reps., 1967-76; mem., vice chair Ark. Constnl. Conv., 1979-80. Author: Carpenter From Conway, 1993, Am. Assn. for State and Local History award 1994; co-author: Arkansas Becomes a State, 1985, The Arkansas Plan, 1979. 1st lt. U.S. Army, 1955-57. Named Educator of Yr. Fedn. Women's Clubs, 1968; Writing Excellence award Ark. Bar Assn., 1985. Mem. West Little Rock Rotary Club (pres. 1987-88). Democrat. Presbyterian. Office: Univ Ark Little Rock 2801 S University Little Rock AR 72204

LEDBETTER, DEIDRE LEDAY, special education educator; b. New Orleans, Oct. 16, 1959; d. Felton Clark Augusta and Frances Ada (Norman) Provost; m. Robert Leday, June 8, 1975 (dec. Aug. 1976); 1 child, Demetria Marie; m. George Dallas Ledbetter, Jr., Feb. 7, 1981. B Gen. Studies in Behavioral Scis., U. Southwestern La., 1982, BA in Spl. Edn., 1993, MEd in Guidance and Counseling, 1996. Resource tchr. Iberia Parish Sch. Bd., New Iberia, La., 1982-94, link cons., 1994—; mem. core com. Very Spl. Arts Festival, New Iberia, 1990-94. Active Coun. for Exceptional Children. Named Tchr. of Yr., Lee Street Elem. Sch., 1994. Mem. NEA, La. Assn. Educators, Iberia Assn. Educators (sec. 1989-90), Order Ea. Star, Order of Cyrene (royal Magdalene 1991—), Heroines of Jericho (vice ancient matron 1990—). Democrat. Methodist. Home: 1007 Bank Ave New Iberia LA 70560 Office: Iberia Parish Spl Edn Dept PO Box 200 New Iberia LA 70560

LEDBETTER, PAUL MARK, lawyer, writer; b. San Francisco, Oct. 14, 1947; s. John Paul and Joyce (Mayo) L.; m. Jerald Ann Broyles, Sept. 18, 1971; children: Paul Mark, Sarah Broyles. BA in English, Ouachita Bapt. U., 1970; JD, U. Ark., 1973. Bar: Ark. 1974, Tenn. 1995, U.S. Dist. Ct. (ea. dist.) Ark. 1974, U.S. Ct. Appeals (8th cir.) 1974, U.S. Ct. Appeals (6th cir.) 1991, U.S. Dist. Ct. (mid. dist.) Tenn. 1995. Assoc. Frierson, Walker, Snellgrove & Laser, Jonesboro, Ark., 1974-77, ptnr., 1977-82; pres. Mark Ledbetter, P.A., Jonesboro, 1982-86; ptnr. Gerber, Gerber & Agee, Memphis, 1986-89, Taylor, Halliburton, Ledbetter & Caldwell, Memphis, 1989—. Author: The Hearing, 1994. Co-founder St. Mark's Episcopal Day Sch., Jonesboro, 1978; mem. vestry St. Mark's Episcopal Ch., 1979; mem. Forum Commn. City of Jonesboro, 1978-80. Conservation Found. grantee, 1976; Rotary Internat. grantee, Japan, 1979. Mem. Am. Bd. Trial Advs. (assoc.), Tenn. Bar Assn., Ark. Bar Assn. (mem. tort reform com. 1980, ho. of dels. 1979-80), Ark. Trial Lawyers Assn. (chmn. amicus curiae com. 1980-81, gov. 1980—), Tenn. Trial Lawyers Assn., Jonesboro C. of C. (bd. dirs. 1978-80). Office: Taylor Halliburton Ledbetter & Caldwell 44 N 2nd St Ste 200 Memphis TN 38103-2220 also: Ledbetter & Caldwell 1804 Executive Square Jonesboro AR 72401

LEDBETTER, SHARON FAYE WELCH, educational consultant; b. L.A., Jan. 14, 1941; d. James Herbert and Verdie V. (Mattox) Welch; m. Robert A. Ledbetter, Feb. 15, 1964; children: Kimberly Ann, Scott Allen. BA, U. Tex.-Austin, 1963; learning disabilities cert. Southwestern U., Tex., 1974; MEd, Southwest Tex. State U., 1979, prin. cert., 1980, supt. cert., 1984. Speech pathologist Midland Ind. Sch. Dist., Tex., 1963, Austin Ind. Sch. Dist., Tex., 1964-72; speech pathologist, asst. prin. Round Rock Ind. Sch. Dist., Tex., 1972-84; prin. Hutto Ind. Sch. Dist., 1984-88; asst. dir. div. mid. sch. edn. Tex. Edn. Agy., 1989-94; educational cons. 1994—. Pres. Berkman PTA, 1983-84; sponsor Jr. Woman's Club, 1980-82; mistress ceremonies Hutto Beauty Pageant, 1986, 87. Recipient Appreciation award Round Rock Sch. Dist., 1984, St. Judes Children's Research Hosp., 1985, Soc. Disting. Am. High Sch. Students, 1985, Disting. Svc. award Tex. Edn. Agy, 1994. Mem. ASCD, Nat. Mid. Sch. Assn., Tex. Mid. Sch. Assn., Tex. Assn. Secondary Sch. Prins., Phielta Kappa. Avocations: spectator sports. Home: 43 Woodland Loop Round Rock TX 78664-9776

LEDE, RICHARD, investment company executive; b. N.Y.C., Mar. 9, 1946; s. Joseph Henry Lede and Anna Mae (O'Donnell) Lede Nichols; m. Maribeth Ann Foster, Nov. 24, 1983; 1 stepchild, Lauren C. Kruta. BA, U. Tampa, 1968; student, Stetson U., 1968. Guest rels. staff Nat. Broadcasting Co., 1968-69; pres. Howle Film Prodns. Ltd., N.Y.C., 1969-73, also bd. dirs.; pres. Delmar Entertainment Corp., N.Y.C., L.A., 1973-83, also bd. dirs.; v.p. Fundamental Brokers U.K., London, 1983-86, MKI Securities Corp., London, 1986-88, Liberty Brokerage, N.Y.C., 1988-92; exec. v.p. S.E. Regional Securities, West Palm Beach, Fla., 1992-93, also bd. dirs.; exec. v.p. Hillman, Lede and Co. Inc., Wets Palm Beach, 1993—, also vice chmn. bd. dirs.; mng. dir. Seaboard Securities Inc., 1994—; pres. Crown Fin. Assocs., Palm Beach, Fla., 1995—. Mem. West Palm Beach C. of C., Palm Beach Yacht Club, Mayacoo Lakes Country Club (bd. govs.), Moor Park Gold Club, Sigma Phi Epsilon. Home: 2452 Seaford Dr West Palm Beach FL 33414-6241 Office: Crown Fin Assocs 250 Royal Palm Way Palm Beach FL 33480

LEDERER, PAUL EDWARD, landscape architect; b. Paradise, Nova Scotia, Can., Mar. 2, 1942; came to U.S., 1946; s. Emil and Edith (Kann) L. BS, Rutgers U., 1964; B of Land Architecture, U. Mass., 1965, M of Land Architecture, 1969. Registered landscape architect, Mass., N.J., Va., Md., Ala. Landscape architect John Rahenkamp & Assoc, Phila., 1965, Nat. Park Svc., Phila., 1965, 67-69; landscape architect, planner Nat. Park Svc., Washington, 1969—; civil engring. aid Soil Conservation Svc., Northampton, Mass., 1967. Mem. Com. of 100 on Fed. City D.C., 1987. Mem. Am. Soc. Landscape Architects, Am. Planning Assn., Nat. Trust for Hist. Preservation, Nat. Park and Recreation Assn. Jewish. Office: Nat Park Svc 6245 Leesburg Pike Falls Church VA 22044-2106

LEDFORD, DENNIS KEITH, physician; b. Johnson City, Tenn., May 10, 1950; s. Lawrence and Dorothy Ruth (Swatzell) L.; m. Jennifer L. Shelton, June 15, 1974; 3 children. BCE, Ga. Inst. Tech., 1973; MD, U. Tenn., 1976. Med. intern U. Tenn. Hosps., Memphis, 1977, asst. and assoc. resident, 1978-79; chief resident City of Memphis Hosps., 1979-80; fellow in clin. immunology and rheumatology NYU, N.Y.C., 1980-82; fellow in clin. allergy and immunology U. South Fla., Tampa, 1983-85, asst. prof. medicine, 1985-91, assoc. prof. medicine, 1991—; instr. dept. medicine U. Tenn. Ctr. Health Scis., Memphis, 1979-80; clin. assoc. internal medicine U. South Fla., 1983-85, dir. tng. program in clin. and lab. immunology, 1992—; mem. AIDS adv. com. James A. Haley VA Hosp., 1987—; mem. infection control com. Univ. Cmty. Hosp., 1987—; mem. adv. com. Blue Cross/Blue Shield, 1987—; med. dir. Asthma and Allergy Clinic of Judeo-Christian Clinic, 1988—. Mem. med. adv. coun. Fla. chpt. Nat. Hemophilia Found., 1990-92; mem. AIDS edn. adv. coun. Hillsborough County Sch. Bd., 1992—. Recipient Outstanding Spkr. award Marion County Med. Assn., 1987, Vol. of Yr. award Vol. Ctr. Hillsborough County, 1994. Mem. AMA, ACP, Am. Soc. Internal Medicine, Am. Rheumatism Assn. (Fellowship award 1981), Am. Coll. Allergy and Immunology (mem. ann. meeting postgrad. program com. 1996—), Am. Acad. Allergy and Immunology (mem. continuing med. edn. com. 1987-90, chmn. 1989-90, mem. AIDS com. 1989—, postgrad. edn. planning com. 1992-93, mem. core curriculum com. for clin. and diagnostic lab. immunology tng. programs 1993—, co-chair, bd. rev. course 1996—), Fla. Allergy and Immunology Soc. (sec. 1989-90, v.p. 1990-91, pres. 1991-93). Office: U South Fla Coll Medicine VA Med Ctr 13000 Bruce B Downs Blvd # 111D Tampa FL 33612-4745

LEDFORD, JANET MARIE SMALLEY, real estate appraiser, consultant; b. Willimantic, Conn., June 1, 1951; d. Harold Eugene and Elizabeth Louise (Loehr) Smalley; m. Timothy Eugene Ledford, Jan. 23, 1988. AA, Young Harris (Ga.) Coll., 1971; BS, W. Ga. Coll., 1973; MEd, U. Ga., 1978. Math. tchr. secondary schs., Atlanta and, V.I., 1973-82; assoc. appraiser Childers Assoc., Atlanta, 1985-87, Am. Realty Concepts, Atlanta, 1987-88; owner, appraiser, cons. Ledford & Assoc., Atlanta, 1988—.

LEDLEY, TAMARA SHAPIRO, earth system scientist, climatologist; b. Washington, May 18, 1954; d. Murray Daniel and Ina Harriet (Gordon) Shapiro; m. Fred David Ledley, June 6, 1976; children: Miriam Esther, Johanna Sharon. BS, U. Md., 1976; PhD, MIT, 1983. Rsch. assoc. Rice U., Houston, 1983-85, asst. rsch. scientist, 1985-90, sr. faculty fellow, 1990—; assoc. rsch. scientist Tex. A&M U., 1995—; mem. Alaska SAR facility archive working team NASA, Pasadena, Calif., 1988, McMurdo SAR facility sci. working team, 1990; participant workshop of Arctic leads initiative Office Naval Rsch., Seattle, 1988, 1st DeLange Conf. on Human Impact on Environ., Houston, 1991; cons. Houston Mus. Natural Sci., 1989-90, Broader Perspectives, Houston, 1989; dir. weather project for tchr. tng. program George Obs., Rice U., 1990-92; co-dir. Rice Houston Mus. Natural Sci. Summer Solar Inst., 1993; mem. rev. panels NSF, 1993, 95. Contbr. articles to profl. publs. Spl. judge Houston Area Sci. and Engring. Fair, 1985; judge S.W. Tex. Region H.S. Debates, 1986, Houston Area Sci. and Engring. Fair, 1990, 91, 92, 95; guest expert Great Decisions '88 Polit. Discussion Group, 1988; participant U.S. Global Change Rsch. Program's Climate Modeling Forum, 1994. Fellow sci. computing Nat. Ctr. for Atmospheric Rsch., 1978, Fed. Jr. fellow, 1972-74; senatorial scholar State of Md., 1972-76; grantee NSF, 1985-87, 89-92, 92-94, 94—, Tex. Higher Edn. Coordinating Bd., 1988-90, 90-92, Univ. Space Rsch. Assn., NASA, 1991-93, 92-94. Mem. AAAS (mem. electorate nominating com. 1995—), Am. Geophys. Union (com. global environ. change 1993-96, assoc. editor Jour. Geophys. Rsch.-Atmospheres 1993-96), Am. Meteorol. Soc., Oceanography Soc., Sigma Xi, Phi Beta Kappa, Phi Kappa Phi, Alpha Lambda Delta. Office: Rice U Dept Space Physics & Astronomy 6100 Main St Houston TX 77005-1827

LEDO, MARLENE, dialysis staff nurse; b. Miami Beach, Fla., Dec. 21, 1963; d. Manuel and Georgina (Sobrino) L.; m. Anthony Quinones, Apr. 24, 1992. Nursing diploma with honors, Jackson Meml. Hosp., 1991; AS, Miami Dade C.C., 1991; BSN with honors, Fla. Internat. U., 1996. AACN, BLS, ACLS; cert. nephrology nurse, clin. nurse II. Nursing asst. Mercy Hosp., Miami, Fla., 1980-83; sec. Palm Springs Hosp., Hialeah, Fla., 1983-85, Wilfredo Alvarez, M.D., Hialeah, 1985-87; ICU sec. Bapt. Hosp., Miami, 1988-91, ICU staff nurse, 1991-93, dialysis staff nurse, 1993—; adv. bd. Bapt. Hosp. of Miami, 1993-95, adj. faculty, 1996, clin. practice coun., 1996. Named to Am. acad. of Disting. Students, 1996; Nephrology Nursing Cert. Bd. Career Mobility scholar, 1996. Mem. AACN, Am. Nephrology Nurses Assn. (sec. 1994-96, pres.-elect 1996, ESRD seminar coord. 1995—). Republican. Roman Catholic. Home: 10615 SW 129th Ct Miami FL 33186 Office: Bapt Hosp of Miami 8900 N Wendall Dr Miami FL 33176

LEDOUX, JOHN CLARENCE, law enforcement official; b. Muskogee, Okla. Oct. 19, 1944; s. Clarence Watson and Nedra Ruth (Dayton) LeD.; m. Anne Marie Sommervold, Aug. 8, 1970; children: Matthew Watson, Justin William Clay. BA, U. Md., 1967; M. Criminal Justice, Auburn U., 1977, EdD, 1980. Spl. agt. FBI, Albany, N.Y., 1971, Binghamton, N.Y., 1972, Opelika, Ala., 1972-80, supervisory spl. agt., Quantico, Va., 1980—; tng. lt. Aguia Harbour Rescue Squad, 1994—; instr. law enforcement, martial arts. Author: (with others) A Study of Factors Influencing the Continuing Education of Law Enforcement Officers, 1982, The Microcomputer Tutor: A Manager's Guide To Personal Computers, 1991; editor Law Enforcement Tng. Network, 1983-89. Mem. Stafford County Parks and Recreation Commn., Stafford, Va., 1982—, chmn., 1983, 85-89, 90; co-chmn. Stafford Citizens for Parks and Librs., 1989—; mem. Stafford County Drug Task Force, 1990-92, Aquia Harbor Rescue Squad, 1992—; EMT FBI Acad., 1990—; CPR instr., 1993—; coun. mem. St. Peter's Ch.; chmn. speakers bureau Stafford Citizens for Parks. Capt. USMC, 1967-71, Vietnam. Recipient Jeffersonian award U. Va., 1982. Mem. Acad. Criminal Justice Scis., Law Enforcement Martial Arts Assn. (instr. 1987—), Assn. for Devel. of Computer-Based Instructional Systems (editor), Internat. Assn. Computer Investigative Specialists, Nat. Recreation and Park Assn., Stafford Recreational Soccer League (coach 1983-86, commr. 1986—, chmn. referees 1991-1994), Rappananock Referees Assn., Spotsylvania Soccer Assn. (coach 1987-91). Lutheran. Avocations: Tae Kwon Do, soccer, tennis, magic, golf. Office: FBI FBI Acad Quantico VA 22135

LEDWITH, SISTER MARGARET CHRISTINE, nun, counselor; b. Longford, Ireland, Dec. 19, 1935; came to U.S., 1990; SRN, Whipps Cross Hosp., London, 1963; SCM, Dublin Nat. Maternity Hosp., Dublin, 1964; postgrad., London Hosp. and Royal Coll., 1967-69; M in Pastoral Counseling, Loyola Coll., Balt., 1991; postgrad. in urban ministry and CPE, Emmanuel Coll., 1991-92; postgrad. in Spanish, Maryknoll Inst., Bolivia, 1992—; clin. pastoral edn., Shannon Hosp., San Angelo, Tex., 1993, Meth. Hosp., Lubbock, Tex., 1994-95. Joined Missionary Sisters of the Holy Rosary, Roman Cath. Ch., 1955; cert. Coll. of Chaplains; cert. Nat. Assn. Cath. Chaplains.qq. Tutor midwifery Missionary Sisters of Holy Rosary, Nigeria, 1964, sr. ward sister, 1964-67; adminstr. pers. Missionary Sisters of Holy Rosary, Ireland, 1972-78, superior gen., 1978-89; chaplain Med. Ctr. Hosp., Odessa, Tex., 1993—; adminstr. nursing Tembisa Hosp., Johannesburg, South Africa, 1969-72; clin. pastoral edn. Shannon Hosp., San Angelo, Tex., 1993, Meth. Hosp., Lubbock, Tex., 1994-95. Fellow Coll. of Chaplains; mem. Am. Assn. Pastoral Counselors. Address: Missionary Sisters of Holy Rosary 14 Marquee West 1111 W 13th St Odessa TX 79763 Office: Missionary Sisters of Holy Rosary 741 Polo Rd Bryn Mawr PA 19010

LEE, AMY FREEMAN, artist, educator; b. San Antonio, Oct. 3, 1914; d. Joe and Julia (Freeman) Freeman; grad. St. Mary's Hall, 1931; student U. Tex., 1931-34; student Incarnate Word Coll., 1934-42, Litt.D. (hon.), 1965; m. Ernest R. Lee, Oct. 17, 1937 (div. Jan., 1941). Art critic San Antonio Express, 1939-41; staff art critic radio sta. KONO, 1947-51; lectr. Eng. dept., Incarnate World Coll., San Antonio, 1955-56, Tex., lectr. on art humanities dept. Trinity U., San Antonio, 1954-56, San Antonio Art Inst., 1955-56; lectr. art Our Lady of Lake Coll., San Antonio, 1969-71, The Humane Soc., Am. Inst. Architects, Washington, numerous others, 1991—; elected to San Antonio Women's Hall of Fame, 1991, Ark. chpt. Am. Inst. Architecture, Hot Springs, 1991, Austin, Tex., 1993, Inst. Tex. Cultures, 1993, Ann. Windcrest Christmas Contest, San Antonio, others. One man shows, 1947—, including U. Tex., 1970, 73, Tex. Tech. U., 1970, Del Mar Coll., Corpus Christi, Tex., 1970, Southwestern U., Georgetown, Tex., 1971, 79, Pioneer Meml. Libr., Fredricksburg, Tex., 1971, U. Tex. Student Union, 1972, Ojo del Sol Gallery, El Paso, 1972, Shook-Carrington Gallery, San Antonio, 1972, 1st Repertory Theatre, San Antonio, 1974, Sol del Rio Galleries, San Antonio, 1976, 87, 89, Oakwell Libr., San Antonio, 1976, U. Central Ark., Conway, 1977, NE La. State U., Monroe, 1978, Our Lady of the Lake U., San Antonio, 1978, Univ. Art Gallery, N. Tex. State U., Denton, 1979, L & L Gallery, Longview, Tex., 1980, 93, Meredith Long Galleries, Houston, 1980, Incarnate Word Coll., San Antonio, 1981, St. Mary's Hall, San Antonio, 1981, Sol del Rio Gallery, San Antonio, Tex., 1987, 1989, 35th Anniversary Exhbn. Art, A.C., Monterrey, Mex., 1990, McNay Art Mus., 1991, others, Tex. and Calif.; exhibited works in numerous group shows U.S. and Europe, including Nat. Soc. Painters in Casein, N.Y.C., 1969-79, Tex. Watercolor Soc., San Antonio, 1974-77, Nat. Watercolor Soc., 1978, 79, Silvermine Guild, New Canaan, Conn., 1974-75, Art Mus. S. Tex., Corpus Christi, 1975-76, Nat. Tour Am. Drawings, Smithsonian Instn., 1965-66, S.W. Tex. Watercolor Soc., 1976, 79, Tex. Watercolor Soc., 1980, Silvermine Guild Artists, New Canaan, Conn., 1980, Sol del Rio Gallery, San Antonio, 1982, 83, 85, McNay Art Mus., San Antonio, 1983, 85, Incarnate Word Coll., San Antonio, 1984, 85, Bright Shawl Gallery, San Antonio, 1985, also ann. exhbns. San Antonio Art League, 1986, St. Mary's Hall Libr., 1988, Arte, A.C., Monterrey, 1992, L&L Gallery, Longview, Tex., 1993, nat. art socs., galleries, confs.; represented in permanent collections. Pres., mem. exec. bd. San Antonio Blind Assn.; jury mem. children's poetry contest San Antonio Libr. System, apptd. by mayor libr. found., 1983-84; judge numerous art and lit. competitions; elected lifetime chmn. Young Pegasus Poetry Contest Jury, 1984, judge 1992-93; elected mem. adv. bd. Mex. Cultural Inst., San Antonio, 1990; elected mem. adv. coun. The Tex. Ctr. for Legal Ethics and Professionalism, 1991; apptd. by the Supreme Ct. of Tex. to Tex. Lawyer Discipline Commn., by gov. Tex. to Tex. Com. on Humanities, 1992; hon. chair San Antonio State Hosp. Centennial; chmn. bd. trustees Incarnate Word Coll., San Antonio; bd. dirs., nat. sec., mem. adv. bd. Gulf States Regional Office; nat. trustee, nat. sec. Humane Soc. U.S.; judge San Antonio Public Schs., 1987, lectr. in field; bd. dirs. Man and Beast, Inc.; fine arts adv. coun. U. Tex.; pres. Friends San Antonio Public Libr., 1969-70; mem. com. on grievance oversight Tex. State Bar, 1979-90; designated dir. emeritus Man and Beast Inc., San Antonio, 1986, hon. pres., 1980, hon. dir., 1985-87; mem. steering com. 100th Anniversary Celebration Healy-Murphy Ctr., 1988; trustee Inst. Humanities at Salado, Tex., 1993, Tex. Ctr. Legal Ethics and Professionalsim, Austin, 1993. Recipient awards, 1960—, including: 1st prize Contemporary Artists Exhbn., San Antonio, 1973; Women in Art award San Antonio Bus. and Profl. Women's Club, 1975; Drought award Local Artists Exhbn., San Antonio, 1977, drawing award, 1978, M.J. Kaplan award Nat. Soc. Painters in Casein and Acrylic, 1978; numerous other art awards; Hon. Stagescrew award, drama dept. San Antonio Coll., 1975; Service award Providence High Sch., San Antonio, 1976; Gold medal Incarnate Word Coll., San Antonio, 1978; Disting. Alumna medal St. Mary's Hall, 1981, Spl. recognition award Tex. Ednl. Theater Assn., 1982, Arts and Letters award Friends of San Antonio Library, 1985, The Joseph Wood Krutch medal Humane Soc. of U.S., 1985, Harold Vagtborg award Council of Research and Acad. Libraries (San Antonio), 1986, Hors de Concourt award Tex. Watercolor Soc., 1989, Spirit of Am. Women award J.C. Penny, 1990, citiation City of San Antonio, 1991; named Woman of Distinction, Baylor U., 1967, Texas Art Collector, McNay Mus., 1991, Tex. Women's Hall Fame, Gov.'s Tex. Commn. for Women, 1984, Hon. RN-Nursing Divsn. San Antonio Coll., 1992; Amy Freeman Lee AAUW Ednl. Found. Fellowship named, 1973; honored for 45 yrs. of disting. service to Madonna Ctr., San Antonio, 1986. Fellow Tex. Art Edn. Assn. (charter mem.), 1993; mem. Am. Fedn. Arts, Nat. Soc. Painters in Casein, Artists Equity Assn., Boston Soc. Ind. Artists (Smith Coll. purchase prize 1950), San Antonio Art League (adv. bd. of presidents, 6th v.p.), Nat. Soc. Arts and Letters, San Antonio Chamber Music Soc. (dir.), Philos. Soc. Tex., Defenders of Wildlife, Am. Anti-Vivisect. Soc. (life), World Fedn. for Protection Animals (life), Nat. Assn. for Advancement Humane Edn., Tex. Art Educators, Humane Soc. U.S. (v.p. Earthkind, 1992), Woman's Aux. Santa Rosa Hosp. (founder), St. Mary's Hall Alumni Assn., San Antonio Conservation Soc., Poetry Soc. Am., Am. Soc. for Aesthetics, Assn. Internationale des Critiques d'Art, Paris, Contemporary Artists Group San Antonio (dir.), Southwest Watercolor Soc. (purchase prize 1967, Harwood K. Smith award 1969), Tex. Watercolor Soc. (founder, pres., dir., purchase prize 1963, 64, 69, 74, 79, 80, emeritus charter mem. 1994), Nat. Watercolor Soc. (Figure painting award 1967), Calif., Los Angeles, San Antonio watercolor socs., Tex. Art Edn. Assn., Coll. Art Assn. Am. , Silvermine Guild Artists, S. Tex. Print Soc., Tex. Fine Arts Assn. (adv. council), Tex. Art Alliance, Artists Fellowship of N.Y., Assn. Governing Bds. Univs. and Colls., Internat. Platform Assn., Bus. and Profl. Women's Club (hon.), AAUP, AAUW, Internat. Soc. for Edn. Through Art, Cum Laude Soc. (hon.), Kappa Pi (hon.), Delta Delta Delta, Tau Sigma Delta (hon.), Delta Kappa Gamma (hon.), numerous other groups. Author: Hobby Horses, 1940; A Critic's Notebook, 1943; Remember Pearl Harbor, 1945; contbg. editor S.A. mag. and Radio Sta. KTSA, San Antonio, 1977. Address: 127 Canterbury Hill St San Antonio TX 78209-5421

LEE, ANN MCKEIGHAN, secondary school educator; b. Harlan, Iowa, Nov. 18, 1939; d. Earl Edward and Dorothy Elizabeth (Kaufman) McK.; m. Duane Edward Compton, Aug. 13, 1960 (div. 1985); children: Kathleen, David, Anne-Marie, John. Cert. in med. tech., Creighton U., 1960; BA in Art History, Ind. U., 1984; MA, U. South Fla., 1992, postgrad. Cert. secondary tchr., Fla.; cert. med. technologist. Realtor Savage/Landrian Realty, Indpls., 1978-84; lectr. Marian Coll., Indpls., 1987-88; tchr. Sarasota (Fla.) County Schs., 1989-92, rep. faculty coun., 1991-92; lectr. curriculum & instrn. U. South Fla., 1993—; docent Historic Spanish Point, Osprey, Fla., 1989-93, Ringling Mus. Art, 1993—; presenter panel Bibliographic Intstruction in Art History. Contbr. articles to profl. jours. V.p. fin. LWV, Indpls., 1971-73; v.p dist. IV aux. ADA, 1976-78, comptroller, 1978-89; coord. Gold Coun. and Ambs. U. South Fla., 1990-92. Recipient Silver Svc. award Crossroads Guild, 1981. Mem. AAUW, Coll. Art Assn., Soc. Archtl. Historians, Gulf Coast Heritage Assn. (co-chmn. pub. rels.), Sarasota Arts Coun. (tchr. rep. 1990), Phi Kappa Phi, Phi Delta Kappa. Roman Catholic. Home and Office: 3617 Shady Brook Ln Sarasota FL 34243-4840

LEE, ARMISTEAD MASON, economics consultant; b. Anking, China, Apr. 2, 1916; (parents Am. citizens); s. Edmund Jennings IV and Lucy Mitchell (Chaplin) Lee; m. Eleanore Ruggles Cobb, June 20, 1942; children: Eleanore Lee Elson, Rebecca Lee Samanci, Jeffrey Armistead. BA, Yale U., 1938, MA in Internat. Rels., 1941; Rhodes scholar, Oxford (Eng.) U., 1938-39; MPA in Econs., Harvard U., 1957. Reporter, editorial writer Roanoke (Va.) World News, summer 1940, 41; fgn. svc. officer Dept. State, Toronto, 1943, Dakar, 1944-45, Melbourne, Australia, 1946-48, Wellington, New Zealand, 1948-51, Washington, 1951-54, 63-67, Jamaica, 1954-56, Reykjavik, 1957-59, Brussels, 1959-63; dep. dir. Office Ctrl. Africa Affairs Dept. State, 1963-67; ret., 1967; dir. econ. rsch. Pharm. Mfrs. Assn., Washington, 1967-82; ret., 1982, econ. cons., 1982—; econ. cons. various pharm. cos., 1982—; lectr. on fgn. policy, 1985—. Contbr. articles to profl. jours. Pres. Soc. of the Lees of Va., Alexandria, 1972-86; sec. Com. for Peaceful Progress in South Africa, Washington, 1986—. Mem. Am. Fgn. Svc. Assn. (mem. retirees adv. com. 1992—), Diplomatic and Consular Officers Ret. (mem. program com. 1992—), Nat. Economists Club (sec. 1976-77, v.p. 1978). Democrat. Unitarian. Home: 2367 N Kenmore St Arlington VA 22207-4481 Office: Goodwin House # 932 4800 Fillmore Ave Alexandria VA 22311

LEE, B. KYUN, mechanical engineer, educator; b. Taegu, Kyung-Boog, Republic of Korea, Sept. 20, 1952; came to U.S., 1982; s. Jung-Ha and Il-Jin (Kim) L.; m. Misook Park, Oct. 3, 1980; children: Eun-Gi, Nathan. BSME, Young-Nam U., Taegu, 1980; MSME, Oreg. State U., 1984; MA, N.W. Christian Coll., 1988; PhD, Oreg. State U., 1988; MDiv, New Orleans Bapt. Theol. Sem., 1994. Registered profl. engr., Tex. R&D engr. Hyun-Dai Motor Co., Ulsan, Republic of Korea, 1980-82; engr. Evanite Fiber Co., Corvallis, Oreg., 1987-88; assoc. prof. LeTourneau U., Longview, Tex., 1988—; prin. investigator Colt Friction Products, Longview, 1989-90; co-investigator GRACO Children's Products, 1990-91; cons. Stemco Co., Longview, 1990-91; prin. investigator Capacity of Tex., Longview, 1991—; researcher LeTourneau U., Longview, 1988—. Author sci. papers. Mem. ASME, Am. Soc. Engring. Edn., Soc. Mfg. Engr., Phi Kappa Phi. Baptist. Home: 1805 Rodden St Longview TX 75604-2459 Office: LeTourneau U PO Box 7001 2100 S Mobberly Ave Longview TX 75602-3564

LEE, BETTE GALLOWAY, accountant; b. Charlotte, N.C., Oct. 5, 1927; d. William Lawson and Bertha (Christenbury) Galloway; m. Joe Lee, June 11, 1949 (div. Sept. 1968); children: Carolyn Jean, William Patterson, Perry Galloway. AA, Carolina Bus. Coll., Charlotte, 1948; student, Cen. Piedmont Community Coll., Charlotte, 1974—. Clk. accounts receivable Associated Transport, Charlotte, 1948-49; bookkeeper J.E. Elrod Lumber Co., Charlotte, 1949-54; acct. F.W. Faires Co., Charlotte, 1954-56, Boise-Cascade Bldg. Materials, Charlotte, 1971-74, D.W. Flowe & Son Grading Co., Charlotte, 1974-83; office mgr. and acct. BBC Tax Svcs., Charlotte, 1963-71; prin. B.G. Lee Bookkeeping Svc., Charlotte, 1983—; cons. various small bus.'s, 1985—; leader seminars fin. analyses, 1985—. Asst. leader local troop U.S. Girl Scouts, 1963-70; active on Rep. Presdl. Task Force, Washington, 1989. Mem. Am. Soc. Women Accts., Women Bus. Owners, Charlotte C. of C. (BG Network), Beta Sigma Phi (Iota chpt.). Presbyterian. Home and Office: 2600 Commonwealth Ave Charlotte NC 28205-5305

LEE, BETTY REDDING, architect; b. Shreveport, La., Dec. 6, 1919; d. Joseph Alsop and Mary (Byrd) Redding; m. Frank Cayce Lee, Nov. 22, 1940 (dec. Aug. 1978); children: Cayce Redding, Clifton Monroe, Mary Byrd (Mrs. Kent Ray). Student La. State U., 1936-37, 37-38, U. Calif. War Extension Coll., San Diego, 1942-43; student Centenary Coll., 1937; attended Roofing Industry Ednl. Inst., 1980-82, 84, 86-88, 89-90, 93, Better Understanding Roofing Systems Inst., 1989. Sheetmetal worker Consol.-Vultee, San Diego, 1942; engring. draftsman, 1943-45; jr. to sr. archtl. draftsman Bodman & Murrell, Baton Rouge, 1945-55; sr. archtl. draftsman to architect Post & Harelson, Baton Rouge, 1955-58; assoc. arch. G. Ross Murrell, Jr., Baton Rouge, 1960-66; staff arch. Charles E. Schwing & Assos., Baton Rouge, 1966-71, Kenneth C. Landry, Baton Rouge, 1971, 73-74; engring., design draftsman Rayner & McKenzie, Baton Rouge, 1972-73; cons. arch. and planner Office Engring. and Cons. Svcs., La. Dept. Health and Human Resources, Baton Rouge, 1974-82; sr. arch. roofing and waterproofing sect. La. Dept. Facility Planning and Control, 1982-96; pvt. consulting practice, Baton Rouge, 1996-96; Betty Redding Lee, Architect, 1996; Author Instructions to Designers for Roofing Systems for Louisiana Public Buildings; co-author: Building Owners Guide for Protecting and Maintaining Built-Up Roofing Systems, 1981; designed typical La. country store for La. Arts and Sci. Ctr. Mus. Recipient Honor award Schuller BURSI Group, 1989, 90, 91, 92, 93. Mem. La. Assn. Children with Learning Disabilities, 1967-69, Multiple Sclerosis Soc., 1963—, CPA Aux., 1960-69, PTA, 1953-66; troop leader Brownies and Girl Scouts U.S.A., 1959-60; asst. den mother Cub Scouts, 1955-57. Licensed architect. Mem. ASTM, Nat. AIA, AIA La., AIA Baton Rouge (first woman mem.), DAR, Constrn. Specifications Inst. (charter mem. Baton Rouge chpt.) So. Bldg. Code Congress Internat., Miss. Roofing Contractors Assn. (first woman hon.), Nat. Roofing Contractors Assn., La. Inst. Bldg. Scis. (founding mem. 1980), Roof Cons. Inst. (profl. mem.), Inst. Roofing and Waterproofing Consultants, Internat. Jr. League Baton Rouge, Le Salon du Livre Club, Kappa Delta. Republican. Episcopalian. Home: 1994 Longwood Dr Baton Rouge LA 70808-1247 Office: 881 Kenmore Ave Baton Rouge LA 70806-5521

LEE, BRENDA B., critical care nurse; b. Picayune, Miss., Dec. 7, 1947; d. James Thomas K. and Dorothy Pearl (Thrash) L. AD, Pearl River Jr. Coll., 1967. RN, La., Miss.; cert. gastroenterology RN; cert. ACLS. Staff and charge nurse, supr. Crosby Meml. Hsop., Picayune; staff and charge nurse Meth. Hosp., New Orleans, St. Joseph Hosp., Asheville, N.C.; oper. rm. aand endoscopy nurse Biloxi (Miss.) VA Med. Ctr. Mem. AORN (sec.), AACN, Soc. Gastrointestinal Nurses and Assocs.

LEE, CATHY CALLANS, nonprofit management executive; b. Birmingham, Ala., Dec. 15, 1950; d. Charles William and Bernice Ann (Colafrancesco) Callans; m. Robert Oscar Lee, July 29, 1972; 1 child, Amanda. BA cum laude, St. Mary's Dominican Coll., New Orleans, 1972; post-grad., Birmingham-So. Coll., 1978. Cert. fund raising exec. Tchr. psychology, English and theology John Carroll High Sch., 1977-83; mktg. coord. Gresham, Smith and Ptnrs., Architects, 1983-87; devel. cons. LWV, Ala. Friends of Adoption, B.A.Y. Theater, 1985-90; devel. officer U. Ala., Birmingham, 1987-92; v.p. for devel. and comms. Discovery 2000, Inc., 1992—. Contbr. to anthology collection Alalitcom, 1982, 90, 92. Past state bd. dirs. Ala. Friends of Adoption; past bd. dirs. Network Birmingham. Mem. Nat Soc. Fund Raising Execs., Toastmasters, Ala. Writers' Conclave.

Roman Catholic. Home: 2217 Shelterwood Rd Birmingham AL 35226-1049 Office: Discovery 2000 Inc 1320 22nd St S Birmingham AL 35205-4108

LEE, CHANGNAM, education educator; b. Kohung, Chonnam, Korea, July 23, 1955; came to U.S., 1987; s. Kun-Hee and Won-Oak (Kim) L.; m. Soojung Jongshil Choi, July 22, 1987; children: Eumeen, Eunice. BA, Chonnam Nat. U., Kwangju, Korea, 1979, MA, 1984; PhD in Spl. Edn., U. Oreg., 1993. Tchr. Han-Sung H.S., Seoul, Korea, 1979, Kum-Ho H.S., Kwangju, 1980-84; instr. So-Kang Jr. Coll., Kwangju, 1984-87; grad. tchr. fellow U. Oreg., Eugene, 1991-93, rsch. asst., 1993-95; curriculum evaluator 4J Sch. Dist., Eugene, 1993; asst. prof. Union U., Jackson, Tenn., 1996—. Contbr. articles, monograph to profl. publs. Mem. ASCD, Assn. for Direct Instrn., Coun. for Exceptional Children. Office: Union U 2447 Us Highway 45 Byp Jackson TN 38305-2002

LEE, CLIFFORD LEON, II, lawyer; b. Savannah, Ga., Aug. 16, 1957; s. Leo Mack and Marjean S. (Williams) L.; m. Harriette E.P. Howard, Aug. 16, 1986 (div. Dec. 1988); 1 child, Leonette Lowri Marie; m. Alisha Blackmon, Dec. 1990; children: Ronald A. Walker, Clifford Leon III; 1 stepchild, Kiara Ellison. BS, Tuskegee Inst., 1979; JD, So. U., Baton Rouge, La., 1982. Bar: La. 1983, U.S. Ct. Mil. Appeals 1983, Nebr. 1985, U.S. Supreme Ct. 1986. N.C. 1988. Special asst. to chancellor Delta Theta Phi Law Frat., Worthington, Ohio, 1981-83, 85-87; ptnr. Barton & Lee, Fayetteville, 1988-94, The Lee Law Firm, Fayetteville, 1994—. Served to capt. U.S. Army, 1983-86. Named one of Outstanding Young Men Am., 1979. Mem. ABA, Nat. Bar Assn., Assn. Trial Lawyers Am., Fed. Bar Assn., NAACP (life), Kapp Alpha Psi. Democrat. Baptist.

LEE, DAN M., state supreme court justice; b. Petal, Miss., Apr. 19, 1926; s. Buford Aaron and Pherbia Ann (Camp) L.; m. Peggy Jo Daniel, Nov. 27, 1947 (dec. 1952); children, Sheron, Lee Anderson; m. Mary Alice Gray, Sept. 30, 1956; 1 child, Dan Jr. Attended, U. So. Miss., 1946; LLB, Jackson Sch. Law, 1949; JD, Miss. Coll., 1970. Bar: Miss. 1948. Ptnr. Franklin & Lee, Jackson, Miss, 1948-54, Lee, Moore and Countiss, Jackson, Miss., 1954-71; county judge Hinds County, Hinds County, 1971-77; cir. judge Hinds-Yazoo Counties, Hinds-Yazoo Counties, 1977-82; assoc. justice Miss. Supreme Ct., Jackson, 1982-87, presiding justice, 1987-95, chief justice, 1995—. With U.S. Naval Air Corps, 1944-46. Mem. ABA, Hinds County Bar Assn., Miss. State Bar Assn., Aircraft Owners and Pilots Assn., Am. Legion, VFW. Democrat. Baptist. Lodges: Masons, Odd Fellows.

LEE, DANIEL KUHN, economist; b. Kyoto, Japan, Dec. 18, 1946; came to U.S., 1977; s. Chu G. and Myung N. (Lee) L.; m. Kaye K.S. Kwon, Apr. 10, 1976; children: David, Alexander. BS, Kyoto U., Japan, 1970; MA, Seoul Nat. U., Seoul, Republic of Korea, 1973, SUNY, Stony Brook, 1979; PhD, Iowa State U., 1981. Postdoctoral rsch. assoc. Iowa State U., Ames, 1981-82, instr., 1982; sr. economist Miss. Rsch. and Devel. Ctr., Jackson, 1982-88; dir. of econs. Miss. Insts. of Higher Learning, Jackson, 1988-95; sr. fiscal advisor Barents Group, KPMG Peat Marwick, 1995—; adj. prof. Jackson State U., 1986-88; advisor Gov.'s Econ. Task Force, Jackson, 1982-84. Author: A Study of Mississippi Input-Output Model, 1986; contbr. articles to profl. jours. Exec. dir. So. Regional Assn., Washington, 1992—; elder Presbyn. Ch. USA, 1991—. Travel grantee UN Indsl. Devel. Orgn., Vienna, Austria, 1986. Mem. So. Regional Sci. Assn., North Am. Regional Sci. Assn., Am. Econ. Assn., So. Econ. Assn., Gamma Sigma Delta. Office: Barents Group KPMG Peat Marwick 2001 M St NW Washington DC 20036-3310

LEE, HIEN QUANG, religious organization executive. Pres. Vietnamese Cath. Fedn. in U.S. Address: PO Box 1419 Gretna LA 70053-1419

LEE, HOWARD DOUGLAS, academic administrator; b. Louisville, Ky., Mar. 15, 1943; s. Howard W. and Margaret (Davidson) L.; m. Margaret Easley, Nov. 20, 1965; children: Gregory Davidson, Elizabeth Anna. BA in English, U. Richmond, 1964; ThM, Southeastern Seminary, Wake Forest, N.C., 1968; PhD in Religion, U. Iowa, Iowa City, 1971. Prof. religion, devel. dir. Va. Intermont Coll., Bristol, 1971-73; dir. univ. relations Wake Forest (N.C.) U., 1973-78; v.p. devel. Stetson U., DeLand, Fla., 1978-80, v.p. planning and devel., 1980-83, exec. v.p., 1984-86, pres.-elect, 1986-87, pres., 1987—. Contbr. articles to profl. jours. Founding dir. Atlantic Ctr. for Arts, New Smyrna Beach, Fla., 1978—; chmn. DeLand C. of C., 1994; chair Volusia Vision Com., 1994-96. Named Cen. Fla. Fundraiser of Yr. Nat. Assn. Fundraising Execs. 1985. Mem. So. Assn. Colls. and Schs. (exec. coun. 1993-94), Rotary, Deland Country Club, Omicron Delta Kappa. Office: Stetson U Campus Box 8258 421 N Boulevard Deland FL 32720

LEE, JAMES A., health facility finance executive; b. Red Level, Ala., Dec. 19, 1939; s. H. Alton Lee; m. Charlotte Phillips, Dec. 19, 1963 (div. July 1971); children: Phillip, Michele, Jenifer; m. Melanie Cooper, Dec. 14, 1973; children: Christopher, Amanda. BBA in Acctg., Jacksonville State U., 1964; MS in Hosp. and Health Adminstrn., U. Ala., 1980. CPA, Ala. Sr. acct. Macke, Eldredge, McIntosh, Birmingham, Ala., 1964-67, Touche, Ross, Bailey & Smart, Birmingham, 1967-68; bus. functions mgr. Druid City Hosp., Tuscaloosa, Ala., 1968-71; sr. assoc. adminstr., fin. Univ. Ala. Hosp., Birmingham, 1971-94; CFO Montgomery Cardiovasc. Assocs., PC, 1994—; asst. prof. health services adminstrn. Univ. Ala. Birmingham, 1980—; asst. prof. Dept. Pub. Health, Univ. Ala. Birmingham, 1984—. Mem. Health Care Fin. Mgmt. Assn., Ala. Soc. CPA's, Am. Inst. CPA's, Am. Hosp. Assn. Republican. Baptist. Home: 109 Pemberton Pl Pelham AL 35124-2817

LEE, JAMES ASHLEY, writer, film producer; b. Baton Rouge, Aug. 2, 1948; s. James Eli and Evelyn Franklin L.; divorced; children: David Ashley, Jonathan Michael. BA in English Lit., U. of Southwestern La., 1987. Mechanic Stark Candy Co., Thibodaux, La., 1971-72; sales mgr. Sears, Pocatello, Idaho, 1977; salesperson photog. equipment J.C. Penny, Baton Rouge, 1977; freelance photographer Creative Images, Baton Rouge, 1977-78; exec. producer Cinevision Pictures, Lafayette, La., 1989-90. Editor: (newsletter) The Vet Gazette (Vietnam), 1983 (Outstanding Achievement Award 1985). Mem. Beacon Club, Lafayette, 1981-87. Sgt. USAF, 1968-71, Vietnam. Baptist. Home: PO Box 1083 Many LA 71449-1083 Office: Cinevision Pictures 240 Pinecrest St Many LA 71449

LEE, JEFFREY EDWIN, surgeon; b. Queens, N.Y., July 6, 1957; s. Edwin Joseph and Miriam Magdalene (Niedhammer) L.; m. Laura Norma Dietch, May 19, 1984 (div. Dec. 9, 1988); m. Joy Kay McFate, Apr. 6, 1991; children: Caitlin Elizabeth, Alicia Colleen. AB magna cum laude, Dartmouth Coll., 1979; MD, Stanford U., 1984. Lic. physician Tex., Hawaii, Calif.; diplomate Am. Bd. Surgery, Nat. Bd. Med. Examiners. Rsch. asst. dept. chemistry Dartmouth Coll., Hanover, N.H., 1978-80; rsch. asst. div. epidemiology dept. family, community and preventive medicine Stanford U., 1981-82; intern dept. surgery Stanford U. Med. Ctr., 1984-85, resident div. gen. surgery, 1985-91, postdoctoral rsch. fellow dept. surgery and pediatrics, 1987-89; clin. fellow gen. surg. oncology dept. gen. surgery U. Tex. M.D. Anderson Cancer Ctr., Houston, 1991-93, postdoctoral rsch. fellow depts. gen. surgery/immunology, 1992, asst. prof. dept. surgical oncology, 1993—; lectr. in field. Contbr. articles to profl. jours. Rufus Choate scholar, 1975-76; NIH Nat. Rsch. Svc. award, 1987-89. Mem. AMA, ACS, Am. Soc. Clin. Oncology, Soc. Surgery of Alimentary Tract, Am. Pancreatic Assn., Am. Assn. Endocrine Surgeons, Soc. Surg. Oncology, Assn. Acad. Surgery, Internat. Assn. Pancreatology, S.W. Surg. Congress, Tex. Med. Assn., Harris County Med. Soc., Houston Surg. Soc., Am. Heart Assn. (cert.), Am. Assn. Cancer Rsch., Am. Gastroenterol. Assn. Home: 3646 Glen Haven Blvd Houston TX 77025-1308 Office: U Tex M D Anderson Cancer Dept Surg Oncology 106 1515 Holcombe Blvd Houston TX 77030-4009

LEE, JEROME ODELL, minister; b. Chgo., July 28, 1955; s. Myrtle Carllillian Lee; m. Andrea Yvette White, Apr. 27, 1991; 1 child, Jasmine Tyler. Student, Loop Jr. Coll., Chgo., 1973-75; BA, Bishop Coll., 1978; MDiv, Va. Union U., 1982, D in Ministry, 1995. Ordained to ministry Nat. Bapt. Conv. U.S.A., 1979; lic. min. So. Bapt. Conv., 1974, Shiloh Missionary Bapt. Ch., 1994. Pastor Pleasant Plain Bapt. Ch., Drewyville, Va., 1980-81, Spring Creek Bapt. Ch., Midlothian, Va., 1985—; instr. Christian edn. leadership teaching team Bapt. Gen. Conv. of Va., Richmond, 1981-85, Evans-Smith Leadership Inst., Va. Union U., Richmond, 1983-85. Del. Dem. State Conv., Richmond, 1989. Mem. Richmond Bapt. Assn., Tuckahoe Bapt. Assn., Bapt. Gen. Conv. Va. (asst. sec. clergy div. 1990-92, pres. African-Am. Fellowship), African-Am. Fellowship Va. (pres.), Bapt. Gen. Assn. Va./So. Bapt. Conv., Bapt. Min. Conf. Richmond, Alpha Phi Alpha (Xi Delta Lambda chpt., intake coord. 1993-96, rec. sec. 1992-94). Office: Spring Creek Bapt Ch 11900 Genito Rd Midlothian VA 23112-3652

LEE, JIMMY CHE-YUNG, city planner; b. Canton, China, May 29, 1946; came to U.S., 1969.; s. Chi Dui and Fong-Lee (Leung) L.; m. Annie On-lin Chan, Nov. 29, 1970 (div. 1987); m. Eileen Oi Ping Cheung, Dec. 16, 1987 (div. 1990); m. Sara Yeuk Siu, June 21, 1994. Grad., Sir. Robert Black Coll. Edn., Hong Kong; BA, U. Tex., 1973, MA, 1975. Tchr. English and Chinese Asbury Meth. Primary Sch., Hong Kong, 1966-69; asst. mgr. Trader Vic's Restaurant Dallas Hilton Inn, 1971-75; planner Dallas County Community Action Agy., 1975, dir. projects and resource devel. div., 1975—; pres. U-Asia Corp., Hong Kong, 1975; owner Dragon Inn Restaurant, 1975; contr. food and beverage div. Plaza of Am. Hotel, 1979-82; comptr. Carlyle Hotels & Restaurants Inc., Harold Farb Cos., 1982; founder, chief exec. officer Lee & Lee Fine Linens, Inc., 1982—; v.p. Asiatex Inc., 1987—, Titan Real Estate Devel. & Investment Group, Inc., 1993—; bd. dirs. Crown Chpt. Nat. Bank Dallas. Pres. North Tex. Cantonese Assn., 1986-88, hon. pres., 1989—; dir. Dallas chpt. Friends of Hong Kong and Macau; v.p., dir. North Tex. Chinese Culture Divination Soc. Mem. Am. Inst. Planners (assoc.), Tex. Assn. Community Action Agys., Hong Kong Registered Tchrs. Assn., Oakcliff C. of C. Baptist. Home: 10115 Chisholm Trl Dallas TX 75243-2511 Office: 4846 Alexander Ln Dallas TX 75247-6504

LEE, JIN SOO, oncologist, educator; b. Cheonbuk-Do, Republic of Korea, Nov. 19, 1950; came to U.S., 1978; m.; 4 children. Premed. degree, Seoul Nat. U., 1970, MD with honors, 1974, MPH, 1976. Diplomate Am. Bd. Internal Medicine. Intern Seoul Nat. U. Hosp., 1975-76; staff physician Koje Community Health Care Corp., Kyunngnam-Do, Republic of Korea, 1976-78; resident St. Joseph Hosp., Chgo., 1979-82; fellow U. Tex. M.D. Anderson Cancer Ctr., Houston, 1982-84, faculty assoc., 1984-85, instr. medicine, asst. internist, 1985-87, asst. internist, asst. prof. medicine, 1987-92, assoc. internist, assoc. prof. medicine, 1992—; teaching experience U. Tex., 1984, St. Joseph Hosp., Chgo., 1979-82, Seoul Nat. U. Sch. Pub. Health, 1978, Koje Community Health Care Corp., 1976-78, Seoul Nat. U. Med. Sch., 1975-76. Contbr. articles to profl. jours.; patentee in field. Recipient Changhee scholarship, 1971-73, NIH grants, 1987-90, 1988-92, 1991-95, 1992-94, 1993-96. Mem. AAAS, ACP, AMA, Am. Assn. for Cancer Rsch., Am. Soc. Clin. Oncology, Harris County Med. Soc., Tex. Med. Assn. Office: MD Anderson Cancer Ctr U Tex 1515 Holcombe Blvd Houston TX 77030-4009

LEE, JOHN FRANCIS, surgeon; b. Chgo., Apr. 3, 1942; s. Robert Emmett and Kathryn Irene (Winke) L.; m. Naomi Sharon Prinz, June 26, 1965 (dec. June 1991); children: Gina Marie, Christopher, Brendan, Patrick; m. Dorothea Boulter Bowers, Mar. 14, 1992; children: Jacquelyn, Alexander, Zachary, Mackenzie, William Edward. MD, Loyola U., Chgo., 1967. Diplomate Am. Bd. Surgery, Am. Bd. Gen. and Vascular Surgery. Intern in surgery U. Chgo., 1967-68, resident in surgery, 1968-72, chief resident and instr. in surgery, 1972-73; fellow in vascular surgery Henry Ford Hosp., Detroit, 1973-74; pvt. practice St. Petersburg, Fla., 1974—; pres., CEO, bd. dirs. 1st Fla. Med. PA, St. Petersburg, 1992; founder, past dir. vascular lab. St. Anthony's Hosp., St. Petersburg, 1977-85, pres-elect med. staff, 1983-85, pres. med. staff, 1985-88; chief of surgery, 1990-94; active Edward H. White II Meml. Hosp., St. Petersburg, 1976—, Bayfront Med. Ctr., 1991—, VA Hosp., Bay Pines, Fla., 1985. Contbr. articles to profl. jours. Mem. Fla. Com. on Cost of Med. Care, Jacksonville, 1978-82. Fellow ACS; mem. Fla. Med. Assn., Fla. Assn. Gen. Surgeons, Fla. Physicians' Assn., Pinellas County Med. Soc. (bd. govs. 1976-81), Southeastern Surg. Congress, Frederick A. Coller Surg. Soc., So. Assn. for Vascular Surgery. Republican. Roman Catholic. Home: 114 Rafael Blvd NE Saint Petersburg FL 33704-3740 Office: Lee and Williams 1111 7th Ave N Saint Petersburg FL 33705-1348

LEE, JOHN THOMAS, finance educator, financial planner; b. Cleve., May 31, 1942; s. Harry C. and Lucille B. (Varnell) L.; children: Andrea, Joanne. BS in Econs., Tenn. Tech U., 1964; MS in Fin., U. Tenn., 1966; PhD in Fin., U. Ga., 1977. CFP. Instr. fin. Tenn. Tech U., Cookeville, 1966-71, asst. prof., 1973-78, assoc. prof., 1978-84; teaching asst. U. Ga., Athens, 1971-73; prof. fin. Mid. Tenn. State U., Murfreesboro, 1984—, Weatherford prof. fin., 1984-91, chmn. dept. econs. and fin., 1991—; mem. faculty 5th Ann. Cash Mgmt. Inst. Nat. Forum, 1984, Grad. Sch. Banking of South, La. State U., 1986, 88, 89, Tenn. Bankers Sch., Vanderbilt U., 1985; spkr., discussant, moderator, presenter numerous profl. orgns. Contbr. numerous articles to profl. jours. Recipient Outstanding Faculty award Tenn. Tech. U. Coll. Bus. Found.; named Prof. of Yr. Coll. of Bus. Mid. Tenn. State U., 1988, 91; Ayers fellow ABA Stonier Grad. Sch. Banking, summer 1987. Mem. Inst. CFP's, Internat. Assn. for Fin. Planning (pres. greater Tenn. chpt. 1995-96), Fin. Mgmt. Assn., So. Fin. Assn., Ea. Fin. Assn., Midwest Fin. Assn., Southwestern Fin. Assn., Mid-South Acad. Econs. and Fin. (2d v.p. 1990-91, 1st v.p. 1991-92, pres. 1993-94), Mid. Tenn. Soc. CFP's (charter), Civitan (pres. Cookeville 1983-84, Stones River 1990-91, lt. gov. Valley dist.), Beta Gamma Sigma (pres. Mid. Tenn. State U. chpt. 1986-87, 92-94), Omicron Delta Epsilon, Sigma Iota Epsilon, Alpha Kappa Psi, Phi Delta Theta. Baptist. Home: 2522 Tomahawk Trce Murfreesboro TN 37129-6502 Office: Mid Tenn State U E Main St Murfreesboro TN 37132

LEE, JOHNSON Y., financial executive; b. Rangoon, Burma, June 10, 1955; came to U.S., 1968; s. Tat K. Lee and Thoy Lin (Ng); m. Lorraine Tran, June 29, 1981; children: Kent F., K. Ming. AA, City Coll., San Francisco, 1975; student, U. Calif., Berkeley, 1976. Cert. fin. planner. Agt. Prudential Ins. Co., Daly City, Calif., 1976-78; mgr. Prudential Ins. Co., Menlo Park, Calif., 1978-79; cons., pres. J.Y. Lee Pension Cons., L.A., 1979-83; broker Dean Witter, L.A., 1983-84; pres. Sun Cal Fin. Group, Inc., Pasadena, 1986—; v.p. TransCapital, Alexandria, Va., 1984-95;, 1991-94; pres. Sun-Cal Fin. Group Inc., Internat. Trading, Universal Gateways, Inc.; west coast dir. Telecommunication Internat.; dir. Biotek Solutions, Inc., 1995-96. Cons. Ming-Ye Buddhist Found., L.A., 1987—. Recipient Presdl. Citation Prudential Ins. Co., 1976-77. Home: 3004 E Charlinda St West Covina CA 91791-2904 Office: Trans Capital Corp Ste 206 11130 Sunrise Valley Dr 206 Reston VA 22091

LEE, JOSEPH EDWARD, history educator; b. Chester, S.C., Sept. 24, 1953; s. Tyre Douglas and Martha Ola (Bankhead) L.; m. Ann-Franklin Hardy, Sept. 24, 1983; 1 child, Elizabeth. BA, Presbyn. Coll., Clinton, S.C., 1975; MA, Winthrop U., 1983; PhD, U. S.C., 1987. Instr. Adult Edn. Program, Chester, 1975-81; ctr. dir. Project Head Start, Chester, 1975-76; edn. coordinator Project Head Start, Rock Hill, S.C., 1978-81, Rock Hill, 1978-81; tchr., coach Chester Sch. Dist., 1976-78; personnel dir. Carolina Community Actions, Rock Hill, 1981-82; grad. asst. Winthrop U., Rock Hill, 1982-83; teaching asst. U. S.C., Columbia, 1983-85; hist. prof. U. N.C., Charlotte, 1985-94; prof. history Winthrop U., Rock Hill, S.C., 1994—; adj. prof. U. S.C., 1985-88, Belmont Abbey Coll., 1987-95; cons. S.C. Com. on the Humanities, Columbia, 1983, N.C. Humanities Coun., 1991; guest lectr. Sacred Heart Coll., Belmont, N.C., 1987. Author: The New Muckrakers, 1996; contbr. articles to profl. jours. Mem. Chester City Council, 1979-83; treas. Chester County Dem. Orgn. 1984-86, vice-chmn. 1976-82; v.p. S.C. Young Democrats, 1982-83; election com. City of Chester, 1976-79; lectr. N.C. Commn. on the Bicentennial of the Const., Charlotte, 1986. Recipient Sen. Olin D. Johnston award, S.C. Dem. Orgn., R. Means Davis Fellow in So. Hist., U. S.C., 1983-85. Mem. So. Hist. Assn., S.C. Hist. Assn. (bd. dirs.), S.C. Hist. Soc., So. Caroliniana Soc., Order of Omega, Friends of Historic Brattonsville, Mus. of York County, Yorkville Hist. Soc., Kiwanis, Sertoma (v.p. Chester club 1981-82), Moose, Phi Alpha Theta, Phi Beta Delta, Kappa Alpha Order, Omicron Delta Kappa. Democrat. Presbyterian. Home: 202 W Madison St York SC 29745

LEE, JOSEPH KING TAK, radiologist, medical educator; b. Shanghai, China, Mar. 17, 1947; came to U.S., 1968; s. S.Y. (Zee) Lee; m. Christina Y.M. Tsai, June 2, 1973; children: Alexander, Betsy, Catherine. BSc, Chinese U. of Hong Kong, 1968; MD, Washington U., St. Louis, 1973. Diplomate Am. Bd. Radiology. Intern Washington U. Sch. Medicine, St. Louis, 1973-74, resident, 1974-77, instr. radiology, 1977-78, asst. prof. radiology, 1978-82, assoc. prof. radiology, 1982-86, prof. radiology, 1986-91; prof. radiology, chair dept. radiology U. N.C., Chapel Hill, 1991—; editor Topics in MRI, 1988—. Author, editor: Computed Body Tomography, 1983, Computed Body Tomography with MRI Correlation, 1989, Pocket Atlas of Normal CT Anatomy, 1984, Manual of Clinical Magnetic Resonance Imaging, 1985. Fellow Am. Coll. Radiology; mem. Am. Roentgen Ray Soc., Soc. Uroradiology (bd. dirs. 1988-90), Soc. Computed Body Tomography/MR (pres. 1993-94), Soc. of Chairmen of Acad. Radiology, Radiology Soc. N.Am. Protestant. Office: Univ North Carolina CB 7510 Chapel Hill NC 27599

LEE, KAMEE ANGELA, financial analyst; b. Hong Kong, Sept. 4, 1961; d. Yick-Kun and Fan-Yuk (Ho) L.; m. Hei-Wai Lee, May 23, 1988; 1 child, Jonathan. BA magna cum laude, Whittier Coll., 1984; MS in Fin., U. Ill., 1986, M of Acctg. Sci., 1989; student, U. Mich., 1996—. CPA, Fla.; cert. mgmt. acct. Tax assoc. Price Waterhouse, Miami, Fla., 1989-90; staff acct. Humana Health Care Plans, Tampa, Fla., 1990-92; mgr. finance and accounting Humana Health Care Plan, Tampa, Fla., 1992-94; mgr. data analysis and reporting Access Care, Tampa, 1994-96. Recipient Wall Street Journ. Student Achievement award, 1984, Barr scholar, Moss scholarship in acctg., 1987, Whittier Coll. scholarship, 1981-84, Acad. Achievement award, 1983. Mem. AICPA, Fla. Inst. CPA, Inst. of Mgmt. Accts., Phi Kappa Phi. Home: 44071 Dartmouth St Canton MI 48188

LEE, KATIE BROOKS, songwriter, entertainer; b. Louisville, Ky., Mar. 29, 1958; d. Hugh Ballard and Carolyn Ann (Bowling) Brooks; m. Dickey Lee, July 19, 1991. BS, Pa. State U., 1980. Entertainer Pa. and Tenn., 1980—; published songwriter Polygram, Famous Music, Crossfield Music, Lisa Glenn Music, Coal Miner's Music, Pal Time Music, 1988—; vocalist Boots Randolph Band, Nashville. Touring appearances (The Katie Brooks Show): Camp David for Pres. Jimmy Carter, Appalachian Jubilee Headliner, Jamboree USA (regular appearances Sta. WWVA radio), The Ralph Emery Show (WSMV-TV), The Tennessee Barn Dance (KNOX radio), IAAPA Internat. Showcases, USO, Re-Creation USA for Vets. Hosps., Banquets and Convs.: IBM, AMWAY, GE/RCA, Armstrong, Coachmen, NRPA, FFA; appearances for fraternal orgns., amusement parks, numerous others; choreographer: Re-Creation USA, high sch., university and community theatre prodns. including: West Side Story, Guys and Dolls, South Pacific, Carousel; choreographer ind. rock 'n roll and gospel bands, country line dances for video tapings; TV spokesperson Rea and Derick Drug Store Chain; reader The Talking Library-WPLN radio, Nashville. Vol. counselor Crisis Pregnancy Support Ctr., Nashville, 1993—; reader for blind Sta. WPLN radio, Nashville, 1994—. Pa. State Talent winner Jr. Miss Program Am., 1976, Center County Jr. Miss, State Coll. Pa., 1976; recipient svc. award VA, 1986. Republican. Baptist.

LEE, KENNETH STUART, neurosurgeon; b. Raleigh, N.C., July 23, 1955; s. Kenneth Lloyd and Myrtie Lee (Turner) L.; m. Cynthia Jane Anderson, May 23, 1981; children: Robert Alexander, Evan Anderson. BA, Wake Forest U., 1977; MD, East Carolina U., 1981. Diplomate Nat. Bd. Med. Examiners, Am. Bd. Neurol. Surgeons; med. lic. N.C., Ariz. Intern then resident in neurosurgery Wake Forest U. Med. Ctr., Winston-Salem, N.C., 1981-88; fellow Barrow Neurol. Inst., Phoenix, 1988-89; clin. asst. prof. neurosurgery East Carolina U., Greenville, N.C., 1989-93; clin. assoc. prof. neurosurgery, 1994—. Assoc. editor Current Surgery, 1990—; contbr. 30 articles to profl. jours. and 5 chpts. to books. Mem. Ethicon Neurosurgical Adv. Panel, 1989—. Bucy fellow, 1988. Fellow ACS, Am. Heart Assn. (stroke coun.); mem. AMA, N.C. Med. Soc., Am. Assn. Neurol. Surgeons, Am. Soc. Stereotactic and Functional Neurosurgery, So. Med. Assn., Congress Neurol Surgeons, N.C. Neurosurg. Soc. (sec.-treas. 1991-93, pres. 1994-95), Alpha Omega Alpha. Democrat. Baptist. Home: 3600 Baywood Ln Greenville NC 27834-7630 Office: Ea Carolina Neurosurg 2325 Stantonsburg Rd Greenville NC 27834-7534

LEE, LELA ANN, dermatology educator, researcher; b. Gorman, Tex., Sept. 7, 1950; d. J.H. and Pauline (Lemaster) L.; m. Norman Erling Wikner, June 24, 1984. BA, Rice U., 1972; MD, Southwestern Med. Sch., Dallas, 1976. Diplomate Am. Bd. Internal Medicine, Am. Bd. Dermatology. Resident in medicine Temple U. Hosp., Phila., 1976-79; resident in dermatology U. Colo., Denver, 1980-83, immunodermatology fellow, 1983-85, asst. prof. dermatology and medicine, 1985-91; staff physician V.A. Hosp., Denver, 1985-91; prof. dermatology U. Okla. Sch. of Medicine, 1991—; mem. test com. Am. Bd. Dermatology, 1993—. Contbr. articles to med. jours.; chief assoc. editor: Jour. Investigative Dermatology, 1990-92. Recipient Stelwagon award Coll. Physicians of Phila., 1983, Clin. Investigator award NIH, 1985-90; VA merit rev. grantee, 1991—; Bill Reed Traveling fellow Friends of Bill Reed Com., 1984; named Carl Herzog Prof. of Dermatology, 1991. Mem. Soc. Investigative Dermatology (bd. dirs. 1985-87), Am. Acad. Dermatology, Am. Assn. Immunologists, Am. Dermatol. Assn. Office: U Okla Sch Medicine 619 NE 13th St Oklahoma City OK 73104-5001

LEE, LESLIE W., truck parts manufacturing company executive; b. 1926. Student, U. Mo., 1945-48. Various sales positions Lee-Smith Internat. Inc., Chattanooga, 1959-65, v.p., 1965-72, pres., CEO, 1972—; pres. Lesco Inc., Chattanooga, 1960—. With U.S. Army, 1944-45. Office: Lee Smith Internat Inc 2600 8th Ave Chattanooga TN 37407-1156

LEE, LILLIAN ALDRIDGE, music educator; b. Greenwood, Miss., Mar. 29, 1934; d. Joseph Everette and Virginia (Gillespie) Aldridge; m. Robert G. Lee, June 24, 1956; children:Virginia Louise Lee McMurray, Dicey Gay Lee. B in Mus. Edn. magna cum laude, Miss. U. for Women, 1956; MusM, Miss. Coll., 1971, MusM in Vocal Performance, 1976. Music edn. tchr. Van Winkle and Clinton Blvd. Elem. Schs., Jackson, 1956-57, Terry (Miss.) Consol. Sch., 1962-70; choral dir. Jackson (Miss.) Preparatory Sch., 1970-77, First Presbyn. Day Sch., Jackson, 1978-96; pvt. instr. voice and piano, Jackson and Terry, Miss., 1956-84; instr. voice Miss. Coll., summer 1973; dir. children's choir and youth choir Ctrl. Presbyn. Ch., Jackson, 1976-80; guest condr. Hinds County Elem. Music Festival, 1991, Miss. Pvt. Sch. Edn. Assn. State Jr. High Choral Festival, 1991; coord. children's choirs First Presbyn. Ch., Jackson, 1982-84, dir. Minnesingers Women's Ensemble, 1985-93, dir. jr. high choir, 1987-90. Soprano soloist Ctrl. Presbyn. Ch., Jackson, 1974-82. Mem., soloist Jackson Choral Soc., 1972-75; asst. dir. Miss. Youth Chorale Summer Tour to Europe, 1976-78; active St. Andrews Chamber Soc., 1977-78, Miss. Opera Chorus, 1977-78; judge Capital City Jr. Miss Program, 1982. Recipient Miss. Music Educator of Year award, 1995. Mem. Am. Choral Dirs. Assn., Miss. Music Educators Assn. and Music Educators Nat. Conf. (dist. VI choral chmn. 1964-65, elem. textbook selection com. 1965-66, dist. VI elem. chmn. 1966-67, state choral chmn. 1969-70, state sec. 1970-71, state treas. 1993-95), Miss. Pvt. Sch. Edn. Assn. (state choral chmn. high sch. divsn. 1971-72, 72-73, 76-77, state choral chmn. jr. high divsn. 1984-85), Sigma Alpha Iota, Kappa Delta Pi. Republican. Methodist. Home: 1329 Simwood Pl Jackson MS 39211-6352

LEE, MARY VIRGINIA, artist; b. Clinton, Okla., Nov. 19, 1924; d. Thomas Joseph and Opal Corbin (Sights) Lee; m. Angelo Marelli, June 29, 1959; children: Luciana Powell, Thomas Giuseppe Marelli. Student, Corcoran Art Gallery, Washington, 1940-41; student, Am. U., Phillips Meml. Gallery, Washington, 1943-45, U. N.Mex., 1947; pvt. study, Scuola Beato Angelico, Milan, Italy, 1958-59. V.p. Marelli-Lee, Inc., Italy, N.Mex., Okla., 1961-94; mem. of fellowship Phillips Meml. Gallery, 1945-46; artist-in-residence Camp Galilee, Lake Tahoe, Nev., 1953, 56; guest instr. Clinton (Okla.) Elem. Sch., 1983. One-man shows include AAUW, Boulder City, Nev., 1950, Okla. Art Ctr., Oklahoma City, 1951, Nev. State Art Gallery, Reno, 1952, N.Mex. State Art Gallery, Santa Fe, 1954; group shows include N.Mex. State Traveling Collection, 1955; painter 2 murals parish ch. Montalto, Parma, Italy, mural St. Joseph's Ch., Hong Kong, 1993, 15 paintings St. Mary's Ch., Clinton, 1979, 14 paintings Epiphany Ch., Oklahoma City, 1984, double icon, 1984; designer 14 enamels St. Lawrence Cathedral, Amarillo, Tex., 1975, 2 hanging banners St. Mary's Ch., Clinton, 1983, 2 stained glass windows St. Peter's Ch., Guyman, Okla., 1985. Mem. DAR, Nat. Assn. Women Artists, Kappa Pi (hon.). Home: PO Box 132 Clinton OK 73601-0132

LEE, MELVIN JOSEPH, minister; b. New Orleans, Dec. 25, 1929; s. John and Isabelle (Green) L.; m. Dorothy Peterson, June 5, 1971; children: Betty, Barbara, Joseph, Edward. BS in Chemistry, So. U., New Orleans, 1970;

MDiv, Union Bapt. Theol. Sem., New Orleans, 1988, ThM, 1989. Ordained to ministry Bapt. Ch., 1984. Assoc. min. 3d Missionary Bapt. Ch., St. Bernard, La., 1984-87, pastor, 1987—, chair deacon bd., 1974-84; coroner's investigator Orleans Parish, New Orleans, 1982—; bd. dirs. So. Gen. Missionary Bapt. Assn., New Orleans, 1987—, chmn. bldg. com., 1988-92. Author: What Baptists Should Know, 1991; contbr. articles to profl. jours. Chmn. St. Bernard Cmty. Devel. Corp., 1988-93. Sgt. USAF, 1947-52. Democrat. Home: 7514 Dwyer Rd New Orleans LA 70126-4220 Office: 3d Missionary Bapt Ch 206 Armstrong Rd PO Box 1012 Saint Bernard LA 70085

LEE, NELDA S., art appraiser and dealer, film producer; b. Gorman, Tex., July 3, 1941; d. Olan C. and Onis L.; A.S. (Franklin Lindsay Found. grantee), Tarleton State U., Tex., 1961; B.A. in Fine Arts, N. Tex. State U., 1963; postgrad. Tex. Tech. U., 1964, San Miguel de Allende Art Inst., Mexico, 1965; 1 dau., Jeanna Lea Pool. Head dept. art Ector High Sch., Odessa, Tex., 1963-68. Bd. dirs. Odessa YMCA, 1970, bd. dirs. Am. Heart Assn., Odessa, 1975; fund raiser Easter Seal Telethon, Odessa, 1978-79; bd. dirs. Ector County (Tex.) Cultural Center, 1979—, Tex. Bus. Hall of Fame, 1980-85; bd. dirs., mem. acquisition com. Permian Basin Presdl. Mus., Odessa, 1978; bd. dirs., chairperson acquisition com. Odessa Art Mus., 1979—; pres. Mega-Tex. Prodns., TV and movie producers; pres. Ector County Democratic Women's Club, 1975, Nelda Lee, Inc., Odessa; appointee Tex. Commn. Arts, 1993—. Group exhbns. include El Paso, Tex., New Orleans. Recipient Designer-Craftsman award El Paso Mus. Fine Arts, 1964. Mem. Am. Soc. Appraisers (sr.), Nat. Tex. Assn. Art Dealers (pres. 1978—), Odessa C. of C. Contbr. articles to profl. jours. Office: Nelda Lee Inc PO Box 4268 Odessa TX 79760-4268

LEE, PETER JAMES, bishop; b. Greenville, Miss., May 11, 1938; s. Erling Norman and Marion (O'Brien) L.; m. Kristina Knapp, Aug. 28, 1965; children: Stewart, Peter James Jr. AB, Washington and Lee U., 1960; MDiv, Va. Theol. Sem., 1967; postgrad. Duke U. Law Sch., 1963-64; DD (hon.), Va. Theol. Sem., 1984, St. Paul's Coll., Lawrenceville, Va., 1985, U. of the South, 1993. Ordained priest Episc. Ch., 1968, bishop, 1984. Newspaper reporter, editor Pensacola, Fla., Richmond, Memphis, 1960-63; deacon St. John's Cathedral, Jacksonville, Fla., 1967-68; asst. min. St. John's Ch. LaFayette Sq., Washington, 1968-71; rector Chapel of the Cross, Chapel Hill, N.C., 1971-84; bishop coadjutor Episcopal Diocese of Va., Richmond, 1984-85, bishop, 1985—; pres. trustees of the funds Diocese of Va., 1985—; dir. Presiding Bishop's Fund for World Relief, 1986-93. Rector bd. trustees Episcopal H.S., Alexandria, Va., 1985—; chmn. Meml. Trustees, Richmond, trustee Wash. Nat. Cathedral. Mem. Phi Beta Kappa, Omicron Delta Kappa. Office: Diocese Va 110 W Franklin St Richmond VA 23220-5010

LEE, ROBERT JUSTIN, information systems programmer and analyst; b. Petersburg, Va., Aug. 5, 1945; s. Robert Logan and Nelda Glee (Bradley) L.; m. Mary Eunice Precise, Sept. 9, 1972; children: Charles Nathan, Mary Rachel, Robert Justin Jr. BA, David Lipscomb Coll., 1968; MPA, Tenn. State U., 1980. Systems analyst Human Svcs. (State of Tenn.), Nashville, 1979-82; infosystems programmer and analyst Gen. Svcs. (State of Tenn.), Nashville, 1982—; lectr. World War II artifacts history classes. Author: Fascinating Relics of the Third Reich, 1985; contbr. articles to various publs. Mem. Coun. Conservative Citizens, mem. nat. adv. bd., 1994—. Mem. Tenn. Mil. Collectors Assn. (pres. 1976-77, chmn. bd. dirs. 1982-87), Hupmobile Club, Vintage Motor Bike Club. Mem. Ch. of Christ. Home: PO Box 465 Franklin TN 37065-0465 Office: Gen Svcs TN Towers 3d Fl Nashville TN 37243

LEE, RUTH DAVIDSON, tax collector; b. Jackson County, Ind., July 15, 1935; d. Miles and Elsie M. (George) Davidson; m. Robert Alexander Lee, Sept. 8, 1956; children: Joan Reneé Weeks, Robyn Ann Lorenz, Robert Anthony. Student, Fla. Jr. Coll., 1979, 80, 82, Jacksonville U., 1989-90. Cert. tax collector. Clk. Prudential Ins. Co., Jacksonville, Fla., 1955-56; office staff Green Cove Hosiery Co., Green Cove Springs, Fla., 1956-59; asst. tax collector Clay County Tax Collector's Office, Green Cove Springs, 1959-84; tax collector Clay County, 1985—. Bd. dirs. Area Coun. Aging, Clay County, 1991—, Am. Cancer Soc., Orange Park, Fla., 1992—, Clay County Cmty. Svcs., 1992—, Penney Retirement Cmty., Penney Farms, Fla., 1992—; past bd. dirs. Green Cove Bus. Coun., current mem.; chair precinct Clay County Dem. Exec. Com.; mem. 4-H "500" Club Clay County 4-H Club Found., Green Cove Springs; patron life mem. Clay County Fair Bd. Recipient Super Server award Leukemia Soc. Am., 1991, Celebrity Waiters award Am. Cancer Soc., 1988, Presdl. award Green Cove Bus. Coun., 1985. Mem. Orange Park C. of C. (past dir., Govt. Affairs award 1985-88, past v.p.). Baptist. Home: 734 Myrtle Ave Green Cove Springs FL 32043-3071

LEE, SARA NELL, lay worker, small business owner; b. Amarillo, Tex., Oct. 31, 1934; d. Oscar Rand and Lois Peninah (Verner) Jackson; m. William Franklin Lee, Aug. 24, 1956 (div. Jan. 1979); children: David William, Melinda Jean. Student, Hardin Simmons U., 1954, U. Tex., El Paso, 1955-56. Pres., owner Am. Ch. Lists Inc., Arlington, Tex., 1971—. Mem. devel. com. ARC, Ft. Worth, 1986-89; co-chmn. adv. com. Welcome House Teen Crisis Ctr., Arlington, 1988-90; chmn., bd. dirs. Family Svc. Tarrant County, Tex. Mem. Christian Mgmt. Assn., Direct Mktg. Assn. North Tex. (sec. 1981), Direct Mktg. List. Coun., Arlington Postal Customer Coun., Arlington C. of C., Soroptimists (pres. Arlington chpt. 1983-85). Baptist. Office: Am Ch List Inc 1981 Stadium Oaks Ct Ste 100 Arlington TX 76011-7825

LEE, SEUNG-DONG LEIGH, economics and statistics educator; b. Andong, Korea, May 2, 1947; s. Eung-Rak and Jeung-Kyo (Lee) L.; m. Soon Duk Song, Nov. 26, 1977; children—Lyndon, Michelle. B.A., Korea U., 1970; M.A., Korea U., 1974; M.A. in Econs., So. Meth. U., 1976, Ph.D. in Econs., 1979. Teaching asst. Korea U., Seoul, 1970-72; instr. Korea Mil. Acad., Seoul, 1972-74; research asst. So. Meth. U., Dallas, 1974-76, teaching asst., 1976-79; asst. prof. econs. and stats. U. Ala.-Birmingham, 1979-85, assoc. prof., 1986—, acting chmn. dept. econs., 1993—. Assoc. editor Rev. of Regional Studies, 1979—. Research economist Urban Ala. Bus. Newsletter, 1984—. Contbr. articles to profl. jours. Mem. Am. Econ. Assn., Can. Econ. Assn., Korean Scientists and Engrs. Assn. in Am., Korean Assn. Greater Birmingham (pres. 1985-86, prin. Korena Lang. sch.), Omicron Delta Epsilon. Avocations: golf, tennis, jogging. Office: Dept Econs U Ala-Birmingham University Station Birmingham AL 35294

LEE, SHUNG-MAN, nephrologist; b. Canton, Peoples Republic of China, Feb. 22, 1949; came to the U.S., 1968; s. Ning-Woo and Shui-Fong Lee; m. Ellen Poon, Aug., 1976; 1 child, Andrew. BS, U. Toronto, 1972, MD, 1976. Diplomate Am. Bd. Nephrology, Am. Bd. Internal Medicine, Nat. Bd. Med. Examiners. Intern Sunnybrook Med. Ctr. U. Toronto, 1976-77, resident, 1977-78; resident Jewish Gen. Hosp. McGill U., Montreal, 1978-79; clin. fellow in nephrology Billings Hosp. U. Chgo., 1979-81, rsch. fellow, 1981-82; pres., med. dir. Biotronics Kidney Ctr., Beaumont, Tex., 1990—; cons. nephrologist, mem. med. staff St. Elizabeth Hosp., Beaumont, Bapt. Hosp. S.E. Tex., Beaumont, Beaumont Med. Surg. Hosp., 1982-90; med. dir. Cmty. Dialysis Svcs., Beaumont, 1986-90; cons. nephrologist, mem. courtesy staff Dr.'s Hosp., Groves, Tex., Bapt. Hosp., Orange, Tex., Park Place Hosp., Port Arthur, Tex.; clin. asst. prof. U. Tex. Med. Br. at Galveston, 1991—; founder, owner Biotronics Kidney Ctr. Beaumont, Inc.; founder, Lake Charles (La.) Dialysis Ctr. Contbr. articles to profl. jours. Organizer, founding mem. Adult Indigent Clinic for S.E. Tex., Beaumont, 1992—. Rsch. fellow Chgo. Heart Assn., 1981; rsch. scholar Ontario Cancer Soc., 1974, Ann Shepard Meml. scholar in biology, 1970. Fellow ACP; mem. AMA, Internat. Soc. Nephrology, Internat. Soc. Peritoneal Dialysis, Am. Soc. Nephrology, Jefferson County Med. Soc., So. Med. Assn., Am. Soc. Internal Medicine, Tex. Med. Assn., Chinese-Am. Soc. Nephrology (pres.), New Century Health Care Internat. (pres.). Office: Biotronics Kidney Ctr 2688 Calder St Beaumont TX 77702-1917

LEE, SILAS, III, sociologist, public opinion research consultant; b. New Orleans, July 24, 1954; s. Silas Hilton Jr. and Henrietta (Johnson) L. BA, Loyola U., 1976; MS, U. New Orleans, 1979. Cert. expert in social and econ. status of blacks, La. Prof. Sociology Xavier U., New Orleans, 1978—; pres. Silas Lee and Assocs., Pub. Opinion Research Co., New Orleans, 1983—; instr. sociology Xavier U., New Orleans. Methodist. Office: Silas Lee and Assocs 2300 S Claiborne Ave New Orleans LA 70125-3916

LEE, SOONG HYUN, psychiatrist, educator; b. Kwang-Joo, Republic of Korea, Mar. 5, 1938; came to U.S., 1966; Grad., Seoul Nat. U., 1959, MD, 1963; PhD in Epidemiology, U. N.C., 1990. Diplomate Am. Bd. Psychiatry and Neurology. Intern St. Louis City Hosp., 1966-67; resident in psychiatry Duke U. Med. Ctr., Durham, N.C., 1967-70, fellow in cmty. psychiatry, 1970-71, asst. clin. prof. psychiatry, 1974-86; clin. dir. Edgecombe-Nash Mental Health Ctr., Rocky Mount, N.C., 1975-76; pvt. practice, Rocky Mount, 1977—; asst. clin. prof. East Carolina U., Greenville, N.C., 1991-95; assoc. med. dir. Coastal Plain Hosp., Rocky Mount, 1991-93, med. dir., 1993-95. Contbr. articles to profl. jours. Bd. dirs. Meals on Wheels of Rocky Mount Inc., 1978-83, 86-90, Covenant Homes Inc., 1982-85; mem. bd. deacons First Presbyn. Ch., 1977-80, 88-91. With Korean Army, 1963-66. Mem. N.C. Med. Soc., Am. Psychiat. Assn., N.C. Neuropsychiat. Assn., N.C. Med. Soc. Home: 1220 Cheshire Ln Rocky Mount NC 27803-1205 Office: 106 Nash Med Arts Mall Rocky Mount NC 27804-5721

LEE, SUSAN, dentist, microbiologist; b. Jellico, Tenn., June 2, 1943; d. Roy Pickerell and Florida Maybell (Weaver) Savage; m. Joseph James Lee, Dec. 30, 1969 (dec. Dec. 1980); 1 child, Susan. BS, Cumberland Coll., 1965; DMD, U. Louisville, 1976. Lic. real estate agt., Ky. Asst. head dept. microbiology Norton Children's Hosp. (formerly Norton Meml. Infirmary, Louisville, 1964-69; head dept. microbiology St. Anthony's Hosp., Louisville, 1969-72; mgr. office, cons. Drs. Med. Plaza, Louisville, 1976-82; dentist Office Richard S. Bonn, DMD, Louisville, 1982-86; hygienist, dentist, cons. Office James Lewis, DMD, Louisville, 1986—; cons. in field, 1982—. Named Hon. Order Ky. Cols. Mem. Louisville Soc. Physicians and Surgeons (sec., treas.), So. Med. Soc., Fraternal Order Police. Republican. Baptist. Home and Office: 6303 Crest Creek Ct Louisville KY 40241-5801

LEE, TERRENCE ALLAN, analytical chemist, chemistry educator, researcher; b. Akron, Ohio, Nov. 12, 1955; s. Melvin Jellison and Ruth Marie (Skinner) L.; m. Lisa Ann Riggenbach, Apr. 23, 1983; 1 child, Krista Diane. BS in Chemistry, Fla. Inst. Tech., 1979; MS, U. Akron, 1987, PhD in Chemistry, 1991. Teaching asst. U. Akron, 1981-82, 87-90, vis. instr., 1990-91; chemist Stock Equipment Co., Chagrin Falls, Ohio, 1982-86; asst. prof. chemistry Middle Tenn. State U., Murfreesboro, 1991—; cons. SMithers Analytical Svcs, Akron, 1990, Firestone Rubber Co., Akron, Mr. Coffee, Inc., Cleve., Swann Pharms., Smyrna, Tenn. Author: Freshman Laboratory Manual, 1988; contbr. articles to profl. jours. Mem. Am. Chem. Soc. Republican.

LEE, THOMAS ALEXANDER, accountant, educator; b. Edinburgh, Scotland, May 18, 1941; s. Thomas Henderson and Dorothy Jane (Norman) L.; m. Ann Margaret Brown, Sept. 14, 1963; children: Sarah Ann, Richard Thomas. Chartered acct., Inst. Chartered Accts.Scotland, Edinburgh, 1964; tax acct., Inst. Tax, Glasgow, Scotland, 1965; MS, U. Strathclyde, Glasgow, Scotland, 1969, DLitt, 1984. Audit asst. Edinburgh, 1959-64, Glasgow, 1964-66; lectr. U. Strathclyde, 1966-69, U. Edinburgh, 1969-73; prof. U. Liverpool, Eng., 1973-76, U. Edinburgh, 1976-90; dir. rsch. Inst. Chartered Accts. Scotland, 1983-84; prof. U. Ala., 1990—, dir. PhD program, 1991—; vis. prof. U. Md., 1986, U. Utah, 1987-88, U. Edinburg, Scotland, 1991-94, Deakin U., 1994—; hon. prof. U. Dundee, Scotland, 1995—. Editor: Internat. Jour. Auditing; assoc. editor Brit. Acctg. Rev.; mem. editl. bd. various jours., 1971—. Trustee Acad. Acctg. Historians, v.p., 1996—. Mem. Fellow Royal Soc. Arts; mem. Inst. Chartered Accts. Scotland (coun. 1989-90), Inst. Taxation. Presbyterian. Office: U Ala PO Box 870220 Tuscaloosa AL 35487-0220

LEE, TOM STEWART, judge; b. 1941; m. Norma Ruth Robbins; children: Elizabeth Robbins, Tom Stewart Jr. BA, Miss. Coll., 1963, JD cum laude, U. Miss., 1965. Ptnr. Lee & Lee, Forest, Miss., 1965-84; pros. atty. Scott County, Miss., 1968-71; judge Scott County Youth Ct., Forest, 1979-82; mcpl. judge City of Forest, 1982; judge U.S. Dist. Ct. (so. dist.) Miss., Jackson, 1984—. Asst. editor: Miss. Law Jour. Deacon, Sunday sch. tchr. Forest Bapt. ch.; pres. Forest Pub. Sch. Bd., Scott County Heart Assn.; bd. visitors Miss. Coll. Law Sch.; lectr. Miss. Coll., 1993. Served to capt. USAR. Named one of Outstanding Young Men Am. Mem. Miss. Bar Assn., Scott County Bar Assn., Hinds County Bar Assn., Fed. Bar Assn., Fed. Judges' Assn., Forest C. of C. (bd. dirs.), Forest Jaycees (past pres., Disting. Service award), Ole Miss. Alumni Assn. (pres.), Miss. Coll. Alumni Assn. (bd. dirs.), Am. Legion. Office: US Dist Ct 245 E Capitol St Ste 110 Jackson MS 39201-2409

LEE, TUNG-KWANG, pathologist, cancer researcher; b. Wuchang, China, Oct. 6, 1934; came to U.S., 1980; s. Jie-Tsai Lee and Chong-Wen Ding; m. You-An Sun, Jan. 30, 1974; 1 child, Hao. MD, Shanghai First Med. Coll., 1955. Resident in surgery and pathology Yubei Med. Sch., Henan, China, 1957-60, tchr. pathology, 1960-78, assoc. prof., 1979-80; Bradshaw fellow Bowman Gray Sch. of Medicine, Winston-Salem, N.C., 1980-81, rsch. assoc., 1981-85; rsch. instr. East Carolina U. Sch. Medicine, Greenville, N.C., 1985-87, rsch. asst. prof., 1988-95, rsch. assoc. prof., 1996—; researcher and speaker in field. Author: (with others) Rheumatology, 1985, Ovarian Tumors, 1984, Clinical Cytology, 1981; contbr. over 60 articles to profl. jours. Bd. dirs., chmn. membership com. Eastern Carolina Multicultural Ctr., Greenville, 1992—. Brown F. Finch Found. grantee 1993. Mem. Am. Assn. Cancer Rsch., Radiation Rsch. Soc., Internat. Acad. Cytology, Internat. Soc. Comparative Oncology, Sigma Xi. Home: 1403 Evergreen Dr Greenville NC 27858-4612 Office: Dept Radiation Oncology Sch of Medicine Leo W Jenkins Cancer Ctr Greenville NC 27834

LEE, WEN-HWA, medical educator; b. Taiwan, June 1, 1950; came to U.S., 1978; s. Suen-Yi and Chen-Jen (Shu) L.; m. Eva Y.H. Pan, Sept. 12, 1975; children: Sou-Ying, Allen. BS, Nat. Taiwan Normal U., 1972; MS, Nat. Taiwan U., 1977; PhD, U. Calif., Berkeley, 1981. Tchr. Nankung Mid. Sch., Taipei, Taiwan, 1972-73; teaching asst. Inst. Biochemistry, Nat. Taiwan U., Taipei, 1977-78; rsch. scientist Cetus Corp., Berkeley, Calif., 1982-83; asst. prof. U. Calif., San Diego, 1984-87, assoc. prof., 1987-90, prof., 1990-91; prof. pathology U. Tex. Health Sci. Ctr., San Antonio, 1991—, prof. cellular and structural biology, 1991—, chair grad. program molecular medicine, 1993—, Alice P. McDermott Disting. U. chair, prof. and dir. Ctr. Molecular Medicine/Inst. Biotech., 1991—; vis. scientist Lawrence Berkeley Lab., 1983-84; vis. prof. Inst. Molecular Biology, Sinica Academia, Taipei, 1987-88; adj. prof. Chinese U. Sci. and Tech., Hefei, China, 1991-94; chmn. sci. adv. bd. Canji, Inc., San Diego, 1990-95; dir., lectr. NIH, 1991; mem. bd. sci. advisors Hong Kong Cancer Inst., 1994—; sci. advisor for search com. Arthur G. James Cancer Hosp., Columbus, Ohio, 1994—; advisor on life scis. World Sci. Pub. Co., Singapore, 1995—. Jr. lt. Taiwan Army, 1973-75. Postdoctoral fellow U. Calif., 1981-82; Outstanding Sci. Achievement in Bioscis. award Cheng-Hsing Med. Found. and Soc. Chinese Bioscientists in Am., 1992, Rsch. award Alcon, 1994. Mem. AAAS, Am. Soc. Microbiology, Am. Soc. Human Genetics, Am. Assn. Cancer Rsch., Internat. Assn. Comparative Rsch. on Leukemia and Related Diseases, Assn. Rsch. in Vision and Ophthalmology, Soc. Chinese Bioscientists in Am., N.Y. Acad. Sci., Academia Sinica (elected). Office: Ctr for Molecular Medicine/Inst Biotech 15355 Lambda Dr San Antonio TX 78245

LEE, WILLIAM CHRISTOPHER, vocational school educator; b. Louisville, May 14, 1966; s. Alvie E. and Wilma Ruth (Johnson) L. BA, Western Ky. U., 1989, MAE, 1992. Tchr. math. Ky. Advanced Tech. Ctr., Bowling Green, 1989-90, Learning Assistance Ctr., Bowling Green, 1989-90; tchr. math. learning resource ctr. Elizabethtown (Ky.) State Vocat.-Tech. Sch., 1990—. Mem. Nat. Coun. Tchrs. Math., Vocat. Indsl. Clubs Am. Home: 306 N Main St Leitchfield KY 42754-2231 Office: Elizabethtown State Vocat-Tech Sch 505 University Dr Elizabethtown KY 42701-3149

LEEBER, SHARON CORGAN, art consultant; b. St. Johns, Mich., Oct. 1, 1940; d. Michael Henry and Virginia Eileen (Robinson) Corgan; children: Mark, Tracy, Greg. Student, U. Wyo., 1958-61; BFA in Sculpture, Am. U., 1961; MFA in Sculpture, U. Colo., 1962, postgrad., 1970-72. Instr. sculpture El Centro Coll., Dallas, 1971-77, instr. and developer dept. photography, 1977-81; instr. sculpture U. Tex., Dallas, 1976-77; pres. Archtl. Arts Co., Dallas, 1980—; ptnr. Art Assets, a N.Y. Corp., 1993-95; lectr. Nat. Campus Planning Symposium, Baylor U., Waco, Tex., 1982, Am. Soc. Landscape Architects, Tex., 1983, 84, Nat. Soc. Campus and Univ. Planners, New Orleans, 1982, Wash. State Arts Alliance Forum, Seattle, 1985, Les Femmes du Monde, Dallas, 1988, West Palm Beach Devel. Seminar, 1990, Architects and Landscape Architects, Johannesburg, South Africa, 1990, Wyo. Econ. Devel. Sesion, Denver, 1990, Young Pres. Assn., Pasadena, Calif., Urban Land Inst., Boston, 1993, Nucleo Radio Mill, 1993; curator/juror a traveling exhbn. of The Contemporary Artists of Mont. for 1993—; curator Ted Waddell and a Few Friends, 1994—, Dale chihuly at Gerald Peters Gallery, Dallas, 1994, The Texas Show at Parchman Stremmel Gallery, San Antonio, 1995; reviewer Nat. Grad. Fellow, 1987; curator/co-curator various mus. shows; instr. annual jewelry workshp SWEST, 1972-84; mem. Rotogravure Com., Inc., 1996; spkr. in field; coord. The Hart Window (Linda and Mitch Hart) Dallas Mus. Art, 1994-95, 96, supr. poster project, 1995. Author: Selecting and Acquiring Art for Your Development Project, 1987; one-woman shows include Barnwell Art Ctr., Shreveport, La.; permanent collections include Dallas Mus. Fine Arts, Barnwell Art Ctr., Shreveport, La., Del Mar Coll., Corpus Christi, Tex., Incarnate Word Coll., San Antonio, U. Tex., Dallas, U. Tex., Arlington, Brookhaven Coll., Dallas, Renaissance Ctr., Detroit, Arlington (Tex.) City Libr., Internat. Sculpture Park, Liberty Hill, Tex., Barnwell Art Ctr., Dallas; contbr. articles to profl. jours.; sculpture featured in film Logan's Run. film The History fo Masks based on contemporary. Curriculum advisor Dallas Magnet Sch. Sys., 1975; bd. dirs. Program for Talented and Gifted Children, Dallas, 1978-79, Tex. Sculpture Symposium, 1984-85, also fundraising chmn., City of Dallas Parks and Recreation/The Bathhouse Cultural Ctr., 1984-85, Florentine Art Found., 1985-86; membership com. Internat. Women's Forum, 1992-93, global com., 1993-94; mem. adv. com. Dallas Pub. Art, 1992-94; mem. small scale devel. coun. Urban Land Inst., 1985-92; active Dallas Forum, 1991—, others; participant Mayor's Trade Mission to South Africa, 1996. Mem. Dallas Women's Forum (membership com. 1994), Internat. Women's Forum (global com. co-chmn. 1993-94, program chair 1995-96, spring retreat art tour presentation 1993, membership com. 1992-92), Greater Dallas Chamber (internat. trade dept. Middle eAst and African task force 1996, internat. bus. execs. 1996).

LEEDS, ROBERT, dentist; b. Newark, Sept. 8, 1930; s. William David and Gertrude (Greene) L.; m. Joyce Sumner, Nov. 28, 1960; children: Deborah Joyce, Robin Elizabeth. AA, U. Fla., 1950; DDS, Emory U., 1954. Gen. practice dentistry, Miami, Fla. Patentee herpes simplex method of therapy. Served to maj. USAF, 1954-56. Mem. ADA, East Coast Dental Assn., Miami Dental Soc., South Dade Dental Soc. Club: Coral Gables Country (Fla.). Lodges: Shriners, Masons. Avocations: sailing; water skiing; snow skiing. Office: 6437 Bird Rd Miami FL 33155-4827

LEEK, JAY WILBUR, management consultant; b. Albany, Ind., Apr. 24, 1928; s. Cecil and Hazel (Lindley) L.; m. Geneva Adams, June 30, 1948; children: Roderick Jay, Stacy LeAnn, Scott Lee, Timothy Lane, Debra Jan, Marilynn Sue, James Jay. BS in Indsl. Engring., Pacific Western, 1969, MS in Mgmt., 1976, D in Bus. Adminstrn., 1980. Registered profl. engr., Calif. Mgr. Nutone, Inc., Cin., 1951-53, Bulova Watch Co., N.Y.C., 1953-59, Martin Marietta Corp., Orlando, Fla., 1959-75; v.p. Northrop Corp., L.A., 1975-80; pres., COO Philip Crosby Assocs., Winter Park, Fla., 1980-87, also bd. dirs.; mgmt. cons., Ft. Myers, 1987-1991; bd. dirs. So. Bank, Longwood, Fla., Electro-World, Orlando. Author: Workmanship Standards, 1974; co-author: (with others) AMA Management Handbook, 1986, Quality Management Handbook, 1986. Trustee Orlando Sports Inc., 1985-87, Fla. State Univ. Found., Tallahassee, 1986—; bd. dirs. Fla. Citrus Sports Assn., Orlando, 1984-90. With USN, 1944-46. Recipient Academician award Internat. Acad. for Quality, Grobenzell, Fed. Republic Germany, 1985; Named to Wall of Fame, Am. Mgmt. Assn., 1979. Fellow Am. Soc. Quality Control (pres. 1980-81), Black Diamond Ranch Country Club, Sapphire Lakes Country Club, Masons, Shriners. Republican. Home and Office: 3297 Pebble Beach Ct Lecanto FL 34461

LEEKS, ARNOLD BERNARD, military executive; b. Leesburg, Fla., Nov. 24, 1958; s. Raymond and Ruby (Dickson) L.; m. Dorcas Johnson, Sept. 17, 1983; 1 child, Devona Simone. BS in BA, Bethune Cookman Coll., Daytona Beach, Fla., 1982. Office clk. Bethune-Cookman Coll., Daytona Beach, 1978-82; pub. rels./customer svc. rep. Fla. Power and Light Co., Daytona Beach, 1982-96; aide to adjutant gen. Fla. Dept. Mil. Affairs, St. Augustine, Fla., 1994-96; EEO specialist, equal opportunity advisor Fla. N.G., St. Augustine, 1996—; exec. officer 156th Med. Co., St. Augustine, 1990-94, ambulance platoon leader, 1987-92. Co-chmn. adv. bd. Volusia County March of Dimes, Daytona Beach, 1983, team capt., 1992-93; co-chmn. cmty. affairs Bethune-Cookman Coll., 1979-80. Capt. N.G., 1976—. Decorated Army Commendation medal; named to Outstanding Young Men of Am., 1984, 87; recipient Presdl. Award of Honor, Daytona Beach Jaycees, 1983. Mem. N.G. Assn. U.S., N.G. Assn. Fla., Assn. U.S. Army, St. Augustine Officers Club, Daytona Beach Sunrise Lions (pres. 1991-92, Lion of the Yr. 1990). Baptist. Home: 1515 Casey Ln Port Orange FL 32119

LEEPER, DORIS MARIE, sculptor, painter; b. Charlotte, N.C., Apr. 4, 1929; d. Ernest R. Leeper and Pauline A. (Fry) Leeper Harrison. B.A., Duke U., 1951. With graphic arts dept. Charlotte Engraving, 1951-55; artist, salesperson, designer So. Engraving, Atlanta, 1955-61; mem. adv. panels Fla. Arts Council, 1975-93. One-woman shows include Hunter Mus. Art, Chattanooga, 1968, 75, 79, Jacksonville Art Mus., Fla., 1968, 76, Mint Mus. Art, Charlotte, 1968, 76, Duke U. Mus., Durham, N.C., 1969, High Mus. Art, Atlanta, 1975, Greenville County Mus. Art, S.C., 1976, Columbia Mus. Art, S.C., 1976, Ringling Mus. Art, Sarasota, Fla., 1976, Miss. Mus. Art, Jackson, 1979, Mus. Arts and Scis., Daytona Beach, Fla., 1980, LeMoyne Art Found., Tallahassee, 1980, Anniston Mus., Natural History, Ala., 1980, G. McKenna Gallery, Charlotte, 1983, Foster Harmon Galleries, Sarasota, 1984, Atlantic Ctr. for the Arts, New Smyrna Beach, 1984, Albertson Peterson Gallery, Winter Park, 1993, Cornell Fine Arts Mus., Winter Park, 1995; group shows include Jacksonville Art Mus., 1971-72, 72, Albright-Knox Gallery, Buffalo, 1972-73, Miss. Mus. Art, 1978, Am. Acad. and Inst. Arts and Letters, N.Y.C., 1979, N. Miami Mus., Fla., 1984, Ctr. Arts, Vero Beach, Fla., 1986, Sampson Art Gallery, Stetson U., DeLand, 1990, Cornell Fine Arts Mus., Rollins Coll., Winter Park, 1990, Appalachian State U., Boone, N.C., 1990, 91, 2d Internat. Ephemeral Sculptures Exhbn., Fortaleza, Brazil, 1991, Duncan Gallery of Art, DeLand, 1991, Cummer Gallery of Art, Jacksonville, 1992, Cornell Fine Arts Mus., Rollins Coll., Winter Park, 1992, Samuel P. Harn Mus. of Art, Gainesville, 1993, Hodgell Gallery, Sarasota, 1995, Arts on Douglas, New Smyrna Beach, Fla., 1996; commns. include Fla. State Legis. Bldg., IBM, Atlanta, Orlando Internat. Airport, Fla., others; represented in permanent collections Hunter Mus. Art, Chattanooga, Jacksonville Art Mus., Columbus Mus. Art, Ohio, Duke U., Durham, Greenville County Mus. Art, Ill. Wesleyan U., Mint Mus. Art, Miss. Mus. Art, Mus. Arts and Scis., Daytona Beach, Nat. Mus. Am. Art, Washington, Stetson U., Deland, Fla., U. S. Fla., Tampa, Wadsworth Athenaeum, Hartford, Conn., others. Founder Atlantic Ctr. for Arts, New Smyrna Beach, Fla., 1977-78, trustee, 1979-86, adv. coun. 1986-92; trustee Mus. Arts and Scis., Daytona Beach, 1977-78, Fla. Conservation Found., 1981-85; mem. adv. commn. Canaveral Nat. Seashore, 1975-85; bd. dirs. Coastal Ednl. Broadcasters, Inc., New Smyrna Beach, 1983-90; mem. internat. adv. bd. La Napoule Art Found., France, 1987-94. Nat. Endowment Arts fellow, 1972; Fla. Fine Arts Council fellow, 1977; Rockefeller Found. fellow, 1977; recipient Humanist Arts award Am. Humanist Assn., 1990, Fla. Arts Recognition award 1993, Outstanding Alumnae award Zeta Tau Alpha, 1994. Avocations: reading; tennis; environmental affairs. Home: 806 N Peninsula Ave New Smyrna Beach FL 32169-2318

LEEPER, HAROLD HARRIS, arbitrator; b. Kansas City, Mo., July 29, 1916; s. Truman Elmer and Bess Mayburn (Harris) L.; m. Maribelle Potts, Sept. 21, 1941; children: Robert Chester, Marilyn Anne. BSBA, U. Mo., 1937; JD, Oklahoma City U., 1956. Bar: Okla. 1957, U.S. Supreme Ct. 1969. Regional pers. officer VA, Oklahoma City, 1946-52; state adminstrv. officer IRS, Oklahoma City, 1952-56; pers. officer FAA, Oklahoma City, 1956-63; from hearing officer to chief hearing officer FAA, Washington, 1963-71; adminstrv. law judge Social Security Adminstrn., Dallas, 1971-73; freelance labor mgmt. arbitrator Dallas, 1974—. Pres., bd. dirs. Way Back House, Inc., Dallas, 1975-77; chmn. pers. com. Wesley Rankin Community Ctr., Dallas, 1989-95. 1st lt. U.S. Army, 1943-46, lt. col. Res. ret. Mem. Fed. Bar Assn. (pres. Dallas chpt. 1982-83), Nat. Acad. Arbitrators (regional chmn. 1990-92), Mil. Order World Wars (comdr. D.C. chpt. 1969-70), Mason, Shriner. Democrat. Methodist. Home and Office: 6256 Glennox Ln Dallas TX 75214-2144

LEEPER, ZANE H., automotive company executive, consultant; b. Monogah, W.Va., Sept. 27, 1922; s. Igor Michelovich and Yetela Prokovna (Marenkoff) Leepa; m. Helen Irene Showalter, Nov. 13, 1942; 1 child, Robert Allen. BS in Broadcasting, U. Fla., 1971; JD, Fla. State U., 1974. Communications dir. Hercules Powder Co., Baraboo, Wis., 1941-48; radio announcer Mutual Broadcasting System, N.Y.C., 1948-52; pub. rels. dir. Allen Distbg. Co., Richmond, Va., 1952-55; pres. Globe Records, Roanoke, Va., 1955-67; mgmt. cons. Formann-Bennes Assocs., Zurich, Switzerland, 1967-69; legis. analyst Adminstrv. Procedures Com. State of Fla., Tallahassee, 1974-89; pres., chief exec. officer Lambda Automotive, Tallahassee, 1984—; bd. dirs. Grupo Lambdamex S.A. de C.V., Guadalajara, Mex., Automotriz Lambda S.A., Colima, Mex. Mem. Rep. Nat. Com., Washington, 1980—. Mem. Kappa Tau Alpha, Phi Kappa Phi. Roman Catholic. Home: 1810 Tamiami Dr Tallahassee FL 32301-5849 Office: Lambda Automotive 5132 Woodlane Cir Tallahassee FL 32303-6812

LEES, ANTHONY PHILIP, business consultant; b. Bramhall, Cheshire, Eng., Apr. 20, 1930; came to U.S., 1980; s. Philip Newark and Joan Mary (Barber) L.; m. Ann Fitton, Dec. 5, 1964; children: Joanna Frances, Victoria Ann, David Anthony. BA in Mech. Scis., Cambridge (England) U., 1953, MA, 1957. Rsch. engr. Ferodo Ltd., Chapel-En-Le-Frith, England, 1953-56; devel. engr. Borg Warner Ltd., Letchworth, England, 1956-59; resident cons. then sr. cons. PA Mgmt. Cons. Ltd., Manchester, England, 1959-67; mgr. PA Consultores de Direccion, Madrid, 1967-70; survey cons. PA Mgmt. Cons., Manchester, 1970-76; dir. mfg. Brit. Driver-Harris Co., Stockport, England, 1976-79; assoc. cons. PA Mgmt. Cons., London, 1979-80; prin. cons., mng. cons. PA Cons. Group, Inc., Hightstown, N.J., 1980-94; independent mfg. cons. Wilmington, N.C., 1994—. Mem. com. Conservative Assn., Wilmslow, England, 1978-79. Fellow Brit. Inst. Mgmt.; mem. Inst. Mgmt. Cons., Soc. Mfg. Engrs. (sr., chapter planning com. 1986, computer & automated systems assn. 1986). Episcopalian. Home and office: 6410 Timber Creek Ln Wilmington NC 28405-7465

LEFEVER, ALAN JEFFREY, archivist; b. Andrews AFB, Md., Sept. 22, 1962; s. Walter Donald and Jacqueline (Dotson) L.; m. Sara Elizabeth Goode, June 29, 1985. BA, Baylor U., 1984; MDiv, Southwestern Bapt. Theol. Sem., Fort Worth, 1988, PhD in Ch. History, 1992; cert. of archives adminstrn., U. Tex., Arlington, 1990. Assoc. coll. minister First Bapt. Ch., Waco, Tex., 1983-84; asst. archivist Southwestern Bapt. Theol. Sem., Ft. Worth, 1985-91, archivist, 1991—, adj. prof., 1991—. Author: (book) Fighting the Good Fight: The Life and Work of Benajeh Harvey Carroll, 1994 (2 writing awards 1995); assoc. editor: Flowers and Fruits, 1993; contbr. The Handbook of Texas, 1996, A Cloud of Witnesses, 1996, Teaching, Then..., 1996. Recipient Robert A. Baker award Southwestern Bapt. Theol. Sem., 1988, Davis C. Woolley award, So. Bapt. Hist. Commn., 1995. Mem. So. Bapt. Hist. Soc. (v.p. 1995—), Tex. Bapt. Hist. Soc. (sec.-treas. 1991—), Acad. Cert. Archivists (cert.), Soc. Am. Archivists, Nat. Assn. Bapt. Religion Profs., Tex. State Hist. Assn. Home: 6145 Whitman Ave Fort Worth TX 76133 Office: Tex Bapt Hist Collection Box 22000 2001 W Seminary Dr Fort Worth TX 76122

LEFEVRE, DAVID E., lawyer, professional sports team executive; b. Cleve., Oct. 25, 1944; s. Fay A. and Mary (Eaton) LeF. B.A., Yale U., 1966; J.D., U. Mich., 1971. Bar: N.Y., U.S. Dist. Ct. (so. and ea. dists.) N.Y. Assoc. Reid & Priest, N.Y.C., 1971-78, ptnr., 1979-92; owner Houston Astros Baseball Club, 1979-84, Cleve. Indians Baseball Club, 1984-86; gov., dir. Tampa Bay Lightning, NHL; bd. dirs. Lightning Arena, Inc., TDC (USA), Inc., NHL Pension Soc.; chmn. bd. dirs. Chertsey Corp.; bd. govs. NHL, 1992—; bd. dirs. Fla. Sports Found., 1996—. Bd. dirs. Tampa Downtown Partnership; vol. Peace Corps, Uruguay, 1966-68. Recipient Spl. award Tampa Sports Club.; named Hon. Alumnus, Cleve. State U., 1985. Mem. ABA, Canyon Club (pres. Armonk, N.Y. 1986—), Nippon Club, Japan Soc., Alexis de Tocqueville Soc., Univ. Club of Tampa. Office: Tampa Bay Lightning 501 E Kennedy Blvd Tampa FL 33602-5200 also: 303 E 57th St Apt 39G New York NY 10022-4001

LEFEVRE, RICHARD J., art educator, graphic designer, illustrator; b. Rochester, N.Y., Feb. 11, 1931; s. Harold John and Mary Lou (Geitener) LeF.; m. Shirley Bryant, June 14, 1952 (div. 1976); children: Corey J., Amy J., Geoffrey P.; m. Carol Ann Summers, Dec. 11, 1976. AAS, Rochester Inst. Tech., 1952, BS, 1955, MFA, 1967. Designer, Todd Co., Rochester, 1954-55, S.M. Crossett, Rochester, 1955-58, LeFevre Studios Inc., Rochester, 1958-65; prof. art U. Tenn., Knoxville, 1967—; free lance designer, Knoxville, 1967—; also painter. Adviser Tenn. Arts Commn., Nashville, 1973-75, Knoxville, 1981. Served with USN, 1952-54. Recipient over 50 awards in painting and design. Episcopalian. Avocation: folk singing with guitar. Home: PO Box 281 Seymour TN 37865-0281

LEFLER, LISA JANE, anthropologist and social sciences educator; b. Gastonia, N.C., Jan. 21, 1959; d. Buddy Allen and Jean (Nations) L. AA in Liberal Arts, Montreat-Anderson Coll., 1979; BA in Psychology, Appalachian State U., 1981; MA in Edn., Western Carolina U., 1988, EDS, 1991; PhD Anthropology, U. Tenn. Instr. social scis. Southwestern C.C., Sylva, N.C., 1988-93, Haywood C.C., Clyde, N.C., 1990-96; instr. history Western Carolina U., Cullowhee, N.C., 1989, 93, vis. instr. anthropology Dept. Continuing Edn., 1990, instr. dept. anthropology, continuing edn. instr., 1990-96, instr. regional history, 1990-96, lectr. new beginning program, 1989-92, instr. anthropology, 1991—; also counselor asst. upward bound program Western Carolina U., 1989, lectr. new beginning program, 1989-92; chem. dependency curriculum writer, grant writer, lectr. Unity Regional Treatment Ctr./Indian Health Svc., Cherokee, N.C., 1990, 93—; adjunct asst. prof. Anthropology, U. Okla., 1996; grant writer Indian Health Promotion Dept., U. Okla., 1996; mem. subcom. Project Healthy Cherokee. Chair Mountain Heritage Ctr. Mus. Vols.; former bd. dirs. Catch the Spirit of Appalachia, Inc. Tennis scholar Montreat-Anderson Coll., 1977-79. Mem. Am. Anthrop. Assn., Southeastern Anthrop. Soc., Appalachian Studies Assn. Mem. Worldwide Ch. of God. Home: PO Box 662 Dillsboro NC 28725

LEFTON, LESTER ALAN, dean, psychology educator; b. Brookline, Mass., July 27, 1946; s. Bernard and Sylvia (Bernstein) L.; m. Linda J. Levine, June 7, 1969; children: Sarah, Jesse. BA in Psychology, Northeastern U., 1969; PhD in Psychology, U. Rochester, N.Y., 1974. Asst. to assoc. prof. psychology U. S.C., Columbia, 1972-80, prof., 1980—, dir. grad. studies, 1982-84, dir. undergrad. edn., 1985-87, chmn. dept., 1986-94, dean, 1994—; mem. Harvard Univ.'s Mgmt. Devel. program; mem. Coun. Acad. Deans; mem. Coun. Colls. Arts and Scis. Author: Introductory Psychology, 6th edit., 1996; co-author: Mastering Psychology, 4th edit., 1992. Pres. Tree of Life Congregation, Columbia, 1983-84. Fellow APA; mem. Optical Soc. Am., Psychonomic Soc., Southeastern Psychol. Assn. Jewish. Home: 124 Pebble Creek Rd Columbia SC 29223-3113 Office: U SC Office of Dean Coll Liberal Arts Columbia SC 29208

LEFTWICH, CYNTHIA SHELTON, commercial interior designer; b. Childress, Tex., Sept. 12, 1951; d. Thomas Lee and Joann (Goff) Shelton; m. Jack Wilson Leftwich, July 27, 1974 (div. Aug. 1986); children: Jack Wilson II, Charles Shelton, Nancy Kristina. Student, U. Tex., Arlington, 1970-71, Clarendon Jr. Coll., Clarendon, Tex., summers 1970-73, Tex. Tech U., 1971-74, 1989—. Registered interior designer, Tex. Designer/drafts person Lubbock Ind. Sch. Dist., Tex., 1975-80; project mgr. M. Verner Interiors, Lubbock, Tex., 1975-79; pres. Shelton-Leftwich, Inc. dba Leftwich & Assocs., Lubbock dba, 1980—; prin. Shelton-Leftwich, Inc. Prin. design works include: (renovation) Lubbock Cotton Exch., First Nat. Bank of Lubbock; (new contrn.) McInturff Conf. Ctr. at Univ. Med. Ctr., Med. Office Plz. at Univ. Med. Ctr., Leadership Bank of Oklahoma City, United Bank of Midland, ER & radiology expansion Univ. Med. Ctr., Lexus Dealership of Lubbock, Butler Ob-gyn. Clinic; pub.: 100 Designers Favorite Rooms, Vol. I, 1992, II, 1994. Bd. dirs. Lubbock Symphony Guild, Lubbock Mcpl. Arts Com.; mem. Lubbock Cultural Affairs Coun. Recipient Achievement award Lubbock Historical Soc., 1986. Mem. Internat. Interior Design Assn., Am. Soc. Interior Designers (state bd.), Nat. Coun. for Interior Design Qualifications, Tex. Assn. Interior Designers, Lubbock C. of C. Republican. Methodist. Office: Leftwich & Assocs 1711 Avenue S Ste 108 Lubbock TX 79401-4816

LEFTWICH, RUSSELL BRYANT, allergist, immunologist, consultant; b. Glasgow, Ky., Nov. 1, 1951; married; 2 children. BSChemE, Arizona State U., 1974; MD, Vanderbilt U., 1978. Diplomate Am. Bd. Allergy and Immunology, Am. Bd. Internal Medicine, Nat. Bd. Med. Examiners. Resident dept. internal medicine Vanderbilt U., Nashville, 1978-81, clin. asst. prof. medicine, 1984—; staff physician Green Hosp., La Jolla, Calif., 1981-83; dir. allergy ctr. Bapt. Hosp.; mem. group practice in allergy and clin. immunology, 1983-84, pvt. practice, 1985—; chief divsn. allergy U. Tenn.-Bapt. Hosp. Internal Medicine Residency, 1989—. Contbr. articles to profl. jours. Summer Rsch. grantee Ariz. Heart Assn., 1974; fellow Scripps Clinic and Rsch. Found., 1981-83, chief clin. fellow, 1982-83. Fellow Am. Acad. Allergy and Immunology (sinusitis com., vice chmn. computers and tech. com.), Am. Coll. Chest Physicians; mem. AMA, Am. Coll. Allergy and Immunology (mem. pub. rels. com., regional coord. pub. rels. network, chmn. computers and tech. com. 1994—), Tenn. Med. Assn. (del. ho. dels. 1990—), Tenn. Soc. Allergy and Immunology (pres. 1989-92), Nashville Acad. Medicine (chmn. young physicians com. 1990-91, mem. comm. and pub. svc. com.), Nashville Soc. Internal Medicine, Nashville Allergy Soc., Southea. Soc. Allergy and Immunology, So. Med. Assn., Alpha Omega Alpha, Tau Beta Pi. Office: Allergy & Asthma Assocs 300 20th Ave N Ste 100 Nashville TN 37203-2132

LEGA, NICHOLAS ROBERT, information systems specialist; b. Louisville, Sept. 20, 1960; s. Bertrand A. and Patricia Ann (Reilly) L. AA, Bellarmine Coll., 1982, BA, 1982. From acct. to data analyst Dairymen, Inc., Louisville, 1982-87; data analyst U. Louisville, 1987-89; info. analyst Humana, Inc., Louisville, 1989—. Treas. Just Creations, Louisville, 1993-95, chmn. bd. 1995-96. Roman Catholic. Home: 1512 S Pope Lick Rd Louisville KY 40299-4620

LEGAN, ROBERT WILLIAM, securities analyst; b. Eugene, Oreg., Mar. 9, 1936; s. John William and Mertha Evelyn (Bagent) L.; m. Janis Carolyn Fosnaugh, Apr. 28, 1957; children: Tracy Legan Kurtz, Lori Legan Mondshine, Dale William. BS, Oreg. State U., 1959, MS in Nuclear Engring., 1965; PhD ChemE, U. Idaho, 1969. Registered profl. engr., Tex. Engr. GE, Richland, Wash., 1959-64, Battelle Northwest, Richland, 1959-71, Phillips Petroleum, Idaho Falls, Iowa, 1964-67; v.p. Houston Rsch., 1973-77, Subsurface Disposal Co., Houston, 1977-79; pres., owner Photox Internat. Inc., Texas City, Tex., 1979-87; commodity and stock market analyst, Texas City, 1987—; pub. The Oracle Stock and Commodity newsletters; presenter investment seminars. Developer computer program forcasting price and time for markets. Republican. Home and Office: PO Box 2639 Texas City TX 77592-2639

LEGASPI, JESUSA CRISOSTOMO, agricultural scientist, entomologist; b. Pasay, Manila, Philippines, Oct. 26, 1958; came to U.S., 1987; d. Benjamin Buencamino and Rosalinda Nieto (Manikis) Crisostomo; m. Benjamin Antonio Legaspi Jr., Jan. 2, 1987; 1 child, Michelle Elaine. BS, U. Philippines, Los Banos, 1978; MSc, U. Newcastle-Upon-Tyne, Eng., 1984; PhD, Purdue U., 1991. Rsch. asst. Philippine Coun. for Agr., Los Banos, 1980-82, Internat. Rice Rsch. Inst., Los Banos, 1985-86; grad. rsch. asst. Purdue U., West Lafayette, Ind., 1987-91; rsch. assoc. USDA, Weslaco, Tex., 1992-95; asst. prof. Tex. Agrl. Experiment Sta., Weslaco, 1995—. Contbr. articles to profl. jours. Sci. judge Jackson Elem. Sch., McAllen, Tex., 1992; vol. Ind. State Fair, Indpls., 1990; mem. Fil-Am Assn., Rio Grande Valley, Tex., 1993. David Ross fellow Purdue U., 1987; Colombo Plan scholar Brit. Coun., 1982. Mem. Entomol. Soc. Am., Philippine Assn. of Entomologists, Sigma Xi, Gamma Sigma Delta. Roman Catholic. Office: Tex Agrl Experiment Sta 2415 E Hwy 83 Weslaco TX 78596-8344

LEGG, LARRY BARNARD, biology educator; b. Laurel, Miss., Aug. 19, 1941; s. Walter H. and Lillian (Stringer) L.; m. Katherine Sue Bynum, May 30, 1965; 1 child, Elizabeth. BS, U. So. Miss., 1965; MS, Northwestern State U. of La., 1970. Tchr. biology Vidalia (La.) High Sch., 1966-69; instr. biology NW State U. of La., Natchitoches, 1969-70, Mountain View Coll., Dallas, 1970—; broker Tex. Real Estate Commn.; presenter League of Innovation in C.C. Conf. on Computing, 1988-94. Author: Microbiology, 1973, Breeds of Animals, 1975, Biological Science I, 1982, 4th ed. 1989, Biological Science II, 1984, 4th ed., 1990. Mem. Mountain View Coll. Faculty Assn. (v.p. 1986-90, 95, chmn. welfare and benefits 1989-90), Tex. Assn. of Advisers to Health Profession, Lions (pres. Red Bird/Dallas chpt. 1976-77, pres. Duncanville Noon chpt. 1982-83, editor newspaper 1984-85, 87-88, Lion of Yr. 1979-80, life advisor 1989, Gov. Spl. Appreciation award 1983, 87-88, 89, 100% Dep. Dist. Gov. 1987-88, 100% Dist. Cabinet sec.-treas. 1988-89. Home: 1512 Wyndmere Dr De Soto TX 75115-7808 Office: Mountain View Coll 4849 W Illinois Ave Dallas TX 75211-6503

LEGG, RAYMOND ELLIOTT, JR., English language educator; b. Charleston, W.Va., Feb. 24, 1949; s. Raymond E. Legg Sr. and Madge E. (Hoffman) Hartman; m. Margaret Anne Reece, Sept. 9, 1972; 1 child, Joshua Arthur. Student, U. Arkon, 1976-77; Bible/Theology diploma, Moody Bible Inst., Chgo., 1980; BA, Northeastern Ill. U., 1981; MDiv, Trinity Evang. Div. Sch., 1985; MA, U. Tenn., 1993; ArtsD, Middle Tenn. State U., 1996. Instr., adj. faculty Bryan Coll., Dayton, Tenn., 1987-95; asst. prof. English Bryan Coll., Dayton, 1995—, dir. external programs, 1990-91; pastor Daisy Cmty. Ch., Soddy-Daisy, Tenn., 1989—; tutor in English athletic dept. U. Tenn., Chattanooga, 1992-93; instr., adj. faculty Chattanooga State Tech. C.C., 1993-94; grad. tchg. asst. Middle Tenn. State U., Murfreesboro, 1994-95. With USN, 1967-71. Decorated Viet Nam Nat. Def. medal USN, 1970, Viet Nam Svc. medal USN, 1970, Meritorious Unit citation USN, 1970. Mem. MLA, South Atlantic MLA, Nat. Coun. Tchrs. English, Kiwanis Internat. (v.p. 1996—), Sigma Tau Delta. Republican. Home: 418 Haywood St Dayton TN 37321 Office: Bryan Coll PO Box 7753 Dayton TN 37321

LEGG, REAGAN HOUSTON, lawyer; b. Kaufman, Tex., Nov. 18, 1924; s. Edward and Mary Alta (Coon) L.; m. Norma Jean Eden, July 16, 1949 (div. 1976); children—John, Ellen, Emily, Reagan Houston. BBA, U. Tex.-Austin, 1947, LLB, 1948. Bar: Tex. 1948, U.S. Dist. Ct. (we. dist.) Tex. 1951, U.S. Dist. Ct. (no. dist.) Tex. 1957, U.S. Ct. Appeals (5th cir.) 1960, U.S. Supreme Ct. 1961. County atty. Midland County (Tex.), 1951-55; ptnr. Legg, Saxe & Baskin, Midland, Tex., 1955-79, Legg, Aldridge & Carr, Midland, 1980-84, pvt. practice law, Midland, 1984-89, Kaufman, Tex., 1989—. Trustee Midland Coll., 1971-86 , pres. bd., 1972-75; bd. dirs. Permian Basin Regional Planning Commn., 1977-86 ; pres. Leadership Midland, 1978-80, Tex. Community Coll. Trustees and Adminstrs., 1980-81, Nat. Assn. Community Coll. Trustees, 1982-83. With USN, 1942-46. Named Boss of Yr. Midland Legal Secs. Assn., 1969; recipient M. Dale Ensign Leadership award Assn. Community Coll. Trustees, 1977. Fellow Tex. Bar Found.; mem. ABA, Tex. Bar Assn. (chmn. com. group legal svcs. 1968-74), Midland C. of C. (bd. dir. 1968-73, 78-81), Midland County Bar Assn. (pres. 1967-68). Democrat. Methodist. Clubs: Cedar Creek Country, Masons. Office: PO Box 227 Kaufman TX 75142-0227

LEGGETT, DAVID JOHN, federal agency adminstrator, lawyer; b. Pitts., Jan. 15, 1961; s. John Milton and Ellin North Leggett; m. Julia Hsiang-Ning Chu, June 13, 1992. BA, Washington and Jefferson Coll., 1983; JD, Dickinson Sch. Law, 1986. Bar: Mass. 1986. Pres. Leggett Reprodns./Restorations, Nantucket, Mass., 1986-91; lobbyist Bonner & Assocs., Washington, 1991-92; program analyst USDA Food and Consumer Svc., Alexandria, Va., 1992—. Author vestry resolution on Episcopal visitation Diocese of Washington, 1996. Mem. choir St. Paul's Episc. Ch., Nantucket, vestryman, 1988-90; mem. choir St. Paul's Parish, Washington, vestryman, 1995-96; mem. zoning bd. appeals Town of Nantucket, 1988-90; active Nantucket Conservation Found., 1984—, Nantucket Hist. Assn., 1984—, Madaket Conservation Assn., 1984—. Mem. Phi Beta Kappa, Omicron Delta Epsilon, Phi Alpha Theta, Delta Theta Phi. Republican. Home: 1020-263 S Barton St Arlington VA 22204-4837 Office: USDA Food and Consumer Svc 3101 Park Center Dr 5th Fl Alexandria VA 22302

LEGGETT, DONALD YATES, academic administrator; b. Windsor, N.C., Oct. 31, 1935; s. Turner Carter Leggett and Ruby (Harden) Lanier; m. Nancy Lou Porter, Aug. 17, 1980; 1 stepson, Clayton Porter Johnston. BS in Phys. Edn., Social Studies, East Carolina U., 1958, MA in Edn., 1962; postgrad., N.C. State U., 1966-67. Tchr., coach Benhaven (N.C.) High Sch., 1958-59, Buies Creek (N.C.) High Sch., 1959-64; coach, tchr., Needham B. Broughton High Sch., Raleigh, N.C., 1964-66; asst. prin. Needham B. Broughton High Sch., Raleigh, 1966-70; dir. alumni affairs East Carolina U., Greenville, N.C., 1970-73; dir. alumni affairs and founds. East Carolina U., Greenville, 1973-79, dir. alumni rels., 1979-85, asst. to vice chancellor for instl. advancement, 1985-92, assoc. vice chancellor for alumni rels., 1992—, acting dir. Regional Devel. Inst., 1993; driver tng. coord. Raleigh City Sch. System, 1964-66; mem. numerous coms. at East Carolina U., 1970—. Editor East Carolina U. Alumni pubs. 1979-85; contbr. articles to alumni pubs. Past mem. bd. dirs. Pitt County Boys Club, Pitt-Greenville Arts Coun. (past mem. steering com.); former bd. dirs. Ea. N.C. village of Yesteryear; vice chmn. Pitt-Greenville Conv. and Visitors Authority. Named Boss of Yr. Greenville Jaycees, 1976. Mem. Coun. for Advancement and Support of Edn., East Carolina U. Pirate Club, Pitt-Greenville C. of C., Kiwanis Club (charter mem., past bd. dirs. Univ. City), Greenville Golf and Country Club, Phi Kappa Phi, Phi Delta Kappa. Baptist. Home: 113 Belle St Greenville NC 27858

LEGGETT, EUGENIA HARRIS, college director; b. Henderson, N.C., Oct. 27, 1960; d. Clarence Yates Jr. and Alice Jean (Brewer) H.; m. Calvin William Leggett, Apr. 8, 1996; 1 child, Lydia Elaine. AA, St. Mary's Coll., 1980; BS in Edn., U. Va., 1982; Cert. Non-Profit Mgmt., Duke U., 1996—. Educator Vance County Pub. Schs., Henderson, N.C., 1982-85, Wake County Pub. Schs., Raleigh, N.C., 1985-87, Crawford for Lt. Gov., Raleigh, N.C., 1987-88; field dir. Pines of Carolina Girl Scout Coun., Raleigh, N.C., 1988-91, program dir., 1991-93, dir. devel., 1993-95; dir. planned and annual giving Peace Coll., Raleigh, N.C., 1995—. Bd. dirs. SAFE Child of Wake County, Raleigh, N.C., 1996—; mem. program com. Alice Aycoch Poe Ctr. Health Edn., Raleigh, 1994-95; mem. Hudson Meml. Presbyn. Ch. Named Outstanding Young Tchr. of Yr. Jr. Women's Club, N.C., 1985. Mem. Nat. Soc. Fund Raising Execs. (dir. nat. philanthropy day 1995—), U. Va. Alumni Assn., St. Mary's Coll. Alumnae Assn. Home: 5408 Alpine Dr Raleigh NC 27609 Office: Peace Coll 15 E Peace St Raleigh NC 27604

LEGGETT, NANCY PORTER, university official; b. Greenville, N.C., Aug. 14, 1952; d. Earl Lindeburgh and Louise (Adams) Porter; m. Ted Clayton Johnston, Nov. 19, 1971 (div. Dec. 1979); 1 child, Clayton Porter; m. Donald Yates Leggett, Aug. 17, 1980. Student, East Carolina U., 1971-73, Pitt C.C., Greenville, 1975-76. Sec./coord. grad. ext. and tchr. edn. programs Divsn. Continuing Edn., East Carolina U., Greenville, 1971-80; sect. sec. ambulatory pediatrics Sch. Medicine, East Carolina U., Greenville, 1981-83; adminstrv. sec. to chmn. dept. pediatrics Esat Carolina U., Greenville, 1983-94; resource person dept. pediatrics Sch. Medicine, East Carolina U., Greenville, 1984-94, exec. asst. to chmn. dept. pediatrics, 1994—; mem. traffic appeals com. East Carolina U., Greenville, 1995-96, chair benefits com., 1995—. Mem. Greenville Cmty. Appearance Commn., 1990-94, Greenville Mus. Art, 1980-82; com. mem. N.C. Symphony, Greenville, 1988-89; mem., mem. steering com. Children's Miracle Network Telethon, Greenville, 1986-90; vol. Friends of Children's Hosp. Greenville, 1986-88; mem. Nat. Scleroderma Found., 1987-88, Hist. Hope Found., Windsor, N.C., 1990—; bd. dirs. Rose H.S. Acad. Boosters, 1994-95. Mem. Greenville Country Club, Kiwanis (charter mem., bd. dirs. 1990-91). Baptist. Home: 113 Bells St Greenville NC 27858 Office: East Carolina Univ Sch of Medicine Dept Pediatrics Greenville NC 27858

LEGLER, MITCHELL WOOTEN, lawyer; b. Alexandria, Va., June 3, 1942; s. John Clarke and Doris (Wooten) L.; m. Harriette Dodson; children: John Clarke, Dorothy Trumbull, Harriette Holland. BA in Polit. Sci. with honors, U. N.C., 1964; JD, U. Va., 1967. Bar: Va. 1967, Fla. 1967. Pres. Commander, Legler, Werber, Dawes, Sadler & Howell, Jacksonville, Fla., 1976-91; mng. ptnr. Foley & Lardner, Jacksonville, 1991-95; chmn. Fla. Bar Consumer Protection Law Com. Editorial bd. Va. Law Rev., 1966-67. Mem. Va. Bar Assn., Fla. Bar Assn. (lectr. continuing legal edn.), Order of Coif, Phi Beta Kappa, Phi Eta Sigma, Delta Upsilon, Delta Theta Phi. Office: Mitchell W Legler PA 1 Independent Dr Ste 3104 Jacksonville FL 32202-5026

LEGUE, LAURA ELIZABETH, resort and recreational facility executive; b. Towanda, Pa., Oct. 11, 1954; d. William Frederick and Frances Lorraine (Cease) Goeckel; m. Stephen Wheeler, Nov. 9, 1974 (div. June 1989); m. Brian E. Legue, Mar. 17, 1990 (div. July 1996). AA, Mt. Ida Jr. Coll., Newton Ctr., Mass., 1974. Gen. mgr. Towanda Motel & Restaurant, Inc., 1974-82; mgr. Wilson's Suede & Leather, Lawrenceville, N.J., 1982-83; front office mgr. Park Shore Resort Hotel, Naples, Fla., 1985-87; property mgr. World Tennis Ctr. and Resort, Naples, 1987—; pres. World Tennis Club, Inc., Naples, 1991-95, World Tennis Cmty. Assn., Inc., 1994—; notary pub. State of Fla., 1987—. Mem. Collier County Hotel Assn. (sec. 1988, v.p. 1989), Fla. Vacation Rental Mgrs. Assn., Naples Area Accomodations Assn., Hospitality Sales and Mktg. Assn. Internat. (lic. cmty. assn. mgr.). Office: World Tennis Ctr. 4800 Airport Rd Naples FL 33942

LEHFELDT, MARTIN CHRISTOPHER, nonprofit consulting company executive; b. N.Y.C., Aug. 18, 1940; s. Martin Rudolf and Amanda Hermine (Schneider) L.; m. Anne Russell, 1963 (div. 1970); children: Elizabeth Anne, Conrad Peter; m. Ann Ashford, 1972 (dec. 1988); m. Linda Graham, 1989. BA, Haverford Coll., 1961; M Div., Union Theol. Sem., 1965. Program dir. Woodrow Wilson Nat. Fellowship Found., Princeton, N.J., 1965-69; v.p. devel. Clark Coll., Atlanta, 1969-76; dir. devel. Atlanta Univ. Ctr., 1976-79; pres. Lehfeldt and Assocs., Inc., Atlanta, 1979-90, The Lehfeldt Co., Atlanta, 1990—. Author: (play) Can You Hear Me in the Back Pew, 1981, (play) Back to Bethlehem, 1973. Mem., past chmn., bd. dir. Acad. Theatre, Atlanta, 1972—, Lit. Action, Inc., Atlanta, 1972-86; mem. Ctrl. Atlanta Progress, 1986—; bd. dirs. Johnson C. Smith Theol. Sem., 1991—, The Sullivan Ctr.; bd. chmn. Ctr. for Positive Aging. Presbyterian. Office: The Lehfeldt Co 127 Peachtree St NE Ste 805 Atlanta GA 30303-1809

LEHIGH, GEORGE EDWARD, medical group consultant, management consultant; b. Graettinger, Iowa, Feb. 3, 1927; s. Earl F. and Rachel F. (Baker) L.; m. Karla Bair; children: Bruce V., Susan Paige. Student, N.D. State U., 1944-45, W.Va. U., 1945; BA, Buena Vista Coll., 1948; postgrad., Drake U., 1949-50. Tchr. secondary schs., Iowa, 1953-54; prin. secondary schs., Iowa and Minn., 1948-51, 57-58; jr. exec. World Ins. Co., 1951-54; field cons. Profl. Mgmt. Midwest, Waterloo, Iowa, 1954-57; bus. adminstr. Mankato (Minn.) Clinic, 1958-70; adminstr. Austin (Tex.) Diagnostic Clinic, 1970-75, Jackson (Tenn.) Clinic, P.A., 1975-77; exec. adminstr. Thomas-Davis Clinic, P.C., Tucson, 1977-80; dir. adminstrn. law firm Brown, Maroney, Rose, Baker & Barber, Austin, 1980-82; exec. adminstr. Capitol Anesthesiology Assn., Austin, 1982-89; pres. A.P.S. Practice Mgmt., Inc., 1984-85; dir., treas. Profl. Health Services, Inc., Tucson, 1977-80. Bd. dirs. Credit Bur., Mankato, 1960-70, pres., 1967. Fellow Am. Coll. Med. Practice Execs.; mem. Med. Group Mgmt. Assn., Austin-Cen. Tex. Assn. Legal Adminstrs. (pres. 1981-82), Anesthesia Adminstrn. Assembly (chmn. 1983-85). Republican. Methodist.

LEHMAN, DOUGLAS KENT, librarian; b. Decatur, Ind., Apr. 24, 1953; s. William E. and Carolyn R. (Lewton) L.; m. Mayra Casas, Oct. 21, 1978 (div. July 1982); 1 child, Arwen Kristin. BA, Miami U., Oxford, Ohio, 1975; MLS, Ind. U., 1978. Cataloger, libr. Robert J. Kleberg Pub. Libr., Kingsville, Tex., 1978-79; state documents libr. Ohio Hist. Soc., Columbus, 1979-81, catalog libr., 1980-81; reference libr. Miami (Fla.)-Dade C.C., 1981-84, dir. libr. tech. svcs., 1984—; pres. SEFLIN, Inc., Ft. Lauderdale, 1995-96, also bd. dirs.; mem. adv. bd. Coll. Ctr. for Libr. Automation, Tallahassee, 1990—; mem. users coun. OCLC, Inc., Columbus, 1992—. Contbg. author: Community College Reference Services, 1992. Mem. ALA, Orgn. Am. Historians, Fla. Libr. Assn., Soc. for Am. Baseball Rsch., Assn. Coll. and Rsch. Librs. (chair cmty. and jr. coll. librs. sect. 1996-97). Office: Miami-Dade CC Libr Tech Svcs 11380 NW 27th Ave Miami FL 33167-3418

LEHMAN, JAMES ORTEN, library director; b. Apple Creek, Ohio, Dec. 22, 1932; s. Willis Albert and Sarean Aldula (Amstutz) L.; m. Dorothy Anna Amstutz, Sept. 5, 1953; children: Lynn, Orval, Gerald, Beverly, Alan. BA, Ea. Mennonite Coll., Harrisonburg, Va., 1959; MLS, Kent State U., 1965, cert. advanced studies in libr. sci., 1969. Prin., tchr. Sonnenberg Mennonite Sch., Kidron, Ohio, 1955-57, 59-60; libr., tchr. Cen. Christian High Sch., Kidron, 1961-68; asst. libr. Ea. Mennonite Coll. and Sem., 1969-73, dir. librs., 1973—; mem. hist. com. Mennonite Ch., Goshen, Ind., 1973-77, 87-93; chmn. hist. com. Va. Mennonite Conf., Harrisonburg, Va., 1975—; chmn.

Ea. Mennonite Assoc. Librs. and Archives, Lancaster, Pa., 1977-89; various positions Sonnenberg Mennonite Ch., Lindale Mennonite Ch., 1955—. Author congl. and community histories in Ohio, 1969, 74, 75, 78, 80, 86, 90; contbr. numerous articles to religious jours. Served alt. mil. duty Univ. Hosp., Cleve., 1953-55. Mem. ALA, Va. Libr. Assn., Am. Assn. for State and Local History, Ohio Hist. Soc., Mennonite Ch. Hist. Assn., Lancaster Mennonite Hist. Soc., Mennonite Historians Ea. Pa., Kidron Community Hist. Soc., Shenandoah Valley Mennonite Historians. Office: Ea Mennonite Univ Libr 1200 Park Rd Harrisonburg VA 22801-2462

LEHMAN, WILLIAM LOUIS, JR., orthopaedic surgeon; b. Portland, Oreg., Feb. 17, 1951; s. William Louis and Josephine (Miller) L.; m. Joanne Louise Mauch, Oct. 26, 1985; 3 children, Andrew, Brett, Sandia. BS in Biology with distinction, Stanford U., 1973; MD, Case Western Res. U., 1977. Diplomate Am. Bd. Family Practice, Am. Bd. Orthopaedic Surgery. Resident in family practice U. Colo., Denver, 1977-80, resident in orthopaedic surgery, 1981-84, chief resident, 1985; assoc. dir. U. Colo. Family Practice Residency, Ft. Collins, 1980-81; pvt. practice, Rock Hill, S.C., 1985—; med. vol., Indonesia, 1972-73; adj. prof. edn. Winthrop U., Rock Hill, 1987-88. Contbr. articles to med. jours. Maj. USAR, 1982—. Fellow Am. Acad. Orthopaedic Surgery; mem. AMA, S.C. Med. Assn. York county Med. Soc. (pres. 1995), Chester County Med. Soc., Lancaster county Med. Soc., Rock Hill. C. of C. Democrat. Presbyterian. Office: Carolina Ortho Surgery Assocs 370 S Herlong Ave Rock Hill SC 29732-1179

LEHMANN, C. RICHARD, financial editor; b. Rotha, Germany, Aug. 6, 1942; came to U.S., 1950; s. Richard H. and Annemarie (Henke) L.; m. Sarah A. Lynagh, Aug. 17, 1968; children: Katherine, Richard, Andrew. BS, U. Richmond, Va., 1963; MBA, Columbia U., N.Y.C., 1965. CPA 1967, N.Y.C. Sr. acct. Price Waterhouse & Co., N.Y.C., 1965-67; mgr. Price Waterhouse & Co., Sao Paulo, Brazil, 1968-70; internat. controller Ingersoll Rand Co., Woodcliff Lake, N.J., 1970-82; pres. Bond Investors Assn., Miami, 1983—; pres. USID, Inc., a/b/a Stamp Finder. Author, editor: Bond Investors Assn., 1983-93, Defaulted Bonds Newsletter, 1985-94, High Yield Securities Jour., 1992-94; author: A Guide to Investing, 1992, The Handbook of Municipal Bonds, 1994. Office: Bond Investors Assn 6175 NW 153rd St Ste 221 Hialeah FL 33014-2435

LEHMANN, CLIFFORD PAUL, media center director; b. St. Louis, Sept. 22, 1936; s. Wilford Richard and Mary Christine (Maddox) L. BA in Art, Okla. Bapt. U., 1974; MEd, U. Okla., 1979. Sr. patternmaker Internat. Shoe Co., St. Louis, 1958-70; student photographer Okla. Bapt. U., Shawnee, 1970-74; asst. mgr. Cen. Hardware, St. Louis, 1970-74; dir. Media Ctr. Okla. Bapt. U., summers 1975—; mem. Media Ctr. adv. bd. Gordon-Cooper Vo-Tech., Shawnee, 1990—. Author: (booklets) The Media Center and You, 1984, Operations Manual of Selected Audio Visual Equipment, 1984. Mem. exec. bd. Pottawatamie County Hist. soc., Shawnee, 1986-94, spl. activities bd. C. of C., Shawnee, 1989-91, edn. task force, 1977-79; deacon First Bapt. Ch., Shawnee, 1989—. Named Choir Mem. of Yr., First Bapt. Ch., Shawnee, 1989; recipient award for Creative Set Design, Jim Paul Dance Studio, Shawnee, 1990. Mem. Assn. for Edn. Comms. and Technology. Democrat. Baptist. Home: 1932 N Bell Shawnee OK 74801-3712 Office: Oklahoma Bapt Univ 500 W University Shawnee OK 74801-2558

LEHMANN-CARSSOW, NANCY BETH, educator, coach; b. Kingsville, Tex., Sept. 9, 1949; d. Valgene William and Ella Mae (Zajicek) Lehmann; m. William Benton Carssow, Jr., Aug. 1, 1981. BS, U. Tex., 1971, MA, 1979. Freelance photographer, Austin, Tex., 1971—; geography tchr., tennis coach Austin Ind. Sch. Dist., Tex., 1971—; salesperson, mgr. What's Going On-Clothing, Austin, 1972-78; area adminstr. Am. Inst. Fgn. Study, Austin, 1974-81; area rep. World Encounters, Austin, 1981—, tour guide, Egypt, Kenya, 1977, 79, 81, 87, 92; participant 1st summer inst. Nat. Geog. Soc., Washington, 1986; tchr. Leader for People in Soviet Union, 1989, 90; vol. First Internat. Environ. Expedition to Antarctica. Author curriculum materials; photographer (book) Bobwhites, 1984. Recipient Merit award Nat. Coun. Geog. Edn., 1975, Creative Teaching award Austin Assn. Tchrs., 1978; Fulbright scholar, Israel, 1983; recipient study grant to Malaysia & Indonesia, 1990. Mem. NEA, Nat. Coun. Social Studies, Nat. Coun. Geog. Edn., Earthwatch (participant archaeol. dig. in Swaziland 1984), World Wildlife Fund, Rotary, Delta Kappa Gamma (pres. 1986-88), Phi Kappa Phi. Democrat. Roman Catholic. Avocations: stained glass, photography, tennis, gardening, needlepoint. Home: 1025 Quail Park Dr Austin TX 78758-6749 Office: Lanier High Sch 1201 Payton Gin Rd Austin TX 78758-6616

LEHRMAN, DAVID, orthopedic surgeon; b. N.Y.C., June 12, 1936; s. Irving and Bella (Goldfarb) L.; m. Sandra Rich, Dec. 18, 1958 (div. 1969); m. Linda Schwartz, Nov. 27, 1970; children: Richard, Michael, Steven, Robert. BA, Brandeis U., 1958; MD, U. Miami, 1962. Diplomate Am. Bd. Orthopaedic Surgery. Intern Lenox Hill Hosp., 1962-63; resident in gen. surgery Manhattan VA Hosp., N.Y.C., 1963-64; resident in orthop. Bklyn. Jewish Brookdale Med. Ctr., N.Y.C., 1964-67; mem. assisting attending med. staff Dept. Orthopaedics, Tulane U. Med. Sch., New Orleans, 1967-68; dep. chief orthop. surgery U.S. Pub. Health Hosp., New Orleans, 1968-69; chief orthop. surgery U.S. Pub. Health Hosp., Boston, 1968-69; orthop. surgeon Miami Beach, Fla., 1969—; chmn. dept. orthopedics South Shore Hosp., Miami Beach, 1975-78, pres. med. staff, 1978-81; chmn. dept. orthopedics St. Francis Hosp., Miami Beach, 1983—; chmn. Human Performance Technology, Miami Beach, 1988—, pres., med. dir. Lehrman Back Systems, Miami Beach, 1988—, Baxter Physiotherapy Ctr., Miami Beach, 1992—; pres. Backaid Systems, Miami Beach, 1984—; cons. Waterbed Health Orgn., L.A., 1987—, contbr. spine cons. Krames Communication, San Francisco, 1989—. Columnist Better Health and Living mag., 1987, creator videotape on back exercises, 1986, software Back Typing, 1989; inventor back support pillows Backaid. Mem. Mayor's Safety com. City of Miami Beach, 1975-78, Mayor's Health adv. bd., 1991—. With USPHS, 1967-69. Fellow ACS, Am. Acad. Orthopaedic Surgeons, Internat. Coll. Surgeons; mem. Am. Arthroscopy Assn., Internat. Arthroscopy Assn., Am. Pain Soc., Nat. Back Found., Am. Back Soc. (bd. dirs., treas.), N.Am. Spine Soc., Am. Occupational Med. Assn., Am. Coll. Sports Medicine. Republican. Jewish. Office: 1680 Michigan Ave Miami Beach FL 33139-2538

LEIB, LUIS, physician; b. El Paso, Dec. 3, 1931; s. Irving and Anna (Diamond) L.; m. June Rosenberg, June 12, 1955; children: Bruce G., Nancy G., Thomas E. BA, Tex. Western Coll., El Paso, 1950; MD, U. Tex., Dallas, 1957. Diplomate Am. Bd. Ob-Gyn. Intern VA Hosp., Dallas, 1957-58; resident St. Paul Med. Ctr., 1958-59, 61-63; pvt. practice, Dallas, 1963—; chief ob-gyn. dept. St. Paul Med. Ctr., Dallas, 1972—, pres. med. staff, 1987—. Capt. USAF, 1959-61. Fellow Am. Coll. Ob-Gyn., Am. Soc. Reproductive Medicine, Dallas County Med. Soc. (bd. dirs., pres. 1986-93), S.W. Gynecol. Assembly (treas. 1981-84, pres. 1989). Republican. Jewish. Home: 4530 Melissa Ln Dallas TX 75229 Office: Dallas Ob-Gyn Assocs 5939 Harry Hines Blvd # 503 Dallas TX 75235

LEIBACH, FREDERICK HARTMUT, biochemist, educator; b. Kitzingen, Germany, Sept. 21, 1930; came to U.S., 1955; s. Johann Karl Ernst and Hedwig Gertrude (Geuder) L.; m. Diane Cooper, Mar. 17, 1961 (dec. Dec. 1988); children: John G., Maria C., James W. BS, S.W. Mo. State U., 1959; PhD, Emory U., 1964. Rsch. assoc. NASA, Moffett Field, Calif., 1964-67; asst. prof. Med. Coll. Ga., Augusta, 1967-73, assoc. prof., 1973-79, prof., 1979—, chmn.; guest prof. U. Wuerzburg, Germany, 1976. Contbr. 200 articles to profl. jours. Mem. grant rev. panel NIH, NSF, Nat. Kidney Found., VA Merit Rev. Bd. Rotary Internat. scholar, 1956-59; Brown Hazen fellow, 1959-64; grantee NIH, Nat. Kidney Found., 1967—. Mem. Am. Soc. Biochemistry and Molecular Biology, Am. Physiol. Soc., Am. Soc. Nephrology, Sigma Xi. Home: 2916 Stratford Dr Augusta GA 30909-3528 Office: Med Coll Ga 1120 15th St Augusta GA 30901-3157

LEIBOWITT, SOL DAVID, lawyer; b. Bklyn., Feb. 18, 1912; s. Morris and Bella (Small) L.; BA, Lehigh U., 1933; LLB, Harvard U., 1936; m. Ethel Leibowitt, June 18, 1950 (dec. Aug. 1985); m. Babs Lee Dec. 28, 1986. Bar: N.Y. 1937, Conn. 1970. Pvt. practice, N.Y.C., 1937-84, Stamford, Conn., 1970-78, Milford, Conn., 1978-79; gen. counsel New Haven Clock and Watch Co., 1955-59, pres., 1958-59; pres. Diagnon Corp., 1981-83, vice chmn., 1983-86; chmn. Card Tech. Corp., 1983-85; dir. Data Card Internat. Corp., Hevant, Eng., 1977-79. Pres. Ethel and David Leibowitt Found.; dir. Am. Com. for Weizmann Inst. Sci.; mediator family law Supreme Ct. State Fla. 15th Jud. Ct., 1990—; arbitrator Am. Arbitration Assn., Fla.; chmn. Israel Cancer Assn. USA. Recipient Human Relations award Anti-Defamation League, 1969, Ethel Leibowitt Fund Johns Hopkins U. Sch. Medicine, Meml. award Anti-Defamation League, 1971, Tikvah award Israel Cancer Assn., 1995. Mem. ABA, Assn. Bar N.Y.C., N.Y. State bar Assn, Anti-Defamation League (commr.), Am. Soc. for Technion U. (mem. bd., v.p., Conn. pres.), Lotos Club, Harvard Club (N.Y.C.), Banyon Country Club (West Palm Beach, Fla.).

LEICHNETZ, GEORGE ROBERT, anatomy educator; b. Buffalo, Oct. 15, 1942; s. George and Alberta G. (Black) L.; m. Athalie Joan Archibald, Sept. 2, 1967; children: Keri Elizabeth, Geoffrey Scott, Joel Ethan. BS in Zoology, Wheaton Coll., 1964; MS in Anatomy, Ohio State U., 1966, PhD in Anatomy, 1970. Instr. Ohio State U., Columbus, 1969-70; asst. prof. anatomy Med. Coll. Va., Va. Commonwealth U., Richmond, 1970-78, assoc. prof., 1978-85, prof., dir. anatomy dept. grad. program, 1985—. Contbr. 50 articles to profl. publs. Active Richmond Symphony Chorus. NSF grantee, 1978-93. Mem. Am. Assn. Anatomists, Cajal Club Neuroanatomy, Soc. Neurosci. Republican. Baptist. Home: 2200 Banstead Rd Midlothian VA 23113-4101 Office: Va Commonwealth U Med Coll Va Dept Anatomy Box 980709 Richmond VA 23298-0709

LEICHTER, JULIAN CHARLES, periodontist; b. N.Y.C., June 12, 1948; s. Morty J. and Thelma Beatrice (Diamond) L.; m. Nancy Pamela Miller, July 18, 1970; children: Marissa Joy, Jana Martine. BS in Biology, SUNY, Stony Brook, 1970; DMD, Tufts U., 1974; postgrad., Harvard Sch. Dental Medicine, 1975-76. Diplomate Am. Soc. Osseointegration, Am. Congress Oral Implantologists; cert. in periodontology and oral medicine, periodontal prosthesis, prosthetic surgery and implant dentistry, implantology, spl. jaw reconstrn., guided tissue regeneration, laser applications in oral maxillofacial dentistry; lic., Mass., Conn., Fla., N.Y. Resident periodontology West Roxbury VA Hosp., 1974-76; vis. resident periodontology Brockton VA Hosp., 1975-76; chief resident Boston VA Outpatient Clinic, 1975-76; assoc. multi-office periodontal practice Natick, Mass., 1976-77; assoc.multi-specialty practice East Boston, Mass., 1976-78; assoc. periodontal practice North Miami Beach, Fla., 1978-79; assoc. group practice Pompano Beach, Fla., 1978-80; assoc. pvt. practice Plantation, Fla., 1979-80; pvt. practice Boca Raton, Fla., 1980—; co-chmn. periodontics sect. Atlantic Coast Dental Rsch. Clinic, 1991—; clin. instr. periodontology Tufts U. Sch. Medicine, 1976-78; cons. periodontology West Roxbury VA Hosp., 1976-78; dir. lecture series in periodontology, periodontal-prosthetic dental residency program West Roxbury VA Hosp., 1976-78; clin. instr. periodontology Harvard Sch. Dental Medicine, 1977-78; mem. staff Delray Community Hosp., West Boca Med. Ctr. Mem. ADA, Acad. Advanced Oral Reconstrn. and Esthetics, Acad. Osseointegration, Am. Acad. Periodontology, Am. Assn. Implant Dentistry, Am. Coll. Oral Implantology, Am. Soc. Osseointegration, Atlantic Coast Dist. Dental Assn., East Coast Dist. Dental Assn., Fla. Dental Assn., Fla. Soc. Periodontists, Internat. Congress Oral Implantologists, South Palm Beach County Dental Assn., So. Acad. periodontology. Office: 7000 W Camino Real Boca Raton FL 33433-5551

LEICHTER, STEVEN BRUCE, endocrinologist; b. N.Y.C., Dec. 31, 1944; s. Isidore and Marion (Goodman) L.; m. Sydney Lee Glover, July 12, 1991; children: Matthew, Andrew, Meagan, Mack, Michael. AB, Columbia U., 1966; MD, U. Va., Charlottesville, 1970. Intern Michael Reese Hosp., Chgo., 1970; resident Barnes Hosp., St. Louis, 1972-73; fellow Wash. U., St. Louis, 1973-75; chief endocrinologist Travis AFB USAF, Fairfield, Calif., 1975-77; asst. prof. Endocrinology U. Ky., Lexington, 1977-82; dir. Ky. Diabetes Found., Lexington, 1982-88; prof. Endocrinology Ea. Va. Med. Sch., Norfolk, 1988—; clin. dir. The Diabetes Inst., Norfolk, 1988—; cons. Cancer Treatment Ctr., Arlington Heights, Ill., 1993—, U.S. Atty.'s Office, Norfolk, 1993—, co-dir. Columbus Metabolic Found. and West Ga. Ctr. for Metabolic Disorders, Columbus, Ga., 1995—; partner Endocrine Consultants, 1995—. Contbr. articles to profl. jours. Basketball coach Virginia Beach (Va.) Recreation League, 1992-95. Fellow ACP, Am. Coll. Endocrinology. Office: Columbus Metabolic Found 500 18th St Columbus GA 31901-1536

LEIDY, ROSS BENNETT, research scientist, educator; b. Newark, Ohio, June 1, 1939; s. Myron Willis and Marigold Olga (Hall) L.; m. Nancy Elaine Antoine, May 1, 1971; BS in Physiology, Tex. A&M U., 1963, MS in Radiation Biology, 1966; PhD in Biochemistry, Auburn U., 1972. Chemist Dow Chem. Co., Freeport, Tex., 1960-61, Pennwalt Chem. Co., Bryan, Tex., 1961-63; grad. rsch. asst. Radiation Biology Labs., Tex. A&M U., College Station, 1963-66; instr. U.S. Army Chem. Ctr. and Sch., Ft. McClellan, Ala., 1966-68; grad. rsch. asst. biochemistry Auburn U. (Ala.), 1968-72; NIH rsch. fellow N.C. State U., Raleigh, 1972-73, prof., dir. Pesticide Residue Rsch. Lab., 1974—; supr. Pesticide Residue Lab. Dept. Human Resources, State of N.C., Raleigh, 1973-74; cons., mem. faculty toxicology dept. N.C. State U. Served to col. Chem. Corps, USAR, 1963-93. Mem. Am. Chem. Soc., N.Y. Acad. Scis., Sigma Xi, Gamma Sigma Delta. Contbr. tech. reports, articles and textbook chpts. to profl. lit. Home: 5128 Norman Pl Raleigh NC 27606-2223 Office: NC State U Pesticide Rsch Lab 3709 Hillsborough St Raleigh NC 27607-5464

LEIGH, JAMES HENRY, marketing educator; b. Midland, Tex., Feb. 6, 1952; s. John Marshall Leigh and Ethel Elizabeth (Eppright) Davis; m. Jane Ellen Hudson, Dec. 26, 1979; children: James Daniel, Robert Scott. BBA with honors, U. Tex., 1974, MBA, 1976; PhD, U. Mich., 1981. Research assoc. U. Mich., Ann Arbor, 1977-79; asst. prof. mktg. Ea. Mich. U., Ypsilanti, 1980-81; asst. prof. Tex. A&M U., College Station, 1981-87, assoc. prof., 1987—. Co-founder, co-editor: Jour. Current Issues and Research in Advt., 1978—; reviewer: Jour. Advt., 1983—, Jour. Mktg. Rsch., 1982, 86—, Jour. Pub. Policy and Mktg., 1986—, Jour. Mgmt., 1987-89, Internat. Jour. Retailing, 1987; regular contbr. Advt. and Mktg. Jours. Mem. Acad. Mktg. Sci., Am. Acad. Advt., Am. Mktg. Assn., Soc. for Consumer Psychology, Assn. Consumer Rsch., So. Mktg. Assn. Home: 605 Ivy Cv College Station TX 77845-6300 Office: Tex A&M U Dept Mktg College Station TX 77843-4112

LEIGH-MANUELL, ROBERT ALLEN, training executive, educator; b. Bay Shore, N.Y., Oct. 4, 1942; s. Darrell B. and Rose A. (Sanders) L.-M.; m. Diane W. Frisbee, Mar. 28, 1964 (div. May 1982); children: Nancy D., Timothy J., Charles R.; m. Donna M. McGrath, Oct. 25, 1982; children: Michael N., David A. Student, Kans. State U., 1960-61; BS, SUNY, Oswego, 1964; postgrad., Hofstra U., 1965-66; MA, NYU, 1977. Cert. secondary sch. tchr., N.Y.; cert. sch. adminstr., N.Y. Tchr. Sachem Cen. Sch. Dist., Holtsville, N.Y., 1964-67; tng. mgr. Deutsch Relays, North Port, N.Y., 1967-68; instructional systems engr. Sperry Gyroscope, Great Neck, N.Y., 1968-74; cons. Mind, Inc., N.Y.C., 1974; tchr. Wantagh Sch. Dist., Wantagh, N.Y., 1974-76; adminstrv. intern Mamaroneck (N.Y.) Sch. Dist., 1976; adminstr. Westchester B.O.C.E.S., Port Chester, N.Y., 1976-79; tng. mgr. Data Communication, Farmingdale, N.Y., 1979-84; mgr. program devel. The Southland Corp., Dallas, 1984-92; ind. cons., owner Monarch Assocs., Dallas, Tex., 1992—; com. mem. Commr.'s Task Force for technology in edn. Tex. Edn. Agy., Austin, 1987-88. Mem. Huntington (N.Y.) Sch. Dist. Bd. Edn., 1973-79, pres., 1975-77; vol. fireman West Sayville (N.Y.) Fire Dept., 1960-70. Named an Outstanding Young Man in Am., Jaycees, 1974. Republican. Baptist. Home: 3439 Meadow Creek Ln Sachse TX 75048-4181 Office: Monarch Assocs Ste 119 9319 Lyndon B Johnson Fwy Dallas TX 75243-3453

LEIGHTNER, JONATHAN EDWARD, economist, educator; b. Fort Wayne, Ind., Aug. 16, 1957; s. Paul Edward and Lois Ann (Michael) L.; m. Sandra Dylene Friend, Feb. 28, 1981; 1 child, Luke Justice. BA in Philosophy, Baylor U., 1980, MA in Philosophy, 1982; PhD in Econs., U. N.C., 1989. Tchr. ESL Lampang (Thailand) Coll. Commerce and Tech., 1981-82; instr. philosophy, econs. Cameron U., Lawton, Okla., 1983-84; instr. econs. U. N.C., Chapel Hill, 1986-87, N.C. State U., Raleigh, 1988-89; asst. prof. Augusta (Ga.) Coll., 1989-93, assoc. prof., 1993—; Author: The Impact of Yonok College and ASHA's Seed Money on Lampang, Thailand, 1992; contbr. articles to profl. jours. Grantee Bell South, 1993-95, EGAT of Thailand, 1994, USDA, 1991, Ford Found., 1989. Mem. Internat. Network for Econ. Method, Am. Econ. Assn., Assn. Comparative Econs., So. Econ. Assn. Methodist. Office: Augusta Coll 2500 Walton Way Augusta GA 30904-2200

LEIGHTON, FRANCES SPATZ, writer, journalist; b. Geauga County, Ohio; m. Kendall King Hoyt, Feb. 1, 1984. Student, Ohio State U. Washington corr. Am. Weekly; corr. and Washington editor This Week Mag.; Washington corr. Met. Group Sunday Mags.; contbg. editor Family Weekly; free-lance journalist Metro Sunday Group, Washington; lectr. summer confs. Dellbrook-Shenandoah Coll., Georgetown U., Washington. Author over 30 books on hist. figures, celebrities, Hollywood, psychiatry, the White House and Capitol Hill, 1957—; (with Louise Pfister) I Married a Psychiatrist, 1961, (with Francois Rysovy) A Treasury of White House Cooking, 1968, (with Frank S. Caprio) How to Avoid a Nervous Breakdown, 1969, (with Mary B. Gallagher) My Life with Jacqueline Kennedy, 1969, (with Traphes Bryant) Dog Days at the White House, 1975, (with William Fishbait Miller) Fishbait—the Memoirs of the Congressional Doorkeeper, 1977, (with Lillian Rogers Parks) My 30 Years Backstairs at the White House (made into TV mini-series), 1979, (with Hugh Carter) Cousin Beedie, Cousin Hot--, My Life with the Carter Family of Plains, Georgia, 1978, (with Jerry Cammarata) The Fun Book of Fatherhood-or How the Animal Kingdom is Helping to Raise the Wild Kids at Our House, 1978, (with Natalie Golos) Coping with Your Allergies, 1979, (with Ken Hoyt) Drunk Before Noon—The Behind the Scenes Story of the Washington Press Corps, 1979, (with Louis Hurst) The Sweetest Little Club in the World, The Memoirs of the Senate Restaurateur, 1980, (with John M. Szostak) In the Footsteps of Pope John Paul II, 1980, (with Lillian Rogers Parks) The Roosevelts, a Family in Turmoil, 1981, (with June Allyson) June Allyson, 1982, (with Beverly Slater) Stranger in My Bed, 1985 (made into TV movie, 1987), (with Oscar Collier) How to Write and Sell Your First Novel, 1986, The Search for the Real Nancy Reagan, 1987, (with Oscar Collier) How To Write and Sell Your First Nonfiction Book, 1990, (with Stephen M. Bauer) At Ease at the White House, 1991; contbr. numerous feature stories on polit., social and govtl. personalities to various publs. Bd. dirs. Nat. Found., from 1963. Recipient Edgar award, 1961. Mem. Senate Periodical Corr. Assn., White House Corr. Assn., Am. News Women's Club, The Writers Club, Nat. Press Club, Writers League of Washington (pres.), Washington League Am. Pen Women (pres.), Washington Ind. Writers, Smithsonian Assocs., Nat. Trust Historic Preservation, Lake Barcroft Women's Club, Delta Phi Delta, Sigma Delta Chi. Unitarian. Office: Lake Barcroft 6336 Lakeview Dr Falls Church VA 22041-1331

LEIGHTON, KIM GREGORY, information systems specialist; b. St. Louis, May 13, 1952; s. James Leland and Rosemary Dolores (Schroll) L. BA in Biology, U. Mo., 1974, MBA, 1976, MS in Mgmt. Info. Systems, 1986. CPA, Mo. Auditor Ernst & Whinney, St. Louis, 1976-79; sr. auditor Anheuser-Busch Cos., St. Louis, 1979-81; fin. analyst Seven-Up Co., St. Louis, 1981-82, mgmt. info. systems field coordinator, 1982-85; asst. controller Amedco, Inc., Chesterfield, Mo., 1985-86, dir. acctg. and adminstrn., 1986-87, dir. infosystems and tech., 1987-88; MIS dir. York Products, Inc., Houston, 1988-90, The York Group Inc., Houston, 1990—; cons. Cen. Med. Ctr., St. Louis, 1979-80, Seven-Up Co., 1985-86. Mem. Backers of St. Louis Repertory Theatre, Friends of St. Louis Art Mus., Friends of St. Louis Zoo, Mo. Bot. Garden, Laumeier Sculpture Park. Mem. AICPA, Inst. Econometric Rsch., Mensa, U. Mo. at St. Louis Alumni Assn., Beta Gamma Sigma, Beta Alpha Psi. Republican. Roman Catholic. Home: 2851 Wallingford Dr Apt 307 Houston TX 77042-3427 Office: The York Group Inc 9430 Old Katy Rd Houston TX 77055-6368

LEIGHTON, LESLIE STEVEN, gastroenterologist; b. N.Y.C., Jan. 18, 1952; s. Fred Victor and Sitty (Hess) L.; m. Deborah Gilda Perl, Apr. 25, 1982; children: Andrew David, Lauren Sophia, Jennifer Ellen, Rachel Johanna. BA with high distinction, U. Va., 1974; MD, Johns Hopkins U., 1978. Diplomate Am. Bd. Internal Medicine, Am. Bd. Gastroenterology. Intern, then resident in medicine NYU-Bellevue Hosp., N.Y.C., 1978-81; gastroenterology fellow Brigham and Women's Hosp., Boston, 1981-84; teaching asst. NYU Sch. Medicine, N.Y.C., 1980-81; clin. fellow Harvard Med. Sch., Boston, 1981-83, rsch. fellow, 1983-84; pvt. practice Peachtree Gastroenterology, P.C., Atlanta, 1984—; clin. instr. Emory U. Sch. Medicine, Atlanta, 1986-90, clin. asst. prof. medicine, 1990—; chmn. dept. internal medicine Ga. Bapt. Med. Ctr., 1991-94; asst. clin. prof. medicine Med. Coll. Ga., 1992—; staff physician Piedmont Hosp., Atlanta, 1984—. Vice chmn. Nat. Found. Ileitis and Colitis, Atlanta, 1989-91, chmn., 1991-93. Mem. AMA, Med. Assn. Atlanta, Am. Gastroenterol. Assn., Am. Coll. Physicians, Am. Coll. Gastroenterology, Druid Hills Golf Club, Buckhead Club. Office: Peachtree Gastroenterol PC 95 Collier Rd NW Ste 4075 Atlanta GA 30309-1721

LEIGHTON, MIRIAM, artist, consultant; b. N.Y.C.; d. Nathan and Rose (Unger) Kaback; m. Bruce Leighton, Feb. 22, 1965 (dec.); children: Elayne Joyce, Jo-Ann Helene. Student, NYU, 1934, 45. Cons. Saks Fifth Ave., N.Y.C., 1954-56; freelance cons. Ft. Lee, N.J., 1973-80; cons. in field; rep. Artists and Sculptors, N.J., 1984—. Active vol. various charitable orgns. Honored by Am. Cancer Soc., Technion, Univ. of Tech., United Jewish Community of Bergen County, Holly Ctr. (adv. for abused children), others.

LEIGHTY, DIANE CAROL, secondary education educator; b. East Orange, N.J., Feb. 21, 1951; d. Paul and Miriam Ruth (Thrall) Kraeuter; m. James Larry Leighty, June 24, 1972; children: Jocelyn Rebecca, Steven James. BA in Math. magna cum laude, Grove City (Pa.) Coll., 1973; MA in Math., U. Va., 1993. Cert. secondary math. instr., Va. Tchr. math. Stonewall Jackson H.S., Charleston, W.Va., 1973-74; substitute tchr. Cleve. City Schs., 1974-75; substitute tchr. Spotsylvania (Va.) Schs., 1981-83, tchr. math., 1983-84; tchr. math. Manchester H.S., Chesterfield County, Va., 1984-95; tchr. math., curriculum writer Math and Sci. H.S. at Clover Hill, Midlothian, Va., 1995—; sophomore class adv. Manchester H.S., Midlothian, 1985-90, ecology club adv., 1992-95; tech. trainer Chesterfield County Schs., 1993—; presenter in field. Author: The Statistical Analysis of Compositional Data, 1993. Cmty. adv. coun. mem. Manchester H.S., Midlothian, 1990-92; youth dir. Christ King Luth. Ch., Richmond, Va., 1993-96, mem. ch. coun., 1993-95; mem. ch. choir. Grantee Grove City Coll., 1969-72; Manchester H.S. PTA scholar, 1992. Mem. Nat. Coun. Tchrs. Math., Va. Coun. Tchrs. Math., Greater Richmond Coun. Tchrs. Math. (mem. com. 1984—). Lutheran. Home: 11930 Silbyrd Dr Midlothian VA 23113 Office: Math and Sci HS at Clover Hill 13900 Hull St Rd Midlothian VA 23112

LEISE, ESTHER MARCIA, biology educator; b. Washington, May 13, 1953; d. David and Phyllis Rhea (Fleitman) L. BS in Zoology, U. Md., 1975; PhD in Zoology, U. Wash., 1983. Teaching asst. U. Wash., Seattle, 1975-82, rsch. asst., 1977-79; rsch. assoc. U. HAwaii, Honolulu, 1990-91; asst. prof. U. N.C., Greensboro, 1991—. Recipient USPHS nat. rsch. svc. award NIH, 1985-88; postdoctoral fellow U. Calif., Davis, 1983-88; Ga. State U., 1988-90; rsch. grantee NSF, 1990-91. Mem. Soc. for Integrative and Comparative Biology (pub. affairs com. 1992-94), Soc. Neurosci., Roy Scot Country Dance Soc., Phi Beta Kappa, Sigma Xi. Office: U NC Dept Biology Greensboro NC 27412

LEISNER, ANTHONY BAKER, publishing company executive; b. Evanston, Ill., Sept. 13, 1941; s. A. Paul and Ruth (Solms) L.; BS, Northwestern U., 1964, MBA, 1983; children: Justina, William, Sarah; m. Patricia Anne Leisner, 1996. Salesman, Pitney Bowes Co., 1976-77; with Quality Books Inc., Lake Bluff, Ill., 1968—, v.p., 1972—, gen. mgr., 1979—; adj. faculty Lake Forest (Ill.) Sch. Mgmt., 1983—, Kellogg Grad. Sch. Mgmt. Northwestern U., Evanston, Ill.; assoc. prof. internat. mktg. Schiller Internat. U., Dunedin, Fla., 1995—; head global strategic planning, spl. asst., CEO Dawson Group, Folkestone, Eng. pres. Watersedge Properties Inc., Tarpon Springs, Fla.; ptnr. Wikle Properties Mgmt., Palm Harbor, Fla.; bd. dirs. PLK Inc., Washington, Highland Properties, Inc., Palm Harbor, Fla. Bank of Commerce, Palm Harbor. Pres. bd. dirs. Lake Villa (Ill.) Pub. Libr., 1972-78; bd. dirs. No. Ill. Libr. Systems, 1973-78, Fla. Bank of Commerce, Palm Harbor; chmn. Libertarian Party Lake County (Ill.), 1980-81; probation officer Lake County CAP, 1981. Mem. ALA (councilor, del. pub. com., White House conf. on librs. and info. svcs.), Ill. Libr. Assn. (Gerald L. Campbell award 1980), Am. Booksellers Assn., Acad. Mgmt., Am. Mktg. Assn., World Future Soc., World Isshin Ryu Karate Assn. Author: Official Guide to Country Dance Steps, 1980; also articles. Home and Office: 1350 Riverside Ave Tarpon Springs FL 34689

LEISS, ERNST LUDWIG, computer science educator; b. July 7, 1952; m. Benigna N. Cortés, 1979; 1 child, Ernst A.C. M of Math. in Computer Sci., U. Waterloo, Ont., Can., 1974; Dipl.-Ing., Tech. U. Wien, Vienna, 1975,

Dr.tech. in Math., 1976. Teaching asst. dept. computer sci. U. Waterloo, 1973-74, postdoctoral fellow dept. computer sci., 1976-77; profesor investigador U. Chile, Santiago, 1978; vis. asst. prof. computer sci. U. Ky., Lexington, 1979; asst. prof. computer sci. U. Houston, 1979-85, asst. chmn. dept. computer sci., 1985-86, assoc. prof. computer sci., 1985-92, dir. W. M. Keck Rsch. Computation Lab., 1985-93, prof. computer sci., 1992—; vis. faculty, mem. sci. com. Master in Computer Sci. Sch., Pordenone, Italy, 1991, 92; vis. prof. U. Campinas, Brazil, 1987, U. Udine, Italy, 1990, U. Rio Grande do Sul, Porto Alegre, Brazil, 1991; cons. The Houston Chronicle, Teltech, Mobil R&D, various venture capital cos.; invited spkr. at various instns. including IBM, U. Calif. Berkeley, UCLA, U. Erlangen, Germany, U. Bologna, Italy, U. Rio de Janeiro, Russian Acad. Scis., Moscow, many others; grant reviewer NSF, Nat. Rsch. Coun., mem. REU panel, 1993; mem. program com. Internat. Conf. on Computer Sci., Santiago, Chile, 1982, 84, 86, 90, 94, chair, 1983; fin. chair 10th Internat. Conf. on Data Engring., Houston, 1994; visitor Computer Sci. Accreditation Commn., 1988-89, 89-90, 90-91, team chair, 1991-92, 96-97. Author: Principles of Data Security, 1982, Software Under Siege: Viruses and Worms, 1990, Parallel and Vector Computing, 1995; editor: W. M. Keck Research Computation Laboratory Annual Progress Report, Vols. 2-8, 1986-92; contbr. chpts. to books, numerous papers to conf. procs., profl. jours. Grantee U. Houston, 1989, 90, 93, NSF, 1983-86, Teledyne Rsch. Assistance Program, 1988-89, Mobil R&D, 1989-90, State of Tex., 1989-93, U.S. Dept. Energy, 1989-92, Nat. Rsch. Coun. Italy, 1990, Consortium of Indsl. Cos., 1985-86, 86-87, 87-88, 88-89, 89-90, 90-91, 91-92, 92-93, Sandia Nat. Labs., 1994-96. Mem. IEEE (sr.), IEEE Computer Soc. (chmn. Houston chpt. 1982-96), Assn. Computing Machinery (advisor U. Houston student chpt., nat. spkr. 1991-97, SIGACT, SIGARCH, rev. computing revs.), EATCS, SEG. Office: Univ of Houston Dept Computer Sci Houston TX 77204-3475

LEISY, WILLIAM BERNARD, management consultant; b. Washington, Jan. 24, 1957; s. Roland H. and Therese E. (Kelley) L.; m. Claire Elizabeth Davis, May 10, 1987; children: Davis, Katherine, Ridley. BA, Wake Forest U., 1980; MBA, Ga. State U., 1983. Mgr. Wilson Trucking, Greensboro, N.C., 1980-81; compensation analyst Yellow Freight Systems, Overland Park, Kans., 1983-84; staff cons. Ernst & Young, Atlanta, 1984, sr. cons., 1985, mgr., 1985-87, sr. mgr., 1987-91, ptnr., nat. dir. healthcare compensation cons., 1991—. Contbr. articles to profl. jours. Mem. Am. Compensation Assn. (cert. compensation profl.), Am. Soc. Pers. Adminstrs. (Profl. Human Resources Specialist), Cobb C. of C. Republican. Roman Catholic. Home: 4741 Talleybrook Dr Kennesaw GA 30144-5483 Office: Ernst & Young 600 Peachtree St Atlanta GA 30308

LEITHEAD, R. JAMES, lawyer; b. Pueblo, Colo., June 1, 1930; s. Ross F. and Merna O. (Johnston) L.; m. Ann A. Clammer, June 1954 (div. 1969); children: Karen, Jeff, David, James. BA in Geology, U. Colo., 1950, LLB, 1953; Cert. Bus. Adminstrn., Columbia U., 1971. Bar: Colo. 1953, Okla. 1954. Pvt. practice Pueblo, 1953-54, Tulsa, 1954-55; law clk. to presiding justice U.S. Dist. Ct., Tulsa, 1955; atty. Cities Svc. Oil Co., Bartlesville, Okla., 1956-69; asst. gen. counsel Cities Svc. Co., Tulsa, 1970-79, Cities Svc. Gas Co., Oklahoma City, 1980-82; pvt. practice Tulsa and Oklahoma City, 1983-89. Mem. ABA, Okla. Bar Assn., Colo. Bar Assn., Fed. Energy Bar Assn., Tulsa County Bar Assn.

LEITNER, GREGORY MARC, lawyer; b. Chattanooga, Apr. 19, 1957; s. Paul Revers and Suzanne Joy Leitner; m. Sheryl Leitner; children: Gregory Marc, Ashley Meredith. BA cum laude, Memphis State U., 1978; JD, U. Tenn., Knoxville, 1980. Bar: Tenn. 1981, U.S. Dist. Ct. (ea. dist.) 1981, U.S. Ct. Appeals (6th cir.) 1983, U.S. Ct. Appeals (11th cir.) 1988. Ptnr. Leitner, Warner, Moffitt, Williams, Dooley, Carpenter & Napolitan, Chattanooga, 1986—. Mem. ABA, Tenn. Bar Assn., Pi Sigma Alpha, Phi Delta Phi. Republican. Methodist. Home: 6259 Forest Trl Signal Mountain TN 37377-2807

LEITZ, ROBERT CHARLES, III, English language educator; b. New Orleans, Oct. 28, 1944; s. Robert Charles Jr. and Mildred Mary (Kurz) L.; m. Ann Marie Vicknair, May 25, 1968. BA, U. New Orleans, 1967; MA, Tex. A&M U., 1969, PhD, 1973. Asst. prof. English, La. State U., Shreveport, 1973-77, assoc. prof., 1977-82, prof., 1982—; curator J.S. Noel Collection Noel Meml. Libr., La. State U., Shreveport, 1994—. Editor: Selected Letters of W.D. Howells, 1980, The Letters of Jack London, 1988, Critical Essays on George Santayana, 1990, Complete Short Stories of Jack London, 1993; Am. lit. editor South Ctrl. Rev., 1985-87. Rsch. grantee Am. Philos. Soc., 1975, 78, 80, Henry E. Huntington Libr., San Marino, Calif., 1978-79, NEH, 1980-81. Mem. Nat. Assn. Scholars, Assn. for Documentary Editing (bd. dirs. 1986-88), Am. Lit. Assn., Frank Norris Soc. (pres. 1987—), Jack London Soc. (bd. dirs. 1990—). Republican. Mem. United Ch. of Christ. Home: 680 Southern Trace Pky Shreveport LA 71106-9323 Office: La State U 1 University Pl Shreveport LA 71115-2301

LELAND, JOHN LOWELL, humanities educator; b. Bowling Green, Ohio, Mar. 11, 1950; s. Lowell Pond and Virginia Thornton (Everett) L.; m. Carol A. Howard, Sept. 23, 1995. BA, Bowling Green State U., 1972; MA, Yale U., 1973, PhD, 1979. Teaching fellow Pikeville (Ky.) Coll., 1980-81; vis. asst. prof. Bowling Green State U., 1982, 86, 89, Millersville (Pa.) U., 1983-84, U. Nebr., Lincoln, 1985; vol. in mission Keimyung U., Taegu, Korea, 1987-88; assoc. prof. humanities Salem (W.Va.) Teikyo U., 1990—. Contbr. articles to profl. jours. Mem. exec. com. Wood County Dem. Com., Bowling Green, 1990. Mem. Am. Hist. Assn., Medieval Acad. Am., Assn. Lit. Scholars and Critics, Tchrs. ESL, Soc. for Creative Anachronism (Master of Laurel award 1971, knighthood 1972), Mensa, Phi Alpha Theta, Phi Kappa Phi. Episcopalian. Home: 163 E Main St Salem WV 26426-1244 Office: Salem Teikyo U University Blvd Salem WV 26426

LEMAHIEU, JAMES JOSEPH, business consultant; b. Milw., Feb. 23, 1936; s. Harold William and Genieveve Azalea (Christman) LeM.; m. Barbara M. Pratt, July 3, 1989; children: Paul George, Ann Genieveve, Charles William. BS, Yale U., 1958; MBA cum laude, Boston U., 1969. Cert. prodn. and inventory mgmt. mgr. System analyst USM Co., Beverly, Mass., 1961-68; system cons. IMF, Inc., Waltham, Mass., 1968-70; mgr. inventory, prodn. control Gorton Group div. Gen. Mills, Gloucester, Mass., 1970-77, dir. forecasting, 1977-91; cons. in field, Derry, N.H., 1965—. Chmn. Derry (N.H.) Sch. Survey Com., 1963-66; active Derry Sch. Bd., 1964-79; coach, organizer Derry Recreation Prog., 1974-80; trustee, pres. Pinkerton Acad., Derry, 1980-91. Mem. Beta Gamma Sigma, Kiwanis. Home: 12627 El Palacio San Antonio TX 78233-6312

LE MAISTRE, CHARLES AUBREY, internist, epidemiologist, educator; b. Lockhart, Ala., Feb. 10, 1924; s. John Wesley and Edith (McLeod) LeM.; m. Joyce Trapp, June 3, 1952; children: Charles Frederick, William Sidney, Joyce Anne, Helen Jean. BA, U. Ala., 1943, LLD (hon.), 1971; MD, Cornell U., 1947; LLD (hon.), Austin Coll., 1970; DSc (hon.), U. Dallas, 1978, Southwestern U., 1981; D honoris causa, U. Guadalajara (Mex.), 1989. Intern, then resident medicine N.Y. Hosp., 1947-49; research fellow infectious diseases Cornell U. Med. Coll., 1949-51, mem. faculty, 1951-54, asst. prof. medicine, 1953-54; mem. faculty Emory U. Sch. Medicine, 1954-59, prof. preventive medicine, chmn. dept., 1957-59; prof. medicine U. Tex. Southwestern Med. Sch., 1959-78, assoc. dean, 1965-66; vice chancellor health affairs U. Tex. System, Austin, 1966-68; exec. vice chancellor U. Tex. System, 1968-69, dep. chancellor, 1969-70, chancellor, 1971-78, prof. medicine, 1978—; pres., internist U. Tex. M.D. Anderson Cancer Ctr., 1978-96; cons. epidemiology Communicable Disease Center, USPHS, 1953—; cons. medicine VA, 1954-59; area med. cons. VA (Atlanta area), 1958-59; vis. staff physician Grady Meml. Hosp., Atlanta, 1954-59, Emory U. Hosp., 1954-59; sr. attending staff mem. Parkland Meml. Hosp., Dallas, 1959-66; med. dir. chest div. Woodlawn Hosp., Dallas, 1959-65; mem. Surgeon Gen.'s Adv. Com. Smoking and Health, 1963-64, AMA-Edn. Research Found. com. research tobacco and health, 1964-66; chmn. Gov. Tex. Com. Tb Eradication, 1963-64; cons. internal medicine Baylor U. Med. Center, Dallas, 1962-66, St. Paul Hosp., Dallas, 1966; cons. div. hosp. and med. facilities USPHS, 1966; mem. N.Y.C. Task Force on Tb, 1967; cons. Bur. Physician, HEW, 1967-70; mem. grad. med. edn. nat. adv. com. Health Resources Adminstrn., 1977-80; mem. Tex. Legislature Dept. Health, Edn. and Welfare, 1967, Tex. Legislature Com. on Organ Transplantation, 1968, Carnegie Commn. on Non-Traditional Study, 1971-73; mem. bd. commrs. Nat. Commn. on Accrediting, 1973-76; mem. joint task force on continuing competence in pharmacy Am. Pharm. Assn.-Am. Assn. Coll. in Pharmacy, 1973-74; mem. exec. com. Legis. Task Force on Cancer in Tex., 1984-86; adv. bd. 6th World Conf. on Smoking and Health. Contbr. med. jours.; contbg. author: A Textbook of Medicine, 10 and 11th edits, 1963, Pharmacology in Medicine, 1958; Translating author: The Tubercle Bacillus, 1955; mem. editorial bd. Am. Rev. Respiratory Diseases, 1955-58. Mem. President's Commn. White House Fellows, 1971; chmn. subcom. on diversity and pluralism Nat. Council on Ednl. Research, 1973-75; bd. dirs. Assn. Tex. Colls. and Univs., 1974-75; mem. devel. council United Negro Coll. Fund, 1974-78; mem. nat. adv. council Inst. for Services to Edn., 1974-78; mem. exec. com. Assn. Am. Univs., 1975-77; mem. Project HOPE com. on Health Policy, 1977; chmn. steering com. Presbyn. Physicians for Fgn. Missions, 1960-62; mem. Ministers Cons. Clinic, Dallas, 1960-62; trustee Austin Coll., 1979-83, Stillman Coll., 1978-84; bd. dirs. Ga. Tb Assn., 1955-59; bd. dirs. Damon Runyon-Walter Winchell Cancer Fund, 1976-85, chmn. exec. com., v.p., 1978, pres., 1979-83; trustee Biol. Humanics Found., Dallas, 1973-82; chmn. health manpower com. Assn. Am. Univs., 1975-78; sec. Council So. Univs., Inc., 1976-78, pres., 1977-78; hon. life trustee Menninger Found.; Host com. Houston Econ. Summit, 1990. Recipient Cornell Univ. Alumni of Distinction award, 1978, Disting. Alumnus award U. Alabama Sch. Medicine, 1982, Pres.' award Am. Lung Assn., 1987, Gibson D. Lewis award for Excellence in Cancer Control Tex. Cancer Coun., 1988, award of Honor Am. Soc. Hosp. Pharmacists, 1988, Svc. to Mankind award Leukemia Soc. Am. Tex. Gulf Coast chpt., 1991, People of Vision award Tex. Soc. to Prevent Blindness, 1991, Outstanding Tex. Leader award 7th Ann. John Ben Sheppard Pub. Leadership Forum, 1991; Inst. Religion's Caring Spirit Tribute, 1993, AMA Disting. Svc. award, 1995; named Houstonian of Yr. Houston Sch. for Deaf Children, 1987. Mem. AMA, (Disting. Svc. award 1995), NASA, NIH (chair joint adv. com. behavioral rsch. 1992), Am. Thoracic Soc. (past v.p.), So. Thoracic Soc. (past pres.), Nat. TB Assn., Tex. Med. Assn., Ga. Med. Assn., Soc. Assn. Oncology (bd. dirs.), Am. Cancer Soc. (tex. bd. dirs. 1977-89, med. and sci. com. 1974, chmn. study com. on tobacco and cancer 1976—, pub. edn. com. 1976-87, chmn., mem. various nat. coms., v.p., pres. 1986, med. dir.-at-large 1977-89), Houston C. of C. (dir. 1979-89), Philos. Soc. Tex. (pres. 1980-81), Greater Houston Ptnrship (bd. dirs. 1989—), Alpha Omega Alpha. Presbyterian. Home: 13104 Travis View Loop Austin TX 78732-4928*

LEMAN, ROBERT BURTON, cardiology educator; b. Upper Darby, Pa., Dec. 23, 1947; s. William Walter and Ruth Cordelia Leman; m. Patti Ruth Pennington, June 9, 1973; children: Brian Burton, Heather Michelle. BS, Ursinus Coll., 1969; MD, U. Ark., 1976. Diplomate Am. Bd. Internal Medicine; cert. internal medicine, cardiovascular disease, cardiac electrophysiology; lic. physician, S.C. Intern Med. U. of S.C., Charleston, 1976-77, resident, 1977-79, fellow, 1979-81, instr., 1971-72, dir., 1982—, asst. prof., 1983-89, assoc. prof., 1989—; dir. pacemaker surveillance Med. U. S.C., Charleston, 1982—, dir. adult electrophysiology medicine, 1988—; dir. Cath. Lab., Charleston VA, 1986-92; lectr. in field. Contbr. articles to profl. jours. Active Hibben Meth. Ch.; bd. dirs. Trident Fishing Tournament of Charleston County Park. Grantee Wyeth-Ayerst Labs., 1990, G.D. Searl & Co., 1991, Pfizer, Inc., 1992, 93. Fellow ACP, Am. Coll. Cardiology; mem. Am. Heart Assn. (fellow coun. in clin. cardiology), N.Am. Soc. Pacing and Electrophysiology, Charleston County Med. Soc., Hobcaw Yacht Club, Sea Island Sportfishing Soc., Alpha Omega Alpha. Office: Med U SC 816 CSB 171 Ashley Ave Charleston SC 29425-0001

LEMASTER, ROBERT ALLEN, mechanical engineer; b. Troy, Ohio, Sept. 18, 1953; s. Robert Milton and Betty Jean (Reynolds) LeM.; m. Debbie Lou Hinton, Apr. 6, 1974; 1 child, Michael Allen. BSME, Akron U., 1976; MS in Engring. Mechanics, Ohio State U., 1978; PhD in Engring. Sci., U. Tenn., 1983. Engr. Hissong Cons., Mt. Vernon, Ohio, 1976-77; program engr. W.J. Schafer & Assocs., Dayton, Ohio, 1988-89; engr. AEDC Group Arnold Engring. Devel. Ctr. Group Sverdrup Tech. Inc., Tullahoma, Tenn., 1978-83; project engr. tech. group Sverdrup Tech. Inc., Tullahoma, Tenn., 1983-88; dept. mgr. MSFC Group Sverdrup Tech. Inc., Huntsville, Ala., 1989—. Contbr. tech. papers to profl. publs. Mem. budget com., fundraising com. Bob Jones H.S. Athletic Booster Club, Madison, Ala., 1989-93. Mem. ASME, AIAA (structures tech. com.), ASCE (advisor, electric transmission structures com.). Republican. Baptist. Home: 116 Silver Creek Cir Madison AL 35758-7637 Office: Sverdrup Tech Inc MSFC Group 620 Discovery Dr NW Huntsville AL 35806-2802

LEMASTER, SHERRY RENEE, fundraising administrator; b. Lexington, Ky., June 25, 1953; d. John William and Mary Charles (Thompson) LeM.; BS, U. Ky., 1975, MS in Higher Edn. Adminstrn., Bryn Mawr Coll. Inst. for Women, 1984. Cert. fund raising exec. Lab. technician in virology, serology Cen. Ky. Animal Disease Diagnostic Lab., Lexington, 1975-76; grant coord., environ. specialist Commonwealth Ky. Dept. for Natural Resources and Environ. Protection, Frankfort, 1976-78; coord. residence hall program Murray (Ky.) State U., 1978-80; dean students Midway (Ky.) Coll., 1980-81, v.p. devel., alumnae affairs, 1981-86; dir. devel. Wilderness Road Coun. Girl Scouts U.S., Lexington, 1986-88, Coll. of Agr. and Life Scis. Va. Tech., Blacksburg, Va. 1988-94; sr. major gifts officer Bowman Gray Sch. Medicine Wake Forest U. and N.C. Baptist Hosp., Inc., Winston-Salem, N.C., 1994—. amb. U. Ky. Coll. Agr.; cons. U.S. Dept. Edn., 1987—; chmn. Midway chpt. Am. Heart Assn., 1981; mem. adminstrv. bd. First United Meth. Ch., Lexington, 1982-84, 87; mem. Coun. for Advancement and Support Edn., 1981—, chmn. Ky. conf., 1982; planning com. charter mem. Nat. Disciples Devel. Execs. Conf., 1984; mem. East Ky. First Quality of Life Com., 1987-88. Recipient Young Career Woman award Bus. and Profl. Women's Club, Frankfort, 1981; named to Hon. Order of Ky. col., 1977, hon. sec. state, 1984. Mem. Nat. Soc. Fund Raising Execs. (bd. dirs. Lexington chpt. 1986), Advancement Women in Higher Edn. Adminstrn. (former state planning com. Ky.), U. Ky. Alumni Assn. (life), P.E.O. (charter, chpt. X-Ky., sec. chpt. AU-Va. 1991-93, Va. state chpt., amendments and accommodation com. 1990-92), Ninety-Nines Internat. Assn. Women Pilots (vice chmn. Ky. Bluegrass chpt. 1986-87, chmn. and chmn. bd. 1987-88), Kentuckians N.Y., Jr. League, Nat. Agriculture Alumni and Devel. Assn. (awards com. 1992-94), Pi Beta Phi Nat. Alumnae Assn. (alumnae province pres. 1980-81, sec. bd. dirs. Ky. Beta chpt. 1982-84, pres. Va. Zeta chpt. house corp. 1991-94). Avocations: private pilot, needlecrafts, swimming, equitation, racquetball. Office: Bowman Gray Baptist Hosp Wake Forest U The Med Ctr Medical Center Blvd Winston Salem NC 27157

LEMAY, SONLEY ROBERT, JR., otolaryngologist; b. Dallas, Nov. 6, 1933; m. Nancy LeMay; children: Diana, Robert, Darlene. BA, So. Meth. U., 1953; MD, U. Tex. Southwestern Med. Sch., 1957. Diplomate Am. Bd. Otolaryngology, Tex. State Bd. Med. Examiners. Commd. 2d lt. U.S. Army Med. Corps., 1958; advanced through grades to col. USAMC, 1972, ret., 1978; intern Meth. Hosp., Dallas, 1957-58; resident in otolaryngology Brooke Gen. Hosp., Ft. Sam Houston, Tex., 1959-62; fellow in otolaryngic pathology Armed Forces Inst. Pathology, Washington, 1964-66; asst. clin. prof. surgery U. Tex. Health Sci. Ctr., San Antonio, 1970-78; clin. asst. prof. dept. otolaryngology U. Tex. Southwestern Med. Sch., 1978—; staff appointment Navarro Regional Hosp., Corsicana, Tex., chief of staff, 1992; courtesy staff appointment Baylor Med. Ctr., Ennis, Tex.; adj. prof. Health Sci., Baylor U., 1976-78. Fellow ACS, Am. Acad. Otolaryngology, Am. Laryngolica, Rhinological and Otological Soc., Am. Acad. Facial Plastic and Reconstructive Surgery; mem. AMA, Tex. Otolaryn. Assn. (pres. 1995-96), Tex. Assn. Otolaryngology-Head and Neck Surgery (pres. 1995-96); Navarro County Med. Soc. (pres. 1987), Tex. Med. Assn. (chmn. sect. otolaryngology 1994, sec. 1993), Soc. Mil. Otolarynologists (pres. 1977-78). Home: 2024 Glenwood Cir Corsicana TX 75110-3420 Office: Med Arts Clinic 301 Hospital Dr Corsicana TX 75110-2471

LEMBKE, JANET NUTT, writer; b. Cleve., Mar. 2, 1933; d. Joseph Randolph and Sarah Howell (East) Nutt. AB in Classics, Middlebury Coll., 1953. Author: River Time, 1989, Looking for Eagles, 1990, Dangerous Birds, 1992, Skinny Dipping, 1994, Dipping, 1994, Shake Them Simmons Down, 1996; translator: Aeschylus, 1981, Euripides, 1991, 94; poet: Bronze and Iron, 1973; contbr. articles and poems to profl. jours. Mem. PEN Am. Ctr. Home: 210 N Madison St Staunton VA 24401-3359

LEMENS, WILLIAM VERNON, JR., banker, finance company executive, lawyer; b. Austin, Tex., Oct. 26, 1935; s. William Vernon and Lylia (Engberg) L.; m. Jean Lemens, May 31, 1959; children: William Vernon III, Shandra Christine. BA, U. Tex., 1958, LLB, 1962, JD, 1962. Bar: Tex. 1962; lic. real estate broker, Tex. Pvt. practice Austin, 1962—; pres. Standard Fin. Co., Austin, 1963-67, First State Loan, Austin, 1967—; chief exec. officer Southwest Computer Svcs., Inc., Austin, 1965—; pres., chief instr., mgmt. cons. Decision Dynamics, Inc., Austin, 1965-75; exec. v.p., atty. Northwest Savs. Assn., Austin, 1975-78; chmn. bd. First State Bank, Jarrell, Tex., 1975-87; pres., chief exec. officer First Am. Fin. Co., Ft. Worth, 1982—, Eagle Bank, Jarrell, 1987—. Author: Elements of Objective Orientation, 1971, SSAM-The Power of Perfect Decisions, 1972, Successful Financial Institution Operation, 1978, National Standard Financial Company Operations, 1981. Pres. Ballet Austin, 1967, Southwest Regional Ballet Assn., 1968; deacon Univ. Bapt. Ch., Austin, 1979—. Mem. State Bar Tex., Austin Bd. Realtors, Tex. Fin. Inst. (bd. dirs. 1975—), Tex. Consumer Fin. Asns. (bd. dirs. 1995—). Office: 1509 Guadalupe St Ste 200 Austin TX 78701-1608

LEMERISE, ELIZABETH ANN, psychology educator; b. Berlin, N.H., Sept. 27, 1952; d. William Paul and Claire Lucille (Boucher) L.; m. Joseph Bilotta, Oct. 16, 1982. BA in Psychology cum laude, Bates Coll., 1974; MA in Psychology, New Sch. for Soc. Rsch., N.Y.C., 1976, PhD in Personality & Social Psychology, 1988. Rsch. coord. Bklyn. Coll. CUNY, 1978-84, rsch. assoc., 1984-87, lectr., 1981-85; rsch. assoc. Vanderbilt U., Nashville, Tenn., 1987-91, lectr., 1988-90; asst. prof. Western Ky. U., Bowling Green, 1991-95, assoc. prof., 1995—. Contbr. articles to profl. jours. Rep. Alumni in Admissions, Bates Coll., Maine, 1983—, coord., N.Y.C., 1985-87. Mem. APA, AAUW, Soc. Rsch. Child Devel., Internat. Soc. Infant Studies, Ky. Acad. Sci., Phi Beta Kappa. Office: Western Ky Univ Dept Psychology Bowling Green KY 42101

LEMING, W(ILLIAM) VAUGHN, electronics engineer; b. Pawhuska, Okla., Dec. 11, 1945; s. William Dalton Leming and Mattie Cornelia (Hatfield) Kafer; m. Janis Diana Lee (div.); children: Heather Lynne, Hilary Ann; m. Donna Faye Sartor, May 18, 1975; 1 child, Chandra Paige. Student, U. Okla., 1964-67. 68-70, U. Tulsa, 1967-68; cert., diploma, DeVry Inst. Tech., Chgo, 1977; cert., diploma with highest honors, Nat. Radio Inst., Washington, 1981. FCC Gen. Radio telephone, Naber Cert., IHF Consumer Audio Assoc. Spl. instr. Tri County Vocat.-Tech. Sch., Bartlesville, Okla., 1975-76; pres., chief exec. officer Fantasia Sound Systems, Inc., Jenks, Okla., 1976-87; announcer KWON Radio, Bartlesville, 1980-81; chief electronics technician The Sound Centre, Bartlesville, 1978-81; electronic technician 1A Burlington No. R.R. Co., Tulsa, 1981-92; founder, CEO FeS2 Pictures, 1991—. Musician, actor, entertainer, 1966—; bassist The New Orleans Jazz Band, Jenks, Okla., 1979—; actor: (films) The Outsiders, 1982, Rumble Fish, 1983, Fandango, 1984, Schizophrenia, 1989; dir., editor: (documentary) Adjuvant Nutrition in Cancer Treatment Symposium; photographer (campaign exhibit) Picture What Women Do, Lifetime TV, 1994. Recipient Gold Medal in Electronics, U.S. Skill Olympics, Lawton, Okla., 1976. Home: 523 E E St Jenks OK 74037-3326 Office: FeS2 Pictures PO Box 772 Jenks OK 74037-0772

LEMOINE, SANDRA MARIE, health and physical education educator; b. New Orleans, Aug. 11, 1943; d. Allen Joseph and Odell (Branch) L.; 1 child, Nicole Marie. BA, La. Tech. U., 1978, MA, 1979; PhD, U. So. Miss., 1984. Mem. Arabian Am. Oil Co. Schs., Dhahran, Saudi Arabia, 1976-77; instr. U. So. Miss., Hattiesburg, 1979-81; assoc. prof. La. Tech. U., Ruston, 1981-92; dept. chair kinesiology Shenandoah U., Winchester, Va., 1992—; summer faculty fellow NASA Johnson Spac Center, 1992; dir. Fitness Inst. of Tech. Ruston, 1987-90. Contbr. articles to Aviation, Space and Environ. Medicine, Lahperd Jour., 1984-95; spkr. internat. and nat. profl. orgns. and many civic groups Ruston, 1981-91. Sec. Am. Heart Assn., Ruston, 1991. Grantee Spl. Edn. and Rehab. Svcs., Hattiesburg, 1980-82, State Dept. Edn. Spl. Edn., Ruston, 1987, La. Tech. U., 1988, 90; fellow NASA Johnson Space Ctr., Houston, summer 1992. Mem. Am. Alliance for Health, Phys. Edn., Recreation and Dance, Va. Alliance for Health, Phys. Edn., Recreation and Dance, Am. Coll. Sports Medicine. Office: Shenandoah Univ 1460 University Dr Winchester VA 22602

LEMON, ROBERT SHELDON, JR., art history educator; b. Pittsburg, Kans., Oct. 1, 1938; s. Robert Sheldon and Lois Margaret (Wise) L.; m. Julia Nancy Claugus, Dec. 29, 1967; children: Rebecca, Robert III. BA, U. Mo., 1962; MA, Ohio U., 1969, PhD, 1975. Asst. dean Coll. Fine Arts Ohio U., 1969-70; instr. to full prof. Rollins Coll., Winter Park, Fla., 1973—, art dept. chair, 1983—. Author: The Figurative Pretext, 1980; author exhbn. catalogues. Bd. dirs. Southeastern Coll. Art Conf., Chapel Hill, 1981-84, 87-93, v.p. 1993-96, pres. 1996—; v.p., bd. dirs. Maitland (Fla.) Art Ctr., 1976-80; art selection com. Orlando Aviation Authority, Orlando Internat. Airport, 1982-89. With U.S. Army, 1962-65. Rsch. grantee State of Fla. Arts Coun., 1995, Nat. Endowment for the ARts, 1988, Fla. Art Coun., 1988. Office: Rollins Coll Box 2684 1000 Holt Ave Winter Park FL 32789

LEMON, WILLIAM JACOB, lawyer; b. Covington, Va., Oct. 25, 1932; s. James Gordon and Elizabeth (Wilson) L.; m. Barbara Inez Boyle, Aug. 17, 1957; children: Sarah E. Lemon Ludwig, William Tucker, Stephen Weldon. BA, Washington & Lee U., 1957, JD, 1959. Bar: Va. 1959. Assoc. Martin, Martin & Hopkins, Roanoke, Va., 1959-61; ptnr. Martin, Hopkins & Lemon, Roanoke, 1962—; pres. Liberty Nursing Homes, Inc., Roanoke, 1965-81; trustee Washington & Lee U., Lexington, Va., 1988—. Trustee North Cross Sch., Roanoke, 1995—; pres. Specific Reading and Learning Difficulties Assn. Shedd Early Learning Ctr., 1985-86. Cpl. U.S. Army, 1952-54, Austria. Mem. ABA, Va. Bar Assn., Roanoke Bar Assn. (pres. 1982-83), Va. State Bar, Shenandoah Club. Presbyterian. Office: Martin Hopkins Lemon First Union Tower 10 S Jefferson St Ste 1000 Roanoke VA 24011 also: PO Box 13366 Roanoke VA 24033-3366

LEMONS, ALBERT LEE, principal, musician; b. San Francisco, Dec. 29, 1944; s. Albert Renger and Vera (Mancy) L. BS, Tex. So. U., 1968, MA, 1976, MEd, 1979; PhD, Bapt. Theol. Sem., 1977. Cert. reading specialist. 4th grade tchr. Fairchild Elem. Sch., Houston, 1967-68; 4th-6th grade tchr. Oates Elem. Sch., Houston, 1968-83; reading specialist Holland Middle Sch., Houston, 1983-89; tchr. vocat. enrichment lab., acting dean instruction Jefferson Davis Sr. High Sch., Houston, 1989-90; prin. Atherton Elem. Sch., Houston, 1990—; asst. dir. Youth Enrichment Program, Houston, 1987-90; reading clinic tchr. Tex. So. U. Weekend Coll., Houston, 1987-90; tchr. youth opportunities program Prairie View A&M U., 1983-87. Co-editor: (sch. newspaper) Atherton Owl, 1991. Bd. dirs. Gospel Melody Enterprize, Houston, 1988—; bd. dirs. scholarship com. First Morning Star Bapt. Ch., Houston, 1991; active PTA, Houston, 1973—; asst. choir dir. New Pleasant Grove Bapt. Ch., 1990-94; musician Lilly Grove Bapt. Ch., 1990-93; organist Fifth Ward Missionary Bapt. Ch., 1978-90; min. of music Miles Chapel CME Ch., 1994—; cheerleader and booster sponsor Holland Mid. Sch., 1984-89; cheerleader sponsor Jefferson Davis Sr. High Sch., 1989-91. Recipient Career Ladder III award Houston Ind. Sch. Dist., 1978, Leadership award, 1990, Community Svc. award Mayors Office, Houston, 1980, Exceptional Musical Ability award Nevarro Music Studio, 1991, Men on the Move in the 90's award Sigma Gamma Rho Sorority, 1992; named Man of the Yr. Nat. Women of Achievement, 1994, Principal of the Yr. Better Way Youth, Inc., 1994. Mem. Shriners (sec. 1983-86, Outstanding Svc. award 1983), Masons (Civic Svc. award 1978), Phi Delta Kappa (bd. dirs. 1979). Democrat. Home: 10530 Rockaway Dr Houston TX 77016-3335 Office: Atherton Elem School 2011 Solo St Houston TX 77020-4223

LE MONS, KATHLEEN ANN, portfolio manager, investment broker; b. Trenton, N.J., Apr. 6, 1952; d. Albert Martin and Veronica Grace (Kerr) LeM.; m. Walter Everett Faircloth, Apr. 15, 1978 (div. Dec. 1988); m. Jeffery West Benedict, June 29, 1991. Attended, Rollins Coll., 1970-71, Fla. State U., 1971-76; BSBA magna cum laude, Christopher Newport U., 1995; post-grad., Coll. William and Mary, 1995—. Registered rep. NASD/NYSE, investment advisor; cert. portfolio mgr. Sci. rsch. assoc. NASA, Hampton, Va., 1973-76; fin. cons. Merrill Lynch Pierce Fenner Smith, Hampton, 1985-88; cert. portfolio mgr. Wheat First Butcher Singer, Newport News, Va., 1988—. Pres. James Landing Assn., 1991-95; life mem. Capital Dist. Found., 1992; mem. exec. panel fund distbn. Va. Peninsula United Way, 1996—; Hampton Rds. chair March of Dimes Walk Am., 1996—. George F. Hixson fellow Kiwanis Internat., 1996. Mem. Am. Mktg. Assn., Va. Peninsula C. of C. (transp. task force 1993—, govtl. affairs task force 1993—), Oyster Point Kiwanis (charter), Coll. of William and Mary Part-

Time MBA Assn. (charter, curriculum com. chair 1995—, v.p. 1996—), Christopher Newport U. Pres.' Coun., Christopher Newport Univ. Alumni Soc. (bd. dirs. 1996—), James River Country Club (9-hole golf group), Alpha Chi. Republican. Home: 61 Queens Ct Newport News VA 23606-2034 Office: Wheat First Butcher Singer 11817 Canon Blvd Newport News VA 23606-2569

LENARD, LLOYD EDGAR, financial consultant; b. West Monroe, La., July 29, 1922; s. James Edward and Doshie (Boyette) L.; m. Betty-Jo Sawyer, Dec. 23, 1947; children: Carla Dawn, Brian Drury, Lloyd E. BA in Journalism, La. State U., 1943; MA in Advt. and Mktg., U. Mo., 1947. CLU, ChFC. News reporter Shreveport (La.) Times, 1946; exec. trainee Neiman-Marcus, Dallas, 1947-48; advt. mgr. Sta. KNOE, Monroe, La., 1948-52; life ins. agt. Aetna Life, Monroe, 1952-53; asst. agy. mgr. Aetna Life, Shreveport, 1953-56; agy. mgr., owner Pan Am. Life, Shreveport, 1956-80; freelance fin. cons. Shreveport, 1980—; county commr. Caddo Parish Commn., Shreveport, 1983—. Author fiction and non-fiction books; contbr. articles to profl. jours. Chmn. Reps., Caddo Parish, La., 1975; chmn. Reps. five parish area; treas. La. Rep. Party; mem. Rep. State Ctrl. Com., Heart Assn. Named Young Man of Yr. Jr. Chamber, 1956, Gen. Agt. of Yr. Pan Am. Life, 1963; recipient various speech trophies. Mem. Nat. Assn. County Govts. (taxation and fin. steering com.), Kiwanis, Mid-City Kiwanis Club Sport (dist. lt. gov. 1978). Republican. Baptist. Home and Office: Ind Fin Cons 6122 River Rd Shreveport LA 71105-4834

LENARD, PETER DENNIS, general surgeon; b. Hungary, Dec. 25, 1942; came to U.S., 1949; m. Margaret Knapik, June 8, 1968; children: Elizabeth Ann, P. Dennis, Stephen H., David G. Student, Emory Univ., 1961-63, Emory Coll., 1959-61; BS, George Washington Univ., 1964, MD, 1968. Diplomate Am. Bd. Surgery. Surgical intern Univ. Rochester, N.Y., 1968-69, surgical resident, 1969-70; surgical resident Georgetown Univ., Washington, 1970-74; pvt. practice McLean, Va., 1974—. Trustee Blue Cross Blue Shield Nat. Capitol Area, Washington, 1981-93. Capt. U. S. Army, 1975-81. Fellow Am. Coll. Surgeons; mem. Fairfax County Medical Soc. (exec. com. 1987-89). Home: 6964 Kyleakin Ct Mc Lean VA 22101-1556 Office: 1485 Chain Bridge Rd Mc Lean VA 22101-4501

LENGOMIN, JUAN A., educational administrator; b. Havana, Cuba, Apr. 8, 1953; came to U.S., 1962; s. Juan Evaristo and Hortensia Andrea (Ocána) Lengomín; m. Raquel Gonzalez, June 20, 1975; children: Javier, Sergio, David. BA, Fla. Internat. U., 1974; MS, Nova U., 1978. Classroom tchr. Skyway Elem. Sch., 1974-82; pers. cord. Bur. Pers. Mgmt., 1982-86; asst. prin. Airbase Elem. Sch., 1986-87; prin. intern North Glade Elem. Sch., 1987; prin. Springview Elem. Sch., 1987-92; dir. pers./contract mgmt. Region III Ops Dade County Pub. Schs., Miami, 1992—; mem. Dade County Pub. Schs./United Office Pers. of Dade Collective Bargaining Team, 1993; pers. recruiter Dade County Pub. Schs., 1990-94, mem. Region III Tchr. of Yr. Com., 1990; Fulbright Tchr. Exch. liaison Dade County Pub. Schs. and USIA, Washington, 1982-86; mem. North Cen. Area Paraprofl. of Yr. Selection Com., 1988-89, North Cen. Area Tchr. of Yr. Luncheon Com., 1989-91. Mem. Dade County chpt. PTA, North Cen. Area Beautification Com., 1987; grad. Leadership Miami, 1990. Recipient Bros. to Rescue Hon. pin, 1994, Miami Coral Park Sr. H.S. Ram Price plaque and cert., 1994, Orden Cultural 12 de Octubre de 1492, Instituto de Cultura Hispanic, 1991, Assn. Scholarship award Dade County Coun. Parent Tchr. Assn., 1989, D.A.R.E. Drug Abuse Resistance Edn. plaque Police Dept., City of Miami Springs, 1992, Metro Dade key to County; named Person of Day, Sta. WQBA, 1990; Juan Lengomin Day named in his honor City of Miami. Mem. ASCD, Nat. Assn. Sch. Adminstrs., Am. Fedn. Sch. Adminstrs., Nat. Assn. Elem. Sch. Prins., Am. Hispanic Educators Assn. of Dade, Fla. Assn. Elem. Sch. Adminstrs., Fla. Assn. Sch. Adminstrs., Fla. Congress Parents and Tchrs. (Cert. Hon. life mem. 1992), Cuban Tchrs. in Exile Orgn. (Plaque of hon. mem. 1992), Dade County Sch. Adminstr.'s Assn. (bd. dirs. 1994-95, adminstr.'s profl. devel. com. 1991), Dade Assn. Sch. Adminstrs. (legis. com. 1994), Greater Miami C. of C., The Club at Doral-Country Club (legends mem.). Home: 115 SW 135th Ave Miami FL 33184 Office: Dade County Pub Schs Region III Ops 1080 LaBaron Dr Miami FL 33166

LENK, CHRISTA C., lawyer; b. Heidelberg, Germany, Feb. 8, 1950; d. Walter Ernst and Theresia (Schuster) L. BA, St. Mary's U., 1972; MSW, Our Lady of the Lake, 1975; JD, Tex. So. U., 1981. Bar: Tex. 1983. Pvt. practice San Antonio. Office: 200 E Main Plz Ste 200 San Antonio TX 78205-2736

LENNON, A. MAX, food products company executive; b. Columbus County, N.C., Sept. 27, 1940; m. Ruth Carter; children—Daniel Ray, Robin LuRay. AA, Mars Hill Coll., 1960; BS, N.C. State U., 1962, PhD, 1970. Owner, operator crop and livestock farm, 1962-66; grad. asst. N.C. State U., Raleigh, 1966-70; asst. prof. animal sci. Tex. Tech U., Lubbock, 1970-72, assoc. prof., 1972, prof., chmn. dept. animal sci., 1974-77; asst. dean, dir. rsch. Coll. Agrl. Scis., Tex. Tech U., 1977-79, assoc. dean, dir. rsch., 1979; sr. swine nutritionist Central Soya Co., Decatur, Ind., 1973; dir. swine feeds rsch. Cen. Soya Co., Decatur, Ind., 1974; chairperson dept. animal husbandry U. Mo.-Columbia, 1980, dir. agrl. experiment sta., dean coll. agr., 1980-83; v.p. for agrl. adminstrn., exec. dean for agr., home econs. and natural resources Ohio State U., Columbus, 1983-86; pres. Clemson (S.C.) U., 1986-94; pres., CEO Ea. Foods Inc., Atlanta, 1994—; Seaman A. Knapp lectr. Dallas, 1988; past co-chmn. Ohio Gov.'s Commn. on Agr.; past chmn. N. Cen. region Coun. of Adminstrv. Heads of Agr.; bd. dirs. First Union Corp., Delta Woodside Industries, Inc., Duke Power Co., Escuela Agricola de la Region Tropical Humeda, Baptist Med. Ctr. Found.; past bd. govs. Am. Royal; E.T. York Disting. lectr. Auburn U., 1991. Contbr. articles to profl. jour. Mem. S.E. regional adv. bd. Inst. Internat. Edn.; adv. com. for task force on agriculture devel. and cooperation, Internat. Devel. Agy.; co-chair policy adv. com. Competitive Rsch. Grants; bd. dirs. Farm Found., Nat. Dropout Prevention Fund Devel. Coun., Greenville Tech. Coll. Fed. Devel. Coun., Fellowship Christian Farmers Internat. State Panel, S.C. Women in Higher Edn.; mem. Dept. Def. Clothing & Textile Bd., Adv. Com. for Task Force on Agrl. Devel. and Cooperation; trustee Palmetto Partnership, Found. for Drug Abuse Prevention, adv. bd. McDonald's Initiative , So. Assn. Coll. and Schs. Com. on Intercollegiate Athletics, Internat. Assn. of Agribus; mem. Congl. Office Tech. Assessment Coun., So. Assn. Colls. and Schs., Commn. on Colls. Class of 1994, rep. S.C.'s Exec. Coun.; bd. dirs. Bapt. Med. Ctr. Found. Recipient Disting. Alumnus award Coll. Agr. and Life Scis., N.C. State U., 1989, Nat. 4-H Alumni award, 1989, Thomas Green Clemson medallion Clemson U., 1991. Mem. AAAS, Am. Soc. Animal Sci., Internat. Assn. Agribus., Coun. for Agrl. Sci. and Tech., Farm House Assn., Internat. Devel. Agy., Alpha Zeta, Phi Sigma, Phi Kappa Phi, Gamma Sigma Delta.

LENNOX, EDWARD NEWMAN, holding company executive; b. New Orleans, July 27, 1925; s. Joseph Andrew and May Alice (Newman) L.; B.B.A., Tulane U., 1949; m. Joan Marie Landry, Sept. 3, 1949; children: Katherine Sarah, Anne Victoria, Mary Elizabeth, Laura Joan. Mktg. service clk. Shell Oil Co., New Orleans, 1949; with W.M. Chambers Truck Line, Inc., 1950-60, exec. v.p., 1954-60; v.p., gen. mgr. Radcliff Materials, Inc., New Orleans, 1961-71; v.p. Office Pub. Affairs, So. Industries Corp., 1971-88; v.p. Dravo Natural Resources Co., 1982-91, Dravo Corp., 1989-91, ret., 1992; pres. Tidelands Industries, Inc., 1982-85; bd. dir. Home Savings & Loan Assn., 1979-89, pres., 1982-88, chmn., 1984-89; cons. Martin-Marietta Aggregates, 1995—. Pres., La. Tank Truck Carriers, 1954-55; mem. La. Bd. Hwys., 1965-67; chmn. New Orleans Aviation Bd., 1965-66; bd. dirs. Travelers Aid Soc., 1966-68, Met. Area Com., 1967-80, Constrn. Industry Legis. Coun., 1968-85, Miss. Valley Assn., 1969-72; pres. bd. levee commrs. Orleans Levee Dist., 1969-72; pres. Met. New Orleans Safety Coun., 1969-71; bus. and fin. adviser Congregation Sisters of Immaculate Conception; vice chmn. transp. task force Goals for La., 1969-72; mem. New Orleans Bd. Trade, 1971-89; mem. Ala. Gov.'s Adv. Coun. on Econs., 1971-72, Gov.'s Adv. Com. River Area Transp. and Planning Study, 1971-72; area v.p. Pub. Affairs Rsch. Coun. La., 1972-73; mem. exec. com. La. Good Roads Assn., 1972-74; industry del. La. Constl. Conv., 1973; mem. exec. com. Miss. Valley World Trade Coun., 1973-74; bd. dirs., exec. com. Pendleton Meml. Meth. Hosp., 1963-81, dir. emeritus, 1981—; bd. dirs. Boys' Clubs Greater New Orleans, 1973-79; bd. dirs., mem. exec. bd. Goodwill Industries Greater New Orleans, Inc., 1975-79, 81—, treas., 1984-85, first v.p., 1987-88, chmn. 1989-90; bd. dirs. Americanism Forum, 1975—, Tragedy Fund, Inc., 1976—; bd. govs. La. Civil Svc. League, 1974—, pres., 1977-78; dir. chmn. bd. trustees La. Found. Pvt. Colls., 1980-83. Capt. AUS, 1943-46. Recipient Industry Svc. award Assoc. Gen. Contractors Am., 1967, Cert. of Appreciation Constrn. Industry Assn. New Orleans, 1972, New Orleans Jaycees award, 1960, Cert. of Merit Mayoralty of New Orleans, 1964, 67, Monte M. Lemann award La. Civil Svc. League, 1976; named Hon. Life Chmn., 1980, hon. Citizen and Amb. at Large City of Jacksonville, 1966. Mem. NAM (pub. affairs steering com. So. div. 1979—), La. Motor Transport Assn. (pres. 1963-64), Ala. Trucking Assn. (v.p. 1956-60), So. Concrete Masonry Assn. (pres. 1963-68), Greater New Orleans Ready Mixed Concrete Assn. (pres. 1966-68), La. Shell Producers Assn. (pres. 1966-68), C. of C. New Orleans Area (bd. dir. 1968-73, 75-77, pres. elect 1973), Internat. House (bd. dir. 1977-79), Traffic Club New Orleans, Lakeshore Property Owners Assn. (bd. dir. 1974-86 , pres. 1976-77, 79-80), Tulane Alumni Assn., Mobile Area C. of C. Club: Metairie Country (bd. govs. 1976-82, 89-92, pres. 1980-81). Home: 862 Topaz St New Orleans LA 70124-3626 Office: 120 Mallard St Ste 150 Saint Rose LA 70087-9452

LENOIR, GLORIA CISNEROS, small business owner, business executive; b. Monterrey, Nuevo Leon, Mex., Aug. 18, 1951; came to U.S., 1956, naturalized; d. Juan Antonio and Maria Gloria (Flores) Cisneros; m. Walter Frank Lenoir, June 6, 1975; children: Lucy Gloria, Katherine Judith, Walter Frank IV. Student, Inst. Am. Univs., 1971-72; BA in French Art, Austin Coll., 1973, MA in French Art, 1974; MBA in Fin., U. Tex., 1979. French tchr. Sherman (Tex.) High Sch., 1973-74; French/Spanish tchr, dept. chmn. Lyndon Baines Johnson High Sch., Austin, 1974-77; legis. aide Tex. State Capitol, Austin, Tex., 1977-81; stock broker Merrill Lynch, Austin, 1981-83, Schneider, Bernet and Hickman, Austin, 1983-84; bus. mgr. Holleman Photographic Labs., Inc., Austin, 1984-87, 88-90; account exec., stock broker Eppler, Guerin & Turner, 1987-88; ind. distbr. Austin, 1990-93; owner, cons. Profl. Cons. Svcs., Austin, 1991—; adj. faculty Spanish , internat. bus. St. Edwards U., 1991—; group counselor, organizer Inst. Fgn. Studies, U. Strasbourg, France, summer 1976; mktg. intern IBM, Austin, summer 1978; mktg. cons. Creative Ednl. Enterprises, Austin, 1980-81; hon. speaker Mex.-Am. U. of Tex., Austin, 1984; speaker various orgns., bus. classes, Austin, 1981-84; speaker, coord. small bus. workshops, 1985. Photographs pub. in Women in Space, 1979, Review, 1988; exhibited in group shows throughout Tex., 1979, 88-89. Neighborhood capt. Am. Cancer Soc., Austin, 1982-86, 90, Am. Heart Assn., 1989; active PTA, 1989—, mem. Bryker Woods Elem. PTA Bd., 1990-92, pres., 1990-91, mem. Kealing Jr. H.S. PTA Bd., 1992-94, chair 50th anniversary celebration com., 1990, hospitality chmn., 1st grade coord., Austin, 1986, mem. legis. com. Tex. State, 1990-92; vol. liaison leads program Austin Coll., 1983—; mem. advantage Austin, 1988; peer panelist Major Art Insts. Austin, 1989-90; co-chair fin. Ctrl. Presbyn. Ch., elder, 1988-90, session clk., 1989, chair membership com., 1990, mem. staff com., 1991-92; megaskills leader Austin Ind. Sch. Dist., 1991—; bd. dirs. Magnet Parents Coalition, 1995—; mem. Austin City coun. PTA Bd., 1991-96, Dist. 7 PTA Bd., 1996—. Recipient Night on the Town award IBM, 1978. Mem. Tex. Congress Tchrs. and Parents (chair cultural arts dist. 13 1996—). Republican. Home and Office: 1202 W 29th St Austin TX 78703-1917

LENOX, ROGER SHAWN, lawyer; b. Prescott, Ark., June 27, 1961; s. Ollie and Mae Lenox; m. Patricia Mickens; children: Mariah, Maya. BSN cum laude, U. Ala., Huntsville, 1987; JD, U. Mich., 1991. Bar: Tex. 1992, D.C. 1993, U.S. Ct. Appeals (D.C. cir.) 1993, U.S. Dist. Ct. (no., so., ea. and we. dists.) Tex. 1994, U.S. Ct. Appeals (5th cir.) 1995; RN, Ala. Summer assoc. Dykema Gossett, Detroit, 1989-90; assoc. Fulbright & Jaworski, L.L.P., Dallas, 1991-95; pvt. practice Dallas, 1995—. Firm rep. Dallas Black C. of C., 1992-95, The Sci. Place, Dallas, 1993-95; spkr. Greater Tex. chpt. Nat. Assn. Pediatric Nurse Practitioners and Assocs., 1995; atty. mentor for Criminal Cts. Day, Youth Leadership Dallas, 1994; Career Day spkr. Dallas Bus. Magnet H.S., 1993. Lt. (j.g.) USN, 1987-91. Recipient Faculty Award for Clin. Excellence, U. Ala., Huntsville, 1987, Nat. Collegiate Nursing award U.S. Achievement Acad., 1987; U. Mich. Law Sch. Clarence Darrow scholar, 1988-91. Mem. ABA, Am. Assn. Nurse Attys., Tex. Bar, No. Tex. Soc. for Healthcare Risk Mgmt., D.C. Bar, Dallas Bar Assn., J.L. Turner Legal Assn., Sigma Theta Tau. Home: 842 Clear Fork Dr Dallas TX 75232 Office: PO Box 222128 Dallas TX 75222

LENT, NORMAN FREDERICK, JR., former congressman; b. Oceanside, N.Y., Mar. 23, 1931; s. Norman Frederick and Ellen (Bain) L.; m. Barbara Ann Morris, Aug. 4, 1979; children from previous marriage: Norman Frederick 3d, Barbara Anne, Thomas Benjamin. BA, Hofstra U., 1952; LLB, Cornell U., 1957; LLD (hon.), Kyung Hee U., Seoul, Republic of Korea, 1975, Molloy Coll., 1985, Hofstra Coll., 1988. Bar: N.Y. 1957, Fla. 1976. Assoc. police judge East Rockaway, N.Y., 1958-60; confidential law sec. to N.Y. State Supreme Ct., 1960-62; mem. N.Y. State Senate, 1963-70, chmn. joint legislative com. public health, 1966-70; mem. 92nd Congress 5th Dist. N.Y., 1971-73; mem. 93rd-102d Congresses 4th Dist. N.Y., 1973-93; vice chmn. Energy and Commerce com. 100th-102nd Congresses U.S. Ho. Reps., 1986-93, vice chmn. Mcht. Marine subcom., 1987-93; cons. Lent & Scrivner, Washington, 1993—; Rep. exec. leader, East Rockaway, N.Y., 1968-70. Mem. bd. visitors U.S. Mcht. Marine Acad., Kings Point, N.Y. With USNR, 1952-54. Recipient George Estabrook Disting. Service award Hofstra U., 1967, Israeli Prime Minister's medal, 1977, Disting. Achievement medal N.Y.C. Holland Soc., 1987, Tree of Life award Jewish Nat. Fund., 1987, Anatoly Sharansky Freedom award L.I. Com. for Soviet Jewry, 1983. Mem. Fla. Bar Assn. Office: Lent & Scrivner 555 13th St NW Ste 305 E Washington DC 20004-1109

LENTZ, EDWIN LAMAR, art historian; b. Houston, Mar. 31, 1951; s. Edwin Lonzo and Gerald Dwain (Flack) L. BA, U. Tex., 1973, MA, 1991. Spl. asst. to Harry H. Ransom Harry Ransom Humanities Rsch. Ctr., U. Tex., Austin, 1971-73, curator Coral Maud Oneal Rm., 1975—; mus. registrar Lyndon Baines Johnson Libr. and Mus., Austin, 1974-75; asst. to registrar Mus. Fine Arts, Houston, 1975-76; curator/assoc. mng. dir. Festival-Inst. at Round Top, Tex., 1976—. Author (catalog): Cora Maud Oneal Room, 1979, 85; contbr. articles to profl. jours. Ransom Ctr. rsch. grantee, 1985, 86, 88; Victorian Soc. Am. scholar, 1992. Mem. Coll. Art Assn. (mem. mus. com. 1993—), Am. Friends of Attingham, Victorian Soc. Am., Phi Kappa Phi. Office: Festival-Inst at Round Top PO Box 89 Round Top TX 78954-0089

LEON, BRUCE FREDERICK, environmental scientist; b. L.A., Nov. 6, 1952; s. Herman I. and Carol (Waterstone) L.; m. Linda Gail Gross, Jan. 7, 1990. BS, U. Mich., 1974; MA, Princeton U., 1976, PhD, 1979. Cert. sr. ecologist; profl. wetland scientist. Environ. scientist Ecol Scis., Inc., Milw., 1978-80; asst. prof. landscape architecture and planning U. Ill., Urbana, 1981-85; mgr. environ. planning Quadrant Cons. Inc., Houston, 1985-90; mgr. environ. studies Brown & Root, Houston, 1990—. Contbr. articles in field to ecol. jours. NSF postgrad. fellow, 1975-78; U. Ill. rsch. grantee, 1983. Mem. Ecol. Soc. Am. Home: 12050 Sugar Springs Dr Houston TX 77077-4929

LEÓN, EDUARDO A., diplomat, business executive; b. Santiago de los Caballero, Dominican Republic, Oct. 13, 1920; s. Eduardo and Maria León Jimenes; m. Ana Tavares, Feb. 16, 1946. Student, O'Sullivan Bus. Coll., Montreal, Can., 1937; BBA, McGill U., 1939. Under sec. of state Industry and Commerce Ministry, Santo Domingo, Dominican Republic, 1953, Fgn. Affairs Ministry, Santo Domingo, Dominican Republic, 1954; ministry of comml. affairs Embassy of Dominican Republic, Washington, 1955; envoy extraordinary and minister Plenipotenciary of Dominican Republic, London, 1956, Otawa, Can., 1957; pres. E. León Jimenes, C. por A., Santiago de los Caballero, 1939—; ambassador extraordinary Plenipotenciary of Dominican Republic, Washington, 1986-89, Plenipotenciary at Large, Dominican Republic, 1989—. Named to Order of Duarte, Sánchez and Mell in the Grade of Grand Cross, Order of Christopher Columbus in the Grade of Comdr., Order of Cuban Red Cross in Grade of Grand Cross, Decoration of Christopher Columbus in Grade of Grand Cross Silver Plate, 1995; recipient Paul Harris medal Rotary Internat., Gold Ring Philip Mo rris Inc. Mem. Nat. Coun. Businessmen, Assn Industries of Dominican Republic, Ctrl. Bank Dominican Republic, Bank of Agriculture and Industry, State Coun. of Sugar, Rotary, Met. Club N.Y., Union League Club, Internat. Golf Club, Centro Espanol Club. Roman Catholic. Office: EPS Esp No B 101 PO Box 02 5360 Miami FL 33102-5360

LEONARD, ANGELA MARIE, editor; b. Galax, Va., Nov. 6, 1961; d. Bobby Jefferson and Mary Evelyn (Bunn) Beamer; m. Richard Sheldon Leonard, Oct. 24, 1992; children: Genesis, Ethan. BS, Radford U., 1982. Sub. tchr. Carroll County Schs., 1979-83; tchr. Head Start, 1983; staff writer The Gazette, Galax, Va., 1983-89, news editor, 1989-93, staff writer, 1993-94; news editor The Declaration, Independence, Va., 1994; free lance writer Galax, Va., 1994—; staff writer The Mount Airy News, Mount Airy, N.C., 1995—; editor Simple Pleasures, Mt. Airy, 1995—. Mem. exec. bd. Surry County Children's Ctr. Recipient 2d pl. News Writing award Landmark Comty. Newspapers, Inc. 1983, 2d pl. Excellence in News Photography, 1988, 2d pl. Excellence in Editorial Writing, 1990, 3rd pl. Excellence in Feature Writing, 1993; 2d pl. Editorial Writing award Va. Press Assn., 1984, 2d pl. Display Advt.,1985, 2d pl. Feature Photo, 1986, 1st pl. Combination Pictures and Story, 1987, 3d pl. Photo-Illustration, 1988, 2d pl. Gen. News Writing, 1990, 1st pl. Gen. News Writing, 1991, 3d pl. Spot News Writing, 1993. Mem. Order of Ea. Star. Home: 514 Chestnut Dr Galax VA 24333-4505

LEONARD, CAROLE J., community health nurse; b. Normetal, Que., Can., Aug. 15, 1947; d. Andre Dupuis and Theresa Theriault; m. Roy Leonard, Dec. 6, 1980; children: Michael, Kimberly, Wendy. Practical nursing program grad., Burbank Hosp. Sch., 1967; ADN, Mt. Wachuselt Com. Coll., 1980. Charge nurse Fla. Med. Ctr., Lauderdale Lakes, nursing supr., patient care adminstr.; inpatient team dir. Hospice Inc., Lauderdale Lakes; patient care mgr. Vitas Healthcare Corp., Ft. Lauderdale; dir. clin. projects West Coast region Vitas Healthcare Corp., Orange, Calif.; dir. nurses Vitas Healthcare Corp., San Gabriel, Calif. Home: 1653 Eucalyptus St Brea CA 92621

LEONARD, DAVID MORSE, lawyer; b. Akron, Ohio, Dec. 4, 1949; s. Frank O. and Barbara J. (Morse) L.; m. Sharon Elaine Quati, May 7, 1977; children: Michael Morse, Lindsey Marie. BS in Chem. Engrng., Purdue U., 1972; JD, Emory U., 1975. Bar: Ga. 1975, U.S. Ct. Appeals (4th, 5th and 11th cirs.), U.S. Dist. Ct. (no., mid. and so. dists.) Ga., U.S. Dist. Ct. (so. dist.) Ala., U.S. Dist. Ct. (we. dist.) La.; cert. mediator, cert. mediation tng. Assoc. Montet & Smith, Atlanta, 1975-79; assoc. Hurt, Richardson, Garner, Todd & Cadenhead, Atlanta, 1979-83, ptnr., 1983-85; of counsel Lord, Bissell & Brook, Atlanta, 1985-87, ptnr., 1987—; mem. panel of arbitrators Am. Arbitration Assn., 1995—. Mem. ABA (litigation sect., tort and ins. practice sect.), Profl. Liability Underwriting Soc., Atlanta Lawyers Club, Atlanta C. of C., Am. Arbitration Assn. (panel of arbitrators). Home: 4152 Club Dr NE Atlanta GA 30319-1116 Office: Lord Bissell & Brook Ste 3700 1201 W Peachtree St NW Atlanta GA 30309-3421

LEONARD, GUY MEYERS, JR., international holding company executive; b. Bluefield, W.Va., Sept. 22, 1926; s. Guy Meyers and Mabel (Bonham) L.; AB, BS, Morris Harvey Coll., 1949; BDiv, Southwestern Bapt. Sem., 1952; STM, Harvard U., 1957; m. Pat Kirby, June 28, 1949; children: Calvin David, Dinah Lynn. Commd. ensign U.S. Navy, 1952, advanced through grades to capt., 1968, ret., 1972; dir. R & D Ency. Britannica Ednl. Corp., Chgo., 1972-76; pres. Communication Programming Svcs., Inc., Charleston, S.C., 1976—; pres., CEO First Don Trading Co., 1982—; chmn., CEO Transocean Ltd., internat. holding co., 1982-86; pres. GHL, Inc., Pacific rim, Africa, 1991—; cons. drug control programs for schs., cons. Ency. Britannica, Home Mission Bd. and Brotherhood Commn. So. Bapt. Conv. Sec., U.S. Power Squadron, Charleston, 1969; chmn. Spl. Commn. on Drug Abuse for Armed Forces, 1970-72; active Comn. coun. Boy Scouts Am., 1959-62; chmn. stewardship com. Episc. Diocese of S.C., 1994-95. Served with USN, 1943-72. Decorated Legion of Merit, Meritorious Svc. medal, Navy Commendation medal, Disting. Svc. Medal; recipient Disting. Svc. award City of Louisville, 1963. Mem. Harvard Club S.C., C. of C., Trident Chamber (Charleston), Navy League U.S., Ret. Officers Assn. Club: Kiwanis (spl. projects chmn., 1964-65). Designer, produced with Harvard U. and sta. WGBH, Boston, mediated coll. curriculum leading to B.S. degree for use by naval personel.

LEONARD, MARGARET BEASLEY, gerontology nurse; b. Nash County, N.C., Nov. 3, 1946; d. Archie and Lucille (Johnson) Beasley; m. Phillip Leonard, June 18, 1988; 1 child, Kimberly; stepchildren: Jonathan, Joshua. ADN, Wake Tech. Coll., 1981. Gerontology nurse THS Nursing Facility, Knightdale, N.C., 1996—. Patentee wheel chair abduction pillow. Recipient Great 100 award for nursing excellence, 1989.

LEONARD, PAUL HARALSON, retired lawyer; b. Houston, Mar. 4, 1925; s. Paul Haralson and Dovie Lore (Shuler) L.; m. Barbara Ann Underwood, Nov. 26, 1948; children: Leslie Ann, Scott Paul. BA, Rice U., 1948; JD, South Tex. Coll. of Law, 1957. Bar: Tex. 1957, U.S. Patent and Trademark Office 1960, U.S. Ct. Appeals (10th cir.) 1963, U.S. Ct. Mil. Appeals 1965, U.S. Supreme Ct. 1965, U.S. Ct. Appeals (5th cir.) 1981, U.S. Ct. Appeals (Fed. cir.) 1982. Acct. Highland Oil Co., Houston, 1948-50; statis. acct. Union Oil and Gas Corp. of La., Houston, 1953-59; assoc. Hayden & Pravel, Houston, 1959-61; patent atty. Halliburton Co., Duncan, Okla., 1961-69; div. patent atty. Ethyl Corp., Baton Rouge, 1969-87; v.p. Cen. Foods, Inc., Baton Rouge, 1979-90, bd. dirs. V.p. Plato Dependent Sch. Dist., Duncan, Okla., 1966-67, pres., 1968. Served to lt. comdr., USNR, 1942-67. Me. Tex. Bar Assn., Masons. Republican. Home and Office: 10639 Rondo Ave Baton Rouge LA 70815-4847

LEONARD, RICHARD DOUGLAS, army officer; b. Greenville, S.C., Feb. 16, 1956; s. Robert Dunbar and Jimmie Magdoline (Robinson) L.; m. Shani Ann Diggs, July 7, 1978 (div. 1980); m. Vender Lee Tedder Grimes, Nov. 22, 1985; 1 child, Zachary Douglas. BS, The Citadel, 1978, MS, 1983. Commd. 2d lt. U.S. Army, 1981, advanced through grades to maj., 1994; platoon leader 112 Signal Co., North Charleston, S.C., 1981-85; signal officer 1st of 263 Armour Bn., Mullins, S.C., 1985-86; with 163d Support Bn., Hampton, S.C., 1986-90; with 122d Engring. Bn., Edgefield, S.C., 1990—, bn. adminstrv. officer, combat engr., 1995—. Decorated Meritorious Svc. medal, U.S. Army Commendation medal, U.S. Army Achievement medal. Mem. SCV, Edgefield Soccer League (coach, pres.), N.G. Assn. S.C., Masons. Republican. Presbyterian. Office: 122d Engr Bn 225 Augusta Rd Edgefield SC 29824

LEONARD, SUSAN RUTH, psychologist, consultant; b. Mineola, N.Y., June 15, 1955; d. Donald Edward Leonard and Jane (Solomon) Hertzberg. BA, L.I. U., 1977; MA, U. N.C., 1980, PhD, 1985. Lic. psychologist, N.C. From instr. to asst. prof. psychology dept. Wake Forest U., Winston-Salem, N.C., 1984-86, staff psychologist counseling ctr., 1985-89; clin. psychologist Manoogian Psychol. Assocs., Winston-Salem, 1986—; cons. Ctr. for Creative Leadership, Greensboro, N.C., 1985-92. Vol. United Way, Winston-Salem, 1990-91; mem. adv. com. Family Svcs., Family Violence, Winston-Salem, 1987-90; trustee Resource Ctr. for Women and Ministry in South, 1989-91; bd. dirs. AIDS Task Force, Winston-Salem, 1989-92, Youth Opportunities Inc., Winston-Salem, 1990-92, 93—, AIDS Care Svc., Winston-Salem, 1991-95, Cancer Svcs., Winston-Salem, 1996—. Mem. APA, AAUW, Assn. Women in Psychology, N.C. Psychol. Assn. Office: Manoogian Psychol Assocs 1338 Ashley Sq Winston Salem NC 27103

LEONARD, TIMOTHY DWIGHT, judge; b. Jan. 22, 1940; s. Dwight and Mary Evelyn Leonard; m. Nancy Louise Laughlin, July 15, 1967; children: Kirstin Dione, Ryan Timothy, Tyler Dwight. BA, U. Okla., 1962; JD, 1965; student Mil. Naval Justice Sch., 1966. Bar: Okla. 1965, U.S. Dist. Ct. (no. and we. dists) Okla. 1969, U.S. Ct. Appeals (10th cir.) 1969, U.S. Supreme Ct. 1970. Asst. atty. gen. State of Okla., 1968-70, senator, 1979-88; ptnr. Blankenship, Herrold, Russell et al, Oklahoma City, 1970-71, Trippet, Leonard & Kee, Beaver, 1971-88; of counsel Huckaby, Fleming, et al., Oklahoma City, 1988-89; U.S. atty. Western Dist. Okla., 1989-92; judge U.S. Dist. Ct. (we. dist.) Okla., 1992—; guest lectr., tchr. Oklahoma City U., 1988-89. Mem. U.S. Atty. Gen.'s Adv. Com., 1990-92, chmn. office mgmt. and budget subcom., 1990-92. Co-author: 4 Days, 40 Hours, 1970. Rep. lt. gov. candidate Okla.; minority leader Okla. State Senate, 1985-86; white ho. mil. aide, Washington, 1966-67. Lt. USN, 1965-68, Washington. Named Outstanding Legislator Okla. Sch. Bd. Assn., 1988. Mem. ABA, Okla. Bar Assn., Phi Alpha Delta, Beta Theta Pi. Republican. Methodist. Avocations: basketball, running, reading. Home: PO Box 54587 Oklahoma City OK 73154-1587 Office: 200 NW 4th St Ste 5102 Oklahoma City OK 73102-3031

LEONARD, VENELDA HALL, writer; b. Tifton, Ga., Jan. 7, 1914; d. Alonza Clayton and Bessie Lee (Shiver) Hall; m. James W. Leonard, Mar. 7, 1953; children: James W. Leonard, Jr., Doris Delle Carr, Joan Le Mai Kyser. AA, Gulf Coast C.C., Panama City, Fla., 1964; BS, Fla. State U., 1965, MS, 1966. Instr. English, journalism Mosley H.S., Panama City, Fla., 1969-78; instr. remedial English Gulf Coast C.C., Panama City, 1979. Author: Sourwood, 1995. Mem. Phi Theta Kappa. Home: 2302 Country Club Dr Lynn Haven FL 32444

LEONHARDT, DEBBIE ANN, counselor, writer, minister; b. Valdese, N.C., June 11, 1953; d. Douglas Franklin and Jettie Arcena (Stilwell) L. BA, Lenoir-Rhyne Coll., 1975, MA, 1986; MDiv, Southeastern Bapt. Theol. Sem., 1977. Cert. Nat. Bd. Cert. Conselors, N.C. Bd. Licensed Profl. Counselors; ordained to ministry Bapt. Ch., 1983. Min. edn. Front St. Bapt. Ch., Statesville, N.C., 1978-80; assoc. min. First Bapt. Ch., Taylorsville, N.C., 1980-85; sch. counselor Alexander County Pub. Schs., Taylorsville, N.C., 1985—; pres. Alexander Counseling and Consulting Svcs., Inc., Taylorsville, N.C., 1994—; instr. cont. edn. Catawba Valley C.C., Hickory, N.C., 1993—; cons., seminar leader Catawba County Family Support Network, Hickory, N.C., 1996. Author: Survival Kit: A Guide for Brain Injured Patients, 1995; contbr. article to profl. jour., poems to collection. Vol. chaplain Catawba Meml. Hosp., Hickory, N.C., 1994-95; mem. Smart Start Partnership Task Force, Alexander County, N.C., 1995-96; mem., cons. Catawba County Traumatic Brain Injury Resource Com., Hickory, N.C., 1996. Name Young Career Woman Bus. and Profl. Women's Club, 1984. Mem. Nat. Brain Injury Assn., Nat. Bd. Cert. Counselors (test item writer Master Addictions Counselor, test item review com. 1996), N.C. Bd. Licensed Profl. Counselors, N.C. Sch. Counslors Assn., N.C. Brain Injury Assn. Democrat. Home: Rt 2 Box 443 Curtis Ln Hiddenite NC 28636 Office: Alexander Counseling & Cons Svcs 125 Wilkesboro Rd Taylorsville NC 28681

LEPERA, DARLA CRAFT, English language educator; b. Littlefield, Tex., Dec. 24, 1939; d. Russell and Alice LeVona (McFarlin) Craft; m. Terry Alan LePera; children: Stephen Damian, Anne Catherine. BS, U. Tex., El Paso, 1961; MEd, James Madison U., 1971. Cert. tchr. K-8 Va., ESL endorsed. 1st grade tchr. El Paso (Tex.) Pub. Schs., 1961-62; 1st and 2d grade tchr. St. Paul Pub. Schs., 1962-66; 2d grade tchr. Las Cruces (N.Mex.) Pub. Schs., 1966-68; from kindergarten aide to ESL tchr. K-5 Harrisonburg (Va.) City Schs., 1978—. Author: Texas Tales: An Oral History, 1994. Pres. Waterman Elem. PTA, Harrisonburg, 1977-78; commr. Harrisonburg Parks and Recreation Dept., 1980-88; religious edn. tchr. Blessed Sacrament Ch., Harrisonburg, 1980-83. Mem. NEA, TESOL, Va. Edn. Assn., Harrisonburg Edn. Assn. (sch. rep. 1993-94). Democrat. Roman Catholic. Home: 318 6th St Harrisonburg VA 22801 Office: Harrisonburg City Schs 400 Mountain View Dr Harrisonburg VA 22801

LEPOSKY, GEORGE C., editor; b. Chgo., Mar. 25, 1943; s. Howard C. and Florence G. (Goldenberg) L.; m. Rosalie E. Miller, Sept. 2, 1973; children: Marjory E., Edward D. (Teddy). BA in Polit. Sci., Washington U., St. Louis, 1963, MA in Polit. Sci., 1964. Registered resort profl., Am. Resort Devel. Assn. Reporter City News Bur., Chgo., 1964-65, Chgo. American (later Chgo. Today), 1965-69; account exec. Dale O'Brien & Co., Chgo., 1969-71; publs. mgr. Mt. Sinai Med. Ct., Miami Beach, Fla., 1975-76; dir. pub. rels. Mercy Hosp., Miami, Fla., 1976-78; mng. editor Vacation Industry Rev., Miami, 1985-91, editor, 1991—; dir. comm. Interval Internat., Miami, 1991—; editor Ampersand Comm., Miami, 1980—; freelance writer and photographer Miami; fellow advanced sci. writing program Grad. Sch. Journalism, Columbia U., N.Y.C., 1967-68; tech. writer for physicians, engrs., architects and other profls.; ind. cons., 1971-75, 78-91; adj. instr. Miami-area colls. and univs., 1981—; contest judge Mark Twain awards Midwest Travel Writers Assn., 1985-86; guest lectr. dept. med. comm. Southeastern Coll. Osteo. Medicine, North Miami Beach, Fla., 1985-88. Video scriptwriter: The Best of Travel Florida/State and National Parks, 1989; author: An Employer's Guide to Preferred Provider Organizations, 1984, Technical Writing for Fun and Profit, 1992, Business Writing for Fun and Profit, 1995; co-author: Fodor's 89 Florida, 1988, Fodor's 89 Greater Miami, Fort Lauderdale, Palm Beach, 1988, Fodor's 90 Florida, 1988, Fodor's 90 Greater Miami, Fort Lauderdale, Palm Beach, 1988, AEI Resource Manual, 1991; contbr. articles to profl. jours., chpts. to books; contbg. editor: Hotel and Resort Industry, 1987-90, Inland Architect, 1968-72. Recipient MacEachern awards Acad. Hosp. Pub. Rels., advt. and pub. rels. awards Sarasota-Bradenton-Venice Advt. Club, Fla. Hosp. Assn. Pub. Rels. Coun., Internat. Assn. Bus. Communicators, Miami chpt., journalistic awards ADA, Fla. Mag. Assn., Nat. Soc. Med. Rsch., Am. Resort Devel. Assn., Am. Psychol. Found., photographic awards Izaak Walton League, Mt. Sinai Med. Ctr. Arts and Crafts Exhbn. Mem. Internat. Assn. Bus. Communicators (officer, bd. dirs. South Fla. chpt.). Home: 2311 S Bayshore Dr Miami FL 33133-4728 Office: Vacation Industry Rev Penthouse One 6262 Sunset Dr Miami FL 33143-4843

LEPPLA, DAVID CHARLES, pathology educator; b. Denver, July 22, 1953; s. Charles Frederick and Lucille Josephine (Schneider) L. BS, Seattle U., 1975; MD, Colo. U., 1979. Diplomate Am. Bd. Pathology. Intern in internal medicine U. Tex. Health Sci. Ctr., Dallas, 1979-80, fellow in mineral metabolism and endocrinology, 1980-82, rsch. assoc., 1982-83; resident in pathology Marshall U. Sch. Medicine, Huntington, W.Va., 1984-87, chief resident in pathology, 1987-88, asst. prof., 1988—. Fellow Am. Soc. Clin. Pathology (alt. to adv. com. 1990); mem. AAAS, Alpha Omega Alpha. Office: Marshall U Sch Medicine 1542 Spring Valley Dr Huntington WV 25704-9388

LERNER, THEODORE RAPHAEL, dentist; b. Bklyn., Sept. 28, 1932; s. Meyer and Tillie (Brimberg) L.; student Washington and Jefferson Coll., 1950-53; DDS, U. Pa., 1957; m. Barbara Ellen Bernstein, June 29, 1974; children by previous marriage: Andrea Holly, Evan Andrew. Practice dentistry, specializing in endodontics, Bklyn., 1957-93, Forest Hills, N.Y., 1968-93, Boca Raton, Fla., 1992—. Diplomate Am. Bd. Endodontics. Fellow Internat., Am. colls. dentists, Am. Assn. Endodontists; mem. ADA, 2d Dist. Dental Soc. (pres. 1971), Dental Soc. State of N.Y. (pres. 1983), Fla. Dental Assn. Home: 7040 Lions Head Ln Boca Raton FL 33496-5931 Office: 2499 Glades Rd Ste 204 Boca Raton FL 33431-7201

LEROY, MISS JOY, model, designer; b. Riverdale, Ill., Sept. 8, 1927; d. Gerald and Dorothea (Wingebach) Reasor. BS, Purdue U., 1949. Model, sales rep. Jacques, Lafayette, Ind., 1950; book dept. sales rep. Loebs, Lafayette, 1951-52; window trimmer Marshall Field's and Co., Evanston, Ill., 1952-53; sales and display rep. Emerald Ho., Evanston, 1954-55; model, narrator, designer J.L. Hudson Co., GM Corp., Coca Cola Co., Hoover Vacuum Co., Jam Handy Orgn., Am. Motors Corp., Speedway Petroleum Corp., Ford Motors Tractor & Implement Divsn.-The Sykes Co., Detroit, 1958-61; tour guide, model The Christian Sci. Publ. Soc., spl. events coord. Prudential Ins. Co., model Copley 7, Boston, 1962-70. Author: Puzz-its, 1986-96. Founding angel Asolo Theatre, Sarasota, 1960s; mem. Ft. Lauderdale Internat. Film Festival, 1990, Mus. of Art, 1978, Fla. Conservation Assn., Rep. Senatorial Com. Inner Cir., 1990, Congl. Com., 1990, Nat. Trust for Hist. Preservation, 1986, Fla. Trust for Hist. Preservation, 1987, Nat. Wildflower Rsch. Ctr., 1992; one of founding friends 1000 Friends of Fla., 1991; mem. Rep. Presdl. Task Force, 1993; founding mem. Rep. Campaign Coun., 1994, Grand Club Rep. Party Fla., 1996. Mem. Purdue U. Gold Coast Club, Stratford Shakespearean Festival of Am., USS Constn. Mus. (charter mem. 1993), Purdue U. Alumni Assn., Walt Disney's Magic Kingdom Club, Wilderness Soc., Magic Kingdom Entertainment Club, Maupin Alumni, Heritage Found., Soc. Honorary Mariners, Heralds of Nature Soc., Ducks Unltd., Paddlewheel Steamboatin' Soc. Am., Cunard World Club, Skald Club, Yacht Club, The Crystal Soc., The Cousteau Soc., Covette Club, Coastal Conservation Assn., Captain's Cir., Intravler Club, Internat. Marine Animal Trainers Assn., Am. Queen Inaugural Soc., Zeta Tau Alpha. Home: 2100 S Ocean Ln Apt 2104 Fort Lauderdale FL 33316-3827

LERSCH, DELYNDEN RIFE, computer engineering executive; b. Grundy, Va., Mar. 22, 1949; d. Woodrow and Eunice Louise (Atwell) Rife; m. John Robert Lersch, May 9, 1976; children: Desmond, Kristofer. BSEE, Va. Poly. Inst. and State U., 1970; postgrad. Boston U., 1975—. With Stone & Webster Engring. Corp., 1970-91, elec. engr., supr. computer applications, Boston, 1978-80, mgr. computer graphics, 1980-84, mgr. engring. systems and computer graphics, 1984-87, div. chief info. techs., 1987-90, v.p., 1990-91; chief A.D.P. officer Univ. Rsch. Assocs., 1991-94; CARE Pvt. Mortgage Ins. Sys. Corp. account mgr. Perot Sys. Corp., Dallas, 1994—. Named Stone and Webster's Woman Engr. of Yr., 1976, 79; Mass. Solar Energy Research grantee, 1978; honored by Engring. News Record mag. for contbns. to constrn. industry, 1983. Mem. IEEE (sr.), Assn. Women in Sci., Soc. Women Engrs. (sr.), Women in Sci. and Engring., Energy Communicators, Nat. Computer Graphics Assn., Profl. Council New Eng., Women in Energy (dir. Mass. chpt. 1978, New Eng. region 1979), LWV, Rotary (Rotarian of Yr. 1993-94). Congregationalist. Club: Boston Bus. and Profl. Women's. Author: Cable Schedule Information Systems As Used in Power Plant Construction, 1973, 2d edit., 1975; Information Systems Available for Use by Electrical Engineers, 1976; contbr. articles in field of computer aided design and engring. Home: 1106 Bristol Cir De Soto TX 75115-2818 Office: Perot Sys Corp 12377 Merit Dr Ste 1100 Dallas TX 75251-3233

LESAK, JOANNE HELEN, artist; b. Watertown, Wis., Feb. 4, 1939; d. Joseph John and Martha Leslie (Sorensen) Reuter; divorced; children: Ralph Michael, Rachelle Theresa, Craig Owen. Student, U. Wis., 1957-59, Meredith Coll., 1974; BFA, Maryville Coll., 1974; MFA, East Carolina U., 1990. Cert. Nat. Coun. Interior Design Qualification. Prin. JoAnn LeSak Designs (formerly LeSak Interiors), various cities, N.C., 1974—; co-owner Plum Tree Gallery, Goldsboro, N.C.; assoc. of Artist Artisan and Assocs., Goldsboro; grad. tchr. environ. design dept. Sch. Art, East Carolina U., 1989; vis. faculty art and interior design depts. Halifax C.C., Weldon, N.C., 1990—; developer, presenter interior design seminars; tchr. pvt. painting. One-woman shows include Halifax C.C., Carteret C.C., Goldsboro Art Ctr., Rocky Mount Art Ctr., Bertie County Arts Ctr.; designer, builder residential propotype for sr. citizens Lake Gaston, 1995; exhibited Native Am. painting series throughout N.C., 1995; represented in permanent collection at Appalachian State U. Active Downtown Goldsboro Hist. Revolving Fund, Goldsboro New Neighbors. Recipient award of merit for hist. preservation for Downtown Goldsboro Devel. Corp., Plum Tree Gallery, 1996. Mem. Durham Art Guild, Greensboro Arts League, Rocky Mount Artists League. Home and Studio: 106 S George St Goldsboro NC 27530

LESCH, ALMA WALLACE, fiber artist; b. McCracken County, Ky., Mar. 19, 1917; d. Rollie Elmo and Gela Ruth (Burnley) Wallace. BS in Edn., Murray (Ky.) State U., 1941; MEd, U. Louisville, 1962. Tchr. Louisville Pub. Schs., 1941-48; tchr., head textile dept. Louisville Sch. of Art, 1961-78; adj. prof. fine arts U. Louisville, 1975-82; fiber artist Shepherdsville, Ky.; tchr. textiles Arrowmont Sch. Crafts, Gatlinburg, Tenn., summers, 1970-77, Haystack Mountain Craft Sch., Deer Isle, Maine, summers, 1966, 71, Chgo. Art Inst., 1973; tchr. natural dyeing Phila. Coll. Textiles, 1967, U.S. Indian Sch., Santa Fe, N.Mex., 1972; tchr. needlework N.E. Am. Crafts Coun., Washington, 1979. Author: Vegetable Dyeing, 1970; many large commns. in fiber art, 1962—. Sec. Planning and Zoning Commn., Shepherdsville, 1959-62; chmn. blood donor mobile ARC, Bullitt County, Ky., 1950-55; vol. restoration projects Shaker Mus., South Union Ky., J.B. Speed Art Mus., Louisville. Recipient Artist award Ky. Gov. Martha Layne Collins, 1987; named Master Craftsman, World Crafts Orgn., 1974. Mem. Am. Crafts Coun. (Ky. state rep. 1964-68), Ky. Guild Artists and Craftsmen (charter, hon. fellow 1986), Louisville Craftsmen's Guild (life), Ky. Art and Craft Found. (Lifetime Contbn. award 1996). Home and Office: PO Box 67 Shepherdsville KY 40165-0067

LESLIE, LYNN MARIE, secondary education educator; b. Lake City, Fla., Nov. 17, 1948; d. Billy Verlyn Spooner and Dorothy Marie (Odom) Loomis; m. Roy Hamner Leslie, Nov. 25, 1967; children: Kim Ball, Billy Leslie, Dodi Leslie. BS in Edn., Trevecca U., 1970; ME in Spl. Edn., Tenn. State U., 1987. Cert. career ladder III, Tenn. Tchr. Leesburg (Fla.) Elem. Sch., 1970-71, Wessington Pl. Elem. Sch., Hendersonville, Tenn., 1974-87, Knox Doss Mid. Sch., Hendersonville, 1987—; mem. Sumner County Ins. Trust, Gallatin, Tenn., 1991-96. Mem. Sumner County Edn. Assn. (pres. 1991-92, 95-96, sec. 1992-95, sec./treas. 1996—). Mem. Ch. of Nazarene. Home: 1032 Carriage Hill Pl Hendersonville TN 37075-8728

LESLIE, MAE SUE, writer; b. Forrester, Ark., Dec. 22, 1940; d. Doyle Joseph and Ruby Estelle (Stewart) Davis; m. Gerald Robert Leslie, Sept. 2, 1967; children: Neal R., Denise. Student, Instituto Allende, San Miguel Allende, Mex., 1960-61; BA in Journalism, Sam Houston State U., 1966. Cert. nursing home social worker, Tex. Sec. Am. Gen. Ins. Co., Houston, 1966-67; social worker Harris County, Houston, 1968; sec. temp. agys.. Houston, 1977-81; freelance writer, 1981—. Pianist, Sunday sch. tchr. Riverside (Tex.) Bapt. Ch., 1963-65. Recipient 3d pl. for article Fla. State Writing Competition, 1994, 2d pl. for short story Manuscripts Guild, 1994, 3d pl. for nonfiction, 1994. Mem. Nat. Writer's Union, Houston Screenwriters. Democrat. Baptist. Home: 802 Carol St Bellaire TX 77401

LESOURD, NANCY SUSAN OLIVER, lawyer, writer; b. Atlanta, Aug. 22, 1953; d. Carl Samuel and Jane (Meadows) Oliver; m. Jeffrey Alan LeSourd, Oct. 18, 1986; children: Jeffrey Luke, Catherine Victoria. BA in Polit. Sci., Agnes Scott Coll., 1975; MA in History, Edn., Tufts U., 1977; JD, Georgetown U., 1984. Bar: Pa. 1985, D.C. 1986, Va. 1992, Fed. Cir. Ct. Appeals., 1988, U.S. Claims Ct., 1988. Instr. Newton (Mass.) High Sch., 1976-78, The Stony Brook (N.Y.) Sch., 1978-81; assoc. Gammon and Grange, Washington, 1984-88; ptnr. Gammon and Grange, P.C., 1988—; legal commentator (radio shows) UPI News, Washington, 1985-91, Focus on the Family (Washington corr.), Colorado Springs, Colo., 1987-94; legal columnist Christian Mgmt. Rev., Downers Grove, Ill., 1987-90; spkr. numerous confs. Author: No Longer The Hero, 1992; editor: Georgetown Law Jour., 1982-84; contbr. articles to profl. jours. Bd. dirs. Arlington County Equal Employment Opportunity Commn., 1985. William Robertson Coe fellow SUNY, Stony Brook, 1978. Mem. D.C. Bar Assn., Va. Bar Assn., Christian Legal Society (bd. dirs. 1990-93). Republican. Home: 2624 New Banner Ln Herndon VA 22071-2659 Office: Gammon and Grange PC 8280 Greensboro Dr Fl 7 Mc Lean VA 22102-3807

LESSARD, RAYMOND W., bishop; b. Grafton, N.D., Dec. 21, 1930. Student, St. Paul Sem., Am. Coll., Rome. Ordained priest Roman Cath. Ch. Mem. staff Congregation for Bishops, Roman Curia, 1964-73; consecrated bishop, 1973; bishop Diocese of Savannah Diocese of Savannah, Ga., 1973-95. Office: Catholic Pastoral Ctr 601 E Liberty St Savannah GA 31401-5118

LESSES, GLENN, philosophy educator; b. Buffalo, Sept. 7, 1951; s. Milton Aaron and Lois (White) L.; m. Claire Fund. BA, U. Rochester, 1973; MA, Ind. U., 1977, PhD, 1980. Vis. asst. prof. U. Tex., Arlington, 1980-82, Tex. Christian U., Ft. Worth, 1982-83; asst. prof. philosophy Spring Hill Coll., Mobile, Ala., 1983-86; asst. prof. philosophy Coll. of Charleston, S.C., 1986-91, assoc. prof., 1991—; vis. scholar Brown U., Providence, 1987-88, Harvard U., Cambridge, Mass., 1993-94. Contbr. articles to profl. jours. NEH fellow, 1987-88; Am. Coun. Learned Socs. grantee, 1987. Mem. Am. Philos. Soc., Soc. for Ancient Greek Philosophy, Internat. Plato Soc. Office: Coll of Charleston Dept Philosophy Charleston SC 29424

LESSIS, GARY PAUL, engineer, sales executive; b. Dayton, Ohio, Apr. 23, 1960; s. George P. and Irene (Sopronyi) L. BS in Engring., U. Cin., 1983; MS in Computer Sci., U. So. Calif., 1986; MBA, Pepperdine U., 1990. Engr. Northrop Corp., Hawthorne, Calif., 1983-85; systems analyst Tektronix Inc., Woodland Hills, Calif., 1985-86, sales engr., 1986-90; sales mgr. Auto-Trol Tech. Corp., Irvine, Calif., 1990-93, Open Connect Systems, Cin., 1993-94; dist. mgr., pres. Dicom, Inc., Lexington, Ky., 1994—.

LESTER, JAMES CURTIS, computer scientist; b. Oklahoma City, May 8, 1961; s. James Curtis and Edythe Louise (Peck) L.; m. Tammy Jane Roy, May 28, 1983; children: Katherine Louise, Christopher Adam. BA in History in honors with distinction, Baylor U., 1983; BA in Computer Sci. with highest honors, U. Tex., Austin, 1986, MS in Computer Sci., 1988, PhD in Computer Sci., 1994. Grad. rsch. asst. dept. computer sci. U. Tex., Austin, 1988-94; asst. prof. dept. computer sci. N.C. State U., Raleigh, 1994—; lectr. in field. Contbr. articles to profl. jours. U. Tex.-Austin doctoral fellow, 1986-88. Mem. Assn. for Computing Machinery, Am. Assn. Artificial Intelligence, Cognitive Sci. Soc., Phi Beta Kappa, Upsilon Pi Epsilon. Office: NC State U Dept Computer Sci PO Box 8206 Raleigh NC 27695-8206

LESTIN, ERIC HUGH, real estate investment banking executive; b. Rochester, N.Y., Sept. 4, 1950; s. Charles Benjamin and Elise (Rosenbaum) L.; m. Jani Fox, Feb. 20, 1982; children: Jill, Abby, Lauren. BA, U. Rochester, 1972. Lic. real estate broker, Tex. V.p. Home Leasing Corp., Rochester, N.Y., 1973-79; sr. v.p. Henry S. Miller Co., Houston, 1979-81, Jones Lang Wootton, Houston, 1981-85; sr. v.p., gen. mgr. Landauer Assocs. Inc., Houston, 1985-89; pres. Lestin Advisors Inc., Houston, 1989-96, Trione & Gordon, Houston, 1996—; guest lectr. in field; prof. Houston Bapt. U., 1986-88. Contbr. articles to profl. jours. Bd. dirs. Associated Bldg. Svcs. Co., Houston, 1980—, Crime Stoppers Inc., Houston, 1989—; mem. devel. bd. Tex. Spl. Olympics, Houston, 1988-90; vol. Am. Heart Assn. Guild, Houston, 1990—. Mem. Nat. Assn. realtors, Tex. Assn. Realtors, Houston Bd. Realtors (assoc.), Urban Land Inst. (assoc.). Republican. Jewish. Office: Trione and Gordon Ste 1200 1900 W Loop South Houston TX 77027

LESTINA, ROGER HENRY, English language educator; b. Yosemite Nat. Pk., Calif., Apr. 7, 1940; s. Henry Francis and Mary Roselyn (O'Brien) L.; m. Linda Jeanne Fish, Aug. 24, 1963; children: Deanna, Joseph, Nicholas, Daniel. BA in English, Loyola U., L.A., 1962; MA in English, U. Alaska, 1974. Cert. secondary education tchr., Calif. Commd. 2d lt. USAF, 1962, advanced through grades to maj., 1974, ret., 1984; instr. USAF Acad., Colorado Springs, Colo., 1975-79; parish adminstr. St. John's Cath. Ch., Edmond, Okla., 1984-90; lead instr. Freshman Compostion I and II Okla. State U., Oklahoma City, 1990—. Co-author: (textbook) The Freshman Writer: Finding, Organizing, and Supporting Ideas, 1996; editor: (handbook) The Conservation Officer's Guide to Collection and Preservation of Evidence, 1995. Ch. cantor/choir mem. St. John the Bapt., Edmond, Okla., 1979—. Recipient Nat. Inst. for Staff and Organizational Devel. Excellence in Tchng. award, 1996. Mem. MLA, AAUP (sec. OSU-OKC chpt. 1995—), Nat. Coun. Tchrs. English, S.W. Regional Conf. on English. Republican. Roman Catholic. Home: 708 Concord Cir Edmond OK 73003 Office: Okla State U Oklahoma City 900 N Portland Ave Oklahoma City OK 73107

LESTINGER, ALAN, company executive. Pres., COO, vice chmn. Barnett Banks. Office: 50 N Laura St Jacksonville FL 32202-3664

LESZCZYNSKI, JERZY RYSZARD, chemistry educator, researcher; b. Tomaszow, Poland, May 26, 1949; cam to U.S., 1986; s. Leslaw and Hanna (Kaptur) L.; m. Danuta, June 25, 1972; children: Rafal, Magda. MS, Tech. U. Wroclaw (Poland), 1972, PhD, 1975. Lectr. chemistry Tech. U. Wroclaw, 1976-86; vis. sci. U. Fla., Gainesville, 1986-88; rsch. assoc. U. Ala., Birmingham, 1988-90; from asst. to assoc. prof. Jackson (Miss.) State U., 1990-95, prof., 1995—; conf. chmn. organizing com. Current Trends in Computational Chemistry, 1992-96; presenter in field. Author chpts. to books; editor: Computational Chemistry, Reviews of Current Trends, 1995; co-author: Computational Quantum Chemistry, 1988, Combustion Efficiency and Air Quality, 1995, Interaction of DNA Bases and the Structure of DNA, 1996; editor: Electronic Jour. of Theoretical Chemistry; guest editor: Structural Chemistry, 1995; referee: Jour. Am. Chem. Soc., Internat. Jour. Quantum Chemistry, Chem. Physics Letters, Structural Chemistry, Jour. Phys. Chemistry, Jour. Molecular Structure, Jour. Computational Chemistry, Jour. Biomolecular Structure and Dynamics; mem. editl. bd. Structural Chemistry; contbr. articles to profl. jours. Recipient Outstanding Faculty award AT&T, 1992. Mem. Am. Chem. Soc., Internat. Soc. Quantum Biology and Pharmacology (exec. com. 1995—), Miss. Acad. Sci. Office: Jackson State U Dept Chemistry 1400 Lynch St Jackson MS 39217-0002

LETSON, RUTH STAFFORD, librarian; b. Oak Ridge, Tenn., Oct. 21, 1944; d. Claude E. and Lillie (White) Stafford; m. G. Paul Letson, June 13, 1970; children: Stacey Rene, Danielle Michelle, Todd Shane. BS, East Tenn State U., 1966; MLS, George Peabody Coll., 1972. Tchr. Holston High Sch., Blountville, Tenn., 1966-67; tech. svcs. libr. Joint Univ. Librs., Nashville, 1968-77; serials libr. Tenn. State U., Nashville, 1977; libr. II Tenn. Dept. Transp., 1978—. Treas. LaVergne (Tenn.) H.S. Band Boosters, 1992-93. Mem. Tenn. Libr. Assn. (treas. 1991-92). Office: Tenn Dept Transp Libr JK Polk Bldg Ste 300 Nashville TN 37243

LETSOU, GEORGE VASILIOS, cardiothoracic surgeon; b. Boston, 1958; s. Vasilios George and Helen (Valacellis) L.; m. Jane Elizabeth Carter, June 1, 1985; children: Christopher George, Philip Taylor, John Carter. AB magna cum laude, Harvard U., 1979; MD, Columbia U., 1983. Diplomate Am. Bd. Surgery, Am. Bd. Thoracic Surgery. Resident in gen. surgery Yale-New Haven Hosp., 1983-88, chief resident and instr. surgery, 1987-88, clin. fellow in cardiothoracic surgery, 1988-89, Cystic Fibrosis Found. fellow in cardiopulmonary transplantation, 1988-89, Winchester scholar in cardiothoracic surg. rsch., 1989-90, resident in cardiothoracic surgery, 1990-91; chief resident in cardiothoracic surgery, 1991-92; Houston; attending surgeon Yale-New Haven Hosp., 1992-95; instr. surgery Yale U., New Haven, 1987-88, 91-92, asst. prof. surgery, 1992-95; attending surgeon Yale-New Haven Med. Ctr., 1992-95; Meth. Hosp., Ben Taub Hosp., Houston, 1995—; assoc. prof. surgery Baylor Coll. Medicine, Houston, 1995—. Mem. AMA, ACS, Am. Coll. Cardiology, Am. Coll. Chest Physicians, Soc. Thoracic Surgeons. Office: Dept Surgery One Baylor Plaza Ste 4040 Houston TX 77030

LEUKEFELD, CARL GEORGE, researcher, educator; b. Lake Forest, Ill., May 14, 1943; s. Karl Frederick and Berta (Link) L.; BS, Mo. Valley Coll., 1965; MSW, U. Mich., 1967; DSW, Cath. U. Am., 1975; cert. Harvard Sch. Public Health, 1980; m. Sara Ann Huffstutler, Aug. 13, 1966; children: Sarabeth, Karl Austin, Marianne. Program dir. Boys Club, Pontiac, Mich., 1966; commd. lt. USPHS, 1967, advanced through grades to capt. 1980; mental health officer, L.A., 1967-71; mental health adv., Rockville, Md., 1971-73; staff asst., then spl. asst. Nat. Inst. on Drug Abuse, USPHS, Rockville, Md., 1975-77, dep. dir., acting dir. div. of resource devel., 1978-81, dep. dir., then dir. div. prevention and treatment devel., 1981-82, acting dir., dep. dir. div. clin. rsch., 1982-90; prof. psychiatry, dir. Ctr. Drug and Alcohol Rsch. U. Ky., Lexington, 1990—; principal investigator NIH, Aids Rsch., 1993, Inst. for Women Substance Abuse Treatment, 1993, Ctr. for Substance Abuse Treatment, 1993, Ky. State Substance Abuse Needs Assessment, Drug Addictions Treatment, 1995; detailed to Naval Mil. Personnel Command, 1983, chief health svcs. officer USPHS, 1984-89; fellow mental health career devel. program NIMH, 1973-75. Mem. social work career devel. com. USPHS, chair. social work career devel. com., 1982, chairperson social work profl. adv. subcom. 1983; mem. Intra-Agy. Task Force Emergency Preparedness, 1987-90; adj. faculty Va. Commonwealth U., 1986-90. Editor jour. National Health Line, Health and Social Work, Jour., 1987-90, AIDS Edn. and Prevention, 1989—; cons. editor Jour. Primary Prevention; mem. editorial bd. Jour. Social Work Rsch., 1990-93, Jour. Mental Health Adminstrn., Substance Use and Misuse; co-editor books including Responding to AIDS: Psychosocial Initiatives, 1987, 89, Improving Drug Abuse Treatment, 91, Treatment in Prisons and Jails, 1992, Cocaine Treatment: Research and Clinical Perspective, 1992, Getting Funded, 1994, Prevention Research, 1995; contbr. articles to profl. jours. Decorated Commendation medal, 1978, 83, Outstanding Service medal, Meritorious Service medal, 1987, Pub. Health Svc. citation, 1988, 90; recipient Torch award Am. Humanics Found., 1978, Disting. Alumni award Cath. U. of Am., 1994; named to Honorable Order of Ky. Cols. State of Ky., 1991. Mem. Nat. Assn. Social Workers (chmn. commn. on health and mental health 1985-87, co-chair fund devel., Whitham/Knee awards), Acad. Cert. Social Workers, AAAS, Nat. Acads. Practice, Am. Public Health Assn., Assn. Mil. Surgeons (chmn. med. service corp. sect. 1987), Commd. Officers Assn. USPHS (bd. dirs. 1984-90), Alcohol and Drug Abuse Problems Am., Social Work Coun., Am. Pub. Health Assn., Am. Correctional Assn., Soc. Clin. Social Workers (bd. dirs. Bluegrass chpt. 1990-92), Am. Probation and Parole Assn., Tau Kappa Epsilon, Alpha Phi Omega, Pi Gamma Mu. Presbyterian (elder). Home: 1121 Sheffield Pl Lexington KY 40509-2018 Office: U Ky Coll Medicine Annex 2 Rm 210 Lexington KY 40536-0080

LEUPP, EDYTHE PETERSON, retired education educator, administrator; b. Mpls., Nov. 27, 1921; d. Reynold H. and Lillian (Aldridge) Peterson; m. Thomas A. Leupp, Jan. 29, 1944 (dec.); children: DeEtte (dec.), Patrice, Stacia, Roderick, Braden. BS, U. Oreg., 1947, MS, 1951, EdD, 1972. Tchr. various pub. schs. Idaho, 1941-45, Portland, Oreg., 1945-55; dir. tchr. edn. Northwest Nazarene Coll., Nampa, Idaho, 1955-61; sch. adminstr. Portland Pub. Schs., 1963-84; dir. tchr. edn. George Fox Coll., Newberg, Oreg., 1984-87; ret., 1987; vis. prof. So. Nazarene U., Bethany, Okla., 1988-95; adj. prof. Warner Pacific Coll., Portland, 1996—; pres. Portland Assn. Pub. Sch. Adminstrs., 1973-75; dir.-at-large Nat. Coun. Adminstrv. Women in Edn., Washington, 1973-76; state chmn. Oreg. Sch. Prins. Spl. Project, 1978-79; chair Confdn. Oreg. Sch. Adminstrs. Ann. Conf.; rschr. 40 tchr. edn. programs in colls. and univs.; designer tchr. edn. program George Fox Coll. Author tchr. edn. materials. Pres. Idaho State Aux. Mcpl. League, 1957, Nampa PTA, 1958, Nampa unit AAUW, 1956; bd. dirs. Portland Fedn. Women's Clubs, 1963. Recipient Golden Gift award; named Honored Tchr. of Okla.; Hazel Fishwood scholar; Idea fellow Charles Kettering Found., 1978, 80, 87, 91, 92, 93, 94. Mem. Delta Kappa Gamma (pres. Alpha Rho). Republican. Nazarene. Home: 8100 SW 2nd Ave Portland OR 97219-4602

LEUTZE, JAMES RICHARD, academic administrator, television producer and host; b. Charleston, S.C., Dec. 24, 1935; w. Willard Parker and Magdalene Mae (Seith) L.; m. Kathleen Shirley Erskine, Feb. 13, 1960; children—Magdalene Leigh, Jay Erskine, James Parker. B.A., U. Md., 1957; M.A., U. Miami, 1959; Ph.D., Duke U., 1968. Legis. asst. U.S. Senator Hubert Humphrey, Washington, 1963-64; prof. history U. N.C., Chapel Hill, 1968-87, chmn. curriculum peace, war, and def., 1979-87, Bowman and Gordon Gray prof., 1982, Dowd prof. Peace and War, 1986; TV host-producer N.C. Ctr. for Pub. TV, Chapel Hill, 1984—; pres. Hampden-Sydney (Va.) Coll., 1987-90; chancellor U. N.C. at Wilmington, 1990—. Author: Bargaining for Supremacy: Anglo-American Naval Collaboration, 1937-41, 1977 (Bernath prize 1978), A Different Kind of Victory: The Biography of Admiral Thomas C. Hart, 1981 (John Lyman Book award 1981); editor: London Journal Gen. Raymond E. Lee, 1972, The Role of the Military in a Democracy, 1974; contbr. articles to profl. jours. Served to capt. USAF, 1960-63. Recipient Standard Oil award for teaching U. N.C., 1971, Tanner award for teaching, 1978, Order of Golden Fleece award, 1983. Mem. Orgn. Am. Historians, Royal U.S. Inst. (London), Am. Hist. Assn., Univ. Club (N.D.), George C. Marshall Found., Phi Beta Kappa. Democrat. Episcopalian. Office: U NC 601 S College Rd Wilmington NC 28403-3201

LE VAN, DANIEL HAYDEN, gas industry executive; b. Savannah, Ga., Mar. 29, 1924; s. Daniel Hayden and Ruth (Harner) LeV. Grad., Middlesex Sch., 1943; BA, Harvard U., 1950; postgrad., Babson Inst., 1950-51. Underwriter Zurich Ins. Co., N.Y.C., 1951-52; co-owner, dir. Overseas Properties, Ltd., N.Y.C., 1970—; dir. Colonial Gas Co., Lowell, Mass., 1973—. With AUS, 1943-46. Mem. Harvard Club (N.Y.C. and Boston).

LEVELL, EDWARD, JR., city official; b. Jacksonville, Ala., Apr. 2, 1931; m. Rosa M. (Casellas) L. Aug. 3, 1951; children: Edward III (dec.), Ruben C., Kenneth W., Randy C., Raymond C., Cheryl D. Levell Rivera, Michael K. BS, Tuskegee Inst., 1953; MA in Urban Sociology, U. No. Colo., 1972; M in Mgmt., Indsl. Coll./Air War Coll., 1974. Commd. 2d lt. USAF, 1953, advanced through grades to col., 1978, various flight tng., air ops. and command positions, 1953-69; comdr. cadet group, then dep. commandant cadet wing USAF Acad., 1969-73; dep. comdr., wing comdr., vice comdr. 1st spl. ops. wing USAF, 1973-77, wing comdr. 58th tactical air command tng. wing, 1977-78, col., vice comdr., comdr. 20th air divsn., 1978-83, ret., 1983; dep. commr. aviation City of Chgo. Dept. Aviation, 1983-89; dep. dir. aviation, fin. and adminstrn. City of New Orleans Dept. Aviation, 1989-90, dep. dir. aviation, ops. and maintenance, 1990-92, dir. aviation, 1992—. bd. dirs. Tourist & Conv. Commn., New Orleans; trustee Dryades YMCA, New Orleans; mem. transp. com. World Trade Ctr. Decorated Legion of Merit, D.F.C. (2), Meritorious Svc. Medal (2), Air Medal (8), Air Force Commendation Medal; recipient Disting. Svc. award Jacksonville, Ala., 1974, State of Fla. Commn. Human Rels. award for spl. recognition, 1977, Air Force Assn. Spl. Citation of Merit, 1977, Disting. Svc. award City of Chgo. Dept. Aviation, 1986, 87, 88; inducted in Tuskegee Univ. Hall of Fame, 1991. Mem. Airport Ops. Coun. Internat. (task force chmn. ann. conf. New Orleans 1991), Am. Assn. Airport Execs., Gulf Coast Internat. Hispanic C. of C. Home: 1500 W Esplanade Ave Apt 46F Kenner LA 70065-5346 Office: New Orleans Aviation Bd New Orleans Intl Airport Box 20007 New Orleans LA 70141

LEVENDUSKI, CRISTINE MARIE, American literature and culture educator; b. Duluth, Minn., Feb. 17, 1953; d. Daniel Frank and Mary Clara (Bee) L. BA in Interdisciplinary Studies, U. Minn., Duluth, 1975, BS in English, 1975, MA in English, 1978; PhD in Am. Studies, U. Minn., Mpls., 1989. Teaching asst. U. Minn., Duluth, 1975-78, vis. instr., 1978-81; teaching assoc. U. Minn., Mpls., 1981-88; asst. prof. Emory U., Atlanta, 1988-95, assoc. prof., 1995—. Author: Peculiar Power: A Quaker Woman Preacher in Eighteenth-Century America, 1996; contbr. several articles to profl. jours. Office: Emory U Dept English Atlanta GA 30322

LEVENSON, MARIA NIJOLE, retired medical technologist; b. Kaunas, Lithuania, Mar. 24, 1940; came to U.S., 1948; d. Zigmas and Monika (Galbuogis) Sabataitis; m. Coleman Levenson, Nov. 21, 1975. BA, Annhurst Coll., 1962. Sr. rsch. technician Case Western Res. U., Cleve., 1962-69; phys. sci. technician Nat. Oceanographic Data Ctr., Washington, 1969-70; biologist NIH, Bethesda, Md., 1970-76; nuclear medicine technologist VA Med. Ctr., New Orleans, 1977-79; paramed. examiner Hooper Industries, New Orleans, 1980-82; assoc. chemist Computer Scis. Corp., Stennis Space Ctr., Miss., 1982-83; med. technologist VA Med. Ctr., New Orleans, 1984-96; sec. Lithuanian Cath. Youth Assn., Putnam, Conn., 1960-62, Lithuanian Club, Annhurst Coll., South Woodstock, Conn., 1960-62. Participant Freedom Movement for Baltic Independence, Slidell, La., 1990-91; counselor Life with Cancer, Slidell, 1989—. La. State Nursing Sch. scholar, 1989. Mem. Daus. of Lithuania, Internat. Platform Assn. Home: PO Box 593 Dauphin Island AL 36528-5130

LEVERING, RALPH BROOKS, history educator; b. Mt. Airy, N.C., Feb. 27, 1947; s. Samuel R. and Miriam Farson (Lindsey) L.; m. Patricia Irene Webb, June 3, 1967; children: Matthew, Brooks. BA in History, U. N.C., 1967; MA in History, Princeton U., 1969, PhD in History, 1972. Instr. history George Mason U., Fairfax, Va., 1971-72; from asst. to assoc. prof. history Western Md. Coll., Westminster, Md., 1972-81; assoc. prof. history Earlham Coll., Richmond, Ind., 1981-86; assoc. prof. history Davidson (N.C.) Coll., 1986-92, prof. history, 1992—. Author: American Opinion and the Russian Alliance, 1939-45, 1976, The Public and American Foreign Policy, 1918-1978, 1978, The Cold War: A Post-Cold War History, 1994; co-author: The Kennedy Crises, 1983. Mem. selection com. Morehead Found., Chapel Hill, N.C., 1988-90; bd. dirs. Am. Freedom Assn., Charlotte, N.C., 1992-94. Recipient NEH fellowship, 1976-77. Mem. Soc. Historians Am. Fgn. Rels., Orgn. Am. Historians, Am. Hist. Assn., Conf. on Peace Rsch. in History, Phi Beta Kappa. Democrat. Mem. Soc. of Friends. Office: Davidson Coll PO Box 1719 Davidson NC 28036-1719

LEVI, MICHAEL ALAN, newspaper executive, publisher; b. N.Y.C., May 2, 1946; s. Henry C. and Marilyn (Rosenberg) L.; m. Vicki L. Volan, May 22, 1994; children: Michelle Messier, Ben Levi. BS, Northeastern U., Boston, 1969. Media analyst Compton Advt. Agy., N.Y.C., 1969-70; asst. adj. U.S. Army, 1970-72; gen. mgr. Stuart News Mirror Publs., Stuart, Fla., 1972-88; pres., pub. Destin (Fla.) Log, 1988—; mem. White Wilson adv. bd., Destin, 1993-95. Pres. Stuart C. of C., 1981, Destin C. of C., 1992. Mem. Fla. Press Assn. (bd. dirs.), Rotary (bd. dirs. Stuart chpt. 1986, Destin chpt. 1989). Office: Destin Log PO Box 957 1225 Airport Rd Destin FL 32540

LEVI, MOSHE, nephrologist, medical educator, researcher; b. Istanbul, Turkey, Feb. 16, 1950; came to U.S., 1969; s. Hayim and Sara (Amira) L.; m. Marilyn Eckstein, June 26, 1976; children: Jessica, Jonathan. BSChemE, Northwestern U., 1973; MSChemE, Stanford U., 1974; MD, Albert Einstein, 1977. Intern, resident Cornell U. Med. Sch., Manhasset, N.Y., 1977-80; renal fellow U. Colo. Med. Ctr., Denver, 1980-83; asst. prof. U. Tex. Southwestern Med. Ctr., Dallas, 1984-91, assoc. prof., 1991-96, prof., 1996—; chief hemodialysis Dallas VA Med. Ctr., 1984-87, chief home dialysis, 1987-91, chief renal sect., 1991—; pres. med. adv. bd. Nat. Kidney Found. Tex. Author: numerous chpt. in books; contbr. articles to numerous med. jours. Pres. Shaare Tefilla, Dallas, 1986-88. Mem. Am. Soc. Nephrology, Internat. Soc. Nephrology, Am. Soc. Cell. Biology, Am. Heart Assn., Am. Physiol. Soc., Am. Soc. Biochemistry, Biophys. Soc. Jewish. Office: Dallas VA Med Ctr 4500 S Lancaster Rd Dallas TX 75216-7167

LE VIEUX, JANE STUART, pediatrics nurse; b. Washington, May 1, 1956; d. Richard Stuart and Jane Marie (O'Connell) Le V.; m. Gary B. Elliott, Sept. 4, 1982; children: Julianne, Aimée. BSN, U. South Ala., 1979; MS in Child Devel., U. North Tex., 1989, MEd in Counseling and Play Therapy, 1991. Lic. profl. counselor; registered play therapist, Tex. Staff nurse ICU Children's Med. Ctr., Dallas, 1979-81, RN cardiac cath lab., 1981-84, bone marrow transplant child life specialist, 1991—; supr. cardiac cath lab. Humana Hosp.-Medical City, Dallas, 1984-86, pediatric clin. nurse educator, 1986-87; child and family therapist The Caring Ctr., Dallas, 1992—; children's grief therapist and cons. Family Hospice, 1993—; clin. instr. Tex. Woman's U. Coll. Nursing, 1995—; therapist Grief Camp El Tesoro De La Vida, First Tex. coun. Camp Fire Girls, 1995. Active Weekend to Wipe Out Cancer, Dallas, Children's Cancer Fund, Jr. League of Dallas; bd. dirs. Trinity Ministry to the Poor. Author: (with others) A Handbook for Practitioners, 1993. Mem. Assn. for Play Therapy, ANA, Tex. Nurses Assn., Child Life Coun., Assn. for Care of Children's Health, Phi Delta Kappa. Roman Catholic. Home: 4815 Royal Ln Dallas TX 75229-4208 Office: The Caring Ctr 8222 Douglas Ave Ste 777 Dallas TX 75225-5938

LEVIEUX-ANGLIN, LIZETTE LOUISE, pediatric nurse, nursing educator; b. Washington; d. Richard Stuart and Jane Marie (O'Connel) LeV.; m. David Lee Anglin, Aug. 31, 1985; 1 child, Ethan. BSN, U. Tex., 1981; MS in Pediat. Nursing, Ohio State U., 1992. RN, Tex., Ohio; CPR; ABLS. Staff, preceptor nurse PICU Children's Med. Ctr., Dallas, 1982-85; staff, charge nurse Santa Rosa Children's Hosp., San Antonio, 1985-87; pvt. duty pediat. nurse Primary Care Nursing Svc., Dublin, Ohio, 1987-89; nurse clinician, pediat. cons. Caremark, Inc., Columbus, 1987-92; clin. instr. pediat. nursing Ctrl. Ohio Tech. Coll., Newark, 1991, 92; field nurse Children's Homecare Svcs., Columbus, 1991-92; clin. nurse specialist dept. surgery corp. divsn. pediat. surgery Columbus Children's Hosp., 1992-94; clin. instr. pediat. nursing Sch. Nursing U. Tex., Austin, 1995—. Contbr. articles to profl. jours. Recipient Student Appreciation award USAF, 1981. Mem. Am. Pediat. Surg. Nurses Assn., Soc. Pediat. Nurses, Sigma Theta Tau (Epsilon chpt.). Home: 1117 Elder Cir Austin TX 78733 Office: U Tex Sch Nursing 1700 Red River Austin TX 78701-1499

LEVIN, DAVID HAROLD, lawyer; b. Pensacola, Fla., Nov. 19, 1928. A.B., Duke U., 1949; J.D., U. Fla., 1952. Bar: Fla. 1952. Asst. county solicitor Escambia County (Fla.), 1952; sr. ptnr. Levin, Middlebrooks, Mabie, Thomas, Mayes & Mitchell, Pensacola; chmn. 1st Jud. Circuit Fla. Jud. Nominating Commn., 1976-78; chmn. Fla. Pollution Control Bd., 1971-74. Chmn., Escambia County Cancer Crusade, 1963-65; pres. Escambia County unit Am. Cancer Soc., 1964-65; bd. dirs. W. Fla. Heart Assn., 1966-69; chmn. United Jewish Appeal Escambia County, 1967-68; former mem. human rights commn. W. Fla. Hosp. Mem. Fla. Alumni Assn. (pres. chpt. 1960), U. Fla. Alumni Assn. (dist. v.p. 1961-62), Blue Key. Recipient Good Govt. award Pensacola Jaycees, 1972; Service award Fla. Council for Clear Air, 1974; Francis Marion Weston award Audubon Soc., 1974; commendation Gov. Fla., 1974. mem. Am. Acad. Matrimonial Lawyers (pres. Fla. chpt. 1987-88). Home: 3632 Menendez Dr Pensacola FL 32503-3133 Office: PO Box 12308 Pensacola FL 32581-2308

LEVIN, HERVEY PHILLIP, lawyer; b. Chgo., Oct. 22, 1942; s. Julius L. and Gertrude (Cohen) L.; m. Madeleine J. Raskin, Sept. 22, 1970; children: Arianne, Nicole, David. BBA, U. Mich., 1964, MBA, 1968; JD, DePaul U., 1969. Bar: Ill., 1969, Tex., 1979, U.S. Dist. Ct. (no. dist.) Ill. 1970, U.S. Ct. Appeals (5th cir.) 1981, U.S. Ct. Appeals (7th cir.) 1971, U.S. Supreme Ct. 1972. Assoc. Potts Randall & Horn, Chgo., 1969-70, Randall Horn & Pyes, Chgo., 1970-71; assoc., jr. ptnr. Mehlman, Ticho, Addis, Susman, Spitzer, Randall, Horn & Pyes, Chgo., 1971-75; sole practice, Chgo., 1975-78, Dallas, 1979—; dir. Leedal Inc., Chgo.; cons. in workers' compensation, occupational disease and gen. practice. Bd. dirs. Solomon Schecter Acad. of Dallas, 1979—, Cong. Shearith Israel, Dallas, 1981-88, Am. Jewish Congress, Dallas, 1980-85, Nat. Assn. Mortgage Planners, 1995—. Named Ky. Colonel. Mem. Chgo. Bar Assn., Ill. Bar Assn., Dallas Bar Assn., Tex. Bar Assn., ABA (workers compensation com. torts and ins. practices sect., chmn. 1989-90, sr. vice chair, 1990—, coun. mem. torts and ins. practices sect. 1995—, various adminstrv. coms., torts and ins. practices sect. 1990—, mem. torts and ins. practices sect. coun., 1995—, liaison to Internat. Assn. Indsl. Accident Bds. and Commns. 1989—, cons. labor standards subcom., house edn. and labor com., U.S. Congress, chair solo and small firm practices com., 1994-95). Office: 6918 Blue Mesa Dr Ste 115 Dallas TX 75252-6140

LEVIN, JERRY WAYNE, cosmetics executive; b. San Antonio, Tex., Apr. 18, 1944; s. Bernard H. and Marion (Bromberg) L.; m. Carol Lee Motel, Dec. 18, 1966; children—Joshua, Abby. B.S.E.E., U. Mich., 1966, B.S.E. in Math., 1966; M.B.A., U. Chgo., 1968. With Tex. Instruments, Dallas, 1968-72; with Marsh & McLennan, Chgo., 1972-74; with The Pillsbury Co., Mpls., from 1974, exec. v.p. corporate devel., treas., from 1985, exec. v.p. corp. devel., chmn. Haagen-Dazs div., 1987-88; exec. v.p. corp. devel. and chmn. S&A Restaurant Corp., from 1988; chmn. Burger King Corp., 1988-89; exec. v.p. MacAndrews Forbes, N.Y.; chmn., CEO, Revlon Inc., N.Y.C., 1995—; bd. dirs. Apogee Enterprises, Inc., Coleman, Ecolabs, First Bank Sys., Paradise Kitchens, Meridian. Bd. dirs. United Way, N.Y.C., N.Y. Hillel, N.Y. Fedn., N.Y. Philharm., U. Mich. Engring. Sch. Mem. U. Chgo. Alumni Bd., Oak Ridge Country Club, Ventana Canyon Country Club, Minneapolis Club. Home: 15 E 70th St New York NY 10021-4907 Office: Revlon Inc 625 Madison Ave New York NY 10022-1801

LEVIN, JORDAN G., journalist; b. New Haven, Dec. 25, 1959; d. G. Roy and Marty (Trent) L. BA in Dance and Liberal Arts with honors, Sarah Lawrence Coll., 1981. Dancer N.Y.C., 1981-87; arts presenter Tigertail Prodns., Miami, Fla., 1988-91; freelance writer Miami Beach, 1991—; founding mem. The Field, N.Y.C., 1985-87; talent coord. 4D Club, N.Y.C., 1986; mgr. bartender 8BC Club, N.Y.C., 1984-85; mktg. dir. Fla. Dance Festival, Tampa, 1991; presenter in field; program coord. Wolfson campus Miami-Dade C.C., 1989-90; adminstrv. coord. New Music Am.-Miami Festival, 1988. Contbr. to profl. jours. and newspapers (Miami Herald, LA Times, Variety, Interview, Billboard, Am. Theatre, Dance Mag.).

LEVIN, RICHARD C., lawyer; b. Dallas, June 15, 1945; s. Paul Michael and Yetta Gail (Caplan) L.; m. Kay Robins, June 18, 1982; children: Edward C., Henry A. BA, Tulane U., 1967; JD, Georgetown U., 1970. Bar: Tex. 1975. Law clerk 5th cir. U.S. Ct. Appeals, 1970-71; assoc. Sulivan & Cromwell, N.Y.C., 1971-74; assoc. Akin, Gump, Strauss, Hauer & Feld L.L.P., Dallas, 1974-77, ptnr., 1978—; with Dallas Mgmt. com., 1989—; co-head litigation sect. Akin, Gump, Strauss, Hauer & Feld, head antitrust sect., internat. litigation sect.; spkr. in field. Contbr. articles to profl. jours. Former mem. exec. bd. Dallas Opera; former mem. bd. govs. Dallas Symphony; corp. com. Dallas Mus. Fine Arts; former mem., v.p. bd. trustees Hist. Preservation League; former mem. Landmark Com. City Dallas, bd. trustees Arts Magnet Sch.; former mem., dep. vice chmn., mgmt. com. Arts Dist. in Dallas; former chmn. Task Force Multi-Purpose Performing Arts Hall Dallas Opera, Dallas Ballet; bd. dirs. Dallas Opera, Salzburg Music Festival. Mem. Dallas Bar Assn. (coun. mem. Antitrust, Trade Regulation sect. 1987—, internat. law sect. 1990—). Jewish. Home: 4408 Saint Johns Dr Dallas TX 75205-3825 Office: Akin Gump Strauss Hauer & Feld 1700 Pacific Ave Ste 4100 Dallas TX 75201-7322

LEVIN, WILLIAM COHN, hematologist, former university president; b. Waco, Tex., Mar. 2, 1917; s. Samuel P. and Jeanette (Cohn) L.; m. Edna Seinsheimer, June 23, 1941; children: Gerry Lee Levin Hornstein, Carol Lynn Levin Cantini. B.A., U. Tex., 1938, M.D., 1941; M.D. (hon.), U. Montpellier, 1980. Diplomate: Am. Bd. Internal Medicine. Intern Michael Reese Hosp., Chgo., 1941-42; resident John Sealy Hosp., Galveston, Tex., 1942-44; mem. staff U. Tex. Med. Br. Hosps., Galveston, 1944—, assoc. prof. internal medicine, 1948-65, prof., 1965—; Warmoth prof. hematology U. Tex. Med. Br., 1968-86, Ashbel Smith prof., 1986—, pres., 1974-87; past chmn., past mem. cancer clin. investigation rev. com. Nat. Cancer Inst., past. mem. Bd. Sci. Counselors. Exec. com., mem. nat. bd. Union Am. Hebrew Congregations; trustee Houston-Galveston Psychoanalytic Found., 1975-78, Menil Found., 1976-83. Recipient Nicholas and Katherine Leone award for adminstrv. excellence, 1977; decorated Palmes Académiques France. Fellow ACP, Internat. Soc. Hematology; mem. Am. Fedn. Clin. Research, Central Soc. Clin. Research, Am. Soc. Hematology, Phi Beta Kappa, Sigma Xi, Alpha Omega Alpha. Office: Am Indemnity Co PO Box 1259 Galveston TX 77553-1259

LEVINE, AARON M., physiatrist; b. Bronx, N.Y., Mar. 5, 1947; s. David and Dorothy (Moshman) L.; m. Susan F. Labelle, Sept. 4, 1983; children: Danielle, Robert, Phillip, Ethan. BS, U. Pitts., 1967, MD, 1971. Diplomate Am. Bd. Phy. Medicine and Rehab., Am. Bd. Electodiagnostic Medicine. Intern gen. surgery U. Ill. Chgo., 1971-73; resident orthopaedics Hosp. Joint Diseases, N.Y.C., 1973-76; resident phys. medicine Baylor Coll. Medicine, Houston, 1978-80, asst. prof., 1980-84; staff physician MacGregor Clinic, Houston, 1984-86; med. dir. Harris Meth. Hosp., Ft. Worth, 1986-87; pvt. practice Ft. Worth, 1987-88; asst. med. dir. Mt. Sinai Hosp., Hartford, Conn., 1988-90; med. dir. Meml. Inst. Rehab., Houston, 1990—. Asst. editor Postgraduate Medicine, 1986-90. Maj. U.S. Army, 1976-78. Mem. Tex. Med. Assn. (del. rehab. div.). Home: 4210 Misty Heather Ct Houston TX 77059-5521 Office: Meml Inst of Rehab 11914 Astoria Blvd Houston TX 77089-6064

LEVINE, HAROLD, lawyer; b. Newark, Apr. 30, 1931; s. Rubin and Gussie (Lifshitz) L.; children: Brenda Sue, Linda Ellen Levine Gersen, Louise Abby, Jill Anne Levine Zuvanich, Charles A., Cristina Gussie, Harold Rubin II; m. Cristina Cervera, Aug. 29, 1980. B.S. in Engring., Purdue U., 1954; J.D. with distinction, George Washington U., 1958. Bar: D.C. 1958, Va., 1958, Mass. 1960, Tex. 1972, U.S. Patent Office, 1958. Naval architect, marine engr. U.S. Navy Dept., 1954-55; patent examiner U.S. Patent Office, 1955-58; with Tex. Instruments Inc., Attleboro, Mass., 1959-77, asst. sec., Dallas, 1969-72, asst. v.p. and gen. patent counsel, 1972-77; ptnr. Sigalos & Levine, Dallas, 1977-93; prin. Levine & Majorie LLP, 1994—; chmn. bd. Vanguard Security, Inc., Houston, 1977—; chmn. Tex. Am. Realty, Dallas, 1977—; lectr. assns., socs.; del. Geneva and Lausanne (Switzerland) Intergovtl. Conf. on Revision, Paris Pat. Conv., 1975-76. Mem. U.S. State Dept. Adv. Panel on Internat. Tech. Transfer, 1977. Mem. ABA (chmn. com. 407 taxation pats. and trdmks. 1971-72), Am. Patent Law Assn., Dallas Bar Assn., Assn. Corp. Pat. Csl. (sec.-treas. 1971-73), Dallas-Fort Worth Patent Law Assn., Pacific Indsl. Property Assn. (pres. 1975-77), Electronic Industries Assn. (pres. pat. com. 1972), NAM, Southwestern Legal Inst. on Patent Law (planning com. 1971-74), U.S. C. of C., Dallas C. of C., Alpha Epsilon Pi, Phi Alpha Delta. Republican. Jewish. Club: Kiwanis. Contbr. chpt. to book, articles to profl. jours. Editor: George Washington U. Law Rev., 1956-57; mem. adv. bd. editors Bur. Nat. Affairs, Pat., Trdmk. and Copyright Jour., 1979-87. Office: Levine and Majorie LLP 12750 Merit Dr Ste 1000 Dallas TX 75251-1243

LEVINE, JOHANAN SIDNEY, neurologist; b. N.Y.C., May 16, 1947; s. Julius and Shirley Levine; m. Rashalee Swichkow, June 1, 1969 (div. Sept. 1988); 1 child, Dee Dee; m. Yolanda Lopez, 1995. BS, Yale Coll., 1968; MD, Albert Einstein, 1972. Diplomate Am. Bd. Pediatrics, Am. Bd. Psychiatry and Neurology with spl. competence in child neurology. Pediatric intern Albert Einstein Coll. of Medicine, Bronx, N.Y., 1972-73, pediatric resident, 1973-74, neurology fellow, 1974-77; pvt. practice Neurology Assocs. of El Paso, Tex., 1979—; clin. assoc. prof. Tex. Tech U., El Paso, 1979—; governing bd. Rio Vista Rehab. Hosp., El Paso, 1991-95. Med. dir. El Paso Rehab. Ctr. for Children; dir. Muscular Dystrophy Assn. Clin., El Paso. Maj. U.S. Army, 1977-79. Fellow Am. Acad. Neurology, Am. Acad. Pediatrics; mem. AMA, Child Neurology Soc., Am. Epilepsy Soc., Am. Soc. Neuroimaging, Am. Acad. Cerebral Palsy and Devel. Medicine, Tex. Med. Assn., El Paso County Med. Soc. Jewish. Office: Neurology Assocs El Paso 10400 Vista Del Sol Dr El Paso TX 79925-7923

LEVINE, LAURENCE BRANDT, investment banker; b. N.Y.C., Dec. 17, 1941; s. Martin and Beulah (Brandt) L.; m. Laura Lynn Vitale; 1 child, Blair Brandt. BA (Francis Biddle prize 1961), Princeton U., 1964; LLB, Stanford U., 1967. V.p., voting shareholder Drexel Burnham Lambert, N.Y.C., 1968-71; corp. planning officer Office of Chmn., Ogden Corp., N.Y.C., 1971-73; pres. Investment Research Assos., West Chester, Pa., 1973-80; sr. v.p., dir. investment banking Kramer Capital Cons., Inc., N.Y.C., 1981; exec. v.p. Henry Ansbacher Inc., N.Y. and London, 1982-84; sr. v.p. Rothschild Inc., N.Y., 1984-86; exec. v.p. and dir. corp. fin. Smith New Ct. Inc., N.Y. and London, 1986-90; chmn. Blair Corp., N.Y. and London, 1990—, dir. First Internat. Fin. Group, Hamburg, London and Bermuda, Landmark Funds Svcs., Inc., N.Y.C.; dir., vice chmn. Signature Fin. Group, Boston; Bd. visitors Stanford U. Law Sch., 1968-71, exec. com., 1970; dir. Musica Sacra, N.Y., 1981-86, Concert Artists Guild, N.Y., 1989-92, Ballet Fla., 1992—; pres. Palm Beach Sch. Arts Found., 1993—; adv. bd. Kravis Ctr., 1991—. Office: 250 Royal Palm Way Ste 205 Palm Beach FL 33480-4315

LEVINE, PAUL ALBERT, head and neck surgeon; b. Bklyn., Nov. 4, 1947; s. Bernard and Saralee (Rothman) L.; m. Susan Lyn Stahl, Nov. 13, 1971; children: Marc Lawrence, Ross Stephen. BS in Biology, Rensselaer Polytech. Inst., 1956-69; MD, Albany Med. Coll., 1969-73. Diplomate Am. Bd. Med. Examiners; lic. Conn., Calif., Va. Intern. gen. surgery, asst. resident Yale New Haven (Conn.) Hosp., 1973-74, asst. resident dept. surgery sect. otolaryngology, 1974-76, chief resident, 1976-77; head and neck surgery fellow Stanford (Calif.) U. Med. Ctr., 1977-78, asst. prof., assoc. chief dept. otolaryngology, 1978-84; assoc. prof., vice chmn. U. Va. Med. Ctr., Charlottesville, 1984-87, dir. head and neck surg. oncology, 1984—, prof., vice chmn., 1987—; guest examiner Am. Bd. Otolaryngology Oral Exam., Chgo., 1990, 91, 93; mem. numerous coms. Santa Clara Valley Med. Ctr., 1978-84, U. Va. Health Scis. Ctr., 1984—. Abstract editor Head and neck Surgery, 1984-86; assoc. editor Otolaryngology Head and Neck Surgery, 1987-94; reviewer Archives of Otolaryngology, 1992—, Head and Neck, 1991—, Skull Base Surgery, 1992—; presenter in field; contbr. articles to profl. jours. Grantee Triton Bioscis., 1986, 87, Am. Acad. Facial Plastic and Reconstructive. Fellow Am. Acad. Otolaryngology (Honor award 1986, mem. numerous coms.), Am. Soc. Head and Neck Surgery (mem. numerous coms.), Am. Acad. Facial Plastic and Reconstructive Surgery); mem. AMA, Calif. Med. Assn. (standard nomenclature com. 1982-84), Va. Soc. Otolaryngology (legis. com. 1992-93), Soc. Univ. Otolaryngologists (nom. com.), Am. Broncho-Esophogol. Assn., Am. Coun. Otolaryngology, Peninsula ENT Soc., Albermarle County Med. Soc., Med. Soc. Va., Deafness Rsch. Found., N.Am. Skull Base Soc. Office: U Va Health Sci Ctr PO Box 430 Charlottesville VA 22902-0430

LEVINE, PAUL JACOB, writer, screenwriter; b. Williamsport, Pa., Jan. 9, 1948; s. Stanley Howard and Sally (Kazdoy) L.; m. Alice E. Holmstrom, Aug. 22, 1975 (div. July 1991); children: Wendy Michelle, Michael Johannes. BA in Journalism, Pa. State U., 1969; JD cum laude, U. Miami, 1973. Bar: Fla. 1973. Atty., ptnr. Morgan, Lewis and Bockius, Miami, Fla., 1978-87; of counsel Spence, Payne, Masington, Grossman, Miami, Fla., 1987-89, Grossman & Roth, Miami, Fla., 1989-91; writer Miami, Fla., 1991—. Author: To Speak for the Dead, 1990, Night Vision, 1991, False Dawn, 1993, Mortal Sin, 1994, Slashback, 1995, Fool Me Twice, 1996, Flesh and Bones, 1997. Mem. devel. coun. Pa. State U., 1982-85, alumni coun. Commn. Coll., 1988-91, alumni fellow, 1993. Recipient John D. MacDonald award for fiction JDM Bibliophile, 1994. Home and Office: 3155 Mary St Miami FL 33133

LEVINE, ROBERT MARTIN, historian; b. N.Y.C., Mar. 26, 1941; s. David S. and Ruth (Fried) L.; m. Peggy A. Phillips, May 5, 1983; children: Joseph, David. BA, Colgate U., 1962; PhD, Princeton U., 1967. From instr. to prof. SUNY, Stony Brook, 1966-80; prof., chair history dept., dir. Latin Am. studies U. Miami, Coral Gables, Fla., 1981—; chair Nat. Coun. Brazilian Studies, 1982-83, Columbia U. seminar on Brazil, N.Y.C., 1984-86. Author: The Vargas Regime: The Critical Years, 1934-1938, 1970, Pernambuco in the Brazilian Federation, 1889-1937, 1978, Images of History: Nineteenth and Early Twentieth Century Latin American Photographs as Documents, 1989, Vale of Tears: The Canudos Massacre in Northeast Brazil Revisited, Tropical Diaspora, 1902-1992, 1993, Cinderela Negra: A Saga de Carolina Maria de Jesus, 1994, Father of the Poor, 1997, Brazilian Legacies, 1997. NEH fellow, 1989, 94; Fulbright grantee, 1981. Mem. Harbor Club, Phi Beta Kappa. Office: History Dept U Miami PO Box 248107 Coral Gables FL 33124-8107

LEVINE, RONALD H., physician, state official; b. N.Y.C., Mar. 30, 1935; m. Elizabeth P. Kanof; children—Mitchell, Rebecca Ann. BS, Union Coll., Schenectady, N.Y., 1955, DSc (hon.), 1990; MD, SUNY-Bklyn., 1959; MPH, U. N.C., 1967. Officer USPHS, Raleigh, N.C., 1963-65; chief communicable disease br. N.C. State Bd. Health, Raleigh, 1965-67, chief community health sect., 1968-73; asst. dir., dep. dir. N.C. Div. Health Services, Raleigh, 1974-

81, state health dir., 1981—. Recipient Stevens award N.C. Assn. Local Health Dirs., 1982. Fellow Am. Acad. Pediatrics, Am. Pub. Health Assn., Am. Coll. Preventive Medicine, mem. N.C. Pub. Health Assn. (pres. 1974-75, Reynolds award 1973), Wake County Med. Soc. (pres. 1978), N.C. Med. Soc. Office: Dept Environ Health & Natural Resources PO Box 27687 512 N Salisbury St Raleigh NC 27604-1118

LEVINE, STEVEN NEIL, endocrinologist; b. N.Y.C., June 10, 1946; s. Milton and Miriam (Gerofsky) L.; m. Laurie Rita Winkler, July 27, 1969; children: Amy, Karen, Jonathan. BA in Gen. Sci. with distinction, U. Rochester, 1968; MD, NYU, 1971. Diplomate Am. Bd. Internal Medicine. Intern N.C. Meml. Hosp., Chapel Hill, 1971-72, resident in medicine, 1972-74; fellow in endocrinology U. N.C. Sch. Medicine, Chapel Hill, 1976-79, clin. instr. medicine, 1976-79; asst. prof. medicine La. State U. Med. Ctr., Shreveport, 1979-84, assoc. prof. medicine, chief sect. endocrinology, 1984-91, prof. medicine, chief sect. endocrinology, 1991—; instr. dept. medicine N.C. Meml. Hosp., Chapel Hill, 1976-79; staff physician La. State U. Med. Ctr., 1979, Shreveport VA, 1979; courtesy staff Schumpert Med. Ctr., Shreveport, 1980, Highland Hosp., Shreveport, 1981. Reviewer Archives of Internal Medicine, 1981—, Jour. Clin. Endocrinology and Metabolism, 1985—, Obstetrics and Gynecology, 1985—, Clin. Toxicology, 1985—, Biochem. Pharmacology, 1991—; contbr. numerous articles to profl. jours.; also abstracts. Recipient 1st ann. Outstanding Attending award House Staff of Dept. Internal Medicine, La. State U. Med. Ctr., 1990; grantee Am. Heart Assn.-La. Inc., 1981-82, 83-84, 84-85, 85-88,, 89-91, NIH, 1976-79, 81-82, 82-83, Edward P. Stiles Trust Fund, 1979-80, 82-83, 85-87, La. State Bd. Regents, 1984-85, VA Rsch. Adv. Group, 1987-89, Am. Diabetes Assn, 1988-89. Fellow ACP; mem. Shreveport Med. Soc., La. State Med. Soc., Am. Fedn. Clin. Rsch., Am. Diabetes assn. (N.W. La. chpt. bd. dirs. 1980-83, pres. 1983-84), Endocrine Soc. (program dirs. com. 1988—), Am. Heart Assn. (basic sci. coun. 1984—), Alpha Omega Alpha. Office: La State U Med Ctr PO Box 33932 1501 Kings Hwy Shreveport LA 71130

LEVINE, SUSAN MICHELLE, social worker; b. Bklyn., July 29, 1963; d. Norman and Barbara Ellen (Fishman) L.; life ptnr. Karen J. Docherty, Dec. 14, 1993. BA in Psychology, SUNY, Stony Brook, 1986, MSW, 1990; MPA, Ga. State U., 1993. Lic. clin. social worker, Ga. Foster care worker Angel Guardian Home, Bklyn., 1986-87; child protective svcs. worker N.Y.C. Dept. Human Resources, 1987-88; cmty. asst. Chapin Apt. Complex, Stony Brook, 1989-90; sr. caseworker Fulton County Family and Children's Svcs., Atlanta, 1991-92; clin. social worker Ga. Mental Health Inst., Atlanta, 1992—; guest lectr. Ga. State U. Dept. Mental Health, 1994; clinician mobile crisis psychiat. assessment team Brawner Hosp., 1995, Charter Peachford, 1996. Disaster mental health counselor ARC, Atlanta, 1996. Mem. NASW (continued edn. com. 1991—, legis. com. 1992, panel mem. com. on inquiry Ga. chpt. 1995—, counselor for depression hotline 1992), Am. Soc. Pub. Adminstrs., Pi Alpha Alpha. Office: Ga Mental Health Inst 1256 Briarcliff Rd Atlanta GA 30306

LEVINGSTON, ERNEST LEE, engineering company executive; b. Pineville, La., Nov. 7, 1921; s. Vernon Lee and Adele (Miller) L.; m. Kathleen Bernice Bordelon, June 23, 1944; children: David Lewis, Jeanne Evelyn, James Lee. BME, La. State U., 1960. Gen. foreman T. Miller & Sons, Lake Charles, La., 1939-42; sr. engr., sect. head Cities Service Refining Corp., Lake Charles, 1946-57; group leader Bovay Engrs., Baton Rouge, 1957-59; chief engr. Augenstein Constrn. Co., Lake Charles, 1959-60; pres. Levingston Engrs., Inc., Lake Charles, 1961-85, gen. mgr. SW La., Austin Indsl., 1985-88; pres. Levingston Engrs., 1989-96, chmn. bd., 1996—. Mem. Lake Charles Planning and Zoning Commn., 1965-70; mem. adv. bd. Sowela Tech. Inst., 1969—; mem. Regional Export Expansion Council, 1969-70, chmn. code com., 1966—; mem. La. Bd. Commerce and Industry, 1978—; bd. dirs. Lake Charles Meml. Hosp.; bd. dirs., regional chmn. La. Chem. Industry Alliance, 1990—. With USNR, 1942-46. Named Jaycee Boss of Year, 1972. Registered profl. engr., La., Tex., Miss., Ark., Tenn., Pa., Md., Del., N.J., D.C., Okla., Colo. Mem. La. Engring. Soc. (pres. 1967-68, state bd. dirs. 1967-68, 90-91), Nat. Inst. Cert. Engring. Technologists (past trustee, mem. exam. com.), La. Assn. Bus. and Industry, Lake Area Industries/McNeese Engring., Lake Charles C. of C. (dir. 1969-73). Baptist (deacon 1955—). Office: PO Box 1865 Lake Charles LA 70602-1865

LEVIN-WIXMAN, IRENE STAUB, librarian; b. Bklyn., Sept. 30, 1928; d. Harry and Regina (Klein) Staub; BA, Hunter Coll., CUNY, 1949; MLS, L.I. U., 1969; m. Harold E. Levin, Nov. 19, 1950 (dec. June 1984); children: Alan, Leslie, Kim, Paula; m. Lee Wixman, June 5, 1989.. Reference librarian and young adults Henry Waldinger Library, Valley Stream, N.Y., 1969-87, program coordinator public relations, 1976-87; free-lance info. specialist, Boynton Beach, Fla., 1988—; cons. on Jewish books and libraries; librarian Judaica Libr. Temple Emanu El, Palm Beach., Fla., 1988—; active Palm Beach Libr. Adv. Bd., 1993—; lectr. books with Judiac themes. Trustee, Sisterhood Temple B'nai Israel of Elmont, 1969-71, 87, Temple B'nai Israel of Elmont, 1982; libr. Temple Emanuel, Palm Beach, Fla., 1988—. Recipient Library Public Relations Council award, 1973. Mem. Assn. Jewish Librs. (editor Bull. 1973-83, Newsletter 1978—, Fanny Goldstein Merit award 1992), Am. Mizrachi Women, Hadassah. Contbr. to Contemporary Literary Criticism, Vol. 13, 1979.

LEVISON, ANDREW HUGH, author, information specialist; b. N.Y.C., Sept. 20, 1948; s. Stanley David and Beatrice (Merken) L.; m. Judith Luna, Mar. 19, 1974; children: Anthony, David. BA in Psychology, U. Wis., Madison, 1970. Pres. Anston Realty Corp., N.Y.C., 1975-82, Am. Micro Export, Atlanta, 1982-89, Electronic Info., Atlanta, 1989—; bd. advisors Martin Luther King Ctr. for Nonviolent Social Change, Atlanta; assoc. McPherson Assocs., Phila. Author: Working Class Majority, 1974, The Full Employment Alternative, 1979, Atlanta Constitution, 1992, Online Database Magazine, 1992-93, Atlanta Computer Currents, 1991—. Office: Electronic Information 786 Wildwood Rd NE Atlanta GA 30324-4942

LEVIT, HELOISE B. (GINGER LEVIT), arts administrator, fine arts and media consultant; b. Phila., Apr. 2, 1937; d. Elmer and Claire Frances (Schwartz) Bertman; m. Jay Joseph Levit, July 14, 1962; children: Richard Bertman, Robert Edward, Darcy Francine. BA in French Literature, U. Pa., 1959; MA in French Literature, U. Richmond, 1975; Cert., Alliance Française, Paris, 1991, Chambre de Commerce et d'Industrie de Paris, 1991, La Sorbonne, Paris, 1994, Instituto Lorenzo di Medici Firenze, Italy, 1996; post grad., art history, Commonwealth U., Richmond. Arts broadcaster Richmond, Va., 1976-82; dir. Fine Arts Am., Inc., Richmond, 1982-84; tchr. Henrico County Pub. Schs., Richmond, 1984-88; dir. devel. Sta. WVST-FM Va. State U., Petersburg, 1987-88; mgr., dir. devel. Richmond Philharm. Orch., 1988-94; fine arts and media cons. Art-I-Facts, Richmond, 1988—. Author: Moments, Monuments & Monarchs, 1986 (Star award 1986); arts writer Richmond Rev., 1989-90; anchor, producer (syndicated radio series) Va. Arts Report, 1978-83, Va. Women, 1984 (Va. Press Women award 1986). V.p. Va. Mus. Collector's Cir., Richmond, 1986-91, mem. steering com.; pres. Richmond Area Dem. Women's Club, 1992-93; mem. Va. Mus. Coun., Richmond; mem. Richmond Symphony Orch. League. Mem. Am. Assn. Tchrs. of French, Va. Capitol Corrs. Assn., Va. Press Women, U. Pa. Alumni Club (v.p. 1980-90, Ben Franklin award 1990), Am. Symphony Orch. League, Amicale Francaise, Alliance Francaise (cert. 1989, 91), La Table Francaise (pres. 1996), Va. Writers Club. Home and Office: Art-I-Facts 1608 Harborough Rd Richmond VA 23233-4720

LEVIT, JAY J(OSEPH), lawyer; b. Phila., Feb. 20, 1934; s. Albert and Mary Levit; m. Heloise Bertman, July 14, 1962; children: Richard Bertman, Robert Edward, Darcy Francine. AB, Case Western Res. U., 1955; JD, U. Richmond, 1958; LLM, Harvard U., 1959. Bar: Va. 1958, D.C. 1961, U.S. Supreme Ct. 1961. Trial atty. U.S. Dept. Justice, Washington, 1960-64; sr. atty. Gen. Dynamics Corp., Rochester, N.Y., 1965-67; ptnr. Stallard & Levit, Richmond, Va., 1968-77, Levit & Mann, Richmond, 1978—; instr. U. Mich. Law Sch., Ann Arbor, 1964-65; adj. assoc. prof. U. Richmond Law Sch., 1974-77; adj. lectr. Va. Commonwealth U., Richmond, 1970-85; lectr. in field. Contbg. editor The Developing Labor Law-Bur. Nat. Affairs, 1974—. Mem. ABA (labor com.), Va. Bar Assn. (labor com.), Fed. Bar Assn. (labor com.). Home: 1608 Harborough Rd Richmond VA 23233-4720 Office: Levit & Mann Hamilton Pl Ste 100 1301 N Hamilton St Richmond VA 23230

LEVITAS, MIRIAM C. STRICKMAN, events coordinator, realtor, television producer; b. Phila., Aug. 3, 1936; d. Morris and Bella (Barsky) Cherrin; m. Bernard Strickman, June 3, 1956 (dec. 1975); children: Andrew, Brian, Craig, Deron; m. Theodore Clinton Levitas, Apr. 25, 1976; children: Steven, Leslie, Anthony. Student Temple U., 1953-56, LaSalle U., Chgo., 1968; cert. in Gerontology Ga. State U., 1988, coord. Intergenerational Connections, State of Ga., 1989—. V.p. programming interior design Nat. Home Fashions League, Atlanta, 1974-75; Ga. Bd. Realtors, 1971—; adminstr. Stanley H. Kaplan Ednl. Ctr., Atlanta, 1974-84; owner, pres. Levitas Svcs., Inc. (Internat. Destinations), Atlanta, 1984-85; owner, v.p. Nat. Travel Svcs. and Internat. Destinations, Atlanta, 1984-85; realtor Philip White Properties Inc./Sotheby's Internat. Realty, 1985-91; realtor Coldwell Banker Previews, 1991—. Exec. producer, host community svc. videos TV cable broadcast, Atlanta, 1988—; solo pianist Paul Whiteman TV, Phila. Youth Orch., Frankford Symphony Orch., 1950. Pres. Ahavath Achim Sisterhood, Atlanta, 1977-79, co-pres., 1996—; bd. dirs. Jewish Family Svcs., 1993-96, Atlanta chpt. Nat. Osteoporosis Found., 1990-91, Outings in the Park, 1989-91; chmn. Tea at the Ritz Scottish Rite Children's Med. Ctr., 1987-90, women's div. Israel Bond, Atlanta, 1987, 88, 89, mem. aux.; chmn. Who's Bringing in the Great Chefs Scottish Rite Childrens Med. Ctr., 1990, 91, 92; mem. Atlanta Symphony, High Mus. Art, Nat. Mus. of Women in Arts (charter), Alliance Theater Atlanta. Phila. Bd. Edn. scholar, 1952, Atlanta Hist. Ctr.-Atlanta Hist. Soc., Alliance No. Dist. Dental Soc.; charter mem. U.S. Holocaust Mus.; bd. dirs. Jewish Family Svcs., nat. bd. advisors Brevard Music Ctr., 1993—. Named Woman of Achievement, Atlanta Jewish Fedn., 1993. Mem. Ga. Gerontology Soc., Atlanta Bd. Realtors, Spl. Children of the South (chmn. 1991-93), Internat. Furnishings and Design Assn. (Atlanta chpt.), Women in Film, Am. Women in Radio and TV, Children's Med. Ctr. Aux., Brandeis Nat. Women (life), Hadassah (life), Nat. Council Jewish Women (life), B'nai Brith (life), Scots (life).

LEVITCH, HARRY HERMAN, retail executive; b. Memphis, Dec. 24, 1918; s. Samuel Arthur and Lena (Feingold) L. LLB cum laude, So. Law U. (now Memphis State U.), 1941; m. Frances Wagner, May 31, 1940; 1 child, Ronald Wagner. Mdse. mgr. Perel & Lowenstein, Inc., 18 yrs.; pres. Harry Levitch Jewelers, Inc., Memphis, 1955—, also treas.; past lectr. on diamonds Memphis State U., Shelby State U. Now hon. Pres. Leo N. Levi Nat. Arthritis Hosp., Hot Springs Nat. Park, Ark.; del. Conf. on Am.'s Cities, Washington, Regional Conf. U.S. Fgn. Policy, Louisville, Conf. of U.S. Dept. State and So. Center for Internat. Studies, 1989; pub. B'nai B'rith Voice newspaper of Dist. 7; mem. exec. com. Anti Defamation League B'nai B'rith, Southeastern region, elected hon. life mem., 1989; apptd. mem. U.S. Holocaust Meml. Coun., B'nai B'rith Found.; bd. dirs. B'nai B'rith Home and Hosp. for Aged, Memphis, West Tenn. chpt. Arthritis Found.; now hon. life chmn. Internat. Commn. on Community Vol. Services; bd. dirs. West Tenn. chpt. March of Dimes, NCCJ; lt., spl. dept. sheriff Shelby County (Tenn.). Appointee U.S. Holocaust Meml. Council by Pres. Reagan, 1988—. Served with JAGC, USAAF, 1943-46. Recipient Outstanding Civic Service award City of Memphis; Outstanding Leadership award Christian Bros. Coll.; col. a.d.c. Gov. Tenn.; named Hon. citizen Tex., Ala., Ark., New Orleans; named one of 150 Outstanding Vols. in the World B'Nai B'Rith, 1994. Mem. Memphis Area C. of C., Retail Jewelers of Am., Jewelers Vigilance Com., Nat. Assn. Jewelry Appraisers (sr. appraiser), Internat. Soc. Appraisers, Am. Soc. Appraisers, Diamond Council Am. (cert. gemologist), Jewelry Industry Council, B'nai B'rith (internat. v.p., hon. life mem. Nat. Commn. Anti-Defamation League, Parent Power-Keeping Our Kids Drug Free award Community Vol. Svcs. commn. 1990, David M. Blumberg award Outstanding Mem. Dist. 7, 1990), Rotary, Summit, Masons, Shriners. Jewish. Home: 4972 N Peg Ln Memphis TN 38117-2070 Office: Harry Levitch Jewelers Inc 5100 Poplar Ave Ste 111 Memphis TN 38137-0113 also: Levi Arthritis Hosp 300 Prospect Ave Hot Springs National Park AR 71901-4003

LEVITT, GREGORY ALAN, education educator; b. Memphis, Jan. 12, 1952; s. Robert Riley and Martha Lorraine (Swincher) L.; m. Billie Diane Tomblin (div. June 1985); 1 child, Joshua Paul; m. Yueping Guo, June 3, 1994; 1 child, Maya Guo. BA, Capital U., Columbus, Ohio, 1975; MA, Ohio State U., 1988, PhD, 1990. Cert. secondary sch. tchr., adminstr., Ohio; cert. tchr. Chinese lang. Beijing Lang. Inst. Tchr. Wehrle H.S., Columbus, 1975-85; grad. teaching assoc. Ohio State U., Columbus, 1985-90; cons./rschr. CBS News, Beijing, China, 1989; dir. fgn. tchrs. Beijing U. of Aero. and Astron. Engring., 1988-90; assoc. prof. U. New Orleans, 1990—; assoc. dir. Ctr. for the Pacific Rim, New Orleans, 1990—; dir. A World of Difference Inst., New Orleans, 1994—. Mem. editl. rev. bd. Teaching About Asia Jour., 1993—; contbr. articles to profl. jours., chpts. to books and computer software. Bd. dirs. Tyomey Ctr. for Peace Through Justice, New Orleans, 1994—; mem. cmty. bd. Success Dropout Prevention, New Orleans, 1990—; coll. organizer AIDS Walk, U. New Orleans, 1993-94. Grantee U.S. Dept. Edn., 1994, East-West Ctr., Honolulu, 1994, La. Endowment for Humanities, 1993. Mem. ASCD, Nat. Coun. for the Social Studies, Assn. for Asian Studies, Nat. Assn. for Multicultural Edn., La. Coun. for the Social Studies, La. Ednl. Rsch. Assn., Phi Beta Delta, Phi Delta Kappa (advisor 1994—). Home: 5421 Hewes St New Orleans LA 70125 Office: Univ of New Orleans Coll of Edn Dept of C&I New Orleans LA 70148

LEVITZ, JOHN BLASE, investment manager, consultant; b. Miami, Fla., June 4, 1956; s. John Robert and Barbara Jean (Schwab) L.; m. Mayra Aleida Lopez, Mar. 31, 1990. BA, Fla. State U., 1978; MBA with honors, Barry U., 1993. Cert. fund specialist; cert. investment mgmt. analyst. V.p., investment cons. Levitz Electric Co., Inc., Miami, 1979-86; v.p., retirement plan investment cons. S.E. Fla. Electric, Inc., Miami, 1986-90; pres., chief investment officer Levitz Investment Mgmt., Inc., Miami, 1991-94; investment cons. Smith Barney, Coral Springs, Fla., 1994—. Mem. Investment Mgmt. Cons. Assn., Inst. Cert. Fund Specialists, Barry Univ. Alumni Assn. (bd. dirs.). Office: 3111 N University Dr Ste 900 Coral Springs FL 33065-5061

LEVITZKY, MICHAEL GORDON, physiology educator; b. Elizabeth, N.J., Jan. 3, 1947; s. Edward and Shirley Edith (Worfman) L.; m. Ellen M. de Roxtro (div. Dec. 1984); m. Elizabeth Seeliger Gouaux, Mar. 13, 1985; children: Edward Benjamin, Sarah Elizabeth. BA, U. Pa., 1969; PhD, Albany Med. Coll., Union U., 1975. Instr. physiology Albany (N.Y.) Med. Coll., 1974-75; asst. prof. physiology La. State U. Med. Ctr., New Orleans, 1975-80, assoc. prof., 1980-85, prof., 1985—; adj. prof. Tulane U. Med. Ctr., New Orleans, 1990—. Author: Pulmonary Physiology, 1982, 2d edit., 1986, 3d edit., 1991, 4th edit., 1995; co-author: Introduction to Respiratory Care, 1990. Nat. Heart, Lung and Blood Inst. grantee, 1976-78, 78-86. Mem. Am. Physiol. Soc. (edn. com. 1988-91), Am. Thoracic Soc., N.Y. Acad. Scis., Soc. for Exptl. Biology and Medicine, Sigma Xi. Office: La State U Med Ctr Dept Physiology 1901 Perdido St New Orleans LA 70112-1328

LEVSTIK, FRANK RICHARD, archivist; b. Chgo., Mar. 3, 1943; s. Frank Richard and Anna Katherine (Dickman) L.; m. Linda Suzanne Thoms, June 15, 1968; children: Jeremy, Jennifer. BA in History, Pikeville Coll., 1966; MA in History, Va. Polytech. Inst., 1968; PhD in History, Ohio State U., 1981. Archives specialist Ohio Hist. Soc., Columbus, 1969-72, asst. state archivist, 1972-76, state archivist, 1976-82; prin. archivist Ky. Dept. Librs./Archives, Frankfort, 1982-83, 85-87, archives & records adminstr., 1987—; libr. U. Ky., Lexington, 1983-85; treas. Soc. Ohio Archivists, Columbus, 1980-82; state hist. records adv. bd. Ohio State Hist. Soc., Columbus, 1976-82; chmn., sec. State Records Commn., Columbus, 1972-82. Author: Kentucky Historical Records Needs Assessment Report, 1983; co-author: Union Bibliography of Ohio Printed State Documents, 1974. 2d v.p. Bluegrass Assn. Retarded, Lexington, 1992—; bd. dirs. Southside Settlement House, Columbus, 1980-82. Mem. Hist. Confedn. Ky. (treas., bd. dirs. 1985—), Ky. Coun. Archives (bd. dirs.). Presbyterian. Home: 1042 Forest Lake Dr Lexington KY 40515 Office: Ky Dept Librs & Archives 300 Coffee Tree Rd Frankfort KY 40601-9267

LEVY, DANIEL, economics educator; b. Tschakaia, Georgian Republic, Georgia, Nov. 13, 1957; came to U.S., 1983; s. Shabtai and Simha (Levi-ashvili) L.; m. M. Sarit Adler, Spet. 10, 1981; children: Avihai, Eliav. BA, Ben-Gurion U., Beer-Sheva, Israel, 1982; MA, U. Calif., Irvine, 1989, PhD, 1990. Lectr. U. Minn., Mpls., 1983-88, St. Olaf Coll., Northfield, Minn., 1986-88, The Coll. St. Catherine, St. Paul, 1987-88; prof. Pepperdine U., Irvine, 1989-90, U. Calif., Irvine, 1990-91, Union Coll., Schenectady, N.Y., 1991-92, Emory U., Atlanta, 1992—; computer software programmer Mac Cartuli, 1989. Contbr. articles to profl. jours. Treas. Minn. Student Orgn., 1984-85. Mem. Internat. Inst. Forecasters, Am. Econ. Assn., Soc. Econ. Dynamics and Control, Econometric Soc., Western Econ. Assn., Mensa. Office: Emory U Dept Economics Atlanta GA 30322

LEVY, ELLIOT GENE, physician; b. Kansas City, Mo., Oct. 15, 1946; s. Jerry and Sarah A. (Lesser) L.; m. Deborah Lynn Benovitz, Aug. 24, 1971; children: Jonathan, Emily, Daniel. BS, Northwestern U., 1967, MD, 1971. Intern U. Pa., Phila., 1971-72; resident Washington U., St. Louis, 1972-74; pvt. practice North Miami Beach, Fla., 1975—. Fellow ACP; mem. Am. Diabetes Assn., Am. Thyroid Assn., Endocrine Soc., Thyroid Found. Am. Republican. Jewish. Office: 2110 Biscayne Blvd # 203 Miami FL 33137-5014

LEVY, H. NATHAN, III, science foundation executive; b. Torrance, Calif., Nov. 26, 1955. BS, Southeastern La. State U., 1977; MS, La. State U. Sr. chemist Hydro-Chem Analytical, Inc., 1978-79; pres., tech. consulting chemist, CEO A & E Testing, Inc., Baton Rouge, 1979—. Mem. ASTM, Am. Chem. Soc., Water Pollution Control Fedn. Office: 1717 Seaboard Dr Baton Rouge LA 70809

LEVY, HAROLD BERNARD, pediatrician; b. Shreveport, La., Apr. 27, 1918; s. Phillip and Ida (Sperling) L.; m. Betty Ann Friedenthal, Nov. 29, 1942; children—James, Charles, Roger, Judy Levy Harrison. B.S., La. State U., 1937; M.D., 1940. Diplomate Am. Bd. Pediatrics. Intern, Tri-State Hosp., Shreveport, 1940-41; resident in pediatrics Shreveport Charity Hosp., 1946-48; practice medicine specializing in pediatrics, Shreveport, La., 1948—; co-med. dir. Caddo Found. for Exceptional Children, 1953—; founder, dir. spl. clinic for learning disabilities La. Handicapped Children's Services, 1955—; clin. assoc. prof. pediatrics La. State U. Med. Sch., Shreveport, 1973—; faculty mem. Nat. Coll. Juvenile Justice, Reno, 1975—; mem. staff Schumpert, Willis-Knighton, Doctors, La. State U. hosps.; Pres., Shreveport Summer Theater, 1953; pres. Caddo-Bossier Safety Council, 1959-60. Served to maj. M.C., USAAF, 1942-46. Recipient Brotherhood citation NCCJ, 1976; Spl. recognition award La. Assn. Children with Learning Disabilities, 1976; Axson-Choppin award La. Pub. Health Assn., 1983. Mem. Am. Acad. Cerebral Palsy and Devel. Medicine (pres. 1983), Am. Acad. Pediatrics, La. Med. Soc., So. Med. Assn., AMA, Orton Dyslexia Soc., Sigma Xi. Republican. Jewish. Club: East Ridge Country. Author: Square Pegs, Round Holes, The Learning Disabled Child in the Classroom and at Home, 1973; contbr. articles to profl. jours. Home: 6026 Dillingham Ave Shreveport LA 71106-2131 Office: 865 Margaret Pl Ste 316 Shreveport LA 71101-4542

LEVY, MAURICE, education educator, researcher; b. Chgo., Aug. 15, 1933; s. Eugene and Jean Belle (Anshel) L.; m. Loris Belle Rissman, Sept. 11, 1955; children—Arden Lynn, Andrea Hilary, James Michael. B.S., U. Ill., 1956, Ed.M., 1959; Ed.D., U. Ga., 1968. Asst. prof. Ga. State U.-Atlanta, 1968-69; postdoctoral fellow U. So. Calif., Los Angeles, 1969-70; assoc. prof. Med. Coll. Ga., Augusta, 1970-73, prof. ednl. research, dir., 1976-86, prof. pediatrics, 1986—, assoc. dean faculty devel., 1990; prof., dir. So. Ill. U. Sch. Medicine, Springfield, 1973-76. Author: Introduction to Pediatric Cardiology, 1975, Physicians Assistants Exam Review, 1980; contbr. articles to profl. jours. Bd. dirs. Am. Cancer Soc., Springfield, Ill., 1974, Health Info. Services, Virginia Beach, Va., 1982—; trustee Augusta County Day Sch., 1972-80; chmn. Med. Coll. Ga. United Fund, Augusta, 1980. Recipient Outstanding Sci. Exec. award Am. Acad. Family Practice, 1974; Gold Cert. award Am. Acad. Pediatrics, 1973; Boss of Yr. award Am. Bus. Women's Assn., 1978. Mem. Am. Acad. Phys. Assts. (bd. advisors 1975-85, Significant Contbns. award 1980-83), Health Scis. Commn. Assn. Jewish. Clubs: Augusta Track, Torch (vice chmn. 1972-73). Home: 703 Woodgate Ct Augusta GA 30909-3122 Office: Med Coll Ga 1120 15th St Augusta GA 30912-0004

LEVY, MICHAEL HOWARD, environmental management professional; b. Newburgh, N.Y., Oct. 2, 1947; s. Max and Helen (Rankell) L.; m. Judith Linenbroker, Aug. 28, 1971; children: Matthew, Andrew. BS in Civil Engring., Rensselaer Polytech. Inst., 1969, ME in Environ. Engring., 1972; post-grad., Fairleigh Dickinson U., 1977-78. Registered profl. engr., N.Y.; cert. environ. auditor. Jr. civil engr. N.Y. State Dept. Transp., Albany, 1969-72; asst. sanitary engr. N.Y. State Dept. Environ. Conservation, Albany, 1972-73, sr. air pollution engr., 1973-76; environ. engr. Allied Chem. Co. div. Semet Solvay, Morristown, N.J., 1976-78; supt. environ. and quality control div. Allied Chem. Co., Detroit, 1979; with Mobil Chem. Co./Mobil Corp., 1979-83; mgr. environ. affairs Mobil Chem. Co./Mobil Corp., Pittsford, N.Y. and Princeton, N.J., 1984-87; mgr. legis. and regulatory affairs Mobil Chem. Co./Mobil Corp., Fairfax, Va., 1987-89; v.p. Franklin Assocs., Ltd., McLean, Va., 1990-92; pres. Environ. Strategies & Solutions, Inc., McLean, Va., 1993—; dir. energy and materials policy Am. Forest & Paper Assn., Washington, 1993-94; exec. dir. Polystyrene Packaging Coun. & Formed Polystyrene Alliance, Washington, 1994—. Sports vol. McLean (Va.) Youth, Inc., 1988-89; registrar troop 128, Boy Scouts Am., 1985—. Sgt. USAR, 1970-76. Mem. ASCE, Am. Soc. Assn. Execs., Air Pollution Control Assn., Water Pollution Control Fedn., Profl. Engring. Soc., Phi Sigma Kappa (alumni pres. 1969-71). Lutheran. Home: 744 Ridge Dr Mc Lean VA 22101-1623

LEVY, RALPH M., cardiologist; b. Barranquilla, Colombia, Oct. 18, 1960; came to U.S., 1984; s. Steven Armand and Helena (Naimark) L.; m. Deborah M. Winslow, Mar. 28, 1987; children: Natan, Joel, Gabriel. Student, Colombo-Hebrew Sch., Bogota, 1971-77; MD, U. Rosario, 1983. Diplomate Am. Bd. Internal Medicine, Am. Bd. Cardiovascular Disease; lic. physician, N.Y., Fla. Surg. intern Lincoln Med. Ctr., Bronx, N.Y., 1984-85; intern, resident internal medicine SUNY Health Scis. Ctr., Bklyn., 1985-88, instr. medicine, 1988-89; attending physician med. emergency rm. Kings County Hosp., 1988-89; clin. fellow cardiology Mount Sinai Med. Ctr., N.Y.C., 1989-91; attending physician South Broward Cardiology Cons., Hollywood, Fla., 1991—; mem. staff Meml. Hosp. West, Meml. Hosp. E., Hollywood Med. Ctr. Fellow Am. Coll. Cardiology; mem. AMA, ACP, Broward County Med. Assn. Jewish. Office: 1150 N 35th Ave Hollywood FL 33021-5424

LEVY, ROBIN CAROLE, elementary guidance counselor; b. Berlin, Apr. 13, 1964; parents Am. citizens; d. Kenneth and Henrietta Nan (Weithorn) Kaplan; m. Guy Glickson Levy, July 27, 1986; 1 chld, Clare Sydney. BS, Fla. State U., 1986; MEd, Coll. William and Mary, 1991. Cert. tchr. Pre-sch. tchr. Talent House Pvt. Sch., Fairfax, Va., 1986-87; 4th grade tchr. Mt. Vernon Elem., Tabb, Va., 1987-92; elem. counselor Bethel Manor Elem., LAFB, Va., 1992-95; family mediator Dispute Settlement Ctr., Norfolk, Va., 1993—, Dispute Resolution Ctr., Richmond, Va., 1994—. Past pres., v.p. Denbigh Jaycees, Va., 1987-94 (Project Mgr. of Yr. 1991, 93, Outstanding Local Pres. 1994), sec., treas. Mem. ASCD, ACA, Va. Counselors Assn., Va. Sch. Counselors Assn., Peninsula Counselors Assn. Democrat. Jewish. Home: 463 Cheshire Ct Newport News VA 23602-6404

LEVY-MYERS, ERIC, management consultant; b. Harvey, Ill., Aug. 17, 1960; s. Donald A. and Dixie L. (Ashton) Myers; m. Helen Obermayer; 1 child, Reuben. Student, U. Chgo., 1978-80; BA, Creighton U., 1984; PhD, Tufts U., 1996. Field ops., and adv. Dukakis for President, Boston, 1987-88; dir. info. syss. The Fletcher Sch. Tufts U., Medford, Mass., 1990-93; pres. elm consulting Am. Mgmt. Syss., Fairfax, Va., 1993-95. Office: Am Mgmt Syss 12701 Fair Lakes Cir Fairfax VA 22033

LEW, D(UKHEE) BETTY, physician; b. Seoul, Korea, June 1, 1952; came to U.S., 1972; d. H.S. and M.S. Lew. BS, Temple U., 1976, MD, 1980. Intern, resident Shands Med. Ctr., Gainesville, Fla., 1980-83; fellow Nat. Jewish Ctr. for Immunology and Respiratory Medicine, Denver, 1983-86; asst. prof. U. Tenn., Memphis, 1986-92; assoc. prof. U. Tenn., 1992—. Grantee Am. Lung Assn., 1991—, Am. Lung Assn. Tenn., 1990-91; recipient 1st award NIH, 1991—. Mem. Am. Acad. Allergy & Immunology, Am. Coll. Allergy & Immunology, Ten. Soc. Allergy & Immunology, Tenn. Thoracic Soc., Soc. Pediat. Rsch., Soc. Leukocyte Biology. Methodist. Home: 2490 Ayrshire Cv Memphis TN 38119-7506 Office: LeBonheur Children's Med Ctr 1 Children's Plz Memphis TN 38105

LEW, EDWIN WAYNE, chemist; b. Phoenix, June 20, 1950; s. Gin Yuen and Szeto Ting (Ting) L.; m. Alice Suet Ching, July 6, 1980; children: Melissa Robin, Michael Wayne. BA, U. Ariz., 1972. Research & devel. chemist Rubatex Corp., Bedford, Va., 1973-79, Belding Corticelli, Bedford, 1980-82, Bedford Weaving Mills, Inc., 1982—; bd. dirs. Cen. Va. Planning Dist. Waste Mgmt., Lynchburg, Va., 1978-79. Mem. Am. Assn. Textile Chemists and Colorists. Republican. Baptist. Home: 1127 Smith St Bedford VA 24523-3009 Office: Bedford Weaving Mills Monroe St Bedford VA 24523

LEW, LAWRENCE EDWARD, chemical engineer; b. Santa Monica, Calif., June 11, 1952; s. Robert Joseph and Evelyn (Joy) L.; m. Doris Schaefer, May 28, 1976; children: Katherine, Henry. BSChE and Petroleum Refining Engring., Colo. Sch. Mines, 1974. Registered profl. engr., Okla. Process/constrn. engr. Natural Resources Group Phillips, Teesside, Eng./Emden, Germany, 1975-78; process engr. corp. engring. Phillips, Bartlesville, Okla., 1978-80, process engr. refining div., 1980-84, prin. engr. catalytic processes, 1984-89, supr. residual oil rsch., 1989-90, tech. planning dir., 1990-91, mgr. process modeling, hydrotreating and catalytic cracking br., 1991—. Contbr. articles to profl. jours. Mem. AIChE, NSPE, Nat. Petroleum Refiners Assn. (screening com. 1988-96). Democrat. Roman Catholic. Office: Phillips Petroleum Co 154 PDC Bartlesville OK 74004

LEW, SALVADOR, radio station executive; b. Camajuani, Las Villas, Cuba, Mar. 6, 1929; came to U.S., 1961; s. Berko and Clara (Lewinowicz) L.; m. Laura F. Lew; 1 child, Esther Maria. JD magna cum laude, U. Havana, 1952. Editor Sch. Mural Newspaper, Camajuani, Cuba, 1941-43; pres. youth sect. and nat. sec. Cuban People's Party, Cuba, 1948-53; Latin Am. cons. Walters, Moore & Costanzo, Miami, Fla., 1961-72; news dir. Sta. WMIE and Sta. WQBA, Miami, 1961-70; gen. mgr., news dir. Sta. WRHC, Miami, 1973-89; host talk show, 1989—; pres. adv. bd. Cuba Broadcasting, 1992.Trustee, dir. United Way, 1985—. Recipient Lincoln Marti award Sec. HEW, 1964; FBI Award for Community Svcs., 1983; community svc. awards various orgns., 1973-84. Mem. Cuban Lawyers Assn. Exile. Jewish. Home: 2863 SW 23rd St Miami FL 33145-3309

LEWANDO, ALFRED GERARD, JR., oceanographer; b. Boston, Apr. 17, 1945; s. Alfred Gerard and Marie Helen (Coughlin) L.; m. Carol Ann Kologe, Nov. 8, 1969; children: Jennifer Ann, Christina Marie. BS in Earth Sci., State Coll. Boston, 1967; MBA, U. So. Miss., 1986, MS in Polit. Sci., 1989, MS in Pub. Rels., 1990, MEd in Adult Edn., 1991. Lic. real estate broker and notary pub., Miss. Staff oceanographer Naval Oceanographic Office, Washington, 1967-76, head fleet support br., 1976-80; dir. tactical analysis div. Naval Oceanographic Office, Bay St. Louis, Miss., 1980-86, dir. oceanographic programs div., 1986-88; dep. asst. chief of staff for ops. Naval Oceanography Command, Stennis Space Ctr., Miss., 1988-94; asst. chief staff for command mgmt. and inspector gen. Naval Meteorology and Oceanography Command, Stennis Space Center, 1994—; mem. policy bd. Ctr. of Higher Learning, Stennis Space Ctr., Miss., 1990—; mem. adv. com. Cape Fear Jr. Coll., Wilmington, N.C., 1974—, Miss. State U. Rsch. Ctr., 1988—; mem. steering com. Summer Indsl. fellowships for Gulf Coast Tchrs., 1990—; mem. organizing com. 44th Internat. Sci. and Engring. Fair, 1993. Contbr. articles to profl. publs. Commr., City of Long Beach (Miss.) Port Authority, 1986-88. Govt. Sr. Exec. fellow Harvard U., 1996. Mem. Miss. Acad. Scis., Gamma Theta Upsilon. Home: 553 Mockingbird Dr Long Beach MS 39560-3105 Office: Naval Meteorology and Oceanography Command Stennis Space Center MS 39529-5000

LEWCOCK, RONALD BENTLEY, architect, educator; b. Brisbane, Australia, Sept. 27, 1929; s. Harry Kingsley and Ena (Orrock) L.; m. Barbara Sansoni, Aug. 8, 1981. Student, U. Queensland, 1947-49; BArch, Capetown U., South Africa, 1951; PhD, U. Cape Town, South Africa, 1961; MA, Cambridge U., Eng., 1970; Eliza Howard vis. fellowship, Columbia U., 1963. Pvt. practice architecture, 1951—; Whitehead research fellow Clare Hall, Cambridge U., Eng., 1970-72, ofcl. fellow, 1976-84; research officer Middle East Centre, Cambridge, 1973-80; Aga Khan prof. architecture for Islamic culture, dir. program in architecture for Islamic socs. MIT, Cambridge, 1984-91; chmn. Aga Khan program for Islamic architecture MIT and Harvard U., 1985-87; prof. architecture Ga. Inst. Tech., Atlanta, 1991—; cons. UNESCO, Habitat, World Bank, British Coun., Am. Rsch. Cen., Egypt, 1976—; lectr. U. Natal, 1952-57, sr. lectr., 1958-69; lectr., examiner Cambridge U., 1973-85; unit leader design in developing world Archtl. Assn., London, 1977-81; lectr. Archtl. Assocs. Sch., London, 1971-82; vis. prof. grad. sch. architecture Ga. Inst. Tech., 1979-84, Harvard, 1984, Louvain U., 1984; vis. Aga Khan prof., MIT, 1991-93, UQT, Australia, 1996. Author: Early 19th Century Architecture in South Africa, 1963, Traditional Architecture in Kuwait and the Northern Gulf, 1978, 2d edit. 81, Wadi Hadramawt and the Walled City of Shibam, 1986, The Old World City of San'a', 1986, The Architecture of an Island—Sri Lanka, 1996; editor: (with R.B. Serjeant) San'a' an Arabian Islamic City, 1983; contbr. articles to profl. jours., Architecture in the Islamic World, 1976, New Grove Dictionary of Music and Musicians, 1980, 97. Mem. coun. Inst. History and Archaeology East Africa, London, 1976-86, Middle East Centre, Cambridge, Eng., 1981-88, British Sch. Archaeology in Jerusalem, London, 1981—; tech. coord. Internat. Campaign for the Conservation of Sana'a in Yemen Arab Rep. and Shibam and Wadi Hadramaut in Peoples Dem. Rep. of Yemen, 1978-93, UNESCO/UNDP Campaign for Conservation of Monuments and Cities in Uzbekistan, 1994—; steering com. mem. Aga Khan award, 1990-93, Aga Khan Trust for Culture, Geneva, 1993—. Mem. Royal Inst. British Architects (assoc.).

LEWIS, ANNA, legal secretary, writer; b. Forrest City, Ark., Sept. 9, 1958; d. Leroy Gates and Willie Ella (Walker) Mathis; children: Sholanda Drone Walker, Yolanda Drone, Arvester Carading Jr. Grad., Benjamin Franklin H.S., Rochester, N.Y., 1977. Mgr. Homeland News, Forrest City, 1992-95; legal sec. Simes & Simes Law Firm, Forrest City, 1995—. Home: 1026 Robinson Forrest City AR 72335

LEWIS, BILLY MAC, newspaper executive; b. Clinton, N.C., Jan. 22, 1933; s. Morrison Edwin and Myrtle Lee (Bruce) L.; m. Rachel Jeanette Walters, Sept. 11, 1953; children: Timothy Grant (dec.), Jennifer Christine. Grad. high sch. Printer, compositor The Robesonian, Lumberton, N.C., 1951-55; advt. sales staff The Robesonian, Lumberton, 1956-63, advt. mgr., 1965-82, gen. mgr. editor, 1990-96; exec. editor The Robesian, Lumberton, 1996—; advt. sales staff Daily News Tribune, Fullerton, Calif., 1963-64; advt. mgr. Nash Finch Co., Lumberton, 1983-86; gen. mgr., owner Lewis Advt. Svcs., Lumberton, 1987—; cons. Nashville (N.C.) Graphics, 1987-89. Mem., dir. C. of C., Lumberton, 1991-93, United Way, Lumberton, 1991-93. With U.S. Army, 1953-54. Mem. Rotary, Kiwanis. Home: PO Box 1162 704 W 22nd St Lumberton NC 28359 Office: The Robesonian 121 W 5th St Lumberton NC 28359

LEWIS, BLAINE, JR., surgeon; b. Ashland, Ky., Sept. 6, 1919; s. Blaine and Hallie Maud (Heal) L.; m. Belle Johns, 1939; 1 child, Martha Sue. BS, Morehead State U., 1940; MD, U. Louisville, 1943. Diplomate Am. Bd. Surgery. Clinical instr. in surgery U. Louisville, 1947-51, instr. in surgery, 1951-63, asst. clinical prof. surgery, 1963-83, assoc. clinical prof. surgery, 1983—; surgical staff position various Louisville Hosps. Capt. U.S. Army Medical Corps., 1944-46, ETO, PTO, Japan. Fellow Am. Coll. Surgeons; mem. Louisville Surgical Soc. (sec.-treas. 1957-60, pres. 1961), Louisville Soc. Medicine (sec.-treas. 1958-59), Ky. Surgical Soc. (sec.-treas. 1962-68, pres. 1970), AMA, Internat. Soc. Surgery, Jefferson County Medical Soc., Ky. Medical Assn., Southern Medical Assn. Home: 1052 Alta Vista Rd Louisville KY 40205-1758

LEWIS, CARL EDWIN (DJINN), artist, photographer, designer; b. N.Y.C., June 1, 1951; s. Roman and Mabel Gertrude (Prescott) L.; m. Julia Jane Brown (div. 1974); m. Dorena Renise Rachall, Apr. 30, 1977. Student, U. Ariz., 1977-78; grad., Cathedral Choir Sch. of St. John the Divine. Designer Apple Unltd., Tucson, 1977-80; photographer The Grey Scale, Hartford, Conn., 1980-83; photographer/designer Zen D'Zins, Dallas, 1984-92, . . .And Lewis, Too?!, Dallas, 1993—; mem. pub. art com. City of Dallas, 1996—; dir. mktg. Global Environ. Group, 1996—; mem. Tex. Commn. on the Arts; artist-in-edn. dir. Skate Away From Violence; cons. Tex. Network of Youth Svcs. Project coord. Kente, the Sight and Sound, 1994; dir. Everybody Skate!, 1993; co-author Captured Light; exhibited in shows at Paul Mellon Art Ctr., Wallingford, Conn., 1984, 87, Mayor's Gallery, Stamford, Conn., 1990, U. Tex. at Dallas, 1991, Visions in Black Gallery, Bath House Cultural Ctr., 1993, Conduit Gallery, 1993, Amon Carter Mus., 1994, Houston Mus. Fine Arts, 1994, Irving Art Ctr., 1996others; represented in collections at U. Wis., Madison, Cathedral Choir Sch. of St. John the Divine, N.Y.C., San Antonio Mus. Art, Bklyn. Mus., Amon Carter Mus., Houston Mus. Fine Arts, Schomburg Ctr. Rsch. into Black Culture, African Am. Mus. at the Smithsonian Tex. Instruments. Served with USAF, 1971-76, Turkey. Recipient scholarships and awards; fellow Internat. Biog. Ctr., Cambridge, Eng. Mem. Royal Photography Soc. Office: . . .And Lewis Too?! PO Box 820813 Dallas TX 75382-0813

LEWIS, CHARLES ROBERT, newspaper columnist; b. Cumby, Tex., Mar. 18, 1929; s. John Bunyan and Blanche (Devall) L.; m. Gale Miller Lewis, Feb. 20, 1960; 1 child, Charles Devall. BJ, U. Tex., 1951; M of Interdisciplinary Studies, U. Tex., Tyler, 1988. Newspaper editing and mgmt. Dallas-Ft. Worth, 1955-67; newspaper mgmt. Concord, Calif., 1967-71; owner, mgr. advt. and pub. rels. agy., Concord, 1971-74; in newspaper pub. Kilgore, Tex., 1974-78; owner advt. and pub. rels. agy., Tyler, Tex., 1978-91; instr. history Tyler Jr. Coll., 1991—. Author: Discovery Well, 1993. Lt. (j.g.) USNR, 1951-55, Korea. Recipient Column Writing award Tex. Press Assn., 1956, Edtl. Writing award Dallas Press Club, 1962. Mem. Tex. United Press Editors assn. (pres. 1966-67). Home: 1604 Tanglewood Dr E Lindale TX 75771-5150

LEWIS, CHRISTINA LYNN, human services administrator; b. Brook Park, Ohio, June 19, 1963; d. Albert Joseph and Gail Ann (Kohler) Urbas; m. Timothy Allen Lewis, Aug. 3, 1989; 1 child, Cherie Ann. AA, Pasco Hernando C.C., Brooksville, Fla., 1996; student, Thomas Edison State Coll., 1996—. Owner, operator Spl. Touch Day Care, Olmsted Twp., Ohio, 1986-89, Spring Hill, Fla., 1989-94; dir., tng. coord. United Cerebral Palsy, Brooksville, 1994-96; mentor, tng. advisor child care outreach program United Cerebral Palsy, Brooksville, Fla., 1993—; advisor, instr. Child Devel. Assn. Credential Program, Brooksville, 1991—; coun. mem. Pre-K Interagy. Coun., Brooksville, 1994—; CPR, First Aid instr. ARC, 1994—; area supr. Head Start, Inverness, Fla., 1996—. Author (tng. packet) CDA: Everything You Need to Know to Get Started, 1992. Dep. registrar Supr. Elections, Hernando County, 1994; vol. instr. ARC. Recipient Resolution 91-70 award Hernando County Commr., Brooksville, 1991. Mem. Nat. Assn. for the Edn. Young Children, Assn. for Better Child Care (founding mem., newsletter editor 1990, sec., resource and referral 1989-93, Tchr. of Yr. 1990), Phi Theta Kappa. Republican. Home: 9063 Spring Hill Dr Spring Hill FL 34608-6241 Office: Childhood Devel Svcs 613 US 41 Inverness FL 34450

LEWIS, CLINTON, federal agency administrator; b. Eastman, Ga., Sept. 24, 1931; s. Theo and Lucy Victoria (Smith) L.; m. Jane Ivelyn Cadwell Evans, Aug. 18, 1950 (div. Aug. 1967); children: Jerry Thomas, David Theo; m. Ruth Grace Waller, June 19, 1969; children: Gwendolyn Elaine Gay, Clinton Jr. BBA, Ga. Coll., 1973; diploma, Air War Coll., 1979. Chief mgmt. evaluation office USAF, Robins AFB, Ga., 1971-73, supt. aircraft components repair, 1973, chief aircraft scheduling, inventory br., 1973-74, chief aircraft planning, engring. br., 1974-75, chief indsl. products and life support sys. divsn., 1975-76, dep. chief aircraft divsn., 1976-81, dep. dir. directorate of distbn., 1981-84, dep. dir. directorate of maintenance, 1984-90, dir. tech. and indsl. support directorate, 1990—. Chmn. Civilian Non-Appropriated Funds Coun., Robins AFB, 1988—; treas. Parkerson Bapt. Ch., Eastman, Ga, 1978—. Recipient Presdl. Rank of Meritious Exec., Pres. of U.S., 1988, Disting. Civilian Svc. award Dept. of Def., 1995, Vocat. award for Civil Svc., Warner Robins, Ga. Rotary Club, 1996. Mem. Air Force Assn., Fed. Mgrs.' Assn. (Outstanding Fed. Mgr. of Yr. 1995), Sr. Exec. Svc. Home: Rt 4 Eastman GA 31023 Office: WR-ALC/TI 420 2nd St Ste 100 Robins AFB GA 31098-1640

LEWIS, CLYDE A., author, counselor; b. San Gabriel, Calif., July 25, 1948; s. A.B. and Mary Anna (Brown) L.; 1 child, Clint A. BBA, Oklahoma City U., 1971, JD, 1976; MBA, U. Okla., 1991. Bond underwriter USF&G, Oklahoma City, 1972-73, bond dept. mgr., 1973-79; law assoc. Harbor & Leonard, Oklahoma City, 1978-79; ptnr. Harbor Leonard & Lewis, Oklahoma City, 1979-80; pvt. practice Clyde Lewis & Assocs., Oklahoma City, 1980-95; lectr. Networking Ptnrs., Dallas, 1993-95; author, counselor, lectr. Drug Recovery Inc., Oklahoma City, 1996—; cons. Red Rock Mental Health, Oklahoma City, Eagle Ridge Inst., Oklahoma City, Green Valley Mental Health, Tulsa, State Mental Health, Oklahoma City. Author: Encounter with a Prophet, 1995, Chronicles of Chaos, Book I, 1996, Book II, 1996, Book III, 1996. Vol. counsel Drug Recovery Inc., 1971-95; advisor El Reno Prison, Yukon, 1994. Office: Drug Recovery Inc 415 NW 8th Oklahoma City OK 73102

LEWIS, DELBERT O'NEAL, disability consultant, former state official; b. Searcy, Ark., Oct. 15, 1947; s. Scott and Viola Marie (Hodges) L. BA in Psychology and Sociology, Harding U., 1969; 2M Rehab. Counseling, Ark. State U., 1972. Cert. rehab. counselor. With divsn. rehab. svcs. Ark. Dept. Human Svcs., Little Rock, 1972-90, planning specialist, 1978-90; ret., 1990, cons. on disability issues to govt., legal, ednl., and pvt. orgns., 1990—; former staff and advisor Ark. Com. on Equal Access for Handicapped, Interdeptl. Task Force on Rights of Handicapped; former rehab. specialist Disability Determination Svcs. Social Security Adminstrn., Little Rock; former mem. planning coun. CETA and Job Tng. Partnership Act, Little Rock and Pulaski County; guest lectr. on disability issues U. Ark., Little Rock; founding mem., past pres. Ark. Environ. Barriers Coun.; mem. Ark. Adv. Com. to U.S. Commn. on Civil Rights; cons. Emerging Issues Project Inst. for Info. Studies, Washington. Contbr. articles to profl. publs. First pub. mem. Ark. Bd. Architects; former bd. dirs. OurWay, Inc., Little Rock; active Ark. Child Find to Implement Edn. for Handicapped Children Act., others. Recipient plaque of appreciation for svcs. as pres. Ark. br. Nat. Rehab. Counseling Assn., 1976, certs. City of Little Rock, 1975-85, First Mover and Shaker award Ark. Gov.'s Commn. on People with Disabilities, 1978, recognition of svc. plaque Ark. Rehab. Assn., 1990, dedicated svc. plaque Ark. Divsn. Rehab. Svcs. Consumer Adv. Coun., 1990, pub. svc. plaque ARKLA Gas Co., 1991, Cert. of Svc. award U.S. Commn. on Civil Rights, Washington, 1995. Fellow Internat. Biog. Assn.; mem. Found. for Sci. and Disability, Gazette Internat. Networking Inst.-Internat. Polio Network, Drug Policy Found., Rehab. Tech. Assn. Home and Office: 2400 Riverfront Dr Apt 12-f Little Rock AR 72202

LEWIS, FORBES DOWNER, computer scientist, educator; b. New Haven, Apr. 15, 1942; s. Taylor D. Lewis and Clara (Bartholow) Hall. BS, Cornell U., 1967, MS, 1969, PhD, 1970. Asst. prof. Harvard U., Cambridge, Mass., 1970-75; assoc. prof. SUNY, Albany, 1975-78; from assoc. prof. to prof. U. Ky., Lexington, 1978—; vis. asst. prof. Yale U., New Haven, 1973; vis. prof. U. Calif., Berkeley, 1985-86; program dir. NSF, Washington, 1992-94; adv. Fond du Lac Tribal Coll., Cloquet, Minn., 1995—, U. P.R., 1996—. Served in U.S. Army, 1960-63. Mem. IEEE Computer Soc., Assn. Computing Machinery. Office: U Ky Dept Computer Sci Lexington KY 40506

LEWIS, GLADIUS, mechanical engineer, educator; b. Freetown, Sierra Leone, Aug. 29, 1945; came to U.S., 1983; s. William Benjamin and Gladys (Johnson) L. BSc in Mech. Engring., U. London, 1972; PhD in Materials Sci. and Engring., U. Nottingham, Eng., 1976. Lectr. U. Zambia, Lusaka, 1976-81, U. Zimbabwe, Harare, 1981-83; asst. prof. U. Ala., Huntsville, 1983-86; assoc. prof. dept. mech. engring. U. Memphis, 1987-93; prof. Memphis State U., 1993—; vis. scholar Pa. State U., University Park, summer, 1993, 95. Author: Engineering Materials: Theory, Worked Examples and Problems, 1981, Selection of Engineering Materials, 1990. Mem. Assoc. Rural Devel. Internat., Memphis, 1988—. Faculty Rsch. Participation awardee Argonne Nat. Lab., summer 1990; Fulbright-Hays scholar, 1979. Mem. ASME, Tenn. Acad. Sci. Office: U Memphis Dept Mech Engring Memphis TN 38152

LEWIS, GLADYS SHERMAN, nurse, educator; b. Wynnewood, Okla., Mar. 20, 1933; d. Andrew and Minnie Elva (Halsey) Sherman; R.N., St. Anthony's Sch. Nursing, 1953; student Okla. Bapt. U., 1953-55; AB, Tex. Christian U., 1956; postgrad. Southwestern Bapt. Theol. Sem., 1959-60, Escuela de Idiomas, San Jose, Costa Rica, 1960-61; MA in Creative Writing, Central (Okla.) State U., 1985; PhD in English Okla. State U. 1992; m. Wilbur Curtis Lewis, Jan. 28, 1955; children: Karen, David, Leanne, Cristen. Mem. nursing staff various facilities, Okla., 1953-57; instr. nursing, med. missionary Bapt. mission and hosp., Paraguay, 1961-70; vice-chmn. edn. commn. Paraguay Bapt. Conv., 1962-65; sec. bd. trustees Bapt. Hosp., Paraguay, 1962-65; chmn. personnel com., handbook and policy book officer Bapt. Mission in Paraguay, 1967-70; trustee Southwestern Bapt. Theol. Sem., 1974-84, chmn. student affairs com., 1976-78, vice-chmn. bd. 1978-80; ptnr. Las Amigas Tours, 1978-80; writer, conference leader, campus lectr., 1959—; adj. prof. English Cen. State U., Okla. (name changed to U. Cen. Okla.), 1990-91; faculty mem., asst. prof. English U. Cen. Okla., 1991-95, assoc. prof., 1996—. Active Dem. com., Evang. Women's Caucus, 1979-80; leader Girl Scouts U.S.A., 1965-75; Okla. co-chmn. Nat. Religious Com. for Equal Rights Amendment, 1977-79; tour host Meier Internat. Study League, 1978-81. Mem. AAUW, Internat. and Am. colls. surgeons women's auxiliaries, Okla. State, Okla. County med. auxiliaries, Am. Nurse Assn., Nat. Women's Polit. Caucus, 1979-80. Author: On Earth As It Is, 1983; Two Dreams and a Promise, 1984, Message, Messenger and Response, 1994; also religious instructional texts in English and Spanish; editor Sooner Physician's Heartbeat, 1979-82; contbr. articles to So. Bapt. and secular periodicals. Home: 14501 N Western Ave Edmond OK 73013-1828

LEWIS, GORDON GILMER, golf course architect; b. Shawnee, Okla., Sept. 7, 1950; s. Ted Eugene and Janet Garvin (Panner) L.; m. Karen Louise McKenzie, June 2, 1973 (div. Dec. 1981); children: Melanie Marie Lewis-Lehr, Katie McKenzie Lewis-Lehr; m. Susette Mamie London, June 11, 1988; children: London Marshall, Sarah June Victoria. B of Landscape Architecture, Kans. State U., 1974. Registered landscape architect, Ala., Kans., Fla. Golf course architect David Gill, St. Charles, Ill., 1974-75, Charles M. Graves Orgn., Atlanta, 1975-78, Gordon G. Lewis, Naples, Fla., 1978—. Prin. works include Meadowbrook Links, Rapid City, S.D. (Top 50 Pub. Courses in U.S.), The Hulman Links at Los Creek, Terre Haute, Ind. (Top 50 Pub. Courses in U.S.), Lagoon Park, Montgomery, Ala. (Top 75 Pub. Courses in U.S.), The Forest, Ft. Myers, Fla. (Top 50 Courses in Fla.), The Vines, Estero, Fla. (Golf Digest One of Top New Courses 1986), Worthington, Bonita Springs, Fla., Tsai-Hsing, Taipei, Taiwan, others. Republican. Presbyterian. Home: 5098 2nd Ave SW Naples FL 34119-2528

LEWIS, HAROLD E(UGENE), association executive; b. Dodge City, Kans., July 7, 1933; s. Eugene Paul and stepson Gladys M. (Davis) L.; m. Fern E. Snowbarger, June 8, 1953; children: Carla Lewis Gleason, Annette Lewis Fields, Eldon, Monica Lewis Morgan, Bonita Lewis Simmons. B.S. in Edn., Pittsburg (Kans.) State U., 1956, M.S. in Vocat. Tech. Edn., 1965. Cert. secondary tchr., Kans.; accredited conf. mgr.; cert. assn. exec. Am. Soc. Assn. Execs. Secondary and jr. high sch. tchr., 1956-68; prodn. and design supr. Adventure Line Mfg. Co., Parsons, Kans., 1960-63; asst., then acting state supr. trade and indsl. edn. Kans. Dept. Edn., 1968-74; dir. Skills U.S.A. Vocat. Indsl. Clubs Am., Leesburg, Va., 1974—; organizer Internat. Skill Olympics, Atlanta, 1981; project dir. Nat. Standards for Trade and Insdl. Edn. U.S. Dept. Edn., 1984; leader workshops and tng. confs. on vocat. edn.; ofcl. rep. of U.S., Internat. Orgn. for Promotion of Vocat. Edn., 1982—, Internat. Youth Skill Olympics. Pres. Topeka chpt. Gideons Internat., 1968-71; assoc. Parsons YMCA, 1960-65; bd. dirs. Nat. Safety Council, 1985-87. Recipient Disting. Service award Kans. Vocat. Indsl. Clubs Am., 1974; ann. award for nat. project, Nat. Assn. Industry Edn. Cooperation, 1980, Meritorious Achievement award Pitts. State U., 1991; named to Dodge City Community Coll. Hall of Fame, 1988. Mem. Am. Vocat. Assn., Kans. Vocat. Assn., Nat. Assn. Trade and Indsl. Edn., Nat. Assn. Industry Edn. Cooperation (ann. award 1980), Am. Welding Soc. (edn. com., 1983-89). Mem. Ch. of Nazarene. Office: 3600 NE 68th Ter Gladstone MO 64119-1315

LEWIS, JOHN EDWARD, psychologist, educator; b. Kingston-on-Thames, Surrey, Eng., Mar. 16, 1949; came to U.S., 1990; s. Edward Thomas and Gloria June (Simmonds) L.; children: Jessica Catherine, Alexander John Hugh. BA, Queen's U., Kingston, Ont., Can., 1972; BEd, Queen's U., 1973, MEd, 1981; PhD, Syracuse U., 1991. Tchr., counselor Frontenac Sch. Bd., Kingston, Ont., Can., 1976-80; counselor/psychologist Correctional Svcs. Can., Kingston, 1981-85; prof. Brandon (Man. Can.) U., 1985-88, McGill U., Montreal, Can., 1988-91, Nova U., Fort Lauderdale, Fla., 1991—; assoc. dir. Southeast Inst. for Multicultural Studies, Fort Lauderdale, 1992—. Co-author: Assessment and Placement of Minority Students, 1991. Mem. APA. Office: Nova Univ Ctr for Psychol Studies 3301 College Ave Fort Lauderdale FL 33314-7721

LEWIS, JOSEPH BRADY (JAY LEWIS), lawyer; b. Shreveport, La., Nov. 27, 1946; s. Joseph Peter and Gwendolyn (Pate) L.; m. Wanda Gayle Holland Marshall, Mar. 4, 1988. Student, U. So. Miss., 1964-67; BS summa cum laude, Troy State U., 1982; JD magna cum laude, Jones Sch. Law, Montgomery, Ala., 1991. Bar: Ala. 1992. News reporter Sta. WDAM-TV, Hattiesburg, Miss., 1968-69, Sta. KTVT-TV, Ft. Worth, Tex., 1969-70, Sta. WFAA-TV, Dallas, 1970-72; news anchor Sta. KTOK/Okla. News Network, Oklahoma City, 1972-74; editorial dir. Sta. WSFA-TV, Montgomery, Ala., 1974-77; pres. Ala. Info. Network, Montgomery, 1977-80, Amendment One, Inc., Montgomery, 1980-82; owner Lewis Comm., Montgomery, 1977-92; comm. dir. Augat Inc., 1983-92; cons. Gen. TV Network, Montgomery, 1980-83; v.p., dir. Am. Community TV Assn., Montgomery, 1980-82. Contbr. articles to jours. and newspapers. Pres. Community Counseling and Guidance Ctr., Oklahoma City, 1973; trustee Ft. Toulouse Found., Montgomery. Named Communicator of Yr., Ala. Wildlife Fedn., 1977. Mem. ABA, Ala. Bar Assn., Ala. Criminal Def. Lawyers Assn., Ala. Trial Lawyers Assn., Montgomery County Trial Lawyers Assn., Montgomery County Bar Assn., Soc. Profl. Journalists (pres. chpt. 1974, 75, 78, Nat. Disting. Svc. award 1974, 78), Mensa, Citizens Against Fgn. Control of Am. (pres.), Alpha Epsilon Rho, Sigma Delta Kappa. Republican. Roman Catholic. Home: 3628 Bankhead Ave Montgomery AL 36111-2020 Office: 619 S Perry St Montgomery AL 36104-5819

LEWIS, MARTHA ANNE, nurse executive; b. New Orleans, May 13, 1942; d. William West and Eulala (Estes) Miller; m. Carl E. Lewis (div.); children: Carl Jr., Timothy. Diploma, Gilfoy Sch. Nursing, Jackson, Miss., 1963; BS in Nursing, U. So. Miss., 1980, MS in Nursing Adminstrn., 1985. Staff nurse Miss. Hosp. Sch. for Cerebral Palsy, Jackson, 1963; staff nurse Lafayette County Hosp., Oxford, Miss., 1964; clinic nurse U. Miss. Student Infirmary, Oxford, 1964-65; pediatric head nurse, pediatric/nursery supr. Miss. Bapt. Hosp., Jackson, 1965-67; staff nurse-operating room psychiatry and obstetrics Miss. Bapt. Hosp., 1967; from pediatric clinic nurse to charge nurse ICU-burn unit Univ. Med. Ctr., Jackson, 1967-68; head nurse pediatric endocrine pulmonary, oncology Univ. Med. Ctr., 1969-71; asst. dir. nursing svc. Riley Meml. Hosp., Meridian, Miss., 1971-75; from dir. nursing svc. to asst. exec. dir. Riley Meml. Hosp., Meridian, 1976—; mem. adv. com. Meridian Community Coll., 1980-89, MHA-MNA-MSMA-MHCC liaison com, 1982-84, Deans and Dirs. Liaison Com., 1982-84. Bd. dirs. Meridian Symphony League, 1983-88, hon. bd., 1988—; mem. Ednl. Coun.-Concern for Dying, Meridian, 1985, Lauderdale County Interagency Coun., Meridian, 1985-87, Meridian Indsl. Found., 1989-93, ARC. Mem. Am. Orgn. Nurse Execs., Mental Health Assn. (bd. dirs. 1994-99), Am. Nurses Assn. (In Search of Excellence award 1989), Miss. Hosp. Assn.-Orgn. Nurse Execs. (chmn. communications com. 1980-84, 88—, pres. 1982-83), bd. dirs. 1980-84, 88-91, chmn. recognition com. 1984, Miss. orgn. exec. 1991 recognition award), Miss. Nurses Assn (state Health affairs com. 1985-86, del. to convs., fin. com. 1990-92, membership com., program com. v.p., bd. dirs. Nurse of Yr. award dist. 16, 1983, Adminstrv. Nurse of Yr. award 1987, MBH-Gilfoy Alumni Assn. 1993-97). Republican. Baptist. Home: 194 Skyland Dr Meridian MS 39301-9708 Office: Riley Meml Hosp 1102 Constitution Ave Meridian MS 39301-4001

LEWIS, MARTHA NELL, expressive arts therapist, massage therapist; b. Atlanta, Mar. 4, 1944; d. Clifford Edward and Nell (Shropshire) Wilkie; m. Jeffrey Clark Lewis, Aug. 20, 1966 (div. Aug. 1986); children: John Martin, Janet Michelle Teal. BA, Tex. Tech. U., 1966; massage therapy, The Winters Sch., 1991; MA, Norwich U., 1994. Registered expressive therapist, massage therapist, therapeutic massage and bodywork, massage therapist instr. Geophys. analyst Shell Oil Co., Houston, 1966-68; photogravity specialist Photogravity, Inc., Houston, 1972-80; tchr. music Little Red Sch. House, Houston, 1974-75; sec., treas. Lewis Enterprises, Inc., Houston, 1976-83; regulatory supr. Transco Energy Co., Houston, 1983-92; expressive arts therapist Shalom Renewal Ctr., Splendora, Tex., 1995—, River Oaks Health Alliance, Houston, 1995—; nat. exec. dir., pres. Music for Healing and Transition Program, Houston, 1994—; massage therapist, Houston,

1991—. Advisor youth Corpus Christi Ch., Houston, 1970-80; vocalist, instrumentalist Sounds of Faith Folk Group, Houston, 1978—; harpist Houston Harpers Harp Ensemble, 1990-92; instr. exercise, body awareness Transco Energy Co. Fitness Ctr., Houston, 1990-92; vol. The Inst. for Rehab. and Rsch., Houston, 1989-90, Houston Hospice, 1992—, Houston Healing Healthcare Project, 1993—; vol. Healing Environ. Coun. St. Luke's Episc. Hosp., 1993—, lay chaplain, 1994—; founder The Winters Sch. Massage Therapy Care Team, Houston, 1991—. Mem. Internat. Expressive Arts Therapy Assn., Am. Holistic Nurses Assn., Am. Harp Soc., Internat. Folk Harp Assn., Am. Massage Therapy Assn., Nat. Soc. Fund Raising Execs., Exec. Dir.'s Forum, Space City Ski Club (asst. trip coord. 1991-92), Houston Sigma Kappa Found. (bd. dirs.), Sigma Kappa Alumnae Assn. (pres. Houston chpt. 1974-76, nat. collegiate province officer 1981-85, Houston Alumnae of Yr. 1981, Tex. Alumnae of Yr. 1980, Pearl Ct. award 1991). Roman Catholic. Home: 6400 Christie Ave # 4202 Emeryville CA 94608

LEWIS, MARY CAROL, early childhood educator; b. Cin., June 6, 1964; d. Joseph William and Georgia Ann (Elberg) Utter; m. Lawrence Edward Lewis Jr., Jan. 7, 1984; children: Keith, Katie. BS in Edn., Western Ky. U., 1990. Cert. tchr., Ky. Tchr. Fort Knox (Ky.) Cmty. Schs., 1990—; owner, dir., pres. Granny's Appleseed Child Enrichment Ctr., Inc., Radcliff, Ky., 1994—. With U.S. ANG, 1981-83. Mem. NEA, ASCD. Office: Grannys Appleseed Child Enrichment Ctr Inc 605 S Wilson Rd Radcliff KY 40160-1629

LEWIS, MYRON, physician; b. Memphis, Oct. 16, 1937; s. Joseph and Louise Elizabeth (Ottenheimer) L.; m. Edith Gail Haupt, Nov. 30, 1963; children: Robin, Tracey, Joelle. BA magna cum laude, Dartmouth Coll., 1959; MD, Columbia U., 1963. Cert. in medicine, gastroenterology. Intern, resident Vanderbilt U., Nashville, 1963-65; resident Cornell and Bellvue, N.Y.C., 1965-67; fellow U. Tenn., Memphis, 1969-70, assoc. prof. dept. medicine, 1980—. Asst. editor The Gastroenterologist, 1993—. Lt. comdr. USPHS, 1967-69. Fellow Am. Coll. Physicians, Am. Coll. Gastroenterology (master, pres. 1987-88), Phi Beta Kappa. Office: Memphis Gastro Group PC 80 Humphreys Ctr Ste 220 Memphis TN 38120-2352

LEWIS, NANCY LOUINE LAMBERT, school counselor; b. Austin, Tex., Jan. 28, 1938; d. Claud Standard and Audrey Louine (Jackson) Lambert; m. Raymond Clyde Lewis, Dec. 27, 1958; children: Laura Lewis Maloy, John Lambert. BA in English with highest honors, U. Tex., 1958, MEd in Guidance and Counseling, 1964. Lic. tchr. secondary English, counselor; lic. profl. counselor. Tchr. English Allan Jr. High Sch. Austin Ind. Sch. Dist., 1958-62, counselor Univ. Jr. High Sch., 1963-65; counselor Gary Job Corps Ctr., San Marcos, Tex., 1965-67; supr. student tchrs. English dept. curriculum and instrn. U. Tex., Austin, 1968-69, editor, writer, group leader Ctr. Pub. Sch. Ethnic Studies, 1969-76; counselor Allan Jr. High Sch. Austin Ind. Sch. Dist., 1976-80, counselor Martin Jr. High Sch., 1980-86, counselor Fulmore Mid. Sch., 1986-87, counselor Mendez Mid. Sch., 1987—; instr. corr. studies U. Tex., Austin, 1968—. Contbr. articles to profl. jours. Vol. Dem. party, Austin, 1973—, First United Meth. Ch., Austin, 1955—; mem. Mayor's Task Force on Gangs, Crime and Drugs, City of Austin, 1990-91. Mem. ACA, NEA, Am. Sch. Counselors Assn. (editl. bd. Sch. Counselor 1989-96), Tex. State Tchrs. Assn., Tex. Sch. Counselors Assn. (senator 1981-84, pres. 1985-86, chair counseling advocacy com. 1991-93, Mid. Sch. Counselor of Yr. 1993), Tex. Counseling Assn. (senator 1981-84, publs. com. chair 1981-84, membership com. chair 1994-96), Ctrl. Tex. Counseling Assn. (pres. 1982-83), Austin Assn. Tchrs. (cons. com. 1990-93, Human Rels. award 1989-90), Pathways (bd. dirs.), Delta Kappa Gamma (pres. Lambda Iota chpt. 1990-92), Phi Beta Kappa, Phi Delta Kappa. Home: 1427 Salem Meadow Cir Austin TX 78745-2911 Office: Mendez Mid Sch 5106 Village Square Dr Austin TX 78744-4462

LEWIS, OVID C., dean, law educator, lawyer; b. 1932. J.D., Rutgers U.-Newark, 1960, A.B., 1962; LL.M., 1962; J.S.D., Columbia U., 1970. Bar: N.J. 1961. Jud. clk. Superior and County Ct., N.J., 1960-61; asst. prof. Western Res. U., 1962-64, assoc. prof., 1965-68, prof., 1968-76; prof. No. Ky. S.C.-Chase, 1976, assoc. dean and interim dean, 1978; dean, prof. Nova U. Ctr. for Study Law, 1979—; hearing examiner Ohio Civil Rights Com., 1965—; cons. in field. Mem. Assn. Trial Lawyers Am. (co-chmn. automated data retrieval com. 1970-71), Omicron Delta Kappa. Past mem. editorial bd. Rutgers Law Rev. Office: Nova U Ctr for Study Law 3301 College Ave Fort Lauderdale FL 33314-7721*

LEWIS, PHILIP C., company executive; b. 1942. BSME, U. Tex., 1965, MBA, 1971. With Cameron Iron Works, Houston, 1965-68, Tex-Tube, Houston, 1968-69; with Armco Inc, Houston, 1969-73, with subs., 1973—; with Spax Inc., Houston, 1984—, pres. Office: Spax Inc 6307 Toledo St Houston TX 77008

LEWIS, RICHARD, SR., securities broker, consultant; b. Macon, Ga., Jan. 18, 1930; s. William Chapman and Florida (Zelius) L.; m. Iris Joy Clements, Sept. 10, 1949; children: Richard Jr., Linda Lee. Cert. investments securities broker, pistol and rifle instr. State trooper Fla. Hwy. Patrol, various cities, 1951-72; pres. Gateway Shooters Supply, Inc., Jacksonville, Fla., 1972-82; broker Global Investments Securities Inc., Miami, 1985-86, Investacorp, Inc., Miami Lakes, Fla., 1986-89. Lobbyist Fla. Assn. of State Troopers, Tallahassee, 1988-89. With U.S. Army, 1952-54. Recipient cert. of appreciation, State of Fla., Tallahassee, 1972; Demolay Cross of Honor, Internat. Coun., Kansas City, Mo., 1973; cert. of commendation, State of Fla., 1972. Mem. NRA (life), Fla. Assn. State Troopers (legis. chmn. retirees 1987), V.F.W., Jacksonville Pistol Club (pres. 1968-72), Marion Dunn Masonic Lodge, Elks, Sons Am. Revolution, Sons Confederate Vets., Mil. Order Stars and Bars, Fraternal Order Police, Scottish Rite, Nobles Mistic Shrine (Ambassador-at-large). Republican. Methodist. Home: 461 High Meadow Tr Cleveland GA 30528

LEWIS, RICHARD HARLOW, urologist; b. San Diego, May 14, 1951; s. Charles William Jr. and Gene (Harlow) L.; m. Deanna Elma Boggs, March 14, 1950; children: Richard Harlow Jr., Sara-Grace Dean. BS, Guilford Coll., 1973; MD, Duke U., 1977. Intern Bethesda (Md.) Naval Hosp., 1977-78, residence, 1978-82, chief urology, 1982-85; pvt. practice McIver Clinic, Jacksonville, Fla., 1985—; mng. ptnr. McIver Clinic divsn. Urology Clinic of Fla., Jacksonville, 1994—. Mem. Christian Coalition, Duval County, Fla., 1987—; Rep. precinct rep., Duval County, 1987-90. Lt. comdr. USNR, 1973-85. Winner, Karl Storz Endoscope Photography Contest Karl Storz Corp., 1983. Fellow ACS, Am. Soc. Laser Medicine Surgery, Am. Bd. Laser Surgery, S.E. Surg. Soc.; mem. Am. Urol. Assn. Home: 4900 Arapahoe Ave Jacksonville FL 32210-8336 Office: McIver Clinic 710 Lomax St Jacksonville FL 32204-4004

LEWIS, RICHARD JAY, marketing educator, university dean; b. Marion, Ohio, July 14, 1933; s. Harley Franklin and Christina Mary (Anderson) L.; m. Patricia Ruth Montgomery, Sept. 17, 1955; children: Pamela Kay, Gregory Carl, Scott Alan. BS, Miami U., Oxford, Ohio, 1957, MBA, 1959; DBA, Mich. State U., 1964. Mem. faculty Mich. State U., East Lansing, 1964-93, prof. mktg., 1970-93, dean Coll. Bus., 1975-93; dean Faculty of Bus. U. Nigeria, Enugu, 1966-67; mem. faculty, dean Coll. Mgmt., N.C. State U., Raleigh, 1993—; bd. dirs. First of Mich. Corp., Detroit, First of Mich. Capital Corp., Am. Assembly Collegiate Schs. Bus. Author: Logistical Information System for Marketing Analysis, 1970, (with B. von H. Gilmer) Industrial and Organizational Psychology, 1971. Bd. dirs. Edward W. Sparrow Hosp., 1985—. Served with U.S. Army, 1953-55. Decorated Commendation medal. Mem. Am. Mktg. Assn., Lansing Regional C. of C. (bd. dirs. 1980-83), Am. Assembly Collegiate Schs. Bus. (pres. elect 1990, pres. 1991), Golden Key, Sigma Xi, Beta Gamma Sigma (bd. govs. 1976-82, nat. pres. 1980-82), Sigma Beta Delta (exec. coun.), Omicron Delta Epsilon. Home: 6100 Heatherstone Dr Raleigh NC 27606-8701 Office: NC State U Coll Mgmt Raleigh NC 27606-8614

LEWIS, ROBERT EARL, city traffic engineer; b. Suffolk, Va., Dec. 19, 1962; s. Floyd Benjamin and Carol Jean (Darden) L.; m. Rachel Ann Wright. BS in Engring., Va. Poly. Inst. and State U., 1985. Engring. technician Va. Dept. Transp., Suffolk, 1986-87; city traffic engr. City of Suffolk, 1987—. Vol. com. chmn. Suffolk Peanut Fest, 1987—; asst. scoutmaster Boy Scouts Am., Suffolk, 1990—. Mem. Internat. Mcpl. Signal Assn., Am. Soc. Agrl. Engrs., Inst. Transp. Engrs. Baptist. Office: City of Suffolk 441 Market St Suffolk VA 23434

LEWIS, ROBERT HENRY, lay worker; b. Chillicothe, Tex., Oct. 16, 1921; s. William Arnet and Minnie Easter (Stuckey) L.; m. Miriam Agnes Kothgassner, Mar. 10, 1946; children: Cindy Kaye Lewis Shaw, Pamela Jo Lewis Owens. BSin Elec. Engring., Tex. Tech U., 1952; postgrad., U. Ala., 1965-70. Registered elec. engr. Tex., Ala. Retired engr., 1981; treas. Willowbrook Bapt. Ch., Huntsville, Ala., 1981—; Deacon Willowbrook Bapt. Ch., 1981. Mem. Rep. Presdl. Task Force. With U.S. Army, 1942-46. Mem. IEEE, Nat. Assn. Investors Corp., Nat. Assn. Investment Clubs (pres. Ala. coun.). Home: PO Box 220 Laceys Spring AL 35754-0220 Office: Willowbrook Bapt Ch 7625 Bailey Cove Rd SE Huntsville AL 35802-2759

LEWIS, ROBERT KAY, JR., fundraising executive; b. Danville, Ky., Aug. 10, 1935; s. Robert K. and Mona (Hyden) L.; m. Wendy Gardiner, June 18, 1960; children: Mary Elizabeth, Mona Hyden, Robert K. III. BA, Ctr. Coll., Danville, 1957; MS, George Washington U., 1972. Advanced through ranks to lt. U.S. Navy, 1958-63; alumni/annual giving dir. Ctr. Coll., 1963-67; served to capt. U.S. Navy, 1967-81; alumni/pub. affairs dir. Ctr. Coll., 1981-83; pub. affairs dir. Va. Tech., Blacksburg, 1983-87; sr. v.p. Host Comm., Lexington, 1987-89; pres. Ky. C. of C., Frankfort, 1990, Global Advancement, Lexington, Ky., 1991—. Trustee Severn Sch., Severna Park, Md., 1979-83; bd. visitors McCallie Sch., Chattanooga, 1983-86; bd. dirs. Ky. Advocates for Higher Edn., Lexington, 1990—. Mem. Nat. Soc. Fund Raising Execs. (bd. dirs. Lexington chpt. 1991—), Henry Clay Found. (bd. dirs. Lexington, 1994—), Nat. Press Club, Coun. Advancement and Support of Edn. (Ky. bd. dirs. 1991—). Presbyterian. Home: Forest Hill Farm 2667 Lexington Rd Danville KY 40422 Office: Global Advancement 333 W Vine St Ste 300 Lexington KY 40507-1626

LEWIS, RON, congressman; b. Greenup County, Ky., Sept. 14, 1946; m. Kayi Gambill, 1966; children: Ronald Brent, Allison Faye. Student, Morehead State U.; BA in History and Polit. Sci., U. Ky., 1969; MA in Higher Edn., Morehead State U., 1981; student, USN Officer Candidate Sch. Ordained to ministry Bapt. Ch. With Ky. Hwy. Dept., Ea. State Hosp.; with sales various cos.; tchr. Watterson Coll., 1980-85; pastor White Mills Bapt. Ch.; owner small bus. Elizabethtown, Ky.; mem. 103d-104th Congresses from 2d Ky. Dist., 1994—; mem. mil. procurement and mil. pers. subcoms., nat. security com., mem. risk mgmt. and splty. crops and resource conservation, rsch. and forestry subcoms., agr. com. Past pres. Hardin and Larue County Jail Ministry. Named Guardian of Srs.' Rights, Tax Fairness Srs.; honoree U.S. Term Limits, League Pvt. Property Rights, Coun. Citizens Against Govt. Waste, Nat. Fed. Ind. Bus. Mem. Severus Valley Ministerial Assn., Elizabethtown C. of C. Office: US Ho of Reps 223 Cannon House Office Bld Washington DC 20515-1702

LEWIS, RONALD CHAPMAN, record company executive; b. Louisville, Aug. 20, 1950; s. William June and Mildres A. (Lewis) Miller; m. Laquetta W. Lewis; 1 child, Keith. A. in Music, Jeff Community Coll., Louisville, 1975. Pres. Mr. Wonderful Prodns., Inc., Louisville, 1984—, Louisville Assn. Music Performers, 1987—. Served with USN, 1969-71. Home and Office: Mr Wonderful Prodns Inc 1730 Kennedy Rd Louisville KY 40216-5110

LEWIS, RONALD WALTER, artist; b. Atlanta, Jan. 27, 1945. BS, U. Montevallo, 1967. Exhibited with Am. Watercolor Soc., Water Color U.S.A., Dixieland Watercolor and Drawing Soc., Rocky Mountain Watercolor Soc., others; one-man shows include Istean Gallery, Tokyo, 1993; represented in permanent collections Birmingham (Ala.) Mus. Art, Columbus (Ga.) Mus., Fine Arts Mus. South, Mobile, Ala.; illustrator: (books) My Country Roads, Papa's Old Trunk.

LEWIS, RONALD WAYNE, lawyer; b. Buffalo, Wyo., May 13, 1943; s. George Weber and Marianne (Parsons) L.; m. Melissa Cory Byron, June 3, 1983; children: Stephen Lee, Joshua Byron, Kristopher Byron, Katherine Byron. AB, Dartmouth Coll., Hanover, N.H., 1965; MAT in French, Harvard U., 1969; JD, U. Miss., Oxford, 1978. Bar: Miss. 1978, U.S. Dist. Ct. (no. dist.) Miss. 1978, U.S. Ct. Appeals (5th cir.) 1979, U.S. Dist. Ct. (so. dist.) Miss. 1985, U.S. Supreme Ct. 1990, U.S. Claims Ct. 1991. Pvt. practice Oxford, 1978-81; assoc. Hill, Lewis & Bell, Oxford, 1981-83, Hill & Lewis, Oxford, 1983-86, Holcomb, Dunbar, Connell, Chaffin & Willard, Oxford, 1986-88; pvt. practice Oxford, 1988—; CJA criminal def. tng. coord. No. Jud. Dist., Miss., 1991—, CJA panel rep. to nat. confs., 1995, 96. Mem. Lafayette County Dem. Exec. Com., Oxford, 1985-96, chmn., 1987-91; bd. dirs. ACLU of Miss., 1989-90, Miss. Assn. for Children with Learning Disabilities, 1990-91. Mem. ABA, ATLA, Nat. Assn. Criminal Def. Lawyers, Miss. Trial Lawyers, Miss. Bar, Lafayette County Bar Assn., Am. Inn. of Ct. Ill. (bencher). Office: 1001 Jackson Ave E Oxford MS 38655-3905

LEWIS, RUSSELL CARL, JR., family nurse practitioner; b. Charlotte, N.C., Nov. 8, 1946. AS, Cen. Piedmont Community Coll., Charlotte, 1972. Cert. family nurse practitioner, BCLS, ACLS. Adminstr., healthcare provider, owner Downtown Med. Ctr., Charlotte; staff nurse, mem. emergency room computer com. Carolinas Med. Ctr., Charlotte; prin. in design of downtown med. ctr. With USNR, 1964-70.

LEWIS, TED ADAM, political science educator; b. Fort Worth, Tex., Mar. 7, 1960; s. Lawrence Adams and Josephine (Brooks) L. BA, Tex. Wesleyan U., 1982; MS, U. North Tex., 1990. Assoc. prof. polit. sci. Collin County C.C., McKinney, Tex., 1988-91, prof. polit. sci., 1991—, evening adminstr., 1992—; coord. polit. sci. dept. Collin County C.C., Frisco, Tex., 1995—; host call in radio show Denton County Party Line, 1990-94; panelist talk show To the Point, 1993—; mem. Collin County C.C. Faculty Senate, 1991—. Author: Texas Democratic County Chairs Manual, 1994. Campaign dir. Denton County Dem. Party, 1988, chmn., 1990—; mem. committeeman Tex. Dem. Exec. Com., 1994—; pres. Tex. Dem. County Chairs Assn., 1994—; pres. Young Dem. Club, Tex. Wesleyan U., 1982. Elliot R. Richardson scholar U. North Tex., 1987. Mem. Denton C. of C., Denton Rotary Club, Tex. Jr. Coll. Tchrs. Assn., Phi Theta Kappa, Pi Kappa Alpha (pres. 1981-82), Pi Sigma Alpha (pres. 1981). Baptist. Home: 1245 Dallas Dr Denton TX 76205 Office: Collin County C C Preston Ridge Campus 9700 Wade Blvd Frisco TX 75034

LEWIS, THOMAS ALLISON, writer; b. Farmington, Minn., May 20, 1942; s. Myron David and Mildred Louise (Gronnerud) L.; children: Jason, Kimberly, Andrew. BA, U. Sask., 1963. Gen. assignment reporter WTOP Radio and TV, Washington, 1965-66, 68-69; editor, pub. Shenandoah Valley weekly newspaper, New Market, Va., 1970-73; dir. news and pub. affairs, anchor WHSV-TV, Harrisonburg, Va., 1973-78; sr. editor Time-Life Books, Alexandria, Va., 1980-85; contract editor Time-Life Books, Alexandria, 1985—. Author: The Shenandoah in Flames: The Valley Campaign of 1964-65, 1987, The Guns of Cedar Creek, 1988, For King and Country: The Maturing of George Washington 1748-1760, 1993; roving editor: Nat. Wildlife and Internat. Wildlife Mags., Nat. Wildlife Fedn., 1985—; editor: Civil War Mag., 1988-93; contbr. articles to profl. jours. Trustee Cedar Creek Battlefield Found.; chmn. Civil War Soc., 1989-93; founder, convener Commonwealth Coalition. With U.S. Army, 1966-68. Decorated Army Commendation medal, 1968; recipient George Washington Medallion for editorial writing Freedoms Found. at Valley Forge, 1972, Artie award Shenandoah Valley Arts Coun., 1989. Home: 1542 Dry Run Rd Fort Valley VA 22652

LEWIS, THOMAS PROCTOR, law educator; b. Ashland, Ky., Mar. 26, 1930; s. Blaine and Hallie Maud (Heal) L.; m. Nancy Ann Magruder, Sept. 27, 1949; children: Jean, Catherine, Jennifer, Blaine. A.B., U. Ky., 1959, LL.B., 1954; S.J.D., Harvard U., 1964. Asst. prof. law U. Ky., 1957-59, assoc. prof., 1959-60, prof., 1961-65, acad. asst. to pres., 1964-65, dean Coll. of Law, 1976-82, prof., 1982—; prof. law U. Minn., 1965-72, Boston U., 1972-76; of counsel Wyatt, Tarrant & Combs, 1982-86 ; vis. prof. U. Chgo., 1962, U. Wash., 1963-64; labor arbitrator, 1965—; spl. justice Ky. Supreme Ct., 1995. Author: (with R. Levy, P. Martin) Social Welfare and the Individual, 1971; contbr. articles to law jours. Served with USNR, 1954-57. Mem. Ky., Mass. bar assns., Nat. Acad. Arbitrators, Am. Law Inst. Office: U Ky Law Coll Lexington KY 40506

LEWIS, TOLA ETHRIDGE, JR., state agency administrator, martial arts instructor; b. Columbia, S.C., July 7, 1945; s. Tola Ethridge and Hettie (Willets) L.; m. Frances Rebecca Coggins, July 10, 1965 (div. Jan., 1978); m. Martha E. Cartwright, Mar. 24, 1978; children: Toby Isaac, Charles Andrew. AB, East Carolina U., 1972. Dist. vets. svc. officer N.C. Div. Vets. Affairs, Elizabeth City, 1972—; instr. karate. Contbr. articles to martial arts jours. With USN, 1964-66, retired USNR, 1989. Mem. Am. Legion (comdr. dist., chmn. oratorical contest), Nat. Karate and Jujitsu Union (dir. 1989—). Republican. Baptist. Home: PO Box 1331 Elizabeth City NC 27906-1331 Office: NC Div Vets Affairs 1023 Us Highway 17 S Ste 2 Elizabeth City NC 27909-9666

LEWIS, VERNA MAE, physiatrist; b. Texarkana, Tex., May 31, 1951; d. John Davis and Gladys Vern (Brown) L.; m. Samuel Dubois Robinson, Feb. 20, 1988. BS in Biology, U. Houston, 1972, MS in Microbial and Plant Biochemistry, 1974; MD, Baylor Coll. of Medicine, 1984. Diplomate Am. Bd. Phys. Medicine and Rehab. Rsch. asst. U. Houston, 1973; sr. rsch. asst. Baylor Coll. of Medicine/VA Hosp., Tex. Med. Ctr., Houston, 1975-80; resident in phys. medicine and rehab. Mayo Grad. Sch. of Medicine, Rochester, Minn., 1984-88; chairperson, med. dir. dept. phys. medicine and rehab. Lewis-Gale Hosp., Salem, Va., 1988—; student asst. dept. edn. U. Houston, 1972-79; guest lectr. annual meeting Am. Coll. Rheumatology, 1990; med. dir., chairperson, Lewis-Gale Regional Rehab. Ctr., Salem.; mem. instl. rev. bd. Lewis-Gale Clinic. Contbr. articles to profl. jours. Active exec. com., utilization rev. com. Lewis-Gale Hosp., 1990—, trustee, 1991—; bd. dirs. Tomorrow's Teacher's Program, Roanoke, Va., 1991, ARC, Roanoke, 1991, Girl Scouts Am., Roanoke, 1993; active Va. Med. Polit. Action Com., Richmond, Va., 1993, Roanoke Continentals. Microbiology Teaching fellow U. Houston, 1973, Immunology Teaching fellow, 1974, Gen. Biology Teaching fellow, 1974, Teaching and Rsch. fellow, 1973-74; Rsch. grantee Mayo Found., 1986-88. Fellow Am. Acad. phys. Medicine and Rehab. (Am. Cong. Rehab. Medicine); mem. AMA, Nat. Med. Assn., Am. Med. Women's Assn., Va. Soc. Phys. Medicine and Rehab., Assn. Acad. Physiatrists, Roanoke Acad. Medicine. Baptist. Office: Lewis Gale Hosp 1900 Electric Rd Salem VA 24153-7456

LEWIS, WILLIAM HEADLEY, JR., manufacturing company executive; b. Washington, Sept. 29, 1934; s. William Headley and Lois Maude (Bradshaw) L.; BS in Metall. Engring., Va. Poly. Inst., 1956; postgrad. Grad. Sch. Bus. Adminstrn., Emory U., 1978; m. Carol Elizabeth Cheek, Apr. 22, 1967; children: Teresa Lynne, Bret Cameron, Charles William, Kevin Marcus. Various positions Lockheed Corp., Marietta, Ga. 1956-1987; mgr. engring. tech. services, 1979-83, dir. engring. Getex div., 1983-86; gen. mgr. Inspection Systems div. Lockheed Air Terminal, Inc., 1986-87; pres., CEO Measurement Systems Inc., Atlanta, 1987—; chmn. Lockheed Corp. Task Force on NDE, 1980-86; mem. Com. to Study Role of Advanced Tech. in Improving Reliability and Maintainability of Future Weapon Systems, Office of Sec. of Def., 1984-85; co-founder, dir., exec. v.p. Applied Tech. Svcs., Inc., 1967—; pres. CEO Applied Tech. Fin. Corp., Atlanta, 1993—; mng. ptnr. Tech. Fin. Co., LLC; lectr. grad. studies and continuing edn. Union Coll., Schenectady, 1977-82. Served to 1st lt. USAF, 1957-60. Registered profl. engr., Calif. Fellow Am. Soc. for Non-destructive Testing (nat. dir. 1976-78, chmn. nat. tech. council 1977-78, chmn. aerospace com. 1972-74, nat. nominating com. 1982-83, 1984-85); mem. Am. Inst. Aeronautics and Astronics, Am. Soc. for Metals, Nat. Mgmt. Assn., NAS (mem. com. on compressive fracture 1981-83), Brotherhood of the Knights of the Vine, St. Ives Country Club, Country Club Sapphire Valley. Editor: Prevention of Structural Failures: The Role of Fracture Mechanics, Failure Analysis, and NDT, 1978; patentee detection apparatus for structural failure in aircraft. Home: 3127 St Ives Country Club Pky Duluth GA 30155-2038 Office: 2262 Northwest Pky Ste B Marietta GA 30067-9306

LEWIS, WILLIAM S., JR., educator; b. Moultrie, Ga., Sept. 8, 1949; s. William S. Sr. and Helen Grace (Lasseter) L.; m. Ann Ruth Burns, Dec. 11, 1971; children: William S. III, Annie Burns, John Burns. BBA in Acctg., Valdosta State U., 1974, MEd in Bus. Edn., 1991; MEd in Bus. Edn., Valdosta State U., 1991; EdD in Occupl. Edn., U. Ga., 1994. V.p. Lewis Supply Co., Moultrie, Ga., 1974-88; pres. Century 21 Lewisco Realty, Moultrie, 1988-89; computer instr. Grady County Sch. Sys., Cairo, Ga., 1989-90; acctg. instr. Southeastern Tech. Inst., Vidalia, Ga., 1990-95, dir. instrn., 1996—; vice chmn. Lewis-Smith Supply, Dothan, Ala., 1975-82; mem. adv. bd. bus. programs Vidalia H.S., 1994—. Deacon First Bapt. Ch., Vidalie, 1993—. Sgt. USMC, 1968-70. Named Tchr. of Yr. 1st dist. Ga. Bus. Edn. Assn., 1992-93, Commr.'s Outstanding Instr. Ga. Dept. Tech. and Adult Edn., 1995. Mem. ASCD, Am. Vocat. Assn., Nat. Bus. Edn. Assn., Am. Ednl. Rsch. Assn., Lions, Kappa Delta Pi, Omicron Tau Theta. Office: Southeastern Tech Inst 3001 E 1st St Vidalia GA 30474

LEWTER, ALICE JENKINS, history and political science educator; b. Roanoke Rapids, N.C., Aug. 16, 1946; d. Thomas George and Parthenia (Jones) Jenkins; m. Dennis Lacon Lewter, Oct. 3, 1980; 1 child, Sonya Desett Jenkins. BA, N.C. Ctrl. U., 1969, MA, 1975; EdD, N.C. State U., 1995. Cert. tchr. adult and c.c. adminstrn. Instr. Halifax County (N.C.) Schs., 1969-70, Durham (N.C.) City Schs., 1970-72; adminstrv. asst. Found. for Rsch. and Edn. in Sickle Cell Disease, N.Y.C., 1972-73; instr. history/polit. sci. Halifax C.C., Weldon, N.C., 1973—, divsn. chair, 1986-90; program dir. MSIP U.S. Dept. Edn., Washington, 1986-89; adj. prof. Chowan Coll., Murfreesboro, N.C., 1994—; advisor African-Am. Soc., Weldon, 1990-93. Coauthor: American History: An Introduction, 1996. Judge Precinct #11, Bd. of Elections, Halifax County, 1978-87; coord. 5-A-Day program Black Chs. United for Better Health, Raleigh, 1992—. Named Educator of the Yr., Halifax-Northampton Opportunities Indsl. Corp., 1994; U.S. Dept. Edn. Minority Sci. Improvement grantee, 1986-89. Mem. Am. Coll. and Univ. Women, Am. Assn. Polit. Scientists, Am. Assn. Women in C.C.'s, The Smithsonian Club, Alpha Kappa Alpha. Democrat. Baptist. Home: 120 Carmichael Cir Roanoke Rapids NC 27870 Office: Halifax Community College PO Drawer 809 Weldon NC 27890

LEWTER, HELEN CLARK, elementary education educator; b. Millis, Mass., Jan. 14, 1936; d. Waldimar Kenville and Ida Mills (Currier) Clark; m. Alvin Council Lewter, June 18, 1966; children: Lois Ida, David Paul, Jonathan Clark. BA, U. Mass., 1958; MS, Old Dominion U., 1978. Post-grad. profl. cert. reading specialist, sociology, elem. grades 1-7. Tchr. Juniper Hill Sch., Framingham, Mass., 1960-63, Aragona Elem. Sch., Virginia Beach, Va., 1963-65, Park Elem., Chesapeake, Va., 1965-67; edn. specialist Riverview Sch., Portsmouth, Va., 1977-78; reading tchr. Truitt Jr. H.S., Chesapeake, 1979-83; reading resource tchr. Southeastern Elem., Chesapeake, 1983-86; tchr. Deep Creek Elem. Sch., Chesapeake, 1986—; pers. task force Chesapeake (Va.) Pub. Schs., 1984-85, textbook adoption com., 1984-85, employee handbook com., 1986-87, K-6 writing curriculum com., 1988-89. Tchr., workshop leader, dir., mem. various coms. Fairview Heights Bapt. Ch., Deep Creek Bapt. Ch., Va. So. Bapt. Retreats, 1968—; mem. mayor's adv. coun. City of Chesapeake, Va., 1988-89; mem. summer missionary Va. So. Bapts., 1993; active PTA. Mem. NEA, Va. Edn. Assn., Chesapeake Edn. Assn., Chesapeake Reading Assn. (v.p., pres., honor and merit coun., chmn. various coms.), Internat. Reading Assn., Va. Reading Assn., Delta Kappa Gamma (legis. chmn.), Kappa Delta Pi, Phi Kappa Phi. Republican. Home: 428 Plummer Dr Chesapeake VA 23323-3116 Office: Deep Creek Elem Sch 2809 Forehand Dr Chesapeake VA 23323-2005

LEX, ANGELA KAY, oncological nurse; b. Ft. Worth, July 6, 1963; m. Lamar M. Lex, Nov. 13, 1982. Student, Mesa (Ariz.) Community Coll., Tex. Woman's U.; BSN cum laude, U. N.D., 1987. RN, Tex. Staff oncology charge nurse Bethania Regional Health Care Ctr., Wichita Falls, Tex., 1988-89; staff nurse Hospice of Wichita Falls, Inc., 1989-91; quality resource mgr. Bethania Regional Health Care Ctr., Wichita Falls, Tex., 1991-92; RN supr. Sr. Life Care, Inc., Arlington, Tex., 1994-95; staff nurse, pres. Expressly Natural, Ft. Worth, 1994—.

LI, CHUNG-LI JASON, scientist; b. L.A., Oct. 28, 1960; s. Ching-Chung Li and Shiu-Fong Yang; m. Chi-Yin Gina Wu, Sept. 21, 1990; children: Catherine Y.F. Li, Marian J.C. Li. BS in Pharmacy, Taipei Med. Coll., 1984; PhD in Pharm. Scis., U. Fla., 1993. Postdoctoral rsch. assoc. U. Nebr. Med. Ctr., Omaha, 1993-95, U. Fla., St. Augustine, 1995—. Author publs. in field. Mem. Internat. Soc. for Study of Xenobiotics, AAAS, Am. Assn.

Pharm. Scientists. Office: The Whitney Lab/Univ Fla 9505 Oceanshore Blvd Saint Augustine FL 32086-8610

LI, HUA HARRY, computer scientist; b. Tianjin, People's Republic of China, Nov. 22, 1956; came to U.S., 1982; s. Hua Sheng and Bao Ai Li; m. Maiying Lu, Nov. 4, 1982; children: Alen Lee, Kevin Lee. BS in Elec. and Computer Engring., Tianjin U., 1982; MSECE, U. Iowa, 1984, PhD in ECE, 1989. Lectr. Tianjin U., 1982; asst. prof. computer science Tex. Tech U., Lubbock, 1989-95, assoc. prof. computer sci., 1995—; computer cons., 1990—. Author, editor: Vision Computing with VLSI Circuits, 1994, Fuzzy Logic and Intelligent Systems, 1995, Video Compression, 1996, (prototype system) Realtime Fuzzy Controller, 1994 (Neural Network award). Mem. IEEE. Home: 5102 78th St Lubbock TX 79424 Office: Tex Tech U Computer Sci Dept University Ave Lubbock TX 79409

LI, SHU, business executive. Chief rsch. officer Polytronics Inc., Richardson, Tex. Office: Polytronics Inc 805 Alpha Dr Richardson TX 75081

LIAN, ERIC CHUN-YET, hematologist, educator; b. Tainan Hsien, Taiwan, China, Nov. 11, 1938. Student, Nat. Taiwan U. Sch. of Medicine, 1957-64, MD, 1964. Intern Newark City Hosp., 1965-66; resident in internal medicine U.S. VA Hosp., N.Y.C., 1966-68; fellow in clin. hematology D.C. Gen. Hosp., Georgetown U. Svc., 1968-69; rsch. assoc. Beth Israel Hosp., Harvard Med. Sch., Boston, 1971-73; hematology rsch. fellow U. Miami, Fla., 1969-71, asst. prof. medicine, 1973-78, assoc. prof. medicine, 1978-87, prof. medicine, 1987—; surgeon Army of Nationalist China, 1964-65; rsch. dir. Jon Eric Hemophilia Clinic, 1973-75; staff physician VA Med. Ctr., Jackson Meml. Hosp., U. Miami Hosp., 1973—; dir. hemostasis lab. U. Miami, 1976—, Comprehensive Hemophilia Diagnostic and Treatment Ctr., Miami, 1976—; cons. TTP Working Com., NIH, 1986, mem. hematology study sect. grant rev., 1992; mem. Peer Rev. Sci. Com., 1992—; ad hoc referee in field. Contbr. articles to profl. jours. Mem. AAAS, ACP, Am. Heart Assn. (coun. thrombosis 1983—), Am. Chem. Soc., Am. Soc. Hematology, Am. Fedn. Clin. Rsch., Am. Soc. Biochemistry and Molecular Biology, Internat. Soc. Thrombosis and Hemostasis, World Fedn. Hemophilia, Fla. Med. Assn., Dade County Med. Assn. Office: U Miami Divsn Hematology/Oncology 1475 NW 12th Ave Miami FL 33136-1002 also: U Miami Sch Medicine PO Box 016960 Miami FL 33101 also: VA Med Ctr 1201 NW 16th St Miami FL 33125-1624

LIAN, KARL, corporate educator; b. Falam, Burma, Mar. 29; came to U.S., 1981; s. Lal Tin Khup and Khuang Thluai. BS, Ga. State U., 1985; MS, Fla. Internat. U., 1989; PhD, Va. Tech. U., 1995. Gen. mgr. Athens Pizza & Restaurants, Atlanta, 1981-88; mgr. The Ritz-Carlton Hotels, Atlanta, 1989-91, Donaldson Brown Hotel, 1992-93; prof. Lynn U., Boca Raton, Fla., 1993-94, Ga. State U., Atlanta, 1994-95; exec. v.p., COO Internat. Hosp. & Tourism Inst., Atlanta, 1995—; adv. UN, N.Y.C., 1994—. Author: International Hospitality Tourism Dictionary, 1996. Mem. Am. Hotel & Motel Assn. (found. award 1985), Mtg. Profls. Internat. Assn. (grantee 1994), Profl. Conv. Mgmt. Assn., Travel & Tourism Rsch. Assn. (pres., chmn. 1992-94). Office: IHTI PO Box 620162 Atlanta GA 30362

LIANG, QINGJIAN JIM, petroleum engineer; b. Dalian, China, Apr. 18, 1957; came to U.S., 1988; s. Jishun Liang and Shuzhen Sui; m. Huang Xiaozhong, Apr. 14, 1983; 1 child, Zheng Liang. BS, Daqing (China) Petroleum Inst., 1982; MS, Mont. Coll. Mineral Sci./Tech., 1989; DEng, La. Tech. U., 1993. Drilling engr. Daqing No. 3 Drilling Co., Daqing, 1982-87; rsch. asst. La. Tech. U., Ruston, 1989-93; divsn. engr. Sonat Offshore Drilling Inc., Morgan City, La., 1993—. Assoc. mem. SPE. Office: Offshore Turnkey Ventures Inc Corporate Plaza 110 Capital Dr Ste 100 Lafayette LA 70508

LIAO, WARREN SHAU-LING, biochemistry and molecular biology educator; b. Tainan, Republic of China, Nov. 22, 1951; came to U.S., 1969; s. Ting-Chung and Chun-Yu (Hou) L.; m. Jennifer Yueh-Chin, Dec. 29, 1984. BS, Pa. State U., State College, 1974; MS, Pa. State U., Hershey, 1976, PhD, 1980. Postdoctoral fellow Hershey Med. Ctr. Pa. State U., 1980-81, Stanford (Calif.) U., 1981-85; vis. scientist Imperial Cancer Rsch. Fund, London, 1985; asst. prof. U. Tex. M.D. Anderson Cancer Ctr., Houston, 1985-92, assoc. prof. biochemistry and molecular biology, 1992—; vis. prof. Beijing Med. Sch., 1988, Académica Sinica, Shanghai, 1988. Mem. AAAS, Am. Microbiology Soc. Office: MD Anderson Cancer Ctr Dept Biochem & Mol Biology 1515 Holcombe Blvd Houston TX 77030

LIBBEY, DARLENE HENSLEY, artist, educator; b. La Follettee, Tenn., Jan. 9, 1952; d. Charles Franklin and Geneva (Chitwood) Hensley; children: Michael Damon McLaughlin, Marina Auston. BFA in Painting, San Francisco Art Inst., 1989; MFA in Painting/Drawing, U. Tenn., 1994. Grad. asst. Alliance of Ind. Colls., N.Y.C., 1989; gallery asst. Holley Solomon Gallery, N.Y.C., 1989; teaching assoc., instr. U. Tenn., Knoxville, 1991-94; lectr., instr. U. Tex.-Pan Am., 1994—, South Tex. Cmty. Coll., 1995—; curator Belleza Salon, Knoxville, 1993—; invitational rep. San Francisco Art Inst., N.Y. Studio Program, Alliance Ind. Colls., 1989; organizer Multi-Media Group Exhbn.; lectr., instr. South Tex. C.C., McAllen. One-woman shows include U. Tex.-Pan Am., 1995, 96; exhibited in group shows at San Francisco Art Inst., 1985, 86, 87, 88, 89, Pacific Ctr., San Francisco, 1988, alliance of Ind. Colls., N.Y.C., 1989, San Francisco Mus. Modern Art, 1990, Bluxom Studios, San Francisco, 1991, Gallery 1010, Knoxville, 1991, 92, Ewing Gallery, U. Tenn., Knoxville, 1991, 92, 93, 94, SUNY, Syracuse, 1992, Printers Mark, Knoxville, 1993, Unitarian Ch., Knoxville, 1993, Tomato Head, Knoxville, 1994, Belleza Salon, Knoxville, 1994, U. Pan Am., 1995, 96; group show Museo Historico de Reynosa, Tamalipus, Mex., 1996. Vol. San Francisco Mus. Modern Art, 1990-91; founding mem. Grad. Student Union, U. Tenn., Knoxville, 1993; vol. instr. Knox County Schs., Knoxville, 1992-93; vis. artist Marin County Schs., San Anselmo, Calif., 1989. Tuition scholar San Francisco Art Inst., 1987; materials grantee U. Tenn., 1993, grantee Buck Found., 1987-89. Mem. Coll. Art Assn. Democrat. Unitarian. Home: 1118 W Upas Ave Mcallen TX 78501 Office: U Tex-Pan Am Art Dept 1201 W University Dr Edinburg TX 78539-2909

LIBBY, GARY RUSSELL, museum director; b. Boston, June 7, 1944; s. Charles W. and Sylvia P. L. BA, U. Fla., 1967, MA (NDEA fellow), 1968; MA, Tulane U., 1972. Instr. English Tulane U., 1968-71; asst. prof. Stetson U., Deland, Fla., 1972-77, vis. prof., 1977-86; dir. Mus. Arts and Scis., Daytona Beach, Fla., 1977—; reviewer Inst. Mus. Svcs., mem. panel Mus. Assessment Program; reviewer Accreditation Commn. of Am. Assn. of Mus. Author: Two Centuries of Cuban Art, 1985; editor: Archipenko: Themes and Variations, 1989, Chihuly: Form From Fire, 1994 (Southeastern Mus. Conf. award 1994), A Century of Jewelry and Gems, 1995, Celebrating Florida, 1995. Trustee Cuban Found.; mem. visual arts panel, youth and children's mus. panel, sci. mus. panel A.D.A. statewide panel Fla. Arts Coun.; panelist Challenge Grant Program; panelist Cultural Instns. Program; mem. hist. mus. grants panel Fla. Divsn. History. Mem. Fla. Art Mus. Dirs. Assn. (govt. liaison 1990, pres. 1995-96), Fla. Assn. Mus. (bd. dirs. 1992—, sec. 1995-96), Fla. Cultural and Ednl. Alliance (bd. dirs. 1995), Am. Assn. Mus. (accreditation commn. 1994—). Home: 419 Jessamine Blvd Daytona Beach FL 32118-3740 Office: Mus of Arts & Scis 1040 Museum Blvd Daytona Beach FL 32114-4510

LIBERMAN, MICHAEL, metallurgist, researcher; b. Gomel, USSR, June 24, 1938; came to U.S., 1980; s. David Liberman and Tsivya Goldberg; m. Alla Itkin, Feb. 23, 1963; 1 child, Vladimir. MS, Poly. Inst., Minsk, USSR, 1961; PhD, Poly. Inst., Leningrad, USSR, 1974. Process engr. Machinery Plant, Gomel, 1961-63; sr. scientist Inst. of Alumnium, Leningrad, 1963-79; sr. rsch. assoc. N.J. Inst. Tech., Newark, 1980-81; metall. engr. Exxon Enterprises, Greer, S.C., 1981; metallurgist Steel Heddle Mfg. Co., Greenville, S.C., 1981-82, tech. svcs. mgr., 1982-87, chief metallurgist, 1987-89; R&D mgr. Memtec Am. Corp., Deland, Fla., 1989—; cons. Siege Corp., Greenville, 1981-83. Contbr. 30 articles to profl. jours.; patentee in field. Mem. ASTM, Am. Soc. Metals (abstractor), The Metall. Soc. Home: 1505 Covered Bridge Dr Deland FL 32724-7931

LICALZI, MICHAEL CHARLES, county official; b. Washington, May 12, 1949; s. Phillip S. Licalzi and Arlene L. (Hemphill) Webb; m. Patricia Ann Roth, Nov. 28, 1970; 1 child, Michael Scott. AAS in Computer Info. Systems, No. Va. C.C., 1990; BBA, Averett Coll., 1995. Wireman Traffic Signal Supply Corp., Alexandria, Va., 1973-91; field troubleshooter Hawkins Electric Co., Inc., College Park, Md., 1973-80; traffic signal field tech. Arlington County, Va., 1980—. Bd. dirs. Internat. Mcpl. Signal Assn. Edn. Found., Ft. Worth, 1995. With USN, 1967-71. Mem. Am. Pub. Works Assn., Mid. Atlantic Signal Assn. (pres. 1985-95), Am. Legion. Office: Arlington County Traffic 4300 S 29th St Arlington VA 22206

LICK, DALE WESLEY, academic administrator; b. Marlette, Mich., Jan. 7, 1938; s. John R. and Florence M. (Baxter) L. (dec.); m. Marilyn Kay Foster, Sept. 15, 1956; children: Lynette (dec.), Kitty, Diana, Ronald. BS with honors, Mich. State U., 1958, MS in Math, 1959; PhD in Math, U. Calif., Riverside, 1965. Research asst. physics Mich. State U., East Lansing, 1958; teaching asst. math. Mich. State U., 1959; instr., chmn. dept. math. Port Huron (Mich.) Jr. Coll., 1959-60; asst. to comptroller Mich. Bell Telephone Co., Detroit, 1961; instr. U. Redlands, 1961-63; teaching asst. math. U. Calif., Riverside, 1964-65; asst. prof. math. U. Tenn., Knoxville, 1965-67; postdoctoral fellow Brookhaven Nat. Lab., Upton, N.Y., 1967-68; assoc. prof. U. Tenn., 1968-69; assoc. prof., head dept. math. Drexel U., Phila., 1969-72; adj. assoc. prof. dept. pharmacology Med. Sch., Temple U., Phila., 1969-72; v.p. acad. affairs Russell Sage Coll., Troy, N.Y., 1972-74; prof. math. and computing scis. Old Dominion U., Norfolk, Va., 1974-78; also dean Old Dominion U. (Sch. Scis. and Health Professions); pres., prof. math. and computer sci. Ga. So. Coll., Statesboro, 1978-86; pres., prof. math. U. Maine, Orono, 1986-91; pres., prof. math. Fla. State U., Tallahassee, 1991-93, univ. prof., 1993—; Cert. in tng., mng. orgnl. change. Author: Fundamentals of Algebra, 1970; contbr. articles to profl. jours. Bd. dirs. Statesboro/Coll. Symphony, 1978-86, Statewide Health Coordinating Coun. Va., 1976-78; chmn. higher edn. adv. bd. Reorganized Ch. of Jesus Christ of Latter Day Sts., 1986—; mem. planning com. Bulloch Meml. Hosp., 1979-86; active Coastal Empire coun. Boy Scouts Am., 1982-86, Katalidin coun., 1986-91; bd. dirs. Health Care Ctrs. Am., Virginia Beach, Va., 1978, Ea. Va. Health Systems Agy., 1976-78; chmn., bd. dirs. Assembly Against Hunger and Malnutrition, 1977-78, pres., 1977-78. Mem. AAUP, AAAS, Am. Math. Soc., Math. Assn. Am., Am. Assn. Univ. Adminstrs., Am. Soc. Allied Health Professions, Am. Assn. State Colls. and Univs. (chmn. com. agr. resources and rural devel. 1981-86), Am. Assn. Higher Edn., Sigma Xi, Phi Kappa Phi, Pi Mu Epsilon (governing coun. 1972-77), Beta Gamma Sigma, Pi Sigma Epsilon. Mem., high priest Reorganized LDS Ch. Office: Learning Systems Inst 205 Dodd Hall Tallahassee FL 32306-4041

LICKLE, WILLIAM CAUFFIEL, banker; b. Wilmington, Del., Aug. 2, 1929; m. Renee Carpenter Kitchell, Nov. 24, 1950; children: Sydney L., Garrison duPont, Ashley L. O'Neil, Kemble L. O'Donnell. BA, U. Va., 1951, LLB, 1953. Bar: Va. 1953. Chmn., CEO Laird, Bissell & Meeds, Inc., 1952-73; sr. v.p., dir. Dean Witter & Co. Inc., 1973-77; chmn., CEO Del. Trust Co., Wilmington, 1977-88; chmn. J.P. Morgan Fla., 1989-93, J.P. Morgan Internat. Holdings, 1989-92; pres. Thomasson Grant & Lickle Pub., 1996—; vice chmn. M.P. Morgan Del., 1989-92; chmn. Register Transfer Co., 1963-65; bd. dirs. Marvin Palmer Assoc., Ashbridge Investment Mgmt. Bd. dirs., treas. Blue Cross-Blue Shield Del., 1963-68; commr. New Castle County (Del.) Airport, 1964-67, New Castle County Transp. Commn., 1967-69; bd. vice chmn., founder Better Bus. Bur. Del., 1966-72; hon. dir. Boys' Club Wilmington, 1963—; trustee Thomas Jefferson U., Phila., 1971-78, Med. Ctr. Del., 1965—, Breeder's Cup Ltd., Lexington, Ky., 1984-95, Winterhur Mus., 1989-94; mem. Pres. Reagan's Export Coun., 1988-89; pres. U. Va. Alumni Assn., 1987-94; spl. asst. Gov.'s Econ. Devel. for State of Del., 1987-91; bd. dirs. Raymond F. Kravis Ctr., Palm Beach, Fla., 1990-95. Clubs: Vicmead Hunt (Del.); Everglades, Bath and Tennis (Palm Beach, Fla.); Saratoga Golf and Polo, Reading Room (Saratoga, N.Y.); Springdale Hall (Camden, S.C.). Home: 568 Island Dr Palm Beach FL 33480-4747

LIDE, NEOMA JEWELL LAWHON (MRS. MARTIN JAMES LIDE, JR.), poet; b. Levelland, Tex., Apr. 1, 1926; d. Charles Samuel and Juel (Yeager) Lawhon; Secretarial cert. Draughon's Bus. Coll., 1943; student U. Tex., 1944-46; R.N., Jefferson-Hillman Sch. Nursing, 1950; m. Martin James Lide, Jr., Nov. 12, 1950; children: Martin James, III, Brooks Nathaniel, Gardner Lawhon. Writer column Baldwin Times, Bay Minette, Ala., 1964-68, Shades Valley Sun newspapers, Birmingham, Ala., 1974-75; v.p., sec. Martin J. Lide Assocs., Inc., Birmingham, 1977-81; R.N. supr. St. Martin's in the Pines, 1984.Mem. Mountain Brook Political Scis. Club, 1954; bd. Leagues of Women Voters, 1954-56; Pride of the Valley Sun Newspaper, 1954, Mem. (Pelham chapt.), Charter bd., (Sally Jones chapt.U.D.C., 1950), Ala. State bd., Children of the Am., Revolution, sr. pres., Reuben Rogers Soc., 1959-65; Good Citizens com. chmn., (William Speer chapt.), NSDR, ear, 1960, pres. advisory com., Cabana Girls Scouts coun., 1963-64. Mem. def. adv. com. Women in Services, for Ala., 1961-63; coordinator women's activities Nat. Vets. Day, Birmingham, 1961-68; diating guests, vets. award Dinner and the World Peace Luncheon, 1963-64; hon. mem. IV U.S. Army Corps, 1964; Original 1st chmn., an original 1st pres., Women Auxiliary for Patriotic Events, 1968; mem. exec. com., 1968-70; Charter mem., 1964; exec. bd. Women's Com. of 100 for Birmingham, 1964-65, 84-85; Best original column divsn., AAla. Press Assn. better Newspaper Contest, 1964-65, 66. PTA bd., Cherokee Bend Elementary Sch., 1971-72; spkr. (Poetry), Mountain Brook Junior High Sch.,(Videotape shown in English Classes), 1974 spkr. Arlington Hist. Assn., 1983; mem. Gorgas bd. U. Ala., Tuscaloosa, 1959. Recipient citation Merit, Muscular Dystrophy Assn. Am., 1961. Mem. Christian Women's Soc. Mountain Brook (bd. dirs. 1993-95), Nat. Soc. DAR (regent Princess Sehoy chpt. 1983-85, 91-92, chpt. spkr. 1988, 92, chpt. exec. bd. 1991-95), The Salvation Army Women's Auxiliary, Birmingham, 1995-96; Cauldron Club (spkr. 1989, 2d v.p. 1992-93, 95). Author: Home Sweet Homecoming, (musical skit),1954, (poetry) Instead of Sunset, 1973; (narrative) Life of Service-These are My Jewels, 1979; Music in the Wind - The Story of Lady Arlington, 1980; Brother James Bryan-Hope Lives Eternal, 1981; Music of the Soul, 1982; The Past and Psyche of Arlington, 1983, The Light Side of Life in the American Colonies, 1988, The American Woman, 1989, revised, 1992, The Lawhons of Texas, 1995. Home: 3536 Brookwood Rd Birmingham AL 35223-1446

LIDSTROM, PEGGY RAY, mental health administrator, psychotherapist; b. Oxford, N.C., Apr. 8, 1949; d. Robert Marsh and Margaret (O'Brian) Ray; m. Paul D. Lidstrom (div.); 1 child, Kristin. BA, Stratford Coll., Danville, Va., 1971; MSW, Norfolk (Va.) State U., 1979. Lic. clin. social worker, Va.; cert. social worker; diplomate in clin. social work. Coord. social work Tidewater Psychiat. Inst., Norfolk, 1983-85; dir. substance abuse Southside Community Svc. Bd., South Boston, Va., 1985-88; dir. mental health svcs. Hampton (Va.) Newport News Community Svcs. Bd., 1988-95; clin. mgr., psychotherapist Chessen and Assocs., Newport News, Va., 1995—; adj. prof. St. Leo Coll., Langley AFB, Hampton, Va. Named Boss of Yr., Am. Bus. Women's Assn., 1986; Va. Gov.'s Coun. on Substance Abuse grantee, 1988. Fellow Am. Bd. Managed Care Providers; mem. NASW, Peninsula Mental Health Assn. (pres. 1991-92, Rollins award 1996), Mental Health Assn. Va. (pres. 1996—), C.G. Jung Soc. of Tidewater. Quaker. Office: Chessen and Assocs 12420 Warwick Blvd Ste C Newport News VA 23606-3001

LIEBERMAN, LAURA CROWELL, arts administrator, artist, critic; b. Oak Ridge, Tenn., Apr. 7, 1952; d. Bernard and Lisbeth (Crowell) L.; m. William R. Gignilliat, III, Mar. 20, 1984; children: William R. Gignilliat, IV, Elizabeth Ann Gignilliat. BA in English Lit., Swarthmore Coll., 1974. Tchr. remedial reading Paulding County Schs., Dallas, Ga., 1974-75; critic, writer Atlanta, 1976-77, 89-92; artist-in-residence Atlanta Women's Art Collective, 1977-78; editor-in-chief Art Papers, Atlanta, 1979-84; arts editor So. Accents Mag., Atlanta, 1985-88; dir. Arts Clearinghouse Bur. Cultural Affairs, Atlanta, 1992—; publicist Gt. Am. Gallery, Atlanta, 1988-92; lectr. Ala. Attists Gallery, Montgomery, 1991; cons., juror, panelist and lectr. in field. Contbr. articles to Afterimage, Atlanta Mag., Am. Ceramics, Atlanta Jour.-Constn., Fulton County Daily Report, So. Homes, So. Accents, Southpoint, others. Bd. dirs., newsletter editor Whittier Mills Village Neighborhood, 1990-92; founding bd. dirs. S.E. Arts Exch., 1984-85; bd. dirs. Atlanta Art Workers Coallition, others. Home: 3 Spring Cir NW Atlanta GA 30318-1024

LIEBERMAN, PHILLIP LOUIS, allergist, educator; b. Memphis, Mar. 20, 1940; m. Barbara; children: Ryan, Lee, Jay. Student, London Sch. Econs., 1961; BA in Sociology, Tulane U., 1962; MD, U. Tenn., 1965. Intern City of Memphis Hosp. U. Tenn., 1965-66, asst. resident internal medicine, 1966-67, assoc. resident internal medicine, 1967-68, chief resident, 1968-69; fellow in allergy, immunology Northwestern U., Evanston, Ill., 1969-71; asst. prof., chief div. allergy, immunology U. Tenn., 1971-74, assoc. prof., chief div. allergy, immunology, 1974-79, prof., chief div. allergy, immunology, 1979—; instr. internal medicine U. Tenn., 1968-69; mem. exec. bd. Joint Coun. of Allergy & Immunology, 1985-90, AAAI rep., 1990; AAAI rep. Mothers for Asthmatics, 1990. Co-editor: Asthma Edition: Abstract-a-Card System, 1991—; contbr. numerous articles, abstracts to profl. publs.; author numerous presentations in field, book chpts., revs. Exec. bd. dirs. Asthma and Allergy Found. of Am., 1990—, mem. med. scientific coun., 1987, chmn., 1990—. Served to cpt. USAR, 1965-71. Mem. Am. Acad. Allergy (com. on alternative forms of therapy, 1980—), Am. Acad. Allergy and Immunology (exec. com. 1983-91, constitution and by-laws com. 1984-87, also chmn. 1985, undergraduate com. 1985, pres.-elect. 1987-88, pres. 1988-89, nominating com. 1987, also chmn. 1989, program com. 1987), Am. Coll. Allergists, Am. Assn. Allergists (sec. 1985), Am. Assn. Certified Allergists (2d v.p. 1986-87, pres. 1989-90), Am. Bd. Allergy and Immunology. Office: U Tenn 300 S Walnut Bend Rd Cordova TN 38018-7293 also: Allergy Assocs 920 Madison Ave Ste 909N Memphis TN 38103-3451

LIEBERMAN, ROBERT, radio chemist; b. Columbus, Ohio, Apr. 9, 1924; s. Benjamin Harry and Goldie (Pass) L.; m. Lorraine Harris Lieberman, Feb. 3, 1962; children: Bruce, Suzanne, Stephen. BA in Biochemistry, Ohio State U., 1948, MSc in Chemistry, 1952. Devel. chemist Hudson Foam Plastics, Yonkers, N.Y., 1953-55; polymer and radiochemist Battelle Meml. Inst., Columbus, 1955-67; chief phys. sci. U.S. EPA, Montgomery, Ala., 1967-88, quality assurance coord., 1967-88, sr. radiochemist, 1967-88; cons. radiochemist Sanford Cohen & Assocs., Montgomery, 1988—; cons. chemist S. Cohen & Assocs., Montgomery, 1988—. Editor: Radiochemistry Procedure Manual, 1984; contbr. articles to profl. jours.; inventor foamed polyester material. With AUS, 1943-45. Jewish. Home: 3707 Laconia Ln Montgomery AL 36111

LIEBERMAN, ROCHELLE PHYLLIS, relocation company executive; b. Bklyn., June 27, 1940; d. Solomon and Freda (Shapiro) Beller; m. Melvyn Lieberman, June 10, 1961; children—Eric Neil, Marc Evan. B.A., Bklyn. Coll., 1961; M.Ed., Duke U., 1977. Tchr., Bklyn. pub. schs., 1961-64; instr. Carolina Friends, Durham, N.C., 1967-70; grad. intern Duke U., Durham, 1974-75, faculty adviser, 1975-76; sales assoc. Kelly Matherly, Durham, 1978-81; pres. Shelli, Inc., Durham, 1981—. Treas. Duke Forest Assn., Durham, 1980-85. Mem. LWV, Durham and Chapel Hill Bd. Realtors, Women's Council of Realtors (sec. 1980-81), Duke U. Eye Ctr. adv. bd., Kappa Delta Pi. Republican. Jewish. Clubs: Duke Faculty, Duke Campus (Durham). Avocations: piano; walking; knitting; writing; reading. Office: Shelli Inc 1110 Woodburn Rd Durham NC 27705-5738

LIEBMANN, SEYMOUR W., construction consultant; b. N.Y.C., Nov. 1, 1928; s. Isidor W. and Etta (Waltzer) L.; m. Hinda Adam, Sept. 20, 1959; children: Peter Adam, David W. BSME, Clarkson U. (formerly Clarkson Coll. Tech.), 1948; grad. Indsl. Coll. Armed Forces, 1963, U.S. Army Command and Gen. Staff Coll., 1966, U.S. Army War Coll., 1971. Registered profl. engr., N.Y., Mass., Ga. Area engr. constrn. div. E.I. DuPont de Nemours & Co., Inc., 1952-54; constrn. planner Lummus Co., 1954-56; prin. mech. engr. Perini Corp., 1956-62; v.p. Boston Based Contractors, 1962-66; v.p. A.R. Abrams, Inc., Atlanta, 1967-74, pres., 1974-78, also bd. dirs.; founder Liebmann Assocs., Inc., Atlanta, 1979—; mem. nat. adv. bd. Am. Security Council. Author: Military Engineer Field Notes, 1953, Prestressing Miter Gate Diagonals, 1960; contbr. articles to publs. Mem. USO Council, Atlanta, 1968—, v.p., 1978, mem. exec. com., 1975-79; mem. Nat. UN Day Com., 1975; sr. army coord., judge Sci. Fair, Atlanta Pub. Schs., annually 1979-88, 92-96; asst. scoutmaster troop 298 Atlanta area council Boy Scouts Am., 1980-87, Explorer advisor, 1982-86, unit commr., 1985, dist. commr. North Atlanta Dist., Atlanta Area Council, 1988-90, asst. coun. commr., 1990-95, mem. faculty Commrs. Coll., 1985-88, 92, mem. North Atlanta Dist. com. BSA, 1996—; mem. alumni adv. com. Clarkson Coll. Tech., 1981—, alumni bd. govs., 1983-94, Disting. Alumni Golden Knight award, 1983; mem. exec. com., zoning chmn. neighbor planning unit City of Atlanta, 1982—, chmn., 1988, 95, 96, vice-chmn., 1989; pres. West Paces/Northside Neighborhood Assn., 1991—; apptd. civil engr. mem. to City of Atlanta Water and Sewer Appeals Bd., 1992—; apptd. mem. to Mayor's Bond Oversight Com. City of Atlanta, 1995—. Col. AUS Ret. Corps Engrs., 1948-52, Korea, Germany. Decorated Legion of Merit, Meritorious Service medal, U.S. Army Res. medal, 1975; elected to Old Guard of Gate City Guard, 1979; recipient cert. of Achievement Dept. Army, 1978, USO Recognition award, 1979, Order of Arrow award Boy Scouts Am., 1983, 87, Scouters Key Boy Scouts Am., 1988, North Atlanta Dist. Merit award Boy Scouts Am., 1989, Silver Beaver award, 1991, Disting. Commn. award, 1991, Engring. Profl. award Am. Inst. Plant Engrs., 1987; named Met. Atlanta Engr. of Yr. in Pvt. Practice Ga., 1991, Engr. of Yr. in Pvt. Practice, 1991. Fellow Soc. Am. Mil. Engrs. (bd. dirs. 1986—, chmn. readiness com. 1986-88, program chmn. Atlanta post 1980-81, v.p. 1982, pres. 1983, program chmn. 1988 nat. meeting, asst. regional v.p. for readiness So. region 1991—, Nat. award of Merit 1982-83, Atlanta post Leadership award 1988, life dir. Atlanta Post, 1994, elected nat. dir. 1994—, James Lucas Chair Atlanta Post, 1994, life mem.); mem. ASTM, NSPE, Am. Cons. Engrs. Coun. (state and nat. pub. rels. coms., nat. ethics com., state legis. liaison com.), Am. Concrete Inst., Soc. 1st U.S. Inf., Res. Officers Assn. (life mem.), U.S. Army War Coll. Found. (life mem.), Nat. Def. Univ. Found., U.S. Army War Coll. Alumni Assn. (life), Ga. Soc. Profl. Engrs. (bd. dirs. Buckhead chpt., state ethics com.), Engrs. Club Boston, Assn. U.S. Army, Def. Preparedness Assn., Am. Arbitration Assn. (panel arbitrators 1979—, constrn. adv. com. 1984—), Cobb C. of C., Downtown Atlanta Kiwanis, Mil. Order World Wars, Order of Engr., Army Engr. Assn. (life), Appalachian Trail Conf., Benyton Mackaye Trail Assn., Ga. Conservancy, Atlanta Hist. Soc., NRA. Republican. Jewish. Clubs: Ft. McPherson Officers; Ga. Appalachian Trail. Lodges: Masons (32 deg.), Shriners, Nat. Sojourners, Heros of '76, Elks, Civitan. Home: 3260 Rilman Dr NW Atlanta GA 30327-2224 Office: Ste 700 210 Interstate North Pky NW Atlanta GA 30339-2120

LIESENFELD, VINCENT JOSEPH, English language educator; b. St. Paul, Feb. 16, 1947; s. Vincent Edward and Agnes Lillian (Schaaf) L.; children: Patricia, Peter. BA summa cum laude, U. Minn., 1970; student, U. Reading, Eng., 1973-74; PhD, U. Wis., 1978; JD summa cum laude, Oklahoma City U., 1996. Writer Minn. State Employment Svc., St. Paul, 1970, U. Wis. News and Publs., Madison, 1972; asst. prof. English U. Okla., Norman, 1977-83, assoc. prof., 1983-96; vis. scholar UCLA, 1980; contbg. writer Am. Coll. Testing Program, Iowa City, 1982; rsch. cons. civil rights cases, Norman, 1982—. Author: The Licensing Act of 1737, 1984; editor: The Stage & the Licensing Act, 1981; contbr. articles and revs. to profl. jours. Vol. Spl. Olympics, Norman, 1990. Fulbright scholar, 1973-74; Woodrow Wilson fellow, 1969, W.A. Clark Libr. fellow, 1980, Rsch. fellow NEH, 1980-81; Rsch. grantee U. Okla., 1978, 79, 81. Mem. ABA, Am. Radio Relay League, Amnesty Internat., South Cen. Soc. for 18th Century Studies, (exec. bd. 1979-80), Greenpeace, Phi Beta Kappa, Phi Delta Phi, Phi Kappa Phi. Home: 1633 Westbrooke Ter Norman OK 73072-6020

LIGHT, ARTHUR HEATH, bishop; s. Alexander Heath and Mary Watkins (Nelson) L.; m. Sarah Ann Jones, June 12, 1954; children: William Alexander, Philip Nelson, John Page, Sarah Heath. BA, Hampden-Sydney Coll., 1951, DD, 1987; M.Div., Va. Theol. Sem., 1954, DD, 1970; DD, St. Paul's Coll., 1979. Ordained priest Episcopal Ch., 1955. Rector West Mecklenburg Cure, Boydton, Va., 1954-58, Christ Ch., Elizabeth City, N.C., 1958-63, St. Marys Ch., Kinston, N.C., 1963-67, Christ and St. Luke's Ch., Norfolk, Va., 1967-79; bishop Diocese of Southwestern Va., Roanoke, 1979—; pres. Province III Episcopal Ch., 1984-93; mem. adv. coun. to presiding bishop, 1985-93; nominating com. 25th presiding bishop of the Episcopal Ch., 1994-97. Author: God, The Gift, The Giver, 1984. Bd. dirs. United Communities Fund, 1969-79, Norfolk Seamen's Friends Soc., 1969-79, Tidewater Assembly on Family Life, 1970-79, Friends of Juvenile Ct., 1975-79, Va. Inst. Pastoral Care, 1971-72; bd. dirs., mem. exec. com. Va. Coun. Chs., 1979—; bd. dirs. Roanoke Valley Coun. of Community Svcs., 1980-83, Virginians Organized for Informed Community Effort (VOICE), 1981—; bd. dirs. Appalachian People's Svc. Orgn., 1981-91, pres., 1981-85, v.p., 1989-91; mem. bio-med. ethics com. Ea. Va. Med. Sch., 1973-79, Lewis Gale Hosp., Salem, 1988—, Community Hosp. Roanoke Valley, 1990-94; trustee Va. Episc. Sch., Lynchburg, 1979—, Episc. High Sch., Alexandria, 1979—, Boys' Home, Covington, 1979—, Stuart Hall Sch., Staunton, 1979—, St. Paul's Coll., Lawrenceville, 1979-88; chmn. com. on continuing edn. Va. Theol. Sem., Alexandria, 1985—, v.p. bd. trustees, 1987—; bd. dirs., co-chair rural residency program Appalachian Ministries Ednl. Resource Ctr., Berea, Ky., 1985-87; mem. coordinating cabinet, Va. Counc. Churches, 1988—, chair com. on church and society, 1989-92; mem. Am. com. Kiyosato Ednl. Experiment Project, 1990—, v.p., 1991—; mem. Gen. Conv. Standing Com. on World Mission, 1988-94, chair, 1991-94; trustee Kanuga Conf. Ctr., 1991—. Named Young Man of Yr., Jaycees, 1961, 63; fellow St. George's Coll., Jerusalem, 1978, 89, fellow in biomed. ethics U. Va., 1989. Democrat. Office: PO Box 2068 1000 1st St SW Roanoke VA 24009

LIGHT, JO KNIGHT, stockbroker; b. DeQueen, Ark., Mar. 15, 1936; d. Donald R. and Auda (Waltrip) Knight; m. Jerry T. Light, June 21, 1958 (dec. 1979); m. Victor E. Menefee Jr., Nov. 18, 1981; 1 child, Jerry T. BA cum laude, U. Ark., 1958. Cert. fin. planner. Travel cons. Comml. Nat. Bank, Little Rock, 1971-76; dist. mgr. Am. Express Co., N.Y.C., 1976-82; account exec. Dean Witter Reynolds, N.Y.C., 1982—, v.p. investments, 1987—, registered investment advisor, 1996—. Mem. Jr. League of Little Rock; vol. Happiness Singers. Mem. Inst. Cert. Fin. Planners, Internat. Assn. Fin. Planners (bd. dirs. 1992-98, pres. bd. 1995-96), U. Ark. Alumni Assn. (bd. dirs. 1974-77), Little Rock Country Club, Razorback Club, Phi Beta Kappa, Kappa Kappa Gamma. Office: Dean Witter Reynolds 401 W Capitol Ave Ste 101 Little Rock AR 72201-3437

LIGHT, RUSSELL JEFFERS, lawyer; b. Dallas, Sept. 8, 1949; s. Marion Russell and Isabel (Jeffers) L.; m. Mary Louise Allen, July 20, 1979; children: Erin, Brendan, Justin. BA, So. Meth. U., 1971, JD, 1975. Bar: Tex. 1976. Instr. legal writing So. Meth. U., Dallas, 1975-76; briefing atty. to assoc. justice Ct. of Civil Appeals, Austin, Tex., 1976-77; law clk. U.S. Dist. Ct., Ft. Worth, 1977-78; atty. Union Pacific Resources Co., Ft. Worth, 1978—; chmn. air task force of subcom. on environment and health law Am. Petroleum Inst., 1987-89. Author: (poetry) Nirvana, 1971 (recipient Dallas Poetry award 1971); actor, dir. (film) A Child's Garden, 1971 (recipient D.W. Griffith award 1971). Mem. Calif. Coun. Environ. and Econ. Balance, Dallas Bar Environ. Com. Mem. ABA (vice chmn. air com. natural resources sect. 1987-93, environ. controls corp. banking sect. 1987-89), Tex. Mid-Continent Oil and Gas Assn. (environ. law com.), Ft. Worth Petroleum Club, Ridglea Country Club, Ft. Worth Club. Home: 3705 Streamwood Rd Fort Worth TX 76116-9316 Office: Union Pacific Resources Co 801 Cherry St Fort Worth TX 76102-6803

LIGHT, WILLIAM RANDALL, lawyer; b. Lynchburg, Va., Sept. 11, 1958; s. John Leftwich and Patricia (Wilson) L.; m. Lisa Burcher, Apr. 27, 1991; children: William Randall II, Madeline Gibson. BA, Emory and Henry Coll., 1980; JD, Nova U. Bar: Va. 1985, U.S. Dist. Ct. (we. dist.) Va. 1985, U.S. Ct. Appeals (4th cir.), U.S. Supreme Ct. Assoc. Killis T. Howard, a profl. corp., Lynchburg, 1984—; spl. justice Commonwealth of Va. 24th Jud. Dist., Lynchburg, 1987—; adj. prof. Lynchburg Coll., 1989, 91. Bd. dirs. Lynchburg Mental Health Assn.; vice chmn. Rep. com. City of Lynchburg, 1986-90, acting chmn., 1990-91; capt. Va. Def. Force, 1994—. Mem. ABA, Lynchburg Bar Assn. (v.p. young lawyers sect. 1984-88, pres. 1989-90), Va. Trial Lawyers Assn., Masons (Master 1991), Phi Alpha Delta. Republican. Episcopalian. Home: 23 W Princeton Cir Lynchburg VA 24503-1434 Office: Killis T Howard PC 712 Court St PO Box 99 Lynchburg VA 24505

LIGHTBURN, FAYE MARIE, genealogist; b. Oakland, Calif., Aug. 9, 1928; d. Lloyd Michael and Alma Leone (Dennis) Brown; m. Jesse Leon Lightburn, Apr. 2, 1946; children: Sandra Jean Lightburn Stein (dec.), Steven Douglas, Marcia Faye Lightburn Scarborough, Janet Lightburn Powers. Student, Sacramento Jr. Coll., Mercy Hosp. Nursing, Sacramento. Food svc. mgr. Duval County Sch. Bd., Jacksonville Beach, Fla., 1964-86. Compiler and editor: Revolutionary Soldier Samuel Brown and some of His Family, 1993, supplement, 1994; compiler: The Palms Presbyterian Church History 1956-1996. Mem. DAR, Nat. Geneal. Soc., Mo. Geneal. Assn., Howard County Geneal Soc., St. Augustine Geneal. Soc., Federated Geneal. Soc., Va. Geneal. Soc., Assn. Profl. Genealogists. Democrat. Presbyterian.

LIGHTNER, A. LEROY, JR., advertising agency executive; b. Wyomissing, Pa., Apr. 26, 1921; s. Angus LeRoy and Grace Darling (Thompson) L.; A.B., Franklin and Marshall Coll., 1942; m. Betty Pauline Jenkins, July 22, 1950 (dec. 1994); children—Karen, Kevin, Laura Lightner Gorham. Prodn. supr. N.W. Ayer & Son, Inc., Phila., 1942-47, account exec., Boston, 1947-52, Phila., 1956-60, account supr., 1961-69, v.p., account supr., N.Y.C., 1970-80; nat. dir. United Meth. Ch. TV Presence and Ministry Campaign, Nashville, 1980-81; sr. v.p. mktg. Carden & Cherry Advt. Agy., Nashville, 1982—. Mem. Nat. Assn. Conf. Lay Leaders United Meth. Ch., 1973—; trustee Morristown Coll., 1977-87; pres. alumni council Franklin and Marshall Coll., 1960-62, chmn. alumni fund, 1962-70; sec. bd. trustees, chmn. devel. com. McKendree Village, 1988—. Mem. Geneal. Soc. Pa., Soc. Genealogists (London), Utility Communicators Internat., Am. Gas Assn., New Brunswick Genealogical Soc., Maine Genealogical Soc. (life), Berks County Genealogical Soc., New Eng. Hist. Geneal. Soc. (trustee 1996—), Tulpehocken Settlement Geneal. Soc., SAR, Blue Key, Druids, Lambda Chi Alpha, Pi Gamma Mu. Methodist (lay leader Eastern Pa. Conf. 1971-74, pres. Conf. Bd. Missions and Ch. Extension, 1965-69; pres. Northeastern Jurisdiction Bd. of Laity 1979-80, lay leader No. N.J. Conf. 1976-80, Cumberland dist. lay leader Tenn. Ann. Conf. 1992—). Author: Jenkins-Berry Ancestry, 1970, Lightner-Thompson Family, 1969. Home: Box 501 11450 Asbury Circle Solomons MD 20688 Office: Carden & Cherry Advt Agy 1220 Mcgavock St Nashville TN 37203-3130

LILES, MALCOLM HENRY, stockbroker; b. Tampa, Fla., Sept. 21, 1950; s. Henry J. and Frances (Bingham) L.; m. Marion Townsend McDougal, May 24, 1975; children; M. Leighton, William N. Student, Valdosta State Coll., 1969-70; BBA, U. Ga., 1972. Mortgage officer Citizens & So. Nat. Bank, Atlanta, 1973-76; v.p., regional mgr. Investors Mortgage Group, Nashville, 1976-81; 1st v.p., mem. chmn.'s coun. The Robinson-Humphrey Co., Nashville, 1981—; trustee Arthur & Sylvia Lee Scholarship Found., Brentwood, Tenn., 1986—. Sustaining membership chmn. Mid. Tenn. Explorer Scouts, Nashville, 1986; bd. dirs. Alive Hospice Inc., Nashville, 1986-93, United Cerebral Palsy of Nashville, Battle of Nashville Preservation Soc. Mem. Internat. Assn. Fin. Planning (past pres., bd. dirs. Nashville chpt.), Am. Funds Group (chmn.'s adv. coun.), Exchange Club (bd. dirs. 1986-87), Sons Confederate Vets. (camp 28). Home: 3506 Echo Hill Rd Nashville TN 37215-2010 Office: The Robinson-Humphrey Co Fl 9 Suntrust Bank Building Nashville TN 37219

LILLER, KAREN DESAFEY, health education educator; b. Pitts., Nov. 18, 1956; d. Thomas and Irene (Cenderelli) DeSafey; m. David Allen Liller, Aug. 30, 1980; children: Matthew Thomas Allen, Rebecca Irene Rose. BS, W.Va. U., 1978; MA, U. South Fla., 1982, EdS, 1986, PhD, 1988. Med. technologist Fla. Hosp., Altamonte Springs, 1978-81; lab. instr. Tampa (Fla.) Med. Coll., 1982-83; edn. dir. Sch. of Med. Tech. Tampa Gen. Hosp., 1983-85; sci. advisor Mylan Pharms., Inc., Tampa, 1986-87; postdoctoral fellow Coll. of Pub. Health U. South Fla., Tampa, 1988-90, asst. prof. Coll. of Pub. Health, 1990-96; assoc. prof. U. South Fla., 1996—. Contbr. articles to profl. jours. Mem. Am. Soc. Clin. Pathologists, Assn. for the Advancement of Health Edn., APHA. Home: 16509 Cayman Dr Tampa FL 33624-1065 Office: U South Fla Coll Pub Health 13201 Bruce B Downs Blvd Tampa FL 33612

LILLEY, EVELYN LEWIS, operating room nurse; b. Jackson, Miss., Jan. 10, 1962; d. Robert B. and Clara Mae (Thompson) Lewis; m. Bobby Frank Lilley, Mar. 16, 1985 (dec. Sept. 1991); children: Phillip James, Latasha Nicole. BSN, Miss. Coll., 1987. RN, Miss.; cert. nurse operating rm. Med-surg. staff nurse Miss. Bapt. Med. Ctr., Jackson, 1987-88; operating rm. staff nurse U. Miss. Med. Ctr., Jackson, 1988-90; staff nurse Nightingale Nursing Agy., Jackson, Miss., 1991-92; staff devel. instr. U. Miss. Med. Ctr., Jackson, 1992-94; head nurse U. Miss. Med. Ctr., 1994—. Dir. youth choir Mt. Hood Ch. Mem. Assn. Oper. Rm. Nurses (bd. dirs. 1995—), Elizar Pillar Nurses Assn. (Toastmasters Internat. (pres. local chpt. 1995-96, competent toastmaster, advanced toastmaster). Baptist. Home: 112 Casa Grande Dr Clinton MS 39056 Office: U Miss Med Ctr 2500 N State St Jackson MS 39216-4500

LILLEY, MILI DELLA, insurance company executive, entertainment management consultant; b. Valley Forge, Pa., Aug. 29; d. Leon Hanover and Della Beaver (Jones) L. MBA, Tex. Christian U., 1957, PhD, 1959. Various positions G & G Cons. Inc., Ft. Lauderdale, Fla., 1971-75; v.p. AMEX, Inc., Beverly Hills, Calif. and Acapulco, Mex., 1976-80; pres. The Hanover Group, Ft. Lauderdale, 1981—; personal and bus. mgr. entertainers including Ink Spots, Ft. Lauderdale, 1984—, Lanny Poffo, Ft. Lauderdale, 1990—, The Dixie Hummingbirds, 1996—; dist. agt. ITT Life Ins. Corp., also other leading cos. Named to All Stars Honor Roll Nat. Ins. Sales Mag., 1989. Mem. Fla. Assn. Theatrical Agents, Fla. Guild of Talent Agts., Mgrs., Producers and Orchestras. Office: The Hanover Group PO Box 70218 Fort Lauderdale FL 33307-0218

LILLY, ARNYS CLIFTON, JR., physicist; b. Beckley, W.Va., June 3, 1934; s. Arnys Clifton and Ella Vay (McKeehan) L.; m. Agnes Madeline Micou, June 9, 1956; children: Gregory Alan, Diane Renee, James Clifton. BS in Petroleum Engring., Va. Poly. Inst., 1957, PhD in Physics, 1989; MS in Physics, Carnegie-Mellon U., 1963. Rsch. physicist Gulf Rsch. and Devel. Co., Pitts., 1957-65; prin. scientist Philip Morris Rsch. Ctr., Richmond, Va., 1965—, research fellow, 1984, dir. tech. assessment, 1988. Mem. Am. Phys. Soc., Sigma Xi. Contbr. articles to physics jours.; patentee in field. Home: 9641 Waterfowl Flyway Chesterfield VA 23838-8905 Office: Philip Morris Rsch Ctr 4201 Commerce Rd Richmond VA 23234-2269

LILLY, GREGORY ALAN, economics educator, researcher; b. Pitts., Oct. 23, 1957; s. Arnys Clifford and Agnes Madeleine (Micou) L.; m. Karen Lu Sanford, June 2, 1994; children: Adam Gregory & Jackson Smith. BA in Econs., Washington and Lee U., 1979; PhD in Econs., Duke U., 1988. Asst. prof. Wake Forest U., Winston-Salem, N.C., 1987-90, Elon Coll., Elon College, N.C., 1990—. Contbr. articles to profl. jours. Recipient Instrumentation and Lab. Improvement award NSF, 1993. Mem. Am. Econ. Assn., Am. Statis. Assn. Office: Elon Coll Dept of Econs Elon College NC 27244-2010

LILLY, NANCY COBB, civic worker; b. Durham, N.C., Sept. 17, 1930; d. Collier and Emma (Estes) C.; m. Edward Guerrant Lilly, Jr., Nov. 25, 1961; children: Penelope Read, Edward III, Collier Cobb (dec.), Steven Clay. BA, Randolph-Macon Woman's Coll., 1952. Asst. calendar clk. N.C. State Legislature, Raleigh, 1953, 55; sec. to dir. Met. Mus. Art, N.Y.C., 1956-61; tchr. Chapin Sch. for Girls, N.Y.C., 1961. Pres. Women of Ch., White Meml. Presbyn. Ch., Raleigh, 1986-88, bd. deacons 1991—; bd. dirs. ARC, Wake County, Raleigh, 1988-92, Friends of Libr. U. N.C., Chapel Hill, N.C. com. Nat. Mus. Women in Arts, N.C. Soc.; mem. Tyron Palace Commn., New Bern, N.C., 1988-92; regent Gunston Hall Plantation, Lorton, Va., 1988—; pres. bd. N.C. Art Soc., 1983-84; bd. visitors Peace Coll. Mem. Jr. League, Raleigh Fine Arts Soc. Republican. Presbyterian. Home: 612 Scotland St Raleigh NC 27609-6950

LILLY, TAMARA FAITH, psychiatric and geriatric nurse; b. Augusta, Ga., Apr. 9, 1957; d. Norman and Louise (Moore) L. BSN, Med. U. S.C., Charleston, 1979; postgrad., Ga. State Coll., Atlanta, 1980. Cert. dir. nursing adminstrn. long term care. Supr. Manor Care, Sarasota, Fla., 1986-87; DON Raleigh Hills Hosp., Las Vegas, Nev.; substance abuse prog. dir. The Montavista Ctr., Las Vegas; DON The Shores, Bradenton, Fla., 1987-96; dir. clin. svcs. Integrated Health Svcs., Inc, Integrated Living Cmty., Inc., 1996—; conductor seminars in field. Mem. Nat. Assn. DON Adminstrn., Fla. Assn. DON Adminstrn.

LILLY, WESLEY COOPER, marine engineer, surveyor; b. Phila., May 23, 1933; s. Richard Gladstone and Margaret Jane L.; m. Barbara Joan Newton, Mar. 15, 1953 (div. Nov. 24, 1978); children: Pamela Lynn, Barbara Joan. BS in Engring., Pa. Mil. Coll., 1956-61. Apprentice machinist Phila. Naval Shipyard, 1951-53, prodn. shipbuilding, 1955-66, planning, design divsn., 1966-68; engring. specifications Naval Weapons Svc. Office, 1968-70; procurement prodn. Navy Dept. Navsea, Washington, 1970-86; pres., owner Marine Assocs., St. Augustine, Fla., 1972—; pres., founder Saturn Marine Engring., St. Augustine, Fla., 1986-96; programmer Fortran and Cobol rev. bus. computech programs. Inventor, patentee in field. Served with U.S. Army, 1953-55. Mem. Soc. Naval Archs. and Marine Engrs. (chmn. com. for small and medium shipyards/shipbuilding), Tech. Exch. Marine Profls., Putnam Co. Computer Group, Palatka Yacht Club, Navy Dept. Computer Club. Republican. Episcopalian. Home: 2727 1st Ave Fernandina Beach FL 32034 Office: Marine Assocs 1960 S US Rt 1 Ste 114 Saint Augustine FL 32086

LIM, ALEXANDER RUFASTA, neurologist, clinical investigator, educator, writer; b. Manila, Philippines, Feb. 20, 1942; s. Benito P. and Maria Lourdes (Cuyegkeng) L.; m. Norma Sue Hanks, June 1, 1968; children: Jeffrey Allen, Gregory Brian, Kevin Alexander, Melissa Gail. AA, U. Santo Tomas, Manila, Philippines, 1959, MD, 1964. Intern Bon Secours Hosp., Balt., 1964-65; resident in internal medicine Scott and White Clinic, Temple, Tex., 1965-67; resident in neurology Cleve. Clinic, 1967-69, chief resident in neurology, 1969-70, fellow clin. neurophysiology, 1970-71, clin. assoc. neurologist, 1971-72; neurologist, co-founder, co-mng. ptnr. Neurol. Clinic, Corpus Christi, Tex., 1972—; pres., CEO Neurology, P.A., Corpus Christi, 1972-92; chief neurology Meml. Med. Ctr., Corpus Christi, 1975-90, Spohn Hosp., Corpus Christi, 1974-90, Reynolds Army Hosp., Ft. Sill, Okla., 1990-91; clin. assoc. prof. Sch. Medicine U. Tex. Health Sci. Ctr., San Antonio. Mem. editl. bd. Coastal Bend Medicine, 1988-95; cons., reviewer Tex. Medicine, 1995—. Lt. col. Med. Corps, 1990-91. Recipient Army Commendation medal, 1991, Nat. Def. medal U.S. Army, 1991. Mem. AMA, Tex. Med. Assn. (chmn. neurology 1985-86, cons. Tex. Medicine jour. 1995—), Tex. Neurol. Soc. (sec. 1986-88, pres. 1989-90), Am. Acad. Neurology, Am. Epilepsy Soc., Am. Acad. Clin. Neurophysiology, Am. Electroencephalographic Soc., So. Electroencephalographic Soc., Am. Acad. Pain Mgmt., Physician Com. Responsible Medicine, Doctors of the World, Am. Legion, Internat. Platform Assn., KC. Republican. Roman Catholic. Home: 4821 Augusta Cir Corpus Christi TX 78413-2711 Office: The Neurological Clinic 3006 S Alameda St Corpus Christi TX 78404-2601

LIM, HWA AUN, research geneticist, bioinformaticist, consultant; b. Alor Setar, Kedah, Malaysia, July 29, 1957; came to U.S., 1981; s. Keng Hoon and Beng See (Tan) L. BSc (hons.), Imperial Coll. of Sci. & Tech., London, 1981; MA, U. Rochester, 1982, PhD, 1986. Rsch. asst. Imperial Coll. of Sci. & Tech., London, 1978-81, U. Rochester, Rochester, N.Y., 1981-85; medical asst. Strong Meml. Hosp., Rochester, N.Y., 1985-86; rsch. assoc. Lab. for Laser Energetics, Rochester, N.Y., 1986-87; rsch. assoc. Fla. State U., Tallahassee, 1987-89, univ. faculty, 1989-95; dir. bioinformatics HYSEQ, Sunnyvale, Calif., 1995—; adj. prof. St. Johns Fisher Coll., Rochester, 1986-87; vis. academician USSR Acad. Scis., Moscow, Kiev, Tbilisi, 1989; prin. investigator Fla. State U., 1989-95. Co-author: Computer Analysis of Genetic Macromolecules: Structure, Function and Evolution, 1994; editor: Electrophoresis, Supercomputing and Genome, 1991, Bioinformatics, Supercomputing and Genome, 1993, Isozymes: Roles in Evolution, Genetics and Physiology, 1994, Bioinformatics and Genome Research, 1994, Gene Families: Structure, Function, Genetics and Evolution, 1996; mng. editor Internat. Jour. Genomic Rsch., 1989—; assoc. editor Internat. Jour. Modern Physics C: Physics and Computers, 1989—; editor Jour. Modelling and Scientific Computing, 1991—; contbr. articles to profl. jours. Mem. rev. panel NSF, Arlington, Va., 1992, Nat. Cancer Inst., Bethesda, Md., 1994; bioinformatics expert UN, Daejon, Korea, Rome, Washington, 1993. Recipient numerous grants. Mem. AAAS, N.Y. Acad. Scis., Internat. Assn. Math. & Computer Modelling, Internat. Human Genome Orgn., Soc. Chinese Bioscientists in Am. (life). Office: HYSEQ 670 Almanor Ave Sunnyvale CA 94086-3513

LIM, JEFFREY JAMES, internist; b. Manila, The Philippines, Apr. 8, 1963; came to U.S., 1990; s. Henry Co and Emily (Weesit) L. BS in Biology, U. of the Philippines, 1984, MD, 1989. Diplomate Am. Bd. Internal Medicine. Intern SUNY, Bklyn., 1990-91, resident, 1991-93; clin. asst. instr. SUNY Health Scis. Ctr., Bklyn., 1990-93; attending physician Meml. Hosp. of Texas County, Guymon, Okla., 1994—, Cimarron Meml. Hosp., Boise City, Okla., 1994—; cons. physician MHTC Home Health, Guymon, 1994—. Mem. ACP, AMA, Am. Soc. Internal Medicine, Soc. Critical Care Medicine, Am. Coll. Chest Physicians, Okla. Med. Assn., Okla. Soc. Internal Medicine. Roman Catholic. Office: Regional Health Care Ctr 1309 N East St Guymon OK 73942

LIMA, BOB, broadcasting company executive, radio consultant; b. Havana, Cuba, May 5, 1946; came to U.S., 1947; s. Rene and Carmen (Gonzalez) L.; m. Stella Maria Hankin, Aug. 5, 1967; children: Michelle, Julie. AA in Bus. Adminstrn., Miami-Dade Jr. Coll., 1967; student, U. So. Miss., 1979. Announcer Sta. WIII, Homestead, Fla., 1966-67, Sta. WAEZ, Miami Beach, Fla., 1967-68; prodr. news Sta. WKAT, Miami Beach, 1968; asst. program dir. Sta. WGMA, Ft. Lauderdale, Hollywood, Fla., 1968-70; program dir. Sta. WVMI, New South Comm., Biloxi, Miss., 1970-74, Sta. WQID, 1974-80; ops. mgr. Stas. WVMI and WQID, Biloxi, 1976-87; v.p., gen. mgr. Sta. WKNN, So. Starr, Biloxi, 1987-92; v.p., gen. mgr. Sta. WGNE-FM, SFX Broadcasting, Daytona Beach, Fla., 1992—; owner Qualitech Bus. Computers, Inc., Gulfport, Miss., 1980-89; ptnr. The Prodn. Co., Biloxi, 1982-87; bd. dirs. Sta. WNSL-FM, Laurel, Miss., 1983-87. Bd. dirs. Miss. Gulf Coast C.C., Gulfport, 1985-92, Miss. Coast Crimestoppers, Inc., Biloxi, 1988-91; bd. trustees Miss. Gulf Coast Jr. Coll., 1984-92. Recipient gold record awards Bang/B. Tree Records, 1974, 76, silver medal Am. Advt. Fedn., 1992. Mem. Nat. Assn. Broadcasters, Am. Advt. Fedn. (Daytona Beach chpt.), Radio Assn. Broadcasters, Daytona Beach C. of C. Office: Sta WGNE-FM 340 S Beach St Daytona Beach FL 32114-5035

LIMBRICK, MARJORIE, critical care nurse; b. Tex., June 7, 1933; d. Elbert W. Sr. and Victoria N. (Baynes) Owens; m. T.J. Limbrick, Apr. 1954; children: Lois, Joyce, Tanya, Lawana. AAS, Angelina Coll., 1975. RN, Tex.; ACLS; BCLS. Charge nurse ICCU Meml. Med. Ctr. E. Tex., Lufkin, Tex., 1975-79, 83-86, 1989-94, catheterization lab. coord., 1987-89, staff nurse ICCU, catheterization lab., 1970-75, 80-83, catheritization lab. staff, 1990-92, staff nurse acute long term care, 1994—.

LIMEHOUSE, HARRY BANCROFT, JR., real estate developer; b. Charleston, S.C., Dec. 3, 1938; m. Frankie Fennell, Jan. 18, 1961; children: Chip, Brien, Barry, Brad. BA in English, The Citadel, 1960. Lic. real estate broker and broker-dealer, S.C. Mgmt. trainee Deering-Millikin, 1960-61; agt. Prudential Ins. Co., Charleston, 1962-67; mgr. Prudential Ins. Co., W. Palm Beach, Fla., 1967-69; dir. campaign mgmt. divsn. Rep. Nat. Com., Washington, 1967-69; pres., founder Limehouse Properties, Charleston, 1970—; bankruptcy trustee U.S. Trustee's Office, Columbia, S.C., 1988—. Mem. Pub. Rys. Commn. S.C., 1989-93, chmn., 1992-93; past pres. Carolina chpt. Real Estate Securities Inst.; charter pres. Charleston chpt. Comml. Income Properties Coun.; founding pres. Palmetto State Games; chmn. So. Govs. Conf., 1992; chmn. S.C. Dept. Transp. Commn., 1994—. Named hotelier of Yr. S.C. Hospitality Assn., 1994; named to Order of the Palmetto, 1995; S.C. Transportation and Policy Counc., 1995, Man of the Year, 1996—; S.C. Wildlife Federation, Conservationist of the Year, 1996—; S.F. Taxpayers Assn., Man of the Year. Mem. Nat. Assn. Realtors, Aircraft Owners and Pilots Assn., S.C. Waterfowl Assn., Hibernian Soc., Harbour Club, Downtown Athletic Club. Office: Limehouse Properties 8 Cumberland St Charleston SC 29401-2602

LIN, JACK EYIH, chemist; b. Taipei, Taiwan, Jan. 8, 1941; came to U.S., 1967; m. Susan Su-Mei Tu, Sept. 7, 1968; children: Thomas, Connie. BS in Chemistry, Nat. Cheng Kung U., Tainan, Taiwan, 1964; MBA, Kennedy-Western U., Agoura Hills, Calif., 1986; PhD in Chemistry, U. Mo., Kansas City, 1972. Cert. clin. chemistry, lab. inspector, lab. dir., N.Y., Fla., Tenn., Maine. Chemist, asst. dir. clin. labs. Helen Keller Meml. Hosp., Sheffield, Ala., 1972-86; tech. dir. Shoals Med. Lab., Inc., Florence, Ala., 1987-88; lab. dir. Roche Biomed. Labs., Inc., Southaven, Miss., 1988-96, LabCorp., Memphis, 1996—. Contbr. articles to profl. jours. Fellow Nat. Acad. Clin. Biochemistry; mem. AAAS, Am. Chem. Soc., Am. Assn. Clin. Chemistry (Clin. Chemist Recognition award 1993), Soc. Applied Spectroscopy, Soc. Forensic Toxicology. Home: 7870 Elm Leaf Dr Germantown TN 38138-7129 Office: LabCorp 4022 Willow Lake Blvd Memphis TN 38118

LIN, MING-CHANG, physical chemistry educator, researcher; b. Hsinpu, Hsinchu, Taiwan, Oct. 24, 1936; came to U.S., 1967, naturalized, 1975; s. Fushin and Tao May (Hsu) L.; m. Juh-Huey Chern, June 26, 1965; children: Karen, Linus H., Ellena J. BSc, Taiwan Normal U., Taipei, 1959; PhD, U. Ottawa, Ont., Can., 1966. Postdoctoral rsch. fellow U. Ottawa, 1965-67; postdoctoral rsch. assoc. Cornell U., Ithaca, N.Y., 1967-69; rsch. chemist Naval Rsch. Lab., Washington, 1970-74, supervisory rsch. chemist, head chem. kinetics sect., 1974-82, sr. scientist for chem. kinetics, 1982-88; Robert W. Woodruff prof. phys. chemistry Emory U., Atlanta, 1988—; mem. adv. bd. Internat. Jour. Chem. Kinetics, 1990-93, Chemistry, World Sci. Pub. Co., Singapore, 1991—, Inst. Atomic and Molecular Sci., Taipei, 1991—; mem. young presdl. award com. NSF, Washington, 1990. Contbr. over 300 articles to profl. jours. 2d lt. Taiwan ROTC, 1960-62. Recipient Civilian Meritorious award USN, 1979, Humboldt award Humboldt Found., 1982, prize in sci. tech. Taiwanese-Am. Found., 1989; Guggenheim fellow, 1982. Mem. Am. Chem. Soc. (Hillebrand prize 1975), Combustion Inst., Am. Vacuum Soc., Materials Rsch. Soc., N.Am. Taiwanese Profs. Assn., Sigma Xi (Pure Sci. award 1976 Naval Rsch. Lab. chpt.). Office: Emory Univ Dept Of Chemistry Atlanta GA 30322

LIN, TU, endocrinologist, educator, researcher, academic administrator; b. Fukien, China, Jan. 18, 1941; came to U.S., 1967; s. Tao Shing and Jan En (Chang) L.; m. Pai-Li, July 1, 1967; children: Vivian H., Alexander T., Margaret C. MD, Nat. Taiwan U., Taipei, 1966. Diplomate Am. Bd. Internal Medicine, Am. Bd. Endocrinology and Metabolism. Intern Episcopal Hosp.-Temple U., Phila., 1967-68; resident in medicine Berkshire Med. Ctr., Pittsfield, Mass., 1968-70; fellow in endocrinology Lahey Clinic, Boston, 1970-71, Roger Williams Gen. Hosp.-Brown U., Providence, 1971-73; rsch. fellow in med. sci. Brown U., 1971-73; chief, endocrine sect. WJB Dorn Vet. Hosp., Columbia, S.C., 1975—; asst. prof. U. S.C. Sch. Medicine, Columbia, 1976-80, assoc. prof., 1980-84, prof. medicine, 1984—, prof., dir. divsn. endocrinology, diabetes and metabolism, 1992—; mem. Merit Review Bd. of Endocrinology, Dept. Vet. Affairs, 1990-94. Author: (book chpt.) Disorders of Male Reproductive Function, 1996; mem. editl. bd. Biology of Reproduction, 1990-95, Jour. of Andrology, 1993-96; contbr. articles to med. and profl. jours. Recipient Disting. Investigator award U. S.C. Sch. Medicine, 1981, 88, 95. Fellow ACP; mem. Endocrine Soc., Am. Soc. Andrology (chmn. ann. meeting, coun. 1993-96), Soc. for the Study of Reproduction. Office: U SC Sch Medicine Med Library Bldg Ste 316 Columbia SC 29208

LINCECUM, JERRY BRYAN, English language educator; b. Seale, Tex., Feb. 15, 1942; s. John Auben and Mildred Maurice (Jones) L.; m. Etta Mae Sanders, Dec. 30, 1960 (div. Mar. 1985); children: David, Deborah, Douglas; m. Peggy Ann Redshaw, Sept. 28, 1985. BA, Tex. A&M U., 1963; AM, Duke U., 1964, PhD, 1967. Asst. prof. English, Austin Coll., Sherman, Tex., 1967-72, assoc. prof., 1972-77, prof., 1977—, Piper prof., 1981; dir. Telling Our Stories Project, Sherman, 1990—. Author: Adventures of G.H.M., 1990, Adventures of a Frontier Naturalist, 1994; newspaper columnist The Good Humor Man, 1990—; editor newspaper column Telling Our Stories, 1990—. Recipient Silver award of merit Daus. of Republic of Tex., 1996; grantee Tex. Coun. for Humanities, 1978, 90, 91, 92, Sherman Coun. on Arts and Humanities, 1993, 94, 95. Mem. Nat. Coun. Tchrs. English, Friends Sherman Libr. Home: 608 N Cleveland Ave Sherman TX 75090-4604 Office: Austin Coll 900 N Grand Ave Sherman TX 75090-4440

LINCK, CHARLES EDWARD, English language educator; b. Lowemont, Kans., June 6, 1923; s. Charles Edward and Grace Elizabeth (Miller) L.; m. Alice Eugenie Meyer (div. Feb. 1964); 1 child, Charles Edward Lincoln; m. Ernestine Marie Porcher Sewell, Aug. 23, 1970. AB magna cum laude, St. Benedict's Coll., Atchison, Kans., 1951; MS, Kans. State Coll., 1953; PhD in English, U. Kans., 1962. Prof. English East Tex. State U., Commerce, 1958-91, prof. emeritus, 1991—; owner, pub. Cow Hill Press. Author, editor: Edgar Rye: North Central Texas Cartoonist and Journalist, 1972; co-editor: Bibliography of Evelyn Waugh, 1984; editor, pub. Evelyn Waugh in Letters by Terence Greenridge. With USN, 1943-46, PTO. Mem. MLA, Tex. Coll. English Assn. (pres. 1972), Am. Studies Assn., Tex. Folklore Soc. (pres. 1984). Democrat. Roman Catholic. Home: PO Box 3002 E T Sta Commerce TX 75429-3002

LINCOLN, BLANCHE LAMBERT, congresswoman. Mem. from Ark. U.S. Ho. of Reps., Washington. Office: US Ho of Reps 1204 Longworth Ho Off Bldg Washington DC 20515

LINCOLN, TIMOTHY DWIGHT, library director; b. Norfolk, Nebr., June 12, 1955; s. Dwight Adelbert and Betty Lee (Carlson) L.; m. Laura Marie Vaught, Aug. 6, 1982; children: Micah Timothy, Abby Christine. BA, Concordia Coll., Moorhead, Minn., 1976; MDiv, Yale U., 1981; MS, Simmons Coll., 1992. Asst. pastor Trinity Luth. Ch., Detroit Lakes, Minn., 1982-89; assoc. libr. Maryknoll (N.Y.) Sch. Theology, 1992-94; dir. Stitt Libr., Austin (Tex.) Presbyn. Theol. Sem., 1994—. Contbr. articles to theol. and ecumenical publs. Bd. dirs. Minn. Coun. Chs., 1982-84; del. Luth. World Fedn., Budapest, Hungary, 1984; mem. ecumenical ministries com. Southwestern Tex. synod Evang. Luth. Ch. in Am., 1995—. Mem. Am. Theol. Libr. Assn., Southwestern Theol. Libr. Assn., Beta Phi Mu. Office: Austin Presbyn Theol Seminary Stitt Libr 100 E 27th St Austin TX 78705

LINDELOF, WILLIAM CHRISTIAN, JR., financial company executive; b. Wheeling, W.Va., June 21, 1946; s. William Christian and Ruth Elizabeth (Perkins) L.; m. Virginia Lee Partezana, May 5, 1973; children: Erik Christian, Alan Brent, Heather Catherine. AA, Ohio Valley Coll., Parkersburg, W.Va., 1967; BS, West Liberty State Coll., 1970. Cert. credit union exec. Salesman Univ. Guaranty Life Ins., Youngstown, Ohio, 1972-73; asst. mgr. Household Fin. Corp., Youngstown, 1974-76; loan officer 1st Wetzel Savs. and Loan (later 1st Wetzel Nat. Bank), New Martinsville, W.Va., 1976-79; mgr. Mobay Employees Fed. Credit Union, New Martinsville, 1979-85; pres., chief exec. officer First Flight Fed. Credit Union, Havelock, N.C., 1985—; chmn. exec. com. Gen. Sys. Users Group, New Martinsville, 1984-85; bd. dirs., sec. Marine Credit Union Network, 1988-91. Mem. citizen's adv. coun. Adena Industries Workshop for Handicapped, New Martinsville, 1981-84; deacon, tchr. Bible class Morehead City (N.C.) Ch. of Christ; v.p. Carteret County chpt. Parents for Advancement Gifted Edn., 1987-91. With U.S. Army, 1969-71. Recipient Medal of Merit, Ohio Valley Coll., 1989. Mem. Credit Union Exec. Soc., N.C. Credit Union League (bd. dirs. East Carolina chpt. 1986-91, v.p. 1987-88, pres. 1988-90, edn. com. 1989-90, annual meeting com. 1995-96), Nat. Assn. Fed. Credit Unions (regulatory com. 1990-95, comm. com. 1996—), Am. Legion (vice comdr. 1974-76), Havelock C. of C. (govtl. affairs com. 1990-95, bd. dirs. 1991-94, v.p. 1991-92, pres. 1992-93), Morehead City C. of C. (co-chmn. blueprint task force for Carteret C.C., mem. spkrs. bur., mil. liaison 1990-92), Navy League, Delta Sigma Pi (life). Republican. Home: 3515 Meadow Dr Morehead City NC 28557-3013 Office: First Flight Fed Credit Union 1208 E Main St Havelock NC 28532-2405

LINDENMUTH, RICHARD ALAN, electronics company executive; b. Phila., Dec. 28, 1944; s. Ralph Lester and Evelyn Josephine (Zimmerman) Dedel L.; m. Mary-Beth Anthony, Nov. 9, 1994; children: Michael, Carol Anne. BA in Internat. Affairs, U. Colo., 1970; MBA, Wharton Sch., U. Pa., 1971. Gen. mgr. North and West Africa Singer, Beirut, Lebanon, 1972-77; dir. internat. ops. Bendix Corp., Southfield, Mich., 1978-80; pres. Lexar Bus. Communications, Inc., Woodland Hills, Calif., 1980-82; v.p., gen. mgr. Imaging Systems div. Burroughs Corp., Danbury, Conn., 1982-83; pres. Bus. and Consumer Communications div. ITT, Raleigh, N.C., 1983-86; pres., CEO Robinson Nugent Inc., New Albany, Ind., 1986-90, InterPacific, 1991—; pres. The Lindenmuth Group, 1990-91; pres., CEO Interpacific, 1991—. Mem. nat. adv. bd. Ctr. Study Presidency, N.Y.C., 1982—; bd. dirs. Internat. Trade, Raleigh, 1983—; cons. on middle east U.S. Govt., 1982-83, Interpacific, San Francisco, 1990—. With USN, 1962-66. Republican. Presbyterian. Club: Capital City (Raleigh). Avocations: flying, sailing, travel, tennis. Office: Twin Forks Office Plz 6040 Six Forks Rd Ste 190 Raleigh NC 27609-8601

LINDER, ANN LAURA, marketing administrator; b. Meridian, Miss., Dec. 3, 1936; d. Percy McCay and Beatrice (McCraine) Lum; m. Lionel Linder, Jan. 23, 1965 (dec. Dec. 1992); children: Lesley John, Laura Ann. BS, Northwestern U., 1959. TV promoter WTOP-TV, Washington, 1961-65; mktg. adminstr. Guardsmark, Inc., Memphis, 1993—. Bd. dirs. Memphis Brooks Mus. Art, 1995—; past bd. dirs. Memphis Symphony League, Brooks Mus. League, Woman's Exch. of Memphis. Mem. Memphis Rotary Club, Memphis Hunt and Polo Club, Memphis Area C. of C. (bd. dirs. 1995—). Home: 3878 St Andrews Green Memphis TN 38111 Office: Guardsmark Inc 22 S 2nd St Memphis TN 38103-2629

LINDER, BRUNO, chemist, educator; b. Sniatyn, Poland, Sept. 3, 1924; s. Elias and Feiga (Kleinman) L.; m. Cecelia Fahn, Feb. 14, 1953; children: William H., Diane T., Richard A., Nancy M., Carolyn B. B.S., Upsala Coll., 1948; M.S., Ohio U., 1950; Ph.D., UCLA, 1955. Asst. research chemist, engring. dept. UCLA, 1955; research asso. U. Wis. Naval Research Lab., 1955-57; asst. prof. Fla. State U., 1957-61, asso. prof., 1961-65, prof. chemistry, 1965—, chmn. chem. physics program, 1971-73, 75-83, assoc. chmn. Chemistry dept., 1980-83; research participant Oak Ridge Nat. Lab., summers 1958, 59, 61; vis. asso. prof. U. Wis., summer 1964, U. Amsterdam, 1964-65; vis. prof. Hebrew U. of Jerusalem, 1973. Guggenheim fellow, 1964-65. Mem. Am. Phys. Soc., Southeastern Theoretical Chemistry Assn. (co-founder, chmn. 1969-72, program chmn. 1974-76, 83-87, 90—), Sigma Xi, Phi Lambda Upsilon, Phi Mu Alpha. Office: Fla State U Dept Chemistry Tallahassee FL 32306

LINDER, HARVEY RONALD, lawyer, arbitrator, mediator; b. Pitts., July 23, 1949; s. Charles Joseph and Rose (Ruben) L.; m. Reva Rebecca Vertman, Aug. 14, 1971; children: Zalman F., Seth A. BA, Duquesne U., 1971, JD, 1975. Bar: Pa. 1975, U.S. Dist. Ct. (we. dist.) Pa. 1975, U.S. Supreme Ct. 1979. Legal intern Dist. Atty.'s Office, Pitts., 1974-75; asst. mgr. arbitration U.S. Steel, Pitts., 1975-80, mgr. labor rels., 1980-81; supt. employee rels. U.S. Steel, Clairton, Pa., 1981-83; corp. dir. employee rels. U.S. Steel Agri-Chemicals, Atlanta, 1984-86; corp. dir. law and human resources LaRoche Industries Inc., Atlanta, 1986-88, v.p., gen. counsel, 1988-96; arbitrator, mediator, 1996—; pres. A.C.I.R.A., 1987-90. Contbr. poetry and photography to Duquesne Literary Mag., 1968-74. Exec. cons. Jr. Achievement, Pitts., 1978-83; head coach Atlanta Jewish Cmty. Ctr., Dunwoody, Ga., 1984—, bd. dirs., 1991—; pres. B'nai Torah Synagogue, 1995—, Hunter's Woods Homeowners' Assn., Dunwoody, 1986-87; commr. Baseball & Soccer Leagues; bd. dirs. Atlanta Jewish Fedn., 1995-96. Steel fellow Am. Iron and Steel Inst., 1977-85. Mem. ABA, Allegheny County Bar Assn., Indsl. Rels. Rsch. Assn., Duquesne U. Law Sch. Alumni Assn. (bd. dirs. 1980-84), B'nai B'rith (local v.p. 1975-80), Amer-Israel C. of C. (bd. dirs. 1993—). Democrat. Home and Office: 365 Waters Bend Way Alpharetta GA 30202-8014

LINDER, JOHN E, congressman, dentist; b. Deer River, Minn., Sept. 2, 1942; s. Henry and Vera Elizabeth Davis L.; m. Lynne Leslee Peterson, 1963; children: Kristine Kerry, Matthew John. BS, U. Minn., 1963, DDS, 1967. Pvt. practice Atlanta, Ga., 1967-82; mem. Ga. Ho. of Reps., 1975-80, 82-90; pres. Linder Fin. Corp., 1977-92; mem. 103d-104th Congress from 4th Ga. Dist., 1993—, 105th Congress from 11th Ga. Dist., 1996—; house rules com., subcom. on legis. process, Rep. steering com., NRCC exec. com. U.S. Ho. of Reps. Founder I Care, 1970. Capt. USAF, 1967-69. Mem. ADA, Ga. Dental Assn., No. Dist. Dental Soc., Rotary. Republican. Presbyterian. Office: US Ho of Reps 1318 Longworth Bldg Washington DC 20515-0004

LINDGREN, CARL EDWIN, educational consultant, antiquarian, photographer; b. Coeburn, Va., Nov. 20, 1949; s. Carl and Ruby (Corder) L.; m. Lynn Stewart, 1976 (div. 1979); m. Penelope Bolton, 1990. A in Edn. with honors, N.W. Jr. Coll., 1970; BA in Edn., U. Miss., 1972, MEd, 1977; MH, Emerson Coll., Toronto, Ont., Can., 1991; EdS, U. Miss., 1993; postgrad., U. South Africa. FCP, Coll. of Preceptors, London, 1993. Coord. dept. edn. Delta Hills Edn. Assn., 1976-79; lectr. photography U. Miss., 1979-81; instr. health edn. Batesville Job Corps Ctr. U.S. Dept. Labor, 1980-82; pres., dir. Edn. Cons. of Oxford, Ltd., London, England and Courtland, Miss., 1981—; Faulknerian landscape photographer, 1989—; adj. faculty univs. in U.S., Can., and Eng.; ind. cons. staff tng. and rsch. inst. for distance edn. Indira Gandhi Nat. Open U. Contbr. over 200 articles to profl. jours. and mags.; author 9 books; mem. several adv., rev. and editorial bds. including London Inst. Sci. Tech., Ednl. Forum, Introductions, others; one-man shows and exhbns. U.S., Eng. and India. Recipient Acad. Achievement award, 1970; EDPA fellow, 1973; Robert A. Taft fellow, 1977; Hon. Life Fellowship award (Jnana Ratna) World Janana Sadhak Soc., Calcutta, 1978; Cert. of Excellence and Svc. Associateship award India Internat. Photog. Coun., New Delhi, 1991; Mahatma Gandhi Meml. award, 1994; named to Order of Good Templars; assoc. Brotherhood of St. Gregory, Brotherhood of Blessed Gerard. Fellow Royal Soc. arts, Royal Soc. Health, Royal Asiatic Soc., Soc. Antuquaries of Scotland, Coll. Preceptors of Essex; mem. Royal Hist. Soc., Orders and Medals Soc. Am., History of Edn. Soc., Humanitarian Soc., Medieval Acad. Am., Photog Soc. Am. (Bronze Star Editorial award 1991, 92, 93), Asiatic Soc. Calcutta (affiliate), Parapsychol. Assn. (affiliate), Phi Alpha Theta, Phi Delta Kappa, Kappa Delta Pi, Phi Theta Kappa. Republican. Home: Avalon Woods Rte 2 Box 88A Courtland MS 38620-9801 Office: PO Box 8161 University MS 38677-8161

LINDIG, BILL M., food distribution company executive; b. 1936; married. Attended, U. Tex. With Sysco Corp., Houston, 1969—, exec. v.p., from 1984, COO, 1984—, now pres., COO.; chmn. Sysco Avard Food Svcs., Inc., Union City, Calif., Santa Fe Pacific Corp., Schaumburg, Ill. Office: Sysco Corp 1390 Enclave Pky Houston TX 77077-2025*

LINDLEY, BARRY DREW, medical educator; b. Orleans, Ind., Jan. 25, 1939; s. Paul Lemuel and Martha (Drew) L.; m. Sondra Patterson, June 20, 1964 (div. 1980); children: Theodore Drew, Matthew Bishop, Sarah Jeannette; m. Elizabeth Price, Apr. 24, 1982. BA, DePauw U., 1960; PhD, Western Res. U., 1964. Postdoctoral fellow Karolinska Inst., Stockholm, 1964-65; asst. prof. Western Res. U., Cleve., 1965-68; assoc. prof. Case-Western Res. U., Cleve., 1968-84, prof. physiology, 1984-93, assoc. dean, 1985-93, acting chmn. of anatomy, 1988-93; vice chancellor for acad. affairs U. Ark. for Med. Scis., Little Rock, 1993—, dean Grad. Sch., prof. physiology and biophysics, 1993—; vis. scientist ARC unit of Invertebrate Physiology, Cambridge, Eng., 1972, Duke U. Marine Lab., Beaufort, N.C., 1973; mem. physiology study sect. NIH, Bethesda, Md., 1975-79; com. mem. Nat. Bd. Med. Examiners, Phila., 1986-91; bd. visitors DePauw U., Greencastle, Ind., 1989-92; faculty fellow Liaison Com. on Med. Edn., 1988; vis. lectr. in med. illustration Cleve. Inst. Art, 1993-94; adj. prof. applied health scis. Tulane U. Sch. Pub. Health and Tropical Medicine, 1994—; mem. sci. adv. bd. Nat. Ctr. for Toxicol. Rsch., 1995—; cons.-evaluator North Ctrl. Assn. Colls. and Schs., 1996—. Contbr. numerous articles to sci. jours. Deacon Calvary Presbyn. Ch., Cleve., 1971; asst. scoutmaster Cleve. area Boy Scouts Am., 1987, supernumerary Cleve. Opera, 1988-93; bd. dirs. Kenneth J. Pennebaker Ctr., 1994—. Recipient Med. Faculty award Lederle Found., 1967-70, Career Devel. award NIH, 1971-76; disting. scholar Camille and Henry Dreyfus Found., DePauw U., 1983. Mem. Am. Physiol. Soc. (membership com. 1973-76), Biophys. Soc., Soc. Gen. Physiologists, Assn. Anatomy Chmn., MidSouthern Watercolorists, 1994—. Office: U Ark for Med Scis 4301 W Markham St # 541 Little Rock AR 72205-7199

LINDLEY, LESTER GALE, legal and constitutional historian; b. Bloomington, Ill., Mar. 16, 1937; s. Austin Raitt and Rosabella (Ford) L.; m. Letty Ellen Adamson, Aug. 4, 1963; children: Austin Harold, Philip Richard. BA, So. Ill. U., Carbondale, 1964; MA, U. Ill., 1966; PhD, Rice U., 1971; JD, DePaul U., Chgo., 1985. Bar: Ill. 1986. Asst. prof. Union Coll., Barborville, Ky., 1970-75; vis. asst. prof. U. Notre Dame, Ind., 1975-76; assoc. prof. Kendall Coll., Evanston, Ill., 1976-89, Nova Southeastern U., Ft. Lauderdale, Fla., 1989—; part-time lawyer Chgo. area law firms, 1986-88. Author: The Constitution Faces Technology, 1975, Impact of the Telegraph on Contract Law, 1991, Contract, Economic Change and the Search for Order in Industrializing America, 1993. Mem. ABA, Orgn. Am. Historians, Am. Soc. Legal History, Ill. Bar Assn.

LINDNER, JOHN M., publisher, editor, minister; b. Jackson, Miss., July 20, 1937; s. Harold A. and Anna E. (Hahn) L.; m. Jo Ann Vaclavik, Aug. 13, 1960; children: Jeanne, Joyce, Jill, John Jr. AA, Jackson (Miss.) C.C., 1957; BA, Elmhurst Coll., 1959; BD, Lancaster Theol. Sem., 1962. Pastor St. John's United Ch. of Christ, Marine City, Minn., 1962-67, Zion United Ch. of Christ, New Bremen, Ohio, 1967-70, Faith Alliance Ch., New Bremen, Ohio, 1970-73; elder Ch. at Celina (Ohio), 1973-76; pastor, elder Kenton (Ohio) Faith Fellowship, 1976-79; minister, elder Ch. Blue Ridge, Afton, Va., 1980—; v.p. Christian Aid Mission, Charlottestville, Va., 1980—. Contbr. articles to Charisma mag., Nat. Religious Braodcaster, Christian Mission mag. Mem. No. Va. Christian Writers, Evang. Press Assn. Mem. Evang. Ch. Home: 3995 William Ct Charlottesville VA 22903 Office: Christian Aid Mission 3045 Ivy Rd Charlottesville VA 22903

LINDQUIST, LEO ANSELM, surgeon; b. Paavola, Mich., Feb. 26, 1927; s. Karl Edward and Ida L.; m. Nancy Lou Townsend, Aug. 4, 1956 (dec. Feb. 1987); children: Leo A. Jr., Amy M., Karl J., Kurt P. BS, Wayne U., 1949; MD, U. mich., 1953. Diplomate Am. Bd. Surgery. Intern Phila. Gen. Hosp., 1953-54; resident, clin. instr. U. Hosp., Ann Arbor, Mich., 1954-58; pvt. practice, surgery Marquette, Mich., 1958-64, Redlands, Calif., 1964-66; dir. surg. edn. San Joaquin Gen. Hosp., Stockton, Calif., 1966-71; pvt. practice Owosso (Mich.) Med. Group, 1971-72, Danville, Va., 1972-73, 75-94; dir. surg. edn. York (Pa.) Hosp., 1973-75; acting chief of surgery Lake City (Fla.) Vet. Affairs Med. Ctr., 1994—; faculty VA Univ. Fla., 1994—. With USN, 1945-46. Fellow ACS; mem. Southeastern Surg. Congress, F.A. Coller Surg. Soc., So. Med. Assn. Office: VA Med Ctr 801 N Marion St Lake City FL 32055-2853

LINDQVIST, GUNNAR JAN, management consultant, international trade consultant; b. Stockholm, July 12, 1950; s. Bengt Olof Sigfrid and Greta (Nyberg) L.; m. Mary Grady, June 23, 1984; children: Greta Louise, Mary Kerstin. Grad. with honors, Stockholm Sch. Econs., 1974. Lic. realtor, Ga. Asst. acctg. mgr. Granges Shipping, Stockholm, 1975-77; asst. budget mgr. Dynapac AB, Stockholm, 1978-79; asst. treas., contr. Peeples Industries, Savannah, Ga., 1980-83; owner, pres. Cash Mgmt., Inc., Savannah, 1983—. Mem. The Carpenter's Order, Stockholm, 1978—. Served with Swedish Army. Mem. Scandinavian-Am. Found. of Ga. (bd. govs. 1988—), Savannah Area C. of C. (chmn. subcom. Small Bus. Coun. 1984-89), Swedish-Am. C. of C. Home and Office: 6800 Sandnettles Dr Savannah GA 31410-2317

LINDSAY, DAVID MICHAEL, pharmacist; b. Waynesburg, Pa., Jan. 28, 1957; s. Walter David and Ann Eleanor Lindsay. BS in Pharmacy, U. N.C., 1980. Lic. pharmacist. Pharmacist Wake Med. Ctr., Raleigh, N.C., 1980-89, Columbia/HCA Raleigh Cmty. Hosp., 1989—; relief pharmacist Western Wake Med. Ctr., Cary, N.C., 1990-95, Holly Hill Hosp., Raleigh, 1981-85. Mem. Am. Soc. Health Sys. Pharmacists, Am. Soc. Parenteral and Enteral Nutrition, Am. Pharm. Assn., N.C. Soc. Hosp. Pharmacists, N.C. Pharm. Assn. Home: 8005 McGuire Dr Raleigh NC 27604

LINDSAY, JOHN, IV, principal; b. Trenton, N.J., Oct. 31, 1960; s. John III and Dolores (Hambright) L.; m. Mandy Jane Ablitt, Aug. 23, 1982; children: John V, James Stirling, Cameron Sinclair. BS, Trenton State Coll., 1982; MS, U. North Tex., 1993. Cert. tchr., adminstr., Tex., N.J. Tchr. Dallas Ind. Sch. Dist., 1984-91, asst. prin. Pearl C. Anderson Mid. Sch., 1991-95; prin.Aledo (Tex.) Elem. Sch. Aledo Ind. Sch. Dist., 1995—; demonstration tchr. Project CARE, Dallas, 1985-88; team leader Leadership Devel. Acad. Dallas Ind. Sch. Dist., 1989. Mem. ASCD, Tex. State Tchrs. Assn., Phi Delta Kappa. Home: 213 Scenic Trail Willow Park TX 76087 Office: Aledo Elem Sch 12 Vernon Rd Aledo TX 76008

LINDSAY, MICHAEL KENNETH, obstetrics and gynecology educator; b. Norfolk, Va., Oct. 1, 1953; s. George Alfred and Lillie Mae Lindsay; m. Lorna Eileen Douglas, June 2, 1979; children: Jonathan, Kenneth. BS, Morehouse Coll., 1975; MD, Yale U., 1979; MPH, Emory U., 1991. Diplomate Am. Bd. Med. Examiners, Am. Bd. Obstetrics and Gynecology, Am. Bd. Maternal Fetal Medicine. Intern St. Louis U. Hosps., 1979-80; resident in ob.-gyn. Boston City Hosp., 1980-83; fellow in maternal fetal medicine U. Cin. Med. Ctr., 1983-85; asst. prof. gynecology and obstectrics Emory U., Atlanta, 1985-92, assoc. prof. gynecology and obstetrics, 1993—; cons. Emory U. Regional Perinatal Ctr., Grady Meml. Hosp., Atlanta, 1986—, cons. maternal and infant care project, 1986—, chmn. med. ethics fetal and neonatal review com., 1988-90; mem. Ga. Divsn. Pub. Health Syphillis Adv. Com., Atlanta, 1989-90, Women's Health Com. AIDS Clin. Trials Group, 1991—, Women and HIV Disease Subcom. Agy. for Health Care Policy and Rsch., 1991—. Author: (with others) Obstetric and Gynecology Physical Therapy, 1988, Clinical Obstetrics and Gynecology, 1993; contbr. articles to profl. jours. Grantee Ctrs. for Disease Control, 1988—, NIH, 1991-92. Mem. ACOG, Atlanta Med. Assn., Soc. Perinatal Obstetricians, Nat. Minority AIDS Coun., Internat. AIDS Coun., Nat. Med. Assn., So. Med. Assn. Home: 3461 Fox Hound Run Lithonia GA 30038-1606 Office: Emory U Sch Medicine Dept Gynecology/Obstetrics 80 Butler St SE Atlanta GA 30303-3031

LINDSEY, DOTTYE JEAN, marketing executive; b. Temple Hill, Ky., Nov. 4, 1929; d. Jesse D. and Ethel Ellen (Bailey) Nuckols; m. Willard W. Lindsey, June 14, 1952 (div.). BS, Western Ky. U., 1953, MA, 1959. Owner, Bonanza Restaurant, Charleston, W.Va., 1965; tchr. remedial reading Alice Waller Elem. Sch., Louisville, 1967-75, tchr., 1953-67, 1975-84, contact person for remedial reading, 1968—; regional mgr. A.L. Williams Fin. Mktg. Co., 1988—; profl. model Cosmo/Casablancas Modeling Agy., Louisville, 1984-89; with Primerica Fin. Svcs. (formerly A.L. Willams Fin. Svcs.), Louisville, 1988—; model, 1984-89; regional mgr. Primerica Fin. Svcs., 1988—. Treas. Met. Louisville Women's Polit. Caucus, 1980-88, Ky. Women's Polit. Caucus, 1988-91; bd. sponsor ROTC Western Ky. U., 1950; local precinct capt., 1987—; election officer, 1984—; treas. Ky. Women's Polit. Caucus, 1988-91. Named Miss Ky., 1951. Mem. NEA, Ky. Edn. Assn., Jefferson County Tchrs. Assn., various polit. action coms., Internat. Reading Assn., Am. Childhood Edn. Assn. Democrat. Baptist.

LINDSEY, JAMES KENDALL, civil engineer; b. Poteau, Okla., Jan. 15, 1924; s. Ray Vernett and Mattie Frances (Kendall) L.; m. Lady Joyce Crowley, July 14, 1946; children: Marcia Gay Morgan, Mark Ray, James Neill, John Kendall. AS, Clemson U., 1944; BCE, Okla. State U., 1948; MS in Pub. Health, U. Mich., 1950. Registered profl. engr., Okla.; registered land surveyor, Okla. Mobile labs. engr. Okla. State Dept. Health, Oklahoma City, 1947-49, dist. engr., 1949-53; cons. engr. USA Ops. Mission, Addis Ababa, Ethiopia, 1954-55, various water and pollution control facilities, Okla., 1955—; mem. environ. health com. Okla. Health Planning Coun., Oklahoma City, 1968-75. With U.S. Army, 1943-46. Named Okla. Water Pioneer Gov. of Okla., 1994. Mem. NSPE, Am. Waterworks Assn. (Okla. trustee 1958), Water Environ. Fedn., Okla. Water and Pollution Control Assn. (sec. 1948-53, pres. 1957), Lions (pres. Tahlequah club 1964-65), Tahlequah (Okla.) C. of C. Home and Office: 1630 N Vinita Ave Tahlequah OK 74464-6222

LINDSEY, LAWRENCE BENJAMIN, economist, federal official; b. Peekskill, N.Y., July 18, 1954; s. Merritt Hunt and Helen Ruth (Hissam) L.; m. Susan Ann McGrath, Aug. 28, 1982; 2 children. AB magna cum laude, Bowdoin Coll., Brunswick, Maine, 1976; MA, Harvard U., 1981, PhD, 1985; JD (hon.), Bowdoin Coll., 1993. Economist Coun. Econ. Advisers, Washington, 1981-84; from asst. prof. to assoc. prof. Harvard U., Cambridge, Mass., 1984-90; faculty rsch. fellow Nat. Bur. Econ. Rsch., Cambridge, 1984-89; from assoc. dir. to spl. asst. to Pres., Office of Policy Devel., The White House, Washington, 1989-91; gov. Fed. Res. Bd., Washington, 1991—. Author: The Growth Experiment, 1990; contbr. articles to profl. jours. Recipient Walter Wriston award Manhattan Inst., 1988. Mem. Phi Beta Kappa. Office: Fed Res Bd 20th & C Sts NW Washington DC 20551

LINDSEY, LIBBY, editor, graphic designer; b. Corsicana, Tex., Dec. 7, 1971; d. W.L. and Margaret Ann (Fulton) L. Student, Navarro Coll., 1990-92; BA in English, Tex. A&M U., 1994. Reporter, mem. composition dept. Teague (Tex.) Chronicle, 1994; editor, graphic design layout person Prufrock Press, Waco, Tex., 1994—. Editor: Brain Bogglers, 1995, CPS for Kids, 1996, Be A Problem-Solver, 1996, Scamper and Scamper On, 1996. Mem. Editl. Press Assn.. Office: Prufrock Press PO Box 8813 Waco TX 76714

LINDSEY, LYDIA, education educator, researcher; b. Trenton, N.J., Jan. 10, 1951; d. Charles and Ollie S. Lindsey. BA, Howard U., 1972, MA, 1974; PhD, U. N.C., 1992. Asst. prof. N.C. Ctrl. U., Durham, 1974-92, archivist, 1992—; adj. prof. U. N.C., Chapel Hill, 1992—; cons. A Philip Randolph Ednl. Found., 1975-78; rsch. assoc. U. Warwick, Coventry, Engr., 1985-86; Rockefeller doctoral fellow Duke-U.N.C. Women's Studies Rsch. Ctr., 1985-886; bd. dirs. Carolina Wren Press, Durham, Stagville Plantation, 1992—; minority postdoctoral fellow U. N.C., 1994-96, participant in nat. land interaction confs. Contbr. articles to profl. jours. Campaign mgr. Beverly Jones Sch. Bd., Durham, 1991-92; active People's Alliance, Durham, 1991-92, Durham Hist. Preservation Soc., 1991-92. Recipient DAR History award; N.C. Minority Postdoctoral fellow, 1994—, N.C. Bd. Gov.'s Doctoral fellow, 1986-87, NEH fellow for coll. tchrs. of historically black colls., 1985-86, U. N.C.-Chapel Hill Reynolds Overseas Grad. fellow, 1985-86, Rockefeller fellow from Duke-U. N.C. Women's Studies Rsch. Ctr. Doctoral fellow, 1985-86; N.J. State scholar, 1968-72, Fulbright scholar, 1995; NEH grantee, 1979. Mem. Assn. Black Women Historians, Assn. for Study African, Caribbean and Asian Culture in Britain, Assn. for Study of Afro-Am. Life and History, Assn. Caribbean Studies, Assn. So. Women Historians, Assn. Social and Behavioral Scis., Collegium for African Am. Studies, Am. Hist. Assn., Nat. Coun. Black Studies, Nat. Coun. Black Women, Carolina Symposium Brit. Study, So. Confs. Brit. Studies, Golden Key (hon.), Delta Sigma Theta, Pi Gamma Mu, Phi Alpha Theta. Democrat. Baptist. Home: 2210 Alpine Rd Durham NC 27707-3970 Office: NC Ctrl U Durham NC 27707

LINDSLEY, JOHN MARTIN, chemical engineer; b. Syracuse, N.Y., Sept. 4, 1914; s. Floyd Adelbert and Katherine Agusta (Birch) L.; m. Lois Dorothy Eshleman, May 6, 1939; children: Katherine Virginia Lindsley Scherer, Nancy Sarah Morris, Karen Jean Knowles. Diploma, Mechanics Inst. (now R.I.T.), 1940; certificate, John Huntington Polytech. Inst, 1940-41; student, U. Pitts., 1944-46. Registered profl. engr., N.Y. Pipe fitter, design draftsman Eastman Kodak Kodak Park, Rochester, N.Y., 1935-40; design engr. chem. plant Carbide and Carbon Chems., South Charleston, W.Va., 1940-42; engr. design Koppers Co., Pitts., 1942-46; new plant ops. Buffalo, Houston, Granite City, Ill., 1943-45; project engr. Eastman Kodak, Kodak Park, Rochester, 1947-55, dept. head construction & maintaince div., 1955-67, dept. head utilities, waste disposal solid and liquid, 1967-75; design ops. assignment Kodak Carbide Carbon, Oak Ridge, Tenn., 1951-54; chair subcom. incineration Mfg. Chemist Assn., Washington, 1968-75; vice chmn. Monroe County Sewer Agy./Pure Waters Agy, 1964-73. Mem., chair Gates, Chili Ogden Sch. Bd., Monroe County, Rochester, 1959-68; rep. dist. 21 Republican Party, St. Lucie County, Fla., 1980-85, chair exec. com., 1983-85; mem. Gates Town Planning Bd., Monroe County, 1956-62, 67-75, Monroe County Pure Waters Bd., 1973-75, St. Lucie County Water/Sewer Authority, 1986-92. Mem. AIChE (cert., emeritus).

LINDSTROM, DONALD FREDRICK, JR., priest; b. Atlanta, July 18, 1943; s. Donald Fredrick Sr. and Elizabeth (Haynes) L.; m. Marcia Pace, Dec. 30, 1983; children: Christopher, Eric, Ashley, Ellison. ABJ, U. Ga., 1966; MDiv, Va. Theol. Sem., 1969; JD, Woodrow Wilson Coll. Law, 1977; postgrad., U. West Fla., 1984. Lic. marriage and family therapist. Broadcast journalist radio and TV Atlanta and N.Y.C., 1961-68; priest Episcopal ch., 1969—; rector Episcopal Ch. Mediator, Meridian, Miss., 1991—; pvt. practice as marriage and family therapist, Pensacola, Fla., 1983-91; ecumenical officer Diocese of Ctrl. Gulf Coast, 1989-91, Miss., 1992—; bd. visitors Kanuga Conf. Ctr., 1993—; guest chaplain U.S. Ho. of Reps., 1994; mem. ecumenical staff gen. conv. Episcopal Ch., 1994. Writer, producer The Cry for Help, The Autumn Years. Chaplain Atlanta Police Dept., 1975-78, Meridian Police Dept., 1995—; pres. N.W. Fla. chpt. Nat. Kidney Found., 1987-88; mem. Leadership Atlanta, 1975; bd. dirs. Leadership Pensacola; trustee Fla. Trust for Hist. Preservation. Mem. Am. Assn. for Marriage and Family Therapy (clin.), Mental Health Assn. (life, bd. dirs. Pensacola 1986-88), Navy League, Order of Holy Cross (assoc.), Regional Chambellan, Confrerie de la Chaine des Rotisseurs, Bailli, Bailliage de Meridian, Alpha Tau Omega, Sigma Delta Chi, Delta Gamma Kappa. Office: Episcopal Ch Mediator 3825 35th Ave Meridian MS 39305-3617

LINDSTROM, ERIC EVERETT, ophthalmologist; b. Helena, Mont., Nov. 28, 1936; s. Everett Harry and Nan Augusta (Johnson) L.; BS, Wheaton Coll., 1958; MD, U. Md., 1963; MPH, Harvard U., 1966; m. Nancy Jo Alexander, July 24, 1960; children: Laura Ann, Eric Everett. Intern, Madigan Army Med. Center, Tacoma, Wash., 1963-64; resident in aerospace medicine Sch. Aerospace Medicine, Brooks AFB, Tex., 1966-68, resident in ophthalmology Brooke Army Med. Ctr., Ft. Sam Houston, Tex., 1972-75; surgeon 12th combat aviation group U.S. Army, Vietnam, 1968-69, chief profl. svcs. and aviation medicine Beach Army Hosp., Ft. Wolters, Tex., 1969-72; asst. chief ophthalmology clinic Madigan Army Med. Center, Tacoma, 1975-76; now with Lindstrom Eye Clinic; med. dir. Palo Pinto County (Tex.) Mental Health Clinic., 1970-72; cons. Tex. State Rehab. Com., 1971-72; chmn. bd. trustees South Cen. Regional Med. Ctr.; sr. aviation med. examiner, FAA; flight surgeon Miss. ANG, ret. Deacon First Bapt. Ch., Laurel, 1978—; bd. dirs. Laurel Salvation Army. Decorated Bronze Star, Air medal with 2 oak leaf clusters, Meritorious Svc. medal. Diplomate Am. Bd. Preventive Medicine, Am. Bd. Ophthalmology. Fellow ACS, Am. Coll. Physician Execs., Am. Coll. Preventive Medicine, Aerospace Med. Assn. (assoc.), Am. Acad. Ophthalmology; mem. AMA, FAA (sr. aviation med. examiner), Am. Acad. Cataract and Refractive Surgery, New Orleans Acad. Ophthalmology, Miss. Med. Assn. (trustee), Miss. EENT Assn., South Miss. Med. Soc., Southern Med. Assn., La.-Miss. EENT Assn., Flying Physicians Assn., Soc. Mil. Ophthalmologists, Soc. of USAF Flight Surgeons, Alliance of Air N.G. Flight Surgeons, Aircraft Owners and Pilots Assn., Nu Sigma Nu. Club: Kiwanis. Home: 809 Cherry Ln Laurel MS 39440-1651 Office: Lindstrom Eye Clinic PO Box 407 Laurel MS 39441-0407

LING, LILY HSU-CHIANG, real estate executive, accountant; b. Taipei, Republic of China, May 29, 1952; came to U.S., 1974; d. John Y. and Sophia (Siu-ho) Liu; m. William Chong-Seng Ling, Dec. 23, 1976; 1 child, Johnathan. B of Bus., Chengchi U., Republic of China, 1974; MBA, Fla. State U., 1975. CPA, Tex. Acct. The Lummus Co., Houston, 1978-79; gen. ledger acct. Black, Sivalls & Bryson Inc., Houston, 1979-81; pres. Lily H. Ling & Co., Houston, 1981—; sales mgr. Robert William Homes, Inc. and L. William Homes, Houston, 1991—. Bd. dirs. Tex. Buddhist Assn., Houston, 1985-90. Mem. AICPA, Tex. Soc. CPAs, Houston Bd. Realtors, Houston Soc. Chinese-Am. CPAs, Chengchi U. Alumni Assn. (pres. Houston chpt. 1984). Office: Lily H Ling & Co 7011 Harwin Dr Ste 178 Houston TX 77036-2121

LINGERFELT, B. EUGENE, JR., minister; b. Highland Park, Mich., Dec. 18, 1955; s. Beecher Eugene and Nellie Beatrice (Sampson) L.; m. Suzanne Marie Martin, Aug. 7, 1976; children: Austin Stuart, Krystina Marie. BA, Cen. Bible Coll., Springfield, Mo., 1976; MDiv, Tex. Christian Univ., 1980; D of Ministry, Southwestern Bapt. Theol. Seminary, Ft. Worth, 1984. Ordained min. Cathedral of Praise Ch., 1984. Assoc. pastor Bethel Temple, Ft. Worth, 1978-82; missionary, guest lectr. East Africa Sch. of Theology, Nairobi, Kenya, 1982-83; marriage enrichment seminar speaker, 1983; founder and sr. pastor Cathedral of Praise, Arlington, Tex., 1984—; founder Cathedral Christian Acad., 1988—; founder Overcoming Faith TV, 1994—. Co-author: Money: A Spiritual Force, 1985, The Spirit of Excellence, 1994, Compromise in the Church, 1995; contbr. articles to religious jours. Named to Outstanding Young Men of Am., 1980. Republican. Office: Cathedral of Praise PO Box 121234 Arlington TX 76012-1234

LINK, RAYMOND ROGER, property broker, natural resource consultant; b. Mineola, N.Y., Sept. 22, 1943; s. Otto and Elizabeth (Greube) L. BA in Conservation Biology, Fla. Atlantic U., 1972. Field biologist Fla. Bd. Trustees of Internal Improvement Trust Fund, 1972; staff biologist Wilson, Miller, Barton, Soll & Peek, Inc., Naples, Fla., 1973-75; natural resources cons. Naples, 1976—; pres. Glass-Link & Assocs., Inc., Naples, 1982—. Active Collier County Environ. Adv. Coun., 1978-88; mem. Collier County Planning Commn., 1988-92, sec., 1992; precinct committeeman Collier County Rep. Com., 1984. With USAR, 1969-71. Lutheran. Home: 5770 12th Ave SW Naples FL 33999-4908 Office: Glass Link & Assocs Inc 1020 8th Ave S Ste I Naples FL 34102-6959

LINK, ROBERT JAMES, lawyer, educator; b. Washington, May 25, 1950; s. Robert Wendell and Barbara Ann (Bullock) L.; m. Cheryl Ann Brillante, Apr. 22, 1978; children: Robert Edward, Holden James. BA, U. Miami, 1972, JD, 1975. Bar: Fla. 1975, U.S. Dist. Ct. (mid. dist.) Fla. 1980, U.S. Ct. Appeals (5th cir.) 1980, U.S. Ct. Appeals (11th cir.) 1981, U.S. Supreme Ct. 1984, U.S. Dist. Ct. (no. dist.) Fla. 1989. Asst. pub. defender City of Miami, Fla., 1975-78, City of Jacksonville, Fla., 1978-82; ptnr. Greenspan, Goodstein & Link, Jacksonville, 1982-84, Goodstein & Link, Jacksonville, 1984-85; sole practice Jacksonville, 1985-88; assoc. Howell, Liles & Milton, Jacksonville, 1988-89; ptnr. Pajcic & Pajcic P.A., 1990—; guest instr. U. Miami, 1976, U. Fla., 1979-88, Stetson Law Sch., 1984, Jacksonville U., 1987-88, U. North Fla., 1991. Atty. legal panel ACLU, Jacksonville, 1982-88; bd. dirs. Jacksonville Legal Aid, 1990-92. Mem. Fla. Bar Assn. (chmn. com. for representation of indigents criminal law sect. 1980, cert. criminal trial lawyer 1989), Jacksonville Bar Assn. (criminal law sect.), Nat. Assn. Criminal Def. Lawyers (vice-chmn. post conviction com. 1990), Fla. Pub. Defender Assn. (death penalty steering com. 1980-82, instr. 1979-89). Democrat. Methodist. Home: 3535 Carlyon St Jacksonville FL 32207-5836 Office: 1900 Independent Sq Jacksonville FL 32202-5013

LINK, WILLIAM ALLEN, history educator; b. Evanston, Ill., Aug. 18, 1954; s. Arthur Stanley and Margaret McDowell (Douglas) L.; m. Susannah Hopkins Jones, June 21, 1980; children: Percy Anne, Margaret Dorothy, Josephine McDowell. BA, Davidson Coll., 1976; MA, U. Va., 1979, PhD, 1981. Asst. prof. history U. N.C., Greensboro, 1981-86, assoc. prof. history, 1986-92, prof. history, 1992—, assoc. dean, Coll. Arts and Scis., 1995—; editl. bd. History of Education Quarterly, 1994-96. Author: A Hard Country and a Lonely Place: Schooling, Society, and Reform in Rural Virginia, 1870-1920, 1986, The Paradox of Southern Progressivism, 1880-1930, 1992, William Friday: Power, Purpose, and American Higher Education, 1995. Elder, Starmount Presbyn. Ch., Greensboro, 1996—. Recipient Mayflower prize, N.C. Lit. and Hist. Assn., 1993, 95. Mem. Am. Hist. Assn., Hist. Edn. Soc., So. Hist. Assn., Hist. Soc. N.C., Phi Beta Kappa. Presbyterian. Home: 219 S Tremont Dr Greensboro NC 27403 Office: U NC Coll Arts and Sciences 105 Foust Bldg Greensboro NC 27412

LINKONIS, SUZANNE NEWBOLD, pretrial case manager, counselor; b. Phila., Aug. 24, 1945; d. William Bartram and Kathryn (Taylor) Newbold; m. Bertram Lawrence Linkonis, May 29, 1966; children: Robert William, Deborah Anne, Richard Anthony. AA in Psychology, Albany (Ga.) Jr. Coll., 1979; BA in Psychology, Albany (Ga.) State Coll., 1981; MS in Indsl. Psychology, Va. Commonwealth U., 1986. Office mgr., media buyer Long Advt. Agy., Richmond, Va., 1981-84; media mgr. Clarke & Assocs., Richmond, 1984-85; human resources asst. Continental Ins., Richmond, 1985; rsch. assoc. Signet Bank, N.A., Richmond, 1986-87; program coord. Med. Coll. Va., Richmond, 1988; personnel mgr. Bur. Microbiology, Richmond, 1988; pers. specialist Va. State Dept. Corrections, Richmond, 1989-90; human rights adv. Va. State Dept. Youth and Family Svcs., Richmond, 1990-92, rehab. counselor, 1992-94, sr. rehab. counselor, 1994; pre-trial case mgr./counselor Henrico County Govt., 1995—; future dir., cons. Mary Kay Cosmetics, Springfield, Va., 1975-77. Mem. NAFE, APA. Republican. Roman Catholic. Home: 401 Saybrook Dr Richmond VA 23236-3621 Office: 8600 Dixon Powers Dr Richmond VA 23228-2737

LINNEHAN, PAUL JOSEPH, English language educator; b. Cambridge, Mass., Sept. 2, 1946; s. Leonard Joseph and Ruth Elizabeth (Power) L.; m. Genevieve Angus, Nov. 24, 1973; children: Andrew, Meredith. Student, Jesuit Sem., 1964-72; BA magna cum laude, Boston Coll., 1970; PhD in English and Comparative Lit., Washington U., St. Louis, 1975. Teaching asst. Washington U., 1973-75; writer Sears, Roebuck Advt., Chgo., 1976; tchr. English Jesuit High Sch., Tampa, Fla., 1976-89, chmn. English dept., 1979-87; Fulbright exch. tchr. Richard-Wagner Gymnasium, Bayreuth, Germany, 1987-88; instr. English Hillsborough C.C., Tampa, 1989; assoc. prof. English U. Tampa, 1989—, dir. first year writing, 1995—; cons. great books program Mitchell Elem. Sch., Tampa, 1989—, nonfiction editor Tampa Review, 1994—; judge essay contests Hillsborough County Schs., Tampa, 1989—; contbr. lectrs., presentations, films for honors program U. Tampa, coord. steering com. devel. studies program, mem. curriculum devel. studies program, mem. curriculum com., 1991—, mem. William Stewart Scholarship com., 1991—, mem. faculty publs. coms., 1992—, mem. honors com., 1989-90, mem. steering com. on enhancement of teaching, 1989-91; presenter in field. Co-author: The Best Test Preparation for the CLAST, 1994; translator: The Tampa Rev., 1992, nonfiction editor, 1994—. Coord. Sun City Center (Fla.) Lectr. Series, 1992-93; tutor Time-to-Read Program, Tampa, 1992-93; interpreter World Championship Challenge Boxing, Tampa, 1992; asst. coach Bayshore Little League, Tampa, 1991-93; vol. editorial work Tampa Mus. Art; lay minister all-mem. canvassing dr. St. John's Episcopal Ch., Tampa, 1990. Fulbright Exch. grantee U. Tampa, 1992, 93, 94. Mem. MLA, Nat. Coun. Tchrs. English, Fla. Coll. English Assn., Conf. on Coll. Composition, Fla. Coll. English Assn. (bd. dirs. 1994—). Home: 2515 W Palm Dr Tampa FL 33629-7313 Office: U Tampa 401 W Kennedy Blvd Tampa FL 33606-1450

LINNSTAEDT, JOHN BYRON, retired military officer, operations researcher; b. Ft. Worth, July 13, 1945; s. George Adolph Linnstaedt and Nona Mae (Floyd) Watson; m. Susan Beatrice Tree, Feb. 24, 1974; children: David J., Andrew J., Sarah D., Richard M. BS in Chem. Engring., U. Houston, 1969; MS in Ops. Mgmt., U. Ark., 1976; MS in Sys. Tech., Naval Postgrad. Sch., Monterey, Calif., 1984. Registered profl. engr., Tex. Commd. 2d lt. USAF, 1969, advanced through grades to maj., ret., 1989. With USMC, 1995-96.

LINTHICUM, JAMES HAROLD, principal; b. Independence, Kans., Mar. 9, 1944; s. Lovell Thornton and Elsie May (Honeywell) L.; m. Betty Lois Gaines, Aug. 15, 1964; 1 child, Melinda Lois. BS, Tex. Tech. U., 1968; MEd, Sul Ross State U., 1978. Cert. tchr., sch. adminstr., Tex. Rsch. technician Tex. A&M Rsch. Ctr., Lubbock, 1967-68; sales mgr. Procter & Gamble Distbn. Co., Lubbock, 1968-70; tchr. Seminole (Tex.) High Sch., 1970-82, 85-87; gen. mgr. Tusha Bldgs., Inc., Lubbock, 1982-83; communications cons. Motorola Communications & Electronics, Lubbock, 1983-85; asst. prin. Seminole Jr. High Sch., 1987-94; prin. Seminole H.S., 1994—; dist. dir. Drug Free Schs. Team, Seminole, 1987—. Producer, dir. video presentation on edn. County chmn. Congl. election com., Seminole, 1975, county election counting sta. judge and mgr., 1981-94. Mem. Nat. Assn. Secondary Sch. Prins., Tex. Assn. Secondary Sch. Prins. (Region XVII Outstanding Prin.-Vice Prin. of Yr., 1993-94, Tex. State Tchrs. Assn. (life), Seminole Area C. of C. (bd. dirs. 1984-86), Tex. Edn. Agy. State Accreditation Team, Seminole Lions Club (bd. dirs. 1984-90, pres. 1991-92). Republican. Methodist. Home: 2117 NW Avenue C Seminole TX 79360-3004 Office: Seminole Ind Schs 2201 Hobbs Hwy Seminole TX 79360

LINTO, NANCY, nursing case manager; b. Madison, Wis., Dec. 30, 1959; d. Roger H. and Ann L. (Coyle) Rebholz; m. Johnnie Linto Jr., June 27, 1987; children: William, Emily. BSN, Viterbo Coll., La Crosse, Wis., 1982. Cert. in EKG monitoring, ACLS, med./surg. nursing. Staff nurse Sacred Heart Hosp., Eau Claire, Wis.; traveling nurse Boswell Meml. Hosp., Sun City, Ariz., McLeod Regional Med. Ctr., Florence, S.C., Lubbock (Tex.) Gen. Hosp., Morton F. Plant Hosp., Clearwater, Fla., Meml. Med. Ctr., Savannah, Ga.; Healthmaster Home Health, Augusta, Ga.; asst. dir. med., C.A.R.E. coord. Lanier Park Regional Hosp., Gainesville, Ga.

LINTZ, CHRISTOPHER RAY, archaeologist; b. Bryn Mawr, Pa., Aug. 20, 1948; s. Joseph and Mary Avis (Powell) L.; m. Roberta Ann Kleykamp, Oct. 24, 1969; children: Cynthia A., Patrick R., Andrew J. BA, Ariz. State U., 1970; MA, U. Okla., 1975, PhD, 1984. Archaeol. tech. Pueblo Grande Mus./Park, Phoenix, 1970, Okla. River Basin Survey, Norman, Okla., 1971; teaching asst. dept. anthropology U. Okla., Norman, 1972-73, rsch. archaeologist archaeol. rsch. mgmt. ctr., 1978-80, acting dir., 1983-84; archaeol. coord. Earth Sci. Obs., Norman, 1973-75; field archaeologist Okla. Archaeol. Survey, Norman, 1978-80; rsch. archaeologist Okla. Conservation Commn., Norman, 1980-82, 84-85; rsch. prof. ctr. for archaeol. rsch. U. Denver, 1985-86; project mgr. cultural resources MARIAH Assocs., Albuquerque, 1986-89; cultural resource program dir. MARIAH Assocs., Austin, Tex., 1989—; Author: Archaeology of Gus Fruh Park, 1995; contbr. articles to books and profl. jours. Active in providing expert testimony to various legis. subcoms., Tex., 1994, 95. Mem. Plains Anthrop. Soc. (pres. 1994, bd. dirs., sec. 1991-93), Tex. Hist. Commn. (adv. bd. dept. antiquities protection 1994-96), Coun. Tex. Archaeologists (sec.-treas. 1991-93), Okla. Coun. Profl. Archaeologists (pres., v.p. 1981-82), mem. numerous state, regional and nat. archaeol. socs., Toughlove Internat. (group leader Austin chpt. 1995). Home: # 193 8617 Spicewood Springs Rd Austin TX 78759 Office: TRC-MARIAH Assocs 3939 Bee Caves Rd C-100 Austin TX 78746

LINZ, GERHARD DAVID, psychologist; b. Waltershausen, Thuringia, Germany, Jan. 5, 1927; came to U.S., 1936; s. Leopold and Rita (Nussbaum) L.; m. Frances Ann Pierson; children: Christopher, Michael, Stephanie, Peter. B in Elec. Engring. with honors, Ga. Inst. Tech., 1948, MS, 1949; BDiv, Episcopal Theol. Sem. S.W., Austin, Tex., 1956; PhD, U. Tex., Austin, 1966. Diplmate Am. Bd. Profl. Psychology, Counseling Psychology. Rsch. engr. RCA Labs., Princeton, N.J., 1949-51; rsch. engr., Engring. Experiment Sta. Ga. Tech., Atlanta, 1951-53; rsch. engr., Def. Rsch. Lab. U. Tex., Austin, 1953-56; vicar All Saints Episcopal Ch., Warner Robins, Ga., 1956-59; assoc. rector Christ Ch. Episcopal, Macon, Ga., 1959; Episcopal chaplain U. Tex., Austin, 1960-66; asst. prof. Counseling Ctr. Mich. State U., East Lansing, 1966-70; from assoc. prof. to prof., assoc. dir. Counseling Ctr. Ga. State U., Atlanta, 1970-93, Alumni Disting. prof., 1984; pvt. practice Decatur, Ga., 1971—; mem. dept. Christian Edn., Episcopal Diocese of Atlanta, 1957-59; bd. dirs. Inst. for Marital and Family Therapy, Atlanta. Author: Novice Notes-An Introduction to Cryptanalysis, 1990; contbr. articles to profl. jours. Chaplain Civitan Club, Warner Robins, Ga., 1958-59. With U.S. Army, 1945-46, ATO. Mem. Assn. Counseling Ctr. Tng. Agts. (v.p. 1979-85), Am. Psychol. Assn., Soc. for Clin. and Exptl. Hypnosis, Southeastern Psychol. Assn., Ga. Psychol. Assn., Ga. Coll. Pers. Assn. Episcopalian.

LIPCON, CHARLES ROY, lawyer; b. N.Y.C., Mar. 20, 1946; s. Harry H. and Rose Lipcon; m. Irmgard Adels, Dec. 1, 1974; children: Lauren, Claudia. B.A., U. Miami, 1968, J.D., 1971. Bar: Fla. 1971, U.S. Dist. Ct. (so. dist.) Fla. 1971, U.S. Ct. Appeals (5th cir.) 1972, U.S. Supreme Ct. 1976, U.S. Ct. Appeals (D.C. cir.) 1980, U.S. Dist. Ct. (so. dist.) Tex. 1982, U.S. Ct. Appeals (11th cir.) 1994. Pvt. practice, Miami, Fla., 1971—; lectr. U. Miami Sch. Law; moderator Am. On Line section on Admiralty Law. Author: Help for the Auto Accident Victim, 1984, Seaman's Rights in the United States When Involved in An Accident, 1989. Named Commodore of High Seas, Internat. Seaman's Union. Mem. Fla. Bar Assn., Am. Trial Lawyers Assn., ABA, Fla. Trial Lawyers, Dade County Bar Assn., Dade County Trial Lawyers. Club: Rotary (Key Biscayne). Contbr. articles to profl. jours. Office: 2 S Biscayne Blvd Ste 2480 Miami FL 33131-1801

LIPE, LINDA BON, lawyer; b. Clarksdale, Miss., Jan. 10, 1948; s. William Ray and Gwendolyn (Strickland) Lipe. BBA in Accountancy, U. Miss., 1970, JD, 1971. Bar: Miss. 1971, Ark. 1976, U.S. Dist. Ct. (no. dist.) Miss. 1971, U.S. Dist. Ct. (ea. dist.) Ark. 1976, U.S. Ct. Appeals (8th cir.) 1985. Sr. tax acct. Arthur Young & Co., San Jose, Calif., 1971-74, A.M. Pullen & Co., Knoxville, Tenn., 1975; legal counsel to gov. State of Ark., Little Rock, 1975-79; dep. pros. atty. 6th Jud. Dist. Ark., Little Rock, 1979-80; chief counsel Ark. Public Service Commn., Little Rock, 1980-83; asst. U.S. atty. Eastern Dist. Ark., Dept. Justice, Little Rock, 1983—. Mem. ABA, Miss. State Bar, Ark. State Bar Assn., Ark. Bar Assn. Episcopalian. Office: US Attys Office PO Box 1229 Little Rock AR 72203-1229

LIPHAM, WILLIAM PATRICK, principal, educator; b. Franklin, Ga., Oct. 15, 1950; s. William Taft and Claudie Evelyn (McCord) Lipham; m. Jane King, Aug. 11, 1973; children: Leslie Ann, William Brian. BA, West Ga. Coll., 1972, MEd, 1979, EdS, 1990. Cert. in secondary sci., adminstrn./supervision, Ga. Tchr. Heard County Bd. Edn., Franklin, Ga.; asst. prin. Heard County Bd. Edn., prin. With U.S. Army Nat. Guard, 1972-78. Recipient Dave Edelson award, Boy Scouts Am., 1982, Dist. award of Merit, 1980. Mem. Ga. Assn. Educators, (v.p., pres., treas.), Ga. Assn. Edn. Leaders. Home: 2727 Ga 34 Hwy Franklin GA 30217 Office: Heard Elem Sch 150 Alford Dr Franklin GA 30217-6345

LIPKOVIC, PETER, chief medical examiner; b. Novisad, Yugoslavia, July 14, 1934; came to U.S., 1962; s. Dragutin and Anica (Klauser) L.; m. Lida M. Kovacevic, Oct. 11, 1964; children: Myrna Leilani, Vesna Maile. MD, U. Beograd, Yugoslavia, 1960. Intern Meml. Hosp., Phoenix, 1963-64; resident in pathology Maricopa County Hosp., Phoenix, 1964-65, Kuakini Hosp., Honolulu, 1965-66, St. Francis Hosp., Honolulu, 1966-68; forensic pathologist Med. Examiners Office, Balt., 1969-70; asst. prof. U. Hawaii, Honolulu, 1968-69; asst. prof., lectr. Johns Hopkins U., Balt., 1969-73; asst. prof. U. Md., Balt., 1969-73; asst. med. examiner State of Md., Balt., 1969-73; chief med. examiner 4th dist. State of Fla., Med. Examiner's Office, Jacksonville, 1973—; clin. prof. dept. pathology U. Fla., Gainesville, 1973-90. Recipient Good Govt. award, Jr. C. of C., Jacksonville, 1977-78. Fellow Am. Acad. Forensic Sci.; mem. Nat. Assn. Med. Examiners, Fla. Assn. Med. Examiners (pres. 1986-92). Republican. Roman Catholic. Office: Med Examiners Office 2100 Jefferson St Jacksonville FL 32206-3534

LIPMAN, IRA ACKERMAN, security service company executive; b. Little Rock, Nov. 15, 1940; s. Mark and Belle (Ackerman) L.; m. Barbara Ellen Kelly Couch, July 5, 1970; children: Gustave K., Joshua S, M Benjamin. Student, Ohio Wesleyan U., 1958-60; LLD (hon.), John Marshall U., Atlanta, 1970. Salesman, exec. Mark Lipman Svcs. Inc., Memphis, 1960-63; v.p. Guardsmark, Inc., Memphis, 1963-66; pres. Guardsmark, Inc., 1966—, CEO, 1968—, chmn. bd., 1968—; bd. dirs. Nat. Coun. on Crime and Delinquency, 1975—, chmn. fin. com., treas., 1978-79, vice chmn. bd. dirs., 1982-86, chmn. exec. com., 1986-93, chmn. bd. dirs., 1993-94, chmn. emeritus, 1995—; bd. dirs. Greater Memphis Coun. Crime and Delinquency, 1976-78, entrepreneurial fellow Memphis State U., 1976; mem. environ. security com., pvt. security adv. coun. Law Enforcement Assistance adminstrn., 1975-76; mem. conf. planning com. 2d Nat. Law Enforcement Explorer Conf., 1980. Author: How to Protect Yourself From Crime, 1975, 3d edit., 1989; contbr. numerous articles to profl. jours., mags. and newspapers. Bd. dirs. Memphis Jewish Cmty. Center, 1974, Memphis Shelby County unit Am. Cancer Soc., 1980-81, Memphis Orchestral Soc., 1980-81, Memphis Jewish Fedn., 1974-83; chmn. Shelby County com. U.S. Savs. Bonds, 1976; mem. president's coun. Memphis State U., 1975-79;, mem. visual arts coun., 1980-82; Memphis met. chmn. Nat. Alliance Businessmen, 1970-71; mem. task force Reform Jewish Outreach, Union Am. Hebrew Congregations, 1979-83; mem. young leadership cabinet United Jewish Appeal, 1973-78, mem. S.E. regional campaign cabinet, 1980; exec. bd. Chickasaw council Boy Scouts Am., 1978-81; bd. dirs., exec. com. Tenn. Ind. Coll. Fund, 1979; trustee Memphis Acad. Arts, 1977-81; mem. president's club Christian Bros. Coll., 1979; bd. dirs. Future Memphis, 1980-83, 83-86; nat. trustee NCCJ, 1980-92, exec. com., 1981-92, nat. Jewish co-chmn., 1985-88, nat. chmn., 1988-92, hon. chmn., past nat. chmn. nat. conf. Christians and Jews, 1992—; bd. dirs. Memphis chpt., 1980-85, life bd. dirs. Memphis chpt. 1985—; group II chmn. for 1982 campaign United Way Greater Memphis, 1981; v.p. exec. com. Internat. Coun. Christians and Jews, 1992-94; bd. govs. United Way of Am., 1992—, bd. gov.'s liaison, 1991-92, chmn. ethics com., 1992—, mem. exec. com., 1992—, co-chmn. vol. involvement com., 1992—, mem. strategic planning com., 1994—; chmn. UWLC steering com. 1995—; mem. Alexis de Tocqueville Soc. Nat. Leadership Coun., 1992—, mem. Second Century Initiative Vol. Involvement com., 1987-91; chair Task Force on Critical Markets, 1987-91, mem. exec. cabinet, 1990-91; trustee Memphis Brooks Mus. Art, 1980-83, Yeshiva U.; trustee Simon Wiesenthal Ctr., 1982—, chmn. campaign com., 1983—, mem. fin. and audit com., 1993—; bd. dirs. Nat. Alliance against Violence, 1983-85, Nat. Ctr. Learning Disabilities, 1989-94, United Way of Greater Memphis, 1984-85, gen. campaign chmn., 1985-86; founder, bd. overseers B'nai Brith, 1980; bd. dirs. Tenn. Gov.'s Jobs for High Sch. Grads. Program, 1980-83; trustee Ohio Wesleyan U., 1988—; vice chmn. spl. task force on endowment growth Ohio Wesleyan U., 1990—; mem. bd. overseers Wharton Sch., U. Pa., 1991—, devel. com., 1995—; assoc. trustee U. Pa., 1991—; mem. exec. com. Am. Israel Pub. Affairs Com., 1991—. Recipient Humanitarian of Yr. award NCCJ, 1985, Outstanding Cmty. Sales award Sales and Mktg. Execs. Memphis, 1987, Jr. Achievement Master Free Enterprise award, 1987, Alexis de Tocqueville Soc. award, 1995; one of 10 cited as Best Corp. Chief Exec. of Achievement, Gallagher Pres.'s Report, 1974. Mem. Internat. Assn. Chiefs Police, Am. Soc. Criminology, Internat. Soc. Criminology, Am. Soc. Indsl. Security (cert. protection profl.), 100 Club, B'nai B'rith, Ridgeway Country Club, Racquet Club, Summit Club, Econ. Club (bd. dirs. 1980-85, v.p. 1983-84, pres. 1984-85, chmn. exec. com. 1984-85), Internat. Club (Washington). Republican.

LIPPITT, ALAN BRUCE, orthopedic surgeon; b. Norwich, Conn., June 22, 1941; s. Harold and Ruth Shirley (Sakowitz) L.; m. Ellen Wessler, Jan. 1967 (div. 1974); m. Linda Nathanson, Aug. 1, 1975; children: Melanie, Karen, Scott, Elizabeth, Jennifer, Daniel. BS, Trinity Coll., 1963; MD, N.Y. Med. Coll., 1969. Diplomate Am. Bd. Orthop. Surgery. Intern then resident Hosp. Joint Diseases, N.Y.C., 1969-74; pvt. practice Atlanta, 1976—; clin. instr. Ga. Bapt. Orthop. Residency Program; sanctioned second opinion orthop. surgeon Nat. Football League Player's Assn., 1994—; chmn. orthop. quality assurance com. Ga. Bapt. Med. Ctr.; attending physician Northlake Regional Med. Ctr.; presenter in field. Contbr. articles to profl. jours. Maj. U.S. Army Med. Corps., 1974-76. Mem. So. Med. Assn., So. Orthop. Assn., Am. Assn. Orthop. Medicine (bd. dirs. 1992-94, sec., treas. 1993-95), Am. Back Soc., Internat. Spinal Injection Soc. Home: 1327 Paces Forest Dr NW Atlanta GA 30327 Office: 315 Boulevard Ste 336 Atlanta GA 30312

LIPPMAN, ALFRED JULIAN, retired real estate executive; b. Newark, May 7, 1900; s. Lewis Isaac and Henrietta (Meyer) L. With L. Bamberger & Co. Dept. Store, Newark, 1912-22; buyer Symons Dry Goods Co., Butte, Mont., 1922-26; asst. mdse. mgr. Stix, Baer & Fuller Co., St. Louis, 1926-28; mdse. mgr. Union Co., Columbus, Ohio, 1928; supr. N.J. br. offices Eisele & King, mems. N.Y. Stock Exchange, 1928-38; owner real estate bus., 1928-38; salesman, broker Feist & Feist, Newark, 1938-41; ptnr. real estate firm John E. Sloane & Co., Newark, 1941-45; owner, pres. successor firm Alfred J. Lippman Inc., 1945-80; pres. Fereday & Meyer Co. Inc. Contractors, Newark, 1938-80; exec. dir. Latin Am. Devel. and Ops. Co. V.p. Aerovias Latino Americanos, S.A. of Mexico, 1951-52; N.J. rep. to 3 presdl. inaugurations in Mexico; mem. N.J. Planning Bd., 1936-43; chmn. Sea Bright (N.J.) State Park Commn., 1938; mem. Mcpl. Sanitation Commn., 1952; vice chmn. solid wastes tech. com. N.J. Dept. Health; dir. Children to Children Orgn.; dir. extension course on solid wastes disposal Rutgers U., 1962-71. Served with USN, World War I, USCGR, World War II. Decorated Order of Aztec Eagle (Mexico), 1952, L'Ordre Internacional du Bien Public Comandeur, comdr. Order Holy Cross Jerusalem; named Man of Yr., Acapulco, Mexico, 1971; recipient Disting. Achievement award Advt. Club N.Y., 1964, diploma and gold medal for extraordinary contbn. Mexican Nat. Tourist Coun., 1967, Gold medallion Port Authority N.J. and N.Y., 1975, Order of Lafayette, 1959; named Outstanding Citizen N.J., K.P., 1955, hon. consul Mex., 1957-77, consul-gen., 1977-78, others. Mem. Am. Legion (life), Soc. Solid Waste Technicians (pres.), Circus Saints and Sinners (nat. v.p.), Nat. Sweepstakes Regatta of Red Bank, N.J. (past rear commodore), Mex. Acad. Internat. Law, Mex. C. of C. of U.S. (pres. 1962-78, chmn. bd. 1978-89), N.J. World Trade Com., Consular Corps Coll. Home: 4748 S Ocean Blvd Boca Raton FL 33487-5367

LIPPMAN, SCOTT MICHAEL, oncologist; b. Columbia, S.C., Apr. 2, 1955; s. Melvyn and Nanette (Gwirtzman) L.; m. Mary Elizabeth Marsh, Feb. 27, 1987; children: Kyle Andrew, Elizabeth Pauline. BS, U. Calif., 1977; MD, The Johns Hopkins U., 1981. Diplomate Am. Bd. Internal Medicine, Am. Bd. Oncology and Hematology. Clin. dir., faculty mem. cancer prevention control program U. Ariz., Tucson, 1987-88; asst. prof. medicine U. Tex. M.D. Anderson Cancer Ctr., Houston, 1988-92, assoc. prof. medicine, 1992-96, prof. medicine, chair dept. clin. cancer prevention, 1996—; chmn. chemoprevention subcom. Radiation Therapy Oncology Group, Phila., 1990—; mem. spl. rev. com. Nat. Cancer Inst., Bethesda, Md., 1992—. Author: (with others) Cancer Medicine, 1993; co-editor: Molecular Markers of Early Detection of Cancer, 1992; author, assoc. editor: Jour. of Nat. Cancer Inst., 1995; editl. bd. Nat. Cancer Inst., PDQ, 1995. Recipient Career Devel. award Am. Cancer Soc., 1989-92; hon. professorship La Universidad de Guadalajara, Mex., 1993; grantee Nat. Cancer Inst., 1991—. Fellow ACP; mem. Am. Soc. Clin. Oncology (mem. cancer prevention com. 1993—, program com. 1995, Travel award 1985), Am. Soc. Preventive Oncology, Am. Assn. Cancer Rsch. (membership com. 1993—), Am. Assn. Cancer Edn., Am. Soc. Hematology. Home: 2420 Locke Ln Houston TX 77019-6323 Office: U Tex MD Anderson Cancer Ct 1515 Holcombe Blvd # 80 Houston TX 77030-4009

LIPSCOMB, GUY FLEMING, JR., artist, manufacturer, chemist, educator; b. Clemson, S.C., Apr. 11, 1917; s. Guy Fleming Sr. and Adelin (Schroder) L.; m. Margaret Fant, June 30, 1942; children: Margaret, Louise, Georgia, Elizabeth. BS, U. S.C., 1938, DFA (hon.), 1988. Pres. Anchor Continental & Cont. Chem., Columbia, S.C., 1955-75, chmn. bd., 1975-79; pvt. practice Columbia, 1979-96, tchr. art, 1978-91; mem. adv. bd. 1st Nat. Bank of S.C., Columbia, 1955-70. Painter (watercolors, water-based medium), exhibits include 30 one-man shows. Pres. Columbia Mus. of Art, chmn. bd. dirs., 1972-74; chmn. bd. dirs. S.C. State Mus., Columbia, 1975-96. Recipient Outstanding Alumnus award U. S.C. Order of the Palmetto.

Mem. Rotary (pres. 1957). Home: 1717 W Buchanan Dr Columbia SC 29206-2850

LIPSCOMB, OSCAR HUGH, archbishop; b. Mobile, AL, Sept. 21, 1931; s. Oscar Hugh and Margaret (Saunders) L. S.T.L., Gregorian U., Rome, 1957; Ph.D., Cath. U. Am., 1963. Ordained priest Roman Cath. Ch., 1956; consecrated bishop Roman Cath. Ch., 1980. Asst. pastor Mobile, 1959-65; tchr. McGill Inst., Mobile, 1959-60, 61-62; vice chancellor Diocese of Mobile-Birmingham, 1963-66, chancellor, 1966-80; pastor St. Patrick Parish, Mobile, 1966-71; lectr. history Spring Hill Coll., Mobile, 1971-72; asst. pastor St. Matthew Parish, Mobile, 1971-79, Cathedral Immaculate Conception, Mobile, 1979-80; adminstr. sede vacante Diocese of Mobile, 1980, now archbishop; pres. Cath. Housing Mobile, Mobile Senate Priests, 1978-80; chmn. com. on doctrine Nat. Conf. Cath. Bishops, 1988-91. Author articles, papers in field. Pres. bd. dirs. Mobile Mus., 1966-76; trustee Ala. Dept. Archives and History, Cath. U. Am., Washington, 1983—, Spring Hill Coll., Mobile; chmn. NCCB Com. on Ecumenical and Interreligious Affairs; chmn. bd. govs. N.Am. Coll., Rome, 1982-85. Mem. Am. Cath. Hist. Assn., So. Hist. Assn., Ala. Hist. Assn. (pres. 1971-72, exec. com. 1981-88), Hist. Mobile Preservation Soc., Lions. Address: PO Box 1966 36633 400 Government St Mobile AL 36602-2332

LIPSET, SEYMOUR MARTIN, sociologist, political scientist, educator; b. N.Y.C., Mar. 18, 1922; s. Max and Lena (Lippman) L.; m. Elsie Braun, Dec. 26, 1944 (dec. Feb. 1987); children: David, Daniel, Carola; m. Sydnee Guyer, July 29, 1990. BS, CCNY, 1943; PhD, Columbia U., 1949; MA (hon.), Harvard U., 1966; LLD (hon.), Villanova U., 1973, Hebrew U., 1981, U. Buenos Aires, 1987, Free U., Brussels, 1990, U. Judaism, 1991, Hebrew Union Coll., 1993, Boston Hebrew Coll., 1993, U. Guelph, 1996. Lectr. U. Toronto, 1946-48; asst. prof. U. Calif., Berkeley, 1948-50; asst., then assoc. prof. grad. faculty Columbia U., 1950-56, asst. dir. Bur. Applied Social Research, 1954-56; prof. sociology U. Calif., Berkeley, 1956-66, dir. Inst. Internat. Studies, 1962-66; vis. prof. social rels. and govt. Harvard U., 1965-66, prof. govt. and sociology, exec. com. Ctr. Internat. Affairs, 1966-75, George Markham prof. Ctr. Internat. Affairs, 1974-75; sr. fellow Hoover Inst. Stanford U., 1975—, prof. polit. sci. and sociology, 1975-92, Caroline S.G. Munro prof., 1981-92; Hazel prof. pub. policy George Mason U., Fairfax, Va., 1990—; Henry Ford vis. research prof. Yale U., 1960-61; Paley lectr. Hebrew U., 1973; Fulbright program 40th Anniversary Disting. lectr., 1987; vis. scholar Russell Sage Found., New York, 1988-89. Author: Agrarian Socialism, 1950, (with others) Union Democracy, 1956, (with R. Bendix) Social Mobility in Industrial Society, 1959, expanded edit., 1991, Political Man, 1960, expanded edit., 1981, The First New Nation, 1963, expanded edit., 1979, Revolution and Counter Revolution, 1968, expanded edit., 1988, (with Earl Raab) The Politics of Unreason, 1970, expanded edit., 1978, Rebellion in the University, 1972, (with Everett Ladd) Academics and the 1972 Election, 1973, Professors, Unions and American Higher Education, 1973, The Divided Academy, 1975, (with David Riesman) Education and Politics at Harvard, 1975, (with I.L. Horowitz) Dialogues on American Politics, 1978, (with William Schneider) The Confidence Gap, 1983, expanded edit., 1987, Consensus and Conflict, 1987, Continental Divide: The Institutions and Values of the United States and Canada, 1990, The Educational Background of American Jews, 1994; (with Earl Raab) Jews and the New American Scene, 1995, American Exceptionalism: A Double-Edged Sword, 1996; co-editor: Class, Status and Power, 1953, Labor and Trade Unionism, 1960, Sociology: The Progress of a Decade, 1961, Culture and Social Character, 1961, The Berkeley Student Revolt, 1965, Class, Status and Power in Comparative Perspective, 1966, Social Structure, Mobility and Economic Development, 1966, Elites in Latin America, 1967, Party Systems and Voter Alignments, 1967, Students in Revolt, 1969, Issues in Politics and Government, 1970, Failure of a Dream? Essays in the History of American Socialism, 1974, rev. edit., 1984; co-editor: Democracy in Developing Countries, 3 vols., Africa, Asia and Latin America, 1988, 89, Politics in Developing Countries, 1990, 95, The Encyclopedia of Democracy, 4 vols., 1995; co-editor Public Opinion mag., 1977-89, Internat. Jour. Pub. Opinion Rsch., 1989—; editor: Students and Politics, 1967, Politics and Social Science, 1969, Emerging Coalitions in American Politics, 1978, The Third Century, 1979, Party Coalitions in the Eighties, 1981, Unions in Transition, 1986, American Pluralism and the Jewish Community, 1990; adv. editor: various jours. including Sci., Comparative Politics. Mem. Bd. Fgn. Scholarships, 1968-71; bd. dirs. Aurora Found., 1985—, U.S. Inst. Peace, 1996—; nat. chmn. B'nai B'rith Hillel Found., 1975-79, chmn. nat. exec. com., 1979-84; assoc. pres. Am. Profs. for Peace in the Middle East, 1976-77, nat. pres., 1977-81; co-chmn. exec. com. Internat. Ctr. Peace in Middle East, 1982-92; co-chmn. Com. for Effective UNESCO, 1976-81; chmn. Com. for UN Integrity, 1981-83; chmn. nat. faculty cabinet United Jewish Appeal, 1981-84; pres. Progressive Found., 1991-95. Recipient Gunyar Myrdal prize, 1970, Townsend Harris medal, 1971, 125th Anniversary alumni medal CCNY, 1963, M.B. Rawson award, 1986, No. Telecom. Gold Medal for Can. Studies, 1987, Marshall Sklare award Assn. Social Sci. Study of Jewry, 1993; fellow Social Sci. Rsch. Coun., 1945-46, Ctr. Advanced Study Behavioral Sci. fellow, 1971-72, Woodrow Wilson Ctr. for Internat. Scholars fellow, 1995-96. Fellow NAS, AAAS (v.p. 1974-78, chmn. sect. on econ. and social sci. 1975-76, 95-96), Nat. Acad. Edn., Am. Sociol. Assn. (coun. 1959-62, MacIver award 1962, pres. 1992-93), Japan Soc.; mem. Sociol. Rsch. Assn. (exec. com. 1981-84, pres. 1985), Am. Polit. Sci. Assn. (coun. 1975-77, pres. 1981-82, Leon Epstein prize 1989), Internat. Polit. Sci. Assn. (coun. 1981-88, v.p. 1982-88), Internat. Soc. Polit. Psychology (pres. 1979-80), Internat. Sociol. Assn. (chmn. com. polit. sociology 1959-71), World Assn. Pub. Opinion Rsch. (v.p. and pres.-elect 1982-84, pres. 1984-86), Am. Philos. Soc., Finnish Acad. Sci. (hon.), Paul Lazarsfeld Gesellschaft (social rsch. 1994—), Soc. for Comparative Rsch. Office: George Mason U Inst of Policy Studies Pohick Module Fairfax VA 22030 also: Stanford U 213 Herbert Hoover Meml Bu Stanford CA 94305

LIPSHUTZ, ROBERT JEROME, lawyer, former government official; b. Atlanta, Dec. 27, 1921; s. Allen A. and Edith (Gavronski) L.; m. Barbara Sorelle Levin, Feb. 16, 1950 (dec.); children: Randall M., Judith Ann, Wendy Jean, Debbie Sue; m. Betty Beck Rosenberg, Feb. 10, 1973; stepchildren: Robert, Nancy Fay. J.D., U. Ga., 1943. Bar: Ga. 1943, D.C. 1980. Practice in Atlanta, 1947-77, 79—; ptnr. firm Lipshutz, Greenblatt & King, 1979—; counsel to Pres. U.S., Washington, 1977-79. Past vice chmn. Ga. Bd. Human Resources; treas., legal counsel Jimmy Carter Presdl. campaign com., 1976; trustee The Carter Ctr. Capt. AUS, 1944-46. Mem. Am., Ga., Atlanta, D.C. bar assns., Atlanta Lawyers Club, Atlanta., B'nai B'rith (past pres.). Jewish (past pres. The Temple). Office: Lipshutz Greenblatt & King Harris Tower Peachtree Ctr Ste 2300 Atlanta GA 30303

LIPTON, ALLEN DAVID, retail executive; b. Bklyn., Aug. 10, 1940; s. Moses Meyer and Pearl (Schiff) L.; m. Nanci Mayer, Feb. 24, 1963 (div. 1991); 1 child, Dawn Natalie; m. Vicky Jordan, Sept. 9, 1995. AAS, N.Y.C. Community Coll., 1961. Salesman Bakers Shoe Store, N.Y.C., 1961, Fabrex, N.Y.C., 1962-63, Sporteens, N.Y.C., 1963; asst. buyer Hammacher & Schlemmer, N.Y.C., 1961-62, Gimbels Dept. Store, N.Y.C., 1963-65; area mgr. Gimbels Dept. Store, Paramus, N.J., 1965-69; corp. buyer Stone & Thomas Dept. Store, Charleston, W.Va., 1969—; seminar spokesperson Draperies & Window Coverings Mag., N. Palm Beach, Fla., 1984; chmn. steering com. Fredrick Atkins Wholesale Buying Office. Author: Drapery and Curtain Department Store Training Manual, 1972, Buying Curtains and Draperies, 1987, Buying Carpet, Broadloom and Orental Rugs, 1991. Firefighter, Parsippany-Troy Hills (N.J.) Vol. Fire Assn., 1966-69. With N.Y. Nat. Guard, 1962-68. Recipient Leadership award Kirsch Co., 1983. Mem. Kanawha Valley Aquarium Soc. (pres. 1972, v.p. 1973, treas. 1975), Lions Club (v.p. Charleston 1996-97), Phi Kappa Rho (sec. 1960). Democrat. Jewish. Home: 1619 Quarrier St Apt A Charleston WV 25311-2136 Office: Stone & Thomas Dept Store Lee at Dickinson Charleston WV 25326

LIPTON, CLIFFORD CARWOOD, retired glass company executive; b. Huntington, W.Va., Jan. 30, 1920; s. Clifford Carwood and Zerelda (Adkins) L.; m. Alyce Jo Anne Eckley, Jan. 3, 1943 (dec. July 1975); children: Clifford Carwood III, Thomas Denton, Michael Forrester; m. Marie Hope Mahoney, May 26, 1976. B in Engring. Sci., Marshall U., 1948; postgrad. exec. mgmt. program, Pa. State U., 1959. Staff engr. Owens-Ill. Inc., Huntington, 1948-52; supr. engring. Owens-Ill. Inc., Streator, Ill., 1952-55; chief engr. divsn. Owens-Ill. Inc., Toledo, 1955-66; gen. mgr. Giralt Laporta SA, Madrid, 1966-71; dir. mfg. United Glass Ltd., London, 1971-74; mfg. and tech. dir. Owens-Ill. Internat., Geneva, 1974-82; dir. internat. devel. Owens-Ill. Inc., Toledo, 1982-83; ret., 1983; cons. Owens-Ill., Inc., China, Greece and U.S., 1983-85, Internat. Exec. Svc. Corps., 1986—. Mem. sch. bd. Am. Sch., Barcelona, Spain, 1966-67, Madrid, 1967-70; pres. Highland Trails Homeowners Assn., Southern Pines, N.C., 1987-93. 1st lt. Parachute Inf., U.S. Army, 1942-45. Mem. Benevolent and Protective Order Elks, 101st Airborne Divsn. Assn. Republican. Presbyterian. Home: 104 Selkirk Trl Southern Pines NC 28387-7230

LIS, JANET C., visual artist, writer/illustrator. BFA, Ohio U.; student (scholarship), Cleveland Inst. of Art. Exhibited in group shows at Pensacola (Fla.) Mus. (Mitchell Graphics award), Butler Inst. Am. Art (Top award Midyear Show), Youngstown, Ohio, San Diego Watercolor Soc., Southeastern Ctr. for Contemporary Art, Winston-Salem, N.C. (Purchase award), Columbus (Ga.) Mus., Springfield (Mo.) Mus., Ky. Watercolor Soc., Frankfort, Scottsdale (Ariz.) Ctr. for Arts, Soc. of Four Arts Exhbn., Palm Beach, Fla. (Hon. Mention), Lauren Rogers Mus., Laurel, Mich. (Purchase award), Grand Ctrl. Galleries, N.Y.C., Mint Mus. Art, Charlotte, N.C., Hanson Gallery, New Orleans, Miami-Dade C.C., U. New Orleans, Miami Met. Mus. and Art Ctrs., Soho 20, N.Y.C., Arts Assembly of Jacksonville, Fla., Mus. of Gt. Plains, Lawton, Okla., U. Ea. N.Mex., Portales, Springville (Utah) Mus. Art, Edison C.C., Ft. Myers, Fla. (Hon. Mention), Deep South Artists & Writers Conf., Baton Rouge (Hon. Mention), Southeastern Art Exhbn., Panama City, Fla. (3d Grand award), Jacksonville (Fla.) Jus. (Cash award); represented in collections at Savannahs Clubhouse, Merrit Island, Fla., Fla. Regional Office Bldg., Miami, Southeastern Ctr. for Contemporary Art, Laruen Rogers Mus., Hollywood (Fla.) Mus. Art, Holy Cross Hosp., Ft. Lauderdale, Fla., Ft. Lauderdale Symphony Orch., Internat. Inst. Human Rights, Strasbourg, France, Gen. Bldrs. Corp., Pompano Beach, Fla., Ohio U., Athens, Nat. Red Cross., Cleve., 1st United Meth. Ch., Pompano Beach, 1st Ch. of the Nazarene, Pompano Beach. Recipient Internat. Women's Yr. award Ford Found. Mem. So. Arts. Federation, Fla. Watercolor Soc., So. Watercolor Soc. Home: 12 Sunset Ln Pompano Beach FL 33062-7304

LISENBY, DORRECE EDENFIELD, realtor; b. Sneads, Fla., Dec. 2, 1942; d. Neal McLendon and Linnie (McCroan) Edenfield; m. Wallace Lamar Lisenby, Nov. 18, 1961; children: Pamela Ann, Wallace Neal. BS in Tech. Bus. magna cum laude, Athens (Ala.) State Coll., 1991. Stenographer State of Fla., Tallahassee and Miami, Fla., 1960-62, Gulf Oil Corp., Coral Gables, Fla., 1962-64, Gulf Power Co., Pensacola, Fla., 1965-68; loan svc. asst. First Fed. Savs. and Loan Assn., Greenville, S.C., 1969-70; various real estate positions Greenville, 1978-85; adminstrv. asst. Charter Retreat Hosp., Decatur, Ala., 1986-91; realtor assoc. Ferrell Realty Plus, Inc., Tallahassee, Fla., 1995—. Mem. Am. Legion (Citizenship award 1957), Tallahassee Symphony Soc., Avondale Forest Cmty. Club (pres. Taylors, S.C. chpt. 1969), Taylor's Garden Club (pres. Taylor's chpt. 1975-76), P.E.O. Sisterhood, Killearn Ladies Club. Republican. Baptist. Home: 2925 Shamrock St S Tallahassee FL 32308-3226

LISHAK, LISA ANNE, secondary education educator; b. Berlin, Nov. 27, 1960; (parents Am. citizens); d. Richard Edward Brogdon and Martha (Shuman) Gault; m. Robert Stephen Lishak, Apr. 22, 1989; 1 child, Trent Stephen. BS, Auburn U., 1989; postgrad., Ala. State U., 1996—. Cert in early adolescence/generalist category, Ala.; nat. bd. cert. tchr. Nat. Bd. for Profl. Tchg. Stds. Substitute tchr. Lee County, Auburn, Opelika Schs., Ala., 1989; tchr. math. Lanett (Ala.) Jr. High Sch., 1989-91, Opelika (Ala.) Mid. Sch., 1992-95. Usher Trinity Luth. Ch., Auburn, Ala., 1989—. Master sgt. USAF, 1978-84, mem. Res. Recipient plaque of appreciation Math-A-Thon, St. Jude's Children's Hosp., 1991; Ala. Power grantee, 1993-94, site-based mgmt. grantee Opelika Mid. Sch., 1994-95. Mem. NEA, Nat. Coun. Tchrs. Math., Chattahoochee Coun. Tchrs. Math., Ala. Edn. Assn., Columbia Regional Math. Collaborative, Air Force Sgts. Assn., Phi Kappa Phi, Kappa Delta Pi, Pi Lambda Theta. Home: 789 Annabrook Dr Auburn AL 36830-7529

LISK, ANNE MURRAY, daycare owner, administrator, educator; b. Wilmington, N.C., Mar. 13, 1956; d. Edward and Martha Sherman (Everett) Murray; m. David Wayne Lisk, Aug. 27, 1977; children: David Wayne, Jr., Steven Murray, Bradley Sherman. BA in English, Winthrop U., 1994, MA in History, 1996. Tchr. Charlotte (N.C.) - Mecklenburg Schs., 1978-79; exec. asst. to v.p. Independence Assocs., Inc., Charlotte, 1979-80, exec. asst. to pres., 1980-82; dir., tchr. Pleasant Hills CDC, Inc., Ft. Mill, S.C., 1983-94, exec. dir., 1994—; trainer Dept. Social Svcs., Columbia, S.C., 1983—; nurture com. chair St. Andrews UMC, Charlotte, 1994—; grad. asst. history dept. Winthrop U., Rock Hill, S.C., 1994, 95, 96. Mem. United Meth. Women, Sigma Tau Delta, Phi Alpha Theta, Pi Mu. Republican. Methodist. Home: 10843 Caroline Acres Rd Fort Mill SC 29715

LISTER, MARK WAYNE, clinical laboratory scientist; b. Panama City, Fla., June 30, 1954; s. Heamon Lee and Virginia (Hughes) L.; m. Elizabeth Ann Steger, Oct. 4, 1984; 1 child, Andrew Mark. Student med. tech. program, Monaco Med. Labs., Panama City, Fla., 1973-75; grad. with honors, Gulf Coast Coll., Panama City, Fla., 1976-79. Cert. med. technologist, Fla.; clin. lab. scientist, Nat. Cert. Agy. Lab. dir. Calhoun Gen. Hosp., Blountstown, Fla., 1979-82; evening shift supr. Hosp. Lab. Devel. Corp., Plantation, Fla., 1982-83; med. technologist Margate (Fla.) Gen. Hosp., 1983-84, Las Olas Hosp., Ft. Lauderdale, Fla., 1984; blood bank supr., coord. continuing edn. Fla. Med. Ctr., Lauderdale, Fla., 1984-89; evening shift supr. hosp. and reference lab. Westside Regional Med. Ctr., Plantation, 1989—, coord. continuing edn., 1989—, coord. ancillary blood glucose testing program, 1989—; mem. Broward County Tech. Adv. Com.; coord. continuing edn.; inspector Coll. Am. Pathologists; presenter 10th Internat. Conf. on AIDS, Yokohama, Japan, 1994. Rschr. in human immunodeficiency virus; rsch. in immunology. Active Christ Ch. United Meth., Ft. Lauderdale, 1990—, Imperial Point Homeowners Assn., Ft. Lauderdale, 1991—; host parent Westminster Acad., Ft. Lauderdale, 1993. Mem. Am. Assn. Blood Banks, Fla. Assn. Blood Banks, Am. Med. Technologist, Fla. Soc. Med. Technologist. Home: 2125 NE 56th Pl Fort Lauderdale FL 33308-2504

LITTEN, DEBORAH JEAN, elementary school educator; b. Quicksburg, Va., Jan. 1, 1961; d. Edwin LeRoy and Barbara Ruth (Click) Litten; m. Gregory Allen Litten, July 9, 1983. BA, Bridgewater (Va.) Coll., 1983; MEd, James Madison U., 1996. Tchr. Shenandoah County Pub. Schs., Woodstock, Va., 1983—. Mem. ASCD, Phi Delta Kappa. Home: 120 Cooper St Edinburg VA 22824

LITTLE, GREGORY DON, mental health services professional; b. Corinth, Miss., Nov. 10, 1954; s. Howard Henry and Annie Earling (Setliff) L.; m. Pamela Regina Zumwalt, Mar. 9, 1985; children: Patrick Gregory, Drew Christopher (dec.). BS, Miss. State U., 1977; MEd, U. So. Miss., 1980, PhD, 1992; postgrad., Miss. State U., U. Miss. Cert. therapeutic recreational specialist. Recreational therapist, unit dir. Miss. Bur. Mental Retardation, Jackson, 1977-84; health facilities surveyor Miss. State Dept. Health, Jackson, 1984-89; expressive therapist Pine Grove Recovery Ctr., Hattiesburg, Miss., 1989-93; quality assurance coord. Ellisville (Miss.) State Sch., 1994-95; coord. restorative therapy Miss. State Hosp., Whitfield, 1995—; profl. spkr., motivator Therapeutic Cons. Group, Ellisville, 1989—. Contbr. articles to profl. jours.; contbg. author: Therapeutic Recreation: Cases and Exercises, 1992. Mem. Ellisville Toastmasters (pres. 1994-95), Miss. Recreation and Park Assn. (Profl. of Yr. 1987, pres. 1986-87), Miss. Therapeutic Recreation Soc. (chair 1985, Therapeutic Recreator of Yr. 1985, 86), Compassionate Friends (bd. dirs. 1996—), Miss. Head Injury Assn., Miss. Gerontol. Soc. Republican. Baptist. Office: Miss State Hosp PO Box 292 Whitfield MS 39193

LITTLE, JON WARREN, materials executive; b. Fabens, Tex., Aug. 11, 1952; s. Roscoe Orin and Laura Louise (Cleghorn) L.; m. Dorothy Patricia McCarthy, Aug. 20, 1977; children: Dorothy Margaret, Patricia Erin, Timothy Jon. BBA, Tex. Tech U., 1974; MBA, U. Tex., Arlington, 1982. Pers. mgr. USAF Res., Robins AFB, Ga., 1975-76; mgr. McDonald's Restaurant, Lubbock, Tex., 1974-75, Jackson, Miss., 1976-77; mgr. Bonanza Internat., Dallas, 1977-78; inventory mgr. Sweetheart Cup Corp., Dallas, 1979-84; mgr. prodn. control Snapper Power Equipment, Ft. Worth, 1984-86; dir. prodn. control Snapper Power Equipment, McDonough, Ga., 1986-94; materials mgr. Onan Corp., Huntsville, Ala., 1994—. Mem. Am. Prodn. and Inventory Control Soc. (cert. mgr.). Roman Catholic. Home: 125 Springwater Dr Madison AL 35758-1392 Office: Onan Corp PO Box 240004 646 James Record Rd Huntsville AL 35824

LITTLE, MARK MCKENNA, financial management executive; b. Hoisington, Kans., Mar. 30, 1957; s. Freed Sebastian Little and Jana Vaye (Jones) Hansen; m. Peggy Louise Kelly, Jan. 24, 1988. B of Gen. Studies, Tex. Christian U., 1980. Account exec. Liberty Mut. Ins. Co., San Antonio, 1981-83; cons. M. Little Fin. Enterprises, San Antonio, 1983-89; chmn., chief exec. officer Wall St. Svcs., Inc., San Antonio, 1989—; pres./CEO Waterhouse Fin. Mgmt. Group, Inc., 1995—. Bd. dirs. Mental Health Assn. in Greater San Antonio, United Way, 1988-92, pres., chmn., 1990, KLRN TV Cmty. Adv. Bd., San Antonio, 1990-94, pres., 1992-93; bd. dirs. N.E. Ind. Sch. Dist., Kids Involvement Network, San Antonio, 1990—, chmn., 1990-93; bd. dirs. N.E. Ind. Sch. Dist.-Wide adv. bd., 1991—, pres., 1991-92; del., bd. dirs. Jaycees Internat., Taipei, Taiwan, 1983; elected del. Tex. State Rep. Conv., 1992; elected del. White House Conf. Small Bus., mem. exec. coun. Tex. del.; mem. bd. trustees N.E. Ednl. Found.; vice chair allocattions panel United Way, San Antonio, 1994; del. Tex. Gov.'s Conf. on Small Bus., 1996. Mem. San Antonio Area Coun. Pres., Greater San Antonio C. of C., North San Antonio C. of C. (bd. dirs. 1991—, vice chmn. bd. 1991-92, 95, chmn. bd. elect 1996, Edith Caldwell award 1995), San Antonio Jaycees (bd. dirs. 1982-83), North San Antonio Toastmasters (pres. 1990-91, world affairs coun. 1992-93), Delta Tau Delta (Larry Abrahms award). Office: Wall St Svcs Inc 12042 Blanco Rd Ste 330 San Antonio TX 78216-5438

LITTLEFIELD, DANIELLE JOAN, renal nutritionist; b. Tacoma, Feb. 22, 1952; d. Daniel Gustav and Bernice Elizabeth (Nordlund) Anderson; m. Jay Mitchell Littlefield, Nov. 13, 1976; children: David, Rachel, Paul. BS, Va. Poly. Inst., 1974; MS, U. Md., 1975. Registered dietitian, Va. Therapeutic dietitian Samaritan Hosp., Troy, N.Y., 1976; renal dietitian BMA/Nat. Med. Care, Washington, 1977—; cons. Fairfax, 1985—; rep. network coordinating coun. Nat. Kidney Found., Chevy Chase, Md., 1980-84; chmn. BMA Dietitians Group, Washington, 1980—. Contbr. articles to profl. jours., mags. Del. Va. Rep. Party, Vienna, 1982. Mem. Am. Dietetic Assn., No. Va. Dietetic Assn. Republican. Office: BMA of Arlington 8316 Arlington Blvd Fairfax VA 22031-5216

LITTLEJOHN, MARK HAYS, radiologist, b. Detroit, Apr. 11, 1936; s. Maurice Mark and Elizabeth Dowell (Metcalf) L.; children from previous marriage: M. Hays, Sara J.; m. Karla Ann McGinnis, Apr. 16, 1983; 1 stepchild, Bradford D. Schwartz. BS, Northwestern U., 1958, MD, 1961. Diplomate Am. Bd. Radiology, Am. Bd. Nuclear Medicine. Intern, Luth. Hosp., Ft. Wayne, Ind., 1961-62; resident VA Rsch. Hosp., Chgo., Northwestern U. Med. Sch., Chgo., 1962-65; staff radiologist Ireland Army Hosp., Ft. Knox, Ky., 1965-66, chief radiology, 1966-67; staff radiologist St. Mary Nazareth Hosp., Chgo., 1968-80, chief nuclear medicine, 1975-80; instr. in radiology Northwestern U. Med. Sch., 1968-71; dir. dept. radiology Cannon Meml. Hosp., Banner Elk, N.C., 1980—, chief of staff, 1987-89; cons. 1st U.S. Army, 1966-67. Served to capt. U.S. Army, 1965-67. Mem. AMA (Physician's recognition award 1971, 74, 77, 80, 84, 90, 93, 96), Am. Coll. Radiology, Am. Coll. Nuclear Physicians, (charter), Am. Inst. Ultrasound in Medicine, Radiology, Soc. N.Am., Soc. Nuclear Medicine, Pi Kappa Epsilon. Avocations: sculpture, painting. Home: PO Box 188 Blowing Rock NC 28605-0188 Office: PO Box 1167 Banner Elk NC 28604-1167

LITTLETON, ISAAC THOMAS, III, retired university library administrator, consultant; b. Hartsville, Tenn., Jan. 28, 1921; s. Isaac Thomas Jr. and Bessie (Lowe) L.; m. Dorothy Etta Young, Aug. 12, 1949; children—Sally Lowe Littleton Phillips, Thomas Young, Elizabeth Ann. B.A., U. N.C., Chapel Hill, 1943; M.A., U. Tenn., Knoxville, 1950; M.S.L.S., U. Ill., Champaign-Urbana, 1951, Ph.D., 1968. Circulation librarian, asst. librarian U. N.C., Chapel Hill, 1951-58; asst. dir. then dir. libraries N.C. State U., Raleigh, 1959-87; emeritus dir. libraries N.C. State U., 1987—; mem. N.C. Libr. Networking Steering Com., Raleigh, 1982-85; bd. dirs. Southeastern Libr. Network, Atlanta, 1973-74, 83-86, chmn., 1985-86; chmn. Assn. Southeastern Rsch. Librs., 1969-71; mem. com. Gov.'s Conf. on Libr. and Info. Svcs., 1990. Author: The Literature of Agricultural Economics, 1969, State Systems of Higher Education and Libraries, 1977, D.H. Hill Library: An Informal Historu, 1993; editor: N.C. Union List of Scientific Serials, 1967. Bd. dirs., treas. Theater in Park, Raleigh, 1982-85, Friends of Wake County Pub. Librs.; sec. N.C. State U. Friends of Libr., Raleigh, 1964-87, bd. dirs., 1990-94; pres. Friends of N.C. Libr. for Blind and Physically Handicapped, 1989-93, bd. dirs. 1993—; v.p. Wake County UN Assn., 1994-95. Lt. (j.g.) USN, 1943-46, PTO. Council on Library Resources fellow, Washington, 1975-76. Mem. Southeastern Library Assn. (exec. bd. 1974-78), N.C. Library Assn. (exec. bd. 1969-71, hon. life). Mem. Community United Ch. of Christ. Club: Torch (pres. Raleigh, N.C. 1974-75). Home: 4813 Brookhaven Dr Raleigh NC 27612-5706

LITTLETON, NAN ELIZABETH FELDKAMP, mental health services professional; b. Covington, Ky., Oct. 23, 1942; d. William Albert and Norma Elizabeth (Smith) Feldkamp; m. O.W. Littleton, Oct. 4, 1969 (div. 1979). AAS, No. Ky. U., 1976, BS, 1978; MACE, Morehead State U., 1981; MA, U. Cin., 1986, PhD, 1995. Prof. No. Ky. U., Highland Heights, 1976—, dir. women's studies program, 1996—; officer, pres. Holly Hill Children's Home, Cold Spring, Ky., 1980-86; cons. Attituding Healing Ctr., Cin., 1990-94. Bd. dirs. Coun. for Stds. in Human Svc. Edn., Chgo., 1990-96, Cancer Family Care, Cin., 1992-96. Mem. APA, Am. Psychol. Soc., Nat. Orgn. Human Svc. Edn., So. Orgn. Human Svc. Edn. (state rep. 1991-95), Nat. Assn. Women in Edn., Nat. Women's Studies Assn. Home: 333 W 17th Covington KY 41014 Office: No Ky U HC 206 Highland Heights KY 41099-2104

LITTON, ROBERT CLIFTON, marine engineer, consultant; b. Banner Elk, N.C., Jan. 11, 1934; s. Hailey Clifton and Edna (Walsh) L.; m. Michele Louise Gennette, July 1, 1961. B in Mech. Engring., U. Va., 1957; MS in Mech. Engring., Rensselaer Polytech. Inst., 1963. Commd. ensign USN, 1957, advanced through grades to capt., ret., 1984; pvt. practice marine engring. cons. Great Falls, Va., 1985-94; sr. cons. engr. Mech. Tech., Inc., Latham, N.Y., 1988-95; program mgr. Innovative Tech., Inc., McLean, Va., 1988-89, Sachse Engring. Assocs., Inc., San Diego, 1989-90; bus. area mgr. naval engring. RGS Assocs., Arlington, Va., 1994-96; v.p. ops. New Dawn Universal Power Corp., Arlington, 1996—; v.p. ops. New Dawn Universal Power Corp., 1996—. Mem. Soc. Naval Archs. and Marine Engrs., Am. Soc. Naval Engrs., U.S. Naval Inst., Naval Sub. League. Republican. Home and Office: 10334 Eclipse Ln Great Falls VA 22066-1730

LITZSINGER, ORVILLE JACK, aerospace technology executive; b. Richmond Heights, Mo., Sept. 11, 1936; s. Orville Frank and Irma Helen (Krisay) L.; m. Frances Elaine Shepard, June 14, 1958; children: Karen Elaine, Cheryl Denise. BS, U. Mo., 1958; MBA, Auburn U., 1972. Commd. USAF, 1958-82, advanced through grades to col.; ret., 1982; ICBM program dir. USAF, Ogden, Utah, 1979-82; pres., cons. OJL Inc., Alexandria, Va., 1982-85, 92—; v.p. Alliance for Am. Innovation Inc., 1994—; cons. Textron, Titan Systems, Aerojet, Washington, 1985-92, NASA HQ, 1992, Dept. Energy, USAF, 1993-94, United Inventors Assn. U.S.A., 1993-94, Info. Systems & Networks Corp., 1993-94. Pres. Clermont Woods Cmty. Assn., Fairfax County, Va., 1980-81. Recipient Key to City of Omaha, 1967, City of San Bernardino, Calif., 1970. Mem. AIAA, Am. Space Transp. Assn. (bd. dirs. 1991—, vice chmn. 1992-94), Air Force Assn., Tech. Transfer Soc., U. Mo. Alumni Assn. (bd. dirs. 1993-96, pres. state soc. 1994-96. Home and Office: 5824 Wessex Ln Alexandria VA 22310-1437

LIU, CHARLES CHUNG-CHA, transportation engineer, consultant; b. Ping-Tung, Taiwan, Oct. 6, 1953; came to U.S., 1977; s. Lian-Chyan and Sheue-Er (Chien) L.; m. Ing-Ing Tsai, Aug. 19, 1979; children: Alexander Charles, Andrew Huey. BSCE, Nat. Taiwan U., 1975; MSCE, Purdue U., 1979, PhD, 1982. Registered profl. engr., Tenn. Instr. Chinese Army Engr. Sch., Taipei, Taiwan, 1975-77; grad. instr. Sch. Civil Enging. Purdue U., West Lafayette, Ind., 1977-82; asst. prof. civil engring. Tenn. State U., Nashville, 1982-84; prin. engr. SRA Techs., Inc., Alexandria, Va., 1984-89; on-site automatic data processing contract mgr. Turner-Fairbank Hwy. Research Ctr., Fed. Hwy. Adminstrn., McLean, Va., 1988—; dir. transp. engring. AEPCO, Inc., Rockville, Md., 1989-95; pres., LENDIS Corp., McLean, Va., 1992—; adj. assoc. prof. civil engring. The Cath. U. Am.,

Washington, 1995—; cons. Cumberland Tectonics, Inc., Nashville, 1984, Engring. Directions Internat., Leesburg, Va., 1986-92, UN Devel. Program People's Republic of China, 1991, Vicor Assoc., Manassas, Va., 1988-96, Sci. Tech., Inc., Gaithersburg, Md., 1995—. Contbr. articles to profl. jours. Mem. ASCE (referee Jour. of Transp. Engring. 1989—), Inst. Transp. Engrs. (Past Pres.'s award 1988), Ops. Soc. Am., Sigma Xi, Omega Rho. Office: LENDIS Corp 6300 Georgetown Pike Rm F-111 Mc Lean VA 22101

LIU, DANXIA, neurochemistry educator, biophysicist; b. Shanxi, China, Dec. 24, 1940; d. Lin Liu and Dong Su; children: Haitao, Hailan. BS, Beijing (China) U., 1963, MS, 1965, PhD, 1982; grad., Chinese Acad. Mil. Med. Sci., Beijing, 1966. Asst. investigator Biology Rsch. Inst., Beijing, 1966-77; assoc. investigator Cancer Rsch. Inst. Beijing Med. U., 1977-79; asst. prof. biology dept. Beijing U., 1982-86; postdoctoral rsch. assoc. U. Tenn., Memphis, 1986-87; postdoctoral researcher dept. pharmacology Ohio State U., Columbus, 1987-88; vis. scientist Marine Biomed. Inst. U. Tex. Med. Br., Galveston, 1988-90, asst. prof. dept. human biol. chemistry and genetics, 1990-96, assoc. prof. dept. surgery, 1996—. Contbr. articles to profl. jours. Grantee Paralyzed Vets. of Am. Spinal Cord Rsch. Found., 1991-95, Am. Paralysis Assn., 1991-93, The Amyotrophic Lateral Sclerosis Assn., 1995—, Tex. Higher Edn. Coordinating Bd., 1996—, NIH, 1996—. Mem. AAAS, Am. Peptide Soc. (charter), Internat. Soc. Neurochemistry, Neurotrauma Soc., Soc. for Neurosci. Office: U Tex Med Br Dept Surg Galveston TX 77555-1143

LIU, DAVID T., librarian, writer; b. Zhong-shan City, China, Dec. 6, 1936; came to U.S., 1961; s. Chung-Ling and Ging-Wa (Vong) L.; m. Agnete M.C. Shih, Dec. 15, 1962; children: Nadine, Austin W.T. Student, Tamkang English Coll., Taipei, Taiwan, 1954-55; BA, Nat. Taiwan U., Taipei, 1959; postgrad., Nat. Normal U., Taipei, 1960-61, U. Wash., 1962; MA in Libr. Sci., George Peabody Coll. for Tchrs., 1963. Interpreter, officer Chinese Air Force Hdqrs., Taipei, 1960-61; cataloger Chgo. Pub. Libr., 1963-64; chief adult svcs., reader's advisor Joliet (Ill.) Pub. Libr., 1964; head libr., asst. prof. polit. sci. Bay de Noc C.C., Escanaba, Mich., 1964-73; libr. dir. Pharr (Tex.) Meml. Libr., 1973—; pres. libr.'s adv. coun. Hidalgo County Libr. System, McAllen, Tex., 1980. Author: Taiwan Revisited, 1985. Recipient 20-Yr. Disting. Svc. award City of Pharr, 1993. Mem. ALA, Chinese-Am. Librs. Assn. (pres. 1981-82), Asian/Pacific-Am. Librs. Assn. (chair recruitment & scholarship com. 1993-94). Home: 311 S Cypress Cir Pharr TX 78577-5950 Office: Pharr Memorial Library 200 S Athol St Pharr TX 78577-4806

LIU, SUYI, biophysicist; b. Dalian, Liaoning, People's Republic of China, May 23, 1955; came to U.S., 1983; s. Hanzhou and Yiying Liu; m. Wei Sun, July 27, 1985; 1 child, Andrew. BS, Tsinghua U., Beijing, 1982; PhD, U. Ill., 1990. Postdoctoral rsch. assoc. U. Ill., Urbana, 1990; dir. R&D World Precision Instruments, Sarasota, Fla., 1990—. Contbr. articles to Biophys. Jour., Photochem. Photobiol. Mem. Biophys. Soc. Office: World Precison Instruments 175 Sarasota Center Blvd Sarasota FL 34240-9258

LIVELY, H(OWARD) RANDOLPH, JR., retail company executive; b. Atlanta, Nov. 24, 1934; s. Howard R. Sr. and Nelle (Everett) L.; m. Barbara Fortun, June 3, 1958 (div. Apr. 1975); children—Bonnie, Dana, Andrea, Mindy, John; m. Fran Antone, Apr. 3, 1976. B.A., La. State U., 1957. Cert. consumer credit exec. With Sears Roebuck and Co., 1960-81, asst. credit mgr., New Orleans, 1960-63, statis. analyst, Atlanta, 1963-64, credit field supr., 1964-66, asst. gen. credit mgr., 1966-69, spl. research asst., Chgo., 1969-71, dir. public affairs, 1971-77, gen. credit mgr. Southwest Territory, Dallas, 1978-80, gen. credit mgr. Eastern Territory, Phila., 1981; pres. Jewelers Fin. Services Div., Zale Corp., Dallas, 1981-84, exec. v.p. Zale Corp., Dallas, 1984-85, ret., 1993; owner Via Real, Inc., 1987—, Kokopelli by Via Real, Dallas, Tex., Via Real, Irving, Tex.; pres., CEO Am. Fin. Svcs. Assn., Washington, 1994—. Chmn. Bd. Jr. Achievement Dallas, Inc., 1991-92, bd. dirs., 1989-95, CEO Fine Jewelers Guild div., 1986-91; chmn. bd. First Bank/Las Colinas, Irving, Tex.; pres. Merchants Research Council, Chgo., 1982-84. Contbr. articles in field to profl. pubs. Exec. advisor (indsl. film) A Day at the Fair 1975 (Best Indsl. Film Indsl. Film Producers Assn. 1977). Chmn., Zale PAC, 1983—; mem. legis. com. Am. Retail Fedn., 1972—; mem. Ill. State Electronic Funds Transfer Study Commn., 1976-77. Served to E-5 U.S. Army, 1957-59. Recipient Disting. Service to Retail Industry award Merchants Research Council, 1977; President's Cup Zale Corp., 1984. Mem. Credit Research Ctr. Purdue U. (exec. com. 1985—), mem. Columbia U. Fin. Services Mgmt. Program Alumni Assn., Nat. Retail Merchants Assn. (chmn. credit mgmt. div. 1984—, bd. dirs. 1985—), Internat. Credit Assn. (bd. dirs. 1982—). Republican. Methodist. Clubs: Las Colinas Sports, La Cima (Irving, Tex.). Avocations: home computing; swimming.

LIVELY, PIERCE, federal judge; b. Louisville, Aug. 17, 1921; s. Henry Thad and Ruby Durrett (Keating) L.; m. Amelia Harrington, May 25, 1946; children: Susan, Katherine, Thad. AB, Centre Coll., Ky., 1943; LL.B., U. Va., 1948. Bar: Ky. 1948. Individual practice law Danville, Ky., 1949-57; mem. firm Lively and Rodes, Danville, 1957-72; judge U.S. Ct. Appeals (6th cir.), Cin., 1972—, chief judge, 1983-88; now sr. judge; Mem. Ky. Commn. on Economy and Efficiency in Govt., 1963-65, Ky. Jud. Advisory Com., 1972. Trustee Centre Coll. Served with USNR, 1943-46. Mem. ABA, Am. Judicature Soc., Order of Coif, Raven Soc., Phi Beta Kappa, Omicron Delta Kappa. Presbyterian. Office: US Ct Appeals PO Box 1226 Danville KY 40423-5226 also: US Courthouse Rm 418 Cincinnati OH 45202

LIVENGOOD, CHARLOTTE LOUISE, employee development specialist; b. L.A., June 18, 1944; d. James Zollie and Zela (Cogburn) L. BS in Secondary Edn., Tex. A & I U., 1968; MEd in Pers. Guidance and Counseling, North Tex. U., 1971. Cert. secondary teaching, Tex.; cert. counselor, Tex. Counselor Gus Grissom H.S., Huntsville, Ala., 1971-72; tchr. West Springfield H.S., Springfield, Va., 1972-73; edn. specialist U.S. Dept. Def., El Paso, Tex., 1975-78; instr. El Paso (Tex.) C.C., 1977-78; employee devel. specialist U.S. Office Pers. Mgmt., Dallas, 1978-79; pers. mgmt. specialist Dept. Vets. Affairs, Houston, 1979-87; labor rels. specialist Dept. Vets. Affairs, VA Med. Ctr., Houston, 1987-89; pers. staffing specialist Dept. Vets. Affairs, Houston, 1989-90; employee devel. specialist, acad. tng. officer HUD, Ft. Worth, 1990-95; assoc. prof. Ariz. State U., 1995—; Bur. of Engraving and Printing univ. tng. officer Dept. Treasury, Ft. Worth, 1995—; EEO investigator Dept. Vet. Affairs, 1984-87, fed. women's program mgr., 1984-85; mem. standing panel for pers. specialists/fed. suprs./mgrs. Merit Systems Protection Bd., 1996—; speaker in field. Editor: (monthly office newspaper) Pipeline, 1980-87. Chairperson, forensics coach Jr. High Sch. Speech Dept., 1968-69; tchr. S. Grand Prairie H.S., 1969-71; mem. Dallas/Ft. Worth Quality Control Coun., Tex. War on Drugs Com., 1990—; hon. mem. Dallas/Ft. Worth Fed. Exec. Bd., 1993-94. Recipient Future Secs. of Am. scholarship, 1962. Mem. ASTD, AAUW, Am. Pers. and Guidance Assn., Assn. for Quality Participation, Internat. Transactional Analysis Assn., Tex. State Tchrs. Assn., Tex. Classroom Tchrs. Assn., Fed. Bus. Assn., VA Employee Assn., Intergovernmental Tng. Assn., Intergovernmental Tng. Coun. (chairperson 1993-94), Federal Women's Program Mgr., Merit Sys. Protection Bd. Standing Panel for Personnel Specialists, Federal Supv., Mgrs. Mem. Church of Christ. Office: US Dept Treasury Bur Engraving & Printing Western Currency Facility 9000 Blue Mound Rd Fort Worth TX 76131-3304

LIVERMAN, LYNDA M., community health nurse; b. Bogalusa, La., Mar. 26, 1941; d. Warren LeRoy and Verdine jane (McTaggart) Mizell; m. Merlin C. Liverman, Jan. 28, 1962; children: David, Debra, Donna. Student, La. State U., 1959-61, Our Lady Holy Cross Coll., 1972-74; ADN, Northwestern State U., 1979. Cert. care mgmt. Staff nurse Schumpert Med. Ctr., Shreveport, La., 1979; staff, charge nurse North Caddo Meml. Hosp., Vivian, La., 1979-81, Highland Hosp., Shreveport, 1982-85; patient care supr. for home health MAS Nursing, Shreveport, 1985-87, dir. pers., Medicare adminstr., 1987-89; br. mgr. Kimberly Quality Care, Shreveport, 1989-92; established Premier Family Healthcare, Inc., Shreveport, La., 1992—, Glen Home Health, Inc. (subs. Premier Healthcare Mgmt. Inc.), Shreveport, La., 1995—; v.p. clin. svcs. Premier Healthcare Mgmt., Inc., Shreveport, La., 1995—. Mem. Riverside Bapt. Ch. Named Nurse of the Yr. Shreveport Dist. Nurses Assn., 1989. Mem. ANA, NAHC, Shreveport Dist. Nurses Assn., Am. Soc. Parenteral and Enteral Nutrition, Ark.-La.-Tex. Assn. Home Health and Hospice Agys., Homecare Assn. La.

LIVINGSTON, MARGARET GRESHAM, civic leader; b. Birmingham, Ala., Aug. 16, 1924; d. Owen Garside and Katherine Molton (Morrow) Gresham; m. James Archibald Livingston, Jr., July 16, 1947; children: Mary Margaret, James Archibald, Katherine Wiley, Elizabeth Gresham. Grad. The Baldwin Sch., Phila., 1942; AB, Vassar Coll., 1945; MA, U. Ala., 1946. Acting dir. Birmingham Mus. Art, 1978-79, 81, chmn. bd. dirs., 1978-86; bd. dirs. Birmingham Civic Ctr. Authority, 1988-95; bd. dirs. Altamont Sch., Birmingham, 1963—, chmn. bd. 1986. Named Woman of Yr., Birmingham, 1986; named to Ala. Tennis Hall of Fame, 1994. Mem. Am. Assn. Mus. Episcopalian. Clubs: Jr. League, Ala. State Tennis Assn.

LIVINGSTON, PAMELA JANELLE, insurance company executive; b. Vinita, Okla., Jan. 7, 1956; d. Charles Thalbert and Mildred Joan (Rumsey) L.; m. Dale R. Vennes, June 16, 1984. BA in Journalism, U. Okla., 1977; MBA in Fin., Oklahoma City U., 1996. Tech. dir. CBS TV, Inc., N.Y.C., 1982-93; sr. promotions prodr. KJRH-TV, Tulsa, 1993-96; owner Farmer's Ins. Group, Tulsa, 1996—. Recipient Emmy award Acad. TV Arts and Scis., 1992. Mem. Tulsa 99's. Office: Farmer's Ins Group 1515 E 71st St #202 Tulsa OK 74136

LIVINGSTON, PATRICIA DIANNE, secondary education educator; b. Berekley, Calif., Dec. 7, 1945; d. Waldene Mignon (Hatchett) Littleton; m. Robert Allen Livingston (div.); children: Felicia Mignon Livingston. Degree, Hartnell Jr. Coll., Salinas, Calif., 1965; BS, Paul Quinn Coll., Waco, Tex., 1970. Tchr., coach West Columbia (Tex.) Jr. H.S., Freeport (Tex.) Intermediate Sch., 1979—. Active Jr. Svc. League, Lake Jackson, Tex., 1995—. Mem. Tex. State Tchr. Assn., Tex. Girls Coaches Assn., Tex. H.S. Coaches Assn., Tex. Assn. for Health, Phys. Edn., Recreation and Dance, Tex. Mid. Sch. Assn., Brazoport Edn. Assn. (past pres. 1982-95). Democrat. Baptist. Home: 909 Magnolia Lake Jackson TX 77566

LIVINGSTON, PETER GASKILL, entrepreneur, consultant; b. Phila., Mar. 16, 1954; s. N.B. Jr. and Marion Gaskill (Gaskill) L.; m. Debra Graves, June 25, 1977; children: Neal, Meredith, Natasha, Joshua, Noah. BS in Edn., Ohio State U., 1976. Sales rep. McNeil Pharm., Spring House, Pa., 1978-80, dist. mgr., 1981-83, dir. new bus. devel., 1984-86; dir. mktg. & bus. devel. biotech. divsn. Phillips Petroleum Co., Bartlesville, Okla., 1986-88; pres., CEO Eagle Techs., Bartlesville, Okla., 1989-90, Symex Corp., Tulsa, 1990-93, ZymeTx, Inc., Oklahoma City, Okla., 1993—; cons. Okla. Med. Rsch. Found. Virology Rsch., Oklahoma City, 1993—. Contbr. articles to profl. jours.; patent pending on diagnostic methods for detecting viruses. Mem. devel. com. Christian Heritage Acad., Del City, Okla., 1994—; Sunday sch. tchr. First Southern Bapt. Ch., Del City, 1995—. Republican. Baptist. Office: ZymeTx Inc 800 Research Pkwy Ste 100 Oklahoma City OK 73104

LIVINGSTON, ROBERT LINLITHGOW, JR. (BOB LIVINGSTON, JR.), congressman; b. Colorado Springs, Colo., Apr. 30, 1943; s. Robert L. and Dorothy (Godwin) L.; m. Bonnie Robichaux, Sept. 13, 1965; children: Robert Linlithgow, III, Richard Godwin, David Barkley; SuShan Alida. BA in Econs., Tulane U., 1967, JD, 1968; postgrad., Loyola Inst. Politics, 1973. Bar: La. 1968. Ptnr. Livingston & Powers, New Orleans, 1976-77; asst. U.S. atty., dep. chief criminals divsn. U.S. Attys. Office, 1970-73; chief spl. prosecutor, chief armed robbery divsn. Orleans Parish Dist. Atty.'s Office, 1974-75; chief prosecutor organized crime unit La. Atty. Gen.'s Office, 1975-76; mem. 95th-104th Congresses from 1st La. Dist., 1977—; chair appropriations com., 1996—; Mem. nat. adv. bd. Young Ams. for Freedom. Mem. nat. adv. bd. Young Ams. for Freedom; bd. suprs. Smithsonian Inst.; bd. dirs. Internat. Rep. Inst. Ctr. for Democracy. Named Outstanding Asst. U.S. Atty., 1973. Mem. ABA, Fed. Bar Assn., La. Bar Assn., New Orleans Bar Assn., Navy League, Am. Legion. Roman Catholic. Home: 111 Veterans Memorial Blvd Metairie LA 70005-3028 Office: US Ho of Reps 2406 Rayburn HOB Washington DC 20515*

LIVINGSTONE, ALAN SAMUEL, surgeon; b. Montreal, Que., Can., Apr. 4, 1947; came to U.S., 1974; married. BSc, McGill U., Montreal, 1969, MD, 1971, MSc in Exptl. Surgery, 1974. Diplomate Am. Bd. Surgeons. Asst. prof. surgery U. Miami (Fla.) Sch. Medicine, 1976-80, assoc. prof., 1980-86, prof., 1986—; acting chmn. dept. Surgery acting chmn. dept., 1993-94; vice chmn. dept. U. Miami (Fla.) Sch. Medicine, 1994—; staff surgeon gen. surg. svc./peripheral vascular svc. Jackson Meml. Hosp., Miami, 1976—; staff surgeon Sylvester Comprehensive Cancer Ctr., Miami, 1992—, chief divsn. surg. ocology, 1995—; assoc. v.p. med. affairs, med. dir. U. Miami Med. Group, 1996—. Contbr. chpts. to books, articles to profl. jours. Med. Rsch. Coun. of Can. fellow, 1973. Fellow ACS (Schering scholar 1974), Royal Coll. Surgeons, Royal Coll. Medicine; mem. Assn. Acad. Surgery, Am. Assn. for the Study of Liver Diseases, Am. Gastroenterol. Assn., Soc. for Surgery of Alimentary Tract, Collegium Internationale Chirurgiae Digestivae. Home: PO Box 016310 Miami FL 33101-6310 Office: Dept Surgery U Miami Sylvester Comprehensive Cancer Ctr Divsn Surg 1475 NW 12 Ave Rm 3550 Miami FL 33136

LIVINGSTONE, JOHN LESLIE, accountant, management consultant, business economist, educator; b. Johannesburg, Republic of South Africa, Aug. 29, 1932; m. Trudy Dorothy Zweig, Aug. 7, 1977; children: Roger Miles, Adrienne Jill, Graham Ross, Robert Edward. B in Commerce, U. Witwatersrand, South Africa, 1956; MBA, Stanford U., 1963, PhD, 1966. C.P.A., N.Y., Tex. Budget dir. Edgars Stores Ltd., South Africa, 1958-61; asso. prof. Ohio State U., Columbus, 1966-69; Arthur Young Disting. prof. Ohio State U., 1970-73; Fuller E. Callaway prof. Ga. Inst. Tech., Atlanta, 1973-78; mem. exec. bd. Ga. Inst. Tech., 1976-78; ptnr. Coopers & Lybrand, N.Y.C., 1978-81; prin., v.p. Mgmt. Analysis Center, Inc., Cambridge, Mass., 1975-90; prof., chmn. div. acctg. and law Babson Coll., 1985—; cons. FPC, SEC, HEW, also maj. corps. Author 10 books including Accounting for Changing Prices: Replacement Cost and General Price Level Adjustments, 1976, Management Planning and Control, 1987, The Portable MBA: Finance and Accounting, 1992; assoc. editor: Decision Scis., 1973-78; mem. editl. bd. The Acctg. Rev., 1969-72, 76-78, Acctg., Orgns. and Socs., 1975-78, Jour. Acctg. and Pub. Policy, 1983-95; contbr. numerous articles to profl. jours. Mem. AICPA, Fla. Inst. CPAs, N.Y. Soc. CPAs, Am. Acctg. Assn., Acad. of Experts, Nat. Assn. for Forensic Econs., Nat. Assn. Bus. Economists, Tex. Soc. CPAs, Am.Arbitration Assn., Palm Beach Nat. Golf and Country Club, Breakers Club (Palm Beach), Govs. Club (Palm Beach). Office: 2300 Palm Beach Lakes Blvd West Palm Beach FL 33409-3303

LIVINGSTONE, TRUDY DOROTHY ZWEIG, dancer, educator; b. N.Y.C., June 9, 1946; d. Joseph and Anna (Feinberg) Zweig; m. John Leslie Livingstone, Aug. 7, 1977; 1 child, Robert Edward. Student, Charles Lowe Studios, N.Y.C., 1950-52, Nina Tinova Studio, N.Y.C., 1953-56, Ballet Russe de Monte Carlo, N.Y.C., 1956-57, Bklyn. Coll., 1964-66; BA in Psychology cum laude, Boston U., 1968, MEd, 1969; postgrad., Serena Studios, Carnegie Hall Ballet Arts, N.Y.C., 1973-74. Tchr. Millis (Mass.) Pub. Schs., 1969-72, Hebrew Acad. Atlanta, 1974-76; profl. dancer various orgns. including Rivermont Country Club, Jewish Community Ctr., Callanwolde Performing Arts Ctr., Atlanta, 1974-84; founder, owner, instr. dance Sasha Studios, Atlanta, 1974-77; owner Trudy Zweig Livingstone Studios, Wellesley, Needham, Mass., 1987-88, Palm Beach, Fla., 1989—; judge dance competition Atlanta Council Run-Offs, 1976. Vol. League Sch., Bklyn., 1965, Kennedy Meml. Hosp., Brighton, Mass., 1969, Nat. Affiliation for Literacy Advances, Santa Monica, Calif., 1982. Mem. Am. Alliance for Health, Phys. Edn., Recreation and Dance, Poets of the Palm Beaches, L.A. Athletic Club, Wellesley Coll. Club, Governor's Club (West Palm Beach).

LLEWELLYN, CHARLES ELROY, JR., psychiatrist; b. Richmond, Va., Jan. 16, 1922; s. Charles Elroy and Pearl Ann (Shield) L.; m. Grace Eldridge, Sept. 25, 1948; children: Charles Elroy III, George E. (dec.), Richard S. BS, Hampden-Sydney Coll., 1943; MD, Med. Coll. Va., 1946; MS in Psychiatry, U. Colo., 1953. Diplomate Am. Bd. Psychiatry and Neurology; lic. marriage and family therapist, N.C. Intern psychiatry Tucker Hosp., Inc., Richmond, 1946-47, asst. to staff, 1948-50; intern gen. medicine Bellevue Hosp., N.Y.C., 1947-48; fellow psychiatry Colo. Psychopathic Hosp. and U. Colo. Med. Ctr., Denver, 1950-53; assoc. dept. psychiatry Duke U., Durham, N.C., 1955-56, asst. prof., 1956-63, assoc. prof., 1963-87; asst. dir. adult psychiat. outpatient clinic Duke U. Med. Ctr., Durham, 1955-56, head adult psychiat. outpatient div., 1956-76, acting head divsn. cmty. and social psychiatry, 1976-81, chief tng. divsn. cmty. and social psychiatry, 1976-85, head divsn. cmty. and social psychiatry, 1985-87; pvt. practice Durham, 1987—; psychiat. cons., supr., seminar dir. pastoral counseling tng. programs Duke U. Med. Ctr., 1965-87, dir. student mental health svc. Duke U., 1959-68; psychiat. cons. N.C. Divsn. Social Svcs., 1955-79, N.C. Medicaid Program, 1971-75, N.C. Med. Peer Rev. Found., Inc., 1975-79; sr. psychiat. cons. Family Cons. Svc., Durham, 1966-87; mem.-at-large N.C. Substance Abuse Profl. Ctr. Bd., 1984-89; part-time cons., med. dir. Durham Substance Abuse Treatment Ctr., 1968-88. Contbr. articles to profl. jours, chpts. to books. Mem. adv. bd. Durham County Drug Counseling and Evaluation Svc., 1972-79; bd. dirs. Family Counseling Svc. Durham, 1973-78, pres., 1975; bd. dirs. United Health Svcs., 1975-84; trustee Epworth United Meth. Ch., 1959-62, dir. cmty. ministries com., 1961-62; cubmaster Boy Scouts Am., 1960-66; mem. ch. campus rels. com. The Meth. Ctr., Duke U., 1964-66. Capt. U.S. Army, 1953-55. Recipient Outstanding Profl. Human Svcs. Am. Acad. Human Svcs., 1974-75; grantee U.S. Inst. Mental Health, 1967-71. Fellow Am. Psychiat. Assn. (life); mem. AMA (life), Am. Group Psychotherapy Assn., Pan Am. Med. Soc. (life), Am. Assn. Marriage and Family Therapy, Carolinas Group Psychotherapy Soc. (treas. 1983-94), N.C. Med. Soc. (life), N.C. Assn. Marriage and Family Therapists, Mental Health Assn. N.C., Durham-Orange County Med. Soc. (life). Office: 3308 Chapel Hill Blvd Ste 110 Durham NC 27707-2643

LLEWELLYN, LEONARD FRANK, real estate broker; b. Harlowton, Mont., Oct. 31, 1933; s. Ralph Emory and Frances Louise (Ewing) L.; m. Patricia Lockrom, Aug. 16, 1951 (div. 1955); m. Corrie J. Spruit, Apr. 21, 1974 (div. 1995). BSEE, Eastern Mont. Coll. Edn., 1955. Enlisted USMC, 1957, advanced through grades to capt., 1960, ret., 1967; owner Capitol Fla. Assn., Inc., Alexandra, Va., 1966-74; pres., owner Fla. Properties, Inc., Balt., 1968-74; chmn. Marco Beach Realty, Inc., Marco Island, Fla., 1975-82, 82—, Cons., Inc. of S.W. Fla., Marco Island, 1982—; served as presdl. pilot for presidents Kennedy and Johnson, 1963-66; bd. dirs. Founders Nat. Bank and Trust Co. Author: (manual) Aero-Gunnery Tactics, 1958. Bd. dirs. Collier County Servancy, 1978-83; trustee Naples (Fla.) Cmty. Hosp., 1980-93, Cmty. Found. Collier County, 1990-94. Named Top Gun, USN, USMC, 1958, Citizen of Yr. Marco Island N.Y. Times and Marco Island Eagle, 1982. Mem. Marco Island Bd. Realtors (pres. 1982), Marco Island C. of C. (pres. 1981-82, pres. emeritus 1984), Naples Forum (pres. 1985-86), Nat. Aviation Club, Nat. Assn. Sales Masters, Rotary Club. Republican. Home: PO Box 825 Marco Island FL 34146-0825 Office: Cons Inc of SW Fla Marco Island FL 33937

LLEWELLYN, THOMAS SYLVESTER, III, radiologist, educator; b. Tulsa, June 13, 1936; s. Thomas Sylvester and Agnes Marie (Quinn) L.; m. Lana Jean Holder, Aug. 7, 1976; children: Bronwen Kay, Deirdre Ann, Cristin Marie. BS, U. Tulsa, 1958; MD, U. Okla., 1961. Diplomate Am. Bd. Radiology. Intern St. John Hosp., Tulsa, 1961-62; resident U. Mo. Med. Ctr., Columbia, 1964-67; instr. U. Mo. Med. Ctr., 1967-68; radiologist St. Francis Hosp., Tulsa, 1968—, clin. prof., 1995—; clin. asst. prof., assoc. prof. U. Okla. Health Sci. Ctr., Tulsa, 1978-95; pres. Radiol. Cons. Tulsa. Bd. dirs. 12 & 12 Transition House, Tulsa. Capt. U.S. Army, 1962-64. Mem. AMA, Okla. Radiol. Soc., Okla. Med. Soc., Am. Soc. Emergency Radiology, Tulsa County Med. Soc., Am. Coll. Radiology, Radiol. Soc. N.Am., Soc. Cardiovasc. and Interventional Radiology, Flying Physicians Assn., Alpha Omega Alpha. Republican. Roman Catholic. Office: St Francis Hosp 6161 S Yale Ave Tulsa OK 74136-1902

LLOYD, CECIL RHODES, pediatric dentist; b. Corpus Christi, Tex., Aug. 18, 1930; s. Cecil Rhodes Hilbun and Cidney W. (Linxwiler) Lloyd; m. Donna Mae Thomas, Dec. 31, 1955 (div. 1973); children: James Michael, Leigh Ann, Lisa Kendall; m. Glenda Sue Williams, Dec. 31, 1979; children: Lauren Cecily, Sutton Rhodes. Student, La. State U., 1949, La. Tech. Inst., 1950, Centenary Coll., 1952-54; DDS, Loyola U., New Orleans, 1958. Pediatric dentist Shreveport, La., 1958—; cons. pediatric dentistry Barksdale AFB, La., 1970—. Chmn. Cen. YMCA, Shreveport, 1974, met. bd., 1969, Ind. Bowl Football Classic, Shreveport, 1984, 85, Fellowship Christian Athletes, 1986; bd. dirs. Riverside Hosp., Bossier, La., 1982-84; pres.-elect Sports Found., 1989, pres., 1990; founder Sports Mus. of Champions, Shreveport-Bossier; interim mem. Shreveport City Coun., 1990. Named Southwestern Handball Hall of Fame, 1996. NW La. Dental Assn., La. Dental Assn., ADA, Am. Acad. Pediatric Dentistry, La. Bd. Dentistry (pres., 1969-70, 77-78, 83-84), Ark.-La.-Tex. Dental Congress (chmn. 1979-80). Republican. Baptist. Office: 927 Shreveport Barksdale Hwy Shreveport LA 71105-2205

LLOYD, FRANCIS LEON, JR., lawyer; b. Winchester, Va., Dec. 1, 1955; s. Francis Leon Sr. and Jeannette Marie (Dove) L.; m. Myra Denise DuBose, Sept. 18, 1982. BA in English and French, U. Richmond, 1978; JD, U. Va., 1981. Bar: Va. 1981, Tenn. 1982, U.S. Dist. Ct. (ea. dist.) Tenn. 1982, U.S. Ct. Appeals (6th cir.) 1984. Assoc. Herndon, Coleman, Brading & McKee, Johnson City, Tenn., 1981-83, 1984-86, ptnr., 1987-88; of counsel The Taylor Group, Ltd., Johnson City, 1983; law clk. to judge U.S. Dist. Ct. (ea. dist.) Tenn., Knoxville, 1988—. Bd. dirs. Assn. Retarded Citizens Washington County, Inc., Johnson City, 1982-88. Home: 8804 Regent Ln Knoxville TN 37923-1640 Office: US Dist Ct 800 Market St Knoxville TN 37902-2312

LLOYD, JACQUELINE, English language educator; b. N.Y.C., Aug. 21, 1950; d. R.G. and Hortense (Collins) L. BA, Fisk U., 1972; MEd, U. North Fla., 1989. Instr. English Edward Waters Coll., Jacksonville, Fla., 1983, 90—. Mem. Nat. Coun. Tchrs. English. Democrat. Presbyterian. Home: 5006 Andrew Robinson Dr Jacksonville FL 32209-1002

LOBB, WILLIAM ATKINSON, financial services executive; b. Arlington, Pa., Apr. 21, 1951; s. Anthony William and Annamarie (Hilpert) L.; m. Maureen Veronique O'Hagan, July 7, 1977; children: William Atkinson III, Anthony Hagan. BS, Georgetown U., 1977. Account exec. Johnston Lemon, Washington, 1977-78; sr. account exec. Merrill Lynch, Alexandria, Va., 1979-83; asst. v.p. E.F. Hutton, Washington, 1983-85; mng. dir., ptnr.-in-charge Oppenheimer and Co., Inc., Atlanta, 1985—. Bd. trustees The Howard Sch.; bd. dirs. Atlanta Charity Clays. Mem. Ga. Rep. Found., Nat. Assn. Securities Dealers (bd. arbitrators), Nat. Securities Traders Assn., Ga. Securities Assn., Am. Arbitration Assn., Univ. Club, Army-Navy Club, Settindown Creek Club, Burge Plantation Hunt Club. Office: Oppenheimer & Co Inc 1200 Monach Plz 3414 Peachtree Rd NE Atlanta GA 30326-1113

LOCKE, ELIZABETH HUGHES, foundation administrator; b. Norfolk, Va., June 30, 1939; d. George Morris and Sallie Epps (Moss) Hughes; m. John Rae Locke, Jr., Sept. 13, 1958 (div. 1981); children: John Rae III, Sallie Curtis. BA magna cum laude with honors in English, Duke U., 1964, PhD, 1972; MA, U. N.C., 1966. Instr. English, U. N.C., Chapel Hill, 1970-72; vis. prof. English, Duke U., Durham, N.C., 1972-73, dir. univ. pubs., 1973-79; corp. contbns. officer Bethlehem Steel Corp., Pa., 1979-82; dir. edn. div. and comm. Duke Endowment, Charlotte, N.C., 1982-96, exec. dir., 1996—; past pres. Comm. Philanthropy, Washington; mem. comms. com. Coun. on Founds., Washington, 1995— . Editor: Duke Encounters, 1977, Prospectus for Change: American Private Higher Education, 1985, (mag.) Issues, 1985-96. Pres., Jr. League, Durham, 1976, Hist. Preservation Soc., Durham, 1977, Pub. Rels. Soc. Am., Charlotte chpt., 1988, Charlotte Area Donors Forum; past pres. Sch. of Arts, Charlotte; bd. visitors Davidson Coll., Charlotte Country Day Sch., Duke U., Johnson C. Smith U. Recipient Leadership award Charlotte C. of C., 1984; Danforth fellow, 1972. Mem. Nat. Task Force, English Speaking Union, The Most Venerable Order of St. John of Jerusalem (officer sister), Phi Beta Kappa. Democrat. Episcopalian. Club: Charlotte City. Office: 100 N Tryon St Ste 3500 Charlotte NC 28202-4000

LOCKE, JOHN HOWARD, lawyer; b. Berryville, Va., Sept. 4, 1920; s. James Howard and Mary Elizabeth (Hart) L.; m. Frances Rebecca Cook, Feb. 23, 1946; children: Anne Locke Evans, Nancy Locke Curlee, Rebecca Locke Leonard. BS, U. Richmond, 1941; LLB, U. Va., 1948. Bar: Va. 1948. Ptnr., Gentry, Locke, Rakes & Moore, Roanoke, Va., ret. 1985. Apptd. Hearing Officer Supreme Ct. Va., 1987; founder, pres. Big Bros., Roanoke, 1960. With USN, 1942-46. Fellow Am. Coll. Trial Lawyers, Internat. Soc. Barristers (pres. 1970); mem. ABA, Va. State Bar, Va. Bar Assn., Roanoke City Bar Assn. (pres. 1970-71), Internat. Assn. Ins. Counsel, 4th Cir. Jud. Conf., Omicron Delta Kappa, Raven Soc. Presbyterian. Club: Shenadoah (Roanoke, Va.).

LOCKE, THOMAS BERNARD, federal agency administrator; b. Bridgeport, Conn., Nov. 3, 1948; s. Bernard Ray and Marion Jewel (Johnson) L.; m. Alice Frances McCabe, Apr. 17, 1971 (div. 1983); children: Thomas John, James Tennant; m. Gina Rae Robinson, May 21, 1983 (div. 1993); 1 child, Erin Brittany; m. Tina Suzanne Gentry, Aug. 28, 1993. AB, Catholic U. Am., 1970. With FBI, 1970-96, 95—; inspector FBI hdqrs., asst. spl. agt. in charge FBI, Knoxville, Tenn., 1987-95; supr. exchange program Drug Enforcement Adminstrn., Washington, 1985-87. Author spl. report Black Tar Heroin in the U.S., 1986. Exec. com. Ea. Dist. Narcotics Unit, Tenn., 1988-95. Recipient Achievement award N.Y.C. Police Dept., 1980; Secret Service plaque U.S. Secret Service, 1984. Mem. Am. Soc. Indsl. Security, FBI Agts. Assn., Hon. Legion of Police Dept. N.Y.C. (Valor award 1986). Republican. Episcopalian. Office: FBI Hdqrs 935 Pennsylvania Ave NW Washington DC 20535-0001

LOCKE, THOMAS J., III, physician; b. Vidalia, Ga., June 22, 1955; s. Thomas Jesse II and Armentha (Harvey) L.; divorced; children: Tahira J., Takeia J., Tschena J. Student, Princeton U., 1972-74; MD with honors, Howard U., 1978. Diplomate Am. Bd. Internal Medicine, Nat. Bd. Med. Examiners, Am. Bd. Emergency Medicine. Intern Howard U. Hosp., Washington, 1978-79; resident George Washington U. Hosp., Washington, 1980-81; practice medicine, specializing in internal medicine Ga., 1981—; bd. dirs. Capitol City Bank & Trust Co. Home: 129 Robinhood Dr Warner Robins GA 31088 Office: Contemporary Med Svcs 131 Russell Pkwy # 202 Warner Robins GA 31088

LOCKE, WILLIAM HENRY, lawyer; b. Eagle Pass, Tex., Nov. 14, 1947; s. William Henry and Genevieve (Moss) L.; m. Michelle Ivy Wilson, Aug. 21, 1971; children: William Henry III, Elizabeth Madeleine. AA with honors, Del Mar Coll., 1967; BA, U. Tex., 1969, JD with honors, 1972. Bar: Tex. 1972; cert. in real estate law. Exec. dir. Kleberg & Head, P.C., Corpus Christi, Tex., 1972—. Author: Seizure of Lender's Collateral Under Drug Enforcement Laws, 1990, Contractual Indemnity in Texas, 1991, Civil Forfeiture Actions, 1993, Shifting of Risk: Contractual Provisions for Indemnity, Additional Insureds, Wavier of Subrogation and Exculpation, 1995, Texas Foreclosure Manual, 1995, Risk Management: Through Contractual Provisions for Indemnity, Additional Insureds Waiver of Subrogation, Releases and Exculpation, 1996; contbg. author: Texas Construction Law, 1988. Chmn. Corpus Christi Planning Commn., 1984-85, Corpus Christi Airport Zoning Commn., 1985; bd. dirs., sec. Leadership Corpus Christi, 1984-85; pres. Palmer Drug Abuse Program, Corpus Christi, 1985-87, pres.-elect. 1996; treas. St. James Episcopal Elem. Sch., 1987-91. Fellow Tex. Bar Bound. (life), Tex. Coll. Real Estate Law (dir. 1990-96), Coll. Law of State Bar Tex. (co-dir. advanced real estate law course 1986-87); mem. ABA, Nueces County Bar Assn. (pres. 1987-88), Rotary (bd. dirs. Corpus Christi 1987-88, sec. 1989, Disting. Svc. Above Self award 1985, Corpus Christi merit award 1987), Beta Theta Pi. Democrat. Episcopalian. Office: Kleberg & Head 500 N Water St Corpus Christi TX 78471-0001

LOCKETT, CORNELIUS RANDOLPH, JR., social science educator; b. West Tocoi, Fla., Aug. 18. BS in Indsl. Arts, Fla. A&M U., 1959, MEd in Indsl. Edn., 1969; Diploma in Cen. Am. Rels., U. Costa Rica, 1992. Cert. adminstrn., supervision, Am. history. Furniture finisher Elkor Furniture Co., Jacksonville, Fla., 1956-57; instr. indsl. arts Bd. Pub. Instrn., Jacksonville, Fla., 1959-69; radio announcer WRHC Radio Sta., Jacksonville, Fla., 1962-69; personnel specialist Corning (N.Y.) Glass Works, 1969-70; dir. continuing edn. Fla. Community Coll., Jacksonville, 1970-86; prof. social sci. Fla. C.C., Jacksonville, 1986-95; chmn. Northwest Quadrant Econ. Devel. Trust Fund, 1991-92. Bd. dirs. Northwest Coun.; mem. Jacksonville Community Coun. Inc. With U.S. Army, 1950-53, Korea. Ford Found. fellow, 1974-75, Nat. Tchrs. fellow, 1975; recipient Outstanding Devel. Educator award C.C.s Fla., 1986, Outstanding Yearbook Advisor for High Schs. award State of Fla., 1967. Mem. NAACP, Fla. Assn. C.C.s, Adult and Community Educators, Fla. Devel. Edn. Assn. (pres. 1981), Nat. Assn. Devel. Educators, Fla. Sheriffs Assn., Jacksonville Urban League, Amvets, Am. Legion, Jacksonville C. of C. (bd. govs. 1985, pres. NW coun. 1985), Flajax Club, Inc. (Outstanding Flajax 1980), Omega Psi Phi (Omega Man of Yr. 1966). Home: 8416 Finch Ave E Jacksonville FL 32219-3699

LOCKEY, RICHARD FUNK, allergist, educator; b. Lancaster, Pa., Jan. 15, 1940; s. Stephen Daniel and Anna (Funk) L.; m. Carol Lee Madill, July 3, 1982; children: Brian Christopher, Keith Edward. B.S., Haverford Coll., 1961; M.D., Temple U., 1965; M.S., U. Mich., 1972. Diplomate Am. Bd. Internal Medicine, Am. Bd. Allergy and Immunology. Intern Temple U. Med. Sch., Phila., 1965-66; asst. resident internal medicine Univ. Hosp. U. Mich., Ann Arbor, 1966-67, resident, 1966-68, fellow in allergy and immunology, 1969-70; asst. prof. medicine U. South Fl. Coll. Medicine, Tampa, 1973-77, assoc. prof. medicine, 1977-83, asst. dir. div. allergy and immunology, 1979-82, dir. allergy and immunology, 1982—, prof. medicine, 1983—, prof. pediats., 1983—, prof. pub. health, 1987—; asst. chief sect. allergy and immunology VA Hosp., Tampa, 1973-82, chief sect. allergy and immunology, 1983—; mem. allergenic adv. com. FDA, 1985-89. Editor: Allergy and Clinical Immunology, 1980; co-editor: (with S.C. Bukantz) Fundamentals of Immunology and Allergy, 1987, (with S.C. Bukantz) Principles of Immunology and Allergy, 1987, JAMA Primer on Allergic and Immunologic Diseases, 1987, (with S. C. Bukantz) Allergen Immunotherapy, 1991, (with M. Levine) Monograph on Insect Allergy, 1995; contbr. articles to profl. jours. and chpts. to books; author monographs. Served to maj. USAF, 1971-73. Named Outstanding Med. Specialist, Town and Country Mag., 1989, Claude P. Brown Meml. lectr. Assn. Clin. Scientists, ADA, 1981, Disting. Visitor Ann. Meeting of Coll. of Medicine, Republic of Costa Rica, 1979, spl. mem. Internat. Sci. Bd. Pharmacia Allergy Rsch. Found., 1992—; recipient Alumni Achievement award Temple U. Sch. of Medicine Alumni Assn., 1990, Outstanding Leadership in Chpt. Devel. and Patient Support, Nat. Asthma and Allergy Found. of Am. award, 1992, Cert. of Appreciation, Fla. Med. Assn., 1992. Fellow ACP, AAAS, AMA, Am. Coll. Chest Physicians, Am. Acad. Allergy and Immunology (chmn. com. on insects 1978-81, chmn. undergrad. and grad. edn. com. 1982-88, com. on occupational lung disease 1982—, chmn. com. on standardization of allergenic extracts 1983-86, exec. com. mem. at large 1986-88, historian 1988-89, sec. 1989-90, treas. 1990-91, pres.-elect 1991-92, pres. 1992-93, Am. Bd. Allergy and Immunology (bd. dirs. 1993—), Soc. Allergy and Immunology of Cordoba, Argentina (hon.), John M. Sheldon U. of Mich. Allergy Soc. (councilor 1977-80, pres. 1980-82), Fla. Allergy and Immunology Soc. (sec.-treas. 1979-80, pres. 1981-82), Southeastern Allergy Assn., Hillsborough County Med. Assn., Joint Coun. Allergy and Immunology, Clin. Immunology Soc., Fla. Thoracic Soc., Univ. Club, Carrollwood Village Club. Clubs: Carrollwood Village (Tampa), University. Home: 3909 Northampton Way Tampa FL 33624-4443 Office: U So Fla VA Hosp 13000 Bruce B Downs Blvd Tampa FL 33612-4745

LOCKHART, LILLIE WALKER, retired primary school educator; b. Anderson, S.C., Mar. 19, 1931; d. Luther James and Katy Lee (Evans) Walker; m. Rufus Nelson Lockhart, Mar. 29, 1953. BA cum laude, Johnson C. Smith U., 1958; MA, Appalachian State U., 1981; Advanced MA, U. N.C., Charlotte, 1986. Cert. primary tchr., N.C. Prin. Airline Sch., Anderson, S.C., 1952-55; tchr. primary sch. Alexander St. Sch., Charlotte, N.C., 1956-60, First Ward, Charlotte, 1961-69, Lansdowne Sch., Charlotte, 1970-88; dir. music Rising Star Missionary Assn., 1988-92; team leader, grade chmn., supr. student tchrs., com. chmn., tchr. Charlotte-Mechlenburg Sch. System, 1958-88. Active Nat. Sunday Sch. Congress Christian Edn. Nat. Bapt. Conv. USA, The Lott Carey Missionary Conv., Gen. Bapt. Conv., N.C., All Bapt. World Alliance; vol. March of Dimes; pres. Mountain and Catawba Missionary Women's Aux., 1960-64, supr., 1965-78; tchr. Fairview Heights Bapt. Ch., Salisbury, N.C., 1980-88; com. chair Womens Home and Fgn. Missionary Convention N.C., 1988-92, chair pres.'s address, 1990-93; pianist, supr., tchr. Sunday sch. Fairview Heights Bapt. Ch., Salisbury, 1978-92, program coord., 1986-93; tchr., pianist Rising Star Sunday Sch. Conv., Thomasville, N.C., 1989-92; tutor Enrichment Program of the Oaklawn Park and McCrocery Heights Cmty. Orgn., Charlotte, N.C. Recipient Svc. award Mountain and Catawba Women's Aux., 1964, Christ Call to Youth, 1970, Womens Home and Fgn. Missionary Conv., 1992, Fairview Heights Bapt. Ch., 1990-92, Recognition cert., 1990, Recognition cert. Time and Place, 1995; named N.C. Minister's Wife of Yr., N.C. Assn. Minister's Wives and Widows Interdenominational, Cert. of Appreciation Salisbury-Rowan County Missionary Union, 1996. Mem. NEA, Assn. Childhood Edn. Internat., Interdenominational Mins. Wives (pres., sec. 1966-76, chair budget com. 1992—, Silver Tray award 1988), Charlotte-Mecklenburg Assn. Educators (sch. rep. 1980-88), Charlotte Ret. Sch. Pers., Alumnae J.C. Smith and Appalachian State Univs., Dean St. Cmty. Club (sec. 1990-92), Order Eastern Star, Am. Diebetic Assn. Democrat. Home: 1315 Dean St Charlotte NC 28216-5132

LOCKHART, MADGE CLEMENTS, educational organization executive; b. Soddy, Tenn., May 22, 1920; d. James Arlie and Ollie (Sparks) Clements; m. Andre J. Lockhart, Apr. 24, 1942 (div. 1973); children: Jacqueline, Andrew, Janice, Jill. Student, East Tenn. U., 1938-39; BS, U. Tenn., Chattanooga and Knoxville, 1955, MEd, 1962. Elem. tchr. Tenn. and Ga., 1947-60, Brainerd High Sch., Chattanooga, 1960-64, Cleveland (Tenn.) City Schs., 1966-88; owner, operator Lockhart's Learning Ctr., Inc., Cleveland and Chattanooga, 1975—; co-founder, pres. Hermes, Inc., 1973-79; co-founder Dawn Ctr., Hamilton County, Tenn., 1974; apptd. mem. Tenn. Gov.'s Acad. for Writers. AuthAor poetry, short stories and fiction; contbr. articles to profl. jours. and newspapers. Pres. Cleveland Assn. Retarded Citizens, 1970, state v.p., 1976; pres. Cherokee Easter Seal Soc., 1973-76, Cleveland Creative Arts Guild, 1980; bd. dirs. Tenn. Easter Seal Soc., 1974-77, 80-83; chair Bradley County Internat. Yr. of Child; mem. panel for grants Coun. Govts. S.E. Tenn. Devel. Dist., 1990-92; mem. Internat. Biog. Centre Adv. Coun., Cambridge, Eng., 1991-92; mem. mayor's com. Mus. for Bradley County, Tenn., 1992—. Recipient Service to Mankind award Sertoma, 1978, Gov.'s award for service to handicapped, 1979; mental health home named in her honor, Tenn., 1987. Mem. NEA (life), Tenn. Edn. Assn., Am. Assn. Rehab. Therapy, S.E. Tenn. Arts Coun., Cleveland Edn. Assn. (Service to Humanity award 1987). Mem. Ch. of Christ. Clubs: Byliners, Fantastiks. Home: 3007 Oakland Dr NW Cleveland TN 37312-5281

LOCKHART, MARY ANN, elementary education educator; b. Joplin, Mo., June 24, 1938; d. Gerald Michael and Mabel (Holman) Kursar; m. Jerry Donald Blalock, Aug. 15, 1954 (div. 1964); children: Elizabeth Ann, Jerry Donald; m. Glenn H. Lockhart, Mar. 6, 1965 (div. 1975); 1 child, Herb Glenn; m. Frank Albert Ristau, Apr. 15, 1979 (dec.); m. Glenn H. Lockhart, July 17, 1994. BS in Elem. Edn., East Cen. State U., 1970; cert. in reading edn., Northeastern Okla. State U., 1976; postgrad., East Tex. State U., 1983—. Tchr. Bowlegs (Okla.) Pub. Sch. Dist., 1970-72; tchr., remedial reading tchr. Okmulgee (Okla.) Pub. Sch. Dist., 1973-78; tchr. Toler Elem. Sch., Garland, Tex., 1979-87, Hillside Acad. Excellence, Garland, 1987—; curriculum devel. specialist Garland Ind. Sch. Dist., 1987-90. Mem. ASCD, Assn. Tex. Profl. Educators. Republican. Presbyterian. Home: 1109 Hamilton Dr Richardson TX 75080-5930 Office: Hillside Acad Excellence 2014 Dairy Rd Garland TX 75041-2001

LOCKLEY, JEANETTE ELAINE, mathematics educator, statistics educator; b. Dallas, Feb. 13, 1933; d. Robert L. and Morita (Williams) Prince; m. Arnold Herbert Lockley, Aug. 5, 1952 (dec. Dec. 1973); 1 child, Geoffrey Lynn Lockley. BS in Math., Wiley Coll., Marshall, Tex., 1953; MS in Math., Tex. So. U., Houston, 1954; MS in Math. Statistics, Stanford (Calif.) U., PhD in Math. Instr. math. Tex. So. U., Houston, 1954-57; prof. math. Merritt Coll., Oakland, Calif., 1958-76; rsch. assoc. Office of Ednl. Rsch., asst. prof. math. and edn. Macalester Coll., St. Paul, Minn., 1969-70; dept. chmn. math, physics, engrin. and philosophy Merritt Coll., 1972-76, divsn. chmn. math., drafting, electronic, welding, machine shop, aviation adminstrn., pilot technology, avionics, 1976-80; prof. math., dept. chmn. Mountain View Coll., Dallas, 1976—; pres. and exec. dir. Inst. Ednl. Rsch. & Devel., Inc., Dallas; adj. prof. math. scis. U. Tex., Dallas; panelist NSF, 1977, 78, 79, 80, Dept. Energy, 1979, 80, MISIP Minority Science Improvement Program U.S. Dept. Edn., 1990, 92, 94. Grantee U.S. Dept. Edn., Washington D.C., 1996. Mem. Links, Inc., Girl Friends, Inc. (pres. 1995), Alpha Kappa Alpha. Episcopal. Office: Mountain View Coll 4849 W Illinois Ave Dallas TX 75211

LODDER, ROBERT ANDREW, chemistry and pharmaceutics educator; b. Cin., May 31, 1959. BS, Xavier U., Cin., 1981, MS, 1983; PhD, Ind. U., 1988. Teaching asst. Xavier U., 1981-83; teaching asst. Ind. U., Bloomington, 1983-85, rsch. asst., 1985-87; asst. prof. chemistry and pharmaceutics U. Ky., Lexington, 1988-94, assoc. prof., 1994—. Contbr. articles to profl. jours.; patentee in field. Recipient 100 award R & D mag., 1988, Tomas Hirschveld award Pitts. Conf., 1988; 1st prize IBM Supercomputing Competition, 1990, NSF New Young Investigator award 1992; Technicon near-infrared analysis rsch. fellow, 1987. Mem. AAAS, ASTM, Coun. for Near-Infrared Spectroscopy (del.-at-large to nat. bd. dirs.), Am. Chem. Soc., Am. Assn. Pharm. Scientists, Am. Pharm. Assn., Ky. Acad. Sci. Office: U Ky Coll Pharmacy Rose St Lexington KY 40536-0082

LODEN, RONALD LYNN, physicist; b. Corpus Christi, Tex., Dec. 23, 1968; s. Kenneth L. and Ethel M. (Sweeten) L. Lab. instr. Tex. A&M U., Kingsville, 1990—. Mem. Soc. Physics Students. Baptist. Office: Tex A&M U Physics Dept CB175 Kingsville TX 78363

LOE, EMMETT BAXTER, social worker; b. Haskell County, Tex., Dec. 28, 1924; s. Stephen Rals and Ellie Lorene (Baker) L.; m. Ruby Nell Ketchersid, Sept. 12, 1946; children: Ronald Wayne, Karen June, Kimberley Grant, Melinda Michelle. Student, Howard Payne U., 1964-66, Amarillo, Coll., 1970-71, West Tex. State U., 1971-72. Ordained to ministry Ch. of Christ, 1961. With Amerada Petroleum Corp., Gaines County, Tex., 1950-61; pastor chs. Brownwood, Tex., 1961-66, Odessa, Tex., 1966-69; chmn. bd. Christian Relief Fund, Amarillo, Tex., 1975—; lectr. in field. Editor Gospel Tidings mag., 1965-75. Bd. dirs. Southwestern Bible Inst., San Angelo, Tex., 1980-83. With USN, 1944-46. Mem. Evang. Council for Fin. Accountability, Amarillo Ministerial Alliance (pres.), Christian Ministries Mgmt. Assn., Rotary (Paul Harris Fellow, pres. Amarillo chpt. 1978-79, chaplain City of Amarillo 1987-89). Republican. Home: 2521 Walnut St Amarillo TX 79107-2047 Office: 4606 River Rd Amarillo TX 79108-5202

LOEFFLER, WILLIAM GEORGE, JR., advertising executive; b. Washington, Feb. 23, 1939; s. William George and Sara Mae (Henderson) L.; children: William Douglas, Sara Cantillon, Michael Christopher; m. Christine Sinclair Tomberlin, Apr. 19, 1991. BA, Washington and Lee U., 1960. Pub. rels. specialist Gen. Electric Co., Schenectady, N.Y. and Winston-Salem, N.C., 1965-68; v.p., account supr. Cargill, Wilson & Acree, Charlotte, N.C., 1968-74; exec. v.p. McConnell and Assocs., Charlotte, 1974-81; pres. Loeffler Ketchum Mountjoy, Charlotte, 1981-90, chmn. 1990—; bd. dirs. First Commerce Bank; mem. Advt. Rev. Bd., Charlotte, 1983—; chmn. Nat. Advt. Agy. Network; judge advt. awards competitions. Bd. dirs. Better Bus. Bur., Charlotte, 1980-81, 89-93; v.p. Play Units for the Severely Handicapped, Charlotte, 1977-84; active Win with Charlotte Com., 1984, Charlotte Basketball Com., 1978-95, pres. 1987; mem. adv. bd. United Carolina Bank, 1995—; bd. dirs. acad. guidance com. Charlotte Christian Sch., 1974-75; bd. dirs. Matthews Athletic Assn., N.C., 1979; comm. chmn. fund drive Arts and Sci. Coun., 1988, bd. dirs. 1991—; bd. visitors mktg. dept. U. N.C., Charlotte. Served to lt. USMCR, 1962-65. Mem. Advt. Club of Charlotte (pres. 1980-81, Silver medal 1984), Bus. and Profl. Advt. Assn., Charlotte Sales and Mktg. Execs., Am. Mktg. Assn., Charlotte C. of C. (mem. bd. advisors 1989—), River Run Country Club (bd. advisors). Republican. Home: 18830 River Wind Ln Davidson NC 28036-8878 Office: Loeffler Ketchum Mountjoy 2101 Rexford Rd Ste 200 E Charlotte NC 28211-3477

LOESCH, MABEL LORRAINE, social worker; b. Annandale, Minn., July 1, 1925; d. Rudolph and Hedwig (Zeidler) Treichler; m. Harold Carl Loesch, Oct. 19, 1945; children: Stephen, Gretchen, Jonathan, Frederick. BS, La. State U., 1972, MSW, 1974. Cert. Acad. Cert. Social Worker, bd. cert. diplomate. Tchr. Am. schs. Tegucigalpa, Honduras, 1960-61, Guayaquil, Ecuador, 1962-66, La Ceiba, Honduras, 1966-67; supr. clin. svc. Blundon Home, Baton Rouge, 1974-81; social worker, cons. Dhaka, Bangladesh, 1981-85; social worker Manna Food Bank, Pensacola, Fla., 1986—; adj. instr. social work dept. Southern U., Baton Rouge, 1976-81. Author: Generations in Germany and America, 1996; editor: Making Do, 1989, Making Do II, 1994, Generations in Germany and America, 1996. Mem. adv. com. Luth. Ministries of Fla., 1993—. Mem. NASW, Mensa (local sec. 1986-90, chair scholarships com.), Phi Kappa Phi. Democrat. Lutheran. Home: 2140 E Scott St Pensacola FL 32503-4957

LOESCHER, BARBARA ANN, auditing executive; b. Mauston, Wis., Aug. 20, 1953; d. Arnold John Loescher and Carol Jeanne (Vinopal) Gross. BS in Bus. and Acctg., Edgewood Coll., 1988. CPA, Wis; cert. internal auditor, fraud examiner. Acct. Harco Ins. Co., Milw., 1977-78; corp. acct. Blunt Ellis and Loewi, Milw., 1978-79; fin. technician Cumis Ins. Soc., Inc., Madison, Wis., 1979-81; budget, tax and cost specialist Cumis Ins. Soc., Inc., Madison, 1981-83, risk mgmt. investment specialist, 1983-84, fraud auditing mgr., 1984-90; asst. to sr. v.p. individual life and health mktg. CUNA Mut. Fin. Svcs. Corp., Inc., Madison, 1990-91; pres., COO, Fin. Standards Group, Inc., Boca Raton, Fla., 1991-94; pres. Loescher & Assocs., Boca Raton, 1994—; lectr. seminars on auditing, risk mgmt. and fraud. Author of numerous articles in field. Mem. AICPA, Wis. Inst. CPAs, Inst. Internal Auditors (sec. 1987), Nat. Assn. Cert. Fraud Examiners. Republican. Roman Catholic. Home: 21479 Sweetwater Ln S Boca Raton FL 33428 Office: 20423 State Road 7 Ste 295 Boca Raton FL 33498-6747

LOEWENSTEIN, DAVID ANDREW, clinical psychologist, neuropsychologist, educator; b. Miami, Fla., Dec. 31, 1959; s. Jack Meyer and Arline (Perry) L.; m. Susan Laurie Berkell, Nov. 15, 1992. BA in Psychology, U. S. Fla., 1981; MS in Clin. Psychology, Fla. State U., 1983, PhD in Clin. Psychology, 1986. Psychol. intern U. Washington Sch. Medicine, Seattle, 1985-86; rsch. asst. prof. U. Miami Sch. Medicine, 1986-90, assoc. prof. psychiatry, 1992—; dir. neuropsychology labs. Wien Ctr. for Alzheimers Disease Mt. Sinai Med. Ctr., Miami Beach, Fla., 1986—; dir. psychol. svcs. dept. psychiatry U. Miami/Mt. Sinai Med. Ctr., Miami Beach, 1990—. Author book chpts.; contbr. numerous articles to profl. jours. Grantee NIMH, 1992-97. Office: Mt Sinai Med Ctr Dept Psych 4300 Alton Rd Miami FL 33140-2849

LOEWENSTEIN, GEORGE WOLFGANG, retired physician, UN consultant; b. Germany, Apr. 18, 1890; m. Johanna Sabath, Nov. 27, 1923; children: Peter F. Lansing (dec.) and Ruth Edith Gallagher (twins). Student, Royal William Coll., Germany, 1909, Friedrich William U., Germany, 1919, London Sch. Tropical Hygiene and Medicine, 1939. Dir. pub. health Neubabelsberg, 1920-24, Berlin, 1924-34; dir. pub. health and welfare City of Berlin, 1923-33; pvt. practice medicine, Chgo., 1940-46, Chebeague and Dark Harbor, Maine, 1947-58; instr. Berlin Acad. Prevention of Infant Mortality, Postgrad. Acad. Physicians; permanent cons., v.p., rep. Internat. Abolitionists Fedn. at ECOSOC, UN, 1947-90; med. cons. German Gen. Consulate, Atlanta, Miami, Fla., 1963; lectr. Morton Plant Hosp., Clearwater, Fla., also Clearwater campus St. Petersburg Jr. Coll.; guest prof. U. Bremen, Berlin, 1981-82. Author: Public Health Between the Time of Imperium and National Socialism, The Destruction of Public Health Reforms of the First German Republic, 1985, others; transl. from the Japanese Origin of Syphilis in the Far East, Static Atony, Sexual Pedagogic; contbr. 300 articles to med. jours. and revs. to books. Served with German Army, 1914-18. Decorated Cross Merit I Class (Germany), 1965; recipient Commendation awards Pres. of U.S., 1945, 70, 65 Year Gold Service Pin, AMA and ARC, 1985, Service to Mankind award Sertoma, 1972-73, Sport award Pres. Carter, 1977, Musicologist award Richey Symphony, 1979, Reconciliation award Germany-U.S.A., 1983, Friendship award Fed. Republic of Germany, USA, 1985, Teaching award Morton Plant Hosp., 1988, 70 Yrs. Svc. Red Cross, others. Fellow Am. Acad. Family Physicians (charter, life, 40-Yr. Svc. award 1986), AAAS, Am. Coll. Sport Medicine (emeritus, charter, life), Am. Pub. Health Assn. (life, 40-Yr. Svc. award 1984), Brit. Soc. (emeritus); mem. World Med. Assn. (life), German Assn. History of Medicine (life), Acad. Mental Retardation (charter, life), Am. Pub. Health Assn. (life, 40 Yr. Svc. award), Fla. Health Assn. (life), Brit. Pub. Health Assn. (life), AMA (hon.), Am. Assn. Mil. Surgeons (life), Acad. Preventive Medicine (life), Steuben Soc., Richey Symphony Soc. (charter, Musicologist 1979), World Peace Through World Law Ctr. Clubs: City (Chgo. chmn. hygiene sect. 1944-46). Lodges: Rotary (life, Harris fellow 1980), Masons (32 deg.), Shriners (comdr., life v.p.). Home: 2470 Rhodesian Dr Apt 34 Clearwater FL 34623-1948

LOFLAND, GARY KENNETH, cardiac surgeon; b. Milford, Del., Mar. 5, 1951; s. Joseph Sudler and Doris Louise (Peters) L.; m. Janice Marie Show, Feb. 3, 1979; children: Kiernan Sudler, Glennis Kathleen. BA cum laude, Boston U., 1969, MD cum laude, 1975. Diplomate Am. Bd. Surgery, Am. Bd. Thoracic Surgery; lic. physician, Va., N.Y., Mont., N.C. Intern, jr. asst. resident in surgery Duke U. Med. Ctr., Durham, N.C., 1975-81; rsch. fellow dept. surgery Duke U. Med. Ctr., Durham, 1979-81, sr. asst. resident in surgery, 1981-84, chief resident in surgery, 1984-85, teaching scholar in cardiac surgery, 1985-86; sr. registrar in cardiothoracic surgery Hosp. for Sick Children, London, 1986-87; dir. cardiovascular surgery Children's Hosp. of Buffalo, 1987-88; asst. prof. surgery SUNY, Buffalo, 1987-88; assoc. prof. surgery/pediatrics, Med. Coll. Va., Richmond, 1988-94, dir. pediatric cardiac surgery/med. dir. cardiac surgery ICU, 1988-94; clin. prof. surgery Georgetown U., Washington, 1994—; dir. Columbia/HCA Ctr. Congenital Heart Disease, Richmond, 1994—. Editorial rev. bd. Progress in Pediatric Cardiology, Year Book of Thoracic Surgery; contbr. articles to profl. jours. Pres. Am. Heart Assn., Richmond; mem. bd. trustees Transplant Found. Lt. comdr. USPHS, 1977-79. Recipient Univ. Hosp. Trustees award, Boston, 1975; HEW/USPHS commendation medal, 1979. Mem. AMA, Am. Heart Assn., Assn. for Acad. Surgery, Internat. Soc. for Heart Transplantation, Med. Soc. Va., Richmond Acad. Medicine, Richmond Surg. Soc., So. Thoracic Surg. Assn., Soc. for Thoracic Surgeons, Congenital Heart Surgeons Soc., , Alpha Omega Alpha. Home: 740 Lee Rd PO Box 126 Crozier VA 23039 Office: Columbia/HCA Ctr Congenital Heart Disease 7602 Forest Ave Ste 208 Richmond VA 23229

LOFT, BERNARD IRWIN, education educator, consultant. BS, West Chester (Pa.) U., 1939; MA in Edn., U. Fla., 1949; Directorate in Health and Safety, Ind. U., 1956, D of Health and Safety, 1957. Ednl. advisor Civilian Conservation Corps, Branchville, N.J., 1940-42; dir. phys. edn., coach Lower Paxton Twp. High Sch., Harrisburg, Pa., 1942; field rep. in safety svcs. ARC, Atlanta, 1946; instr. in biology and phys. edn., coach Andrew Jackson High Sch., Jacksonville, Fla., 1946-48; chmn. safety edn. program, instr. phys. edn., faculty, coach U. Fla., Gainesville, 1948-51; asst. prof. edn. and continuing edn. Mich. State U., East Lansing, 1951-55; prof. Sch. of Health, Phys. Edn. and Recreation, dir. health and safety Ind.U., Bloomington, 1956—, assoc. prof. health and safety, 1957-65; fgn. assignment Cultural Exchange Program Americans Abroad Dept. State, Cambodia, 1961-62; dir. Ctr. fo Safety Studies, prof. health safety edn. Ind.U., Bloomington, 1962-63, prof. emeritus Applied Health Sci., dir., 1981; emeritus prof. health and safety Ind. U., Bloomington, 1981—; ednl. cons. Am. Automobile Assn., Washington, Am. Trucking Assn., Washington; vis. lectr. U. Md., U. N.C., U. Ga., Syracuse (N.Y.) U., Kent (Ohio) State U., U. Miami, Fla. State U., S.C. A&M Coll., Purdue U.; faculty advisor doctoral studies and PhD and EdD degrees, chair health svcs. track Walden U., acad. policies bd.; participant The White House Conf. on Health, 1965, White House Conf. on Occupational Safety, 1956; participant cultural exch. program to Phnom Penh, Cambodia, U.S. Dept. State, Voice of Am. Author: How to Prevent Accidents in the Motor Home, 1978; contbr. articles to profl. jours. Head counselor Camp Ridgedale, Sumneytown, Pa., waterfront dir., counselor; athletic dir. Camp Arthur, Zieglersville, Pa.; waterfront dir. Pocono Highland Camp, Marshall's Creek, Pa., Blue Mountain Camps, East Stroudsburg, Pa., Kitatinny Camps, Dingman's Ferry, Pa., head counselor. Lt. comdr. USN, 1942-46, USNR, 1946-65, World War II, ret., 1965. Recipient Cert. of Appreciation, Ind. U. Student Found., 40 Yr. Svc. Pin, ARC; decorated Cheva'Lier de L'Order du Monisaraphon (Cambodian Govt.). Fellow AAHPERD, Am. Acad. Safety Edn. (charter, pres.), Am. Sch. Health Assn.; mem. NEA, Ind. Mobile Home Assn. (hon. Cert. of Appreciation 1966), Nat. Safety Coun. (gen. chmn. higher edn. sect. 1960-61 Plaque), Ind. Assn. for Health, Phys. Edn. and Recreation (v.p.), Am. Sch. Health Assn. (chmn. sch. safety edn. com., and others), Ind. Coll. Health Assn. (pres. 1958-59), Ind. Tchr.'s Assn., Am. Acad. Safety Edn. (pres., v.p., chmn. membership com., pres. 1967-68), Mid-Am. Coll. Health Assn., Ind. Assn. Health Educator. Office: Walden Univ Liaison Rep to Ind Univ 801 Anchor Rode Dr Naples FL 34103-2751

LOFTIN, MARION THEO, sociologist, educator; b. Coushatta, La., Sept. 10, 1915; s. John Griffin and Ida Estella (Huckaby) L. B.A., Northwestern La. State Coll., 1936; M.A., La. State U., 1941; Ph.D., Vanderbilt U., 1952. Tchr. pub. high schs. Red River Parish, La., 1935-40; asso. prof. Southeastern La. State Coll., 1946-47; faculty Miss. State U., 1949—, Thomas L. Bailey prof. sociology and anthropology, head dept., 1961-67; assoc. dean Miss. State U. (Grad. Sch.), 1965-77, dean, 1977-79, v.p. grad. studies and research, 1980-85, prof. sociology, v.p. grad. studies and research emeritus,

1986—. Served with AUS, 1941-45. Mem. Am. Sociol. Assn., Rural Sociol. Soc., So. Sociol. Soc., Phi Kappa Phi, Omicron Delta Kappa. Home: 1214 Hillcrest cir Starkville MS 39759

LOFTON, KEVIN EUGENE, medical facility administrator; b. Beaumont, Tex., Sept. 29, 1954. BS, Boston U., 1976; M Health Care Adminstrn., Ga. State U., 1979. Adminstrv. resident Meml. Med. Ctr., Corpus Christi, Tex., 1978-79; adminstr. emergency svcs. Univ. Hosp., Jacksonville, Fla., 1979-80, adminstr. material mgmt., 1980-81, asst. exec. dir. ambulatory care, 1981-82, asst. v.p. ambulatory svcs., 1982-83, v.p. profl. svcs., 1983-86; exec. v.p. Univ. Med. Ctr., Jacksonville, 1986-90; exec. dir. Howard Univ. Hosp., Washington, 1990-93; assoc. v.p., exec. dir. U. Ala. Hosp., Birmingham, 1993—. Contbr. articles to profl. publs. Fellow Am. Coll. Health Care Execs. (R.S. Hudgenw award 1993); mem. Am. Hosp. Assn., Nat. Assn. Health Svcs. Execs. (pres.-elect). Home: U Ala Hosp Room 246/OHB 2112 Lake Heather Way Hoover LA 35242 Office: U Ala Hosp 619 19th St S Rm 246/ohb Birmingham AL 35233-1924*

LOFTUS, JILL VINES, civilian military employee; b. Glens Falls, N.Y., Feb. 3, 1954; d. John Lincoln and Jeannette Jean (Gould) Vines; m. Robert Houghwout Jackson Loftus, Sept. 6, 1975; 1 child, Patrick Jackson. BA in English Lit., U. Va., 1975; MBA, U. Calif., Santa Ana, 1989. Contract specialist Dept. of Navy/Space and Naval Warfare, Arlington, Va., 1975-80, contracting ofcr., 1980-82, head, command control contracts, 1982-83, head, surface and submarine contracts, 1983-86, head, tactical aircraft contracts, 1986-91, dir. policy and mgmt., 1991-94, dir. cruise missiles and unmanned aerial vehicle contracts, 1994-96, dep. inspector gen., 1996—; dir. contacts and grants NIH, Bethesda, Md., 1994. Sponsor, uniform dir. Great Falls Little League, Va., 1989-95, mem. sr. exec. svc., 1994—. Recipient various civilian svc. awards Sec.of Navy, 1990, Superior Civilian medal, 1994, 96. Mem. Riverbend Golf and Country Club, U. Va. Alumni Assn. Home: 509 Arnon Ridge Ct Great Falls VA 22066 Office: Dept of the Navy Naval Inspector Gen Bldg 200 Washington Navy Yard Washington DC 20360

LOGAN, DAN, investment professional; b. Chgo., Dec. 10, 1946; s. David S. and Reva (Frumkin) L.; m. Gloria Jean Blasz, July 8, 1973; children: Elizabeth, Andrew. BA, Knox Coll., 1969. Sr. speechwriter, asst. Ill. Gov. Daniel Walker, Springfield, Ill., 1975-76; spl. asst. U.S. Sen. Joseph Biden, Jr., Washington, 1977; speechwriter, cons. U.S. Rep. Max Baucus Senate campaign, Washington, 1978; speechwriter U.S. Sen. Edmund S. Muskie, Washington, 1979, Charles Ferris, chmn. FCC, Washington, 1980; exec. dir. Free Men, Inc., Washington, 1980-87; co-founder Nat. Congress for Men, Washington, 1981; ptnr. Mercury Investments, Chgo., 1988—. Contbr. articles to newspapers. Mem. Nat. Writers Union. Unitarian Universalist.

LOGAN, GORDON BAKER, small business owner; b. Sumter, S.C., Sept. 17, 1946; s. Joseph E. and Myrtis (Baker) L.; m. Bettye Brown, Dec. 4, 1983; children: Gordon Edward, Carolyn Elizabeth. BS in Mech. Engring., MIT, 1968; MBA with Honors, U. Pa., 1976. CPA, Tex. Capt. USAF, 1969, advanced through grades to aircraft comdr., 1972; project engr. Dow Badische, Inc., Williamsburg, Va., 1968-69; mgr. M.A.S. Price Waterhouse & Co., Houston, 1976-80; pres. Austin Style, Inc., 1979—, Texas Style, Inc., Austin, 1980—, Performance Salon Systems, Inc., 1991—, Sport Clips, Inc., 1995—. Pres. Belmont Park Homeowners Assn., Houston, 1978-80, Lost River Homeowners Assn., Georgetown, Tex., 1989-92; bd. dirs. Georgetown Indsl. Found., 1995—. Capt. USAF, 1969-76. Mem. Tex. Soc. CPAs (outstanding achievement award 1978), Internat. Franchise Assn. (Disting. Achievement award 1982), Wharton Alumni Assn. (v.p. 1979-80), Georgetown C. of C. (bd. dirs. 1992-95, v.p. 1993-95), Beta Gamma Sigma, Delta Tau Delta (pres. coun., other offices). Home: 20159 W Lake Pky Georgetown TX 78628-9511

LOGAN, LINDA JO, secondary school educator; b. Houston, May 3, 1968; d. Earl Roger and Louise Delphine (Meyer) L. BS in Secondary English Edn., U. Tex., 1990. Cert. English and reading tchr., Tex. Tchr. reading Northside Ind. Sch. Dist., San Antonio, 1990—; counselor Master Sch., Austin, Tex., summers 1989—. Mem. ASCD, NEA, Tex. Mid. Sch. Assn., Ex-Students Assn. U. Tex. Republican. Roman Catholic. Office: HB Zachry Mid Sch 9410 Timber Path San Antonio TX 78250-4921

LOGAN, MARY CALKIN, volunteer director community relations; b. Washington, Jan. 23, 1941; d. Loren Malcolm and Edith Garrison Calkin; m. Richard Lewis Logan, Jan. 6, 1962; children: Ashley Logan Drews, Austin Lewis. BA, U. Tex., 1963. Tchr. Tex. State Sch. for the Deaf, Austin, 1963-64; exec. sec. Dewar, Robertson & Pancoast, Austin, 1964-69; devel. dir. St. Joseph High Sch., Victoria, Tex., 1989-94; vol. dir. comty. rels. Hospice of S. Tex., Victoria, 1994—; bd. dirs. Victoria Coll. Author, producer video; author script. Vice-chair Govs. Commn. for Women, State of Tex., 1989-90, Victoria County (Tex.) Rep. Orgn., 1988-94; chmn. Tex. Women's Hall of Fame, 1988; v.p. Palmer Drug Abuse Program, 1990-91, Womens Crisis Ctr., Victoria, 1987-89; sec. Boys Club, Victoria, 1981-83; steering com. Nat. Pub. Radio, Victoria, 1992-94. Mem. Jr. League Victoria (pres. 1985-86, Oustanding Sustainer Recognition award 1996), Ct. Six Flags (sec. 1989-90, treas. 1993-94), Victoria Preservation, Inc. (sec., founding mem., pres. 1994—), Victoria Country Club (pres. 1989-90), Settlement Club Austin. Episcopalian. Home: 707 W Stayton Ave Victoria TX 77901-6343

LOGAN, SHARON BROOKS, lawyer; b. Easton, Md., Nov. 19, 1945; d. Blake Elmer and Esther N. (Statum) Brooks; children: John W. III, Troy Blake. BS in Econs., U. Md., 1967, MBA in Mktg., 1969; JD, U. Fla., 1979. Bar: Fla. 1979. Ptnr. Raymond Wilson, Esq., Ormond Beach, Fla., 1980, Landis, Graham & French, Daytona Beach, Fla., 1981, Watson & Assocs., Daytona Beach, 1982-84; prin. Sharon B. Logan, Esq., Ormond Beach, 1984—; legal advisor to paralegal program Daytona Beach Community Coll., 1984—. Sponsor Ea. Surfing Assn., Daytona Beach, 1983—, Nat. Scholastic Surfing Assn., 1987—; bd. dirs. Ctr. for Visually Impaired, Daytona Beach, 1991—; mem. Fla. Supreme Ct. Hist. Soc. Recipient Citizenship award Rotary Club, 1962-63; Woodrow Wilson fellow U. Md., 1967. Mem. ABA, Fla. Bar Assn. (real property and probate sect., cert. real estate atty. 1996), Volusia County Bar Assn. (bd. dirs.), Volusia County Real Property Council, Inc. (bd. dirs. 1987—, sec. 1987-88, v.p. 1988-89, pres. 1989-90, sec. 1990-91), Ducks Unlimited, Mus. Arts and Scis., Volusia County Estate Planning Council, Daytona Beach Area Bd. Realtors, Ormond Beach C. of C., Gator Club, Halifax Club, Tomoka Oaks Country Club, Daytona Boat Club, Md. Club, Beta Gamma Sigma, Alpha Lamba Delta, Phi Kappa Phi, Omicron Delta Epsilon, Delta Delta Delta (Scholarship award 1964), Sigma Alpha Epsilon. Democrat. Episcopalian. Avocations: cooking, sewing, golf, tennis, aerobics. Office: Sharon B Logan Esq 400 S Atlantic Ave Ste 110 Ormond Beach FL 32176-7142

LOGAN, STEPHEN BEAN, III, safety engineer; b. Lexington, Ky., Nov. 1, 1932; s. Stephen Bean II and Minnie Howell (Davies) L.; m. Rayma Jean Sharp; children: Leah, Lori, Lynda, Stephen IV, Jill; stepchildren: Joey, Barry. BSCE, U. Ky., 1959. Registered profl. engr., Calif. Estimator, sales engr. Ferry Bros. Constrn. Co., El Cajon, Calif., 1967-68; regional safety engring. mgr. Allstate Ins. Co., Santa Ana, Calif., 1968-70; resident loss control mgr. Kemper Ins. Group, Washington, 1970-74; mgr. loss control Levi Strauss Co., San Francisco, 1974-75; pvt. practice safety cons. Danville, Calif., 1975-76; corp. safety engr. Morrison-Knudsen Co., Boise, Idaho, 1976-77; pres. Logan & Assocs., Inc., Boise, 1977-80; indsl. safety and fire protection mgr. TVA, Decatur, Ala., 1980-88; corp. environ. and safety mgr. Crain Industries, Ft. Smith, Ark., 1988-90; dir. occupational health and safety Lexicon Inc., Little Rock, 1990—; cons. in field. Contbr. articles to profl. publs. With USAF, 1951-55. Mem. Am. Soc. Safety Engrs. (treas. 1968-70, v.p. Ark. chpt. 1993, pres. 1994), Constrn. Safety Assn. Am. (life, founder, pres. 1971-72, award 1972, 91), Nat. Safety Mgmt. Assn., Nat. Fire Protection Assn., Am. Legion. Democrat. Methodist. Home: 422 Carol Ann Cv Southaven MS 38671-5826 Office: Lexicon Inc 4611 W Bethany Ln N Little Rock AR 72231

LOGANATHAN, BOMMANNA GOUNDER, environmental chemist, biologist, researcher, educator; b. Mettupalayam, Coimbatore, India, Sept. 30, 1954; arrived in U.S., 1990; s. Nanjappa Bommanna Gounder and Periakkal (Subbayan) B.; m. Kalaiselvi Kurunthachalam; children: Sudan, Dheepa. BS in Zoology, U. Madras, India, 1977; MS in Marine Biology, Annamalai U., Porto Novo, India, 1979, PhD in Marine Biology, 1986; PhD in Ecotoxicology/Environ. Chemistry, Ehime U., Matsuyama, Japan, 1990. Rsch. sci. SUNY, Buffalo, 1990-93; asst. prof. Skidaway Inst. Oceanography (U. Ga. sys.), Savannah, Ga., 1993—. Author chpts. to books; mem. rev. panel Environ. Pollution, Marine Pollution Bull., Environ. Toxicology & Chemistry; contbr. articles to profl. jours. Recipient Outstanding Rsch. award, 1991; sr. rsch. fellow Indian Coun. Agrl. Rsch., 1980-83, Govt. India rsch. fellow Dept. Ocean Devel., 1985-86; Monbusho (Japanese Govt.) rsch. fellow, 1986-90; U.S. EPA rsch. grantee, 1993-95. Mem. AAAS, Soc. Environ. Toxicology and Chemistry, Japanese Soc. Environ. Chemistry, Skidaway Marine Sci. Found. Office: U Systems Ga Skidaway Inst Oceanography 10 Ocean Sci Cir Savannah GA 31411

LOGRECO, GERARD ERNEST, industrial engineer; b. New Orleans, May 9, 1951; s. John Joseph Sr. and Rose Mary (Rebaudo) L.; m. Mary Ann Peters, June 29, 1974; children: Jennifer, Melissa, Erin. BS in Bus. Mgmt., Nicholls State U., Thibadoux, La., 1974. Retail mgr. Cullum & Boren, Inc., New Orleans, 1975-79; assoc. indsl. engr. Martin Marietta Manned Space Systems, New Orleans, 1979-80, indsl. engr., 1980-81, sr. indsl. engr., 1981-83, group indsl. engr., 1983-89, total quality mgmt. adminstr., 1989. Coordinator dept. United Way, New Orleans, 1984, 87, U.S. Savs. Bond Drive, New Orleans, 1984; assoc. mem. rev. bd. U.S. Senate Productivity Award Com., New Orleans, 1984-85. Mem. Inst. Indsl. Engrs. (v.p. 1982-83, pres. 1983-85, 90-92, dir. dist. VII 1986-89, award of excellence 1983-85), Tech. Mktg. Soc. Am. Home: 1313 Melody Dr Metairie LA 70002-1919 Office: Martin Marietta Aerospace PO Box 29304 M/S 3652 New Orleans LA 70189

LOHMANN, GEORGE YOUNG, JR., neurosurgeon, hospital executive; b. Scranton, Pa., Aug. 9, 1947; s. George Young Lohmann and Elizabeth (Nichols) Frantzen; m. Joette Calabrese, May 15, 1973 (div. 1981); m. Rosemary Ei-Ling Ma, Sept. 24, 1988; 1 child, Norelle Christa Victoria. AB in Chemistry with honors, Hobart Coll., 1968; MD, SUNY, Buffalo, 1972. Diplomate Am. Bd. Neurol. Surgeons, Am. Acad. Pain Specialists. Resident gen. surgery Wesley Meml. Hosp., Chgo., 1972-73; from jr. resident to chief resident Georgetown U. Hosp., Washington, 1975-79; asst. med. dir. West Side Orgn., Chgo., 1973-74; emergency physician St. James Hosp., Chicago Heights, Ill., 1973-74; pvt. practice Baton Rouge, 1979-81, 81-84; dir. dept. neurosurgery Brookdale Hosp. Med. Ctr., Bklyn., 1984-93; pres. Bklyn. Neurosurg. Svcs., Inc., 1985—; mem. Med. Dir. Com., Risk Mgmt. Com., Exec. Quality Assurance Com., 1987-93; mem. Med. Bd. Com., 1985-93, Exec. Bd. Com., 1984-93, Pain Mgmt. Com., 1988-91. Named to Compton-Connolly Guide to Best Physicians in the New York Met. Area; patentee in field; contbr. articles to profl. jours. Mem. adv. bd. Ctr. Latin Affairs, Baton Rouge, 1982-84; mem. Senatorial Inner Cir., 1988; bd. trustees Christian Victory Ctr., Hempstead, N.Y., 1986-88; fellow Am. Coll. Pain Mgmt. Named Best Doctor in Am. Fellow ACS; mem. AMA, Am. Assn. Neurologic Surgeons (AANS-CNS joint sects.), N.Y. State Neurosurg. Soc., N.Y. Soc. Neurosurgery, Congress Neurologic Surgeons (spine sect., sect. on trauma), Tex. State Med. Soc., So. Med. Soc. Presdl. Roundtable, Shanhai Tiffin Club, Donyin Sister City Assn., Senatorial Inner Circle, Midland C. of C., Midland-Odessa Symphony and Choral Soc.

LOHRMAN, WILLIAM WALTER, investment company executive, consultant; b. Schulkyll Twp., Pa., Aug. 7, 1954; s. Roger Moore and Joan (Powell) L. BS in Environ. Sci., Rutgers U., 1976, MBA, 1979. Exec. intern Mountainside Hosp., Montclair, N.J., 1976-77; rate analyst N.J. Bd. Pub. Utilities, Newark, 1977-79; project cons. Ebasco Bus. Cons. Co., Dallas, 1979-83; edn. cons. Applied Learning, Dallas, 1983; cost ctr. mgr. GTE Sprint, Las Colinas, Tex., 1984-86; mgr. fin. planning and analysis Am. Airlines DMC, Ft. Worth, 1987; project mgr. NCNB Tex., Dallas, 1987-88; mgr. Price Waterhouse, Dallas, 1988-92; sr. fin. analyst CSW Energy Inc., Dallas, 1993-94; mgr. corp. ventures Ctrl. and South West Corp., Dallas, 1994—. Mem. pub. rels. com. Covenant Inn Homeless Project, Dallas, 1988-89; mem. Dallas Coun. on World Affairs, Dallas/Brno Sister City com., Japan Am. Soc. of Dallas/Ft. Worth, Internat. Trade Assn. Dallas/Ft. Worth; bus. advisor to pilot program Jr. Achievement, Prague, Czechoslovakia, summer 1992. Mem. Mensa. Republican. Methodist. Office: Central & South West Corp 1616 Woodall Rodgers Fwy Dallas TX 75202-1234 Address: 1927 Lansdown Ct Carrollton TX 75010

LOICK, WALTER JULIUS, investment company executive; b. N.Y.C., Jan. 26, 1927; s. Stephen and Anna (Lechka) L.; m. Jean Virginia Ault, Aug. 26, 1950 (div. Feb. 1967); m. Rena Heare, May 4, 1968; children: Terri Kenefsky, Harvey Gortner, Sue. BSME, Rensselaer Poly. Inst., 1951. Advt. and sales promotion mgr. Westinghouse, Pitts., 1951-57; data processing sales IBM, Pitts., 1957-59; pvt. practice in real estate sales St. Petersburg, Fla., 1959-62; broker to v.p. Smith Barney, St. Petersburg, Fla., 1962-85; founder, pres. LBS Capital Mgmt., Inc., Clearwater, Fla., 1985—. With U.S. Maritime Svc., 1945-47. Mem. Safety Harbor Spa, Clearwater Club. Office: LBS Capital Mgmt 311 Park Place Blvd Ste 330 Clearwater FL 34619-3923

LOIGNON, GERALD ARTHUR, JR., nuclear engineer; b. N.Y.C., June 25, 1950; s. Gerald Arthur Loignon Sr. and Nancy MacLean (Walker) Bucknell; m. Margaret Mary Hamburger, Aug. 7, 1971; children: Brian MacLean, Matthew Thomas, Teresa Marie. BS in Nuclear Engring., N.C. State U., 1976. Registerd profl. engr., S.C.; lic. sr. reactor operator Nuclear Regulatory Commn. Health physics technician nuclear fuel div. Westinghouse, Columbia, S.C., 1970-72; office equipment technician Cavin's Inc., Raleigh, N.C., 1973-76; quality assurance engr. Met. Edison Co., Reading, Pa., 1976-79; shift tech. advisor Met. Edison Co., Gen. Pub. Utility, Harrisburg, Pa., 1979-81; shift tech. advisor S.C. Electric and Gas Co., Jenkinsville, 1981-83, assoc. mgr. performance and results, 1983-88, shift engr., 1988-91, test unit supr., 1992-95, coord. nuc. ops. project, 1995—, sr. engr., 1996—. Mem. choir, dir. religious edn. St. Marks Parish, Newberry, S.C., 1991—. Mem. Am. Nuclear Soc. (chair S.C. chpt. 1985-86, profl. engring. exam. com. 1987—, cert. appreciation 1985, cert. governence 1986), Profl. Reactor Operator Soc. Roman Catholic. Home: 3137 Jalapa Rd Kinards SC 29355 Office: SC Electric and Gas Co VC Summer Nuc Sta PO Box 88 Jenkinsville SC 29065-0088

LOKMER, STEPHANIE ANN, public relations counselor; b. Wheeling, W.Va., Nov. 14, 1957; d. Joseph Steven and Mary Ann (Mozney) L. BA in Comm., Bethany Coll., 1980; cert., U. Tübingen, Germany, 1980, Sprach Inst. Tübingen, Germany 1980. V.p., Wheeling Coffee and Spice, W.Va., 1981—; pres. Lokmer & Assocs., Inc., McLean, Va., 1986—; pharm. mktg. rep. Bristol Labs., Wheeling, 1982-84, pharm. hosp. mktg. rep., 1984-85; pharm. mktg. rep. Boehringer Ingelheim, Nashville, 1985-87. V.p., bd. dirs. Wheeling Coffee & Spice, 1981—. Mem. Pub. Rels. Soc. Am. (accredited), Pub. Rels. Soc. Am. Internat., Counselors Acad., Zeta Tau Alpha. Republican. Roman Catholic. Avocations: flying, sailing, tennis, reading.

LOLLAR, FRED PAUL, editor; b. Chgo., Feb. 15, 1927; s. Fred Paul Lollar and Ruth Mary (Anselm) Light; m. Virginia Lee Bowman, Sept. 3, 1948; children: Vivian Lee Fontana, Marian Hutson, Michael, Daniel. BA in Polit. Sci., Baylor U., 1950; MA in Journalism, U. Mo., 1981. Night editor Telegraph Herald, Dubuque, Iowa, 1952-53; editor Spectator, Joliet, Ill., 1953-55, Caterpillar Folks, Peoria, Ill., 1955-61; asst. mgr. comm. Chevron Corp., San Francisco, 1961-82; asst. prof. La. Coll., Pineville, 1982-84; assoc. prof. journalism John Brown U., Siloam Springs, Ark., 1984-92; established journalism dept. John Brown U., Siloam Springs, 1984; free-lance writer and editor, 1992—. With USAAC, 1944-47. Mem. Soc. Profl. Journalists, Am. Legion, Nature Conservancy, Mensa. Baptist. Home: PO Box 746 Rogers AR 72757

LOLLEY, WILLIAM RANDALL, minister; b. Troy, Ala., June 2, 1931; s. Roscoe Lee and Mary Sara (Nunnelee) L.; m. Clara Lou Jacobs, Aug. 28, 1952; children: Charlotte, Pam. AB, Samford U., 1952, DD (hon.), 1980; BD, Southeastern Sem., 1957, ThM, 1958; ThD, Southwestern Sem., 1962; DD (hon.), Wake Forest U., 1971, U. Richmond, 1984; LLD (hon.), Campbell U., 1986; LittD (hon.), Mercer U., 1988. Ordained to ministry So. Bapt. Conv., 1951; pastor First Bapt. Ch., Winston-Salem, N.C., 1962-74; pres. Southeastern Bapt. Theol. Sem., Wake Forest, N.C., 1974-88; pastor First Bapt. Ch., Raleigh, N.C., 1988-90; pastor First Bapt. Ch., Greensboro, N.C., 1990-96, ret., 1996. Author: Crises in Morality, 1963, Bold Preaching of Christ, 1979, Servant Songs, 1994. Democrat. Club: Rotary. Home: 3200 W Market St Greensboro NC 27403-1456

LOMAX, JOHN H., financial service company executive; b. Macon, Ga., Mar. 28, 1924; s. John H. and Regis (Garrity) L.; m. Ann E. Davis, Dec. 30, 1947; children: J. Harvey, Jan (Mrs. Ben Teal). BBA, U. Ga., 1948; student, U. N.C., 1962. Exec. v.p. Am. Credit Corp., Charlotte, N.C., 1958-76; exec. v.p. Assocs. Corp. of N.Am., Dallas, 1976-87; dir. Gulf Coast Consol. Office Resolution Trust Corp., Houston, 1989-91, dir. north ctrl. region, 1991-92; v.p. S.W. region Resolution Trust Corp., Dallas, 1992-94; chmn., CEO Policy Funding Corp., Dallas, 1994-95; chmn. Utility Gen. Corp., Dallas, 1997—. Bd. dirs. Dallas Summer Musicals. Capt. USAF, 1942-46. Home: 4215 Glenaire Dr Dallas TX 75229-4140 Office: Utility General Corp 16901 N Dallas Pkwy Dallas TX 75248

LOMBARD, DEBORAH LYNN, nurse midwife; b. Toledo, Ohio, Mar. 15, 1950; d. Raymond S. Jr. and Eleanor K. (Rakestraw) Metzger; m. Bernard E. Lombard, Aug. 7, 1976; children: Travis Alan, Craig Kinkade. BA, Bowling Green State U., 1972; BSN, U. South Fla., 1980; MSN, U. Fla., 1984. RN, Fla.; CNM. Staff RN St. Joseph's Hosp., Tampa, Fla., 1980-81, Tampa (Fla.) Gen. Hosp., 1982-84; nurse midwife Polk Gen. Hosp., Bartow, Fla., 1984-87; nurse midwife-ARNP Hillsborough County. Health Dept., Tampa, 1987-88; nurse midwife Turner & Muir, M.D., PA, Cocoa Beach, Fla., 1988-94, Brevard Ob-Gyn. Assocs., Titusville, Fla., 1994-96, A Place for Women, Inc., Port St. John, Fla., 1996—; adj. faculty, clin. instr. Polk County C.C., Lakeland, Fla., 1985-86, Brevard C.C., Cocoa, Fla., 1989—; adj. faculty, preceptor for masters level nursing students U. Fla., Gainesville, Fla., 1988—; adj. faculty, preceptor for masters level nurse-midwifery students U. Fla., Jacksonville, Fla., 1991—; clin. instr. Polk Gen. Hosp., Bartow, Fla., 1985-86; instr. in childbirth edn. classes Tampa Gen. Hosp., 1982-83. Den leader Cub Scouts Pack 397, Merritt Island, 1993—. Named Best Midwife of Brevard County Fla. Today Newspaper, 1990. Mem. Am. Coll. of Nurse Midwives, Fla. Perinatal Assn., Am. Coll. of Nurse-Midwives (Fla. chpt. scholarship com. 1991—), Sigma Theta Tau. Home: 1830 Newfound Harbor Dr Merritt Island FL 32952 Office: A Place for Women Inc Port Saint John FL 32927

LOMBARD, JUDITH MARIE, human resource policy specialist; b. Harmony, Maine, June 7, 1944; d. Clayton Selden and Helen Mae (Wentworth) L. BA, U. Maine, 1966; MPA, U. So. Calif., 1982, D of Pub. Adminstrn., 1987. Psychodramatist HEW, Washington, 1966-68; creative arts therapist U.S. Health and Human Svcs., Washington, 1968-87; sr. therapist Mental Health Svcs., Washington, 1987-88; tng. officer USDA, Washington, 1988-92; mem. adj. faculty U. So. Calif., L.A., 1988—; sr. mem. adj. faculty Shenandoah U., Winchester, Va., 1993—; employee devel. specialist U.S. Office Personnel Mgmt., Washington, 1992—; pvt. cons., Alexandria, Va., 1988—. Author (book chpt.) How Public Organizations Work, 1991, (handbook) Supervisor's Guide, 1993; contbr. articles to profl. jours. Active Maine State Soc., Washington, 1980—; mem. fundraising bd. doctorial assn. U. So. Calif., Washington, 1986—; active Del Ray Citizens Assn., Alexandria, 1982—. Recipient Dorothy Dix award St. Elizabeth's Hosp., Washington, 1982. Mem. Am. Soc. Pub. Adminstrn., Am. Soc. Tng. and Devel., Nat. Therapeutic Recreation Soc., Am. Therapeutic Recreation Assn. (pres. Washington chpt. 1990), Med. Soc. Washington (pres. 1990), Nat. Recreation and Parks Assn. (elections chair 1990, 91), D.C. Jungian Soc., Chesapeake Bay Orgnl. Devel. Network. Office: US Office Personnel Mgmt 1900 E St NW Washington DC 20415

LOMBARD, MITCHELL MONTE, marketing professional; b. Bronx, N.Y., May 13, 1951; s. Bernard and Dolores (Levy) L.; m. Jennifer Karen Lombard (div.); children: Jordan Ilan, Joseph Taylor; Jennifer K. Lombard. Student, Ohio State U., 1969-72, U. Fla., Miami-Dade Community Coll. V.p. Lombard's Sporting Goods, North Miami Beach, Fla., 1977-83; pres. Bard Internat., Ojus, Fla., 1983-92, Gold Eagle Profl. Golf Products, Dallas, 1992—; real estate broker, Fla.; bd. dirs. Flamingo Bank, Pembroke Pines, Fla. Nominee Rep. Senatorial Inner Circle U.S. Senate; sponsor Diabetes Research Inst., Miami, Fla., 1985-86, AMC Cancer Research Ctr., Shriners Hosp. for Crippled Children. Mem. Sporting Goods Mfrs. Assn., Nat. Buying Syndicate, Nat. Assn. Catalog/Showroom Merchandisers, U.S. Racquet Stringers Assn., U.S. Profl. Tennis Assn., Mensa. Jewish. Lodges: Optimists, Masons (chair), Shriners. Office: Gold Eagle Profl Golf Prods 17480 N Dallas Pkwy # 107 Dallas TX 75287-7303

LOMBARD, RICHARD SPENCER, lawyer; b. Panama Canal Zone, Jan. 28, 1928; s. Eugene C. and Alice R. (Quinn) L.; m. Arlene Olson, Dec. 27, 1952; children: Anne, James. AB, Harvard U., 1949, JD, 1952. Bar: N.Y. 1953, Tex. 1971. Assoc. Haight, Gardner, Poor & Havens, N.Y.C., 1952-55; mem. law dept. Creole Petroleum Corp., Caracas, Venezuela, 1955-65, mgr., 1963-65; gen. counsel Esso Chem. Co., N.Y.C., 1966-69; assoc. gen. counsel Humble Oil & Refining Co., Houston, 1969-71; asst. gen. counsel Exxon Corp., N.Y.C., 1971-72, assoc. gen. counsel, 1972-73, gen. counsel, 1973-93, v.p., 1980-93; counsel Baker & Botts, Dallas, 1993-96; trustee Parker Sch. Fgn. and Comparative Law, Columbia U., 1977—, Southwestern Legal Found., 1978, Practicing Law Inst., 1980. Author: American-Venezuelan Private International Law, 1965. Served with AC AUS, 1946-47. Fellow Am. Bar Found.; mem. ABA, Am. Law Inst., Am. Arbitration Assn. (bd. dirs., chmn. bd. 1983-86), N.Y. State Bar Assn., Assn. Bar City of N.Y., State Bar of Tex., Dallas Bar Assn., Univ. Club (N.Y.C.). Address: 108 Eastbank Ct N Hudson WI 54016 Address: 7401 N Cobblestone Rd Tucson AZ 85718

LOMBARDI, JOHN V., university administrator, historian; b. Los Angeles, Aug. 19, 1942; s. John and Janice P. Lombardi; m. Cathryn Lee; children: John Lee, Mary Ann. B.A., Pomona Coll., 1963; M.A., Columbia U., 1964, Ph.D., 1968. Prof. contratado Escuela de Historia, Universidad Central de Venezuela, Caracas, 1967; lectr. history Ind. U. S.E., Jeffersonville, 1967-68; asst. prof. Ind. U. S.E., 1968-69; vis. asst. prof. Ind. U., Bloomington, 1968-69; asst. prof. history Ind. U., 1969-71, assoc. prof., 1971-77, prof., 1977-87, dir. Latin Am. studies program, 1971-74, dean Internat. Programs, 1978-85, dean Coll. Arts and Scis., 1985-87; prof. history Johns Hopkins U., 1987-89, provost, vp. for acad. affairs, 1987-89; pres. U. Fla., Gainesville, 1989—. Author: (with others) Venezuelan History: A Comprehensive Working Bibliography, 1977, People and Places in Colonial Venezuela, 1976, Venezuela: Search for Order, Dream of Progress, 1982; Mem. editorial bd.: (with others) UCLA Statis. Abstracts Latin Am, 1977—; contbr. (with others) articles to profl. jours. Fulbright-Hayes research fellow, 1965-66. Mem. Am. Hist. Assn., Latin Am. Studies Assn., Pan Am. Inst. Geography and History, Academia Nacional de la Historia (corr. mem .). Office: U Fla Office of Pres Gainesville FL 32611*

LONDON, J. PHILLIP, information technology company executive; b. Oklahoma City, Apr. 30, 1937; s. Harry Riles and Laura Evalyn (Phillips) L.; children: J. Phillip Jr., Laura McLain. BSc, U.S. Naval Acad., 1959; MSc, U.S. Naval Postgrad. Sch., 1967; D in Bus. Adminstrn., George Washington U., 1971. Commd. ensign USN, 1959, advanced through grades to capt., resigned, 1971; program mgr. Challenger Research Inc., 1971-72; mgr. CACI Internat. Inc., Arlington, Va., 1972-76, v.p., 1976-77, sr. v.p., 1977-79, exec. v.p., 1979-82, pres. operating div., 1982-84, pres., chief exec. officer, 1984-90, chmn. bd., 1990—. Recipient Alumni of Yr. award George Washington U. Sch. Govt. & Bus. Adminstrn., Washington, 1987, High Tech Entrepreneur award KPMG Peat Marwick, 1995. Mem. George Town Club (Washington), Cosmos Club (Washington). Episcopalian. Office: CACI Internat Inc 1100 N Glebe Rd Arlington VA 22201-4798

LONDON, JAMES HARRY, lawyer; b. Balt., Dec. 12, 1949; s. Frank and Coral Marie (Calongne) L.; children: Frank T., Charles J. BS, U. Tenn., 1971, JD, 1974. Bar: Tenn. 1974, U.S. Dist. Ct. (ea. dist.) Tenn. 1974, U.S. Ct. Mil. Appeals 1975, U.S. Tax Ct. 1976. Law clk. to judge Joe D. Duncan State Tenn. Criminal Ct., 1971-74; assoc. Bond, Carpenter & O'Connor, Knoxville, Tenn., 1979-80; ptnr. Hogin, London & Montgomery, Knoxville, 1980-91, London Amburn & Thomforde, Knoxville, 1991—; nominated to White House to be fed. dist. judge, 1991; mem. hearing com. Bd. of Profl. Responsibility Tenn. Supreme Ct., 1991-95. Chmn. Bd. Deacons Lake Forest Presbyn. Ch., 1984, clk. of Session, 1985; active state and local Rep. politics. Served to capt. JAGC, USAF, 1974-79. Mem. ABA, Tenn. Bar Assn. (chmn. interdisciplinary rels. com. 1995-96), Knoxville Bar Assn. (chmn. citizenship com. 1983-89), Am. Legion (comdr. post #126 1983-85). Home: 700 Kenesaw Ave Knoxville TN 37919-6462 Office: London Amburn & Thomforde 1716 W Clinch Ave Knoxville TN 37916-2408

LONG, ALFRED B., former oil company executive, consultant; b. Galveston, Tex., Aug. 4, 1909; s. Jessie A. and Ada (Beckwith) L.; student S. Park Jr. Coll., 1928-29, Lamar State Coll. Tech., 1947-56, U. Tex., 1941; grad. Citizens Police Acad.; m. Sylvia V. Thomas, Oct. 29, 1932; 1 child, Kathleen Sylvia (Mrs. E.A. Pearson, II). With Sun Oil Co., Beaumont, Tex., 1931-69, driller geophys. dept., surveyor engring. dept., engr. operating dept., engr. prodn. lab., 1931-59, regional supr., 1960-69, cons., 1969—. Sr.'s bd. dirs. Bapt. Hosp., Beaumont, Tex.; chaplain sr.'s vols. bd. dirs., S.E. Tex. Rehab. Hosp., Beaumont, Seniors-Lawmen Coun.; chaplain; Jefferson County Program Planning Com., 1964; mem. tech. adv. group Oil Well Drilling Inst., Lamar U., Beaumont. Mem. IEEE, Soc. Petroleum Engrs., Am. Petroleum Inst., Am. Assn. Petroleum Geologists, Houston Geol. Soc., Gulf Coast Engring. and Sci. Soc. (treas. 1962-65), U.S. Power Squadron, Soc. Wireless Pioneers, Citizen Police Acad. Recipient Nat. Jefferson award for Outstanding Pub. Svc. Am. Inst. for Pub. Svc., 1992, Community Svc. award Quarter Century Wireless Assn., 1994, Sensational Seniors of the U.S. honor CBS TV, 1994, Hometown Heroes Sta. CH6TV, 1995, Olympic torch bearer, 1996. Inventor oil well devices. Office: PO Box 7266 Beaumont TX 77726-7266

LONG, ALLAN HENRY, electrical engineer; b. Jan. 22, 1958. BS in EE summa cum laude, Memphis State U., 1980, MS in Indsl. Systems Analysis, 1985, MBA, 1993. Registered profl. engr., Tenn. On-site constrn. team engr., power systems engr. Memphis Light, Gas and Water Div., 1980-84; resident project engr. Foster Wheeler Energy Corp., 1981-83; design engr., elec. engring. dept. Memphis Light, Gas and Water Div., 1984-86, lead design engr., electric distbn. engring. dept., gas and water divsn., 1986-87, planner-coord. gas and water divsn., 1987-89, supr. resdl. distbn. engring. gas and water divsn., 1989—. Instr. sailing, CPR, first aid; chmn. small craft tech. adv. group ARC, EMT,; br. chief for sailing and seamanship, flotilla cmdr,. dist. state legis. liaison officer USCG Aux.; dist. cmdr. U.S. Power Squadrons. Mem. NSPE (treas. Memphis chpt. 1994-95, v.p. 1995-96, pres.-elect 1996—), IEEE (chmn. Memphis sect. 1985-88, regional sec. 1991-93, regional awards chmn. 1994-95, U.S. activities bd. awards vice-chair 1996—), Engrs. Club Memphis, Memphis State Alumni Assn., Omicron Delta Kappa (pres.), Tau Beta Pi, Phi Kappa Phi (v.p.). Home: 108 Eastland Dr Memphis TN 38111-6900

LONG, CECIL LENEIR, engineer; b. Philadelphia, Miss., Dec. 8, 1938; s. John Cecil and Sudie Elizabeth (Fulton) L.; m. Wanda Jo Lyle, May 30, 1963; children: John Andrew, Dana Elizabeth. BA in Chemistry, Miss. So. Coll., 1961; postgrad. U. So. Miss., 1971-72; MSEE, Southeast Inst. Tech., 1983. Quality control mgr. Johnson & Johnson Co., Chgo., 1963-65; supr., prodn. supt. May Alumnium Inc., El Campo, Tex., 1965-68; chemist Dow Chem. Co., Russellville, Ark., 1969-70; prodn. supr. Armstrong Rubber Co., Natchez, Miss., 1970-73; quality assurance mgr. Coyne Cylinder Co., Huntsville, Ala., 1973-79; systems analyst Delta Rsch. Inc., Huntsville, 1979-87; sr. engr. CAS, Inc., Huntsville, 1987-91; sr. systems analyst, Johnson Controls, 1992-94; quality assurance cons. Fairbanks Scales, Meridian, Miss., 1994-95; sr. engr. EG&G Spl. Projects, Las Vegas, 1995—. Patentee in field. Served to 1st. lt. U.S. Army, 1961-63. Recipient Disting. Svc. award U. So. Miss., 1983, Alumni Continuous Svc. award, 1989. Mem. NRA, Am. Soc. for Quality Control, Am. Def. Preparedness Assn., Jaycees (past officer El Campo), U. So. Miss. Alumni Assn. (Huntsville chpt. pres. 1982-83, 87-88), Assn. Old Crows, Masons, Kappa Alpha. Republican. Baptist. Home: 6335 Annie Oakley Dr # 247 Las Vegas NV 89120

LONG, CHARLES FARRELL, insurance company executive; b. Charlottesville, Va., Nov. 19, 1933; s. Cicel Early and Ruth Elizabeth (Shifflett) L.; m. Ann Tilley, May 28, 1960; children: C. Farrell, Linda. CLU; chartered fin. analyst. Founder, pres. Casualty Underwriters Inc., Charlottesville, 1959-72; founder, pres. Group Underwriters Inc., Charlottesville, 1959—; trustee P.A.I. Ins. Trust. Mem. Assoc Commn. of U.S., 1975. Bd. dirs. Heart Assn.; mem. U. Va. Student Aid Found. With USN, 1954-58. Mem. Central Va. Estate Planning Council, Am. Soc. CLUs, Central Va. CLUs Assn. (dir.), Va. Press Assn., Inland Press Assn. Chgo., Million Dollar Round Table, Farmington Country Club. Creator Queen's medal for Queen Elizabeth, 1976. Home: 1400 W Leigh Dr Charlottesville VA 22901-7719 Office: Madison Park Charlottesville VA 22903

LONG, CHARLES WILLIAM, child and adolescent psychiatrist; b. Helena, Ark., Sept. 22, 1947; s. Benjamin Asa and Laura Jo (Underwood) L.; m. Heather Barbara Murray, Sept. 19, 1987; children: Charles William 2d, Lindsay Catherine. BS in Biology and Chemistry, Ark. State U., 1969; MD, U. Ark., Little Rock, 1976. Diplomate in gen. psychiatry and child and adolescent psychiatry Am. Bd. Psychiatry and Neurology. Chief resident in psychiatry William S. Hall Psychiat. Inst., Columbia, S.C., 1978-79; from instr. to asst. prof. dept. neuropsychiatry U. S.C. Sch. Medicine, Columbia, 1978-80, asst. clin. prof., 1980-82; chief child and adolescent psychiatry WSHPI, Columbia, 1978-80; pvt. practice Columbia, 1982-88; from vice chief to chief psychiatry Bapt. Med. Ctr., Columbia, 1983-87; med. dir. Psychiat. Health Svcs., Columbia, 1987-88; pvt. practice Charter Hosp. Charleston, S.C., 1988-95, assoc. med. dir., 1994-95; assoc. med. dir. Charter Hosp., Charleston, S.C., 1993-95; pres. med. staff Charter Hosp. Charleston, 1993-95; med. dir. Charter Behavior Health Sys., Charleston, 1995, Behavior Resources, Greenville, S.C., 1995; psychiat. cons. Univ. Devel. Disability, Columbia, 1982-83. Mem. Am. Psychiat. Assn., Am. Acad. Child Psychiatry, Am. Soc. Adolescent Psychiatry, S.C. Med. Assn., Greenville Med. Soc.

LONG, ELLEN ADAIR, publicist; b. Kingsport, Tenn., May 12, 1962; d. Laurence Maxwell and Catherine Bell (House) L. BS, U. Tenn., 1984; MA, U. Ala., 1987. Traveling cons. Alpha Delta Pi, Atlanta, 1984-85; sports info. asst. U. Ala., Tuscaloosa, 1985-87; editor King Pub. Co., Knoxville, Tenn., 1987-88; pub. rels. account exec. J.P. Hogan & Co., Inc., Knoxville, 1988-91; publicist The Dollywood Co., Pigeon Forge, Tenn., 1991—. Feature editor Adelphean mag., 1986—. Vol. Knoxville Zoo, 1990-94, Nat. Found. to Protect Am.'s Eagles, Pigeon Forge, 1992—, East Tenn. chpt. March of Dimes, 1995—, Bicentennial Celebration, Knoxville, 1990-91; bd. dirs. Tanasi Girl Scout Coun., Knoxville, 1991-93. Recipient Creative Writing award Soc. for Tech. Comms., 1992. Mem. Pub. Rels. Soc. Am. (accredited, bd. dirs., membership chair 1992-93, treas. 1993, pres.-elect 1993, pres. Vol. chpt. 1994-95, Creative Writing award 1990, 91, 92, 94, Cmty. Svc. award 1990). Democrat. Presbyterian. Office: Dollywood 1020 Dollywood Ln Pigeon Forge TN 37863-4113

LONG, ERIK L., hospital financial executive; b. Copenhagen, Oct. 30, 1951; s. Guy Oliver and Joy Elizabeth (White) L.; m. Vicki Nanette Arnold, Jan. 21, 1982 (div. 1987); children: Erik M., Kimberley A., Christopher M.; m. Linda Jean Wilson, Apr. 22, 1989. BA, U. South Fla., 1974; MBA, Nova U., 1985. Acct. Fla. Dept. Health and Rehabilitative Services, Sarasota, 1974-78; asst. dir. budget and fin. Sarasota Meml. Hosp., 1978-82; sr. fin. analyst Morton F. Plant Hosp., Clearwater, Fla., 1982-85; controller Manatee Meml. Hosp., Bradenton, Fla., 1985-95; CFO Coral Gables (Fla.) Hosp., 1995—. Mem. Healthcare Fin. Mgmt. Assn., Nat. Assn. Accts. Office: Coral Gables Hosp 3100 S Douglas Rd Coral Gables FL 33134-6914

LONG, FREDERICK DANIEL, editor, publishing executive, writer; b. Hinton, W.Va., June 13, 1946; s. Roy Clarence and Willianna (Hancock) L.; m. Kathleen Mosako Kohaya, Oct. 18, 1969 (div. Jan. 1993); children: Robert-Victor, Seiichi, Gertrude Kiyoko Hancock. Student, Bluefield State Coll., 1971. Salesman Mut. of Omaha, Hinton, W.Va., 1970-79; journalist Hinton News, 1979-82, editor, journalist, 1983-84, editor, publisher, 1984—; cons. dept. anthropology U. Ky., 1982-85. Co-author: The History of Summers County, West Virginia, 1984, Historic Pence Springs Resort, 1987. Post pres. Summers County Hist. Landmark Commn., 1982—; councilman City of Hinton, 1983-87, mgr. pk.; chmn. hist. com. Nat. Pk. Svc. Task Force, Hinton, 1988-89; chmn. Hinton Hist. Landmark Commn., 1989—. With USAF 1966-70, Vietnam. Democrat. Mem. Christian Ch. Office: Hinton News 210 2nd Ave Hinton WV 25951-2404

LONG, H. OWEN, retired economics educator, fiction writer; b. Decatur, Tenn., Mar. 6, 1921; s. Thomas Frank and Mattie Lena (Powers) L.; m. Mary Virginia Patrick, Dec. 20, 1951; children: Belinda Jane Long Stevens, John Owen Long. BA, Maryville (Tenn.) Coll., 1943; MS, U. Tenn., 1945; PhD, Vanderbilt U., 1952. Asst. prof. econs. Carson-Newman Coll., Jefferson City, Tenn., 1947-48; assoc. prof. Maryville Coll., 1948-50; prof., dean Ky. Wesleyan Coll., Owensboro, 1951-60; prof., registrar, dean admissions, scholarship officer Evansville (Ind.) U., 1960-62; prof., head dept. bus. and econs. Pensacola (Fla.) Jr. Coll., 1962-86; ret., 1986, writer fiction, history and econs., 1986—. Author: Long-Told Tales, 1990, The Long Path to the Western Waters, 1991, Tales of the Gulf Coast, 1992, Tales of Pleasant Grove, 1992, Tales with a Smile, 1992, A Medley of Tales, 1992, Tales de Guerre, 1993, Get Three Out..Unto a Land, 1994, Tales of Father Gander, 1994, Outline of the Principles of the Science of Economics: Macro-Economics and Micro-Economics, 1994, More Tales of the Gulf Coast, 1994, Tales of the River Country, 1995, Tales of the 50 States and the D.C., 1996. Named Hon. Order Ky. Cols., 1958. Mem. Am. Econ. Assn. (life), Alpha Beta Gamma (life). Home: 1712 Whaley Ave Pensacola FL 32503-5733

LONG, HENRY ARLINGTON, real estate executive; b. Arlington, Va., May 18, 1937; s. William Armstead and Emily Pearl (Garland) L.; m. Betty Mae Horner, Dec. 28, 1963; children: Andrea Long Selfe, Elissa Long White, Elizabeth Kristen, Henry Arlington II. BS, Va. Poly. Inst., 1959. Cert. comml. investment mem., 1977. Ind. comml. real estate sales Va. and Washington, 1965-68; co-owner Long & Foster Real Estate, Inc., Fairfax, Va., 1968-79; owner Henry A. Long Co., Westfields, Va., 1979—; co-owner Scott, Long Constrn., 1978—; owner Long Property Co., Chantilly, Va., 1992—; mng. gen. ptnr. Snowden Village Assocs., 1972-85, Manassas Forum Assocs., 1973-86, Eskridge Indsl. Assocs., 1974-86, Reston Racquet Club Assocs., 1976-86, Westwood Corp. Ctr. Assocs., 1979—, Westfields Corp. Ctr. Assocs., 1984—, Internat. Conf. Resorts Am., 1987-91. Trustee Potomac Sch., McLean, Va., 1979-85; chmn. fundraising com. Potomac Secondary Sch., 1986-89, Fairfax County chair local govt. George Mason U., 1987—, mem. found. bd., 1989—, also mem. major gifts steering com., spl. advisor for establishment Sch. Real Estate Devel.; trustee Madeira Sch., 1989-92; mem. found. bd. Wolf Trap Assocs., 1986-92; chmn. Wolf Trap Ball, 1993; bd. dirs. Air and Space Heritage Coun., 1987—, Washington Airports Task Force, 1989—; vestryman C. of Epiphany, 1986-89. Recipient award for Mil. Merit, Chgo. Tribune, 1959, Disting. Service award No. Va. Bd. Realtors, 1972, 73. Mem. Nat. Assn. Realtors, Real Estate Securities and Syndication Inst., MIT Ctr. Real Estate Devel., Realtors Nat. Mktg. Inst., No. Va. Bd. Realtors (bd. dirs. 1973-74), Econ. Club, Georgetown Club, Pi Delta Epsilon. Home: PO Box 1827 Middleburg VA 22117-1827 Office: Ste 204 14800 Conference Center Dr Chantilly VA 20151-3806

LONG, JAMES ALVIN, exploration geophysicist; b. Porto Alegre, Brazil, July 13, 1917; s. Frank Millard and Eula (Kennedy) L.; m. Vivienne V. Peratt, Apr. 13, 1940 (dec. 1979); children: Frank, David, Susan, Kathryn; m. Suzanne Nicholas Morrow, Apr. 26, 1994. AB, U. Okla., 1937. With Stanolind Oil & Gas Co., 1937-46; mgr. United Geophys. Co., Venezuela and Brazil, 1946-61; tech. svcs. and divsn. mgr. United Geophys. Co., Pasadena, Calif., 1961-72; sr. geophysicist Tetratech, Houston, also Peru, 1973-74; geophys. adviser Yacimientos Petroliferos Fiscales Bolivianos, Santa Cruz, Bolivia, 1974-77; internat. geophys. cons., Australia, S.Am., U.S., China, 1978-86. Author, editor manuals for United Geophys. Co.; contbr. articles to profl. jours. Fellow The Explorers Club (co-founder, chmn. S.W. Fla. chpt.); mem. Geophys. Soc. Houston (emeritus), Naples North Rotary Club (dir. 1987-88), Country Club Naples, Earthwatch (6 expeditions). Home: 622 Binnacle Dr Naples FL 34103

LONG, JAMES E., state commissioner; b. Burlington, N.C.; s. George A. and Helen L. Long; 2 children. AB, N.C. State U., JD. Pvt. practice law, 1967—; mem. N.C. Ho. Reps., 1970-75, legal counsel to speaker, 1980-84, chmn. N.C. commn. property tax, 1981-84; chief dep. commr. N.C. Dept. Ins., Raleigh, 1975-76, state commr. ins., 1984—; fire marshall State N.C., Raleigh; chmn. N.C. Manufactured Housing Authority, N.C. Arson Awareness Coun., Fire Commn. N.C., Firemen's Pension Fund Bd., N.C. and Capitol Planning Commn. Co-author: Douglas Legal Forms. Named Alumnus of Yr. N.C. State U. Mem. Nat. Assn. Ins. Commrs. (v.p. 1989-90, pres. 1990-91), Legion Honor, Internat. Order Demolay, Tau Kappa Epsilon Internat. Episcopalian. Home: 5000 Birchleaf Dr Raleigh NC 27606-9358 Office: Dept of Insurance PO Box 26387 Raleigh NC 27611-6387*

LONG, JOANN MOREY, publishing company executive, editor; b. Dallas; d. David and Mary Q. Morey; m. James W. Long, Aug. 15, 1946; children: Mary Joan, Michael. BA, So. Meth. U., 1946. Editor, v.p. Hendrick-Long Pub. Co., Dallas, 1969—; bd. dirs., sec. Book Pubs. of Tex., 1980s; bd. dirs., treas. Southwestern Booksellers Assn., 1980s. Bd. dirs. Jr. League of Dallas, 1977-78, Cath. Charities, 1970-79. Mem. Dallas Mus. Art, Dallas Zool. Soc., Dallas County Heritage Soc., Dallas Woman's Club, Pi Beta Phi Alumnae. Roman Catholic. Home: 3513 Villanova St Dallas TX 75225-5008 Office: Hendrick-Long Pub Co 4811 W Lovers Ln Dallas TX 75209-3137

LONG, KENNETH D'VANT, state agency administrator; b. Myrtle Beach, S.C., Mar. 26, 1959; s. J.M. and Judy (Crosland) L.; children: Justin, Kevin. BA in Polit. Sci., U. S.C., 1982, M in Criminal Justice, 1988. Field auditor S.C. Ct. Adminstrn., Columbia, 1984-85; project dir., ctrl. correctional instn. relocation State Reorgn. Com., Columbia, 1985-87, dir. jail/prison overcrowd, 1985-89, sr. project dir., 1989-92, project dir. S.C. restructuring, 1991, dir., 1992—; mem. Commn. on the Future of S.C., Columbia, 1987-88; grad. S.C. Exec. Inst., Columbia, 1992-93. Fundraising vol. Am. Cancer Soc., Columbia, 1979-82; bd. mem. S.C. Big Bro. and Big Sister, Columbia, 1986. Mem. ASPA, Am. Correctional Assn., Am. Evaluation Assn., Nat. Legis. Program Evaluation Soc. Home: 209 Willowood Pkwy Chapin SC 29036 Office: State Reorganization Commn. Ste 228 1105 Pendleton St Columbia SC 29201

LONG, KENNETH HAMMOND, publishing executive; b. Dixon, Ill., Aug. 18, 1946; s. Kenneth Leroy Long and Joan Gracia (Wasson) Phalen; m. Dana Joan Todd, Aug. 3, 1968; children: Beth Ann, Mark Andrew, Megan Todd. BJ, U. Mo., 1968. Asst. mgr. advt. Henry Field Seed and Nursery Co., Shenandoah, Iowa, 1968-69, 71-72; pub. Cuero (Tex.) Daily Record, 1972-84; v.p. Todd Publs., Inc., Austin, Tex., 1972—; pub. Round Rock (Tex.) Leader, 1984—; assoc. pub. Austin Sr. Beacon, 1992-95. Bd. dirs. Bluebonnet Youth Ranch, Yoakum, Tex., 1976-84, chmn. 1984, Round Rock Cmty. Choir, 1984-89; 1st v.p. Williamson County YMCA, Round Rock, 1989-90, 95—; bd. dirs. Round Rock Hosp., 1996—, chair, 1997. With U.S. Army, 1969-70, Vietnam. Recipient Communication award Tex. Bapt. Conv., 1991. Mem. Tex. Press Assn. (dir., officer 1993—), South Tex. Press Assn. (dir., past chmn.), Kiwanis (v.p. 1984—), Round Rock C. of C. (chmn. bd. dirs. 1991). Republican.

LONG, MICHAEL, foundation administrator; b. Princeton, N.J., Dec. 26, 1961; s. Richard Roy and Aurelia Barbara (Matlack) L. AA, Broward Community Coll., 1982; BS, Fla. Atlantic U., 1985. Cert. vocational edn., Fla. Fin. coord. Plantation High Sch., 1986-87, mktg. program coord., 1985-87; acad. adminstr. S. Fla. Regional Office, 1987-89; assoc. dir. Fla. State U., S. Fla. Regional Office, 1989-94; dir. sports devel. Greater Fort Lauderdale (Fla.) C. of C., 1994-95; exec. dir. Business Against Narcotics and Drugs (BAND), Ft. Lauderdale, 1995—. Mktg. edn. adv. com. Sch. Bd. Broward County, 1990—, com. chair 1992-94; code enforcement bd. City of Lighthouse Point, 1993-96, spl. com. Area on Aging, 1990; mem. appearance com. City of Pompano Beach, 1987-88; chair, Youth Leadership Class IX; vice chair Leadership Broward Found., 1994-95, youth leader, curriculum chair, 1994-95; founder Seminole Club Broward; bd. dirs. Fla. Atlantic Univ. Found., 1995—. Mem. Fla. Atlantic U. Nat. Alumni Assn. (bd. dirs. 1989—, v.p. 1994-95, treas., com. chair budget), Ft. Lauderdale C. of C., Leadership Broward Found. (bd. dirs. 1995—), Fla. Atlantic Nat. U. Alumni Assn. (pres. 1995—). Roman Catholic. Home: 2481 NE 21st Ave Lighthouse Point FL 33064-7735 Office: Bus Against Narcotics and Drugs 512 NE 3rd Ave Fort Lauderdale FL 33301-3236

LONG, NICHOLA Y., technical writer; b. Walnut Creek, Calif., Jan. 4, 1955; d. Shogo and Elizabeth (Hughes) Yamaguchi. BS in Indsl. Tech./Electronics, Tuskegee U., 1978. From spl. tech. asst. to tech. writing specialist Western Electric Corp., Winston-Salem, N.C., 1977-86; sr. tech. documentation specialist AT&T Network Systems, Winston-Salem, 1986-96. Friend, The Arts Council, Inc., Winston-Salem, 1984-86. Mem. NAFE, Am. Soc. Profl. and Exec. Women, Tuskegee Nat. Alumni Assn. (pres. Winston-Salem chpt. 1984-85), Alliance Black Telecommunications Employees, Alpha Kappa Mu. Home: 168 Carrisbrooke Ln Winston Salem NC 27104-2528

LONG, RALPH STEWART, clinical psychologist; b. Pitts., Feb. 23, 1926; s. Ralph S. and Virginia (Hawk) L.; m. Vera Lazorchak, June 16, 1951; children: Karen Virginia, Brian Reed, Lauri Michelle. BS, Lock Haven U., 1950; MEd, Pa. State U., 1951; PhD, Washington U., St. Louis, 1965. Lic. psychologist, Tex. Commd. 2d lt. USAF, 1951, advanced through grades to lt. col., 1968; psychologist various hosps. USAF, U.S. and Europe, 1951-71; ret., 1971; dir. psychol. svcs. Community Ctr. Mental Health, Mental Retardation, Wichita Falls, Tex., 1971-72; psychol. cons. Family Counseling Ctr., Wichita Falls, 1972-74; dir. psychol. svcs. Nueces County Mental Health-Mental Retardation Community Ctr, 1974-77; dir. Corpus Christi Counseling Ctr./Physicians-Surgeons Hosp., Tex., 1977-79, Psychol. Cons., Corpus Christi, 1979-82; exec. dir. Personal Dynamics Inst., Corpus Christi, 1982—, dir., 1988—; instr. dept. psychology McKendree Coll., Lebanon, Ill., 1962-63; instr. So. Ill. U., 1962-64; adj. prof. human rels. Webster U., Webster Groves, Mo., 1976-79, 88-93; adj. prof. psychology Del Mar Coll., Corpus Christi, 1977-83, adj. prof. bus. adminstrn., 1991-93; cons. Tex. Dept. Corrections, 1988-90; bd. dirs. Ctr. Creative Living, 1986—; cons., trainer Crisis Svcs., 1980—; profl. adv. bd. North Tex. Regional Coun. Alcoholism, 1971-74, Mental Health Assn. Coastal Bend, 1974-83, Wichita Mental Health Assn., 1965-67, 70-74; adj. prof. Embry-Riddle U., Corpus Christi, 1991-93; consulting psychologist Nueces County Juvenile Justice Ctr., Corpus Christi, 1992—, Warm Springs Rehab. Ctr., Corpus Christi, 1992—, MCC Managed Behavioral Care, Inc., Eden Prairie, Minn., 1992—, Champus Provider, 1972—; bd. dirs. Consumer Credit Counseling Svc. South Tex., 1983-92, emeritus, 1993—. Contbr. to profl. jours.; presenter in field. Charter mem. U.S. Holocaust Meml. Mus.; active Tex. chpt. ARC. With USN, 1944-51. Named Am. Man Sci., 1962. Fellow Soc. Air Force Clin. Psychologists; mem. APA, DAV, VFW, Am. Inst. Hypnosis, U.S. Holocaust Meml. Mus. (charter), Libr. of Congress Assocs. (charter), Tex. Assn. Mental Health (exec. com. 1980-83), Air Force Assn., Nat. Register Health Svc. Providers in Psychology, Smithsonian, Sierra Club, Am. Assn. Ret. Persons, Ret. Officers Assn., Am. Legion, Theosophical Soc. Am., Nat. Wildlife Fedn., Masons, Shriners, Sigma Xi. Office: Personal Dynamics Inst 1819 S Brownlee Blvd Corpus Christi TX 78404-2901

LONG, RICHARD ALEXANDER, English language educator; b. Phila., Feb. 9, 1927; s. Thaddeus B. and Leila (Washington) L. AB, Temple U., 1947, MA, 1948; D, U. Poitiers, France, 1965. Instr. English, W.Va. State Coll., Charleston, 1949-50; instr., asst. prof., then assoc. prof. Morgan State Coll., Balt., 1951-66; prof. Hampton (Va.) Inst., 1966-68; prof. English and Afro-Am. studies Atlanta U., 1968-77; Atticus Haygood prof. Emory U., Atlanta, 1987—. Author: The Black Tradition in American Dance, 1989, African Americans; 1993; co-editor: Afro-American Writing, 1985. Bd. dirs. High Mus., Atlanta, 1980—. Fulbright scholar, Paris, 1957-58. Mem. Soc. Dance History Scholars (bd. dirs. 1992—). Office: Emory U Inst for Liberal Arts Atlanta GA 30322

LONG, RUSSELL CHARLES, academic administrator; b. Alpine, Tex., Oct. 9, 1942; s. Roy Joel and Lovis Lorene (Graham) L.; m. Elaine Gresham, May 8, 1964 (div. Jan. 1986); 1 child, Mark Roy; m. Natrelle Hedrick, Mar. 28, 1986. BS, Sul Ross State U., Alpine, 1965; MA, N.Mex. State U., 1967; PhD, Tex. A&M U., 1977. Assoc. prof. Schreiner Coll., Kerrville, Tex., 1967-69; instr. Tarleton State U., Stephenville, Tex., 1969-72, asst. prof., 1972-77, assoc. prof., 1977-85, prof., 1985-92, asst. v.p. acad. adminstrn., 1987-90, chair dept. English and Lang., 1990-92; provost and v.p. acad. adminstrn. West Tex. A&M U., Canyon, 1992-94, interim pres., 1994-95, pres., 1995—. Office: West Texas A&M Univ WT Sta 2501 4th Ave Canyon TX 79016

LONG, THOMAS, lawyer. BA cum laude, U. Fla., 1977; JD, Wake Forest U., 1980. Bar: Tex. 1984, N.C., 1980; cert. in personal injury trial lawy. Assoc. Eikenburg & Stiles, Houston, 1986-87, Law Offices of Howard Kaffenburger, Houston, 1987-90, Law Offices of Michael R. Ross, Houston, 1990—. Contbr. articles to profl. jours. Capt. U.S. Army, 1980-83. Home: 12910 Sandri Ln Houston TX 77077-5625

LONGACRE, ROBERT EDMONDSON, linguist, educator; b. Akron, Ohio; s. William K. and Sylvia Melissa (Steed) L.; m. Gwendolyn M. Stratton; children: Roberta, William, Stephen, David. BA in Liberal Arts, Houghton Coll., 1943, LLD (hon.), 1969; BDiv, Faith Theol. Sem., 1946; MA in Linguistics, U. Pa., 1953, PhD, 1955. Rschr., cons. Summer Inst. Linguistics, Huntington Beach, Calif., 1946-72; prof. linguistics U. Tex. Arlington, 1972-93, prof. emeritus, 1993—. Author: Grammar Discovery Procedures, 1964, An Anatomy of Speech Notions, 1973, Grammar of Discourse, 1983, rev. edit., 1996, Languages of Philippines, Papua New Guinea, Africa, South America, and India, 1968-90. Mem. Linguistic Soc. Am., Evang. Theol. Soc., Linguistic Assn. Can. and U.S. (pres. 1994), Linguistic Assn. Southwest, Soc. Bibl. Lit. Republican. Presbyterian. Home: 7500 W Camp Wilson Rd Dallas TX 75236

LONGHURST, ROBERT RUSSELL, retired secondary school educator; b. Montgomery, Ala., Feb. 28, 1921; s. Lawrence Alston and Margaret Earlene (King) L.; m. Anne McMahon, Nov. 26, 1952 (div. 1982). BA in Edn., Peabody Coll., 1949, MA, 1950. Cert. tchr., Tenn. Tech. rep. Lockheed Overseas Corp., British Isles, 1943-44; tchr. Nashville Bd. Edn., 1950-77, coordinator vocat. edn., 1977-87; ret., 1987. Served as petty officer USNR, 1944-46, PTO. Mem. NEA, Tenn. Edn. Assn., Met. Nashville Edn. Assn., Am. Vocat. Assn., Pi Gamma Mu. Mem. Ch. of Christ. Home: 2421 Eastland Ave Nashville TN 37206-1101

LONGINO, THERESA CHILDERS, nurse; b. Jacksonville, Fla., Feb. 17, 1959; d. Harold David and Eleanor Theresa (McHarg) Childers; m. Matthew Ray Longino, July 11, 1987. Student, Stetson U., 1977-78; ADN, Fla. C.C., Jacksonville, 1981; student, U. North Fla., 1985—. RN, Fla. RN Meth. Hosp., Jacksonville, 1981, Meml. Med. Ctr., Jacksonville, 1981-86, Good Samaritan Home Health, Jacksonville, 1986, Kimberly Nurses, Jacksonville, 1986, St. Vincents Med. Ctr., Jacksonville, 1986—. Catechist Prince of Peace Cath. Ch., Jacksonville, 1990-91, lectr., reader, 1991—, youth min., 1996. Mem. Jacksonville Jaguars Booster Club. Republican. Roman Catholic. Home: 4135 Hudnall Rd Jacksonville FL 32207-5766

LONGNECKER, BETH ANNE, audiologist; b. Hamilton AFB, Calif., Dec. 17, 1956; d. David Earl and Myrtle Ethel Elizabeth (Bock) L. BA cum laude, Wash. State U., 1978; M Speech Pathology and Audiology, U. Wash., 1980. Cert. audiologist. Trainee VA Med. Ctr., Seattle, 1979-80; clin. fellow in audiology Porterville (Calif.) State Hosp., 1981-82; audiologist El Paso Rehab. Ctr., 1982-85; clin. audiologist El Paso Ear, Nose and Throat Assocs., 1985—; pvt. practice, El Paso, 1982—; workshop presenter, 1982, 86. Sec. El Pasoans for Choice, 1995-96, 96-97; Dem. precinct chair, mem. county conv. rules com., 1992, county conv. credentials and resolution coms., 1994, county conv. resolution com., 1996, vice chair, 1994; mem. Voice for Choice; chmn. steering com., profl. adv. com. Rio Grande cpt. Self-Help Hearing Impaired Persons. Mem. Am. Speech-Lang.-Hearing Assn. (Continuing Edn. award 1987, 90), Tex. Speech-Lang.-Hearing Assn. (hearing impaired task force 1987-88, infant task force 1983-87, hospitality chmn. ann. conv. 1989), El Paso Speech-Lang.-Hearing Assn., Am. Auditory Soc., Am. Acad. Audiology, Gamma Tau, Mortar Bd. Home: 734 N Mesa Hills Dr Apt 184 El Paso TX 79912-5522 Office: El Paso Ear Nose Throat 5959 Gateway Blvd W Ste 160 El Paso TX 79925-3331

LONGO, MARGARET FAY, surgeon; b. Alexandria, La., July 4, 1936; d. Joseph Phillip and Mary Margaret (Cangelosi) L. BA, Our Lady of the Lake, San Antonio, 1958; MD, La. State U., 1962. Diplomate Am. Bd. of Surgery. Pvt. practice Lafayette, La., 1968-89; coord. quality mgmt. Lafayette Gen. Med. Ctr., 1990, v.p. quality mgmt., 1990-92; from v.p. to sr. v.p. med. svcs. Acadian Ambulance Svc., Lafayette, 1992—; mem. Mayo Found. com. on devel., Chgo., 1989-94; advisor Lafayette Cmty. Health Care Clinic, 1993—. Contbr. chpt. Air Medical Physician Handbook, 1994; contbr. articles to profl. jours including Archives of Surgery, Current Surgery, other. bd. dirs. Vol. Ctr. of Lafayette, 1993, Goodwill Industries of Southwest La., 1991—, Acadiana Arts Coun., 1990-93, Eterna, Inc., 1987-92, United Givers Fund of Lafayette, Inc., 1979-81; mem. med. adv. com. Hospice of Acadiana, 1983-90; active Bayou Girl Scout Coun., Lafayette,

1982-85. Recipient Surgical Travel award Mayo Found., 1967; Scholastic scholar Our Lady of the Lake, 1954-58. Fellow ACS (regent Chgo. 1993—); mem. AMA (numerous awards 1977—), Am. Coll. Physicians Execs., Am. Assn. Med. Reviews (cert.), Nat. Assn. EMS Physicians, Air Med. Physicians Assn., Assb, Women Surgeons, Mayo Alumni Assn., Priestly Soc. of Mayo Alumni Assn., Surg. Assn. La., Lafayette Parish Med. Soc., La. State Med. Soc., The Doctors Mayo Soc., Fellows Leadership Soc. (life). Office: Acadian Ambulance Svc Inc 300 Hopkins St Lafayette LA 70501

LONGOBARDI, PAMELA SCOTT DODGEN, artist, educator; b. Montclair, N.J., Oct. 1, 1958; d. Jerome Clyde and Patricia Joy (Gammons) Dodgen; m. Harry Gennaro Longobardi, Apr. 18, 1981 (div. Mar. 1984). BFA, U. Ga., 1981; MFA, Mont. State U., 1985. Freelance sci. illustrator, dept. zoology U. Ga., Athens, 1980-81; sci. illustrator Mus. of the Rockies, Bozeman, Mont., 1982-84; cartographer Red Bluff Archeol. Survey, Mont. Com. for Humanities, Bozeman, 1984-85; conservator prints Permanent Collection, Mont. State U., Bozeman, 1986; printer Teaberry Press, San Francisco, 1986; collaborative printer Exptl. Workshop, San Francisco, 1986; artist in residence Ucross Found., Clearmont, Wyo., 1986; instr. Mont. State U., Bozeman, 1985; assoc. prof. art U. Tenn., Knoxville, 1987—; vis. artist, lectr. Acad. Fine Arts, Helsinki, 1993; vis. artist Fine Arts Inst., Lahti, Finland, 1993; vis. critic Acad. Fine Arts, Bratislava, Slovakia, 1993; vis. lectr. Temple U. Program in Rome, 1993. Exhibited in solo shows Kathryn Sermas Gallery, N.Y.C., 1991, 92, Lowe Gallery, Santa Monica, Calif., 1992, Lowe Gallery, Atlanta, 1991, 93, 94, Instituto de Estudios Norteamericanos, Barcelona, 1991, others; solo multimedia installation at MUUry Gallery of New Media, Helsinki, 1993, Czech Cultural Ctr., Bratislava, 1993. Recipient Artis Prematis award Taller Galeria Fort, Barcelona, 1989, others; U. Tenn. rsch. grantee abroad, 1990, 91, 92, 94, SAF/NEA Visual Artist fellow, 1994, Tenn. States Arts Commn. Visual Artist fellow, 1996. Mem. Coll. Art Assn., So. Graphics Coun. Home: 2524 Jefferson Ave Knoxville TN 37914-5228 Office: U Tenn Knoxville 1715 Volunteer Blvd Knoxville TN 37916-3715

LONGORIA, FRANCISCO ANSELMO, English and Spanish language educator; b. San Benito, Tex., Jan. 11, 1935; s. Francisco and Josefa (Esparza) L.; m. Lucila Lerma, July 31, 1964; 1 child, Rebecca. BS in Edn., S.W. Tex. State U., 1956; MA in Spanish, Tex. A&M U., Kingsville, 1962; PhD in Romance Langs., U. Wash., 1974. Cert. K-12 tchr., Tex. Tchr. Villa Nueva (Tex.) Sch. Dist., 1960-61; Spanish/English tchr. Brownsville (Tex.) H.S., 1961-62; Spanish instr. Tex. A&M U., Kingsville, 1962-64; tchg. assoc. U. Wash., Seattle, 1964-68; prof., dir. internat. programs SUNY, Potsdam, 1968-74, chair fgn. lang. dept., 1974-76; assoc. prof. U. Tex., Arlington, 1976-78; chair dept. English, speech and fgn. langs. Tex. Woman's U., Denton, 1978—; tchr. Cameron County Schs., La Encantada, Tex., 1956-58; cons. in field; citizen rep. North Ctrl. Tex. Coun. Govts., Arlington, 1995—. Author: El arte narrativo de Max Aub, 1977; co-author: (play) Una familia del barrio, 1978; guest editor jour. English in Tex., 1978. With U.S. Army, 1958-60. Mem. Tex. Assn. Chicanos in Higher Edn. (pres. 1980-82, editor), Rotary. Democrat. Roman Catholic. Home: 3916 Winter Park Dallas TX 75244 Office: Tex Woman's U Dept English Speech and Fgn Langs PO Box 425829 Denton TX 76204

LONGSTREET, HAZEL LEE, counselor; b. Memphis, Mar. 8, 1954; d. Ben Franklin and Bettie (Simmons) White; m. John Ervin Longstreet, July 9, 1974 (div. Mar. 1991); children: Kevin, Aqueeta, John D., Lawanda. BS, U. Memphis, 1995. Testing clk. Memphis Correctional Ctr., 1976-86; probation counselor Pretrial Svcs., Memphis, 1986—. Author: Parenting and Communication Skills for African American Families, 1995. Bd. dirs. Parenting Ctr., Memphis, 1989-95, Gov.'s Adv. Com. for Fair Employment, Nashville, 1993—; mem. adv. bd. East Precinct Police Dept., Memphis, 1994—; v.p. Cherokee Elem. Sch. PTO, Memphis, 1987-88; candidate for Tenn. Legislature, 1994; commr. for youth devel. Senator Dixon's Kitchen Cabinet, Memphis, 1989—; pres. Concerned Neighbors United, Memphis, 1991—; vol. Mental Health Soc., Memphis, 1988—; v.p. Blacks in Criminal Justice, Memphis, 1988-91. Recipient Merit of Svc. award Mayor of Memphis, 1996. Mem. Coffee/Dialogue (chmn. 1995-96). Democrat. Home: 2931 Montague Cove Memphis TN 38114 Office: Pretrial Svcs/Probation 201 Poplar Ave Fl 8 Memphis TN 38103-1947

LONGSWORTH, CHARLES R., foundation administrator; b. Fort Wayne, Ind., Aug. 21, 1929; s. Maurice A. and Marjorie K. L.; m. Polly Ormsby, June 30, 1956; children: Amy Porter, Elizabeth King, Laura Cramer, Anne Graybill. B.A., Amherst Coll., 1951; M.B.A., Harvard U., 1953. Mktg. trainee Campbell Soup Co., Camden, N.J., 1955-58; account exec. Ogilvy & Mather, Inc., N.Y.C., 1958-60; asst. to pres. Amherst (Mass.) Coll., 1960-65; chmn. edn. trust Hampshire Coll., Amherst, 1966, v.p., sec., 1966-71, pres., 1971-77, pres. emeritus, 1992; pres., chief operating officer Colonial Williamsburg Found., Va., 1977-79, pres., CEO, 1979-92; chmn. Colonial Williamsburg Found., 1991-94, chmn. emeritus, 1994—; dir. Houghton Mifflin Co., Flight Safety Internat., Crestar Fin. Corp., Caliber Sys. Inc., Saul Ctrs. Inc., Pub. Radio Internat., Va. Ea. Shore Corp. Author: (with others) The Making of a College, 1966, Five Colleges: Five Histories, 1993; contbr. articles to profl. jours. Chmn. bd. trustees Amherst Coll.; trustee Colonial Williamsburg Found., 1977-94, Emeritus Nat. Trust Hist. Preservation; bd. dirs. Ctr. for Pub. Resources, bd. advisors, trustee reservations. Lt. USMC, 1953-55. Mem. Am. Philos. Soc., Am. Antiquarian Soc., Phi Beta Kappa, Univ. Club (N.Y.C.), Century Assn. Club (N.Y.C.), Commonwealth Club (Richmond, Va.). Home: PO Box 567 Davis Hill Rd Athol MA 01331 Office: Colonial Williamsburg PO Box C Williamsburg VA 23187-3707

LONGWELL, H.J., petroleum engineer; b. 1941. Degree in petroleum engring., La. State U. Drilling engr. Exxon, New Orleans, 1963-95, sr. v.p., 1995—. Office: Exxon Corp 225 E John W Carpenter Fwy Irving TX 75062-2298

LOO, MARITTA LOUISE, military officer, nurse; b. Denver, Feb. 6, 1945; d. William Del Rio and Audrey Elaine (Fromholz) Dugan; m. Albert W.S. Loo, June 26, 1971 (div. Apr. 1976). Diploma, St. Mary's, Kansas City, Mo., 1966; BS in Health Svcs. Adminstrn., Calif. U., Navato, 1986; student, Army War Coll., 1986-87. RN, Tex. From staff to head nurse Kansas City Gen. Hosp., Mo., 1966-69; shift charge, emergency nurse St. Mary's Hosp., Kansas City, 1969-71; research nurse office of Dr. J. Willoughby, Kansas City, 1970-71; dir. critical care Dallas-Ft. Worth Med. Ctr., Grand Prairie, Tex., 1974-86; rev. supr. Tex. Med. Found., 1988-92; dir. home health Dallas-Ft. Worth Med. Ctr., Grand Prairie, 1993—; freelance leadership trainer, mgmt. cons., 1985-93; owner, mgr. Masavic Properties, Inc., Ft. Worth, 1979—; co-chmn. Tex. Adj. Gen.'s adv. coun., Austin, 1985-86; spl. advisor Am. Security Coun., Washington, 1985, nat. advisor, 1985-87; rep. Partnership For Peace program, Prague, 1995; mem. Congl. Bd. for candidate selection Annapolis Acad., 1995—; comdr. med. unit Tex. Air N.G., 1996—; rep. Partnership for Peace Program, Prague, 1995; mem. Cong. Bd. for Candidate Selection for Sr. Mil. Acads., 1995—; motivational spkr., 1994—. Contbr. articles to mags., 1984—. Resource coord. ARC, Carlisle, Pa., 1986-87; mem. Cath. Adults, Arlington, Tex. Served to capt. USAF, 1971-74; col. Air N.G., 1975—, Desert Shield, 1990, Desert Storm, 1990-91; comdr. Tex. Air Nat. Guard, 1995—. Recipient honored vol. award ARC, 1982, Profl. Devel. award Tex. Adj. Gen.'s Adv. Coun., 1986, Rare Joint Forces award, 1995; named one of Notable Women of Tex., 1985. Mem. ANA, DAV (bronze leader comdrs. club), AACN (bd. advisors 1983, office Ft. Worth chpt. 1984-86), N.G. Assn. (del. 1984—), Air Force Assn., Am. Legion. Republican. Roman Catholic. Home: 2433 Parkwood Grand Prairie TX 75050-1727

LOOGES, PETER JOHN, systems engineer, architect; b. East Orange, N.J., Mar. 4, 1963; s. Edwin John and Ida Claire (Jacobus) L.; m. Heather Marta Evans, Apr. 6, 1989 (dec.); 1 child, Adrian. BS in Computer Sci., Rensselaer Poly. Inst., 1985; MS in Computer Sci., Old Dominion U., 1991, PhD in Computer Sci., 1992. Commd. ensign USN, 1985, advanced through grades to lt., resigned, 1992; researcher, adj. prof. Old Dominion U., Norfolk, Va., 1992-93; adj. computer sci. prof. Old Dominion U., Norfolk, 1993—; chief engr., asst. v.p. Sci. Applications Internat. Corp., Hampton, Va., 1993—. Contbr. articles to profl. jours. Mem. IEEE, Assn. for Computing Machinery, Software Engring. Inst. Office: Sci Applications Internat Corp 22 Enterprise Pky Ste 200 Hampton VA 23666-5844

LOOMIS, EARL ALFRED, JR., psychiatrist; b. Mpls., May 21, 1921; s. Earl Alfred and Amy Louise (Shore) L.; m. Victoria Malkerson, June 2, 1944 (div.); children: Rebecca Marie Keith, Kathleen Victoria, Jennifer Lee; m. Lucile Meyer, July 1, 1962 (dec. 1967); 1 child, Amy Windeler; m. Anita Muriel Peabody, Mar. 22, 1969. MD, U. Minn., 1945. Diplomate Am. Bd. Psychiatry and Neurology, Am. Bd. Adult and Child Psychiatry. Intern in internal medicine, pediatrics Univ. Hosp., Boston, 1945-46; resident Western Psychiat. Hosp., Pitts., 1946-48, Hosp. U. Pa., Phila., 1948-50; assoc. prof. child psychiatry U. Pitts. Sch. Medicine, 1952-56; prof. psychiatry and religion Union Theol. Sem., N.Y.C., 1956-63; chief div. child psychiatry St. Luke's Hosp., N.Y.C., 1956-62; rsch. fellow U. Geneva (Switzerland) Inst. Jean-jacques Rousseau, 1962-63; med. dir. Blueberry Treatment Ctr./Severly Emotionally Ill Children, Bklyn., 1963-81; prof. psychiatry Med. Coll. Ga., Augusta, 1980-90; pvt. practice, cons. Vet. Hosp., Charter Hosp. of Augusta, 1985-95; cons. U.S. VA Hosp., Augusta, 1985-95; cons. Gracewood Sch. and Hosp., Augusta, 1983-89, Eisenhower Army Med. Ctr., Augusta, 1983—. Author: The Self in Pilgrimage, 1960; contbr. articles to profl. jours. Lt. (j.g.) USNR, 1950-52. Rsch. grant NIMH, 1956-63, travel grant, 1962-63, U.S. Info. Svcs., 1963. Fellow Am. Psychiat. Assn. (chair psychiatry and religion 1955-60); Group for the Advancement of Psychiatry (chair psychiatry and religion 1959-62), Am. Psychoanalytic Assn., Psychoanalytic Study Group of S.C. (founder, pres. 1981-88). Home and Office: 1002 Katherine St Apt 6 Augusta GA 30904-6141 also: PO Box 697 125 Cove Cir Greenport NY 11944

LOOMIS, JACQUELINE CHALMERS, photographer; b. Hong Kong, Mar. 9, 1930 (parents Am. citizens); d. Earl John and Jennie Bell (Sherwood) Chalmers; m. Charles Judson Williams III, Dec. 2, 1950 (div. Aug. 1973); children: Charles Judson IV, John C., David F., Robert W.; m. Henry Loomis, Jan. 19, 1974; stepchildren: Henry S., Mary Loomis Hankinson, Lucy F., Gordon M. Student, U. Oreg., 1948-50, Nat. Geog. Soc., 1978-79, Winona Sch. Profl. Photography, 1979, Sch. Photo Journalism, U. Mo., 1979. Pres. J. Sherwood Chalmers Photographer, Jacksonville, Fla., 1979—, Windward Corp., Washington, 1984—. Contbr. photos to Nat. Geog. books and mag., Fortune mag., Nat. Newspapers, Ducks Unltd., Living Bird Quar., Orvis News, Frontiers Internat., others, also calendars; one-woman show Woodbury-Blair Mansion, Washington, 1980; rep. in pub. and pvt. collections. Trustee Sta. WJCT-TV, Jacksonville, Fla., 1965-73, mem. exec. com., chmn., 1965-66; co-chmn. Arts Festival, Jacksonville, 1970, chmn., 1971; bd. dirs., mem. exec. com. Nat. Friends Pub. Broadcasting, N.Y.C., 1970-73; bd. dirs. Washington Opera, 1976—, Pub. Broadcasting Svcs., Washington, 1972-73, Planned Parenthood of North Fla., 1968-70; bd. dirs. Jacksonville Art Mus., 1968-70, treas., 1968; bd. dirs. Jacksonville Symphony Assn., 1988-94; mem. bd. Children's Home Soc. of Fla., 1988-96. Recipient Cultural Arts award Jacksonville Coun. Arts, 1971, award Easton Waterfowl Festival, 1982, 1st and 2d prizes, 1984. Mem. Profl. Photographers Am. (Merit award 1982), Photog. Soc. Am., Am. Soc. Picture Profls., Jr. League Jacksonville Inc., Fla. Yacht Club (Jacksonville), Amelia Island Plantation Club (Fla.), Timuquana Country Club (Fla.), Chattooga Club (N.C.). Republican. Presbyterian. Avocations: travel, golf, sailing, skiing, riding. Home and Office: 4661 Ortega Island Dr Jacksonville FL 32210-7500

LOOMIS, MELINDA ATKINS, conductor, singer; b. Ft. Worth, Tex., July 31, 1945; d. William Bryan and Margaret (Merrifield) Atkins; m. Paul White Loomis, Dec. 31, 1973; 1 child, Nathaniel Malott. BM, Trinity U., 1967; MA, Stanford U., 1971. Teaching asst. Stanford U., Calif., 1969-71; pvt. voice instr. San Antonio, 1966—; music instr. Castilleja Sch., Palo Alto, Calif., 1971-73; voice instr. preparatory dept. Conservatory of Music, San Francisco, 1973; chapel choir dir. Trinity U., San Antonio, 1981-82; children's choir dir Christ Luth. Ch., Alamo Hts., 1979-85; asst. dir. San Antonio Symphony Mastersingers, 1979-82, San Antonio Master Chorale, 1978-79; mem., sect. leader San Antonio Symphony Mastersingers, 1967-68, 74-82; sect. leader San Francisco Cantata Singers, 1971-74; mem. Tex. Bach Choir, San Antonio, 1976-79, 85-87, San Antonio Choral Soc., 1992. Choir dir. St. Andrew's Episcopal Ch., San Antonio, 1974-75, Tuesday Musical Club, San Antonio, 1985-89; soloist Christ Episcopal Ch., San Antonio, 1988-94, founder and artistic dir. San Antonio Boys Choir, Inc. dba San Antonio Men and Boys Choir, 1987—; min. of music Grace Presbyn. Ch., 1982-86. Mem. Internat. Fedn. Choral Music, Am. Choral Dirs. Assn. (Tex. state chair repertory and stds. com. for boychoirs), Tex. Choral Dirs. Assn., Tex. Music Educators Assn. Home: 321 W Summit Ave San Antonio TX 78212-2807 Office: San Antonio Men/Boys Choir 321 W Summit Ave San Antonio TX 78212-2807

LOONEY, RONALD LEE, investment executive; b. Springfield, Mo., Mar. 5, 1956; m. Robin Marie Ryan, Sept. 2, 1978; children: Jaime Leigh, Sarah Ann, Timothy. BS in Fin., S.W. Mo. State U., 1980; MBA, Drury Coll., 1983. Cert. fin. mgr. With Merrill Lynch, 1980—, sales mgr., 1985-86, 1986-89; resident, v.p. Merrill Lynch, Charleston, W.Va., 1989-93; CEO Pvt. Investments Inc., Springfield, Mo., 1993—. Bd. dirs. Mid-Am. Singers; tchr. S.W. Mo. State U. Mem. Nat. Assn. Security Dealers (arbitrator), Kappa Alpha. Democrat. Home: 1463 S Virginia Ave Springfield MO 65807-1871 Office: Pvt Investments Inc PO Box 4524 Springfield MO 65808-4524

LOOP, ROBERT KENNETH, aerospace engineer; b. Edinburg, Tex., Dec. 28, 1956; s. Kenneth Herman Loop and Elizabeth Claire (Russell) Dugelby; m. Jeanne Honig, Dec. 31, 1978; children: Lauren Kimberly, Melanie Elisabeth. BS in Aerospace Engring., Tex. A&M U., 1979. Registered investment advisor, Tex. State Securities Commn. Engr. aerospace Boeing Co., Seattle, 1980-82; cons. engring. Threshold Engring., San Antonio, 1982-83; engr. Kelly AFB, San Antonio, 1983—; owner Altair Investment Mgmt. Co., Bulverde, Tex., 1994—; ptnr. Demographics for Schs., Bulverde, 1994—. Trustee Comal Ind. Sch. Dist., Comal County, Tex., 1995—. Methodist. Home: 5280 Eagle Claw Bulverde TX 78163

LOOPER, DONALD RAY, lawyer; b. Ft. Worth, Sept. 4, 1952; s. Rudolph Winnard and Margie Lee (Nix) L.; m. Cara Shoen, Oct. 17, 1992; children: Scott Aaron, Cory Michael, Jonathan Reed, L. Quinn. BBA with honors, U. Tex., Austin, 1974, M in Profl. Acctg., 1976; JD cum laude, U. Houston, 1979. Bar: Colo. 1979, Tex. 1981; cert. arbitrator. Assoc. Cohen, Brame, Smith & Krendl, Denver, 1979-81; dir. Reynolds, Allen & Cook, Houston, 1981-85, head tax sect., 1984-85; dir. Looper, Reed, Mark & McGraw, Houston, 1985—; lectr. Houston Soc. CPA's, 1984; acquisition negotiations in Europe, Asia, U.S. and OPEC Countries, 1987—. Coach national champion Women's Softball Team, Houston, 1981-90. Named one of Outstanding Young Men Am., 1980, 84. Mem. ABA, Tex. Bar Assn. (seminar speaker 1983-85, divorce tax com. 1985-86, lectr. tax sect. 1983-86), Houston Bar Assn. (tax sect. coun. 1985-87), Phi Delta Phi (province pres. 1984-86). Republican. Presbyterian. Home: 11264 Memorial Dr Houston TX 77024-7509 Office: Looper Reed Mark & McGraw 9 E Greenway Plz Ste 1717 Houston TX 77046-0903

LOORY, STUART HUGH, journalist; b. Wilson, Pa., May 22, 1932; s. Harry and Eva (Holland) L.; m. Marjorie Helene Dretel, June 19, 1955 (div. July 1995); children: Joshua Alan, Adam Edward, Miriam Beth; m. Nina Nikolaevna Kudriavtseva, Aug. 17, 1995. B.A., Cornell U., 1954; M.S. with honors, Columbia U., 1958; postgrad., U. Vienna, Austria, 1958. Reporter Newark News, 1955-58; Reporter N.Y. Herald Tribune, 1959-61, sci. writer, 1961-63, Washington corr., 1963-64; fgn. corr. N.Y. Herald Tribune, Moscow, 1964-66; sci. editor Metromedia Radio Stas., 1962-64, Moscow corr., 1964-66; sci. writer N.Y. Times, 1966; White House corr. Los Angeles Times, 1967-71; fellow Woodrow Wilson Internat. Center for Scholars, Washington, 1971-72; exec. editor WNBC-TV News, 1973; Kiplinger prof. pub. affairs reporting Ohio State U., Columbus, 1973-75; assoc. editor Chgo. Sun-Times, 1975-76, mng. editor, 1976-80; v.p., mng. editor Washington bur. Cable News Network, 1980-82, Moscow bur. chief, 1983-86, sr. correspondent, 1986, exec. producer, 1987-90; exec. dir. internat. rels. Turner Broadcasting System, Inc., Atlanta, 1988—; editor-in-chief CNN World Report, 1990-91; v.p. CNN, 1990-95; exec. v.p. Turner Internat. Broadcasting, Russia, 1993—; v.p., supervising prodr. Turner Original Prodns., 1995; lectr. in field. Author: (with David Kraslow) The Secret Search for Peace in Vietnam, 1968, Defeated: Inside America's Military Machine, 1973, (with Ann Imse) Seven Days That Shook the World: The Collapse of Soviet Communism, 1991; contbr. articles mags. and encys. Recipient citation Overseas Press Club, 1966; Raymond Clapper award Congl. Press Gallery, 1968; George Polk award L.I.U., 1968; Du Mont award U. Calif. at, Los Angeles, 1968; Distinguished Alumni award Columbia, 1969; 50th Anniversary medal Columbia Sch. Journalism, 1963; Edwin Hood award for diplomatic corr. Nat. Press Club, 1987; Pulitzer traveling scholar, 1958. Jewish. Office: CNN Moscow Box 26 Post International Inc 666 5th Ave Ste 572 New York NY 10103

LOOS, JOHN THOMPSON, business owner; b. West Palm Beach, Fla., Mar. 3, 1947; s. John T. and Margaret (Browning) L.; children: Amy, John, Melissa. BSBA, U. Fla., 1970. Co-founder, v.p., bd. dirs. Am. Mktg. and Mgmt., Inc., Ft. Lauderdale, Fla., 1970-78; pvt. practice real estate investor Ft. Lauderdale, 1978—; bd. dirs. DiMar Industries, Davie, Fla.; pres. Historic Brickell Devel. Corp., 1st Lauderdale Investments-Di-Mar Properties. Active Ft. Lauderdale Riverwalk Com., 1987-91, Jud. Nominating Commn., Broward County, Fla., 1988-92; bd. dirs. Broward County YMCA, 1982—, past pres.; bd. dirs., vice-chmn., chmn. North Broward Hosp. Dist., 1989-93; bd. dirs., vice-chmn. Downtown Devel. Authority, Ft. Lauderdale, 1990, 93, 96, chmn., 1990-94, active, 1988—; chmn., Cmty. Svcs. Bd., Ft. Lauderdale, 1986-90; bd. dirs. North Lauderdale-Progreso Devel. Dist., 1990-91, Broward County Planning Coun., 1993—, Broward County Charter Rev. Com., 1994-96. Republican. Home: PO Box 399 Fort Lauderdale FL 33302-0399

LOOS, RANDOLPH MEADE, financial planner; b. Warren, Ohio, May 22, 1954; s. Donald Ambert and Kathleen Jean (Woods) L.; m. Jolene Lora Turkoc, Aug. 3, 1985. BSBA, U. Fla., 1977. CFP. Rsch. cons. Fla. State U., Tallahassee, 1977-78; exec. sec. Chi Phi Fraternity, Atlanta, 1978-79, nat. dir., 1979-80; systems rep. Burroughs Corp., Chgo., 1980-81, sr. systems rep., 1981-82; account exec. Prudential-Bache Securities, Charlotte, N.C., 1982-84; investment broker A. G. Edwards & Sons, Clearwater, Fla., 1984—, sr. investment broker, 1991-92, v.p. investments, 1992—, trust specialist, 1995—. Musical dir. Toast of Tampa Show Chorus, 1986—, internat. champions 1994. Mem. Inst. CFP. Republican. Office: A G Edwards & Sons Inc 28100 Us Highway 19 N Ste 500 Clearwater FL 34621-2686

LOOSER, DONALD WILLIAM, academic administrator; b. Lufkin, Tex., June 14, 1939; s. William E. and Mildred H. (Wageneck) L.; m. Elsa Jean Albritton, Aug. 20, 1966; 1 child, William Gregory. B in Music Edn., Baylor U., 1962, MusB, 1962; MusM, Northwestern U., 1963; PhD, Fla. State U., 1972. Instr. Miss. Coll., Clinton, 1963-64; asst. prof. Houston Bapt. U., 1964-68, asst. to pres., 1968-72, dean gen. edn., 1972-77, v.p. adminstrv. affairs, 1977-83, v.p. acad. affairs, 1983—; pres. Conf. Deans Faculties and Acad. V.P.s, 1985-86; participant Harvard U. Inst. Edn. Mgmt., 1985; mem. adv. bd. Tex. Edn. Agy., Austin; mem. innovation in undergrad. edn. panel So. Regional Edn. Bd., Atlanta; pres. Nat. Conf. Acad. Deans, 1990-91. Mem. editorial adv. bd. Audio-Visual Inst. Mag.; contbr. articles to profl. jours.; rec. artist A Jubilant Song, 1983. Mem. adv. bd. Houston Symphony Orch., Houston Grand Opera, S.W. Consortium on Internat. Study, Dallas. Mem. Assn. Bapt. Colls. (sec. 1986-87), Am. Assn. Higher Edn., Rotary, Phi Delta Kappa, Omicron Delta Kappa, Pi Kappa Lambda, Kappa Delta Pi.

LOPACKI, EDWARD JOSEPH, JR., lawyer; b. Bklyn., June 4, 1947; s. Edward Joseph and Lillian Jane (Wallace) L.; m. Crystal May Miller, June 21, 1969; children: Edward Joseph III, Elizabeth Jane. BA in sociology, Villanova U., 1971; JD, Vt. Law Sch., 1980. Bar: Fla. 1981, U.S. Dist. Ct. (mid. dist.) Fla. 1983, U.S. Ct. Appeals (11th cir.) 1986. Mgmt. trainee Bankers Trust Co., N.Y.C., 1968-72; counselor N.J. State Employment Svcs., Red Bank, 1972-77; pvt. practice Bradenton, Fla., 1981—; adj. prof. of law Nova U., Ft. Lauderdale, Fla., 1981, Manatee C.C., Bradenton, Fla., 1994-96. Mem. adv. coun. W.D. Sugg Mid. Sch., 1983-87, Martha B. King Mid. Sch., 1986-88, dist. VI adv. coun. Fla. Dept. Health and Rehabilitative Svcs., 1988-92, Manatee County Health Care Adv. Bd., 1993—, Manatee County Coun. on Access for the Disabled, 1994—, Suncoast Ctr. for Ind. Living, 1995—, Fla. Ind. Living Coun.; pres. Cen. Soccer Assn., 1981-82; mem. De Soto Boys Club, 1982-87, sec., 1986-87; chmn. edn. com. Manatee Area c. of C., 1983; mem. Manatee Area Youth Soccer Assn., 1981-82, Manatee Coun. on Aging, 1986-87, Boys' Club Manatee County, 1986-87; bd. dirs. Manatee County G.T. Bray Little League East, 1988-89. Mem. Nat. Orgn. Social Security Claimants Reps., Nat. Assn. Elder Law Attys., Manatee County Bar Assn. (bd. dirs. 1988-89), Elks, KC (advocate 1984-85, 88-91), Lions (pres. Manatee River 1985-86, treas. 1987-88, 90-91, sec. 1988-89, Lion of Yr. award 1988, 94). Democrat. Roman Catholic. Home: 6612 27th Avenue Dr W Bradenton FL 34209-7405 Office: 5515 21st Ave W Ste C Bradenton FL 34209-5601

LOPER, LINDA SUE, learning resources center director; b. Wakefield, R.I., Jan. 28, 1945; d. Delmas Field and Dora Belle (Hanna) Sneed; children: Matthew Lee Mathany, Amanda Virginia Mathany, Morgan Lynnclare Loper. BA, Peabody Coll., Nashville, 1966, MLS, 1979; EdD in Ednl. Adminstrn., Vanderbilt U., Nashville, 1988. Tchr. Parkway Sch., Chesterfield, Mo., 1966-68, Charlotte Mecklenburg Schs., Charlotte, N.C., 1968-71; dir. city libr. Jackson George Regional Libr. System, Pascagoula, Miss., 1979-82; media ctr. specialist Pascagoula Mcpl. Sch. Dist., 1982-83, Moore County Sch. System, Lynchburg, Tenn., 1983-91; ref. libr. Motlow State Community Coll., Tullahoma, Tenn., 1983-85; dir. learning resource ctr. Columbia (Tenn.) State C.C., 1991-96; exec. dir. Tenn. Bd. Regents Media Consortium, 1993-96; pres., CEO Grant Seekers, Inc., 1996—; presenter TLA Ann. Conv., Knoxville, Tenn., LEAP State Dept. Edn. Conf. for Libr., Chattanooga; career ladder participant Tenn. Edn. Dept. Level II; TIM trainer Dept. Edn., Nashville; exec. dir. Tenn. Bd. of Regents Media Consortium, 1993-96. Author: Bibliography for Tennessee Commission on Status of Women, 1979; contbr. article to profl jour. Pres. Moore County Friends of Libr., Lynchburg, Tenn., 1991; bd. dirs. Moore County Hist. and Geneal. Soc., Lynchburg, 1991; mem. Tenn. Bicentennial Com., Giles County; co-dir. So. Tapestry, a Bicentennial oral history project; sec., mem. exec. bd. Hope House Domestic Violence Shelter, 1993-96, mem. adv. bd., 1996—; mem. steering com. Bus., Industry, Edn. Coun. Recipient Gov.'s Acad. award State Dept. of Edn., U. Tenn., 1988, Inst. for Writing Tenn. History, U. Tenn., 1990, Gov.'s Conf. on Info. Sci., Nashville, 1990. Mem. ASCD, ALA, S.E. Libr. Assn., Tenn. Libr. Assn., Moore County Edn. Assn. (treas., chair tchrs. study coun., chair polit. action commn. 1989-91), Giles County Edn. Found. (bus., industry, edn. steering com.), UDC (historian), DAR, Phi Delta Kappa, Beta Phi Mu, Delta Kappa Gamma. Democrat. Methodist. Office: Columbia State Cmty Coll PO Box 1315 Columbia TN 38402-1315

LOPER, LUCIA ANN, retired elementary school educator; b. Albany, Ga., Nov. 11, 1937; d. Andrew and Elizabeth Francis (Bacon) Wurst; m. Leo Gerald Loper (div. Oct. 1984); children: Valecia Ann, Sheri Lee. MusB, Wesleyan Coll., Macon, Ga., 1959. Lic. tchr. music edn. elem., high sch., Fla. Music tchr. Mil. Trail Sch., Palm Beach County Bd., West Palm Beach, Fla., 1959, Cen. Elem. Instrn. Sch., Palm Beach County Bd., West Palm Beach, 1961-65, Jupiter (Fla.) Elem. Sch., Palm Beach County Bd., 1966-70; music tchr. Eisenhower Elem. Sch., Palm Beach County Bd., Lake Park, Fla., 1970-95, ret.; gen. chmn. Devel. of Opera for Schs. with Opera Lyrica, West Palm Beach, 1961-62; co-chmn. North County Music in Our Schs. Performance, Lake Worth, Fla., 1984. Active Music Team for Devel Palm Beach County Music Unified Curriculum, 1984, Palm Beach County Arts Council, 1975-76. Recipient Spotlight award Fla. Music Dir. mag., 1986. Mem. Music Educators Nat. Conf., Fla. Elem. Music Educators Assn. (hostess workshop Tampa), Palm Beach County Elem. Music Educators Assn., Am. Orff Schulwerk Assn., Sigma Alpha Iota. Republican. Home: PO Box 571 Jupiter FL 33468-0571

LOPEZ, ALFREDO SALDIVAR, elementary school educator; b. Sinton, Tex., May 13, 1966; s. Alfredo Nieto and Beatrice Martinez (Saldivar) L. AS, Bee County Coll., 1987; BS, Corpus Christi State U., 1991. Cert. elem., secondary, ESOL, bus., bilingual tchr., Tex. ESOL educator grades 6-12 Brazosport High Sch., Freeport, Tex., 1991-94; bilingual educator grade 5 Delasco Elem. Sch., Freeport, 1994-95; 5th grae sci. and social studies tchr. R. O'Hara Lanier Middle Sch., Freeport, 1995—. Mennonite. Home: 1002 W 8th Freeport TX 77541 Office: Brazosport Ind Sch Dist Drawer Z Freeport TX 77541

LOPEZ, DAVID TIBURCIO, lawyer, educator, arbitrator, mediator; b. Laredo, Tex., July 17, 1939; s. Tiburcio and Dora (Davila) L.; m. Romelia

G. Guerra, Nov. 20, 1965; 1 child, Vianei López Robinson. Student, Laredo Jr. Coll., 1956-58; BJ, U. Tex., 1962; JD summa cum laude, South Tex. Coll. Law, 1971. Bar: Tex. 1971, U.S. Dist. Ct. (so. dist.) Tex. 1972, U.S. Ct. Appeals (5th cir.) 1973, U.S. Dist. Ct. (we. dist.) Tex. 1975, U.S. Ct. Claims 1975, U.S. Ct. Appeals (fed. cir.) 1975, U.S. Supreme Ct. 1976, U.S. Dist. Ct. (ea. dist.) Tex. 1978, U.S. Ct. Appeals (11th cir.) 1981, U.S. Ct. Appeals (9th cir.) 1984; cert. internat. com. arbitrator Internat. Ctr. for Arbitration; mediator tng. Atty.-Mediator Inst. Reporter Laredo Times, 1958-59; cons. Mexican Nat. Coll. Mag., Mexico City, 1961-62; reporter Corpus Christi (Tex.) Caller-Times, 1962-64; state capitol corr. Long News Svc., Austin, Tex., 1964-65; publs. dir. Interam. Regional Orgn. of Workers, Mexico City, 1965-67; nat. field rep. AFL-CIO, Washington, 1967-71, publs. dir. Tex. chpt., Austin, 1971-72; pvt. practice, Houston, 1971—; adj. prof. U. Houston, 1972-74, Thurgood Marshall Sch. Law, Houston, 1975-76; mem. adv. com. nat. Hispanic ednl. rsch. project One Million and Counting Tomas Rivera Ctr., 1989—; mem. adv. bd. Inst. Transnat. Arbitration; charter mem. Resolution Forum Inc.; mem. adv. bd. South Tex. Ctr. Profl. Responsibility. Bd. dirs. Pacifica Found., N.Y.C., 1970-72, Houston Community Coll., 1972-75; mem. bd. edn. Houston Ind. Sch. Dist., 1972-75. With U.S. Army. Mem. ABA (chair sub-com. atty. fees in appeals), FBA, ATLA, Tex. Bar Assn. (dir. State Bar Coll., task force on rules of civil procedures), Houston Bar Assn., Internat. Bar Assn., Interam. Bar Assn., Bar of U.S. Fed. Cir., Mex.-Am. Bar Assn., Inter-Pacific Bar Assn., Tex.-Mex. Bar Assn. (chair labor com.), Hispanic Bar Assn., World Assn. Lawyers (chair com. on law and the handicapped), Resolution Forum Inc., Am. Judicature Soc., Indsl. Rels. Rsch. Assn., Kappa Tau Alpha, Phi Theta Kappa, Sigma Delta Chi, Phi Alpha Delta. Democrat. Roman Catholic. Home: 28 Farnham Ct Houston TX 77024 Office: 3900 Montrose Blvd Houston TX 77006-4959

LOPEZ, JORGE LUIS, physicist, educator; b. Lima, Peru, Sept. 29, 1961; came to U.S., 1984; s. Jorge Guillermo and Emma Irma (Barraza) L.; m. Jacqueline Rosa Crousillat, June 7, 1985; children: Alexis Christine, Rebecca Gisele. BSc, Nat. Engring. U., Lima, 1984; PhD, U. Wis., 1989. Asst. rsch. scientist Tex. A&M U., College Station, 1989-92, adj. asst. prof., 1992-93, vis. asst. prof., 1993-95; instr. physics Rice U., Houston, 1995—; mem. astroparticle physics group Houston Advanced Rsch. Ctr., The Woodlands, Tex., 1989—; mem. Bonner Nuclear Lab., Rice U., 1995—. Editor: Recent Advances in the Superworld, 1994; referee bd. mem. Phys. Rev. D, 1989—, Phys. Rev. Letters, 1989—; contbr. articles to profl. jours. Recipient award for dissertation excellence Sigma Xi, 1989, Gold medal World Lab., Lausanne, Switzerland, 1993, Tex. State Senate proclamation, 1992; Supercollider Nat. fellow Tex. Nat. Rsch. Lab. Commn., 1992. Mem. AAUP. Office: Bonner Nuclear Lab MS315 Rice U 6100 Main St Houston TX 77005

LOPEZ, THOMAS SAMUEL, sociology educator; b. Coatesville, Pa., Feb. 5, 1948; s. Ysabel and Mary Margaret (D'Ambrosco) L.; m. Mary Katherine Murphy, Nov. 6, 1971; children: Korinne Marie, Victoria Andresa. BS, Geneva Coll., 1970; M of Psychosocial Sci., Pa. State U., 1975, PhD, 1988. Exec. dir. Am. Heart Assn., State College, Pa., 1976-78, Norfolk, 1978-81; organizational cons. Norfolk, 1981-86; asst. prof. psychology Tidewater Community Coll., Virginia Beach, Va., 1986-88; asst. prof. sociology Va. Wesleyan Coll., Norfolk, 1988—; lectr. Norfolk Gen. Hosp., 1986—, DePaul Gen. Hosp., 1986-87. Contbr. articles to profl. jours. Faculty rsch. grant Va. Wesleyan Coll., 1990. Mem. Am. Sociol. Assn., Am. Soc. Criminology, Acad. Criminal Justice Scis., Va. Acad. of Sci. (v.p. psychology div. 1989-90), Alpha Kappa Delta. Office: Virginia Wesleyan Coll Wesleyan Dr Norfolk VA 23502

LÓPEZ-CALVO, IGNACIO, foreign language educator; b. Segovia, Spain, Aug. 5, 1968; came to U.S., 1991; s. Gonzalo López-Martínez and Maria Teresa Calvo-Matesanz. BA in English Philology, U. Complutense, Madrid, 1990, Diplomado in French Philology, 1990; MA in Spanish, U. Ga., 1993. Spanish tchg. asst. U. Ga., Athens, 1990—. Author: (poems) Entorno, 1996; contbr. articles to profl. jours. With Spanish Army, 1995-96. Mem. Spanish Profls. in Am., Sigma Delta Pi. Home: 160-6 Phidias Ave Athens GA 30605 Office: University of Georgia 109 Moore College Athens GA 30602

LOPEZ-MUNOZ, MARIA ROSA P., land development company executive; b. Havana, Cuba, Jan. 28, 1938; came to U.S., 1960; d. Eleuterio Perfecto and Bertha (Carmenati Colon) Perez Rodriguez; m. Gustavo Lopez-Munoz, Sept. 9, 1973. Student, Candler Coll., Havana, 1951-53; Sch. Langs., U. Jose Marti, Havana, 1954-55. Lic. interior designer, real estate broker. Pres. Fantasy World Acres, Inc., Coral Gables, Fla., 1970-84, pres., dir., 1984—; sec. Sandhills Corp., Coral Gables, Fla., 1978-85, dir., 1978—. Treas. Am. Cancer Soc., Miami, Fla., 1981, sec. Hispanic Bd., 1987, pres. Hispanic div., 1989, bd. dirs., aux. treas.; bd. dirs. Am. Heart Assn., Miami, 1985, chmn. Hispanic div.; bd. dirs. YMCA, Young Patronesses of Opera, Miami, 1985, Lowe Mus. of U. Miami, 1986—, Linda Ray Infant Ctr.; ex-pres. Ladies Aux. Little Havana Child Care Ctr.; trustee Ronald McDonald House, sec. exec. bd., 1992; mem exec. bd. Young Patronesses of the Opera; cabinet mem. Children's Cardiac Found., New Horizons Cmty. Devel., Transplant Ctr. Sch. Medicine U. Miami-Jackson Meml. Hosp, 1992; dir. Cultura Italiana, Inc.; v.p. Messenger of Peace. Recipient Merit award Am. Cancer Soc., 1980, 81, 82, 83, 84, Dynamic Woman award, 1992; Woman with Heart Award, Am. Heart Assn., 1985, Merit awards, 1980-84, Women of Yr., 1986, Outstanding Ladry award Greater Miami Opera, 1992; named Woman of Yr., Children's Hosp., 1993; named to Gt. Order of José Marti, 1988; named Leading Miami's Beautiful Couples for ACS, 1995. Mem. Real Estate Bd. Realtors, Coral Gables Real Estate Assn. Republican. Roman Catholic. Clubs: YPO, Vail 50, Ocean Reef (Key Largo, Fla.); Opera Guild (Miami); Key Biscayne Yacht; Regine's Internat. Bath Club (Miami Beach). Avocations: yachting, snow skiing, scuba diving, guitar, piano. Office: Fantasy World Acres Inc 147 Alhambra Cir # 22021 Miami FL 33134-4524

LOPEZ-NAKAZONO, BENITO, chemical and industrial engineer; b. Nuevo Laredo, Tam., Mex., Oct. 26, 1946; came to U.S., 1968; s. Benito and Ayko (Nakazono) Lopez-Ramos; m. Anastacia Espinoza, June 22, 1981; children: Benito Keizo, Tanzy Keiko, Mayeli, Aiko Michelle. BSc in Chem. Engring. & Indsl. Engring., ITESM, Monterrey, Mexico, 1968; MS in Chem. Engring., U. Houston, 1971. Prof. chem. engring. ITESM, Monterrey, 1971-72; vessel analytical design engr./process engr. M.W. Kellogg, Houston, 1973-79, 81; product mgr. Ind. Del Alcali, Monterrey, 1980-81; sr. process engr. Haldor Topsoe, Inc., Houston, 1982—. Pres. adminstrv. coun. United Meth. Ch., Houston, 1990-92, lay leader, 96. ITESM fellow, 1963, U. Houston fellow, 1968. Mem. Tex. Soc. Profl. Engrs., Am. Inst. Chem. Engrs., Sigma Xi. Home: 1805 Lanier Dr League City TX 77573-4720 Office: Haldor Topsoe Inc 17629 El Camino Real Ste 302 Houston TX 77058-3051

LOPREATO, JOSEPH, sociology educator, author; b. Stefanaconi, Italy, July 13, 1928; came to U.S., 1952; s. Frank and Marianna (Pavone) L.; m. Carolyn H. Prestopino, July 18, 1954; (div. 1971); children: Gregory F., Marisa S. Schmidt; m. Sally A. Cook, Aug. 24, 1972 (div. 1978). BA in Sociology, U. Conn., 1956; MA in Sociology, Yale U., 1957, PhD in Sociology, 1960. Asst. prof. sociology U. Mass., Amherst, 1960-62; vis. lectr. U. Rome, 1962-64; assoc. prof. U. Conn., Storrs, 1964-66; prof. sociology U. Tex., Austin, 1968—; chmn. dept. sociology U. Tex., 1969-72; vis. prof. U. Catania, Italy, 1974, U. Calabria, Italy, 1980; mem. steering com. Council European Studies, Columbia U., 1977-80; chmn. sociology com. Council for Internat. Exchange of Scholars, 1977-79; mem. Internat. Com. Mezzogiorno, 1986—; Calabria Internat. Com., 1988—. Author: Italian Made Simple, 1959, Vilfredo Pareto, 1965, Peasants No More, 1967, Italian Americans, 1970, Class, Conflict and Mobility, 1972, Social Stratification, 1974, The Sociology of Vilfredo Pareto, 1975, La Stratificazione Sociale negli Stati Uniti, 1945-1975, 1977, Human Nature and Biocultural Evolution, 1984, Evoluzione e Natura Umana, 1990, Mai Più Contadini, 1990; contbr. articles to profl. jours. Mem. Nat. Italian-Am. Com. for U.S.A. Bicentennial; mem. exec. com. Congress Italian Politics, 1977-80. Served to cpl. U.S. Army, 1952-54. Fulbright faculty research fellow, 1962-64, 73-74; Social Sci. Research Council faculty research fellow, 1963-64; NSF faculty research fellow, 1965-68; U. Tex. Austin research fellow, spring 1985, spring 1993; Guido Dorso award for U.S.A., Italy, 1992. Mem. AAAS (behavioral sci. rsch. prize com. 1992-94), Internat. Sociol. Assn., Am. Sociol. Assn., European Sociobiolog. Soc., Evolution and Behavior Soc., So. Sociol. Soc. (assoc. editor Am. Sociol. Rev. 1970-72, Social Forces 1987-90, Jour. Polit. and Mil. Sociology 1980—), Internat. Soc. Human Ethology. Catholic-Episcopalian. Office: Univ of Tex Dept Sociology Austin TX 78712

LORD, DICK, brokerage house executive; b. Fairfield, Calif., Aug. 12, 1941; s. Gibson L. Lord and Joyce (Davis) Belton; m. Ginger Lord, June 20, 1964; children: Joy, Jill. BA in Econs., 1963; MPA, Auburn U., 1976. Registered rep.; lic. ins., real estate. Commd. 2d lt. USAF, 1963, advanced through grades to lt. col.; combat pilot USAF, Vietnam, 1966-67; ret. USAF, 1983; v.p., stockbroker Merrill Lynch, San Antonio, 1983—; mem. speaker's bur. Reese Air Force Base, Lubbock, Tex., Sheppard Air Force Base, Wichita Falls, 1973-80. Usher adminstrv. bd. Meth. Ch. Win Smith fellow, 1987. Mem. Aircraft Owners and Pilots Assn., U.S. Tennis Assn., San Antonio Tennis Assn., Prime Time Tennis Assn., Daedalions, Sonterra, Thousand Oaks Racquet Club (com. chmn.), Majestic Club, Chairmen's Club, Cir. of Excellence, Beta Theta Pi. Republican. Methodist. Home: 14107 Bluff Park Dr San Antonio TX 78216-7964 Office: Merrill Lynch 200 Concord Plaza Dr Ste 100 San Antonio TX 78216-6939

LORD, EVELYN MARLIN, former mayor; b. Melrose, Mass., Dec. 8, 1926; d. John Joseph and Mary Janette (Nourse) Marlin; m. Samuel Smith Lord Jr., Feb. 28, 1948; children: Steven Arthur, Jonathan Peter, Nathaniel Edward, Victoria Marlin, William Kenneth. BA, Boston U., 1948; MA, U. Del., 1956; JD, U. Louisville, 1969. Bar: Ky. 1969, U.S. Supreme Ct. 1973. Exec. dir. Block Blight Inc., Wilmington, Del., 1956-60; mem. Del. Senate, Dover, 1960-62; administrv. asst. county judge Jefferson County, Louisville, 1968-71; corr. No. Ireland News Jour. Co., Wilmington, 1972-74; legal adminstr. Orgain, Bell & Tucker, Beaumont, Tex., 1978-83; v.p. Tex. Commerce Bank, Beaumont, 1983-84; councilman City of Beaumont, 1980-82, mayor pro tem, 1982-84, mayor, 1990-94; tourism chmn. U.S. Conf. Mayors, 1994, mem. adv. bd., chmn. arts, culture and recreation, 1992-94; bd. dirs. Tex. Commerce Bank. Bd. dirs. Symphony Soc. S.E. Tex., 1990—, Beaumont Cmty. Found., 1990-96, S.E. Tex. Art Mus., 1990-96, Lincoln Inst. Land Policy, Beaumont Pub. Schs. Found., Cmtys. in Schs.; trustee, pres. United Way, Beaumont, 1995; exec. bd. Boy Scouts Am., Three Rivers, 1978-84, 89-96; pres. Girl Scouts Am., Louisville, 1966-70, Tex. Energy Mus., 1996-97; active Sister City Commn. Recipient Silver Beaver award Boy Scouts Am., Beaumont, 1979, Disting. Alumni award Boston U., 1983, Disting. Leadership award Nat. Assn. Leadership Orgns., Indpls., 1991, Labor-Mgmt. Pub. Sector award, 1991, Disting. Grad. award Leadership Beaumont, 1993, Rotary Svc. Above Self award, 1994; named Citizen of Yr., Sales and Mktg. Assn., 1990, Beaumont "Man of Yr.", 1993. Mem. LWV (Del. state pres. 1960-62, bd. dirs. Tex. 1978-80), Bus. and Profl. Women Assns. (Woman of Yr. 1983), 100 Club (pres. 1995—), Girl Scouts Am. (life), Rotary (hon.), Sigma Kappa (life), Phi Kappa Phi, Delta Kappa Gamma (hon.), Sigma Iota Epsilon (hon.). Home: 1240 Nottingham Ln Beaumont TX 77706-4316

LORD, JACQUELINE WARD, accountant, photographer, artist; b. Andalusia, Ala., May 16, 1936; d. Marron J. and Minnie V. (Owen) Ward; m. Curtis Gaynor, Nov. 23, 1968. Student U. Ala., 1966, Auburn U., 1977, Huntingdon Coll., 1980, Troy State U., 1980; BA in Bus. Adminstrn., Dallas Bapt. U., 1985. News photographer corr. Andalusia (Ala.) Star-News, 1954-59, Sta. WSFA-TV, Montgomery, Ala., 1954-60; acct., bus. mgr. Reihardt Motors, Inc., Montgomery, 1962-69; office mgr., acct. Cen. Ala. Supply, Montgomery, 1969-71; acct. Chambers Constrn. Co., Montgomery, 1972-75; pres. Foxy Lady Apparel, Inc., Montgomery, 1973-76; acct. Rushton, Stakely, Johnston & Garrett, attys., Montgomery, 1975-81; acctg. supr. Arthur Andersen & Co., Dallas, 1981-82; staff acct. Burgess Co., C.P.A.s, Dallas, 1983; owner Lord & Assocs. Acctg. Svc., Dallas, 1983—; tax acct. John Hasse, C.P.A., Dallas, 1984-86; Dallas Bapt. Assn., 1986—. Vol. election law commr. Sec. of State of Ala. Don Siegelman, Montgomery, 1979-80; mem. Montgomery Art Guild, 1964-65, Ala. Art League, 1964-65, Montgomery Little Theatre, 1963-65, Montgomery Choral Soc., 1965. Recipient Outstanding Achievement Bus. Mgmt. award Am. Motors, 1968. Mem. Am. Soc. Women Accts. (pres. Montgomery chpt. 1976-77, area day chmn. 1978, del. ann. meeting 1975-78), Soroptimists Internat. (pres. elect Montgomery chpt. 1975-76), Nat. Assn. Ch. Bus. Adminstrn. Home: 5209 Meadowside Dr Garland TX 75043-2731

LORD, JOHN STANLEY, JR., lawyer; b. Orlando, Fla., Sept. 9, 1969; s. John Stanley and Carolyn Eunice (Tucker) L. BA, U. Fla., 1990; JD, Duke U., 1994. Bar: Fla. 1994. Assoc. Foley & Lardner, Orlando, 1994—. Staff editor Duke Jour. Gender Law and Policy, 1993-94. Bd. dirs. Hope and Help Ctr. Ctrl. Fla., Winter Park, 1995—. Mem. Fla. Bar, Orange County Bar Assn., Phi Beta Kappa. Office: Foley & Lardner 111 N Orange Ave Ste 1800 Orlando FL 32801

LORD, LESLIE BAIN, management specialist, marketing professional; b. Jackson, Miss., Sept. 3, 1950; s. Frank and Charlotte (Bain) L. BA, Belhaven Coll., 1972; postgrad., Ark. State U., 1972; MPA, George Washington U., 1984; grad., Army Mgmt. Staff Coll., 1994. Occupl. data base tech. Mil. Personnel Ctr. U.S. Army, Alexandria, Va., 1979-80, mil. personnel analyst Soldier Support Ctr., 1980-82; occupl. analyst Soldier Support Ctr. U.S. Army, Alexandria, 1982-85; mil. personnel mgmt. specialist U.S. Total Army Command, Alexandria, 1986—. Co-author: Distribution of Quality Program Handbook, 1987. Disciple Bible study tchr. Fairfax (Va.) United Meth. Ch., 1994-95, adminstrv. bd., 1996; bass sect. rep. Nat. Christian Choir, Rockville, Md., 1990-91; work area chairperson Calvary United Meth. Ch., Arlington, Va., 1986-89; chorus mem. Asaph Ensemble Christian Performing Artists Fellowship, Fairfax, Va., 1992—. Served in U.S. Army, 1973-75. Mem. Am. Soc. Pub. Adminstrn., Masons, Order of the Ea. Star. Mem. United Meth. Ch. Home: 10222 Bushman Dr #8101 Oakton VA 22124 Office: US Total Army Personnel Com 200 Stovall St Alexandria VA 22332

LORENTZ, GEORGE, mathematics educator; b. St. Petersburg, Russia, Feb. 25, 1910; came to U.S., 1953; s. Rudolf Friedrich and Milena (Chegodaev) L.; m. Tanny Belikor, Jan. 20, 1942; children: Rudolph Alexander, Erica Marie, Irene, Olga, Katherine. Candidate phys. math., U. Leningrad, Russia, 1937; PhD, Tubingen U., Germany, 1944, Dr. rer. nat. (honoris causa), 1977. Docent U. Leningrad, Russia, 1936-42; dozent U. Frankfurt, Germany, 1946-48; lectr., asst. prof. U. Toronto, Can., 1949-53; prof. Wayne State U., Detroit, 1953-58, Syracuse (N.Y.) U., 1958-68; prof. U. Tex., Austin, 1968-80, prof. emeritus, 1980—; vis. prof. U. Tokyo, 1962, Calif. Inst. Tech., 1975, 83, U. Stuttgart, Germany, 1973, U. Alberta, Can., 1982. Contbr. articles to profl. jours., chpts. to books. Named Hon. Prof., U. Tubingen, Germany, 1948-49; Lady Davis Found. fellow, 1949-51; recipient A.V. Humboldt Stiftung prize, Germany, 1973. Mem. Am. Math. Soc., Am. Math. Assn., Deutsche Mathematker Vereiniung. Home: 2750 Sierra Sunrise Terr 404 Chico CA 95928 Office: Univ of Texas at Austin Dept of Mathematics R Lee Moore Hall 8.100 Austin TX 78712

LORENTZEN, JAMES CLIFFORD, internist; b. Ardmore, Okla., Apr. 15, 1957; s. Clifford Leslie and Doris Lorraine (Thompson) L.; m. Tracey J. Smith, Apr. 4, 1992. BA, Baylor U., 1979; MD, Baylor Coll. Med., 1983. Diplomate Am. Bd. Internal Medicine. Intern Baylor Coll. of Medicine, 1983-84, resident, 1984-86; staff physician Okla. City Clinic, 1986—; clin. asst. in medicine Med. Sch. U. Okla., 1987—. Mem. AMA, ACP, Am. Soc. Internal Medicine, Phi Beta Kappa, Alpha Omega Alpha, Pi Kappa Alpha. Republican. Baptist. Home: 200 Crown Colony Ct Edmond OK 73034-6615 Office: Oklahoma City Clinic 701 NE 10th St Oklahoma City OK 73104-5403

LORENZ, ALFRED LAWRENCE, communications educator; b. Lakeland, Fla., Apr. 3, 1937; s. Alfred Lawrence and Violet Mae (Redfern) L.; m. Kathleen Ann Condon, Aug. 8, 1970; children: Abigail Joan, Katherine Ann, Patrick Lawrence, Robert Francis, Mary Colleen. BA, Marquette U., 1958; MA, So. Ill. U., 1965, PhD, 1968. Prof. Marquette U., Milw., 1968-80; prof., chmn. N.Mex. State U., Las Cruces, 1980-81; prof. comm. Dept. Communications Loyola U., New Orleans, 1981—; chmn. dept. comm. Loyola U., New Orleans, 1981-94. Author: Hugh Gaine: A Colonial Printer-Editor's Odyssey to Loyalism, 1972; co-author: (with John Vivian) News: Reporting and Writing, 1996; writer/narrator Anatomy of a Newscast video documentary, 1980 (Clarion award 1980). Recipient Research Grant Harry S. Truman Library Inst., 1965. Mem. Soc. Profl. Journalists, Assn. for Edn. in Journalism and Mass Communications, Am. Journalism Historians Assn., Press Club New Orleans (pres. 1984-85), Phi Kappa Phi, Kappa Tau Alpha, Sigma Delta Pi. Roman Catholic. Office: Loyola U Dept Comm 6363 St Charles Ave New Orleans LA 70018

LORENZ, ANNE PARTEE, special education educator, consultant; b. Nashville, Aug. 6, 1943; d. McCullough and Mary Elizabeth (Shemwell) Partee; m. Philip Jack Lorenz, Jr., Nov. 26, 1970; stepchildren: Brenna Ellen, Philip Jack III. Student, Rhodes Coll., 1961-63, 64; BS, George Peabody Coll., 1966; postgrad., Ga. State U., 1967-68; MS, George Peabody Coll., 1969. Clerk Tenn. State Libr. Archives, Nashville, 1963-64; tchr. learning disabilities Howard Sch., Atlanta, 1966-68; prin., tchr. learning disabilities Sewanee (Tenn.) Learning Ctr., 1969-78; tchr. learning disabilities Clark Meml. Sch., Winchester, Tenn., 1978-79; tutor, cons. learning disabilities Anne Partee Lorenz Tutoring Consultation Svc., Sewanee, 1979—; psychol. cons. U. of South, 1974-78; cons. St. Andrew's-Sewanee Sch., Tenn., 1980—; vol. presenter Effective Adv. for Citizens With Handicaps, Inc. workshop, 1986. Active Coun. for Exceptional Children, 1968-79; treas. Franklin County Dem. Party; sec. Sewanee Precinct Dem. Party, 1974-76; del. dist. and state Dem. Conf.; judge John M. Templeton Laws of Life Essay Contest, 1995; vol. Cordelle-Lorenz Obs., U. of the South, 1970—; bd. dirs. Franklin County Adult Activities Ctr., 1979-82; vol. presenter E.A.C.H., Inc. (Effective Advocacy for Citizens with Handicaps), 1986. Recipient letter of commendation Gov. Tenn., 1974. Mem. Tenn. LWV (pres., bd. dirs.), Franklin County LWV (pres.), Learning Disabilities Assn. Tenn. (1st Tchr. Yr. 1975), Children and Adults with Attention Deficit Disorders. Home and Office: 390 Onteora Ln Sewanee TN 37375-2639

LORENZ, HANS ERNEST, photographer; b. Karlsbad, Czechoslovakia, Sept. 11, 1940; s. Hugo and Maria (Gareis) L.; came to U.S., 1950, naturalized, 1954; B.A., Okla. Baptist U., 1962; m. Pamela Marie Carswell, May 27, 1978; 1 child, April Nicole. Tchr. pub. schs., Prince George County, Va., 1964-65; sr. curatorial photographer Colonial Williamsburg Found., Williamsburg, Va., 1965—. Served with USN, 1962-64. Mem. Am. Photographic Hist. Soc., Nat. Stereoscopic Assn., Am. Numismatic Assn. Baptist. Photographs contbr. to numerous books in field of 18th century antiques. Home: PO Box 336 Williamsburg VA 23187-0336 Office: Colonial Williamsburg Found Dept Williamsburg VA 23185

LORENZO, JUAN MANUEL, geophysics educator; b. Leon, Spain, Mar. 25, 1960; s. Juan Manuel and Maria Gertrudis (Fernandez) L.; m. Joanne Ryan, Sept. 15, 1990; 1 child, Simon. MA, Columbia U., 1986, MPhil, 1987, PhD, 1991. Fgn. English tchr. Internat. Ho., Barcelona, Spain, 1978-81; rsch. asst. U. Barcelona, 1981-83; seismic processor Western Geophys., Milan, 1982; field demonstrator Flinders U., Adelaide, Australia, 1991, rsch. fellow, 1990-92; asst. prof. La. State U., Baton Rouge, 1993—; dir. rsch. seismology La. State U., Baton Rouge, 1993—; tectonics panel mem. Internat. Drilling Program, 1993—. Editl. bd. Geo-Marine Letters, 1993—; contbr. articles to profl. jours. Sci. fair judge La. State U., 1994-96. Rsch. scholarship Govt. of Spain, 1979-83, Fulbright scholarship La Caixa, 1983-85; recipient Nat. Oak Ridge award Oak Ridge Associated Univs., 1994. Mem. Geol. Soc. of Am., Am. Assn. Petroleum Geologists, Soc. of Exploration Geophysicists, Am. Geophys. Union, Sigma Xi. Home: 1611 St Rose Ave Baton Rouge LA 70808 Office: La State U Dept Geology & Geophysics Baton Rouge LA 70803

LORIA, ROGER MOSHE, microbiology, virology and immunology educator; b. Antwerp, Belgium, Apr. 19, 1940; came to U.S., 1965, naturalized, 1975; m. Win A. Bailey, Dec. 1978; 3 children. BS in Clin. Microbiology-Biochemistry, Bar Ilan U., Ramat Gan, Israel, 1964; MS in Biochemistry, SUNY, Buffalo, 1968; PhD in Med. Scis., Boston U., 1972. Asst. in clin. and diagnostic mycology Bar Ilan U., 1962-64; asst. in biochemistry SUNY, 1965-68; asst. in neurochemistry, bacteriology and virology Boston U. Sch. Medicine, 1968-72, instr. dept. microbiology, 1972-74, rsch. assoc., 1974-79; asst. prof. dept. microbiology Med. Coll. Va., Richmond, 1974-78, adj. asst. prof. pathology, 1976-78, assoc. prof. microbiology, assoc. prof. pathology, 1978-91; prof. microbiology and immunology, prof. pathology Va. Commonwealth U., Richmond, 1991—; asst. prof. Mass. Coll. Optometry, 1969-70; mem. nutrition adv. subcom. AMA, 1979; instr. pediatrics Harvard Med. Sch., Boston, 1980-82; rsch. fellow infectious disease ctr. Children's Hosp., Boston, 1980-82; advisor to consol. laab. Commonwealth of Va., 1982-86; referee Jour. Infectious Diseases, 1984; Am.-Israeli Binat. Found., 1987—, Diabetes, 1989, Fedn. Am. Socs. for Exptl. Biology Jour., 1989; ad hoc referee Am. Jour. Physiology, 1985—; past external reviewer Wright State U., Dayton, Ohio. Contbr. numerous articles and abstracts to sci. jours., chpts. to books; patents on use of dehydroepiandrosterone to improve immune response, enhancement of immune response, regulation of immune system by androstenediol and androstenetriol. Bd. dirs. Richmond Montessori Sch. With Israeli Army, 1958-60. Recipient numerous rsch. grants, including Richmond Area Heart Assn., 1974-75, NIH, 1975-85, Alexander Med. Found., 1978, Envirosci. Found., 1983, 85, Matrix Rsch. Labs., Inc., 1984, Office Naval Rsch., 1986-89, Neurocrine Biosci. Inc., 1992-97, Ctr. Innovative Tech., 1993-94. Mem. AAAS, AAUP (v.p. Va. Commonwealth U. chpt. 1989, pres. 1990), Am. Inst. Nutrition, Am. Soc. for Clin. Nutrition, Internat. Soc. for Antiviral Rsch., Am. Acad. Microbiology, Am. Soc. Virology (charter), Am. Diabetes Assn., Leukocyte Biology, Fedn. Am. Soc. Exptl. Biology, Am. Heart Assn., Am. Fedn. for Clin. Rsch., Am. Soc. for Microbiology, Neuroimmunology, Sigma Xi. Home: 3219 Brook Rd Richmond VA 23227-4803 Office: Va Commonwealth U PO Box 980678 1101 E Marshall St Richmond VA 23298-0678

LORING, DAVID WILLIAM, neuropsychologist, researcher; b. Richmond, Ind., July 13, 1956; s. Richard William and Janet (Teetor) L.; m. Debra Rogers, Jan. 5, 1980 (div. 1983); m. Sherrill Rabon, July 30, 1988; children: Jason Michael, Sarah Elizabeth, Rachel Erin. BA, Wittenberg U., 1978; PhD, U. Houston, 1982. Diplomate Am. Bd. Profl. Psychology. Postdoctoral fellow dept. neurology Coll. of Medicine Baylor U., Houston, 1982-83; instr. div. neurosurgery U. Tex. Med. Br., Galveston, 1983-85; asst. prof. dept. neurology Med. Coll. Ga., Augusta, 1985-89, assoc. prof. dept. neurology, 1989-94, prof., 1994—; lectr. Parke-Davis Nat. Speakers Bur., 1991—. Author: Amobarbital Effects and Lateralized Brain Function, 1992; cons. editor Clin. Neuropsychologist Jour., 1991—, Jour. Epilepsy, 1991—, Jour. Clin. and Exptl. Neuropsychology, 1993—, Aging and Cognition, 1993—, Jour. Internat. Neuropsychol. Soc., 1994—; contbr. articles to Jour. Clin. and Exptl. Neuropsychology, Neuropsychologia, Archives of Neurology, Neurology. Mem. Internat. Neuropsychol. Soc. (bd. govs. 1991-94), Am. Epilepsy Soc., Am. Psychol. Assn., Am. Acad. Neurology (assoc.). Home: 147 Savannah Pt North Augusta SC 29841-3568 Office: Med Coll Ga Dept Neurology Augusta GA 30912

LORINSKY, LARRY, international trade executive, consultant; b. New Britain, Conn., July 31, 1944; s. Jacob and Bernice Edythe (Horn) L.; BA, U. Conn., 1966, MA, 1968; postgrad. Newport U.; m. Laurie Clark Griffin, June 9, 1968; children: Michael Bliss, Jennifer Bartlett, Jessica Clark. Ops. mgr., then trading mgr. Norwich Iron & Metal Co. (Conn.), 1965-75; ferrous export mgr. Comml. Metals Co., Dallas, 1975-77, br. mgr., San Francisco, 1977-81, West Coast area mgr., 1980-81; exec. v.p. Technalloy Inc., San Jose, Calif., 1981-83; dir. nonferrous alloys David Joseph Co., 1983-84; pres., chief exec. officer Lornat Metals Trading, Inc., 1984-87; project mgr. Mindseed Corp., 1987-89; gen. mgr. Custom Alloy, 1989-90; div. mgr. Ferromet Resources, Inc., 1990-92, pres. 1992; ltd. dir., rep. METALSASIA Internat., 1983—; mng. dir. Ecos Metall. Inc., 1993—. Mem. Nat. Inst. Scrap Recycling Industry, Seaguard Svcs. Inc. (dir.), Locell Assocs. Ltd. (dir. 1983—, dir. bus. devel. 1992—), Brisbane (Calif.) C. of C. (dir. 1977-81), Chickasaw (Ala.) C. of C., Masons. Democrat. Jewish.

LORTIE, JOHN WILLIAM, solar research company executive; b. Chgo., July 11, 1920; s. William Arthur and Alice Marie (McNamee) L.; m. Mary Elaine Sullivan, Sept. 21, 1946; children: Colleen, Kevin, Timothy. Student, Ill. Inst. Tech., 1940-42, U. Ala., 1976. Radar technician Western Electric Co., Westchester, Ill., 1946-50; pres. William A. Lortie & Sons, Westchester, 1950-65, Monark Instant Homes, Ocean Springs, Miss., 1965-75; dir. research Energy Research Corp., Mobile, Ala., 1974-88; pres. Essential Solar Products, Mobile, 1980—; pres. Energy Internat. Innovations, Mobile, Ala., 1981—; solar cons.; bd. dirs. Internat. Solar Acad., 1988—; head dept. solar tech. Carver State Tech. Coll., 1976-81. Served with U.S. Army, 1942-46. Mem. Ala. Acad. Scis., Ala. Solar Energy Assn. (state chmn.), Ala. Solar

Industries Assn. (bd. dirs., pres.), Internat. Solar Energy Soc., Nat. Assn. Solar Contractors. Republican. Roman Catholic.

LOSEY, RALPH COLBY, lawyer; b. Daytona Beach, Fla., May 26, 1951; s. George Spar and Alix (Colby) L.; m. Molly Isa Friedman, July 7, 1973; children: Eva Merlinda, Adam Colby. Student, Inst. European Studies, Vienna, Austria, 1971; BA, Vanderbilt U., 1973; JD cum laude, U. Fla., 1979. Bar: Fla. 1980, U.S. Dist. Ct. (mid. dist.) Fla. 1980. Assoc. Subin, Shams, Rosenbluth & Moran, Orlando, Fla., 1980-84; ptnr. Subin, Rosenbluth, Losey & Brennan, Bittman & Morse, P.A., Orlando, Fla., 1984—. Author: Laws of Wisdom, 1994; contbr. articles to profl. jours., chpt. to book. Pres. Sch. of Wisdom, Fla. Mem. ABA, Fla. Bar Assn., Orange County Bar Assn. Democrat. Home: 1661 Woodland Ave Winter Park FL 32789-2774 Office: Subin Rosenbluth Losey & Brennan PA PO Box 4950 Orlando FL 32802-4950

LOSIER, ANDREW J., writer, missionary; b. Pitts., Aug. 11, 1910; s. Andrew Jackson and Emma Louise L.; m. Dorothy L. Losier, May 16, 1937 (wid.); nine children: m. Imogene Harper, Nov. 28, 1992; two children. BA, Wheaton Coll., 1934; postgrad., Dallas Theol. Seminary, 1934-37, Faith Theol. Seminary and, Bible Coll., Marina, Lagos, Nigeria. Founder, pres. Christian Lit. and Bible Ctr., Inc., Toccoa, Ga., 1952—; missionary to Africa, 1938—. Author 36 Biblical textbooks. Office: Christian Literature and Bible Ctr 1006 Oak Cliff Dr Toccoa GA 30577

LOSIER, THOMAS PHILIP, chemical engineer; b. Nairobi, Kenya, Dec. 12, 1950; s. Andrew Jackson and Dorothy Leona (Lehman) L.; m. Carol Jane Osina, June, 8, 1985. BA in Biblical Edn., Dallas Bible Coll., 1974; BS in Chemistry, U. Tex., Austin, 1978, MSChemE, 1981. Rsch. engr. Exxon Prodn. Rsch., Houston, 1981-86; leader rsch. group BASF Corp., Freeport, Tex., 1986-92; bus. integration analyst BASF Corp., Freeport and Mt. Olive, N.J., 1993—; mem. devel. and curriculum coms. Summer Science Tchrs. Workshop, Freeport, 1991-93. Patentee hydroxyamine catalyst, 1993. Fellow Marathon Oil col, 1978-81. Republican. Home: 214 Live Oak Ln Lake Jackson TX 77566-4630

LOTHROP, THOMAS LOW, environmentalist; b. Portland, Maine, Sept. 1, 1944; s. Cummings Lincoln and Elizabeth (Low) L.; m. Karen Keef, Aug. 27, 1966; children: James, Stephen, Michael. BS in Civil Engring., U. Maine, 1966, MS in Civil Engring., 1968. Registered profl. engr., Fla., Maine. Engring. asst. USPHS, N.Y.C., 1968-70, EPA, Boston, 1970-72; dir. wastewater divsn. Portland Water Dist., 1972-80; sr. engr. Hunter-Ballew Assocs., Falmouth, Maine, 1980-82; project mgr. City of Orlando (Fla.), 1983-85, bur. chief wastewater, 1985-87, dir. environ. svcs., 1987—. Contbr. articles to profl. jours. Bd. dirs. Zoning Bd. for Windham (Maine), 1974-82. With USPHS, 1968-72. Mem. Am. Pub. Works Assn., Fla. Pollution Control Assn., Water Pollution Control Assn., Commd. Officer Assn.-USPHS, New Eng. Water Pollution Control Assn. (2d v.p. 1982-83). Home: 321 Pickering Ct Longwood FL 32779-4524 Office: City of Orlando 5100 L B Mcleod Rd Orlando FL 32811-7407

LOTT, JOHN BERTRAND, English language educator, university dean; b. Aberdeen, Miss., June 27, 1933; m. Sandra Ward; children: Anna, Bertrand, Ward. B.A. with highest honors, Millsaps Coll., 1955; M.A., Vanderbilt U., 1956, Ph.D., 1961. Asst. prof. English, U. Montevallo, Ala., 1959-61, assoc. prof., 1961-64, prof., 1964—, chmn. English dept., 1962-79, dean Coll. Arts and Scis., 1979-90; disting. prof. English and internat. intercultural studies, 1990—. Preparer TV programs in English lit. Past chmn. bd. dirs. First United Methodist Ch. Recipient J. Malone fellowship in Middle Eastern Studies, 1987, 89, 90. Mem. Assn. Coll. English Tchrs. Ala., (past pres.), South Atlantic Modern Lang. Assn., Am. Popular Culture Assn., Ala. Coun. on Internat. Programs (pres.). Office: Montevallo Sta # 6501 Montevallo AL 35115

LOTT, SHERYL L., critical care nurse; b. Owensboro, Ky., Feb. 23, 1953; d. James A. and Margaret Jeroldine (Beavin) Lawhorn; m. Lucian L. Lott, July 8, 1985; children: Christina Renee Armes, Beverly Suzanne Armes. ADN, Elizabethtown (Ky.) Community, 1978. RN, Ky.; cert. advanced cardiac life support. Staff nurse, charge nurse Breckinridge Meml. Hosp., Hardinsburg, Ky., office nurse, supr. oper. rm.; staff nurse critical care unit, ICU Ohio County Hosp., Hartford, Ky.; staff nurse Owensboro-Daviess County Home Health; circulating nurse oper. rm. Owensboro Ambulatory Surg. Ctr.; oper. rm. mgr. Columbia Owensboro Surgery Ctr. Home: 3415 Man O War Loop Owensboro KY 42303-2456

LOTT, TRENT, senator; b. Grenada, Miss., Oct. 9, 1941; s. Chester P. and Iona (Watson) L.; m. Patricia E. Thompson, Dec. 27, 1964; children—Chester T., Jr., Tyler Elizabeth. B.P.A., U. Miss., 1963, J.D., 1967. Bar: Miss. 1967. Assoc. Bryan & Gordon, Pascagoula, Miss., 1967; adminstrv. asst. to Congressman William M. Colmer, 1968-72; mem. 93d-100th Congresses from 5th Miss. dist., 1973-89; Rep. whip 97th-100th Congresses from 5th Miss. dist., mem. Ho. Rules com.; U.S. senator from Miss., 1989—, Senate armed svcs. com., budget com., energy, natural resources com., 102d Congress, sec. Senate Rep. Conf., 103d Congress, majority whip 104th Congress; field rep. for U. Miss., 1963-65; acting alumni sec. Ole Miss Alumni Assn., 1966-67; named as observer from House to Geneva Arms Control talks; chmn. Commerce, Sci. & Transp. subcom. on surface transp. & merchant marine; mem. Senate Republican Policy Com. Recipient Golden Bulldog award, Guardian of Small Bus. award. Mem. ABA, Jackson County Bar Assn., Sigma Nu, Phi Alpha Delta. Republican. Baptist. Lodge: Mason. Office: 487 Russell Senate Office Bldg Washington DC 20510*

LOTT, WAYNE THOMAS, systems engineer; b. Pitts., Mar. 20, 1959; s. Wayne Thomas Lott Sr. and Patricia Julia (Malanowski) Martin; m. Diane Mary Phillips, Sept. 11, 1982; children: Sarah Marie, Justin Thomas. AS in Computer Sci., C.C. Allegheny County, Pitts., 1984; BSBA in Info. Sys., Robert Morris Coll., 1986. Intern, programmer Thrift Drug Co., Pitts., 1986; contract programmer Comsource Tech. Svcs., Pitts., 1986-87; programmer Tippins Inc., Pitts., 1987; initial designer tng. ATT, Herndon, Va., 1988; tech. tester ATT, Herndon, 1988-89; sys. analyst ATT, Herndon, Va., 1989-92; sys. engr. ATT Bell Labs., Herndon, 1992-94, ATT, Herndon, 1995—. Mem. IEEE. Roman Catholic. Home: 12779 Misty Creek Ln Fairfax VA 22033-3102

LOTT, WILLIAM RONALD, contracting company owner; b. Wichita Falls, Tex., Oct. 28, 1956; s. William Frank and Berta B. (Wilson) L. BA in Polit. Sci., Princeton U., 1979. Stockbroker Merrill Lynch, L.A., 1984-86, Paine Webber, L.A., 1986-89; pres., owner Lott Investments, Inglewood, Calif., 1989-92; v.p. Triple L Mgmt. Corp., Shreveport, La., 1992-95; pres., owner The Lott Group, Irving, Tex., 1995—. Author: (screenplays) Running for It, 1994, The Dating Game, 1994. Treas. African Am. Bus. Alliance, Irving, 1995. Mem. African Am. C. of C. (v.p. 1995-96), Irving (Tex.) C. of C., Dallas C. of C. Home: 4311 Caleta Dr # 406 Irving TX 75038 Office: The Lott Group 4311 Caleta Dr # 406 Irving TX 75038

LOTZ, DENTON, minister, church official; b. Flushing, N.Y., Jan. 18, 1939; s. John Milton and Adeline Helen (Kettell) L.; m. Janice Robinson, Mar. 15, 1970; children: John-Paul, Alena, Carsten. BA, U. N.C., 1961; STB, Harvard Div. Sch., 1966; ThD, U. Hamburg, Fed. Republic Germany, 1970; DD (hon.), Campbell U., 1982, Ea. Bapt. Sem., 1991, Alderson-Broadus, 1995. Prof. mission Bapt. Sem., Ruschlikon, Switzerland, 1972-80; dir. evangelism Bapt. World Alliance, McLean, Va., 1980-88, gen. sec., 1988—; fraternal rep. Am. Bapt. Internat. Ministries To Ea. Europe, Valley Forge, Pa., 1970-80. Author, editor: Baptists in the USSR, 1987; editor: Spring Has Returned to China, 1987. V.p. CARE, N.Y.C., 1981. 1st lt. USMC, 1961-63. Mem. Internat. Religious Liberty Assn. (pres. 1990-91). Office: Bapt World Alliance 6733 Curran St Mc Lean VA 22101-3804

LOUCK, LISA ANN, lawyer; b. Davenport, Iowa, July 16, 1963; d. Richard Lane and Jo Ann (Frerkes) L. BSBA, Iowa State U., 1985; JD, South Tex. Coll. Law, 1991. Bar: Tex. 1992. Atty. Woodard, Hall & Primm, Houston, 1994—; mediator Tex. Registry Alt. Dispute Resolution Profls., 1992—. Recipient Am. Jurisprudence award Lawyers Coop. Pub., 1991. Mem. ABA, State Bar Tex., Houston Young Lawyers Assn., Phi Alpha Delta. Office: Woodard Hall & Primm PC 7100 Texas Commerce Tower Houston TX 77002

LOUCKS, NANCY J., association executive; b. Lansing, Mich., Mar. 21, 1957; d. John Robert and Marian Elizabeth (Lemmon) L. BS in Edn., Cen. Mich. U., 1980. Therapeutic counselor Hope Ctr. for Youth, Houston, 1981-82; recreation therapist Mental Health/Mental Retardation Assn., Houston, 1983-86; case mgr. Mental Health/Mental Retardation Assn., 1986-87; area dir. Tex. Spl. Olympics, Houston, 1988-91; program dir. Tex. Spl. Olympics, Austin, Tex., 1991-95; dir. sr. sports Wash. Spl. Olympics, Seattle, 1995—; cons. YMCA, Houston, 1985-87; event dir. Internat. Spl. Olympic Games, Baton Rouge, 1983. Vol. Mental health/Mental Retardation Assn. of Houston, 1988—; spl. friend Tex. Spl. Olympics, 1988. Mem. Assn. Retarded Citizens, Lambda Chi Alpha.

LOUDEN, DAVID BRUCE, classical literature and languages educator; b. Birmingham, Mich., Nov. 8, 1954; s. Robert Kurtz and Anne (Zimmerman) L.; married, July 20, 1986. BA, U. Calif., Santa Cruz, 1977; MA, San Francisco State U., 1983; PhD, U. Calif., Berkeley, 1990. Grad. instr. San Francisco State U., 1982, U. Calif., Berkeley, 1985-90; vis. asst. prof. U. Wis., Madison, 1990-91; asst. prof. U. Tex., El Paso, 1991—. Contbr. numerous articles to profl. jours. Mem. Am. Philol. Assn., Classics Assn. Midwest and South. Home: 4401 Wallington Dr El Paso TX 79902-1415

LOUDEN, VICTORIA ANHALT, public relations professional; b. Las Vegas, Oct. 5, 1968; d. James Robert and Nadia (Banbury) Anhalt; m. Charles Edward Louden Jr., Sept. 23, 1995. BS, Ark. State U., 1991; MA, Webster U., 1996. Asst. dir. pub. rels. Spalding U., Louisville, 1992—. Mem. Pub. Rels. Soc. of Am., Zeta Tau Alpha. Roman Catholic. Office: Spalding Univ 851 S 4th St Louisville KY 40203-2115

LOUDERMILK, PEGGY JOYCE, pediatrics nurse, public health nurse; b. Mar. 1, 1944; d. Marshall Brown and Esther Rebecca (Gaines) Fisher; m. George E. Loudermilk, Dec. 21, 1968; children: Darrell Wayne, Donna Lynn. ADN, Dabney S. Lancaster C.C., 1985. Nursing asst. Alleghany Regional Hosp., Low Moor, Va., 1980-84, nursing extern, 1984-85, staff nurse med./surg., 1985-87, staff nurse ICU, 1987-92; nurse pediatrics Alleghany County/Covington (Va.) Health Dept., 1992—; CPR instr. ARC, Covington, 1984-92. Mem. sch. adv. bd. Alleghany County Sch. System, 1994; local interagy. coun. (State Mandated Orgn.), Clifton Forge, Va., 1993—. Nursing grantee Alleghany Regional Hosp., 1983-85. Fellow Nursing Coun. Alleghany Dist. Republican. Baptist. Home: 2700 Sugar Maple Dr PO Box 52 Low Moor VA 24457

LOUGHRIDGE, JOHN HALSTED, JR., lawyer; b. Chestnut Hill, Pa., Oct. 30, 1945; s. John Halsted Sr. and Martha Margaret (Boyd) L.; m. Amy Claire Booe, Aug. 3, 1980; 1 child, Emily Halsted. AB, Davidson Coll., 1967; JD, Wake Forest U., 1970. Bar: N.C. 1970, U.S. Dist. Ct. 1970, U.S. Ct. Mil. Appeals, 1986. Div. head, v.p., counsel Wachovia Mortgage Co., Winston-Salem, N.C., 1971-79; v.p., counsel Wachovia Corp., Winston-Salem, 1980—, also Wachovia Bank of N.C. Col. JAGC, USAR, 1970—. Mem. ABA (corp., banking and bus. law sect. 1971—), N.C. Bar Assn. (internat. law com. 1984—, fin. instns. com. 1985—, real property sect. governing coun. 1988-91, bus. law sect. 1971—, corp. counsel sect. 1989—, governing coun. 1992—, real property curriculum com. 1990-93), N.C. State Bar, N.C. Coll. of Advocacy, Forsyth County Bar Assn., Am. Corp. Counsel Assn. (v.p., bd. dirs. N.C. chpt. 1988—, comml. law com. 1996—), Mortgage Bankers Assn. of Am. (legal issues com. 1982—, fin. affiliates com. 1988—), Union League (Phila.), Twin City Club (sec. 1990—), Forsyth Country Club, Phi Delta Phi, Phi Delta Theta. Republican. Presbyterian. Avocations: golf, tennis. Home: 615 Arbor Rd Winston Salem NC 27104-2331 Office: Wachovia Corp 100 N Main St Winston Salem NC 27150-0001

LOUIS, WILLIAM ROGER, historian, educator, editor; b. Detroit, May 8, 1936; s. Henry Edward and Bena May (Flood) L.; m. Dagmar Cecilia Friedrich; children: Antony Andrew, Catherine Ann. BA, U. Okla., 1959; MA, Harvard U., 1960; PhD, Oxford U., 1962, DLitt, 1979. Asst. prof., then assoc. prof. history Yale U., 1962-70; prof. history, curator hist. collections Humanities Research Center U. Tex., Austin, 1970-85, dir. Brit. Studies, 1975—, Kerr chair English history and culture, 1985—; supernumerary fellow St. Antony's Coll., U. Oxford, Eng., 1986-96, hon. fellow, 1996—; corr. fellow Brit. Acad., 1993—; Chichele lectr. All Souls Coll., U. Oxford, Eng., 1990; Disting. lectr. London Sch. Econs., 1992; Cust lectr. Nottingham (Eng.) U., 1995; Brit. Acad. Elie Kedorie Meml. lectr., 1996; dir. summer seminars NEH, 1985, 88, 90, 91, 96. Author: Ruanda-Urundi, 1963, Germany's Lost Colonies, 1967, (with Jean Stengers)The Congo Reform Movement, 1968, British Strategy in the Far East, 1919-1939, 1971, Imperialism at Bay, 1977 (History Book Club), British Empire in the Middle East, 1984 (George Louis Beer prize Am. Hist. Assn. and Tex. Inst. Letters award), In The Name of the God Go! Leo Amery and the British Empire in the Age of Churchill, 1992; editor British Documents on the End of Empire, 1988—; editor-in-chief Oxford History of the British Empire, 1993—; editor: (with P. Gifford) Britain and Germany in Africa, 1967, France and Britain in Africa, 1971, The Origins of the Second World War: A.J.P. Taylor and his Critics, 1972, National Security and International Trusteeship in the Pacific, 1972, Imperialism: The Robinson and Gallagher Controversy, 1976, (with William S. Livingston) Australia, New Zealand and the Pacific Islands since the First World War, 1979, (with P. Gifford) The Transfer of Power in Africa, 1982, (with R. Stookey) End of the Palestine Mandate, 1986, (with H. Bull) The Special Relationship: Anglo-American Relations Since 1945, 1986, (with P. Gifford) Decolonization and African Independence, 1988, (with James Bill) Musaddiq, Iranian Nationalism, and Oil, 1988, (with Roger Owen) Suez 1956: The Crisis and Its Consequences, 1989, (with Robert A. Fernea) The Iraqi Revolution of 1958, 1991, (with Robert Blake) Churchill, 1993, Adventures with Britannia, 1995. Woodrow Wilson fellow Harvard U., 1959-60, Marshall scholar Oxford U., 1960-62, NEH fellow, Am. Inst. Indian Studies fellow, Guggenheim fellow, vis. fellow All Souls Coll., U. Oxford, overseas fellow Churchill Coll., U. Cambridge, Eng., fellow Woodrow Wilson Internat. Ctr.; guest scholar Brookings Instn. Fellow Royal Hist. Soc.; mem. Am. Hist. Assn. (life), Coun. on Fgn. Rels. (N.Y.C.), Tex. Inst. Letters, Reform Club (London), Century (N.Y.C.), Met. Club (Washington). Democrat. Office: U Texas Dept History Austin TX 78712

LOUVIERE, JAMES PETER, science foundation administrator, writer, inventor; b. New Iberia, La., Feb. 23, 1937; s. Clarence Justin and Julie (LaFleur) L.; m. Lynn Heintz, Jan. 16, 1971; children: Michelle, Jacques, Remy, Jeanne. BA, Coll. Santa Fe, 1959; MA, St. Mary's U., 1966, NYU, 1972; BS, Regents Coll., 1984; PhD, Columbia Pacific U., 1985. Life cert. edn. adminstrn., La. Tchr. St. Michael's H.S., Santa Fe, N. Mex., 1959-62, 66-67, Archbishop Rummel H.S., Metairie, La., 1962-66, Coll. Santa Fe (N. Mex.), 1967-68, Alexander Hamilton Vocat.-Tech., Bklyn., 1969-71, Rivers Frederick Jr. H.S., New Orleans, 1971-73, County Day Sch., Metairie, La., 1973-74; tchr., adminstr. Dept. Def. Schs., Germany, 1974-95; coord. nat. Sci. Found. phys. sci. program La. State U., Baton Rouge, 1995—; founder Iberia Inst. Profl. Devel., 1995, LouVee Air tm Syss., Baton Rouge, 1996; tchr. rsch. assoc. Argonne Nat. Lab., Idaho Falls, 1993, 94. Co-author: (textbook) S/T/S: Science, Technology and Society, 1984-85, Riskin' It., 1996; contbr. articles to profl. jours.; inventor LouVee Air air car.ž. Mem. AAAS, APS, NSF Leadership Assn., Assn. Supervision and Curriculum Devel., N.Y. Acad. Scis., Nat. Sci. Tchrs. Assn. Office: La State U 107 Peabody Hall Baton Rouge LA 70803

LOUX, JEAN MCCLUSKEY, housewife, registered nurse; b. Phila., Sept. 1, 1953; d. Robert Clyde and Jean Lois (Ashford) McC.; m. Peter Charles Loux, Sept. 27, 1975; children: Tara, Kimberly. Student, West Chester State Nursing Sch, 1971-74; registered nurse diploma, Chester County Sch. Nursing, West Chester, Pa., 1974. RN, Pa., N.Y., Fla. Nursing aide Chester City Hosp., West Chester, Pa., 1971-74; officer tng. U.S. Navy, Newport, R.I., 1974; RN staff, 3 shifts U.S. Navy Nat. Med. Ctr., Bethesda, Md., 1975; RN supr. duty clinic U.S. Navy Clinic, Queens, N.Y., 1975-76; RN med. surg. and pvt. duty Doctors Hosp., Staten Island, N.Y., 1977-78; admstrv. asst. P.C. Loux DO, Huntsville, Ala.; co-mgr. office of P.C. Loux, D.O. and Huntsville (Ala.). Tour guide, helper The Arts Couns. Panoply Art Festival, Huntsville, Ala., 1978, 79.; ARC CPR and First Aid Tng.; Angel, life mem. On-Call Angel, mail out com.; UTCT com. Randolph Sch., Raiders Club, First Aid Rm., printing chmn., 3 Yrs., sec., co-chmn., Capital Campaign and Ann. Giving; chmn. nominating com. St. Marks Luth. Ch., Huntsville, 1993-94, fellowship com. 1993-95, co-chmn. 1991-93, nursery coord. several years, recycling chmn., 1986—, altar guild, 1995—; baby sitting coord. Hope Project, 1995. Lt. USNR, 1973-76. Mem. Madison County Med. Auxiliary (cmty health com.-organ donating edn. sub com. for pub. schs., legis. chmn., spl. projects chmn., scholarship chmn., fashionshow coms., 1996-97, treas. 1993-95. fin. com. 1993-96, long range planning com., 1993-96), Am. Med. Assn. Alliance, Huntsville Hosp. Found., Huntsville-Madison County Botanical Garden Soc.-Found. I and II, Friends of Huntsville Libr., Huntsville Mus. of Art, Madison County Med. Aux., Nat. Children's Advocacy Ctr. Huntsville. Home: 1606 Drake Ave SE Huntsville AL 35802-1057

LOUX, PETER CHARLES, anesthesiologist; b. Phila., Feb. 1, 1949; s. Theodore Clewell and Agnes Elva (Eichelman) L.; m. Jean Alyce McCluskey, Sept. 27, 1975; children: Tara Jean, Kimberly Marie. Student, Ea. Bapt. Coll., St. David's, Pa., 1967-68; BS in Biology, Widener Coll., Chester, P., 1971; DO, Phila. Coll. Osteo. Medicine, 1975. Diplomate Am. Bd. Anesthesiology. Resident USPHS, Staten Island (N.Y.C.), 1975-78; fellowship Milton S. Hershey Med. Ctr. Pa. State U., Hershey, 1978-79, asst. prof. Anesthesiology Milton S. Hershey Med. Ctr., 1979-83; pvt. practice Huntsville, Ala., 1983-95; ptnr. Comprehensive Anesthesia Svcs., Huntsville, 1995—; clin. assoc. prof. Anesthesiology and Surgery U. Ala. Sch. Medicine, Huntsville, 1993—; co-med. dir. Surgery Ctr. of Huntsville, 1985-86; chief divsn. of Anesthesiology Huntsville Hosp., 1986-87. Contbr. articles to profl. jours. Mem. St. Mark's Luth. Ch. (constitution com., 1987, long-range planning com., 1989, fellowship com., 1986). Lt. cmdr. USPHS, 1975-78. Mem. AMA, Am. Soc. Anesthesiologists, Ala. State Soc. Anesthesiologists (pres. 1993-95, alt. del. to Am. Soc. Anesthesiologists 1989, 91, del. 1990, 92), Madison County Med. Soc. (anesthesiology rep. to exec. bd. 1987-92, dist. 5 rep. to Ala. State Soc. Anesthesiologists 1987-92). Soc. Critical Care Medicine, Am. Soc. Regional Anesthesia. Home: 1606 Drake Ave Huntsville AL 35802-1057 Office: Comprehensive Anesthesia Svcs 201 Sivley Rd SW Ste 500 Huntsville AL 35801-5138

LOVE, FRANCES TAYLOR, public relations consultant; b. Salina, Kans., Apr. 25, 1926; d. Harold Sturtz Taylor and Elizabeth Redmon; m. John William Love, July 12, 1947; 1 child, John Taylor. Student, U. Tex., 1947, U. Houston, 1951, Victoria and Albert Mus., London, 1975. Instr. speech Delmar Coll., Corpus Christi, Tex., 1948-49; pub. rels. profl. Houston BBB, 1951-54; pub. La./Tex. Books, 1957—; pub. rels. cons. Frances Love and Assocs., Lafayette, La., 1959—; dir. Art Ctr. Southwestern La., U. Southwestern La., Lafayette, 1965-83; pub. rels. cons., Twinning/City of Poitiers, France, 1977, Twinning/City of Nameur, Belgium, 1979. Author, pub.: My Home Is Austin, Texas, 1958, Here Is South Louisiana, 1965, Louisiana French Furnishings, 1974, 96, Oil People: A Gap of Understanding, 1991; editor: (weekly newspaper) Six Points News, 1947-49; pub. Acadiana Mag., 1982-92, Conv. and Visitors Commn. Ann., 1985-94. Sec. bd. dirs. U. Southwestern La. Found., Lafayette, 1968-83; regional chmn. Bicentennial Commn., La., 1971-76; writer, campaign mgr. La. Citizens of Term Limits, La., 1994—. Presbyterian. Office: Frances Love and Assocs PO Box 51998 Lafayette LA 70505

LOVE, GAYLE MAGALENE, special education educator, adult education educator; b. New Orleans, July 25, 1953; d. Lowell F. Sr. and Nathalie Mae (Adams) L.; children: Nathanael Dillard, Raphael. BMEd, Loyola U., New Orleans, 1975, MMEd, 1981. Cert. learning disabled, emotionally disturbed, gifted-talented, adult edn., mild-moderate, elem.-secondary vocal music, prin., spl. sch. prin., parish/city sch. supr. instrn., supervision of student tchg., supr. adult edn. & spl. edn., child search coord. Dean student svcs. Jefferson Parish Sch. Bd., Harvey, La., chmn. spl. edn. dept., 1990-93; adult educator instr.; chmn. Sch. Bldg. Level Com., 1994-96; presenter St. Joseph the Worker Cath. Ch., 1988, Very Spl. Arts Week Jefferson Parish Pub. Sch. Sys., 1989, 90, 91, 92, 93, 94, 95, 96; mem. spl. edn. alternative curriculum com., 1990—, Urban Ctr. Tchrs. Devel. com. U. New Orleans, 1990-91. Mem. NAFE, ASCD, Coun. Exceptional Children (workshop presenter 1990), Jefferson Assn. Pub. Sch. Adminstrs., East Bank Jefferson Parish Parent Adv. Coun., New Orleans C. of C. (com. Alliance for Quality, small bus. improvement team), La. Assn. Sch. Execs., Jefferson Chamber Leadership Inst., Phi Beta, Kappa Delta Pi, Alpha Kappa Alpha. Home: 1740 Burnley Dr Marrero LA 70072-4522

LOVE, MARY ANGELEAN, company executive; b. Alton, Ill., May 7, 1955; d. Johnes Joel and Fannie Mae Love. Student, L.A. City Coll., 1978-81, U. So. Calif., L.A., 1977-83; BS in Paralegal Studies, U. West L.A., 1986. Lic. paralegal, Calif. Legal asst. pub. fin. Nossaman, Guthner, Knox & Elliott, L.A., 1987-91; quality control auditor Scientific Games, Inc., Alpharetta, Ga., 1995—. Author: Poetry in Regards to the Child, 1995, Poetry for Lovers, 1995, (record cassettes) The Sound of Poetry, 1994 (Merit award 1994), 1995 (Merit award 1995), 1996 (Merit award 1996); songwriter: Star Route U.S.A., 1996, America, 1996. Recipient Editor's Choice award Nat. Libr. Poetry, 1994, 95, 96, Poetic Achievement Cert., The Amherst Soc., 1992, Accomplishment of Merit, Creative arts and Sci. Enterprises, N.Y., 1992. Mem. Internat. Soc. Poets (Poet of Merit 1996). Mem. Ch. of God in Christ, Holiness. Home: 2603 Bronco Trail Duluth GA 30136

LOVE, MILDRED ALLISON, retired secondary school educator, historian, writer, volunteer; b. Moultrie, Ga., Mar. 12, 1915; d. Ulysees Simpson Sr. and Susie Marie (Dukes) Allison; m. George Alsobrook Love, Aug. 24, 1956 (dec. 1978). BSEd, U. Tampa (Fla.), 1941; MS in Home Econs., Fla. State U., 1953; MA in History, U. Miami, Coral Gables, Fla., 1969. Cert. tchr., Fla. Vocat. home econs. tchr. Hamilton County Pub. Schs., Jasper, Fla., 1941-43, Pinellas County Pub. Schs., Tarpon Springs, Fla., 1946-51; vocat. home econs. tchr. Dade County Pub. Schs., Miami, Fla., 1951-61, history tchr., 1961-73; supr. food svcs. Ft. Jackson (S.C.), 1944-46. Chmn. subcoun. for crime prevention Brickell Area, City of Miami, 1983-87; mem. Crisis Response Team, Miami Police Dept., 1983—; vol. VA Hosp., Miami, 1987—; historian, vol. vets affairs VFW Aux., Miami, 1988-89; precinct worker presdl. election, 1976, 80; sponsor history honor soc. Miami Edison Sr. H.S., 1961-73; mem. Mus. of Sci., St. Stephen's Episc. Ch., Coconut Grove, Fla.; mem. Dade Heritage Trust; charter mem. Libr. Congress Assocs.; mem. Arthritis Found., Consumer Union. Mem. AAUW, VFW (aux. post 471 Miami, Fla.), Am. Assn. Ret. Persons, Inst. for Retired Profls., Hist. Assn. S. Fla., U. Miami Alumni Assn., Fla. Ret. Educators Assn., Nat. Wildlife Fedn., Am. Legion (aux. post 29 Miami, Fla.), Nat. Trust Hist. Preservation, Coll. of Arts and Scis. Assn. U. Miami, Fla. Vocat. Home Econs. Tchrs. (pres. 1947), Fla. Vocat. Home Econs. Assn. (pres. 1948-49), Dade Heritage Trust, Woman's Club of Miami Beach, Sierra Club, Phi Alpha Theta. Democrat. Episcopalian. Home: 2411 S Miami Ave Miami FL 33129-1527

LOVE, MILDRED LOIS (JAN LOVE), public relations executive; b. Iowa City, July 9, 1928; d. Joseph R. and Gladys M. (Parsons) Casey; BS in Bus. Adminstrn., U. Iowa, 1951; m. Gerald Dean Love, Apr. 4, 1952; children: Laura Anne Love Parris, Cynthia Love-Hazel, Gregory Alan, Linda Love Mesler, Geoffrey Dare. Vocal soloist Sta. KXEL, Waterloo, Iowa, 1944-46; sec. to lawyer, La Porte City, Iowa, 1944-46; administrv. aide Office of Supt., La Porte City High Sch., 1947-48; office mgr. Minn. Valley Canning Co., Iowa div. offices, LaPorte City, 1947-48; sec. dept. mktg. U. Iowa, 1948-51; asst. dept. pub. rels. Chgo. Bd. Trade, 1949-51; exec. sec. patent dept. Collins Radio Co., Cedar Rapids, 1951-52; vol. VA Hosp., Albany, N.Y., 1965-73; adminstrv. dir. Tri-Village Nursery Sch., Delmar, N.Y., 1960-61; participant Internat. Lang. Teaching Exch., Cambodia, 1961; vol. hosps. in Concord, N.H., 1963-64; vol. Chgo. Maternity Center, 1973-74; mgr. Wolf Trap Assocs. Gift Shop, Vienna, Va., 1975-80; gen. mgr. Travelhost of Washington, 1980-81; cons. mgmt., 1980—; chmn. Nat. Cherry Blossom Festival, Washington. Participant community pageants on local and dist. levels, Iowa, 1950-51; Sunday sch. tchr. Meth. Ch., 1941-61; mem. Flossmoor (Ill.) Planning and Zoning Commn., 1973-74, McLean (Va.) Planning and Zoning Comm., 1975-81; precinct worker in Iowa, 1946-52, N.Y., 1956-61, N.H., 1963-64, Va., 1979-84; pres. I.O.W.A. Inc., Washington, 1980-81; active various community fund raising drives; mem. LWV, Ladies Aux., McCosh Infirmary, Princeton, N.J.; chair pub. rels. Nat. Assistance League/Amador Valley Guild, 1990-93. Mem. AAUW, Am. Mkgt. Assn., NAFE, Nat. Conf. State Socs. (pres. 1983), Ariz. Opera League, Navy League U.S. (life), Princeton

Club, Can. Club, Normanside Country Club, Olympia Fields Winter Club, Kenilworth Club, P.E.O. (Ind.), Delta Zeta.

LOVELACE, GEORGE DAVID, JR., quality engineer; b. Pampa, Tex., Aug. 9, 1952. AS, Clarendon (Tex.) Coll., 1972; BS, Oklahoma City U., 1985, MBA, 1992. Cert. quality engr. Engring. aide Dayton Tire subs. Bridgestone/Firestone, Inc., Oklahoma City, 1973; sr. engring. aide Bridgestone/Firestone, Inc., Oklahoma City, 1973-75, tech. asst., 1975-83, sr. tech. asst., 1983-85, statis. engr., 1985-87, sr. statis. engr., 1987-90; sr. statis. engr. Dayton Tire, Oklahoma City, 1991-92, sect. mgr. quality assurance, 1992—. Mem. bd. of elders Grace Chapel Pentecostal Holiness Ch., Mustang, Okla., 1977—, chmn. 1987—; tchr. Grace Chapel Sunday Sch., Mustang, 1977—. Mem. Am. Soc. for Quality Control (sr., Okla. sect., program chmn. 1984-85, vice chmn. 1985-86, chmn. 1986-87). Democrat. Home: 1101 W Churchill Way Mustang OK 73064-2103 Office: Dayton Tire Div Bridgestone Firestone Inc 2500 S Council Rd # 24011 Oklahoma City OK 73128-9501

LOVELESS, KATHY LYNNE, client services executive; b. Corsicana, Tex., Mar. 7, 1961; d. Vernon Ray and Barbara Alice (Brown) L. BA, Baylor U., 1983. Adminstrv. asst. InterFirst Bank, Dallas, 1983-85; adminstrv. asst. Chaparral Steel Co., Midlothian, Tex., 1985-89, audio/visual coord., 1989-93; freelance computer instr. Duncanville, Tex., 1993-94; tng. specialist U. Tex. Southwestern Med. Ctr., Dallas, 1994-95, supr. client svcs. ctr., 1995—. Pres., v.p. Midlothian Cmty. Theatre, 1990-93, mem., 1987-94; v.p. Lovers Ln. United Meth. Ch. Choir, Dallas, 1994, 95, Adminstrv. Bd., 1995-96; chmn. worship and mem. care com. Elmwood United Meth. Ch., 1990, 91; bd. dirs. Trinity River Mission, Dallas, 1994, 95, 96. Mem. NAFE, AAUW, USA Film Festival, Am. Film Inst. Home: 8903 San Benito Way Dallas TX 75218

LOVELL, RICHARD THOMAS, aquaculture researcher; b. Lockesburg, Ark., Feb. 21, 1934; s. Thomas N. and Henry Etta L.; m. Ganata Jo Nettles, Dec., 21, 1963; children: Thomas Alan, Richard Graves. BS, Okla. State U., 1956, MS, 1960; PhD, La. State U., 1963. From asst. to assoc. prof. food sci. dept. La. State U., Baton Rouge, 1963-69; prof. fisheries dept. Auburn (Ala.) U., 1969—, disting. univ. prof., 1995—; chmn. edit. com. nutritioinal requirements of fish NRC, 1982. Author: Nutrition and Feeding of Fish, 1989, Laboratory Handbook for Fish Feed Analysis and Fish Nutrition Research 1982; contbr. over 275 articles to sci. jours. and publs. Scoutmaster Boy Scouts Am., Stillwater, Okla., 1956-60, chmn. Saugahatchee dist. com., 1980-84; chmn. adminstrv. bd. 1st United Meth. Ch., Opelika, Ala., 1986-88. Recipient profl. sci. award So Assn. Agrl. Scis., 1977, cert. of merit Inst. Food Tech., 1992, dir.'s award Ala. Agrl. Expt. Sta., 1994. Mem. NAS, Am. Fisheries Soc., Am. Inst. Nutrition, Am. Angus Assn., Catfish Farmers Am. (Dist. Svc. award 1978, 80), Ala. Cattlemen's Assn. Home: 622 Terracewood Dr Opelika AL 36801-3851 Office: Fisheries Dept Auburn Univ Swingle Hall Auburn AL 36849

LOVETT, BOBBY LEE, history educator, university dean; b. Memphis, Jan. 19, 1943; s. Edward Kirk and Frances Marie (Wordlaw) L.; m. Elaine Harvey, Dec. 11, 1965 (div. Aug. 1981); children: Todd Allen, Bridgett Franzette, Kenyatta Kirk; m. Lueatrice Green, July 14, 1984; children: Leigh Francine, Catherine Lueatrice. BS in History, Ark. AM&N State Coll., 1967; MA in History, U. Ark., 1969, PhD in History, 1978. Tchr. White State H.S., Memphis, 1969-70; asst. prof. history Eureka (Ill.) Coll., 1970-73; prof. history Tenn. State U., Nashville, 1973—, dean arts and scis., 1983—. Author: Black Man's Dream, 1993; editl. bd. Ark. Hist. Quar., 1993-95. Vice chmn. Met. Hist. Commn., Nashville, 1995—; mem. State Rev. Bd., Tenn., 1995—. Mem. So. Hist. Assn., Assn. for Study of Negro Culture and History, Nashville C. of C. (subcom. on edn. 1995—), Kappa Alpha Psi, Phi Alpha Theta, Phi Kappa Phi, Alpha Delta Mu. Baptist. Home: 1308 Valley Trail White Creek TN 37189 Office: Tennessee State Univ 3500 John A Merritt Blvd Nashville TN 37209-1500

LOVETT, WILLIAM ANTHONY, law and economics educator; b. Milw., Sept. 2, 1934. AB, Wabash Coll., 1956; JD, NYU, 1959; PhD in Econs., Mich. State U., 1969. Bar: N.Y. 1960. Atty. U.S. Dept. Justice, Washington, 1962; economist FTC, Washington, 1963-69; prof. Tulane U., New Orleans, 1969—, dir. internat. law, trade and fin. program, 1985—; Joseph Merrick Jones prof. law and econs., 1991—. Author: Inflation and Politics, 1982, Banking and Financial Institutions Law, 1984, 88, 92, World Trade Rivalry, 1987, U.S. Shipping Policies and the World Market, 1996. Root-Tilden scholar, 1956-59. Mem. ABA, Am. Econs. Assn., Am. Soc. Internat. Law, Phi Beta Kappa. Office: Tulane Law Sch New Orleans LA 70118

LOVING, SUSAN B., lawyer, former state official; m. Dan Loving; children: Lindsay, Andrew, Kendall. BA with distinction, U. Okla., 1972, JD, 1979. Asst. atty. gen. Office of Atty. Gen., 1983-87, first asst. atty. gen., 1987-91; atty. gen. State of Okla., Oklahoma City, 1991-94; with Lester, Loving & Davies, P.L.L.C., Edmond, Okla., 1996—; Master Ruth Bader Ginsburg Inn of Ct.; mem. Truth in Sentencing Policy Adv. Commn., 1995—. Vice chmn. Pardon and Parole Bd., 1995—; mem. Gov.'s Commn. on Tobacco and Youth, 1995—; bd. dirs. Bd. for Freedom of Info., Okla. Inc., Boy Scouts Am., Legal Aid of West Okla., Okla. Com. for Prevention of Child Abuse; mem. med. steering com. Partnership for Drug Free Okla., Inst. for Child Advocacy, 1996—; mem. adv. bd. Law and You Found. Recipient Nat. Red Ribbon Leadership award Nat. Fedn. Parents, Headliner award, By-liner award Okla. City and Tulsa Women in Comm., First Friend of Freedom award, Freedom of Info., Okla., Dir. award Okla. Dist. Attys. Assn. Mem. Okla. Bar Assn. (past chmn. adminstrv. law sect., mem. ho. dels. 1996—, mem. adminstrn. of justice com., mem. profl. responsibility commn.), Phi Beta Kappa. Office: Lester Loving & Davies PLLC Ste 102 601 N Kelly Edmond OK 73003

LOVING, WILLIAM RUSH, JR., public relations company executive, consultant; b. Norfolk, Va., Sept. 14, 1934; s. William Rush and Margaret Elizabeth (Billups) L.; m. Jane Parker, July 1963 (div. Dec. 1987); children: Katharine G., Margaret Borden, Leslie R.; m. Marsha Thaler, June 30, 1989 (div. June 1994). BA, U. Richmond, 1956. Lt. U.S. Army, 1957-59; reporter Richmond (Va.) Times-Dispatch, 1959-62, bus. editor, 1965-69; reporter The Virginian-Pilot, Norfolk, 1962-63; info. coord. Va. Mus. Fine Arts, Richmond, 1963-65; assoc. editor Fortune mag., N.Y.C., 1969-79; asst. dir. U.S. Office Mgmt. and Budget, Washington, 1979-80; pres. Loving Asssocs. Ltd., New Hope, Pa., 1980—, Loving Assocs. Ltd. Va., Alexandria, 1989—; dir. Railway Svc. Corp.; trustee Loving Assocs. Pension and Profit Sharing Funds, New Hope, Pa. Editor: How To Protect What's Yours, 1983; contbr. numerous articles to Fortune mag. Mem. Old Town Civic Assn., Alexandria, 1986—, The Torpedo Factory, Alexandria, 1986—. Mem. Nat. Press Club, R.R. Pub. Rels. Assn., Bucks County C. of C., Va. Hist. Soc. Home: 405 S Lee St Alexandria VA 22314-3815 Office: 519 Oronoco St Alexandria VA 22314-2305

LOVVORN, JOELLA, newspaper editor; b. Pep, Tex., Mar. 20, 1934; d. Alford Marion and Emma (Daniel) L. B.S., Wayland Bapt. Coll., 1969. Ordained non-denominational min. Ch. news editor Plainview (Tex.) Daily Herald, 1957-60, typesetter, proofreader, 1965-67; offset printer, photographer Muleshoe (Tex.) Jours., 1960-64; asst. editor Ariz. Bapt. Beacon, Phoenix, 1964-65; society editor Lamb County Leader-News Littlefield, Tex., 1967-69, editor, 1969—. Bd. dirs. United Way Fund, 1979-88, Salvation Army, 1976—; dir. Lamb County Spelling Bee, Littlefield, 1980-90; judge Regional Spelling Bee, Lubbock, 1980-90; chmn. public info. Am. Cancer Soc., 1968—, Am. Heart Assn., 1976-79; chmn. publicity county chpt. ARC, 1976, retail trade com., 1987—; mem. Lamb County Crime Stoppers Bd., 1990—. Recipient appreciation cert. Am. Cancer Soc., 1974, 80, 83, 86-89, 93, Am. Heart Assn., 1974, appreciation plaque Distributive Edn. Classes Am., 1983-85, appreciation plaque Future Farmers Am., 1985. Mem. Tex. Press Assn., West Tex. Press Assn. (contest chmn. 1970), Littlefield C. of C. (chmn. publicity, named Woman of the Yr. 1988). Republican. Lodges: Woodmen of the World, Rotary Club (Littlefield). Office: Lamb County Leader-News Box 293 Littlefield TX 79339-0293

LOW, EMMET FRANCIS, JR., mathematics educator; b. Peoria, Ill., June 10, 1922; s. Charles Walter and Nettie Alys (Baker) Davis; m. Lana Carmen Wiles, Nov. 23, 1974. B.S. cum laude, Stetson U., 1948; M.S., U. Fla., 1950, Ph.D., 1953. Instr. physics U. Fla., 1950-54; aero. research scientist NACA, Langley Field, Va., 1954-55; asst. prof. math. U. Miami, Coral Gables, Fla., 1955-60; assoc. prof. U. Miami, 1960-67, prof., 1967-72, chmn. dept. math., 1961-66; acting dean U. Miami (Coll. Arts and Scis.), 1966-67, assoc. dean, 1967-68, assoc. dean faculties, 1968-72; prof. math. Clinch Valley Coll., U. Va., 1972-89, dean, 1972-86, chmn. dept. math. scis., 1986-89; emeritus prof. math., 1989—; vis. research scientist Courant Inst. Math. Scis., NYU, 1959-60. Contbr. articles to profl. jours. Mem. Wise County Indsl. Devel. Authority, 1992—, chmn., 1996—. Served with USAAF, 1942-46. Recipient award for excellence in tchg. Clinch Valley Coll., 1988; hon. Ky. Col. Mem. Am. Math. Soc., Math. Assn. Am., Soc. Indsl. and Applied Math., Nat. Council Tchrs. of Math., Southwest Va. Council Tchrs. of Math., AAUP, AAAS, Sigma Xi, Delta Theta Mu, Phi Delta Kappa, Phi Kappa Phi. Clubs: Univ. Yacht (Miami, Fla.); Kiwanis.

LOW, JACLYN FAGLIE, occupational therapist; b. San Antonio, June 26, 1941; d. Jack Claude and Peggy (Smith) Faglie; m. William Bert Low, Dec. 27, 1960; 1 child, Paige Low Gilliam. BS in Occupational Therapy, U. Tex., Galveston, 1973, PhD in Med. Humanities, 1991; MA in Behavioral Scis., U. Houston, Clear Lake City, 1978. Lic. occupational therapist, Tex. Staff therapist pediatric in- and out-patient svcs. U. Tex. Med. Br., Galveston, 1973-75, supr. pediatric in-patient svc., 1975-83; instr. dept. occupational therapy U. Tex. Sch. Allied Health Scis., Galveston, 1975-78, asst. prof. clin. occupational therapy, 1978-82, asst. prof. assoc. health occupations, 1979-80, asst. prof. dept. occupational therapy, 1982-89, assoc. prof., 1989—; chair ad interim dept. occupational therapy, 1994—; occupational therapy cons. Hospice of Galveston County, 1983-93. Contbr. articles to profl. jours. Trustee Hospice of Galveston County, 1984-94, v.p. fin., 1985-89, pres. elect, 1988-89, pres., 1989-94. recipient Outstanding Tchr. in Dept. Occupational Therapy award U. Tex. Sch. Allied Health Scis., 1986, 89, Outstanding Alumni award dept. occupational therapy, 1986, Community Svc. award, 1990, Sch. of Allied Health Scis. Faculty Excellence award, 1991, Lillian Hoyle Parent award dept. occupational therapy U. Tex. Med. Br. at Galveston, 1992. Mem. Am. Occupl. Therapy Assn., Tex. Occupl. Therapy Assn. (edn. chmn. Gulf Coast ea. dist. 1984-89, devel. chmn. 1994—, letter of appreciation 1984, Disting. Svc. award 1985), LWV (bd. dirs. 1994—), Krewe of Hygeia (sec. 1986-88), Knights of Regina, Tex. Occupl. therapy Polit. Action Com. (bd. dirs. 1994—). Office: U Tex Med Br Sch Allied Health Scis Dept Occupational Therapy Galveston TX 77555-1028

LOW, MORTON DAVID, physician, educator; b. Lethbridge, Alta., Can., Mar. 25, 1935; s. Solon Earl and Alice Fern (Litchfield) L.; m. Cecilia Margaret Comba, Aug. 22, 1959 (div. 1983); children—Cecilia Alice, Sarah Elizabeth, Peter Jon Eric; m. Barbara Joan McLeod, Aug. 25, 1984; 1 child, Kelsey Alexandra. M.D., C.M., Queen's U., 1960, M.Sc. in Medicine, 1962; Ph.D. with honors, Baylor U., 1966. From instr. to asst. prof. Baylor Coll. Medicine, Houston, 1965-68; assoc. prof. medicine U. B.C., Vancouver, Can., 1968-78, prof. medicine, 1978-89, clin. assoc. dean, 1974-76, assoc. dean rsch. and grad. studies, 1977-78, coord. health scis., 1985-89; creator Health Policy Rsch. Unit U. B.C., Vancouver, 1987; pres. U. Tex. Health Sci. Ctr., Houston, 1989—, prof. neural scis. Grad. Sch. Biomed. Scis., 1989—, dir. Health Policy Inst., 1990—; prof. neurology U. Tex. Med. Sch., Houston, 1989—; prof. health policy and mgmt. Sch. Pub. Health U. Tex., 1989—; cons. in neurology U. Hosp. Shaughnessy site, Vancouver, 1971-89, U. B.C. site, Vancouver, 1970-89; dir. dept. diagnostic neurophysiology Vancouver Gen. Hosp., 1968-87; cons. in EEG, 1987-89; exec. dir. Rsch. Inst., 1981-86; mem. med. sci. adv. com. USIA, 1991-93. Mem. editorial bd. numerous jours.; contbr. articles to profl. jours. Bd. dirs. Greater Houston Ptnrship., 1994—; mem. governing bd. Houston Mus. Natural Sci., 1991—; trustee Kinkaid Sch., Houston, 1991—. Med. Rsch. Coun. Can. grantee, 1968-80; recipient Tree of Life award Jewish Nat. Fund, 1995, Caring Spirit award Inst. Religion, 1995. Fellow Am. EEG Soc., Royal Coll. Physicians (Can.), Royal Soc. Medicine (London); mem. AMA, Tex. Med. Assn. (coun. on med. edn. 1990—), Can. Soc. Clin. Neurophysiology, Internat. Fedn. Socs. for EEG and Clin. Neurophysiology (rules com. 1977-81, sec. 1981-85), Assn. Acad. Health Ctrs. (task force on access to care and orgn. health svcs. 1988—, chmn. 1992, task force on instnl. values 1989—), Harris County Med. Soc., Am. Coun. Edn., Forum Club of Houston (governing bd. 1991—). Office: U Tex-Houston Health Sci PO Box 20036 Houston TX 77225-0036

LOWDER, NED EDWARD, JR., army officer; b. Anderson, S.C., Jan. 6, 1969; s. Ned Edward Sr. and Diane (Lewis) L.; m. Kristen Anne Graves, Mar. 12, 1994. BBA in Fin., North Ga. coll., 1991. Commd. 2d lt. U.S. Army, 1991, advanced through grades to capt., 1994; logistics officer 2-17 Cavalry, Ft. Campbell, Ky., 1995—. Decorated Army Commendation medal (2), Army Achievement medal. Mem. Army Aviation Assn. Am., Assn. U.S. Army. Home: 113 Peggy Dr Clarksville TN 37042

LOWE, CAMERON ANDERSON, dentist, endodontist, educator; b. Alcester, S.D., Dec. 19, 1932; s. Richard Barrett and Emma Louise (Anderson) L.; m. Doris Teresita Franquez, Dec. 23, 1957; children: Barrett, Steven, Leslie. Student, George Washington U., 1951-53, U. Va., 1955-56; DDS, Georgetown U., 1956-60; cert. residency in endodontics, U.S. Naval Dental Sch., 1967-69. Commd. lt. (j.g.) U.S. Navy Dental Corps, 1953, advanced through grades to capt., 1976, ret., 1978; pvt. practice endodontist Newport News, Va., 1978-81; assoc. prof. dentistry emeritus Old Dominion U., Norfolk, Va., 1991, asst. chair Sch. Dental Hygiene, 1985-89; adj. asst. prof. Med. Coll. Va.-Va. Commonwealth U. Sch. Dentistry, Richmond, 1979-81. Contbr. articles to profl. jours. Tutor adult literacy, 1994-96; coord. Neighborhood Watch, 1994-96; pack and troop chmn. Boy Scouts Am., Guam, 1969-72, Virginia Beach, Va., 1972-78. With USN, 1953-55. Mem. Assn. Mil. Surgeons of U.S., Am. Assn. Endodontists, Am. Acad. Oral Medicine, Am. Dental Assn., Va. Acad. Endodontics, USN Assn. Endodontists, Peninsula Dental Soc., Sigma Alpha Epsilon, Delta Sigma Delta, Sigma Phi Alpha (Dental Hygiene Honor Soc.). Republican. Methodist. Home: 1497 Wakefield Dr Virginia Beach VA 23455-4541

LOWE, CAROLYN ELIZABETH, librarian; b. Knoxville, Tenn., May 26, 1964; d. John Maxwell and Rebecca Kay (Osborn) L. BS, Johnson Bible Coll., 1986; MSLS, U. Tenn., 1993. Libr. asst. Johnson Bible Coll., Knoxville, 1991-93, libr., 1993—. Mem. ALA, Assn. Christian Librs., Assn. Coll. and Rsch. Librs., East Tenn. Libr. Assn., Phi Kappa Phi, Beta Phi Mu. Home and Office: Johnson Bible Coll 7900 Johnson Dr Knoxville TN 37998

LOWE, DOUGLAS HOWARD, architect; b. Akron, Ohio, Nov. 1, 1952; s. Howard Bernard and Dorothy Rachael (Nowag) L.; m. Mary Louise Folk, Jan. 1, 1975; children: Ashley Marie, Austin Douglas, Andrea Catherine. BA in Pre Architecture with honors, Clemson U., 1974, MArch, 1976. Registered profl. architect, Tex., interior designer, Tex. Archtl. programmer Lockwood, Andrews, Newnam, Houston, 1978-80; sr. assoc. Planning Design Research Corp., Houston, 1980-82; v.p., head interior architecture and programming 3D/Internat., San Antonio, 1982-88, exec. v.p., chief ops. officer 3D/M subs., 1988-92; founder, pres. Facility Programming and Consulting, San Antonio, 1992—; co-founder, v.p. Facility Consulting Group, San Antonio, 1994-95. Mem., elder First Presbyn. Ch., San Antonio; mem. legis. com. Alamo Heights Ind. Sch. Dist.; mem. Friends of the McNay. Mem. AIA, Tex. Soc. Archs., Internat. Facility Mgmt. Assn., Nat. Coun. Archtl. Registration Bds., Nat. Trust Hist. Preservation, Soc. for Coll. and Univ. Planning, Rotary Club San Antonio, Town Club San Antonio, Phi Kappa Phi, Tau Sigma Delta. Republican. Presbyterian. Office: Facility Programming & Cons 100 W Houston St Ste 1170 San Antonio TX 78205-1457

LOWE, HAROLD GLADSTONE, JR., photojournalist, small business owner, farmer; b. Nashville, Aug. 3, 1933; s. Harold Gladstone and Kathrine (Rice) L.; m. Anne Poteat, Feb. 26, 1957 (div. 1962); 1 child, Harold Guy; m. Linda Susan Brown, Mar. 14, 1976. Student, Vanderbilt U., 1951-52, 53-54, U. of the South, 1952-53. Pres., owner Campus Cameras, Inc., Nashville, 1953-55; photographer Nashville Tennessean Newspaper, 1960-65; photo corr. UP Internat., Nashville, 1961-65; photographer, reporter Sta. WSM TV News, Nashville, 1965-71; staff photographer, editor Senator Howard Baker, Nashville, 1971-72; freelance photographer and reporter Nashville, 1973-76; photographer, reporter Sta. WTVF-TV News, Nashville, 1976-78; photographic supr. State of Tenn., Nashville, 1978-81; photographer, owner CHSS Newspix-Capitol Press, Nashville, 1981—; pres. Campbell-Brown Farms, Inc., Dyersburg, Tenn., 1969—. Photographer Spot News, 1962 (1st Pl. award 1962); photographer, editor (documentary) United Givers Fund, 1970 (Diamond award 1970). Photographer Gov. Lamar Alexander, Nashville, 1979-80, col. aide de camp, 1979, Gov. Ned Ray McWherter, 1986. Mem. Nat. Press Photographers Assn., Tenn. Capitol Press Corps, SDX Soc. Profl. Journalists, Sports Car Club Am., Masons, Sigma Nu. Democrat. Anglican. Home: 1113 Lipscomb Dr Nashville TN 37204-4121 Office: CHSS Newspix Capitol Press 28 Legislative Pla Nashville TN 37219

LOWE, JOE ALLEN, minister; b. Midland, Tex., Dec. 20, 1945; s. Homer Allen and Theresa (Lowry) L.; m. Shirley Christy, Apr. 9, 1965; children: Robert Allen, John David, Steven Scott. BS, Howard Payne Coll., 1968; MDiv, Tex. Christian U., 1976; postgrad, Princeton Theol., 1990. Cert. secondary tchr.; ordained to the ministry Christian Ch., 1976. Tchr. Bible history Midland (Tex.) Ind. Sch. Dist., 1968-74; assoc. min. First Christian Ch., Denison, Tex., 1974-76; campus min. United Campus Ministries, Warrensburg, Mo., 1976-78; nurture min. Meml. Christian Ch., Midland, Tex., 1978-84; assoc. min. 1st Christian Ch., Corpus Christi, Tex., 1984-91; sr. min. South Shore Christian Ch., Corpus Christi, 1991—; chmn. Cen. Area Youth Coun., Tex., 1980-84; moderator Youth Ministry Coun. S.W., 1984-87, Bluebonnet Area Youth Coun., 1988-92; advisor Gen. Youth Coun., U.S. and Can., 1985-87; vice moderator Bluebonnet Area of Christian Ch. in S.W., 1994—. Mem. IMPACT, 1974-82, Nat. Peace Acad., 1973-78; coach YMCA basketball, 1980-81, Little League, Youth Flag Football teams, Denison and Midland, 1967-68, 70, 74; ethics commn. City of Corpus Christi, 1994—. Recipient Friend of Youth City award, 1989; O.H. Karr Ministerial scholar Tex. Christian U., 1975-76. Mem. Youth Ministry Coun. (moderator 1989-93), Ministerial Alliance. Home: 7130 Everhart Rd Apt 8 Corpus Christi TX 78413-2469 Office: South Shore Christian Ch 4710 S Alameda St Corpus Christi TX 78412-2331

LOWE, PETER STEPHEN, non-profit company executive; b. Lahore, Pakistan, Oct. 23, 1958; s. Eric and Margaret Winnifred (Bradshaw) L.; m. Tamara Angela Forte, May 9, 1987. BA, Carleton U., Ottawa, Ont., Can., 1986. Pres. Lifemasters Tng. Co., Vancouver, B.C., Can., 1981-87, Global Achievers, New Orleans, 1987-90; pres., chief exec. officer Peter Lowe Internat., Inc., Tampa, Fla., 1990—. Mem. Nat. Speakers Assn., Nat. Christian Speakers Assn. (founder), Internat. Platform Assn. Office: 8405A Benjamin Rd Tampa FL 33634

LOWE, ROBERT CHARLES, lawyer; b. New Orleans, July 3, 1949; s. Carl Randall and Antonia (Morgan) L.; m. Theresa Louise Acree, Feb. 4, 1978. 1 child, Nicholas Stafford. BA, U. New Orleans, 1971; JD, La. State U., 1975. Bar: La. 1975, U.S. Dist. Ct. (ea. dist.) La. 1975, U.S. Ct. Appeals (5th cir.) 1980, U.S. Dist. Ct. (we. dist.) La. 1978, U.S. Supreme Ct. 1982. Assoc. Sessions, Fishman, Rosenson, Boisfontaine, and Nathan, New Orleans, 1975-80, ptnr., 1980-87; ptnr. Lowe, Stein, Hoffman, Allweiss and Hauver, 1987—. Author: Louisiana Divorce, 1984; mem. La. Law Rev., 1974-75; contbr. articles to profl. jours. Mem. ABA, La. State Bar Assn. (chmn. family law sect. 1984-85), La. Assn. Def. Counsel, New Orleans Bar Assn. (chmn. family law sect. 1991-92), La. State Law Inst., La. Trial Lawyers Assn., Order of Coif, Phi Kappa Phi. Republican. Home: 9625 Garden Oak Ln River Ridge LA 70123 Office: 701 Poydras St Ste 3600 New Orleans LA 70139-3600

LOWELL, JEANNE, nursing educator, psychiatric-mental health nurse; b. Duncan, Okla., July 3, 1946; d. E.O. and Abbie Louise (Wood) Meeks. AS in Nursing, Cameron U., Lawton, Okla., 1970; BS in Edn., Cen. State U., Edmond, Okla., 1976; MS in Nursing, Tex. Woman's U., 1981; postgrad., U. Okla. Cert. in psychiat. nursing. Instr. nursing Cameron U., 1980-82; asst. prof. nursing U. Okla., Oklahoma City, 1982-86; dir. nursing Community Mental Health Ctr., Norman, Okla., 1986-89; prof. nursing Oklahoma City Community Coll., 1989—. Contbr. articles to profl. jours. Mem. Am. Nurses Assn. (cert. psychiat. nurse). Home: 1866 W Robinson St Apt B Norman OK 73069-7323 Office: Oklahoma City CC 7777 N May Ave Oklahoma City OK 73116-3113

LOWERS, GINA CATTANI, process and instrumentation engineer; b. Evanston, Ill., Oct. 16, 1961; d. Lawrence F. and Arlene Bernice (Phillips) Cattani; m. Robert Judson Lowers, Oct. 10, 1984. BS in Math., U. Calif., Riverside, 1984; BS in Physics, Carnegie-Mellon U., 1987, MS in Physics, 1989; postgrad., W.Va. U. Test systems engr. Aerojet Electrosystems Co., Azusa, Calif., 1983-85; instr. calculus Carnegie Mellon U., Pitts., 1986-88; product devel. engr. Philips Lighting Co., Fairmont, W.Va., 1988—; instr. physics Fairmont State Coll., 1990-91, instr. electronics, 1992—. Judge physics and math. orals and presentations W. Va. State Sci. and Engring. Fair, 1989-91, judge physics projects, 1989, 91, 92; chair covenants and restrictions com. Greystone-on-the-Cheat Property Owner's Assn., sec. Mem. Electrochem. Soc., Soc. Mfg. Engrs., Soc. Tech. Comm. Office: Philips Lighting Co RR 3 Box 505 Fairmont WV 26554-9484

LOWERY, ANNE BARROW, business administration dean; b. Tuscaloosa, Ala., Jan. 11, 1958; d. Curtis Fowler and Bonnie Kate (Hollingsworth) Barrow; m. Henry Ellis Lowery, Jr., Aug. 10, 1985; 1 child, Meredith Anne. BS in Econs., U. Ala., Tuscaloosa, 1980; MA in Econs., U. Wis., Milw., 1982; DBA in Bus. Adminstrn., Miss. State U., Starkville, 1990. Adminstrv. asst. Internat. Ins. Soc., Tuscaloosa, 1976-81; teaching asst. U. Wis., Milw., 1981-82; indsl. developer Ala-Tom Regional Commn., Camden, Ala., 1983; instr. Livingston (Ala.) U., 1983-88, dir. Small Bus. Devel. Ctr., 1983-88, asst. prof., 1988-90; assoc. prof. bus. adminstrn. U. Mobile, Ala., 1990—, chair dept. bus. adminstrn., MBA dir., 1994—; dean Sch. Bus. U. Mobile, 1995—; cons. Small Bus. Devel. Ctr., Livingston, 1983-88, Mobile Law Firm, 1991. Editor Bus. and Econ. REv., 1986. Mem. Mayor's Task Force on Econ. Devel., York, Ala., 1986. Mem. Am. Mktg. Assn., Phi Eta Sigma, Beta Gamma Sigma, Gamma Iota Sigma. Baptist. Home: 22120 Mcphillips Rd Loxley AL 36551-8428 Office: U Mobile PO Box 13220 Mobile AL 36663-0220

LOWERY, F(LOYD) LYNN, JR., insurance executive; b. Milan, Tenn., Feb. 9, 1940; s. Floyd L. and Seeley (Moore) L.; m. Dale Turner, Jan. 30, 1960; children: Seeley Anne, F. L. III. BBA, U. Memphis, 1962. Regional mgr. Fidelity and Deposit Co. of Md., Memphis, 1963—. Project chmn. Phoenix Club, Memphis, 1968-75; commr. Meth. Athletic Assn. of Memphis, 1975-76. Mem. Surety Assn. Tenn., Miss. Surety Assn. Republican. Office: Fidelity and Deposit Co Md 50 N Front St 770 Morgan Keegan Tower Memphis TN 38103

LOWERY, LEE LEON, JR., civil engineer; b. Corpus Christi, Tex., Dec. 26, 1938; s. Lee Leon and Blanche (Dietrich) L.; children: Kelli Lane, Christianne Lindsey. B.S. in Civil Engring, Tex. A&M U., 1960, M.E., 1961, Ph.D., 1965. Prof. dept. civil engring. Tex. A&M U., 1960; rsch. engr. Tex. A&M Rsch. Found., 1962—; pres. Pile Dynamics Found. Engring., Inc., Bryan, Tex., 1962—; pres. Tex. Measurements, Inc., College Station, 1965—; pres. Interface Engring. Assos., Inc., College Station, 1969—; dir. Braver Corp. Bd. dirs. Deep Found. Inst. Recipient Faculty Disting. Achievement Teaching award Tex. A&M U., 1979, Zachary Teaching award, 1989, 91, award of merit Tex. A&M Hon. Soc., 1991; NDEA fellow, 1960-63. Mem. ASCE, NSPE, Tex. Soc. Profl. Engrs., Sigma Xi, Phi Kappa Phi, Tau Beta Pi. Baptist. Home: 2905 S College Ave Bryan TX 77801-2510 Office: Tex A&M U Dept Civil Engring College Station TX 77843

LOWERY, RICHARD HARLIN, religious studies educator; b. Springfield, Tenn., Apr. 8, 1957; s. Robert Harlin and Joyce Marie (McDaniel) L.; m. Sharon Elizabeth Watkins, Aug. 22, 1981; children: Bethany Watkins, Christopher Watkins. BA, U. Tenn., 1979; MDiv, Yale U., 1982, MA, 1983, MPhil, 1986, PhD, 1989. Ordained min. Disciples of Christ Ch., 1982. Adj. instr. Hebrew Yale U., New Haven, 1984; reporter, columnist Vidette-Messenger, Valparaiso, Ind., 1986-89; adj. instr. Theology Valparaiso U., 1989; asst. prof., assoc. prof. Bibl. studies Phillips U., Enid, Okla., 1989-94, assoc. prof. Old Testament, 1994—; asst. prof. preaching Phillips Theol. Sem., Enid, 1992—. Author: The Reforming Kings: Cult and Society in First Temple Judah, 1991, Revelation: Hope for the World in Trouble Times, 1994, Daniel and Revelation: Storyteller's Companion to the Bible, 1996; contbr. articles to profl. jours. Dem. nominee Okla. Legis., 1996. Mem. Soc. Bibl. Lit., Disciples Peace Fellowship. Democrat. Mem. Disciples of Christ Ch. Home: 310 N 17th St Enid OK 73701-4531 Office: Phillips Theol Sem Box 2335 Enid OK 73702

LOWERY, WILLIAM HERBERT, lawyer; b. Toledo, June 8, 1925; s. Kenneth Alden and Drusilla (Pfanner) L.; m. Carolyn Broadwell, June 27, 1947; children: Kenneth Latham, Marcia Mitchell. PhB, U. Chgo., 1947; JD, U. Mich., 1950. Bar: Pa. 1951, U.S. Supreme Ct. 1955. Assoc. Dechert Price & Rhoads, Phila., 1950-58, ptnr., 1958-89, mng. ptnr., 1970-72; mem. policy com., chmn. litigation dept., 1962-68, 81-84; of counsel Dechert Price & Rhoads, Phila., 1989—; counsel S.S. Huebner Found. Ins. Edn., Phila., 1970-89; faculty Am. Conf. of Legal Execs., Pa. Bar Inst.; permanent mem. com. of visitors U. Mich. Law Sch. Author: Insurance Litigation Problems, 1972, Insurance Litigation Disputes, 1977. Pres. Stafford Civic Assn., 1958; chmn. Tredyffrin Twp. Zoning Bd., Chester County, Pa., 1959-75; bd. dirs. Paoli (Pa.) Meml. Hosp., 1964-89, chmn., 1972-75; bd. dirs. Main Line Health, Radnor, Pa., 1984-89; permanent mem. Jud. Conf. 3d Cir. Ct. Served to 2d lt. USAF, 1943-46. Mem. ABA (chmn. life ins. com. 1984-85, chmn. Nat. Conf. Lawyers and Life Ins. Cos. 1984-88), Order of the Coif, Royal Poinciana Golf Club, Phi Gamma Delta, Phi Delta Phi. Home: Apt S-4 2777 Gulf Shore Blvd N Naples FL 34103 Office: Dechert Price & Rhoads 4000 Bell Atlantic Tower 1717 Arch St Philadelphia PA 19103-2713

LOWITZ, ROBIN ADELE, nurse administrator; b. Balt., May 29, 1954; d. Irving Robert and Sonia Dean (Krulevitz) L. BSN, U. Md., 1976; postgrad., U. Miami, Fla., 1986; cert. health mgmt., St. Thomas U., Miami, 1995; MS in Mgmt., St. Thomas U., Miami, Fla., 1996. CCRN. Staff nurse Sinai Hosp., Balt., 1976-80, Mt. Sinai Med. Ctr., Miami Beach, Fla., 1980-84; educator critical care Cedars Med. Ctr., Miami, Fla., 1984-85, nurse mgr., 1985-86; nurse pvt. duty Allied Nurses and Health Care Svcs., Miami, Fla., 1986-88, coord. mini ICU, 1988-89, dir. profl. svcs., 1989-91; staff nurse Surg. Park, Inc., Miami, Fla., 1990-91; case mgr. PayMed/Ontario Blue Cross, Bay Harbor Islands, Fla., 1991-92; nursing supr. HRS/Hurricane Andrew Relief Project, Miami, 1992-94; pre-authorization coord. Av Med Health Plan, Miami, 1994-96, mgmt. info. sys. project implementation team mem., 1996—; cons. in field. Mem. AACN, Emergency Nurses Assn. Home: 8315 SW 72nd Ave # 216 Miami FL 33143-7694 Office: AV Med Health Plan 9400 S Dadeland Blvd Miami FL 33156-2823

LOWMAN, RODNEY LEWIS, psychologist, author, educator; b. Oklahoma City, Feb. 10, 1949; s. Raymond Paul and Olga Lowman; m. Linda Richardson, July 21, 1979. B.A. in Psychology with high honors, U. Okla., 1973; B.S. in Bus., Okla. State U., 1969; M.A. in Psychology, Mich. State U., 1975, Ph.D. in Psychology, 1979. Lic. psychologist, Tex., N.C. Asst. prof. psychology, asst. research scientist Inst. Social Research, U. Mich., Ann Arbor, 1979-82; asst. prof., dir. designate Ph.D. program cons. psychology N. Tex. State U., Denton, 1982-86; dir. corp. assistance program and child and family programs, Houston Child Guidance Ctr., 1985-86, clinical faculty, Baylor Coll. and U. Tex., 1986-96, dir. occupational mental health programs Duke U., 1986-89; pres. Lowman, Richardson & Assocs., Fort Worth, 1982-86, Dallas/Fort Worth Orgnl. Psychology Group, 1984-85; CEO Devel. Labs., Houston, 1989-96; adj. full prof. dept. psychology Rice U., Houston, 1990—, dept head, prof., La. Tech. U., Ruston, Calif., 1996—, consulting faculty, Duke U. Med. Ctr., 1986—; cons. in field. Author: Counseling and Psuchotherapy of Work Dysfunctions, The Mental Health Professional's Guide to Managed Care, The Clinical Practice of Career Assessment: Interests, Abilities and Personality, Pre-Employment Screening for Psychopathology; editor The Psychologist-Mgr., 1996—; contbr. articles to profl. jours. Served to capt. USAF, 1969-72. Rochester Area Hosp. Corps. grantee, 1981-82. Fellow Am. Psychol. Assn. (ethics com. 1987-60, chair bd. profl. affairs 1993-94, com. psyuchol. tests and assessments, 1994-97), Soc. Indsl. and Organizational Psychology (head com. profl. affairs), Soc. Psychologists in Mgmt. (pres. 1993-94).

LOWNDES, JOHN FOY, lawyer; b. Medford, Mass., Jan. 1, 1931; s. Charles L. B. and Dorothy (Foy) L.; m. Rita Davies, Aug. 18, 1983; children: Elizabeth Anne, Amy Scott, John Patrick, Joseph Edward. BA, Duke U., 1953, LLB, 1958. Bar: Fla. 1958. pvt. practice, Daytona Beach, Fla., 1958, Orlando, Fla., 1959-69; sr. ptnr., chmn. bd. dirs. Lowndes, Drosdick, Doster, Kantor & Reed, P.A., Orlando, 1969—; mem. dean's adv. coun. Coll. Bus. Adminstrn. U. Cen. Fla.; bd. dirs. First Union Nat. Bank Fla.; mem. bd. trustees Winter Park Meml. Hosp.; former chmn. bd. trustees Orlando Mus. Art; bd. visitors Duke U. Served to capt. USMCR, 1953-55. Republican. Home: 1308 Green Cove Rd Winter Park FL 32789 Office: Lowndes Drosdick Doster Kantor & Reed 215 N Eola Dr Orlando FL 32801-2028

LOWRANCE, PAMELA KAY, medical/surgical nurse; b. Pensacola, Fla., July 17, 1959; d. Carl Boyce and Sara Mae (Wrenn) L. BSN, U. N.C., 1981. RN, N.C.; cert. in chemotherapy adminstrn. Staff nurse Charlotte (N.C.) Meml. Hosp. and Med. Ctr.; asst. nurse mgr. Carolinas Med. Ctr. Mem. ANA, Oncology Nursing Soc., Soc. of Gynecologic Nurse Oncologists, Sigma Theta Tau. Home: 6014 Rose Valley Dr Charlotte NC 28210-3830

LOWRIE, ALLEN, geologist, oceanographer; b. Washington, Dec. 30, 1937; s. Allen and Mary (Green) L.; m. Mildred C. McDaniel, Feb. 2, 1985; 1 child from previous marriage, Tanya Anne. BA, Columbia U., 1962. Cert. profl. geologist. Geologist, Lamont Doherty Geol. Obs., Palisades, N.Y., 1963-68; oceanographer U.S. Naval Oceanographic Office, SSC/NASA, Miss., 1968-81, 83—; geologist Mobil Oil Corp., New Orleans, 1981-83; instr. Tulane U., 1979-82, 90, U. So. Miss., 1984-86; instr. continuing edn., 1985—; cons. Mobil Research & Devel. Corp., Dallas, Sci. Applications Inc., McLean, Va., Geo-Cons Internat., Inc., Kenner, La., Seagull Internat. Exploration Inc., Houston, Planning Systems, Inc., Slidell, La., Corporacion Miners de Cerro Colorado, Republic of Panama, Hotel Drotama, Santa Marta, Colombia, others. Author: Offshore Louisiana Geology, an Offshore Exploration Model, 1988, Gulf of Mexico Salt Tectonics, Associated Processes and Exploration, 1989, Seismic Stratigraphy and Hydrocarbon Traps: Louisiana Onshore and Offshore, 1994; contbr. 60 articles to profl. jours. Mem. Am. Assn. Petroleum Geologists (vis. geologists program 1995—, cert. divsn. profl. affairs), Soc. Econ. Paleontologists and Mineralogists, N.Y. Acad. Scis., Am. Geophys. Union, Sierra Club, Sigma Xi. Episcopalian. Avocations: reading; hiking; ranching. Home: 230 F Z Goss Rd Picayune MS 39466-9458

LOWRIE, WALTER, administrator Orlando Science Ctr. Office: Orlando Sci Ctr Inc Lock Haven Park 810 E Rollins St Orlando FL 32803-1221

LOWRIE, WALTER OLIN, management consultant; b. North Braddock, Pa., Apr. 7, 1924; s. Robert Newell and Laura Rae (Essick) L.; m. Dorothy Ann Williams, Aug. 28, 1948; children: Susan, Allison, James. B.S. in Aero. Engring., MIT, 1948; Dr. Engring. (hon.), U. Central Fla., 1985. With Martin Marietta, 1948-86; v.p., program dir. Viking Program Martin Marietta, Denver, 1972-77; v.p., program dir. Missile X Martin Marietta, 1977-78, v.p. tech. ops. Denver divsn., 1978-80, v.p., gen. mgr. space and electronics, 1980-82; pres. Martin Marietta Orlando, Fla., 1982-86; pvt. practice mgmt. cons. Maitland, Fla., 1986—. Bd. dirs. U. Ctrl. Fla. Found., Orlando, 1983-91; gen. chmn. 42d Internat. Sci. and Engring. Fair, 1991; mayor City of Bow-Mar, Colo., 1964-68; mem. Colo. Gov.'s Adv. Commn. on Corrs., 1979-80; bd. dirs. Indsl. Devel. Commn. Mid-Fla. Inc., Orlando, 1983; chmn. Met. Transp. Authority of Greater Orlando, 1985-86; trustee Orlando Sci. Ctr., 1986—, chmn. bd. trustees, 1994-95. 1st lt. USAAF, 1943-45, ETO. Decorated DFC; decorated Air medal with 6 oak leaf clusters; recipient Disting. Pub. Service award NASA, 1977. Fellow Am. Astronaut. Soc.; assoc. fellow AIAA (Space Systems Engr. of Yr. award 1977). Republican. Presbyterian.

LOWRY, CHRISTINE OSSENBERG, elementary school educator; b. Corning, N.Y., June 13, 1952; d. Harry Paul and Grace Katherine (Kretz) Ossenberg; m. Peter David Lowry, Dec. 17, 1983. AA, St. Petersburg Jr. Coll., 1972; BA, U. South Fla., 1974; MS, Nova-Southea. U., 1987. Cert. elem. sch. tchr., cert. gifted edn. tchr., cert. ednl. adminstr. and supr., Fla. Tchr. Maximo Elem. Sch., St. Petersburg, Fla., 1974—; tchr. elem. gifted edn. Area IV Gifted Ctr., St. Petersburg, 1983—; tchr. gifted edn. Seminole (Fla.) Mid. Sch., 1987-93; resource tchr. Pinellas County Schs. Adminstrn., Largo, Fla., 1993—, acting supr. Magnet/Choice programs, 1996—. Mem. NEA, ASCD, Fla. Tchg. Profession, Delta Kappa Gamma (pres. Beta Omega chpt. 1996-98), Kappa Delta Pi. Home: 5041 Myrtle Ln N Saint Petersburg FL 33708 Office: Pinellas County Schs 301 4th St SW Largo FL 33770

LOWRY, LEO ELMO, former petroleum executive; b. Utopia, Kans., Dec. 4, 1916; s. Nim Roderick and Marticia (Veach) L.; B.A., Okla. A&M Coll., 1937; m. Elizabeth Watson, Sept. 5, 1940; children—Richard Clark, John Christopher, Janet Kaye. With Creole Petroleum Corp., Caracas, Venezuela, 1937-71, exec. v.p., 1961-64, pres., 1964-71; pres. Esso Inter-Am., Inc., Coral Gables, Fla., 1971-77.

LOY, RANDALL ALAN, endocrinologist; b. Mansfield, Ohio, Apr. 10, 1956; s. Ronald David and Nancy Marie (Vitello) L.; m. Julie Ann Gooding, Nov. 14, 1981; children: Jonathan Asher, Jamison Isaac. BA, UCLA, 1978; MD, Med. Coll. Ga., 1983. Diplomate Am. Bd. Ob-Gyn., subspecialty cert. in reproductive endocrinology. Intern in ob-gyn Med. Coll. Ga., Augusta, 1983-84, resident in ob-gyn, 1984-87; fellow in reproductive endocrinology Beth Israel Hosp., Harvard Med. Sch., Boston, ;1987-88, Yale Univ. Sch. Medicine, New Haven, 1988-89; ptnr. Ctr. Infertility Reproductive Medicine, Orlando, Fla., 1989—, Southeastern Reproductive Medicine Assocs., 1996—; med. dir. Orlando Surgery Ctr., 1995—; co-chmn. Am. Reproductive Medicine Specialists, 1996—. Ad hoc rev. Fertility and Sterility, 1989—; contbr. over 20 articles to profl. jours. Bd. dirs. House of Hope, Orlando, 1994-95, Restore Orlando, 1996—. Fellow AMA, ACOG; mem. Am. Soc. Reproductive Medicine, Soc. Reproductive Endocrinologists, Soc. Assisted Reproductive Techs., Fla. Med. Assn., Alaqua Country Club, Heathrow Country Club, Sigma Xi, Alpha Omega Alpha. Republican. Office: Ctr Infertility Reproductive Medicine 3435 Pinehurst Ave Orlando FL 32804-4049

LOYER-DAVIS, SHARON LYNN, social services administrator, author, poet; b. Norfolk, Va., May 23, 1949; d. Alfred Augustine Jr. and Elsie Anne (McBride) Loyer; m. Raymond Grover Davis, June 22, 1968 (div. June 1, 1992); children: Rebecca Ann, Daniel Raymond. AA, Hillsborough C.C., Tampa, Fla., 1983; BS in Mktg. and Distributive Edn., U. South Fla., 1990. Libr. asst. Tampa-Hillsborough County Pub. Libr. System, 1970-71, 75-85; co-owner family bus. Brandon, Fla., 1975-92; clerical asst. Office of V.P., Hillsborough C.C., Tampa, 1990—; case mgr. Dept. of Aging Svcs., Community Care for the Elderly, Tampa, 1990—; info. and referral task force mem. Dept. Aging Svcs., Orlando, 1992, invited presenter conv., 1991, 92; CIRTS steering body mem. Dept. Elder Affairs, State of Fla., 1993—; apptd. alt. del. White House Conf. on Aging, State of Fla., 1995, Info. & Referral Steering Body, Dept. of Elder Affairs, 1995. Poetry pub. in anthologies including A Question of Balance, 1992, Distinguished Poets of the United States, 1993, Galeria, 1992, 93; author various tng. materials. Del. Nat. Issues Forum, Washington, 1993. Recipient Editor's Choice award for 1993 poetry pub. Nat. Libr. Poetry. Mem. Assn. of Info. and Referral Specialists, Fla. Coun. on Aging, Am. Soc. on Aging. Office: Hillsborough Dept Aging Svc 25th Fl 601 E Kennedy Blvd Fl 25 Tampa FL 33602-4932

LOZANO, JOSE, nephrologist; b. San Vicente, El Salvador, Feb. 11, 1941; came to U.S., 1968; s. Jose E. and Transito Maria (Mendez) L.; m. Hilda Berganza, Jan. 27, 1965; children: Jose E., Claudia Maria. MD, U. El Salvador, 1965. Diplomate Am. Bd. Internal Medicine, Am. Bd. Nephrology. Rotating intern Nat. Med. Ctr., San Salvador, El Salvador, 1963-64; asst. resident in internal medicine Rosales Hosp., San Salvador, 1965-66, resident in internal medicine, 1966-67, chief resident in internal medicine, 1967-68; resident in internal medicine Baylor U. Affiliated Hosps., Houston, 1968-70, fellow in nephrology, 1970-71, 73-74; asst. prof. medicine U. El Salvador, 1971-72; internist and nephrologist Social Security Hosp., San Salvador, 1971-72; instr. in medicine Baylor Coll. Medicine, Houston, 1974-75, asst. prof. medicine in nephrology, 1975-76, clin. asst. prof. medicine, 1976-80; mem. staff internal medicine St. Elizabeth Hosp., Beaumont Med./Surg. Hosp., Bapt. Hosp., Beaumont, Tex., 1976; med. dir. Golden Triangle Dialysis Ctr., Beaumont, 1977—, BMA Jasper, Jasper, Tex., 1986, BMA Orange, Orange, Tex., 1987-90; med. dir. Golden Triangle Dialysis Ctr., Beaumont, 1977; med. dir. BMA Jasper, Tex., 1986, Orange, Tex., 1987-90; mem. Kidney Health Care Adv. Com., 1981-82; pesenter in field. Contbr. articles to profl. publs. Mem. AMA, ACP, Am. Soc. Nephrology, Internat. Soc. Nephrology, Tex. Med. Assn., Harris County Med. Soc., Jefferson County Med. Soc., Am. Coll. Physicians Execs., Physicians for A Nat. Health Plan. Home: 4655 Ashdown St Beaumont TX 77706-7723 Office: Beaumont Nephrology Assocs 3282 College St Beaumont TX 77701-4610

LU, DAN, systems analyst, mathematician, consultant; b. Beijing, Jan. 22, 1960; came to U.S., 1981; s. Yingzhong Lu and Huaiqing Chen; m. Hong Lou, Sept. 28, 1994; 1 child, Katherine H. BS in Physics, Beijing U., 1981; MS in Physics, U. Wash., 1983, PhD in Theoretical Physics, 1986. Tchg., rsch. asst. U. Wash., Seattle, 1981-86; postdoctoral rsch. assoc. Washington U., St. Louis, 1986-88; R&D mgr. Yu Feng Internat. Ltd., Hong Kong, 1988-90; sys. cons. Summit Computer Svcs., Charlotte, N.C., 1991-93; sr. sys. cons. Criterion Group, Charlotte, 1993-94; bus. sys. analyst, mathematician CMS, Inc., Winston-Salem, N.C., 1994—. Contbr. articles to profl. publs. China-U.S. Physics Examination and Application fellow, 1981. Mem. Am. Phys. Soc. Home: 325 Craver Pointe Dr Clemmons NC 27012 Office: CMS Inc 2650 Pilgrim Ct Winston Salem NC 27106

LU, MING-HSIUNG, research biologist; b. Taoyuan, Taiwan, Jan. 4, 1937; came to U.S., 1967; s. Chou-Fang Lu and Shen Lin; m. Chun-Hua Chen, July 8, 1969; children: Eugene Lu, Torence Lu, Ellen Lu. BS, Nat. Taiwan U., Taipei, 1960, MS, 1964; PhD, U. Mo., 1972; postdoctoral, Johns Hopkins U., 1978. Teaching asst. Nat. Taiwan U., 1964-66, lectr., 1966-67; rsch. asst. U. Mo., Columbia, 1967-72; rsch. assoc. Med. Health Sci. Ctr. U. Tenn., Memphis, 1972-73; vis. fellow Nat. Inst. Environ. Health Scis., Research Triangle Park, N.C., 1973-76; postdoctoral fellow, teratologist med. sch. Johns Hopkins U., Balt., 1976-78; rsch. teratologist and toxicologist Haskall Lab for Toxicology and Indsl. Medicine, Dupont Co., Newark, Del., 1978-82; sr. teratologist Program Resources Inc./Nat. Ctr. for Toxicological Rsch., Jefferson, Ark., 1983-84; rsch. assoc., adj. instr. U. Ark. for Med. Scis., Little Rock, 1984-87; rsch. biologist, scientist Nat. Ctr. for Toxicological Rsch., Jefferson, Ark., 1987—, Asian/Pacific Islander program rep., 1992-96; adj. asst. prof. dept. pediatrics U. Ark. for Med. Scis., Little Rock, 1996—; participant 3rd Internat. Rad. Biol. Tng., IAEA, Tel-Aviv, Israel, 1967. Author: Biological Oxidation System, Vol. 2, 1990, The Cell Cycle: Regulation Target and Clinical Applications, 1994, Dietary Restriction: Implications for the Design and Interpretation of Toxicity and Carcinogenicity Studies, 1995. 2nd lt. Taiwan Infantry, 1961-62. Scholar U. Mo., 1967-72; grantee Am. Inst. for Cancer Rsch./Nat. Ctr. for Toxicological Rsch., 1994-96. Mem. Am. Assn. for Cancer Rsch., Soc. Toxicology (Mid Atlantic chpt. 1981-83, South Ctrl. chpt. 1983—), Teratology Soc., Sigma Xi. Office: Nat Ctr for Toxicological Rsch 3900 Nctr Rd Jefferson AR 72079-9502

LU, QUN, cell biologist, educator; b. Shanghai, China, Feb. 22, 1960; s. Ding Zong Lu and Li Ying Qian; m. Yan-Hua Chen, Sept. 2, 1986; Yian-Hope Lu, Wendy Lu. BS in Biochemistry, East China Normal U., 1982, MS in Zoology, 1985; PhD in Anatomy and Cell Biology, Emory U., 1993. Rsch. asst. dept. biology U. Iowa, Iowa City, 1986-87; rsch. specialist Emory U., Atlanta, 1987-88, rsch. assoc., rsch. fellow, 1993—; sci. cons. Ga. Biomed. Equipment, Atlanta, 1994; presenter numerous seminars, confs. Contbr. articles, abstracts to profl. jours. Recipient award Marine Biol. Lab., Woods Hole, Mass., 1989, Cold Spring Harbor Lab., N.Y., 1993, rsch. award Sigma Xi, 1992. Mem. AAAS, Am. Soc. Cell Biology (Dorothea C. Wilson Travel award 1991), Am. Soc. Neuroscience, Chinese Soc. Cell Biology, Sigma Xi (Grad. Student Rsch. award 1992). Office: Emory U Sch Medicine Dept Anatomy & Cell Biology 1648 Pierce Dr Atlanta GA 30322

LU, YICHI, materials scientist; b. Shanghai, China, Feb. 20, 1956; came to U.S., 1985; s. Zhongyong Lu and Meide Zhang; m. Nansun Liang, Mar. 7, 1985; 1 child, Binhong. B in Engring., Shanghai Jiaotong U., 1982, M in Engring., 1984; PhD, Northwestern U., 1990. Sr. scientist U. Va., Charlottesville, 1990—. Mem. ASME. Office: U Va Dept Materials Sci Charlottesville VA 22903

LU, YINGZHONG, nuclear engineer, educator, researcher; b. Jiangsu, People's Republic China, June 24, 1926; came to U.S., 1988; s. Zheng and Yi Lu; m. Huaiquing Chen; 1 child, Dan. BSc, Tsinghua U., Beijing, China, 1950. Teaching asst. Tsinghua U., Beijing, 1950-52, lectr., 1952-60, assoc. prof., 1960-79, prof., 1979—, dir. inst. nuclear energy tech., 1960-85, dir. inst. for techno-econs. and energy system analysis, 1985—; tech. advisor Profl. Analysis Inc., Oak Ridge, Tenn., 1990—; advisor Sages' group of energy and environment World Bank, Washington, 1990-91; advisor internat. panel energy program Office of Tech. Assessment, Washington, 1990-92; advisor sci. and tech. panel Global Environment Facility, World Bank, UN Devel. Program and UN Environ. Program, Washington and Nairobi, Kenya, 1991-93. Author: Fueling One Billion--Chinese Energy Policy, 1993, 14 other books and monographs; contbr. more than 60 articles to profl. jours.; patentee in field. Recipient 1st Grade Sci. & Tech. Advance award Chinese Govt., 1988, 3d Grade Sci. & Tech. Advance award, 1987. Mem. Am. Nuclear Soc., China Nuclear Soc.

LUBBS, GRESILDA ANNE TILLEY, secondary school educator; b. Oak Hill, W.Va., June 7, 1946; d. Albert Thurmon and Anna Gresilda (Fox) Tilley; m. Daniel Raymond Lubbs, Jan. 1, 1972; children: Kirsten Elizabeth, Eowyn Gresilda, Peter Christian Daniel. Diploma, U. Salamanca, Spain, 1969; BA, U. Ill., 1969, MS, 1970; postgrad., Hollins Coll., 1990. Cert. Spanish tchr., music tchr., Va. Rsch. asst., teaching asst. U. Ill., Champaign, 1969-70; music tchr. Elgin (Ill.) Pub. Schs., 1972, Spanish tchr., 1972-74; tchr. ESL Ill. Migrant Coun. and YWCA, Elgin and Aurora, Ill., 1971-74; tchr. ESOL Modesto (Calif.) Jr. Coll., 1979-80; choir dir. Oak Grove Ch. of the Brethren, Roanoke, Va., 1983-84; pvt. piano and voice tchr. Roanoke, 1980-88, Mt. Morris, Ill., 1980-88; Spanish tchr. Va. Western C.C., Mt. Morris, 1985-89; Spanish tchr., head dept. Glenvar H.S., Salem, Va., 1988—; piano and voice tchr., Mt. Morris, Ill., 1975-77, Roanoke, 1980-88, Va. Western C.C., Roanoke; cons. Heinle and Heinle Pubs., Boston, 1993-94. Named Roanoke County Tchr. of the Yr., Roanoke County Pub. Sch., 1994; James scholar, 1964-66. Mem. NEA, Va. Edn. Assn., Roanoke Tchrs. Assn., Fgn. Lang. Assn. Va., Am. Assn. Tchrs. Spanish and Portuguese (Va. chpt. v.p.), Alpha Delta Kappa. Democrat. Mem. Ch. of the Brethren. Home: 5007 Mount Holland Dr SW Roanoke VA 24018-1631 Office: Glenvar High Sch 4549 Malus Dr Salem VA 24153-7921

LUBIN, IRA MARTIN, molecular biologist, biochemist; b. Wilmington, Del., Mar. 18, 1959; s. Harry and Helen (Cylinder) L. BS in Chemistry, BA in Biology, U. Del., 1981; PhD in Chemistry, U. S.C., 1986. IRTA fellow NIH, Bethesda, Md., 1986-89; NRSA fellow in cardiology Emory U., Atlanta, 1989-93, instr. in hematology, 1993—. Mem. AAAS. Office: Emory Univ Dept Hematology Drawer AJ Atlanta GA 30322

LUBKER, JOHN WILLIAM, II, manufacturing executive, civil engineer; b. Indpls., Jan. 11, 1943; s. John William and Wilhelmina Jane (Zieglar) L.; m. Kathy Sue Kiel, June 20, 1970; 1 child, John Ryan. BSCE, Purdue U., 1968. Project engr. Amoco Plastics Products, Seymour, Ind., 1968-72; tech. sales rep. Amoco Plastics Products, Seymour, 1972-75; project mgr. venture group Amoco Chem. Co., Chgo., 1975-77; so. sales mgr. Amoco Container Co., Norcross, Ga., 1978-79; mgr. mktg. svcs. Amoco Container Co., Atlanta, 1979-80; plant mgr. Amoco Container Co., Worcester, Mass., 1980-83; project devel. mgr. Amoco Foam Products Co., Atlanta, 1983-85; mgr. new technology Amoco Foam Products Co., Smyrna, Ga., 1986-87; mgr. process devel. Amoco Foam Products Co., Smyrna, 1988-90; mgr. cups Amoco Foam Products Co., Atlanta, 1991-92, mgr. venture team, 1992-93, mktg. mgr. indsl. products, 1994-96; mktg. mgr. Tenneco Bldg. Products, Smyrna, Ga., 1997—. Patentee in field. Mem. Soc. Packaging & Handling Engr., Soc. Plastic Engrs., Nat. Soc. Profl. Engrs., Ga. Soc. Profl. Engrs., Soc. Plastics Inc. Lutheran. Home: 8895 Willowbrae Ln Roswell GA 30076-3572 Office: Tenneco Bldg Products 2907 Log Cabin Dr Smyrna GA 30080-7013

LUCAS, AUBREY KEITH, university president; b. State Line, Miss., July 12, 1934; s. Keith Caldwell and Audelle Margaret (Robertson) L.; m. Ella Frances Ginn, Dec. 18, 1955; children: Margaret Frances, Keith Godbold (dec.), Martha Carol, Alan Douglas, Mark Christopher. BS, U. So. Miss., 1955, MA, 1956; PhD, Fla. State U., 1966. Instr. Hinds Jr. Coll., Raymond, Miss., 1956-57; pres. Delta State U., Cleveland, Miss., 1971-75; asst. dir. reading clinic U. So. Miss., Hattiesburg, 1955-56, dir. admissions, 1957-61, registrar, 1963-69, dean Grad. Sch., 1969-71, pres., 1975-96, pres. emeritus, prof. higher edn., 1997—. Author: The Mississippi Legislature and Mississippi Public Higher Education, 1890-1960; contbg. author: A History of Mississippi, 1973. Bd. dirs. Pine Burr Area coun. Boy Scouts Am., Miss. Inst. Tech. Devel., Miss. Power Co., Miss. Assn. Coll., 1979-80, Miss. Arts Commn., 1977-87, Salvation Army, Pine Burr; mem. gen. bd. Global Ministries, United Meth. Ch., 1984-92, mem. gen. bd. higher edn. and ministry, 1992—; chmn. Miss. Arts Commn., 1983-85; campaign chmn. Forest United Way, 1979, So. U. Conf., 1995—; state chmn. Am. Cancer Soc., 1978; mem. Commn. on Nat. Devel. Postsecondary Edn., 97th Congress; pres. Miss. Econ. Coun., 1982-83; lay leader Miss. Meth. Conf., 1980-88, mem. adminstrv. bd., 1989-92; bd. visitors Air U., 1990-94, chmn., 1991-92; mem. exec. bd. Commn. on Colls. of So. Assn. Colls. and Schs., 1990-93. Mem. So. Assn. Colls. and Schs. (mem. exec. bd. commn. on colls. 1990-93, v.p. commn. on colls. 1993, mem. exec. coun.), Hattiesburg C. of C., Miss. Forestry Assn., Newcomen Soc. N.Am., Am. Assn. State Colls. and Univs. (bd. dirs. 1982-86, chmn. 1984-85), Am. Coun. Edn. (bd. dirs. 1984-86), Miss. Inst. Arts and Letters, Red Red Rose Club, Sigma Phi Epsilon, Omicron Delta Kappa, Phi Kappa Phi, Pi Gamma Mu, Pi Tau Chi, Kappa Delta Pi, Phi Delta Kappa, Kappa Pi. Home: 3701 Jamestown Rd Hattiesburg MS 39402-2336 Office: U So Miss PO Box 5001 Hattiesburg MS 39406-5001

LUCAS, CAROLYN HOLDEN, procurement analyst; b. Madison, Ala., Aug. 12, 1954; d. Thomas Holden and Lizzie Fletcher; m. Willie Lucas (div. Oct. 1982). BS, N.Y. State U., 1991; MS, Fla. Inst. Tech., 1994. Clk. typist U.S. Army Missile Command, Redstone Arsenal, Ala., 1971-72; procurement clk./sec. U.S. Army Corps of Engrs., Huntsville, Ala., 1972-78, purchasing agt., 1978-89; contract specialist U.S. Army Missile Command, Redstone Arsenal, 1982-89; contracting specialist U.S. Army Space Strategic Def. Command, Huntsville, 1989-93, procurement analyst, 1993—. Assoc. min. Union Hill Primitive Bapt. Ch., Huntsville, 1986—, outreach ministry dir., 1986—, alcohol and drug abuse counselor, 1989—; vol. Huntsville Boys and Girls Club, Mason Ct., Huntsville, 1986—; mem. Greater Huntsville Interdenominational Ministerial Fellowship, 1987—. Recipient Comty. Leadership award Twenty Disting. Men, 1995. Mem. Nat. Contract Mgmt. Assn., Nat. Assn. Black Procurement Profls. (pres. pro tem 1995-96). Home: 6215 Colfax Rd Huntsville AL 35810 Office: US Army Space and Strategic Def Command 106 Wynn Dr Huntsville AL 35807

LUCAS, FRANK D., congressman; b. Cheyenne, Okla., Jan. 6, 1960; m. Lynda L. Bradshaw, 1988. BS, Okla. State U., 1982. Mem. Okla. Ho. of Reps., 1989-94, 103d Congress from 6th Okla. Dist., 1994—. Baptist. Office: US Ho of Reps 107 Cannon Bldg Washington DC 20515-0003 Home: Rte 2 Box 136A Cheyenne OK 73628

LUCAS, GREGORY CHARLES, sports announcer; b. Kokomo, Ind., Mar. 3, 1946; s. Charles Edward and Estella Marie (Small) L.; m. Yong Ae (Park) Lucas, Dec. 12, 1972; 1 child, Alexander Charles. BS in Radio and TV, Butler U., 1969; cert., Def. Info. Sch., Dept. Def., 1970. Sports dir./announcer Sta. WMBD-AM-FM-TV, Peoria, Ill., 1975-78; sports/baseball play-by-play announcer Sta. WEBR-AM, Buffalo, 1978-80; sports dir. Sta. WOAI-AM, San Antonio, 1980-83; announcer San Antonio Spurs, 1980-82, Houston Rockets, Sta. KTXH-TV, 1982-85, Ind. Pacers, Indpls., 1986-87; announcer coll. basketball Raycom, Inc., Charlotte, N.C., 1988-94; play-by-play announcer—all sports—Fox Sports Net Fox Sports SW, Houston and Dallas, 1983—; play-by-play announcer Tex. Rangers baseball Home Sports Entertainment, Houston and Dallas, 1988-95; past announcer various sporting events, including World championship tennis, yacht racing, U. Ill. basketball, Bradley U. basketball, others, 1960s through mid 1970s. With U.S. Army, 1969-72, Korea. Recipient Spl. Svcs. to Soccer award Honolulu Soccer Assn., 1973; inducted into Tex. Baseball Hall of Fame, 1994. Mem. Am. Sportscasters Assn., U.S. Basball Fedn., Soc. for Am. Baseball Rsch. Home: 4430 Carnelian Ct Houston TX 77072-1830 Office: Fox Sports SW 5251 Gulfton St Houston TX 77081-2907

LUCAS, JOHN ALLEN, lawyer; b. Washington, Aug. 1, 1943; s. George Luther and Opal (McCollum) L.; m. Carol Kaine, June 7, 1969; children: John Christian, Helen Elizabeth, David Marshall, Kerri Christine. BS, U.S. Mil. Acad., 1969; JD, U. Tex., 1977. Bar: Va. 1978, Tenn. 1984, N.Y. 1986. Assoc. Hunton & Williams, Richmond, Va., 1977-83; ptnr. Hunton & Williams, Knoxville, Tenn., 1984—; prof. law U. Richmond, 1979-80; lectr. various legal seminars, 1979—. Contbr. articles to profl. jours. Bd. dirs. Knoxville Boys Club, 1984-88; bd. dirs. Tenn. Juvenile Diabetes Assn., 1989—. Capt. U.S. Army, 1969-74. Mem. ABA, Va. Bar Assn., Tenn. Bar Assn. Roman Catholic. Office: Hunton & Williams PO Box 951 Knoxville TN 37901-0951

LUCAS, MELINDA ANN, pediatrician, educator; b. Maryville, Tenn., June 27, 1953; d. Arthur Baldwin and Dorthy (Shields) L. BA, Maryville Coll., 1975; MS, U. Tenn., 1976, MD, 1981; postgrad., U. Tenn. Law Sch., 1992-93. Diplomate Am. Bd. Pediatrics; lic. dr. N.Y., Tenn. Intern in pediatrics U. Rochester, N.Y., 1981-82, resident in pediatrics, 1982-84; pvt. practice, Maryville, 1984-85; emergency room pediatrician U. Tenn. Med. Ctr., Knoxville, 1985-90, dir. child abuse clinic, 1987-90, pediatric intensivist, 1987—, acting dir. pediatric ICU, 1990-92, mem. faculty, 1988—; fellow in pediatric critical care U. Mich., Ann Arbor, 1995-96; mem. Pediatric Cons., Inc. Knoxville; physician rep. Project Search Working Symposium, 1990—. Contbr. articles to profl. jours. Mem. Blount County Foster Care Rev. Bd., Maryville, Tenn., 1985-93, Blount County Exec. Bd. Maryville Coll. Alumni Assn., 1988-92. Fellow U. Tenn. Genetics Ctr., 1988-89, pediatric critical care fellow U. Mich., 1995-96; scholar United Presbyn. Ch., 1971, Mary Lou Braly scholar, 1971-74; grantee AAP-NHTSA for Safe Ride Program. Fellow Am. Acad. Pediatrics; mem. AMA (Physician Recognition award 1984-87, 88-91, 91-94, 94-97), Am. Profl. Soc. on Abuse of Children, Tenn. Pediatric Soc. (co-chmn. accident and injury prevention com. 1993-95), Knoxville Area Pediatric Soc., Soc. Critical Care Medicine (abstract reviewer 1991, 92, 93, 94). Methodist. Home: 1608 Mcilvaine Dr Maryville TN 37803-6230

LUCAS-TAUCHAR, MARGARET FRANCES, university official; b. Jackson, Miss., Oct. 24, 1956; d. Aubrey Keith and Ella (Ginn) Lucas; m. Paul Raymond Tauchar, Dec. 29, 1990; children: Michael Lucas, Anna Catherine. BA, Miss. State U., 1978; MA, U. Ala., Tuscaloosa, 1980, PhD, 1985; postgrad., Harvard U., 1989. Community program dir. YMCA, Tuscaloosa, 1978-79; residence hall dir. U. Ala., Tuscaloosa, 1979-80, 80-81, area coord., 1981-83, residence life dir., 1983; asst. dean for student life Miss. State U., Starkville, 1983-86; v.p. for student affairs Baldwin-Wallace Coll., Berea, Ohio, 1986-92; v.p. for campus life Emory U., Atlanta, 1992—. Author: The Partnership Model, 1986, Off To College, 1990, Invisible Leaders: Student Affairs Mid-Managers, 1990. Mem. Am. Coll. Pers. Assn., Assn. Fraternity Advisors, Nat. Assn. Student Pers., Am. Coun. of Edn., Bus. and Profl. Women (pres. Berea 1990). Methodist. Home: 1391 Cedar Post Ct Decatur GA 30033-2123 Office: Emory U Atlanta GA 30322

LUCE, EDWARD ANDREW, plastic surgeon; b. Syracuse, N.Y., Mar. 5, 1940; s. Edward Andrew and Constance Faith (Jones) L.; m. Rebecca Sue Wall; children: Darcie, Michael. BS, U. Dayton, 1961; MD, U. Ky., 1965. Diplomate Am. Bd. Surgery, Am. Bd. Plastic Surgery (chmn. 1990-91). Resident in surgery Barnes Hosp., St. Louis, 1965-71; resident in plastic surgery Johns Hopkins Hosp., Balt., 1971-73, asst. prof. plastic surgery, 1973-75; assoc. prof. plastic surgery U. Ky., Lexington, 1975-87, prof. plastic surgery, 1987-95, chief plastic surgery, 1975-95; chief plastic surgery VA Hosp., 1975-95; Kiehn-DesPrez prof. surgery Case Western Reserve U., Cleve., 1995—; chief plastic surgery U. Hosps. of Cleve., 1995—, VA Hosp., Cleve., 1995—; attending plastic surgeon St. Joseph Hosp., Lexington, 1975-95, Good Samaritan Hosp., Lexington, 1978-95, Humana Hosp., Lexington, 1982-95; Kiehn-DesPrez Prof. and Chief of Plastic Surgery, Case Western Reserve U. and Univ. Hosps. of Cleveland; pres. Assn. Acad. Chmn. of Plastic Surgery, 1989-90, Am. Soc. Maxillofacial Surgeons, 1990-91, Southeastern Soc. Plastic and Reconstructive Surgeons, 1992-93. Pres. U. Ky. Med. Alumni Assn., 1977-78; pres. John Hoopes Plastic Surgery Found., 1993. Recipient Clinician of Yr., Am. Assn. Plastic Surgeons, 1990. Mem. Plastic Surgery Ednl. Found. (pres. 1993-94), Am Coll. Surgeons, Am. Surg. Assn., So. Surg. Assn., Am. Soc. Plastic and Reconstructive Surgeons, Soc. Head and Neck Surgeons. Office: Univ Hosp Lakeside Plastic Surgery 11100 Euclid Ave Cleveland OH 44106-1736

LUCE, THOMAS WARREN, III, former chief justice, lawyer; b. Dallas, June 18, 1940; s. Thomas Warren and Ruth (Hardy) L.; m. Phoebe Ann McCain; children: Ken, Ellen Luce Tucker, Susan. Student, Va. Mil. Inst.; BBA in Acctg., So. Meth. U., 1963, LLB, 1966. Bar: Tex. 1966, U.S. Dist. Ct. (no. dist.) Tex. 1966, U.S. Supreme Ct. 1971, U.S. Ct. Appeals (2d cir.) N.Y. 1976, U.S. Ct. Appeals (5th cir.) La. 1981, U.S. Ct. Appeals (11th cir.) Ga. 1981. Assoc. McKenzie & Baer, Dallas, 1966-67; assoc. then ptnr. Jenkens, Spradley & Gilchrist, Dallas, 1968-73; ptnr. Hughes & Luce, Dallas, 1973—, mng. ptnr., 1973-87; chief justice pro tempore Tex. Supreme Ct., Dallas, 1988. Bd. dirs., trustee So. Meth. U., Dallas; bd. dirs., founding mem. Episcopal Sch. Dallas; bd. dirs. Dallas Citizen Council; chmn. Tex. Nat. Rsch. Lab. Commn., 1987-89. Mem. ABA, Tex. Bar Assn., Dallas Bar Assn. Club: Salesmanship of Dallas. Office: Hughes & Luce 1717 Main St Ste 2800 Dallas TX 75201-7342

LUCIAK, ILJA ALEXANDER, political science educator; b. Gmunden, Austria, May 15, 1956; came to U.S., 1980; s. Gregor and Diane (af Wirsèn) L.; m. Jane E. Goette, May 25, 1991; 1 child, Carl David. LLM, U. Vienna, Austria, 1979; JD, U. Vienna, 1980; MA in Polit. Sci., U. Iowa, 1981, PhD in Polit. Sci., 1987. Vis. prof. polit. sci. U. Ctrl. Am., Managua, Nicaragua, 1984-85; Soc. for Humanities postdoctoral fellow Cornell U., Ithaca, N.Y., 1989-90; assoc. prof. Va. Poly. Inst. and State U., Blacksburg, 1987—; sec. dept. polit. sci. Va. Poly. Inst. and State U., 1987-88, undergrad. course advisor, 1988-89, 90-92, editor dept. newsletter, 1987-89; advisor Va. Poly. Inst. and State U. chpt. Pi Sigma Alpha, 1987-89, 90—; cons. Swedish Internat. Devel. Authority, Nicaragua, 1989-90; participant, presenter various profl. confs., 1985—. Author: The Sandinista Legacy: Lesons From a Political Economy in Transition, 1995; contbr. chpt. to: Understanding the Central American Crisis: Sources of Conflict, U.S. Policy, and Options for Peace, 1991; contbr. articles to conf. procs., articles and revs. to profl. jours., including Latin Am. Perspectives, Scandinavian Jour. Devel. Alts., Jour. Latin Am. Studies; article referee Legis. Studies Quar., Rev. of Internat. Polit. Economy. Named Outstanding Prof. of Yr., Va. Poly. Inst. and State U. chpt. Pi Sigma Alpha, 1993—; recipient NEH Summer Inst. award Cornell U., 1990; Austrian Govt. fellow, 1975-79, Swedish Govt. Internat. postgrad. fellow, 1979-80. Mem. Am. Polit. Sci. Assn. (panel chairperson/discussant ann. meeting 1988, fgn. travel grantee 1983), Internat. Polit. Sci. Assn., Latin Am. Studies Assn. (panel co-organizer internat. congress 1989), Internat. Studies Assn. (panel co-chairperson ann. meeting 1990), Nordic Assn. for Rsch. on Latin Am., Oesterreichische Gesellschaft fuer Politikwissenschaft. Office: Va Poly Inst and State U Dept Polit Sci Blacksburg VA 24061

LUCIER, JAMES ALFRED, advertising executive; b. Grand Forks, N.D., Feb. 5, 1920; s. Alfred Joseph and Mildred Perry (Fahar) L.; BA, U. Minn., 1946; postgrad. U. So. Methodist, 1965; m. Juliann K. Dunlap, July 26, 1991; children: Edward, Kelley, John, Jane, Teddi, James. Sales exec. Times, Ft. Smith, Ark., 1946-47; sales mgr. KRKN, Ft. Smith, 1947-48; dir. advt. Times, Fayetteville, Ark., 1948-51; sales exec. Express, San Antonio, 1952-53; mgr. Sunday mag. Times, Dallas, 1953-65; dir. advt. and advt. and pub. rels. Home Furniture Co., Dallas, 1965-81; advt. mgr. Smith Furniture Co., Dallas, 1981-85; v.p./gen. mgr. Home Furnishings Internat. Assn., 1985—; owner Lucier Assocs. Advt., Dallas, 1965—. Assoc. pub. Home Furnishings Rev., 1986—. Unit chmn. United Way, 1965-81; precinct chmn. Democratic Party, 1974-85; mem. bd. Dem. Forum, 1974-75; pres. bd. dirs. Dallas coun. USO; mem. orgns. com. Greater Dallas Sesquicentennial Com., 1983-86. Served with inf., AUS, 1942-44, USAAF, 1944-45, USAF, 1951-52. Decorated Air medal with 2 oak leaf clusters. Mem. Retail Furniture Assn. Greater Dallas (pres. 1971-72, pres. 1983-84, dir. 1972-85), Sigma Delta Chi, Theta Chi. Episcopalian. Clubs: Exchange (pres. E.Dallas 1967, pres. Tex. dist. 1969-70, nat. dir. 1970-72, chmn. nat. edn. com. 1974-76, fin. com. 1976-80), U. Minn. Alumni (past pres.), Vagabond, Dallas Magic Circle (past pres.). Home: 4345 Meadowdale Ln Dallas TX 75229-5339 Office: Home Furnishings Internat Assn 110 World Trade Ctr Dallas TX 75258

LUCIO, EDUARDO ANDRES, JR., former state senator; b. Brownsville, Tex., Jan. 20, 1946; s. Eduardo Andres Sr. and Josefa (Liendo) L.; m. Herminia Cerda, Feb. 21, 1968; children: Lynda Anne, Eddie III. BS in Edn., Pan Am. U., 1972. County treas. Cameron County, Brownsville, 1971-78, county commr., 1979-82; state rep. Ho. of Reps., Brownsville, 1987-90; state senator Tex. State, Brownsville, 1991-92; state pres. County Treas. Assn. Tex., Brownsville, 1976. Past pres. West Brownsville Lions Club; active Civil Air Patrol, Brownsville. Recipient Jose Maria Morelos de Pavon award Assn. Newspaper Editors of Mex., 1989, Legis. Leadership award Tex. C. of C., 1991; named Legislator of Yr. Tex. Mcpl. League, 1991, South Tex. Tort Reformer of Yr. Tex. Civil Justice League, 1991. Mem. Nat. Fedn. Ind. Bus. Democrat. Roman Catholic. Office: Tex Senate Office 33 N Park Dr Brownsville TX 78520-4326

LUCK, GREGORY MATTHEW, lawyer; b. Lubbock, Tex., Jan. 21, 1960; s. Bill Joe and N.L. Luck. BS, Tex. A&M U., 1982; JD with honors, South Tex. Coll., 1986. Bar: Tex. 1986, U.S. Dist. Ct. (no. dist.) Calif. 1988, U.S. Dist. Ct. (so. dist.) Calif. 1990, Calif. 1993, U.S. Dist. Ct. (ea. dist.) Calif. 1993, U.S. Dist. Ct. (no. dist.) Tex. 1993; registered Cen. States Patent and Trademark Office 1987. Assoc. Arnold, White and Durkee, Houston, 1985-90, Lyon & Lyon, L.A., 1990-92; ptnr. Sankey & Luck, LLP, Houston, 1995—. Contbr. articles to profl. jours. (award 1988). Mem. ABA, Am. Intellectural Property Law Assn., Houston Intellectural Property Assn., Houston Young Lawyers Assn., Dallas Bar Assn. Republican. Methodist. Home: 11507 Del Monte Houston TX 77077 Office: Sankey & Luck LLP 6500 Tex Comm Tower 600 Travis Houston TX 77002

LUCKES, MARY HELEN B., mental health nurse; b. Nashville; d. George Armistice and Vivian E. Baum; m. Douglas S. Luckes. ADN, Brunswick Jr. Coll., 1970; BSN, Armstrong State Coll., 1977; MSN, Med. Coll. Ga., 1986. RN, Ga., Fla., S.C.; cert. C.S. in adult psychiat., mental health nursing, ANA. Sr. staff nurse Med. Coll. Ga., Augusta; clin. nurse specialist U. Hosp. Jacksonville (Fla.), William S. Hall Psychiat. Inst., Columbia, S.C. Mem. S.C. Nurses Assn., Sigma Theta Tau (Alpha Xi chpt.). Home: 205 Cherry Stone Dr Columbia SC 29223

LUCKTENBERG, GEORGE HAZARD, classical musician; b. Columbus, Ohio, June 30, 1930; s. Dewey and Kathryn (Okey) L.; m. Jerrie Marie Girard Cadek, June 7, 1953 (div. 1985); children: Judith L. Arrants, Kathryn L. Pologe, G. Ted. BMus, U. Ill., 1952, MMus, 1953; diploma, State Acad. Music, Vienna, Austria, 1957; DMus, Fla. State U., 1965. Instr. music U. Ala., Tuscaloosa, 1953-56; asst. prof. music U. Chattanooga, 1957-60; prof. music Converse Coll., Spartanburg, S.C., 1960-90, Clayton State Coll., Morrow, 1991-94; artist-in-residence, adj. prof. music Reinhardt Coll., Waleska, Ga., 1994—; tchr. piano, harpsichord, piano lit. Interlochen (Mich.) Arts Camp, 1953—; exec. dir. Alienor Harpsichord Composition Awards, 1981—. Grantee Fulbright Found., Vienna, 1956-57. Mem. S.C. Music Tchrs. Assn. (founding pres. 1960-63), Music Tchrs. Nat. Assn. (2d v.p., v.p., pres. 1963-70), Southeastern Hist. Keyboard Soc. (founding pres. 1981-84), Ga. Music Tchrs. Nat. Assn., Music Educators Nat. Conf., Atlanta Music Club, Midwestern Hist. Keyboard Soc., Am. Musical Instrument Soc., Coll. Music Soc., Am. Musicol. Soc., Nat. Guild Piano Tchrs., Amis du Musee, Conservatoire Nationale (France), Ruckers Genootschap (Belgium), Pi Kappa Lambda. Office: Dept Music Reinhardt Coll Waleska GA 30183

LUDDEN, GEORGE CLEMENS, metallurgical engineer; b. Washington, Sept. 18, 1945; s. Clemens Pratt and Velma Laverne (Talley) L.; m. Elizabeth Garrett, Aug. 1, 1970; children: Brett Joseph, Jeffrey Clemens, Mark Garrett. BS, Mich. State U., 1967; MBA, Baldwin-Wallace Coll., 1977. Registered profl. engr., Va., Ohio, Calif. Engr. Mare Island Naval Shipyard, Vallejo, Calif., 1967-69, Charleston (S.C.) Naval Shipyard, 1969-73; engr. Davy McKee, Independence, Ohio, 1973-80, proposal mgr., 1980-82; system engr. Va. Power, Richmond, 1982-95; computer specialist St. Mary's Hosp., Richmond, VA, 1996—; utility advisor Electric Power Rsch. Inst., Palo Alto, Calif., 1982-87; lectr. nuclear safety Czechoslovakia, 1987, 89. Contbr. articles on welding design and fabrication to profl. jours. Mem. vol. staff Nat. Air Show, Cleve., 1979, World Cup USA, 1991-94; World Cup amb., 1994; 1996 Olympic vol. staff, 1996; first aid chmn. ARC, Cleve., 1980-82; mem. Va. Coop. Grad. Engring. Program Adv. Com., Richmond, 1988-90. Mem. Edison Electric Inst. (task force officer 1985-95), Am. Soc. for Metals (chpt. chmn. 1971-72), Internat. Metallographic Soc., Richmond Joint Engrs. Coun. (chmn. 1988-89). Home: 2102 Planters Row Dr Midlothian VA 23113-2266 Office: Saint Mary's Hospital 5801 Bremo Rd Richmond VA 23226

LUDDEN, JOHN FRANKLIN, retired financial economist; b. Michigan City, Ind., May 6, 1930. BS in Econs., U. Wis., 1952, MS in Econs., 1955; postgrad., U. Mich., 1955-59. Wage and hour investigator U.S. Dept. Labor, 1960, mgmt. intern, 1960-61, labor economist, 1963; economist, instr. U.S. Bur. of Labor Statis., 1961-63; economist Office of Internat. Ops. IRS, 1963-68, fin. economist Audit div., 1968-86, fin. economist Office of the Asst. Commr. Internat., 1986-95; ret. Office of the Asst. Commr. Internat., 1995. With U.S. Army, 1952-54. Recipient spl. svc. award U.S. Dept. Treasury, 1967, 68, 87, spl. achievement award, 1984, Spl. Act award, 1990, Albert Gallatin award, 1995. Mem. Am. Econ. Assn.

LUDDINGTON, BETTY WALLES, library media specialist; b. Tampa, Fla., May 11, 1936; d. Edward Alvin and Ruby Mae (Hiott) L.; m. Robert Morris Schmidt, Sept. 20, 1957 (div. Dec. 1981); children: Irene Schmidt-Losat, Daniel Carl Schmidt. AA, U. South Fla., 1979, BA in Am. Studies and History, 1980, MA in Libr., Media and Info. Studies, 1982, EdS in Gifted Edn., 1986. Cert. tchr. media and gifted edn., Fla. Media intern Witter Elem. Sch., spring 1982; media specialist Twin Lakes Elem. Sch., 1982-84, Just Elem. Sch., 1984-87, Blake Jr. H.S., 1987-88, Dowdell Jr. H.S. (now named Dowell Mid. Sch.), 1988—; educator Saturday enrichment program for gifted children U. South Fla., springs 1980, 84, 85; participant pilot summer program in reading and visual arts Just Elem. Sch., 1987; educator gifted edn. program in visual and performing arts Kingswood Elem. Sch., summers 1985, 86, gifted edn. program in video camera Apollo Beach Elem. Sch., summer 1989. Author: (book of poetry) Aaron Tippin: A Hillbilly Knight, 1993; contbr. articles and poems to various books and periodical publs., 1986—. Parent vol. media ctr. Witter Elem. Sch., 1976-78; tchr. sponsor Storytelling Club, Dowdell Jr. H.S., 1994-95; news media liaison, tchr. vol. Dowdell Jr. H.S., 1993-96. Recipient Parent award for continuing support of Fla. chpt. # 39 Am. Indsl. Arts Student Assn., 1987-88, Editor's Choice awards for outstanding achievement in poetry Nat. Libr. of Poetry, 1996; nominee Tchr. of Month, Sta. WTSP-TV, 1994; recognized for contbn. of motivational activity for Sunshine State Young Reader's Award program Fla. Assn. for Media in Edn., Inc., 1985; named to Internat. Poetry Hall of Fame, 1996. Mem. Internat. Soc. Poets (Disting. mem. 1995), Hillsborough Classrm. Tchrs. Assn. (grantee 1988, 90), Hillsborough Assn. Sch. Libr. Media Specialists, Clan Wallace Soc. (life), Phi Kappa Phi, Kappa Delta Pi, Phi Alpha Theta (pres., v.p., rep. to honors coun. 1980, 81, Outstanding Student award), Omicron Delta Kappa (treas., chairperson, del., mem. selection com. 1981, Leslie Lynn Walbolt book award), Pi Gamma Mu. Episcopalian. Home: 1032 E Robson St Tampa FL 33604

LUDEKE, AARON KIM, geographic information systems manager, educator; b. Vernon, Tex., Aug. 11, 1951; s. James Milton and Mary Joreen (Kocurek) L.; m. Quana Lynn Childs, Dec. 21, 1985. BA with honors, U. Tex., 1973; PhD in Recreation and Resources Devel., Tex. A&M U., 1987. Park ranger US Army Corp. of Engrs., Coleman, Tex., 1977-78; park mgr. US Army Corp. of Engrs., Abiquin, N.Mex., 1978-80; instr. Tex. A&M U., 1981-83, rsch. assoc., 1983-85; mgr. geog. info. sys. Tex. Natural Resources Info. Sys., Austin, 1988-93, Tex. Parks and Wildlife, Austin, 1993—; instr. U. Tex., 1991-95, instr. PC ARC info., 1995—. Contbr. articles to profl. jours. including Jour. of Environ. Mgmt., Revista Geografica, Biological Conservation. Vol. Peace Corps, Grenada, 1987-88, Austin City Limits. Tom and Ruth Rivers Scholar World Leisure and Recreation Assn., 1987. Mem. Am. Soc. of Photogramettric Engring. and Remote Sensing, Soc. of Conservation Biology, Tex. Acad. of Sci. Home: 3507 Windsor Rd Austin TX 78703 Office: Tex Parks and Wildlife Dept 4200 Smith Sch Rd Austin TX 78744

LUDEMAN, KATE, human resources consultant; b. San Antonio, Aug. 14, 1946; d. Ben and Annette (Martin) L.; 1 child from previous marriage, Catherine. BS in Engring., Tex. Tech U., 1967, MA in Psychology, 1972; postgrad., U. Tex., 1974-76; PhD in Psychology, Saybrook Inst., 1979. Project leader Control Data, Saigon, Socialist Republic of Vietnam, 1970-71; cons. Dallas, 1972-79; interviewer morning news ABC Sta. WFAA-TV, Dallas, 1976-77; mgr. tng. and devel. Shaklee Corp., San Francisco, 1979-81; mgr. human resources Impell Corp., San Francisco, 1981-83; corp. v.p. human resources KLA Instruments, Santa Clara, Calif., 1984-88; pres. Worth Ethic Tng. Co., 1988—; developer profl. stress mgmt. conf. for use in Dallas, Albuquerque, and Atlanta. Author: Worth Ethic: How to Profit from Changing Values of the New Work Force, 1989, Earn What You're Worth, 1995, The Corporate Mystic, 1996; contbr. articles to profl. jours. Chemstrand & Am. Dyers scholar Tex. Tech U., 1965-67. Mem. Am. Soc. Personnel Adminstrs., Am. Soc. Tng. and Devel., Tau Beta Phi. Office: Worth Ethic Corp 4210 Spicewood Springs 205 Austin TX 78759

LUDFORD, GEOFFREY WAYNE, psychotherapist, counselor, educator; b. Norfolk, Va., Mar. 16, 1948; s. Aaron Lee and Virginia Nancy (Lee) L. BPE, Coll. William and Mary, 1970; postgrad., Pasadena City Coll., 1975-76, Santa Monica (Calif.) C.C., 1977-79, Golden Gate U., 1984-86; M in Agency Counseling, Coll. William and Mary, 1989, Specialist Degree, 1990, Doctoral degree in Counseling, 1994. Major account rep., district sales mgr. U.S. Sprint, L.A., 1987; counselor Commonwealth Profl. Svcs., Richmond, Va., 1989, PACES Family Counseling Ctr., Williamsburg, Va., 1989-94; dir. client svcs. Tidewater AIDS Crises Taskforce, Norfolk, Va., 1994—; pvt. practice North Beach Counseling Svcs., Virginia Beach, Va.; adj. prof. Hampton (Va.) U.; counselor, adj. prof. Christopher Newport Coll.; tchr. coord. Coll. William and Mary; cons. Wasmund Group, Fredericksburg, Va.; therapist Mary Immaculate Hosp. Program, 1995—; presenter in field. Home: 98 Hopkins St Newport News VA 23601

LUDOVICE, PETER JOHN, chemical engineer; b. Des Plaines, Ill., Apr. 1, 1962; s. William Peter and Mary Jane (Unger) L.; m. Jennifer Davis Clair, May 29, 1993. BSChemE, U. Ill., 1984; PhDChemE, MIT, 1989. Rsch. assoc. ETH-Zurich, Switzerland, 1988-89; vis. scientist IBM Almaden Rsch. Ctr., San Jose, Calif., 1989-91, NASA Ames Lab., Moffett Field, Calif., 1989-91; polymer product mgr. Polygen Inc., Waltham, Mass., 1991-92, Molecular Simulations Inc., Burlington, Mass., 1992-93; asst. prof. Ga. Inst. Tech., Atlanta, 1993—; tech. cons. Molecular Simulations, Inc., Burlington, Mass., 1992—; faculty mem. Polymer Edn. Rsch. Ctr., Atlanta, 1993—, Ga. Tech Bioengring. Program, Atlanta, 1994—. Mem. editorial bd. Chem. Design Automation News, N.Y.C., 1992—. Mem. AIChE, Am. Chem. Soc. (Sherwin Williams award 1988). Office: Ga Inst of Technology Sch of Chem Engring Atlanta GA 30332-0100

LUDWICK, MIKE JOHN, secondary education educator; b. St. Louis, Nov. 23, 1962; s. Ronald Michael and Mary Ann (Sarhage) L.; m. Marie Renee Schneider, Oct. 13, 1990; 1 child, Erin Jacob. BS in History, East Carolina U., 1985; MS in Tchg., U. N.C., 1991. Cert. tchr., adminstr., cert. mentor tchr., N.C. Tchr. social studies East Wake H.S., Wendell, N.C., 1986—, coach soccer/cross country, 1986—; presenter in field. Active Wake County's Future Leaders Program, Raleigh, N.C., 1995-96. Mem. ASCD, KC, Nat. Con. for the Social Studies, N.C. Coun. for the Social Studies. Republican. Roman Catholic. Home: 1120 Buttercup Wake Forest NC 27587 Office: Wast Wake High Sch 5101 Rolesville Rd Wendell NC 27591

LUDWIG, ORA LEE KIRK, coal company executive; b. Morgantown, W.Va., June 25, 1925; d. Thomas Jefferson and Nora Belle (Browning) Johnson; m. Eugene P. Kirk, Dec. 6, 1947 (div. 1957); children: E. Phillip, Lisa Ann Kirk Wiese; m. August J. Ludwig, May 17, 1983. AA, Mt. State Coll., Parkersburg, W.Va. With Rosedale Coal Co., Morgantown, W.Va., 1945—; corp. sec. Rosedale Coal Co., 1954, v.p., 1971, pres., 1980—; with Mon Valley Coal & Lumber Co., Morgantown, 1945—; pres. Mon Valley Coal & Lumber Co., 1983—; with Mon-Valley Mining Co., 1945—, pres., 1980—. Pres. Monongalia Arts Ctr., Morgantown, 1960-83; bd. dirs., com. chmn. W.Va. Hosp. Aux., 1990—; treas. United Way, 1991—; bd. dirs. Lakeview Theatre. Mem. Tri-State Coal Assn., W.Va. Coal Assn., W.Va. Hosp. Assn. (exec. bd. aux., treas. 1991—), Morgantown C. of C. (treas. 1989-90), Women's Alliance, Rotary, White Shrine of Jerusalem, Order Eastern Star. Methodist. Home: 940 Riverview Dr Morgantown WV 26505-4634 Office: Rosedale Coal Co Morgantown WV 26507-0676

LUEBBERS, LESLIE LAIRD, museum director; b. Upland, Calif., June 13, 1945; d. Frank Whitley and Frances Georgina (Metz) Laird; m. James Arnold Luebbers, Aug. 10, 1968 (div. Dec. 1986); 1 child, Laird Browning. AB, Wellesley Coll., 1967; MAT, Johns Hopkins U., 1969; MA, NYU, 1987. Tchr. Patterson High Sch., Balt., 1968-71; editor Libr. Am. Lit., Chgo., 1971-73; freelance artist Riverside, Calif., 1973-75, San Francisco, 1976-78; asst. dir. World Print Coun., San Francisco, 1978-79, dir./curator, 1980-84; free lance curator Internat. Art Projects, N.Y.C., 1985-90; dir. Art Mus., U. Memphis, 1990—. Author, curator: (book/exhbn.) American Woodcuts: Revival & Innovation, 1988, Min & Matter: New American Abstraction, 1990; contbr. articles and revs. to profl. jours. Mem. Am. Assn. Muss., Memphis Arts Coun. (grant reviewer). Office: Art Museum U Memphis 3750 Norriswood Ave Memphis TN 38111-5943

LUECKE, CONRAD JOHN, aerospace educator; b. Escanaba, Mich., Dec. 30, 1932; s. John Frederick and Rose Margaret (Jaeger) L.; m. Shirley Kerfoot, Dec. 30, 1969 (dec. 1978); m. Freida Belle Shell, Dec. 15, 1979; 1 child, B. Michael. BA, Albion Coll., 1954. Commd. 2d lt. USAF, 1954, advanced through grades to maj., command pilot, 1969, ret., 1977; instr. orbiter systems Lockheed Space Ops. Co., Titusville, Fla., 1984-95; ret.; instr. celestial navigation U.S. Power Squadron, Cocoa Beach, Fla., 1984—; trainer emergency egress shuttle astronauts NASA, Kennedy Space Ctr., Fla., 1984-95. Decorated Silver star, Air medal with 5 oak leaves. Democrat. Baptist. Home: 655 Doral Ln Melbourne FL 32940-7601

LUEDECKE, WILLIAM HENRY, engineer; b. Pittsburg, Tex., Apr. 5, 1918; s. Henry Herman and Lula May (Abernathy) L.; B.S., U. Tex., 1940; m. Mary Anne Copeland, June 3, 1939; children—William Henry, John Copeland. Mech. engr. Columbian Gasoline Corp., Monroe, La., 1940-41; supr. shipbldg., mech. engr. USN, Orange, Tex., 1941-42; gen. supr. factory mgrs. N. Am. Aviation Co., Dallas, 1944-46; mech. engr., charge Chrysler Airtemp. div. Chrysler Corp., Los Angeles, 1946-50; owner Luedecke Engring. Co., Austin, Tex., 1950—, also Luedecke Investment Co.; chmn. bd. dirs. Mut. Savs. Instn., Austin; dir. City Nat. Bank, Austin, 1st Tex. Fin. Corp., Dallas. Bd. dirs. Travis County Heart Fund, Austin YMCA. Named Man of Year, Tex. Barbed Wire Collectors Assn.; registered profl. engr., Tex. Mem. Am. Soc. Heating, Refrigerating and Air Conditioning Engrs. (dir., pres. Austin chpt.), Tex., Nat. socs. profl. engrs., C. of C., Econ. Devel. Council, Better Bus. Bur., Nat. Fedn. Ind. Bus. (nat. adv. council). Lutheran. Clubs: Rotary, Austin, Westwood Country (treas., dir.). Home: 15 Woodstone Sq Austin TX 78703-1159 Office: 1007 W 34th St Austin TX 78705-2008

LUELLEN, CHARLES J., retired oil company executive; b. Greenville, S.C., Oct. 18, 1929; s. John B. and Dorothy C. (Bell) L.; m. Jo S. Riddle, July 11, 1953; children: Margaret L. Briggs, Nancy L. Bissell. B.S., Ind. U., 1952. Sales rep. Ashland Oil, Inc., Ky., 1952-70, v.p. sales, 1970-72, group v.p. sales, 1972-80, pres., chief operating officer, 1986-92; also dir. emeritus Emeriti-Ashland, Inc., Ky.; pres. Ashland Petroleum Co., 1980-86; bd. dirs. Tosco Corp., Stamford, Conn. Bd. dirs. Kings Daus. Hosp., Ashland, 1981-87, Ashland Area YMCA, 1980-92, Nat. Chamber Found., Washington, 1987-92; trustee Centre Coll., Danville, Ky., 1988, Joint Coun. for Econ. Edn., N.Y.C. Mem. Beta Gamma Sigma. Home: 3409 Monte Vista Dr Austin TX 78731-5722 Office: Ashland Inc PO Box 391 Ashland KY 41105-0391 also: Ashland Inc 1000 Ashland Dr Russell KY 41169

LUEPNITZ, ROY ROBERT, psychologist, consultant, small business owner, entrepreneur; b. Ft. McClellan, Ala., June 3, 1955; s. Carl A. and Helen Elizabeth (Brown) L.; m. Mary Kinloch Bush, Dec. 18, 1981; 1 child, Noel. BA cum laude, Southwestern U., 1979; MS in Counseling Psychology, U. So. Miss., 1981; PhD in Counseling Psychology, Tex. A & M U., 1985. Diplomate Am. Bd. Forensic Examiners; cert. health svc. provider in psychology, Tex.; cert. travel agt.; registered treator of sex offenders; bd. cert. forensic examiner. Intern, vol. Austin (Tex.) State Hosp., 1978-79; counselor Univ. Counseling Psychology Clinic, Hattiesburg, Miss., 1980; master level psychologist Pine Belt Mental Health Ctr., Hattiesburg, 1981, Tex. Rehab. Commn., Bryan, 1981-82; grad. tchr. Tex. A & M Univ., College Station, 1982-83; psychologist Brazos Valley MHMR Authority, Bryan, 1983-84;

mental health dir. Brazes Valley MHMR Authority, Bryan, 1984-86; pvt. practice psychologist College Station, 1987—; cons. Dept. Human Svcs., Bryan, 1987—, Brazos Valley MHRA, Bryan, 1987—, Sandstone Psychiatry, College Station, 1990—, HCA Greenleaf Hosp., College Station, 1991—, various chs., schs., govt. agys., 1983—; Noel's Wonderful World of Travel, Village Square Office Park. Sec. Miss. APGA, 1979-81; active sex offender's assessment/treatment program. Mem. Assn. Treatment of Sexual Abuses, Am. Assn. Christian Counselors, Nat. Register Health Svc. Providers in Psychology, Tex. Psychol. Assn., Brazos Valley Psychol. Assn. Republican. Methodist. Home: 1200 Noel Ct College Station TX 77845-3803 Office: Brazos Valley Christian Counseling 2748 Longmire Dr College Station TX 77845-5424

LUJAN, ROSA EMMA, bilingual specialist, trainer, consultant; b. El Paso, Tex., May 17, 1949; d. Rosendo G. and Petra (Rubalcava) López; m. Daniel Lujan, Feb. 21, 1976; children: Lorena Janel, Daniel Omar, Carina Viani, Crystal Rose. BA in Elem. Edn., U. Tex. El Paso, 1972, MS in Edn., 1978, postgrad., 1988; postgrad., N.Mex. State U. Tchr. Ysleta Ind. Sch. Dist., El Paso, 1972-74, bilingual tchr., 1974-90, immigrant tchr., 1990-94; cons. Internat. Acad. Coop. Learning, 1994; mem. Tex. Task Force on Profl. Preparation and Profl. Devel.; nat. bd. dirs. profl. tchg. stds. com. English as a New Lang., 1994; cooperating tchr. U. Tex. El Paso, 1978—; tchr. tnr. Ysleta Ind. Sch. Dist., 1980—; rschr. tnr. Johns Hopkins, U. Tex. El Paso, Haifa U., Israel, 1988—; mentor tchr. U. Tex. El Paso, El Salvador C.A., Boise, Idaho, 1990—; bd. dirs. Nat. Bd. for Profl. Tchg. Stds. Editor: (bilingual newsletter) El Chisme Bilingüe, 1986—. Pres. Ysleta Assn. Bilingual Edn., 1975-76, SW Assn. Bilingual Edn., El Paso, 1990-91; mem. Mt. Carmel Sch. Bd., El Paso, 1991-94, Tex. Com. Student Learning, Austin, 1992—. Named Tex. Tchr. of Yr., Tex. Edn. Agy., 1991-92, Tex. Elem. Tchr. of Yr., 1991-92. Mem. NEA, AAUW, ASCD, Nat. Assn. Bilingual Edn., Tex. Assn. Bilingual Edn., Tex. State Tchrs. Assn., Delta Kappa Gamma, Kappa Delta Pi. Democrat. Roman Catholic. Home: 1933 Sea Gull Dr El Paso TX 79936-3602 Office: Ysleta Ind Sch Dist 9600 Sims Dr El Paso TX 79925-7200

LUKER, JEAN KNARR, school system administrator; b. St. Petersburg, Fla., May 4, 1944; d. Harry M. Jr. and Mary M. (Insley) Knarr; m. Maurice S. Luker Jr., Mar. 1, 1976; children: Maurice S. III, Amy Luker Cloud, Marc A. Miller. AA, Manatee Jr. Coll., 1964; BS in Edn., Fla. State U., 1966; MS in Edn., U. Va., 1982. Tchr., 1st grade Sarasota (Fla.) County Pub. Schs., 1966-70, tchr. emotionally disturbed, 1974-76; tchr. mentally retarded Washington County Schs., Abingdon, Va., 1978-82; tchr. learning disabled Washington County Schs., 1982-89; coord. gifted secondary Washinton County Schs., 1990-91, coord. instructional technology, gifted, 1991—; chair, bd. dirs. Southwest Va. Edn. & Tng. Network, Abingdon, 1993—; founding mem. Electronic Village of Abingdon; mem. VESIS Bd., Richmond, Va., 1993—. Co-author, illustrator: Of Clay Metal and Stone: Objects for Life and Death in Ancient Palestine, 1979. Mem. Va. Assn. Edn. of Gifted, Delta Kappa Gamma (scholar com. chair 1991—, AK7 Founders scholar), Phi Delta Kappa, Kappa Delta Pi, Phi Theta Kappa. Methodist. Home: 216 Stonewall Hts NE Abingdon VA 24210-2924 Office: Washington County Schs 220 Stanley St Abingdon VA 24210-2346

LUMBY, BETTY LOUISE, music educator, organist, composer; b. Detroit; d. Avery Lewellyn and Besse Alena (Baker) L. MusB, Detroit Inst. Mus. Art; MusB summa cum laude, U. Detroit, 1947; MusM, U. Mich., 1949; D of Sacred Music, Union Theol. Sem., 1956. Instr. Detroit Inst. Mus. Art, Detroit; asst. prof. Music Howard Coll., Brimingham, Ala.; prof. music, organist U. Montevallo, Ala., 1956—; titular organist St. Bernard Abbey, Cullman; concert organist, lectr. Composer: To Play the Organ—From Spinette to Full-sized Console, vol. I/II, 1993, rev. 2d edit., 1994; mus. compositions: Metaphors on Mystery for Corpus Christi, 1990, Music for the Hallowing of a Church, 1990, The Wise Men, 1990, Lullaby for a Winged Church Mouse, 1990, To Play the Organ—A Method, 1989-90, Greetings for a Cathedral, 1991, Mass of St. Mary Magdalene, 1991, Vesper Hymn on Ar Hyd y Nos, 1991, Translucences on the Holy, 1991, Cecilian Allegories for the Feast of a Martyr, 1991, Questing Paradigms, 1992, Exsultet for Easter Vigil for Flute and Organ, 1995, Luminary on The Green Blade Riseth for Organ, 1996, Durations: 7 Studies on Time for Organ, 1996, (baritone and organ) Songs of Theophilus, 1996, 3 Songs of Theophilus, 1996. Fulbright scholar West Germany, 1956. Fellow The Am. Guild of Organists; mem. Ala. Music Tchrs. Assn. Music Tchrs. Nat. Assn., Soc. of Composers Inc., Southeastern Composers' League, Southeastern Hist. Keyboard Soc., Delta Omicron, Pi Kappa Lambda, Phi Kappa Phi. Home: PO Box 357 Montevallo AL 35115-0357

LUMPKIN, ALVA MOORE, III, electrical engineer, marketing professional; b. Columbia, S.C., Dec. 4, 1948; s. Alva Moore Jr. and Willodene Evelyn (Rion) L. Student, Washington and Lee U., 1967-68; BS in Applied Math., U. S.C., 1976; MSEE, Ga. Inst. Tech., 1980; student, Rice U. Lic. real estate broker, Ga. Teaching asst. U. S.C., Columbia, 1977, Ga. Inst. Tech., Atlanta, 1978-80; rsch. engr. Ga. Tech. Rsch. Inst., Atlanta, 1980-82; microwave engr., project mgr. Electromagnetic Scis., Inc., Norcross, Ga., 1982-85; pres. A.M. Lumpkin, Inc., Atlanta, 1985—; sales engr. Gentry Assocs., Inc., Orlando, Fla., 1988-90; corp. sec. Gentry Electronics and Instrumentation, Inc., Orlando, 1990-93, also bd. dirs. Mem. IEEE, Antennas and Propagation Soc., Microwave Theory and Techniques Soc., Aerospace and Electronics Systems Soc., Am. Inst. Physics, Assn. Old Crows, Ga. Tech. Alumni Assn., Sigma Pi Sigma, Sigma Alpha Epsilon. Episcopalian.

LUMPKIN, ANNE CRAIG, retired television and radio company executive; b. DeValls Bluff, Ark., Apr. 3, 1919; d. Claude Cleo and Lou (Craig) L. Student, Little Rock Bus. Sch., 1938-39, Patricia Stevens, 1953. Adminstrv. asst. to pres. Sta. KVLC (S.W. Broadcasting), Little Rock, 1949-52, Sta. KGKO (Lakewood Broadcasting), Dallas, 1952-54, Sta. KTLN, Inc., Denver, 1954-58; asst. mgr. Sta. KLRA, Inc., Little Rock, 1958-83; asst. dir. fin. affairs KLRT-TV, Little Rock, 1983-91; retired, 1991. Mem. Ark. Arts Ctr., Little Rock, Fine Arts Club, Little Rock, Nat Audubon Soc., Pulaski County Hist. Soc., Little Rock. Mem. Am. Women in Radio-TV, Am. Bus. Women's Assn., Little Rock Club. Baptist.

LUMRY, WILLIAM RAYMOND, physician, allergist; b. Coronado, Calif., Feb. 17, 1951; s. Raymond Harley and Evelyn (Bamson) L.; m. Rozalia Nadel, May 18, 1980; children: Ariel Martina, Randall Bamson. BS, Tex. A&M U., 1973; MD, U. Tex., Galveston, 1977. Diplomate Am. Bd. Internal Medicine, Am. Bd. Allergy and Immunology. Intern Jewish Hosp., St. Louis, 1977-78, resident in internal medicine, 1978-80; fellow in allergy/immunology Scripps Clinic and Rsch. Found., La Jolla, Calif., 1980-82; physician Dallas Allergy Clinic, 1982-96; assoc. clin. prof. Southwestern Med. Sch., U. Tex., Dallas, 1982—; med. dir. Children's Lung Disease, Dallas, 1985—, Better Breathing Club, Med. City, Dallas, 1985—. Contbr. articles to profl. jours. Recipient Alcoa award Alcoa Found., 1976. Fellow Am. Coll. Physicians, Am. Coll. Allergists, Am. Acad. Allergy and Immunology. Republican. Methodist. Office: Allergy & Asthma Spec Dallas Ste 525 9900 N Central Expressway Dallas TX 75231

LUNA, CHERRY MARTIN, marketing professional; b. Norfolk, Va.; d. Paul Edward and Betty Lou (Crawford) Martin; m. Larry Alan Luna, Mar. 8, 1986; 1 child, Ryan A. BS, Baylor U., 1978. Sales rep. Met. Life, Dallas, 1981-84, Home Life, Dallas, 1984-85; dist. mgr. Continental Ins., Dallas, 1985-86; sr. mkg. rep., employee benefits profl. Provident Life, Dallas, 1990-96. Poll watcher Rep. Party, Dallas, 1983; mem. Rep. Nat. Com.; del. Tex. Gen. Bapt. Conv., Austin, 1985, So. Bapt. Conv., New Orleans, 1990, Tex. Gen. Bapt. Conv., Waco, 1991. Mem. Nat. Assn. Health Underwriters, Women's Life Underwriters Confedn., Tex. Assn. Health Underwriters (bd. dirs.), Dallas Assn. Health Underwriters, Liberty Found., Concerned Women for Am. Republican. Baptist. Home: 6303 Black Berry Ln Dallas TX 75248-4912

LUNA, PATRICIA ADELE, marketing executive; b. Charleston, S.C., July 22, 1956; d. Benjamin Curtis and Clara Elizabeth (McCrory) L. BS in History, Auburn U., 1978, MEd in History, 1980; MA in Adminstrn., U. Ala., 1981, EdS in Adminstrn., 1984, PhD, ABD in Adminstrn., 1986. Cert. tchr., Ga., Ala. History tchr. Harris County Middle Sch., Ga., 1978-79, head dept., 1979-81; residence hall dir. univ. housing U. Ala., 1981-83, asst. dir. residence life, 1983-85; intern Cornell U., Ithaca, N.Y., 1983; dir. of mktg. Golden Flake Snack Foods, Inc., Birmingham, Ala., 1985-89; sr. v.p. Quest U.S.A., Inc., Atlanta, 1989-90; pres. Promotion Mgmt. Group, Inc., 1990—; cons., lectr. in field. Author: Specialization: A Learning Module, 1979, Grantsmanship, 1981, Alcohol Awareness Programs, 1984; University Programming, 1984; Marketing Residential Life, 1985; The History of Golden Flake Snack Foods, 1986; Golden Flake Snack Foods, A Case Study, 1987, Cases in Strategic Marketing, 1989, Cases in Strategic Management, 1990, Frequency Marketing, 1992. Fundraiser, U. Ala. Alumni Scholarship Fund, Tuscaloosa, 1983, Am. Diabetes Assn., Tuscaloosa, 1984, Urban Ministries, Birmingham, 1985-88; fundraiser, com. chmn. Spl. Olympics, Tuscaloosa, 1985; fundraiser Am. Cinema Soc., 1988; chmn. Greene County Relief Project, 1982-89; bd. dirs. Cerebral Palsy Found., Tuscaloosa, 1985-86; lay rector and com. chmn. Kairos Prison Ministry, Tutwiler State Prison, Ala., 1986—; lobbyist, com. chmn. task force Justice Fellowship, 1988-91; bd dirs. Internat. Found. Ewha U., Seoul, Korea, 1988-91; chmn. bd. dirs. Epiphany Ministries, 1991—; bd. dir. Hunting Coll. of Fine Arts. Recipient Dir. of Yr. award U. Ala., 1982, 83; Skeets Simonis award, U. Ala., 1984, nat. award Joint Coun. on Econ. Edn., 1979, rsch. award NSF, 1979; named to Hon. Order Ky. Cols. Commonwealth of Ky., 1985—, Rep. Senatorial Inner Circle, 1986—; Com. chmn. Emmaus Ministry, 1985—; chmn. Chrysalis steering com., 1995-96. Mem. Sales and Mktg. Execs. (chmn. com. 1985-86), Leadership Ala. (pres. 1982-83), Am. Mktg. Assn. (Disting. Leadership award 1987, Commemorative Medal of Honor 1988), Assn. Coll. and Univ. Housing Officers (com. chmn. 1983-85), Nat. Assn. Student Personnel Officers, Snack Food Assn. (mem. mktg. com. and conf. presenter), Internat. Coun. Shopping Ctrs. (Merit award 1991, program com.), Commerce Exec. Soc., Snow Skiing Club, Sailing Club, Omega Rho Sigma (pres. 1983-84), Omicron Delta Kappa, Phi Delta Kappa, Kappa Delta Pi, Phi Alpha Theta. Republican. Methodist. Avocations: skiing, racquetball, tennis, community work, public speaking.

LUNA PADILLA, NITZA ENID, photography educator; b. San Juan, P.R., Mar. 13, 1959; d. Luis and Carmen Iris (Padilla) Luna. BFA, Pratt Inst., 1981; MS, Brooks Inst., 1985. Instr. U. P.R., Carolina, 1981-82, Cultural Inst., San Juan, 1988; asst. prof. photography U. Sacred Heart, Santurce, P.R., 1987—; assoc. dir. communication ctr. U. Sagrado Corazon, Santurce, P.R., 1989-90. Contbr. articles to profl. publs.; one-woman shows P.R. Inst. Culture, 1988, Art and History Mus., San Juan, 1989, 94, 96, U. P.R., 1989, 90, Brooks Inst. Phototography, Santa Barbara, Calif., 1990, Miriam Walsh Gallery, Glenwood Springs, Colo., 1991, Mus. Ponce, 1991; exhibited in group shows Santa Barbara Mus. Art, 1987, Coll. of Santa Fe, N.Mex., 1988, Durango (Colo.) Arts Ctr., 1988, 90, Laband Art Gallery, L.A., 1989, Cultural Ctr., Vercelli, Italy, 1989, Univ. Union Gallery Calif. Poly. State U., 1990, Coconino Ctr. Arts, Flagstaff, Ariz., 1990, Centro Cultural Washington Irving, Madrid, 1991, L.A. County Fair, 1991, Museo del Grabado Latinoamericano, San Juan, 1992, 93, 94, P.R. Inst. Culture, 1994, Hostos Art Gallery, N.Y.C., 1996, others; in permanent collections; juror Fotografia de prensa "Mandin,", 1991-92. MacDowell Colony grantee, Instituto de Cultural Puertorriqueña grantee, 1993, 94, 96. Mem. Soc. Photog. Edn., Friends of Photography. Roman Catholic. Office: U Sagrado Corazón PO Box 12383 San Juan PR 00914-0383

LUND, FREDERICK HENRY, aerospace and electrical engineer; b. Seattle, June 2, 1929; s. Henry George and Minnie (Wilbern) L.; m. Joyce Pauline Mon Pleasure, Sept. 8, 1950; children: Frederick Bradley, Christopher Michael, Peter Andrew, Andrea Leslie. BSEE, U. Wash., Seattle, 1951; postgrad., U. Calif., L.A., 1954-56, 57-59; MS in Aeros., MIT, 1957. Registered profl. engr., Fla. Electronics engr. U.S. Naval Air Missile Test Ctr., Point Mugu, Calif., 1951, 53-56; head systems employment br., aero. rsch. engr. U.S. Naval Missile Ctr., Point Mugu, 1957-61, head plans and analysis group, gen. engr., 1961-65; sr. rsch. engr. Stanford Rsch. Inst., Menlo Park, Calif., 1965-69; mem. profl. staff Martin Marietta Missile Systems, Orlando, Fla., 1969-93; P.E. cons., 1994-95; electronics engr. Naval Aviation Dept, Jacksonville, Fla., 1995—. Chmn. com. Ventura area Coun. Boy Scouts Am., Camarillo, Calif., 1962-65, asst. dist. commr., Stanford area coun., Los Altos, Calif., 1967-69, instnl. rep. Cen. Fla. counc., Orlando, 1972-74; mem. pres.'s coun. U. Fla., Gainesville, 1987—. 1st lt. C.E., USAR, 1951-53. USN Bur. Aeros. scholar, 1956-57. Mem. AIAA (missile sys. tech. com. 1987-91), IEEE (life, sect. chmn. 1962-63), Aerospace and Electronics Systems Soc. of IEEE (chpt. chmn. 1972-73), Mil. Ops. Rsch. Soc. (dir. 1962-66), Assn. Old crows (sec. 1973, club dir. 1986—), Adelphi (sub-chpt. pres. 1948-51), Wesley, Kiwanis, Sigma Xi. Home and Office: 28 Montrano Ave Saint Augustine FL 32084-3819

LUND, RITA POLLARD, aerospace consultant; b. Vallscreek, W.Va., Aug. 28, 1950; d. Willard Garfield and Faye Ethel (Perry) Pollard; m. James William Lund, Dec. 30, 1969. Student, Alexandria Sch. Nursing, 1989-90, Columbia Pacific U., 1989-91. Confidential asst. U.S. Ho. of Reps., Washington, 1975-76; exec. asst. White House Domestic Policy Staff, Washington, 1977-82, White House Sci. Office, Washington, 1982-83; asst. to pres. Telecom Futures Inc., Washington, 1983-84, v.p. for adminstrn., 1985-86; internat. accounts mgr. TFI Ltd., McLean, Va., 1987-89; ind. cons. telecom. Washington, 1989-90, aerospace cons., 1990—; rep. Scott Sci. & Tech., Washington, 1992—; cons. Vanguard Space Corp., Washington, 1992—; exec. dir. Puckett Bros. Co., Washington, 1995—; sec. ELS Corp., 1992; Washington rep. Scott Sci. & Tech., 1992—; cons. Vanguard Space Corp., 1992—; exec. dir. Puckett Brothers Corp., 1995—. Mem. AIAA, NAFE, Women in Aerospace, Am. Space Transp. Assn., Competitive Alliance Space Enterprise. Republican. Methodist. Home: 9020 Patton Blvd Alexandria VA 22309-3334

LUNDBERG, JON CLARK, news anchor, reporter; b. Royal Oak, Mich., June 26, 1961. BS in Mass Communications, U. So. Colo., 1983. Dir. Sta. KTSC-TV, Pueblo, Colo., 1982-83; account exec. Sta. KCBN/KRNO, Reno, 1983; news anchor Sta. KRDO-TV, Colorado Springs, Colo., 1984-85; news anchor, reporter Sta. KVMT-FM, Vail, Colo., 1985, Sta. KSPN-TV, Aspen, Colo., 1985, Sta. KSNW-TV, Wichita, Kans., 1985-87; news anchor, mng. editor Sta. WCYB-TV, Bristol, Va., 1988-94; pres., CEO The Corporate Image, Inc., Bristol, 1994—. With USNR. Recipient 1st place award Colo. Broadcasters Assn., 1985, Sports Program award Kans. Assn. Broadcasters, 1987, 2nd pl. award Tenn. Assn. Broadcasters, 1989. Mem. Soc. Profl. Journalists, Pub. Rels. Soc. of Am. Home: 124 Skyline Dr Bristol TN 37620 Office: 522 State St Ste 204 Bristol TN 37620

LUNDBERG, WILLIAM ALBERT, artist, educator; b. Albany, Calif., May 23, 1942; s. Leo Holgar and Marian Alvina (Swanson) L.; m. Regina Maria da Motta Vater, Jan. 11, 1989. BA, San Jose State U., 1964; MA, U. Calif., Berkeley, 1966. Instr. Parsons Sch. Design, N.Y.C., 1984-85; assoc. prof. U. Tex., Austin, 1985—; film and video juror Guggenheim Found., N.Y.C., 1982-85. Guggenheim fellow, 1981, Fulbright fellow, 1992, NEA fellow, 1991; grantee N.Y. Coun. on the Arts, 1984. Home: 4901 Caswell Ave Austin TX 78751 Office: U Tex Dept Art & Art History Austin TX 78751

LUNDE, ANDERS STEEN, demographer; b. Bridgeport, Conn., Dec. 10, 1914; s. Anders and Cecilia (Steen) L.; m. Eleanor Sheldon, Sept. 9, 1939; children: Erik Sheldon, Peter Steen, Anne Louisa. BA, St. Lawrence U., 1938; MA, Columbia U., 1947, PhD, 1955. Lectr. Rutgers U., New Brunswick, N.J., 1948-51; assoc. prof. St. Lawrence U., Canton, N.Y., 1951-55; prof. Gallaudet Coll., Washington, 1955-60; chief natality statis. br. Nat. Ctr. for Health Statis., Washington, 1962-64, asst. dir. nat. vital statis. div., 1964-67; dir. Office of State Svcs. Nat. Ctr. for Health Statis., Research Triangle Park, N.C., 1967-74; assoc. dir. Nat. Ctr. for Health Statis., Washington, 1974-77; adj. prof. biostatis. Sch. Pub. Health U. N.C., Chapel Hill, 1977—; cons., author Internat. Inst. Vital Registration and Statis., Bethesda, Md., 1977-80. Author: Whirligigs: Design and Construction, 1982, reprinted (under title Easy-to-Make Whirligigs), 1996, More Whirligigs: Large Scale and Animated Figures, 1984, Whirligigs in Silhouette, 1989, Whirligigs for Children: Young and Old, 1992; contbr. numerous articles to profl. jours. Mem. adv. com. Ret. Sr. Vol. Program, Chapel Hill, 1983-89; bd. dirs., treas. N.C. Art Soc., 1978-82; bd. dirs., 1st v.p. N.C. Botanical Garden Found., 1984-90. Recipient First award Durham (N.C.) Art Guild, 1982, Hon. Mention, N.C. Mus. History, 1983. Fellow AAAS, APHA, Am. Statis. Assn.; mem. Am. Population Assn. (sec.-treas. 1965-68, bd. dirs. 1968-71). Democrat. Episcopalian. Home: 1120 Sourwood Dr Chapel Hill NC 27514-4915

LUNDE, KATHERINE LAMONTAGNE, educational consultant; b. Kankakee, Ill., May 3, 1947; d. James Armond and Frances Elizabeth (Maas) LaMontagne; m. Walter A. Lunde Jr., June 15,1969; children: Lisa Christine, Walter James. BS, No. Ill. U., 1969; postgrad., Jacksonville (Fla.) U., 1972. Cert. elem., secondary and early childhood educator. Tchr. 1st grade Kenwood Elem. Sch., Ft. Walton Beach, Fla.; kindergarten tchr., supr. Orange Park (Fla.) Kindergarten; asst. dir. Stoneway Sch., Stoneway Pvt. Sch., Plano, Tex.; former dir. Westminster Preschool and Kindergarten, Dallas; dep. gov. Am. Biog. Rsch. Inst. (life); internat. motivational spkr. spkr.'s bur. Assn. Childhood Edn. Internat. Track coach Spl. Olympics, 1981-83; learning disabilities tutor, 1978-85; bd. dirs. Mi Escuelita Preschs., Inc., 1985-90, v.p. bd. dirs., 1989-90. Grantee Sewell Fund, Lard Trust; recipient Christa McAuliffe Outstanding Educator award, 1994. Mem. ASCD, Nat. Assn. Edn. Young Children (life), Dallas Assn. Edn. Young Children, Kappa Delta Pi.

LUNDGREN, CLARA ELOISE, public affairs administrator, journalist; b. Temple, Tex., Mar. 7, 1951; d. Claude Elton and Klara (Csirmaz) L. AA, Temple Jr. Coll., 1971; BJ, U. Tex., 1973; MA, Columbia Pacific U., 1986. Reporter Temple Daily Telegram, 1970-72; news editor Austin (Tex.) Am.-Statesman, 1972-75; mng. editor Stillhouse Hollow Pubs., Inc., Belton, 1975-77; pub. affairs officer Darnall Army Community Hosp., Ft. Hood, Tex., 1978-80; editor Ft. Hood Sentinel III Corps, 1980-85; command info. officer Pub. Affairs Office III Corps, Ft. Hood, 1985-87, community relations officer, 1987-88, dep. pub. affairs officer, 1988-94; pub. info. dir. Texas Dept. Transp., Austin, 1994—. Recipient Nat. Observer Journalistic Achievement award Dow Jones & Co., 1971, Superior Civilian Svc. award Dept. Army, 1989, Meritorious Civilian Svc. award, 1992, Exceptional Civilian Svc. award, 1994. Mem. Exec. Women in Tex. Govt., Women in the Pub. Sector (pres.), Nat. Assn. Govt. Communicators, Tex. Good Rds./Transp. Assn. Home: 2513 W 45th St Austin TX 78756-2901 Office: Pub Info Office Dept Transp 125 E 11th St Austin TX 78701-2409

LUNDIN, ANN FRANCES, chemist, medical technologist; b. Dallas, Pa., Sept. 22, 1941; d. Walter Stanley and Frances Evelyn (Sholes) Black; m. Lars Norman Lundin, June 10, 1967; children: Lori, Terri, Wendy. BS in Chemistry, Coll. Misericordia, 1963; MS in Chemistry, Villanova U., 1967. Chem. asst. Worcester Found. for Exptl. Biology, Shrewsbury, Mass., 1963-67; research chemist Dow Chem. Co., Wayland, Mass., 1967-71; chem. technologist Children's Hosp., Boston, 1975-80, VA Med. Ctr., San Francisco, 1980-83; quality control chemist Nobel Sci., Alexandria, Va., 1983-84; chemist Nat. Health Labs., Englewood, Colo., 1984-91, chemistry supr., 1991-93; chemist Smith Kline Beecham Labs., Tucker, Ga., 1993—; cons. sci. projects Randolph Mass., 1975-80,. Sec. Jr. League of Swedish Charitable Soc., Boston, 1970-72. Grantee NSF, 1959. Mem. Am. Chem. Soc. Democrat. Roman Catholic. Club: Gen. Fedn. Womens. Lodge: Order of Eastern Star, Ind. Order Vikings. Home: 635 Sullivan Rd Newnan GA 30265-1722 Office: Smith Kline Beecham Labs Tucker GA 30084

LUNDY, VICTOR ALFRED, architect, educator; b. N.Y.C., Feb. 1, 1923; s. Alfred Henry and Rachel Lundy; m. Shirley Corwin, 1947 (div. 1959); children: Christopher Mark, Jennifer Alison; m. Anstis Manton Burwell, Sept. 19, 1960; 1 child, Nicholas Burwell. BArch, Harvard U., 1947, MArch, 1948. Registered architect, Tex., N.Y., Calif. Pvt. practice architecture Sarasota, Fla., 1951-59, N.Y.C., 1960-75; prin. Victor A. Lundy & Assocs., Inc., Houston, 1976-84; design. prin., v.p. HKS Inc., Dallas, 1984—; vis. prof. Grad. Sch. Design, Harvard U., Sch. Architecture, Yale U., Columbia U., U. Calif., Berkeley, Calif. Poly. State U. San Luis Obispo, U. Houston, U. Rome, others; U.S. specialist-architect in U.S.I.A. exhibit, USSR, 1965. Responsible for design St. Paul's Luth. Ch., Sarasota, 1959, new sanctuary, 1970, 1st Unitarian Ch. of Fairfield County, Westport, Conn., 1961, 1st Unitarian Congl. Soc., Hartford, Conn., 1964, Ch. of Resurrection, East Harlem Protestant Parish, N.Y.C., 1966, exhbn. bldg. and exhibit for AEC in S.Am. (Buenos Aires, Rio de Janeiro, Bogota, Santiago), 1967 (Silver medal for exhbn. Archtl. League N.Y. 1965), recreation shelters for Nat. Mus. History and tech., Smithsonian Instn., Washington, 1967, U.S. States Tax Ct. bldg. and pla., Washington, 1976, U.S. Embassy, Colombo, Sri Lanka, for Office of Fgn. Bldgs., Dept. State, 1983 (U.S. Presdl. Design Awards Program 1988, Fed. Design Achievement award), Austin Centre-Omni Hotel, Austin, Tex., 1984, One Congress Pla., Austin, Tex., 1984, Walnut Glen Tower, Dallas, 1985, Mack Ctr. II, Tampa, Fla., 1990, Greyhound Corp. Ctr., Phoenix, 1991, GTE Telephone Ops. World Hdqrs., Irving, Tex., 1991, others; archtl. work represented in Berlin Internat. Archtl. Exposition, 1957, Sao Paulo Internat. Biennial Exposition, 1957, 5th Congress Union Internat. Des Architectes, Moscow, 1958, Expo '70 Exhbn., Osaka, Japan, 1970, travelling exhbn. of architecture in S.Am. Sgt. inf. U.S. Army, 1943-46, ETO. Decorated Purple Heart; recipient Gold medal award Buenos Aires Sesquicentennial Internat. Exhbn., 1960, Gold medal award Buenos Aires Sesquicentennial Interntl.Exhbn., 1960; Silver medal Archtl. League N.Y., 1965; Charles Hayden Meml. Scholastic scholar, 1939-43, Edward H. Kendall scholar Harvard U., 1947-48, Rotch travelling scholar Boston Soc. Architects, 1948-50; travelling fellow Harvard U., 1948-50; Dept. State grantee, 1965. Fellow AIA. Home: 701 Mulberry Ln Bellaire TX 77401-3805 Office: HKS Inc 1111 Pla of the Americas N Ste LB 307 Dallas TX 75201

LUNGER, JAMES BROWN, secondary school administrator; b. Clifton Forge, Va., Sept. 19, 1933; s. Walter Floyd and Genevieve (Brown) L.; m. Janet Dell Corbin, Aug. 14, 1965; children: Robert Clarkson, Margaret Corbin. BA, Washington & Lee U., 1956; MEd, U. Va., 1960, postgrad., 1961—. Tchr. Waynesboro (Va.) Pub. Schs., 1956-57, sci. supr., 1962-70, elem. prin., 1970-83, gen. supr., 1983-92, secondary supr., 1992—; tchr., asst. prin. Clifton Forge (Va.) Pub. Schs., 1957-62; adv. com. Ctrl. Shenandoah Valley Gov.'s Sch., Fisherville, 1993—; adv. bd. Blue Ridge Cmty. Coll., Waynesboro Bd., 1990—. Mem. Ch. Coun., Waynesboro, 1985; mem. Selective Svc. Bd., Waynesboro, 1968. NSF fellow, 1959-60. Mem. ASCD, Waynesboro Rotary Club (pres.-elect, dir.), Rotary Internat. (Paul Harris fellow), Vocat. Assn. Am., Assn. Testing Dirs., Phi Delta Kappa. Office: Waynesboro Pub Schs 301 Pine Ave Waynesboro VA 22980

LUNSFORD, RICHARD EARLY, biology educator; b. Arlington, Va., Oct. 25, 1945; s. Elmer Early and Sarah Edmonston (Wallace) L.; m. Joan Carol Hemmerich, Aug. 9, 1980; children: Teresa Ann, Thomas Jay, Andrew Lee. BS in Biology, Coll. of William and Mary, 1968. Tchr. biology Falls Church (Va.) High Sch., 1973-92, Centreville (Va.) High sch., 1992—; assoc. tchr. student tchrs. George Mason U., 1987, 88; mem. Curriculum Devel. Com. for Adopting Biology for ESL Students; cons. in field. Mem. Gov.'s Sch. Selection Com., Va., 1986-92. Recipient Tandy Scholars Most Outstanding Tchr. award, 1992. Mem. Nat. Assn. Biology Tchrs., No. Va. Soc. of Alumni of Coll. of William and Mary. Home: 6033 Forest Run Dr Clifton VA 20124-2319 Office: Centreville High Sch 6001 Union Mill Rd Clifton VA 22024-1128

LUOMA, KEITH ELLIOTT, mathematics educator; b. Detroit, Dec. 13, 1961; s. Alvin William and Mary Lou Vivian (Burton) L.; m. Linda Carol Johnson, Aug. 11, 1984; children: Lauren Anne, Rachel Lynn. BS, U. Detroit, 1984; MS, George Mason U., 1988. Asst. prof. Augusta (Ga.) Coll., 1988—; instr. Bellsouth, Augusta, 1993; mem. task force on tchg./learning, Augusta, 1995—. Co-founder, editor Mathematical Connections, 1992; contbr. articles to profl. jours. Mem. U.S. Track and Field; judge local/regional sci. fairs, 1989-90. Mem. Humanistic Math Network, Internat. Study Group on History and Pedagogy of Math, Pi Mu Epsilon, Omega Rho, Phi Delta Kappa. Lutheran. Office: Augusta Coll 2500 Walton Way Augusta GA 30904

LUPBERGER, EDWIN ADOLPH, utility executive; b. Atlanta, June 5, 1936; s. Adolph and Esma L.; m. Mary Jane McAlister Redmon, Jan. 6, 1989; children by previous marriage: David Todd, Edward Townsend. A.B. in Econs, Davidson (N.C.) Coll., 1958; M.B.A., Emory U., 1963. Asst. v.p. Southern Co. Services, Inc., Atlanta, 1963-69; v.p., treas. Gulf Power Co., Pensacola, Fla., 1969-77; sr. v.p. fin. Indpls. Power & Light Co., 1977-79; sr. v.p., chief fin. officer Middle South Utilities, Inc., New Orleans, 1979-85; chmn., CEO Entergy Corp., New Orleans, 1985—. Ensign USN, 1960. Mem. Edison Electric Inst., Univ. Club, Met. Club. Presbyterian. *

LUPO, ROBERT EDWARD SMITH, real estate developer and investor; b. New Orleans, May 27, 1953; s. Thomas Joseph and Alvena Florence (Smith) L.; m. Mary Lynn Puissegur, June 16, 1980; children: Robert Thomas Smith, Francesca Marfese Smith. BArch, Tulane U., 1977. Owner Robert Edward Smith Lupo Properties, New Orleans, 1976—; cons. various firms, New Orleans, 1977—; COO Commodore Thomas J. Lupo Enterprises, Williams-Lupo, Smith-Lupo, New Orleans, 1981—; pres. Hedwig, Inc., Zephyr, Inc., Noroaltom Devel. Co., Inc., New Orleans, 1981—; cons. Mrs. Thomas J. Lupo properties. Grad. Met. Area Leadership Forum, New Orleans, 1980; bd. dirs., pres. New Orleans Mcpl. Yacht Harbor, 1989-93; life mem. Friends Audubon Zoo, 1983—; bd. dirs. New Orleans Met. Area Com., 1985-90, Orleans Levee Dist. Commn.; guardian mem. Boy Scouts Am., 1991—; mem. capital projects oversight com. Orleans Parish Sch. Bd., 1995—; mem. bd. commrs. Orleans Levee Dist., 1996—. Recipient Gov.'s award State of La., 1980, Tulane Assocs. award Tulane U., 1986; named One of 10 Best Dress Men, Men of Fashion, 1983, named to Hall of Fame, 1991. Mem. Aquarium Ams. (life), Assn. Naval Aviation (charter), Sigma Alpha Epsilon (founding). Republican. Roman Catholic. Club: Semreh. Office: 145 Robert E Lee Blvd New Orleans LA 70124-2552

LUPTON, MARY HOSMER, retired small business owner; b. Olympia, Wash., Jan. 2, 1914; d. Kenneth Winthrop and Mary Louise (Wheeler) Hosmer; student Gunston Hall Jr. Coll., 1932-33; BS in Edn., U. Va., 1940; m. Keith Brahe-Wiley, Oct. 12, 1940 (dec. Apr. 1955); children: Sarah Hosmer Wiley Guise, Victoria Brahe-Wiley; m. Thomas George Lupton, Nov. 27, 1965 (dec. Feb. 1989); 1 stepson, Andrew Henshaw. Ptnr., Wakefield Press, Earlysville, Va., 1940-55; owner, operator Wakefield Forest Bookshop, Earlysville, 1955-65, Forest Bookshop, Charlottesville, 1965-85, Wakefield Forest Tree Farm, 1955-85. Contbr. articles to profl. mags. Corr. sec. Charlottesville-Albemarle Civic League, 1963-64; sec. Instructive Vis. Nurses Assn., Charlottesville, 1961-62; chmn. pub. info. Charlottesville chpt. Va. Mus. Fine Arts, 1970-77; mem. writers' adv. panel Va. Center for Creative Arts, 1973-75, chmn. pub. info., 1976-77; mem. Albemarle County Forestry Com., 1961-62; bd. dirs. Charlottesville-Albemarle Mental Health Assn., 1980-82, 89-91. Mem. AAUW, DAR (Am. Heritage com. chmn. 1983-85, 89-91), Assns. of U. Va. Libr., New Eng. Hist. Geneal. Soc., Conn. Soc. Genealogists, Geneal. Soc. Va., Albemarle County hist. socs., Va. Soc. Mayflower Descs. (asst. state historian 1979-82), LWV, Soc. Mayflower Descs., Am. Soc. Psychical Research, Brit. Soc. Psychical Rsch., Nature Conservancy, Charlottesville Soc. of Friends, Jefferson Soc., Cornerstone Soc. (charter), Lawn Soc. (charter), Chi Omega. Unitarian. Address: 2600 Barracks Rd Apt 361 Charlottesville VA 22901-2195

LURIER, PETER BRUCE, marketing professional; b. Worcester, Mass., Oct. 2, 1961; s. Howard Ralph and Dorothy Lois (Feingold) L.; m. Kimberley Ann Bell, Nov. 3, 1990; children: Joshua, Jeremy. BA in Communications, U. Mass., Amherst, 1983. Account exec. WMRE Radio (NBC affiliate), Boston, 1983-84, Dun and Bradstreet Mktg. Svcs., Tampa, Ft. Lauderdale, Fla., 1984-88; sr. account exec. Dun and Bradstreet Info. Svcs., Ft. Lauderdale, 1988-93, nat. account exec., 1993—, asst. v.p. bus. mktg., 1995—; cons. IBM, UPS, MCI, Citicorp, Office Depot, Inc., Miami Econ. Devel., 1987—; spkr. Seminar Direct Mktg. to Bus., 1990-92, Commencement Ft. Lauderdale Art Inst., 1995, FDMA Database Mktg., 1995. Mem. Am. Mktg. Assn., Fla. Direct Mktg. Assn. (v.p., bd. dirs. 1990—, pub. Bus. to Bus. Mktg. Strategies), Humane Soc. Broward County. Republican. Office: Dun & Bradstreet Info Svcs 200 S Park Rd Ste 300 Hollywood FL 33021-8542

LURIX, PAUL LESLIE, JR., chemist; b. Bridgeport, Conn., Apr. 6, 1949; s. Paul Leslie and Shirley Laurel (Ludwig) L.; m. Cynthia Ann Owens, May 30, 1970; children: Paul Christopher, Alexander Tristan, Einar Gabrielson. BA, Drew U., 1971; MS, Purdue U., 1973; postgrad., 1973—. Tech. dir. Analysts, Inc., Linden, N.J., 1976-77; chief chemist Caleb Brett USA, Inc., Linden, 1977-80; v.p. Tex. Labs., Inc., Houston, 1980-82; pres. Lurix Corp., Fulshear, Tex., 1982—; cons. LanData, Inc., Houston, 1980-88, Nat. Cellulose Corp., Houston, 1981-88, Met. Transit Authority, Houston, 1981—, Phillips 66, Houston, 1986—, Conoco, Inc., Houston, 1988—, Caronia Corp., Houston, 1988—, Compaq Computer, 1996—, M&H Engring., 1994—, WBC Holdings, Inc., 1989-96; dir. research and devel. Stockbridge Software, Inc., Houston, 1986-88; v.p. Diesel King Corp., Houston, 1980-82. Contbr. articles to profl. jour. Patentee distillate fuel additives. Fellow Am. Inst. Chemists; mem. Am. Chem. Soc., ASTM, AAAS, Soc. Applied Spectroscopy, N.Y. Acad. Sci., Phi Kappa Phi, Phi Lambda Upsilon, Sigma Pi Sigma. Republican. Methodist. Lodge: Kiwanis (pres., 1970-71). Current work: Infrared spectroscopy; data base programming for science and industrial applications. Subspecialties: Infrared spectroscopy; Information systems, storage, and retrieval (computer science). Avocations: tennis, golf, piano.

LUSK, CHARLES MICHAEL, III, real estate professional; b. Houston, Apr. 7, 1948; s. Charles Michael and Ursula Josephine (Guseman) L.; m. Kathleen Frances Carroll, Nov. 24, 1973; children: Andrew Stephen, Lauren Carroll. AA, Schreiner Inst., 1969; BA in English, Baylor U., 1971. Cert. real estate broker, Tex. Broker, salesman Coldwell Banker Company, Houston, 1971-74; owner, operator Lusk Properties, Houston, 1975—; v.p. Mortgage & Trust, Inc., Houston, 1977-86; exec. v.p. Commonwealth Fed. Savings Assn., Houston, 1986-89; prin., pres. Realty Adv. Group, Inc.; trustee J & J Drilling Co., Lulling, Tex., 1989-95; contractor Resolution Trust Corp., Houston, 1990—; trustee Gen. Homes Liquidating Trust, Houston, 1991—. Active Houston Livestock Show & Rodeo, Houston, 1989—; exec. com. West Univ. Party, Houston, 1989-93. Mem. Am. Soc. Real Estate Counselors, Tex. Bd. Realtors, Houston Bd. Realtors, Urban Land Inst., The Briar Club (various offices, 1984—), Breakfast Club Houston (various offices 1980—). Republican. Presbyterian. Home: 3718 Chevy Chase Houston TX 77019 Office: Realty Adv Group, Inc One W Loop South Ste 690 Houston TX 77027

LUSK, GLENNA RAE KNIGHT (MRS. EDWIN BRUCE LUSK), librarian; b. Franklinton, La., Aug. 16, 1935; d. Otis Harvey and Lou Zelle (Bahm) Knight; m. John Earle Uhler, Jr., May 26, 1956; children: Anne Knight, Camille Allana; m. 2d, Edwin Bruce Lusk, Nov. 28, 1970. BS, La. State U., 1956, MS, 1963. Asst. librarian Iberville Parish Library, Plaquemine, La., 1956-57, 1962-68; tchr. Iberville Parish Pub. Schs., Plaquemine, 1957-59, Plaquemines Parish Pub. Schs., Buras, La., 1959-61; dir. Iberville Parish Library, Plaquemine, 1969-89; chmn. La. State Bd. Library Examiners, 1979-89; pres. Camille Navarre Gallery, Ltd., Zachary, La., 1989-94. Mem. Iberville Parish Econ. Devel. Council, Plaquemine, 1970-71; sec. Iberville Parish Bicentennial Commn., 1973—; mem. La. Bicentennial Commn., 1974; bd dirs. McHugh House Mus., 1991-92. Named Outstanding Young Woman Plaquemine, La. Jr. C. of C., 1970. Mem. La. (sect. chmn. 1967-68), Riverland (sec. 1973-74) libraries assns., Capital Area Libraries (chmn. com. 1972-74). Republican. Episcopalian. Author: (with John E. Uhler, Jr.) Cajun Country Cookin', 1966, Rochester Clarke Bibliography of Louisiana Cookery, 1966, Royal Recipes from the Cajun Country, 1969, Iberville Parish, 1970. Home: 22736 Plainsland Dr Zachary LA 70791-9764

LUSK, LISA MARIE, lawyer; b. Tucson, Feb. 17, 1957; d. Robert Fearn Lusk and Kay (Tollett) MacLeod; m. Thomas Edward Drasites, Jan. 27, 1979; children: Andrea Lee, Mark David, Alexa Nicole. BA, U. Miami, 1977, JD, 1980. Bar: Fla. 1980; U.S. Dist. Ct. (so. dist.) Fla. 1980, U.S. Dist. Ct. (mid. dist.) Fla. 1986; U.S. Ct. Appeals (5th and 11th cirs.) 1980; cert. real estate law, 1991. Intern Legal Svcs. of Miami, Fla., 1979-80; assoc. and law clk. Curry, Shamas & Elias, Miami, 1980; assoc. Barry Kutun, Miami, 1980-81, Robert L. Ratliff, Cape Coral, Fla., 1981-82; ptnr. Lusk, Drasites & Tolisano, P.A., Cape Coral, 1982—. Mem. Real Property Lawyers (v.p. Ft. Myers, Fla. chpt. 1986-87), Phi Alpha Delta (v.p. 1978-79). Republican. Office: Lusk Drasites & Tolisano PA 202 Del Prado Blvd S Cape Coral FL 33990-1726

LUSSKY, WARREN ALFRED, librarian, educator, consultant; b. Chgo., Apr. 16, 1919; s. Arthur W. and Alma (Proegler) L.; B.A., U. Colo., 1946; M.A., U. Denver, 1948; student U. Ill., 1941-42; m. Mildred Joann Island, June 12, 1948. Asst. libr. Pacific Luth. Coll., Parkland, Wash., 1948-49; libr. Hopkins Transp. Libr., Stanford, 1950, Rocky Mountain Coll., Billings, Mont., 1950-55; head libr. Nebr. Wesleyan U., Lincoln, 1955-56; dir. libr., assoc. prof. Tex. Luth. Coll., Sequin, 1956-85; libr. cons.; mem. accrediting team Tex. Edn. Agy., 1961, 84. Mem. Am. Libr. Assn., Tex. Libr. Assn. (dist. vice chmn. 1965, chmn. 1966), S.W. libr. Assn., Council Research and Acad. Librs. (bd. dirs. 1968-85, pres. 1976-78). Prin. contbr. to design new Tex. Luth. Coll. Libr.; research and publs. on design and functions coll. libr. bldgs. Home: 357 Irvington Dr San Antonio TX 78209-4221

LUST, BARBARA LOUISE, nursing educator, health facility administrator; b. Columbus, Ohio, Dec. 11, 1938; d. Herbert Leroy and Mabel Louise (Wurm) L. Diploma in Nursing, Christ Hosp. Sch. Nursing, Cin., 1959; BSN, Ohio State U., 1961, MS, 1967; PhD, U. Tex., 1981. RN, Tex. Ohio. Instr. Mt. Carmel Sch. Nursing, Columbus, 1964-71; asst. prof. San Antonio Coll., 1976-78; assoc. dean students U. Tex. Health Sci. Ctr. Sch. Nursing, San Antonio, 1978—; researcher in field. Contbr. articles to profl. jours. With U.S. Army, 1971-76, col. USAR, 1976-92. Decorated Army Commendation with four oak leaf clusters, Meritorious Svc. medal; recipient Fed. Tranieeship, 1966-67, 78-79; grantee Chem. Abuse and Substance Abuse Prevention Program U.S. Dept. Edn. Drug Prevention Program, 1988-92, Divsn. Nursing for Disadvantaged Students, 1991-94. Mem. ANA, Nat. League for Nursing, Tex. League for Nursing (mem. CBHDP bd. rev., bd. dirs., past pres.), Tex. Nurses Assn. (dist. #8 recognition award 1981, 85), Sigma Theta Tau. Home: 4922 Tiffany Ln Cibolo TX 78108-2142

LUTES, BENJAMIN FRANKLIN, JR., investor; b. Chavies, Ky., Nov. 1, 1927; s. Benjamin F. Sr. and Leona Marguerite (Knox) L.; m. Delphia Weddle, Sept. 1, 1950; children: Benjamin F. III, Elizabeth Ann Benners. BS, U. Ky., 1950. Acct. Magnolia Petroleum Co., Dallas, 1953-60; sr. acct. Magnolia Pipe Line Co., Dallas, 1960-66; sr. systems analyst Mobil Pipe Line Co., Dallas, 1966-76, sect. head acct., 1976-77; systems supr. Mobil Overseas Pipe Line Co., Dallas, 1977-78, sect. head acctg. and fin., 1978-85; sect. head acctg. Mobil Alaska, Mobil Eugene Island, Dallas, 1982-85; Wolverine Pipe Lines, Dallas, 1982-85. Spl. agt. CIC, 1946-47. Recipient Recognition for Svc. in Constrn. of Saudi Arabian Pipe Line, 1980, Recognition of Svc. in Ops. Saudi Arabian Pipe Line, 1982. Home: 11008 Fernald Ave Dallas TX 75218-1206

LUTHER, GEORGE ALBERT, truck brokerage executive; b. Pulaski, N.Y., Feb. 16, 1926; s. Leslie Leon and Bertha Adelaide (Kind) L.; m. Lucile Pauline Lane, May 26, 1945; children: John Paul, Roger Lane. Grad., Ithaca (N.Y.) High Sch., 1943. Driver Mayflower Van Lines, Ithaca, 1946-47, Red Star Express, Auburn, N.Y., 1947-52; owner, operator B&L Trucking, Locke, N.Y., 1952-56; transport broker Cross Country Truck Svc. Inc., Lakeland, Fla., 1956-61, Horne Distbrs., Inc., Sanford, Fla., 1961-62; office mgr., broker Cross Country Truck Svc., Inc., Lakeland, 1962-67; office mgr., broker Haines City (Fla.) Truck Brokers, Inc., 1967-84, co-owner, 1984-88; pres. Nat. Agrl. Transp. League, Tavares and Leesburg, Fla., 1966-67, 75-77; v.p. Fla. Watermelon Growers & Distbrs. Assn., Lakeland, 1972-74, Nat. Watermelon Growers & Distbrs. Assn., Morven, Ga., 1974-75. Editor, writer Luther Family newsletter, 1986—; pub. Luther Family in Am., 1976; contbr. articles to mags. Sec., chief exec. officer, genealogist Luther Family Assn., Lakeland, 1986—. Home: 2531 Lakeview St Lakeland FL 33801-2556

LUTHER, JOHN M., business executive; b. 1949. With Gracewood, Inc., Vero Beach, Fla., 1970—; officer Gracewood Fruit Co., Inc., Vero Beach, Fla., 1971—; gen. mgr. Belair Packing HSE Joint Venture, Vero Beach, Fla., 1983—. Office: Belair Packing HSE Joint Venture 1626 90th Ave Vero Beach FL 32966-6614

LUTHER, MARK ALAN, electrical deisgn engineer; b. Newport News, Dec. 9, 1963; s. Edward Morris and Brenda Lucille (Hill) L.; m. Anna Bessie Belt, Oct. 5, 1991; 1 child, Jessica Victoria. BSEE, Old Domionion U., Norfolk, Va., 1987. Elec. test engr. Newport News Shipbldg. and Drydock Co., 1990-92; design engr. Texcom, Inc., Portsmouth, Va., 1992—. Mem. Moose (legionnaire). Home: 527 Beech Dr Newport News VA 23601 Office: Texcom Inc 801 Water St # 500 Portsmouth VA 23704

LUTHER, SUSAN MILITZER, poet; b. Lincoln, May 28, 1946; d. Walter Ernest and Sarah Clementine (Newman) Militzer; m. Robert Norman Luther, July 18, 1971; stepchildren: Carol Charlene Luther Lay, Robert N. Jr. BA in English, La. State U., 1969; MA in English, U. Ala., 1976; PhD in English, Vanderbilt U., 1986. Faculty mem. U. Ala., Huntsville, 1986-92; adj. asst. prof. English U. Ala., 1990-92; presenter in field. Author of poems. Teaching fellow Vanderbilt U., 1976-79. Mem. Nat. Assn. Poetry Therapy, Nat. Coalition Ind. Scholars, N.Am. Soc. Study Romanticism, South Atlantic Modern Lang. Assn., Ala. Writers' Forum, Ala. State Poetry Soc., Modern Lang. Assn. Home: 2115 Buckingham Dr SW Huntsville AL 35803-2017

LUTHRA, GURINDER KUMAR, osteopath; b. Jullundur, Punjab, India, June 18, 1964; s. Satya Pal and Suraksha (Kumari) L.; m. Bhawna Narang, Mar. 20, 1989. BS in Biology with honors, U. Tex., Arlington, 1987; DO with honors, Tex. Coll. Osteo. Medicine, 1991. Rsch. technician U. Tex. Health Sci. Ctr., Houston, 1982-84, Tex. Coll. Osteo. Medicine, Ft. Worth, 1987; internal medicine resident U. Tex. Med. Br., Galveston, 1991-94, acad. faculty in dept. internal medicine, 1994-95, fellowship in gastroenterology, 1995-97. Scholar Houston Osteo. Found., 1988-91, Acad. scholar U. Tex., Arlington, 1985-87. Mem. Tex. Osteo. Med. Assn., Am. Osteo. Assn., Student Osteo. Med. Assn., Psi Sigma Alpha (Membership award 1988-91). Home: 17010 Sailors Moon Ct Friendswood TX 77546 Office: U Tex Med Br 301 University Blvd Galveston TX 77550-2708

LUTON, MARY KATHRYN, hospital patient relations administrator; b. Oklahoma City, Apr. 3; d. Marvin Linwood and Irene Allen Briggs; m. James Polk Luton, Feb. 17, 1946; 1 child, Virginia Ann Luton Manahan. Grad. high sch., Okla. City; student coll. courses, Pvt. Tutor, 2 yrs. Copy writer Halliburton's, Oklahoma City, 1944-46; exec. dir. Okla. Soc. to Prevent Blindness, Oklahoma City, 1965-72; dir. patient relations Presbyn. Hosp., Oklahoma City, 1978—. Mem. LWV, 1947; founder Okla. Soc. to Prevent Blindness, 1965, Hosp. Hospitality House, Oklahoma City, 1979; sec. Nat. Soc. to Prevent Blindness, 1987-89; developed Presbyn. Hosp. Patient Rep. program, 1978. Named Outstanding Layman award Okla. State Med. Assn., 1980, Woman of Vision Founder-Okla. Society to Prevent Blindness, 1980; recipient Ark. Traveler award, 1980, Honor award Channel 5 Who Care, 1983, Ladies in the News award Okla. Hospitality Club, 1986, Achiever award Pearl M. and Julia J. Harmon Found., 1989; Mary Kathryn Luton Hosp. Hospitality House named in her honor, 1986. Mem. Nat. Soc. Patient Representation & Consumer Affairs, Okla. Soc. Patient Representation (pres. 1987-88). Democrat.

LUTTER, CHARLES WILLIAM, JR., lawyer; b. Kenosha, Wis., July 12, 1944; s. Charles William and Eva (Kuyawa) L.; m. Carol Hamilton Ewing, July 13, 1974; children: Charles William III, Scott. BS, U. Wis., 1966; postgrad., U. Tex., 1972; JD, St. Mary's U., 1976. Bar: Tex. 1976, U.S. Dist. Ct. (no. dist.) 1977, U.S. Dist. Ct. (so. dist.) 1981, U.S. Dist. Ct. (we. dist.) 1985, U.S. Ct. Appeals (5th and 11th cir.) 1981. Gen. atty. fin. SEC, Atlanta, 1976-80; chief regulations br. SEC, Houston, 1980-83; ptnr. Byrnes & Martin, Houston, 1983-84, Martin, Shannon & Drought, Inc., San Antonio, 1984-87; sr. corp. atty. LaQuinta Motor Inns, Inc., San Antonio, 1987-90; v.p., assoc. gen. counsel, sec. United Svcs. Advisors, Inc., 1991-93; v.p., spl. counsel, sec. United Svcs. Advisors, Inc., San Antonio, 1993-95, legal/operational cons., 1995—; mem. planning com. Ann. Securities Regulation Conf., SEC, Tex. Securities Bd., State Bar Tex., U. Tex. Law Sch., 1986—; mem. initial exec. com. San Antonio Tech. Adv. Group, 1985-87; mem. target '90 Goals for San Antonio Sci. and Tech. Venture Task Force, 1985-90, exec. com. for forum on entrepreneurship, 1985-87; mem. estate planning coun. Southwest Found. Biomed. Rsch., San Antonio, 1987—; arbitrator Nat. Assn. Securities Dealers, N.Y. Stock Exchange, Mcpl. Securities Rulemaking bd. Contbr. articles to profl. jours. Bd. dirs. Boysville, San Antonio, 1989—; scout leader Alamo Area coun. Boy Scouts Am., 1988—. Capt. USAF, 1966-71. Decorated Air medal (6). Mem. ABA, State Bar Tex. (securities and investment banking com. 1984—, ad hoc subcom. on securities activities of banks 1987-89, subcom. on rules of fair practce for Tex. broker-dealers 1990), Internat. Assn. for Fin. Planning (bd. dirs. and regulatory coord. San Antonio chpt. 1987—), Investment Co. Inst. (SEC rules com. 1993-95), San Antonio Bar Assn., San Antonio Bar Found., U. Wis. Alumni Assn., Air Force Assn., John M. Harlan Soc., Kiwanis, Phi Delta Phi. Home: 103 Canyon Oaks Dr San Antonio TX 78232-1305 Office: care United Svcs Advisors 7900 Callaghan Rd San Antonio TX 78229-2327

LUTTIG, J. MICHAEL, federal judge; b. 1954. BA, Washington and Lee U., 1976; JD, U. Va., 1981. Asst. counsel The White House, 1981-82; law clk. to Judge Antonin Scalia U.S. Ct. of Appeals D.C. Cir., 1982-83; law clerk to chief justice Warren Burger Supreme Ct. of U.S., 1983-84, spl. asst. to chief justice Warren Burger, 1984-85; assoc. Davis Polk & Wardwell, 1985-89; prin. dep. asst. atty. gen., office of legal counsel U.S. Dept. of Justice, 1990-90, asst. atty. gen., office of legal counsel, counselor to atty. gen., 1990-91; judge U.S. Cir. Ct. (4th cir.), McLean, Va., 1991—. Mem. Nat. Adv. Com. of Lawyers for Bush, 1988, Lawyers for Bush Com., 1988. Mem. ABA, Va. Bar Assn., D.C. Bar Assn. Office: Circuit Ct 8280 Greensboro Dr Ste 780 Mc Lean VA 22102-3807

LUTTRELL, WILLIAM ERNEST, naval officer,industrial hygienist, toxicologist; b. Oceanside, Calif., Jan. 5, 1952; s. Robert Landon Sr. and Opal Charlene (Wheeler) L.; m. Sarah Beth Woodson, July 28, 1973; children: Daniel Robert, Janna Marie. BS in Chemistry, U. Louisville, 1975; MS in Chemistry, Old Dominion U., 1983; PhD in Toxicology, Ea. Va. Med. Sch., 1993. Commd. ensign Med. Svc. Corps USN, 1977, advanced through grades to comdr., 1993; indsl. hygiene officer Navy Environ. and Preventive Medicine Unit No. 2, Norfolk, Va., 1977-81; head indsl. hygiene dept. Naval Hosp., Portsmouth, Va., 1981-84, Navy Environ. and Preventive Medicine Unit No. 2, Norfolk, 1987-90; dir. occupl. health and preventive medicine U.S. Naval Hosp., Yokosuka, Japan, 1990-93; dir. safety & occ. health program, fleet indsl. hygiene off. Comdr. in Chief, U.S. Atlantic Fleet, Norfolk, 1993-95; dir. environ. programs Navy Environ. Health Ctr., Norfolk, 1995—; indsl. hygiene and toxicology cons. WELAIR, Inc., Norfolk, 1989—. Contbr. articles to profl. jours. Mem. AAAS, Soc. Toxicology, Internat. Occupational Hygiene Assn., Am. Indsl. Hygiene Assn. (pres. Tidewater sect. 1982), Am. Conf. Govtl. Indsl. Hygienists, Navy Indsl. Hygiene Assn. Home: 1349 Llewellyn Ave Norfolk VA 23517-2266 Office: Navy Environ Health Ctr 2510 Walmer Ave Norfolk VA 23513-2617

LUTTS, RALPH HERBERT, museum administrator, scholar, educator; b. Quincy, Mass., Jan. 7, 1944; s. Herbert Warren Lutts and Jean May (MacKenzie) Easton. BA in Biology, Trinity U., San Antonio, 1967; EdD, U. Mass., 1978. Curator, educator Mus. Sci., Boston, 1967-73; naturalist Hampshire Coll., Amherst, Mass., 1973-80; natural sci. faculty Hampshire Coll., 1976-84; dir. Blue Hills Trailside Mus., Mass. Audubon Soc., Milton, 1980-90; dir. edn. Va. Mus. Natural History, Martinsville, 1990-92, dir. outreach div., 1992-94, rsch. assoc., 1994—; assoc.faculty Goddard Coll., Plainfield, Vt., 1995—; pres. Alliance for Environ. Edn., 1988-89; founding pres. New Eng. Environ. Edn. Alliance, 1980-84; assoc. Ctr. for Animals and Pub. Policy, Tufts U. Sch. Vet. Medicine, North Grafton, Mass., 1989-90; dept. dir. mid-atlantic region Global Network of Environ. Edn. Ctrs., 1993-95, bd. dirs., 1994—. Author: The Nature Fakers: Wildlife, Science and Sentiment, 1990; founding editor New Eng. Jour. Environ. Edn., 1985-88; contbr. articles to profl. jours. Pres. Hitchcock Ctr. for Environ., Amherst, Mass., 1977-79; treas. Mass. Environ. Edn. Soc., 1982-84; mem. Blue Hills citizens' adv. com. Met. Dist. Commn., 1988-89, mgmt. adv. com., 1989-90; mem. sec.'s adv. group on environ. edn. Mass. Exec. Office for Environ. Affairs, 1989-90. Recipient New Eng. Regional awrd for achievement New Eng. Environ. Edn. Alliance, 1989; Paul Harris fellow Rotary Internat. Mem. AAAS, Am. Soc. Environ. History, Assn. for Study of Lit. and Environ., Internat. Soc. Environ. Ethics, Forest History Soc. (Ralph W. Hidy award 1993), N.Am. Assn. Environ. Edn., Am. Nature Study Soc. (bd. dirs. 1990—, pres. 1995—), Authors Guild Popular Culture Assn. (area chair 1993-95), Nat. Writers Union, Rotary.

LUTZ, FRANK WENZEL, education administration educator; b. St. Louis, Sept. 24, 1928; s. Vincent J. and Helen M. (Scrivens) L.; m. Susan Virginia Bleikamp, July 12, 1958; children: Paul E., Andrew C., Lynn S. AA, Harris Tchrs. Coll., 1948; BS, Washington U., 1950, MS, 1954, EdD, 1962. Instr. Washington U., St. Louis, 1961-62; from asst. to assoc. prof. NYU, N.Y.C., 1964-68; dir. div. policy studies Pa. State U., State College, 1968-73; prof. edn. adminstrn. Pa. State U., 1974-80; dean Sch. Edn. Eastern Ill. U., 1980-82, asst. to v.p., 1982-83; prof., dir. Ctr. Policy Studies Tex. A&M (formerly East State U.), Commerce, Tex., 1983—, prof. edn. adminstrn., 1991—; sr. nat. lectr. Nova S.W. U., 1991—; mem., pres. Pattonville (Mo.) Sch. Bd., 1960-62; mem. adv. com. Opportunities Acad. Mgmt. Tng., Phila., 1975-90. Author seven books, numerous book chpts. in field; contbr. over 100 articles to profl. jours. Deacon 1st Presbyn. Ch., Commerce, Tex., 1989-91. Doctoral fellow Washington U., 1960-61; grantee U.S. Office Edn., OEO. Mem. Am. Ednl. Rsch. Assn. (sec. Div. 1970-72, dir. rsch. pre-session 1969, program com. 1970), Commerce Rotary (pres. 1991-92, chair internat. svc. 1994-96), Phi Delta Kappa (life, pres. Washington U. chpt. 1960, 1st v.p. East Tex. State U. chpt. 1985, Lafferty Faculty Senate Disting. scholarship award 1996). Home: PO Box 51 Nederland CO 80466-0051 Office: East Tex State U Edn North Building Rm 214 Commerce TX 75428

LUTZ, GRETCHEN KAY, English language educator; b. Ft. Worth, Tex., Jan. 6, 1948. BA, Tex. Christian U., 1970; MA, U. Houston, 1974, Rice U., 1995; postgrad., Dartmouth Coll., 1994; MA, Rice U., 1995. High sch. and mid. sch. tchr. English Galveston and Deer Park (Tex.) Sch. Dists., 1970-77; instr. ESL and English Schreiner Coll., Kerrville, Tex., 1979-80; instr. English San Jacinto Coll. Ctr., Pasadena, Tex., 1981—; tchr. English Sch. of the Talented and Gifted Magnet High Sch., Dallas. Contbr. articles to profl. jours. Mem. MLA, Nat. Symposium for Coherence in Liberal Arts, C.C. Humanities Assn., Am. Culture and Popular Culture Assn., U.S. European Command Mil. to Mil. Program Conf., Am. Studies Assn. Tex., South Ctrl. MLA, Conf. Coll. Tchrs. English (exec. coun.), S.W. Conf. Christianity and Lit., Western Soc. 18th Century Studies, Tex. Folklore Soc., S.W. Regional Conf. English in Two-Year Colls., Tex. Voices Sesquicentennial Series, Rice English Symposium, San Jacinto Coll. Faculty Symposium. Home: 3946 Sherwood Forest #135E Dallas TX 75220

LUTZ, ROBERT BRADY, JR., engineering executive, consultant; b. Akron, Ohio, Nov. 17, 1944; s. Robert Brady and Kathryn Mae (Vallen) L.; m. Anna Lee Burns, Aug. 26, 1967. BS in Engring. Mgmt., Rensselaer Polytech., 1970. Reg. profl. engr., Hawaii, Tex., Okla. Resident engr. Goodkind & O'Dea, Inc., Montclair, N.J., 1967-69; project engr. to program control cons. Parsons, Brinckerhoff, Quade & Douglas, Inc., Portland, Oreg., and internat. cities, 1970-81; constrn. mgr. CH 2M Hill, Portland, Oreg., 1981-83; project engr. Bechtel Constrn., Inc., Portland, 1983-84; asst. exec. dir., dir of facilities engring. & constrn. Dallas Area Rapid Transit, 1984-88; v.p., transp. sect. mgr. HDR Engring., Inc., Dallas, 1988-96; v.p., dir. Tex. ops. Morrison Knudsen Centennial, Dallas, 1996—. Bd. dirs. Garland (Tex.) Civic Theater, 1985-87. Mem. Am. Soc. Civil Engrs. (urban transp. com. 1988—) Am. Assn. Cost Engrs. (coun., bd. dirs., 1982-84, v.p. Oreg. sect. 1984), Am. Bus. Clubs (v.p. Duck Creek chpt., Garland Tex., 1986). Democrat. Home: 3705 Oakridge Cir Garland TX 75040-3559 Office: MK Centennial 8333 Douglas Ste 1500 Dallas TX 75225

LUU, QUYEN NGOC, physician, educator; b. Saigon, Vietnam, June 13, 1956; came to U.S., 1982; m. Thomas William Price, June 15, 1985; children: Katherine Claire, Kathleen Elizabeth, Christopher Reagan. Faculte de Medecine, Rene Descartes, Paris, 1975; BS in Biology cum laude with honors, Ga. State U., 1978; MD, Med. Coll. Ga., Augusta, 1982. Diplomate Am. Bd. Internal Medicine, Am. Bd. Infectious Diseases; cert. ACLS, advanced trauma life support. Intern Med. Coll. Ga., 1982-83, resident in internal medicine, 1983-85, fellow in infectious disease, 1986-88; asst. prof. sch. medicine Mercer U., Macon, Ga., 1988—; med. dir. Response Techs., Inc., Macon, Ga., 1991-94; physician St. Joseph Urgent Care Ctr., Augusta; regional med. dir. ABC Home Health Svcs., mem. ethics com., 1993-94; vice-chmn. infection control com. HCA Coliseum Med. Ctr., Macon, 1990-94, chmn. pharmacy and therapeutics com. 1993—; mem. pharmacy and therapeutics com. Med. Ctr. Ctrl. Ga., Macon, 1990-94, mem. antibiotics subcom. 1990—, chmn. infection control com. 1992—; mem. infeciton control com. Charter Northside Hosp., Macon; mem. adv. bd. Local Pointe Women, Macon, 1991—. Contbr. articles and abstracts to publs. Fellow ACP; mem. Infectious Disease Soc. Am., Infectious Disease Soc. Ga., Med. Assn. Ga., So. Med. Assn., Bibb County Med. Soc., Mortar Bd., Blue Key, Phi Kappa Phi. Home: 133 Hampton Ridge Dr Macon GA 31210-7828 Office: 133 Hampton Ridge Rd Macon GA 31220-4007

LUXENBERG, STEVEN NEUWAHL, physician; b. Miami, Fla., July 11, 1964; s. Malcolm N. and Sandra R. Luxenberg. BS, Emory U., 1986; MD, Med. Coll. Ga., 1990. Intern and resident in internal medicine Med. Coll. Va., Richmond, 1990-93; with CompHealth/Kron, Salt Lake City, 1993-94; fellow in med. informatics Columbia U., N.Y.C., 1994—. Mem. AMA, ACP, Am. Med. Informatics Assn.

LUZA, RADOMIR VACLAV, historian, educator; b. Prague, Czechoslovakia, Oct. 17, 1922; s. Vojtech V. and Milada (Vecera) L.; m. Libuse Ladislava Podhrazska, Feb. 5, 1949; children: Radomir V., Sabrina. JuDr, U. Brno, Czechoslovakia, 1948; MA, NYU, 1958, PhD, 1959. Assoc. prof. modern European history La. State U., New Orleans, 1966-67; prof. history Tulane U., New Orleans, 1967—; scholar-in-residence Rockefeller Found., Bellagio Study Ctr., 1988; prof. gen. history Masaryk U., Brno, 1993—. Author: The Transfer of the Sudeten Germans, 1964, History of the International Socialist Youth Movement, 1970, (with V. Mamatey) A History of the Czechoslovak Republic, 1918-1948, 1973, Austro-German Relations in the Anschluss Era, 1975, Österreich und die Grossdeutsche Idee in der NS-Zeit, 1977, Geschichte der Tschechoslowakischen Republik 1918-1948, 1980, A History of the Resistance in Austria, 1938-1945, 1984, Der Widerstand in Österreich, 1938-1945, 1985, La Rèpublique Tchècoslovaque 1918-1948, 1987; mem. editl. bd. East European Quar., Contemporary Austrian Studies. With Czechoslovak Resistance, 1939-45. Recipient all Czechoslovak mil. decorations; prize Theodor Körner Found., Vienna, 1965, J. Hlavka Hon. medal Czechoslovak Acad. Arts and Scis., 1992; grantee Social Rsch. Coun., Am. Philos. Soc., Coun. Learned Socs., Fulbright Com., NEH. Mem. Am. Hist. Assn., Conf. on Slavic and East European History,Czechoslovak History Conf., So. Conf. Slavic Studies, Am. Assn. Advancement Slavic Studies, Am. Com. to Promote Studies of Habsburg Monarchy. Home: 18 Golf Club Dr Langhorne PA 19047-2163 Office: Tulane U Dept History New Orleans LA 70118

LY, RAYMOND HOA BINH, physician; b. Kompongcham, Cambodia, Jan. 29, 1943; came to U.S., 1979; s. Hiep Binh and Hieu Thi (Tong) L.; m. Kathryn Diep Nguyen, Dec. 20, 1972; children: Quynh, Lien, Lan. Pre-med. cert., U. Saigon, Vietnam, 1962-63; MD, U. Saigon, 1971; cert. emergency resuscitation, Cong-Hoa Gen. Mil. Hosp., Saigon, 1972. Chief med. aero. sect. Phu-Cat Air Base, Vietnam Air Force, Binh-Dinh, 1972-74; attending physician Tan-Son-Nhat Med. Aero. Sect., Saigon, 1974-75; vis. fellow diagnostic radiology VA Hosp West L.A., Calif., 1983-85; clin. officer of day, emergency room physician Fla. State Hosp., Chattahoochee, Fla., 1985-89; staff physician Polk Gen. Hosp., Bartow, Fla., 1989—. Mem. AMA, Vietnamese Med. Assn. Fla., Assn. Vietnamese Physicians of Free World (mem. organizing com. 4th internat. conv. 1993). Republican. Buddhist. Office: Paxon Primary & Family Care Ctr 1718 Edgewood Ave N Jacksonville FL 32254-1757

LYCAN, REBECCA TATUM, professional dog handler; b. Atlanta, Oct. 10, 1960; d. Clement Marduke and Ruth (Davenport) Tatum; m. Glenn Eugene Lycan, July 14, 1984. BS in Microbiology, U. Ga., 1982. Lab. technician Optimal Systems, Inc., Norcross, Ga., 1982-84; asst. dog handler Canine Country Club, Chattanooga, 1984-86; profl. dog handler Leading Edge Kennel, Griffin, Ga., 1986—. Nominee for Best New Female Profl. Handler, Kennel Rev. and IAMS, 1989, 90. Mem. Profl. Handlers Assn., Dog Handlers Guild, Griffin Kennel Club, Griffin Kennel Club (show chmn. Fall shows 1990-92), Conyers Kennel Club. Office: Leading Edge Kennel PO Box 849 Griffin GA 30224-0849

LYERLY, ELAINE MYRICK, advertising executive; b. Charlotte, N.C., Nov. 26, 1951; d. J.M. and Annie Mary (Myrick) L.; m. Marc Rauch, Jan. 17, 1987. AA in Advt. and Comml. Design, Cen. Piedmont Community Coll., 1972. Freelance designer Sta. WBTV, Charlotte, N.C., 1972; fashion illustrator Matthews Belk, Gastonia, N.C., 1972-73; designer Monte Curry Mktg. and Communication Svcs., Charlotte, 1973-74, exec. v.p., 1974-77; pres. Repro/Graphics, Charlotte, 1975-77, Lyerly Agy. Inc., Charlotte, 1977—; bd. dirs. SouthTrust Bank. Illustrator: Mister Cookie Breakfast Cookbook, 1985. Chmn. regional blood com. ARC, chmn. Greater Carolinas chpt., 1990-93, mem. nat. implementation com., 1991; bd. dirs. United Way; mem. exec. com. Ptnrs. in Quality. Named Bus. Woman of Yr., Shearson Lehman Hutton/Queens Coll., 1989, N.C. Young Careerist Bus. and Profl. Women's Club, 1981; recipient ACE award Women in Comms., 1993. Mem. Women Execs. (bd. dirs.), Women Bus. Owners (adv. coun., Leadership award 1990, Woman Bus. Owner of Yr. award 1994), Pub. Rels. Soc. Am. (Counselors Acad. 1985—), Charlotte C. of C. (bd. dirs., diversity coun., long-range planning com., Bus. Woman of Yr. award 1985), Hadassah. Republican. Jewish. Office: Lyerly Agy Inc 4819 Park Rd Charlotte NC 28209

LYERLY, HERBERT KIM, surgical oncology educator, researcher; b. San Diego, Aug. 26, 1958; s. Albert Elliot and Mitsu (Kinoshita) L. BS, U. Calif., Riverside, 1980; MD, UCLA, 1983. Diplomate Am. Bd. Surgery. Intern Duke U., Durham, N.C., 1983, resident, 1990-94, from asst. prof. to assoc. prof. surgery, 1990—, asst. prof. pathology, 1991—, clin. dir. molecular therapeutics, 1993—, asst. prof. immunology, 1995—. Editor: Surgical Intensive Care, 2d edit., 1989, co-editor: Surgical Intensive Care, 3d edit., 1991, Companion, 1992, Essentials of Surgery, 1994. Mem. Assn. Acad. Surgery, Soc. Surg. Oncology, Soc. Univ. Surgeons, Am. Coll. Surgeons. Office: Duke U Hosp Box 2606 Durham NC 27710

LYGAS, MARJORIE MACGREGOR, critical care nurse; b. Cornwall, Ont., Canada, Oct. 14, 1942; came to U.S., 1966; d. James Clifton and Helen Isabel (McDonnell) MacGregor; m. Edward Allan Lygas, Nov. 13, 1965 (div. Oct. 1979); children: Marnie Elizabeth Krause, Andrew Walter Lygas. Diploma in nursing, St. Joseph Sch. Nursing, Cornwall, Ont., 1963; BSN, Tex. Woman's U., 1992. RN, Tex.; cert. CEN; cert. ACLS instr., TNCC; cert. emergency nurse. Surg. fl. staff nurse King Edward VII Meml. Hosp., Hamilton, Bermuda, 1964-66; ICU staff nurse Upstate Med. Ctr., Syracuse, N.Y., 1966-68; critical care staff nurse Meml. City Med. Ctr., Houston, 1973-79, emergency staff nurse, 1979-81, emergency dept. coord., 1981-94; trauma coord. LBJ Hosp. of Harris County Hosp. Dist., Houston, 1994—; guest lectr. Houston C.C. ADN program, 1990—. Mem. Soc. Trauma Nurses, Trauma Coords. Forum, Am. Trauma Soc., Emergency Nurses Assn., Sigma Theta Tau. Home: 10610 Holly Springs Houston TX 77042 Office: LBJ Hosp 5656 Kelley St Houston TX 77042

LYLE, JAMES ARTHUR, real estate broker; b. Charlottesville, Va., Mar. 9, 1945; s. James Aaron and Sallie (Tuthill) Lyle; m. Martha Lee Gale, Jan. 28, 1978; children: Cory Jackson, Martha Jessica. BS in Indsl. Mgmt., Ga. Inst. Tech., 1968. Cert. comml. investment mem. Mktg. rep. IBM, Atlanta, 1970-71; investment cons. La Salle Ptnrs., El Paso, Tex., 1971-76; owner James Arthur Lyle and Assocs., El Paso, 1976—; v.p., bd. dirs. Hueco Mountain Estates, Inc., 1983-94; bd. dirs. Vista Hills Townhomes, 1977-78; bd. dirs. Southwestern Savs., 1984-86. Chmn., vice-chmn. El Paso City Plan Commn., 1978-82; vice-chmn. Internat. Airport Bd., 1982; adv. bd. El Paso Bikeway, 1986-88; active El Paso County Planning Commn., 1986-96; bd. dirs. NCCJ, 1978-82, Southwestern Gen. Hosp., 1979-83, El Paso Econ. Devel. Bd., 1980-82; bd. dirs. Am. Heart Assn., 1989-93. 1st lt. U.S. Army, 1968-70. Named Bus. Assoc. of Yr., Am. Bus. Womens Assn., 1984, S.W. Challenge Series Champion, 1991-96, Ironman World Triathlon Championship, 1992. Mem. SAR (dist. v.p., Bronze Good Citizenship medal, Cert. of Disting. Svc.), Nat. Assn. Realtors, Realtors Nat. Mktg. Inst., Nat. Assn. Indsl. and Office Parks, Tex. Property Exchangors (Best Exch. 1979), Tex. Assn. Realtors, Tex. Real Estate Polit. Action Com. (life), El Paso Bd. Realtors (bd. dirs. 1975-88, cert. comml. investment mem. 1975—, El Paso-West Tex. cert. comml. investment mem., pres., sec.-treas. 1975—, comml.-investment real estate coun. 1971—), El Paso Indsl. Devel. Bd., El Paso Investment Exch. Svc., Sons Confederate Vets, Sunturians (life), Half Fast Track Club (v.p. multisports), USA Triathlon (bd. dirs. 1995-96), Team El Paso. Republican. Episcopalian. Home: 626 Blacker Ave El Paso TX 79902-2711 Office: James Arthur Lyle & Assocs 6028 Surety Dr Ste 204 El Paso TX 79905-2024

LYLE, ROBERT EDWARD, chemist; b. Atlanta, Jan. 26, 1926; s. Robert Edward and Adaline (Cason) L.; m. Gloria Gilbert, Aug. 28, 1947. B.A., Emory U., 1945, M.S., 1946; Ph.D., U. Wis.-Madison, 1949. Asst. prof. Oberlin Coll., Ohio, 1949-51; asst. prof. U. N.H., Durham, 1951-53; assoc. prof. U. N.H., 1953-57, prof., 1957-76; prof., chmn. dept. chemistry U. North Tex., Denton, 1977-79; v.p. chemistry, chem. engr. S.W Rsch. Inst., San Antonio, 1979-91; v.p. GRL Cons., San Antonio, 1992—; vis. prof. U. Va., Charlottesville, 1973-74, U. Grenoble, France, 1976; adj. prof. Bowdoin Coll., Brunswick, Maine, 1975-79, U. Tex., San Antonio, 1985—. Mem. editorial bd. Index Chemicus, 1976—. USPHS fellow Oxford U., Eng., 1965; recipient honor scroll award Mass. chpt. Am. Inst. Chemistry, 1971; Harry and Carol Mosher awardee, 1986. Fellow AAAS; mem. Am. Chem. Soc. (councilor 1965-84, 86-92, medicinal chemistry divsn.), Royal Soc. Chemistry, Alpha Chi Sigma (editor Hexagon 1992—). Methodist. Office: GRL Cons 12814 Kings Forest St San Antonio TX 78230-1511

LYLE, VIRGINIA REAVIS, retired archivist, genealogist; b. Nashville, Apr. 19, 1926; d. Damon Ashley and Nellie Alice (Vaughan) R.; m. John Reid Lyle, Sept. 25, 1943; 1 child, Judith L. Haggard. BA, Vanderbilt U., 1974, MLS, 1975. Cert. genealogist, archivist. Administrv. officer Commerce Union Bank, Nashville, 1961-70, 75-78; rsch. asst. R.C.H. Mathews, Jr., Nashville, 1970-75, 78-79; genealogist Nashville 1980; archivist Metro Nashville-Davidson County Archives, Nashville, 1981-93; ret., 1993; organizing sec. Friends of Metro Archives, 1994-95. Sec. Homecoming '86 Metro Steering Com. for Tenn., 1986; mem. Pub. Libr. Bd., 1978-81; historian Dalewood United Meth. Ch., 1995—. Mem. AAUW, Tenn. Archivists, Nat. Geneal. Soc., DAR, Ladies Hermitage Assn., Soc. Am. Archivists, Acad. Cert. Archivists, Woman's Club of Nashville (adv. bd.). Methodist. Home: 1421 Eastland Ave Nashville TN 37206-2626

LYLE, WILLIAM FREDERICK, III, computer science educator; b. Charleston, W.Va., Oct. 26, 1950; s. William Frederick Jr. Lyle and Frances Adele (Murray) Lyle Dumpel; m. Judith Denise Rogers, Aug. 11, 1973. BS, Davidson (N.C.) Coll., 1972; MS, Clemson U., 1974, PhD, 1977. Asst. prof. math. Columbia (S.C.) Coll., 1977-81; asst. prof. computer sci. Murray (Ky.) State U., 1981—, dept. chair, 1982-83, 86-88. Mem. IEEE, Assn. Computing Machinery. Home: 104 S 9th St Murray KY 42071-2429 Office: Murray State U PO Box 9 Murray KY 42071-0009

LYLES, MARTIN DALE, secondary school educator; b. Macon, Ga., May 12, 1954; s. William Clifford and Jean (Clark) L.; m. Virginia Jean Henninger, June 17, 1978; 1 child, Grayson Henninger. BFA in Drama and Theatre, U. Ga., 1976; MEd in Media Edn., West Ga. Coll., 1984. Tchr. Ctrl. H.S., Newnan, Ga., 1977-79, East Coweta H.S., Senoia, Ga., 1979-80; media specialist East Coweta H.S., Sharpsburg, Ga., 1980—; artistic dir. Newnan Cmty. Theatre Co., 1978—; choir dir. Newnan Presbyn. Ch., 1993—; ednl. writer Turner Ednl., Atlanta, 1988-95; instr. Ga. Gov.'s Honors Program, Valdosta, 1984—; mem. remote staff Am. Online, 1990—. Mem. ASCD, Theatre Comm. Group. Office: East Coweta HS 400 McCollum-Sharpsburg Sharpsburg GA 30277

LYLES-ANDERSON, BARBARA DUNBAR, civil engineer; b. Columbia, S.C., June 2, 1954; d. Thomas McDonald and Barbara Ann (Dukes) L.; m. John Bristow Anderson, Feb. 20, 1988. BSCE magna cum laude, Clemson (S.C.) U., 1976. Registered profl. engr., S.C. Engr. Davis & Floyd Engrs., Inc., Greenwood, S.C., 1976-80; project mgr. Life Cycle Engrng., Inc., Charleston, S.C., 1980-88; v.p. Jordan, Jones & Goulding Engrs., Atlanta, 1988—; corp. mgr. Fulton County Arts Coun., 1992—. Vice-pres. Greenwood Ballet Guild, 1978; bd. dirs. Jr. League of Atlanta, 1991-92. Recipient John M Ford Meml. award, Walter Lowry award. Mem. ASCE (Charleston chpt. co-chmn. Mathcounts 1986), NSPE (bd. dirs.), S.C. Soc. Profl. Engrs. (Charleston chpt. bd. dirs. 1986-87), Soc. Women Engrs., Am. Waterworks Assn. (com. 1980—), Water Pollution Control Fedn. (com. 1980—), Nat. Assn. Counties (bd. dirs. 1995), Fulton County Roundtable on Children, Lords Proprietors Soc., Jr. League of Atlanta (bd. dirs. 1991-92). Episcopalian. Home: 2980 Howell Mill Rd NW Atlanta GA 30327-1606 Office: Jordan Jones & Goulding Inc 2000 Clearview Ave Atlanta GA 30340-2100

LYLISTON, WILLIAM PHILIP, writer, poet; b. Hampton, Va., Apr. 14, 1955; s. William D. and Aurelia M. LyL. Student, U. Richmond, 1973, Christopher Newport U., 1977-79, 84-86. Dept. store, grocery store clk., shipyard laborer, freelance writer, 1975—. Author: (sci. fiction) All Living Things, 1982, Live Wires, 1985, A Time for Caring, 1986, A Voyage to the Stars and Beyond, 1989, A World United in Endeavor, 1990, Writing Poetry for the Fun of It, 1990, Concert on a Far Planet, 1991, The Example of Jesus Christ, 1992, Scenes From the American Blue Ridge, 1992, Lament of an Artificial Intelligence, 1994, Reflections, 1996. Mem. Va. Democratic Orgn., poll-worker, office worker, poll-organizer, state conv. del., 1992;. Mem. Internat. Soc. Poets. Methodist.

LYMAN, GARY HERBERT, epidemiologist, cancer researcher, educator; b. Buffalo, Feb. 24, 1946; s. Leonard Samuel and Beatrice Louise L.; children: Stephen Leonard, Christopher Henry. BA, SUNY-Buffalo, 1968, MD, 1972; MPH, Harvard U., 1982. Diplomate: Am. Bd. Internal Medicine (med. oncology, hematology). Resident in medicine U. N.C.-Chapel Hill, 1972-74; fellow in oncology Roswell Park Meml. Inst., Buffalo, 1974-77; rsch. instr. medicine SUNY Med. Sch.-Buffalo, 1974-77; mem. faculty U. South Fla. Coll. Medicine, Tampa, 1977—, assoc. prof. medicine, 1980-86, prof. medicine, 1986—, dir. div. med. oncology, 1979-93, chief medicine H. Lee Moffitt Cancer Ctr. and Rsch. Inst., prof. epidemiology and biostats., 1988—. Co-author: Geriatric Oncology, 1992; contbr. articles to profl. jours., chpts. to books. Spl. fellow Leukemia Soc. Am., 1976-77; postdoctoral fellow biostats. Harvard U., 1981-82; spl. clin. fellow Roswell Park Meml. Inst., Buffalo, 1975-76. Fellow ACP, Am. Coll. Preventive Medicine, Am. Coll. Clin. Pharm.; mem. Am. Soc. Clin. Oncology. Current work: Cancer clinical trials, biostatistics, epidemiology, clinical decision analysis. Office: 12902 Magnolia Dr Tampa FL 33612-9416

LYNCH, ALLEN CHARLES, political science researcher; b. N.Y.C., Aug. 17, 1955; s. Allen John and Eileen Patricia (McCartin) L.; m. Tullia Mary Maffei, May 16, 1987; 1 child, Thomas Gregory. BA in History with high honors, SUNY, Stony Brook, 1977; M in Internat. Affairs, cert., Russian Inst., Columbia U., 1979; PhD in Polit. Sci., Columbia U., 1984. Rsch. assoc. Inst. for East-West Security Studies, N.Y.C., 1984-87, dep. dir. of studies, 1987-89; exec. v.p. Feris Found. Am., Mt. Kisco, N.Y., 1988—; asst. dir. W. Averell Harriman Inst. for Advanced Study of Soviet Union Columbia U., N.Y.C., 1989-92; lectr. Dept. Polit. Sci., Columbia U., 1990-92; assoc. prof. Woodrow Wilson dept. govt. and fgn. affairs U. Va., Charlottesville, 1992—, dir. ctr. Russian and East European studies, 1993—; rapporteur Soviet study group Coun. on Fgn. Rels., N.Y.C., 1978-79; cons. Ford Found. Office of European and Internat. Affairs, N.Y.C., 1980; mem. U.S.-Soviet steering com. Am. Ctr. for Internat. Leadership, Balt., 1986-89; bd. dirs. Feris Found. Am., Mt. Kisco, N.Y. Author: The Soviet Study of International Relations, 1987 (Marshall D. Shulman award 1988), (monographs) Political and Military Implications of the Nuclear Winter Theory, 1987, Gorbachev's International Outlook, 1989, The Cold War is Over Again, 1992, The Disintegration of the USSR and U.S. Foreign Policy, 1992, Europe from the Balkans to the Urals, 1996; editor: Building Security in Europe-Confidence-Building Measures and the CSCE, 1986, Soviet-and-post-Soviet Russia in a World of Change, 1994. Named All-Am. Football Kicker, Nat. Club Football Assn., 1975; fellow Columbia U. Sch. Internat. Affairs, 1977-79, Ford Found., 1979-80; Pres. fellow Columbia U., 1979-80; Albert Gallatin fellow Feris Found. Am., 1981-82; status of visitor Russian Rsch. Ctr., Harvard U., 1980-81; vis. scholar RFE/RL Rsch. Inst., Munich, 1993-94. Office: U Va Dept Govt/Fgn Affairs 232 Cabell Hall Charlottesville VA 22901

LYNCH, CAROLE YARD WORTHINGTON, lawyer; b. Knoxville, Tenn., Aug. 29, 1951; d. Charles R. and Alma (Allred) Yard; m. Robert F. Worthington Jr., Sept. 14, 1996; 1 child, Allison Kathleen. BA, U. Tenn., 1972, JD, 1977. Bar: Tenn. 1977, Ga. 1982. Assoc. Thomas, Leitner, Mann, Warner & Owens, Chattanooga, 1977-78, Thomas, Mann & Gossett, Chattanooga, 1978-81, ptnr., v.p., 1981-86; ptnr. Grant, Konvalinka & Harrison, P.C., 1987—. Author: Estate Planning Tennessee Practice, 1992; asst. editor Tenn. Law Rev., 1976-77. Vice chmn. allocations United Way of Chattanooga, 1985, vice chmn. pilot campaign, 1986; active Jr. League of Chattanooga, 1981-92; mem. alumnae adv. coun. U. Tenn. Coll. Law, 1983-92, chair 1990-92, dean's circle, 1989—; bd. dirs. Mental Health Assn. Chattanooga Inc., 1986-92, 1st v.p. 1988-89, sec. 1989-92; trustee St. Nicholas Sch., 1992-95. Recipient Alumni Leadership award U. Tenn. Coll. Law, 1988, 92. Fellow Am. Bar Found., Tenn. Bar Found. (hearing com. mem, Tenn. bd. profl. responsibility 1992-95, bd. govs. 1994—), Chattanooga Bar Found.; mem. ABA (assembly del. 1991—, com. on legal aid and indigent defendants 1994-95, select com. of the house 1994—), Chattanooga Bar Assn. (bd. govs. 1982-89, sec.-treas. 1985-86, pres. 1987-88), Tenn. Bar Assn. (chair long range planning com. 1995—, vice chair comml. law, banking and bankruptcy 1988-90, unified bar study com. 1990-91, chair bar leadership conf. 1990, editorial bd. Tenn. Bar Jour. 1991-94, bd. govs. 1994—), Ga. Bar Assn., Nat. Conf. Lawyers and Realtors (ABA del. 1990-92), Nat. Conf. Bar Pres.'s (exec. coun. 1989-92, treas. 1992-93, sec. 1993-94, pres. elect 1994-95, pres. 1995-96), Phi Alpha Delta. Episcopalian. Home: 807 Woodland Ct Knoxville TN 37919 Office: Grant Konvalinka & Harrison PC PO Box 1626 2303 Riverview Tower Knoxville TN 37919

LYNCH, CATHERINE GORES, social work administrator; b. Waynesboro, Pa., Nov. 23, 1943; d. Landis and Pamela (Whitmarsh) Gores; BA magna cum laude and honors, Bryn Mawr Coll., 1965; Fulbright scholar, Universidad Central de Venezuela, Caracas, 1965-66; postgrad. (Lehman fellow), Cornell U., 1966-67; m. Joseph C. Keefe, Nov. 29, 1981; children: Shannon Maria, Lisa Alison, Gregory T. Keefe, Michael D. Keefe. Mayor's intern, Human Resources Adminstrn., N.Y.C., 1967; rsch. asst. Orgn. for Social and Tech. Innovation, Cambridge, Mass., 1967-69; cons. Ford Found., Bogota, Colombia, 1970; staff Nat. Housing Census, Nat. Bur. Statistics, Bogota, 1971; evaluator Foster Parent Plan, Bogota, 1973; rsch. staff FEDESARROLLO, Bogota, 1973-74; dir. Dade County Advocates for Victims, Miami, Fla., 1974-86; asst. to dep. dir. Dept. Human Resources, Miami, 1986-87, computer liaison, 1987-88, asst. adminstr. placement svcs. program, 1988-89; exec. dir. Health Crisis Network, 1989-96; liaison HIV cmty. svc. State of Fla. Disease Prevention and Control, 1996—; guest lectr. local univs. Participant, co-chmn. various task forces rape, child abuse, incest, family violence, elderly victims of crime, nat., state, local levels, 1974-86; developer workshops in field; participant, chair, co-chair task forces on HIV/AIDS impact, long term care, children and AIDS, AIDS orgnl. issues, 1991—; mem. gov.'s task force on victims and witnesses, gov.'s task force on sex offenders and their victims, gov.'s Red Ribbon panel on AIDS, 1992-93, gov.'s interdepartmental work group, 1993—; mem. ednl. review com. Am. Found. AIDS Rsch., 1991-96; vice chair Metro-Dade HIV Svcs. Planning Council, 1991-93; active Fla. HIV Svcs. Adv. Coun., 1991-94; review panel Fed. Spl. Projects of Nat. Significance; adv. coun. Metro Dade Social Svcs., 1995-96; cert. expert witness on battered women syndrome in civil and criminal cts. Recipient various public svc. awards including WINZ Citizen of Day, 1979, Outstanding Achievement award Fla. Network Victim Witness Svcs., 1982, Pioneer award Metro-Dade Women's Assn., 1989; cert. police instr. Mem. Nat. Orgn. of Victim Assistance Programs (bd. dirs. 1977-83; Outstanding Program award 1984). Fla. Network of Victim/Witness Programs (bd. dirs., treas., 1980-81), Nat. Assn. Social Workers, Am. Soc. Public Adminstrs., Dade County Fedn. Health and Welfare Workers, Fla. Assn. Health and Social Svcs. (Dade County chpt., treas., 1979-80), LWV (bd. dirs. Dade County chpt. 1989-92). Contbr. writings in field to publs. Office: Fla. HRS Office Dist Adminstr N-1007 401 NW 2d Ave Miami FL 33128

LYNCH, CHARLES THEODORE, SR., materials science engineering researcher, consultant, educator; b. Lima, Ohio, May 17, 1932; s. John Richard and Helen (Dunn) L.; m. Betty Ann Korkolis, Feb. 3, 1956; children: Karen Elaine Ostdiek, Charles Theodore Jr., Richard Anthony, Thomas Edward. BS, George Washington U., 1955; MS, U. Ill., 1957, PhD in Analytical Chemistry, 1960. Group leader ceramics div. Air Force Materials Lab., Wright-Patterson AFB, Ohio, 1962-66; lectr. in chemistry Wright State U., Dayton, Ohio, 1964-66; chief advanced metall. studies br. Air Force Materials Lab., Wright-Patterson AFB, Ohio, 1966-74, sr. scientist, 1974-81; head materials div. Office of Naval Rsch., Arlington, Va., 1981-85; pvt. practice cons. Washington, 1985-88; sr. engr. space ops. Vitro Corp., Washington, 1988-95; cons. Burke, Va., 1996—; USAF liaison mem. NMAB Panels on Solids Processing, Ion Implantation and Environ. Cracking, Washington, 1965-68, 78, 81; U.S. rep. AGARD structures and materials panel NATO, 1983-85. Co-author: Metal Matrix Composites, 1972; editor, author: Practical Handbook of Materials Science, 1989; editor: (series) Handbook of Materials Science, vol. I, 1974, vol. II, 1975, vol. III, 1975; vice chmn. editorial bd. Vitro Corp. Tech. Jour., 1989-92, chmn., 1993; contbr. articles to profl. jours. including Jour. Am. Ceramics Soc., Analytical Chemistry, Sci., Transactions AIME, Corr. Jour., Jour. Inorganic Chemistry, SAMPE, Jour. Less Common Metals. Mem., soloist George Washington U. Traveling Troubadours, Washington, 1950-55; choir dir. Trinity United Ch. of Christ, Fairborn, Ohio, 1966-81, Univ. Bapt. Ch., Champaign, Ill., 1957-60, Chapel II, Wright-Patterson AFB, Ohio, 1960-64; pres. Pub. Sch. PTO, 1967-69. 1st lt. USAF, 1960-62. Bailey scholar U. Ill., 1958-60; recipient Commendation medal USAF, 1962, Outstanding Achievement cert. NASA, 1992, award Soc. for Tech. Comm. Publ., 1993. Mem. Am. Chem. Soc. (treas. 1966-67, chmn. audit sect. 1967-68), ASM Internat. (sec. oxidation and corrosion com. 1980-81, chmn. 1981-82). Presbyterian. Home and Office: 5629 Kemp Ln Burke VA 22015-2041

LYNCH, FRAN JACKIE, investment advisory company executive; b. Bklyn., Dec. 15, 1948; d. William R. and Ruth (Slaiman) Diamondstein; m. James P. Lynch, Jan. 8, 1969; children: Cheryl Ann, Christopher, Kevin. BA, Bklyn. Coll., 1969; student, Suffolk Community Coll., Brentwood, N.Y., 1980-82; postgrad, L.I. U., 1983. V.p. Castle Capital Corp., N.Y.C., 1971-74; agt. Jerome Castle Found., N.Y.C., 1970-74; dir. office services Penn-Dixie Industries, N.Y.C., 1970-74; exec. asst. Med. Fin. Advisor, N.Y.C., 1974; v.p. Sept. Capital Corp., Glen Cove, N.Y., 1977-80; controller Bobgar Inc., Wallweaves Inc. and N.Y. Twine, Syosset, N.Y., 1980-86, The Kapson Group, Commack, N.Y., 1987-91, Westbury Transport ETAL, Astoria, N.Y., 1991-93; ptnr. Econometric Capital Advisors Inc., Miami, Fla., 1992—; bus. mgr. Am-Pro Protective Agy., Columbia, S.C., 1994-96; cons. Women's Times, Queens, N.Y., 1987. Sec. Elwood Booster Club, East Northport, N.Y., 1987; mem. Harley Ave. PTA, 1980-87; coach Northport Youth Soccer, 1982; tchr. Confraternity Christian Doctrine Project St. Elizabeth's Ch., 1972-80, bd. dirs. Parish council, S. Huntington, N.Y., 1978-80. Home: 216 Camden Chase Columbia SC 29223-8416

LYNCH, GEORGE CUNINGGIM, art director; b. Hillsborough, N.C., Sept. 29, 1924; s. George Calvin and Cora Elizabeth (Litchfield) L.; m. Margot Dawn Monk (div.); children: Elizabeth Dawn, Charles Mark; m. Elizabeth Suzanne Peninger, Oct. 1, 1977. Student, Duke U., 1944-45, Ringling Sch. Art, Sarasota, Fla., 1945-47, Island City Sch. Art, Key West, Fla., 1947-48, U. Ga., 1948-49. Med. illustrator Duke U., Durham, N.C., 1949-54; instr. med. illustration Duke U., Durham, 1954; from asst. prof. to prof. med. illustration Bowman Gray Sch. Medicine, Winston-Salem, N.C., 1954-88; prof., emeritus prof. biomed. comm. Bowman Gray Sch. Medicine, Winston-Salem, 1991; art dir. George Lynch Studios, Winston-Salem, 1991—. Portraits represented in numerous collections including Bowman Gray Sch. Medicine, Duke U., U. Ga. Med. Coll., Forsyth Meml. Hosp., Reynolds Tobacco Co., High Point Coll., N.C. Bapt. Hosp.; contbr. illustrations to textbooks; contbr. articles to profl. jours. Bd. govs. Vesalius Trust for Health Scis. Comm. Edn., 1991—, fellow, 1992—, v.p., 1994-95. Mem. Assn. Biomed. Comm. Dirs. (bd. dirs. 1977-78, 83-86, treas. 1983-85, pres. 1986-87, jour. editor 1988-90), Health Scis. Comm. Assn., Biol. Photographic Assn. (bd. govs. 1983-86), Inst. Med. and Biol. Illustration, Assn. Med. Illustrators (chmn. bd. 1964-65, pres. 1968-69, fellow 1988, Life Achievement award 1992). Home and Office: 141 Lamplighter Cir Winston Salem NC 27104-3416

LYNCH, JAMES CHARLES, security consultant; b. Newark, Jan. 15, 1919; s. Bernard and Bridget (Fitzsimmons) L.; BS in BA, Rutgers U., 1940; cert. Indsl. Coll. of Armed Forces, 1964; m. Mary Delia Powell, June 29, 1959; 1 child, Brian Joseph; 1 stepchild, Maria Nannette. Insp. P. Ballantyne & Son, Newark, 1940-42; investigator Retail Credit Co., Newark, 1946; night mgr. Robert Richter Hotel, Miami Beach, 1946-47, night auditor, 1947-48; hotel asst. mgr. Sans Souci Hotel, Miami Beach, Fla., 1948-50; pres., chmn. bd. Asset Protection Assocs., Inc., Huntsville, Ala., 1973-91; cons. in intelligence and security, Huntsville, 1991—; chief Intelligence and Security div. Redstone (Ala.) Arsenal, 1950-60; security adv. NATO Hawk Prodn. Orgn., Paris, 1960, security program chief, until 1964; security specialist U.S. Army Missile Command, Redstone Arsenal, 1964-68; chief Security Office, U.S. Army Safeguard Systems Command, Huntsville, Ala., 1968-72; guest lectr. U. Ala., Birmingham, 1979-80, Jefferson State U., Birmingham, 1979-80, U.

Fla., Huntsville, 1984-85. Served with U.S. Army, 1942-46; ETO. Decorated Silver Star with oak leaf cluster, Bronze Star medal with oak leaf cluster, Purple Heart; inducted into Madison County Hall of Honor, Huntsville, 1987. Cert. protection profl., 1978. Mem. Huntsville-Madison County C. of C. (chmn. internat. trade com. 1976-78), Am. Soc. Indsl. Security (nat. treas. 1984, bd. dirs. 1982-84), Assn. U.S. Army, Smithsonian Assocs., Am. Security Council, VFW, Am. Legion, Security and Intelligence Assn. Republican. Roman Catholic. Clubs: Huntsville Country, Burning Tree Country, Elks, KC. Contbr. articles to profl. jours. Home and Office: 403 Zandale Dr SW Huntsville AL 35801-3462

LYNCH, JOHN ELLSWORTH, hospital administrator; b. Fargo, N.D., June 8, 1935; s. John Joseph and Mary Louise (Paulson) L.; m. Beth Margaret Pallas, July 14, 1956; children—John Ellsworth, Michael, Kevin. B.S. in Bus. Adminstrn, U. N.D., 1959; M.B.A., U. Mo., 1969; doctorate in Pub. Adminstrn., Nova U., 1980; LL.D. (hon.), Campbell U., 1983. Fin. mgr. U.S. Steel Corp., Chgo., 1959-63; controller Decatur (Ill.) and Macon County Hosp., 1963-65; asst. exec. dir. Research Hosp. and Med. Center, Kansas City, Mo., 1965-70; pres., chief exec. officer N.C. Baptist Hosps., Winston-Salem, 1970—; mem. exec. com., chmn. fin. com. dir. 1st Home Fed. Savs. and Loan Assn.; bd. dirs. Sun Alliance, SunHealth Care Plans, Inc.; chmn. Piedmont Associated Industries; mem. nominating com. and retirement com. Blue Cross/Blue Shield N.C. Hon. life mem. Forsyth County chpt. ARC; bd. dirs. Amos Cottage; trustee N.C. Hosp. Assn. Served with AUS, 1954-57. Mem. Am. Coll. Hosp. Adminstrs., N.C. Hosp. Assn. (budget com., council on mgmt.), Beta Gamma Sigma, Beta Alpha Psi. Republican. Baptist. Club: Rotary. Home: 430 Staffordshire Rd Winston Salem NC 27104-1514 Office: NC Bapt Hosp 300 S Hawthorne Rd Winston Salem NC 27157-0002

LYNCH, JOSEPH PATRICK, radio broadcaster; b. Mobile, Ala., Aug. 5, 1950; s. Joseph Richard and Dorothy (Rodwell) L. Talk show host Sta. KSPO, Spokane, Wash., 1980-83, Sta. KARN, Little Rock, 1983—; polit. columnist Ark. Gazette, Little Rock, 1991, Ark. Bus., Little Rock, 1990—, Daily Record, Little Rock, 1992—; editorial writer Spectrum, Little Rock, 1990. Radio commentator: Lynch at Large, 1984-93 (AP Features award 1985, Gold Apple award Little Rock Classroom Tchrs. Assn. 1985), Pat Lynch News and Comments, 1993— (on 30 radio stas. of the Ark. Radio Network), Pat Lynch Show Comcast Cablevision, 1995—. Mem. ACLU (bd. dirs. 1989-95), Soc. Profl. Journalists, Founders Lions Club. Office: Sta KARN 4021 W 8th St Little Rock AR 72204-2029

LYNCH, KAREN LEE, insurance rehabilitation specialist; b. Troy, N.Y., May 5, 1955; d. Richard and Laura Mae (Metcalf) Seib; m. J. Timothy Lynch, May 8, 1976; children: Kelly, Kristy, Katie. Diploma in Nursing, Albany (N.Y.) Sch. Nursing, 1976; BS in Health Care Adminstrn., St. Joseph's Coll., Standish, Maine, 1981; Paralegal Cert. with honors, Sch. Paralegal Studies, Atlanta, 1993. Cert. rehab. nurse. Rehab. nurse Liberty Mutual, Binghamton, N.Y., 1979; sr. rehab. nurse, medex supr. Intracorp, Greenville, S.C., 1980-85; rehab. nurse specialist RMS, Greenville, 1985; clin. rev. specialist SC-PRO, Upstate, S.C., 1986-87; staff nurse Brierwood Hosp., Greer, S.C., 1985-87; clin. nursing instr. Greenville Tech. Coll., 1990-91; clin. nurse III St. Francis Hosp., 1987-91; ob-gyn. nurse Dr. Neeta Rana, Spartanburg, S.C., 1992-93; ins. rehab. nurse, triage nurse Liberty Mutual, Spartanburg, 1993—. Mem. exec. bd. PTA, Buena Vista Elem. Sch., Greer, 1989-92; religious edn. tchr. St. Mary's Cath. Ch., Greenville, 1990-93; classroom vol. Ctr. for Developmental Pediatrics, Greenville, 1991-92. Recipient Preceptor award Bob Jones U., Divsn. Nursing, Greenville, 1991, Golden Touch award St. Francis Hosp., Greenville, 1990, Outstanding Svc. award Office of Solicitor, 13th Judicial Cir., Greenville, 1987. Mem. Assn. Rehab. Nurses. Roman Catholic. Home: 108 Middle Brook Rd Greer SC 29650-3405 Office: Liberty Mutual 775 Spartan Blvd Spartanburg SC 29301-1370

LYNCH, MARY BRITTEN, artist, educator; b. Pruden, Ky., Sept. 30, 1931; d. Fred Clarence and Mary Virginia (Strange) Hill; m. James Walton Lynch, Oct. 6, 1956; 1 child, Holly Kristen. BA, U. Tenn.-Chattanooga, 1956. Art instr. Hunter Mus. Art, Chattanooga, 1954-56, 65-95; Chattanooga Christian High Sch., Chattanooga, 1979-85; apptd. panel mem. Tenn. Arts Commn. Visual Arts Adv. Panel, 1972-76. Exhibited in group shows throughout U.S., 1974-77; represented by Art South, Inc., Phila. and Montgomery, Ala., Trinity Artgroup, Atlanta; featured in numerous art mags. & books, 1983-96. Founder Tenn. Watercolor Soc., 1969, Lenoir City Spring Arts Festival, Tenn., 1963; v.p. Hamilton County Republican Women's Club, 1969; bd. dirs. Chattanooga Symphony Guild, 1968-73, Little Miss Mag Day Nursery, 1977-85, Chattanooga Nature Ctr., 1983-84. Recipient award for Outstanding Contbn. to the State of Tenn. Tenn. Arts Commn., 1978, numerous purchase and cash awards Tenn. State Mus., Anchorage Mus., 1995, Agueous '96 purchase award Ky. Watercolor Soc., Grumbacher Gold Medallion award. Mem. Am. Watercolor Soc., Nat. Watercolor Soc. (top award 1995). Episcopalian. Home: 1505 Woodnymph Trl Lookout Mountain GA 30750-2633

LYNCH, MARY PATRICIA, insurance sales executive; b. Chgo., Oct. 31, 1932; d. Thomas and Nora Marie (Cooney) Lavelle; m. Terrence Brons Lynch, Oct. 9, 1954 (div. 1985); children: Patrice M., Michael J., Thomas F., Teresa J. Student, Loyola U., Chgo., 1951-53, U. Calif., Sacramento, 1956, Rollins Coll., 1981, Valencia Community Coll., 1982; cert., Am. Coll., Bryn Mawr, Pa., 1980-86. CLU, chartered fin. cons. Office mgr. Guardian Life Ins. Co. Am., Orlando, Fla., 1971-80; ptnr. Macsay, Lynch & Assocs., Casselberry, Fla., 1980-85; owner, operator Mary "Pat" Lynch, CLU, Chartered Fin. Cons. & Assocs., Longwood, Fla., 1985—; moderator Life Underwriter Tng. Course, Orlando, 1989-91. Vice pres. Govt. Point Homeowners Assn., 1990, pres., 1991. Mem. Ctrl. Fla. Soc. CLUs and ChFCs (chmn. Huebner Sch. 1983-84, Golden Key chair 1994-95, pub. rels. chair 1995-96), Ctrl. Fla. Women's Life Underwriters (bd. dirs. 1985-91), Women's Life Underwriters Confdn. (bd. dirs. 1985—). Democrat. Roman Catholic. Home: 436 Evesham Pl Longwood FL 32779-3390 Office: 2917 State Road 434 W Ste 141 Longwood FL 32779-4884

LYNCH, MILDRED VIRGINIA, lead company executive; b. Sharp's Chapel, Tenn., Jan. 10, 1928; d. Charles Lafayette and Mossie Edith (Needham) Ousley; m. William Theodore Lynch, July 15, 1948; children: Pat Bryan, Penny Beth. Student, Maryville Coll., 1945-46, U. Tenn., 1946-47. Math. tchr. Horace Maynard High Sch., Maynardville, Tenn., 1948; sec., treas. Nuclear Lead Co. Inc., Oak Ridge, Tenn., 1977-83, v.p., 1983—. Pres. PTA, Farragut Elem. and High Sch., Knoxville, 1967-69, hon. life mem., 1970; pres. Farragut Adv. Bd., 1970, Farragut Hills Estate Home Owners Assn., 1987-91; past mem. coun. and regional v.p. Knox County PTA; pres. Women's Guild, Inskip Meth. Ch., Knoxville, 1959-61; chmn. Women's Circle, Concord United Meth. Ch., also past mem. numerous coms., trustee; mem. Knox County Rep. Exec. Com.; bd. dirs. Oak Square Condominium, Gatlinburg, Tenn.; pres. Volunteer Rep. Woman's Club, 1981-83. Named Woman of Yr., Volunteer Rep. Women's Club, 1983. Mem. Am. Rose Soc. (nat. life judge, nat. life judge emeritus 1995), Knoxville Rose Soc. (pres. 1972-74), DAR (regent Rev. Philip Ausmus chpt. 1976-79, Tenn. state flag chmn. 1983-86), Farragut Garden Club (organizing), Psi Psi Psi (pres. U. Tenn. 1978). Home: 350 David Ln Knoxville TN 37922-3209

LYNCH, PATRICIA M., dietitian; b. Springfield, Mass., Dec. 22, 1954; d. Robert Richard and Mary Patricia Lynch. Student, Springfield Tech. C.C., 1972-73; BS in Food Sci.-Nutrition with honors, U. Mass., 1976; MS in Mgmt. for Health Profls., Ga. State U., 1983. Dietetic intern Emory U. Sch. Medicine, Atlanta, 1976-77; clin. nutrition specialist Ga. Bapt. Med. Ctr., Atlanta, 1977-84; clin. nutrition specialist diabetes treatment ctr. HCA West Paces Ferry Hosp., Atlanta, 1984-88; mgr. clin. svcs. Diabetes Treatment Ctrs. Am., Nashville, 1988-91, dir. clin. svcs., 1992-95, sr. dir. clin. svcs., 1995—. Editor: Current Trends in Diabetes Management, 1993. Vol. St. Patrick's Shelter, Nashville, 1992—. Mem. Am. Dietetic Assn. (registered, former co-chmn. award com. diabetes care and edn. practice group, former mem. edn. com.), Am. Diabetes Assn. (cert. diabetes educator), Juvenile Diabetes Found., Internat. Diabetes Found., Sierra Club, Westside Athletic Club. Office: Diabetes Treatment Ctrs Am One Burton Hills Blvd Nashville TN 37215

LYNCH, SAMUEL CURLEE, JR. (SAMI LYNCH), painter, sculptor, writer; b. Salisbury, N.C., July 31, 1953; s. Samuel and Mae (Alexander) L. Student, Windsor (Ont., Can.) U., 1970-73, Acad. for Arts, N.Y.C., 1978, Raymond Duncan Acad., Paris, 1981, Writers Inst., Mamaroneck, N.Y., 1991-92. Registered Soc. N.AM. Artists. Artist Windsor Sun, 1973-74; artist, editor asst. Akwesasne Notes, St. Regis, Que., Can., 1974; graphic artist Art Leadley, Windsor, 1974; counseling asst. S.W. REgional Centre, Cedar Springs, Ont., 1974-76; art dir., set. designer Video Variety, N.Y.C., 1977-79; instr. painting and sculpture Waterworks, Salisbury, 1980; artist, fashion designer DHR/555 Import-Export, N.Y.C. and Montreal, 1985-86; artist, writer, inventor, designer Landis, N.C., 1986—; v.p. Native Cultural Centre, Windsor, 1974; mem. Rowan Art Guild, Salisbury, 1980. Inventor art material Wings Easel, 1983; illustrator/editor The Oracle, 1985-87; works include Wedding Party/On a Summer's Night, Storm Shelter, mini-pastels, 1985-86, watercolor, oils; commemorative art of Princess Grace for Royal Family of Monaco/Consul de Monaco; exhibited in numerous shows in U.S. and abroad. Artist, Landis Heritage Day Com., 1987-94. Decorated knight Royal Order (Hutt River Principality); recipient Bronze Medallion of Paris, Acad. Raymond Duncan, 1981, Prix du Centennaire, Musèo Duncan, 1981, Salon d'Aout award, 1981, Archtl./Landscape Design Outstanding Artistic Ability award, 1966, Art award, 1970; Royal Patronage, Hutt River Province Principality, 1994, others. Mem. Societe des Amis de la Fondation Maeght. Roman Catholic. Office: Sami Lynch PO Box 331 Landis NC 28088-0331

LYNCH, SHERRY KAY, counselor; b. Topeka, Kans., Nov. 20, 1957; d. Robert Emmett and Norma Lea Lynch. BA, Randolph-Macon Woman's Coll., 1979; MS, Emporia State U., 1980; PhD, Kans. State U., 1987. Vocat. rehab. counselor Rehab. Services, Topeka, 1980-81, community program cons., 1981-86. Mem. exec. com. Sexual Assault Counseling Program, Topeka, 1983-86, recruitment coordinator, 1983-86, counselor, 1981-86, Nat. Singles Conf. Planning Com., Green Lake, Wis., 1987-90; area admissions rep. Randolph-Macon Woman's Coll., Lynchburg, Va., 1981-87; counseling intern, Winthrop Coll., Rock Hill, S.C., 1986-87; counselor Ripon (Wis.) Coll., 1987-90, mem. Student Outreach Svcs. coun. Northbrooke Hosp., 1988-90; counselor Va. Poly. Inst. and State U., 1991—, mem. Student Affairs Staff Devel. com., 1991-94, chairperson, 1992-94, mem. Sexual Assault Victim Edn. and Support com., 1991-95, Wellness com., 1993—, Leadership Resource team, 1994—; bd. dirs., sec. Ripon Chem. Abuse and Awareness program, 1987-90; bd. dirs. Montgomery County Community Shelter, 1992—, also sec., 1993—, Haymarket Sq. Homeowners Assn., 1992—, also treas., 1993—; chairperson ch. and soc. com. Blacksburg United Meth. Ch., 1992-94, mem. coun. ministries, 1992-94. Recipient Kans. 4-H Key award Extension Service of Kans. State U., 1974; named Internat. 4-H Youth Exchange Ambassador to France, 1977. Mem. Nat. Rehab. Counseling Assn. (bd. dirs. 1982-88, chairperson br. devel. subcouncil 1982-87, chairperson policy and program council 1987-88), Gt. Plains Rehab. Counseling Assn. (newsletter editor 1982-85, bd. dirs. 1983-87, pres. 1984-85, sec. 1986-87), Gt. Plains Rehab. Assn. (bd. dirs. 1983-85, awards chairperson 1984-85), Kans. Rehab. Counseling Assn. (bd. dirs. 1983-86, pres. 1984-85), Kans. Rehab. Assn. (bd. dirs. 1982-85, advt. chairperson 1983-85), Topeka Rehab. Assn. (bd. dirs. 1982-85, sec. 1982-83, pres. 1983-84), Am. Assn. Counseling and Devel., Am. Coll. Personnel Assn. (chair-elect commn. VII counseling and psychol. svcs., 1995-96, chair, 1996—, directorate body, 1990-93, 95—, membership commn. 1990-93), Wis. Coll. Personnel Assn. (bd. dirs. 1988-90), Assn. for Specialists in Group Work, Va. Coll. Pers. Assn. Republican. Methodist. Avocation: tennis. Home: 2700 Newton Ct Blacksburg VA 24060-4112 Office: Va Tech U Counseling Ctr 152 Henderson Hall Blacksburg VA 24061

LYNCH, WAYNE ALAN, broadcasting executive; b. Pitts., Jan. 30, 1950; s. Norbert Ernest and Rita Ann (Ciancio) L.; m. Karen Joyce Miller, July 10, 1971; 1 child, Matthew. BA in Radio-TV Journalism, Kent State U., 1971. Reporter Akron (Ohio) Beacon Jour., 1971-72, WTVN-TV, Columbus, Ohio, 1972-74; reporter, anchor WMAR-TV, Balt., 1974-81, exec. prodr. news, 1981-84, mng. editor news, 1984-87; news dir. WRIC-TV, Richmond, Va., 1987-91; news dir. Allnewsco, Inc., Springfield, Va., 1991-95, v.p. news and programming, 1995—. Recipient Outstanding News Operation award Va. AP Broadcasters, 1988, Outstanding News Operation award Va. Assn. Broadcasters, 1989, 90. Mem. Radio-TV New Dirs. Ass., Soc. Profl. Journalists (chair journalism edn. com. 1988, Md. chpt. pres. 1986, 87, Outstanding Chpt. award 1987). Office: Allnewsco Inc 7600 Boston Blvd # D Springfield VA 22153-3136

LYNCH, WILLIAM WRIGHT, JR., investment executive, engineer; b. Dallas, Aug. 26, 1936; s. William Wright Sr. and Alma Martha (Hirsch) L.; m. June 11, 1960; children: Mary Margaret, Katherine. BSEE, U. Ariz., 1959; MBA, Stanford U., 1962. Pres. Ins. Bldg. Corp., Dallas, 1965-84; ptnr. Estacado Ptnrs., Dallas, 1985—, Encino Co., Dallas, 1970—, Cimarron Properties Co., Tucson, 1972-83; pres., bd. dirs. Argus Realty Corp., Dallas, 1972—; bd. dirs. Lynch Properties Inc., Dallas, Lynch Investment Co., Dallas, G.P. Bourrous Trucking Co., Inc., Dallas, Tex. Metal Works, Inc., Beaumont, Tex.; adv. dir. Sun Valley Fruit Co., Albuquerque, Patent Smith Tech., LTD, Enersyst Devel. Ctr., Inc., Dallas, 1995—. Bd. dirs. Dallas Symphony Orch., 1966-74, Dallas Civic Music, 1970-77, Ednl. Opportunities Inc., Dallas, 1973-90, Dallas Coun. World Affairs, 1990—; trustee W. W. Lynch Found., Dallas, 1968—. Capt. U.S. Army, 1959-60. Mem. Brook Hollow Club, Verandah Club, M.O. Club (Tuscon). Republican. Episcopalian. Office: Lynch Investment Co 1845 Woodall Rodgers Fwy Dallas TX 75201-2287

LYNE, JAMES COLEMAN, JR., magazine editor, magazine writer; b. Greenville, Ky., Feb. 5, 1944; s. James Coleman Lyne and Lucy Mae (Linton) Locke; m. Laura Conway, July 15, 1991; stepchildren: Adam, Piper. BA in History, U. Ky., 1966, MA in Communications, 1970. Coord. sch.-community rels. Louisville Pub. Sch. System, 1970-77, editor Daybreak, 1971-77; commentator Ky. Ednl. TV, Lexington, 1978-79, Cable News Network, Atlanta, 1980-82; freelance journalist Atlanta, 1982-83; editor, mgr. editorial/prodn. dept. Site Selection Mag., Conway Data, Atlanta, 1984—; bd. dirs. Conway Data; featured speaker N.C. State Japan Ctr. Ann. Conf., 1993; panel moderator World Devel. Coun. Global Super Projects Conf., Singapore, 1993, Barcelona, 1994. Sponsor Global Super Projects Conf., Barcelona, 1994. Recipient Golden Lamp award Ednl. Press Assn. of Am., 1974. Mem. Descendants of George Washington, Magna Charta Barons, Order Ky. Cols., Omicron Delta Kappa. Office: Conway Data Inc 40 Technology Park Norcross GA 30092-2906

LYNK, DEENA HANCOCK, public information professional; b. Morehead City, N.C., June 9, 1968; d. Charles Michael and Drexell Layton (Bryant) Hancock; m. Noah Michael Lynk, Oct. 17, 1992; 1 child, Tanner Michael. BA, U. N.C., 1990, MA, 1992. Instr. English U. Md. Ea. Shore, Princess Anne, 1992-95, Wor-Wic Tech. C.C., Salisbury, Md., 1992-95; instr. comm. Salisbury State U., 1992-95; instr. English Ea. Shore C.C., Melfa, Va., summer 1994; instr. English Carteret C.C., Morehead City, 1990-92, pub. info. officer, 1995—; pub. rels. cons. Hancock & Grandsons, Inc., Beaufort, N.C., 1992—. Counselor, Helpline Carteret County, Beaufort, 1991-92. Mem. Carteret C.C. Assn. Ednl. Office Profls., Carteret Writers. Democrat. Mem. LDS Ch. Home: 195 Lewis St Harkers Island NC 28531 Office: Carteret CC 3505 Arendell St Morehead City NC 28551

LYNN, CAROLYN HUGHES, editor; b. Lexington, Ky., Oct. 27, 1940; d. James Stanley and Ruth Russell (Jarvis) Hughes; m. Robert Charles Lynn, June 30, 1962; children: Melanie D., Bart P., Ruth R. BA, Transylvania U., Lexington, 1962; MA, Georgetown Coll., 1983. Cert. secondary edn. tchr., Ky. Tchr. Scott County H.S., Georgetown, Ky., 1962-65; seasonal clerk to editor Ky. Dept. Fish and Wildlife Resources, Frankfort, 1982—. Author: Kentucky Wildlife Viewing Guide 1994 (Ky. Assn. Govtl. Communicators award 1995); editor Ky. Afield, Ky. Afield Outdoor Calendar. Mem. Assn. Conservation Info. Office: Ky Dept Fish Wildlife Resources 1 Game Farm Rd Frankfort KY 40601-3909

LYNN, DAVID F., transportation design engineer; b. Chgo., Mar. 20, 1964; s. Robert H. and Valmere (Reeves) L. BA in English, U. of Rochester, 1986; BS in Transp. Design, Art Ctr. Coll. of Design, Pasadena, Calif., 1990. Sr. project designer John David Mooney Studio, Chgo., 1990; asst. design and engring. dir. Downing Atlanta (Ga.), Inc., 1991; dir. of design and engring. Downing Atlanta, Inc., 1992—; Body Designer, Evans Automobiles, Scottdale, Ga., 1992—. Affiliate mem. Soc. of Automotive Engrs. Office: Downing Atlanta, Inc. 5096 Peachtree Rd Atlanta GA 30341

LYNN, MARK WAYNE, secondary school educator, administrator; b. Daytona Beach, Fla., Dec. 14, 1965; s. Richard Patrick and Marie Joan (Amodio) L. BA, St. John's U., Jamaica, N.Y., 1986, MA, 1988. Tchr. Xavier High Sch., N.Y.C., 1986-91, chmn. dept., 1989-91; prin. Our Lady Queen of Martyrs Sch., Ft. Lauderdale, Fla., 1991-93; tchr., chmn. dept. Father Lopez High Sch., Daytona Beach, Fla., 1993—, asst. prin., 1996—. Mem. ASCD, NAESP, Nat. Cath. Edn. Assn., K.C., Theta Alpha Kappa.

LYNN, SHEILAH ANN, service executive, consultant; b. Anderson, Ind., Jan. 28, 1947; d. John Benton and Kathleen (Taylor) Bussabarger; m. John Hoftyzer, Dec. 21, 1968 (div. June 1982); children: Melanie Kay, John Theo; m. Guy C. Lynn, May 20, 1984. BS, Ind. U., 1969; postgrad., U. N.C., Greensboro, 1970, Webster U., 1994; diploma, Data Processing Inst., Tampa, Fla., 1983; MS, Ctrl. Mich. U., 1993. Bookkeeper John Hancock Life Ins. Co., Greensboro, 1970-72; freelance seminar leader and devel. Dhahran, Saudi Arabia, 1978-82; dir. programming Fla. Tech. Inst., Jacksonville, 1983-84, instr. in computer sci., 1984-85; real estate sales assoc. Fla. Recreational Ranches, Gainesville, 1985; instrnl. program coord., workforce tng. coord. Fla. C.C., Jacksonville, 1986—; handwriting analyst, cons. Sheilah A. Lynn & Assocs., Jacksonville, 1989—; cons. programmer, analyst Postmasters Co., Jacksonville, 1986—; pres. Options Cons., Jacksonville, 1986-89, Sheilah A. Lynn & Assocs., Jacksonville, 1989—; 6L cons. assocs. Dacum facilitator and curriculum developer. Mem. Jacksonville Community Council, Inc., 1986-87, Fla. Literacy Coalition, 1986-87. Mem. NAFE, ASTD, Fla. Assn. Ednl. Data Systems, Bus. and Profl. Women, Jacksonville C. of C. (bd. dirs. south coun. 1987, sec. 1989, treas. 1990, v.p. 1991, pres. 1992). Democrat.

LYNN, TONY LEE, import company executive; b. Burke City, N.C., Oct. 13, 1939; s. Craig and Marie (Lowman) L.; m. Cindy Robson; 1 child, Gretchen. Student, Lenoir Rhyne Coll., 1958-62, N.C. Sch. Banking, 1972, Sch. Banking of South, Baton Rouge, 1972-75, Am. Inst. Banking, 1976. Dist. mgr. Am. Credit Co., Atlanta, 1961-66; v.p. First Nat. Bank Catawba County, Hickory, N.C., 1966-76; exec. v.p. Dixie Boat Works, Newton, N.C., 1976-82; founder, pres. Friitala Am., Hickory, 1982—. Named one of Outstanding Young Men of Am., 1975. Mem. Am. Inst. Banking (past bd. dirs., pres. Hickory unit), Nat. Ski Patrol Alumni Assn. (lifetime mem., tng. officer, sr. profl.), Catawba County C. of C. (lifetime hon. mem.). Home: 5670 37th St NE Hickory NC 28601-9703 Office: Friitala Am 231 10th St NW Hickory NC 28601-4857

LYON, GILES A., artist; b. N.Y.C., June 30, 1967. Student, Sch. Visual Arts, N.Y.C., 1984-85, Vt. Studio Sch., 1985, Rochester Inst. Tech., 1985-86; BFA, R.I. Sch. Design, 1989. vis. artist./lectr. R.I. Sch. Design, Providence, 1990, San Jacinto Coll., Houston, 1993; vis. critic sculpture dept. U. Houston, 1990; artist-in-residence Edward F. Albee Found., Montauk, N.Y., 1991. One-person shows include Lynn Goode Gallery, Houston, 1992, 94, 96, Mus. of Art Guise, Houston, 1992, Nina Freudenheim Gallery, Buffalo, 1994, Queretaro Cultural Art Ctr., Mex., 1996; exhibited in group shows at Moxy Logic Gallery, Providence, 1988, Bert Gallery, Providence, 1989, Hiram Butler Gallery, Houston, 1990, GVG Gallery, 1990, Amarillo (Tex.) Art Ctr., 1991, Mus. Fine Arts, Houston, 1991,, 93, Blaffer Gallery, Houston, 1992, Laguna Gloria Art Mus., Austin, Tex., 1992, Nina Freudenheim Gallery, Buffalo, 1992, 94, Deutser Gallery, The Jewish Comty. Ctr. Houston, 1993, Michael Walls Gallery, N.Y.C, 1993, DiverseWorks, Houston, 1993, 94, Lawndale Art and Performance Ctr., Houston, 1994, Jan Abrams Gallery, L.A., 1994, Mitchell Algus Gallery, N.Y.C., 1994, Art Mus. South Tex., Corpus Christi, 1995, Artpace, San Antonio, 1995, Galveston (Tex.) Art Ctr., 1996, Arena Gallery and Pierogie 2000 Gallery, N.Y.C., 1996, O'Hara Gallery, N.Y.C., 1996; represented in pvt. collections Archie Rand, N.Y.C., Walter Hopps, Houston, Christophe de Menil, N.Y.C., The Barrett Collection, Dallas, Edward Albee, N.Y.C.; represented in pub. collections Mus. Fine Arts, Houston, Std. Ins., Detroit; featured in publs. including Houston Post, New Orleans Picayune, Mus. and Arts Mag., N.Y. Times, Houston Chronicle, Buffalo News, ArtNews, Art in Am., ArtForum, Dallas Morning News. Core fellow Glassell Sch. Art, Mus. Fine Arts, Houston, 1989-91; Mid-Am. Arts Alliance/NEA grantee, 1994. Home: 212 Northwood St Houston TX 77009

LYON, ISOLDA YVETTE, dietitian; b. Managua, Nicaragua, Nov. 10, 1954; came to U.S., 1982; naturalized citizen 1989; d. Lauriston Edmund and Teresa del Carmen (Rodriguez) Burey; m. Ward Burton Lyon, Mar. 25, 1983; children: Jessica Yvette, Angelica Isolda. BS in Nutrition and Dietetics, U. San Carlos, Guatemala, 1978. Registered dietitian; lic. dietitian; cert. food and beverage mgr., correctional officer. Nutritionist Health Ministry, Managua, Nicaragua, 1975-77; cons. Welfare Ministry and Health Ministry, Managua, Nicaragua, 1978-79; prof. faculty Ctrl. Am. U., Managua, Nicaragua, 1981; dietitian Nestle Co., Managua, Nicaragua, 1979-82; nutritionist Harris County Hosp. Dist., Houston, 1983-85; food svc. dir. Carnegie Gardens Nursing, Melbourne, Fla., 1985-86; food svc. supr. Wuesthoff Hosp., Rockledge, Fla., 1986-87; sgt., food svc. mgr. Tex. Dept. of Corrections, Rosharon, Tex., 1987-88; dir. dietary svcs. Washington Sq. Devel. Svcs. Inc., Titusville, Fla., 1988—. Mem. Dem. Party, Managua, 1981-82. Named Employee of Yr., Carnegie Gardens, 1985, Intelligent Employee of the Yr., Devel. Svcs., 1992. Mem. Am. Dietetic Assn., Dietetics in Devel. and Psychiat. Disorders, Clin. Nutrition Mgmt., Dietetics in Phys. Medicine and Rehab., Space Coast Dietetic Assn. (pres. 1995-96), Nicaraguan Nutritionist and Dietetic Assn. (treas. 1979-82), Ctrl. Am. and Panama Nutritionist Dieticians Assn. Republican. Roman Catholic. Home: 847 Tiffany Pl Rockledge FL 32955 Office: Washington Sq Devel Svcs 1401 N Us Highway 1 Titusville FL 32796-1310

LYON, MARTHA SUE, research engineer, retired military officer; b. Louisville, Oct. 3, 1935; d. Harry Bowman and Erma Louise (Moreland) Lyon. BA in Chemistry, U. Louisville, 1959; MEd in Math., Northeastern Ill. U., 1974. Cert. tchr. Ill., Ky. Rsch. assoc. U. Louisville Med. Sch., 1959-61, 62-63; commd. ensign, USNR, 1965, advanced through grades to comdr., 1983; instr. instrumentation chemistry Northwestern U., Evanston, Ill., 1968-70; tchr. sci., chemistry, gifted math. Waukegan (Ill.) pub. schs., 1970-75; phys. scientist Libr. of Congress, Washington, 1975-76; rsch. engr. Lockheed Missiles & Space Co., Sunnyvale, Calif., 1976-77; instr., assoc. chmn. dept. physics U.S. Naval Acad., Annapolis, Md., 1977-80; analyst Systems Analysis Div., Office of Chief of Naval Ops. Staff, Washington, 1980-81; comdg. officer Naval Res. Ctr., Stockton, Calif., 1981-83; mem. faculty Def. Intelligence Coll., 1983-85; program mgr. Space and Naval Warfare Systems Command, 1985-86, commanding officer PERSUPPACT Memphis, 1986-88; program mgr. Space and Naval Warfare Sys. Command, 1988-91; sect. chief Def. Intelligence Agy., 1991-95. Chief marching divsn. Nat. Homecoming Parade and N.Y.C. Regional Parade Task Force Desert Storm, 1991-95. Grantee Am. Heart Assn., 1960-62, NSF, 1971, 72. Mem. Am. Chem. Soc., Soc. Women Engrs., Am. Fedn. Musicians, Am. Statis. Assn., Am. Soc. Photogrammetry, Internat. Conf. Women in Sci. Engring. (protocol chair), Internat. Soc. Bassists, Mensa, Zeta Tau Alpha, Delta Phi Alpha. Club: Order of Ea. Star. Developer processes used in archival photography, carbon-14 analyses; presenter of papers at profl. confs.

LYON, PHILIP K(IRKLAND), lawyer; b. Warren, Ark., Jan. 19, 1944; s. Leroy and Maxine (Campbell) L.; children by previous marriage: Bradford F., Lucinda H., Bruce P., Suzette P., John P., Martin K., Meredith J.; m. Jayne Carol Jack, Aug. 12, 1982. JD with honors, U. Ark., 1967. Bar: Ark. 1967, U.S. Supreme Ct. 1970, Tenn. 1989. Sr. ptnr., dir. ops. House, Wallace, Nelson & Jewell, P.A., Little Rock, 1967-86; pres. Jack, Lyon & Jones, P.A, Little Rock & Nashville, 1986—; instr. bus. law, labor law, govt. bus. and collective bargaining U. Ark., Little Rock, 1969-72, lectr. practice skills and labor law, U. Ark. Law Sch., 1979-80; bd. dirs. Southwestern Legal Found., 1978—; editorial bd. dirs. Entertainment Law & Fin., 1993—. Coauthor: Schlei and Grossman Employment Discrimination Law, 2d edit., 1982; editor-in-chief: Ark. Law Rev., 1966-67, bd. dirs., 1978-93, v.p., 1990-92; editor: Ark. Employment Law Letter, 1995. Fellow Coll. Labor and Employment Lawyers; mem. ABA (select com. liason office fed. contract compliance programs 1982—, select com. liason EEOC 1984—, select com. immigration law, forum com. entertainment and sports industries), Ark. State C. of C. (bd. dirs. 1984-88), Greater Little Rock C. of C. (chmn.

community affairs com. 1982-84, minority bus. affairs 1985-89), Ark. Bar Assn. (chmn. labor law com. 1977-78, chmn. labor law sect. 1978-79, chmn. lawyers helping lawyers com. 1988-94), Tenn. Bar Assn. (labor sect., lawyers helping lawyers com. 1989—), Nashville Bar Assn. (entertainment law com., lawyers concerned for lawyers com., editor Ark. Employment Law Letter 1995—), Pulaski County Bar Assn., Country Music Assn., Acad. of Country Music, Nashville Entertainment Assn., Nashville Songwriters Assn. Internat., Copyright Soc. of South, Capitol Club. Recipient Golden Gavel award Ark. Bar Assn., 1978, Writing Excellence award Ark. Bar Found., 1980. Home: 350 Ardsley Pl Nashville TN 37215-3247 also: 17 Heritage Park Cir North Little Rock AR 72116-8528 Office: Jack Lyon & Jones PA 11 Music Cir S Nashville TN 37203-4335 also: Jack Lyon & Jones PA 425 W Capitol 3400 TCBY Tower Little Rock AR 72201

LYON, WILFORD CHARLES, JR., insurance executive; b. Blackfoot, Idaho, June 1, 1935; s. Wilford Charles and Nellie Anna (Estenson) L.; m. Eleanor Perkins, Aug. 23, 1957; children: Katherine Ann, Wilford Charles III. BS, Ga. Inst. Tech., 1958; MA in Actuarial Sci., Ga. State Coll., 1962. Asst. v.p. Ind. Life and Accident Ins. Co., Jacksonville, Fla., 1963-69, asst. v.p., dir. methods and planning dept., 1969-70, v.p., home office coordinator, 1970-79, pres., chief adminstrv. officer, 1979-84, chmn. bd., chief exec. officer, 1984-96; trustee, mem. exec. com. Edward Waters Coll., Jacksonville, 1983-96, chmn., bd. visitors, 1993-96. Trustee Gator Bowl Assn., Jacksonville, 1981—, pres., 1981; pres. Jacksonville C. of C., 1984; trustee community TV, Inc., Jacksonville, 1980-93, chmn., 1991-92; trustee Univ. Hosp., Jacksonville, Inc., 1985-86; bd. dirs. YMCA Fla.'s First Coast, 1985—, sec., 1986, vice chmn., 1987, chmn., 1988 (Svc. to Youth award 1991); chmn. 1991 Nat. Vol. Week, Vol. Jacksonville, Inc. Recipient Disting Svc. award Jacksonville Jaycees, 1972, Jack Donnell award Outstanding Businessman of the Year, 1983, Dick Hutchinson award Sertoma Club South Jacksonville, 1972, Svc. to Mankind award, 1972, Boss of Yr. award Profl. Secs. Internat., 1972-73, Victory Crusade award Fla. Cancer Soc., 1969, Ins. Industry Community Svc. award Jacksonville Assn. Life Underwriters, 1986, C.G. Snead Meml. award Jacksonville Assn. of Life Underwriters, 1991, Top Mgmt. award Sales and Mktg. Execs. of Jacksonville, 1990, Clanzel T. Brown award Jacksonville Urban League, 1991, Svc. to Youth award YMCA of Fla.'s First Coast, 1991, Humanitarian award NCCJ, 1994. Mem. Life Insurers Conf. (exec. com. 1981-91, chmn. membership com. 1981-86, sec. 1984-85, vice chmn. 1985-86, chmn. 1986-87), Am. Coun. Life Ins. (Fla. state v.p. 1981-96, bd. dirs. 1987-88, bd. dirs. Polit. Action Com. 1988-94), Southeastern Actuaries Club, Rotary Club Jacksonville (pres. Mandarin club 1977-78, Paul Harris fellow, dist. gov. 697 1985-86), Masons, York Rite, Scottish Rite Bodies, Shriners (potentate Morocco Temple 1973). Republican. Presbyterian. Home: 1129 Mapleton Rd Jacksonville FL 32207-5342

LYONS, CHARLES HENRY, academic director; b. Boston, July 20, 1941; s. John Laurence and Adelaide (English) L.; m. Anne Warner Nason, Nov. 30, 1968; children: Mary Littlefield, Paul Laurence, Charles Philip. BA, Harvard U., 1963, MA in Tchg., 1964; PhD, Columbia U., 1970. Lectr. Syracuse (N.Y.) U., 1969-70; asst. to assoc. prof. Tchrs. Coll., Columbia U., N.Y.C., 1970-76; dir., overseas liaison Am. Coun. on Edn., Washington, 1976-82; exec. dir. Fulbright Found., Monrovia, Liberia, 1982-85; dir. internat. rsch. U. Ill., Chgo., 1985-87; dir. internat. affairs Conn. State U., New Britain, 1987-91; dir. internat. programs U. N.C., Greensboro, 1991—; cons. U.S. AID, Washington, 1980-82. Author: To Wash An Aethiop White, 1975. Vol. U.S. Peace Corps, Nigeria, 1964-66; bd. dirs. Nat. Coun. Returned Peace Corps Vols., Washington, 1980-82; chmn. edn. com. Conn. World Trade Assn., Hartford, 1988-90. Recipient fellowship Fulbright Program, Germany, 1989. Home: 4628 Brompton Dr Greensboro NC 27407

LYONS, CLEM V., lawyer; b. Huntington, N.Y., Sept. 4, 1931; s. Clarence Cornelius and Margaret Marie (Donovan) L.; m. Stephanie Virginia Harville; children: Robin Kathleen, Kelly Eileen, Sean Michael. BS in Pharmacy, St. John's U., Bklyn., 1954; LLB, St. Mary's U., San Antonio, 1962. Bar: Tex. 1962; registered pharmacist, N.Y., Tex.; cert. personal injury law; diplomate Am. Bd. Profl. Liability Attys. Asst. dist. atty. Bexar County, Tex., 1962-66; ptnr. Lyons and Rhodes Inc., San Antonio; advocate Am. Bd. Trial Advocates. With U.S. Army, 1954-56. Fellow Internat. Soc. Barristers, Internat. Acad. Trial Lawyers; mem. ABA, Am. Judicature Soc., Assn. Trial Lawyers Am., Am. Soc. for Pharmacy Law, State Bar Tex., Tex. Bar Found., San Antonio Bar Assn., San Antonio Bar Found., Tex. Trial Lawyers Assn. Office: Lyons & Rhodes Inc 126 Villita St San Antonio TX 78205-2735

LYONS, CYNTHIA DIANNE, special education educator, lecturer; b. Munich, Germany, Aug. 20, 1954; d. Jackson Clinton and Theda Rose (Chelette) Thomas; m. Don Carson Lyons, Apr. 8, 1982. BA, McNeese State U., 1981, MEd, 1992. Cert. supr. in instrn., tchr. spl. edn., tchr. grades 1-8, La. Spl. edn. tchr. Calcasieu Parish, Sulphur, La., 1982; Spl. edn. tchr. Jefferson Davis Parish, Welsh, La., 1982-87, dir. Jefferson Davis Parish Sch. Exceptional Children, 1987-90; spl. edn. tchr. Welsh (La.) Elem. Sch., 1990—; lectr. grad. level McNeese State U., Lake Charles, La., 1993—; Presenter 11th, 12th annual superconf. La. spl. edn., 1992, 93. Author, editor: Cookbook for Handicapped Individuals, 1989. Treas., coach, vol. Jeff Davis Parish (La.) Spl. Olympics, 1984—; leader handicapped individuals Girl Scouts Am., S.W. La., 1988-90; Sunday sch. tchr. Bible sch. Houston River Bapt. Ch., Sulphur, La., 1991—; asst. troop leader handicapped boys Boy Scouts Am., S.W. La., 1988-90. Recipient Green Angel award Girl Scouts Am., 1988, Great Expectation Class Act Tchr. KPLC TV and area industries, 1992. Mem. La. Fedn. Teachrs., Associated Profl. Educators La., Alpha Delta Kappa (Alpha Tau chpt. historian 1994-96). Democrat. Baptist. Home: 508 Bankens Rd Sulphur LA 70663 Office: 222 E Bouregois St Welsh LA 70591

LYONS, FRANK DANIEL, retired oil company executive; b. Springfield, Mo., July 27, 1926; s. Francis Daniel and Gladys Mary (Packer) L.; m. Joan Dishman, Aug. 5, 1950; children: Daniel, Susan. AB, Drury Coll., 1948; BS, U. Mo., 1950. Registered profl. engr. Mo., Okla., Ark. Sr. engr. Mo. Dept. Transp., Jefferson City, 1950-61; dir. Okla. Dept. Transp., Oklahoma City, 1961-67; prin. Howard Samis Lyons Architects and Engrs., Oklahoma City, 1967-68; pres. engrng. svcs. divsn. Kerr McGee Corp., Oklahoma City, 1968-90.; bd. dirs. U. Okla. Rsch. Inst., Okla. State U. adv. bd., Stillwater. Exec. reservist Nat. Emergency Planning Commn.; bd. dirs. Boy Scouts Am., Oklahoma City. Recipient alumni achievement award U. Mo., 1965. Fellow Am. Soc. Civil Engrs.; mem. NSPE, Oklahoma County Hist. Soc., Am. Road Builders Assn. (past nat. dir.), Am. Assn. State Hwy. Ofcls. (exec. com.), Soc. Am. Mil. Engrs. (dir., pres.), Sigma Nu. Home: 3037 Willowbrook Rd Oklahoma City OK 73120

LYONS, NATALIE BELLER, family counselor; b. Habana, Cuba, Apr. 3, 1926; d. Herman Lawrence and Jennie (Engler) B.; widowed, Apr. 18, 1986; children: Anne, Sara. BS in Surveying and Land Appraising, Inst. Vedado, Habana, Cuba, 1943; BA, U. Mich., 1946; MEd, U. Miami, Fla., 1967. Family counselor, mem. staff furniture design and mfg. co. George B. Bent, Gardner, Mass., 1953-58; tchr. H.S., Winchendon, Mass., Hollywood, Fla., 1962; tchr. parochial sch., Ft. Lauderdale, Fla., 1963-64; family counselor Miami, 1967—; project dir. Cen. Am. fisheries program Peace Corps, 1972-74; counselor Svc. Corp. of Ret. Execs., Miami, 1993, bd. dirs., 1994—; bd. dirs., mem. Com. for Accuracy in Mid East Reporting, 1990—. Pres. Miami region Hadassah, 1989-91; bd. dirs. Greater Miami Jewish Fedn., 1985—, mem. women's divsn., mem. cmty. rels. coun., 1985—; bd. dirs. Miami Civic Music Assn., 1985—; mem. nat. bd. dirs. nat. women's divsn. Am. Soc. for Technion, 1991—, pres. 1984-86; co-chair Pro-Israel Rally, Tri County, 1991, Joint Action Com., Miami, 1989-91; tng. dir. Los Amigos de las Ams., 1975—; founder, dir. Cmty. Inst. Jewish Studies, Hollywood, Fla., 1962-64. Recipient Leadership award Hadassah, 1987, honoree Am. Soc. for Technion Scholarship Fund, 1991; named Woman of Yr., Hadassah, 1991. Democrat.

LYONS, PHILLIP MICHAEL, SR., insurance accounting and real estate executive; b. Gueydan, La., Nov. 22, 1941; s. Joseph Bosman and Elder (Richard) L.; children from previous marriage: Phillip M., Wilton J.; m. Regina Zoe (Malloy) Johnson, Aug. 15, 1991; stepchildren: Jennifer R. Johnson, Tracey L. Johnson. Student, McNeese State Coll., 1959-62, Alvin Jr. Coll., 1964, Coll. of Mainland, 1974; BBA, U. Houston, 1977, postgrad., 1984. CPA. Adminstrv. trainee Am. Nat. Ins. Co., Galveston, Tex., 1965, asst. mgr., acting mgr. policy issue dept., 1966-67, mgr., 1967-68, mgr. preissue dept., 1968-71, systems analyst, 1971-72, divsn. mgr., policyholder's svc. divsn., 1972-74, dir. ordinary policyholder's svc., 1974-76, dir. combination policy records, 1976-77; supervising acct. materials acctg. comptr.'s dept. Aramco Svcs. Co., Houston, 1977-79, ins. adviser treas.'s dept., 1979-80, adminstr. risk mgmt. and ins. div., treas.'s dept., 1980—; ptnr. Lyons Real Estate, Sulphur, La., 1966—, L&L Enterprises, Sulphur; bd. dirs. Studio B, Inc., Houston. Solicitor United Fund, 1966-69. Fellow Life Mgmt. Inst.; mem. Risk and Ins. Mgmt. Soc. (assoc. in risk mgmt.), Internat. Found. Employee Benefit Plans, Jr. C. of C. (bd. dirs. 1972, state bd. dirs. 1972—, Sparkplug of Yr. 1972-73, Roadrunner or Yr. 1972-73), Masons, Order of Ea. Star, Shriners, KC. Home: 223 W Sherwood Dr Alvin TX 77511-5109 also: 1012 S Stanford St Sulphur LA 70663-4824 Office: PO Box 4536 Houston TX 77210-4536

LYONS, ROGER MICHAEL, physician; b. Prince Albert, Can., May 1, 1943. MD, U. Man., Can., 1967. Diplomate Am. Bd. Internal Medicine, Am. Bd. Hematology; cert. Med. Coun. Can.; lic. physician, Tex., New South Wales. Chief therapeutics plasmaperesis com. S.W. Tex. Meth. Hosp., 1983—; chief hematology/oncology sect. Humana Hosp., San Antonio, 1985; chief computer com. S.W. Tex. Meth. Hosp., 1985, vice chief dept. medicine, 1987-88, chief dept. medicine, 1989-90; pres. Hematology Oncology Assoc. South Tex., 1980—; clin. prof. medicine Health Sci. Ctr. U. Tex., San Antonio, 1994—; trustee South Tex. Regional Blood Bank, 1986-93; med. audit com., medicine quality assurance com., therapeutic plasmapheresis com., instl. rev. bd., cancer com., exec. com., cancer and blood disease long-term planning com. S.W. Tex. Meth. Hosp. Contbr. chpts. to books, articles to profl. jours. Fellow Internat. Acad. Clin. and Applied Thrombosis and Hemostasis; mem. ACP, AMA, Am. Soc. Hematology, Am. Fedn. Clin. Rsch., Bexar County Med. Soc., Am. Soc. Internal Medicine, Am. Soc. Clin. Oncology, Internat. Soc. Hematology, Internat. Soc. Thrombosis and Haemostasis, Tex. Soc. Med. Oncology. Office: South Tex Med Ctr Methodist Plaza Bldg 4499 Medical Dr Ste 233 San Antonio TX 78229-3712

LYTLE, CHARLES FRANKLIN, biology educator; b. Crawfordsville, Ind., May 13, 1932; s. Robert Earl and Rose May (Caplinger) L.; m. Carol Helen Cottingham, Jan. 22, 1955; children: Charles G., Eric, Stephen, Victoria Lytle Utesch, Thomas. AB, Wabash Coll., 1953; MA, Ind. U., 1958, PhD, 1959. Rsch. assoc. Ind. U., Bloomington, 1959-60; asst. prof. zoology Tulane U., New Orleans, 1960-62; rsch. analyst U.S. Army, Washington, 1962-64; assoc. prof. Pa. State U., State College, 1964-69; prof. biology, coord. biol. scis. N.C. State U., Raleigh, 1969-93, coord. biology outreach programs, 1994—; vis. prof. Duke U., Durham, N.C., 1972, 76, 88, mem. adv. com., 1971-84; vis. prof. Fla. Atlantic U., 1988, U. Ala., summers, 1988—, Jacksonville U., 1988—, The Bolles Sch., Jacksonville, Fla., summers, 1988—, Millsaps Coll., summer, 1992, Thammasat U., Thailand, summer, 1996; cons. Coll. Bd., Atlanta, 1990—, N.C. Wildlife Resources Commn., Raleigh, 1980-87, Ednl. Testing Svc., 1977—, Carolina Biol. Supply Co., Burlington, N.C., 1988—; bd. dirs. Sci.; N.C., Quantum Rsch. Svcs., Inc. Author: A Laboratory Guide to Biology, 1987, General Zoology Laboratory Guide, 1996; co-author: Laboratory Investigations in Biology, 1995, (videodisc) The Biology Encyclopedia; author, dir. 40 instrnl. programs on videotape and film; contbr. articles to profl. jours. Recipient Pub. Svc. award N.C. Optometric Soc., 1975, Outstanding Tchr. award N.C. State U., 1982, Disting. Svc. award N.C. Acad. Sci., 1991, Disting. Svc. in Sci. Edn. award N.C. Sci. Tchrs. Assn., 1991, Disting. Svc. award Nat. Assn. Acads. Sci., 1995, Sci. Star award SCIENCE: N.C., 1995. Fellow AAAS; mem. ASCD, NSTA, Nat. Assn. Biology Tchrs. (cons.), Am. Inst. Biol. Scis., Internat. Platform Assn., Nat. Assn. Acad. Sci., Nat. Sci. Leadership Assn., Nat. Speakers Assn., Text and Acad. Authors Assn., Sigma Xi. Home: 102 Carmel Ct Cary NC 27511-5560 Office: NC State Univ Biol Scis Box 7611 Raleigh NC 27695

LYTLE, MICHAEL ALLEN, academic administrator, consultant; b. Salina, Kans., Oct. 22, 1946; s. Milton Earl and Geraldine Faye (Young) L.; divorced; 1 child, Eric Alexander. BA, Ind. U., 1973; grad. cert. Sam Houston State U., Huntsville, Tex., 1977; MEd, Tex. A&M U., 1978, postgrad., 1978-80, Nat. Def. U., 1988. Diplomate Am. Bd. Forensic Examiners. Substitute high sch. tchr., Butler County, Kans., 1969; instr. criminal justice Cleveland State Community Coll., Tenn., 1974-77; adj. instr. criminal justice U. Tenn., Chattanooga, 1975-76; teaching asst. Tex. A&M U., 1977-80, intern adminstrv. asst. Office Vice Chancellor Legal Affairs and Gen. Counsel, Tex. A&M U. System 1980, staff assoc. Office Chancellor, 1980-81, asst. to chancellor, 1981-83, asst. dir. govt. relations, 1983-84, spl. asst. to Chancellor for fed. relations, 1984-87; dir. research devel. and spl. asst. to v.p. for research and grad. studies, Syracuse U., 1987; exec. dir. for Govt. Relations, 1987-89, dir. fed. rels., 1989-92; prin. and sr. counsel The Erik Alexander Group, 1992-93; adj. prof. internat. bus. studies Syracuse U., 1990-92; sr. rsch. assoc. Tech. and Info. Policy Program Maxwell Sch. Citizenship and Pub. Affairs Syracuse U., 1987-92; exec. dir. instl. devel. U. Tex. Brownsville, 1993—; rep. Council on Fed. Rels., Assn. of Am. Univs.; instl. rep. Research Univs. Network; exec. dir. Tex. Com. for Employer Support of the Guard and Res., 1982-86, N.Y. com., 1987-89; mem. US Mexico Com. Philanthropy and the Border, 1994—. Mem. editorial bd. Jour. Tech. Transfer, 1987—. Mem. militarily critical techs. adv. com. U.S. Internat. Trade Adminstrn.; bd. advisers Ctr. Internat. Bus. Studies Tex. A&M U., 1986-87; Res. asst. army attache to Republic of Ireland, 1986-87; mem. exec. com. N.E. Parallel Architectures Ctr.; mem. Sec. of Army's adv. panel on ROTC affairs, 1988-92. Contbr. articles to profl. jours. Trustee Brownsville Hist. Mus. Assn., 1994-96. Served with USAR. Decorated Bronze Star, Army Commendation medal with 4 oak leaf clusters, Meritorious Service medal with 2 oak leaf clusters, Tham Muu Boi Tinh medal; Inter-Univ. Seminar Armed Forces and Soc. fellow, 1979; assoc. Ctr. NATO Studies, Kent State U. Mem. AAAS (bd. advisors nat. security and sci. comm. project, mem. award selection panel sci. freedom and responsibility), N.Y. Acad. Scis., Tech. Transfer Soc., Nat. Assn. State Univs. and Land-Grant Colls. (vet. affairs and nat. service com.), Pub. Rels. Soc. Am., Council on European Studies, Nat. Soc. Fund-Raising Execs., Am. Soc. for Pub. Adminstrn. (exec. com. sect., past chair on Nat. Security and Def. Analysis), Internat. Assn. Bus. Communicators, Atlantic Coun. U.S. (councilor), Army and Navy Club, Capitol Hill Club, Sigma Xi, Phi Delta Kappa. Republican. Episcopalian. Office: U Tex Instl Devel The Regiment House 80 Fort Brown St Brownsville TX 78520-4956

LYTTON, LINDA ROUNTREE, marriage and family therapist, test consultant; b. Suffolk, Va., Mar. 30, 1951; d. John Thomas and Anne Carolyn (Edwards) Rountree; m. Daniel Michael Lytton, June 23, 1973; 1 child, Seth Daniel. BS, Radford U., 1973; MS, Va. Poly. Inst. and State U., 1992. Collegiate profl. cert. Tchr., cons. Fauquier County Pub. Schs., Warrenton, Va., 1973-74, Chesterfield County Pub. Schs., Richmond, Va., 1974-78, Williamsburg (Va.)-James City Pub. Schs., 1979-83, Prince William County Pub. Schs., Manassas, Va., 1983-89; hist. area interpreter Colonial Williamsburg Found., 1978-79; outpatient therapist Prince William County Community Svcs. Bd., 1989-91, emergency svcs. therapist, therapist cons., 1991-93; marriage and family therapist Employee Assistance Svc., Inc., Manassas, 1993—; pvt. practice Ashton Profl. Ctr., 1996—; cons. Horizons for Learning, Inc., Richmond, 1989—. Great Books Leader, 1993—. Mem. Am. Assn. Marriage and Family Therapy, Va. Assn. Marriage and Family Therapy, Internat. Assn., Marriage and Family Counselors, Sigma Kappa (life). Home: 12046 Market Square Ct Manassas VA 20112-3214

LYTTON, ROBERT LEONARD, civil engineer, educator; b. Port Arthur, Tex., Oct. 23, 1937; m. Robert Odell and Nora Mae (Verrett) L.; m. Eleanor Marilyn Anderson, Sept. 9, 1961; children: Lynn Elizabeth, Robert Douglas, John Kirby. BSCE, U. Tex., 1960, MSCE, 1961, PhD, 1967. Registered profl. engr., Tex., La.; registered land surveyor, La. Assoc. Dannenbaum and Assocs., Cons. Engrs., Houston, 1963-65; U.S. NSF fellow U. Tex., Austin, 1965-67, asst. prof., 1967-68; NSF postdoctoral fellow Australian Commonwealth Sci. & Indsl. Rsch. Orgn., Melbourne, Australia, 1969-70; assoc. prof. Tex. A&M U., College Station, 1971-76, prof., 1976-90, Wiley chair prof., 1990-95, dir. ctr. for infrastructure engrng., 1991—, Benson chair prof., 1995—; divsn. head Tex. Transp. Inst., 1982-91, head infrastructure and transp. divsn. civil engring. dept., 1993-95; bd. dirs. MLA Labs., Inc., Austin, Trans-tec, Inc., Austin, Lyric Tech., Llc., Houston; v.p. bd. dirs. MLAW Cons., Inc., Austin, 1980—, ERES Cons., Inc., Champaign, Ill., 1981-95; prin. investigator strategic hwy. rsch. program A005 rsch. project, 1990-93. Patentee for sys. identification and analysis of subsurface radar signals. Mem. St. Vincent de Paul Soc., Houston, 1963-65, Redemptorist Lay Mission Soc., Melbourne, Australia, 1969-70. Capt. U.S. Army, 1961-63. Recipient SAR medal of honor St. Mary's U., 1957, Soc. Am. Mil. Engrs. Outstanding Sr. cadet U. Tex., 1959, Disting. Mil. grad. award, 1960, Hamilton Watch award Coll. Engring., 1960, Disting. Achievement award Tex. A&M U. Assn. Former Students. Fellow ASCE; mem. NSPE, Transp. Rsch. Bd. (chmn. com. A2LO6 1987-93), Internat. Soc. for Soil Mechanics & Found. Engrng. (U.S. rep. tech. com. TC-6 1987—, keynote address 7th internat. conf. on expansive soils 1992, keynote address 1st internat. conf. on unsaturated soils 1995), Assn. Asphalt Paving Technologists, Post-Tensioning Inst. (adv. bd.), Tex. Soc. Profl. Engrs., Internat. Soc. Asphalt Pavements, Sigma Xi, Phi Kappa Delta, Chi Epsilon, Tau Beta Pi, Phi Kappa Phi. Roman Catholic. Office: Tex A&M U 508G CE/TTI Bldg College Station TX 77843

MA, MICHAEL JOHN, legal assistant; b. Cleve., July 2, 1966; s. Jong Kyu and Carol Ann (Kleffman) Hong; m. Stephanie N. Hunt Ma, Feb. 19, 1994. BS in Polit. Sci., U.S. Naval Acad., 1988; MA in Nat. Security Studies, Georgetown U., 1989; postgrad., George Washington U. Naval officer USN, 1988-94; law clk. U.S. State Dept., Washington, 1995—. Vol. Carpenter Shelter, Alexandria, Va., 1993—, Friends of Nat. Zoo, Washington, 1993—, Habitat for Humanity, Alexandria, 1994—. Mem. Am. Legion, Phi Delta Phi. Presbyterian. Home: 1201 Braddock Pl #911 Alexandria VA 22314 Office: US Dept State Washington DC 20520

MAAR, ROSINA, medical organization executive. BS, Ga. Inst. Tech., 1984; MD, Morehouse Sch. Medicine, 1988. Bd. cert. in internal medicine; lic. Ga., N.C. Intern and resident in internal medicine Emory U. Sch. Medicine, Atlanta, 1991; physics lab. instr. Ga. Inst. Tech., Atlanta, 1981-84; rsch. asst. Emory U., Atlanta, 1985-86; med. evaluator maternal and infant project Grady Meml. Hosp., Atlanta, 1987-88; contract physician Wesley Woods Geriatric Hosp., Atlanta, 1989-90; contract physician, program dir. Piedmont Hosp./Spinal Shepard Ctr., Atlanta, 1989-91; med. dir. Cellcor, Inc., Atlanta, 1991-92; corp. med. dir. Cellcor, Inc., Newton, Mass., 1992-93; med. scientist med./regulatory svcs. Quintiles, Inc., Research Triangle Park, N.C., 1993-94, dir. med. svcs., 1994-95, v.p. clin. ops., 1995—. Contbr. articles and abstracts to med. jours. Mem. ACP, AMA, Am. Bd. Internal Medicine (diplomate). Office: Quintiles Inc PO Box 13979 Research Triangle Park NC 27709

MAASOUMI, ESFANDIAR, economics educator; b. Tehran, Iran, Mar. 5, 1950; came to U.S., 1977; s. Ahmad and Sharifeh (Fakhri) M. BS in Econs., U. London, 1972, MS in Stats., 1973, PhD in Econometrics, 1977. Lectr. London Sch. Econs., 1975-76, U. Birmingham, Eng., 1976-77; asst. prof. U. So. Calif., L.A., 1977-81; assoc. prof. Ind. U., Bloomington, 1982-86, prof., 1986-89; Robert and Nancy Dedman prof. econs., adj. prof. stats. So. Meth. U., Dallas, 1989—; vis. scholar MIT, Boston, 1981; vis. prof. U. Calif., Santa Barbara, 1987-88; mem. adv. bd. N.Am. Free Trade Agreement; presenter over 100 lectures and seminars. Editor Econometric Revs., 1987—; contbr. over 50 books, articles and revs. Rsch. grantee NSF, 1980-82; fellow Jour. Econometrics, others. Fellow Royal Statis. Soc.; mem. Econometric Soc. (conf. organizer 1983), Am. Statis. Assn., Inst. Math. Stats. Office: So Meth U Dept Economics Dallas TX 75275

MABE, R. KEITH, marketing executive; b. Reidsville, N.C., Aug. 6, 1954; s. Aubrey Dennis and Ruby Elizabeth (Taylor) M.; m. Sharon Mabe, May 22, 1976. BS in Geography, U. N.C., Greensboro, 1976; MS in City Planning, Va. Poly. Inst. and State U., 1978; MBA, Wake Forest U., 1989. Cmty. planner State of Va., Richmond, 1978-79; dir. devel. Albemarle County, Charlottesville, Va., 1979-81; asst. dir. City of Virginia Beach, Va., 1981-85; dir. devel. City of Waynesboro, Va., 1985-87; asst. brand mgr. Sara Lee Hosiery, Winston-Salem, 1989-91, dir. mktg., 1996—; v.p. mktg. Kayser Roth, Greensboro, 1991-96. Mem. AIDS Task Force, Winston-Salem, 1996—. Mem. Am. Mktg. Assn. Home: 145 Whitley Mill Ct Clemmons NC 27012

MABE, SHARON RUSSELL APPLEGATE, academic official; b. Dayton, Ohio, Oct. 4, 1954; d. Gerald Richard and Anne Cly (Russell) Applegate; m. R. Keith Mabe, May 22, 1976. BA in Studio Art cum laude, U. N.C., Greensboro, 1976. Pub. info. asst. Publs. Office, U. N.C., 1977-78, 79-80; forms coord. Ctrl. Fidelity Bank, Richmond, Va., 1980; legal asst. Stuart Carwile, atty., Charlottesville, 1981; dir. rsch. U. Va., Charlottesville, 1981-84; program coord. Muscular Dystrophy Assn., Virginia Beach, Va., 1984-85; real estate rschr., analyst Realty Adv. Group, Virginia Beach, 1985-86; dir. grants Mary Baldwin Coll., Staunton, Va., 1986-87; dir. prospect rsch. Devel. and Alumni Affairs Office, Bowman Gray Sch. Medicine-N.C. Bapt. Hosp. Med. Ctr., Winston-Salem, 1988-92; adminstrv. asst. to chancellor N.C. Sch. Arts, Winston-Salem, 1987-88, dir. rsch. Devel. Office, 1992—. Bd. dirs. Forsyth Humane Soc., 1995—. Alumni scholar U. N.C., 1972-76. Mem. Am. Prospect Rsch. Assn., Carolinas' Assn. Profl. Rschrs. for Advancement (bd. dirs. 1992—, pres. 1994-96). Democrat. Home: 145 Whitley Mill Ct Clemmons NC 27012 Office: NC Sch Arts PO Box 12189 Winston Salem NC 27117-2189

MABEL, SCOTT EDWARD, military officer; b. Ft. Hood, Tex., Nov. 15, 1968; s. Richard I. and Debra (Greenblatt) M. BBA, U. Mass., 1990; postgrad., Troy State U., 1996—. Commd. 2d lt. U.S. Army, 1990, advanced through grades to capt., 1994; platoon leader U.S. Army, South Korea, 1991-93; co. comdr. U.S. Army, Ft. Riley, Kans., 1994-95; strategic plans officer U.S. Army, Ft. Rucker, Ala., 1996—. Mem. Army Aviation Assn. Am. Home: 116 Foxhill Dr Enterprise AL 36330

MABERRY, JOE MICHAEL, federal agency administrator; b. Waco, Tex., Nov. 17, 1946; s. William Thomas and Eula Monetta (Alexandex) M.; m. Linda Joan Stout, May 12, 1973; children: Misty Dawn, Shane Micah. BS, U. Tex., Arlington, 1982. Detective, tng. officer Dallas (Tex.) Police Dept., 1971-92; fingerprint specialist Drug Enforcement Adminstrn., Dallas, 1992—; cons. Forensic Cons. Svcs., Fort Worth, 1985-92. Contbr. sci. papers to profl. jours. Pres. Ovilla (Tex.) Lions Club, 1991-92, 95-96, Lions Sight and Tissue Found., 1995-96. Sgt. USMC, 1967-71, Vietnam. Recipient Cert. of merit Dallas (Tex.) Police Dept., 1991. Fellow Fingerprint Soc. of the U.K.; mem. Internat. Assn. for Identification (cert. latent print examiner 1991—, sr. crime scene analyst 1991—, crime scene cert. bd. 1992—), Tex. Divsn. Internat. Assn. for Identification (2d v.p. 1992-93, pres. 1994-95), Am. Acad. Forensic Scientists, Southwestern Assn. Forensic Scientists, Homicide Investigators Tex. (life), Internat. Assn. Bloodstain Pattern Analysts. Democrat. Baptist. Home: 411 Shadowwood Trl Ovilla TX 75154-1425 Office: Drug Enforcement Adminstrn South Ctrl Lab 1880 Regal Row Dallas TX 75235-2302

MABROUK, SUZANNE THERESA, chemistry educator; b. Peoria, Ill., Nov. 15, 1964; d. Ahmed and Barbara Elaine (Ford) M.; m. Stephen Stanford Jones. AB, Wheaton Coll., Norton, Mass., 1986; PhD, U. Mass. at Amherst, 1994. Asst. prof. chemistry The Citadel, Charleston, S.C., 1993—. Author: The Organic Chemistry Survival Manual, 1996; co-author: Organic Metallic Synthesis, 1988. Mem. Am. Chem. Soc., Coun. on Undergraduate Rsch. Office: The Citadel 171 Moultrie St Charleston SC 29409

MABRY, CATHY DARLENE, elementary school educator; b. Atlanta, Dec. 9, 1951; d. German William and Erma Isabel (Lyons) M. BA in Sociology and Psychology, U. Ga., 1975; Cert. in Edn., Oglethorpe U., Atlanta, 1983, MA in Elem. Edn., 1990. Cert. in early childhood edn., Ga. Charge account svcs. staff C&S Nat. Bank, Atlanta, 1974-75; with Rich's, Decatur, Ga., 1975-76, 79-84; mgr. trainee sales Sears Roebuck & Co., Decatur, 1974-75, 76-78; intermediate clk. Superior Ct. of DeKalb County, Decatur, 1978-81; paraprofl. kindergarten DeKalb County Sch. Sys., Decatur, 1979-81, tchr., 1984—; mem. sch.-based mgmt. com. Hooper Alexander Sch., Decatur, 1991-92, strategic planning com., 1990—; mem. social studies curriculum com. DeKalb County Sch. Sys., 1990-91, tchr. forum rep., 1992—. Author poetry in Am. Poetry Anthology, 1986. Sec. Lithonia Civic League, Inc., 1987—, Teen Scene, Inc., Lithonia, 1993-94; chair bd. dirs. DeKalb Econ. Opportunity Authority, Decatur, 1991-92, 93—; mem. Teach Well Wellness Program, Emory U. Sch. Pub. Health, 1994; active PTA. Mem. NAACP, Nat. Coun. of Negro Women, Inc., Nat. Geog. Soc., DeKalb Assn. Educators, Zeta Phi Beta. Democrat. Baptist. Home: 7109 Rhodes St Lithonia GA 30058-4235 Office: Hooper Alexander Sch 3414 Memorial Dr Decatur GA 30032-2708

MABRY, DOROTHY MAE, elementary school principal; b. Ellerslie, Ga., Dec. 23, 1947; d. Johnny King McGhee and Elizabeth Odessa (Taylor) Jackson; m. Howard Mabry, Aug. 27, 1968. BS, Ft. Valley (Ga.) State Coll., 1969; MEd, Southwestern Okla. State Coll., Weatherford, 1978. Cert. elem. adminstrn., Okla. 3d yr. tchr. Carver Elem. Sch., Hamilton, Ga., 1969-70, Harris County Elem. Sch., Hamilton, 1970-72, Pershing Pk. Elem. Sch., Killeen, Tex., 1973-74, Susie E. Allen Elem. Sch., Phenix City, Ala., 1974-75, Ridgecrest Elem. Sch., Phenix City, 1975-76; 2d, 3d, 4th, 5th, 6th yr. tchr. Crosby Pk. Elem. Sch., Lawton, Okla., 1977-95; asst. prin. Lawton Pub. Schs., 1995-96; prin. Lee Elem. Sch., Lawton, 1996—. Named Tchr. of Today, Masonic Lodge, Lawton, 1995. Mem. NAACP, NEA, Assn. Supervision and Curriculum Devel., Okla. Educators Assn., Lawton Area Reading Coun., Lawton Assn. Elem. Sch. Prins., Delta Sigma Theta (Soror of Yr. 1992), Kappa Kappa Iota, Phi Delta Kappa. Home: 7611 Baldwin Ave Lawton OK 73505

MABRY, RICHARD LEE, otolaryngologist; b. Decatur, Tex., July 7, 1936; s. George D. and Ina Rachel (Lambert) M.; m. Cynthia Ann Surovik, July 17, 1959; children: Allen, Brian, Ann Elizabeth. BA, North Tex. State U., 1956; MD, U. Tex. Southwestern Med. Sch., 1960. Diplomate Am. Bd. Otolaryngology-Head and Neck Surgery. Intern VA Hosp., Dallas, 1960-61, resident, 1961, 64-67; pvt. practice medicine specializing in otolaryngology, Dallas, 1968-93; clin. prof. otolaryngology U. Tex. Southwestern Med. Ctr., Dallas, 1984-93, prof. otorhinolaryngology, 1993—; cons. Dallas VA Hosp., 1968-80; mem. expert adv. panel otolaryngology U.S. Pharmacopoiea. Author, editor numerous med. textbooks. Office: U Tex Southwestern Med Ctr Dept Otorhinolaryngology 5323 Harry Hines Blvd Dallas TX 75235-9035

MABSON, ROBERT LANGLEY, clergyman, librarian; b. New Orleans, Apr. 17, 1931; s. Eugene Beall and Eva Louise (Lea) M.; m. Minnie Augusta Lewis, Dec. 22, 1953; children: Lewis, Susan Jane, Laura Lea. BA, Tulane U., 1952; postgrad., Union Theol. Sem., 1952-55; M. of Religious Edn., Pres. Sch. Christian Edn., 1955; MS, La. State U., 1964. Ordained to ministry Presbyn. Ch., 1955. Pastor, Mt. Pleasant Presbyn. Ch., Sinks Grove, W.Va., 1955-57; dir., Christian edn. Barbee Larger Parish 1957-59; pastor, 1st Presbyn. Ch., Perry (Mo.), 1957-59; pastor, 1st Presbyn. Ch., Talihina, Okla., 1959-63, Eastland Presbyn. Ch., Memphis, 1966-78, Ebenezer Presbyn. Ch., Strong, Ark., 1983-84, Sulphur Springs Cumberland Presbyn. Ch., Louann, Ark., 1984-88; chaplain USPHS Hosp., Talikina, Okla., 1959-63, Calvary Colony Alcoholic Rehab. Ctr., also Kings Daus. and Sons Home, Memphis, 1979-83; head librarian, prof. Meth. Coll., Fayetteville, N.C., 1964-66; asst. libr. Memphis Theol. Sem., 1967-74; active Presbyn. Coun. Evangelism, 1959-63, Covenant Presbytery, 1973-84, stated clk., 1973-75, moderator, 1976, Mound Prairie Presbytery, 1984-88, Ark. Presbytery, 1989. Author: Presbyterian Missionary Labors in Kiamichi Valley, Oklahoma, 1850-1960. Recipient Congl. Cmty. Svc. award, 1978. Mem. ALA (life). Address: PO Box 92 Mount Holly AR 71758-0092

MACALUSO, JAMES, accountant, estate planner; b. Paterson, N.J., Oct. 14, 1943; s. Vincent J. and Virginia (Pasqualetti) M.; m. Carol A. Levesque, Feb. 14, 1979; children: James M., Michael C., Christopher J. AA, St. Petersburg Jr. Coll., 1968; BA, U. S.Fla., 1970. Owner James Macaluso E.A., St. Petersburg, Fla., 1973-76; pres. Macaluso Demaree & Carter, St. Petersburg, 1976-87; gen. mgr. Carter & Cartier CPAs, St. Petersburg, 1987-91; pres. Macaluso & Co., P.A., St. Petersburg, 1991—; dir., chmn. audit com. Marine Bank, St. Petersburg, 1987—; instr. and lectr. in the field of estate and trust taxation. Pres. N.E. Exch. Club, St. Petersburg, 1974, Dragon Club of St. Petersburg, 1996. Mem. Nat. Assn. Enrolled Agts., Nat. Soc. Tax Profls., Nat. Soc. Pub. Accts., Accreditation Coun. for Accountancy, St. Pete Yacht Club, Dragon Club, Phi Kappa Phi, Gold Key Honor Soc. Republican. Roman Catholic. Home: 1045 39th Ave N Saint Petersburg FL 33703-4521 Office: Macaluso & Co PA 3839 4th St N Ste 450 Saint Petersburg FL 33703-6112

MACBETH, HUGH JAMES, data processing executive; b. N.Y.C., Jan. 19, 1947; s. John Brown and Josephine Earl (Olsen) Macb. BA, Hiram Coll., 1968. Gen. mgr. 9-20 Inc., Great Barrington, Mass., 1971-73; acct. Chem. Constrn. Corp., N.Y.C., 1973-75; owner, gen. mgr. The Fairfield Inn, Great Barrington, 1975-78; v.p. Am. Agy. Data Systems, Merritt Island, Fla., 1978-80; pres. Advanced Info. Mgmt., Cocoa Beach, Fla., 1980—; mgr. info. systems and telecomm. Greater Orlando (Fla.) Aviation Authority, 1981—; pres. Exec. Info. Svcs., Cocoa Beach, 1985—; mem. adv. coun. Bellcore Pub. Comm.; mem. Internat. Air Transport Assn. Passenger Svcs. Automation Com., Joint Airport Passenger Svcs. Automation Strategy Group; mem. AT&T customer adv. coun.; chmn. bd. Scott Laurent Galleries, Winter Park, Scott Laurent Galleries Internat., Scott Laurent & Assocs. Columnist: Orlando Bus. Jour., 1984—. Mem. U.S. working party to UN Jt. Commn. on Electronic Document Interchange; treas., bd. dirs. Orlando Gay Chorus. Mem. Airport Ops. Internat. (chmn. info. sys. sub-commn. 1985-86, chmn. internat. airport ops. computer fair, 1988, chmn. 1990 fair, chmn. MIS/Telecom. com. 1995), Am. Assn. Airport Execs. (chmn. computer com.). Republican. Episcopalian. Home: 2815 S Atlantic Ave Apt 102 Cocoa Beach FL 32931-2170 Office: Orlando Internat Airport Greater Orlando Aviation Orlando FL 32837

MACCONKEY, DOROTHY I., academic administrator; b. New Brunswick, N.J.; d. Donald Thurston and Dorothy Bennett (Hill) Ingling; m. Joseph W. MacConkey, June 19, 1949 (dec. Aug. 1975); children: Donald Franklin, Diane Margaret, Dorothy Frances; m. Karl Schmeidler, May 26, 1994. BA, Beaver Coll., 1947; MA, Wichita State U., 1953; PhD, U. Md., 1974; LLD (hon.), Beaver Coll., 1988. Lectr. Wichita (Kans.) State U., 1950-51; rsch.-campaign assoc. United Fund and Council, Wichita, 1951-62; rsch.- com. coordination Health and Welfare Council of Nat. Capital Area, Washington, 1963-65; exec. dir. multi-program agy. Prince Georges County Assn. for Retarded Children, Hyattsville, Md., 1965-66; prof. George Mason U., Fairfax, Va., 1966-76, asst. vice pres., acting dean, 1976-82; v.p., dean of coll. Hiram (Ohio) Coll., 1982-85; pres. Davis & Elkins (W.Va.) Coll., 1985—; bd. dirs. Davis Trust Co., Elkins, 1987—; adv. bd. George Mason U. Found., Fairfax, 1976-95; trustee Beaver Coll., Glenside, Pa., 1971-87; cons., evaluator North Cen. Assn., Chgo., 1985—, commr., 1993—; mem. exec. com., pres. Assn. Presbyn. Colls. and Univs.; mem. bd. Svc. Opportunity Colls., Presbyn. Found., trustee, 1993—; chmn. North Area Cen. Com.; treas. Coun. of Ind. Colls. Pres. County Chasers of Am., 1985—. Recipient Citizen award for service to handicapped, Fairfax County, 1981, Woman of Yr. in Edn. award W.Va. Fedn. Women's Clubs, 1986. Mem. Coun. of Pres.', Nat. Assn. Intercollegiate Athletics, Coun. Ind. Colls. (bd. dirs.). Office: Davis and Elkins Coll Office of Pres 100 Campus Dr Elkins WV 26241-3971

MACCUISH, DONALD ALEXANDER, educational products manager; b. Stoneham, Mass., May 10, 1945; s. W. Francis and Geneve (Brigham) MacC.; m. Joan Van Horn, Jan. 30, 1971. BA in History, Va. Mil. Inst., 1968; MEd in Ednl. Psychology, Wayne State U., 1973; diploma in leadership, U.S. Army Command and Gen. Staff Coll., 1980; EdD in Curriculum and Instrn., U. Ctrl. Fla., 1990. Cert. secondary sch. guidance counselor, cert. secondary sch. history tchr., Mass.; cert. rescue diver Profl. Assn. Diving Instrs. Secondary sch. tchr., adminstr. spl. edn. Essex Agrl. and Tech. H.S., 1974-77; ops. and mktg. mgr. Warner Comm. Corp., Belmont, Mass., 1977-81; mgr. ednl. svcs. Analytic Sys. Engring. Corp., 1981-83, Orlando (Fla.) Aerospace divsn. Martin Marietta, 1983-85; dir. instrnl. sys. devel. Deterline Corp., Orlando, Fla., 1985-86; gen. mgr., spl. asst. to v.p. Online Computer Sys., Orlando, 1986-90; rsch. assoc. dept. psychology Coll. Arts and Scis. U. Cen. Fla., Orlando, 1990-92; mgr. testing products and svcs. internat. divsn. Harcourt Brace and Co., Orlando, 1992-95; pres. Ednl. and Psychol. Svcs. Internat., Oviedo, 1995—; pres., CEO Alsan, Oviedo, 1995—; adj. prof. Coll. Bus. Adminstrn. U. Sarasota, 1990-92, Coll. Edn. U. Cen. Fla., 1991—, Coll. Bus. Adminstrn. Nova U., 1990, Coll. Edn., 1992—, dept. edn. grad. sch. Rollins Coll., 1992—; cons. Datacom Cable Sys., Inc., 1981-82, True Cable TV Corp., 1982-84; condr. profl. seminars and workshops, 1985—; presenter profl. confs. and symposia, most recently Cen. Asia Coun. Internat. Schs., Taipei, Taiwan, East Asia Region Adminstr.'s Conf., Singapore, Near East South Asia Ednl. Adminstr.'s Conf. Contbr. articles to profl. jours. and conf. procs., 1984—. Mem. bd. trustees U. Tampa, 1993—, pres. parent's coun., 1993-94; mem. parents' adv. coun. Lyman H.S., Seminole County Schs., Fla., 1992-93, vice chmn. adv. com. Casselberry Elem. Sch., 1984-88, mem. tech. infusion action team, 1992-93; judge behavioral and social scis. divsn. Internat. Sci. and Engring. Fair, Orlando, 1991, Orange County Regional Sci. and Engring. Fair, 1991, 92; mem. governing bd., elder Winter Springs Alliance Ch., 1984-88; alt. precinct committeeman Seminole County Rep. Exec. Com., 1990-93, mem. edn., pub. rels., membership subcoms. With U.S. Army, 1968-74, lt. col. res. 1974—. Rsch. grantee, FAA, several, 1992, Naval Tng. Sys. Ctr., 2, 1990-91, Office Naval Rsch., 1990-93, Spencer Fellowship, 1990-91, U.S. Dept. Edn., 1982-83, 90-91. Mem. ASCD, Am. Ednl. Rsch. Assn., Fla. Ednl. Rsch. Assn., Nat. Dropout Prevention Network, Soc. Automotive Engrs. (mem. aviation tng. subcom. 1992-94), Internat. Test Commn., Kappa Delta Pi, Psi Chi. Baptist. Home: 200 Forest Trl Oviedo FL 32765-6756

MACCURDY, JOHN A., real estate appraiser, consultant; b. Ft. Worth, Mar. 6, 1947; s. Robert Earl and Constance (Pontius) MacC.; m. Kathryn Blitch, Feb. 11, 1967; 1 child, Kristen. BBA, U. Miami, 1974; MSM, Fla. Internat. U., 1977. Supr. Fed. Res. Bank, Miami, Fla., 1971-73; realtor, assoc. Chas. SandeFur Realty, Miami, 1963-75; grad. asst. Fla. Internat. U., Miami, 1975-77; appraiser Jos. J. Blake & Assoc., Inc., Miami, 1977-80; exec. v.p. Chas. V. Failla & Assoc., Inc., Coral Gables, Fla., 1980-87; pres. J.A. MacCurdy & Assoc., Inc., Boca Raton, Fla., 1987—; spl. master Palm Beach (Fla.) County Property Appraisal Adjustment Bd., 1987, 88. Mem. Boca Forum, Palm Beach County Devel. Bd. Sgt. USAF, 1966-70, Korea. Mem. Am. Real Estate Soc., Am. Real Estate and Urban Economic Assn., Am. Inst. Real Estate Appraisers, Fin. Mgmt. Assn., Urban Land Inst., Boca Raton Bd. Realtors, Boca Raton C. of C. Republican. Presbyterian. Office: 315 SE Mizner Blvd Boca Raton FL 33432-6004

MACDONALD, CAROLYN HELMS, gifted education educator; b. Leesburg, Va., Oct. 15, 1941; d. Edmund Davis and Mary Irene (Peters) Helms; m. John Mount MacDonald, July 27, 1963 (div. Dec. 1984); children: Christina Hope, Heather Laurel, Katherine Anne. BS, East Tenn. State U., 1964; MS, Nova U., 1979. Cert. elem. tchr., jr. coll. tchr., gifted tchr., Fla. Elem. tchr. Shoemaker Elem. Sch., Gate City, Va., 1964-65, Bakersfield Elem. Sch., Aberdeen, Md., 1965-66, Brookview Elem. Sch., Jacksonville, Fla., 1966-68, Holiday Hill Elem. Sch., Jacksonville, Fla., 1968-69, Arlington Annex 5th Grade Ctr., Jacksonville, 1972-73; elem. tchr., social studies, lang. arts specialist Loretto Elem. Sch., Jacksonville, 1973-81, tchr. gifted, 1981—; mem. steering com. for gifted edn. Duval County Sch. Bd., 1982-85; del to Murmansk, USSR, 1991, ESOL trainer, 1995—. Pres. Mandarin Cmty. Club, Jacksonville, 1980; mem. Panel on Sewage Treatment Problems, 1979, Neighborhood Cancer Drive Com., 1979-84, Com. to Assess Cmty. Recreation Needs, Jacksonville, 1981-82; sponsor ARC. Recipient placque Mandarin Community Club, Jacksonville, 1974-77; named Outstanding Safety Patrol Sponsor North Fla., 1993. Mem. Fla. Jr. Coll. Woman's Club (v.p. 1969-71, pres. 1971-72, Outstanding Young Woman Am. 1971), Southside Jr. Woman's Club (v.p. 1970-73), Phi Mu Alumnae (v.p. 1989-90), Delta Kappa Gamma. Democrat. Methodist. Home: 9439 San Jose Blvd Apt 228 Jacksonville FL 32257 Office: Loretto Elem Sch # 30 3900 Loretto Rd Jacksonville FL 32223-2055

MACDONALD, ELEANOR JOSEPHINE, epidemiology educator, cancer epidemiology consultant; b. Boston, Mar. 4, 1906; d. Angus Alexander and Catharine Pauline (Boland) M. AB, Radcliffe Coll., 1928; postgrad., Harvard, 1930-36. Epidemiologist divsn. cancer Mass. Dept. Pub. Health, Boston, 1930-41; tchr. Tufts Coll. Sch. Dentistry, 1930-45, Harvard Sch. Pub. Health, 1936; epidemiologist in cancer Conn. State Dept. Health, 1941-48; epidemiologist, prof., head dept. epidemiology M.D. Anderson Cancer Hosp. and Tumor Inst. U. Tex., Houston, 1948-74, emeritus epidemiologist, 1974-82; cons. Meml. Sloan Kettering, 1944-48, Nat. Adv. Cancer Coun., 1946-48; cancer epidemiology cons., 1982—. Co-author: (with Evelyn Heinze) The Epidemiology of Cancer in Texas 1944-1966, 1978, (with Wellington and Wolf) Cancer Mortality: Environmental and Ethnic Factors, 1979; contbr. 220 articles to profl. jours. Recipient Myron Gordon award for work on melanoma Pigment Cell Growth Assn., 1971, Disting. Alumna award Radcliffe Coll., 1973. Fellow APHA (sec. 1954-64, pres. 1964-64), Am. Radium Soc.; mem. Am. Assn. for Cancer Rsch. Roman Catholic. Home: 2107 University Blvd Houston TX 77030

MACDONALD, SHEILA DE MARILLAC, transaction management company executive; b. Santa Monica, Calif., Jan. 17; d. William Alan and M. Jane (Crotty) M. BS, Stanford U.; BA, U. San Francisco; MBA, Harvard U. Prin. Tex. Transaction Mgmt. Co., Houston, 1990—. Mem. Harvard Club N.Y., Met. Club, Petroleum Club.

MACDONALD, THOMAS COOK, JR., lawyer; b. Atlanta, Oct. 11, 1929; s. Thomas Cook and Mary (Morgan) MacD.; m. Gay Anne Everiss, June 30, 1956; children: Margaret Anne, Thomas William. B.S. with high honors, U. Fla., 1951, LL.B. with high honors, 1953. Bar: Fla. 1953. Practice law Tampa, 1953—; mem. firm Shackleford, Farrior, Stallings & Evans, 1953—; spl. counsel Gov. of Fla., 1963, U. Fla., 1972—; del. 5th cir. Jud. Conf., 1970-81; mem. adv. com. U.S. Ct. Appeals (5th cir.), 1975-78, (11th cir.), 1988-93; mem. Fla. Jud. Qualifications Commn., 1983-88, vice chmn., 1987, chmn., 1988; mem. judicial nominating com. Fla. Supreme Ct., 1995—. Mem. Fla. Student Scholarship and Loan Commn., 1963-67; bd. dirs. Univ. Cmty. Hosp., Tampa, 1968-78, Fla. West Coast Sports Assn., 1965-80, Hall of Fame Bowl Assn., 1989-93, Jim Walter Corp., 1979-87; mem. Hillsborough County Pub. Edn. Study Commn., 1965; lic. lay eucharistic min. Episcopal Ch., 1961—; chancellor Episcopal Diocese of S.W. Fla., 1990-93; bd. dirs. U. Fla. Found., 1978-86, Shands Tchg. Hosp., U. Fla., 1981-95; counsel Tampa Sports Authority, 1983-94. Recipient Disting. Alumnus award U. Fla., 1976, George C. Carr award Fed. Bar Assn., 1991, Fla. Bar Presdl. award of Merit, 1995, Goldburg award Hillsborough County Bar Assn. Trial Lawyers, 1995. Fellow Am. Coll. Trial Lawyers (chmn. state com. 1990-91), Am. Bar Found., Fla. Bar (chmn. com. profl. ethics 1966-70, bd. govs. 1970-74, bar mem. Supreme Ct. com. on stds. conduct governing judges 1976, Fla. bd. cert. appellate lawyer); mem. ABA (com. on ethics and profl. responsibility 1970-76), Am. Law Inst. (life), 11th Cir. Hist. Soc. (trustee 1982-95, pres. 1989-95), U. Fla. Nat. Alumni Assn. (pres. 1973), Phi Kappa Phi, Phi Delta Phi, Fla. Blue Key, Kappa Alpha. Episcopalian. Home: 1904 S Holly Ln Tampa FL 33629-7004 Office: PO Box 3324 Tampa FL 33601-3324

MACDUFFEE, ROBERT COLTON, family physician, pathologist; b. Princeton, N.J., Apr. 23, 1923; s. Cyrus Colton and Mary Augusta (Bean) MacD.; m. Elizabeth Ann Jessup, Aug. 30, 1984; children: Martha, Jennifer, Susan. BS, U. Chgo., 1944, MD, 1946. Diplomate, Am. Bd. Pathology, Am. Bd. Family Practice. Asst. prof. pathology Hahnemann Med. Sch., Phila., 1959-60; chief clin. pathologist Grad. Hosp. U. Pa., Phila., 1960-63; pathologist Lock Haven (Pa.) Hosp., 1963-64; pathologist, chief Altoona (Pa.) Hosp., 1964-71; pathologist, assoc. SmithKline Labs., Tampa, Fla., 1971-84; dir. walk-in clinic Naples (Fla.) Med. Ctr., 1984-93; ret., 1994. Maj. MC, U.S. Army, 1946-54, Korea. Fellow Coll. Am. Pathologists. Presbyterian.

MACE, MARY ALICE, coal company administrator; b. Charleston, W.Va., Nov. 21, 1949; d. John Robert Leake and Georgia Alice (Wilhelm) Crist; m. Charles Michael Mace, May 20, 1968; 1 child, Christina Michelle. Student, U. Charleston, 1990—. Sec. Capitol Paper Supply, Inc., Charleston, 1967-68, Persingers, Inc., Charleston, 1968-77; benefits coordinator Elk Run Coal Co., Inc., Sylvester, W.Va., 1981—; notary public. Sec. PTA, Pettus, W.Va., 1981-83, pres. 1983-85. Mem. NAFE, Health Benefits Group, Women of Moose. Democrat. Home: 2741 Rose Lane Dr Charleston WV 25302-4923 Office: Elk Run Coal Co Inc PO Box 497 Sylvester WV 25193-0497

MACE, TERESA ANN, geriatrics nurse; b. San Diego, Mar. 10, 1967; d. E Clayton Knight and Patricia Lee (Doggette) Humphries; married; children: Steven J., Clayton Alexander. Diploma in nursing, Moultrie Area Tech. Sch., 1992. LPN, Ga., Va.; cert. BLS Am. Heart Assn. Patient care coord. Horizon Health Ctr., Athens, Ga., 199294; LPN charge nurse Beverly Manor of Portsmouth, Va., 1994, Mannings Convalescent Home, Portsmouth, Va., 1994—. Leader Girl Scouts U.S., Moultrie, 1988-89; vol. ARC, Ga., 1991-93, 94-95. Mem. Nat. Fedn. LPN. Democrat. Baptist.

MACFARLAND, MIRIAM KATHERINE, computer science consultant, writer; b. Trenton, N.J., June 21, 1949; d. James and Merrianne (Collins) MacF.; children: Bridget Lorraine MacFarland, Chloe Merrianne Griffin. Student in computer scis., student in lit., Rutgers U., 1976-78; student in computer scis., U. Pa., 1981-83, U. Okla., 1986-88, Oxford U., Eng., 1988. Programmer-analyst Naval Air Devel. Ctr., Warminster, Pa., 1977-81; programmer, analyst NASA/Ames Rsch. Ctr., Moffett Field, Calif., 1978; writer BancTec, Inc., Oklahoma City and Dallas, 1983-95; cons. engr. BancTec, Inc., Dallas, 1983-95; cons. engr., writer MCI Comm. Internat., Rye Brook, N.Y., 1984-86; cons. engr. Western Union Internat., N.Y.C., 1984, RCA Global Comm., Fort Lee, N.J., 1985; cons. engr., writer Siemens Med. Sys., Iselin, N.J., 1988—; guest spkr. Okla. State U., Edmond, 1994. Author numerous lit. revs., CONTACT/II Lit. Rev., 1989-92; The Bloomsbury Rev., 1993—; contbr. articles to jours. and mags. Democrat. Protestant. Home and Office: 2323 Blue Creek Ct Norman OK 73071

MACFARLANE, ALASTAIR IAIN ROBERT, business executive; b. Sydney, Australia, Mar. 7, 1940; came to U.S., 1978; s. Alexander Dunlop and Margaret Elizabeth (Swan) M.; m. Madge McCleary, Sept. 24, 1966; children: Douglas, Dennis, Robert, Jeffrey. B in Econs. with honours, U. Sydney, 1961; MBA, U. Hawaii, 1964; postgrad., Columbia U., 1964; AMP, Harvard U., 1977. Comml. cadet B.H.P. Ltd., Australia, 1958-62; product mgr. H.J. Heinz Co., Pitts., 1965-66; gen. mgr. new products div. H.J. Heinz Co., Melbourne, Australia, 1967-72; ptnr., dir., gen. mgr. Singleton, Palmer & Strauss McAllan Pty. Ltd., Sydney, 1972-73; dir., gen. mgr. successor co. Doyle Dane Bernbach Internat. Inc., Sydney, 1973-77; group sr. v.p. Doyle Dane Bernbach Internat. Inc., N.Y.C., 1978-84; pres., chief exec. officer PowerBase Systems, Inc., 1984-85, Productivity Software Internat. L.P., N.Y.C., 1985-86; div. pres., pub. Whittle Comm. L.P., Knoxville, Tenn., 1987-88; chmn., CEO Phyton Techs. Inc., Knoxville, 1988-94; pres., CEO Knox Internat. Corp., Knoxville, 1988-94; chmn., CEO Mich. Bulb Co., Grand Rapids, 1988-94; chmn., CEO Lansinoh Labs., Inc., Oak Ridge, Tenn., 1994—; lectr. Monash U., Melbourne, 1970-71; ind. mgmt. cons., Melbourne, 1970-72; dir. Univ. of Sydney USA Found., 1994—. Author papers in field. V.p. Waverley Dist. Cricket Club, 1975-77. East-West Ctr. fellow, 1962-64; Australian Commonwealth scholar, Australian Steel Industry scholar, 1961. Fellow Australian Inst. Mgmt. (assoc.); mem. Australian Soc. Accts. (assoc.), Harvard Club N.Y.C., Cherokee Country Club. Home: 5210 Rio Vista Ln Knoxville TN 37919-8987 Office: 5201 Rio Vista Ln Knoxville TN 37919-8987

MACFARLANE, DAVID GORDON, defense systems design and development executive; b. Portland, Oreg., June 2, 1947; s. Gordon August and Virginia Lorraine (Thompson) F.; m. Zella Mae Garber, Jan. 24, 1969 (div. Feb. 1987); children: Carol Anne, Nancy Jane; m. Kathryn June Kuhfahl, May 13, 1991; 1 stepson, Chad Patrick Hughes. BGS in Bus. Adminstrn., U. Nebr., Omaha, 1976; MBA, U. Nebr., 1980. Computer operator and programmer Data Systems, Inc., Portland, 1967-68; computer programmer Far West Fed. Savs. & Loan, Portland, 1968; programmer, system analyst PRC Data Svcs. Co., Virginia Beach, Va., 1970-71, San Diego, 1971-72; systems analyst PRC Info. Scis. Co., Bellevue, Nebr., 1972-81, project mgr., 1981-85; dept. mgr. PRC Govt. Info. Systems, Bellevue, 1985-90; ops. ctr. mgr. PRC Inc., 1991-93, v.p., gen. mgr., 1994-95; v.p. EER Systems, Inc., Seabrook, Md., 1995—. Bd. dirs., past pres. Bellevue Swim Club, 1979-84. With U.S. Army, 1968-70. Mem. Armed Forces Communications and Electronics Assn., U.S. Space Found., Air Force Assn., Omaha Press Club. Republican. Methodist. Office: EER Systems Inc 10289 Aerospace Rd Seabrook MD 20706-2280

MACGOWAN, CHRISTOPHER JOHN, literature educator; b. London, Aug. 6, 1948; came to U.S., 1976; s. James Oliver Patrick and Patricia Kathleen (East) MacG.; m. Catherine Margaret Levesque, July 10, 1988. BA with honors, Cambridge U., Eng., 1976; MA, Princeton U., 1979, PhD, 1983. Asst. prof. Coll. William and Mary, Williamsburg, Va., 1984-90, assoc. prof., 1990—. Author: William Carlos Williams Early Poetry: The Visual Arts Background, 1984; editor: Collected Poems of William Carlos Williams, 1939-62, 1988, Paterson, 1992; co-editor: Collected Poems of William Carlos Williams, 1909-1939, 1986; mem. editorial bd. William Carlos Williams Rev.; contbr. articles to profl. jours. Recipient summer stipend NEH, Washington, 1986, fellowship, 1990-91. Mem. Modern Lang. Assn., William Carlos Williams Soc. (pres. 1989-91). Office: Coll of William and Mary Dept English PO Box 8795 Williamsburg VA 23187-8795

MACHANIC, ROGER, real estate developer; b. Burlington, Vt.; A.B. in Econs., Harvard U., 1955; m. Grace Wishart Manly, Apr. 20, 1963. Founder, past owner, Devel. Resources Inc.; now pres. Montgomery Real Estate Corp. (all Alexandria, Va.); dir. Allied Capital Mortgage Co. LLC. Trustee Emeritus George Mason U. Found.; past chmn. First Commonwealth Savs. and Loan Assn., Alexandria, 1984-86. Mem. Alexandria C. of C. (past pres.), Va. C. of C. (past v.p., bd. dirs.), Alexandria Bldg. Industry Assn. (past pres.), No. Va. Builders Assn. (dir. 1967-70, past v.p.). Clubs: Belle Haven Country, Rotary (Alexandria); Harvard (Washington). Office: 300 Montgomery St Alexandria VA 22314-1516

MACHOL, FREDERICK BERNHARD, mining engineer; b. Cleve., June 12, 1916; s. Bernhard and Elsydeane (Steele) M.; m. Mary Louise Peyton, Dec. 18, 1943 (dec. May 1951); children: Katherine, JoAnn, Deborah, Mary Louise, John; m. Anne Jane Prisel, June 4, 1952; children: Patricia, Ann Marie, Margaret, Michael, Carole, Mary Andre, Joseph. B in Engring., Ohio State U., 1938. Jr. engr. Ky. Natural Gas, Owensboro, 1938-39, Standard Oil of Ohio, Allegan, Mich., 1939-40; treas., v.p. Solvent Svc., Inc., Painesville, Ohio, 1946-63; mktg. mgr. Bendix Ultrasonics, Davenport, Iowa, 1963-66; sales mgr. CCI Pumps, Inc., Houston, 1966-70; CEO Acme Cleaning Equipment, Inc., Houston, 1970—. Author: They Are NOT Cheaper by the Dozen, 1962. Lt. col. U.S. Army, 1940-46. Mem. VFW, Bay Area Exch. Club. Republican. Roman Catholic. Home: 605 Bay Club Dr Seabrook TX 77586 Office: Acme Cleaning Equipment 6839 Piccadilly Houston TX 77061

MACIAS, GLORIA PATRICIA, editor; b. El Paso, Tex., July 11, 1973; d. Camilo Victor and Gloria Maria (Gonzalez) M. BS, U. Tex., El Paso, 1995. Mng. editor Ctr. for Inter-Am. and Border Studies, El Paso, 1991—. Mem. Kiwanis Internat. Family, El Paso. Democrat. Roman Catholic. Home: 4128 Olympic Ave El Paso TX 79904 Office: University of Texas-El Paso Ctr Interamerican/Border St 103 Benedict Hall El Paso TX 79968

MACILROY, JOHN WHITTINGTON, lawyer; b. Natchez, Miss., Jan. 15, 1946; s. John Cunnington and Mildred (Whittington) MacI.; m. Linda Susan Pierson, Apr. 11, 1987; 1 stepson, Jeffrey Lee Walters. BA, Yale U., 1968; MPA, Harvard U., 1980; JD, U. Va., 1974; postgrad., Princeton U., 1970. Bar: Va. 1975, U.S. Dist Ct. Va. (ea. and we. dists.) 1976, U.S. Ct. Appeals (4th cir.) 1976. Asst. atty. gen. Office of the Atty. Gen., Commonwealth of Va., Richmond, 1975-77; legis. counsel and spl. asst. to Sen. Byrd U.S. Senate, Washington, 1977-80; legis. counsel and gen. atty. Union Pacific Corp., Omaha, 1980-85; sr. mem. nat. outreach faculty Lesley Coll., Cambridge, Mass., 1985—; cons., exec. asst. for policy Commonwealth of Va., Richmond, 1985-88; cons. faculty U. Va., 1989—; v.p., counsel Va. Mfrs. Assn., 1988-90, pres., 1990—; mem. sci. and tech. task force, 1994-95; adv. com. Va. Adminstrv. Code Commn., 1995—; adv. com. U. Va., 1995—. Creator exec. seminars and acad. programs. Bd. dirs. Blue Ridge Leadership Conf., 1995—. Lt. (j.g.) USNR, 1968-71. Named War Meml. scholar, 1964, Rhodes scholarship candidate 1972, Nat. Merit scholar, 1963. Mem. ABA, Va. State Bar Assn., Am. Mgmt. Assn. (assoc.), U. Va. Alumni Assn. (life), Magna Carta Soc., Harvard Faculty Club (Cambridge), Brandermill Country Club, York River Yacht Club (Gloucester Point, Va.), Mory's Assn. (New Haven), Bull and Bear Club, Yale Club (N.Y.C.). Episcopalian. Home: 11004 Lansdowne Ter Midlothian VA 23113-1362

MACINTYRE, DUGALD STEWART, physician, educator; b. El Paso, Tex., Aug. 23, 1941; s. Dugald Stewart and Elizabeth Bracelin (Davis) M.; m. Maria Theresa Rodriguez, July 5, 1968; children: Ann Therese, Dugald Stewart III. BS, Yale Univ., 1963; MD, Univ. Mich., 1967. Diplomate Am. Bd. Internal Medicine, Am. Bd. Infectious Disease. Intern U. Oreg., 1967-68; resident in medicine U. Mich., Ann Arbor, 1968-71; fellow in infection disease U. Miami, 1973-75; asst. prof. U. Miami, Miami, Fla., 1973-79; pvt. practice Mercy Hosp., Miami, 1979—; clin. assoc. prof. Univ. Miami, 1979-94, clin. prof., 1994—; medical staff Cedars Medical Ctr., 1979—, Miami VA Medical Ctr., 1979—; divsn. chief infectious disease Mercy Hosp., 1988—.

Contbr. articles to profl. jours. Maj. U.S. Army, 1971-73. Mem. Infectious Disease Soc. Am., Am. Soc. Microbiology, Assn. Practioners in Infection Ctr. (dir. 1979-81). Office: Mercy Prof Bldg # 604 3661 S Miami Ave Miami FL 33133-4236

MACIONE, JOE, JR., television broadcasting executive; b. Arcola, Miss., Mar. 30, 1937; s. Joe and Pauline (Nabers) M.; m. Annette Pritchett, Apr. 30, 1960; children: Kimberly Caldwell, Kyle P. BBA, U. Miss., 1958. CPA, Miss., Ark., La. CPA Peat Marwick, Jackson, Miss., 1960-64; pvt. practice Leland, Miss., 1964-69; ptnr., co-founder Sayle & Macione, CPAs, Greenville, Miss., 1969-83; gen. mgr., co-founder Sta. WXVT-TV, CBS affiliate, Greenville, 1983-90; exec. v.p., gen. mgr. Sta. WCYB-TV, NBC affiliate, Bristol, Va., 1990—; founder, co-founder Hollandale Cable Co., Athletes Foot, Greenville, Country Gentleman, Travel Unltd., Big River Barge Co., Choctaw Barge Co., Deer Creek Barge Co., Commonwealth Cornerstone, Inc., Roanoke, Va.; bd. dirs. Wellmont Health System, Wellmont Physician Svcs. Chmn. bd. dirs., treas., Paramount Found.; bd. dirs. Bristol United Way, Bristol Regional Med. Ctr. bd. dirs. Wellmont Health Sys.; mem. Pres.' Round Table King Coll.; mem. King Coll. Campaign for Kins Coll, co-chair of East TN/SWV mem. Commn. on Future S.W. Va.; bd. dirs., vice chmn. govt. rels. com. Greenville Planning Coun.; trustee Greenville Found.; mem. adv. bd. Greenville Jr. Achievement, Allied Enterprises divsn. Miss. Dept. Rehab. Svcs.; mem. adv. coun. U. Miss. Acctg. Sch.; pres., founder Leland Acad.; vice chmn. Govt. Rels. Commn.; active East Tenn. State Univ. Found. Mem. AICPA, Va. Assn. Broadcasters (bd. dirs.), Miss. Assn. Broadcasters (pres.), Nat. Assn. Broadcasters (UHF com., Legis. liaison com., 100 TV com.), Miss. TV Mgrs. Assn. (treas.), Miss. Soc. CPAs, Bristol C. of C. (chmn., chmn. visitors and conv. bur.), Kingsport C. of C. (bd. dirs.), Nat. Ctr. Quality (bd. dirs.), Greater Tri Cities Bus. Alliance (bd. dirs.), Sullivan county Tenn. Indsl. Commn., N.E. Tenn. S.W. Va. C. of C. Coalition (organizer, bd. dirs.), Country Club Bristol, U. Miss. Alumni Assn. (bd. dirs), Leland C. of C. (pres.), Greenville C. of C. (v.p. mktg. divsn.), Rotary (bd. dirs. Bristol chpt., pres. Leland chpt.). Home: 118 Phlox Crk Bristol TN 37620-4757

MACK, CONNIE, III (CORNELIUS MACK), senator; b. Phila., Oct. 29, 1940; s. Cornelius Mack and Susan (Sheppard) McGillicuddy; children: Debra Lynn, Cornelius Harvey. Degree in bus., U. Fla., 1966. Mgmt. tng. Sun Bank, Cape Coral, Fla., 1966-68; v.p. bus. devel. First Nat. Bank, Ft. Myers, 1968-71; sr. v.p., dir. Sun Bank, Cape Coral, Fla., 1971-75; pres., dir. Fla. Nat. Bank, Cape Coral, 1975-82; mem. U.S. Ho. of Reps. from 13th Dist. Fla., Washington, 1983-89; U.S. Senator from Fla., 1989—, sec. Rep. conf. 104th Congress. Bd. dirs., chmn. Palmer Drug Abuse Program, Cape Coral; bd. dirs. Cape Coral Hosp. Mem. Met. Ft. Myers C. of C., Cape Coral C. of C. Republican. Roman Catholic. Office: US Senate 517 Senate Hart Bldg Washington DC 20510*

MACK, MARK PHILIP, chemical company executive; b. Buffalo, Jan. 14, 1950; s. Stanley Joseph and Florence M. (Kopacz) M.; m. Jean Ann Merrick, June 2, 1984; 1 child, Hannah Elizabeth. BS in Chemistry, Buffalo State Coll., 1971; PhD in Chemistry, SUNY, Buffalo, 1976. Rsch. assoc. Duke U., Durham, N.C., 1975-77; rsch. chemist Conoco Inc., Ponca City, Okla., 1977-80; group supr. Conoco Inc., Ponca City, 1980-81; group leader Conoco/DuPont, Ponca City, 1982-85; sr. supr. DuPont Polymer Products, Wilmington, Del., 1985-89; rsch. mgr. OxyChem, Houston, 1989-90; dir. tech. Occidental Chem. Corp., Houston, 1990-95, Lyondell Petrochemical Co., Houston, 1995—. Patentee in field; contbr. articles to profl. jours. Recipient Linus Pauling award SUNY-Buffalo, 1971, Outstanding Student in Chemistry award Western N.Y. Sect. Am. Chem. Soc., 1971, Samuel B. Silbert Fellowship SUNY-Buffalo, 1974-75, Conoco Patent award, 1983. Mem. Am. Chem. Soc., Soc. Plastics Engrs., N.Y. Acad. Sci., Am. Mgmt. Assn., Sigma Xi. Home: 14602 Wisteria Hollow Ln Houston TX 77062-2309

MACK, SANDRA LEE, secondary school educator; b. Charleston, S.C., Feb. 8, 1953; d. Arthur and Lucille (Brown) M. BS in Edn., Knoxville Coll., 1976; MA in Edn., Western Ky. U., Bowling Green, 1977. Cert. tchr., Va. Tchr. Richmond (Va.) Public Schs., 1977—. 4-H vol. Va. Coop. Ext. Svcs., Richmond, 1984—, svc. award, 1990; spl. event coord. West End Svc. unit Commonwealth Girl Scout Coun. of Va., Inc., 1994—, svc. award, 1990, vol. of yr. award, 1995; pres. new mem. com. Trinity Bapt. Ch., Richmond, 1984; head judge Miss Black Am. Richmond pageant, 1990, 91; mem. local PTA; vol. Black History instr. Minority Youth Appreciation Soc., Inc. Learning Ctr., Richmond. Recipient Creighton Ct.'s Youth Sponsor award Richmond Redevel. and Housing Authority, 1990, Cmty. Svc. award, 1994, Vol. of Yr. Gardner-Robinson Youth Svc. award, 1994, Outstanding Vol. award Girl Scout Coun. Va., Inc., 1991, J.C. Penney Golden Rule award for Vol. Excellence in Edn., 1994. Mem. NEA (Va. and Richmond chpts.), Va. Geographic Soc., Va. Socal Studies Coun. (Tchr. of Yr. award 1988), Alpha Kappa Mu.

MACK, SUSAN PRESCOTT, critical care nurse; b. Milton, Fla., Apr. 12, 1957; d. John Hansel and Dorothy Lawrence (Wise) Prescott; 1 child from previous marriage, Heather Denise Phillips; m. Willie Mack; 1 child, Dakota Suzanne. Cert. of practical nursing with honors, Pensacola Jr. Coll., 1976; ADN, Jefferson Davis Jr. Coll., 1980; BSN, U. South Ala., 1989, postgrad., 1994—. RN, Fla., Ala.; CEN. Jay Hosp., 1976-80, Santa Rosa Med. Ctr., 1980-92; Relief staff nurse Am. Nurses Svcs., Inc., Pensacola, Fla., 1992—; ICU staff Atmore Cmty. Hosp., 1994—; home health nurse Advance Home Health, 1996—; adj. in nursing Pensacola Jr. Coll., 1992—. Home: 5711 Pine Dr Milton FL 32583

MACKAY, KENNETH HOOD (BUDDY MACKAY), state official, former congressman; b. Ocala, Fl, Mar. 22, 1933; m. Anne Selph; children: Ken, John, Ben, Andy. B.S., B.A., U. Fla., 1954, LL.B. with honors, 1961. Bar: Fla. 1961. Pvt. practice Raymond, Wilson & Karl, Daytona Beach, Fla., 1963; sole practice 98th-100th Congresses from 6th Dist. Fla., Ocala, Fla., 1963—; mem. Fla. Ho. of Reps. state of Fla., 1968-74; mem. Fla. State Senate, 1974-80, mem. U.S. Ho. Reps. from 6th dist. Fla., 1985-89; lt. gov. State of Fla., 1990—. Elder Ft. King Presbyn. Ch. With USAF 1955-58. Recipient Nat. Legis. Leadership award, 1976; named Most Valuable Freshman Ho. Mem., 1968, Most Valuable Legislator St. Petersburg Times, 7 times; recipient Allen Morris award. Mem. ABA, Kiwanis. Democrat. Office: Office of Lt Gov The Capitol PL05 Tallahassee FL 32399-0001

MAC KENZIE, JAMES DONALD, clergyman; b. Detroit, Nov. 17, 1924; s. James and Ida Catherine (Conklin) M.; student Moody Bible Inst., 1946-49, Union Theol. Sem., 1952; m. Elsie Joan Kerr, May 7, 1960; children—Janet Eileen, Kayly Kathleen, Christy Carol, Kenneth Kerr. Ordained to ministry Presbyn. Ch., 1953; pastor Calvary Ch., Swan Quarter, N.C., Edenton (N.C.) Presbyn. Ch., 1952-60, Kirkwood Ch., Kannapolis, N.C., 1960-64, Barbecue and Olivia Ch., Olivia, N.C., 1964-71, Elise Ch., Robbins, N.C., 1971-87, Horseshoe Presbyn. Ch., Carbonton, N.C., 1971—. Columnist The Chowan Herald, Edenton, N.C., 1952-60, The Robbins (N.C.) Record, 1971-86, The Pilot, Southern Pines, N.C., 1987—. Historian, Fayetteville Presbytery, 1975—, chmn. hist. com., 1983—, moderator, 1978. Founder, Conf. on Celtic Studies, Campbell Coll. (now Campbell U.), Buies Creek, N.C., 1972—; councillor Conf. on Scottish Studies (Can.), 1968-75. With AUS, 1943-45, ETO. Decorated Purple Heart, Bronze Star, Combat Inf. Badge; recipient Disting. Citizen award, Robbins, 1983. Fellow Soc. Antiquaries Scotland; mem. N.C. Presbyn. Hist. Soc. (pres. 1972-74, Author's award 1970, 75, Cert. Merit 1975), Harnett Hist. Soc. (pres. 1968-71, Distinguished Service award 1970), Irish Uilleann Pipers Soc., Gaelic Soc. of Inverness, An Comunn Gaidhelach (life). Author: Colorful Heritage, 1970; editor: The Uilleann Piper, 1974—; contbr. articles to profl. jours. Home and Office: PO Box 867 Robbins NC 27325-0867

MACKENZIE, JOHN, retired oil industry executive; b. 1919. B.S., N.Y. U., 1948. Accountant S.Am. Devel. Co., N.Y.C., 1938-41; financial comptroller French Oil Ind. Agy.-Groupment D'Achat des Carburants, N.Y., 1946-53; v.p., treas. George Hall Corp., 1954-56; asst. treas. Am. Petrofina, Inc., 1956-61, sec., 1961-64, v.p., sec., 1964-68, sr. v.p., sec., 1968-84; ret., 1984. Decorated comdr. Order of Crown (Belgium). Address: 1304 Pagewynne Dr Plano TX 75093-2630

MACKENZIE, MALCOLM ROBERT, personnel management consultant; b. Revere, Mass., Oct. 12, 1924; s. Malcolm John and Helen Margaret (Pelrine) MacK.; m. Chieko Yoshida, Nov. 4, 1954; 1 child, Kenneth Andrew. BA, Tufts U., 1945; Japanese Lang. cert. Sophia U., Tokyo, 1951; Advanced Mgmt. Program U. Hawaii, 1966. Dep. civilian pers. dir. U.S. Army, Camp Zama, Japan, 1959-63, civilian pers. dir., Fort Shafter, Honolulu, 1963-65, chief employee mgmt. U.S. Army Pacific Hdqrs., 1965-69, civilian pers. dir. electronics command, Fort Monmouth, N.J., 1969-76; command civilian pers. mgr. Naval Edn. and Tng., Naval Air Sta, Pensacola, Fla., 1976-81; pers. mgmt. cons., Gulf Breeze, Fla., 1981—. Mem. Human Rights Advocacy Com., Dist. I, Pensacola, 1982-84; asst. dist. dir. Fla. Spl. Olympics, Pensacola, 1982-86; bd. dirs. Pensacola Penwheels, Employ the Handicapped, Pensacola, 1983—; pres. Pensacola Spl. Steppers retarded dancers, 1983; mem. Fla. Gov.'s Com. on Employment of Handicapped, 1983; co-chmn. com. for handicapable dancers United Square Dancers Am., 1984—; active Handicapped Boy Scouts, Pensacola; pres. Assn. Retarded Citizens-Escambia, Pensacola, 1985-87, Fla. State Assn. for Retarded Citizens, 1987-90; mem. Fla. Developmental Disability Coun., 1992—; state bd. dirs. Fla. Blueprint for Sch. To Community Transitions, 1993-96. With USNR, 1943-45, PTO. Recipient Commemorative medallion Tokyo Met. Govt., 1963, cert. Appreciation, Chief of Staff, Ground Office, Defense Agy., Japan, 1963, dir. fgn. affairs. Kanagawa Prefecture, Japan, 1963, dir. fgn. affairs, Saitama Prefecture, Japan, 1963. Mem. Internat. Pers. Mgmt. Assn. (pres. far east chpt. 1960-63, Honolulu chpt. 1964-65, N.J. chpt. 1973-74), Am. Soc. Pub. Adminstrn., Fed. Pers. Coun. Pacific (chmn. 1965-66), Fed. Pers. Coun. N.J. (chmn. 1972-73), Gulf State Fed. Pers. Coun. (vice-chmn. 1980-81), Indsl. Rels. Rsch. Assn., Am. Soc. Tng. and Devel., Fla. Pub. Pers. Assn., Eastern Regional Orgn. for Pub. Adminstrn., Am. Arbitration Assn. (mem. comml. and trade panels), Northwest Fla. Area Agy. on Aging (adv. coun. 1990-92), Parent Edn. Network (cert. trainer 1989-93). Democrat. Roman Catholic. Lodges: KC, Civitan, Elks (treas. 1976-78). Avocations: bowling; golf. Home and Office: 2652 Venetian Way PO Box 280 Gulf Breeze FL 32562

MACKEY, ROSALYN GALE, organization official, consultant; b. Kansas City, Kans., Nov. 11, 1956; d. Sidney and Dela Mildred Ann (Brown) Durham; m. Charles Mackey, Oct. 25, 1982 (div. Jan. 1990). AA in Gen. Edn., Longview (Mo.) Coll., 1982; BS in Math. and Computer Sci., U. Tex., Richardson, 1991. Meeting planner Coun. on Career Devel. for Minorities, Inc., Dallas, 1984-91; mgr. exhibits and meetings Am. Coll. Emergency Physicians, Irving, 1992-94; meeting planner, cons. RGM MicroSolutions, Irving, Tex., 1991—; exhibits mgr. HR S.W.-Human Resources Corp. & Expn., Dallas, 1994—. Bd. dirs. Dallas Urban League, 1986-91; mem. adv. bd. United Way, Dallas, 1987-89. Mem. Am. Soc. Assn. Execs., Profl. Conv. Mgmt. Assn., Internat. Assn. for Expn. Mgmt., Assn. Expn. Mgmt. (cert. meeting planner and expn. mgr.), Ad Hoc Group. Office: HR SW Human Resources Corp & Expn 1230 River Bend Dr Ste 220 Dallas TX 75247

MACKEY, THOMAS CLYDE, historian; b. Radford, Va., Aug. 17, 1956; s. Howard and Blanche M. BA, Beloit Coll., 1978; PhD, Rice U., 1984. Golieb postdoctoral fellow NYU Sch. Law, N.Y.C., 1984-85; vis. asst. prof. Mich. State U., East Lansing, 1985-86; asst. prof. U. Nebr., Lincoln, 1986-88, Ea. Mont. Coll., Billings, 1988-89; vis. asst. prof. Kans. State U., Manhattan, 1989-90, asst. prof., 1990-91; asst. prof. history, adj. asst. prof. law U. Louisville, 1991-95, assoc. prof. history, adj. prof. law, 1995—. Author: Red Lights Out: A Legal History of Prostitution, Disorderly Houses and Vice Districts, 1870-1917, 1987. NEH travel grantee, 1992. Mem. Am. Soc. Legal History, Soc. Historians of the Gilded Age and Progressive Era (com. mem.), Orgn. Am. Historians (com. mem.), Am. Hist. Assn., So. Hist. Assn. Democrat. Office: U Louisville Dept History Louisville KY 40292

MACKIE, DONALD JOHN, JR., real estate developer; b. Ashland, Wis., July 29, 1944; s. Donald John and Mary Eleanor (Berglund) M.; m. Sara Nelle Lowrey, Apr. 6, 1974; children: Anna Kathleen, Douglas Lowrey. BBA in Urban Land Econs., U. Wis., 1969. Project mgr. Bliss & Laughlin Industries, Oak Brook, Ill., 1969-72; pres. Green Mark, Inc. subs. Gerald D. Hines, Houston, 1972-78; mng. ptnr. Mill Creek Golf & Country Club, Salado, Tex., 1978—, Mill Creek Properties, Salado, 1978—; pres. Salado Water Supply Corp., 1993—; chmn. Anchor Industries, Gatesville, Tex., 1996—. Sponsor, dir. Cen. Tex. Area Mus., Salado, 1980—, Bell County Rehab Tournament, Salado, 1984—, Table Rock Festival, Salado, 1985—. Served to 1st lt. U.S. Army, 1962-66. Recipient Environ. award, City of Houston, 1977, Design award, Am. Inst. Architects, 1976. Mem. Urban Land Inst. (residential, recreation, indsl., office couns. 1970-87), Nat. Assn. Indsl. and Office Parks, Nat. Assn. Home Builders (Profl. Mktg. award 1976), Nat. Golf Course Owners Assn. Episcopalian. Lodge: Lions. Home: 806 Hilltop Salado TX 76571-9566 Office: Mill Creek Golf & Country Club PO Box 67 Salado TX 76571-0067

MAC'KIE, PAMELA S., lawyer; b. Jackson, Miss., Jan. 2, 1956; d. Charles Edward and Betty Jo (Moore) Spell; children: John Greene IV, Ann Katherine. BS, Delta State U., Cleveland, Miss., 1978; JD, U. Miss., Oxford, 1984. Bar: Miss. 1984, Fla. 1986. Assoc. Cummings & Lockwood, Naples, Fla., 1985-93; prin. Pamela S. Mac'Kie, P.A., Naples, 1993-95, pres., 1995—. Pres. Naples Better Govt., 1992-95; pres.-elect Women's Rep. Club, Naples, 1994; county commr. Collier County Bd., Naples, 1994—; dir. Youth Haven, 1992, YMCA, 1993, Collier County Women's Polit. Caucus, 1992—. Recipient Pro Bono award Fla. Bar, 1990, Leadership Collier C. of C., Naples, 1991. Recipient Pro Bono award Fla. Bar, 1990; grad. Leadership Collier, Naples, 1991, Leadership S.W. Fla., 1995. Republican. Episcopalian. Office: No Trust Bldg Ste 320 4001 Tamiami Tr N Ste 320 Naples FL 34103 Office: Ste 201 4001 Tamiami Trl N # 320 Naples FL 34103-3556

MACKORELL, JAMES THEODORE, JR., entrepreneur, small business owner; b. Chapel Hill, N.C., Nov. 6, 1959; s. James Theodore and June (Andrews) M.; m. Wendy LeVeau, June 25, 1983 (div.); children: Andrew James, Ashley Nicole; m. Stacy Conn, Oct. 5, 1996. BS, Appalachian State U., 1982. Owner Makoto's of Boone, N.C., 1981-87; treas. Mendenmack, Inc., Boone, 1985-86; sec., treas. Mackenall Enterprises, Inc., Boone, 1986-87; owner Makato's of Tenn., Tenn., 1987-91; founder, owner, mgr. Mackorell Group, Inc., Boone, 1989—; cons. Food Mgmt., Inc., Boone, 1982-86. Organizer fund raising Boone Citizens Com. for Legal Control, 1986; trustee E.B. Andrews Meml. Found.; mem. Appalachian State U. Chancellors Com. Recipient Eagle Scout award Boy Scouts Am., 1976. Mem. Nat. Restaurant Assn. (Cert. of Achievement 1984), N.C. Restaurant Assn., High Country Host, Boone Area C. of C., Nat. Eagle Scout Assn. (life), Chancellors Club (Appalachian State U. com. mem.). Republican. Methodist. Clubs: Deer Valley Racquet, Yosef (Boone). Home: 626 Windwood Ln Boone NC 28607-9437 Office: The Mackorell Group Inc 2124 Blowing Rock Rd Boone NC 28607-4865

MACLAREN, NEIL MOORLEY, JR., musician, music educator; b. Cambridge, Mass., July 12, 1932; s. Neil Moorley and Elsie Violet (Elmes) MacL.; m. Mary Peloquin, Oct. 5, 1989. MusB, Westminster Choir Coll., 1957, MusM, 1959; MusD (hon.), Geneva-St. Albans Theol. Coll., 1976. Organist, choir dir. First Presbyn. Ch., Bordentown, N.J., 1957-59; choir dir., accompanist N.J. State Reformatory, Bordentown, 1957-59; pvt. tchr. piano, voice, organ and electronic keyboard, 1959—; organist, choir dir. Deerfield (N.J.) 1st Presbyn. Ch., 1959; min. music, organist, soloist First Bapt. Ch., Fall River, Mass., 1959-64; organist., ch. and sch. mus. dir. St. Mark's Episc. Ch. and Sch., Ft. Lauderdale, Fla., 1964-72; organist, choirmaster St. Peter's Am. Episc. Ch., Deerfield Beach, Fla., 1973-86; faculty piano tchr. Sch. Arts Second Presbyn. Ch., Ft. Lauderdale, 1976-77; organist Temple Kol Ami, Plantation, Fla., 1979-82; tchr. piano, organ, electronic keyboard Suniland Music Shoppe, Plantation, 1981-91; mus. dir. Hawaiian Gardens Choral Group, 1986-93; organist First Ch. Christ Scientist, Pompano Beach, Fla., 1986—; faculty tchr. piano Sch. Arts Coral Ridge Presbyn. Ch., Ft. Lauderdale, 1991-93; tenor soloist Phila. area chs., 1957-59; mus. dir. lenten choir and summer daily vacation Bible studies and camp Greater Fall River Coun. Chs., 1959-64; part time tchr. music Henry Lord Jr. H.S., James Morton Jr. H.S., 1959-64; tchr., piano, organ, voice First Bapt. Ch., 1959-64; organist high holy days Temple Beth-El, Fall River, 1959-64; charter mem. Gold Coast Symphony Chorus, 1973-74; part time tchr., chorus dir., accompanist Fla. Oaks Sch., Ft. Lauderdale, 1980-82; village chorus accompanist John Knox Village, Pompano Beach, 1992—; judge Gwen Bari Talent Show, 1980-82. Mem., tenor soloist R.I. Civic Chorale, 1959-64; mem. U. Miami Civic Chorale, 1969-74. With U.S. Army, 1953-55. Mem. Am. Guild Organists (dean Ft. Lauderdale chpt. 1967-69, Svc. Playing cert. 1989), Fla. State Music Tchrs. Assn. (corr. sec. 1993-95), Broward County Music Tchrs. Assn. (parliamentarian 1987-89, pres. 1991-93, yearbook editor, newsletter editor 1991-95, 2d v.p. 1993—), Toastmasters Internat. (area IV gov. 1978, Outstanding Gov. of Dist. 47, Dist. Toastmaster 1981), Kiwanis. Republican. Episcopalian. Home: 1861 SW 6th Ave Pompano Beach FL 33060-9019

MACLAREN, WILLIAM GEORGE, JR., engineering executive; b. Chgo., May 6, 1928; s. William George Sr. and Dorothy Pauline (Costello) MacL.; m. Marie Lorraine Logan, Sept. 15, 1951 (div. Dec. 1977); children: Vanessa Ann MacLaren-Wray, Jon Mark, Scott William; m. Mary Patricia Loftus, Dec. 22, 1977 (div. Oct. 1995). BS in Indsl. Engring., U. Pitts., 1951; MS in Indsl. Engring., Syracuse U., 1958; PhD in Indsl. Mgmt., Columbia Pacific U., 1989. Commd. 2nd lt. USAF, 1951, advanced through grades to major gen., 1974; comdr. 5BW Minot AFB, N.D., 1972-74; chief of staff, 1975; comdr. Pacific Comm. Area, 1975-78; vice comdr. Air Force Comm. Command, 1978-79; dir. Command Control and Comm. Hdqs. USAF, 1979-81; dir. Comm. and Info. Sys. NATO, 1981-84; ret. USAF, 1984; v.p. Gia, Inc., Arlington, Va., 1984-90, 93—; dir. gen. NATO/NATO Air Command and Control Mgmt. Agy., Brussels, 1990-93. Contbr. articles to profl. jours. Regional bd. dirs. Boy Scout Am., Minot, N.D., 1972-74. Named Disting. Engring. Alumnus U. Pitts., 1986. Mem. AIAA, Inst. Indsl. Engrs., Air Force Assn., Armed Forces Comm. and Electronics Assn. (regional v.p. 1975-78, Gold medal 1983), Am. Def. Preparedness Assn., Order of Daedalians (chpt. pres. 1976-78, merit award 1979), Rotary. Republican. Home: 438 N Park Dr Arlington VA 22203-2344 Office: GIA Inc 1800 Diagonal Rd Ste 510 Alexandria VA 22314

MACLEOD, DONALD MARTIN, corporate professional; b. N.Y.C., May 21, 1929; s. John and Annie Campbell (Martin) MacL.; m. Beverly Ann Thomson, Feb. 16, 1952 (div. Nov. 18, 1979); children: James Donald, Terry Ann; m. Harriet Elaine Hoff, Feb. 17, 1989 (dec. Mar. 1993). BS in Mech. Engring., Rensselaer Poly. Inst., 1951. Engr. IBM Corp., Endicott & Kingston, N.Y., 1951-54; supr. quality control Ronson Corp., East Stroudsburg, Pa., 1954-55; pres. Manco Specialties, Apalachin, N.Y., 1955-58; engring. supr. Link Aviation, Binghamton, N.Y., 1958-59; sales mgr. Universal Instruments Corp., Binghamton, 1959-61; mktg. mgr. Xerox Corp., Rochester, N.Y., 1961-71; pres. Industry Search Inc., Rochester, 1971-83; gen. mgr. Consler Sci. Design, Inc., Tampa, Fla., 1983-88; pres. Industry Tech, Oldsmar, Fla., 1989—. Mem. Tech. Assn. of the Pulp and Paper Industry. Home: 110 Lesley Ln Oldsmar FL 34677-2090 Office: Industry Tech 188 Scarlet Blvd Oldsmar FL 34677-3002

MACLEOD, JOHN DANIEL, JR., religious organization administrator; b. Robbins, N.C., Mar. 16, 1922; s. John Daniel Sr. and Sarah Cranor (McKay) MacL.; m. Helen Frances Boggs, Sept. 18, 1945 (dec. Aug. 1990); children: Sarah MacLeod Owens, Mary Marget MacLeod Silberstein, John Daniel III, William Boggs. AB, Davidson (N.C.) Coll., 1942; MDiv, Union Theol. Sem., Richmond, Va., 1945, ThM, 1949, ThD, 1952; DD (hon.), St., Andrews Presbyn. Coll., Laurinburg, N.C., 1992. Ordained to ministry Presbyn. Ch., 1945. Pastor Carolina Beach (N.C.) Presbyn. Ch., 1945-48, Brett-Reed Presbyn. Ch., Sweet Hall, Va., 1949-53, Keyser (W.Va.) Presbyn. Ch., 1953-63; exec. Appomattox Presbytery, Lynchburg, Va., 1963-67, Norfolk (Va.) Presbytery, 1967-76, Westminster Presbytery, St. Petersburg, Fla., 1976-81; exec. Synod of N.C., Raleigh, 1981-88, ret., 1988; interim exec. Coastal Carolina Presbytery, Fayetteville, 1991-93, Holston Presbytery, Kingsport, Tenn., 1993; interim parish assoc. White Meml. Presbyn. Ch., Raleigh, N.C., 1994; interim exec. Western N.C. Presbytery, Morganton, 1995, interim assoc. exec., 1996—; mem., chmn. various local and nat. Presbyn. Ch. Coms. Trustee Warren Wilson Coll., 1985-89, N.C. Presbyn. Hist. Soc., 1981—, Mary Baldwin Coll., 1960-68, Davis and Elkins Coll., 1955-61, Massanetta Springs Conf. Ctr., 1956-62, Barium Springs Children's Home, 1995—; active Mineral County Redevel. Commn., Keyser, 1960-63; mem. N.C. Gov's. Adv. com. on Citizen Affairs, Raleigh, 1983-84; bd. advisors Wake Forest U. Div. Sch., 1991—. Nominee moderator Presbyn. Ch. USA Gen. Assembly, 1987, moderator Synod of Va., 1969, Synod of Mid-Atlantic, 1990. Fellow Soc. Antiquaries (Scotland); mem. St. Andrews Soc. (Southern Pines, N.C. chpt., bd. dirs. Tampa, Fla. chpt. 1976-81), N.C. Scottish Heritage Soc. (pres. 1992—), Clan MacLeod Soc. (chaplain, bd. dirs. 1994). Democrat. Home: 114 Silver Creek Rd Morganton NC 28655-4205

MACMANAMY, GARY ALLAN, minister; b. Pontiac, Mich., Apr. 17, 1946; s. Allan Alden and Sue Ann (Carlton) MacM.; m. Janine McKinley, June 18, 1971; children: Sarah Gayle, James Colin. BBA, East Tex. State U., 1970; MDiv, Southwestern Bapt. Theol. Sem., 1980. Ordained to gospel ministry Southern Bapt. Conv., 1981. Youth min. Evang. Meth. Ch., Duncanville, Tex., 1976-78; chaplain Police Dept., Duncanville, 1979-80; pastor First Bapt. Ch., Bloomington, Tex., 1981-85, Calvary Bapt. Ch., Lawton, Okla., 1986-91, Country Estates Bapt. Ch., Midwest City, Okla., 1991—; trustee, vice chair and chair exec. com. Sunday Sch. Bd., Nashville, 1989—; trustee So. Bapt. Found., Nashville, 1990—; moderator Capital Bapt. Assn., 1993-95. Steering com. Task Force for A Drug Free Community, Lawton, Okla., 1990—; chmn. prog. com. Baptist Gen. Convention of Okla., 1994. Mem. Commanche Cotton Bapt. Assn. (moderator 1989-91), Am. Bus. Club. Republican. Home: 12433 Hastings Rd Oklahoma City OK 73130-4929 Office: Country Estates Bapt Ch 1000 S Midwest Blvd Oklahoma City OK 73110-4731

MACMULLEN, JEAN ALEXANDRIA STEWART, nurse, administrator; b. N.Y.C., Feb. 21, 1945; d. John Douglas and Isabella Stewart (Park) MacM. Diploma in nursing, Lenox Hill Hosp., N.Y.C., 1965; BS in Nursing, Adelphi U., 1969, MS in Nursing, 1971; MA in Anthropology, U. South Fla., 1978. Nurse renal disease unit N.Y. Hosp., N.Y.C., 1971-72; clin. nurse specialist VA Hosp., Tampa, Fla., 1972-76, med./surg. coord., 1976-82; assoc. chief nurse VA Med. Ctr., Gainesville, Fla., 1982-93; assoc. med. ctr. dir. nursing VA Med. Ctr., Montgomery, Ala., 1993—. Jour. editor Am. Assn. Nephrology Nurses, Pitman, N.J., 1980-82, referee, adviser, 1983—; contbr. numerous articles to profl. publs. Mem. Fla. Nurses Assn. Republican. Episcopalian. Office: VA Med Ctr 215 Perry Hill Rd Montgomery AL 36109-3725

MACNUTT, FRANCIS SCOTT, religious organization administrator; b. St. Louis, Apr. 22, 1925; s. Joseph Scott and Agnes (Cady) MacN.; m. Judith C. Sewell, Feb. 9, 1980; children: Rachel, David. BA, Harvard U., 1948; MFA, Cath. U. Am., 1950; PhD, Aquinas Inst. Theology, 1958. Ordained priest Roman Cath. Ch., 1956. Prof. homiletics Aquinas Inst. Theology, Dubuque, Iowa, 1960-66; exec. sec. Cath. Homiletic Soc., St. Louis, 1966-69; dir. Thomas Merton Found., St. Louis, 1970-80; dir. Christian Healing Ministries, Clearwater, Fla., 1981-87, Jacksonville, Fla., 1987—; founder, bd. mem. Assn. Christian Therapists, Laurel, Md., 1975-80; bd. mem. nat. svc. com. Cath. Charismatic Renewal, Notre Dame, Ind., 1975-80. Author: Gauging Sermon Effectiveness, 1960, Healing, 1974, Power to Heal, 1977, The Prayer That Heals, 1981, Overcome By the Spirit, 1990, Deliverance From Evil Spirits, a Practical Manual, 1994; co-author: Praying for Your Unborn Child, 1988; editor Preaching, A Jour. of Homiletics, 1966-70. Cpl. U.S. Army, 1944-46. Recipient 19th ann. Franciscan award, Prior Lake, Minn., 1977. Mem. First Coast Harvard Club (Fla.), Audubon Soc., Nature Conservancy, Common Cause, Amnesty Internat., Network. Democrat. Roman Catholic. Office: Christian Healing Ministries PO Box 9520 Jacksonville FL 32208-0520

MACON, JANE HAUN, lawyer; b. Corpus Christi, Tex., Sept. 26, 1946; d. E.H. and Johnnie Mae (De Mauri) Haun; m. R. Laurence Macon, Sept. 6, 1969. BA in Internat. Studies, U. Tex., 1967, JD, 1970. Bar: Tex. 1971, Ga. 1971, U.S. Dist. Ct. (we. dist.) Tex. 1973, U.S. Ct. Appeals (5th and 11th cirs.) 1973. Legal staff Office Econ. Opportunity, Atlanta, 1970-71; trial atty. City of San Antonio, 1972-77, city atty., 1977-83; ptnr. Fulbright & Jaworski, LLP, San Antonio, 1983—; pres. Internat. Women's Forum, Washington, 1987-89; mem. Com. of 200, 1988—; bd. dirs. Thousand Oaks Nat. Bank, San Antonio. Legal counsel Nat. Women's Polit. Caucus, 1981—; bd. dirs. Alamo council Boy Scouts Am., San Antonio, 1977—. Named to San Antonio Hall of Fame, 1984; named one of Rising Stars, 1984. Fellow Tex. Bar Found., Tex. Bar Assn. (chmn. women and the law

1984-85, client security fund com.), Southwest Research Found.; mem. San Antonio Bar Assn., San Antonio Young Lawyers Assn., Women Lawyers Tex. (pres. 1984-85), Tex. Banking Bd., Bexar County Women's Bar Assn. Democrat. Baptist. Home: 230 W Elsmere Pl San Antonio TX 78212-2349 Office: Fulbright & Jaworski LLP 300 Convent St Ste 2200 San Antonio TX 78205-3723

MACPHAIL, DEBORAH, mission service volunteer, educator; b. Gettysburg, Pa., June 14, 1951; d. John Archie and Jeanne Alma (Spangler) MacP. BS in Music Edn., Gettysburg Coll., 1973; MEd in Tng. and Devel. Pa. State U., Harrisburg, 1993; postgrad. Louisville Presbyn. Theol. Sem. Selection/tng. coordinator Commonwealth Nat. Bank, Harrisburg, Pa., 1978-79; safety tng. mgr. Ralston Purina Co., Mechanicsburg, Pa., 1979-81; data processing edn. coordinator Hamilton Bank, Lancaster, Pa., 1981-82, dir. mgmt. devel., 1982-83; asst. v.p., dir. manpower devel. Hamilton Bank, subs. CoreStates, Lancaster, 1982-85; asst. v.p., dir. corp. devel. CoreStates Fin. Corp., Phila., 1985-86; asst. v.p. personnel, tng. coordinator, Consumer Banking Group Phila. Nat. Bank, 1986-87, v.p., personnel and tng. coordinator, Consumer Banking Group, Phila. Nat. Bank, 1987, v.p., cluster sales mgr., 1988-90; cons. in leadership devel. affiliated with Tandem Group, 1990-93; exec. dir. Community Music Sch., York, Pa., 1992-93; mission vol. Presbyn. Ch. USA at Sheldon Jackson Coll., Sitka, Alaska, 1993-94; women's ctr. coord. Louisville Presbyn. Theol. Sem., 1994-95; tchr. ESL/global mission vol. Gymnazium S.A. Komensky, Kosice, Republic of Slovakia, 1995—; mem. corp. adv. bd. Lebanon Valley Coll., Annville, Pa., 1985-88; instr. Am. Inst. Banking, Lebanon, 1983-90; mem. tng. degree adv. com. Pa. State U., Middletown, Pa., 1983-84; mem. state edn. exec. adv. com. Pa. Am. Inst. Banking, Harrisburg, 1982; lectr. in field; bd. dirs. ARI. Co-dir. The Last Supper, Cornwall (Pa.) Meth. Ch.; music dir. Spoon River Anthology, Sheldon Jackson Coll., Sitka Cmty. Players. Mem. finance com. Del. County Chpt. Girl Scouts, 1989-90; mem. exec. bd. Susquehanna Chorale, 1991-92; pres. Profiles in Excellence, 1992; choir dir. 1st Presbyn. Ch., Sitka, 1993. Mem. Am. Soc. Tng. and Devel. (chpt. pres. 1981, Leigh Woehling Meml. award 1985, mem. exec. com. human resource devel. careers 1986-87, Outstanding Leadership award 1990, project coord. CATER initiative 1990—), Adminstrv. Mgmt. Soc. (bd. dirs. 1991), Gettysburg Coll. Alumni Assn. (exec. com. 1992-93), Recorder Soc. Avocations: reading, gardening, hiking, camping.

MADDEN, ARTHUR ALLEN, nuclear pharmacist, educator; b. Atlanta, Sept. 19, 1960; s. Arthur Allen and Lillian Brandon (Vaughan) M.; m. Rebecca Kaye Teague, June 25, 1988; 1 child, Kelley Vaughan. BA in English, U. of the South, Sewanee, Tenn., 1982; BS in Pharmacy, U. S.C., 1988, PharmD, 1990. Registered pharmacist, N.C., S.C.; bd. cert. nuclear pharmacist, 1994. Poison control specialist Palmetto Poison Ctr., Columbia, 1988-90; relief pharmacist Wal-Mart, Columbia, 1989-91; dir. S.C. Nuclear Pharmacy, Columbia, 1990-91; nuclear pharmacist Syncor Internat. Corp., Columbia, S.C., 1991-95; radiation safety cons. Syncor Internat. Corp., Columbia, 1990-95; dir. Cosource Nuclear Pharmacy Geodax Tech., Inc., Columbia, 1995—; mem. faculty U. S.C. Sch. Medicine, Columbia, 1990—, asst. prof. Coll. Pharmacy, 1990—; third party ins. expert, Columbia, 1983-93; mem. ad hoc com. for infectious disease policy. Mem. Am. Pharm. Assn., Am. Soc. Hosp. Pharmacists, S.C. Nuclear Medicine Soc., S.C. Sch. Medicine Hemotology/Oncology Jour. Club, Bd. Pharm. Specialties-Nuclear Pharmacy, Phi Lambda Sigma (sec. 1987-89), Order of the Thistle, Order of the Highlander. Home: 4626 Reamer Ave Columbia SC 29206-1541 Office: Cosource Nuclear Pharmacy 2501 Main St Columbia SC 29201

MADDEN, DAVID, author; b. Knoxville, Tenn., July 25, 1933; s. James Helvy and Emile (Merritt) M.; m. Roberta Margaret Young, Sept. 6, 1956; 1 son, Blake Dana. B.S., U. Tenn., 1957; M.A., San Francisco State Coll., 1958; postgrad., Yale Drama Sch., 1959-60. Faculty Appalachian State Tchrs. Coll., Boone, N.C., 1957-58, Centre Coll., Danville, Ky., 1960-62, U. Louisville, 1962-64, Kenyon Coll., Gambier, O., 1964-66, Ohio U., Athens, 1966-68; writer-in-residence La. State U., Baton Rouge, 1968-92, dir. creative writing program, 1992-94, dir. U.S. Civil War Ctr., 1992—; alumni prof. La. State U., 1994. Author: (novels) Cassandra Singing, 1969, Bijou, 1974, The Suicide's Wife, 1978, Pleasure Dome, 1979, On the Big Wind, 1980, (stories) The Shadow Knows (Nat. Coun. on Arts selection), 1970, The New Orleans of Possibilities (lit. criticism) Wright Morris, 1964, Poetic Image in Six Genres, 1969, James M. Cain, 1970, A Primer of the Novel, 1980, Writers' Revisions, 1981, Cain's Craft, 1985, Revising Fiction, 1988, Rediscoveries II, 1988; asst. editor: The Kenyon Rev., 1964-66; editor: Remembering James Agee, 1974; co-editor: (with P. Bach) Classics of Civil War Fiction, 1991, Sharpshooter, 1996. Served with AUS, 1953-55. Recipient Rockefeller grant in fiction, 1969; John Golden fellow in playwriting, 1959. Mem. Authors League, Associated Writing Programs (bd). Democrat. Office: US Civil War Ctr La State U Raphael Semmes Dr Baton Rouge LA 70803

MADDEN, MARIE FRANCES, marketing professional; b. Weatherby, Mo., Sept. 27, 1928; d. Truman E. and Hazel (Tiller) Wilford; m. Mertice A. Madden, July 20, 1974. Grad. high sch., Cameron, Mo. Cert. personnel cons. Office mgr. Bechtel Corp., San Francisco, Lawrence, Kans., 1948-52; adminstrn. asst. Milton P. Allen, Atty., Lawrence, 1952-56, Philip T. Sharples, Entrepreneur, Phila., 1956-74; corp. sec. Madden Aircraft Sales Corp., Dallas, 1974-81; pres., owner Madden Co., Inc. of Dallas, Dallas, 1981-89; exec. dir. TPC Madden Mktg. Group, Dallas, 1989-91; owner, pres. Madden Mktg. and Design Group, Dallas, 1991—; ptnr. Madden-Otterbine Tng., Dallas, 1994—. Mem. Metroplex Assn. Personnel Cons. (bd. dirs. 1986-87), Tex. Assn. Personnel Cons. (bd. dirs. 1987-89). Home: 2822 Oak Point Dr Garland TX 75044 Office: 12001 N Central Expy Dallas TX 75243-3700

MADDEN, ROBERTA MARGARET, association program developer; b. Council Bluffs, Iowa, Nov. 9, 1936; d. Charles Theodore and Mary Elizabeth (Moffatt) Young; m. Jerry David Madden, Sept. 6, 1956; 1 child, Blake Dana. BA in Govt. summa cum laude, Ohio U., 1968. Editor Ky. Labor News, Louisville, 1962-64, La. State U. Press, Baton Rouge, 1969-72; dir. Consumer Protection Ctr., Baton Rouge, 1972-76; agt. Mut. Benefit Life Ins. Co., Baton Rouge, 1977-79; dist. mgr. U.S. Census Bur., Baton Rouge, 1979-80; exec. dir. YWCA, Baton Rouge, 1980-83, program devel., 1994—; field dir. Common Cause, Baton Rouge, 1983-90; exec. dir. Am. Diabetes Assn., Baton Rouge, 1990-93; mem. adv. com. U.S. Consumer Product Safety Commn., 1973-75; mem. Pub. Affairs Rsch. Coun., Baton Rouge, 1992—. Editor/dir. (oral history project) Remembering the Struggle, 1983; freelance writer/editor, 1966-71. Candidate La. State Senate, Baton Rouge, 1979; mem. state adv. com. U.S. Civil Rights Commn., La., 1981—; founding mem. Capital Area Network, Baton Rouge, 1978—; mem. Early Risers Kiwanis Club, Baton Rouge, 1993—, pres.-elect, 1996—; chmn. race rels. Baton Rouge Coun. on Human Rels., 1993—; grad. Leadership Greater Baton Rouge, 1992. Recipient Advancement of Women award NOW, 1975, Humanitarian award Baton Rouge Human Rels., 1985. Mem. AAUW, LWV, Common Cause, Kiwanis, Phi Beta Kappa. Democrat. Unitarian. Home: 614 Park Blvd Baton Rouge LA 70806-5331 Office: YWCA PO Box 66435 Baton Rouge LA 70896-6435

MADDEN, TERESA DARLEEN, insurance agency owner; b. Dallas, Aug. 4, 1960; d. Tommy Joe Frederick Dodd and Mary Helen (Sterner) Smith; m. Kim Ashley Madden, June 2, 1989. Student, Tex. Tech U., 1978-81. Cert. ins. counselor. With personal lines svc. Charles R. Ervin Ins., Midland, Tex., 1981, Bryant Scalf Ins., Richardson, Tex., 1981-82; with comml. ins. svc. Street & Assocs. Inc., Dallas, 1982-84; with comml. ins. sales/svc. Hotchkiss Ins., Dallas, 1984-85; mgr. sales Abbott-Rose Ins. Agy., Dallas, 1985-89; owner Glenn-Madden & Assocs. Ins., Dallas, 1990—. Methodist. Office: Glenn Madden & Assocs Inc Ste 1470 9330 Lyndon B Johnson Fwy Dallas TX 75243-3436

MADDOCK, LAWRENCE HILL, language educator, writer; b. Ogden, Utah, July 14, 1923; s. Lawrence J. and Nellie (Hill) M. Student, U. Fla., 1941-42; BA, George Peabody Coll., 1946, PhD, 1965; MA, U. So. Calif., 1949. Tchr. pub. schs. Jacksonville, Fla., 1949-52; instr. U. Fla., Gainesville, 1952-53; asst. prof. California (Pa.) State Coll., 1955-56, assoc. prof., 1956-64; assoc. prof. N.E. La. State Coll., Monroe, 1964-67, U. West Fla., Pensacola, 1967-90. Author: The Door of Memory, 1974, John Maddock: Mormon Pioneer, 1996; contbr. chpts. to books and articles to profl. jours. Mem. MLA (bibliographer 1978-93), Thomas Wolfe Soc., Mormon History Assn. Republican. Mormon. Home: 1012 Gerhardt Dr Pensacola FL 32503-3222

MADDOX, ALVA HUGH, state supreme court justice; b. Andalusia, Ala., Apr. 17, 1930; s. Christopher Columbus and Audie Louella Maddox; m. Virginia Roberts, June 14, 1958; children: Robert Hugh, Jane Maddox. AB in Journalism, U. Ala., Tuscaloosa, 1952, JD, 1957. Bar: Ala. 1957. Law clk. to Judge Aubrey Cates, Ala. Ct. Appeals, Montgomery, 1957-58; field examiner Chief Atty.'s Office, VA, Montgomery, 1958-59; law clk. to Judge Frank M. Johnson, U.S. Dist. Ct., Montgomery, 1959-61; pvt. practice, Montgomery, 1961-65; cir. judge, spl. cir. judge Montgomery Cir. Ct., 1963, asst. dist. atty., 1964; legal advisor to govs. State of Ala., Montgomery, 1965-69; assoc. justice Supreme Ct. Ala., Montgomery, 1969—; mem. adv. bd. JUSTEC Rsch. Author: Alabama Rules of Criminal Procedure, 1991, supplements, 1992—. Founder youth jud. program YMCA, Montgomery, 1987, also mem. metro. bd. dirs. 2d lt. USAF, 1952-54, col. USAF Res. ret. Recipient Man of Yr. award YMCA, 1988, Disting. Program Svc. award, 1989. Mem. ABA, Ala. Bar Assn., Inst. Jud. Adminstrn., Christian Legal Soc., Federalist Soc. (bd. dirs.), Montgomery County Inns of Ct. (charter, founding), Ala. Law Inst., Am. Jud. Soc., Kiwanis (past bd. dirs. Montgomery). Democrat. Baptist. Office: Supreme Ct Ala 300 Dexter Ave Montgomery AL 36104-3741

MADDOX, HUGH, state supreme court justice. Justice Ala. Supreme Ct., Montgomery. Office: Ala Supreme Ct 300 Dexter Ave Montgomery AL 36104-3741

MADDOX, ROBERT ALAN, atmospheric scientist; b. Granite City, Ill., July 12, 1944; s. Robert Alvin and Maxine Madeline (Elledge) M.; m. Rebecca Ann Speer, Dec. 27, 1967 (dec. Oct. 1995); children—Timothy Alan, Jason Robert. Student Purdue U., 1962-63; B.S., Tex. A&M U., 1967; M.S. in Atmospheric Sci., Colo. State U., 1973, Ph.D. in Atmospheric Sci., 1981. Meteorologist, Nat. Weather Service, Hazelwood, Mo., 1967; research meteorologist Geophys. Research & Devel. Corp., Ft. Collins, Colo., 1975-76; research meteorologist Atmospheric Physics and Chemistry Lab., NOAA-Environ. Research Labs., Boulder, Colo., 1976-79, meteorologist Office Weather Research and Modification, 1979-82, program mgr. weather analysis and storm prediction, 1982-83, dir. weather research program, 1983-84, program mgr. mesoscale studies, 1984-86; dir. Nat. Severe Storms Lab., Norman, Okla., 1986—; participant numerous sci. workshops; tchr. weather analysis, forecasting, mesoscale phenomena; presenter workshops on mesoscale analysis and heavy precipitation forecasting Nat. Weather Service Forecast Offices; cons. in field. Served to capt. USAF, 1967-75. Decorated Air Force Commendation medal with oak leaf cluster; recipient Superior Performance award NOAA, 1981, Outstanding Sci. Paper award, 1984. Fellow Am. Meteorol. Soc. (councilor 1989-92, chmn. severe storms com. 1991-92, Clarence Leroy Meisinger award 1983, co-editor, assoc. editor Monthly Weather Rev., assoc. editor Weather & Forecasting); mem. Nat. Weather Assn. (award for outstanding contbns. to operational meteorology 1981, co-editor Nat. Weather Digest, Mem. of Yr. award 1992, Silver medal, 1994), Sigma Xi, Phi Kappa Phi, Chi Epsilon Pi. Contbr. articles to profl. pubis. Office: NOAA/ERL Nat Severe Storms 1313 Halley Cir Norman OK 73069-8480

MADDOX, ROGER WAYNE, minister; b. Sayre, Okla., Apr. 22, 1950; s. Earnest Clifford and Wilma Nell (Walkup) M.; m. Judith Ellen Mann, Aug. 23, 1968; 1 child, Deidra. AA in Gen. Edn., Sayre Jr. Coll., 1970; BA in Comml. Art, Southwestern Okla. State U., 1972, MEd in Art Edn., 1982; MDiv, Southwestern Bapt. Theol. Sem., 1989, postgrad., 1994—. Ordained to ministry So. Bapt. Ch., 1989. Cert. tchr. Okla., 1979, Tex., 1987. Evangelist Wedgwood Bapt. Ch., Ft. Worth, 1984-86; Mardi Gras evangelist New Orleans, 1985-86; physical plant journeyman Southwestern Bapt. Theol. Sem., Ft. Worth, 1984-87; mission pastor Wedgwood Bapt. Ch. to Oak Park Chapel, Ft. Worth, 1985-86; pastor First Bapt. Ch., Arnett, Okla., 1989-93, Pleasant Glade Bapt. Ch., Colleyville, Tex., 1994—. Exhibited in juried shows, 1982; represented in Shorney Art Gallery, 1981—. Recipient Excellence in Teaching award Ft. Worth Ind. Sch. Dist., 1987-88; featured artist Art Gallery Mag., 1982. Republican. Home and Office: Pleasant Glade Bapt Ch 3708 Glade Rd Colleyville TX 76034-4827

MADDUX, GREG(ORY ALAN), professional baseball player; b. San Angelo, Tex., Apr. 14, 1966. Grad. high sch., Las Vegas. Baseball player Chicago Cubs, 1984-92, Atlanta Braves, 1992—. Recipient Cy Young award Baseball Writers' Assn. Am., 1992, 93, 94, 95; named to All-Star team, 1988, 92, 94-5; recipient Gold Glove Award, 1990-94; Sporting News All-Star Team, 1992-94; named Nat. League Pitcher of Yr., Sporting News, 1993; Nat. League Innings Pitched Leader, 1991-92, earned run avg., 1995, fielding percentage, 1990-95. Office: Atlanta Braves PO Box 4064 Atlanta GA 30302-4064*

MADIGAN, RICHARD ALLEN, museum director; b. Corning, N.Y., Oct. 29, 1937; s. Myles L. and Rebekah M. (Bacon) M.; AB, Drew U., 1959; m. Mary Jean Smith, June 11, 1960 (div. 1975); children: Richard Allen, Dana Smith, Reese Jennings; m. 2d, Alice Sturrock, Sept. 6, 1975 (div. May 1978); m. 3d, Cara Montgomery, Aug. 5, 1978 (div. July 1987); 1 son, James Myles. Pub. contact rep. Corning Glass Center, 1959, supr. visitor rels., 1959-60; dir. Andrew Dickson White Mus. Art, Cornell U., 1960-63; asst. dir., asst. sec. Corcoran Gallery Art, Washington, 1963-67; dir. N. Tex. Museums Resources Council, 1967-68, Bklyn. Children's Mus., 1968-69; exec. dir. Wave Hill Center Environ. Studies, 1969-74; instr. anthropology dept. Lehman Coll., 1968-74; dir. Norton Gallery and Sch. Art, West Palm Beach Fla., 1974-89; sec. Norton Gallery and Sch. of Art, Inc., 1974-80; pvt. art cons., 1989-91; columnist Palm Beach Daily News, 1990-91; contbr. Calif. mag.; exec. dir., CEO Atlantic Ctr. for Arts, New Smyrna Beach, Fla., 1990-91; dir. Decorative Arts Study Ctr., San Juan Capistrano, 1992-93, dep. dir., N.Y. Transit Mus. 1994—; past instr. art dept. George Washington U.; bd. dirs. Palm Beach Festival; lectr. Fgn. Svc. Inst., Dept. State. Mem. Am. Assn. Museums (chmn. coll. and univ. museums sect. 1962-63), Museums Council N.Y.C. (chmn. 1970-71), Fla. Art Mus. Dirs. Assn. (pres. 1978-79, 83-84), S.E. Museums Conf., Assn. Art Mus. Dirs., Palm Beach C. of C. (dir. 1979-91), West Palm Beach C. of C. (dir. 1981-82). Author: The Sculpture of Michael Schreck, 1983. Office: New York Transit Mus 130 Livingston St 9th Fl Box E Brooklyn NY 11201-5106

MADISON, JANET ELAINE, geriatrics nurse; b. Chgo., Feb. 9, 1958; d. George C. and Ercel (Scott) Bowles; children: Amanda Reed, Angie Steffanie. Cert. CPR, Rich Mountain C.C., 1978, LPN, 1987. LPN, Ark.; cert. EMT. Pvt. duty nurse Mena, Ark., 1988; LPN, staff nurse, night charge nurse Rich Mt. Nursing Home, Mena, 1989-92; pvt. duty nurse, 1993-94; nurse Area Agy. of Aging, 1994—. Baptist. Home: 5134 Highway 8 W Mena AR 71953-9514

MADISON, MIRIAM FRANCES, educational administrator; b. Starkville, Miss., Nov. 29, 1937; d. Leonard and Minnie (Smith) Green; children: Harriet Madison Tuggle, Michael, Keshea L. BS, Stillman Coll., 1960; MS, Fort Valley State Coll., 1971; Cert. L6 Specialist Adminstrn., U. Ga., 1982. Tchr. Starkville Separate Mcpl., 1960-63; tchr. Pearl Stephens Elem. Sch., Warner Robins, Ga., 1964-87, prin., 1991-94; prin. Watson Elem. Sch., Warner Robins, Ga., 1988-91; coord. parent and family svcs. Houston County Sch. System, Perry, Ga., 1994—. Vice pres. Presbyn. Women, 1991, pres. Mem. AAUW, Profl. Assn. Educators, Nat. Assn. Elem. Prins., Ga. Assn. Educators, Phi Delta Kappa. Democrat. Presbyterian. Home: 9342 Feagin Rd Macon GA 31206-7944 Office: 305 Watson Blvd Warner Robins GA 31093-3405

MADISON, OCTAVIA DIANNE, mental health services professional; b. Lynchburg, Va., Mar. 28, 1960; d. Raymond Barlow Sr. Madison and Doreatha Madison Anderson. BA, Hampton U., 1982; MEd, Lynchburg Coll., 1983; postgrad., George Mason U., Fairfax, Va., 1989-94, Va. Poly. Inst. and State U., 1994—. Lic. profl. counselor, addiction counselor. Resource counselor Lynchburg Community Action Group, 1983, placement specialist, 1984; program mgr. Lynchburg 70001 Program, 1985; therapist, case mgr. Cen. Va. Community Svcs., Lynchburg, 1985-88; substance abuse counselor II Fairfax County Govt., 1988—; therapist Women's Ctr. No. Va., Vienna, 1990—; psychotherapist Dr. Carolyn Jackson-Sahni-Assocs., 1993; mental health therapist Arlington County Dept. Human Svcs., 1994—; grad. asst. Va. Polytechnic Inst. and State U., 1994. Asst. sec. So. Christian Leadership Conf., Lynchburg, 1983-84; mem. single ministry, asst. chair youth adv. bd. Mt. Pleasant Bapt. Ch., Alexandria, Va., 1991—; bd. examiners Profl. Counselors, 1991—. Recipient 2-Star award United Way (coord.), 1989. Mem. Am. Assn. for Counseling and Devel., Women's Ctr. Career Network, Advs. for Infants and Mothers, Inc., Nat. Black Alcoholism Coun., Va. Counselor's Assn., Washington Met. Area Addictions Counselors, Nat. Bd. Cert. Counselors, Psi Chi, Beta Kappa Chi. Home: 3890 Lyndhurst Dr Apt 303 Fairfax VA 22031-3722

MADORY, JAMES RICHARD, hospital administrator, former air force officer; b. Staten Island, N.Y., June 11, 1940; s. Eugene and Agnes (Gerner) M.; m. Karen James Clifford, Sept. 26, 1964; children: James E., Lynn Anne, Scott J., Elizabeth Anne, Joseph M. BS, Syracuse U., 1964; MHA, Med. Coll. Va., 1971. Enlisted USAF, 1958; x-ray technician Keesler Area Med. Ctr., Biloxi, Miss., 1959-62; commd. 2d lt. USAF, 1964, advanced through grades to maj., 1979—; x-ray technician Keesler Area Med. Ctr., Biloxi, Miss., 1959-62; adminstr. Charleston (S.C.) Clinic, 1971-74, Beale Hosp., Calif., 1974-77; assoc. adminstr. Shaw Regional Hosp., S.C., 1977-79; ret. USAF, 1979; asst. adminstr. Raleigh Gen. Hosp., Beckley, W.Va., 1979-81; adminstr., dir., sec. bd. Chesterfield Gen. Hosp., Cheraw, S.C., 1981-87; pres., CEO Grand Strand Hosp., Myrtle Beach, S.C., 1987-95, trustee, 1987-95; elected vice chairman Horry County Planning Commn., 1996—; cons. Healthcare Adminstrn., 1995—; mem. adv. bd. Cheraw Nursing Home, 1984-85. Contbr. articles to profl. publs. Chmn. bd. W.Va. Kidney Found., Charleston, 1980-81; chmn. youth bd. S.C. TB and Respiratory Disease Assn., Charleston, 1972-73; county chmn. Easter Seal Soc., Chesterfield County, S.C., 1984-85; campaign crusade chmn. Am. Cancer Soc., Chesterfield County, 1985-86; chmn. dist. advancement com. Boy Scouts Am., 1987-90; bd. dirs. Horry County United Way, 1989-95, Horry County Access Care, 1989-91; trustee Cheraw Acad., 1982-85, Grand Strand Gen. Hosp., 1987-94, Coastal Acad., 1988-90; commr. Horry County Planning Commn., 1995—, vice chmn., 1996—. Decorated Bronze Star, Vietnamese Cross of Gallantry, Vietnamese Medal of Honor; named to S.C. Order of Palmetto Gov. David Beasley, 1995. Fellow Am. Coll. Hosp. Adminstrs., Am. Coll. Health Care Execs; mem. S.C. Hosp. Assn. (com on legislation 1984-86, trustee 1989-94), Am. Acad. Healthcare Adminstrs., Cheraw C. of C. (bd. dirs. 1982-83), Rotary (pres. 1984-85). Republican. Roman Catholic. Home and Office: 3710 Kinloch Dr Myrtle Beach SC 29577

MADREN, DON ATHRON, pharmaceutical executive, researcher; b. Charleston, Nov. 9, 1955; s. Kenneth Vander and Babylee (Burnette) M.; m. Kathleen Irene Cahill, May 6, 1989; 1 child, Bradley Thomas. BS in Biology, Coll. Charleston, 1979; BS in Pharmacy, Med. U. S.C., 1984; MBA, Kennesaw State U., 1996. Registered pharmacist, S.C. Pharm. sales rep. Pharmacia and Upjohn, Inc., Columbia, S.C., 1984-85, pharm. sales splst., 1985-88; hosp. sales splst. Pharmacia and Upjohn, Inc., Winston-Salem, N.C., 1988-90; medm. scis. liaison Pharmacia and Upjohn, Inc., Marietta, Ga., 1990—; profl. scis laison Agouron Pharmaceuticals Inc., 1996—. Served in USMC, 1973-75. Mem. Am. Med. Informatics Assn., Am. Soc. Microbiology, AAAS, Am. Mgmt. Assn., Atlanta Track Club, Beta Gamma Sigma, Rho Chi. Methodist. Home: 4703 Hallford Way Marietta GA 30066

MADRID, OLGA HILDA GONZALEZ, retired elementary education educator, association executive; b. San Antonio, May 4, 1928; d. Victor A. and Elvira Ardilla Gonzalez; m. Sam Madrid, Jr., June 29, 1952; children: Ninette Marie, Samuel James. Student, U. Mex., San Antonio, St. Mary's U., San Antonio; BA, Our Lady of Lake U., 1956, MEd, 1963. Cert. bilingual tchr., adminstr., Tex. Sec. Lanier High Sch. San Antonio Ind. Sch. Dist., 1945-52, tchr. Collins Garden Elem. Sch., 1963-92; tutor Dayton, Ohio, 1952-54; bd. dirs., sch. rep. San Antonio Tchr.'s Coun., 1970-90; chair various coms. Collins Garden Elem., 1970-92. Elected dep. precinct, senatorial and state Dem. Convs., San Antonio, 1968—; apptd. commr. Keep San Antonio Beautiful, 1985; life mem., past pres. San Antonio YWCA; bd. dirs. Luth. Gen. Hosp., NCCJ, Cath. Family and Children's Svcs., St. Luke's Luth. Hosp.; nat. bd. dirs. YWCA, 1985—, also mem. exec. com.; mem. edn. commn. Holy Rosary Parish, 1994—; mem. bus. assocs. com. Our Lady of the Lake U., 1995—. Recipient Outstanding Our Lady Lake Alumni award Our Lady Lake U., 1975, Guadalupana medal San Antonio Cath. Archdiocese, 1975, Yellow Rose Tex. citation Gov. Briscoe, 1977; Olga H. Madrid Ctr. named in her honor, YWCA San Antonio and San Antonio City Coun., 1983; Lo Mejor De Lo Nuestro honoree San Antonio Light, 1991, honoree San Antonio Women's History Month Coalition, 1996. Mem. San Antonio Bus. and Profl. Women, Inc. (mem. exec. com.), Salute Quality Edn. (honoree 1993), Delta Kappa Gamma (Theta Beta chpt., mem. exec. com.). Home: 2726 Benrus Blvd San Antonio TX 78228-2319

MADRY-TAYLOR, JACQUELYN YVONNE, educational administrator; b. Jacksonville, Fla., Sept. 27, 1945; d. Arthur Chester and Janie (Cowart) Madry; 1 child, Jana LeMadry. BA, Fisk U., 1966; MA, Ohio State U., 1969; EdD, U. Fla., 1975. Cert. Inst. for Ednl. Mgmt., Harvard U., 1981. Tchr. Spanish Terry Parker Sr. High Sch., Jacksonville, 1967-72; instr. U. Fla., Gainesville, 1972-75; asst. to v.p. for acad. affairs. Morris Brown Coll., Atlanta, 1975-76; dean for instructional svcs. No. Va. Community Coll., Annandale, Va., 1976-83; dean undergrad. studies Bridgewater (Mass.) State Coll., 1983-92, exec. asst. to acting pres., 1988, acting v.p. acad. affairs, 1988-90; dir. Acad. Leadership Acad. Am. Assn. State Coll. and Univs., Washington, 1992-94; dir. ednl. programs and svcs. United Negro Coll. Fund Hdqs., 1994—; cons. W.K. Kellog Found., 1993—; bd. dirs. Bridgewater State Coll. Early Learning Ctr., 1984-88; evaluator U.S. Dept. State/Fgn. Svc., Washington, 1982—, U.S. Dept. Edn., 1989—; cons. in field. Vice chmn. No. Va. Manpower Planning Coun., Fairfax County, Va., 1981. Recipient Cert. Achievement Bridgewater State Coll. Black Alumni, 1988, Women Helping Women award Soroptimist Internat., 1983, Outstanding Young Women Am. award, 1976, 78; named Personalities of South, 1977; recipient Outstanding Tchr./Student Rels. Humanitarian award B'nai B'rith, 1972. Mem. Pub. Mem. Assn. U.S. Fgn. Svc., Soroptimist Internat., Boston Club (v.p. 1986-88), Jack and Jill of Am., Inc., Pi Lambda Theta, Phi Delta Kappa, Alpha Kappa Alpha, Links Inc. (Reston, Va. chpt.). Methodist. Home: 12274 Angel Wing Ct Reston VA 22091 Office: United Negro College Fund PO Box 10444 8260 Willow Oaks Corp Dr Fairfax VA 22031-4511

MADU, LEONARD EKWUGHA, lawyer, human rights officer, newspaper columnist; b. Ibadan, Nigeria, Mar. 17, 1953; came to U.S., 1977; s. Luke E. and Grace (Dureke) M.; m. Jaculine Stephanie Turner, June 4, 1980; children: Christine, Oscar. BA, Marshall U., 1980; JD, U. Tenn., 1988; MA, Sch. Internat. Svc., Am. U. Rsch. assoc. Lamberts Publs., Washington, 1980-82; data specialist Govt. Employees Ins. Co., Washington, 1982-85; law intern Knoxville (Tenn.) Urban League, 1986-88; cons. Morris Brown Coll., Atlanta, 1988; staff atty. East Carolina Legal Svc., Wilson, N.C., 1989-90; cons. youth devel. Nat. Crime Prevention Coun., Washington, 1990; contract compliance officer Walters State C.C., Morristown, Tenn., 1990; examiner Dept. of Human Svc., Nashville, 1990-93; human rights officer Human Rights Commn., Nashville, 1993—; pres. Panafrica, Nashville, 1994—; CEO Madu and Assoc. Internat. Bus. Cons., 1996—; polit. cons. Embassy of Nigeria, Washington, 1995; cons. Embassy of Swaziland, Washington, 1995, Embassy of Sierra Leone, Washington, 1995, Healthcare Internat. Mgmt. Co., 1996—; bd. dirs. Peace and Justice Ctr., Nashville. Editor: African Nations Handbook, 1994, Directory of African Universities and Colleges, 1994; editor-in-chief Panafrican Digest, 1994, Panafrican Jour. of World Affairs, 1994; columnist Met. Times, Nashville, 1991—, The African Herald, Dallas, 1995—, U.S./African Voice, Balt., 1995—, African Sun Times, 1995—, The Nigerian and African, 1995—. Co-chmn. Clergy and Laity Concerned, Nashville, 1992—; mem. curriculum and character com. Met. Sch. Bd., Nashville, 1994—; vice chmn. Nigerian Network Leadership awards N.Y., 1996; chmn. Internat. Women's Expo, Knoxville, Tenn., 1996; co-chairperson Miss Nigeria Internat. Beauty Pageant, Washington, 1995, Miss Africa Internat. Beauty Pageant, Nashville, 1996, Igbo Union Chieftaincy Coronation Ceremony, Nashville, 1995. Recipient World Hunger Devel. Program award Marshall U., 1978, 79, Hall of Nations scholar Am. U., 1980, 82, Mary Strohbel award United Way, 1994, 95, Nonprofit Vol. award Nat. Conf. of Christians and Jews, 1994. Mem. NAACP, U.S. Com. on Fgn. Rels., Soc. Profl. Journalists, UN Assn., Orgn. African Natonals (pres. 1994). Office: Panafrica 1016 18th Ave S Nashville TN 37212-2105

MAESTRIPIERI, DARIO, research scientist; b. Rome, July 31, 1964; came to U.S., 1992; Degree in biology, U. Rome, 1987, PhD in Biology, 1992. Rsch. fellow Nat. Rsch. Coun., Rome, 1990-91; vis. scholar U. Cambridge, Eng., 1991-92; postdoctoral rsch. assoc. Emory U., Atlanta, 1992—. Contbr. articles to scientific jours. Grantee L.S.B. Leakey Found., 1993; recipient B. Grassi as Best Young Investigator in Zoology Acad. Nat. Dei Lincei, 1991. Office: Emory U Yerkes Primate Ctr 2409 Taylor Ln Lawrenceville GA 30243-2921

MAFICO, TEMBA LEVI JACKSON, Old Testament and Semitic languages educator, clergy; b. Chipinge, Zimbabwe, Jan. 28, 1943; came to U.S., 1987; s. Mafico Ntondoyo Jackson Mhlanga and Lucy (Siqalaba Mpofu) Mafico Mhlanga; m. Thecla Chiza, Aug. 31, 1963; 1 child, David. AB, U. London, Salisbury, Rhodesia, 1970; ThM, Harvard U., 1973, MA, 1977, PhD, 1979. Ordained minister United Ch. of Christ, 1964. Ch. minister United Ch. of Christ, Harare, Zimbabwe, 1963-70; sch. chaplain Chikore High Sch., Chipinge, 1971; sr. lectr. U. Zimbabwe, Harare, 1979-86, univ. chaplain, 1979-86; prof. O.T. and Semitic langs. Interdenominational Theol. Ctr., Atlanta, 1988—; cons. globalizaion of theol. schs. Assn. Theol. Schs., 1988—; trustee U. Zimbabwe Evening Sch., 1987—. Contbr. articles to profl. jours. Sec.-treas. Student Christian Movement, Zimbabwe, 1965-70, Manicaland Devel. Assns., Zimbabwe, 1980-86; founder, dir. Univ. Evening Sch., Zimbabwe, 1980-86. Recipient Scholarship award Harvard U., 1971-78; grantee U. Zimbabwe, 1982, 86, Interdenominational Theol. Ctr., Atlanta, 1989, 90, Gammon Theol. Sch., Atlanta, 1990. Mem. Soc. Bibl. Lit., Internat. Assn. Mission Studies, Atlanta O.T. Colloquium (chmn.). Office: Interdenominational Theol Ctr 671 Beckwith St SW Atlanta GA 30314-4112

MAGDOVITZ, LAWRENCE MAYNARD, real estate executive, lawyer; b. Clarksdale, Miss., Aug. 21, 1937; s. Harry David and Lenabel (May) M.; m. Kerin Coffey, June 25, 1972 (dec. Apr. 1994); children: Beth, Larry. BA, Vanderbilt U., 1959, JD, 1961. Bar: Tenn. 196l, Miss. 196l, Ky. 1962. Trust officer First Nat. Bank, Mayfield, Ky., 1961-62; sole practice law Clarksdale, 1962—; br. office Collierville, Tenn., 1984-95; realtor Valley Realty Co., Clarksdale, 1962—, Magdovitz Agy., Inc., Clarksdale, 1972—, First, Inc., Clarksdale, 1973—; ins. exec. Mid-Am. Agy., Clarksdale, 1985—. Mem. Miss. State Bar Assn., Ky. State Bar Assn., Tenn. State Bar Assn., Memphis Bar Assn., Clarksdale Bd. Realtors. Republican. Jewish. Lodges: B'nai Brith (pres. Clarksdale br. 1979-82), Elks. Office: 112 E 2nd St Clarksdale MS 38614-4206

MAGEE, THOMAS ESTON, JR., minister; b. DeRidder, La., Aug. 9, 1947; s. Thomas Eston and Doris Maxine (Gallion) M.; m. Linda Ruth Lewis, Nov. 9, 1967. Student, McNeese State U., 1966-69; BTh, Tex. Bible Coll., 1972. Ordained to ministry United Pentecostal Ch., 1973. Asst. pastor United Pentecostal Ch., Pasadena, Tex., 1969-72; instr. Tex. Bible Coll., Houston, 1970-72, dean of women, 1970-71; evangelist United Pentecostal Ch., various locations, U.S., 1972-77; pastor 1st United Pentecostal Ch., Ragley, La., 1977—; sect. youth dir. La. Dist. United Pentecostal Ch., Ragley, 1979-83; sect. Sunday Sch. dir., 1984-86; sect. sec.-treas., 1989—. Named col., La. Gov., 1975. Democrat. Home: 800 First Pentecostal Church Rd Longville LA 70652-5407 Office: 1st United Pentecostal Ch PO Box 44 Ragley LA 70657-0044

MAGGIO, THERESA GRIFFIN, librarian, consultant; b. Shreveport, La., May 27, 1952; d. James Henry and Annie Laurie (Rosenblath) Griffin; m. Edward James Maggio, July 2, 1977; 1 child, Kelli Suzanne. BS in Social Studies Edn., La. State U., 1975, MLS, 1980; PhD in Libr. and Info. Studies, Fla. State U., 1988. Librarian La. State Library, Baton Rouge, 1980-82; med. library cons. 7th Ward Hosp., Hammond, La., 1984-86; med. librarian Lallie Kemp Hosp., Independence, La., 1982-85; reference libr. Roddenbery Meml. Libr., 1988-89; dep. dir., pub. svcs. libr. SW Ga. Regional Libr., Bainbridge, 1989—. Recipient Baker and Taylor Grassroots award, 1980; La. Library Assn. scholar, 1979, Title IIB fellow, 1985-86. Mem. ALA. Democrat. Roman Catholic. Avocation: horse racing. Home: 3255 Capital Cir NE Apt 8A Tallahassee FL 32308-3746 Office: SW GA Regional Library Shortwell & Monroe Sts Bainbridge GA 31717

MAGGIOLO, ALLISON JOSEPH, lawyer; b. New River, N.C., Aug. 29, 1943; s. Allison and Florence Celeste (Vago) M. Cert., U. Paris-Sorbonne, 1965; AB, Brown U., 1966; JD, U. Louisville, 1975. Bar: Ky. 1976, U.S. Dist. Ct. (we. dist.) Ky. 1981. Ops. mgr., stockbroker Bache & Co., Louisville, 1970-73; ptnr. Reisz, Blackburn, Manly & Treitz, Louisville, 1976-78, Greenebaum Boone Treitz Maggiolo & Brown, Louisville, 1978-91, Wyatt, Tarrant & Combs, Louisville, 1991—; workshop panelist Fin. Adv. Coun., 1994; panelist Seminar on Defaulted Bond Issues, 1987-89, Bond Counsel and the Corp. Trustee, 1990-92, Defaults and Workouts, 1993. Author: Indenture Trustee Liability and Defaulted Bond Issues, 1987, Minimizing Indenture Trustee Liability and Defaulted Bond Issues, 1991, Bond Default Resolution, 1993; co-author: The legal Aspects of Doing International Business in Kentucky, 1990. Exec. com. Louisville Com. Fgn. Rels., 1979—, chmn., 1991-96; bd. dirs. Ky. Opera, Louisville, 1978-91, mem. hon. coun., 1991—; bd. dirs. Ky. Show, Louisville, 1980-88. 1st lt. U.S. Army, 1966-69, Vietnam. Decorated Bronze Star. Mem. Internat. Bar Aassn., Nat. Assn. Bond Lawyers, Bond Attys. Workshop (planning com. 1991-93), Pendennis Club, Wynn Stay Club, Jefferson Club. Office: Wyatt Tarrant & Combs Citizens Pla Louisville KY 40202

MAGID, ANDY ROY, mathematics educator; b. St. Paul, May 4, 1944; s. William Eli and Marion Ethel (Mintz) M.; m. Carol Ann King, Aug. 21, 1966; children: Sarah, Samuel. BA, U. Calif., Berkeley, 1966; PhD, Northwestern U., 1969. Instr. Columbia U., 1969-72; prof. math. U. Okla., Norman, 1972—. Author: The Separable Galois Theory of Commutative Rings, 1974, Module Categories of Analytic Groups, 1983, Applied Matrix Models, 1985, Lectures on Differential Galois Theory, 1994. Mem. Am. Math. Soc., Math. Assn. Am., Am. Stat. Assn., Nat. Coun. Tchrs. Math. Democrat. Jewish. Home: 1025 Connelly Ln Norman OK 73072-6314 Office: U Okla Dept Math 601 Elm Rm 423 Norman OK 73019

MAGILL, DODIE BURNS, early childhood education educator; b. Greenwood, S.C., July 10, 1952; d. Byron Bernard and Dora Curry B.; m. Charles Towner Magill, May 4, 1974; children: Charles Towner II, Emily Curry. BA, Furman U., 1974; MEd, U. S.C., 1978. Cert. tchr., early childhood, elementary, elementary principal, supv., S.C. Kindergarten tchr. Sch. Dist. Greenville County, 1974-83; early childhood edn. instr. Valdosta (Ga.) State Univ., 1983-84; dir. lower sch. Valwood Sch., Valdosta, 1984-86; kindergarten tchr. Sch. Dist. Greenville County, 1986—; tchr.-in-residence S.C. Ctr. for Tchr. Recruitment, Rock Hill, 1993, mem. policy bd.; workshop presenter and lectr. in various schs. and sch. dists. throughout U.S., 1974—; chmn. S.C. Pub. Kindergarten Celebration, 1994; giv. S.C. State Readiness Policy Group; mem. Southeastern Region Vision for Edn. Adv. Bd., S.C. Coun. Ednl. Collaboration. Demonstration tchr. S.C. ETV (TV show) Sch. Begins with Kindergarten. Mem. Gov. of S.C.'s State Readiness Policy Group, Southeastern Regional Vision for Edn. Adv. Bd., South Carolina Ctr. Tchr. Recruitment Policy Bd. Recipient Ralph Witherspoon award S.C. Assn. for Children Under Six; named Tchr. of Yr., Greenville County, 1992, 93, State of S.C., 1993, S.C. Tchr. of Yr. Coun. of Chief State Sch. Officers, 1993, 94. Mem. Assn. for Childhood Edn. Internat., S.C. Tchr. Forum (chmn. 1993-94), S.C. Early Childhood Assn., Alpha Delta Kappa. Presbyterian. Office: Mountain Park Elem Sch 1500 Pounds Rd SW Lilburn GA 30247

MAGNUM, WYATT D., entertainment consulting company executive; b. Washington, Jan. 16, 1961; s. William Duncan Magnum and Myrtle (Glynn) Eaton. Student, U. Tex., Arlington, 1982-83. Music programmer McFaddin Ventures, Houston, 1982-85; dir. Core Music Svcs., Houston, 1985—; moderator panel discussions various seminars, Las Vegas, Nev., Atlantic City, San Francisco. contbr. articles to profl. publs. Office: Core Music Svcs 2323 S Shepherd Ste 1104 Houston TX 77019-6117

MAGRATH, C. PETER, educational association executive; b. N.Y.C., Apr. 23, 1933; s. Laurence Wilfrid and Giulia Maria (Dentice) M.; m. Deborah C. Howell, 1988; children: Valerie Ruth, Monette Fay. BA summa cum laude, U. N.H., 1955; PhD, Cornell U., 1962. Mem. faculty Brown U., Providence, 1961-68, prof. polit. sci., 1967-68, assoc. dean grad. sch., 1965-66; dean Coll. Arts and Scis. U. Nebr., Lincoln, 1968-69, dean faculties Coll. Arts and Scis., 1969-72, interim chancellor univ., 1971-72, prof. polit. sci., 1968-72, vice chancellor for acad. affairs, 1972; pres. SUNY, Binghamton, 1972-74, prof. polit. sci., 1972-74; pres. U. Minn., Mpls., 1974-84, U. Mo. System, 1985-91, Nat. Assn. State Univs. and Land Grant Colls., Washington, 1991—. Author: The Triumph of Character, 1963, Yazoo: Law and Politics in the New Republic, The Case of Fletcher v. Peck, 1966, Constitutionalism and Politics: Conflict and Consensus, 1968, Issues and Perspectives in American Government, 1971, (with others) The American Democracy, 2d edit., 1973, (with Robert L. Egbert) Strengthening Teacher Education, 1987; contbr. articles to profl. jours. Served with AUS, 1955-57. Mem. Assn. Am. Univs. (chmn. 1985-86), Phi Beta Kappa, Phi Kappa Phi, Pi Gamma Mu, Pi Sigma Alpha, Kappa Tau Alpha. Office: Nat Assn State U and Land Grant Colls 1 Dupont Cir NW Ste 710 Washington DC 20036-1110

MAGRINO, PETER FRANK, lawyer; b. New Rocelle, N.Y., Nov. 13, 1952; s. Daniel William and Gloria (Faiola) M.; m. Kathleen Ann Kearney, Apr. 5, 1986 (div. 1995). AS, Miami (Fla.) Dade Community Coll., 1972; BA, Biscayne Coll., Miami, 1980; JD, Nova Law Ctr., Ft. Lauderdale, Fla., 1982. Bar: Fla. 1983. Dep. sheriff Dade County, Miami, 1974-76; police officer Miami Shores Police Dept., 1976-83; asst. state atty. State of Fla., Ft. Lauderdale, 1983—; spl. asst. U.S. atty. strike force Ft. Lauderdale, 1990—. Served to cpl. USMC, 1970-72. Mem. ABA, Am. Trial Lawyers Assn., Fla. Assn. Police Attys., Nat. Dist. Atty's Assn., Fraternal Order Police. Democrat. Roman Catholic. Office: Broward State Atty's Office Homicide Div 201 SE 6th St Fort Lauderdale FL 33301-3303

MAGUIRE, BLANCHE JOAN (MAGGIE MAGUIRE), watercolorist; b. N.Y.C., July 5, 1922; m. Joseph Thomas Maguire; children: Thomas Joseph, Kathleen Julie. BA, U. Tex., El Paso, 1971, postgrad., 1972-73. Cert. art teacher. Chmn. Allied Military Host Family Program, Ft. Bliss, Tex., 1970-73. Named Woman Yr. El Paso Herald Post, 1971; recipient honor Allied Military Host Family Program Past Gen., 1970-73. Mem. ARC, Nat. Soc. Arts Letters (chmn. El Paso chpt. 1970-72), El Paso Art Assn., Discover El Paso (bd. dirs.), C. of C. Home: 5120 Camino De La Vista Dr El Paso TX 79932-2202

MAGUIRE, CHARLOTTE EDWARDS, retired physician; b. Richmond, Ind., Sept. 1, 1918; d. Joel Blaine and Lydia (Betscher) Edwards; m. Raymer Francis Maguire, Sept. 1, 1948 (dec.); children: Barbara, Thomas Clair II. Student, Stetson U., 1936-38, U. Wichita, 1938-39; BS, Memphis Tchrs. Coll., 1940; MD, U. Ark., 1944. Intern, resident Orange Meml. Hosp., Orlando, Fla., 1944-46; resident Bellevue Hosp. and Med. Ctr., NYU, N.Y.C., 1954, 55; instr. nurses Orange Meml. Hosp., 1947-57, staff mem., 1946-68; staff mem. Fla. Santarium and Hosp., Orlando, 1946-56, Holiday House and Hosp., Orlando, 1950-62; mem. courtesy and cons. staff West Orange Meml. Hosp., Winter Garden, Fla., 1952-67; active staff, chief dept. pediatrics Mercy Hosp., Orlando, 1965-68; med. dir. med. svcs. and basic care Fla. Dept. Health and Rehab. Svcs., 1975-84; med. exec. dir., med. svcs. divsn. worker's compensation Fla. Dept. Labor, Tallahassee, 1984-87; chief of staff physicians and dentists Ctrl. Fla. divsn. Children's Home Soc. Fla., 1947-56; dir. Orlando Child Health Clinic 1949-58; pvt. practice medicine Orlando, 1946-68; asst. regional dir. HEW, 1970-72; pediat. cons. Fla. Crippled Children's Commn., 1952-70, dir., 1968-70; med. dir. Office Med. Svcs. and Basic Care, sr. physician Office of Asst. Sec. Ops., Fla. Dept. Health and Rehab. Svcs.; clin. prof. dept. pediat. U. Fla. Coll. Medicine, Gainesville, 1980-87; mem. Fla. Drug Utilization Rev., 1983-87; real estate salesperson Investors Realty, 1982—; bd. dirs. Stavros Econ. Ctr. Fla. State U., Tallahassee; mem. pres.'s coun. Fla. State U., U. Fla., Gainesville. Mem. profl. adv. com. Fla. Center for Clin. Services at U. Fla., 1952-60; del. to Midcentury White House Conf. on Children and Youth, 1950; U.S. del from Nat. Soc. for Crippled Children to World Congress for Welfare of Cripples, Inc., London, 1957; pres of corp. Eccleston-Callahan Hosp. for Colored Crippled Children, 1956-58; sec. Fla. chpt. Nat. Doctor's Com. for Improved Med. Services, 1951-52; med. adv. com. Gateway Sch. for Mentally Retarded, 1959-62; bd. dirs. Forest Park Sch. for Spl. Edn. Crippled Children, 1949-54, mem. med. adv. com., 1955-68, chmn., 1957-68; mem. Fla. Adv. Council for Mentally Retarded, 1965-70; dir. central Fla. poison control Orange Meml. Hosp.; mem. orgn. com., chmn. com. for admissions and selection policies Camp Challenge; participant 12th session Fed. Exec. Inst., 1971; del. White House Conf. on Aging, 1980. Mem. AMA (life), Nat. Rehab. Assn., Am. Congress Phys. Medicine and Rehab., Fla. Soc. Crippled Children and Adults, Ctrl. Fla. Soc. Crippled Children and Adults (dir. 1949-58, pres. 1956-57), Am. Assn. Cleft Palate, Fla. Soc. Crippled Children (trustee 1951-57, v.p. 1956-57, profl. adv. com. 1957-68), Mental Health Assn. Orange County (charter mem.; pres. 1949-50, dir. 1947-52, chmn. exec. com. 1950-52, dir. 1963-65), Fla. Orange County Heart Assn., Am. Med. Women's Assn., Am. Acad. Med. Dirs., Fla. Med. Assn. (chmn. com. on mental retardation), Orange County Med. Assn., Orange Med. Soc. (life), Fla. Pediatric Soc. (pres. 1952-53), Fla. Cleft Palate Assn. (counselor-at-large, sec.), Nat. Inst. Geneal. Rsch., Nat. Geneal. Soc., Assn. Profl. Genealogists, Tallahassee Geneal. Soc., Fla. State U. Found. Inc. (bd. dirs. Stavoris Ctr. for Econ. Edn.). Club: Governors. Home: 4158 Covenant Ln Tallahassee FL 32308-5765

MAGUIRE, D.E., electronics executive. CEO Kemet Electronic Corp., Greenville, S.C. Office: Kemet Electronic Corp PO Box 5928 Greenville SC 29606

MAGUIRE, KEVIN, travel management consultant; b. Austin, Tex., Dec. 27, 1951; parents Jack R. and Pat (Horton) M.; m. Jimmy Gay Freeze, June 15, 1974; children: Christopher, Shannon. BA, BJ in Pub. Rels., U. Tex., 1974. Sr. rep. for youth and student sales Pan Am. World Airways, Houston, 1970-74; asst. v.p. United Bank of Tex., Austin, 1974-76; sr. program developer State Bar of Tex. Comprehensive Offender Manpower Program, Austin, 1976-79; pres. Travel Place of Austin, Inc., 1979-83; gen. mgr. Tex. br. IVI Travel, Inc., Chgo., 1983-86; owner, mgr. KM Travel Mgmt. Co., Austin, 1976—; pres., CEO The Expedition Devel. Co. Internat. Bus. & Resource Group, 1991—; exec. dir. sales S.W. region Total Travel Mgmt. Inc., Austin, 1994-95; travel mgr. Tokyo Electron Am., Inc., Austin, 1995—; travel and mktg. cons. IBM Tex. Employees Fed. Credit Union, Austin, 1982-88; travel cons. to compt. pub. accts. State of Tex., 1986—, U. Tex. Med. Ctr., San Antonio, 1986-87. Contbr. articles to mags. Sustaining mem. Salvation Army, Austin, 1980; mem. Austin Cultural and Bus. Exch., 1987. Recipient Disting. Svc. award Tex. Corrections Assn., 1976. Mem. Nat. Bus. Travelers Assn., Austin Bus. Travelers Assn., Ex-Students Assn. (life). Home: 7010 Narrow Oak Trl Austin TX 78759-4625 Office: 2400 Grove Blvd Austin TX 78744

MAHADEVA, MANORANJAN, financial executive; b. Colombo, Sri Lanka, Feb. 12, 1955; came to U.S., 1977; s. Kandiah and Rupavathy (Ponniah) M.; m. Donna Sue Martin, May 12, 1986; 1 child, Danielle. BBA, U. Tex., 1981; MBA, N. Tex. State U., 1985. Notary pub., Tex. Asst. contr. Presbyn. Village North, Dallas, 1981-84; CFO Dallas Meml. Hosp., 1984-86; exec. dir. Associated Orthopedics & Sports Medicine, Plano, Tex., 1986-95; CFO Access Med. Supply Inc., Plano, 1988-95; mng. dir. YNM Corp., Plano, 1987-95; practice adminstr. Tex. Orthopaedic Assocs., Dallas, 1995—; chief fin. officer Access Med. Supply, Inc., 1988—; bd. dirs. Gibraltar Mgmt. Enterprises, Dallas, 1982—. Mem. Leadership Plano Class 8, 1990—, bd. dirs., mem. exec. bd., 1991—, chmn. exec. bd., 1992-93; mem. Mental Health Assn. Collin County; bd. dirs. Nat. Assn. Cmty. Leadership, Am. Heart Assn.; bd. dirs., treas. Crisis Ctr. of Collin County; chmn. emergency svcs. Coalition of Collin County. Recipient Nat. Disting. Leadership award, 1994; Presdl. scholar Wayne (Nebr.) State U., 1977-78. Mem. Nat. Assn. Accts. (bd. dirs. North Dallas chpt. 1985-86), Am. Hosp. Assn., Internat. Students Assn., Nat. Assn. for Cmty. Leadership (bd. dirs., vice chair 1996—), Plano C. of C. (chmn. cmty. edn. com.), Leadership Plano Alumni Assn. (bd. dirs.), Plano Talkers Toastmasters, Lions (past pres. Plano Early Club), Rotary (sec., program chmn., pres. Plano Met. 1996-97), Rotarian of Yr. award 1995), Delta Sigma Pi. Home: 3313 Claymore Dr Plano TX 75075-6267 Office: PBI Ste 416 8210 Walnut Hill Ln Dallas TX 75231

MAHAN, SHIRLEY JEAN, nursing educator; b. Corbin, Ky., July 19, 1937; d. Jacob Monroe and Geneva Samantha (Pennington) Lloyd; m. Clarence Edward Mahan, Mar. 28, 1954; children: Clarence Sandy, Randall Barry. AS in Nursing, Ea. Ky. U., 1985, BSN, 1989. Staff nurse Knox County Gen. Hosp., Barbourville, Ky., 1983-87, Bapt. Regional Med. Ctr., Corbin, Ky., 1987-93; mem. faculty Lincoln Meml. U., Harrogate, Tenn., 1989—. Mem. ANA, Ky. Nurse Assn., Nazarene Health Care Fellowship. Home: PO Box 8 Corbin KY 40702-0008

MAHANES, JOANNE RIDOB, assistant dean; b. Calgary, Alberta, Can., Aug. 5, 1955; d. William and Anne (Saluk) Ridob; m. Clifford Barclay Mahanes, May 28, 1988. BA in Psychology and Sociology, Hofstra U., 1977, MS in Edn., 1979, Profl. Diploma in Counseling, 1982. Cert. counselor. Admissions counselor Hofstra U., Hempstead, N.Y., 1977-78, asst. dir. admission, 1978-82; asst. dir. internat. admissions Fla. Atlantic U., Boca Raton, 1984, dir. admissions, 1984-87; extern coord. U. Va., Charlottesville, 1987-89, asst. dean Coll. Arts and Scis., 1989—; adj. instr. Broward C.C., Coconut Creek, Fla., 1983-84, Hofstra U., 1981-83. Contbr. articles to profl. jours. Elder and session mem. Olivet Presbyn. Ch., Charlottesville, 1990-93. Mem. So. Career Planning Assn., Va. Career Planning Assn., Jefferson Counselors Assn. (pres. elect 1992). Presbyterian. Home: PO Box 8162 Charlottesville VA 22906-8162

MAHANES, MICHAEL WAYNE, audio-visual electronics company executive; b. Fulton, Mo., Jan. 18, 1956; s. Paul W. and Betty Catherine (Kelsey) M.; m. Cynthia Anne Ward, June 13, 1981; children: Catherine Anne, Michael Wayne Jr. BFA, Westminster Coll., 1977. Tchr. William Woods Coll., Fulton, 1978-79; dir. audio-visual studio Daniel/Flour Internat., Fulton, 1979-81; dir. audio-visual dept. and Lifelong Learning Ctr., tng. coord. MEMC Electronics Materials Co., Spartanburg, S.C., 1981—; mem. com. Malcolm Baldrige Nat. Quality Award; dir. Skills Enhancement Ctr., Next Step Program, Life-Long Learning Ctr.; master trainer Zenger Miller; cons. in field, 1982—. Writer, dir., cameraman (video) Collective Works of Michael Mahanes, 1979—; writer, editor over 500 videos; co-inventor electronic data gathering indsl. problem solving method, 1981. Pre-sch. tchr. Southside Bapt. Ch., Spartanburg, 1982—; pre-sch. tchr. Southside Bapt. Ch., Spartanburg, 1986—, deacon, chmn. broadcast sound; active ARC; mem. Edn. Consensus Project, 1992—. Mem. Am. Soc. Tng. and Devel., Internat. TV Assn., Carolina Soc. Tng. and Devel. Republican. Office: MEMC Electronic Materials Hwy 221 S PO Box 5397 Spartanburg SC 29304-5397

MAHANNAH, JAMES, engineering company executive. V.p. S.C. Nars Engrng. Corp., Boca Raton, Fla. Office: SC Nars Engrng Corp 951 Broken Sound Pkwy NW Boca Raton FL 33487-3531

MAHARG, MEREDITH MCCLINTOCK, education director; b. Bartlesville, Okla., June 5, 1938; d. Edward Curtis and Margaret Lamb McClintock; m. John Wendell Maharg, June 25, 1966; children: John Andrew, Mary Elizabeth. AA, Stephens Coll., 1958. Master craftsman in canvas work, Embroiderers' Guild of Am. Founding pres. Permian Basin Needle Arts, Odessa, Tex., 1982-84, regional rep., 1984-85; new chpt. liaison South Cen. Region Embroiderer's Guild of Am., 1985-87, asst. dir., 1987-88, dir., 1988-91, mem. faculty seminar, 1987, 90, 91—; dir. edn. Embroiderer's Guild of Am., Inc., 1991—. Author: American Needlepoint Guild, 1991, Needle Arts mag.; designer, tchr. original embroidery. Recipient first place ribbons and rosettes, Permian Basin Fair, 1981-88, Best in Div. plaques, 1984-88, first place and hon. mention, Odessa Art Assn., 1987, hon. men., 1988. Mem. Embroiderer's Guild of Am. (bd. dirs. 1988-93), Council of Am. Embroiderers, Odessa Art Assn., Am. Needlepoint Guild. Republican. Episcopalian. Home and Office: Dear to My Heart 1615 Englewood Ln Odessa TX 79761-3235

MAHER, STEPHEN TRIVETT, lawyer, educator; b. N.Y.C., Nov. 21, 1949; s. William John and Jean Dorothy (Trivett) M.; m. Sharon Leslie Wolfe, Nov. 22, 1981; children: Meaghan Wolfe, Caitlin Wolfe. BA, NYU, 1971; JD, U. Miami, Coral Gables, Fla., 1975. Bar: Fla. 1975, U.S. Dist. Ct. (so. dist.) Fla. 1976, D.C. 1979, U.S. Dist. Ct. (no. dist.) Fla. 1979, U.S. Supreme Ct. 1980, U.S. Ct. Appeals (5th and 11th cirs.) 1981, U.S. Dist. Ct. (so. dist.) Fla. 1982, U.S. Dist. Ct. (mid. dist.) Fla. 1983. Assoc. Chonin & Levey, Miami, 1975; staff atty. Legal Svcs. of Greater Miami, Inc., 1975-81; assoc. Finley, Kumble, Wagner et al, Miami, 1981-84; dir. clin. program Sch. of Law U. Miami, Coral Gables, 1984-90, assoc. prof. law Sch. of Law, 1984-92; pvt. practice Stephen T. Maher, P.A., Miami, Fla., 1992—; mem. Fla. Bar/Fla. Bar Found. Joint Commn. on Delivery Legal Svcs. to the Indigent, Tallahassee, 1990-91, chair, organizer Seventh Adminstrv. Law Conf., Tallahassee, 1990, Conf. on the Fla. Constn., 1995; cons. on in-house legal edn. Contbr. articles to profl. jours. Fellow Fla. Bar Found. (life, bd. dirs. 1984-91); mem. ABA, Fla. Bar (chair adminstrv. law sect. 1993-94, chair coun. of sects. 1996—), Dade County Bar Assn. Home: 1015 Sevilla Ave Miami FL 33134-6328 Office: 1500 Miami Ctr 201 S Biscayne Blvd Miami FL 33131-4332

MAHER, WILLIAM JAMES, investment executive; b. Chgo., Feb. 23, 1937; s. Alexander E. and Merle G. M.; B.B.A., Marquette U., 1961. Merchandising exec. Montgomery Ward & Co., Inc., Chgo., 1962-68; mgmt. cons. Cresap, McCormack & Paget, N.Y.C., 1968-69; v.p., treas. Solar Prodns., Inc., L.A., 1969-72; v.p., sec., treas. Creative Mgmt. Assocs., L.A., 1972-74; v.p., dir. Josephson Internat., Inc., L. A., 1975-83; pres. Tipperary Prodns., Inc., Beverly Hills, Calif., 1983-88; pres. Winter Park Capital Assets, Inc., 1989—. Office: Winter Park Capital Assets Inc 1031 W Morse Blvd Winter Park FL 32789-3715

MAHESH, VIRENDRA BHUSHAN, endocrinologist; b. India, Apr. 25, 1932; came to U.S., 1958, naturalized, 1968; s. Narinjan Prasad and Sobhagyawati; m. Sushila Kumari Aggarwal, June 29, 1955; children: Anita Rani, Vinit Kumar. BSc with honors, Patna U., India, 1951; MSc in Chemistry, Delhi U., India, 1953, PhD, 1955; DPhil in Biol. Sci, Oxford U., 1958. James Hudson Brown Meml. fellow Yale U., 1958-59; asst. rsch. prof. endocrinology Med. Coll. Ga., Augusta, 1959-63, assoc. rsch. prof., 1963-66, prof., 1966-70, Regents prof., 1970-86, Robert B. Greenblatt prof., 1979—, chmn. endocrinology, 1972-86, chmn., Regents prof. physiology and endocrinology, 1986—, chmn. physiology and endocrinology, 1986—; dir. Ctr. for Population Studies, 1971—; mem. reproductive biology study sect. NIH, 1977-81, mem. human embryology and devel. study sect. NIH, 1982-86, 90-93, chmn., 1991-93. Contbr. articles to profl. jours., chpts. to books; editor: The Pituitary, a Current Review, Functional Correlates of Hormone Receptors in Reproduction, Recent Advances in Fertility Research, Hirsuitism and Virilism, Regulation of Ovarian and Testicular Function, Excitatory Amino Acids: Their Role in Neuroendocrine Function; mem. editl. bd. Steroids, 1963—, Jour. of Clin. Endocrinology and Metabolism, 1976-81, Jour. Steroid Biochemistry and Molecular Biology, 1991—, Assisted Reproductive Tech./Andrology, 1993—; mem. adv. bd. Maturitas, 1977-81. Recipient Rubin award Am. Soc. Study Sterility, 1962, Billings Silver medal, 1965; Best Tchr. award freshman class Sch. Medicine, Med. Coll. Ga., 1969, Outstanding Faculty award Sch. Medicine, 1992, Outstanding Faculty award Sch. Grad. Studies, 1981, 94, Disting. Teaching award, 1988, Excellence in Rsch. award Grad. Faculty Assembly, 1987-91, 93-95; Disting. Scientist award Assn. Scientist Indian Origin in Am., 1989, rsch. grantee NIH, 1960—. Mem. Chem. Soc. (Eng.), Soc. Biochem. and Molecular Biol., Soc. Neurosci., Endocrine Soc., Soc. for Gynecologic Investigation, Internat. Soc. Neuroendocrinology, Soc. for Study Reproduction (Carl G. Hartman award 1996), Am. Physiol. Soc., Internat. Soc. Reproductive Medicine (pres. 1980-82), Soc. Exptl. Biology and Medicine, Am. Fertility Soc., Am. Assn. Lab. Animal Sci., N.Y. Acad. Scis., AAUP, Sigma Xi. Office: Med Coll of Ga Dept Physiology & Endocrinology Augusta GA 30912-3000

MAHLAN-DITCH, MICHELLE T., maternal/child home health nurse; b. Queens, N.Y., Apr. 22, 1960; d. Charles F. Jr. and Elizabeth (Schell) Mahlan; m. Robert L. Ditch, Apr. 5, 1988. BSN, Molloy Coll., Rockville Centre, N.Y., 1981. RN, Tex., N.Y., Hawaii, Va.; cert. BCLS instr., EMT. Commd. USAF, 1981, advanced through grades to maj., 1994; asst. charge nurse, nurse corps USAF, Tampa, Fla., 1987-88; family advocacy nurse, U.S. Civil Svc. USAF, Honolulu, 1988-90, triage/advice nurse, Kaiser Permanente; pub. health nurse II City of Austin, 1990-93; aero. flight nurse 32d AEG, Kelly AFB, Tex., 1990-93; nurse APSS (name now Aeromedical Staging Squadron), Lawrence, N.Y., 1993-95; maternal/child home health nurse Riverside RMC Home Health Agy., Newport News, Va., 1995—. With USAF Res., Saudi Arabia. Mem. ANA, Assn. Mil. Surgeons U.S.,

Nat. Flight Nurses Assn., Air Force Assn., Res. Officers Assn. Office: 11833 Canon Blvd Ste 120 Newport News VA 23606

MAHON, ELDON BROOKS, federal judge; b. Loraine, Tex., Apr. 9, 1918; s. John Bryan and Nola May (Muns) M.; m. Nova Lee Groom, June 1, 1941; children: Jana, Martha, Brad. B.A., McMurry Coll., 1939; LL.B., U. Tex., 1942. Bar: Tex. 1942. Law clk. Tex. Supreme Ct., 1945-46; county atty. Mitchell County, Tex., 1947; dist. atty. 32d Jud. Dist. Tex., 1948-60, dist. judge, 1960-63; v.p. Tex. Electric Service Co., Ft. Worth, 1963-64; mem. firm Mahon Pope & Gladden, Abilene, Tex., 1964-68; U.S. atty. U.S. Dist. Ct. (no. dist.) Tex., Ft. Worth, 1968-72, judge, 1972—, now sr. judge. Pres. W. Tex. council Girl Scouts U.S.A., 1966-68; Trustee McMurry Coll. Served with USAAF, 1942-45. Named an outstanding Tex. prosecutor Tex. Law Enforcement Found., 1957. Mem. ABA, Fed. Bar Assn., Ft.-Worth-Tarrant County Bar Assn., Am. Judicature Soc., State Bar Tex. Methodist (past del. confs.). Office: US Courthouse 501 W 10th St Rm 502 Fort Worth TX 76102*

MAHONEY, KEVIN A., historian, consultant. BA in Anthropology, George Washington U., 1973; MA in Econs., Georgetown U., 1983. Cons. asst. F.L. Mahoney & Assocs., Westfield, N.J., 1974-79; mgr. Nat. Capital Historical Sales, Springfield, Va., 1979-83; litigation support specialist Arlington, Va., 1983-86; mgr. fin. and data base Holy Trinity Parish, Washington, 1986-87; cons. military history Washington, 1987—; cons. Holocaust Meml. Mus., Ctrl. Armed Forces Mus., Moscow, Peter Batty Prodns., Eng., Discovery Channel, TimeWatch, Eng.; rschr., cons. Time Life Books, Third Reich series. Editor: 1945: The Year of Liberation, 1995, In Pursuit of Justice, 1996; contbr. articles to mags. and jours. Home and Office: PO Box 13110 Arlington VA 22219-3110

MAHONEY, LINDA KAY, mathematics educator; b. Bay Shore, N.Y., June 8, 1951; d. James Nathaniel and Katherine Pauline (Booth) Palmer Jr.; m. Peter Allan Mahoney, Jr., June 5, 1976; children: Matthew J., Michael J., Patrick A. BS, U. Md., 1972; MEd, 1979; postgrad., R.I. Coll., 1988-89, Providence Coll., 1989-90. Tchr. math. Prince George's County Pub. Schs., Benjamin Tasker Jr. High, Bowie, Md., 1973-76; tchr. substitute Warwick (R.I.) Pub. Schs., 1987-90, tchr. math., 1990-91; tchr. math. Ctrl. Tex. Coll., P.R., 1992-96; lectr. U. Tenn., Knoxville, 1996—. Vol. Sherman Elem. Sch., Warwick, 1989-90, Rohr Elem. Sch., Chula Vista, Calif., 1985-87. Mem. Nat. Coun. Tchrs. Math., ASCD, The Math. Assn. Am. Republican. Lutheran.

MAIDIQUE, MODESTO ALEX, academic administrator; b. Havana, Cuba, Mar. 20, 1940; s. Modesto Maidique and Hilda Rodriguez; m. Ana Hernandez, July 18, 1981; children: Ana Teresa, Mark Alex. BS, MIT, 1962, MS, 1964, PhD, 1970. Instr. MIT, Boston, 1976-79; v.p., gen. mgr. Analog Devices Semiconductor, Boston, 1970-76; asst. prof. Harvard U., Boston, 1976-81; assoc. prof. Stanford U., Palo Alto, Calif., 1981-84; sr. ptnr. Hambrecht and Quist Venture Ptnrs., Palo Alto, Calif., 1981-86; co-founder, dir. U. Miami (Fla.) Innovation and Entepreneurship Inst., 1984-86; pres. Fla. Internat. U., Miami, 1986—. Mem. Pres.'s Edn. Policy Adv. Com.; chmn. Beacon Coun., 1992-93. Recipient Citizenship award HEW, 1973, Teaching award Stanford U., 1983. Mem. IEEE, Assn. Cuban Engrs. Republican. Roman Catholic. Home: 6821 SW 104th St Miami FL 33156-3253 Office: Fla Internat U Office of President Miami FL 33199

MAIER, ANNE MARIE MCDONALD, journalist; b. Houston, Mar. 16, 1954; d. Terrence and Patricia Jean (Whitfield) McDonald; m. Frederick W. Maier, June 26, 1975 (div. Mar. 1989); children: Maximilian, Nicholas. BJ, U. Tex., 1976; JD, U. Houston Law Ctr., 1990. Adminstrv. asst. U. Tex. M.D. Anderson Cancer Ctr., Houston, 1976-77; staff corr. People Mag., Time Inc., Houston, 1981-91; regional bur. chief People Mag., Time Inc., 1991—; pub. rels. cons. St. Rose of Lima Sch., Houston, 1984-88; pvt. practice law, Houston, 1990—. Author: Mother Love, Deadly Love, 1992. Office: People Mag 2500 Etc Jester # 645 Houston TX 77008

MAIER, KARL GEORGE, estate and financial planner; b. N.Y.C., Jan. 4, 1937; s. Karl and Frieda (Kraft) M.; m. Magaret A. Sandner, Apr. 30, 1994; children: Karl Douglas, Suanne Charlotte, Tanya Charlotte. AA, St. Petersburg (Fla.) Jr. Coll, 1959; BA, Fla. State U., 1961, MS, 1971. With Bartkeys, Treasure Island, Fla., 1955-56, Ray Jackson Wine House, Redington Beach, Fla., 1956-57; dormatory counselor Fla. State U., Tallahassee, 1962-64, rsch. asst. dept. psychology, 1962; counselor Vocat. Rehab., Pinellas Park, Fla., 1964-68, supervising counselor, 1968-86; exec. dir. Nat. Safety Coun. P.C.C., Inc., Clearwater, Fla., 1986-91; mem. approvals bd. driving under the influence office State of Fla., 1988—; porpoise trainer, Marine Arena, Madeira Beach, Fla., 1957-64; instr. in field; cons. U. Bogota, Min. Spl. Edn., Columbia, S.Am., 1973-85, Medellin Drug Rehab. Program, 1985—. Bd. dirs. Suncoast Epilepsy Assn., Pinellas Park, 1973—, pres., sec.; bd. dirs. Caring and Sharing Ctr. for Ind. Living, Inc., Fla. Assn. DUI programs, 1987-91, sec.-treas.; adv. bd. mem. Masters Chamber Music Soc., Inc., Palm Harbor, Fla., 1991—; vol. Pinellas Country Fla. Sch. NSF rsch. grantee, 1962. Mem. Am. Soc. Assn. Execs., Am. Soc. Safety Engrs., Operation Lifesaver Coun., Fla. Fedn. for Safety, Epilepsy Found. Am., Fla. Safety Coun., Execs. Assn. (pres., sec., treas., 1989-91), Suncoast Crime Prevention Assn., Inc., Cmty. Blood Bank, Breakfast Optimists, Elks. Home and Office: 9716 62nd Ave N Saint Petersburg FL 33708-3508

MAIER, ROBERT HENRY, real estate executive; b. Greenville, Tex., Nov. 19, 1932; s. William Lokey and Charlsie Lorraine (Nation) M.; m. Ruth Jean Chapman, Mar. 1, 1968; children: Alice, Joy Kupp. BA, So. Meth. U., 1964. Pers. dir. Atlantic Richfield Co., Dallas, 1954-69; v.p. adminstrn. ETMF Freight System, Dallas, 1969-78; chief pers. officer Varo, Inc., Garland, Tex., 1978-80; corp. v.p. adminstrn. Comml. Metals Co., Dallas, 1980-88; pres., COO The Staubach Co., Dallas, 1988-93; pres., CEO, bd. dirs. Cornerstone Mgmt. Co., 1993—, also bd. dirs.; exec. dir. HFTH. Bd. dirs. Victims Outreach. Mem. Am. Soc. Pers. Adminstrn., Am. Soc. Advancement of Mgmt. (chpt. pres.), Dallas Pers. Assn. Republican. Rotary, Masons. Office: PO Box 802421 Dallas TX 75380-2421

MAIER, RUDOLPH JOSEPH, neurologist; b. Oak Park, Ill., Feb. 17, 1939; m. Diana J. Wheeler. MD magna cum laude, Stritch Sch. Medicine, 1963. Diplomate Am. Bd. Psychiatry and Neurology, Am. Bd. Electrodiagnostic Medicine. Intern Phila. Gen. Hosp., 1963-64; resident in internal medicine Lakeside VA Hosp., Chgo., 1964-65; resident in neurology Northwestern U., Chgo., 1965-69, Albany (N.Y.) Med. Ctr., 1969-70; neurologist Lovelace Clinic, Albuquerque, 1971-74, Neurology Cons., Ltd., Albuquerque, 1974-75, pvt. practice, Albuquerque, 1975-81, Norte Vista Med. Ctr., Hobbs, N.Mex., 1981-83, Whittaker Corp., King Abdul Aziz Meml. Hosp., Tabuk, Saudi Arabia, 1983-84, Coastal Neuro-Psychiat. Assocs., 1985-90, pvt. practice, Goldsboro, N.C., 1990—; clin. assoc. neurology U. N.Mex., 1971-81; neurologist USPHS Indian Hosps., Gallup and Zuni, N.Mex., 1974-81, Lea Regional and Nor-Lea Hosp., Lea County, N.Mex., 1981-83, Carrie Tingley Hosp. for Crippled Children, Truth or Consequences, N.Mex., 1981-83, Guadalupe Meml. Hosp., Carlsbad, N.Mex., 1981-83, Craven Regional Med. Ctr., New Bern, N.C., 1985-90, Lenoir Meml. Hosp., Kinston, N.C., 1985-90, Onslow Meml. Hosp., Jacksonville, N.C., 1985-90, Wayne Meml. Hosp., Goldsboro, 1990-93, O'Berry Ctr., Goldsboro, 1991-95, Sampson County Meml. Hosp., Clinton, N.C., 1991-95, Cherry Hosp., Goldsboro, 1992, St. Joseph's Hosp., Presbyn. Hosp., Anna Kaseman Hosp., Bataan Meml. Hosp., Santa Fe Meml. Hosp., Hdqs. Gen. Hosp. Mem. AMA, Am. Acad. Neurology, Am. Acad. Pain Mgmt., Am. Assn. Electromyography and Electrodiagnosis, N.C. Med. Assn. Office: 1138 Tommys Rd # C Goldsboro NC 27534-8273

MAILLARD, ALBERT ACHILLES JOSEPH, head and neck surgeon, educator; b. Santiago, Chile, Aug. 8, 1943; s. Albert Joseph and Amanda (Holtheuer) M.; 1 child, John David. BS, U. Houston, 1968; MD, U. Tex., Galveston, 1972. Cert. Tex. State Bd. Med. Examiners, Nat. Bd. Med. Examiners, Am. Bd. Otolaryngology. Resident gen. surgery U. Tex. Med. Sch., Houston (Tex.) Affiliated Hosps., 1972-73, U. Tex. Southwestern Med. Sch., Affiliated Hosp., 1973-74; resident gen. surgery U. Tex. Med. Sch. Houston Affiliated Hosp., 1974-75, resident otolaryngology head and neck surgery, 1975-77; resident U. Tex. Med. Sch. Houston, M.D. Anderson Hosp. & Tumor Inst., 1977-78; instr. otolaryngology U. Tex. Med. Sch., Houston, 1978-82, clin. asst. prof. otolaryngology, head and neck surgery, 1982-84, clin. assoc. prof. otolaryngology, head and neck surgery, 1984—, clin. prof. dept. family practice, 1993—, cons. dept. oncology, 1989—; mem. St. Joseph Hosp. Quality Assurance Rev. Com.-Gen. Surgery, 1989-93, Quality Assurance Rev. Com.-Otolaryngology-Head and Neck Surgery, 1989-93, Bylaws Rev. Com., 1990, Hermann Hosp. Credentials Com., 1990, Hermann Hosp. Tissue Com., 1993, Sci. and Tech. Com., 1993—; bd. dirs. Physicans, Inc., Tex.; pvt. practice, 1979-94; lectr. and presenter in field. Contbr. articles to profl. jours. Charter mem. The Statue of Liberty Found., N.Y., 1983-86, Ellis Island Found., N.Y., 1985-92, Market Sq. Restoration, Houston, 1991. Fellow ACS, Am. Acad. Otolaryngology-Head and Neck Surgery, Am. Soc. for Head & Neck Surgery; mem. AAAS, AMA, Tex. Med. Assn., Harris County Med. Soc., M.D. Anderson Surg. Alumni Assn., The Deafness Rsch. Found., Nature Conservancy, Phi Beta Pi. Roman Catholic. Home: 2038 Suffolk Dr Houston TX 77027-3801 Office: AAJ Maillard MD 6410 Fannin St Ste 1508 Houston TX 77030-5306

MAILLIARD, MARK E., medical educator; b. Washington, Oct. 6, 1956; m. Mary Wagoner, Nov. 12, 1982; children: James, Andrew. BA in Chemistry, Northwestern U., 1977; MD, U. Nebr., 1980. Diplomate Am. Bd. Internal Medicine. House officer dept. internal medicine U. Nebr. Med. Ctr., Omaha, 1980-83, rsch. fellowship in gastroenterology liver-study unit, 1983-84; acad. fellowship in gastroenterology dept. medicine U. Fla., Gainesville, 1984-87, asst. prof. dept. medicine, 1987-92, assoc. prof. medicine dept. medicine, 1992-95; prof. medicine Tex. Tech. HSC/U. Med. Ctr., Lubbock, 1995—; on staff Shands Hosp., U. Fla., Gainesville VA Med. Ctr.; adj. faculty dept. biochemistry and molecular biology U. Fla., Gainesville, 1990-95. Contbr. articles to profl. jours. Recipient Am. Liver Found. fellowship Liver-Study Unit, U. Nebr. Med. Ctr., 1983-84, Nat. Rsch. Svc. award NIH, Dept. Medicine, U. Fla., 1984-86, fellowship in the lab. Michael S. Kilberg PhD, Dept. Biochemistry and Molecular Biology, U. Fla. Coll. Medicine, 1986-87, Clin. Investigator award NIH, NIDDK, 1988-93, Rsch. Devel. award U. Fla., 1988-90. Mem. ACP, Am. Gastroenterol. Assn., Am. Fedn. for Clin. Rsch., Am. Assn. for the Study of Liver Disease, Fla. Gastroenterol. Soc. (chmn. acad. affairs com. 1990-95). Office: Tex Tech Univ Health Sci Ctr Dept Medicine 3601 4th St Lubbock TX 79430

MAIN, EDNA (JUNE) DEWEY, education educator; b. Hyannis, Mass., Sept. 1, 1940; d. Seth Bradford and Edna Wilhelmina (Wright) Dewey; m. Donald John Main, Sept. 9, 1961 (div. Dec., 1989); children: Alison Teresa Main Ronzon, Susan Christine Main Leddy, Steven Donald Main. Degree in Merchandising, Tobe-Coburn Sch., 1960; BA in Edn., U. North Fla., 1974, MA in Edn., 1979, M. Adminstrn. and Supervision, 1983; PhD in Curriculum and Instrn., U. Fla., 1990. Asst. buyer Abraham & Straus, Bklyn., 1960-61; asst. mdse. mgr. Interstate Dept. Stores, N.Y.C., 1962-63; tchr. Holiday Hill Elem. Sch., Jacksonville, Fla., 1974-86; mem. adv. coun. Coll. Edn., U. North Fla., 1982—, instr. summer sci. inst., 1984-92, prof., 1990-92; assoc. prof. Jacksonville U., 1992—, also coord. masters program in integrated learning and ednl. tech.; instr. U. Fla., 1987-90. Co-author: Developing Critical Thinking Through Science, 1990. Rep. United Way, 1981-86; tchr. rep., chpt. leader White House Young Astronaut Program, 1984-85; team leader NSF Shells Elem. Sci. Project. Mem. ASCD, Nat. Sci. Tchrs. Assn. (sci. tchrs. achievement recognition award 1983), Coun. Elem. Sci. Internat., Fla. Assn. Sci. Tchrs., Phi Kappa Phi, Phi Delta Kappa, Delta Kappa Gamma, Kappa Delta Pi. Republican. Episcopalian. Office: Jacksonville U 2800 University Blvd N Jacksonville FL 32211-3321

MAIRE, BARBARA JEAN, volunteer; b. Chgo., Feb. 23, 1932; d. Eldee W. and Emilie (Gadecki) Sayre; m. L. Thomas Maire, July 25, 1953. Student, Art Inst., Chgo., 1946-50. Officer mgr., asst. sec., cost acct. Buchen Advt., Inc., Chgo., 1952-72; with pub. rels. dept. Sebring (Fla.) Internat. Raceway, 1986—. Bd. mem. Sebring Internat. Raceway Adv. Coun., 1986—; bd. dirs. Lake Briarwood Homeowners Assn., Arlington Heights, Ill., 1976-80; active Citizens for Utility Rate Equity, Sebring,, 1989-92, SE div. Adminstr. Race Control, Sports Car Club Am., 1989—; coord. Highlands County, Fla. Lakewatch, 1991—; mem. code enforcement bd. City of Sebring, 1993—. Mem. Fla. Steinmetz Alumni Assn., Sports Car Club Am. (bd. govs. 1985-92, chmn. race ofcl. licensing 1986-91, Race Ofcl. of Yr. 1988), MG Car Club Am. (officer 1962-67, Mem. of Yr. 1966), Am. Model Yachting Assn. (exec. sec. 1977-87), Sebring Country Club. Democrat. Home and Office: 104 W Lake Drive Blvd Sebring FL 33872-5021

MAITLAND, CARLA LOVE, history educator, program coordinator; b. Memphis, June 5, 1947; d. Richard Enloe Jr. and Evelyne Francis (Wallace) Love; m. William Kent Fortson, Dec. 31, 1967 (div. July 1974); children: William Kent Jr., Russell Louis; m. Charles Dean Maitland, Apr. 6, 1984; 1 child, Charles Dean Jr. BA, U. Memphis, 1970. Cert. tchr. history, French. History and French tchr. Glenmore Acad., Memphis, 1973-82; dir. of donor svcs. Life Blood, Memphis, 1982-84; history tchr. Lanier Jr. High Sch., Memphis, 1984-89; coord. of internat. studies Craigmont High Sch., Memphis, 1989—; elected mem. site-based mgmt. coun. Craigmont High Sch., Memphis, 1994—, mid. sch. facilitator, 1993—, pub. info. newspaper in edn. coord., 1992—; mid. sch. adv. coun. Memphis City Schs., 1993—. Author: (handbooks) How to Have a Blood Drive, 1983, Help Yourself Publications, 1993-94. Mem. World Affairs Coun., Memphis, 1989—, Am. Forum for Global Edn., N.Y.C., 1989—. Named Tchr. of the Yr., The Commercial Appeal, Memphis, 1993; recipient Cmty. Contbg. awards Memphis City Coun., 1990-91, 91-92, 92-93, 93-94, 94-95, 95-96. Mem. Nat. Assn. Middle Schs., Nat. Geographic Alliance, Greater Memphis Assn. of Social Studies Tchrs., Tenn. Assn. Middle Schs. Office: Craigmont High Sch 3333 Covington Pike Memphis TN 38128-3902

MAJEWSKI, THEODORE EUGENE, chemist; b. Boonton, N.J., July 5, 1925; s. Witold Charles and Felixa (Tkacz) M.; m. Cynthia Ann Davis, Sept. 26, 1953; children: Andrea, Theodore, Steven, Felicia, Cynthia, Melissa. BA, Syracuse U., 1951; MS, U. Del., 1953, PhD, 1960. Chemist Dow Chem. Co., Midland, Mich., 1957-69; rsch. chemist Philip Morris USA, Richmond, Va., 1969-92; ret., 1992; cons. Herald Pharmacal, Richmond, 1979-81. Contbr. articles to profl. jours.; patentee in field. Bd. dirs. Boy Scouts Am., Richmond, 1957-91. With USN, 1943-46, PTO. Recipient Silver Beaver award Boy Scouts Am., 1980. Mem. Am. Chem. Soc., AAAS, Alpha Ci Sigma. Home: PO Box 8117 Kitty Hawk NC 27949-8117

MAJMUDAR, BHAGIRATH, medical educator; b. Nadiad, India, Jan. 29, 1938; came to U.S., 1967; s. Nanubhai and Pramilaben (Trivedi) M.; m. Uma Mehta, May 24, 1962; children: Nija, Sangini. MB BS, B.J. Med. Coll., Ahmedabad, India, 1962, MD, 1966. Diplomate Am. Bd. Pathology; ordained Hindu priest. Asst. prof. pathology B.J. Med. Coll., 1966-67; chief resident in pathology Salem (Mass.) Hosp., 1967-69; instr. in pathology Ohio State U., Columbus, 1971-75; asst. prof. pathology Emory U., Atlanta, 1971-75, assoc. prof. pathology, 1975-85, assoc. prof. ob-gyn, 1978—, prof. pathology, 1985—; lectr., trainer S.E. Regional Tng. Ctr., Atlanta, 1988—; mem. cervical cancer com. Ga. State Health Dept., Atlanta, 1988—; chief surg. pathology Grady Health Sys., Atlanta, 1992—; lectr. in field. Contbr. articles to profl. publs. Mem. Interfaith Com., State of Ga., 1991-94, Interfaith Com. for Olympic Games, Atlanta, 1992-96; pres. India Am. Cultural Assn., Atlanta, 1976, chmn. bd. dirs., 1979. Recipient Outstanding Cmty. Svc. award India-Am. Cultural Assn., 1982. Fellow Coll. Am. Pathology, Internat. Acad. Pathology; mem. Soc. Med. Assn. (sec., chmn. 1992-95), Internat. Soc. for Study of Vulvovaginal Diseases, Arthur P. Soc. Surg. Pathologists, Internat. Soc. Gynecol. Pathology, Alpha Omega Alpha. Home: 3220 Olde DeKalb Way Atlanta GA 30340 Office: Grady Health Sys Pathology Dept 80 Butler St SE Atlanta GA 30335

MAJOR, DON LINDBERGH, management educator; b. Nassau, The Bahamas, July 14, 1952; s. Stanley Alfred and Ruby Charlotte (Rookwood) M.; m. Feb. 28, 1982; 1 child, Don Lindbergh. BSBA, BA in English, Oakwood Coll., Huntsville, Ala., 1972; student, Ohio State U., 1972-73, MPA, 1973-74; MBA, Ala. A&M U., 1983; postgrad., U. Miami, 1990. Lectr. Coll. of The Bahamas, Nassau, 1975-77; tchr. Ministry of Edn. and Culture, Nassau, 1977-78; asst. prof. internat. bus. and strategic mgmt. Fla. A&M U., Tallahassee, 1990—; revenue officer, mgr. Bahamas Water and Sewerage Corp., Nassau, 1978-85; mgr. human resources, dir. pers. Citibank NA/Cititrust Ltd., Nassau, 1985-86; tchr., chmn. pub. rels. com. Bahamas Acad., 1987; gen. mgr. Bahamas Mgmt. Assn., 1986-87; bd. dirs. Caribbean-Am. Bus. Network, Inc., chmn. com. on emergening and minority bus. devel.; cons. and spkr. in field. Contbr. articles to profl. jours. First elder Johnson Park Seventh Day Adventist Ch., Nassau, 1983-86, local elder Coconut Grove Ch., Miami; elder, long-range planning com. Capital Cir. Seventh Day Adventist Ch.; bd. edn. Fla. Conf. Seventh Day Adventists; adv. bd. Neurofibromatosis Found., Big Bend. Faculty scholar U. Miami, 1987; OAS fellow, 1988. Mem. Internat. Studies Assn., Internat. Trade and Fin. Assn., Acad. Internat. Bus., Assn. for Global Bus., Assn. Mgmt., Bus. Assn. Latin Am. Studies, Toastmasters Internat. (area gov.), Bahamas Acad. Alumni Assn. (pres.), Maranatha Chorus (treas., charter), Chambers Singers, Nassau Amateur Operatic Soc., Consumer Protection Assn., Omicron Delta Kappa. Office: Fla A&M U Sch Bus One SBI Plz Tallahassee FL 32307

MAJORS, ROBERT POWELL, JR., surgeon; b. Charlotte, N.C., Oct. 13, 1935; s. Robert Powell and Dorothy (Fortune) M.; m. Helen Rose Palmer, June 20, 1959; children: Andrew Grier, Elizabeth Ann Majors Smith, Susan Leigh Majors Flynn. BS, Davidson Coll., 1957; MD, George Washington U., 1961. Intern Naval Hosp., Portsmouth, Va., 1961-62; commd. ensign USN, 1961, advanced through grades to comdr., 1970, ret., 1971; resident in surgery Washington Hosp. Ctr., 1965-66, resident in ear, nose and throat, 1966-67; resident in ear, nose and throat Naval Hosp., Bethesda, Md., 1967-69; chief ear, nose and throat svc. Naval Hosp., Portsmouth, 1969-71; pvt. practice as otorhinolaryngologist Raleigh (N.C.) ENT-Head and Neck Surgery, Inc., 1971—. Fellow Am. Acad. Otolaryngology, Soc. Mil. Otolaryngologists; mem. Royster Med. Soc. (sec., pres. 1983—), Wake County Med. Soc. (v.p. 1971—), AMA, N.C. Med. Soc., Nat. Ry. Hist. Soc., Am. Philatelic Soc., Wilderness Med. Soc. Methodist. Home: 3508 Williamsborough Ct Raleigh NC 27609-6354 Office: Raleigh Ear Nose and Throat 3010 Anderson Dr Raleigh NC 27609-7720

MAK, KAI-KWONG, hazardous waste company executive, engineer; b. Kowloon, Hong Kong, Oct. 21, 1948; s. Ping-Cheung and Siu-Hung (Young) M.; m. Chan-Chen; 1 child, Larry Wei. BScChemE, Nat. Taiwan U., Taipei, Republic of China, 1972; MScChemE, Ga. Inst. Tech., 1973. Registered profl. engr., Ont., Can. Process engr. Midrex Corp., Charlotte, N.C., 1974-76; chief process engr. Sudbury Metals, Sudbury, Ontario, Can., 1976-78; sr. process engr. Allis-Chalmers Corp., Milw., 1978-85; project mgr. Internat. Tech. Corp., Knoxville, Tenn., 1985-94; mgr. engring. OHM Corp., 1994—. Inventor method and apparatus for treating waste organics, process for the treatment of hot waste gas containing hydrogen chloride, thermal treatment process for organic material. Mem. AICE, AIME. Office: OHM Remediation Svcs 5335 Triangle Pky Ste 450 Norcross GA 30092-2556

MAKINS, JAMES EDWARD, retired dentist, dental educator, educational administrator; b. Galveston, Tex., Feb. 22, 1923; s. James and Hazel Alberta (Morton) M.; m. Jane Hopkins, Mar. 4, 1943; children: James E. Jr., Michael William, Patrick Clarence, Scott Roger. DDS, U. Tex.-Houston, 1945; postdoctoral, SUNY-Buffalo, 1948-49. Lic. dentist, Tex. Practice dentistry specializing in orthodontics, Lubbock, Tex., 1949-77; dir. clinics Dallas City Dental Health Program, 1977-78; dir. continuing edn. Baylor Coll. Dentistry, Dallas, 1978-92, ret., 1992, prof. emeritus Baylor Coll. Dentistry. Author: (book chpt.) Handbook of Texas, 1986. Chmn. profl. div. United Fund, Lubbock, 1958; pres. Tex. State Bd. Dental Examiners, Austin, Tex., 1968; instl. chmn. United Way, Dallas, 1983. Served to lt. comdr., USNR, 1945-47. Recipient Community Service award W. Tex. C. of C., Abilene, 1968, Clinic award Dallas County Dental Soc., 1981. Fellow Am. Coll. Dentists, Internat. Coll. Dentists; mem. Tex. Dental Assn. (life, v.p. 1954, Goodfellow 1973), West Tex. Dental Assn. (pres. 1955), Am. Assn. Dental Examiners, Park City Club, Rotary, Omicron Kappa Upsilon. Methodist. Avocation: dental history.

MAKI-WALLACE, SUSAN, anthropology educator; b. Corpus Christi, Tex., Oct. 20, 1950; d. Gerald Albert and Susan Elizabeth (Bostwick) Lutz; m. Richard S. Maki (div. 1991); children: Samuel J., Margaret E.; m. Jacky Arthur Wallace, Aug. 26, 1995. BA, U. Tex., 1986, MA, 1987, PhD, 1990. Lectr. U. Tex., San Antonio, 1990-91; asst. dir. Primate Found., Mesa, Ariz., 91-92; asst. prof. Baylor U., Waco, Tex., 92—; forensic anthropologist Am. Acad. Forensic Sci. Contbr. articles to profl. jours. Mem. Am. Acad. Forensic Sci., Am. Soc. Primatologists, Animal Behavior Soc., Am. Assn. Phys. Anthropologists, Assn. for Anthropology and Gerontology. Office: Baylor U Po Box 97326 Waco TX 76798

MAKSI, GREGORY EARL, engineering educator; b. Wilkes-Barre, Pa., May 9, 1939; s. Stephen Cedric and Laura Victoria (Pytell) M.; children: Sabrina, Jared, Joshua. BSME, Ga. Inst. Tech., 1961, MS in Indsl. Mgmt., 1964; PhD in Edn. Adminstrn., U. Miss., 1983. Registered profl. engr., Tenn. Mech. engr. Ellicott Machine Corp., Balt., 1961-62; project engr. Celanese Corp., Rock Hill, S.C., 1964-67; assoc. prof. State Tech. Inst., Memphis, 1967-71, prof., 1971-73, program chmn. of indsl. engring., 1973-90, dept. chmn. mech. engring./indsl. engring., 1990—; cons. Tenn. Ednl. Alliance, Nashville, 1994—, U. Ark., Millington, Tenn., 1988, instr., 1988—; curriculum coord. Memphis City H.S., 1993—; quality-productivity adv., 1990—; CAD/CAM cons., 1995—. Hon. sheriff Shelby County Sheriff's Office, 1991; hon. state legis. Tenn. Ho. Reps., Nashville, 1992. Named Disting. Engr. Memphis Engrs. Coun., 1986. Mem. SME, Inst. of Indsl. Engrs., World Future Soc., Tenn. Profl. Engrs. Soc. Office: State Tech Inst Memphis 5983 Macon Cv Memphis TN 38134-7642

MALAMUD, FERNANDO, oncologist; b. Rosario, Argentina, Nov. 13, 1963; arrived in U.S., 1987; s. Roberto and Ligia Maria Isabel (Garcia) M.; m. Chandra Elise Furches. Secondary, Inst. Dante Alighieri, Rosario, 1980; MD, U. Nat. De Rosario, Rosario, 1987. Diplomate Am. Bd. Internal Medicine, Diplomate Am. Bd. Medical Oncology. Internal medicine intern Tex. Tech. U., El Paso, Tex., 1990-91; resident in internal medicine Tex. Tech. U. Health Scis. Ctr., El Paso, Tex., 1991-93; fellow hematology-oncology U. Utah, Salt Lake City, 1993-94; fellow in med. oncology U. Miss., Jackson, Miss., 1994-95, asst. prof. medicine, 1995—; med. oncologist VA Med. Ctr., Jackson, 1996—. Active Temple Beth Israel, Jackson, 1996. Mem. ACP, Am. Soc. Internal Medicine, S.W. Oncology Group, Am. Soc. Clin. Oncology, Optimist Club. Republican. Jewish. Home: 318 Wildwood Blvd Jackson MS 39212 Office: VA Med Ctr 1500 E Woodrow Wilson Dr Jackson MS 39216

MALASRI, SIRIPONG, engineering educator; b. Bangkok, Oct. 17, 1953; came to U.S., 1978; s. Wong (dec.) and Nongluck (Hutamongkol) M.; m. Kriangchitt Banphabutr, June 1, 1978; children: Kriangsiri, Jittapong, Pongsakorn. B Engring., Chulalongkorn U., Bangkok, 1975; M Engring., Asian Inst. Tech., Bangkok, 1977; PhD, Tex. A&M U., 1982. Registered profl. engr., Fla. Asst. prof. U. Miami, Coral Gables, Fla., 1982-88; assoc. prof. engring. Christian Bros. U., Memphis, 1988-95, prof. engring., 1995—, head dept. civil & environ. engring., 1992—. Guest editor spl. issue Internat. Jour. Applied Engring. Edn., also mem. editorial bd.; contbr. articles to jours., books, conf. procs. Mem. ASCE, Am. Soc. Engring. Edn., Nat. Soc. Profl. Engrs., Tau Beta Phi, Phi Kappa Phi, Chi Epsilon. Office: Christian Bros U 650 E Parkway S Memphis TN 38104-5519

MALCOM, JOSEPH ADAMS, military officer; b. Social Circle, Ga., Oct. 29, 1944; s. Archie Preston Malcom and Sarah Rebecca (Adams) Malcom-Anderson; m. Mary Carol Anderson, May 7, 1967; children: Mary Elizabeth, Susan Rebecca. BBA, North Ga. Coll., 1966; MS in Econs., Clemson U., 1968; grad., Command and Gen. Staff Coll., 1984. Commd. 2d lt. U.S. Army, 1966; advanced through grades to lt. col., 1985; chief, financial mgr. U.S. Army Inventory Control Ctr., Long Binh, Vietnam, 1971; instr., inventory mgt. U.S. Army Quartermaster Sch., Ft. Lee, Va., 1972-73; co. commdr. XVIII Airborne Corps, Ft. Bragg, N.C., 1974-77; asst. prof. U. Tenn., Martin, 1977-80; finance officer 3d Infantry Divsn., Wuerzburg, Germany, 1980-83; chief executive divsn. U.S. Army Logistics Ctr., Ft. Lee, 1984-88; chief logistics assistance officer 82nd Airborne Divsn., Ft. Bragg, 1989-93; adj. prof. U. Richmond, Ft. Lee, 1970, Chapman Coll., Ft. Lee, 1972-74, U. Md., Wuerzburg, 1980-82. Author: Civil War Organization, 1979; editor: Civil War Press Corps newsletter, 1980-87. Decorated Bronze Star (2), Meritorious Svc. medal (4), Army Commendation medal (3). Mem. SAR, SCV, Assn. U.S. Army, Soc. Civil War Necrologists, Assn. Quartermaster Officers, Assn. for Gravestone Studies, 3d Inf. Divsn. Marne Assn. Republican. Baptist. Home: PO Box 722 Social Circle GA 30279-0722 Office: USA AMC LSE Bldg 200 Ft McPherson Atlanta GA 30330-6000

MALDONADO, NORMAN I., academic administrator, physician educator; b. Adjuntas, P.R., Nov. 3, 1935; s. Herminio and Esther (Simon) M.; m. Mary Anne Maldonado, July 2, 1960; children—Norman H., Michael A., Maria B., Luis F., Ana E. B.A., Inter Am. U., San Germán, P.R., 1955; M.D., U. P.R., San Juan, 1959. Intern D.C. Gen. Hosp., Washington, 1959-60; resident in internal medicine Univ. Hosp. of San Juan, 1960-61, 64, fellow in hematology, 1964-65; fellow in hematology New Eng. Ctr. Hosp., 1966; chief hematology sect. U. P.R. Med. Sch., San Juan, 1966-73; med. dir. San Juan City Hosp., 1973-76; undersec. health Commonwealth of P.R., San Juan, 1977-78; chancellor med. scis. campus U. P.R., San Juan, 1978-85, prof. medicine, 1985—; now pres. U P.R. Sys., San Juan; cons. hematology VA Hosp., Tchrs. Hosp., San Juan, 1968—. Contbr. articles to profl. jours. Bd. dirs. P.R. chpt. ARC, San Juan, 1973—; pres. fund raising Soc. for Crippled Children and Adults, San Juan, 1980; pres. adv. bd. Antiaddiction Services Dept., San Juan, 1982-84; mem. adv. bd. P.R. Planning Bd., San Juan, 1983-84. Served to capt. U.S. Army, 1962-63. Named Outstanding Young Man in Medicine, P.R. Jr. C. of C., 1972, Outstanding Man in Medicine, P.R. Jr. C. of C., 1983, hon. prof. U. Madre Maestra, Dominican Republic, 1985. Fellow ACP; mem. Am. Soc. Hematology, Internat. Soc. Hematology, P.R. Soc. Hematology (pres. 1983-85), Alpha Omega Alpha. Roman Catholic. Home: Granada 1610 Torrimar Guaynabo PR 00657 Office: U PR Sys Office of the Pres PO Box 364984 San Juan PR 00936*

MALDONADO, OTMARA LINA, university administrator; b. Caimanera, Cuba, May 12, 1944; came to U.S., 1962; d. Abelardo Miguel and Otmara (Motes) Navarro; divorced; children: Lina Maria Pertierra, Pedro Miguel Pertierra; married, Nov. 16, 1985 (div. Dec. 1988). Grad. high sch., Havana, Cuba; student, Barry U., 1982; BS in Communication, U. Miami, 1993. Clk. Title Ins. and Trust Co., L.A., 1962-65, Black and Red Transfer and Storage, Miami, Fla., 1965; clk., asst. to supr. Airwork Internat., Miami, 1965-66; acctg. clk. fin. affairs div. Med. Sch. U. Miami, 1967-74, staff coord II fin. affairs div. Med Sch., 1974-77, staff coord. III dept. anesthesiology, 1977-80, adminstrv. asst. Dept. Medicine, 1980-84, adminstrv. asst. fin., acad. and Latin Am. affairs, 1984-88, adminstr. divsn. hematology, asst. dir. Latin Am. tng. program, 1984-88, adminstr. divsn. hematology, 1989-92, asst. dir. L.Am. tng. program, 1992—. Lay min. Archdiocese of Miami, 1995. Mem. Am. Soc. Notaries. Republican. Roman Catholic. Office: U Miami 1600 NW 10th Ave Rm 7099 Miami FL 33136-1015

MALECKI, JEAN MARIE, public health director; b. Miami, Mar. 27, 1953; d. Raymond Edward and Patricia Ann (Diehl) Mortimer; m. Peter John Malecki, Apr. 11, 1981; 1 child, Heather Marie. BS, Fairfield U., 1971; MD, N.Y. Med. Coll., 1975; MPH, U. Miami Sch. Medicine, 1985. Diplomate Nat. Bd. Medical Examiners, Am. Bd. Preventive Medicine and Pub. Health. Acting med. dir. HRS Palm Beach County Pub. Health Unit, Lake Worth Br., Lake Worth, Fla., 1983—; dir. Grad. Programs in Pub. Health, 1989—; med. dir. HRS/Palm Beach County Pub. Health Unit, West Palm Beach, Fla., 1989—; adj. asst. prof. dept. epidemiology and pub. health U. Miami Sch. Medicine, 1988—; chairperson Residency Adv. Com. Gen. Preventive Medicine and Pub. Health, 1986-89; pres. Healthy Start Coalition of Palm Beach County, 1992—; lectr. in field. Contbr. articles to profl. jours. Recipient Up and Comer award, 1990, Citation for Scholastic Achievement Am. Med. Women's Assn., 1979, Cor Et Manus award N.Y. Med. Coll., 1979, award Alpha Omega Alpha. Mem. AMA, APHA, Am. Cancer Soc. (Vol. of Yr. award 1991), Fla. Med. Assn., Fla. Pub. Health Assn., Palm Beach County Med. Soc. Office: HRS Palm Beach County PO Box 29 West Palm Beach FL 33402-0029

MALEK, FREDERIC VINCENT, finance company executive; b. Oak Park, Ill., Dec. 22, 1936; s. Fred W. and Martha (Smickilas) M.; m. Marlene A. McArthur, Aug. 5, 1961; children: Fred W., Michelle A. BS, U.S. Mil. Acad., 1959; MBA, Harvard U., 1964; D of Humanities (hon.), St. Leo Coll., St. Petersburg, Fla., 1970. Assoc. McKinsey & Co., Inc., L.A., 1964-67; chmn. exec. com. Triangle Corp., Columbia, S.C., 1967-69; dep. under sec. HEW, Washington, 1969-70; spl. asst. to Pres. U.S., Washington, 1970-73; dep. dir. U.S. Office of Mgmt. and Budget, Washington, 1973-75; with Marriott Corp., Washington, 1975-88, sr. v.p., 1975-77, exec. v.p., 1978-88; pres. Marriott Hotels and Resorts, 1981-88; pres. Northwest Airlines, Mpls., 1989-90, vice chmn., 1990-91, also bd. dirs.; campaign mgr. Bush-Quayle '92, 1991-92; co-chmn. CB Comml. Real Estate Group, 1989—; chmn. Lodging Opportunities Fund, 1991—, Thayer Capital Ptnrs., 1992—, Thayer Hotel Investors, 1994—; chmn. 1996 Rep. Presdl. Trust, 1995—; bd. dirs. Automated Data Processing Corp., Am. Mgmt. Sys. Inc., Avis Inc., ICF Kaiser Inc., Nat. Edn. Corp., N.W. Airlines, FPL Group Inc., Paine Webber Funds, Manor Care Inc.; dir. with rank of amb., 1990 Econ. Smuuit, 1989—; adj. prof. U. S.C., 1986-89; lectr. Kennedy Sch. Govt., Harvard U., 1976. Mem. Pres.'s Commn. on White House Fellows, 1971-75, White House Domestic Coun., 1974-75, Pres.'s Commn. on Pers. Interchange, 1974-76; dep. dir. com. for Re-election of Pres., 1972; Pres.'s Commn. on Pvt. Sector Initiatives, 1982-85, dir. conv. Bush for Pres., 1988; mem. Nat. Coun. on Surface Transp. Rsch., 1993-95; nat. adv. bd. Nat. Ctr. Econ. Edn. of Children, 1980-82; mem. Pres.'s Coun. on Phys. Fitness and Sports, 1986-91. Mem. Am.-Israel Friendship League (bd. trustees 1991—), Aspen Inst. (bd. trustees 1996—). Episcopalian. Office: 901 15th St NW Washington DC 20005-2327

MALENICK, DONALD H., metals manufacturing company executive; b. 1939. Steel bander, slitting machine operator, later prodn. mgr. Worthington Industries, Inc., Columbus, Ohio, 1958-67, v.p. mfg., 1967-72, exec. v.p., 1972-76, pres., 1976—, chief operating officer, from 1976, also bd. dirs. Office: Worthington Industries Inc 1345 Hall Spencer Rd Catawba SC 29704

MALIK, RAJEEV, physician; b. New Delhi, India, Dec. 7, 1954; came to U.S., 1977; s. Baikunth Nath and Santosh Kumari (Tuli) M.; m. Ravinder Kaur, Jan. 5, 1977; children: Ryan, Robin. BS, Ramjas Coll.; MD, Maulana Azad Med. Coll. Intern, 1978, resident, 1980, fellow, 1992; Asst. prof. medicine, dept. family practice U. S.C. Sch. Medicine, Columbia, 1982—; pres. Anderson (S.C.) Oncology Hematology CLinic, 1983—. Fellow Am. Coll. Physicians; mem. Am. Assn. Clin. Oncologists, S.C. Oncology Assn., Anderson County Med. Soc. (pres. 1994), Reid Oncology Assn.

MALIN, HOWARD GERALD, podiatrist; b. Providence, Dec. 2, 1941; s. Leon Nathan and Rena Rose (Shapiro) M. AB, U. R.I., 1964; MA, Brigham Young U., 1969; BSc, Calif. Coll. Podiatric Medicine, 1969, DPM, 1972; MSC, Pepperdine U., 1978; postgrad. in classic, U. So. Calif., 1983—. Diplomate Am. Bd. Podiatric Pub. Health, Am. Bd. Podiatric Orthopedics. Extern in podiatry VA Med. Ctr., Wadsworth, Kans., 1971-72, Marine Corps Res. Dept., San Diego, 1972; resident in podiatric medicine and surgery N.Y. Coll. Podiatric-Medicine, N.Y.C., 1972-73; resident in podiatric surgery, instr. in podiatric surgery N.Y. Coll. Podiatric Medicine, N.Y.C., 1973-74; pvt. practitioner in podiatric medicine and surgery Bklyn., 1974-77; mem. staff Prospect Hosp., Bronx, N.Y., 1974-77; chief podiatry service, mem. staff, cons. sports medicine David Grant U.S. Air Force Med. Ctr., Travis AFB, Calif., 1977-80; chief podiatric sect., mem. staff VA Med. Ctr., Martinsburg, W.Va., 1980—; instr. ednl. devel. program VA Med. Ctr., Martinsburg, W.Va., 1980—; clin. prof. med. sci. Alderson-Broaddus Coll., U. Osteopathic Medicine and Health Scis.; adj. prof. Barry U. Sch. Podiatric Medicine; dir. extern program Pa. Coll. Podiatric Medicine. Editorial rev. bd. Jour. Contemporary Podiatric Physician, 1991—. Lt. col. USAF, 1977-80, with Res. Fellow Am. Coll. Foot Orthopedics, Am. Coll. Podiatric Physicians, Am. SOc. Podiatric Medicine (past pres., archivist), Am. Soc. Podiatric Radiologists (v.p., archivist, pres. elect), Royal Soc. Health; mem. Am. Acad. Podiatric Sports Medicine (assoc.), Assn. Mil. Surgeons U.S. (life), Am. Coll. Podiatric Surgery (assoc.), Am. Assn. Podiatric Med. Writers (archivist), Phi Kappa Theta, Phi Kappa Psi. Home: 210 Shenandoah Rd Apt 2D Martinsburg WV 25401-3723 Office: VA Med Ctr Dept Podiatry Martinsburg WV 25401

MALINAUSKAS, MARK JEROME, communication and theatre educator; b. Ashley, Pa., Sept. 11, 1939; s. Anthony Andrew and Stella Ann (Greyscavage) M.; m. Barbara Karen Hansen, Apr. 3, 1966; children: Deidre, Sean, Megan. BA, King's Coll., 1961; MA, N.Mex. Highlands, 1962; PhD, U. Oreg., 1970. Instr. U. Oreg., Eugene, 1967-70; asst. prof. Lawrence U., Appleton, Wis., 1970-76, Earlham Coll., Richmond, Ind., 1976-78; prof. Murray (Ky.) State U., 1978—. Co-author: The Theatre Experience, 1989, Assessing Communication Education, 1994, Foundations of Theatre, 1995. Named hon. Ky. col. Mem. Nat. Collegiate Honors Conf., Southern Regional Honors Conf., Southeastern Theatre Conf. (treas. 1995-96), Ky. Theatre Assn. (pres. 1986), Ky. Arts Adminstr (sec./treas. 1985), Alpha Chi, Phi Eta Sigma, Omicron Delta Kappa. Episcopal. Office: Murray State U PO Box 9 Murray KY 42071

MALINCONICO, S. MICHAEL, librarian, educator; b. Bklyn., Mar. 12, 1941; s. Gennaro and Rosaria (Pappalardo) M.; child from previous marriage: Michael Gennaro. BS in Physics, Bklyn. Coll., 1962; MA in Physics, Columbia U., 1964, MLS, 1983. Lectr. Bklyn. Coll., 1965-67; data/systems analyst NASA, Greenbelt, Md., 1967-69; asst. chief systems analysis and data processing N.Y. Pub. Library, N.Y.C., 1969-78; assoc. dir. N.Y. Pub. Library, 1978-87; dean Sch. Computer, Info. & Library Sci., Pratt Inst., Bklyn., 1987-89; EBSCO prof. sch. libr. and info. studies U. Ala., Tuscaloosa, 1989—; adj. prof. Columbia U. Sch. Libr. Sci., 1985-86; mem. com. to study Dept. Navy info. resource mgmt. NRC, 1989-90. Author: Future of the Catalog, 1979, Nature of the Catalog, 1979; contbr. articles to profl. jours. J.C. Pfister fellow, Columbia U., 1966-67; NSF fellow, 1963-66; Esther J. Piercy award, ALA, 1978. Mem. IEEE, ALA, Internat. Fedn. Libr. Assns. (standing com. 1987-96, adv. bd. 1987-93), Libr. and Tech. Assn., Am. Soc. Info. Sci., Ala. Libr. Assn., Spl. Librs. Assn., Assn. for Sys. Mgmt. Home: 1931 Manassas Ave Tuscaloosa AL 35406-1744

MALIXI, EDWIN CAMACHO, family physician, navy officer; b. Abucay, Bataan, The Philippines, Aug. 13, 1947; came to U.S., 1975; s. Marcelino Tengonciang and Filomena Soriano (Camacho) M.; m. Nora Bangco DeLeon, Apr. 19, 1975; children: Marvin Glenn, Merrille Carl, Meverly Annette, Maynard Conrad, Myron Edwin. BS, U. Philippines, Quezon City, 1968; MD, U. Philippines, Manila, 1973. Diplomate Am. Bd. Forensic Examiners; cert. in forensic medicine. Commd. officer USN, 1979, advanced through grades to lt. comdr.; chief clin. svcs. br. hosp. USMC Air Sta., Iwakuni, Japan, 1980-82; with BMC Naval Sta., Norfolk, Va., 1993—. Vol. Spl. Olympics, Virginia Beach, Va., 1991-93; euchristic min. St. Luke Cath. Ch., Virginia Beach, 1994-96. Recipient physician recognition award AMA, 1979-95. Fellow Am. Acad. Family Physicians; mem. Am. Coll. Emergency Physicians, Assn. Mil. Surgeons U.S., KC (trustee, grand knight 1992-93). Republican. Home: 4608 Mistral Ln Virginia Beach VA 23456

MALKIN, ROBERT ALLEN, biomedical engineer; b. Cleveland, Mar. 28, 1962; s. Irving and Charllotte (Cohen) M.; m. Alexandra Sarah Gruber, May 9, 1993; 1 child, Rebekah. BS in Computer Engring., U. Mich., 1984, BS in Elec. Engring., 1984; MS, Duke U., 1993, PhD in Elec. Engring., 1993. Cons. Sarns Corp., Ann Arbor, Mich., 1982-84; design engr. Cordis Corp., Miami, Fla., 1984-86, EM Microelectronics, Neuchatel, Switzerland, 1986-89; asst. prof. CCNY, 1993-95; asst. prof. biomed. engring. U. Memphis, 1995—. Recipient Young Investigator award Computers in Cardiology, 1994. Mem. IEEE. Office: U Memphis Biomed Engring ET330 Memphis TN 38152

MALKIN, ROGER D., agricultural products executive; b. 1931. With Federal Compress & Warehouse Co., Memphis, 1968-69, Southwide Inc., Scott, Miss., 1968-69; now chmn. bd. dirs., CEO Delta & Pine Land Co., Scott, Miss., 1972—. Office: Delta & Pine Land Co 1 Cotton Row Scott MS 38772*

MALLAN, FRANCIS SCOTT, accounting manager; b. Ft. Gordan, Ga., Oct. 24, 1964; s. Edward Michael and Connie Elizabeth (Taylor) M. Student, U. S.C., 1982-83, 85-88. Night mgr. Chick-Fil-A, Columbia, S.C., 1980-82; asst. mgr. Showbiz Pizza, Columbia, 1983-85; credit mgr. Cir. City Stores, Inc., Columbia, 1985-89, ops. mgr., 1989-90; fin. analyst Policy Mgmt. Systems, Columbia, 1990-92; acctg. mgr. Food Svc. Inc., Lexington, S.C., 1992-93; dir. fin. ops. Kappa Sigma Frat., Charlottesville, Va., 1993—. Pres. S.C. chpt. Students Against Multiple Sclerosis, 1989-90. Mem. Fraternity Execs. Assn. Inst. Mgmt. Accts., Assn. for Soc. Pers. Adminstrs., Am. Mgmt. Assn., Kappa Sigma (pres. 1988-89, v.p. 1987-88, alumnus advisor, Treas. Efficiency award 1987). Home: PO Box 4353 Charlottesville VA 22905

MALLEN, BRUCE, real estate developer, educator, producer, economist, consultant; b. Montreal, Que., Can., Sept. 4, 1937; Came to the U.S., 1978; s. Mitchell and Mary Mallen; m. Carol Klein; children: Howard Eliot, Jay Leslie, Reesa Lynn. BA in Philosophy, B of Commerce, Sir George Williams U., Montreal, 1958; MS, Columbia U., 1959; MBA, U. Mich., 1960; PhD, NYU, 1963; DSc (hon.), Pacific Western U., 1993. Registered fin. planner; cert. realtor; lic. real estate broker, Calif. Sr. cons., dir. econ. and market rsch. P.S. Ross & Ptnrs., Montreal, 1961-64; pres. Bruce Mallen & Assocs., Inc., Montreal, 1964-79; assoc. prof. Concordia U., Montreal, 1965-67, chmn. dept. mktg., 1965-71, prof. mktg., 1967-79, founding chmn. grad. studies commerce, 1968-75, acting dean faculty of commerce and adminstrn., 1970-71; pres. Filmcorp Entertainment Fins., Inc., Montreal, L.A., 1979-96; dean Coll. Bus. Fla. Atlantic U., Boca Raton, 1996—; econ. cons. Consulate Gen. Japan, Montreal, 1966-78; vis. prof. mktg. Laval U., 1968-70; vis. scholar Grad. Sch. Mgmt., UCLA, 1978-79; vis. prof. U. So. Calif., 1979-81. Author: The Costs and Benefits of Evening Shopping to the Canadian Economy, 1969, Principles of Marketing Channel Management, 1977; co-author: Marketing Canada, 1968 (2d edit.), Marketing in the Canadian Environment, 1973, Principles of Marketing in Canada, 1979, Distribution of Canadian Feature Films in the U.S. Market, 1979, and others; founder, 1st editor-in-chief The Can. Marketer; mem. editorial rev. bd. The Jour. of Mktg.; mem. editorial bd. Internat. Jour. of Phys. Distbn.; contbr. articles to profl. jours.; developer Sony Pictures Plz., Culver City, Calif.; prodr. sev. feature films. Ford Found. fellow, 1961-62; recipient Founders Day award, 1963, Alumni Achievement award for distinction in the entertainment industry, 1990. Mem. Am. Mktg. Assn. (past internat. dir., past pres. Montreal chpt.), Prodrs. Guild Am., Acad. Can. Cinema, Assn. of Indsl. Marketers and Advertisers (past pres. Montreal chpt.), Mktg. and Sales Execs. (past dir.), L.A. Arts Coun.(past dir.), Advt. and Sales Execs., Montreal Club (past dir.), Culver City C. of C. (past dir. entertainment industry coun.), Beverly Hills Bd. Realtors.

MALLENBAUM, SIDNEY, neurologist; b. Milford, Conn., July 14, 1960; s. Victor Mallenbaum; m. Rita Hixson, June 15, 1986; children: Joshua John, Isaac Chaim. BSc, McGill U., Montreal, Que., Can., 1982; MD, U. N.C., 1986. Diplomate Am. Bd. Psychiatry and Neurology, Am. Bd. Electrodiagnostic Medicine. Intern in internal medicine Royal Victoria Hosp., Montreal, 1986-87; resident in neurology Montreal Neurol. Inst. and Montreal Neurol. Hosp., 1987-90, chief resident, 1989; active staff and cons. neurologist Virginia Beach (Va.) Gen. Hosp., 1990—; pvt. practice, Virginia Beach, 1990—; cons. neurologist Sentara Bayside Hosp., Virginia Beach, 1990—; prin. investigator Stroke Treatment with Ancrod Trial, Lubeluzole in Acute Ischemic Stroke Study, Thrombolytic Therapy in Acute Ischemic Stroke Trial; electrodiagnostic cons. Dynamic Engring. Corp., Madison, Wis., 1992—; lectr. Va. Pediat. Soc., Virginia Beach, 1993. Univ. scholar McGill U., 1978-79, faculty scholar, 1979-80. Fellow Am. Assn. Electrodiagnostic Medicine; mem. Am. Acad. Neurology, Virginia Beach Med. Soc. Office: Neurol Cons Va Beach Inc 1008 First Colonial Rd Ste 101 Virginia Beach VA 23454-3002

MALLET, ALEXIS, JR., construction company executive; b. New Iberia, La., Nov. 9, 1951; s. Alexis Sr. and Adelia Maria (Comeaux) M.; m. Brenda King (div.); children: Lorphy, Devlin, Casey, Reagan; grandchildren: Edward Alexis; m. Sarah Elizabeth Roach, Oct. 24, 1987 (div.); children: Thomas Wilson, Alexis III, Joseph Taylor. BA, U. S.W. La., 1975. Bookkeeper A & A Home Supplies, New Iberia, 1969-71; with sales staff Voorhies Supply Co., New Iberia, 1972-74; CEO Royal Constrn. Co., New Iberia, 1974—; bd. dirs. 1st Gen. Enterprises, Ft. Lauderdale, Fla., Jackie Edgar Ford, Inc., Jackie Edgar RV Ctr., Inc.; CEO First Gen. Svcs., South La., 1990; legal constrn. cons. various attys. and ins. cos., La., Miss., 1978-93. Prodr. (record album) Fourth Hour, 1982. Recipient Sales Achievement award Southern Structures, La., 1987, Superior Performance award Southern Structures, 1984, Facility award U.S. Tennis Assn., 1982. Mem. Iberia Bldg. Assn. (v.p., past bd. dirs.), Inst. Inspection Cleaning and Restoration (cert. fire restoration specialist), Assn. Specialists in Cleaning and Restoration (cert. fire restoration specialist), Lafayette C. of C. Republican. Roman Catholic. Office: 113 Flagg Blvd Ste 201 Lafayette LA 70508-7066

MALLETT, T.C., government financial administrator, rancher; b. Florence, Tex., Oct. 31, 1942; s. Thomas Hardin and Alberta (Preslar) M.; m. Virgie Ann Klein, May 29, 1965; children: Michelle, Michael, Melissa, Mark. BBA, U. Tex., 1967. Acct. fuels tax divsn. Comptr. Pub. Accounts, Austin, 1966-71, procedures specialist, 1971-72, acct. acctg. divsn., 1973-82, dir. fund acctg. divsn., 1982-90, dir. fiscal mgmt., 1991—; mem. Senate Com. on Agy. Svcs. Mgmt., Austin, 1986, Senate Com. on Agy. Funds Mgmt., Austin, 1984; mem. adv. mem. Legis. Com. on Budget, Austin, 1986. Mem. Assn. Govt. Accts. (cert. govt. fin. mgr.), Tex. State Agy. Bus. Adminstrs. Assn. (pres. 1989-90, Adminstr. of Yr. 1991). Home: 3209 Silverleaf Dr Austin TX 78757 Office: Tex Comptr Pub Accounts 111 E 17th St Austin TX 78757

MALLEY, MARJORIE CAROLINE, science and mathematics educator, historian; b. Bristol, Conn., Feb. 5, 1941; d. Raymond Thomas and Alice Caroline Strauss (Wight) M.; m. James Michael Hornell, Nov. 16, 1963; children: Tara Maureen C. Hornell, Kristin Maria M. Hornell. BS in Physics and Philosophy, MIT, 1962; AMT in Sci. Teaching, Harvard U., 1963; PhD in History, U. Calif., Berkeley, 1976. Cert. secondary tchr. Tchr. physics and math. Vallejo, Calif.; tchr. physics and phys. sci. Independence, Mo.; founder, tchr. Fun with Sci. Bartlesville, Okla., 1984-87; sci. cons. Bartlesville Pub. Schs., 1986-89; spl. cons. Soc. for History of Tech., 1991, Biol. Scis. Curriculum Study, Colorado Springs, Colo., 1990-91; instr. Rogers U., Bartlesville, 1992—; mem. planning com. Green Country Regional Sci. Tchrs. Workshop, 1987-95; vol. tchr. several local orgns. Contbr. articles to profl. jours. Mem. curriculum com. Bartlesville Assn. Gifted and Talented, 1981-82, 84-87, 92, coord. summer and winter enrichment classes, 1985, v.p., 1986, pres., 1987, bd. dirs., 1993—. Rsch. grantee NSF, 1971, 87-88. Mem. AAUW, AAAS, History of Sci. Soc. (com. on edn. 1992—, chair 1996-97), Osage Gem and Mineral Club, Midwest Junto History of Sci. (coun. 1996-98), Mo. State Tchrs. Assn., Nat. Coun. Tchrs. Math., Nat. Sci. Tchrs. Assn., Okla. Sci. Tchrs. Assn. Home: 1934 S Dewey Ave Bartlesville OK 74003-6226

MALLEY, RAYMOND CHARLES, retired foreign service officer, industrial executive; b. Cambridge, Mass., Dec. 22, 1930; s. William and Evangeline (Vautour) M.; m. Rita Ann Masse, May 26, 1951 (dec. June 1989); children: Keith, Bruce, Gregory; m. Josette Lucile Vidril Murphy, Aug. 11, 1995. AA, Boston U., 1950, BS, 1952; MA Equivalent, U. Geneva, Switzerland, 1955; MA and PhD A.B.D., Fletcher Sch. Law & Diplomacy (Tufts U. and Harvard U.), Medford, Mass., 1956. Economist, fin. analyst Texaco, Inc., N.Y.C., 1957-61; fgn. svc. officer U.S. Dept. State/A.I.D., Washington & fgn. posts, 1961-82; dir. U.S. Trade and Devel. Program, Washington, 1980; v.p. Silopress, Inc., Sioux City, Iowa, 1982-87; cons., advisor Labat-Anderson Internat., Arlington, Va., 1988-92; sr. group advisor, N. Am. rep. Halla Bus. Group, Seoul (Korea), N.Y.C., Washington, 1991—. Mem. exec. bd. Coll. of Mgmt., Long Island U., Brookville, N.Y., 1994. Major U.S. Air Force, 1952-54, Korea; active reserve 1954-70. Mem. Acadian Cultural Soc., Am. Fgn. Svc. Assn., U.S. Profl. Tennis Registry, Ft. Myer Officers Club, Arlington, Va., Harvard Club, Boston. Roman Catholic. Home: 6224 Loch Raven Dr McLean VA 22101 Office: Halla Bus Group 60 Oxford Dr Moonachie NJ 07074

MALLIA, MARIANNE HAGAR, medical writer; b. Davenport, Iowa, Feb. 14, 1948; d. Norman Bramblett and Mary Jane (Hilkemeyer) Hagar; m. Michael P. Mallia; 1 child, Lindsay Sharyn Kneipp. BA in English, U. Iowa, 1970. Cert. tchr. Tchr. tech. writing Houston Ind. Sch. Dist., 1970-76; med. writer Tex. Heart Inst., Houston, 1976—; editorial cons. Tex. Heart Inst. Jour., 1977-87, head sci. publs., 1986-94, sr. med. writer, 1994—; instr. Sch. of Allied Health Scis., Sch. of Pub. Health, U. Tex., 1990-94. Editor: (with Denton A. Cooley) Surgical Treatment of Aortic Aneurysms, 1985; Reflections and Observations, Essays of Denton A. Cooley, M.D., 1985; Techniques in Cardiac Surgery, 1984, Heart Owner's Handbook, 1995. Fellow Am. Med. Writers Assn. (editor, writer core curriculum 1985, instr. 1988—, honor roll workshop leaders 1992—, pres. S.W. chpt. 1995-96, bd. dirs. 1996—); mem. Friends and Neighbors of Trial Lawyers, Coun. of Biology Editors, Women in Communications (Matrix First Place award 1996), Tex. Trial Lawyers Assn., Houston Trial Lawyers Assn. (sec 1995—), Pi Beta Phi. Home: 3779 Tangley St Houston TX 77005-2031 Office: Tex Heart Inst PO Box 20345 Houston TX 77225-0345

MALLIK, MUHAMMAD ABDUL-BARI, soil microbiologist; b. Pabna, Bangladesh, Mar. 15, 1927; s. Monsur Ali and Ataharun-Nisa Mallik; m. Rowshan Jahan Hamida, Sept. 24, 1966; 1 child, Abds-Sami. BSc, Rajshahi (Bangladesh) Coll., 1949; MSc, Dhaka (Bangladesh) U., 1952; MS, Minn. U., 1961; PhD, Okla. U., 1964. Lectr. botany U. Karachi, Pakistan, 1956-59, asst. prof., 1964-68, 69-72; vis. scholar dept. botany Baghdad (Iraq) U., 1968-69; asst. prof. Dhaka (Bangladesh) U., 1973-74; rsch. assoc. dept. botany and microbiology u. Okla., Norman, 1974-75; assoc. rsch. prof. agrl. rsch. program Langston (Okla.) U., 1975-82, rsch. prof. agrl. rsch. program, 1982—. Author: Introduction to Fungi, 1973; contbr. articles to profl. and popular publs. Fulbright scholar Minn. U., St. Paul, 1961; rsch. grantee Pakistan Agrl. Rsch. Coun., Karachi, 1968-69, USDA, Langston, 1982—. Mem. Am. Soc. Agronomy, Internat. Allelopathy Soc., Okla. Acad. Sci., Bangladesh Bot. Soc. Democrat. Muslim. Home: 2611 S Oxford Dr Stillwater OK 74074 Office: Langston Univ Agrl Rsch Program PO Box 730 Langston OK 73050

MALLON, WILLIAM JAMES, orthopaedic surgeon, sports historian; b. Paterson, N.J., Feb. 2, 1952; s. John William and Evelyn (Schoe) M.; m. Karen Jane Kurtz, June 11, 1977; children: Kamper, Kelly, Mickey. AB in Math., Physics, Duke U., 1973, MD, 1984. Diplomate Am. Bd. Orthopaedic Surgery. Profl. golfer PGA Tour, 1975-79; resident in orthopaedic surgery Duke U. Med. Ctr., Durham, N.C., 1984-90; fellow in shoulder surgery U. Western Ont., London, 1990; orthopaedic surgeon Triangle Orthopaedic Assocs., Durham, 1990—; asst. consulting prof. orthopaedic surgery Duke U. Med. Ctr., Durham, 1990—. Author: Quest for Gold, 1984, Orthopaedics for the House Officer, 1990, Guinness International Who's Who of Sport, 1993, Golden Book of the Olympic Games, 1993, The Golf Doctor, 1996, Historical Dictionary of the Olympic Movement, 1995; editor: Medical Aspects of Golf, 1994. Liaison com. N.C. Indsl. Commn., Raleigh, N.C., 1994—. Mem. Internat. Soc. Olympic Historians (sec.-gen. 1991-96, v.p. 1996—), Treyburn Country Club, Framingham Country Club (hon. life). Office: Triangle Orthopaedic Assocs 2609 N Duke St Ste 301 Durham NC 27704-3048

MALLORY-YOUNG, SHIRLEY, religion educator; b. Bronwood, Ga., July 15, 1942; d. Clarence and Lula (Perry) Mallory. BA, Bethune Cookman Coll., 1964; MEd, Stetson U., 1981; PhD, Fla. State U., 1985; D in Ministry, Logos Grad. Sch., 1993. Instr. Jesus Ministries-Bible Coll., Miami, Fla., 1989-90; founder, pres. Christian Dynamics Internat., Inc., Ft. Lauderdale, Fla., 1986—; founder, chancellor Evangel Ctr. Internat., Inc., Ft. Lauderdale; dir. Christian edn. H.O.P.E. Ministries, Lauderhill, Fla.; founder, pres. Christian Dynamics Bible Coll. and Grad. Sch. Author religious ednl. materials: Lord, Teach Us Me to Pray, 1986, Putting on the Whole Armour of God, 1990, Family Altar Prayer Guide, 1991; seminar: Management of Today's Church, 1989. Mem. Delta Sigma Theta, Inc., Phi Delta Kappa, Inc., Kappa Delta Pi. Democrat. Home: 2144 NW 56th Ave Fort Lauderdale FL 33313-3058 Office: PO Box 491224 Fort Lauderdale FL 33349-1224

MALLOY, PHEOBE SMALLS, secondary school educator; b. Charleston, S.C., Oct. 9, 1954; d. James and Evelina (Jenkins) Singleton; m. Edward Lamar Smalls, July 9, 1977 (div. Dec. 1983); 1 child, Ashanti Lamar; m. Frank Walter Malloy Jr., Mar. 10, 1984; children: Maggie Blythwood, Rowland Malcolm. BA, Johnson C. Smith U., Charlotte, N.C., 1976; MEd, The Citadel, 1979; postgrad., The Union Inst., Cin. Cert. tchr. educable mentally handicapped, learning disabilities. Intern Ctr. for Human Devel., Charlotte, 1975-76; tchr. for educable mentally handicapped Bapt. Hill High Sch., Charleston, 1976-81; resource tchr. for students with learning disabilities, corr. pub. rels. Burke High Sch., Charleston, 1981—, chair exceptional children's month, 1982-86, chair black history month, 1982-86, co-chair sch. based mgmt. team, 1985—, co-chair self-study team for So. Assn. Accreditation, 1986—; est. Spanish programs James Simmons Elem. Sch., Charleston, 1985—; co-owner Malloy's Ctr. for Desktop Pub.; owner Malloy's Designs, Lena's Cmty. Residential Care Facility, LLC; asst. mgr. Low

Country Postal Specialties. Liaison editorial staff Handbook for Tchrs., 1982; contbr. articles to profl. jours. Mem. pub. relations com. Burke PTA, 1985-87, co-chair ways and means com., 1986-87; sec. dist. 20 City Council PTA, Charleston, 1986-87. Named Disting. Corr., Burke High Sch., 1986-87, Disting. Vol., Charleston County Schs., 1987, Disting. Vol., James Simons Elem. Sch., 1987. Mem. Council for Exceptional Children, Div. for Learning Disabilities, Cath. Women Orgn., Eta Phi Beta (sec. 1983-84, 1st v.p. 1984-86). Office: Burke High Sch 244 President St Charleston SC 29403-4742

MALM, RICHARD LEWIS, forester; b. N.Y.C., July 24, 1948; s. Harold Stanley and Marie Louise (Palmer) M.; m. Patricia Ann Cox, June 14, 1970; children: Michael, Elizabeth, Matthew. BS in Forestry, W.Va. U., 1970; MS in Forestry, U. N.H., 1972; MBA, U. North Fla., 1977. Registered forester, Ga., S.C., N.C. Tech. forester ITT Rayonier, Inc., Fernandina Beach, Fla., 1974-75, area forester, 1975, tax specialist, 1976-78, asst. controller, 1978, contr., 1979-80; fin. analyst Union Camp Corp., Savannah, Ga., 1980-81; procurement supt. Union Camp Corp., Waycross, Ga., 1982; region mgr. Union Camp Corp., Savannah, 1983-89, tech. dir., 1989-90; region mgr. Union Camp Corp., Franklin, Va., 1989—; mem. adv. com. sch. forestry, Va. Polytechnic Inst., Blacksburg, 1989—. Forest econ. Peace Corps, Ghana, 1973-74; chmn. Project Learning Tree Program, Ga., 1987-89; bd. dirs. St. Andrews Sch., Savannah, 1985-86; asst. scoutmaster Boy Scouts Am., Richmond Hill, Ga., 1987-89. Mem. Am. Forest Coun. (resource com. 1986-88, rsch. com. 1989-90, Best New PLT Program 1989), Nat. Coun. Paper Industry for Air and Stream Improvement (forest health com. 1989-90), Ga. Forestry Assn. (bd. dirs., exec. com. 1986-89, chmn. reforestation com. 1986-89, forest health com. 1989-90, publicity award 1988), Soc. Am. Foresters, Forest Devel. Com., S.C. Forestry Assn. (environ. com. 1989-90), Va. Forestry Assn. (bd. dirs. 1992—), Cypress Cove Country Club. Democrat. Episcopalian. Home: 4748 Barn Swallow Dr Chesapeake VA 23321-1233 Office: Union-Camp Corp 206 E 2nd Ave Franklin VA 23851-1506

MALM, RITA H., securities executive; d. George Peter and Helen Marie (Woodward) Pellegrini; student Packard Jr. Coll., 1950-52, N.Y. Inst. Fin., 1954, Wagner Coll., 1955; m. Robert J. Malm, Apr. 19, 1970. Sales asst. Dean Witter & Co., N.Y.C., 1959-63, asst. v.p., compliance dir., 1969-74; v.p., dir. Securities Ind. Assocs., N.Y.C., 1969-72; chief exec. officer Muriel Siebert & Co., Inc., N.Y.C., 1981-83; pres., founder Madison-Chapin Assocs., N.Y.C., 1984-89; pres. Hayward Malm Securities, Ltd., 1989-93; pres., founder Concord Stuart, Inc., 1993—; art mktg. cons. Author: Dying On Wall Street, 1996. Mem. NAFE (bd. dirs), Am. Cancer Soc. (bd. dirs. Jupiter/Tequesta chpt. 1992-95), Profl. Women's Network (founder Palm Beach and Martin Counties 1991), Women's Bond Club N.Y. (dir., v.p., program chmn., pres. 1980-82), Cornell U. Club Ea. Fla. (bd. dirs. 1992—). Office: 1061 E Indiantown Rd Ste 410 Jupiter FL 33477-5143

MALONE, CAROLYN DELORIS, elementary education educator; b. Birmingham, Ala., Aug. 6, 1946; d. J.D. and Ethel (Brown) Cockrell; m. Lawrence Malone, Oct. 12, 1969 (dec. May 1991); 1 child, Chelsea Camille. BS in Elem. Edn., Rust Coll., 1968; M of Elem. Edn., Jackson State U., 1975, EdS in Elem. Edn., 1979. Elem. edn. tchr. Laurel, Miss., 1968—. Mem. NEA, Miss. Edn. Assn., Laurel Edn. Assn. Office: Stainton Elem Sch 795 S 19th Ave Laurel MS 39440-4849

MALONE, DAN F., journalist; b. Dallas, Jan. 22, 1955; s. Charles Ted and Ela Grace (Darden) M.; m. Kathryn Jones, June 27, 1981. BJ, U. Tex., 1978. Editor-in-chief The Daily Texan, Austin, Tex., 1977-78; intern Harte-Hanks Austin Bur., 1978-79; staff writer Corpus Christi (Tex.) Caller-Times, 1979-81, Ft. Worth Star-Telegram, 1981-85; staff writer Dallas Morning News, 1985—, Ft. Worth bureau chief, 1992—; Fox fellow Nat. News Coun., N.Y.C., summer 1978. Recipient Pulitzer prize for investigative reporting, 1992, 1st Place Freedom of Info. Category award Tex. AP Mng. Editor's Assn., 1992, 1st Place Investigative Reporting Inst. Southern Studies, 1992. Office: Dallas Morning News 500 Main St Ste 800 Fort Worth TX 76102-3939

MALONE, DAVID, healthcare company executive; b. 1941. Active Hosp. Corp. Am., Nashville, 1968-81, v.p., 1981—.

MALONE, DAVID CLAY, computer specialist, retired police officer; b. Duluth, Minn., June 27, 1948; s. Jeune Darwin and Dorothea (Snebold) M.; 1 child, Christopher Bowden. BA, Tex. Wesleyan U., 1973. Lic. security support person, Tex. Cadet, police officer Ft. Worth Police Dept., 1966-70, police officer, sgt., lt., 1972-86; ret., 1986; computer operator Alarm Specialist, Inc., Arlington, Tex., 1986—. With U.S. Army, 1970-72. Mem. Am. Legion. Baptist.

MALONE, DAVID ROY, state senator, university administrator; b. Beebe, Ark., Nov. 4, 1943; s. James Roy and Ila Mae (Griffin) M.; m. Judith Kaye Huff, June 20, 1965 (div. Feb. 1990); 1 child, Michael David. BSBA, U. Ark., 1965, JD, 1969, MBA, 1982. Bar: Ark. 1969, U.S. Dist. Ct. (we. dist.) Ark. 1969, U.S. Tax Ct. 1972, U.S. Ct. Appeals (8th cir.) 1972, U.S. Supreme Ct. 1972. Pvt. practice Fayetteville, Ark., 1969-72; atty. City of Fayetteville, 1969-72; asst. prof. bus. U. Ark., Fayetteville, 1972-76, asst. dean law, 1976-91; mem. Ark. Ho. of Reps., 1980-84, Ark. Senate, 1984—; exec. dir. U. Ark. Found., 1991—; bd. dirs. Bank of Elkins, S.W. Edn. Devel. Lab., Austin, Tex., 1988-94; legal adv. coun. So. Regional Edn. Bd., Atlanta, 1991—. Contbr. articles to profl. jours.; bd. dirs. Ark. Law Rev., 1978-92; contbg. author U. Ark. Press, 1989. Mayor City of Fayetteville, 1979-80; mem. Jud. Article Task Force, Little Rock, 1989-91; chair Motor Voter task force, 1994-95; bd. dirs. Music Festival Ark., 1989-91, Washington County Hist. Soc., 1993—; chmn. bd. Walton Arts Ctr. Found., 1994—; chmn. bd. dirs. Washington County Law Libr., 1970-84. Recipient Svc. award Ark. Mcpl. League, 1980, Disting. Service award U. Ark., 1988. Mem. Ark. Bar Assn. (ho. of dels. 1977-81, award of merit 1980, exec. 1981-82, Outstanding Lawyer-Citizen award 1990), Washington County Bar Assn., Ark. Inst. Continuing Legal Edn. (bd. dirs. 1979-88), Fayetteville C. of C. (bd. dirs. 1984—), Ark. Genealogy Soc. (bd. dirs. 1990—). Democrat. Methodist. Home: 1928 Austin Dr Fayetteville AR 72703-2713 Office: PO Box 1048 Fayetteville AR 72702-1048

MALONE, JAMES HIRAM, graphic artist, painter, writer; b. Winterville, Ga., Mar. 24, 1930; s. Ralph and Sarah Lena (Echols) M.; m. Mary Louise Liebaert, 1972 (div. 1982); children: Andrew Ralph, Matthew Martin. Student, Morehouse Coll., 1949-50, Coll. Art and Design, 1959-62. Art dir., prodn. mgr. Better Brochures, Inc., Detroit, 1963-65; graphics mgr. Fed. Dept. Stores, Detroit, 1965-69; sr. art cons. Northgate Ad Agy., Detroit, 1969-75; sr. graphics designer Montgomery Ward Regional Hdqs., Southfield, Mich., 1975-80; layout/prodn. designer K-Mart Internat. Hdqs., Troy, Mich., 1980-83; ad/promotions creative dir. Atlanta Jour./Constitution, 1983-90; fine art prodr., painter Bianco Art Collections of Atlanta, Marietta, Ga., 1990-92; cartoonist, newspaper columnist/reporter Atlanta News Leader, Union City, Ga., 1992—. Author, artist: Brother, 1970, Malone's Atlanta, 1986, No-Job Dad, 1992, The Cart, 1994; artist: (literacy drawings) Say (Simply Apply Yourself), 1988, (paintings) BIG (Black Inventors Gifts), 1991; one-man shows include AAA Art Gallery, Detroit, 1963-67, Richard Russell Hall Gallery, Atlanta, 1985, C. W. Hill Gallery, Atlanta, 1990, Walker St. Gallery, Atlanta, 1992, Alma Simmons Gallery, 1986-94, The Atlanta Project Collaboration Ctr., 1994; exhibited in group shows at Red Cross European Exchange Touring Art Exhbn., 1949, Atlanta U. Art Exhbn., 1949, 53, 54, 55, Contemporary Art Studio Gallery, Detroit, 1962, 64, 65, 66, 67, 75, Detroit Mus. Art, 1968, Wayne State Coll. Cmty. Gallery, Detroit, 1969, Kumarsi Mart Art Gallery, Detroit, 1970, Scarab Club Mus., Detroit, 1974, United Auto Workers, Detroit, 1977, Salon Internat. De La Caricature, Montreal, Can., 1980, 81, 82, 83, 85, 86, 88, Artistic Directions Gallery, Atlanta, 1983, Nexus Gallery, Atlanta, 1984, 89, Ctr. Creative Studies Coll. Art and Design Alumni Exhibits, Detroit, 1986-92, Spelman Coll., Atlanta, 1987, Mattress Factory, 1987, Nat. Black Arts Festival, Atlanta, 1988-92, Ga. State U., 1989, Ruth Hall Hodges Gallery, Atlanta, 1990-93, TULA Galleries, Atlanta, 1990, EarthFactory, Atlanta, 1991, Art Station, Atlanta, 1991, Atlanta Life, 1992, Trinity Art Gallery, 1992, Samari Art Gallery, 1993, Mobile (Ala.) Coll., 1993-94, Albany Mus. of Art, 1994, Alma Simmons Gallery, Atlanta, 1994, Atlanta Project Hdqs., 1994; Buttermilk Bottom Art Proj., 1995, 96, Alma Simmons Gallery, 1995, 96, Atlanta's Auburn Ave Rsch. Libr., African Am. Culture and History Gallery, 1996, City Hall East Gallery, 1996; represented in numerous permanent collections including Atlanta U., Hatch-Billups, N.Y., Ga. Artists Register, Atlanta, Bianco Collections, Ga. Rsch. library of African-American culture and history, 1995, neighborhood schs. mentor Fed. Dept. Stores, Detroit, 1964-69; motivator, sch. lectr. Atlanta Jour./Constitution, 1983-90, minority job fairs guide, 1985; bd. drs. Neighborhood Planning Unit J, Atlanta, 1984—, Bankhead Hwy. Revitalization Project, Atlanta, 1990—; arts cons. Fulton County Arts Task Force, Atlanta, 1990—; com. chmn. Jimmie Carter's West Fulton and Douglass Atlanta Cluster Project, 1992—; active Feed The Homeless, Inc., Atlanta Olympics Com. Sgt. 1st class Spl. Svcs., U.S. Army, 1950-59. Recipient George H. Clapp Meml. Found. award Art Inst. Pitts., 1949, Nat. Art award (first Ga. recipient) Scholastic Art Awards Contest, Atlanta U. Nat. Art award (youngest winner), 1949, Nat. Cartoonist Soc. scholarship, 1958, Editorial Cartoon award Nat. Newspapers Pubs. Assn., 1973, Bronze Jubilee Cmty. award WPBA TV, Atlanta, 1986, Alumni Art award Ctr. Creative Studies, Coll. Art and Design, Detroit, 1986, Youth Motivation award Merit Employment Assn., 1987, 88, 89, So. Drawl Art Exhbn. award, 1993; grantee Atlanta Jour./Constitution, 1986, Nexus Family History Artbook Project, 1994. Mem. High Mus. Art, 1st World Writers (v.p. 1993-94), Internat. Black Writers (cons., v.p. 1993—), Atlanta Writing Resource Ctr., Nat. Conf. Artists, Friends of Atlanta/Fulton County Libr., Buttermilk Bottom Cmty. Assn. (cons., v.p. 1996), Individual Visual Artists' Coalition. Democrat. Unitarian. Home: 1796 North Ave NW Atlanta GA 30318-6441

MALONE, PATRICIA LYNN, artist; b. Kansas City, Mo., Dec. 3, 1930; d. Ralph John and Frances Juanita (Hopkins) Lynn; m. Charles E. Malone, Apr. 13, 1958; children: Kerry, Lisa, Lori. Student, Kansas City Jr. Coll., 1947-48, Art Inst., Kansas City, 1948-51, U. Tulsa, 1978-80. Represented by Final Touch Gallery, Tulsa, M.A. Doran Gallery, Tulsa, Am. Legacy Gallery, Kansas City, Mo., Talisman Gallery, Bartlesville, Okla. Exhibited in group shows at Wichita (Kans.) Art Mus., Tweed Mus., Duluth, Minn., Tucson Mus. Art, Ariz., Talisman Gallery, Bartlesville, Okla., Spiva Art Ctr., Joplin, Mo., Sloan Gallery, Tulsa, Okla., Salmagundi Gallery, N.Y.C., Neville Pub. Mus., Green Bay, Wis., Nat. Art Club, Nat. Acad. Gallery, N.Y.C., Midland Ctr. for Arts, Mich., House Gallery, Oklahoma City, Okla., Grants Pass Mus. Art, Oreg., Galleria Meml. Art Ctr., Atlanta, Ga., Frye Mus. Art, Seattle, Flint Inst. Arts, Mich., Dailey Ctr. Council for Fine Arts, Chgo., Cox Gallery Drury Coll, Springfield, Mo., Chouteau Gallery U. Tulsa, Okla., Center Art Gallery, Tulsa, Canton Art Inst., Canton, Ohio, Brea Cultural Ctr., Calif., Bath House Cultural Ctr., Dallas, Anchorage Fine Arts Mus., Alaska; represented in permanent collections at U. Tulsa, Transco Energy Corp., Okla. Art Ctr., Hallmark-Crown Ctr., Florentine's, Bovaird Supply, Inc. Mem. Am. Watercolor Soc., Nat. Watercolor Soc., Midwest Watercolor Soc., Watercolor Okla. Home: 2807 E 48th St Tulsa OK 74105-5310

MALONE, PERRILLAH ATKINSON (PAT MALONE), retired state official; b. Montgomery, Ala., Mar. 17, 1922; d. Odolph Edgar and Myrtle (Fondren) Atkinson. BS, Oglethorpe U., 1956; MAT, Emory U., 1962. Asst. editor, then acting editor Emory U., 1958-64; asst. project officer Ga. Dept. Pub. Health, Atlanta, 1965-68; asst. project dir. Ga. Ednl. Improvement Coun., 1968-69, assoc. dir., 1970-71; dir. career svcs. State Scholarship Commn., Atlanta, 1971-74; rev. coord. Div. Phys. Health, Ga. Dept. Human Resources, Atlanta, 1974-79; project dir. So. Regional Edn. Bd., 1979-81; specialist Div. Family and Children Svcs., Atlanta, 1982-91, ret., 1991; mem. Gov.'s Commn. on Nursing Edn. and Nursing Practice, 1972-75, Aging Svcs. Task Force, Atlanta Regional Commn., 1985-95; book reviewer Atlanta Jour.-Constn., 1962-79. Recipient Recognition award Ga. Nursing Assn., 1976, Korsell award Ga. Ga. League for Nursing, 1974, Alumni Honor award Emory U., 1964. Mem. APHA, Ga. Gerontology Soc. (editor GGS Newsletter 1988-92, Lewis Newmark award 1991). Methodist. Home: 1146 Oxford Rd NE Atlanta GA 30306-2608

MALONE, VIRGINIA, educational measurement professional; b. Houston, Nov. 16, 1940; d. Frank Joseph and Myrtle Virginia (Eidelbach) Stalmach; m. Robert Norman Malone, Aug. 13, 1965; 1 child, Dale Samuel. BS in Edn., S.W. Tex. State U., 1962. Cert. tchr., Tex. Tchr. Kenedy (Tex.) Ind. Sch. Dist., 1962-63, North East Ind. Sch. Dist., San Antonio, 1963-68, Northside Ind. Sch. Dist., San Antonio, 1973-86; mgr. ednl. measurement The Psychol. Corp., San Antonio, 1986—; cons. AMU, College Station, Tex., 1992, U. of Tex. at Austin, 1990-91, S.W. Tex. State U., 1993; co-leader NSF Inst., St. Mary's U., San Antonio, 1984-85. Chairperson sci. adv. com. Witte Mus., San Antonio, 1993—; adv. bd. TAMU, College Station, 1992-93; panel mem. for proposal evaluation NSF, Washington, 1991. Recipient Pres.'s Circle of Excellence Harcourt Brace Corp., Orlando, Fla., 1993, Tex. Mid. Sch. Tchr. of the Yr. Sci. Tchrs. Assn. of Tex., 1982. Mem. ASCD, Tex. Earth Sci. Tchrs. Assn. (conf. dir. 1983), Sci. Tchrs. Assn. of Tex., Nat. Sci. Tchrs. Assn., Nat. Assn. of Geology Tchrs., Tex. Assn. of Biology Tchrs. (pres.). Home: 1791 US Hwy 90 East Hondo TX 78861 Office: The Psychol Corp 555 Academic Ct San Antonio TX 78204

MALONE, WALLACE D., JR., bank executive; b. Dothan, Ala., 1936; married. BS, U. Ala., 1957; MBA, U. Pa., 1960. With First Nat. Bank, 1959-71; with SouthTrust Corp., Birmingham, Ala., 1972—, now chmn., chief exec. officer, dir. Office: SouthTrust Corp 420 N 20th St PO Box 2554 Birmingham AL 35290*

MALONE, WILLIAM GRADY, lawyer; b. Minden, La., Feb. 19, 1915; s. William Gordon and Minnie Lucie (Hortman) M.; m. Marion Rowe Whitfield, Sept. 26, 1943; children: William Grady, Gordon Whitfield, Marion Elizabeth, Helen Ann, Margaret Catherine. BS, La. State U., 1941; JD, George Washington U., 1952. Bar: Va. 1952, U.S. Supreme Ct 1971. Statis. analyst Dept. Agr., Baton Rouge, 1941; investigator VA, Washington, 1946-59; legal officer, dep., gen. counsel, asst. gen. counsel VA, 1959-79; pvt. practice law Arlington, Va., 1979—. Editor: Fed. Bar News, 1972-73. Pres. Aurora Hills Civic Assn., 1948-49; spl. asst. to treas. Com. of 100, 1979-81, chmn., 1982-83; pres. Children's Theater, 1968-69; trustee St. George's Episc. Ch., 1979—; chmn. Arlington County Fair Assn., 1979-83. Lt. col. AUS, 1941-46, ETO. Decorated Legion of Merit; recipient Disting. Svc. award, 1979, 3 Superior Performance awards, 1952-72, Outstanding Alumni award George Washington Law Sch., 1978. Mem. Fed. Bar Assn. (pres. D.C. chpt. 1970-71, nat. pres. 1978-79), Va. Bar Assn., Arlington County Bar Assn., Nat. Lawyers Club (dir.), Arlington Host Lions, Ft. Myer Officers Club. Home: 224 N Jackson St Arlington VA 22201-1253 Office: 2060 14th St N Ste 310 Arlington VA 22201-2519

MALONEY, FRANCIS PATRICK, physiatrist, educator; b. Pitts., Mar. 4, 1936; s. Francis Barrington and Esther Elizabeth (Kuhn) M.; m. Kathryn Brassell Anderson, June 25, 1960 (dec. June 6, 1987); children: Timothy J., Kevin P., J. Christopher; m. Billie Barbara Galloway, Feb. 14, 1990. BA, St. Vincent Coll., 1958; MD, U. Pitts., 1962; MPH, Johns Hopkins U., 1966. Diplomate Am. Bd. Phys. Medicine and Rehab., Am. Bd. Preventive Medicine, Am. Bd. Med. Mgmt. Intern St. Francis Hosp., Pitts., 1962-63; resident gen. preventive medicine Johns Hopkins U. Sch. of Hygiene & Pub. Health, Balt., 1965-67; fellow medicine, med. genetics Johns Hopkins U. Sch. of Medicine, Balt., 1966-68; resident phys. medicine and rehab. U. Minn., Mpls., 1968-70; staff physician Sister Kenny Inst., Mpls., 1970-72; asst. clin. prof. U. Minn., Mpls., 1970-72; asst. prof. phys. medicine and rehab., assoc. prof. U. Colo., Denver, 1972-78, 78-84; prof. head div. of rehab. medicine U. Ark., Little Rock, 1984-91, prof., chmn. dept. phys. medicine and rehab., 1991—; med. dir. Bapt. Rehab. Inst., Little Rock, 1985—; chief rehab. medicine svc. VA Med. Ctr., Little Rock, 1984—. Editor: Interdisciplinary Rehabilitation of Multiple Sclerosis and Neuromuscular Disease, 1984; editor, author: Physical Medicine & Rehabilitation State of the Art Reviews, 1987, Primer on Management, 1987, Rehabilitation of Aging, 1989, Management for Rehabilitation Medicine II, 1993; alt. editor: Archives of Physical Medicine and Rehabilitation, 1989-93. Mem. exec. bd. Greater No. Colo. Chpt. of Muscular Dystrophy Assn. of Am., 1972-82; spl. edn. adv. com. Cherry Creek Sch. Dist., Denver, 1975, vice chmn., 1976, chmn., 1977; med. advisor Denver Commn. on Disabled and Coun. on Aging, Denver, 1980-82, Denver Commn. on Human Svcs., 1982-84; external examiner King Saud U. Med. Sch., Saudi Arabia, 1983; med. adv. bd. Ark. Multiple Sclerosis Soc., Little Rock, 1985-88; chmn. chmn's. coun. Assn. Acad. Physiatrists, Indpls., 1992-94. Fellow Am. Acad. Phys. and Rehab.; mem. AMA, Am. Congress of Rehab. Medicine, Am. Acad. Cerebral Palsy, Am. Pub. Health Assn., Am. Bd. Physical Medicine and Rehbilitation (dir. 1988—), Soc. for Exptl. Biology and Medicine, Assn. Acad. Physiatrists, Ark. Med. Soc., Pulaski County Med. Soc., Soc. for Neuroscis. Office: U Ark Med Scis 4301 W Markham Slot #602 Little Rock AR 72205

MALONEY, J. PATRICK, minister, educator, seminary administrator; b. Pitts., Feb. 19, 1929; s. James Deasy and Helen (Crouse) M.; m. Bettie Jean Silvus, Dec. 1, 1953; children: Sharon Shakespeare, Lori Spencer, Mitzi Kelley. BA, Jacksonville U., 1961; BD, New Orleans Bapt. Theol. Sem., 1964; PhD, St. Marys Sem. and U., Balt., 1973. Ordained to ministry So. Bapt. Conv., 1960. Pastor Fairfield Bapt. Chapel, Jacksonville, Fla., 1958-61, 1st Bapt. Ch., Thomas, La., 1963-64, Hayne Boulevard Bapt. Ch., New Orleans, 1964-67, Kent Bapt. Ch., Landover, Md., 1969-77, Fisher Rd. Bapt. Ch., 1977-83, Mission Oaks Bapt. Ch., East Ridge, Tenn., 1983—; prof. Sem. Extension So. Bapt. Conv., Nashville, 1973—; acad. v.p. Oxford Grad. Sch., Dayton, Tenn., 1982-86; dir. Mission Oaks Sem. Extension Ctr., East Ridge, 1990—; corr. sec. Bapt. Mins. Conf. Chattanooga, 1991-94. Mem. Soc. Bibl. Lit., Cath. Theol. Soc. Am., Evang. Theol. Soc., Near East Archaeol. Soc., Oxford Soc. Scholars. Home: 1210 John Ross Rd Chattanooga TN 37412-1466

MALONEY, JAMES EDWARD, lawyer; b. Hackensack, N.J., Apr. 28, 1951; s. Edward James Maloney and Kathleen Elizabeth (Lamont) Leaf. BA, Yale U., 1972; JD, Harvard U., 1975. Bar: Tex. 1975, U.S. Dist. Ct. (no., so., ea. and we. dists.) Tex., U.S. Ct. Appeals (2d, 3d, 5th, 9th and D.C. cirs.), U.S. Supreme Ct. Assoc. Baker & Botts, Houston, 1975-82, ptnr., 1982—; chmn. bd. dirs. Fotofest, Inc.; bd. dirs. Houston Ctr. for Photography. Trustee Woodberry Forest (Va.) Sch., 1991—. Mem. ABA, Tex. Bar Assn., Tex. Bar Found., Houston Bar Assn., Houston Bar Found., Yale Club (Houston, Assn. Yale Alumni rep. 1984-86). Republican. Episcopalian. Home: 2129 Tangley St Houston TX 77005-1640 Office: Baker & Botts 3000 One Shell Plz 910 Louisiana St Houston TX 77002

MALONEY, MICHAEL JAMES, allergist, pediatrician; b. Ft. Stewart, Ga., Apr. 15, 1956; s. Charles Shaw and Martha Sue (Drake) M.; m. Sherry Lea De Loach, Dec. 17, 1983; children: Jacob Michael, Luke James, Grace Ellington. AA, Emory U., 1975, BA in Chemistry, 1977; MD, Med. Coll. Ga., 1981. Diplomate Am. Bd. Pediatrics, Am. Bd. Allergy and Immunology. Intern Charlotte Meml. Hosp., 1981-82, resident in pediats., 1982-83; resident in pediats. Med. Coll. Ga., Augusta, 1983-84, fellow allergy and immunology, 1984-86; with Lanier Pk. Regional Hosp. and N.E. Georgia Med. Ctr., Gainesville, Ga.; pvt. practice Gainesville, 1986—. Contbr. articles to med. jours. Fellow Am. Acad. Allergy and Immunology, Am. Coll. Allergists; mem. AMA, Ga. Thoracic Soc., Kiwanis. Republican. Methodist. Home: 520 Jesse Jewell Pky Gainesville GA 30501-3779

MALONEY, ROBERT B., federal judge; b. 1933. BBA, So. Meth. U., 1956, Postgrad., 1960. Asst. dist. atty. County of Dallas, 1961-62; ptnr. Watts, Stallings & Maloney, 1962-65, Maloney, Miller & McDowell, 1966-75, Maloney & McDowell, 1976-78, Maloney & Hardcastle, 1979-80, Maloney & Maloney, 1981-84; assoc. judge Tex. Ct. Appeals (5th cir.), Tex., 1983-85; judge U.S. Dist. Ct. (no. dist.) Tex., Dallas, 1985—. State rep., Austin, Tex., 1973-82. Mem. Tex. Bar Assn. Office: US Dist Ct 1100 Commerce St, Rm 15 E 26 Dallas TX 75242-1027*

MALONEY, SEAN ROBERT, physician, biomedical engineer; b. L.A., Feb. 21, 1949; s. Robert Edward and Virginia Elizabeth (Walsh) M.; m. Susan Marie Howard, Aug. 15, 1981; children: Michael Patrick, Matthew Robert. BSChemE, BS in Phys. Scis., U. Calif., Davis, 1975; MD, Emory U., 1980; MS in Mech. Engring., Stanford U., 1984. Diplomate Am. Bd. Electrodiagnostic Medicine, Nat. Bd. Med. Examiners, Am. Bd. Phys. Medicine and Rehab. Process control engr. Atlantic Richfield and Hanford (Wash.) Co., 1975-76; intern/resident phys. medicine and rehab. Stanford (Calif.) U., 1980-83; asst. med. dir., dir. spinal cord injury unit Thoms Rehab. Hosp., Asheville, N.C., 1984-85; pvt. med. practice Asheville, 1985—; sole proprietor, biomedical engr. Sean R. Maloney & Co., Asheville, 1989—; asst. clin. prof. surgery orthop./rehab. Bowman Gray Sch. Medicine, 1995—; presenter in field. Article reviewer Archives Phys. Medicine & Rehab., 1988—; patentee intraoral controller. Col. Asheville Buncombe County Christian Mission Free Med. Clinic, 1992—. With U.S. Army, 1968-72. Grantee Nat. Inst. Neurol. Disorders and Stroke, 1990, 92-93, 96—, Bapt. Hosp. Inc., 1995—. Fellow AICE, Am. Assn. Electrodiagnostic Medicine, Am. Acad. Phys. Medicine and Rehab., Am. Med. Soc. Democrat. Roman Catholic. Home: 405 Sondley Woods Pl Asheville NC 28805-1156 Office: Sean R Maloney & Co 60 Livingston St Ste 300 Asheville NC 28801-4400

MALORZO, THOMAS VINCENT, lawyer; b. Rome, N.Y., Jan. 10, 1947; s. Helen Adeline (Grande) M.; m. CAtherine Marie Healy, Dec. 28, 1968; children: Amy, Craig, Mary, Thomas Jr. BA, Walsh U., Canton, Ohio, 1969; JD, Cleve. State U., 1979. Bar: Ohio 1979, Tex. 1981, U.S. Dist. Ct. (no. dist.) Ohio 1980, U.S. Dist. Ct. (no. dist.) Tex. 1981, U.S. Patent Office 1980, U.S. Ct. Appeals (7th cir.) 1994. Environ. regulations analyst Diamond Shamrock Corp., Dallas, 1979-81; ind. adv. counsel Southwestern Corp., Dallas, 1981-83; staff atty. NCH Corp., Irving, Tex., 1983-89; gen. counsel Wormald US, Inc., Dallas, 1989-90; patent atty. Otis Engring. Corp., Carrollton, Tex., 1990-93; pvt. practice Addison, Tex., 1993-95; ptnr. Falk, Vestal & Fish LLP, 1995-96; pvt. practice Addison, Tex., 1996—; asst. prof. law Dallas/Ft. Worth Sch. Law, Irving, Tex., 1990-92. Dist. com. Circle 10 Boy Scouts Am., Dallas, 1985—; first aid team ARC, Cleve., 1972-80. Mem. State Bar Tex. (chmn. trademark com. intellectual property sect. 1989). Office: 15800 Addison Rd Ste 112 Dallas TX 75248

MALOUF, EDWARD WAYNE, lawyer; b. Dallas, Oct. 14, 1957; s. Edward Malouf and Marie Moossy; m. Marianne M. Walder, Feb. 11, 1984; children: Natalie, Anastasia, Monica. BA in English, St. Mary's U., San Antonio, 1980, JD, 1986; MA in Social Scis., U. Chgo., 1987. Bar: Tex. 1987, U.S. Ct. Appeals (5th cir.) 1990, U.S. Supreme Ct. 1990, U.S. Dist. Ct. (no. dist.) Tex. 1991. Tchr. Bishop Lynch High Sch., Dallas, 1983; briefing atty. to Justice Blair Reeves Ct. Appeals (4th cir.), San Antonio, 1986-87; atty. Brock & Kelfer, P.C., San Antonio, 1987-89, Milgrim, Thomajan & Lee, Dallas, 1989, Hutchison, Boyle, Brooks & Fisher, Dallas, 1989-91; pvt. practice Dallas, 1991—. Editor, writer Air Force News Svc., 1981. Chmn. bd. of advocates St. Mary's U. Sch. of Law, 1985. Mem. State Bar Tex. (jour. com. 1988-92), Nat. Order of Barristers (E. Davila Jr. award for Excellence in trial advocacy 1986). Office: 2651 N Harwood St Ste 360 Dallas TX 75201-1563

MALSEED, LYNN MARIE, child and adolescent psychiatrist; b. Houston, Nov. 15, 1951; d. William A. Malseed and Jeanne Marie (Carter) Bowen; m. J.R. Mayo, 1978 (div. 1980); 1 child, James David Mayo; m. Joseph Charles Luspin, Aug. 18, 1990; children: Jason, Audra, David. BA summa cum laude, Rice U., 1973; MD, U. Tex. Med. Br., 1977. Eligible diplomate Am. Bd. Gen. Psychiatry. Resident in pediatrics U. Tex. Health Sci. Ctr., Houston, 1977-79, fellow in child devel., 1979-80; chief pediatrics Dyess AFB, Abilene, Tex., 1980-81, Bergstrom AFB, Austin, Tex., 1981-82; fellow in child and adolescent psychiatry Baylor Coll. Medicine, Houston, 1983-85, resident in adult psychiatry, 1985-87; med. dir. attention deficit hyperactivity disorder svcs. Cypress Creek Hosps., Houston, 1987-90; svc. chief ADHD programs Baywood Hosp., Houston, 1991-93, svc. chief Therapeutic Sch., 1992-93; child and adolescent psychiatrist Wetcher Clinic, Houston, 1991-95; psychiatrist for Mental Health Svcs. MHMRA of Harris County, 1995—; unit dir. Youth Dual Diagnosis Clinic, 1995—; lectr. in field; speaker A.M. Houston TV show, 1993. Contbr. rsch. articles to med. jours. Capt. USAF-M.C., 1980-82. Mem. Tex. Attention Deficit Assn. (lectr.), Harris County Med. Soc., Bay Area Power Squadron, Phi Beta Kappa, Mu Delta Pi. Republican. Roman Catholic. Office: MHMRA of Harris County 2850 Fannin Houston TX 77002

MALT, CAROL NORA, art museum director; b. Glenridge, N.J., Dec. 3, 1942; d. George E. and Hazel Marie (Yarboro) Tubb; m. Harold Lewis Malt; 1 child, Nora. BA, U. Miami, Coral Gables, Fla., 1978, MA, 1980, PhD, 1986. Asst. dir. Gulf Am. Galleries mus., Miami, Fla., 1965-69; gallery owner Hotchkiss Galleries, Miami, 1969-70; registrar, curator Lowe Art Mus., Coral Gables, 1970-78; dir. Art and Culture Ctr. of Hollywood, Fla., 1979-86, Albany (Ga.) Mus. Art, 1987-90, Pensacola Mus., 1991—; bd. dirs.

Ctr. for Design Planning, Washington, 1978—; grant reviewer So. Arts Fedn., Atlanta, 1982—, IMS, State of Fla.; spkr. various civic and youth groups, Leadership Pensacola. Author over 30 mus. catalogs, 1973—; curator over 60 exhbns., 1973—; contbr. articles, revs. to art jours. and mags.; editor Arts & the Islamic World, 1982—. Vol. Miami Pub. Libr., 1974-83; hostess visitor program svc. Meridian House Internat., Washington, 1980-86; bd. dirs. Folk Art Ctr. for the Americas, Miami, 1985—. Fellow, Explorers Club, 1985. Mem. Ga. Assn. Mus. and Galleries, Southeast Mus. Coun. (com. mem. 1988-89), Am. Assn. Mus., Internat. Coun. Mus. (Ga. rep. 1989), DAR, AAM, FAMDA.

MALVIN, FREDERICK BAGE, accountant; b. Syracuse, N.Y., Oct. 3, 1932; s. Robert Bage and Mary (Ross) M.; children: Cynthia Cameron, Robert Bage. BA, Coll. William and Mary, 1955; MA, George Washington U., 1970, Naval War Coll., 1975; postgrad., Marshall Wythe Law Sch., Williamsburg, 1983-85. Pres., CEO Century Devel. Co., Norfolk, Va., 1970-90; v.p. Hampton Rds. Wholesalers, Newport News, 1988-90; mng. ptnr., acct. Malvin, Riggins & Co., Newport News, 1986—; tax ptnr. Hall Cotman, Newport News, 1984-86. Chmn. bd. Peninsula Drug Rehab. Svcs., Inc., Newport News, 1986-90; pres. Friends of the Homeless, 1987-93; treas. St. Stephen's Ch. Found., 1987-90; v.p. Boys Club of Va. Peninsula, 1985-96. Cmdr. USN, 1956-79. Mem. AICPA's, Va. Soc. CPA's, Peninsula Soc. CPA's. Episcopalian. Office: Malvin Riggins & Co 12350 Jefferson Ave Ste 160 Newport News VA 23602-6951

MAMMEN, SAM, publishing executive, entrepreneur; b. Kerala, India, June 22, 1949; came to U.S., 1972; s. K.O. and Mariamma M.; m. Lori J. Hummel, Dec. 20, 1973; children: Sarah Nalini, Suzanne Kamala, Christopher Ashok. BS in Biology and Chemistry, U. Kerala, 1969; MA in English Lit., Kanpur (India) U., 1971; MA in Edn., U. Tex., San Antonio, 1979. Cert. profl. supr., Tex. Edn. Agy. Tchr. St. James Sch., San Antonio, 1973-76, St. Gerard Sch., San Antonio, 1976-77, Comal Ind. Sch. Dist., Bulverde, Tex., 1978-83; owner Ednl. Cons. Svc., San Antonio, 1982-86; pres. ECS Learning Systems, Inc., San Antonio, 1986—; coach Tex. Future Problem Solving Program State Finals, 1981-83. Founding pres. Assn. Educators Gifted Students, San Antonio, 1980-81; pres. San Antonio Assn. for Gifted and Talented Children, San Antonio, 1987-88. Teaching grantee Tex. Assn. for the Improvement Reading, 1978, Tchr. Tng. grantee Tex. Dept. Human Resources, 1986; Grad. Student scholar Nat. Assn. for Gifted Children, 1983. Mem. Ednl. Press Assn. Am. (regional rep. 1993-94), Am. Creativity Assn., Ednl. Dealers and Suppliers Assn., Nat. Sch. Supply and Equipment Assn., India/Asia Entrepreneur's Assn., Tex. Assn. for the Gifted and Talented (charter mem., 2d v.p. 1981-82, exec. bd. dirs. 1979-82). Office: ECS Learning Systems Inc PO Box 791437 San Antonio TX 78279-1437

MAMMINO, JERE JOSEPH, dermatologist; b. Lowr Merion, Pa., Dec. 12, 1956; s. Joseph John and Dorothy Emma Mammino; m. Wendy Sencenbach, June 21, 1980; children: Julie, Jennifer, Jason. BS in Biochemsitry cum laude, Albright Coll., 1978; DO, Phila Coll. Osteo. Medicine, 1982. Diplomate Am. Bd. Dermatology, Am. Osteo. Bd. Dermatology, Nat. Bd. Osteo. Examiners; lic. N.J., Ohio, Fla., N.C. Intern Kennedy Meml. Hosps. U. Med. Ctr., Voorhees, N.J., 1982-83; resident Nat. Naval Med. Ctr., Bethesda, Md., 1986-89; asst. clin. prof. dept. dermatology Wright State U. Sch. Medicine, Dayton, Ohio, 1989-91; clin. dermatologist pvt. practice, Greensboro, N.C., 1991-92, Winter Park, Fla., 1992—; dir. dermatology residency program Fla. Hosp., Orlando, 1994—. Contbr. articles to profl. jours. Maj. USAF, 1983-91. Decorated Air Force Commendation medal with Oak Leaf Cluster. Fellow Am. Acad. Dermatology, Am. Osteopathic Coll. Dermatology (vice chmn. tng. examination com. 1990—, mem. edn. evaluating com. 1992—); mem. Am. Osteopathic Assn., Ctrl. Fla. Soc. Dermatology (treas. 1994-95). Home: 753 Bear Creek Cir Winter Springs FL 32708-3892 Office: Advanced Dermatology Ctr 1410 W Broadway St Ste 102 Oviedo FL 32765-6537

MANAKER, ARNOLD MARTIN, mechanical engineer, consultant; b. N.Y.C., Feb. 11, 1947; s. Paul Bernard and Rose Norma (Malakoff) M.; m. Ellen Conant, Nov. 21, 1970; children: Ryan Scott, Heidi Cora, Jana Ashley. BSME, Newark Coll. of Eng., 1968; MS in Mech. Engring., U. Mass., 1970, PhD in Mech. Engring., 1973. Asst. to plant engr. J. Wiss & Sons Co., Newark, 1965-68; rsch. asst. Dept. Mech. and Aerospace Engring., U. Mass., Amherst, 1968-73, teaching asst., 1970-72; pvt. practice cons., 1972—; staff engr., Clinch River Breeder Reaction Project TVA, Oak Ridge, 1976-77; mech. engr. TVA, Chattanooga, 1977-79, project mgr. adv. energy, 1979, project mgr. AFBC R & D, 1979-81, project mgr. AFBC Demonstration Plant, 1984-88, AFBC devel. project engr., 1988-91, mgr. NOx/CEMS projects, 1991—; adminstrv. asst. NASA, 1968-69; rsch. asst. NSF, 1971-73. Contbr. numerous articles to profl. jours. Vol. United Way Leadership Club, 1987-92, Friends Always Indian Guide Program/YMCA, 1988-92. Named Engr. of Yr., TVA, 1989; recipient Product Champion award EPRI, 1992. Fellow ASME (officer coms.). Jewish. Home: 9420 Mountain Shadows Dr Chattanooga TN 37421-3444 Office: TVA PO Box 2000 Stevenson AL 35772-2000

MANCINI, MARY CATHERINE, cardiothoracic surgeon, researcher; b. Scranton, Pa., Dec. 15, 1953; d. Peter Louis and Ferminia Teresa (Massi) M. BS in Chemistry, U. Pitts., 1974, MD, 1978; postgrad. in Anatomy and Cellular Biolog, La. State U. Med. Ctr., 1994—. Diplomate Am. Bd. Surgery (speciality cert. critical care medicine), Am. Bd. Thoracic Surgery. Intern in surgery U. Pitts., 1978-79, resident in surgery, 1979-87; fellow pediatric cardiac surgery Mayo Clinic, 1987-88; asst. prof. surgery, dir. cardiothoracic transplantation Med. Coll. Ohio, Toledo, 1988-91; assoc. prof. surgery, dir. cardiothoracic transplantation La. State U. Med. Ctr., Shreveport, 1991—. Author: Operative Techniques for Medical Students, 1983; contbr. articles to profl. jours. Rsch. grantee Am. Heart Assn., 1988; recipient Pres. award Internat. Soc. Heart Transplantation, 1983, Charles C. Moore Tchg. award U. Pitts., 1985, Internat. Woman of Yr. award Internat. Biog. Inst., Eng., 1992-93, Internat. Order of Merit award, 1995, Nina S. Braunwald Career Devel. award Thoracic Surgery Found. Fellow ACS, Am. Coll. Chest Physicians, Internat. Coll. Surgeons (councillor 1991—); mem. Assn. Women Surgeons, Rotary (gift of life program 1991). Roman Catholic. Office: La State U Med Ctr 1501 Kings Hwy Shreveport LA 71103-4228

MANDA, JOSEPH ALEXANDER, III, veterinary consulting executive; b. Orange, N.J., Jan. 17, 1952; s. Joseph Alexander and Caroline (Barnes) M. BS in Edn., Okla. State U., 1973, BS, 1978; MS, Rutgers U., 1979; DVM, Universidad Nacional de Pedro Henriquez Urena, Santo Domingo, Dominican Republic, 1981; MBA, Hood Coll., Frederick, Md., 1989; cert. in veterinary practice adminstrn., Purdue U., Am. Animal Hosp. Veterinarian Cameron Animal Hosp., Montclair, N.J., 1981-82; veterinarian, mgr. Whitesburg (Ky.) Animal Clinic, 1982-83; rsch. assoc. Coll. Vet. Medicine, U. Wis., Madison, 1983-84; vet. researcher W.Va. U. Sch. Medicine, Morgantown, 1984-86; sr. veterinarian/prin. investigator Hazelton Labs./Am., Rockville, Md., 1986-90; pres., CEO Vet. Consulting Corp., Gainesville, Fla., 1984—; asst. dir. U. Fla. Biotech. Inst., Gainesville, 1990-93; adj. prof. Coll. Vet. Medicine, U. Fla., Gainesville, 1990—; lectr. various profl. orgns., 1986—; radio talk show host WPAZ Radio. Author: Problems in Management, 1992; contbr. articles to profl. jours. Grantee Bionetics Corp., Rockville, Md., 1986-90, NIH, Rockville, 1986-90, USDA/State Fla., Alachua, 1990-93. Mem. Am. Vet. Medicine Assn., Am. Assn. Lab. Animal Sci. (nat. steering com., editorial rev. bd. jours. 1991—), Am. Assn. Lab. Animal Practitioners, Am. Heartworm Soc., Am. Animal Hosp. Assn. (nat. mgmt. com. 1992), Gainesville Area Innovation Network. Office: care 28 Battle Hill Rd Basking Ridge NJ 07920

MANDANIS, ALICE SUBLEY, academic official. V.p. acad. affairs Marymount Coll. Va., Arlington, until 1987; provost Marymount U., Arlington, 1987—. Mem. Southern Assn. Colls. and Schs. (bd. trustees). Office: Marymount U School of Arts & Sciences 2807 N Glebe Rd Arlington VA 22207-4224*

MANDEL, MARILYN, community planner, medical assistant; b. Norfolk, Va., Jan. 2, 1943. BS in Urban Studies, Ga. State U., 1979; postgrad., Old Dominion U., 1980-81; AS in Med. Assisting, Keiser Coll., Ft. Lauderdale, Fla., 1996. Adminstrv. mgr. Howard, Needles, Tammen & Bergendoff, Richmond, Va., 1975-76; adminstrv. mgr., urban environ. specialist Howard, Needles, Tammen & Bergendoff, Atlanta, 1976-79; legis. asst. Va. Gen. Assembly-Ho. Dels., Richmond, 1980-85; planning/policy analysis mgr. Va. Dept. Labor and Industry, Richmond, 1985-94; mem. EEO adv. com. Va. Dept. Labor and Industry, 1991-93, chmn., 1991-93. Chpt. pres. Women's Am. ORT, 1971-73, regional v.p., 1972-73; vol. Va. Opera-Children's Opera Theater, Norfolk, 1979-84; mem. U.S. Com. for Israel's Environ., 1980-83; gov.'s loaned exec. United Way Svcs., Richmond, 1990; v.p. Regency Woods Condo Assn., Richmond, 1992-93, pres., 1993-94. Recipient Cert. of Appreciation, Cen. Va. Safety Coun., 1987, 88. Mem. Commonwealth Mgrs. Assn. (treas. 1992-95).

MANDELKER, LESTER, veterinarian; b. Memphis, July 31, 1945; s. Maurice and Alice (Herman) M.; m. Brenda Conger, Oct. 21, 1989; children: Zev and Blakelee (twins). BS, Mich. State U., 1968, DVM, 1969. Assoc. veterinarian Yarbrough Animal Hosp., Miami, Fla., 1969-71, Gulf Bay Animal Hosp., Clearwater, Fla., 1971-72; owner, dir. Cmty. Vet. Hosp., Largo, Fla., 1972—; mem. Am. Bd. Vet. Practitioners; mem. adv. bd. Vet. Forum, N.Y.C., 1980—, Vetoquinol USA, Inc., Tampa, Fla., 1996—; computer specialist, pharmacology operator Network of Animal Health, Chgo., 1995—. Author: Veterinary Practice Tips I, 1980, II, 1985, Pharmaceutical Index, 1994. Founder, past pres. Class Inc., Clearwater, 1973-80. Mem. AVMA, Am. Animal Hosp. Assn., Pinellas County Vet. Med. Soc. (past pres.). Jewish. Office: Cmty Vet Hosp 1631 W Bay Dr Largo FL 33770

MANDELL, HAROLD LANCE, internist, hematologist; b. Wiesbaden, Germany, Jan. 21, 1964; arrived in U.S., 1964; s. Harold and Frances Elaine (Oliver) M.; m. Susan Catherine Cohen, Aug. 6, 1989. BS magna cum laude in Computer Sci., Tex. A&M U., 1986; MD, Baylor U., 1990. Diplomate Am. Bd. Internal Medicine. Resident internal medicine Baylor Coll. Medicine, Houston, 1990-93, clin. instr., 1993-95, chief resident internal medicine, 1994, fellow hematology, 1993-95; pvt. practice Atlanta, 1995-96, Ft. Worth, 1996—. Pres. endowed scholar Tex. A&M U., College Station, 1982-86. Mem. Am. Coll. Physicians, Am. Soc. Hematology, Am. Soc. Internal Medicine. Office: Ft Worth Clinic Ste 300 909 9th Ave Fort Worth TX 76104

MANDELSTAMM, ALLAN BERYLE, economics educator, consultant; b. Saginaw, Mich., Oct. 18, 1928; s. Jonas and Helen G. (Weinburg) M.; m. Maria T. Buhlmeyer, Sept. 1, 1967. B.A., U. Mich., 1950, M.A., 1951, Ph.D., 1962. Instr. Northwestern U., Evanston, Ill., 1957-59; asst. prof. Vanderbilt U., Nashville, 1959-63; assoc. prof. Mich. State U., East Lansing, 1963-67, prof., 1967-74; prof. econs. Va. Poly. Inst. and State U., Blacksburg, 1974-90, prof. emertus, econ. cons., 1990—; vis. prof. Dartmouth Coll., 1970, U. Fla., 1972; cons. Dept. State, AID, U.S. Dept. Labor, others. Contbr. articles to profl. jours. and encys. Recipient Disting. Teaching award Mich. State U., 1968, Best Prof. award U. Fla., 1972, Va. Poly. Inst., 1976, 77, Sporn award, 1987; Rockefeller Found. grantee, 1958-62. Mem. AAUP, Am. Econ. Assn., Indsl. Rels. Rsch. Assn., Acad. Polit. Sci., Va. Assn. Scholars (treas.). Home: 600 Landsdowne Dr Blacksburg VA 24060-5926

MANDOR, LEONARD STEWART, real estate company executive; b. Bklyn., Oct. 2, 1946; s. Harris and Helen (Roth) M.; m. Yolande Rosario, June, 1973; children: Samantha, Melissa; m. Sandra Doolittle, Apr. 9, 1983 (div. 1990); 1 child, Gregory. BBA, Kent State U., 1968. Tchr. Pub. Sch. 3, Jersey City, 1969-70; exec. and sales mgr. Paragon Securities, N.Y.C., 1971-72; acct. exec. Merrill Lynch, N.Y.C., 1972-74; exec., mgr. E.N.I. Corp., Seattle, 1974-75; chmn. bd. Stonhenge Capital Corp., N.Y.C., 1975-81; chmn. bd. Concord Assets Group, Boca Raton, Fla., 1981—, also CEO, pres. With U.S. Army, 1970-71. Mem. United Jewish Appeal. Office: Concord Assets Group 5200 Town Center Cir Boca Raton FL 33486-1015*

MANDRAKE, MARK WAYNE, actor; b. Ft. Worth, Dec. 8, 1954; s. Joe Burkett and Viola Marie (Wooten) Mapes. Student, U. Tex., Arlington, 1973-74, Harkness House Ballet, 1974. Dancer Dallas Met. Ballet, Ft. Worth, 1970-75; actor, film, stage Dallas, 1975—; rec. engr. Phil York's 24-track, Dallas, 1987. Author: (poetry) Whatever Face, 1991; logos: I Am the Word, Noel and Leon, 1990, A Cheerful Earful; writer plays and screenplays, composer (rock musical) Playing It By Ear, 1989; producer, performer (record album) It's Time to Fly, 1987 (1st album produced, performed by deaf man); lyricist, composer over 200 songs. Deaf activist, Dallas, AIDS activist, Dallas. Harkness House Ballet scholar, N.Y.C., 1974. Mem. Broadcast Music Inc. Democrat. Office: PO Box 190248 Dallas TX 75219-0248

MANDRI, DANIEL FRANCISCO, psychiatrist; b. Camaguey, Cuba, Apr. 22, 1950; came to U.S., 1962; s. Adalberto Froilan and Estrella (Pereiro) M.; m. Monica A. Ruffing, May 21, 1983; children: Nicholas, Natalie. MD, U. Cen. Del Este, Dominican Republic, 1977. Diplomate Am. Bd. Psychiatry and Neurology. With internal medicine PGY-1 Christ Hosp., Oak Lawn, Ill., 1979-80; with psychiatry PGY 2 plus 3 U. Miami/Jackson Meml. Hosp., Miami, Fla., 1980-82, chief resident psychiatry, 1982-83; pvt. practice psychiatry Coral Gables, Fla., 1983-86; dir. acute care unit Broward County Mental Health Div., Hollywood, Fla., 1986-87; dir. psychiat. svcs. Douglas Gardens Community Mental Health Ctr., Miami, 1987—, Douglas Gardens Home and Hosp. for the Aged, Miami, 1989-92; asst. instr. psychiatry dept. of psychiatry U. Miami, 1982-83. Mem. N.Y. Acad. Scis., Am. Psychiatry Assn., World Psychiat. Assn., World Fedn. for Mental Health, Am. Assn. Community Psychiatrists. Office: Douglas Gardens Cmty Mental Health Ctr 701 Lincoln Rd Miami FL 33139-2879

MANESS, DIANE MEASE, pediatrics nurse; b. McDowell County, N.C., Oct. 8, 1958; d. C. Nelson Jr. and Rose Marie (Dover) Mease; m. Edwin Clinton Maness III, July 17, 1981; 1 child, Mackenzie Brooke. ADN, Western Piedmont Community Col, 1979; BSN, U. N.C., Charlotte, 1989. RN, N.C. Pediatric staff nurse Grace Hosp., Morganton, N.C., 1979-80; staff nurse neonatal ICU Scott and White Hosp., Temple, Tex., 1981; staff nurse pediatric and newborn svcs. Glen R. Frye Meml. Hosp., Hickory, N.C., 1981; coord. neonatal and pediatric home care Presbyn. Hosp., Charlotte, 1986-88, primary, staff and charge nurse pediatrics, neonatal ICU, 1982-94; nurse pediatric neurosurgery Charlotte Neurosurg. Assoc., 1990; neonatal ICU nurse Mercy South, Charlotte, 1993-94; presenter workshop in field. Mem. Sigma Theta Tau.

MANGAN, PATRICIA ANN PRITCHETT, research statistician; b. Hammond, Ind., Feb. 4, 1953; d. Edward Clayton and Helen Josephine (Mills) Pritchett; m. William Paul Mangan, Aug. 30, 1980; 1 child, Ryan Christopher. BS in Maths. and Stats., Purdue U., 1975, MS in Applied Stats., 1977. Tobacco devel. statistician R.J. Reynolds Tobacco Co., Winston-Salem, N.C., 1978-82, R&D statistician, 1982-86, sr. R&D statistician, 1986-90, sr. staff R&D statistician, 1990-93; dir. software devel. ARJAY Equipment Corp., Winston-Salem, N.C., 1993—; cons. Lab. for Application of Remote Sensing, West Lafayette, Ind., 1976-77; statis. engr. Corning Glass Works, Harrodsburg, Ky., 1977. Editor Jour. of Sensory Studies, 1992—; contbr. articles to sci. jours. Rep. United Way, Winston-Salem, 1985. Recipient G.R. DiMarco award, 1990, Excaliber award for Outstanding Performance, 1991, 93. Mem. Am. Statis. Assn., Wash. Statis. Assn., Purdue Alumni Assn. Office: RJ Reynolds PO Box 1487 Winston Salem NC 27102-1487

MANGANARIS, STEFANOS, computer scientist; b. Patras, Greece, Sept. 24, 1966; came to U.S., 1989; s. Panayotis and Heleni (Kalligeris) M.; m. Theodosia A. Kalfa, June 15, 1994. Diploma in computer engring. with honors, U. Patras, Greece, 1989; MS in Computer Sci., Vanderbilt U., 1991, PhD in Computer Sci., 1996. Operator Computer Tech. Inst., Patras, 1986-87, sys. adminstr., 1987-88, sys. programmer, 1988-89; cons. Pvt. Sch., Patras, 1988; lab. asst. Vanderbilt U., Nashville, 1989-90, tchg. asst., 1991, rsch. asst., 1990-91, 92-95; cons. air ops. divsn., info. svcs. Fed. Express Corp., Memphis, 1990; assoc. rsch. scientist Honeywell, Inc. Sys. & Rsch. Ctr., Mpls., 1992-93; summer intern Artificial Intelligence Br. NASA Ames Rsch. Ctr., Moffett Field, Calif., 1992, 93; sr. analyst data mining solutions IBM Almaden Rsch. Ctr., San Jose, Calif., 1996—; participant various presentations, panels, tutorials. Contbr. articles to profl. jours. Mem. IEEE, Computer Soc. of IEEE, Assn. Computing Machinery, Am. Assn. Artificial Intelligence. Office: IBM Data Mining Solutions Almaden Rsch Ctr Dept N3LC/D2 650 Harry Rd San Jose CA 95120 also: Computer Sci Dept Vanderbilt U Box 1679 Sta B Nashville TN 37235

MANGAPIT, CONRADO, JR., manufacturing company executive; b. Cavite, Philippines, Oct. 17, 1946; s. Conrado Lebang Sr. and Amparo Ajuste (Odion) M.; m. Rosalinda Martinez Travis, Dec. 19, 1970; 1 child, Regina. BEE, U. So. Calif., Los Angeles, 1969; MA in Human Resource Mgmt., Pepperdine U., 1978. Commd. ensign USN, 1969, advanced through grades to lt. comdr., resigned, 1979; project engr. Continental Can Co., Houston, 1979-80; applications engr. Toshiba Houston Internat. Corp., 1980-83, asst. mktg. mgr., asst. product mgr., 1983, mgr. mktg., products, 1983-89, mgr. power apparatus div., 1989-96, mktg. mgr. packaging group, 1995-96, dir. ops.-contract, 1995-96, mktg. mgr. switchgear products group, 1996—. Advisor Filipino-U.S. Mil. Assn., Guam, 1977-78; co. rep. Japan-Am. Soc., Houston, 1985—. Recipient Humanitarian Service medal U.S. Dept. Def., 1978; named Outstanding Young Man of Am. U.S. Jaycees, 1980. Mem. IEEE, Am. Mgmt. Assn. Republican. Roman Catholic. Clubs: Mission Bend Homeowners Assn. (Houston). Office: Toshiba-Houston Internat 13131 W Little York Rd Houston TX 77041-5807

MANGENA, VENKATA S. MURTY, microbiologist, researcher; b. Lakkavaram, India, Sept. 15, 1959; came to U.S., 1990; s. V. Gopala Rao and Anantha Lakshmi (Valavala) M.; m. Lakshmi M. Mangena, Mar. 23, 1988; children: Anantha Sameera, Viswanath D. BS in Biology and Chemistry, Andhra U., India, 1980, MS in Biochemistry, 1983; PhD in Chemistry, Indian Inst. Tech., Madras, 1989. Indian Coun. for Agr. Rsch. rsch. fellow Indian Inst. Tech., 1984-89, ad hoc rsch. asst., 1990; rsch. assoc. dept. chem. engring. and Sch. Biol. Scis., U. Ky., Lexington, 1993—. Author: Biological Degradation and Bioremediation of Toxic Chemicals, 1994; mem. editl. bd. Jour. Ind. Microbiology; contbr. articles and abstracts to sci. jours. Nat. merit scholar Govt. of India, 1980-82, sr. rsch. scholar Indian Inst. Tech., 1989; travel grantee Royal Soc., Eng., 1986, grantee U.S. Dept. Energy, 1992—. Mem. AAAS, Am. Soc. for Microbiology, Am. Chem. Soc. Home: D108 Shawneetown Dr Lexington KY 40503 Office: U Ky Dept Chem Engring 163 Anderson Hall Lexington KY 40506-0046

MANGIAPANE, JOSEPH ARTHUR, consulting company executive, applied mechanics consultant; b. N.Y.C., Aug. 1, 1926; s. Michael and Rose D'Amico M.; m. Marcia Balut, Oct. 30, 1954 (div. Apr. 1974); children: Rosemarie, Michael, Diana, Joseph J., Susan. BS, Fordham U., 1950. Stress analyst Republic Aviation, Farmingdale, N.Y., 1951-55; pvt. practice tech. cons., 1955-58; sect. mgr. Aerojet-Gen., Sacramento, 1958-61; project engr. Pratt & Whitney Aircraft, East Hartford, Conn., 1961-71; pvt. practice tech. cons., 1971-79; pres. Joseph A. Mangiapane & Assocs., Inc., Tampa, Fla., 1979-92. Author numerous tech. reports. Served as cpl. USAAF, 1945-47, ETO. Assoc. fellow AIAA; mem. Pine Acres Club (Wethersfield, Conn.) (pres. 1968-69). Republican. Roman Catholic. Home: 4713 W San Rafael St Tampa FL 33629-5507

MANGINO, STEPHEN JOSEPH, protective services official; b. Easton, Pa., May 23, 1960; s. Stephen Dominic and Dorothy Elaine (Wieser) M.; m. Griselda Leticia Mendosa, Oct. 18, 1992; children: Matthew, Stephen. BA in Journalism, Moravian Coll., 1982. Mgr. Clinton (N.J.) Racquet & Fitness, 1982-86; carrier U.S. Post Office, Phillipsburg, N.J., 1986-88; agt. U.S. Border Patrol, Laredo, Tex., 1988—; instr. Fed. Law Enforcement Tng. Ctr., 1994—. Dir. Williams Twp. Athletic Assn., Easton, 1979-82. Mem. Phi Alpha Theta.

MANGUS, CARL WILLIAM, technical safety and standards consultant, engineer; b. Broken Bow, Okla., Aug. 20, 1930; s. Nathaniel M. and Eva Tennessee (Johnson) M.; m. Dorotha Marie Wood; children: Steven Neal, Roy Gene, Carla Anne. BSME, Okla. State U., 1958. Registered profl. engr., La. Various positions, 1948-63; project mgr. Chalkley Gas Processing Plant, 1964; project devel. Seven Natural Gas Plants, 1965; project mgr. N. Terrebonne Plant Expansion & Dual 36 Pipeline Loop, 1966-67; with Project Devel.-Two Natural Gas Plants, 1967-68; project mgr. Calumet Gas Processing Plant, 1968, offshore engring. sect. leader facilities, 1969; offshore prodn. supt. Maintenance and Operating Standards, 1970; with tech. safety rev. & approval engring. procedures Plus Regulations and Industry Standards, 1971; mgr. regulatory affairs Shell Offshore Inc., 1982, sr. staff tech. safety specialist, 1985; pvt. practice tech. safety and standards Lacombe, La., 1986—; com. mem. Am. Bur. Shipping, N.Y.C., 1974-88; Dept. State cons. Internat. Maritime Orgn., London, 1975-79; Am. Petroleum Inst. rep. to Exploration/Prodn. Forum, London, 1979-83; com. mem. NAS, Washington, 1979-84; mem. spl. adv. ad hoc com. Internat. Assn. Drilling Contractors, Houston, 1978, human resources com., 1978-80; past mem. offshore operators com. Am. Petroleum Inst., New Orleans; past U.S. industry rep. safety code for constrn. offshore structures, ILO, Geneva. Staff sgt. USAF, 1951-55. Recipient Am. Petroleum citation for svc. Am. Petroleum Inst., 1987. Mem. La. Engring. Soc., Am. Soc. Safety Engrs., Gulf Coast Safety & Tng. Group, Soc. Petroleum Engrs., Pine Island Club. Republican. Home and Office: 59131 Cypress Bayou Ln Lacombe LA 70445-0250

MANHART, MARCIA Y(OCKEY), art museum director; b. Wichita, Kans., Jan. 14, 1943; d. Everett W. and Ruth C. (Correll) Yockey; children: Caroline Manhart Sanderson, Emily Alexandrea Morrison. BA in Art, U. Tulsa, 1965, MA in Ceramics, 1971. Dir. edn. Philbrook Art Ctr., Tulsa, 1972-77, exec. v.p., asst. dir., 1977-83, acting dir., 1983-84; exec. dir. Philbrook Mus. Art (formerly Philbrook Art Ctr.), Tulsa, 1984—; instr. Philbrook Art Ctr. Mus. Sch., Tulsa, 1963-72; gallery dir. Alexandre Hogue Gallery, Tulsa U., 1967-69; NEH Challenge Grant panelist, 1991, presenter to AAM Conv., 1991; MAAA Craft Fellowship panelist, 1988, 93, NEA Craft Fellowship panelist, 1990; curator nat. touring exhibit Nature's Forms/Nature's Forces: The Art of Alexandre Hogue, 1984-85; co-curator internat. exhbn.: The Eloquent Object, 1987-90; curator Sanford and Diane Besser Collection exhbn., 1992. Vis. com. Smithsonian Instn./Renwick Gallery, Washington, 1986; cultural negotiator Gov. George Nigh's World Trade Mission (Okla.), China., 1985; com. mem. State Art Coll. of Okla., 1985—; mem. Assocs. of Hillcrest Med. Ctr., 1983-88, exec. com., 1985-88; com. mem. Neighborhood Housing Services, 1985-87; mem. Mapleridge Hist. Dist. Assn., 1982—; steering com. Harwelden Isnt. for Aesthetic Edn., 1983; com. mem. River Parks Authority, 1976; mem. Jr. League of Tulsa Inc., 1974-78; adv. panel mem. Nat. Craft Planning Project, NEA, Washington, 1978-81; craft adv. panel mem. Okla. Arts and Humanities Council, 1974-76; juror numerous art festivals, competitions, programs; reviewer Inst. Mus. Services, Washington, 1985, 88, 92; auditor Symposium on Language & Scholarship of Modern Crafts, NEA and NEH, Washington, 1981; nominator MacArthur Fellows Program, 1988. Recipient Harwelden award for Individual Contbrn. in the Arts, 1989, Gov.'s award State of Okla., 1992. Mem. Assn. Am. Mus., Assn. Art Mus. Dirs., Art Mus. Assn. Am., Mountain Plains Assn. Mus., Am. Craft Coun., Okla. Mus. Assn., Rotary. Office: Philbrook Mus Art PO Box 52510 Tulsa OK 74152-0510

MANIERI-HARVEY, MICHELE DAWN, elementary school educator, musician; b. Melbourne, Fla., Apr. 25, 1955; d. Ettore Don and June Laclaire (Spaur) Manieri; m. Joseph Howard Harvey, May 27, 1989. AA, U. Fla., 1976, B in Music Edn., 1978; M in Early Childhood and Elem. Edn., Nova U., 1983; M in Guidance and Counseling, U. South Fla., 1993. Cert. tchr., Fla. Profl. vocalist Fla., 1973—; vocal tchr. in pvt. practice Gainesville, Fla., 1978-80; substitute tchr. Alachua Sch. Bd., Gainesville, 1978-79; music specialist Levy County Sch. Bd., Williston, Fla., 1979-82, kindergarten tchr., 1982-83; tchr. 2d grade Hernando County/Moton Elem., Brooksville, Fla., 1983-84, tchr. 1st grade, 1984-86, music specialist with integrated counseling concepts and basic skills, 1986—; chair calendar plus com. Moton, 1994—; adj. prof. St. Leo Coll., 1984—; Fla. cert. observer and peer tchr., 1986—; mem. Hernando County Fine Arts Curriculum Writing Team, 1994-96. Featured vocalist Hernando Symphony Orch., Spring Hill, Fla., 1992, 95, 96, Nature Coast Festival Singers Messiah, 1994, 96, Brooksville Music Club Christmas Ho., 1987, 94; dir., prodr. 14 sacred cantata-dramas, 40 children's musicals. Music dir. 1st Bapt. Ch., Brooksville, 1989—. Named 1994 Hernando County Tchr. of Yr., 1994, Best Musical Actress, Stage West, 1995, Best Musical Supporting Actress, Outstanding Young Woman of Am., 1981. Mem. FTP-NEA, Nat. Music Educators Assn., Fla. Music Educators Assn., Fla. League Tchrs., Fla. Counseling Assn., Hernando Counseling Assn. (Counseling Advocate of Yr. 1994), Hernando County Bd. Fine Arts Coun., Hernando Edn. Found. (sec. 1995-

96), Hernando Classroom Tchrs. Assn. (exec. bd. 1985-86), Hernando Acad. Tchrs. (vice chair 1994-95, chair 95-96), Alpha Delta Kappa Internat. Educators Hon. Fraternity (1985-96). Office: Moton Elem Sch 7175 Emerson Rd Brooksville FL 34601-5752

MANITSAS, NIKITAS CONSTANTIN, career officer, automotive executive; b. Batavia, N.Y., Oct. 18, 1923; s. George Gabriel and Thalia (Sitara) M.; m. Ursula Suzanne Klar, Mar. 5, 1949 (dec. Aug. 1960); m. Hildegard Wessel, Dec. 26, 1963. Student, Dartmouth Coll., 1940-42; BS in Mil. Engring., U.S. Mil. Acad., 1945; MS in Engring., U. Ill., 1950; MS in Interna . Rels., George Washington U., 1964. Commd. 2d lt. U.S. Army, 1945, advanced through grades to brig. gen., 1971; engring. exec. Parsons Corp., Washington, 1976-81; exec. v.p. H.B.L., Inc., Vienna, Va., 1981-87; pres. Lantzsch-Andreas Enterprises, Inc., Vienna, Va., 1987-93; pvt. practice as mgmt. cons. McLean, Va., 1994—; bd. dirs. Lantzsch-Andreas Enterprises, Inc., Vienna, H.B.L., Inc., Vienna. Decorated Disting. Svc. medal, 3 Legions of Merit, Army Commendation medal. Mem. Army Navy Country Club, Tower Club. Greek Orthodox. Home and Office: 1333 Pine Tree Rd Mc Lean VA 22101-2417

MANJURA, BONNIE DOREEN, marketing and advertising executive, educator; b. Duluth, Minn., Mar. 2, 1956; d. Maximilian Karl and Charlotte Erna (Jaeschke) M.; m. Daniel Charles Boody, Jan. 31, 1984; 1 child, Robert Maximilian Bonafide Manjura-Boody. BA, Rollins Coll., 1977, MA, 1979. Internat. promotion specialist dept. commerce State of Fla., Tallahassee, 1979-80; motion picture liaison dept. econ. devel. State of Fla., Orlando, 1981-85; dir. tourism devel. Greater Orlando C. of C., 1980-85; exec. dir. Centerra Group, Heathrow, Fla., 1985-91; pres. small bus. Longwood, Fla., 1989-91; exec. dir. spl. project Heathrow Land & Devel. Corp., A'tamonte Springs, 1985-90; vice chmn. JFP & Assocs. Fla., Inc., Sanford, Fla., 1988-90; CFO, pres. Gilbert & Manjura Mktg. and Advt., Longwood, Fla., 1991—; mem. Christopher Columbus Quincentennial Core Commn., 1992; prof. MBA program Webster U., 1994—, mentor mktg. dept., 1994—. Contbg. editor Lake Mary Progress, 1988-90. Mem. golf tournament com. Internat. Embassy House, 1992-93; ACS 125 Com., 1991-93, Seminole C.C. Bus. and Industry Coun., 1988-93; bd. dirs. Hospice of the Comforter, 1994-95; pub. rels. com. Orlando Day Nursery, 1995—; cmty. trustee Seminole Visions, 1996. Recipient Scholarship award Notre Dame Cen. Fla. Soc. Assn. Execs., 1984, Dictionary of Internat. Biography, 1991, Silver Addy for Creative Excellence, 1994; named Up & Comers Finalist Price Waterhouse & Orlando Bus. Jour., 1988, One of the Movers and Shakers Cen. Fla. mag., 1987, Grand Patron-Tunon Internat. Sch., 1986. Mem. Vis. Nurses Assn. (adv. bd. 1988—), Am. Diabetes Assn. (bd. dirs. 1987-89), Internat. Visitors Coun. (bd. dirs. 1987-89), Internat. Visitors Coun. (bd. dirs. 1987-90), Leukemia Soc. (bd. dirs. Ctrl. Fla. chpt. 1986-88), Fla. Motion Picture and TV Assn., Greater Orlando C. of C. (steering com. on suburban mobility 1991), Seminole County C. of C. (CEO's roundtable 1988), Variety Club Internat. (bd. dirs. 1988-90), Seminole Ornament Soc. (pres. 1988—). Republican. Presbyterian. Office: 346 Freeman St Longwood FL 32750

MANK, RODNEY LAYTON, lawyer; b. Miami, Fla., Jan. 2, 1937; s. Philip Jameson and Margaret (Layton) M.; m. Mary Stuart Patton, July 17, 1982; children: Stephen, Christopher, Julie Courtright, Bentley Courtright. BA in Polit. Sci., U. Fla., 1959, JD, 1962. Bar: Fla. 1962; diplomate Am. Bd. Trial Advs. Atty. Wilson, Elser, Moskowitz, Edelman & Dicker, Miami, 1995—; sec. Fla. Blue Key, Gainesville, 1962. Contbr. articles to profl. jours. Bd. dirs. Mus. of Sci., Miami, 1976; pres. Hist. Assn. So. Fla., Miami, 1977-79. Capt. U.S. Army, 1962-65. Decorated Army Commendation medal U.S. Army, Hawaii, 1965; recipient Good Guy award United Way, Miami, 1967, Exceptional Svc. award Def. Rsch. Inst., Chgo., 1979. Mem. Fedn. Ins. and Corp. Counsel, Dade Def. Bar Assn. (pres. 1977), Riviera Country Club, Biscayne Bay Yacht Club. Home: 1457 Certosa Ave Coral Gables FL 33146-1919 Office: Wilson Elser Moskowitz Edelman & Dicker 100 SE 2nd St Miami FL 33131-2100

MANKILLER, WILMA PEARL, tribal leader; b. Stilwell, Okla., Nov. 18, 1945; d. Charley and Clara Irene (Sitton) M.; m. Hector N. Olaya, Nov. 13, 1963 (div. 1975); children: Felicia Marie Olaya, Gina Irene Olaya; m. Charlie Soap, Oct. 13, 1986. Student, Skyline Coll., San Bruno Coll., 1973, San Francisco State Coll., 1973-75; BA in Social Sci., Union Coll., 1977; postgrad., U. Ark., 1979; DHL (hon.), U. New Eng., 1986; PhD in Pub. Svc. (hon.), R.I. Coll., 1989; DHL (hon.), Yale U., 1990; PhD (hon.), Dartmouth Coll., 1991; LLD (hon.), Mills Coll., 1992. Cmty. devel. dir. Cherokee Nation, Tahlequah, Okla., 1977-83, dep. chief, 1983-85, prin. chief, 1985-95; Montgomery fellow Darmouth Coll., 1996; mem. exec. bd. Coun. Energy Resource Tribes; bd. dirs. Okla. Indsl. Devel. Commn. Author: Mankiller: A Chief and Her People, 1993. Bd. dirs. Okla. Acad. for State Goals, 1985—. Recipient Donna Nigh First Lady award Okla. Commn. for Status of Women, 1985, Am. Leadership award Harvard U., 1986; inducted Okla. Women's Hall of Fame, 1986. Mem. Nat. Tribal Chmn. Assn., Nat. Congress Am. Indians, Cherokee County Dem. Women's Club. Home: PO Box 308 Park Hill OK 74451

MANLEY, LANCE FILSON, data processing consultant; b. Atlanta, Dec. 8, 1945; s. Vern Paul Manley and Beth (Filson) Morgan; m. Sandra Faye Parris, Oct. 31, 1964 (div. 1967); 1 child, Lance Filson Jr.; m. Elizabeth Jane Wallace, Oct. 31, 1968; children: Jeffrey Lance, Heather Leigh. Student, John Marshall Law Sch., 1964-66, Shorter Coll., Rome, Ga., 1967-68, Brevard Coll., Cocoa, Fla., 1968-69, U. Mid Fla., 1972-74; tech. cert., Programming Systems Inst., Atlanta, 1967, RCA Edn. Ctr., L.A., 1968, Burroughs Edn. Ctr., Detroit, 1973, Honeywell Edn. Ctr., Atlanta, 1976, Info. Sci., San Antonio, 1977, IBM Edn. Ctr., Atlanta, 1978, Emory U., 1988, Platinum Tech., Atlanta, 1993, 96. Sr. computer operator Fed. Elec. Corp., Cape Kennedy, Fla., 1966-68, Universal Studios, Universal City, Calif., 1968-70; program analyst State of Fla., Jacksonville, 1970-73, Fla. Nat. Bank, Jacksonville, 1973-76; sr. program analyst Fulton Nat. Bank, Atlanta, 1977-78, 1st Nat. Bank Atlanta, 1978-80; cons. Ins. Systems Am., Atlanta, 1980, Cotton States Ins., Atlanta, 1981, State of Ga., Atlanta, 1981-83, Decatur Fed., Atlanta, 1981, C&S Bank, Atlanta, 1982, Cox Communication, Atlanta, 1983, Emory U., Atlanta, 1984-88; staff cons. So. Co. Svcs., Atlanta, 1988-93; sr. info. sys. software engr. Ga. Bapt. Med. Ctr., 1993-96; sr. analyst State of Ga. Dept. Adminstrv. Svcs., Atlanta, 1996—. Home: 3033 Langley Rd Loganville GA 30249-2227 Office: ASAP 3834 Cardinal Dr Tucker GA 30084

MANLEY, NANCY JANE, environmental engineer; b. Ft. Smith, Ark., Sept. 13, 1951; d. Eugene Hailey and Mary Adele (Chave) M. BSE, Purdue U., 1974; MSE, U. Wash., 1976; postgrad., U. Minn., 1976-77; grad., Air Command and Staff Coll., 1984, Exec. Leadership Devel. Program Dept. Def., 1988. Lic. profl. engr., Ga. Sanitary engr. Minn. Dept. Health, Mpls., 1976-77; sanitary engr. water supply EPA, Chgo., 1977; leader primacy unit water supply EPA, Atlanta, 1977-79, leader tech. assistance team, 1979-82; chief environ. and contract planning, project mgr. Grand Bay Range design USAF, Moody AFB, Ga., 1982-84; dep. base civil engr. USAF, Carswell AFB, Tex., 1984-86, Scott AFB, Ill., 1986-89; mem. tech. adv. com. Scott AFB master plan study USAF, Belleville, Ill., 1986-89; dep. base civil engr. USAF, Robins AFB, Ga., 1989-91, acting chief engr., 1990-91, chief pollution prevention divsn., dir. environ. mgmt., 1991-93; chief engr. divsn. 78 Civil Engr. Group, Robins AFB, Ga., 1993—; mem. Fla. Tech. Adv. Com. for Injection Wells, Tallahassee, 1980-82, Nat. Implementation Team for Underground Injection Control Program, Washington, 1979-82, tech. panel Nat. Groundwater Protection Strategy Hearings, 1981; judge Internat. Sci. and Engring. Fair, 1986. Active various ch. support activities, 1969-74; sec. Perry Area Hist. Soc., 1991-93; vol. Meals-on-Wheels, Girl Scouts U.S., others, various locations, 1982—; founder, crisis intervention counselor Midwest Alliance, West Lafayette, Ind., 1970-74; active St. Louis Math. and Sci. Network Day, 1989, Adopt-a-Sch. Program, Lebanon, Ill., 1987-89; scientist by mail Boston Mus. Sci., 1989—. Recipient Presdl. Point of Light award USAF, 1991, Disting. Govt. Svc. award Dallas/Ft. Worth Fed. Exec. Bd., 1986, Lady of the Black Knights award 19th Air Refueling Wing, 1991. Mem. NSPE (v.p. local chpt. 1994-95, pres.-elect local chpt. 1995-96, pres. 1996—), ASCE, Soc. Women Engrs. (regional mem.-at-large rep. 1990-93, sr. mem. local officers 1979-82, 84-86), Am. Women in Sci., Soc. Am. Mil. Engrs. (local membership and contingency coms.), Internat. Platform Assn. Office: 78 CEG/CEC Robins AFB GA 31098-1864

MANLEY, WALTER WILSON, II, lawyer; b. Gainesville, Fla., Mar. 16, 1947; s. Walter Wilson and Marjorie Iley (Watkins) M.; children: Marjorie, Benjamin. BA, Fla. So. Coll., 1969; JD, Duke U., 1972; MBA, Harvard U., 1975. Atty. Blackwell, Walker & Gray, Miami, Fla., 1972-75; pvt. practice law Lakeland, Fla., 1975-84; prof. bus. adminstrn. Fla. State U., Tallahassee, 1985—; ptnr. MacFarlane, Ferguson, Allison & Kelly, Tallahassee, 1991-94; vis. prof. bus. adminstrn. Ridley Hall Coll. and Cambridge Fedn. Theol. Colls., Eng., 1988-90, Cambridge U. Faculties of Mgmt. Studies, Philosophy, Law, Social and Polit. Scis. and Divinity, 1989-90; pres. Exeter Leadership Cos. Inst., Inc., Tallahassee, 1989-94, Fla. North Shore Tech. Ctrs., Inc., 1995—. Author: Critical Issues in Business Conduct, 1990, Executive's Handbook of Model Business Conduct Codes, 1991, Handbook of Good Business Practice, 1992, What Florida Thinks, 1996, The History of the Supreme Court of Florida and Its Predecessor Courts, 1821-1917, 1997. Pres. Fla. Endowment Found. for Vocat. Rehab., 1991-93; bd. dirs. Fla. Real Property and Casualty Joint Underwriters Assn., 1987-91, Consumer Coun. Fla., 1992—; bd. visitors Duke U. Sch. Law, 1991—; trustee The Webb Sch., BellBuckle, Tenn., 1983-92, nat. fund chmn., 1982; pres. Polk County Legal Aid Soc. Mem. ABA, Fla. Bar Assn. (Pres.' Pro Bono Svc. award 1985), Lakeland Bar Assn. (pres.), Capital Duke Club (pres.), Tallahassee Quarterback Club Found. (chmn., Biletnikoff award), Psi Chi, Omicron Delta Kappa, Sigma Alpha Epsilon, Phi Delta Phi. Episcopalian. Home: 2804 Rabbit Hill Rd Tallahassee FL 32312-3137

MANLY, SAMUEL, lawyer; b. Louisville, Aug. 8, 1945; s. Samuel III and Nell Thornton (Montgomery) M.; m. Tacie Jarrett Bond, Aug. 8, 1970 (div. 1978); children: Julie Elder, Elizabeth Meriwether. BA cum laude, Yale U., 1967; JD, U. Va., 1970. Bar: Ky. 1971, U.S. Dist. Ct. (we. and ea. dists.) Ky. 1972, U.S. Dist. Ct. (so. dist.) Ind. 1972, U.S. Dist. Ct. (we. dist.) Mich. 1995, U.S. Ct. Appeals (6th cir.) 1972, U.S. Dist. Ct. (so. dist.) Miss. 1989. Pres. Madison House, U. Va., Charlottesville, 1968-70; assoc. Greenebaum Doll & McDonald, Louisville, 1970-76; ptnr. Reisz Blackburn Manly & Treitz, Louisville, 1976-78; sr. ptnr. Manly & Sears, Louisville, 1978-81, Manly & Heleringer, Louisville, 1981-84; pvt. practice Law Offices of Samuel Manly, Louisville, 1984—; sec., gen. counsel Gibbs-Inman Co., Louisville, 1972-78; contract atty. FDIC, Washington, 1976-84; counsel Winston Products Co., 1988—; dir. defender svcs. U.S. Dist. Ct. (we. dist.) Ky., 1992-94. Contract atty. Jefferson County, 1977-78, City of Louisville, 1978-83. Capt. USAR, 1967-86. Fellow Ky. Bar Found. (life); mem. ABA (com. on products liability, subcom uninsured mfrs. sect. ligitation, com. on self-insurers and risk mgrs. sect. tort and ins. law practice), Ky. Bar Assn. (com. on legal ethics 1978-84, 96—), Louisville Bar Assn., Ky. Assn. Criminal Def. Lawyers (bd. dirs., exec. com., chmn. criminal rules com.), Nat. Assn. Criminal Def. Lawyers, Ky. Acad. Trial Lawyers, Fed. Bar Assn., Comml. Law League of Am., Assn. Trial Lawyers of Am., Am. Judicature Soc., Louisville Boat Club. Republican. Home: 407 S Sherrin Ave Louisville KY 40207-3817 Office: Law Offices of Samuel Manly 239 S 5th St Louisville KY 40202-3213

MANN, DONALD CAMERON, marketing company executive; b. Memphis, Jan. 31, 1949; s. Cameron Mann and Jane Snowden (Treadwell) Martin; m. Natacha Luba Plotnikoff, June 1, 1972; 1 child, Cameron Alexander. BA, Brown U., 1971; MBA, Columbia U., 1978. Assoc. pub. Portfolio Mag., N.Y.C., 1978-80; mktg. dir. Bloom & Gelb, N.Y.C., 1980-82; gen. mgr. Malmo Dir. Advt., Memphis, Tenn., 1982-88; pres. Fusion Mktg. Group, Memphis, 1988—; spkr. Fin. Inst. Mktg. Assn., Chgo., 1988-90, Bank Mktg. Assn., Database Mktg. Conf., 1995, OKRA Mktg. User Conf., Tampa, Fla., 1989-94, Customer Insights Corp. Conf., 1989, Bank Mktg. Assn. Argentina, Buenos Aires, 1994, Strategic Rsch. Inst., N.Y., 1994-95; founder, dir. Advanced Fin. Database Mktg. Sch. Northwestern U., Chgo., 1990—. Editor, author: (book) The New Age of Financial Marketing, 1991. Bd. dirs. Concerts Internat., Memphis, 1989; mem. Leadership Memphis, 1993; mem. adv. bd. Case-in-Point, Axciom Corp., 1995—. Recipient Cert. Merit Direct Mktg. Assn., 1983, Fin. Inst. Mktg. Assn., 1987, ADDY, Am. Assn. Advt. Agys., 1988. Mem. The Univ. Club, The Porsche Club Am., The Dixon Gallery and Gardens. Office: Fusion Mktg Group 88 Union Ave Memphis TN 38103-5100

MANN, EDWINA WALLS, medical librarian; b. Little Rock, Ark., Jan. 7, 1941; d. Joseph Edward and Mary Armorial (Gravette) W. BSE, Ouachita Bapt. Coll., 1962; MLS, Vanderbilt U., 1982. Bookmobile libr. S.E. Ark. Reg. Libr., Monticello, 1962-63; libr. asst. serials La. State U. Libr., Baton Rouge, 1963-65; serials asst. U. Ark. Med. Ctr. Libr., Little Rock, 1965-66; asst. ref. libr. U. Ark. Med. Ctr. Libr., 1966-69, chief technical svcs., 1970-72, ref. libr., 1972-74; chief technical svcs. U. Ark. for Med. Scis. Libr., Little Rock, 1974-78; chair hist. rsch. ctr. U. Ark. for Med. Scis. Libr., 1978—. Contbr. articles to profl. jours. Mem. Med. Libr. Assn. (mem. com. 1982-83), Ark. Libr. Assn. (legis. com. 1994-95), Soc. S.W. Archivists (bd. mem. 1982-84, 1988-91, nom. com. 1994-95), South Ctrl. Cpt. Med. Libr. Assn. (treas. 1982), Archivists & Libr. in the History of Health Sci. (sec. 1991-93), Ark. Hist. Assn. (bd. dirs. 1988-95), Pulaski County Hist. Soc. (pres. 1992-93, bd. dirs. 1992-95). Democrat. Baptist. Office: UAMS Libr Slot 586 4301 W Markham Little Rock AR 72205

MANN, HARVEY BLOUNT, retired banker; b. Raleigh, N.C., Sept. 19, 1930; s. Harvey Blount Sr. and Margaret Mann; m. Florence Potter, June 25, 1958; children: Laura Bradford, Virginia Lee. BS, N.C. State U., 1953; MBA, U. N.C., 1956. Tchr. agr. N.C. Sch. System, Moyock, N.C., 1953-54; grain merchandiser Cargill, Inc., Mpls., 1956-63; pvt. practice Virginia Beach, Va., 1963-69; trust officer Va. Nat. Bank (and predecessor firms), Norfolk, 1969-80; v.p. Nations Bank (formerly Sovran Bank), Norfolk, 1980-93; ret., 1993; sec., treas. Am. Realty & Fin., Portsmouth, Va., 1980-89. Bd. dirs., exhibits chmn. 1st Ann. Virginia Beach Country Classic, 1994. Mem. Rotary Internat. (pres. Virginia Beach chpt. 1973-74), Broad Bay Point Greens Country Club, Masons, Shriners. Republican. Episcopalian. Home: 2601 Sandy Valley Rd Virginia Beach VA 23452-7724

MANN, JACK MATTHEWSON, bottling company executive; b. Marshall, Tex., Apr. 14, 1932; s. Jack Slater and Mary (Matthewson) M.; m. True Sandlin, Sept. 4, 1954 (div. 1989); children: Jack, Robert, Daniel, Nathaniel. Student, N.Mex. Mil. Inst., 1952; BBA, U. Tex., 1954; MBA, Harvard U., 1960. Credit analyst Republic Nat. Bank, Dallas, 1959; chem. coord. Humble Oil and Refining Co., Baytown, Tex., 1960-61; asst. sales mgr. The Made-Rite Co., Marshall, Tex., 1957-58; asst. gen. mgr. The Made Rite Co., Marshall, Tex., 1961-63; gen. mgr. The Made Rite Co., Longview, Tex., 1963—, pres., 1972—, owner, chmn., 1982—; v.p. Longview Econ. Devel. Corp., 1994—, treas., 1995-96, pres., 1996—; bd. dirs. Longview Nat. Bank; mem. pres.'s adv. coun. Le Trouneau U., 1994—. Exec. com. Rep. Party Tex., 1962-65; mem. exec. bd. Episcopal Diocese Tex., Houston, 1974-76; mem. small bus. adv. com. Tex. Dept. Commerce, 1988-91. Mem. Tex. Soft Drink Assn. (pres. 1972), Nat. Dr. Pepper Bottlers Assn. (pres. 1983-85), Longview C. of C. (dir. 1965-68, 84-86). Club: Summit (Longview) (gov. 1982-94). Home: 45 Stonegate Dr Longview TX 75601-3600 Office: The Made Rite Co PO Box 3283 Longview TX 75606-3283

MANN, JAMES DARWIN, mathematics educator; b. Lambric, Ky., Feb. 27, 1936; s. Glinn W. and Wanda (Collins) M.; 1 child, Terry Brian. BS, Morehead State U., 1962; M in Math., U. S.C., 1965; postgrad., Ind. U., 1968-69, Obelin Coll., 1968. High sch. tchr. math., 1962-64; instr. math. Presbyn. Coll., Clinton, S.C., 1965-66; assoc. prof. math. Morehead (Ky.) State U., 1966—. Fundraiser United Way, 1977-78; vol. coach Little League Baseball, 1973-76; coach Babe Ruth Baseball, 1977; chmn. N.E. Ky. Sci. Fair Rules, 1969-76; judge N.E. Ky. Sci. Fair, 1967, 68, 77, 79, 80, 81. NSF grantee U. S.C., 1964-65, Vanderbilt U., 1967, Oberlin Coll., 1968, N.C. State U., 1972; recipient Outstanding Alumni award Ky. Zeta chpt. Sigma Phi Epsilon, 1977. Mem. Math. Assn. Am., Nat. Coun. Tchrs. Math. Baptist. Home: 4200 Christy Crk Morehead KY 40351-9075 Office: Morehead State U PO Box 1231 Morehead KY 40351-5231

MANN, JAMES ROBERT, congressman; b. Greenville, S.C., Apr. 27, 1920; s. Alfred Cleo and Nina (Griffin) M.; m. Virginia Thomason Brunson, Jan. 15, 1945; children—James Robert, David Brunson, William Walker, Virginia Brunson. B.A., The Citadel, 1941, LL.D. (hon.), 1978; JD, U. S.C., 1947. Bar: S.C. 1947, U.S. Ct. Appeals (4th cir.) 1948, U.S. Supreme Ct. 1970. Practice in Greenville, 1947—; del. S.C. Ho. of Reps. from, Greenville County, 1949-52; solicitor 13th Jud. Circuit, 1953-63; mem. 91st-95th Congresses 4th Dist., S.C. Sec. Greenville County Planning Commn., 1963-67; Trustee Greenville Hosp. System, 1965-68; bd. govs. Greenville Shriners Hosp., 1983-90. Served to lt. col. AUS, 1941-46; col. USAR ret. Mem. Am., S.C., Greenville County bar assns., Am. Judicature Soc., Greater Greenville C. of C. (pres. 1965), V.F.W. (dep. comdr. 1951-52), Am. Legion. Democrat. Baptist. Lodges: Mason; Shriners; Kiwanis; Elks; Woodmen of World. Office: 812 E North St Greenville SC 29601-3102

MANN, MEL, food products company executive; b. New Orleans, Jan. 10, 1955. BS, Miss. State U., 1977; MS, W.Va. U., 1983; MBA, Memphis State U., 1993. Researcher Chem. Lab. Miss. State U., Starkville, 1977-78; lab. mgr. W.Va. U., Morgantown, 1980-84; project mgr. Standard Meat Co., Ft. Worth, 1984-88; project leader Sara Lee Applied Tech., Traverse City, Mich., 1988-89; sr. rsch. and devel. project mgr. Jimmy Dean Foods, Cordova, Tenn., 1989-95, mktg. mgr., 1995-96, dir. product devel., 1996—. Editor (newsletter) Jimmy Dean Link Letter, 1992-93; contbr. articles to profl. jours. Instr. Adult Continuing Edn., Morgantown, 1983. Mem. Inst. Food Technologists (mem. coun. 1992-93), Am. Meat Sci. Assn., Am. Mgmt. Assn., The Nature Conservancy, Earthwatch, Sigma Xi. Office: Jimmy Dean Foods 8000 Centerview Pky Ste 400 Cordova TN 38018-4240

MANN, STEPHEN ASHBY, financial counselor; b. Richmond, Va., Feb. 20, 1947; s. Milton Ashby and Rebecca (George) M.; m. Patricia Ann Kofron, Aug. 25, 1982; 1 child, Michael Joseph Ashby; stepchildren: Christine Ferguson, Tracy Kofron. BS in Gen. Bus., Va. Poly. Inst. and State U., 1970. CLU; Life Underwriters Tng. Coun. Fellow, 1990. Supr. mfg. Brown & Williamson Tobacco Corp., Petersburg, Va., 1970-72; pres. Cumberland (Va.)) Woodyard, 1972-79; mgr. Ragland Woodyards, Goochland, Va., 1980-81; advt. mgr., rep. Gazette Newspapers, Goochland, 1982-85; fin. counselor, ins. and fin. planner Peoples Security Ins. Co., Mechanicsville, Va., 1986—. Pres. Millquarter Property Owners Assn., Powhatan, Va., 1987. Named to All-Star Honor Roll, Ins. Sales mag., 1989, 90. Mem. Nat. Assn. Life Underwriters (Nat. Quality award 1986—, Nat. Sales Achievement award 1986—, Nat. Health Inst. award 1986—), Am. Soc. CLU and ChFC (student mem.), Golden Key Soc. (com. mem. 1991-96), Assn. Health Inst. Agts., Richmond Assn. Life Underwriters (bd. dirs. 1989-92), SCV (comdr., lt. comdr. Powhatan 1980-82, insp. gen. state divsn. 1981, nat. a.d.c. 1982-83), Sons of the South Motorcycle Club (pres. 1993—), Masons (master 1990, 94Va. 16th dist. blood coord. 1995-96, Samis Grotto, treas. 1991-93). Republican. Baptist. Home: 1433 E Overlook Dr Powhatan VA 23139 Office: Peoples Security Ins Co 5980 Chamberlayne Rd Mechanicsville VA 23111-2511

MANN, TRUE SANDLIN, psychologist, consultant; b. Longview, Tex., Aug. 4, 1934; d. Bob Murphy and Stella True (Williams) Sandlin; m. Jack Matthewson Mann, Sept. 4, 1954 (div. Dec. 1989); children: Jack Matthewson Jr., Bob Sandlin, Daniel Williams, Nathaniel Currier. BS, Stephen F. Austin State U., Nacogdoches, Tex., 1973, MA, 1977; PhD, East Tex. State U., 1982. Lic. psychologist, Tex., Ark. Instr. Stephen F. Austin State U., 1975-76, vis. asst. prof. psychology, 1986-87; instr. East Tex. State U., Commerce, 1980-81; postdoctoral fellow Southwestern Med. Sch., Dallas, 1982-83; pvt. practice, Longview, Tex., 1983-92; psychologist dept. family practice U. Tex. Health Sci. Ctr., Tyler, 1990-92; dir. psychol. svcs. St. Michael's Hosp., Texarkana, Tex., 1992-93; cons. psychologist, Longview, 1993—; weekly newspaper columnist HARBUS, Cambridge Mass., 1959-60; cons. Made-Rite Co., Longview, 1989—. Mem. candidate com. Assoc. Reps. Tex., Austin, 1990—; bd. dirs. Mental Health Assn. Tex., 1977-82, 84-92, Longview Symphony, 1995, Longview Mus. of Art, 1995; mem. Leadership Tex., 1988—. Mem. APA, Tex. Psychol. Assn. Episcopalian. Home: 1309 Inverness St Longview TX 75601-3548 Office: 1203 Montclair St Longview TX 75601-3565

MANN, WILLIAM JOSEPH, JR., gynecologic oncologist; b. Wilkes Barre, Pa., Apr. 13, 1947; s. William Joseph and Irene Bertha M.; m. Katie Gallagher, Aug. 8, 1980; children: William Joseph Mann III, Kelly Catherine Rena. BA cum laude, Amherst Coll., 1969; MD, Pa. State U., 1973. Diplomate Am. Bd. Ob-Gyn. Intern, resident M.S. Hershey Med. Ctr., Hershey, Pa., 1973-78; ACOG-Ortho fellow M.S. Hershey Med. Ctr., 1976-77; fellow in gynecol. oncology U. Ala., Birmingham, 1978-80; assoc. prof., dir. gynecol. oncology SUNY, Stony Brook, 1980-91; dir. ob-gyn. residency Riverside Regional Med. Ctr., Newport News, Va., 1991—; prof. ob-gyn. Med. Coll. of Va., Richmond, 1993—; prof. clin. ob-gyn. Ea. Va. Med. Sch., Norfolk; cons. Mary Immaculate Hosp., Newport News, Williamsburg Community Hosp., Sentara Hampton Gen. Hosp. Contbr. numerous articles to profl. jours., chpts. in books, revs. in various publs. Coach Smithtown Kickers soccer league, 1988-89, Rugby Club, SUNY at Stony Brook, 1980-87; vol. fireman Nissequogue Fire Dept., St. James, N.Y., 1988-91, Setauket (N.Y.) Vol. Fire Dept., 1983-88. Recipient Silver Sword award Am. Cancer Soc., 1991. Fellow ACS, Am. Coll. Ob-Gyn.; mem. Soc. Gynecol. Oncologists, Assn. Profs. Ob-Gyn., So. Med. Soc., So. Oncology Assn. (founding), Gyn. Urology Soc., Am. Soc. for Colposcopy and Cervical Pathology, Suffolk County Soc. Ob-Gyns., Internat. Gyn. Cancer Soc., Am. Soc. for Laser Medicine and Surgery, Inc., Newport News Med. Soc., Va. Ob-Gyn. Soc., Am. Soc. for Parenatal and Enteral Nutrition, Mid-Atlantic Gyn. Oncologic Soc. Office: Riverside Regional Med Ctr 314 Main St Ste A Newport News VA 23601-3813

MANNERS, PAMELA JEANNE, middle school educator; b. Holyoke, Mass., Mar. 20, 1951; d. Francis Edward and Helen Mary (Kurtyka) Herbert; div. 1985; children: Tracy, Kristen. BA, U. So. Miss., 1986, MEd, 1993. Cert. elem. edn. K-3, 4-8, secondary Eng., Social Studies; cert. elem. prin., secondary prin., elem. and secondary adminstrn. Registrar Michel Mid. Sch., Biloxi, Miss., 1987-88, tchr. Eng. and Social Studies, 1988-90, tchr. reading/law related edn., 1990-95; curriculum coord. Biloxi Pub. Schs., 1995—; dir. ABA Reading Cirriculum Program; law-related edn. trainer Miss. Law-Related Edn. Ctr., Jackson, 1990—; law-related trainer Ctr. Civic Edn., Calabasas, Calif., 1993; law-related trainer Constitutional Right Found., 1994—. Participant program Lawyer in Every Class Miss. Bar Assn., Jackson, 1990-93. On-site target grantee Miss. Bar/Dept. Justice, 1992; A+ Site recognition U.S. Dept. Edn. Mem. NEA, Miss. Edn. Assn., Leadership Gulf Coast C. of C. Roman Catholic. Office: Curriculum Office Biloxi Pub Schs 1424 Father Ryan Ave Biloxi MS 39530-3523

MANNING, CHARLES W., academic administrator; b. Mar. 18, 1943; s. Charles Manning; m. Sharon Fischer; children: Shannon, Charles, Kelly. BS in Chemistry, Western Md. Coll., 1965; PhD in Analytical Chemistry, U. Md., 1969; postgrad., Inst. Anorganische und Kernchemie, Johannes Gutenberg U., Mainz, Germany, 1969-70. Sr. staff assoc. Nat. Ctr. Higher Edn. Mgmt. Systems, Boulder, Colo., 1971-74; asst. provost, asst. prof. chemistry U. Mo., Kansas City, 1974-79; assoc. exec. dir. acad. affairs Colo. Commn. Higher Edn., Denver, 1979-81, dep. exec. dir., 1982-88; v.p. acad. affairs U. No. Colo., Greeley, 1981-82; exec. vice chancellor Okla. State Regents for Higher Edn., Oklahoma City, 1988-90; chancellor U. System W.Va., Charleston, 1991—; cons. as v.p. for planning and fin. Fed. U. Ceara, Brazil, 1976-77; presenter in field. Contbr. articles to profl. jours. Capt. U.S. Army, 1970-71. Mem. Rotary. Office: U System WVa 1018 Kanawha Blvd E Ste 700 Charleston WV 25301-2827

MANNING, KIM DODD, legislative staff member; b. New Orleans, Mar. 23, 1969; d. Alvin Gerald and Florence Dodd; m. James Lealon Manning, Aug. 4, 1990. BA, La. State U., 1994. Rsch. analyst, webmaster La. Senate, Baton Rouge, 1994—; mem. Senate Info. Coord. Com., Baton Rouge, 1996. Mem. Nat. Conf. State Legislatures, La. State U. Alumni Assn. Roman Catholic. Office: La State Senate 900 Riverside Mall Baton Rouge LA 70804

MANNING, NANCY ANNE, law librarian; b. Tulsa, Aug. 9, 1949; d. Joseph Eugene and Virginia Louise (Johnston) Small; m. Carl D. Smith, Aug. 13, 1971 (div. Apr. 1975); 1 child, Erik Zachary; m. Clifford Allen Manning, May 1, 1992 (dec. June 12, 1993); 1 child, Michael S. BFA, U. Okla., 1976, MLS, 1977. Libr. clk. U. Okla. Law Libr., Norman, 1971-72, 77; libr., acquisitions/serials U. Tex. Law Libr., Austin, 1978-80; libr., head tech. svcs., Oklahoma City U. Law Libr., 1980—. Mem. Am. Assn. Law Librs., Southwestern Assn. Law Librs., Mid-Am. Assn. Law Librs. Office: Okla City U Law Library 2501 N Blackwelder Oklahoma City OK 73106-1402

MANNING, WALTER SCOTT, accountant, former educator, consultant; b. nr. Yoakum, Tex., Oct. 4, 1912; BBA, Tex. Coll. Arts and Industries, 1932; MBA, U. Tex., 1940; m. Eleanor Mary Jones, Aug. 27, 1937; children: Sharon Frances, Walter Scott, Robert Kenneth. Asst. to bus. mgr. Tex. Coll. Arts and Industries, Kingsville, 1932; tchr. Sinton (Tex.) High Sch., 1933-37, Robstown (Tex.) High Sch., 1937-41; prof. Tex. A&M U., College Station, 1941-77; cons. C.P.A., Tex. Walter Manning Outstanding Jr. and Outstanding Sr. awards at Coll. Bus. Adminstrn., Tex. A&M U. named in his honor. Mem. AICPA, AAUP, Am. Acctg. Assn., Tex. Soc. CPAs, College Station C. of C. (past pres.), Tex. Assn. Univ. Instrs. Acctg. (pres. 1963-64), SAR (independence chpt. past pres.), Knights York Cross of Honor, Alpha Chi, Beta Gamma Sigma, Beta Alpha Psi. Democrat. Presbyterian (elder). Clubs: Masons, (32 degree), Shriners, K.T., Kiwanis (past pres., past lt. gov. div. IX Tex. Okla. dist., Kiwanis Internat. Legion of Honor). Home: 405 Walton Dr College Station TX 77840-2224

MANNING, WALTER SCOTT, JR., veterinarian; b. Bryan, Tex., Mar. 3, 1945; s. Walter Scott and Eleanor Mary (Jones) M.; m. Mary Ann Hurliman, Mar. 11, 1972; children: Adrienne Emily, Walter Scott III. BS, Tex. A&M U., 1967, 76; MS, East Tex. State Univ., 1972; DVM, Tex. A&M U., 1977, PhD, 1986. Mixed practitioner Benton (Ark) Veterinary Hosp., 1977-81; veterinary clin. assoc. Coll. Veterinary Medicine Tex. A&M U., College Station, Tex., 1981-84; regional animal care specialist USDA Animal and Plant Health Inspec. Svc., Regulatory Enforcement Animal Care, Ft. Worth, 1986-89; clin. veterinarian Alcon labs., Inc., Ft. Worth, 1989-90, mgr., 1990-94, asst. dir., 1995—. Com. chmn. troop 431 Santa Fe Dist., Longhorn Coun., Boy Scouts Am. Mem. AVMA, Tex. Vet. Med. Assn., Tarrant County Vet. Med. Assn., Dallas County Vet. Med. Assn., Am. Soc. Lab. Animal Practitioners, Am. Assn. Lab. Animal Sci., Tex. Br. Lab. Animal Sci., Assn. Primate Veterinarians, Nat. Eagle Scout Assn., SAR, Beta Beta Beta, Phi Eta Sigma. Lutheran. Home: 2055 Mary Ann Ln Burleson TX 76028-9470 Office: Alcon Labs Inc 6201 South Freeway (R3-12) Fort Worth TX 76134

MANNON, CAROLYN SUE, elementary school educator, reading specialist; b. Wagoner, Okla., Nov. 23, 1950; d. Earl Franklin and Inez Ella (Dodson) Casebolt; m. Dennis Wayne Mannon, Aug. 4, 1972; 1 child, Kristen Dawn. BS in Elem. Edn., Northeastern State U., Tahlequah, Okla., 1972, MS in Edn., 1976. Cert. elem. edn., reading specialist, lang. arts. jr. high, democracy, geography, sociology/anthropology, social studies jr. high, psychology. 6th grade tchr. Moseley Elem. Sch., Siloam Springs, Ark., 1972-74; regional supr. Coweta Ctr. Ctr. for Study of Lit., Northeastern State U., Tahlequah, 1990-91; 2nd grade tchr. Coweta (Okla.) Pub. Schs., 1974-78, reading specialist, 1978—; mem. Tulsa County Reading Coun. Bd., 1994—. Mem. NEA, ASCD, Internat. Reading Assn., Okla. Edn. Assn., Okla. Reading Coun. (bldg. rep.), Coweta Edn. Assn. (v.p. 1994—, pres. 1995—), Tulsa County Reading Coun. (treas. 1995—), Chpt. I Spl. Interest Group. Lutheran. Home: 11608 S 272nd East Ave Coweta OK 74429-5924

MANNS, LINDA GREENE, community health nurse coordinator; b. Bklyn., May 21, 1951; d. Gaston A. and Cleopatra (Frier) Greene; m. Nov. 25, 1978 (div. 1984); 1 child, Temeca E. AAS, Bronx Community Coll., 1971; BSN, Hunter Coll., 1973; MSN, U. Va., 1988. Staff nurse Kings County Hosp., Bklyn., 1971-73; charge nurse St. John's Episcopal Hosp., Bklyn., 1974-78; pub. health nurse Dept. Health, Bklyn., 1973-78; staff nurse Roanoke (Va.) Meml. Hosp., 1979; staff nurse VA Med. Ctr., Salem, Va., 1979-83, primary nurse oncology clinic, 1983-84, weekend nurse supr., 1986-87, community health nurse, 1984-90, community health nurse coord., 1990—. Coord. Community Awareness Health Fair, High St. Bapt. Ch., 1987; vol. coord. Roanoke City Health Dept. Cardiovascular Risk Reduction Program. Mem. Va. Pub. Health Assn., Roanoke Valley Black Nurses' Assn. (treas.), Sigma Theta Tau. Home: 3103 Northside Rd Roanoke VA 24019-2709

MANOCCHIO, VIVIENNE CINDA (VICKI LANE), vocalist, composer; b. Bklyn., Mar. 11, 1949; d. Victor David and Victoria (Allawas) M. Student, U. Miami (Fla.), 1967-69. Internat. singer appeared with Bob Hope, Don Rickles, Merle Haggard, Lou Rawls, others; performed in Japan, S.Am., N.Am., Europe; performed for Presidents Ronald Reagan and Jimmy Carter; actress, singer, dancer summer stock theater, 1961-65; mem. Jackie Gleason Dancers, 1965-70; singer Boca Raton (Fla.) Symphonic Pops, London Philharm., 1989; albums Vicki Lane, With Love, Off the Top of My Head, Pompadour; composer Madame de Pompadour; composer, featured in Lincoln Mercury TV comml. Performer Multiple Sclerosis TV Telethon, Cerebral Palsy Telethon, Parkinson's Disease Telethon. Named Miss Italian Am. Italian Am. Orgn., 1965, Miss Treadway World Miss World Contst, 1970. Roman Catholic. Home: 4400 N Ocean Dr Hollywood FL 33019-4104

MANOS, DENNIS MICHAEL, science educator; b. Cleve., Nov. 7, 1947; s. Nicholas Anthony and Frances Ann (Hofer Svitek) M.; m. Cynthia Ann Ziebro, Dec. 27, 1969; children: Jonathan, Elizabeth. BS in Chemistry, Case Inst. Tech., 1968; PhD in Phys. Chemistry, Ohio State U., 1976. Postdoctoral fellow U. Toronto, Ont., Can., 1976-78; rsch. scientist Aerochem Rsch. Labs, Princeton, N.J., 1978-80; prin. rsch. physicist, br. head surface physics plasma physics lab. Princeton U., 1980-86, 88-92; v.p. tech. Materials Rsch. Corp., Orangeburg, N.Y., 1987; v.p. Princeton Sci. Cons., Inc., 1981-90, pres., chmn., 1990-92; CSX prof. applied sci. and physics, dir. applied sci. Coll. William and Mary, Williamsburg, Va., 1992-95, chmn. dept. applied sci., 1995—; cons. Eaton Corp., ATT, SAIC, IBM, U.S. Army, MRC, USAF, Directed Techs., SEMATECH, others, 1980-92; chmn. DT materials bd. Dept. Energy, 1987-92. Co-author: Plasma Materials Interactions, 1986; co-author, editor: Plasma Etching: An Introduction, 1987; contbr. articles to profl. jours.; patentee coatings, beam production methods. Mem. adv. bd. Va. Space Grant Consortium, 1993—. With U.S. Army, 1969-71. Mem. IEEE, Am. Vacuum Soc. (program chmn. 1992), Am. Phys. Soc., Optical Soc. Am. Home: 101 Thorpes Parish Williamsburg VA 23185-5119 Office: Coll William and Mary Applied Science Williamsburg VA 23185

MANSELL, JOYCE MARILYN, special education educator; b. Minot, N.D., Dec. 17, 1934; d. Einar Axel and Gladys Ellen (Wall) Alm; m. Dudley J. Mansell, Oct. 31, 1954; children: Michael, Debra Mansell Richards. BS, U. Houston, 1968; MEd, Sam Houston State U., 1980. Cert. provisional elem. tchr. 1-8, provisional mentally retarded tchr., provisional lang. and/or learning disabilities tchr., profl. elem. tchr. gen. 1-8, profl. reading specialist. 1st grade tchr. Johnson Elem. Sch., 1968-72, 2nd grade tchr., 1972-76, 3rd grade tchr., 1976-77; spl. edn. tchr. mentally retarded/learning disabled Meml. Parkway Jr. H.S., 1982-86, Waller Mid. Sch., 1986-90; spl. edn. tchr. mentally retarded Royal Mid. Sch., Tex., 1990-95, Royal H.S., 1995-96; ret., 1996; tchr. Am. sign lang. for retarded students Holy Three and One Luth. Ch. of Deaf. Lutheran. Home: 2155 Paso Rello Dr Houston TX 77077-5622

MANSEN, STEVEN ROBERT, manufacturing company executive; b. Chgo., Nov. 26, 1955; s. Robert Lee and Dorothy Nora (Nichols) M.; m. Leesa, May 7, 1988; children: Ambur, Christopher. B in Indsl. Adminstrn., Gen. Motors Inst., 1978. Data processing system analyst in traffic Gen. Motors Corp., Oklahoma City, 1979-81, premium freight system coordinator, outbound distbn. rate analyst in traffic, 1981-83; sr. mfg. system analyst Tech. Oil Tool Co. div. Baker Internat., Norman, Okla., 1983-86; v.p. mgmt. infosystems W. Pat Crow Forgings, Inc., 1986-88; material mgr., Aerospace Technologies, Inc. div. Alco Standard Group, Ft. Worth, 1988-89; mgr. infosystems, Wynn-Kiki div. Diesel-Kiki (name changed to Zexel Tex., Inc. div. Zexel Corp.), Grand Prairie, Tex., 1989—. Mem. S.W. States ASK Users Group (v.p. 1984-86, pres. 1986, Hewlett Packard liaison 1992). Home: 2214 Diamond Point Dr Arlington TX 76017-4517 Office: Zexel Tex Inc 1102 N Carrier Pky Grand Prairie TX 75050-3364

MANSFIELD, JAMES NORMAN, III, lawyer; b. Chattanooga, Feb. 15, 1951; s. James Norman and Doris June (Hilliard) M.; m. Terry Ann Thomas, Dec. 28, 1975; children: Seth Thomas, James Norman, Scott Michael. BA, U. Tenn., Chattanooga, 1973; MA, La. State U., 1976, JD, 1979. Bar: La. 1979, U.S. Dist. Ct. (we. dist.), La. 1979. Shareholder Liskow and Lewis, Lafayette and New Orleans, La., 1979—. Pres. Raven Soc., Chattanooga, 1973. Mem. ABA, La. Bar Assn., Am. Assn. Profl. Landmen, Lafayette Assn. Petroleum Landmen, Order of Coif. Roman Catholic. Home: 103 Asbury Circle Lafayette LA 70503 Office: Liskow & Lewis PO Box 52008 Lafayette LA 70505-2008

MANSFIELD, KARLA JEAN, financial executive; b. Elmhurst, Ill., Aug. 4, 1950; d. Alfred B. and Marian V. (Caniff) M. B in Bus., Western Ill. U., 1971; M in Mgmt., Northwestern U., 1984. CPA, Ill. Sr. auditor Price Waterhouse, Chgo., 1971-74; mgr. acctg. Admiral group Rockwell Internat., Schaumburg, Ill., 1974-78; program mgr. Automatic Electric div. GTE, Northlake, Ill., 1978-81; dir. planning McGraw-Edison Co., Rolling Meadows, Ill., 1981-82; v.p. fin. and planning Aon Risk Svcs., Chgo., 1983-90; v.p., regional contr. AON Risk Svcs., Chgo., 1990-96; v.p., contr. CNA Excess & Select, Chgo., 1996—. Mem. AICPAs, N.C. Assn. CPAs, Planning Forum, Ill. Soc. CPAs, Sigma Iota Epsilon, Beta Gamma Sigma. Office: CNA CNA Plz 255-0 Chicago IL 60685

MANSFIELD, NORMAN CONNIE, bookkeeper; b. Rayle, Ga., Apr. 27, 1916; s. Boykin Carswell and Cleo (Norman) M.; m. Ila Ruth Poss, Jan. 3, 1943; children: Jonathan Norman, Jerry Carswell. Cert., U. Ga. Notary Pub., Ga. Mgr. Railway Express Agy., Washington, Ga., 1943-78; semi-retired bookkeeper Russell Transfer Co. Inc., Washington, 1979—; mgr. Rwy. Express. Exec. bd. mem. Ga. Carolina Coun.; deacon First Baptist Ch., Washington; cubscout master, Washington, Ga., 1962. With USNG. Recipient Baseball and Little League award Coca Cola Co., Washington, Ga., 1951, 68, Woodmen of World award Life Ins. Soc., Augusta, Ga., 1978; named Boy Scout of Yr., Ga. Carolina Coun., Thomson, 1956. Mem. Masons (Shriner, worship master 1984), Order of Eastern Star (worthy patron), Woodman of the World (pres.), Lions (pres.), Washington (Ga.) Country Club, Ida Cason Callaway Found., Ga. Sheriffs Assn. Home: 209 Hudson Dr Washington GA 30673-1527 Office: The News-Reporter 116 W Robert Toombs Ave Washington GA 30673-1664

MANSFIELD, PHILIP DOUGLAS, veterinary medicine educator; b. Glasgow, Ky., Mar. 30, 1941; s. William Arnold and Zada Mae (Proffitt) M.; m. Sheila Lynn Poynter, Aug. 6, 1969; children: Tamara Lynn, Kimberly Brooke. Student, Ea. Ky. State U., 1967-69; DVM, Auburn U., 1967. Diplomate Am. Bd. of Vet. Practitioners. Assoc. vet. practitioner Glasgow Animal Clinic, 1967-69; vet. practitioner ptnr. Mansfield Animal Hosp., Hopkinsville, Ky., 1969-72, 72-78; asst. prof. Auburn (Ala.) U., 1978-96, assoc. prof., 1996—; owner Mansfield Animal Hosp., 1969-78; pres. Am. Bd. Vet. Practitioners, Nashville, 1995—. Author: (with others) Emergency Medicine and Critical Care in Practice, 1992; contbr. articles to profl. jours. Chmn. cmty. outreach Auburn United Meth. Ch., 1994-96. Recipient Grace Kemper Rsch. award 1983; grantee Scott-Ritchey Rsch. Ctr., 1985, 89, Auburn U., 1983, Am. Animal Hosp. Assn., 1993-95. Mem. AVMA, Opelika Performing Arts Assn., Auburn Rotary Club (dir. vocat. svcs. 1995-96, v.p. 1996-97), Univ. Club (sec. 1994-96), Elks. Methodist. Office: Dept of Animal Surgery Auburn U Coll of Vet Med Auburn AL 36849-5523

MANSFIELD, TOBI ELLEN, psychologist; b. Miami Beach, Fla., Oct. 4, 1949; d. Murray Irwin and Rose Turner (Plansky) Mantell; 1 child, Mia Michelle. BA, U. Miami, Fla., 1974; MA, Norwich U., Montpelier, Vt., 1982; PhD, Union Inst., Cin., 1987. Mental health counselor South Dade Crisis Intervention, Miami, Fla., 1978-80; adj. faculty Miami Dade Community Coll., 1977-80; clin. assoc. Miami Psychotherapy Inst., 1980-88; adj. faculty Nova U., 1984-87, U. Miami Med. Sch., 1988-90; psychologist, dir. Miami Wellness Ctr., 1987—; mem. med. staff South Fla. Inst. for Reproductive Medicine. Contbr. articles to profl. jours. Mem. APA, Am. Bd. Med. Psychotherapists (assoc.), Royal Soc. Medicine, Am. Soc. for Reproductive Medicine. Office: Miami Wellness Center Ste # 106 9150 SW 87th Ave Miami FL 33176-2311

MANSMANN, PARIS TAYLOR, medical educator; b. Pitts., Feb. 19, 1957; s. Herbert Charles Jr. and Margaret Marshal (Miller) M.; m. Leslie Ann Windstein, July 8, 1978; children: Erin Hart, Paris Corey, Maureen Ellyse. Student, Lafayette Coll., 1975-76; BS in Math., St. Joseph's U., Phila., 1980; MD, Jefferson Med. Coll., 1984. Diplomate Am. Bd. Medicine, Am. Bd. Internal Medicine, Am. Bd. Pediatrics, Am. Bd. Allergy and Immunology. Resident in medicine, pediatrics Geisinger Med. Ctr., Danville, Pa., 1984-88, chief resident, 1987-88; fellow in allergy, immunology Duke U. Med. Ctr., Durham, N.C., 1988-90; asst. prof. medicine and pediat. W.Va. U., Morgantown, 1990-93, asst. prof. medicine, 1990-95, assoc. prof. medicine, 1995—; program coord. medicine, pediat., W.Va. U., Morgantown, 1990-93. Author: (with others) Current Pediatric Therapy, 1994; contbr. articles to profl. jours. Recipient Outstanding Commitment award Vis. Clinicians, 1990. Fellow Am. Acad. Pediatrics, Am. Coll. Allergy and Immunology; mem. ACP, Am. Acad. Allergy and Immunology, European Acad. Allergy and Clin. Immunology, W.Va. Allergy Soc. (pres. 1992—). Republican. Roman Catholic. Office: WVa U Sch Medicine Box 9167 Health Scis Ctr Morgantown WV 26506-9167

MANSO, GILBERT, physician; b. Havana, Cuba, Dec. 16, 1942; s. Gilberto F. and Gricelda (Jimenez) M.; m. Dana Manso; came to U.S., 1959, naturalized, 1968; BA, U. Tex., Austin, 1965; MD, U. Tex. Med. Br., Galveston, 1969; student U.S. Air Force Sch. Aerospace Medicine, 1970; children from previous marriage: Wayne, Tammy, Seth. Cert. comml., multiengine, instrument rated pilot. Rotating intern Meml. Bapt. Hosp., Houston, 1969-70; chief of staff Cochran Meml. Hosp., Morton, Tex., 1974-76; health officer Cochran County, Tex., 1974-76; chmn. med. care evaluation com. Tidelands Hosp., Channelview, Tex., 1976-77, vice-chief of staff, 1977-78, chief of staff, 1978—; mem. faculty U. Tex. Health Science, Houston, asst. prof. dept. family medicine; pres. The Whole Health Ctr., Houston, 1976—. Pres., Manso Airmotive; bd. dirs. The Living Ctr. one of the pioneers in wholistic medicine in Tex., Houston; med. adv. bd. Am. Reflexology Assn. Author: The Diabetes & Hypoglycemia Cope Book. Served to maj. MC USAF, 1970-75, Vietnam 1970-71. Decorated Air medal and 2 oak leaf clusters. Diplomate Am. Bd. Family Practice. Fellow Am. Acad. Family Practice; mem. AMA, Tex. Med. Assn., Harris County Med. Soc., Am. Holistic Med. Assn., Internat. Wine and Food Soc. (bd. dirs. 1981-84), Houston Acad. Family Practice, Am. Coll. Emergency Physicians, Chaine de Rotisseurs, New Warriors. Republican. Office: 5177 Richmond Ave Ste 125 Houston TX 77056-6736

MANSON, KEITH ALAN MICHAEL, lawyer; b. Warwick, RI, Oct. 26, 1962; s. Ronald Frederick and Joan Patricia (Reardon) M.; m. Jennifer Annette Stearns; children: Kristin Elizabeth, Michelle Nicole. BA, R.I. Coll., 1985; cert. computer info. systems, Bryant Coll., 1988; cert. law, U. Notre Dame, London, 1990; JD, Thomas M. Cooley Law Sch., 1991. Bar: Ind. 1991, U.S. Dist. Ct. (no. dist.) Ind. 1991, U.S. Dist. Ct. (so. dist.) Ind. 1991, U.S. Dist. Ct. (so. dist.) Ga. 1992, U.S. Dist. Ct. Mil. Appeals 1991. Spl. asst. U.S. atty. U.S. Dist. Ct. Ga., Brunswick, 1992-93; pvt. practice Fernandina Beach, Fla., 1994—; cons. The Law Store Ltd. Paralegal Svcs., Fernandina Beach., 1994—. Contbr. articles to profl. jours. Commnr. Fla. coun. Boy Scouts Am., Jacksonville, 1993—; com. mem. sea scout ship 660 St. Peter's Ch., Fernandina Beach, 1994—; chmn. Scouting for Food Dr., Nassau County, Fla., 1994. Lt. USN, 1985-86, 90-94. F.C. Tanner Trust, Fed. Products Inc. scholar, Providence, 1981-85, Esterline Corp. scholar, Providence, 1986. Mem. ABA, Judge Advocate Assn., Jacksonville Bar Assn., Navy League U.S., Rotary (project mgr. Webster-Dudley Mass. chpt. 1986-88), Phi Alpha Delta. Home and Office: 1908 Reatta Ln Fernandina Beach FL 32034-8936

MANSON, LEWIS AUMAN, energy research executive; b. Cleve., July 12, 1918; s. Lewis Frederick and Ina Josephine (Auman) M.; m. Alva Anne London, Sept. 3, 1960 (div. 1982); children: Anita, Howard; m. Shirley Anne Traeger, Jan. 27, 1982; children: Lewis, Jean, Phillip, Edward. Student, Gen. Motors Tech. U., 1943-44, Purdue U., 1942-43, Rice U., 1950-54. Cons. numerous oil, gas, and mining cos., 1951-57; cons. The Space Agy., Washington, 1958-59, Douglas Aircraft, El Segundo, Calif., 1964; dir. Copper Range Mines, Wyo., 1965; dir. explorations, cons. Nico Internat., S.A. de C.V., Mex., 1968-71; builder Spring, Tex., 1971-74; dir., conductor explorations Minerals of the Sun, S.A. de C.V., Honduras, 1975; dir. Asheville Petroleum Corp., Ill., 1976; conductor explorations Neozoic Minerals & Petroleum, Ltd., Colo., N.Mex., Tex., 1976-77; conductor explorations, dir. Primal Energy Rsch. Found., Houston, 1982—; pres. Transzoic Orebody Locators, Ltd., Vancouver, B.C., Pleiades Petroleum Corp., Lexington, Tenn. and Houston; lectr. grade schs., high schs., Kiwanis, and Rotary, 1962—. Author: The Primal Energy Transverter, 1966, Birth of the Moon, 1978, Origins of Solar Flares and Keys to Predicting Them, 1978, Automatic Recording of Deep Space (interplanetary) Gravity, 1978, Arriving Ionospheric High Energy (Solar Generated), 1978, Out of the Grey Mist, 1992, Life's Continuum, 1992, The Real Origin of Stellar Energy, 1993, The Great Mystery, 1994; patentee in field; inventor Quakaster, Affinity Sys., The Cradle System equipment to prevent and/or cure decubitis ulcers by "ocean motion." Scoutmaster Boy Scouts Am., Houston, 1956-63; cubmaster Cub Scouts, Pasadena, Calif., 1962. With Ind. NG, 1942-43. Republican. Office: Primal Energy Rsch Found Apt 113 11250 Taylor Draper Ln Austin TX 78759-3976

MANTEY, ELMER MARTIN, food company executive; b. Malone, Tex., July 20, 1926; s. Edward G. and Margaret H. Mantey; m. Donna May Scritsmier, Dec. 27, 1948; children: Patricia, Carol Mantey Callis, Cynthia Mantey Stockdale. BS in Chemistry with honors, Bradley U., 1949. Chemist, plant mgr. Am. Petrochem. Co., Mpls., 1949-63, v.p. ops., 1963-66; v.p. Polychem. Group, Whittaker Corp., L.A., 1966-69, pres. textile div., 1969-71; chief exec. officer Flavorite Labs. Inc., Memphis, 1971-89, also chmn. bd. dirs.; bd. dirs. Craig-Hallum Corp., A.M. Todd Co., The Dupps Co.; chmn. bd. trustees Crichton Coll.; bd. dirs. John Brown U. Served with USN, 1944-46. Mem. Inst. Food Techs., Pres.' Assn., Am. Mgmt. Assn. Evang., Am. Spice Trade Assn. (chmn. manufactured products com.), Meat Industry Suppliers Assn. (chmn.), Nat. Seasoning Mfrs. Assn. Clubs: Rotary (Memphis), Summit; Farmington Country. Home: 6925 Sugar Maple Cv Memphis TN 38119-5619 Office: PO Box 1315 Memphis TN 38101-1315

MANTHEY, FRANK ANTHONY, physician, director; b. N.Y.C., Dec. 2, 1933; s. Frank A.J. and Josephine (Roth) M.; m. Douglas Susan Falvey, Sept. 14 1958 (div. 1979, dec. 1989); children: Michael P., Susan M., Peter J.; m. Doris Jean Pulley, Oct. 11, 1979. BS, Fordham U., 1954; MD, SUNY, Syracuse, 1958. Diplomate Am. Bd. Anesthesiology, Am. Bd. Med. Examiners. Intern Upstate Med. Ctr., Syracuse, 1958-59; resident in anesthesiology Yale-New Haven Med. Ctr., 1962-64; physician Yale-New Haven Hosp., 1964-75; pvt. practice medicine Illmo, Mo., 1975-79; dir. Manthey Med. Clinic, Elkton, Ky., 1979—; clin. instr. anesthesiology Yale U. Med. Sch., New Haven, 1964-69, asst. clin. prof. anesthesiology, 1969-75; cons. Conn. Dept. Aeros., Hartford, 1969-70; sr. med. examiner Fed. Aviation Adminstrn., Illmo, 1975-79. Contbr. articles to profl. jours. Chmn. gen. works Little Folks Fair, Guilford, Conn., 1967-71; mem. Rep. Town Com., Guilford, 1969-75; chmn. Guilford Sch. Bldg. Com., 1973-75. Capt. USAF (M.C.), 1956-62. Mem. Ky. Med. Assn., Aerospace Med. Assn. (assoc. fellow 1973-75), Flying Physicians Assn. (v.p. NE chpt. 1973-75, v.p. nat. 1974-75, 79-80, bd. dirs. 1970-73, 75-78, bd. dirs. nat. 1975-78), Aircraft Owners and Pilots Assn., Mercedes Benz Club Am., Alpha Kappa Kappa. Home: 105 Sunset Dr Elkton KY 42220-9257 Office: Manthey Family Practice Clinic 203 Allensville St PO Box 368 Elkton KY 42220

MANUEL, DAVID P., university dean; b. Thibodaux, La., Mar. 1, 1947; s. Oliver J. and Leona M. (Meancon) M.; m. Betty Coe Cruzen, Dec. 21, 1974; children: Edward, Robert. BA in Econs., Nicholls State U., 1970; MA in Econs., U. Miss., 1972, PhD in Econs., 1975. Asst. prof. econs. U. S.W. La., Lafayette, 1974-77, assoc. prof. econs., 1977-83, prof. econs., 1983-90, dean Coll. bus., 1986-90; dean Sch. Bus. St. Mary's U., San Antonio, 1990—. Contbr. articles to profl. publs. Bd. dirs. Am. Heart Assn., San Antonio, 1992—, Bus. Expansion and Retention Ctr., San Antonio, 1995—; co-chair Leadership San Antonio, 1993-94; chair bus. adv. coun. Bus. Careers H.S., San Antonio, 1994-96. Mem. Rotary. Home: 13810 Bluff Top San Antonio TX 78216 Office: Saint Mary's U Sch Bus San Antonio TX 78228

MANUELLA, FRANK, art and design educator; b. N.Y.C.. BFA, Cooper Union U., 1963; M in Comm. Design, Pratt Inst., 1982. Pres. Manuella & Assocs., N.Y.C., 1963-82; prof. art & design U. Tex., Edinburg, 1982—; asst. prof. design Pratt Inst., N.Y.C., 1975-82; adv. bd. U. Tex. Press, 1982—, coun. mem., 1989-92, officer Phi Kappa Phi, 1990-92, faculty senator, 1986-93. Solo exhbns. include U. Tex. Gallery, 1991, 92, Reynosa, Mex., 1993, McAllen Internat. Mus., 1994. Recipient gov.'s award for acad. excellence, State of Tex., 1989; Fulbright grantee, 1993. Office: U Tex Dept Art 1201 W University Dr Edinburg TX 78539-2909

MANUTI, ANNABELLE THERESA, advertising agency financial executive; b. Bklyn., Sept. 11, 1928; d. Decio Dan and Anna Michelle (Vanacore) Assorto; m. John Thomas Manuti, Dec. 31, 1958. Student, Hunter Coll., 1950, postgrad. in real estate sch. Continuing Edn., 1980-82. Lic. real estate broker, N.Y. Statis. auditor Am. Fore Ins. Group, N.Y.C., 1950-55; bookkeeper Picard Advt., N.Y.C., 1955-60; supr. dept. acctg. Moquel Williams & Saylor Advt., N.Y.C., 1960-65; comptroller's asst. Frolich Advt., N.Y.C., 1965-70; supr. accounts payable Miller Advt., N.Y.C., 1970-80; v.p. fin. Jaffe Communications, N.Y.C., 1980-90; free-lance, 1990—. Roman Catholic.

MAO, HO-KWANG, geophysicist, educator; b. Shanghai, China, June 18, 1941; came to U.S., 1964; s. Sen and Tak-chun (Hu) M.; m. Agnes Liu, Feb. 10, 1968; children: Cynthia, Linda, Wendy. BS, Nat. Taiwan U., Taepei, 1963; MS, U. Rochester, 1966, PhD, 1968. Rsch. asst., teaching asst. U. Rochester, N.Y., 1964-67, rsch. assoc., 1967-68; postdoctoral fellow Geophys. Lab., Carnegie Instn., Washington, 1968-70, rsch. assoc., 1970-72, geophysicist, 1972—. Recipient Bridgman Gold medal Internat. Assn. for Advancement of High Pressure Sci. and Tech., 1989. Fellow Am. Geophys. Union, Am. Phys. Soc., Mineral Soc. Am. (award 1979); mem. AAAS, NAS (Arthur L. Day prize and lectureship 1990), Academia Sinica, Sigma Xi. Home: 11322 Edenderry Dr Fairfax VA 22030-5441 Office: Carnegie Inst Geophysics Lab 5251 Broad Branch Rd NW Washington DC 20015-1305*

MAO, JINTONG, physicist; b. Shanghai, People's Republic of China, May 12, 1944; came to U.S., 1981; s. Enpei Mao and Jiuru Qiao; m. Junhua Wang, Apr. 19, 1971; 1 child, Jie Mao. BA in Mech. Engring., Huazhong Inst. Tech., Wuhan, People's Republic of China, 1967; MSEE, Tech. and Sci. U. China, Beijing, 1981; PhD in Physics, U. Fla., 1987. Engr. electronics and automatic control Wuhan Iron and Steel Co., 1968-78; teaching and rsch. asst. dept. physics and radiology U. Fla., Gainesville, 1981-87; rsch. assoc. dept. radiology Columbia U., N.Y.C., 1987-88, asst. prof. dept. radiology, 1988-96; assoc. prof. Columbia U., 1996—. Contbr. articles to profl. jours. Recipient Prin. Investigator grant Whitaker Found., 1993—. Mem. Soc. Magnetic Resonance. Office: U Fla Dept Radiology PO Box J-374 Gainesville FL 32610

MAPLE, HOWARD DONALD, organbuilders association executive, organist; b. Peoria, Ill., Apr. 8, 1959; s. Donald F. and Bonnie L. (Rankin) M. Student, Cornell Coll., 1977-78, U. Iowa, 1978-81. Pipe organ builder Visser-Rowland Assocs., Houston, 1981-87; exec. sec. Am. Inst. Organbuilders, Houston, 1989—. Recipient Music scholarship Cornell Coll., 1977. Mem. Am. Guild of Organists. Office: Am Inst Organbuilders PO Box 130982 Houston TX 77219-0982

MAPLE, MARILYN JEAN, educational media coordinator; b. Turtle Creek, Pa., Jan. 16, 1931; d. Harry Chester and Agnes (Dobbie) Kelley; B.A., U. Fla., 1972, M.A., 1975, Ph.D., 1985; 1 dau., Sandra Maple. Journalist various newspapers, including Mountain Eagle, Jasper, Ala., Boise (Idaho) Statesman, Daytona Beach (Fla.) Jour., Lorain (Ohio) Jour.; account exec. Fredericks & Co., N.Y.C.; producer hist. films Fla. State Mus., Gainesville, 1967-69; writer, dir., producer med. and sci. films and TV prodns. for six medically related colls. U. Fla., Gainesville, 1969—; pres. Media Modes, Inc., Gainesville. Recipient Blakslee award, 1969, spl. award, 1979, Monsour Lectureship award, 1979. Mem. Health Edn. Media Assn. (dir., awards, 1977, 79), Phi Delta Kappa, Kappa Tau Alpha. Author: On the Wings of a Butterfly; columnist: Health Care Edn. mag.; contbr. Fla. Hist. Quar. Home: 1927 NW 7th Ln Gainesville FL 32603-1103 Office: U Fla PO Box 16J Gainesville FL 32602-0016

MAPLE, TIMOTHY MICHAEL, chemical company executive; b. Owensboro, Ky., Jan. 24, 1936; s. T.M. Maple and Lucille (Coons) Lambert; m. Wilda Jo Atherton, Apr. 20, 1957 (div. 1979); children: Timothy Michael II, Kimberly Jo, David Kyle. BLS, U. Evansville, 1984. Truck driver PB&S Chem. Co., Henderson, Ky., 1960-63, supr. solvents, 1963-67, supr. vehicle maintenance, 1967-69, adminstv. asst. to v.p., 1969-77, corp. fleet mgr., 1977-89, asst. to exec. v.p., 1989-94; cons., 1994—; mem. task force com. Chlorine Inst., N.Y.C., 1979. Author: Operations Procedures, 1984. Fund raiser United Way, Henderson, 1972, YMCA, Henderson, 1968-72; bd. dirs. Hugh Edward Sandefur Tng. Ctr., 1973-74. Named Boss of Yr., Profl. Sec. Internat., 1980-81. Mem. Pvt. Truck Council Am. Democrat. Baptist. Avocations: landscaping, gardening. Home: 2243 Book Dr Henderson KY 42420-9259

MAPLES, DAN, golf course designer; b. Pinehurst, N.C., 1947. Degree in landscape architecture, U. Ga. Golf. profl., supt. Palmetto Country Club, Aiken, S.C.; prin. Dan Maples Design, Inc., Pinehurst, N.C. Prin. works include Marsh Harbor, Oyster Bay, The Pit. Mem. Am. Soc. Golf Course Archs. (pres. 1990). Office: Dan Maples Design Inc PO Box 5769 77 Cherokee Rd Pinehurst NC 28374

MARBLE, MELINDA SMITH, writer, editor; b. Ponca City, Okla., June 17, 1960; d. Monte Gene and Dorothy Worthington Smith; m. Sanford Marble. BA with high hons., spl. hons. English, U. Tex., 1984. Mktg. Data Base Publs., Austin, Tex., 1986-87; assoc. editor Austin Area Bus. Women Directory, 1987-88; asst. pub. Travelers' Times, Austin, 1988-89; assoc. editor Tex. Bar Jour., Austin, 1989-95; freelance editor, Austin, 1989-95, novelist, freelance journalist, Morristown, N.J., 1995—. Contbr. articles to newspapers and profl. jours. Recipient Gold Quill award of merit Internat. Assn. Bus. Communicators, 1993, Gold Quill Excellence award for First Person Articles, 1995; Best of Austin 4 Color Mag. award, 1993, 2 awards of merit, 1995, Presdl. Citation, State Bar of Tex., 1993, Nat. Assn. Govt. Communicators award of Honor 4 Color Mag., 1994, Best of Austin Feature Writing award, 1995, Best of Austin Advocacy Writing award, 1995.

MARBUT, ROBERT GORDON, communications and broadcast executive; b. Athens, Ga., Apr. 11, 1935; s. Robert Smith and Laura Gordon (Powers) M.; m. Margo Susan Spitz, Sept. 24, 1989; children: Robert Gordon, Laura Dodd, Michael Powers, Marcy Lizbeth. B Indsl. Engring., Ga. Inst. Tech., 1957; MBA with distinction, Harvard U., 1963. Registered profl. engr., Calif. Engr. Esso Standard Oil Co., Baton Rouge, 1957; corp. dir. engring. and plans Copley Press, La Jolla, Calif., 1963-70; v.p. named changed to Harte-Hanks Newspapers, Inc., San Antonio, 1970-71; pres., CEO named changed to Harte-Hanks Comm., Inc., San Antonio, 1971-91, also dir., 1971-91, vice chmn. bd. dirs., 1991; founder, chmn., CEO Argyle Comm., Inc, San Antonio, 1992—; founder, CEO, dir. Argyle TV Holding, Inc., San Antonio, 1993-95; co-founder, chmn., CEO Argyle TV, Inc., San Antonio, 1994—; dir. AP, 1979-88, vice chmn. 1987-88; chmn. Newspaper Advt. Bur., 1988-90, exec. com. dir. 1974-80, 82-90; bd. dirs Tupperware, Inc., Diamond Shamrock, Inc., Tracor, Inc., Katz Media Group; pres. adv. bd. U Ga. Henry W. Grady Sch. Journalism, 1975—, mem. adv. Found. for Comm. Sch. U. Tex., 1975—; bd. dirs. Tex. Rsch. League, 1975—, Salzburg Inst. Am. Studies, 1978-81; mem. adv. bd. Ga. Tech., 1978-81; founding mem. Am. Bus. Conf., 1981-89; mem. U. Tex. Centennial commn., 1981-83; pres. adv. coun. U. Tex. Coll. Comm., 1982-83; bd. dirs. Up With People, 1983—, exec. com., 1984—; instr. Armstrong Coll., 1951, Calif. State, Los Angeles, 1964, Woodbury Coll., 1964. Author: (with Healy, Henderson and others) Creative Collective Bargaining, 1965; also articles in mags., jours.; frequent spkr. Coordinating chmn. San Antonio Target 90 commn., 1983-84; campaign chmn. United Way, San Antonio, 1985, chmn. bd. dirs., 1988-89; vice chmn. Tex. select com. on Tax Equity, 1987-89; mem select com. Tex. Revenues, 1991-92; mem. Tex. World Trade Coun., 1986-87. Served with USAF, 1958-61. Recipient Isaiah Thomas award Rochester Inst. Tech., 1980, EXCEL award in comm., 1987, People of Vision award, 1991; selected to Acad. Disting. Engring. Alumni Ga. Tech., 1995. Mem. Am. Newspaper Pubs. Assn. Rsch. Inst. (exec. com. 1973—), Am. Newspaper Publs. Assn. (chmn. task group on future, chmn. telecomm. com. 1974—, bd. dirs. 1976—, chmn. future task group), So. Newspaper Pubs. Assn. (pres. 1979-80, dir. 1975-81, treas. 1977, chmn. bus. and adminstrn. com. 1976), Am. Newspaper Pubs. Assn. Found. (trustee 1976—), Tex. Daily Newspaper Assn. (pres. 1979, Tex. Newspaper Leader of Yr., 1981), Greater San Antonio C. of C. (chmn. long range planning task force, dir. 1979—, exec. com. 1981—, chmn., 1984), Delta Tau Delta, Omicron Delta Kappa, Phi Eta Sigma. Protestant. Club: San Antonio Country, Argyle. Office: Argyle Communications 200 Concord Plz Ste 700 San Antonio TX 78216

MARBUT, ROBERT GORDON, JR., sports organization executive; b. Savannah, Ga., May 5, 1960; s. Robert Gordon Sr. and Berta (Dodd) M.; m. Mary M. Hartman, July 27, 1985; 1 child, Amanda Marie. BA in Econs., Polit. Sci. and Psychology, Claremont Men's Coll., 1983, MA in Criminal Justice, 1985; student, Air War Coll., Maxwell AFB, Ala., 1991. Dir. campaign ops. Com. to Re-elect Mayor Henry Cisneros, San Antonio, 1984-85, campaign mgr., 1986-87; asst. to Mayor Henry Cisneros for spl. projects and politics City of San Antonio, 1987-88, adminstrv. asst., 1987-88; pres. AAU Jr. Olympics Games Com., San Antonio, 1988-89, San Antonio Sports Found., 1990-91, U.S. Olympic Festival '93, San Antonio, 1991-93, SAOne; fellow Nat. Svc. Office White House, Washington, 1989-90; bd. dirs. U.S. Olympic Com., 1992—; active U.S. Olympic Com. Nat. Sports Festival (now called U.S. Olympic Festival), 1978, 79, 81, U.S. Olympic Tng. Squad, 1972-82; cons., coord. to polit. campaigns, 1988—. Weekly guest Sta. WOAI Jay Howard Sports Talk Show, 1987-88; bd. dirs. Austin area br. Orton Dyslexia Soc., 1988-89; youth dir. La Verne Heights Presbyn. Ch., 1981-84; bd. dirs., advisor The Winston Sch. for Dyslexics, 1986-89, 91—; pres. San Antonio Amateur Sports Found., 1986-88; Sunday sch. tchr. Madison Sq. Presbyn. Ch., 1988-92, ruling elder, 1991-93, budget and finance chair, 1991-92, usher capt., 1991—, stewardship chair, 1991; vol. Vance Jackson Neighborhood Recycling Ctr., 1992-93; bd. advisors Schreiner Coll., 1994—; active Bexar County Red Cross Emergency Disaster Relief Teams, 1978, 80, also shelter mgr., 1980, Martin Luther King Jr. Meml. City/County Commn., 1986-88, Alamodome Design Adv. Com., 1989, transition/departure com. George Bush for President, 1992. Rhodes scholar finalist, 1983; recipient Bronze medal U.S. Olympic Festival, 1979; named Live Wire, Tex. Bus., 1986. Mem. U.S. Penthathlon Assn. (v.p. 1992-94, mem. exec. com., bd. dirs. 1992—, pres. 1994—), Rotary Club San Antonio. Home: 10203 Vernlyn Dr San Antonio TX 78230-4134 Office: San Antonio Sports Found PO Box 830386 San Antonio TX 78283-0386

MARCADIS, ABRAHAM S., plastic surgeon; b. Tampa, Fla., Sept. 29, 1954; s. Sam Abraham M.; m. Elizabeth Zack. BA in Chemistry, Emory Univ., 1975, MD, 1979. Diplomate Am. Bd. Plastic Surgeons. Recipient AOA Emory Sch. Medicine, 1979. Fellow Am. Coll. Surgeons; mem. Am. Soc. Plastic and Reconstructive Surgeons, Phi Beta Kappa. Office: 508 S Habana Ave Ste 300 Tampa FL 33609-4144

MARCANO, CONCHITA SOLTERO, Spanish language educator; b. San Juan, P.R., Nov. 21, 1934; d. Rafael Soltero-Peralta and Conchita (Rinaldi) de Soltero; m. Rafael A. Marcano, July 3, 1958; children: Maria C., Rafael, Francisco Javier, Maria del Carmen. Secretarial diploma cum laude, U. P.R., 1957, BA in Edn. cum laude, 1959, MA in Edn., 1975; PhD summa cum laude, U. de Santiage de Compostela, Spain, 1990. Cert. profl. sec., 1986. Mem. bus. faculty U. P.R., Rio Piedras, 1961-66, 73-75; instr. bus. Spanish and secretarial sci. econs. dept. Interam. U., Hato Rey, P.R., 1975-82, Bayamon, P.R., 1982-83; assoc. prof. Spanish dept. U. P.R. Coll., Bayamon, 1983—; condr. seminars govt. and pvt. enterprises. Mem. Eastern Bus. Edn. Assn., Asociacion Puertorriquena de Profesores de Educacion Comercial, Cath. Bus. Edn. Assn., Am. Bus. Communications Assn., Assn. Wives P.R. Med. Assn., Am. Assn. Tchrs of Spanish and Portuguese (treas. local chpt.). Home: 1801 Santa Marta St El Pilar Rio Piedras PR 00926

MARCH, JACQUELINE FRONT, retired chemist; b. Wheeling, W.Va.; m. A.W. March (dec.); children: Wayne Front, Gail March Cohen. BS, Case Western Res. U., 1937, MA, 1939; postgrad. U. Chgo., U. Pitts. (1942-45), Ohio State U. Clin. chemist, Mt. Sinai Hosp., Cleve.; med. rsch. chemist U. Chgo.; rsch. analyst Koppers Co., also info. scientist Union Carbide Corp., Carnegie-Mellon U., Pitts.; propr. March Med. Rsch. Lab., etiology of diabetes, Dayton, Ohio; guest scientist Kettering Found., Yellow Springs, Ohio; Dayton Found. fellow Miami Valley Hosp. Rsch. Inst.; chemistry faculty U. Dayton, computer/chem. info. scientist Rsch. Inst. U. Dayton; on-base prin. investigator Air Force Info. Ctr. Wright-Patterson AFB, 1969-79; chem. info. specialist Nat. Inst. Occupl. Safety and Health, Cin., 1979-90; propr. JFM Cons., Ft. Myers, Fla., 1990-93; ret., 1993; designer info. sys., spkr. in field. Contbr. articles to profl. publs. Active Retired & Sr. Vol. Program Lee County Sch. Dist., 1992-93, Lee County Hosp. Med. Libr., Rutenberg County Libr., Wyeth Gastrointestinal fellow med. rsch. U. Chgo., 1940-42. Mem. AAUP (exec. bd. 1978-79), Am. Soc. Info. Sci. (treas. South Ohio chpt. 1973-75), Am. Chem. Soc. (emeritus, Fla. chpt., pres. Dayton 1977), Dayton Engring. Soc. (hon.), Soc. Advancement Materials & Process Engring. (Fla. chpt., pres. Midwest chpt. 1977-78), Dayton Affiliated Tech. Socs. (Outstanding Scientist and Engr. award 1978), Sigma Xi (emeritus, Fla. chpt., pres. Cin. fed. environ. chpt. 1986-87). Home: 1301 SW 10th Ave F-203 Delray Beach FL 33444-1280

MARCH, WALLACE EUGENE, dean, religious studies educator; b. Dallas, July 8, 1935; s. Wallace Walter March and Helen Maud (Thompson) Dickey; m. Margaret Ann Spencer, June 8, 1957; children: Judith Elizabeth March Kelley, Katherine Anne. BA, Austin Coll., 1957; BD, Austin Presbyn. Theol. Sem., 1960; PhD, Union Theol. Sem., N.Y.C., 1966. Ordained to ministry Presbyn. Ch., 1964. Tutor Union Theol. Sem., 1961-64; asst. prof. Old Testament Austin (Tex.) Presbyn. Theol. Sem., 1966-70, assoc. prof. Old Testament, 1970-74, prof. Old Testament, 1974-82; A.B. Rhodes prof. Old Testament Louisville Presbyn. Theol. Sem., 1982—, dean faculty, 1993—; sec., vice chairperson Appalachian Ministry Ednl. Resources Ctr., Berea, Ky., 1992—; mem., chairperson coun. theology and culture Presbyn. Ch. U.S.A., Atlanta and Louisville, 1979-88. Author: Basic Bible Study, 1978, Israel and the Politics of Land, 1994, From the Conquest to the Kingdom, 1994; contbr. articles to profl. publs. Mem. Louisville Orch. Assn. and Fund for the Arts, 1983—; pres. parent assn. Winn Elem. Sch., Austin, 1979-81, Pierce Jr. H.S., Austin, 1981-82, Atherton H.S., Louisville, 1983-87. Rsch. grantee Assn. Theol. Schs., Pitts., 1980; Rockefeller fellow, rsch. grantee Rockefeller Found., N.Y.C., 1964-65; named Disting. Alumnus, Austin Coll., Sherman, Tex., 1995. Mem. Am. Acad. Religion, Soc. Bibl. Lit. (regional pres. 76-77), Am. Schs. of Oriental Rsch., S.W. Commn. on Religious Study (pres. 1977-78). Democrat. Office: Louisville Presbyn Theol Sem 1044 Alta Vista Rd Louisville KY 40205-1758

MARCHAM, TIMOTHY VICTOR, pharmacist; b. New Britain, Conn., June 15, 1943; s. John Nelson and Eileen Agnes (Mannings) M. BS in Pharmacy, U. Conn., 1966. Diplomate Am. Bd. Forensic Examiners. Staff pharmacist Kensington (Conn.) Pharmacy, Inc., 1968-72, New Britain Meml. Hosp., 1972-75; cons. pharmacist Health Care Cons. Corp., West Hartford, Conn., 1976-85; staff pharmacist Conn. Dept. Mental Health/Cedarcrest Regional Hosp., Newington, 1978-85; dir. pharmacy Conn. Dept. Mental Health/Cedarcrest Regional Hosp., 1985-91, N.C. Dept. Corrections, 1992—; corporator New Britain (Conn.) Gen. Hosp., 1974—. Radiol. officer Civil Preparedness/Emergency Mgmt. Div., Town of Plainville, Conn., 1965-91; life mem. New Britain Gen. Hosp. Aux.; pres. New Britain Meml. Hosp. Credit Union, 1974-75; provider, SAC officer Health Systems Agy. of North Cen. Conn., 1976-82. Capt. CAP, 1974—. Fellow Am. Soc. Cons. Pharmacists; mem. Am. Pharm. Assn., Am. Soc. Hosp. Pharmacists, Conn. Pharm. Assn. (awards and scholarship), Conn. Soc. Hosp. Pharmacists, Pharmacy Alumni Assn. U. Conn. (life), N.C. Pharm. Assn., N.C. Soc. Hosp. Pharmacists, Moore County Pharm. Assn. Republican. Episcopalian. Home: 106 Atwater Ct 612 Sun Rd Aberdeen NC 28315

MARCOTTE, DAVID BACON, psychiatrist; b. Glen Ridge, N.J., Sept. 3, 1936; s. Robert Louis and Ruth Mabel (Bacon) M.; m. Eugenia Gullick, July 22, 1978; children: David, Melissa, Michele, Margot, Margaret. BS, St. Lawrence U., 1958; MD, Cornell U., 1963. Diplomate Am. Bd. Psychiatry and Neurology. Assoc. dept. psychiatry Med. U. S.C., Charleston, 1970-75, from asst. to assoc. prof. psychiatry, 1975-78, prof. psychiatry and family medicine, 1978-81; med. dir. Mandala Hosp., Winston-Salem, N.C., 1981-84, Cumberland Hosp., Fayetteville, N.C., 1984-89; prin. Marcotte & Assocs., Fayetteville, 1993—; psychiatrist Carolina Neuropsychiat. Assocs., 1985-93. Contbr. chpts. to books, articles to profl. jours. Maj. USAR, 1968-70. Office: Marcotte & Assocs 210 Fairway Dr Fayetteville NC 28305-5512

MARCOTTE, MICHAEL STEVEN, municipal administrator; b. New Orleans, Jan. 17, 1951; s. Steven Stephen and Gloria Catherine (DeValcourt) M.; m. Mary Jane Kilgore, May 28, 1972; children: Matthew David, Margaret Katherine. BA, M of Environ. Engring., Rice U., 1973. Cert. profl. engr., Tex., Colo.; diplomate Am. Acad. Environ. Engrs. Engr., sr. engr., mgr. Turner, Collie & Braden, Inc., Houston, 1973-82; chief maintenance engr. water div. City of Houston, 1982-83, mng. engr. water div., 1984-85, asst. to the dir. pub. works dept., 1985-87, exec. asst. to the dir. pub. works dept., 1987-88, acting dir. dept. planning and devel., 1988-89; dir. Dallas Water Utilities, 1989-95; dir. econ. devel. City of Dallas, 1995—. Mem. NSPE, ASCE, Water Resources Coun., Am. Water Works Assn. (trustee Rsch. Found.), Water Environ. Fedn., North Ctrl. Tex. Coun. Govts., Tex. Water Conservation Assn. (bd. dirs.). Presbyterian. Home: 9718 Shoreview Rd Dallas TX 75238-4239 Office: City of Dallas/Economic Devel 1500 Marilla St 5CS Dallas TX 75201-6318

MARCUM, JAMES WALTON, library director, educator; b. Crystal City, Tex., June 8, 1940; s. Clarence Edwin and Caroline (Koonce) M.; m. Judith Higginbotham, June 23, 1963 (div. 1986); children: Virginia Ann Marcum Lindhurst, Jessica Marcum; m. Rebecca Beavers, Feb. 14, 1987. BA, MA, Tex. A&I Coll., Kingsville, 1960, 61; PhD, U. N.C., 1970; MPA, U. Okla., 1978; MLS, U. North Tex., 1991. History tchr. Donna (Tex.) High Sch., 1961-62; reporter-photographer Taylor (Tex.) Daily Press, 1962-63; instr. Pfeiffer Coll., Misenheimer, N.C., 1963-65; asst., assoc., prof. History Okla. Bapt. U., Shawnee, 1967-80; ptnr. Marcum Pontiac, Buick, GMC, Toyota. Pampa, Tex., 1980-81, owner, 1981-84; fin. cons. Shearson Lehman, Oklahoma City, 1984; owner, operator Fee Internat., Oklahoma City, 1985-86, Marcum Chrysler Dodge, Pampa, 1987-90; adj. prof. History U. North Tex., Denton, 1990-91; dir. libr. svcs., assoc. prof. history Centenary Coll., Shreveport, La., 1991-96; dir. libr.sr. lect. History, 1996—; chair corp. faculty Okla. Bapt. U., 1979-80; instr. U. N.C., Chapel Hill, 1969-70; vis. prof. U. Okla., Norman, 1976-77; dir. continuing edn. Okla. Bapt. U., 1977-80, chair divsn. social scis., 1974-76, chair dept. History and Polit. Sci., dir. European study program, 1970-74. Contbr. articles, revs. to profl. jours. Mem. Shawnee Human Rels. Commn., 1970s; Dem. chair 4th Congl. Dist. Okla., 1975-77; chair resources com. Cmty. Partnerships, Shreveport, 1993—, West Tex. C. of C., Okla. Hist. Records Adv. Bd. Okla. Humanities grantee, 1975, 78. Mem. ALA, La. Libr. Assn., Am. Assn. for Advancement of Slavic Studies, World Future Soc. Democrat. Office: U Tex Permian Basin 49012 University Odessa TX 09762

MARCUS, BERNARD, retail executive; b. 1929; married. BS, Rutgers U., 1954. V.p. Vornado Inc., 1952-68; pres. Odell Inc., 1968-70; v.p. Daylin Inc., 1970-73; with Handy Dan Home Improvement, Los Angeles, 1972-78; with Home Depot Inc., Atlanta, 1978—, now chmn., chief exec. officer, sec., also bd. dirs. Office: Home Depot Inc 2727 Paces Ferry Rd NW Atlanta GA 30339-4053*

MARCUS, HEATHER, artist, sculptor; b. Kansas City, Mo., Mar. 20, 1939; d. Allen Lee and Una Adele (Hodson) Johnson; m. Richard Cantrell Marcus, Mar. 23, 1968 (div. 1997); children: Catherine Marcus Rose, Charles Allen. BFA in Sculpture with distinction, U. Kans., 1961. Prin. works include Carrollton (Tex.) City Hall, 1987, Meth. Hosp., Dallas, 1991, Schumpert Meml. Hosp., Shreveport, La., 1992, GTE Corp., Irving, Tex., 1994; one-woman shows include Nimbus Gallery, Dallas, 1984, DW Gallery, Dallas, 1986, Janet Steinberg Gallery, San Francisco, 1986, Marvin Seline Gallery, Austin, Tex., 1987, 90, U. Tex. of the Permian Basin, Odessa, 1987, The U. Tex. at Tyler, 1988, Jan Weiner Gallery, Kansas City, 1988, 90, 93, Barbara Gillman Gallery, Miami, Fla, 1990, 94, Jaffe-Baker Gallery, Boca Raton, Fla., 1991; numerous group exhbns.; represented in permanent collections Neiman Marcus Co., Short Hills, N.J., Hall Fin. Group, Dallas, Howard Hughes Corp., Las Vegas, U.S. Trust, Dallas, GTE Corp., Irving, Gateway Tower, Dallas, Edwin Ulrich Mus. Art at Wichita (Kans.) State U., Pagenet Corp., Dallas, Schumpert Meml. Hosp., Shreveport, No. Telecom, Richardson, Tex., Meth. Hosp., Dallas, Equitable Real Estate Co., Atlanta, Security Benefit Group, Topeka, Kans., Winning Ways, Lenexa, Kans., Citigas Co., Miami, Steak and Ale Corp., Dallas, Hillcrest Bank, Kansas City, City of Carrollton, Bloom Cos., Dallas, The Galleria, Dallas, Hubler Roseberg, Inc., Dallas, Lewis and Ptnrs., Advt., San Francisco, Flynn, Steinberg, Dick and Lee, San Francisco, Joel Lewis and Assocs., San Francisco, The Alpert Corp., Dallas, U. Tex. at the Permian Basin, Yellow Freight, Kansas City, Hallmark, Inc., Kansas City. former bd. dirs. Dallas Artists' Rsch. and Exhbns., Dallas KERA Pub. Radio, Tex. Sculpture Assn., Dallas chpt. Cystic Fibrosis Found., Dallas Film Festival, Dallas Opera; former chmn. Beaux Arts Ball Dallas Mus. Art; former trustee St. Marks Sch. for Boys; former mem. Internat. Coun. San Francisco Museums of Fine Arts; former mem. bd. advisors Sch. Fine Arts U. Kans. Mem. Dallas Charter 100, Dallas Forum. Office: 1415 Slocum Ste 105 Dallas TX 75207

MARCUS, JAMES ELBERT, manufacturing company executive; b. Helena, Ala., July 3, 1949; s. James Edward and Ora Dee (Shanks) M.; m. Willie Mae Murry, June 30, 1980; children: Charsie Latrice, Chareka Lenita, Carlisle Lamar. BS in Biology, Chemistry, Tuskegee U., 1971. Soft drink technician Custom Canners, Inc., Norcross, Ga., 1972-73; comml. inventory supr. Washington Inventory Svc., Inc., Atlanta, 1973-76; shipping and receiving specialist Norrell Temporary Svc., Atlanta, 1977-78; enology lab. technician Monarch Wine Co., Atlanta, 1978-80; R & D technician Pave-Mark Corp., Atlanta, 1980-82; mfg. tech. support specialist Dynatron Bondo Corp., Atlanta, 1982-85; equipment operator Circuit City, Inc., Atlanta, 1985-86; air filter technician Comml. Air Filter Co., Atlanta, 1987-88; owner, pres. Marcus Industries, Atlanta, 1989—, Group 38 Transp. Svcs., Inc., Atlanta, Group 38 Medical Claims Processing, Atlanta. Prin. developer pavement marking material, 1981. Cub scout master Southeastern dist. Traveler's Rest Bapt. Ch. Boy Scouts Am., 1988, 89, 90. Mem. Nat. Hon. Soc. Pershing Rifles, Oxford Club, Highlander Club. Democrat. Baptist. Home: 2788 Tee Rd SW Atlanta GA 30311-1516

MARCUS, JOY JOHN, pharmacist, consultant; b. Charleston, S.C., Aug. 13, 1951; d. John Basil and Penelope (Polizos) M. AS, Anderson (S.C.) Jr. Coll., 1971; BS in Health and Phys. Edn., U. S.C., 1976; MS in Sports Adminstrn., St. Thomas U., Miami, 1987; BS in Pharmacy, Southeastern U., Miami, 1992. Assoc. prof. Miami Dade C.C. N, 1987—; pharmacy technician/intern Bay Rexall Drug Store, Miami, 1974-91; intern Eckerd's Pharmacy, Miami, 1991-92, extern and intern, 1991-92; pharmacist Eckerd's Pharmacy, 1992—; lab. instr. Southeastern Coll. of Pharmacy, 1991, asst. prof. pharm. sci., pharmacy practice, 1992-94; cons. pharmacist, 1992—; mem. com. admissions Nova Southeastern Coll. Pharmacy, 1995—, interview com., 1995—; adj. prof. St. Thomas U., 1988. Treas., Miami Shore Bus. Assn., 1985; Sunday sch. tchr. Recipient award for Campuses Addressing Substance Abuse, 1991, Women in Pharmacy Leadership, 1993; recipient several grants. Mem. Am. Pharm. Assn. (state del. for nat. conv. ho. of dels. 1994, 96, liaison info. networking and knowledge 1994-95), Nat. Assn. Retail Druggists; Fla. Pharmacy Assn. (mem. exec. com. 1991-92, mem. futuristic com. 1992-94, mem. orgnl. affairs com. 1994-96, pub. affairs com. 1996-98), Dade County Pharmacy Assn. (mem. resolution com. 1992-94, mem. exec. com. 1992—, chairperson membership com. 1992-94, del. Fla. Pharmacy Assn. con. 1993—, pres. elect 1993-94, pres. 1994-95, chmn. bd. dirs. 1995-97, Kiwanis Club, Phi Lambda Sigma (sec., treas. 1991-92), Alpha Zeta Omega (v.p. 1989-90, sec. 1990-91). Republican. Greek Orthodox. Home: 13105 Ixora Ct Apt 317 Miami FL 33181-2322

MARCUS, LEE EVAN, business consultant; b. Cleve., 1953; s. Morton and Bluma Marcus. BA in English, Amherst Coll., 1975. CPA, Fla. Audit staff acct. Arthur Andersen, Tampa, 1976-78; tax mgr. Price Waterhouse, Miami, Fla., 1978-83; controller Williams Island Assocs., Ltd., North Miami Beach, Fla., 1983-84; corp. contr. Suncoast Land Devel. Co., Inc., and Affiliates, Stuart, Fla., 1984-85; fin. officer, contr. Haydn Cutler Cos., Ft. Worth, 1985-89; pres., cons. Global Solutions Co., Coconut Creek, Fla., 1989—. Mem. World Future Soc.

MARCUS, M. JEFFREY, physician; b. Providence, R.I., July 21, 1946; s. Stanley Raymond and Beatrice (Perry) M.; m. Judith Wally London, Aug. 31, 1975; children: Michelle Lynn, Cherie London, Melanie Perry, Marshall Bernard. BS, Yale U., 1968; MD, U. Va., 1971. Diplomate Am. Bd. Otolaryngology. Intern Cornell Med. Ctr., N.Y.C., 1971-72; surgery resident Boston U. Hosp., 1972-73; otolaryngology resident U. Miami, 1973-76; pvt. practice Inverness, Fla., 1978—; pres. Citrus County Med. Soc., 1997; chief of staff Citrus Meml. Hosp., Inverness, 1991-92, chmn. med. records com., 1992-93, chief of staff med. staff, 1990-91, chmn. exec. com. 1990-91, chmn. exec. credentials com., 1990-91, v.p. med. staff, 1989-90, sec.-treas. med. staff, 1988-89, mem. quality assurance utilization rev. com., 1986-87; courtesy staff Seven Rivers Community Hosp., Crystal River, Fla.; clin. asst. prof. dept. Otolaryngology-Head and Neck Surgery, U. Fla. Coll. Medicine. Contbg. editor (med. mag.) The Doctor's Office, 1991-93, Fla. Healthcare News, 1991-94, Country Lifestyles Mag., 1990-92. Lt. comdr. USN, 1976-78. Fellow AMA, ACS, Am. Acad. Otolaryngology, Am. Acad. Facial Plastic and Reconstructive Surgery, Am. Acad. Otolaryngologic Allergy, Am. Coll. Allergy and Immunology, Skin Cancer Found. (hon.); mem. Fla. Med. Assn., Citus County Med. Soc. Office: 3733 E Gulf To Lake Hwy Inverness FL 34453-3206

MARCUS, STANLEY, federal judge; b. 1946. BA, CUNY, 1967; JD, Harvard U., 1971. Assoc. Botein, Hays, Sklar & Herzberg, N.Y.C., 1974-75; asst. atty. U.S. Dist. Ct. (ea. dist.) N.Y., 1975-78; spl. atty., dep. chief U.S. organized crime sect. Detroit Strike Force, 1978-79, chief U.S. organized crime sect., 1980-82; U.S. atty. So. Dist. of Fla., Miami, 1982-85; judge U.S. Dist. Ct. (so. dist.) Fla., Miami, 1985—. Office: US Dist Ct 301 N Miami Ave Miami FL 33128-7702*

MARCUS, WALTER F., JR., state supreme court justice; b. New Orleans, July 26, 1927; married; children: Walter III, Adam, Barbara Ann. B.A., Yale U.; J.D., Tulane U. Bar: La. 1955. Mem. New Orleans City Council, 1962-66; judge Civil Dist. Ct., 1966-73; assoc. justice Supreme Ct. La., 1973—. Mem. ABA. Office: Supreme Ct La 301 Loyola Ave New Orleans LA 70112-1800*

MAREADY, WILLIAM FRANK, lawyer; b. Mullins, S.C., Sept. 13, 1932; s. Jesse Frank and Vera (Sellers) M.; m. Brenda McCanless, Nov. 3, 1979. AB, U. N.C., 1955, JD with honors, 1958. Bar: N.C. 1958, U.S. Dist. Ct. N.C. 1960, U.S. Ct. Appeals (4th cir.) 1962, U.S. Supreme Ct. 1968. Assoc. Mudge, Stern, Baldwin & Todd, N.Y.C., 1958-60, Hudson, Ferrell, Carter, Petree & Stockton, Winston-Salem, N.C., 1960-65; ptnr. Petree, Stockton & Robinson, Winston-Salem, 1965-92, Robinson, Maready, Lawing & Comerford, 1992—; N.C. chmn. Winston-Salem/Forsyth County Bd. Edn., 1968-70, chmn., bd. dirs. and mem. exec. com. N.C. State Port Authority, 1984—. Served with Green Berets, U.S. Army, 1952-54. Recipient Disting. Svc. award N.C. Sch. Bds. Assn. Fellow Am. Coll. Trial Lawyers, Am. Bar Found.; mem. ABA (chmn. standing com. on aero. law 1979-82, chmn. forum com. on air and space law 1982-86), N.C. Bar Assn. (chmn. litigation sect. 1981-82, adminstrn. of justice com. 1981-82), Nat. Parent Tchr. Assn. (life), Order of Coif, Phi Delta Phi, Phi Beta Kappa. Republican. Methodist. Clubs: Forsyth County. Lodge: Rotary of Winston Salem. Office: 370 Knollwood St Ste 600 Winston Salem NC 27103-1835

MAREE, ELIZABETH GOODWIN, psychiatric mental health nurse; b. Winston-Salem, N.C., June 3, 1954; d. Russell McClyde and Mary Watkins (Baird) Goodwin; m. Franklin Kenyon Maree, June 18, 1977; children: Kenyon Russell, Ryon Baird. BSN magna cum laude, U. N.C., Greensboro, 1977; MSN, Med. U. S.C., Charleston, 1993. RN, S.C., N.C., La. Supr. West Jefferson Gen. Hosp., Marrero, La., 1979-81; clin. instr. Touro Sch. Nursing, New Orleans, 1982; team leader Charter Hills Hosp., 1982-83; clin. mgr. psychiatry West Jefferson Gen. Hosp., 1983-84; mental health nurse II Guilford County Mental Health Ctr., 1986; Baylor nurse Charter Hosp. of Greensboro, N.C., 1987-90; clin. specialist II High Point (N.C.) Mental Health Ctr., 1988-89; shift coord. Med. U. S.C. Inst. Psychiatry, Charleston, 1990-94; outcome mgr. adult gen. svcs. MUSC Inst. of Psychiatry, Charleston, S.C., 1994-95; outcome mgr. Med. U. S.C. Inst. Psychiatry, 1995—; facilitator patient/family support groups Hollings Cancer Ctr., Med. U. S.C.; facilitator CARENET caregiver support group, 1995—. Mem. Low Country Coalition for Cancer Survivorship; mem. admissions and recruitment com. S.C. Govs. Sch. for Sci. and Math. Mem. ANA (cert. specialistain adult psychiat.-mental health nursing, polit action com.), S.C. Nurses Assn., Am. Psychiat. Nurses Assn., U. N.C. at Greensboro Sch. Nursing Alumni Assn., The Great 100, Charleston Scottish Soc., Charleston Running Club, Sigma Theta Tau. Democrat. Presbyterian. Home: 55 Fort Royal Ave Charleston SC 29407-6000 Office: Med U SC Inst Psychiatry 3N-#339A 171 Ashley Ave Charleston SC 29425-0001

MAREE, WENDY, painter, sculptor; b. Windsor, Eng., Feb. 10, 1938. Student, Windsor & Maidenhead Coll., 1959; studied with Vasco Lazzlo, London, 1959-62. Exhibited in group shows at Windsor Arts Festival, San Bernardino (Calif.) Mus.; one-woman shows include Lake Arrowhead (Calif.) Libr., 1989, Amnesty Internat., Washington, 1990, Phyllis Morris Gallery, Many Horses Gallery, L.A., 1990, Nelson Rockefeller, Palm Springs, Calif., 1992, 94, Stewart Gallery, Rancho Palos Verdes, Calif., Petropavlovsk (Russia) Cultural Mus., Kamchatka, Russia, 1993, Coyle-Coyle Gallery, Blue Jay, Calif., 1995, La Quinta Sculpture Park, Calif., 1995, Avante-Garde Gallery, Palm Springs, 1996, Avante-Garden Gallery, La Jolla, Calif., 1996, Avante Garde Gallery, La Jolla, 1996, others; represented in pvt. collections His Royal Highness Prince Faisal, Saudi Arabia, Gena Rowlands, L.A., John Cassavetes, L.A., Nicky Blairs, L.A., Guilford Glazer, Beverly Hills, Calif., June Allyson, Ojai, Calif., Amnesty Internat., Washington. Recipient award San Bernardino County Mus., 1988, Gov. Kamchatka of Russia, 1993. Mem. Artist Guild of Lake Arrowhead.

MARGED, JUDITH MICHELE, middle school educator; b. Phila., Nov. 27, 1954; d. Bernard A. and Norma Marged. Student, Drexel U., 1972-73; AA in Biology, Broward Community Coll., Ft. Lauderdale, Fla., 1975; BA in Biology, Fla. Atlantic U., 1977, BA in Exceptional Edn., 1980, MEd in Counseling, 1984; EdD in Early and Middle Childhood, Nova U., 1991. Cert. tchr., Fla. Tchr. Coral Springs (Fla.) Mid. Sch., 1979-80, Am. Acad., Wilton Manors, Fla., 1980-83, Ramblewood Mid. Sch., Coral Springs, 1984—; creator programs for mid. sch. students. Author: A Program to Increase the Knowledge of Middle School Students in Sexual Education and Substance Abuse Prevention, An Alternative Education Program to Create Successful Learning for the Middle School Child At-Risk. Mem. NSTA, AACD, ASCD, Am. Sch. Counselors Assn., Nat. Assn. Sch. Psychologists, Fla. Assn. Sch. Psychologists, Fla. Assn. Sci. Tchrs., Fla. Assn. Counseling and Devel., Am. Sch. Health Assn., Fla. Sch. Health Assn., Phi Delta Kappa. Democrat. Jewish. Home: 9107 NW 83rd St Tamarac FL 33321-1509 Office: Ramblewood Mid Sch 8505 W Atlantic Blvd Pompano Beach FL 33071-7456

MARGER, EDWIN, lawyer; b. N.Y.C., Mar. 18, 1928; s. William and Fannie (Cohen) M.; m. Kaye Sanderson, Oct. 1, 1951; children: Shari Ann, Diane Elaine, Sandy Ben; m. L. Suzanne Smyth, July 5, 1968; 1 child, George Phinney; m. Mary Susan Hamel, May 6, 1987; 1 child, Charleston Faye. BA, U. Miami, 1951, JD, 1953. Bar: Fla. 1953, Ga. 1971, D.C. 1978. Sole practice, Miami Beach, Fla., 1953-67, Atlanta, 1971—; gen. counsel Physicians Nat. Risk Retention Group, 1988-91, Physicians Reliance Assn., 1988-91, Physicians Nat. Legal Def. Corp., 1988-91; spl. asst. atty. gen. Fla., 1960-61; of counsel Richard Burns, Miami, 1967—. Tchr. Nat. Inst. Trial Advocacy. Mem. Miami Beach Social Svc. Commn., 1957; chmn. Fulton County Aviation Adv. Com., 1980—; trustee Forensic Scis. Found., 1984-88, v.p., 1986-88; lt. col., a.d.c. Gov. Ga., 1971-74, 80-84; col., a.d.c. Gov. La., 1977-87; Khan Bahador and mem. exiled King of Afghanistan Privy Council, 1980—. Served with USAAF, 1946-47. Fellow Am. Acad. Forensic Scis. (chmn. jurisprudence sect. 1977-78, sec. 1976-77, exec. com. 1983-86); mem. ABA, Fla. Bar Assn. (aerospace com. 1971-83, bd. govs. 1983-87, 90-94, exec. com. 1993-94), State Bar Ga. (chmn. sect. environ. law 1974-75, aviation law sect. 1978), Ga. Trial Lawyers Assn., Nat. Assn. Criminal Def. Lawyers, Ga. Assn. Criminal Def. Lawyers, Assn. Trial Lawyers Am., Am. Judicature Soc., Am. Arbitration Assn. (comml. panel 1978—), Inter-Am. Bar Assn. (sr.), World Assn. Lawyers (founding), Advocates Club, Lawyer-Pilots Bar Assn. (founding; v.p. 1959-62),Vets. of Foreign Wars, Rotary. Contbr. articles to legal jours. Office: 44 N Main St Jasper GA 30143-1516

MARGOLIN, SOLOMON BEGELFOR, pharmacologist; b. Phila., May 16, 1920; s. Nathan and Fannie (Begelfor) M.; m. Gerda Levy, Jan. 17, 1947 (div. Feb. 1985); children: David, Bernard, Daniel; m. Nancy A. Cox, Apr. 30, 1987. BSc, Rutgers U., 1941, MSc, 1943, PhD, 1945. Asst. Rutgers U., New Brunswick, N.J., 1943-45; rsch. biologist Silmo Chem. Co., Vineland, N.J., 1947-48; rsch. pharmacologist Schering Corp., Bloomfield, N.J., 1948-52, dir. pharmacology dept., 1952-54; chief pharmacologist Maltbie Labs., Belleville, N.J., 1954-56; chief pharmacologist Wallace Labs, Carter-Wallace, Inc., Cranbury, N.J., 1956-60, dir. pharmacology dept., 1960-64, v.p. biol. rsch., 1964-68; pres. AMR Biol. Rsch., Inc., Princeton, N.J., 1968-78; from prof., chmn. pharmacology dept. to emeritus prof. St. George's (Grenada) U. Sch. Medicine, 1978—; pres. MARNAC, Inc., Dallas, 1990—. Author: Harper's Handbook Therapeutic Pharmacology, 1981; author: (with others) Physiological Pharmacology, 1963, World Review, Nutrition & Dietetics, 1980; contbr. over 50 articles to profl. jours. including Annals of Allergy, Proc. Soc. Exptl. Biol. & Med., Nature. Mem. AAAS, Endocrino Soc., Am. Chem. Soc., Soc. Exptl. Biology and Medicine, Am. Soc. Pharmacology and Exptl. Therapeutics, N.Y. Acad. Scis., Drug Information Assn. Home: 6723 Desco Dr Dallas TX 75225-2704 Office: Marnac Inc 6723 Desco Dr Dallas TX 75225-2704

MARGOLIS, JAMES ROBINEAU, cardiovascular physician, educator; b. Chgo., Apr. 10, 1943. BS, U. Wis., 1966; MD, U. Ill., 1968. Diplomate Nat. Bd. Medicine Examiners, Am. Bd. Internal Medicine; lic. physician, Mass., N.C., Mo., Fla. Fellow in pathology Michael Reese Hosp. and Med. Ctr., 1966; fellow in cardiology Serafimerlasaret Karolinska Inst., 1967; intern in medicine Barnes Hosp., 1968-69; rsch. assoc. Nat. Heart and Lung Inst., Framingham, Mass., 1969-71; physician Framingham Union Hosp., 1970-71; asst. resident in medicine Barnes Hosp., 1971-72; fellow in myocardial infarction rsch. unit Duke U. Med. Ctr., Durham, N.C., 1972-73, fellow cardiovascular lab., 1973-74, assoc. in medicine, 1974-75, dir. cardiovascular follow-up clinic, 1974-76; dir. cardiovascular lab. South Miami Hosp., 1976-91, Miami Heart Inst., 1991—; instr. medicine Washington U., 1968-69, 71-72; instr. medicine Duke U. Med. Ctr., 1972-74, asst. prof. medicine, 1975-76; clin. asst. prof. medicine U. Miami, 1976-78, clin. prof. medicine, 1979—; mem. sci. adv. bd. Schneider-Shiley, 1987—; mem. clin. adv. bd. Advanced Cardiovascular Systems, 1988—. Mem. editorial bd Circulation; contbr. articles to profl. jours. Bd. govs., pres. Am. Heart Assn. of Greater Miami, 1988—, chmn. rsch. com., chmn. profl. edn. com.; chmn. profl. edn. com. Fla. Heart Assn. With USPHS, 1969-71. Thord-Gray fellow Am. Scandinavian Found.; clin. scholar Robert Wood Johnson Found. Fellow Am. Coll. Cardiology, Coun. Clin. Cardiology; mem. Am. Soc. Internal Medicine. Office: Miami Heart Inst Cardiovasc Lab 4701 N Meridian Ave Miami FL 33140-2910

MARIER, ROBERT L., hospital administrator; b. Mar. 29, 1943; m. Joanne Marier; 2 children. AB, Boston Coll., 1965; MD, Yale U., 1969; MHA, Tulane U., 1990. Diplomate Am. Bd. Internal Medicine. Intern in internal medicine Mass. Gen. Hosp., Boston, 1969-70, asst. resident in medicine, 1970-71; epidemic intelligence svc. officer Nat. Ctr. Disease Control USPHS, Atlanta, 1971-73; clin. rsch. fellow in inflammatory disease Yale U., New Haven, Conn., 1973-75, asst. prof. medicine, 1975-78; assoc. prof. medicine La. State U., New Orleans, 1978-83, acting head sect. infectious disease, 1982-83, dir. intro. to clin. medicine, 1982-85, dir. residency program, 1982-86, prof. medicine, 1983—; dir. adult closed care Charity Hosp., New Orleans, 1982-83, dir. office infection control, 1982—, asst. dean, 1986—, assoc. med. dir., 1986-88; Dean LSU School of Med, New Orleans, 1989—; vis. physician Yale-New Haven Hosp., 1975-78; mem. La. State AIDS Task Force, 1985—; mem. Met. Hosp. Coun. New Orleans, 1988—; physician advisor La. Health Care Review, New Orleans, 1991—. Mem. editorial bd. Infections in Surgery, 1983-88, Jour. Orthopedics, 1983—, AHPS Drug Info. Monographs, 1986—. Remsey Meml. scholar Yale U., 1968—; rsch. fellow in infectious disease NIH, 1975-77. Fellow ACP, Infectious Disease Soc. Am.; mem. AMA, Am. Soc. Microbiology, Am. Fedn. Clin. Rsch., So. Soc. Clin. Investigation, La. State Med. Soc., Orleans Parish Med. Soc., Alpha Omega Alpha. Office: La State U Med Ctr 1542 Tulane Ave New Orleans LA 70112-2825*

MARINI, ELIZABETH ANN, civilian military executive; b. Dubuque, Iowa, Feb. 8, 1940; d. Cletus Nicholas and Catherine Margaret (Blasen) Freiburger; m. John J. Marini, Jan. 12, 1980. BA, Carinal Stritch Coll., 1962; MPA, George Washington U., 1982. Claims examiner Social Security Adminstrn., Chgo., 1962-64; supply systems analyst Navy Electronic Supply Office, Great Lakes, Ill., 1964-67; investment rep. Investors Planning Corp. Am., N.Y.C., 1967; supply systems analyst Naval Electronic Systems Command, Washington, 1968-76, head Saudi naval expansion program, 1976-80, head def. security assistance office internat. program, 1979-80; chief East Asia/Latin Am. divsn. Office of Sec. of Def. Def. Security Assistance Agy., Washington, 1980-84; chief East Asia Pacific divsn. Office of the Sec. of Def., DSAA, Washington, 1984-90; chief arms coop. and policy analysis divsn. Office of the Sec. of Def., Def. Tech. Security Adminstrn., Washington, 1990—. Tchr. religion classes Blessed Sacrament Ch., Alexandria, Va., 1972-73. Mem. Kappa Gamma Pi, Pi Alpha Alpha. Roman Catholic. Office: Def Tech Security Adminstrn 400 Army Navy Dr Arlington VA 22202-2884

MARINIS, THOMAS PAUL, JR., lawyer; b. Jacksonville, Tex., May 31, 1943; s. Thomas Paul and Betty Sue (Garner) M.; m. Lucinda Cruse, June 25, 1969; children—Courtney, Kathryn, Megan. B.A., Yale U., 1965; LL.B., U. Tex., 1968. Bar: Tex. Assoc. Vinson & Elkins, Houston, 1969-76, ptnr., 1977—. Served with USAR, 1968-74. Fellow Tex. Bar Found; mem. ABA (sec. taxation sect. 1984-85), Tex. Bar Assn. (chmn. taxation sect. 1986-87). Clubs: Houston Country, Houston Ctr., Coronado.

MARINO, ANN DOZIER, real estate agent; b. Durham, N.C., Apr. 22, 1944; d. Walter Joseph and Ellen G. (Cheek) Dozier; m. John Harrison Marino, Oct. 15, 1966 (div. Jan. 1981); children: John Harrison Jr., Ann Southerlyn. BA, Salem Coll., 1966. Sales assoc. Rector Assocs. Realtors, Alexandria, Va., 1984—. Vol. Jr. League, Chgo., 1970-74; bd. dirs. Jr. League, Washington, 1979-95, Vol. Clearing House, Washington, Project Open Rd., Chgo., Fire and Burn Inst., Washington; mem. parents coun. Burgundy Farm Sch., 1983; mem. parish coun. St. Mary's, Oldtown, 1977-80. Recipient Rookie of Yr. award No. Va. Bd. Realtors, 1985, Lifetime Top Producer award, Million Dollar Club, No. Va. Bd. Realtors, 1985-94. Mem. Salem Coll. Alumnae Club (pres. Chgo. chpt. 1970-73), Million Dollar Club (life). Republican. Roman Catholic. Office: Rector Assocs 211 N Union St Ste 250 Alexandria VA 22314-2643

MARINO, DANIEL CONSTANTINE, JR., professional football player; b. Pittsburg, Sept. 15, 1961. BA, communications, U. Pitts., 1983. Profl. football player Miami Dolphins, NFL, 1983—. Named All-America team quarterback, The Sporting News, 1981; Rookie of the Year, The Sporting News, 1983, NFL All-Pro team, The Sporting News, 1984-86, MVP, Nat. Football League, 1984-85; named to Pro Bowl Team, 1983-87, 91-92. Office: care Miami Dolphins Joe Robbie Stadium 2269 NW 199th St Opa Locka FL 33056-2600*

MARINO, LOUIS JOHN, mathematics educator; b. Whitestone, N.Y., May 3, 1949; s. Lewis F. and Lillian (Sheilds) M.; m. Sheila Burris, Dec. 19, 1969; children: Sheila Noelle, Heather Michelle. BS, U. Tenn., 1971, MS, 1975; MA in Teaching, U. S.C., 1977; AS in Engring., Piedmont Tech. Coll., 1981. Cert. tchr., S.C. Salesman Harper Bros., Inc., Greenwood, S.C., 1971-72; tchr. Orangeburg County (S.C.) Sch. Dist. 5, 1975-76, Greenwood County (S.C.) Sch. Dist. 50, 1976-77; mgr. Burger King, Greenwood, 1977-79; tchr. Laurens County (S.C.) Sch. Dist. 55, 1980-94; math. tchr. Long Cane Acad., McCormick, S.C., 1994—; adj. prof. Limestone Coll., Spartanburg, S.C., 1978-79, Piedmont Tech. Coll., Greenwood, 1979-81. S.C. Dept. Edn. grantee, 1986. Mem. NEA, Mktg. Educators Assn., Am. Vocat. Assn., Laurens County Edn. Assn. (pres. 1991-92, sec. 1980-83, 90-91, assn. rep. 1984-94, mem. svcs. 1984-86, chmn. membership com. 1988-89), S.C. Edn. Assn., Shelby Am. Automobile Club, Mustang Club Am., Foothills Mustang Club, Distributive Clubs Am., Phi Delta Kappa. Democrat. Presbyterian. Home: 103 Essex Ct Greenwood SC 29649-9561

MARINO, MICHAEL FRANK, lawyer; b. Little Falls, N.Y., Feb. 19, 1948; s. Michael Frank and Betty (Roberts) M.; m. Catherine Viladesau, Aug. 31, 1970; children: Michael John, Lisa Kathryn, Matthew Christopher. BS, Cornell U., 1971; JD, Syracuse U., 1974; LLM, Georgetown U., 1982. Bar: D.C. 1975, U.S. Dist. Ct. D.C. 1975, U.S. Ct. Mil. Appeals 1975, N.Y. 1976, U.S. Dist. Ct. (ea. and we. dists.) Va. 1977, U.S. Dist. Ct. Md. 1980, U.S. Ct. Appeals (4th cir.) 1982, Va. 1982, U.S. Ct. Appeals (9th cir.) 1994. Civilian employee head rels. br. Office of the Judge Adv. of the Navy, Washington, 1975-76; spl. asst. to the gen. counsel Office of Sec. of Navy, Washington, 1977; asst. gen. counsel labor and employment Office of the Gen. Counsel of the Navy, Washington, 1978; assoc. Pierson, Ball & Dowd, Washington, 1978-81; ptnr. Boothe, Prichard & Dudley, Fairfax and Mc Lean, Va., 1981-87, McGuire, Woods, Battle & Boothe, Mc Lean, 1987-89, Reed, Smith, Shaw & McClay, Mc Lean, 1989—; labor group head, Washington, Va.; mng. ptnr. McLean Office. Author: Virginia Employer's Guide to Labor Law, 1982; co-author: New York Employer's Guide, 1989, 92-94, Fla. Labor and Employment Law, 1994, Labor Employment Law in Pa., 1994. Mem. planning com. SMU Multi State labor Law Conf., Dallas; chmn. Arlington (Va.) Chamber Employee Rels. Com.; bd. dirs. Arlington Chamber Bd. of Dirs.; mem. Va. Chamber Mgmt. Rels. Com. Richmond, 1980—. Capt. USMC, 1971-78. Named Best Lawyer in Am., 1986-95. Mem. ABA (labor law com. 1974—), D.C. Bar Assn. (labor law com. 1974—), Va. Bar Assn. (labor law com. 1974—, sec.-treas. labor law sect. 1995), N.Y. Bar Assn. (labor law com. 1974—), Westwood Country Club. Roman Catholic. Office: Reed Smith Shaw & McClay 8251 Greensboro Dr Ste 1100 Mc Lean VA 22102-3809*

MARINO, RUCHE JOSEPH, district court judge; b. New Orleans, Jan. 22, 1936; s. Ruche and Amy L. M.; m. Juanita Duplantis, Jan. 25, 1958; children: Mark, Yvette, Mollie, Justin, Ruche, Juanita R. LLB, JD, La. State U., 1962. Dist. ct. judge State of La., 1971—. With USMC, 1956. Mem. ABA, Les Judges, Am. Judges Assn., Juvenile Judges. Democrat. Roman Catholic. Office: PO Box 129 Norco LA 70079

MARION, GAIL ELAINE, reference librarian; b. Bloomington, Ill., May 31, 1952; d. Ralph Herbert and Norma Mae (Crump) Nyberg; m. David Louis Marion, May 13, 1972 (div. Apr. 1983). AA in Liberal Arts, Fla. Jr. Coll., 1976; BA in U.S. History, U. North Fla., 1978; MS in Libr. and Info. Sci., Fla. State U., 1985. Law libr., legal rschr. Mathews Osborne et al, Jacksonville, Fla., 1979-82; reference libr. City of Jacksonville-Pub. Librs., 1982—. With U.S. Army, 1970-72, maj. U.S. Army Res., 1978—, with Fla. Army N.G., 1974-78. Named to Outstanding Young Women of Am., 1985; N.G. Officers Assn. scholar, 1980. Mem. ALA, WAC Vets. Assn., Adj. Gen. Regimental Corps, Res. Officers Assn., Fla. Libr. Assn., Fla. Paleontol. Soc., Jacksonville Gem and Mineral Soc. Republican. Methodist. Home: 3200 Hartley Rd Apt 70 Jacksonville FL 32257-6719 Office: Jacksonville Pub Librs 122 N Ocean St Jacksonville FL 32202-3314

MARION, JEFF DANIEL, poet, educator; b. Rogersville, Tenn., July 7, 1940; s. Jefferson Daniel and Eloise (Gladson) M.; m. Lana Marie Collins, Sept. 1, 1962 (div. Feb. 1984); children: Stephen Daniel, Rachel Lana. BS, U. Tenn., 1962, MA in English, 1966; postgrad., U. So. Miss., 1969, U. Ala., 1984. Asst. prof. Carson-Newman Coll., Jefferson City, Tenn., 1966-68, William Carey Coll., Hattiesburg, Miss., 1968-69; assoc. prof. Carson-Newman Coll., 1969—, poet-in-residence, 1980—; poet-in-residence Gov.'s Sch. Humanities, U. Tenn., 1985—; dir. Appalachian Ctr. Carson-Newman Coll., 1990—. Author of poems, (children's book) Hello Crow, 1992. Tenn. Arts Literary fellow, Tenn. Arts Commn., 1978. Home: 1604 Old River Rd New Market TN 37820 Office: Appalachian Ctr Carson-Newman Coll Russell St Jefferson City TN 37760

MARIOTTO, MARCO JEROME, psychology educator, researcher; b. Ill., Oct. 21, 1946; s. Marco Anibele and Sally (Hughes) M.; m. Danita Irene Czyzewski, May 4, 1985; children: Ana-Sofia Antonia, Marco Luca. BS, U. Ill., 1968, PhD, 1974. Diplomate Am. Bd. Sexology, Am. Bd. Forensic Examiners; lic. psychologist; cert. sex therapist, cert. health svcs. provider. Asst. rsch. dir. Adolf Meyer Ctr. Rsch. Units, Decatur, Ill., 1972-74; psychologist U.S. Army Acad. Health Scis., San Antonio, 1974; asst. prof. Purdue U., West Lafayette, Ind., 1975-79; assoc. prof. U. Houston, 1979-90, supervisory psychologist, 1979—, prof., 1990—, dept. chmn., 1994—; cons. NIMH, Bethesda, Md., 1977—, NSF, Washington, 1980-84, Nat. Inst. Drug Abuse, Bethesda, 1986-89; adj. prof. U. Tex. Health Scis., Houston, 1980—. Contbr. chpts. to books and articles to profl. jours.; also rsch. monographs and tech. reports. Forensic cons. Harris County Dist. Atty.'s Office, Houston, 1988—, ABA, 1989—; founding mem. Gulf Coast Consortium on Mental Health, Houston and Galveston, Tex., 1989. Capt. U.S. Army, 1968-74. Named one of top 35 Young Scientist Profls. Jour. Cons. and Clin. Psychology, 1988; David Ross fellow Purdue U., 1977. Mem. APA, Am. Psychol. Soc.; mem. AAAS, Midwestern Psychol. Assn. (local rep. 1979—), Sigma Xi. Office: U Houston Dept Psychology Houston TX 77004

MARIS, STEPHEN S., lawyer, educator; b. Dallas, Dec. 19, 1949; m. Bronwyn Holmes; children: Shane, Kara. BS, Stephen F. Austin State, 1971; JD, So. Meth. U., 1975. Bar: U.S. Dist. Ct. (no. dist.) Tex. 1975, U.S. Dist. Ct. (ea. dist.) Tex. 1986, U.S. Dist. Ct. (so. dist.) Tex. 1992, U.S. Ct. Appeals (5th cir.) 1980, U.S. Ct. Appeals (11th cir.) 1981, U.S. Supreme Ct. Tex. 1975. Assoc. Passman & Jones, Dallas, 1975-80, ptnr., 1980-87; ptnr. Fulbright & Jaworski, Dallas, 1987—; prof. So. Ill. U., 1979-80, So. Meth. U., Dallas, 1980—; mem. faculty Nat. Inst. Trial Advocacy, 1980—. Editor: Southwest Law Journal, 1973-75. Mem. ABA, State Bar Tex., Dallas Bar Assn., Barristers, Order Coif, Phi Delta Phi. Office: Fulbright & Jaworski 2200 Ross Ave Ste 2800 Dallas TX 75201-6773*

MARK, DANIEL BENJAMIN, internist, cardiologist, medical educator; b. Boston, Aug. 1, 1953. BA, Hampshire Coll., Amherst, Mass., 1974; MD, Tufts U., 1978; MPH, Harvard U., 1979. Diplomate Am. Bd. Internal Medicine. Resident in internal medicine U. Va. Med. Ctr., Charlottesville, 1979-82; fellow in cardiology Duke U. Med. Ctr., Durham, N.C., 1982-85, assoc. in medicine, 1985-86, assoc. dir. sec. clin. epidemiology, biostatistics, 1985—, asst. prof. medicine, 1987-92, co-dir. Cardiac Care Unit, 1987—, assoc. prof., 1993—, dir, Outcomes Rsch. and Assessment Group, 1994—. Author: (textbook) Basic Dopplar Echocardiography, 1986; editor: Acute Coronary Care, 1994; contbr. over 90 articles to profl. jours. Rsch. grantee NIH, AHCPR, 1978—. Fellow ACP, Am. Coll. Cardiology, Am. Heart Assn., Am. Fedn. for Clin. Rsch., Assn. for Health Svcs. Rsch., Soc. for Med. Decision Making. Office: Duke U Med Ctr Box 3485 Durham NC 27710

MARK, PETER, director, conductor; b. N.Y.C., Oct. 31, 1940; s. Irving and Edna M.; m. Thea Musgrave, Oct. 2, 1971. BA (Woodrow Wilson fellow), Columbia U., 1961; MS, Juilliard Sch. Music, 1963. Prof. music and dramatic art U. Calif., Santa Barbara, 1965-94; fellow Creative Arts Inst., U. Calif., 1968-69, 71-72; guest condr. Wolf Trap Orch., 1979, N.Y.C. Opera, 1981, L.A. Opera Theater, 1981, Royal Opera House, London, 1982, Hong Kong Philharm. Orch., 1984, Jerusalem Symphony Orch., 1988, Tulsa Opera, 1988, Companía Nacional de Opera, Mexico City, 1989, 92, N.Y. Pops, Carnegie Hall, 1991. Concert violist U.S., S.Am., Europe, 1961-67; artistic dir., condr. Va. Opera, Norfolk, 1975—, gen. dir., 1978—; condr.: Am. premier of Mary, Queen of Scots (Musgrave), 1978; World premier of A Christmas Carol (Musgrave), 1979, of Harriet, the Woman Called Moses (Musgrave), 1985, of Simon Bolivar (Musgrave), 1984, Porgy and Bess, Buenos Aires, Mexico City and São Paulo, 1992, Orlando Opera co., 1993, Richmond Symphony, 1993, Krakow Opera, 1995, Pacific Opera Victoria (Can.), 1996, Cleve. Opera, 1996, Festival Pucciniano-Torre del Lago, Italy, 1996. Recipient Elias Lifchey viola award Juilliard Sch. Music, 1963; named hon. citizen of Norfolk (Va.). Mem. Musicians Union, Phi Beta Kappa. Office: Va Opera PO Box 2580 Norfolk VA 23501-2580

MARKESBERY, WILLIAM R., neurology and pathology educator, physician; b. Florence, Ky., Sept. 30, 1932; s. William M. and Sarah E. (Tanner) M.; m. Barbara A. Abram, Sept. 5, 1958; children—Susanne Hartley, Catherine Kendall, Elizabeth Allison. B.A., U. Ky., 1960; M.D. with distinction, U. Ky. Med. Coll., 1964. Diplomate Am. Bd. Neurology and Psychiatry Diplomate Am. Bd. Pathology. Intern U. Hosp., Lexington, KY, 1964-65; resident neurology Presbyn. Hosp., N.Y.C., 1965-67; fellow neuropathology Coll. Physicians and Surgeons, Columbia U., N.Y.C., 1967—; asst. prof. pathology, neurology U. Rochester, N.Y., 1969-72; assoc. prof. pathology, neurology U. Ky., Lexington, 1972-77, prof. neurology, pathology, anatomy, 1977—, dir. Ctr. on Aging, 1979—, prof. neurology, pathology, dir., 1977—; mem. pathology study sect. NIH, Washington, 1982-85, nat. adv. coun. NIH, 1990-94; chmn. Med. Sci. Adv. Bd., Chgo., 1989-94, Nat. Alzheimer's Assn., Chgo., 1985-86, adv. panel on dementia U.S. Congress of Tech., Washington, 1985-86; dir. Alzheimer's Disease Research Ctr., 1985—, Alzheimer's Diseases Program Project Grant, 1984—. Mem. editorial bd. Jour. Neuropathology and Exptl. Neurology, 1983-86, 89—, Neurobiology of Aging, 1986—, Ann. Neurology, 1990—; contbr. numerous articles to profl. jours. With U.S. Army, 1954-56. Recipient Disting. Achievement award Ky. Research Found., Lexington, 1978; named U. Ky. Disting. Alumni prof., 1985, Disting. Research prof., U. Ky., 1977, Disting. Alumni U. Ky. Coll. Medicine, 1993; inductee U. Ky. Disting Alumni, 1989; prin. investigator NIH, Washington, 1977—. Mem. Am. Acad. Neurology, Am. Assn. Neuropathologists (exec. com. 1984-86, pres1991—), Soc. Neurosci., Am. Neurol. Assn., Alpha Omega Alpha. Home: 1555 Tates Creek Rd Lexington KY 40502-2229 Office: U Ky Coll Med Dept Neurology & Pathology 800 Rose St Lexington KY 40536-0024*

MARKHAM, CAROLE PILLSBURY, medical-surgical nurse educator; b. Beaumont, Tex., Aug. 18, 1951; d. Walter Earl and Leatrice Joy (Wall) P.; divorced; children: Ryan Vance, Reed Taylor. AS, Tyler Jr. Coll., 1972; diploma of nursing, Tex. Ea. Sch. of Nursing, 1973; BSN, U. Tex., Tyler, 1993. RN, Tex. Charge nurse, staff nurse Meth. Hosp., Houston, 1973-79; mem. staff emergency dept. Baylor U. Med. Ctr., Dallas, 1979-80; heart catheter nurse Schumpert Med. Ctr., Shreveport, La., 1989-91; mem. staff emergency dept. Mother Frances Hosp., Tyler, Tex., 1992-93, med.- surg. nurse educator, 1993—, staff devel. educator, 1995—; chair Nurse Oncology Edn. Program, 1994, co-chair 1996. Charter mem. La. Child Passenger Safety, Shreveport, 1983-87; sustainor Jr. League of Shreveport. Mem. AAUW, ANA, Tex. Nurse Assn. (dist. 19), Emergency Nurse Assn., Sigma Theta Tau. Presbyterian. Home: 4920 Pine Knoll St Tyler TX 75703-2624 Office: Trinity Mother Frances Health Sys 800 E Dawson St Tyler TX 75701-2036

MARKHAM, MEELER, retired minister; b. Ft. Worth, Tex., Mar. 8, 1914; s. Henry Nathan and Mattie V. (Sanders) M.; m. Myrtie L. Manlove, June 18, 1937; 1 child, Edwin Meeler. Student, Howard Payne U., 1934, 35, U. Tex., Austin, 1936, 37; BA, TCU, 1942; ThM, Southwestern Sem., 1947. Ordained to ministry Baptist Ch., 1941. Technician Soil Conservation Svc., Kenedy, Tex., 1937-40; chief inspector Quartermaster Corps, Ft. Worth, 1941-43; assoc. pastor 1st Bapt. Ch., Beeville, Tex., 1945; pastor First Bapt. Ch., Carrizo Springs, Tex., 1945-51, Mercedes, Tex., 1951-55; dir. missions Lower Rio Grande Assn., Harlingen, Tex., 1955-60; missions sec. Kans.-Nebr. Conv., Wichita, Kans., 1960-65; editor Home Mission Bd., SBC, Atlanta, 1966-76; dir. missions Frio River Assn., Devine, Tex., 1976-81; pastor Trinity Bapt. Ch., Lytle, Tex., 1981-83; pres. Alto Frio Bapt. Encampment, Leakey, Tex., 1953-57, S. Tex. Bible Conf., Corpus Christi, 1959-60; moderator Frio River Assn., Tex., 1946-48, 83-84; interim pastor Black Creek Bapt. Ch., Devine, 1985—; featured speaker at encampments, convs., nat. confs. Author: This Confident Faith, 1968 (Readers Plan award 1968), History of the WMU, 1980, Centennial History: Frio River Association, 1981, History of Co. 874, CCC, 1993; co-author: Five Minutes with God, 1969, Selected Poems by the MM's, 1991. Pres. Rotary, Mercedes, 1954-55. Mem. Masons. Home: 214 Harralton Cir Devine TX 78016-2309

MARKHAM, WILLIAM, county official; b. Pitts., Feb. 11, 1940; s. Charles Robert and Madolyn Jeanette (Pickett) M.; m. Sharon Rhodes, Nov. 22, 1972; children: James Rhodes, Robert William. BA, Ctr. Coll. of Ky., Danville, 1962; D in Commerce (hon.), Ft. Lauderdale (Fla.) Coll., 1982. Cert. Fla. Appraiser, Am. Sr. Appraiser. Mem. mktg. staff Am. Oil Co., Atlanta, 1963-67; property appraiser (elected) Broward County, Ft. Lauderdale, Fla., 1968—. Sgt. USMC Res. Recipient Good Govt. award Jaycees, Disting. Svc. award; recipient Damon award Knights of Pythias, Am. Sportsman award Nat. Football Hall of Fame, Great Am. Traditions award B'nai B'rith, 7 nat. awards for outstanding work in assessment profession; named Man of Yr. City of Hope Margate chpt. 1148. Mem. Internat. Assn. Assessing Officers (bd. dirs. 1974—, exec. bd. 1982-84), Tax Assessors' Assn. Fla. (pres. 1972-73). Home: 58 Cayuga Rd Sea Ranch Lakes FL 33302 Office: Broward County Property Appraiser 115 S Andrews Ave Rm 111 Fort Lauderdale FL 33302

MARKLEY, ARNOLD ALBERT, IV, English language educator; b. Greenville, S.C., Mar. 29, 1964; s. A.A. III and Julia (Dent) M. BA in English and Classics with honors, Guilford Coll., Greensboro, N.C., 1986; MA in English, U. N.C., 1990, PhD in English, 1996; postgrad., U. Pa., 1987-88. Rsch. asst. dept. medicine U. N.C., Chapel Hill, 1989-91, instr. composition and Brit. lit., 1991-96; adj. faculty dept. English Durham (N.C.) Tech. C.C., 1990-91; faculty Coll. Gifted Programs, Summer Inst. for Gifted, Bryn Mawr, Pa., 1991—; asst. prof. English Pa. State U., Media, 1996—. Contbr.

articles to profl. jours. Bd. trustees Carolina Friends Sch., Chapel Hill, 1992-95; reading tutor Orange County Literacy Coun., Carrboro, N.C., 1988-89; vol. group facilitator Outright, Durham, 1994; admissions assoc. Guilford Coll., 1986-92; co-convenor pubs. com. and newsletter editor Chapel Hill Friends Meeting, 1988-92. McLaurin Dissertation fellow for rsch. abroad U. N.C. Dept. English, London and Lincoln, Eng., 1993; Guilford Coll. Honors scholar, 1985. Mem. MLA, Tennyson Rsch. Soc., Keats-Shelley Assn. Democrat. Soc. of Friends. Home: 11 Walnut Rd Newtown Square PA 19073 Office: Dept English Pa State Delaware County 25 Yearsley Mill Rd Media PA 19063

MARKOE, ARNOLD MICHAEL, radiation oncologist; b. N.Y.C., Apr. 15, 1942; s. Joseph Markoe and Claire (Hershkowitz) Markoe Berger; m. Tana Kates, Sept. 3, 1967; 1 child, Zaharah. BA, Adelphi U., 1963; MS, U. Rochester, 1966; ScD, U. Pitts., 1972; MD, Hahnemann U., 1977. Diplomate, Am. Bd. Radiology (Therapeutic Radiology). Rsch. assoc. Albert Einstein Coll. Medicine, Bronx, N.Y., 1966-69; USPHS postdoctoral fellow Allegheny Gen. Hosp., Pitts., 1972-73; Am. Cancer Soc. spl. postdoctoral fellow Hahnemann Med. Coll., Phila., 1975-77; from sr. instr. to assoc. prof. radiation oncology Hahnemann U., Phila., 1977-89; staff physician Jackson Meml. Hosp., Miami, Fla., 1990—; mem. Sylvester Comprehensive Cancer Ctr., Miami, 1990—; assoc. prof. radiation oncology U. Miami, 1989-92, prof., 1992—, interim chmn. radiation oncology Sch. Medicine, 1994-96; chmn., 1996—; staff physician U. Miami Hosp. & Clinics, 1990—, VA Hosp., Miami, 1996—; cons. Anna Bates Leach Hosp. of Bascom-Palmer Eye Inst., 1990—, Cancergrams Info. Ventures, Inc., Phila., 1989-92; spl. site vis. radiation oncology Accreditation Coun. for Grad. Med. Edn., 1986—; adv. bd. radiation therapy tech. tng. program Gwynedd-Mercy Coll., Gwynedd Valley, Pa., 1988-89, Miami Dade C.C./Jackson Meml. Hosp. Consortium, 1989—, med. advisor, 1995—; adv. panel Radiation Oncology Self-Assessment Program, 1992—. Mem. editl. bd. Am. Jour. Clin. Oncology, 1991—, Radiation Oncology Investigations, 1992—; rev. Cancer, 1994—, Jour. Neuro-Oncology, 1994—; contbr. articles to profl. jours., chpts. to med. textbooks. Grantee, Soc. Nuclear Medicine, 1976; named One of Best Drs. in Am., 1996. Mem. Am. Radium Soc., Am. Soc. Clin. Oncology, Am. Coll. Radiology, Am. Coll. Radiation Oncology, Am. Soc. Therapeutic Radiation Oncology, So. Med. Soc., Fla. Med. Soc., Dade County Med. Soc., Fla. Soc. Clin. Oncology, Alpha Omega Alpha, Beta Beta Beta.

MARKS, B. E., JR., company executive; b. 1947. With Philip Morris, Richmond, Va., 1968-78; dir. Peanut Growers Coop. Mktg. Assn., Franklin, Va., 1978-88; with Va. Carolina Farmers Assn., Franklin, 1988—. Office: VA Carolina Farmers Assn 31380 General Thomas Hwy Franklin VA 23851-5124

MARKS, BONITA L., physiologist, researcher, educator; b. Munhall, Pa., Nov. 2, 1954; d. William Louis and Evelyn (Seeley) M.; m. Laurence M. Katz, July 27, 1986. BS, U. Pitts., 1977, PhD, 1989; MA, Columbia U., 1979. Cert. excercise specialist Am. Coll. Sports Medicine. Intern Cardio-Fitness Syss., Inc., N.Y.C., 1978-79; adult fitness coord. Jewish Cmty. Ctr., Pitts., 1979-81; grad. asst. U. Pitts., 1982-83, rsch. assoc., 1985-88; rsch. assoc. Hebrew Rehab. Ctr. for the Aged, Boston, 1988-89; postdoct. fellow U. Mass. Med. Ctr., Worcester, 1989-90; dir., owner Exercise Cons. Svcs., Pitts., 1990-93; asst. prof. Fla. Atlantic U., Boca Raton, Fla., 1993-96, U. N.C., Chapel Hill, 1996—; cons. Human Performance Resources, Boston, 1990—. Reviewer (textbook) Human Kinetic Book Publishers, Champaign, Ill., 1995; referee Medicine Sci. and Sports and Excercise, 1991—, Medicine, Excercise, Nutrition and Sports Jour., 1992—; contbr. articles to profl. jours. Physical fitness assessment coord. Seminole Tribe of Fla., Big Cypress, 1995; fall liaison Heartscore 95 AHA, Boca Raton, Fla., 1995; coord. Greater Pitts. Fitness Coun. Pa. Govt. Coun. on Physical Fitness and Sports, Pitts., 1992. Seed grant Mercy Hosp. Found., Pitts., 1992. Fellow Am. Coll. Sports Medicine (ad hoc com. Healthy People 2000 1977—, Healthy People 2000 grantee 1995, S.E. chpt. lectr. cir. coord. 1993—); mem. Am. Alliance Health, Phys. Edn., Dance, Nat. Strength and Conditioning Assn. Office: U NC CBA 8700 Fetzer Gym Chapel Hill NC 27514

MARKS, CHARLES DENNERY, insurance salesman; b. New Orleans, Nov. 22, 1935; s. Sidney Leroy Marks and Melanie Dennery; m. Gillian E. Otter, Sept. 1, 1963; children: Elizabeth Dennery, Richard Dennery. BA, Yale U., 1957. CLU, ChFC. With Charles Dennery, Inc., 1959-63; sales rep. Prudential Ins. Co., New Orleans, 1964—; v.p. Mgmt. Compensation Group, New Orleans, 1985—. Past bd. dirs. Boys Club Greater New Orleans, Big Bros. Greater New Orleans, United Way; past pres. Goodwill Rehab. Ctr.; vice chmn. Jr. Achievement; active Temple Sinai Synagogue. 1st lt. U.S. Army, 1957-59. Recipient award Volunteer Activist, 1983. Mem. Am. Soc. CLU and ChFC (pres. New Orleans chpt. 1984-85), Assn. Advanced Life Underwriting, Life Underwriters Pol. Action Com. (diplomat, sec./treas. 1982-87), La. Assn. Life Underwriters (Life Underwriter of Yr. 1985, 87, pres. 1986-87), New Orleans Estate Planning Coun. (pres. 1986-87), New Orleans Life Underwriters Assn. (Life Underwriter of Yr. 1981, pres. 1982-83), Million Dollar Round Table (Top of the Table 1986-89, exec. com. 1990-94, pres. 1993) Nat. Assn. Life Underwriters (vice chmn. fin. com. 1993—), Life and Health Found. for Edn. (life, chmn. 1996—). Republican. Home: 1525 Eleonore St New Orleans LA 70115-4242 Office: Mgmt Compensation Group 1250 Poydras St Ste 325 New Orleans LA 70113-1804

MARKS, HENRY LEWIS, poultry scientist; b. Waynesboro, Va., Sept. 6, 1935; s. Charles Alexander Jr. and Mabel Elizabeth (Batten) M.; m. Shirley Anita Reasor, Dec. 27, 1959; 1 child, Daniel Steven. BS, Va. Polytech. Inst., 1958, MS, 1960; PhD, U. Md., 1967. Poultry husbandman, rsch. geneticist USDA, Beltsville, Md., 1960-67; rsch. geneticist USDA, Athens, Ga., 1967-95; head dept. poultry sci. U. Ga., 1995—. Contbr. chpts. in books and articles to profl. jours. Mem. World Poultry Sci. Assn (bd. dirs. U.S. br.), Poultry Sci. Assn. (bd. dirs., 2d v.p. 1992-93, 1st v.p. 1993-94, pres. 1994-95, Rsch. award 1969, Merck Achievement award 1987), Phi Kappa Phi, Sigma Xi. Office: 117 Livestock-Poultry Bldg Univ Georgia Athens GA 30602-2772

MARKS, JENNIFER BYRNE, internist, endocrinologist, educator; b. Salem, Mass., Oct. 8, 1950; d. Frank Edward Byrne and Priscilla Arlene (Hawes) Gillis; m. Stanley William Marks, June 27, 1982; children: Darren Brett, Darryl Alan Anderson. BSN magna cum laude, U. Maine, 1974; MD, U. Miami, 1984. Diplomate Am. Bd. Internal Medicine, Nat. Bd. Med. Examiners, Am. Bd. Diabetes, Endocrinology, and Metabolism. Intern in internal medicine Jackson Meml. Hosp./U. Miami Affiliated Hosps., 1984-85, resident in internal medicine, 1985-87, chief resident internal medicine, 1987-88, clin. fellow endocrinology and diabetes, 1988-89, rsch. and clin. fellow endocrinology, diabetes, 1989-90; clin. instr. dept. medicine U. Miami Sch. Medicine, 1987-88, instr. dept. medicine divsn. endocrinology, 1990-91, assoc. prof. medicine dept. medicine divsn. endocrinology, 1996—, asst. dir. clin. rsch. Behavioral Medicine Rsch. Ctr., 1992—; mem. residency selection com. Jackson Meml. Hosp./U. Miami Affiliated Hosps., 1987-94, intern adv. program, 1988-90; mem. com. to restructure Profl. Income Plan U. Miami Sch. Medicine, 1993, com. on dept. medicine future, 1993, rev. com. Clin. Rsch. Ctr., 1993—, exec. promotions com., 1993—; lectr. continuing med. edn. Pembroke Pines Gen. Hosp., 1989, Coral Springs Med. Ctr., 1993; preceptor Cmty. Lab. Rsch. program Dade County Pub. Schs., 1990-91; presenter in field. Rev. editor Internat. Diabetes Monitor, 1989—, Clin. Diabetes, 1992—; sci. reviewer Am. Jour. Med. Scis., Jour. Diabetes and its Complications, 1992-93; contbr. over 28 articles, papers and abstracts to profl. jours. Vol. physician Camillus House Health Concern Clinic for Homeless, Miami, 1993—. HRS Tng. grantee NIH, 1989-91, grantee 1993—; grantee Nat. Heart, Lung and Blood Inst/NIH, 1986-91, 91—, Boehringer Mannheim Pharms., 1989, Xoma Corp., 1989-90, Nat. Heart, Lung and Blood Inst./USPHS, 1989-91, Pfizer/Roerig Pharms., 1991-94, Wyeth-Ayerst Rsch., 1991-93, Parke-Davis Rsch., 1992, Stanley Glaser Rsch. Found., 1993-94. Fellow ACP; mem. AMA, Am. Med. Womens Assn. (vol. lectr. 1993, Woman Rsdient of Yr. U. Miami chpt. 1986), Am. Diabetes Assn., Am. Fedn. for Clin. Rsch., Am. Assn. Clin. Endocrinologists, Endocrine Soc., Fla. Endocrine Soc. Home: 3390 Dockside Dr Cooper City FL 33026-3780 Office: U Miami Dept Endocrinology 1500 NW 12th Ave Fl W Miami FL 33136-1051

MARKS, MARILYN, company executive; b. 1952. BS, U. Tenn., 1975. Acct. Ernst & Ernst, Chattanooga, 1975-76; with Deloitte, Haskins & Sells, Chattanooga, 1976-79; v.p. corp. planning The Dorsey Corp., Chattanooga, 1979-87; pres., chmn. of bd., CEO Dorsey Trailers, 1987—. Office: Dorsey Corp 2727 Paces Ferry Rd NW Atlanta GA 30339-4053*

MARKS-DEMOURELLE, KAREN, diabetes nurse; b. Opelousas, La., Apr. 3, 1963; d. Bernard and Jane (Quebedeaux) Marks; m. Steven DeMourelle, Oct. 7, 1989. BSN, U. Southwestern La., 1986. RN, La. Staff nurse med./surg. unit Dr.'s Hosp., Opelousas, 1986; staff nurse gen. medicine unit Baton Rouge Gen. Med. Ctr., 1986-88, diabetes edn. coord., 1988-95; diabetes clin. mgr., 1995—. Mem. ANA, Am. Diabetes Assn., Am. Assn. Diabetes Educators, Sigma Theta Tau.

MARKUN, FRANK O., food services executive; b. Des Moines, Oct. 22, 1947; s. Frank Oliver and Grace Ellen (Marshall) M.; m. Milagros Macuja, Dec. 29, 1971; children: Michael Allen, Jeffrey Patrick. BS, Iowa State U., 1969; MBA, Eastern Mich. U., 1974. Registered dietitian; disting. health care food svc. adminstr. Dietitian II, South Quadrangle U. Mich., Ann Arbor, 1969-71, food svc. supr. II Bursley Hall, 1971-77, food svc. mgr. II, Residential Coll., 1977-80, food svc. mgr. II, West Quadrangle Complex, 1980-81; dir. food svcs. Cabell Huntington (W.Va.) Hosp., 1981-89, St. Mary's Hosp., Huntington, 1990—; participant various nat. recipe contests; Statler Found. scholar, 1965. Contbr. articles to profl. jours. Mem. Am. Dietetic Assn., W.Va. Dietetic Assn. (pres. 1984-85, adv. bd. 1985-88, 90-91, various com. 1981—, Outstanding W.Va. dietition 1983-84), W.Va.-Ohio-Ky. Dist. Dietetic Assn. (chmn. coun. on practice 1981, pres. 1982-83, 96—, chmn. nominating com. 1984-85, various coms. 1985-88, 90—), Am. Soc. Hosp. Food Svc. Adminstrs. (pres. W.Va. chpt. 1985-86, dir. region III 1990-91, nat. pres.-elect 1991-92, nat. nominating com. 1988-89, nat. legis. com. 1987-88, nat. publs. com. 1988-90, com. mem. Nat. APEX 1992-94, com. chmn. 1994—, various coms. W.Va. chpt. 1986—, pres.-elect W.Va. chpt. 1994-95, pres. 1995-96). Republican. Roman Catholic. Home: 54 Twin View Ln Huntington WV 25704-9607 Office: St Marys Hosp 2900 1st Ave Huntington WV 25702-1271

MARKWELL, DICK R(OBERT), retired chemist; b. Muskogee, Okla., Feb. 20, 1925; s. Alex J. and May (Albright) M.; m. Virginia Ann Gass, Aug. 28, 1949; children: Steven R., Scot L., Eric R., Cheryl F. BS, Wichita State U., 1948, M.S., 1950; PhD, U. Wis., 1956. Commd. 2d lt. U.S. Army, 1951, ret. lt. col., 1967, with Office Chief Rsch. and Devel.; assoc. prof. chemistry San Antonio Coll., 1967-74; chemist Corpus Christi Dept. Health, 1975-77; supr. chemistry sect. lab. div. San Antonio Met. Health Dist., 1977-87. With USMC, 1942-45. Mem. Am. Chem. Soc. Home: PO Box 34834 San Antonio TX 78265-4834

MARKWELL, NOEL, psychology educator; b. Covington, Ky., May 24, 1933; s. Quentin Roosevelt and Lelia Rose (Workman) M. AB, Lafayette Coll., 1955; MS, Purdue U., 1958, PhD, 1959. Lic. psychologist, Md. Psychologist Warley Hosp., Brentwood, Essex, Eng., 1960-61, D.C. Gen. Hosp., 1962-66, Law Sch. Georgetown U., Washington, 1967-72; cons. Gen. Acctg. Office, Washington, 1980-81; pvt. practice clin. psychology Md., 1972-1990; prof. Union Inst. Grad. Sch., Cin., 1980—; pres., bd. dirs. Inst. for Victims of Trauma, Washington, 1987—; cons.-sr. reviewer, Nat. Register of Health Svc. Providers in Psychology, Washington, 1975—. Dissertation Rsch. grant U.S. Office of Edn., Purdue U., 1958-59; Am.-Scandinavian Found. scholar U. Stockholm, 1959-60. Mem. Internat. Soc. of Polit. Psychology (founder, treas. 1986—); mem. APA, World Fedn. for Mental Health. Home: 4737 Country Oaks Blvd Sarasota FL 34243-4316

MARLAND, MELISSA KAYE, judge; b. Beckley, W.Va., Feb. 16, 1955; d. James Robert and Fannie Evelyn (Cook) M. BA in Polit. Sci., W.Va U., 1976, JD, 1979. Bar: W.Va. 1979, U.S. Dist. Ct. (so. dist.) W.Va. 1979, U.S. Supreme Ct. 1983. Law clk. Pub. Svc. Commn. W.Va., Charleston, 1979-82, hearing examiner, 1982-87, dep. chief adminstrv. law judge, 1987-89, chief adminstrv. law judge, 1989—; faculty mem. ann. regulatory studies program Nat. Assn. Regulatory Commrs./Inst. Pub. Utilities, Mich. State U., 1994—. Assoc. editor: West Virginia Digest of Public Utility Decisions, vols. 1-7, 1986-91; contbr. articles to profl. jours. Mem. ABA, NAFE, W.Va. State Bar (com. on corp., banking and bus. law 1987—), Nat. Assn. Regulatory Commrs. (chmn. subcom. on adminstrv. law judges 1991-95), Phi Beta Kappa, Phi Alpha Delta, Pi Sigma Alpha. Democrat. Office: Pub Svc Commn WVa 201 Brooks St Charleston WV 25301-1827

MARLAR, JANET CUMMINGS, public relations officer; b. Burnsville, Miss., Dec. 22, 1942; d. James E. and Juanita (Hale) Cummings; m. David C. Linton, May 21, 1961 (div. 1984); 1 child, Jeffory Mark; m. Thomas Gilbert Cupples, Mar. 5, 1984 (div. 1990); m. Fredrick Marlar, Nov. 19, 1994. Student, NE Miss. Jr. Coll., 1960-61, Memphis State U., 1975-76, Sheffield Tech. Ctr., Memphis, 1984-85. Property owner, Burnsville, 1974—, Glen, Miss., 1993—; mem. bus. adv. com. Sheffield Tech. Ctr., 1996—; with Scott Child Devel. Ctr., Oxford, Miss., 1989—; exec. bd. Internat. Heritage Commn., Memphis, 1987-92; pub. rels. officer Interant. Heritage Ethnic Festival, Memphis. Co-editor Internat. Heritage Bull./Newsletter. Vol. Memphis Brooks Mus. Art, 1980—; mem. exec. com., pub. info. officer Bldg. Bridges for A Better Memphis, 1985—; pres. Eagle Watch Assn.; founder Janet C. Cupples Citizenship awards, Memphis City Inter-City Sch., 1975, Student Leadership award, Memphis City Schs.; founder, chair women's com. on crime, City of Memphis, 1985—, chair Heritage-City of Memphis, chair internat. heritage program, 1987, 88—, Ethnic Outreach Neighborfest, 1988; hon. mem. city council, 1987; donor, exec. com. Women of Achievement, Inc., Memphis, 1986; mem. speakers bur. United Way of Greater Memphis, Friends of Shelby County Library, 1986—, YWCA; chair ethnic outreach com. Neighborfest, Memphis, 1987, chairperson exec. com. 1988; amb. Memphis Internat. Heritage Commn., 1988; youth mentor Memphis Youth Leadership Devel. Inst.; internat. coord. Neighborfest '88; chairperson Internat. Heritage City of Memphis, 1987, Ethnic Outreach Neighborfest, 1988. Contbr. articles to newspapers. Mem. community coun. Memphis City Schs., Memphis Cablevision Edn. Task Force; appointed col. aide de camp to staff of Gov. Ned McWherter of Tenn., 1988; sec. Shelby County Dem. Women, 1991; sec. safety com. St. Francis Hosp., 1992; participant Vol. Miss. Food Network Distbn. For Disabled Persons, 1996. Recipient 10 certs. of recognition Memphis City Council, 1986-89, Outstanding Service to Pub. Edn. award, 1986, merit award City of Memphis, 1987; named Outstanding Female Participant, Neighborhood, Inc., 1987; named Woman of Achievement 1988; honored by Pres. George Bush as Outstanding Vol., 1989; featured one of top 1000 Vols. in Mid-South, 1989; Svc. award Cummings Sch., 1993; apptd. Hon. Memphis City Councilwoman, 1995-96; recipient Royal award HRH Prince Kevin, 1996. Mem. NAFE, NOW (2d v.p. Memphis chpt. 1987, del. nat. conf. 1987, 2d v.p.), Network Profl. Women's Orgn., NCCJ, Rep. Career Women, Memphis Peace and Justice Ctr., Women's Polit. Caucus Tenn., Nat. Children's Cancer Soc. (friend 1995-96). Methodist. Avocations: community service, writing, teaching.

MARLAR, JOHN THOMAS, environmental engineer; b. Jackson, Ala., Sept. 24, 1939; s. John Thomas and Ada Jean (Hamilton) M.; m. Maryjo Borges, June 22, 1963 (div. 1979); children: John Thomas III, Jeannine Marie, Jennifer Joanne; m. Joyce A. Moon, Aug. 12, 1988; children: Regina Etheridge, Preston E. Moon. Student Miss. So. Coll., 1957-58; B.C.E., Auburn U., 1963; M.S., Ga. Inst. Tech., 1968. Coop. student U.S. Army C.E., Mobile, Ala., 1958-63; staff engr. Fed. Water Pollution Control Adminstrn., Atlanta, 1967-68, Alameda, Calif., 1968-69; supervisory sanitary engr. Fed. Water Quality Adminstrn., San Francisco, 1969-71; chief tech. assessment unit U.S. EPA, Atlanta, 1971-73, chief tech. support br., 1973-76, chief water quality planning br., 1976-81, chief facilities performance br., 1981-91, chief environ. complance branch, 1991-96, 96—, sr. tech. authority internat. program-Ukraine. With USPHS, 1963-66. Recipient Bronze medal EPA, 1973, 86, 94, Silver medal, 1985, Gold medal, 1988; Alcoa scholar, 1962-63. Mem. Water Pollution Control Fedn., Sigma Xi, Chi Epsilon, Phi Kappa Phi. Home: 85 Sims Rd Winder GA 30680-3567 Office: EPA Environ Svc Divsn College Station Rd Athens GA 30605

MARLER, ADDIE KAREN, elementary school educator; b. Dothan, Ala., Nov. 5, 1950; d. James Luther and Beulah Lee (Clenney) Savell; m. Thomas Franklin Marler, June 15, 1967; children: Jeffery, Jamie, Pamela. AA, Pasco Hernado C.C., 1981; BA, St. Leo Coll., 1985, postgrad. 6th and 7th grade lang. arts tchr. Moore Mickens Mid. Sch., Dade City, Fla., 1985-86, 7th grade gifted class tchr., 1985-86; developmental kindergarten tchr. Pasco Elem. Sch., Dade City, 1986-88, tchr. 6th grade self-contained class, 1988-89, 1st grade tchr., 1989-90, 1st/2d grade tchr., 1990-91, primary house K-2d grade tchr., 1991-93, intermediate house 3d-5th grade tchr., 1993-94, ESOL resource tchr., 1994—; migrant lead tchr. Pasco Elem. Sch., 1990-92, ESL tchr., 1994-95, ESOL resource tchr., 1994-96; dist. curriculum writer Pasco County Schs., 1991-93; ednl. cons., 1990—. Mem. adv. bd. Fla. League of Tchrs./Fla. Dept. Edn.; mem. Heritage Arts Assn., Dade City. Named 20th Anniversary Ambassador, Edn. Ctr. N.C., 1993-94. Mem. Fla. Assn. Childhood Edn., Alpha Delta Kappa (historian, scholarship chmn. 1990-93 Alpha Phi chpt.). Republican. Baptist. Office: Pasco Elem 37350 Florida Ave Dade City FL 33525-4041

MARLER, CHARLES HERBERT, journalism educator, historian, consultant; b. Garfield, Ark., Apr. 13, 1933; s. William Owen and Velma Valentine (Poe) M.; m. Peggy Lucille Gambill, Dec. 30, 1954; children: David Owen, Todd Alan, Scott Ladd. BA, Abilene Christian U., 1955, MA, 1968; PhD, U. Mo., 1974. Publicity asst. Abilene (Tex.) Christian U., 1955-56, sports info. dir., 1958-63, assoc. dir. devel., 1963-64, dir. info. and pubs., 1964-71, prof. journalism, 1974—, chmn. dept. journalism and mass comm., 1987—; rsch. asst. U. Mo., Columbia, 1973-74. Editor: Horizons, 1963-71, Lone Star Christmas, 1989; cons. Parenting Today, Christian Woman, Gospel Advocate, IdeaShop, Christian Chronicle; mem. editl. bd. Am. Journalism, Southwestern Mass Comm. Jour.; contbr. articles to profl. jours. Elder Univ. Ch. Christ, Abilene, 1977—; trustee Christian Village of Abilene, 1981—, Members of Chs. of Christ for Scouting, Abilene, 1985—, nat. chmn., 1989-91; mem. coun. bd. Boy Scouts Am., Abilene, 1981—. With U.S. Army, 1956-57, Germany. Frank Luther Mott Hist. Rsch. fellow U. Mo., Columbia, 1972-74, Cullen Fund grantee, 1982-84, 85-87; recipient Improvement award Time/Life Alumni Mag., 1966, Journalism Excellence award 20th Century Christian Mag., 1968, Clinton H. Denman Freedom of Info. Writing award U. Mo., 1974, Scoutmaster's key Boy Scouts Am., 1981, Dist. Merit award, 1982, Keith Ware award U.S. Army Journalism Competition, 1985, Silver Beaver award Boy Scouts Am., 1988, Christian Journalism award The Christian Chronicle, 1993; named Advisor of Yr., Tex. Intercollegiate Press Assn., 1982, Faithful Servant, Chs. Christ for Scouting, 1990. Mem. Am. Journalism Historian Assn. (bd. dirs. 1985-88, chmn. pub. com. 1983-87, 95-96, chmn. election and site com. 1987-90), Nat. Conf. Editorial Writers, S.W. Edn. Coun. for Edn. in Journalism and Mass Comm. (pres. 1988-89), Soc. Newspaper Design, Soc. Profl. Journalists (dep. dir. journalism edn. 1988-90, mem. nat. journalism edn. com. 1988-90). Home: 818 Radford Dr Abilene TX 79601-4613 Office: Dept Journalism and Mass Comm ACU Box 27892 Abilene Christian U Abilene TX 79699-7892

MARLER, SUSAN ANN, cardiology nurse, educator; b. Henryetta, Okla., Aug. 23, 1946; d. Grover E. and LouCille M. (Whippo) M. Nursing diploma, Hillcrest Med. Ctr., Tulsa, 1967. Staff nurse ICU Hillcrest Med. Ctr., Tulsa, 1967-71, head nurse ICU, 1971-80, critical care clinician, 1980-86, critical care edn. specialist, 1986-92; patient svcs. mgr. Okla. Heart, Inc., Tulsa, 1992-93; cons., lectr., owner Cardiovasc. Ednl. Svc., Tulsa, 1993—; BLS instr. trainer, 1991-92, 93—, ASLC instr., 1989—. Author, cons.: (film strip series) Critical Care Skills, 1982; cons.: (video series) Neurological Critical Care, 1985; revising author: (ind. learning packet) Basic Electrocardiography, 1991. Mem. AACN (CCRN 1976-89, bd. mem. Greater Tulsa Area Chpt. 1974-81). Republican. Baptist. Home and Office: 1809 S 91st East Ave Tulsa OK 74112-8422

MARLIN, ARTHUR EDWARD, pediatric neurosurgeon, educator; b. Boston, Jan. 28, 1947; s. Herman and Eva Marlin; m. Bebby Marlin; children: Sarah Jane, Tamara Eve, Evan Seth. BSc with distinction, McGill U., 1968, MD, 1972. Diplomate Am. Bd. Neurol. Surgery; lic. surgeon, N.Y., Tex. Surg. intern U. Minn. Hosps., 1972-73; resident NYU Med. Ctr., 1973-78; clin. instr. neurosurgery NYU Sch. Medicine, 1978; asst. prof. surgery/neurosurgery, asst. prof. pediatrics U. Tex. Health Sci. Ctr., San Antonio, 1978-80, clin. asst. prof. surgery/neurosurgery, 1980-84, clin. asst. prof. pediatrics, 1980-82, clin. assoc. prof. pediatrics, 1982-91, clin. assoc. prof. orthopedics, 1985—, clin. prof. pediatrics, 1991—; chief sect. pediatric neurosurgery Santa Rosa Childrens Hosp., San Antonio, 1984—; mem. adv. bd. South Tex. Organ Bank, 1987-90; mem. tech. adv. com. to gen. program Crippled Children's Svcs., Tex. Dept. Health, Austin, 1983-84. Author: Handbook of Pediatric Neurology and Neurosurgery, 1993; editor: Concepts in Pediatric Neurosurgery, Vol. VII, 1987, Vol. VIII, 1988, Vol. IX, 1989, Vol. X, 1990, Vol. XI, 1991, Shortcuts, 1989-91; mem. editl. bd. Clin. Neurosurgery, 1981, 82, 83; ann. meeting editor Jour. Pediatric Neurosurgery, 1992—, mem. editl. bd., 1992—; prodr. movies Brain Retraction Pressure Monitoring, 1983, The Use of Surgical Isolation Bubble, 1986; contbr. articles to profl. jours. Fellow ACS, Am. Acad. Pediatrics; mem. AMA, Bexar County Med. Soc., Tex. Med. Assn., Internat. Soc. Pediatric Neurosurgery, Congress Neurol. Surgeons, San Antonio Pediatric Soc., Soc. Neurosurg. Anesthesia and Neurol. Supportive Care, Am. Soc. Pediatric Neurosurgery (chmn. edn. com. 1986-91), Tex. Pediatric Soc., Am. Assn. Neurol. Surgeons (chmn. pediatric sect. 1993-95, chmn. surg. policy com. 1990-91), Am. Acad. Pediatrics (neurology sect.), Am. Acad. Cerebral Palsy and Devel. Medicine. Office: 4499 Medical Dr Ste 397 San Antonio TX 78229-3713

MARLIN, STERLING, professional race car driver. Winner Daytona 500, 1994, 1995. Office: NASCAR PO Box 2875 Daytona Beach FL 32120-2875*

MARLOW, JAMES ALLEN, lawyer; b. Crossville, Tenn., May 23, 1955; s. Dewey Harold and Anna Marie (Hinch) M.; m. Sabine Klein, June 9, 1987; children: Lucas Allen, Eric Justin. BA, U. Tenn., 1976, JD, 1979; postgrad., Air War Coll., Maxwell AFB, Ala., 1990-91, Internat. Studienzentrum, Heidelberg, Fed. Republic Germany, 1985-86. Bar: Ga. 1979, D.C. 1980, Tenn. 1980, U.S. Dist. Ct. (mid. dist.) Tenn. 1984, U.S. Ct. Fed. Claims 1987, U.S. Ct. Internat. Trade 1988, U.S. Tax Ct. 1987, U.S. Ct. Mil. Appeals 1980, U.S. Ct. Appeals (fed. cir.) 1987, U.S. Supreme Ct. 1987. Assoc. Carter & Assocs., Frankfurt, Fed. Republic Germany, 1984-85; chief internat. law USAF, Sembach AFB, Fed. Republic Germany, 1986-96; adj. prof. Embry-Riddle Aero. U., Kaiserslauten, Fed. Republic Germany, 1985—; judge advocate USAFR, Ramstein Air Base, Fed. Republic Germany, 1984—. Capt. USAF, 1980-84. Mem. Phi Beta Kappa. Home and Office: 5746 Hwy 127 South Crossville TN 38555

MARLOW, ORVAL LEE, II, lawyer; b. Denver, May 1, 1956; s. Jack Conger and Barbara A. (Stolzenburg) M.; m. Paige Wood, June 8, 1985; children: Lorri Wood, Orval Lee III. BA, U. Nebr., 1978, JD, 1981. Bar: Tex. 1981, U.S. Dist. Ct. (so. dist.) Tex. 1984, U.S. Ct. Appeals (5th cir.) 1984. Assoc. Krist & Scott, Houston, 1981-82; prin. Marlow & Assocs., Houston, 1982-83; ptnr. Lendais & Assocs., Houston, 1983-91; dir. Morris, Lendais, Hollrah & Snowden, 1992—. Mem. ABA, Internat. Bar Assn., Tex. Bar Assn., Houston Bar Assn., Phi Delta Phi. Lutheran. Office: Morris Lendais Hollrah & Snowden Ste 700 1980 Post Oak Blvd Houston TX 77056-3807

MARMION, WILLIAM HENRY, retired bishop; b. Houston, Oct. 8, 1907; s. Charles Gresham and Katherine (Rankin) M.; m. Mabel Dougherty Nall, Dec. 28, 1935; children: William Henry, Roger Mills Nall. B.A., Rice U., 1929; M.Div., Va. Theol. Sem., 1932, D.D. (hon.), 1954. Ordained to ministry Episc. Ch., 1932. Priest-in-charge St. James, Taylor, Tex., and Grace Ch., Georgetown, Tex., 1932-35; asso. rector St. Mark's Ch., San Antonio, 1935-38; rector St. Mary's-on-the-Highlands, Birmingham, Ala., 1938-50, St. Andrew's Ch., Wilmington, Del., 1950-54; bishop Episcopal Diocese of Southwestern Va., Roanoke, 1954-79, ret., 1979; Former dir. diocesan camps for young people in, Tex. and Ala., headed diocesan youth work, several yrs; dep. to Gen. Conv. Episcopal Ch., 1943, 46, alternate dep., 1949, 52; del. to Provincial Synod; mem. exec. council Episcopal Ch., 1963-69; chmn. Ala. Com. on Interracial Cooperation, 4 yrs. Trustee Va. Theol. Sem., Va. Episc. Sch., St. Paul's Coll.; pres. Appalachian Peoples Svc. Orgn.; interim warden Coll. of Preachers, 1981-82, diocesan coord. of pastoral ministry to retired clergy and families, 1990—. Home: 2730 Avenham Ave SW Roanoke VA 24014-1527

MARMOR, ROBERT RUBEN, drilling contracting executive, petroleum engineer; b. Buenos Aires, Argentina, Apr. 21, 1926; came to U.S., 1941; s.

Mauricio and Fay (Schuster) M.; m. Roberta Joan Konczak, Dec. 28, 1951; children: Michael, Katherine, Gary. BS in Petroleum Engring., Okla. U., 1951. Registered profl. engr., Tex. Chief engr. internat. ops. Sinclair Internat. Oil, N.Y.C., 1951-69; v.p. internat. ops. Tex. Internat., Oklahoma City, 1969-71; ops. mgr. Delhi Internat. Oil Corp., Adelaide, Australia; chmn. South Tex. Drilling and Exploration, San Antonio, 1980—. Served with U.S. Army, 1944-46, ETO. Home: 4313 Shavano Woods St San Antonio TX 78249-1845 Office: South Tex Drilling & Exploration Inc 9310 Broadway St San Antonio TX 78217-5906

MARNEY, SAMUEL ROWE, physician, educator; b. Bristol, Va., Feb. 15, 1934; m. Elizabeth Ann Bingham, Oct. 1, 1966; children: Samuel Rowe III, Annis Morison. BA in Chemistry, U. Va., 1955, MD, 1960. Staff physician VA Hosp., Nashville, 1968-69, clin. assoc., 1969-71, clin. investigator, 1971-74, staff physician, infectious disease and allergy cons., 1974—; asst. prof. medicine Med. Ctr. Vanderbilt U., Nashville, 1971-76, assoc. prof., 1976—, dir. allergy and immunology, 1974—; vis. investigator Scripps Clinic and Rsch. Found., La Jolla, Calif., 1973-74. Capt. USAF, 1962-64, Korea. Fellow ACP, Am. Acad. Allergy and Immunology, Am. Coll. Allergy and Immunology; mem. Southeastern Allergy Assn. (pres. 1986-87, Hal M. Davison Meml. award, 1981), Tenn. Soc. Allergy and Immunology. Home: 4340 Sneed Rd Nashville TN 37215-3242 Office: Vanderbilt U Med Ctr Allergy & Immunology 1500 21st Ave S Ste 3500 Nashville TN 37212

MAROCKIE, HENRY R., state school system administrator. Instr., rsch. assoc., asst. to dean W.V. Univ., Morgantown, 1968; asst. supt. Fin., Secondary Schs., Parkersburg, W.V., 1971; supt. Ohio County Schs., Wheeling, W.V., 1972-89; state supt. schs. Charleston, W.V., 1989—; chair Nat. gov. bd. Project Use It, W.V. Literacy Coun.; co-chair Learning Techs. com. Coun. Chief State Sch. Officers; pres. W.V. Sch/ Bldg. Authority; exec. com. mem. W.V. Edn. Fund; past officer W.V. Bd. Edn.; dir. reorgn. W.V. Dept. Edn., new evaluation systems tchrs., adminstrs.; launched Tobacco Control Policy W.V. schs.; est. Student, Tchr. Code Conduct, policies to modernize curriculum to State Bd., Gov's, Am. 2000 goals. Contbr. articles to profl. jours. Officer W.Va. Bd. Dirs., W.Va. Bd. Trustees, W.Va. Gov.'s Honors Acad., W.Va. Profl. Devel. Ctr., W.Va. Joint Commn. Vocat., Tech., Occupational Edn. Recipient W.Va. Supt. Yr. award, W.Va. Leader Learning award Dept. Edn., 1984, Supt. Yr. award W.Va. Assn. Music Educators, 1986, Leadership award Coll. Human Resources and Edn., W.Va. U., 1988, Alumni Achievement award West Liberty State Coll., 1985, citation edn. excellence W.Va. Ho. of Dels., 1982, Disting. Svc. award Nat. Alliance Health/Phys. Edn. Mem. W.V. Bd. Pub. Works, Ednl. Broadcasting Authority, Labor Mgmt. Coun., Tchrs. Retirement Bd., Drug Control Policy Bd., State Job Tng. Coord. Coun., Private Ind. Coun. W.V. Inc. Office: State Dept Edn 1900 Kanawha Blvd E Charleston WV 25305-0002*

MAROHN, ANN ELIZABETH, health information professional; b. Grand Rapids, Mich., Feb. 26, 1946; d. Luther Alfonse and Mary Inez (Pinkstaff) M. BS, Ind. U., 1968; MS, SUNY, Buffalo, 1978. Asst. med. record dir. Highland Park (Mich.) Gen. Hosp., 1968-70; asst. dir. med. record svcs. Meml. Hosp., Elmhurst, Ill., 1970-73; dir. med. record tech. program Alfred (N.Y.) State Coll., 1974-76; mem. faculty med. record adminstrn. dept. Lincoln Coll., Melbourne, Australia, 1977-78, Kean Coll., Union, N.J., 1984-85, Med. U. S.C., Charleston, 1985-87; mem. faculty health record dept. Ferris State Coll., Big Rapids, Mich., 1979-80; dir. health info. mgmt. Armstrong State Coll., Savannah, Ga., 1980-84; dir. med. record dept. Tucson Gen. Hosp., 1988-89, N.D. State Hosp., Jamestown, 1990-92; cons. Prospective Payment Specialists, Tucson, 1992-93; health info. mgr. Sierra Med. Ctr., El Paso, Tex., 1993-94; dir. health info. mgmt. program Southern U., Shreveport, La., 1994—; cons. Oglethorpe Ctr., Savannah, 1983-84. Columnist Australian Med. Record Jour., 1981-87, Communique, 1981-84, Palmetto Breeze, 1985-87, Progress Notes, 1984-85. Recipient disting. mem. award Ga. Med. Record Assn., 1984. Mem. NAFE, Am. Health Info. Mgmt. Assn., Ariz. Health Info. Mgmt. Assn. (program chmn. 1988-89, sec. 1989—), Tex. Health Info. Mgmt. Assn. (dist. III v.p.), La. Health Info. Mgmt. Assn., N.W. La. Health Info. Mgmt. Assn., Assembly on Edn. Episcopalian. Home: 215 Sand Beach Blvd 1205 Shreveport LA 71105

MAROHN, MARY LYNN, anesthesiologist; d. William Leroy and Josephine Genevieve (Repa) Dailey; m. Michael Robert Marohn, Dec. 17, 1988. MD, Uniformed Svcs. U. Intern gen. surgery, 1981-82, resident anesthesiology, 1985-87, advanced track anesthesiology fellow, 1987-88; commd. officer USAF, 1977, advanced through grades to lt. col., 1993; anesthesiologist MGMC/SGHSA, Andrews AFB, Md.; pain mgmt. fellow, 1995—. Vol. pediat. anesthesiologist Operation Smile Internat., Naga, The Philippines, 1992, 93, chief anesthesiologist, Nairobi, Kenya, 1993. Home: 1510 Dairy Rd Charlottesville VA 22903

MARONEY, JOHN EDWARD, environmental scientist; b. Medford, Mass., Aug. 6, 1937; s. Edward William and Evelyn Margaret (Finegan) M.; m. Patricia Maria Folsom, July 16, 1960; children: Timothy John, Kevin John, Terry Ann. Student, MIT, 1955-57; BA in Govt., Tufts U., 1959; MA in Govt., Ohio U., 1972; postgrad., Ohio State U., 1975-76. Registered environ. assessor, Calif.; qualified environ. profl. Multifamily mortgage servicing specialist U.S. Dept. HUD, Columbus, Ohio, 1972-73; coord. local air agy. programs Ohio EPA, Columbus, 1973-75, chief local air agy. sect., 1975-76; mgr. air quality mgmt. sect. EPA Air Pollution Tng. Inst., Northrop Svcs., Inc., Rsch. Triangle Pk., N.C., 1976-81; environ. mgmt. specialist Northrop Svcs. Inc., Rsch. Triangle Pk., 1981-89; tech. writer Manpower Tech. Temporary Svcs., Wilson, N.C., 1989-90; sci. writer, editor Rsch. & Evaluation Assocs., Chapel Hill, N.C., 1990-91; environ. cons. Chapel Hill, 1991-92; environ. scientist Environ. Resource Ctr., Cary, N.C., 1992—. Co-author: Air Pollution Control Orientation Course, 3d edit., 1981, Principles and Practices of Air Pollution Control: Instructor's Guide and Student Workbook, 1982, Hazardous Materials Management: Compliance with the New DOT Requirements, 1993; author: Overview of PSD Regulations, 1982, Air Pollution Control Orientation Course, 3d edit., 1991, Overview of the Human Health Evaluation Process in the RI/FS, 1991, Environmental Assessments for Real Property Transfers, 1994. Capt. USAF, 1959-72. Decorated Air medal with 2 oak leaf clusters. Mem. ASTM, ASPA (chpt. pres. 1983-84, sec. 1980-81, chpt. coun. 1979-86), Air and Waste Mgmt. Assn. (chpt. bd. dirs. 1991-94), Am. Mensa (local sec. 1979-81), Ea. N.C. exec. com. 1979-83, Columbus (Ohio) area exec. com. 1971-76), Triangle Computer Soc., Triangle Macintosh Users' Group, Universala Esperanto-Asocio, Esperanto Ligo por N.Am., Celtic Soc. of Chapel Hill (founding mem.), Raleigh Friends of Ireland. Democrat. Roman Catholic. Home: 409 Landerwood Ln Chapel Hill NC 27514-2340 Office: Environ Resource Ctr 101 Center Pointe Dr Cary NC 27513-5706

MAROSCHER, BETTY JEAN, librarian; b. Ashland, Ky., Aug. 12, 1934; d. Raymond and Virginia Dell (Staten) Boggs; student Columbus Coll. (Ga.), 1963-64; B.S., Hardin-Simmons U., 1967; M.S. in L.S., Our Lady of Lake U., San Antonio, 1970; M.Ed., Trinity U., 1975; m. Albert G. Maroscher Mar. 21, 1955 (dec.). Tchr., McAllen (Tex.) Ind. Sch. Dist., 1967-68; tchr. Northside Ind. Sch. Dist., San Antonio, 1968-69, librarian, 1969-71; reference librarian ednl. media Trinity U., San Antonio, 1971-76; reference librarian St. Philip's Coll., San Antonio, 1976, audiovisual librarian, mgr. audiovisual dept., 1977-86; librarian, coordinator Learning Resources Ctr., 1986—; lectr., cons. in field; chmn. subcom. programming and scheduling Univ. and Fine Arts Cable TV Com., 1980-81, sec. 1984-85. Active ARC; sec., trustee Compañia de Arte Español, 1982-84; sec. Council of Research and Academic Libraries, 1988-89. Recipient Minter/Medal Hardin-Simmons U., 1965, 66. Mem. Tex. Library Assn., Bexar County Library Assn., ALA, Tex. Jr. Coll. Tchrs. Assn., Tex. Assn. Chicanos in Higher Edn. (sec. St. Philip's chpt. 1982-84), Instructional Media Services Group, Council Research and Acad. Libraries Coop. Circulation Group (sec.-treas. 1977-79), Pi Gamma Mu (sec. chpt. 1965-67), Alpha Chi (historian 1965-67), other orgns. Republican. Home: 5230 Galahad Dr San Antonio TX 78218-2823 Office: 1801 Martin Luther King Dr San Antonio TX 78203-2027

MARPLE, MARY LYNN, software engineer, environmental scientist; b. Norristown, Pa., July 4, 1951; d. M. Robert and Elsie Alice (Lawton) M.; m. Cyrus Duncan Cantrell, Nov. 18, 1972; children: Katherine Anne and Sarah Montgomery Marple Cantrell. BA in Math., Swarthmore Coll., 1973; MS in Biology, U. N.Mex., 1975, PhD, 1979. Environ. scientist N.Mex. Environ. Improvement Agy., Santa Fe, 1974-75, Los Alamos (N.Mex.) Nat. Lab., 1975-79, French AEC, Paris, 1980; environ. quality specialist Tex. Dept. Health, Austin, 1981-83; software engr. Tele-Drill Inc., Richardson, Tex., 1983-86, Merit Tech., Dallas, 1986-89, Halliburton Reservoir Svcs., Carrollton, Tex., 1989-92, Superconducting Super Collider, Dallas, 1992-93, SBS Sensor Sys., Farmers Branch, Tex., 1994-95; with No. Telecom., Richardson, Tex., 1995—. Contbr. articles to profl. jours. Mem. class XI, Leadership Richardson. Mem. IEEE, Soc. Petroleum Engrs., Computer Soc., Dallas Accueil, Health Physics Soc., Canyon Creek Country Club, Sigma Xi (treas. 1986-87). Home: 2409 Lawnmeadow Dr Richardson TX 75080-2342 Office: No Telecom 2201 Lakeside Blvd Richardson TX 75082

MARQUARDT, MARY MEYERS, critical care nurse, educator; b. Austin, Tex., Mar. 9, 1959; d. Joseph Louis and Gladys Therese (New) Meyers; m. Michael Paul Marquardt, Feb. 23, 1985; children: Patricia Marie, Stephen Michael. BSN cum laude, Incarnate Word Coll., San Antonio, 1981; postgrad., Tex. Women's U., 1994—. CCRN, RN, Tex.; cert. ACLS instr., pediatric advanced life support instr. Staff nurse, charge nurse Scott and White Meml. Hosp., Temple, Tex., 1982-83; staff nurse, charge nurse Olin E. Teague Vets. Ctr., Temple, Tex., 1983-87, head nurse geriatric/rehab. unit, 1987-88, critical care coord., 1988-89; staff devel./edn. coord. Nan Travis Meml. Hosp., Jacksonville, Tex., 1989-90; staff nurse critical care St. Joseph's Health Ctr., Bryan, Tex., 1991—, quality assessment analyst, 1994; instr. nursing students Blinn C.C., Bryan, 1994—; critical care lectr., Bryan/College Station, Tex., 1991—. Co-author: Pocket Guide to Critical Care Assessment, 1989, 2d edit., 1994; contbg. author: Principles and Practices of Adult Health Nursing, 1989, Health Assessment, 4th edit., 1989. Mem. AACN (pres.-elect Lond Star chpt. 1994-95, pres. Lone Star chpt. 1995-96), ANA, Tex. Nurses Assn., Alpha Chi. Methodist. Office: Blinn CC ADN Program 1905 S Texas Ave Bryan TX 77802-1832

MARQUARDT, ROBERT RICHARD, lawyer; b. Columbus, Ohio, Aug. 22, 1943; s. Robert Gustave and Ethel M. (Augur) M.; m. Alice Grant, Sept. 9, 1966 (div. 1985); children: Theresa, Robert, Christopher; m. Patricia Moore Peek, Sept. 3, 1989. BS in Commerce, Rider Coll., 1965; MBA, Fairleigh Dickinson, 1966; JD, U. Ark., 1973; LLM, Temple U., 1977. Bar: Iowa 1973, Ark. 1973, U.S. Dist. Ct. (ea. dist.) Ark. 1973, N.J. 1975, U.S. Supreme Ct. 1979. Counsel RCA Corp., Camden, N.J., 1973-77; assoc. counsel Occidental Chem. Corp., Niagara Falls, N.Y., 1977-79, div. counsel, 1979-80, counsel, 1980-81, assoc. gen. counsel, 1981-87, v.p., gen. counsel electrochems. and specialty products grp., 1987-91, assoc. gen. counsel, mng. atty., 1991—; instr. bus. law Niagara U., 1978-82. Contbr. legal essays to profl. publs. Chmn. Youngstown (N.Y.) Environ. Com., 1980-84; mil. chmn. UN Operation Horseshoe, Niagara Falls, 1981; staff judge adv. USAFR, 1974-89. Served to lt. col. USAFR, 1967-89. Recipient United Way awards, 1968-76, Corp. award Am. Jurisprudence, 1972; named Judge Adv. of Yr., USAFR, 1980. Office: 5005 LBJ Freeway Dallas TX 75244

MARQUEZ, HOPE, school system worker, educator; b. Winters, Tex., Sept. 12, 1948; d. Richard Ruiz and Candelaria (Medrano) Palomo; m. Arthur G. Marquez Jr.; children: Beverly Ruth Gonzales, Lytha Maria Mendoza, Hope. Bus driver, office asst., safety officer Ft. Worth Ind. Sch. Dist., 1977-90; ops.mgr., in charge bus driver tng. and cert. Ednl. Svc. Ctr., Ft. Worth, 1990—, coord., 1994. Vol. Ft. Worth Fire Dept. Relief, 1987, sec., 1991. Mem. Tex. Assn. for Pupil Transp. (region XI reporter 1995, 96, chmn. poster contest 1995). Office: Edn Svc Ctr Region XI 3001 North Fwy Fort Worth TX 76106-6526

MARR, DAVID FRANCIS, television announcer, former professional golfer, journalist; b. Houston, Dec. 27, 1933; s. David Francis and Grace Anne (Darnell) M.; m. Caroline Elizabeth Dawson, Sept. 25, 1972; children by previous marriage: Elizabeth S., David Francis III, Anthony J. Student, Rice U., 1950-51, U. Houston, 1951-52. Profl. golfer, 1953—, tour player, 1960-72, part-time tour player, 1973—; golf announcer ABC Sports, 1970-91, BBC Sports, 1992—; dir. Nabisco-Dinah Shore Tournament, 1981-86. Elected to Coll. golf Hall of Fame, 1981, Tex. Golf Hall of Fame, 1981; named to Ryder Cup Team, 1965. Mem. Profl. Golfers Assn. (nat. champion 1965, Player of Year 1965), AFTRA. Roman Catholic. Clubs: Lochinvar Golf (Houston); Houston City; Champions Golf (Houston); Brae-Burn Country. Office: care Hans Kramer IMG 1 Erieview Plz Ste 1300 Cleveland OH 44114-1715

MARRACK, DAVID, pathologist; b. Sawbridgeworth, Herts., England, Dec. 25, 1922; came to U.S., 1961; s. John Richardson and Alice May (Milward) M.; m. Patricia Franklin, June 1949; children: Jane, Paul, Mary. BS, MB, U. London, England, 1947, MD, 1952. Rsch. fellow Royal Postgrad. Med. Sch., London, 1951-53; travelling fellow Washington U., St. Louis, 1953-54; assoc. prof. pathology U. Tex. M.D. Anderson Hosp., Houston, 1961-68; pathologist Harris County Hosp., Houston, 1965-75; with Fort Bend Med. Clinic, Houston. Contbr. articles to profl. jours. With RAF, 1949-51. Mem. Air Waste Mgmt. Assn., Am. Soc. Clin. Pathology, Audubon Soc. Office: Fort Bend Med Clinic PO Box 271907 Houston TX 77277-1907

MARRESE, BARBARA ANN, nurse, educator, program planner; b. Dover, N.J., Mar. 24, 1936; d. Andrew A. and Eleanor C. (Connelly) Brown; m. Thomas G. Marrese, Nov. 27, 1959; children: Guy A., Holly A. Karker. BA, Jersey City State Coll., 1973; MS, East Stroudsburg (Pa.) U., 1989. Scrub nurse Orange (N.J.) Meml. Hosp., 1956-58; head scrub nurse Columbus Hosp., Newark, 1959-60; sch. nurse/tchr. Mt. Olive Twp. Bd. of Edn., Budd Lake, N.J., 1964-90; asst. supr. Childrens Med. Svcs., Ft. Lauderdale, Fla., 1990-92; program planner Sch. Dist. Palm Beach County, Fla., 1992—. Mem. AAHPERD, Am. Sch. Health Assn., Fla. Sch. Health Assn., Fla. Nurses Assn., Fla. Assn. Health, Phys. Edn., Recreation, Dance and Driver Edn., Morris County Ret. Tchrs. Assn. Republican. Roman Catholic. Home: 2142 NW 60th Cir Boca Raton FL 33496-2647

MARRIOTT, SUSAN, virology educator; b. Ft. Madison, Iowa, Mar. 31, 1959; d. Richard S. and H. Irene (Garner) M. BS in microbiology, Iowa State U., 1981; PhD, Kans. State U., 1986, postgrad., 1986-87; postgrad., NIH, 1987-91. Asst. prof. divsn. molecular virology Baylor Coll. Medicine, Houston, 1991—; mem. faculty recruitment com. Baylor Coll. Medicine, 1992—, grad. student recruitment com. Contbr. chpts. in books; contbr. articles to profl. jours.; speaker at numerous confs. Recipient Cora M. Downs award for Excellence in sci. rsch. Mo. Valley Br. Am. Soc. Microbiology, 1982; NIH fellow, 1985-86; rsch. grantee Sci. Rsch. Soc., 1986. Mem. Am. Assn. Advancement of Sci., Am. Soc. Virology, Am. Soc. Microbiology, Sigma Xi (bd. dirs. 1992—). Office: Baylor Coll Medicine Div Moleculat Violgy One Baylor Plaza Houston TX 77030

MARRS, JAMES F. (JIM), JR., author, journalist, educator; b. Ft. Worth, Dec. 5, 1943; s. James Marrs; m. Carol Ann Worcester, May 25, 1968; children: Cathryn Nova Ayn, Jayme Alistar. BA in Journalism, North Tex. State U., 1966; postgrad., Tex. Tech. Coll., 1967-68. Editor/owner Magpie Mag., 1963-64; sports/news writer, cartoonist Denton (Tex.) Record Chronicle, 1965-66; reporter, copy editor, cartoonist and photographer Lubbock (Tex.) Avalanche-Jour., 1967-68; news and feature writer, cartoonist, photographer Lubbock Sentinel, 1968; reporter, feature writer, photographer, cartoonist Ft. Worth Star-Telegram, 1968-80; prodr. "Texas Roundup" Sammons Cable TV, Ft. Worth, 1982-83; scriptwriter Spindletop Prodns., Dallas, 1982-83; pub. rels. cons. The Mktg. Group, Dallas, 1982-83; pubr., co-owner The Springtown (Tex.) Current, 1983-84; comm. dir. Continental State Bank, Springtown, 1985—; editl. page editor Campus Chat, North Tex. State U., 1965-66; part-time copywriter, pub. rels. dir., cartoonist Jerre R. Todd & Assocs., 1972-74, dir. spl. projects, account exec., pub. rels. dir., 1980-81; editor/pub. and co-owner Cowtown Trails, Ft. Worth, 1983-84; faculty Office Continuing Edn. U. Tex., Arlington, 1976—; comm. dir. N.E. HealthCare Ctr., Hurst, Tex., 1985-86. Contbr. articles to profl. jours.; author: Crossfire: The Plot That Killed Kennedy, 1992; scriptwriter, dir. video: Fake, 1991, The Many Faces of Lee Harvey Oswald, 1992. Prodr. Tex. Gridiron Show, Ft. Worth, 1978-79, dir., 1980; chmn. pub. info. subcom. Ft. Worth Mayor's Com. on Employment of Handicapped, 1979-82; co-chmn. Springtown Centennial Com., 1984; workshop tchr. Operation CLASP, Neighborhood Adv. Coun., Community Devel. Block Grant, City of Ft. Worth, 1984; community rels. cons. All Church Home for Children, Ft. Worth, 1984—. With USAR, 1969-70. Recipient White Helmet award Ft. Worth Fire dept., 1969, 71, Assoc. Press writing awards, 1969-76, Nat. Writing award Aviation/Aerospace Writers Assn., 1972, Human Rights Leadership award Freedom Mag., 1993; named Arts and Entertainment Newsmaker of the Yr., Tex. Gridiron Club, Soc. Profl. Journalists, 1991. Mem. Tex. Mil. Hist. Soc., Springtown Optimist Club, Delta Sigma Phi, Sigma Delta Chi. Libertarian. Methodist. Home and Office: Wise Comms PO Box 189 Springtown TX 76082-0189

MARSCH, ANDREW JOHNSON, III, university dean; b. Painesville, Ohio, Sept. 12, 1959; s. Andrew Johnson II and Marlene Thalia (Maier) M.; m. Sharon Anne Kebbel, Nov. 3, 1990; children: Andrew Johnson IV, Adam Everett. BA, The Coll. of Wooster, Ohio, 1982; MA, Miami U., Oxford, Ohio, 1983. Grad. asst. recreational sports Miami U., Oxford, Ohio, 1982-83; dir. intramural and recreational sports U. Ala., Birmingham, 1983-89, asst. dean student affairs, 1988-90, assoc. dean student affairs, 1990—. Diversity trainer Leadership for Diversity Initiative, Birmingham, 1995—; mem. scout svcs. com. U. Ala., Birmingham; mem. student devel. task force Birmingham area, 1994—; mem. leadership devel. class C. of C., Birmingham, 1993. Named hon. mem. Golden Key Nat. Honor Soc., 1989. Mem. Student Assn. for Coll. Student Affairs (chair time/place com. 1994—, mem. conf. program com. 1993, chair local arrangements 1992), Order of Omega (hon.), Omicron Delta Kappa. Lutheran. Home: 525 Currie Way Birmingham AL 35209 Office: The U of Ala at Birmingham 110 HUC 1400 University Blvd Birmingham AL 35233-1515

MARSDEN, KEITH LYNN, minister, counselor; b. Carbondale, Pa., Dec. 13, 1951; s. George Emerson and June Elizabeth (Stouffer) M.; m. Dianne West, June 18, 1977; children: Gretchen Kimberly, Jesse West. BA in Sociology, N.C. Wesleyan Coll., Rocky Mount, 1974; MDiv, Wesley Theol. Sem., 1977; postgrad., Columbia Pacific U., San Rafael, Calif., 1994—. Ordained to ministry, Meth. Ch., 1975. Minister So. N.J. Conf. United Meth. Ch., Trenton, 1975-81; exec. dir. outdoor edn. Wyo. Conf. United Meth. Ch., Binghamton, N.Y., 1981-83; minister United Meth. Ch., Binghamton, 1983-88; dir. aftercare The Children's Home, Inc., Winston-Salem, 1988—; bd. dirs. Contact Teleministries, USA, Trenton, 1977-81, also trainer, counselor; bd. dirs. Pastoral Counseling Ctr. Northeastern Pa., Scranton, 1986-88. Mem. steering coun. of Mayor's Violence Reduction Task Force, Winston-Salem, 1993-95. Democrat. Office: The Childrens Home Inc 1001 Reynolda Rd Winston Salem NC 27104

MARSEL, ROBERT STEVEN, law educator, mediator, arbitrator; b. N.Y.C., July 23, 1947; s. Bernard and Vivian (Gilbert) M. J.D., U. Calif., 1971. Bar: N.Y., D.C., U.S. Supreme Ct. Mem. Worcester Coll., Oxford, Eng.; vis. lectr. Faculty Law, U. Auckland N.Z.; spl. asst. U.S. atty., San Francisco; legal officer U.S. Supreme Ct., Washington; vis. asst. prof. law U. Miami, 1983-84; prof. South Tex. Coll. Law, Houston, 1984—; chmn. com. on privacy and confidentiality U.S. Dept. Commerce, 1973-75; trainer, lectr. on mediation; mediator pro bono Houston Dispute Resolution Ctr.; faculty mem. Ctr. for Legal Responsibility. U. Calif. hon. traveling fellow, 1971-72. Fellow Houston Bar Found.; mem. Am. Arbitration Assn., Tex. Assn. Mediators, Tex. Accts. and Lawyers for the Arts (bd. dirs. mediation com.), Soc. Profls. in Dispute Resolution. Office: 3032 San Felipe Houston TX 77019

MARSH, CHARLES CLIFTON, pharmacist, educator; b. DeWitt, Ark., Feb. 28, 1953; s. Kile F. and Betty Jo (Gabe) M.; m. Nancy Smith, Dec. 21, 1974 (div. 1985); children: Austin K. Marsh, Spencer G. Marsh; m. Cynthia Ann English, Oct. 21, 1991. BS in Pharmacy, U. Ark. Med. Sci., 1980; PharmD, Med. U. S.C., 1984. Bd. cert. pharmacotherapy specialist Bd. of Pharm. Specialties. Staff pharmacist St. Mary's Hosp., Russellville, Ark., 1980-82; drug and poison info. specialist Med. U. S.C., Charleston, 1982-84; ambulatory care resident VA Hosp., Madison, Wis., 1984-85; asst. prof., clin. coord. VA Med. Ctr., Salt Lake City, 1985-87; asst. prof. Coll. Medicine U. Ark. Med. Scis., Little Rock, 1987—, asst. prof. Coll. Pharmacy, 1987-93, assoc. prof. Coll. Pharmacy, 1993—; dir. clin. pharmacy Area Health Edn. Ctr., Ft. Smith, Ark., 1987—; rsch. com. Ark. chpt. Am. Heart Assn., 1993—; cons. Bost Human Devel., Ft. Smith, 1988-95; mem. S.W. Regional Cholesterol Coun., Memphis, 1992-95. Author: Magill's Survey of Science, 1994; contbr. articles, book revs. to profl. jours. Dir. M*A*S*H program, Ft. Smith, 1990, 92. Fellow Am. Soc. Cons. Pharmacists; mem. Am. Coll. Clin. Pharmacy, Am. Assn. Colls. Pharmacy, Am. Soc. Hosp. Pharmacists, Mid-South Coll. Clin. Pharmacy, Soc. Tchrs. Family Medicine. Office: AHEC Family Med Ctr 612 S 12th St Fort Smith AR 72901-4702

MARSH, ELLA JEAN, pediatrician; b. Chgo., Dec. 16, 1941; d. Charles and Eleanor (Canfield) M.; BA, St. Mary of Woods (Ind.) Coll., 1963; DO, Chgo. Coll. Osteo. Medicine, 1971. Intern, Doctor's Hosp., Columbus, Ohio, 1971-72; resident in pediatrics, then asst. prof. Chgo. Coll. Osteo. Medicine, 1972-78, assoc. prof. pediatrics, 1978-82; assoc. prof. W.Va. Coll. Osteo. Medicine, 1975—; chmn. pediatric and newborn nursery, 1982-94, assoc. dir. med. edn. Orlando (Fla.) Gen. Hosp., 1985-88; assoc. clin. prof. Nova Southeastern Coll. Osteo Medicine, 1984; mem. staff Arnold Palmer Children's Hosp., Fla. Hosp., Humana Hosp.-Orlando Gen. Hosp., Winter Park Hosp., Health Ctr.; pediatric cons. Nat. Bd. Osteo. Examiners; lectr., cons. in field. Bd. dirs. St. Mary of Woods Coll., 1992-95, Ctrl. Fla. Primary Care. Donald Bucknar Moore scholar, 1963; diplomate Am. Coll. Osteo. Pediatricians (chmn. evaluating com. 1981-89), Nat. Osteo. Bds. Fellow Am. Coll. Osteo. Pediatrics (v.p. 1986, pres. 1988); mem. AMA, Am. Osteo. Assn., Fla. Osteo. Assn., Fla. Med. Soc., Orange County Med. Soc., Cen. Fla. Pediatric Soc., Chgo. Coll. Osteo. Medicine Alumni Assn. Roman Catholic. Home: 8210 Imber St Orlando FL 32825-8233 Office: 7824 Lake Underhill Rd Orlando FL 32822-8201

MARSH, JOSEPH VIRGIL, commercial real estate and investment broker, consultant; b. Winston-Salem, N.C., Apr. 28, 1952; s. Gilliam Hughes and Dovie Elizabeth (Watson) M.; student Surrey C.C., 1970-72; Coop. Engring. Program, U.S. Govt. Schs., Md., S.C., Washington, 1972-74; BSEE, U. Md., 1976; grad. N.Y. Inst. Fin., 1978, NYU, 1978, MBA, 1980. With Joint Armed Svcs. Tech. Liaison, Washington, 1974-75; cons. U.S. Govt., 1975-76; corr., cons. individuals, bus. on tech. matters, Ararat, N.C., 1977—; registered adviser SEC, 1981—. Mem. U.S. Presdl. Task Force, 1981—; tech. liason NASA, 1992. Comml. real estate broker, N.C.; founder The Marsh Found., 1989. Recipient Presdl. Medal of Merit Pres. of U.S., 1988, 90. Mem. Internat. Entrepreneurs Assn., VFW (hon.), Armed Forces Assn., Ind. Cons. Assn., Internat. Assn. Sci. Devel., Council Civilian Tech. Advisers. Republican. Office: RR 1 Box 12 Ararat NC 27007-9703

MARSH, MALCOLM ROY, JR., electronics engineer; b. Bedford, Va., Oct. 12, 1932; s. Malcolm Roy and Mildred (Overstreet) M.; BEE, U. Va., 1956; children: Lauranne Ashton, James Overstreet. Elec. engr. Sperry Piedmont, Inc., Charlottesville, Va., 1957-58, Martin Orlando Co., Orlando, Fla., 1958-60; electronic engring. cons., Orlando, 1960—. Served with U.S. Army, 1958. Mem. IEEE. Methodist. Home and Office: 2609 Tradewinds Trl Orlando FL 32805-5840

MARSH, MILES L., textile company executive; b. 1947. With various divsns. Dart & Kraft Inc., Gen. Foods USA; chmn., CEO, Pet Inc., St. Louis, until 1995; pres., CEO, James River Corp. Va., Richmond, 1995—, chmn. bd., 1996—. Office: James River Corp Va 120 Tredegar St Richmond VA 23219

MARSH, NELSON LEROY, military officer; b. Ft. Worth, Tex., Sept. 27, 1937; s. Edward Donald and Joyce Estelle (Taif) M.; m. Janice Ferguson, Nov. 20, 1960 (div. 1965); m. Anne Schreiweis, Sept. 6, 1966; children: Michele Maria, Sharon Catherine, Glenn Edward. BA, Tex. Christian U., 1959; law cert., LaSalle U., Chgo., 1973; cert., Nat. War Coll., 1980, Army Command & Gen. Staff Coll, 1973. Commd. 2nd lt. U.S. Army, 1959, advanced through grades to col., 1979; office dep. dir. office of chief of pers. U.S. Army, Washington, 1965-68; div. personnel officer 101st Airborne Div. U.S. Army, Bien Hoa, Vietnam, 1968-69; adjutant gen. 3rd infantry div. U.S. Army, Wuerzburg, Fed. Republic of Germany, 1969-72; comdr. 3d infantry div. Rear U.S. Army, Wuerzburg; editor in chief Soldiers Mag. U.S. Army, Alexandria, Va., 1973-75; commdr. various battalions U.S. Army, Chgo., Frankfurt, 1975-79; dir. various offices U.S. Army, Washington, San Antonio, 1980-86; dir. Army/Air Force News Service U.S. Army, San Antonio, 1986-89; owner NLM Income Tax Svc., San Antonio, 1987-95; bd. dirs. Bright Eyes Vision, Babylon Grill, Inc, Starbuck Svc.; pres., CEO NLM

Tax Svc. Inc., 1995-96. Author, editor: Army Enlisted Management, 1965; contbr. articles to mags. and newspapers. Block dir. Stone Oak Community Orgn., San Antonio, 1986-90; vol. Lyndon B. Johnson for Senator campaign, Ft. Worth, 1954; pres. Armed Forces Pub. Affairs Council, San Antonio, 1987-88. Decorated Bronze Star (3 awards), Legion of Merit (5 awards), Meritorious Svc. medal (3 awards), Army Commendation medal (5 awards). Mem. Order of Mil. Med. Merit, Tex. Christian U. Alumni Assn., VFW, Stamp Collectors Club, Phi Alpha Theta. Democrat. Presbyterian. Home: 18003 Green Knls San Antonio TX 78258-3418

MARSH, OWEN ROBERT, education educator; b. Springfield, Ill., Oct. 4, 1935; s. Owen Rainey and Dorothea Nell (Frutiger) M.; m. Evelyn Joyce Mathews, Aug. 19, 1958; children: Jeffrey, John, Thomas. BS in Edn., Ill. State Normal U., 1957, MS in Edn., 1958; EdD, Ill. State U., Normal, 1967. Tchr. Galesburg (Ill.) Pub. Schs., 1958-61; instr. edn. Western Ill. U., Macomb, 1962-64, Ill. State U., Normal, 1967; rsch. assoc. Ill. Bd. Higher Edn., Springfield, 1967-69; registrar U. Ill., Springfield, 1969-72; dean of admissions and records Tex. Ea. U., Tyler, 1972-80; registrar U. Tex., Tyler, 1980-89, assoc. prof., 1989—. Author: Illinois Board of Higher Education, 1969; contbr. articles to mags. Pres. Springfield Lions Club, 1967-72, Tyler Evening Lions, 1979-80, 86-87; treas. Assn. of Retarded Citizens, Springfield, 1971-72; mem. Human Rights Com., Tyler, 1992—. Served with USAF, 1961-62. Recipient Roy A. Clark scholarship Ill. State U., 1967. Mem. St. Louis Performance Coun., Kappa Delta Pi (counselor 1992-95, area rep. 1994—). Methodist. Home: 3613 Glendale Dr Tyler TX 75701-8642 Office: Univ Tex Tyler 3900 University Blvd Tyler TX 75799

MARSH, WILLIAM DOUGLAS, lawyer; b. Sikeston, Mo., Feb. 22, 1947; s. Ray Carl and Mary Louis (Buchanan) M.; m. Georgia Kay Trigg, June 3, 1967; children: Kristin Elizabeth, Kelly Anne. BSBA, S.E. Mo. State U., 1971; JD, U. Mo., Kansas City, 1973. Bar: Fla. 1974, U.S. Dist. Ct. (no., mid. and so. dists.) Fla., U.S. Ct. Appeals (5th and 11th cir.). Shareholder Emmanuel, Sheppard & Condon, Pensacola, Fla., 1973—. Contbr. articles to profl. jours.; reviewer Fla. Torts, 1990. Active numerous polit. campaigns/polit. action groups. 1st lt. U.S. N.G., 1967-73. Mem. ABA (litigation sect., torts and ins. practice sect., com. on auto. law), Assn. Trial Lawyers Am. (diplomate), Acad. Fla. Trial Lawyers (sustaining), Am. Bd. Trial Advocacy (cert. trail lawyer), Fla. Bar Assn. (rules of civil procedure com. 1991—, trial lawyers sect. exec. coun. 1979-88, sec. 1984-85, editor trial sect. newsletter 1982-83, chmn. 1986-87). Democrat. Methodist. Office: Emmanuel Sheppard & Condon 30 S Spring St Pensacola FL 32501-5612

MARSHAK, LISA RACHEL, special education educator; b. Augusta, Ga., Nov. 1, 1969; d. Stephen Howard and Elizabeth Susan (Lefrak) M. BA in History, U. Mass., 1992; MEd, Wesley Coll., 1994. Cert. tchr. 5-9 social studies, N-9 moderate spl. needs, therapeutics crisis intervention, Mass. Tchr. social studes/moderate spl. needs New Eng. Home for Little Wanderers, Watertown, Mass., 1993-94; tchr. learning disabilities Mark Twain Mid. Sch., Alexandria, Va., 1994—; adj. faculty Lesley Coll., Cambridge, Mass., 1993-94; team leader, yearbook advisor Twain Mid. Sch., Alexandria, 1994—. Mem. ASCD, Nat. Orgn. Fetal Alcohol Syndrome, Va. Mid. Sch. Assn. Office: Twain Mid Sch 4700 Franconia Rd Alexandria VA 22310

MARSHALL, ALLEN WRIGHT, III, communications executive, consultant; b. Griffin, Ga., Dec. 4, 1941; s. Allen Wright, Jr. and Evelyn Louise (Halliburton) M.; m. Carole Anne Moore, Dec. 24, 1964; 1 child, Allen Wright IV. BA in Journalism, U. Ga., 1964; diploma Elkins Inst. Radio, Atlanta, 1964; postgrad. Ga. State U., 1968, MBA Ga. State U., 1988; cert. Coll. Fin. Planning, Denver, 1991. 1st class radio telephone lic. FCC; cert. fin. planner. Pres., Sta. WKEU-AM-FM, Griffin, Ga., 1954-86; co-founder, v.p. Griffin Cable TV, 1971-74; co-founder, pres. Custom Services, Inc., Griffin, 1974—; co-founder, v.p. Cobbwells Marshall, Inc., Griffin, 1982-87, Page One, Griffin, 1983-87; co-founder, pres. Toolware, Inc., Griffin, 1993—; co-founder, sec./treas. Magnolia Broadcasting, Inc., LaGrange, Ga., 1993-95; founder, mng. mem. Spalding Speculators LLC, Griffin, 1995—; dir. First Union Nat. Bank, Griffin; bd. dirs. Goals for Griffin and Spalding Counties, Inc., 1981-92, pres., 1991. Author radio programs, editorials (Ga. AP awards 1969-84); also articles; speaker in field. Mem. adv. com. Griffin Vocat.-Tech. Sch., 1982-87; bd. dirs. Jr. Achievement, Griffin, 1977-87; chmn. Griffin-Spalding Indsl. authority, 1984; mem. Gov.'s Adv. Com. on Area Planning and Devel. Commns., 1971-72; bd. dirs. McIntosh Trail Area Planning and Devel. Commn., Ga., 1971-73; founding trustee, vice chair, dir. St. George's Episc. Sch., 1995—; treas., trustee Nat. Episc. Radio/TV Found., 1986-93. Sgt. U.S. Army, 1966-68. Named Man of Yr., Exchange Club of Griffin, 1984. Mem. Ga. Assn. Broadcasters (bd. dirs. 1970-74, Radio Sta. of Yr. 1977), Griffin Area C. of C. (bd. dirs. 1980, chmn. indsl. com. 1980, 81). Episcopalian. Clubs: Country (charter mem. 1966). Lodge: Rotary (pres. 1976-77). Avocations: photography, landscape design, archtl. renovation. Home and Office: 1800 Maple Dr Griffin GA 30223-7405

MARSHALL, BRUCE, artist, writer; b. Athens, Tex., Dec. 29, 1929; s. Litten B. and Myrtis (Hoover)M.; m. Ann Smith, Sept. 30, 1962; children—Susanne, Randolph, Cody. Student Univ. Ariz., 1950-52, So. Ariz. Sch. Art, 1952-54. Writer Jour. Commerce, N.Y.C., 1959-64, Houston Post, 1964-66; artist, Austin, Tex., 1970—. One-man shows include Bank Douglas, Tucson, 1953, Old Overland Trail Mus., Ft. Davis, Tex., 1972, 74, 1st Cavalry Mus., Ft. Hood, Tex., 1972, Univ. Ariz., Tucson, 1973, Hidalgo County Hist. Mus., Edinburg, Tex., 1972, Ft. Bend County Hist. Mus., Richmond, Tex., 1974, 76, Star Republic Mus., Washington, Tex., 1978, San Jacinto Monument, Deer Park, Tex., 1978, Llano Estacado Mus., Plainview, Tex., 1975, Heard Natural Sci. Mus. and Wildlife Sanctuary, McKinney, Tex., 1975, Rotunda Tex. State Capitol, 1975, 76, 84, Panhandle-Plains Mus., Canyon, Tex., 1977, Mus. Big Bend, Alpine, Tex., 1977, Chamizal Nat. Monument, El Paso, 1977, John E. Conner Mus., Kingsville, Tex., 1985-86, U. Tex. Health Sci. Ctr., San Antonio, 1991-92, Rotunda Cannon Ho. Office Bldg., Washington, 1991-92, War Meml. Mus. Va., Newport News, 1991-92; exhibited in group shows at Smithsonian Instn., Washington, 1953, Tex. State Archives & Library, Austin, 1978, Le Musee de L'Histoire de l'Homme, Brussels, 1983, Rotunda Tex. State Capitol, Austin, 1991; represented in permanent collections 1st Cavalry Mus., Univ. Tex. Inst. Texan Cultures, San Antonio, Nat. Infantry Mus., Ft. Benning, Ga., San Jacinto Monument, Dick Dowling Sch., Houston, Wings Club, N.Y.C., Confederate Research Ctr. Hill Coll., Hillsboro, Tex., Laredo (Tex.) Nat. Bank, Capital Bank, Dallas, Dallas Pub. Library, Houston Pub. Library, The Alamo, San Antonio; executed mural Tex. Citizen Soldier, Nat. Infantry Mus., 1976; mural The Patriots for Dallas Baptist Univ., 1994, illustrator various books and publs. Vice-comdr. Mil. Order of the Stars & Bars, N.Y.C., 1962-64. Named to knighthood King Peter II of Yugoslavia, 1966; named Artist of 65th Legislature, State of Tex., 1977, Artist of Confederacy Tex. div. United Daughters Confederacy, 1974, Nat. Artist Confederate States Am., Sons of Confederate Vets., 1976, Lt. Col. Gov. Lester Maddox's Staff State of Ga., 1967; recipient Jefferson Davis medal United Daus. of Confederacy 1974, Alamo award Daus. Republic of Tex., 1979. Mem. Hood's Tex. Brigade Assn. (pres. 1967-69), Tex. State Hist. Assn., Sons Confederate Vets. (comdr. Trans-Miss. dept. 1970-72). Presbyterian. Avocation: writing. Office: Westart PO Box 161616 Austin TX 78716-1616

MARSHALL, DONALD BRUCE, political science educator; b. Portland, Maine, Apr. 15, 1931; s. John T. and Olive (Schultz) M.; m. Betty Rodes, Aug. 10, 1953 (dec.); children: Susan, Clifton, Olivia, John; m. Susan Winkler Dunn, Aug. 17, 1967 (div.); children: Margaret, Elizabeth, Richard. BA, Yale U., 1952, MA, 1953, PhD, 1968. Instr. Ohio State U., Columbus, 1956-64; lectr. Smith Coll., Northampton, Mass., 1964-67; prof. U. S.C., Columbia, 1967—; exec. sec. Conf. Group on French Politics and Soc., 1973-77; vis. prof. U. Paris, France, 1984-85; exec. bd. Conf. on European Problems, Kansas City, Mo., 1988—. Named Fulbright scholar U.S. Govt., France, 1954-55, Nat. fellow Hoover Instn., Stanford, 1971. Mem. Am. Polit. Sci. Assn., Internat. Studies Assn., Inst. Francais de Rels. Internats. Office: Dept Govt/Internat Studies Univ SC Columbia SC 29208

MARSHALL, DOYLE, real estate executive; b. Frederick, Okla., July 22, 1932; s. Dallas H. and Sally Vada (Hicks) M.; m. Glenda Ruth Pawley, May 7, 1955; children: William Donald, Sheryl Ruth, David Weston. AS, U. Tex., Arlington, 1957. Realty specialist Corps Engrs., Ft. Worth, 1955-70; realty officer Gen. Svcs. Adminstrn., Ft. Worth, 1971—, dep. dir. real estate sales, 1981—; pub. Annetta Valley Farm Press, Aledo, Tex., 1987—. Author: Aledo Country Sketchbook, 1987, A Cry Unheard, 1990, The Liveoak Tree School, 1994; contbr. articles to mags. and newspapers. Scoutmaster Boy Scouts Am., Ft. Worth, 1969-72. Mem. Tex. State Hist. Assn., West Tex. Hist. Assn., various county hist. assns. Baptist.

MARSHALL, FREDRICK L., protective services official. Police chief Charleston, W.Va. Office: Police Dept 501 Virginia St E Charleston WV 25301

MARSHALL, GAILEN DAUGHERTY, JR., physician, scientist, educator; b. Houston, Sept. 9, 1950; s. Gailen D. and Evelyn C. (Gresham) M.; m. Elizabeth M. Marek, Nov. 5, 1978; children: Sarah Elizabeth, Jonathan David, Rebecca Marie. BS, U. Houston, 1972; MS, Tex. A&M U., 1975; PhD, U. Tex., 1979, MD, 1984. Rsch. sci. U. Tex., Galveston, 1981-84; rsch. fellow U. Iowa, Iowa City, 1985-86; lab. dir. Biotherapeutics Inc., Memphis, 1986-88; chief med. resident Bapt. Meml. Hosp., Memphis, 1988-89; assoc. dir. Rsch. for Health Inc., Houston, 1989-90; clin. asst. prof. medicine U. Tex., Houston, 1990-91, asst. prof. medicine, 1991-94, assoc. prof. medicine and pathology, 1994—, dir. divsn. allergy and immunology, 1990—; mem. sci. adv. com. Carrington Labs., Dallas, 1992-94. Mem. editl. bd. Molecular Biotherapy, 1992-93, Cancer Biotherapy, 1994—, Allergy Proceedings, 1994—; contbr. articles to profl. jours. Judge Greater Houston Sci. Fair, 1992—. Fellow ACP, Am. Coll. Allergy and Immunology, Am. Acad. Allergy-Immunology (chair com.); mem. Tex. Allergy-Immunology Soc. (chair com.), Greater Houston Allergy Soc. Republican. Baptists. Office: U Tex Houston Med Sch 6431 Fannin St # 4044 Msb Houston TX 77030-1501

MARSHALL, GILLY ANTHONY, air force officer; b. New Orleans, Feb. 23, 1948; s. Henry Gilbert and Joanna Rose (Almerico) Marshall Callahan; m. Lisa Marie Hebert, Sept. 20, 1978; children: Anthony G. (dec. 1994), Emelia Rosa. BS, La. State U., 1974, MA, 1983; MS, U. Southern Miss., 1988; postgrad., Squadron Officer's Sch., 1979, Air Command and Staff Coll., 1985, Air War Coll., 1994. Aviation electronics tech. U.S. Coast Guard, 1968-73; Comd. officer USAF, 1977, advanced through grades to lt. col., 1992; communications computer staff officer USAF, Kelly AFB, Tex., 1987-89; communications squadron comdr. USAF, Crete, Greece, 1989-91; deputy comdr. logistics 693d Intelligence Wing, Air Force Intelligence Command, Kelly AFB, Tex., 1991-93; 6960 electronic security group comdr. USAF, Kelly AFB, Tex., 1993-95; 67 Support Squadron comdr. USAF, Kelly AFB, 1995-96; 692 Intelligence Support Squadron comdr. USAF, Hickam AFB, Hawaii, 1996—; seminar leader Air Command and Staff Coll., Crete, 1984; instr. history, U. Md., Crete, 1984-85. Contbr. articles to profl. jours. Vol. Spl. Olympics, Baton Rouge, La., 1976, Biloxi, Miss., 1982. Decorated 3 Air Force Commendation medals, 3 Meritorious Svc. medals. Mem. Armed Forces Communications Electronics Assn., Freedom Through Vigilance Assn., La. State U. Alumni Assn., Hickory Officers Club. Roman Catholic.

MARSHALL, GRACE THOMPSON, court clerk; b. Lunenburg County, Va., July 8, 1929; d. Charles Nicholas and India Love Thompson; m. LeRoy Edward Marshall Jr., Jan. 20, 1962 (dec. Sept. 1978); 1 child, LeRoy Edward III. BS, Longwood Coll., 1951. Tchr. City of Richmond (Va.) Schs., 1951-53; bookkeeper Peebles Dept. Stores, Kenbridge, Va., 1953-54; mgr. Thompson's Grocery, Kenbridge, 1955-56; dep. clk. Lunenburg County Cir. Ct., Lunenburg, Va., 1956-89, clk., 1989—. Sec. adminstrv. bd. Kenbridge United Meth. Ch., 1985—; mem. grants com. Va. State Libr., Richmond, 1990-92. Mem. Va. Assn. Govt. Archives and Records Adminstrn., Va. Ct. Clk.'s Assn., Inc., Nat. Ct. Clk.'s Assn., Va. Assn. Constnl. Officers Officers, Rotary. Home: 611 S Broad St Kenbridge VA 23944 Office: Lunenburg County Cir Ct Lunenburg VA 23952

MARSHALL, JAMES ARTHUR, chemistry educator; b. Oshkosh, Wis., Aug. 7, 1935; s. Claude Wendal and Alice (Rodat) M.; m. Elizabeth Binder, Aug. 3, 1983; children: Amy Sue, Andrew Robert, Samantha Leigh. B.S., U. Wis., 1957; Ph.D., U. Mich., 1960; postdoctoral research, Stanford U., 1962. Mem. faculty Northwestern U., 1962-80, prof. chemistry, 1968-80; faculty, prof. chemistry U. S.C., 1980-95, Guy Lipscomb prof., 1984-95; prof. associaté Univ. Paris, 1991; prof. associate U. Jos Fourier, Grenoble, 1994; faculty, Thomas Jefferson prof. chemistry U. Va., 1995—; cons. to industry; mem. com. phys. scis. NRC, 1969; mem. U.S.-Brazil grad. edn. in chemistry study group, 1971—; lectr. Am. Swiss Found., 1972; Mobay lectr., 1981; Merck-Frosst lectr., 1989, 90; Monsanto lectr., 1989; FACS lectr., 1990, 94; mem. NIH Study Sect. on Fertility and Human Welfare, 1972-75; chmn. U.S.-Japan Conf. on Organic Synthesis, 1973; mem. medicinal chemistry study sect. USPHS, 1977-81; mem. adv. com. chemistry NSF, 1981-84; mem. devel. therapeutics rev. com. USPHS; chmn. Gordon Rsch. Conf. on Stereochemistry, 1990. Author papers in field; mem. editl. bd. Organic Reactions, 1970-77, adv. bd., 1977—; editl. bd. Jour. Organic Chemistry, 1972-76, assoc. editor, 1993—; editor Synthetic Communications, 1972-93. Named Depth Charger of Yr., 1978; Alfred P. Sloan fellow, 1967-68. Fellow AAAS, ACS (lectr. 1989), Japan Soc. Promotion of Sci.; mem. Am. Chem. Soc. (mem. exec. com. organic divsn. 1978—, chmn. organic divsn. 1992, Ernest Guenther award 1979, Russell award 1985, Stone award Piedmont sect. 1986, com. on nomenclature 1979—, Govs. award 1991), Chem. Soc. (London), Brazilian Acad. Scis. (corr.). Home: 1987 N Pantops Rd Charlottesville VA 22911

MARSHALL, JERRY ALLYN, dentist, mayor; b. Brady, Tex., June 27, 1938; s. Floyd Leslie and Beth (Watkins) M.; m. Mary Ann Parks, Aug. 16, 1959; children—Jerilyn, Mark. A.S., Tarleton State U., 1958; student Tex. Tech U., 1958-59; D.D.S., U. Tex.-Houston, 1963. Gen. practice dentistry, Rotan, Tex., 1966—. Sec. Rotan Ind. Sch. Dist., mem. bd. trustees, 1969-80; councilman City of Rotan, 1980-84, mayor, 1985—; pres. West Ctrl. Tex. Coun. Govts., 1996; adminstrv. bd. First United Methodist Ch., Rotan, 1970—; pres. Rotan C. of C., 1970. Served to lt. Dental Corps, USN, 1963-66; Viet Nam. Recipient Vietnam Vets. Community Service award Pres. Jimmy Carter, 1979. Mem. ADA, Tex. Dental Assn. Democrat. Lodge: Lions (sec. 1975—, dist. 2T2 region chmn. at large 1992—). Home: 912 E Johnston St Rotan TX 79546-4010 Office: 212 E Snyder Ave Rotan TX 79546-4613

MARSHALL, JOHN HARRIS, JR., geologist, oil company executive; b. Dallas, Mar. 12, 1924; s. John Harris and Jessie Elizabeth (Mosley) M.; BA in Geology, U. Mo., 1949, MA in Geology, 1950; m. Betty Eugenia Zarecor, Aug. 9, 1947; children: John Harris III, George Z., Jacqueline Anne Marshall Leibach. Geologist, Magnolia Oil Co., Jackson, Miss., 1950-59, assoc. geologist Magnolia/Mobil Oil, Oklahoma City, 1959-63, dist. and divsn. geologist Mobil Oil Corp., L.A. and Santa Fe Springs, Calif., 1963-69, divsn. geologist, L.A. and Anchorage, 1969-71, exploration supt., Anchorage, 1971-72, western region geologist, Denver, 1972-76, internat. and offshore geol. mgr., Dallas, 1976-78, chief geologist Mobil Oil Corp., N.Y.C., 1978-81, gen. mgr. exploration for Western Hemisphere, 1981-82; chmn. Marshall Energetics, Inc., Dallas, 1982—; dir. exploration Anschutz, 1985-91; pres. Madera Prodn. Co., 1992—, Summit Oil and Gas Worldwide, 1993-96; CEO Marshall Energetics Ltd., 1994—; active Geology Devel. Bd. U. Mo., 1982—; pres. Coll. Arts and Sci. Leaders Devel. Coun., U. Mo., 1996—. Councilman, City of Warr Acres (Okla.), 1962-63; various positions United Meth. Ch., 1951—, Boy Scouts Am., 1960-68; Manhattan adv. bd. Salvation Army, 1980-82; trustee The Sci. Place., Dallas, 1995—. Served with U.S. Army, 1943-46. Recipient U. Mo. Bd. Curators medal, ROTC Most Outstanding Student, 1949, Disting. Alumni Svc. award U. Mo., 1996; registered geologist, Calif., Wyo., Ky. Mem. Am. Assn. Petroleum Geologists (Pacific sect.), Am. Geol. Inst., Petroleum Exploration Soc. N.Y., Dallas Geol. Soc., Rocky Mountain Assn. Geologists, Alaska Geol. Soc., Oklahoma City Geol. Soc., N.Y. Acad. Sci., L.A. Basin Geol. Soc. (pres. 1969-70), Am. Sci. Affiliation, Assn. Christian Geologists, Meth. Men Club, Denver Petroleum Club, Sigma Xi. Democrat. Office: Marshall Energetics Inc 12720 Hillcrest Rd Ste 105 Dallas TX 75230-9999

MARSHALL, JOHN TREUTLEN, lawyer; b. Macon, Ga., Nov. 1, 1934; s. Hubert and Gladys (Lucas) M.; m. Katrine White, May 1, 1959; children: Allison, Rebecca, Paul, Mary Anne. BA, Vanderbilt U., 1956; LLB, Yale U., 1962. Bar: Ga. 1962, U.S. Dist. Ct. (no., mid. and so. dists.) Ga. 1962, U.S. Ct. Appeals (5th cir.) 1962, U.S. Supreme Ct. 1978, U.S. Ct. Appeals (11th cir.) 1982. Ptnr. Powell, Goldstein, Frazer & Murphy, Atlanta, 1962—; adj. prof. law Emory U. Sch. Law, 1968-86, mem. coun.; chmn. No. Dist. Ga. Bar Coun., 1989; chmn. Ga. State Commn. on Continuing Lawyer Competency, 1991-93. Bd. editors: Yale Law Jour. Bd dirs. Atlanta Legal Aid, 1972-73; trustee Ga. Inst. Continuing Legal Edn., 1983-90; chmn. adv. bd. Atlanta Vol. Lawyers Found. Recipient S. Phillip Heiner award Atlanta Vol. Lawyers Assn., 1992, A. Gus cleveland award Ga. Commn. on Continuing Edn., Tradition of Excellence award State Bar Ga., 1995. Fellow Am. Coll. Trial Lawyers (state chmn. 1985-86), Am. Acad. Appellate Lawyers, Am. Bar Found., Ga. Bar Found.; mem. ABA (ho. of dels. 1976-86, Harrison Tweed award 1986), Atlanta Bar Assn. (pres. 197475, Charles E. Watkins Jr. award 1988), Ga. Inst. Trial Advocacy (chmn. 1982-830, Cherokee Town and Country Club, 191 Club, Layers Club. Office: Powell Goldstein Frazer & Murphy 191 Peachtree St NE 16th Fl Atlanta GA 30303-1741

MARSHALL, KENNETH ALAN, anesthesiologist, consultant; b. Latrobe, Pa., Dec. 22, 1955; s. Donald E. and Mary Y. (Yafchak) M.; m. Martha Jane File, Apr. 21, 1984; children: Ryan Kenneth, Katherine Christine. BA, Earlham Coll., 1978; MD, U. Pa., 1982. Diplomate Nat. Bd. Med. Examiners; lic. physician, Fla., N.C., Ohio, Pa. Resident internal medicine Presbyn. U. Hosp./U. Pitts., 1982-85; med. dir., physician Cleve. Dept. Health, 1985-87; chief profl. svcs. HMO We. Pa., New Kensington, 1987-89; med. dir., physician Homestead (Pa.) Family Medicine Ctr., 1989; resident anesthesiology Mercy Hosp., Pitts., 1989-91; staff anesthesiologist We. Pa. Hosp., Pitts., 1992; fellow pain mgmt. N.C. Bapt. Hosp./Bowman Gray Sch. Medicine, Winston-Salem, 1992-93; cons. anesthesiology and pain mgmt. Mayo Clinic, Jacksonville, Fla., 1993—. Contbr. articles to profl. jours. Mem. ACP, Internat. Assn. Study of Pain, Internat. Anesthesia Rsch. Soc., Am. Soc. Anesthesiologists, Am. Pain Soc., Am. Soc. Regional Anesthesia, Phi Beta Kappa.

MARSHALL, LAURIE, artist, educator; b. Chgo., Nov. 19, 1949; d. Stanley Charles and Alice (Zindel) M.; m. Rory Donaldson, Nov. 25, 1969 (div. 1974); m. Rex Kennedy Slack, Aug. 18, 1981; children: Jeremy, Daniel. BA, Antioch Coll., 1971; MA, Beacon Coll., 1980. Cert. tchr., Va. Curriculum designer, tchrs. gifted/talented Rappahannock County Schs., 1979-81; affiliate artist Va. Mus., Richmond, 1987-88; artist-in-residence "Web of Life" Rappahannock Elem. Sch., Sperryville, Va., 1989; artist-in-residence Geography Mural Fauquier (Va.) Jr. H.S., 1993-94; artist-in-residence ancestor drama Middleburg (Va.) Elem. Sch., 1994-95; adj. faculty art history and studio art Lord Fairfax C.C., Warrenton, Va., 1988—; founder Middle Street Gallery, Washington, 1986—. Author: I Will Survive, 1994; artist, writer, choreographer: Dreaming and the Pursuit of Light, 1990; co-author, dir.: The Ties That Bind, 1990, Stories From the Dust in the Corner, ; dir., choreographer, prodr.: (multi-media dance drama, book, video) of Dust in the Corner, 1995-96. Mem. Internat. Ctr. for Conflict Resolution, Pitts., 1990-96. Home: 4 Skyline Ln Washington VA 22747

MARSHALL, LINDA LANTOW, pediatrics nurse; b. Tulsa, Dec. 13, 1949; d. Lawrence Lee and Lena Mae (Ross) Lantow; m. David Panke Hartson, Aug. 25, 1970 (div. 1982); children: Michael David, Jonathan Lee; m. Roger Nathan Marshall, Dec. 11, 1985; 1 child, Sarabeth Megan. A, U. Okla., 1970; BSN, U. Tulsa, 1983. Cert. pediatric nurse. Pediats. nurse Youthcare, Claremore, Okla., 1983-85, 87—; staff nurse ICU Doctors Hosp., Tulsa, 1985-87. Bd. dirs. PTA Barnard, Tulsa, 1993-95; leader Brownie troop Girl Scouts U.S., Tulsa, 1994-95, leader jr. scouts, 1995—. Mem. Sigma Theta Tau. Home: 2628 E 22nd St Tulsa OK 74114-3123 Office: Youth Care of Rogers County 525 E Blue Starr Dr Claremore OK 74017-4401

MARSHALL, MARGO, artistic director; b. Louisville, Nov. 3, 1934; d. Irving Robert and Elizabeth (Greenleaf) Lisbony; m. Jay C. Marshall, 1952 (div. 1971); 1 child, Dennis. BA, U. Houston, 1953. Pvt. tchr. dance Houston, 1950-58, owner, operator pvt. dance sch., 1958—; guest tchr. Joffrey Sch., N.Y., Internat. Acad. Dance, Portugal, Louisville Ballet, Boston Ballet's Summer Workshops, 1981-85, The Place, London, and others; part-time faculty mem. High Sch. for the Performing and Visual Arts, Houston; tchr. dance U. Houston, Sam Houston State U. Artistic dir. City Ballet Houston, 1967—; mem. dance panel Cultural Arts Coun. Houston; advisor Tex. Commn. on the Arts. Recipient Adjudicator for Mid-States Regional Ballet Assn., 1986. Mem. Southwestern Regional Ballet Assn. (officer 1965—), Houston Grand Opera (trustee). Office: City Ballet 9902 Long Point Rd Houston TX 77055-4116

MARSHALL, MARILYN JOSEPHINE, lawyer; b. Dayton, Ohio, May 31, 1945; d. Foy Wylie and Inez Virginia (Smith) Gard; m. Alan George Marshall, June 13, 1965; children: Gwendolyn Scott, Brian George. Student, Northwestern U., 1963-65; BA, Stanford U., 1967; cert. in teaching, U. B.C., Vancouver, 1977; JD, Capital Law Sch., Columbus, Ohio, 1985. Bar: Ohio 1985, Fla. 1993, U.S Dist. Ct. (so. dist.) Ohio 1986, U.S. Dist. Ct. (no. dist., mid. dist. and so. dist.) Fla. 1994, U.S. Ct. Appeals (6th cir.) 1986, U.S. Ct. Appeals (11th cir.) 1994. Tchr. Sutherland Secondary Sch., North Vancouver, B.C., 1977-79; instr. Brit. Col. Inst. Tech., Burnaby, B.C., 1979-80; assoc. Crabbe, Brown, Jones, Potts & Schmidt, Columbus, Ohio, 1985-86; clk. to judge U.S. Dist. Ct. (so. dist.) Ohio, Columbus, 1986-88; clk. to justice Ohio Supreme Ct., 1988-89; assoc. Squire, Sanders & Dempsey, 1989-92; with Columbus City Atty.'s Office, Columbus, Ohio, 1992-93; asst. atty. gen. civil divsn. State of Fla., Tallahassee, 1994-96; pvt. practice Tallahassee, 1996—. Mem. ABA, Ohio Bar Assn., Fla. Bar Assn., Tallahassee Bar Assn., Tallahassee Women Lawyers Assn., Capital U. Law Sch. Alumni Assn. Republican. Office: 561 E Sixth Ave Tallahassee FL 32303

MARSHALL, MARY ELIZABETH, secondary school English educator; b. Stoughton, Mass., Mar. 1, 1969; d. Peter John and Edith Jane (Wallis) M. BA in Psychology, Bates Coll., 1991; MEd, George Washington U., D.C., 1996. Cert. secondary sch. English tchr., D.C. Bd. Edn. Tutor Androscoggin City Jail, Auburn, Maine, 1990; music. tchr. Montello and Pettingill Elem. Schs., Lewiston, Maine, 1991; nature tchr. The Family Sch., Brewster, Me., summer 1991; ESL tchr. Internat. Lang. Sch., Budapest, Hungary, 1991-93; exec. asst. Inst. for Ednl. Leadership, Washington, 1993-96; 8th grade English tchr. Longfellow Mid. Sch., Falls Church, Va., 1996—. Organist and choir dir. St. Andrews Episcopal Ch., Readfield, Maine, 1988, 6th Street Congrgational Ch., Auburn, Maine, 1988-89, Trinity Episcopalian Ch., Lewiston, Maine, Spring 1991; accompanist Va., Budapest, Hungary, Maine, 1987—. Mem. Nat. Coun. Tchrs. of English. Home: 6568 Flagmaker Ct Falls Church VA 22042

MARSHALL, NANCY HAIG, library administrator; b. Stamford, Conn., Nov. 3, 1932; d. Harry Percival and Dorothy Charlotte (Price) Haig; m. William Hubert Marshall, Dec. 28, 1953; children—Bruce Davis, Gregg Price, Lisa Reynolds, Jeanine Haig. B.A., Ohio Wesleyan U., 1953; M.A.L.S., U. Wis., 1972. Dir. Wis. Inter Libr. Svcs., Madison, 1972-79; Reference librarian U. Wis., Madison, 1972, assoc. dir. univ. libraries, 1979-86; dean univ. librs. Coll. William and Mary, Williamsburg, Va., 1986—; mem. adv. com. Copyright Office, Washington, 1978-82; dir. USBE, Inc., Washington, 1983-86; trustee OCLC, Inc., Dublin, Ohio, 1982-88. Contbr. articles to profl. jours. Mem. ALA (coun. 1980-88, 90-93), Wis. Libr. Assn. (Libr. of the Yr. award 1982), Va. Libr. Assn., Beta Phi Mu. Office: Coll William and Mary E G Swem Libr Williamsburg VA 23185

MARSHALL, NATHALIE, artist, writer, educator; b. Pitts., Nov. 10, 1932; d. Clifford Benjamin and Clarice (Stille) Marshall; m. Robert Alfred Van Buren, May 1, 1952 (div. June 1965); children: Christine Van Buren Popovic, Clifford Marshall Van Buren, Jennifer Van Buren Lake; m. David Arthur Nadel, Dec. 30, 1976 (div. Oct. 1995). AFA, Silvermine Coll. Art, New Canaan, Conn., 1967; BFA, U. Miami, Coral Gables, 1977, MA, 1982, PhD in English and Fine Art, 1982. Instr. humanities Miami Ednl. Consortium, Miami Shores, Fla., 1977-79, Barry U., Miami Shores, 1979-81, U. Miami, Coral Gables, 1977-81; sr. lectr. Nova U., Ft. Lauderdale, Fla., 1981-84, assoc. prof. humanities, 1985-86; prof. art, chair dept. art. Old Coll., Reno, Nev., 1986-88; chief artist Rockefeller U., N.Y.C., 1973-75; asst. registrar Lowe Art Mus., Coral Gables, 1976-78; co-founder, dir. The Bakehouse Art Complex, Miami, 1984-86; advisor, bd. mem. NAH YAH EE (Indian children's art exhibits), Weimar, Calif., 1984—; mem. adv. bd. New World Sch. Arts, Miami, 1985-86. One-woman shows include Silvermine Coll. Art, New Canaan, Conn., 1968, Ingber Gallery, Greenwich, 1969, Capricorn Gallery,

N.Y.C., 1969, Pierson Coll. at Yale U., New Haven, 1970, The Art Barn, Greenwich, 1972, Art Unltd., N.Y.C., 1973, Benevy Gallery, N.Y.C., 1974, Richter Libr., U. Miami, 1985, Nova U., Ft. Lauderdale, 1985, Ward Nasse Gallery, N.Y.C., 1985, Old Coll., Reno, 1986, Washoe County Libr., Reno, 1987, Sabal Palms Gallery, Gulfport, Fla., 1992, Ambiance Gallery, St. Petersburg, 1995, 96, Gulfport Libr., 1996; group shows include: Capricorn Gallery, N.Y.C., 1968, Ingber Gallery, Greenwich, 1968, Compass Gallery, N.Y.C., 1970, Optimums Gallery, Westport, Conn., 1970, Finch Coll. Mus., N.Y.C., 1971, Town Hall Art Gallery, Stamford, Conn., 1973, 74, Jewish Community Ctr., Miami Beach, 1981, Continuum Gallery, Miami Beach, 1982, South Fla. Art Inst., Hollywood, Fla., 1984, Met. Mus., Coral Gables, Fla., 1985, Ward Nasse Gallery, N.Y.C., 1985, Brunnier Mus., Iowa State U., Ames, 1986, Nat. Mus. of Women in The Arts Libr., Washington, 1987, 89, U.S. Art in Embassies Program, 1987-88, UN World Conf. Women, Nairobi, 1987, Raymond James Invitational, St. Petersburg, Fla., 1989-92, Arts Ctr., St. Petersburg, 1990, 91, 92, Global Gallery, Tampa, Fla., 1990, 91, Sabal Palms Gallery, Gulfport, Fla., 1992, No. Nat. Nicolet Coll., Rhineland, Wis., 1992, Internat. Biennale, Bordeaux, France, 1993, Salon de Vieux Colombier, Paris, 1993, Synchronicity Space, N.Y.C., 1993, Women's 1st Internat. Biennal of Women Artists, Stockholm, 1994-95 (gold medal), Tampa Arts Forum, Fla., 1995, 96, Salon Internat. des Seigneurs de l'Art, Aix-en-Provence, France, 1995 (silver medal), World's Women Online Internet Installation Ariz. State U. 1995-96, UN 4th Conf. on Women, Beijing, 1995-96, Artemisa Gallery, Chgo., 1995-96; author, artist: Vibrations on Revelations, 1973, The Firebird, 1982, Homage to John Donne's Holy Sonnets 10 & 13, 1987, Tidepool, 1995; numerous artist books, 1968—; author: Be Organized for College, 1980; artist: (children's book) The Desert: What Lives There?, 1972; editor, designer: Court Theaters of Europe, 1982; writer, dir. T.V. programs Moutain Mandala: Autumn, Mountain Mandala: Winter, The Unexpected, 1992; contbr. poems to poetry mags., articles to profl. jours. Recipient Sponsor's award for Painting Greenwich Art Soc., 1967; Steven Buffton Meml. award Am. Bus. Women's Assn., 1980; grantee Poets & Writers, 1993; one of 300 global artists in Internat. Hope and Optimism Portfolio, Oxford. Mem. MLA, Coll. Art Assn., Nat. Women's Studies Assn., Women's Caucus for Art (nat. adv. bd. 1983-88, pres. Miami chpt. 1984-86, southeast regional v.p. 1986). Address: 5444 1/2 30th Ave S # 5C Gulfport FL 33707-5207

MARSHALL, ROSALIND RENEÉ, communications educator, television producer; b. Bronx, N.Y., Feb. 15, 1964; d. Ralph Reco Marshall and Gail Maxine (Clark) Johnson. BA in Journalism, So. U., 1992; postgrad., La. State U. Police officer Baton Rouge Police Dept., 1984-90; reporter, editor Baker Observer, 1988-89; asst. assignments editor, field prodr. Sta. WBRZ-TV, Baton Rouge, 1989-91; prodr. Sta. WLOX-TV, Biloxi, Miss., 1991; equity field specialist bur. ednl. support and divsn. spl. projects La. Dept. Edn., Baton Rouge, 1992; instr. A&M coll. La. State U., Baton Rouge, 1992—, acad. counselor acad. ctr. athletes, 1993—; prodr. Sta. WAFB-TV, Baton Rouge, 1994—; advisor La. State U. chpt. Nat. Assn. Black Journalists, 1992—; co-advisor Sta. WLSU-TV, 1993—; speaker in field; weekend exec. prodr. WBRC-TV, Birmingham, Ala., 1995—. Vol., reader Beachwood Elem. Sch., 1992-93; elem. sch. tutor, 1993-94; hon. bd. dirs. Sickle Cell Anemia Found.; active Heritage. Mem. NAACP, La. State U. Black Faculty and Caucus, Soc. Profl. Journalists. Home: 104 Woodmere Creek Rd Birmingham AL 35226 Office: La State U Manship Sch Mass Comm 222 Journalism Baton Rouge LA 70803-7202

MARSHALL, WAYNE KEITH, anesthesiology educator; b. Richmond, Va., Feb. 9, 1948; s. Chester Truman and Lois Ann (Tiller) M.; m. Dale Claire Reynolds, June 18, 1977; children: Meredith Reynolds, Catherine Truman, Whitney Wood. BS in Biology, Va. Poly. Inst. and State U., 1970; MD, Va. Commonwealth U., 1974. Diplomate Am. Bd. Anesthesiology, Nat. Bd. Med. Examiners; bd. cert. in pain mgmt. Surg. intern U. Cin., 1974-75, resident in surgery, 1975-77; resident in anesthesiology U. Va. Coll. Medicine, Charlottesville, 1977-79, rsch. fellow, 1979-80; asst. prof. anesthesia Pa. State U. Coll. Medicine, Hershey, 1980-86, assoc. prof., 1986-95, assoc. clin. dir. oper. rm., 1982-95, dir. pain mgmt. svc., 1984-95, chief divsn. pain mgmt., 1992-95; prof., chmn. dept. anesthesiology Med. Coll. Va., Richmond, 1995—; med. dir. operating rms. MCV Hosp., 1995—; moderator nat. meetings. Mem. editorial bd. Am. Jour. Anesthesiology, 1987—, Jour. Neurosurg. Anesthesiology, 1988—; contbr. articles and abstracts to med. jours. Recipient Antarctic Svc. medal NSF, 1980. Mem. AMA, Soc. Neurosurg. Anesthesia and Critical Care (sec.-treas. 1985-87, v.p. 1987-88, pres. 1989-90, bd. dirs. 1985-91), Assn. Univ. Anesthetists, Am. Soc. Anesthesiologists (del. ASA ho. of dels. 1990-92), Internat. Anesthesia Rsch. Soc., Pa. Soc. Anesthesiology. Republican. Baptist. Office: VCU Med Coll Va Dept Anesthesiology PO Box 980695 Richmond VA 23298-0695

MARSHALL, WILLIAM LEITCH, chemist; b. Columbia, S.C., Dec. 3, 1925; s. William Leitch and Georgia (Kittrell) M.; m. Joanne Fox, Apr. 16, 1949; children: Nancy Diane, William Fox. BS, Clemson U., 1945; PhD, Ohio State U., 1949. Tchg. asst. Clemson U., 1944-45, Ohio State U., 1945-46; Naval rsch. fellow Ohio State U., 1947-49; mem. sr. rsch. staff (chemistry) Oak Ridge Nat. Lab., 1949-89, guest scientist, 1990—, rsch. group leader, 1957-75; Plenary lectr. internat. congresses on oceanography, electrochemistry, geochemistry, high temperature water chemistry, high pressure fluids; mem. orgn. coms. internat. sci. congresses. Guggenheim fellow van der Waals Lab., U. Amsterdam, 1956-57. Contbr. articles to profl. jours. Patentee in field. Mem. Am. Chem. Soc. (nat. coun. 1968-83, nat. membership affairs com. 1980-82, nat. coun. com. chem. edn. 1970-80, nat. com. chem. edn. 1980-82, chmn. nat. subcom. on h.s. chem. edn. 1970-75, mem. nat. h.s. chemistry com. 1978-81, nat. congl. sci. counselor 1974-83, nat. com. tchr. tng. guidelines 1975-77, Charles Holmes Herty Gold medal 1977), AAAS, Geochem. Soc., Am. Geophys. Union, Sigma Xi (v.p. chpt. 1974-75), N.Y. Acad. Sci., Tenn. Acad. Sci. (vis. scientist program 1975), Internat. Assn. Properties of Water and Steam (working groups 1975—), Internat. Platform Assn., Phi Kappa Phi. Achievements include research on water solutions over wide ranges of temperature and pressure of basic (thermodynamics, solubility, ionization, solvation, critical phenomena, geochemistry, oceanography, origin of life) and applied (desalination, geothermal, nuclear, and fossil fuel power plants) interests. Home: 101 Oak Ln Oak Ridge TN 37830-4046 Office: Oak Ridge Nat Lab Chem and Analytical Scis Divsn MS 6201 PO Box 2008 Oak Ridge TN 37831-6201

MARSTON, EDGAR JEAN, III, lawyer; b. Houston, July 5, 1939; s. Edgar Jr. and Jean (White) M.; m. Graeme Meyers, June 21, 1961; children: Christopher Graham, Jonathan Andrew. BA, Brown U., 1961; JD, U. Tex., 1964. Bar: Tex. 1964. Law clk. to presiding justice Supreme Ct. Tex., Austin, 1964-65; assoc. Baker & Botts, Houston, 1965-71; ptnr. Bracewell & Patterson, Houston, 1971-89, of counsel, 1990-96, ptnr., 1996—; exec. v.p., gen. counsel Southdown, Inc., Houston, 1996—, also bd. dirs. Mem. ABA, Tex. Bar Assn., Tex. Bar Found., Houston Bar Assn., Houston Country Club, Coronado Club. Episcopalian. Office: Bracewell & Patterson 711 Louisiana Ste 2900 Houston TX 77002-4401

MARTELL, ARTHUR EARL, chemistry educator; b. Natick, Mass., Oct. 18, 1916; s. Ambrose and Dorina (Lamoureaux) M.; m. Norma June Saunders, Sept. 2, 1944; children: Stuart A., Edward S., Janet E., Judith S., Jon V., Elaine C.; m. Mary Austin, 1965; children: Helen E., Kathryn A. B.S., Worcester Poly. Inst., 1938, D.Sc. (hon.), 1962; Ph.D., NYU 1941. Instr. Worcester Poly. Inst., 1941-42; mem. faculty Clark U., 1942-61, prof. chemistry, 1951-61, chmn. dept., 1959-61; prof. chemistry, chmn. dept. Ill. Inst. Tech., 1960-66; prof. chemistry Tex. A&M U., College Station, 1966—; Disting. prof. Tex. A&M U., 1973—, dept. head, 1966-80, adv. to pres., 1980-82; rsch. on chem equilibria, kinetics, catalysis, metal chelate compounds in solution. Author: (with M. Calvin) Chemistry of the Metal Chelate Compounds, 1952, (with S. Chaberek, Jr.) Organic Sequestering Agents, 1959, (with L.G. Sillen) Stability Constants, 1964; supplement, 1971, (with M.M. Taqui Khan) Homogeneous Catalysis by Metal Complexex, 2 vols., 1973, (with R.M. Smith) Critical Stability Constants, Vol. 1, 1974, Vol. 2, 1975, Vol. 3, 1977, Vol. 4, 1976, Vol. 5, 1982, Vol. 6, 1989, (with R.J. Motekaitis) Determination and Use of Stability Constants, 1989, 2nd edit., 1992, (with R.D. Hancock) Metal Complexes in Aqueous Solutions, 1996; editor: ACS Monograph on Coordination Chemistry, Vol. 1, 1973, Vol. 2, 1978, ACS Symposium Series 140, inorganic Chemistry in Biology and Medicine, 1980, Jour. Coordination Chemistry, 1970-80; mem. editl. bd. Bioinorganic Chemistry, Jour. Inorganic and Nuclear Chemistry, Inorganic Chemisty; contbr. articles to profl. jours. Mem. sch. bd. Northborough, Mass., 1958-61, chmn., 1959-61. Research fellow U. Calif. at Berkeley, 1949-50; Guggenheim fellow U. Zurich, Switzerland, 1954-55; NSF sr. postdoctoral fellow, also fellow Sch. Advanced Studies Mass. Inst. Tech., 1959-60; NIH Spl. fellow U. Calif. at Berkeley, 1964-65. Fellow N.Y. Acad. Scis. (hon. life); mem. AAAS, Am. Chem. Soc. (chmn. ctrl. Mass. sect. 1957-58, chmn. Tex. A&M sect. 1990-91, S.W. Regional award 1976, Nat. award for Disting. Svc. 1980, Patterson-Crane award 1995), Am. Acad. Arts and Scis., Japan Soc. for Analytical Chemistry (hon.), Sigma Xi, Phi Lambda Upsilon (hon.). Home: 9742 Myrtle Dr College Station TX 77845-6786

MARTELL, DENISE MILLS, lay worker; b. Newberry, S.C., Apr. 8, 1965; d. Wyman Harman and Evangeline (Berry) Mills; m. Marty Martell, FEb. 29, 1992. Grad., Newberry High Sch., 1983. Tchr. Vacation Bible Sch., Newberry, 1984-95, Sun. Sch., Newberry, 1989-92; dir. Bapt. Young Women, Newberry, 1989-92; sec. Sunday Sch. Bapt. Ch., Newberry, S.C., 1993-95, Sun. Sch. tchr. 1-3 grades, 1995-96; tchr. mission trips, various locations, 1987-89; tchr. Mission Friends, Newberry, 1987-96, mem. choir, 1986—, mem. Newberry Cmty. choir, 1992-95, tchr. children's choir, 1993-95; leader Weekday Bible Club, 1990-92, missionary to Bolivia, South Am., 1996. Active March of Dimes Walk Am., Am. Diabetes Assn. Bike-a-thon. Home: 8769 Monticelle Rd Columbia SC 29203-9708 Office: Shakespeare E and F Newberry SC 29108

MARTENS, JOHN DALE, telecommunications company executive; b. Wayne, Nebr., Nov. 12, 1943; s. Leonard William and Irma Bertha (Von Seggern) M.; m. Laura Elizabeth Price, Dec. 28, 1966. BSBA, U. Colo., 1966; MS, Thurderbird Grad. Sch. Internat. Mgmt., 1972; postgrad. Queen Mary Coll., U. London, 1976. Analyst overseas ops. Ford Motor Co., Dearborn, Mich., 1972-73; internat. mktg. ofcl. Agrico Chem. Co., Tulsa, 1973-76; tech. and comml. devel. ofcl. Resource Scis. Co., Tulsa, 1976-78, planning and corp. devel. ofcl., 1978-80; chief exec. officer, pres., treas., dir. Sterling Oil of Okla., Inc., Tulsa, 1980-82; dir. strategic devel. MCI Communications Corp., Washington, 1983-84, v.p. corp. devel., 1984-86; v.p. mktg. So. New Eng. Telecommunications Co. Inc., New Haven, 1986-92; sr. v.p. comml. sales, Williams Telecom. Group, Inc., Tulsa, 1992-93; founder, pres. Corp. Devel. Co., Tulsa, 1993—. Capt. USAF, 1967-70. Mem. Tulsa Country Club. Episcopalian.

MARTIKAINEN, A(UNE) HELEN, retired health education specialist; b. Harrison, Maine, May 11, 1916; d. Sylvester and Emma (Heikkinen) M.; AB, Bates Coll., 1939, DSc (hon.), 1957, Smith Coll., 1969; MPH, Yale, 1941; DSc, Harvard U., 1964. Health edn. sec. Hartford Tb and Public Health Assn., 1941-42; cons. USPHS, 1942-49; chief health edn. WHO, Geneva, 1949-74; chair internat. affairs N.C. div. AAUW, 1986-94. Trustee Bridgton Acad., North Bridgton, Maine; mem. N.C. Women's Forum, 1984—; bd. dirs. N.C. Ctr. of Laws Affecting Women, Inc.; bd. dirs. West Triangle chpt. UNA-USA; mem. program com. and health and social svcs. coms. Carol Woods Retirement Cmty. Recipient Delta Omega award Yale U.; Nat. Adminstrv. award Am. Acad. Phys. Edn.; Bates Key award; Internat. Service award, France, 1953; Prentiss medal, 1956; spl. medal, certificate for internat. health edn. service Nat. Acad. Medicine for France, 1959; Profl. award Soc. Pub. Health Educators, 1963, Benjamin Elijah Mays award Bates Coll. Alumni Assn., 1989. Fellow APHA (chmn. health edn. sect., Excellence award 1969); mem. AAUW, LWV (Chapel Hill, N.C. br. 1987—), Women's Internat. League for Peace and Freedom, U.S. Soc. Pub. Health Educators, Internat. Union Health Edn. (Parisot medal, tech. adviser), Acad. Phys. Edn. (assoc.), N.C. Coun. Women's Orgns. (mem. coun. assembly 1988-92, Women of Distinction award 1989), Phi Beta Kappa. Home: 3113 Carol Woods 750 Weaver Dairy Rd Chapel Hill NC 27514

MARTIN, ALOISE MARIE BRITTEN, school nurse; b. Groom, Tex., Jan. 25, 1939; d. Harry Francis and Mary Veronica (Drerup) Britten; m. Chester Bruce Martin Jr., Oct. 14, 1960; children: Kenneth, Joe, Larry, Robert. AA, Amarillo Coll., 1959; diploma in nursing, St. Anthony's Hosp., 1960. RN, Tex. Head nurse Highland Gen. Hosp., Pampa, Tex., 1960-61, 64-71, pvt. duty nurse, 1961-64, insvc. dir., 1970-71; sch. nurse White Deer (Tex.) Ind. Sch. Dist., 1971—; office nurse Porviance Clinic, Pampa, summers 1971-84; med. chmn. Carson County Cancer Bd., Panhandle, Tex., 1990—. Mem. Nat. Assn. Sch. Nurses, Tex. Assn. Sch. Nurses, Region XVI Nurses Assn. Republican. Roman Catholic. Home: PO Box 158 White Deer TX 79097-0158

MARTIN, ANDREW AYERS, lawyer, physician, educator; b. Toccoa, Ga., Aug. 18, 1958; s. Wallace Ford and Dorothy LaTranquil (Ayers) M. BA, Emory U., Atlanta, 1980, MD, 1984; JD, Duke U., 1988. Bar: Calif. 1989, La. 1990, D.C. 1991; diplomate Am. Bd. Pathology, Nat. Bd. Med. Examiners; lic. physician, La. Intern in pediatrics Emory U./Grady Meml. Hosp., Atlanta, 1984; intern Tulane U./Charity Hosp., New Orleans, 1989-90, resident in anatomic and clin. pathology, 1990-94; law clk. Ogletree, Deakins, Smoak, Stewart, Greenville, S.C., summer 1986, Thelen Marrin Johnson Bridges, L.A., summer 1987, Duke Hosp. Risk Mgmt., 1987-88; assoc. Haight Brown Bonesteel, Santa Monica, Calif., 1988; pvt. practice L.A., 1989; physician/atty. Tulane Med. Ctr./Charity Hosp., New Orleans, 1989-94, Baylor Coll. Medicine/Tex. Med. Ctr., Houston, 1994-95; lab. dir., sr. ptnr. King's Daus. Hosp., Greenville, Miss., 1995—; bd. dirs. Martin Bldrs., Inc., Toccoa; mem. AIDS Legis. Task Force for La.; case cons. Office of Tech. Assessment, Washington; tech. cons. and autopsy extra Oliver Stone's "JFK"; adj. clin. faculty Moorhead Coll. Contbr. articles to profl. jours.; author: Reflections on Rusted Chrome (book of poetry). Fellow Coll. Am. Pathologists, Coll. Legal Medicine, La. State Med. Soc. (del. meeting 1992-93). Home: 935 Lake Hall Rd Lake Village AR 71653 Office: Kings Daughters Hosp PO Box 1857 Greenville MS 38702-1857

MARTIN, ANDREW DELLENEY, life and health underwriter, financial and employee benefits consultant; b. Dallas, Aug. 23, 1963; s. William David and Nina Jo (Delleney) M.; m. Carissima Pineda Liwanag, Jan. 4, 1991; children: Connor Andrew, Corbin Alesandro. Life Underwriters Tng. Coun. fellow designation; registered fin. cons. Fin. cons. New England Life Ins. Co., New England Securities Corp., Houston, 1988-94; bus. and estate planning staff Mass. Mutual Life Ins. Co., MML Investor Svcs. Inc., Houston, 1994—; ptnr. Corp. Fin. Assocs., Houston, 1996—. Contbr. articles to profl. publs. Fundraiser Literacy Advance, Houston, 1992, Houston Young Profl. Reps., 1992; exec. bd. mem., com. chmn. Rep. Nat. Conv.; vol. Boys & Girls Club, Houston, 1993. Mem. Internat. Assn. Registered Fin. Cons., Nat. Assn. Life Underwriters (nat. quality award), Nat. Assn. Securities Dealers, New Eng. Leaders Assn., Tex. Assn. Life Underwriters, Houston Assn. Life Underwriters, Clear Lake C. of C. (ambassador), Million Dollar Roundtable, Tex. Leaders Roundtable, Internat. Assn. Registered Fin. Cons. Office: Corp Fin Assocs Mass Mutual Life Ins Co 333 Clay St Ste 300 Houston TX 77002-4004

MARTIN, ANDREW DOUGLAS, investment broker; b. Nashville, Jan. 21, 1960; s. James Bell and Deborah (Bair) M.; m. Kathleen Ann Cochrane, June 8, 1985. BBA, Belmont U., 1982. With Merrill Lynch, Nashville, 1982-85; fin. cons. Merrill Lynch, N.Y.C., 1985-86, Nashville, 1986-90; investment broker J.C. Bradford, Nashville, 1990-91; regional sales mgr. Hornor Townsend & Kent, 1991-95; br. mgr., regional prin. Sentra/Spelman, Nashville, 1995—; investment com. bd. dirs. Cockroft Forum for Free Enterprise, Nashville, 1990—. Chmn. Fin. Profls. for Bush/Quayle, Tenn., 1992; tchr. Jr. Achievement, Nashville, 1989, 92-93; founding mem. Nat. Alumni Advancement Bd., Belmont U.; assoc. trustee Belmont U., Nashville. Mem. Inst. CFP (assoc.). Republican. Episcopalian. Office: Sentra/Spelman 611 Commerce St Ste 3002 Nashville TN 37203-3742

MARTIN, ANGELA CARTER, nursing educator; b. Reidsville, N.C., June 24, 1957; d. R. Philip and Carol (Walker) Carter; m. Dale Martin, Apr. 3, 1976; children: Melissa, Christopher. BSN, U. N.C., Greensboro, 1979; MS in Nursing, U. N.C., Chapel Hill, 1983. Cert. family nurse practitioner, N.C. Dir. Children's Med. Clinic Person-Chatman-Caswell County Health Dept., Yanceyville, N.C., 1983; family nurse practitioner Nat. Health Svc. Corps, Atlanta, 1983-86; asst. prof. dept. family and community medicine Med. Coll. Hampton Rds., Norfolk, Va., 1986—; asst. prof., coord. family nurse practitioner program Sch. Nursing, Old Dominion U., Norfolk, 1987-92, 94—; cons. in field. Contbr. articles to profl. publs. Mem. ANA, Va. Nurses Assn., Nat. Orgn. Nurse Practitioners Faculties (bd. dirs. 1992-93), Am. Acad. Nurse Practitioners (state award for excellence 1992), Sigma Theta Tau (Rsch. award 1988, award for excellence Epsilon Chi chpt.). Home: 3228 Pineridge Dr Chesapeake VA 23321-5404

MARTIN, BECCA BACON, editor, journalist; b. Ontario, Oreg., Nov. 26, 1957; d. Raymond A. and Ruth (Wilson) Bacon; m. Daniel P. Martin, Sept. 1, 1984; adopted daughter, Amanda Kathryn. AA, Allen County Coll., Iola, Kans., 1978; student, U. Ark., 1990. Wire and page 1 editor Iola Register, 1979-84; asst. mng. editor Benton County Daily Record, Bentonville, Ark., 1985-87, news editor, 1987-88; editor living, entertainment and weekend mag. Morning News of N.W. Ark., Springdale, 1988-96; freelance writer, photographer, cons. Fayetteville, Ark., 1996—. Editorial asst. Arkansas County Judges Mag., 1989; founding editor (monthly mag.) Bella Vista Village Voice, 1985; contbr. investigative reports to Ark. Bus. mag., 1988; author spl. arts sect. U. Ark. Alumni Mag., 1990; play producer Ozark Stage Works, 1990. Former mem. adv. bd. Fayetteville West Campus Child Care/Parenting Ctr.; troop leader Girl Scouts U.S.A., Farmington, Ark., 1988-89; mem. adv. bd. Ark. Better Chance, Fayetteville, 1991-92; chmn. publicity Miss N.W. Ark. Pageant, Springdale, 1990—; charter mem. Altrusa Internat., Springdale, 1994. Recipient Excellence in Journalism award Am. Cancer Soc., 1990-95, award AP Mng. Editors, 1991, 94, WISE award Northwest Ark. Women's Festival and Conf., 1995; named Best Humorous Column Ark. Press Assn., 1992-94, Best Family Pages in Ark., APA, 1995, 2d place in both humorous and serious col. categories, 1995; Writing grant Nat. League Am. Pen Women, 1995. Mem. Internat. Thespian Soc. (hon.), Nat. League Jr. Cotillions Washington County (adv. bd.), Alpha Psi Omega (hon.). Home: 173 S Hill Ave Fayetteville AR 72701-5768 Office: Morning News PO Box 7 Springdale AR 72765-0007

MARTIN, BILLY C., advertising executive; b. 1925. Pres. Martin, White & Mickwee, Inc., Birmingham, Ala., 1959-77; chmn., CEO Martin Advertising, Inc., Birmingham, 1977—. Office: Martin Advt Inc 2801 University Blvd Birmingham AL 35233-2846*

MARTIN, BOB, airport executive. V.p., asst. sec. Memphis-Shelby County Airport Authority; v.p. ops. Memphis Internat. Airport. Office: Memphis Internat Airport Memphis-Shelby County Airport Authority PO Box 30168 Memphis TN 38130-0168*

MARTIN, BOYCE FICKLEN, JR., federal judge; b. Boston, Oct. 23, 1935; s. Boyce Ficklen and Helen Artt M.; m. Mavin Hamilton Brown, July 8, 1961; children: Mary V. H., Julia H.C., Boyce Ficklen III, Robert C. G. II. AB, Davidson Coll., 1957; JD, U. Va., 1963. Bar: Ky. 1963. Law clk. to Shackelford Miller, Jr., chief judge U.S. Ct. Appeals for 6th Circuit, Cin., 1963-64; asst. U.S. atty. Western Dist. Ky., Louisville, 1964; U.S. atty. Western Dist. Ky., 1965; pvt. practice law Louisville, 1966-74; judge Jefferson Circuit Ct., Louisville, 1974-76; chief judge Ct. Appeals Ky., Louisville, 1976-79; judge U.S. Ct. Appeals (6th cir.), Cin. and Louisville, 1979-96, chief judge, 1996—; mem. judicial coun. U.S. Ct. Appeals (6th cir.), 1979-96, chmn., 1996—, judicial conf. of U.S., 1996—. Mem. vestry St. Francis in the Fields Episcopal Ch., Harrods Creek, Ky., 1979-83; bd. visitors Davidson (N.C.) Coll., 1980-86, trustee, 1994—; trustee Isaac W. Bernheim Found., Louisville, 1981—, chmn., 1982-95; trustee Blackacre Found., Inc., Louisville, 1983-94, chmn., 1986-94; trustee Hanover (Ind.) Coll., 1983—, vice chmn., 1992—; mem. exec. bd. Old Ky. Home coun. Boy Scouts of Am., 1968-72; pres. Louisville Zool. Commn., 1971-74. Capt. JAGC U.S. Army, 1958-66. Fellow Am. Bar Found.; mem. Inst. Jud. Adminstrn., Am. Judicature Soc., Fed Bar Assn., ABA (com. effective appellate advocacy Conf. Appellate Judges), Ky. Bar Assn., Louisville Bar Assn. Office: US Ct Appeals 209 US Courthouse 601 W Broadway Louisville KY 40202-2238

MARTIN, BRYAN LESLIE, allergist, immunologist; b. Macomb, Ill., June 25, 1954; s. George Albert and Vernal Louise (Stutsman) M.; m. Deborah Ann Schettig, June 22, 1979; children: Emily, Stephanie, Scott. BA, St. Vincent Coll., 1976; postgrad., Ohio U., 1976-79; DO, U. Osteo. Medicine/Hlth. Scis., 1984; M of Mil. Art and Sci., Command & Staff Officer Coll., 1994. Diplomate Am. Bd. Internal Medicine, Am. Bd. Allergy and Immunology, Nat. Bd. Osteo. Med. Examiners. Commd. 2d lt. U.S. Army, 1980, advanced through grades to lt. col., 1996—, comdr. med. troop 3d armored cavalry regiment, 1990-91; resident in internal medicine William Beaumont Army Med. Ctr., 1987-90, chief med. resident, 1990-91; with U.S. Army Command and Gen. Staff Coll., 1993-94. Student body pres. U. Osteopathic Medicine and Health Scis., Des Moines, 1981-82. Allergy/immunology fellow Fitzsimons Army Med. Ctr., Aurora, Colo., 1991-93; Health Professions scholar U.S. Army, 1980-84; decorated Bronze star. Fellow Am. Coll. Allergy, Asthma and Immunology (fellow-in-tng. rep. to bd. regents 1991-93, chmn. fellow-in-tng. sect. 1992-93); mem. ACP, AMA (del. resident physicians sect. 1991-93, young physicians sect. 1993—), Am. Acad. Allergy and Immunology, Am. Osteo. Assn. (del. 1981-83), Dustoff Assn., Nat. Med. Vets. Soc., Sigma Sigma Phi. Office: SW Allergy and Asthma Ctr Ste 901 7711 Louis Pasteur Dr San Antonio TX 78229

MARTIN, CAROL JACQUELYN, educator, artist; b. Ft. Worth, Tex., Oct. 6, 1943; d. John Warren and Dorothy Lorene (Coffman) Edwards; m. Boe Willis Martin, Oct. 6, 1940; children: Stephanie Diane, Scott Andrew. BA summa cum laude, U. N. Tex., 1965; MA, U. Tex., El Paso, 1967. Tchr. Edgemere Elem. Sch., El Paso, Tex., 1965-66, Fulmore Jr. H.S., Austin, 1966-67, Monnig Jr. H.S., Ft. Worth, 1967-68, Paschal H.S., Ft. Worth, 1968-69; instr. Tarrant County Jr. Coll., Ft. Worth, 1968-69, 71-72; press sec. U.S. Sen. Gaylord Nelson, Washington, 1969-71; instr. Eastfield C.C., Dallas, 1981, Richland C.C. Dist., 1982. Editor The Avesta Mag., 1964-65; exhibited in group shows at City of Richardson's Cottonwood Park, 1970-86, Students of Ann Cushing Gantz, 1973-85, Art About Town, 1979, 80, shows by Tarrant County and Dallas County art assns. Active Dallas Symphony Orch. League, Easter Seal Soc., Dallas Hist. Soc., Women's Bd. of the Dallas Opera, Dallas Arboretum and Garden Club, Dallas County Heritage Soc. Mem. Internat. Platform Assn., Mortar Bd., Alpha Chi, Sigma Tau Delta, Kappa Delta Pi, Delta Gamma. Democrat. Methodist. Address: 4435 Arcady Ave Dallas TX 75205-3604

MARTIN, CAROLYN STEWART, school system administrator, counselor; b. Pitts., May 16, 1951; d. Robert Thomas and Mary (Schoenecker) Stewart; m. Bradley W. Ritter, Feb. 14, 1973 (div. 1979); m. Scott Harwood Martin, July 29, 1983; 1 child, Carrie Lee. BS, Calif. State U., 1972; MA, Ohio State U., 1978; postgrad., Stetson Univ., DeLand, Fla., 1985-87. Tchr. Garrett County Schs., Oakland, Md., 1972-74, Little Darlings Sch., Columbus, Ohio, 1974-75, Colegio Nueva Granada, Bogota, Colombia, 1978-80; bilingual tchr. Othello (Wash.) Sch. Dist., adminstr. title VII, 1981-82; primary specialist, counselor Lake County Sch. Dist., Fla., 1982-84; tchr. Volusia County Sch. Dist., Deltona, Fla., 1984-85; guidance counselor Volusia County Schs., Deltona, Fla., 1989-96; ind. parenting instr., DeLand, 1988; chair Volusia Mental Health Assn., Daytona, 1987; mem. Fla. State Dept. Edn. Task Force, Orlando, 1989; presenter at profl. confs.; guest speaker Women Volusia Conf., 1989. Co-author: Survival Spanish for Teachers, 1982; presenter, guest speaker in field. Bd. dirs. S.W. Volusia YMCA, 1988-93, House Next Door I-CARE Counseling Ctr., 1991-96; chpt. coord. C.H.A.D.D., West Volusia, 1993-95. Named Elem. Counselor of Yr., Volusia/Flagler Counties, 1995-96. Mem. ASCD, Fla. Assn. for Counseling and Devel., Voluusia Assn. for Counseling and Devel., AAUW. Republican. Episcopalian. Office: Timbercrest Sch 2401 Eustace Ave Deltona FL 32725-1763

MARTIN, CHARLES WADE, pastor; b. Athens, Ga., June 7, 1952; s. William Edward and Winifred (Maxwell) M.; m. Rebecca Hankins, May 26, 1973; children: John Wade, Elizabeth Lynn. BA, Asbury Coll., 1974; MDiv, Asbury Theol. Sem., 1977, MA in Religion, 1977; postgrad. in hist. geography of Palestine, Inst. Holy Land Studies, 1977; postgrad. in audience psychology and behavior, Wheaton Coll., 1981, postgrad. in principles of rsch., 1982-83; DMin in Preaching and Worship, Fuller Theol. Sem., 1982; postgrad. in missiology and cultural anthropology, Trinity Evangelical Div. Sch., 1986-87, D in Missiology, 1989; postgrad. in missiology and cultural anthropology, Ft. Wayne Bible Coll., 1987. Lic. to preach by United Meth. Ch., 1972; ordained deacon United Meth. Ch., 1975; ordained elder United Meth. Ch., 1978; ordained to ministry First Bapt. Ch., 1983. Pulpit supply preacher Statesboro Dist. United Meth. Ch., 1970-72, pulpit supply preacher Ky. Annual Conf., 1972-77; pastor Mt. Moriah United Meth. Ch., Matthews, Ga., 1977-80; staff min. in youth work and leadership devel. First United Meth. Ch., Sylvania, Ga., 1981-83; co-pastor Black Creek United

Meth. Ch., Newington, Ga., 1982-87; interim pastor Little Horse Creek Bapt. Ch., Woodcliff, Ga., 1986-87, pastor, 1987-96; exec. dir. Evan. Ministries of Sylvania, Inc., 1978—; tour escort to Israel, 1979, Israel and Egypt, 1981, Greece, 1982; interim Bible tchr., First Bapt. Ch., Sylvania, 1983-84. Contbr. articles to profl. jours. Home: 206 Pinecrest Dr Sylvania GA 30467-1664 Office: Evang Ministries Sylvania PO Box 1664 Sylvania GA 30467-1664

MARTIN, COLLEEN E., medical/surgical, oncological, post-anesthesia nurse, emergency room nurse; b. Oklahoma City, July 10, 1955; d. Wm. D. and Dona Jean (O'Day) M. Student, Oklahoma State U., Stillwater, 1973-75, Rose State Coll., Midwest City, Okla., 1988; BSN, U. Okla., 1979. Cert. in med.-surg. nursing. Charge nurse Okla. Meml. Hosp., Oklahoma City; staff and charge nurse Midwest City Regional Hosp., head ambulatory surgery unit; Assoc. Med. Profls., 1994—. Mem. ANA, Am. Soc. Post Anesthesia Nurses, Okla. Soc. Post Anesthesia Nurses.

MARTIN, DANIEL C., surgeon, educator; b. St. Louis, Apr. 7, 1946; s. Dan Allen and Ruth Keel (Fields) M.; m. Glenn Ann Blakemore, July 7, 1970; children: Josh, Adam. BS in Physics, Emory U., 1968, MD, 1972. Diplomate Am. Bd. Ob-Gyn. Rsch. asst. physics and radiology Emory U., Atlanta, 1968-69; intern, resident, fellow, instr. The Johns Hopkins Med. Instns., Balt., 1972-77; from asst. prof. to clin. asst. prof. U. Tenn., Memphis, 1977-90, clin. assoc. prof., 1990—; surgeon Reproductive Surgery, P.C., Memphis, 1977—; reproductive surgeon Bapt. Meml. Hosp., 1977—; dir. gynecologic laser and endoscopy workshops, 1982-93. Editor: (textbooks) Lasers in Endoscopy, 1990, Laparoscopic Appearance of Endometriosis, 1990, Manual of Endoscopy, 1990, Atlas of Endometriosis, 1993, Endoscopic Management of Gynecologic Disease, 1996. Basketball coach Grace St. Luke's Ch., Memphis, 1992-95. Picker Found. fellow Emory U., 1969; Tex. Assn. Ob-Gyn. hon. fellow, 1989; recipient Bridges trophy for athletics Emory U., 1968, Codman surg. award, 1982, 83, Video award Am. Fertility Soc., 1992; named one of Best Drs. Am. Woodward and White Inc., 1992. Mem. ACOG (sect. chair jr. fellows Md.), Tenn. Med. Assn., Memphis and Shelby County Med. Soc. (comm. com.), Am. Nat. Std. Inst. (subcom. on laser safety in med. facility), Am. Assn. Gynecol. Laparoscopists (pres. 1990-91, Videoendoscopy award 1993), Gynecologic Surgery Soc. (pres. 1994-96), Sigma Pi Sigma. Office: Reproductive Surgery PC # 100 1717 Kirby Pkwy Ste 100 Memphis TN 38120-4331

MARTIN, DAVID ALAN, law educator, government official; b. Indpls., July 23, 1948; s. C. Wendell and Elizabeth Bowman (Meeker) M.; m. Cynthia Jo Lorman, June 13, 1970; children: Amy Lynn, Jeffrey David. BA, DePauw U., 1970; JD, Yale U., 1975. Bar: D.C. Law clk. Hon. J. Skelly Wright U.S. Ct. Appeals (D.C. cir.), 1975-76; law clk. Hon. Lewis F. Powell U.S. Supreme Ct., Washington, 1976-77; assoc. Rogovin, Stern & Huge, Washington, 1977-78; spl. asst. bur. human rights and humanitarian affairs U.S. State Dept., Washington, 1978-80; from asst. prof. to assoc. prof. U. Va. Sch. Law, Charlottesville, 1980-86, prof., 1986-91, Henry L. & Grace Doherty prof. law, 1991—, F. Palmer Weber Rsch. prof. civil liberties and human rights, 1992-95; on leave U.S. Immigration and Naturalization Svc., Washington, 1995—; cons. Adminstrv. Conf. U.S., Washington, 1988-89, 91-92, U.S. Dept. Justice, 1993-95; gen. counsel U.S. Immigration and Naturalization Svc., 1995—. Author: Immigration: Process and Policy, 1985, 2d edit., 1991, 3d edit., 1995, Asylum Case Law Sourcebook, 1994, The Endless Quest: Helping America's Farm Workers, 1994; editor: The New Asylum Seekers, 1988; contbr. numerous articles to profl. jours. Mem. nat. governing bd. Common Cause, Washington, 1972-75; elder Westminster Presbyn. Ch., Charlottesville, 1982-84, 89-92. German Marshall Fund Rsch. Fellow, Geneva, 1984-85. Mem. Am. Soc. Internat. Law (ann. book award 1986), Internat. Law Assn. Democrat. Office: Immigr & Naturaliz Svc Rm 6100 425 I St NW Washington DC 20536

MARTIN, DAVID C., advertising exective; b. 1952. With Gillis Advertising, Birmingham, Ala., 1973-77; pres. Martin Advertising Agy., Birmingham, 1977—. Office: Martin Advt Inc 2801 University Blvd Birmingham AL 35233-2846*

MARTIN, DAVID D., electronics executive; b. 1939. BA, Wesleyan U., 1960; MS, So. Methodist U., 1963, MSEA, 1968. With Tex. Instruments, 1966—, v.p., 1984—. Office: 13500 N Central Expy Dallas TX 75243-1108*

MARTIN, DAVID HUGH, private investigator, business executive, writer; b. Ft. Worth, Mar. 24, 1952; s. Joseph Morgan Jr. and Jane Maurine (Harriss) M.; children: David Christian, Thomas Joshua, Michael Morgan. Ordained to ministry Meth. Ch., 1979; lic. pvt. investigator, Tex. CEO Woodland West Corp., Houston, 1977-84; owner D. H. Martin & Assocs. Investigations, Austin, Tex., 1980—; fin. mgr. The Williams Trust, Austin, 1982—; chmn. Biologic, Inc., Austin, 1983—; exec. dir. Grace Ministries, Austin, 1980—. Author: Rain Music, 1990; albums include Voice of a Child, 1987. Recipient Prism award Nat. Homebuilders Assn., 1979, 80, 82. Mem. MENSA, SAG, Tex. Assn. Lic. Investigators, Tex. Assn. Nurserymen, Rep. Nat. Com. Office: DH Martin & Assocs PO Box 5581 Austin TX 78763-5581

MARTIN, DAVID LANCE, botanist; b. Phila., June 1, 1950; s. Edward Ransom M. BS, Pa. State U., 1971; MS, U. N.C., 1974; postgrad., U. Ga., 1977-78. Biol. tech. U.S. Fish & Wildlife Svc., Gainesville, Fla., 1976-77; botanist Bur. Land Mgmt., Worland, Cody, Wyo., 1978-84, U.S. Fish & Wildlife Svc., Jacksonville, Fla., 1984—. Mem. Am. Soc. Plant Taxonomists, Calif. Botanical Soc. Office: US Fish & Wildlife Svc Ste 310 6620 Southpoint Dr S Jacksonville FL 32216-0912

MARTIN, DEBORAH ANN, intensive care nurse, educator; b. Chester, Pa., June 4, 1957; d. Clarence Hayden and Freida Florence (Hubacher) Williams; m. Gary Gene Martin, Aug. 14, 1982; children: Sean, Jeremy, Kyle. BSN, U. Del., 1979; MSN, U. Ctrl. Ark., 1994. RN, Ark.; cert. ACLS. Staff RN renal transplant and surg. ICU Hosp. U. Pa., Phila., 1979-81; staff RN burn treatment ctr., charge nurse ICU relief Crozer-Chester Med. Ctr., Upland, Pa., 1981-83; staff RN ICU, ICU clin. educator Bapt. Med. Ctr., Jacksonville, Fla., 1983-85; staff nurse ICU Med. Pers. Pool and Staff Builders, Tampa, Fla., 1985-88; staff RN ICU Berwick (Pa.) Hosp., 1988-89; staff RN ICU, spl. recovery, relief cardiac/diabetes educator, instr. dysrhythmia and pacemaker instr. St. Edward's Mercy Med. Ctr., Ft. Smith, Ark., 1990—; part-time faculty Westark C.C., Ft. Smith, 1996—. Mem. AACN, Sigma Theta Tau. Home and Office: 7515 Bear Hollow Rd Fort Smith AR 72916-7408

MARTIN, DONNIS LYNN, educational analyst; b. Knox City, Tex., Sept. 7, 1948; s. Derrell Lee Martin and Audie Lee (Qualls) Kempe; m. Karen Marie Hanzevack, Dec. 24, 1988; children: Christina, Dustin, Shara. BA, Met. State Coll. Denver, 1979; MA in Mgmt., U. Phoenix, 1990; EdD, N.C. State U., 1991. Cert. tchr. lang. arts. Program supr. wind energy systems Rockwell Internat., Golden, Colo., 1980-83, mgr. plant tng., 1983-84, prin. orgn. devel. specialist, 1984-87; mgr. computer-based tng. courseware devel. No. Telecom, Inc., Raleigh, N.C., 1987-88, program mgr. documentation, 1988-89; edn. program specialist N.C. Dept. Community Colls., 1991-92; pres. ERC Assocs., Cary, N.C., 1992—. Contbr. articles to profl. jours. With USAF, 1973-80. Fellow Acad. Human Resource Devel.; mem. Am. Soc. for Tng. and Devel., Am. Ednl. Rsch. Assn., Am. Vocat. Edn. Rsch. Assn., Nat. Soc. for Performance and Instrn., Soc. for Tech. Comm. (sr.), Omicron Tau Theta. Home: 110 Talon Dr Cary NC 27511-8604 Office: ERC Assocs 110 Talon Dr Cary NC 27511-8604

MARTIN, EDYTHE LOUVIERE, business educator; b. Breaux Bridge, La., Dec. 30, 1940; d. James Ivy and Volna Mary (Landry) L.; m. James Henry Martin, Aug. 23, 1969; 1 child, Lois Elizabeth. BS in Bus. Edn., U. Southwestern La., 1972; MEd in Supervision, La. State U., 1977, Specialist Degree in Ednl. Adminstrn., 1988, postgrad studies in Ednl. Adminstrn., 1989—. Geol. sec. Sohio Petroleum Co., Lafayette, La., 1960-67, Bintliff Oil & Gas Co., Lafayette, 1967-69; bus. tchr. Cottonport (La.) H.S., 1972-74; bus. instr. Acadian Tech. Coll., Crowley, La., 1975—; team leader, mem. accrediting teams So. Assn. Colls. and Schs., 1978—, chmn. of steering com. for Acadian Tech. evaluation, 1991; speaker, presenter at meetings and seminars of educators. Publicity chairperson Miss Eunice (La.) Pageant, 1981-88; chairperson Eunice Lady of Yr. award, 1982; organizer chairperson, St. Jude Children's Hosp., Fund Raiser, Memphis, Eunice, 1985-91; PTC sec. St. Edmund Sch., Eunice, 1982-84; vol. March of Dimes, 1995-96. Mem. Office Occupations Assn., La. Vocat. Assn. Inc., La. Vocat. Assn. (trade and indsl. divsn.). Democrat Roman Catholic. Home: 750 Viola St Eunice LA 70535-4340 Office: Acadian Tech Coll 1933 W Hutchinson Ave Crowley LA 70526-3215

MARTIN, GEORGE M., food products executive; b. 1938. Prin. George M. Martin atty., Corsicana, Tex., 1965-77; owner Navarro Pecan Co., Inc., Corsicana, 1977—. Office: Navarro Pecan Co Inc 2131 E Highway 31 Corsicana TX 75110-9077

MARTIN, GREGORY KEITH, lawyer; b. Conway, S.C., Nov. 7, 1956; s. George Henry Martin and Julia Ann (Johnson) M. Land. BS in Fin. Mgmt., Clemson U., 1979; JD, U. S.C., 1983. Bar: S.C. 1983. Intern U.S. Senate, 1980; law clk. to presiding judge 15th Jud. Cir. Ct., Conway, 1983; assoc. Johnson & Martin, Conway, 1983-88, ptnr., 1988-93; mayor City of Conway, 1995—. Commr. Conway Planning Commn., 1986-89, chmn., 1989; bd. dirs. Conway-Main St. U.S.A., 1986-90, chmn., 1988; mem. Conway Bd. Appeals, 1987-89, Horry County Bd. Archtl. Rev., 1987-90; mem. First United Meth. Ch. of Conway, Conway City Coun., 1991-94; pres., Horry County Hist. Soc., 1988, 90, mayor pro tem, 1994; mem. adv. bd. Pee Dee Heritage Ctr., 1988—. Named Outstanding Young Man Am., 1987. Mem. ABA, S.C. Bar Assn., Horry County Bar Assn., Sigma Nu, Phi Delta Phi. Home: 706 Elm St Conway SC 29526-4373

MARTIN, HARRY CORPENING, lawyer, retired state supreme court justice; b. Lenoir, N.C., Jan. 13, 1920; s. Hal C. and Johnsie Harshaw (Nelson) M.; m. Nancy Robiou Dallam, Apr. 16, 1955; children: John, Matthew, Mary. A.B., U. N.C., 1942; LL.B., Harvard U., 1948; LL.M., U. Va., 1982. Bar: N.C. 1948. Sole practice Asheville, N.C., 1948-62; judge N.C. Superior Ct., Asheville, 1962-78, N.C. Ct. Appeals, Raleigh, 1978-82; justice N.C. Supreme Ct., 1982-92; ptnr. Martin & Martin, Attys., Hilllsborough, N.C., 1992—; adj. prof. U. N.C. Law Sch., 1983-92, Dan K. Moore disting. vis. prof., 1992—; sr. conf. atty. U.S. Ct. Appeals for 4th Cir., 1994—; adj. prof. Duke U., 1990-91. Served with U.S. Army, 1942-45, South Pacific. Mem. U.S. Supreme Ct. Hist. Soc., N.C. Supreme Ct. Hist. Soc. (pres.). Democrat. Episcopalian. Home: 702 E Franklin St Chapel Hill NC 27514-3823 Office: U NC Law Sch Van Hecke-Wettach Hall Chapel Hill NC 27599

MARTIN, HARRY W., sociologist, educator; b. Phenix City, Ala., Oct. 22, 1916; s. Edward Warren Martin and Eva Izora Shepherd; m. Margaret Patricia Horne, June 24, 1951; children: Margaret Holmes, Jonathan Edward. BA, U. Ga., 1949, MA, 1959-68; PhD, U. N.C. Instr. Salem Coll., Winston-Salem, N.C., 1950-52; rsch. fellow Inst. for Social Rsch. U. N.C., 1950, project dir. behavioral sci. and nursing edn. Sch. Nursing, 1957; from asst. prof. to prof. dept. psychiatry U. Tex. Southwestern Med. Sch., Dallas, 1959-68; prof., chief divsn. sociology dept. psychiatry U. Tex. Health Sci. Ctr., San Antonio, 1968-84, dir. Health Svcs. Rsch. Inst., prof. dept. comty. dentistry, 1973-84, prof. dept. family practice, 1977-84; adj. prof. U. Tex. Sch. Pub. Health, San Antonio; mem. geriatrics task force U. Tex. Med. Sch.-San Antonio, 1976-79, chmn. geriatrics task force, 1976-77, mem. curriculum rev. com., 1969-72, chmn. curriculum rev. com., 1972, mem. 1st yr. promotions com., 1968-72, chmn. 1st yr. promotions com., 1970-71; mem. promotions and tenure com. U. Tex. Health Sci. Ctr.-San Antonio, 1980-83, com. on coms., 1973-78, chmn. com. on coms., 1974-76, grad. exec.com., 1970-74, chmn. curriculum rev. com., 1972. Assoc. editor: Sociological Inquiry, 1962-67; adv. editor: Family Systems Medicine, 1983-86; contbr. articles to profl. jours. Bd. dirs. Dallas County Mental Health Ctr., 1964-68; v.p. Easter Seal Soc. for Crippled Children, San Antonio, 1970-71. Home: 10510 Mount Marcy San Antonio TX 78213-1612

MARTIN, J. LANDIS, manufacturing company executive, lawyer; b. Grand Island, Nebr., Nov. 5, 1945; s. John Charles and Lucile (Cooley) M.; m. Sharon Penn Smith, Sept. 23, 1978; children: Mary Frances, Sarah Landis, Emily Penn. BS in Bus. Adminstrn., Northwestern U., 1968, JD cum laude, 1973. Bar: Ill. 1974, D.C. 1978, Colo. 1982. Assoc. Kirkland & Ellis, Chgo., 1973-77; ptnr. Kirkland & Ellis, Washington, 1978-81; mng. ptnr. Kirkland & Ellis, Denver, 1981-87, firm com. mem., Chgo., 1983-87; pres., CEO NL Industries Inc., Houston, 1987—; also bd. dirs. NL Industries Inc.; chmn., CEO Baroid Corp., Houston, 1987-94; chmn. bd., pres., CEO Tremont Corp., 1990—, also bd. dirs.; dir. Dresser Industries, Dallas, Aimco. Editor-in-chief: Exchange Act Guide to SEC Rule 144, 1973; articles editor Northwestern U. Law Rev., 1972-73. Pres Ctrl. City Opera House Assn., Denver, 1986-88, chmn. 1987; pres. Ctrl. City Opera House Endowment Fund, 1992—; vis. com. Northwestern U. Sch. Law, 1987—; mem. exec. com. Houston Grand Opera, 1991—, sr. v.p. devel. 1992—, pres. 1993-95, chmn. 1995—; bd. trustees Denver Art Mus., 1994—, Graland Country Day Sch., 1992—. With U.S. Army, 1969-71. Mem. ABA, Ill. Bar Assn., Colo. Bar Assn., D.C. Bar Assn. Clubs: Chevy Chase (Md.), John Evans (Evanston, Ill.), Denver, Denver Country, Castle Pines Golf. Office: NL Industries Inc 16825 Northchase Dr Ste 1200 Houston TX 77060-2544*

MARTIN, JAMES GRUBBS, medical research executive, former governor; b. Savannah, Ga., Dec. 11, 1935; s. Arthur Morrison and Mary Julia (Grubbs) M.; m. Dorothy Ann McAulay, June 1, 1957; children: James Grubbs, Emily Wood, Arthur Benson. BS, Davidson Coll., 1957; PhD, Princeton U., 1960. Assoc. prof. chemistry Davidson (N.C.) Coll., 1960-72; mem. 93d to 98th Congresses from N.C., 1973-85; gov. State of N.C., 1985-92; v.p. rsch. Carolinas HealthCare System, Charlotte, N.C., 1993—; mem. Mecklenburg (N.C.) Bd. County Commrs., 1966-72, chmn., 1967-68, 70-71; v.p. Nat. Assn. Regional Couns., 1971-72; pres. N.C. Assn. County Commrs., 1970-71; mem., tuba player Charlotte Symphony, 1961-66. Danforth fellow, 1957-60. Mem. Beta Theta Pi (v.p., trustee 1966-69, pres. 1975-78), Masons (33 deg.), Shriners. Presbyterian. Office: Carolinas Med Ctr PO Box 32861 Charlotte NC 28232-2861*

MARTIN, JAMES HARBERT, school administrator, retired Air Force officer; b. Sparta, Tenn., Jan. 5, 1941; s. Harbert Rogers and Monia Gladys (Grissom) M.; m. Madoline Carter, Sept. 14, 1963; children: Erin Dawn, Ann Farley, John Harbert. MSBA, Tenn. Tech. U., 1963; MBA, Auburn U., 1975. CPA; cert. profl. logistician. Commd. USAF, 1963, advanced through ranks to col., 1983; dep. program mgr. B1B System Program Office, 1982-84; dir. logistics Aero. Systems Div., Wright-Patterson AFB, Ohio, 1984-86; dep. comdr. resources Incirlik Air Base, Adana, Turkey, 1986-88; comdr. Tyndall AFB, Panama City, Fla., 1988-90; vice comdr. Air Force Engring. and Svcs. Ctr., Tyndall AFB, 1990; ret., 1990; exec. dir. Lookout Mountain (Ga.) Golf Club, 1991-94; CFO Riverside Mil. Acad., Gainesville, Ga., 1994—. Mem. exec. bd. Gulf Coast coun. Boy Scouts Am., Pensacola, Fla., 1989-92; chmn. Bay County WalkAmerica (March of Dimes), Panama City, 1990. Decorated Legion of Merit (2). Mem. Air Force Assn., Masons. Republican. Methodist. Office: Riverside Mil Acad Box 565 2001 Riverside Dr Gainesville GA 30501

MARTIN, JAMES KIRBY, historian, educator; b. Akron, Ohio, May 26, 1943; s. Paul Elmo and Dorothy Marie (Garrett) M.; m. Karen Wierwille, Aug. 7, 1965; children: Darcy Elizabeth, Sarah Marie, Joelle Kathryn Garrett. B.A. summa cum laude, Hiram Coll., 1965; M.A., U. Wis., 1967, Ph.D., 1969. Asst. prof. history Rutgers U., New Brunswick, N.J., 1969-73, assoc. prof., 1973-79, prof., 1979-80, asst. provost, 1972-74, v.p. acad. affairs, 1977-79; vis. prof. Rutgers Ctr. of Alcohol Studies, 1978-88; prof. history U. Houston, 1980—, chmn. dept., 1980-83; vis. prof. history Rice U, 1992; chmn. bd. sponsors Papers of Thomas Edison Project, 1977-80; mem. editorial adv. bd. Papers of William Livingston Project, 1973-80. Author: Men in Rebellion, 1973, In the Course of Human Events, 1979, (with M.E. Lender) A Respectable Army: The Military Origins of the Republic, 1982 (contemporary mil. reading list), Drinking in America: A History, 1982, rev. edit. 1987, (with others) America and Its Peoples, 1989, 2d edit., 1993, concise edit. 1995; editor: Interpreting Colonial America, 1973, 2d edit. 1978, The Human Dimensions of Nation Making, 1976, (with K. Stubaus) The America Revolution, Whose Revolution?, 1977, 81, (with M.E. Lender) Citizen-Soldier: The Revolutionary War Journal of Joseph Bloomfield, 1982 (R.P. McCormick prize), Ordinary Courage: The Revolutionary War Adventures of Joseph Plumb Martin, 1993; mem. bd. editors Houston Rev., 1981, N.J. History, 1986, Conversations with the Past Series, 1993-95; gen. editor Am. Social Experience Series, 1983—. Recipient N.J. Soc. of the Cin. prize for Disting. Achievement in Am. History, 1995, Hiram Coll. Alumni Achievement award, 1996. Mem. Tex. Assn. for Advancement History (bd. dirs. 1981-93, v.p. 1986-90), Inst. for Internat. Bus. Analysis (adv. coun. 1982-86), Am. Hist. Assn. (Beveridge-Dunning prize com. 1990-93), Orgn. Am. Historians, So. Hist. Assn., Soc. Historians Early Am. Republic (adv. coun. 1985-88), Phi Beta Kappa, Phi Kappa Phi, Pi Gamma Mu, Omicron Delta Kappa, Phi Alpha Theta. Office: U Houston Dept History 4800 Calhoun Rd Houston TX 77204-3785

MARTIN, JAMES NEAL, lawyer; b. Glasgow, Ky., Jan. 11, 1950; s. J. Jack and Olive Katherine (Conover) M.; 1 child, Amelia Anne. BA, U. Louisville, 1972, JD, 1980. Bar: Ky. 1980, U.S. Dist. Ct. (ea. dist.) Ky. 1988. Pvt. practice Tompkinsville, Ky., 1980-82; spl. commr. Cumberland Cir. Ct. for 29th Jud. Cir. Ky., Burkesville, 1982-84; ptnr. Martin & Martin, Richmond, Ky., 1984-89; pvt. practice, Richmond, 1989—; asst. county atty., prosecutor, criminal div. Office Madison County Atty., Richmond, 1986. Bd. dirs. Richmond Little League, Inc., 1987—, chmn. exec. bd., 1988-89. Mem. ABA, Ky. Bar Assn., Ky. Assn. Hosp. Attys., Ky. Acad. Trial Attys., Ky. Assn. Criminal Def. Lawyers, Madison County Bar Assn., Richmond C. of C. (legis. affairs com. 1986-88), Rotary (bd. dirs. Richmond 1986, v.p., pres. 1991-92). Office: PO Box 828 Richmond KY 40476-0828

MARTIN, JAMES WILLIAM, lawyer; b. Turlock, Calif., Dec. 20, 1949. Student, Ga. Inst. Tech., 1967-69; BS, Stetson U., 1971, JD, 1974. Bar: Fla. 1974, U.S. Dist. Ct. (mid. dist.) Fla. 1974, U.S. Ct. Appeals (5th cir.) 1974, U.S. Ct. Appeals (11th cir.) 1987, U.S. Supreme Ct. 1978. Ptnr. Brickley & Martin, St. Petersburg, Fla., 1974-79; pres. James W. Martin, P.A., St. Petersburg, 1979—; Author: West's Florida Corporation System, 1984, West's Legal Forms, rev. edit., Non-Profit Corporations, 1991, 92, 93, 94, 96, West's Florida Legal Forms, Business Organizations, Real Estate, Specialized Forms, 1990, 91, 92, 93, 94; contbr. articles to Word Perfect mag. Author: West's Florida Corporation System, 1984, 84, West's Legal Forms, 2d edit., Non-Profit Corporations, 1991, 92, 93, 94, West's Florida Legal Forms, Business Organizations, Real Estate, Specialized Forms, 1990, 91, 92, 93, 94, 95; contbr. articles to Word Perfect mag. City councilman, St. Petersburg, 1982-83; active Leadership St. Petersburg; active charter class Leadership Tampa Bay; founding trustee, sec., counsel Salvador Dali Mus., 1980—; founding dir., sec., counsel Fla. Internat. Mus., 1992-94. Recipient Outstanding Young Man award Jaycees, 1982, Outstanding Contbn. to City award St. Petersburg C. of C., 1980. Mem. Fla. Bar (chmn. coordinating com. tech. 1992-93), St. Petersburg Bar Assn., St. Petersburg C. of C. (gen. counsel 1991-92, arts task force 1987, chmn. parking com., chmn. Urban Solutions coun. 1992-93, chmn. downtown coun. 1993-94), Pres. Club (founder, hon. bd. dirs. 1985-91).

MARTIN, JANICE LYNN, special education educator; b. Louisville, Feb. 24, 1952; d. Thomas Joseph and Agnes Marie (Singhiser) Duddy; m. Reed Ammerman Martin Jr., Aug. 14, 1976; children: Susan, John. BS magna cum laude, U. Ga., 1974; MEd, U. Louisville, 1976, grad. dean's citation, 1984; cert., Western Ky. U., 1984. Tchr. Jefferson County Pub. Schs., Louisville, 1974—; mem. curriculum coun. Jefferson County Pub. Schs., 1979-82. Mem. St. Joseph Cath. Orphan Soc., Louisville, 1981—; mem., adult asst. Troop 513 Girl Scouts U.S., Louisville, 1988—. Recipient Grad. Dean's citation U. Louisville, 1976, Achievement in Edn. award Middletown Optimist Club, 1989, Eisenhower Title II math. and sci. grant, 1992, 93, Appalachian Ednl. Lab. Eisenhower Math. Grant Project, 1994. Mem. NEA, ASCD, Ky. Edn. Assn., Coun. for Exceptional Children (Outstanding Spl. Edn. Tchr. of Yr. 1990), Louisville Coun. Tchrs., Ky. Coun. Tchrs. of Math., Nat. Coun. Tchrs. Math., Jefferson County Tchrs. Assn., AAUW, Internat. Reading Assn., Alpha Delta Kappa, Phi Kappa Phi, Phi Delta Kappa, Sigma Kappa. Democrat. Home: 9005 Cardiff Rd Louisville KY 40242-3362 Office: Jefferson County Pub Schs Middletown Elem 218 N Madison Ave Louisville KY 40243-1018

MARTIN, JERRY HAROLD, bank examiner; b. Richwood, W.Va., Apr. 28, 1945; s. Weaver Eugene and Hazel Lee (Adkins) M.; m. Phyllis Lowe, Apr. 26, 1967 (div. 1980); m. Deborah Ann Perry, June 6, 1983 (div. 1994); children: Marlene, Renee. BA in Econs., U. Charleston (W.Va.), 1967; Cert. Banking, La. State U., Baton Rouge, 1980. Asst. examiner Comptroller of the Currency, Charleston, 1969-74, bank examiner, 1974-77, examiner-in-charge, 1977-84, field mgr., 1984—. With U.S. Army, 1967-69. Recipient Cert. of Appreciation, Comptroller of Currency, 1986. Methodist. Home: PO Box 3934 Charleston WV 25339-3934 Office: 102 Capitol St Charleston WV 25301-2610

MARTIN, JOHN CHARLES, judge; b. Durham, N.C., Nov. 9, 1943; s. Chester Barton and Mary Blackwell (Pridgen) M.; m. Margaret Rand; children: Lauren Blackwell, Sarah Conant, Mary Susan. BA, Wake Forest U., 1965, JD, 1967; postgrad. Nat. Judicial Coll., Reno, 1979. Bar: N.C. 1967, U.S. Dist. Ct. (mid. dist.) N.C. 1967, U.S. Dist. Ct. (ea. dist.) N.C. 1972, U.S. Dist. (we. dist.) N.C. 1975, U.S. Ct. Appeals (4th cir.) 1976. Assoc., Haywood, Denny & Miller, Durham, N.C., 1970-72; ptnr. Haywood, Denny & Miller, 1973-77; resident judge Superior Ct. 14th Jud. Dist. N.C., Durham, 1977-84; judge N.C. Ct. Appeals, Raleigh, 1985-88, 93—; ptnr. Maxwell & Hutson, P.A., Durham, 1988-92; mem. study com. rules of evidence and comparative negligence N.C. Legis. Research Commn., 1980; mem. N.C. Pattern Jury Instrn. drafting com., 1978-84, N.C. Trial Judge's Bench Book Drafting Com., 1984-87; mem. bd. visitors Wake Forest U. Sch. Law, 1985—; mem. alumni coun. Wake Forest U., 1993-96; mem. state/fed. Judicial Council of N.C., 1985-87, chmn. 1987. Mem. Durham City Council, 1975-77. With U.S. Army, 1967-69. Recipient Disting. Service award Durham Jaycees, 1976. Mem. ABA, N.C. Bar Assn. (chmn. adminstrn. of justice study com. 1990-92, bench, bar and law sch. com. 1987-91, adminstrn. justice task force 1996—, conv. planning com.), Durham County Bar Assn. (bd. dirs. 1991-92), Wake County Bar Assn., 10th Jud. Dist. Bar Assn., Braxton Craven Inn of Ct., Hope Valley Country Club, Phi Delta Phi. Democrat. Methodist. Office: PO Box 888 Raleigh NC 27602-0888

MARTIN, JOHN DAVID, finance educator, researcher, author; b. Ruston, La., Oct. 1, 1945; m. Sally Johnson; children: Marcus David, Jesse John. BS cum laude in Bus. Adminstrn., La. Tech. U., 1967, MBA, 1968; PhD in Fin., Tex. Tech U., 1973. Instr. econs., La. Tech. U., Ruston, 1968-69; instr. fin. Tex. Tech U., Lubbock, 1969-73; assoc. prof. fin. Va. Poly. Inst. and State U., Blacksburg, 1973-77; assoc. prof. fin., Tex. A&M U., College Station, 1977-79; assoc. prof. fin. U. Tex., Austin, 1980-83, prof. fin., 1984-86, First Republic Bank centennial prof. bus. adminstrn., 1987-88, Margaret and Eugene McDermott prof. banking and fin., 1989—, PhD program advisor, 1984-86; chmn. grad. studies com., 1984-86, mem. univ. coms. including exec. com. of operating bd. of trustees of Tex. Student Publs., 1984-88, fac. sen. and univ. coun, 1992-94. Contbg. author: Study Guide and Workbook to Fundamentals of Financial Management, 3rd edit., 1977; Guide to Financial Analysis, 2nd edit., 1988, Spanish transl., 1982; Cases in Financial Management, 3d edit., 1992; Readings in Financial Management, 1981; Personal Financial Management, 1982; The Theory of Finance: Evidence and Applications, 1988; Study Guide and Workbook to Basic Financial Management, 7th edit., 1996; Basic Financial Management, 7th edit., 1996; Cases in Finance, 2d edit., 1983; editor for fin. Jour. Bus. Rsch., 1977-82; assoc. editor Advances in Fin. Planning and Forecasting, 1982—, Jour. Small Bus. Fin., 1991—, Jour. Internat. Econs. and Fin., 1991—; assoc. editor for fin. Jour. Fin. Rsch., 1980-81; editorial bd. Jour. Bus. Rsch., 1975-76; contbr. articles to publs. in field. Recipient Outstanding Rsch. award Coll. Bus. Adminstrn., Tex. A&M U., 1979. Mem. Fin. Mgmt. Assn. (dir. doctoral seminar 1983, chmn. editor selection com. Fin. Mgmt. 1984, bd. dirs. 1991-92), So. Fin. Assn. (bd. dirs. 1978-80, 84-86), Southwestern Fin. Assn. (pres. 1980-81), Phi Kappa Phi, Beta Gamma Sigma, Phi Kappa Alpha. Office: U Tex Dept Fin Austin TX 78712

MARTIN, JOHN LEWIS, army officer; b. Richmond, Va., Oct. 27, 1965; s. Richard Lewis and Beatrice Frances (Tomes) M.; m. Kemberly Leigh Thorn, June 27, 1988; 1 child, John Richard. AA in Bus. Adminstrn., Rappahannock C.C., Warsaw, Va., 1986; BS in Polit. Sci., James Madison U., 1988. Sales rep., staff writer Rappahannock Times, Tappahannock, Va., 1988; commd. 2d lt. U.S. Army, 1988, advanced through grades to capt., 1993; served in Ft. Sill, Okla./Ft. Hood, Tex., 1988-95; co. comdr., recruiting Corinth, Miss., 1996—. Organizer, v.p. Young Reps., Tappahannock, 1986-

88. Decorated Bronze Star, Army Commendation medal (2). Mem. Assn. U.S. Army, The Alliance. Episcopalian. Office: US Army Corinth Recruiting Co 515 Franklin St Corinth MS 38834-4842

MARTIN, JOHNNY BENJAMIN, accountant; b. Gainesville, Ga., June 9, 1947; s. John Daniel and Helen Amanda (Meeks) M.; m. Mary Sue West, June 8, 1969; 1 child, Tammy Michelle. BBA, U. Ga., Athens, 1969, MA, 1971. CPA, Ga. Tchr. high sch. Hall County Sch. Systems, Gainesville, 1969-70; instr. in acctg. Austin Peay State U., Clarksville, Tenn., 1972-76; instr. in bus. Gainesville Jr. Coll., 1976-77; controller Home Fed. Savs. and Loan, Gainesville, 1977-83; ptnr. Kendrick & Jessup, CPA's, Gainesville, 1983-92; pvt. practice, Gainesville, 1992—. Mem. Am. Inst. CPAs, Ga. Soc. CPAs, Tenn. Soc. CPAs, Phi Kappa Phi, Beta Gamma Sigma. Democrat. Baptist. Lodge: Civitan (bd. dirs., treas. 1981-82, treas. 1986-87). Home: 3751 Robinson Dr Oakwood GA 30566-3408

MARTIN, JUDY BRACKIN HEREFORD, higher education administrator; b. York, Ala., May 25, 1943; d. Julian Byron and Willie Lee (Aiken) B.; m. Roy Nichols Hereford, Jr., Apr. 1, 1962 (dec. Mar. 1988); children: Leanne, Roy Nichols III, Rachel, Samantha; m. John Lawrence Martin Sr., Nov. 23, 1988. BA, Judson Coll., 1964. Co-owner, ptnr. Hereford Haven Farms, Faunsdale, Ala., 1962-93; ptnr. The Mustard Seed, Demopolis, Ala., 1974-76; ptnr., sales mgr. Hereford & Assocs. Auction Co., Faunsdale, Ala., 1967-91; alumnae dir., dir. admissions Judson Coll., Marion, Ala., 1988-90, asst. to pres., 1990-94, interim v.p. for instnl. advancement, 1996—; exec. sec.-treas. Ala. Women's Hall of Fame, Judson Coll., Marion, 1991—; exec. dir. Ala. Rural Heritage Found., Thomaston, 1991-95. Officer Marengo County Red. Cross, 1987-88; mem. Marengo County Hist. Soc., Econ. Devel. Assn. Ala., 1991—; com. mem. Marengo Dem. Exec. Com.; bd. dirs. Dept. Human Resources, Marengo County, 1987-95, Marengo County Farmers Fedn. Bd., 1985-95; mem. So. Arts Fedn. Adv. Coun., 1994-95; mem. steering com. Leadership Marengo, 1994; chmn. bd. Faunsdale United Meth. Ch., 1989-91. Mem. Blackbelt Tourism Coun. (bd. dirs. 1991), Judson Coll. Alumnae Assn. (treas. 1992-96). Methodist.

MARTIN, JULIE WARREN, sculptor; b. Knoxville, Tenn., Jan. 4, 1943; d. Millard Robert and Sarah (Lytle) Warren; 1 child, Andrea Elizabeth Martin. BFA, U. Tenn., 1965. One-woman shows include Hunter Mus. Chattanooga, 1969, 80, 83, Tyco Art Gallery, Nashville, 1974, Cheekwood Fine Arts Ctr., Nashville, Byck Gallery, Louisville, 1981, Ann Jacob Gallery, Atlanta, 1983, Lagerquist Gallery, Atlanta, 1986, 88, Albers Fine Art Gallery, Memphis, 1989, 92, 93, 94, Knoxville Opera Co., 1989, 90; group exhbns. include Art Expo, 1987, N.Y.C., Laumeier Invitational, St. Louis, 1988; commns. include Glaxo Inc., Rsch. Triangle Park, N.C., U. Tenn., Knoxville, Nations Bank, Charlotte, N.C., Memphis Cancer Ctr.; many pvt./corp. collections. Elder 2nd Presbyn. Ch., Knoxville, chmn. bldg. and ops. com., many other coms.; vol. buyer East Tenn. Children's Gift Shop; trustee Knoxville Mus. of Art, 1983-93, co-chmn. 1991 mem. drive; bd. dirs. Ewing Gallery, U. Tenn., Knoxville, mem. Chancellor's Assocs., Tenn. Women's Forum, Leadership Knoxville, Class of 90. Mem. Phi Kappa Phi. Office: 6006 Walden St Knoxville TN 37919-6337

MARTIN, KENNETH FRANK, insurance company executive; b. Milw., Feb. 27, 1948; s. John Fred Martin and Paula Christine (Lochstampfer) Rodgers; m. Patricia Ann Liggett, Dec. 23, 1970; children: Theodore Dieter, Oliver Derek. Student, U. Wis., Oshkosh, 1966-69, Career Acad. Broadcasting, Milw., 1969. Lic. Tex. ins. group I, HMO; registered health underwriter. Radio announcer Sta. KRGI, Grand Island, Nebr., 1970, Sta. WLVA, Lynchburg, Va., 1970-71; freelance writer Milw., 1971-73; radio journalist Stas. WRIT, WBCS, Milw., 1973-74, Sta. KTRH, Houston, 1974-75; with ins. sales staff Combined Am. Ins. Co., Houston, 1975-77; with office equipment sales staff Pitney Bowes, Houston, 1977-80; owner Bayou Benefits Group (formerly The Ken Martin Co.), Houston, 1980-96, Sr. Security of Tex., Houston, 1995-96; pres. Bayou Benefits Group, Inc., Houston, 1996—; corr. Moscow Bus. Jour. Report, Open Radio AM 918, 1993. Nation chief, pres. Indian Guides Westside Family YMCA, Houston, 1987-89, trail guide, pres. Trailblazers, 1990-96; judge Westside Swim League, Houston, 1990; umpire, coach, mgr. Meml. Ashford Little League, 1993—; bd. dirs. Greater Houston YMCA Camping Svcs., 1991-95. Named Vol. of Yr. YMCA of Greater Houston Area, 1989. Mem. Nat. Assn. Life Underwriters, Nat. Assn. Health Underwriters (named to Pres.'s Coun. Leading Prodrs. Round Table 1991-96, Nat. Conv. master of ceremonies Atlanta 1996), Houston Assn. Life Underwriters, Tex. Assn. Life Underwriters (bd. dirs. 1991-92, 2d v.p. 1992-93, pres.-elect 1993-94, pres. 1994-95, immediate past pres. 1995-96, trustee 1996—), Tex. Assn. Health Underwriters (bd. dirs. 1996—). Office: Bayou Benefits Group Inc Ste 200 2000 S Dairy Ashford St Houston TX 77077-5719

MARTIN, KENNETH PAUL, social services administrator; b. Washington, Aug. 23, 1964; s. William Robert and Alice Lucille (Long) M. BA in Polit. Sci., Pa. State U., 1986, BS in Computer Sci., 1986, postgrad., 1986-93. Grad. housing asst. Pa. State U., 1989-91, tchg. asst., rsch. asst., instr., grader, 1986-91, reviewer ADA compliance for Univ. Health Svcs., 1993; LSAT supr. Coll. Bd., 1986-89; libr. asst., clk. Am. Philatelic Soc., 1985-86; group health ins. adminstr. Grad. Student Assn., 1988-93; pres. Continuing Care, Inc., Sarasota, Fla., 1993—; presenter various workshops; coord. Grad. Fair, 1988-93. Editor The Philatelic Observer, 1987, The Guide to Grad. Life, 1988-92, GSA Newsletter, 1987-88, 91-92, GSA Tax Guide, 1990-93, Univ. Student Adv. Bd. Notebook, 1989-93, State Coll. Area Child Care Facilities, 1989-93; columnist The Wall Jour., 1989-90; book reviewer The Am. Philatelist; author phamphlets for Internat. Cultures Interest House and Interest House Coun.; contbr. articles to profl. jours. Grad. student rep. Pa. State bd. trustees, 1988-91; vol. Am. Philatelic Rsch. Libr., 1982-84; mem. Johnstown Regional Adv. Com. ARC, 1990-93, coord. GSA Blood Drives, 198-93, chair Pitt Penn State Challenge Adv. Com., 1990, vol., 1987-93; vol. Habitat for Humanity, 1993; mem. Mayor's Action Network, 1988-91, Mayor's Student Leadership Task Force, 1988-91, 92-93; vol. Shaver's Creek, 1993; Pa. State Games vol. Spl. Olympics, 1989, 91; ptnr. of conscience Amnesty Internat., 1988—; vol. various stamp fairs. Recipient Justham award ARC, Johnstown Blood Region, 1992. Mem. ACLU, NAACP, Pa. State Alumni Assn. (exec. bd. 1988-91, coun. 1988-91), Nat. Assn. Grad. Profl. Students, Am. Polit. Sci. Assn. (presidency rsch. sect., women's issues sect. 1987—), Ctr. for Study of Presidency, Common Cause, Nat. Geographic Soc., So. Poverty Law Ctr., Valley Friends Meeting, Worldwatch Inst., Jr. Philatelists Am., Inc. (immediate past pres., exec. com. 1987-89, stamp identification dir. 1983-90), Coun. Philatelic Orgns. (exec. com. bd. dirs. 1987-89), Sarasota Philatelic Club (mem. Sarasota Nat. Stamp Exhbn. Com. 1993—), Venice Stamp Club, Am. Assn. Philatelic Exhibitors, Am. First Day Cover Soc., Am. Philatelic Congress, Am. Philatelic Rsch. Libr., Am. Philatelic Soc. (writer's unit), Am. Topical Assn. (map study unit), Bur. Issues Assn., Errors, Freaks, Oddities Collector's Club, Internat. Philatelic Press Club, Internat. Soc. Worldwide Stamp Collectors, Modern Postal History Soc., Philatelic Computing Study Group, Plate Number Coil Collectors Club, Precancel Stamp Soc.

MARTIN, LELAND MORRIS (PAPPY MARTIN), history educator; b. Patrick Springs, Va., Aug. 8, 1930; s. Rufus Wesley and Mary Hilda (Biggs) M.; m. Mildred Greer, May 12, 1956; children: Lee Ann Martin Powell, Mitzi Jo. AB, Berea Coll., 1953; MS, U. Tenn., 1954; grad., Air War Coll., Maxwelll AFB, Ala., 1978; MA in History, U Tex. Pan-Am., 1993. Enlisted USAF, 1954, advanced through grades to col., 1977; comdr. RAF, Greenham Common, Welford, 1974-76; comdt., comdr. Mil. Airlift Command Noncommisioned Officers Acad., McGuire AFB, N.J., 1976-79; vice comdr., comdr. RAF Mildenhall and RAF Chicksands, Eng., 1979-83; chief staff 21st Air Force, McGuire AFB, 1983-84; pres. Air Force Phys. Evaluation Bd., Randolph AFB, N.J., 1984-86; ret., 1986; dep. exec. dir. Confederate Air Force, Harlingen, Tex., 1986-88; exec. dir. Am. Airpower Heritage Found., Harlingen, 1986-88; tchg. asst., lectr. in history Pan Am. dept. U. Tex., Edinburg, 1989-93; adj. prof. history Tex. State Tech. Coll., Harlingen, 1994—; co-chair (with Sir Douglas Bader) 1976 Internat. Air Tatoo at RAF Greenham Common; chair Air Fete 80 and 81, RAF Mildenhall, Eng. Co-editor: History of Military Assistance Command, Vietnam, 1970. Decorated Legion of Merit with two oak leaf clusters, Bronze Star; Cross of Gallantry (Vietnam); recipient Amb.'s award Ct. St. James, London, 1974, 83. Mem. Air Force Assn., Am. Watchmakers Inst., Nat. Assn. Watch and Clock Collectors, Brit. Officers Club Phila. (hon.), Rotary (gov. internat. dist. 5930 1995-96), Order of Daedalians, Phi Alpha Theta, Phi Kappa Phi. Republican. Presbyterian. Home: 3001 Emerald Lake Dr Harlingen TX 78550-8621 Office: Tex State Tech Coll Dept History Harlingen TX 78550-3697

MARTIN, LESLIE EARL, III, marketing executive; b. Madison, Wis., Sept. 19, 1955; s. Leslie Earl Jr. and Dorothy Mae (Clark) M. BBA, U. Wis., 1978. Agt. Conn. Mut. Life Ins. Co., Madison, Wis., 1978-81; dir. mktg. Strand Assocs., Inc., Madison, Wis., 1981-85; bus. devel. Balcor/Am. Express, San Francisco, 1985-86; v.p. sales QualiCorp. Fin., Inc., Tampa, Fla., 1986-88, Calvert Group, Bethesda, Md., 1988-91; v.p. mktg. SRI Group, Inc., Atlanta, 1991, IDEX Mut. Funds, Clearwater, Fla., 1992—. Mem. Internat. Assn. Fin. Planning (chmn. 1993-94). Office: IDEX/Western Reserve Life 201 Highland Ave NE Largo FL 33770-2512

MARTIN, LOUIS FRANK, surgery and physiology educator; b. Troy, N.Y., Nov. 7, 1951; s. Eugene Lavern and Lois Jane (Perkins) Martin; m. Deborah Lynn Tjarnberg, Mar. 12, 1977; children: Jesse Tjarnberg, James Casey, Tyler Gene. BA, Brown U., 1973, MD, 1976; MS in Health Adminstrn., U. Louisville, 1993. Diplomate Am. Bd. Surgery. Resident in gen. surgery U. Wash. Affiliated Hosps., Seattle, 1977-78; resident in gen. surgery U. Louisville, 1978-83, rsch. fellow trauma rsch. and health care ednl. adminstrn., 1980-82; asst. prof. surgery Pa. State U., Hershey, 1983-88, asst. prof. physiology, 1986-88, assoc. prof. surgery and cellular and molecular physiology, 1988-92; prof. surgery, assoc. chmn. dept. La. State U., New Orleans, 1992—, prof. health svcs. rsch./pub. health, 1994—; prof. neurosci., 1995—; med. dir. St. Charles Weight Mgmt. Ctr. La. State U., New Orleans, 1995—; vis. scientist INSERM, Poste ORange, France, 1990-91; cons. TENET Health Care Corp. MEd. Affairs Dept., 1995—. Mem. editorial bd. Shock, 1994; contbr. articles to newspapers and profl. jours. Recipient Loyal Davis Traveling Surg. scholar ACS, 1990, Clin. Investigator award NIH, 1985-90. Mem. ACS, Am. Coll. Critical Care Medicine, Am. Coll. Physician Execs., Am. Physiol. Soc., Assn. for Acad. Surgery (councilman 1988-90), Collegium Internat. Chirurgiae Digestivae, Soc. Internat. Chirurgie, Soc. Univ. Surgeons. Home: 3005 Palm Vista Dr Kenner LA 70065-1560 Office: La State U Dept Surgery 1542 Tulane Ave New Orleans LA 70112-2825

MARTIN, MARGARET (HILL), vocational school educator; b. N.Y.C., July 26, 1948; d. William Oliver and Marie Terese (Donovan) Hill; m. John Knox Martin, July 24, 1976; children: Troy Wade, Hope Ann, Chris Kyle, John William. BA in Bus. Edn., U. So. Fla., 1972; MEd, Lynchburg Coll., 1992; student, Va. Poly. Inst. and State Univ, 1995—. Cert. tchr., Va. Investigative sec. State Atty.'s Office, Clearwater, Fla., 1972-76, St. Petersburg, Fla., 1978-79; radio dispatcher Pinellas County Sheriff's Dept., Largo, Fla., 1981-86; data entry clk. Mid Coast Mental Health, Rockland, Maine, 1986-87; correctional officer Knox County Sheriff's Dept., Rockland, Maine, 1987, Va. Dept. Corrections, Rustburg, Va., 1988-91; vocat. tchr. Old Dominion Job Corps, Monroe, Va., 1991-95; grad. tng. asst. Va. Tech., Blacksburg, Va., 1995—; adj. faculty Nat. Bus. Coll., Lynchburg, Va., 1992-94. Bd. dirs. Tabor Retreat Ctr., Lynchburg, Va., 1994—; lector, eucharistic min. Holy Cross Ch., Lynchburg, 1993—. Mem. Am. Vocat. Assn., Am. Vocat. Rsch. Assn., Omicron Tau Theta (Va. Tech.), Kappa Delta Pi (pres. 1991—). Roman Catholic. Home: 105 Rainbow Forest Dr Lynchburg VA 24502 Office: Va Tech 214 Lane Hall Blacksburg VA 24061-0254

MARTIN, MARTA N., special education educator; b. Miami, Fla., Apr. 30, 1952; d. Martin Nemerof and Rita Auletta. BA in Psychology, Fla. Atlantic U., 1975; MA, Nova U., Ft. Lauderdale, 1985; student, U. Tenn., 1970-73. Specific learning disability instr. Univ. Sch. of Nova U., 1980-85; dir. edn. Sylvan Learning Ctr., Palm Beach Gardens, Fla., 1987-89; specific learning disabilities tchr. Palm Beach Gardens Elem. Sch., 1989-92; owner, dir. Tutoring and Ednl. Counseling, 1990-96.

MARTIN, MARY COATES, genealogist, writer, volunteer; b. Gloucester County, N.J.; d. Raymond and Emily (Johnson) Coates; m. Lawrence O. Kupillas (dec.); m. Clyde Davis Martin (dec.); 1 child, William Raymond. Contbg. editor Md. & Del. Genealogist, St. Michaels, Md., 1985—. Author: The House of John Johnson (1731-1802) Salem County, N.J. and His Descendants, 1979, Fifty Year History of Daughters of Colonial Wars in the State of New York, 1980, 350 Years of American Ancestors: 38 Families: 1630-1989, 1989, Colonial Families: Martin and Bell Families and Their Kin: 1657-1992, Clifton--Coates Kinfolk and 316 Allied Families, 1995. Pres. Washington Hdqrs. Assn., 1970-73, bd. dirs., 1962—; Centennial pres. Sorosis, Inc., 1966-68; bd. dirs. Soldiers Sailors Airmen's Club, N.Y.C., 1976-81, Yorkville Youth Coun., N.Y.C., 1954-60; co-chmn. Colonial Ball, N.Y.C., 1965-67; rec. sec. Parents League of N.Y., Inc., 1954-57; mem. com. Internat. Debutante Ball, N.Y.C., 1977-81; mem. Am. Flag Inst., N.Y.C., 1963-72. Mem. Hereditary Order of Descendants of Colonial Govs. (gov. gen. 1981-83), Nat. Soc. Colonial Dames of Seventeenth Century (N.Y. State pres. 1977-79, parlimentarian 1979-81), Nat. Soc. Daus. of Colonial Wars (N.Y. State pres. 1977-80), Nat. Soc. DAR (regent 1962-65, pres. roundtable 1964-65, N.Y. State chaplain 1968-71, parliamentarian 1980-83, nat. platform com. 1970-76, certificate of award 1971, nat. vice chmn. lineage rsch. com. 1977-80, geneal. com. 1980-83), Nat. Soc. New Eng. Women (dir. gen. 1972-77, nat. vice chmn. helping hand disbursing fund 1968-71), Order of Crown of Charlemagne U.S.A. (corr. sec. gen. 1985-88, 3rd v.p. 1988-89, 2nd v.p. 1989-91), Nat. Soc. Children Am. Revolution, Nicasius de Sille Soc. (pres. 1960-62), Order Ams. of Armorial Ancestry (1st v.p. gen. 1985-88, councillor gen. 1988—), Nat. Gavel Soc., Nat. Soc. Magna Carta Dames, Descendants of Soc. of Colonial Clergy, Huguenot Soc. Am., Descendants of a Knight of Most Noble Order Garter, Nat. Soc. Daus. Am. Colonists, Nat. Soc. U.S. Daus. 1812, Order of Descendants of Colonial Physicians and Chirurgiens, Plantagenet Soc., Vt. Soc. Colonial Dames, Del. Geneal. Soc., Huguenot Hist. Soc., DuBois Family Assn. (1st v.p.), Cumberland County N.J. Hist. Soc., Gloucester County N.J. Hist. Soc., Md. Hist. Soc., Hist. Soc. Del., Salem County N.J. Hist. Soc., Woodstown-Pilesgrove N.J. Hist. Soc., Hereditary Order First Families of Mass., Inc. Home: Hague Towers # 1815 330 W Brambleton Ave Norfolk VA 23510-1307

MARTIN, MARY EVELYN, advertising, marketing and business writing consultant; b. Lexington, Ky.; d. George Clarke and Georgann Elizabeth (Bovis) M. BA magna cum laude, Lindenwood Coll., 1980; MA with honors, U. Ky., 1991. Asst. to pres. The Hamlets, Ltd/Park Place Country Homes, Louisville, 1984-85; advt. designer, copywriter Park Place Country Homes, Anchorage, Ky., 1985-86; creative dir. of advt., mktg., v.p., treas. Park Place Country Homes/Park Place Properties, Anchorage, Ky., 1986—; founder, pres. Good Help Cons. Svcs., Louisville and Lexington, Maison Marche Advt. & Promotions, Louisville, 1989; instr. dept. English U. Ky., 1989-91; adj. prof. composition U. Louisville, 1991-96; vis. lectr. lit. Bellarmine Coll., Louisville, 1992; adj. prof. humanities Ind. U. S.E., 1991-95; prof. arts and humanities McKendree Coll., Louisville, 1993-96; writer, historian Home Builders Assn. Louisville, 1996. Editor: (poetry mag.) The Griffin, 1979-80; contbr. series to mag., 1996. Mem. People for the Am. Way, Greenpeace. Recipient Spahmer creative writing award, 1979; Haggin fellow U. Ky., 1987; grantee U. Louisville, 1992-95. Mem. Am. Film Inst., Nat. Assn. Home Builders (affiliate), Internat. Platform Assn., Ky. Film Artists Coalition. Democrat. Home: PO Box 23282 Anchorage KY 40223-0282 Office: Park Place Country Homes PO Box 23226 Anchorage KY 40223-0226

MARTIN, MICHAEL REX, lawyer; b. Lawton, Okla., Feb. 16, 1952; s. Rex R. and Mary L. (Smith) M.; m. Janet E. Becker, Aug. 25, 1979; children: Katy, Donnie, Melissa. BS in Bus. Adminstrn., Tulsa U., 1974, JD, 1979. Bar: Okla. 1979, U.S. Dist Ct. (we. dist.) Okla. 1984. Ptnr. Musser, Musser & Martin, Enid, Okla., 1981-85, Crowley, Pickens & Martin, Enid, Okla., 1985—. Republican. Methodist. Office: PO Box 3487 Enid OK 73702-3487

MARTIN, NEIL, lawyer; b. Centralia, Ill., Oct. 9, 1942; s. Robert Floyd and Virginia Dare (Rice) M.; m. Judy Ann Parker, Aug. 29, 1964; children: Lori Ann, Brett Tyson. BBA, Baylor U., 1964, JD, 1967. Bar: Tex. 1967, U.S. Dist. Ct. (no., so. and we. dists.) Tex. 1967, U.S. Ct. Appeals (5th cir.) 1971, U.S. Supreme Ct. 1972. Spl. agent FBI, Birmingham, Ala., 1968-69, St. Louis, 1969-70; assoc. Fulbright & Jaworski, Houston, 1970-77, ptnr., 1977-93; ptnr. Gardere, Wynne, Sewell & Riggs, Houston, 1993—. Mem. ABA, Tex. Bar Assn., Houston Bar Assn., Baylor Alumni Assn, Baylor Law Sch. Alumni Assn. (counselor). Baptist. Office: Gardere Wynne Sewell & Riggs LLP 333 Clay Ave Ste 800 Houston TX 77002

MARTIN, NORMA ANNE HOLMES, electronic technician; b. Long Branch, N.J., May 19, 1948; d. George Washington Holmes and Lillian Dove Wall Collins; m. Jimmie Martin, July 2, 1966 (dec. June 1990); children: Karen Anne, Cynthia Annette Martin Bridges. Student, Brookdale Coll., Lincroft, N.J., 1975-80. Electronic tester Atlantic Semiconductor, Asbury Park, N.J., 1966-68, Intco Telecomms., Neptune, N.J., 1978-80; electrician Port Authority of N.Y. and N.J., N.Y.C., 1980-82; cable tv sales rep. Ultracom Cablevision, Ocean Twp., N.J., 1983-84, Harte Hanks Cable TV, Ocean Twp., N.J., 1984-86; elec. tech. United Telecontrol Electronics, Asbury Park, N.J., 1986-88; pres. Norma's Home Electronic Cons., Richmond, Va., 1992-93; warehouse shipping/receiving Va. Automotive Svc. Corp., Richmond, 1993—. Inventor in field. Mem. Va. Orgn. Composers and Lyricists, Internat. Soc. Poets (disting.). Mormon. Home: 2000 Riverside Dr #9H Richmond VA 23225

MARTIN, PAMELA JANE, educational educator, adminisrator; b. Ft. Worth, Dec. 26, 1958; d. Harold Frank and Mary Jane (Wallace) M. BA, Sam Houston State U., 1981, postgrad., 1984-86. Cert. provisional tchr., Tex., elem. tchr., Tex., secondary tchr., Tex. Tchr. Tomball (Tex.) Ind. Sch. Dist., 1981-84; sec. Tex. A & M U., Coll. Station, 1987-89; tchr. Covenant Christian Sch., Conroe, Tex., 1989-90; vol. tchr. Samoa Bapt. Acad., Pago Pago, Am. Samoa, 1990-91; tchr. Brazos Bus. Coll., Conroe, Tex., 1991-93; tchr. jr. h.s. social studies, bus. Nordheim (Tex.) Ind. Sch. Dist., 1993-95; tchr. jr. h.s. lang. arts Runge (Tex.) Ind. Sch. Dist., 1995-96; owner Tejas y Mas, Goliad, Tex., 1996—; faculty adv. Collegiate Secs. Internat., Conroe, Tex., 1992-93. Dir. (one act play) U. Interscholastic League. Vol. youth dir. First Bapt. Ch., Runge, Tex., 1996—. Mem. Assn. Tex. Profl. Educators (unit pres. 1995—), Goliad County C. of C., Singing Women of S. Tex. Mem. So. Baptist Ch. Home: PO Box 186 232 W Oak Goliad TX 77963 Office: Tejas y Mas PO Box 186 130 N Courthouse Sq Golidad TX 77963

MARTIN, PAUL EDWARD, lawyer; b. Atchison, Kans., Feb. 5, 1928; s. Harres C. and Thelma F. (Wilson) M.; m. Betty Lou Crawford, Aug. 28, 1954; children: Cherry G., Paul A., Marylou. BBA, Baylor U., 1955, LLB, 1956; LLM, Harvard U., 1957. Bar: Tex. 1956, Pa. 1958. Assoc. Ballard, Spahr, Andrews & Ingersoll, Phila., 1957-58; ptnr. Fulbright & Jaworski, Houston, 1959-77; shareholder Chamberlain, Hrdlicka, White, Williams & Martin, 1977—; instr. in estate planning U. Houston. Exec. com. Met. Houston March of Dimes, 1980-82 ; chmn. deacons West Meml. Bapt. Ch., 1979-80; trustee Baylor U., 1970-89, Meml. Hosp. Sys., 1975—, Fgn. Mission Bd., So. Bapt. Conv.; pres. Baylor U. Devel. Coun., 1973-74. Lt. comdr. USN, 1947-53. Fellow Am. Coll. Trust and Estate Coun.; mem. ABA (sect. real property, probate and trust law and sect. taxation), State Bar Tex., Houston Bar Assn., Houston Estate and Fin. Forum (pres. 1965-66), Houston Bus. and Estate Planning Coun., Houston Club, Phi Delta Phi. Republican. Co-author: How to Live and Die with Texas Probate. Office: Chamberlain Hrdlicka White Williams & Martin 2 Allen Ctr 1200 Smith St Houston TX 77002

MARTIN, PAUL LEE, building contractor, consultant; b. Lunchburg, Va., Mar. 28, 1960; s. James Howard and Melinda Florence (Cousins) M.; m. Aleida Elizabeth White, July 23, 1986 (div. 1992); children: Michael Shane, Kaitlan Elizabeth; m. Terrace Anne Martin, July 28, 1993. Student, W.Va. U. Asst. supt. Deltona Constrn. Corp., St. Augustine, Fla., 1980-83; supt. RBT & Assocs., Chantilly, Va., 1983-85; owner So. Craftsman, Lynchburg, Va., 1985-91; bldg. cons. Richmond, Va., 1991—; cons. Youth Devel. Svcs. Inc., Lynchburg, 1985-87. Author songs and poetry. Mem., vol. Food Bank, Lynchburg, 1988-91; vol. Salvation Army Thrift Store, Lynchburg, 1988-91; bd. dirs. Youth Devel. Svcs., Inc., 1984-87; tutor Literacy Vols. Am., Fla., 1982-83, Va., 1983-91; mem. Dem. Nat. Com., 1995—; mem. Clinton/Gore Re-election Steering Com., 1995—. Cpl. USMC, 1977-80. Mem. Vietnam Vets. Am., Cosntrn. Specifications Inst., Am. Soc. Sanitaiton Engrs., marine Corps Assn. Roman Catholic.

MARTIN, PHILIP LEE, ophthalmologist, surgeon; b. Asheboro, N.C., Jan. 21, 1948; s. Paul Edward and Elizabeth (Lee) M. BA, U. N.C., Chapel Hill, 1970, MD, 1973. Intern Geisinger Med. Ctr., Danville, Pa., 1974; resident fellow U. N.C., Chapel Hill, 1975, resident in ophthalmology, 1977-80; fellow in diseases and surgery of the eye Baylor Coll. Medicine, Houston, 1980-81; physician Biscoe Med. Clinic and Montgomery Meml. Hosp., Troy, N.C., 1975-77; ophthalmologist Carolina Eye Assocs., Southern Pines, N.C., 1982; owner, physician, surgeon Carolina Retina Clinic, Raleigh, N.C., 1982-84; owner, physician, surgeon So. Eye Assocs., P.A., Raleigh, N.C., 1984—, owner, dir., surgeon Ophthalmic Surgery Ctr., 1991—; examiner class I Fed. Aviation Med. Examiners, 1981—; clin. asst. prof. dept. ophthalmology Sch. Medicine, U. N.C., Chapel Hill, 1982-90. Contbr. articles to profl. jours. Fellow Internat. Coll. Surgeons, Am. Acad. Ophthalmology; mem. AMA (Physician's Recognition award 1992—), Internat. Assn. Ocular Surgeons (charter), Am. Diabetes Assn., Inc., N.C. Soc. Ophthalmology, N.C. Med. Soc., Montgomery County Med. Soc. (sec. 1975-78), Durham/Orange County Med. Soc., Moore County Med. Soc., Wake County Med. Soc., Alpha Epsilon Delta, Alpha Chi Sigma. Office: So Eye Assocs PA Ophthalmic Surgery Ctr 2801 Blue Ridge Rd Ste 200 Raleigh NC 27607-6474

MARTIN, RALPH HARDING, investor; b. Youngstown, Ohio, Dec. 22, 1923; s. Walter H. and Helen Jane (Metcalf) M.; m. N. Suzanne Scott, July 7, 1945 (div. Sept. 1994); children: Lois Elizabeth Cooper-Martin, Jeffrey Scott. BSChemE, Carnegie Inst. of Tech., 1944, MSChemE, 1948. Cert. profl. engr., Pa. Rsch. and devel. engr., supr. Pitts. Consolid. Coal Co., Library, Pa., 1947-55; gen. mgr. Pitts. Consolid. Chem. Co., Newark, 1955-58; asst. to pres. and v.p. Standard Packaging Corp., N.Y.C., 1958-64; exec. v.p., dir. The Dexter Corp., Windsor Locks, Conn., 1964-85; pvt. investor Stuart, Fla., 1985—. Lt. (j.g.) USNR, 1944-46. Runner-up, Sr. Better Ball, Conn. State Golf Assn., Conn., 1991, runner-up, Sr. Amateur Champion, 1992. Mem. Hartford Sr. Golf Club. (Sr. Champion 1991, 93), Willoughby Golf Club, So. Srs. Golf Assn. Republican. Home and Office: 4439 SE Haig Point Ct Stuart FL 34997-5677

MARTIN, RICHARD KELLEY, lawyer; b. Tulsa, June 30, 1952; s. Richard Loye and Maxine (Kelley) M.; m. Reba Lawson, June 12, 1993; children from previous marriage: R. Kyle, Andrew J. BA, Westminster Coll., 1974; JD, So. Meth. U., 1977. Bar: Tex. 1977, U.S. Tax Ct. 1979. Ptnr. Akin, Gump, Strauss, Hauer & Feld, LLP, Dallas, 1977-95; prnt. Haynes and Boone LLP, Dallas, 1995—. Bd. dirs. Goodwill Industries, Dallas, 1986—, v.p., 1986-91; bd. dirs. Greater Dallas Youth Orchs., 1987-90; bd. dirs., v.p., pres. Big Bros. and Sisters Met. Dallas, 1988-91; bd. dirs. Tejas coun. Girl Scouts U.S. Mem. Tex. Bar Assn., Salesmanship Club Dallas. Republican. Methodist. Office: Haynes and Boone LLP 3100 NationsBank Plz 901 Main St Dallas TX 75202-3714

MARTIN, ROBERT LESLIE, physician; b. Abilene, Tex., Oct. 28, 1934; s. Leslie Resa and Garnet Iva (Brown) M.; m. Henrietta Montgomery, 1956; children: Randal, Christopher. BA, U. Kans., 1956, MD, 1960. Diplomate in clin. pathology Am. Bd. Pathology; diplomate Nat. Bd. Med. Examiners; lic. physician, Calif., Fla. Intern U. Kans., 1960-61, resident and fellow in pathology, 1964-67; asst. prof. pathology Case We. Res. U., Cleve., 1967-78; dir. clin. labs. Univ. Hosps. of Cleve., 1972-76; assoc. prof. pathology U. South Fla., Tampa, 1978-82; chief clin. pathology James A. Haley Vets. Hosp., Tampa, 1978-82; project mgr. Scott Sci. & Tech., Albequerque, N.Mex., 1982-83; physician advisor Profl. Found. for Health Care Inc., Tampa, 1984-89; primary care physician Tampa, Fla., 1986—. Contbr. articles to profl. jours. Fellow Coll. Am. Pathologists; Alpha Omega Alpha, Phi Gamma Delta. Republican. Episcopalian. Home: 15840 Sanctuary Dr Tampa FL 33647-1075

MARTIN, ROBERT O., cardiologist; b. Meridian, Miss., July 9, 1951. MD, Georgetown Sch. of Medicine, 1977. Intern U. Tex., 1977-78; resident Southwestern Med. Sch., 1978-80; cardiology fellow Georgetown U. Med. Ctr., Washington, 1982-84; cardiologist E. Tenn. Heart Cons., Knoxville, 1984—. Fellow Am. Coll. Cardiology; mem. ACP, AMA, Knoxville Acad. Medicine, Tenn. Med. Assn., Alpha Omega Alpha. Office:

E Tenn Heart Cons PC 300 Baptist Med Twr 101 Blount Ave Knoxville TN 37920

MARTIN, ROBERT WILLIAM, econometrician; b. Elizabeth, N.J., Nov. 14, 1961; s. Edward Robert Martin and Vivienne Angela Schaul. BA in English, U. N.C., 1984, BA in Econs., 1985; MA in Econs., Clemson U., 1989. Rsch. asst. dept. econs. Clemson (S.C.) U., 1988-89, lectr., policy analyst Ctr. Policy Studies, 1989-90; econometrician, exec. mgr. Bd. Econ. Advisors, Columbia, S.C., 1990—; cons. Clemson U., 1990; adj. instr. Midlands Tech. Coll., Columbia. Contbr. articles to profl. jours. Mem. Am. Econ. Assn., Nat. Assn. Bus. Economists (Carolinas chpt. regional v.p. and sec.), Omicron Delta Epsilon, Sigma Tau Delta. Home: 933 Paces Run Ct Columbia SC 29223-7951 Office: Bd Econ Advisors Rembert Dennis Buildin Ste 446 Columbia SC 29201

MARTIN, RON, newspaper editor-in-chief. Editor Atlanta Journal-Constitution, Ga. Office: Atlanta Jour-Constn 72 Marietta St PO Box 4689 Atlanta GA 30302-5502*

MARTIN, SHEREE (TAMELA MARTIN), lawyer; b. Russellville, Ala., Nov. 28, 1962; d. Jimmy Colin and Peggy Sue (Aycock) M. BA, U. Ala., Tuscaloosa, 1984, JD, 1987; LLM in Taxation, U. Fla., 1989. Bar: Fla. 1987, Ala. 1988. Atty. Potts & Young, Florence, Ala., 1987-88, Tanner & Guin, Tuscaloosa, 1989, Rosen, Cook, Sledge, Davis, Carroll & Jones, Tuscaloosa, 1992—; sole practice Florence, 1989-92. Chmn. bd. Frank Lloyd Wright Rosenbaum House Found., Florence, 1991-92; bd. dirs. Down Town Florence Unltd., 1991. Mem. Tuscaloosa C. of C. (grad. leadership 1992-93), Tuscaloosa Estate Planning Coun., Delta Zeta (dir. collegiate chpt. 1994—). Republican. Baptist. Office: Rosen Cook Sledge Davis Carroll & Jones 1020 Lurleen B Wallace Blvd N Tuscaloosa AL 35401-2225

MARTIN, SHIRLEY BOGARD, maternal/women's health nurse administrator; b. Samuels, Ky., Sept. 30, 1941; d. Vernie D. and Eliza (Snawder) Bogard; m. Weldon Martin, Aug. 24, 1962; children: Jospeh Kevin, Jeffery Scott. Grad., Louisville Gen. Hosp., 1962; BSN, Bellarmine Coll., 1980; postgrad., U. Louisville. Cert. perinatal nurse. Charge nurse obstetrics Meth. Evang. Hosp., Louisville; continuing edn. coord. Louisville Gen. Hosp.; dir. CareTenders Children's Clinic, Louisville; leadership team Jefferson County Bd. Edn., Louisville, 1980—; lectr. in field. Adv. bd. Link Project-Drug and Alcohol Program for Pregnant Women, Fairdale Edn. Complex Youth Svc. Ctr.; health adv. com. Jefferson County Pub. Schs.; vol. Teenage Parent Program, Ky. Coalition Teenage Pregnancy. Mem. AWHONN, ANA, Ky. Nurses Assn., Dist. Nurses Assn., Internat. Childbirth Educators Assn., Nat. Orgn. Adolescent Pregnancy/Parenting, Alexander Graham Bell Assn. for the Deaf, Nat. Assembly on Sch. Based Health, Sigma Theta Tau. Home: 3125 Pomeroy Dr Louisville KY 40220-3001 Office: 8800 Westport Rd Louisville KY 40242-3124

MARTIN, STACEY, accountant; b. Dallas, Dec. 5, 1951; d. Orval Calvin and Adella Aloise (Morgan) M.; m. Bryan Keith Ellis, Jan. 31, 1987; children: Martin Harrison, Morgan Houston Ellis. BA in Bus. Adminstrn., Austin Coll., 1973; MBA in Acctg., So. Meth. U., 1974. CPA, 1982. Jr. acct. MacIver & Bell, CPA's, Dallas, 1974-76; staff acct. Steak & Ale Restaurants, Inc., Dallas, 1975-76; internal auditor Columbia Gen. Corp., Dallas, 1976-80; tax specialist MARC, Inc., Dallas, 1981—; owner Sallie's Baby, Infant & Toddler Knitwear, 1988—. Mem. Greenland Hills Neighborhood Assn., Dallas, 1983-94, Dallas Heritage Soc., 1987, Dallas Arboretum Soc., 1987. Mem. AICPA, Tex. Soc. CPA's, DAR (treas. White Oak chpt. 1990—), Daus. Republic of Tex. (treas. Peter James Bailey chpt. 1993—). Presbyterian. Office: MARC Inc 7850 N Belt Line Rd Irving TX 75063-6064

MARTIN, THOMAS SHERWOOD, history and political science educator; b. Athens, Ohio, May 18, 1938; s. William Oliver and Grace Dean M.; m. Nancy Joyce Coggeshall, Sept. 12, 1964 (div.). BA, Georgetown U., 1960; MA, Yale U., 1964, U. Chgo., 1965; PhD, U. Toronto, 1972. Lic. real estate profl., Fla. Prof. history and polit. sci. Champlain Coll., Lennoxville, Que., Can., 1972-73; edn. cons. Cape Coral, Fla., 1993—; head dept. history and polit. sci. Champlain Coll., 1972-75; resp. Provincial History Curriculum Com., Que., Can., 1972-92, Provincial Polit. Sci. Curriculum Com., Que., 1980-92; mem. curriculua, hiring coms., Champlain, 1972-92. Editl. bd. The Canadian Forum mag., 1968-70; creator/cons. simulation games, 1972-92; contbr. articles to profl. jours. Mem. Rep. Nat. Com., Washington, 1995-96. Scholar French Govt., Aix-en-Provence, France, 1960-61; fellow Yale U., New Haven, Conn., 1962-64, Earhart fellow Relm Found., U. Chgo., 1964-65, Can. Coun. fellow Can. govt., London, Eng., 1969-71. Mem. Cape Coral Sailing Club (speaker's bur. 1993-96), Ft. Myers Sailing Club (bd. govs. 1993-95). Episcopalian. Home and Office: 617 SE 47th St #6 Cape Coral FL 33904

MARTIN, ULRIKE BALK, laboratory analyst; b. Kelheim, Germany, Oct. 28, 1965; d. Gunther Anton and Elfriede Babette (Eiser) Balk; m. Kent Daniel Martin, May 1, 1988. BS summa cum laude, Stephen F. Austin State U., Nacogdoches, Tex., 1992; MS, 1994. Lab. analyst Eastman Chem. Co., Longview, Tex., 1994—. Author: An Analysis of Heavy Metals on Forest Stream Ecosystems Receiving Run Off from an Oil Field, 1992. Mem. Tex. Acad. Sci., Sigma Xi. Home: 3019 B Tryon Rd Longview TX 75605

MARTIN, VIRVE PAUL, licensed professional counselor; b. Tallinn, Estonia, Nov. 19, 1928; came to U.S., 1949; d. Walter Gerhard and Alice (Haas) Paul; m. Albert Lynn Martin Jr., May 31, 1952; children: Lynda Lee, Elaine Lynne, Monique Louise. Student, U. Heidelberg, Germany, 1948-49; BA, Wesleyan Coll., Macon, Ga., 1952; MA, U. Minn., 1970. Cert. profl. counselor, Ga. Interpreter Internat. Refugee Orgn., Nuremberg, Frankfurt, Heidelberg, Fed. Republic of Germany, 1947-49; bookkeeper, receptionist DeKalb Nat. Bank, Atlanta, 1955-56; rsch. asst. Kenny Inst., Mpls., 1966-67; vocat. evaluator Dept. Human Resources, Atlanta, 1970-73, rehab. counselor, 1973—; interpreter Mpls. C. of C., 1963-65, Dem. Nat. Conv., Atlanta, 1988; attaché Estonian Olympic Com. 1996 Olympics, Atlanta. Writer, editor World Pen Pals, 1964-66. V.p., bd. dirs. Ms. JCs, Minn., 1959-62; pres. Valley View Mothers' Club, Bloomington, Minn., 1961-62. Mem. AAUW, Nat. Rehab. Assn., Ga. Rehab. Assn. (membership chair 1988), Ga. Mental Health Counselors Assn. Home: 1106 Norwich Cir NE Atlanta GA 30324-2908 Office: Dept Rehab Svc 1800 Peachtree St NW Ste 444 Atlanta GA 30309-2505

MARTIN, WAYNE A., clinical social worker; b. N.Y.C., Jan. 26, 1945; s. Bernard and Juliet (Aurbach) M.; m. Barbara Jo Goodman, Aug. 16, 1970; 1 child, Jason David. BA in Social Sci., Fla. State U., 1966; MS, Columbia U., 1968; postgrad. Old Dominion U., 1978—. Lic. clin. social worker, Va., cert. diplomate. Day camp dir. Jewish Cmty. Ctr., Norfolk, Va., 1968-71, children's dept. dir., 1968-69, youth dept. dir., 1969-71; psychiat. social worker Psychiat. Assocs., Ltd., Portsmouth, Va., 1971-77; clin. social worker Human Resource Inst., Norfolk, 1977-79; part-time caseworker Cath. Home Bur., Hampton, Va., 1977-78; primary therapist Charter Colonial Inst., Newport News, Va., 1980-91; pvt. practice clin. social work, Virginia Beach, Norfolk and Newport News, 1980—; program coord. for adolescent psychiat. unit Peninsula Psychiat. Hosp., Hampton, Va., 1979-80; field supr. Va. Commonwealth U. Sch. Social Work, 1978-84, Norfolk State U. Sch. Social Work, 1982—; chmn. adv. com. Upjohn Health-care Svcs., 1979-80; dir. social svcs. Colonial Hosp., Newport News, 1995—; oral examiner/adviser Va. Bd. Social Work. Chmn., Crisis Ctr., 1977-78; pres. Arnold Gamsey Lodge of B'Nai B'rith, 1975-77; 1st v.p. B'nai Brith, Va. State Assn., 1977-78, pres., 1979-80, mem. B'Nai B'rith dist. 5 bd. govs., 1978—, 3d v.p./treas. dist. 5, 1983-84, 1st v.p., 1985-86, pres.-elect 1986-87, pres. 1987-88, chmn. dist. 5 personnel com., bd. govs. B'nai B'rith Internat., 1986-88, 94—; chmn. Hillel Found. for State of Va., 1978-79, 90—; bd. dirs. Jewish Community Ctr., Norfolk, 1973-79, Anti-Defamation League; exec. bd. Temple Israel Synagogue, 1981-84, pres. Men's Club, 1981-82, temple sec., 1982-84. Recipient Charles Olshansky Lodge Svc. award B'nai Brith, 1991, Outstanding Svc. Presdl. citation, 1991; named Outstanding Lodge Pres., B'nai Brith, 1977, Outstanding State Pres., 1980, Man of Yr., Va. State Assn. B'nai B'rith, 1980. Mem. NASW (v.p. Hampton Roads unit 1974-76, dist. chmn. 1982-83 state dir. 1977-83), Va. Soc. Clin. Social Work (bd. dirs. Ea. Va. chpt. 1989-96, pres. 1991-95), Nat. Fed. Socs. Clin. Social Work (bd. dirs. 1991-95), Acad. Cert. Social Workers (bd. cert. diplomate), ACLU, Kappa Delta Pi, Phi Alpha Theta, Pi Sigma Alpha. Democrat. Jewish. Club: Mogul Ski (v.p. 1970-71) (Norfolk). Home: 1827 Longdale Dr Norfolk VA 23518-4943 also: Colonial Practice Assocs 708 Mobjack Pl Newport News VA 23606

MARTIN, WAYNE MALLOTT, lawyer; b. Chgo., Jan. 9, 1950; s. Mallott Caldwell and Helen (Honkisz) M.; m. Jo Ann Giordano, Mar. 18, 1978; 1 child, Bradley. BA, Drake U., 1972; JD, DePaul U., 1977. Bar: Ill. 1978, U.S. Dist. Ct. (7th dist.) Ill. 1978. Dir. sales Inland Real Estate Corp., Chgo., 1977-78; asst. v.p. Inland Real Estate Corp., Oak Brook, Ill., 1979; v.p. Inland Real Estate Corp., 1980-81; pres. Inland Property Sales Corp., Palatine, Ill., 1981-85; sr. v.p. Inland Investment Corp., Oak Brook, 1985-86, Bramar Mortgage Corp., Long Grove, 1987-90; prin. IMA Ltd., Stuart, Fla., 1990—. Trustee, Chgo. Realtors Polit. Action Com. Mem. ABA, Ill. Bar Assn., Chgo. Bar Assn., Nat. Assn. Realtors, Ill. Assn. Realtors, Chgo. Bd. Realtors (bd. dirs. 1986-88), West Side Real Estate Bd. (bd. dirs. 1982-84, pres. 1984-88, gen. counsel 1988-90), Chicagoland Assn. Real Estate Bds. (chmn. 1987-88), Fla. Assn. Realtors, Martin County Bd. Realtors. Office: IMA Ltd 1806 Glenview Rd Glenview IL 60025-2910

MARTIN, WILLIAM COLLIER, hospital administrator; b. Atlanta, Aug. 16, 1926; s. William Henry and Lillian (Collier) M.; BS, U. Ga., 1950; diploma Charlotte Meml. Hosp., 1952; postgrad. U. Okla., 1969; m. Alice Elizabeth Nickle, Jan. 12, 1952; children: Mary Anne, Patricia Jean, William Collier, Nancy Lee. Operating room technician Athens (Ga.) Gen. Hosp., 1949-50; hosp. adminstrn. intern/resident Charlotte (N.C.) Meml. Hosp., 1950-52; hosp. adminstr. Rockmart-Aragon Hosp., Rockmart, Ga., 1952-54; asst. hosp. adminstr. St. Agnes Hosp., Raleigh, N.C., 1954-56; hosp. adminstr. Florence-Darlington Tb. Sanitorium, Florence, S.C., 1956-58; commd. 1st lt. MSC, U.S. Army, 1959, advanced through grades to lt. col.; adj. U.S. Army Hosp., Ft. Campbell Ky., 1959; comdg. officer med. co. U.S. Army Hosp., 1959-61; comdg. officer U.S. Army Med. Svc. Detachment, Ft. Gulick, C.Z., 1961-64; exec. officer 5th Evacuation Hosp., Ft. Bragg, N.C., 1964, comdg. officer, 1964-65; adj. personnel officer 55th Med. Group, Ft. Bragg, 1965-66, Qui Nhon, Republic Vietnam, 1966-67; comdg. officer 47th Gen. Hosp., Fitzsimons Gen. Hosp., Denver, 1967-68; exec. officer Evans Health Care Facility, Ft. Buckner, Okinawa, 1968-69; dir. security plans and ops. U.S. Army Med. Ctr., Camp Kue, Okinawa, 1969-71; med. ops. officer VII Corps, Moehringen, W.Ger., 1971-73; chief tng., exercises and readiness U.S. Army Med. Command, Europe, Heidelberg, W.Ger., 1973-74; dir. security plans and tng. Fitzsimons Army Med. Ctr., 1974-77, ret., 1977; guest lectr. health care adminstrn. U.S. Army Med. Command in Europe, 1973-74; exec. dir. Thomas Rehab. Hosp., Asheville, N.C., 1977-78; chmn. Pub. Health Trust of Escambia County, Pensacola, Fla., 1979-86; guest lectr. to profl. assns., civic orgns. and mil. units, 1965—; mem. N.C. Gov.'s Adv. Com. on Rehab. Ctrs., 1977-78; mem. regional Hospice Program for NW Fla., Inc., 1979-80, chmn., bd. dirs., 1980-83, exec. dir., 1983-85; mgmt. cons. Pensacola (Fla.) Habatat for Humanity, Inc., 1986-88, Niceville (Fla.) Mktg. Resources, 1986-87, Dan Laumpking Mgmt. Cons., Fairhope, Ala., 1986-87. Mem. Pres.'s Com. on Employment of the Handicapped, 1978; sec. United Meth. Bd. Pastoral Care and Counseling, 1988-90; mem., v.p., bd. ministries Pensecola Dist. United Meth. Ch., Inc., 1988—; dir. lay speaking, bd. laity, council on ministries Ala.- West Fla. Conf. United Meth. Ch., 1988—; mem. Health and Human Services task force of citizens goals for Pensacola, 1981-86; vice chmn. adminstrv. bd. Pine Forest United Meth. Ch., Pensacola, 1979-86; mem. fin. com., 1979-86; dir. for lay speaking Pensacola Dist. United Meth. Ch., 1985-88; bd. dirs. Hispanic Minorities, Inc., 1986-93, Meth. Homes for the Aging, Inc., 1988—, Pastoral Counseling, Care and Tng., Inc., 1990-95. Served with USN, 1944-46. Decorated Legion of Merit, Bronze Star; Vietnam Royal Cross of Gallantry with bronze palm; cert. lay speaker of United Meth. Ch. Fellow Am. Acad. Med. Adminstrs.; mem. Am. Soc. Tng. and Devel. (dir. 1977-78), Ret. Officers Assn., Assn. of U.S. Army (dir. Denver-Centennial chpt. 1974-77, Greater Gulf Coast chpt. 1979-86), U.S. Power Squadrons, V.F.W., Phi Delta Theta. Democrat. Club: Masons.

MARTIN, WILLIAM HAYWOOD, ecologist, scientist; b. Bath Springs, Tenn., Nov. 29, 1938; s. William Haywood and Mary (Isbell) M.; m. Julia Frances Silbar; children: Thomas, Marianne. BS, Tenn. Tech. U., 1960; MS, U. Tenn., 1966, PhD, 1971. Prof. Eastern Ky. U., Richmond, 1969—; adminstr. Ea. Ky. U., 1977—; commr. Ky. Dept. Natural Resources, Frankfort, 1992-96; cons. The Nature Conservancy, Arlington, Va., 1975, U.S. Nat. Park Svc., 1976-83, U.S. Forest Svc., 1988—. Editor: Biodiversity of the Southeastern United States, 1993. Mem. Ky. River Authority, Frankfort, 1992—; co-chair Ky. Biodiversity Task Force, 1994-95. Named Ky. Wildlife Conservationist of Yr., League of Ky. Sportsmen, 1977; recipient Disting. award Ky. Assn. Conservation Dists., 1995, Pub. Svc. Earth Day award Ky. Environ. Quality Commn., 1996. Mem. Ecol. Soc. Am., Assn. Southeastern Biologists (pres. 1988-89), Southern Appalachian Botanical Soc. (pres. 1985-86), Freemasons, Scottish Rite, Shriners. Democrat. Home: 3508 Trails End Lexington KY 40517-2017 Office: Dept Natural Resources 663 Teton Trl Frankfort KY 40601-1758

MARTIN, WILLIAM RAYMOND, retired financial manager; b. Phila., Oct. 16, 1939; s. Clyde Davis and Mary Anna (Coates) M.; m. Michaela Smink, Sept. 8, 1962 (div. 1969); 1 child, James; m. Margaret Scouten, Oct. 16, 1970 (div. 1983); children: Mary Frances, Susanna; m. Joan Friedman Kennedy, Jan. 29, 1988. BSME, Lehigh U., 1960; MBA, U. Pa., 1973. Mem. engring. staff Pa. R.R., 1960-65; asst. gen. mgr. Excelsior Truck Leasing, Phila., 1965-71; sr. analyst Assn. Am. R.R.s, Washington, 1973-76, mgr. engring. econ., 1976-78; mgr. fin. analysis So. Ry., Washington, 1978-83; dir. fin. planning Norfolk So. Corp., Va., 1984-92; asst. v.p. fin. Norfolk So. Corp., 1992-95. Contbr. articles to profl. jours. Bd. dirs. The Williams Sch., Norfolk, 1988-96, pres., 1992-96, bd. dirs. Va. Stage Co., Norfolk, 1995—. Mem. ASME, Soc. Automotive Engrs., The Harbor Club. Home: 2725 River Rd Virginia Beach VA 23454-1210

MARTIN, WILLIAM ROBERT, accountant; b. Cocoa, Fla., Nov. 26, 1927; s. Roy Nmi and Ella (Barton) M.; m. Lurline Lillian Powell, Apr. 30, 1954; children: Lurline Lillian, Nancy Louise, William Robert, Jr. BA in Acctg., Stetson U., 1949. CPA, Fla. Staff acct. Potter, Loucks & Bower, CPAs, Orlando, 1949-51; in-svc. auditor Army Audit Agy., Atlanta, 1951-53; sr. acct. Potter, Bower & Co., CPAs, Orlando, 1954-55; ptnr. Kurtz and Martin, CPAs, Orlando, 1956-68, Osburn, Henning & Co., CPA, Orlando, 1968-92; mem. Bd. of Accountancy Dept. Profl. Regulation, 1987-92, vice chmn. 1989, chmn. 1990; adj. faculty Valencia Community Coll. Acctg. Founding treas., past bd. dirs. Orlando Opera Co., Inc.; bd. dirs., fin. advisor Open Door Mission, Inc.; treas. Bill McCollum for Congress, 1982—; v.p., bd. dirs. Cen. Fla. Crew Boosters Assn., Inc., 1979-81; charter dir. Cen. Fla. Crime Watch Program, Inc., 1977-79; mem. Fla. Symphony Orch., Inc., Assoc. Bd., 1959-72; active Indsl. Devel. Commn. Mid-Fla., 1977-89; past treas., bd. dirs. United Cerebral Palsy Orange County, 1960-64, We Care, Inc., 1971. Mem. AICPA (mem. legis. key contact program), Fla. Inst. CPAs (founding chmn., local practitioners com., chmn. pub. rels. com., 1984-85), Nat. Assn. Bds. Accountancy administrv. and fin. com. 1991—), Greater Orlando C. of C. (bd. dirs. 1985, asst. v.p. fin. 1986, v.p. fin. 1987). Republican. Presbyterian. Office: Osburn Henning & Co CPAs 617 E Colonial Dr Orlando FL 32803-4602

MARTIN, WILLIAM ROYALL, JR., association executive; b. Raleigh, N.C., Sept. 3, 1926; s. William Royall and Edith Ruth (Crocker) M.; m. Betty Anne Rader, June 14, 1952; children: Sallie Rader Martin Busby, Amy Kemp Martin Lewis. AB, U. N.C., 1948, MBA, 1964; BS, N.C. State U., 1952. Chemist Stamford (Conn.) rsch. labs. Am. Cyanamid Co., 1952-54; chemist Dan River Mills, Danville, Va., 1954-56, Union Carbide Corp., South Charleston, W.Va., 1956-59; rsch. assoc. Sch. Textiles N.C. State U., 1959-63; tech. dir. Am. Assn. Textile Chemists and Colorists, Research Triangle Park, N.C., 1963-73, exec. dir., 1974-96; adj. asst. prof. Coll. Textiles, N.C. State U., 1966-88, adj. assoc. prof., 1989—; del. Internat. Orgn. Standardization, Pan Am. Standards Commn. With USNR, 1944-46. Fellow Am. Inst. Chemists, Soc. Dyers and Colourists, Textile Inst.; mem. Am. Chem. Soc., Coun. Engring. and Sci. Soc. Execs. (past pres. 1992-93), Fiber Soc., Am. Assn. Textile Chemists and Colorists, Masons, Rotary, Phi Kappa Phi, Phi Gamma Delta. Methodist. Home and Office: 224 Briarcliff Ln Cary NC 27511-3901

MARTINDALE, CARLA JOY, librarian; b. Ladysmith, Wis., Sept. 9, 1947; d. Howard Walter and Audrey Elizabeth (Stanton) M. BA, Mt. Senario Coll., 1970; MLIS, U. South Fla., 1990. Sch. librarian Blackhawk Schs., South Wayne, Ind., 1975-79; librarian Osceola County Libr., Kissimee, Fla., 1989-90, Fla. Tech. Coll., Orlando, 1991-92, Orlando Coll. South, 1993—; chair for libr. 21st curriculum Phillips Coll., Orlando, 1995, acad. com., 1993—, accreditation steering com., 1996. Library named in her honor Orlando Coll. South, 1995. Mem. Fla. Libr. Assn. Home: 705 Bear Way Kissimmee FL 34759 Office: Orlando Coll South 2411 Sand Lake Rd Orlando FL 32809-7641

MARTINEAU, JULIE PEPERONE, social worker; b. Kilgore, Tex., Oct. 31, 1956; d. Angelo Gerad and Jane Margaret (Reppel) Peperone; m. Russell Joseph Martineau, Dec. 30, 1950; children: Adria Helen, Brittany Jane. AA, Marymount Palos Verdes Coll., Calif., 1976; BA, Calif. State U., Long Beach, 1979. Staff cons. United Way of L.A., 1979-83; group mgr. United Way of the Tex. Gulf Coast, Houston, 1983; dir. cmty. devel. Tri-County Mental Health and Mental Retardation Svcs., Conroe, Tex., 1984-87; exec. dir. Montgomery County Com. on Aging, Conroe, 1987—; chmn. South Montgomery County Healthier Cmty. Forum, Conroe, 1996—; chmn. Project CARE Monitoring Coun., Conroe, 1989—; mem. long term care task force Tex. Health and Human Svcs. Commn., Austin, 1993-95; mem. aging programs adv. coun. Houston-Galveston Area Coun., 1987—; mem. aging and disabled adv. coun. Dept. Human Svcs., Houston, 1993—. Bd. dirs. Conroe Regional Med. Ctr., 1993—, United Way of Montgomery County, Conroe, 1984-87; congl. del. 1995 White House Conf. on Aging; chmn. Leadership Montgomery County, 1995—; v.p. Bluebonnet chpt. Nat. Charity League. Named Oustanding Woman of Yr., YWCA of Montgomery County, 1990, recipient awards. Mem. John Ben Sheperd Leadership Forum, Leadership Conroe, Area Agy. on Aging Execs. Network, South Montgomery C. of C. (chmn. bd. 1992-93), LWV of Montgomery County (pres. 1990-92, v.p. 1995—). Roman Catholic. Office: Montgomery County Com Aging 39 W Mistybreeze The Woodlands TX 77381

MARTINELLI, LAWRENCE PHILLIP, infectious diseases physician; b. Sacramento, Sept. 11, 1959; s. Phillip C. and Eva M. (Taverna) M.; m. Brigitte Curtis, June 25, 1985. BS in Biology, U. Santa Clara, 1981; MD, Med. Coll. Wis., 1985. Intern St. Joseph Hosp., Denver, 1985-86, resident in internal medicine, 1986-88; fellow in infectious diseases Med. U. S.C., Charleston, 1988-90; infectious diseases physician Med. Assoc., p.a., Charleston, 1990-93, Cons. in Infectious Diseases, Lubbock, Tex., 1993—; chmn. pharmacy and therapeutics com. Roper Hosp., Charleston, 1993; asst. clin. prof. medicine Tex. Tech. Health Scis. U., Lubbock, 1993—. Active task force on AIDS S.C. Med. Assn., Columbia, 1991-92. Mem. AMA, ACP, Am. Soc. for Microbiology, Infectious Diseases Soc. Am., Alpha Sigma Nu, Alpha Omega Alpha. Office: Cons in Infectious Diseases PO Box 16327 Lubbock TX 79490-6327

MARTINEZ, CHRISTOPHER DAMON, journalist, novelist; b. Orange, Calif., Feb. 18, 1960; s. Manuel Oliver and Angela Marie (Perko) M. AA, Hillsborough Community Coll., 1980; BA, U. South Fla., 1991. Reporter, photographer Oracle Newspaper, Tampa, Fla., 1979-80, Laker Newspaper, Land O'Lakes, Fla., 1980-84; acting news dir. WDCF-AM, Dade City, Fla., 1983-84; corrs. Fla. Catholic Newspaper, St. Petersburg, Fla., 1980-84; bureau chief Fla. Catholic Newspaper, Pensacola, Fla., 1984-93; free-lance journalist, 1993—. Author: Come The Dawn, 1994. Recipient 1st Place award Catholic Press Assn., 1992, 2nd Place award Best Feature, 1993. Republican. Roman Catholic. Home and Office: 22117 River Rock Dr Land O'Lakes FL 34639-4631

MARTINEZ, ERNESTO, III, sales professional; b. Brownsville, Tex., Sept. 15, 1953; s. Ernesto Jr. and Irene (Mendez) M.; m. Joslyn Elaine Snider, June 15, 1974; children: Eric Wayne, Adam Eugene. AA, San Antonio Coll., 1975. Salesman Sears Roebuck and Co., San Antonio, 1973-90; sales mgr. Am. Remodeling Inc., 1990—. Participated in Sears tng. video The Sales Pros, 1987. Bd. of elders Concordia Luth. Ch., San Antonio, 1987. Recipient Great Salesperson award Hall of Fame, 1987-88, Top Five award Sears Roebuck & Co.; named Sales Mgr. of Yr. Am. Remodeling Inc., 1993; mem. Million Dollar Sales Club, 1986-87. Mem. Exec. Sales Club Home Improvement Products and Services. Home: 1405 Vista Del Monte San Antonio TX 78216-2236 Office: Am Remodeling Inc 3031 Interstate Dr San Antonio TX 78219-1708

MARTINEZ, JOE LOUIS, JR., neurobiologist; b. Albuquerque, Aug. 1, 1944; s. Joe Louis and Maria Elena (Werner) M.; m. Janice Susanna Hepner, Sept. 17, 1967 (div. Oct. 1987); children: Adan, Adria, Aric; m. Kimberly Smith, Dec. 2, 1990; 1 child, Ariel. BA, U. San Diego, 1966; MS, N.Mex. Highlands U., 1968; PhD, U. Del., 1971. From asst. to assoc. prof. Calif. State U., San Bernardino, 1971-75; assoc. researcher U. Calif., Irvine, 1975-82; prof. U. Calif., Berkeley, 1982-94; prof., dir. divsn. life scis. U. Tex., San Antonio, 1994—. Mem. AAAS (lifetime mentor award 1994), APA (pubs. and comms. bd. 1993—). Office: U Tex San Antonio 6900 N Loop 1604 W San Antonio TX 78249

MARTÍNEZ, LUÍS OSVALDO, radiologist, educator; b. Havana, Cuba, Nov. 27, 1927; came to U.S., 1962, naturalized, 1967; s. Osvaldo and Felicita (Farinas) M.; children: María Elena, Luís Osvaldo, Alberto Luis; m. Nydia M. Ceballos. MD, U. Havana, 1954. Intern Calixto García Hosp., Havana, 1954-55; resident in radiology Jackson Meml. Hosp., Miami, Fla., 1963-65, fellow in cardiovascular radiology, 1965-67; instr. radiology U. Miami, 1965-68, asst. prof., 1968, clin. asst. prof., 1968-70, assoc. prof., 1970-76, prof., 1976-91, clin. prof., 1991-94; chief radiol. svcs. VA Med. Ctr., 1991—; assoc. dir. dept. radiology Mt. Sinai Med. Ctr., Miami Beach, Fla., 1969-91, chief div. diagnostic radiology, 1970-91, dir. residency program in diagnostic radiology; dir. Spanish Radiology Seminar. Reviewer Am. Jour. Radiology, Radium Therapy and Nuclear Medicine, 1978; contbr. articles to profl. jours. Former pres. League Against Cancer. Recipient Gold medal Interam. Coll. Radiology, 1975, Carlos J. Finlay Gold medal Cuban Med. Convb., 1990, Honors Achievement award, Cert. of Merit Mallinckrodt Pharms., 1972-74. Mem. AMA (Physician's Recognition award 1971, 74-83), AAUP, Radiol. Soc. France (hon. 1991), Internat. Soc. Lymphology, Interam. Coll. Radiology (pres.), Internat. Coll. Surgeons, Internat. Coll. Angiology, Internat. Soc. Radiology, Cuban Med. Assn. in Exile, Am. Coll. Chest Physicians (assoc.), Radiol. Soc. N.Am., Am. Coll. Radiology, Am. Roentgen Ray Soc., Am. Assn. Fgn. Med. Grads., Am. Profl. Practice Assn., Am. Thoracic Soc., Pan Am. Med. Assn., Am. Assn. Univ. Radiologists, Brit. Inst. Radiology, Am. Heart Assn. (mem. council cardiovascular radiology), Faculty Radiologists, Soc. Gastrointestinal Radiologists, Am. Geriatrics Soc., Am. Coll. Angiology, Royal Coll. Radiologists, Am. Soc. Therapeutic Radiologists, Assn. Hosp. Med. Edn., Am. Coll. Med. Imaging, Interasma, So. Med. Assn., N.Y. Acad. Scis., Fla. Thoracic Soc., Fla. Radiol. Soc., Dade County Med. Assn., Greater Miami Radiol. Soc., Cuban Radiol. Soc. (sec.), Can. Assn. Radiologists, Soc. Thoracic Radiologists (founding mem.), Emeritus mem., Am. Coll. of Angiology, 1989, Emeritus mem., Am. Heart Assn., 1992; hon. mem. numerous med. socs. of Mex., Cen. and S.Am. Roman Catholic. Office: 1201 NW 16th St Miami FL 33125-1624

MARTINEZ, MARIA DOLORES, pediatrician; b. Cifuentes, Cuba, Mar. 16, 1959; d. Demetrio and Alba Silvia (Perez) M.; m. James David Marple, Apr. 25, 1992. MD, U. Navarra, Pamplona, Spain, 1984. Med. diplomate. Resident in pediatrics Moses Cone Hosp., Greensboro, N.C., 1986-89; pvt. practice Charlotte, N.C., 1989-93, Mooresville, N.C., 1993-96; pediat. pulmonary fellow Univ. Med. Hosp., Tucson. Mem. AMA, Am. Acad. Pediatrics, N.C. Med. Soc., Mecklenburg County Med. Soc. Republican. Roman Catholic. Office: Univ Med Hosp 1501 Campbell Ave Tucson AZ 85741

MARTINEZ, MARIA LEONOR, translator, counselor, educator; b. Cali, Colombia, Mar. 12, 1948; came to U.S., 1960, naturalized, 1984; d. Alfonso Martinez-Arizabaleta and Angela Esther (Rengifo) Martinez. BA, Inst. Cath. Paris, Madrid, 1976; MA in Community Counseling, Barry U., Miami Shores, Fla., 1992; postgrad., F.I.U., 1994. Asst. to owner export-import firm Navios Madrid, 1978; med. staff coord. dept. oncology U. Miami, Fla., 1978-79; mgr. travel wholesale ops. OK Tours, Miami Beach, Fla., 1979-80; sec., pharmacist asst. Miami Heart Inst., Miami Beach, 1980-81; computer operator Investors', Inc., Coral Gables, Fla., 1981-82; asst. to pres. Barcelo

Internat. Corp. subs. Fontes & Fontes Assocs. Inc., Miami, 1983-87; owner Polypholologie Trans. Svcs., Miami Beach, 1986—; legal sec. Alan M. Fisher Law Firm, South Miami, Fla., 1988; exec. officer, translator Servihotels Corp. subs. Fontes & Fontes Assocs. Inc., Miami, 1988-90; asst. to internat. area mgr. Parfums Givenchy, Miami, 1990—; part-time French tchr. Holy Cross Acad., 1991-93; counselor intern Regis House Adolescent Treatment Ctr., Miami, 1992; case mgr. Youth Co-Op, Inc., Tng. and Employment Coun., Miami, 1994—. Mem. ACA, Dade County Counselor's Assn., Club Campestre de Cali (hon.), Sacred Heart Alumni Assn. Roman Catholic. Home and Office: 3440 Garden Ave Miami FL 33140-3824

MARTINEZ, MELQUIADES R. (MEL MARTINEZ), lawyer; b. Sagua La Grande, Cuba, Oct. 23, 1946; came to U.S., 1962, naturalized, 1971; s. Melquiades C. and Gladys V. (Ruiz) M.; m. Kathryn Tindal, June 13, 1970; children: Lauren Elizabeth, John Melquiades, Andrew Tindal. BA, Fla. State U., 1969, JD, 1973. Bar: Fla. 1973, U.S. Dist. Ct. (mid. dist.) Fla. 1973, U.S. Supreme Ct. 1979, U.S. Dist. Ct. (so. dist.) Fla. 1986; cert. Nat. Bd. Trial Advocacy, civil trial atty. Fla. Ptnr., Martinez, Dalton, Dellecker and Wilson, P. (and predecessor firms), Orlando, Fla., 1973—. Bd. dirs. Cath. Social Svcs. Orlando, 1978-86; chmn. Mayor's Hispanic Adv. Com., Orlando, 1981-82; chmn. bd. commrs. Orlando Housing Authority, 1983-86; commr. Orlando Utilities Commn., 1992—, pres., 1995—. Mem. Fla. Bar (bd. govs. young lawyers sect. 1980-81), Acad. Fla. Trial Lawyers (dir. 1981-85, treas. 1986-87, pres. 1988-89), 9th Jud. Cir. (jud. nomination commn. 1986). Roman Catholic. Office: 719 Vassar St Orlando FL 32804-4920

MARTINEZ, PETE R., beverage company executive; b. San Antonio, July 8, 1937; m. Aurora Valadez; children: Shirley Jeanne, Peter Roland, Frieda Ann, Ruben Jay and Lynn Virginia (twins). A in Mgmt., San Antonio Coll., 1974. Various positions Coca-Cola Bottling Co. of S.W., San Antonio, 1952-79, v.p., 1979, BEVTEX gen. mgr., 1979-84, spl. events/concessions/ youth market depts. mgr., 1984-86, spl. events/concessions/ice/youth market/cold drink telephone sales and cooler depts. mgr., 1986-87, v.p. govt. and cmty. rels., 1987—; chmn. U.S. Hispanic Bus. Bilateral Commn. on Free Trade Agreement, 1990—. Vol. United Way San Antonio, 1979, bd. dirs. 1989-96; mem. adv. com. San Antonio Coll. Mgmt., 1984-91; bd. dirs. Leukemia Soc. Am., 1985, v.p., 1986, pres. S.W. Tex. chpt., 1987, 88, 89; chmn. nat. hispanic leukemia televent, 1990, treas., 1990-91, nat. bd. trustee class A, 1988-92; bd. dirs. Goodwill Industries of San Antonio, 1985-90, vice chmn., 1991-94, bd. chmn., 1995-96; bd. dirs. Jr. Achievement South Tex., 1985-94, chmn., 1995, Keep San Antonio Beautiful, 1987-94, chmn. legis. com., 1990; chmn. found. bd. dirs. Alamo Cmty. Coll. Dist., 1985, 94, vice chmn., 1986-95; commr. San Antonio Fiesta Commn./Ann. Fiesta Week, 1986-91, v.p., chmn. pub. rels. com., 1989, mem. exec. bd. presdl. appointee, 1990, mem. exec. bd. treas. and chmn. finance com., 1991, mem. exec. bd. sr. v.p.-chmn., 1992, mem. pers. com., pres. 1993, mem. exec. bd. cmty. rels. and nominating com., 1994; mem. distribution com. San Antonio Area Found., 1985-92, treas. exec. com., 1994-95; so. sector task force chmn. City of San Antonio, 1985-86, bd. dirs. Citizens for Dome, 1988-89, bd. dirs. Inst. Ams.; mem. fgn. trade and transp. com. San Antonio Target Commn. 1983-84; mem. awards selection panel J.C. Penny Golden Rule Awards, Bexar County, Tex., 1988, 89; bd. dirs. North San Antonio Chamber, 1988-91, vice chmn. cmty. devel., 1989, 91, YMCA of San Antonio & Hill Country, 1989-90, vice chmn. pub. policy 1990, vice chmn. bd. devel., 1991, vice chmn. ptnrs. in youth 1992-94, bd. chmn. 1993, 94; mem. pub. policy com. YMCA of Tex., 1989-94, bd. dirs. YMCA of U.S.A., 1994-96; Assumption Sem. Press area chmn. Papal Visit Pope John Paul II, 1989; mem. corporate adv. coun. to sch. bd. Ursuline Acad., 1989-91. Recipient Leadership award Jr. Achievement San Antonio, 1989, Corporate Sponsor of Yr. award Keep San Antonio Beautiful, 1989. Mem. Tex. Soft Drink Assn., San Antonio Mex.-Am. Profl. Men's Assn. (bd. dirs. 1985, 86, v.p. 1987), U.S. Hispanic C. of C. (bd. dirs. 1980, mem. adv. bd. 1981, Member of Yr. award 1984, Corp. Adv. of Yr. award 1990), Tex. Assn. Mex. C. of C. (San Antonio rep. 1976-92, chmn. conv. 1980, 92, state chmn. bd. dirs. 1980-81, 86-87, 87-88, spl. advisor to chmn. 1989-92, Pres. award 1980), San Antonio Hispanic C. of C. (bd. dirs. 1975-77, 81, 82, 84, 1st v.p. 1978, 3d v.p. 1979, 2d v.p. 1980, co-chmn. conv. 1985, 86, adv. to chmn. bd. dirs. 1987-91, bd. historian 1992, bd. chair advisor 1996), Greater San Antonio C. of C. (mem. Internat./Mex. Day Stock Show com. 1976-93, chmn. com. 1980-85, mem. steering com. econ. devel. coun. 1980, 81), San Antonio Downtown Rotary. Office: Coca-Cola Bottling Co SW 1 Coca Cola Pl San Antonio TX 78219-3712

MARTINEZ, RICHARD DANIEL, computer programmer; b. Jersey City, July 14, 1964; s. Delfin and Delia Marta (Bitocchi) M.; m. Ana Marin, May 27, 1989. AA in Chemistry with highest honors, Miami-Dade C.C., 1989; B Computer Sci. with highest honors, Fla. Internat. U., 1992. Chem. analyst Panair Lab., Miami, Fla., 1987-90; rsch. asst. Fla. Internat. U., Miami, 1990-92; programmer Voice Rite, Inc., Miami, 1992-94, IBM Corp., Miami, 1994—. Roman Catholic. Home: 5501 Doemont Dr Apex NC 27502 Office: IBM Bldg 502 Rm E118 4205 S Miami Blvd Research Triangle Park NC 27709

MARTINEZ, ROBERT E., state official. Sec. transp. State of Va., Richmond. Office: Va State Office Transp 1401 E Broad St Rm 414 Richmond VA 23219-2000

MARTINEZ-GLANDER, PATRICIA ANN, artist; b. New Rochelle, N.Y., Nov. 17, 1942; d. David Clyde Waters and Kathleen (Parsons) Glanders; m. Martin W. Taplin, Jan. 30, 1965 (div. July 1985); children: Jennifer Taplin, Andrew Taplin, Kristopher Taplin; m. Roberto Martinez, May 5, 1987. Student, New Sch. of Fine Arts, Met. Mus. Coral Gables, Art and Culture Mus. Hollywood, Photographic Inst. of Miami. Actress, 1955-65, artist, 1966—. One-woman shows include Virginia Miller Galleries, Coral Gables, Fla., Art and Culture Ctr. of Hollywood, Fla.; exhibited in group shows at Gallery Exposures, Coral Gables, Soc. of The Four Arts Palm Beach, Fla., Deer Art Gallery, Tyler, Tex., Mus. of Arts, Ft. Lauderdale, Fla., Southeastern Women's Caucus for Art Resource Ctr., Gainesville Ctr. of Modern Art, Micanopy, Fla., Thomas Ctr. Gallery, Gainesville; appeared in TV series Flipper, TV commls. Home: 995 N Venetian Dr Miami FL 33139-1014 Studio: Cast Iron Bldg 67 E 11th St Apt 317 New York NY 10003-4615

MARTINEZ ROGERS, NORMA ELIA, nursing educator; b. San Antonio, Jan. 15, 1943; d. Jesse R. and Estella (Chavez) Martinez; widowed Oct. 4, 1968; children: Sean W. Rogers, Scott L. Rogers. BS, Incarnate Word Coll., 1965; MA, St. Mary's Univ., 1968; MS, U. Tex. Health Sci. Ctr., 1978; PhD, U. Tex., 1995. RN, Tex. Counselor, tchr. Edgewood Ind. Sch. Dist., San Antonio, 1972-76; assoc. prof. San Antonio Coll., 1978-88; dir. psychiat. nursing Villa Rosa Hosp., San Antonio, 1988-90; dir. nursing Charter Palms Hosp., McAllen, Tex., 1991-92; quality assurance coord. Austin (Tex.)/ Travis County Health & Human Svcs., 1992-94; faculty U. Tex. Health Sci. Ctr., San Antonio, 1994—; cons. Nueva Frontera, San Antonio, 1993-95. Maj. U.S. Army Nurse Corps, Ft. Bliss, Tex., 1991. Mem. Sigma Theta Tau. Home: 232 W Wildwood San Antonio TX 78212

MARTINSON, JACOB CHRISTIAN, JR., academic administrator; b. Menomonie, Wis., Apr. 15, 1933; s. Jacob Christian and Matilda Kate (Wisner) M.; m. Elizabeth Smathers, Apr. 29, 1962; children—Elizabeth Anne, Kirsten Kate. BA, Huntingdon Coll., Ala., 1954, LLD (hon.), 1993; MDiv, Duke U., 1957; DDiv, Vanderbilt U., 1972; grad., Inst. Ednl. Mgmt., Harvard U., 1981. Ordained elder United Methodist Ch. Minister Trinity United Meth. Ch., Lighthouse Point, Fla., 1960-67; sr. minister First United Meth. Ch., Winter Park, Fla., 1967-71; supervising instr. Vanderbilt U. Div. Sch., Nashville, 1971-72; pres. Andrew Coll., Cuthbert, Ga., 1972-76, Brevard Coll., N.C., 1976-85, High Point (N.C.) U., 1985—; bd. dirs. First Union Nat. Bank, High Point, chmn. 1989; lectr. St. Mary's Theol. Soc., U. St. Andrews, Scotland. Bd. advisors Uwharrie coun. Boy Scouts Am. Glen Slough scholar Vanderbilt U., 1971; Z. Smith Reynolds grantee Harvard U. Inst. Ednl. Mgmt., 1981; hon. fellow Westminster Coll., Oxford, Eng., 1994. Mem. Nat. Assn. Schs. and Colls. United Meth. Ch. (bd. dirs. 1982-85, 87-90, chmn. fin. com.), So. Assn. Colls. and Schs. (commn. on colls.), Ind. Coll. Fund. N.C. (trustee), N.C. Ctr. Ind. Higher Edn. (bd. dirs.) Brevard C. of C. (pres. 1979), High Point C. of C. (chmn. 1992), Piedmont Ind. Coll. Assn. (chmn. 1991-93), Carolinas Intercollegiate Athletic Conf. (pres. 1991-93), Rotary, Phi Theta Kappa. Methodist. Home: 1109 Rockford Rd High Point NC 27262-3607 Office: High Point U Office of Pres High Point NC 27262-3598

MARTOCCIA, CHARLES THOMSON, psychology educator; b. Daytona Beach, Fla., Dec. 28, 1930; s. Lionel J. and Frances (Brower) M.; m. Carol Martoccia, July 25, 1965; children: Douglas, Randall. BA, U. Va., 1952; PhD, U. Fla., 1960. Prof. psychology E. Carolina U., Greenville, N.C., 1961—. Mem. AAUP, AAAS, Am. Psychol. Soc. Office: E Carolina U Dept Psychology Greenville NC 27858

MARULLO, MICHAEL ANTHONY, marketing consultant; b. Rochester, N.Y., July 13, 1947; s. Anthony Francis and Rosemarie (Iacona) M.; m. Barbara G. Clark, Dec. 22, 1967 (div. Aug. 1986); 1 child, Marc David; m. Kimberly M. Groetsch, Oct. 30, 1988. Grad. high sch., Rochester. Lab technician Gen. Dynamics Electronics, Rochester, 1969-70; shift leader Gen. Dynamics-Stromberg, Rochester, 1969-70; engring. aide TANO Corp., New Orleans, 1970-71, systems engr., 1971-74, product line mgr., 1974-78; regional sales mgr. Logicon, Inc., Fairfax, Va., 1978-79; v.p. sales and mktg. Quantum Systems, Inc., New Orleans, 1980-84; pres. TECH-MARC, New Orleans, 1984-96; mng. dir., CEO cfar internat. ltd., Kenner, La., 1996—; cons. various U.S. and fgn. corps. Founder, Supplier Profiles Directory; editorial advisor SCADA Letter. Served with USAF, 19-69. Mem. IEEE, Instrument Soc. Am. (sr.), Am. Water Works Assn., AM/FM Internat. (exec coun.), SCADA Forum (charter mem.), New Orleans Sports Car Club (v.p. 1976-77). Republican. Methodist. Office: cfar international ltd PO Box 641177 Kenner LA 70064

MARUPUDI, SAMBASIVA RAO, surgeon, educator; b. Chintalapudi, India, July 1, 1952; came to U.S., 1976; s. Venkateswarlu and Nagendramma (Gaddipati) M.; m. Usha Nandipati, Mar. 25, 1976; children: Neena, Neelima. MB, BS, Guntur (India) Med. Coll., 1974. Diplomate Am. Bd. Surgery, Am. Bd. Colon and Rectal Surgery. Rotation intern St. Clare's Hosp., Schenectady, 1976-77; resident in gen. surgery. St. Agnes Hosp., Balt., 1977-78, Franklin Square Hosp., Balt., 1978-82; fellow in colon and rectal surgery U. Tex. Health Scis. Ctr., Houston, 1982-83; pvt. practice, Amarillo, Tex., 1983—; clin. asst. prof. dept. surgery Tex. Tech U Health Scis. Ctr., Amarillo, 1984—. Fellow ACS, Am. Soc. Colon and Rectal Surgeons, Internat. Coll. Surgeons; mem. AMA, Tex. Med. Assn., Potter-Randall County Med. Soc. Democrat. Hindu. Office: 3501 Soncy Rd Ste 103 Amarillo TX 79121-1738

MARVEL, KENNETH ROBERT, lawyer, corporate executive; b. July 5, 1952; s. Robert and Kay Marvel. AB, Dickinson Coll., 1974; JD, Harvard U., 1977. Bar: Tex. 1977. Ptnr. Jenkens & Gilchrist, Dallas, 1977-85; chmn., chief exec. officer Fitz & Floyd Silvestri Inc., Carrollton, Tex., 1985-96; mng. dir., chief operating officer Dallas Inst. of Humanities and Culture, 1996—; hon. consul Republic of Korea, 1994—. Bd. dirs. USA Film Festival, Dallas, 1984-85; bd. advisers Dickinson Coll., Carlisle, Pa., 1989-94, trustee, 1994—; bd. dirs., past pres. Nat. Tabletop Assn.; trustee Dallas Inst. Humanities and Culture; bd. dirs. Dallas Citizens Coun., 1995-96; bd. dirs. So. Dallas Devel. Corp., 1993—. Mem. Tex. Bar Assn., Dallas Bar Assn., Dallas Arboretum, Kimball Mus. Home: 7220 Tokalon Dr Dallas TX 75214-3560 Office: Dallas Inst of Humanities and Culture 2719 Routh St Dallas TX 75201

MARVIN, CHARLES ARTHUR, law educator; b. Chgo., July 14, 1942; s. Burton Wright and Margaret Fiske (Medlar) M.; m. Elizabeth Maureen Woodrow, July 4, 1970 (div. July 1987); children—Colin, Kristin. B.A., U. Kans., 1964; postgrad. (Fulbright scholar) U. Toulouse (France), 1964-65; J.D., U. Chgo., 1968, M.Comparative Law, 1970. Bar: Ill. 1969. Legal intern EEC, Brussels, 1970; lectr. law U. Kent, Canterbury, Eng., 1970-71; asst. prof. law Laval U., Quebec City, Que., Can., 1971-73; legal adv., constl., internat. and adminstrv. law sect. Can. Dept. Justice, Ottawa, Ont., 1973-76; assoc. prof. law U. Man., Winnipeg, Can., 1976-77; dir. adminstrv. law project Law Reform Commn. Can., Ottawa, 1977-80; prof. law Villanova (Pa.) U., 1980-83; dir. Adminstrv. Law Reform Project, Can. Dept. Justice, 1983-85; prof. law Ga. State U., 1985—; assoc. dean, 1987-89; legal advisor on administrv. code revision to Govt. of Kazakhstan, 1993; law faculty devel. adviser to Bulgaria, 1993. Bd. trustees Glenn Meml. United Meth. Ch. Summerfield scholar, 1961-64; Fulbright fellow, 1964-65; U. Chgo. scholar, 1965-68; Ford Found. Comparative Law fellow, 1968-70. Mem. ABA, Ill. Bar Assn., Chgo. Bar Assn., Am. Soc. Internat. Law, Am. Fgn. Law Assn., Internat. Bar Assn., Internat. Law Assn., Can. Bar Assn., Can. Council on Internat. Law, Phi Beta Kappa, Omicron Delta Kappa, Phi Beta Delta, Phi Delta Phi. Office: Ga State U Coll Law PO Box 4037 Atlanta GA 30302-4037

MARVIN, ROBERTA MONTEMORRA, musicologist; b. Everett, Mass., July 29, 1953; d. Anthony Joseph and Iris Assunta (Lemme) Montemorra; m. Conrad Albert Marvin, June 30, 1973. BM, Boston Cons., 1975; MA in Musicology, Tufts U., 1986; PhD in Musicology, Brandeis U., 1992. Lectr. in music Tufts U., Medford, Mass., 1991-92; asst. prof. music Boston U., 1992-93; asst. prof. music history U. Ala., Tuscaloosa, 1993—. Contbr. articles to profl. publs.; editor score: The Works of Giuseppe Verdi: (I masnadieri). Grantee Fulbright Found., 1988-89, NEH, 1992, Am. Philos. Soc., 1992; recipient Premio internazionale Giuseppe Verdi, Instituto nazionale di studi verdiani, 1991; Fulbright rsch. fellow Coun. for Internat. Exch. of Scholars, 1993. Mem. Am. Musicol. Soc., Royal Musical Assn., Coll. Music Soc., N.Am. Soc. for Study of Romanticism, Am. Bach Soc. Office: U Ala Sch of Music Tuscaloosa AL 35487

MARVIN, WILBUR, real estate executive; b. Jamaica, N.Y., Apr. 8, 1921; s. Benjamin and Rose L. (Salmow) M.; m. Shirley G. Marvin, Mar. 18, 1945 (div. 1977); children: Michael F., Anne E. Marvin Swanson, Richard A.; m. Livia Seigho, Feb. 1980. BA, Harvard U., 1941; postgrad., U.S. Naval Acad., 1945-46. V.p. Third & Laurel Corp., N.Y.C., 1946-52; pres. Comml. Properties Devel. Corp., Baton Rouge, 1953—; bd. trustees Internat. Coun. Shopping Ctrs., N.Y.C. Contbr. articles to profl. jours. Comdr. USN, 1941-45. Decorated Purple Heart. Mem. Masons (bd. dirs.), Temple B'Nai Israel, Temple B'Nai Brith. Democrat. Jewish. Home: 18835 Beaconwoods Dr Baton Rouge LA 70817-1808 Office: Comml Properties Devel Corp 1906 Beaumont Dr PO Box 1693 Baton Rouge LA 70821 Office: Guaynabo S Ctr PO Box 8459 SR 20 KM 3 5 Santurce PR 00910

MARX, JOHN NORBERT, chemistry educator; b. Columbus, Ohio, Oct. 31, 1937; s. John Norbert and Cecelia Evelyn (Noziska) M.; m. Charmaine Prudence Mueller, Dec. 27, 1968 (div. 1974); m. Patricia Colleen Loyd, Dec. 21, 1974; children: Ruth Elizabeth, Samuel John Loyd. BS, St. Benedict's Coll., Atcheson, Kans., 1962; PhD, U. Kans., 1965. Postdoctoral assoc. Cambridge (Eng.) U., 1965-66, Johns Hopkins U., Balt., 1966-67; asst. prof. Tex. Tech. U., Lubbock, 1967-74, assoc. prof. dept. chemistry, 1974—. Contbr. articles to profl. jours. Asst. scoutmaster Boy Scouts Am., Lubbock, 1990—. Rsch. grantee Robert A. Welch Found., Houston, 1968—. Mem. Am. Chem. Soc. (treas. South Plains sect. 1983—). Office: Tex Tech U Dept Chem Biochemistry Lubbock TX 79409

MARX, MELVIN H., psychologist, educator; b. Bklyn., June 8, 1919; m. Kathleen Kendall, Sept. 5, 1948; children: Diana, Christine, Ellen, James. AB, Washington U., 1940, MA, 1941, PhD, 1943. Instr. to prof. U. Mo., Columbia, 1944-84; sr. rsch. scientist Ga. State U., Atlanta, 1985-89; vis. prof. Fla. Inst. Tech., Melbourne, 1990—; disting. vis. prof. Western Carolina U., Cullowhee, N.C., 1991—. Author: Introduction to Psychology: Problems, Procedures, Principles, 1976; co-author: Systems and Theories in Psychology, 1963, 4th edit., 1987; editor: Psychological Theory, 1951; co-editor: Fundamentals and Applications of Learning, 1977. Recipient numerous Rsch. grants NIMH U. Mo., 1950-84, NSF U. Mo., USAF U. Mo., Army Rsch Inst., 1974-82. Fellow APA (mem. council), Am. Psychological Soc.; mem. Midwest Psychological Assn. (pres. 1965), Psychonomic Soc., Sigma Xi. Home: HC 66 Box 233 Cullowhee NC 28723-9721

MARX, MORRIS LEON, academic administrator; b. New Orleans, May 21, 1937. BS in Math., Tulane U., 1959, MS in Math., 1963, PhD, 1964. Asst. prof. math. Vanderbilt U., 1966-69, assoc. prof., 1969-77, dir. grad. studies in math., 1970-72; prof. math., chmn. dept. U. Okla., 1977-81, assoc. dean coll. of arts and scis., 1981-84, interim dean coll. of arts and scis., 1984-85; vice chancellor acad. affairs, prof. math. U. Miss., 1985-88; pres., prof. math. U. West Fla., Pensacola, 1988—. 1st lt. U.S. Army, 1964-65, capt., 1965-66. Office: U West Fla 11000 University Pkwy Pensacola FL 32514-5750*

MARX, RICHARD BENJAMIN, lawyer; b. N.Y.C., June 17, 1932; s. Samuel and Veronica (Baer) M.; m. Doriann Belzer, Nov. 28, 1992; children: Jennifer, Bruce. BA, Hobart Coll., 1954; JD, NYU, 1957. Bar: N.Y. 1958, Fla. 1965, U.S. Dist. Ct. (so. dist.) Fla., U.S. Dist. Ct. (no. dist.) Fla., U.S. Ct. Appeals (2d, 5th, 8th, 9th, and 11th cirs.), U.S. Supreme Ct. Sole practice Miami, 1965—. Named one of top 25 criminal attys. in U.S. Town & Country mag., Miami, 1985. Mem. ABA, Dade County Bar Assn., Nat. Assn. Criminal Def. Attys., Acad. Fla. Trial Lawyers, Dade County Trial Lawyers Assn. Clubs: Jockey, Palm Bay, Grove Isle (Miami). Office: 1221 Brickell Ave Ste 1010 Miami FL 33131-3258

MARYNICK, SAMUEL PHILIP, physician, educator; b. Dallas, Aug. 6, 1945; s. Teophil and Ruth (Barnes) M.; m. Sharon Kay Marynick, Aug. 8, 1969; children: Ashley Suzanne, Samuel Laird, Mark Philip. BA cum laude, U. South Sewanee, 1967; MS with honors, Tulane U., 1968; MD, U. Tex., Dallas, 1972. Diplomate Am. Bd. Internal Medicine, Am. Bd. Endocrinology, Am. Bd. Bioanalysis in High Complexity Lab. Testing, Nat. Bd. Med. Examiners, Tex. State Bd. Med. Examiners, Md. Bd. Med. Examiners. Fellow in environ. biology NIH, 1967-68; intern in internal medicine Parkland Meml. Hosp., Dallas, 1972-73, resident in internal medicine, 1973-74; fellow in endocrinology & metabolism Nat. Inst. Child Health & Human Devel.-NIH, Bethesda, Md., 1974-77; with dept. internal medicine Baylor U. Med. Ctr., Dallas, 1977-86, co-dir. Collins Diabetes Ctr., 1983-86, med. dir. Baylor Ctr. for Reproductive Health, 1989—, chmn. instrn. rev. bd. for human protection, 1989—; pvt. practice Dallas, 1986—; clin. assoc. prof. internal medicine U. Tex. Southwestern Med. Sch., Dallas. Contbr. articles to profl. jours. Advocate for reproductive legis. Resolve and Tex. Assisted Reproduction Tech. and In Vitro Fertilization Group, 1986—. Lt. comdr. USPHS, 1974-77. Fellow ACP, Am. Coll. Endocrinology; mem. Tex. Med. Assn., Dallas County Med. Soc., Endocrine Soc., Am. Fertility Soc., Am. Fedn. for Clin. Rsch., Dallas Acad. Internal Medicine, Am. Soc. Internal Medicine, Soc. Reporductive Endocrinologists, European Soc. Embryology & Human Reproduction, Am. Assn. Clin. Endocrinologists, Am., Assn. Bioanalysts, Tex. Med. Found., Alpha Omega Alpha. Presbyterian. Office: 3707 Gaston Ave Ste 325 Dallas TX 75246-1520

MARZ, LOREN CARL, environmental engineer, chemist; b. Jamestown, N.Y., June 11, 1951; s. Maurice Carl and Dorothy May (Anderson) M.; m. Sharon Lee Mekus, June 2, 1979; children: Brandon, Stephen. BS, Gannon U., Erie, Pa., 1975; MS, SUNY, Fredonia, 1990. Registered environ. profl. Profl. baseball player Milw. Brewers Class A Team, Newark, N.Y., 1973; analyst chem. lab. Dunkirk (N.Y.) Ice Cream Co., 1975-80, Ralston-Purina Co., Inc., Dunkirk, 1980-84; environ. engr. CPS, Dunkirk, 1985-89; environ. scientist U.S. Army Med. Rsch. Inst. Chem. Def., Aberdeen Proving Ground, Md., 1989-91; environ. engr. U.S. Dept. Energy, Oak Ridge, Tenn., 1991—; site operator Nat. Atmospheric Deposition Program-Nat. Trends Network, Ft. Collins, Co., 1987-89. Mem. Mayville (N.Y.) Emergency Planning Com., 1988-89. Mem. AAAS, Am. Meteorol. Soc. Baptist. Home: 410 Jefferson Ln Clinton TN 37716-5741 Office: Dept Energy PO Box 2001 Oak Ridge TN 37831-8723

MARZIALE, ANTONIO, investment company executive; b. Rome, Apr. 30, 1959; came to U.S., 1982; s. Paolo and Liliana (Barsotti) M. Lic. in Enterprise Mgmt., Ecole Hautes Etudes Commercial, Lausanne, Switzerland, 1981. Fin. analyst Paribas Bank, Geneva, 1981-82; ptnr. The Core Co., Houston, 1983-85; mng. ptnr. Marco Investments, Houston, 1985—; mng. dir. Heptagon Investments, Ltd., Tortola, Brit. V.I., 1992—. Founding mem. Tex. Heart Inst. Assocs., Houston, 1988—. Office: Heptagon Capital Mgmt Inc Ste 950 5847 San Felipe Ste 4540 Houston TX 77057-3011

MARZIO, PETER CORT, museum director; b. Governor's Island, N.Y., May 8, 1943; s. Francis and Katherine (Mastroberte) M.; m. Frances Ann Parker, July 2, 1979; children: Sara Lon, Steven Arnold. B.A. (Neva Miller scholar), Juniata Coll., Huntingdon, Pa., 1965; M.A., U. Chgo., 1966, Ph.D. (univ. fellow, Smithsonian Instn. fellow), 1969. Research asst. to dir., then historian Nat. Mus. History and Tech., Smithsonian Instn., 1969-73, asso. curator prints, 1977-78, chmn. dept. cultural history, 1978; dir., chief exec. officer Corcoran Gallery Art, Washington, 1978-82; dir. Mus. Fine Arts, Houston, 1982—; instr. Roosevelt U., Chgo., 1966-68; assoc. prof. U. Md., 1976-77u; adv. coun. Anthrop. Film Ctr., Archives Am. Art; mem. adv. bd. Smithsonian Inst. Press; bd. dirs. First Interstate Bank of Tex. Author: Rube Goldberg: His Life and Works, 1973, The Art Crusade, 1976, The Democratic Art: An Introduction to the History of Chromolithography in America, 1979; editor: A Nation of Nations, 1976. Mem. adv. council Dumbarton Oaks, 1979-86; trustee, mem. exec. com., pres. Texart 150, Tex. Commn. on the Arts, Tex. Assn. for Promotion of Art, 1990-91. Sr. Fulbright fellow Italy, 1973-74. Mem. Print Council Am., Am. Print Council, Dunlap Soc., Assn. Art Mus. Dirs. (pres. 1988-89), Am. Assn. Mus. (exec. com.), Am. Fedn. of the Arts (trustee), Young Pres. Orgn. Club: Cosmos (Washington). Home: 101 Westcott St Houston TX 77007 Office: Mus Fine Arts PO Box 6826 1001 Bissonet St Houston TX 77005

MASCAVAGE, JOSEPH PETER, sales executive; b. Allentown, Pa., July 7, 1956; s. John Joseph and Florence M.; m. Jo Ellen Huhnke, Aug. 8, 1981; children: Lauren Christine, Gregory Joseph. BS in Environ. Resource Mgmt., Pa. State U., 1978. Tech. sales rep. Am. Cyanamid Co., Los Angeles, 1978-82; supr. utilites application Am. Cyanamid Co., Azusa, Calif., 1982-83; asst. to mktg. mgr. Am. Cyanamid Co., Wayne, N.J., 1983; dist. sales mgr. Am. Cyanamid Co., Houston, 1984-86; mgr. sales tng. Am. Cyanamid Co., Wayne and Charlotte, N.C., 1986-91; mgr. comml. tng. Am. Cyanamid Co., Charlotte, 1991-93; exec. Cytec Industries, Charlotte, 1993-94, mgr. of tng. and employee devel., 1994-96, mgr. corp. edn., 1996—. Editor: Safe Driving newsletter, 1990—; author: Cytec Sales Manual, 1993. Office: Cytec Industries 8309 Wilkinson Blvd Charlotte NC 28214-9052

MASELLI, JOSEPH, distribution company executive; b. Newark, May 30, 1924; s. Frank Paul and Mary Assunta (Iannetti) M.; m. Antoinette Cammarata, Sept. 8, 1946; children: Joseph, Jr., Frank Michael, Jan Maria, Michael Gerard. Diploma in Acctg., Tulane U., 1950. Acctg. and tax svc. prof. New Orleans, 1946-50, distbn. co. profl., 1950—; mng. ptnr. Car Wash Ctr., New Orleans, 1955-75; real estate developer New Orleans, 1960-90; advisor Bank of New Orleans, 1965-80; vice-chmn. New Orleans Aviation Bd., 1990-96; bd. dirs. Tulane Med. Sch., New Orleans. Author: (booklet) Ethnicity - Year 2000, 1993, Vanishing Minority, 1990; editor/pub.: Italian Am. Digest, 1990-96. Founder Am. Am. Italian Renaissance Found., New Orleans, 1973, Am. Italian Fedn./SE, La., Miss., Ala., 1972-96; vice-chmn. Nat. Itlian Am. Found., Washington, 1980-96. Recipient Ellis Island Medal of Honor, N.Y.C., 1990, Primo Dorso U. of Naples, Italy, Italian Am. of Yr., GNOICS, New Orleans, 1977. Mem. Jewish-Italian Civic Assn. (co-chmn. 1992-96), Am. Italian Civic Affairs (co-chmn. 1970-96). Democrat. Roman Catholic. Office: 1608 South Salcedo St New Orleans LA 70125

MASHBURN, DONALD EUGENE, middle school educator; b. Johnson City, Tenn., June 10, 1944; s. Harvey and Martha (McNeese) M.; m. Mary Juanita McKee, May 30, 1970; 1 child, Donna Sue. BS, East Tenn. State U., 1965, MS, 1971. Tchr. Cocke County High Sch., Newport, Tenn., 1965-66, John S. Battle High Sch., Bristol, Va., 1966-94, Wallace Mid. Sch., Bristol, 1994—; adj. faculty Northeast State Tech. Community Coll., Blountville, Tenn., 1984—. Mem. Va. Assn. Student Coun. Advisers (v.p. 1983-85), Ruritan (sec. 1986-91, pres. 1985, 92, 93, dist. treas. 1993). Republican. Methodist. Home: 195 Mashburn Rd Telford TN 37690-3132 Office: Wallace Mid Sch 13077 Wallace Pike Bristol VA 24202-3601

MASHBURN, GUERRY LEONARD, marketing professional; b. Hawkinsville, Ga., Mar. 14, 1952; s. Marvin Butler Mashburn Sr. (dec.) and Ruby Geneva (Brown) Greenway; m. Gloria Michelle Jones, June 1, 1975. AA, Middle Ga. Coll., 1972; BS, Ga. Southwestern Coll., 1974. Sales assoc. A. Cohen & Sons, Americus, Ga., 1973-77; mng. prin. The Bell Co., Americus, Ga., 1977-82; exec. mgmt. Maier & Berkele, Inc., Atlanta, 1982-85; v.p. Trosby Contracts, Inc., Atlanta, 1985-87; dir. sales and mktg. Ernest Gaspard & Assocs., Atlanta, 1987-94, Atlanta Decorative Arts Ctr., 1994; v.p.

mktg. CEO Internat., Atlanta, 1994—; chmn. industry com. Decorators' Show House of Atlanta Symphony Orch., 1991, mem. hon. com., 1992; adv. bd. Interior Design dept. U. Ga., 1992-94. Bd. dirs. Am. Cancer Soc., Americus, 1977-80, ARC, Americus, 1978-80; divsn. chmn. United Way campaign, Americus, 1978-82; pres. Americus Merchants Assn., 1980-82; mem. task force Unified Voice, 1988—; mem. adv. bd. Ronald McDonald House, Scottish Rite Children's Hosp., Atlanta, 1991—; bd. dirs. Atlanta Interfaith AIDS Network, 1994; host com. Dining for Friends Makes Cents, 1993, co-chmn., 1994; co-chmn. publicity Atlanta Symphony Ball, 1994. Mem. Internat. Soc. Interior Designers (trade liaison Ga. chpt. 1987-89, internat. exec. coun., trade devel. chmn., internat. industry resource liaison 1990, v.p. industry affairs 1992), Ga. Alliance for Interior Design Profls. (industry chmn. 1992, sec. 1994, mem. candidacy rsch. com. 1994), Americus & Sumter County C. of C. (bd. govs. 1980-82), Nat. Trust for Hist. Preservation, Ga. Trust for Hist. Preservation (chmn. preview party 1992), Buckhead Towne Club, Inland Yacht Club, High Mus. of Art, Sigma Chi Alumni (pres. 1978-80). Republican. Presbyterian. Home: 409 Peachtree Hills Cir Atlanta GA 30305-4240

MASHBURN, JAMAL, professional basketball player; b. N.Y.C., Nov. 29, 1972. Grad., Ky. Coll. Forward Dallas Mavericks, 1993—. Named to NBA All-Rookie First Team, 1994. Office: Dallas Mavericks Reunion Arena 777 Sports St Dallas TX 75207*

MASHBURN, JOHN WALTER, quality control engineer; b. Athens, Tenn., Oct. 17, 1945; s. Edgar Newton and Grace Victoria (Ellis) M.; m. Lillian Loyall Tauxe, Sept. 17, 1965; children: Samuel Louis, Laura Jean. BS in Engring. Physics, U. Tenn., 1966, MS in Physics, 1970. Registered profl. engr., Tenn.; cert. quality engr., quality auditor, quality sys. auditor, profl. mgr. Sr. prodn. engr. EG&G ORTEC, Oak Ridge, Tenn., 1966-75; nuclear engr. TVA, Knoxville, Tenn., 1975-86; v.p. mfg. Delta M Corp., Oak Ridge, 1986-89; cons. engr. LTM Cons., Knoxville, 1982-89; quality engr. Martin Marietta Energy Systems, Oak Ridge, 1989-95, Lockheed Martin Energy Rsch., Oak Ridge, 1995—. Chmn. Gulf Park Civic Assn., Knoxville, 1978. Mem. IEEE (sr., chair East Tenn. sect. 1990-91), Am. Nuclear Soc. (sr., sect. chair 1986-87), Am. Phys. Soc., Am. Soc. Quality Control, Tau Beta Pi. Home: 920 Venice Rd Knoxville TN 37923-2098

MASHBURN, SYLVIA ANITA SMITH, public relations specialist; b. McRae, Ga., Mar. 28, 1964; d. Alexander Peterson and Sylvia Ann (Hartman) Smith; m. Thomas Matthew Mashburn, May 18, 1991; 1 child, Melissa Anne. BA, Vanderbilt U., Nashville, 1986; MA, Ga. State U., 1994. Cert. assoc. pub. mgr., Ga. Staff asst. U.S. Info. Agy., Washington, 1986-88; newspaper reporter The Courier-Herald, Dublin, Ga., 1989; pub. rels., info. specialist Ga. Dept. Transp., Atlanta, 1989-93, sr. pub. rels., info. specialist, 1993—. Vol. DeKalb Amb., Decatur, Ga., 1992—. Recipient Better Newspaper Contest award Ga. Press Assn., 1993, 94, 1st pl. award, 1995, Publ. Excellence award Ga. Milepost, 1991, 93. Mem. Pub. Rels. Soc. Am., Ga. Soc. Cert. Pub. Mgrs. Methodist. Office: Ga Dept Transportation Public Affairs Office 2 Capitol Sq SW Atlanta GA 30334-9003

MASLOV, VADIM (YURYEVICH), computer scientist; b. Novosibirsk, Russia, June 20, 1965; came to U.S., 1992; s. Yuriy Nikolaevich and Tamara (Selipanova) M.; m. Marina Serebriakova, Mar. 8, 1992. MSc in Applied Math., Moscow State U., Russia, 1987, PhD in Computer Sci., 1992. Programmer, system designer GAMMA Software, Moscow, 1988-89, sr. programmer, analyst, 1989-92; sr. programmer-analyst U. Md., College Park, 1992-94; sr. sys. analyst Info. Analysis Inc., 1994-95; sr. software devel. specialist Landmark Sys., Vienna, Va., 1995-96; tech. specialist Cybercash Inc., Reston, Va., 1996—. Contbr. articles to profl. jours. Mem. Assn. for Computing Machinery. Home: 2902 Rock Manor Ct Herndon VA 22071 Office: Cybercash Inc 2100 Reston Pkwy Ste 300 Reston VA 22091

MASON, AIMEE HUNNICUTT ROMBERGER, retired philosophy and humanities educator; b. Atlanta, Nov. 3, 1918; d. Edwin William and Aimee Greenleaf (Hunnicutt) Romberger; m. Samuel Venable Mason, Aug. 16, 1941 (dec. 1988); children: Olivia Elizabeth (Mrs. Mason Butcher), Christopher Leeds. BA, Conn. Coll., 1940; postgrad. Emory U., 1946-48; MA, U. Fla., 1979, PhD, 1980, MA, Stetson U., 1968. Jr. exec. merchandising G. Fox & Co., Hartford, Conn., 1940-41; air traffic contr. CAA, Atlanta, 1942; ptnr. Coronado Concrete Products, New Smyrna Beach, Fla., 1953-81; adj. faculty Valencia Jr. Coll., Orlando, Fla., 1969; instr. philosophy and humanities Seminole Community Coll., Sanford, 1969, ret. Area cons. ARC, 1947-50; del. Nat. Red Cross, Washington, 1949; founding mem. St. Joseph Hosp. Aux., Atlanta, 1950-53; v.p., treas. New Smyrna Beach PTA 1955-60; bd. dirs. Atlanta Symphony Orch., Fla. Symphony Orch., 1954-59; mem. Code Enforcement Bd., Edgewater, Fla., 1992-94. Lt. USCGR, 1943-46. Recipient award in graphics Nat. Assn. Women Artists, 1939, 41. Mem. AAUP, AAUW (founding mem. New Smyrna Beach, exec. bd. 1984-85, chmn. scholarship com. 1984-87, coll./univ. liaison 1987-91, citizen's code enforcement bd. Edgewater 1992-94), DAV, Am. Philos. Assn., Fla. Philos. Assn. (exec. coun. 1978-79), Collegium Phenomenologicum, Soc. Existential and Phenomenological Philosophy, Soc. Phenomenology in Human Scis., Merleau-Ponty Circle, Fla. Assn. Community Colls. Home: 511 N Riverside Dr Edgewater FL 32132-1631

MASON, ANDREA LEE, physical education educator; b. Savannah, Ga., June 7, 1971; d. Andrew S. and Barbara L. Mason. BS in Health and Phys. Edn., Armstrong State Coll., 1993. Cert. tchr., Ga. Tchr. Chatham County Bd. Edn., Savannah, 1994—; coach softball Myer's Mid. Sch., Savannah, 1994, sponsor Kiwanis Builder's Club, 1994-95; mem. Wellness Team, Savannah, 1994. Vol. Spl. Olympics, Savannah, 1992, Olympic Regatta, Savannah, 1994. Kiwanis scholar, 1989, athletic scholar Armstrong State Coll., 1989-93. Baptist. Home: 108 C Magnolia Ave Savannah GA 31419

MASON, BENJAMIN PAGE, director of vocational education; b. Nassawadox, Va., June 25, 1946; s. O. Page and Margaret (Houston) M.; m. Shirley Hall, Aug. 31, 1968; children: Wendy M. Roache, James Christopher. BS in Acctg., Old Dominion U., 1969, MS in Edn., 1982. Bus. edn. tchr. Accomock (Va.) County Schs., 1969-75, chmn. bus. edn. dept., 1975-82; prin. T.H. Badger Tech. Ctr., 1982-83, dir. vocational edn., 1983—; vice chmn. Region IV Vocat. Adminstrn., Norfolk, Va., 1993-96. Treas. Emmanuel Episcopalian Ch., Jenkins Bridge, Va., 1981-96. Mem. Parksky Lions Club (treas. 1993—). Office: Accomack County Schs 26350 Lankford Hwy Onley VA 23418

MASON, ELLSWORTH GOODWIN, librarian; b. Waterbury, Conn., Aug. 25, 1917; s. Frederick William and Kathryn Loretta (Watkins) M.; m. Rose Ellen Maloy, May 13, 1951 (div. Oct. 1961); children: Kay Iris Maurice, Joyce Iris Lande; m. Joan Lou Shinew, Aug. 16, 1964; 1 son, Sean David. B.A., Yale U., 1938, M.A., 1942, Ph.D., 1948; L.H.D., Hofstra U., 1973. Cert. Inst. Children's Lit., 1996. Reference asst. Yale Library, 1938-42; export license officer Bd. Econ. Warfare, 1942-43; instr. English Williams Coll., 1948-50; instr. humanities div. Marlboro (Vt.) Coll., 1951-52; serials libr. U. Wyo. Libr., 1952-54; reference libr. Colo. Coll. Libr., Colorado Springs, 1954-58; lectr., libr. Colo. Coll., 1958-63; prof., dir. libr. svcs. Hofstra U., Hempstead, N.Y., 1963-72; prof., dir. U. Colo. Librs., Boulder, 1972-76; freelance writer children's lit., 1995—; adj. prof. U. Ill., Urbana, 1968; pres. Mason Assocs., Ltd., 1977—; rsch. assoc. U. Calif.-Berkeley, 1965; vis. lectr. Northwestern U., 1961, Colo. Coll., 1965, Syracuse U., 1965-68, Elmira Coll., 1966, Columbia U., 1966-68, U. Ill., 1972, Lincoln U., 1969, U. B.C. (Can.), 1969, U. Toronto, 1970, U. Tulsa, 1971, 76, Rutgers U., 1971, Colgate U., 1972, Simmons Coll., 1972, U. Oreg., 1973, Hofstra U., 1974, U. N.C., 1976, U. Ala., 1976, Ball State U., 1977, U. Lethbrige, Can., 1977, U. Ariz., 1981, Ariz. State U., 1981, Victoria U., New Zealand, 1983, U. Canterbury, New Zealand, 1983, U. Nev. Las Vegas, 1992, Remember Pearl Harbor Assn., 1993, 94; libr. cons., 1958—, libr. value engr., 1992—. Editor: (with Stanislaus Joyce) The Early Joyce, 1955, Xerox U.M. edit., 1964, (with Richard Ellmann) The Critical Writings of James Joyce, 1959, 2d edit., 1989, Critical Commentary on A Portrait of the Artist as a Young Man, 1966; translator: Recollections of James Joyce (S. Joyce), 1950, Essais de J. Joyce, 1966, Escritos Criticos de James Joyce, (Portuguese edit.), 1967, (Spanish edit.), 1973, 75, James Joyce's Ulysses and Vico's Cycle, 1973, Kritische Schriften v. James Joyce, 1975, Mason on Library Buildings, 1980, (with Walter and Jean Shine) A MacDonald Potpourri, 1988, The University of Colorado Library and Its Makers, 1876-1972, 1994; contbr. Contemporary Authors, 1988—; editor: Colorado College Studies, 1959-62; editor and compiler: Focus on Robert Graves, 1972-88; adv. editor: Focus on Robert Graves and His Contemporaries, 1988—; editor: The Booklover's Bounty, 1977—; mem. editorial bd. Serial Slants, 1957-59, The Serials Librarian, 1977—, Choice, 1962-65, Coll. and Rsch. Librs., 1969-72. Mem. exec. bd. U. Ky. Libr. Assocs., 1991-94—. Served with USNR, 1943-46. Recipient Harry Bailly spkr.'s award Assn. Colls. of Midwest, 1975; fellow Coun. on Libr. Resources, 1969-70; grantee Am. Coun. Learned Socs., Edn. Facilities Labs., Hofstra U., U. Colo.; named Ky. Col., 1993. Mem. ALA (councillor-at-large 1961-65), Colo. Libr. Assn. (pres. so. dist. 1960-61), Bibliog. Soc. Am., Libr. Assn. (London), N.Z. Libr. Assn., MLA, Pvt. Librs. Assn., Alcuin Soc. Vancouver, Conf. Editors Learned Jours., N.Z. Royal Forest and Bird Protection Soc., Colo. Book Collectors (founder, pres. 1975-86—), Inst. Vio Studies, James Joyce Found. (chmn. sect. on translation from Joyce, 2d Internat. James Joyce Symposium, Dublin 1969), Black America's PAC, Caxton Club, Archons of Colophon, Ghost Town Club, Alpha Sigma Lambda, Sigma Kappa Alpha (pres. 1969-70). Home: 736 Providence Rd Lexington KY 40502-2267 also: 39 Discovery Dr, Whitby New Zealand

MASON, FRANK HENRY, III, automobile company executive, leasing company executive; b. Paris, Tenn., Nov. 16, 1936; s. Frank H. and Dorothy (Carter) M.; children—Robert C., William C. B.E.E., Vanderbilt U., 1958; M.S. in Indsl. Mgmt., MIT, 1965. With Ford Motor Co., 1965-71, asst. controller Ford Brazil, Sao Paulo, Brazil, 1971-74, mgr. overseas financing dept., Dearborn, Mich., 1974-76, asst. controller engine div., 1976-78, mgr. facilities and mgmt. services, 1978-81; controller Ford Motor Credit Co., Dearborn, 1981-87; dir. finance Ford Fin. Services Group, Dearborn, 1987-89; exec. v.p., chief fin. officer U.S. Leasing, Internat., San Francisco, 1989-92; ret. 1992. Served to lt. USN, 1958-63.

MASON, JAMES MICHAEL, geneticist, researcher; b. Vancouver, Wash., Apr. 14, 1949; s. Charles Edward and Eugenia Eliza (Kinzer) M.; m. Verna Georgine Schlink, Sept. 8, 1970; children: George Edward, Stuart Michael. BA in Biology, U. Calif., San Diego, 1971; PhD in Genetics, U. Wash., 1976. Postdoctoral fellow U. Calif., Davis, 1976-78; staff fellow Nat. Inst. Environ. Health Scis., Research Triangle Park, N.C., 1978-80, geneticist, 1980—; mem. ad hoc com. NIH Biomed. Fellowship Study Sect., 1984-85; mem. Interagy. Aneuploidy Data Rev. Com., 1984-85; invited participant Symposium on Aneuploidy: Etiology and Mechanisms, Washington, 1985; chair task group on Drosophila assays Am. Soc. Testing and Materials on Biol. Effects and Environ. Fate, 1986; chair work group on Drosophila assays Workshop on Relationship Between Short-Term Test Info. and Cardinogenicity, Williamsburg, Va., 1987; chair session Genome Structure and Function Nat. Drosophila Conf., Chgo., 1991; mem. Gene-Tox Phase III Com. Drosophila Mutagenesis Assays, 1991-92; speaker in field. Mem. editorial bd. Environ. and Molecular Mutagenesis, 1993—. Cubmaster Boy Scouts Am., Pittsboro, N.C., 1992-94. Mem. AAAS, Environ. Mutagen Soc. (chair session Drosophila Mutagenesis meeting 1991, chair session Mutation Spectra meeting 1992), Genetics Soc. Am., N.C. Drosophila Users Group (founder, chair 1991-93). Office: Nat Inst Environ Health Sci PO Box 12233 # 06 Research Triangle Park NC 27709

MASON, JOHN, research and consulting company executive, mayor; b. Springfield, Mass., Jan. 27, 1935; s. Anders G. and Magda (Peick) M.; m. Jeanette Funk, June 11, 1963; children: John Jr., Joanna, Jeffrey. BA, U. Mass., 1956; MA, NYU, 1970. Commd. 2d lt. U.S. Army, 1956, advanced through grades to col., 1978, ret.; v.p. Sci. Applications Internat. Corp., McLean, Va., 1978—. Mem. Fairfax (Va.) Planning Commn., 1980-86, chmn., 1984; mem. Fairfax City Coun., 1986-90, No. Va. Transp. Commn., 1990-94, Nat. Capital Region Transp. Planning Bd., 1990—; mem. Met. Washington Coun. Govts., 1990—, pres., 1996; mem. Met. Washington Air Quality Com., 1992-96, vice chmn. Va., 1992-96; bd. dirs. nat. capital area chpt. ARC, 1996—, Fairfax (Va.) Spotlight on the Arts, Inc., 1992—; chmn. Patawomeck dist. nat. area coun. Boy Scouts Am., 1996—. Home: 3548 Queen Anne Dr Fairfax VA 22030-1852 Office: Sci Applications Internat Corp 1710 Goodridge Dr Mc Lean VA 22102-3701

MASON, MITCHELL GARY, emergency nurse; b. Nelsonville, Ohio, Aug. 11, 1957; s. Homer Frank and Margaret Louise (Lehman) M. Student, Capital U., Columbus, Ohio, 1975-76; BSEd, Ohio U., Athens, Ohio, 1981; ADN, Hocking Tech. Coll., Nelsonville, Ohio, 1985; postgrad., Barry U., Miami Shores, Fla., 1991. Instr. med. terminology Hocking Tech. Coll., Nelsonville, 1984-85; staff nurse Hocking Valley Community Hosp., Logan, Ohio, 1974-86; trauma nurse specialist, assoc. head nurse Jackson Meml. Hosp., Miami, Fla., 1986—. Home: 316 W 194th Ave Pembroke Pines FL 33029-5456

MASON, RAY, company executive. Dir. R & D, Telematic Internat., Ft. Lauderdale, Fla. Office: Telematic Internat 1201 W Cypress Creek Rd Fort Lauderdale FL 33309-1912

MASON, ROBERT LESTER, engineer, small business computer consultant; b. Urbana, Ill., Oct. 24, 1945; s. Curtis Leonel and Mary Eleanor (Funkhouser) M.; m. Shirley Coggins, June 5, 1971. AS, Va. Commonwealth U., 1973; BA, N.C. State U., Raleigh, 1978; student, L.R.W.G., 1996. Cen. office switchman Chesapeake & Potomac Telephone Co., Richmond, Va., 1970-71; asst. engr. Gen. Telephone (GTE), Durham, N.C., 1973-74; design engr. Gen. Electric, Mebane, N.C., 1978-79; application engr. Cornell Dublier Electronics, Sanford, N.C., 1980; field support engr. No. Telecom, Inc., Research Triangle Park, N.C., 1980-82, customer service rep., 1982-86, technical accounts rep., 1986-87, customer service engr., 1987-88; pres. RLM Enhancers Inc., Chapel Hill, N.C., 1989—, pres., CEO, computer cons., 1989—; authorized sales rep. Telecom Solutions, Inc., 1992-93; vice chair Northern Telecom Employee Club, Research Triangle Park, 1983; delktop pub. and computer/telecom cons.; Aptiva support tech., IBM, 1996—. Patentee electronic burglar alarm, 1975. Mem. Orange County Econ. Devel. Coun., 1990-92. With USN, 1966-70, Vietnam. Mem. Am. Assn. Individual Investors, No. Telecom Inc. Mgmt. Assn. (facility rep. 1986-87, treas. 1987-88), Nat. Trust for Historic Preservation, Postal Commemorative Soc., Nat. Geog. Soc., World Futurist Soc., Navy League U.S., U.S. Navy Meml., VFW (jr. vice comdr. 1986-87), Chapel Hill-Carrboro C. of C., Chapel Hill-Carrboro Kiwanis (bd. dirs., newsletter editor, pres.-elect 1996-97).

MASON, STEPHANIE OLIVE, medical/surgical nurse, educator; b. St. Thomas, V.I., Apr. 6, 1966; d. Anthony P. and Cecilia (Danet) Olive; m. Timothy Lee Mason, June 17, 1989; children: Brandon Lee, Patrick James, Kelsey Leigh. BSN, Emory U., 1988. Cert. med.-surg.; cert. ACLS. Nurse Crawford Long Hosp. of Emory U., Atlanta; clin. instr. Lansing (Mich.) Community Coll., 1989; nurse Edward W. Sparrow Hosp., Lansing, 1990, asst. dept. mgr. surg. specialities unit, 1992; staff nurse critical care unit Satilla Regional Med. Ctr., Waycross, Ga.; asst. head nurse surg. unit St. Thomas (V.I.) Hosp., 1993, asst. head nurse ICU, 1994—; instr. CPR. Mem. Mich. Nurses Assn., V.I. Nurses Assn., Sigma Theta Tau. Home: 39 Aa-2 Estate Pearl PO Box 307473 Charlotte Amalie VI 00803 Office: St Thomas Hosp ICU Sugar Estate Charlotte Amalie VI 00801

MASON, WILLIAM CORDELL, III, hospital administrator; b. Montgomery, Ala., June 7, 1938; s. William C. and Sibyl (Evans) M.; m. Mona Holloway, Jan. 5, 1957 (div. June 1992); children: Michael C., Rebecca Mason Malone, Stephen E., Holly M.; m. Juliette Baldwin Woodruff, Apr. 17, 1993. B.S., U. Southwestern La., 1961; M. Hospital and Health Care, Trinity U., 1971. Hosp. rep. Eaton Labs., Norwich, N.Y., 1962-66; fgn. service officer U.S. Dept. State, Manila and Saigon, 1966-69; chief exec. officer Bapt. Hosp. of East Africa, Mbeya, Tanzania, 1971-74, Bapt. Hosp., Bangalore, India, 1974-78; chief operating officer Bapt. Med. Ctr., Jacksonville, Fla., 1978-84, vice chmn., CEO, 1984-95; pres., CEO Bapt./St. Vincent's Health Sys. Inc., Jacksonville, Fla., 1995—; mem. adj. faculty U. No Fla. Jacksonville, 1985—; cons. So. Bapt. Fgn. Mission Bd., Richmond, Va., 1980-85; bd. dirs. Sun Bank of North Fla., N.A., SunHealth Corp., sec. exec. com., 1990-94. Contbr. articles to profl. jours. Chmn. deacons Hendricks Ave. Bapt. Ch., Jacksonville, 1984-85, Calvary Bapt. Ch., Bangalore, 1976-77; treas. Karnataka State Bapt. Conv., Bangalore, 1975-77; trustee Jacksonville Symphony Orch.; bd. dirs. U. No. Fla.Assn. Vol. Hosps., 1986, Med. Assistance Program Internat., 1986-87, United Way, 1990; chmn. Greater Jacksonville Area Hosp. Coun., 1985, Mayor's Health Econ. Devel. Coun., 1986-87, Greater Jacksonville U.S. Savs. Bond Campaign, 1987; mem. adv. coun. Jacksonville U. Sch. Bus., 1986-88; chmn. area devel. coun. So. Bapt. Fgn. Mission Bd., 1987-91. Fellow Am. Coll. Hosp. Execs.; mem. Am. Hosp. Assn., Fla. Hosp. Assn. (trustee 1982, 83-85, 86), Fla. Hosp. Assn. (chmn. 1992-93, trustee 1994—), Healthcare Exec. Study Soc., Jacksonville C. of C. (vice chmn. exec. com. 1988-89, chmn. health econ. devel. 1992-95, chmn. cornerstone econ. devel. initiative), Epping Forest Yacht Club (bd. govs. 1990—), Beta Sigma Gamma, Rotary. Home: 947 Greenridge Rd Jacksonville FL 32207-5203 Office: Bapt/St Vincent's Health Sys Inc 1301 Riverplace Blvd, Ste 1700 Jacksonville FL 32207*

MASSAD, STEPHEN ALBERT, lawyer; b. Wewoka, Okla., Dec. 20, 1950; s. Alexander Hamilton and Delores Jean (Razook) M.; m. Amy S. Massad, Jan. 13, 1979; children: Caroline, Sarah, Margaret. AB, Princeton U., 1972; JD, Harvard U., 1975. Bar: Tex. 1975. Assoc. Baker & Botts, Houston, 1975-82, ptnr., 1983—. Office: Baker & Botts 3000 One Shell Plz 910 Louisiana St Houston TX 77002

MASSARO, MARK V., civil engineer; b. Totowa, N.J., Oct. 5, 1952; s. Vincent M. and Patricia (Baer) M.; m. Wanda Sue Massaro, June 28, 1981; children: Jennifer, Vincent. BS in Civil Engring., Ind. Inst. Tech., 1975; MPA, Ind. U., 1984. Registered profl. engr., Ind., Fla. Staff engr., traffic engr., signal engr., hwy. lighting engr Ind. Hwy. Commn., Indpls., 1976-82; city engr./dir. pub. works City of Noblesville, Ind., 1982-84; staff engr., sr. design engr., traffic dept. mgr., hwy. main Orange County Pub. Works, Orlando, Fla., 1984—. Chmn. Orange County Cmty. Traffic Safety Program, Orlando, 1994-95, M.P.O. Tech. Com., Orlando, 1995; facility chmn. YMCA Camp Wewa, Orlando, 1994. Fellow Fed. Hwy. Adminstrn., 1987. Mem. ITE (sec. 1987), APWA, Fla. Prof. Soc. Roman Catholic. Home: 3314 Heathgate Ct Orlando FL 32812 Office: Orange County Hwy Maintenance Dept 4200 S John Young Pkwy Orlando FL 32839-8659

MASSELL, SAM, civic organization executive. BCS, Ga. State U.; LLB, Atlanta Law Sch. Cert. travel counselor. Chief of pubs. Nat. Assn. Women's and Children's Apparel Salesmen, Inc., 1949-51; with Allan-Grayson Realty Co., Atlanta, 1951-69, v.p., 1955-69; instr. real estate Smith-Hughes Atlanta Vocat. Sch., 1956; v.p. Mallin Developers, Inc. a Fla. Corp., 1956-65; pres. Allan-Grayson Devel. Assocs., Atlanta, 1974-75, Aditus, Inc. (d/b/a Your Travel Agt. Sam Massell), Atlanta, 1975-88, Buckhead Coalition, Inc., Atlanta, 1988—. Councilman City of Mountain Park, Ga., 1950-52; sec. Atlanta City Exec. Com., 1953-61; pres. Bd. of Aldermen, vice mayor City of Atlanta, 1962-69, mayor, 1970-74; dir. Metro Atlanta Rapid Transit Authority, 1988-91; former pres. Nat. League Cities; dir., past pres. Buckhead Bus. Assn.; dir. Buckhead YMCA, North Atlanta Sch. Arts, Atlanta Internat. Sch., Atlanta Conv. and Visitors Bur., Atlanta Com. for the Olympic Games. With USAF, 1946-47. Mem. Standard Club, Travel Industry Assn. of Ga., Ga. Downtown Devel. Assn. Democrat. Jewish. Office: Buckhead Coalition Inc Ste 560 3340 Peachtree Rd NE Atlanta GA 30326-1059

MASSEY, DONALD WAYNE, microfilm consultant, small business owner; b. Durham, N.C., Mar. 7, 1938; s. Gordon Davis and Lucille Alma (Gregory) M.; m. Violet Sue McIlvain, Nov. 2, 1958; children: Kimberly Shan (dec.), Leon Dale, Donn Krichele, Anthony Donn Prestarri. Student, U. Hawaii, 1959, U. Ky., 1965, 66, U. Va., 1970, Piedmont C.C., 1982. Head microfilm sect. Ky. Hist. Soc., Frankfort, 1961; dir. microfilm ctr. U. Ky., Lexington, 1962-67; dir. photog. svcs. and graphics U. Va., Charlottesville, 1967-73; pres. Micrographics II, Charlottesville, Va. & Charleston, S.C., 1973—; owner Roseraie Nursery Ctr., 1988—; instr. U. Va. Sch. Continuing Edn., 1971-72, Central Va. Piedmont Community Coll., 1976; cons. Microform Systems and Copying Centers; owner Massland Farm, Shadwell, Va.; basketball coach Rock Hill Acad., 1975-77; chaplain Cedars Nursing Home, Charlottesville, 1992-94; chaplain Colonnades Charlottesville, Va., 1994—. Pub.: Micropublishing Series, 18th Century Sources for Study of English Lit. and Culture, Women Authors 18th and 19th Centuries, 1993, Va. Colonial History, 1994—, Theology in the 18th and 19th Centuries, 1995; author: Episcopal Churches in the Diocese of Virginia, 1989, A Catechism for Children, 1995, A Guide to Colonial Churches in Virginia, 1996, The Christian Philosophy of Patrick Henry, In Memoriam to the Rt. Rev. William Meade, Third Bishop of Virginia, 1996, Jamestown, the Beginning of the Church in Virginia, 1996, Christ Episcopal Church, Monticello Parish, Charlottesville, Va. The First 100 years, 1924-1924, 1996. Chmn. bd. dirs. Park St. Christian Ch., 1970, 75; pres., Rock Hill Acad. Aux., 1975-76; pres. bd. Workshop V for handicapped, Charlottesville, Va., 1972-73; bd. chmn. Park St. Christ Ch., 1969-73; mem. Emmanuel Episc. Ch., Greenwood, Va., Grace Episc. Ch., Cismont, Va.; pres. region XV Episc. Diocese of Va.; chalice bearer St. Luke's Chapel Simeon, Va., Christ Ch., Charlottesville, 1992, lay eucharistic min., 1993—; lay reader eucharistic minister Christ Episcopal Ch., Charlottesville, Va.; chaplain Cedars Nursing Home, Charlottesville, 1991—; rep. Senatorial Inner Circle, 1990, George Bush Rep. Task Force, 1990; eucharistic min. Grace Episc. Ch., Cismont, 1995—. With USMCR, 1957-63. Named Ky. Col.; recipient Key award Workshop V. Mem. Am. Libr. Assn., Va. Libr. Assn. Soc. Reprodn. Engrs., Nat. Microfilm Assn. (libr. rels. com. 1973—), Va. Microfilm Assn. (pres. 1971-72, v.p. 1973-74, program chmn. ann. conf. 1974, Pioneer award 1973, Fellow award 1976), Ky. Microfilm Assn. (Outstanding award 1967, pres. 1964-67), Assn. for Info. and Image Mgmt., Va. Gamebird Assn., Thoroughbred Owners and Breeders Assn., Am. Rose Soc., Thomas Jefferson Rose Soc. (charter), Nat. Rifle Assn. Contbg. editor Va. Librarian, 1970-71, Micro-News Va. Microfilm Assn., 1970-71, Plant & Print Jour., 1983-85; contbr. articles to profl. publs. Home and Office: 3304 Keswick Rd Keswick VA 22947

MASSEY, JANICE MUNN, neurology educator; b. Middleton, Tenn., Dec. 10, 1946; d. Walton T. and Mildred Elizabeth (Watson) Munn; m. Edward Wayne Massey, Aug. 22, 1967; children: Patrick, Austen, Elizabeth. BA in Math and Biology, Abilene (Tex.) Christian U., 1968; MD, Georgetown U., 1978. Diplomate Nat. Bd. Med. Examiners, Am. Bd. Psychiatry and Neurology, Am. Bd. Electrodiagnostic Medicine. Tchr. math. Ball High Sch., Galveston, Tex., 1967-70; intern Sch. Medicine Georgetown U., Washington, 1978-79; resident in neurology Duke U. Med. Ctr., Durham, N.C., 1979-82, fellow in electromyography and neuromuscular disease dept. medicine divsn. neurology, 1982-83, dir. neurology residency tng., 1983-84, assoc. divsn. neurology, 1983-85, asst. dir. EMG Lab., 1983—, asst. prof. dept. medicine divsn. neurology, 1985-92, assoc. prof., 1992—; mem. com. on women Duke U. Sch. Medicine, 1990—, com. on admissions, 1991—, subcom. on patient and clinic flow Med. Pvt. Diagnostic Clinic, 1992-93; examiner Am. Bd. Psychatry and Neurology, 1987, 89, 90, 91, 92, 94; cons. grant reviewer Orphan Products Devel. Office, U.S. FDA, 1990—; Delozier Meml. lectr. Ohio State U., 1988; cons. NIH, 1993—. Contbr. over 115 articles and abstracts to sci. and profl. jours. Bd. trustees AGAPE N.C., 1987-92, vice chmn., 1989-91, chmn., 1991-92; nat. bd. trustees Abliene Christian U., 1990—. Welch Found. fellow, 1971-73; NIH fellow, 1974; recipient Alumni Citation award Abilene Christian U., 1985; grantee Abbott Labs., 1987 (2 grants), Sandoz Rsch. Inst., 1987, 89, (two grants), Muscular Distrophy Assn., 1987 (2 grants), 89, Benign Essential Blepharospasm Rsch. Found., 1989, U.S. FDA, 1990-93, SyntexúSynergan Neurosci. Joint Venture, 1993 (2 grants), N.C. Neurological Soc., 1993, Allergan Pharms., 1994. Fellow Am. Acad. Neurology (continuing edn. com. 1985-92, session chmn. 40th ann. mtg. 1988, ad hoc com. on assessment 1989, ad hoc com. on regional and fgn. continuing med. edn. programs 1989—, councillor exec. bd. 1991-95, non-neurologist edn. subcom. 1991—, rep. to AMA nat. adv. com. on family violence 1992-94, chair women in neurology sect. 1992-93, chair task force on women 1992-94, bylaws com. 1993—); mem. AMA, Am. Assn. Electrodiagnostic Medicine (examiner 1985, 87, tng. program rev. com. 1987-89, joint mtgs. com. 1990-91, mem. com. 1991-94, chair mem. com. 1992-94, liaison to Am. Acad. Neurology 1992-93, ethics and peer rev. com. 1993—), Nat. Spasmodic Torticollis Assn. (med. adv. bd. 1989—), Soc. Clin. Neurology, N.C. Neurol. Soc., Myasthenia Gravis Found. (med. adv. bd. 1986—, program com. 1990—). Mem. Ch. Christ. Office: Duke U Med Ctr PO Box 3403 Durham NC 27702-3403

MASSEY, LEWIS, state official; b. Gainesville, Ga.; s. Abit and Kayanne M.; m. Amy Massey; children: Chandler, Cameryn. BBA in Finance, U. Ga.

Mem. campaign staff Ct. Appeals Judge Robert Benham; mgr. reelection campaign Gov. Joe Frank Harris; dir. election campaigns various first time candidates apptd. by Gov. Joe Frank Harris; spl. asst. Gov. Joe Frank Harris; campaign mgr. Pierre Howard for Lt. Gov.; chief of staff Lt. Gov. Pierre Howard; v.p. Bank South Securities Corp.; sec. of state. State of Ga., 1996—. Elder Peachtree Presbyn. Ch.; mem. bd. dirs. Am. Cancer Soc., Eagle Ranch Home For Boys. Recipient Blue Key ALumnus of the Yr. award U. Ga., Outstanding Young Alumnus Bus. Sch. U. Ga. Office: Office of Sec of State State Capitol Rm 214 Atlanta GA 30334

MASSEY, PATTI CHRYL, elemetary school educator; b. Electra, Tex., Nov. 18, 1952; d. Francis Leon and Violet V. (Inabinette) Perry; m. William S. Massey, July 18,1986. BS, Midwestern U., 1974; MEd, Southwest Tex. State U., 1979. Cert. lifetime elem. educator, reading specialist, coop. learning trainer, reading recovery tchr. Tchr. East Central ISD, San Antonio, 1975-89, San Antonio ISD, 1990—. Vol. Tex. Spl. Olympics, San Antonio, 1975—, Jimenez Thanksgiving Sr. Citizens Dinner, San Antonio, 1983—, Amateur Athletic Union Jr. Olympics, San Antonio, 1989, Amateur Athletic Union Nat. Basketball Tournament, San Antonio, 1990, U.S. Olympic Festival, San Antonio, 1993, Alzheimer's Memory Walk, 1992-95. Named One of Outstanding Young Women in Am., 1983. Mem. NEA, San Antonio Tchrs. Coun., Tex. State Tchrs. Assn., PTA (hon. life, sec. 1982-84), Internat. Reading Assn., Alamo Reading Coun., Tex. State Reading Assn., Reading Recovery Coun. N.Am., Kappa Delta Pi, Alpha Delta Kappa, Sigma Kappa (Outstanding Alumna 1988, 91, Pearl Ct. award 1990, Outstanding Regional Alumna 1991). Democrat. Methodist. Home: 4527 Black Oak Woods San Antonio TX 78249-1478

MASSEY, WILLIAM WALTER, JR., sales executive; b. Lawrenceburg, Tenn., Sept. 21, 1928; s. William Walter and Bess Ann (Brian) M.; m. Virginia Claire Smith, Aug. 16, 1952; children: William Walter III, Laura Ann, Lynn Smith, Lisa Claire. BBA, U. Miami, Fla., 1949; BFA, U. Fla., 1969. Exec. v.p., dir. Massey Motors, Inc., Jacksonville, Fla., 1950—; v.p., dir. Atlantic Discount Co. Inc., Jacksonville, 1954-64; pres. Owners Surety Corp., Jacksonville, 1959—, General Svcs. Corp., Jacksonville, 1960-69, Owners Guaranty Life, Phoenix, Ariz., 1960-64, Securities Guaranty Life, Phoenix, Ariz., 1961-64, Fla. Properties, Inc., Jacksonville, 1961-66, Chi-Cha, Inc., Jacksonville, 1965-70, Univ. Square Properties, Jacksonville, 1969-80; v.p., bd. dir. Southside Country Day School, Jacksonville, 1963-68; bd. dirs. Southside Atlantic Bank, Jacksonville, 1965-93. Exhibited in group shows at Internat., N.Y., 1970, Ball State U., 1972. Lt. USAF, 1950-1952. Mem. Ponte Vedra Club, River Club, Epping Forest Club, Sigma Chi. Methodist.

MASSEY, W(ILMET) ANNETTE, nurse, former educator; b. Big Chimney, W.Va., June 30, 1920; d. Robert Lee and Twila Augusta (Pringle) M.; student Morris Harvey Coll., 1938-39; diploma, Phila. Gen. Hosp. Sch. Nursing, 1943; BS in Edn., U. Pa., 1948; MSN, Yale U., 1959. Nurse cadet instr. U.S. Cadet Nurse Corps, Huntington (W.Va.) Meml. Hosp., 1943-45; nurse instr. St. Mary's Sch. Nursing, Huntington, 1948-51; WHO nurse cons. Govt. Ceylon, 1951-55; staff nurse instr. VA Hosp., Ft. Thomas, Ky., 1955-57; asst. prof. nursing Brigham Young U., Provo, Utah, 1959-61; assoc. prof. nursing W.Va. U., Morgantown, 1961-83, chmn. dept. psychiat. nursing, 1968-72, ret.; cons. Appalachian Regional Hosp., Beckley, W.Va., W.Va. Dept. Mental Health, Charleston, Valley Community Mental Health Center, Kingwood, W.Va.; group leader med.-nursing group to India, Expt. Internat. Living, Brattleboro, Vt., 1965. Mem. Appalachian Trail, Morgantown Hospice, Rep. Nat. Com., Drummond Chapel United Meth. Ch., United Meth. Women, health adv. com. Coun. Mins., ARC, Nat. Coun. Sr. Citizens, Monongalians Srs., Rails to Trail, W.Va. Highlands Conservancy, W.Va. Citizens Action, Cooper's Rock Found. NIMH grantee, 1964-75. Mem. ANA, League Nursing, Am. Orthopsychiat. Assn., Internat. Transactional Analysis Assn., Am. Counseling Assn. (dir. 1981-82, v.p. 1982), Am. Soc. Profl. and Exec. Women, Environ. Def. Fund, Nat. Parks and Conservation Assn., Nat. Trust for Hist. Preservation, Tarrytown Group, Nat. Registry Psychiat. Nurse Specialists (edn. and resources com.), Internat. Acad. Cancer Counselors and Cons., Nat. Alliance Family Life, Inc. (founding), AAUP, Nat. Hist. Soc., Hastings Ctr., Nat. Wildlife Fedn., Smithsonian Assos., Phila. Gen. Hosp. Sch. Nursing Alumni, U. Pa., Yale U., W.Va. U. Sch. Nursing (hon.) Alumni Assns., 20/20 Vision Winterthur Guild, Empower Am., Pub. Citizen, Friends of the Earth, W.Va. Pub. Theatre, Am. Rivers, Project Vote Smart, W.Va. Rivers Coalition, World Learning, Wash. Nat. Cathedral, So. Property Law Ctr., Am. Red Cross, Am. Farmland Trust, Sierra Club, Lakeview Resort Club, Appalachian Trail, Sigma Theta Tau. Clubs: Alpine Lake Recreation Cmty.(Terra Alta, W.Va.), Penn (N.Y.C.). Home: 432 Western Ave Morgantown WV 26505-2135

MASSIE, ANN MACLEAN, law educator; b. South Bend, Ind., Sept. 17, 1943; d. John Allan and Gladys Sherill (Wilkie) MacLean; m. Kent Belmore Massie, Aug. 25, 1973; children: Allan Barksdale, Laura Sherrill. BA, Duke U., 1966; MA in English, U. Mich., 1967; JD, U. Va., 1971. Bar: Ga. 1971. Assoc. Alston, Miller & Gaines, Atlanta, 1971-73, Long and Aldridge, Atlanta, 1974-76; staff atty. regional office FTC, Atlanta, 1973-74; law clk. to Hon. J. Harvie Wilkinson III U.S. Ct. Appeals (4th cir.), Charlottesville, Va., 1984-85; adj. prof. law Washington & Lee U., Lexington, Va., 1985-88, asst. prof. law, 1988-93; assoc. prof. law Washington & Lee U., Lexington, 1993—. Contbr. articles to law jours. Deacon Waynesboro (Va.) Presbyn. Ch., 1986-88; bd. dirs., v.p. Hosp. Aux., Waynesboro, 1986-88; elder Lexington Presbyn. Ch., 1995—. Named Prof. of Yr., Women Law Students Orgn., 1993. Mem. Am. Soc. Law, Medicine and Ethics, Hastings Ctr., Choice in Dying. Home: PO Box 1076 Lexington VA 24450-1076 Office: Washington and Lee U Sch of Law Lexington VA 24450

MASSIE, ANNE ADAMS ROBERTSON, artist; b. Lynchburg, Va., May 30, 1931; d. Douglas Alexander and Annie Scott (Harris) Robertson; m. William McKinnon Massie, Apr. 30, 1960; children: Anne Harris, William McKinnon, Jr. Grad., St. Mary's Coll., Raleigh, N.C., 1950; BA in English, Randolph Macon Woman's Coll., 1952. Tchr. English E.C. Glass High Sch., Lynchburg, 1955-60; juror Ctrl. Va. Watercolor Guild, 1996. Represented in permanent collectsions at Hotel de Ville, Rueil-Malmaison, France, Randolph Macon Womans Coll., Lynchburg Coll., Va. Episcopal Sch., Va. Sch. of Arts, Va. State Bar Assn., Richmond, St. John's Episcopal Ch. Bd. dirs. Lynchburg Hist. Found., 1968-81, 91-95, pres., 1978-81; bd. dirs. Lynchburg Fine Arts Ctr., 1992—; bd. dirs. Point of Honor Mus., 1988—, chmn. accessions com., 1989—; bd. dirs. Amazement Sq. Children's Mus., 1996; trustee Va. Episcopal Sch., Lynchburg, 1983-89. Mem. Am. Watercolor Soc. (signature, Dolphin fellow 1993, Gold medal Honor 1993), Nat. Watercolor Soc. (signature, Artist's Mag. award), Nat. League Am. Pen Women (pres. 1987, Best in Show 1994), Knickerbocker Artists (signature, Silver medal Watercolor 1993), Watercolor USA Honor Soc., Watercolor West (signature), Catharine Lorrilard Wolfe Art Club (signature), Southern Watercolor Soc (signature), Va. Watercolor Soc. (artist mem., Best in Show 1992, chmn. exhbns. 1986, pres. 1995-96), Colonial Dames Am. (chmn. 1987-90), Hillside Garden Club (pres. 1974-76), Jr. League (editor 1953-72), Lynchburg Art Club (bd. dirs. 1995—, chmn. 1981-84), Antiquarian Club. Episcopalian. Home: 3204 Rivermont Ave Lynchburg VA 24503-2028

MASSIN, STEVEN SCOTT, business education educator; b. Falls City, Nebr., June 25, 1944; s. Sy and Hariette Ann (Medlock) M. BJ, U. Mo., Columbia, 1966; JD, U. Nebr., 1971. Mem. bus. faculty U. No. Colo., Greeley, 1972-77, Ill. State U., Normal, 1977-85, Emory U., Atlanta, 1985—; mem. adv. bd. West Pub. Co., Mpls., 1990—. Author: Business Law Manual, 1976; contbr. articles to profl. publs. Pres. Rocky Mountain Bus. Law Assn., 1975-76. Mem. Am. Acad. Mgmt., Soc. for Bus. Ethics, Southeastern Acad. Legal Studies in Bus., Acad. Legal Studies of Bus. Home: 1483 Oakridge Ct Decatur GA 30033 Office: Emory U 228 Rich Bldg 1602 Mizell Dr Atlanta GA 30322

MASSINGILL, HARRY BRADFORD, JR., retired association administrator; b. Beaumont, Tex., Apr. 8, 1932; s. Harry Bradford and Ivy Regina (Newman) B.; m. Mary E. Grey, Apr. 23, 1954; children: Kathryn E. Manck, Harry Bradford III, Laura A. Nurse, David. AA in Engring., Lamar Jr. Coll., Beaumont, Tex., 1951. Commd. 2nd lt. USAF, 1954, advanced through grades to lt. col., sr. navigator, 1961-69; master navigator USAF, Ramey AFB, P.R., 1969-72; ret. USAF, 1972; dist. chmn. Boy Scouts Am., Ramey AFB, 1970-72; dist. exec. South Plains Coun. Boy Scouts Am., Lubbock, Tex., 1973-94. Bd. dirs. Festivals, Inc., Lubbock, 1992—, Univ. Ministries, Lubbock, 1990—, Presbyn. Clinic, Lubbock, 1980-84;. Mem. Ret. Officers Assn., Air Force Assn., Lions (Lubbock club), Rotary (dir. Ralls chpt. 1978-83), Alpha Phi Omega. Republican. Presbyterian. Home: 3603 77th Dr Lubbock TX 79423-1215

MASSOUD, SAMIA LAMIE, mathematics educator, computer systems analyst; b. Cairo, Egypt, July 1, 1959; d. Lamie and Lyla F. (Saad) M.; m. Erian A. Baskharone, Sept. 24, 1978; children: Richie, Bobby. BS, U. Garunis, Cairo, 1978; MS, U. Cin., 1980; PhD, Tex. A&M U., 1989. Cert. tchr., Ariz. Math. instr. U. Cin., 1979-80, Ariz. State U., Tempe, 1980-82; math. and computer sci. instr. Maricopa County Coll., Phoenix, 1982-85; systems analyst Tex. A&M U., College Station, 1987—, math. instr., 1992—; computer cons. Garrett Turbine Engine Co., Phoenix, 1984-85; presenter Conf. on Innovation, Phoenix, Coll., 1985, Am. Assn. Adult and Continuing Edn. Conf., Hollywood, Fla., 1986, Computer Literacy in Community, Tex. A&M U., 1990. Author: (software package) Steps in Solving Word Problems, 1983, (textbook) Calculus with Maple, 1994, Calculus with Mathematica, 1995; asst. editor: Computer Assisted Instruction, 1985, Lifelong Learning, 1986; contbr. articles to profl. jours. Instrnl. design coord. Maricopa County Coll. Dist., Phoenix, 1983. Grantee Funds for Improvement of Postsecondary Edn., 1984, Dist. Edn. and Devel. Projects, 1985. Mem. Am. Math. Soc., Assn. Computing Machinery, Acad. Computer Assn. Office: Tex A&M U Computing Info Sys College Station TX 77843

MASTEN, W. YONDELL, nursing educator; b. Alexandria, La., Sept. 7, 1940; d. Kelly and Alyne (Shankles) Bingham; m. Larry Burce Masten, May 27, 1960; children: Gordon, Larry Bryan, John, Lari. BS in Math., West Tex. State U., 1973, BSN, 1977; MS in Nursing, U. Tex., 1981; MS, Tex. Tech. U., 1978, PhD, 1985. Prof. Tex. Tech. U. Health Scis. Ctr. Sch. Nursing; women's health nurse practitioner, instr. Meth. Hosp. Sch. Nursing, Lubbock; head nurse Meth. Hosp., Lubbock; faculty Tex. Tech. U., Lubbock. Contbr. articles to profl. jours. Mem. ANA, Assn. Women's Health Obstet. and Neonatal Nurses, Nat. League for Nursing, Human Factors Soc., Inst. Indsl. Engrs., Internat. Childbirth Edn. Assn., Sigma Theta Tau, Iota Mu.

MASTERS, BETTIE SUE SILER, biochemist, educator; b. Lexington, Va., June 13, 1937; d. Wendell Hamilton and Mildred Virginia (Cromer) Siler; m. Robert Sherman Masters, Aug. 6, 1960; children: Diane Elizabeth, Deborah Ann. B.S. in Chemistry, Roanoke Coll., 1959, D.Sc. (hon.), 1983; Ph.D. in Biochemistry, Duke U., 1963. Postdoctoral fellow Duke U., 1963-66, advanced research fellow, 1966-68, assoc. on faculty, 1967-68; mem. faculty U. Tex. Health Sci. Ctr. (Southwestern Med. Sch.), Dallas, 1968-82; assoc. prof. biochemistry U. Tex. Health Sci. Ctr. (Southwestern Med. Sch.), 1972-76, prof., 1976-82, research prof. surgery, dir. biochem. burn research, 1979-82; prof. biochemistry, chmn. dept. Med. Coll. Wis., Milw., 1982-90; Robert A. Welch prof. chemistry, dept. biochemistry U. Tex. Health Sci. Ctr., San Antonio, 1990—; mem. pharmacology-toxicology rsch. rev. com. Nat. Inst. Gen. Med. Scis., NIH, 1975-79; mem. bd. sci. counselors Nat. Inst. Environ. Health Scis., 1982-86, chmn., 1984-86; mem. adv. com. on biochemistry and endocrinology Am. Cancer Soc., 1989-92, chmn., 1991-92; mem. phys. biochemistry study sect. NIH, 1989-90; vis. scientist Japan Soc. for Promotion Sci., 1978. Mem. editl. bd. Jour. Biol. Chemistry, 1976-81, 96—, Archives Biochemistry and Biophysics, 1991—; contbr. chpts. to books and articles, revs. and abstracts to profl. jours. Recipient Merit award Nat. Heart, Lung and Blood Inst., 1988-97, grantee, 1970—; recipient Excellence in Sci. award Fedn. Am. Socs. for Exptl. Biology, 1992; postdoctoral fellow Am. Cancer Soc., 1963-65, advanced rsch. fellow Am. Heart Assn., 1966-68, established investigator, 1968-73; rsch. grantee NIH, 1970—, Nat. Heart Lung Blood Dist., 1970—, Nat. Inst. Gen. Med. Scis., 1980—, Robert A. Welch Found., 1971-82, 90—. Mem. AAAS, Am. Soc. Biochemistry and Molecular Biology (nominating com. 1983, coun. 1985-86, awards com. 1992—, fin. com. 1993—, publs. com. 1994—), Am. Soc. Pharmacology and Exptl. Therapeutics (exec. com. drug metabolism divsn. 1979-81, chmn. exec. com. 1993-94, bd. publs. trustees 1982-87), Am. Soc. Cell Biology, Am. Chem. Soc., Internat. Union Biochemistry and Molecular Biology (vice chair U.S. nat. com. 1994—, nominating com. 1995—), Sigma Xi, Alpha Omega Alpha. Office: U Tex Health Sci Ctr Dept Biochemistry 7703 Floyd Curl Dr San Antonio TX 78284-6200

MASTERS, CLAUDE BIVIN, lawyer; b. Cleburne, Tex., July 25, 1930; s. Claude Pinkney and Ola Mae (Rollins) M.; m. Jenita Whites, June 1, 1949 (div.); children: C. Thomas, C. Danette Masters McClanahan, Teresa Masters Lebeck; m. Cynthia McCormack, Nov. 4, 1983. BS, U. Houston, 1953, JD, 1969, LLM, 1985. Bar: Tex. 1969, U.S. Dist. Ct. (so. dist.) Tex. 1971, U.S. Dist. Ct. (we. dist.) Tex. 1972, U.S. Ct. Appeals (5th cir.) 1971, U.S. Ct. Appeals (11th cir.) 1983, U.S. Supreme Ct. 1978. Ptnr. Martin & Masters, Houston, 1971-73; v.p., gen. counsel Summit Ins. Co. N.Y., N.Y.C., 1973-75; sr. atty. Ashland Oil Co., Ky., 1975-78; v.p. Houston Oil & Minerals Co., Houston, 1978-84; assoc. Dunnam & Strong, Houston, 1984-85; risk-mgmt. cons. Masters & Assocs., Houston, 1975—; bd. dirs. Alford & Assocs., Houston; adj. prof. law U. Houston, 1984—. Dir.-gen. Tex. Safety Assn., Austin, 1959. Served with U.S. Army, 1946-47. Named Outstanding Speaker, Southwest Ins. Info. Service, Dallas, 1961-62. Fellow Tex. Bar Found; mem. Jaycees (bd. dirs. Tulsa 1962; named Outstanding Mem. Tex. 1960), Phi Delta Phi. Republican. Mem. Ch. of Christ. Home: 5605 Saint Moritz St Bellaire TX 77401-2617 Office: 675 Bering Dr #300 Houston TX 77057-2128

MASTERS, DAVID LEE, pediatrician; b. Kankakee, Ill., Nov. 22, 1964; s. David Romey and Deborah Lynn (Dietrich) M.; m. Trician Deanne Kinsey, May 20, 1995. Student, Coll. Lake County, Grayslake, Ill., 1985-88; BA in Biology, U. N.C., Greensboro, 1991; MD, East Carolina U., 1995. Operating room technician Moses H. Come Meml. Hosp., Greensboro, 1988-91; resident in pediat. Duke Univ. Med. Ctr., Durham, N.C., 1995—; mem. pediat. house staff adv. com. Duke Univ. Med. Ctr., Durham, 1995—. With USN, 1985-88. Mem. AMA (resident sect., editor), N.C. Med. Soc., Phi Beta Kappa, Phi Theta Kappa. Democrat. Baptist. Home: 2810 Shaftsbury St Durham NC 27704 Office: Duke Univ Med Ctr Fulton & Erwin St Durham NC 27710

MASTERS, RONALD G., dentist, educator; b. Hannibal, Mo., Jan. 24, 1947; s. Gilbert D. and Beulah E. (Lewton) M.; m. Mary Jane Boulware; children: Alex, Jake, Jessica, Anna. AB in Zoology and Microbiology, Ind. U., 1969; DDS, U. Mo., 1974. From dental student to LTJG USNR, Camp Lejeune, N.C., 1970-74, lt., 1974-76; tchr. sci. Hazelwood (Mo.) Sch. Dist., 1969-70; med. lab. technician Downtown Hosp., Branch of Rsch. Hosp., Kansas City, Mo., 1971-74; pvt. practice, 1976-83; chief of dental svc. State Hosp. Number 1, Fulton, Mo., 1980-84; staff dentist, dir. dental programs for geriatrics and long term care VA Med. Ctr., Houston, 1984—; clin. asst. prof. stomatology, gen. and cmty. dentistry U. Tex. Dental Branch, Houston, 1991—. Contbg. editor for gerodontics Huffington Ctr. forAging, Baylor Coll. Medicine, Home Page/Internet. Mem. ADA, Greater Houston Dental Soc., Assn. Mil. Surgeons U.S. Home: 14 Martins Way Sugar Land TX 77479-2484 Office: VA Med Ctr 2002 Holcombe Blvd Houston TX 77030-4211

MASTERSON RAINES, JUDITH AMANDA, marketing executive; b. Chgo., Aug. 18, 1952; d. Thomas Robert and Dorothy Jean Masterson; m. Stephen S. Raines, July 18, 1981; stepchildren: Jennifer, Jeffrey. BA with honors, Emory U., 1974. Dir. advt. Alex Cooley Presents, Atlanta, 1974-79; gen. mgr. Theatre League of Atlanta, 1981-94, Chesapeake Concerts, Atlanta, 1979-94; v.p. Nat. Franchise Assocs., Atlanta, 1983—; pres. M&R Advt., Atlanta, 1986—. Author/editor Franchise News, 1991—; contbr. articles to profl. jours. Mem. Ga. Com. on Music Industry, Atlanta, 1989-93; local press rep. Nat. Black Arts Festival, Atlanta, 1990, The Phantom of the Opera, Atlanta, 1991; organizer benefits NAPWA/Aid Atlanta, Zoo Atlanta, UNICEF, Atlanta Food Bank. Recipient 20th Century Award of Achievement Internat. Biog. Ctr., 1995. Mem. AAUW, NOW, NAFE, Nat. Wildlife Fund, Atlanta C. of C., Phi Beta Kappa. Office: M&R Advertising Ste 201 3473 Satellite Blvd Duluth GA 30136

MATA, ELIZABETH ADAMS, language educator, land investor; b. Raleigh, N.C., Jan. 11, 1946; d. John Quincy Adams and Beulah Honeycutt; m. Juan Mata, June 21, 1968; children: Laura, Juan, Daniel. Student, Sweet Briar Coll., Paris, 1966-67; BA in French, Randolph-Macon Women's Coll., 1968; tchr. cert. in French and Spanish, N.C. State U., 1981; postgrad., U. Salamanca (Spain), summers 1983-86, Fordham U., 1994; MA in Spanish, NYU, 1986; cert. mentor tchr., N.C. State U., 1989; postgrad., U. N.C., 1995—. Lic. real estate agt., N.C. ESL tchr. Am. Inst., Madrid, 1968-69; English tchr. Ay J Garriques, Madrid, 1968-74, pvt. classes, Madrid, 1975-78; French tchr. Wake County Schs., Cary, N.C., 1982; tchr. Spanish, Wake County Schs., Apex, N.C., 1994; chmn. sch. improvement team Wake County Schs., Apex, 1991-93. Named Tchr. of Yr., Apex H.S., 1992-93. Mem. NAFE, Am. Assn. Tchrs. Spanish and Portuguese, Univ. Coun. on Edn., Alpha Kappa Delta. Democrat. Home: 643 Kings Fork Rd Cary NC 27511-5711

MATA, ZOILA, chemist; b. Galveston, Tex., Aug. 8, 1937; d. Francisco Zuniga and Leonarda (Sustaita) M. BS in Biology, Chemistry, Tex. A&I U., 1975. Office asst. Galveston Pub. Health Nursing Service, 1959-63; draftswoman Wilson Real Estate Index and Pub, Houston, 1964-65; bookkeeper City Products Corp, Galveston, 1966-67; research asst. U. Tex. Med. Br., Galveston, 1967-70; clk. State Dept. Pub. Welfare, Houston, 1971-72, Quinby Temporary, Houston, 1972-76; research technician Baylor Coll. Medicine, Houston, 1976; sr. chemist Nalco Chem. Co., Sugarland, Tex., 1976-94, Nalco/Exxon Energy Chemicals, LP, Sugarland, 1994—. Active Rep. Nat. Hispanic Assembly of Tex. (chair membership credentials 1986—), Rep. Nat. Hispanic Assembly of Harris (vice chair 1986, treas. 1991—), Iota Sigma Pi. Named one of Notable Woman of Tex., 1984-85. Mem. Am. Chem. Soc. (rubber div.), Amigas de las Americas, Nat. Chicano Health Orgn. Home: 7733 Dixie Dr Houston TX 77087-5507 Office: Nalco/Exxon Energy Chemicals LP PO Box 87 Sugar Land TX 77487-0087

MATARELLI, STEVEN ANTHONY, health facility administrator; b. Urbana, Ill., Dec. 1, 1962; s. Michael Anthony and Mary Kathryn (Carnahan) M.; m. Joan Carey, Dec. 22, 1984 (div. June 1987). A., Ill. Cen. Coll., 1985; diploma in nursing, Meth. Med. Ctr., Peoria, Ill., 1985; BSN, SUNY, Albany, 1990; MSN, Tex. Women's U., 1994. RN, Tex., Okla.; CCRN; cert. clin. nurse specialist. Staff/charge nurse Vanderbilt U. Med. Ctr., Nashville, 1985-88, Baylor U. Med. Ctr., Dallas, 1988-91; practice coord. Presbyn. Hosp. Dallas, 1991-94; asst. hosp. adminstr. clin. ops. Vencor Hosp., Oklahoma City, 1994—; gen. ptnr. Med.-Legal Assocs., Dallas, 1991-94; guest lectr. multiple orgns., Dallas, 1988—. Mem. AACN, Emergency Nurses Assn. Home: 113 NW 13th Loft 207 Oklahoma City OK 73103 Office: Vencor Hosp 1407 N Robinson Oklahoma City OK 73103

MATAS, MYRA DOROTHEA, interior architect and designer, kitchen and bath designer; b. San Francisco, Mar. 21, 1938; d. Arthur Joseph and Marjorie Dorothy (Johnson) Anderson; m. Michael Richard Matas Jr., Mar. 15, 1958; children: Michael Richard III, Kenneth Scott. Cert. interior design, Canada Coll.; cert. interior design, Calif. Owner, operator Miquel's Antiques Co., Millbrae, Calif., 1969-70, Miguel's Antiques & Interiors Co., Burlingame, Calif., 1970-79, Country Elegance Antiques & Interiors Co., Menlo Park, Calif., 1979-84, La France Boutique Co., 1979-84, Myra D. Matas Interior Design, San Francisco, 1984—, Lafayette, La., 1994—; mgr. La France Imports, Inc., 1982-92; pres., gen. contractor Artisans 3 Inc., Burlingame, 1988-92; gen. contractor Matas Constr., Millbrae, 1993—; instr. interior design dept. Canada Coll. Mem. Calif. Coun. Interior Design. Contbr. articles in field to profl. jours. Office: 101 Henry Adams St Ste 348 San Francisco CA 94103-5213 also: 324 rue Jefferson Lafayette LA 70501

MATEKER, EMIL JOSEPH, JR., geophysicist; b. St. Louis, Apr. 25, 1931; s. Emil Joseph and Lillian (Broz) M.; m. Lolita Ann Winter, Nov. 25, 1954; children: Mark Steven, Anne Marie, John David. BS in Geophys. Engring., St. Louis U., 1956, MS in Rsch. Geophysics, 1959, PhD in Seismology, 1964. Registered geologist and geophysicist, Calif. Assoc. prof. geophysics Washington U., St. Louis, 1966-69; mgr. geophys. rsch. Western Geophys. Co. of Am., Houston, 1969-70; v.p. R & D Western Geophys. Co. of Am., 1970-74; pres. Litton Resources Sys., Houston, 1977, Litton Westrex, Houston, 1974-79; pres. Aero Svc. div. Western Geophys. Co. of Am., 1974-87, v.p., 1974-90; v.p. Western Atlas Internat., Inc., Houston, 1987—; pres. Aero Svc. div. Western Atlas Internat., Inc., Houston, 1987-90; v.p. tech. Western Geophys. div. Western Atlas Internat., Inc., Houston, 1990-93; pres. Western Atlas Software Divsn. Western Atlas Internat. Inc., Houston, 1993-94; sr. v.p. tech. Western Atlas Internat. Inc., 1994—; mem. State of Calif. Bd. Registration for Geophysicists, Sacramento, 1974—, State of Calif. Bd. Registration for Geologists, Sacramento, 1974—. Author: A Treatise on Modern Exploration Seismology, 2 vols., 1965; contbr. articles to profl. jours.; asst. editor Geophysica, 1969-70. Baseball mgr. Westchester High Sch., 1969-74; soccer coach Spring Forest Jr. High Sch., Houston, 1974; bd. dirs. St. Agnes Acad., Houston, 1977-82, pres. bd. dirs., 1996-97; pres. Strake Jesuits Booster Club, Houston, 1977-78. 2nd lt. U.S. Army, 1951-54. Recipient St. Louis U. Alumni award, 1976. Mem. AAAS, Am. Geophys. Union, Seismological Soc. Am., Geophys. Soc. Houston, European Assn. Exploration Geophysicists, Soc. Exploration Geophysicists (chmn. 1974). Roman Catholic. Home: 419 Hickory Post Ln Houston TX 77079-7430 Office: Div Western Atlas Internat 10205 Westheimer Rd Houston TX 77042-3115

MATELAN, MATHEW NICHOLAS, software engineer; b. Stephenville, Tex., Aug. 21, 1945; s. Mathew Albert and Mary Frances (Hardwick) M.; m. Lois Margaret Waguespack, Apr. 5, 1975; children: Evelyn Nicole, Eleanor Gillian. BS in Physics, U. Tex., Arlington, 1969; MS in Computer Engring., So. Meth. U., 1973, PhD in Computer Sci., 1976. Sr. aerospace engr. Gen. Dynamics, Ft. Worth, 1969-75; sys. engr. Lawrence Livermore (Calif.) Labs., 1975-76; group mgr. Gen. Dynamics, Ft. Worth, 1976-78; computer R&D mgr. United Techs./Mostek, Carrollton, Tex., 1978-82; chief sys. arch. Honeywell Comm., Dallas, 1982-83; pres., CEO, chmn., co-founder Flexible Computer Corp., Dallas, 1983-90; chief arch. Matelan Software Sys., Dallas, 1991-94; chief engr. Expertware, Santa Clara, Calif., 1991-94; chief tech. officer Learn Techs. Interactive, N.Y.C., 1994—; cons. Bendix Flight Controls Divsn., Teterboro, N.J., 1974-75; founding dir. Picture Telephone, Boston, 1984-86, Spectrum Digital, Washington, 1984-86; adv. bd. Axavision, N.Y.C., 1993—. Contbr. articles to profl. jours. Libr. automation bd. So. Meth. U., Dallas, 1985-86. Devel. grantee U.S. Energy Dept., 1975, NASA, 1985. Mem. IEEE (sr. mem.), Assn. for Computing Machinery. Home: 3969 Courtshire Dr Dallas TX 75229 Office: Learn Techs Interactive 3530 Forest Ln S 61 Dallas TX 75234

MATER, MAUD E., federal agency administrator, lawyer. BA in English, Case Western Reserve U., 1969, JD, 1972. Asst. gen. counsel Fed. Home Loan Mortgage Corp., 1976-78, assoc. gen. counsel, 1978-79, dep. gen. counsel, 1979-81, v.p., dep. gen. counsel, 1981-84, sr. v.p., gen. counsel, sec., 1984—. Mem. ABA, Fed. Bar Assn., Ohio Bar Assn., D.C. Bar Assn., Washington Met. Corp. Counsels Assn. (dir., sec.). Office: Fed Home Loan Mortgage Corp 8200 Jones Branch Dr Mc Lean VA 22102-3107

MATEUS, LOIS, manufacturing executive; b. 1946. Grad., U. Ky., 1968. Asst. mgr. advt. Begley Drug, 1969-70; staff writer Commonwealth of Ky., 1970-72; dir. pub. rels. Ky. Dem. Party, 1973-75; exec. dir. Hist. Events Celebration Commn., 1976; free-lance writer, 1977-79; press sec., various other adminstrv. positions Gov. John Y. Brown of Ky., 1979-82; sr. v.p. corp. communications and corp. svcs. Brown-Forman Corp., Louisville, 1982—. Office: Brown-Forman Corp 850 Dixie Hwy Louisville KY 40210-1038*

MATHAVAN, SUDERSHAN KUMAR, nuclear power engineer; b. Muzfrabad, Kashmir, India, Aug. 18, 1945; came to U.S., 1968; s. Kartar Chand and Ram Rakhi (Makoli) M.; m. Alka Rani Ajrawat, Oct. 23, 1979; children: Erik, Sarita, Manika, Ketan. BS, Kasmir U., Srinagar, India, 1967; MS, U. Miami, 1970, PhD, 1977. Registered profl. engr., Fla. Engr. Ground Support Engring., Miami, Fla., 1969-73, Smith, Korach A/E, Miami, 1973-75; cons. engr. U. Miami, Coral Gables, Fla., 1975-77; sr. engr. Duke Power, Charlotte, N.C., 1977-79; prin. engr. Fla. Power & Light Co., West Palm Beach, 1979—; mem. analysis subcom. Westinghouse Owners Group, Pitts., 1983—. Contbr. articles to profl. jours. Pres. India Soc., Miami, 1984-86; sec. Hindu Temple, Ft. Lauderdale, Fla., 1986—. Mem. Am. Nuclear Soc. Democrat. Home: 1130 Fairdale Way Wellington FL 33414-9038 Office: Fla Power & Light Co Universe Blvd North Palm Beach FL 33408

MATHAY, MARY FRANCES, marketing executive; b. Youngstown, Ohio, July 26, 1944; d. Howard E. and Mary C. (Siple) M.; m. Thomas Stone Withgott, Dec. 20, 1969 (div. June 1973). BA in English Lit. and Composition, Queens Coll., 1967; grad. in bus., Katharine Gibbs Sch., 1968. Corp. mktg. mgr., assoc. Odell Assocs., Inc., Charlotte, N.C., 1973-90; dir. pub. rels. and spl. events Charlotte (N.C.)-Mecklenburg Arts and Sci. Coun., 1990-92; pres. Mathay Comm., Inc., Charlotte, 1992—; speakers bur. chmn. Hospice at Charlotte, Inc., 1980-83; pub. rels. and advt. dir. "Chemical People" program PBS, Charlotte, 1983-84. Author: Legacy of Architecture, 1988; editor: Mint Mus. Antiques Show Mag., 1980, editorial advisor Crier, 1987-92; producer Charlotte's Web, 1977. Bd. dirs. Jr. League of Charlotte, Inc., 1978-79, mem. 1968—; bd. dirs. ECO, Inc., Charlotte, 1979-86, Queens Coll. Alumni, Charlotte, 1984-87, Learning How, Inc., Charlotte, 1988-91; bd. dirs. on adolescent pregnancy Mecklenburg County Coun., 1986-88; vol. tchr. ABLE Cen. Piedmont C.C., 1987-90; comm. com. vol. Am. Cancer Soc., 1994—, Charlotte-Mecklenburg Edn. Found., 1992-94, Charlotte-Mecklenburg Sr. Ctrs., 1994-95; bd. dirs. Arches, 1996-98. Mem. Pub. Rels. Soc. Am. (bd. dirs. 1989—, pres. 1995), Charlotte Pub. Rels. Soc. (bd. dirs. 1986-89, 92-93), Olde Providence Racquet Club, Tower Club. Republican. Presbyterian.

MATHENY, CHARLES WOODBURN, JR., retired army officer, retired civil engineer, former city official; b. Sarasota, Fla., Aug. 7, 1914; s. Charles Woodburn Sr. and Virginia (Yates) M.; m. Jeanne Felkel, July 12, 1942; children: Virginia Ann, Nancy Caroline, Charles Woodburn III. BSCE, U. Fla., 1936; grad., Army Command and Gen. Staff Coll., 1944. Lic. comml. pilot. Sanitary engr. Ga. State Dept. Health, 1937-39; civil engr. Fla. East Coast Ry., 1939-41; commd. 2d lt. F.A., USAR, 1936, 2d lt. F.A. U.S. Army, 1942, advanced through grades to col., 1955; comdr. 351st Field Arty. Bn., 1945, commr., 33rd Field Arty. Bn., 1st Inf. Divsn., 1945, coaan.staff officer, 1947; gen. staff G-3 Plans Dept. Army, 1948-51; qualified Air Force liaison pilot, 1951; qualified Army aviator, 1952; aviation officer 25th Inf. Div., Korea, 1952-53; sr. Army aviation advisor Korean Army, 1953; dep. commdt., dir. combat devel. Army Aviation Sch., 1954-55; dep. dir. research, dep. dir. dept. tactics Arty. Sch., 1955-57; aviation officer 7th U.S. Army, Germany, 1957-58; Munich sub area comdr. So. Area Command, Europe, 1958-59, qualified sr. army aviator, 1959, dep. chief staff for info. So. Area Command, 1960; Mich. sector comdr. VI Army Corps, 1961-62; ret., 1962; asst. dir. Tampa (Fla.), Dept. Pub. Works 1963-77, asst. to dir., 1977-81, ret., 1981. During World War II, Germany Commd., 31st field artillery Battalion in combat and occupation, 1945, also 33d field artillery battalion, 1st Infantry Divsn., in occupation, 1947. Inititator tact use of helicopters in Army and army warrant officer aviator program, 1949, army combat units equipped with helicopter mobility, 1950; pilot 1st combat observation mission in army helicopter, Korea, 1952; organizer, comdr., helicopter pilot 1st Army combat ops. using helicopter mobility to support inf. and engr. front line units 25th Inf. Div., Korea, 1952; pilot 100 combat observation missions, Korea, 1952-53; author 1st state legis. to establish profl. sch. civil engring. for state of Fla., 1974. Contbr. numerous articles on tactical use of helicopter aerial vehicles to mags. Mem. troop com. Boy Scouts Am., 1965-73; active various community and ch. activities; patron Tampa Art Mus., 1965-83, Tampa Community Concert Series, 1979-82; bd. dirs. Tampa YMCA, 1967-71, Fla. Easter Seal Soc., 1978, Easter Seal Soc. Hillsborough County, 1971-84, hon. bd. dirs. 1984—, treas., 1973-76, pres., 1977. Decorated Bronze Star with oak leaf cluster, Air medal with three oak leaf clusters, Recipient of the Eagle Scout award, 1928; named to U. Fla. Student Hall of Fame, 1936. Mem. ASCE (pres. West Coach br., dir. Fla. sect. 1973, Engr. of Yr. award West Coast br. Fla. sect. 1979, life mem. 1980), Am. Soc. Profl. Engrs., Fla. Engring. Soc., Am. Pub. Works Assn. (pres. West Coast br. Fla. chpt. 1972, exec. com. Fla. chpt. 1972-77, v.p. 1977, pres. 1978), Ret. Officers Assn., Army Aviation Assn., Am. Thoracic Soc., SAR, Fla. Blue Key, Alpha Tau Omega. Episcopalian. Lodge: Kiwanis. Home: 4802 W Beachway Dr Tampa FL 33609-4836

MATHENY, PAUL DUANE, minister, theological researcher; b. Conroe, Tex., July 13, 1953; s. Robert Duane and Norma Elizabeth (Cheverton) M.; m. Mary Cevilla Nebelsick, May 30, 1983; child: Rachel Marie. BA, Clark U., 1975; MDiv, Princeton Theol. Sem., 1982; STM, Yale U., 1983; ThD magna cum laude, U. of Heidelberg, Germany, 1989. Ordained to ministry Christian Ch. (Disciples of Christ), 1982. Univ. chaplain UCM at Rutgers U., New Brunswick, N.J., 1983-84; assoc. of divsn. overseas ministry Christian Ch. (Disciples of Christ), Heidelberg, Germany, 1985-88; interim pastor Corydon (Ind.) Christian Ch., 1989-90; asst. prof. of religion Barton Coll., Wilson, N.C., 1990-91; sr. min. Westhampton Christian Ch., Roanoke, Va., 1991—; pres. dist. III, Christian Ch. in Va., 1994-96, mem. com. on Ecumenical and Comm. Witness, 1993—, stewardship adv., 1993—. Author: Dogmatics and Ethics, 1990; editor: Renaissance and Reformation,1992; contbg. editor Karl Barth Soc. Newsletter, 1990—; ed. bd. translation project Internat. Bonhoeffer Soc., 1993—; contbr. articles to profl. jours. Rep. Va. Council of Churches, 1994—; bd. dirs. Roanoke Valley Min. Conf., 1995—, Roanoke Area Ministries, 1991—. Disciples House scholar, Disciples Divinity House, U. Chicago, 1980-81. Mem. Am. Acad. of Religion, Am. Philos. Assoc., Gesellschaft für Ev. Theologic, Karl Barth Soc., Internat. Bonhoeffer Soc. Office: Westhampton Christian Ch 2515 Grandin Rd SW Roanoke VA 24015

MATHER, DONNA COTTRELL, secondary school educator; b. Hodgenville, Ky., Nov. 13, 1951; d. Arvin Elwood and Opha Lena (Bennett) Turner; children: Michael Shannon Cottrell, Kendrick O'Bryan Mather. AAS with distinction, Elizabethtown (Ky.) C.C., 1988; BS cum laude, Western Ky. U., 1991, MA, 1992. Cert. tchr., Ky. Owner/operator Cottrell's Svc. Stas. and Wholesale Warehouse, Elizabethtown, 1968-79; purchasing agt. Phelps Dodge, Elizabethtown, 1979-83; pres. DTC Inc. dba Country Villa, Hodgenville, 1983-88; tchr. Hardin County Bd. Edn., Elizabethtown, 1994-95, LaRue County Bd. Edn., Hodgenville, 1995—; part-time instr. McKendree Coll., Radcliff, Ky., 1993—. Mem. NEA, Ky. Edn. Assn., Ky. Mid. Sch. Assn., Golden Key, Delta Pi Epsilon, Phi Beta Lambda, Phi Theta Kappa. Baptist. Home: 2850 Parkers Grove Rd Magnolia KY 42757-7818

MATHER, HAL FREDERICK, management consultant; b. London, Oct. 2, 1935; came to U.S., 1966; s. Stanley Arthur and Elizabeth (Gibson) M.; m. Jean Richardson, Oct. 6, 1956; 1 child, Carol Ann. BSc, Southall Tech. Coll., 1956. Design engr. Fairey Aviation, Hayes, Eng., 1952-58, Dartmouth, N.S., Can., 1958-66; materials mgr. Nat. Rsch. Corp., Boston, 1966-69, Gilbarco Inc., Greensboro, N.C., 1969-73; v.p. Mather & Plossl, Atlanta, 1973-78; pres. Hal Mather Inc., Atlanta, 1978—. Author: Bills of Materials, 1982, How To Really Manage Inventories, 1984, Competitive Manufacturing, 1988; contbr. articles to profl. jours. Fellow Instn. Mech. Engrs., Am. Prodn. and Inventory Control Soc.; mem. Soc. Mfg. Engrs. (sr.), Inst. Indsl. Engrs., Assn. for Mfg. excellence. Home: 40 Marsh Creek Rd Fernandina Beach FL 32034

MATHER, ROLAND DONALD, administrative law judge; b. New Albany, Ind., Oct. 1, 1939; s. Howard Milton and Elizabeth Ann (Fisher) M.; m. Elizabeth Vivian Fuqua, Dec. 26, 1966. BS, Ind. State U., 1963; MA, Ball State U., 1967; JD, Ind. U., 1972; postgrad., Nat. Jud. Coll., 1977-92; grad., Ind. Jud. Coll., 1981. Bar: Ind. 1972, U.S. Dist. Ct. 1972. Tchr. Richmond (Ind.) Community Schs., 1963-67, Indpls. Pub. Schs., 1967-68; asst. dir. consumer protection div. Ind. Atty. Gen., Indpls., 1970-72, asst. atty. gen., dir. consumer protection div., 1972-75; county judge Montgomery County, Crawfordsville, Ind., 1976-84; U.S. adminstrv. law judge Office of Hearing and Appeals, Pitts., 1986-88, Louisville, 1988—. Mem. ABA, Ind. Bar Assn., Assn. Adminstrv. Law Judges. Republican. Methodist. Home: 6106 Partridge Pl Floyds Knobs IN 47119-9427 Office: Office Hearing Appeals 332 W Broadway Ste 1402 Louisville KY 40202-2119

MATHER, RUTH ELSIE, writer; b. Waverly, Wash., Feb. 14, 1934; d. James Orrin and Leona Ezthelda (Mather) Tallman; m. Mike Nicholas Dakis, Apr. 20, 1958 (div. Nov. 1971); children: Cynthia Michelle, Martin Nicholas; m. Fred Junior Morgan, Nov. 20, 1971. BA with highest honors, Brigham Young U., 1961, MA, 1965; postgrad., U. Miss., 1977-78. Cert. secondary tchr., Idaho, cert. elem. tchr. and secondary tchr. grades 7-14, Calif. English tchr. Lemhi County Schs., Leadore, Idaho, 1962-66; English instr. Yonsei U., Seoul, Republic of Korea, 1973-74, U. Md. Far East Divsn., Seoul, 1975-77, Boise (Idaho) State U., 1978-79, Coll. of the Redwoods, Eureka, Calif., 1980-81; writer hist. video scripts History West Pub. Co., Oklahoma City, 1990—; screenwriter Frontier Images, Canyon Country, Calif., 1994—; cons. on hist. video for PBS, A La Carte, San Francisco, 1994-95, guest expert on Secrets of the Gold Rush-PBS, 1995. Author: Hanging the Sheriff: A Biography of Henry Plummer, 1987, John David Borthwick: Artist of the Gold Rush, 1989, Gold Camp Desperadoes: Study of Crime & Punishment on Frontier, 1990, Vigilante Victims, 1991; contbr. short stories, book revs., articles to encys. and profl. jours. Local campaign dir. Dem. Party, Arcata, Calif., 1969-70. Mem. Nat. Outlaw and Lawman Assn., Western Outlaw and Lawman Assn. Office: History West Pub Co PO Box 23133 Oklahoma City OK 73123

MATHERLEY, STEVE ALLEN, cost accountant; b. Hixson, Tenn., July 15, 1954; S Frank Heilman and Shirley Belle (Clements) M.; m. Gina Anne Baker, Jan. 24, 1981; children: Steve Allen Jr., Mekeesha Anne. Student, David Lipscomb Coll., 1972, 73-75, Tenn. Tech. U., 1973, Fla. Atlantic U., 1976; BS in Bus. Adminstrn. and Acctg., U. Tenn., 1978. Cost acct. Cavalier Corp., Chattanooga, Tenn., 1978-82; pvt. practice bookkeeper Chattanooga, 1982-83, 84-86; contr. Robert M. Davenport Co., Chattanooga, 1983-84; sr. staff acct. Carter Ltd., Inc., Fayetteville, Tenn., 1986-88; mgr. acctg. and fin., Ctr. Space Transp. and Applied Rsch. U. Tenn. Space Inst., Tullahoma, Tenn., 1988-94; cost acct. Tenn. Apparel Corp., Tullahoma, 1994-96, Samuel Shipping Systems, Wincehster, Tenn., 1996—; ind. cons. Engring. Rsch. & Cons., Inc., 1989-94. Mem. loan policy com. Arnold Eng. Devel. Ctr., Fed. Credit Union, 1989-90; adult vol./leader Boy Scouts Am., 1991-95; preacher Ch. of Christ, 1990—; vol., instr. cmty. CPR and first aid ARC, 1993—. Mem. NRA, Nat. Contract Mgmt. Assn., Kiwanis Internat. Republican. Office: Samuel Strapping Systems 110 Wilton Cir Winchester TN 37398

MATHERS, DANIEL EUGENE, musician, educator; b. Tallahassee, Sept. 22, 1962; s. Gale Levy and Alice (Metcalf) M. BMus, Fla. State U., 1984, MMus, 1989. Piano accompanist dept. dance Fla. State U., Tallahassee, 1989, 95; piano accompanist dept. dance Cin. Conservatory Music, 1990, instr. sophomore theory, 1989-91, instr. hons. theory, 1991-93; vis. instr.music theory Coll.-Conservatory of Music, Cin., 1995-96; music dir. So. Acad. Ballet Arts, Tallahassee, 1987—, Pas de Vie Ballet Co.; tenor saxophonist, U.S. Collegiate Wind Band, 1980; pianist in premieres of works by local musicians, Cin., 1989—; various pub. piano recitals. Contbr. articles to profl. publs. Recipient summer rsch. fellowship, Cin. Conservatory Music, 1991, Univ. Grad. Scholarship, 1989—. Mem. Am. Musicological Soc., Soc. Music Theory, Golden Key, Sonneck Soc. Am. Music, Pi Kappa Lambda. Home: 3603 Derwood Ln Apt T4 Alexandria VA 22309

MATHERS, NORMAN WAYNE, minister; b. Dec. 1, 1946; m. Norma J. Payne, July 1, 1972; children: Robert T., Ruthlyn Elizabeth, Rachel Noreen, Victoria Grace. BA, Wilfred Laurier U., Waterloo, Ont., Can., 1972; ThM, Dallas Theol. Sem., 1976; MA, Calif. State U., Carson, 1985; PhD, Columbia Pacific U., 1989. Ordained to ministry Trinity Bible Ch., 1976. Min. Mathers Home Fellowship Ch., Willow Springs, N.C., 1993—; author, pub., distbr. Norman W. Mathers, ATS Publs., Willow Springs, N.C., 1993—; vis. instr. Faith Theol. Sem., Elkins Park, Pa., 1989-90; rschr. Author: Beyond Desert Storm, 1993. Mem. Am. Philos. Assn. Home and Office: 62 Chase Cir Willow Springs NC 27592

MATHES, DOROTHY JEAN HOLDEN, occupational therapist; b. Paterson, N.J., Mar. 13, 1953; d. Cornelius Fred and Dorothy Johanna (Ferguson) Holden; m. Clayton Derald Mathes, May 26, 1973 (div. Dec. 1984); children: Christy, Carl, Chuck, Chad; m. Elie Youssef Hajjar, Oct. 4, 1989. BS in Occupational Therapy, Tex. Woman's U., Denton, Tex., 1988; MA in Occupational Therapy, Tex. Woman's U., 1995. Lic. occupational therapist, Tex.; cert. pediatric occupational therapist. Occupational therapy cons. Lakes Regional-SOCS Early Childhood Intervention, 1988—. Mem. Am. Occupational Therapy Assn., Tex. Occupational Therapy Assn. Home: 2608 Woodhaven St Denton TX 76201-1340 Office: Lakes Regional SOCS-ECI 3969 Teasley Lane Denton TX 76205

MATHES, EDWARD CONRAD, architect; b. New Orleans, Mar. 10, 1943; s. Earl L. and Margaret (Gash) M.; m. Anne M. Ergenbright, Mar. 1, 1964; children: Margaret Elizabeth, Anne Catherine. BArch, U. Southwestern La., 1968. Registered architect, La., Miss., Fla., Tex., Ala. Tchr. U. Southwestern La., Lafayette, 1968-69; asst. to mng. architect Rogers, Taliaferro, Kostritsky & Lamb, Balt., 1969; pres. Mathes, Bergman & Assocs., Inc., New Orleans, 1969-82, The Mathes Group, New Orleans, 1982—. Chmn. Orleans Svc. Ctr., ARC, 1993-94; bd. dirs. City Park Improvement Assn., 1996—. Recipient Am. Sch. and Univ. award 1983, 85, Honor award La. Architects Assn., New Orleans, 1986. Mem. AIA (Inst. scholar 1968-69, honor award New Orleans chpt. 1982, 89, pres. 1989), Constrn. Industry Assn. (pres. 1984-85, Honor award 1993), Pickwick Club, Metairie Country Club, City Energy Club, Rotary (pres. New Orleans 1985-86). Republican. Presbyterian. Home: 4130 Vendome Pl New Orleans LA 70125-2739 Office: The Mathes Group 201 Saint Charles Ave 23d Fl New Orleans LA 70170-2300

MATHEW, JOY, biochemist, educator; b. Muttuchira, Kerala, India, June 4, 1956; s. Varkey and Thressiamma M.; m. Leela Cherian, Mar. 11, 1985; 1 child, Fred. BS, Kerala U., Trivandrum, Kerala, India, 1977; MS, M.S. Univ., Baroda, Gujarat, India, 1980; PhD, Madras U., Madras, Tamil Nadu, India, 1986. Jr. rsch. fellow Christian Med. Coll. Hosp., Vellore, Tamil Nadu, India, 1980-82, sr. rsch. fellow, 1982-86; rsch. assoc. Tex. A&M U., Coll. Sta., 1986-88, 88-90; rsch. assoc. U. Houston, 1990-91, asst. prof., 1991—. Contbr. papers, revs. to profl. publs. and chpts. to books. Recipient Individual Rsch. fellowship Indian Coun. Med. Rsch., 1985-86, Young Investigator Travel award Am. Soc. for Neurochemistry, 1991, Rsch. grant RGD Found., 1991-92. Mem. Soc. for Neurosci., Am. Soc. for Neurochemistry, Am. Soc. for Biochemistry & Molecular Biology, Rsch. Soc. for Alcoholism. Roman Catholic. Home: 10602 Plainfield St Houston TX 77031-1006 Office: U of Houston 4800 Calhoun Rd Houston TX 77004-2610

MATHEW, PORUNELLOOR ABRAHAM, molecular biologist, educator; b. Alleppey, Kerala, India, Dec. 13, 1952; came to U.S., 1987; s. Porunelloor and Mary (Philipose) Abraham; m. Annamma Abraham Mathew, July 30, 1981; children: Anoop, Anisha. BS, U. Kerala, India, 1974; MS, U. Poona, India, 1979, PhD, 1987. Govt. of India fellow Ahmednagar (India) Coll., 1980-81, lectr., 1981-87; Am. Cancer Soc. postdoctoral fellow N.J. Med. Sch., Newark, 1987-88; Robert Welch postdoctoral fellow U. Tex. Southwestern Med. Ctr., Dallas, 1988-90, asst. instr., 1990-91, instr., 1991-92, asst. prof. pathology, 1993—. Author: Current Topics in Cell Biology, 1992; contbr. articles to profl. jours. Mem. AAAS.

MATHEWS, CHRIS J., financial executive; b. Bayonne, N.J., Aug. 15, 1959; s. Christopher Arthur and Ann Lois (Lambert) M.; m. Laura Ann Nesbitt, July 13, 1985; children: Sarah Elizabeth, Marissa Kyle. Student, Tex. A&M U., 1981. Asst. v.p. Allied Bank of Tex., Houston, 1981-86; sr. analyst Beacon Mgmt. Corp., Houston, 1986-89; v.p., CFO, CIO Nationwide Recovery Systems, Carrollton, Tex., 1989—. Republican. Roman Catholic. Home: 410 Winter Oaks Dr Houston TX 77079 Office: Nationwide Recovery Systems 50 Briar Hollow Ln #330W Houston TX 77027

MATHEWS, FRED LEROY, librarian; b. New Kensington, Pa., Apr. 20, 1938; s. Fred Lyman and Mabel (Vivola) M.; m. Glenda Carolyn Zorn, Dec. 2, 1988; l child, Eric. Student, U. Md., European Div., 1968-69; AA, Weber State Coll., Ogden, Utah, 1981, B Gen. Studies, 1983; MSLS, Clarion U. Pa., 1985. Enlisted man USAF, 1957, advanced through grades to master sgt., 1977; coord. subscriber svcs. 1920th Communications Group, Washington, 1970-73; noncommd. officer-in-charge phys. therapy USAF, Bitburg, Fed. Republic Germany, 1976-79; supt. phys. medicine USAF, Carswell AFB, Tex., 1979-80; ret., 1980; asst. systems libr. Maxwell AFB, Montgomery, Ala., 1985-86; refrence libr. Hdqrs. Tng. and Doctrine Command Libr., Ft. Monroe, Va., 1986-89; trainer, asst. systems libr. Hdqrs. Tng. and Doctrine Command Libr. and Info. Network, Ft. Monroe, 1989-91; systems adminstr. Strategic Def. Command Libr., Huntsville, Ala., 1991—. Recipient U.S. Army Achievement medal Hdqrs. Tng. and Doctrine Command, 1990. Mem. ALA, Assn. U.S. Army, Air Force Sgts. Assn., Beta Phi Mu. Office: US Army Strategic Def Command Libr PO Box 1500 Huntsville AL 35807-3801

MATHEWS, GEOFFREY KEVIN, advertising executive; b. London, Eng., Oct. 18, 1936; came to U.S., 1979; s. Arthur Bruce and Vera Edna (Morgan) M.; m. Angela Withnal Mathews, Sept. 8, 1968 (dec. Sept. 1970); m. Pamela Jean Leslie Thomas Mathews, May 22, 1977. BS in Econ., London Sch. Econ., 1957. Prodn. trainee Shell Petroleum Co., London, 1960-62; sales rep. Petrofina S.A., Brussels, Belgium, 1962-68; branch mgr. Murphy Oil Corp., Eldorado, Ark., 1968-70; sales dir. Mktg. Design, N.Y.C., 1970-72; mng. dir. G.K.M. Internat., London, 1973-79; chmn. G.K.M. Internat., Miami, Fla., 1979—, Tung Li, Singapore, 1979—; cons. Lloyds Bank Ltd., London, Royal Bank of Scotland, Edinburgh, 1980-85, 85—. Officer RAF, 1957-60. Mem. Bal Harbour Club, St. Stephens Club, Rotary Club, Guild of Air Pilots and Navigators, Royal Air Force Club. Republican. Roman Catholic. Home: 10190 Collins Ave Bal Harbour FL 33154-1611 Office: GK Mathews Internat, 3245 Claydon Ct, Tung Li Singapore

MATHEWS, JAMES HAROLD, minister; b. Longview, Tex., Nov. 28, 1946; s. James Harold Sr. and Ruth Mildred (Gaines) M.; m. Carol Elaine Hartin, Aug. 2, 1969; children: Katherine Mathews Curlee, Patrick Alan, Suzanne Elaine. Student, Howard Payne U., 1965-73, Southwestern Bapt. Theol. Sem., 1984-87. Minister of music and youth Goldthwaite, Tex., 1973-75, Freeman Heights Bapt. Ch., Garland, Tex., 1975-78, N.W. Bapt. Ch., Austin, Tex., 1978-81, First Bapt. Ch., Marshall, Tex., 1981-85; minister of music First Bapt. Ch., West Columbia, Tex., 1985-95, Glen Meadows Bapt. Ch., San Angelo, Tex., 1995—; pres. bd. Tex. Bapt. Encampment, Palacios, 1989-90. Bd. dirs. Cen. Emergency Med. Svcs., West Columbia, Tex., 1986-91, v.p., 1989-90; pres. Howard Payne U. Alumni bd. dirs., 1992-94. Mem. Soda Lake Assn. (assist team Marshall chpt. 1983-86), Mills Assn. (assoc. music dir. Goldthwaite chpt. 1969-73), Austin Assn. (assoc. music dir. Austin chpt. 1978-80), Rotary (bd. dirs. West Columbia chpt. 1987-90, sec. 1990-91). Home: 2620 W Twohig San Angelo TX 76901 Office: Glen Meadows Bapt Ch 6002 Knickerbocker Rd San Angelo TX 76904

MATHEWS, PATRICIA SPANIOL, outpatient services coordinator; b. Cin., Oct. 24, 1943; d. Lyna Sadd; m. Moses Levon Mathews, Mar. 1, 1993; children: Frank Spaniol, Rodger Spaniol, Cyndi Spaniol. AA, Somerset (Ky.) C.C., 1984; BA in Edn., U. Ky., 1987; MA in Edn. and History, Ea. Ky. U., 1990; postgrad., Fla. State U., 1990—. Instr., coord., counselor Somerset C.C., 1984-88; regional tng. coord. Ea. Ky. U., Richmond, 1988-90; instr. Lexington C.C., 1989-90; grant mgr., tng. coord. Apalachee Ctr. for Human Svcs., Tallahassee, 1990-92; juvenile justice coord. HRS/Alcohol & Drug Abuse Office, Tallahassee, 1992-96; outpatient svcs. coord. Apalachee Ctr. for Human Svcs., Tallahassee, 1996—. Mem. Juvenile Justice Trainers Assn., Kappa Delta Pi, Phi Theta Kappa, Phi Delta Kappa. Democrat. Roman Catholic. Home: 6802 Chisholm Ct W Tallahassee FL 32311-8775

MATHEWS, SHARON WALKER, artistic director, secondary school educator; b. Shreveport, La., Feb. 1, 1947; d. Arthur Delmar and Nona (Frye) Walker; m. John William (Bill) Mathews, Aug. 14, 1971; children: Rebecca, Elizabeth, Anna. BS, La. State U., 1969, MS, 1971. Dance grad. asst. La. State U., Baton Rouge, 1969-71, choreographer, 1975-76; 6th grade tchr. East Baton Rouge Parish, 1971-72, health phys. edn. tchr., 1972-74; dance instr. Magnet High Sch., Baton Rouge, 1975—; artistic dir. Baton Rouge Ballet Theatre, 1975—; dance dir. Dancers' Workshop, Baton Rouge, 1971—; choreographer Baton Rouge Opera, 1989-94. Named Dance Educator of Yr., La. Alliance for Health, Physical Edn., Recreation and Dance, 1986-87. Mem. Southwestern Regional Ballet Assn. (bd. dirs. 1981—, treas., exec. bd. dirs. 1989-92), La. Assn. for Health, Phys. Edn., Recreation and Dance (dance chairperson 1995). Republican. Baptist. Office: Baton Rouge Ballet Theater 10745 Linkwood Ct Baton Rouge LA 70810-1608

MATHEWSON, KENT, II, geography educator; b. Lenoir, N.C., Aug. 6, 1946; s. Kent and Mariana Worth (Moore) M.; m. Kathleen Elsa Kennedy, Nov. 30, 1991. Secondary diploma, The Lawrenceville Sch., 1965; BA, Antioch Coll., 1970; MA, U. Wis., 1976, PhD, 1987. Instr. U. Wis. System, Rockville, 1975, Baraboo, 1976; instr. Winona (Minn.) State U., 1977; vis. lectr. Inst. Mil. Geography, Quito, Ecuador, 1978, Escuela Politecnica del Litoral, Guayaquil, Ecuador, 1980, Va. Commonwealth U., Richmond, 1982-83; lectr. U. Wis., Madison, 1984-86; vis. asst. prof. U. N.C., Chapel Hill, 1986-88; asst. prof. geography La. State U., Baton Rouge, 1988-94, assoc. prof. geography, 1994—. Author: Irrigation Horticulture in Highland Guatemala, 1984; co-editor: Pre-Hispanic Agricultural Fields in the Andean Region, 1987, ReReading Cultural Geography, 1994, Concepts in Human Geography, 1996; editor: Culture, Form, and Place, 1993. Fellow NDEA, 1977-78, Fulbright-Hays fellow, Ecuador, 1979-80, fellow NSF, Ecuador, 1979-80. Fellow Am. Geog. Soc.; mem. Assn. Am. Geographers (chmn. cultural ecology sect.1994-96, chmn. L.Am. sect. 1991-92), Conf. L.Am. Geographers (bd. dirs. 1990-93, book rev. editor 1993-96). Episcopalian. Home: 4112 Palm St Baton Rouge LA 70808-3786 Office: La State U Dept Geography-Anthropology Baton Rouge LA 70803

MATHIA, MARY LOYOLA, parochial school educator, nun; b. Hempstead, N.Y., Sept. 14, 1921; d. Paul John and Laura Marie (Linck) Mathia. BA, Coll. Mt. St. Joseph, 1953; M in Pastoral Studies, Loyola U.-Chgo., 1980. Joined Sisters of Charity of Cin., Roman Cath. Ch., 1941. Tchr. various schs. Ohio and Mich., 1943-62, St. John Bapt. Sch., Chillum, Md., 1962-63; social studies tchr. and dept. chmn. Holy Name High Sch., Cleve., 1963-69; ednl. cons. Diocese of Cleve., 1970-78; dir. edn. St. Benedict Ch., Crystal River, Fla., 1979-86; founding prin. Cen. Cath. Sch. of Citrus County, Lecanto, Fla., 1985-90, v.p. devel. and pub. rels., 1990-91; parish cons. and dir. adult edn., 1986—. Republican. Office: St Scholastica Ch 4301 W Homosassa Trl Lecanto FL 34461-9106

MATHIAS, ALYCE ANN, advertising and graphic design executive; b. East Liverpool, Ohio, June 23, 1947; d. John F. and Mary M. (Cunningham) M.; 1 child, Ian. BFA, Youngstown State U., 1976. Creative dir., pres. Studio Graphics, Naples, Fla., 1988—; instr. Internat. Coll. Naples, 1991-92. Pub., editor Naples Guide Mag., 1995—. Recipient Shopping Catalog award, 1985-87, Ad Awards Newspaper and Mag., 1985, 86, 90, 91, 92, 93, Direct Mail awards, 1992, 93, 94, 95, Newsletter award, 1993, 94, 95, Logo Design award, 1991, 93, 94, Stationary Package award, 1994, 95, CD Cover award, 1995, Menu Design award, 1986, 90, Invitation award, 1994, Mag. Cover award, 1995, Best Advt. Promotion award, 1985-87, 90, 93, Editl. Illustration award, 1986, Illustration Editl. Mag. award Art Dirs. Club of N.Y., 1987, Christmas Theme Catalog award, 1987, Sales Media Kit award, 1985-87, 93, Spl. Invitation award, 1991, Gen. Excellence award Fla. Mag. Assn., 1985-87, Best Cover award, 1985-87, Best Spl. Issue award, 1987, Best Circulation, CD/Cassette Album, 1995, Mag. Cover, 1995. Mem. Advt. Fedn. S.W. Fla. (Addy award 1985, 86, 87, 90, 91, 92, 93, 94, 95), Fla. Pub. Rels. Assn., S.W. Fla. Pub. Rels. Assn., Naples Area Accommendation Assn., Fla. Mag. Assn. Democrat. Office: Studio Graphics and Naples Guide 947 4th Ave S Naples FL 34102-6402

MATHIAS, JOHN ROBERT, gastroenterologist; b. Rapid City, S.D., Dec. 9, 1942; s. Johnny and Genevieve (Mabbott) M.; m. Lynne Jane Martin, June 1, 1963; children: Stephanie Anne, Emily Lynne. BS, U. S.D., 1965; MD, Temple U. Sch. Medicine, 1968; postgrad., U. Pa., 1975. Prof. medicine U. Fla. Coll. Medicine, Gainesville, 1975-86, U. Va. Sch. Medicine, Charlottesville, 1986-87, U. Tex. Med. Br., Galveston, 1987—; edit. bd. Postgrad. Medicine, Mpls., 1991—. Co-author: Handbook of Physiology: Bacterial Toxins and Motility, 1989. Maj. U.S. Army, 1971-73. Recipient Komarov award Rsch., Phila. Rsch. Forum, 1976. Mem. Am. Gastroent. Assn., Am. Soc. Clinical Investigation. Republican. Episcopalian.

MATHIS, BILLIE FRITZ, artist; b. Lindale, Ga., Apr. 16, 1936; d. George Franklin and Willie Velma (Jailette) Fritz; m. Guy Ferman Mathis, June 24, 1954; children: Janet D. Mathis Smith, G. Timothy, Gregory T. Student, Art Instrn., Inc., Mpls., 1962; studies in painting, Paris. Exhibited in group shows: Allied Artist Exhbn., N.Y., Butler Inst. Am. Art Mus., Youngstown, Ohio, Okla. Nat. Watercolor Exhibit, La. Internat. Water Color Soc. Nat. Exbiit, Md. Fedn. Nat. Watercolor Soc. Nat. Exhibit, Visual Arts Atlanta, FrameWorks, Albany (N.Y.) U., Cultural Exch. Am. and Que., Abstein Gallery, Cobb Country C. of C., Ga. Watercolor Soc. Nat. Exhibit, Gallery 300/SAGA, Atlanta, Can./U.S. Visual Arts Exhibit, Marietta-Cobb Mus. Art; featured artist Masterpiece Ball; work featured in Ga. Artists, Mountain Prodns., Atlanta Homes, cover for Airborne Mag., Marietta/Cobb Collection Tours, other collections. Selected one of ten outstanding artists of the Southeast for exhibition in SAGE. Atlanta. Mem. Am. Watercolor Soc. (assoc.), Nat. Watercolor Soc. (assoc.), Ga. Watercolor Soc. (signature mem., bd. dirs. 1991—), Women of the Arts (charter), Am. References, Cobb ARTS Coun., Atlanta Artist Soc. Home: 1665 Hasty Rd Marietta GA 30062-1947

MATHIS, JANE ANN, nursing educator, safety and legal consultant; b. Fort Ord, Calif., Jan. 7, 1950; d. Allen Wayne Nicola and Bonnie May Rynkiewitz; m. Terry Lee Mathis, Dec. 21, 1968; children: Scott, Sean, Christopher, Lori, Traci, Daniel. BSN, W. Tex. State, 1990; MSN, Tex. Tech. U., 1992. Cert. childbirth educator, in-patient obstetrics. Nurse St. Mary's of the Plains Hosp., Lubbock, Tex., 1985-87; staff nurse, parent educator Meth. Hosp., Lubbock, 1987-91; instr. Meth. Hosp. Sch. of Nursing, Lubbock, 1991-93; faculty San Jacinto Coll. Ctrl., Pasadena, Tex., 1993-96, North Harris C.C., 1996—; cons. Behavioral Sch. Tech., Ojai, Calif., 1993, Panhandle Edn. for Nurses, Lubbock, 1993-94; mem. com., adv. coun. on edn. Tex. State Bd. Nurse Examiners, 1996—; safety and legal cons., 1993—; guest lectr. Contbr. articles to profl jours. Bd. dirs. PTA, Lubbock, 1991-92; com. mem. Boy Scouts Am., Lubbock, 1988-92. Mem. ANA (dist. fund chair 1991-93), Assn. for Women's Obstet., Health and Neonatal Nursing, Sigma Theta Tau. Home: 2010 Wilderness Point Dr Kingwood TX 77339-2247

MATHIS, LARRY LEE, health care administrator; b. Lincoln, Nebr., May 29, 1943; s. Henry William George and Berneta Lucille (Van Laningham) M.; children—Julie, Jennifer. B.A. in Social Scis., Pittsburg State U., Kans., 1965; M.H.A., Washington U., St. Louis, 1972; postgrad. health systems mgmt., Harvard U., 1978, advanced mgmt. program, 1982. Adminstrv. resident Meth. Hosp., Houston, 1971-72, adminstrv. asst., 1972, asst. to pres., 1972-74, v.p., 1974-78, sr. v.p., 1978-80, exec. v.p., chief operating officer, 1980-83, pres., CEO, 1983—. Contbr. articles to profl. jours. Health svcs. chair U.S. Savs. Bond Vol. Com. Gulf Coast, Diagnostic Ctr. Hosp., Am. Hosp. Istanbul; mem. various coms. St. Luke's United Meth. Ch., Houston, 1972—; mem. bd. global ministries Tex. Conf. United Meth. Ch., 1984—; chmn., bd. dirs. Greater Houston Hosp. Coun. Rsch. and Edn. Found., 1985—. Capt. U.S. Army, 1965-70, Vietnam. Decorated Bronze Star, Vietnamese Cross of Gallantry; recipient Alumni Meritorious Achievement award Pittsburg State U., 1984. Fellow Am. Coll. Healthcare Execs. (gov. 1990-94); mem. Am. Hosp. Assn. (chmn. 1993, spkr. Ho. Dels. 1994), Healthcare Execs. Study Soc., Assn. Univ. Programs in Health Adminstrn., Assn. Am. Med. Colls. (various coms. coun. on tchg. hosps.), Tex. Hosp. Assn. (trustee 1984-90, chmn. 1988-89), Washington U. alumni Assn. (pres. 1988-90), Houston C. of C., Greater Houston Hosp. Coun. (chmn. bd. dirs. 1983-84), Petroleum Club, Ramada Club, Drs. Club, Harvard Bus. (bd. dirs. 1986-87), Houston City. Home: 3037 Reba Dr Houston TX 77019-6203 Office: Meth Hosp Sys 6565 Fannin St D-200 Houston TX 77030-2704*

MATHIS, MARSHA DEBRA, software company executive; b. Detroit, Dec. 22, 1953; d. Marshall Junior and Anita Willene (Biggers) M. BS, Fla. State U., 1978; MBA, Miss. Coll., 1982. With telecommunications dept. Fla. State Dept. Safety, Tallahassee, 1973-76; asst. to chmn. Tallahassee Savs. and Loan Assn., 1976-78; sales engr. Prehler, Inc., Jackson, Miss., 1978-82; mktg. mgr. Norand Corp., Arlington, Tex., 1982-87; v.p. mktg. and sales Profl. Datasolutions, Inc., Irving, Tex., 1987-88; v.p. mktg. and sales, ptnr. Target Systems, Inc., Irving, 1988-89, also bd. dirs.; v.p. mktg. Profl. Datasolutions, Inc., Temple, Tex., 1990—. Contbr. articles to industry trade jours. Advisor Am. Diabetes Assn., Jackson, 1983—. Mem. Internat. Platform Assn., Nat. Adv. Group, Nat. Assn. Convenience Stores (Industry Task Force 1987-88). Republican. Roman Catholic. Home: 325 Old York Rd Irving TX 75063-4247 Office: Profl Datasolutions Inc 3407 S 31st St Temple TX 76502-1921

MATHIS, ROBERT REX, church administrator, educator; b. Harrison, Ark., Dec. 27, 1947; s. Rex Clayton and Jannie Fay (Garner) M.; m. Maryln Odene Floyd, Aug. 23, 1968; 1 child, Karissa Trotti. BA, Wayland Bapt. Coll., 1969; MEd, U. Tex., El Paso, 1976; MRE, Southwestern Theol. Sem., 1979; PhD, Southwestern Bapt. Theol. Sem., 1984; EdD, U. So. Miss., 1994. Min. edn. Mountain View Bapt. Ch., El Paso, Tex., 1974-77, Ridglea Bapt. Ch., Ft. Worth, 1977-81; assoc. pastor 1st Bapt. Ch., Santa Fe, N.Mex., 1981-86; min. of edn. Metairie (La.) Bapt. Ch., 1987-93; assoc. prof. ednl. founds., chmn. divsn. Christian edn. New Orleans Bapt. Theol. Sem., 1986—. Contbr. articles to profl. jours. Sgt. U.S. Army, 1971-74. Recipient Albert Marsh award Southwestern Bapt. Theol. Sem., 1981, rsch. award So. Bapt. Rsch. Fellowship, 1996. Mem. Nat. Assn. Ch. Bus. Adminstrs., Southern Bapt. Rsch. Fellowship, Southern Bapt. Religious Edn. Assn. Office: New Orleans Bapt Theol Sem 3939 Gentilly Blvd New Orleans LA 70126-4858

MATHIS, SHARON ANN, home health nurse, mental health nurse, consultant, columnist, entrepreneur; b. Normangee, Tex., Sept. 29, 1957; d. James Ezekiel Sr. and Rosie Mae (Stovall) M. BS in Nursing, Prairie View A&M U., 1980; MPA, Tex. So. U., 1987. RN, Tex. Staff nurse AMI Twelve Oaks Hosp., Houston, 1980-81; staff nurse, charge nurse Sisters of Charity-St. Joseph Hosp., Houston, 1981-84; coord. West Oaks Hosp., Houston, 1984-86, dir., 1986-88; dir. nursing HCA Beaumont (Tex.) Neurol. Hosp., Houston, 1988-89, adminstr. directions of nursing svcs., 1989-90, CEO, dir. nursing svcs., 1990-95; pres., CEO Fiesta Home Health and Cmty. Support Svcs., Inc., 1995—; mem. U. Tex. Health Sci. Ctr. Needs Assessment, 1993-94; founder health care mgmt., edn. and consulting bus., 1989; pub. speaker in field. Contbg. author: Tales from 50 Nurses in Business; pub., editor Choices; health care columnist Houston Chronicle. Pub. spkr., Hong Kong, Beijing, Turpan, Guangzhou, Urumaqi, China; mem. The Mayor's Drug Needs Assessment and Treatment Com., ARC, 1989-90, The Mayor's Houston Homeless Coalition, 1989-90; mem. peer rev. Beaumont Ind. Sch. Dist., 1988-89; citizen amb. People to People. Mem. ANA, NAFE, ARC, Am. Evaluation Assn., Chinese Nursing Assn., S.E. Tex. Assn. Psychiat. Nurses, Tex. Nurses Assn. (dist. 9 nominating com., pres., publicity com., strategic planning com., multi culture com.), Houston Assn. Psychiat. Nurses, Am. Nurses in Bus. Assn. (founder, pres.), Nat. Assn. Hispanic Nurses, Tex. Nurses in Bus. Assn. (founder), Houston Chronicle Adv. Bd., Impaired Nurse Advs., Empowered Women, Health BUS-NET, Prairie View A&M Alumni Assn. (life), Carter G. Woodson Alumni Assn. (pres. 1987), Sigma Theta Tau. Office: PO Box 741384 Houston TX 77274-1384

MATHISEN, RALPH WHITNEY, ancient history educator; b. Ashland, Wis., Feb. 17, 1947; s. Arnold Howard and Barbara Louise (Varner) M.; m. Rita M. Rhodes, July 26, 1980; children: Katherine Whitney, David Arthur. MS in Mech. Engring., Rensselaer Poly., 1972; BS in Astronomy and Physics, U. Wis., 1969, MA in Classics, 1973, PhD in Ancient History, 1979. Computing analyst United Aircraft Rsch., East Hartford, Conn., 1969-71; systems analyst Travelers Ins., Hartford, Conn., 1971-72; project asst. Space Medicine Lab., Madison, Wis., 1971-79; vis. asst. prof. U. Ill., Chgo., 1979-80; prof. U. S.C., Columbia, 1980—; v.p. Byzantine Studies Conf., 1994-96. Author: Ecclesiastical Factionalism and Religious Controversy in Fifth-Century Gaul, 1989, Studies in the History, Literature and Society of Late Antiquity, 1991, Roman Aristocrats in Barbarian Gaul: Strategies for Survival in an Age of Transition, 1993, Shifting Frontiers in Late Antiquity, 1996; mem. editl. bd. Medieval Prosopography, 1993—; editor Lake Antiquity Newsletter, 1996—; contbr. numerous articles to profl. jours. Pres. S.C. Neighborhood Coalition, 1992-96, Columbia Coun. of Neighborhoods, 1991-92; active Quality Housing Task Force, Columbia, 1987, Columbia Neighborhood Redevel. Com., 1991-92. Rsch. grantee NEH, 1990-95; Howard fellow, 1988, Am. Coun. Learned Soc. fellow, 1980; recipient Russell award for rsch. U. S.C., 1993. Fellow Am. Numismatic Soc.; mem. Am. Philol. Soc., Assn. for Ancient Historians, Soc. for Ancient Numismatics, U.S. Com. for Byzantine Studies, Assn. for History Computing, U.S. Byzantine Studies Conf. (v.p. 1994-96, pres. 1996—). Methodist. Home: 2517 Kiawah Ave Columbia SC 29205-3109 Office: U SC Dept History Columbia SC 29208

MATHISON, JAMES ANTHONY (TONY MATHISON), mathematics educator; b. Sacramento, Oct. 2, 1958; s. James Ira and Mary Louise (Smith) M.; m. Carolyn Denise Brown, Nov. 3, 1979; 1 child, Cayla DeAnn. AA, Weatherford (Tex.) Coll., 1980; BGS, Tex. Christian U., 1982; MEd, U. North Tex., 1987. Cert. tchr. Tex., Fla. Math. tchr., football coach Italy (Tex.) Jr. H.S., 1982-83; math. tchr., tennis coach Peaster (Tex.) H.S., 1983-84; computer programming tchr., football coach Aledo (Tex.) Mid. Sch., 1984-86; math. tchr., football coach La Marque (Tex.) H.S., 1986-89; tchr. students-at-risk, football coach Putnam County Schs., Palatka, Fla., 1989-90; pro-football coach Arena Football League, Dallas, 1990-91; tchr. students-at-risk, football coach Clay County Schs., Green Cove Springs, Fla., 1991-94; calculus tchr., football coach Wilmer-Hutchins H.S., Dallas, 1995-96; tchr. students-at-risk Venus (Tex.) Middle Sch., 1996—. Author: (book) The South Finally Won, 1994. Bus. dir. Southside Bapt. Ch., Weatherford, 1976-77; pres. Christ on Campus, Weatherford, 1974-77; active Big Brother program Venus Bapt. Ch., 1996—. Recipient Master Tchr.'s scholarship Dallas Bapt. U., 1996. Mem. Tex. H.S. Coaches Assn., Delta Psi Kappa, Phi Delta Kappa. Democrat. Baptist. Office: Venus Mid Sch Box 364 Venus TX 76084

MATHUR, KAILASH, nutritionist, educator; b. Jodhpur, India, Feb. 21, 1934; came to the U.S., 1962; s. Vijey Mal and Mohan Kaur Mathur; m. Savita Mathur, July 29, 1964; children: Shikha, Sameer. BS, Jaswant Coll., Jodhpur, 1955; DVM, Vet. Coll., Bikaner, India, 1960; MS, N.C. State U., 1964; PhD, U. Ill., 1975. Mgr. coll. clinics Vet. Coll., Bikaner, 1960-62; assoc. prof. dairy sci. S.C. State U., Orangeburg, 1965-71, project dir. human nutrition rsch., 1971-80, prof., advisor to nutritional scis. grad. program, 1982—; tech. Southeastern Consortium for Internat. Devel., Kenya, 1980-82; specialist, cons. for nutrition edn. project, vis. prof. food sci. Clemson (S.C.) U., 1979-80; field dir. health measurements program sch. pub. health U. S.C., Columbia, 1976-77; local project officer Head Start Orangeburg Com. for Econ. Progress, 1968; adj. prof. nutrition Med. U. S.C., Charleston. Contbr. articles to profl. jours. Bd. dirs. Orangeburg divsn. Am. Heart Assn.; mem. adv. bd. assoc. degree in nursing divsn. Orangeburg Calhoun Tech. Coll. Recipient Gov.'s Disting. Prof. award, 1991; apptd. by Pres. Clinton to Nat. Nutrition Monitoring Adv. Coun. Mem. Am. Dietetic Assn., S.C. Dietetic Assn. (bd. dirs. 1986-87, 90—, chmn. licensure and legis. network coord.), Edisto Dietetic Assn. (pres. 1986-87), Am. Soc. Microbiology, Nutrition Today Soc., Soc. for Nutrition Edn., S.C. Acad. Scis., S.C. Soc. Microbiology (pres. awards com.), S.C. State Nutrition Coun. (mem. exec. bd., chmn. nominating com.), S.C. Pub. Health Assn., S.C. Soc. Allied Health Professions (sec.-treas. 1976-77), Greater Orangeburg C. of C. (chmn. health care nutrition com.). Home: 610 Alexander Dr NW Orangeburg SC 29115-2202 Office: SC State U 300 College St NE Orangeburg SC 29117-0001

MATHUR, RUPA AJWANI, former state official, risk management consultant; b. Khairpur, Sind, India, Nov. 2, 1939; came to U.S., 1980; d. Menghraj Lalchand and Giani Ajwani; m. Ramesh Saran Mathur, Mar. 2, 1967; children: Sanjay Saran, Seema. BA with honors, Bombay U., 1962, LLB, 1965. CPCU. Lawyer High Ct., Bombay; with GM, U.K., Lindus & Horton, U.K.; welfare staff Brit. High Commn., Africa, 1977-78; English tchr. Thailand, 1978-80; ins. specialist, analyst Met. Transit Authority, Houston, 1980-83; ins. analyst Coastal Corp., Houston, 1983-84; dir. ins. and employee benefits Houston Ind. Sch. Dist., 1984-88; dir. risk mgmt. and benefits Harris County, Houston, 1988-94; dir. State Risk Mgmt., Austin, 1994—; pres. Rupa Mathur & Assocs.; bd. dirs. Surplus Line; owner Health Environ. and Risk Mgmt. Co. (HER Inc.); team leader risk mgmt. del. People to People, Ea. Europe and Russia, 1993, China, 1994; instr. CPCU and accredited advisor ins. courses U. Houston Sch. Inst. Mktg. and Fin., 1985-88; speaker in field. Author: Managing Occupational Injury Costs, 1993; contbr. articles to profl. jours. Chmn. Multi Cultural Soc., Ft. Bend County, Tex., 1992, Indian Cmty.-Equal Opportunity, Houston, 1990; bd. dirs. Children at Risk, Ft. Bend Sch. Dist., 1990, mem. task force Multi Culture Ctr., 1993; co-founder Internat. Gourmet Club, 1976; sec.-treas. Internat. Ladies Club, 1976; tchr. English, YMCA, Thailand, 1976; founder Indian Am. Orgn. for Equal Opportunity; bd. dirs. India Culture Ctr., 1993-94, Surplus Lines Stamping. Recipient Honor award Tex. Safety Assn., 1993, Woman on the Move award Houston Post and KPRC/Channel 2, 1993. Mem. Profl. Women in Govt., Risk and Ins. Mgrs. Soc. (com.), Pub. Risk and Ins. Mgmt. Assn. (past pres. Tex. chpt., mem. internat. com.), World Safety Orgn. (cert. safety exec., appreciation award 1991, Concerned Safety Profl. award 1993), CPCU's (edn. com.), State and Local Govt. Benefits Assn., Nat. Safety Coun. (safety awards), Profl. Devel. Inst. (past officer), Internat. Hospitality Coun. (bd. dirs.), People to People Orgn. (Austin chpt.). Home: 3400 Pace Bend Rd Spicewood TX 78669

MATIAS, PATRICIA TREJO, secondary education educator; b. Havana, Cuba; came to U.S., 1967; d. Juan Mario and Maria (Rexach) Trejo; m. Miguel Matias, Mar. 20, 1972; children: Michael George, Mark Patrick. BA in French/Spanish, Ga. Coll., 1973; MAT in Spanish Edn., Ga. State U., 1985, EdS in Fgn. Lang. Edn., 1991. Cert. Spanish tchr., Ga. Spanish lead tchr. Wheeler High Sch., Marietta, Ga., 1980—; mem. adv. bd. So. Conf. Lang. Teaching, Ga., 1987—; part-time instr. Kennesaw State Coll., 1991—. VIP guest svc. goodwill amb. Olympics Games Com., Atlanta, 1995-96. Mem. AAUW, ASCD, Am. Assn. Tchrs. Spanish and Portuguese, Profl. Assn. Ga. Educators, Fgn. Lang. Assn. Ga., Kappa Delta Pi, Sigma Delta Pi (hon.). Office: Wheeler High Sch 375 Holt Rd Marietta GA 30068-3560

MATRAGRANO, MARGHERITE PAULA, medical librarian; b. Bklyn., May 3, 1947; s. Joseph Rocco and Angelina Mary (Ragonesi) Salerno; m. Martin C. Matragrano, Aug. 18, 1973. Student, Cornell U., 1965-67; BA in Polit. Sci., Ga. State U., 1974; M Librarianship, Emory U., 1975. Adminstrv./faculty sec. Mercer U. Law and Med. Schs., Macon, Ga., 1983-85; cataloger, coll. libr. Ga. Coll., Milledgeville, 1985-87; dir. med. libr. Med. Ctr. Ctrl. Ga., Macon, 1987—. Mem. Med. Libr. Assn. (hosp. librs. sect., tech. svcs. divsn.). Roman Catholic. Home: 306 Westcliff Center Warner Robins GA 91093 Office: Med Ctr Ctrl Ga 777 Hemlock St Hosp Box 147 Macon GA 31201

MATSON, VIRGINIA MAE FREEBERG (MRS. EDWARD J. MATSON), retired special education educator, author; b. Chgo., Aug. 25, 1914; d. Axel George and Mae (Dalrymple) Freeberg; m. Edward John Matson, Oct. 18, 1941; children: Karin (Mrs. Donald H. Skadden), Sara M. Drake, Edward Robert, Laurence D., David O. BA, U. Ky., 1934; MA, Northwestern U., 1941. Spl. edn. tchr. area high schs., Chgo., 1934-42, Ridge Farm, 1944-45; tchr. high schs. Lake County (Ill.) Pub. Schs., 1956-59; founder Grove Sch., Lake Forest, Ill., 1958-87, ret., 1987; instr. evening sch. Carthage Coll., 1965-66. Author: Shadow on the Lost Rock, 1958, Saul, the King, 1968, Abba Father, 1970 (Friends Lit. Fiction award 1972), Buried Alive, 1970, A School for Peter, 1974, A Home for Peter, 1983, Letters to Lauren, A History of the Methodist Campgrounds, Des Plaines, 1985; contbr. many articles to profl. publs. Mem. Friends of Lit. Dem. Recipient Humanitarian award Ill. Med. Soc. Aux. Home: 4133 Mockingbird Ln Suffolk VA 23434-7186

MATTERA, TONY, sporting company executive. CEO Gary Koch Golf. Address: PO Box 272807 Tampa FL 33688-2807

MATTESON, THOMAS DICKENS, aeronautical engineer, consultant; b. Mpls., Oct. 16, 1920; s. Herbert Sumner and Edna Gertrude (Dickens) M.; m. Rosemary Ann Hamilton, Jan. 11, 1947; children: Ann Claire, John Thomas. B Aero. Engring., U. Minn., 1942; MBA in Mgmt., NYU, 1956. Various managerial positions Pan Am. Airways, N.Y.C., San Francisco, 1946-59; asst. to exec. v.p. Pacific div. Pan Am. Airways, San Francisco, 1959-60; various managerial positions United Airlines, San Francisco, 1960-70, dir. maintenance planning, 1970-75, v.p. maintenance adminstrn., 1975-78; sr. cons. Am. Mgmt. Systems, Arlington, Va., 1978-85; cons. engr., Flat Rock, N.C., 1978—; guest lectr. U. Calif. Ext., Berkeley, L.A., 1966, 70; IBM vis. disting. scholar Northeastern U., Boston, 1983; chmn., mem. maintenance program planning coms. for B727, B737, B747; cons. on nuc. reactor maintenance programs EPRI/NRC; mem. sr. rev. panel Savannah River PRA, 1985-93; lectr./advisor on applications of reliability-centered maintenance to paper mfg., 1992, CNO, NAVSEA, NAVAIR on improving aircraft and ship maintenance mgmt., 1993, EPRI on applications to electric power sub-stations, 1995. Author: NAVSEA Reliability-Centered Maintenance Handbook, 1980; contbr. numerous articles on aircraft, naval ship and nuclear systems maintenance mgmt. to profl. publs. Team leader Grace Commn., Washington, 1982. Lt. USNR, 1942-46, PTO. Assoc. fellow AIAA (chmn. tech. com. 1964-66, Systems Effectiveness and Safety medal 1976); mem. Western N.C. for United We Stand Adm. (com. coord. 1993-94). Home and Office: 1933 Little River Rd Flat Rock NC 28731-9766

MATTHEWS, BRUCE RANKIN, professional football player; b. Arcadia, Calif., Aug. 8, 1961. BS in Indsl. Engring., U. So. Calif., 1983. Center, guard Houston Oilers, 1983—. Named NFL All-Pro Team Guard by Sporting News, 1988-90, 92, Leader, 1993. Office: Houston Oilers 8030 EL Rio Houston TX 77054*

MATTHEWS, CLARK J(IO), II, retail executive, lawyer; b. Arkansas City, Kans., Oct. 1, 1936; s. Clark J. and Betty Elizabeth (Stewart) M.; children: Patricia Eleanor, Pamela Elaine, Catherine Joy. B.A., So. Meth. U., 1959, J.D., 1961. Bar: Tex. 1961. Trial atty. Ft. Worth Regional Office, SEC, 1961-63; law clk. to chief U.S. dist. judge No. Dist. Tex., Dallas, 1963-65; atty. Southland Corp., Dallas, 1965-73; v.p., gen. counsel Southland Corp., 1973-79, exec. v.p., chief fin. officer, 1979-83, sr. exec. v.p., chief fin. officer, 1983-87, exec. v.p., chief fin. officer, 1987-91, pres., chief exec. officer, 1991—. Mem. ABA, Tex., Dallas, Bar Assns., Am. Judicature Soc., Alpha Tau Omega, Pi Alpha Delta. Methodist. Club: DeMolay. Home: 7005 Stefani Dr Dallas TX 75225-1747 Office: Southland Corp 2711 N Haskell Ave Dallas TX 75204-2911

MATTHEWS, DAN GUS, lawyer; b. Jacksonville, Tex., Feb. 6, 1939; s. Agustus Newcomb and Charlie (Morton) M.; m. Mary Ellen Whittredge, Dec. 12, 1959; children: Mark Henderson, Daniel William. BS in History and English, Stephen F. Austin U., 1960; LLB, U. Houston, 1964. Bar: Tex. 1964, U.S. Dist. Ct. (so. dist.) Tex. 1964, U.S. Ct. Appeals (5th cir.) 1965, U.S. Ct. Appeals (11th cir.) 1981, U.S. Supreme Ct. 1967, U.S. Dist. Ct. (ea. dist.) Tex. 1990. Briefing clk. Fed. Judge Ben C. Connally, Houston, 1964-66; assoc. firm Fulbright & Jaworski, Houston, 1966-73; ptnr. Fulbright & Jaworski, Houston and San Antonio, 1973—. Bd. dirs., exec. com., chmn. membership coun. Los Compadres de San Antonio, Missions Nat. Hist. Pk., 1988—; deacon, elder Presbyn. Ch. Mem. ABA, State Bar Tex., Houston Bar Assn., San Antonio Bar Assn. Office: Fulbright & Jaworski 300 Convent St Ste 2200 San Antonio TX 78205-3723*

MATTHEWS, DANE DIKEMAN, urban planner; b. Memphis, Dec. 19, 1950; d. Neil Jude and Virginia Ann (Turnbull) Dikeman; m. John Wesley Matthews, Dec. 28, 1971. BA with distinction, U. Okla., 1972, M of Regional and City Planning, 1974. Planner Hudgins, Thompson & Ball, Inc., Tulsa, 1975-76; econ. devel. planner Tulsa Metro. Area Planning Commn., 1976-77; planner II Tulsa Met. Area Planning Commn., 1977-80; prin. regional planner Indian Nations Coun. Govts., Tulsa, 1980—. Project dir. Kendall-Whittier Neighborhood Master Plan, 1992. Bd. dirs. Met. Tulsa Urban League, 1993-95, Parkside Cmty. Mental Health Ctr., Tulsa, 1986—; bd. dirs., chair house com. Arts and Humanities Coun., Tulsa, 1991—; div. chair Tulsa Area United Way, 1988-96. Recipient Spl. Recognition award Downtown Tulsa Unltd., 1988. Mem. Am. Inst. Cert. Planners (cert.), Am. Planning Assn. (Okla. chpt. pres. 1988-89, Master Plan award 1992, Outstanding Profl. Planner 1991), Phi Beta Kappa. Democrat. Episcopalian. Office: INCOG 201 W 5th St Ste 600 Tulsa OK 74103-4278

MATTHEWS, DAVID, clergyman; b. Indianola, Miss., Jan. 29, 1920; s. Albert and Bertha (Henderson) M.; m. Lillian Pearl Banks, Aug. 28, 1951; 1 dau., Denise. A.B., Morehouse Coll., Atlanta, 1950; student, Atlanta U., 1950, Memphis Theol. Sem., 1965, Delta State U., Cleveland, Miss., 1969, 71, 72; D.D. (hon.), Natchez (Miss.) Jr. Coll., 1973, Morris Booker Meml. Coll., 1988. Ordained minister Nat. Baptist Conv. U.S.A., 1946; pastor chs. in Miss., 1951—, Bell Grove Baptist Ch., Indianola, 1951—, Strangers Home, Greenwood, 1958—; tchr., chmn. dept. social sci. Gentry H.S., Indianola, 1958-83; moderator Sunflower Bapt. Assn., 1957—; v.p. Gen. Bapt. Conv. Miss., 1958—, former lectr., conv. congress religious edn.; v.p. Nat. Bapt. Conv. U.S.A., 1971-94; del. to Nat. Coun. Chs., 1960, supr. oratorial contest, 1976; pres. Gen. Missionary Bapt. State Conv. Miss., 1974—. Mem. Sunflower County Anti-Poverty Bd., 1965-71, Indianola Bi-Racial Com., 1965—; mem. Gov.'s Advisory Com.; col. on staff Gov. Finch, 1976-80; mem. budget com. Indianola United Fund, 1971—; chmn. bd. Indianola FHA, 1971—; trustee Natchez Jr. Coll.; mem. Miss. Gov.'s Research and Devel. Council, 1984—; apptd. mem. So. Govs. Ecumenical Coun. Infant Mortality, 1987. Served with U.S. Army, 1942-45, PTO. Recipient citation Morehouse Coll., 1950, citation Miss. Valley State Coll., 1956; J.H. Jackson Preaching award Midwestern Baptist Laymen Fellowship, 1974; Gov.'s Merit award, 1975. Mem. NEA, Miss., Indianola Tchrs. Assns., Am. Bible Soc. (adv. coun. 1991—, student reform theol. sem. centennial edn. 1990—). Democrat. Home: PO Box 627 Indianola MS 38751-0627*

MATTHEWS, ED C., internist; b. Garberville, Calif., Jan. 2, 1955; s. Robert Thomas and Rae C. (Thomas) M.; m. Cynthia S. Smith; children: Nicholas, Brady, Dave. BS, U. Calif., Davis, 1978; BS Physician Assoc. with distinction, U. Okla., 1984; MD, Albany (N.Y.) Med. Coll., 1990. Diplomate Am. Bd. Internal Medicine. Commd. USAF, 1980—, advanced through grades to maj.; staff internist Wilford Hall Med. Ctr., Lackland AFB, Tex., 1993—. Mem. AMA, ACP, Soc. of Air Force Physicians, Alpha Omega Alpha. Home: 4000 Horizon Hill Apt 1909 San Antonio TX 78229

MATTHEWS, FRANCES KELLER, retired real estate agent, researcher; b. Honesdale, Pa., July 19, 1925; d. Abram and Fanie (Koenig) Keller; m. William D. Matthews, Nov. 27, 1951. Student, St. Petersburg Jr. Coll., 1944, Lamar U., 1977. Real estate agt./broker Frances K. Matthews Real Estate, St. Petersburg, Fla., 1960-76; real estate agt. Junction Realty, Liberty and Pasadena, Tex., 1980-87; ret., 1987; rschr., social justice adv., writer, networker Ideas at Work, Liberty, 1992—. Local contact United We Stand, 1992-94; networking vol. Am. Soc. for Quality Control, Milw., 1993-94, Psychologists for Social Responsibiity, Washington, mem. divsn. # 48 Psychologists for Peace, divsn. #9 Psychologists for Study of Social Issues; active Libr. of Congress Assocs. Mem. NAFE, NOW, Tex. Libr. Assn., U.S. Golf Assn., Project Vote Smart, Amnesty Internat., Bread for the World, So. Poverty Law Ctr., Soc. Profl. Journalists, Alliance for Comty. Media, African Violet Soc., S.E. Tex. Orchid Soc., Am. Orchid Soc., U.S. C. of C., Nat. Coun. for the Social Studies, Gospel Music Assn., Am. Assn. Ret. Persons, Sisterhood is Global, Internat. Tng. in Comm.

MATTHEWS, GEORGE BOSTERT, engineering educator; b. Johnstown, Pa., 1927. BSME, Carnegie Inst. Tech., 1948, MSME, 1949; MA, Princeton U., 1954, PhD in Aeronautical Engring., 1957. Aeronautical rsch. engr. Office of Naval Rsch., Washington, 1957-60; assoc. prof. dept. aerospace engring. Sch. of Engring. and Applied Sch. U. Va., Charlottesville, 1960-69, chmn. dept. of aerospace engring., 1962-65, prof. dept. aerospace engring./engring. physics, 1969-77, asst. to the dean engring. and applied sci., 1972-73, asst. dean engring. and applied sci., 1974-75, dean of admissions undergrad., 1973-75, prof. dept. mech. and aerospace engring., 1977—; lectr. cons. NASA Langley Rsch. Ctr., 1963-64; resident cons. engr. Kaman Nuclear divsn. Kaman Aircraft Corp., Colorado Springs, 1964; lectr. and resident cons. Bio-Space Tech. Tng. Program, 1967-68; vis. prof., lectr. Dept. Aeronautics and Astronautics, Southampton U., U.K., 1970-71; expert Aero. Sys., Air Combat divsn., U.S. Army, Nat. Ground Intelligence Ctr., Charlottesville, Va., 1984—; program evaluator Naval Aviation Exec. Inst., 1984, program coord.; vis. prof. Coll. Aeronautics, Cranfield (U.K.) Inst. Tech., 1988; cons. Texaco Experiment Inc., Richmond, Va., 1963-65, Teledyne Avionics, Charlottesville, 1984-85, Daedalus Rsch., Inc., Petersburg, Va., 1987. Contbr. articles to profl. jours. Recipient Ralph R. Teetor award for outstanding educator Soc. of Automotive Engrs., 1984. Fellow AIAA (assoc., editor student jour. 1966-69, Disting. Educator award region I, 1984, Outstanding Faculty award 1988), Acad. of Model Aeronautics, Soc. Automotive Engrs., Am. Helicopter Soc., Tau Beta Pi, Pi Tau Sigma, Sigma Gamma Tau, Sigma Xi. Office: U Va Mech Aerospace/Nuclear Eng Charlottesville VA 22903

MATTHEWS, GERALD, association administrator. Exec. dir. Fla. Assn. Realtors, Orlando. Office: Fla Assn Realtors PO Box 725025 Orlando FL 32872-5025

MATTHEWS, HAROLD DOWNS, author, consultant; b. Waco, Tex., Mar. 24, 1925; s. Harold Jackson and Sophie Grace (Downs) M.; m. Mary Byers Riley, Nov. 22, 1948 (div. Oct. 1971); children: Mark Allen, Elizabeth

Ann Matthews Inman; m. Marianne Reeder, Nov. 22, 1971. BA in Journalism, U. Tex., 1947. Coord. employee comm. Schlumberger Well Svcs., Houston, 1948-68; editor Exxon USA mag. Exxon Co., U.S.A., Houston, 1968-86; freelance writer, cons., Houston, 1986—. Author: How to Manage Business Publications, 1987, Polar Bear Cubs, 1989, Skimmers, 1990, Arctic Summer, 1992, Wetlands, 1993, Polar Bear, 1993, Arctic Foxes, 1994; contbr. numerous feature articles to publs. Fellow Internat. Assn. Bus. Communicators; mem. Travel Journalists Guild, Outdoor Writers Assn. Am., Am. Soc. Journalists and Authors, Am. Orchid Soc. Home and Office: 3501 Underwood St Houston TX 77025-1903

MATTHEWS, HERBERT R., transportation company executive; b. 1930. With GMAC, Atlanta, 1952-57; with Benton Express Inc., Atlanta, 1957—, chmn. bd.; officer Air Van Inc., Atlanta, 1961—, Benton Film Forwarding Co. Inc., Atlanta, 1973—. Office: Benton Express Inc 1045 S River Industrial Atlanta GA 30315

MATTHEWS, HEWITT WILLIAM, science educator; b. Pensacola, Fla., Dec. 1, 1944; s. Hewitt W. and Jestine Texas (Lowe) M.; m. Marlene Angela Mouzon, June 21, 1969; children: Derrick Hewitt, David Paul. BS in Chemistry, Clark Coll., 1966; BS in Pharmacy, Mercer U., 1968; MS in Pharm. Biochemistry, U. Wis., 1971, PhD in Pharm. Biochemistry, 1973. From asst. to assoc. prof. medicinal chemistry so. sch. pharmacy Mercer U., Atlanta, 1973-81, prof. pharm. scis., 1981—, Hood-Myer Alumni Chair prof., 1982—, dir. rsch., 1975-79, asst. to dean, 1979-80, asst. dean svcs., 1980-83, asst. provost, 1983-85, assoc. dean, 1985-89, acting dean, 1989-90, dean, 1990—; rsch. chemist Ctr. Disease Control, Atlanta, 1976, vis. scientist hosp. infectious disease program, 1987, 88; pharmacist Dr.'s Meml. Hosp., Atlanta, 1978-80; vis. assoc. prof. Tex. So. U., Houston, 1979; lectr. pharmacology sch. anesthesia Ga. Bapt. Med. Ctr., 1979-85; lectr. advanced nutrition dept. allied healths Clark Coll., 1980-82, mem. adv. bd. sci. enrichment and rsch. program, 1986—; item writer Nat. Assn. Bds. Pharmacy Licensure Examinations, 1981, 83-87; mem. Ga. State Bd. Pharmacy Continuing Edn. Tripartite Com., 1986-89, Gov.'s Adv. Coun. Sci. and Tech. Devel., 1992-93; mem. various coms., advisor various univ. orgns. Mercer U.; presenter in field. Mem. editorial adv. bd. Jour. Nat. Pharm. Assn., 1981-83, reviewer, 1989, U.S. Pharmacist, 1982-83; mem. editl. bd. Pharmacy Today, Am. Pharm. Assn., 1995—; contbr. articles to profl. jours. Assoc. pastor Fellowship Faith Ch., Internat.; coach Little League Baseball, Fayette County 10 & Under Basketball; score keeper Fayette County Athletic Assn.; mem. Fayette C. of C. Project Fayette Housing and Labor Task Force; bd. dirs. met. Atlanta chpt. ARC, 1986—. Recipient Friend of Acad. Student Pharmacists award, 1991-92; named Outstanding Citizen of State of Ga., Ga. Ho. of Reps., 1992; grantee Bristol Labs., 1974, Pfeiffer Found., 1976-80, Hoechst-Roussel, 1982-91, Smith Kline Beckman Corp., 1986, Am. Cyanamid Co., 1987, Glaxo, Inc., 1988, Sandoz Pharm. Co., 1988, 89; fellow Am. Found. Pharm. Edn., 1968, pre-doctoral fellow NIH, 1970-73. Mem. Am. Soc. Hosp. Pharmacists, Am. Pharm. Assn., Am. Assn. Hosp. Pharmacists, Am. Assn. Colls. Pharmacy (chmn. profl. affairs com. 1984-85, rsch. and grad. affairs com. 1986-87, GAPS grant reviewer 1987, reviewer mgmt. systems manuel minorities 1988-89, coun. deans nominating com. 1990-91), Nat. Pharm. Assn. (v.p. 1994—, Recognition award 1990), Ga. Soc. Hosp. Pharmacists (continuing edn. com. 1986-87, strategic planning com. 1991), Ga. Pharm. Assn. (com. colls. 1984-85, continuing edn. com. 1986-87, commn. pharm. care 1991—), Tenn. Pharmacists Assn., Atlanta Acad. Instl. Pharmacists, Beta Kappa Chi, Kappa Epsilon (assoc.), Phi Kappa Phi, Phi Lambda Sigma, Rho Chi, Sigma Xi. Home: 120 Hanover Cir Fayetteville GA 30214-1233 Office: Mercer U So Sch Pharmacy 3001 Mercer Univ Dr Atlanta GA 30341*

MATTHEWS, J. ROSSER, historian, educator; b. Williamsburg, VA, Sept. 27, 1964; s. John Rosser and Barbara Brand (McCaskill) M. AB, Coll. of William & Mary, 1985; MA, Duke U., 1988, PhD, 1992. Vis. lectr. N.C. State U., fall 1992, 93; vis. asst. prof. history Duke U., spring 1993; vis. asst. prof. history of sci. U. Okla., spring 1994; adj. prof. interdisciplinary studies Coll. William and Mary, 1997; mem. Local Arrangements com. for the 1997 meeting of Am. Assn. for the History of Medicine in Williamsburg, 1995-97. Author: Quantification and the Quest for Medical Certainty, 1995; contbr. articles to scholarly publs. Mem. History of Sci. Soc., Phi Beta Kappa. Home: 200 Captain Newport Circle Williamsburg VA 23185

MATTHEWS, JAMES GORDON, JR., obstetrician, gynecologist; b. Bridgeport, Conn., Jan. 22, 1916; s. James G. and Sue Gay (Short) M.; m. Gladyce Lorraine Carlberg, Apr. 4, 1942; children: Suzanne, James III, Barbara, William, Christine, Thomas. BS, Ea. Mich. U., 1937; DO, Kirksville Coll Osteo Mecidine, 1942. Diplomate ob-gyn. Am. Osteo. Bd. Intern-resident ob-gyn. Detroit Osteo. Hosp., Highland Park, Mich., 1942-45, sr. ob-gyn., chmn., 1947-68; chmn. ob-gyn. Bicounty Community Hosp., Warren, Mich., 1970; sr. attending ob-gyn. Doctor's Hosp., Columbus, Ohio, 1971-75; chair ob-gyn. Doctor's Hosp., Columbus, 1974-75, Dallas Ft. Worth Med. Ctr., Grand Prairie, Tex., 1975-90; clin. prof. ob-gyn. Tex. Coll. Osteo. Medicine, Ft. Worth, 1975—, Okla. State U. Coll. Osteo. Medicine, Tulsa, 1984—; dir. resident tng. ob-gyn. Dallas Ft. Worth Med. Ctr., Grand Prairie, 1984-94; retired, 1994; lectr. in field; cons. sex edn. Bd. Edn., Berkley, Mich. Contbr. articles to profl. jours. Mem. Grand Prairie YMCA Bd. Mgmt., 1977—; sustaining campaign chmn. YMCA, Grand Prairie, 1989; pres. Rotary Club, Grand Prairie, 1988-89. Named Pub. Servant of Yr., Grand Prairie C. of C., 1988, Vol. of Yr., Dallas Met. YMCA, 1989, Physician of Yr., Dallas/Ft. Worth Med. Ctr. Found., 1990. Fellow Am. Coll. Osteo. Ob-Gyn. (disting., pres. 1964); mem. Am. Osteo Assn. (life), Am. Menopause Soc., Am. Bd. Sexology (diplomate), Tex. Osteo. Med. Assn. (life), Assn. Reproductive Health Profls., Grayline Game Club (pres.), Red Run Golf Club (life), Mich. Inter-Club Swimming Assn. (pres.), Rotary Internat. (Paul Harris fellow). Methodist.

MATTHEWS, JAY ARLON, JR., publisher, editor; b. St. Louis, Apr. 13, 1918; s. Jay Arlon and Mary (Long) M.; student San Jose State Coll., 1939-41, U. Tex., 1946-47; BLS St. Edward's U., 1994; m. May Clark McLemore, Jan. 16, 1944; children—Jay Arlon III, Emily Cochrane, Sally McLemore. Asst. dir. personnel Adj. Gen.'s Dept. Tex., 1947-53, dept. adj., 1957-65, mil. support plans officer, 1965-69, chief emergency operations, 1965-71; pub. Presidial Press, Mil. History Press. Past Dir. Civil Def., Austin; mem. adv. bd. Confed. Research Center, Hill Jr. Coll.; mil. historian 65th Legislature, Tex., 1977-78. Served with AGC, Tex. N.G., 1946—, brig. gen. ret., 1973. Named to Tex. Nat. Guard Hall of Honor, 1990. Fellow Co. Mil. Historians (gov. 1981-84); mem. Austin (state v.p. 1951-52), U.S. Jaycees (chmn. nat. security com. 1952-53), N.G. Assn. U.S. (chmn. publicity 81st Gen. Conf.), Instituto Internationale de Historia Militar (hon. life), Mil. Order World Wars (comdr. Austin chpt. 1980). Episcopalian. Club: Exchange (pres. Austin chpt. 1982-83). Editor: Mil. History of Tex. and S.W. Quar., 1961-88; editor emeritus Mil. Hist. of the West, 1989. Home: 1807 Stamford Ln Austin TX 78703-2939 Office: 407-B E 6th St Ste 200 Austin TX 78701

MATTHEWS, JEANNE PEARSON, logistic support analyst, company executive; b. Marietta, Ga., July 2, 1941; d. Silas Leon and Edith Mae (Rich) Pearson; m. William Dean Bottoms, Apr. 2, 1960 (div. 1973); 1 child, William Dave; m. William Glenn Matthews, Sept. 4, 1976. Typist, stenographer, sec. Lockheed-Ga. Co., Marietta, 1962-82, gen. acct., price estimator, 1982-84, logistic support analyst, 1984—; pres. J&B Office Service, Inc., Villa Rica, Ga., 1984-87. Mem. Nat. Platform Com. Named Hon. Lt. Col. Aide-de-Camp Ala. State Militia, 1976; named Ms. Lockheed, Lockheed-Ga. Co., 1972, 74. Mem. Nat. Assn. Female Execs., Nat. Film Inst., Nat. Assn. Mature People, Paulding County C. of C., AFL-CIO (recording sec. Lodge 709 1973-79). Democrat. Baptist. Clubs: Kennesaw Mountain Beagle (sec.-treas. Dallas, Ga. 1980—), Atlanta Braves Fan. Lodge: Order Eastern Star. Avocations: Beagles; baseball; swimming. Home: 2565 Townsend Rd Villa Rica GA 30180-3635

MATTHEWS, JOHN CARROLL, manufacturing executive; b. Galax, Va., Dec. 25, 1933; m. Freida Felts; children: Jason, Justin. BSBA, Appalachian State U., 1959. Plant employee Carolina Mirror Co., North Wilkesboro, N.C., 1959-60, scheduling employee, 1960-66, salesman, 1967-77, sales promotion profl., 1978-88, nat. sales mgr., 1989-90, v.p., 1991—; bd. dirs. First Citizens Bank, seminar spkr., trade show mgr. Nat. Assn. Mirror Mfrs., Potomac, Md. Contbr. articles to profl. jours. Mem. YMCA; mem. adminstrv. bd. First United Meth. Ch., North Wilkesboro; pres. PTA, North Wilkesboro; chmn. Wilkes County Cancer Soc., North Wilkesboro; coach YMCA Little League, North Wilkesboro. With U.S. Army, 1956-58. Mem. Nat. Glass Assn. (bd. dirs., seminar spkr.), Appalachian State U. Alumni Assn., Rotary (charter, past pres. North Wilkesboro chpt.), Oakwoods Country Club. Office: Carolina Mirror Co Hwy 268 E North Wilkesboro NC 28659

MATTHEWS, LINDA NELL, secondary school educator; b. Decatur, Ala., May 12, 1948; d. Clinton Van and Lela Magdalene (Pressnell) Bowers; m. David Latrell Matthews, Sept. 4, 1971; children: Amy Leanne, Lorrie Suzanne. BS in Edn., Athens State Coll., 1991; postgrad., U. North Ala., 1991—. Cert. tchr. elem. edn., early childhood, mid. sch. lang. arts, social sci., 7-12 English, Ala., Tenn. Sales assoc. Longaberger Baskets, Athens, Ala., 1988-92; substitute tchr. Giles County and Limestone County, Ala. and Tenn., 1991-92; tchr. English Elkton (Tenn.) Elem. Sch., 1992-93; tchr. English Limestone County Bd. Edn. West Limestone H.S., Athens, 1993—; beauty cons. Mary Kay Cosmetics, Athens, 1984—. Vol. tutor Laubach Literacy Action, 1991-93; participant Ptnrs. for Drug-Free Edn. Orgn., Athens, 1991-93; pres. West Limestone PTO, Lester, Ala., 1991-93. NEH grantee, 1993, Ala. Humanities Found. grantee, summer 1996. Mme. Phi Theta Kappa, Kappa Delta Pi (pres. 1992-93). Mem. Ch. of Christ. Home: 15283 Hobbs Rd Athens AL 35614 Office: West Limestone HS 10945 W School House Rd Lester AL 35647-3635

MATTHEWS, SHERMAN ERVIN, JR., social services administrator; b. Chattanooga, May 4, 1948; s. Sherman J. and Mary K. (Powell) M.; m. Brenda Jones, May 2, 1970; children: Kimberly Diane, Erika Lannette. BA in Sociology, Ky. State U., 1971; postgrad., U. Tenn., Chattanooga, 1974-76. Emergency substitute tchr., Chattanooga, 1971; family counselor Assn. Day Care Agy., Chattanooga, 1971-72; drug counselor day program Community Action Agy., Chattanooga, 1972-73; juvenile probation officer Tenn. Dept. Correction, Chattanooga, 1973-86, supervisory probation officer III, 1986-88, mgr. juvenile probation I, 1988-89; regional dir. SE region Tenn. Dept. Youth Devel., Chattanooga, 1989—; adj. prof. U. Tenn., 1978. Bd. dirs. Operation PUSH; mem. adv. bd. and steering com. PUSH-Excel Program, Chattanooga, 1979, now bd. dirs.; mem. Unity Group, Chattanooga; mem. Chattanooga Pub. Sch. Bd. Edn. Dist. 5, 1990—. Recipient award Excel Adv. Bd., 1983, Key to City, City of Chattanooga, 1988. Mem. NAACP (bd. dirs. Chattanooga 1989), Masons (32 degree, master mason), Shriners, Kappa Alpha Psi, Alpha Phi Omega. Democrat. Baptist. Home: 2808 Terry Ct Chattanooga TN 37411-1065 Office: Tenn Dept Youth Devel 540 Mccallie Ave Chattanooga TN 37402-2089

MATTHEWS, SUZETTE, lawyer; b. Morristown, N.J., July 8, 1953; d. Stanley and Agnes (Loprete) M.; m. Arthur Donald Bernstein, Mar. 22, 1986. BA, Cornell U., 1975, JD, 1978. Bar: Va., D.C. Assoc. Galland, Kharasch, Morse & Garfinkle, Washington, 1978-83; dir. Straus & Matthews, Washington, 1984; gen. counsel Air Traffic Control Assn., Arlington, Va., 1984—; ptnr. Bernstein & Matthews, Marshall, Va., 1984—. Editor Jour. of Air Traffic Control, Arlington, Va., 1994—. Mem. Phi Beta Kappa. Home: 5649 John Barton Payne Rd Marshall VA 22115

MATTHEWS, WADE HAMPTON BYNUM, consul, consultant; b. Winston-Salem, N.C., June 29, 1933; s. Marshall Lawrence and Mary Preston (Bynum) M.; m. Betty Morgan, May 5, 1961; children: Deborah Preston, Pamela Morgan Matthews Klinger, Wade H.B. Jr. BA, U. N.C., 1954; student, U. Fla., 1956-57, Stanford U., 1969-70. Dep. amb. U.S. Embassy, Georgetown, Guyana, 1974-76, Santiago, Chile, 1982-85; dep. dir. U.S. Mission Orgn. Am. States, Washington, 1976-77; dir. Office Ctrl. Am. Affairs U.S. Dept. State, Washington, 1977-79, sr. insp., 1987-90, mem. Fgn. Svc. Res. Corps, 1990—; consul gen. U.S. Consulate Gen., Guayaquil, Ecuador, 1980-82; prof. strategy and policy U.S. Naval War Coll., Newport, R.I., 1985-87; internat. cons. Global Bus. Assocs., Ltd., Washington, 1990—. Author: Human Rights and the National Interest: U.S. Policy in Central America and the Phillippines, 1980. Dean Consular Corps, Guayaquil, 1981-82, bd. dirs. Sarasota Audubon Soc., 1992—, com. chair. Mem. UN Assn. (pres. Sarasota-Manatee chpt. 1995—, vice chmn. 1993-95), Fgn. Affairs Assistance Corps (bd. dirs. 1990-92), Fgn. Svc. Retirees Fla. (vice chmn. 1993-95). Office: Wade Matthews and Assocs 5152 Admiral Pl Sarasota FL 34231-4202

MATTHIES, MARY CONSTANCE T., lawyer; b. Baton Rouge, Mar. 22, 1948; d. Allen Douglas and Mazie (Poche) Tillman. B.S., Okla. State U., 1969; J.D., U. Tulsa, 1972. Bar: Okla. 1973, U.S. Ct. Appeals (10th cir.) 1974, U.S. Ct. Appeals (8th and D.C. cirs.) 1975, U.S. Supreme Ct. 1976. Assoc., ptnr. Kothe, Nichols & Wolfe, Inc., Tulsa, 1972-78; pres. sr. prin. Matthies Law Firm, P.C., Tulsa, 1978—; guest lectr. U. Tulsa Coll. Law, U. Okla. Sch. Law, Oral Roberts U. Sch. Contbr. articles to profl. jours; mem. staff Tulsa Law Jour., 1971-72. Law. Mem. Women's Task Force, Tulsa Community Rels. Commn., 1972-73. Recipient Tom Brett Criminal Law award, 1971, Am. Jurisprudence awards, 1971. Mem. ABA (mem. spl. subcom. for liaison with EEOC, 1974—, spl. subcom. for liaison with OFCCP, 1979—, mgmt. co-chmn. equal employment law subcoms. on nat. origin discrimination 1974-75, class actions and remedies 1975-80), Okla. Bar Assn. (coun. mem. labor law sect. 1974-80, chmn. 1978-79), Women's Law Caucus, Phi Delta Phi. Presbyterian. Office: Thompson Bldg 20 E 5th St Ste 310 Tulsa OK 74103-4435

MATTHIESEN, LEROY THEODORE, bishop; b. Olfen, Tex., June 11, 1921; s. Joseph A. and Rosa (Englert) M. BA, Josephinum Coll., Columbus, Ohio, 1942; MA, Cath. U., Washington, 1961; LittD, Register Sch. Journalism., Denver, 1962. Ordained priest Roman Cath. Ch., 1946. Editor West Tex. Cath., Amarillo diocese, from 1948; prin. Alamo Cath. High Sch, from 1969; pastor St. Francis parish, from 1972; ordained bishop of Amarillo, Tex., 1980—. Office: 1800 N Spring St PO Box 5644 Amarillo TX 79117-5644*

MATTICE, HOWARD LEROY, education educator; b. Roxbury, N.Y., Sept. 23, 1935; s. Charles Pierce and Loretta Jane (Ellis) M.; m. Elaine Grace Potts, Feb. 4, 1956; children: Kevin, Stephen. BA, King's Coll., 1960; MA, L.I. U., 1965, NYU, 1969; cert., CUNY, 1972; EdD, NYU, 1978. Cert. tchr. N.Y., clin. educators trainer, Fla. Dept. Edn. Social studies tchr. N.Y.C. Bd. Edn., 1961-90, mid. and jr. H.S. asst. prin., 1970-72, 73-75; assoc. prof. edn. and history Clearwater (Fla.) Christian Coll., 1990-92, chmn. divsn. of edn., prof. edn. and history, 1992—; adj. lectr. history S.I. C.C., CUNY, 1969-75; curriculum writer N.Y.C. Bd. Edn., 1985; program reviewer Fla. Dept. Edn., Tallahassee, 1994—; item writer GED Testing Svc., Washington, 1988-92; mem. So. Assn. Colls. and Schs. Accreditation Team H.S., 1995—. Chmn. bd. New Dorp Christian Acad., S.I., 1973-90; chmn. bd. deacons New Dorp. Bapt. Ch., S.I., 1981-90. Mem. ASCD, Assn. Tchr. Educators, Nat. Coun. Social Studies, So. Assn. Colls. and Schs. (h.s. accreditation review team 1995—). Office: Clearwater Christian Coll 3400 Gulf To Bay Blvd Clearwater FL 34619-4514

MATTINGLY, L. SHARON, elementary principal; b. Henderson, Ky., July 16, 1953; d. George Muir Jr. and Ida Mae (Slaughter) M. AS, Henderson C.C.; BA in Elem. Edn. Adminstrn. & Supervisn., U. Evansville; MA in Elem. Edn., Western Ky. U. Elem. tchr. Henderson County Sch., 1975-95, prin., 1995—. Home: 5371 US 41 Alternate Henderson KY 42420

MATTIS, GEORGE EVANS, JR., librarian; b. Providence, Feb. 28, 1954; s. George Evans and Rita (Kenyon) M.; m. Brenda Jean Thornhill, June 1, 1984; children: Jason, Jeremy, Justin, Joshua. AA, R.I. Jr. Coll., 1974; BA, Rogers Williams Coll., 1976; MLS, George Peabody Coll., 1977. Catalog libr. Miss. State Univ., 1978-80; humanities cataloger Va. Polytechnic Inst. and State U., Blacksburg, Va., 1980-83; catalog libr. Radford (Va.) U., 1983-86; asst. libr. Wytheville (Va.) C.C., 1986—. Mem. Wythe County Hist. Soc., Loyal Order of the Moose. Republican. Roman Catholic. Home: 1105 W Franklin St Apt 2 Wytheville VA 24382 Office: Wytheville CC Libr 1000 E Main St Wytheville VA 24382

MATTISON, GEORGE CHESTER, JR., health and environmental company executive, consultant; b. Eutaw, Ala., May 9, 1940; s. George Chester and Martha Pauline (Chilton) M; m. Barbara Peppenhorst, Aug. 20, 1963 (div. 1979); children: Mary Martha, George Chester III, William Grant; m. Linda Morris, May 23, 1987; step-daughter, Lisa Anne. MBA, Winthrop U., 1989. Shift chemist Gulf States Paper Corp., Demopolis, Ala., 1960-66; lab. technician Ala. Kraft Co., Mahrt, 1966-68; sales rep. Drew Chem. Co., Boonton, N.J., 1968-70, Betz Labs., Trevose, Pa., 1970-73; dist. mgr. Nalco Chem. Co., Naperville, Ill., 1976-85; regional mgr. Sandoz Chem. Co., Charlotte, N.C., 1985-89, Procomp (DuPont/Eka Nobel), Marietta, Ga., 1989-90; pres. OmniKem, Rock Hill, S.C., 1990-93, Mattison Enterprises, Inc., Rock Hill, 1993—; bd. dirs. Mattison Enterprises, Inc.; adv. bd. Haas Corp., Phila., 1990-93, Horizon Industries. Mem. adv. bd. Rock Hill High, 1985; mem. Rep. Re-election com., Rock Hill, 1990; coach YMCA Pee-Wee Football, Rock Hill, 1973-78. Mem. TAPPI, Paper Industry Mgmt. Assn., Nat. Eagle Scout Assn., Nat. MBA Assn., Shriners, Masons, Rock Hill C. of C. Baptist. Home: 441 Lakeside Dr Rock Hill SC 29730-6105 Office: Mattison Enterprises Inc 141 Oakland Avenue Rock Hill SC 29732

MATTOCKS-WHISMAN, FRANCES, nursing administrator, educator; b. Cedar Vale, Kans., Dec. 20, 1945; d. Thomas Emerson and Lavonna Laura (Myers) McKinney; m. Jim L. Whisman, Nov. 6, 1981; stepchildren: Toni Zweigart, Gay Asbell, Jenny Watts, Beth Whisman. Diploma, William Newton Sch. Nursing, Winfield, Kans., 1966; student, Tulsa Jr. Coll., Cen. State U., Edmond, Okla., Graceland Coll., Lamoni, Iowa, 1989—. RN; cert. operating room nurse. Operating room nurse Hillcrest Med. Ctr., Tulsa, 1968-72, 74-76; office mgr. Myra A. Peters, M.D., 1972-76; pvt. duty nurse Homemakers Upjohn, Inc., Tulsa, 1976-77; staff nurse, head nurse, insvc. instr. Doctors Med. Ctr., Inc., Tulsa; co-dir. Sch. Surg. Tech. Tulsa County Area Vo-Tech. Sch., 1981-89; asst. dir. transplantation/retrievals Tulsa chpt. ARC, 1989; staff nurse, infection control coord. Wetumka (Okla.) Gen. Hosp., 1989-91; dir. nurses Bristow (Okla.) Meml. Hosp., 1991-93; br. mgr. Columbia Homecare of Okla., Sapulpa, Okla., 1993—; br. supr. Sapulpa and Mannford offices Doctors Homecare, 1994-95; instr. Wes Watkins Area Vo-Tech. Sch., Wetumka, 1989-90; cons. ARC, Tulsa chpt. Transplantation, 1990. Contbr. articles to profl. jours. Active ARC. Mem. NEA, Nat. Assn. Orthopedic Nurses, Nat. League for Nursing, Am. Vocat. Assn., Okla. Vocat. Assn., Okla. Edn. Assn., Concerned Oklahomans for Nurse Edn., Assn. Operating Rm. Nurses, Infections Control. Nurses. Home: 1418A E 71st St Tulsa OK 74136 Office: Columbia Homecare-Okla 405 S Main Sapulpa OK 74066

MATTOX, RONALD EUGENE, counselor; b. Farmville, Va., Aug. 22, 1948; s. David Madison Jr. and Ruth (Allen) M.; m. Anita Russell Hardy, July 19, 1970; children: James Russell, Jason Dean, Joseph Edward. Diploma in higher acctg., Phillips Bus. Coll., 1968; BS cum laude, Campbell U., 1973; MS, Longwood Coll., 1978; cert. of advanced grad. studies, Va. Polytech. Inst., 1991. Cert. nat. counselor. Fin. aid officer Southside Va. Community Coll., Keysville, Va., 1973-78, counselor, 1978-93, coord. of counseling, 1993—. Bd. dirs. Friends of Victoria (Va.) Pub. Libr., 1976-80, Victoria-Lunenburg County Community Ctr., Inc., 1976-80; trustee Victoria Bapt. Ch., 1985—; coun. mem. Town of Victoria, 1976-80, vice mayor, 1978-80; coach Dixie Youth League Baseball, Victoria, 1986-88; mem. Piedmont Dist. Humanities Coun., Farmville, Va., 1987-89. With U.S. Army, 1968-71, Vietnam. Named Outstanding Va. Chpt. Sponsor, Phi Theta Kappa of Va., 1985; named to Hall of Honor for Sponsors, Phi Theta Kappa Internat., 1985, Fred Baker Scholar, 1986, Top Ten Advisor, 1988. Mem. AACD, Am. Coll. Pers. Assn., Southside Pers. and Guidance Assn. (treas. 1977-78, v.p. 1978-79, pres.-elect 1979-80, pres. 1980-81, Outstanding Chpt. Mem. award 1983, Coll. Counselor of Yr. award 1991), Va. Counselors Assn., Va. Assn. Student Pers. Adminstrs., Va. Assn. Collegiate Registrars and Admissions Officers, VFW, Chi Sigma Iota, Epsilon Pi Eta. Baptist. Home: RR 1 Box 300 Victoria VA 23974-9650 Office: Southside Va CC RR 1 Box 15 Keysville VA 23947-9703

MATTOX, THOMAS FORREST, county official; b. San Antonio, Nov. 24, 1939; s. Thomas Matlock and Ruby Norma Mattox; m. Edith Louise Burge; children: Connie E., Christopher T. AS, U. S.C., Beaufort, 1990; BSBA in Mgmt., U. S.C., Aiken, 1991. Gen. mgr., purchasing agent, buyer various pvt. sector cos.; chief procurement officer City of Lake Charles, La., 1982-87, City of Beaufort, S.C., 1987—; mem. profl. devel. com. Beufort County Constrn. and Ins. Coms. Dir. finance, chmn. stewardship, outreach leader, usher Bapt. Ch. Mem. Nat. Inst. Govt. Purchasing (cert. pub. purchasing ofcl. 1990), Nat. Assn. Purchasing Mgmt. (cert. purchasing mgr. 1988), S.C. Assn. Govtl. Purchasing Officers (profl. devel. com., Scholarship award 1991). Office: Beaufort County PO Box 1228 Beaufort SC 29901-1228

MATTSON, JAMES STEWART, lawyer, environmental scientist, educator; b. Providence, July 22, 1945; s. Irving Carl and Virginia (Lutey) M.; m. Carol Sandry, Aug. 15, 1964 (div. 1979); children: James, Birgitta; m. Rana A. Fine, Jan. 5, 1983. BS in Chemistry, U. Mich., 1966, MS, 1969, PhD, 1970; JD, George Washington U., 1979. Bar: D.C. 1979, Fla. 1983, U.S. Dist. Ct. D.C. 1979, U.S. Dist. Ct. (so. dist.) Fla. 1984, U.S. Ct. Appeals (D.C. cir.) 1979, U.S. Ct. Claims 1985, U.S. Supreme Ct. 1985, U.S. Ct. Appeals (11th cir.) 1985, U.S. Ct. Appeals (5th cir.) 1987, U.S. Ct. Appeals (fed. cir.) 1990. Staff scientist Gulf Gen. Atomic Co., San Diego, 1970-71; dir. R & D Ouachita Industries, Inc., Monroe, La., 1971-72; asst. prof. chem. oceanography Rosenstiel Sch. Marine & Atmospheric Sci., U. Miami (Fla.), 1972-76; phys. scientist NOAA, Washington, 1976-78; mem. profl. staff & congl. liaison Nat. Adv. Commn. on Oceans and Atmosphere, 1978-80; ptnr. Mattson & Pave, Washington, Miami and Key Largo, Fla., 1980-86, Mattson & Tobin, Key Largo, 1987—; adj. prof. law U. Miami, 1983-93; cons. Alaska Dept. Environ. Conservation, 1981-91. Author: (with H.B. Mark) Activated Carbon: Surface Chemistry and Adsorption from Solution, 1971; editor (with others): Computers in Chemistry and Instrumentation, 8 vols., 1972-76; The Argo Merchant Oil Spill: A Preliminary Scientific Report, 1977, (with H.B. Mark) Water Quality Measurement: Modern Analytical Techniques, 1981; contbr. articles to profl. jours. Candidate dist. 120 Fla. Ho. of Reps., 1994. Fellow Fed. Water Pollution Control Adminstrn., 1967-68; recipient Spl. Achievement award U.S. Dept. Commerce, 1976-77; Regents Alumni scholar U. Mich., 1963. Mem. ABA, Am. Chem. Soc. (chmn. Symposium on Oil Spill Indentification 1971), Am. Trial Lawyers Assn., Order of Coif. Office: Mattson & Tobin PO Box 586 Key Largo FL 33037-0586

MATUSZKO, ANTHONY JOSEPH, research chemist, administrator; b. Hadley, Mass., Jan. 31, 1926; s. Joseph Anthony and Katherine (Narog) M.; m. Anita Colley, Oct. 26, 1956; children—Martha, Mary, Stephen, Richard. BA, Amherst Coll., 1946; MS in Chemistry, U. Mass., 1951; PhD in Chemistry, McGill U., 1953. Demonstrator in chemistry McGill U., Montreal, Que., Can., 1950-52; from instr. to assoc. prof. chemistry Lafayette Coll., Easton, Pa., 1952-58; head fundamental process div. Naval Propellant Lab., Indian Head, Md., 1958-62; program mgr. in chemistry Air Force Office Sci. Research, Washington, 1962-89; cons., Annandale, Va., 1989—. Contbr. articles to tech. jours. Patentee in field. Pres. Forest Heights PTA, Md., 1967. Served with U.S. Army, 1946-48. Named Hon. Fellow in Chemistry, U. Wis.-Madison, 1967-68, recipient Superior Performance award USAF, Outstanding Career Svc. award U.S. Govt. Fellow AAAS, Am. Inst. Chemists (life); mem. Am. Chem. Soc., Cosmos Club, Sigma Xi. Home: 4210 Elizabeth Ln Annandale VA 22003-3654

MAU, SHENG TAUR, engineering educator; b. Chungking, China, Jan. 19, 1943; M. Sein-Ming Gerry Pei, Aug. 24, 1968; children: I-Fan Ted, I-Min Mike. BS, Nat. Taiwan U., Taipei, 1965, MS, 1967; PhD, Cornell U., 1971. Chmn. dept. civil engring. Nat. Taiwan U., 1973-79, prof. civil engring., 1977-84; vis. prof. dept. civil and environ. engring. U. Houston, 1984-85, assoc. prof., 1985-89, prof., 1989—, chmn. dept. civil and environ. engring., 1993-96. Co-author: Elementary Theory of Structures, 4th edit., 1994. Fellow ASCE (Moissieff award 1989), Am. Concrete Inst. Office: U Houston Dept Civil and Environ Engring 4800 Calhorn Houston TX 77204-4791

MAUCK, WILLIAM M., JR., executive recruiter, small business owner; b. Cleve., Mar. 30, 1938; s. William M. and Elizabeth Louise (Stone) M.; m. Paula Jean Mauck, Aug. 15, 1969 (div. Mar. 1983); children: Brian, David; m. Jeanne Lee Mauck, May 21, 1987. BS in Bus., Ind. U., 1961. Sales engr. Inland Container Corp., Louisville, 1961-69; sales mgr. Dixie Container Corp., Knoxville, Tenn., 1969-70, gen. mgr., 1970-75; v.p., ptnr. Heidrick & Struggles, Inc., Houston, 1975-81; pres. Booker & Mauck, Inc., Houston, 1981-85; ptnr. Ward Howell Internat. Inc., Houston, 1985-88; prin. William

M. Mauck, Jr., Houston, 1988—; owner Pepe Engring., Inc., Houston, 1990—; mem. adv. bd. Women's Sports Found., N.Y.C., 1985—. Mem. Plaza Club (Houston) (chmn. bd. govs. 1987-88), Sertoma Club (Knoxville 1972-75) (pres. 1974-75). Republican. Methodist. Home: 5203 Norborne Ln Houston TX 77069-1537 Office: 9950 Cypresswood Dr Ste 300 Houston TX 77070-3400

MAUK, AMY MARGARET, purchasing agent; b. Lubbock, Tex., Mar. 1, 1963; d. Clarence Delmar and Anna Mary (Ripper) House; children: Ashley Denise, Brittney Elise. BBA, Baylor U., 1986. Office mgr. Roming & Porter Engrs., Temple, Tex., 1986-90; dir. mgmt. svcs. City of Belton, Tex., 1990-94; purchasing agt. City of Temple, Tex., 1994—. Loaned exec. United Way, Temple, 1992-94, bd. dirs., 1994—; mem. Leadership Temple, 1995-96. Mem. Nat. Inst. Govt. Purchasing, Tex. Purchasing Mgmt. Assn., Ctrl. Tex. USTI Software Group (v.p. 1990-94), Nat. Assn. Purchsing Mgrs. Republican. Baptist. Home: 1019 Westgate I Rd Eddy TX 76524 Office: City of Temple 2 N Main Ste 302 Temple TX 76501

MAUKE, LEAH RACHEL, counselor; b. Newport, R.I., Aug. 29, 1924; d. Louis and Annie (Price) Louison; m. Otto Russell Mauke, June 18, 1950. BSBA, Boston U., 1946, MBA, 1948. Teaching fellow Boston U., 1946-48; head advt. dept. Endicott Coll., Beverly, Mass., 1948-66; guidance counselor Vineland (N.J.) Sr. High Sch., 1966-69; guidance counselor Black Horse Pike Regional Sch. Dist., Blackwood, N.J., 1969-86, ret., 1986. Vol. ARC, Vero Beach, Fla., 1988—. Boston U. fellow 1946. Mem. AAUW (life, pres. North Shore br. 1955-59, state fellowship chmn. 1957-58), NEA, N.J. Edn. Assn., Camden County Pers. and Guidance Assn. (sec. 1972). Home: 2119 E Lakeview Dr Sebastian FL 32958-8519

MAUL, KEVIN JAY, financial consultant; b. York, Pa., Jan. 11, 1968; s. Peter Henry Jr. and Patricia Louise (Young) M. BA, Shippensburg U., 1990; MA, U. Va., 1992. Economist USDA Econ. Rsch. Svc., Washington, 1991-92; fin. cons. Coopers & Lybrand LLP, Washington, 1992—. Author: The Handbook of Mortgage Banking, 1993. Mem. Am. Econ. Assn. Lutheran. Home: 909-A S Rolfe St Arlington VA 22204 Office: Coopers & Lybrand LLP 1751 Pinnacle Dr Mc Lean VA 22102

MAULDEN, JERRY L., utility company executive; b. North Little Rock, Ark., 1936; married. B.S., U. Ark., Little Rock, 1963. Acct. Dyke & Assocs., Inc., 1959-61; sr. auditor Madigan James & Co., C.P.A.'s, 1961-62; asst. controller Dillard Dept. Stores, Inc., 1962-65; asst. to treas. Ark. Power & Light Co. a company of Middle South Utilities, Inc., Little Rock, 1965-68, asst. controller, 1968-71; controller, asst. sec., asst. treas. and later spl. asst. to pres. Ark. Power & Light Co., Little Rock, 1971-73, sec.-treas., 1973-75, v.p. fin. svcs., sec., treas., 1975-79, pres., chief exec. officer, 1979-89, chmn. bd., chief exec. officer, 1989—, also dir.; former sr. v.p. Entergy Corp., Little Rock; v.p. Entergy Corp., New Orleans; sr. v.p. Mid. South Utilities, 1990; chmn., chief exec. officer Miss. Power & Light, also dir. Office: Entergy Corp PO Box 551 Little Rock AR 72203-0551

MAULDIN, JEAN ANN, controller; b. Ft. Chaffee, Ark., Oct. 12, 1957; d. Lawrence Ray and Antoinette Marie (Tusa) Mitchell; 1 child, Michele L. Carter. BBA in Acctg., U. Ctrl. Ark., 1979, MBA, 1985. Cost acct. FMC Automotive Svc. Divsn., Conway, Ark., 1979-82, mgr. cost acctg., 1982-85, divsnl. fin. analyst, 1985, plant contr., 1985-86, divsn. contr., 1986-88; mgr. cost acctg. Columbian Chems. Co., Atlanta, 1988-90, dir. field acctg., 1990-92, No. Am. contr., 1992-93, corporate controller, 1993-94; v.p., CFO Accuride Corp., Henderson, Ky., 1995—. Recipient Young Career Woman award Bus. and Profl. Women, 1986. Mem. Inst. Mgmt. Accts. (cert., v.p. adminstrn. 1993-94). Republican. Roman Catholic.

MAULDIN, JOHN INGLIS, lawyer; b. Atlanta, Nov. 6, 1947; s. Earle and Isabel (Inglis) M.; m. Cynthia Ann Balchin, Apr. 15, 1967 (div. Dec. 1985); children: Tracy Rutherford, Abigail Inglis. BA, Wofford Coll., 1970; JD, Emory U., 1973. Bar: S.C. 1974, U.S. Ct. Appeals (4th cir.) 1974, U.S. Dist. Ct. S.C. 1975, U.S. Supreme Ct. 1978. Asst. pub. def. Defender Corp. Greenville County, S.C., 1974-76; ptnr. Mauldin & Allison, Greenville, 1977-92; pub. defender Greenville County, S.C., 1992—; chair S.C. Commn. on Indigent Def., 1993-96; adj. prof. Greenville Tech. Coll., 1975-80; sec., treas. Def. Corp. Greenville County, 1979-92, bd. dirs. Bd. dirs. Speech Hearing and Learning Ctr., Greenville, 1977-90, pres., 1982, Save our Sons, 1995—. Named S.C. Atty. Yr. ACLU, S.C., 1986. Mem. Nat. Assn. Criminal Def. Attorneys, S.C. Trial Lawyers Assn., Rotary, Sigma Delta Phi. Democrat. Methodist. Club: Harlequins (Greenville) (pres. 1978-79). Lodge: Sertoma. Office: PO Box 10264fs Greenville SC 29603

MAULDIN, MARY POWER, academic adminstrator; b. Laurens, S.C., Apr. 28, 1951; m. Michael Stephen Mauldin. BA, Columbia Coll., 1973; MEd, U. S.C., 1974, U. Ga., 1993. Spl. edn. tchr. Charleston County Schs., S.C., 1974-80, spl. edn. cons., 1981-91; dir. edn. tech. lab. Med. U. S.C., Charleston, 1993—; surrogate parent Charleston County Sch. Dist., 1994—; presenter in field. Contbr. articles to profl. jours.; project mgr. (CD-ROM) Enviro Quest, ROC-CD, MedSource, 1994—. Vol. Crisis Ministries, Charleston, 1985—; guardian ad litem Gov.'s Office, Charleston, 1995—. Mem. Assn. for Ednl. Comms. and Tech., Assn. for Multimedia Profls., Phi Kappa Phi. Office: Med U SC 435 Admin Bldg 171 Ashley Ave Charleston SC 29425

MAULDIN, ROBERT RAY, banker; b. China Grove, N.C., Jan. 15, 1935; s. Raymond Ray and Hazel Inez (Luther) M.; m. Patricia Crain Jarman, Aug. 29, 1959; children—John Clayton, Patricia Crain, Elizabeth Jarman, Anne Luther, Katherine Purnell. Student, N.C. State U., 1953-54; B.S., U. N.C., 1959. Trainee, asst. trust officer Nations Bank, Charlotte, 1959-62; cashier Bank of York, S.C., 1962-65; v.p. Colonial Am. Nat. Bank, Roanoke, Va., 1965-69; exec. v.p. Peoples Bank & Trust Co., Rocky Mount, N.C., 1969-81; pres. Peoples Bank & Trust Co., 1981-85, chmn., chief exec. officer, 1985-90; chmn., CEO Centura Banks Inc., 1993—. Pres. Rocky Mount United Cmty. Svcs., 1974-75; mem. Rocky Mount City Schs. Bd., 1979-83, Commn. for Competitive N.C., 1994—; trustee N.C. Wesleyan Coll., 1993—, Va. Episc. Sch., 1993—; bd. dirs. N.C. Citizens Assn., N.C. Pub. TV Found., Global Tranpark Found., N.C. Partnerships for Children, N.C. Cmty. Found.; chmn. bd. Carolinas Gateway Partnership; mem. adv. bd. Kenan Flaglar Bus. Sch. U. N.C., 1994—. Mem. Am. Inst. Banking, N.C. Young Bankers (pres. 1974-75), N.C. Bankers Assn. (dir. 1984-95), Robert Morris Assocs., Rocky Mount C. of C. (dir. 1975-80, pres. 1978-79), Kiwanis (pres. Rocky Mount 1976-77), Chi Phi. Presbyn. Home: 109 Essex Ct Rocky Mount NC 27803-1207 Office: Centura Bank 134 N Church St Rocky Mount NC 27804-5401

MAULION, RICHARD PETER, psychiatrist; b. Rosario, Argentina, Sept. 2, 1949; s. Peter Henry and Vivien Ormsby (Gough) M.; m. Renee Vander Hayden de Maulion, July 24, 1982; 1 child, Maximillian. BS, Colegio Salesiano San Jose, Rosario, ARgentina, 1967; MD, U. Nacional de Rosario, 1980. Diplomate Am. Bd. Psychiatry and Neurology, Am. Acad. Psychoanalysis, Am. Acad. Addiction Medicine, Am. Acad. Pain Mgmt., Am. Bd. Forensic Examiners. Intern Kans. U., Kansas City, 1981-82; resident in psychiatry Tulane U., New Orleans, 1983-86, fellow in psychoanalytic medicine, 1984-87; pvt. practice gen. psychiatry Covington, La., 1986-87; pvt. practice psychiatry Ft. Lauderdale, 1987—; founder, med. dir. The Rose Inst., Ft. Lauderdale Fla., 1988—; sec. med. exec. com., chmn. quality assurance com., The Retreat Hosp., Sunrise, Fla., 1994—; med. dir. Anxiety and Depression prog., CPC Ft. Lauderdale Hosp., 1989-90; med. dir. Acad. Medicine and Psychology, Ft. Lauderdale, 1988-89, CEPHAS Prog., HSA Greenbrier Neuropsychiat. Hosp., Covington, La., 1986-87, chief med. staff, 1987; clin. instr. psychiatry Tulane U. Med. Ctr., 1986-87; pres. med. exec. com., chief med. staff, chmn. quality assurance com. Retreat Hosp., 1992—; workshop speaker; radio program host The Rose Institute Hour; lectr. in field; cons. in field. Host ednl.-cmty. svc. radio program The Rose Inst. Hour, 1995—. Mem. pub. health com. for the Health and Human Svcs. Bd., Dist. 10; mem. alochol, drugs and mental health com.. Fellow Am. Acad. Psychoanalysis, Am. Bd. Forensic Examiners, Interam. Coll. Physicians and Surgeons; mem. AMA, Am. Psychiat. Assn., Am. Acad. Psychoanalysis, Am. Soc. Clin. Hypnosis, Fla. Med. Assn. (Med. Speaker of Yr. award, 1st pl. radio, 2nd pl. t.v., 1990, del. 1993—), Fla. Psychiat. Soc. (coun. mem. 1993-94), Broward County Psychiat. Soc. (med. exec. com., pres. 1994-95), Broward County Med. Assn. (chmn. physicians recovery network com., bd. dirs.), Broward County Psychiat. Soc. (pres. 1993—), M.I.N.D. Home: PO Box 350033 Fort Lauderdale FL 33335-0033

MAUMUS, CRAIG W(ALTHER), psychiatrist, consultant; b. New Orleans; m. Priscilla Guderian; 1 child, Michael Fletcher. BS, Tulane U., 1968, MD, 1972. Diplomate Am. Bd. Psychiatry and Neurology. Pvt. practice Metairie, La., 1976—; chief day programs VA Med. Ctr., New Orleans, 1995—; clin. assoc. prof. psychiatry Tulane Med. Ctr. Stadium, basketball and regatta coms. Sugar Bowl, New Orleans, 1971-76. Fellow Am. Psychiat. Assn. (chair newsletter subcom. 1993—); mem. AMA, So. Med. Assn., La. State Med. Soc., La. Psychiat. Med. Assn. (newsletter editor, mem. exec. coun. 1979—), Tulane Psychiatry and Neurology Alumni Assn. (newsletter editor, mem. exec. com. 1990—), So. Yacht Club. Office: # 402 4051 Veterans Meml Blvd Metairie LA 70002

MAURER, VIRGINIA GALLAHER, law educator; b. Shawnee, Okla., Nov. 7, 1946; d. Paul Clark Gallaher and Virginia Ruth (Watson) Abernathy; m. Ralph Gerald Maurer, July 31, 1971; children: Ralph Emmett, William Edward. BA, Northwestern U., 1968; MA, Stanford U., 1969, JD, 1975. Bar: Iowa 1976. Tchr. social studies San Mateo (Calif.) High Sch. Dist., 1969-71; spl. asst. to pres. U. Iowa, Iowa City, 1976-80, adj. asst. prof. law, 1979-80; affiliate asst. prof. law U. Fla., Gainesville, 1981, asst. prof. bus. law, 1980-85, assoc. prof., 1985-93, prof., 1993—, dir. MBA Program, 1987, chair dept. mgmt., 1994—; vis. prof. Wolfson Coll., Cambridge, 1994, SDA Bocconi U., Milan, 1994, 95; cons. Gov.'s Com. on Iowa 2000, Iowa City, 1976-77, Fla. Banker's Assn., Gainesville, 1982. Contbr. articles to profl. jours.; jr. editor Am. Bus. law Jour., 1989-90, mng. editor, 1990-91, editor-in-chief, 1992-94. Bd. dirs. Gainesville Chamber Orch., 1990-93; mem. fundraising com. Pro Arte Musica, Gainesville, 1980-84; sr. warden, mem. vestry, Holy Trinity Episc. Ch., 1991-93; bd. dirs. Holy Trinity Found., Gainesville, 1991-93; mem. com. charter and canon law Episc. Diocese Fla., 1994—; bd. dirs. Samaritan Ctrs. of North Ctrl. Fla., inc., 1995—. Mem. ABA, Acad. Legal Studies in Bus. (ho. of dels., 1989-90, exec. com. 1992), Southeastern Bus. Law Assn. (Proc. editor 1984-87, treas. 1985-86, v.p. 1986-87, pres.-elect 1987-88, pres. 1988-89), Iowa Bar Assn., LWV, U. Fla. Athletic Assn. (bd. dirs. 1982-88; v.p., chmn. fin. com.), Gainesville Womens' Forum (bd. dirs. 1988-91), Fla. Women' Network (bd. dirs. 1995—), Beta Gamma Sigma, Kappa Alpha Theta, Delta Sigma Pi, Univ. Women's Club (Gainesville, Fla.), Rotary (bd. dirs. 1989-91). Home: 2210 NW 6th Pl Gainesville FL 32603-1409 Office: U Fla Grad Sch Bus Gainesville FL 32611

MAURER, YOLANDA TAHAR, publisher; b. Tuuis-Tunisia, North Africa, Oct. 8, 1922; d. Joseph Tahar and Oro (Sidi) Tahar; m. William S. Maurer, Jan. 5, 1966; 1 child, Larry. Columnist Ft. Lauderdale News, 1948-65; pub. Pictorial Life, 1965-71; edtl. writer Ft. Lauderdale News, 1971-80; pub., 1980-86. Author: The Best of Broward, 1986, Ode To the City, 1995. Bd. mem. Miami City Ballet, Performing Arts Ctr., 1985-89, Fla. Philharm. Orch., Opera Guild Ft. Lauderdale. Recipient First Prize Fla. Mag., Fla. Newspaper Assn., 1958, George Washington award Freedoms Found., 1975; named Woman of Yr., Am. Cancer Soc., 1983, Woman of Style and Substance, Philharm. Soc., 1996, Woman of Yr., Women in Comms., 1967, 83. Republican. Home: 1811 SE 14th St Fort Lauderdale FL 33316 Office: Lauderdale Life 11 NE 12th Ave Fort Lauderdale FL 33301-1603

MAURITSON, DAVID RICHARD, cardiologist, flight instructor; b. Cleve., July 28, 1948; s. Donald Forsyth and Janet Elizabeth (Howard) M.; m. Eleanora Margaret Buchanan, June 30, 1973; children: Amy Eleanora, Eric Buchanan. BA, Westminster Coll., 1970; MD, Harvard U., 1974. Diplomate Am. Bd. Internal Medicine and Cardiovascular Diseases. Resident in internal medicine Parkland Meml. Hosp./Southwestern Med. Sch., Dallas, 1974-77, fellow in cardiology, 1979-81; fellow in emergency medicine Moffitt Hosp./U. Calif., San Francisco, 1977-79; cardiologist, pres. Cardiology Assocs. of West Ala., Northport, 1981—; assoc. prof. Coll. Community Health Scis., Tuscaloosa, Ala., 1981—. Fellow Am. Coll. Cardiology, Am. Coll. Physicians; mem. Aircraft Owners and Pilots Assn., Nat. Assn. Flight Instrs., Exptl. Aircraft Assn. Unitarian. Home: 22 Indian Hills Tuscaloosa AL 35406-2276 Office: Cardiology Assocs West Ala 1325 Mcfarland Blvd Northport AL 35476-3270

MAURO, GEORGE THEODORE, corporate executive; b. N.Y.C., Mar. 7, 1938; s. Peter Terzo and Bella (Cohn) M.; m. Mary Ann Stoehr, Feb. 15, 1964; children: Mary Patricia, Christine. BA, U. N.H., 1959; MBA, U. Pa., 1972. Sr. cons. Booz, Allen & Hamilton, Inc., Phila., 1972-75, v.p., 1975-77; dir. Asset Value Analysis, U.S. Ry. Assn., Washington, 1977-79; sr. assoc. Temple Barker & Sloane, Inc., Lexington, Mass., 1979-83; dir. transp. FMC Corp., Chgo., 1984-85, dir. logistics, 1985-89, dir. mfg. automotive svcs. equipment divsn., Conway, Ark., 1989-91; v.p. ops. Delta Consol. Industries, Jonesboro, Ark., 1991-92, exec. v.p. ops., Raleigh, N.C., 1994-96; exec. v.p., gen. mgr. So. Case Inc., Raleigh, N.C., 1992-93; v.p. ops. Interpane Glass Co., Clinton, N.C., 1996—. Served with USAF, 1960-70. Decorated Meritorious Service medal Dept. Def., Air Force Commendation medal. Mem. Soc. Plastics Engrs., Council Logistics Mgmt., Assn. for Mfg. Excellence, Beta Gamma Sigma, Tau Kappa Alpha, Psi Chi, Pi Kappa Alpha.

MAUTZ, KARL EMERSON, engineering executive; b. Columbia, Mo., Sept. 30, 1957; s. Wayne Albert Mautz and Imogene (Embrey) Whitten; m. Pamela Dawn Quillen, Mar. 12, 1988; children: Alyssa Mae, Brandon Tyler. BS in Chemistry, U. Tex., El Paso, 1979, BS in Geology, 1983; MS in Chemistry, Ariz. State U., 1985, PhD, 1987. Process engr. Motorola, Inc., Mesa, Ariz., 1980-87; mem. tech. staff Motorola, Inc., Austin, Tex., 1988—; cons. Motif, Inc., Portland, Oreg., 1994. Contbr. articles to profl. jours.; patentee in field of semiconductor processes; numerous patents pending. Mem. recycling com. Homeowners Assn., Austin, 1992. Mem. Electrochem. Soc., Am. Chem. Soc. Office: Motorola Inc 1 Tex Ctr Ste 1050 505 Barton Springs Rd Austin TX 78704

MAUZY, OSCAR HOLCOMBE, lawyer, retired state supreme court justice; b. Houston, Nov. 9, 1926; s. Harry Lincoln and Mildred Eva (Kincaid) M.; m. Anne Rogers; children: Catherine Anne, Charles Fred, James Stephen. BBA, U. Tex., 1950, JD, 1952. Bar: Tex. 1951. Practiced in Dallas, 1952-87; pres. Mullinax, Wells, Mauzy & Baab, Inc. (P.C.), 1970-78; mem. Tex. Senate from 23d Dist., 1967-87, chmn. edn. com., 1971-81, chmn. jurisprudence com., 1981-87, pres. pro tempore, 1973; justice Tex. Supreme Ct., 1987-93; pvt. practice Austin, 1993—; Mem. Tex. Adv. Commn. Intergovtl. Relations, Nat. Conf. State Legislators, Edn. Commn. of the States, Am. Edn. Finance Assn., 1971-87. Vice chmn. judiciary com. Tex. Constl. Conv., 1974; nat. committeeman Young Democrats, 1954. Served with USNR, 1944-46. Home: 5000 Crestway Dr Austin TX 78731-5404

MAVEETY, NANCY LOIS, political science educator; b. Belleville, N.J., July 11, 1960; d. Donald John and Joan (Campbell) M. BA in Polit. Sci., Ariz. State U., 1982; MA in Polit. Sci., Johns Hopkins U., 1984, PhD in Polit. Sci., 1987. Asst. prof. Tulane U., New Orleans, 1986-92, assoc. prof., 1992—. Author: Justice Sandra Day O'Connor: Strategist on the Supreme Court, 1996. Mem. Am. Polit. Sci. Assn. Office: Tulane U Dept Polit Sci New Orleans LA 70118

MAVROS, GEORGE S., clinical laboratory director; b. Adelaide, Australia, Oct. 14, 1957; came to U.S., 1970; s. Sotirios George and Angeliki (Korogiannis) M.; m. Renee Ann Cuddeback, June 24, 1979. BA in Microbiology, U. South Fla., 1979, MS in Microbiology, 1987; MBA, Nova U., 1991; PhD in Health Sci. Mgmt., LaSalle U., 1995. Cert. lab. dir. Nat. Certifying Agy. for Clin. Lab. Pers.; diplomate Am. Coll. Health Care Execs. Med. technologist Jackson Meml. Hosp., Dade City, Fla., 1979-81; microbiology supr. HCA Bayonet Point-Hudson Med. Ctr., Hudson, Fla., 1981-82, dir. labs., 1982-88; lab. mgr., adminstrv. and tch. dir. Citrus Meml. Hosp., Inverness, Fla., 1988—; lab. cons. HCA Oak Hill Hosp., Spring Hill, Fla., 1983-84; cons. lab. info. systems Citation Computer Systems, St. Louis, 1983—, Hosp. Corp. of Am., Nashville, 1986; instr. Microbiology Pasco Hernando Com. Coll., New Port Richey, Fla., 1986-88, Inst. Biolog. Scis. Cen. Fla. Community Coll., Lecanto, 1989—; bd. dirs. Gulf Coast chpt. Clin. Lab. Mgrs. Assn., Tampa, Fla., 1987, pres., 1987-89. Parish pres. Greek Orthodox Ch. of West Cen., Inverness, Fla.; chmn. Bayonet Point Hosp. Good Govt. Group, Hudson, 1986-88. Mem. APHA, Am. Mgmt. Assn., Am. Soc. Microbiology, Am. Soc. Clin. Pathologists (cert. in lab. mgmt.), Am. Soc. Med. Technologists (cert.), Fla. Soc. Med. Technologists, Clin. Lab. Mgmt. Assn. (pres. Gulf Coast chpt. 1988-90), Am. Assn. Clin. Chemists, Am. Acad. Microbiology (cert.), Fla. State Bd. Clin. Lab. Pers. (chmn. 1994). Democrat. Clubs: Greek Orthodox Youth Am. (Clearwater, Fla.). Lodges: Order of DeMolay, Sons of Pericles (sec.). Home: 6 Byrsonima Ct W Homosassa FL 34446-4610 Office: Citrus Meml Hosp 502 W Highland Blvd Inverness FL 34452-4720

MAWHINNEY, KING, insurance company executive; b. Richmond, Va., Sept. 13, 1947; s. John A. and Ellen E. (King) M.; m. Jeanne Dale Smothers, June 8, 1976 (div. Oct. 1984); m. Cathryn C. Morley, Nov. 15, 1986. AB, Davidson Coll., 1971; MA, Pacific Lutheran U., 1973; MEd, U. Tex., 1992. CLU; ChFC; FLMI; ALHC; registered health underwriter; assoc. customer svc., health ins. assoc., devel. mgr. Prudential Ins. Co., Newark, 1977-80; sr. sales rep. USAA Life Ins. Co., San Antonio, 1980-81, sales tng. adminstr., 1981-82, dir. procedures and tng., 1983-85, dir. group/bus. sales, 1985-86, sr. dir. USAA Ednl. Services, 1986-88, exec. dir. life sales, FSD Mktg., 1989-90, asst. v.p. life sales, 1990-91; asst. v.p. health sales Life Gen. Agy., 1991-92, asst. v.p. health ins., 1992-94, v.p. health ins., 1994—. Mem. choir Alamo Heights Presbyterian Ch., 1981-83, deacon, 1982-83; mem. Univ. United Meth. Ch., 1991—, mem. adminstrv. bd., 1992-93; mem. bd. gov's. San Antonio Estate Planners Coun., 1988-92; with U.S. Olympic Festival, 1993; chmn. Dreams for Youth Project. Capt. U.S. Army, 1972-77; Korea. Mem. Life Office Mgmt. Assn. (coun. mem. 1988-91, 1993-96, chmn. soc. com. 1988-91), Davidson Coll. Alumni Assn. (chpt. pres. 1983-94), San Antonio Chpt. C.L.U. (bd. dirs., v.p. programs, v.p. fin., v.p. adminstrn., pres.-elect, pres.), FLMI Soc. So. Cen. Tex. (chpt. pres. 1986, bd. dirs. 1987-88), Leadership San Antonio (class XVII 1991-92), Phi Kappa Phi, Sigma Nu, Kappa Delta Pi. Republican. Avocations: sports cards, walking. Home: 23744 Up Mountain Trl San Antonio TX 78255-2000 Office: USAA Life Ins Co 9800 Fredericksburg Rd San Antonio TX 78288-0001

MAX, BUDDY (BORIS MAX PASTUCH), musician; b. Jan. 25; m. Freda Max; 1 child, John. Musician, performer as America's Singing Flea Market Cowboy: albums include: Many Styles and Sounds of Buddy Max, 1980, The Great Nashville Star, 1984, The Story of Freda and Bud, 1985, Cowboy Junction Stars, 1985, Tribute to Challenger's Crew of 7, 1986, With Our Friends at Cowboy Junction, 1989, Little Circle B, 1990, Together-Our Masterpiece, 1991, The Life to Fame and Fortune, 1992, Orange Blossom Special, 1996, Hall of Fame, Gold Record Award Winning Buddy Max, 1996; composer songs include When the Magnolia Tree Blooms in Lecanto, The Story of Barney Clark, Hang My Guitar on the Wall, John F. Kennedy, The Challenger, Where the Maple Syrups Flow, Little Circle B, Way Up on the Mountain, Desert Storm, When Do I Love You, The Pretty Girl on TV. Recipient numerous trophies, awards for benefit and non-profit shows Am. Heart Assn., Am. Lung Assn., Girl Scouts Am., Citizens of Citrus County Fla., Deaf Svcs. of Citrus County, others. Address: care Cowboy Junction Hwy 44 & Jct 490 3949 W Gulf To Lake Hwy Lecanto FL 34461-9232

MAX, ERNEST, surgeon; b. Vienna, Austria, Mar. 3, 1936; m. Silvia Neger, Mar. 18, 1964; children: Yvette Rosa, Oliver Fredrick. MD, U. Chile, 1961. Diplomate Am. Bd. Surgery, Am. Bd. Colon and Rectal Surgeons, Am. Bd. Laser Surgery. Intern Hosp. San Borja, Santiago, Chile, 1960-61, resident, 1962-63; fellow in gen. surgery, colon and rectal surgery Lahey Clinic Found., Boston, 1969-70; resident Sinai Hosp., Balt., 1971-72, The Western Pa. Hosp., Pitts., 1972-74; resident in colon and rectal surgery Hermann Hosp., Houston, 1974-75; staff Hermann Hosp., 1975—, Park Plz. Hosp., 1975—, Meml. Hosp. Southwest, 1975—, Meml. NW Hosp., 1975—, Diagnostic Ctr. Hosp., 1975—, The Methodist Hosp., 1976—, Meml. City Hosp., 1976—, Woman's Hosp., 1976—, HCA Spring Br., 1976—, Houston NW Med. Ctr., 1976—, Sam Houston Meml. Hosp., 1977—, St. Luke's Episcopal Hosp., 1981—, Cypress Fairbanks, 1983—; chief of staff Meml. Hosp., 1983; staff HCA Med. Ctr., 1986—, Meml. Hosp. Southeast, 1994—; CEO Colon and Rectal Clinic PA, 1989—; clin. assoc. prof. surgery Baylor Coll. Medicine; clin. instr. surgery U. Tex. Med. Sch., Houston. Author: (with others) Current Diagnosis, 1971. Recipient Walter A. Fansler Travel Edn. award Am. Soc. Colon and Rectal Surgeons, 1974, Harriet Cunningham award Tex. Med. Assn., 1988, Best of the Best award Tex. Med. Assc., 1989; The Purdue Fredrick fellow Am. Soc. Colon and Rectal Surgeons, 1974. Mem. Am. Coll. Surgeons, Tex. Med. Soc., Harris County Med. Soc., Tex. Soc. Colon and Rectal Surgeons (pres. 1982-83), Am. Soc. Laser Medicine and Surgery, Internat. Soc. Univ. Colon and Rectal Surgeons, Lahey Clinic Alumni Assn., Am. Soc. Colon and Rectal Surgeons, Tex. Gulf Coast Colon and Rectal Surgical Soc. (sec. treas. 1992—), Colombian Soc. Colo-Proctology (hon. mem.). Office: Colon & Rectal Clinic PA 6550 Fannin St Ste 2307 Houston TX 77030-2723

MAX, RODNEY ANDREW, lawyer, mediator; b. Cin., Jan. 28, 1947; s. Howard Nelson and Ruth Max; m. Laurie Gilbert; children: Adam Keith, Jeffery Aaron. Student, Am. U.; BA, U. Fla., 1970; JD cum laude, Cumberland Sch., 1975. Bar: Ala. 1975, Fla. 1975, U.S. Ct. Appeals (5th and 11th cirs.) 1975, U.S. Supreme Ct. 1982. From assoc. to ptnr. Najjar Denaburg PC, Birmingham, Ala., 1975-94; ptnr. Sirote & Permutt, P.C., Birmingham, 1994—; with Ala. State Adv. Com., U.S. Civil Rights Commn., 1985—; lectr. in field. Officer, bd. dirs. Jewish Cmty. Ctr., Birmingham, 1980—, Family and Child Svcs., Birmingham, 1984—; trustee Temple Emanu-El, sec. 1990-93, v.p., 1992—; active Summer Youth Task Force; mem. Camp Birmingham adv. com. Leadership Birmingham, 1989-90, mem. alumni bd., 1990-93; bd. dirs., mem. exec. com. NCCJ, 1989—; co-chmn. cmty. affairs com. Operation New Birmingham, pres. exec. com.; bd. dirs. PATH; founder A-Plus; co-chmn. Coalition Against Hate Crimes, 1992—; v.p., mem. exec. com. Mountain Brook City Sch. Found., 1992—. Nominated Citizen of Yr. award Young Bus. Club, 1989; recipient Peggy Spain McDonald award Birmingham Bd. of Edn., 1993. Mem. ABA, ATLA, Ala. Bar Assn. (chmn. task force for alternatives to dispute resolution, co-chmn. increased minority participation, chmn. fee dispute resolution task force), Ala. Trial Lawyers Assn., Ala. Def. Lawyers Assn., Am. Arbitration Assn. (arbitrator, mediator, chmn. Ala. adv. coun.), Birmingham Bar Assn. (trustee legal aid 1985-88, mem. exec. bd. 1989-92, sec.-treas. 1993), Am. Acad. Atty. Mediators, Newcomen Soc. U.S., Kiwanis, B'nai B'rith (pres., bd. govs. 1978-85). Democrat. Office: Sirote & Permutt 2222 Arlington Ave S Birmingham AL 35205-4004

MAXEY, NIGEL AARON, publisher; b. Rock, W.Va., Nov. 29, 1945; s. Aaron Burr and Ruth Aretta (Wiley) M.; m. Linda Sharon Boyd, Oct. 29, 1971. BA, Concord Coll., 1969; MA, W.Va. U., 1987. Reporter Princeton (W.Va.) Times, 1963-64, mng. editor, 1965; editor Mall Order Bus. Mag., Bluefield, W.Va., 1972-77; pub. Small Pub. Mag., Pineville, W.Va., 1993—; with W.Va. Dept. Human Svcs., Pineville, 1970—. Author: How to Successfully Publish and Market Your Own Book, Publishing 101, Government Open for Business-Working People Not Served. Home: PO Box 1620 Pineville WV 24874-1620 Office: 92 C Cedar Ave Pineville WV 24874

MAXEY, WANDA JEAN, geriatrics nurse practitioner, consultant; b. Chandler, Okla., Dec. 1, 1934; d. Martin Luther and Juanita Clover (Hesser) Henderson; m. Wendell P. Maxey, Jan. 26, 1983 (dec.); children: Dennis, Jeffrey, Renee. ADN, Okla. State Tech. Inst., 1971; BS, Cen. State U., Edmond, Okla., 1976, MSEd in Gerontology, 1986; cert. family nurse pracitioner, U. Okla., 1977. RN, Okla. Asst. dir. nursing Lora Lane Nursing Home, Oklahoma City; dir. nursing North East Nursing Home, Oklahoma City; nursing cons. to several nursing homes Oklahoma City, 1977—; dir. nursing svc., v.p. nursing Amity Care Corp., Oklahoma City, 1977—. Mem. Nat. Geriatric Nurses Assn. Home: 8211 Laura Ln Oklahoma City OK 73151

MAXFIELD, ANNE M., sales executive; b. Cin., Apr. 18, 1961; d. Howard B. and Nancy C. (O'Connell) M.; m. William Eugene Lege. BA, No. Ky. U., 1994; cert., Inst. Orgn. Mgmt., 1990, Salesability, 1991. Supr. St. Elizabeth Med. Ctr., Covington, Ky., 1979-86; v.p. No. Ky. C. of C., Covington, 1986-90; account rep. Olsten STaffing Svcs., Florence, Ky., 1990—; bd. dirs. New Perceptions, Inc., Edgewood, Ky., 1990-96, chair nominating com., 1992; mem. workforce preparation task force No. Ky. C. of C., 1996—; mem. pers. com. No. Ky. U., 1996—, mem. legislation task force, 1995—. Advocacy mgr. W)od Hudson Cancer Rsch., Newport, Ky., 1988-90; chmn. small bus. sect. Cin. United Way, 1990; cmty. chair Fine Arts

Fund, 1990-94; vol. AIDS Vols. of No. Ky., 1996—; mem. devel. com. Villa Madonna Acad., 1995—. Mem. Nat. Assn. Temp. Svcs., Ky. Assn. Temp. Svcs., No. Ky. C. of C. (chmn. bus. svcs. com.). Democrat. Office: Olsten Staffing Svcs 5 Spiral Dr Florence KY 41042-1395

MAXFIELD, MARY CONSTANCE, management consultant; b. Washington, Mar. 16, 1949; d. Orville Eldred and Rose Mary (Stiarwalt) Maxfield; m. Robert Charles Kneip, III, Aug. 21, 1971 (div. Apr. 1981); 1 child, Stephanie Alexandra; m. Richard Howard Cowles, May 16, 1981 (dec.); m. Phillip Walker, July 25, 1985 (div. June 1991). BA in History and Spanish, Va. Tech., 1970; MS in Occupl. Tech. U. Houston, 1996. Clk.-typist HEW, Social Security Adminstrn., New Orleans, 1971-72, svc. rep., 1972-73; mgmt. analyst Office Comptroller of Currency, Treasury Dept., Washington, 1974-77; dir. mgmt. analysis divsn. U.S. Customs, New Orleans, 1978-80, mgmt. analyst, Houston, 1980-81, program analyst, 1981-82, chief data processing br., 1982-83, chief mgmt. analysis br., 1983-85; pres. Constance Walker Assocs., Inc., 1985-91, Maxfield Productivity Cons., Inc., 1991—; co-founder Supplier Registry. Author: MBO Handbook, 1979, Professional Problem Solving, 1985, The Productivity Ascent, 1987, Participative Problem Solving: A Guide for Work Teams, 1988; (with others) Program Management Handbook, 1983, Introduction to Employee Involvement, 1985, Team Approach to Problem Solving, 1991, Quality School Facilitator Training, 1992, Gender Awareness Training, 1992, Interpersonal Communications Skills, 1992, Introduction to Total Quality Schools, 1992, Tex. Leadership Ctr. DuPont LDP Tng., TQM Module, 1993, Introduction to ISO 9000, 1993, Total Quality Management, 1993, Benchmarking, 1994, Effective Facilitation Skills, 1995, Strengthening Team Development, 1995, Internal Auditing to ISO 9000 Standards, 1995, Personnel Management in Food Service, 1995, Successfully Leading Change, 1996, Leading Change Through Site-Based Teams, 1996, Quality Tools 101, 1996, Advanced Facilitation Skills, 1996; contbr. numerous articles to profl. jours. Mem. Friends of Stehlin Found., 1982-88, Friends of the Cabildo, 1978-80. Named Customs Woman of Yr., U.S. Customs, 1979, recipient Outstanding Performance award, 1979, 80, 81, 82, 83, 84, 85; named Fed. Exec. Bd. Woman of Yr., 1979; recipient Outstanding Service award Office of Sec. of Treasury, 1976, Key to City, New Orleans, 1990; Cora Bell Wesley scholar, UDC, 1969. Mem. DAR, Am. Soc. for Quality Control, Assn. for Quality and Participation, Treasury Hist. Assn., Daus. Rep. of Tex., Daus. 1812. UDC, Va. Tech. Alumni Assn., Austin Old 300 (founding mem.), Delta Zeta. Episcopalian. Home and Office: Maxfield Productivity Cons Inc 8007 Liberty Elm Ct Spring TX 77379-6125

MAXWELL, CYNTHIA NEAGLE, mitigation professional; b. Charlotte, N.C., July 15, 1953; d. Emmett Orr and Nettie Prue (McCaslin) Neagle; m. L.A. Waggoner III, Apr. 30, 1977 (div. Aug. 1987); 1 child, Margaret "Rett" Emma Waggoner; m. Kirby Ben Maxwell, June 19, 1991; stepchildren: Rachel Meredith, Jennifer Lauren Maxwell. BA in Psychology, U. N.C., 1975. Health care techician II, asst. recreational therapist Gaston-Lincoln Area Mental Health, Gastonia, N.C., 1975-77; social worker I Mecklenburg County Mental Health Svcs., Charlotte, N.C., 1978; vol. svcs. coord. Mecklenburg County Mental Health Svcs., Charlotte, 1978-79, dir. community rels., 1979-81; exec. dir. Heart Soc. Gaston County, Inc., Gastonia, N.C., 1983-85; product rep. Perma-Bound, Jacksonville, Fla., 1984-86; dist. adminstr. Guardian Ad Litem Program, Gastonia, N.C., 1985-91; v.p., food products exec. Maxwell Assocs., 1991—; criminal law mitigation expert; jury selection specialist. Author: Volunteer Manual, 1979; author, editor: Gaston County Bar Assn., 1993. bd. dirs., chmn., exec. com., personnel com., search com., pub. rels. com., sec., program com., fin. com., by laws com., Gaston-Lincoln Area Mental Health, Mental retardation and Substance Abuse Program, 1978-87; search com., by laws com., rep., pres. bd. dirs., 1983-87; co-chair, chair, exec. by laws chair, Jr. League Gaston County, N.C., 1980-91; CPR instr. Gaston County Red Cross, 1985—; mem. devel. chair. Civitans, 1986-90; mem. planning and zoning bd., Belmont, N.C., 1994-95; dir. Alliance Healthier Babies. Named Vol. of Yr. Gaston County C. of C., 1982, Gaston County Mental Health Assn., 1983; N.C. Col. of Yr. N.C. Coun. of Community Mental health Programs, 1983. Mem. Gaston County C. of C., United Meth. Women, Humane Soc. Gaston County, Gaston County Commn. of Family. Democrat. Methodist.

MAXWELL, DANIEL GARETH, psychotherapist; b. Phoenix, Ariz., Apr. 11, 1957. BA in Anthropology summa cum laude, Chapman Coll., 1979, BA in Art, 1979; MA in Psychology, U.S. Internat. U., San Diego, 1990; PhD in Psychology, U.S. Internat. U., 1995. Planner Phelps Dodge Corp., Morenci, 1979-80; ceramic sculptor/designer Stoneware Unltd., Inc., Santa Ana, Calif., 1980-86; dir. adminstrn. Alternative Ways Inc., Long Beach, Calif., 1986-87; video editor Belmont Prodns., Long Beach, 1988-90; instr. Loyola Marymount U., L.A., 1990; case mgr. St. John's Hosp., Santa Monica, Calif., 1990-93; clin. supr. Jefferson Alcohol and Drug Abuse Program, Louisville, 1994-96; clin. mgr. chem. dependency unit Bapt. East Hosp., Louisville, 1996—; dir. edn. Fellowship of Pachamama, 1989—. Editor, art dir. (video documentary) For Love and For Life, 1988, A Shaman's World, 1989. Mem. APA, Nat. Assn. Alcohol and Drug Abuse Counselors, Ky. Psychol. Assn.

MAXWELL, DIANA KATHLEEN, early childhood education educator; b. Seminole, Okla., Dec. 16, 1949; d. William Hunter and ImoJean (Mahurin) Rivers; m. Clarence Estel Maxwell, Jly 3, 1969; children: Amanda Hunter, Alexandra Jane. BS, U. Md., 1972; M of Secondary Edn., Boston U., 1974; PhD, U. Md., 1980. Cert. tchr., counselor, Tex. Tchr. Child Garden Presch., Adelphi, Md., 1969-71; tchr., dir. PREP Edn. Ctr., Heidelberg, Germany, 1972-74; tchr. N.E. Ind. Schs. Larkspur, San Antonio, 1974-77, 89-90, Headstart, Boyds, Md., 1978; dir., founder First Bapt. Child Devel. Ctr., Bryan, Tex., 1982-84; instr. English lang. Yonsei Med. Ctr., Seoul, Republic of Korea, 1985-87; asst. prof. Incarnate Word Coll., San Antonio, 1987-89; tchr. kindergarten Fairfax County Pub. Schs., Kings Park, Va., 1990-94; tchr. Encino Park, San Antonio, Tex., 1994-95; lectr. U. Tex., San Antonio, 1995—; cons. Sugar N'Spice Child Devel. Ctr., Kilgore, Tex., 1980-90; bd. dirs. Metro Area Assn. for Childhood Edn. Internat., 1991-93. Author: (book revs.) Childhood Education, 1979, 80, 92. Block chairperson March of Dimes, 1991, 92, 93, Am. Heart Assn., Fairfax, Fa., 1991, 92, Am. Diabetes Assn., Fairfax, 1992; judge speaking com. Burke Optomists, 1992, 93l judge writing competition N.E. Ind. Sch. Dist., 1996; sec. Cole H.S. Cougar Club, Ft. Sam Houston, San Antonio, 1996-97; Bible tchr. 1st Bapt. Ch., Alexandria, Va., 1992-94; tchr. kindergarten Trinity Bapt. Ch., San Antonio, 1995—. Named one of Outstanding Young Women of Am., 1983; Md. fellow State of Md., 1978, 79; grantee San Antonio, 1990, Springfield, 1991. Mem. ASCD, Internat. Reading Assn., Assn. Profl. Tchr. Educators, Edn. Internat., Assn. for Childhood Edn. Internat. (v.p., pres.-elect), Tex. Assn. Childhood Edn., Bexar County and Surrounding Areas Assn. Childhood Edn. Home: 106 Artillery Post Rd San Antonio TX 78234 Office: U Tex Divsn Edn 6900 North Loop 1604 San Antonio TX 78249-0616

MAXWELL, DONALD POWER, JR., ophthalmologist, physician, educator; b. Lawton, Okla., Aug. 13, 1955; s. Donald Power and Beverly Sue (Schilling) M.; m. Karen Sue Carringer, May 14, 1982. BS, U. Okla., 1977, MD, 1982. Diplomate Am. Bd. Ophthalmology, Nat. Bd. Med. Examiners. Intern U. Okla. Tulsa Med. Br., 1982-83; resident in ophthalmology U. Kans., Kansas City, 1983-86; vitreo-retinal fellow Tulane Med. Ctr., New Orleans, 1986-88, clin. instr., 1986-88, asst. prof., 1988-92, assoc. prof., 1992—; adv. mem. curriculum com. Tulane Med. Ctr., 1993—, mem. admissions com., 1993—. Contbr. articles to profl. jours. Fellow ACS, Am. Acad. Ophthalmology; mem. AMA (physician's recognition award 1986—), Retina Soc. Vitreous Society, Am. Acad. Opthalmology-Honor Award-1996, Comm. on Ophthalmic Procedure Assessment-Retina Panel Chmn., SAR, Soc. of Cincinnati, Soc. Colonial Wars; Sons of revolution, Soc. War 1812, Col. Soc. Americans Royal Descent, Order of American Armorial Ancestry, Col. Order of the Crown, Internat. Soc. of Charlemagne. Office: Tulane Med Ctr 1430 Tulane Ave New Orleans LA 70112-2699

MAXWELL, FREDRIC ALAN, writer, library activist; b. Birmingham, Mich., June 17, 1954; s. Jack Erwin and Mignonne Marie (Addis) M. Student, U. Md., 1973-75; BA, Albion Coll., 1978; postgrad., U. Mich., 1979, U. Va., 1982; cert., Stanford Prof. Publ. Course, 1983; postgrad., U. Georgetown, 1987. Ind. researcher, 1981—, ind. writer, author, journalist, 1986—. Author: The State of the Lake, 1988, Romanic Depressive, 1989, Letters to Myself, 1990; editor, publisher The Maxwell Report, 1982-84; contbr. articles to profl. jours. and national publs. Founder The Vietnamese Meml. Assn., 1992-93. With U.S. Navy, 1973-75. Recipient Nat. Def. medal, 1973. Home: 3001 S Ocean Dr Ste 12-T Hollywood FL 33019

MAXWELL, ROBERT EARL, federal judge; b. Elkins, W.Va., Mar. 15, 1924; s. Earl L. and Nellie E. (Rexstrew) M.; m. Ann Marie Grabowski, Mar. 29, 1948; children—Mary Ann, Carol Lynn, Ellen Lindsay, Earl Wilson. Student, Davis and Elkins Coll., LLD (hon.), 1984; LL.B., W.Va. U., 1949; LLD (hon.), Davis and Elkins Coll., 1984. Bar: W.Va. 1949. Practiced in Randolph County, 1949, pros. atty., 1952-61; U.S. atty. for No. Dist. W.Va., 1961-64; judge U.S. Dist. Ct. (no. dist.) W.Va., Elkins, 1965—, Temp. Emergency Ct. of Appeals, 1980-89; past chmn. budget com. Jud. Conf. U.S.; former mem. exec. com. Nat. Conf. Fed. Trial Judges; former mem. adv. bd. W.Va. U. Mem. bd. advisors W.Va. U., past chmn.; bd. advisors Mary Babb Randolph Cancer Ctr. Recipient Alumni Disting. Svc. award Davis and Elkins Coll., 1969, Religious Heritage Am. award, 1979, Outstanding Trial Judge award W.Va. Trial Lawyers Assn., 1988, Order of Vandalia award W.Va. U., Outstanding Alumnus award, 1992, Tenured Faculty Mem. Recognition award Bd. Govs., Def. Trial Coun., W.Va., 1992, Cert. of Merit, W.Va. State Bar, 1994, Justitia Officium award Coll. of Law, W.Va. U., 1994. Mem. Nat. Conf. Federal Trial Judges, Dist. Judges Assn. 4th Cir. (past pres.), Moose (life), Lions (life), Beta Alpha Beta (merit award), Elkins-Randolph County C. of C. (citizen of yr. 1994). Office: US Dist Ct No Dist PO Box 1275 Elkins WV 26241-1275

MAXWELL, SARA ELIZABETH, psychologist, educator, speech pathologist; b. DuQuoin, Ill., Jan. 23; d. Jean A. (Patterson) Green; m. David Lowell Maxwell, Dec. 27, 1960 (div. Mar. 1990); children: Lisa Marina, David Scott. BS, So. Ill. U., 1963, MS, 1964, MEd, 1965; MEd, Boston Coll., 1982; attended, Harvard U., 1983; PhD, Boston Coll., 1992. Cert. and lic. speech./lang. pathologist, early childhood specialist, guidance counselor, sch. adjustment counselor, EMT. Clin. supr. Clin. Ctr. So. Ill. U., Carbondale, 1964-65, grad. clin. instr., 1965-66; speech/lang. pathologist, sch. adjustment counselor Westwood (Mass.) Pub. Schs., 1967-93; grad. faculty Emerson Coll., Boston, 1979-81; cons. Mass. Dept. Mental Health, Boston, 1979-82; grad. clin. supr. Robbins Speech/Hearing Ctr., Emerson Coll., Boston, 1979-82; cons. Westwood Nursery Preschs., 1989-93; devel. and clin. staff psychologist S. Shore Mental Health Ctr., Hingham and Quincy, Mass., 1989-93; emergency svcs. team and respite house manager S. Shore Mental Health Ctr., Quincy, Mass., 1990-93; pvt. practice Twin Oaks Clin. Assocs., Westwood, Mass. 1986-88, S. Coast Counseling Assocs., Quincy, 1989-93; cons. local collaboratives and preschs., Westwood, 1980-83; profl. workshops presenter Head Start, 1980; predoctoral intern in clin. psychology S. Shore Mental Health Ctr., Quincy, 1985-86; program specialist speech, lang., learning Broward County (Fla.) Schs., 1993—; adj. prof. grad. sch. of psychology Nova Southeastern U., 1995—; presenter Head Start, ASHA, CEC, APSC, IALP and other profl., nat. and state confs., 1980-93; invited del. to Sino-Am. Conf. on Exceptionality, Beijing Normal U., People's Republic of China, 1995. Contbr. articles to profl. jours., chpts. to textbooks. Mem. adv. coun. Westwood Bd. Health, 1977-80; emergency med. technician Westwood Pub. Schs. Athletic Dept., 1981. Vocat. Rehab. fellow So. Ill. U., 1964; Merit scholar Perry County, Ill., 1959-64, Gloria Credi Meml. scholar So. Ill. U., 1964. Mem. Am. Speech & Hearing Assn. (nat. schs. com., nat. chairperson Pub. Sch. Caucus 1985-87), Am. Psychol. Assn., Assn. Psychiat. Svcs. for Children, Coun. Exceptional Children, Internat. Assn. of Logopedics, Rio Vista Civic Assn., Boston Coll. Alumni Assn., Harvard Club. Episcopalian. Office: Nova Southeastern U Ctr for Psychol Studies College Ave Fort Lauderdale FL 33314-7721

MAXWELL, STEVEN ROBERT, social studies educator; b. Coral Gables, Fla., Oct. 1, 1951; s. David Gregor and Thelma Antoinette (Clayton) M.; m. Catherine Templeton, May 25, 1985. BA, U. Fla., 1975; MPA, U. Dayton, 1976; EdS, Fla. State U., 1982. Lectr. Sinclair C.C., Dayton, Ohio, 1976-77; social studies instr. Lee County Sch. Bd., Ft. Myers, Fla., 1978-80, 85—. Mem. editl. bd. Pub. Adminstrn. Quar., 1989, 94, Jour. Pub. Adminstrn. Edn., 1995. Mem. adv. bd. Lee County Human Rels. Rev. Bd., Ft. Myers, 1994. Mem. ASPA (exec. bd. dirs., pub. adminstrn. edn., profl. and orgnl. devel. sects. 1990—), Rotary (Paul Harris fellow 1993). Home: 19741 N River Rd Alva FL 33920-3317

MAXWELL, WILLIAM, food products executive; b. 1949. Grad., Clemson U., 1971. Prin. Maxwell and Suber, Quincy, Fla., 1973—; pres. Gadsden Tomato Co., Quincy, Fla., 1983—. Office: Gadsden Tomato Co 218 Graves St Quincy FL 32351-2100

MAY, ALBERT LOUIS, III, journalist; b. Oakland, Calif., Dec. 28, 1948; s. Albert Louis Jr. and Elivia Charles (Clodfelter) M.; m. Jan Hayes, Apr. 29, 1978 (div. Mar. 1992); m. Carol Cameron Darr, Dec. 19, 1992. BA in History, U. Mo., 1970; MA in Polit. Sci., U. Mo. Sch. Pub. Adminstrn., 1974; MA, U. Mo. Sch. Journalism, 1974. Reporter The Ark. Dem., Little Rock, 1975-78; chief capitol corr. The News & Observer, Raleigh, N.C., 1978-83, Washington corr., 1983-87; capitol bur. chief The Atlanta Jour.-Constitution, 1987-90, nat. polit. reporter, 1991-93, govt. pub. affairs editor, 1993—. Lt. (j.g.) USNR, 1970-72. Nieman fellow Harvard U., 1986-87; recipient Jacob Sherr award U. Mo., 1974. Mem. Kappa Tau Alpha. Home: 4473 Jett Rd NW Atlanta GA 30327-3563 Office: The Atlanta Jour 72 Marietta St NW Atlanta GA 30303-2804

MAY, BEVERLY, elementary school educator; b. Marshall, Tex., Sept. 11, 1939; d. Carl Glendon and Omie Louise (Berry) Brewster; m. William Raymond May, Sept. 19, 1958; children: William Jr., Karri, David. BS in Elem. Edn., U. Houston, 1969, MEd, 1978. Cert. elem. tchr., profl. reading specialist, profl. supr., Tex. Clerical, secretarial Houston Ind. Sch. Dist., 1957-64, tchr. grades 2, 3, 7, elem. reading ctr., 1969-90, ret., 1990; ednl. materials rep. World Book/Childcraft, Houston, 1975-90; reading cons. Region IV Edn. Svc. Ctr., Houston, 1977-83; supr. reading lab. downtown campus U. Houston, 1985; clk. sec. Houston Ind. Sch. Dist., 1957-64, tchr. grades two, three, seven Elem. Reading Ctr., 1969-90; pvt. reading skills and study skills specialist, 1975—; cons., presenter workshops in field. clerical/secretarial (1957-64). gr 2,3,7, elem. reading center, 1969-90. Participant TV-Radio broadcast ministries workshop 1st Bapt. Ch., Houston, 1988. Mem. Inspirational Writers Alive, Soc. Children's Book Writers and Illustrators, Internat. Reading Assn., Greater Houston Area Reading Coun. Home: 2102 Du Barry Ln Houston TX 77018-5060

MAY, DEBORAH LYNN, secondary school educator; b. Minot, N.D., July 2, 1971; d. Edward George III and Sharon Lee (Gierach) Schussler; m. Eric Ronald May, June 25, 1994. BS in Edn., Ind. U., 1993. Cert. English, history and sociology tchr., Tenn. English tchr. Wilson County Schs., Mt. Juliet, Tenn., 1993-94, Brentwood (Tenn.) H.S., 1994—. Vol. Middleway House Shelter, Bloomington, Ind., 1991-93. Mem. Nat. Coun. Tchrs. English. Home: 713 McKays Ct Brentwood TN 37027 Office: Brentwood HS Murray Ln Brentwood TN 37027

MAY, JACKSON CAMPBELL, real estate developer, writer; b. Danville, Ky., June 19, 1936; s. Earl Campbell and Emmalee (Fleming) M.; m. De Lena Inez Courtney, Nov. 26, 1965 (div. 1981); children: Jackson Campbell II (dec.), Geoffrey Courtney; m. Juanita Lucielee Sarver, June 16, 1984; children: Winston Augustus, Emmalee Annabella. BS, U.S. Mil. Acad., 1958. Commd. 1st lt. U.S. Army, 1958, with airborne, ranger and mountain sects. 82d Airborne Divsn., 1958-61; founder The May Cos., Gainesville, Fla., 1961—; Bd. dirs. First City Bank, Gainesville, Nat. Apt. Devel. Coun.; internat. explorer, safari photographer, mountain climber, 1950—; founder Pub. Partnerships for Investment, U.S., Germany, Italy, 1993—; presenter numerous seminars. Contbr. articles to profl. jours. Patron Jacksonville Symphony, Hippodrome State Theatre, Performing Arts Ctr. U. Fla., World Wildlife Fund; advisor dept. classics U. Fla. Named to Honorable Order Ky. Cols. Mem. Alumni Assn. U. Fla., Gator Boosters U. Fla., Assn. Grads. West Point, Chevaliers du Tastevin (Palm Beach), Explorers Club (N.Y.), Gainesville Country Club, Gator Hunt Club, The Heritage Club (Gainesville), Lodge and Bath Club (Ponte Verde Beach), Mensa, River Club (Jacksonville), Safari Club Internat., The Seminole Club (Jacksonville), Poinciana Club (Palm Beach), Societe de Bons Vivants, Sports Car Club Am., Univ. Club (Orlando), Soc. Colonial Wars, Circumnavigators Club (N.Y.), Am. Mus. Nat. History, Cousteau Soc., Ducks Unltd., Smithsonian. Republican. Baptist. Office: The May Cos PO Box 140600 Gainesville FL 32614-0600

MAY, JAMES D., physiologist. Supervisory rsch. physiologist Miss. State U. Address: PO Box 5367 Mississippi State MS 39762

MAY, JOHN ANDREW, petrophysicist, geologist; b. Lawrence, Kans., July 4, 1952; s. Donald Lawrence and Marie Jean (McCartney) M.; m. Aurelia Angela Szyfer, Nov. 23, 1988; children: Sean, Thomas, Daniel, Krystyna. BS in Geology, U. Kans., 1974. Sr. geologist Cities Svc. Oil Co., Tulsa, 1974-80; div. geologist Exxon, Denver, 1980-85; mgr. exploration systems Sci. Software-Intercomp, Denver, 1985-88; sr. staff geologist Kerr-McGee, Oklahoma City, 1985—; mem. quality assurance com. Internat. MWD Soc., Houston, 1994—. Mem. Am. Assn. Petroleum Geologists (cert., Cert. of Merit award 1993), Soc. Petroleum Engrs., Soc. Profl. Well L.A. (publs. com. 1995—), Okla. SPWLA (pres. 1993-94, v.p. tech. 1994-95). Democrat. Roman Catholic. Home: 403 Hunters Ct Edmond OK 73034 Office: Kerr McGee 123 Robert S Kerr Oklahoma City OK 73102

MAY, JOHN M., sales and marketing executive, consultant; b. San Diego, Jan. 11, 1948; s. James W. and Ruth I. (Lester); widower; 1 child, Alicia D. BSME, U.S. Merchant Marine Acad., 1971; MBA, U. New Haven, 1982. Installation and svc. engr. GE, N.Y.C., 1971-72; mgr. Bargain Supply Co., Danielson, Conn., 1972-75; western regional sales mgr. Novenco, Inc., Simsbury, Conn., 1975-78; product mgr. Flakt, Inc., Old Greenwich, Conn., 1978-82; dir. AEC mktg. Pall Corp., Ocala, Fla., 1982-86; owner, mgr. John May Cons., Ocala, 1986-87; mgr. sales and mktg. Gen. Air Div. Zurn Industries, Inc., Erie, Pa., 1987-92; pres. John May Cons., Clermont, Fla., 1987—. Editor newsletters, 1984-85, 89—; contbr. articles to profl. jours. Masons, Shriners. Republican. Presbyterian. Office: 215 Broad St Ste A Danielson CT 06239

MAY, JOSEPH LESERMAN (JACK), lawyer; b. Nashville, May 27, 1929; s. Daniel and Dorothy (Fishel) M.; m. Natalie McCuaig, Apr. 12, 1957 (dec. May 1990); children: Benjamin, Andrew, Joshua, Maria; m. Lynn Hewes Lance, June 10, 1994. BA, Yale U., 1951; JD, NYU, 1958; postgrad., Harvard Bus. Sch., 1969. Bar: Tenn. 1959. Prodr. Candied Yam Jackson Show, 1947-51; with CIA, 1951-55; pres. Nuweave Socks, Inc., N.Y.C., 1955-59, May Hosiery Mills, Nashville, 1960-83, Athens Hosiery Mills, Tenn., 1966-83; v.p. Wayne-Gossard Corp., Chattanooga, 1972-83; pvt. practice law Nashville, 1984—; bd. dirs. Convertible Holdings, Princeton, N.J., World Income Fund, Princeton, Merrill Lynch Growth Fund; adv. group Civil Justice Reform Act U.S. Dist. Ct., 1991; adv. bd. Asian Strategies Group, 1994. Bd. dirs. Vanderbilt Cancer Ctr., 1994—; pres. Jewish Cmty. Ctr., 1969; chmn. Guardianship and Trust Corp., 1994-96; trustee Tenn. Hist. Soc., 1996—. With USN, 1947-53, U.S. Army, 1954. Mem. Tenn. Bar Assn., Nashville Bar Assn., Tenn. Hist. Soc. (trustee 1996), Eagle Scout Assn., Shamus Club, Old Oak Club, Yale Club N.Y., Rotary (pres. Nashville 1971). Home: 2136 Golf Club Ln Nashville TN 37215-1224 Office: Box 190628 424 Church St Ste 2000 Nashville TN 37219-0628

MAY, JOY ELAINE, recreational facility executive; b. Mobile, Ala., Nov. 23, 1947; d. Allen Clark and Catherine (Finch) May. BS In English, U. So. Miss., 1970, MEd, 1971. Asst. dir. communications and devel. St. Mary's Hosp., Galveston, Tex., 1980-81; dir. communications and pub. rels. Galveston C. of C., 1981-82; dir. pub. relations and sales Galveston Arts!, 1982-83; exec. dir., v.p. Col. Paddlewheel Boat, Galveston, 1985—, also bd. dirs.; reserve faculty Galveston Coll., 1978—. Author: Journal of Creative Behavior, 1978. Bd. dirs. Col. Mus., Inc., Moody Found.; founder, bd. dirs. Galveston Acad. Booster Club, 1977; bd. dirs. Clean Galveston, 1981, 87, Jr. League Galveston County, 1981—, Mental Health Assn., 1983, Galveston Attractions Assn., 1986, pres., 1990; chmn., founder, Galveston Island Jazz Festival, trustee Galveston Park Bd., 1987-93, chmn., 1993. Recipient Outstanding Tchr. Galveston Ind. Sch. Dist., Evening Optimists, 1978. Mem. Nat. Tour Assn., Tex. Soc. Asst. Execs., Rotary, Delta Kappa Gamma. Episcopalian. Home: 5525 Palm Cir Galveston TX 77551-5567 Office: Col Paddlewheel Boat 1 Hope Blvd Galveston TX 77554-8928

MAY, KENNETH NATHANIEL, food industry consultant; b. Livingston, La., Dec. 24, 1930; s. Robert William and Mary Hulda (Caraway) M.; m. Patsy Jean Farr, Aug. 4, 1953; children: Sherry Alison (dec.), Nathan Elliott. BS in Poultry Sci., La. State U., 1952, MS in Poultry Sci., 1955; PhD in Food Tech., Purdue U., 1959, DAgr, 1988. Asst. prof. U. Ga., Athens, 1958-64, assoc. prof., 1964-67, prof., 1967-68; prof. Miss. State U., State College, 1968-70; dir. rsch. Holly Farms Poultry, Wilkesboro, N.C., 1970-73, v.p., 1973-85, pres., 1985-88, chmn., CEO, 1989; bd. dirs. Hudson Foods, Inc., Embrex, Inc., Alcide Corp.; adj. prof. N.C. State U., 1975. Contbr. over 60 articles to profl. jours.; patentee treatment of cooked poultry. Bd. trustees Appalachian State U., 1987-94, chmn., 1989-90. Recipient Industry Service award Poultry and Egg Inst. Am., 1971, Meritorious Service award, Ga. Egg Commn., 1964, Disting. Service award Agribus. N.C., 1986; named to Am. Poultry Hall of Fame, 1992. Fellow Poultry Sci. Assn.; mem. Nat. Poultry Hist. Soc. (bd. dirs. 1982-83), Inst. Food Technologists. Methodist.

MAY, WILLIAM E., association administrator. V.p. ops. and adminstrn. Am. Cotton Exporters Assn., Memphis. Office: Am Cotton Exporters Assn PO Box 3366 Memphis TN 38173

MAYBERRY, JULIUS EUGENE, realty company owner, investor; b. Qulin, Mo., July 3, 1935; s. Julius E. and Mabel L. (Gunnells) M.; m. Nettie Sue Burden, Dec. 8, 1953; children: Michael Eugene, Cynthia E. Copeland, Karen Sue Mayberry-Lee. AS, Ga. Mil. Acad., 1973; postgrad., Augusta Coll., 1976. Enlisted U.S. Army, 1957, advanced through grades to first sgt., 1973, ret., 1979; salesperson TIPS Realty Co., Augusta, Ga., 1979—, owner, broker, 1984—. Scoutmaster Boy Scouts of Am., Ft. Gordon, Ga., 1961-67. Decorated Bronze medal, Purple Heart. Mem. Augusta Bd. Realtors, Multiple Listing Service Augusta. Republican. Baptist. Lodge: Optimist (v.p. 1987). Home: 2327 Lumpkin Ct Augusta GA 30906-3090 Office: TIPS Realty Co 2327 Lumpkin Ct Augusta GA 30906-3090

MAYBERRY, RODNEY SCOTT, dentist; b. Salt Lake City, Oct. 12, 1947; s. R.C. and Virginia (Hood) M.; m. Zellor Juanita Sears, May 30, 1970; children: Christopher, Matthew, Lauren. BA in Biology, U. Richmond, 1974; DDS, Med. Coll. Va., 1978. Pvt. practice dentistry Salt Lake City, 1979-89, McLean, Va., 1989—; cons. Artech Corp., Chantilly, Va., 1991—; exec. producer CD-ROM Dental Edn. Corp. With U.S. Army, 1967-69, Vietnam. Fellow Am. Acad. Implant Dentistry, Internat. Congress Oral Implantologists; mem. ADA, Am. Acad. Implant Prosthodontics, Am. Dental Soc. Anesthesiology, Acad. Gen. Dentistry, Va. State Dental Assn., No. Va. Dental Implant Study Club (founder). Mormon. Office: 8353A Greensboro Dr Mc Lean VA 22102-3530

MAYBURY, P(AUL) CALVIN, chemistry educator; b. Rio Grande, N.J., July 20, 1924; s. Byron Harris and Mildred Abigail (Bower) M.; m. Rebecca Lillian Palmer, July 27, 1949; children: Paul Calvin, James Palmer, Anne Elizabeth Maybury Krumrei, Lynn Marie, Susan Gail Maybury Mackay. BS, Ea. Nazarene Coll., 1947; PhD, The Johns Hopkins U., 1952. Sr. staff chemist Applied Physics Lab., Silver Spring, Md., 1951-52; rsch. assoc. The Johns Hopkins U., Balt., 1952-54; asst. prof. Ea. Nazarene Coll., Quincy, Mass., 1954-57, chmn., assoc. prof., 1957-61; assoc. prof. U. South Fla., Tampa, 1961-63, prof., 1963-92, chmn. chemistry dept., 1963-74; v.p., dir. rsch. and devel. Belmac Corp., St. Petersburg, Fla., 1980-88; v.p. Fluid Life Systems Inc., Laguna Niguel, Calif., 1989-91; pres. Biorelease Corp., 1991-93; chmn. Health Svcs. of Am. Corp., 1992-96; cons. Diamond Products Inc., Sefner, Fla., 1979-88, Valcor Sci. Ltd., St. Petersburg, 1986-89. With U.S. Army, 1944-46, PTO. Grantee U.S. AEC, 1961-62, Thiokol Corp., 1978. Fellow Am. Inst. Chemists; mem. Am. Chem. Soc., Sigma Xi. Republican. Home: 4102 Cypress Bayou Dr Tampa FL 33624-5323

MAYCOCK, WILLIAM W., lawyer; b. Salt Lake City, Nov. 13, 1952. BS cum laude, Brigham Young U., 1975; JD, U. Utah, 1978. Bar: D.C. 1978, Utah 1978, Ga. 1980. Law clk. Hon. Frank Q. Nebeker D.C. Ct. Appeals, 1978-79; ptnr. Smith, Gambrell & Russell, Atlanta. Assoc. editor Utah Law Rev., 1977-78. Mem. ABA (litigation and pub. utility law sects.), State Bar Ga. (chair adminstrv. law sect. 1990-92, antitrust and adminstrv. law sects.),

D.C. Bar, Order of Coif. Office: Smith Gambrell & Russell Promenade II 1230 Peachtree St NE Ste 3100 Atlanta GA 30309-3592

MAYER, LLOYD D., allergist, immunologist, physician, medical educator; b. Bklyn., Nov. 6, 1921; s. Morris and Leonore (Sullivan) M.; m. Marie Faith Puntney, Feb. 2, 1957 (dec. Sept. 1981); children: Michael, Fredrick, Loren, Lee; m. Carol Smith, Dec. 21, 1985. BA, U. Louisville, Ky., 1941, MD, 1944. Diplomate Am. Bd. Internal Medicine, Am. Bd. Internal Medicine Alergy, Am. Bd. Allergy and Immunology. Rotating intern Coney Island Hosp., Bklyn., 1944-45; resident in contagious diseases Kingston Ave Hosp., Bklyn., 1945-46; resident in pathology Long Island Coll. Hosp., Bklyn., 1946-47; resident in medicine Montefiore Hosp., Pitts., 1947-48; teaching fellow in allergy U. Pitts., 1948-49; resident in medicine VA Hosp., Pitts., 1949-50; instr. in allergy medicine U. Pitts., 1950-52; staff St. Joseph Hosp., Good Samaritan Hosp.; staff Ctrl. Baptist Hosp., chmn. dept. internal medicine, 1972-74; staff Humana Hosp.; clin. prof. medicine, allergy U. Ky. Med. Ctr., Lexington, Ky., 1962—; cons. in allergy medicine VA Hosp.; chmn. respiratory therapy com. Good Samaritian Hosp., Ctrl. Baptist Hosp., 1970-74; chmn. nursing care com. Ctrl. Baptist Hosp., 1979;bd. dirs. Allergy Clinic, VA Hosp., Adult Allergy Clinic, U. Ky. Med. Ctr. 1994—. Contr. to profl. jours. Lt. US Army, 1941-46. Recipient cert. Appreciation Coll. Allied Health and Nursing Eastern Ky. U., Am. Acad. Family Practice award, 1979. Fellow Am. Coll. Physicians, Am. Acad. Allergy, Am. Coll. Allergists; mem. AMA, Fayette County Med. Soc., Ky. State Med. Assn., Ky. Thoracic Soc. (sec. 1962), Am. Assn. Cert. Allergists, Mason (pres. 1961), Scottish Rite Masonic Shriner (pres. 1962). Home: 470 Woodlake Way Lexington KY 40502-2570 Office: 2368 Nicholasville Rd Lexington KY 40503-3004

MAYER, MARION SIDNEY, research entomologist; b. New Orleans, July 25, 1935; s. Marion Sidney and Jewel (Colvin) M.; m. Martha Anne McLemore, June 17, 1967; children: Melissa, Ellen. BS, La. State U., 1957; MS, Tex. A&M U., 1961, PhD, 1963. Rsch. entomologist ARS, USDA, Gainesville, Fla., 1963—. Author: Insect Pheromones and Sex Attractants, 1990. Office: ARS USDA 1700 SW 23rd Dr Gainesville FL 32608-1069

MAYERS, HANS JOSEPH, systems programmer; b. Baton Rouge, Jan. 5, 1955; s. Alton Edmund Mayers and Gladys Louise Bohnhoff Mayers Spinato; m. Sharron Ann Brown, Apr. 17, 1953; children: Jonathan Joseph, Jennifer Addie. Student, La. State U., U. So. La.; diploma, Baton Rouge Sch. of Computers, 1984. Transit operator Am. Bank, Baton Rouge, 1974-76; lead operator United Cos., Baton Rouge, 1980-81; EDP technician II Baton Rouge Water Co., 1981-83, 85-90; system programmer Baton Rouge Water Co., Baton Rouge, 1990-95; system adminstr. Baton Rouge Water Co., 1995—. Speaker on alcohol and drug abuse, Baton Rouge, 1988—. Fellow Nat. Assn. System Programmers, GUIDE. Roman Catholic. Home: 5235 Lost Oak Dr Baton Rouge LA 70817-2718 Office: Baton Rouge Water Co 8755 Goodwood Blvd Baton Rouge LA 70806-7916

MAYES, GLENN, social worker; b. Aug. 23, 1955; s. Johnny and Lillie (Hopper) M. BS, Cameron U., 1977; MSW, U. Okla., 1984. Cert. profl. healthcare quality; lic. social worker, Okla.; bd. cert. diplomate clin. social worker. Dir. spl. svcs. Jim Taliaferro C.M.H.C., Lawton. Mem. NASW (S.W. chpt. br. chmn. nominations and leadership com.), Nat. Assn. Healthcare Quality, Acad. Cert. Social Workers. Home: 6112 NW Birch Ave Lawton OK 73505-4442

MAYES, STEVEN L., art educator, artist; b. Glendale, Calif., Nov. 7, 1939; s. Wayne L. and Alma L. (Swenson) M.; m. Pamela K. Shelden, Aug. 14, 1965; children: Erin E., Eric L. BFA, Wichita State U., 1963, BAE, 1963, MFA, 1965. Asst. prof. U. S.D., Springfield, 1966-71; assoc. prof. S.D. State U., Brookings, 1971-77; prof. West Tex. State U., Canyon, 1977-88, Ark. State U., Jonesboro, 1988—. Exhibited in shows at Pratt Inst., N.Y.C., 1987, Bronx (N.Y.) Mus., 1987. Bd. dirs. Amarillo (Tex.) Art Ctr., 1978-83. Mem. Jonesboro C. of C. (bike lane com. 1991—). Office: Ark State U Dept Art PO Box 1920 State University AR 72467

MAYFIELD, J. W., police official; b. Hubbard, Tex., Nov. 5, 1937; s. William L. and Othella (Olsson) M.; m. Alma Louise McMahon, Oct. 10, 1958; children: Jana D., Shari Ann Mayfield Harrison, Joseph R. AA, Abilene Christian U., 1972, BS, 1974, MS, 1978. Licensed peace officer, Tex. Police officer, asst. police chief City of Garland (Tex.) Police Dept., Garland, Tex., 1960-93; chief of police City of Electra, Tex., 1993-96; instr. criminal justice, Abilene Christian U., Garland, 1974-80. With USAF, 1956-60. Named Officer of the Yr., Garland Jaycees, 1976; chmn. awards com. Garland Optimist Club, Garland, 1977-78. Mem. Internat. Assn. Chiefs of Polics, Law Enforcement Officers Tex. (bd. dirs.), Garland Police Officers Assn., Tex. Law Enforcement Intelligence Units Assn., Abilene Christian U. Alumni Assn., Garland Police Assn. (sec. 1978-80), Garland Country Music Assn. Republican. Missionary Baptist. Home: 718 Eastern Star Dr Garland TX 75040-5178

MAYFIELD, WILLIAM CARY, personnel executive; b. Atlanta, Feb. 6, 1958; s. George R. Mayfield and Janie (Hillman) Evans; m. Melanie Carter, Nov. 7, 1977 (div. 1980); m. Kathy M. Michel, May 5, 1984. BBA, Augusta Coll., 1981. cert. profl. in human resources. Personnel mgr. Temple-Eastex, Inc., Thomson, Ga., 1979-85; purchasing mgr. Temple-Eastex, Inc., 1982-85, office mgr., 1985; personnel mgr. J.P. King Mfg.-div. Spartan Mills, Augusta, Ga., 1985—; mem. Ga. Dept. Labor Adv. Coun., 1986—. Chmn. bd. dirs. King Mill Savs. and Credit, Augusta, 1987—; bd. dirs. Augusta Credit Union, Metro Adult Literacy Coun., Augusta. Mem. Soc. Human Resource Mgmt., Mensa, Cen. Savannah River Area (pres. personnel assn. 1989-90). Republican. Methodist. Home: 2435 Castlewood Dr Augusta GA 30904-3391 Office: JP King Mfg 1701 Goodrich St Augusta GA 30904-3054

MAYHEW, AUBREY, music business executive; b. Washington, Oct. 2, 1927; s. Aubrey and Verna June (Hall) M.; m. Carol de Onis, May 10, 1962 (div. 1971); children: Lawrence Aubrey, Michael Aubrey, Parris Mitchell, Casey Aran. Student, Wilson Tchs. Coll., 1948. Dir. Sta. WWVA, Wheeling, W.Va., 1947-54, Sta. WCOP, Boston, 1954-56; asst. to pres. MGM Records, N.Y.C., 1957-58; v.p. mktg. Capitol Records, Los Angeles, 1958-60; prodr., dir. Sta. KCAM-TV Prodns., Nashville, 1981—; pres., founder John F. Kennedy Meml. Ctr., 1968; authority on John F. Kennedy life and memorabilia. Author: (books) Commandants Marine Corps, 1953, World Tribute to John F. Kennedy, 1965; composer (music) Touch My Heart, 1966 (Broadcast Music, Inc. award, 1967); record producer, artist mgmt., 1947—; music pub., 1954—; developed careers numerous entertainers including Johnny Paycheck, Jeannie C. Riley, Bobby Helms. Served to cpl. U.S. Army Signal Corps, 1945-48. Named Govs. Aide, Nashville, 1978. Mem. Country Music Assn., Broadcast Music Inc., Manuscript Soc., N.Y. Numismatic Soc., Gospel Music Assn. Republican. Episcopalian. Home: 827 Meridian St Nashville TN 37207-5856 Office: Amcorp Music Group 827 Meridian St Nashville TN 37207-5856

MAYHEW, KENNETH EDWIN, JR., transportation company executive; b. Shelby, N.C., Sept. 27, 1934; s. Kenneth Edwin and Evelyn Lee (Dellinger) M.; m. Frances Elaine Craft, Apr. 7, 1957; 1 dau., Catherine Lynn Prince. A.B., Duke U., 1956. CPA, N.C. Sr. auditor Arthur Andersen & Co., Atlanta, 1956-58, 60-63; controller Trendline, Inc., Hickory, N.C., 1963-66; with Carolina Freight Corp., Cherryville, 1966-93; treas., 1969-74; v.p. Carolina Freight Carriers Corp., Cherryville, 1971-72, exec. v.p., 1972-85, pres., chief oper. officer, 1985-89, dir., 1968-93, chmn., pres., CEO, 1989-93; pres., dir. Robo Auto Wash Shelby Inc., 1967-73, Robo Auto Wash Cherryville, Inc., 1968-73; dir. Cherryville Nat. Bank, Kenmar Bus. Group, Inc. Mem. Bus. Adv. Bd., Fuqua Sch. Bus., Duke U.; bd. dirs., vice-chmn. Gaston Meml. Hosp.; trustee Pfeiffer Coll. With AUS, 1958-60. Mem. AICPA, Am. Trucking Assn. (dir., v.p.), N.C. Trucking Assn. (dir., chmn.), Gaston County C. of C. (v.p. pub. affairs), Lions (pres. Cherryville 1972-73), Phi Beta Kappa, Omicron Delta Kappa, Phi Eta Sigma. Methodist. Home: 507 Spring St Cherryville NC 28021-3540

MAYHUGH, JOEL OGDEN, JR., financial executive; b. Little Rock, Nov. 9, 1941; s. Joel Ogden Sr. and Jessie Olin (Hall) M.; m. Caroline Elizabeth Boellner, Nov. 5, 1966; 1 child, Katherine Elizabeth. BA in Social Scis., U. Little Rock, 1969. Sales rep. Kraft Foods, Little Rock, 1964-66, 68-72; sr. fin. cons. Merrill Lynch, Little Rock, 1972-92; asst. v.p. Merrill Lynch, Hot Springs, Ark., 1992—. Co-chmn. North Little Rock Port Authority, 1982; pres. Ark. affiliate Am. Diabetes Assn., Little Rock, 1980, North Little Rock Kiwanis Club, 1977; bd. dirs. YMCA, North Little Rock, 1983. With U.S. Army, 1966-68. Named Outstanding Kiwanian of Yr. Kiwanis Club, 1976, Outstanding Stock Broker in the U.S. Money Mag., 1987. Mem. Hot Springs Jazz Soc., Little Rock C. of C. (bd. dirs. 1977-78), Hot Springs C. of C., North Hills Country Club (greens com. 1975-76), Ark. State Golf Assn., Ark. Fly Fishing Assn., Ark. Wilde Life Assn., Ducks Unltd., Merrill Lynch Presidents Club. Baptist. Home: 1340 Rock Creek Rd Hot Springs National Park AR 71913-9283 Office: Merrill Lynch Inc PO Box 205 Hot Springs National Park AR 71951-0205

MAYNARD, GEORGE FLEMING, III, hospital administrator; b. Tupelo, Miss., Mar. 29, 1947; s. George Fleming Jr. and Shirley Lindsey (Russell) M.; m. Janie White, Aug. 16, 1969; children: George Fleming IV, Benjamin Hoyle. BA in Sociology, U. Miss., 1969; MS in Social Work, U. Tenn., 1972. Child welfare supr. Miss. Dept. Pub. Welfare, Pontotoc, 1972-74; exec. dir. Lift, Inc., Tupelo, 1974-77; dir. devel. and pub. relations North Miss. Med. Ctr., Tupelo, 1977-82; v.p. pub. affairs United Health Svcs., Binghamton, N.Y., 1982-87; exec. v.p. Orlando (Fla.) Regional Healthcare Found., 1987—. Contbr. articles to profl. jours. Mem. Miss. Econ. Coun., Jackson, 1981-82; mem. exec. com. Bayhill Invitational, Orlando, 1987—; bd. dirs. Broome County Cmty. Charities, Endicott, N.Y., 1984-87; mem. Leadership Miss., 1980, Leadership Orlando, 1988, Econ. Devel. Commn.; Eagle scout Boy Scouts Am.; elder Metro Ch. of Christ; lay missionary Varna Bulgaria. Recipient MacEachern award Am. Soc. Hosp. Pub. Relations, 1979. Fellow Assn. Healthcare Philanthropy; mem. Health Systems Devel. Network (pres. 1994-97), Planned Giving Coun. Ctrl. Fla. (pres. 1994-95), Rotary (pres. Tupelo chpt. 1980-82). Home: 451 Longmeadow Ln Longwood FL 32779-6011 Office: Orlando Regional Healthcare 1414 Kuhl Ave Orlando FL 32806-2008

MAYNARD, MICHAEL SCOTT, toxicologist; b. Rome, N.Y., Sept. 18, 1951; s. William Charles and Mary Louise (Costello) M.; m. Katherine Grace Kearney, May 27, 1984; children: Healther Dawn, Jarod Paul Kearney. BS in Chemistry, U. Calif., Riverside, 1976; PhD in Pharmacology, UCLA, 1982. Diplomate Am. Bd. Toxicology. Chem. technician dept. Entomology U. Calif., Riverside, 1976-77; sr. rsch. chemist Merck & Co. Inc., Three Bridges, N.J., 1982-88; project scientist CIBA-GEIGY Corp., Greensboro, N.C., 1988-92, product toxicologist, 1992, mgr. product toxicology dept. Tech. Svc., 1992—; adj. prof. pharmacology Bowman Gray Med. Sch., Wake Forest U., 1995—. Contbr. articles to profl. jours. U. Calif. Alumni Assn. Undergrad. Rsch. grantee, 1976, NCI Toxicology and Chem. Carcinogenesis grantee, 1979-82. Mem. AAAS, Am. Chem. Soc., Soc. Toxicology, Am. Acad. Clin. Toxicology, Soc. Environ. Toxicology and Chemistry, Genetic Toxicology Assn., Internat. Soc. of Regulatory Toxicology and Pharmacology. Office: CIBA Crop Protection PO Box 18300 Greensboro NC 27419-8300

MAYO, CLYDE CALVIN, organizational psychologist, educator; b. Robstown, Tex., Feb. 2, 1940; s. Clyde Culberson and Velma (Oxford) M.; m. Jeanne Lynn McCain, Aug. 24, 1963; children: Brady Scott, Amber Camille. BA, Rice U., 1961; BS, U. Houston, 1964, PhD, 1972; MS, Trinity U., 1966. Lic. psychologist, Tex. Mgmt. engr. LWFW, Inc., Houston, 1966-72, sr. cons., 1972-78, prin., 1978-81; ptnr. Mayo, Thompson, Bigby, Houston, 1981-83, founder Mgmt. and Personnel Systems, Houston, 1983—; counselor Interface Counseling Ctr., Houston, 1976-79; dir. Mental Health HMO Group, 1985-87; instr. St. Thomas U., Houston, 1979—, U. Houston Downtown Sch., 1972, U. Houston-Clear Lake, 1983-88, U. Houston-Central Campus, 1984—; dir. mgmt. devel. insts. U. Houston Woodlands and West Houston, 1986-1991, adj. prof. U. Houston, 1991—. Author: Bi/Polar Inventory of Strengths, 1978, LWFW Annual Survey of Manufacturers, 1966-1981. Coach, mgr. Meyerland Little League, 1974-78, So. Belles Softball, 1979-80, S.W. Colt Baseball, 1982-83, Friends of Fondren Library of Rice U., 1988—; charter mem. Holocaust Mus. Mem. Soc. Indsl. Organizational Psychologists, Tex. Indsl. Orgnl. Psychologists (founder, bd. dirs. 1995—), Houston Psychol. Assn. (membership dir. 1978, sec. 1984), Tex. Psychol. Assn., Am. Psychol. Assn., Bus. Execs. for Nat. Security, Houston Area Indsl. Orgnl. Psychologists (bd. dirs. 1989-92), Forum Club. Methodist. Club: Meyerland (bd. dirs. 1988-92, pres. 1991). Home: 8723 Ferris Dr Houston TX 77096-1409 Office: Mgmt and Personnel Systems 4545 Bissonnet St Bellaire TX 77401

MAYO, LOUIS ALLEN, corporation executive; b. Durham, N.C., Nov. 27, 1928; s. Louis Allen and Amy Earl (Overton) M.; student Calif. State Poly. Coll., 1948-50; BA in Criminology, Calif. State Coll., Fresno, 1952; MA in Pub. Adminstrn., Am. U., 1960, PhD in Pub. Adminstrn., 1983; postgrad. U. So. Calif., 1960-62; m. Emma Jean Minshew, Oct. 31, 1953 (div.); children: Louis Allen III, Robert Lawrence, Carolyn Jean; m. 2d, Myrna Ann Smith, Feb. 16, 1980 (div.). Spl. agt. U.S. Secret Svc., Treasury Dept., L.A., 1956-58, 60-63, White House, Washington, 1958-60, 63-66; program mgr. law enforcement Office Law Enforcement Assistance, Justice Dept., 1967-68; acting chief Rsch. Ctr., rsch. program mgr. Nat. Inst. Law Enforcement and Criminal Justice, 1968-74; alternate assoc. mem. Fed. Coun. on Sci. and Tech., White House, 1973-74; dir. tng. and testing div. Nat. Inst. Justice, 1975-87; pres. Murphy, Mayo & Assocs., Alexandria, Va., 1987—; lectr. criminology Armed Forces Inst. Tech., 1954-55; professorial lectr. Am. U., 1974-82; adj. prof. August Vollmer U., 1990-95. 2d lt. to 1st lt. USAF, 1952-56. Mem. Am. Police Assn. (pres., co-founder), Internat. Assn. Chiefs of Police, Am. Soc. Pub. Adminstrn. (nat. chmn. sect. on criminal justice adminstrn. 1975-76), Acad. Criminal Justice Scis., Police Exec. Rsch. Forum, Soc. Police Futurists Internat., Am. Soc. Indsl. Security, Pi Sigma Alpha. Methodist. Home and Office: 5200 Leeward Ln # 101 Alexandria VA 22315-3944

MAYO, MARTI, art historian, curator; b. Bluefield, W. Va., Oct. 17, 1945; d. Robert J. and Kathryn Ann (Kearns) Kirkwood; m. Edward K. Mayo, May 13, 1974 (div. 1983); 1 child, Nesta. BA, Am. U., 1970, MFA, 1974. Asst. dir. Jefferson Place Gallery, Washington, 1973-74; coordinator exhbns. Corcoran Gallery Art, Washington, 1974-80; curator Contemporary Arts Mus., Houston, 1980-86; dir. Blaffer Gallery U. Houston, 1986—. Author: Robert Morris Selected Works: 1970-80, 1981, Other Realities: Installations for Performance, 1981, Arbitrary Order: Paintings by Pat Steir, 1983, (with others) Robert Rauschenberg, Work from Four Series: A Sesquicentennial Exhibition, 1985, Joseph Glasco 1948-1986: A Sesquicentennial Exhibition, 1986, Six Artists/Six Idioms, 1988. Mem. Am. Assn. Museums, Coll. Art Assn.

MAYO, ROBERT BOWERS, art company owner; b. Phoenixville, Pa., Apr. 26, 1933; s. Newton Tabb and Mary Eugenia (Dabney) M.; m. Margaret Gwynn Thomas, Dec. 1, 1956; children: Pamela Mayo Rogansky, Mary-Beth Mayo Johnson, Margaret Bingham. BFA, Richmond Profl. Inst., 1959. Dir. interpretation Jamestown (Va.) Festival Park, 1959-61, Archives and History, Raleigh, N.C., 1961-66; dir. Valentine Mus., Richmond, Va., 1966-75; ptnr. Val-Glare Studio, Richmond, 1975-77; owner art gallery Gallery Mayo, Inc., Richmond, 1977—. Served with USN, 1951-55, Korea, Mediterranean. Methodist. Office: Gallery Mayo Inc 5705 Grove Ave Richmond VA 23226-2345

MAYO, ROBERT MICHAEL, nuclear engineering educator, physicist; b. Phila., Sept. 23, 1962; s. Robert Norman and Joan Ann (Oeschner) M.; m. Judith Ann Hopkins, June 24, 1989. BS, Pa. State U., 1984; MS, Purdue U., 1987, PhD, 1989. Rsch. asst. Argonne (Ill.) Nat. Lab., 1984; rsch. asst. Los Alamos (N.Mex.) Nat. Lab., 1985, physicist, 1989-91; instr. Purdue U., West Lafayette, Ind., 1986, rsch. asst., 1984-86; rsch. asst. Princeton (N.J.) U., 1986-88; asst. prof. N.C. State U., Raleigh, 1991—; faculty advisor ANS, N.C. State U., 1991-95. Contbr. articles to profl. jours. Recipient David Ross fellowship Purdue U., 1986-88. Mem. Am. Phys. Soc., Am. Nuclear Soc. (R.A. Daniels Meml. scholar Purdue U. 1988), Fusion Power Assocs., Sigma Xi, Sigma Pi Sigma, Tau Beta Pi. Office: NC State U Dept Nuclear Engrng Box 7909 2101 Burlington Labs Raleigh NC 27695-7909

MAYR, LINDA HART, internal medicine nurse; b. Orange, Tex., July 15, 1951; d. Richard Gail and Gwendolyn (Condrey) Hart; m. Julius Charles Mayr, Nov. 20, 1987; children: Christopher Feazel, Keith Feazel, Kimberly Feazel, Christina Duke, Thomas Mayr. Diploma, North Harris County Coll., Houston, 1980. Newborn nursery and neonatal ICU nurse Houston N.W. Med. Ctr., 1980-81, 1982-84; pvt. nurse Frederick Hill, D.O., Houston, 1981-82; nurse FM 1960 Pediatric Ctr., Houston, 1984-85; nurse ob-gyn. Steven Zarzour, M.D., Houston, 1985-86; office mgr. Bert Williams, D.C., Houston, 1986-87; office nurse Ronald E. Sims, M.D., Houston, 1987—; allied health profl. Meth. Hosp., Houston, 1987—. Mem. Am. Assn. Office Nurses, Assn. Nurses AIDS Care, The Care Group, Inc. (profl. adv. com.). Home: 206 E Oak St Deer Park TX 77536-4104

MAYROSE, MONA PEARL, critical care nurse, flight nurse, educator; b. Levittown, N.J., Nov. 3, 1961; d. William Joseph and Sarah (Tanne) Tillis; m. Alan Gary Mayrose, Nov. 1, 1987; 1 child, Kattey; stepchildren: Dale, Brian. BA, NYU, 1982; MSN, Pace U., 1986. Cert. critical care nurse, trauma nurse, staff devel. nurse; instr. ACLS and critical care. Nursery nurse No. Westchester Hosp. Ctr., Mt. Kisco, N.Y., 1987-88; ICU nurse Meth. Hosp., Houston, 1988-89; dir. nursing Golden Age and Winslow Nursing Homes, Houston, 1989; hospice case mgr. Vis. Nurse Assn., Houston, 1989-91; critical care charge nurse Woodlands (Tex.) Meml. Hosp., 1990-92; commd. 1st lt. USAF, 1992, advanced through grades to capt., 1992; charge nurse surg. ICU 59th Med. Wing USAF, Lackland AFB, Tex., 1992-94, critical care educator, 1994-95; flight nurse 23d Aeromed. Evacuation Squadron, Pope AFB, N.C., 1996—. Mem. AACN (bd. dirs. San Antonio chpt.), Nat. Nurses Staff Devel. Orgn., Air Force Assn., Aerospace Med. Assn., Sigma Theta Tau. Jewish. Home: 853 Foxcroft Dr Fayetteville NC 28311

MAYS, CATHY CASH, development officer; b. Lynchburg, Va., Aug. 8, 1962; d. Alvin Marks Cash and Alverta Geraldine (Patterson) Hensley; m. Neal Anderson, July 7, 1984; 1 child, Jason Van. AB in Anthropology/Sociology, Sweet Briar Coll., 1984. Cert. bus. mgmt. Sales clk. Leggett Dept. Store, Lynchburg, Va., summer 1981; spl. computer program mgr. Sweet Briar (Va.) Coll., 1984-87, rsch. asst., 1987-89, assoc. dir. annual fund, 1989-90, dir. annual fund, 1990-92, dir. prospect rsch., 1992-94, dir. stewardship and rsch., 1994-95; assoc. dir. devel., 1995—; workshop presenter Nat. Soc. Fund Raising Execs., Roanoke, Va., 1991. Acteens leader Ctrl. Bapt. Ch., Lowesville, Va., 1989-91, 93-94, fin. com., 1990-91, Mission Friends Leader, 1996—; mem. fin. deve. com. ARC Met. Lynchburg Chpt. Mem. Coun. for Advancement and Support of Edn., Assn. Profl. Rschrs. for Advancement, Nat. Soc. Fund Raising Execs. (Va. Piedmont chpt.), Pi Gamma Mu. So. Bapt. Home: RR 4 Amherst VA 24521-9804 Office: Sweet Briar Coll Box G Devel Office Sweet Briar VA 24595

MAYS, DAVID ARTHUR, agronomy educator, small business owner; b. Waynesburg, Pa., Apr. 17, 1929; s. Arthur Lynn and Edith N. (Breakey) M.; m. Betty Ann Sellers, Aug. 7, 1954; children: Gregory D., Laurie Ann. MS in Agronomy, Pa. State U., 1959, PhD in Agronomy, 1961. Cert. profl. agronomist. Asst. county agrl. agt. Pa. State, Washington, Pa., 1954-57; grad. rsch. asst. Pa. State U., University Park, Pa., 1957-61; asst. agronomist Va. Polytech. Inst. & State U., Middleburg, 1961-63; rsch. agronomist TVA, Muscle Shoals, Ala., 1963-88; prof. agronomy Ala. A&M Univ., Normal, Ala., 1989—. Editor: Forage Fertilization, 1974; Contbr. articles to profl. jours. and chpts. to books, 1959—. 1st lt. U.S. Army, 1951-54, Korea. Mem. Am. Soc. Agronomy, Am. Forage and Grassland Coun. (Merit Cert. award 1976), Ala. Turfgrass Assn. Presbyterian. Home: 114 Kathy St Florence AL 35633-1428 Office: Ala A&M U Dept Plant and Soil Sci PO Box 1208 Normal AL 35762-1208

MAYS, GLENDA SUE, retired education educator; b. Freer, Tex., July 18, 1938; d. Archie Richard and Helen Hildred (Morgan) Cox; m. Dewey William Mays, Sept. 7, 1963; children: Rose Marie, Teresa Sue, Frank Dewey. BS, Tex. Tech. U., 1959, MA, 1961; PhD, North Tex. State U., 1969. Cert. tchr., supr., prin. Tchr. Lubbock (Tex.) Pub. Schs., 1959-61, Amarillo (Tex.) Pub. Schs., 1961-62, Austin (Tex.) Pub. Schs., 1962-63; curriculum intern/rsch. asst., elem. coord. U. Tex. at Austin, Hurst, Tex., 1963-65; asst. prof. McMurry U., Abilene, Tex., 1965-67; assoc. prof. Dallas Bapt. U., 1968-71; reading resource tchr., dept. chair Ft. Worth (Tex.) Ind. Sch. Dist., 1971-74, reading specialist, 1974-82, instructional specialist, 1982-95, ret., 1995; spkr. lang. acquisition and reading 7th World Congress in Reading, Hamburg, Germany, 1978. Advisor/writer (English textbook): McDouglas Littel Language, 1985-86; writer: Bilingual Stories for Ft. Worth Ind. Sch. Dist., 1979-80. Patron Kimbell Mus. Art, Ft. Worth, 1994—; mem. Nat. Cancer Soc., Ft. Worth, 1980—. Fulbright-Hays scholar, Kenya, Africa, 1970; grantee in fgn. langs. Nat. Endowment Arts U. Ark., 1987, Ft. Worth Ind. Sch. Dist. Study grantee U. London, 1978. Fellow ASCD, NEA, Tex. State Tchrs. Assn., Ft. Worth Edn. Assn., Internat. Reading Assn. (hostess 1st Tex. breakfast 1969), Nat. Geog. Soc., Smithsonian Instn., Libr. of Congress, Ft. Worth Reading Assn., Nat. Coun. for Social Studies spkr. social studies symposium N.Y.C. 1970, Tex. Elem. Prins. and Suprs. Assn. (sec. 1971-72). Home: 1225 Clara St Fort Worth TX 76110-1009

MAYS, JOSEPH BARBER, JR., lawyer; b. Birmingham, Ala., Dec. 15, 1945; s. Joseph B. and Elizabeth (Tiller) M.; m. June Blackwell, June 13, 1970; 1 child, Mary-Elizabeth. BA, Tulane U., 1967; MA, Cornell U., 1969; JD, U. Ala., 1978. Bar: Ala. 1978, U.S. Ct. Appeals (5th, 4th, 6th, 11th cir.) Ala., U.S. Supreme Ct., U.S. Tax Ct. Ala. Tchr. Indian Springs Sch., Helena, Ala., 1969-75; assoc. Bradley, Arant, Rose & White, Birmingham, 1978-84, ptnr., 1984—; tchr. Birmingham Sch. Law, 1979—. Contbr. articles to profl. jours. Recipient Woodrow Wilson fellowship Woodrow Wilson Found., 1968-69. Mem. ABA, Nat. Assn. Criminal Def. Lawyers, Ala. State Bar Assn., Birmingham Bar Assn., Phi Beta Kappa. Episcopalian. Home: 3514 Country Club Rd Birmingham AL 35213-2824 Office: Bradley Arant Rose & White 2001 Park Place North, Ste 1400 Birmingham AL 35203*

MAYS, KATE S., primary education educator; b. Beaumont, Tex., May 27, 1950; d. James Alvin and Lera L. (Williams) Sartain; m. James Dominey, Apr. 20, 1973 (div. Oct. 1983); children: Newton, Tad; m. James K. Mays, June 10, 1988. BA, Sam Houston State U., 1971. Math. tchr. 7-12th grades New Caney (Tex.) Ind. Sch. Dist., 1972-73; tchr. remedial reading 3rd-6th grades Silsbee (Tex.) Ind. Sch. Dist., 1973-74; tchr. reading 7th grade, math. 9th grade and 4th grade Tyler (Tex.) Ind. Sch. Dist., 1974-78; tchr. 2d grade East Tex. Christian Acad., Tyler, 1981-82, tchr. 6th and 7th grades, 1987-88; tchr. kindergarten Knoxville (Tenn.) Christian Sch., 1988-89; tchr. 1st grade Knox County Schs., Knoxville, 1990-95, tchr. 2nd grade, 1995—. Mem. NEA, ASCD, Coun. for Exceptional Children, Tenn. Edn. Assn., Knox County Edn. Assn., Smoky Mountain Reading Coun., Smoky Mountain Math. Coun. Republican. Mem. Ch. of Christ. Home: 5529 Timbercrest Trl Knoxville TN 37909-1838 Office: Cedar Bluff Primary 705 North Cedar Bluff Rd Knoxville TN 37923

MAYS, LESTER LOWRY, broadcast executive; b. Houston, July 24, 1935; s. Lester T. and Virginia (Lowry) M.; m. Peggy Pitman, July 29, 1959; children: Kathryn Mays Johnson, Linda Mays McCaul, Mark P., Randall T. BS in Petroleum Engring., Tex. A&M U., 1959; MBA, Harvard U., 1962. Comml. recorder San Antonio; with Sta. KTTU-TV, Tucson, Sta. KOKI/KTFO-TV, Tulsa, Sta. WMPI/WJTC-TV, Mobile and Pensacola, Okla., Sta. WAWS-TV, Jacksonville, Fla., Sta. KSAS-TV, Wichita, Kans., Sta. KLRT/KASN-TV, Little Rock, Sta. WFTC-TV, Mpls., Sta. WFTC-TV, WLMT/WMTU-TV, WLMT/WMTU TV, Memphis, Sta. WXXA, Albany, Sta. WQUE-AM-FM, New Orleans, Clear Channel Sports, Des Moines, Okla. News Network, Oklahoma City, Va. News Network, Stas. KJYO and KTOK, Oklahoma City, Sta. KEBC, Oklahoma City, Sta. WELI, New Haven, Sta. WKCI-WAVZ, New Haven, Sta. KPEZ, Austin, Tex., Stas. KHYS, KALO, KBXX, KMJQ, KPRC, KSEV and KYOK, Houston and Point Arthur, Tex., KMOD & KAKC, Tulsa, KTAM & KORA, Bryan and College Station, Tex., WHAS & WAMZ, Louisville; with radio and TV broadcasting WOAI, KQXT, and KAJA, San Antonio; pres., CEO Clear Channel Comms., Inc., San Antonio; past chmn. bd. CBS Radio Affiliates Bd. Bd. dirs., trustee Tex. Rsch. Pk.; bd. dirs., mem. exec. com. United Way; chmn. United Way San Antonio and Bexar County, 1995; regent emeritus Tex. A&M U. Sys.; trustee Tex. Rsch. and Tech. Found.; mem. deve. bd. U. Tex. Health Sci. Ctr.; adv. dir. Permanent Univ. Fund Tex. Mem. Nat. Assn. Broadcasters (past chmn. joint bd.), Greater San Antonio C. of C. (past chmn.), Rotary. Home: 400 Geneseo Rd San Antonio TX

78209-6127 Office: Clear Channel Comms., Inc PO Box 659512 San Antonio TX 78265-9512*

MAZA, RICHARD KAZDIN, internist; b. Toledo, Oct. 20, 1944; s. Harry and Gertrude (Schwartz) M.; m. Nancy H. Kander, May 11, 1969; children: Stephanie Elyse, Emily Rebecca, Michael Aaron. BS, U. Toledo, 1965; MD, Ohio State U., 1969. Diplomate Am. Bd. Internal Medicine. Intern Balt. City Hosps., 1969-70, resident in internal medicine, 1971-72; with U.S. Pub. Health Svc., Kalamazoo, Mich., 1972-74; med. dir., internist Family Health Ctr., Kalamazoo, 1974-80; med. dir. INA Healthplan, Tampa Bay, Fla., 1980-81; internist Mease Health Care, Dunedin, Fla., 1982—; pres. Mease Clinic, Dunedin, 1985-86, bd. trustees; bd. dirs. Mease Hosp. Found., Morton Plant Mease Health Care, Baycare (formerly Care First). Vol. physician Clearwater Fla. Free Clinic, 1980—. Lt. comdr. USPHS, 1969-72. Johns Hopkins Hosp. fellow, 1969-72. Mem. AMA, ACP, Am. Soc. Internal Medicine, Fla. Med. Assn., Fla. Soc. Internal Medicine, Pinellas County Med. Assn. Office: 3253 N Mcmullen Booth Rd Clearwater FL 34621-2010

MAZANEC, GEORGE L., natural gas company executive; b. Chgo., May 30, 1936; s. Charles and Catherine (Traczyk) M.; m. Elsa Weiffenbach, Oct. 1, 1960; children: Robert A., John C. AB in Econs., DePauw U., 1958; MBA, Harvard U., 1960. Various positions Internorth Inc., 1964-82; exec. v.p., CFO Tex. Gas Resources Corp., Owensboro, Ky., 1982-85; CFO, v.p. fin. Duquesne Light Co., 1985-87; formerly sr. v.p. Tex. Ea. Corp.; formerly pres. TETCO; group v.p. Panhandle Ea. Corp., Houston, 1989-91, exec. v.p., 1991-93, vice chairman, 1993—; bd. dirs. Panhandle Ea. Corp., TEPPCO Ltd., Associated Electric Gas Ins. Svcs. Ltd. Mem. Am. Gas Assn. (bd. dirs.), Houston Mus. of Natural Sci. (bd. dirs.), Houston Grand Opera (bd. dirs.), Ramada Club, Houston Country Club, Old Baldy Club. Home: 302 Fall River Ct Houston TX 77024-5611 Office: Panhandle Ea Corp PO Box 1642 Houston TX 77251

MAZZARELLA, DAVID, newspaper editor; b. 1938. With AP, Lisbon, N.Y.C., Rome, 1962-70, Daily American, Rome, 1971-75, Gannett News, D.C., 1976-77, The Bridgewater, Bridgewater, N.J., 1977-83; now editor USA Today, Arlington, Va. Office: USA Today 1000 Wilson Blvd Arlington VA 22209-3901

MAZZARELLA, MARIO DOMENIC, history educator; b. Providence, May 7, 1941; s. Philip Fermino and Catherine (Luca) M.; m. Mary Kathleen Mazzarella, June 19, 1971 (div. 1983); children: Thomas Mario, Haley Kathleen. AB, Providence Coll., 1962; MA, U. R.I., 1965; PhD, Am. U., 1977. From instr. to prof. history Christopher Newport U., Newport News, Va., 1969-91, exec. asst. to pres., 1991-94, prof. history, 1994—. Del. Va. State Dem. Conv., 1984. Capt. U.S. Army, 1965-67. Grantee Nat. Endowment for Humanities, 1978, Fulbright-Hays, 1989. Mem. AAUP, Am. Hist. Assn., NAACP, Ams. for Peace Now, Amnesty Internat., Appalachian Trail Conf., Tidewater Appalachian Trail Club, Phi Alpha Theta. Democrat. Roman Catholic. Office: Christopher Newport U Dept History Newport News VA 23606

MAZZONI, BARBARA JEAN, advice nurse; b. Cumberland, Md., July 23, 1949; d. Robert Taylor and Loretta (Miller) McLaughlin; m. Robert A. Mazzoni, Feb. 17, 1979; 1 child, Michael. Diploma, Ch. Home/Hosp. Sch. Nursing, 1971; BS in Nursing, U. Md., 1976. Advice nurse Kaiser Permanente, Lutherville, Md., 1989—; clin. mgr. Greater Balt. Med. Ctr., Towson, Md., 1987-89; nurse clinician U. Md. Hosp., 1978-87. Mem. Md. State Emergency Nurses Assn. (founder; past pres. Met. Balt. chpt.). Home: 670 Post Ln Rock Hill SC 29730-6028

MBUH, REBECCA NEH, university administrator; b. Bamenda, NW, Cameroon, June 11, 1962; came to U.S., 1983; d. Isaac and Margaret M. BA, Allen U., 1987; MEd, U. S.C., 1989, PhD in Higher Edn., 1993. Grad. rsch. asst. U. S.C., Columbia, 1987-90; grad. tchg. asst. U. S.C., 1990-93; contbg. writer S.C. Black Media Group, Columbia, 1989—; dir. institutional rsch. and effectiveness Allen U., Columbia, 1993—; mem. exec. bd. S.C. Higher Edn. Assessment Network, Rock Hill Winthrop U., 1994—; chief editor It's Allen Newspaper, 1993-95. Mentor Big Bros./Big Sisters, Columbia, 1986; bd. dirs. Cmty. Focus Youth Group, Inc., Columbia, 1994. Mem. NAACP, Phi Delta Kappa, Delta Sigma Theta Sorority, Inc. Presbyterian. Home: 521 Sheridan Dr Columbia SC 29223 Office: Allen U 1530 Harden St Columbia SC 29204

MCABEE, THOMAS ALLEN, psychologist; b. Spartanburg, S.C., Mar. 31, 1949; s. Thomas Walker and Doris Lee (Gillespie) McA. Student Ga. Inst. Tech., 1967-69; BA, Furman U., 1971; MA, U. S.C., 1975, PhD, 1979. Clin. counselor Adolescent Inpatient Service, William S. Hall Psychiat. Inst., Columbia, S.C., 1971-73; counselor children's therapeutic camp Columbia Area Mental Health Center, 1974; co-dir. community problems survey Eau Claire Community Project, Columbia, 1975; asst. aging services planner Central Midlands Regional Planning Council, Columbia, 1976; instr. U. S.C., 1976; NSF intern S.C. State Legislature, 1978; research dir. S.C. Legis. Gov.'s Com. on Mental Health and Mental Retardation, Columbia, 1979-80; co-dir. TV project "Feelings Just Are," Columbia Area Mental Health Center, 1980-89, cons., 1977-79; cons. S.C. Protection and Advocacy System for Handicapped Citizens, 1980, 81, S.C. Dept. Mental Health, 1981; psychologist, S.C. Dept. Mental Retardation, 1982-93, S.C. Dept. Disabilities and Spl. Needs, 1993—; mem. deinstitutionalization task force S.C. Developmental Disabilities Council, 1979-80; mem. subcom. State Commr.'s Ad Hoc Com. to Study and Develop Work/Lodge System for S.C., S.C. Dept. Mental Health, 1979-80; mem. Media Task Force of Gov.'s Adv. Com. on Early Childhood Devel. and Edn., 1980-81; chmn. primary prevention public media com. S.C. Dept. Mental Health, 1979-81. Recipient Palmetto Pictures Photography award, 1977; NIMH fellow, 1976-77. Mem. Am. Psychol. Assn., S.C. Psychol. Assn. Home: Rivergate # 821 3900 Bentley Dr Columbia SC 29210-7980 Office: 8301 Farrow Rd Columbia SC 29203-3245

MC ADOO, DAVID JOHN, neurochemist; b. Washington, Pa., Aug. 11, 1941; s. Donald Wayne and Helen Louise (Bromely) Mc A.; m. Martha Cole Hervey, May 20, 1967; children: Catherine Lynn, Matthew David. BA in Chemistry, Lafayette Coll., 1963; PhD in Chemistry, Cornell U., 1970. Chemist U.S. Dept. Agr., Phila., 1963-64, Union Carbide, Tarrytown, N.Y., 1966-67; postdoctoral fellow Johns Hopkins U., Balt., 1970-71; sr. scientist Jet Propulsion Lab., Pasadena, Calif., 1971-73; prof. U. Tex., Galveston, 1973—. Contbr. articles to profl. jours. With U.S. Army, 1964-66. Mem. AAAS, Soc. Neurosci., Neurotrauma Soc., Am. Soc. Mass Spectrum, Sigma Xi. Democrat. Office: Univ Tex Med Br 301 University Blvd Galveston TX 77555-1069

MCADORY, JEFFREY KENT, picture editor; b. Forest, Miss., Sept. 28, 1957; s. James Travis and Grace Truman (Rushing) McA. BA in Journalism, U. So. Miss., Hattiesburg, 1979. Staff photographer/picture editor The Clarion-Ledger/Jackson Daily News, Jackson, Miss., 1979-82; staff photographer The Commercial Appeal, Memphis, 1984-89; picture editor The Commercial Appeal, 1989—. Editor: I Am a Man: Photographs of the 1968 Memphis Sanitation Strike and Dr. Martin Luther King Jr., 1993. Recipient Photographer of Yr. award Scripps Howard Newspapers, 1987; Guggenheim fellow, 1983. Mem. Nat. Press Photographers Assn. Office: The Commercial Appeal 495 Union Ave Memphis TN 38103-3242

MCAFEE, LYLE VERNON, chemistry educator; b. Harlowton, Mont., Aug. 8, 1956; s. Lyle Elwood and Florence McA. BS, Ea. Mont. Coll., Billings, 1979; PhD, Oreg. State U., 1985. Postdoctoral rsch. assoc. U. N.Mex., Albuquerque, 1985-86, Trinity U., San Antonio, 1986-88; asst. prof. chemistry The Citadel, Charleston, S.C., 1988-93, assoc. prof. chemistry, 1993—. Mem. Am. Chem. Soc., Sigma Xi, Phi Lambda Upsilon. Office: The Citadel Dept Chemistry Charleston SC 29409-0001

MCALLISTER, CHARLES JOHN, nephrologist, medical administrator; b. Bklyn., Dec. 1, 1947; s. John Anthony and Lillian Marceline McAllister; m. Diane Dolores, Aug. 22, 1970; children: Jill, Kelly, Myles. BS magna cum laude, St. Francis Coll., 1969; MD with honors, SUNY, Buffalo, 1973. Pres. Nephrology Assocs., Clearwater, Fla., 1978—; med. dir. clin. affairs Community Dialysis Ctrs. of U.S., Laguna Hills, Calif., 1992—; chief of medicine Morton Plant Hosp., Clearwater, 1991-92; v.p. med. affairs Vivra Renal Care; med. dir. VRC, Clearwater, Palm Harbor. Contbr. articles to sci. and profl. jours. Comdr. USNR, 1981-90. Republican. Roman Catholic. Home: 1001 S Keene Rd Clearwater FL 34616-4633 Office: Nephroogy Assocs 1124 Lakeview Rd Clearwater FL 34616-3524

MCALLISTER, DAVID FRANKLIN, computer science educator; b. Richmond, Va., July 2, 1941; s. John Thompson and Dorothy (Waits) McA.; 1 child, Timothy Walt. BS, U. N.C., 1963; MS, Purdue U., 1967; PhD, U. N.C., 1972. Instr. computer sci. U. N.C., Greensboro, 1967-72; asst. prof. N.C. State U., Raleigh, 1972-76, assoc. prof., 1976-83, prof., 1983—; grad. adminstr. dept. computer sci. N.C. State U., 1984-86. Author: Discrete Mathematics in Computer Science, 1977; editor: Stereo Computer Graphics, 1993. Lt. (j.g.) USNR, 1963-65. Lt. (j.g.) USNR, 1963-65. Mem. IEEE, AAUP, Assn. for Computing Machinery, Soc. Photgrammetric Instrumentation Engring., Soc. for Info. Displays. Home: 3905 Meadow Field Ln Raleigh NC 27606-4470 Office: NC State U Computer Sci Dept Raleigh NC 27695-8206

MC ALLISTER, GERALD NICHOLAS, retired bishop, clergyman; b. San Antonio, Feb. 23, 1923; s. Walter Williams and Leonora Elizabeth (Alexander) McA.; m. Helen Earle Black, Oct. 2, 1953; children—Michael Lee, David Alexander, Stephen Williams, Elizabeth. Student, U. Tex., 1939-42, Va. Theol. Sem., 1948-51; D.D. (hon.), Va. Theol. Sem., 1977. Rancher, 1946-48; ordained deacon Episcopal Ch., 1953, priest, 1954; deacon, priest Ch. of Epiphany, Raymondville, Ch. of Incarnation, Corpus Christi, St. Francis Ch., Victoria, all Tex., 1951-63; 1st canon Diocese of W. Tex., 1963-70; rector St. David's Ch., San Antonio, 1970-76; consecrated Episcopal bishop of Okla., Oklahoma City, 1977-89, ret., 1989; bishop-in-residence Episcopal Theol. Sem., Austin, Tex., 1990-93; trustee Episcopal Theol. Sem. of S.W., 1961—, adv. bd., 1974—; mem. Case Commn. Bd. for Theol. Edn., 1981-82; pres. Tex. Council Chs., 1966-68, Okla. Conf. Chs., 1980-83; bd. dirs. Presiding Bishop's Fund for World Relief, 1972-77, Ch. Hist. Soc., 1976—; chmn. Nat. and World Mission Program Group, 1973-76; mem. Structure of Ch. Standing Commn., 1979, mem. standing com. on Steward-ship/Devel., 1979-85; founder Chaplaincy Program, Bexar County Jail, 1968; mem. governing bd. nat. council Ch. of Christ, 1982-85; chmn. standing commn. on stewardship Episcopal Ch., 1983-85; v.p., trustee The Episc., Episc. Theol. Sem. of Soutwest, 1987—, chmn. bd. trustees, 1993—. Author: What We Learned from What You Said, 1973, This Fragile Earth Our Island Home, 1980. Bd. dirs. Econ. Opportunity Devel. Corp., San Antonio, 1968-69; mem. exec. com. United Way, 1968-70, vice-chmn., 1970. Served with U.S. Mcht. Marines, 1942; to 1st lt. USAAF, 1942-45. Recipient Agudas Achim Brotherhood award, 1968. Address: 507 Bluffestates San Antonio TX 78216-7930

MCALLISTER, NANCY HARDACRE, music academy administrator; b. Highland Park, Ill., Feb. 24, 1940; d. Milton Joseph Jr. and Virginia Letitia (Engels) Hardacre; m. Claude Huntley McAllister, Sept. 5, 1970. MusB, B Music Edn., Denison U., 1962; MA, U. N.C., 1967, M Music Edn., 1968. Cert. in music edn., violin performance, composition. Organist, choir dir. St. Mark's Episcopal Ch., Barrington, Ill., 1957-58; orch. dir. Adrian (Mich.) Pub. Schs., 1964-66, Luther Coll., Decorah, Iowa, 1966-67; orch. dir., tchr. New Hanover Pub. Schs., Wilmington, N.C., 1964-87; dir., owner Wilmington Acad. Music, 1987—; grad. asst. U. N.C., Chapel Hill, 1962-66; violinist Columbus (Ohio) Symphony Orch., 1961-62, Acad. Music Chamber Trio, Wilmington, 1987—; concertmaster Wilmington Symphony Orch., 1987-92; condr. Acad. Music Orch., 1987-96, Cape Fear Symphony Orch., 1996—. Composer: Sonata in A Major for violin and piano, 1961, Suite for Horn and Strings, 1961 (2d place Priz de Rome 1965). Mem. Am. String Tchrs. Assn. (sec. 1987-91), Music Educators Nat. Conv., Nat. Sch. Orch. Assn., Wilmington C. of C., P.E.O. Episcopalian. Office: Wilmington Acad Music 1635 Wellington Ave Wilmington NC 28401-7758

MCALLISTER, WALTER WILLIAMS, III, insurance company executive; b. San Antonio, Apr. 9, 1942; s. Walter Williams Jr. and Edith McAllister; m. Lida Picton Suttles, Nov. 2, 1963; children: Lida Picton, Walter Williams IV. BA in Bus. Adminstrn. cum laude, Tex. U., 1963; postgrad., Ind. U., 1971, So. Calif., 1972. Dir. Savs. & Loan Inst., 1971-74; pres. Southwestern S&L Conf., 1981-82; adv. dir. PMI Ins. Co., 1983-87; dir. Fed. Asset Disposition Assn., 1987-89, Fed. Home Loan Bank of Dallas, 1988-89; chmn. bd., CEO San Antonio Savs. Assn., First Gibraltar; chmn. bd. San Antonio Fed. Savs. Bank, Tex. Ins. Agy., Inc., San Antonio, US Delivery Corp. (formerly Security Courier Corp.), 1994—; pres. San Antonio chpt. Savs. & Loan Inst.; com. chmn. FSLIC Recapitalization Task Force, 1986-87, sub-com. on regional problems; trustee Found. for Savs. Assns.; pres. Tex. Savs. & Loan League, 1986-87; exec. com. U.S. League Savs. Inst., 1984-87. Chmn. Consumer Credit Counseling Svc., 1974, Met. YMCA, 1976-77, San Antonio River Authority, 1979-83; co-chmn. Urban Affairs Coun., 1981, Mayor's Drainage Task Force, 1981-84; treas. United Way, 1980; bd. dirs. St. Luke's Luth. Hosp., 1977-82, v.p., 1981; pres. San Antonio/Austin chpt. Young Pres.'s Orgn.; bd. dirs. Boy Scouts; chmn elect Sta. KLRN-Alamo Pub. Telecomm. Coun.; trustee St. Mary's Hall. 1st lt. U.S. Army, 1963-65. Named one of Outstanding Young Men in Am., 1973. Mem. San Antonio C. of C. (exec. com. 1979, 80, 82, 83, chmn. govt. affairs com.), San Antonio German Club (pres. 1977), San Antonio Country Club, The Argyle, Tex. Cavaliers, Order of the Alamo. Office: Tex Ins Agy Inc Ste 700 7550 IH-10 W San Antonio TX 78229-5814

MCALLISTER, WILLIAM ALEXANDER, JR., manufacturing company executive; b. Phila., Oct. 30, 1928; s. William Alexander and Evelyn Eunice (Kidd) McA.; m. Jean Carol Dungan, Apr. 22, 1950; children: Martha Jill, Margaret Louise, William Alexander III. AA, Ohio U., 1995. Salesman Del. Asbestos & Rubber Co., Phila., 1946-62; v.p. DAR Indsl. Products Inc., Phila., 1962-72, pres., 1972—; pres. DARCO So., Inc., Independence, Va., 1976—; treas. McAllister Mills, Inc., Independence, 1980—; bd. dirs. Thermofab, Inc., Toronto, Ont., Can. Chmn. bd. Twin County Regional Healthcare, Galax, Va., 1982—; bd. dirs. Wytheville (Va.) C.C., 1986-93. Mem. Fluid Sealing Assn. (past pres. and bd. dirs.). Home: 81 Sea Marsh Rd Amelia Island FL 32034 Office: DARCO So Inc 253 DARCO Dr Independence VA 24348

MCALOON, EDWARD JOSEPH, oncologist; b. Chgo., Jan. 19, 1948; s. Joseph Francis and Elizabeth (Bell) McA.; m. Pamela Ann Wolf, July 12, 1975; children: Courtney Ann, Kelly Katherine, Edward Joseph Jr. BS in Chemistry, U. Fla., 1970; MD, U. Miami, 1974. Diplomate Am. Bd. Internal Medicine, Am. Bd. Med. Oncology. Intern U. Fla., 1974-75, resident, 1975-77, fellow oncology hematology, 1977-79; oncology physician Mease Clinic, Dunedin, Fla., 1979-92, Fla. Community Cancer Ctrs., Dunedin, 1992—; asst. clin. prof. dept. of medicine U. South Fla.; chmn. cancer com. Mease Health Care, Dunedin, 1991-92. Recipient physician recognition award AMA, 1993. Roman Catholic. Home: PO Box 6765 Ozona FL 34660-6765 Office: Fla Cmty Cancer Ctrs 725 Virginia St Dunedin FL 34698-6615

MCAMIS, EDWIN EARL, lawyer; b. Cape Girardeau, Mo., Aug. 8, 1934; s. Zenas Earl and Anna Louise (Miller) McA.; m. Malin Eklof, May 31, 1959 (div. 1979); 1 child, Andrew Bruce. AB magna cum laude, Harvard U., 1956, LLB, 1959. Bar: N.Y. 1960, U.S. Dist. Ct. (so. dist.) N.Y. 1962, U.S. Supreme Ct. 1965, U.S. Ct. Appeals (2d and 3d cirs.) 1964, U.S. Ct. Appeals (D.C. cir.) 1981. Assoc. law firm Webster, Sheffield & Chrystie, N.Y.C., 1959-61, Regan Goldfarb Powell & Quinn, N.Y.C., 1962-65; assoc. law firm Lovejoy, Wasson, Lundgren & Ashton, N.Y.C., 1965-69, ptnr., 1969-77; ptnr. Skadden, Arps, Slate, Meagher & Flom, N.Y.C., 1977-90, spl. ptnr., pro bono, 1990-93; adj. prof. law Fordham U., 1984-85, Benjamin N. Cardozo Sch. Law, N.Y.C., 1985-90. Bd. dirs. Aston Magna Found. for Music, Inc., 1982-93, Cmty. Rsch. Initiative N.Y., 1988-89; mem. Lambda Legal and Edn. Fund, 1991-95. With U.S. Army, 1961-62. Mem. ABA, Selden Soc. Home: 4110 Kiaora St Coconut Grove FL 33133

MCANELLY, ROBERT D., physiatrist, researcher; b. Austin, Tex., Jan. 31, 1958; s. Robert C. and Betty J. McAnelly; m. Suzanne Marie Blickhan, Aug. 18, 1990. BS in Engring., Calif. Inst. Tech., 1979, BS in Physics, 1980; MD, U. Tex., 1987. Diplomate Am. Bd. Phys. Medicine and Rehab. Aerospace engr. Vought Corp., Dallas, 1980-82; resident U. Kans., Kansas City, 1987-91, chief resident, 1990-91; asst. prof. U. Tex. Health Scis. Ctr., San Antonio, 1991-94; dir. movement analysis lab. U. Tex., San Antonio, 1994—; staff physician, univ. liaison Warm Springs Rehab. Hosp., San Antonio, 1993-94. Contbr. chpt. Physical Medicine and Rehabilitation, 1996, Cancer Rehabilitation, 1994. Mem. Assn. Acad. Psysiatrists (mem. com. 1993—), N.Am. Soc. Gait and Clin. Movement Analysis, Paralyzed Vets. Am. Office: U Tex Health Sci Ctr 7703 Floyd Curl Dr San Antonio TX 78284-6200

MC ANINCH, ROBERT DANFORD, philosophy and government affairs educator; b. Wheeling, W.Va., May 21, 1942; s. Robert Danford and Dorothy Elizabeth (Goudy) McA.; 1 child, Robert Michael; m. Helen M. Perry, June 5, 1993. AB, West Liberty State Coll., 1969; MA, W.Va. U., 1970; MA, Morehead State U., 1975; postgrad. U. Hawaii, U. Ky. Engring. technician Hydro-Space Rsch., Inc., Rockville, Md., 1965-66; prof. govt., philosophy Prestonsburg (Ky.) Community Coll., 1970—; v.p. Calico Corner, Inc.; dir. Chase-Options, Inc., Medisin, Inc. Bd. dirs. Big Sandy Area Community Action Program, Inc., 1973-76; chmn. Floyd County Solid Waste, Inc.; mem. War on Drug Task Force. Served with AUS, 1962-65. Recipient Great Tchr. award Prestonsburg Community Coll., 1971; named Ky. col., 1977. Mem. Am. Polit. Sci. Assn., Am. Philos. Soc., Ky. Philosophy Assn., Ky. Assn. Colls. and Jr. Colls. Achievements include designed Cosmic ray chamber, artificial human circulatory system, Wilson type cloud chamber, TOTO 1, 2. Home: Bert Combs Dr Prestonsburg KY 41653

MCARDLE, SALLY SCHAFER, association executive; b. Wheeling, W.Va., June 19, 1967; d. Joseph Robert and Sarah jean (Hughes) Schafer; m. Peter Edward McArdle. BS in Journalism, Bowling Green State U., 1989. Dir. devel. PUSH Am., Charlotte, N.C., exec. dir. Bd. dirs. Cmty. Health Svcs., Charlotte, 1995—, Charlotte Pub. Rels. Soc., 1990-96; com. mem. Nat. Soc. F/R Execs. Republican. Roman Catholic. Office: PUSH Am PO Box 241226 Charlotte NC 28224

MC ARTHUR, GEORGE, journalist; b. Valdosta, Ga., July 15, 1924; s. George and Ann (Johnson) McA.; m. Eva Kim, Sept. 17, 1979. B.A. in Journalism, U. Ga., 1948. With AP, 1948-69; corr. AP, Korea, 1950-54, Paris, 1954-60; bur. chief AP, Cairo, 1960-63, Manila, 1963-65; corr. AP, Saigon, 1966-68; bur. chief AP, 1968-69; with Los Angeles Times, 1969-83; bur. chief Los Angeles Times, Saigon, 1970-75; corr. for Southeast Asia Los Angeles Times, Bangkok, 1975-79; diplomatic corr. U.S. News & World Report, 1983-85. Served with USNR, 1943-45. Recipient citation for fgn. reporting Overseas Press Club, 1973. Mem. Sigma Delta Chi. Clubs: Fgn. Corrs. (Hong Kong); Glen Arven Country (Thomasville, Ga.); River Bend Country (Gt. Falls, Va.). Address: 506 E Creek Ct Vienna VA 22180-3578

MCARTHUR, GERALD, credit union executive. Chmn. bd. dirs. Monsanto Employees Credit Union, Pensacola, Fla. Office: Monsanto Employees Credit Union 220 E Nine Mile Rd Pensacola FL 32534-3121

MCATEER, DEBORAH GRACE, travel executive; b. N.Y.C., Nov. 3, 1950; d. Edward John and Ann Marie (Cassidy) McAteer; m. William A. Helms, Feb. 5, 1948 (div. 1993); children: Elizabeth Grace, Kathleen Marie, Margaret Ann. Student, Montgomery Coll., 1969, Am. U., 1972. Sec. Polinger Co., Chevy Chase, Md., 1969-72, Loews Hotels, Washington, 1972-73; adminstr. asst. Am. Gas Assn., Arlington, Va., 1973-75; mgr. Birch Jermain Horton Bittner, Washington, 1975-77; asst. mgr. Travel Services, McLean, Va., 1977-79; founder, pres. Travel Temps, Washington, Atlanta, Phila., Miami and Ft. Lauderdale, Fla., 1979—; pres. Diversified Communications, Atlanta, 1990—; tchr. Ga. State U., Atlanta, 1996; tchr. Montgomery Coll., Rockville, Md., 1980-84, Ga. State U., 1996. Mem. Christ Child Soc., Washington, 1975—. Mem. Internat. Travel Soc. (pres. 1983-84), Am. Soc. Travel Agts., Pacific Area Travel Assn., Inst. Cert. Travel Cons. (cert., life mem.), Nat. Assn. Women Bus. Owners (chair membership com. 1983-84), Women Bus. Owners Atlanta (bd. dirs. 1991—, pres. 1994), Women's Commerce Club, PROST (v.p. 1991), Atlanta Women in Travel. Republican. Roman Catholic. Home: 7390 Twin Branch Rd NE Atlanta GA 30328-1771 Office: Travel Temps 7390 Twin Branch Rd NE Atlanta GA 30328-1771

MCAULAY, LOUISE SALZMAN, library administrator; b. Chgo., Aug. 20, 1940; d. Edward Simon and Ruth (Stern) Salzman; m. David L. McAulay, Apr. 26, 1967; children: Suzanne, Dianne. BA, U. Ill., 1962, MS, 1965. Asst. libr. Gen. Atomic/Gen. Dynamics, La Jolla, Calif., 1965-67; cataloger U. Tenn., Knoxville, 1967-69; head cataloging dept. U. Wis., Milw., 1969-70; asst. libr. Northwestern Mut. Life Ins. Co., Milw., 1983-84; dir. Marion County Libr., Marion, S.C., 1984-91, Aiken-Bamberg-Barnwell-Edgefield Regional Libr. System, Aiken, S.C., 1991-96; exec. dir. Suburban Libr System, Burr Ridge, Ill., 1996—; NEH grant adminstr. Assn. Pub. Libr. Adminstrs. S.C., 1990-92. Mem. sch. bd. Whitnall Sch. Dist., Greenfield, Wis., 1981-84; mem. bd. control Co-Op Edn. Svc., Milwaukee and Ozaukee Counties, Wis., 1983-84. Named Outstanding Libr. for S.C., S.C. Libr. Assn., 1990. Mem. ALA (libr. adminstrn. and mgmt. sect., mem.-at-large exec. bd. 1993-95, chair libr. adminstrn. and mgmt.-pub. rels.-govt. advocacy 1993-94), Assn. Pub. Libr. Adminstrs. S.C. (treas. 1990-95, pres. 1995-96). Home: 481 Old Surrey Rd Hinsdale IL 60521 Office: Aiken-Bamberg-Barnwell-Edgefield Regional Libr Sys 314 Chesterfield St S Aiken SC 29801-7117

MCAULEY, VAN ALFON, aerospace mathematician; b. Travelers Rest., S.C., Aug. 28, 1926; s. Stephen Floyd and Emily Floree (Cox) McA. BA, U. N.C., Chapel Hill, 1951; postgrad. U. Ala., Huntsville, 1956-57, 60-63. Mathematician Army Ballistic Missile Agy., Huntsville, Ala., 1956-59; physicist NASA, Marshall Center, Huntsville, 1960-61, research mathematician, 1962-70, mathematician, 1970-81. Contbr. articles to profl. jours. Served with U.S. Army, 1944-46. Recipient Apollo achievement award NASA, 1969, cost savs. award, 1973, Skylab achievement award, 1974, Outstanding Performance award, 1976. Mem. AAAS, Am. Math. Soc., N.Y. Acad. Scis., Phi Beta Kappa. Patentee for aerospace control invention; publ. method for solution of polynomial equations; devised methods for numerical solution of heat flow partial differential equations. Home: 3529 Rosedale Dr NW Huntsville AL 35810-2573

MCAUSLAND, RANDOLPH M. N., arts administrator; b. Phila., Oct. 9, 1934; s. John Randolph and Helen (Neal) McA.; m. Marilynn Kemp, July 10, 1965 (div. 1976); children: Andrew, Sean; m. Jan E. Tribbey, May 9, 1986. AB, Princeton U., 1957. Copy editor Wall Street Journal, N.Y.C., 1960-61; editor, publisher Stowe Reporter, 1961-63; consulting editor Interpub. Group Cos., 1963-67; creative dir. The Progress Group, N.Y.C., 1967-70, gen. mgr., 1970-75; dir. mktg. Billboard Pubs., N.Y.C., 1975-77; asst. to pres. Macmillan Mag., Stamford, Conn., 1977-80; editor The New Satirist, New Canaan, Conn., 1980-82; pres. Design Pubs. Inc., N.Y.C., 1983-89; dir. Design Arts Program, NEA, Washington, 1989-90; dep. chmn. programs NEA, Washington, 1990-93; writer, arts cons. Richmond, Va., 1993-94; founder, dir. Design History Found., N.Y.C., 1988-89. Author: Supermarkets: History of an American Institution, 1980; contbr. articles to profl. jours. Bd. dirs. Hand Wodkshop, Richmond, 1993-94, Richmond Choral Soc., 1994, Worldesign Found., 1994—, Fla. Friends Librs., 1995—. With U.S. Army, 1957-60. Recipient Commendation N.Y.C. Police Dept., 1971, Pres. Cup Am. Comedy Club N.Y., N.Y.C., 1974, Bronze Apple award Indsl. Design Soc., 1987. Mem. Am. Ctr. For Design (hon.), Coalition Ind. Scholars, Ivy Club. Home: 2708 NE 37th Dr Fort Lauderdale FL 33308-6327

MCBATH, DONALD LINUS, osteopathic physician; b. Chgo., May 19, 1935; s. Earl and Phyllis (Michalski) McB.; m. Ruth Southerland, Jan. 18, 1956; children: Donald L. Jr., Donna Ruth McBath Bassett, Daniel P. BA in Polit. Sci., U. Fla., 1957, BS in Pre Med., 1962; DO, Kansas City (Mo.) Coll. Osteopathy and Surgery, 1969; MA, St. Leo Coll., 1981. Diplomate Nat. Bd. Examiners; cert. family practice Am. Osteo. Bd. Family Physicians, Correctional Health Profl. Med. Med. dir. various orgns., Dade City, Fla., 1971; chief of staff Jackson Meml. Hosp., Dade City, Fla., 1969—; past chief of staff, med. dir. East Pasco Med. Ctr., Zephyrills, Fla.; med. dir. Pasco County, Hernando County Prison Sys/.Fla.; bd. dirs. East Pasco med. Ctr., Zephrillis; mem. adv. bd. Prudential Health Plan; trustee, pres., exe.c com. Fla. Osteo. Med. Assn.; sports physician Pasco Comprehensive H.S.; med. examiner FAA; Dade City grand marshall, past chmn. adv. coun.; pres., trustee East Pasco Med. Ctr. Found.; assoc. prof. clin. sci. Nova Southeastern U. Health Scis., Miami, Fla. Trustee St. Leo (Fla.) Coll.; adv. dir. First Union Nat. Bank Fla., Dade City; com. chmn. Hall of Fame Bowl, Pasco County, Fla., 1987. Recipient Pump Handle award Pasco County Health Authority, 1988, Outstanding Contbn. award H.R.S. Pasco County Pub. Health Unit, 1988, Outstanding Svc. award Fla. Interscholastic Athletic Adminstrs. Assn., 1994; named Gen. Practitioner of Yr., Fla. Acad. Gen. Practice, 1990-91. Fellow Am. Coll. Osteo. Family Physicians; mem. Am. Osteo. Assn. (nat. program conv. chmn., conv. com., exhibit adv. com., mem. ho. of dels., coun. on predoctoral edn.), Fla. Soc. Am. Coll. of Gen. Practitioners (nat. conv. com., bd. dirs. 1989-90, pres. 1991-92), Rotary (Dade City chpt. past pres., Paul Harris fellow). Roman Catholic. Home and Office: McBath Med Ctr 13925 17th St Dade City FL 33525-4603

MCBEE, FRANK WILKINS, JR., industrial manufacturing executive; b. Ridley Park, Pa., Jan. 22, 1920; s. Frank Wilkins and Ruth (Moulton) McB.; m. Sue U. Brandt, Apr. 10, 1943; children: Marilyn Moore, Robert Frank. BSME, U. Tex, 1947, MSME, 1950; PhD (hon.), St. Edward's U., Austin, 1986. Instr. to asst. prof. mech. engring. U. Tex., Austin, 1946-53, supr. mech. dept. Def. Research Lab., 1950-59; co-founder Tracor, Inc., Austin, 1955, treas., sr. v.p., 1955-67, exec. v.p., 1967-70, pres., 1970-86, chief exec. officer, 1970-88, chmn. bd., 1972-88, exec. cons., 1988-91; bd. dirs. MCorp, Dallas, Radian Corp., Austin, Rsch. Applications, Inc., Austin. Sr. active mem. adv. coun. U. Tex. Engring. Found.; mem. chancellor's coun. U. Tex.; bd. dirs. St. Edward's U.; mem. bd. dirs. Tex. Nature Conservancy, Audubon Soc., Smithsonian Instn.; chmn. adv. bd. Discovery Hall; devel. com. mem. U. Tex. Dept. Computer Scis.; hon. chmn. Allan Shivers Radiation Therapy Ctr.; fin. coun. Seton Med. Ctr., Seton N.W.Corp. Campaign; past chmn. Austin Area Rsch. Orgn.; trustee emeritus S.W. Tex. Pub. Broadcasting Coun.; sustaining mem. Friends of Archer M. Huntington Art Gallery, Austin; contbg. mem. N.Y. Met. Mus. Art; sr. advisor Tex. Lyceum; trustee Headliners Found.; chmn. Headliners Club; patron Ctr. for Battered Women, Austin; dir., chmn. bd. SW Rsch. Inst., San Antonio; past dir. Paramount Theatre for Performing Arts. Capt. USAAF, 1944-46. Recipient Benefactor award Austin Community Found., 1980, Spl. award Austin C. of C. Econ. Devel. Council, 1982, Clara Driscoll award Laguna Gloria Art Mus., 1987, Disting. Alumnus award U. Tex. Coll. Engring., 1978, Austinite of Yr. award Austin C. of C., 1986, Disting. Alumnus award U. Tex., 1988, Hist. Preservation awards 1964, 75, Walter Bremond House, 1990, Raymond Todd Civic award Austin Community Found., 1989, Allan Shivers Jr. award Bus. Com. for the Arts, Greater Austin C. of C., 1989, Brotherhood award Nat. Conf. Christians and Jews, 1981; named to Stephen F. Austin High Sch. Hall of Honor, 1981, Tex. Bus. Hall of Fame, 1990, Bus. Stateman of Yr. Harvard Bus. Sch. Club, 1990, Man of Yr. Air Force Assn. (Austin chpt.), 1977. Mem. NAE (life), NSPE, Tex. Soc. Profl. Engrs. (Outstanding Engr. of Yr. 1983), Tex. Assn. Bus., Tex. Taxpayers Assn. (bd. dirs.), Austin Heritage Soc. (life), Austin History Ctr. Assn. (founding), Nat. Trust for Hist. Preservation (sustaining mem.), Nat. Acad. Engring., Tex. Bus. Hall of Fame, U. Tex. Pres.'s Assocs., Austin C. of C., U. Tex. Ex-Students Assn. (life), 100 Club, Tau Beta Pi, Sigma Xi, Pi Tau Sigma, Austin Yacht Club (former commodore, vice chmn.). Office: 705 San Antonio St Austin TX 78701-2823

MCBRIDE, JUANITA LOYCE, oncological nurse; b. Memphis, Feb. 16, 1947; d. Albert Woodrow Sr. and Anita Mae McBride. Diploma, Bapt. Meml. Hosp. Sch. Nursing, Memphis, 1973; BS in Psychology, Belmont Coll., Nashville, 1970; BSN, U. Tenn., Memphis, 1977. RN, Tenn. Nurse educator Fgn. Mission Bd., SBC, Richmond, Va.; hospice/oncology coord. St. Francis Hosp., Memphis. Mem. Memphis Area Ostomy Group (historian). Home: 749 Loeb St Memphis TN 38111-7538

MCBRIDE, KEITH L., investment banker; b. Steubenville, Ohio, Dec. 22, 1947; s. Charles E. and Catherine T. (Woodstuff) McB.; m. Mary Therese Samodell, June 11, 1971; children: Cameron K., Evan C., Brandon C., Amber T. BA, Case Western Res. U., 1974, MS in Mgmt., 1975; postgrad., U. Pa., 1981. Mgr. mktg. Indsl. Distbns., Atlanta, 1975-76; co-owner McDonald & Co., Cleve., 1976-85; sr. v.p. Underwood Neuhaus & Co., Houston, 1985-90, sec., 1987-89, also bd. dirs.; sr. v.p. structured fin. group Oppenheimer & Co., Inc., Houston, 1993—; bd. dirs. Underwood Neuhaus Fin. Corp., Houston, Underwood Neuhaus Corp., Gateway Fin. Corp., Commodities Future Corp; mem. partnership coun. Prudential Securities Inc., 1992-93. Sgt. N.G., 1972-78. Mem. Mcpl. and Govt. Bond Club Houston, Cleve. Bond Club (bd. govs. 1982-85, pres. 1984-85), Securities Industry Assn., Pub. Securities Assn., N.Y. Stock Exch. (allied mem.). Republican. Office: Oppenheimer & Co Inc 333 Clay St Houston TX 77002-4000

MCBRIDE, KENNETH EUGENE, lawyer, title company executive; b. Abilene, Tex., June 8, 1948; s. W. Eugene and I. Jean (Wright) McB.; m. Peggy Ann Waller, Aug. 7, 1969 (div. 1980); m. Katrina Lynne Small, June 1, 1985; children: Katherine Jean, Kellie Elizabeth. BA, Central State U., 1971; JD, Oklahoma City U., 1974. Bar: Okla. 1974. Assoc. Linn, Helms & Kirk, Oklahoma City, 1974-76; city atty. City of Edmond (Okla.), 1976-77; v.p., gen. counsel Am. First Land Title Ins., Oklahoma City, 1977-81; pres. Am. First Abstract Co., Norman, Okla., 1981-90, Lawyers Title of Oklahoma City, Inc., 1990—; CEO Am. Eagle Title Ins. Co., 1994—; pres. Okla. Land Title Assn., 1987-88, LT Exch. Corp., 1996—; bd. dirs. Okla City Met. Assn. Realtors. Bd. dirs. Norman Bd. Adjustment, 1982-85, Leadership Okla., Inc., 1986-94, pres., 1989-90, 93-94. Fellow Okla. Bar Found.; mem. ABA, Okla. Bar Assn. (bd. dirs. Real Property Sect. 1992-94), Oklahoma County Bar Assn., Oklahoma City Met. Assn. Realtors, Oklahoma City Title Attys. Assn., Leadership Norman Alumni. Democrat. Presbyterian. Office: Lawyers Title Oklahoma City Inc 1141 N Robinson Ave Oklahoma City OK 73103-4929

MCBRIDE, SANDRA TEAGUE, critical care nurse; b. Corinth, Miss., Sept. 13, 1958; d. Clarence R. and Alice (Ingram) T. AAS, Shelby State Community Coll., 1983; BSN, U. North Ala., 1987. RN, Miss., Tenn. Nurse supr. Alcorn County Care, Inc., Corinth, Miss., 1985-87; staff nurse Bolivar (Tenn.) Community Hosp., 1988-90; staff nurse West Tenn. High Security Facility Tenn. Dept. of Corrections, Ripley, 1990-91; staff nurse U.S. Med. Ctr. for Fed. Prisoners, Springfield, Mo., 1991-92, Western Mental Health Inst., Bolivar, 1992—.

MCBRIDE, SHARAN SCHMIDT, English language educator; b. Houston, Dec. 26, 1944; d. Merle Aubrey and Bernice Ann (Davis) Schmidt; m. Maury Gibson, June 25 1966 (div. June 1976); m. William Henry McBride, July 20, 1991. BA, U. Houston, 1966, MA, 1968, PhD, 1992. English tchr. Spring Branch Ind. Sch. Dist., Houston, 1969—. Book reviewer of fiction/nonfiction The Houston Chronicle, 1986—. Mem. NEA, Spring Branch Edn. Assn. Democrat. Office: Northbrook Sr High Sch #1 Raider Cir Houston TX 77080

MCBRIDE, WANDA LEE, psychiatric nurse; b. Dayton, Ohio, Dec. 13, 1931; d. Owen Francis Staup and Ruby Madonna (Campbell) Inscore; m. Richard H. McBride, July 28, 1951 (div. Mar. 1966); children: Kathleen Kerns, Kimberlee Haley. Diploma, Christ Hosp. Sch., Cin., 1953; student, U. Cin., 1954-55. Cert. psychiat. mental health nurse ANA. Various healthcare positions, 1953-66; from supr. 4 acute male units to supr. outpatient dept. Cen. Ohio Psychiat. Hosp., Columbus, 1966-77; supr. hosp., head nurse urology and respiratory diseases flr. St. Anthony Hosp., Okla., 1977-83; shift supr. and coord. child program Willowview Hosp., Spencer, Okla., 1983-88; adminstrv. nursing supr. Grant Ctr. of Deering Hosp., Miami, 1988—, assessment specialist, 1995—; disabilities case mgr. Kemper Nat. Svcs., Plantation, Fla., 1996—. Mem. Gov.'s Com. for Mental Health and Retardation, 1963-66, Logan County Mental Health League, Ohio, 1963-66. Named Nurse of Yr., 1983-90. Mem. Nat. League for Nursing, Mental Health League (past pres.), Lioness Club (past pres.). Republican. Episcopalian. Home: 304 Lakeside Ct Fort Lauderdale FL 33326-2117

MCBRIDE, WILLIAM A., psychiatrist, educator; b. Shreveport, La., Apr. 2, 1921; m. Opal Fussell, Oct. 6, 1945; children: William A. III, Patti. BS, La. Poly. Inst., 1942; postgrad., La. State U., 1942-45, U. Tenn., 1960, Columbia U., 1962. Diplomate Am. Bd. Psychiatry and Neurology. Intern Willis Knighton Meml. Hosp., Shreveport, 1945; family medicine and surgery physician Willis Knighton Clinic, Shreveport, 1948-54; pvt. practice family practice Shreveport, 1949-54, pvt. practice neurology and psychiatry, 1957-87; ret., 1987; chief Mental Hygiene Clinic VA Med. Ctr., Alexandria, La., 1987-88, 88—; chief psychiatry VA Med. Ctr., Shreveport, 1990-94; clin. prof. psychiatry La. State U. Med. Ctr., Shreveport, 1994—; head dept. psychiatry Confederate Meml. Med. Ctr., Shreveport, 1957-59, part-time, 1959-63; cons. Barksdale AFB Hosp., Va. Hosp., Shreveport, Vocat. Rehab. Svc., Shreveport, others; bd. dirs. Riverside Hosp., Bossier City, La.; founders com. La. State U. Med. Ctr. Planning Coms., Brentwood Hosp., Shreveport, Riverside Hosp., Bossier City; mem. pharmacy and therapeutic com., mental health coun., clin. exec. bd., others Overton Brooks VA Med. Ctr., Shreveport; others. Contbr. articles to profl. jours. Active Cmty. Coun., Shrevport Art Guild, La. Wildlife Fedn., Our Cmty. Theatre, Shreveport Art Guild, Am. Rose Found., Shreveport Beautification Soc., St. Paul's Episcopal Ch. Lt. (j.g.) USNR, 1946-48. Fellow Am. Psychiat. Assn. (life), Am. Acad. Psychosomatic Medicine (life), So. Psychiat. Assn. (life), So. Med. Assn. (vice-councilor); mem. AMA, AAUP, La. Psychiat. Assn. (sec. 1975-77, pres. 1979-80, others), North La. Psychiat. Assn. (past pres.), Am. Group Psychotherapy Assn., La. Group Psychotherapy Assn., New Orleans Soc. for Adolescent Psychiatry, N.W. La. Area Wide Health Planning Coun., Inc., So. Assn. Geriatric Medicine, La. State Med. Soc. (del. 1976-78, 85-90, geriatric com., others), Shreveport Med. Soc. (bd. dirs. 1986-87, others), World Fedn. Mental Health, Am. Cancer Soc., Am. Heart Assn., Nat. Rehab. Assn., Inst. Religion and Health (charter), Nat. Assn. Disability Examiners, New Orleans Grad. Assembly, Nat. Coun. Alcoholism (bd. dirs., past pres.), La. Assn. Mental Health (hon. bd. dirs.), Am. Acad. Religion and Psychiatry, La. Assn. Family Physicians (former La. state v.p.), Family Rels. Coun. La., Am. Acad. Psychotherapists, United Fund (past chmn. med. divsn.), Arthritis Found., Am. Assn. Social Psychiatry, So. Assn. Geriatric Medicine, U.S. Power Squadron, Ducks Unltd., Barksdale AFB Officer's Club, Shreveport Club. Republican. Episcopalian. Office: Overton Brooks VA Med Ctr 510 E Stoner Ave Shreveport LA 71101-4243

MCBRIDE, WILLIAM MICHAEL, historian, educator; b. Cleve., Oct. 9, 1952; s. William Albert and Bernice Margaret (Wagner) McB.; m. Sally Chase Gorman, Sept. 11, 1987; children: William Gorman, Emily Woods, Kylie Chenault. BSc in Naval Architecture, U.S. Naval Acad., 1974; MSc, Va. Tech., 1985; PhD, Johns Hopkins U., 1989. Commd. ensign U.S. Navy, 1974, advanced through grades to lt., 1980, resigned, 1980; process engr., assembly div. Gen. Motors, Fremont, Calif., 1981-82; civilian naval architect Office of Naval Intelligence, Washington, 1982-83; sr. naval architect John J. McMullen Assocs., Arlington, Va., 1983-85; John M. Olin fellow Yale U., New Haven, 1989-90; prof. history James Madison U., Harrisonburg, Va., 1990-95, U.S. Naval Acad., Annapolis, Md., 1995—; mem. U.S. Commn. on Mil. History; fellow Inter-Univ. Seminar on Armed Forces and Society; mem. nat. adv. bd. Protect Historic Am. Author, editor: Good Night Officially: The Pacific War Letters of a Destroyer Sailor, 1994 (selection of Mil. Book Club); contbr. articles to Tech. and Culture (Soc. of Historians of Gilded Age and Progressive Era Biennial prize 1994, also internat. awards), Jour. of Mil. History, Jour. of Strategic Studies, others; broadcast interviews. Recipient Inaugural Edna T. Shaeffer Disting. Humanist award James Madison U., 1993, IEEE Life Mem.'s prize Soc. History of Tech., 1993, Moncado prize for excellence Soc. for Mil. History, 1993; Inaugural Rear Adm. John D. Hayes fellow Naval Hist. Ctr., 1977-78, U.S. Senator Roman Hruska fellow, 1988, Madison fellow, 1993; Hoover Presdl. scholar, 1988-89; numerous rsch. grants. Mem. Soc. for Mil. History, Soc. for History of Tech. (Robinson prize com.), History of Sci. Soc., DAV.

MCBROOM, DIANE CRAUN, accountant, horse trainer; b. Gettysburg, Pa., Jan. 2, 1962; d. Edward Kenneth and Suzanne (Catchings) Craun; m. Stephen Cushing, June 3, 1993; children: Emily, Michael Ross. AAS, Piedmont Va. C.C., 1983; BA in Environ. Sci. with distinction, U. Va., 1985, MS in Taxation with distinction, 1990. CPA, Va., Md.; notary public, Va. Rsch. asst. U. Va. Hosp., Charlottesville, 1980-86; instr. The Miller Sch. of Albemarle, Charlottesville, 1986-88; adj. prof. U. Va., Charlottesville, 1987-90; tax assoc. Deloitte & Touche, N.Y.C., 1990-91, Coopers & Lybrand, Roanoke, Va., 1991-92; acct. Owl Hollow Farm, Floyd, Va., 1992—; horse trainer Owl Hollow Farm, Floyd, 1980—. Asst. editor: (instrnl. book) Lotus 1-2-3, 1987. Leader Jr. Achievement, Roanoke, 1991-92; exec. dir. Boy Scouts Am., Charlottesville, 1986-90. Edmund P. Berkely scholar Commonwealth of Va., 1982. Mem. AICPA, Va. Soc. CPAs, U.S. Equestrian Team, U.S. Combined Tng. Assn., U.S. Dressage Fedn., Am. Horse Shows Assn. Republican. Episcopalian. Home and Office: Owl Hollow Farm RR 4 Box 212 Floyd VA 24091-9117

MCBROOM, THOMAS WILLIAM, SR., utility manager; b. Atlanta, Mar. 29, 1963; s. William Ralph and Ethel Irene (Bradley) McB.; m. Susan H.; 1 child, Thomas William Jr. B in Mech. Engring., Ga. Tech., 1985, MS in Mech. Engring., 1987; JD, Ga. State U., 1992, MBA, 1992. Bar: Ga. 1993, D.C. 1994, U.S. Tax Ct. 1993, U.S. Supreme Ct. 1996; registered profl. engr., Ga.; lic. comml. pilot and flight instr. Mfg. engr. AT & T Techs., Norcross, Ga., 1985-86; energy systems engr. Atlanta Gas Light Co., 1987-89, sales engr., 1989-90, dir. power systems markets, 1991-94, sr. corp. planning analyst, 1994-95, mgr. maj. accounts, 1995—. Mem. Leadership Coweta, 1996, Coverdell Rep. Leadership Inst., 1997. Mem. ASHRAE, Ga. Bar Assn., Ga. Soc. Profl. Engrs. (treas. 1990-91, sec. 1991-92, pres. 1992-93, Young Engr. of Yr. 1991), Newnan-Coweta C. of C. (transp. com. 1996), Toastmasters Internat. (treas. 1996—), Phi Delta Phi (exchequer 1991). Home: 15 Culpepper Way Newnan GA 30265-2217 Office: Ga Natural Gas Co PO Box 698 Newnan GA 30264

MCBRYDE, JOHN HENRY, federal judge; b. Jackson, Oct. 9, 1931; m. Betty Vinson; children: Rebecca McBryde Dippold, Jennifer, John Blake. BS in Commerce, Tex. Christian U., 1953; LLB, U. Tex., 1956. Bar: Tex. 1956, U.S. Ct. Appeals (5th cir.) 1958, U.S. Dist. Ct. (no. dist.) 1958, U.S. Dist. Ct. (ea. dist.) 1989, U.S. Supreme Ct. 1972. Assoc. Cantey, Hanger, Johnson, Scarborough & Gooch, Ft. Worth, 1956-62; ptnr. Cantey & Hanger and predecessor firm, Ft. Worth, 1962-69, McBryde, Bennett and predecessor firms, Ft. Worth, 1969-90; judge U.S. Dist. Ct. (no. dist.) Tex., Ft. Worth, 1990—. Fellow Am. Bar Found., Tex. Bar Found. (life), Am. Coll. Trial Lawyers. Office: US Dist Ct US Courthouse Rm 401 501 W 10th St Fort Worth TX 76102-3637

MCBURNEY, CHARLES WALKER, JR., lawyer; b. Orlando, Fla., June 6, 1957; s. Charles Walker McBurney and Jeane (Brown) Chappell. BA, U. Fla., 1979, JD, 1982. Bar: Fla. 1982, U.S. Dist. Ct. (mid. dist.) Fla. 1983, U.S. Ct. Appeals (11th cir.) 1984. Assoc. Mathews, Osborne, McNatt, Gobelman & Cobb, Jacksonville, Fla., 1982-84; asst. state's atty. State's Atty.'s Office, Jacksonville, 1984-90, civil atty., 1987-88, sr. trial atty., 1988-90; ptnr. Fischette, Owen & Held, Jacksonville, 1990—; dir. Serious or Habitual Juvenile Offender Program, 1986. Bd. dirs. Civic Round Table, 1988-92, treas., 1988-89, pres. 1989-90; chmn. com. congl. campaigns, Jacksonville, 1982, 84, 88; mem. Mayor's Bicentennial Constnl. Commn., 1989-91; treas. Internat. Rels. and Mktg. Devel. Commn. for Jacksonville; bd. dirs. Am. Heart Assn. N.E. Fla., 1990-92. Mem. ABA, Jacksonville Bar Assn., Nat. Dist. Atty.'s Assn., Fla. Jaycees (legal counsel 1987-88, most outstanding local pres. award 1987), Jacksonville Jaycees (pres. 1986, Jaycee of yr. 1984), Jacksonville C. of C. (bd. govs. 1987), Summit Civitans (judge adv. 1991-93, ctrl. civitan 1991—, bd. dirs. 1992—), Masons, Bull Snort Club (chmn. bd.). Republican. Presbyterian. Home: 1551 1st St S Apt 503 Jacksonville FL 32250-6350 Office: Fishette Owen & Held Gulf Life Building Ste 1916 Jacksonville FL 32207

MCBURNEY, ELIZABETH INNES, physician, educator; b. Lake Charles, La., Dec. 24, 1944; d. Theodore John and Martha (Caldwell) Innes; divorced, 1980; children: Leanne Marie, Susan Eleanor. BS, U. Southwestern La., 1965; MD, La. State U., 1969. Diplomate Am. Bd. Internal Medicine, Am. Bd. Dermatology. Intern Pensacola (Fla.) Edn. Program, 1969-70; resident in internal medicine Boston U. and Carney Hosps., 1970-72; resident in dermatology Charity Hosp., New Orleans, 1972-74; staff physician Ochsner Hosp., New Orleans, 1974-80; assoc. head of dermatology Ochsner Clinic, New Orleans, 1974-80; clin. asst. prof. Sch. Medicine La. State U., New Orleans, 1976-79, clin. assoc. prof., 1979-90, clin. prof., 1990—; clin. asst. prof. Sch. Medicine Tulane U., New Orleans, 1976-88, clin. assoc. prof., 1988-91, clin. prof., 1991—; mem. staff Northshore Regional Med. Ctr., Slidell, La., 1985—, Slidell Meml. Hosp., 1988—, chmn. CME courses, 1988—; regional dir. Mycosis Fungoides Study Group, Balt., 1974-94. Author: (with others) Dermatologic Laser Surgery, 1990; contbr. articles to profl. jours. Bd. dirs. Slidell Art Coun., 1988—, Camp Fire, New Orleans, 1979-83, Cancer Assn. New Orleans, 1978-83; juror Art in Pub. Places, Slidell, 1989. Fellow ACP; mem. Am. Soc. Dermatologic Surgery (treas. 1991-94, bd. dirs. 1988-91, pres. elect 1995-96, pres. 1996—), Am. Acad. Dermatology (bd. dirs. 1994—), Am. Bd. Laser Medicine & Surgery (bd. dirs. 1991-96), La. Dermatologic Soc. (pres. 1989-90), St. Tammary Med. Soc. (pres. 1988), Phi Kappa Phi, Alpha Omega Alpha. Office: 1051 Gause Blvd Ste 460 Slidell LA 70458-2950

MCCABE, HELEN ANN, school system administrator; b. San Angelo, Tex., Sept. 5, 1939; d. Howard Stacy and Marjorie (Ritter) Becknell; m. Douglas Truitt McCabe, June 27, 1957 (dec. June 1984); children: Michael Truitt, Douglas Terry, Howard Jerry, John Todd. BA, U. Tex. Permian Basin, 1976, MEd, 1980. Cert. elem. tchr., reading specialist, mid-mgmt., supt. Elem. tchr. Andrews ISD, Tex., 1976-84, tchr. appraiser, 1987-88, elem. prin., 1988-91, dir. pers., 1991-94; asst. supt. Snyder ISD, Tex., 1994—; dir. First Nat. Bank, Andrews, 1984-90, Andrews Sch. FCU; grad. and curriculum chairperson Leadership Andrews, 1990-92. Pres. Andrews County United Way, 1991-92, bd. dirs., 1991-94; pres. Andrews County C. of C., 1994; mem. adv. bd. Scurry County Sr. Ctr., Synder, 1994—; bd. dirs. Scurry County C. of C., 1996—. Recipient Family of Yr. award Andrews County 4-H, 1996. Mem. ASCD, Tex. Assn. Sch. Pers. Adminstrs. (dist. VI rep. 1994), Tex. Assn. Sch. Adminstrs., Tex. Assn. Gifted and Talented, West Tex. Sch. Pers. Adminstrs. Methodist. Home: PO Box 1326 Snyder TX 79550

MCCABE, ROBERT HOWARD, college president; b. Bklyn., Dec. 23, 1929; s. Joseph A. and Kathryn (Greer) McC.; m. Arva Moore Parks, June 1992. BEd, U. Miami (Fla.), 1952; MS, Appalachian State U., Boone, N.C., 1959; PhD, U. Tex., Austin, 1963; LLD (hon.), Barry U., 1986, U. Miami, 1990, Fla. Internat. U., 1990. Asst. to pres. Miami-Dade C.C. (Fla.), 1963-65, v.p., 1965-67, exec. v.p., 1969-80, pres., 1980-95 pres. Essex County Coll., Newark, 1967-69; sr. fellow League for Innovation in the C.C., 1995—; exec. com. So. Regional Edn. Bd., Atlanta, 1981-83; trustee Coll. Bd., chmn., 1988-90; vice chair The Miami Coalition for a Drug-Free Cmty., 1989-93. Recipient Disting. Svc. award Fla. Congl. Del., 1983, Spirit of Excellence award The Miami Herald, 1988, Harold W. McGraw Jr. prize in Edn., 1991, The Coll. Bd. medal, 1995; named Outstanding Grad., Coll. Edn., U. Tex., 1982, named one of the 18 Most Effective Chief Exec. Officer in Am. Higher Edn. Bowling Green U., 1988; Disting. Svc. award, Dade County, Fla., 1983; Kellogg fellow, 1962-63, MacArthur fellow John D. and Catherine T. MacArthur Found., 1992. Fellow League for Innovation in the C.C. (dir. exec. com. 1985—, disting. svc. award 1995); mem. Am. Assn. C.C. (bd. dirs. 1991—, disting. svc. award 1995), Am. Assn. Higher Edn. (dir. 1973-75), Am. Assn. for Environ. Edn. (pres. 1970-73), Am. Coun. on Edn., Commn. on Higher Edn. Issues, Higher Edn. Consortium, Am. Coun. Edn. (bd. dir. 1983-85, 92—), Southeast Fla. Edn. Consortium (chmn. bd. 1981-83). Episcopalian. Author: Man and Environment, 1971; contbr. articles to profl. jours.; editor Jour. Environ. Edn.; cons. editor Change Mag., 1980—. Home: 1601 S Miami Ave Miami FL 33129

MCCABE, THOMAS EDWARD, lawyer; b. Washington, Jan. 22, 1955; s. Edward Aeneas and Janet Isabel McCabe; m. Kelly Marie McCarthy; children: Edward Charles, Benjamin Patrick, Adrienne Marie, Therese Eileen, Luke Stevens, Nicholas Joseph. AB, Georgetown U., 1977; MBA, U. Notre Dame, 1981, JD, 1981. Bar: D.C. 1982, U.S. Dist. Ct. D.C. 1983, U.S. Ct. Appeals (D.C. cir.) 1983, Va. 1989, U.S. Supreme Ct. 1990. Law clk. U.S. Dist. Ct. Judge Hon. Charles R. Richey, Washington, 1981-82; assoc. Reavis & McGrath, Washington, 1982-84, Venable Baetjer Howard & Civiletti, Washington, 1984-85, McCarthy & Durrette, Washington, 1985-88; ptnr. McCarthy & Burke, Washington, 1988-91; sr. v.p., gen. counsel, sec. GRC Internat., Inc., Vienna, Va., 1992—. Republican. Roman Catholic. Office: GRC Internat Inc 1900 Gallows Rd Vienna VA 22182-3865

MCCABE, TOM, advertising executive; b. 1942. With Travelers Ins. Co., Valley Forge, Pa., 1963-72; owner Internat. Mktg. Group, McLean, Va., 1972-84; pres. Killion, McCabe & Assocs., Dallas, 1984—. Office: Killion McCabe & Assoc 12001 N Central Expy, STW 900 Dallas TX 75243-3700*

MCCACHREN, JO RENEE, musicologist, theorist, pianist, educator; b. Eugene, Oreg., July 22, 1955; d. Hoyt McKee and Minnie Lodina (Alexander) McC. MusB magna cum laude, U. N.C., Greensboro, 1977; MusM, U. North Tex., 1979, PhD, 1989. Piano instr. Coble's Luth. Ch., Julian, N.C., 1975-77; assoc. prof. Catawba Coll., Salisbury, N.C., 1984—, dir. freshman program, 1996—; prin. keyboardist Salisbury Symphony, 1986—; instr. Catawba Cmty. Music, 1986-90; presenter profl. cons.; grad. teaching fellow U. North Tex., 1977-84; Am. Field Svc. exch. student, Patras, Greece, 1972; del. music educators Citizen Ambassador Program of People to people Internat., Indonesia, summer, 1990, Russia, summer, 1993, Eastern Europe, 1994. Contbr.: Beethoven: The Age of Revolution and Restoration, NEH Inst., 1991, Beethoven String Quartets, NEH Summer Seminar for Coll. Tchrs., Harvard U., 1993; assoc. editor: THEORIA, 1984, 85; contbr. articles to profl. jours. Elder Presbyn. Ch., 1987-90; mem. faculty senate Catawba Coll., 1990—, sec., 1991-95, hearing com., 1991-92, vice chair, 1995-96. Named one of Outstanding Young Woman of Am., Am. Keyboard Artist, 1989; first place winner Young Artists Competition, Salisbury Symphony Orch., 1980; Reynolds scholar U. N.C., 1973-77, Piano Pedagogy Inst. scholar Columbia U., 1987; NEH grantee, 1991, 93. Mem. AAUW (sec. Salisbury 1985-87, exec. bd. 1989-91, pub. policy chmn. 1994—), N.C. Fedn. Music Clubs (parliamentarian 1992-96, dist. jr. counselor 1991-95), Coll. Music Soc., Soc. Music Theory, Salisbury Music Club (program coord. steering com. 1985-86, performer, adjudicatur 1984-85, dist. jr. counselor 1991-95), Music Theory S.E. (steering com. 1991, exec. com. 1992-95, program com. 1991-92, pres. 1996—), Pi Kappa Lambda, mu Phi Epsilon. Democrat. Presbyterian.

MCCAFFREY, KEVIN JOHN, small business owner; b. Newark, Sept. 6, 1950; s. John Joseph and Ellen (Devery) McC. Student, Spring Hill Coll., 1968-72. Editor, reporter Mobile (Ala.) Press Register, 1972-73; editor news North Dade Jour., North Miami, Fla., 1973-75; asst. mgr. Doubleday Bookshop, New Orleans, 1975-76; mgr. Waldenbooks, New Orleans, 1977-82; asst. mgr. U. New Orleans Bookstore, 1982-87, mgr., 1987-88; owner Children's Hour Books, New Orleans, 1986-94; pres. Booksellers, Inc., New Orleans, 1994—; v.p. Booksellers Pub., Inc., N.Y.C., 1988-90, also bd. dirs. Contbr. articles to profl. jours. Bd. dirs. Tennessee Williams New Orleans Lit. Festival, 1986-90, treas., 1988-90; trustee New Orleans Children's Mus., 1990—. Mem. Am. Booksellers Assn. (bd. dirs. 1986-92), Assn. Booksellers for Children (bd. dirs. 1995—), New Orleans Booksellers Assn. (charter pres. 1985-86), La. Assn. Coll. Stores (bd. dirs. 1987-88), Nat. Assn. Coll. Stores, New Orleans Chess Club (pres. 1977-78). Democrat. Home: 216 Chartres St # 3 New Orleans LA 70130-2215 Office: 3308 Magazine St New Orleans LA 70115-2411

MCCAIN, BETTY LANDON RAY (MRS. JOHN LEWIS MCCAIN), political party official, civic leader; b. Faison, N.C., Feb. 23, 1931; d. Horace Truman and Mary Howell (Perrett) Ray; student St. Marys Jr. Coll., 1948-50; AB in Music, U. N.C., Chapel Hill, 1952; MA, in Music Columbia U., 1953; m. John Lewis McCain, Nov. 19, 1955; children: Paul Pressly III, Mary Eloise. Courier, European tour guide Ednl. Travel Assocs., Plainfield, N.J., 1952-54; asst. dir. YWCA, U. N.C., Chapel Hill, 1953-55; chmn. N.C. Democratic Exec. Com., 1976-79 (1st woman); mem. Dem. Nat. Com., 1971-72, 76-79, 80-85, chmn. sustaining fund, N.C., 1981, 88-91, mem. com. on Presdl. nominations (Hunt Commn.), 1981-82, mem. rules com., 1982-85, mem. cabinet Gov. James B. Hunt, Jr., sec. dept. cultural resources 1993—; mem. Winograd Commn., 1977-78; pres. Dem. Women of N.C., 1971-72, dist. dir., 1969-72; pres. Wilson County Dem. Women, 1966-67; precinct chmn., 1972-76; del. Dem. Nat. Conv., 1972, 88; mem. Dem. Mid-term Confs., 1974, 78, mem. judicial council Dem. Nat. Com., 1985-89; dir. Carolina Tel. & Tel. Co. (now Sprint), 1981— (1st woman). Sunday sch. tchr. First Presbyn. Ch., Wilson, 1970-71, 86-88, 90-92, mem. chancel choir, 1985—, deacon, 1986-92, elder, 1992-95, chmn. fin. com., 1990-91; treas. Wilson on the Move, 1990-92; mem. Council on State Goals and Policy, 1970-72, Gov.'s Task Force on Child Advocacy, 1969-71, Wilson Human Relations Commn., 1975-78, chmn. Wilson-Greene Morehead scholarship com., 1986-89; mem. career and personal counseling service adv. bd. St.

Andrews Coll.; charter mem. Wilson Edn. Devel. Council; active Arts Council of Wilson, Inc., N.C. Art Soc., N.C. Lit. and Hist. Assn.; regional v.p., bd. dirs. N.C. Mental Health Assn.; pres., bd. dirs., legis. chmn. Wilson County Mental Health Assn.; bd. dirs. U. N.C. Ctr. Pub. TV, 1993—, Country Doctor Mus., 1968-93, Wilson United Fund; bd. govs. U. N.C., 1975-81, personnel and tenure com., 1985-91, chmn. budgets and fin. com. 1991-93; bd. regents Barium Springs Home for Children; bd. dirs., pres. N.C. Mus. History Assocs., 1982-83, membership chair, 1987-88; co-chmn. Com. to Elect Jim Hunt Gov., 1976, 80, co-chmn. senatorial campaign, 1984; mem. N.C. Adv. Budget Com., 1981-85 (1st woman); chmn. State Employees Combined Campaign N.C., 1993; bd. visitors Peace Coll., Wake Forest U. Sch. Law, U. N.C., Chapel Hill; co-chmn. fund drive Wilson Community Theatre; state bd. dirs. N.C., Am. Lung Assn., 1985-88; bd. dirs. Roanoke Island Commn. 1994—, USS/NC Battleship Commn., 1993—. Recipient state awards N.C. Heart Assn., 1967, Easter Seal Soc., 1967, Community Service award Downtown Bus. Assocs., 1977, award N.C. Jaycees, 1979, 85, Women in Govt. award N.C. and U.S. Jaycettes, 1985, Alumni Disting. Svc. award U. N.C., Chapel Hill, 1993, Flora Mac Donald Scottish Heritage award, 1995, Carpathian award N.C. Equity, 1995; named to Order of Old Well and Valkyries, U. N.C., 1952; named Dem. Woman of Yr., N.C., 1976. Mem. U. N.C. Chapel Hill Alumni Assn. (dir.), St. Marys Alumni Assn. (regional v.p.), AMA Aux. (dir., nat. vol. health services chmn., aux. liaison rep. AMA Council on Mental Health, aux. rep. Council on Vol. Health Orgns.), N.C. (pres., dir., parliamentarian) med. auxs., UDC (historian John W. Dunham chpt.), DAR, N.C. Found. for Nursing (bd. dirs. 1989-92), N.C. Agency Pub. Telecoms.(bd. dirs. 1993—), Info. Resources Mgmt. Commn. N.C. (bd. dirs. 1993—), N.C. Symphony (bd. dirs. 1993—), N.C. Soc. Internal Medicine Aux. (pres., bd. dirs. N.C. Equity), N.C. Sch. Arts (bd. trustees 1993—), Pi Beta Phi. The Book Club (pres.), Little Book Club , Wilson Country Club. Contbg. editor History of N.C. Med. Soc. Home: 1134 Woodland Dr Wilson NC 27893-2122

MCCAIN, LYNNE ANNETTE, counselor; b. St. Augustine, Fla., July 13, 1961; d. Robert George and Mildred (Cone) McC. BSN, Duke U., 1983. Cert. BCLS, RN, Ga. Nurse hemotology/oncology to nurse plastic surgery Emory Clinic, Atlanta, 1985-91, patient counselor, educator, 1991—; founder, coord. Image Reborn, 1988—. Contbr. articles to profl. jours. Founder, coord. Image Reborn Nat. Support Group, 1988—. Recipient 2d place writing award Plastic Surgery Nursing Jour. Mem. Am. Soc. Plastic and Reconstructive Surgery Nurses (co-chmn. southeastern dist. 1990, exec. bd. 1995, 96, Nurse of Yr. 1994). Office: Emory Clinic Bldg B Ste 2100 1327 Clifton Rd NE Atlanta GA 30307-1013

MC CAIN, MAURICE EDWARD, investment firm executive, former uniform company executive; b. Denver, Feb. 14, 1909; s. Thomas C. and Fannie (Burke) McC.; m. Florence Inez Snowden, Dec. 27, 1927 (dec. Apr. 1978); m. Ruth Barnhill Hinkle. Grad. high sch. With McCain Tailoring Co., 1927-32; mgr. uniform dept. Yielding's, 1932-39; with McCain Uniform Co., Inc., Birmingham, Ala., 1939-83, pres., 1954-83; pres. McCain Investment Co., Inc., 1983—; v.p., bd. dirs. Decatur (Ala.) Transit Trucklines, 1954-61; chmn. bd. dirs. Banner Uniform Co., Atlanta, Macon, 1962-78; v.p., dir. Burke Uniform Co., Houston, 1967-80. Trustee Bapt. Med. Ctrs., Birmingham, 1978-88. Served with USAAF, 1943-45. Mem. Nat. Assn. Uniform Mfrs. and Distbrs. (bd. dirs. 1965-78). Clubs: City Salesmen's (pres. 1967-68, Man of Yr. 1977), Vestavia Country, The Club. Lodges: Masons, Shriners, Rotary. Home: 3756 Locksley Dr Birmingham AL 35223-2757 Office: 2208 3rd Ave N Birmingham AL 35203-3814

MCCALEB, JOE WALLACE, lawyer; b. Nashville, Dec. 9, 1941; s. J.W. McCaleb and Majorie June (Hudson) DePriest; m. Glenda Jean Queen, June 26, 1965. BA, Union U., 1964; JD, Memphis State U., 1970; MSEL cum laude, Vt. Law Sch., 1995. Bar: Tenn. 1971, U.S. Dist. Ct. (mid. dist.) Tenn. 1977, U.S. Ct. Appeals (6th cir.) 1984, U.S. Supreme Ct. 1978. Law clk. to presiding justice Tenn. Supreme Ct., Memphis, 1970-71; staff atty. Tenn. Dept. of Pub. Health Bur. Environ. Svcs., Nashville, 1971-77; pvt. practice Hendersonville, Tenn., 1977-94, 96—. Chmn. Hendersonville Recycling Com., 1990-91. Mem. ABA, Tenn. Bar Assn., Sierra Club (chmn. local chpt. 1980-81, chmn. mid.-Tenn. group 1989-90, 93-94, chmn. water quality com., co-chmn. forestry com.), Tenn. Environ. Coun. (v.p. 1987-88, conservation adv. 1991-92), Hendersonville Exch. Club (sec. 1983, pres. 1985-86). Democrat. Home and Office: 100 Colonial Dr Hendersonville TN 37075-3205

MCCALISTER, MICHAEL EUGENE, pharmaceutical and medical product sales executive; b. Farmington, Mo., Nov. 29, 1951; s. Eugene Womack and Mary Joyce (McClure) McC.; 1 child, William Michael Eugene. BS in Natural Scis., S.E. Mo. State U., 1974; postgrad., Command and Gen. Staff Coll., 1990; PhD in Mgmt., The Union Inst., 1994; student, Air War Coll., 1996. Pharm. rep. USV Corp., 1974-76; sr. pharm. rep. Boehringer Ingelheim Corp., 1976-92; hosp. med. rep. Abbott Labs., 1993-94; dist. mgr. Syncom Pharmaceutical, 1995, zone mgr., 1996—; faculty Fla. A&M U., 1990-92. Served to Lt. Col. Mo. Army, N.G. Decorated Valley Forge Cross; recipient Eagle Scout God and Country award Boy Scouts Am. Mem. 35th Engring. Brigade Officers Assn. (pres.), 1140th Engring. Bn. Officers Assn. (pres.), Mo. N.G. Assn. (state v.p.). Home: 31177 US Hwy 19N #1001 Palm Harbor FL 34684

MC CALL, CHARLES BARNARD, health facility executive, educator; b. Memphis, Nov. 2, 1928; s. John W. and Lizette (Kimbrough) McC.; m. Carolyn Jean Rosselot, June 9, 1951; children: Linda, Kim, Betsy, Cathy. B.A., Vanderbilt U., 1950, M.D., 1953. Diplomate: Am. Bd. Internal Medicine (pulmonary diseases). Intern Vanderbilt U. Hosp., Nashville, 1953-54; clin. assoc., sr. asst. surgeon USPHS, Nat. Cancer Inst., NIH, 1954-56; sr. asst. resident in medicine U. Ala. Hosp., 1956-57, chief resident, 1958-59; fellow chest diseases Nat. Acad. Scis.-NRC, 1957-58; instr. U. Ala. Med. Sch., 1958-59; asst. prof., then assoc. prof. medicine U. Tenn. Med. Sch., 1959-69, chief pulmonary diseases, 1964-69; mem. faculty U. Tex. System, Galveston, 1969-75, prof. medicine med. br., 1971-73; assoc. prof. medicine Health Sci. Center, Southwestern Med. Sch., Dallas, 1973-75, also assoc. dean clin. programs, 1973-75; dir. Office Grants Mgmt. and Devel., 1973-75; dean, prof. medicine U. Tenn. Coll. Medicine, 1975-77, Oral Roberts U. Sch. Medicine, Tulsa, 1977-78; interim assoc. dean U. Okla. Tulsa Med. Coll., 1978-79; clin. prof. medicine U. Colo. Med. Sch., Denver, 1979-80; prof. medicine, assoc. dean U. Okla. Med. Sch., 1980-82; exec. dean and dean U. Okla. Coll. Medicine, 1982-85; v.p. patient affairs, prof. medicine U. Tex. M.D. Anderson Cancer Ctr., 1985-94; chief of staff VA Med. Center, Oklahoma City, 1980-82; cons. in field; physician cons. Fla. Cancer Network, M.D. Anderson Cancer Ctr., Orlando. Contbr. articles to med. jours. Fellow ACP, Am. Coll. Chest Physicians; mem. AMA, Am. Thoracic Soc., So. Thoracic Soc. (pres. 1968-69), Am. Fedn. Clin. Rsch., Sigma Xi, Alpha Omega Alpha. Baptist. Home: 17056 Crossgate Dr Jupiter FL 33477-5851

MCCALL, CLYDE SAMUEL, JR., petroleum engineer; b. Memphis, May 29, 1931; s. Clyde Samuel and Marguerete (Rogers) McC.; m. Patricia Dean Boswell, Sept. 5, 1989; children: Clyde Samuel III, Amy Woolsey McDonald, John Porter Boswell, Vivienne Boswell (Mrs. Robert Clayton Mays), Elise Boswell, Edith Annlouise Boswell. BS in Commerce, Washington and Lee U., 1953; BS in Petroleum Engring., U. Tex.-Austin, 1959. Registered profl. engr., Tex. Engr. to sr. petroleum engr. Amoco Prodn. Co., Andrews and Midland, Tex., 1959-69; cons. petroleum engr., Midland, Tex., 1969-73; petroleum engr. James A. Lewis Engring., Dallas, 1973-81, exec. v.p. 1974-76, pres., 1977-81; exec. v.p. McCord-Lewis Energy Svcs., Dallas, 1981-83; petroleum cons., pres. Cenesia Petroleum Corp., 1983—. With U.S. Army, 1954-56. Mem. Soc. Petroleum Engrs., Ind. Petroleum Assn. Am., Soc. Ind. Profl. Earth Scientists, Dallas Mus. Fine Arts, Kappa Alpha Order, Idlewild Club, Terpsichorean Club, Steeplechase Club, Dallas Petroleum Club, Brook Hollow Golf Club, Confriere des Chevalier du Tastavin., Commanderie de Bordeaux. Address: 2 Energy Sq 4849 Greenville Ave Ste 648 Dallas TX 75206-4124

MCCALL, DANIEL THOMPSON, JR., retired judge; b. Butler, Ala., Mar. 12, 1909; s. Daniel Thompson and Caroline Winston (Bush) McC.; m. Mary Edna Montgomery, Apr. 3, 1937; children: Mary Winston McCall Laseter, Daniel Thompson III, Nancy McCall Poynor. A.B., U. Ala., 1931, LL.B., 1933, LL.D. (hon.), 1981. Bar: Ala. 1933, U.S. Supreme Ct. 1960. Practice law Mobile, 1933-60; ptnr. Johnston, McCall & Johnston, 1943-60; cir. judge Mobile County, 1960-69; assoc. justice Supreme Ct. Ala., 1969-75; dir. Title Ins. Co., 1959-69; pres. Jr. Bar Ala., 1937. Author McCall Reprot on U. Ala. Hosps. Elected to Mobile County Bd. Sch. commrs., 1950-56, 58-60; co-founder, trustee Julius T. Wright Sch. Girls, 1953-63; dir. U. Ala. Law Sch. Found., Ala. Bar. Commrs., 1957-60; trustee U. Ala., 1965-79, nat. alumni pres., 1963, pres. Mobile chpt., 1961, Disting. Alumnus award, 1995. Lt. USNR, World War II. Named to Ala. Acad. of Hon.; recipient Dean's award, U. Ala. Law Sch., 1974, Julius T. Wright Sch. Disting. Svc. award, 1979, M.O. Beale Scroll Merit, 1979, U.M.S. Preparator Sch. Outstanding Alumnus award, 1980. Mem. ABA, Ala. Bar Assn. (grievance com. 1954-57), Mobile Bar Assn. (pres. 1953), Am. Judicature Soc., Farrah Law Soc. (charter), Cumberland Law Sch. Order Jurisprudence, Inst. Jud. Adminstrn., Nat. Trust Hist. Preservation, Hist. Mobile Preservation Soc., Navy League U.S. (co-founder, pres. Mobile chpt. 1963-65), Am. Legion, Ala. Hist. Soc., Res. Officer's Assn. U.S., 40 and 8, U. Tuscaloosa Club, Omicron Delta Kappa, Phi Delta Phi, Sigma Nu. Democrat. Episcopalian. Home: 2253 Ashland Place Ave Mobile AL 36607-3242

MCCALL, JOHN PATRICK, college president, educator; b. Yonkers, N.Y., July 17, 1927; s. Ambrose V. and Vera E. (Rush) McC.; m. Mary-Berenice Morris, June 15, 1957; children: Claire, Anne, Ambrose, Peter. AB, Holy Cross Coll., 1949; MA, Princeton U., 1952, PhD, 1955; DHL, Knox Coll., Galesburg, Ill., 1993. Instr. Georgetown U., 1955-57, asst. prof. English, 1957-62, asso. prof., 1962-66; prof. U. Cin., 1966-82, head dept. English, 1970-76, sr. v.p., provost, 1976-82; pres. Knox Coll., 1982-93, pres. emeritus and prof. emeritus English, 1993—; vol. Peace Corps, Turkmenistan, 1993-95; vis. prof. Turkmen State U., 1994-95; vice chmn. Gov.'s Task Force on Rural Ill., 1986; pres. Associated Colls. Ill., 1986-88; chmn. Associated Colls. of M.W., 1991-92; mem. edn. com. Ill. Bd. Higher Edn., 1985, 90; mem. rural libr. panel, State of Ill., 1992. Author: Chaucer Among the Gods: the Poetics of Classical Myth, 1979; contbr. articles to profl. jours.; research in medieval lit. and Chaucer's poetry. With Signal Corps, U.S. Army, 1952-54. Am. Coun. Learned Socs. fellow, 1962-63; John Simon Guggenheim Meml. Found. fellow, 1975; Fulbright grantee, 1962. Mem. Medieval Acad. Am. MLA, AAUP. Democrat. Roman Catholic. Home: 1404 3d St New Orleans LA 70130

MCCALL, MARVIN MATHER, III, internist, educator; b. Charlotte, N.C., May 5, 1931; s. Marvin Mather Jr. and Pauline Baker (Early) McC.; m. Beverly Belle Bryant, June 20, 1953; children: Erin Lee, Melanie Bryant. BS in Medicine, U. N.C., 1953, MD, 1956. Diplomate Am. Bd. Internal Medicine. Intern Grady Meml. Hosp., Atlanta, 1956-57, from jr. asst. resident to chief resident, 1959-62; pvt. practice Charlotte, 1962-67; chmn. dept. internal medicine, dir. residency program, chief cardiology Carolinas Med. Ctr., Charlotte, 1967-95; clin. prof. internal medicine U. N.C., Chapel Hill, 1972—; chmn. dept. clin. cardiology Carolinas Heart Inst.; dir. project CPR Course for Physicians. Contbr. articles to profl. jours. Bd. dirs. Charlotte Mecklenburg Health Svcs. Found., 1985-95, sec., 1985-87, pres., 1987-95; mem. rsch. rev. com. United Meth. Rsch. Found. N.C. Capt. M.C., U.S. Army, 1957-59. Fellow ACP, Am. Coll. Cardiology (gov. N.C. 1978-81); mem. AMA, Am. Heart Assn. (bd. dirs. 1978-82, med. and community program com. 1978-82), N.C. Heart Assn. (past pres., bd. dirs., med. and community program coun.). Episcopalian. Home: 4404 Nesbit Rd Monroe NC 28112-7533 Office: Carolinas Med Ctr 1000 Blythe Blvd Charlotte NC 28203-5812

MCCALL, PATRICIA ALENE, elementary and secondary music education educator; b. Cleve., June 17, 1957; d. James Henry and Ada (Johnson) McC. BM, U. Wis., 1979; MM, U. Miami, 1982. Cert. tchr., Ga. Music tchr. Bibb County Pub. Schs., Macon, Dade County Pub. Schs., Miami, Fla., 1981-85; violinist Macon (Ga.) Symphony and String Quartet, Chromatic Duo, Baronyx Trio; string coach Macon (Ga.) Symphony Youth Symphony, 1990-96; dir. Mid. Ga. String Orch., Macon, 1996—; freelance violinist, Ga.; part-time prof. Mercer U., Miami Beach, Fla., 1979-85; pvt. instr. Recipient Superior and Excellent medals Dist. II Ensemble Festival, 1986-95. Mem. NEA, NAFE, AAUW, Music Tchrs. Nat. Assn. Musicians Union, Am. Viola Soc., Music Educators Nat. Conf., Am. String Tchrs. Assn., Ga. Edn. Assn., Ga. Music Educators Assn., Nat. Sch. Orch. Assn., Macon Morning Music Club, Macon Music Tchrs. Assn.

MCCALLA, JON P., federal judge; b. 1947; m. Mary R. McCalla; children: Marjorie Katherine, Elizabeth Clair. BS, U. Tenn., 1969; JD, Vanderbilt U., 1974. Law clk. to Hon. Bailey Brown U.S. Dist. Ct. (we. dist.) Tenn., 1974-75; assoc. Armstrong, Allen, Braden, Goodman, McBride & Prewitt, 1975-80; ptnr. Armstrong, Allen, Prewitt, Gentry, Johnson & Holmes, 1980-87, Heiskell, Donelson, Bearman, Adams, Williams & Kirsch, 1987-92; fed. judge U.S. Dist. Ct. (we. dist.) Tenn., Memphis, 1992—. Mem. Fed. Bar Assn., Tenn. Bar Assn., Memphis Bar Assn. Office: US Dist Ct 167 N Main St Ste 907 Memphis TN 38103-1828*

MCCALLA, SANDRA ANN, principal; b. Shreveport, La., Nov. 6, 1939; d. Earl Gray and Dorothy Edna (Adams) McC. BS, Northwestern La. State U., 1960; MA, U. No. Colo., 1968; EdD, Tex. A&M U., 1987. With Caddo Parish Sch. Bd., Shreveport, 1960-88; asst. prin. Capt. Shreve H.S., 1977-79, prin., 1979-88, 94—; dir., dean divsn. edn. Northwestern State U., Natchitoches, La., 1988-94; instr. math. La. State U., 1979-81. Named Educator of Yr. Shreveport Times-Caddo Tchrs. Assn., 1966, La. H.S. Prin. of Yr., 1985, 87; recipient Excellence in Edn. award Capt. Shreve H.S., 1982-83; Danforth fellow, 1982-83. Mem. adv. bd. Sta. KDAQ Pub. Radio, 1985-89. Mem. Shreveport Women's Commn., 1983-89. Mem. Nat. Assn. Secondary Sch. Prins., La. Assn. Prins. (Prin. of Yr. 1985), La. Assn. Sch. Execs. (Disting. Svc. award 1983), Times-Caddo Educators Assn. (Educator of Yr. 1984), Rotary Internat., Phi Delta Kappa, Kappa Delta Pi. Democrat.

MCCALLEY, HEATHER BARNHILL, bank executive; b. Tuscaloosa, Ala., Nov. 1, 1966; d. Charles William Bd. and Doris Carolyn (Bell) Hatch; m. Winston Tilley McCalley, Jan. 28, 1995; 1 child, Carolyn Davis. AB in Econs., Duke U., 1988. Comml. officer Phila. Nat. Bank, 1988-92; asst. v.p. comml. loans 1st Comml. Bank, Birmingham, Ala., 1992-95; sch. coord. Ala. Young Bankers Assn., Birmingham, 1993-94. Asst. editor: Jr. League of Birmingham newsletter, Between the Lines, 1995-96, editor, 1996-97. Active Jr. League, Birmingham, 1992—, Phila., 1990-92; mem. bldg. team Habitat for Humanity, 1993-94, Bethel Ensley Action Task, 1994; advisor, founder Cahaba Girl Scouts Career Interest Group, Birmingham, 1993-96; mem. Duke Ann. Fund Gifts Com., 1993-95; mem. advisory com. Duke Alumni Admissions, 1990—. Named to Dean's List Duke U., 1987. Mem. Country Club Birmingham. Episcopalian. Home: 3049 Cambridge Rd Birmingham AL 35223

MC CALLUM, CHARLES ALEXANDER, university official; b. North Adams, Mass., Nov. 1, 1925; s. Charles Alexander and Mabel Helen (Cassidy) McC.; m. Alice Rebecca Lasseter, Dec. 17, 1955; children: Scott Alan, Charles Alexander III, Philip Warren, Christopher Jay. Student, Dartmouth Coll., 1943-44, Wesleyan U., Middletown, Conn., 1946-47; DMD, Tufts U., 1951; MD, Med. Coll. Ala., 1957; DSc (hon.), U. Ala., 1975, Georgetown U., 1982, Tufts U., 1988, Chulalongkorn U., Thailand, 1993, U. Medicine and Dentistry, N.J., 1993. Diplomate Am. Bd. Oral Surgery (pres. 1970). Intern oral surgery Univ. Hosp., Birmingham, Ala., 1951-52, resident oral surgery, 1952-54, intern medicine, 1957-58; mem. faculty U. Ala. Sch. Dentistry, 1956-96, prof., chmn. dept. oral surgery, 1959-65, dean sch., 1962-77; prof., dept. surgery U. Ala. Sch. of Medicine, 1965-96; v.p. for health affairs, dir. U. Ala. Med. Center, Birmingham, 1977-87; pres. U. Ala., Birmingham, 1987-93, chief sect. oral surgery Sch. Dentistry, 1958-65, 68-69; prof., 1959-93, disting. prof., 1993—; mem. nat. adv. dental rsch. coun. NIH, 1968-72; mem. Joint Commn. on Accreditation of Hosps., 1980-91, vice chmn., 1985, chmn., 1986-88. Fellow Am. Coll. Dentists, Internat. Coll. Dentists; mem. ADA (council on dental edn. 1970-76), Am. Assn. Dental Schs. (pres. 1969), Ala. Acad. of Honor, AMA, Am. Soc. Oral Surgeons (trustee 1972-73, pres. 1975-76), Southeastern Soc. Oral Surgeons (pres. 1970), Inst. of Medicine of Nat. Acad. of Scis., Assn. Acad. Health Ctrs. (chmn. bd. dirs. 1984-85), Omicron Kappa Upsilon, Phi Beta Pi. Home: 2328 Garland Dr Birmingham AL 35216-3002 Office: Univ Ala at Birmingham 107 MJH Birmingham AL 35294-2010

MCCALLUM, CORRIE, painter, printmaker; b. Sumter, S.C., Mar. 14, 1914; m. William Halsey. Cert. in fine arts, U. S.C., 1936; studies with Karl Zerbe, Boston Mus. Sch. Curator art edn. Charleston County Gibbes Art Gallery, 1960-69; instr. painting and drawing Newberry (S.C.) Coll., 1969-71; instr. painting, drawing and printmaking Coll. Charleston, 1971-79; represented by Kunstsalon Wolfsberg, Zurich, Switzerland, Sound Shore Gallery, Crossriver, N.Y.; printmaker emertitus So. Graphics Coun., 1984. One-woman shows include Concourse Gallery, State St. Bank, Boston, 1971; exhibited in group shows at Greenville Mus., Gibbes Mus. Art, 1994-95, State Mus., Columbia, S.C., 1995; co-author: A Travel Sketchbook, 1971; illustrator: Dutch Fork Farm Boy and 50 Years Along the Way, 1968. Recipient Purchase prize for drawing Mint Mus. Graphics Ann., 1964; internat. travel and study grantee Sci. Edn. Found., 1968. Mem. Coll. Art Assn. Am., Guild S.C. Artists (pres. 1961, painting award 1965), Copley Soc. (Boston). Home: 26 Archdale St Charleston SC 29401-1961

MCCALLUM, RODERICK EUGENE, microbiologist; b. Denver, Aug. 14, 1944; s. Thomas H. and Elizabeth M. (Matheson) McC.; m. Cheryl A. Ortmann, Aug. 20, 1967; children: Christopher, David. BA, U. Kans., Lawrence, 1967, PhD, 1970; postdoctoral study, U. Tex., 1970-72. Instr. U. Tex., Austin, 1970-72; asst. prof. microbiology U. Okla., Oklahoma City, 1972-75, assoc. prof., 1975-84, prof., 1984-92; prof., head dept. med. microbiology and immunology Health Sci. Ctr. Tex. A&M U., College Station, 1992—, dir. Inst. Molecular Pathogenesis and Therapeutics, 1993—; guest prof. U. Heidelberg, Germany, 1980, 85; reviewer BM-2 study sect. NIH, Bethesda, Md., 1986-90; lectr. Mid-Am. States Univ. Assn., 1988. Contbr. articles to profl. jours. Instr. STD & AIDS pub. schs., College Station, 1992—; coalition mem. Shots Across Tex., College Station, 1993—. Fellow Am. Acad. Microbiology; mem. AAAS, Am. Soc. Microbiology (editor Infection and Immunity 1992—), Internat. Endotoxin Soc., Tex. Infectious Disease Soc., Soc. Leukocyte Biology, Shock Soc. Democrat. Lutheran. Office: 407 Reynolds Bldg Tex A&M U Health Sci Ctr College Station TX 77843

MCCALLY, CHARLES RICHARD, construction company executive; b. Dallas, Oct. 5, 1958; s. Richard Holt and Elizabeth Ann (Webster) McC.; m. Shirley Elizabeth Avant, Aug. 18, 1979 (div.); children: Charles Richard Jr., Meredith Holt; m. Judy Lynn Tackett, June 24, 1993. BSME, So. Meth. U., 1981. Engr. McCally Co., Dallas, 1977-83; owner, v.p. DRT Mech. Corp., Dallas, 1983-95; owner McCally Svc. Co., Inc., Dallas, 1995—. Active Young Reps., Dallas, 1980—. Mem. NSPE, ASME, ASHRAE, Am. Soc. Plumbing Engrs. (membership com. 1983-89), Tex. Soc. Profl. Engrs., So. Meth. U. Alumni Assn., SMU Mustang Club, Bent Tree Country Club (Dallas), Oaktree Country Club (Garland, Tex.) (bd. dirs. 1986-89), Sigma Chi. Home: 4832 Sandestin Dr Dallas TX 75287 Office: McCally Svc Co Inc 2850 Congressman Ln Dallas TX 75220-1408

MCCANDLESS, CARLA JEAN, rehabilitation nurse, consultant, corporate trainer; b. Galveston, Tex., Mar. 20, 1956; d. Dana Lee and Joan Adell (Miller) Inbody; m. David McCandless III, Aug. 24, 1982. BSN, U. Tex., 1989. CRRN, CCM. Shift supr. Healthcare Rehab. Ctr., Austin, Tex., 1989-91; cons.-in-charge Crawford & Co., Austin, 1991-95; tng. specialist Crawford & Co., Atlanta, 1995—; presenter workshop: Walking Wounded, Mild TBI, 1994. Chairperson Austin Case Mgmt. Assn., 1992-93, Health-care Rehab. Ctr., 1990. Mem. Assn. Rehab. Nurses, Tex. Head Injury Assn., Tex. Nurses Assn. (newsletter editor 1990-91). Home: 4509 Wedewer Way Woodstock GA 30188 Office: Crawford & Co 5620 Glenridge Dr NE Atlanta GA 30342

MCCANN, ANDREW HUGHES, dance consultant, journalist; b. San Antonio, June 3, 1933; s. Hughes Sanford and Marie (Andrew) McC.; m. Alice Carolyn Hamlin (div.); children: Steven Andrew, Stephanie Alicia; m. Kristal Sue Fitzgerald. Registered adjudicator Nat. Dance Coun. Am. Dance dir. Dale Dance Studios, Phoenix, 1955; co-mgr. Fred Astaire Studios, Dallas, 1964, Tyler, Tex., 1965; mgr. Fred Astaire Studios, Memphis, 1968, Arthur Murray Studios, Arlington, Va., 1977; nat. dance dir. Dance World USA Studios, Inc., 1978; regional devel. coord. Md. area Fred Astaire Internat., Inc., 1980. Contbr. DanScene mag., Ballroom Dancing USA mag., Dance Action Internat. mag.; columnist Amateur Dancer. Soloist Arlington (Va.) 7th Day Adventist Ch.; judge Va. Commonwealth Games, Roanoke, 1995-96. With U.S. Navy, 1950-54, Korea. Mem. Dance Educators Am., U.S. Ind. Dance Coun., Profl. Dancers Fedn., N.Am. Dance Tchrs. Assn. Democrat. Home and Office: Amuse-a-Mood Co 128 Hancock Pl NE Leesburg VA 20176

MCCANN, JAMES TODD, marketing professional; b. San Antonio, Aug. 17, 1946; s. James E. and Clara (Cravens) McC.; m. Robin Myers; 1 child, Kimberly L. BS in Edn., S.W. Tex. State U., 1989. Cert. secondary tchr., Tex. Supr. Nat. Data Network, San Antonio, 1986-87; owner McCann Writing & Cons., Austin, 1987—; telemarketer Select Mktg., Austin, Tex., 1993—; substitute tchr. Austin Ind. Sch. Dist., 1990-93. Eidtor newsletter Communter News, 1988; contbr. articles to profl. jours. Leader Boy Scouts Am., Albuquerque, 1970. With USN, 1965-85. Mem. Ctrl. Tex. Writers Assn. (chmn. market rsch. 1987-89), Golden Key, Kappa Delta Pi, Phi Alpha Theta. Home: 1124 Rutland Dr Apt 15 Austin TX 78758-6354 Office: J McCann Writing/Cons 1124 Rutland Dr #15 Austin TX 78758

MCCANN, MARY CHERI, medical technologist, horse breeder and trainer; b. Pensacola, Fla., July 29, 1956; d. Joseph Maxwell and Cora Marie (Underwood) McC.; m. Robert Lee Spencer, July 20, 1977 (div. Nov. 1983). AA, Pensacola Jr. Coll., 1975; student, U. Md., 1977-78; BS in Biology, Troy State U., 1979; postgrad., U. Fla., 1979. Med. technologist Cape Fear Valley Med. Ctr., Fayetteville, N.C., 1981-85, Doctors Diagnostic Ctr., Fayetteville, 1985-86; sales rep. Waddell & Reed, Fayetteville, 1985-86; med. technologist Roche Biomed. Lab., Burlington, N.C., 1986-87; lab. mgr. Cumberland Hosp., Fayetteville, 1987-89, Naval Hosp., Pensacola, 1989-90, chemistry supr., 1990-96, night shift supr., 1996—. With U.S. Army, 1976-77. Mem. NAFE, Am. Soc. Clin. Pathologists (registrant), Am. Quarter Horse Assn., Japan Karate Assn., Pinto Horse Assn. Am. Republican. Avocations: horses, karate, guns, oil painting. Home: 300 Dogwood Dr Pensacola FL 32505-5323 Office: Naval Hosp Pensacola Lab US Hwy 98 Pensacola FL 32512

MCCANN, THOMAS RYLAND, JR., minister; b. Columbus, Miss., May 28, 1944; s. Thomas Ryland and Shirley Elizabeth (Jones) McC.; m. Beverly Jane Marshall, Nov. 26, 1966; children: Jane, Thomas Scott, Stephen. Student, U. Hawaii, 1962-64; BA in Polit. Sci., U. Richmond, 1966; MPA, U. N.C., Chapel Hill, 1971; MDiv, Southeastern Sem., 1985, DMin, 1990. Ordained to ministry So. Bapt. Conv., 1983. Pastor Wakefield Cen. Bapt. Ch., Zebulon, N.C., 1983-86; pastor 1st Bapt. Ch., Dunn, N.C., 1986-91, Martinsville, Va., 1991—; mem. gen. bd. Bapt. State Conv., Cary, N.C., 1990, mem. coun. on Christian life and pub. affairs, 1990, svcs.-rendered com., 1990; sec. Dunn Ministerial Assn., 1989—; v.p. Mcpl. Advisors, Inc., Virginia Beach, Va., 1975-82; county adminstr. James City County, Va., 1973-75; budget dir. Alexandria, Va., 1970-73; dep. dir. Model Cities, Winston-Salem, N.C., 1967-70; mem. strategy planning com. Baptist Gen. Assn. of Va.; bd. trustees Baptist Theological Seminary, Richmond, Va. Co-chmn. Evening in the Park Com., Dunn, 1987—; mem. City Planning Bd., Dunn, 1989—; chmn. Dunn (N.C.) Drug Abuse Task Force, 1989—; mem., chmn. City Planning Commn., Martinsville, 1993—. Mem. Pi Sigma Alpha. Office: 1st Bapt Ch 23 Starling Ave Martinsville VA 24112-2921

MCCANN, WILLIAM DONALD, journalist, public relations specialist; b. Pitts., Aug. 3, 1942; s. William Donald Sr. and Gertrude Mary (Thompson) McC.; m. Susan Toomey Frost, June 1, 1941; children: Melissa, Corinne. BA in Journalism, Pa. State U., 1964. Sci. editor Am. Edn. Publs., Middletown, Conn., 1965-67; sci. writer Cleve. Plain Dealer, 1969-74; spl. asst. Nat. Commn. on Water Quality, Washington, 1974-76; pub. info. officer Energy R&D Adminstrn., Washington, 1976-78; editor Energy Conservation Digest, Washington, 1978-80; tech. info. mgr. U.S. EPA, Washington, 1980-81; staff writer Austin (Tex.) Am.-Statesman, 1982-90; sr. writer Austin Bus. Jour., 1990-91; mgr. corp. comm. Lower Colo. River Authority, Austin, 1992—. Author (periodical) State of the River, 1993; editor (periodical) State of the River, 1995; contbr. articles to profl. jours. With USN, 1968-69. Recipient Small Bus. Writer of Yr. award Austin C. of C., 1990, Comm. Team of Yr. award Tex. Pub. Power Assn., 1996. Mem. Soc. Profl. Journalists (pres. Austin chpt. 1988-89), Internat. Assn. Bus. Communicators. Office: Lower Colo River Authority Box 220 Austin TX 78767

MCCANTS, CLYDE TAFT, minister; b. Anderson, S.C., Jan. 9, 1933; s. Edwin Clyde and Mary Rachel (Taft) McC. AB, Erskine Coll., 1954; MA, Duke U., 1956; M of Div., Erskine Theol. Sem., 1970; D of Ministry Columbia Theol. Sem., 1987. Ordained to ministry, 1970. English faculty Elon Coll., N.C., 1955-60, Erskine Coll., Due West, S.C., 1960-65; faculty English and dept. chmn. Gaston Coll., Gastonia, N.C., 1965-67; pastor Lauderdale Ch., Lexington, Va., 1970-73; dir. ch. extension Gen. Synod, Assoc. Ref. Presbyn. Ch., 1973-77; pastor First A.R. Presbyn. Ch., Burlington, N.C., 1977-78; asst. and assoc. prof. ministry Erskine Theol. Sem., 1978-82; pastor Greenville A.R.P. Ch., Greenville, S.C., 1982-93, Bethel A.R.P. Ch., Winnsboro, S.C., 1993—; trustee Erskine Coll., 1973-78; moderator Gen. Synod of Assoc. Ref. Presbyn. Ch., 1978-79; chmn. Presbyn. Coun. on Chaplains and Mil. Personnel, Washington, 1983-84; chmn. bd. Friends of Fairfield County Libr., 1995—; bd. dirs. Fairfield County Libr. Bd., 1996—. Author: The God Who Makes History, 1976, David, King of Israel, 1978; contbr. articles to profl. jours. Democrat. Home: 120 Walnut St Winnsboro SC 29180-1040 Office: PO Box 639 Winnsboro SC 29180

MCCARL, HENRY N., economics and geology educator; b. Balt., Jan. 24, 1941; s. Fred Henderson and Mary Bertha (Yaeger) McC.; m. Louise Becker Rys, June 8, 1963 (div. 1986); children: Katherine Lynne, Patricia Louise, Fredrick James; m. Mary Frederica Rhinelander, Jan. 31, 1987; 1 stepchild, Francesca C. Morgan. BS in Earth Sci., MIT, 1962; MS in Geology, Pa. State, 1964, PhD in Mineral Econ., 1969. Cert. profl. geologist. Market rsch. analyst Vulcan Materials Co., 1966-69; asst. prof. econs., asst. prof. geology U. Ala., Birmingham, 1969-72, assoc. prof. econs., 1973-77, assoc. prof. econs. and geology, 1978-91, prof. econs. and geology, 1991-95, prof. econs., edn. and geology, 1995—, dir. Ctr. for Econ. Edn., Sch. Bus., 1987—, prof. econs., edn., geology, 1995—; chief econs. div. Ala. Energy Mgmt. Bd., Montgomery, 1973-74; sr. lectr. in energy econs. Fulbright-Hays Program, Bucharest, Romania, 1977-78; mng. dir. McCarl & Assocs., Birmingham, 1969—; vis. fellow Grad. Sch. Arts and Scis., Harvard U., Cambridge, Mass., 1987. Co-author: (book) Energy Conservation Economics, 1986; Introduction to Energy Conservation, 1987; contbr. articles to profl. jours. Mem. Zoning Bd. of Adjustments, Birmingham, 1974-79, Birmingham Planning Commn., 1974-86, chmn. 1980-86; dist. commr. Boy Scouts Am., Birmingham, 1988-94. Mem. SAR (nat. trustee 1996—, nat. soc. sec. fin. com. 1995—, Birmingham chpt. pres. 1994-96, Ala. soc. pres. 1995-96), Soc. Mining Engrs. of AIME (bd. dirs. 1978-80), Am. Inst. Profl. Geologists (sect. pres. 1981-83), Mineral Econs. and Mgmt. Soc. (pres. 1992-93), Ala. Geol. Soc., Nat. Assn. Econ. Educators, St. Andrews Soc. of Mid-South (sec. 1996—). Democrat. Episcopal. Home: 1828 Mission Rd Birmingham AL 35216-2229 Summer home: 1828 Mission Rd Vestavia Hls AL 35216-2229 Office: U Ala Sch Bus Dept Econs Birmingham AL 35294-4460

MCCARLEY, ROBERT EDWARD, real estate executive, real estate appraiser; b. Memphis, Apr. 19, 1943; s. Bernie Bryant and Mildred (Clark) McC.; m. Anne Weatherford Hyatt, Oct. 23, 1971; children: Hyatt, Clark, John. BS in Bus. Adminstrn., U. Ark., 1965. Pres. McCarley & Co., West Memphis/Little Rock, Ark., 1966—; v.p. The Hathaway Group, Little Rock, 1986-89; sec.-treas. The Title Co., West Memphis, 1992—. Dir. Bank of West Memphis, Ark., 1973-86. Mem. Appraisal Inst. (regional committeeperson 1990—, pres. Ark. chpt. 1989), Country Club of Little Rock. Presbyterian. Home: 5614 Edgewood Rd Little Rock AR 72207-5314

MCCARRON, ROBERT FREDERICK, II, orthopedic surgeon; b. Hot Springs, Ark., Oct. 31, 1952; s. Robert Frederick and Irene (Shanks) McC.; m. Vicki Lynn Nichols, June 10, 1977; children: Elizabeth, Jennifer. BS, La. Tech. U., 1974; MD, U. Ark., 1977. Diplomate Am. Bd. Orthopedic Surgery. Intern U. Ark., Little Rock, 1977-78; resident Tex. Tech U., Lubbock, 1978-82, instr. dept. orthopedics, 1983-84, asst. prof., 1984-88; trauma fellow Kantonspittal, Basel, Switzerland, 1982; spine fellow St. Vincent's Hosp., Melbourne, Australia, 1983; pvt. practice orthopedic surgery Conway (Ark.) Orthopaedic and Sports Medicine Clinic, P.A., 1988—; cons. physician U. Cen. Ark., Conway, 1989; chief of surgery Conway Regional Med. Ctr., 1991-94; presenter, exhibitor in field. Contbr. articles to profl. publs. Bd. dirs. Clifton Day Care Ctr., chmn. 1994-95; pres. Conway Regional Physician Hosp. Orgn., 1996, sec., 1995. Fellow Am. Acad. Orthopedic Surgeons, Am. Orthopedic Foot and Ankle Soc.; mem. Ark. Med. Soc., Faulkner County Med. Soc., Ark. Orthopedic Soc., Conway Area C. of C., Sigma Nu. Republican. Mem. Christian Ch. (Disciples of Christ). Office: Conway Orthopaedic Clinic 525 Western Ave Ste 202 Conway AR 72032-4967

MC CARTHY, EDWARD, JR., lawyer; b. Jacksonville, Fla., Jan. 17, 1931; s. Edward and Margaret R. (Durkee) McC.; A.B., Princeton U., 1953; LL.B., U. Colo., 1956; m. Julie Beville Fant, May 18, 1962; children—Mitchell Fant, Beville Durkee, Edward III. Bar: Colo. 1956, Fla., 1959. Ptnr. firm Strang & McCarthy, Montrose, Colo., 1956-59, McCarthy, Adams & Foote, Jacksonville, 1959-68, Freeman, Richardson, Watson, Slade, McCarthy & Kelly, P.A., Jacksonville, 1968-80; sole practice law, 1980—; dir. First Guaranty Bank & Trust Co. Jacksonville. Bd. dirs., past pres. Riverside Hosp. of Jacksonville; trustee Edna Sproull Williams Found.; trustee Eunice Pitt Odom Semmes Found. Mem. Am., Fla., Jacksonville bar assns. Republican. Episcopalian. Clubs: Timuquana Country, Florida Yacht, Univ., Highlands Country (N.C.). Home: 4710 Apache Ave Jacksonville FL 32210-7612 Office: 1238 Frederica Pl Jacksonville FL 32205-7604 also: PO Box 2257 Highlands NC 28741

MC CARTHY, JOHN EDWARD, bishop; b. Houston, June 21, 1930; s. George Gaskell and Grace Veronica (O'Brien) McC. Student, St. Mary's Sem., Houston, 1949-56; M.A., St. Thomas U., Houston, 1979. Ordained priest Roman Catholic Ch., 1956; served various Houston Cath. parishes; exec. dir. Nat. Bishops Com. for Spanish speaking, 1966-68; asst. dir. Social Action Office, U.S. Cath. Conf., 1967-69; exec. dir. Tex. Cath. Conf., Houston, 1973-79; ordained aux. bishop Diocese of Galveston-Houston, 1979-86; installed third bishop of Austin, 1986—; Bd. dirs. Nat. Center for Urban Ethnic Affairs, Mexican-Am. Cultural Center, Sisters of Charity of the Incarnate Word, Houston, from 1981, St. Thomas U., Houston, from 1980. Mem. Cath. Conf. for Urban Ministry. Democrat. Office: Chancery N Congress &16th PO Box 13327 Austin TX 13327*

MCCARTHY, MARGARET R., German language and literature educator; b. Phila., Feb. 21, 1963; d. Thomas Noble and Ruth Gow (Patterson) McC.; m. Joachim Ghislain, June 17, 1996. BA, Conn. Coll., 1985; MA, U. Rochester, 1991, PhD, 1996. Prof. German Davidson (N.C.) Coll., 1995—; lectr. and presenter in field. Contbr. articles to profl. jours. Fulbright scholar, 1985-86; AATG grantee, 1989; Austrian Fed. Ministry rsch. grantee, 1991; Heinrich-Hertz-Stiftung grantee, 1991-92; DAAD rsch. grantee, 1995. Mem. MLA, Am. Assn. Tchrs. German, Coll. Lang. Assn., German Studies Assn., Women in GErman. Democrat. Office: Davidson Coll Dept German Davidson NC 28036

MCCARTHY, MARY ELIZABETH, psychologist; b. N.Y.C., Feb. 22, 1937; d. Timothy and Bridget (Hester) McC. BA in Polit. Sci./Psychology, Hunter Coll., 1964; MS in Guidance and Counseling, Fordham U., 1965; PhD in Clin. Psychology, U. Santo Tomas, 1970, MA in Philosophy, 1971; MBA in Mgmt./Mktg., Golden Gate U., 1990. Tchr., dir. guidance Notre Dame Acad., N.Y.C., 1965-66; career guidance counselor Bklyn. Coll., 1966-68; asst. prof. Ateneo de Manila U., Quezon City, Philippines, 1968-71; dir. Epoch House Friends Med. Sci. Rsch. Ctr., Inc., Balt., 1971-72; lectr. U. ILE-IFE, Nigeria, 1972-73; assoc. prof. psychology U. V.I., St. Thomas, 1973-80; program dir. Santa Rosa Geriat. Residential Ctr., Milton, Fla., 1981; dir. Regional Alcohol Rehab. Program West Tidewater Community Svcs. Bd., Suffolk, Va., 1982-83; from clin. svcs. mgr. to cmty. rels. coord. Chesapeake (Va.) Cmty. Svcs. Bd., 1983—; adj. prof. Troy State U., Norfolk, Va., 1992—, Old Dominion U., Norfolk, 1991—, Golden Gate U., Va. and N.C., 1984-91, St. Leo Coll., Va., 1983-87, Norfolk State U., 1983-86; cons. Peninsula Alcohol Svcs., Newport News, Va., 1982-83. Author: An Assessment of the Unique Needs of the Elderly Offender, 1980, When Someone You Love Goes to Prison, 1992, (with Jerome McElroy) An Assessment of the Needs of the Older Adult in the U.S. Virgin Islands, 1979; editor: Gerontology in the Virgin Islands: Readings and Research, 1978; Procs. of the First Gerontology Institute, 1979; contbr. articles to profl. jours., chpts. to books. Bd. dirs. V.I. coun. Alcoholism, 1975-79, v.p., 1976-78; bd. dirs. St. Dunstan's Episc. Ch., St. Croix, V.I., 1977, Antilles Sch., St. Thomas, 1979; sr. Companion Program Adv. Coun., 1985-89; advisor gerontology curriculum Tidewater C.C., 1985-87; mem. task force refugee resettlement, Tidewater, 1985-87; bd. dirs. Alzheimer's Disease and Related Disorders Assn., Hampton Rds., Va., 1983-90, pres. 1987-90, grantee 1985; corr. sec. Headstart Policy Coun., 1984-85, vice chair, 1987-88, bd. dirs., 1984-89; mem. long term care coun. City of Chesapeake, 1983-89; bd. dirs. Am. Cancer Soc., 1986-95, chairperson svcs. and rehab. com., 1988-89, 2d v.p., 1990-91, pres. 1992-94; mem. planning com. Chesapeake Guardianship, 1993—. Fellow USPHS, 1979-80; grantee U.S. Dept. Edn., 1976, V.I. Commn. of Aging, 1978-79, Va. Dept. Corrections, 1984, 85, Commonwealth of Va., 1985-86, State of Va. and City of Chesapeake, 1985; recipient Cert. Appreciation Philippine Guidance and Pers. Assn., 1968, Philippine Mental Health Assn., 1971, Am. Cancer Soc. for Patient Svcs., 1987, 88, 89, 90-91, 91-92, Alzheimer's Assn., 1984, 90, Peer Recognition award Chesapeake Cmty. Svcs. Bd., 1990, Vol. Yr. award Am. Cancer Soc., 1993, Star Performer award City of Chesapeake, 1993, 95, Jefferson award Outstanding Cmty. Svc., 1994. Mem. APA, Am. Marriage and Family Therapy, Nat. Assn. Mental Health Info. Officers (Pub. Rels./Writing award 1990, 91, 92, 94, 95), Bioethics Network of Southwestern Va., Chesapeake Guardianship Com. Roman Catholic. Home: 5639 Picadilly Ln Portsmouth VA 23703-1649 Office: Chesapeake Cmty Svcs Bd 1417 Battlefield Blvd N Chesapeake VA 23320-4516

MCCARTHY, MICHAEL FITZMICHAEL, business executive; b. Boston, May 5, 1944; s. Michael Fitzmichael and Stella Mary (Krajewski) McC. BA in Comm., Harvard U., 1963; MS in Psychology, U. Miami, 1972. Audio engr. Scripps-Howard Broadcasting, Palm Beach, Fla., 1972-73; field svc. engr. Xerox Corp., West Palm Beach, Fla., 1973-84; mng. broker Croton Plaza Realty, Palm Beach, 1984-88; dep. clk. of cts. Palm Beach County, West Palm Beach, 1989-93; ptnr. G2 Resources, Inc., North Palm Beach, Fla., 1993—. State vice chmn. Teen Dems. for Kennedy, West Palm Beach, 1960; del. at large Dem. Nat. Conv., Chgo., 1968. Lt. col. USAF, 1963-68. Mem. Soc. for Tech. Commn., Poinciana Club of Plam Beach, Govs. Club, Palm Beach Yacht Club, Masons, Mensa. Democrat. Anglican. Home: 5200 Poinsettia Ave #2105 West Palm Beach FL 33407 Office: G2 Resources Inc 760 US Highway 1 #206 North Palm Beach FL 33408

MCCARTHY, PATRICK A., English language educator; b. Charlottesville, Va., July 12, 1945; s. Thomas Blair and Virginia Rose (Feuerstein) McC.; children: Keely, Cailin, Brendan. BA, U. Va., 1967, MA, 1968; PhD, U. Wis., Milw., 1973. Asst. prof., English U. Miami, Coral Gables, Fla., 1976-81, assoc. prof., 1981-84, prof., 1984—; dir. grad. studies English dept. U. Miami, 1986-95; manuscript cons. various univ. presses. Author: The Riddles of Finnegans Wake, 1980, Olaf Stapledon, 1982, Ulysses: Portals of Discovery, 1990, Forests of Symbols: World, Text, and Self in Malcolm Lowry's Fiction, 1994; editor: Critical Essays on Samuel Beckett, 1986, Critical Essays on James Joyce's Finnegans Wake, 1992, Malcolm Lowry's La Mordida: A Scholarly Edition, 1996; co-editor: The Legacy of Olaf Stapledon, 1989. Travel grantee Am. Coun. Learned Socs., 1977; recipient Max Orovitz summer stipend U. Miami, 1980, 82, 85, 90, 92, gen. rsch. support grant, 1990, 92, 93. Mem. MLA, Assn. Lit. Scholars and Critics, South Atlantic MLA, Internat. James Joyce Found., Am. Coun. Irish Studies. Office: U Miami Dept English Coral Gables FL 33124

MCCARTHY, TIMOTHY J., company executive; b. 1944. With Combustion Engring., Stamford, Conn., 1959-90; CEO Mullite Co. of Am., Andersonville, Ga., 1990—. Office: Mullite Co of Am Off State Hwy 49 Andersonville GA 31711

MCCARTNEY, MITCHELL DAVID, electron microscopist, anatomist; b. Guelph, Ont., Can., Sept. 3, 1955; s. George Mitchell and Agnes Margret (Morton) McC.; m. Patricia Dianne Goodwin, Nov. 26, 1983; 1 child, Colleen Amanda. BS in Biol. Sci. with honors, U. Guelph, Ont., Can., 78; MS in Anatomy, U. Western Ont., London, Can., 1980; PhD in Anatomy, Dalhousie U., N.S., Can., 1985. Postdoctoral rsch. assoc. dept. anatomy and neurobiology U. Tenn., Memphis, 1985-87; postdoctoral rsch. assoc. dept. ophthalmology Ky. Lions Eye Rsch. Inst., U. Louisville, 1988; mgr. electron microscope rsch. unit Alcon Labs., Inc., Ft. Worth, 1988-91, asst. tech. dir. phys. sci. rsch., 1992-94, dir. biology rsch., 1994—; adj. asst. prof. dept. anatomy and cell biology U. North Tex. Health Sci. Ctr., Ft. Worth, 1993—; mem. faculty North Tex. Eye Rsch. Inst., 1993—; presenter in field. Reviewer Current Eye Rsch., 1987—, Investigative Ophthalmology and Visual Sci., 1989—; contbr. articles, papers to profl. jours. Grad. fellow Dalhousie U., 1981-85; grantee Bapt. Meml. Hosp. Clin. Innovations Fund, 1986-88. Mem. Can. Assn. Anatomists, Tex. Soc. Electron Microscopy (program chair 1994-95, pres.-elect 1995-96, pres. 1996-97), Microscopy Soc. Am., Microscopical Soc. Can., Assn. Rsch. in Vision and Ophthalmology. Office: Alcon Labs Inc 6201 South Fwy Fort Worth TX 76134-2001

MCCARTY, DAVID LEWIS, emergency physician; b. Commerce, Tex., June 20, 1950; s. Billy Edward McCarty and Laura Ruth (Parker) Simpson; m. Deborah Jean Turner,Sept. 1, 1971 (div. Mar. 1976); m. Lauralyn Eloise Phillips, June 1, 1976 (div. July 1991); children: Anthony David, Alexander Morgan. BS in Chemistry and Zoology with honors, East Tex. State U., 1968-72; MD, Baylor Coll. of Med., 1972-76. Intern U.S. Pub. Health Svc. Hosp., San Francisco, 1976-77; gen. practioner, nat. health svc. corps. U.S. Pub. Health Svc., Tishomingo, Okla., 1977-78; emergency physician Texoma Med. Ctr., Denison, Tex., 1978-81, emergency room dir., 1980-81; emergency physician Tex. Emergency Physicians P.A., Dallas, 1981-86; dir. urgent care dept. Central Okla. Med. Group, Oklahoma City, 1986-88; asst. prof. surgery, sect. of emergency med. U. Okla., Oklahoma City, 1988—, rsch dir., sect. of emergency med., 1989-90, assoc. prof., 1994—; safety com. B.B. Owen Hosp., 1984-86, Okla. Meml. Hosp., 1989-90; cons. Pediatric Emergency Trends, 1989-92, Okla. Poison Control Ctr., 1989—; vice chmn. Pharmacy & Therapeutics Com., Okla. Meml. Hosp., 1990—. Author: (with others) Annals of Emergency Medicine, 1989, Emergency Medicine Pretest Self Assessment and Review, 1990; co-author: (with Surpure) Indian Jour. Pediatrics, 1990; co-author: Emergency Medicine, 1992. Tribal chief YMCA Indian Guides, Edmond, Okla., 1989-90; adult med. dir. Mediflight Okla., 1992—. USPHS scholar, 1975-76; recipient DuPont Toxicology Tutorial award N. Poison Ctr., 1989, Moody C. Bettis award, 1976; Am. Coll. Emergency Physicians teaching fellow, 1990-91. Fellow Am. Coll. Emergency Physicians (Okla. alternate counselor 1989-93, editor newsletter 1989-90); mem. AMA, Okla. State Med. Assn. (coun. of state legis. and regulation 1988—, com. legis. 1988—, Okla. alternate del. 1990—, coun. domestic violence 1993—), Okla. Coll. Emergency Physicians (chmn. govt. affairs com.), Am. Trauma Soc. (chpt. chmn. legis. affairs com. 1990-92), s. Soc. for Acad. Emergency Medicine, Okla. County Med. Soc. (emergency care com. 1990—). Office: U Okla Health Ctr PO Box 26307 Oklahoma City OK 73126-0307

MCCARTY, DORAN CHESTER, religious organization administrator; b. Bolivar, Mo., Feb. 3, 1931; s. Bartie Lee and Donta Marian (Russell) McC.; m. Gloria Jean Laffoon, June 14, 1952; children: Gaye, Risë, Marletta, Leslie. AA, Southwest Bapt. Coll., 1950; AB, William Jewell Coll., 1952; BD, So. Bapt. Theol. Sem, 1956, PhD, 1963. Pastor 1st Bapt. Ch., Switz City, Ind., 1956-62, Pleasant Hill, Mo., 1962-65; pastor Susquehanna Bapt. Ch., Independence, Mo., 1965-67; prof. Midwestern Bapt. Theol. Sem., Kansas City, Mo., 1967-81, Golden Gate Bapt. Theol. Sem., Mill Valley, Calif., 1981-87; coord. Northeastern Bapt. Sch. Ministry, N.Y.C., 1987-94; exec. dir. Sem. Ext., Nashville, 1988—; cons. Bapt. Home Mission Bd., 1981—; assoc. dean So. Bapt. Theol. Sem., Louisville, 1989. Author: Rightly Dividing the Word, 1973, Teilhard de Chardin, 1976, The Supervision of Ministry Students, 1978, The Supervision of Mission Personnel, 1983, The Inner Heart of Ministry, 1985, Working With People, 1987, Leading the Small Church, 1991, Supervision: Developing and Directing People on Mission, 1994; editor: Key Resources, 5 vols., Broadman Leadership Series, 16 vols., The Practice of Ministry: A Sourcebook, 1995. Recipient Life Service award Southwest Bapt. U., Bolivar, 1973, William Jewell Coll. Achievement citation, 1987. Mem. Assn. for Theol. Field Edn. (chairperson 1979-81), Inst. Theol. Reflection (exec. dir. 1978-86), Fellowship In Service Guidance Dirs. (pres. 1986-87, Lewis Newman award 1988). Home: Sem Ext 116 Del Lago Ln Saint Augustine FL 32084

MCCARTY, JENNIFER LEWIS, fraternal organization administrator; b. Peru, Ind., Dec. 31, 1958; d. John Vincent and Joyce Lee (Bradley) Lewis; m. Timothy Paul McCarty, Sept. 29, 1984; children: John maxwell, Jacob Morris. BS, U. Ill., Urbana, 1982. Case worker Devel. Svcs. Ctr., Champaign, 1982-83; devel. assoc. U. Ill. Found., Champaign, 1983-86; asst. dir. annual giving Kalamazoo Coll., 1986-87; dir. alumni rels. Nazareth Coll., Kalamazoo, 1987-88; asst. dir. alumni rels. Ind. U. Alumni Assn., Indpls., 1988-90; dir. planning and asst. to exec. dir. Ind. U. Alumni Assn., Bloomington, 1990-94; dir. alumni rels. Ga. State U., Atlanta, 1994—. Mem. Jr. League Kalamazoo, 1987-93; mem. spl. events com. Jerusalem House, Atlanta, 1994—, co-chair publs. com., 1994—; vol. Grady Hosp., Atlanta, 1994—. Mem. U. Ill. Alumni Assn. (Loyalty award 1990), Commerce Club. Office: Ga State U Office Alumni Rels University Plz Atlanta GA 30303-3083

MCCARTY, LISA ANN, elementary and early childhood educator; b. Wichita, Kans., July 27, 1963; d. James Harold and Sharen Adele (Motzner) McC. BS in Edn. cum laude, Concordia Tchrs. Coll., Seward, Nebr., 1988. Cert. tchr. Ala., Tenn., La., Miss. 4th grade tchr., band dir. Trinity Luth Sch., Faribault, Minn., 1988-89; kindergarten tchr., band dir. St. Paul Luth Sch., Harlingen, Tex., 1989-90; kindergarten tchr., band dir., extended care supr. Concordia Luth. Sch., Harlingen, 1990-93; kindergarten tchr., extended care supr. Believer's Life Christian Acad., Harvey, La., 1993-94; kindergarten tchr. Valley Fellowship Christian Acad., Huntsville, Ala., 1995; substitute tchr. Huntsville City Schs., 1994-95, Madison County and Huntsville City Schs., 1995; cert. permanent substitute tchr. Madison Crossroads Sch., 1995-96, Chapman Elem. Sch., Madison, Ala., 1996. Author: (poetry) The Secret Place, 1995. Mem. Valley Fellowship Sidewalk Sunday Sch., Huntsville, Ala. Mem. ASCD. Republican. Home: 693 Crestview Dr Madison AL 35758

MC CARTY, RAYMOND M., lawyer, poet; b. Council Bluffs, Iowa, July 27, 1908; s. Cecil and Eva Frances (Wilson) M.; student S.W. Mo. State Tchrs. Coll., 1931-33; LL.B., So. Law U., Memphis, 1948, Memphis State U., 1967; m. Margaret Esther Burton, Mar. 23, 1942 (div. Mar. 31, 1995). Chief clk. State Social Security Commn., Springfield, Mo., 1937-39; admitted to Tenn. bar 1948; with U.S. Army C.E., Memphis, 1939-72, chief planning and control br. Real Estate div., 1953-72; pvt. practice law, Memphis, 1972-90 . Served with AUS, 1942-43. Recipient Countess d'Esternaux Gold medal award for poetry, 1950. Mem. Poetry Soc. Tenn. (hon. mem., organizer 1953, 1st pres., poet laureate 1977-78), World Poetry Soc. Intercontinental (Disting. citation for Poetry 1970, honoree Mid-South Poetry Festival 1983), Avalon World Arts Acad. (hon.), Ala. Writers Conclave, Nat. Fedn. State Poetry Socs., Acad. Am. Poets, Ala. State Poetry Soc., Am. Legion, Tenn. Bar Assn., Fed. Bar Assn. (sec. Memphis chpt. 1971-72), Nat. Assn. Ret. Fed. Employees. Baptist (deacon, chmn. deacons 1965-66). Author: Harp in a Strange Land, 1973; Trumpet in the Twilight of Time, 1981; The Wandering Jew, 1984; contbr. poems to profl. jours. and poetry mags. Home and Office: 1247 Colonial Rd Memphis TN 38117-6159

MCCARY, ANNE MARGARET, trauma nurse, medical case management service professional, nurse practitioner; b. Anniston, Ala., Sept. 26, 1967; d. Elvin Columbus and Margaret Pauline (Waters) McC. BSN, Birmingham So. Coll., 1989; MSN, U. Ala., Birmingham, 1991, 95. RN, Ala.; CEN; cert. FNP, ANCC; cert. case mgr., ins. rehab. specialist. Staff nurse AMI Brookwood Med. Ctr., Birmingham, 1989-90, preceptor, 1990-91, clin. nurse specialist, 1992-94; clin. nurse specialist U. Ala. Hosp., Birmingham, 1992-94; case mgr. Directions Mgmt. Svcs. Inc., 1994-95; nurse practitioner dept. rehab. medicine U. Ala. Sch. Medicine, Birmingham, 1995—. Mem. ANA, Emergency Nurses Assn., Am. Assn. Spinal Cord Injury Nurses, Sigma Theta Tau. Episcopalian. Home: 411 Skyview Dr Apt A Birmingham AL 35209-3037 Office: 1717 6th Ave N Birmingham AL 35203-2014

MCCASKEY, NANCY ANN, English language educator; b. Gulfport, Miss., July 26, 1963; d. Joe Mack and Virginia Ann Hancock; m. Thomas Carl McCaskey, June 14, 1986. BA in English, Miss. State U., 1985; MA in Lit., Fla. State U., 1996. Various positions State of Fla., Tallahassee, 1988-92; asst. to homeless coord. Fla. Dept. Edn., Tallahassee, 1992-94; entrepreneur Tallahassee, 1995-96; dir. ops. Active Images, Tallahassee, 1996—; tchg. intern Tallahassee C.C., 1994. Sec. Big Bend Bird Club, Tallahassee, 1990-92, United Meth. Women, Tallahassee, 1994; mem. Tallahassee Jaycees, 1991-92, Tallycomm, Tallahassee, 1993—. Mem. MLA, Nat. Coun. Tchrs. English, Sigma Tau Delta. Home: 925 E Magnolia Dr #K-3 Tallahassee FL 32301

MCCASKILL, BARBARA ANN, African American literature educator; b. Ft. Dix, N.J., Sept. 14, 1960; d. John Lansdon and Inez (Owens) McC. PhD in English, Emory U., 1988. Grad. asst. and composition tutor Emory U., Atlanta, 1983-84, teaching asst. dept. English, 1984-87; lectr. English U. Albany, 1988-89, asst. prof. English dept., 1989-92; asst. prof. English U. Ga., Athens, 1992—; participant various confs.; founding co-dir. Womanist Studies Consortium. Editor: (with Suzanne Miller) Multicultural Literature and Literacies: Making Space for Difference, 1993; founding co-editor Womanist Theory and Rsch.; adv. editor Langston Hughes Rev.; editor Spl. Focus: Women Writers of Caribbean for Thirteenth Moon: A Feminist Mag.; contbr. articles and book revs. to profl. jours., chpts. to books. Ford Found. seminar fellow, 1991, Lilly Found. fellow, 1993; Schomburg Ctr. scholar, 1992. Fellow AAUW; mem. MLA, Coll. Lang. Assn., Am. Lit. Assn., Soc. for Study of the Multi-Ethnic Lit. of U.S., Assn. for Study of Afro-Am. Life and History, Middle Atlantic Writers Assn. Office: University of Georgia Park Hall # 343 Athens GA 30602

MCCASKILL, JAMES H., secondary education educator, consultant; b. Pinehurst, N.C., May 18, 1937; s. J. Hubert and Neva Louise (Carter) McC. PhB, Wayne State U., 1967; MA, U. N.C., 1968. Cert. secondary tchr., administr., Va. Staff mem. Congressman Charles B. Deane, Washington, 1955-57; various Arlington (Va.) Pub. Schs., 1968—; mem. Vocat. Gender Equity Proposal review com. Va. Dept. Edn., 1990; cons. European Inst. Tech., Verona, Italy, 1988—. Pres. Arlington Civic Fedn., 1978, 79. With U.S. Army, 1957-64. Named Citizen of the Yr. Washington Star (Arlington), 1979. Mem. NEA (Internat. Rels. Com. 1976-77), Va. Edn. Assn., Arlington Edn. Assn. (pres. 1972), Coun. Exceptional Children, Kiwanis (pres. South Arlington chpt.), Phi Delta Kappa. Office: Arlington Career Ctr 816 S Walter Reed Dr Arlington VA 22204-2376

MCCASLIN, F. CATHERINE, consulting sociologist; b. Chattanooga, Feb. 21, 1947; d. John Jacob and Elizabeth Dorothy (Johnson) McC. AB, Hollins Coll., Roanoke, Va., 1969; MA, Ga. State U., 1972; PhD, UCLA, 1979. Assoc. dir. Ga. Narcotics Treatment Program, Atlanta, 1972-73; research assoc., dir. research Health Care Delivery Services, Inc., Los Angeles, 1974-76; sr. survey analyst Kaiser Found. Health Plan, Los Angeles, 1978-80; program officer The Robert Wood Johnson Found., Princeton, 1980-84; faculty U. Pa. Sch. Medicine, Phila., 1984-86; ptnr. Schuhmacher & McCaslin Assocs., Phila., 1986—; exec. dir. The H.F. Lenfest Found., Pottstown, Pa., 1988-89; dir. rsch. Beaufort (S.C.) County Sch. Dist., 1992—; adj. faculty sociology U. S.C., Beaufort, 1992—; mem. adv. bd. Nat. Childhood Asthma Project, NHBLI, Washington, 1982-84; adv. com. mem. Statewide Adolescent Pregnancy, New Brunswick, 1981-84; trainee NIH, 1973-79; cons. in field. Mem. editorial bd. Jour. Health & Social Behavior, 1988—; editor Med. Sociology newsletter, 1984—; contbr. articles to profl. jours. Fellow NIMH, 1975; grantee Spl. Action Office for Drug Abuse Prevention, 1972, Robert Wood Johnson Found., 1984. Mem. Am. Sociol. Assn. (nat. council med. sociology sect. 1984—). Am. Pub. Health Assn., Sociologists for Women in Soc. Democrat. Episcopalian. Home: Mossy Oaks Rd Ste K-1 Beaufort SC 29902 Office: Beaufort County Sch Dist 1300 King St Beaufort SC 29902-4936

MCCAUGHRIN, WILLIAM CASS, health management educator; b. Detroit, Mar. 16, 1948; s. Harold William John and Madelyn Helen (Widlaski) McC.; m. Carol Ann Oldenburg, June 20, 1981 (div. July 1983). AB, U. Mich., 1970, MPH, 1979, PhD, 1991; MS in Edn., U. Pa., 1972. English and journalism instr. Abington (Pa.) High Sch., 1972-77; dir. membership affairs Greater Detroit (Mich.) Area Health Coun., 1979-84; health edn. specialist Oakwood Hosp., Dearborn, Mich., 1984-85; occupational health svcs. mgr. Heritage Hosp., Taylor, Mich., 1986; teaching asst. dept. psychology U. Mich., 1988, 1989; instr. dept. orgnl. behavior and human resources mgmt. Sch. Bus. Adminstrn., U. Mich., 1988-89; teaching asst. dept. health svcs.

mgmt. and policy Sch. Pub. Health, U. Mich., 1989-90; asst. prof. dept. health care adminstrn. Trinity Univ., San Antonio, 1991—; exec. com. faculty devel. com. Trinity U., 1992—, faculty search com. dept. health care adminstrn., 1992—, mem. faculty senate, 1996—, budget com., 1995—; vis. scholar Inst. for Social Rsch., U. Mich., 1992-95; bd. dirs. Pub. Forum and Ctr. for Health Policy, San Antonio, 1992—; bd. mem. Incarnate Word Motherhouse and Retirement Cmty., San Antonio, 1993—; presenter in field. Ad hoc reviewer Acad. of Mgmt. Jour., 1992—, Hosp. and Health Svcs. Adminstrn., 1992—; contbr. articles to profl. jours. Mem. friends com. Mus. of Art, U. Mich., 1979-85. Recipient Faculty Publ. of the Yr. award Am. Acad. Med. Adminstrs., 1992. Mem. APHA (program planning chair Med. Care Sect. 1993—), Assn. for Univ. Programs in Health Adminstrn. (chair orgn. theory behavior forum 1992—). Democrat. Home: 919 W Lynn St Austin TX 78703-9999 Office: Trinity Univ Health Care Adminstrn 715 Stadium Dr San Antonio TX 78212-3104

MCCAUL, EUGENE WILLIAMSON, JR., meteorologist; b. Richmond, Va., Feb. 19, 1948; s. Eugene Williamson and Mary Ursula (Fuller) McC. BA in Physics, U. Va., 1970; MArch, U. Pa., 1979; MS in Meteorology, U. Okla., 1985, PhD in Meteorology, 1989. Structural designer Keast and Hood Co., Phila., 1979-81; rsch. asst. U. Okla., Norman, 1981-89; postdoctoral fellow Nat. Ctr. Atmospheric Rsch., Boulder, Colo., 1989-90; rsch. scientist Univs. Space Rsch. Assoc., Huntsville, Ala., 1990—; adj. prof. U. Ala., Huntsville, 1996—; lectr. Nat. Weather Svc., Raleigh, N.C., 1995, also various emergency mgmt. assns., Ala. and Tenn., 1993-95; instr. project LASER, NASA, Huntsville, 1991, 92; co-investigator Project VORTEX, 1992-95. Contbr. articles to profl. publs.; contbr. photographs to Audubon Society Field Guide to North American Weather, 1991. Mem. U. Okla. Found., Norman, 1995—; mem. Transition Verification Com., Huntsville, Ala., 1993-95. Sgt. USAF, 1970-73. Recipient Best Front Page award Riverside County (Calif.) Press Assn., 1972. Mem. Am. Meteorol. Soc., Nature Photography. Office: Global Hydrology and Climate Ctr 977 Explorer Blvd NW Huntsville AL 35806-2807

MCCAULEY, CLEYBURN LYCURGUS, lawyer; b. Houston, Feb. 8, 1929; s. Reese Stephens and Elizabeth Ann (Burleson) McC.; m. Elizabeth Kelton McKoy, June 7, 1950; children: Stephens Francis, Lillian Elizabeth, Cleyburn, Lucy Annette. BS, U.S. Mil. Acad., 1950; MS in Engring. Econ., Statistical Quality Control and Indsl. Engring., Stanford U., 1959; JD, Coll. William and Mary, 1970. Bar: D.C. 1971, Va. 1970, Tex. 1970, U.S. Ct. Claims 1971, U.S. Tax Ct. 1971, U.S. Supreme Ct. 1973. Commd. 2d lt. U.S. Air Force, 1950, advanced through grades to lt. col., 1971, ret., 1971; pvt. practice law, Washington, 1975—. Mem. Fed. Bar Assn., Va. Bar Assn., Tex. Bar Assn., D.C. Bar Assn., IEEE, AIAA, Am. Soc. Quality Control, Phi Alpha Delta. Home: 402 S 3rd St Wilmington NC 28401-5102

MCCAULEY, DAVID W., lawyer, educator; b. Wheeling, W.Va., June 29, 1958; s. David A. and Patricia S. (Clark) McC.; children from previous marriages: Ashley Lynn, Connor Bryan. BA, U. W.Va., 1980, JD, 1983. Bar: W.Va. 1983, U.S. Dist. Ct. (no. and so. dists.) W.Va. 1983. Assoc. Coleman & Wallace, Buckhannon, W.Va., 1983-86, ptnr., 1986-94; city atty. City of Buckhannon, 1983—; instr. bus. law W.Va. Wesleyan Coll., Buckhannon, 1983-94, asst. prof., 1994—, dir. MBA program, 1994—, gen. legal counsel, 1993—; spkr. W.Va. Mcpl. League Conv., 1989. Sec. Upshur-Buckhannon Main St. Project, 1987-89, pres., 1989-90; bd. dirs., legal counsel W.Va. Strawberry Festival, 1986—; Upshur County United Way, Buckhannon, 1986-89, v.p., 1987; v.p. Buckhannon-Upshur Work Adjustment Ctr., 1990—. Mem. ABA, W.Va. Bar Assn., W.Va. State Bar Assn., Upshur County Bar Assn. (pres. 1990-93), Nat. Inst. Mcpl. Law Officers W.Va. Trial Lawyers Assn., W.Va. U. Alumni Assn., Mountaineer Athletic Club (Upshur County chpt.), Lions (pres. Buckhannon club 1988), Nat. Assn. of Bus. Schs. and Programs. Home: 10 Meade St Buckhannon WV 26201-2630 Office: WVa Wesleyan Coll Box 121 Buckhannon WV 26201-0518

MCCLAIN, BENJAMIN RICHARD, music educator, educational administrator; b. Highland Park, Mich., May 20, 1931; s. Benjamin Richard and Julia (Hockett) McC.; m. Tahlia Helen Ruth Carter, Feb. 9, 1952 (div.); children: Terrence, Gerald, Sharalyn, Marilyn; m. Shirley Ann Brown, June 16, 1982; stepchildren: Keith, Sheila, Kenneth Hall. BMus, U. Mich., 1959, MusM, 1967, PhD, 1972. Cert. tchr., Mich., Fla., Wash. Jr. high sch. tchr. Inkster (Mich.) Pub. Schs., 1959-62; high sch. tchr. Dearborn Heights (Mich.) Pub. Schs., 1962-67, attendance officer, 1967-68, asst. high sch. prin., 1968-69; high sch. prin. Robichaud High Sch., Dearborn Heights, 1969-72; cons. State Dept. of Edn., Lansing, Mich., 1973-74; prof. Fla. Atlantic U., Boca Raton, 1974-79; academic dean Fla. Meml. Coll., Miami, 1979-80; prof. U. North Fla., Jacksonville, 1980-82, Gonzaga U., Spokane, Wash., 1982-85; with Seattle Pub. Schs., 1985-88; CEO MELT and Assocs., 1985-88; prof. Valdosta (Ga.) State U., 1988—. Editorial bd. The Western Jour. of Black Studies, 1984; contbr. numerous articles to profl. jours. Co-chmn. Athletic Booster Club, Boca Raton, 1977. Recipient Lafayette Allen Sr. Disting. Svc. award, 1973; Mott fellowship U. Mich., 1971-72, Regents Alumni scholarship, 1949-53. Mem. NAACP, Nat. Community Edn. Assn. (human rels. chair), Kiwanis, Phi Delta Kappa, Kappa Alpha Psi. Democrat. Baptist. Office: Valdosta State Univ EDL Dept Valdosta GA 31698

MCCLAIN, GREGORY DAVID, minister; b. Anderson, S.C., June 6, 1957; s. Lemuel David and Mary Josephine (Hawkins) McC.; m. Anne Leigh Blackwell, May 21, 1983; children: Jonathan David, Sean Gregory. AS, Anderson Coll., 1977; BA, Erskine Coll., 1979; MDiv, Southeastern Bapt. Theol. Sem., Seminary, Wake Forrest, N.C., 1982; D of Ministry, Wesley Theol. Sem., Washington, 1996. Ordained Boulevard Bapt. Ch., 1983. Chaplain extern Bapt. Med. Ctr., Columbia, S.C., 1982; assoc. pastor First Bapt. Ch., South Boston, Va., 1983-86; minister Corrottoman Bapt. Ch., Lancaster, Va., 1986-93, Colonial Beach (Va.) Bapt. Ch., 1993—; pres. Dan River Bapt. Pastors, Halifax, Va., 1984-85; preacher-jr. high weekend, Va. Bapt. Gen. Assn., 1986, faculty youth week, 1984-88; v.p. Lancaster Ministerial Assn., 1987-88. Active CROP walk, South Boston, Va., 1984-85; coach youth soccer, South Boston, 1985, Westmoreland County, Va., 1995, 96; merit badge counselor Boy Scouts Am., Lancaster, 1990-93; mem. Lancaster Ednl. Task Force, 1988. Mem. Ruritan Club (chaplain 1990-93). Office: Colonial Beach Bapt Ch PO Box 27 Colonial Beach VA 22443-0027

MCCLAIN, JONI LYNN, medical examiner; b. Oklahoma City, May 9, 1957; d. John Norman and Mary Ann (Johnson) McC. BS in Chemistry, Cen. State U., Edmond, Okla., 1979; MD, U. Okla., 1983. Resident pathology U. Okla., 1983-87; fellow forensic pathology Ind. U., 1987-88; dep. med. examiner Office of the Armed Forces Med. Examiner, Washington, 1988-92; med. examiner Southwestern Inst. Forensic Scis., Dallas, 1992—. Med. examiner Nat. Disaster Med. System (D-MORT Team VI), Rockville, Md., 1992—. Recipient joint svc. achievement medal Dept. Def., 1991, joint svc. commendation medal, 1992, def. meritorious svc. medal, 1992. Fellow Am. Acad. Forensic Scis.; mem. Nat. Assn. Med. Examiners (bd. dirs. 1993—). Office: SW Inst Forensic Scis PO Box 35728 Dallas TX 75235-0728

MCCLAIN, KATE ANNE, trade association administrator; b. Cambridge, Eng., Nov. 14, 1967; d. Frank Mauldin and Mary Lee (McGinnis) McC. AA, Ray Vogue Coll. of Design, 1989. Dir. Regional Investment Bankers Assn., Charleston, S.C., 1992—. Office: Regional Investment Bankers Assn 171 Church St Ste 260 Charleston SC 29401

MCCLAIN, LARRY FRENCH, lumber company executive; b. Knoxville, Tenn., Mar. 4, 1937; s. French Charles McClain and Jean (Vineyard) Duff; children: Jennifer, Callie. BA, Baylor U., 1959. Sr. v.p. Enmmet Vaughn Lumber Co., Knoxville, 1963—. Mem. allocation com. United Way, Knoxville, 1987—, del. at large, 1993—; bd. dirs. YMCA Cen., Knoxville, 1975-85, Vol. Helpers Inc., Knoxville, 1987—; vestry Episcopal Ch., 1979-81, sr. warden, 1981. With U.S. Army, 1960-62. Mem. Antique Auto Club of Am. (nat. judge 1980—), Rotary (bd. dirs. Knoxville chpt. 1988, v.p. 1994-95, Man of Yr. 1987). Home: 1855 Cherokee Bluff Dr Knoxville TN 37920-2216 Office: Emmet Vaughn Lumber Co 3932 Martin Mill Pike Knoxville TN 37920-2457

MCCLAIN, MARILYN RUSSELL, admission and retention counselor; b. Laurelton, N.Y., Aug. 18, 1956; d. Russell H. and Lillian A. (Yarbrough) McC.; 1 child, Amy Lynne Roberts. BS in Social Work, Harding U., 1977; postgrad., Okla. State U. Career counselor Foothills Vo-Tech Sch., Searcy, Ark., 1977-78; social worker Dept. of Social Svcs., Tulsa, Okla., 1978-79; owner, operator, instr. Spl. Deliveries Childbirth Preparation Ctr., Tulsa, 1980-85; mgr. One Hour Moto Photo, Tulsa, 1986-89; area mgr. Mervyn's, Tulsa, 1989-92; admission/retention counselor Rogers State Coll., Claremore, Okla., 1992—; primary advisor Adult Students Aspiring to Prosper, Claremont, Okla., 1993—; pres. RSC Staff Assn., 1995—; parent educator Parenting Ptnrs., Claremore, 1994—. Sec. Oologah-Talala Sch. Found., 1994-95, pres., 1995—; mem. statue and hotel coms. Rogers County Hist. Soc., Claremore, 1994—; mem. planning com. Leadership Claremore, 1994—; mem. Oologah PTA, 1990—. Mem. Okla. Acad. Advising Assn. (comm. com. 1994—), Am. Assn. for Adult and Continuing Edn. Republican. Home: 3612 N Oaklawn Dr Claremore OK 74017-1828 Office: Rogers State Coll Will Rogers & College Hill Claremore OK 74017

MCCLANAHAN, JOHN D., painting and design educator; b. Salina, Kans.. BFA, Bethany Coll., 1960; MFA, U. Iowa, 1964. Teaching fellow U. Iowa, Iowa City, 1962-64; asst. prof. painting and drawing Stephen F. Austin State U., Nacogdoches, Tex., 1964-67, dir. grad. program dept. of art, 1965-67; assoc. prof. painting and drawing Queens Coll., Charlotte, N.C., 1967-76, chair dept. art, 1975-76; prof. painting and design Baylor U., Waco, Tex., 1976—, acting chair dept. art, 1985-89, chair dept. art, 1989—. One-man shows include Upstairs Gallery, Iowa City, 1964, Mint Mus. Art, Charlotte, 1971, Tex. Luth. Coll., Seguin, 1982, Baylor U., Waco, 1983, 94, McCreary Gallery, Cultural Activities Ctr., Temple, Tex., 1993; exhibited in group shows at Sophia Art Ctr., Tokyo, 1964, N.C. Mus. Art, Raleigh, 1974, E. Tex. State U., 1990, La. Coll., Weathersby Fine Arts Gallery, Pineville, 1994, and others; represented in permanent collections Hong Kong Bapt. Univ., Mint Mus. Art, Charlotte, Baylor U., Waco, U. Iowa, Iowa City, and others. Recipient Purchase prize, Mint Mus. Art, Charlotte, N.C., 1968, Merit award N.C. Mus. Art, Raleigh, 1973, Purchase prize Second St. Gallery, Charlottesville, Va., 1976, Seguin (Tex.) Art Ctr., 1977, 82, Gates Gallery, Port Arthur, Tex., 1979. Mem. Coll. Art Assn. Am., Tex. Fine Arts Assn., Tex. Watercolor Soc., Tex. Assn. Schs. of Art. Office: Baylor U Dept Art PO Box 97263 Waco TX 76798-7263

MCCLANAHAN, LELAND, academic administrator; b. Hammond, Ind., Mar. 14, 1931; s. Alonzo Leland and Eva (Hermanson) McC.; m. Lavaughn Adell Meyrer, June 5, 1954; children: Lindel, Loren. Diploma, Ctrl. Bible Coll., 1954; PhBB, Nat. Postgrad. Bible Acad., 1969; BA, Southwestern Coll., 1973; MA, Fla. State Christian Coll., 1964, ThD, 1970; PhD, Faith Bible Coll. and Sem., Ft. Lauderdale, Fla. and Marina, Lagos, Nigeria, 1969; MA, Bapt. Christian U., 1988; PhD, Freedom U., 1989; ThD, Bapt. Christian U., 1989, DLitt, 1990, PsyD, 1991; PhD, Freedom U., 1989; PhD (hon.), Hawaii U., 1995; DEd, Bapt. Christian U., 1992, D in Bus. Adminstrn., 1993; DD (hon.), Internat. Evangelism Crusades, 1969, Trinity Union Coll., 1991; LLD, La. Bapt. U., 1994; StD, PhD, Trinity Internat. U., 1994; HHD (hon.), La. Bapt. U., 1995; LittD (hon.), Cambridge Theol. Sem., 1995; PhD, LittD, PsyD, DBA, LLD, EdD, U. Hawaii, 1995; LittD(hon.), The Messianic Coll. of Rabbinical Studies. Diplomate Nat. Bd. Christian Clin. Therapists; ordained pastor, Christian Ch., 1950. Founder, pastor Evangel Temple, Griffith, Ind., 1954-73, Abundant Life Temple, Cocoa, Fla., 1974-77; mgr. ins. divsn. United Agys., Cocoa, Fla., 1979-81; assoc. pastor Merritt Assembly of God, Merritt Island, Fla., 1982-85, Palm Chapel, Merritt Island, 1987-89, 1990-93; founder Hawaii U., Merritt Island Offices, Merritt Island, Fla., 1990—; chancellor Hawaii U. Merritt Island Offices, 1995—; dir. Fla. Hawaii U. Schs.; founder, dir. Griffith Youth Ctr., 1960-70, Todd Nursery Sch., Griffith, 1971-73; founder, chancellor Ind. Bible Coll., Griffith, 1971-73; dir. Chapel Counseling Ctr., Merritt Island, 1990-94; mem. national accreditation com. Hawaii U. Author: Is Divine Healing For Today?, 1989, Truths From the Gospel of St. John, 1991, An Outline of the Revelation, 1993, Numbers in the Bible, 1994, An Outline of the Acts of the Apostle, 1995; author 142 coll. courses and books. Recipient Disting. Svc. award U.S. Jaycees, 1966; named Hon. Lt. Col., Gov. Guy Hunt, 1988. Fellow Am. Biog. Inst. (life); mem. Internat. Platform Assn., Order of Internat. Fellowship (life), Am. Inst. Clin. Psychotherapists, Am. Assn. christian Counselors, Nat. Christian Counseling Assn. (assoc., lic.), Internat. Assn. Pastoral Psychologists (lic.), Order of St. John, Knight of Malta (comdr. 1990). Republican. Office: Hawaii U Merritt Island Offices 670 N Courtenay Pkwy Ste 15 Merritt Island FL 32953-4770

MCCLANAHAN, PATSY HITT, women's health nurse practitioner; b. Pasadena, Tex., Sept. 17, 1954; d. Clifton Lee and Doris Allene (Edwards) Hitt; m. George Terrell McClanahan, Nov. 26, 1980; children: Terry Lee, Jennifer Allene. BSN, N.E. La. U., 1976; Ob/gyn. Nurse Practitioner Cert., U. Tex., Dallas, 1987; MSN, Northwestern State U., 1990. Lic. RN/advanced nurse practitioner, ob-gyn. sonography, NAACOG. Nurse dir. Columbia (La.) State Sch., 1976-77; staff nurse Caldwell Meml. Hosp., Columbia, La., 1977-79; instr. N.E. La. U., Monroe, 1979; staff nurse Schumpert Med. Ctr., Shreveport, La., 1979; dir. nurses Citizens Med. Ctr., Columbia, La., 1980-84; pub. health nurse III Caldwell Parish Health Unit, Columbia, La., 1984-88; nurse II E.A. Conway Hosp., Monroe, La., 1988; regional pub. specialist Regional Pub. Health, Monroe, La., 1988-89; instr. dept. ob/gyn La. State U. Med. Ctr., Monroe, La., 1989—; mem. La. State Bd. Nursing, 1996—. Dir. youth Music Fellowship Bapt. Ch., Columbia, 1990-92; youth Sunday sch. tchr. Fellowship Bapt. Ch., 1995-96, softball coach Caldwell Parish Dixie Youth, Columbia, 1989-90. Mem. ANA, La. Nurse Practitioners (N.E. regional rep. 1990-95, prescriptive task force 1992-94, treas. 1995—), Assn. Women's Health, Obstet. and Neonatal Nurses, Am. Inst. Ultrasound Medicine, Am. Acad. Nurse Practitioners (State award for Excellence 1991), Am. Acad. Nurse Practitioners (state rep. 1995), La. Coalition for Maternal and Infant Health, Sigma Theta Tau. Democrat. Baptist. Home: 1780 Blankston Rd Monroe LA 71202 Office: La State U Med Ctr E A Conway Divsn 4864 Jackson St Monroe LA 71202-6400

MCCLANE, ROBERT SANFORD, bank holding company executive; b. Kenedy, Tex., May 5, 1939; s. Norris Robert and Ella Addie (Stockton) McC.; m. Sue Nitschke, Mar. 31, 1968; children: Len Stokes McClane Brown, Norris Robert. BS in Bus. Adminstrn., Trinity U., San Antonio, 1961. With Ford Motor Co., Detroit, 1961-62; with Frost Nat. Bank, San Antonio, 1962—, mem. staff, 1962-68, v.p., 1968-78; exec. v.p. Cullen/Frost Bankers, Inc., 1976—, pres., dir., 1985—; bd. dirs. Frost Nat. Bank, San Antonio. Crusade chmn. Baxar County chpt. Am. Cancer Soc., 1974; bd. dirs. Bexar County ARC, 1969-72; sr. warden St. Luke's Episopal Ch., San Antonio, 1980; trustee Alamo Pub. Telecomms. Coun., San Antonio, 1981-88, Trinity U., 1990—; chmn. San Antonio Econ. Devel. Found., 1987-89, exec. com. 1985-91. Mem. Greater San Antonio C. of C. (chmn. leadership San Antonio 1975-76, bd. dirs. exec. com. 1994—, chmn. 1996), Trinity U. Alumni Assn. (pres. 1968-69, disting. alumnus 1987), San Antonio German Club, Order Alamo, Tex. Cavaliers, Argyle Club, Town Club, Plaza Club (bd. dirs. 1973-92). Episcopalian. Office: Cullen/Frost Bankers Inc 100 W Houston St San Antonio TX 78205-1457

MCCLARD, JACK EDWARD, lawyer; b. Lafayette, La., May 13, 1946; s. Lee Franklin and Mercedes Cecile (Landry) McC.; m. Marilyn Kay O'Gorman, June 3, 1972; 1 child, Lauren Minton. BA in Hist., Rice U., 1968; JD, U. Tex., 1974. Bar: Va. 1974, U.S. Dist. Ct. (ea. and we. dists.) Va. 1974, D.C. 1981, U.S. Dist. Ct. D.C. 1981, N.Y. 1985, U.S. Dist. Ct. (so. and ea. dists.) N.Y. 1985, U.S. Ct. Appeals (4th cir.) 1978, U.S. Ct. Appeals (D.C. cir.) 1980, U.S. Ct. Appeals (5th cir.) 1993. Assoc. Hunton & Williams, Richmond, Va., 1974-81; ptnr. Hunton & Williams, Richmond, 1981—. Contbr. articles to profl. jours. Served to lt. (j.g.) USN, 1968-71. Mem. ABA, Va. Bar Assn., Richmond Bar Assn., Va. Trial Lawyers Assn., 5th Cir. Bar, John Marshall Inns of Ct. Democrat. Episcopalian. Home: 100 Trowbridge Rd Richmond VA 23233-5724 Office: Hunton & Williams Riverfront Plz E. Tower 951 Byrd St Richmond VA 23219-4074

MCCLARON, LOUISIANNA CLARDY, retired secondary school educator; b. Clarksville, Tenn., Dec. 12, 1929; d. Abe and Chinaster (Simpson) Clardy; m. Joe Thomas McClaron, July 17, 1965. BS, Tenn. State U., 1952; MA, Ohio State U., 1956; EdS, Tenn. State U., 1977; PhD, Vanderbilt U., 1981. Cert. secondary tchr., sch. adminstr., supr., Tenn. Tchr. Madison County Bd. Edn., Normal, Ala., 1952-58, Metro Nashville Bd. Edn., 1958-94; ret., 1994; presenter workshops in field. Mem. NEA, Tenn. Edn. Assn., Metro Nashville Edn. Assn. (exec. bd., dist. dir.), Tenn. Bus. Edn. Assn., Nat. Bus. Edn. assn., Am. Vocat. Assn., Delta Pi Epsilon (former v.p. Omega chpt., now pres.), Alpha Kappa Alpha, Alpha Delta Omega Chpt. Found. (housing treas.).

MCCLARTY, JACK LEE, academic administrator; b. Kalispell, Mont., July 11, 1938; s. Homer J. and Beryl Thelma (Elwood) McC.; m. Wilma K. Doering, June 3, 1962; children: Julie, Stacey. BA in Music Edn., U. Mont., 1960; MA in Music Edn., Andrews U., Berrien Springs, Mich., 1964; EdD, U Mont., 1968. Cert. fund raising exec. Dir. bands Conrad (Mont.) H.S., 1960-61, Milo (Oreg.) Acad., 1962-63; dir. bands and Phys. Edn. Kingsway Coll., Oshawa, Ont., Can., 1964-66; dir. bands S.W. Union Coll., Keene, Tex., 1968-72; dir. bands So. Coll. (now So. Adventist U.), Collegedale, Tenn., 1972-79, v.p. devel., 1980—; coach Softball League for H.S. Age, Collegedale, Tenn., 1991—; bd. dirs. Tenn. Wellness Coun. Recipient AIM award Coun. for Support of Edn., 1991, award of excellence, 1994. Mem. Nat. Soc. Fund Raising Execs. (pres. S.E. Tenn. chpt.). Home: PO Box 544 Collegedale TN 37315-0544 Office: So Adventist Univ PO Box 370 Taylor Cir Collegedale TN 37315

MCCLARY, JIM MARSTON, accounting executive, consultant; b. Nashville, Feb. 26, 1949; s. Joseph Patrick and Daisy Wynell (Marston) McC.; m. Billie Sue Gwinn, Feb. 27, 1970; children: Traci Gwinn, Matthew Ryan. BSBA with honors, U. Tenn., 1974. CPA, Tenn.; cert. personal fin. specialist. Staff acct. Price Waterhouse & Co. CPAs, Nashville, 1974-76; sr. acct. Bradley & Crenshaw, CPAs, Nashville, 1976-77; controller Holder & No. Lumber Sales, Inc., Nashville, 1977-78; pres. Retirement Plans, Inc., Nashville, 1978-80; ptnr. McClary, Yeary & Howell, CPAs, Brentwood, Tenn., 1980-85; cons. Franklin, Tenn., 1985—; pres. Employee Benefit Svcs. Inc., Brentwood, 1985—; ops. prin. Advanced Fin. Planning Securities Corp., Brentwood, 1985—, cons. 1985—. Served with USAF, 1968-69. Mem. AICPA, Tenn. Soc. CPAs, U.S. C. of C. Democrat. Office: Employee Benefit Svcs Inc 5038 Thoroughbred Ln Brentwood TN 37027-4225

MCCLAY, HARVEY CURTIS, data processing executive; b. Houston, Jan. 2, 1939; s. Clarence and Agnes E. McC.; m. Patricia Lott, Jan. 8, 1961; children: James, John, Susan, Robert. BA in Math., Rice U., 1960. Field engr. Western Electric Co., Marysville, Calif., 1960-62; analyst math. Litton Data Systems Co., Canoga Park, Calif., 1962-63; mgr. programming Lockheed Electronics Co., Houston, 1967-75; systems mgr. City of Houston, 1975-77; project mgr. fin. systems devel. Brown & Root, Houston, 1977-81; mgr. data processing Nat. Supply, Houston, 1981-84; project mgr. Computer Scis. Corp., Houston, 1984-92, Grumman Tech. Svcs., Houston, 1992-95; exec. dir., applications Houston Ind. Sch. Dist., 1996—; part-time instr. data processing and mgmt. Houston Community Coll. Home: 2911 Huckleberry Ln Pasadena TX 77502-5409

MCCLAY, WILFRED MARK, history educator, writer; b. Champaign, Ill., Dec. 7, 1951; s. Clarence Harvey and Mary Rosalie (Bear) McC.; m. Julie Louise Holt, July 8, 1983; children: Mark, Barbara. BA cum laude, St. John's Coll., 1974; MA, John's Hopkins U., 1982, PhD, 1987. Legis. aide Md. Gen. Assembly, Annapolis, 1974-75; tchr. St. Mary's H.S., Annapolis, 1975-76; editor U.S. Naval Inst., Annapolis, 1976-78; dir. pubs. Folger Shakespeare Libr., Washington, 1978-80; vis. instr. history Towson (Md.) State U., 1985-86; asst. prof. history U. Dallas, Irving, Tex., 1986-87; asst. prof. history Tulane U., New Orleans, 1987-93, assoc. prof. history, 1993—. Author: The Masterless: Self and Society in Modern America, 1994 (Merle Curti award Orgn. Am. Historians 1995); mem. editl. bd. Continuity: A Journal of History, 1995—. Mem. exec. bd. Crescent City Youth for Christ, New Orleans, 1995—. Danforth fellow Danforth Found., 1980-84, Richard Weaver fellow Intercollegiate Studies Inst., 1982-83, Spencer postdoct. fellow Nat. Acad. Edn. Stanford U., 1993-94, Howard fellow Howard Found. Brown U., 1993-94. Mem. Am. Hist. Assn., Orgn. Am. Historians, Social Sci. History Assn. Office: Tulane U Dept History New Orleans LA 70118

MCCLELLAN, CHARLES WAYNE, history educator, researcher; b. Bklyn., June 16, 1945; s. Charles H. and Cecilia (Müller) McC. BSE, Emporia State U., 1967; MA, Mich. State U., 1971, PhD, 1978. Vol. U.S. Peace Corps, Ethiopia, 1967-70; instr. humanities Mich. State U., East Lansing, 1976-77, instr. Am. thought and lang., 1978; instr. humanities Lansing (Mich.) C.C., 1977; asst. prof. Murray (Ky.) State U., 1979, SUNY, Plattsburgh, 1979-80; prof. history Radford (Va.) U., 1980—; vis. prof. East Tenn. State U., Johnson City, 1988; observer (Ethiopian elections) Joint Internat. Observer Group, Washington, 1992. Author: State Transformation and National Integration: Gedeo and the Ethiopian Empire, 1988; editl. bd. African Studies Assn., 1981-82; contbr. articles to profl. jours. U. Fla. Rsch. grantee, summer 1983, NEH grantee, 1984, Am. Coun. Learned Socs. grantee, 1989; Fulbright-Hays fellow, 1990. Mem. AAUP, African Studies Assn., S.E. Region Seminar in African Studies, Nat. Coun. of Returned Peace Corps Vols., Pi Gamma Mu, Omicron Delta Kappa. Office: Radford Univ PO Box 6941 Radford VA 24142

MCCLELLAN, RICHARD AUGUSTUS, small business owner; b. Gainesville, Fla., Sept. 13, 1930; s. Marion Theodore Sr. and Cornelia (Hampton) McC.; m. Thelma Watson, May 19, 1947 (dec. Mar. 1980); children: Richard A., Wayne Theodore, Viola Patricia, Michael Ray; m. Betty Lee Snow, Dec. 12, 1980 (div. July 1991); children: Claranell Y., Juanita F., Johnnie C.; m. Geraldine C. Williams, Aug. 14, 1993. Diploma, Nat. Inst. Drycleaning, 1975, Napoleon Hill Found., 1994. Drycleaner S & S Cleaners, Gainesville, 1958—. Mem. Am. Soc. Notaries (govt. relations com. 1984, pub. relations com. 1989), Notary Pub. Assn. State Fla., Nat. Notary Assn., United Methodist Ch. Democrat. Home and Office: 625 SE 15th St Gainesville FL 32641-3116

MCCLELLAN, ROGER ORVILLE, toxicologist; b. Tracy, Minn., Jan. 5, 1937; s. Orville and Gladys (Paulson) McC.; m. Kathleen Mary Dunagan, June 23, 1962; children: Eric John, Elizabeth Christine, Katherine Ruth. DVM with highest honors, Wash. State U., 1960; M of Mgmt, U. N.Mex., 1980. diplomate Am. Bd. Vet. Toxicology, cert. Am. Bd. Toxicology. From biol. scientist to sr. scientist Gen. Electric Co., Richland, Wash., 1957-64; sr. scientist biology dept. Pacific N.W. Labs., Richland, Wash., 1965; scientist med. research br. div. biology and medicine AEC, Washington, 1965-66; asst. dir. research, dir. fission product inhalation program Lovelace Found. Med. Edn. and Research, Albuquerque, 1966-73; v.p., dir. research adminstrn., dir. Lovelace Inhalation Toxicology Research Inst., Albuquerque, 1973-76, pres., dir., 1976-88; chmn. bd. dirs. Lovelace Biomedical and Environ. Research Inst., Albuquerque, 1988—; pres. Chem. Industry Inst. Toxicology Research, Triangle Park, N.C., 1988—; mem. research com. Health Effects Inst., 1981-92; bd. dirs. Toxicology Lab. Accreditation Bd., 1982-90, treas., 1984-90; adj. prof. Wash. State U., 1980—, U. Ark., 1970-88; clin. assoc. U. N.Mex., 1971-85, adj. prof. toxicology, 1985—; adj. prof. toxicology and occupational and environ. medicine Duke U., 1988—; adj. prof. toxicology U. N.C. Chapel Hill, 1989—; adj. prof. toxicology N.C. State Univ., 1991—; mem. dose assessment adv. group U.S. Dept. Energy, 1980-87, mem. health and environ. research adv. com., 1984-85; mem. exec. com. sci. adv. bd. EPA, 1974-95, mem. environ. health com., 1980-83, chmn., 1982-83, chmn. radionuclide emissions rev. com., 1984-85, chmn. Clean Air Sci. Adv. Com., 1987-92, chmn. rsch. strategies adv. com., 1992-94; mem. com. on toxicology NAS-NRC, 1979-87, chmn., 1980-87; bd. dirs. Lovelace Anderson Endowment Found.; mem. com. risk assessment methodology for hazardous air pollution NAS-NRC, 1991-94, com. biol. effects of Radon NAS NRC, 1994—; mem. com. on environ. justice Inst. of Medicine, 1996—; pres. Am. Bd. Vet. Toxicology, 1970-73; mem. adv. council Ctr. for Risk Mgmt., Resources for the Future, 1987—; council mem. Nat. Council for Radiation Protection, 1970—; bd. dirs. N.C. Assn. Biomedical Rsch., 1989-91, N.C. Vet. Medical Found., 1990-95, pres., 1993-94; bd. govs. Rsch. Triangle Inst., 1994—. Contbr. articles to profl. jours. Editorial bd. Jour. Toxicology and Environ. Health, 1980—, assoc. editor, 1982—; editorial bd. Fundamental and Applied Toxicology, 1984-89, assoc. editor, 1987-89; editorial bd. Toxicology and Indsl. Health, 1984—; editor CRC Critical Revs. in Toxicology, 1987—; assoc. editor Inhalation Toxicology Jour., 1987—; mem. edit. bd. Regulatory Toxicology and Pharmacology, 1993—. Recipient Herbert E. Stokinger award Am. Conf. Govtl. Indsl. Hygienists, 1985, Alumni Achievement award Wash. State U., 1987, Disting. Assoc. award Dept. Energy, 1987, 88, Arnold Lehman award Soc. Toxicology, 1992; co-recipient Frank R. Blood award Soc. Toxicology, 1989. Fellow AAAS, Am. Acad. Vet. and Comparative Toxicology, Soc. Risk Analysis; mem. Am. Chem. Soc., Inst. Medicine (elected), NAS, Radiation Research Soc. (sec.-treas. 1982-84, chmn. fin. com. 1979-82), Health Physics Soc. (chmn. program com. 1972, Elda E. Anderson award 1974), Soc. Toxicology (v.p.-elect to pres. 1987-90; inhalation specialty sect. v.p. to pres. 1983-86, bd. publs. 1983-86, chmn. 1983-85), Am. Assn. Aerosol Research (bd. dirs. 1982-94, treas. 1986-90, v.p. to pres. 1990-93), Am. Vet. Med. Assn., Gesellschaft fur Aerosolforschung, Sigma Xi, Phi Kappa Phi, Phi Zeta Republican. Lutheran. Home: 1111 Cuatro Cerros Trl SE Albuquerque NM 87123-4149 also: 2903 Bainbridge Dr Apt Q Durham NC 27713-1448 Office: Chem Industry Inst Toxicology PO Box 12137 Research Triangle Park NC 27709

MCCLELLAND, JAMES RAY, lawyer; b. Eunice, La., June 21, 1946; s. Rufus Ray and Homer Florene (Nunn) McC.; m. Sandra Faye Tate, Feb. 6, 1971; children: Joseph Ray, Jeffrey Ross. B.S., La. State U., 1969, M.B.A., 1971, J.D., 1975. Bar: La. 1975, U.S. Ct. Appeals (5th cir.) 1976, U.S. Dist. Ct. (ea. dist.) La. 1976, U.S. Dist. Ct. (we. dist.) La. 1976, U.S. Dist. Ct. (mid. dist.) La. 1994. Assoc. Aycock, Horne & Coleman, Franklin, La., 1975-78, ptnr., 1978—; dir. Bayou Bouillon Corp., Cotten Land Corp. Mem. exec. com. Democratic Party, St. Mary Parish, 1980-88; del. La. Dem. Party, 1982, 84, bd. govs., 1995—, ho. of dels., 1982-95, law reform com., 1984-86. Mem. La. State Bar Assn. (ho. of dels. 1982-95, law reform com. 1984-86, bd. govs. 1995—), St. Mary Parish Bar Assn. (pres. 1978-79), Order of Coif. Club: Rotary (pres. 1981-82). Home: PO Box 268 Franklin LA 70538-0268 Office: PO Box 592 Franklin LA 70538-0592

MCCLENDON, DENNIS EDWARD, retired military officer; b. Nashville, July 8, 1922; s. Dennis Eugene and Loralee (Aswell) McC.; m. Vivian Eunette Youmans, May 13, 1944 (dec. 1989); children: Denise Diane Chastain, Lisa Linda Sims, Dennis Edward Jr. BS in Journalism, U. Houston, 1952. Commd. 2d lt. USAAF, 1942; advanced through grades to lt. col. USAAF, 1966; pub. info. officer U.S. Strike Command, MacDill AFB, Fla., 1975-80; ret. USAAF, 1967; dir. pub. info. St. Leo (Fla.) Coll., 1967-68; dir. info. svcs. U. South Fla., Tampa, 1968-73; pub. info. dir. Fla. Regional Med. Program, Tampa, 1973-75. Author: Lady Be Good, Mystery Bomber of WWII, 1962; co-author: Legend of Colin Kelly, First American Hero of WWII, 1995. Journalism scholar U. Houston, 1951; decorated Legion of Merit, Joint Svc. Commendation medal, Air medal, Air Force Commendation medal (2). Mem. Air Force Assn. (past chpt. pres., life), Ret. Officers Assn. (life), Order of Daedalians (life), Fla. Pub. Rels. Assn. (past chpt. pres.). Democrat. Home: 354 Inverness Dr SW Huntsville AL 35802

MCCLENDON, FRED VERNON, real estate professional, business consultant, equine and realty appraiser, financial consultant; b. Vernon, Tex.; s. Guy C. and Lexie M. (Johnson) Mc C.; m. Dorothy J. Seibert, June 1943 (div. 1953); children: Cathy, Kent, Tracy; m. Ethel R. Cherry, Sept. 15, 1959; children: Tess, Rob, J.T. Assoc. degree, Hannibal La Grange Coll., 1947; BBA, Baylor U., 1949; MBA, Harvard U., 1951, postgrad. in law, 1951; postgrad. in banking, Colo. U., 1951-52; postgrad., Denver U., 1951-52. Lic. ins. agt., Tenn.; cert. real estate broker, Tenn.; sr. cert. valuer. Asst. cashier U.S. Nat. Bank, Denver, 1951; gen. mgr. Nat. Paper Band Co., Denver, 1952-53; personnel mgr. Houston Fire & Casualty Co., Ft. Worth, 1954-56; gen. sales mgr. City Lincoln/Mercury, Dallas, 1957-58; owner INS-Bank Personnel Agy., Dallas, 1959-61; mng. ptnr. Allen & Mc Clendon Ins., Dallas, 1959-63; owner, broker Mc Clendon Real Estate, Dallas, 1959-63; pres. Mc Clendon Realty Co., Hampton, Tenn., 1961—; gen. mgr. Eagle Nest Ranch, Roan Mountain, Tenn., 1963-88, Mile High Ranch, Roan Mountain, 1988—; pres. FMV Appraisal Co., Hampton, 1988—; cons. Gen. Adjustments Bur., 1981—, Debourdieux Corp., 1985—, Wachesaw Corp., 1985—, Hidden Lakes Devel. Corp., various ins. cos. and law firms in U.S. and Can., IRS, U.S. Marshals Svc., U.S. Customs, 1993—; exec. cons. El Dorado Ranch, 1991—; cons. IRS; lectr. to lodges and assns.; gen. ptnr. Flexnet Investments, Ltd., Dallas, 1988—; pres. Bus. Realty Internat. Cons., Roan Mountain, Tenn., 1990—; exec. v.p. OmniVue, Inc., S.C., 1992—; chmn. AmeriFund Ventures, Inc., Tenn., 1995—; pres. U.S. Med-Am. Fin. Svcs., 1995—. Contbr. articles to profl. jours. Recipient W.T. Grant fellow Harvard U., 1950-51. Mem. Am. Quarter Horse Assn. (life), Australian Appaloosa Assn., Appaloosa Horse Club U.S., Tenn. Walking Horse Breeders Assn., Am. Paint Horse Assn., Am. Soc. Equine Appraisers, Am. Horse Coun., Am. Soc. Appraisers (Accredited sr. appraiser, bd. examiners 1990—), Internat. Real Estate Inst., Nat. Assn. Real Estate Appraisers, Environ. Assessment Assoc. (cert. insp. 1991—), Appraisers Assn. Am. (cert. sr. appraiser). Republican. Mem. Seventh Day Adventists. Home: Mile High Ranch PO Box 190 Roan Mountain TN 37687-0190 Office: FMV Appraisal Co PO Box 330 Hampton TN 37658-0330

MCCLENDON, MAXINE, artist; b. Leesville, La., Oct. 21, 1931; d. Alfred Harry and Clara (Jackson) McMillan; student Tex. U., 1948-50, Tex. Woman's U., 1950-51, Pan Am. U., 1963-64; m. Edward Edson Nichols, Mar. 28, 1967; children—Patricia Ann, Joan Terri, Christopher, Jennifer. Instr. McAllen Internat. Mus., 1987-90, in studio, Mission, Tex., 1990—. Drawing tchr., 1991—. One-woman shows include: Art Mus. S. Tex., Corpus Christi, 1971, McAllen (Tex.) Internat. Mus., 1976, Amarillo (Tex.) Art Center, 1982, U. Tex., Pan American, 1994; group shows in Wichita, Kans., 1972, Marietta, Ohio, 1975, Dallas, 1977; represented in permanent collections: Mus. Internat. Folk Art, Santa Fe, Ark. Mus. Fine Art, Little Rock, McAllen Internat. Mus., Lauren Rogers Mus., Laurel, Miss.; commns. include: Caterpillar Corp., Peoria, Ill., Union Bank Switzerland, N.Y.C., Crocker Bank, Los Angeles, Tarleton U., Tex., Hyatt Regency, Ft. Worth Forbes Inc., San Francisco, First Savs. & Loan, Shreveport, La., Continental Plaza, Ft. Worth. curator Mexican folk art McAllen Internat. s., 1974-80. Recipient judges award 4th Nat. Marietta, 1975, numerous others. Mem. World Crafts Council, Am. Crafts Council (Tex. rep. 1976-80), Tex. Designer/Craftsmen (pres. 1973-74). Christian Scientist. Home and Studio: 2018 Sharyland St Mission TX 78572

MCCLENDON, SUSAN K., secondary education educator; m. Greg McClendon, Dec. 19, 1992. Tchr. Goddard Jr. High Sch., Midland, Tex., 1991-93; tchr. social studies, team leader Abell Jr. High Sch., Midland, Tex., 1993—. Recipient Sallie Mae First Yr. Tchr. award, 1992. Office: Abell Jr H S 3201 Heritage Blvd Midland TX 79707-5001*

MC CLENDON, WILLIAM HUTCHINSON, III, lawyer; b. New Orleans, Feb. 19, 1933; s. William H. and Eleanor (Eaton) McC.; m. Eugenia Mills Slaughter Feb. 6, 1960; children: William Hutchinson, IV, Virginia Morris, Eleanor Eaton, Bryan Slaughter. B.A., Tulane U., 1956, LL.B., 1958. Bar: La. 1958, U.S. Supreme Ct. 1964. Atty. Humble Oil & Refining Co., 1958-60; with firm Taylor, Porter, Brooks & Phillips, Baton Rouge, 1960—; ptnr. Taylor, Porter, Brooks & Phillips, 1966—; instr. comml. law and negotiable instruments Am. Inst. Banking, 1963-74; lectr. movable Property La. Bar Assn. Bridging the Gap Inst., 1965; lectr. La. State U. LAw Sch. and Real Estate Seminar chmn., 1972, 74, 76, 80, 82, 85, 87, 95, La. Soc. of Profl. Surveying, 1989, La. Soc. CPA's, 1991, Banking Seminar, 1995; adj. prof. La. State U. Legal Negotiation, 1983—. Contbr. articles to legal jours. Bd. dirs. Cancer Soc. Baton Rouge, 1968-71; trustee Episcopal High Sch., 1976-78; mem. Dean's council Tulane U. Law Sch., 1984-88. Served to capt. AUS. Mem. ABA, Am. Judicature Soc., La. Bar Assn. (chmn. sect. trust estates, probate and immovable property law 1969-70, Meml. award article 1987), Baton Rouge Bar Assn. (chmn. title standards com. 1968-69), Tulane Alumni Assn. Greater Baton Rouge (pres. 1968-69), Baton Rouge Green (bd. dirs. 1991-93), Hilltop Aboretum (bd. dirs. 1993-95), La. Civil Svc. League (pres. 1992-94), La. Tulane Law Alumni (treas., 2d v.p. 1964-65), Kappa Alpha. Republican. Episcopalian (vestry, sr. warden 1975, 81, 84, diocesan standing com. 1985-89). Clubs: Baton Rouge Assembly (treas. 1983); Toastmasters (Baton Rouge) (pres. 1970), Baton Rouge Country (Baton Rouge), Camelot (Baton Rouge); Pickwick (New Orleans). Lodge: Rotary (bd. dirs. Baton Rouge club 1972). Home: Oakland at Gurley 6165 Highway 963 Ethel LA 70730-3615 Office: 451 Florida St, 8th Fl Baton Rouge LA 70801-1700*

MCCLINTON, JAMES LEROY, city administrator; b. Longview, Wash., Oct. 14, 1949; s. James Delmer and Norma Jean (Ammons) McC.; m. Carmen Lassaphine Amador, Nov. 7, 1983; children: James Andrew, Ian Tyler, Kevin Riley. AA, SUNY, Albany, 1973; BA, Upper Iowa U., 1974; MA, Calif. State U., Carson, 1984; PhD, Calif. Coast U., 1985. Cert. mgr. Inst. Cert Profl. Mgrs. Non-commd. officer USCG, various locations, 1967-72, commd. officer, 1972-89; comdr. (ret.) USCG; bur. mgr. adminstrv. svcs. Charleston (S.C.) County Sheriff's Office, 1989—; spkr. pro tem S.C. Criminal Justice Acad., Columbia, 1989—; mem. auditor selection com. Charleston County Govt., 1989—, computer users action com., 1989—; mem. various coms. County Govt. and Sheriff's Office, Charleston, 1989—. Editor (newsletter) The Badge, 1989—; contbr. articles to profl. jours. Mem. Charleston Police Pipes and Drums, 1994—; grad. Leadership S.C., 1993. Recipient Achievement award Nat. Assn. Counties, Washington, 1993, 96, Golden Pen award The Post and Courier Newspaper, Charleston, 1996. Mem. ASPA, S.C. Law Enforcement Officers Assn. Republican.

MCCLINTON, WENDELL C., religious organization administrator; b. Waco, Tex., Jan. 10, 1933; s. Clyde E. and Gertrude (Cotton) McC.; m. Beverly A. Harrison, Oct. 19, 1954; children: Kent, Jana, Lori, Meg. BBA, Baylor U., 1960. Exec. dir. Gideons Internat., Nashville.

MCCLOUD, MARVIN LYNN, state agency administrator; b. Kingsport, Tenn., Mar. 21, 1954; s. Clarence Marvin and Jewell Lynn (Messick) McC.; m. Deborah Gail Kidder, Feb. 11, 1984; children: Kaitlin Robin, Kelly Lynn, Emily Amanda. BS in Gen. Studies, La. State U., 1978. Prison classification officer Hunt Correctional Ctr. La. Dept. Pub. Safety and Corrections, Baton Rouge, 1979-87, transfer officer, 1987-88, corrections internal affairs officer, 1988-92; dir. classification Washington Corp. Inst. La. Dept. Pub. Safety and Corrections, Angie, 1992—; mem. jail monitoring team La. Dept. Pub. Safety and Corrections, Baton Rouge, 1993-96. Exec. editor Chainlink Chronicle, 1994-96. Recipient Svc. award WCI Inmate Welfare Fund, Washington Correctional Inst., 1995. Mem. Am. Corrections Assn. (Program Recognition award 1996), Corrections Edn. Assn., Correctoins Accreditation Mgrs. Assn., Bogalusa Sports Assn. Home: 318 Montgomery St Bogalusa LA 70427 Office: Washington Correctional Inst 27268 Hwy 21 Angie LA 70426

MCCLOUD, NEDRA, English language educator; b. Ft. Worth, Tex., June 10, 1940; d. James William and Nita (Hunter) Dyer. BA, North Tex. State U., 1970; MA, Sam Houston State U., 1974, U. North Tex., 1983; postgrad., Tex. Tech. U. English tchr. various univs., Middle East, 1984-94; owner, founder Windsor Audios, Lubbock, Tex., 1995—; teaching fellow English Dept. Texas Tech. U., 1995—. Mem. MLA, TESOL, South Central MLA. Republican. Methodist. Home: 2400-44th St #243 Lubbock TX 79412

MC CLUNG, JIM HILL, light manufacturing company executive; b. Buena Vista, Ga., Nov. 8, 1936; s. Jim Hill and Marjorie (Oxford) McC.; m. Jo Patrick, July 5, 1958; children—Jim Hill, Karen Mareese. B.A., Emory U., 1958; M.B.A., Harvard U., 1964. With Lithonia Lighting div. Nat. Svc. Industries, Inc., Conyers, Ga., 1964—; now pres., assoc. dir. Lithonia Lighting div. Nat. Svc. Industries, Inc. Served with USAF, 1958-62. Mem. Illuminating Engring. Soc. N.Am. (vice chmn. lighting rsch. and edn. fund), Nat. Elec. Distbrs. Assn. (mfrs. bd.), Nat. Elec. Mfrs. Assn. (nat. lighting bur., bd. dirs., vice chmn.), Intelligent Bldgs. Inst. (bd. dirs.), Lighting Rsch. Inst. (bd. dirs.), Elec. Mfrs. Club, World Pres.'s Orgn. Methodist. Office: Lithonia Lighting Div PO Box A Conyers GA 30207-0067

MCCLURE, ANN CRAWFORD, lawyer; b. Cin., Sept. 5, 1953; d. William Edward and Patricia Ann (Jewett) Crawford; m. David R. McClure, Nov. 12, 1983; children: Kinsey Tristen, Scott Crawford. BFA magna cum laude, Tex. Christian U., 1974; JD, U. Houston, 1979. Bd. cert. in family law and civil appellate law Tex. Bd. Legal Specialization. Assoc. Piro and Lilly, Houston, 1979-83; pvt. practice El Paso, Tex., 1983-92; ptnr. McClure and McClure, El Paso, 1992-94; justice Eighth Ct. of Appeals, El Paso, 1995—; former mem. Tex. Bd. Law Examiners, Bd. Disciplinary Appeals; mem. Family Law Specialization Exam Com., 1989-93. Contbr. articles to profl. jours.; past editor The Family Law Forum; contbg. editor: Texas Family Law Service; mem. editl. bd. Tex. Family Law Practice Manual, 1982-93. Mem. State Bar Tex. (dir. family law sect. 1987-91, treas. 1993-94, vice-chair 1995-96, chair-elect 1996—, dir. appellate & advocacy sect. 1991-95, treas. 1996—), Tex. Acad. Family Law Specialists (past dir.). Democrat. Presbyterian.

MCCLURE, CHRISTOPHER EWART, architect; b. Washington, Oct. 31, 1943; s. Harlan Ewart and Virginia Withers (Varney) McC.; m. Joyce Leigh Davis, Aug. 11, 1974; children: Andrew Ewart, Virginia Leigh. BA in Polit. Sci., The Citadel, 1965; BFA, R.I. Sch. Design, 1972, BArch, 1973. Registered arch., N.C., Va., S.C. Prin. NBBJ N.C., Inc., Raleigh, 1975-94; architect O'Brien/Atkins Assocs., Research Triangle Park, NC, 1994—. Elder St. Giles Presbyn. Ch., Raleigh, 1985—; commr. N.C. Child Day Care Commn., 1990—, chmn., 1993—. Capt. U.S. Army, 1967-70, Vietnam. Decorated Bronze Star. Mem. AIA (sect. sec. 1982-83), Am. Correctional Assn., N.C. Vietnam Vets., Inc., Citadel Alumni Assn., Citadel (life), Spl. Forces Assn. (life), Am. Mensa Soc., Aircraft Owners and Pilots Assn., Alpha Rho Chi (award 1973). Office: OBrien Atkins Assocs PO Box 12037 Research Triangle Park NC 27709

MCCLURE, CONNIE DIANE, elementary school educator; b. Huntsville, Tex., July 4, 1956; d. Albert Joseph and Alpha Lee (Ash) Davis; m. Ronnie Preston McClure, May 20, 1978; children: Micah Lindsay, Matthew Christopher. BS in Edn., Howard Payne U., 1978; MS in Art Edn., U. North Tex., 1996. Cert. elem. tchr., Tex. Tchr. Brownwood (Tex.) Ind. Sch. Dist., 1980-82; interviewer Tex. Employment Commn., Ft. Worth, 1983-85, investigator, 1985-87, job search tng. seminar facilitator, 1987-89; elem. art tchr. Ft. Worth Ind. Sch. Dist., 1989—; instr. North Tex. Getty Inst. Visual Arts Edn., 1992—. Vol. Brownwood Community Cultural Affairs Commn., 1980-82. Marcus fellow Sch. Visual Arts, U. North Tex., 1995-96. Mem. NEA, NAEA, Ft. Worth Classroom Tchrs. Assn., Fort Worth Art Edn. Assn., Alpha Rho Tau (sec. 1976-77). Republican. Baptist. Office: 1809 NE 36th St Fort Worth TX 76106-4607

MCCLURE, DANIEL M., lawyer; b. Enid, Okla., Feb. 5, 1952; s. Larry M. and Marie Dolores (Sarver) McC.; m. Judy Lynn Pinson, Jan. 3, 1976; children: Andrew Mead, Mark William, Kathleen Claire. BA with highest hons., U. Okla., 1974; JD cum laude, Harvard U., 1978. Bar: Tex. 1978, U.S. Dist. Ct. (so. dist., ea. dist.) Tex. 1979, U.S. Ct. Appeals (5th cir., 11th cir.) 1981. Assoc. Fulbright & Jaworski, Houston, 1978-86, ptnr., 1986—. Fellow Tex. Bar Found.; mem. ABA, Nat. Health Lawyers Assn., Nat. Assn. R.R. Trial Counsel, Tex. Bar Assn., Houston Bar Assn. (cert. civil trial law), Harvard Law Sch. Assn. Home: 2 Long Timbers Ln Houston TX 77024-5445 Office: Fulbright & Jaworski 1301 McKinney St Houston TX 77010*

MCCLURE, DAVID H., industrial engineer, utilities company manager; b. Kennesaw, Ga., Apr. 29, 1948; s. Benjamin H. and Katherine E. (Reece) McC.; 1 child, Charissa Diane. B in Indsl. Engring. Tech., So. Coll. Tech., 1976. Assoc. engr. Western Electric Co., Atlanta, 1972-75; jr. acct. Jack McPherson, CPA, Acworth, Ga., 1975-76; div. materials planner Southwire Co., Carrollton, Ga., 1976-78, indsl. engr., 1978-79; process engr. Alcan Cable, Tucker, Ga., 1979-82; rsch. specialist Ga. Power Co., Forest Park, 1982-86, staff rep., 1986-87, staff services engr., 1987—, head of quality assurance sect., 1982-91, mgr. quality and support, 1991—. Chmn. bd. dirs. Am. Diabetes Assn. Ga. Affiliate, Inc., Atlanta, 1985-87, nat. bd. dirs., 1988-91, mem. nat. com. on affiliate assocs., 1986-89, vice chmn., 1988-89, chmn. 1991-92, nat. So. region liaison, 1987-89; chmn. Nat. Com. on Fund Raising, 1989-91; nat. bd. mentor, 1989—, ctr. for equality excellence adv. coun., 1987—, chmn., 1989-90; chmn. Southeastern Quality Conf. Program, 1989, 90, 91, chmn. arrangements, 1992; mem. Ga. Dept. Human Resources Diabetes adv. com., 1989-92. Staff sgt. USAF, 1968-72. Named Vol. of Yr., Am. Diabetes Assn. Ga. Affiliate, Inc., 1983-84, 84-85. Mem. Inst. Indsl. Engrs. (sec. 1976-77, v.p. seminars 1977-78), Am. Soc. Quality Control (cert. quality engr. 1983—, chmn. bd.-elect Greater Atlanta sect. exec. bd. 1989-92), Nat. Mgmt. Assn. (LDR chpt., profl. devel. com. 1989-91), Capital Area Kiwanis Club (bd. dirs. 1989—, pres. elect 1990-91, pres. 1991-92). Baptist. Home: RR 2 Box 249R Jasper GA 30143-9568

MCCLURE, JOHN EDWARD, research biomedical scientist, virologist; b. El Campo, Tex., Nov. 20, 1944; s. John and Tillie Margaret (Cervenka) McC.; m. Mary Sue Raymond, Mar. 11, 1973; children: Jonathan Allan, Jennifer Karin. BSc in Chemistry, U. Tex., 1967; PhD in Molecular Virology, Baylor Coll. Medicine, 1994. Rsch. assoc. biochemistry U. Ariz., Tucson, 1968-71, Baylor Coll. Medicine, Houston, 1971-72, U. Tex. Med. Sch., Galveston, 1973-78, George Washington U. Med. Sch., Washington, 1978-82; rsch. assoc. pediatrics Baylor Coll. Medicine, Houston, 1982-85, rsch. instr. pediatrics, 1985—; rsch. scientist immunology Tex. Children's Hosp., Houston, 1985-94; R & D scientist Ramco Labs., Inc., Houston, 1994-96; rsch. cons. Hoffmann-LaRoche Inc., Nutley, N.J., 1975-79. Contbr. articles to profl. Jour. Immunology, Cancer Rsch., Cellular Immunology, Molecular Cellular Probes, Prog. in Med. Virology. Mem. Jr. C. of C. (Jaycees), LaMarque, Tex., 1981-82. Co-grantee Nat. Cancer Inst., NIH-USPHS, 1981-82. Mem. AAAS, Am. Soc. for Microbiology, Am. Chem. Soc., N.Y. Acad. Sci. Democrat. Lutheran. Office: 902 FM 518 Kemah TX 77565

MCCLURE, PAMELLA ANNE, drama educator, stage director; b. Charlotte, N.C., Jan. 15, 1956; d. Joe Stuart and Virginia Dell Houser (Sperry) McC.; m. John Steven Baker, Oct. 23, 1993. BA with honors, Davidson Coll., 1978. Program dir. Sta. WLOQ-FM, Winter Park, Fla., 1978-80; freelance stage dir. Atlanta, 1980—, freelance journalist, 1980—; program dir. Ga. Radio Reading Svc. for the Blind and Print Handicapped, Atlanta, 1985-86; exec. dir. Atlanta Theatre Coalition, Atlanta, 1986-89; writer, editor Life Office Mgmt. Assn., Atlanta, 1989-92; company mgr. Carl Ratcliff Dance Theatre, Atlanta, 1992; creative drama tchr. A.R.T. Station, Atlanta, 1992—; theatre lit. mgr., dir. edn., facilitator I.T.C. playwrights project; pres. bd. dirs. ACME Theatre Co., Atlanta, 1985-91; bd. dirs. Atlanta Theatre Coalition, 1986-90; theatre community rep. Ctrl. Atlanta Progress Arts and Recreation Task Force, Atlanta, 1987-89; panelist emerging arts fund Met. Atlanta Community Found., Atlanta, 1988-89. Dir. (play) Math and Aftermath, 1987, Living Color, 1989, Georgie Nobody, 1991, Gethsemane, 1993 (Best New Atlanta Play 1993). Affiliated artist Performing Artists for Nuclear Disarmament, Atlanta, 1981—; advisor S.E. Playwrights Project, Atlanta, 1986-90; coord. Atlanta Theatre Coalition's Ann. Holiday Show for Homeless Children, Atlanta, 1989-94. Grantee Atlanta Bur. Cultural Affairs, 1989. Mem. Alternate Roots. Democrat. Buddhist. Home: 2655 W Main St NW Atlanta GA 30318-1148

MCCLURE, ROGER JOHN, lawyer; b. Cleve., Nov. 22, 1943; s. Theron R. and Colene (Irwin) McC. BA, Ohio State U., 1965, JD cum laude, 1972; MA, Northwestern U., 1966. Bar: U.S. Ct. Appeals (D.C. cir.) 1974, U.S. Supreme Ct. 1978, Va. 1983, Md. 1983, Ohio, U.S. Ct. Appeals (4th, 5th & 10th cirs.). Asst. atty. gen. State of Ohio, Columbus, 1972; trial atty. FTC, Washington, 1972-76; sr. assoc. Law Offices of A.D. Berkeley, Washington, 1976-81; pvt. practice, Alexandria, Va., 1981-86; pres. Roger J. McClure, P.C., Alexandria, 1987—; del. Va. Gen. Assembly, 1992—; adj. prof. Antioch Sch. Law, Washington, 1982-84; mem. adv. bd. Va. Commerce Bank; host talk show Sta. WRC Radio, 1987-93, Sta. WPGC, 1993-94. Co-author: Winning the Syndication Game, 1988; bd. editors Ohio State U. Law Rev., 1970-72; contbr. numerous articles to profl. jours. Bd. dirs. No. Va. Cmty. Found., 1995—. Served with U.S. Army, 1967-69. Decorated Bronze Star. Fellow Esperti-Peterson Inst.; mem. D.C. Bar Assn. (real estate steering com. 1982-84, chmn. antitrust divsn. 1975-76), No. Va. Apt. Assn. (bd. dirs. 1988—, 1st v.p. 1987-88, pres. 1988-89), Nat. Network Estate Planning Attys., Dulles Area Transp. Assn. (bd. dirs.). Office: 500 N Washington St Alexandria VA 22314-2314

MCCLYMONDS, MARITA PETZOLDT, musicologist; b. St. Louis, Dec. 4, 1935; d. Adie Sylvester and Elda Louise Engert Petzoldt; m. Clarence Milton McClymonds, June 15, 1957; children: James Taylor, Julie Rose McClymonds Smith. BA, Culver-Stockton Coll., 1956; MA, U. Calif., 1971, PhD, 1978. Music dir. Edina (Mo.) Pub. Schs., 1955-57; music tchr. Jr. High Sch., Quincy, Ill., 1957-60; lectr. U. Calif., Berkeley, 1979; mgr. Berkeley Conservatory Ballet, Berkeley, 1979; dir. Ind. Learning Sch., Berkeley, 1980-81; asst. prof. dept. music U. Va., Charlottesville, 1981-86, assoc. prof., 1986—, chair dept. music, 1988-95; co-founder, contbr. Commedia dell'Opera, Berkeley, 1980-81; cons. A.Co.M. Sub-Project Catalogo dei libretti Sele Sistemi, Venice, Italy, 1990; mem. U. Va. Summer Rsch. Awards in the Humanities and Socials Scis. com., 1991—, chair, 1995—). Author: Niccolò Jommelli: The Last Years 1769-1774, 1980; area advisor, maj. contbr.: The New Grove Dictionary of Opera, 1987-92, The New Grove Dictionary of Music and Musicians, 1993—; co-editor: Opera and the Enlightenment, 1995; contbr. articles to profl. jours. Bd. dirs. League of Women Voters, Quincy, Ill., 1960-62, Denver, 1964-68; exec. chair Classical Chorale, Denver, 1965-68; co-founder, 1st pres. S.W. Denver Human Rels. Coun., 1967-68; mem. artistic com. Ashlawn Highlands Summer Festival Bd., 1991—. Recipient Disting. Alumna award for profl. achievements Culver-Stockton Coll., 1996; Am. Coun. Learned Socs. fellow, 1984; grantee Va. Found. Humanities and Pub. Policy, 1983, 84, 86, Dept. Edn., 1987, 89, NEH Travel, 1989, NEH Access, 1990-92. Mem. Am. Musicological Soc. (mem. nat. coun. 1984-87, mem. program com. 1987-88, newsletter editor 1990-93, mem. 50 fellowship com. 1995-98, chair nominations com. 1997), Am. Handel Soc., Am. Assn. Italian Studies, Am. Soc. 18th Century Studies (jour. adv. editor), women's Faculty and Profl. Assn. (mem. steering com. 1987-92), Internat. Jommelli Gesellschaft Stuttgart (founding mem. 1993), Internat. Musicological Soc., Inst. Advanced Mus. Studies (U.K.), Early Music Am., Coll. Music Soc., Sonneck Soc., Societa Italiana di Musicologia. Home: 701 Locust Ave # A Charlottesville VA 22902-4912 Office: McIntire Dept Music U Va 112 Old Cabell Hall Charlottesville VA 22903

MCCOLL, HUGH LEON, JR., bank executive; b. Bennettsville, S.C., June 18, 1935; s. Hugh Leon and Frances Pratt (Carroll) McC.; m. Jane Bratton Spratt, Oct. 3, 1959; children: Hugh Leon III, John Spratt, Jane Bratton. B.S. in Bus. Adminstrn, U. N.C., 1957. Trainee NCNB Nat. Bank, Charlotte, 1959-61, officer, 1961-65, v.p., 1965-68, sr. v.p., 1968, div. exec., 1969, exec. v.p., 1970-73, vice chmn. bd., 1973-74, pres., 1974-83, also dir.; chmn., CEO NationsBank Corp., Charlotte, 1983—; bd. dirs. Sonoco Products Inc., Hartsville, S.C., CSX Corp., Richmond, Va., Jefferson-Pilot Corp., Greensboro, N.C. Trustee Heineman Found., Charlotte, 1976—, Queens Coll., Charlotte; bd. visitors Grad. Sch. Bus. U. N.C. at Chapel Hill; chmn. Charlotte Uptown Devel. Corp., 1978-81, 85. 1st lt. USMCR, 1957-59. Mem. Bankers Roundtable (mem. trialateral commn.), Am. Bankers Assn., N.C. Bankers Assn. (pres. 1974). Democrat. Presbyterian. Office: NationsBank Corp 100 N Tryon Charlotte NC 28255*

MCCOLLEY, BEVERLY ALICE, English language educator; b. East Orange, N.J., May 31, 1942; d. James Edward and Jessie Donaldson (Morrow) Brown; m. John Allen McColley, Apr. 27, 1963 (div. Oct. 1977); children: Elizabeth Alice, Laura Anne. AB in English, Rutgers U., 1966; Ma in English, Middlebury Coll., 1989. Tchr. Latin, humanities Gayle Jr. High Sch., Stafford, Va., 1971-73; tchr. English Broadwater Acad., Exmore, Va., 1975-77, Plaza Jr. High Sch., Virginia Beach, Va., 1977-78; tchr. Latin, English Brandon Jr. High Sch., Virginia Beach, Va., 1978-87, Green Run High Sch., Virginia Beach, Va., 1988-89; tchr. English Salem High Sch., Virginia Beach, Va., 1989-90; tchr. Latin Virginia Beach Jr. High Sch., 1990-91, Great Neck Jr. High Sch., Virginia Beach, 1990-91; tchr. English Norfolk (Va.) Acad., 1991-95, tchr. Latin, 1995-96, instructional libr., 1996—; fellow in creative writing St. Andrews U., Scotland, 1995; presenter, cons. in field. Author of poems; contbr. articles to profl. publs. Recipient Alice Sherry Meml. Poetry 1st pl. prize Poetry Soc. Va., 1993, Karma Deane Ogden Meml. Poetry prize 2d pl. Poetry Soc. Va., 1994, 3rd pl., 1995; Nancy Byrd Turner Meml. Poetry prize 2d pl. Poetry Soc. Va., 1996; Summer Poetry Inst. fellow U. Va., 1986, Ruth E. Admas fellow Assn. Alumnae Douglass Coll., 1989; Virginia Beach Reading Coun. scholar, 1987, Lyndhurst scholar Middlebury Coll., 1985, 87, 88, 89. Mem. Am. Classical League, Nat. Coun. Tchrs. English, Va. Assn. Tchrs. English (Svc. award 1983, 85, V-Bate Tchr. of Yr. 1990), Harvard Tchrs. Network, Tidewater Classical Symposium, Phi Delta Kappa. Episcopalian. Office: Norfolk Acad 1585 Wesleyan Dr Norfolk VA 23502-5512

MCCOLLOCH, MURRAY MICHAEL, lawyer; b. Los Angeles, June 9, 1926; s. Carrick L. and Irma (Shelton) McC.; m. Jane Frye, Oct. 17, 1953; children: Sidney Michael, Mark Lindsey. BA, U. Md., 1949; JD, Harvard U., 1952. Bar: U.S. Dist. Ct. D.C. 1953, U.S. Ct. Appeals (D.C. cir.) 1953, U.S. Ct. Claims 1953, U.S. Ct. Customs and Patent Appeals 1953, U.S. Tax Ct. 1953, Calif. 1954, U.S. Dist. Ct. (so. dist.) Calif. 1954, Va. 1963, Tex. 1979, U.S. Dist. Ct. (no. dist.) Tex. 1980. Law clk. to presiding judge U.S. Ct. Appeals, Washington, 1952-53; atty. subcom. adminstrn. internal revenue laws U.S. Ho. Reps., Washington, 1953; assoc. Gray, Binkley & Pfaelzer, Los Angeles, 1953-55; asst. counsel Occidental Life Co. Calif., Los Angeles,

1955-62; v.p. and counsel Fidelity Bankers Life Ins. Co., Richmond, Va., 1962-67; v.p., sec. and counsel J.C. Penney Life Ins. Co. subs. J.C. Penney Co., Inc., N.Y.C., 1967-76; sr. v.p., sec. and counsel J.C. Penney Life Ins. Co. subs. J.C. Penney Co., Inc., Plano, Tex., 1982-94, J.C. Penney Life Ins. Co., Great Am. Res. Ins. Co., Dallas, 1976-82; of counsel Thompson, Coe, Cousins & Irons, L.L.P., Dallas, 1994—; chmn. industry adv. com. Conf. Ins. Legis., 1982-83; chmn. legal sect. Am. Coun. Life Ins., 1985; chmn. Fla. Ins. Coun., 1990-91. Author: Group Insurance Trusts, 1962. Bd. dirs. Plano Chamber Orch. Served as cpl. AC U.S. Army, 1944-45. Mem. ABA, Dallas Bar Assn., Assn. Life Ins. Counsel, Plano Bar Assn. Republican. Methodist. Home: 3516 Robin Rd Plano TX 75075-7818 Office: Thompson Coe Cousins & Irons LLP 200 Crescent Ct 11th Fl Dallas TX 75201-1840

MCCOLLOUGH, MICHAEL LEON, astronomer; b. Sylva, N.C., Nov. 3, 1953; s. Stribling Mancell and Vivian Hazel (Bradley) McC. B.S., Auburn U., 1975, M.S., 1981; PhD, Ind. U., 1989. Lab. instr. Auburn (Ala.) U., 1974-75, grad. asst., 1975-77, lab. technician, 1977-78; assoc. instr. Ind. U., Bloomington, 1978-86; ops. astronomer Computer Scis. Corp., Balt., 1988-90, sci. planning and scheduling system dep. br. chief, 1990-92; data processing and distbn. mgr. U.S. ROSAT Sci. Data Ctr., 1992-93; asst. system mgr. BATSE Data Analysis System, 1993—; vis. lectr. Okla. State U., 1986-87; vis. asst. prof. U. Okla., 1987-88. Recipient Achievement award Space Telescope Sci. Inst., 1990, 91, Pub. Svc. Group Achievement award NASA, 1991, Cert. Recognition, 1991, 93. Mem. Am. Astron. Soc., Royal Astron. Soc., Astron. Soc. Pacific, Am. Phys. Soc., Soc. Physics Students, Sigma Xi (assoc.), Sigma Pi Sigma. Baptist. Home: 201 Water Hill Rd Apt G13 Madison AL 35758-2919 Office: NASA/MSFC Code ES84 Huntsville AL 35812

MC COLLOUGH, NEWTON CLARK, III, orthopaedic surgeon; b. Butler, Pa., July 17, 1934; s. Newton C. and Margaret Elizabeth (Mattocks) McC.; m. Mary Eva Semanski, Feb. 22, 1968; children—Peter Scott, Amy Marie. B.A., Duke U., 1956; M.D., U. Pa., 1959. Diplomate: Am. Bd. Orthopaedic Surgery. Intern Jackson Meml. Hosp., Miami, Fla., 1959-60; resident in orthopaedic surgery Jackson Meml. Hosp., 1960-64; dir. orthopaedic resident edn. Orange Meml. Hosp., Orlando, Fla., 1965-66; asst. prof. orthopaedics and rehab. U. Miami Sch. Medicine, 1968-72, assoc. prof., 1972-76, prof., vice chmn. dept., 1976-78, prof., chmn. dept., 1978-86; dir. rehab. Jackson Meml. Hosp., Miami, 1972-82, chief orthopedics and rehab., 1978-86; dir. med. affairs Internat. Shriners Hosps. for Crippled Children, Tampa, Fla., 1986—; dir. Am. Bd. for Certification in Prosthetics/Orthotics, 1974-77; mem. Health Planning Council So. Fla. Task Force on Long Term Patient Care, 1974-77; asst. med. dir. Div. of Children's Med. Services, State of Fla., 1975-86; chmn. Statewide Com. for Spinal Cord Injury, 1976-78. Trustee Jour. Bone and Joint Surgery, 1992—, vice chmn., 1996—; contbr. articles to med. jours. Served to lt. comdr. M.C. USNR, 1966-68. Decorated Legion of Merit. Mem. ACS, AMA, Am. Acad. ORthopaedic Surgeons (bd. dirs. 1978-79, 87-92, 2d v.p. 1987-88, 1st v.p. 1988-89, pres. 1989-90), Fla. Orthopaedic Soc. (mem. exec. com. 1978—), Miami Orthopaedic Soc. (v.p. 1978-79), Am. Acad. Orthotists and Prosthetists (hon.), Fla. Med. Soc. Hillsborough County Med. Assn., Am. Congress Rehab. Medicine, Nat. Rehab. Assn., Scoliosos Rsch. Soc., Internat. Soc. Prosthetics and Orthotics, Am. Orthopaedic Assn., Orthopaedic Rsch. and Edn. Found. (trustee 1991—, sec. 1995—), Internat. Soc. Prosthetics and Orthotics (dir. 1980—), Assn. Children's Prosthetic and Orthotic Clinics (pres. 1983-84), Rehab. Engring. Soc. N.Am. (dir. 1980—), Am. Spinal Injury Assn., Internat. Med. Soc. Paraplegia, Pediatric Orthopaedic Soc. (dir. 1983-84, pres. 1984-85), 20th Century Orthopaedic Assn. (treas. 1984-89), Am. Acad. Pediatrics, Phi Beta Kappa, Alpha Omega. Republican. Lutheran. Home: 3206 Mermaid Ct New Port Richey FL 34652-3045 Office: Internat Shriners Hosps for Crippled Children 2900 N Rocky Point Dr Tampa FL 33607-1435

MC COLLUM, IRA WILLIAM, JR. (BILL MC COLLUM), congressman; b. Brooksville, Fla., July 12, 1944; s. Ira William and Arline Gray (Lockhart) McC.; m. Ingrid Mary Seebohm, Sept. 25, 1971; children: Douglas Michael, Justin Randolph, Andrew Lockhart. BA, U. Fla., 1965, JD, 1968. Bar: Fla. 1968. Ptnr. Pitts, Eubanks & Ross (P.A.), Orlando, Fla., 1973-80; mem. 97th-102nd Congresses from 5th Dist. Fla., 1981-92, 103d-104th Congresses from 8th Dist. Fla., 1993—; ranking minority mem., mem. banking and fin. svcs. subcom. on fin. instns. supervision, mem. regulation and deposit ins. com., chmn. judiciary subcom. on crime, mem. select com. on intelligence; vice chair House Rep. Conf. 101st-103d Congresses. Chmn. Rep. Exec. Com. Seminole County, Fla., 1976-80; county chmn.'s rep. 5th Dist. Fla. State Rep. Exec. Com., 1977-80; co-chmn. rep. platform com., 1992. With USN, 1969-72. Mem. Fla. Bar, Naval Res. Assn., Res. Officers Assn., Orange County Bar Assn. (exec. coun. 1975-79), Am. Legion, Mil. Order World Wars, Fla. Blue Key, Phi Delta Phi, Omicron Delta Kappa, Kiwanis. Episcopalian. Office: 2266 Rayburn HOB Washington DC 20515*

MCCOLLUM, JAMES FOUNTAIN, lawyer; b. Reidsville, N.C., Mar. 24, 1946; s. James F. and Dell (Frazier) McC.; m. Susan Shasek, Apr. 26, 1969; children: Audra Lynne, Amy Elizabeth. BS, Fla. Atlantic U., 1968; JD, Fla. State U., 1972. Bar: U.S. Ct. Appeals (5th cir.) 1973, Fla. 1972, U.S. Ct. Appeals (11th cir.) 1982. Assoc. Kennedy & McCollum, 1972-73; prin. James F. McCollum, P.A., 1973-77, McCollum & Oberhausen, P.A., 1977-80, McCollum & Rhoades, Sebring, Fla., 1980-86; pres. Highlands Devel. Concepts, Inc., Sebring, 1982—; sec. Focus Broadcast Communications, Inc., Sebring, 1982-87; mng. ptnr. Highlands Investment Service. Treas. Highlands County chpt. ARC, 1973-76; vestryman St. Agnes Episcopal Ch., 1973—, chancellor, 1978—; mem. Fla. Sch. Bd. Atty.'s Assn., 1974—, bd. dirs., 1989—, pres., 1995-96; mem. Com. 100 of Highlands County, 1975-83, bd. dirs., 1985-87, chmn., 1991-92; chmn. Highlands County High Speed Rail Task Force; chmn. bd., treas. Ctrl. Fla. Racing Assn., 1976-78; chmn. Leadership Sebring: life mem., past pres. Highlands Little Theatre, Inc.; bd. dirs. Palms of Sebring Nursing Home, 1988-90, Palms Estate Mobile Home Park, Sebring Airport Authority, 1988-90, treas., 1988, chmn. indsl. com., 1988, vice-chmn., 1989-90, chmn., 1990-91, Highlands County High Speed Rail Task Force, 1986-89; bd. dirs. Highlands County Family YMCA, 1985-93, pres. Sebring br., 1992-93, chmn. bldg. com., 1992-94. Recipient ARC citation, 1974, Presdl. award of appreciation Fla. Jaycees, 1980-81, 82, 85, Outstanding Svc. award Highlands Coun. of 100, 1988, Most Valuable Player award Highlands Little Theatre, Inc., 1986, Zenon Significant Achievement award, 1991; named Jaycee of Year, Sebring Jaycees, 1981, Outstanding Local Chpt. Pres., U.S. Jaycees, 1977. Outstanding Service award Highlands Council of 100, 1988. Mem. ABA, ATLA, Comml. Law League Am., Am. Arbitration Assn. (comml. arbitration panel), Nat. Assn. Retail Credit Attys., Fla. Bar (jour. com.), Highlands County Bar Assn. (past chmn. legal aid com.), Fla. Sch. Bd. Attys. Assn. (dir. 1989—, v.p. 1993-94, pres. 1994-95), Greater Sebring C. of C. (dir. 1982-89, pres. 1986-87, chmn. transp. com. 1986—, Most Valuable Dir. award 1986, 87), Fla. Jaycees (life mem. internat. senate 1977—), Lions (bd. dirs. 1972-73, v.p. 1994—, Disting. award 1984). Republican. Episcopalian. Office: 129 S Commerce Ave Sebring FL 33870-3602

MCCOLLUM, NANCY EDWARDS, vocational educator; b. Monroe, N.C., May 30, 1942; d. James William and Edna Louise (McLaughlin) Edwards; 1 child, John Bennett. BSHE, U. N.C., Greensboro, 1964; MEd in Counseling, Winthrop U., Rock Hill, S.C., 1982; Adminstrv. Cert., U. N.C., Charlotte, 1983. Tchr. Prince William County Schs., Manassas, Va., 1968-69, Forsyth County Schs., Winston-Salem, 1964-67, 70-71, Monroe (N.C.) City Schs., 1967-68, 75-86; spl. populations coord. Union County Schs., Monroe, 1986-88, industry edn. coord., 1988—; cons. PACE Learning Sys., Ala., 1987-89. Pres. Union Diversified Ind., Monroe, 1992-93. Mem. Union County C. of C. (com. mem. 1990-96), N.C. Vocat. Assn. (pres. guidance divsn. 1996—). Baptist. Office: Union County Career Ctr 600 Brewer Dr Monroe NC 28112

MCCOLLUM, SARAH, artist; b. May 16, 1955. BS in Arch., U. Va., 1977. vis. artist Indiana (Pa.) U. Pa., 1990. Appeared in shows Balt., 1987-93, West Springfield, Mass., 1987-93, Mesa, Ariz., 1988, others; exhbns. include Buffalo State U., 1985, Ivy (Va.) Gallery (Honor award), 1986, U. Fla., Gainesville, 1986, Craft Alliance, St. Louis, 1986, Sansar, Washington, 1981, 86, 87, 88, Showplace Design Ctr., San Francisco, 1988, Key Gallery, Richmond, 1992, Springfield (Ill.) Art Assn., 1993, Arrowmont Gallery, Gatlinburg, Tenn., 1993, Main Line Arts Ctr., Haverford, Pa., 1994; represented in pvt. collections. Office: PO Box 18 Free Union VA 22940-0018

MCCOMAS, GARY, fire chief. Chief Lexington Fire Dept. Office: Fire & Emergency Svcs Div 219 E 3rd St Lexington KY 40508-1827

MCCOMBS, CANDACE CRAGEN, medical educator; b. Springfield, Ill., Jan. 30, 1947; d. Francis H. and Blanche Cragen; m. Joseph P. Michalski, Dec. 22, 1963; children: Jeanette R., Zachary P. Michalski. BS in Biology, AB in Psychology, Stanford U., 1969; PhD in Genetics, San Diego State U./U. Calif., Berkeley, 1974. Postdoctoral rsch. fellow dept. medicine U. Calif., San Francisco, 1974-78; postdoctoral rsch. fellow, assoc. rsch. immunologist VA Med. Ctr., Long Beach, Calif., 1978-82; asst. prof. medicine La. State U. Med. Ctr., New Orleans, 1982-84, assoc. prof. medicine, 1984-88, prof. medicine, 1988-80; prof. medicine, chief divsn. exptl. medicine U. South Ala., Mobile, 1990—; mem. instl. rev. bd., rsch. and career devel. com., Rostov-U.S.A. med. exch. com. U. South Ala.; adj. asst. prof. medicine U. Calif., Irvine, 1978-82; vis. prof. Univ. Coll., Galway, Ireland, 1988-89; mem. peer rev. panel health rsch. La. Bd. Regents Rsch. and Devel. Panel, 1983; reviewer study sessions NIH, 1992-96, peer reviewer, 1992; reviewer rsch. proposals VA Ctrl. Office. Patentee immunosorbent Assay for alpha-1-antirypsin, kit employing said assay, monoclonal antibody to alpha-a-antirypsin, hybridoma for producing said monoclonal antibody; ad hoc reviewer profl. jours.; contbr. over 86 articles and abstracts to med. and profl. jours. Nat. Merit scholar; rsch. fellow USPHS, 1974-77, Arthritis Found., 1978-81; recipient Rsch. Career Devel. award NIH, 1981-86; Fogarty Sr. Internat. fellow, 1988-89; grantee Am. Behcet Found., 1980-81, Am. Heart Assn., 1977-81, 81-82, Am. Lung Assn. Calif., 1981-82, NIH, 1981-86, 83-84, 84-87, 86-89, 87-88, 88-92, 92-93, Kroc Found., 1984, Cancer Crusaders, 1984-85, Edward G. Schlieder Ednl. Found., 1986, La. Edn. Quality Support Fund, 1987-92, Thrasher Rsch. Fund, 1988-89, Merck Sharp/Dohme Rsch. Labs., 1993. Mem. AAAS, Am. Assn. Immunologists (Travel award 1983), Am. Soc. Human Genetics, Fedn. Am. Socs. for Exptl. Biology, So. Soc. for Clin. Investigation. Office: U South Ala CCCB # 486 Mobile AL 36688

MCCONNELL, ADDISON MITCHELL, JR. (MITCH MCCONNELL, JR.), senator, lawyer; b. Tuscumbia, AL, Feb. 20, 1942; s. Addison Mitchell and Julia (Shockley) McC.; children: Eleanor Hayes, Claire Redmon, Marion Porter; m. Elaine Chao, Feb. 6, 1993. B.A. with honors, U. Louisville, 1964; J.D., U. Ky., 1967. Bar: Ky. 1967. Chief legis. asst. to Senator Marlow Cook, Washington, 1968-70; sole practice Louisville, 1970-74; dep. asst. U.S. atty. gen. Washington, 1974-75; judge Jefferson County, Louisville, 1978-85; U.S. Senator from Ky., 1985—, chmn. select com. on ethics 104th Congress. Chmn. Jefferson County Republican Com., 1973-74; co-chmn. Nat. Child Tragedies Coalition, 1981; chmn., founder Ky. Task Force on Exploited and Missing Children, 1982; mem. Pres.'s Partnership on Child Safety. Recipient commendation Nat. Trust on Hist. Preservation in U.S., 1982, Conservationist of Yr. award League Ky. Sportsmen, 1983, cert. of appreciation Am. Correctional Assn., 1985. Mem. Ky. Assn. County Judge Execs. (pres. 1982), Nat. Inst. Justice (adv. bd. 1982-84). Republican. Baptist. Office: SR-120 Russell Office Bldg Washington DC 20510-1702*

MCCONNELL, ALBERT LYNN, college educator; b. Springfield, Ohio, Oct. 20, 1946; s. Jack Pershing and Betty Ann (Venema) M.; m. Cathy Jo Garland, July 24, 1986; children: Alisha Marcel, Nickolas Alan, Ciara Lynn. BA, Cen. State U., 1969; MA, Webster U., 1983; MS, USACGSC, 1984. Commd. 2d. lt. U.S. Army, 1969, advanced through grades. to maj., 1980; ret., 1989; served as inf. bn. intelligence officer Schofield Barracks, Hawaii, 1970-71; inf. co. comdr., asst. ops. officer, inf. bn. Schofield Barracks, 1971; intelligence analyst and briefer U.S. Mil. Assistance Command, Schofield Barracks, 1972-73; instr. U.S. Army Intelligence Sch., Ft Huachuca, Ariz., 1973-77; served in 3rd Armored Div., Frankfurt, West Germany, 1980-81; project officer Combined Arms Ctr., Ft. Leavenworth, Kans., 1981-83, comdr. spl. security detachment, 1981-83; dir. intelligence, asst. chief staff for intelligence U.S. Army South, Ft. Clayton, Panama, 1984-85; mng. exec. officer U.S. Army South, Ft. Davis, Panama, 1985-86; tactical intelligence officer, chief adminstrv. svcs. U.S. Army Air Def. Arty. Sch., Ft. Bliss, Tex., 1986-87, dep. directorate chief, 1987-88, sr. intelligence officer, dept. div. chief, 1988-89; ops. analyst RAM Inc., Sierra Vista, Ariz., 1989-92; prof. So. Ohio Coll., Columbus, 1992, Bliss Coll., Columbus, 1993; store mgr. Circle K Corp., Yuma, Ariz., 1993-94; tchr. Glendale (Ariz.) Union H.S., 1994-95; mgr. Dexter Book Store, 1995-96; instr. Ariz. Inst. Bus. & Tech., Phoenix, 1996—; instr. Mansfield Bus. Sch., El Paso, Tes., 1987-89; adj. prof. Chapman U., Sierra Vista, 1990-92; tax preparer H&R Block, Sierra Vista, 1990-92. Treas. Antioch Missionary Bapt. Ch., Huachuca City, Ariz., 1991-92. Decorated Bronze Star. Mem. Assn. U.S. Army, Air Force Assn., Ret. Officers Assn., Assn. Old Crows, Scabbard and Blade, Phi Alpha Theta, Iota Beta Sigma. Republican. Baptist.

MCCONNELL, JAMES JOSEPH, internist; b. Lynchburg, Va., Sept. 4, 1946; s. Willis Samson and Hope (Lewis) McC.; m. Pamela Marie Sabatino, Apr. 7, 1979. BS, Lynchburg Coll., 1968; MD, Med. Coll. Va., 1972. Diplomate Am. Bd. Internal Medicine. Intern USN, Portsmouth, Va., 1972-73; dir. occupational medicine Norfolk Naval Shipyard, Portsmouth, Va., 1973-75; resident internal medicine USN, Portsmouth, Va., 1975-78; dir. internal medicine clinic Naval Amphibian Base, Virginia Beach, Va., 1978-79; physician internal medicine Wythe Med. Assn., Wytheville, Va., 1979-80; private practice Wytheville, Va., 1981—; bd. dirs. Spl. Care Svcs., Wytheville, Echo Vascular Lab., Advanced Cardiac Life Support. Recipient Outstanding Citizenship award M.T. Rodgers, 1982, Woodsmen of World, 1984. Mem. AMA, Am. Coll. Physicians, Am. Soc. Internal Medicine, Am. Heart Assn. (Va. faculty). Home: 625 S 9th St Wytheville VA 24382-3213 Office: 365 W Ridge Rd Wytheville VA 24382-1008

MCCONNELL, JOHN DOWLING, urologist, educator; b. Independence, Kans., Oct. 16, 1953; m. Melinda Bohr, 1975; 1 child, Cara. BA with honors in Biochemistry, U. Kans., 1975; MD magna cum laude, Loyola U., 1978. Diplomate Am. Bd. Urology. Intern in surgery Parkland Meml. Hosp., Dallas, 1978-79, resident in surgery, 1979-80; resident in urology U. Tex. Southwestern Med. Sch. Affiliated Hosps., Dallas, 1980-84; asst. prof. divsn. urology U. Tex. Southwestern Med. Ctr., Dallas, 1984-91, assoc. prof. divsn. urology, 1991-94, dir. Prostate Disease Ctr., 1992—, prof., chmn. divsn. urology, 1994-96, prof., chmn. dept. urology, 1996—; staff physician Parkland Meml. Hosp., Zale Lipshy U. Hosp., VA Med. Ctr., St. Paul, Children's Med. Ctr., 1984—; chief urology svc. VA Med. Ctr., Dallas, 1986-91; mem. dir. U. Tex. Southwestern Outpatient Surgery Ctr., Aston, 1986-90, U. Tex. Southwestern Urology Clinic, Aston, 1993—; mem. coms., study sects. NIH, 1990—; mem. numerous hosp. coms.; cons., lectr in field. Author: (with others) Common Problems in Infertiligy and Impotemce, 1989, Harrison's Principles of Internal Medicine, 12th edit., 1991, Infertility in the Male, 3d edit., 1996, Reproductive Issues and the Aging Male, 1992, Textbook for Reproductive Medicine, 1993, Principles of Surgery, 6th edit., 1993; editor: Technical Report: Guidelines for the Diagnosis and Treatment of BPH, 1994, Clinical Guidelines for the Diagnosis and Treatment of BPH, 1994; asst. editor The Jour. of Urology, 1988-92, reviewer, 1986—; mem. editorial bd. Jour. Andrology, 1990-93, World Jour. of Urology, 1990—, Urology, 1992—; reviewer Biology of Reproduction, 1988—, The Prostate, 1988—, Jour. Andrology, 1989—; contbr. articles to profl. jours. Recipient Fellowship award Nat. Kidney Found., 1989-90, Edwin Beer award N.Y. Acad. of Medicine, 1989-91; instl. grantee U. Tex. Southwestern Med. Ctr., 1985-86, Merit Rev. grantee VA, 1989-92, Clin. Investigation grantee Am. Cancer Soc., 1991-93, grantee Agy. Health Care Policy and Rsch., 1990-92, 92—, NIH, 1992—, 93—, Merck Rsch. Labs., 1987-91, 88—, Merck Sharp & Dohme Rsch. Labs., 1990-92, 90—, 92—, others. Fellow ACS (program chmn. North Tex. chpt.); mem. AMA (diagnostic and therapeutic tech. assessment com. 1992—), AAAS, Am. Urological Assn. (South Ctrl. sect., Scholar Alumni Assn., mem. numerous coms., 2d prize Clin. Rsch. Essay 1982, Rsch. scholar 1984-86, Gold Cystoscope award 1991), Am. Soc. Andrology (membership com. 1987-89), Am. Soc. Cell Biology, Am. Diabetes Assn., Am. Fertility Soc., Am. Fedn. Clin. Rsch., Tex. Med. Assn. (sec. urologic sect. 1985-86, pres. 1986-87), Tex. Urol. Soc. (exec. com. 1989-92), Tex. Assn. Genitourinary Surgeons, Dallas County Med. Soc., Soc. for the Study of Reproduction, Soc. Univ. Urologists, Soc. Basic Urology Rsch., Urologic Rsch. Soc., Nat. Urologic Forum, Tex. Surg. Soc., Urol. Investigator's Forum, Phi Beta Kappa, Alpha Omega Alpha. Home: 4326 Enfield Dr Dallas TX 75220-3810 Office: U Tex Southwestern Med Ctr Dept Urology 5323 Harry Hines Blvd Dallas TX 75235-9110

MCCONNON, LORENA ANNA, secondary education educator; b. Camp Lejeune, N.C., Jan. 1, 1957; d. James Elgin and Era McConnon; 1 child, James Joseph. AA, East Ark. C.C., 1977; BS in Edn., Ark. State U., 1993, MS in Edn., 1994. Cert. secondary English tchr. with mid. sch. endorsement, Ark. Tchr. English, Forrest City (Ark.) H.S., 1994—. Mem. Nat. Coun. Tchrs. English, Kappa Delta Pi, Gamma Beta Phi. Home: PO Box 1977 Forrest City AR 72336 Office: Forrest City HS 467 Victoria Forrest City AR 72335

MCCORD, BETTY J., reading specialist; b. Bowman, S.C., Mar. 4, 1940; d. Permon Walter and Pauline S. (Glover) Smith; m. Nathaniel McCord, Feb. 19, 1959 (div. May 1981); children: Nathan Anthony, Carla Tajuan, James Edward. BA, Jersey City State Coll., 1975, MA, 1979. Cert. tchr. social studies K-12, reading specialist. Home instr. Jersey City, 1975-78; grad. asst. Jersey City State Coll., 1978-79, spl. tchr. reading, 1979-81; reading specialist Denmark (S.C.) Tech. Coll., 1982—; Cons., Gov.'s Work Force Specialist, Denmark, 1989—; tutor, coord. Reading in Industry, Denmark, 1989. Author: (poetry) Hugo, 1989. Liaison, Police and Community Rels., Jersey City, 1978-79; former pres. New Castle West Community Orgn., Columbia, S.C., 1987—; asst. dir. tutoring program 2d Nazareth Bapt. Ch., Columbia, 1989—. Recipient service and appreciation awards. Mem. NAACP, AAUW, Internat. Reading Assn., S.C. Tech. Edn. Assn., S.C. Internat. Reading Assn., S.C. Assn. Devel. Educators, Wil Lou Gray Adult Reading Coun. (rec. sec. 1989), Kappa Delta Pi. Democrat. Home: 319 Carterhill Dr West Columbia SC 29172-3106 Office: Denmark Tech Coll PO Box 327 Denmark SC 29042-0327

MCCORD, GLORIA DAWN HARMON, music educator, choral director, organist; b. Jacksonville, Fla., June 14, 1949; d. Earl H. and C. Grace (Lupo) Harmon; m. Mark L. McCord, Sr., Aug. 7, 1971; children: M. Lance, Ian H. BMus in Edn., Fla. State U.; MMus in Choral Conducting, La. State U.; postgrad., U. New Orleans, U. Ga. Cert. tchr., Ga. Classroom music tchr. Nassau County (Fla.) Bd. Edn., 1971, Orange County (Fla.) Bd. Edn., 1971-74; choral dir., gen. music tchr. Fulton County (Ga.) Bd. Edn., 1974-75; dir. music Aldersgate United Meth. Ch., Slidell, La., 1978-86; tchr. for gifted and talented in music St. Tammany Parish Schs., La., 1988-91; asst. prof. arts and scis. Brenau U., Gainesville, Ga., 1991—; registrar, pub. rels. dir., choral dir. Firespark Summer Sch. for Students Gifted in Arts, 1992—; organist Riverside Mil. Acad., 1994—; presenter, adjudicator North Gwinnett Piano club, 1992, North Gwinnett Federated Festival, 1993, 95, 96, Ga. Music Educators Edn. Piano Festival, 1993; choir dir. Ga. Music Educators Dist. IX Honor Choir, 1993, others; series dir. radio broacast Panorama; adjudicator West Gwinnett Fed. Piano, 1995. Interim organist 1st United Meth. Chancel Choir, 1993, other positions; evaluator United Meth. Ch.; sec. Gainesville H.S. Band Boosters, Gainesville H.S. PTA, 1992-94. Recipient Lake Como (Orange county, Fla.) NEA Tchr. of the Yr., 1973. Mem. Am. Choral Dirs. Assn., United Meth. Am. Guild of Organists, Music Educators Nat. Assn (seminar facilitator 1993), Music Tchrs. Nat. Assn., Ga. Music Tchrs. Assn., Ga. Music Educators, Sigma Alpha Iota. Office: Brenau Univ 1 Centennial Cir Gainesville GA 30501-3668

MC CORD, GUYTE PIERCE, JR., retired judge; b. Tallahassee, Sept. 23, 1914; s. Guyte Pierce and Jean (Patterson) McC.; student Davidson Coll., 1933-34; B.A., J.D., U. Fla., 1940; m. Laura Elizabeth Mack, Dec. 16, 1939; children: Florence Elizabeth, Guyte Pierce III, Edward LeRoy. Admitted to Fla. bar, 1940; practiced in Tallahassee, 1940-60; dep. commr. Fla. Insl. Commn., 1946-47; pros. atty. Leon County, 1947-48; asst. gen. counsel Fla. Public Service Commn., 1949-60; judge 2d Jud. Circuit Fla., Tallahassee, 1960-74; judge Ct. Appeal 1st Dist. Fla., 1974-83, chief judge, 1977-79; mem. Fla. Senate Pres.'s Council on Criminal Justice 1972; mem. appellate ct. rules com. Fla. Supreme Ct., 1977-78, mem. appellate ct. structure commn. 1978-79. Pres., Murat House Assn., Inc., 1967-69; bd. dirs. Fla. Heritage Found., 1969-70, mem. exec. com., 1965-69; mem. Andrew Jackson staff of Springtime Tallahassee, 1973-74, 84-86, Andrew Jackson, 1987. Served to comdr. USNR, 1942-46, 52-53. Mem. Ret. Officers Assn., ABA, Fla. Bar, Tallahassee Bar Assn., Fla. Conf. Circuit Judges (sec.-treas. 1970, chmn. 1972), Fla. State U. Pres. Club, Phi Delta Phi, Sigma Alpha Epsilon. Presbyterian (elder 1960—, ch. trustee 1981-86). Club: Kiwanis (dir. 1958-59). Home: 502 S Ride Tallahassee FL 32303-5164 Office: PO Box 4121 Tallahassee FL 32315-4121

MCCORD, J. WILLIAM, anesthesiologist; b. Winchester, Tenn., Aug. 27, 1949; s. Joseph William and Sarah Omega (Woodall) McC.; m. Nancy Lee Kincade, Apr. 26, 1982; children: Jim, Mike, Kelly Lee, Megan. BA, U. of the South, 1971; MS magna cum laude, Mid. Tenn. State U., 1973; DO, Kansas City Coll, 1980. Diplomate Am. Bd. Family Practice, Am. Osteo. Bd. Anesthesiology. Intern Flint (Mich.) Osteo. Hosp., 1980-81; resident physician St. Joseph Hosp., Flint, 1981-83; pvt. practice family medicine Winchester, Tenn., 1983-89; resident in anesthesiology Vanderbilt U. Hosp., Nashville, 1989-91, resident physician, 1989-91; asst. prof. anesthesiology Vanderbilt U. Sch. Medicine, Nashville, 1991-94; mem. courtesy staff County Regional Hosp., Columbia, Tenn.; mem. staff Columbia Outpatient Surgery; cons. occupl. health U. Tenn. Space Inst., Tullahoma, 1987-89; cons. to health related bds. Office Gen. Counsel, State of Tenn., Nashville, 1993—; mem. gov.'s task force for rural healthcare Tenn. High Edn. Commn., 1989-90. Fellow Am. Acad. Family Physicians, Fedn State Med. Bds. U.S. (bd. dirs.); mem. Tenn. Bd. Osteo. Examiners (sec. 1993—), Tenn. Osteo. Med. Assn. (pres. 1988, trustee 1989-92), Am. Osteo. Assn., Am. Assn. of Osteo. Examiners (v.p. 1995—), Am. Soc. Antesthesiologists, Am. Osteo. Coll. Anesthesiologists. Mem. Ch. of Christ. Home: 6325 Mapledale Ln Brentwood TN 37027-5601 Office: McCord Med Svcs 6325 Mapledale Ln Brentwood TN 37027-5601

MCCORD, JAMES RICHARD, III, chemical engineer, mathematician; b. Norristown, Ga., Sept. 2, 1932; s. Zachariah Thigpen Houser Jr. and Neilie Mae (Sumner) McC.; m. Louise France Manning, Oct. 1956 (div. 1974); children: Neil Alexander, Stuart James, Valerie France, Kent Richard. Student, Abraham Baldwin Agrl. Coll., Tifton, Ga., 1949-50; BChE with honors, Ga. Inst. Tech., 1955; postgrad., U. Pitts., 1955-56, Carnegie Inst. Tech., 1956-57; MS, MIT, 1959, PhD in Math, 1961. Asst. chem. engr. TVA, Wilson Dam, Ala., 1951-54; assoc. engr. Westinghouse Electric Corp., Pitts., 1955-57; rsch. asst. ops. rsch. MIT, Cambridge, Mass., 1957-59; tchg. asst. dept. math. MIT, Cambridge, 1959-61, rsch. assoc. dept. math., 1961-62, asst. prof., postdoctoral fellow dept. chem. engring., 1962-64, rsch. assoc., 1957-62; sr. engr., project analyst Esso Research and Engring. Co., Florham Park, N.J., 1964-68; asst. prof. Emory U., Atlanta, 1968-71; pvt. practice math. cons. Atlanta, 1971-80; instr. in math. Ga. So. Coll., Statesboro, 1980-81; inventory control Lovett & Tharpe, Inc., Dublin, Ga., 1981-84; Norristown-Adrian, farmer, businessman, 1984—. Contbr. numerous articles to sci. and math. jours. WEBELOS den leader Boy Scouts Am., Dunwoody, Ga., 1969-70; mem., vol. worker Key Meml. Found., Adrian-Norristown, Ga., 1965—. Mem. AIChE, Ga. Tech. Alumni Assn., MIT Alumni Assn., Sigma Xi, Tau Beta Pi. Republican. Methodist. Home and Office: Rt 1 Box 58C Adrian GA 31002-9461

MCCORD, SCOTT ANTHONY, chemistry educator; b. Orlando, Fla., Sept. 15, 1956; s. Randolph John and Genevieve (Sbordone) M. BA in Limnology and Music Edn., U. Ctrl. Fla., 1980; MME, Ind. U., 1982; EdD in Sci. Edn., U. Ctrl. Fla., 1995. Cert. tchr., Fla. Lab./field chemist U. Ctrl. Fla., Orlando, 1977-79; instr. chemistry Titusville (Fla.) High Sch., 1983—; mem. lab. safety com. Brevard County (Fla.) Schs., 1989, chmn., 1991; cons. Space Port Fla. Authority, Cocoa, 1992, co-prin. investigator, 1992; sci. rsch. supr. Bionetics Corp., Kennedy Space Ctr., Fla., 1992; chemistry specialist Lockheed Space Ops., Kennedy Space Ctr., 1993; chmn. Brevard County Clash of Titans Sci. Acad. Competition, 1994, master of ceremonies, 1995; sci. and music adjudicator Nat. Excellence in Acads. Competition, Orlando, 1994. Co-author, editor: Brevard County Laboratory Safety Manual, 1991. Honorary liaison officer USAF Acad., Colorado Springs, 1986—. Named Outstanding Chemistry Tchr. Am. Chem. Soc., 1986-94; recipient various outstanding sci. rsch. teaching awards from industry and cmty. including NASA, Harris and Lockheed Martin Corps. Home: 1720 York Town Ave Titusville FL 32796 Office: Titusville High Sch 150 Terrier Tr Titusville FL 32780

MCCORD, TIM JAMES, telecommunications software engineer; b. Lake Charles, La., Oct. 25, 1955; s. James Wylie and Lorine Sylvia (Busby) McC.; m. Suzanne Scott Wiese, Jan. 15, 1983; children: Cameron Forrest, Keenan Matthew. BSEE, Rice Univ., 1977, MSEE, 1978. Computer scientist Harris Corp., Dallas, 1978-81; software engr. Rockwell Internat., Richardson, Tex., 1981-89; team leader, software engr. Rockwell Internat., Richardson, 1989-91; software engr. Alcatel Network Systems, Richardson, 1991-94; team leader software engring. Data Flow Systems, Dallas, 1994-95; software engr. MCI, Richardson, 1995—. Candidate U.S. Congress Rep. Party, Tex., 1994, 1992. Recipient scholarship Nat. Assn. Corrosion Engrs., 1973. Mem. Inst. Cert. Profl. Mgrs., Collin County Rep. Men's Club (sgt. at arms 1993-94). Lutheran. Home: 203 Riva Ridge Wylie TX 75098 Office: MCI 400 International Parkway Richardson TX 75081

MCCORKINDALE, DOUGLAS HAMILTON, publishing company executive, corporate lawyer; b. N.Y.C., June 14, 1939; s. William Douglas and Kathleen (Miles) McC.; m. Nancy Walsh, Dec. 24, 1991; children by previous marriage: Laura Ann, Heather Jean. BA, Columbia U., 1961, LLB cum laude (Harlan Fiske Stone scholar), 1964. Bar: N.Y. 1964. Assoc. Thacher Proffitt & Wood, N.Y.C., 1964-70, ptnr., 1970-71; gen. counsel, sec. Gannett Co., Inc., 1971-72, v.p., gen. counsel, sec., 1972-77, sr. v.p. fin. and law, 1977-79, sr. v.p., chief fin. officer, 1979-83, pres. diversified media div., 1980-83, exec. v.p., 1983; vice chmn., CFO Gannett Co., Inc., Arlington, Va., 1984—, chief adminstrv. officer, 1986—, dir. all subsidiaries and joint ventures; bd. dirs. Continental Airlines Inc., Frontier Corp., The Global Govt. Plus Fund Inc., Prudential Global Genesis Fund Inc., Prudentual Natural Resources Fund Inc., Prudential Multi-Sector Fund Inc.; trustee Prudential Equity Income Fund, Prudential Allocation Fund, Prudential Mcpl. Bond Fund, Mut. Ins. Co. Ltd. Mem. ABA (chmn. com. Exch. Act of 1934 1971-73), N.Y. State Bar Assn., Newspaper Assn. Am., Nat. Press Club, Oak Hill Country Club, Pine Valley Golf Club, Mid Ocean Club, Burning Tree Club. *

MCCORKLE, JAMES LORENZO, JR., history educator; b. Jackson, Miss., May 17, 1935; s. James Lorenzo and Lois Carolyn (Wilson) McC.; m. De Ann Oborn Dawes, Nov. 24, 1975; 1 child, James Wilson. BA, Ala. Poly. Inst., 1957; MA, U. Miss., 1962, PhD, 1966. From asst. prof. to prof. history Northwestern State U., Natchitoches, La., 1966—. Contbr. articles to profl. jours. Lt. (j.g.) USN, 1957-60. Mem. Am. Hist. Assn., So. Hist. Assn., La. Hist. Assn., Agrl. History Soc., Miss. Hist. Soc., North La Hist. Assn. (pres. 1989-91). Democrat. Presbyterian. Home: 615 Marion St Natchitoches LA 71457-5519 Office: Northwestern State Univ Social Scis Dept Natchitoches LA 71497

MCCORKLE, MICHAEL, electrical engineer; b. Americus, Ga., Mar. 7, 1957; s. Charles Harold and Marjorie Marie (Hamilton) McC.; m. Carroll Leah Crawley, Mar. 21, 1981; children: David Michael, Christopher Adam. BSEE, Ga. Inst. Tech., 1981. Mgr. Powers Ferry Bottle Shop, Atlanta, 1978-81; product specialist Yokogawa Corp. Am., Shenandoah, Ga., 1981-84; application engr. Gould, Inc., Norcross, Ga., 1984-86, sales engr., 1986-92, product sales mgr., 1993-95; sales rep. maj. elec. digital test equipment mfrs., 1995—. Roman Catholic.

MCCORMACK, GRACE LYNETTE, civil engineering technician; b. Dallas, Nov. 2; d. Audley and Janice Meredith (Metcalf) McC. Tech. degree, Durham's Coll., 1958; grad. in civil engring., El Centro Coll., 1972; grad. in advanced surveying, Eastfield, 1975. Cert. sr. engr. technician. Contract design technician various engring firms, Dallas, 1958-70; sr. design engr. technician City of Dallas Survey Div., 1970-80, street light div., 1980-95, ret. 1995. Mem. Unity Ch. Avocations: numerology, astrology, metaphysics, Egyptian-Arabian horses, lighting and designing black and white portrait photography. Home: 1428 Meadowbrook Ln Irving TX 75061-4435

MCCORMICK, CLYDE REECE, II, lawyer, educator; b. San Francisco, May 31, 1940; s. Clyde Reece and Inez (Gambill) McC.; m. Kathryn Ann Sinquefield, Jan. 28, 1963 (div.); children: Shawna L. McCormick Caridi, Mark Shannon; m. Alice Ann Jones, June 2, 1979 (div. 1994); m. Pamela Lynn Garcia, Mar. 17, 1995; 1 child, Jennifer Michelle Garcia. BA, Hendrix Coll., 1964; MA, St. Mary's U., San Antonio, 1979; MBA, JD, Tex. Tech. U., 1987. Bar: Tex. 1987, U.S. Dist. Ct. (no., we. and so. dists.) Tex.; cert. comml. pilot, consumer law by Tex. Bd. Legal Specialization. Commd. 2d lt. USAF, 1964, advanced through grades to major, 1975, ret., 1984; atty. 4th Ct. of Appeals, San Antonio, 1987-88; litigation atty. Brite & Drought, San Antonio, 1988-90, John Dwyre & Assocs., San Antonio, 1990-93; pvt. practice litigation atty. San Antonio, 1993-96; lawyer comml. and bus. litigation Soules & Wallace, 1996—; adj. prof. San Antonio Sch. Law, 1993-95; chair Consumer Law Coun., Pub. Svc. Com., 1990—, Adv. Commn. on Consumer Law, 1991—, San Antonio Bar Legal Edn. Com., 1992—, State Bar of Tex., 1996-97. Contbr. articles to profl. jours. Dir. Samm Housing Corp., San Antonio, 1991-94, pres., 1994; dir. San Antonio (Tex.) Met. Ministries, 1994. Mem. ABA, Feb. Bar Assn., Tex. Bar Assn., San Antonio Bar Assn., Am. Trial Lawyers Assn., Tex. Trial Lawyers Assn., Air Force Assn., Daedalions, Alamo Lodge No. 44 AF & AM (Worshipful Master 1995-96). Office: 100 W Houston St Ste 1500 San Antonio TX 78205-1457

MCCORMICK, DAVID ARTHUR, lawyer; b. McKeesport, Pa., Oct. 26, 1946; s. Arthur Paul and Eleanor Irene (Gibson) McC. BA, Westminster Coll., 1967; JD, Duquesne U., 1973; MBA, U. Pa., 1975. Bar: Pa. 1973, D.C. 1978, U.S. Ct. Appeals (3d cir.) 1977, U.S. Ct. Appeals (4th and D.C. cirs.) 1980, U.S. Supreme Ct. 1980. Asst. commerce counsel Penn Cen. R.R., Phila., 1973-76; assoc. labor counsel Consol. Rail Corp., Phila., 1976-78; atty. Dept. Army, Washington, 1978—. Author various geneal. and hist. works; contbr. articles to profl. jours. Mem. Pa. Bar Assn., Phila. Bar Assn., D.C. Bar Assn., Assn. Transp. Practitioners, Soc. Cin. (Del. chpt.), SAR (Pitts. chpt.), Am. Legion, Res. Officers Assn., Masons, Phi Alpha Delta. Presbyterian.

MCCORMICK, J. PHILIP, natural gas company executive; b. San Antonio, Feb. 21, 1942; s. Eugene Hay and Beulah (Barber) McC.; m. Jo Ann Wendland, July 17, 1965; children; J. Philip Jr., Scott Daniel. BBA, Tex. A&I U., 1964, MS in Bus. and Econs., 1965. CPA, Tex. Sr. acct. Price Waterhouse, Houston, 1965-70; mgr. KMG Main Hurdman, Houston, N.Y.C., 1970-73; ptnr. KMG Main Hurdman, El Paso, Houston, 1973-83; mng. ptnr. KMG Main Hurdman, Houston, 1983-85, mng. ptnr. So. region, 1985-87; mng. ptnr. KPMG Peat Marwick, Austin, Tex., 1987-91; sr. v.p. fin. Lone Star Gas Co., Dallas, 1991-93, sr. v.p. transmission and office of pres., 1994-95; sr. v.p., CFO Enserch Exploration, Dallas, 1995—; bd. dirs. The Dallas Opera; mem. State of Tex. Natural Gas Reliability Coun., 1993-95. Bd. dirs. Austin Symphony, 1988-92, Tex. Bus. Hall of Fame, Houston, 1990-94, Tex. A&I Found., 1989— (chmn. 1992—); fin. coun. Seton Hosp., Austin, 1990-91; search com. bus. sch. dean Tex. A&I U., 1990, Tex. A&I alumni assn. (pres. 1977-78, nat. chmn. ann. alumni fund drive 1978-80), chmn. industry adv. coun. to dean, 1968-69; sec. bbd. regents Univ. System South Tex., Corpus Christi, 1988-89; steering com. St. Edward's U., Austin, 1990-91; founding dir. Escape Ctr. for Prevention Child Abuse, Houston, 1980-89; dir. Exch. Club Child Abuse Prevention Ctr., Dallas, 1993—, others. Named Disting. Alumnus Tex. A&I U., 1991, one of Outstanding Young Men Am., 1971. Mem. Am. Gas Assn. (fin. and adminstrv. sect., acctg. adv. coun. 1991—, mng. com., corp. planning com. 1991-93), AICPA, Tex. Soc. CPAs, Tower Club Dallas, Petroleum Club Houston, Houston Club, Headliners Club Austin, Delta Sigma Pi (life). Office: Enserch Exploration Inc Ste 1000 6688 N Central Expwy Dallas TX 75206-3922

MCCORMICK, JACK RANDALL, environmental engineer; b. Livingston, Tenn., Aug. 15, 1942; s. Jesse Arnold and Henriella (Phillips) McC.; m. Judy Rebecca Shaw, Aug. 9, 1969; children: Jennifer Elise, Clifton Andrew, Sara Catherine. BS in Engring. Sci., Tenn. Tech. U., 1964. Hydraulic engr. U.S. Geol. Survey, Jackson, Miss., 1964, 67-68, Nashville, 1969; mech. engr. U.S. Army Ordinance Corps, White Sands, N.Mex., 1965-66; civil engr. Lester Engring. Co., Jackson, Miss., 1970; sanitary engr. Tenn. Dept. Pub. Health, Nashville, 1971; sanitary engr. Tenn. Dept. Pub. Health, Chattanooga, 1972-73, field office mgr., 1974-80, environ. mgr., 1981—. Mem. Rep. Orgn., Chattanooga, 1975—. With U.S. Army, 1965-66. Mem. Nat. Speleological Soc., Southeastern Cave Conservancy, Nature Conservancy, Tenn. Water and Wastewater Assn., Tau Beta Pi. Republican. Methodist. Home: 8622 Blueberry Ln Ooltewah TN 37363-9251 Office: Tenn Dept Environ & Cons Tenn Divsn Water Supply 540 Mccallie Ave Chattanooga TN 37402-2089

MCCORMICK, JOHN HOYLE, lawyer; b. Pensacola, Fla., July 30, 1933; s. Clyde Hoyle and Orrie Brooks (Frink) McC.; m. Patricia McCall, Dec. 27, 1974. BS, U. Fla., 1955; JD, Stetson U., 1958. Bar: Fla. 1958. Ptnr. McCormick, Drury & Scaff, Jasper, Fla., 1958-74; county atty., 1973—; sr. ptnr. McCormick, Drury & Scaff, Jasper, 1974-91; pvt. practice Jasper, 1991—; county judge, Hamilton County, Fla., 1960-72; local counsel So. Ry. System, 1968—, CSX, Ry., 1972—; atty. Hamilton County Devel. Authority, 1970-91; bd. dirs. 1st Fed. Savs. Bank Fla.; bd. dirs., v.p., atty. Hamilton County Bank. Mayor City of White Springs, Fla., 1959; pres. Hamilton County C. of C., Jasper, 1961. Mem. Phi Delta Phi. Democrat. Methodist. Lodges: Masons. Home: 403 SE 2nd Ave Jasper FL 32052-3242 Office: 215 NE 2nd St Jasper FL 32052-2015 Address: PO Drawer O Jasper FL 32052-0695

MCCORMICK, NANCY CAMPBELL, lawyer; b. Stuart, Fla., Apr. 17, 1947; d. Howard Edwin and Margaret (Servies) McC.; m. Nathan M. Crystal, Aug. 5, 1973; children: Abraham Joseph, Miriam Emily. BA, Duke U., 1968; JD with honors, Emory U., 1971. Bar: Ga. 1971, Mass. 1976, S.C. 1977, U.S. Dist. Ct. S.C., U.S. Ct. Appeals (4th cir.), U.S. Supreme Ct. Mng. atty., staff atty. Atlanta Legal Aid Soc., 1971-74; supervising atty. Boston U. Legal Aid Program, 1974-76; dir., mng. atty. Palmetto Legal Svcs., Columbia, 1976-80; cons. Continuum of Care Project, Columbia, 1982-83; staff atty. S.C. Legal Svcs. Assn., Columbia, 1984-87, dir., 1987-89; gen. counsel Protection & Advocacy for People with Disabilities, Inc., Columbia, 1989—; adj. prof. U.S.C. Sch. of Law, fall 1991, spring 1995; chair legis. subcom. S.C. Bar children's com.; del. USIA/Columbia Coll. exchange program to Cali, Colombia, 1976; presenter in field. Co-editor: S.C. Bar, Representing Children in Family Court: A Manual for Attorneys and Guardians ad Litem, 1995. Past pres. Sistercare, Inc., Columbia; founding bd. dirs. S.C. Alliance for Children, Columbia; vol. guardian ad litem Richland County Family Ct., 1984-90. Mem. Richland County Bar Assn., S.C. Women Lawyers Assn., Order of Coif. Office: SC Protection Advocacy 3710 Landmark Dr Ste 208 Columbia SC 29204-4034

MCCORMICK, ROBERT, hospital food service administrator, dietitian consultant; b. Albuquerque, Dec. 10, 1948; s. Wilfred and Eleanor (Paddock) McC. BS, U. N.Mex., 1971, MS, 1973, BS, 1975. Registered dietitian. Clin. dietitian Tex. Ctr. for Infectious Disease, San Antonio, 1976-79; chief of food svc. San Antonio State Chest Hosp., 1979—; cons. Alcoholic Rehab. Ctgr., San Antonio, 1979—. Treas. Tex. Pub. Employees Assn., San Antonio, 1988-94. Recipient Martin Fleck award U. N.Mex., 1971. Mem. Am. Dietetic Assn., Tex. Dietetic Assn., San Antonio Dist. Dietetic Assn., Phi Kappa Phi, Phi Beta Kappa.

MCCORMICK, ROSCOE, mathematician, educator, career officer, retired; b. Fayetteville, N.C., Aug. 24, 1949; s. Roland Boyd and Ethelyn (McNeil) McC.; m. A. Mechele Dickerson; 1 child, Erika Yolanda. BS, N.C. A&T State U., 1971; MA, Ctrl. Mich. U., 1982; MS in Edn., Old Dominion U., 1994. Commd. 2d lt. U.S. Army, 1971, with, 1971—, advanced through grades to lt. col., 1988; ambulance platoon leader 1st Cavalry Divsn. U.S. Army, Ft. Hood, Tex., 1971-72, clearing platoon leader, 1972, company exec. officer, 1972-73, troop comdr. dept. med. activity, 1973-74; company exec. officer 82nd Airborne Divsn. U.S. Army, Ft. Bragg, N.C., 1974-75, company comdr., 1975-77; patient adminstr. Rader Health Clinic U.S. Army, Ft. Myer, Va., 1977-80; ops. officer 2nd Inf. Divsn. U.S. Army, Korea, 1980-81; pers. counselor Army Med. Dept. Pers. Support Agy. U.S. Army, Washington, 1981-82, regional dir., 1982-83; ops. officer 68th Med. Group U.S. Army, Frankfurt, Wiesbaden, Germany, 1984-86; ops. officer Office of the Surgeon Gen. U.S. Army, Washington, 1986-88, med. plans/ops. officer Joint Chiefs of Staff, 1988-91; ops. officer Tng. and Doctrine Command Surgeon U.S. Army, Ft. Monroe, Va., 1991-95; tchr. math. C. Alton Lindsay Mid. Sch., Hampton, Va., 1995—. Named Tchr. of Yr. for Hampton Schs. Newspaper in Edn., 1996. Mem. Nat. Coun. Math. Tchrs., Va. Coun. Math. Tchrs., Pershing Rifles Soc., Alpha Phi Alpha, Sigma Iota Epsilon, Phi Delta Kappa.

MCCOY, CARROLL PIERCE, retired minister; b. Hennessey, Okla., Sept. 14, 1920; s. Victor Pierce and Mary Ruth (Meyer) McC.; m. Florence Louise Hogle, July 31, 1964. BS, Okla. State U., 1947; BD, S.W. Bapt. Theol. Sem., 1951, MRE, 1952. Min. Christian Ch., Mutual, Okla., 1955-59, 81-89; ret., Buffalo, Okla., 1959-64, Gage, Okla., 1964-71, Arnett, Okla., 1971-80. With USN, 1942-46. Mem. Rotary (past pres. Gage Club), Kiwanis (past sec.-treas. Arnett club). Democrat. Home: RR 2 Box 26 Vici OK 73859-9303

MCCOY, DOROTHY ELOISE, writer, educator; b. Houston, Sept. 4, 1916; d. Robert Major and Evie Letha (Grimes) Morgan; m. Roy McCoy, May 22, 1942; children: Roy Jr., Robert Nicholas (dec.). B., Rice U., 1938; M., Tex. A&I U., 1968; postgrad., Ind. U., 1971, U. Calif., Berkeley, 1972, U. Calif., Santa Cruz, 1977. Cert. secondary tchr. BA Corpus Christi (Tex.) Independent Schs., 1958-84, MA, 1985; freelance writer Corpus Christi, 1987—; co-owner United Iron and Machine Works, Corpus Christi, 1946-82; freelance lectr.; master tchr. Nat. Coun. Tchrs. English, 1971, Nat. Humanities Faculty, Concord Mass., 1977-78; mem. steering com. Edn. Summit, Corpus Christi, 1990-91, mem. summit update, 1991. Author: A Teacher Talks Back, 1990, Let's Restructure the Schools, 1992; contbr. articles and columns to profl. jours. Sr. advisor to U.S. Congress, Washington, 1982-85; trustee Corpus Christi Librs., 1987-90; mem. Corpus Christi Mus.; mem. Friends Corpus Christi Librs., chmn. publicity com., 1988; participant Walk to Emmaus Group, 1990, UPDATE, U. Tex., 1978-92; cons. Libr. Bd. Democracy competition Am. 2000; sec. adminstrv. bd. First United Meth. Ch., 1992-93. Recipient Teacher of Yr. Paul Caplan Humanitarian award, 1981, Advanced Senior Option Program award, 1968. Mem. AAUW, LWV, Phi Beta Kappa. Home and Office: 612 Chamberlain St Corpus Christi TX 78404-2605

MC COY, LEE BERARD, paint company executive; b. Ipswich, Mass., July 27, 1925; d. Damase Joseph and Robena Myrtle (Bruce) B.; student U. Ala., Mobile, 1958-60; m. Walter Vincent de Paul McCoy, Sept. 27, 1943; children: Bernadette, Raymond, Joan, Richard. Owner, Lee's Letter Shop, Hicksville, L.I., N.Y., 1950-56; mgr. sales adminstrn. Basila Mfg. Co., Mobile, Ala., 1957-61; promotion mgr., buyer Mobile Paint Co., Inc., Theodore, Ala., 1961—. Curator, Shepard Meml. Libr., 1972—; bd. dirs. Monterey Tour House, Mobile, 1972-78, Old Dauphin Way Assn., 1977-79, Friends of Mus., Mobile, 1978—, Miss Wheelchair Ala., 1980—; del. Civic Roundtable, 1977-78, bd. dirs., 1980-81, 1st v.p., 1980-81, pres., 1981-82; pres.'s Com. Employment of Handicapped, 1981—; chmn. Mobile, Nat. Yr. Disabled Persons, 1982; chmn. Mobile, Internat. Decade Disabled Persons, 1983—; mem. Nat. Project Adv. Bd., 1983—, Nat. Community Adv. Bd., 1983—, World Com. for Decade of Disabled Persons, 1983—; v.p. Bristol Sister City Soc.; active Mobile Area Retarded Citizens, Am. Heart Assn.; mem. City of Mobile Cultural Enrichment Task Force, 1985—, Mobile United Recreation and Culture Com.; dir. Culture Mobile, 1986—; v.p., bd. dirs. Joe Jefferson Players, 1986; co-chmn. Brit. Faire, 1983; chmn. Mobile Expo, 1990, Culture & Recreation Com. Mobile United, 1989, steering com., 1990. Recipient Honor award Civic Roundtable, 1979, 80; Service award Women's Com. of Spain Rehab. Center, State of Ala., 1980; award Nat. Orgn. on Disability, 1983, Gayfer's Outstanding Career Woman award, 1988; Golden Rule award, 1991. Mem. Spectromatic Assos., Nat. Paint Distbrs., Hist. Preservation Soc., Color Mktg. Group, English Speaking Union (v.p., pres. 1992, 94, 95, 96), U.S. C. of C. (chmn. local cultural enrichment task force 1986), Toastmasters (pres. 1995-96), The Nat. Mus. of Women of the Arts, Washington (charter), Internat. Platform Assn. Methodist. Republican. Clubs: Quota (charter mem. Mobile chpt. dir. 1977—, pres. 1978-80, chmn. numerous coms., recipient Service award Dist. 8, 1979, Internat. award for serving club objectives, 1980, editor Care-Gram, Weekly newsletter for nursing homes 1980—), Bienville; writer 10 books; lectr., worldwide traveler. Home: 1553 Monterey Pl Mobile AL 36604-1227 Office: 4775 Hamilton Blvd Theodore AL 36582-8523

MCCOY, MARY ELIZABETH, primary school educator; b. Stillwater, Okla., Sept. 8, 1947; d. Clarence William and Mary Ruth (Harrison) Lambert; m. Carl Patrick McCoy, June 12, 1971; children: Brian, Keith. BS in Edn., Okla. State U., 1969. Tchr. Oklahoma City Pub. Schs., 1969-71, St. Vincent Cath. Sch., Denver, 1974-75, Starkville (Miss.) Acad., 1987—. Named Best Tchr., Starkville Daily News Readers Survey, 1994. Mem. AAUW, Miss. Pvt. Sch. Assn., Phi Delta Kappa. Roman Catholic.

MCCOY, REAGAN SCOTT, oil company executive, lawyer; b. Port Arthur, Tex., Nov. 25, 1945; s. William Murray and Elizabeth (Gilbert) McC.; m. Pat Kowalski, June 21, 1969; 1 child, Traci. BCE, Ga. Inst. Tech., 1968; JD, Loyola U., 1972. Bar: Tex. 1972, La. 1978; registered profl. engr., Tex., La. Structural engr. McDermott Inc., New Orleans, 1966-72; data processing mgr. McDermott Inc., London, 1972-76; cons. engr. McDermott Inc., New Orleans, 1976-79; adminstrv. mgr. Concord Oil Co., San Antonio, 1979-81, v.p., 1981—; mem. World Affairs Coun., Tex. Luth. Coll. Bus. Sch. Adv. Com. Treas. Countryside San Pedro Recreation Club, 1981-82; bd. dirs. Countryside San Pedro Homeowners Assn., 1984-86; pres. San Antonio Baylor U. Parents League, 1995-96. Fellow Tau Beta Pi; mem. ABA, NSPE, ASCE, Am. Assn. Profl. Landmen (San Antonio chpt. treas. 1990-91, v.p. 1991-93, pres. 1993-94), La. State Bar Assn., Tex. State Bar, San Antonio Bar Assn. (natural resources com. treas. 1986-87, vice chmn. 1987-88, chmn. 1988-89), Tex. Soc. Profl. Engrs., La. Soc. Profl. Engrs., So. Tex. Assn. Divsn. Order Analysts (v.p. 1993, pres. 1994), Fin Execs. Inst. (treas. 1991-92, sec. 1992-93, v.p. 1993-94, pres. 1994-95, bd. dirs. 1995—), Soc. Mining Engrs., Real Estate Fin. Soc. (bd. dirs. 1986-89, v.p. 1987-88, pres. 1988-89, pres. coun.), Adminstrv. Mgmt. Soc. (pres. 1985-86, 89-90), Plz. Club, Sonterra Club, Tex. Ind. Producers and Royalty Owners Assn. Presbyterian. Home: 14103 Bluff Manor Dr San Antonio TX 78216-7976 Office: Concord Oil Co 105 S Saint Marys St Ste 1500 San Antonio TX 78205-2807

MCCOY, SANDRA JO, pharmacist; b. Burkesville, Ky., July 30, 1953; d. Jesse Martin and Wanda Lee (Biggerstaff) McC. BS in Pharmacy, Samford U., 1977; D Pharmacy, 1983. Lic. pharmacist Ala., Ky., Tenn. Staff pharmacist St. Vincent's Hosp., Birmingham, Ala., 1977-83; staff pharmacist St. Thomas Hosp., Nashville, 1983—, ptnrs. in excellence quality leadership process trainer, pharmacy dept. coord., 1992—, drug interaction specialist pharmacy, 1992—, profl. achievement system participant, 1994-95; pres. S.J. McCoy Timber, S.J. McCoy Properties; mem. Consumer Mail Panel, Chgo., 1989—; cons. Clin. Mgmt. Cons., Nashville, 1991—; adv. bd. Town and Country Mag. Mem. Opera Guild, Nashville, 1989, mem. com., standing bd. mem., com. event chair, 1994-95, 95-96; mem. Symphony Guild, Nashville, 1992—, Ballet Guild, 1992—, founding mem. Ballet Friends '92, com. chair, 1993-94, 94-95; mem. Friends of Checkwod, Nashville, 1994—, Tenn. Performing Arts Ctr. Friends, 1994—; founding mem. The Abbey Leix Soc. of the O'more Coll. of Design, 1995; stewarship Ky. Dept. Forestry, Ky. Dept. Fish & Wildlife, 1994. Mem. Am. Soc. Hosp. Pharmacists (midyear presentation 1993, 94, alt. del. state of Tenn. 1994), Mid. Tenn. Soc. Hosp. Pharmacists (bd. dirs. 1987-91, sec. 1987-88, pres. elect 1988-89, pres. 1989-90, scholarship com. 1992, poster presentation 1995), Tenn. Soc. Hosp. Pharmacists (membership com. 1989-90), Nashville Area Pharmacists Assn., Lambda Kappa Sigma (Women in Pharm. Leadership in Am. award 1993). Republican. Home: 3415 W End Ave Apt 608 Nashville TN 37203-1025 Office: St Thomas Hosp Dept Pharmacy 4220 Harding Rd Nashville TN 37205-2005

MCCOY, STUART SHERMAN, manufacturing executive; b. Little Rock, Dec. 16, 1958; s. Gene Guy and Idella Maria Theresa (Brown) McC.; m. Juliet Kathryn Goens, Sept. 9, 1977 (div. Apr. 1986); children: Ashley Nicole, Christopher Sean. Student, U. Ark., Little Rock, 1976, 78. Various positions Ad Craft Ark., Inc., Little Rock, 1976-80, prodn. supr., 1980-82, v.p. prodn., 1982-86, v.p. ops., 1986—; bd. dirs. Subiaco Acad. Alumni Assn. Photojournalist. Team mgr. Red Elk Motorsports, 1990-93, pres., 1991—; v.p. Ark. Dirt Riders, 1991-92, pres., 1992-93. Mem. Am. Advt. Fedn. (10th dist Addy award com. 1989, 10th dist. student compitition com. 1994—, Nat. Addy com., 1994—, constrn. and bylaws com. 1991—), Screen Print Assn. Internat., Ark. Advt. Fedn. (bd. dirs. 1992—), Jaycees (state dist. bd. dirs. Ark. chpt. 1983, state bd. dirs. pub. rels. com. 1984-85), Masons. Republican. Episcopalian. Home: 11940 Southridge Dr Little Rock AR 72212-1740 Office: Ad Craft Ark Inc 1122 W 3rd St Little Rock AR 72201-2008

MCCOY, WILLIAM O., retired telecommunications executive; b. Snow Hill, N.C., Oct. 26, 1933; s. Marcus Cicero and Anna Kathleen (Shirley) McC.; m. Sara Jane Hart, Dec. 18, 1955; children—Laura Jo McCoy Foster, Kathleen Sue. BS, U. N.C., 1955; MS, MIT, 1968. Gen. mgr. South Central Bell, New Orleans, 1973-76; v.p. South Central Bell, Nashville, 1978; exec. v.p. South Central Bell, Birmingham, Ala., 1978-82, vice chmn., 1982-83; asst. v.p. Am. Tel & Tel, Basking Ridge, N.J., 1976-78; vice chmn. BellSouth Corp., Atlanta, 1993—; dir. First Am. Corp., Nashville, Liberty Corp., Greenville. Chmn. Middle Tenn. Heart Assn., Nashville, 1971; div. chmn. Greater New Orleans Fedn. of Chs., 1974; gen. vice chmn. New Orleans Symphony Campaign, 1975; co-chmn. Ala. United Way Campaign, Birmingham, 1982; adv. council Coll. Bus. Adminstrn., Ga. State U., 1983—. Served to capt. USMC, 1955-59. Republican. Methodist. Office: BellSouth 675 Peachtree St NE Atlanta GA 30308-1928 also: U NC Systemsrp PO Box 2688 Chapel Hill NC 27514-2688

MCCRACKEN, ALEXANDER WALKER, pathologist; b. Motherwell, Lanarkshire, Scotland, Nov. 24, 1931; came to U.S., 1968; s. William and Mary Snedden (Walker) McC.; m. Theresa Credgington, June 4, 1960; children: Fiona Jane, Claire Louise. MD, U. Glasgow, Scotland, 1956. Resident in surgery Glasgow Royal Inf., 1956-57; resident in pathology Royal Air Force, U.K., 1957-61, pathologist, 1962-68; fellow in pathology Royal Postgrad. Med. Sch., London, 1961-62; assoc. prof. Med. Sch., U. Tex., San Antonio, 1968-72; prof. Med. Sch., U. Tex., Houston, 1972-73; dir. of microbiology Baylor U. Med. Ctr., Dallas, 1973-81; pres. med. staff, dir. of labs. Meth. Hosps. of Dallas, 1982—; pres. med. staff Meth. Med. Ctr., 1994-95; adj. prof. pathology Baylor U. Coll. Dentistry, Dallas, 1982—; clin. prof. U. Tex. Southwestern Med. Sch., Dallas, 1986—. Author: Pathologic Mechanisms of Human Disease, 1985, Oral and Clinical Microbiology, 1986, Pathology, 1990, (play) Mister Gilbert, 1985, 89. With Royal Air Force, 1957-68. Decorated Gen. Svc. medal. Fellow Royal Coll. Pathologists, Coll. Am. Pathologists; mem. AAAS, AMA, Am. Soc. Microbiology, Tex. Med. Assn., Dallas County Med. Soc., Tex. Soc. Infectious Diseases, Tex. Med. Found., Assn. of Clin. Chemists, Masons. Republican. Anglican. Home: 607 Kessler Lake Dr Dallas TX 75208-3943 Office: Lab Physicians Assn 221 W Colorado Blvd Dallas TX 75208-2363

MCCRACKEN, JOHN ROBERT, library science educator; b. Victoria, Tex., Jan. 4, 1941; s. Robert Elwin and Olive Bernice (Olsen) McC.; m. Barbara Lou Williams, June 21, 1976 (div. Dec. 1988); 1 child, Laurea Elizabeth. BA in Scandinavian, U. Calif., Berkeley, 1967; MA, U. Denver, 1968; MPA, U. Ariz., 1980; PhD in Libr. Sci., Tex. Woman's U., 1992. Cert. pub. libr. profl. Dir. Main Libr., Tucson Pub. Libr., 1970-74; dir. libr. svcs. Yuma (Ariz.) City-County Libr., 1974-78; dir. dept. mgmt. svcs. City of Yuma, 1978; grad. asst. U. Ariz. Coll. Bus. and Pub. Policy, Tucson, 1979-80; owner, mgr. McCracken & Assocs., libr. planners and cons., Ft. Worth, Tucson, 1980—; mgr. bus. and tech. Ft. Worth Pub. Libr., 1982-84; dir. libr. devel. br. Okla. Dept. Librs., Oklahoma City, 1984-87; libr. dir. Shasta County Libr., Redding, Calif., 1987-88; vis. prof. Tex. Woman's U., Denton, 1988—, vis. prof. Sch. Libr. and Info. Studies, 1992-94; libr. dir. Carnegie-Stout Pub. Libr., Dubuque, Iowa, 1994—; presenter in field; cons. Yuma Union High Sch. Dist., 1977, U. Okla. Sch. Libr. and Info. Studies, 1985, Navajo Nation Libr. and Info. Svcs. Br. Libr., Dept. Recreational Resources, Window Rock, Ariz., 1982; mem. com. on accreditation, vis. team U. Tenn., 1973, U. Iowa, 1974, Western Mich. U., 1975, St. John's U., 1975, U. North Tex., 1976; mem. nat. adv. bd. Tng. and Assistance for Indian Libr. Svcs., 1985-87; evaluator U.S. Dept. Edn., 1976-78, 85-93. Contbr. articles and book revs. to various publs. Bd. dirs. Yuma County Guidance Clinic, 1977-79, pres., 1978-79; pres. Yuma County Coordinating Coun., 1976-77; mem. adv. bd. dirs. Yumohave Regional Libr., 1976-78; chmn. subcom. for comty. needs Tucson Area Libr. Coun., 1971-73; finalist judge Dubuque Fine Arts Players, Nat. One-Act Play Competition, 1995-96. Mem. ALA, Am. Indian Libr. Assn., Am. Soc. for Pub. Adminstrn., Libr. Adminstrn. and Mgmt. Assn., Pub. Libr. Assn. (interlibr. loan com. 1977-79), Tex. Libr. Assn., Westerners Internat., U. Denver Grad. Libr. Sch. Alumni Assn. (pres. 1976-77). Home: 2955 Timberline St Dubuque IA 52001-1865 Office: Carnegie-Stout Pub Libr 11th and Bluff Sts Dubuque IA 52001

MCCRACKIN, BOBBIE HUMENNY, economist; b. Pitts., Sept. 25, 1944; d. Harry and Helen (Carlin) Humenny; m. Charles Alexander McCrackin, July 1, 1967; children: Jordan Evan, Miriam Owen. BA, U. Pa., 1966; MA, Bryn Mawr Coll., Phila., 1967; PhD, Emory U., Atlanta, 1980. Teaching asst. Emory U., Atlanta, 1976; rsch. assoc. Dean Rusk Ctr., U. Ga., Athens, 1980-82; economist Fed. Res. Bank, Atlanta, 1982-87, pub. info. officer, 1987-91, v.p., pub. affairs officer, 1991—. Contbr. articles to profl. jours. Mem. Harper Adv. Bd. Magnet Sch., Atlanta, 1990—; mem. Leadership Atlanta, 1992-93; trustee Ga. Coun. Econ. Edn., 1990—; mem. adv. bd. Ga. Tech. Ctr. for Internat. Bus. Edn. and Rsch., 1993—; bd. dirs. Consumer Credit Counseling Svc., 1994—. Fulbright scholar Ind. U., 1965. Mem. Nat. Assn. Bus. Economists, Am. Econ. Assn., Atlanta Econs. Club (pres., v.p., sec.-treas. 1986-89). Office: Fed Res Bank Atlanta 104 Marietta St NW Atlanta GA 30303-2706

MCCRARY, SHARON HASH, medical and surgical nurse; b. Manassas, Va., Nov. 6, 1960; d. Fred and Ilene (Walker) Hash; m. Walter Larry McCrary, July 20, 1979. ADN, Polk Community Coll., Winter Haven, Fla., 1986. Nurse Hardee Meml. Hosp., Wauchula, Fla.; gen. nurse Erlanger Med. Ctr., Chattanooga, trauma stepdown nurse; med.-surg. nurse Fla. Hosp., Wauchula.

MC CRAY, EVELINA WILLIAMS, librarian, researcher; b. Plaquemine, La., Sept. 1, 1932; d. Turner and Beatrice (Gordon) Williams II; m. John Samuel McCray, Apr. 7, 1955; 1 child, Johnetta McCray Russ. BA, So. U., Baton Rouge, 1954; MS in Library Sci., La. State U., 1962. Librarian, Iberville High Sch., Plaquemine, 1954-70, Plaquemine Jr. High, 1970-75; proofreader short stories, poems Associated Writers Guild, Atlanta, 1982-86; library cons. Evaluation Capitol High Sch., 1964, Iberville Parish Educators Workshop, 1980, Tchrs. Core/Iberville Parish, 1980-81. Contbr. poetry New Am. Poetry Anthology, 1988, The Golden Treasury of Great Poems, 1988, Acres of Diamonds A Collection of Poetry, The Power and the Glory, A Collection of Poetry, Favorite Poems Southern Poetry Association, 1996. Vol. service Allen J. Nadler Library, Plaquemine, 1980-82; librarian Local Day Care Ctr., Plaquemine, 1978-79; mem. adv. bd. Iberville parish Project Independence, 1992—. Mem. ALA, La. Library Assn., Nat. Ret. Tchrs. Assn., La. Ret. Tchrs. Assn. (cons. ann. workshops 1986—, state appointee to informative and protective svcs. com. 1988-92), Iberville Ret. Tchrs. Assn. (info. and protective services dir. 1981—), Internat. Soc. Poets, So. Poetry Assn. (asst. coll. State Arts Mus. Miss., Blue Ribbon award 1989, SPA's Finest award 1992). Democrat. Baptist. Home: PO Box Q Plaquemine LA 70765-0220

MCCREA, MICHAEL ANDREA, manufacturing company executive; b. Kingstree, S.C., Apr. 6, 1957; s. Sammie Armstrong and Frances (Brown) McC.; m. Connie Sue Pate, Feb. 22, 1986; children: Christian, Brannon (dec.), Cameron (dec.). Student, Williamsburg Tech. Coll., 1982-84, Taguchi Design of Experiments. With Tri-County Tractor Inc., Kingstree, S.C., 1975-84; supt. plant Colonial Rubber Works Inc., Kingstree, 1984-94; plant supt. Firestone Bldg. Products Co., Kingstree, 1994—. Republican. Presbyterian. Home: RR 1 Box 137-a Kingstree SC 29556-9801

MCCREADY, DOROTHY JANE, post-anesthesia nurse; b. Alexandria, La., July 26, 1948; d. Robert Bruce Jr. and Dorothy Louise (Frisch) Wallace; m. Edward Benjamin Scheps, Sept. 14, 1968 (div. 1989); 1 child, Mary Louise Scheps; m. Walter Stephen McCready, Jan. 9, 1991. BA in English, Parsons Coll., 1970; BSN, William Carey Coll., 1975. Cert. post anesthesia nurse, ACLS. Staff nurse surg. ICU So. Bapt. Hosp., New Orleans, 1975-77; staff nurse ICU Our Lady of Lourdes, Lafayette, La., 1978, 82-90, head nurse post anesthesia care unit, 1990-92, staff nurse post anesthesia care unit, 1992—. Mem. Am. Soc. Post Anesthesia Nurses, La. Assn. Post Anesthesia Nurses, Atchafalaya Assn. Post Anesthesia Nurses (founder, pres. 1994). Republican. Methodist. Home: 101 Bocage Cir Lafayette LA 70503-4354 Office: Our Lady of Lourdes 611 St Landry Lafayette LA 70502

MCCREERY, JAMES ALLAN, business services company executive; b. Muncie, Ind., Nov. 21, 1933; s. Herman and Margaret Allena (McKinley) McC.; m. Carolyn Henderson, Dec. 18, 1954; children: Lynn, Julie. BS, Ball State U., 1956. Asst. buyer Ball Stores, Muncie, 1956-59; asst. sales svc. mgr. closure div. Ball Corp., Muncie, 1959; salesman Stecks Inc., Muncie, 1959-61; terr. sales mgr. Western AutoSupply Co., Fort Wayne, Ind., 1961-63; customer svc. mgr. Western AutoSupply Co., Fort Wayne, 1964-65, mgr. new store sales, 1965-66; mktg. analyst Western AutoSupply Co., Kansas City, Mo., 1965; mgr. wholesale sales Western AutoSupply Co., Fort Wayne, 1966-68; v.p. sales Straton Baldwin Hardware Co., New Orleans, 1969-70; v.p. mktg. Klumb Cos., Biloxi, Miss., 1970-78; dir. Klumb Lumber Co., 1976-78; owner, operator Western Auto Store, 1978-80; Midwest sales mgr. Southern Importers, Greensboro, N.C., 1980-83; sales mgr. Millburn Peat Co., LaPorte, Ind., 1983-84, Klumb Co., Jackson, Miss., 1984-86; v.p., gen. mgr. Klumb Co., Jackson, 1987-88; pres., chief oper. officer Klumb Co., Jackson, Miss., 1989—. Elder Presbyn. Ch.; chmn. Downtown Franklin Improvement Com.; active Boy Scouts Am., United Fund; bd. dirs. Timbers II Homeowners Assn., Brandon, 1994-96. Recipient Packaging award Greater Jackson Area Advt. Club, 1971, Nat. Bark Mktg. award Forest Products Rsch. Soc., 1972; named to Honorable Order of Ky. Cols. Mem. Franklin Mchts. Assn., Nat. Bark Producers Assn. (membership chmn. 1973-76, program chmn. ann. conv. 1974, 76, pres. 1976-78, bd. dirs. 1974-78, packaging award 1972, membership award 1972), Franklin C. of C. (bd. dirs.), Rotary (bd. dirs. North Jackson 1977-78), Masons, Shriners. Conservative. Home: 208 Old Oak Cir Brandon MS 39042-2611 Office: Klumb Co PO Box 55949 Jackson MS 39296-5949

MC CREERY, JAMES F., air transportation executive; b. 1912. With Wilson Meat Co., Chgo., 1935-41; various mgmt. positions Mc Creery Aviation Co., Inc., McAllen, Tex., 1946—, now chmn.; officer Airport Car Rental, Inc., McAllen, 1965—. Office: Mc Creery Aviation Co Inc 2400 S 10th St Mcallen TX 78503*

MCCREERY, ROBERT J., air transportation executive; s. James F. McC. Pres., CEO Mc Creery Aviation Co. Inc., McAllen, Tex. Office: McCreery Aviation Co Inc PO Box 1659 Mcallen TX 78505-1659

MCCRERY, JAMES (JIM MCCRERY), congressman; b. Shreveport, LA, Sept. 18, 1949; m. Johnette Hawkins, Aug. 3, 1991; children: Claiborne Scott, Otis Clark. BA, La. Tech. U., 1971; JD, La. State U., 1975. Bar: La. 1975. Pvt. practice Leesville, La., 1975-78; asst. city atty. City of Shreveport, 1979-80; mem. staff U.S. Rep. Buddy Roemer, 1981-84; regional mgr. Ga.-Pacific Corp., 1984-88; mem. 100th-103rd Congresses from 4th (now 5th) La. dist., 1988—; mem. ways and means com. Office: US Ho of Reps 225 Cannon Ho Ofc Bldg Washington DC 20515

MCCRIMMON, BARBARA SMITH, writer, librarian; b. Anoka, Minn., May 3, 1918; d. Webster Roy and Jessie (Sargeant) Smith; m. James McNab McCrimmon, June 10, 1939; children—Kevin Mor, John Marshall. B.A., U. Minn., 1939; M.S.L.S., U. Ill., 1961; Ph.D., Fla. State U., 1973. Asst. librarian Ill. State Nat. Hist. Survey, Champaign, Ill., 1961-62; research assoc. Bur. Community Planning, U. Ill., Champaign, 1962-63; librarian Ill. Water Survey, Champaign, 1964-65; librarian Am. Meteorol. Soc., Boston, 1965-67; editorial asst. Jour. Library History, Tallahassee, 1967-69, 73-74; adj. asst. prof. Sch. Library Sci., Fla. State U., Tallahassee, 1976-77. Author: Power, Politics and Print, 1981, Richard Garnett: The Scholar as Librarian, 1989; editor: American Library Philosophy, 1975; contbr. articles to profl. jours. Mem. ALA, Pvt. Libraries Assn., Beta Phi Mu, Manuscript Soc. Democrat.

MCCRORY, SARAH GRAYDON, church lay leader, retired lawyer; b. Columbia, S.C., Sept. 30, 1921; d. Clinton Tompkins and Raven (Simkins) Graydon; m. Marvin Lowery McCrory, Dec. 15, 1944; children: Clinton, Raven McCrory Wallace, Margie McCrory Hicks, Alice McCrory Felts, Elliott. AB, Hollins Coll., 1942; LLB, U. S.C., 1944. Bar: S.C. Vestrywoman, jr. warden, sr. warden St. Martin's Parish, Columbia, 1972-75, tchr. adult edn., chmn. long range planning, 1975-88, coord. adult ministries, 1988-95; past mem. Episcopal Radio and TV Bd., Atlanta; past chmn. Total Ministry Conf., dep. Diocesan Conv., mem. constn. and canons com. Episcopal Diocese of Upper S.C.; dep. Gen. Conv., Nat. Episcopal Ch., 1973-79—, past mem. constn. and canons com., chmn. Gen. Conv. Consecration of Bishops, 1988, mem. Nat. Commn. on Racism, 1989-95, mem. com. on Canon III, 1981; bd. dirs. Kanuga Confs., N.C., 1983-88, mem. program com., 1986-91, archivist, 1989-95, also mem. minorities com. Past chmn. bd. dirs. Speech and Hearing Clinic, Columbia, Sci. Mus., Columbia; past mem. bd. dirs. Columbia Mus. Art; former precinct officer Columbia Dem. Com.; former mem. Habitat for Humanity, Columbia; former mem. bd. dirs. Columbia Day Care. Named Vol. of Yr., Woodman of World, 1973. Mem. Fortnightly Book Club (past pres.), Phi Beta Kappa. Home: 5036 Wittering Dr Columbia SC 29206-2923

MCCUBBIN, JAMES ALLEN, psychologist and researcher; b. Ft. Smith, Ark., July 27, 1952; s. Harry James and Vera (McMillan) McC.; m. Donna Lee Williams, Aug. 16, 1986; 1 child, Corey James. BA, U. N.C., 1974, PhD, 1980; MA, Wake Forest U., 1976. Lic. psychologist, N.C. Postdoctoral fellow Biol. Scis. Rsch. Ctr. U. N.C., Chapel Hill, 1980-82, instr. dept. psychology, 1980; rsch. assoc. dept. psychiatry Duke U. Med. Ctr., Durham, N.C., 1982-84, asst. med. rsch. prof. med. psychology, 1984-88; asst. prof. dept. behavioral sci. U. Ky. Coll. Medicine, Lexington, 1988-90, assoc. prof., 1990-96, dir. Behavioral Physiology Core Lab.; prof. U. Ky. Coll., 1996—; contract reviewer Nat. Heart, Lung and Blood Inst., 1991-92; behavioral medicine study sect. DRG-NIH, 1990, 92, 95—, VA Career Devel. Program, 1992. Editl. cons. Psychophysiology, Hypertension, Psychobiology, Jour. Behavioral Medicine, Psychopharmacology, Behavior Therapy, Archives of Gen. Psychiatry, Jour. of Cardiovasc. Electrophysiology, Health Psychology, Physiology and Behavior, Psychosomatic Medicine, Jour. of Cons. and Clin. Psychology; contbr. articles to profl. jours.; editor: Stress, Neuropeptides and Systemic Disease, 1991. NIH grantee, 1985-89—, NIDA, 1991—, John D. and Catherine T. MacArthur Found., 1982-88. Fellow Acad. of Behavioral Medicine Rsch., Soc. for Behavioral Medicine; mem. APA, AAAS, Soc. for Neurosci., Soc. for Psychophysiol. Rsch., Trout Unltd. Presbyterian. Office: U Ky Coll Medicine Office Bldg Dept Behavioral Sci Lexington KY 40536

MCCULLAR, BRUCE HAYDEN, oral and maxillofacial surgeon; b. Memphis, June 19, 1953; s. Robert Hayden and Virginia Maria (Daniel) McC; m. Jennifer Hunt, Feb. 15, 1974; 1 child, Michael. BS in Vertebrate Zoology with honors, Memphis State U., 1976; DDS with honors, U. Tenn., 1979. Diplomate Am. Bd. Oral and Maxillofacial Surgery. Intern then resident U. Tenn. Hosp., Memphis, 1980-82; pvt. practice oral and maxillofacial surgery Memphis, 1983—; assoc. prof. dept. oral and maxillofacial surgery U. Tenn., Memphis, 1987—; div. cons. for oral and maxillofacial surgery LeBonheur Children's Med. Ctr. Mem. editorial adv. panel Jour. Dental Econs., 1988. Instr. ACLS, Am. Heart Assn., 1982—. Comdr. USNR, 1985—. Fellow Am. Assn. Oral and Maxillofacial Surgeons, Am. Soc. Dental Anesthesiology, Am. Coll. Oral and Maxillofacial Surgeons, Southeastern Soc. Oral and Maxillofacial Surgeons; mem. ADA, Tenn. Dental Assn., Memphis Dental Soc. (Outstanding New Mem. 1987), Tenn. Soc. Oral and Maxillofacial Surgeons (sec.-treas. 1990-92, v.p. 1993-95, pres. 1996), Memphis Soc. Oral and Maxillofacial Surgeons (pres. 1991-92, sec.-treas. 1990-91), Naval Res. Assn., Assn. Mil. Surgeons of U.S., Memphis C. of C., Rotary Club (East Memphis br.), Chickasaw Country Club, Mensa, Intertel, Psi Omega, Omicron Kappa Upsilon. Republican. Episcopalian. Home: 6597 Oak Estate Dr Memphis TN 38119-6623 Office: 805 Estate Pl Ste 2 Memphis TN 38120-0647

MCCULLOUGH, FRANK WITCHER, III, lawyer; b. New Orleans, Dec. 13, 1945; s. Frank Witcher Jr. and Kathleen Elizabeth (Van Pelt) McC.; m. Barry Jean Bock, Mar. 7, 1981; children: William David Oat, Frank Witcher IV, Elizabeth Layton. BA, Stetson U., 1967; JD, W.Va. U., 1970. Bar: W.Va. 1970, Tex. 1970, U.S. Dist. Ct. (so. dist.) W.Va. 1970, U.S. Dist. Ct. (so. dist.) Tex. 1972, U.S. Ct. Appeals (5th cir.) 1972, U.S. Supreme Ct. 1980, U.S. Dist. Ct. (no. dist.) Calif. 1983, U.S. Dist. Ct. (we. dist.) Tex. 1987, U.S. Dist. Ct. (ea. dist.) Tex. 1993. Indsl. rels. specialist Continental Oil Co., Houston, 1970-72; asst. U.S. atty. U.S. Atty.'s Office, Houston, 1972-75; assoc. Baker & Botts, Houston, 1975-76, Austin, Tex., 1985-89; ptnr. Weiner Strother & Lamkin, Houston, 1983-85; regional counsel GATX Leasing Corp., Houston, 1976-78; ptnr. Walsh Squires Tompkins & McCullough, Houston, 1978-82; shareholder Sheinfeld, Maley & Kay, Austin, 1989—. Spl. commr. Harris County, Houston, 1982; mem. Bellaire (Tex.) Bd. Adjustment, 1982; bd. dirs. Big Bros. and Big Sisters of Austin, 1991-94. Mem. State Bar Tex. (grievance com. 1979-87, 95—), chmn. unauthorized practice law com. 1984-87), Met. Club, SAR. Republican. Episcopalian. Home: 6707 Bridge Hill Cv Austin TX 78746-1338 Office: Sheinfeld Maley & Kay 301 Congress Ave Austin TX 78701-2456

MC CULLOUGH, JOHN PHILLIP, management consultant, educator; b. Lincoln, Ill., Feb. 2, 1945; s. Phillip and Lucile Ethel (Ornellas) McC.; B.S., Ill. State U., 1967, M.S., 1968; Ph.D., U. N.D., 1971; m. Barbara Elaine Carley, Nov. 29, 1968; children—Carley Jo, Ryan Phillip. Adminstrv. mgr. McCullough Ins. Agy., Atlanta, Ill., 1963-68; ops. supr. Stetson China Co., Lincoln, 1967; asst. mgr. Brandtville Service, Inc., Bloomington, Ill., 1968; instr. in bus. Ill. Cen. Coll., 1968-69; research asst. U. N.D., Grand Forks, 1969-71; assoc. prof. mgmt. West Liberty State Coll., 1971-74, prof., 1974—, chmn. dept. mgmt., 1974-82, dir. Sch. Bus., 1982-86, dean Sch. Bus., 1986—, dir. Small Bus. Inst., 1978—; mgmt. cons., Triadelphia, W.Va., 1971—; instr. Am. Inst. Banking, 1971—; lectr. W.Va. U., 1971—; adj. prof. MBA program Wheeling Coll., 1972—, U. Steubenville, 1982—; lectr. Ohio U., 1982—; profl. asso. Inst. Mgmt. and Human Behavior, 1975—; v.p. West Liberty State Coll. Fed. Credit Union, 1976—; rep. W.Va. Bd. Regents Adv. Council of Faculty. Team leader Wheeling div. Am. Cancer Soc.; coordinator Upper Ohio Valley United Fund, 1972-74; instr. AFL-CIO Community Services Program, Wheeling; project dir. Ctr. for Edn. and Research with Industry; bd. dirs. Ohio Valley Indsl. and Bus. Devel. Corp., Inc., Labor Mgmt. Inst. Wheeling Salvation Army, Progress, Inc., Recipient Service award Bank Adminstrn. Inst., 1974, United Fund, 1973; Acad. Achievement award Harris-Casals Found., 1971. Mem. Soc. Humanistic Mgmt. (nat. chmn.), Orgn. Planning Mgmt. Assn. (exec. com.), Spl. Interest Group for Cert. Bus. Educators (nat. dir.), Soc. Advancement Mgmt. (chpt. adv.), Acad. Mgmt., Adminstrv. Mgmt. Soc. (cert.), Am. Soc. Personnel Adminstrn. (cert.), Nat. Bus. Honor Soc. (Excellence in Teaching award 1976, dir. 1974—), Alpha Kappa Psi (Dist. Service award 1973, Civic award 1977, chpt. adv. 1971—), Merit found. W.Va. Ednl. Excellence award, Delta Mu Delta, Delta Pi Epsilon, Delta Tau Kappa, Phi Gamma Nu, Phi Theta Pi, Pi Gamma Mu, Pi Omega Pi, Omicron Delta Epsilon. Author: (with Howard Fryette) Primer in Supervisory Management, 1973; contbr. articles to profl. jours. Home: 68 Elm Dr Triadelphia WV 26059-9620

MCCULLOUGH, KATHRYN T. BAKER, social worker, utility commissioner; b. Trenton, Tenn., Jan. 5, 1925; d. John Andrew and Alma Lou (Wharey) Taylor; m. John R. Baker, Sept. 30, 1972 (dec. Oct. 1981); m. T.C. McCullough, May 14, 1988. BS, U. Tenn., 1945, MSW, 1954; postgrad., U. Chgo., 1950, Vanderbilt U., 1950-51. Lic. social worker, Tenn.; emeritus diplomate in clin. social work Am. Bd. Examiners. Home demonstration agt., agrl. extension svc. U. Tenn., Hardeman County, 1946-49; Dyer County, 1949-50; dir. med. social work dept. Le Bonheur Children's Hosp., Memphis, 1954-57; chief clin. social worker clinic mentally retarded children U. Tenn. Dept. Pediatrics, Memphis, 1957-59; clin. social worker Children's Med. Ctr., Tulsa, 1959-60; dir. med. social work dept. Coll. of Medicine U. Tenn., Memphis, 1960-69; dir. community svcs. regional med. program Coll. of Medicine, 1969-76; dir. regional clinic program Child Devel. Ctr. Coll. of Medicine, 1976-85; mem. faculty Coll. of Medicine, Coll. of Social Work U. Tenn., Memphis, 1960-85; social worker admissions rev. bd. Arlington Devel. Ctr., Memphis, 1976—. Author 14 books. Active Gibson County Fedn. Dem. Women, 1987—; commr. Dist. I, Gibson Utility Dist., 1990—. Fellow Am. Assn. Mental Retardation (life); mem. NASW, AAUP, Acad. Cert. Social Workers, Tenn. Conf. on Social Welfare, Sigma Kappa Alumni. Mem. Ch. of Christ. Home: 627 Riverside Yorkville Rd Trenton TN 38382-9513

MCCULLOUGH, LAURENCE BERNARD, medical educator, consultant; b. Phila., Aug. 2, 1947; s. Henry Joseph and Marie J. (Burns) McC.; m. Linda Jean Quintanilla, May 14, 1977. AB, Williams Coll., 1969; PhD, U. Tex., 1975. Postdoctoral fellow Hastings Ctr., Hastings-on-Hudson, N.Y., 1975-76; Asst. prof. med. humanities and philosophy Tex. A&M U., College Station, 1976-79; asst., assoc. prof. community and family medicine Georgetown U., Washington, 1979-88; prof. medicine, community medicine, med. ethics Baylor Coll. Medicine, Houston, 1988—; adj. prof. ethics in ob-gyn., Cornell U. Med. Coll., N.Y.C., 1988—. Co-author: Ethics in Obstetrics & Gynecology, 1994, Medical Ethics, 1984, Spanish transl., 1987, Japanese transl., 1992; author: Leibniz on Individuals and Individuation, 1996. Office: Baylor Coll Medicine Ctr for Ethics One Baylor Plz Houston TX 77030-3411

MCCULLOUGH, R. MICHAEL, management consultant; b. Springfield, Ohio, Dec. 31, 1938; s. Jerome Edward and Sara Amelia (Fitzsimmons) McC.; m. Frances P. Kelly, Nov. 24, 1962; children: Jeanne M., Michael F., Colleen T., Brian A., Kathleen H., Christopher E., Brendan P. B.S. in Elec. Engring., U. Detroit, 1962. Engr. Gen. Electric Co., Washington, 1962-65; engr., rsch. dir. Booz Allen & Hamilton, Bethesda, Md., 1965-71, ptnr., 1971-73, mng. ptnr., 1973-84; chmn., chief exec. officer Booz Allen & Hamilton, New York, N.Y., 1984-91; sr. chmn. Booz Allen & Hamilton, McLean, Va., 1991—; bd. dirs. Profl. Svcs. Coun., Washington, pres., 1983-84; bd. dirs. Interstate Hotels, Caterair Internat., O'Sullivan Corp. Mem. adv. coun. Stanford U., 1985-91; bd. dirs. Wolf Trap Found., 1989—; trustee U. Detroit Mercy, 1990, U.S. - Panama Bus. Coun., U.S. - Russia Bus. Coun. Club: Columbia Country (Chevy Chase, Md.); Burning Tree Country (Bethesda, Md.); Country of Fla. (West Palm Beach); Robert Trent James Golf Club (Manassas, Va.); Pine Valley (N.J.) Golf Club. •

MCCULLOUGH, ROBERT DALE, II, osteopath; b. Tulsa, June 2, 1937; s. Robert Dale and Roberta Maud (Purdy) McC.; m. Lindell Arlene Wilcox, Sept. 28, 1963; children: Robert Mark, Lori Lindell. Student, Wheaton (Ill.) Coll., 1955-57; BS, N.E. Mo. State U., 1958; DO, Kansas City (Mo.) Coll. Osteopathy, 1958-62. Cert. Am. Osteo. Bd. Internal Medicine, Internal Medicine and Med. Oncology. Gen. practice McCullough Clinic, Tulsa, 1963-68; internal medicine resident Detroit Osteo. Hosp., 1968-71; internal medicine Baker-Todd-McCullough-Sutton, Tulsa, 1971-74; fellow med. oncology M.D. Anderson Hosp., Houston, 1974-75; internal medicine-med. oncology Baker-Todd-McCullough-Sutton, Tulsa, 1975-90; pvt. practice Tulsa, 1990-93; attending staff mem. VA Outpatient Clinic, Tulsa, 1993-94; assoc. med. dir. Blue Cross/Blue Shield of Okla., Tulsa, 1994—; trustee Tulsa Regional Med. Cttr., 1983-88, 90-93; bd. dirs. Okla. Blue Cross Blue Shield, Tulsa, 1983-92, vice chmn., 1991-92; mem. adv. coun. Okla. State U. Coll. Osteo. Medicine, 1988-94, chmn., 1988-90. Mem. bd. of editors Patient Care Magazine, Montvale, N.J., 1988-93. Mem. Okla. State Bd. Health, Oklahoma City, 1983-87, Tulsa City/County Bd. Health, 1988-95, chmn., 1993. Mem. Am. Osteo. Assn. (vice speaker Ho. of Dels. 1986-92, trustee 1993—), Am. Coll. Osteo. Internists, Am. Soc. Clin. Oncology, Okla. Osteo. Assn. (pres. 1982-83), Tulsa Downtown Lions Club, Soc. for Preservation and Encouragement of Barbershop Quartet Singing in Am. Republican. Southern Baptist. Home: 2300 Riverside Dr 10F Tulsa OK 74114-2404 Office: 1215 S Boulder Tulsa OK 74119

MCCULLY, MICHAEL JOHN, economics educator; b. Shawano, Wis., Aug. 23, 1960; s. John James and Donna (Lang) McC. BA in Econs., Austin Coll., 1982; MA in Econs., U. Notre Dame, 1985, PhD in Econs., 1989. Vis. asst. prof. econ. Ohio Wesleyan U., Delaware, 1987-90, St. Norbert Coll., De Pere, Wis., 1990-92, U. Wis., River Falls, 1992-93; asst. prof. econ. High Point (N.C.) U., 1993—. Instr. adult edn. local chs., Ohio, Wis., 1988-90. Nat. Merit scholar Austin Coll., 1978-82, Schmitt Grad. fellow U. Notre Dame, 1982-83. Mem. Am. Econ. Assn. Office: High Point U Sch Bus Montlieu Ave High Point NC 27262

MCCURDY, DAVID KEITH, former congressman, lawyer; b. Canadian, Tex., Mar. 30, 1950; s. Thomas L. and Aileen (Geis) McC.; m. Pamela Mary Plumb, Aug. 14, 1971; children: Josh, Cydney, Shannon. BA, U. Okla., 1972, JD, 1975; postgrad., U. Edinburgh, Scotland, 1977-78. Bar: Okla. 1975. Asst. atty. gen. State of Okla., 1975-77; assoc. Luttrell, Pendarvis & Rawlinson, Norman, Okla., 1978-79; pvt. practice Norman, 1979-80; mem. 96th-103rd Congresses from 4th Okla. dist., Washington, 1980-94; mem. armed svcs. com., sci., space and tech. com. Chmn. Nat. Dem. Leadership Coun. Fellow Internat. Rotary Club; recipient Disting. Svc. award U. Okla., 1991. Mem. Okla. State Bar Assn., Norman C. of C., Omicron Delta Kappa, Rotary. Office: McCurdy Group 1320 Old Chain Bridge Rd Mc Lean VA 22101•

MCCURDY, LAYTON, medical educator; b. Florence, S.C., Aug. 20, 1935; m. Gwendolyn A. McCurdy, 1958; children: Robert Jr., David Barclay. BS, U. N.C., 1956; MD, Med. U. S.C., 1960. Dimplomate Am. Bd. Psychiatry and Neurology (bd. dirs. 1983-91, pres. 1990); lic. psychiatrist, S.C., N.C., Md., Ga., Pa. Resident in psychiatry N.C. Meml. Hosp., Chapel Hill, 1961-64; with psychiatry tng. br. NIMH, Bethesda, Md., 1964-66; asst. prof. dept. psychiatry Sch. Medicine Emory U., Atlanta, 1966-68; prof., chmn. dept. psychiatry and behavioral scis. Med. U. S.C., 1968-82, v.p. med. affairs, dean, 1990—; prof. psychiatry Sch. Medicine U. Pa., Phila., 1982-90; psychiatrist-in-chief Inst. of Pa. Hosp., Phila., 1982-90; vis. colleague Inst. Psychiatry, U. London, 1974-75; nat. adv. mental health coun. NIMH, 1980-83; apptd. Pa. Adv. Com. for Mental Health and Mental Retardation, 1984-87; chmn. consensus panel on panic disorder NIH, 1991. Recipient Disting. Alumnus award Med. U. S.C., 1988, George C. Ham. Soc., 1990; rsch. fellow NIMH, 1974-75. Fellow Am. Coll. Psychiatrists (bd. regents 1987-90, v.p. 1990-93, pres. 1993-94), Am. Psychiat. Assn. (joint commn. pub. affairs 1981-84, chmn. com. on diagnosis and assessment 1988-94), So. Psychiat. Assn. (bd. regents 1977-80, chmn. bd. regents 1979-80), Royal Coll. Psychiatrists (U.K.); mem. AMA, Assn. for Acad. Psychiatry (pres. 1970-72), S.C. Med. Assn., Charleston County Med. Soc. (exec. com.), Waring Libr. Soc. (pres. 1979-80), Cosmos Club (Washington)., Alpha Omega Alpha. Office: Med U SC Coll Medicine 171 Ashley Ave Ste 601 Csb Charleston SC 29425-0001

MCCURDY, PAMELA PARIS, linguistics educator; b. Burlington, Vt., June 30, 1943; d. Franklyn Guy and Greta Mae (Boardman) Paris; m. Jim McCurdy, Nov. 30, 1963. BA in French, U. Tex., Arlington, 1972, MA in Linguistics, 1973; PhD in Applied Linguistics, U. Tex., Dallas, 1978. Dir. English Lang. Inst., Irving, Tex., 1979-81; lectr. dept. linguistics U. Tex., El Paso, 1981-84, dir. English Lang. Inst., 1982-84; asst. prof. English U. Tex.--Pan Am., Edinburg, Tex., 1987—; pres. Ednl. Svcs., Inc., Llano, Tex., 1984-87. Contbr. articles to profl. jours. Vol. trainer Literacy Ctr., San Benito, Tex., 1993-94. Mem. TESOL (sec., program chair regional affiliate 1987-88), Nat. Assn. for Bilingual Edn. Democrat. Mem. Disciples of Christ Ch. Home: 474 N Reagan St San Benito TX 78586-4648 Office: U Tex Pan Am Dept English 1201 W University Dr Edinburg TX 78539-2909

MCCURLEY, CARL MICHAEL, lawyer; b. Denton, Tex., July 15, 1946; s. Carl and Geneva McC.; m. Mary Jo Trice, June 5, 1983; 1 child, Melissa Renee. BA, N. Tex. State U., 1968; JD, So. Meth. U., 1972. Bar: Tex. 1972, U.S. Dist. Ct. (no. dist.) Tex. 1972, U.S. Dist. Ct. (ea. dist.) Tex. 1974, U.S. Supreme Ct. 1977. Ptnr. McGuire, Levy & McCurley , Irving, Tex., 1972-82, Koons, Fuller, McCurley & Vanden Eykel, Dallas, 1982-92, McCurley, Kinser, McCurley & Nelson, 1992—. Contbr. articles to profl. jours. Mem. Family Law Council (chmn. 1991-93), Dallas Bar Assn., Am. Acad. Matrimonial Lawyers (treas. 1990-93, v.p. 1993-96, pres.- elect 1997), Internat. Acad. Matrimonial Lawyers. Home: 4076 Hanover Ave Dallas TX 75225-7009 Office: McCurley Kinser McCurley & Nelson 1201 Elm St Ste 4242 Dallas TX 75270-2133

MCCUSKER, J. STEPHEN, zoo director; b. Chgo., Apr. 18, 1946; s. Richard Joseph and Hilda Mary (Grudgings) McC.; m. Jonolyn E. Wilson. BS, Mich. State U., 1969; MS, Tex. Christian U., 1976. Curator New Eng. Regional Primate Rsch. Ctr., Southboro, Mass., 1969-70; asst. curator Ft. Worth Zool. Pk., 1970-76; gen. curator Washington Pk. Zoo, Portland, Oreg., 1976-86; dir. Reid Pk. Zoo, Tucson, 1986—; cons. Stanley Pk. Zoo, Vancouver, B.C., 1984-87, Larson Co., Tucson, 1987—. Author 14 published papers, articles or chpts., 1971—. Recipient Winston Churchill Traveling fellowship English Speaking Union, British Isles, 1977, several rsch. grants Tex. Christian U., 1974-75. Fellow Am. Assn. of Zool. Pks. and Aquariums, Am. Soc. Mammalogists; mem. Centurions Club (Tucson). Office: Reid Pk Zoo 1100 S Randolph Way Tucson AZ 85716-5835

MCCUSKER, JOHN J., history educator, economist; b. Rochester, N.Y., Aug. 12, 1939; s. John James and Helen Ida (Esse) McC.; m. Ann L. Van

Pelt; children from a previous marriage: John J. III, Patrick W., Margaret E. BA, St. Bernards Coll., 1961; MA, U. Rochester, 1963; postgrad., Univ. Coll. London, 1966-67; PhD, U. Pitts., 1970. Lectr. St. Francis Xavier U., Antogonish, N.S., 1965-66; from lectr. to prof. U. Md., College Park, 1968-92; Ewing Halsell disting. prof. Am. history, prof. econs. Trinity U., San Antonio, 1992—; vis. rsch. assoc. Smithsonian Instn., 1969-70; vis. asst. prof. Coll. William and Mary, Williamsburg, Va., 1972-73; vis. rsch. prof. Katholieke Universteit Leuven, Belgium, 1984-85; adj. prof. early Am. history U. Tex., Austin, 1994—. Author: Money and Exchange in Europe and America, 1600-1775, 1978, European Bills of Entry and Marine Lists: Early Commercial Publications and the Origins of Business Press, 1985, The Economy of British America, 1607-1789, 1985, (with Russell R. Menard) The Economy of Early America: The Revolutionary Period, 1763-1790, 1988, The Beginnings of Commercial and Financial Journalism: The Commodity Price Currents, Exchange Rate Currents and Money Currents, 1991 (with Cora Gravesteijn) Rum and the Am. Revolution: The Rum Trade and the Balance of Payments of the Thirteen Continental Colonies, 1989, How Much Is That in Real Money: A Historical Price Index for Use as a Deflator of Money Values in the Economy of the United States, 1992; mem. editl. bd. Bus. History rev., 1980—, Econ. Hist. Assn., 1984-89; contbr. articles to profl. jours., chpts. to books. Advisor/participant talented and gifted program Prince George's County, Md., 1973-82; counselor merit badges on Am. bus., Boy Scouts Am., 1979-83; judge sci. fair Oxon Hill Sr. High Sch., Prince George's County, Md., 1981-83; seminar leader in-svc. day for social studies tchrs., Balt., 1985; bd. dirs. Chamber Music Soc., San Antonio, 1993—. Grantee Am. Philos. Soc., 1969, 70, 72, 75, 82, Am. Coun. Learned Socs., 1977, 86; fellow Inst. Early Am. History and Culture, 1971-73, NEH, 1976-77, 78-79, Guggenheim Found., 1982-83, Fulbright-Hays Program, 1984-85, St. Catharine's Coll., Oxford U., 1985; vis. sr. Mellon scholar Am. History, U. Cambridge, 1996—, Fulbright Sr. scholarship, 1996—; Helen Cam fellowship Girton Coll., U. Cambridge, 1996—, Leverhulme Trust vis. fellowship, 1996—, fellow Eccles Ctr. for Am. Studies, The British Libr., 1996—, John Adams fellow Inst. of U.S. Studies, U. London, 1996—. Fellow Royal Hist. Soc.; mem. Am. Hist. Assn., Orgn. Am. Historians, Am. Antiquarian Soc. (Fred Harris Daniels fellow 1980-81, editl. bd. 1989—), Am. Assn. Netherlandic Studies, Am. Soc. Eighteenth-Century Studies, Internat. Maritime Econ. History Assn., Economisch-Historisch Vereniging, Nederlandse Vereniging voor Zeegeschiedenis, Koninklijk Instituut voor Taal-, Land-en Volkenkunde, Brit. Assn. Am. Studies, Inst. U.S. Studies, Soc. Nautical Rsch., Econ. History Soc., Société Française d'Histoire d'Outre-Mer, Assn. Caribbean Historians, Barbados Mus. and Hist. Soc., Société d'Histoire de la Guadeloupe, Hist. Soc. Pa. (publs. com. 1980-93), N.Y. State Hist. Assn., Md. Hist. Soc., Washington Area Econ. History Seminar, Va. Hist. Soc., Assocs. Inst. Early Am. History and Culture (coun. mem. 1995-98), Assocs. John Carter Brown Libr., Assocs. James Ford Bell Libr., Econ. History Assn. (nominating com. 1985-86, 92-93, audit com. 1988, 94—), Cliometrics Soc., Cosmos Club, Phi Alpha Theta. Office: Trinity U Dept History 715 Stadium Dr San Antonio TX 78212-3104

MCCUTCHEN, CHARLES WILLIAM, chemical engineer; b. Wichita Falls, Tex., Nov. 20, 1928; s. William Urlin and Karis (Jameson) McC.; m. Joyce Forse, June 10, 1956; children: David William, Karis Ann. BSChE, MIT, 1949. Engring. trainee Dow Chem. Co., Midland, Mich., 1949; R&D engr. Dow Chem. Co., Freeport, Tex., 1949-68; sr. process engr. Dow Chem. Co., —, —, 1968-79, internal process cons., 1979-86; ret., 1986. Mem. AIChE. Home: 109 Blossom St Lake Jackson TX 77566

MCCUTCHEON, ELWYN DONOVAN, minister; b. Paden, Miss., Sept. 14, 1912; s. Samuel Powell and Callie Americus (Gipson) McC.; m. Hattye Gertrude White, July 21, 1940; 1 child, Martha Sue McCutcheon Perry. Grad. high sch., Chillicothe Bus. Coll. Ordained to ministry Primitive Bapt. Ch., 1948. Pastor Bethel Primitive Bapt. Ch., Bruce, Miss., 1948-49, Laodicea Primitive Bapt. Ch., Springs (Thaxton), Miss., 1949—; dir. Harmony Valley Singing Sch., Pontotoc, Miss., 1970-90. Author: (booklets) Doctrine of Grace, 1965, This We Believe, 1982, From Sonship to Discipleship, 1990; contbr. articles to profl. publs. Home: PO Box 35 2260 Hunter Rd Thaxton MS 38871-0035

MCCUTCHEON, IAN EARLE, neurosurgeon; b. London, Ont., Can., June 4, 1959; came to U.S., 1962; s. Otty Earle and Selma Maureen (Burrows) McC.; m. Sylvie Bonnier, May 19, 1984; children: Noëlle, Nicolas. BA, Yale U., 1978; MD, McGill U., 1984. Diplomate Am. Bd. Neurol. Surgery. Rsch. fellow Heart Rsch. Lab. U. Oreg. Health Scis. Ctr., Portland, 1978-80; intern in gen. surgery Cedars-Sinai Med. Ctr./UCLA, 1984-85; resident in neurosurgery Montreal (Can.) Neurol. Inst., 1985-87, 89-91; med. staff fellow Surg. Neurology Br. NIH, Bethesda, Md., 1987-89; asst. prof. neurosurgery U. Tex. M.D. Anderson Cancer Ctr., Houston, 1991—; dep. chmn. dept. neurosurgery U. Tex. M.D. Anderson Cancer Ctr., 1995—; cons. surgeon VA Med. Ctr., Houston, 1994—; clin. asst. prof. neurosurgery Baylor Coll. Medicine, Houston, 1991—. Contbr. numerous articles to profl. jours., chpts. to books; mem. editl. bd. Annals of Surg. Oncology, 1995—, PDQ Cancer Database, 1996—. Trustee Alliance Francaise, Houston, 1992-95; bd. dirs. Neartown Youth Baseball League, Houston, 1996—. Lt. comdr. USNR, 1988—. Fellow Soc. Surg. Oncology, Royal Coll. Surgeons Can.; mem. Am. Assn. Neurol. Surgeons (chmn. young neurosurgeons com. 1995-96), Congress Neurol. Surgery, Can. Neurosurg. Soc., Am. Assn. Cancer Rsch., The Pituitary Soc. Home: 1748 Marshall St Houston TX 77098 Office: U Tex M D Anderson Cancer Ctr 1515 Holcombe Blvd Houston TX 77030

MCCUTCHEON, MARY SHAW, museum consultant; b. July 13, 1947; d. John T. and Susan Micheline (Dart) McC. BA in Anthropology, Rice U., 1969; PhD in Anthropology, U. Ariz., 1981. Cons. on Micronesian mus. Guam and Palau; adj. prof. dept. anthropology George Mason U., Fairfax, Va., 1991—; asst. prof. U. Guam, 1981-83; mgr. tropical island collection Smithsonian Instn., 1988-91; curator numerous exhbns.; book reviewer; reviewer, panelist Office of Tech. Assessment, NEH, NSF; panelist 14th Ann. Meeting Mid-Atlantic Regional Assn. for Asian Studies, Washington, 1986; mem. adv. bd. Micronesian Resource Survey Nat. Park Svc. and Micronesia Inst. Sec. North Highlands Citizens Assn., Arlington, Va., 1980-81, v.p., 1988-89, pres. 1989-90, 91—; mem. Arlington County Bicyclist Adv. Commn., 1988-90; chair survey com. Arlington Hist Affairs and Landmarks Rev. Bd. 1992—, mem. 1991—, vice chmn. 1993, chmn. 1994; bd. dirs. Arlington Hist. Soc., 1993—, newsletter editor, 1992—. Home: 2115 N Rolfe St Arlington VA 22209-1029

MCDANIEL, BENNY JOE, automotive executive; b. Andalusia, Ala., Aug. 21, 1936; s. Harless Almer and Mrytice B. (Hicks) McD.; m. Barbara Grace O'Gwynn, Mar. 25, 1959; children: Thomas Lee, Susan McDaniel Davis, Linda McDaniel McCooey, Patricia McDaniel McVicker.. BS in Indsl. Mgmt, Engring., Auburn U., 1958. Technician So. Radiator, Brake & Elec. Co., Montgomery, Ala., 1959-64, sec.-treas., gen. mgr., 1965-68; sec.-treas., gen. mgr. O'Gwynn, Inc. (name change), Montgomery, Ala., Ala.; pres., gen. mgr. O'Gwynn, Inc., Montgomery, 1978—. Contbr. articles to automotive jours. Mem. SCV, Soc. Automotive Engrs., Automotive Wholesales Assn. Ala. (chmn., bd. dirs. state assn. 1986-88, treas. 1973-76, 79-82, 90-92), Nat. Inst. for Automotive Svc. Excellence (cert. master auto & truck technician), Jaycees, Shriners (chief Nomad Unit 1975), Ala. Geneal. Soc. (newsletter editor 1985-86), Montgomery Geneal. Soc. (pres. 1985). Republican. Baptist. Home: 1520 Meriwether Rd Montgomery AL 36117-3457 Office: O'Gwynn Inc 303 Mildred St # 1068 Montgomery AL 36104-3920

MCDANIEL, DAVID GLENN, business owner, author; b. Tampa, Fla., June 4, 1967; s. Jerry Glenn and Beverly Mitzi (McCullough) M. Student, Chgo. City Coll. Owner, pres. GSI Security, Tampa, Fla., 1992—. Author: (fiction) Godkill, 1996. With USN, 1985-91. Mem. Redman Christian Migrant Assn. (hon.). Republican. Scientologist. Office: GSI 1204 W Reynolds #204 Plant City FL 33566

MCDANIEL, GEORGE WILLIAM, historic site administrator, historian, educator; b. Cherry Point, N.C., Sept. 18, 1944; s. James George and Marguerite (Hodnett) McD.; m. Mary Sue Nunn, June 7, 1980; children: George H., James N. BA in History, U. of the South, 1966; MAT in History, Brown U., 1972; PhD in History, Duke U., 1979. Lectr. Hist. Preservation Program George Washington U., Washington, 1978; hist. sites surveyor Md. Hist. Trust, Annapolis, 1978-80; dir. rsch. and special projects Ctr. for Southern Folklore, Memphis, 1980-85; dir. edn, interpretation and pub. programs Atlanta Hist. Soc., 1985-89; field reviewer Inst. Mus. Svcs., Washington, 1990-93; evaluator Mus. Assessment Program Am. Assn. Mus., Washington, 1990-94; exec. dir. Drayton Hall Nat. Trust for Hist. Preservation, Charleston, S.C., 1989—. Author: Hearth and Home: Preserving a People's Culture, 1982 (honor award); contbg. author: Dictionary of Afro-American Slavery, 1988, Encyclopedia of Southern Culture, 1989. Vol. Rural Community Devel., U.S. Peace Corps, Togo, West Africa, 1968. With U.S. Army, 1969-70, Vietnam. Smithsonian Instn. fellow, 1975-76; recipient Honor award Nat. Trust for Hist. Preservation, Washington, 1982, Disting. Alumnus award The Lovett Sch., Atlanta, 1989, Burroughs award Coastal Carolina U., 1995. Mem. Am. Hist. Assn., Am. Assn. State and Local History, Orgn. Am. Historians. Office: Drayton Hall 3380 Ashley River Rd Charleston SC 29414-7105

MCDANIEL, GERALDINE HOWELL, geriatrics rehabilitation nursing consultant; b. Como, N.C., Feb. 21, 1943; d. Jarvis Littleton and Nell Carson (Daughtley) Howell; m. Paul G. McDaniel; children: Christopher Louis Winstead, Kimberley Ann Winstead. Student, Old Dominion U., 1961-62; diploma, RN, Norfolk (Va.) Gen. Hosp. Sch., 1964. RN, Va.; cert. nurse adminstr. ANA; cert. rehab. RN Am. Rehab. Assn. Office nurse ob-gyn. Dr. A.R. Garnett, Norfolk, Va., 1964; staff nurse Radford (Va.) Cmty. Hosp., 1965-66, Med. Coll. Va., Richmond, 1965; student health nurse Union Coll., Schenectady, N.Y., 1966-69; DON Confederate Home for Women, Richmond, 1975-80; clin. coord. Catawba (Va.) Hosp. Mental/Geriatric, 1981-86; DON Friendship Manor, Roanoke, Va., 1986-89, Avanté of Roanoke, Va., 1989-92, Va. Vets. Care Ctr., Roanoke, 1992-94; rehab. nurse cons. Mariner Rehab., Chapel Hill, N.C., 1994—; mem. Task Force to Study How Regulations Affect Patient Outcomes in Long Term Care, Roanoke, 1994; state coord. for parish nursing Va. Bapt. Women's Missionary Union. Sunday sch. tchr., com. chairperson, mission trips to Argentina, Mexico, Peru First Bapt. Ch., Roanoke, 1987—. Mem. ANA (cert. nurse adminstr.), Am. Rehab. Assn. (cert. rehab. RN), Assn. Rehab. Nurses, Va. Bapt. Nurses Fellowship (sec., treas., area rep. 1993—), Noble Dirs. Nurses S.W. Va., Va. Nurses Assn., Va. Dirs. Nurses Long Term Care (past dist. rep.). Baptist.

MCDANIEL, GRACIE SWAIN, nursing administrator; b. Hernando, Miss., Nov. 5, 1958; d. Edgar Ernest and Margarite Jane (Calvert) Swain; m. David Kenneth McDaniel, July 28, 1978; children: Bethany, Patrick. ADN, N.W. C.C., 1979; postgrad., Miss. State U., 1991-93. RN, Tenn., Miss., Ala., Ga., La. Staff nurse LeBonheur Children's Med. Ctr., Memphis, 1979-84, North Panola Regional Hosp., Sardis, Miss., 1984-90; home health nurse Miss. Dept. Health, 1990—; instr. N.W. C.C., Senatobia, Miss., 1991-94; DON, Dixie Home Care, Batesville, Miss., 1994—. Mem. ANA, Miss. Nurses Assn. Democrat. Baptist. Home: 117 S Pocahontas St Sardis MS 38666-1624 Office: Dixie Home Care PO Box 686 Batesville MS 38606

MCDANIEL, JAMES ROOSEVELT, municipal official; b. St. Petersburg, Fla., Jan. 10, 1947; s. James M. and Rosa L. (McDaniel) Smith; m. Lessie Kay Sams, Mar. 2, 1979; children: Alexcia K. Wiggins, Michael A. BA, U. South Fla., 1971, MA, 1992. Mgr. Radio Shack, Capitol Heights, Md., 1971-72; br. rep. Household Fin. Corp., Annapolis, Md., 1972-73; mng. ptnr. Fried Grease Enterprises, Hampton, Va., 1973-75; cmty. devel. dir. City of Plant City, Fla., 1977—. Bd. dirs. South Fla. Baptist Hosp., Plant City, 1992—, United Way East Hillsborough, Plant City, 1989—; mem. Hillsborough City Census Commn., 1980, 90; task force chmn. Hillsborough City Needs Assessment, 1990-91; coord. Mayor's Substance Abuse Task Force, Plant City, 1986-89; subcom. chmn. Affordable Housing Commn., Plant City, 1990-92. Sgt. U.S. Army, 1967-69, Korea. Recipient ann. svc. award Hillsborough Cmty. Coll., 1991; named outstanding young man of Am., Jaycees, 1982. Mem. Kiwanis (disting. Kiwanian 1994). Democrat. Baptist. Home: 507 S Allen St Plant City FL 33566 Office: City of Plant City PO Box C Plant City FL 33564

MCDANIEL, KAREN JEAN, university library administrator; b. Newark, Nov. 16, 1950; d. Alphonso Cornell Cotton Jr. and Maude Jean (Smoot) Cotton Bledsoe; m. Rodney McDaniel Sr., Aug. 25, 1971; children: Rodney Jr., Kimberly Renee, Jason Bradley. BSBA, Berea Coll., 1973; MS in Libr. Sci., U. Ky., 1975, postgrad., 1977-78; postgrad., Ky. State U., 1979-83, Ea. Ky. U., 1983. Asst. libr., instr. reference studies Paul G. Blazer Libr.-Ky. State U., Frankfort, 1975-79, asst. libr., instr. cataloging, 1980-83, head cataloging and classification, 1983; program coord. libr. svcs. Ky. Dept. Pub. Advocacy, Frankfort, 1983-85, libr. sr., 1985-87, program coord. state publs., 1987-89; dir. libr. svcs. Paul G. Blazer Libr.-Ky. State U., Frankfort, 1989—; bd. dirs. Solinet; mem. adv. bd. African Am. Ednl. Archives Initiative, Wayne State U.; mem. faculty adv. bd. Ctr. of Excellence for Study of Ky. African Ams.; mem. subcom. on target groups Ky./White House Conf. on Libr. and Info. Svcs. II, chair, 1990-91. Mem. State of Ky. Textbook Commn., 1993—; mem. Nat. Coun. Negro Women; adult membership Girl Scouts Am., 1987—, asst. troop leader, 1991-93; active Frankfort H.S. PTA, 1994—, Hearn Elem. Sch. PTA, 1983-94, Elkhorn Mid. Sch. PTA, 1991—, Friends of Paul Sawyer Libr.; active St. John AME Ch.; mem. bd. Frankfort YMCA, 1995—. Mem. ALA, AAUP, NAACP, Assn. Coll. and Rsch. Librs., Black Caucus of ALA (affirmative action com.), Southeastern Libr. Assn. (planning and devel. com. 1991—, preservation round table 1993—), Land Grant and Tuskegee Libr. Dir.'s Assn. (editor Libline 1993—, vice-chair, chair 1994—), State Assisted Acad. Libr. Coun. Ky. (sec. 1991-92, sec. 1992-93), Ky. Libr. Assn. (sec. acad. sect. 1990-91), Ky. Coun. Archives, Ky. Assn. Blacks in Higher Edn., Alpha Delta Kappa, Delta Sigma Theta. Democrat. African Methodist Episcopalian. Home: 147 Northwood Rd Frankfort KY 40601-1477 Office: Ky State U Paul G Blazer Libr Frankfort KY 40601

MCDANIEL, LINDA ELKINS, English language and literature educator; b. Perry County, Miss., Sept. 3, 1942; d. Ernie Willis and Maxine Eliot (Courtney) Elkins; m. Johnny Braxton McDaniel, Dec. 23, 1966. BS in English, U. So. Miss., 1964, MA in Am. Lit., 1970, postgrad., 1977-82; postgrad., U. Miss., 1981-82; PhD in Am. Lit., U. S.C., 1989. Grad. teaching asst. U. So. Miss., 1964-65, instr. in composition and lit., 1965-69, vis. instr., 1986-90, adminstr. asst. to dir. NEH Faulkner seminar, 1990-91; instr. in composition and lit. Delta State U., 1973-79; grad. teaching asst. U. S.C., 1982-83; rsch. and editorial asst. to editors Miss. Quar., 1983-85; adj. prof. English and lit. William Carey Coll., Hattiesburg, Miss., 1993—. Author book on Faulkner; contbr. articles to profl. publs. Leader Girl Scouts U.S.A., Cleveland, Miss., 1972-80; vol. Nat. Cancer Inst., Hattiesburg, 1992-94, Am. Heart Assn., Hattiesburg, 1994. John R. Welsh Meml. fellow, 1982-83, Euphemia McClintock-Susan Markey Fickling-Mary Simms Oliphant fellow, 1985. Mem. MLA, Soc. for Study of So. Lit., Miss. Philol. Assn., Simms Soc., Am. Quilter's Soc., Delta Kappa Gamma. Home: 315 S 23rd Ave Hattiesburg MS 39401-7310 Office: William Carey Coll 498 Tuscan Ave Hattiesburg MS 39401-5461

MCDANIEL, LYNN, small business owner; b. charleston, S.C., Jan. 26, 1954. Student, Harding Coll., Searcy, Ark., 1973-75; AA in Acctg. and Mgmt., Trident tech. Coll., Charleston, S.C., 1979. Adminstrv. specialist Med. U. S.C., Charleston, 1980-95; owner West Ashley Word Processing, Charleston, 1995—; salesperson Avon Co. Author: Conversational Journies and the Word of God, 1996. Named Profl. Handicapped Woman of the Yr., Pilot Club of Charleston, 1981; recipient Spirit award Avon Products, Inc., 1995, Pres.'s Club award, 1995, 96. Mem. Charleston Assn. Female execs. Mem. Ch. of Christ. Home and Office: 1526 Joan St Charleston SC 29407

MCDANIEL, MICHAEL CONWAY DIXON, bishop, theology educator; b. Mt. Pleasant, N.C., Apr. 8, 1929; s. John Henry and Mildred Juanita (Barrier) McD.; m. Marjorie Ruth Schneiter, Nov. 26, 1953; 1 son, John Robert Michael. B.A., U. N.C., 1951; B.D., Wittenberg U., 1954; M.A., U. Chgo., 1969, Ph.D., 1978; D.D. (hon.), Lenoir-Rhyne Coll., 1983; LL.D., Belmont Abbey Coll., 1984. Ordained to ministry United Lutheran Ch. in America, 1954. Pastor Faith (N.C.) Luth. Ch., 1954-58, Ch. of the Ascension, Savannah, Ga., 1958-60; assoc. dir. evangelism United Luth. Ch. in Am., N.Y.C., 1960-62; sr. pastor Edgebrook Luth. Ch., Chgo., 1962-67; pastor, guest lectr. Wittenberg U., Springfield, Ohio, 1970-71; prof. Lenoir-Rhyne Coll., Hickory, N.C., 1971-82, Raymond Morris Bost disting. prof., 1982, dir., prof. Ctr. for Theology, 1991—; bishop N.C. Luth. Ch. in Am., Salisbury, 1982-87, Evang. Luth. Ch. Am., Salisbury, 1988-91; chmn. humanities div. Lenoir-Rhyne Coll., 1973-82; cons., grant coord. NEH, 1977-79; master tchr. Hickory Humanities Forum, 1981—; chmn. task force on ecumenical and interfaith relationships Commn. Forming a New Luth. Ch., 1983-87; rep. Luth. Orthodox Dialogue In U.S.A., 1983-89;; chmn., cons. bishops governing coun. Evang. Luth. Ch. Am., 1987-89. Author: Welcome to the Lord's Table, 1972. Mem. Englewood Human Relations Council, N.J., 1959-60; pres., bd. trustees Edgebrook Symphony, Chgo., 1965-67; sec. Chgo. Astron. Soc., 1966-67; pres. Community Concerts Assn., Hickory, N.C., 1977-80. Served to sgt. U.S. Army, 1946-48, Korea. Luth. World Fedn. fellow, 1967-69, Mansfield Coll. fellow U. Oxford, 1989; recipient Disting. Alumnus award Trinity Luth. Sem., 1990. Home: 125 42nd Avenue Cir NE Hickory NC 28601-9012 Office: Lenoir-Rhyne Coll Hickory NC 28603

MCDANIELS, DAVID MARTIN, aerospace engineer, researcher; b. Camden, N.J., May 29, 1962; s. Theodore Charles and Margaret Lucrece (Longfellow) McD.; m. Karan Ann Click, June 23, 1990; 1 child, Griffin Major. BS in Aerospace and Ocean Engring., Va. Poly. Inst. and State U., 1984; MS in Aerospace Engring., U. Tenn., Tullahoma, 1986. Aerospace engr. NASA, Marshall Space Flight Ctr, Ala., 1987—. Home: 405 N Edgemont Cir Huntsville AL 35811-1364 Office: NASA ED34 Huntsville AL 35812

MC DAVID, GEORGE EUGENE (GENE MC DAVID), newspaper executive; b. McComb, Miss., June 30, 1930; s. O.C. and Inez S. McDavid; m. Betty Ernestine Tinsley, Sept. 24, 1949; children: Carol McDavid, Martha Gene Newman. B.B.A. cum laude, U. Houston, 1965. Owner, publisher Wilk Amite Record, Gloster, Miss., 1949-58; with Houston Chronicle, 1958—, prodn. mgr., 1967-74, v.p. ops., 1974-85, v.p., gen. mgr., 1985-90, pres., 1990—; adv. bd. Am. Press Inst.; past pres. bd. dirs. S.W. Sch. Printing Mgmt. Chmn. Greater Houston chpt. ARC, nat. bd. govs.; mem. pres.'s counsel Houston Bapt. U.; vice-chmn. Sam Houston Boy Scouts Am., United Negro Coll. Fund, Asia Soc. Goodwill Industries, YMCA; bd. dirs., Greater Houston Partnership, Nat. Conf. Christians and Jews, Houston region Am. Cancer Soc.; bd. dirs., pres. Houston Symphony; bd. dirs., v.p. Books of the World; mem. devel. bd. U. Houston; spl. deacon Second Bapt. Ch., Houston. Recipient Franklin award U. Houston, 1961, Disting. Alumnus award, 1990, Taggart award Tex. Newspaper, 1992, Man of Yr. award NCCJ, 1993; named Outstanding Ex-Citizen Gloster, 1973, Hon. Father of Yr., 1996. Mem. Am. Newspaper Pubs. Assn. (chmn. newsprint com.), So. Newspaper Pubs. Assn. (pres.) Tex. Daily Newspaper Assn. (pres.), Houston C. of C. (Houston Citizen's Community Svc. award 1993), Phi Kappa Phi, Beta Gamma Sigma. Clubs: Houston, Houstonian, Texas, Pine Forest Country. Home: 403 Hunters Park Ln Houston TX 77024-5438 Office: Houston Chronicle 801 Texas Ave Houston TX 77002-2906*

MCDAVID, MARION FOY JR., journalist; b. Knoxville, Tenn., Oct. 28, 1944; s. Marion Foy Sr. and Caroline Kelley (Okey) McD. BS in Comm., U. Tenn., 1979. Utilities editor Common Sense, an alternative paper, Knoxville, 1971-73; columnist Nashville Independent Weekly, 1971-72; jr. eligibility counselor Tenn. Dept. Human Svcs., Knoxville, 1974-77; co-founder, mng. editor Sevier County Sun weekly newspaper, Sevierville, Tenn., 1980; mng. editor Campbell County News weekly newspaper, Jacksboro, Tenn., 1980-82; Tenn.-Ala. corr. The Ripon Forum mag., Washington, 1970—; writer Coal Today mag., Ky.; editor County Newsletter and News Svc., Knoxville, 1983—. Campaign mgr. Tex Ritter for U.S. Senate, U. Tenn. Knoxville campus, 1970; vol., editl. writer Lamar Alexander for Gov., Knoxville, 1978, pollster Randy Tyree orgn., Matt Reese & Assocs., Knoxville, 1982; vol., office worker Goldwater for Pres., Baker for U.S. Senate, Chattanooga, 1964. With USN, 1965-69, Vietnam. Mem. Investigative Reporters and Editors, Ripon Soc., Inc. (nat. gov. bd. 1980s, pres. Ripon study group U. Tenn. 1970s), Young Americans for Freedom (East Tenn. bd. dirs. 1964-65). Republican. Methodist. Home and Office: 515 Renford Dr #B515 Knoxville TN 37919-4305

MCDAVID, SARA JUNE, librarian; b. Atlanta, Dec. 21, 1945; d. William Harvey and June (Threadgill) McRae; m. Michael Wright McDavid, Mar. 23, 1971. BA, Mercer U., 1967; MLS, Emory U., 1969. Head librarian Fernbank Sci. Ctr., Atlanta, 1969-77; dir. rsch. libr. Fed. Res. Bank of Atlanta, 1977-81; mgr. mem. services SOLINET, Atlanta, 1981-82; media specialist Parkview High Sch., Atlanta, 1982-84; ptnr. Interncontinental Travel, Atlanta, 1984-85; librarian Wesleyan Day Sch., Atlanta, 1985-86; mgr. info. svcs. Internat. Assn. Fin. Planning, Atlanta, 1986-90; dir. rsch. Korn Ferry Internat., Atlanta, 1990-95; rschr. Lamalie Amrop Internat., Atlanta, 1995—; bd. dirs. Southeastern Library Network, Atlanta, 1977-80, vice chmn. bd., 1979-80. Contbr. articles to profl. jours. Pres., mem. exec. com. Atlanta Humane Soc., 1985-86, bd. dirs. aux., 1978-90. Mem. Ga. Library Assn. (v.p. 1981-83), Spl. Libraries Assn. Home: 1535 Knob Hill Dr NE Atlanta GA 30329-3206 Office: Lamalie Amrop Internat 191 Peachtree St Ste 800 Atlanta GA 30303-1747

MCDERMOTT, CECIL WADE, mathematics educator, educational program director; b. Parkin, Ark., Aug. 19, 1935; s. Joe E. and Myrtle L. (Davis) McD.; m. Nelda Grace Lyons, June 4, 1961; children: Kevin Scott, Stephen Kyle. BS in Math., U. Ark., 1957; MS in Stats., Purdue U., 1962; EdD in Math. Edn., Auburn (Ala.) U., 1967. Cert. tchr. math., gen. sci., phys. sci., curriculum specialist supr., designated ind. fee appraiser, rsch. analyst. Instr. math. Sikeston (Mo.) H.S., 1957-59; state math. supr. Ark. Dept. Edn., Little Rock, 1959-65; ednl. cons. Auburn U., 1965-67; chmn., prof. math. Hendrix Coll., Conway, Ark., 1967-83; program dir. IMPAC Learning Sys., Inc., Little Rock, 1983—; co-dir. NSF Inst. Tulane U., New Orleans, summers 1967-71; residential appraiser Morrilton (Ark.) Savs. & Loan, summers 1977-82; cons. Okla. Legis. Coun., Oklahoma City, 1987, America 2000 Project, Dallas, 1991; mem. tchr. tng. panel Office Tech. Assessment, 1994; pres. Ark. Intercoll. Conf. Faculty Rep., 1974-84. Author: (audio-tutorial film) Primary School Mathematics, 1975; co-author: Modern Elementary Mathematics, 1978, Landmarks, Rudders and Crossroads, 1993; designer: (computer courseware) Mathematics/Basic Skills, 1989, 93. Plan coord. Gov.'s Task Force on Telecomm. Planning, 1991-95. Rsch. grantee U.S. Office Edn., Washington, 1972-73, Rockefeller Found., Little Rock, 1983-85; recipient Cert. of Merit award Electronic Learning, 1987, Endowment Scholarship Hendrix Coll., Conway, Ark., 1987. Mem. Ark. Amateur Union (chmn. state long distance running program 1969-72), Ark. Coun. Tchrs. Math. (chmn. regional conf. 1970), Am. Math. Soc., Math. Assn. Am. (pres. Okla./Ark. 1976-77), Phi Delta Kappa, Phi Kappa Phi, Pi Mu Epsilon. Episcopalian. Home: 1204 Hunter St Conway AR 72032-2716 Office: IMPAC Learning Sys Inc 501 Woodlane Dr Ste 122 Little Rock AR 72201-1024

MC DERMOTT, ROBERT FRANCIS, insurance company executive; b. Boston, July 31, 1920. BS, U.S. Mil. Acad., 1943; MBA, Harvard U., 1950. Commd. USAF, 1943, advanced through grades to brig. gen.; faculty dean USAF Acad., 1956-68, ret.; with United Svcs. Auto. Assn., San Antonio, Tex., 1968—, now chmn., CEO, atty.-in-fact; CEO, pres. La Cantera Devel. Co., La Cantera Hospitality, Inc., Fiesta Tex. Showpark, Inc., HTO, Inc. Author articles in field. Office: United Svcs Automobile Assn 9800 Fredericksburg Rd San Antonio TX 78240*

MCDERMOTT, ROBERT JAMES, academic administrator; b. Madison, Wis., Mar. 6, 1953; s. Austin John and Rosemary (McGilligan) McD.; m. Kay Marie Sonnemann McDermott, June 20, 1981. BS, U. Wis., Madison, 1975; MS, 1977, PhD, 1981. Asst., assoc. prof. So. Ill. U., Carbondale, 1981-86; assoc. prof., prof. Univ. S. Fla. Coll. Pub. Health, Tampa, 1986—; cons. U.S./Russia Commn. on Econ. and Technol. Devel., Washington, 1996—. Author: Health Education Evaluation and Measurement, 1993, Connections for Health, 1996; contbr. articles to profl. jours. Mem. Leadership Tampa Bay, 1995—, New Tampa Cmty. Coun., 1995—. Recipient Mabel Lee award AAHPERD, Reston, Va., 1988. fellow, mem. Am. Sch. Health Assn.; mem. APHA, Soc. for Social Mktg., Hunter's Green Country Club. Office: Univ S Fla Coll Pub Health 13201 Bruce B Downs Blvd Tampa FL 33612-3805

MCDERMOTT, VICTORIA ANN ELIZABETH, sales executive; b. Queens, N.Y., Dec. 8, 1968; d. Kevin Francis and Mary Jane McDermott. BA in Speech Comm., George Mason U., 1990, JD, 1993.

Sales mgr. Phantom Products, Virginia Beach, Va., 1996—. Republican. Office: Phantom Products PO Box 5950 Virginia Beach VA 23471

MCDERMOTT, WILLIAM THOMAS, accountant, lawyer; b. New Orleans, Jan. 3, 1945; s. William Thomas and Delia Ethel (Belden) McD.; m. Geraldine Dorothy Constantine, Nov. 20, 1965; children: Lisa Anne, Shannon Marie. BSBA, Am. U., 1969, MBA, 1971; JD (with hon.), George Washington U., 1974; grad. exec. mgmt. program, J.L. Kellogg Grad. Sch. CPA, Va.; cert. mgmt. acct.; fellow Life Mgmt. Inst. Ptnr. for tax Ernst & Young, Richmond, Va., 1969—; co-chmn. U. Va. Fed. Tax Conf., Charlottesville, 1981—; apptd. by Gov. of Va. to Commn. on Competitive and Equitable Tax Policy, 1996. Contbr. articles to profl. jours. Past chmn. bd. dirs. Richmond br. Tuckahoe YMCA, 1984; mem. citizens promotion bd. Henrico County Police Dept., Richmond, 1985; bd. dirs. Greater Richmond YMCA, 1983-84, Theater Va., Richmond, 1982—; treas., bd. dirs., mem. exec. com. Arts Coun. of Richmond, 1988-96, Children's Home Soc., Richmond, 1987—; apptd. mem. Gov.'s Commn. on Competetive and Equitable Tax Policy, 1996. Recipient Cert. Appreciation award Henrico County Police Dept., 1985, Karl B. Wagner Service award Tuckahoe YMCA, 1986. Mem. ABA, AICPA (individual tax com. 1990-93, chmn. interest expense task force 1993-96), Inst. Mgmt. Accts. (nat. v.p. 1991-92, nat. dir. 1987-89, 95—, chmn. nat. ethics com., prin. Va. Coun. 1987-88), Va. Soc. CPAs, D.C. Inst. CPAs, Downtown Club. Roman Catholic. Home: 1701 Locust Hill Rd Richmond VA 23233-4149 Office: Ernst & Young 901 E Cary St Richmond VA 23219-4057

MCDILDA, WAYNE ALLEN, systems programmer; b. Lincoln, Nebr., Dec. 20, 1960; s. Robert Kenneth and Mary Lou (Guthrie) McD.; m. Melanie Denise Freeman, June 7, 1980 (div. 1988); 1 child, Kenneth James. Student, U. Tex., El Paso, 1979, U. Tex., Austin, 1980-85, Park Coll., 1989-94. Computer operator, programmer Info Now Inc., Austin, 1981-82, Brydon Life Ins. Co., Austin, 1981-82; delivery coord., then programmer Mr. Gatti's, Inc., San Antonio, Austin, 1982-85; computer operator, shift leader Tracor Aerospace, Inc., Austin, 1984-87, systems programmer, 1987-90; equip. operator Tex. Purchasing and Gen. Svcs. Commn., Austin, 1986-90; computer operator Tex. Med. Found., Austin, 1988—; network specialist Dept. Info. Resources, 1990—, systems analyst VI; cons. Ralph Moreland Restaurants, 1984—, Short-Stop Internat., 1985—, J&M Tng. Systems, 1985—. Leader Houston area Boy Scouts of Am., 1970-77; instr. Corp. Adopt-A-Sch., Austin, 1987; mem. Austin Symphonic Band, 1989—. Mem. Austin Area Macintosh Developers, Nat. Eagle Scout Assn., Digital Equipment Computer Users Soc., Masons. Methodist. Home: 1816 Heatherglen Ln Austin TX 78758-3542 Office: Dept Info Resources PO Box 13564 Austin TX 78711-3564

MCDONAGH, KATHLEEN, theology educator, researcher; b. Dublin, Ireland, Aug. 12, 1930; came to U.S., 1947; d. Francis Columba and Charlotte Honoria Maria (Duignan) McD. BA, Incarnate Word Coll., San Antonio, 1963; MS, Marquette U., 1967; MA, St. Mary's U., 1972. Cert. tchr., Tex.; entered Sisters of the Incarnate Word, Roman Cath. Ch. Elem. sch. tchr. Incarnate Word Acad., Corpus Christi, Tex., 1949-53; jr. high tchr. Incarnate Word Acad., Brownsville, Tex., 1953-61; prin. Blessed Sacrament Sch., Laredo, Tex., 1961-63; tchr. Villa Maria H.S., Brownsville, 1963-66, prin., 1967-69; instr. theology Incarnate Word Convent, Corpus Christi, 1970—, Diocese of Corpus Christi, 1983—; assoc. dir. religious Diocese of Corpus Christi, 1988—; gen. adminstr. Sisters of Incarnate Word, Corpus Christi, 1982-96: ex-officio mem. Coun. of Religious (assoc. dir 1988—); mem. exec. coun. Region X Vocation Coun., 1985-92; chmn. subcom. on spiritual Corpus Christi Diocesan Synod, 1986-88;. Editor: 100 Letters from the Correspondence of Jeanne de Matel, 1994; contbr. articles to profl. jours. NSF grantee, 1959, 64-66. Home and Office: Sisters of Incarnate Word 2930 S Alameda Corpus Christi TX 78404

MCDONALD, ALICE COIG, state agency administrator; b. Chalmette, La., Sept. 26, 1940; d. Olas Casimere and Genevieve Louise (Heck) Coig; m. Glenn McDonald, July 16, 1967; 1 child, Michel. B.S., Loyola U., New Orleans, 1962; M.Ed., Loyola U., 1966; cert. rank I sch. adminstrn., Spalding Coll., 1975. Tchr. St. Bernard Pub. Schs., Chalmette, La., 1962-67; counselor, instructional coordinator Jefferson County Schs., Louisville, 1967-77; ednl. adviser Jefferson County Govt., Louisville, 1977-78; chief exec. asst. Office of Mayor, Louisville, 1978-80; dep. supt. pub. instrn. Ky. Dept. Edn., Frankfort, 1980-83, supt. pub. instrn., 1984-88; bd. dirs., com. mem. Ky. Coun. on Higher Edn., 1984-88, Ky. Juvenile Justice com., 1984-88, Ky. Ednl. TV Authority, 1984-88, So. Regional Coun. Ednl. Improvement, 1984-88. Mem. Pres.'s Adv. Com. on Women, 1978-80; active Dem. Nat. Conv., 1972, 76, 80, 84; pres. Dem. Woman's Club Ky., 1974-76, mem. exec. com., 1977-88; bd. dirs. Ky. Found. for Blind; exec. dir. Ky. Govtl. Svcs. Ctr., 1996—. Mem. NEA, Coun. Chief State Sch. Officers, Women in Sch. Adminstrn., Ky. Edn. Assn., River City Bus. and Profl. Women. Home: 6501 Gunpowder Ln Prospect KY 40059-9334 Office: 4th Fl W Acad Bldg Ky State Univ Frankfort KY 40601

MC DONALD, ANDREW J., bishop; b. Savannah, Ga., Oct. 24, 1923; s. James Bernard and Theresa (McGrael) McD. AB, St. Mary's Sem., Balt., 1945, STL, 1948; JCB, Cath. U. Am., 1949; JCD, Lateran U., Rome, 1951. Ordained priest Roman Cath. Ch., 1948. Consecrated bishop, 1972; curate Port Wentworth, Ga., 1952-57; chancellor Diocese of Savannah, 1952-68; vicar gen., from 1968, vice oficialis, 1952-57, oficialis, 1957; pastor Blessed Sacrament Ch., 1963; named papal chamberlain, 1956, domestic prelate, 1959; bishop Diocese of Little Rock, 1972—. Office: Diocese of Little Rock PO Box 7239 2415 N Tyler St Little Rock AR 77217*

MCDONALD, BARBARA JEAN, real estate broker; b. Oklahoma City, Apr. 6, 1941; d. William C. and Juanita Fletcher (Kane) Hightower; m. David N. McDonald, 1965 (div. 1991); children: Neal, Marci. BA, So. Meth. U., 1963. Tchr. Dallas Ind. Sch., 1963-66; real estate salesperson Amarillo, Tex., 1984-90; broker assoc. Jane Elliott Realtors, Amarillo, Tex., 1990—. Bd. dirs. Amarillo Little Theatre and Bravo Opera Assn. Mem. Potter Randall County Med. Aux. (pres. 1989-90).

MCDONALD, BENNA J., nursing educator, critical care nurse; b. Denton, Tex., Aug. 18, 1943; d. Beno C. and Imogene M. (Talkington) Sawyers; children: Russell, Bobbie Sue, Thomas. Diploma, Kilgore (Tex.) Coll., 1980; lic. vocat. nurse, Petit Jean Voc.-Tech., Morrilton, Ark., 1973. RN, Tex.; cert. emergency med. technician-paramedic. Dir. edn. Henderson (Tex.) Meml. Hosp. Mem. Am. Heart Assn. (affiliate faculty), Safety Specialist. Home: 551 CR 223N Henderson TX 75652-3043

MCDONALD, CHARLES EDWARD, lawyer; b. El Paso, Tex., Nov. 13, 1957; s. Carlos and Armida (Adauto) McD.; children: Miranda Lee, Ashley Lee Ann. BA in Philosophy, U. St. Thomas, Houston, 1980; JD, South Tex. Coll. Law, 1985. Bar: Tex. 1985, U.S. Ct. Appeals. (5th cir.) 1991, U.S. Supreme Ct. 1992. Prin. Law Office Charles E. McDonald, El Paso, 1985—. Comms. liaison Coleman Re-election Cong. Campaign, El Paso, 1984, 86. Mem. ATLA, Tex. Trial Lawyers Assn., State Bar Tex., El Paso County Bar Assn. Roman Catholic. Office: Law Office Charles E McDonald 4100 Rio Bravo #117 El Paso TX 79902

MCDONALD, CHARLES EUGENE, lawyer; b. Canyon, Tex., Feb. 21, 1927; s. Bryan Eugene and Mary Pickett (Davidson) McD.; m. Edna Gail Chapman, July 5, 1947; children: Mary Conner, Charles E. McDonald Jr., Wesley Monroe McDonald, Patrick Sean McDonald. BS, West Tex. State Tchr.'s Coll., Canyon, 1948; JD, U. Tex., 1953. Bar: Tex. 1953. Coach Idalou (Tex.) ISD, 1947-48; tchr. Midland (tex.) ISD, 1948-50; pvt. practice Midland, 1953-65, Alpine, Tex., 1965-67, Bangs, Tex., 1967—. Midland county sch. supt., 1954-58; pres. Bangs Lions Club, 1983. Mem. State Bar Tex., Brown County Bar Assn. (pres. 1991-93). Methodist. Office: 101 S 1st St Bangs TX 76823

MCDONALD, DEBORAH HALCOMB, state agency consultant; b. Ky., July 11, 1949; d. Thurston Clay and Berniece (Cole) Halcomb; m. Richard Curtis McDonald (dec.); 1 child, Ty. Student, Sue Bennett Coll., London, Ky., 1967-69; BA, Ea. Ky. U., 1972, MA, 1973, postgrad., 1982. Cert. tchr., ednl. adminstrn., Ky. Tchr. McKee (Ky.) Mid. Sch., 1973; tchr. math., chmn. dept. Clark-Moores Mid. Sch., Richmond, Ky., 1974-92, Madison Mid. Sch., Richmond, 1992-93; ednl. cons. in sch. improvement Ky. Dept. Edn., Frankfort, 1993—; curriculum and assessment cons. Region 6 Svc. Ctr., Corbin, Ky., 1993; trainer Ky. Effective Schs. Network, Frankfort, 1990—; mem. Ky. Gov.'s Adv. Bd. dor Title II Funding; rep. curriculum com. Madison County (Ky.) Bd. Edn.; mgmt. dir. Nat. Cheerleader's Assn., Dallas, summers; conf. presenter on effective schs. and practical arts. Mem. Ky. Task Force for Missing and Exploited Children; former treas., v.p., pres., exec. advisor, edn. chmn., del. to state conv. Richmond Younger Woman's Club; treas., mem. coms. charity ball Pattie A. Clay Hosp. Aux.; chmn. mother's march Kidney Found.; chmn., treas. Madison County Jr. Miss Program. Named Ky. Disting. Educator, Ky. Dept. Edn., 1993. Mem. ASCD, Nat. Coun. Tchrs. Math., Ky. Coun. Tchrs. Math., Ky. Mid. Sch. Assn., Ky. Edn. Assn., Madison County Edn. Assn., Richmond Women's Investment Group (treas.), Beta Sigma Phi, Alpha Kappa Delta, Phi Delta Kappa. Baptist. Home: 1014 Devane Frankfort KY 40601

MCDONALD, GARY HAYWOOD, mechanical engineering educator; b. Nashville, June 27, 1955; s. Haywood and Hallie Bea (Black) McD.; stepmother Virginia Nell (Hart) McD.; m. Shirley Ann Cantrell; 1 child, Emily Ann. BSME, Tenn. Technol. U., 1977, MSME, 1979, PhD in Engring., 1984. Registered profl. engr., Tenn. Grad. tchg. asst. Tenn. Technol. U., Cookeville, 1977-79, grad. instr., 1979-84; asst. prof. mech. engring. U. Tenn., Chattanooga, 1985-92, assoc. prof., 1992—, U. Chattanooga Found. prof., 1992. Contbr. articles to profl. jours. Recipient Young Engr. of Yr. award Chattanooga Engrs. Week, 1989, Outstanding Prof. award Student Govt. Assn., U. Tenn., Chattanooga, 1991-92. Mem. ASME, NSPE, Am. Soc. Engring. Edn. (soc./NASA summer faculty fellow 1987, 88, 90, 91), Chattanooga Engrs. Club. Republican. Methodist. Home: 6508-B Still Meadows Ln Harrison TN 37341 Office: Univ Tenn Grote Hall 615 Mccallie Ave Chattanooga TN 37403-2504

MCDONALD, JACQUELYN MILLIGAN, parent and family studies educator; b. New Brunswick, N.J., July 28, 1935; d. John P. and Emma (Mark) Milligan; m. Neil Vanden Dorpel; five children. BA, Cornell U., 1957; MA, NYU, 1971; MEd, Columbia U., 1992, EdD, 1993. Cert. in behavior modification, N.J.; cert. tchr. grades K-8, N.J.; cert. family life educator. Instr. Montclair (N.J.) State Coll., 1982-93, Edison C.C., Naples, Fla., 1994—; mem. steering com. Fla. Gulf Coast U. Family Ctr.; parent vol. tng. project coord. Montclair Pub. Schs., 1984-86; coord. Collier County IDEAS for Parenting, Inc., Naples, 1993—. Chairperson Interfaith Neighbors Juvenile Delinquency Prevention, N.Y.C., 1960-68; support family Healing the Children, 1970-90; founder The Parent Ctr., Montclair, 1983, Essex County N.J. Fair Housing Coun., 1990. Mem. Pre-Sch. Interagy. Couns., Family Svc. Planning Team, Raven and Serpent Hon. Soc. (pres. 1956). Psi Chi, Kappa Detla Pi. Home: 27075 Kindlewood Ln Bonita Springs FL 33923-4370

MCDONALD, JAMES, science foundation executive. Pres. Sci.-Atlanta, Inc. Address: One Technology Pkwy S Norcross GA 30092-2967

MCDONALD, JAMES PATRICK, county official; b. Fairmont, W.Va., Mar. 30, 1942; s. Romeo Tell and Ouida Emma (Stonestreet) McD.; Mary Anne Bevan, Feb. 21, 1969; children: Andrew Bevan, Laura Stonestreet. BS, U. Pa., 1963, M of Govtl. Adminstrn., 1965; D of Pub. Adminstrn., George Washington U., 1976. Dep. county exec., chief fin. officer Fairfax (Va.) County Govt., 1967—. Capt. U.S. Army, 1965-67. Robert Lincoln McNeill scholar U. Pa., 1959-63, Samuel S. Fels fellowship, 1963-65; decorated Bronze star. Home: 3902 Picardy Ct Alexandria VA 22309

MCDONALD, JEFFERY BLAKE, youth ministries administrator, educator; b. Houston, Sept. 27, 1962; s. Orville E. and JoEllen (Sterken) McD.; m. Lenée Suzanne Walker, Aug. 17, 1991; 1 child, Bailey Suzanne. AA in English, San Jacinto Coll., Houston, 1984; BA in Edn., Centenary Coll., Shreveport, La., 1986; MA in History, Stephen F. Austin State U., 1993. Youth dir. First United Meth. Ch., Lake Jackson, Tex., 1986-90, Lufkin, Tex., 1990-96; adj. prof. history Angelina Coll., Lufkin, 1993—96; youth dir. Christ United Meth. Ch., Sugar Land, Tex., 1996—; vice chmn. divsn. of youth State Conf., United Meth. Ch., Houston, 1993-95 dist. coord. Nacogdoches (Tex.) dist., 1990-95. Author and presenter in field. Mem. East Tex. AIDS Consortium, Lufkin; bd. dir. Habitat for Humanity, Lufkin, 1994—. Mem. Kiwanis Club. Home: 2315 Ridgemont Missouri City TX 77489 Office: Christ United Meth Ch 3300 Austin Pkwy Sugar Land TX 77479

MCDONALD, LESLEY SCOTT, clinical nurse specialist; b. Toronto, Jan. 29, 1946; d. Louis Johnstone and Frances Elizabeth (Pruder) McD.; m. Richard Eldon Jacobson, May 26, 1984. Grad. in nursing, Health Scis. Ctr., Winnipeg, Man., Can., 1969; BA, U. Winnipeg, 1974; MS, Johns Hopkins U., 1984. RN, Md., Wis., Ill., Tenn.; cert. neurosci. RN, ANCC. Neuro nurse clinician, staff nurse Johns Hopkins Hosp., Balt., 1974-83; neuro clin. nurse specialist Madison (Wis.) Gen., 1983-84, St. Anthony Med. Ctr., Rockford, Ill., 1984-90, Nashville Meml., 1990-94; neuro charge nurse Vanderbilt-Stallworth, Nashville, 1994—; lectr. No. Ill. U. Sch. Nursing, Rockford, 1989-90, Austin Peay State U. Sch. Nursing, Clarksville, Tenn., 1991-94. Mem. AACN, Am. Assn. Neurosci. Nurses (Madison chpt. pres. 1983-84, Rockford chpt. pres. 1986-90). Home: 147 Flat Rock Rd Lebanon TN 37090-9217

MCDONALD, MALCOLM S., banker; b. 1938. BBA, U. Minn., 1960. Asst. v.p. Irving Trust Co., N.Y.C., 1960-70; with Signet Banking Corp., Richmond, Va., 1970—; exec. v.p. Signet Banking Corp., 1981-85, sr. exec. v.p., 1985-86, vice chmn., 1986-90; pres., dir. Signet Banking Corp., Richmond, Va., 1990—; chief ops. officer Signet Banking Corp., 1991—, also pres., CEO. Trustee WETA pub. TV, Washington, mem. exec. com. Arts Coun. Richmond, bd. dirs. Sci. Mus. Va. Found., Inc. Mem. Met. Richmond C. of C., Assn. Res. City Bankers (gov. rels. com. mem.), Valentine Mus., Va. Bankers Assn., Japan-Va. Soc. (chmn. bd.), Initiaties Support Corp. (adv. com.). Office: Signet Banking Corp PO Box 25970 Richmond VA 23260-5970

MCDONALD, PATRICIA HAMILTON, insurance agency administrator, real estate broker; b. Raleigh, N.C., Sept. 15, 1952; d. Marvin Stancil Hamilton and Josephine (Blake) Rummage; m. Thomas Wayne McDonald, Jan. 22,1972; children: Wendi Dannette, Thomas Wayne. Diploma, Inst. of Ins., Phila., 1987. Cert. in gen. ins., agy. mgmt.; cert. profl. ins. woman; real estate broker. Sr. comml. lines account rep. Tomlinson Insurors, Fayetteville, N.C., 1970-76, Wachovia Ins. Agy., Fayetteville, 1976--78; agy. mgr., sec.-treas. Ins. Svc. Ctr., Fayetteville, 1978-91, Assoc. Ins. Agy. of Fayetteville, Inc., 1991—; instr. continuing edn. N.C. Dept. Ins., Raleigh, 1990-91; agts. adv. coun. Seibels Bruce Ins. Co., 1991-92, 94—; ins. agts. pre-licensing instr., CPCU instr. Fayetteville Tech. C.C., 1993, 94. Bd. dirs. Fayetteville Tech. Community Coll., 1990—. Recipient State award Cystic Fibrosis Found., 1988. Mem. Ind. Ins. Agts. (assoc., bd. dirs. 1989—), Fayetteville Assn. Ins. Profls. (pres. 1989—, chmn. edn. 1987-89, chmn. pub. rels. 1988, Ins. Woman of Yr. 1989), N.C. Assn. Ins. Women (chmn. edn. 1990, Edn. award 1989, Gen. Excellence award 1991, 92, state treas. 1992-93), Nat. Assn. Ins. Women (dec. 1985—), Ind. Ins. Agts. N.C. (trainer 1986—), Home Builders Assn. Fayetteville (Life Spike award), N.C. Foresters Assn., N.C. Grange, Hope Mills Kiwanis Club (treas. 1994—, bd. dirs. 1994—), Kiwanis Internat., Hope Mills Assn. Ins. Profls. (edn. chmn. 1992-93, long-range planning chmn. 1992-93), Fayetteville Area C. of C. Republican. Baptist. Office: Assoc Ins Agy Fayetteville 2547 Ravenhill Dr Ste 101 Fayetteville NC 28303-5461

MCDONALD, PEGGY ANN STIMMEL, retired automobile company official; b. Darbyville, Ohio, Aug. 25, 1931; d. Wilbur Smith and Bernice Edna (Hott) Stimmel; missionary diploma with honor Moody Bible Inst., 1952; B.A. cum laude in Econs. (scholar), Ohio Wesleyan U., 1965; M.B.A. with distinction, Xavier U., 1977; m. George R. Stich, Mar. 7, 1953 (dec.); 1 son, Mark Stephen (dec.); m. Joseph F. McDonald, Jr., Feb. 1, 1986. . Missionary in S. Am., Evang. Alliance Mission, 1956-61; cost acct. Western Electric Co., 1965-66; acctg. mgr. Ohio Wesleyan U., 1966-73; fin. specialist NCR Corp., 1973-74, systems analyst, 1974-75, supr. inventory planning, 1975, mgr. material planning and purchasing control, 1976-78; materials mgr. U.S. Elec. Motors Co., 1978; with Gen. Motors Corp., 1978-92, shift supt. materials, Lakewood, Ga., 1979-80, gen. ops. supr. material data base mgmt. Central Office, Warren, Mich., 1980, dir. material mgmt. GM Truck and Bus. div., Balt., 1980-91; dir. edn. & tng. GM Truck and Bus, Linden, N.J., 1991-92; ret., 1992. vis. lectr. Inst. Internat. Trade, Jiao Tong U., Shanghai, China, 1985, Inst. Econs. and Fgn. Trade, Tianjin, China, 1986-87; part time instr. Towson (Md.) State U., 1986-87. Capt. USCG. Mem. Am. Prodn. and Inventory Control Soc., Am. Soc. Women Accts., AAUW, Balt. Exec. Women's Network, Balt. Council on Fgn. Relations, Presbyterian. Avocation: sailing. Home: 455 N Alt 19 S Apt 182 Palm Harbor FL 34683-5931

MCDONALD, ROBERT IRVING, secondary education mathematics and science educator; b. Lakeland, Fla., Jan. 16, 1958; s. William Lee and Mary Frances (Emerson) McD. BS in Animal Industries, Clemson U., 1980. Cert. secondary tchr., S.C., metric specialist. Tchr., chmn. math. dept. Timmonsville (S.C.) High Sch., 1985—, also former chmn. governing bd.; mem. sch. improvement coun., mem. of writing team for Pee Dee Math. Curriculum, Grades K-8; also sports coach. Mem. Nat. Coun. Tchrs. Math., Math. Assn. Am., S.C. Sci. Coun. Home: PO Box 701 Lamar SC 29069-0701 Office: Timmonsville High Sch Market St Ext Timmonsville SC 29161

MCDONALD, WYLENE BOOTH, former nurse, pharmaceutical sales professional; b. Kinston, N.C., Sept. 29, 1956; d. Wiley Truett and Hilda Grey (Brinson) Booth; m. Robert H. McDonald; stepchildren: Stephanie Lynn, Robin Leigh. BSN, Barton Coll., 1979; MSN, East Carolina U., 1984. Pub. health nurse Sampson Co. Health Dept., Clinton, N.C., 1979-81; pub. health coord. New Hanover Co. Health Dept., Wilmington, N.C., 1981-83; med. ctr. liaison Cape Fear Valley Med. Ctr., Fayetteville, N.C., 1984-85; profl. sales rep. Merck, Human Health Div., West Point, Pa., 1985-88; hosp. specialist sales rep. Human Health divsn. Merck, West Point, Pa., 1988-90, sr. prostate health specialist rep., 1990-94; exec. cardiovascular specialist Human Health divsn. Merck, West Point, Pa., ž, 1995—; speaker Coastal Area Perinatal Assn., 1983, Career Week, U. N.C. Sch. Bus., Wilmington, 1987, 88, 89, 93. Fundraiser March of DImes, Fayetteville, 1987, Wilmington, 1991, Am. Heart Assn., Wilmington, 1991-93. Named one of Outstanding Young Women of Am., 1981. Mem. ANA, AAUW, N.C. Nurses Assn., N.C. Pub. Health Assn., Sigma Theta Tau. Home and Office: 108 Seapath Estate Wrightsville Beach NC 28480-1964

MCDONALD-GREEN, A. MICHELLE, critical care nurse; b. Beaumont, Tex., Nov. 26, 1963; d. Arthur George and Billie Jean (Harrison) McDonald; m. Jeffery Scott Green, June 7, 1986. BS, Lamar U., 1988. Cert. in basic arrythmia, critical care, ACLS. Past staff nurse St. Elizabeth Hosp., Beaumont, 1988-89. Home: 102 Oak Creek Lumberton TX 77657

MCDONALD-WEST, SANDI M., headmaster, consultant; b. Lowell, Mass., May 8, 1930; d. Walter Allan and Celina Louise (Lalime) MacLean; m. Thomas D. McDonald, Sept. 8, 1951 (div.); children: Todd F. McDonald, Brooke McDonald Killian, Ned M. McDonald, Reid A. McDonald, Heather McDonald Acker. BA, DePauw U., 1951; MA, Fairleigh Dickinson U., 1966; MEd, North Tex. State U., 1980. Cert. in Montessori teaching. Tchr., adminstr. Hudson (Ohio) Montessori Sch., 1966-68, Berea (Ohio) Montessori Sch., 1968-70, Creative Learning Ctr., Dallas, 1970-71; tchr., head of lower sch. The Selwyn Sch., Denton, Tex., 1971-83; tchr., headmaster Cimarron Sch., Enid, Okla., 1983-87; cons. Corpus Christi (Tex.) Montessori Sch., 1987-89, Azlann-Eren Horn Montessori Sch., Denton, 1989-95, Highland Meadow Montessori Acad., Southlake, Tex., 1994—; ednl. dir., pres. Southwestern Montessori Tchg. Ctr., Inc., Denton, 1974—; adj. prof. North Tex. State U., Denton, 1979-80; cons., lectr. Am. Montessori Soc., N.Y.C., 1970—, Japanese Montessori Soc., 1978—, also pub. and pvt. schs., 1972—; chair commn. for accreditation Montessori Accreditation Coun. Tchr. Edn., Denton, 1991—. Developer various Montessori materials; contbr. articles to profl. jours. Mem. Am. Montessori Soc., No. Ohio Montessori Assn. (pres. 1968-70), Assn. Montessori Internat., N.Am. Montessori Tchrs. Assn., Wheat Capital Assn. for Children Under Six (pres. 1986-87), LWV. Mem. Am. Montessori Soc., No. Ohio Montessori Assn. (pres. 1968-70), Assn. Montessori Internat., N.Am. Montessori Tchrs Assn., Wheat Capital Assn. for Children Under Six (pres. 1986-87), LWV, Concerned Scientists. Home: 2005 Marshall Rd Denton TX 76207-3316

MCDONNELL, JEAN-MARIE, writer, public relations educator; b. Mobile, Ala., Oct. 15, 1956; d. Thomas Henry "Harry" and Ruth Lourine (Mell) McD. BA in Bio-Psychology, Eckerd Coll., St. Petersburg, Fla., 1979; MA in Print Journalism, U. Mo., Columbia, 1983. Adjunct prof. Spring Hill Coll., Mobile, Ala., 1988-89; assoc. editor Gulf Coast Newspapers, Baldwin County, 1989-92; adjunct prof. U. W. Fla., Pensacola, 1994-95; Univ. S. Ala., Mobile, 1995-96; pub. rels. coord. instr. Mobile (Ala.) Mus. Art, 1995-96; owner, pres. McDonnell Comms., Daphne, Ala., 1992—; asst. editor Progress Report, Alexandria, Va., 1984-86; county editor St. Albans (Vt.) Messenger, 1983-84; English as a second lang. tchr. East/West Lang. Inst., Chiba, Japan, 1979-81, Swany Corp., Shirotori, Japan, 1979-80; coord. Ea. Shore Literacy Coun., 1996—. Author: Mobile, A Gulf Coast Treasure, 1994; editor: Gulf Coast Newspapers, 1989-92. Vestry mem. St. Paul's Episcopal Ch., Daphne, Ala., 1994-96. Recipient Douglas L. Cannon award Med. Assn. Ala., 1990, 91, Gen. Excellence award 3rd place, 1991, 92, Best Feature award 3rd place, 1992, Best Lifestyle Family Pages award 1st place, 1991, 92, 2nd place, 1993, Best Use of Photographs in Editl. Content award 2nd place 1991, Best Bus. Pages award 1st place, 1992, Ala. Press Assn. Better Newspaper Contest. Mem. Pub. Rels. Coun. Ala. Episcopalian.

MCDONOUGH, PAUL GERARD, obstetrician-gynecologist, educator; b. Scranton, Pa., May 1, 1930; s. Gerard A. and Mary E. (Gannon) McD.; m. Nicole Moreau, Sept. 9, 1959; children: Diana, Michel, Jean Paul. BS in Biology magna cum laude, Holy Cross Coll., Worcester, Mass., 1952; MD, Thomas Jefferson U., 1956. Diplomate: Am. Bd. Ob-Gyn. Intern Phila. Gen. Hosp., 1956-57; resident in diagnostic and therapeutic radiology U. Calif. Med. Center, San Francisco, 1960-61; resident in ob-gyn Phila. Gen. Hosp., 1961-64; research fellow Med. Coll. Ga., 1964-66, asst. prof. ob-gyn, 1966-67, assoc. prof., 1970-75, prof., chief reproductive endocrine div., 1975-83, acting dir. Human Genetics Inst., 1983—; cons. Dwight D. Eisenhower Army Med. Center, Univ. Hosp., Meml. Med. Center, Savannah, Ga., Columbus (Ga.) Med. Center, Greenville (S.C.) Gen. Hosp. Contbr. articles to profl. jours., chpts. in books. Served to capt. M.C. USAF, 1957-60. Recipient Billings Silver medal AMA, 1965, Aesculapius award Med. Assn. Ga., cert. of award So. Med. Assn., 1969. Fellow Am. Coll. Ob-Gyn; mem. Ga. Ob-Gyn Soc., Am. Fertility Soc. (dir.), Med. Assn. Ga., Richmond County Med. Soc., So. Med. Assn., Endocrine Soc., South Atlantic Assn. Obstetricians and Gynecologists, Am. Soc. Human Genetics, Am. Assn. Gynecol. Laparoscopists, Atlanta Genetics, Soc., AAUP, Ga. Perinatal Assn., Internat. Soc. Pediatric and Adolescent Gynecology (exec. com.), Internat. Fedn. Infantile and Juvenile Gynecology (v.p. U.S. sector), Alpha Omega Alpha. Roman Catholic. Office: Med Coll Ga Dept Ob-Gyn 1120 15th St Augusta GA 30901-3157*

MCDOUGAL, IVAN ELLIS, artist; b. Lometa, Tex., June 29, 1927; s. Ellis and Bertha (Robbins) McD.; m. Gloria Deal, Dec. 17, 1949; children: Dana Marlene, Celia Annette, Lea Elaine. Student, Schreiner Inst., 1947-48, Trinity U., 1948-49, Am. Acad. Art, 1949-50. Illustrator Express-News, San Antonio; advtsg. art dir. San Antonio Light, 1954-74, advtsg. promotion mgr., 1974-84; art tchr. Jewish Cmty. Ctr., San Antonio. Featured in (book) The Texas Hill Country Interpretations by 13 artists , 1981, Pecos to the Rio Grande Interpretations by 18 Artists, 1983; permanent collections include McNay Art Mus., San Antonio. Served in USN, 1945-47. Recipient Best of Show award 1st We. Fedn. Exhbn., 1976, Top 100 Nat. Arts for the Parks Exhbn., 1990, 92. Mem. Tex. Watercolor Soc. (7 awards 1972-91), San Antonio Watercolor Group (3 awards 1980-84), San Antonio Art League (Artist of the Yr. 1978, 7 awards 1965-96). Home: 6850 Oxford Pl San Antonio TX 78240

MCDOUGAL, LUTHER LOVE, III, law educator; b. Paris, Tex., Oct. 19, 1938; s. Luther Love and Dorothy Harriet (Atkinson) McD.; m. Mary Anne McDougal, Apr. 12, 1959; children—Luther IV, Katherine, Kim, Mark, Myres. Student, Vanderbilt U., 1956-58; B.A., U. Miss., 1959, LL.B., 1962; LL.M., Yale U., 1966. Assoc. Blair & Anderson, Tupelo, Miss., 1962; ptnr. Riley & McDougal, Tupelo, 1963-64; prof. law U. Miss., Oxford, 1964-70, U. Ariz., Tucson, 1970-74; W. R. Irby prof. law Tulane U., New Orleans, 1974—; chmn. bd. N. Miss. Rural Legal Services, Oxford, 1967-70, Ctr. for

Legal Studies of Intergovtl. Relations, New Orleans, 1982-86. Author: Property, Wealth, Land: Allocation, Planning and Development, 1981, Cases on American Conflicts Law, 1982, 2d edit., 1989, American Conflicts Law, 1986, Louisiana Oil and Gas Law, 1988; contbr. articles to profl. jours. Mem. Am. Law Inst. Democrat. Office: Tulane U Law Sch 6329 Freret St New Orleans LA 70118-5670*

MCDOW, RUSSELL EDWARD, JR., surgeon; b. Waynesboro, Va., Mar. 14, 1950; s. Russell Edward and Estelle (Vereen) McD.; m. Anne Stewart, June 24, 1972 (div. 1982); children: Mary Stewart, Sinclair Russell; m. Linda Stack, May 27, 1984; 1 child, Erin Laney. BS, Duke U., 1972; MD, U. Va., 1976. Diplomate Am. Bd. Surgery. Chmn. dept. surgery Loudoun Hosp. Ctr., Leesburg, Va., 1985-89, chief staff, 1989—. Fellow ACS. Home: RR 1 Box 898 Waterford VA 22190-9703 Office: Loudoun Gen Surgery Ctr 211 Gibson St NW # 207 Leesburg VA 22075-2115

MCDOWELL, RONALD RUSSELL, geologist; b. Boscobel, Wis., Apr. 2, 1949; s. Ronald Russell and Virginia Nellie (Kessler) McD. BSEE, U. Wis., 1972; MS in Geology, U. Kans., 1982; PhD in Geology, Colo. Sch. Mines, 1987. Rsch. asst. geohydrology br. Kans. Geol. Survey, Lawrence, 1981-82; tchg. asst., instr. dept. geology Colo. Sch. Mines, Golden, 1982-85; profl. programmer, instr. computing ctr. Colo. Sch. Mines, 1986-88; project geologist Potter Mine, Inc., Littleton, Colo., 1986-89; dir. product devel. Interactive Concepts Inc., Lawrence, 1989-91; mathematical geologist W.Va. Geol. and Econ. Survey, Morgantown, 1991-94, sr. rsch. geologist, 1994—; instr. Fairmont State Coll., 1994—; adj. asst. prof. W.Va. U., 1995—. Mem. AAAS, Internat. Assn. Mathematical Geologists, Assn. Exploration Geochemists, Am. Assn. Petroleum Geologists, Can. Soc. Petroleum Geologists, Soc. Econ. Paleontologists and Mineralogists, Paleontol. Soc. Office: WVa Geol Survey PO Box 879 Morgantown WV 26507-0879

MCDOWELL, THEODORE NOYES, public relations consultant; b. Washington, Oct. 20, 1925; s. Ralph Walker McDowell and Ruth Noyes Sheldon; m. Mildred Bowen, Mar. 5, 1945; children: Patricia B., Janet Ruth Curtis, Theodora McDowell Herskovitz, Theodore Noyes Jr. BA, Duke U., 1947. Reporter Washington Star Newspaper, 1947-51, asst. promotion mgr., 1951-53; account exec. Evening Star Broadcasting Co., Washington, 1953-55, TV program mgr., 1955-62, gen. mgr. news and pub. affairs and sec., 1962-70; dir. office of pub. affairs U.S. Dept. Transp., Washington, 1970-71; regional rep. of the sec. U.S. Dept. Transp., Atlanta, 1971-76; self-employed media cons. Hilton Head Island, S.C., 1976—. Former mem. and vice chmn. governing bd. Nat. Cathedral Sch., Washington; former bd. dirs. Children's Hosp., Washington, chmn. Pres.'s Cup Regatta, 1960-61; elder Presbyn. Ch. With USN, 1943-46. Recipient Meritorious Achievement award Sec. Transp., 1971, Sec.'s award, 1973, Nat. Def. Transp. Assn. award, 1972-73. Mem. Radio TV News Dirs. Assn. (former bd. dirs.), AP Radio/TV Assn. (bd. dirs., past pres.), Soc. Profl. Journalists, Broadcast Pioneers, Toastmasters. Presbyterian (elder). Home and Office: 29 Ruddy Turnstone Rd Hilton Head Island SC 29928-5704

MCDUFFIE, ADELINA FERRARO, pediatrics nurse; b. N.Y.C., Mar. 16, 1958; d. Thomas Joseph and Justine Rita (Condello) Ferraro; m. Ernest Paul McDuffie, Sept. 21, 1991. BSN, Georgetown U., 1980; MS, U. Mich., 1984. Staff nurse Concord (N.H.) Hosp., 1980; ICU staff nurse Boston Children's Hosp., 1981-82, staff nurse, 1984-85; nursing cons. Children's Ctr. U. Mich., Ann Arbor, 1982-83, tchr. asst. Sch. Nursing, 1983-84; pediatric clin. instr. Cleve. Clinic Found., 1985-87; clin. nurse specialist Rainbow Babies & Children's Hosp., Cleve., 1987-89; GI/nutrition clin. specialist Children's Hosp. of The King's Daus., Norfolk, Va., 1989—. Contbr. articles to profl. publs. Grantee U.S. Dept. HHS, 1982-84. Mem. ANA, Am. Soc. Parenteral and Enteral Nutrition (cert. nutrition support nurse), Pediatric Gastroenterology and Nutrition Nurses. Office: Children's Hosp of King's Daus 601 Childrens Ln Norfolk VA 23507-1910

MCEACHRAN, ANGUS, newspaper editor; b. Memphis, Aug. 24, 1939; s. Angus G. and Maxine (Taylor) McE.; m. Ann Blackwell; children: Angus G. III, Amanda Simmons. Student, George Washington U., 1958-59, Memphis State U., 1959-61. Reporter The Comml. Appeal, Memphis, 1960-63, asst. city editor, 1963-65, metro editor, 1965-69, asst. mng. editor, 1969-77; exec. editor Birmingham (Ala.) Post-Herald, 1977-78, editor, 1978-82; exec. editor The Pitts. Press, 1982-83, editor, 1983-92; editor The Commercial Appeal, Memphis, Tenn., 1993-94, editor, pres., 1994—; corr. N.Y. Times, Wall St. Jour., Newsweek, The Nat. Observer. Mem. Am. Soc. Newspaper Editors, Pa. Soc. Newspaper Editors (bd. dirs.), Sigma Delta. Roman Catholic. Home: 872 River Park Dr Memphis TN 38103 Office: Commercial Appeal 495 Union Ave Memphis TN 38103-3242

MCELDOWNEY, RENE, health care educator, consultant; b. Denver, Mar. 31, 1956; d. Raymond James and Barbara Louise (McNeal) Polanis; m. George Adams McEldowney Jr., June 1, 1984. AB, Morris Harvey Coll., Charleston, W.Va., 1977; BS, W.Va. State Coll., 1983; MBA, Marshall U., 1987; PhD, Va. Tech. U., 1994. X-ray technologist Charleston Area Med. Ctr., 1977-79, nuc. medicine technologist, 1979-84; asst. to v.p. acad. affairs Marshall U., Huntington, W.Va., 1984-87, mgmt. instr., 1987-89; asst. prof. Auburn (Ala.) U., 1992—; rsch. cons. Netherland Sch. Govt., Das Hagg, Holland, 1990—; physics cons. Health Physics & Assocs., Roanoke, Va., 1991-92. Founder Food Search, Charleston, 1987-89; mem. Score, Huntington, 1988-89; literacy vol. Ala. Literacy Coun., Montgomery, Ala., 1993—; mem. Montgomery Jr. League, 1992—. Recipient scholarship Oxford U., 1991. Mem. ASPA, Am. Acad. Mgmt., Mortar Bd., Kappa Kappa Gamma. Office: Auburn U 1224 Haley Ctr Auburn AL 36849

MCELGUNN, PEGGY, management executive; b. Chgo., Jan. 25, 1962; d. Edwin Paul and Patricia Louise (Klein) Moldof; m. Sean Edward McElgunn, May 24, 1987. BA in Polit. Sci., cert. internat. rels., U. Rochester, 1984; JD, George Mason U., 1990. Bar: Va. 1990; 4th cir. 1990. Meeting specialist Smith Bucklin and Assocs., Washington, 1984-86; govt. affairs specialist Hauck and Assocs., Washington, 1986-87; land use coord. Nat. Manufactured Housing Fedn., Washington, 1988-89; v.p. Internat. Mgmt. Group, Washington, 1989-92; exec. dir. Soc. Environ. Toxicology and Chemistry, Washington, 1989-90, Nat. Soc. Cardiovascular Technology/Pulmonary Technology, Washington, 1989—; exec. v.p. The Am. Surety Assn., Washington, 1991-92, 94—; owner, exec. v.p. TriCorp Mgmt., Fredericksburg, Va., 1992—. Bd. dirs. Fairview Preservation Assn., Fredericksburg, Va., 1990. Mem. Am. Soc. Assn. Execs., Va. Bar Assn., Fredericksburg Area Svc. League. Home: 104 Chinaberry Dr Fredericksburg VA 22407-8012 Office: TriCorp Mgmt 120 Falcon Dr # 3 Fredericksburg VA 22408

MC ELHANEY, JOHN HESS, lawyer; b. Milw., Apr. 16, 1934; s. Lewis Keck and Sara Jane (Hess) McE.; m. Jacquelyn Masur, Aug. 4, 1962; children—Scott, Victoria. B.B.A., So. Meth. U., 1956, J.D., 1958. Bar: Tex. bar 1958. Pvt. practice law Dallas, 1958—; shareholder Locke Purnell Rain Harrell, 1976—; lectr. law So. Meth. U., 1967-76. Contbr. articles to legal jours. Trustee St. Mark's Sch. Tex., 1980-86. Fellow Am. Coll. Trial Lawyers; mem. Am. Bd. Trial Advs., ABA, Tex. Bar Assn., So. Meth. U. Law Alumni Assn. (pres. 1972-73, dir. 1970-73), Town and Gown Club (pres. 1981-82). Presbyterian. Home: 5340 Tanbark Dr Dallas TX 75229-5555 Office: Locke Purnell Rain Harrell 2200 Ross Ave Ste 2200 Dallas TX 75201-6766

MCELHANEY, RICHARD FRANKLIN, quality assurance nursing coordinator; m. Lynne E. Mcelhaney, 1972; children: Richard Franklin Jr., Virginia Lynne. Student, U. of So. Miss., 1963-66; BSN, William Carey Coll., 1974; postgrad., U. South Ala., 1988-90; MSN, U. Mobile, Ala., 1994. RN, Ala., Miss.; cert. nursing adminstr. ANCC. Scrub nurse in surgery So. Bapt. Sch., New Orleans, 1972-74; med. surg. nurse U. South Ala. Med. Ctr., Mobile, 1974; instr. nursing Mobile (Ala.) Infirmary Sch. of Nursing, 1974-75; dir. inservice edn. Springhill Meml. Hosp., Mobile, 1975-76; staff nurse U. South Ala. Med. Ctr., Mobile, 1977, head nurse surgery, asst. dir. nursing, 1977-78, 78-80; nursing supr. surg. unit Singing River Hosp., Pascagoula, Miss.; dir. staff devel., head nurse ICU and psychiat. svcs. Doctors Hosp. of Mobile, 1982-89; quality assurance coord., nurse mgr. Knollwood Pk. Hosp., 1990-92, CQI coord., 1990—, with quality mgmt., 199—. Tech. sgt. USAF, 1966-70. Mem. Nat. Assn. Quality Assurance Profls. (Gulf Coast Coun.), Ala. Org. Nurse Execs., Gulf Coast Assn. for Health Care Quality (treas.), U. Mobile Nursing Honor Soc. (pres.). Republican. Methodist. Home: 1006 Uster Dr Mobile AL 36608-4112 Office: Univ S Ala 5500 Girby Rd Mobile AL 36693-5040

MCELROY, ANNIE LAURIE, nursing educator, administrator; b. Quitman, Ga., Dec. 30, 1945; d. Frank H. Sr. and Ina Mae (Carpenter) McElroy; children: Laurie, Matt. Grad., Ga. Baptist Sch Nursing, 1966; BS, Valdosta State Coll., 1988, MEd, 1989, postgrad., 1991; PhD, Ga. State U., 1994. Health aid, then head nurse Presbyn. Home, Quitman, 1960-63, 68-70; owner, bookkeeper Maddox Drugstore, Quitman, 1970-80; instr. health occupations Brooks County High Sch., Quitman, 1981-88, instr. nurses aides, 1983; instr. health occupations Lowndes High Sch., Valdosta, Ga., 1988-89; instr. dept. vocat. edn. Valdosta State Coll., 1989-92; dir. practical nursing program Thomas Tech. Inst., Thomasville, Ga., 1992—. Mem. ASCD, NEA, Ga. Edn. Assn., Nat. Assn. Educators, Ga. Assn. Educators, Am. Vocat. Assn., Ga. Vocat. Assn., Assn. Indsl. and Tech. Tchr. Educators, Internat. Tech. Edn. Assn., Phi Delta Kappa, Phi Kappa Phi. Home: 607 N Laurel St Quitman GA 31643-1221

MCELROY, EMILIE LIN, mental health professional; b. San Francisco, Jan. 10, 1954; d. Earl Edwin and Carolyn Ardell (Brickley) McE.; m. Robert Louis HItsman Jr., Feb. 25, 1984; children: Lynda Nicole, Devin Joseph, Jennifer Maighdlin, Rachel Siobhan, Ian Jeremiah, Elizabeth Ailis. Student, U. Calif., Davis, 1986, U. Louisville, 1986—; BS, NYU, 1990. Artistic dir., gen. mgr. Sunshine Children's Theatre, Davis, 1977-83; counselor Progress Ranch, Inc., Davis, 1981-83; youth worker shelter house YMCA, Louisville, 1983-84, house coord., 1984-85; house dir. Schizophrenia Found. Ky., Louisville, 1985-91; dir. Creative Cons., Lyndon, Ky., 1985—; advocate, counselor Louisville Rape Relief Ctr., 1984—. Organizer Calif. Dem. State Conf., 1982; apptd. spl. adv. Jefferson County (Ky.) Juvenile Ct. Dependency Docket; commd. layminister Ctrl. Ky. Cath. Ch., 1995. Mem. NAFE, Psi Chi. Roman Catholic. Home and Office: 9110 Farnham Dr Lyndon KY 40242-3431

MCELVEEN, JOHN THOMAS, JR., physician, medical educator; b. Columbia, S.C., Dec. 17, 1974. BS in Biology, Davidson Coll., 1974; MD, U. N.C., 1978. Bd. cert. Am. Bd. Otolaryngology. Intern U. Utah Med. Ctr., Salt Lake City, 1978-79; otolaryngology resident Stanford (Calif.) Med. Ctr., 1979-82; rsch. fellowship neurotology House Ear Inst., L.A., 1982; clin. fellowship otology and neurotology Otologic Med. Group, Inc., L.A., 1983; assoc. House Ear Clinic, 1983-87; staff mem. Hosp. of the Good Samaritan, L.A. County/U. So. Calif. Med. Ctr., St. John's Hosp., Raleigh Comty. Hosp.; head of otology/neurotology dept. surgery divsn. otolaryngology Duke U. Med. Ctr., 1987-93; clin. asst. prof. dept. otolaryngology USC Sch. Medicine; clin. asst. prof. USC Sch. Dentistry; attending staff Raleigh Comty. Hosp.; attending staff Rex Healthcare & Wake Med. Ctr.; rschr. in field. Assoc. editor: Neurological Surgery of the Ear, 1992; contbr. chpts. to books and articles to profl. jours. Fellow Am. Acad. Otolaryngology (head and neck surgery), Am. Neurotology Soc., Triologic Soc.; mem. AMA, Calif. Med. Assn., N.C. Med. Soc., N.C. Soc. Otolaryngology and Maxillofacial Surgery, L.A. County Med. Assn., Durham/Orange County Med. Soc., Wake County Med. Soc., Alumni Fellowship Group of the House Ear Inst. Office: Carolina Ear & Hearing Clinic PC Inc Ste 303 3404 Wake Forest Rd Raleigh NC 27609-7317

MCELVEEN-COMBS, GAIL MARIE, middle school educator; b. Houston, May 16, 1954; d. William Conlee and Evelyne Lily (Brautigam) McE. BS in Biology, Sam Houston State U., Huntsville, Tex., 1977, cert. in teaching, 1982; ThM, Logos Bible Coll., 1991. Cert. biology and English tchr., Tex. Tchr. biology Harlandale Ind. Sch. Dist., San Antonio, 1984-93, tchr. comparative religions, 1989-90; sponsor, tchr. El Shaddai Bibl. Studies Club, San Antonio, 1990-91, writer life sci. curriculum, 1989-91, mem. prin.'s adv. com., 1985-90; tchr. 6th grade sci. Page Mid. Sch., San Antonio, 1993—. Recipient Outstanding Sci. Educator award Sigma Xi, 1991. Republican. Charismatic Christian. Home: 130 Sage San Antonio TX 78148

MCENTEE, GRACE ELIZABETH, language educator; b. Fairfield, Ala., Jan. 28, 1948; d. Philip Jerome Jr. and Mary Augusta (McGowan) McE.; m. Raymond Lee Jones, Dec. 26, 1970 (div. 1987). BA, Ga. Coll., 1970; MA in Libr. Sci., U. Denver, 1975; MA, U. Ala., 1985, PhD, 1987. From libr. to adminstrv. head Cody Libr. Southwestern U., Georgetown, Tex., 1975-81; from lectr. to asst. prof. dept. Eng. Appalachian State U., Boone, N.C., 1987-92, assoc. prof. dept. Eng., 1992—; edit. bd. South Atlantic Rev., 1993—; assoc., mng. editor Focuses, 1990-93; asst. editor Coll. Eng., 1986-87, Focuses, 1987-90; fiction reviewer Libr. Jour., 1980-81; presenter in field. Contbr. articles to profl. jours. Recipient Calvert award Assn. Coll. Eng. Tchrs. Ala.; Grad. Coun. Rsch. fellow, 1985-87. Mem. MLA, Nat. Coun. Tchrs. English, South Atlantic MLA. Office: Appalachian State Univ Dept English Boone NC 28608

MCEVILLY, MICHAEL JAMES, civil engineer; b. Newburgh, N.Y., Sept. 29, 1958; s. William George and Mary Elizabeth (Waye) McE.; m. Mary Ellen Hilton, May 23, 1980; children: Melissa Renee, Michael Patrick. BS in Civil Engring., U. Mo., Rolla, 1980, MS in Engring. Mgmt., 1981. Registered profl. engr., Tex. Prodn. engr. Cities Svc. Co., Houston, 1981-84, sr. prodn. engr., 1984-85; sr. constrn. engr. Anadarko Petroleum Corp., Houston, 1985-92, staff constrn. engr., 1992-94, divsn. constrn. supr., 1994—; offshore platform staff Cities Svc. Co., Houston, 1981-85; facilities, pipeline design, fabrication, installation and commissioning Gulf of Mex., onshore Gulf Coast, Alaska and internat. Anadarko Petroleum Corp., Houston, 1985—. Mem. Little League Umpires, Spring, Tex., 1988—. Named Young Engr. of Yr., Tex. Soc. Profl. Engrs., Houston, 1992. Mem. NSPE, ASCE, Am. Welding Soc., Soc. Petroleum Engrs., Am. Soc. Nondestructive Testing, Masters, Warden and Secs. Assn. (sec. 1993—), Order Ea. Star (patron, v.p.), Masons (pres. 1992-93, master, dist. instr.), Lions Club, Shriners, Elks. Republican. Presbyterian. Home: 5210 Nodaway Ln Spring TX 77379-8048 Office: Anadarko Petroleum Corp 17001 Northchase Dr Houston TX 77060-2139

MCEVILY, DANIEL VINCENT SEAN, lawyer, author; b. N.Y.C., June 25, 1944; s. Patrick Vincent and Margaret Dolores (Hawley) McE.; m. Adele Carroll Daly, Sept. 1, 1973 (div. Nov. 1986); 1 child, Kathleen Kerry. BS in Fgn. Svc., Georgetown U., 1966; JD, Cath. U., 1972. Bar: D.C. 1973, Tex. 1994, U.S. Supreme Ct. 1976. Assoc., ptnr. Hamilton and Hamilton, Washington, 1973-81; ptnr. Foley & McEvily, Washington, 1981-89, Alexander & McEvily, Houston, 1991—. Author: Anthem for No Nation, 1989, A Tangled Woven Web, 1990. Capt. USMC, 1966-69, Viet Nam. Decorated 13 personal and unit decorations USMC, 1967. Mem. Am. Legion (post #1 Paris, counsel 1990—). Roman Catholic. Office: Alexander & McEvily 24th Flr 5 Post Oak Park Houston TX 77027-3413

MCFADDEN, CHERYL ELLEN, health care professional; b. Wilkinsburg, Pa., Jan. 24, 1955; d. Robert John and Lois Evelyn (Butler) Worbois; m. Danny Earl McFadden, Aug. 2, 1980; children: Robert Dean, James Michael. Diploma in practical nursing, Westmoreland County C.C., Youngwood, Pa., 1978; BSN, N.W. Okla. State U., 1989; MS, U. Okla., 1996. RN, Okla.; cert. ACLS instr., Okla. Staff nurse Montifiore Hosp., Pitts., 1978-79, Enid (Okla.) Meml. Hosp., 1979-86; staff nurse critical care unit Mercy Health Ctr., Oklahoma City, 1986-89; nurse, edn. coord. N.W. Area Health Edn. Ctr., Enid, 1989-90; nurse, dir. insvc. Enid Regional Meml. Hosp., 1990-92; relief nurse ICU, house supr. Bass Meml. Bapt. Hosp., Enid, 1992—; instr. nursing N.W. Okla. State U., Alva, 1992-95; mem. trauma systems planning coalition Okla. State Dept. Health, Oklahoma City, 1994, trauma systems regional adv. coun., 1994; health care finder Found. Health Fedn. Svcs., Tricare Svc. Ctr., Vance AFB, Enid, Okla., 1995—. Co-author grants Teen Pregnancy Prevention Project, 1990, N.W. Area Health Edn. Ctr. Continuation Grant, 1990. Phone bank personnel Gary Maxey for Sit. #40 Ho. of Reps., Enid, 1990, John McPhail for Dist. Judge, Enid, 1994. Mem. Okla. Nurses Assn. (chairperson govt. activities 1991-92, bd. dirs. 1990-92, nurse of day Okla. State Legislature 1990, 92), Alpha Epsilon Lambda (Delta chpt.), Sigma Theta Tau (Beta Delta chpt.). Democrat. Baptist. Home: 2109 N Meadowbrook Dr Enid OK 73701-2568 Office: Found Health Fed Svcs Tricare Svc Ctr Vance AFB Enid OK 73705

MCFADDEN, FRANK HAMPTON, lawyer, business executive, former judge; b. Oxford, Miss., Nov. 20, 1925; s. John Angus and Ruby (Roy) McF.; m. Jane Porter Nabers, Sept. 30, 1960; children—Frank Hampton, Angus Nabers, Jane Porter. B.A., U. Miss., 1950; LL.B., Yale U., 1955. Bar: N.Y. 1956, Ala. 1959. Assoc. firm Lord, Day & Lord, N.Y.C., 1955-58; assoc. firm Bradley, Arant, Rose & White, Birmingham, Ala., 1958-63, partner, 1963-69; judge U.S. Dist. Ct. No. Dist. Ala., Birmingham, 1969-73; chief judge U.S. Dist. Ct. No. Dist. Ala., 1973-81; sr. v.p., gen. counsel Blount, Inc., Montgomery, Ala., 1982-91, exec. v.p. adminstrn. and govt. affairs, 1991, exec. v.p. legal affairs, 1991-93, exec. v.p., gen. counsel, 1993-95; mem. Capell, Howard, Knabe & Cobbs, P.A., Montgomery, 1995—; chmn. Blount Energy Resource Corp., Montgomery, 1983-88. Mem. jud. panel CPR Inst. for Dispute Resolution, 1985—. Served from ensign to lt. USNR, 1944-49, 51-53. Fellow Am. Coll. Constrn. Lawyers; mem. Am. Corp. Counsel Assn. (bd. dirs. 1984-93, chmn. 1989). Office: Capell Howard Knabe 57 Adams Ave Montgomery AL 36104-4001

MC FADDEN, JOSEPH MICHAEL, academic administrator; b. Joliet, Ill., Feb. 12, 1932; s. Francis Joseph and Lucille (Adler) McF.; m. Norma Cardwell, Oct. 10, 1958; children: Timothy Joseph, Mary Colleen, Jonathan Andrew. B.A., Lewis Coll., 1954; M.A., U. Chgo., 1961; Ph.D., No. Ill. U., 1968. Tchr. history Joliet Cath. High Sch., 1957-60; mem. faculty history dept. Lewis Coll., Lockport, Ill., 1960-70, asso. prof., 1967-70, v.p. acad. affairs, 1968-70; prof. history, dean sch. Nat. and Social Sci., Kearney (Nebr.) State Coll., 1970-74; prof. history, dean Sch. Social and Behavioral Scis., Slippery Rock (Pa.) State Coll., 1974-77; pres. No. State Coll., Aberdeen, S.D., 1977-82, U. S.D., Vermillion, 1982-88, U. St. Thomas, Houston, 1988—. Served with USNR, 1954-56. Roman Catholic. Office: U St Thomas Office of Pres 3812 Montrose Blvd Houston TX 77006-4626

MCFARLAND, GARY LANE, fire protection engineer, consultant; b. Memphis, Apr. 21, 1952; s. Jasper Anderson Jr. and Maxine (Hardy) McF.; m. Terry Lorraine Moore, Aug. 20, 1970 (div. July 1984); children: Joshua, Jeremy, Justin. Student, Air Force C.C., Gulfport, Miss., 1985-86, Nat. Inst. for Cert. in Engring. Techs., Memphis, 1988-89. Electrician AC Electric, Memphis, 1970-72; owner, mgr. McFarland & Son, Hickory Valley, Tenn., 1973-81; draftsman McFarland & Assocs., Memphis, 1981-85, cons., 1991—; engr. LASCO Fire Protection, Memphis, 1986-88; owner, engr. Bi-Mac Cons., Memphis, 1988-89; engr. Grinnell Fire Protection Corp., Memphis, 1989-90, salesman, 1990-93, dist. mgr., 1993—; cons., Jones, MAH, Gaskil, Rhodes Architecture, Memphis, 1988—, Belz Investment Corp., Memphis, 1987—, Boyle Investment Corp., Memphis, 1991—. Sec. Ruritan Civic Club, Hardeman County, Tenn., 1981; rep. Small Farmers Am., Bolivar, Tenn., 1975. Staff sgt. Tenn. Army N.G., 1985-92. Mem. Soc. Fire Protection Engrs., Nat. Fire Protection Assn., Comml. and Indsl. Assn., Memphis C. of C., Memphis Zool. Soc. Republican. Home: 1048 Marshall Brighton TN 38011

MCFARLAND, JAMES WILLIAM, real estate development company executive; b. Montgomery, Ala., Sept. 7, 1948; s. Ward Wharton and Frances Adelia (Morrow) McF.; B.S., U. Ala., 1970; m. Miriam Melinda Webster, Feb. 20, 1971; children—James William, Mimi Morrow. Dir. real estate for Ky., Ind. and Tenn., Winn-Dixie Stores, Inc., Louisville, 1970-72; v.p. Ward McFarland, Inc., Tuscaloosa, Ala., 1972—, also dir. Mem. Coun. for Devel. of French in La., 1976—, Friends of Libr., 1975—; commr. Dept. Mental Health, 1987-89; ; Rep. nominee U.S. Congress Ala. 7th Dist., 1986; young churchmen adviser Episcopal Diocese Ala., 1976—, conv. del.; charter investor, chair of real estate U. Ala.; chmn. Ala. Rapid Rail Transit Commn.; vice chmn. La.-Miss.-Ala. Rapid Rail Transit Commn., 1983-84, chmn., 1984—; state advisor Congl. Adv. Com., Am. Security Coun.; sr. warden Christ Episc. Ch., 1984; bd. dirs. Tuscaloosa Kidney Found.; mem. Rep. State Exec. Com., 1991—; commr. Dept. Mental Health State of Ala.; chmn. Tuscaloosa County Reps., 1991—; flotilla staff officer USCG Aux., 1994—. Named hon. citizen of Mobile and New Orleans, hon. mem. mayor's staff, Mobile. Mem. Nat. Assn. Realtors, Tuscaloosa Bd. Realtors, Nat. Small Bus. Assn., U. Ala. Commerce Execs. Soc., U. Ala. Alumni Assn., Nat. Assn. R.R. Passengers, Ala. Assn. R.R. Passengers (pres. 1982, 90, 91), North River Yacht, Kiwanis of Greater Tuscaloosa, Delta Sigma Pi. Home: 4714 7th Ct E Tuscaloosa AL 35405-4104 Office: 325 Skyland Blvd E Tuscaloosa AL 35405-4030

MCFARLAND, JANET CHAPIN, consulting company executive; b. New Castle, Pa., Jan. 5, 1962; d. Robert Chapin McFarland and Dorothy Jean (Heade) Jost; m. Steven Mitchell Walters, July 30, 1994. BS in Imaging Sci. and Engring., Rochester Inst. Tech., 1985; MBA in Innovation Mgmt. and Mktg., Syracuse U., 1990. Rsch. engr. Shipley Co., Inc., Newton, Mass., 1985-88; mktg. cons. Syracuse (N.Y.) U. Sch. Mgmt., 1988-90; market rsch. coop. AT&T Consumer Comms. Svcs., Basking Ridge, N.J., summer 1989; tech. analyst DynCorp Meridian, Alexandria, Va., 1991-93; dir. studies and analysis Tech. Strategies & Alliances, Burke, Va., 1993-94; pres. ArBar, Inc., Alexandria, Va., 1994—; presenter in field. Mem. Internat. Soc. Optical Engrs., Soc. Mfg. Engrs. (chpt. chair 1995), Beta Gamma Sigma, Alpha Mu Alpha. Office: ArBar Inc 312 S Washington St Ste 5B Alexandria VA 22314

MC FARLAND, MARTHA ANN, education educator; b. Natchitoches, La., Aug. 6, 1940; d. Charles I. and Virginia (Watson) McF. BA, Northwestern State U., 1967; MEd, U. Miss., 1971; postgrad. W. Va. U., 1972-73; PhD, Fla. State U., 1979. With Caddo Parish Sch. Bd., Shreveport, La., 1967-70; tchr. W. Shreveport Acad., 1970, Natchitoches (La.) Acad., 1971; regional dir. early childhood Region VI, Ednl. Service, Wheeling, W.Va., 1971-73; instr. edn., dir. kindergarten Berry Coll., Mt. Berry, Ga., 1973-78; prof. edn. Liberty U., Lynchburg, Va., 1979-87, Miss. Coll., Clinton, 1987—; tchr. NCATE Elem. Portfolios State Dept. Edn. Miss.-cert. standards, early childhood, spl. edn., preschool; chairperson Am. 2000-Goal-1, Clinton, Miss.; reviewer ednl. portfolios; condr. numerous workshops, W.Va., Ga., La., Miss. Mem. ASCD, Assn. Childhood Edn. Internat., Miss. Assn. Childhood Edn., Leon County Assn. Childhood Edn., Nat. Assn. Edn. Young Children, Miss. Assn. Curriculum and Devel., Miss. Assn. Children Under Six, Ga. Assn. Young Children, So. Assn. Children Under Six, Piedmont Area Assn. Young Children (pres. 1986-88), Assn. Christian Educators of Tchrs., Clinton C. of C. (chairperson America 2000-Goal-1), W.Va. Assn. Childhood Edn. (v.p. infants 1972-73), Miss. Educators Assn., Delta Kappa Gamma (v.p. II 1995-96, pres. Beta chpt. 1996—), Phi Delta Kappa. Contbr. articles to profl. jours. Office: Miss Coll PO Box 4165 Clinton MS 39058

MC FARLAND, TERRY LYNN, construction company executive; b. Knoxville, Tenn., July 8, 1947; s. Jacob E. and Virginia Kay (Allen) McF.; student Ind. U., 1969-70, Wickes U., 1977-79; m. Hazel C. Davis, Nov. 1, 1975; Prodn. control staff R.R. Donnelley & Sons, Warsaw, Ind., 1965-68; insp. Bendix Corp., South Bend, Ind., 1968-69; mgr. Wickes Bldgs. div. Wickes Corp., Argos, Inc., 1970-71, Crawfordsville, Ind., 1971-73, Macon, Ga., 1973-76, dist. mgr. Midwest, 1976-78, regional mgr., 1978-80; v.p., gen. mgr. Douglass Bldg. div. of Stanley Smith & Sons, Columbia, S.C., 1980-81; ter. mgr. Butler Mfg. Co., Kansas City, Mo., 1981-84, southeastern area mgr., 1984-89; dist. mgr., Varco-Pruden Bldgs div. United Dominion Industries, Memphis, 1989-96; dist. sales mgr. Nucor Bldg. Systems divsn. Nucor Corp., Charlotte, N.C., 1996—. Served with U.S. Army, 1966-68; Korea. Mem. Am. Legion, Nat. Geog. Soc., Nat. Rifle Assn. Democrat. Clubs: Moose, Masons (Scottish Rite), Shriners. Home: 741 Springdale Woods Dr Macon GA 31210-1530 Office: 200 Whatstone Rd West SC Hwy #3 Swansea SC 29160 also: PO Box 2858 Winston Salem NC 27102-2858

MCFARLAND, VICTOR ALAN, toxicologist; b. Crescent City, Calif., Oct. 10, 1937; s. Victor Marion McFarland and Anna Jean (Endert) Castanos; m. Dwilette Gambrell; children: Frederick Marshall, Daniel Leonard McFarland. BS in Psychology, St. Mary's Coll., 1959; BS in Pharmacy, Oreg. State U., 1964; PhD in Pharmacology/Toxicology, N.E. La. U., 1994. Cert. environ. profl. Rsch. assoc. U. Calif., Bodega Marine Lab., 1972-78; rsch. biologist, prin. investigator, rsch. team leader USAE Waterways Experiment Sta., Vicksburg, Miss., 1978—; mem. U.S. EPA/U.S. Army C.E. Joint Tech. coms. on dioxin, sediment quality criteria, bioaccumulation, 1992—; tech. reviewer of programs, proposals and reports. Editor sediment toxicology sect. Quintessence, 1994-95. Recipient R&D Tech. Achievement award Dept. Army, 1988. Mem. Soc. of Environ. Toxicology and Chemistry (Miss.

state councilman South Ctrl. chpt. 1986, ad hoc founding com. 1986-87, tech. reviewer 1987—), Nat. Assn. of Environ. Profls., Sigma Xi, Rho Chi.

MCFARLAND, WILLIAM CHANDLER, advertising executive; b. 1936. V.p. Ogilvy & Mather, N.Y.C., 1962-70; pres. Mike Sloan Inc., Miami, Fla., 1970-77; with Ryder & Schild, Miami, 1977-79; sec.-treas., chmn., bd. dirs. McFarland & Drier Inc., Miami, 1979—. Office: HMS Partners 1201 Brickell Ave Fl 5 Miami FL 33131-3207*

MCFARLANE, WALTER ALEXANDER, lawyer, educator; b. Richlands, Va., May 4, 1940; s. James Albert and Frances Mae (Padbury) McF.; m. Judith Louise Copenhaver, Aug. 31, 1962; children: Brennan Alexander, Heather Copenhaver. BA, Emory and Henry Coll., 1962; JD, T.C. Williams Sch. Law, U. Richmond, 1966. Bar: Va. 1966, U.S. Supreme Ct. 1970, U.S. Ct. Appeals (4th cir.) 1973, U.S. Ct. Appeals (D.C. cir.) 1977, U.S. Dist. Ct. (ea. dist.) Va. 1973. Asst. atty. gen. Office Va. Atty. Gen., Richmond, 1969-73, dep. atty. gen., 1973-90; exec. asst. chief counsel, dir. policy Gov.'s office, Commonwealth Va., 1990-94; supt. Dept. Correctional Edn. Commonwealth of Va., 1994—. prof. adj. staff U. Richmond, 1978—. Contbr. articles to profl. jours. Chmn. transp. law com. Transp. Research Bd., Nat. Research Bd. Nat. Acads. Scis. and Engring., Washington, 1977-85, 88-94, chmn. legal affairs com., 1978-85, chmn. environ., archeological and hist. com., 1985-90; mem. State Water Commn., 1994-96; mem. exec. com., bd. govs. Emory and Henry Coll., 1985—; pres. Windsor Forest Civic Assn., Midlothian, Va., 1975-76; bd. dirs. Greater Midlothian Civic League, 1981-86, v.p., 1980; instr. water safety ARC, 1962-87; chmn. bldg. com. Mt. Pisgah United Meth. Ch., 1980-85, pres. men's club, 1980-81; bd. dirs. cen. Va. chpt. Epilepsy Assn. Va., 1988-91, Woodland Pond Civic Assn., 1988-89; mem. State Criminal Justice Svcs. Bd., 1994—. Capt. JAGC, USAF, 1966-69. Recipient J.D. Buscher Disting. Atty. award Am. Assn. State Hwy. and Transp. Ofcls., 1983, John C. Vance legal writing award Nat. Acads. Sci. and Engring., 4th ann. outstanding evening lectr. award Student Body U. Richmond, 1980. Mem. Chesterfield Bar Assn., Richmond Bar Assn. (bd. dirs. 1989-93), Richmond Scottish Soc. (bd. dirs. 1980-82), Emory and Henry Coll. Alumni Assn. (chpt. pres. 1971-73, regional v.p. 1974-77, pres. 1981-83), Meadowbrook Country Club. Home: 9001 Widgeon Way Chesterfield VA 23838-5274 Office: 101 N 14th St Richmond VA 23219

MCGARITY, GINGER G., medical/surgical nurse; b. West Point, Miss., Dec. 4, 1965; d. John E. Jr. and Loretta F. (Woods) McGarity. BSN, Miss. U. for Women, 1988, postgrad. Cert. med./surg. nurse. Nursing asst. Clay County Med. Ctr., West Point, 1987-88, staff nurse, 1988-89; staff nurse North Miss. Med. Ctr., Tupelo, Miss., 1989—. Mem. Miss. Nurses Assn.

MCGARR, CHARLES TAYLOR, accountant; b. Greenwood, Miss., Nov. 5, 1956; s. William Ithamar and Mary (Taylor) McG.; m. Kathryn Augusta Reed, July 21, 1979; children: Charles Taylor II, Annie Flynn. BS in Bus. Adminstrn., La. State U., 1978. CPA, Tex., La. Acct., auditor Arthur Andersen and Co., Houston, 1979-82, Lafayette, La., 1982-85; audit mgr. Arthur Andersen and Co., Houston, 1985-86; sec., treas. L.A. Frey and Sons, Inc., Lafayette, 1986-87; asst. sec., controller Waste Mgmt. Baton Rouge, 1987-88; asst. treas., tax mgr. Copolymer Rubber and Chem. Corp., Baton Rouge, 1988-93; divsn. v.p., contr. Waste Mgmt. La., Walker, 1993—. Mem. Am. Inst. CPA's, Tex. Soc. CPA's (Houston chpt.), La. Soc. CPA's, Delta Tau Delta (treas. 1976-77). Republican. Baptist. Office: Waste Mgmt La 29340 Woodside Dr Walker LA 70785-5823

MCGARRY, CHARLES WILLIAM, lawyer; b. Mt. Kisco, N.Y., June 23, 1957; m. Lori J. Voss. BA in Philosophy, SUNY, Binghamton, 1979; JD, U. Tex., 1982. Bar: Tex. 1983. Law clk. Atty. Gen. of Tex., Austin, 1980-82; briefing atty. Tex. Ct. of Appeals, Dallas, 1982-83; pvt. practice, 1984-93, 95—; chief justice Tex. Ct. Appeals, Dallas, 1993-94; mediator Dallas County Juvenile Dept., 1984-93; arbitrator Better Bus. Bur., Dallas, 1985-93. Editor: Aviation Litigation, 1986. Chmn. Irving (Tex.) Dems., 1987-91; pres. Dallas Jazz Orch., 1990-92. Mem. Tex. Bar Assn., Dallas Bar Assn., Irving Bar Assn. Democrat. Roman Catholic. Home: 612 Brookhaven Dr Irving TX 75061-7949 Office: 714 Jackson St Ste 200 Dallas TX 75202

MCGARRY, MARCIA LANGSTON, community service coordinator; b. Washington, Dec. 9, 1941; d. Emil Sylvester and Bernice B. (Bland) Busey. BS, Morgan State U., 1964. Cert. tchr., law enforecment officer, Fla. Payroll clk., jr. acct. U.S. Dept. Labor, Washington, 1964-65; English tchr., Taiwan, 1968-70; tchr. Monroe County Sch. Bd., Key West, Fla., 1971-81; exec. dir. Monroe Assn. Retarded Citizens, Key West, 1977-79; dep. sheriff Monroe County Sheriff's Dept., Key West, 1979-83, 1986-90; probation/parole officer Fla. State Dept. Corrections, Key West, 1983-91; law enforcement instr. Fla. Keys C.C., 1983-91; cmty. svc. coord. City of Bradenton, 1991—; mem. rev. bd. City of Bradenton Police Dept., 1996—, mem. cmty. rels. com. 1996. Active local polit. campaigns; co-founder day schs. for under-privileged children; former mem. Big Bros./Big Sisters Am., mem. com. 1985-86, former bd. dir., Spouse Abuse, former bd. dirs.; bd. dirs. Adv. Coun. Orange-Ridge Elem., 1991-93; bd. dirs. mayor's com., chmn. task force Drug Free Communities, 1991-94, bd. dirs. 1996—; bd. dirs. Human Rels. Commn., 1991-93, Drug Free Schs. and Cmty. Adv. Coun., 1991—; former mem. adv. coun. Byrd Edn. Found., Sweet Adelines Internat., 1992-94, commr. 12th Jud. Nominating Commn. 1992—, cons., facilitator Cultural Diversity Conflict Resolution Workshops, Manatee County High Schs. and Bradenton Police Dept.; attendance avd. com. Bayshore High, 1993, multicultural com., 1994, former rep. Women's Forum; former dir. Choir, Lutheran Ch.; founding mem. Comprehensive Neighborhood Support Network; mem. adv. bd. Manatee County Sheriff's Dept., 1994—. Recipient Appreciation cert. Lions Club, 1978, 79, Career Week award Harris Elem. Sch., 1981, Glynn Archer Elem. Sch., 1989, Trainers award Probation/Parole Acad., 1987, cert. of acknowledgement for cmty. svc. AAUW, 1995, Vol. Army for the War on Drugs. Mem. NAFE, Fla. Police Benevolent Assn., Fla. Women in Govt. (mem. Manatee County chpt.), Ecumanical Luth. Ch. of Am. (elected consultation con. Fla. Synod 1989), Key West Profls., Luth. Ch. Women, Delta Sigma Theta (v.p. 1990-91, corr. sec. 1993-95). Office: City of Bradenton Caller Svc 25015 Bradenton FL 34206

MCGARRY, SUSAN HALLSTEN, magazine editor; b. Mpls., June 27, 1948; d. Clarence Albert and Evelyn Mildred (Nelson) Hallsten; m. Stephen Joseph McGarry, Aug. 11, 1978. BA, U. Minn., 1973, MA, 1978. Editor-in-chief S.W. Art Mag., Houston, 1979—; freelance writer, author M. Hal Sussmann & Assocs., Houston. Author: West of Camelot: The History Paintings of Kenneth Riley, 1993; author, editor: Taking Stock, The Art of G. Harvey, 1986; author: (with others) The Cowboy Artists of America, 1988, (catalog) Wilson Hurley, 1988, New Art of the West, 1991. Mem. Western Writers Am. Home: 2930 Ella Lee Ln Houston TX 77019-5908 Office: SW Art Mag 5444 Westheimer Rd Ste 1440 Houston TX 77056-5306

MCGAW, KENNETH ROY, wholesale distribution executive; b. Parry Sound, Ont., Can., Aug. 25, 1926; s. Dalton Earnest and Grace (Crockford) McG. Student, Denison U., 1946-48; B.A., Western Res. U., 1949. With Bigelow Carpets, N.Y. and Ohio, 1949-53; representing Frederick Cooper Lamps, Inc., Chgo., 1953—; home furnishing salesman Gates Mills, Ohio, 1958-74, Fort Lauderdale, 1974-77, Dallas, 1978-79; pres. Ken McGaw, Inc., Dallas, 1979—; factory rep. for maj. furniture and furniture accessory mfrs. Bd. dirs. Big Bros. Cleve., 1963-65, Dallas Opera Co., 1981-92; v.p. Nat. Council on Alcoholism, Cleve., 1972-74; chmn. fundraising drive Wholesale div. Dallas Industry for Dallas Opera, 1982-83; ruling elder 1st Presbyterian Ch., Dallas., 1981—. Served to 2d lt. U.S. Army, 1944-46. Mem. Greater Dallas Home Furnishings Assn. (bd. dirs. 1985-86), S.W. Homefurnishings Assn., S.W. Roadrunners Assn., Internat. Homefurnishings Reps. Assn. Lodge: Rotary. Home: 8360 E San Bernardo Dr Scottsdale AZ 85258-2430

MCGEE, HAROLD JOHNSTON, academic administrator; b. Portsmouth, Va., Apr. 13, 1937; s. Harold Valentine McGee and Clara Mae (Johnston) Webber; m. Mary Frances Eure, Mar. 22, 1959; children: Harold Johnston, Mary Margaret, Matthew Hayden; m. Linda Gayle Stevens, Apr. 3, 1976; 1 child, Andrew Meade. BS, Old Dominion U., 1959; MEd, U. Va., 1962, EdD, 1968. Tchr. Falls Church (Va.) City Schs., 1959-62; asst. dean, then dean of admissions Old Dominion U., Norfolk, Va., 1962-65; field rep., program officer, sr. program officer U.S. Office Edn. Bur. Higher Edn., Charlottesville, 1965-70; provost Tidewater Community Coll., Portsmouth, 1970-71; founding pres. Piedmont Va. Community Coll., Charlottesville, 1971-75; various offices including dean grad. sch., asst. to pres., v.p. student affairs, v.p. adminstrv. affairs, sec. bd. visitors James Madison U., Harrisonburg, Va., 1975-86; pres. Jacksonville (Ala.) State U., 1986—; bd. dirs. Marine Environ. Scis. Consortium, Dauphin Island, Ala., Gulf South Conf. Conf., chmn. 1990-92; bd. dirs. Birmingham Calhoun County C. of C., vice chmn. 1988-90; chmn. Ala. Coun. Univ. Pres., 1991-93; mem. Gov.'s Tax Reform Task Force, 1991-92; bd. dirs. Trans America Athletic Conf., 1995—, Southland Footbill League, 1995—. Author: Impact of Federal Support, 1968, The Virginia Project, 1976. Mem. United Way of Calhoun County Ala. 1986-92, Knox Concert Series Adv. Bd., Anniston, Ala., Leadership Ala., Anniston Mus. Natural History Found. Mem. NCAA (coun. 1991-95), ACA, Soc. Coll. and Univ. Planning Am. Assn. Higher Edn., Capital City Club (Montgomery, Ala.), Rotary, Phi Delta Kappa. Episcopalian. Office: Jacksonville State U Office of Pres Jacksonville AL 36265

MCGEE, HUMPHREY GLENN, architect; b. Hartsville, S.C., June 26, 1937; s. James Gladney and Elizabeth Adams (Williams) McG.; BArch, Clemson U., 1960. Designer, Clark, McCall & Leach, Hartsville-Kingstree, S.C., 1961; Designer prodn. A. G. Odell & Assocs., Charlotte, N.C., 1962; chief designer Clark, McCall & Leach, Hartsville-Kingstree, S.C., 1963; sr. designer LBC & W, Inc., Columbia, S.C., 1965-69, pres., 1969-76, sr. v.p. client services and design, 1976; pres. CEDA, Inc., Columbia, S.C., 1976-86; pres., treas. McGee-Howle & Assocs., Vero Beach, Fla, 1986—. With USAR, 1961-67. Mem. Am. Inst. Architects, Nat. Soc. Interior Designers (award 1972), Am. Soc. Interior Designers (chmn. S.C. chpt. com. on Found. Interior Design Edn. and Rsch. 1976). Published: Who's Who in Interior Design, 1993-95; cited in 100 Designer's Favorite Rooms, 1993, 94, 95. Home: 251 Johns Island Dr Indian River Shores FL 32963-3238 Office: 2801 Ocean Dr Ste 302 Vero Beach FL 32963-2025

MCGEE, JAMES EDWARD, sales executive; b. Winchester, Mass., July 13, 1958; s. Kenneth Gerard and Anne Marie (Donoghue) McG.; m. Deborah Jean Heppel, Jan. 8, 1983; children: Matthew Alan, Patrick Gerard, Christopher James. BS, U. Cen. Fla., 1979. Pharm. sales rep. Boehringer Ingelheim Ltd., Ridgefield, Conn., 1979-81; radioimmuno assay sales rep. New Eng. Nuclear, North Billerica, Mass., 1981-82; territory mgr. Baxter, Deerfield, Ill., 1982-85, nat. acctg. specialist, 1985-86, diabetes specialist, 1986-89; regional sales mgr. MediSense, Inc., Cambridge, Mass., 1989-92; area sales mgr. MediSense, Inc., Cambridge, 1992-93; regional sales mgr. Command Med. Products, Ormond Beach, Fla., 1993-94; regional sales dir. Home Med. Supply, Hollywood, Fla., 1994-95; dir. sales and mktg. Command Med. Products, Ormond Beach, Fla., 1995—. Spl. min. Holy Eucharist, Roman Cath. Ch., Orlando, Fla., 1981-87, catechist, adv. catachist. Republican. Home: 1445 Canal Point Rd Longwood FL 32750-4550 Office: Command Med Products 15 Signal Ave Ormond Beach FL 32174-2984

MCGEE, LINDA MACE, lawyer; b. Marion, N.C., Sept. 20, 1949; d. Cecil Adam and Norma Jean (Hogan) Mace; m. B. Gary McGee, Dec. 19, 1970; children: Scott Adam, Jeffrey Sean. BA, U. N.C., 1971, JD, 1973. Bar: N.C. 1973. Exec. dir. N.C. Acad. Trial Lawyers, Raleigh, 1973-78; assoc. Finger, Watson & di Santi, Boone, N.C., 1978-80; ptnr. Finger, Watson, di Santi & McGee, Boone, 1980-89, di Santi, Watson & McGee, Boone, 1989—; mem. trustee panel U.S. Bankruptcy Ct., Greensboro, N.C., 1980—; bd. dirs. Legal Services of N.C., Raleigh, 1980-84. Vice-chairperson Watauga County Council on Status of Women, Boone, 1979-82; trustee Caldwell Community Coll. and Tech. Inst., Hudson, N.C., 1980-89; mem. exec. bd. N.C. Assn. Community Coll. Trustees, 1983-85. Mem. N.C. Assn. Women Attys. (charter, treas. 1980-84), N.C. Bar Assn. (bd. govs. 1983-86), ABA, N.C. Acad. Trial Lawyers (editor legal mag. 1973-78), N.C. State Bar, Assn. Trial Lawyers Am., Boone C. of C. (bd. dirs. 1982-85), N.C. Bus. and Profl. Womens Clubs (chair polit. action com. 1982-83; named Young Career Woman 1980), N. C. Bd. Law Examiners, Boone Bus. and Profl. Women's Club (Woman of Yr. 1980), N.C. Women's Forum, AAUW, LWV. Democrat. Presbyterian. Home: 1041 16th Avenue Pl NW Hickory NC 28601-2344 Office: di Santi Watson & McGee PO Box 193 Boone NC 28607-0193

MCGEE, LYNNE KALAVSKY, principal; b. Jersey City, N.J., July 25, 1949; d. Michael V. and Ann (Fedowitz) K.; m. Thomas Robert, Aug. 12, 1972; children: Todd Michael, Ryan Thomas. BS, St. Francis Coll., Loretto, Pa., 1971; MEd, Seton Hall U., 1972; EDS, Fla. Atlantic U., 1978, EdD, 1986. Cert. tchr., Fla., Ill., prin., Fla. Asst. prin. for curriculum, math instr. Palm Beach County (Fla.) Bd. Edn., 1980-82, asst. prin. for student svcs., 1982-86, asst. prin. for adminstrn., 1986-91; prin. Belle Glade (Fla.) Elem. Sch., 1991-94, New Horizons Elem. Sch., Wellington, Fla., 1994—; adj. prof. grad. Nova U., 1991—. Mem. Assn. Supervision and Curriculum Devel., Phi Kappa Phi. Office: New Horizons Elem Sch 13900 Greenbriar Blvd Wellington FL 33414-7718

MCGEE, THOMAS LEE, industrial automation specialist, engineer; b. Shelbyville, Tenn., July 8, 1960; s. Dan Dryden and Margaret (Hathcock) McG.; m. Caroline Diane Campbell, Mar. 8, 1986; children: Jonathan Thomas, James Daniel, Joel Campbell. BSEE, U. Tenn., 1983. Registered profl. engr., Tenn. Mgr. bus. devel. SSOE, Inc., Nashville, 1987-89; sr. sales engr. Richardson Elec., Inc., Brentwood, Tenn., 1989-90; indsl. automation specialist Stuart C. Irby Co., Nashville, 1990—; judge Internat. Sci. and Engring. Fair, Nashville, 1992. Vol., fundraiser Williamson County (Tenn.) Rep. Com., 1992; mem. Heritage Found., Washington, 1992—, Rutherford Inst., Charlottesville, Va., 1992—. Mem. IEEE, Instrument Soc. Am., Soc. Mfg. Engrs., Exchange Club (dir. 1988-90), Tau Beta Pi. Republican. Presbyterian. Home: 1006 Woodside Dr Brentwood TN 37027-5502 Office: Stuart C Irby Co 490 Allied Dr Nashville TN 37211-3315

MCGEHEE, JAMES E., air transportation executive; b. 1937. Chmn. bd. dirs. Memphis Shelby County Airport Authority, Memphis; prin. James E. McGehee & Co., Inc., Memphis, 1958—. Office: Memphis-Shelby County Airport Authority 665 Oakleaf Office Ln Memphis TN 38117-4813*

MCGEHEE, THOMAS RIVES, paper company executive; b. Jacksonville, Fla., July 12, 1924; s. Clifford Graham and Ray (Sutton) McG. Student Davidson Coll., 1942-43, BS in Chemistry, U. Ala. 1948; m. Delia Houser, Nov. 3, 1950; children: Delia McGehee II, Thomas R. Jr. V.p. Jacksonville Paper Co., 1948-56, pres., 1956-64, Mac Papers, Inc., Jacksonville, 1964-79, co-founder, chief exec. officer, chmn. bd., 1979—; co-chmn., chief exec. officer Mac Papers Converters, Inc., 1965—, pres., North Fla. TV-47, Inc., 1979-90; pres. Higley Pub. Co., 1968-90; bd. dirs. Barnett Bank of Jacksonville, 1961-89; chmn. exec. com. Sta. WTLV-TV 12, 1972-78; numerous real estate interests. Chmn. and founder Greater Jacksonville Community Found., 1964-84, trustee, 1964-89; trustee Jacksonville U., 1959—, vice chmn., 1962-65, chmn., 1991-92; trustee Regent U., 1996—; mem. U. Fla. Pres.' Coun., U. Fla. Health & Sci. Ctr.; mem. post secondary edn. planning commn. State of Fla., 1987-90; bd. dirs. Dreams Come True, pres. and founder 1984-90, chmn. emeritus, 1990—; bd. dirs. Bapt. Hosp. Found., 1986-90; vice chmn. Every Home For Christ, 1987—; past mem., officer numerous other community orgs. Served with U.S. Army, 1943-46, ETO. Recipient 3 Battle Stars, Fla. Gov.'s award, 1962. Mem. NAM (dir. 1964-66), Asso. Industries Fla. (dir. 1961-63), Nat. Paper Trade Assn., So. Paper Trade Assn., Nat. Assn. Broadcasters, Fla. State C. of C., Phi Gamma Delta (pres. 1948). Republican. Episcopalian. Clubs: River (dir. 1980-83), Fla. Yacht, Timuquana Country, Ponte Vedra, Plantation Country, Blowing Rock Country (bd. dirs. 1991-94). Home: Park Plz Condominiums 505 Lancaster St Condo 6 Jacksonville FL 32204-4136 Office: MAC Papers Inc 3300 Phillips Hwy PO Box 5369 Jacksonville FL 32247

MCGEHEE, THOMAS RIVES, JR., wholesale distribution company executive; b. Jacksonville, Fla., Aug. 25, 1959; s. Thomas Rives Sr. and Delia (Houser) McG.; m. Terri Ross, Nov. 30, 1985; children: Courtney Leigh, Ashley Ann. BS in Mgmt., U. Fla., 1981. Sales rep. Mac Papers, Inc., Jacksonville, Fla., 1981-82; gen. mgr. Mac Papers, Inc., Columbus, Ga., 1982-83; ops. mgr. Mac Papers, Inc., Montgomery, Ala., 1983-85; v.p. Mac Papers, Inc., Jacksonville, 1985—. Bd. dirs. ABC Bancorp, Moultrie, Ga., 1987-92, United Way of NE Fla., Jacksonville Chpt. of Navy League; exec. com. mem., sr. v.p. YMCA Bd. of Mgmt., 1992—. Mem. Jacksonville C. of C. (mil. affairs/armed svcs. com., small bus. exec. coun. 1991-92, small bus. purchasing task force 1992-93), River Club, Fla. Yacht Club (bd. govs. 1993—), Plantation Country Club, Ponte Vedra Inn and Club. Republican. Office: Mac Papers Inc PO Box 5369 Jacksonville FL 32247-5369

MCGERVEY, TERESA ANN, technology information specialist; b. Pitts., Sept. 27, 1964; d. Walter James and Janet Sarah (Donehue) McG. BS in Geology, Calif. U. Pa., 1986, MS in Earth Sci., 1988. Phys. sci. technician U.S. Geol. Survey, Reston, Va., 1989-90; editor, indexer Am. Geol. Inst., Alexandria, Va., 1990-91; cartographer Def. Mapping Agy., Reston, 1991-93; tech. info. specialist Nat. Tech. Info. Svc., Springfield, Va., 1993—; intern Dept. Mineral Scis., Smithsonian Instn., summers 1985, 1986.

MCGHEE, VICKI GUNTER, home health nurse, pediatrics psychiatry, alcohol and Drug rehabilitation; b. Ga., May 23, 1956; d. James Wesley Gunter and Flora Gunter LeDrew; m. Roger Lane McGhee, Sept. 8, 1984; (div. 1991). Diploma, Pickens Technical Inst., Jasper, Ga., 1975; student, Ga. Bapt. Hosp., Atlanta, 1976; ASN, Floyd Coll., Rome, Ga., 1978; student, Pickens Technical Inst., 1996—. RN, Ga., 1979. Primary staff nurse Woodstock (Ga.) Hosp., Atlanta; home health nurse Med. Personnel Pool, Atlanta; nurse Etowah Nursing Care, Inc., Marietta, Ga., Med. Temps, Marietta, Ga; pvt. duty nurse Acworth, Ga. Home: Bethesda Trail Box 830 Ball Ground GA 30107

MCGIBBON, DONALD BRUCE, public relations executive; b. Oak Park, Ill., Mar. 2, 1935; s. Edward William and Sylvia Louise (Lueker) McG.; m. Kathryn Ruth Walker, Sept. 25, 1965; 1 child, Brian Scott. BSME, BA in English, Valparaiso (Ind.) U., 1958; postgrad., U. Ala., Huntsville, 1959-60. Tech. editor Hallicrafters Co., Chgo., 1960-62; assoc. editor Electronic Packaging and Prodn. Mag., Chgo., 1962-64, Meat Processing Mag., Chgo., 1965-67; account exec. Griswold-Eshleman Co., Chgo., 1967-71, Hoffman-York Inc., Chgo., 1971-73; from account exec. to v.p. Hill and Knowlton, Inc., Chgo., 1973-84; v.p. Hill and Knowlton, Inc., Tampa, Fla., 1984—; competition judge Am. Cancer Soc., Tampa, 1993, Bateman competition Pub. Rels. Student Soc. Am., N.Y.C., 1992. Editor/author: Electronic Packaging and Prodn., 1962-64, Meat Processing, 1965-67. Bd. dirs., sec. Trails Homeowners Assn., Roselle, Ill., 1977-81; bd. dirs. Older Adult Svcs. (Oasis), Tampa, 1987-88. With U.S. Army, 1958-60. Mem. Pub. Rels. Soc. Am. (dir. 1991-93, 95, accreditation chmn. 1990-93, Presdl. All-Star award Tampa Bay chpt. 1993), Greater Tampa C. of C. Democrat. Lutheran. Home: 16631 Vallely Dr Tampa FL 33618-1132 Office: Hill and Knowlton Inc 201 E Kennedy Blvd Ste 1611 Tampa FL 33602-5829

MCGILL, CATHY BROOME, gifted and talented education educator; b. Gastonia, N.C., Sept. 26, 1945; d. Harold Beeler and Christine (Hicks) Broome; m. Paul Furman McGill, July 5, 1969; children: Paul Bryan, Harold Marcus. BA, Mars Hill Coll., 1967; MA, Appalachian State U., 1968. Tchr. 6th grade Victory Elem., Gastonia, N.C., 1968-69; lang. arts, social studies & music tchr. Northside Mid. Sch., West Columbia, S.C., 1969-71, Fulmer Mid. Sch., West Columbia, 1972-76; tchr. Pine View Elem. Sch., West Columbia, 1978-81; sci. & lang. arts tchr. Heiskell Sch., Atlanta, 1981-82; lang. arts & gifted tchr. Fulmer Mid. Sch., 1982-85; itinerant gifted educator Lex II, West Columbia, 1985—; in-svc. presenter Lex II, 1992-95. Pianist Holland Ave. Baptist Ch., Cayce, S.C., 1970—, vacation Bible sch. dir., 1982-93, youth choir dir., 1982-85; neighborhood solicitor Arthritis Found., Columbia, S.C., 1993-95. Mem. Nat. Assn. for Gifted Children, Palmetto State Tchrs. Assn., Alpha Delta Kappa (chaplain 1993—). Republican. Home: 100 Sweetgum Dr Cayce SC 29033-1930

MCGILL, FORREST, art museum director, art historian; b. East Orange, N.J., Oct. 25, 1947; s. Oscar Forrest and Gladys Lee (Autrey) McG. BA, Cornell U., 1969; MA, U. Mich., 1972, PhD, 1977. Asst. dir. Huntington Art Gallery U. Tex., Austin, 1980-84; dir., curator of Asian Art, adj. assoc. prof. Mus. Art & Archaeology-U. Mo., Columbia, 1984-89; asst. dir. Arthur M. Sackler Gallery, Smithsonian Inst., Washington, 1989-91; dir. Mary Washington Coll. Galleries, Fredericksburg, Va., 1992—. Fulbright fellow U.S. Govt., 1975-76. Office: Mary Washington Coll Galleries Fredericksburg VA 22401-5837

MCGILL, JOHN KNOX, lawyer; b. Charlotte, N.C., Aug. 25, 1956; s. John Charles and Mabel (Hamilton) Mc.; m. Elizabeth Roxanne Bondurant. BS in Bus. cum laude, Erskine Coll., 1978; MBA, U. N.C., 1982, JD, 1982. Bar: N.C. 1983; CPA, N.C. Ptnr., tax atty. Garland & Alala, P.A., Gastonia, N.C., 1982-86; tax atty., pub. Blair, McGill & Co., Inc., Charlotte, N.C., 1986—; chmn., bd. dirs. Specter Broadcast Corp., Charlotte, N.C., Blair, McGill & Co., Inc., Charlotte; bd. dirs., founder, Advanced Pension Systems, Inc., Charlotte. Tax editor: Dental Economics Mag., 1982—; editor-in-chief: (newsletter) The Blair, McGill Advisory; contbr. editor: (textbook) Contemporary Marketing (4th edition, 1983. Bd. dirs. Assoc. Reformed Presbyn. Found.; treas. First Assoc. Reformed Presbyn. Ch., Gastonia, N.C., 1989-94, deacon, 1989-94, elder, 1995—. Recipient Tax Law scholarship, Touche, Ross & Co., CPA's, 1982. Mem. ABA, N.C. Bar Assn., Am. Inst. CPA's, N.C. Assn. CPA's, Sertoma Club (Disting. Svc award, Kings Mt. N.C., 1983). Republican. Home: 3418 Thoroughbred Ct Gastonia NC 28056-1686 Office: Blair McGill & Co Inc 4601 Charlotte Park Dr Ste 230 Charlotte NC 28217-1900

MCGILL, JUDY ANNELL MCGEE, early childhood and elementary educator; b. Kosciusko, Miss., Oct. 16, 1949; d. Reeves and Martha Lee (Thompson) McGee; m. Ronald Eugene McGill, June 5, 1971; 1 child, Thomas Eugene. Student, U. Colo., 1979, James Madison U., 1974; BS, Miss. State U., 1971; MEd, Northeast La. U., 1984. 4th grade tchr. Harrison County Schs., Gulfport, Miss., 1971; 1st and 2d grade tchr. Oktibbeha County Schs., Starkville, Miss., 1971-72; 4th grade tchr. Natchez-Adams (Miss.) County Schs., 1972-74; 2d and 3d grade tchr. Shenandoah County Schs., Woodstock, Va., 1974-78; elem. tchr. Jefferson County Schs., Lakewood, Colo., 1980-81; 7th and 8th grade tchr. Ouachita Parish Schs., Monroe, La., 1982; elem. sch. tchr. Union Parish Schs., Farmerville, La., 1982-85; early childhood and elem. tchr. Ouachita Parish Schs., Monroe, La., 1985-95; master tchr., intern assessor Quachita Parish Schs., Monroe, La., 1993-95; elem. tchr. Scottsboro (Ala.) City Schs., 1995—; in-svc. instr. Natchez-Adams County Schs., 1972-74, Shenandoah County Schs., 1974-78; trainer Sci. Rsch. Assocs., Woodstock, 1978; chairperson curriculum revision Ouachita Parish Schs., 1986-92, staff devel. trainer, 1990-92. Den leader Boy Scouts Am., West Monroe, La., 1986-88. La. Quality in Sci. and Math. grantee, 1994-95, grantee Jr. League Monroe, 1994-95. Mem. NEA, ASCD, Am. Assn. Young Children, Nat. Assn. Edn. Young Children, So. Early Childhood Assn., La. Assn. on Children Under Six (Jane Herrin grantee 1987, v.p., program chair 1988-94), N.E. La. Reading Coun. (chairperson grants 1987-88, Reading Tchr. of Yr. 1987-88), Internat. Reading Assn. Methodist. Home: 106 Colonial Dr Scottsboro AL 35768

MCGINLEY, EDWARD STILLMAN, II, naval officer; b. Allentown, Pa., June 9, 1939; s. Edward Stillman and Dorothy Mae (Kandle) McG.; m. Connie Lee Mayo, July 1, 1962; children: Amanda Lee, Edward Stillman III. BS, U.S. Naval Acad., 1961; advanced degree in naval architecture, MIT, 1970; MSA, George Washington U., 1972; cert. exec. program, U. Va., 1981. Commd. ensign USN, 1961, advanced through grades to rear adm., 1990, various positions in submarine engring., 1962-76; repair officer USN, Rota (Spain) and Charleston, S.C., 1976-83; ops. mgr. Mare Island Naval Shipyard, Vallejo, Calif., 1983-87; comdr. Norfolk Naval Shipyard, Portsmouth, Va., 1987-90; maintenance officer U.S. Pacific Fleet, Honolulu, 1990-93; comdr. Naval Surface Warfare Ctr., Washington, 1993-94; vice-comdr. Naval Sea Sys. Command, Washington, 1994-96. Contbr. articles to profl. jours. Recipient Environ. award Sec. of Navy, 1987, Productivity Improvement award Inst. Indsl. Engrs., 1988, Quality Improvement award Office Mgmt. and Budget, 1989, Productivity award U.S. Senate, 1990. Mem. Am. Soc. Naval Engrs. (nat. counselor), Soc. Naval Arch. and Marine Engrs., U.S. Naval Inst., Am. Soc. for Quality Control, Rotary, Sigma Xi, Tau Beta Pi. Republican. mem. United Church of Christ. Home: PO Box 16502 Arlington VA 22215

MCGINLEY, SUZANNE, enrivonmental and civil engineer; b. Jamaica Queens, N.Y., Aug. 24, 1964; d. John Joseph and Bobbie Sue (Herron) McG. BSCE, SUNY, Buffalo, 1986; MS in Environ. Engring., U. Tenn., 1996. Registered profl. engr., N.Y., Ala., Ky., Tenn. Civil engr. Nelson & Pope Engrs., Melville, N.Y., 1986-91; environ. engr. Advanced Scis. Inc., Oak Ridge, Tenn., 1992-94; project mgr., engr., lead engr. Geraghty &

Miller, Inc., Oak Ridge, 1994-95. Mem. ASCE (tech. rep. WATTec com. 1996—, sec.-treas. Knoxville chpt. 1996-97), NSPE. Home: 3227 Riverside Dr Knoxville TN 37914

MCGINN, DONALD JOSEPH, English language educator; b. Indian Lake, N.Y., Apr. 1, 1905; s. James and Mary Elizabeth (McCarthy) McG.; m. Margaret Mary Howley, June 27, 1940 (dec. 1979); children: Kathleen McGinn Spring, Donald J. Jr. AB, Cornell U., 1926, MA, 1929, PhD, 1930. Tchr. Rutgers Prep., New Brunswick, N.J., 1930-36, Rutgers U., 1936-73; prof. English Georgian Court Coll., Lakewood, N.J., 1945-93, ret., 1993. Author: Shakespeare's Influence on the Drama of His Age, 1938, The Admonition Controversy, 1949, (with George Howerton) Literature as a Fine Art, 1959, John Penry and the Marprelate Controversy, 1966, Thomas Nashe, 1981. Home: PO Box 387 Saint Petersburg FL 33731-0387

MCGINNES, PAUL R., environmental chemist; b. Detroit, Mar. 23, 1946; s. Harold P. and Elizabeth J. (Stubbs) McG.; m. Marilyn Thomas, Dec. 27, 1966 (div. Aug. 1979); children: Christen, John; m. Diane E. Johnson, July 14, 1990. BS, Wheaton (Ill.) Coll., 1968; MS, U. Ill., 1971, PhD, 1974. Registered profl. engr., Fla. Pres. McGinnes Labs., Inc., West Palm Beach, Fla., 1974—. Supr. Soil and Water Conservation Bd., Palm Beach County, Fla., 1990. Mem. Am. Chem. Soc., Fla. Engring. Soc. (Engr. of Yr. 1988). Office: McGinnes Labs Inc 711 W Indiantown Rd Ste B3 Jupiter FL 33458-7570*

MCGINNIS, PATRICK BRYAN, mental health counselor; b. Bellville, Ill., June 17, 1948; s. Raymon Lee and Virginia B. (Wiggins) McG.; 1 child, Patrick Bryan II. BS, Rollins Coll., 1977, MS in Criminal Justice, 1981; MA in Counseling Psychology, Norwich U., 1996. Cert. hypnotherapist, criminal justice addictions profl., criminal justice specialist-master addictions counselor. Ct. liaison officer, probation officer, classification spec. State of Fla. Dept. Corrections, Polk County, 1975-87; victim intervention program coord./therapist Peace River Ctr. for Personal Devel., Inc., Lakeland, Fla., 1987-90; clin. social worker State of Fla. Dept. Corrections/South Fla. Reception Ctr., Miami, 1991-92; counselor CareUnit of Coral Springs' Carepsychcenter, Coral Springs, Fla., 1992-93; psychotherapist Ctr. for Human Potential, Ft. Lauderdale, Fla., 1993—; counselor Unity Counseling Ctr./Unity Ch. of Ft. Lauderdale, 1993-94; vocat. rehab. counselor Fla. Divsn. Vocat. Rehab., Ft. Lauderdale, 1995—; adjunct faculty Broward C.C., Ft. Lauderdale, Fla., 1996—; counselor Unity of Hollywood Counseling Ctr., 1996—. With USAF, 1968-69. Recipient State of Fla. Clinician of Yr. award Fla. Coun. for Cmty. Mental Health, 1990; named Clinician of Yr., Peace River Ctr. for Personal Devel., 1980 Law Enforcement Officer of Yr., Greater Lakeland Area Am. Legion. Home: 8560 NW 20th Ct Sunrise FL 33322-3802 Office: Ctr for Human Potential 1881 NE 26th St Ste 103 Fort Lauderdale FL 33305

MCGINNIS, RICHARD PROVIS, chemical educator; b. Woodland, Calif., Dec. 24, 1941; s. Richard Adams and Olive Verna Ruth (Provis) McG. BS in Basic Chemistry with honors, U. Calif., Berkeley, 1963; AM in Chemistry, Harvard U., 1965, PhD in Chemistry, 1971. Mem. chemistry faculty Tougaloo (Miss.) Coll., 1969—, prof., 1977—, chair dept., 1978-79, 81-82, 96—, chair natural sci. divsn., 1979-81, 89-91, 96—, acting v.p. acad. affairs, 1985; Woodrow Wilson Teaching intern, 1969-72; vis. scientist Joint Inst. Lab. Astrophysics Nat. Bur. Stds. and U. Colo., 1982-83; vis. prof. Brown U., 1978; head tutor health careers summer program and intensive summer studies program Harvard U., summer, 1969, tutor, summers 1966-69, head teaching asst., summer 1965, teaching fellow chemistry, 1963-67; coord. Title III program Tougaloo Coll., 1987-88; project dir. Health Career Opportunity Program Pre-Health Program, 1973-76, 77—. Contbr. articles to profl. jours. Prin. investigator Ala. Alliance for Minority Participation, 1991—. Named Pre-Med. Adviser of Yr. Minority Med. Edn. Found., 1976, Prof. of Year Phi Beta Sigma, Tougaloo chpt., 1977; recipient award Tougaloo Coll. Alumni, 1979, Disting. Svc. award Nat. Assn. Med. Minority Educators, 1985. Home: 103 Magnolia St Edwards MS 39066 Office: Tougaloo Coll 500 W County Line Rd Tougaloo MS 39174

MCGINNIS, ROBERT WILLIAM, electronics company executive; b. Modesto, Calif., Oct. 31, 1936; s. George Crawford and Lola May (Provis) McG.; BS in Elec. Engring. with highest honors, U. Calif., Berkeley, 1962; postgrad. NYU, 1962-63; m. Sondra Elaine Hurley, Mar. 1, 1964; children—Michael Fredrick, Traci Anne, Patrick William. Mem. tech. staff Bell Telephone Labs, Murray Hill, N.J., 1961-63; devel. engr., engring. mgr., product mgr., ops. mgr. Motorola Semiconductor Group, Phoenix, 1963-73, ops. mgr. for hybrid circuits group, communications div., Fort Lauderdale, Fla., 1973-76, solar ops. mgr., 1976-79; v.p., gen. mgr. Photowatt Internat., Inc., Tempe, Ariz., 1979-83; gen. mgr. SAFT Electronic Systems Div., 1983-85, pres., Safe Power Systems, Inc., Tempe, 1985-88; gen. mgr. Advanced Energy Systems Acme Electric Corp., 1988-93; product mgr. energy products divsn. Motorola Worldwide, Plantation, Fla. and Motorola, Lawrenceville, Ga., 1993—. Mem. Ariz. Solar Energy Commn., 1977-83; chmn. photovoltaic subcom. Am. Nat. Standards Inst., 1978-83; mem. coordinating council Solar Energy Research Inst. Standards, 1977-82. Served with USNR, 1955-58. Mem. IEEE, Phi Beta Kappa, Tau Beta Pi, Eta Kappa Nu. Republican. Methodist. Contbr. articles in field to profl. jours. Home: 1320 Wilmington Way Grayson GA 30221-1900 Office: Motorola Energy Products 1700 Belle Meade Ct Lawrenceville GA 30243-5854

MCGLAMRY, MAX REGINALD, lawyer; b. Wilcox County, Ga., Sept. 12, 1928; s. Edgar Lee and Allie Bea (Faircloth) McG.; m. Jean Louise Hilyer, Dec. 28, 1950; children: Sharon Kay McGlamry Hendrix, Michael Lee. BS, Auburn U., 1948; LLB cum laude, Mercer U., 1952, JD cum laude, 1970. Bar: Ga. 1953, U.S. Dist. Ct. (mid. dist.) Ga. 1954, U.S. Dist. Ct. (no. dist.) Calif. 1988, U.S. Dist. Ct. (nc. dist.) Ga. 1989, U.S. Ct. Appeals (5th cir.) 1964, U.S. Ct. Appeals (11th cir.) 1981, U.S. Ct. Appeals (4th cir.) 1985, U.S. Supreme Ct. 1972. Pvt. practice Columbus, Ga., 1953-64; from ptnr. to officer Swift, Pease, Davidson & Chapman (name changed to Page, Scrantom, Harris, McGlamry, & Chapman, P.C.), Columbus, 1964-85; ptnr. Pope, Kellogg, McGlamry, Kilpatrick & Morrison, Columbus, 1985-90, Pope, McGlamry, Kilpatrick & Morrison, Columbus, 1990—. Mem. exec. com. Muscogee County Dem. Orgn., Columbus, 1956-60; bd. dirs. Columbus Jr. C. of C. With USN, 1948-49. Am. Coll. Trust & Estate Counsel fellow, 1973, Ga. Bar Found., hon. fellow, 1983. Mem. ABA, ATLA, State Bar Ga., Ga. Trial Lawyers Assn., Assn. U.S. Army, Metro Columbus Urban League, Inc., Columbus Lawyers Club (pres. 1964-65), Lions (Columbus chpt. pres. 1967-68), Chattahoochee River Club, Green Island Country Club, Phi Kappa Phi, Alpha Epsilon Delta, Phi Alpha Delta, Pi Kappa Alpha. Democrat. Methodist. Home: 2937 Lynda Ln Columbus GA 31906-1337 Office: Pope McGlamry Kilpatrick & Morrison PO Box 2128 318 11th St 2nd Fl Columbus GA 31902

MCGLENNON, JOHN JOSEPH, political science educator; b. Bay Shore, N.Y., July 23, 1949; s. Thomas A. and Agnes P. (Mellon) McG.; m. Terry L. Urbanski, May 17, 1986; children: Andrew P., Colin P. BA, Fordham U., 1971; MA, Johns Hopkins U., 1974, PhD, 1977. From asst. prof. to prof. Coll. of William & Mary, Williamsburg, Va., 1974—; chmn. dept. govt. Coll. William & Mary, 1993—, pres. faculty assembly, 1992-93. Co-editor: Life of the Parties, 1986; contbr. articles to profl. jours. Chair 1st Congl. Dist. Dem. Com., Va., 1985—. Roman Catholic. Home: 2817 Mockingbird Ln Williamsburg VA 23185 Office: Coll William & Mary Dept Govt PO Box 8795 Williamsburg VA 23187

MCGLONE, JOHN JAMES, biologist; b. New Rochelle, N.Y., Oct. 27, 1955; s. John Thomas and Maura (Scanlon) McG.; m. Barbara Rose Rattie McGlone, June 12, 1976; children: Molly, Kerry Rose. BS, Wash. State U., 1977, MS, 1979; PhD, U. Ill., 1981. Asst. prof. U. Wyo., Laramie, 1981-84, Tex. Tech. U., Lubbock, 1984-89; assoc. prof. Tex. Tech. Health Sci. Ctr., Lubbock, 1990-95, prof., 1995—; assoc. prof. Tex. Tech. U., Lubbock, 1989—; editorial bd. Jour. Animal Sci., ASAS, Champaign, Ill., 1985-90. Author: Guidelines for Swine Husbandry, 1988, 96, Animal Health, 1990; contbr. articles to profl. jours. Advisor Econ. Devel. for Pork Industry, Tex., 1989—; tchr. St. Elizabeth's Cath. Ch., Lubbock, Tex., 1986—. Recipient Undergraduate Rsch. award Washington St. U., Pullman, Wash., 1976, Presdl. Acad. Achievement award Tex. Tech. U., Lubbock, 1990, Harry Frank Guggenheim Rsch. award N.Y.C., 1983, Outstanding Researcher, Coll. Agrl. Sci., Lubbock, Tex., 1992. Mem. Am. SOc. Animal Scis., Soc. For Neuroscience, Animal Behavior Soc. Democrat. Roman Catholic. Home: 2225 86th St Lubbock TX 79423-3307 Office: Texas Tech University Dept Animal Sci & Food Tech Lubbock TX 79409

MCGONIGLE, RICHARD THOMAS, lawyer; b. Columbus, Ohio, Jan. 29, 1951; s. Francis Phillip and Mary Lou (Daughtery) McG.; m. Janet Christine Bowser, Aug. 17, 1974; children: Richard K., Michael P., Robin C. BA, St. Leo Coll., 1978; JD, Duquesne U., 1981. Bar: Pa. 1981, Okla. 1986, U.S. Supreme Ct. 1994, U.S. Dist. Ct. (we. dist.) Pa. 1981, U.S. Dist. Cts. (ea., we., and no. dists.) Okla. 1985, U.S. Ct. Appeals (5th and 10th cirs.) 1985. Police officer City of Hilliard, Ohio, 1973-74, City of Virginia Beach, Va., 1974-78; atty. Eckert Seamans Cherin & Mellot, Pitts., 1981-85, Hall, Estill, Tulsa, Okla., 1985-95; of counsel Ronald D. Wood & Assocs., Tulsa, 1995—; faculty mem., co-author seminar materials Nat. Bus. Inst., 1992. Author: (case notes) Duquesne Law Rev., 1979. Pres. Eastwood Lake Homeowners Assn., Owasso, Okla., 1993-96; mem. Associated Builders & Contractors, Inc., Tulsa, 1994. Recipient Acad. Achievement award Franklin County Sheriff's Acad., Columbus, 1973, Honor Grad. award Fraternal Order of Police Assn., Norfolk, Va., 1975, Best Oralist award Mugel Nat. Tax Moot Ct., Buffalo, N.Y., 1980. Mem. ABA, Okla. Bar Assn., Pa. Bar Assn., Tulsa County Bar Assn., Muscogee (Creek) Nation Bar Assn. Republican. Roman Catholic. Home: 18432 E 90th St N Owasso OK 74055-8019 Office: Ronald D. Wood & Assocs 2727 E 21st St Ste 500 Tulsa OK 74114

MCGOVERN, JOHN PHILLIP, physician, educator; b. Washington, June 2, 1921; s. Francis and Lottie (Brown) McG.; m. Kathrine Dunbar Galbreath, 1961. BS, Duke U., 1945, MD, 1945; postgrad., London and Paris, 1949; hon. degrees: Ricker Coll., Union Coll., Kent State U., U. Nebr., Ill. Coll. Podiatric Medicine, Lincoln Coll., Emerson Coll., Ball State U., Huston-Tillotson Coll., John F. Kennedy U., Limestone Coll., Southeastern U., Tex. Christian U., Georgetown U., William Penn Coll., Catawba Coll., Fla. State U., Lamar U., Alaska Pacific U., Houston Grad. Sch. Theology, Troy State U., Pan Am. U., Thomas Jefferson U., U. of City of Manila. Intern in pediats. Yale-New Haven Gen. Hosp., 1945-46; resident pediatrics Duke U. Hosp., Durham, N.C., 1948; resident Guy Hosp., London, 1949; chief resident Children's Hosp., Houston, 1949-50, chief out-patient dept., 1950-51; John and Mary R. Markle scholar med. sci., asst. prof. pediatrics George Washington U. Sch. Medicine, Washington, 1950-54; chief George Washington U. pediatric div. D.C. Gen. Hosp., 1951-54; assoc. prof. pediatrics Tulane U., New Orleans, 1954-56; vis. physician Charity Hosp., New Orleans; pvt. practice medicine specializing in allergy/immunology, Houston, 1956-88; chief of allergy svc. Tex. Children's Hosp., Houston, 1957-74; founder, McGovern Allergy Clinic, 1956; clin. prof. pediats. (allergy), adj. prof. dept. of microbiology Baylor Coll. Medicine, Houston; prof., chmn. dept. history of medicine U. Tex. Grad. Sch. Biomed. Sci., 1970-81, prof. history and philosophy of biol. sci., 1981—, clin. prof. allergy, 1956-70, adj. prof. M.D. Anderson Hosp. and Tumor Inst., 1976—; fellow Green Coll. Oxford (Eng.) U.; disting. adj. prof. health and safety edn. Kent (Ohio) State U., 1972—; adj. prof. dept. environ. sci. Sch. Public Health, U. Tex., 1978—, clin. prof. Sch. Medicine, 1978—; cons. USPHS, New Orleans, 1954-56; regional cons. Lackland AFB, San Antonio; regional cons. nat. med. adv. council Asthmatic Children's Found., 1963—, bd. dirs., 1967-79, chmn., bd. dirs. Tex. Allergy Rsch. Found., 1961-86. Pres., bd. dirs. John P. McGovern Found., 1986—; bd. dirs. Allergy Found. Am., 1962-74, McGovern Fund for Behavioral Scis., 1988—; bd. regents Nat. Libr. Medicine, 1970-74, cons., 1975—; mem. Nat. Adv. Coun. on Alcohol Abuse and Alcoholism, 1987—. Served to capt. M.C., AUS, 1946-48. Recipient numerous awards including Disting. Alumni award Duke U. Sch. Medicine, 1976, John P. McGovern award Tex. Sch. Health Assn., 1977, President's citation Pres. Reagan, 1985, Royal Medallion of the Polar Star (Sweden), 1988, l'Ordre national du Merite (France), 1988, Pres.'s Medal U. Texas Health Sci. Ctr., Houston, 1987, Meritorious Svc. award AMA, 1988, Surgeon Gen.'s Medallion (Koop), 1989. Diplomate Nat. Bd. Med. Examiners, Am. Bd. Pediatrics, subsplty. pediatric allergy, Am. Bd. Allergy and Immunology. Fellow Am. Coll. Allergy and Immunology (pres. 1968-69), Am. Acad. Allergy and Immunology, Am. Acad. Pediatrics, Am. Coll. Chest Physicians (Tex. chpt. pres. 1966-67), Am. Assn. Study Headache (pres. 1963-64); mem. AMA, ACP, Am. Assn. Immunologists, Soc. Exptl. Biology and Medicine, Am. Med. Writers Assn., Assn. for Rsch. in Nervous and Mental Diseases, Am. Assn. Hist. Medicine, So. Med. Assn. (life mem.), Tex. Pediatric Soc., Assn. Convalescent Homes and Hosps. for Asthmatic Children (pres. Tex. chpt. 1969-70), Duke U. Med. Alumni Assn. (pres. 1968-69), Am. Assn. Cert. Allergists (pres. 1972-73), Am. Osler Soc. (pres. 1973-74), Am. Sch. Health Assn., Sociedad de Alergia y Ciencias Afines (Mexico, hon.), La Sociedad Mexicana de Alergia e Inmunologia (hon.), Westchester (hon.), Canadian (hon.) allergy socs., Asociacion Argentina de Alergia e Inmmunologia (hon.), Royal Coll. Physicians (London) (hon.), Phi Beta Kappa, Alpha Omega Alpha, Sigma Xi (mem. com. on membership-at-large, editor newsletter 1970-71, dir. 1972-73), Sigma Pi Sigma, Pi Kappa Alpha. Clubs: Cosmos, Army-Navy Country (Washington), Osler (London), Vintage (Calif.). Author: (with Mandel) Bibliography of Sarcoidosis (1876-1963), 1964; (with James Knight) Allergy and Human Emotions, 1967; (with Charles Roland) Wm. Osler: The Continuing Education, 1969; (with Gordon Stewart) Penicillin Allergy: Clinical and Immunological Aspects, 1970; (with Chester Burns) Humanism in Medicine, 1974; (with Glenn Knotts) School Health Problems, 1975; (with Earl Nation and Charles Roland) An Annotated Checklist of Osleriana, 1976; (with Michael Smolensky and Alain Reinberg) Chronobiology in Allergy and Immunology, 1977; (with others) Recent Advances in the Chronobiology of Allergy and Immunology, 1980; editor; A Way of Life (Osler), 1969; Davison Memorial Addresses, 1976; (with E.F. Nation) Student and Chief: The Osler-Camac Correspondence, 1980; (with J. Arena) Davison of Duke - His Reminiscences, 1980; (with C. Roland and J. Barondess) The Persisting Osler, 1985; (with C. Roland) The Collected Essays of Sir William Osler, Vols. I, II, III, 1985; (with J. Vay Eys) The Doctor as a Person, 1988, (with P.L. Starck) The Hidden Dimension of Illness: Human Suffering, 1992; assoc. editor Annals of Allergy, 1965-80; mem. editorial bd. Psychosomatics, Headache, Internat. Corr. Soc. Allergists; assoc. editor Jour. Asthma Research; editor Am. Lecture Series in Allergy and Immunology; assoc. editor Jour. Sch. Health, 1977-80; editorial adv. bd. Chronic Disease Mgmt., 1967-74; editorial bd. Forum on Medicine, 1978-81, The Classics of Medicine Library, 1978—; mem. editorial bd. Acad. Achievement, 1967-75, Geriatrics, 1974-78, numerous others. Office: 2211 Norfolk, Ste 900 Houston TX 77098*

MCGRATH, HUGH, medical educator; b. Mamaroneck, N.Y., Oct. 15, 1936; s. Hugh Aloysius and Marion Elizabeth (Hogan) McG.; m. Carolyn Marie White, Apr. 15, 1967; children: Catherine Anne, Timothy Michael. BS in Biology, Georgetown U., 1954-58, MD, 1966. Diplomate Am. Bd. Internal Medicine, Am. Bd. Rheumatology; lic. physician Mass., N.C., La. Prof. medicine Washington Hosp. Ctr., 1966-67, med. resident, 1967-68; med. resident St. Vincent Hosp., Worcester, Mass., 1968-69; med. resident, chief resident Lahey Clinic Found., Boston, 1969-70; gen. internist Meml. Hosp., Worcester, 1972-74; clin. assoc. in medicine U. Mass. Med. Ctr., Worcester, 1973-76; gen. internist Presbyn. Hosp., Meml. Hosp., Mercy Hosp., Charlotte, N.C., 1976-77; clin. and rsch. fellow in rheumatology U. Va. Med. Ctr., Charlottesville, 1977-80; asst. prof. medicine sch. medicine La. State U., New Orleans, 1980-88, assoc. prof. medicine, 1988—; active staff internal medicine Hotel Dieu Hosp., New Orleans, 1980—; prof. medicine La State U., New Orleans, 1995—; coord. rheumatology svc. Charity Hosp., New Orleans, 1980—; peer reviewer grant proposals NIH, Bethesda, Md., 1993—, U.S.-Israel Binat. Sci. Found., Jerusalem, 1994, Internat. Sci. Found., Washington, 1994; lectr., invited presenter in field. Contbr. 3 chpts. to books, 22 articles to med. and profl. publs. Internist U.S. Army Med. Corps, 1970-72. Grantee Arthritis Found., 1981, 84, 85, 87, NIH, 1981-82, 83-84, 91-93, 93-94, 94—, Am. Cancer Soc., 1985, Lupus Found. Am., 1987, La. Edn. Quality Support Fund, 1989, 90, 91-92. Mem. Am. Coll. Rheumatology, Am. Fedn. for Clin. Rsch., Am. Soc. for Photobiology, Am. Assn. for Immunologists, Nat. Lupus Founs., La. Lupus Found. (grantee 1982-83, 83, 83-84, 85, 88, 91, med. adv. bd. 1990—), La. Arthritis Found. (med. adminstrv. com., startegic planning com.). Office: La State U Sch Medicine 1542 Tulane Ave New Orleans LA 70112-2825

MC GRAW, DARRELL VIVIAN, JR., state attorney general; b. Mullens, W.Va., Nov. 8, 1936; s. Darrell Vivian and Julia (ZeKany) McG.; m. Jorea Marple; children: Elizabeth, Sarah, Darrell, Elliott. AB, W.Va. U., 1961, JD, 1964, MA, 1977. Bar: W.Va. 1964. Gen. atty. Fgn. Claims Settlement Commn., U.S. Dept. State, 1964; counsel to gov. State of W.Va., 1965-68; pvt. practice Charleston, Shepherdstown and Morgantown, 1968-76; judge W.Va. Supreme Ct. Appeals, Charleston, 1977-88, chief justice, 1982, 83; atty. gen. State of W.Va., Charleston, 1996—. Served with U.S. Army, 1954-57. Fellow W.Va. U., Nat. Ctr. Edn. in Politics/Ford Found. Fellow Am. Polit. Sci. Assn. Democrat. Office: Office of Atty Gen Bldg 1 Rm E-26 1900 Kanawha Blvd E Charleston WV 25305-0220

MCGREEVY, MARY, retired psychology educator; b. Kansas City, Kans., Nov. 10, 1935; d. Donald and Emmy Lou (Neubert) McG.; m. Phillip Rosenbaum (dec.); children: David, Steve, Mariya, Chay, Allyn, Jacob, Dora. BA in English with honors, Vassar Coll., 1957; postgrad., New Sch. for Social Rsch., NYU, 1958-59, Columbia U., 1959-60, U. P.R., 1963-65, U. Mo., 1965-68, U. Kans.; PhD, U. Calif., Berkeley, 1969. Formerly exec. Doubleday & Co., N.Y.C., 1957-60; chief libr. San Juan Sch., P.R., 1962-63; NIMH drug rschr. Russell Sage Found., Clinico de los Addictos, Rio Piedras, P.R., 1963-65; psychiat. rschr. U. P.R. Med. Sch., 1963-65; psychiat. researcher U. Kans. Med. Ctr., Kansas City, 1966-68; rsch. assoc. Ednl. Rsch., 1968-69; assoc. prof. U. Calif., Berkeley, 1968-69, disting. prof., ret., 1969; yacht owner Encore; lectr. in philosophy. Author: (poetry) To a Sailor, 1989, Dreams and Illusions, 1993, Coastings, 1996, also articles, poems, book revs. Founder, exec. dir. Dora Achenbach McGreevy Poetry Found., Inc.; active Fla. Atlantic U. Found., 1993—; vol. Broward County Hist. Commn., 1990—, Friends of the Libr., Ft. Lauderdale and Main Broward County Librs., 1969—; mem. Am. Friends of Bodleian Libr., Oxford, Eng., Frances Loeb Lehman Art Gallery, Vassar Coll., Ctr. de las Artes, Miami, Fla., Friends of Modern Mus. Art, Friends of the Guggenheim, Friends of Met. Mus. Art, Nelson-Atkins Mus. Art, Friends of U. Mo. Libr., Johnson County Mental Health Assn., Ft. Lauderdale Philharm. Soc., St. Anthony's Cath. Women's Club, Women's Rsch. Inst., Nova Southea. U., Davie, Fla.; mem. fundraising com. Ednl. Found., 1994—. Recipient Cert. for Svc. Broward County Hist. Commn., 1994, Nat. Women's History Project award, 1995, Status of Women award Broward County Women's History Coalition, 1996; Sproul fellow, Bancroft Libr. fellow, Russell Sage Found. fellow; postdoctoral grantee U. Calif. Mem. AAUW (corr. sec. 1991-95, bd. dirs. 1991—, honoree Ednl. Found. Fund 1993, Jeanne Faiks meml. scholarship fund com. 1992—, chairperson cultural events 1995—, Women of History awards), Pres.'s Coun., Broward Women's History Coalition (bd. dirs. 1991—, archivist, mem. ad hoc com.), Am. Philos. Assn., Women in Psychology, Union of Concerned Scientists, South Fla. Poetry Inst. (yearly poetry anthology 1991—), S.W. Philos. Assn. (hon.), Poets of the Palm Beaches (yearly poetry anthology 1992, 93—, 1st prize free verse ann. contest 1996), Mo. Sociol. Assn., Fla. Philosophy Assn. (spkr. 1991, 93, chairperson self in philosophy 1994), Vassar Alumni Assn. (class historian), Oxfam Am., Pem-Hill Alumni Assn., Sierra Club (newspaper reporter, mem. environ. com., archivist 1993-95, co-chairperson beach clean-up 1993), Alliance Francoise (faculty mem. U. Calif. 1969—), Secular Humanists (bd. dirs. 1992—, program chairperson 1995—), Fla. Women's Consortium, Vassar Club Kansas City, Vassar Alumni Assn. N.Y. Home: PO Box 900 Fort Lauderdale FL 33302-0900

MCGREEVY, TERRENCE GERARD, lawyer; b. Flushing, N.Y., Aug. 15, 1932; s. Martin Gerard and Eileen (O'Connor) McG.; m. Elizabeth Ann Connelly, Sept. 6, 1958; children: Terrence G., Elizabeth C., Martha E., Connelly T., Daniel M. BS in Econs., Fordham U., 1954; LLB, U. Tex., 1959. Mem. firm Vinson & Elkins, Houston, 1959—, ptnr., 1968—. Bd. dirs. St. Joseph Hosp. Found., Houston chpt. NCCJ. Capt. USAF, 1955-57. Mem. ABA, Tex. Bar Assn., Houston Bar Assn., Houston Country Club. Roman Catholic. Office: Vinson & Elkins 3611 First City Tower 1001 Fannin St Houston TX 77002*

MCGREGOR, FRANK BOBBITT, JR., district judge; b. Waco, Tex., Dec. 30, 1952; s. Frank Bobbitt Sr. and Doris (Mason) McG.; m. Brenda Ruth Battles, Apr. 5, 1974; children: Jason Bobbitt, Aaron Lee. BS, Baylor U., 1974; MEd, Tarleton State U., 1976; JD, South Tex. Coll. of Law, 1979. Bar: Tex. 1980, U.S. Dist. Ct. (so. dist.) Tex. 1980, U.S. Dist. Ct. (we. dist.) Tex. 1981, U.S. Ct. Appeals (5th and 11th cirs.) 1981, U.S. Dist. Ct. (no. dist.) Tex. 1983, U.S. Supreme Ct. 1984. Mem. staff banker Citizens Nat. Bank, Waco, 1971-74; tchr. West Tex. and Columbus (Tex.) ISD's, 1974-77; pres. McGregor, McGregor & Carmichael Inc., P.C., Hillsboro, Tex., 1979-93; dist. judge 66th Dist. Ct. Tex., 1993—; mem. devel. bd. Hill Coll., Hillsboro; mem. State Bar Admission Com., Austin, 1983—, State Bar Unauthorized Practice of Law Com., 1989-91. Coun. exec. bd. Boy Scouts of Am., 1989-91. Named Personality of South, 1981; recipient Am. Jurisprudence award Lawyers coop. Pub. Co., 1979. Mem. ABA, State Bar of Tex., Hill County Bar Assn. (pres. 1981), Am. Acad. Hosp. Attys., Lions (pres. and dep. dist. gov. Hillsboro 1987). Baptist. Office: PO Box 284 Hillsboro TX 76645-0284

MCGREGOR, JAMES HARVEY SPENCE, comparative literature educator; b. Frostburg, Md., Oct. 1, 1946; s. James Harvey and Mary (Twigg) McG.; 1 child, Raphael Harvey Gais; m. Sarah Spence, May 25, 1985; 1 child, Edward Isham Spence. BA, Princeton U., 1968, PhD, 1975. Assoc. prof. dept. comparative lit. U. Ga., Athens, 1980—; vis. prof. dept. English Colgate U., Hamilton, N.Y., 1979-80; vis. prof. dept. Italian U. Calif., Berkeley, 1984-85. Author: Image of Antiquity, 1991, Shades of Aeneas, 1991; editor, translator: Sack of Rome, 1993. Rome Prize fellow in post-classical humanistic studies Am. Acad. in Rome, 1981-82. Mem. MLA, Am. Assn. Italian Studies, Internat. Assn. for Study of Italian Lang. and Lit., Am. Boccaccio Assn. Office: U Ga 127 Park Ave Athens GA 30601-1721

MCGREGOR, JANET EILEEN, elementary school educator; b. Pittsfield, Mass., Jan. 6, 1949; d. Joseph Patrick and Edith Cecilia (Wendell) Feeley; m. Ronald Lee McGregor, Jan. 21, 1972; children: Joshua, Jason. BS in Elem./Early Childhood Edn., Fla. State U., 1971; MEd, U. South Fla., 1996. Tchr. 4th grade South Lake Elem. Sch., Titusville, Fla., 1971-74; tchr. 1st and 2d grades Peace River Elem. Sch., Port Charlotte, Fla., 1974-90; tchr. 1st grade Deep Creek Elem. Sch., Punta Gorda, Fla., 1990—; workshop presenter Charlotte County Schs., Port Charlotte, 1989—; cons. Lee County Schs., Ft. Myers, Fla., 1993; seminar presenter (level 3 interns) U. South Fla., Ft. Myers, 1992-94; presenter in field. Co-author: Charlotte's Arithmetic Basic Skills, 1980. Religious edn. tchr. Sacred Heart Ch., Punta Gorda, 1988—, lector, 1994—; Brownie leader Girl Scouts U.S., Port Charlotte, 1976; bd. dirs. Swim Team, Lane 4, Punta Gorda, 1991-93, cert. stroke and turn official, 1995—. Recipient Nat. Presdl. award for excellence in teaching math. NSF/Nat. Coun. Tchrs. Math., 1994, State Presdl. award for excellence in teaching math., 1993; named Charlotte County Tchr. of the Yr., Charlotte County Schs., 1993; profiled on Disney Presents the Am. Teacher, 1994; Disney/Am. Tchr. Honoree in Maths., Disney Corp. along with Campbells Soup Co., 1994. Mem. Nat. Coun. Tchrs. Math., Fla. Coun. Tchrs. Math., Coun. of Presdl. Awardees in Math., Fla. League Tchrs., Phi Delta Kappa, Alpha Delta Kappa. Democrat. Roman Catholic. Home: 3114 Newbury St Pt Charlotte FL 33952-7100 Office: Deep Creek Elem Sch 26900 Harbor View Rd Punta Gorda FL 33983-3601

MCGREGOR, SCOTT DUNCAN, optometrist, educator; b. Berkeley, Calif., Sept. 5, 1953; s. Duncan Charles and Catherine Wala (Guthrie) McG.; m. Michele Rae Gates, Mar. 7, 1981; children: Brittany Erin, Brent Duncan, Shane Donovan. AS magna cum laude, Reynolds Coll., Richmond, Va., 1976; BS, Coll. William and Mary, 1980; OD, So. Coll. Optometry, Memphis, 1986. Lic. optometrist, Tex., Va., Tenn.; cert. Nat. Contact Lens Examiners. Paramedic, EMT-A, City of Newport News, 1974-76; instr. nursing CNC-Riverside Sch. Nursing, Newport News, 1976-80; optician White Med. Ctr., Newport News, 1976-80; pvt. practice, Dallas, 1986—; adj. prof. So. Coll. Optometry, 1987—; dir. optometric svcs. Optometric Eye Assn., Dallas, 1989—. Inventor ocular cancer detector. Team physician Tex. Spl. Olympics, Dallas, 1991—. Fellow Nat. Acad.; mem. Am. Optometric Assn., Tex. Optometric Assn. (legis. cons. 1987, legis. advisor 1987—), Am. Acad. Optometric Physicians, North Tex. Optometric Assn. Office: Preston Doctors Ctr 8215 Westchester Dallas TX 75255-1666

MCGREW, JOHN GILBERT, computer science educator; b. Charleston, W.Va., July 30, 1943; s. John Gilbert and Jessie Alma (Given) McG.; m. Barbara Anne Ivy, May 22, 1978; 1 child, Robert John. BA in Chemistry, Cornell U., 1965; MS in Computer Sci., U. North Tex., 1987; PhD in Organic Chemistry, U. Mich., 1972. Asst. prof. chemistry Macalester Coll., St. Paul, 1971-73; instr., rsch. assoc. dept. chemistry U. Va., Charlottesville,

1973-75; asst. prof. chemistry Alderson-Broaddus Coll., Philippi, W.Va., 1975-80; rsch. chemist, project leader Gulf R&D Co., Harmarville, Pa., 1981-84; software design engr. Tex. Instruments Co., Plano, 1986-90; asst. prof. computer sci. East Ctrl. U., Ada, Okla., 1996-96, assoc. prof. computer sci., 1996—. Contbr. articles to profl. jours.; presenter in field. Mem. IEEE, Assn. for Computing Machinery, Okla. Acad. Scis. Episcopalian. Office: East Ctrl U Ada OK 74820

MCGREW, MICHAEL BRUCE, music minister; b. N.Y.C., Nov. 11, 1950; s. Palmer Whittemore and Dorothy Jean (Thorsen) McG.; m. Peggy Joan McGuffie, Nov. 21, 1970; children: Jennifer Dawn, Jeremy Michael. B in Music Edn., Stetson U., 1979; M of Ch. Music, Southwestern Bapt. Theol. Sem., Ft. Worth, 1981. Ordained to ministry So. Bapt. Conv., 1981. Min. youth 5th Ave. Bapt. Ch., St. Petersburg, Fla., 1983-87; min. music Pinecrest Bapt. Ch., Sanford, Fla., 1976-79, Univ. Bapt. Ch., Arlington, Tex., 1979-81, Main St. Bapt. Ch., Leesburg, Fla., 1981-83, Palma Sola Bay Bapt. Ch., Bradenton, Fla., 1987—; music chmn. Outreach Manatee, Bradenton, 1990—; mem. Dominica mission team Fgn. Mission Bd., So. Bapt. Conv., 1985. James Parrish scholar Stetson U., 1978-79. Mem. Choristers Guild, Am. Choral Dirs. Assn., So. Bapt. Ch. Conf., Fla. Bapt. Ch. Conf., Fla. Bapt. Singing Men. Home: 9604 Carter Rd W Apt 436 Bradenton FL 34210 Office: Palma Sola Bay Bapt Ch 4000 75th St W Bradenton FL 34209-6512

MCGRIFF, FRED (FREDERICK STANLEY MCGRIFF), baseball player; b. Tampa, Oct. 31, 1963. Grad. high sch., Tampa. Baseball player N.Y. Yankees, 1981-82, Toronto Blue Jays, 1982-90, San Diego Padres, 1990-93, Atlanta Braves, 1993—. Named to Sporting News All-Star team, 1989, 92, 93; recipient Silver Slugger award, 1989, 92, 93; mem. Nat. League All-Star Team, 1992, 94; Am. League Home Run Leader, 1989; Nat. League Home Run Leader, 1992. Office: Atlanta Braves PO Box 4064 Atlanta GA 30302*

MCGRUDER, KENNETH GENE, healthcare administrator; b. New Orleans, Feb. 27, 1949; s. Lionel and Wilhelmina (Francis) McG.; m. Patricia Fredia Lymous, July 12, 1969; children: Lashona, Kenneth Jr., Darlene, Patrick. BS, So. U. at New Orleans, 1985; MPA, U. New Orleans, 1996. Cert. supervisory techniques, La. Acct. La. State U. Med. Ctr., New Orleans, 1978-88, bus. mgr., 1988—. Cubmaster Boy Scouts Am., New Orleans, 1987-90. With U.S. Coast Guard, 1969-75. Named Boss of Yr. Orleans Parish Sch. Bd., New Orleans, 1995; recipient Cert. Appreciation New Orleans Parish Sch. Bd., 1994. Mem. Med. Group Mgmt. Assn., Assn. Mgrs. Gyn.-Obs. (bd. dirs. 1990-91), Nat. Forum Black Pub. Adminstrs. (treas. 1995-96). Democrat. Baptist. Home: 917 Gordon St New Orleans LA 70117 Office: La State U Ob/Gyn Dept 1542 Tulane Ave New Orleans LA 70112

MCGUINN, MICHAEL EDWARD, III, retired army officer; b. Spartanburg, S.C., Feb. 22, 1925; s. Michael Edward Jr. and Margaret Cordelia (Shackleford) McG.; m. Betty Gay Corn, 1948 (div. 1951); m. Phyllis Fryer, Oct. 7, 1952; childen: Michael Edward IV, Carol Ann McGuinn Branch. Student, Clemson U., 1941-43, 46, Coll. William and Mary, 1962-63. Served with U.S. Navy, PTO, 1943-46; commd. 2d lt. U.S. Army, 1949, advanced through grades to col., 1971; asst. mil. attache Am. Embassy, Copenhagen, 1958-61; posted to svc. British Army, Longmoor, Eng., 1964-66; served on U.S. Dept. Army Gen. Staff, Washington, 1966-68; comdr. 10th Transp. Bn. U.S. Army, Vietnam, 1968-69; chief transp. div. U.S. Readiness Command, MacDill AFB, Fla., 1969-72; ret. U.S. Army, 1972; state govt. svc. various locations, 1972-82; chief of staff Ga. State Def. Force, an Agy. of the State of Ga., Atlanta, 1987-95. Decorated Legion of Merit (2), Army Commendation medal (2), Naval Commendation medal. Mem. U.S. Army Transp. Mus., The Old Guard of the Gate City Guard. Home and Office: 6420 Tanacrest Ct NW Atlanta GA 30328-2837

MCGUIRE, BRIAN LYLE, health science facility consultant, educator; b. Mobile, Ala., June 13, 1959; s. Frank Ludlow, Jr. and Mary Lyle (Davidson) McG.; m. Jean Ellen Marler, June 18, 1983. BS in Acctg., U. S. Ala., 1982, MBA, 1990; PhD, U. Ctrl. Fla., 1996. CPA, Ala.; cert. mgmt. acct. Staff acct. Smith, Dukes & Buckalew, CPA's, Mobile, 1983-86; corp. acct. So. Med. Health Systems, Mobile, 1986, dir. corp. ops, 1987-88; exec. dir. Med. Arts Clinic, Inc. subs. So. Med. Health Systems, Foley, Ala., 1986-88; adminstr. Mobile Heart Ctr., 1988-91; acctg. instr. U. Ctrl. Fla., Orlando, 1991-95; asst. prof. acctg. U. So. Ind., Evansville, 1995—. Jr. asst. scoutmaster Boy Scouts Am., Birmingham chpt., unit commr. Buffalo Trace Coun., 1996—. Recipient Eagle Scout Order of Arrow Boy Scouts Am., 1977; named one of Outstanding Young Men of Am., 1982. Mem. AICPA, Inst. Mgmt. Accts. (chpt. bd. dirs. 1983-85, pres. 1987-88, nat. bd. dirs. 1989-91, 92-93, pres. regional coun. 1992-93, nat. com. mem. 1993—, Remington Rand trophy), Med. Group Mgmt. Assn., Ala. Soc. CPAs, Mobile Jaycees (treas. 1983-84, v.p. adminstrn. 1984-85, presdl. citation 1984), Alumni Assn. U. South Ala., Hist. Mobile Preservation Soc., Lake Forest Yacht and Country Club, Athelstan Club, Pi Kappa Phi, Phi Kappa Phi, Beta Gamma Sigma. Episcopalian. Office: U So Ind Dept Acctg and Bus Law 8600 University Blvd Evansville IN 47712-3534

MCGUIRE, DIANNE MARIE, psychotherapist; b. Houston, Feb. 22, 1950; d. Sidney A. and Shirley Lee (Ward) Schwartz; m. Walter Fred McGuire, May 7, 1983; children: Christopher C., Emily Nicole, Robert L. AA, San Jacinto Coll., Pasadena, Tex., 1984; BS in Psychology, U. Houston, 1986, MSW, 1988. Cert. social worker, advanced clin. practitioner, trauma resolution therapist, chem. dependency specialist, Tex. Pvt. practice Clear Lake, Pasadena and Deer Park, Tex., 1990—; adj. mem. faculty U. Houston, Clear Lake; presenter in field. Active Multiple Sclerosis Soc. Mem. NASW, Houston Live Stock Show and Rodeo (life), U. Houston Alumni Orgn. (life), U. Houston Clear Lake Alumni Orgn., Psi Chi, Phi Theta Kappa, Alpha Chi. Home: 16910 Pleasant Trace Ct Houston TX 77059-4039 Office: U Houston Clear Lake 2700 Bay Area Blvd Ste 2-529 Houston TX 77058-1002

MCGUIRE, EDWARD DAVID, JR., lawyer; b. Waynesboro, Va., Apr. 11, 1948; s. Edward David and Mary Estelle (Angus) McG.; m. Georgia Ann Charuhas, Aug. 15, 1971; children: Matthew Edward, Kathryn Ann. BS in Commerce, U. Va., 1970; JD, Coll. William and Mary, 1973. Bar: Va. 1973, D.C. 1974, Md. 1990, Pa. 1995, U.S. Dist. Ct. (ea. dist.) Va. 1974, U.S. Dist. Ct. D.C. 1974, U.S. Dist. Ct. Md. 1990, Ct. Appeals (4th cir.) 1974, U.S. Ct. Appeals (D.C. cir.) 1974, U.S. Supreme Ct. 1993. Assoc. Wilkes and Artis, Washington, 1973-78; gen. corp counsel Mark Winkler Mgmt., Alexandria, Va., 1978-80; sr. contracts officer Amtrak, Washington, 1980-81; sr. real estate atty., asst. corp. sec. Peoples Drug Stores, Inc., Alexandria, 1981-88; of counsel Cowles, Rinaldi & Arnold, Ltd., Fairfax, Va., 1989-91; sr. assoc. Radigan, Rosenberg & Holmes, Arlington, Va., 1991; pvt. practice, Annandale, Va., 1992—. Bd. dirs. Dist. XVI Va. Student Aid Found., 1978-85, George Washington dist. Boy Scouts Am., 1986; active William and Mary Law Sch. Assn., bd. dirs., pres., 1987-88, treas., 1990-91. Capt. JAGC, USANG, 1973-79. Mem. ABA, Va. Bar Assn., Va. State Bar, D.C. Bar, Md. State Bar Assn., Fairfax Bar Assn., Arlington County Bar Assn., Va. Trial Lawyers Assn., Nat. Network Estate Planning Attys., William and Mary Alumni Soc. (bd. dirs. D.C. chpt. treas. 1992-94), U. Va. Club of Washington (schs. com. chmn. 1995—), Rotary (treas. Springfield chpt. 1985-86, sec. 1986-87, pres.-elect 1987, chmn. World Affairs Conf. 1985-88, 93-94, Dist. 7610 youth leadership awards chmn. 1994—, Outstanding Rotarian award 1985). Greek Orthodox. Home: 31 W Myrtle St Alexandria VA 22301-2422 Office: 4306 Evergreen Ln Ste 103 Annandale VA 22003-3217

MCGUIRE, JOHN ALBERT, dentist; b. Warren, Ohio, June 20, 1950; s. Bernard Leo and Lucille Ann (Guarnieri) McG.; m. Pamela Kay Muter, May 30, 1969; children: John, Jessica. BS, Ohio State U., 1972, DDS, 1975. Dentist, capt. USAF, Bellevue, Nebr., 1975-77; dentist pvt. practice Dayton, Tenn., 1977-83, Knoxville, Tenn., 1983—. Author: (short story) Stirs, 1990. Mem. Sertoma Club, Knoxville, 1983-86, Jaycees, Dayton, 1978-81; vol. United Meth. Ch., Tilaran, Costa Rica, 1985. Recipient Scholarship, Fred M. Roddy Found., 1990. Mem. Phi Kappa Phi. Home: 301 Grandeur Dr Knoxville TN 37920-6325 Office: 6017 Chapman Hwy Knoxville TN 37920-5932

MCGUIRE, KATIE ELIZABETH, dancer, choreographer, performing company executive; b. Dallas, Mar. 28, 1946; d. Alfred G. and Gladys N. (Horn) McG. BFA cum laude, So. Meth. U., 1971, MFA, 1977; postgrad. dance divsn., U. Utah, 1971-72. Dir./founder Katie McGuire's Creative Dance Theatre, Inc., Berkeley, Calif., 1978-91, Mendocino, Calif., 1988-91, Dallas, 1991—; mem. faculty dance, Children's Creative Dance U. Utah, Salt Lake City, 1972, U. Alaska, Fairbanks, summer 1989; guest tchr. Mills Coll., Goucher Coll., U. N.D., Towson Coll., U. Calif., Berkeley and Hayward, Tex. Tech U., N.D. State U.; cons. Calif. Arts Commn., San Francisco Mus. Art; dance therapist Oakland (Calif.) Children's Hosp., Berkeley Psychomatic Inst., Calif. Assn. Neurologically Handicapped; cons. dance specialist Artists in Schs. NEA 1972-79; lectr. Calif. Dance Educators Assn., Calif. Assn. Neurologically Handicapped Children-Good Teaching Practices Conf., 1975, 76, N.D. State Legislature, 1974. Choreographer (modern dance) Pendulums, 1975-76, Orbits, 1991, (dance theatre prodns.) Roses are Red, Broadway Dreams, Oz Fantasy, Jazzy Nutcrackers, 1993-96; tv prodr. Seaside Village, 1993, A Dancer Prepares, 1994; prodr., moderator tv show Art Cafe, 1995-96. Mem. Dallas Dance Coun. Mem. ASCAP, Artists Helping Artists. Office: Creative Dance Theatre Inc 3610 N Josey Ln # 207 Carrollton TX 75007-3150

MCGUIRE, SANDRA LYNN, nursing educator; b. Flint, Mich., Jan. 28, 1947; d. Donald Armstrong and Mary Lue (Harvey) Johnson; m. Joseph L. McGuire, Mar. 6, 1976; children: Matthew, Kelly, Kerry. BS in Nursing, U. Mich., 1969, MPH, 1973, EdD, 1988. Staff nurse Univ. Hosp., Ann Arbor, Mich., 1969; pub. health nurse Wayne County Health Dept., Eloise, Mich., 1969-72; instr. Madonna Coll., Livonia, Mich., 1973; pub. health coord. Plymouth Ctr. for Human Devel., Northville, Mich., 1974-75; asst. prof. cmty. health nursing U. Mich., Ann Arbor, 1975-83; asst. prof. U. Tenn., Knoxville, 1983-88, assoc. prof., 1990—; dir. Kids Are Tomorrow's Srs. Program, 1988—; resource person Gov.'s Com. Unification of Mental Health Services in Mich.; speaker profl. assns. and workshops; bd. dirs. Ctr. Understanding Aging, 1987-93, v.p. 1995—. Author: (with S. Clemen-Stone and D. Eigsti) Comprehensive Family and Community Health Nursing, 1981, 4th edit. 1995. Bd. dirs. Mich. chpt. ARC, 1980-83, Knoxville chpt., 1984-85; founder Knoxville Intergenerational Network, 1989. USPHS fellow, 1972-73, Robert Woodruff fellow, Emory U., 1996—. Mem. APHA, ANA, Tenn. Nurses Assn., Nat. League Nursing, Tenn. League Nursing, Tenn. Pub. Health Assn., (chmn. mental health sect. 1976) Mich. Pub. Health Assn. (dir., co-chmn. residential services com. 1976-79, chmn. health services 1979-82), Nat. Coun. on Aging, Ctr. for Understanding Aging (v.p., 1994-95), Plymouth (chmn. residential services com. 1975-77) Tenn. Assn. Retarded Citizens, So. Nursing Rsch. Soc., Sigma Theta Tau, Pi Lambda Theta, Phi Kappa Phi. Home: 11008 Crosswind Dr Knoxville TN 37922-4011 Office: 1200 Volunteer Blvd Knoxville TN 37916-3806

MCHALE, MICHAEL JOHN, lawyer; b. N.Y.C., Apr. 14, 1960; s. Michael Joseph and Mary Beatrice (Graddy) McH. BA, U. of the South, 1982; JD, Samford U., 1985. Bar: Ala. 1986, U.S. Dist. Ct. (no., mid. and so. dists.) Ala. 1986, U.S. Ct. Appeals (11th cir.) 1986, Fla. (cert. admiralty and maritime law) 1991, U.S. Dist. Ct. (mid. and so. dists.) 1991, U.S. Supreme Ct. 1991; cert. admiralty and maritime lawyer. Assoc. Wagner, Nugent, Johnson, Roth, Romano, Eriksen & Kupfer, West Palm Beach, Fla., 1989-92; ptnr. Whalen & McHale, West Palm Beach, Fla., 1992-95, Daves, Whalen, McHale & Considine, West Palm Beach, Fla., 1995—. Author: Strategic Use of Circumstantial Evidence, 2nd edit., 1991, Evaluating and Settling Personal Injury Claims, 1992, supplement through present, Making Trial Objections, 1993, supplement through present, Expert Witnesses: Direct and Cross Examination, 1993, supplement through present; editor, author: Litigating TMJ Cases, 1993 and yearly supplements. Named one of Outstanding Young Men of Am., 1988. Mem. ABA (mem. admiralty com.), ATLA, Am. Acad. Fla. Trial Lawyers, Maritime Law Assn. U.S., Southeastern Admiralty Law Inst., Fla. Bar (admiralty law com. editl. bd.), Palm Beach Bar Assn., Sigma Nu Phi. Home: 23018-D Oxford Pl Boca Raton FL 33433 Office: Daves Whalen McHale & Considine 301 Clematis St Ste 200 West Palm Beach FL 33401-4601

MCHENRY, WILLIAM IRVIN, marketing executive; b. Gary, Ind., July 25, 1949; s. Chester Marion and Charlotte M. (Hamilton) McH.; m. Karen Anne Day, Sept. 1, 1973; 1 child, Kristine Lynn. BS in Aero. and Astronautical Engring., Purdue U., 1971; MS in Systems Mgmt., U. So. Calif., 1978. Sr. engr. Gen. Dynamics, Ft. Worth, Tex., 1980-81, project engr., 1981-82, mktg. mgr., 1982-85, dir. program devel., 1990-94; dir. mktg. Lockheed (purchased Gen. Dynamics), Ft. Worth, 1985-90. Mem. adminstrv. bd. Trinity United Meth. Ch., Arlington, Tex., 1989-92, 94—. Comdr. USN, 1971-79, PTO. Home: 7203 Saquaro Lake Ct Arlington TX 76016-4154 Office: Lockheed Martin Co Lockheed Blvd Fort Worth TX 76101

MCHUGH, ELIZABETH ANN, infection control occupational health nurse; b. Hazleton, Pa., Apr. 9, 1934; d. Stephen and Elizabeth (Shinko) Machesko; m. Edward J. McHugh, June 15, 1957. BS, Coll. St. Francis, Joliet, Ill., 1985; postgrad., Hunter Coll., N.Y.C. Staff nurse surg. svcs. Union Meml. Hosp., Balt.; staff nurse operating rm. Greater Balt. Med. Ctr., Towson, Md.; dir. staff devel.-social svcs. Guest House of Slidell (La.); coord. infection control-employee health AMI Highland Park Hosp., Covington, La., Slidell (La.) Meml. Hosp., 1989-93; nurse infection control/employee health Lakeview Regional Med. Ctr., Mendeville, La., 1993-95; pvt. cons. infection control/employee health issues Slidell, 1995—; mem. Speakers' Bur. on Infection Control; contract QM nurse So. La. Hosp., Manderville, La., 1995—. Bd. dirs. Northlake AIDS Network. Mem. ANA, Assn. Practitioners in Infection Control (past pres. Greater New Orleans chpt.).

MCHUGH, THOMAS EDWARD, state supreme court justice; b. Charleston, W.Va., Mar. 26, 1936; s. Paul and Melba McHugh; m. Judith McHugh, Mar. 14, 1959; children: Karen, Cindy, James, John. AB, W.Va. U., 1958, LLB, 1964. Bar: W.Va. 1964. Pvt. practice law Charleston, 1964-66, 69-74; law clk. to presiding judge Harlan Calhoun W.Va. Supreme Ct. of Appeals, 1966-68; chief judge Cir. Ct. (13th cir.) W.Va., Charleston, 1974-80; assoc. justice W.Va. Supreme Ct., Charleston, 1980—; chief justice W. Va Supreme Ct, Charleston, WV, 1984, 88, 92—. Served to 1st lt. U.S. Army, 1958-61. Mem. W.Va. Jud. Assn., W.Va. Bar Assn., Order of the Coif. Democrat. Roman Catholic. Office: WVa Supreme Ct East Wing Rm 302 State Capitol Charleston WV 25305-0001*

MCHUGH-BARBEN, KAREN LYNNE, architectural resource consultant; b. Tacoma, Wash., Feb. 21, 1960; d. Thomas Edward and Judith (Hill) McHugh. BS, W.Va. U., 1982. Resource coordinator GN Design Assocs., N.Y.C., 1982-88; prin. Archtl. Resources, Inc., Winter Haven, Fla., 1988-91; designer Straughn-Furr Assocs., Lakeland, Fla., 1991-92; interior designer Fla., 1992—. Mem. Am. Soc. Interior Designers, Inst. Bus. Designers, Assn. Resource Specialists (founding mem.). Republican. Presbyterian. Home: PO Box 219 Avon Park FL 33826-0219 Office: PO Box 1846 135 Main St Dundee FL 33825

MCILMOIL, L. N., association executive; b. Jacksonville, Fla., Mar. 12, 1948; s. Neil William and Margaret E. (Wright) M.; children: Neil William II, Tara Alana, Rory Devin, Colin Shea. BS, Western Ill. U., 1985. Dir. mem. svcs. Metal Treating Inst., Jacksonville Beach, 1988—. Bob Fossee scholar Fla. Soc. Assn. Execs., 1996. Office: Metal Treating Inst 1550 Roberts Dr Jacksonville Beach FL 32250

MCILROY, WILMER LEE, chamber of commerce executive; b. Louisiana, Mo., Aug. 30, 1931; s. Wilmer Lee and Julia Beth (Whiteside) McI.; m. Margareta Anna Forster, Aug. 14, 1958; children: Robert Lee, Anne McIlroy Wilson. BS, U.S. Mil. Acad., 1955; MPA, Shippensburg (Pa.) State Coll., 1975. Commd. 2d lt. U.S. Army, 1955, advanced through grades to col., 1976; served in U.S. Army, Korea and Vietnam, others; ret. U.S. Army, 1980; membership dir. S.C. C. of C., Columbia, 1980-85, sr. v.p., gen. mgr., 1985-94; pres. McIlroy & Assocs., Columbia, 1994—; sec.-treas. S.C. Travel and Tourism Forum, Columbia, 1986-94. Mem. Assn. Membership Execs. (pres. 1984-85), S.C. Assn. C. of C. Execs. (sec.-treas. 1980-94, Richland Sertoma Club (pres. 1989-90), Assn. U.S. Army, Ret. Officers Assn., Spl. Forces Assn. Presbyterian. Home and Office: 2401 Bermuda Hills Rd Columbia SC 29223-6825

MCILVEEN, WALTER RONALD, architectural engineer; b. London, Sept. 9, 1950; came to U.S., 1959; s. Walter and Margaret Theresa (Ruane) McI.; m. Barbara Lee O'Neill, June 8, 1974 (div. June 1993); 1 child, Daniel Walter. BS in Mech. Engring., Worcester (Mass.) Poly. Inst., 1972; MS in Mech. Engring., Rensselaer Poly. Inst., Hartford, Conn., 1975; MBA, Wayne State U., 1979. Registered profl. engr., Conn., Fla., Tenn., Ga., Mich., Ala. Design engr. Walter McIlveen Assocs., Avon, Conn., 1972-77, project engr., 1977; project engr. Smith Hinchman & Grylls Assocs., Detroit, 1977-78, divsn. discipline head, 1978-81; divsn. mgr. Diaz Seckinger Assocs., Tampa, 1981-84; chief mech. and elec. engr. Archtl. Engring. Inc., Palm Harbor, Fla., 1984—; pres. Archtl. Engrs., Inc., Palm Harbor, 1993—. Mem. ASHRAE, NSPE, Nat. Fire Protection Assn., Nat. Coun. Engring. Examiners, Inc., So. Bldg. Code Congress Internat. Inc., Greater Tampa C. of C. Leadership Tampa. Republican. Roman Catholic. Home: 3526 Shoreline Cir Palm Harbor FL 34684-1743 Office: Archtl Engring Inc 3442 E Lake Rd Palm Harbor FL 34685-2406

MCILWAIN, CLARA EVANS, agricultural economist, consultant; b. Jacksonville, Fla., Apr. 5, 1919; d. Waymon and Jerusha Lee (Dickson) Evans; m. Ivy McIlwain, May 15, 1942 (dec. 1987); children: Ronald E., Carol A. McIlwain Edwards, Marilyn E. McIlwain Ross, Ivy J. McIlwain Lindsay. BS, U. D.C., 1939; M Agrl. Econs., U. Fla., 1972. Notary pub., Va.; lic. life and health ins. agt., Md., Va., D.C. Statis. asst. Hist. and Statis. Analysis Div., Washington, 1962-67; statistician Econ Devel. Div. USDA, Washington, 1967-70, 72, agrl. economist, 1972-74; program analyst Office Equal Opportunity, USDA, Washington, 1974-79; staff writer Sci. Weekly, Chevy Chase, Md., 1988-89; ins. agt. A.L. Williams, Primerica, Camp Springs, Md., 1990—; workshop coord. Author: Steps to Eloquence, 1989; contbr. to profl. publs. Coord., instr. Youth Leadership and Speechcraft, Toastmasters Internat., Washington area, 1972-78; tchr., bd. dirs. Sat. Tutorial Enrichment Program, Arlington, Va., 1988-89; mem. network Christian women, mem. women's fellowship com. Christ Fellowship Ministries. Rockefeller Found. scholar, 1970-72. Mem. Toastmasters Internat. (past pres. Potomac Club, Gavel award 1976, Able Toastmaster award 1978), Am. Assn. Notaries, So. Assn. Agrl. Economists, Nat. Assn. Agrl. Econs., Internat. Platform Assn. Office: Evans Unlimited 8350 Greensboro Dr Mc Lean VA 22102-3533

MCINERNEY, MICHAEL JOSEPH, microbiology educator; b. Chgo., Feb. 5, 1952; s. Joseph Thomas and Della (Morris) McI.; m. Cynthia Francis Reyner, Aug. 17, 1974; children: Mary Christine, Matthew Joseph. BS in Biology summa cum laude, No. Ill. U., 1973; MS in Microbiology, U. Ill., 1977, PhD in Microbiology, 1980. Asst. ecologist Dames and Moore Environ. Cons., Park Ridge, Ill., 1973-75; teaching asst. U. Ill., Urbana, 1975-76, rsch. asst., 1976-79; post-doctoral rsch. assoc. U. Ga., Athens, 1979-81; asst. prof. U. Okla., Norman, 1981-87, assoc. prof., 1987-92, prof., 1992—; grant reviewer, mem. rev. panel U.S. Dept. Energy, 1989—; ad hoc reviewer Bioengring. and Biotech., Environ. Sci. and Tech., 1992-93; Assocs. Disting. lectr. U. Okla., Norman, 1985-86, 86-87, 88-89; panelist NSF, 1990-91. Vol. editor: Manual for Environmental Microbiology, 1992-93; mem. editorial bd. Applied and Environ. Microbiology, 1986—; author book chpts., govtl. reports, conf. procs. and jour. articles. Coach Norman Youth Soccer Assn., 1990—. Recipient Ill. State scholarship, U. Ill. fellowship, Watts scholarship award, Superior Teaching award U. Okla. Bd. Regents, Norman, 1991, Rsch. and Creative Activity award U. Okla. Bd. Regents, Norman, 1993; Sarkey's Energy Ctr. fellow U. Okla., 1991-92. Mem. Am. Soc. Microbiology (judge student paper competition 1988-89, session chair at ann. meeting 1991-92, 92-93, mem. Sci. Edn. Network), Sigma Xi (Rsch. award). Home: 4513 Briarcrest Dr Norman OK 73072-3419 Office: Univ of Okla Dept Botany and Microbiology 770 Van Vleet Oval Norman OK 73019-6130

MCINTEER, JIM BILL, minister, publishing executive, farmer; b. Franklin, Ky., June 16, 1921; s. William Thomas and Mary Edna (Rutherford) McI.; m. Betty Bergner, July 20, 1943; children: MariLynn McInteer Canterbury, Mark Martin. Cert., David Lipscomb Coll., Nashville, 1940; BA, Harding U., 1942; LLD (hon.), Pepperdine U., 1980, Harding U., 1991; degree (hon.) Okla. Christian Coll. Ordained to ministry Ch. of Christ, 1938. Minister Ch. of Christ, Sheridan, Ark., 1942-46, Isabel, Kans., 1947, Locust Grove, Ky., 1948-52, Grace Ave. Ch., Nashville, 1952-56, West End Ch., Nashville, 1956-86; nat. evangalist, 1986—; bus. mgr., pres., pub. 20th Century Christian, Nashville, 1947—; farmer, Franklin,, 1948—. Author: Tiny Tot's Bible Reader, 1956, Great Preachers of Today, 1966. Bd. dirs. Harding U., Searcy, Ark., 1950—, Potter Children's Home, Bowling Green, Ky., 1960—, Fanning Found., Nashville, 1975—, Campbell Trust Fund, Nashville, 1978—. Recipient Alumnus of Yr. award David Lipscomb Coll., 1985, Diakonia award David Lipscomb U., 1990, Disting. Christian Svc. award Pepperdine U., 1991, Disting. Alumnus award Harding U.; named Christian Writer of Yr., Okla. Christian Coll. Mem. SAR. Lodge: Civitan Internat. (dist. chaplain 1975). Avocations: photography, woodcutting, vegetable gardening. Home: 1100 Belvedere Dr Nashville TN 37204-3916 Office: 20th Century Christian Inc 2809 Granny White Pike Nashville TN 37204-2507

MCINTIRE, WESLEY KEVIN, private investigator; b. Dallas, Oct. 22, 1958. AS, Collin County C.C., Plano, Tex., 1994. Chief investigator McIntire & Assoc., Plano, 1978—. Republican. Home and Office: McIntire & Assoc PO Box 861870 Plano TX 75086-1870

MCINTOSH, DENNIS KEITH, veterinary practitioner, consultant; b. Newark, June 12, 1941; s. Sheldon Weeks and Enid Nicholson (Casey) McI.; m. Rachel McIntosh; children: Rebecca, Kevin, Jamie. BS in Animal Sci., Tex. A&M U., 1963, BS in Vet. Sci., 1967, DVM, 1968. Asst. county agrl. agt., Cleburne, Tex., 1963-65; owner, operator Park North Animal Hosp., San Antonio, 1970-75, El Dorado Animal Hosp., San Antonio, 1973—; co-chmn. vet. tech. adv. coun. Palo Alto Coll. tchr. Animal Health Tech., San Antonio Coll., 1985-95; pres., mgr. Bexar County Emergency Animal Clinic, Inc., 1978-81; cons. vet. practice mgmt., mktg., client relations; speaker for vet. meetings, assns.; vet. mem. Tex. Bd. Health, 1984-89, chmn. disease control com., personnel com.; mem. environ. health, hosps. com. Team capt. Alamo Roundup Club and Pres.' Club of San Antonio C. of C., 1970-75; mem. Guadalupe County Youth Fair Bd., 1978-80; 1st v.p. No. Hills Lions Club, 1972-73. Served with Vet. Corps, USAF, 1968-70. Recipient Alumnus award Guadalupe County 4-H Club, 1979, Outstanding Service award San Antonio Coll., 1986-87, Outstanding Bus. Ptnrs. award N.E. Ind. Sch. Dsit., 1995-96. Mem. Tex. Vet. Med. Assn. (pres., chmn. bd.), Tex. Acad. Vet. Practice (pres.), Am. Assn. Human-Animal Bond Vets., AVMA, Vet. Hosp. Mgrs. Assn., San Antonio C. of C. (Life), Tex. County Agrl. Agts. Assn. (4th v.p. 1964), Delta Soc. (pres. San Antonio chpt. 1989-90). Contbr. articles to profl. jours. Office: 13039 Nacogdoches Rd San Antonio TX 78217-1960

MCINTOSH, JOSEPH WILLIAM, health administration consultant; b. Marion, Ind., July 1, 1936; s. Joseph Dawson and Maxine A. (Coffel) McI.; children: Mark Joseph, Marchelle Dawn. AB, U. Indpls., 1958; MS in Pub. Health, U. N.C., 1959; D of Health Sci., Ind. U., 1970; MS, Troy (Ala.) State U., 1983. Cert. health edn. specialist. adminstr. Dept. Pub. Health/Health and Hosp. Corp., Indpls., 1959-70; pub.health cons. Inst. Community and Area Devel., U. Ga., Athens, 1970-73; asst. prof. health edn. U. Ga., Athens, 1970—; chair dept. allied health Columbus (Ga.) Coll., 1973—, dir. Regional Health Professions Edn. Ctr., 1970. Author project report and monograph. Bd. dirs. Wagon Wheel Gun Club, Geneva, Ga., 1975-85, Columbus Symphony, 1983-90; ombudsman West Ctrl. Ga. Coun. on Aging, Columbus, 1983-85. Named to Outstanding Young Men of Am., 1968. Mem. Natural Resource Def. Fund, Nat. Environ. Health Assn., Ind. Environ. Health Assn. Office: Wellness Assocs 2850 Hamilton Rd Columbus GA 31904-8739

MCINTOSH, MICHAEL LORENZO, principal; b. Raeford, N.C., Dec. 24, 1960; s. Mabel Elizabeth McIntosh; m. Sofia Silverthorne McIntosh, June 17, 1990; 1 child, Jennell Sharise. BA, U. N.C., 1983; MS, N.C. A&T State U., 1992; DEd, U. N.C., 1996. Cert. tchr., N.C. Tchr., counselor Upward Bound Program, Chapel Hill, N.C., 1985-87; counselor Boys & Girls Club, Charlotte, N.C., 1987-88; tchr. Char/Mecklenburg Schs., Charlotte, 1988-90, Gilford County Schs., Greensboro, N.C., 1990-92; counselor Ednl. Talent Search, Columbia, S.C., 1992-93; lead tchr. Phoenix Alternative Sch., Danville, Va., 1993-94; prin. Noel C. Taylor Learning Acad., Roanoke, Va.,

1994—; cons. Ednl. Concepts, Greensboro, 1990-96. Bible study instr. Newlight Bapt. Ch., Greensboro, N.C., 1994-95; tutor, vol. Fairfield Sr. H.S., Winnsboro, S.C., 1992-93; fin. aid workshop presenter Ednl. Concepts, S.C., Va., N.C., 1989-96. With U.S. Army, 1983-85. Recipient Coach of Yr. Char/Meck Athletic Assn., 1989. Mem. NEA, Nat. Alliance Black Sch. Educators, Va. Educators Assn., Nat. Assn. of Secondary Prins., Phi Beta Sigma. Home: 4415 Brandt Ridge Dr Greensboro NC 27410

MCINTOSH, ROBERTA EADS, retired social worker; b. Milw., Oct. 1, 1936; d. Robert Howard and Carlene (Rosboro) Eads; m. James Stuart Cameron McIntosh, Sept. 19, 1959; children: Ronald Stuart, Ian Robert, Peter Cameron. BA, Bucknell U., 1958; MS in Social Adminstrn., Case Western Reserve U., 1977. Lic. social worker, Ohio, Fla. Foster care caseworker Monroe County Child Welfare, Rochester, N.Y., 1958-63; group home counselor Betterway, Inc., Elyria, Ohio, 1974-75; group program coord. Elyria YWCA, 1975; caseworker, group home supr. Lorain County Children's Svcs., Elyria, 1977-83; treatment counselor Glenbeigh Adolescent Hosp., Cleve., 1984-86; youth dir. Washington Ave. Christian Ch., Elyria, 1984-85; outreach counselor Spouse Abuse Shelter Religious Community Svcs., Clearwater, Fla., 1986-93; pvt. practice Dunedin, Fla., 1993—; expert witness in domestic violence. Bd. pres. Elyria YWCA, 1972-75; sec., pres. Community Coordinated Child Care, Lorain County, 1970-72. Named Friend of Guidance Guidance Counselors Assn., 1982, Woman of Interest Elyria YWCA & City of Elyria, 1985. Mem. NASW, Acad. Cert. Social Workers, Fla. Coalition Against Domestic Violence (v.p. bd. 1993-94), Nat. Coalition Against Domestic Violence, Leadership Pinellas, Deaf Svc. Ctr. (bd. dirs. 1991-94), Victim Rights Coalition Pinellas County (v.p. bd. 1992-93), Fla. Network Victim Witness Svcs., Ctrl. Christian Ch. Christian Womens Fellowship (pres. 1988-90), Delta Zeta. Democrat. Home: 1501 Pleasant Grove Dr Dunedin FL 34698-2341 Office: PO Box 32 Dunedin FL 34697-0032

MCINTOSH, RUTH LYNNE, maternal, pediatric nurse; b. Mexico City, Mar. 8, 1956; came to the U.S., 1956; d. John Baldwin and Cordelia Genevieve (Hartshorn) McI. Student, LeTourneau U., 1975-78; BSN cum laude, U. Tex., Arlington, 1980, postgrad., 1981; postgrad., Our Lady of the Lake U., 1991. RN, Tex., Calif. Staff nurse newborn nursery Grim-Smith Hosp., Kirksville, Mo., 1980; staff nurse ICU Grim-Smith Hosp., Kirksville, 1981; staff nurse med.-surg. Intercommunity Hosp., Arlington, Tex., 1981-82; staff nurse post partum unit David Grant USAF Med. Ctr., Travis AFB, Calif., 1982; staff nurse combined obstet. unit George AFB Hosp., Victorville, Calif., 1986; asst. dept. nursing edn. Wilford Hall USAF Med. Ctr., Lackland AFB, Tex., 1987; cons. mil. med. care Concerned Ams. for Mil. Improvements, Pompano, Fla., 1988—; mem., RN cons. Fibromyalgia Support Group, San Antonio, 1991—, Chronic Pain Support Group, San Antonio, 1992—; demo artist All Night Media Rubber Stamps, San Raphael, Calif.; instr. (2) craft classes Lackland AFB Skills Devel. Ctr., Northside Ind. Sch. Dist. Adult Cmty. Edn. Mem. Calvary Ch., Santa Ana, Calif., 1980—; RN, vol. ARC, Travis AFB and Lackland AFB, 1984, 87-92; mem. air transportable hosp. team 831st Combat Support Group, George AFB, Calif., 1986. 1st lt. USAF, 1982-91. Mem. Soc. Ret. Air Force Nurses (outreach com. 1987-88), Endometriosis Assn., Air Force Assn. (life), Am. Legion, Disabled Am. Vets., Sigma Theta Tau. Republican. Baptist. Home: 7407 Micron Dr San Antonio TX 78251-2103

MCINTYRE, CHARLES EARL, insurance executive; b. L.A., Mar. 28, 1944; s. Donald Earl and Helen (Walker) McI.; m. Linda W. McIntyre, Oct. 17, 1969; children: Amanda, Margaret. BA, U. Redlands, Calif., 1966. CLU, ChFC. With Ray C. Watson Co., L.A., 1966-70; dir. human resources Leadership Housing, Newport Beach, Calif., 1970-75; agt. Northwestern Mut. Life, Ft. Lauderdale, Fla., 1975-80, dist. agt., 1980-85, gen. agt., 1985—. Bd. dirs. Bonnet House, Ft. Lauderdale, 1993—; bd. advisors Fla. Atlantic U., Ft. Lauderdale, 1994. Mem. Gen. Agts. and Mgrs. Assn. (pres. 1989-90, Master Agy. award 1987—), Gen. Agts. Assn. (bd. dirs. 1988—), Broward County Life Underwriters, Chartered Life Underwriters Assn. Republican. Episcopalian. Office: Northwestern Mutual Life 2101 W Commercial Blvd Ste 5100 Fort Lauderdale FL 33309-3055

MCINTYRE, DOUGLAS CARMICHAEL, II, lawyer; b. Lumberton, N.C., Aug. 6, 1956; s. Douglas Carmichael and Thelma Riley (Hedgpeth) McI.; m. Lola Denise Strickland, June 26, 1982; children: Joshua Carmichael, Stephen Christopher. BA, U. N.C., 1978, JD, 1981. Bar: N.C. 1981, U.S. Dist. Ct. (ea. dist.) N.C. 1984, U.S. Dist. Ct. (mid. dist.) N.C. 1985, U.S. Ct. Appeals (4th cir.) 1987, U.S. Supreme Ct., 1987. Assoc. Law Office Bruce Huggins, Lumberton, 1981-82, McLean, Stacy, Henry & McLean, Lumberton, 1982-86; ptnr. Price & McIntyre P.A., Lumberton, 1987-89; prin. McIntyre Law Firm, P.A., Lumberton, 1989—; mem. law-focused edn. adv. com. N.C. Dept. Pub. Instrn., 1986-87. Del. Dem. Nat. Conv., N.Y.C., 1980, N.C. Dems., Raleigh, 1974—; pres. Robeson County Young Dems., Lumberton, 1982; sec.-treas. 7th Congl. Dist. Young Dems., N.C., 1983, chmn., 1984; 2d vice chmn. 7th Congl. Dist. Dems. So. N.C., 1986-89, 1st vice chmn., 1989; mem. state adv. bd. North Carolinians Against Drug and Alcohol Abuse, Raleigh, 1984-85; chmn. Morehead Scholarship Selection Com., Robeson County, 1985-94; deacon, elder Presbyn. Ch.; active Boy Scouts Am., Lumberton, 1983; mem. N.C. Commn. on Children and Youth, 1987-89, N.C. Commn. on the Family, 1989-91; mem. Young Life Lumberton com., 1987-89; chmn. Robeson County U.S. Constn. Bicentennial com., 1986-87; mem. lawyers' adv. com. to N.C. Commn. on Bicentennial of U.S. Constn., 1986-89; bd. dirs. Robeson County Group Home, Lumberton, 1984-87, Lumberton Econ. Advancement for Downtown, Inc., 1987-90, pres., 1988-89, 89-90; chmn. legis. affairs com. C. of C., 1991, 92, 93, bd. dirs., 1992-94; mem. N.C. Mus. of History Assocs., 1987-89; mem. regional selection com. Gov.'s Award for Excellence in Teaching Social Studies, 1991. Morehead Found. scholar, 1974-78; named one of Outstanding Young Men in Am., 1981, 84, 85, 88; Outstanding Young Dem. Robeson County Young Dems., 1984-85; one of State's Outstanding Young Dems. Young Dems. N.C., 1984, 85; recipient Algernon Sydney Sullivan award U. N.C., 1978, Outstanding Young North Carolinian award N.C. Jaycees, 1988, Outstanding Young North Carolinians, Heart Robeson Jaycees, 1988, Nat. Bicentennial Leadership award for Individual Achievement Coun. for Advancement of Citizenship and Ctr. for Civic Edn., Washington, 1987, Gov.'s Outstanding Vol. Svc. award, 1989. Mem. ABA (exec. com. citizenship edn. com. 1985-87, nat. cmty. law week com. 1982-83), Internat. Platform Assn., N.C. Bar Assn. (chmn. youth edn. and constn. bicentennial com. 1986-87, youth edn. com., exec. coun. young lawyers divsn. 1986-87), Robeson County Bar Assn. (founder, chmn. citizenship edn. com. 1982—, law day com.), 16th Jud. Dist. Bar Assn., N.C. Acad. Trial Lawyers, N.C. Coll. Advocacy, Christian Legal Soc. (state adv. bd. 1986-90, state pres. 1987), Lumberton C. of C. (bd. dirs. 1992-94), Order of Old Well, Lumberton Rotary Club (bd. dirs. 1995-96), Phi Beta Kappa, Phi Eta Sigma. Home: 1701 N Chestnut St Lumberton NC 28358-3839 Office: 102 Elizabethtown Rd Lumberton NC 28358-4856

MCINTYRE, JOHN ARMIN, physics educator; b. Seattle, June 2, 1920; s. Harry John and Florence (Armin) McI.; m. Madeleine Forsman, June 15, 1947; 1 son, John Forsman. B.S., U. Wash., 1943; M.A., Princeton U., 1948, Ph.D., 1950. Mem. faculty elec. engring. Carnegie Inst. Tech., Pitts., 1943; radio engr. Westinghouse Elec. Co., Balt., 1944; research asso. Stanford, 1950-57; mem. faculty Yale, 1957-63, asso. prof., 1960-63; prof. physics Tex. A&M U., College Station, 1963-95, emeritus prof., 1995—; asso. dir. Cyclotron Inst., 1965-70; Mem. council Oak Ridge Assn. Univs., 1964-71. Fellow Am. Phys. Soc., Am. Sci. Affiliation (exec. council 1968-73); mem. AAAS. Presbyn. Home: 2316 Bristol St Bryan TX 77802-2405 Office: Tex A&M U Dept Physics College Station TX 77843

MCINTYRE, RICHARD RAWLINGS, II, elementary school educator; b. Houston, Nov. 20, 1946; s. Richard Rawlings and Emma Ruth (Blossom) McI.; m. Bonnie Antoinette Kimball, Dec. 23, 1973; 1 child, Richard Rawlings III. BA in History, Trinity U., San Antonio, 1969; MEd, Columbus (Ga.) Coll., 1983. Cert. tchr., phys. edn. coach, tech. specialist. Mgmt. trainee Deering Miliken, Manchester, Ga., 1972; tchr. Meriwether County Pub. Schs., Manchester, 1972—; instr. adult edn., Greenville, Ga., 1985-89. Editor newsletter Per Ardua, 1985-91. Coord. Jump Rope for Heart, Am. Heart Assn., Manchester Elem. Sch., 1985—; del. State Dem. Convs.; mem. State Dem. Com., 1990—; pres. Meriwether County Heart Assn, 1991-92. Capt. U.S. Army, 1969-72, Vietnam. Decorated Bronze Star; Nat. Presbyn. scholar, 1965-67. Mem. Meriwether Assn. Educators (past pres., treas., pres. 1996-98), Ga. Assn. Educators (chmn. state spelling bee com. 1987—, legis. contact team and polit. action com.), NEA, Ga. Supporters of Gifted, Warm Springs Merchants Assn. (pres. 1993-95), Jaycees, Clan MacIntyre Assn. (treas. 1994-96), Scottish Am. Mil. Soc. Home: RR 1 Box 175A Woodland GA 31836-9719 Office: Manchester Elem Sch 201 Perry St Manchester GA 31816-1347

MCINTYRE-IVY, JOAN CAROL, data processing executive; b. Portchester, N.Y., Mar. 1, 1939; d. John Henry and Molly Elizabeth (Gates) Daugherty; m. Stanley Donald McIntyre, Aug. 24, 1957 (div. Jan. 1986); children: Michael Stanley, David John, Sharon Lynne; m. James Morrow Ivy IV, June 1, 1988. Student, Northwestern U., 1956-57, U. Ill., 1957-58. Assoc. editor Writer's Digest, Cin., 1966-68; instr. creative writing U. Ala.-Huntsville, 1975; editor Strode Pubs., Huntsville, 1974-75; paralegal Smith, Huckaby & Graves (now Bradley, Arant, Rose & White), Huntsville, 1976-82; exec. v.p. Micro Craft, Inc., Huntsville, 1982-85, pres., 1985-89, chief exec. officer, chmn. bd., 1989—, also dir. and co-owner. Author numerous computer-operating mans. for law office software, 1978-88; co-author: Alabama and Federal Complaint Forms, 1979; Alabama and Federal Motion and Order Forms, 1980; also numerous articles, short stories, poems, 1955-88. Editor: Alabama Law for the Layman, 1975. Bd. dirs. Huntsville Lit. Soc., 1976-77. Hon. scholar Medill Sch. Journalism, Northwestern U., 1956. Republican. Methodist. Office: Micro Craft Inc 6703 Odyssey Dr NW Ste 102 Huntsville AL 35806-3308

MCKAY, JOEL GARDNER, Benedictine monk, musician; b. Winchester, Mass., Jan. 17, 1950; s. William Whitford and Freda Coy (Gardner) McK. B in Music, U. N.H., 1972; M in Music, U.vNorth Tex., 1975. Organist and choir dir. The Durham (N.H.) Comm. Ch., 1972-73; chapel organist St. Paul's Sch., Concord, N.H., 1973-76; supply organist N.H., Tex., Fla., 1973-76, 87; organist, choirmaster St. Wilfred's Ch., Sarasota, Fla., 1977-78; sexton Ch. Redeemer, Sarasota, Fla., 1981-86; adminstr. St. Leo Abbey, 1987—, choir master, formation dir., 1994—; dean Sarsota-Manattee Ch. Am. Guild of Organ, Sarsota, 1981-82. Mem. St. Leo Oratorio Soc. (soloist), Gloria Musicae (charter). Home: 33601 SR 52 Saint Leo FL 33574-2007 Office: PO Box 2157 Saint Leo FL 33574-2157

MCKAY, JOHN JUDSON, JR., lawyer; b. Anderson, S.C., Aug. 13, 1939; s. John Judson and Polly (Plowden) McK.; m. Jill Hall Ryon, Aug. 3, 1961 (div. Dec. 1980); children: Julia Plowden, Katherine Henry, William Ryon, Elizabeth Hall; m. Jane Leahey, Feb. 18, 1982; children: Andrew Leahey, Jennifer McFaddin. AB in History, U. S.C., 1960, JD cum laude, 1966. Bar: S.C. 1966, U.S. Dist. Ct. S.C. 1966, U.S. Ct. Appeals (4th cir.) 1974, U.S. Supreme Ct. 1981, U.S. Dist. Ct. (so. dist.) Ga. 1988, U.S. Ct. Appeals (11th cir.), 1990. Assoc. Haynsworth, Perry, Bryant, Marion & Johnstone, Greenville, S.C., 1966-70; ptnr. Rainey, McKay, Britton, Gibbes & Clarkson, P.A., and predecessor, Greenville, 1970-78; sole practice, Hilton Head Island, S.C., 1978-80; ptnr. McKay & Gertz, P.A., Hilton Head Island, 1980-81, McKay & Mullen, P.A., Hilton Head Island, 1981-88, McKay & Taylor, Hilton Head, 1988-91; pvt. practice, 1991—. Served to lt. (j.g.) USNR, 1961-64; lt. comdr. Res. (ret.). Mem. ABA, S.C. Bar Assn. (pres. young lawyers sect. 1970, exec. com. 1971-72, assoc. mem. grievance and disciplinary com. 1983-87), S.C. Bar, Beaufort County Bar Assn., Hilton Head Bar Assn., Assn. Trial Lawyers Am., S.C. Trial Lawyers Assn., S.C. Bar Found. (pres. 1977), Blue Key, Wig and Robe, Phi Delta Phi. Episcopalian. Clubs: Poinsett (Greenville). Editor-in-chief U. S.C. Law Rev., 1966; contbr. articles to legal jours. Home: 17 Foxbriar Ln Hilton Head Island SC 29926 Office: 203 Watersedge Hilton Head Island SC 29928-3541

MCKAY, MARILYNNE, medical educator; b. Tulsa, Sept. 25, 1942; d. Byrd C. and Josephine (Staley) McK.; m. Ronald S. Hosek, Nov. 27, 1980; children: William W., Benjamin R. BS, U. N.Mex., 1964, MD, 1976; MS, Okla. State U., 1965. Diplomate Am. Bd. Dermatology. Intern Mercy Hosp. & Med. Ctr., San Diego; dermatology resident U. Miami/Jackson Meml. Hosp., Miami, Fla.; asst. prof. dermatology Emory U., Atlanta, 1980-85, assoc. prof. dermatology and gynecology, 1985-94, prof. dermatology and gynecology, 1994—; exec. dir. Cont. Med. Edn. & Biomed. Media, Atlanta, 1996—. Editorial bd. The Female Patient, 1989—, Jour. Reproductive Medicine, 1992—, Contemporary Internal Medicine, 1993—. Pres. Interstate Postgrad. Med. Assn., Madison, Wis., 1993. Fellow Am. Acad. Dermatology, Internat. Soc. for Study of Vulvar Disease (sec. gen. 1985-87, 91—); mem. Assn. Profs. of Ob-Gyn., Sherlock Holmes Soc., Womens Dermatology Soc. (bd. dirs. 1996—). Office: Emory Clinic 1365 Clifton Rd NE Atlanta GA 30307-1013

MCKAY, RENEE, artist; b. Montreal, Que., Can.; came to U.S., 1946, naturalized, 1954; d. Frederick Garvin and Mildred Gladys (Higgins) Smith; m. Kenneth Gardiner McKay, July 25, 1942; children: Margaret Craig, Kenneth Gardiner. BA, McGill U., 1941. Tchr. art Peck Sch., Morristown, N.J., 1955-56; one woman shows: Pen and Brush Club, N.Y.C., 1957, Cosmopolitan Club, N.Y.C., 1958; group shows include: Weyhe Gallery, N.Y.C., 1978, Newark Mus., 1955, 59, Montclair (N.J.) Mus., 1955-58, Nat. Assn. Women Artists, Nat. Acad. Galleries, 1954-78, N.Y. World's Fair, 1964-65, Audubon Artists, N.Y.C., 1955-62, 74-79, N.Y. Soc. Women Artists, 1979-80, Provincetown (Mass.) Art Assn. and Mus., 1975-79; traveling shows in France, Belgium, Italy, Scotland, Can., Japan; represented in permanent collections: Slater Meml. Mus., Norwich, Conn., Norfolk (Va.) Mus., Butler Inst. Am. Art, Youngstown, Ohio, Lydia Drake Library, Pembroke, Mass., many pvt. collections. Recipient Jane Peterson prize in oils Nat. Assn. Women Artists, 1954, Famous Artists Sch. prize in watercolor, 1959, Grumbacher Artists Watercolor award, 1970; Solo award Pen and Brush, 1957; Sadie-Max Tesser award in watercolor Audubon Artists, 1975, Peterson prize in oils, 1980; Michael Engel prize Nat. Soc. Painters in Casein and Acrylic, 1983. Mem. Nat. Assn. Women Artists (2d v.p. 1969-70, adv. bd. 1974-76), Audubon Artists (pres. 1979, dir. oils 1986-88), Artist Equity (dir. 1977-79, v.p. 1979-81), N.Y. Soc. Women Artists, Pen and Brush, Nat. Soc. Painters in Casein and Acrylic M.J. Kaplan prize 1984, Nat. Arts Club, Provincetown Art Assn. and Mus., Key West Art Assn. Club: Cosmopolitan. Home: 5 Carolina Meadows # 206 Chapel Hill NC 27514-8522

MC KAY, SAMUEL LEROY, clergyman; b. Charlotte, N.C., Oct. 15, 1913; s. Elmer Ranson and Arlena (Benfield) McK.; AB cum laude, Erskine Coll., 1937; BD cum laude, Erskine Theol. Sem., 1939; postgrad. U. Ga., 1941-42, Union Theol. Sem., 1957; m. Martha Elizabeth Caldwell, Apr. 29, 1939; children: Samuel LeRoy, Mary Louise, William Ranson. Ordained to ministry of Presbyn. Ch., 1940; pastor Prosperity Assoc. Ref. Ch., Fayetteville, Tenn., 1942-46, Bethel Assoc. Ref. Ch., Oak Hill, Ala., 1946-50, 1st Asso. Ref. Ch., Salisbury, N.C., 1950-53, 1st Ch. U.S., Dallas, N.C., 1953-60, First Ch., Kernersville, N.C., 1960-66, Cooleemee (N.C.) Presbyn. Ch., 1966-69, Broadway (N.C.) Presbyn. Ch., 1969-80, Cape Fear Presbyn. Ch., 1983-91, Sardis Presbyn. Ch., 1984-86; stated clk. Gen. Synod Assoc. Ref. Presbyn. Ch., 1950-53; commr. Gen. Assembly Presbyn. Ch. U.S., 1960, 69; permanent clk. Winston-Salem Presbytery, 1961-69, chmn. leadership edn. com., 1962-66, chmn. Christian edn. com., 1967-68; chmn. nominations com. Fayetteville Presbytery, 1977-79; mem. hunger task force Fayetteville Presbytery, 1984-88, chmn. com. on Bangladesh, 1985-87; supr. chaplaincy program Davie County Hosp., 1968-69. Pres. Dallas PTA, 1955-56; bd. mgrs. Kernersville YMCA, 1962-66, chmn. membership com., 1963, treas., 1964, pres., 1965-66; bd. dirs. Winston-Salem-Forsyth County YMCA, 1965-66. Mem. Kernersville Area Ministers Assn. (pres. 1963-64), N.C. Poetry Soc. (dir. 1971—, chmn. poetry contests 1970-72, 83-88, editor ann. book Award-Winning Poems 1970-90; pres. 1971-74), Clan MacKay Soc. N.Am. (pres. 1971-75, chaplain 1976-90—, coun. 1983-90, honored guest, prin. speaker 1985 internat. gathering Glasgow, Scotland 1985, speaker at Clan Mackay Soc. Centenary Celebration, Edinburgh, Scotland, 1988, elected hon. mem. 1988, keynote speaker at meeting, Atlanta 1994). Lodge: Lions. Author: (poems) Harbinger, 1992; contbr. articles and sermons to periodicals and publs.

MCKECHNIE, JOHN CHARLES, gastroenterologist, educator; b. Louisville, Feb. 1, 1935; s. Albert Hay and Edna Scott (Johnson) M.; children: Steven Keith, Kevin Stuart. BA, U. Louisville, 1955; MD, Baylor Coll. Medicine, 1959. Diplomate Am. Bd. Internal Medicine, Am. Bd. Gastroenterology. Intern Jefferson Davis Hosp., Houston, 1959-60; resident in internal medicine Baylor Affiliated Program, Houston, 1960-61, 65-66; gen. practice medicine, Benham, Ky., 1964; practice medicine specializing in gastroenterology, Houston, 1966—; clin. instr. Baylor Coll. Medicine, Houston, 1966-69, asst. prof., 1969-72, assoc. prof., 1972-77, prof., 1977—; mem. staff Methodist Hosp.; cons. Ben Taub Hosp., St. Luke's Episcopal Hosp. Served to capt. USMC, 1962-64. Fellow Am. Coll. Gastroenterology (gov. Tex. 1979-80, trustee 1981-84), ACP; mem. AMA, So. Med. Assn., Tex. Med. Assn., Am. Gastroent. Assn., Digestive Disease Found., Am. Soc. Gastrointestinal Endoscopy, Tex. Soc. Gastrointestinal Endoscopy, Houston Gastroent. Soc. (pres. 1983), Alpha Omega Alpha. Republican. Baptist. Contbr. numerous articles to profl. jours. Office: 6560 Fannin St Ste 1630 Houston TX 77030-2710

MCKEE, ADELE DIECKMANN, retired church music director, educator; b. Atlanta, Oct. 29, 1928; d. Christian William and Emma Pope (Moss) D.; m. Dean Greer McKee, Nov. 14, 1972 (dec. July 1987). BA summa cum laude, Agnes Scott Coll., 1948; MA, Wellesley Coll., 1949; M in Sacred Music magna cum laude, Union Theol. Sem., N.Y.C., 1955. Tchr. Latin and music theory, chapel organist The Northfield Schs., East Northfield, Mass., 1949-53; tchr. Latin and English Westminster Schs., Atlanta, 1955-58; dir. music, organist Trinity Presbyn. Ch., Atlanta, 1955-83; asst. organist Cathedral St. Philip, Atlanta, 1984-85; organist, choir master St. Luke's Presbyn. Ch., Atlanta, 1985-89; ret., 1989; dir. Montreat Conf. on Worship and Music, 1968; chmn. new music commns. Am. Guild of Organists Nat. Convention, Atlanta, 1992—. Choral reviewer The Am. Organist, 1967-71; contbr. articles to Reformed Liturgy mag., 1970—. Mem. City of Decatur Hist. Preservation Task Force, 1989-90. Fellow Am. Guild Organists (nat. councillor 1967-70, dean 1964-66, 76-78, program chmn. nat. conv. 1966); mem. Choristers Guild (nat. bd. dirs. 1976-79), Decatur Book Lovers' Club (pres. 1991), Young Singers Callanwolde (pres. bd. 1994—).

MCKEE, JEWEL CHESTER, JR., electrical engineer, educator, academic administrator; b. Madison, Wis., Nov. 4, 1923; s. Jewel Chester and Carolyn Reid (Ezell) McK.; m. Rachel McIntosh Magruder, Aug. 30, 1947 (dec. Sept. 1968); children: William M., George C., Catherine M., Jeanne Christopher McKee; m. Barbara Jo Sims, Nov. 1, 1969; 1 dau., Sarah Margaret. Student, Miss State U., 1941-43, Tulane U., 1943-44; BS, Miss. State U., 1944; MS, U. Wis., 1949, PhD (Gen. Edn. Bd. fellow), 1952. Instr. Miss. State U., 1946, asst. prof. elec. engring., 1949-52, asso. prof., 1952-56, prof., 1956-79, prof. emeritus, 1979—, head dept., 1957-62; dean Miss. State U. (Grad. Sch.), 1962-69, v.p. research and grad. studies, 1969-79, v.p. emeritus, 1979—; pres. Conf. So. Grad. Schs., 1974, exec. bd. dirs., 1973-78, chmn., 1977; dir. associateships NRC, NAS, 1979-83, dir. associateship and fellowship program, 1983-89, NRC program cons., 1989-93; exec. dir. ORAU/NSF Grad. Rsch. Fellowship Programs, Oak Ridge Associated Univs., 1993-95. Contbr. articles to profl. and ednl. jours. Exec. dir. Miss. Gov.'s Emergency Council for Camille disaster, 1969-70; dist. chmn. Boy Scouts Am., 1976; bd. dirs. Miss. Heart Assn., 1973-76. Served as engring. officer Naval Amphibious Force, 1944-46. Mem. Nat., Miss., Va. socs. profl. engrs., AAAS, Am. Soc. Engring. Edn., IEEE, Sigma Xi, Sigma Chi, Eta Kappa Nu, Omicron Delta Kappa, Tau Beta Pi, Phi Kappa Phi. Presbyterian. Home: 1110 Yorkshire Dr Starkville MS 39759

MCKEE, MICHAEL LELAND, computational chemist; b. Hampton, Va., Dec. 21, 1949; s. John William and Geraldine Almira (Smith) McK. BS in Chemistry, Lamar Univ., 1971; PhD in Chem. Physics, U. Tex. at Austin, 1977. Assoc. prof. chemistry Auburn (Ala.) U., 1987-93, prof. chemistry, 1994—. Contbr. chpts. to books and articles to profl. jours. Mem. Am. Chem. Soc. Office: Auburn Univ Dept Chemistry 179 Chemistry Bldg Auburn AL 36849

MCKEE, RONALD GENE, vocational education educator; b. Williamsville, Mo., May 5, 1947; s. Enos Elmer and Elsie Mae (Chiles) McK.; m. Sondra Mae Malone, Dec. 1, 1968; 1 child, David. Student, Pearl River C.C., 1992-94, U. Miss., 1994—. Cert. tchr., Miss. Enlisted man, electronics warfare repairman USAF, 1966-73; enlisted man USCG, 1973, advanced through grades to electronics technician 1st class, 1973-87; ret., 1987; tchr. electronics Picayune (Miss.) Vocat.-Tech. Ctr., 1988-95, Pascagoula (Miss.) Vocat.-Tech. Ctr., 1995—. Mem. Vocat. Indsl. Clubs. Am. Home: 8508 Sundance Dr Gautier MS 39553 Office: Pascagoula HS Vocat-Tech Ctr 2602 Market St Pascagoula MS 39567-5158

MCKEE, TIMOTHY CARLTON, taxation educator; b. South Bend, Ind., Mar. 9, 1944; s. Glenn Richard and Laura Louise (Niven) McK.; m. Linda Sykes Mizelle, Oct. 13, 1984; children: Brandon Richard. BS in Bus. Econs., Ind. U., 1970, MBA in Fin., 1973, JD, 1979; LLM in Taxation, DePaul U., 1980. Bar: Ill. 1980, U.S. Dist. Ct. (no. dist.) Ill. 1980; CPA, Ill., Va.; cert. govt. fin. mgr. Procedures analyst Assocs. Corp., South Bend, Ind., 1969-71; asst. dir. fin. Ind. U., Bloomington, Ind., 1971-79; sr. tax mgr. Peat Marwick Mitchell & Co., Chgo., Norfolk, Va., 1979-84; corp. counsel K & K Toys, Norfolk, 1984; assoc. prof. acctg. Old Dominion U., Norfolk, 1985—, chmn. dept., 1994-95, chmn. acctg., fin. and law dept., 1995; computer coord. Peat, Marwick, Mitchell & Co., 1982-84; micro computer cons. Old Dominion U., 1985-91. Contbr. articles to profl. jours. Mem. Friends of Music, Bloomington, 1978, Art Inst., Chgo., 1981; loaned exec. United Way, Chgo., 1981; telethon chmn. Va. Orch. Group, Norfolk, 1983. Mem. Assn. Govt. Accts., Am. Acctg. Assn., Am. Assn. Atty. CPAs, Inc., Am. Tax Assn., Fin. Execs. Inst. (pres. 1995-96), Hampton Rds. Tax Forum, Inst. Internal Auditors, Beta Alpha Psi. Home: 412 Rio Dr Chesapeake VA 23320-7144 Office: Old Dominion U Hughes Hall # 2065 Norfolk VA 23529-0229

MCKEITHAN, DONNA BOYCE, maternal/child health nurse, nursing educator; b. Suffolk, Va., Apr. 17, 1959; d. Floy Glenn and Hilda Gray (Johnson) Boyce; children: Caren Denise, Kimberly Lynn, Tracy Dawn; m. Jinks Wilson McKeithan Jr., March 6, 1993. ADN, Coll. of Albemarle, 1980; BSN, East Carolina U., 1986, postgrad., 1988—. RN, N.C. Staff nurse Chowan Hosp., Inc., Edenton, N.C., 1979-87; charge nurse Britthaven of Edenton, 1984-85; staff nurse Albemarle Hosp., Elizabeth City, N.C., 1986-87; supr. obs. unit Washington County Hosp., Plymouth, N.C., 1987-89; staff nurse Pitt County Meml. Hosp., Greenville, N.C., 1988-95; instr. ADN program Pitt Cmty. Coll., Greenville, N.C., 1995—; presenter workshops. Mem. N.C. Nurses Assn. (dist. v.p. 1986-89, conv. del. 1986-89, continuing edn. provider 1988-91, coun. nursing mgmt. 1990-93, Coun. on Maternal Child Health 1994-95, Coun. on Continuing Edn. and Staff Devel.). Baptist. Home: 3425 Whitehurst Station Rd Robersonville NC 27871-9802 Office: Pitt Cmty Coll PO Box 7007 Greenville NC 27835-7007

MCKEITHEN, WALTER FOX, secretary of state; b. Columbia, La., Sept. 8, 1946; s. John Jesse and Marjorie (Funderburk) McK.; m. Yvonne May; children: Marjorie, Marianne, Rebecca, John Jesse. B in History and Social Studies, La. Tech. U., 1972. Owner, operator Apparel Mart Dept. Store, Columbia, 1974-83, McKeithen Chem. & Cementing, Columbia, 1979-88; mem. appropriation, natural resources and joint budged coms. La. Ho. of Reps., Baton Rouge, 1983-87; sec. of state State of La., Baton Rouge, 1987—; tchr., coach Caldwell Parish High Sch., Grayson, La., 1975-78; past mem. La. Assn. Educators. Past v.p. Caldwell Parish Jaycees; trustee La. Sch. Employees' Retirement System; mem. La. Tourist Devel. Commn.; second injury bd. La. Workmen's Compensation; mem. State Bd. Election Supervisors and State Bond Commn., La. Farm Bur., Am. Petroleum Inst.; administrv. bd. Broadmoor Meth. Ch. Recipient Outstanding Legislator award La. Assn. Educators, 1985, Golden Apple award La. Fedn. Tchrs., 1986. Republican. Methodist. Office: Dept of State State Capitol 20th Fl PO Box 94125 Baton Rouge LA 70804-9125*

MCKELLIPS, TERRAL LANE, mathematics educator, university administrator; b. Terlton, Okla., Dec. 2, 1938; s. Raymond Orlando and Patrice Lillian (Fuller) McK.; m. Karen Kay Sweeney, Sept. 7, 1958; children: Marty Suzanne, Kyle Bret. B.S in Edn., S.W. Okla. State U., 1961; M.S., Okla. State U., 1963, Ed.D., 1968. Asst. prof. S.W. Okla. State U., Weatherford, 1962-66; prof., dept. chmn. Cameron U., Lawton, Okla., 1968-72, 73-83, prof., dean Sch. Math. Applied Scis., 1983-89, provost 1989—; vis. prof. Okla. State U., Stillwater, 1972-73; dir. Bank of Elgin, Okla., 1983—. Contbr. articles to profl. jours. State coordinator Dept. Leadership Inst., Am. Council Edn., 1982-83. NSF Sci. Faculty fellow, 1966-68. Mem. Math. Assn. Am. (cons. bur. 1975—), Nat. Council Tchrs. Math., Pi Mu Epsilon, Phi Kappa Phi. Democrat. Club: Lawton Country (dir. 1982-89, pres. 1986-89). Avocations: golf, genealogy. Home: 825 NW 44th St Lawton OK 73505-4929 Office: Cameron U 2800 W Gore Blvd Lawton OK 73505-6320

MCKELVY, NICOLE ANDRÉE, librarian; b. Paris, France, Mar. 5, 1932; came to U.S., 1960; d. André François and Marie Léonie (Bihr) Burdeyron; m. Raymond E. Hortness, July, 1958 (div. Jan. 1971); children: Estelle, Raymond Jr., André, Roy, Jeannette, Donald; m. William T. Sean McKelvy, Dec., 1981. Baccalaureat, Coll. de Jeunes Filles, Chateauroux, France, 1949; student, Pan Am. U., 1972-81. Cert. libr., Tex. Chief operator, interpreter U.S. Forces in France, Chateauroux, 1952-60; tchr.'s aide Pharr, San Juan, Alamo (Tex.) Ind. Sch. Dist., 1968-69; income tax preparer, tchr. H&R Block, McAllen, Tex., 1969-83; clk. acquisitions and periodicals Pan Am. U., Edinburg, Tex., 1971-72, sr. clk. acquisitions, 1972-80; adminstrv. supr. interlibr. loan office U. Tex. Pan-Am., Edinburg, 1980-93; dir. Alamo Pub. Libr., 1988—; mem. OCLC panel on Interlibr. Loan, ALA Midwinter Conf., San Antonio, Tex. 1992. Pres. Am. Legion Aux., Pharr/Alamo, 1975—; counselor, vol. Juv. Ct. Coun., Alamo, 1989—. Mem. Tex. Libr. Assn., Valley Libr. Assn. (v.p., pres.). Home: Box 2302 Alamo TX 78516 Office: Lalo Arcaute Pub Libr 502 Duranta St Alamo TX 78516

MCKENNA, PATRICK HAYES, pediatric urologist, educator, naval officer; b. May 17, 1956; s. John J. and Mary Rita (Madden) McK.; m. Linda Siebert; children: Katherine E., Mary Rita, Caroline Emma. BS in Biology, George Washington U., 1978, MD, 1982. Diplomate Am. Bd. Urology, Nat. Bd. Med. Examiners; cert. BLS, pediatric advanced life support instr., advanced trauma life support inst. Commd. ensign USN, 1978, advanced through grades to comdr., 1993; head dept. urology Naval Hosp Guam, Agana, 1987-89; staff urologist Naval Hosp. Charleston, S.C., 1989; clin. and rsch. fellow in pediatric urology Hosp. for Sick Children, Toronto, Ont., Can., 1989-91; rotating intern Naval Hosp. Portsmouth, Va., 1982-83, resident in urology, 1983-86, chief resident, 1986-87; head divsn. pediat. urology Naval Hosp., Portsmouth, 1991-95; pediat. urologist Conn. Children's Med. Ctr., Hartford, 1995—; asst. prof. clin. urology Ea. Va. Med. Sch., 1993-95; assoc. prof. clin. urology U. Conn., 1996—; vis. prof. Kimbrough Nat. Meeting, Balt., 1991, San Diego, 1993, Charleston Naval Hosp., 1991, 92, Naval Hosp., Guam, 1994, Naval Hosp., 1991, 92, Naval Hosp., Guam, 1994, Naval Hosp. Gt. Lakes, Ill., 1994; presenter abstracts at profl. meetings, 1989—. Contbr. articles to med. jours., chpt. to book. Rsch. grantee George Washington U., 1977-78, Hosp. for Sick Children Rsch. Inst., 1990-92, Health Scis. Edn. and Tng. Commd., 1992-94. Fellow ACS, Am. Acad. Pediatrics; mem. AMA, Am. Urol. Assn., Mid-Atlantic Sect. Am. Urol. Assn., Soc. Univ. Urologists, Tidewater Urologic Assn., Soc. Govt. Svc. Urologists, Assn. Mil. Surgeons U.S., Soc. for Transplantation, Soc. for Pediatric Urology, Am. Asssn. for Lab. Animal Sci., Soc. for Fetal Urology. Office: Conn Children's Med Ctr 282 Washington Ave Hartford CT 06102

MCKENTLY, ALEXANDRA H., agricultural biotechnologist, researcher, educator; b. Wilmington, Del., Oct. 17, 1956; d. John E. and Alice (Wisgo) Herman; m. Barry C. McKently, Aug. 30, 1980; children: Heather, Michael. BS, Pa. State U., 1978; MS, U. Fla., 1981, PhD, 1988. Mgr. horticulture The Land Epcot Ctr., Lake Buena Vista, Fla., 1981-87; rsch. scientist plant biotechnology The Land Epcot Ctr., Lake Buena Vista, 1988—; cons. Kraft Gen. Foods, Glenview, Ill. 1988-92. Contbr. articles to profl. jours. Mem. AAAS, Am. Soc. Biotech., Tissue Culture Assn., Inst. Food Technologists, Am. Soc. Agronomy, Crop Sci. Soc. Am., Am. Soc. for Horticultural Sci., Phi Kappa Phi, Gamma Sigma Delta. Roman Catholic. Office: Epcot Ctr Sci and Tech PO Box 10000 Orlando FL 32830-1000

MCKENZIE, CLIF ALLEN, Indian tribe official, accountant; b. Lawton, Okla., Sept. 29, 1942; s. Robert Allen and Rubie (Paukei) Williams; m. Michele Ann Martin, Aug. 4, 1972; children: Kasey Roberta, Kristen Marti. BS in Acctg., U. Okla., 1965; MBA, Pa. State U., 1976. Fin. analyst United Tribes of Okla., Shawnee, 1973-75; credit officer Bur. Indian Affairs, Dept. Interior, Horton, Kans., 1975-77, liaison officer, Syracuse, N.Y., 1977-80, program analyst, Denver, 1980-81; tribal adminstr. Kiowa Tribe of Okla., Carnegie, 1981-82; CEO tribal bus. mgr. Cheyenne and Arapaho Tribe of Okla., Concho, 1982-84; pres. Indian Devel. Corp., Oklahoma City, 1973—; contracting officer Bur. Indian Affairs, Anadarko, Okla., 1984-89, agy. ops. officer, Concho, Okla.; contract specialist, Gen. Svc. Administr., Ft. Worth, 1989-92, Dept. Health Human Svc., Pub. Health Svc., supervisory contract specialist, Oklahoma City, 1992-94; asset mgr. HUD Loan Mgmt. Br., Oklahoma City, 1994—. police commr. City of Horton, 1976-77, city commr., 1976-77; dir. LECO, Inc., Tulsa. Recipient H.M. Hefner First Amendment award Playboy Found., 1985, Nat. Notary Pub. of the Yr. award Nat. Notary Assn., 1996. Life mem. DAV, U. Okla. Alumni Assn.; mem. Kiowa Black Legging Soc., Nat. Assn. Accts., Am. Soc. Notaries (dir. govt. affairs 1975-80), Nat. Taxpayers Investigative Fund (Whistleblower award 1982). Republican. Served to capt. U.S. Army, 1959-68. Lodges: Elks, Moose. Home: 3708 Epperly Dr Del City OK 73115-3610 Office: Indian Devel Corp PO Box 15613 Oklahoma City OK 73155-5613 also: HUD 500 W Main Oklahoma City OK 73102

MCKENZIE, JAMES FRANKLIN, lawyer; b. Mobile, Ala., May 3, 1948; s. Frank L. McKenzie and Mary K. (Crow) McKenzie O'Neal; m. Randy Jo Jones, June 25, 1977; children: Katherine J., J. Alistair. BA magna cum laude, U. W. Fla., 1970; JD with honors, U. Fla., 1973. Bar: Fla. 1973, U.S. Dist. Ct. (no. dist.) Fla. 1973, U.S. Ct. Appeals (5th cir.) 1975, U.S. Ct. Appeals (11th cir.) 1982, U.S. Supreme Ct. 1988. Lectr. bus. law U. Fla., Gainesville, 1972-73; assoc. Levin, Warfield et al, Pensacola, Fla., 1973-76; ptnr. Myrick & McKenzie, P.A., Pensacola, 1976-82, McKenzie & Soloway, P.A., Pensacola, 1982—. Contbr. chpts. to books, articles to profl. jours. Pres. NW Fla. Easter Seal Soc., Pensacola, 1975; bd. dirs. Five Flags Sertoma Club, 1977; trustee Fla. Lawyers Action Group, Tallahassee, 1996—; mem. adv. bd. Lupus Soc., N.W. Fla., 1992. Recipient Am. Jurisprudence award U. Fla., 1971, 72, 73. Mem. ABA, ATLA (sustaining), Acad. Fla. Trial Lawyers (coll. diplomates, Silver Eagle award 1989, ABCD award 1991), 1st Cir. Acad. Trial Lawyers (founding mem., pres. 1984), Fla. Bar Assn. (cert. in civil trial law), Acad. Fla. Trial Lawyers (bd. dirs. 1986-93, exec. com. diplomate), Escambia-Santa Rosa Bar Assn. Nat. Bd. Trial Advocacy (cert. civil trial advocacy), Civil Justice Found. (founding sponsor), Order of Coif, Phi Kappa Phi, Omicron Delta Kappa, Phi Delta Phi. Republican. Presbyterian. Clubs: Pensacola Country, Exec. Home: 12 Tristan Way Pensacola Beach FL 32561 Office: McKenzie & Soloway PA 905 E Hatton St Pensacola FL 32503-3931

MCKENZIE, KATHLEEN ROSE, primary school educator; b. Geneva, Ohio, Apr. 12, 1960; d. Clarence Ray and Helen Elaine Rose; m. Joseph Ray McKenzie, Oct. 6, 1984; children: Joshua Ray, Caitlin Rose. BA, Shorter Coll., 1982; MEd, Columbus Coll., 1987; EdD, U. Tenn., 1994. Cert. tchr., Ga. Project mainstream tutor Ctrl. Tex. Coll., Killeen, 1984-85; tchr. English Copperas Cove (Tex.) H.S., 1985-86; program dir. BSEP Richard Milburn H.S., Schofield Barracks, Hawaii, 1989; prof. English Chaminade U., Honolulu, 1990; project SMART coord. Employment Tng. Ofc., Honolulu, 1990-91; prof. reading, writing U. Hawaii Cmty. Coll., Honolulu, 1991-92; grad. tchg. asst. U. Tenn., Knoxville, 1993-94; tchr. English, drama Gordon Ctrl. H.S., Calhoun, Ga., 1994—; mem. Pellissippi State workforce, Knoxville, 1993-94. Contbr. articles to profl. jours. Mem. Calhoun-Gordon County Arts Coun., 1995—. Recipient STAR Student award State of Ga., 1978. Mem. Ga. Coun. Tchrs. of English, Nat. Coun. Tchrs. of English, Internat. Reading Assn., Phi Delta Kappa. Roman Catholic. Home: 297 Scott Cir NW Calhoun GA 30701

MCKENZIE, MELBA HUGHES, gifted and talented education educator; b. Branchville, S.C., Aug. 11, 1937; d. Bartley and Clara Mae (McLean) Hughes; m. Kenyon F. McKenzie, Mar. 6, 1960; children: Kenyon Bartley, James Gibson. BS, Lander Coll., 1959; MEd, U. S.C. at Columbia, 1984, postgrad. Cert. elem. tchr., elem. prin., elem. supr., in bus. edn., mid. sch. sci., social studies and lang. arts, S.C. Tchr. Patrick Henry Acad., Estill, S.C.; tchr. Hampton (S.C.) North Dist. One; tchr., coord. gifted and talented Hampton Two, Estill Elem. Sch., Estill Middle Schs.; adult edn. dir. Hampton Sch. Dist. Two. Mem. ASCD, NEA, SCASA, S.C. Assn. Supervision and Curriculum Devel., S.C. Edn. Assn., Hampton County Edn. Assn., S.C. Consortium for Gifted Edn. (adv. coun. gifted edn.), Delta Kappa Gamma (Alpha Chi chpt., Alpha Eta State). Home: RR 1 Box 65D Garnett SC 29922-9513

MCKENZIE, MICHAEL K., wholesale executive. Past pres., CEO G.S.C. Enterprises, Inc., Sulphur Springs, Tex., now chmn. bd., CEO, also bd. dirs. Office: GSC Enterprises Inc 130 Hillcrest Dr Sulphur Springs TX 75482*

MCKENZIE, SUSAN SMITH, business writer; b. N.Y.C., Dec. 30, 1964; d. John Brewster and Ida (Hawa) Smith. BA in English, Tex. A&M U., 1986; MA in Journalism, Ind. U., 1988. Parachutist and broadcast journalist 1st Special Ops. Command, Ft. Bragg, N.C., 1989-91; media rels. journalist U.S. Army Parachute Team - Golden Knights, Ft. Bragg, N.C., 1991-92; TV reporter Sta. WLTX-TV, Columbia, S.C., 1992; bus. writer The Herald, Rock Hill, S.C., 1992-94; plant comms. specialist Brunswick Nuclear Plant Carolina Power & Light, Southport, 1994—. With U.S. Army, 1988-92, Panama, Persian Gulf. Recipient South Korean Jump Wings Republic of Korea Spl. Warfare Ctr., 1989. Mem. Women in Communications, Inc., Nat. Press Photographers Assn. Presbyterian. Home: 3917 Mayfield Ct Wilmington NC 28412-0965 Office: Carolina Power & Light PO Box 10429 Southport NC 28461-0429

MCKEOWN, FRANK EDWARD, consumer services executive; b. Phila., Apr. 15, 1943; s. Francis Edward and Regina Catherine (Reigle) McK.; m. Karen Jo Moore, Sept. 27, 1967 (div. May 1987); children: Francis, Michael, Sean, Kyle; m. Cynthia Louise Mitualsky, Oct. 24, 1987. BS in English Lit., St. Joseph's U., Phila., 1965; MBA in Mktg., U. Pa., 1970. Fellow The White House, Washington, 1966-68; mktg. mgr. Peter Paul, Inc., Naugatuck, Conn., 1970-73; mktg. dir. Brown & Williamson, Inc., Louisville, 1973-80; v.p. mktg. and planning Schering-Plough, Inc., Memphis, 1980-83; v.p. mktg. The Southland Corp., Dallas, 1983-87; exec. v.p., COO PCA Internat., Charlotte, N.C., 1987-90; chmn., CEO Cynmarlyn, Inc., Tampa, Fla., 1991—; instr. U. Tampa, 1993. Contbr. articles to profl. jours. Chmn. Rep. Fund Raising, Tampa, 1992. Mem. Tampa (Fla.) C. of C. Office: Cynmarlyn Inc 8901 Magnolia Chase Cir Tampa FL 33647-2220

MCKEOWN, REBECCA J., principal; b. Wayne, Okla., Apr. 4, 1937; d. William S. and Ila Rebekah (Mitchell) Lackey; m. Loren Ferris, Apr. 5, 1958; children: Michael, Thomas, Nancy, David. BS, Okla. State U., 1966; MEd, U. Okla., 1976. Cert. elem. tchr., elem. prin. 6th grade tchr. Ponca City (Okla.) Pub. Schs., 1966-67; 1st and 6th grade tchr. Peru Elem. Sch., Auburn, Nebr., 1967-69; 4th grade tchr. Woodland Hills Sch., Lawton, Okla., 1971-76; asst. prin. Douglass Learning Ctr., Lawton, Okla., 1976-78; prin. Lincoln Elem. Sch., Lawton, Okla., 1978-84, Hugh Bish Elem., Lawton, Okla., 1984—. Recipient Disting. Achievement award Lawton Bd. Edn., 1992, Adminstr. of Yr. award Lawton Area Reading Coun., 1993, Arts Adminstr. of Yr. award Okla. Alliance for Arts, 1993, Nat. Blue Ribbon Sch. Recognition award 1993-94, D.A.R.E. Adminstrn. award Lawton Police Dept., 1993. Mem. ASCD, Okla. Reading Coun., Okla. ASCD, Lawton Area Reading Coun., Elem. Prins. Assn. (pres. 1986-87). Democrat. Methodist. Home: 6 SW 71st St Lawton OK 73505-6615 Office: Lawton Pub Schs 751 NW Fort Sill Blvd Lawton OK 73507-5421

MCKESSON, EDWARD LEE, JR., association executive, small business owner; b. Detroit, Nov. 26, 1936; s. Edward Lee and Anna (Pete) McK.; m. Mary Helen Nottingham; children: Connie Lynn Jenkins, Linda Kay Hunter, Michael Edward. BS in Bus. Adminstrn., Cameron U., Lawton, Okla., 1971. Enlisted U.S. Army, 1955, commd. 2d lt., 1960, advanced through grades to maj., 1969, ret., 1975; sales mgr. Parks-Jones Realtors, Lawton, 1976-84; owner Individual Interiors, Lawton, 1976—, Wichita Falls, Tex., 1995—; mng. broker Keller Williams Realtors, Lawton, 1993-94; exec. v.p. Lawton Bd. Realtors, 1994—. Chmn. Task Force Cert. Cities, Lawton, 1995. Decorated Bronze Star (2), Legion of Merit, Air medal (29), Army Commendation medal, Vietnamese Cross of Gallantry. Mem. Nat. Assn. Realtors. Democrat. Baptist. Home: 1101 NW Cherry Lawton OK 73507

MCKIMMEY, MARTHA ANNE, elementary education educator; b. Uvalde, Tex., Apr. 9, 1943; d. Aubrey Allan and Nellie Grey (Roberts) Stovall; m. Vernon Hobart McKimmey Jr., July 3, 1965; children: Annette Gay, Patrick Allan. BS, Howard Payne Coll., Brownwood, Tex., 1964; MEd, Tex. Christian U., 1969; PhD, Tex. Women's U., 1995. Cert. elem. tchr., Tex. Tchr. Ft. Worth Ind. Sch. Dist., 1964-66, White Lake Sch., Ft. Worth, 1979-80, Meadowbrook Christian Sch., Ft. Worth, 1982-87. Contbr. articles to mags. Mem. ASCD, Internat. Reading Assn. Home: 7104 Jewell Ave Fort Worth TX 76112-5712

MCKINLESS, KATHY JEAN, accountant; b. Augusta, Ga., June 15, 1954; d. Jack M. and Jean K. (Norby) VanderWood; m. Darryl P. Calderon, Mar. 17, 1979 (dec. June 1988); children: Christopher, Jackie; m. Richard T. McKinless, July 1, 1989; children: Ashley, Thomas. BS in Acctg., U. S.C., 1975, MBA, 1978. CPA, D.C. Acct. Clarkson, Harden & Gantt, Columbia, 1975-79; sr. acct. KPMG Peat Marwick, Washington, 1979-80, mgr., 1980-86, ptnr., 1986—; spkr. Mortgage Bankers Assn., Fin. Mgrs. Soc., Nat. Assn. Coll. and Univ. Bus. Officers, Fed. Fin. Insts. Exam. Coun., Diocesan Fiscal Mgrs. Mem. governance com., treas., pres. bd. dirs. Nations Capital coun. Girl Scouts U.S., 1985—; mem. fin. com. Cath. Charities, U.S.A. Mem. AICPAs, D.C. Inst. CPAs. Office: KPMG Peat Marwick 2001 M St NW Washington DC 20036-3310

MCKINLEY, EDWARD HARVEY, history educator, author; b. Alameda, Calif., Apr. 11, 1943; s. Harvey Edward and Lucille Alta (Schofield) McK.; m. Rebecca Martha Paulo, Sept. 17, 1987. BA, U. Calif., Berkeley, 1965; MA, U. Wis., Madison, 1966, PhD, 1970. Faculty mem. Asbury Coll., Wilmore, Ky., 1970—; corps sgt.-maj. The Salvation Army Student Fellowship, Wilmore, Ky., 1975-94. Author: The Lure of Africa, 1974, Marching to Glory, 1980, 2nd edit., 1995, Somebody's Brother, 1985. Councilman Wilmore City Coun., 1988-93, Jessamine County-Wilmore City Planning Commn., 1993—. Recipient Allan Nevins prize Soc. Am. Historians, 1970. Mem. Am. Hist. Assn., Soc. Historians of Am. Fgn. Rels., Am. Soc. Ch. History. Democrat. Office: Asbury College 1 Macklem Dr Wilmore KY 40390-1152

MC KINLEY, JIMMIE JOE, business executive; b. Bertram, Tex., July 23, 1934; s. Joseph Crofford and Velma Anne (Barnett) McK.; B.J., U. Tex., 1955; M.S., U. Ky., 1964. Asst. librarian Bethel Coll., McKenzie, Tenn., 1961-63, reference librarian, 1966-70, acting head librarian, 1970-71; owner, mgr. Longview Book Co. (Tex.), 1974—. Former mem., bd. dirs. Longview-Piney Woods chpt. ARC; trustee Bethel Coll., 1977-86. Mem. ALA, Gregg County Hist. and Geneal. Soc., Burnet County Heritage Soc., Celtic Heritage Soc. of East Tex., East Tex. Hist. Assn., History Club East Tex., East Tex. Oil Mus. Guild, Celtic Heritage Soc. East Tex., East Tex. Knife and Fork Club. Presbyterian. Home: PO Box 2106 Longview TX 75606-2106

MCKINLEY, JOHN HENRY, sales executive; b. Harlan, Ky., Feb. 28, 1939; s. John Henry and Nina (Howard) McK.; m. W. Ruth Young, Aug. 15, 1964; 1 child, Mary Hayes. BS in Textile Chemistry, Ga. Tech U., 1962; postgrad., U. Tenn., 1965, 66, Naval War Coll., 1980, Nat. Def. U., 1982, Army War Coll., 1991. Chemist Eastman Chem. Co., Kingsport, Tenn., 1963-67; lab. mgr. Eastman Chem. Co., Lodi, N.J., 1968-70; sales rep. Eastman Chem. Co., Greensboro, N.C., 1970-73; sr. sales rep. in charge Eastman Chem. Co., L.A., 1974-81; dist. mgr. Eastman Chem. Co., Houston, 1982-86; bus. team analysis Eastman Chem. Co., Kingsport, 1986-88, mgr. nat. distbrs., 1988-89; dir. sales N.Am. Eastman Fine Chems. Bus. Orgn., Kingsport, 1990-91, dir. sales Ams., 1992-93, dir. sales worldwide, 1994—. Bd. dirs. Kingsport (Tenn.) Symphony, 1986-91. Rear admiral USNR, 1961—. Decorate Legion of Merit, Meritorious Svc. medals Pres. of the U.S., 1986, 89, Navy Commendation medals Sec. of Def., 1990. Mem. Am. Assn. Textile Colorists and Chemists (chmn. Pacific chpt. 1975-76), Res. Officers Assn. (v.p. Navy Tenn. 1994—), Naval Inst., Naval Res. Assn., Kingsport C. of C., Kiwanis Club (Kingsport, com. chmn. 1986, 88, 89). Episcopalian. Home: 4 Longview Ln Kingsport TN 37660-4518 Office: Eastman Fine Chems PO Box 451 Kingsport TN 37662-0451

MCKINLEY, SARAH ELIZABETH, journalist; b. Bucyrus, Ohio, Jan. 4, 1952; d. Harold Kemp and Velma Elizabeth (Vollmer) McK.; m. Paul Robert Serrano, Aug. 17, 1993; 1 child, James Ernest Serrano. BA, Ohio State U., 1974. Co-investigator, researcher Women's Action Collective, Columbus, Ohio, 1976-80; editor, cons. The Nisonger Ctr., Columbus, 1981; freelance editor Columbus, 1982-84; journalist Gas Daily, Washington, 1985, Energy Daily, Washington, 1985-86; sr. editor Natural Gas Intelligence (Intelligence Press), Washington, 1986—; conf. dir. Gas Mart: The Nat. Trade Fair Nat. Gas Mktg., 1986—. Creator Simplified Map North American Pipelines, 1990-94, Storage Map of the United States, 1991, 93, 94; editor: The Life's Work of a Minor Poet: Collected Fiction, Journalism and Poetry of Edmund McGranaghan, 1982. Pres., bd. dirs. The Commons of Arlington, Va., 1993-95; pres. Columbia Heights Civic Assn., Arlington, 1990-92. Mem. Soc. Profl. Journalists. Home: # 2 2714 Shawn Leigh Dr Vienna VA 22181-6136

MCKINNEY, BARBARA JEAN, librarian; b. Temple, Tex., Nov. 6, 1944; d. Hoyt and Marcella (Durnie) Williams; m. Carroll Collin McKinney, June 28, 1965. BS in Edn., Ouachita Bapt. U., 1966; MLS, Tex. Woman's U., 1979; MS in Edn., U. Cen. Ark., 1982. Librarian Spaulding Pub. Sch., Waukegan, Ill., 1970-72, Libertyville (Ill.) Pub. Schs., 1972-73; library media specialist Oak Grove High Sch. Pulaski County Spl. Sch. Dist., North Little Rock, Ark., 1975—; lectr. U. Ark., Little Rock, 1982; instr. U. Ctrl. Ark., 1990—; mem. handbook com. for Ark. History/Ark. Dept. Edn., 1986-87. Reviewer: Sparks, 1986—; contbr. articles to profl. jours. Vol. Friends of Cen. Ark. Library System, Little Rock, 1975—. Heloise Griffon scholar Ark. Audio Visual Assn., Conway, 1980; fellow Japan Found. Nat. Council for Social Studies, San Francisco, 1986. Mem. AAUW (sec. Little Rock br., Charlie May Simon book selection com. 1985—), NEA, Ark. Edn. Assn., Pulaski Assn. Classroom Tchrs., Nat. Council Social Studies, Internat. Assn. Sch. Librarianship (presenter 1986), Am. Library Assn., Ark. Library Assn., Am. Assn. Sch. Librarians, Ark. Assn. Sch. Librarians and Media Educators (presenter summer conf. 1985, sec.), Assn. for Ednl. Communications and Tech. (sec. region VII conf. 1981, program planning com. sch. media specialists div. 1982-84), Ark. Audio Visual Assn. (membership chmn. 1981-82, bd. dirs. 1981-86, pres.-elect 1983-84, pres. 1984-85, past pres. 1985-86, co-chmn. student media festival 1987—), Cen. Ark. Media Edn. Orgn. (sec. 1980-81, v.p. 1982-83), Beta Phi Mu. Home: 10607 Breckenridge Dr Little Rock AR 72211-1801 Office: Oak Grove H S 10025 Oakland Dr North Little Rock AR 72118-1942

MCKINNEY, BRENDA KAY, nursing educator; b. Bakerfield, Calif., Sept. 25, 1962; d. Jerry and Linda Sue (Perkins) Murray; m. Carl Dewayne McKinney, Aug. 8, 1980. Diploma, Black River Vo-Tech., Pocahontas, Ark., 1987; ASN, Park Coll., 1994. RN, Ark., Mo.; cert. ACLS. Nursing instr. Black River Tech. Coll., Pocahontas, 1990—. Home: 6062 Hwy 67 N Corning AR 72422-9762

MCKINNEY, CAROLYN JEAN, lawyer; b. Holly Springs, Miss., Sept. 28, 1956; d. Walter H. and Elizabeth (Lawrence) McK. BA in History and Polit. Sci., Rust Coll., Holly Springs, 1977; JD, Harvard U., 1980. Bar: Tex. 1980, U.S. Dist. Ct. (no., ea., so. and we. dists.) Tex. 1980, Ill. 1995. Atty. Gulf Oil Corp., Houston, 1980-84; sr. atty. ARCO, Dallas, 1984-90; atty. Amoco Corp., Houston, 1990-94, 1996—, Chgo., 1994-96; vis. prof., mentor black exec. exch. program Nat. Urban League, 1985—; mem. adv. bd. Nat. Soc. Black Engrs., 1987—. Vol. Meals on Wheels program Vis. Nurse's Assn., 1985, Kid Care, 1992; participant Miss. Gov.'s Leadership Conf. on Youth, 1988. Recipient Outstanding Alumni award Nat. Assn. for Equal Opportunity in Higher Edn., 1989. Mem. ABA. Office: Amoco Corp Rm 5166 501 Westlake Pk Blvd Houston TX 77079

MCKINNEY, CYNTHIA ANN, congresswoman; b. Mar. 17, 1955; d. Billy and Leola McKinney; 1 child, Coy Grandison, Jr. B, U. So. Calif.; postgrad., Ga. State U., U. Wis.; Tufts U. Former instr. Clark Atlanta U., Atlanta Met. Coll.; former mem. Ga. Ho. of Reps.; mem. 103rd Congress from 11th Ga. dist., 1993—, mem. banking and fin. svcs. com. housing and cmty. devel., mem. internat. rels. com. internat. ops. and human rights; instr. Agnes Scott Coll. Diplomatic fellow Spellman Coll. Home: 765 Shorter Ter NW Atlanta GA 30318-7140 Office: US Ho of Reps 124 Cannon Washington DC 20515*

MCKINNEY, DONALD LEE, magazine editor; b. Evanston, Ill., July 12, 1923; s. Guy Doane and Cora Redfield (Brenton) McK.; m. Mary Frances Joyce, Dec. 14, 1958; children—Jennifer Joyce, Douglas Guy. A.B., U. N.C., 1948. Salesman textbooks John Wiley & Sons, N.Y.C., 1949-52; freelance writer mostly comic books with some short articles and fiction, 1952-54; asst. mng. editor True mag., N.Y.C., 1955-62; editor articles Saturday Evening Post, 1962-69; spl. features editor N.Y. Daily News, 1969-70; mng. editor McCalls mag., N.Y.C., 1969-86; Gonzales prof. journalism U. S.C., Beaufort, 1986-90, prof. emeritus, 1990—. Author: Writing Magazine Articles That Sell, 1994; reporter, book reviewer. Served with USNR, 1943-46. Democrat. Home: 9 Spanish Moss Rd Hilton Head Island SC 29928-4412

MCKINNEY, GEORGE HARRIS, JR., training systems analyst; b. Birmingham, Ala., Nov. 23, 1943; s. George Harris and Elizabeth Dickey (Fikes) McK.; m. Lynda Jeanne Ponder, June 26, 1965 (div. Aug. 18, 1992; children: Michael Thomas, Carol Elizabeth; m. Tambri Sue Hillis, Aug. 19, 1992. BS in Polit. Sci., U.S. Air Force Acad., 1965; MS in Psychology, Troy State U., 1977. Commd. 2d lt. U.S. Air Force, 1965, advanced through grades to lt. col., 1981; fighter pilot U.S. Air Force, worldwide, 1965-85; ret. U.S. Air Force, 1985; tng. sys. cons. in pvt. practice, Milton, Fla., 1985—. Author tech. reports. Decorated D.F.C. (5), Air medal (26), Purple Heart, Meritorious Svc. medal (3). Mem. Order of Daedalians, USAFA Assn. Grads., Air Force, Assn., Am. Def. Preparedness Assn. Home: 3101 Chippewa Dr Milton FL 32571-9603

MCKINNEY, JANE-ALLEN, artist and educator; b. Owensboro, Ky., Jan. 8, 1952; d. William Holland and Jane Wilhoit (Moore) McK. BA, Scarritt Coll., Nashville, 1974; MA, Vanderbilt U., 1977; MFA, Memphis Coll. of Art, 1993. Grad. asst. dept. art Peabody Coll. for Tchrs., Vanderbilt U., Nashville, 1975-76; tchr. Smyrna (Tenn.) Comprehensive Vocat. Ctr., 1977-78; pres., bd. dirs. Jane Allen Flighton Artworks Inc., Nashville, 1978—; jeweler Wright's Jewelry Store, Clarksville, Tenn., 1982; tchr. art Belmont U., Nashville, 1984-88, Met. Centennial Park Art Ctr., Nashville, 1988-91, Cheekwood Mus. of Art, Nashville, 1990-94, Nossi Coll. of Art, Nashville, 1991-94, Western Ky. U., Bowling Green, 1991-94; ednl. cons. fine art Nossi Coll. Art, Nashville, 1993—; artist for Women of Achievement awards, sculptures and jewelry YWCA, Nashville, 1992—; artist for Bus. Award Sculpture, C. of C., Nashville, 1990. One and two person shows include Cheekwood Mus. Art, 1981, 93, Owensboro Mus. Fine Art, 1992, Western Ky. U., 1992-94, Belmont U., 1984, others; exhbns. include Watkins Art Inst., Nashville, 1991, Western Ky. U., 1992, Parthenon, Nashville, 1992, Owensboro Mus. Art, 1993, Tenn. Performing Arts Ctr., 1995; invitational and juried exhibits include Sculptors of Mid. Tenn. Arts in the Airport, Nashville, 1996, Nat. Coun. on the Edn. of Ceramics Arts, Rochester, N.Y., 1996, Ceramic Exhibn. Tenn. State U., 1996, and numerous others; represented in permanent collections including City of Chattanooga's Visitors Ctr., IBM, Bapt. Hosp., Nations Bank of Tenn., Mass. Pub. Libr., First Am. Bank Corp., and numerous others. Adv. bd. Belmont U., Nashville, 1984—, Nossi Coll. Art, 1993—; mem edn. com. Nat. Mus. of Women in the Arts, Tenn., 1992—; artist for fundraising sculpture Arthritis Found., Nashville, 1989-90; vol. singer VA Hosp., Nashville, 1989—; bd. dirs. Visual Arts Alliance Nashville, 1996; vol. soloist Vet.'s Hosp., 1991-96; artist for ann. fundraiser YWCA, 1993-96. Recipient Best Tchr. award Nossi Coll. Art, 1992-93; grantee City of Chattanooga Welcome Ctr., 1993, Memphis Arts Festival Spl. Projects, 1994. Mem. AAUW, Assn. of Visual Artists, Soc. of N.Am. Goldsmiths, Visual Artists Alliance of Nashville, Nat. Art Edn. Assn., Internat. Sculpture Ctr., Nat. Coun. on Edn. of the Ceramic Arts, Tenn. Assn. of Craft Artists, Coll. Art Assn. Home: PO Box 120454 Nashville TN 37212-0454

MC KINNEY, MICHAEL WHITNEY, trade association executive; b. San Angelo, Tex., Aug. 23, 1946; s. Wallace Luster and Mitzi Randolph (Broome) McK.; m. Martha LaNan Hooker, Feb. 24, 1973; children: Wallace Blake, Lauren Brooke. BA in Govt., U. Tex., Austin, 1973. Adminstrv. asst. to lt. gov. State of Tex., Austin, 1968-69, adminstrv. asst. to gov., 1969-73, asst. to dir. Tex. Water Quality Bd., Austin, 1973-76; chief of staff Tex. Alcoholic Beverage Commn., 1976-83; v.p. for industry affairs Wholesale Beer Distbrs. Tex., 1984-88, exec. v.p., chief exec. officer, 1989—. Bd. dirs. Tex. Alpha Ednl. Found., Inc., Austin, 1969—; mem. Travis County Zoo Task Force, 1986; mem. Senate Com. on Fees and Grants, 1982-83; bd. dirs.

Friends of Gov.'s Mansion, 1993-97. Mem. Sam Houston Soc., Knights of the Symphony, Austin Assembly, Phi Kappa Psi. Democrat. Presbyterian. Club: Masons (32 deg., K.T.), Austin Country Club, Austin Club (bd. dirs. 1989—, exec. com. 1994—, Mem. of Yr. 1994). Home: 1708 Intervail Dr Austin TX 78746-7630 Office: 823 Congress Ste 1313 Austin TX 78701-2404

MCKINNEY, PAMELA ANNE, elementary principal; b. L.A., Sept. 25, 1947; d. Dave and Helen (Wallace) Shorter; m. Frank Alexander McKinney III, Aug. 24, 1968; children: Frank Alexander IV, Pamela Ann. AA, L.A. Harbor Coll., 1967; BA, Conn. Coll., 1973; MS, Old Dominion U., 1982; cert. in advance grad. studies, Va. Tech. U. & State Inst., 1988. Asst. buyer May Co. Dept. Stores, L.A., 1967-68, Liberty House Dept. Stores, Honolulu, 1968-70; tchr. Norfolk (Va.) Pub. Schs., 1982, Tracy (Calif.) Pub. Schs., 1975-77; tchr. Virginia Beach (Va.) Pub. Schs., 1984-80, asst. prin., 1984-89, prin., 1989—; bd. dirs. Tidewater Prin. Ctr., Norfolk. Tchr. religious edn. Holy Spirit Ch., Virginia Beach, 1986—; bd. dirs. Cath. Family and Children's Svcs., Virginia Beach, 1987—. Mem. NAESP, ASCD, Va. Beach Assn. Elem. Sch. Prins., Va. Assn. Elem. Sch. Prins. Home: 4705 Chalfont Dr Virginia Beach VA 23464-3302 Office: Plaza Elem Sch 641 Carriage Hill Rd Virginia Beach VA 23452-6518

MCKINNEY, SUSAN ANNETTE, university administrator; b. Kansas City, Mo., Apr. 10, 1958; d. Bruce Alan and Patricia Jane (Houston) McK. BA in History and Polit. Sci., Cen. Mo. State U., 1980; MA in Am. History, Duquesne U., 1982. Grad. asst. Duquesne U., Pitts., 1980-82; archival intern Pitts. Pub. Sch. Dist., 1982; archival cons. Trinity Cathedral, Pitts., 1982; field archivist Seton Hall U., South Plainfield, N.J., 1982-83; field dir. Balch Inst. Ethnic Studies, Scranton, Pa., 1983-85; survey dir. U. Fla., Gainesville, 1985-87, dir. records mgmt., 1987—; cons. Gainesville Regional Utilities, 1991—, Am. Automobile Assn., Jacksonville Electric Authority, 1994—; chairperson disaster control task force Univ. Librs., U. Fla., mem. archives and records com.; mem. coun. info. techs. and svc., mem. electronic mail policy com. Standing Com. Adminstrv. computing; presenter in field. Curator (art exhibit) Building a Local Heritage: The Work of Vincent Russoniello, Lucan Ctr. for Arts, Scranton, 1985, A Remembrance of Things Past, Women's Resource Ctr., Scranton, 1985. Asst. coord. steering com. Alachua County Spl. Olympics, Gainesville, 1990-91, coord. steering com., 1991—; mem. conservation com. Fla. Mus. Natural Hist.; active Jr. League Gainesville. Mem. Assn. Info. and Image Mgmt., Assn. Records Mgrs. and Adminstrs. (chairperson steering com. for orgn. of Gainesville/North Cen. Fla. chpt. 1987, chpt. pres. 1987-89, bd. dirs. 1989-91, chairperson program and ednl. instns. industry action coms. 1989-90, Mem. of Yr. 1988), Soc. Fla. Archivists (sec./treas. 1989-90), chairperson nominating com. 1987), Soc. Ga. Archivists, Fla. Records Mgmt. Assn. (chairperson steering com.), Midwest Archives Conf., Pilot Club Gainesville (rec. sec. 1991-92), Fla. Records Mgmt. Assn. (pres. 1991-93), Gamma Sigma Sigma (Mem. of Yr. 1980), Phi Alpha Theta. Democrat. Methodist. Home: 4101 Alpine Dr Gainesville FL 32605-1684 Office: Univ Fla PO Box 117007 Gainesville FL 32611-7007

MCKINNEY, WILLIAM DOUTHITT, JR., sales and engineering company executive; b. Memphis, Sept. 2, 1955; s. William Douthitt Sr. and Virginia (Grisham) McK. BBA, U. Miss., 1978. CLU. Bus. fin. account exec. Met. Life Ins. Co., Memphis, 1978-79; def. back Dallas Cowboys Football, 1979, 80, Carloss Well Supply Co., Memphis, 1980-82, San Francisco 49ers, 1981; pres. McKinney and Assocs., Cordova, Tenn., 1981—; sales and engring. mgr. Bryan Custom Plastics, 1991-92; sales mgr. Dresden Products, 1993-94, No. Techs., 1995—. Mem. Statue of Liberty-Ellis Island Centennial Commn., Presdl. Innercir., 1991—. Recipient Outstanding Young Men of Am. award U.S. Jaycees and Disting. Ams. Bd. Advisors, 1985, A Thousand Points of Light Vol. award U.S. Pres. George Bush, 1989, Internat. Man of Yr. award Internat. Ctr. Bd. Advisors of Cambridge, Eng., 1991-92, Admired Man of Decade award Am. Inst. Humanity, Shield award of Valor, Twentieth Century award for Achievement Internat. Ctr., Cambridge, Eng.; named Man of Achievement Internat. Ctr., Cambridge. Mem. Mfrs. Agts. Nat. Assn., United Assn. Mfrs. Reps., Am. Mktg. Assn., Am. Inst. Chem. Engrs., Soc. Plastic Engrs., Am. Water Ski Assn., U. Miss. Alumni Assn., Presdl. Inner Circle, Dallas Cowboys Alumni Assn., Nat. Football Found. and Coll. Hall of Fame, Phi Kappa Psi, Delta Sigma Pi, Pi Sigma Epsilon. Republican. Presbyterian. Home: 684 Tealwood Ln Cordova TN 38018-6333 Office: McKinney and Assocs 684 Tealwood Ln Cordova TN 38018-6333

MCKINNON, ARNOLD BORDEN, transportation company executive; b. Goldsboro, N.C., Aug. 13, 1927; s. Henry Alexander and Margaret (Borden) McK.; m. Oriana McArthur, July 19, 1950; children: Arnold Borden Jr., Colin McArthur, Henry Alexander. AB, Duke U., 1950, LLB, 1951; grad. Advanced Mgmt. Program, Harvard U., 1972. Bar: D.C. 1951, N.C. 1966. With Norfolk So. Corp. (formerly So. Ry. System), Norfolk, Va., 1951—, v.p. law, 1971-75, sr. v.p. law and acctg., 1975-77, exec. v.p. law and acctg., 1977-81, exec. v.p. law and fin., 1981-82, exec. v.p. mktg., 1982-86, vice chmn., 1986-87, chmn., pres., CEO, 1987-91; chmn., 1991-92, chmn. exec. com., 1992—, also bd. dirs.; bd. dirs. Norfolk Works, Inc. Bd. dirs. Va. Port Authority, Nat. Maritime Ctr. Found., Global Transpark Found., Norfolk Forum, Inc., CADRE Found.; active Mil. Civilian Liaison Group; mem. bus. adv. com. Northwestern U. Transp. Ctr.; trustee Med. Coll. Hampton Roads Found., Va. Union Theol. Sem.; vice chmn. Va. Gov.'s Econ. Adv. Coun.; commr. Norfolk Redevel. and Housing Authority. With U.S. Army, 1946-47. Mem. ABA, N.C. Bar Assn., D.C. Bar Assn., Am. Soc. Corp. Execs., Norfolk Yacht and Country Club, Harbor Club, Chevy Chase Club, Met. Club (Washington), Laurel Valley Golf Club, India House (N.Y.C.), Cedar Point Club (Suffolk, Va.), Rotary. Presbyterian. Home: 552 Mowbray Arch Norfolk VA 23507-2130 Office: Norfolk So Corp 3 Commercial Pl Norfolk VA 23510-2191

MCKINNON, KATHLEEN ANN, software engineer; b. Berwyn, Ill., July 27, 1960; d. James Walter and Linda Lee (Belford) Turek; m. Donald Lee McKinnon, Jr., July 27, 1980; 1 child, Donald Lee III. AA in Computer Sci., Pensacola Jr. Coll., 1980; BS in Computer Sci. and Info. Systems, U. Md., 1986. SIGINT Morse interceptor U.S. Army, Ft. Meade, Md., 1982-86; computer scientist Dept. Def., Ft. Meade, 1986-90; software engr. Harris Corp., Melbourne, Fla., 1990—, group leader, 1994—. Mem. missions com. Pineda Presbyn. Ch., Melbourne, 1991—; moderator Pineda Presbyn. Women, 1995-96. Recipient achievement medal U.S. Army, 1983, spl. achievement award Dept. Def., 1989. Republican.

MCKINNON, THOMAS E., human resources executive; b. 1945. V.p. human resources Unisys Corp., Blue Bell, Pa.; exec. v.p. human resources Ryder System, Inc., 1995—. Office: Ryder Sys Inc 3600 NW 82nd Ave Miami FL 33166

MCKINNON, WILLIAM MITCHELL PATRICK, surgeon; b. Houston, Mar. 17, 1924; s. William M. and Rosina Mary McKinnon; m. Elizabeth Jean Beall, Oct. 3, 1953; children: William, Stuart, Mary, John, Fraser, David (dec.). Student, St. Michael's Coll., Toronto, Can., 1942, Tex. A&M State U., 1943, U. Tex., 1947; BS maxima cum laude, St. Edward's U., Austin, Tex., 1948. Diplomate Am. Bd. Surgery; lic. physician, La., N.Y., Tex. Intern Royal Victoria Hosp., Montreal, Can., 1953; resident in surgery 2d surg. divsn. Bellevue Hosp., 1954; asst. resident thoracic surgery Triboro Hosp. for Chest Disease, 1955; asst. resident in surgery Queens Hosp. Ctr., Jamaica, N.Y., 1955, asst. resident in pathology, 1956, assoc. resident, 1957, asst. surgeon, 1959-61; chief resident surgery, fellow in surg. rsch. Maimonides Hosp. of Bklyn., 1958; asst. attending surgeon Flower & Fifth Ave. Hosps., 1961-64, attending surgeon, 1965-67; staff surgeon Alton Ochsner Found. Hosp., 1968—; staff, dept. surgery Ochsner Clinic, 1968—, assoc. dir., dept. surgery, 1979-84, co-dir., breast screening, 1982—; dir. Breast Ctr., Ochsner Clinic, 1992—; clin. asst. in surgery SUNY Med. Ctr. Coll. Medicine, 1957-59; asst. surgeon Kew Gardens (N.Y.) Gen. Hosp., 1959-61, Jamaica Hosp., 1960-61; vis. surgeon Met. Hosp. and Bird S. Coler Hosp., 1961-66, Tulane divsn. Charity Hosp., 1968—; dist. med. cons. N.Y. State Edn. Dept. of Vocat. Rehab., 1960-67; surg. cons. VA Hosp., Lyons, N.J., 1963-67, E.A. Conway Meml. Hosp., Monroe, La., 1968-79; asst. prof. to assoc. prof. surgery N.Y. Med. Coll., 1961-67; clin. assoc. prof. of surgery Tulane U., 1968-92, clinical prof. dept. surgery, 1992—. Contbr. articles to med. jours. Bd. dirs. Am. Cancer Soc., New Orleans, 1953, Komen Found., New Orleans, 1953. Capt. USAF, 1948-52. Recipient 1st prize for med. writing Queensborough Med. Soc., 1957; USPHS rsch. fellow Nat. Heart Inst., 1958. Fellow ACS; mem. AMA, Soc. for Surgery of Alimentary Tract, So. Med. Assn., Am. Gastroenterol. Assn., Societe Internationale de Chirugie, Collegium Internationale Chirugie Digestivae, So. Surg. Assn., New Orleans Surg. Soc. (pres. 1988), Orleans Parish Med. Soc., Tulane Surg. Soc., Alton Ochsner Surg. Soc. (pres. 1985). Home: 1529 Nashville Ave New Orleans LA 70115-4254 Office: Alton Ochsner Med Found Ochsner Clinic 1514 Jefferson Hwy New Orleans LA 70121-2429

MCKNIGHT, A. J., religious organization executive. Pres. Nat. Black Cath. Clergy Caucus. Address: PO Box 1088 343 N Walnut St Opelousas LA 70571

MCKNIGHT, MASON, III, construction company executive; b. 1955. Contractor McKnight & Co., Martinez, Ga., 1973-86; pres. ACC Constrn. Co., Inc., Augusta, Ga., 1986—. Office: ACC Constrn Co Inc 635 NW Frontage Rd Ste B Augusta GA 30907

MCKNIGHT, PATRICIA MARIE, elementary education educator; b. Jersey City, June 7, 1952; d. John M. and Regina C. (Broderick) O'Connor; m. Reese J. McKnight, June 29, 1974; children: Jason, Gregory. BS, Madison Coll., Harrisonburg, Va., 1974. Tchr. 4th and 5th grades Prince William County Schs., Woodbridge, Va., 1974-80; tchr. 5th grade A.G. Wright Middle Sch., Stafford, Va., 1980-88, Grafton Village Elem., Stafford, Va., 1989—. Mem. NEA, Stafford County Edn. Assn.

MCKNIGHT, STEPHEN ALEN, history educator; b. Mt. Airy, N.C., July 27, 1944; s. Samuel Albert and Macy (Midkiff) McK.; m. Rebecca Gale Semones, June 5, 1965; 1 child, Stephen Alen Jr. BA, U. N.C., 1966; MDiv, Crozer Sem., 1969; PhD, Emory U., 1972. Asst. prof. U. Fla., Gainesville, 1972-77, assoc. prof., 1977-91, prof., 1991—; dir. acad. program US Info. Agy., Washington, 1981-83; dir. summer inst. NEH, 1990; Carol Belk prof. U. N.C., Asheville, 1993. Author: Sacralizing the Secular, 1989, The Modern Age and Ancient Wisdom, 1991, Science, Pseudo Science and Utopianism, 1992; editor: Voegelin's Search for Order, 1977. Mem. History Sci. Soc., Renaissance Soc. Am. Home: 2311 SW 43rd Pl Gainesville FL 32608-4036 Office: Univ Fla 4131 Turlington Gainesville FL 32611

MCKNIGHT, WILLIAM EDWIN, minister; b. Grenada, Miss., Mar. 21, 1938; s. Leslie Spurgeon and Lucy Jennings (Sistrunk) McK.; m Sue Belle Roberts, Aug. 5, 1960; children: Susan Michele, William Roberts. BA, Millsaps Coll., 1960; BD, Lexington (Ky.) Theol. Sem., 1963. Ordained to ministry, 1964. Chaplain intern Grady Hosp., Atlanta, 1963-64; pastor First Christian Ch., Cleveland, Miss., 1964-67, Inverness, Miss., 1964-67; assoc. pastor First Christian Ch., Jackson, Miss., 1967-70; regional minister Christian Ch. (Disciples of Christ) in Miss., Jackson, 1971—; bd. dirs. Nat. City Christian Ch., Washington, Christian Brotherhood Homes, Jackson, So. Christian Svcs., Macon, Ga.; mem. Gen. Bd. the Christian Ch., Indpls., 1969—, bd. dirs. fin. coun., 1979-82; mem. bd. higher edn., St. Louis, 1979-80. Named one of Outstanding Young Men Am. U.S. Jaycees, 1976. Mem. Miss. Religious Leadership Conf. (pres. 1984-85), Conf. Regional Ministers and Moderators (pres. 1985-86). Office: Christian Ch in Miss 1619 N West St Jackson MS 39202-1418*

MCLAIN, DAVID ANDREW, internist, rheumatologist, health facility administrator; b. Chgo., Aug. 16, 1948; s. William Rex and Wilma Lucille (Raschka) McL.; m. Pamela Rose Fullmer, June 15, 1974; children: Edward, Richard. BA, Northwestern U., 1970; MD with Honors, Tulane U., 1974. Diplomate Am. Bd. Internal Medicine, Am. Bd. Rheumatology. Intern Oschner Clinic, New Orleans, 1974-75; resident Barnes Hosp., St. Louis, 1975-77; fellow in rheumatology Washington U., St. Louis, 1977-79, instr. dept. medicine, 1979-81; with VA Hosp., St. Louis, 1979-81; pvt. practice Birmingham, Ala., 1981—; chief rheumatology sect. dept. internal medicine Brookwood Med. Ctr., Birmingham, 1983-87, 89-90, 91-94, med. dir. phys. therapy, 1986—; mem. staff St. Vincent's Hosp., Birmingham, 1981—, Shelby Med. Ctr., Alabaster, Ala., 1982—, Lakeshore Rehab. Hosp., Birmingham, 1983—, HealthSouth Hosp., 1989—; dir. courses continuing med. edn., 1983—. Editor: (jour. series) Internal Medicine; contbr. articles, abstracts to profl. jours. Mem. med. adv. com. Birmingham chpt. Lupus Found. Am., 1982—, co-originator Lupus Day, Brookwood Med. Ctr., 1983—; bd. dirs. north ctrl. br. Arthritis Found., 1982—, organizer, originator Benefit Horse Show and Art Fair, Birmingham, 1985, del. nat. coun., 1987, chmn. med. and sci. com. Ala. chpt., 1988-89; active Nat. Arthritis Found.; med. advisor Sjogren's Syndrome Found., 1988—. Recipient award of Appreciation Ala. Podiatry Assn., 1984, Ala. Chpt. Arthritis Found., 1986, award for Decade of Leadership in Rheumatology, 1992, Excellence in Tchg. award Med. Assn. State of Ala., 1995. Fellow ACP, Am. Coll. Rheumatology (founding mem.); mem. AMA (Physicians Recognition award 1979, 82, 85, 88, 91, 94), Am. Soc. Internal Medicine, Am. Med. Equestrian Assn. (bd. dirs. 1995—), Ala. Soc. Rheumatic Diseases (founding mem., sec.-treas. 1996—), Ala. Soc. Internal Medicine, Med. Assn. State Ala. (Excellence in Tchg. award 1995), Jefferson County Med. Soc., Brookwood Splty. Physicians Assn. (founding incorporator, bd. dirs., pres. 1990—), U.S. Combined Tng. Assn. (area coun., editor newsletter, adult riders com., bd. govs. 1992-94, chmn. safety com. 1992—, chmn. ad hoc coalition to promote equestrian helmet safety 1993-95, ann. meeting com. 1996), U.S. Dressage Fedn. (founder aux. U.S. Tes Callers Assn.), Alpha Omega Alpha. Office: Birmingham Rheumatology McLain Med Assocs 2022 Brookwood Med Ctr Dr Ste 509 Birmingham AL 35209-6807

MCLANE, BOBBIE JONES, retired government executive, genealogist, publisher; b. Hot Springs, Ark., Feb. 19, 1927; d. Julian Everette and Eula (Deaton) Jones; m. Gerald Bert McLane, Aug. 14, 1954 (dec. 1994). Chief clk. Army and Navy Hosp., Hot Springs, 1950-52; adminstrv. asst. Wis. Mil. Dist., Milw., 1952-54; exec. sec. to postmaster U.S. Postal Svc., Hot Springs, 1954-70, supr. employment svcs., 1970-74, dir. employee and labor rels., 1974-80; acting postmaster U.S. Postal Svc., Arkadelphia, Ark., 1978; dir. employee and labor rels. U.S. Postal Svc., Ft. Smith, Ark., 1980-86; ret., 1986. Compiler, author pub. Ark. Ancestors, 72 titles, 1962; editor The Record, 1966—. Organizer, charter mem. Garland County Hist. Soc., Hot Springs, 1960—; bd. dirs., chmn. Ark. History Commn., 1966-80, 90—; charter mem., bd. dirs. Community Players Hot Springs, 1949-55. Recipient award for contbns. to hist. and geneal. rsch. Am. Assn. State and Local History, 1967, Bicentennial award Postmaster Gen. U.S. Postal Svc., 1976; named One of 100 Ark. Women of Achievement, Ark. Press Women, 1980; Am. Assn. State and Local History fellow Vanderbilt U., 1967. Mem. Profl. Genealogists Ark. (bd. dirs. 1988—), Ark. Geneal. Soc. (charter, bd. dirs. 1960—, past pres.). Democrat. Episcopalian. Home and Office: 222 McMahan Dr Hot Springs National Park AR 71913-6243

MCLANE, DRAYTON, JR., professional baseball team executive. Owner, chmn. Houston Astros, 1993—. Office: Houston Astros PO Box 288 Houston TX 77001-0288 Office: McLane Co Inc PO Box 6115 Temple TX 76503-6115*

MCLANE, WILLIAM DELANO, mechanical engineer; b. Ralls, Tex., Aug. 22, 1936; s. Clyde and Lillian Helen (Earp) McL.; m. Mary Ann Clark, Feb. 17, 1962; children: William Devin, Keri, Kristi, Mandy. BSME, Tex. Tech. U., 1961. Profl. engr. Tex. Engr. Texaco Inc., Tulsa, 1961-63; plant engring. mgr. Owens-Corning Fiberglas Corp., Toledo, 1963-72; pres., CEO Tucker-McLane Tire Corp., Waxahachie, Tex., 1972-89; commr. County of Ellis, Waxahachie, 1989-93; engr. Morrison Knudsen Corp., Dallas, 1993-94; MK-Ferguson, Albuquerque, 1994-95, Parsons Brinckerhoff, Dallas, 1995-96; quality control mgr. Sedalco, Inc., Ft. Worth, Tex., 1996—; mem. adv. bd. Guaranty Fed. Bank, Waxahachie, 1993—, Citizens Nat. Bank, Waxahachie, 1991-92, City of Waxahachie, 1990-91. Sec. bd. Waxahachie Sch. Dist., 1979-88; vice chmn. Ctrl. Tex. Econ. Devel. Dist., Waco, 1989-93. Mem. ASME, ASCE, NSPE, Tex. Soc. Profl. Engrs., Waxahachie C. of C. (pres. 1977), Internat. Conf. Bldg. Officials. Republican. Presbyterian. Home: 1612 Alexander Dr Waxahachie TX 75165 Office: Sedalco Inc 2554 E Long Ave Fort Worth TX 76137

MCLAREN, JAMES KEVIN, architect; b. Dallas, May 29, 1960; s. James Knox and Charlotte Ann (Washington) McL.; m. Linda Diane Willis, Nov. 8, 1986; children: Travis James, Lindsay Nicole, Emily Michelle. BArch, U. Tex., 1983. Lic. architect, N.Mex., Idaho, S.C.; cert. Nat. Coun. Archtl. Registration Bds. Intern architect Chris Cons., Inc., Irving, Tex., 1984-87, project architect, 1987-88, v.p., 1988-94, sr. v.p., 1994—; teaching asst. Dale Carnegie Sch., Dallas, 1988, 89. Mem. Park City Club. Republican. Methodist. Home: 4811 Tamanaco Ct Arlington TX 76017-2636 Office: Chris Cons Inc 1520 W Airport Fwy Irving TX 75062-6180

MC LAUGHLIN, (EDWARD) BRUCE, lawyer, actor; b. Omaha, Apr. 2, 1921; s. Charles F. and Margaret (Bruce) McL. BS, Georgetown U., 1943; postgrad., George Washington U., 1950-51; JD, U. Miami, 1953. Bar: Fla. 1955. Announcer Sta. KTSM, El Paso, 1943-44; news editor Sta. KFRE, Fresno, Calif., 1944; with McKesson-Robbins, San Francisco, 1945-46; with radio prodn. Sta. KOSA, Odessa, Tex., 1947-49, Sta. KPHO, Phoenix, 1949; with prodn. Sta. WITV, Miami-Ft. Lauderdale, Fla., 1953-55; sole practice, Miami, until 1982. Editor: Florida Screen Actor, 1974-95, emeritus, 1995—; contbr. articles to profl. jours. Served with Signal Corps, U.S. Army, World War II. Mem. ABA, Fla. Bar Assn., Dade County Bar Assn., Lawyers Club Dade County (bd. dirs. 1969-70), Screen Actors Guild (pres. Fla. br. 1965-69, mem. Fla. council 1962-94, mem. nat. bd. dirs. 1968-95, nat. v.p. 1983-95), AFTRA (bd. dirs. Miami chpt. 1975-88), Profl. Actors Assn. Fla. (bd. dirs. 1986-90), Nat. Writers Assn. (Fla. chpt.), Miami Internat. Press Club, Am. Legion, Gamma Eta Gamma. Democrat. Roman Catholic. Clubs: Coral Gables (Fla.) Country. Home: 7245 SW 126th St Miami FL 33156-5332

MCLAUGHLIN, LISA MARIE, educational administrator; b. Sioux City, Iowa, Dec. 27, 1957; d. Donald James and Shirley Jean (Bartlett) Warden; m. Steven A. McLaughlin, Apr. 22, 1978; children: Mark Alan, Catherine Lynn. BS, Ctrl. State U., Edmond, Okla., 1978, MEd, 1982. Cert. tchr., Okla. Tchr. learning disabilities Putnam City Schs., Oklahoma City, 1979-80, tchr. visually impaired, 1980-81; devel. therapist Child Study Ctr., Okla. Teaching Hosps., Oklahoma City, 1981-83; ednl. cons. Oklahoma City, 1983-85; regional program specialist Okla. State Dept. Edn., Oklahoma City, 1985-87, spl. edn. data cons., 1987-90, tech. assistance officer, 1990-91, asst. state dir. spl. edn., 1991-92; ednl. cons., vision specialist, special edn. adminstr. Edmond, 1992-95, asst. elem. prin., 1995-96, elem. prin., 1996—. Contbr. chpt. to book. Mem. coun. on adminstrn. Ione br. YWCA, Oklahoma City, 1985-88, 92-94; mem.-at-large bd. dirs. Met. br. YWCA, Oklahoma City, 1989-91; mem. adv. com. Okla. Sch. for Blind, 1992—; chmn. Parkview Sch. for Blind Ednl. Found., 1994-96; bd. dirs. Prevent Blindness Okla., 1993—. Mem. Coun. Exceptional Children (v.p. Oklahoma City chpt. 1988-89, Spl. Educator of Yr. 1991), Learning Disabilities Assn., Assn. for Edn. and Rehab. of Blind and Visually Impaired (state pres. Okla. chpt. 1989-90), Advocates and Parents of Okla. Sight Impaired (treas. 1984-87), Okla. Women in Edn. Adminstrn., Delta Kappa Gamma (2d v.p. 1990-92), Kappa Delta Pi. Home: 3901 Michael Rd Edmond OK 73003 Office: 22522 N Pennsylvania Edmond OK 73003

MCLAUGHLIN, RICHARD P., internist, health facility administrator; b. Topeka, Kans., Jan. 14, 1939; s. Ernest Hoyt and Lillian Pearl (Barkhurst) McL.; m. Lynda Jane Anderson, June 9, 1962; children: Shelley Lynne Kelley Leigh. BS, U. Ala., 1961; MD, Med. Coll. Ala., 1965. Diplomate Am. Bd. Internal Medicine, Nat. Bd. Med. Examiners; lic. physician, Ala. Intern Carraway Meth. Med. Ctr., Birmingham, Ala., 1965-66; resident in internal medicine Mayo Grad. Sch. Medicine, Rochester, Minn., 1966-69; fellow internal medicine Mayo Clinic, Rochester, 1966-69; staff physician Norwood Clinic, Birmingham, 1971-94; med. dir. S.E. Health Plan, Birmingham, 1985-92, Quest Care, Birmingham, 1990-93; chief med. dir. Medisphere Corp., Birmingham, 1994-96; chief med. officer Txen Corp. (Nichols Rsch.), Birmingham, 1996—; staff physician Carraway Meth. Med. Ctr., Birmingham, 1971—; courtesy staff St. Vincent's Hosp., Birmingham, 1971—, Brookwood Hosp., Birmingham, 1971—, Bapt. Med. Ctr.-Montclair, Birmingham, 1971—; v.p. Am. Med. Rev., Inc.; founding bd. dirs., med. dir. S.E. Health Plan, 1984-93; med. dir. Fair Haven Retirement Home, 1978-87, Questcare, 1991-94; bd. dirs. Fla. Med. Quality Assurance, Inc.; clin. instr. medicine U. Ala., Birmingham, 1971—. Vice pres., bd. dirs. Ala. Quality Assurance Found., 1982-87, chmn. bd. dirs., 1987-90; adminstrv. bd. Canterbury United Meth. Ch. Maj. M.C. USAF, 1969-71. Mem. ACP, AMA, Am. Coll. Physician Execs., Jefferson County Med. Soc., Med. Assn. of State of Ala., Birmingham Soc. Internists (pres. 1983-84), Am. Med. Peer Rev. Assn. (bd. dirs. 1988-91), Alpha Omega Alpha, Phi Beta Kappa, Omicron Delta Chi, Alpha Epsilon Delta, Phi Eta Sigma, Rho Alpha Tau, Delta Phi Alpha, Delta Chi. Republican. Methodist. Home: 4404 Corinth Dr Birmingham AL 35213 Office: Txen Corp Ste 500 10 Inverness Ctr Pkwy Birmingham AL 35242

MCLAUGHLIN, SHARON GAIL, principal, small business owner; b. Little Rock, Jan. 2, 1946; d. William Harry and Marion Virginia (Johnson) Fowler; m. Elbert Leroy Anderson, Apr. 3, 1969 (div. 1975); 1 child, William Eric; m. James Jerry McLaughlin, Nov. 22, 1986. BA, Baker U., Baldwin City, Kans., 1968; MA, U. Mo., Kansas City, 1976, postgrad., 1996—; EdS, U. Cen. Ark., 1987. Tchr. Kansas City (Mo.) Sch. Dist., 1968-77; dir. recruiting Lincoln U., Jefferson City, Mo., 1977-78; tchr., dept. chmn. Magnet Sch., Kansas City, 1978-79; asst. prin. Pulaski County Sch. Dist., Little Rock, 1979-87; prin. Little Rock Sch. Dist., 1987-91; owner L Image Ltd, Little Rock, 1989—; tchr. broadcast journalism, tv prodn., theatre arts Dallas Ind. Sch. Dist., 1991—; speaker Clinto-Gore Campaign; cons. in field. Producer/dir.: Take: Teen, Bridging the Gap, 1980—; author prog. for women, Prisms, 1980, prog. for youth, Kaleidescope III, 1980. Mem. nat. bd. ethics Mrs. Am. Pageant Sys., 1991; Tex. state chair rsch. and status women of African descent AME Ch., 1992—; mem. workshops/seminars Performing Arts in Worship. Named Outstanding Black Arkansan, Women in Motion, 1988, Outstanding Educator, Ark. PTA, 1988, Mrs. Ark. Am., 1990-91. Mem. NAACP, Nat. Assn. Black Sch. Educators, Student Adminstrs. Assn. (prog. chmn. 1986-87), Nat. Assn. Sec. Sch. Prins., Internat. Platform Assn., Smithsonian Assocs., Urban League of Mo.-Ark., Top Ladies of Distinction (Dallas chpt.), Alpha Kappa Alpha, Phi Delta Kappa. Democrat. Home: SMU Box 754699 Dallas TX 75275

MCLAUGHLIN, TIMOTHY THOMAS, physician; b. Phila., Aug. 2, 1950; s. Charles James and Eleanor May (Low) McL.; m. Constance Wrench, Oct. 2, 1976; children: Timothy T., Stacy Marie. BA, La Salle Univ., 1972; MD, Temple Univ., 1978; postgrad., St. Louis Univ., 1978-83. Diplomate Am. Bd. Medical Oncology. Intern St. Louis U., 1978-79, resident in internal medicine, 1979-81, fellow in med. oncology and hematology, 1981-83; pvt. practice, Tampa, Fla., 1983-84; physician Mease Clinic, Duneton, Fla., 1985-92; pvt. practice, Palm Harbor, Fla., 1992—. Contbr. articles to profl. jours. Sponsor Palm Harbor Youth Rec. League, 1988-92. Mem. Am. Coll. Physicians, Am. Soc. Clinical Oncology, Am. Soc. Internal Medicine. Republican. Roman Catholic. Office: Cornerstone Cancer Ctr 3850 Tampa Rd Palm Harbor FL 34684-3670

MCLAUGHLIN, WILLIAM PRESTON, military officer, educator; b. Charleston, S.C., Oct. 31, 1961; s. John Francis Jr. and Mae Jordan (Dunson) McL.; m. Michelle Renée Conley, Jan. 4, 1986; children: Patrick Conley, Brendan Joseph. BA in Polit. Sci., The Citadel, 1979-83; student, U.S. Army Armor Sch., Ft. Knox, Ky., 1990; M in Mil. Studies, Marine Corps U., 1996. Commd. USMC, 1983; platoon comdr., tng. officer 2d Marine Divsn. USMC, Camp Lejeune, N.C., 1984-86; platoon comdr., XO, sch. ops. officer Security Battalion USMC, Norfolk, Va., 1986-90; comdr. AAV co. 2d AA BN 2nd Marine Divsn. USMC, Camp Lejeune, N.C., 1990-91; comdr. HQ co. 2d AA BN 2nd Marine Divsn. USMC, Camp Lejeune, 1992-93; inspector, instr. 4th AA BN 4th Marine Divsn. USMC, Gulfport, Miss., 1993-95; mil. observer Western Sahara Mission UN, Laayoune, Western Sahara, 1991-92; instr. Amphibious Warfare Sch. Marine Corps U., Quantico, Va., 1996—. Contbr. articles to mags. Cons. Salute to the Mil., Miss. Gulf Coast C. of C., Gulfport, 1993-95; mem. Ptnrs. in Edn., Gulfport, 1993-95. Recipient Navy Commendation with V, Sec. of Navy, 1991. Mem. KC (4th degree), Assn. Citadel Men, Citadel Club of Greater Washington, Marine Corps Assn., LVT Assn., U.S. Armor Assn. Roman Catholic. Home: 4710-A Quarters Quantico VA 22134 Office: AWS 2077 Geiger Rd Quantico VA 22134

MCLAUGLIN, ROBERT BRUCE, software designer; b. Camden, N.J., Aug. 30, 1959; s. Robert Bruce and Patricia Ann (Renner) McL. Programmer/analyst Computron, N.Y.C., 1979-81; systems analyst

Wincester Computer, N.Y.C., 1982-83, Geometric Solutions, N.Y.C., 1983-85; instrument maker Fusion Energy Found., N.Y.C., 1985-87; rsch. engr. Community Computer, Arlington, Va., 1987-89; prin. engr. Pilot Rsch., Vienna, Va., 1989-91; systems architect Unitel Comm., Toronto, Ont., Can., 1991-93; chief scientist Image Telecom, Reston, Va., 1993—; design authority Energis Comm., London, 1993-94; chief scientist Winstar Comm., Vienna, Va., 1994—. Author: Fix Your LAN, 1994, Troubleshooting Your Own LAN, 1992, Fix Your PC, 1989-93; contbr. numerous articles to profl. jours. Mem. IEEE, Assn. Computing Machinery, Soc. of Old Crows, Am. Soc. for Quality Control.

MCLAWHORN, REBECCA LAWRENCE, mathematics educator; b. Newport News, Va., July 13, 1949; d. Marion Watson and Hazel Estelle (Babb) Lawrence; m. James Richard McLawhorn, June 23, 1973 (dec. 1980); 1 child, Susan Annette. BS, East Carolina U., 1971, MEd, 1974. Tchr., coach Greene Cen. High Sch., Snow Hill, N.C., 1972-76, Ridgecroft Sch., Ahoskie, N.C., 1976-78, Gates County High Sch., Gatesville, N.C., 1978-86; prof. Chowan Coll., Murfreesboro, N.C., 1986—. Pianist Gatesville Bapt. Ch., 1977—; active Athletic Boosters Club, Gatesville, 1984-91, 93—, Chowan Coll. Braves Club, 1993—, Chowan Coll. Friends of the Libr., 1993—. Mem. ASCD, Nat. Coun. Tchrs. of Math., N.C. Coun. Tchrs. of Math., Parents for Advancement of Gifted Edn. (sec. 1986-90). Democrat. Office: Chowan Coll Murfreesboro NC 27855

MCLEAN, ALBERT FORBES, retired literature educator; b. Boston, July 2, 1928; s. Albert Forbes and Stella (Larsen) McL.; m. Jean McLeod Mairs, July 29, 1952; children: Stuart Alexander, Cameron Forbes, Janet Louise McLean Shock. BA, Williams Coll., 1951; MA, Harvard U., 1953, PhD, 1960. Instr. Pine Manor Jr. Coll., Wellesley, Mass., 1953-56, Tufts U., Medford, Mass., 1956-60; assoc. prof., then prof. Transylvania U., Lexington, Ky., 1960-67; prof. Point Park Coll., Pitts., 1967-87, disting. prof., 1987-90, acad. dean, v.p., 1967-69, 75-86, prof. emeritus, 1990—. Author: William Cullen Bryant, 1964, 2d edit., 1989, American Vaudeville as Ritual, 1965, Point Park College: The First 25 Years, 1985, Collected Poems, 1994. Bd. dirs. Southwestern Pa. High Edn. Coun., Inc., Pitts., 1974-87, pres., 1983-85. Recipient Fulbright Tchg. award, 1961, Disting. Svc. award S.W. Coun. on Higher Edn., 1987. Mem. MLA, AAUP (pres. Ky. State conf. 1965-67), Melville Soc., Am. Studies Assn. Democrat. Home: 2198 Majestic Ct N Naples FL 34110

MCLEAN, MARK PHILIP, physiologist, educator; b. DeKalb, Ill., Feb. 20, 1957; s. James Fredrick and Kaye (Lyman) McL.; m. Lynn Anne Maday, June 18, 1983; children: Bryan, Alyssa, Michelle. BS, No. Ill. U., 1979, MS, 1981; PhD, U. Ill., Chgo., 1986. From rsch. asst. to rsch. assoc. ob/gyn. dept. U. Ill., Chgo., 1981-90; assoc. prof. ob-gyn., biochemistry, molecular biology U. South Fla., Tampa, 1990—. Contbr. articles to profl. jours. Recipient Nat. Rsch. Svc. award NIH, 1986-89, Young Investigator Serono, 1989, Rsch. award Am. Diabetes Assn., 1983, Pres.'s award Soc. for Gynecologic Investigation, 1992, Robert J. Boucek Rsch. award Am. Heart Assn., 1993. Mem. Am. Soc. Cell Biology, Am. Physiol. Soc., Soc. for Exptl. Biology and Medicine, Soc. for Study Reproduction, Endocrine Soc. (New Investigator award 1989), Soc. for Gynecologic Investigation. Office: U South Fla Dept Ob/Gyn 4 Columbia Dr Tampa FL 33606-3589

MCLEAN, ROBERT ALEXANDER, lawyer; b. Memphis, Oct. 24, 1943; s. Albert A. and Harriet Spencer (Pond) McL.; m. Sydney Ross, July 16, 1977; children: Robert Alexander, Ross Andrew. BA with honors, Rhodes Coll., 1965; MA, Princeton U., 1968, PhD, 1974; JD, U. Memphis, 1978. Bar: Tenn. 1979, U.S. Dist. Ct. (we. dist.) Tenn. 1979, U.S. Dist. Ct. (ea. dist.) Wis. 1985, U.S. Ct. Appeals (5th cir.) 1986, U.S. Dist. Ct. (ea. and we. dists.) Ark. 1990, U.S. Ct. Appeals (8th cir.) 1990, U.S. Ct. Appeals (10th cir.) 1991. Asst. prof. Russian lit. U. Calif., Santa Cruz, 1971-76; staff atty. FCA, Washington, 1979-81; assoc. Wildman, Harrold, Allen, Dixon & McDonnell, Memphis, 1981-88, ptnr., 1988-89; ptnr. McDonnell Boyd, Memphis, 1989-94; mem. McDonnell Dyer, PLC, Memphis, 1994-95; spl. counsel Wolf Ardis, P.C., Memphis, 1995—; asst. city atty. Germantown, Tenn.; adj. asst. prof. Russian lang. Rhodes Coll., Memphis, 1982-86. Translator: Mozart and Salieri, 1973; mem. U. Memphis Law Rev., 1977-78. Mem. session Germantown (Tenn.) Presbyn. Ch., 1988—, chmn. fin. com., 1989-94, also trustee. Charlotte Elizabeth Procter fellow Princeton U., 1968, Fulbright fellow U.S.S.R., 1969, Regents fellow U. Calif., Santa Cruz, 1975. Mem. ABA, Tenn. Bar Assn., Memphis Bar Assn. Republican. Home: 8820 Somerset Ln Germantown TN 38138-7375 Office: Wolf Ardis PC Ste 360 6055 Primacy Pkwy Memphis TN 38119

MCLEAN, SUSAN RALSTON, lawyer, federal government; b. Fayetteville, Tenn., Feb. 28, 1948; d. Joseph Frederick and Clara (Robertson) Ralston; m. Arthur Edward McLean, Apr. 16, 1983. AB, Randolph-Macon Woman's Coll., 1970; MAT in English, Vanderbilt U., 1971; JD, U. Tenn., 1979; LLM in Taxation, So. Meth. U., 1984. Bar: Tenn. 1979, Tex. 1981, Ark. 1984. Assoc. Rose Law Firm, Little Rock, 1984-85, Brice & Mankoff, Dallas, 1986-87; counsel tax divsn. Dept. Justice, Dallas, 1987—. Mem. ABA (tax litigation, bus. law sects., exempt orgn. com. tax sect.), Tex. Bar Assn. (tax and litigation sects.), Dallas Bar Assn., Randolph-Macon Woman's Coll. Alumnae (pres. 1992-94). Republican. Presbyterian. Home: 4025 McFarlin Blvd Dallas TX 75205-1723

MCLEES, AINSLIE ARMSTRONG, French language educator; b. Phila., Feb. 17, 1947; d. Maurice Whitman and Irene (Macdonald) Armstrong; m. John Hill McLees Jr., June 5, 1969; children: Angus Armstrong, Ainslie Heather Armstrong. Diplomes, McGill U. Fr. S.S., Montreal, Quebec, 1966, 67, 68; BA, Ursinus Coll., Collegeville, Pa., 1968; MA, Bryn Mawr Coll., 1969; diplome, U. Sorbonne, 1974, diploma, 1974; diplôme, U. Sorbonne Nouvelle, Paris, 1974. Instr. French Mary Washington Coll., Fredericksburg, Va., 1969-70, Kapiolani C.C., Honolulu, 1970-73, No. Va. C.C., Sterling, 1979-85; teaching asst., instr. U. Va., Charlottesville, 1973-77; lang. cons. Fairfax, Va., 1977-79; adj. prof. U. Richmond, Va., 1985-87; vis. assoc. prof. romance langs. Randolph-Macon Coll., Ashland, Va., 1985-93; fgn. langs. curriculum specialist Regional Gov.'s Sch., Richmond, 1993—; coord. Bryn Mawr Coll. Career Network, Washington, 1979; bd. dirs., editor bull. Fgn. Lang. Assn. Va., 1986-96, editor; project dir. Acad. Alliance in Fgn. Lang. and Lit., Richmond, 1990—. Author: Baudelaire's Argot Plastique, 1989. Sec. Guilford Coll. Parents Assn., Greensboro, N.C., 1989-91. U. Va. and Am. Coun. on Teaching of Fgn. Langs. grantee, 1988. Mem. Am. Pen Women (sec. 1987-88), Fgn. Lang. Assn. Va. (bd. dirs. 1986-96), Am. Assn. Tchrs. of French, MLA, South Atlantic MLA (chair women's caucus disc group II 1992-93, bd. dirs. 1993-96), Va. Writers Club (treas. 1991-92). Home: 1628 Park Ave Richmond VA 23220-2909 Office: Regional Gov Sch 4100 W Grace St Richmond VA 23230-3802

MCLEMORE, JOAN MEADOWS, librarian, consultant; b. Bivens, Tex., Aug. 24, 1929; d. James Leon Jr. and Dell (Crawford) Meadows; m. Kenneth Lyons McLemore, May 6, 1950; 1 child, Ken Malcolm. Student, Miss. State Coll. for Women, 1947-49; BS, U. So. Miss., 1976, MLS, 1983. Libr. Franklin County Pub. Libr., Meadville, Miss., 1976-90, Copiah-Lincoln C.C., Natchez, Miss., 1990—; libr. cons. Chamberlain Hunt Acad., Port Gibson, Miss., 1993—; story teller, presenter conf. The Delta Kappa Gamma Soc. Internat., Louisville, 1991, Nashville, 1994; internat. spkr. Delta Kappa Soc., Red Deer, Can., 1994; mem. faculty Elderhostel, Natchez, Miss., 1990—; presenter Southeastern Regional Conf., Delta Kappa Gamma Soc. Internat., Charleston, S.C. Contbr. articles to profl. jours. Libr. trustee Franklin County, Meadville, 1962-76, Lincoln-Lawrence-Franklin Regional Libr., Brookhaven, Miss., 1971-76; jury commr. Franklin County, Meadville, 1988—. Mem. Miss. Libr. Assn. (com. chair, exec. dir. libr. week activities 1989—), Colonial Dames (gov. George Harlan chpt.), DAR (Homochitlo River chpt.), Dames of the Ct. of Honor, Order of the First Families of Miss.: 1619-1817, Delta Kappa Gamma (pres. 1979-80, 94-96 Rho chpt.). Methodist. Home: RR 2 Box 267 Roxie MS 39661-9565 Office: Copiah Lincoln C C Libr 11 Co-Lin Circle Natchez MS 39120-8446

MCLENDON, DOROTHY, school psychologist; b. Crawfordsville, Ind., Feb. 20, 1918; d. Joseph Newton and Dora (Ryall) Fullenwider; m. Hiram James McLendon, May 23, 1942; 1 child, Hiram James McLendon, Jr. AB, Olivet Coll., Kankakee, Ill., 1942; MA, Boston U., 1945, EdD, 1970. Diplomate Am. Bd. of Profl. Psychology. Spl. edn. tchr. Kingsley Schs., Belmont Jr. High, Boston, 1943-46, 56-57; tchr. Homerton Coll., Cambridge, Eng., 1946-47; sch. psychologist Alameda County Schs., Oakland, Calif., 1949-52, Paris Am. Army Dependent Sch., France, 1957-58, Brookline (Mass.) Pub. Schs., 1958-81; pvt. cons. Cambridge, Mass., 1981—; cons. Cocoa, Fla., 1981—.

MCLEOD, ALEXANDER CANADAY, physician; b. Fayetteville, N.C., Jan. 14, 1935; s. Walter Guy and Vida (Canaday) McL.; m. Dorothy Venning Woods, Aug. 21, 1965; children: Alexander Woods, Dorothy Seward. Cert., Städische Akademie für Tönkunst, 1955; AB, Princeton U., 1956; postgrad., Johns Hopkins U., 1959-60; MD, Duke U., 1960; MBA, Vanderbilt U., 1988. Diplomate Am. Bd. Internal Medicine, Nat. Bd. Med. Examiners. Intern, asst. resident N.Y. Hosp.-Cornell Med. Ctr., N.Y.C., 1960-62; resident in medicine and neurology, fellow Vanderbilt U. Hosp., Nashville, 1964-67; pvt. practice internal medicine Nashville, 1967—; gen. mgr.; assoc. clin. prof. medicine, med. adminstrn. Vanderbilt U. Med. Ctr.; adj. prof. mgmt. Owen Grad. Sch. Mgmt. Vanderbilt U., faculty coord. health care mgmt. Owen Grad. Sch. Mgmt. Contbr. numerous articles to med. jours.; presenter papers to various orgns. Bd. of Trust mem. Friends of Heard Libr. Vanderbilt U., Nashville, 1994—; past trustee, past chmn. Dunvegan Found.; past music com. mem. Westminster Presbyn. Ch., 1989-91; past vestryman, jr. warden St. George's Episcopal Ch.; bd. dirs. Nashville Symphony, 1988-91. With USNR, 1962-64. Recipient Physicians Achievement award AMA, 1971, 74, 77, 81, 84, 87, 90, 93, 96; USPHS Summer fellow in neurology, 1957-58, Mid. Tenn. Heart Assn., 1966-67. Fellow ACP, Soc. Antiquaries of Scotland, Hugenot Soc. Gt. Britain and Ireland; mem. Tenn. Med. Assn., Nashville Acad. Medicine, Am. Acad. Med. Dirs., St. Andrew's Soc. N.C., Heraldry Soc. Scotland, Scottish Soc. Mid. Tenn. (life), Clan McLeod Soc. (life, past pres., past co-chmn. Alasdair Crotach com., exec. v.p.), Coun. of Scottish Clan Assns., Inc. (former trustee), Skye Terrier Club Am., Univ. Club Nashville, Princeton Club N.Y., Princeton Club Nashville (past pres. and trustee), Tower Club Princeton, Farmington Country Club, Belle Meade Country Club, Cumberland Club, Grolier Club. Republican. Presbyterian. Home: 203 Evelyn Ave Nashville TN 37205-3307 Office: 2400 Patterson St Ste 400 Nashville TN 37203-1562

MCLEOD, E. DOUGLAS, real estate developer, lawyer; b. Galveston, Tex., Aug. 6, 1941; s. Vaughn Watkins McL. and Dorothy (Milroy) Burton; m. Sarah Jackson Helms, Mar. 20, 1965 (div. 1979); children: Chanse, Alexandra, Lindsey; m. Joan Margaret Williams, Dec. 26, 1979; 1 child, Joanie; stepchildren: Meg, Libbie. BBA, U. North Tex., 1965; postgrad., So. Meth. U., 1965-66; JD, South Tex. Coll. Law, 1990; LLM, U. Houston, 1993. Lic. real estate broker. Pres., owner McLeod Properties & co., Galveston, Tex., 1967—; tchr. Galveston Ind. Sch. Dist., 1967-69; banker W.L. Moody & Co., Galveston, 1969-72; developer, broker McLeod Properties/Builders, Galveston, 1972-82; developer Moody Found., Galveston, 1982—; bd. dirs. Am. Nat. Ins. Co., Galveston, Nat. Western Life Ins. Co., Austin, Anrem Corp., Galveston, Moody Gardens Inc., Galveston, , chmn., 1984—; bd. dirs. Colonel Inc., Galveston, v.p., 1985—; bd. dirs. Ctr. Transp. & Commerce, Glaveston. Pres., trustee Galveston Ind. Sch. Dist., 1969-73; mayor pro-tem, mem. city coun. City of Galveston, 1973-76; state legislator Tex. Ho. of Reps., Austin, 1976-83; bd. visitors So. Tex. Coll. Law, 1990—; mem. adv. bd. U. Houston, 1986—; bd. dirs. Ronald McDonald House, 1986-93, Trinity Episcopal Sch., 1990—. With USMC, 1961-67. South Tex. Coll. Law fellow, 1990-95. Mem. Granaderos De Galvez, Marine Corps League. Episcopalian. Home: 53 Cedar Lawn Cir Galveston TX 77551-4631 Office: The Moody Found 2302 Post Office St Ste 704 Galveston TX 77550-1936

MCLEOD, HARRY O'NEAL, JR., petroleum engineer, consultant; b. Shreveport, La., Feb. 26, 1932; s. Harry O'Neal Sr. and Odelle Nan (Crow) McL.; m. Sandra Lou Mahaffey, Feb. 6, 1959; children: Kathleen Odelle, Bryan O'Neal. Degree in engring., Colo. Sch. of Mines, 1953; MS in Petroleum Engring., U. Okla., 1963, PhD in Engring. Sci., 1965. Registered profl. engr., Okla. Prodn. engr. Phillips Petroleum Co., 1953-58; rsch. engr. Jersey Prodn. Rsch. Co., Tulsa, 1963-64; sr. rsch. engr. Dowell div. Dow Chem. Co., Tulsa, 1965-69; dir. info. svcs. dept. U. Tulsa, 1969-75; from sr. prodn. engr. to sr. staff engr. Conoco, Inc., Houston, 1975-86, engring. profl., 1986-91, sr. engring. profl., 1992—. 1st lt. U.S. Army, 1954-56. Mem. Soc. Petroleum Engrs. (Prodn. Engring. award 1989, Disting. Mem. award 1995), Sigma Xi. Republican. Methodist. Home: 2006 Southwick St Houston TX 77080-6315 Office: Conoco Inc 600 N Dairy Ashford St Houston TX 77079-1100

MCLEOD, LINDY GALE, music educator; b. McLain, Miss., May 24, 1950; d. Roman and Myrtle (Carter) M.; 1 child, Melody DeVerne. AAA, Sherwood Sch. Music, Chgo., 1976; B.Mus.Edn., William Carey Coll., Hattiesburg, Miss., 1979, M.Mus.Edn., 1980; PhD, Columbia State U., Metarie, La., 1996. Cert. music tchr., Miss. Tchr. music Earl Travillion/Forrest Ctrl. H.S., Hattiesburg, 1978-79; grad. asst. tchr. William Carey Coll., Hattiesburg, 1979-80; tchr. music McLain (Miss.) Attendance Ctr., 1980-81, W.H. Jones Elem. Jr. H.S., Hattiesburg, 1981-82; youth choir dir. Toulminville Warren United Meth. Ch., Mobile, Ala., 1981-85; instr. history Mattie T. Blount H.S., Mobile, 1982-85; proffl. pianist St. Francis Xavier Cmty. Choir, Mobile, 1985-86; chairperson, music dir. Piney Woods (Miss.) Country Life Sch., 1986-94; choral dir., chairperson Coahoma C.C., Clarksdale, Miss., 1994—; minister of music Pineview Presbyn. Ch., Hattiesburg, 1975-81; pvt. piano tchr. McLeod's Music Studeio, Mobile, 1969—; music dir. Toulminville Woman Day Care, Mobile, 1969-85, Myrtle C. McLeod Chorals, Mobile, 1995—. Mem. Cancer crusade, Mobile, 1982—, Heart Fund, Mobile, 1982—; mem., pianist Casher Philharmonic Choir, Mobile, 1969—. Named to Outstanding Young Women of Am., 1978. Mem. Music Educators Nat. Conf. (chairperson 1994-95), Music Choral Assn. (chairperson 1994-95), Mobile Music Tchrs. Assn., Miss. Music Tchrs. Assn., Phi Kappa Phi, Zeta Phi Beta (World Class Svc. award 1994), Alpha Kappa Alpha, Delta Omicron. Democrat. Methodist. Home: 1714 First Ave Mobile AL 36610 Office: Coahoma Community College 3240 Friars Point Rd Clarksdale MS 38614-9359

MCLEOD, MARILYNN HAYES, educational administrator, farmer; b. Lake View, S.C., Jan. 2, 1924; d. Cary Victor and Benna (Price) Hayes; BA, Furman U.; MEd, U. S.C., 1952, EdD, 1986; m. Charles Edward McLeod, Aug. 24, 1947; children: Cary Franklin, Mary Marilynn. Tchr., Hamer-Kentyre Sch., Hamer, S.C., 1944-45, Bennettsville (S.C.) City Schs., 1946-59, Clio (S.C.) Elem. Sch., 1960-63; asst. prof. elem. edn. St. Andrews Presbyn. Coll., Laurinburg, N.C., 1964-67; instr. U. S.C., Florence, 1971; reading supr. Marlboro County Sch. Dist., Bennettsville, S.C. 1967-86; prin. Marlboro County Child Devel. Ctr., 1986-87; asst. prin. Bennettsville High Sch., 1987-89, Marlboro County High Sch., 1989-92; farmer, 1960—; mem. Marlboro County Sch. Dist. Bd., 1992—. Author: The History of Education in Marlboro County, South Carolina, 1737-1895, 1988. Chmn. adminstrv. bd. Trinity United Meth. Ch., 1982—, chmn. pastor-parish relations com., 1979—; trustee Epworth Children's Home, chmn. personnel com., Columbia, S.C., 1982-94. Mem. NEA (life), Internat. Reading Assn., S.C. Edn. Assn., S.C. Reading Assn., Assn. Secondary Prins., S.C. Internat. Reading Assn., Marlboro County Edn. Assn., Pee Dee Internat. Reading Assn., Marlborough Hist. Soc., Marlboro Arts Coun., Marlboro County Assn. For Mental Retardation, Dillon County Farm Bur., Clio Federated Women's Club, Palmetto Book Club, Soc. Internat. outstanding women educators, Delta Kappa Gamma. Democrat. Methodist. Home: PO Box 38 127 S Main St Clio SC 29525 Office: 127 S Main St Bennettsville SC 29512-3103

MCLEOD, STEPHEN GLENN, education educator; b. Pensacola, Fla., Mar. 30, 1949. AA, Pensacola Jr. Coll., 1969; BA, U. West Fla., 1971; MA, Vanderbilt U., 1973; EdD, Nova Southeastern U., 1992. Commd. 2d lt. U.S. Army, 1978, advanced through grades to capt., 1981, resigned, 1984; sr. assoc. prof. mil. edn. program St. Leo Coll., Hurlburt Field, Fla., 1984-92; adj. instr. Pensacola Jr. Coll., 1984-86, 91—; West Fla. cluster coord. programs for higher edn. Nova Southeastern U., Pensacola/Ft. Lauderdale, Fla., 1994—. Contbr. articles to profl. publs. Capt. U.S. Army, 1975-84. Recipient Rsch. award Phi Delta Kappa, 1989. Mem. Southeastern Conf. on English in Two-Yr. Coll. Home: 1313 Wisteria Ave Pensacola FL 32507

MCLEOD, WILLIAM LASATER, JR., judge, former state legislator; b. Marks, Miss., Feb. 27, 1931; s. William Lasater and Sara Louise (Macaulay) McL.; m. Marilyn Qualls, June 16, 1962; children: Sara Nelson Judson, Martha Ellen, Ruth Elizabeth. AB, Princeton U., 1953; JD, La. State U., 1958. Bar: La. 1958, U.S. Supreme Ct. 1980. Sole practice, Lake Charles, La., 1958-62; ptnr. McLeod & Little, Lake Charles, 1976-90; dist. judge Calcasieu Parish, 1991—; mem. La. Ho. of Reps., 1968-76; mem. La. Senate, 1976-90. Chmn. Lake Charles Salvation Army Adv. Bd., 1965-66; pres. Calcasieu Area Coun. Boy Scouts Am., 1978; elder Presbyn. Ch. Served with U.S. Army, 1953-55. Recipient Disting. Service award Lake Charles Jaycees, 1963, Civic Service award S.W. La. C. of C., 1986. Mem. ABA, La. Bar Assn., S.W. La. Bar Assn. (pres. 1980). Democrat. Lodge: Masons. Office: Calcasieu Parish Courthouse 1000 Ryan St Lake Charles LA 70601-5250

MCLINDEN, HUGH PATRICK, editor, writer; b. Hartford, Conn., Dec. 6, 1928; s. Hugh Patrick Sr. and Regina (Lorentz) McL.; m. Mary Margaret Lehman, Jan. 17, 1953; children: James Patrick, John Thomas, Hugh Michael. Student, U. Fla., 1947-50; BA, U. Tenn., Nashville, 1963; postgrad., U. Wis. Prin. cts. reporter Nashville Banner, 1953-61; editor St. Louis Globe-Dem., 1961-67; mng. dir. pub. rels. Am. Automobile Assn., Madison, Wis., 1967-86; dir. communications Fla. Restaurant Assn., Hollywood, 1987-95; ret.; freelance writer-reporter various newspapers and mags., 1947—; writer-editor newsletters for several assns. in so. Fla., 1986—; speech writer for nat. and local polit. candidates, 1963—. Capt. U.S. Army, 1950-52, Europe. Recipient various writing awards AP, St. Louis Press Club, others. Mem. Internat. Assn. Bus. Communicators. Democrat. Roman Catholic. Home: 2301 Saint Andrews Rd Hollywood FL 33021-2943

MCLUSKIE, WILLIAM DEAN, computer scientist; b. Pocatello, Idaho, Feb. 7, 1966; s. Edward Wilford and Janice Louise (Martinz) McL.; m. Brenda Mae, Mar. 10, 1988. BS in Comp. Sci., East Carolina U., 1988; MS in Comp. Info. Systems, Boston U., 1991. Computer programmer, analyst GS-11 USAREUR Vehicle Registry, Heidelberg, Germany, 1989-91; lectr. computer sci. Overseas Program Boston U., Heidelberg, 1991; sr. cons. Abaris Software, Charlotte, N.C., 1991—; LAN adminstr. adminstrv. computing svcs. N.C. State U., 1992-93, sr. rsch. analyst adminstrv. computing svcs., 1993-94; cons. Advanced Tech. Svcs., Inc., Charlotte, N.C., 1994—. mem. Assn. of Computing Machinery, Nat. Eagle Scout Assn., Theta Chi Fraternity Alumni Assn., Gamma Beta Phi. Home: 11413 Vista Haven Dr Charlotte NC 28226-3648

MCMACKIN, F. JOSEPH, III, lawyer; b. N.Y.C., July 23, 1946; s. Frank Joseph and Mary Ann (Dunn) McM.; m. S. Elizabeth Simonton, Jan. 12, 1974; children: Frank Joseph IV, Ian Simonton, James Tyler. AB, Wesleyan U., 1968; JD, U. Miami, Fla., 1973. Bar: Fla. 1973, U.S. Dist. Ct. (so. dist.) Fla. 1973, U.S. Ct. Appeals (5th cir.) 1974, U.S. Ct. Appeals (D.C.), 1975, U.S. Tax Ct. 1981, U.S. Ct. Appeals (11th cir.) 1982, Wis. 1984. Practice law, Fla.; assoc. Spingler & Allen, 1973-77; sole practice as F. Joseph McMackin III, Chartered, Fla., 1977-82; ptnr. Quarles & Brady, Naples, Fla., 1982—, mng. ptnr., 1982—; bd. dirs. Barnet Bank of Naples. Bd. dirs. Telford Found. Served to lt. USN, 1968-70. Mem. Fla. Bar (20th jud. cir. grievance com. "B"), D.C. Bar Assn., Wis. Bar Assn. Republican. Office: Quarles & Brady 4501 Tamiami Trl N Naples FL 34103*

MCMAHON, ANTHONY HUGH, SR., computer program manager, systems integrator; b. Nesbitt, Miss., Nov. 16, 1960; s. Sam Ernest Batmon and Velma Louise (Brown) McMahon; m. Queen Esther Harris Taylor, Sept. 9, 1989 (div. June 1993); children: Anthony Hugh Jr. AS in Bus. Tech. and Acctg., State Tech. Inst., Memphis, 1979. Correspondence tax auditor IRS, Memphis, 1981-84; computer systems analyst IRS, Washington, 1984-88, program analyst, 1988-91; tech. support chief electronic filing sys. IRS, Memphis, 1990-94, program mgr., sys. integrator, 1994—. Recipient spl. achievement cash award IRS, 1986, 89, 91-95, mgr.'s award, 1992, Disting. Performance award, 1992, 93. Mem. Black Data Processing Assocs., Assn. for Improvement of Minorities, Info. Sys. Fed. Users Group. Democrat. Baptist. Home: 5508 Edwin Forest Rd Memphis TN 38141-2411 Office: IRS 5333 Getwell Rd Memphis TN 38118-7703

MCMAHON, DENNIS OWEN, school superintendent. BS in Bus. and Speech, Western Mich. U., 1967, M in Sch. Adminstrn., 1969, EdD in Ednl. Adminstrn., 1986. Tchr. Marysville (Mich.) High Sch., 1967-69; prin. high sch. Climax (Mich.) Scotts Jr./Sr. High Sch., 1969-71, Lowell (Mich.) Pub. Schs., 1971-77; supt. schs. Hopkins (Mich.) Pub. Schs., 1977-79, Vicksburg (Mich.) Cmty. Schs., 1979-84, Brighton (Mich.) Area Schs., 1984-94, Sch. Dist. Five of Lexington and Richland Counties, Ballentine, S.C., 1994—; exec. dir. Vicksburg Sch. Found.; mem. State-Wide Bus. Partnership Task Force, Mich., 1987-89; presenter in field. Mem. allocation bd. Brighton United Way, chairperson campaign, 1987; vice chairperson Livingston County United Way, 1988, chairperson campaign, 1989, bd. dirs., 1990-93; chairperson Econ. Devel. Com. Brighton, 1993; chairperson Vicksburg United Way; asst. dir. Vicksburg Rotary Showboat; eucharistic min., lay reader, mem. ch. coun. Vicksburg Cath. Ch.; v.p. Franklin Cmty. Hosp., Vicksburg; chmn. Lowell United Way; new bldg. and site fund chmn. Lowell Cath. Ch.; trustee St. Patrick Cath. Schs. Found., 1987-91; bd. dirs. Wolverine Area coun. Boy Scouts Am., 1987, 88, Livingston County Econ. Devel. Corp., 1993, Lowell Showboat Corp. Named one of three Most Respected Cmty. Leaders, Vicksburg C. of C.; honored for state wide contbns. on behalf of Sch. Bus. Partnership Program, Mich. Dept. Edn.; resolution passed by Mich. Legislature honoring and recognizing contbns. to Vicksburg Sch. Dist. Mem. ASCD, Am. Assn. Sch. Adminstrs., Nat. Assn. Secondary Prins., Nat. Sch. Pub. Rels. Assn., Mich. Assn. Sch. Adminstrs., Mich. Sch. Pub. Rels. Assn. Office: Lexington SD 5 1020 Dutch Fork Road Ballentine SC 29002*

MCMAHON, DONNA MARIE, travel agency executive; b. Washington, Nov. 15, 1946; d. James Vincent and Agnes Mary (Buzby) Mulvihill; m. Joseph Conrad McMahon, Feb. 12, 1977; children: Jace, James. BA, Marywood Coll., Scranton, Pa., 1968. Tchr. DeKalb County Schs., Atlanta, 1968-69; travel agt. Thompson Travel Bur., Scranton, 1969-71; owner, agt. Thompson Travel/Jim Mulvihill Tours, Scranton, 1971—. Chmn. human devel. St. Ann's Ch., Manlius, N.Y., 1990-91. Mem. Providence Country Club Women's Club (chmn. svc. project 1993-94). Republican. Roman Catholic. Home: 9186 Brushboro Dr Brentwood TN 37027-6131

MCMAHON, JOHN ALEXANDER, law educator; b. Monongahela, Pa., July 31, 1921; s. John Hamilton and Jean (Alexander) McM.; m. Betty Wagner, Sept. 14, 1947 (div. Mar. 1977); children: Alexander Talpey, Sarah Francis, Elizabeth Wagner, Ann Wallace; m. Anne Fountain Willets, May 1, 1977 (dec. June 1996). A.B. magna cum laude, Duke U., 1942; student, Harvard U. Bus. Sch., 1942-43; J.D., Law Sch., 1948; LL.D., Wake Forest U., 1978; D.Sc. (hon.), Georgetown U. Sch. Medicine, 1985. Bar: N.C. 1950. Prof. pub. law and govt., asst. dir. Inst. Govt. U. N.C., 1948-59; gen. counsel, sec.-treas. N.C. Assn. County Commrs., Chapel Hill, 1959-65; v.p. spl. devel. Hosp. Saving Assn., Chapel Hill, N.C., 1965-67; pres. N.C. Blue Cross and Blue Shield, Inc., Chapel Hill, 1968-72, Am. Hosp. Assn., Chgo., 1972-86; chmn. dept. health adminstrn. Duke U., Durham, N.C., 1986-92, exec.-in-residence Fuqua Sch. Bus., 1992—; mem. Chapel Hill bd. N.C. Nat. Bank, 1967-72; bd. govs. Blue Cross Assn., 1969-72; mem. Orange County Welfare Bd., 1956-63; chmn. N.C. Comprehensive Health Planning Coun., 1968-72, Health Planning Coun. of Ctrl. N.C., 1963-69; mem. Pres.' Com. on Health Edn., 1971-72; mem. com. health svcs. industry and health industry adv. com. Econ. Stablzn. Program, 1971-74; mem. adv. coun. Kate Bitting Reynolds Health Care Trust, 1971-95; mem. adv. coun. Northwestern U., 1973-86; mem. med. adv. com. VA, 1975-85; bd. dirs. The Forest at Duke, Durham, N.C. Author: North Carolina County Government, 1959, The North Carolina Local Government Commission, 1960; editor: N.C. County Yearbook, 1959-64, Proceedings of the Annual National Forum on Hospital and Health Affairs, 1993—. Mem. Orange County Dem. Exec. Com., also chmn. Kings Mill Precinct, 1964-68; chmn. bd. trustees Duke U., 1971-83, chmn. emeritus, 1983—; bd. dirs. Rsch. Triangle Found., 1971-83, 92—, Nat. Ctr. for Health Edn., 1974-86; bd. mgrs., mem. exec. com. Internat. Hosp. Fedn., London, 1975-85, pres., 1981-83. With USAAF, 1942-46, col. Res., ret. Mem. N.C. State Bar, Inst. Medicine of NAS, Duke Alumni Assn. (pres. 1968-70), Hope Valley Country Club (Durham), Dunes Golf and Beach Club (Myrtle Beach). Presbyterian. Home: 181 Montrose Dr Durham NC 27707-3929 Office: Duke U Fuqua Sch Bus Durham NC 27708-0120

MCMAHON, MARIA O'NEIL, social work educator; b. Hartford, Conn., Jan. 2, 1937; d. John Joseph and Margaret (Galvin) O'Neil; m. Dennis

Richard McMahon, June 10, 1988; stepchildren: Lezlie, Nora, Kelly, Stacie, Michael. BA, St. Joseph Coll., West Hartford, Conn., 1958; MSW, Cath. U. Am., 1964, D. Social Work, 1978. Supr., child and family therapist Highland Heights Residential Treatment Ctr., New Haven, 1964-71; chair dept. sociolgy and social work St. Joseph Coll., 1971-84; prof. E. Carolina U., Greenville, N.C., 1985—, dean Sch. Social Work, 1985-91; cons. to various univs., 1970—; trainer Conn. Dept. Social Svcs., 1982-84, N.C. Dept. Social Svcs., 1987-89. Author: The General Method of Social Work Practice, 1984, 2d edit., 1990, 3d edit., 1996, Advanced Generalist Practice, With An International Perspective, 1994; editor report in field; contbr. articles, book revs. to profl. publs. Commr. Nat. Coun. Social Work Edn., Alexandria, Va., 1983-85; chair bd. dirs. Ea. N.C. Poverty Com., 1987—, Cath. Social Ministries of Archdiocese of Raleigh (N.C.), 1989-92. Recipient Outstanding Educator award AAUW, 1981, Disting. Alumnae award, Cath. U. of Am., 1994. Mem. Nat. Assn. Social Workers (Outstanding Social Worker of Yr., Conn. chpt. 1981), Acad. Cert. Social Workers, Am. Correctional Assn., Nat. Assn. Women Deans, Nat. Coun. Social Work Edn. Democrat. Roman Catholic. Office: E Carolina U Sch Social Work Ragsdale Hall Greenville NC 27858

MCMAHON, PAMELA SUE, dietitian, educator; b. Jersey City, N.J., Apr. 29, 1948; d. William Louis and Pauline Lucille (Oldenberg) Zogbaum; m. Martin James McMahon, June 26, 1971; children: Conor Martin, Timothy James. BS, Douglass Coll., 1970; MS, Framingham State Coll., 1975; PhD, U. Md., 1992. Registered dietitian. Home economist Thomas J. Lipton, Englewood, N.J., 1970-71; dietitian Waltham (Mass.) Hosp., 1971-72, Boston U., 1972; cons. Arthur D. Little, Cambridge, Mass., 1972-79; prof. nutrition and food sci. U. Ky., Lexington, 1979—; dir., coord. dietetics program U. Ky., Lexington, 1992—. Contbr. articles to profl. jours. Mem. Am. Dietetic Assn., Food Svc. Sys. Mgmt. Edn. Coun. (bd. dirs., regional del. 1986-95), Coun. on Hotel, Restaurant Inst. Edn., Ky. Dietetic Assn. (bd. dirs. 1996-97). Home: 154 Mcdowell Rd Lexington KY 40502-1820 Office: Univ Ky Dept Nutrition and Food Sci 218 Funkhouser Lexington KY 40506

MCMAHON, ROBERT ALBERT, JR., lawyer; b. New Orleans, July 23, 1950; s. Robert Albert and Marie Rose (Kennedy) McM.; m. Cynthia Ann Steffan, June 29, 1979; children: Angela, Jennifer, Robyn. BA cum laude, U. Southwestern La., 1972; JD, Loyola U., 1975. Bar: La. 1975, U.S. Dist. Ct. (ea. dist.) La. 1977, U.S. Ct. Appeals (5th cir.) 1978, U.S. Dist. Ct. (mid. dist.) La. 1985, U.S. Supreme Ct. 1989, U.S. Dist. Ct. (we. dist.) La. 1991. Atty. Brown & Hull, Metairie, La., 1975-76, Stewart Title La., New Orleans, 1976, Duplechin & Assocs., Gretna, La., 1977-80, Zelden & Zelden, New Orleans, 1980-81; ptnr. Bernard, Cassisa & Elliott, Metairie, La., 1982—; vol. New Orleans Pro Bono Project, 1991—. Mem. New Orleans Pachyderm Club, 1992—, NRA-Inst. for Legis. Action, Washington, 1991—; chief YMCA Indian Guide/Princess Program, Metairie, 1988-89. Recipient scholarship U. New Orleans, 1968, U. Southwestern La., 1968. Mem. Def. Rsch. Inst., La. Assn. Def. Counsel, Maritime Law Assn. U.S., Jefferson Bar Assn., La. State Bar Assn.(ho. dels. 1993—), Hibernians, Phi Kappa Theta. Republican. Roman Catholic. Office: Bernard Cassisa and Elliott 1615 Metairie Rd Metairie LA 70005-3926

MCMAHON, ROBERT LEE, JR. (BOB MCMAHON), information systems executive; b. Weatherford, Tex., Feb. 19, 1944; s. Robert Lee Sr. and Gusta Rosann (Collins) McM. AA, Weatherford Coll., 1964; BA, U. Tex., Arlington, 1970; postgrad. in mgmt., Tex. Christian U., 1970-73. Announcer Sta. KZEE, Weatherford, Tex., 1963-65; asst. gen. mgr. Sta. KZEE, Weatherford, 1972-75; programmer Gen. Dynamics, Ft. Worth, 1967-68, sr. programmer, 1968-72, sr. engr., 1975-78, project engr., 1978-79, group supr., 1979-80, sect. chief, 1980-83, dept. mgr., 1983-93; staff specialist Lockheed Ft. Worth Co., 1994-95, retired, 1995; mem. adv. bd. Mfg. Tech. Directorate, USAF, Dayton, Ohio, 1981-91, Automation and Robotics Rsch. Inst., Ft. Worth, 1986-91. Editor: Manufacturing Engineer's Handbook, 1988; mem. editorial bd. Mfg. Engring. mag., 1989-91. Dir. adult edn. program Parker County, Tex., 1972-75; chmn. Weatherford City Charter Revision Commn., 1974-75; mem. Weatherford Planning and Zoning Bd., 1984-88; chmn. 4th precinct Parker County Dem. Com., 1982-92, 27th precinct, 1992—; foreman Grand Jury, 1993. Mem. Soc. Mfg. Engrs., (cert., sr.), Robotic Industries Assn. (sr., bd. dirs. 1984-88), Computer and Automated Sys. Assn. (sr.), Robotics Inst. (sr.), Am. Inst. Indsl. Engrs., Nat. Mgmt. Assn., Masons (33d degree, past master), Phi Theta Kappa (v.p. Weatherford chpt.), Ego Omega, Beta Alpha Psi. Mem. Ch. of Christ. Home: 1418 E Bankhead Dr Weatherford TX 76086-4607

MCMAHON, TERRY CALVIN, psychiatrist, medical educator; b. Oklahoma City, Okla., Aug. 31, 1950; s. Calvin Bernard and Ernestine Louise (Weesner) McM.; m. Shari Ann Williams, Mar. 11, 1978; 1 child, Matthew Ryan. Student, Washington U., 1970; BA, U. Okla., 1972; MD, UCLA, 1976. Diplomate Am. Bd. Psychiatry and Neurology. Resident in psychiatry U. Tex. Health Scis. Ctr., San Antonio, 1976-80; fellow in psychosomatic medicine U. Vt., Burlington, Vt., 1980-82; asst. prof. psychiatry Tex. Tech. U. Health Scis. Ctr., Lubbock, 1982-87, assoc. prof. in psychiatry, 1988-94, asst. dean medical edn., 1989—; prof. psychiatry, 1994—. Contbr. articles to profl. jours. Bd. dirs. Hospice of Lubbock, 1986-89, 89-92, chmn., 1990, South Plans Children Shelter, Lubbock, 1990-92. Fellow Am. Psychiatric Assn., Tex. Soc. Psychiatric Physicians (continuing edn. com., budget com., membership com., pub. mental health svcs. com. AIDS edn. com.); mem. Am. Coll. Psychiatrists, Acad. Psychosomatic Medicine, Am. Soc. Psycho-oncology/AIDS, Assn. Acad. Psychiatrists, Tex. Medical Assn. Democrat. Episcopalian. Home: 9307 Utica Dr Lubbock TX 79424-4821 Office: Tex Tech U Health Scis Ctr Lubbock TX 79430

MCMANUS, JAMES WILLIAM, chemist, researcher; b. Atlanta, Oct. 7, 1944; s. Claude William and Sara Louise (Cook) McM.; m. Ruth Krieger, Apr. 10, 1971; children: Angela Ruth, Meagan Joy. BS in Chemistry, Auburn U., 1971. Mgr. Cook's Grocery Co., Atlanta, 1970-73; analytical chemist North Chem. Co., Atlanta, 1973-74; analytical chemist Merck & Co., Inc., Albany, Ga., 1974-75, staff chemist, 1975-76, sr. staff chemist, 1976-78, sr. chemist, 1978-89, rsch. fellow, 1989-94; bd. dirs. M. Taylor, Inc., Albany, 1988—, chmn. chemistry sect., 1994—. Mem. editorial bd. Process Control and Quality, 1990-95; inventor, patentee in field. Mem. Am. Chem. Soc. (cert.). Republican. Baptist. Office: Merck and Co Inc 3517 Radium Springs Rd Albany GA 31705-9596

MCMANUS, JOSEPH WARN, urban planner, architect; b. Detroit, Mar. 24, 1931; s. Joseph Warn and Margaret Catherine (McNeil) McM.; m. Barbara Ann Luger, June 10, 1961; children: Margaret A. Ballas, Catherine M. Valera, Sarah T. Nielsen. BArch, U. Notre Dame, 1953; M in City Planning, U. Mich., 1963. Registered architect, Mich. Job capt. Haughey & Black, Architects, Battle Creek, Mich., 1954-56, Setter, Leach, Lindstrom, Architects, Mpls., 1956-59, Matson & Wegleitner, Architects, Mpls., 1959-61; prin. planner Barton-Aschman Assocs., Inc., Evanston, Ill., 1963-71; planning supr. Skidmore, Owings & Merrill, Architects, Chgo., 1971-73; planner III City of Miami (Fla.) Planning Dept., 1973-76; asst. dir. City of Miami Planning, Bldg. and Zoning Dept., 1976-92, dep. dir., 1993-95; adminstr. Coconut Grove NET, 1992; cons., 1995—. U. Mich. fellow, 1962. Mem. Am. Inst. Cert. Planners, Am. Planning Assn. (Gold Coast chpt.), Fla. Planning and Zoning Assn. (v.p. So. Fla. chpt. 1983-85, pres. 1986, 95, bd. dirs. 1987—), Emerald Soc. South Fla. (bd. dirs. 1995, v.p. 1996), Country Club of Coral Gables, K.C., Tau Sigma Delta.

MCMASTERS, BOBBY LOWELL, statistician; b. Sacramento, June 12, 1957; s. Jesse Lowell and Minnie Lou (Perkins) McM.; m. Glenetta Gay Klein, Aug. 29, 1981; children: Jesse K., Jonathan D., Joshua G., Joseph L. BSME, Okla. State U., 1979; MEd, U. Ark., 1993, EdD, 1995. Registered profl. engr., Tex. Engr. Halliburton Svcs., Duncan, Okla., 1979-82; sales engr. Cooper Industries, Houston, 1982-89; dist. mgr. Fairbanks Morse Pump Corp., Houston, 1989-91; asst. prof. U. Ark., Fayetteville, 1991-95; tng. mgmt. sys. mgr. Flight Safety Svcs., Altus, Okla., 1995—; co-owner, cons. Environ. Enterprises, Pauls Valley, Okla., 1985—. Sgt. USMC, 1976-78. Mem. Phi Delta Kappa. Republican. Baptist. Home: # 1 Carrie Rd Lawton OK 73501-9313

MCMATH, ELIZABETH MOORE, graphic artist; b. Iredell, Tex., Feb. 20, 1930; d. Fred William and Elizabeth Carol (Smith) Moore; m. Charles Wallis McMath, Jan. 16, 1978 (dec. Dec. 1990); children: Charles Wallis, John Seals. BA, BS in Advt. Design, Tex. Woman's U., Denton, 1951; grad. gemologist, Gemol. Inst. Am., L.A., 1977. Layout artist Leonard's Dept. Store, Ft. Worth, Tex., 1951-52; artist/bookkeeper Bud Biggs Studio, Dallas, 1953; sec./artist Squire Haskins Studio, Dallas, 1953-54; artist/art dir. Dowdell-Merrill, Inc., Dallas, 1954-58; owner/artist Moore Co., Dallas, 1958-90. Mem. Stemmons Corridor Bus. Assn., Dallas, 1988-89. Mem. Dallas/Ft. Worth Soc. Visual Comm. (founder), Tex. Woman's U. Nat. Alumnae Assn., Greater North Tex. Orchid Soc. (treas. 1987), Daylily Growers of Dallas (sec. 1989-90, 1st v.p. and program chmn. 1992), Internat. Bulb Soc., Native Plant Soc. Tex. (publicity chmn. Trinity Forks chpt. 1991-96). Presbyterian. Home: PO Box 1068 Denton TX 76202-1068

MCMILLAN, BETTIE BARNEY, English language educator; b. Fayetteville, N.C., Mar. 14, 1941; d. Booker T. and Sarah Estelle (Barney) McM.; children: Gregory L., Kenneth A., Ronald D., Pamela M., Deirdre Y., Michael A. BA in Psychology/Sociology, Meth. Coll., 1978. Program supr. Adminstrv. Office of the Cts.-Guardian Ad Litem Program, Raleigh, N.C.; English instr. Cmty. Coll., Fayetteville, N.C.; info. specialist, case mgr. Big Bros./Big Sisters, Fayetteville. Author: A Plea For Love, 1995. Leader, nat. officer United Order of Tents, Norfolk, Va., 1982-92; vol. N.C. Guardian Ad Litem, Raleigh, 1992—, Network for Homeless, Fayetteville, 1996—; mem. Atlanta Com. for Olympic Games, 1996. Recipient Copyright award plaque Copywright award, 1996, Poet Merit award Nat. Libr. Congress, 1995. Mem. Internat. Soc. of Poets (Disting. mem., 1995-96, Poets Choice award 1995), Sigma Omega Chi. Baptist. Home: 5506 Ramshorn Dr Fayetteville NC 28303

MC MILLAN, GEORGE DUNCAN HASTIE, JR., lawyer, former state official; b. Greenville, Ala., Oct. 11, 1943; s. George Duncan Hastie and Jean (Autrey) McM.; m. Ann Louise Dial, Nov. 20, 1971; children: George Duncan Hastie, III, Ann Dial. B.A. magna cum laude, Auburn U., 1966; LL.B. (Southeastern Regional scholar), U. Va., 1969. Bar: Ala. bar 1969. Research asst. dept. agronomy Auburn U., summers 1963-65; law clk. firm Lange, Simpson, Robinson & Somerville, Birmingham, Ala., summers 1967-68; law clk. to judge U.S. Dist. Ct. No. Dist. Ala., 1969-70; instr. U. Ala. Law Sch., 1969-70; individual practice law Birmingham, 1970-71; ptnr. firm McMillan & Spratling, Birmingham, 1971-86; of counsel Haskell, Slaughter, Young and Lewis, 1986; ptnr. McMillan, Jones and Assocs., 1987-90; pres. McMillan & Assocs., 1990—; mem. Ala. Ho. of Reps., 1973, Ala. Senate, 1974-78; lt. gov. Ala., 1979-83; vice-chmn. Nat. Conf. Lt. Govs., 1980-82; mem. Permanent Study Commn. on Ala.'s Jud. System, 1975-79. Chmn. Ala. Film Commn., 1976-83; mem. Arts Task Force, Nat. Conf. State Legislatures, 1978-80, Multi-State Transp. Adv. Bd., 1974-79; mem. exec. com. So. Growth Policies Bd., 1974-83, vice chmn., 1981-83; bd. dirs. Campfire, Inc., 1975-82, Met. YMCA, Birmingham, Boys and Girls Ranches, Ala., Positive Maturity, 1987—; chmn. bd., pres. Birmingham Cultural and Heritage Found., 1988—; pres., bd. dirs. Birmingham Repertory Theatre, 1989—; exec. producer City Stages; Served to lt. USAR, 1969. Recipient award Ala. Nurses Assn., 1975; named Legislator of Yr. Ala. Forestry Assn., 1978; Hardest Working Senator Capitol Press Corps, 1976; 1 of 4 Outstanding Young Men Ala. Jaycees, 1977; 1 of 10 Most Outstanding State Legislators Assn. Govtl. Employees, 1977; award Birmingham Emancipation Assn., 1977; award Ala. Hist. Commn., 1978; James Tingle award, 1979, Citizen of Yr. award City of Birmingham, 1990. Mem. Birmingham Bar Assn., Ala. Bar Assn., Am. Bar Assn., Birmingham Jaycees, Ala. Jaycees (dir. 1970-72), Birmingham Urban League, United Negro Coll. Fund. Democrat. Mem. Ch. of Christ. Club: Rotary (Birmingham). Office: Mc Millan & Associates PO Box 11311 Birmingham AL 35202-1311*

MCMILLAN, HOWARD LAMAR, JR., banker; b. Jackson, Miss., Aug. 29, 1939; s. Howard Lamar and Mary Frances (Byars) McM.; m. Mary Eliza Love, July 5, 1964; children: Eliza Love McMillan Garraway, Howard Lamar III. BA in Banking & Finance, U. Miss., Oxford, 1960; postgrad., La. State U., 1966, Harvard U., 1979. With Deposit Guaranty Nat. Bank, Jackson, 1960, v.p., 1972-73, sr. v.p., 1973-77, exec. v.p. corp. div., 1977-81, exec. v.p. state bank div., 1981-84, pres., dir., 1987—; pres., CEO. Deposit Guaranty Corp., Jackson, 1984—. Gen. chmn. United Way, Jackson, 1989—. Mem. Am. Bankers Assn. (bd. dirs. 1988—), Miss. Bankers Assn. (chmn. fed. legis. com.), Jackson C. of C. (bd. dirs. 1989—), Univ. Miss. Alumni Assn. (pres. 1988), 100 Club (Jackson). Office: Deposit Guaranty Nat Bank PO Box 1200 Jackson MS 39215-1200*

MCMILLAN, JAMES ALBERT, electronics engineer, educator; b. Lewellen, Nebr., Feb. 6, 1926; s. William H. and Mina H. (Taylor) McM.; m. Mary Virginia Garrett, Aug. 12, 1950 (dec. Feb. 1990); children: Michael, James, Yvette, Ramelle, Robert. BSEE, U. Wash., 1951; MS in Mgmt., Rensselaer Poly. Inst., 1965. Commd. 2d lt. U.S. Air Force, 1950, advanced through grades to lt. col., 1970; jet fighter pilot Columbus AFB, Miss., Webb AFB, Tex., 1951-52, Nellis AFB, Nev., 1953, McChord AFB, Wash., 1953-54; electronic maintenance supr. Lowry AFB, Colo., 1954, Forbes AFB, Kans., 1954-56, also in U.K. and Morocco, 1956-59; electronic engr., program dir. Wright-Patterson AFB, Ohio, 1959-64; chief space tech. Air Force Aero Propulsion Lab., Wright-Patterson AFB, 1965-70, facilities dir. 1965-70, ret., 1970; instr., div. chmn. Chesterfield-Marlboro Tech. Coll., S.C., 1971-75; instr., chmn. indsl. div., Maysville (Ky.) Community Coll., 1976—, asst. prof., 1977, assoc. prof., 1980, prof. 1986-93, prof. emeritus 1993—; chmn. indsl. tech. program, 1976-93; cons. mgmt. and electronic maintenance, 1970—. Served with U.S. Army, 1943-45. Named to Hon. Order Ky. Cols., 1984; fellow U. Ky., 1993. Mem. IEEE (sr., life), Soc. Mfg. Engrs. (sr.), Nat. Rifle Assn. (life), Sigma Xi (life). Republican. Presbyterian (elder). Clubs: Rotary (Maysville, Ky., pres. 1989-90), Masons (32 deg.), Shriners, Spindletops. Author: A Management Survey, 1965. Home: 6945 Scoffield Rd Ripley OH 45167-8967

MCMILLAN, LEE RICHARDS, II, lawyer; b. New Orleans, Aug. 26, 1947; s. John H. and Phoebe (Skillman) McM.; m. Lynne Clark Pottharst, June 27, 1970; children: Leslie Clark, Hillary Anne, Lee Richards III. BS in Commerce, Washington and Lee U., 1969; JD, Tulane U., 1972; LLM in Taxation, NYU, 1976. Bar: La. 1972. Assoc. Jones, Walker, Waechter, Poitevent, Carrere & Denegre, New Orleans, 1976-79, ptnr., 1979—, sect. head, corp. and securities sect., 1987-90, 94—, exec. com., 1990-94, 96—, chmn. exec. com., 1991-94, 96—; vice-chmn. Mech. Equipment Co., Inc., New Orleans, 1980-86, chmn. bd., 1986—, pres. 1989—; bd. trustees Alton Ochsner Med. Found., 1995—. Trustee New Orleans Mus. Art., 1989-95; bd. dirs. bur. Govt. Rsch. New Orleans, 1987-93, Louise S. McGehee Sch., New Orleans, 1982-88, co-chmn. capital fund dr., 1984-86, pres. bd. dirs., 1986-88; bd. govs. Isidore Newman Sch., New Orleans, 1991-95. Lt. JACG USNR, 1972-75. Mem. ABA (com. on negotiated acquisitions 1986-94), La. State Bar Assn. (chmn. corp. and bus. law sect. 1985-86, mem. com. on bar admissions 1986-87), Young Pres. Orgn., Washington and Lee U. Alumni Assn. (bd. dirs. 1995—). Republican. Episcopalian. Office: Jones Walker Waechter Poitevent Carrere & Denegre 201 Saint Charles Ave New Orleans LA 70170-5100

MCMILLAN, MAE FRANCES, child psychiatrist; b. Austin, Tex., May 12, 1936; d. Ben Sanders Sr. and Annie Mae (Walker) McM. BS with honors, Wiley Coll., 1955; MD with honors, Meharry Med. Coll., 1959. Med. diplomate. Psychiat. resident gen. and child Baylor Coll. Medicine, Houston, 1963-65; resident child psychoanalysis Hampstead Clinic, London, 1967; asst. prof. dept. psychiatry Baylor Coll. Medicine, Houston, 1965-75, assoc. prof., 1975—; asst. dir. divsn. child psychiatry Tex. Rsch. Inst. Med. Scis., Houston, 1968-75, dir. child therapy and clinic for early childhood disorders, 1980-85; unit dir. latency svc. Depelchin Children's Ctr., Houston, 1985-90; pvt. practice child psychiatry Houston, 1985-94; cons. Teen. Parent Svcs. of Inst. Child and Family Psychiatry, Houston, 1990—; bd. mem. cons. Harris County Mental Health Mental Retardation Assn., Houston, 1988—. Author, editor: Child Psychiatry - Treatment and Research, 1970; contbr. articles to profl. jours. Bd. dirs. Living Bank, Houston, 1970-80; bd. mem., treas. Tex. Cmty. Corp., Houston, 1995—; cert. lay speaker Tex. Conf. United Meth. Ch., Houston, 1990—, bd. higher edn.; chairperson work area on edn. Ebenezer United Meth. Ch.; del. 13th Congl. Dist., Houston, 1992. Named Outstanding Woman YWCA, Houston, 1978. Fellow Am. Psychiat. Assn.; mem. Nat. Coun. Negro Women (life, chair Thelma Patten Law Lectureship 1977), Houston Psychiat. Soc. (chair children's com. 1990-94), Tex. Soc. Psychiat. Physicians, Tex. Soc. Child Psychiatry, Nat. Med. Assn., Delta Sigma Theta (Golden life). Democrat. Office: Tex Rsch Inst Dept Child Psychiatry 4114 Cornell St Houston TX 77022-4652

MCMILLAN, MOLLY COLLEEN, educational association administrator; b. Angleton, Tex., Aug. 21, 1956; d. Sara Jane (Redd) McMillan-Luck. B in Environ. Design, Tex. A&M U., 1978. Supr. Youth Conservation Corps, Blue Dome, Idaho, 1978; youth specialist Delmina Woods, Forsythe, Mo., 1978-79; dir. outdoor program Winnacunnet Alternative Sch., Hampton, N.H., 1979-80; co-dir. Student Conservation Assn., Charleston, N.H., 1980; asst. dir. Experience N.E., Jeffersonville, Vt., 1980-81; instr. Hurricane Island Outward Bound Sch., Titusville, Fla., 1981; with Coleman Constrn. Co., Asheville, N.C., 1982; instr. N.C. Outward Bound Sch., Morganton, 1983—; dir. vol. svcs. program, coord. outdoor program Warren Wilson Coll., Swannanoa, N.C., 1988-90, personal devel. coord. Cornerstone Ind. Living program, 1990-92; mem. Youth Alternatives Project; founder, dir. N.C. Outward Bound Youth Alternatives Project, 1986-88; dir. outdoor programs Warren Wilson Coll., 1991—. Foster parent, 1994. Democrat. Home: 478 Bull Creek Rd Asheville NC 28805-8704 Office: Warren Wilson Coll 701 Warren Wilson Rd # R Swannanoa NC 28778-2042

MCMILLEN, DAVID L., psychology educator; b. Columbus, Ohio, Sept. 3, 1941; s. Luen R. and Lela (Miller) McM.; m. Edith C. McMillen, Dec. 28, 1963 (div. 1977); children: Robert, Eleanor, Randall; m. Dixie T. McMillen, Apr. 23, 1988. BS, Memphis State U., 1963; PhD, U. Tex., 1968. Asst. prof. Miss. State U., 1968-72, assoc. prof., 1972-78, 80-85, prof., 1985—; sr. rsch. scientist U. Mich., Ann Arbor, 1978-81, assoc. dir. Ctr. for Rsch. on Learning and Teaching, 1978-81. Contbr. articles to profl. jours. including Addictive Behaviors, Internat. Jour. of the Addictions, and Jour. of Alcohol Studies. Rsch. grant Alcohol Beverage Med. Rsch. Found., Miss. State U., 1991-92, Miss. Alcohol Safety Edn. Program, 1984-87, U. Mich., 1979-81. Mem. AAUP, APS, Southeastern Psychol. Assn., Southeastern Soc. Psychologists. Home: 628 S Montgomery St Starkville MS 39759-3802 Office: Miss State U Dept Psychology PO Box 6161 Mississippi State MS 39762-6161

MCMILLEN, HOWARD LAWRENCE, municipal government official; b. Phoenix, Apr. 8, 1937; s. John Lawrence and Bessie Nora McM.; A.A. in Bus. Adminstrn., Phoenix Coll., 1957; A.A. in Fire Sci., Phoenix Coll., 1965; B.A. in Public Mgmt., St. Mary's Coll., Moraga, Calif., 1977; divorced; children—Linda, Karen. Fireman, Phoenix, 1959-63, fire engr., 1963-68, fire capt., 1968-70, br. chief, 1970-76, div. chief, 1976-78, dep. chief, 1978-80; fire chief, City of Ft. Worth, 1980—; vocat. instr. Ariz. Fire Sci. Curriculum; instr. Calif. Fire Officers Acad., Pacific Grove; fireground comdr., seminar instr. Okla. State U.; chmn. Ariz. Fire Tng. Com., 1974-80. Bd. dirs. Parenting Guidance Ctr., Ft. Worth. Mem. Nat. Fire Protection Assn. (chmn. program com. fire service sect. 1973-80), Internat. Assn. Fire Chiefs, S.W. Fire Chiefs Assn., Tex. Fire Chiefs Assn., Internat. Assn. Fire Instructors, Ariz. Fire Prevention Assn. Methodist. Club: Ft. Worth. Lodge: Rotary Office: Fire Dept Pub Safety Bldg 1000 Throckmorton St Fort Worth TX 76102-6311*

MCMILLEN, ROBERT DOANE, public information government official; b. Covington, Ind., June 3, 1916; s. Wheeler and Edna Dorothy (Doane) McM. BA, Columbia Coll., 1937, MS, 1938. Asst. Sunday editor New Haven Register, 1938; dir. info. Nat. Farm Chemurgic Coun., Columbus, Ohio, 1938-39; Washington editor Farm Jour., 1939-42, 47-54; asst. to sec. U.S. Dept. Agr., 1954-58; dir. info. Corn Refiners Assn., 1959-66, N.J. Dept. Agr., Trenton, 1967-74; confidential asst. to sec. U.S. Dept. Agr., Washington, 1974-77; dir. info. Am. Meat Inst., Washington, 1977-78; chmn. Nat. Farm-City Coun., Washington; pres. Agrl. Rels. Soc., Washington, 1964-65; founder, pres. Communications Officers State Depts. Agr., Trenton; sec. N.J. Farm Electrification Coun. cons. editor Ctr. for Naval Analyses, Arlington, Va., 1979; contbr. articles to profl. jours. Mem. Loudoun County Rep. Com., Leesburg, Va., 1983-90; chmn. rural com. Nat. coun. Boy Scouts Am. Lt. comdr. USNR, 1942-46. Recipient Disting. Svc. award N.J. Agr. Soc., Trenton, 1974, Svc. award Am. Assn. Agrl. Coll. Editors, 1974, Cert. of Merit, U.S. Dept. Agr., Washington, 1975, 76. Mem. Mil. Order World Wars (life), Am. Legion (life), Nat. Future Farmers Am. Alumni Assn. (life), Phila. Soc. Promoting Agr. (life), Cosmos Club. Quaker. Home: RR 1 Box 158B Lovettsville VA 22080-9505

MCMILLIAN, JAMES, protective services official. Police chief Jacksonville, Fla. Office: Office of Police Chief City Hall Jacksonville FL 32202

MCMINN, WILLIAM A., chemicals company executive; b. 1931. With FMC Corp., Chgo., 1967-85, Cain Chemical Co., Kearney, N.J., 1987-88; chmn., dir. Arcadian Corp., Memphis, 1989—; dir. Sterling Chems., Houston. Office: Arcadian Corp 6750 Poplar Ave Ste 600 Memphis TN 38138-7424*

MCMULLAN, JAMES FRANKLIN, financial planner; b. Atlanta, Feb. 24, 1928; s. Jesse James and Ruth Guinn (Thomason) McM.; m. Gladis Jo Anne Lovern, Sept. 13, 1951; children: Anne, Martha Jane (dec.), Lynn, Robert Lovern, Beth. BBA, Emory U., 1949; MS, Am. Coll., 1986. CLU, chartered fin. cons.; cert. fin. planner; registered investment advisor. Emeritus gen. agt. State Mutual Co., Atlanta, 1955—; pres. Strategic Asset Adv. Corp., Atlanta, 1968—; elder, pastor Word of Life Fellowship, East Point, Ga., 1984—. Mem. Atlanta Estate Planning Coun., Nat. Assn. Security Dealers, Am. Soc. CLU and Chartered Fin. Cons., Internat. Bd. Cert. Fin. Planners, Nat. Assn. Life Underwriters. Republican. Home: 2935 Duke Of Gloucester Atlanta GA 30344-5806 Office: Strategic Asset Adv Corp 1751 John Calvin Ave College Park GA 30337-2053

MC MULLIAN, AMOS RYALS, food company executive; b. Jackson County, Fla., Aug. 28, 1937; s. Andrew Jackson and Willie Ross (Ryals) McM.; m. Jackie Williams, Aug. 27, 1960; children: Amos Ryals, Britton Jackelyn. BS, Fla. State U., 1962. Successively asst. controller, data processing coordinator, adminstrv. asst. to gen. mgr., asst. plant mgr., plant mgr. Flowers Baking Co., Thomasville, Ga., 1963-70, pres. Atlanta Baking Co. div., 1970-72, regional v.p. parent co., 1972-74, pres., chief operating officer bakery div., 1974-76, chief operating officer industry, 1976-81, pres., 1976-83, dir., 1981—, chief exec. officer, 1983—, co-chmn. exec. com., 1983—, vice chmn. industry and chmn. exec. com., 1984-85, chmn. bd., CEO, 1985—; bd. dirs. Ga. Rsch. Reliance. Mem. adv. bd. President's Club, Fla. State U.; trustee Southeastern Legal Found.; vestryman, sr. warden Episcopal Ch.; bd. govs. Ga. Pub. Policy Found. With USMC, 1958-61. Named Outstanding Bus. Alumnus, Fla. State U. Mem. NAM (bd. dirs.), Thomasville Landmarks Soc., Atlanta Bakers Club (past pres.), Atlanta Commerce Club, Gridiron Soc. (U. Ga.). Office: Flowers Industries Inc PO Box 1338 Thomasville GA 31799*

MCMURRAY, CAROL DOLBER, human services administrator; b. Marilla, N.Y., July 31, 1948; d. Clinton Charles and Frances Ann (Gilmore) Dolber; m. James Michael McMurray, Oct. 21, 1972; children: Christian, Stefan. BA, SUNY, Binghamton, 1970; MSW, Va. Commonwealth U., 1977. Caseworker Warren County Children Svcs., Lake George, N.Y., 1973-75; social worker Chesterfield (Va.) County Mental Health/MR Svcs., 1977-79; dir. Vol. Emergency Foster Care of Va., 1979-80; regional tng. coord. Va. Bapt. Children's Home and Family Svcs., 1980-82; Va. area program coord. Welcome House Adoption Svcs., Inc., Richmond, Va., 1982-90; child and family trainer, cons., 1988—; adj. faculty Divsn. of Continuing Edn., U. Va., 1992—; trainer Prevent Child Abuse, Va.; pres. Va. Assn. Lic. Child Placing Agys., 1988-90, v.p., 1986-88; mem. trainer Conflict Resolution Team Tng., Richmond Peace Edn. Ctr., Va. Contbr. articles to profl. jours. and mags. Organizer, past pres. Richmond Domestic Violence Project, Richmond, Va., 1977-79; chairperson Bd. of Child Care Ctr., Richmond, 1985-88, Job Study Review Com. of Chs. Profl. Ministerial Staff, Richmond, 1989-90. Mem. ASTD, Acad. Cert. Social Workers, Nat. Assn. Social Workers, Adoption Devel. Outreach Planning Team. Home and Office: 1915 Floyd Ave Richmond VA 23220-4515

MCNABB, DARCY LAFOUNTAIN, medical management company executive; b. Middletown, N.J., Aug. 27, 1955; d. Donald Mark LaFountain and Suzanne (Gilman) LaFountain Westergard; m. Leland Monte McNabb, July 4, 1981 (div. Feb. 1989); 1 child, Leland Monte Jr. BBA in Internat.

Fin. cum laude, U. Miami, 1977. Real estate agent, Grad. Realtor's Inst. Market rsch. asst. Burger King Corp., Miami, Fla., 1975-77; regional mktg. supr. Burger King Corp., Huntington Beach, Calif., 1977-78; mgr., restaurant planning Holiday Inns, Inc., Memphis, 1978-79, mgr., nat. promotions, 1979-83; dir., lodging and travel planning Holiday Corp., Memphis, 1983-86; affiliate broker The Hobson Co., Realtors, Memphis, 1986-88, Crye Leike, Memphis, 1988-92; v.p. comm. and planning Medshares Mgmt. Group, Inc., Memphis, 1991—. Active Friends Pink Palace Mus., Memphis, 1987-91, Family Link/Runaway, Memphis, 1980-88; chmn. Foster Care Rev. Bd., Memphis, 1988—; bd. dirs. Bethany House, Memphis, 1989—, pres., 1995; pres., bd. dirs. Am. Cancer Soc., 1994—; mktg. com. Health Industry Coun., 1994-95. Named Profl. Vol. of Yr., Friends of Pink Palace Mus., Memphis, 1989, 93, U.S. Masters Swimming All-Am., 1993, 94; grad. Leadership Memphis, 1995; named Cmty. Hero for Olympic Torch Relay, 1996. Mem. Le Bonheur Club, Memphis Runners Track Club. Republican. Episcopalian. Home: 1948 Harbert Ave Memphis TN 38104-5216 Office: Medshares Mgmt Group Inc 2714 Union Avenue Ext Memphis TN 38112-4415

MCNABB, DIANNE LEIGH, investment banker, accountant; b. Huntsville, Ala., Sept. 7, 1956; d. Walter David and Mary Josephine (Hawkins) McN.; m. William Roland Lantz, July 1, 1983; 1 child, Sarah Elizabeth. BS in Acctg., U. Ala., Tuscaloosa, 1976. CPA, Ga., Ala. Acct. Lilly Flagg Assocs. & Subsidiaries, Huntsville, 1977-78; mgr. Johnston, Joyce & Wigginton, CPA's, Huntsville, 1978-84; sr. mgr. KPMG Peat Marwick, CPA's, Atlanta, 1984-91; v.p. A.G. Edwards & Sons, Inc., Atlanta, 1991—. Mem. ways and means com. Atlanta Jr. League, 1991—; instr., advisor Jr. Achievement, Atlanta, 1985-88; mem. hospitality com. Dem. Nat. Conv., Atlanta, 1988; vol. Ga. Spl. Olympics, Atlanta, 1989-91. Mem. AICPA, Govt. Fin. Officers Assn. (spl. rev. com. 1991—), Ga. Soc. CPA (govtl. acctg. and auditing com. 1992), Assn. of Govt. Accts. (bd. dirs. Atlanta chpt. 1990-92), Ala. Soc. CPA (sec.-treas. 1984), Am. Soc. Women Accts. (pres. Huntsville chpt. 1983-84), U. Ala. Alumni Assn. (treas. 1983-84), Zeta Tau Alpha (advisor 1988-93, v.p. 1983, treas. 1987-89, pres. 1984, 89-91, panhellenic del. 1988-91, dist. pres. 1993-95, Cert. of Merit 1992, Zeta Lady award 1991, Alum Chum award 1991). Home: 2530 Alpine Way Duluth GA 30136-4440 Office: A G Edwards 3399 Peachtree Rd NE Ste 1270 Atlanta GA 30326-1150

MCNAIR, JOHN FRANKLIN, III, banker; b. Laurinburg, N.C., Apr. 12, 1927; s. John Franklin and Martha (Fairley) McN.; m. Martha Fowler, June 16, 1951; children: John Franklin IV, Elizabeth Fowler. BS, Davidson Coll., 1949; postgrad., U. N.C., 1954-56. Pres. McNair Automotive Co., Inc., Laurinburg, 1949-66, The State Bank, Laurinburg, 1966-68; sr. v.p. Wachovia Bank & Trust, Laurinburg, 1968-70, Raleigh, N.C., 1970-72; exec. v.p. Wachovia Bank & Trust, Winston-Salem, N.C., 1972-77, vice chmn., 1977-85; vice chmn. The Wachovia Corp., Winston-Salem, N.C., 1977-87, pres., chief exec. officer, 1987-90; pres., chief exec. officer Wachovia Bank & Trust Co, 1987-90, also dir.; exec. v.p. First Wachovia Corp., 1986-90; bd. dirs. Piedmont Natural Gas Co.; bd. dirs., pres. N.C. R.R. Co., 1993—. Mem. N.C. State Hwy. Commn., Raleigh, 1965-69, Commn. on future N.C., raleigh, 1981-83; chmn. N.C. Bd. Econ. Devel., 1979-85, N.C. Coun. Econ. Edn., Greensboro, 1980-82, Ind. Coll. Fund N.C., 1989-91, N.C. Citizens for Bus. and Industry, 1988-89; trustee Peace Coll., Raleigh, 1980-89, Davidson Coll., 1985-93; trustee Old Salem, Inc., 1985—, treas., 1990—; trustee Winston-Salem Found., 1983-91, chmn., 1989-91; co-chmn. gov.'s adv. com. Superconducting Supercollider Project, 1988; trustee, mem. exec. com. Rsch. Triangle Found., 1986—, vice chmn., 1990-93, chmn., 1992—; trustee exec. com. Winston-Salem Bus., Inc., 1986—, chmn., 1990-95; mem. govt. performance com. State of N.C., 1991-93; bd. dirs. N.C. Enterprise Corp., 1988-93; chmn. Qual Choice of N.C., Inc., 1994—. With USN, 1945-46. Recipient Young Man of Yr. award Laurinburg Jaycees, 1962, Silver Beaver award Boy Scouts Am., 1967, Disting. Alumni award Davidson Coll., 1994. Mem. Am. Bankers Assn. (state v.p. 1980-81), Res. City Bankers Assn., N.C. Bankers Assn. (pres. 1976-77), Cape Fear County Club (Wilmington, N.C.), Old Town Club, Piedmont Club, St. Andrews Soc., Rotary. Democrat. Presbyterian. Home: 234 NW Pine Valley Rd Winston Salem NC 27104-1808 Office: Wachovia Bank NC PO Box 3099 Winston Salem NC 27150

MCNAIR, JOHN WILLIAM, JR., civil engineer; b. Asheville, N.C., June 17, 1926; s. John William and Annie (Woody) McN.; m. June Clemens Kratz; children—Jeffry, Marsha, Cathy. B.S. in Forestry, Pa. State U., 1950; B.S.C.E., Va. Poly. Inst. State U., 1955; postgrad. in engring. U. Va., 1957-58. Registered profl. engr., Va. and other states. Forester U.S. Forest Service, Flagstaff, Ariz., 1950, U.S. Gypsum Co., Altavista, VA., 1951; mem. engring. faculty U. Va., Charlottesville, 1955-58; prin. John McNair & Assocs., Waynesboro, VA., 1958—; owner Brucheum Group, Waynesboro, 1983—; with Va. Bd. Architects, Profl. Engrs. and Land Surveyors, 1969-79, v.p., 1977-78, pres., 1978-79. Author numerous engring. and land mgmt. study reports. Mem. Waynesboro City Council, 1968-72, vice mayor, 1970-72; chmn. Waynesboro INdsl. devel. Authority, 1984—. Served to capt. AUS, 1944-46, 51-53; France, Okinawa. Recipient Disting. Service cert. Va. Soc. Profl. Engrs., 1971. Fellow ASCE; mem. Acad. Environ. Engrs. (diplomate). Republican. Presbyterian. Lodge: Rotary. Office: John McNair and Assocs Wayne Ave LB & B Bldg Waynesboro VA 22980

MCNAIR, NIMROD, JR., foundation executive, consultant; b. Tuscaloosa, Ala., Nov. 2, 1923; s. Nimrod and Salemma (Flowers) McN.; m. Amy Ernestine Phillips, Apr. 27, 1943; children: Janice Lee McNair Bradd, John Rodney. BSChemE, U. Ala., 1949; MS in Aerospace Engring., Air Force Inst. Tech., 196l. Cert. mgmt. cons. Sales engr. Hunt Oil Co., Tuscaloosa, 1949-5l; commd. officer USAF, 1950, advanced through grades to lt. col., 1966; prof. N.C. State U., Raleigh, 1951-55; command pilot SAC, 1955-59; grad. student USAF Inst. Tech.; dir. space planning Space Div., L.A., 1961-65; dir. mgmt. rsch. and devel. USAF, Dayton, 1969-72; staff officer, Pentagon USAF, Washington, 1965-68; reconnaissance pilot USAF, Vietnam, 1968-69; ret., 1972; pres. Exec. Leadership, Inc., Chgo., 1973-80, Exec. Ministries, Inc., Atlanta, 198l-86; chmn., chief exec. officer, bd. dirs. Environ. Control Atlanta, Inc., Atlanta, 1973—, McNair Assocs., Inc., Atlanta, 1980—, Exec. Leadership Found., Inc., Atlanta, 1986—; bd. dirs. ADA Metals, Inc., Lincolnwood, Ill.; developer, instr. bus. ethics program, U.S., Can., South Am., West Europe, East Europe, U.S.S.R. Trustee Rep. Presl. Task Force; Rep. cand. for Gov., Ga., 1994. Decorated DFC, medal (Vietnam); recipient Gov.'s award State of Ky., State of Ark., Commendation award for bus. ethics program U.S. Pres., Chief Exec. Officer of Fortune 500 Corps., numerous awards for speaking. Mem. Am. Mgmt. Assn. President's Assn., Ret. Officers Assn., Christian Businessmen's Com. U.S.A., Inst. for Absolute Ethics (assoc., bd. dirs.), Air Force Assn., Internat. Platform Assn., Nat. Speakers Assn., Nat. Honor Soc., Tau Beta Pi, Phi Eta Sigma. Baptist. Home: 4090 Northlake Creek Cv Tucker GA 30084-3416 Office: Exec Leadership Found 2193 Northlake Pky Ste 107 Tucker GA 30084-4113

MCNAIRN, PEGGI JEAN, speech pathologist, educator; b. Dallas, Sept. 22, 1954; d. Glenn Alton Harmon and Anna Eugenia (McVay) Hicks; m. Kerry Glen McNairn, Jan. 27, 1979; children: Micah Jay, Nathan Corey. BS in Speech Pathology, Tex. Christian U., 1977, MS in Communications Pathology, 1978; PhD in Ednl. Adminstrn., Kennedy Western U., 1991. Cert. speech pathologist, mid mgmt. Staff speech pathologist, asst. dir. infant program Easter Seal Soc. for Crippled Children and Adults Tarrant County, Ft. Worth, 1978-80; staff speech pathologist, spl. edn. lead tchr. Sherrod Elem. Sch. Arlington (Tex.) Ind. Sch. Dist., 1981-84, secondary speech/lang. specialist, early childhood assessment staff Spl. Services dept., 1984-89; owner, dir. Speech Assocs., 1989-92; mem. state forms com. Arlington (Tex.) Ind. Sch. Dist., 1985-86, chairperson assessment com., 1986-87; cons. augmentative communication Prentke Romich Co., 1992—; adj. prof., clin. supr. Tex. Christian U., Ft. Worth, 1978-79; clin. speech pathologist North Tex. Home Health Assn., Ft. Worth, 1980-92. Author: Quick Tech Activities for Literacy, 1993, Readable, Repeatable Stories and Activities, 1994, Quick Tech Magic: Music-Based Literacy Activities, 1996. Chairperson United Cerebral Palsy Toy Lending Libr., 1989-90; sunday sch. tchr. 1st United Meth. Ch., Arlington, 1982-87; mem. South Arlington Homeowners Assn., Arlington, 1985-87; 3rd v.p. Bebensee Elem. PTA. Recipient Outstanding Svc. to Handicapped Am. Biog. Inst., 1989; Cert. of Achievement John Hopkins U. for computing to assist persons with disabilities, 1991. Mem. Internat. U.S. Tex. Socs. for Augmentative and Alternate Comm. (sec. Tex. branch), Neurodevelopmental Assn., Assn. for Curriculum and Supervision, Am. Speech and Hearing Assn., Tex. Speech-Language-Hearing Assn., Tex. Speech and Hearing Assn. (task force mem for augmentative comm.) Teaching Tex. Tots Consortium, Tex. Christian U. Speech and Hearing Alumni Assn., Kappa Delta Pi, Alpha Lambda Delta. Democrat. Home and Office: 215 Spanish Moss Dr Arlington TX 76018-1540

MCNALLY, JAMES JOSEPH, JR., English language educator; b. Washington, Sept. 30, 1924; s. James Joseph and Goldine Virginia (Kitchen) McN.; m. Margaret Jean Wilson, Aug. 12, 1944 (div. Aug. 1946); m. Mary Elinor Griffith, Dec. 3, 1949; children: Emily Anne, John James. AB, U. Va., 1951, MA in Fgn. Affairs, 1952, MA in English, 1954, PhD in English Lit., 1961. Instr. English Pa. State U., University Park, 1957-58; asst. prof., then assoc. prof., head dept. English Morris Harvey Coll., Charleston, W.Va., 1958-63; from asst. prof. to assoc. prof. Old Dominion U., Norfolk, Va., 1963-69, prof., 1969-92, prof. emeritus, 1992. Contbr. articles to scholarly publs., 1967-87. Pres. Faculty Senate of Va., 1973-75. With USMC, 1943-46, The Philippines, China. Mem. AAUP, MLA, Nat. Coun. Tchrs. of English, Am. Conf. on Irish Studies, Poetry Soc. Va. (pres. 1990-93, Edgar Allan Poe award 1989), Victorian Studies. Democrat. Unitarian.

MCNALLY, JAY MICHAEL, computer company executive, consultant; b. Fall River, Mass., June 18, 1961; s. Alfred Ignacious McNally and Marianne (Russo) Palumbo. BA, Coll. of the Atlantic, 1984. Adminstr. Conley & Hodge Assocs., Boston, 1985-87; pvt. practice cons. Portland, Maine, 1987-89; adminstr. litigation support Jenner & Block, Miami, Fla., 1990-91; exec. dir. ops. Document Automation Corp., Wilkes-Barre, Pa., 1991-92; pres. IBIS Recognition Systems, N.Y.C., Fla., 1992—. Mem. Assn. Image and Info. Mgmt. Office: IBIS Recognition Sys 1140 Ave of the Americas New York NY 10036

MCNAMARA, A. J., federal judge; b. 1936. BS, La. State U., 1959; JD, Loyola U., New Orleans, 1968. Bailiff, law clk. U.S. Dist. Ct., New Orleans, 1966-68, sole practice, 1968-72; ptnr. Monton, Roy, Carmouche, Hailey, Bivens & McNamara, New Orleans, 1972-78, Hailey, McNamara, McNamara & Hall, 1978-82; judge U.S. Dist. Ct. (ea. dist.) La., New Orleans, 1982—. Mem. La. Ho. of Reps., 1976-80. Office: US Dist Ct C-367 US Courthouse 500 Camp St New Orleans LA 70130-3313*

MCNAMARA, GREGORY VAUGHN, English language educator; b. Cambridge, Md., Sept. 7, 1969; s. Gary Vaughn and Barbara Ann (Batz) McN.; m. Melanie Ann Moser, Aug. 5, 1995. BS in English, Sociology, Frostburg State U., 1991; MA in English, W. Va. U., 1993, postgrad. studies, 1994—. Adminstrv. asst. Arts and Sci. Advising W. Va. U., Morgantown, 1992-93; tchg. asst. W. Va. U., Morgantown, 1993—, ops. mgr. Ctr. for Literary Computing, 1993-96; asst. coord., 1996—; webmaster Eberly Coll. Arts and Scis. W. Va. U., Morgantown, 1995—; webmaster exptl. program to stimulate competitive rsch., 1995—; adminstrv. asst. W. Va. exptl. program to stimulate competitive rsch., Morgantown, 1996—; presenter Grad Student Colloquium W.Va. U., Morgantown, 1994, Clinch Valley Coll. Medieval Renaissance Conf., Wise, Va., 1995, 96, W.Va. Shakespeare and Renaissance Assn. Meeting, Montgomery, W.Va., 1994; reader Folger Shakespeare Libr. Vol. Stepping Stones, Morgantown, W. Va., 1996. Steven Crocker scholar Dept. English, W. Va. U., Morgantown, 1993—; John C. and Mildred W. Ludlum Doctoral fellow, 1996. Mem. MLA, W. Va. Shakespeare and Renaissance Assn., English Grad. Student Assn. Morgantown (v.p., editor electronic discussion group 1993-96). Home: 521 Beverly Ave #1 Morgantown WV 26505 Office: W Va U Dept English Box 6296 Morgantown WV 26506

MCNAMARA, MARTIN BURR, lawyer, oil and gas company executive; b. Danbury, Conn., Sept. 10, 1947; s. William Joseph and Geraldine Margaret (Young) McN.; m. Anne Rose Hogan, Jan. 15, 1977. BA in English, Providence Coll., 1969; JD, Yale U., 1972. Bar: N.Y. 1973, U.S. Dist. Ct. (so. and ea. dists.) N.Y. 1973, (no. dist.) Tex. 1993, U.S. Ct. Appeals (2d cir.) 1973, Tex. 1980, U.S. Ct. Appeals (5th and 11th cirs.) 1980. Assoc. Shea & Gould, N.Y.C., 1972-76; asst. U.S. atty. (so. dist.) N.Y., N.Y.C., 1976-79; v.p., gen. counsel, sec. Tex. Oil & Gas Corp., Dallas, 1979-91; gen. counsel, sr. v.p. adminstrn. Delhi Gas Pipeline Corp., Dallas, 1979-91; exec. com. ptnr. Gibson, Dunn & Crutcher LLP, Dallas, 1991—; lectr. State Bar of Tex., Dallas Bar Assn., U. Tex. Corp. Coun. Inst., Okla. Bar Assn. bd. dirs. Sonat Offshore Drilling, Inc.; lectr. State Bar of Tex., Dallas Bar ASsn., U. Tex. Corp. Counsel Inst., Okla. Bar Assn. Mem. exec. com. Yale Law Sch. Assn., 1983-86. Mem. State Bar of Tex. (vice chmn. corp. counsel sect. 1984-86, chmn.-elect 1987-88, chmn. 1988-89), Bar Assn. Fifth Fed. Cir., Assn. Bar. City of N.Y., N.Y. State Bar Assn., Fed. Energy Bar Assn. Republican. Roman Catholic. Club: Petroleum. Office: Gibson Dunn & Crutcher 5500 Bank One Ctr 1717 Main St Dallas TX 75201-4605

MCNAMARA, PATRICIA RAE, religious organization administrator; b. Lima, Ohio, Oct. 24, 1936; d. Raymond Joseph and Hildreth Josephine (Kuhn) McN. AA, St. Catharine Coll., Springfield, Ky., 1959; BA, Siena Coll., 1966; MA, Morehead State U., 1973; MRE Loyola U., Chgo., 1996; cert. devel. edn. specialist Appalachian State U., 1983, cert. English lang. arts tchrs/instr., life-time tchr. cert., Ky. Dominican Sisters of St. Catharine of Siena, Roman Cath. Ch., 1955. Tchr. elem. and jr. high Cath. schs., Springfield, Ky., Memphis, 1956-63; mid. and jr. high tchr. Cath. schs., Forrest City, Ark., McMechen, W.Va., 1963-67; tchr. Cath. high schs., Springfield, Louisville, 1968-79; instr. English St. Catharine Coll., Springfield, 1979-86, chair humanities divsn., 1982-84, part-time instr., 1986-89, dir. community rels., alumni, editor 10 yr. self-study for So. Assn. Accreditation, 1986-89, dir. of parish religious edn. and catechist formation, cochair Parish Coun. Comm. Commn. St. Jerome Ch., Fancy Farm, Ky., 1989-91; dir. parish religious edn. St. Martin Tours Ch., Vine Grove, Ky., 1991—; pres. Greater Louisville High Sch. Press Assn., 1973-75, mem. exec. bd., 1973-79. Ga. State Coll. Newspaper Fund grantee, 1970; Eastern Coll. Am. Studies grantee, 1977. Mem. Ky. Council Internat. Reading Assn. (chmn. coll. reading com. 1983-86, regional leader 1984-85), Nat. Council Tchrs. of English (regional judge, ann. awards in writing 1978-88, 89-90, cons. to Coll. English Edn. Commn. 1984-90), Nat. Cath. Catechists Soc., Greater Louisville English Council (v.p. 1977-79), Ky. Council Tchrs. of English (v.p. 1981-82, pres. 1982-83, exec. bd. 1983-84, Faithful Service plaque, 1984). Democrat. Avocations: creative and newsletter writing, singing in ch. choir and cantoring for liturgies, reading, visiting hist. and literary landmarks. Home: 467 Saint Martin Rd Vine Grove KY 40175-8617 Office: Religious Edn Office 440 Saint Martin Rd Vine Grove KY 40175-8617

MCNAMARA, PAULA RUTH WAGNER, therapeutic recreation programs director; b. St. Louis, Feb. 23, 1925; d. Paul Brooks and Leah Ruth (Dick) Wagner; m. Raymond Edmund McNamara, May 28, 1949; children: Carol Rae, Marla Ann, Cynthia Ruth, Erin Marie, Brian Francis. BFA, Sch. of Art Inst., 1948; MA, W. Va. Grad. Coll., 1988. Cert. therapeutic recreation specialist. Supr. leisure edn. W. Va. Rehabilitaion Ctr., Institute, 1970-91; exec. dir. W. Va. Therapeutic Recreation Assn., Institute, 1992—; rep. Nat. Therapeutic Recreation Assn., Arlington, Va., 1984—. Amb. Friendship Force, 1993—; conf. del. Partners of the Americas, Washington, 1991. Mem. Nat. Therapeutic Recreation Assn., Am. Therapeutic Recreation Assn., W.Va. Therapeutic Recreation Assn. (sec. 1991). Office: WVa Therapeutic Recreation Assn PO Box 554 Institute WV 25112-0554

MCNAMARA, ROBERT PAUL, sociology educator; b. New Haven, Nov. 23, 1960. BS in Criminal Justice, Western Conn. State U., 1986; MS in Sociology and Criminal Justice, So. Conn. State U., 1988; MA in Sociology, Yale U., 1990, MPhil in Sociology, 1991, PhD in Sociology, 1993. Adj. faculty mem. So. Conn. State U., New Haven, 1989-93; acting instr. Yale U., New Haven, 1991; asst. prof. sociology and criminal justice West Ga. Coll., Carrollton, 1993-94; asst. prof. sociology Furman U., Greenville, S.C., 1994—. Author: The Times Square Hustler, 1994; Crime Displacement: The Other Side of Prevention, 1994, The Urban Landscape: Selected Readings, 1995, Sex, Scams, Street Life, 1995. Office: Furman U 3300 Ponsett Hwy Greenville SC 29613

MCNAMARA-RAISCH, M. EILEEN, marketing professional; b. Abington, Pa.; d. Edward J. and Mary L. (Perozze) McNamara; m. Thomas R. Raisch; children: Meghan, Michael. BA, LaSalle U., 1973; postgrad., Temple U., 1978, Dartmouth U., 1990, Tufts U., 1993. Bus. rschr. Bell of Pa., 1974-78; market rschr. AT&T, Parsippany, N.J., 1978-81; div. mgr., dist. mgr. consumer svcs. AT&T, Basking Ridge, N.J., 1981-85, 87-88; dir. consumer lab. AT&T, Basking Ridge, 1988-89, mktg. dir. new bus. devel., 1989-91; transponder svcs. dir. satellite svcs. AT&T, Bedminster, N.J., 1991-93; mktg. dir. bus. comms. AT&T, Bedminster, 1993-94; pres., CEO AT&T Tridom, Marietta, Ga., 1994—. Mem. Electronic Industry Assn. (adv. com. 1987-89), Am. Mktg. Assn., Soc. Satellite Profls. Internat., Soc. Internat. Bus. Fellows, Cobb Chamber Chmn.'s Club, Atlanta C. of C. (internat. divsn.). Home: 4356 Highborne Dr Marietta GA 30066-2429 Office: AT&T Tridom 835 Franklin Ct Marietta GA 30067-8946

MCNAUGHTON, ALEXANDER BRYANT, lawyer; b. Atlanta, Apr. 2, 1948; s. William James and June Florence (Gibson) McN.; m. Susan Mary Knox, Mar. 7, 1981; children: Alexis Loren, Elizabeth Adelyn. BS, Ga. State U., 1974; postgrad., Oxford (England) U., 1980; JD, U. Okla., 1981. Bar: Okla. 1981, U.S. Dist. Ct. (we. dist.) Okla. 1981, U.S. Ct. Appeals (10th cir.) 1982, U.S. Ct. Mil. Appeals 1984, U.S. Supreme Ct. 1985. Social worker State of Ga. Dept. Human Svcs., Bainbridge, 1974-75; farmer MC Farms, Cole, Okla., 1975-81; trial lawyer Mattoon Law Offices, Norman, Okla., 1981-82, Jones, Gungoll, Jackson et al, Enid, Okla., 1982-83, Jones, McNaughton & Blakley, Enid, 1983-85, McNaughton & McNaughton, Enid, 1985-94; Norman, Edem, McNaughton & Wallace, Enid, 1994—; expert cons. in field. Contbr. to book chpt. Scoutmaster Boy Scouts Am., Norman. With U.S. Army, 1966-68. Mem. ABA (litigation med. negligence, tort and ins. sects.), ATLA (sustaianging), Okla. Trial Lawyers Assn. (bd. dirs. 1993-95). Home: 2567 Homestead Rd Enid OK 73703-1647 Office: Norman Edem McNaughton Wallace 110 N Independence Enid OK 73701

MCNEELY, PATRICIA GANTT, journalism educator; b. Winnsboro, S.C., Dec. 2, 1939; d. William Adolphus and Alice (Woodson) Gantt; m. Alfred Raymond McNeely, Apr. 8, 1960; children: Allison Patricia, Alan David. BA, Furman U., 1960; MA, U. S.C., 1975. Reporter Greenville (S.C.) News, 1958-60; reporter Columbia (S.C.) Record, 1960-66, 66-72, news editor, 1979-80; reporter The State, Columbia, 1965-66; prof. journalism U. S.C., Columbia, 1972—; state mgr. Voter News Svc., N.Y., 1972—; workshop dir. Reader's Digest, Pleasantville, N.Y., 1985—. Mem. Assn. for Edn. in Journalism and Mass Comm. (sec. mag. divsn. 1995-96, head newspaper divsn. 1988-89, standing profl. freedom and responsibility com. 1995—). Office: Univ SC Coll Journalism Mass Comm Blossom at Assembly Sts Columbia SC 29208

MCNEIL, HOYLE GRAHAM, JR., pharmacist, administrator, pharmacy management and consulting company executive; b. Knoxville, Tenn., Jan. 29, 1950; s. Hoyle Graham Sr. and Betty Sue (Stone) McN.; m. Kathryn Kimberly Bebb, Aug. 10, 1985. Student U. Tenn., 1968-72; BS in Pharmacy, Mercer U., 1975, PharmD, 1977. Lic. pharmacist, Ga., Tenn. Clin. pharmacist, drug info. coord. U. Tenn. Meml. Hosp., Knoxville, 1976-80; dir. pharmacy, purchasing and ancillary svcs. Peninsula Hosp., Louisville, Tenn., 1980-90; cons. pharmacist Corner-Stone of Recovery, Louisville, 1989-93; bd. dirs. Cornerstone of Recovery, Inc.; ptnr., pres. First Pharmacy Mgmt., Inc., Knoxville, 1985—, Home Health Care Infusion Therapy; asst. hosp. adminstr. Peninsula Hosp., Louisville, Tenn., 1986-89; pharmacy cons. Knox County Detoxification Ctr., 1991—; cons. hosps., nursing homes; bd. dirs. Knox County Bd. Health, Knoxville, 1985—; apptd. co-chmn. Knox County Community Health Agy., 1990-92, pres. elect, 1991; alt. del. Tenn. Community Health Adv. Coun. of Commr. of Human Svcs., 1990—; mem. adv. bd. Ptnrs. Home Healthcare Agy., 1992—; mem. adv. bd. Nat. Arthritis Soc. Smoky Mountain chpt., 1990—, ResCare Home Health Agy., 1991—; dir. pharmacy Oakwood Med. Ctr., 1993-95. Mem. editorial adv. panel Am. Pharmacy, 1990—, mem. adv. bd. Home Healthcare Agy., pharmacy jours. publ. coms.; mem. adv. bd. for publs. Drug Topics, 1991—; contbr. articles to Jour. Am. Pharm. Assn., Urban Health Jour., other publs. Editor newsletter: Drug Info. Update, 1977-81. Pres., 2d yr. profl. class Mercer U., 1973-74. Fellow Am. Soc. Cons. Pharmacists; mem. Knoxville Soc. Hosp. Pharmacists (pres. 1983-84), Knoxville Pharm. Assn. (pres. 1984-85), Tenn. Pharm. Assn. (del. 1983-85, co-chmn. impaired pharmacists com. 1984, Tenn. Pharmacists Assn. (chmn. peer assistance com. 1985-93), Tenn. Soc. Hosp. Pharmacists, Tenn. Hosp. Assn. (psychiat. hosp. task force), Tenn. Healthcare Assn., Am. Pharm. Assn., Am. Soc. Hosp. Pharmacists, Knox County Mental Health Assn., Am. Coll. Utilization Rev. Physicians, Am. Biog. Inst. (research bd. advisors), Nat. Assn. Quality Assurance Profls., Soc. Healthcare Adminstrs., Phi Lambda Sigma, Kappa Psi (pres. Gamma Psi chpt. 1974-75, Brother of Yr., 1975). Avocations: reading, gardening, traveling, spectator sports. Home: 5314 Stone Oak Rd Knoxville TN 37920-5024 Office: First Pharmacy Mgmt Inc PO Box 10586 Knoxville TN 37939-0586

MCNEIL, KENNETH EUGENE, law firm administrator; b. Boston, Jan. 14, 1936; s. Clarence L. and Frances Louise (Waterman) McN.; m. Marilyn Loretta Mayo, Aug. 11, 1956; children: Cheryl L. Kolkhorst, Laurie J. Holland, Brian K. (dec.). BS in Acctg., U. N.H., 1962. CPA, Mass., Maine, Ohio. Supr., sr. acct. and staff acct. Coopers & Lybrand, Boston, 1963-69, audit mgr., 1969-70; resident mgr. Coopers & Lybrand, Portland, Maine, 1970-75; mng. ptnr. Coopers & Lybrand, Portland, 1975-78, Akron, Ohio, 1978-83; dir. adminstrn. Robbins, Gaynor, Burton, Hampp, Burns, Bronstein & Shasteen, St. Petersburg, Fla., 1984-87, Henderson, Franklin, Starnes & Holt, P.A., Ft. Myers, Fla., 1987—; pres. Akron (Ohio) Cascade chpt. Nat. Assn. Accts., 1983; adj. prof. Edison C.C., Ft. Myers, 1991. Fin. chmn., trustee Ohio Ballet, Akron, 1980-83; mem. bd. dirs. Jr. Achievement, Akron, 1980-82. With USN, 1955-57. Named Life mem. U.S. Jaycees, Tulsa, 1970. Mem. ABA (assoc. mem. econs. sect.), Assn. Legal Adminstrs. (past chmn. and current treas. Fla. coun., current sec. S.W. Fla. chpt.), Fla. Bar Assn. (adv. bd. for LOMAS and mem. of Exec. Coun. Practice Mgmt. and Devel. sect.), Univ. Club, S.W. Fla. C. of C. (trustee 1990-94), Rotary Ft. Myers S. (pres.-elect 1994, pres. 1995, bd. mem. Found.), Psi Epsilon, Beta Alpha Psi (hon. life). Home: 14682 Triple Eagle Ct Fort Myers FL 33912-1705 Office: Henderson Franklin Starnes & Holt PA 1715 Monroe St Fort Myers FL 33901-3072

MCNEIL, WILLIAM K., folklorist; b. near Canton, N.C., Aug. 13, 1940; s. William McKinley and Winifred (Rigdon) McN.; m. Grace Joy Taucan Morandarte, July 25, 1994. BA, Carson-Newman Coll., 1962; MA, Okla. State U., 1963, SUNY, Cooperstown, 1967; PhD, Ind. U., 1980. VISTA vol. Office Econ. Opportunity, Barbourville, Ky., 1965-66; historian N.Y. State Dept. Edn., Albany, 1967-70; adminstr., folklorist Smithsonian Inst., Washington, 1975-76; folklorist Ozark Folk Ctr., Mt. View, Ark., 1976—; pres. Ozark States Folklore Soc., 1980-81. Author: American Proverb Literature, 1971, The Charm is Broken, 1984, Ghost Stories from the American South, 1985, On a Slow Train Through Arkansas, 1985, Southern Folk Ballads, 1987, Appalachian Images in Folk and Popular Culture, 1989, Ozark Mountain Humor, 1989, The Life and Adventures of an Arkansaw Doctor, 1989, Arkansas Folklore Sourcebook, 1992, Southern Mountain Folksongs, 1993, Ozark Country, 1995. Fellow Ind. U., 1970. Fellow Am. Folklore Soc. (book rev. editor 1977-80), Mid-Am. Folklore Soc. (sec., treas. 1987—), N.Y. Folklore Soc., Calif. Folklore Soc., Pa. Folklore Soc. Home: PO Box 1097 Mountain View AR 72560-1097 Office: Ozark Folk Ctr PO Box 500 Mountain View AR 72560-0500

MCNEILL, JOAN REAGIN, volunteer consultant; b. Atlanta, July 8, 1936; d. Arthur Edward and Annie May (Busby) Reagin; m. Thomas Pinckney McNeill, Sr., Aug. 3, 1957; childen: Thomas Pinckney, Clyde Reagin. Student, U. Louisville, 1955-57; BA, U. Tenn., Chattanooga, 1976. Founding pres. Family and Children's Svcs. Assocs., Chattanooga, 1987-88; bd. dirs. Chattanooga Symphony and Opera Assn., 1984-88, pres., 1984-87; pres. Chattanooga Ballet Assn., 1986-88; bd. dirs. U. Chattanooga Found., 1986-89; mem. vol. coun. bd. dirs. Am. Symphony Orch. League, Washington, 1986-96; pres.-elect, 1992-93, pres., 1993-95. Recipient Outstanding Svc. award U. Tenn., Chattanooga, 1988. Mem. U. Tenn. Chattanooga Alumni Assn. (pres. 1985-86), Golden Key, Sigma Kappa Found. (trustee 1992—, sec. 1993-94, pres. 1994—, Colby award for volunteerism 1990). Republican. Episcopalian. Office: 7457 Preston Cir Chattanooga TN 37421-1839

MCNEILL, MARY KATHRYN MORGAN, librarian; b. Greenville, S.C., Feb. 22, 1958; d. Harvey Eugene and Mary Anna (Walser) Morgan; m. George Terrence McNeill, May 17, 1980; 1 child, Terrence Morgan. BS,

Winthrop Coll., 1980; MLS, Emory U., 1985. Media specialist Thurston Elem. Sch., Thomaston, Ga., 1980-85; asst. libr. Oxford (Ga.) Coll. Libr. Emory U., 1985-88, dir., 1988—. Sunday Sch. tchr. Thomaston United Methodist Ch., 1981. Mem. ALA, Assn. Coll. and Rsch. Librs., Libr. Adminstrn. and Mgmt. Assn., Southeastern Libr. Assn., Ga. Libr. Assn., Delta Kappa Gamma (sec. chpt. 1992-96, pres. chpt. 1996—). Home: 3303 Sams Way Conyers GA 30208-2250 Office: Emory U Oxford Coll Libr PO Box 1448 Oxford GA 30267-1448

MCNEILL, MAXINE CURRIE, county official; b. Rockingham, N.C., Oct. 17, 1934; d. Daniel Franklin and Lollie Mae (Davis) Currie; m. James Albert McNeill, May 5, 1956; children: James C., David A., Jon S., Ellen F. BSN, Wingate Coll., 1986; MPH, U. N.C., 1991. Cert. nurse practitioner; cert. in ambulatory health care Nat. Cert. Corp. Dir. nursing svc. Hamlet, N.C., 1967-69; sch. nurse Rockingham, N.C., 1970-72; dir. Richmond County Home Health Agy., Rockingham, 1972-74; pub. health nurse Scotland County Health Dept., Laurinburg, N.C., 1974-75, nurse practitioner, 1975-79; nurse practitioner Laurinburg Surg. Clinic, 1979-80; nursing supr. Scotland Count Health Dept., Laurinburg, 1980-82, Richmond County Health Dept., Rockingham, N.C., 1982-88; local health dir. Montgomery County Health Dept., Troy, N.C., 1988-92; nurse practitioner Richmond OBGYN, Rockingham, N.C., 1992-93, Bladen County Health Dept., 1993-95; dir. daily ops. St. Joseph Home Health Agy., Troy, N.C., 1995—; staff nurse, relief supr. Richmond Meml. Hosp., Rockingham, N.C., 1955-67; mem. Maternal-Health Liason Com., 1990-91, N.C. State Pers. Liason Com., 1990-91. Mem. ANA, N.C. Nurses Assn. (disting. achievement award dist. V 1986), N.C. Pub. Health Assn. (dist. 12), N.C. Assn. Local Health Dirs., N.C. Dist. V Perinatal Assn., Kiwanis, Sigma Theta Tau. Democrat. Presbyterian. Home: 5080 Woodrun-on-Tillery Mount Gilead NC 27306

MCNICHOLS, GERALD ROBERT, consulting company executive; b. Cleve., Nov. 21, 1943; s. Charles Wellington and June Beatrice (Kalal) McN.; m. Paula Kay Austin, Dec. 26, 1964; children: G. Robert Jr., Kay Lynn, Melissa Sue. BS with honors, Case-Western Res. U., 1965; MS, U. Pa., 1966; ScD, George Washington U., 1976. Cert. cost estimator/analyst. Sr. ops. analyst Office of Sec., Dept. of Def., Washington, 1970-76; v.p. GenTech, Inc., Bethesda, Md., 1976-77, J. Watson Noah, Inc., Falls Church, Va., 1977-78; pres., chief exec. officer Mgmt. Cons. and Rsch., Inc., McLean, Va., 1978—. Co-author: Operations Research for Decision Making, 1975; editor Cost Analysis, 1984; contbr. articles to profl. jours. Pres. Rondelay Civic Assn., Fairfax Sta., Va., 1985-87. Capt. USAF, 1966-70. Mem. Inst. Cost Analysis (pres. 1985-88), Internat. Soc. Parametric Analysts (bd. dirs. 1982-84), Ops. Rsch. Soc. Am. (chmn. mil. applications sect.), Mil. Ops. Rsch. Soc. (sec., treas. 1986-87, v.p. adminstrn. 1987-88, bd. dirs. 1985-88, 92-96), Soc. Cost Estimating and Analysis (bd. dirs. 1990-93). Home: 23349 Parsons Rd Middleburg VA 22117 Office: Mgmt Cons & Rsch Inc 2000 Corporate Ridge # 400 Mc Lean VA 22102

MCNIDER, JAMES SMALL, III, lawyer; b. Richmond, Va., Aug. 23, 1956; s. James Small Jr. and Phoebe Warwick (Johnston) McN.; m. Anna Mary Van Buren, Apr. 30, 1983; children: Anna Lee, Mary Tyler, James S. IV, Elle Page. BS, Washington & Lee U., 1978, JD, 1981. Bar: Va. 1981, U.S. Tax Ct. 1981, U.S. Dist. Ct. (ea. dist.) Va. 1986. Assoc. Kaufman & Canoles, Norfolk, Va., 1981-85; assoc. Willcox & Savage, Norfolk, 1985-87, ptnr., 1987-95; ptnr. James S. McNider, III P.C., Hampton, Va., 1995—. Author: (with others) ABA Sales and Use Tax Handbook, 1988. Mem. ABA, Va. Bar Assn. (chmn. tax sect. 1993-94), Princess Anne Country Club, Omicron Delta Kappa. Episcopalian. Home: 808 Park Pl Hampton VA 23669-4152 Office: PO Box I 32 E Queens Way Ste B Hampton VA 23669

MCNIVEN, MALCOLM ALBERT, marketing educator; b. Oceanside, N.Y., Dec. 8, 1929; s. William McLellan and Hazel Virginia (Summers) McN.; m. Elaine Rusby Vellacott, June 12, 1954; children: Geoffrey David, Susan Leslie, Jane Elizabeth. BA, Denison U., 1951; MS, Ohio U., 1952; PhD, Pa. StateU., 1955. Lic. psychologist. Prof. psychology U. Md., University Park, 1955-56; supr. psychol. testing Pa. State U., University Park, 1956-57; mgr. advt. rsch. E.I. DuPont de Nemours, Wilmington, Del., 1957-67; v.p. strategic planning The Coca-Cola Co., Atlanta, 1967-74; v.p. mktg. svcs. The Pillsbury Co., Mpls., 1974-80; pres. consumer rsch. divsn. IMS Internat., N.Y.C., 1980-83; sr. v.p. mktg. svcs. Bank of Am., San Francisco, 1983-88; prin. Malcolm A. McNiven & Assocs., Athens, Ga., 1988—; dir. Ctr. Mktg. Studies U. Ga., Athens, 1988—; dir. MARC Group, Dallas, 1988—, Audit Bur. Circulation, Chgo., 1972-80. Author: How Much to Spend for Advertising, 1969. Trustee Denison U., Granville, Ohio, 1971—. Fellow APA, Assn. Nat. Advertisers (dir. 1985-88). Republican. Office: U Ga Ctr Mktg Studies 149 Brooks Hall Athens GA 30602

MCNULLY, LYNNETTE LARKIN, elementary education educator; b. Iowa City, Iowa, Jan. 22, 1966; d. Ernest F. and Karen (Schaeferle) Larkin; m. William S. McNully, May 14, 1988. BA in English, U. Okla., 1987; MEd in Early Childhood Edn., East Tex. State U., 1994. Cert. tchr., Tex. Pre-kindergarten and kindergarten tchr. Dallas Pub. Schs., 1989—; founding mem. site-based mgmt. coun. Arlington Park Sch., 1994—. Vol. North Texas Irish Festival, Dallas, 1992, On the Wing Again, Ferris, Tex., 1993—. Named Tchr. of Yr., Arlington Park Sch., Dallas, 1992; Write, Right! grantee Dallas Jr. League, 1993. Mem. Nat. Assn. for Edn. of Young Children, Assn. for Childhood Edn. Internat., Dallas Quilters Guild, PTA (exec. bd. 1993—), Phi Beta Kappa.

MCNULTY, JAMES ERGLER, finance educator; b. Pitts., Aug. 2, 1944; s. James E. and Mary Jane (Wilson) McN.; m. Kathleen Ann Colquhoun, June 18, 1966; childen: Christine Ann, James Kevin. AB, Coll. William and Mary, 1966; MA, Northwestern U., 1967; PhD, U. N.C., 1975. Economist Fed. Home Loan Bank of Atlanta, 1971-77, asst. sec., economist, 1977-79, asst. v.p., economist, 1979-81, v.p., economist, 1982-89; asst. prof. Fla. Atlantic U., Boca Raton, Fla., 1989-91, assoc. prof., 1991—; cons., expert witness in field, 1989—. Contbr. articles to profl. jours.; reviewer acad. jours. Mem. Fin. Mgmt. Assn., Am. Fin. Assn., So. Fin. Assn., Ea. Fin. Assn. Home: 10714 Sea Clipp Cir Boca Raton FL 33498 Office: Fla Atlantic Univ College of Bus Boca Raton FL 33431

MCNULTY, MARY PAT, library administrator; b. Pitts., Sept. 11, 1938; d. Joseph Charles and Margaret Ruth (Lynn) Werl. BA in Sociology, Wheeling Jesuit U., 1967; MA in LS, U. So. Fla., 1983. Ref. libr. Broward County Libr., Ft. Lauderdale, Fla., 1973-80, cataloguer, 1980-82, programming libr., 1982-84, ref. libr./subject specialist, 1985-92, br. head, 1992—. Bd. dirs. Friends of the Libr., Davie, Fla., 1993-96; vol. West Lake Park Nature Ctr., Hollywood, Fla., 1996. Mem. Davie-Cooper City C. of C., ALA, Leadership Enhancement and Devel. of Broward County, Toastmasters, Beta Phi Mu. Home: 3001 S Ocean Dr #PH-K Hollywood FL 33019 Office: Davie-Cooper City Br Broward County Libr 4600 SW 82d Ave Davie FL 33328

MCNULTY, MATTHEW FRANCIS, JR., health sciences and health services administrator, educator, university administrator, consultant, horse and cattle breeder; b. Elizabeth, N.J., Nov. 26, 1914; s. Matthew Francis and Abby Helen (Dwyer) McN.; m. Mary Nell Johnson, May 4, 1946; children: Matthew Francis III, Mary Lauren. BS, St. Peter's Coll., 1938, DHL (hon.), 1978; postgrad., Rutgers U. Law Sch., 1939-41; grad., Officer Candidate Sch., U.S. Army, 1941, U.S. Army Staff and Command Sch., Ft. Leavenworth, 1945; MHA, Northwestern U., 1949; MPH, U. N.C., 1952; ScD (hon.), U. Ala., 1969, Georgetown U., 1986. Contract writer, mgmt. trainee acturial div. Prudential Life Ins. Co., Newark, N.J., 1938-46; dir. med. adminstrn. VA, Chgo. and Washington, 1946-49; project officer to take over and operate new VA Teaching Hosps. VA, Little Rock, Birmingham, Ala. and Chgo., 1949-54; adminstr. U. Ala. Jefferson-Hillman Hosp., Birmingham, 1954-60; founding gen. dir. U. Ala. Hosps. and Clinics, 1960-66; founding prof. hosp. adminstrn. U. Ala. Grad. Sch., 1954-69, vis. prof., 1969—, founding dir. grad. program health adminstrn., 1964-69; prof. epidemiology and preventive medicine Sch. Medicine U. Ala., 1960-69; founding dean Sch. Health Adminstrn. (now Sch. Health Related Profls.), 1965-69; pres. Matthew F. McNulty, Jr. & Assocs., Inc., 1954-91; founding dir. Coun. Teaching Hosps. and assoc. dir. Assn. Am. Med. Colls., 1966-69; prof. community medicine and internat. health Georgetown U., 1969-89, prof. emeritus 1989—, v.p. med. ctr. affairs, 1969-72, exec. v.p., med. ctr. affairs, 1972-74; chancellor, dir. Georgetown U. Med. Ctr., 1974-86; chancellor emeritus Georgetown U., 1986—; chmn. acad. affairs com., trustee Hahnemann U., Phila, 1987—; trustee Fla. Found. for Active Aging, 1989—; cons. VA Adv. Com. on Geriatrics & Gerontology, 1991—; founding chmn. bd. Univ. D.C. Affiliated Health Plan, Inc., 1974-78; founding chmn. bd. trustees Georgetown U. Community Health Plan, Inc., 1972-80; vis. prof. Cen. U., Caracas, Venezuela, 1957-61; hosp. cons., 1953—; bd. dirs. Kaiser-Georgetown Community Health Plan, Inc., Washington, 1980-85, bd. dirs. Kaiser Health Plans and Hosps., Oakland, Calif., 1980-85, emeritus, 1985—; mem. Statuatory VA Spl. Med. Adv. Group, 1978-89, Higher Edn. Com. on Dental Schs. Curriculum, 1978-79; preceptor hosp. adminstrn. Northwestern U., Washington U., U. Iowa, U. Minn., 1953-69; mem. nat. adv. com. health research projects Ga. Inst. Tech., 1959-65, 73-85; nat. adv. com. health rsch. projects U. Pitts., 1956-60; adv. com. W.K. Kellogg Found., 1960-65; vis. cons., lectr. Venezuelan Ministry Health and Social Welfare, 1967-69; dir. Blue Cross-Blue Shield Ala., 1960-61, 65-68; trustee, mem. exec. com. Blue Cross and Blue Shield Nat. Capital Area, 1973-89, Washington Bd. Trade, 1972-86; mem. feasability study P.R. VA Med. Care, 1949, feasability study Ariz. Med. Edn., 1956. Bd. dirs. Greater Birmingham United Appeal, 1960-66; trustee, chmn. Jefferson County (Ala.) Tb Sanatorium, 1958-64; mem. health services research study sect. NIH, 1963-67; cons. USPHS, 1959-63; mem. White House Conf. on Health, 1965, on Medicare Implementation, 1966, NIH, USPHS and DHEW Commns., 1967-86, others; trustee Nat. Council Internat. Health, 1975-86; pres. Nat. League Nursing, 1979-81. Served to maj. USAAF, 1942-46, lt. col. USAFR, 1946-55. Recipient Disting. Alumnus award Northwestern U., 1973, Disting. Alumnus award U. N.C., John Benjamin Nichol award Med. Soc. D.C., Mayor and D.C. Coun., Matthew F. McNulty, Jr. Unanimous Recognition Resolution of 1986, Centennial award Georgetown U. Alumni Assn. award, 1982, Patrick Healy Disting. Svc. award, 1985, Alumni Life Senator Election award, 1986; named to Hon. Order Ky Cols., 1984. Fellow Am. Pub. Health Assn., Am. Coll. Healthcare Execs. (life, bd. regents and council of regents 1961-67, Disting. Health Sci. Exec. award 1976); mem AAAS, Am. Hosp. Assn. (life, Disting. Service award 1984), Ala. Hosp. Assn. (past pres.), Nat. League for Nursing (past pres.), D.C. League Nursing (past dir.), Nat. Forum Health Planning (past pres., Disting. award, 1987), Council Med. Adminstrn., Internat. Hosp. Fedn., Jefferson County Ala. Vis. Nursing Assn. (past pres., Disting. Service award), Ala. Pub. Health Assn. (past chmn. med. care sect.), Southeastern Hosp. Conf. (past dir.), Birmingham Hosp. Council (past pres.), Hosp. Council Nat. Capital Area (pres. 1985-89, exec. com. 1989—, past pres. 1989-93, treas. 1993—), Assn. Univ. Programs in Hosp. Adminstrn. (Disting. award 1971), Greater Birmingham Area C. of C. (Merit award), Washington Acad. of Medicine, Am. Assn. Med. Colls. (founding chmn. teaching hosp. council 1964-69, Disting. Service Mem.), Royal Soc. Health, Am. Systems Mgmt. Soc. (Disting. award), Orgn. Univ. Health Ctr. Adminstrs., Santa Gertrudis Breeders Internat., Bashkir Curley Horse Breeders Assn., Med. Soc. of D.C. (John Benjamin Nichols award 1982), Univ. Club Ala., Cosmos Club, City Tavern Club, KC (3d degree, coun. 10499 Ocean Springs, 4th degree Francis Deignan Assembly), Knights of Malta, Omicron Kappa Upsilon. Home and Office: Teoc Pentref 3100 Phil Davis Rd Ocean Springs MS 39564-9076

MCNUTT, CHARLES HARRISON, archaeologist, educator; b. Denver, Dec. 11, 1928; s. Charles Hammond and Elizabeth (Johnson) McN.; m. Phoebe Cynthia Russell, Aug. 5, 1955; children: Charles, Elizabeth. BS, U. of South, Sewanee, Tenn., 1950; MA, U. N.Mex., 1954; PhD, U. Mich., 1960. Tech. advisor Nat. Mus. of Can., Ottawa, Ont., summer 1956; archaeologist Smithsonian Inst. RBS, Lincoln, Nebr., 1957-60; asst. prof. archaeology U. Tenn., Knoxville, 1960-62, Ariz. State U., Flagstaff, 1962-64; assoc. prof. to full prof. archaeology U. Memphis, 1964—, dir. Anthropol. Rsch. Ctr., 1964—; pres. Archaeol. Adv. Coun., Conservation, Nashville, 1970-80, vice chair, 1986—. Author: Tesuque By-Pass Site NM, 1969, Duncan Tract Site, Tenn., 1983, Chucalissa, 1988; contbr. articles to profl. jours. Recipient Rockefeller award, 1950; rsch. grantee, NSF, 1954. Fellow Am. Anthropol. Assn.; mem. Southeastern Archaeol. Conf. (pres. 1977-80), So. Anthropol. Assn., Tenn. Archaeol. Soc. (editl. bd. 1979), Soc. for Am. Archaeology, Sigma Xi, Alpha Kappa Delta, Phi Beta Kappa. Episcopalian. Home: 351 Grandview St Memphis TN 38111-7607 Office: U. of Memphis Dept Anthropology Memphis TN 38152

MCNUTT, D. GAYLE, academic administrator; b. Comanche, Tex., Oct. 4, 1936; s. Luther E. and Willie B. (Newby) McN.; m. Esther R. Edwards, June 1, 1958; children: Linda, Gaye, Larry. BA, Tex. A&M U., 1959. Reporter Abilene (Tex.) Reporter-News, 1959-60, The Houston Post, 1960-66; pub. rels. asst. Tex. Mid-Continent Oil & Gas Assn., Dallas, 1966-67; news editor AP-Dow Jones Econ. Report, N.Y.C., 1967-68; press sec. to House Speaker/Lt. Gov. Tex. Austin, 1968-69; asst. dir. for communications Tex. Dept. Mental Health & Mental Retardation, Austin, 1969-70; polit. editor The Houston Chronicle, 1970-74; adminstrv. asst. to U.S. Rep. Bob Casey, 1974-76; Washington rep. Harris County, Tex. and Houston Port Authority, 1976-80; dir. communications Baylor Coll. Medicine, Houston, 1980-89, v.p. pub. affairs, 1989—. Dist. chmn. Boy Scouts Am., Sam Houston Area Coun., 1982-84; chmn. pub. rels. adv. com. Tex. Med. Ctr., Inc., 1983-84; mem. comm. adv. com. Houston C. of C., 1984-88. Recipient award of merit Boy Scouts Am., 1984, Disting. Reporting of Pub. Affairs award Nat. Polit. Sci. Assn., 1962, Tex. Atty. Gen.'s award for pub. svc. 1962, Silver Spur award Tex. Pub. Rels. Assn., 1966, 85, Disting. Svc. award Nat. Asns. Counties, 1980, Gold Quill award of excellence Internat. Assn. Bus. Communicators, 1985. Mem. Assn. Am. Med. Colls. (award of excellence for premier performance in pub. affairs 1985, 86), Assn. Acad. Health Ctrs., Pub. Rels. Soc. Am. (accredited mem., fellow/assembly mem., pres. Houston chpt. 1994, pub. affairs coun., Excalibur Excellence award 1983, 88), Coun. for Advancement & Support of Edn., Soc. Prof. Journalists (pres. Tex. Assn. 1963, pres. Tex. Gulf Coast chpt. 1962, sec. Austin chpt. 1970), South Main Ctr. Assn. (vice chmn. 1995—), Press Club of Houston, Quail Valley Country Club. Office: Baylor Coll Medicine 1 Baylor Plz Houston TX 77030-3411

MCNUTT, JACK WRAY, oil company executive; b. Norphlet, Ark., Sept. 7, 1934; s. Fay D. and Mattie E. (Garner) McN.; m. Jordine Chesshir, Aug. 19, 1955; 1 child, Marsha. BS, Harding Coll., 1956; MS, Columbia U., 1957. Acct. Murphy Oil Corp., El Dorado, Ark., 1957-68, exec. mgmt. asst., 1968-69, exec. v.p., 1981-88, chief operating officer, 1986-88, pres., chief exec. officer, 1988-94; ret., 1994; v.p. planning Murphy Ea. Oil Co., London, 1969-72, pres., 1972-81; bd. dirs. First Nat. Bank El Dorado, Ark. Mem. Am. Petroleum Inst. (dir.), 25 Yr. Club. of Petroleum Industry. Home: 1705 W Cedar St El Dorado AR 71730-5309 Office: 101 W Main St Ste 509 El Dorado AR 71730

MCPEAK, ALLAN, career services director, educator, lawyer, consultant; b. Hot Springs, Ark., Oct. 1, 1938; s. Kenneth L. and Dorothy (Whiteman) McP.; m. Judith L. Mathison, Oct. 26, 1973. BA, U. Fla., 1960, JD, 1965; MS, Nova U., 1984; PhD, Fla. State U., 1987; MS Instructional Systems Fla. State U., 1994. Bar: Fla. 1965, U.S. Supreme Ct. 1980. Sole practice, Naples, Fla., 1965-85; asst. dir. the career ctr. Fla. State U., 1987, assoc. dir., 1989; dir. Career Svcs. U. South Ala., Mobile, 1994—. cons. in human relations, organizational devel. and career devel., Tallahassee, 1984-94, Mobile, 1994—; pres. Lawyers Abstract Sevc., Naples, Fla., 1978-80; organizer Marine Savs. & Loan, Naples, 1980-81; Contbr. articles to profl. jours. Served with U.S. Army, 1960-63. Mem. Nat. Assn. Colls. and Employers, So. Assn. Colls. and Employers, Ala. Assn. Colls. and Employers, Fla. Bar Assn., Blue Key, Pi Sigma Alpha.

MCPHAIL, JOANN WINSTEAD, writer, producer, publisher, art dealer; b. Trenton, Fla., Feb. 17, 1941; d. William Emerson and Donna Mae (Crawford) Winstead; m. James Michael McPhail, June 15, 1963; children: Angela C. McPhail Morris, Dana Denise, Whitney Gold McPhail Casso. Student, Fla. So. Coll., 1959-60, St. John's River Jr. Coll., Palatka, Fla., 1960-61, Houston (Tex.) C.C. With Jim Walter Corp., Houston, 1961-62; receptionist, land lease sec. Oil and Gas Property Mgmt. Inc., Houston, 1962-63; sec. to mng. atty. State Farm Ins. Co., Houston, 1963-64; saleswoman, decorator Oneil-Anderson, Houston, 1973; sec. Law Offices of Ed Christensen, Houston, 1980-82; advt. mgr. Egalitarian Houston (Tex.) C.C. Systems, 1981; fashion display artist, 1985-86; entrepreneur, writer, art agt., playwright Golden Galleries, Houston, 1990—; owner, property mgr. APT Investments, 1994—; lyricist, publisher Anna Gold Classics, 1995—, writer, publisher of song lyrics and music, 1996—; screen playwright, 1996. Freelance writer, photographer: Elegance of Needlepoint, 1970, S.W. Art Mag., A Touch of Greatness, 1973, Sweet 70's Anthology, The Budding of Tomorrow, 1974; columnist, photographer: Egalitarian: The Name Game, Design Your Wall Covering, Student Profile, 1981, National Library of Poetry, Fireworks, 1995; contbr. poetry various publs.; playwright, 1992—; writer, publ. religious drama The Missing Crown, KYND-AM, World Wide Christian Radio, KCBI-FM, and other nat. radio stations, 1995—. Vol. PTO bd. Sharptown Middle Sch.; active ch. leadership activities. Mem. NAFE, ASCAP. Methodist. Home: 2608 Stanford St Houston TX 77006-2928

MC PHEETERS, EDWIN KEITH, architect, educator; b. Stillwater, Okla., Mar. 26, 1924; s. William Henry and Eva Winona (Mitchell) McP.; m. Patricia Ann Foster, Jan. 29, 1950 (div. 1981); children: Marc Foster, Kevin Mitchell, Michael Hunter; m. Mary Louise Marvin, July 21, 1984. B.Arch., Okla. State U., 1949; M.F.A., Princeton U., 1956. Instr. architecture U. Fla., 1949-51; asst. prof. Ala. Poly. Inst., Auburn U., 1951-54; fellow Princeton U., 1955, 81; from asst. prof. to prof. U. Ark., 1956-66; prof. Rensselaer Poly. Inst., 1966-69, dean, 1966-69; prof. Auburn (Ala.) U., 1969-89, dean Sch. Architecture and Fine Arts,, 1969-88, dean, prof. emeritus, 1989—; adj. prof. Frank Lloyd Wright Sch. of Architecture, 1992—; mem. Ala. Bd. Registration for Architects, 1978-87; profl. adviser South Ctrl. Bell Telephone Co., 1977-79, So. Co., 1979-81, Ala. Power Co., 1979-81, Okla. State U., 1983, Ala. Sch. Fine Arts, 1985-86; cons. Taliesin Architects, 1988-92. Served to 2d lt. USAAC, 1943-45; capt. USAFR 1945-57. Fellow AIA (pres. Ala. coun. 1978, Merit award 1976, East Ala. Design awards 1986, 87, 90, 92); mem. Assn. Collegiate Schs. Arch. (bd. dirs. 1970-77, Disting. Prof. 1989), Blue Key, Kappa Sigma, Omicron Delta Kappa, Kappa Kappa Psi, Tau Sigma Delta, Rotary. Episcopalian.

MCPHERON, ALAN BEAUMONT, lawyer; b. McAlester, Okla., July 6, 1914; s. Robert Lee and Jeannette (Kridler) McP.; m. Mary Jane Bass, Apr. 8, 1938; 1 dau., Jill McPheron Wigington. LL.B., U. Okla., 1937. Bar: Okla. 1937, U.S. Dist. Ct. (no., ea. and we. dists.) Okla., U.S. Dist. Ct. (no. dist.) Tex. Asst. county atty., Durant, Okla., 1939-42, county atty., 1942-43; sole practice, Durant, 1946-65, 75—; dist. judge Bryan County, Okla., 1965-75; tchr. bus. law So. Okla. State U., 1970-73. Mem. War Vets Commn. Okla., 1949-51; mem. bd. rev. Okla. Employment Security Commn., 1951-59; mem. Okla. Jud. Nominating Commn., 1983-89, 95—, Ct. on Judiciary Appeal Divsn., 1993—. Served to m/sgt. U.S. Army, 1943-46; ETO. Decorated Bronze Star; Croix de Guerre (France). Mem. ABA, Okla. Bar Assn. (bd. govs. 1990-92), Okla. Trial Lawyers Assn., Am. Judicature Soc., Okla. Criminal Def. Lawyers Assn. (charter mem.). Am. Legion, VFW. Democrat. Presbyterian. Club: Elks. Office: 116 N 3rd Ave Durant OK 74701-4728

MC PHERSON, FRANK ALFRED, manufacturing corporate executive; b. Stilwell, Okla., Apr. 29, 1933; s. Younce B. and Maurine Francis (Strauss) McP.; m. Nadine Wall, Sept. 10, 1955; 4 children. B.S., Okla. State U., 1957. With Kerr-McGeeCorp., 1957—; gen. mgr. Gulf Coast Oil and gas ops., Morgan City, La., 1969-73; pres. Kerr-McGee Coal, 1973-76, Kerr-McGee Nuclear, 1976-77; vice chmn. Kerr-McGee Corp., 1977-80, pres., 1980—, chmn., CEO, 1983—; bd. dirs. Kimberly-Clark Corp. Patentee in field. Bd. dirs. Okla. chpt. Nature Conservancy, U.S. Olympic Com. for Okla., Bapt Med. Ctr. Okla., Okla. Med. Rsch. Found., Okla. State U. Found., Okla. State Fair, Bank of Okla., Boys and Girls Clubs of Am., J.&W., Seligman & Co., Inc.; pres. Okla. Found. Excellence; active Bus. Roundtable; adv. com. U. Okla. Coll. Medicine, Oklahoma City Pub. Schs.; mem. bd. visitors U. Okla. Coll. Engring. Mem. Conf. Bd., Soc. Mining Engrs. Am., Am. Petroleum Inst. (dir.), Nat. Petroleum Council, 25-Yr. Club of Petroleum Industry Oklahoma City C. of C. (dir.), Okla. State C. of C. Republican. Baptist. Office: Kerr-McGee Corp PO Box 25861 Oklahoma City OK 73125-0861

MCPHERSON, GAIL, advertising and real estate executive; b. Fort Worth; d. Garland and Daphne McP. Student U. Tex.-Austin; BA, MS, CUNY. Advt. sales exec. Harper's Bazaar mag., N.Y.C., 1974-76; sr. v.p., fashion mktg. dir. L'Officiel/USA mag., N.Y.C., 1976-80; fashion mgr. Town and Country mag., N.Y.C., 1980-82; v.p. advt. and mktg. Ultra mag., Tex. and N.Y.C., 1982-84; fragrance, jewelry and automotive mgr. M. Mag., N.Y.C., 1984-85; sr. real estate sales exec. Fredric M. Reed & Co., Inc., N.Y.C., 1985-88; AT&T security system rep. Home-Watch Inc., Amarillo, Tex.,1989-92; sales rep. Universal Comm., Dallas, 1992-94; acct. exec. Corporate Mktg., Inc., Dallas, 1994—; Sponsor Southampton Hosp. Benefit Com., N.Y.; mem. jr. com. Mannes Sch. Music, N.Y.C., Henry St. Settlement, N.Y.C. Mem. Fashion Group N.Y., Advt. Women N.Y., Real Estate Bd. N.Y., U. Tex. Alumni Assn. of N.Y. (v.p.), Amarillo C. of C. (Comm. com.). Republican. Presbyterian. Clubs: Corviglia (St. Moritz, Switzerland), Doubles, El Morocco (mem. jr. com. 1976-77), Le Club (N.Y.C.). Home: 10812 Stone Canyon Rd Apt 3143 Dallas TX 75230-4312 Office: 12200 Ford Rd Dallas TX 75234

MCPHERSON, MILTON MONROE, history educator; b. Beatrice, Ala., Oct. 19, 1928; s. Laurence Milton and Annie Mae (Bell) McP.; m. Carolyn Elizabeth Coley, Dec. 16, 1955; children: Milton Jr., Herbert L., Gretchen M. BA, U. Ala., 1950, MA, 1959, PhD in Am. History, 1970. Asst. prof. history Miss. Coll., Clinton, 1959-60, Mercer U., Macon, Ga., 1960-61, Ala. Coll., Montevallo, 1961-62, Pensacola (Fla.) Jr. Coll., 1962-68; assoc. prof. history Troy (Ala.) State U., 1968-87, prof. history, 1987-89; prof. history emeritus, 1989—. Editor: Memories That Lingered: The Life and Times of Laurence Milton McPherson, 1993, Timeless Moments: Essays in American History, 1995. 1st lt. U.S. Army, 1950-53. Mem. NEA, Ala. Hist. Assn., So. Hist. Assn. Home: 206 Sherwood Ave Troy AL 36081

MCPHERSON, SAMUEL DACE, III, computer scientist, instructor, consultant; b. Durham, N.C., May 22, 1957; s. Samuel Dace Jr. and Margaret Courtauld (Finney) McP.; m. Grace Carroll Gilliam, Oct. 11, 1986; children: Stuart Dace, Katherine Finney, Rebecca Banks. BA in Edn., U. N.C., 1979; MEd, U. S.C., 1981. Data entry operator Olsten svcs. No. Telecom, Durham, 1985; computer operator GTE Data Svcs., Durham, 1985-86, sr. computer operator, 1986-87, svc. technician, 1987-88; systems tng. analyst GTE Data Svcs., Tampa, Fla., 1988-90, sr. systems tng. analyst, 1990-92; sr. sales tng. specialist Ascom Timeplex, 1992-93; tech. tng. specialist Fujitsu Network Switching, Raleigh, N.C., 1994-95; founder, pres. Technology Tng. Solutions, Inc., 1995—; presenter pub. and ednl. workshops Wake Tech.; instr./lectr. Am. Rsch. Group. Vol. U.S. Olympic Festival, Durham, 1987, GTE Suncoast Classic, Tampa, 1989-91; instr. Jr. Achievement Tampa, 1989; active Village Presbyn. Ch., Tampa, 1990. Recipient Personal Best Group award GTE, 1992, Quest for Quality award, 1992, Outstanding Achievement award Ascom Timeplex, 1993; Cameron scholar U. N.C., 1978-79. Mem. ASTD (spl. projects com. Suncoast chpt. 1989-90, appreciation award 1989), Data Processing Mgmt. Assn. (dir. mem. edn. 1989-91, presenter local workshop 1991). Republican. Home: 5201 Lovell Ct Raleigh NC 27613-5618 Office: Tech Tng Solutions Inc 5201 Lovell Ct Raleigh NC 27613

MCQUARRIE, CLAUDE MONROE, III, lawyer; b. Ft. Benning, Ga., Oct. 15, 1950; s. Claude Monroe Jr. and Rosanne (Sprinkle) McQ.; m. Patricia Elaine Swanson, Dec. 23, 1977; children: Kevin Andrew, Ryan Christopher, Erin Elizabeth. BS, U.S. Mil. Acad., 1972; JD with distinction, St. Mary's U., San Antonio, 1978. Bar: Tex. 1978, U.S. Dist. Ct. (so. dist.) Tex. 1982, U.S. Ct. Mil. Appeals 1979. Commd. 2d lt. U.S. Army, 1972, advanced through grades to capt., 1976, resigned, 1982; assoc. Fulbright & Jaworski, Houston, 1982-89, ptnr., 1989—. Editor Law Rev., 1977-78. Mem. ABA, Houston Bar Assn., John M. Harlan Soc., Phi Delta Phi. Home: 2802 Eagle Creek Dr Kingwood TX 77345-1311 Office: Fulbright & JaworskiLLP 1301 McKinney St, Ste 5100 Houston TX 77010•

MCQUEEN, REBECCA HODGES, health care executive, consultant; b. Dothan, Ala., July 20, 1954; d. Edward Grey and Shirley Louise (Varner) Hodges; m. David Raymond McQueen, Mar. 5, 1982; children: Matthew David, Owen Grey. BS, Emory U., 1976, MPH, 1979. Research assoc. North Cen. Ga. Health Systems Agy., Inc., Atlanta, 1979-80; assoc. dir. Health Services Analysis, Inc., Atlanta, 1980-82; med. group adminstr. Southeastern Health Services, Inc./Prucare, Atlanta, 1982-84; sr. v.p., COO SouthCare Med. Alliance, Atlanta, 1985-93; pres., CEO, PROMINA N.W. Health Network, Atlanta, 1993-96; sr. v.p. managed care PROMINA Health Sys., Atlanta, 1996—; cons. North Cen. Ga. Health Systems Agy., 1980-81, Region 4 HHS, Atlanta, 1980-82, instr. Applied Stats., Washington, 1980-82;

mem. Health Data com. and Health Cost subcom. Atlanta Healthcare Alliance, 1985—; cons. Atlanta Com. for the Olympic Games, 1992. Contbr. articles to profl. jours. Adviser to med. support panel Atlanta Com. for Olympic Games; mem. Morningside/Lenox Park Civic Assn., Friends of Atlanta-Fulton Pub. Libr., Atlanta Bot. Garden, Planned Parenthood-Atlanta, Ga. Coun. on Child Abuse, Atlanta Wellness Coun. Recipient rsch. award Nat. Conf. on High Blood Pressure Control, 1981; nominee Woman of Achievement award YWCA. Mem. APHA (women's caucus com., presenter 1980, 81), ACLU, NOW, Am. Coll. Healthcare Execs. (diplomate), Women Healthcare Execs., Am. Managed Care and Rev. Orgn. (presenter nat. conf. 1989), Am. Assn. Preferred Provider Orgns., Delta Omega, Delta Delta Delta. Democrat. Methodist. Office: PROMINA Health Sys-Managed Care 2000 S Park Pl Atlanta GA 30339

MCQUEEN-GIBSON, ETHLYN, medical/surgical nurse; b. Cleve., Oct. 28, 1959; d. Joshua and Mary (Johnson) McQueen; m. Carl A. Gibson, Apr. 20, 1988; children: Faith Alysia, Carla Renee. BSN, Ursuline Coll., 1983. RN, Ga.; cert. med.-surg. nurse, ANA. Utilization mgmt. analyst Med. Coll. of Ga. Hosp., Augusta. 1st lt. U.S. Army, 1984-88.

MCQUIGG, JOHN DOLPH, lawyer; b. Abilene, Tex., Oct. 19, 1931; s. John Lyman and Dorothy Elinor (King) McQ.; m. Sandra Elainea Duke, Oct. 18, 1969 (div. 1989); 1 son, John Revel. B.A., Denison U., 1953; LL.B., U. Tex., Austin, 1962. Bar: Fla. 1962, U.S. Supreme Ct. 1971. account exec. San Antonio Light, 1957-59; assoc. Shackleford, Farrior, Stallings & Evans, 1962-66, ptnr. Tampa, Fla., 1966-73; pres. John McQuigg, P.A., Tampa, 1973-80; shareholder Fowler, White, Gillen, Boggs, Villareal & Banker, P.A., Tampa, 1980-92; of counsel, Stephen Rosen, P.A., Tampa, Fla., 1993; pvt. practice. Judge Compensation Claims pro hac vice, 1993; bd. dirs. Fla. Gulf Coast R.R. Mus., Inc., Am. Assn. Pvt. Railroad Car Owners; pres. Fla. Coalition R.R. Passengers, 1990—. 1st lt. USAF, 1953-57. Mem. ABA, Fla. Bar. Episcopalian. Club: Tampa. Home: 1000 W Horatio St Apt 125 Tampa FL 33606-2658 Office: PO Box 2480 Tampa FL 33601-2480

MCQUILKIN, DAVID KARL, history educator; b. Canton, Ohio, Oct. 29, 1940; s. Robert Porter and Helen (Lacey) McQ.; m. Charlette Eve Boburka, Aug. 15, 1964; children: Bradford Ryan, Meredith Lyn. BA, Muskingum Coll., 1962; MA, Kent State U., 1968, PhD, 1973; MLS, Case Western Res. U., 1977. Tchr. social studies Warren (Ohio) City Schs., 1962-65; grad. asst., tchg. fellow Kent (Ohio) State U., 1965-71, temporary instr., 1971-73; instr. polit. sci. Cuyahoga C.C., Parma Heights, Ohio, 1973-74; vis. asst. prof. Kent State U., East Liverpool, 1974-75; instr. U. Akron, Ohio, 1977-80; asst. prof. LaGrange (Ga.) Coll., 1980-84; dir. learning resources Reinhardt Coll., Waleska, Ga., 1984-85; prof. history, polit. sci., dept. chmn. Bridgewater (Va.) Coll., 1985—; polit. analyst WHSV-TV, Harrisonburg, Va., 1989—; advanced placement reader European history, 1995. sec., v.p., pres. Kent Parks & Recreation Bd., 1978-80; bd. sessions Kent United Presbyn. Ch., 1977-80, Bridgewater Presbyn. Ch., 1987-90; deacon LaGrange Presbyn. Ch., 1984; baseball coach, umpire Summer Youth League, 1976—. NEH grantee, 1990, 93, 95, Nat. Found. Humanities grantee, 1981, 90, 93, 95, 96. Mem. Internat. Studies Assn., Assn. Russian-Am. Historians, Phi Alpha Theta, Pi Gammu Mu. Democrat. Office: Bridgewater Coll Bridgewater VA 22812

MC QUILLAN, JOSEPH MICHAEL, finance company executive; b. Meridian, Miss., Aug. 9, 1931; s. John Vincent and Florence (Hoban) McQ.; divorced; children: Joseph Michael, James Vincent, Ann Marie, Tom Charles, Mary Clare, Tim Sean; m. Barbara Crawford, Nov. 25, 1983. B.S., Creighton U., Omaha, 1956. Mgr. Arthur Andersen & Co. (CPAs), Omaha and L.A., 1956-63; comptr. Cudahy Co., Phoenix, 1963-66; exec. v.p., comptr. Assoc. Corp. N.Am., 1969—; sr. exec. v.p. Assoc. Corp. N.Am., South Bend, Ind., 1988—; vice chmn. Assoc. Corp. N.Am., 1991; pres. Assocs. Fin. Svcs. Co. Inc., Dallas, 1991; pres. Ford Consumer Fin. Co., Dallas, 1990. Served with USAF, 1951-55. Mem. Nat. Assn. CPAs, Beta Alpha Pi. Home: 4417 Windsor Ridge Dr Irving TX 75038-6303 Office: Assoc First Capital Corp PO Box 660237 250 Carpenter Frwy Dallas TX 75062-2789

MCRAE, CHARLES R., state supreme court justice. Assoc. justice MS Supreme Ct, Jackson, MS, 1992—. Office: Supreme Court PO Box 117 Jackson MS 39205-0117*

MCRAE, DAVID CARROLL, hospital administrator; b. Winston-Salem, N.C., Apr. 15, 1946; married. B, U. N.C., 1968, MHA, 1975; M, East Carolina U., 1985. Adminstr. Medictr. of Am., Raleigh, N.C., 1971-72, Hillhaven Convalescent Ctr., Raleigh, 1972-76; v.p. Univ. Med. Ctr. Pitt County Meml. Hosp., Greenville, N.C., 1976-84, sr. v.p., 1985-86, sr. v.p., chief oper. officer, 1986-89, pres., chief exec. officer, 1989—. Home: 403 Tatten Ct Greenville NC 27834-7677 Office: Pitt County Meml Hosp-Univ Med East Carolina PO Box 6028 Greenville NC 27835-6028*

MCRAITH, JOHN JEREMIAH, bishop; b. Hutchinson, Minn., Dec. 6, 1934; s. Arthur Luke and Marie (Hanley) McR. B.A., Loras Coll., Dubuque, Iowa, 1956. Ordained priest, Roman Cath. Ch., 1960. Assoc. pastor St. Mary's Ch., Sleepy Eye, Minn., 1960-64, assoc. pastor, 1968-71; pastor St. Michael's Ch., Mickoy, Minn., 1964-67, St. Leo's Ch., St. Leo, Minn., 1967-68; dir. Nat. Cath. Rural Life, Des Moines, 1971-78; vicar gen. Diocese of New Ulm, Minn., 1978-82; bishop Owensboro, Ky., 1982—. Home: 501 W 5th St Owensboro KY 42301-0765 Office: 600 Locust St Owensboro KY 42301-2130*

MCREE, CELIA, composer; b. Memphis; d. John Louis and Leta Gwendolyn (Phillips) McR. Student, Phila. Coll. Art (U. of Arts), 1976-77, Herbert Berghof Studio, 1989, Playwrights Horizon Theater, 1989; cert. with distinction, Nat. Acad. Paralegal Studies, Christian Bros. U., 1992. Pres. Mother Records, Memphis, 1984—, You Should Meet My Mother (Publishing), Memphis, 1984—, Wild Thing Music, Memphis, 1987—, Mother Prodns., Memphis, 1986—; producer, host Indian Talk, WEVL-FM90, Memphis, 1992-95; pres. Dancing Heart Pictures, Memphis, 1996—. Artist, group and solo exhbns. including Eads Gallery, Grover Cleveland Arts Inst., Phila. Mus. Natural History; screenwriter, film scoring; singer, writer (nat. album) including Celia McRee/Back From Under, 1985 (ASCAP Spl. Pop award 1985-86, 86-87), Archives of Modern Music NY., Celia McRee/Passion, 1994; composer, arranger, producer, pub. background and feature music ABC Network, Cable TV and Radio. Entertainer Vets. Bedside Network, N.Y.C., 1981. Recipient cert. of scholarly distinction Nat. Acad. for Paralegal Studies, 1992, cert. of appreciation United Music Heritage, 1990, spl. pop award ASCAP, 1982-84, 87-93, 95-96, 96-97, Henrietta Hickman Morgan writing award DAR; named Female Pop Songwriter and Female Pop Vocalist of Yr., Entertainer Indi-Assn., 1994, Female Vocalist and Female Entertainer of Yr., 1995; named Most Popular Female Entertainer, Indi-Assn., 1996. Mem. AFTRA, ASCAP, NARAS, Broadcast Music Inc. (pub. mem.), N.Y. Acad. Sci., Assn. Am. Indian Affairs, Nat. Mus. of the Am. Indian (charter), Environ. Def. Fund, Animal Legal Def. Fund, Greenpeace, Humane Soc. U.S., Mensa, Memphis Kennel Club. Office: Mother Prodns 5159 Wheelis Dr # 110 Memphis TN 38117-4519

MCREE, JOHN BROWNING, JR., physician; b. Anderson, S.C., Dec. 9, 1950; s. John Browning and Melinda Bratton (Beaty) McR.; m. Melody Lynnn Jennings, May 29, 1976; children: Ansley, Sarabeth. BS, Presbyn. Coll., Clinton, S.C., 1973; MD, Med. U. of S.C., 1977. Diplomate Am. Bd. Family Physicians. Resident Anderson (S.C.) Meml. Hosp., 1977-80; physician Family Practice Assocs., North Augusta, S.C., 1980—; asst. clin. prof. family medicine Med. Coll. Ga., 1982—. Fellow Am. Acad. Family Physicians. Presbyterian. Home: 201 Oakhurst Dr North Augusta SC 29841-9719 Office: Family Practice Assocs 509 W Martintown Rd North Augusta SC 29841-3108

MCREYNOLDS, CHARLES BERTRAM, architect; b. Texas City, Ill., Sept. 26, 1916; s. Samuel Elvis and Mabel L. (Harris) McR.; m. Virginia M. Merriman, Mar. 25, 1971; children: Linda Louise McReynolds Little, Kimberly Marie. BArch cum laude, U. So. Calif., 1952. With Van Dyke and Barnes, 1953; dir. N.Y.C. office Welton Becket Assocs., 1962-70; sr. v.p., dir. L.A. office Becket Internat., 1970-75, pres., 1975-81, also bd. dirs.; owner, operator jewelry store Newport News, Va.; bd. dirs. Welton Becket Assocs., ESPDC Corp. Prin. landscape works include pk. design for City of Monterey Park, Calif. (Excellence in Pk. Design award So. Calif. Producers Coun. 1950, 51); prin. archtl. works include Nile Hilton, Cairo, Manila Hilton, Auckland (New Zealand) IHC Hotel, Juffali Bros. Hdqrs., Jeddah, Saudi Arabia, Nassau (N.Y.) Coliseum, Xerox Sq., Rochester, N.Y., Great Wall Hotel, Beijing. With USNR, 1942-46. Fellow AIA; mem. U. So. Calif. Alumni Assn. (life), Scarab, Skull and Dagger, Union League, James River Country Club, Tau Sigma Delta. Republican. Address: 694 Todd Trl Newport News VA 23602-9037

MCREYNOLDS, DAVID HOBERT, hospital administrator; b. Bristol, Tenn., Dec. 28, 1953; s. Hobart Evans and Lena Mae (Brewer) McR.; m. Cynthia Carole Yambert, Sept. 6, 1974; children: Amy, Joseph, John, Rachel. MS, U. S.C., 1983. CPA, Tenn; cert. mng. care profl. Corp. acct. Gen. Care Corp., Nashville, 1975-80; controller Athens-Limestone Hosp., Athens, Ala., 1980-82; dir. fin. St. Mary's Med. ctr., Knoxville, Tenn., 1982-85; v.p. Archbishop Bergan Mercy Hosp., Omaha, 1985-87, Regional Healthcare, Inc., Brooksville, Fla., 1987-91; exec. dir. Hernando Healthcare, Inc. dba Brooksville Regional Hosp. (formerly Lykes Meml. Hosp.), 1987-91; v.p., corp. controller Peninsula Healthcare System, Knoxville, 1991-93; v.p., adminstr. Peninsula Village, Louisville, Tenn., 1993-96; COO Peninsula Healthcare, Louisville, 1996—. Pres. United Meth. Men., Brooksville, 1988-89; mem. Hernando County Health Adv. Bd., Brooksville, 1988-90; bd. dirs. United Way Hernando County, 1987-90, Hernando Cmty. Blood Bank, 1987-91; treas. Hernando Assn. for Retarded Citizens, 1990-91; mem. Knox County Com. on Spl. Edn., 1993-94. Fellow Healthcare Fin. Mgmt. Assn.; mem. Am. Coll. Healthcare Execs., Inst. Mgmt. Accts., Tenn. Assn. Child Care (bd. dirs. 1996—), East Tenn. Assn. Child Care (pres. 1996—), Rotary (bd. dirs. Brooksville chpt. 1988-89). Presbyterian. Home: 4323 Near Shore Dr Louisville TN 37777-5231

MCREYNOLDS, MARY MAUREEN, municipal environmental administrator, consultant; b. Tacoma, July 15, 1940; d. Andrew Harley and Mary Leone (McGuire) Sims; m. Gerald Aaron McReynolds, Dec. 10, 1964. Student Coll. Puget Sound, 1957-59; BA, U. Oreg., 1961; PhD, U. Chgo., 1966; postgrad. San Diego State U., 1973-75. NIH postdoctoral fellow U. Tex., Austin, 1966-68, mem. adj. faculty, 1980-82, mem. biohazards com., 1981—; research assoc. Stanford U., Calif., 1968-71; chemist assoc. Syva Co., Palo Alto, Calif., 1972; environ. specialist County of San Diego, Calif., 1973-75; dept. head City of Austin, 1976-84, chief environ. officer, 1984-85, utility environ. mgr., 1985-92, mgr. environ. and regulatory support, 1992—; dir. Ctr. for Environ. Rsch., 1992—; part-time mem. faculty Austin Community Coll., 1993—; cons. ecologist Mirassou Vineyards, San Jose, Calif., 1969-72; lectr. Wright Inst., Berkeley, Calif., 1971-72; instr. San Diego State U., 1974-75. Editor Dist. 56 newsletter, 1989-90; contbr. articles to profl. publs. Mem. Austin-Satillo Sister City Assn., 1980—; U.S.-Mexico Sister Cities del., 1983-85; sponsor, chaperone Tex.-South Australia Youth Exchange, 1986; active Leadership Austin, 1987-88; mem. Austin-Adelaide Sister City Com., 1986—, chmn., 1989-91, sec., 1992-96; bd. dirs. Internat. Hospitality Coun. of Austin, 1989-96. USPHS tng. grantee U. Chgo., 1961-64; univ. fellow U. Chgo., 1961-66. Mem. NAFE, AAAS, Water Environment Fedn. (v.p. local chpt. 1988-89, pres.-elect 1989-90, pres. 1990-91, sect. rep. 1991-94), Am. Planning Assn., Am. Inst. Cert. Planners (cert.), Assn. Environ. Profls., Am. Water Resources Assn., Tex. Assn. Met. Sewage Agys. (sec. 1994, v.p. 1995, pres. 1996), Austin Soc. Pub. Adminstrn., Zeta Tau Alpha. Lodges: Soroptimists (dir. Soroptimist Manor 1978-80, 83-85, v.p. chpt. 1983-85, pres. chpt. 1985-87, chpt. dir. 1987-88, rep. youth citizenship award com. 1986-88, chmn. South Cen. region UN com. 1988-90, rep. youth forum com. 1990-92), Toastmasters (club pres. 1981, 88, area gov. 1981-82, div. lt. gov. 1982-83, Able Toastmaster award 1983, Dist. 56 Table Topics award 1986, Disting. Toastmaster award 1987, Outstanding Toastmaster Dist. 56 no. divsn. 1987, Able Toastmaster Bronze award 1990, Able Toastmaster Silver award 1993). Avocations: gourmet food and wine. Office: City of Austin PO Box 1088 Austin TX 78767-8865

MCREYNOLDS, PAMELA KAY, controller; b. Knoxville, Tenn., July 19, 1953; d. Harold Edward and Betty Jane (Badgett) McR. BS, U. Tenn., 1975; MBA, Berry Coll., 1979. Acct. Ala. Kraft Co., Mahrt, 1975; corp. acct. Ga. Kraft Co., Rome, 1979-81, ops. acctg. supr., 1981-86, fin. acctg. mgr., 1987-88; mgr. MIS Holliston Mills, Inc., Kingsport, Tenn., 1988-90, controller, 1991-92; contr. Elo TouchSys., Inc., Oak Ridge, Tenn., 1992-96, dir. fin., 1996—; mem. adv. bd. S.I. Users Group, Boston, 1983-88; seminar leader. Republican. Baptist. Office: Elo Touch Sys Inc 105 Randolph Rd Oak Ridge TN 37830-5028

MCROBERTS, JEFFREY ALAN, nursing administrator; b. Chillicothe, Ohio, Oct. 5, 1955; s. Charles Joseph and Mary Catherine (Coleman) McR. BSN, Barry U. RN, Fla.; cert. TNCC, ACLS, CCRN. Staff nurse Mercy Hosp., Columbus, Ohio, 1983-88, JFK Med. Ctr., Lantanu, Fla., 1988-92; supr. nursing Wellington (Fla.) Regional Med. Ctr., 1988-92; staff nurse Good Samaritan Hosp., West Palm Beach, 1992-94; DON Kelly Assisted Living, 1994-95; dir. critical care Aventura (Fla.) Hosp., 1994—. With USN, 1975-79. Mem. AACN (Broward local chpt.). Roman Catholic. Home: 880 Spring Cir Apt 206 Deerfield Beach FL 33441-7888 Office: Aventura Hosp & Med Ctr Bisqucane Blvd Aventura FL

MCSORLEY, DANNY EUGENE, sales executive; b. Huntington, W.Va., Nov. 26, 1960; s. Bernard Eugene and Doris M. (Newman) McS. BBA, Marshall U., Huntington, W.Va., 1983. Mgmt. trainee Lavalette (W.Va.) State Bank, 1980-83; with Profl. Bank Svc., Louisville, 1983-84; territory mgr. Bunzl Paducah (Ky.), 1984-91; sales mgr. Con-Jel Sales, Huntington, W.Va., 1991—. Mem. Marshall Quarterback Club, Marshall Tipoff Club, Big Green Scholarship Club. Democrat. Baptist. Home: 5229 Mays Branch Rd Lavalette WV 25535 Office: Con-Jel Sales 511 28th St Huntington WV 25702

MCSORLEY, ROBERT, nematology researcher, educator; b. Cin., July 23, 1949; s. Robert Terence and Mary Theresa (Creed) McS.; m. Rosario Silva McSorley, Jan, 17, 1976; 1 child, Teresa. BS, U. Cin., 1971, MS, 1974; PhD, Purdue U., 1978. Asst. prof. U. Fla., Homestead, 1978-83, assoc. prof., 1983-85; assoc. prof. U. Fla., Gainesville, Fla., 1985-88, prof., 1988—; rsch. ctr. dir. U. Fla., Homestead, 1984; vis. scientist Dept. Primary Industries, Brisbane, Australia, 1988. Author in field; contbr. articles to profl. jours. Recipient Best Student Paper award Soc. Nematologists, 1977, Best paper Krome Sect. award Fla. State Hort. Soc., 1984, Spl. awrd Orgn. Nematologists Tropical Am., 1988; named Tchr. Yr. Dept. Entomology and Nematology U. Fla., 1992. Mem. Orgn. Nematologists Tropical Am., Soc. Nematologists, Fla. Nematology Forum. Home: 8744 SW 46th Ln Gainesville FL 32608-4137 Office: Univ Florida PO Box 110620 Gainesville FL 32611-0620

MCSWAIN, RICHARD HORACE, materials engineer, consultant; b. Greenville, Ala., Sept. 27, 1949; s. Howard Horace and La Belle (Henderson) McS.; m. Wanda Lynn Hare, June 9, 1972; children: Rachel Lynn, John Angus, Daniel Richard. BS in Materials Engring., Auburn U., 1972, MS in Materials Engring., 1974; PhD in Materials Engring., U. Fla., 1985. Teaching and rsch. asst. Auburn (Ala.) U., 1972-73; metallurgist So. Rsch. Inst., Birmingham, Ala., 1973-76; materials engr. Naval Aviation Depot, Pensacola, Fla., 1977-88, head metallic materials engring., 1988-90; pres. McSwain Engring., Inc., 1991—; cons. materials engr., Pensacola, 1982-90; presenter in field. Contbr. articles to tech. jours. Mem. ASTM, SAE Internat., ASM Internat. (chpt. edn. chmn. 1975-76), Am. Welding Soc., Nat. Assn. Corrosion Engrs., Electron Microscopy Soc., Internat. Soc. Air Safety Investigators. Presbyterian. Home: 1405 Kings Rd Cantonment FL 32533-8951 Office: McSwain Engring Inc PO Box 10847 Pensacola FL 32524-0847

MCSWEENEY, WILLIAM PATRICK, public relations practitioner; b. Cleve., Jan. 22, 1959; s. Donald William and Patricia Frances (McBride) McS.; m. Jane Taylor Jarrell McSweeney, Mar. 3, 1984; children: David William, John Patrick Francis. BA in Journalism, Ohio State U., 1983. Scholastic sports rewriteman The Plain Dealer, Cleve., 1978-80; sports rewrite, editl. clk. The Columbus (Ohio) Dispatch, 1980-83; morning traffic prodr., news asst. Sta. WNCI-FM, Columbus, Ohio, 1982; weekend anchor, reporter Sta. WOSU-AM-FM, Columbus, Ohio, 1982-83, Sta. WLIO-TV, Lima, Ohio, 1983-84; reporter, spl. projects prodr. Sta. WKEF-TV, Dayton, Ohio, 1984-87; spl. projects prodr. Sta. WTLV-TV, Jacksonville, Fla., 1987-88; prodr. Sta. WJXT-TV, Jacksonville, 1988-89; pub. awareness coord. St. Johns River Water Mgmt. Dist., Palatka, Fla., 1990-94; pub. outreach coord. St. Johns River Water Mgmt. Dist., Paltaka, Fla., 1994-96; sr. pub. outreach coord. St. Johns River Water Mgmt. Dist., Jacksonville, 1996—; media rels. vol. Assn. Tennis Profls., Ponte Vedra Beach, Fla., 1989. Bd. dirs. Am. Diabetes Assn., 1989-94, Friends of Stockton Sch., Jacksonville, 1993—; mem. vestry St. Catherine's Episc. Ch., Jacksonville, 1989-95, sr. warden, 1994. Recipient Distinction award Fla. Pub. Rels. Assn., 1992; Best Poster used in a Pub. Rels. Program, Fla. Pub. Rels. Assn., 1993. Mem. Pub. Rels. Soc. Am. Roman Catholic. Office: St Johns River Water Mgmt Dist 7775 Baymeadows Way Ste 102 Jacksonville FL 32256

MCTEE, CINDY, classical musician, educator; b. 1953. BM, Pacific Luth. U., 1976, studied with David Robbins; MM, Yale U., 1978, studied with Krzysztof Pendereckl, Jacob Druckman, and Bruce MacComble; PhD, U. Iowa, 1981, studied with Richard Hervig; studied with Pendereckl, Marek Stachowski, and Krystyna Moszumanska-Nazar, Higher Sch. Music, Cracow, Poland. Tchr. Pacific Luth. U., Tacoma, Wash., 1981-84; assoc. to full prof. music composition U. North Tex., Denton, 1985—; Fulbright-Hayes Sr. Lectr. fellow in computer music Acad. Music, Cracow, 1990. Recipient comms. from Big Eight Band Dirs. Assn., Voices of Change, Barlow Endowment for Music Composition, Am. Guild Organists, Coll. Band Dirs. Nat. Assn., Phi Kappa Lambda Bd. Regents; works performed by Am. Symphony Orch., Nat. Repertory Orch., St. Louis Symphony, Memphis Symphony, Honolulu Symphony, Pitts. New Music Ensemble, Nat. Symphony Orch. Recipient BMI award; grantee Wash. State Arts Commn.; Composers fellow NEA, Goddard Lieberson fellow AAAL. Home: 1217 Piping Rock St Denton TX 76205-8126 Office: U of North Tex Coll of Music Denton TX 76203

MCTERNAN, ANN CIBUZAR, adult nurse practitioner; b. Brainerd, Minn., Nov. 26, 1950. BS in Family Social Sci., U. Minn., 1973; BSN, U. N.C., Greensboro, 1976; MSN-N.P., George Mason U., Fairfax, Va., 1990. RN, Va., Md., Calif., Minn., Washington; cert. adult nurse practitioner. Mem. nursing staff U.S. Naval Hosp., Beaufort, S.C., 1976-77, Eskaton Monterey Hosp., Monterey, Calif., 1977-78; staff Drug Enforcement Adminstrn., Bangkok, 1978-80; mem. nursing staff US Naval Hosp., Okinawa, Japan, 1981-82; mem. nursing staff. St. Joseph's Med. Ctr., Brainerd, 1986-87, Potomac Hosp., Woodbridge, Va., 1980-81, 87-90, Marymount U., Arlington, Va., 1989-90; low impact/expectant mothers aerobic instr. Saratoga Dance Ctr., Springfield, Va., 1990-94; adult nurse practitioner Prime Care, Annandale, Va., 1991-95; master mem. IDEA Found., San Diego, 1990—; aerobic fitness instr. Am. Coun. on Exercise, San Diego, 1990—. Mem. AAUW, Am. Coll. Sports Medicine, Am. Coun. on Exercise, Exer-Safety Assn., Am. Acad. Nurse Practitioners. Home: care Cibuzar 4222 Cottage Grove Dr # 202 Baxter MN 56425

MCTIGUE, TERESA ANN, biologist; b. Washington, July 9, 1962; d. William Edward and Bernice Ann (Bakajza) McT. BS in Zoology, U. Md., 1984; MS in Marine Sci., U. S.C., 1986; PhD in Wildlife and Fisheries Scis., Tex. A&M U., 1993. Lab. asst. U. Md., College Park, 1981-83; rsch. asst. U. S.C., Columbia, 1984-86; staff biologist Sea Camp, Galveston, Tex., 1988-93; fisheries biologist Nat. Marine Fisheries Svc., Galveston, 1987-93, Lafayette, La., 1993—. Contbr. articles to profl. jours. Recipient Grad. Rsch. award Sea Grant, 1986. Mem. Estuarine Rsch. Fedn., Gulf Estuarine Rsch. Soc. (pres.-elect), Am. Fisheries Soc., Sigma Xi. Democrat. Roman Catholic. Office: NMFS Lafayette Office PO Box 42451 Lafayette LA 70504-2451

MCVAUGH, MICHAEL ROGERS, historian, educator; b. Washington, Dec. 9, 1938; s. Rogers and Ruth (Beall) McV.; m. Julia Augusta Farrelly, Aug. 19, 1961. AB, Harvard U., 1960; MA, Princeton U., 1962, PhD, 1965. Asst. prof. history U. N.C., Chapel Hill, 1964-70, assoc. prof., 1970-76, prof., 1976-96, William Smith Wells prof., 1996—; vis. fellow Clare Hall Cambridge, 1994. Author: Medicine Before the Plague, 1993; co-author: The Elusive Science, 1980; editor: Opera Medica Arnaldi de Villanova, 1975—. Fellow John Simon Guggenheim Meml. Found., 1981-82. Mem. Hist. Sci. Soc. (coun. 1971-73), Am. Assn. Hist. Med. (William H. Welch prize 1994), Medieval Acad. Am. Home: 379 Tenney Cir Chapel Hill NC 27514-7806 Office: U NC at Chapel Hill Cb # 3195 Chapel Hill NC 27599

MCVAY, BARBARA CHAVES, secondary education mathematics educator; b. Dallas, July 6, 1950; d. Joe M. and Dorothy May (Nock) Chaves; m. David Clyde McVay, Dec. 23, 1968; 1 child, Kathryn McVay Hearn. BS in Math., U. Tex., Arlington, 1971. Cert. secondary tchr. math., English, Tex. Tchr. math. C.W. Nimitz High Sch. Irving (Tex.) Ind. Sch. Dist., 1972—; bldg. rep. Dallas Tchrs. Credit Union, 1982—; part time lab. instr. Northlake/Dallas County Community Coll., Irving, 1988—. Tchr. Sunday sch. North Dallas Bapt. Ch., 1971-80; ch. tng. leader 1st Bapt. Ch., Irving, 1981-85. Mem. NEA, Tex. State Tchrs. Assn., Irving Edn. Assn. (rep. 1980—), Nat. Coun. Tchrs. Math., Tex. Coun. Tchrs. Math., Greater Dallas Coun. Tchrs. Math., Math. Assn. Am., Delta Kappa Gamma. Republican. Office: CW Nimitz High Sch 100 W Oakdale Rd Irving TX 75060-6833

MCVAY, MARY FRANCES, portfolio manager; b. Washington, Sept. 17, 1955; d. Joseph J. and Stella F. (Walejko) McVay; m. Theodore R. Rosenberg, Sept. 21, 1991. BS in Acctg., Va. Tech., 1978, MBA, 1981. CPA; CFA. Auditor CIA, Washington, 1975-83; sr. cons. Booz, Allen & Hamilton, Arlington, Va., 1983-85; portfolio mgr. Burney Mgmt. Co., Falls Church, Va., 1985—. Mem. Inst. Mgmt. Accts. (dir. newsletter 1992—, v.p. adminstrn. 1993—, dir. program roster 1994—), Assn. Investment, Mgmt. and Rsch. Office: Burney Mgmt Co 123 Rowell Ct Falls Church VA 22046-3126

MCWETHY, PATRICIA JOAN, educational association administrator; b. Chgo., Feb. 27, 1946; d. Frank E. and Emma (Kuehne) McW.; m. H. Frank Eden; children: Kristin Beth, Justin Nicholas. BA, Northwestern U., 1968; MA, U. Minn., 1970; MBA, George Washington U., 1981. Geog. analyst CIA, McLean, Va., 1970-71; research asst. NSF, Washington, 1972-74, spl. asst. to dir., 1975; assoc. program dir. human geography and regional sci. program NSF, 1976-79; exec. dir. Assn. Am. Geographers, Washington., 1979-84, Nat. Assn. Biology Tchrs., Reston, Va., 1984-95, Nat. Sci. Edn. Leadership Assn., Arlington, Va., 1995—; prin. investigator NSF grant on biotech. equipment edni. resource partnership, 1989-93, NSF funded internat. symposium on "Basic Biol. Concepts: What Should the World's Children Know?", 1992-94; co-prin. investigator NSF grant, 1995—; mem. chmn.'s adv. com. Nat. Com. Sci. Stds. & Assessment, 1992—; mem. Commn. for Biology Edn., Internat. Union Biol. Sci., 1988—; mem. exec. com. Alliance for Environ. Edn., 1987-90, chmn. program com., 1990; condr. seminars in field; lectr. in field. Author monograph and papers in field; editor handbook. NSF grantee, 1989-93, 95—; NSF fellow, 1968-69; recipient Outstanding Performance award, NSF, 1973. Mem. Am. Soc. Assn. Execs., Nat. Sci. Tchrs. Assn., Phi Beta Kappa. Office: PO Box 5556 Arlington VA 22205

MCWHORTER, KATHY MARIE, legal secretary; b. Denver, Oct. 17, 1953; d. Paul Frederick and Phyllis Jean (Vincent) Dontje; m. Leon Phillip McWhorter, June 10, 1972 (div. 1985); children: Phyllis Kay, Sarah Anne. Student, S.W. Assembly of God Coll., 1974-78. Exec. sec. Kelly Svcs., Dallas and Kansas City, Mo., 1977-86; legal sec. to real estate atty. Mo., Kans., Tex. R.R., Dallas, 1986-87; sec. to regional v.p. Res. Life Ins. Co., Dallas, 1987; legal sec. Jones, Day, Reavis & Pogue, Dallas, 1988-89, Gardere & Wynne, Dallas, 1989-94, Jackson & Walker, Dallas, 1994—; minister Assemblies of God, 1976-84. Mem. com., bd. dirs. Dallas Symphony; active adv. bd. Dallas Chamber Orch. Mem. Mensa (area coord. St. Louis br. 1981-84, North Tex. br., 1984—, contbr. column 1985—). Home: 1542 Sunrise Ln Duncanville TX 75137-4051 Office: Jackson & Walker 901 Main St Ste 6000 Dallas TX 75202-3748

MCWILLIAMS, KAREN JOAN, writer; b. Alexandria, La., Oct. 12, 1943; d. Steve Peters and Nettie Beatrice Barricklow; step-father: Paul F. McWilliams; m. Charles F. Slezak, June 16, 1973 (div. 1976); m. Julio Espinosa, July 26, 1980 (div. 1988). BA in Elem. Edn., U. No. Colo., 1966; MA in Ednl. Tech./Libr. Sci., San Diego State U., 1976. Tchr. 2d grade Motherlode Union, Diamond Springs, Calif., 1966-67; tchr. 3d grade Redlands (Calif.) Unified Sch. Dist., 1967-69, Dept. of Def. Overseas Schs., various locations, 1969-77; sch. libr. Dept. of Edn., St. Croix, V.I., 1977-83. Author: Pirates, 1989; contbr. numerous articles to Writer's Digest, The

Writer, others. Soc. of Children's Book Writers grantee, 1985. Mem. The Authors Guild, Soc. of Children's Book Writers and Illustrators.

MCWILLIAMS, MARY ANN, school administrator; b. Shreveport, La., July 5, 1944; d. Joseph Vivian and Helen Claire (McKinney) McW. BS, Northwestern State U., 1966; MEd, U. North Tex., 1989. Cert. composite sci., Tex., adminstrn. cert. Tchr. biology Willapa Valley Schs., Menlo, Wash., 1966-67; med. technologist Meth. Hosp., Houston, 1967-68; tchr. biology Caddo Parish Schs., Shreveport, 1968-74, 77-79; advt. account exec. Sta. KCOZ Radio, Shreveport, 1979-80; coord. tng./documentation Tri-State Computer Svcs., Shreveport, 1980-83; tchr. biology, team leader Plano (Tex.) Ind. Sch. Dist., 1983-94, environ. studies coord., coord. for environ. outdoor sch. camp program, 1994—, coord. for environ. outdoor sch. camp program, 1994—; dir. Holifield Sci. Learning Ctr., Plano, 1994—; chmn. ednl. improvement coun. Plano Ind. Sch. Dist., 1990-94; tchr. trainer Jason V Project, Dallas, 1993-94; dir. Environ. Studies Camp, Plano, 1994—. Mem. Dallas Mus. of Art, 1987—; bd. dirs. Camp Classen, Oklahoma City YMCA, 1996. Named Jane Goodall Environ Educator of Yr., Jane Goodall Inst. and Boreal Labs., Dallas, 1993, one of Outstanding Young Women of Am., 1980. Mem. ASCD, NEA, Nat. Sci. Tchrs. Assn., Sci. Tchrs. of Tex., Jane Goodall Inst. Roots and Shoots. Roman Catholic. Office: Plano Ind Sch Sys 2700 W 15th St Plano TX 75075-7524

MEAD, DANA GEORGE, diversified industrial manufacturing company executive; b. Cresco, Iowa, Feb. 22, 1936; s. George Francis and Evelyn Grace (Derr) M.; m. Nancy L. Cooper, Apr. 12, 1958; children: Dana George, Mark Cooper. B.S. (Disting. Cadet), U.S. Mil. Acad., 1957; Ph.D., M.I.T., 1967. Commd. 2d lt. U.S. Army, 1957, advanced through grades to col., 1974; service in W. Ger. and Vietnam; White House fellow, 1970-71; staff asst. to Pres. Nixon, 1970-72; assoc. dir., then dep. dir. Domestic Council, White House, 1972-74; permanent prof. social sci. dept., dep. head U.S. Mil. Acad., 1974-78; ret., 1978; v.p. human resources Internat. Paper Co., N.Y.C., 1978-81, v.p., group exec., 1981-87; sr. v.p. Internat. Paper Co., Purchase, 1987-89, exec. v.p., dir, 1989-92; pres., COO Tenneco, Inc., Houston, 1992-93, chmn., CEO, 1994—, also bd. dirs.; CEO, chmn. J.I. Case, Racine, Wis., 1992-94, chmn., 1994-96; bd. dirs. Alco Standard, Baker Hughes Corp., Logistics Mgmt. Inst., Washington, Textron, Inc. Author articles on nat. security and domestic policy, business and manufacturing planning. Mem. Pres.'s Commn. on White House Fellowships, West Point Soc., N.Y., 1980—, pres., 1981-83; mem. White House Fellows Assn. and Found., 1981-82; bd. dirs. White House Fellows Found., 1978-83, pres. 1978; mem. MIT Vis. Com. Polit. Scis., bd. dirs. new bus. coun., mem. bus. roundtable, MIT Corp. Decorated Legion of Merit with oak leaf cluster, Bronze Star with oak leaf cluster, Meritorious Service medal, Air medal with 3 oak leaf clusters, Army Commendation medal, Presdl. Service badge, Combat Inf. badge; Vietnam Cross Gallantry with palm, silver and bronze stars. Mem. Nat. Assn. Mfg. (chmn. 1995-96), Coun. Fgn. Rels., Assn. Grads. West Point (trustee), Univ. Club, Met. Club (N.Y.). Republican. Home: 14 Fairway Ln Greenwich CT 06830-4011 Office: Tenneco Inc 1275 King St Greenwich CT 06831

MEAD, FRANK WALDRETH, taxonomic entomologist; b. Columbus, Ohio, June 11, 1922; s. Arlington Alfred and Edith May (Harrison) M.; widowed; children: David Harrison, Gregory Scott. BS, Ohio State U., 1947, MS, 1949; PhD, N.C. State U., 1968. Rsch. asst. dept. physiology Ohio State U., Woods Hole, Mass., summer 1941; rsch. asst. dept. entomology Ohio State U., Columbus, 1948-50; Japanese beetle scout bur. entomology and plant quar. USDA, Columbus, summer 1948, biol. aid bur. entomology and plant quar., 1950-53; entomologist div. plant industry Fla. Dept. Agr., Gainesville, 1953-58, 60, biologist IV, 1983—; rsch. asst. N.C. State U., Raleigh, 1958-60; state survey entomologist Fed.-State Coop. Survey, Gainesville, 1969-80; courtesy assoc. prof. dept. entomology U. Fla., Gainesville, 1973—, Fla. A&M U., Tallahassee, 1977—. Co-editor Tri-ology Technical Report; contbr. articles to profl. jours. Bd. dirs., treas. Alachua Audubon Soc., Gainesville, 1968-75, 77-82; bd. dirs. Alachua County Hist. Soc., Gainesville, 1980-82; mem. steering com. Civitan Regional Blood Bank, Gainesville, 1977-79; vol. photographer P.K. Yonge Devel. Rsch. Sch. U. Fla., Gainesville, 1978—. With U.S. Army, 1943-46, PTO. Ohio Acad. Sci. fellow, 1966. Mem. Entomol. Soc. Am. (bd. dirs. S.E. br. 1978-79), Ga. Entomol. Soc., Fla. Entomol. Soc. (hon., sec. 1968-82, Cert. of Appreciation 1975, 82, 91, Cert. of Merit 1986), Fla. Mosquito Control Assn., Entomol. Soc. Washington, Soc. Systematic Biologists, SAR (Benjamin Franklin chpt. Columbus, Ohio), Fla. Track Club. Home: 2035 NE 6th Ter Gainesville FL 32609-3758 Office: Fla Dept Agr and Cons Svcs Divsn Plant Industry PO Box 147100 Gainesville FL 32614-7100

MEAD, HARRIET COUNCIL, librarian, author; b. Franklin, Va., Jan. 11; d. Hutson and Ollie (Whitley) Council; m. Berne Matthews Mead, Jr., Dec. 2, 1940; children—William Whitley, Charles Council. BA, Coll. William and Mary, 1935; postgrad. Fla. State U., 1958-62, Rollins Coll., 1966, 70, 84. County libr. Carroll County, Hillsville, Va., 1935-36; city libr. Suffolk City Schs., Va., 1936-41; libr., media specialist Orange County Schs., Orlando, Fla., 1961-80. Author: The Irrepressible Saint, 1983, A Family Legacy, 1987, Stained Glass in Cathedral Church of St. Luke, 1994. Contbr. article to mag. Mem. Fla. Hist. Soc., Friends of Libr., Orange County Media Specialists (pres. Greater Orlando 1968-69), Nat. Soc. Colonial Dames, Jr. League of Greater Orlando, Orange County Ret. Educators. Democrat. Episcopalian. Avocation: watercolor painting. Home: 500 E Marks St Orlando FL 32803-3922

MEAD-DONALDSON, SUSAN LEE, librarian, administrator; b. Chungking, China, May 13, 1943; came to U.S., 1968; d. Chung-Hwa and Lin Lee; m. Robert Mead-Donaldson, June 20, 1970; children: Charles L., Richard L. BA, Nat. Taiwan U., Taipei, 1967; MS, Fla. State U., 1970. Departmental libr. Nat. Taiwan U., 1967-68; grad. tchg. asst. Fla. State U., Tallahassee, 1969-70; asst. libr. Fla. A&M U., Tallahassee, 1970-72; lectr. Nat. Normal U., Taipei, 1973; asst. libr. Va. Poly. Inst. and State U., Blacksburg, 1975-78; asst. libr. Fla. Internat. U., North Miami, 1979-81, univ. libr., 1981-90; asst. tech. svcs. adminstr. Miami (Fla.)-Dade Pub. Libr., 1990-91, tech. svcs. adminstr., 1991—. Mem. ALA, Assn. Libr. Collections and Tech. Svcs., Libr. Info. and Tech. Assn., Chinese Am. Librs. Assn., Fla. Libr. Assn., Dade County Libr. Assn. (bd. dirs. 1990—). Office: Miami-Dade Pub Libr Sys 101 W Flagler St Miami FL 33130-1504

MEADE, ANGELA KAYE, special education educator; b. Bryon, Ohio, Mar. 14, 1969; d. Douglas MacAuther and Thelma Judy (Williams) Smith; m. Steven Andrew Meade, June 1, 1991; 1 child, Alexander Jefferson. AA in Edn. summa cum laude, S.W. Va. C.C., 1989, AA in Gen. Studies, 1989; BA in English with distinction, U. Va., 1992, M Tchg. in Spl. Edn., 1992. Cert. K-12 tchr. learning disabilities and mental retardation, Va. Tchr. spl. edn. Newport News (Va.) Pub. Schs., 1992—; yearbook sponsor Newport News (Va.) Pub. Schs., 1992-95, implemented collaborative tchg. program, 1994-95; counselor Summer Yough Program, Lebanon and Richmond, Va., 1993-94. Organizer Spl. Olympics Va., Newport News, 1993-94. Mem. ASCD, Internat. Reading Coun., Newport News Reading Coun. (co-chmn. banquet 1993-95).. Office: Reservoir Mid Sch 301 Heacox Ln Newport News VA 23608-1809

MEADE, MELINDA SUE, geographer, educator; b. N.Y.C., Nov. 2, 1945; d. Melville J. and Katherine Meade. BA, Hofstra U., 1966; MA, Mich. State U., 1970; PhD, U. Hawaii, 1974. Rsch. assoc. Internat. Ctr. Med. Rsch. U. Calif., Kuala Lumpur, Malaysia, 1972-74; asst. prof. UCLA, 1974-76, U. Ga., Athens, 1976-78; asst. prof., assoc. prof., prof. U. N.C., Chapel Hill, 1978—; vol. Peace Corps, Thailand, 1966-68. Author: Medical Geography, 1988. Mem. AAAS (steering com. 1984-87), Assn. Am. Geographers (councillor 1984-87), Assn. Asian Studies (councillor 1981-84), Med. Geography Splty. (sect. chair, councillor 1977-92). Democrat. Office: Univ NC Dept Geography Chapel Hill NC 27599-3220

MEADE, REX LEE, consulting firm executive, counselor; b. Norton, Va., Nov. 8, 1947; s. Willard Jefferson and Cora Mae (Stanfield) M.; m. Wanda Lee Snyder, Aug.22, 1970. BA in Clin. Psychology, East Carolina U., 1970, MA in Clin. Psychology, 1972; postgrad., Columbia U., 1988, U. Mich., 1988. Lic. profl. counselor, S.C. Staff psychologist Greenville (S.C.) Hosp. System, 1972-79; mgr. profl. devel. Daniel Constrn., Greenville, 1979-84; dir. orgn. devel. Fluor-Daniel, Greenville, 1984-85; v.p. human resources Ballenger Group, Greenville, 1985-87; pres. Maxim, Inc., Greenville, 1988—; mgmt. chair Inst. Certifying Profl. Secs., Kansas City, Mo., 1982-89; cons. Behavior Resources, Inc., Greenville, 1990—; co-founder Positive Employee Practices Inst., Mpls., 1988—. Loaned exec. United Way, Greenville, 1982; mem. exec. com. State Job Tng. Coun., Columbia, S.C., 1986-96; bd. dirs. Jr. Achievement, Greenville, 1987-89. Capt. USAF, 1970-78. Recipient scholarship/leadership award Kappa Sigma, 1969, Res. Officer's award Air Force ROTC, 1970; named Exec. of Yr., Profl. Secs. Internat., Greenville, 1987. Mem. ACA, Am. Psychol. Assn. (assoc.), Soc. Human Resource Mgmt., Orgn. Devel. Network, Construction Industry Coop. Alliance, Leadership S.C. (participant, alumni). Lutheran. Home: 109 Glenn Burnie Dr Easley SC 29642-2413 Office: Maxim Inc PO Box 27152 Greenville SC 29616-2152

MEADER, DARRELL LEE, psychologist, disaster health specialist; b. Covington, Ky., Oct. 21, 1941; s. Edward Ogden and Lillian (Hull) M.; m. Deloris Caudill, June 22, 1965; children: Darrell Lee, William Edward. BS, No. Ky. U., 1975, postgrad., 1975-77, AD in Nursing, 1979. RN, Ohio, Ky., Tex., N.C.; cert. scuba diver, advance, open water, search and recovery. With St. Elizabeth Hosp., Covington, Ky., 1968-70; staff Jewish Hosp., Cin., 1970-72, Lakeside Place, Cold Srpings, Ky., 1972-75, Bethesda Hosp., Cin., 1975-78, Children's Hosp., Cin., 1979; team leader Bethesda Hosp., 1979-81; charge nurse burn CCU Univ. Hosp., Cin., 1981—, chaplain critical care areas, 1989—; disaster svcs. MAT team mem. Nat. ARC, Cin., 1968—; cons. Meader Cons. Svcs., Ft. Wright, Ky., 1975—; mental health officer Hurricane Hugo, St. Croix, V.I., 1989; ARC disaster health officer Hurricane Bob, 1991; mayor for a day P.R. Flood, 1992; disaster relief worker Hurrican Andrew, 1992. Contbr. articles to profl. jours. Col. U.S. Army Spl. Forces, 1958. Mem. DAV, British Red Cross Cayman Island Br., Res. Officers Assn., Am. Def. Preparedness Assn., Vietnam Vets. Assn., Spl. Forces Assn. Democrat. Baptist. Home: 800 Kyles Ln Fort Mitchell KY 41017-8122 Office: Meader Cons Svc 800A Kyles Ln Fort Mitchell KY 41017-8122 also: Meader's Lung Chows Kennel 800 Kyles Ln # B Fort Mitchell KY 41017

MEADLOCK, JAMES W., computer graphics company executive; b. 1933; married. BSEE, N.C. State U., 1956. Dept. mgr. IBM, 1956-69; pres. Intergraph Corp., Huntsville, Ala., 1969—; also chmn. bd. dirs. Intergraph Corp., Huntsville; chief exec. officer Intergraph Corp., 1989—. Office: Intergraph Corp Huntsville AL 35894-0001*

MEADOR, CLIFTON KIRKPATRICK, internist, health facility administrator, educator; b. Selma, Ala., Sept. 7, 1931; s. Daniel John and Mabel (Kirkpatrick) M.; m. Helen Allen, June 17, 1955 (div. 1977); children: Clifton Kirkpatrick, Aubrey Allen, Ann Meador Shayne, Elizabeth Meador Driskill; m. Kathleen Sewell, Oct. 27, 1979; children: Mary Kathleen, Graham Kirkpatrick, Rebecca Ingram. BA, Vanderbilt U., Nashville, 1952; MD summa cum, Vanderbilt Sch. Medicine, Nashville, 1955. Diplomate Am. Bd. Internal Medicine, Am. Bd. Endocrinology and Metabolism. Intern, asst. resident Columbia-Presbyn. Hosp., N.Y.C., 1955-57; asst. resident Vanderbilt Hosp., Nashville, 1959-60, NIH fellow endocrinology, 1960-61; asst. prof. U. Ala., Birmingham, Ala., 1962-63; assoc. prof. U. Ala., Birmingham, 1963-65; prof. medicine U. Ala., Birmingham, 1965-68, 1965-73; dean sch. medicine U. Ala., Birmingham, 1968-73; prof. medicine Vanderbilt U., Nashville, 1973-80, U. South Ala., Mobile, 1980-82; med. dir. St. Thomas Hosp., Nashville, 1982—; clin. prof. medicine Vanderbilt U., Nashville, 1982—; adv. coun. Health Svcs. Resident, Washington, 1968-73; editorial bd. So. Med. Jour., Birmingham, 1969-74. Author: Little Book of Doctors' Rules, 1992, Little Book of Nurses' Rules, 1993; contbr. articles to profl. jours. Pres., bd. dirs. Univ. Sch., Nashville, 1977-78. Capt. M.C., U.S. Army, 1957-59. Named Markle scholar, Markle Found., 1962-67. Mem. So. Soc. Clin. Investigation, Tenn. Med. Assn., Endocrine Soc., Phi Beta Kappa, Alpha Omega Alpha. Presbyterian. Home: 1727 Kingsbury Dr Nashville TN 37215-5705 Office: St Thomas Hosp 4220 Harding Rd Nashville TN 37205-2005

MEADOR, DANIEL JOHN, law educator; b. Selma, Ala., Dec. 7, 1926; s. Daniel John and Mabel (Kirkpatrick) M.; m. Janet Caroline Heilmann, Nov. 19, 1955; children: Janet Barrie, Anna Kirkpatrick, Daniel John. B.S., Auburn U., 1949; J.D., U. Ala., 1951; LL.M., Harvard U., 1954. Bar: Ala. 1951, Va. 1961. Law clk. to U.S. Supreme Ct. Justice Hugo L. Black, 1954-55; assoc. firm Lange, Simpson, Robinson & Somerville, Birmingham, 1955-57; faculty U. Va. Law Sch., 1957-66, prof. law, 1961-66; prof., dean U. Ala. Law Sch., 1966-70; James Monroe prof. law U. Va., Charlottesville, 1970-94, prof. emeritus, 1994—; asst. atty. gen. U.S., 1977-79, dir. grad. program for judges, 1979-95; Fulbright lectr., U.K., 1965-66; vis. prof. U.S. Mil. Acad., 1984; Chmn. Southeastern Conf. Assn. Am. Law Schs., 1964-65; chmn. Cts. Task Force Nat. Adv. Commn. on Criminal Justice, 1971-72; dir. appellate justice project Nat. Center for State Cts., 1972-74; mem. Adv. Council on Appellate Justice, 1971-75, Council on Role of Cts., 1978-84; bd. dirs. State Justice Inst., 1986-92. Author: Preludes to Gideon, 1967, Criminal Appeals-English Practices and American Reforms, 1973, Mr. Justice Black and His Books, 1974, Appellate Courts: Staff and Process in the Crisis of Volume, 1974, (with Carrington and Rosenberg) Justice on Appeal, 1976, Impressions of Law in East Germany, 1986, American Courts, 1991, (with J. Bernstein) Appellate Courts in the United States, 1994, His Father's House, 1994, (with Rosenberg and Carrington) Appellate Courts: Structures, Functions, Processes, and Personnel, 1994; editor: Hardy Cross Dillard: Writings and Speeches, 1995; editor Va. Bar News, 1962-65; contbr. articles to profl. jours. Served to 1st lt. AUS, 1951-53. Decorated Bronze Star; IREX fellow German Dem. Republic, 1983. Mem. ABA (chmn. standing com. on fed. jud. improvements 1987-90), Ala. Bar Assn., Va. Bar Assn. (exec. com. 1983-86), Am. Law Inst., Am. Judicature Soc. (bd. dirs. 1975-77, 80-83), Soc. Pub. Tchrs. Law, Am. Soc. Legal History (bd. dirs. 1968-71), Order of Coif, Raven Soc., Phi Delta Phi, Omicron Delta Kappa, Kappa Alpha. Presbyn. Office: U Va Sch Law 580 Massie Rd Charlottesville VA 22903

MEADOR, JOHN MILWARD, JR., university dean; b. Louisville, Nov. 4, 1946; s. John Milward and Ruth Inez (Miller) M.; m. Judith Ann Hay, Dec. 22, 1969; children: John Milward III, Elise Kathleen. BA, U. Louisville, 1968; MA, U. Tex., 1972, MLS, 1973; cert. in pub. adminstrn., U. Utah, 1982. Cert. tchr., Ky., Tex. Stacks supr. U. Louisville Librs., 1965-68; English bibliographer M.D. Anderson Libr. U. Houston, 1973-74, head reference dept. social scis. and humanities, 1974-77, head gen. reference dept., 1977-80; asst. dir. pub. svcs. Marriott Libr. U. Utah, Salt Lake City, 1980-84; dean libr. svcs. S.W. Mo. State U., Springfield, 1984-93; dean librs. U. Miss., Univeristy, 1993—; bd. dirs. Mo. Libr. Network Corp., 1984-90, St. Louis, S.W. Mo. Libr. Network, Springfield; cons. Dayco Corp., Springfield, 1984-86; chmn. Mo. Northwestern Online Total Integrated Systems (NOTIS) Users Group, 1988-89. Co-author: The Robinson Jeffers Collection at the University of Houston, 1975; contbr. articles to profl. jours. Sponsor Community Alternative Svc. Program, Springfield and St. Louis, 1985-93; mem. governing bd. Mo. Rsch. and Edn. Network, MOREnet, 1991-93; With U.S. Army, 1969-71, Vietnam. Recipient Nat. Essay award Propeller Club of U.S., 1964; named to Honorable Order of Ky. Colonels, Gov. Ky., 1978; summer scholar English-Speaking Union, Edinburgh, Scotland, 1968; Apple Computer's Higher Edn. Acad. Devel. Donation Program grantee, 1990. Mem. ALA, Am. Assn. for Higher Edn., Assn. Coll. Rsch. Librs., Bibliog. Soc. Am., Libr. Adminstrn. and Mgmt. Assn., other profl. orgns., English-Speaking Union Club, Rotary (chmn. students guests com. Springfield chpt. 1986-89, chmn. scholarships com. 1989-90, bd. dirs. 1990-91, bd. dirs. Oxford chpt. 1995—). Home: PO Box 787 University MS 38677-0787 Office: U Miss J D Williams Libr University MS 38677

MEADOR, RICHARD LEWIS, school counselor; b. Hinton, W.Va., Nov. 13, 1934; s. George Alfred and Juanita (Shirey) M.; m. Mildred Louise Brown, June 20, 1953; children: Stephen, Debra. BS in Edn., Concord Coll., Athens, W.Va., 1961; MA in Guidance, Ohio State U., 1963. Lic. profl. counselor. Tchr. Summers County Schs., Hinton, 1961-62; tchr./counselor Columbus (Ohio) City Schs., 1963-67, Raleigh County Schs., Beckley, W.Va., 1964-65; tchr./prin. U.S. Forest Svc., Neola, W.Va., 1965-69; counselor Shady Spring (W.Va.) High Sch., 1969—. Mem. Summers County Dem. Exec. Com., Hinton, 1972-88; commr. Summers County Commn., Hinton, 1989—. Mem. NEA, W. Va. Edn. Assn., Raleigh County Edn. Assn., W. Va. Counseling Assn. Democrat. Home: PO Box 37 Jumping Branch WV 25969-0037 Office: Shady Spring H S PO Box 2001 Shady Spring WV 25918

MEADOR, ROY EDWARD, commercial writer; b. Cordell, Okla., Apr. 23, 1929; s. Walter Raymond and Gladys Beatrice (Reed) M. BA, U. So. Calif., 1951; MA, Columbia U., 1972. Advt. mgr. diagnostics divsn. Pfizer, Inc., N.Y.C., 1962-72; advt. mgr. Gelman Scis., Inc., Ann Arbor, Mich., 1972-78; freelance writer Ann Arbor, 1978—. Author: Franklin, Revolutionary Scientist, 1975, Guidelines for Preparing Proposals, 1991, Future Energy Alternatives, 1978, Capital Revenge, 1975, Cogeneration and District Heating, 1981. Mem. adv. bd. Ann Arbor Pub. Libr., 1978-94, mem. pub. rels. com. Democrat. Home and Office: PO Box 2045 Ann Arbor MI 48106

MEADOWS, LOIS, mental health nursing clinician and educator; b. N.Y., Apr. 22, 1940; d. Stanley and Elsie (Hutkay) Casden; m. Allen Meadows; children: Henry, Stanley, Laura, Mack. BA, Hunter Coll., 1961; BSN, Troy State, Ala., 1977; MSN, U. Ala., Birmingham, 1981; MS, Troy State U., Montgomery, 1984, EdS, 1990. RN, Ala.; cert. mental health clin. specialist, reality therapist; lic. profl. counselor. Pvt. practice psychiatric nursing Montgomery; asst. prof. Auburn U., Montgomery; faculty mem. Inst. Control Theory, Reality Therapy and Quality Mgmt.; cons. nursing care ctr., Auburn U., Montgomery. Vol. Counselor Neighbors Who Care, Leadership Montgomery, Montgomery Class XI. Mem. ANA, Mental Health Assn., Montgomery Assn. Autistic Children and Adults, Ala. Nurses Assn. (Rsch. award), Inst. Reality Therapy, Inst. Noetic Scis., Ala. State Nat. Assn. Home: 426 Meadows Dr Lowndesboro AL 36752-3040

MEADOWS, LOIS ANNETTE, elementary education educator; b. Harrisville, W.Va., Jan. 12, 1948; d. Orvle Adam and Una Pauline (Slocum) Ingram; m. David Alan Meadows, June 15, 1969; children: Lynecia Ann, Eric Justin. BA, Glenville State Coll., 1969; MA, W.Va. U., 1980. Cert. music, elem. edn., reading, W.Va. Tchr. grade six Acad. Park-Portsmouth (Va.) City Schs., 1969-73; elem. substitute Wood County Schs., Parkersburg, W.Va., 1973-77; real estate agt. Nestor Realty, Parkersburg, 1974-77; tchr. grade five/music Emerson Elem. Wood County Schs., Parkersburg, W.Va., 1977-78, tchr. grade three, 1978—; edn. cons. World Book, Parkersburg, 1986—; mentor tchr.-trainer Wood County Schs., parkersburg, 1990—; W.Va. S.T.E.P. Test com./trainer W.Va. Dept. Edn., Charleston, 1994—, mem. writing assessment com., 1994—; grant writer and speaker in field; mem. W.Va. Dept. Edn. State Writing Manual Com., 1996—. Author: (reading projects) Operation Blackout, 1986-94 (grant 1994), The Reading Room, 1988 (grant 1990), Storytime at the Mall, 1986— (grant 1994, 95). Life mem. Emerson PTA, Parkersburg, 1977—; Sunday Sch. tchr. North Parkersburg Bapt. Ch., 1976—, children's choir dir., 1976-88; fund raiser local charities, Parkersburg. Women of Excellence and Leadership Timely Honored award, W. Va. State Reading Tchr. of Yr., 1988, Finalist W. Va. State Tchr. of Yr., W.Va. Dept. Edn., 1993, Wood County Tchr. of Yr., 1993, Ashland Oil Golden Apple Achiever award, 1995, Wood Co. PTA Outstanding Educator of Yr. award, 1995-96, award for ann. contbrs. and project work Emerson PTA. Mem. W.Va. Reading Assn. (pres. 1993-94, mem. chmn. 1994—), Internat. Reading Assn., Wood County Reading Coun. (past pres. 1986-88, 90-92), Am. Fedn. Tchrs., Delta Kappa Gamma. Republican. Home: 102 Jo Mar Dr Parkersburg WV 26101 Office: Wood County Schs Emerson Elem 1605 36th St Parkersburg WV 26104

MEADOWS, PATRICIA BLACHLY, art curator, civic worker; b. Amarillo, Tex., Nov. 12, 1938; d. William Douglas and Irene Bond Blachly; m. Curtis Washington Meadows, Jr., June 10, 1961; children: Michael Lee, John Morgan. BA in English and History, U. Tex., 1960. Program dir. Ex-Students Assn., Austin, Tex., 1960-61; co-founder, dir. Dallas Visual Art Ctr., 1981-86, curator, 1987—, founder The Collectors, 1988—; exhbn. dir. Tex. bd. Nat. Mus. Women in Arts, Washington, 1986-91; mem. acquisition com. Dallas Mus. Art, 1988-92; chmn. adv. bd. Oaks Bank and Trust, 1993-96; juror numerous exhibits, Dallas and Tex.; speaker on arts subjects; cons. city, state and nat. projects concerning arts; bd. dirs., mem. exec. com. Uptown Pub. Improvement Dist., 1993-96; chmn. bd. dirs. State-Thomas TIF Zone # 1, 1994—. Author: (art catalogues) Critic's Choice, 1983—, Texas Women, 1989-90, Texas: reflections, rituals, 1991; organizer exhbns. Presenting Nine, D-Art Visual Art Ctr., 1984, Mosaics, 1991—, Senses Beyond Sight, 1992-93. Bd. dirs. Mid-Am. Arts Alliance, Kansas City, Mo., 1989-93, Tex. Bd. Commerce, Austin, 1991-93, Women's Issues Network, Dallas, 1994-96; bd. dirs. Dallas Summit, 1989-95, pres., 1993-94; mem. Charter 100, 1993—, Dallas Assembly, 1993—, Leadership Tex., 1987; co-founder, mem. steering com. Emergency Artists Support League, Dallas, 1992—; mem. originating task force Dallas Coalition for Arts, 1984; also others. Recipient Dedication to Arts award Tex. Fine Arts Assn., 1984, Flora award Dallas Civic Garden Ctr., 1987, James K. Wilson award TACA, 1988, Maura award Women's Ctr. Dallas, 1991, Disting. Woman award Northwood U., 1993, Excellence in the Arts award Dallas Hist. Soc., 1993, Legend award Dallas Visual Art Ctr., 1996. Mem. Tex. Assn. Mus., Tex. Sculpture Assn. (originating task force), Arts Dist. Mgmt. Assn. (bd. dirs., exec. com. 1984-92, Artists Square design com. 1988-90), Artists and Craftsmen Assn. (pres. bd. dirs. 1982-83), Dallas Woman's Club. Presbyterian. Office: 2707 State St Dallas TX 75204-2634

MEAGHER, ELIZABETH STRAPP, librarian; b. Trenton, N.J., Dec. 15, 1947; d. Francis James and Elizabeth Ellen (Dorety) Strapp; m. James Francis Meagher, July 7, 1973; children: Jeffrey James, Elizabeth Kathleen. BA in English, Caldwell Coll., 1970; MS in Libr. Sci., Cath. U., 1971. Asst. libr. Seattle Mcpl. Reference Libr., Seattle, 1971-73; rsch. asst., libr. Pa. State U., Coll. Bus. Adminstrn., State College, Pa., 1973-76; resource coord. Muscle Shoals Regional Libr., Florence, Ala., 1976-77; cataloger U. North Ala., Florence, 1986—. Sec., treas. St. Joseph Sch. Found., Florence, 1986—. Mem. Ala. Libr. Assn., Ala. Assn. of Coll. and Rsch. Librs., OCLC Music Users Group, Online Audio-Visual Catalogues. Home: Rt 8 Box 629 Florence AL 35630 Office: Univ North Ala Campus Box 5028 Florence AL 35632

MEALER, LYNDA REAM, physical education educator; b. Lima, Ohio, Sept. 19, 1946; d. Don A. and Sue (Pringle) Duncan; m. Ben T. Mealer, Aug. 29, 1970; children: Thomas Lee, Theresa Lynn. AA, LaSalle U., Chgo., 1976; BS, La. State U., 1983, 1992. Office mgr. M. Quick Ins., Glenmora, La., 1975-77; ind. bus. owner Glenmora (La.) Exxon, 1977-82; kindergarten tchr. Glenmora (La.) Elem. Sch., 1986-87; 4th grade tchr., 1983-86, 92-94; 6th grade tchr. Forest Hill (La.) Acad., 1989-90; 4th grade tchr. Glenmora (La.) Elem. Sch., 1992-94; phys. edn. tchr., 1994—; intervention strategist Drug Free Schs., Rapides Parish, La., 1994-95; crisis intervention Team Glenmora (La.) Elem. Sch., 1994-95. Author: (poem) Who's Who in Poetry, 1993, Vengeance is Mine, 1988. Sec., pres. Glenmora (La.) Garden Club, 1974-87; sec., pres., legis. chair Bus. and Profl. Women, Glenmora, La., 1981-91. Recipient Student Svc. award Student Govt. Assn., La. State U. 1983, Lifetime mem. Gamma Beta Phi, La. State U., 1983, Scholarship award Sm. Assn. Women, Alexandria, La., 1992, Lifetime/charter mem. Golden Key Hon. Soc., Baton Rouge, La., 1992. Mem. NEA, La. Assn. Educators, Rapides Fedn. Tchrs. Home: PO Box 72 806 Hwy 165 S Glenmora LA 71433 Office: Glenmora Elementary School PO Box 1188 Glenmora LA 71433-1188

MEALOR, PHYLLIS JAYNE, nurse, infection control practitioner; b. Calhoun, Ga., Nov. 20, 1948; d. Charles Lindberg and Alice (Porter) Hall; children: Deanna Glass Bates, Rodney M.; m. Gary Lyn Mealor, Apr. 2, 1992. LPN, Gordon County Sch., Calhoun, 1968; ADN, Dalton Coll., 1979; BSN, West Ga. Coll., 1995. RN, Ga.; cert. respiratory therapy technician, Nat. Bd. Respiratory Therapy; cert. provider and instr. ACLS, cert. provider, instr. and instr. trainer BLS, Am. Heart Assn. Nurse Gordon Hosp., Calhoun, 1968-69, Hamilton Hosp., Dalton, Ga., 1969-80; staff nurse ICU and CCU, adminstrv. nursing supr. Redmond Regional Med. Ctr., Rome, Ga., 1980-87; psychiat. charge nurse, infection control practitioner N.W. Ga. Regional Hosp., Rome, 1987—, coord. nursing quality improvement, 1987—; nursing cons., Ga., 1990-95; poster presenter 3d Ann. Cmty. Nurse Coalition, 1995. Mem. Ga. Infection Control Network, Assn. for Profls. in Infection Control and Epidemiology. Home: 289 Miller Loop Rd Plainville GA 30733

MEANS, MICHAEL DAVID, hospital administrator; b. Lakeland, Fla., Jan. 19, 1950; married. B, U. Fla., 1971, MHA, 1974. Adminstrv. resident Manatee Meml. Hosp., Bradenton, Fla., 1974, adminstrv. asst., 1974-78; asst. dir. Orlando (Fla.) Regional Med. Ctr., 1978-80, assoc. exec. dir., 1980-81, exec. v.p., chief oper. officer, 1981-88; pres., chief exec. officer Holmes Regional Healthcare System, Melbourne, Fla., 1988—, Health First, Melbourne, Fla. Mem. Fla. Hosp. Assn. Home: 1848 River Shore Dr Indialantic FL 32903-4514 Office: Health First 8249 Devereaux Dr Melbourne FL 32940*

MEANS, TERRY ROBERT, federal judge; b. Roswell, N.Mex., July 3, 1948; s. Lewis Prude and Doris Emaree (Hightower) M.; m. JoAnn Huffman Harris, June 2, 1973; children: Robert, MaryAnn, Emily. BA, So. Meth. U., Dallas, 1971; JD, So. Meth. U., 1974. Bar: Tex. 1974, U.S. Dist. Ct. (no. dist.) Tex. 1976, U.S. Ct. Appeals (5th cir.) 1978, U.S. Dist. Ct. (we. dist., ea. dist.) Tex. 1991. Ptnr. Means & Means, Corsicana, Tex., 1974-88; justice 10th Ct. Appeals, Waco, Tex., 1989-90; judge U.S. Dist. Ct. for Northern Dist. Tex., Ft. Worth, 1991—. Chmn. Navarro County Rep. Party, Corsicana, 1976-88; pres. YMCA, Corsicana, 1984. Mem. State Bar Tex., Tarrant County Bar Assn., McLennan County Bar Assn. Baptist. Office: 201 US Courthouse 501 W 10th St Fort Worth TX 76102-3637

MEARA, JAMES FRANCIS, JR., real estate broker, land developer; b. Norman, Okla., June 12, 1960; s. James Francis and Dana Denise (McDougal) M.; m. Lisa Ann Morton, May 29, 1994; 1 child, James Francis III. BBA in Bus. Adminstrn., So. Meth. U., 1982. Lic. real estate broker, Tex. Acquisitions/devel./leasing/mgmt. office technician 1st Dallas Investors, 1982-83; leasing/office bldg. agt. Amberton Ltd., Dallas, 1983-84; owner The Meara Co., Dallas, 1984—; pres. Pi Kappa Alpha Housing Corp., Dallas, 1985—. Named to Outstanding Young Men of Am., 1988. Mem. Internat. Coun. Shopping Ctrs., Nat. Apt. and Home Builders Assn., Home and Apt. Builders Assn. of Metro Dallas, Wylie C. of C., East Dallas C. of C. Roman Catholic. Office: The Meara Co 8344 E RL Thornton #102 Dallas TX 75228-7186

MEASELS, DONALD CLARK, music educator; b. Morton, Miss., Oct. 23, 1952; s. W.J. and Katie Ethel (Peagler) M.; m. Nenette Leatherwood, Aug. 10, 1974. BA, William Carey Coll., 1974, MMus, 1976; M in Ch. Music, So. Baptist Theol. Sem., Louisville, 1980, DMus, 1986. From instr. music to assoc. prof. music Carson-Newman Coll., Jefferson City, Tenn., 1983—; dir. London program Carson-Newman Coll., 1991-94, chair dept. music, 1994—, dean divsn. fine arts, 1996—. Mem. Nat. Assn. Tchrs. of Singing (state gov. 1984-88, regional gov. 1989-92). Democrat. Office: Carson-Newman Coll Box 72048 Jefferson City TN 37760

MEBANE, BARBARA MARGOT, service company executive, studio owner; b. Sylacauga, Ala., July 21, 1947; d. Audrey Dixon and Mary Ellen (Yaikow) Baxley; m. James Lewis Mebane, Dec. 31, 1971; 1 child, Cieson Brooke. Student Brookhaven Coll., Dallas. Line performer J. Taylor Dance Co., Miami, Fla., 1964-65; sales mgr. Dixie Readers Svc., Jackson, Miss., 1965-67; regional sales mgr. Robertson Products Co., Texarkana, Tex., 1967-75; owner, pres. Telco Sales, Svc. and Supply, Dallas, 1976—; owner The Dance Factory, ATS Svcs., Lewisville, Tex., Dancers Workshop, Lewisville; mem. Dance Masters, Miami, 1975—; mgmt. specialist SBA; choreographer music videos for pay/cable TV, 1985, cabarette shows coll. and H.S. musicals; founder, dir. The Dance Factory, Lewisville, Tes.; owner, tchr. Dancers Workshop, 1992—; contract cons. for self-employed women; pub. speaker in field. Author: Paper on Positive Thinking, 1983. Sponsor St. Jude's Rsch. Hosp., Memphis, Cancer Rsch. Ctr., Dallas; active Cancer Rsch. Found.; sponsor Nat. Kidney Found., Dallas. Named Bus. Woman of the Yr., Gov. Anne Richards, Tex., 1994. Mem. Nat. Fedn. Ind. Businesses, Internat. Register of Profiles Cambridge, Eng., Female and Minority Owned Bus. League, PDTA (Dallas Dance Coun.), TITAS, Female Exec. Club N.Y.C. Avocations: working with children, teaching dance, writing. Home: 3701 Twin Oaks Ct Lewisville TX 75028-1244 Office: Dancers Workshop 502 S Old Orchard #150 Lewisville TX 75067

MEBANE, GEORGE ALLEN IV, corporate executive, rancher; b. Greensboro, N.C., Sept. 28, 1929; s. George Allen III and Elizabeth (Armstrong) M.; m. Pat Pannill, Aug. 23, 1950 (dec.); children: George Allen IV, William Michael, Lucy Mebane Webster; m. Marianne Cheek, June 28, 1987. BS, Phila. Coll. Textile and Sci., 1950, D Textiles (hon.), 1986. Supr. Sale Knitting Co., Martinsville, Va., 1950-52; salesman Am. & Efird Mills, Mt. Holly, N.C., 1954-56, Burlington, Ind., Greensboro, 1956-64; pres., chief exec. officer Throwing Corp. Am., Swepsonville, N.C., 1964-67, Universal Textured Yarns, Inc., Mebane, N.C., 1967-71; pres., chief exec. officer Unifi, Inc., Greensboro, 1971-78, chmn., chief exec. officer, 1978-85, chmn., 1985—. Sgt. U.S. Army, 1952-54; Korea. Mem. Am. Synthetic Yarns Assn. (bd. dirs. 1977-80), Am. Textile Mfg. Inst. (bd. dirs. 1986-89), N.C. Textile Assn. (bd. dirs. 1988-90). Democrat. Presbyterian. Office: Unifi Inc PO Box 19109 Greensboro NC 27419-9109*

MEBANE, JOHN SPENCER, language and literature educator, dean; b. Atlanta, Jan. 11, 1946; s. John Harrison and Hannah Price (Kallam) M.; m. Frances Carol Tumlinson, Mar. 20, 1971; children: David Spencer, Alan Tumlinson, Hannah Carol. BA in English summa cum laude, Presbyn. Coll., Clinton, S.C., 1968; MA in English, Emory U., 1973, PhD in English, 1974. Asst. prof. English Troy State U., 1974-84, assoc. prof. English, 1984; asst. prof. English U. Ala., Huntsville, 1984-88, assoc. prof. English, 1988—, chair dept. English, 1990-91, from interim dean to assoc. dean Coll. Liberal Arts, 1991—; speaker in field. Author: Renaissance Magic and the Return of the Golden Age, 1989; contbr. articles to profl. jours. Mem. adv. bd. Huntsville Lit. Assn., 1986-89, mem. exec. bd., 1995—; asst. scoutmaster, mem. troop com. troop 364 Boy Scouts Am., Huntsville, 1987-93. Sgt. U.S. Army, 1968-70, Vietnam. Woodrow Wilson fellow, 1968, Danforth fellow, 1970-74. Mem. MLA, Shakespeare Assn. Am., South Atlantic MLA, Medieval Renaissance Drama Soc., Nat. Coun. Tchrs. English, Southeastern Assn. Pre-Law Advisors, Phi Kappa Phi, Sigma Kappa Alpha. Unitarian. Home: 11314 Mountaincrest Dr SE Huntsville AL 35803-1616 Office: U Ala Huntsville Coll Liberal Arts Huntsville AL 35899

MEDBERY, CLINTON AMOS, III, radiation oncologist, internist; b. Bryan, Tex., Feb. 17, 1948; s. Clinton A., Jr. and Robena Claire (Henley) M.; m. Karen Elizabeth Crow (div. Oct. 1992); children: Ashley Elizabeth, Clinton A., IV; m. Jennie Ann Cavallaro. BS, U. S.C., 1971; MD, Med. U. of S.C., 1976. Diplomate Am. bd. Internal Medicine, Am. Bd. Med. Oncology, Am. Bd. Radiology. Commd. ensign USN, 1971, advanced through grades to cmmdr., physician, 1976-89, res., 1989; pres. Southwest Radiation Oncology, Oklahoma City, 1989—; clin. assoc prof. Okla. U. Health Scis. Ctr., Oklahoma City, 1989—. Mem. AMA. Am. Coll. Radiation Oncology, Okla. State Med. Assn. Presbyterian. Office: Southwest Radiation Onc 700 NE 13th St Oklahoma City OK 73104

MEDDING, WALTER SHERMAN, environmental engineer; b. St. Louis, Mar. 4, 1922; s. Walter Lyman and Elizabeth Steele (Sherman) M.; m. Mary Agnes Patty Johnson, Apr. 22, 1944; children: Jean, Walter, Mauri. BSCE, Va. Poly. Inst., 1947, MS in Sanitary Engring., 1970. Registered profl. engr., Va., N.C., Kans. Various positions U.S. Army, 1942-64; student officer advanced course The Engr. Sch., Ft. Belvoir, Va., 1952-53, head fixed bridges sect., 1953-55; asst. engr. Asmara Eritrea, chief design br. Mediterranean Divsn., Gulf Dist., Tehran, Iran, 1955-57; asst. divsn. engr. 9th Infantry Divsn., Ft. Carson, Colo., 1957-59; resident engr. USACAG, chief constrn. ops. U.S. Army Engring. Command Europe, Frankfurt, Germany, 1959-72; chief contract adminstrn. U.S. Army Engring. Divsn. Europe, Frankfurt, Germany, 1972-75; chief environ. engring. Office, Chif of Engrs., U.S. Army, Washington, 1975-86; sr. engr. Romem Aqua Sys. Co., Woodbridge, Va., 1986—. Co-author: (textbook) Non-standard Military Fixed Bridges, 1954; contbr. articles to profl. jours. Mem. ASCE, Am. Waterworks Assn., Water Environment Fedn., Conf. of Fed. Environ. Engrs. Republican. Episcopalian. Home: 204 Brooke Dr Fredericksburg VA 22408 Office: The Romem Aqua Systems Co 1635-2 Woodside Dr Woodbridge VA 22191

MEDDLETON, FRANCIS CHARLES, elementary and secondary school educator; b. Johnson City, N.Y., Nov. 17, 1942; s. Willett J. and Julia (Curley) M.; m. Linda I. Albright, July 10, 1965; children: Dennis K., Laura D. AA, Cayuga County C.C., Auburn, N.Y., 1964; BS, Old Dominion U., 1969; MEd, U. Va., 1972; MA, U. South Fla., 1978, EdS, 1979; BA, SUNY, Albany, 1986; postgrad., Brigham Young U., 1991, U. Houston, 1991, U. St. Thomas, Houston, 1992-93. Tchr. Pub. Sch. Systems, Va., 1969-72, Fla., 1972-82, Tex., 1982-96; instr. Lee Coll., Baytown, Tex., 1989-94; tchr. specialist Harris County Children Protective Svcs. Houston Ind. Sch. Dist., 1994—; cons. insvc. tng. Galena Park Ind. Sch. Dist., Houston, 1982-83, North Forest Ind. Sch. Dist., Houston, 1983-89, Lee Coll., Baytown, 1989-94, Houston Ind. Sch. Dist., 1994—, San Jacinto Coll., Houston, 1995—. Mem. Rep. Nat. Com., Houston, 1989, Am. Legion, Houston, 1989. With USNR, 1961-67. Decorated Nat. Def. Svc. medal. Mem. NRA, NEA, Tex. Coll. Tchrs. Assn., Tex. Faculty Assn., Tex. State Tchrs. Assn. Roman Catholic. Home: 12811 Woodlite Ln Houston TX 77015-2053

MEDEN, ROBERT PAUL, interior design educator; b. Cleve., Jan. 24, 1950; s. Paul Joseph and Irene Theresa (Chuey) M.; m. Maryellen Hudak, June 22, 1979; children: Christina Rose, Patrick Michael. BArch, Kent State U., 1973, MArch, 1975; DArch, Cath. U. Am., 1989. Registered architect, Ohio, Md., Va., Ind. Planner, draftsman John Roush, Architects, Cleve., 1975; hist. sites restoration coord. hist. preservation div. N.Y. State, Office of Parks and Recreation, Albany, 1976-77; designer, draftsman Robert C. Gaede, Cleve., 1977; interior design instr. Sch. Family and Consumer Studies Kent (Ohio) State U., 1977-79; asst. prof. interior design Mt. Vernon Coll., Washington, 1979-82; asst. prof. architecture Ball State U., Muncie, Ind., 1982-85; dir. preservation programs The Am. Inst. Architects, Washington, 1985; assoc. prof. interior design Marymount. U. Sch. Arts and Scis., Arlington, Va., 1986-90; prof. Marymount U. Sch. Arts and Scis., Arlington, Va., 1990—, program chair, 1989—; hist. architect U.S. Dept. Interior Tech. Preservation Svcs., Washington, 1980; architect Turner Renovations, Inc., Washington, 1979-82, Suburban Contractors, Inc., Vienna,Va., 1986-87; architect, preservation specialist Browning, Day, Mullins, Dierdorf, Inc., Indpls., 1984-85; condr. numerous seminars and presentations. Author: Architectural Character Study of the Buckeye Road District, 1975; co-author and illustrator: History of Housing and Furnishings Handbook, 1977; editor and illustrator: Access to Historic Buildings for the Disabled, 1981. Asst. to dir. Mayfield (Ohio) Recreation Com., 1968-73; basketball coach St. Mary's Ch., Cath. Youth Orgn., Albany, 1976-77, basketball coach St. Lawrence Ch., Cath. Youth Orgn., Muncie, 1982-83, woman's varsity soccer coach Marymount U., 1986-88. Recipient ASID Scalamandre Hist. Preservation award, 1978, Dora Brahms award, 1980, 83, Nat. Endowment for Arts, Design Arts Program, Entering Profl. award, 1981; grantee The Cleve. Found., 1979, The Nat. Endowment for the Arts Design Arts Program, 1981. Mem. AIA, Am. Soc. Interior Designers, Interior Design Educators Coun., Internat. Assoc. Lighting Designers. Roman Catholic. Home: 6013 27th St N Arlington VA 22207-1232 Office: Marymount U 2807 N Glebe Rd Arlington VA 22207-4224

MEDFORD, RUSSELL MARSHALL, physician; b. Bklyn., Jan. 8, 1955; s. Jerome L. and Doris P. (Pinchuk) M.; m. Margaret K. Offermann, May 31, 1986; children: Arielle, Rochelle. BA, Cornell U., 1976; MS, Albert Einstein Coll. Medicine, 1980, PhD in Cell and Molecular Biology, 1982, MD, 1983. Diplomate Am. Bd. Internal Medicine. Instr. dept. medicine Harvard Med. Sch., Boston, 1986-89; assoc. physician cardiology Brigham and Women's Hosp., Boston, 1986-89; asst. prof. medicine Emory U., Atlanta, 1989-94, assoc. prof. medicine, 1994—; dir. molecular cardiology rsch. ctr., 1994—; founding scientist Athero Genics, Inc., Atlanta, 1994—, exec. v.p., 1994—; pres., CEO, 1995—; bd. dirs. Ga. Biomed. Partnership, Atlanta; mem. site vis. rev. com. Nat. Heart, Lung and Blood Inst., 1992—, NIH, 1993—; scientific rev. Am. Jour. Physiology, Jour. Clin. Investigation, Jour. Biol. Chemistry. Contbr. articles to profl. jours. Grantee NIH, 1993, 94, 95, Am. Heart Assn., 1993, 95. Mem. Am. Fedn. Clin. Rsch., Am. Heart Assn., Am. Soc. Microbiology. Office: Emory U Sch of Medicine Divsn Cardiology 1639 Pierce Dr WMB 319/LL Atlanta GA 30345

MEDINA, SUE O'NEAL, librarian; b. Knoxville, Nov. 18, 1945; d. Floyd and Violet Bloomer; m. Albert Medina. BA in History, Fla. State U., 1966, MS in Libr. Sci., 1971, PhD, 1983. Base libr. Ft. Bruckner Spl. Svcs., Ryukyu Islands, 1969; head libr. Kubasaki H.S., Ryukyu Islands, 1970; asst. humanities ref. libr. U. Ga. Librs., Athens, 1971-72; head Cottage Hill br. Mobile (Ala.) Pub. Libr., 1972-74; dir. Ala.-Tombigbee Libr. Sys., Camden, 1975-76; cataloger Fla. State U., 1977; cons. for planning and rsch. Ala. Pub. Libr. Svc., Montgomery, 1977-85; dir. Network of Ala. Acad. Librs., Montgomery, 1985—; reader for preliminary rev. of manuscripts Coll. and Undergrad. Librs., Haworth Press, 1993—, Jour. Interlibr. Loan, Document Delivery and Info. Supply, 1995—; lectr. in field; cons. in field. Contbr. articles to profl. jours.; editor The Golden Nugget, 1992-93, 95—, Inner Space News, 1992—. Mem. ala. Adv. Coun. on Librs., 1985-86; mem. Ala. Union List of Serials Adv. Com., 1989—; vol. Archibald Sr. Ctr. Named to Outstanding Young Women of Am., 1978, 81; recipient Award of Excellence for best article about use of microforms in librs. for "Major Microform Sets: The Alabama Experience", UMI, Inc., 1994; grantee ALA/NEW, 1979-80, Humanities Alliance, 1982-83, NEH, 1983-85, 87-89, U.S. Office of Edn., 1989, Ala. State Coun. on Arts and Humanities, 1990, U.S. Dept. Edn., 1990, 93-94. Mem. ALA, Assn. Specialized and Coop. Libr. Agencies (ex-officio bd. dirs., editor Interface 1983-86), Assn. for Libr. Collections and Tech. Svcs., Southeastern Libr. Assn. (mem. ad hoc com. on SELA/SOLINET coop. 1993), Ala. Libr. Assn. (exec. coun. 1987-88, chair bibliographic com. 1996, legis. devel. com. 1988—, Eminent Libr. of Yr. 1996), Southeastern Libr. Network, Rsch. and Acad. Librs. of Ga., Nat. Soc. Fund Raising Execs., Nat. Speleological Assn. (editor chpt. newsletter), Montgomery Gem and Mineral soc. (editor chpt. newsletter), Beta Phi Mu (Libr. of Yr. 1990). Office: Network of Alabama Academic Libraries PO Box 302000 100 N Union St Montgomery AL 36130-2000

MEDINA, THOMAS JULIAN, information management consultant, educator; b. Denver, July 24, 1928; s. Frank John and Francis Josephine (Grasmuck) M.; m. Maryem McKell, Apr. 16, 1973; children: Kim Jordan, Vickie Jeanne, Michael McKell. AA, Mira Costa Coll., 1968; BA, San Diego State U., 1969; PhD, Pacific Western U., 1982. Lic. computer scientist, career counselor, Calif. Commd. 2d. lt. USMC, 1953, advanced through grades to maj., 1945-65, computer specialist, 1945-66, ret., 1966; owner, mgr. Medina Fish Finding Co., San Diego, 1970-82; instr. entrepreneurship San Diego County Schs., 1972-82, San Diego Unified Schs., 1984-90; computer scientist Computer Scis. Corp., San Diego, 1982-83, Sci. Applications, Inc., San Diego, 1983-84; cons. entrepreneurship Calif. Dept. Edn., 1985-91; owner The Entrepreneur, Livingtston, Tex., 1988—; mem. adv. bd. Internat. U. Sch. Info. Mgmt., Santa Barbara, Calif., 1986—, mem. faculty, 1988-96; condr. rsch. project on rural entrepreneurs in U.S., Can., Southeast Asia, China, 1990—. Calif. Entrepreneur Ednl. grantee, 1986, 87; recipient award for model program in entrepreneurial edn. U.S. Assn. Small Bus. and Entrepreneurship, 1989, W.S. Curran Disting. svc. award San Diego Internat. Trade, 1989, Leavy award Freedoms Found. Valley Forge, 1990, Mag. award Ernst & Young, 1990. Mem. U.S. Assn. for Small Bus. and Entrepreneurship, Am. Entrepreneur Assn. (dir. acad. rels. 1985-88), Assn. Pvt. Enterprise Edn., World Future Soc. (adv. coun. 1988-90), Southwestern Yacht Club (port capt. 1985-86), Thalians. Republican. Mem. LDS Ch.

MEDLEY, DEBORAH LANGLEY, elementary and secondary education educator; b. Shelbyville, Ky., Aug. 13, 1956; d. Bruce Leland and Elizabeth Ann (Hughes) Langley; m. William Keith Medley, Nov. 18, 1978; children: William Benjamin, Carolyn Elizabeth. B in Edn., U. Ky., 1983, Masters degree, 1992. Cert. elem. and secondary tchr., Ky. AFDC caseworker Ky. Dept. of Human Resources, Frankfort, 1979-80; tchr. elem. functional disabilities Shelby County Pub. Schs., Shelbyville, Ky., 1984-89, tchr. secondary functional disabilities, 1989—; mem. Ky. State Assistive-Adaptive Tech. Team, Louisville, 1995-96; coun. mem. Ky. Acad. Village, 1996. Mem. adv. bd. Shelby County Resource Ctr., Shelbyville, 1994-95; mem. adv. coun. Shelby County H.S. honor soc., 1996, coach swim team, 1992—. Mem. Ky. Edn. Assn., Shelby County Edn. Assn. Democrat. Baptist. Home: 413 Forbes Dr Shelbyville KY 40065 Office: Shelby County H.S. 1701 Frankfort Rd Shelbyville KY 40065-9451

MEDLIN, JOHN GRIMES, JR., banker; b. Benson, N.C., Nov. 23, 1933; s. John Grimes and Mabel (Stephenson) M. BS in Bus. Adminstrn., U. N.C., 1956; grad., The Exec. Program, U. Va., 1965. With Wachovia Bank & Trust Co., Winston-Salem, N.C., 1959-93, pres., 1974; pres., CEO Wachovia Bank and Wachovia Corp., Winston-Salem, N.C., 1977-93; chmn. bd. Wachovia Corp., Winston-Salem, N.C., 1987—; bd. dirs. US Air Group, Inc., RJR Nabisco, Inc., Wachovia Corp., BellSouth Corp., Nat. Svc. Industries, Inc., Burlington Industries Inc., Media Gen. Inc., Nabisco Holdings, Inc. Trustee Nat. Humanities Ctr., Wake Forest U., Kenan Inst. Pvt. Enterprise, Kenan Inst. Arts, The Duke Endowment; active numerous civic and svc. orgns. With USNR, 1956-59. Mem. Phi Delta Theta. Office: Wachovia Corp PO Box 3099 100 N Main St Winston Salem NC 27150

MEDLOCK, NORMAN DUDLEY, healthcare company executive; b. Salem, Mo., Feb. 20, 1949; s. Norman Clement and Wanda Valrie (McAnear) M.; m. Janet Mae Ogle, Mar. 29, 1969; children: Travis, Shawn Dee. Student, Three Rivers Community Coll., Poplar Bluff, Mo., 1968-70. Cert. patient account mgr. Bus. office mgr. Doctors Regional Med. Ctr., Poplar Bluff, Mo., 1976-82; bus. svcs. dir. Republic Health Corp., Dallas, 1982-87; pres. D-MED Corp., Dallas, 1987—; pres. D-MEDFin Svcs., 1991—. Author: (book) Hospital Business Office Policies & Procedures, 1990; contbr. articles to profl. pubs. Mem. Am. Guild of Patient Account Mgmt. (chpt. pres. 1979-81, page paten 1980-81), Healthcare Fin. Mgmt. Assn. (bd. dirs. Lone Star chpt.). Office: D-MED Corp. 17304 Preston Rd Ste 555 Dallas TX 75252-5617

MEEHAN, MARK WILLIAM, college executive assistant; b. East Stroudsburg, Pa., Mar. 19, 1967; s. William Thomas and Bernadine (Rudnik) M.; m. Leticia Rose Crawford, Mar. 18, 1989; children: Sarah Leticia, Lydia Gisele. BS in Bible, Columbia Bible Coll., 1994; MEd in Adminstrn., Columbia Internat. U., 1996. Ho. adminstr. Daybreak Crisis Pregnancy Ctr., Columbia, S.C., 1993-94; acad. program coord. Columbia Bible Coll., 1994-95, asst. to head acad. dean, 1995—; rsch. asst. to v.p. corp. planning Columbia Internat. U., 1994—. Sec. diaconate Faith Presbyn. Ch., Ballentine, S.C., 1995-96. Named Outstanding Hon. Faculty Mem., Internat. Inst. for Christian Educators, Columbia, 1995. Republican. Office: Columbia Bible Coll 7435 Monticello Rd Columbia SC 29230-3122

MEEK, CHARLES RONALD, II, human resources professional; b. Odessa, Tex., Sept. 7, 1967; s. Charles Ronald Meek and Jaunice Sharyll (Gray) Gonzales; children from previous marriage: Arika Mari, Ashely Nicole; m. Holly Lynn Willsher, Mar. 14, 1992; children: Charles Ronald III, Conner Reed. AAS, Grayson County Coll., Denison, Tex., 1988; AS, Grayson County Coll., 1993; BA, U. Tex., Dallas, 1994; MS, Tex. A&M U., 1996. Cert. profl. in human resources. Ops. rep. Libby Owens Ford/Automotive Glass Ops., Sherman, Tex., 1988-92; adminstrv. clk. II dept. biology U. Tex., Dallas, 1993-94; transp. fellow North Ctrl. Coun. Govts., Arlington, Tex., 1993-94; human resources mgmt. asst. I Tex. Dept. Transp., Dallas, 1994-95, human resources mgmt. asst. II, 1995—, human resources mgmt. officer II, 1996—; adj. instr. Tex. Dept. Transp., Austin, 1996—; mem. dist. safety com. Tex. Dept. Transp., Dallas, 1995—, vice-chair employees adv. com. Mem. Am. Soc. Pub. Adminstrn., Am. Soc. Tng. and Devel., Assn. Human Resource Sys. Profls., Soc. Human Resource Mgmt., Phi Theta Kappa. Home: Rt 1 Box 342 Bells TX 75414 Office: Tex Dept Transp PO Box 3067 Dallas TX 75221-3067

MEEK, MARY VIRGELIA CLEVELAND, special education administrator, psychologist; b. Frankfort, Ky., Sept. 16, 1937; d. James T. and Agnes (Redden) Cleveland; m. Willoughby F. Meek, Dec. 14, 1957; children: Elizabeth, J.B. AB, Transylvania U., Lexington, Ky., 1958; MA, U. Ark., 1969; EdS, Ga. State U., 1988. Cert. assoc. sch. psychologist Svc. 6, Ga. Coord. presch. Child and Adolescent Psychoednl. Ctr., Dalton, Ga., 1975-90, Whitfield County Schs., Dalton, 1990—; mem. com. Presch. Adv. Task Force, Ga. Dept. Edn., Atlanta, 1991; mem. adj. faculty West Ga. Coll., Carrollton, 1991; mem. continuing edn. faculty Dalton Coll., 1989—. Deacon 1st Presbyn. Ch., Dalton, 1986-89, mem. child care com., 1976—. Mem. Coun. for Exceptional Children, Nat. Assn. Sch. Psychologists, Ga. Assn. Sch. Psychologists, LWV, Lesche Women's Club (officer 1976-94). Office: Whitfield County Schs PO Box 2167 Dalton GA 30722-2167

MEEK, PAUL DERALD, oil and chemical company executive; b. McAllen, Tex., Aug. 15, 1930; s. William Van and Martha Mary (Sharp) M.; m. Betty Catherine Robertson, Apr. 18, 1954; children: Paula Marie Meek Burford, Kathy Diane Meek Hasemann, Carol Ann Meek Miller, Linda Rae Meek. B.S. in Chem. Engring, U. Tex., Austin, 1953. Mem. tech. dept. Humble Oil & Refining Co., Baytown, Tex., 1953-55; with Cosden Oil & Chem. Co., 1955-76, pres., 1968-76; dir. Fina, Inc. (formerly Am. Petrofina, Inc.), Dallas, 1968—, v.p. parent co., 1968-76, pres., chief operating officer, 1976-83, pres., chief exec. officer, 1983-86, chmn. bd., pres., chief exec. officer, 1984-86, chmn. bd., 1986—; apptd. by Gov. Wm. P. Clements, Jr. chmn. Pub. Uitilites Commn. of Tex., 1989-92. Contbg. author: Advances in Petroleum Chemistry and Refining, 1957. Chmn. chem. engring. vis. com. U. Tex., 1975-76; mem. adv. coun. Coll. Engring. Found., U. Tex., Austin, 1979—, U. Tex. Longhorn Found., 1989—, Coll. of NaturalScis. Found., 1989—; life mem.-at-large, bd. visitors McDonald Observatory dept. astonomy U. Tex.; co-chmn. indsl. divsn. United Way of Met. Dallas, 1981-82. Named Disting. Engring. Grad. U. Tex., Austin, 1969. Mem. Am. Petroleum Inst. (bd. dirs.), 25 Yr. Club of the Petroleum Industry, Founders Club of the Petrochem. Industry, Dallas Wildcat Com. (chmn. exec. com. 1987-88). Office: Fina Inc 8350 N Central Expwy PO Box 2159 Dallas TX 75221*

MEEKS, WILLIAM HERMAN, III, lawyer; b. Ft. Lauderdale, Fla., Dec. 30, 1939; s. Walter Herman, Jr. and Elise Walker (McGuire) M.; m. Patricia Ann Rayburn, July 30, 1965; 1 son, William Herman IV; m. 2d, Miriam Andrea Bedsole, Dec. 28, 1971; 1 dau., Julie Marie. A.B., Princeton U., 1961; LL.B., U. Fla., 1964; LL.M. (tax), NYU, 1965. Bar: Fla. 1964, U.S. Dist. Ct. (so. dist.) Fla. 1965, U.S. Tax Ct. 1966, U.S. Ct. Appeals (11th cir.) 1981, U.S. Supreme Ct. 1985. Ptnr. McCune, Hiaasen, Crum, Ferris & Gardner, Ft. Lauderdale, 1964-89, Fleming, O'Bryan & Fleming, Ft. Lauderdale, 1990-95; ptnr. Niles, Dobbins and Meeks, Ft. Lauderdale, 1995—; dir. Attys. Title Services, Inc., 1978-79, Attys. Title Services of Broward County, Inc., 1971—, chmn. 1976-77; mem. Attys. Real Estate Coun. Broward County. Mem. ABA, Fla. Bar Assn., Broward County Bar Assn., Attys. Title Ins. Fund, Ft. Lauderdale Hist. Soc., Ft. Lauderdale Mus., Phi Delta Phi. Democrat. Presbyterian. Clubs: Kiwanis, Lauderdale Yacht, Tower (Ft. Lauderdale). Office: Niles Dobbins and Meeks 4th Fl 2601 E Oakland Pk Blvd POB 11799 Fort Lauderdale FL 33339-1799

MEELHEIM, HELEN DIANE, nursing administrator; b. Charleston, W.Va., Mar. 25, 1952; d. Richard Young and Dolores (Frick) M. BS in Nursing, U. N.C., 1974; MS in Nursing, East Carolina U., 1982; JD, U. N.C., 1992. Bar N.C. 1995. Charge nurse Pitt County Health Dept., Greenville, N.C., 1974-77; nursing adminstr. East Carolina U. Sch. of Med., Greenville, N.C., 1978-89, clin. instr., 1986-92; cons. Eastern Area Health Edn. Ctr., Greenville and Fayetteville, 1989-92; staff emergency room U. N.C. Hosps., Chapel Hill, 1989-92; dir. fin. ops., human resources N.C. Bd. Med. Examiners, 1992—. Maj. Army Nurse Corps, USAR, Oper. Desert Storm/Shield, 1990-91. Mem. ANA (cert. family nurse practitioner, 1987—), Am. Acad. Nurse Practitioners, Nat. Health Lawyers Assn., N.C. Soc. Health Care Attys, Sigma Theta Tau. Episcopalian. Avocation: painting. Home: 4622 Pine Trace Dr Raleigh NC 27613-3316 Office: NC Bd Med Examiners PO Box 20007 Raleigh NC 27619

MEENAN, ALAN JOHN, clergyman, theological educator; b. Belfast, No. Ireland, Feb. 7, 1946; came to U.S., 1970; s. John and Elizabeth (Holland) M.; m. Vicky Lee Woodall, May 6, 1974; children: Kelly Elizabeth, Katie Michelle, Kimberly Brooke. BA, Queen's U., Belfast, 1970; MDiv, Asbury Theol. Sem., Wilmore, Ky., 1972, ThM, 1975; PhD, Edinburgh U., 1981. Ordained to ministry Presbyn. Ch., 1973. Pastor Wilmore Presbyn. Ch., 1972-74; asst. pastor St. Giles' Cathedral, Edinburgh, Scotland, 1974-77; head staff 3d Presbyn. Ch., Richmond, Va., 1977-84, Canoga Park (Calif.) Presbyn. Ch., 1984-89, First Presbyn. Ch., Amarillo, Tex., 1989—; vis. lectr. Nairobi (Kenya) Grad. Sch. Theology, 1983, 89. Contbr. revs. to religious publs., including Asbury Bible Commentary. Tchr. Chogoria High Sch., Meru, Keyna, 1965-66. Yale U. rsch. fellow, 1976-77. Mem. Tyndale Fellowship for Bibl. Rsch., Theta Phi. Office: First Presbyn Ch 1100 S Harrison St Amarillo TX 79101-4214

MEENAN, JAMES RONALD, trade association administrator, retired foreign service officer; b. Providence, Dec. 23, 1941; s. James Joseph and Angie May (Richmond) M.; m. Vera Helena Barretto de Carvalho Lima, May 3, 1968; children: Patrick Allen, John Edward. BBA, Woodbury Coll., 1962; grad., Legis. Inst., 1991. Cert. internal auditor. Acct. Jonathan Club, L.A., 1961-63; prodn. cost analyst USAF Auditor Gen., Santa Monica, Calif., 1963-65; supervisory acct., auditor USAID to Vietnam and Brazil,

Saigon and Rio de Janeiro, 1965-68; sr. budget analyst Strategic Sys. USN, Washington, 1968-69; supr. auditor USAID to Chile and Panama, Santiago, Panama City, 1969-74; program devel. mgr. USAID to Africa Bur., Sri Lanka, the Philippines and Asia-Near East-Europe Bur., Washington,, Columbo and Manila, 1974-90; legis. asst. for internat. trade and econ. devel. to Sen. Max Baucus U.S. Senate, Washington, 1990-93; v.p./advisor internat. markets GeoResearch, Inc., Vienna, Va., 1993—; apptd. to U.S. Industry Sector Advisory Com. for Trade Policy Matters and elected mem. U.S. Industry Functional Adv. Com. for Intellectual Property, 1994—; mem. governing bd. Internat. Sch., Manila, 1985-86. Mem. Fairfax (Va.) Hosp. Assn. Found., 1986—, Dem. Nat. Com., Washington, 1987—. Recipient svc. award, Vietnam. Mem. Am. Fgn. Svc. Assn. (treas. 1977-78, rep. Colombo, Sri Lanka 1979-83), World Affairs Coun. Washington, Soc. for Internat. Devel. (exec. bd. Sri Lanka chpt. 1980-83), Washington Export Coun., Coalition for Employment through Exports, L.A. C. of C., Sri Lanka Hill Club, Mantua Swim and Tennis Club, Elks, K.C. Roman Catholic. Home: 3317 Albion Ct Fairfax VA 22031-3001

MEEZAN, ELIAS, pharmacologist, educator; b. N.Y.C., Mar. 5, 1942; s. Maurice and Rachel (Epstein) M.; m. Elisabeth Gascard, May 14, 1967; children: David, Nathan, Joshua. BS in Chemistry, CCNY, 1962; PhD in Biochemistry, Duke U., 1966. Asst. prof. physiology and pharmacology Duke U., Durham, N.C., 1969-70; asst. prof. pharmacology U. Ariz., Tucson, 1970-75; assoc. prof. U. Ariz., 1975-79; prof., chmn. dept. pharmacology U. Ala., Birmingham, 1979-89, prof., dir. Metabolic Diseases Rsch. Lab., 1989-93, prof. dept. pharmacology, 1993—. Asso. editor: Life Sci, 1973-79. Helen Hay Whitney postdoctoral fellow, 1966-69; recipient NIH Research Career Devel. award, 1977-79. Mem. Am. Soc. Pharmacology and Exptl. Therapeutics, Am. Soc. Biol. Chemistry, AAUP, AAAS, N.Y. Acad. Sci., Assn. Med. Sch.Pharmacology. Democrat. Jewish. Home: 1202 Cheval Ln Birmingham AL 35216-2037 Office: U Ala Dept Pharmacology Birmingham AL 35294

MEGEE, GERALDINE HESS, social worker; b. Newark, Ohio, June 9, 1924; d. A.P. Hess and Ethel Stoyle Luther; children: John Megee, Sarah Martens, Thomas Megee. BS, Northwestern U., 1944; MSEd, Ind. U., 1976, MSW, 1978; PhD candidate, Fielding Inst. Cert. social worker, Ill., Fla.; cert. addictions profl., Fla., criminal justice specialist; diplomate social work. Dir. Foster Care Prog., Webster-Cantrel Hall, Decatur, Ill., 1978-81; owner, dir. Family Systems Ctr., Decatur, 1981—; pvt. practice clinic and employee assistance Decatur, 1981—; dir. Charter Counseling Ctr., Charter Glade Hosp., Naples, Fla., 1985-87; owner FamilyWorks, Naples, 1991—. Mem. NASW, Am. Assn. Marriage and Family Therapists, Am. Acad. Sexologists, Sigma Pi Lambda. Home: 9856 Tonya Ct Bonita Springs FL 33923 Office: 5051 Castello Dr Ste 205 Naples FL 34103-8985

MEGEHEE, JOSEPHINE ZELLER, library administrator; b. Jackson, Miss., Nov. 8, 1936; d. Raymond Bryant and Eleanor Louise (Gehrels) Z.; m. Louis Dan Megehee, June 6, 1957; children: Louis Dan III, Raymond Zeller. BA, U. Miss., 1958; MLS, U. So. Miss., 1981. Sch. libr. Piti (Guam) Elem. Sch., 1968-70; br. libr. W.A. Zeltner Libr., McNeill, Miss., 1978-80; dir. Pearl River County Libr. Sys., Picayune, Miss., 1980—. Registrar Picayune DAR, 1995-96, Pearl River Colonial Dames XVIII, Picayune, 1995-96, pres., 1990-93. Mem. ALA, Miss. Libr. Assn. (sec. 1988), Miss. Assn. Archivists, Nat. geneal. Soc., New Eng. Hist. geneal. Soc. Office: Pearl River County Library System 900 Goodyear Blvd Picayune MS 39466-3224

MEGEHEE, LOUIS DAN, meteorologist; b. Pascagoula, Miss., July 11, 1935; s. Louis Daniel and Mary Conerly (Williams) M.; m. Josephine Eleanor Zeller, June 6, 1957; children: Louis Dan III, Raymond Zeller. BS, Tulane U., 1957; MS, Naval Postgrad. Sch., 1959. Meteorol. watch officer Fleet Weather Ctrl. Kodiak, 1959-61; comm. officer USS Rockbridge, N.Y.C., 1961-63; meteorol. officer Comdr. Amphibious Group Two, N.Y.C., 1963-65; asst. ops. officer Fleet Numerical Weather Ctrl., Monterey, Calif., 1965-68; computer officer Fleet Weather Ctrl. Guam, 1968-70; meteorol. officer USS Franklin D. Roosevelt, 1970-72; officer-in-charge Naval Weather Svc. Detachment, Offutt AFB, Nebr., 1972-76; asst. comdr. Naval Oceanography Command, Stennis Space Ctr., Miss., 1976-81; sr. meteorol. data analyst Computer Scis. Corp., Stennis Space Ctr., 1987—. Exec. sec. United Way of South Pearl River County, Picayune, Miss., 1985-87. Comdr. USN, 1957-81. Mem. Am. Meteorol. Soc., U.S. Naval Inst. (life), Rotary (sec. 1980-87), Sigma Xi (assoc.). Methodist. Home: 217 E Lakeshore Dr Carriere MS 39426

MEGGS, WILLIAM JOEL, internist, emergency physician, educator; b. Newberry, S.C., May 30, 1942; s. Wallace Nat and Elizabeth (Pruitt) M.; m. Susan Nancy Spring, June 11, 1966; children: Jason Nathaniel, Benjamin Maffey, Thomas Clute. BS, Clemson U., 1964; PhD, Syracuse U., 1969; MD, U. Miami, 1979. Diplomate Am. Bd. Internal Medicine; diplomate Am. Bd. Allergy and Immunology; diplomate Am. Bd. Emergency Medicine. Resident in internal medicine Rochester (N.Y.) Gen. Hosp., 1979-82; staff fellow in allergy and clin. immunology Nat. Inst. Allergy and Infectious Diseases, Bethesda, Md., 1982-85; asst. dir. med. edn. emergency dept. Washington Hosp. Ctr., 1985-88; asst. prof. allergy, immunology E. Carolina U. Sch. of Medicine, Greenville, N.C., 1988-91, asst. prof. clin. toxicology dept. emergency medicine, 1991-95; assoc. prof. clin. toxicology E. Carolina U. Sch. Medicine, Greenville, 1995—; chmn., dir. emergency dept. Lenoir Meml. Hosp., Kinston, N.C., 1990-91; mem. Emergency Svcs. Com., Lenoir Meml. Hosp., Kinston, N.C., 1988-92; mem workshop on immune testing, Agy. for Toxic Substances and Diseases Registry, 1992, workshop on equity in environ. health, U.S. EPA, 1992, workshop on multiple chem. sensitivity syndrome, Nat. Rsch. Coun., 1991. Contbr. numerous articles and abstracts to profl. jours. Vol. physician Indigent Clinic E. Carolina U., Pitt County Med.Soc., 1988—, Pitt County Shelter, 1989—; advanced cardiac life support instr. , E. Carolina U. Sch. of Medicine, 1988—, advanced trauma life support instr., 1991—; mem. Pitt County Traffic Injury Prevention Program, 1989—; bd. dirs. Rachael Carson Coun., 1988—; adv. bd. Pamplico Tar River Found., 1990—. Named Woodrow Wilson Hon. Fellow, 1964, NSF post-doctoral fellow, 1969; grantee:N.C. United Way, 1988-89, Greer Labs., 1989-90, Am. Lung Assn. N.C., 1992-93. Fellow Am. Coll. Emergency Physicians; mem. AMA, Am. Acad. Allergy and Immuniology, The Clin. Immunology Soc., Am. Acad. Clin. Toxicology, Pitt County Med. Soc., N.C. State Med. Soc., Soc. for Acad. Emergency Medicine, N.C. Thoracic Soc. (physicians' sect.). Office: E Carolina U Sch Medicine Dept Emergency Medicin Greenville NC 27858

MEGHABGHAB, GEORGE VICTOR, computer scientist, educator; b. Ein Zehalta, Lebanon, July 8, 1957; came to U.S., 1984; s. Victor George and Souad Mary (Layoun) M. MS in Engring., Inst. Superieur d'Electronique, Lille, France, 1980; PhD in Computer Sci., U. Pierre et Marie Curie, Paris, 1983, Fla. State U., 1988. Asst. prof. U. Nantes, France, 1983-84, Valdosta (Ga.) State U., 1988-93; assoc. prof. Valdosta (Ga.) U., 1993—; researcher Fla. State U., Tallahassee, 1986-88, Electricite de France, Paris, 1980-83. Contbr. articles to profl. jours. Grantee Ctr. Nat. de Recherche Sci., Nantes, 1984. Mem. IEEE, Am. Soc. for Info. Sci. (officer 1990—), Am. Assn. for Artificial Intelligence, Assn. Computing Machinery. Roman Catholic. Home: 103 Sunnymead Dr Valdosta GA 31602-6411 Office: Valdosta State U Dept Math Computer Sci Valdosta GA 31698-0001

MEGILL, ALLAN D., historian, educator; b. Regina, Sask., Can., Apr. 20, 1947; came to U.S., 1980; s. Ralph Peter and Jean Tudhope (Dickson) M.; divorced; children: Jason Robert, Jessica Susan, Jonathan David; life ptnr. Rita Felski; 1 child, Maria Megill Felski. BA, U. Sask., 1969; MA, U. Toronto, 1970; PhD, Columbia U., 1975. From instr. to prof. history U. Iowa, Iowa City, 1974-90; prof. history U. Va., Charlottesville, 1990—; rsch. fellow in history of ideas Australian Nat. U., Canberra, ACT, 1977-79, temp. lectr. modern European studies, 1979. Author: Prophets of Extremity, 1985; editor: Rethinking Objectivity, 1994; co-editor: The Rhetoric of the Human Sciences, 1987; cons. editor Jour. of History of Ideas, 1986-89, mem. editl. bd., 1990—; mem. editl. bd. Social Epistemology, 1986—, Rethinking History, 1996—, U. Press of Va., 1991-94; contbr. articles to profl. jours. Chmn. Page-Barbour and Richard Lectures com. U. Va., 1994-96. Mem. Am. Hist. Assn. Office: University of Virginia Corcoran Dept of History Randall Hall # 221 Charlottesville VA 22903-3284

MEGSON, MARY NORFLEET, pediatrician, educator, medical facility administrator; b. Richmond, May 28, 1953; d. Marmaduke William and Mary (Crockett) Norfleet; m. Thmas Edward Megson, July 24, 1982; children: Thomas, H. Will, Julia, Peter. BA, Hollins Coll., 1975; MD, U. Va., 1978. Diplomate Am. Bd. Med. Specialists, Am. Bd. Pediats. Intern Tufts New Eng. Ctr., Boston, 1978-81, resident; ambulatory care fellow Boston Children's Hosp., 1981-82; pediatrician Winston-Salem, N.C., 1982-84; dir. child devel. Children's Hosp., Richmond, 1982—, developmental pediatrician, 1989-92; pediatrician Virginia Beach, Va., 1984-85, Richmond, 1985-87; asst. prof. pediats. Med. Coll. Va., Richmond; Bd. dirs. Meml. Child Guidance Clinic, Richmond, 1987—. Fellow Am. Acad. Pediats., Soc. Developmental Pediats. Presbyterian. Office: Children's Hosp 2924 Brook Rd Richmond VA 23220

MEHAFFEY, JOHN ALLEN, marketing, newspaper management and advertising executive; b. Brainerd, Minn.; m. Mary Jean Mehaffey; children: Mark, Scott, Chris. Student, Minn. Sch. Bus. With Communications Service Co., Inc., Naples, Fla., 1954—, pres., 1969—. Mem. Nat. Newspaper Assn., Newspaper Assn. Am., Ill. Press Assn., Assn. Fee Cmty. Papers, Ind. Free Pubs. Assn., Fla. Advt. Pubs. Assn., Am. Mktg. Assn., Inland Press Assn., Fla. Press Assn., Profl. Journalism Soc., Chgo. Headlinge, Internat. Platform Assn., Sigma Delta Chi. Home and Office: Jam Mktg Inc PO Box 2956 Naples FL 34106-2956

MEHAFFEY, ROBERT ANDERSON, company executive, sales consultant; b. Knoxville, Tenn., May 18, 1925; s. Robert Pleasant and Grace (Anderson) M.; m. Mary Stacy Collins, Sept. 2, 1949; children: Robert Anderson Jr., Stacy Ann. BS in Bus., Ind. U., 1947. Mgr. ea. region GE, Morristown, N.J., 1947-88; pres. Ramco, Inc., Memphis, 1989-96; mgr. bus. devel. Union Planters Bank, Germantown, 1996—. Lt. (j.g.) USNR, from 1943, mem. Res. ret. M. Mem. Sigma Alpha Epsilon (pres., bd. dirs. Memphis area alumni 1989—). Republican. Presbyterian. Home and Office: 9490 S Spring Hollow Ln Germantown TN 38139-5633

MEHENDALE, HARIHARA MAHADEVA, toxicologist, educator; b. Philya, India, Jan. 12, 1942; s. Shinginakodlu Mahadeva Bhat and Narmada M. (Tahmankar) M.; m. Rekha N. Joshi, May 10, 1968; children: Roopa, Neelesh. BSc, Karnataka U., Dharwar, India, 1963; MS in Entomology, N.C. State U., 1966, PhD in Physiology, 1969. Diplomate, Am. Bd. Toxicology (bd. dirs. 1986-90, sec. 1987-90), Acad. Toxicol. Scis. Postdoctoral fellow in toxicology U. Ky., Lexington, 1969-71; vis. fellow Nat. Inst. Environ. Health Sci., 1971-72, staff fellow, 1972-75; asst. prof. dept. pharmacology and toxicology, U. Miss. Med. Ctr., Jackson, 1975-78, assoc. prof., 1978-80, prof., 1980, dir. toxicology tng. program, 1982-92; named Prof. and Kitty DeGree endowed prof. and chair in toxicology Coll. Pharmacy and Health Scis. Northeast La. U., Monroe, 1992—; dir. La. Inst. Toxicology, 1995—; vis. prof. dept. forensic medicine, Karolinska Inst., Stockholm, 1983-84; adj. prof. Geriatric Edn. Ctr., 1986-91. Mem. editorial bds. Fundamental and Applied Toxicology, 1983-86, Jour. Toxicology and Environ. Health, 1986-93, Jour. Biochemical Toxicology, 1988-93, Toxicology and Applied Pharmacology, 1989—, Indian Jour. Environment and Toxicology, 1990-94. Overseas editor Indian Jour. Pharmacology, 1984-94, Toxicology, 1996—; editor-in-chief Internat. Jour. Toxicology, 1997—. Contbr. over 230 articles to profl. jours. Past pres. India Assn. Miss.; bd. dirs. Ctr. for Toxicology, J.J. Coll. Criminal Justice, N.Y.C. Recipient Sr. Fogarty Internat. fellowship, 1983; grantee NIH, EPA, Air Force Office of Scientific Rsch., Burroughs Wellcome Fund, Dept. Energy, Agy. for Toxic Substances and Diesease Registry, Miss. Lung Assn., Miss., Heart Assn. Fellow AAAS; mem. Am. Soc. Pharmacology and Exptl. Therapeutics (chmn. divsn. toxicology 1993-96), Am. Assn. for Study of Liver Disease, Soc. Toxicology (awards com. 1996—, Burroughs Wellcome Toxicology Scholar award, 1988-92, Zeneca Internat. Travel award 1993), Am. Chem. Soc., Am. Coll. Toxicology (coun. mem. 1996—, mem. editl. bd. 1995-96), Internat. Soc. Study Xenobiotics Am. (mem. publ. com. 1991—, chmn. 1994-96), Thoracic Soc., Am. Assn. Colls. of Pharmacy, Internat. Union Pharmacologists, South Central Soc. of Toxicology (v.p. 1986—, pres. 1987—), Assn. Scis. Indian Origin in Am. (founding pres. 1981, Disting. Svc. award 1990, Outstanding Scientist award 1992), Acad. Environ. Biology India (pres. 1990-93), Soc. Toxicology (India), Indian Pharm. Soc., Soc. Neuroscis. (India), Indian Sci. Congress Assn., Entomol. Soc. of India, Miss. Acad. Sci. (Outstanding Contbns. to Sci. award 1986), Miss. Heart Assn. (Ernest G. Spirey award 1988), Hindu Temple Soc. Miss. (life, sec. bd. trustees 1991-92, chmn. bd. trustees 1992-95), Sigma Xi (chpt. v.p. 1981-82, pres. 1982-83). Home: 1030 Inabnet Blvd Apt 203 Monroe LA 71203-7104 Office: Northeast La U Coll Pharmacy and Health Scis Monroe LA 71209

MEHTA, ASHOK VALLAVDAS, pediatric cardiologist; b. Bakor, India, Jan. 16, 1951; arrived in U.S., 1975; s. Vallavdas H. and Sushila V. (Doshi) M.; m. Pragna Sheth, Apr. 2, 1978; 1 child. B of Surgery, B of Medicine, Baroda (India) Med. Coll., 1974. Diplomate Am. Bd. Pediatrics, Am. Bd. Pediatric Cardiology. Intern dept. of pediatrics Baroda Med. Coll., 1975; resident dept. of pediatrics Misericordia-Lincoln-Fordham Hosp., Bronx, N.Y., 1976-78; postdoctoral fellowship divsn. of pediatric cardiology U. Miami Sch. Medicine, 1978-80, spl. rsch. fellowship in cardiac electrophysiology, 1980-81; asst. prof. pediatrics Temple U. Sch. of Medicine, Phila., 1981-86, St. Christopher's Hosp. for Children, Phila., 1981-86; chief divsn. of pediatric cardiology James H. Quillen COM, East Tenn. State U., Johnson City, 1986—, assoc. prof. pediatrics, 1986-93, prof. pediatrics, 1993; vis. prof. divsn. pediatric cardiology U. W.Va. Sch. Medicine, 1985; lectr. in field; dir. pediatric preceptor program, family practice resident, Kingsport, 1986-90; dir. pediatric CME program Holston Valley Hosp. Med. Ctr., Kingsport, 1987-91; dir. Tri-Cities Children's heart Ctr., Kingsport, 1986—; cons. pediatric cardiology Holston Valley Hosp. and Med. Ctr., Johnson City Hosp. and Med. Ctr., Bristol (Tenn.) Meml. Hosp., Indian Path Hosp., Kingsport, Crippled Children's Svc. State of Tenn., Sycamore Shoals Hosp., Elizabethton, Tenn.; dir. pediatric cardiac electro-physiology and pacing fellowship, assoc. pediatric cardiologist St. Christopher's Hosp. Children, Phila., 1981-86; cons. pediatric cardiology Med. Coll. Pa., Phila., 1981-86. Referee reviewer Pediatric Cardiology, Am. Jour. of Diseases of Children; contbr. numerous articles to profl. jours. Fellow Am. Coll. Cardiology, Am. Acad. Pediatrics; mem. AMA (Physician's recognition award 1979—), Am. Heart Assn. (Southeastern Pa. chpt. 1981-86, coun. cardiovascular disease in the young 1992—, bd. dirs. Greater Kingsport chpt. 1990-92, Washington County chpt. 1992—, Young Investigator award Pa. chpt. 1982-84), Cardiac Electrophysiology Soc., Pediatric Cardiac Electrophysiology Soc., S.E. Pediatric Cardiology Soc., Tenn. Pediatric Cardiology Assn., Tenn. Pediatric Soc. (Tenn. chpt. AAP). Republican. Hindu. Home: 1903 Roundtree Dr Johnson City TN 37604 Office: Tri Cities Childrens Heart Ctr 310 St of Franklin Rd Johnson City TN 37604

MEHTA, JAYANT B., internist, health facility administrator; b. Dakor, India, Apr. 6, 1945; married; 3 children. Degree, U. Baroda, India, 1963; MD, Govt. Med. Coll., Baroda, 1969. Diplomate Am. Bd. Internal Medicine, Am. Bd. Pulmonary Medicine. Resident medicine and ob-gyn. Jinja Govt. Hosp., Uganda, East Africa, 1970-71; rotating intern Meth. Hosp., Gary, Ind., 1972; resident in internal medicine VA Hosp., Northport, N.Y., 1973-74, chief resident in internal medicine, 1975-76, fellow divsn. pulmonary medicine, 1975-76; fellow tuberculosis and chest Nat. Jewish Hosp., Denver, 1976-77; med. dir. tuberculosis program First Tenn. Region, Tenn. Dept. of Health and Environ., 1977-87, med. cons., 1981-87; dir., cons. Pulmonary Function Lab., North Side Hosp., Johnson City, 1986—; med. dir. communicable diseases East Tenn. Regional Health Office, Johnson City, 1988-90; asst. dean community health East Tenn. State U., 1986-90, chief divsn. preventive medicine/epidemiology, 1986—; attending med. staff Johnson City (Tenn.) Med. Hosp., 1977—, sec.-treas., 1993—, ad hoc com. for enhancement of joint adv. com. functions, 1993—; cons. VA Med. Ctr., Mountain Home, Holston Valley Hosp.; program dir. pulmonary tchg. svc. Johnson City (Tenn.) Med. Ctr. Hosp., 1990—. Contbr. numerous articles to profl. jours. Med. examiner U.S. Dept. Justice, Immigration and Naturalization Svc. Grantee Pulmonary Rehab. Program from REACHS, 1983-85, Med. Svcs. and Tuberculosis Contract, 1982-86, Hypertension Screening Program, 1982-85, Tuberculosis Control grant, 1977-79; recipient Outstanding Svc. award Rural Health Consortium, 1988, Appreciation award Tenn. Dept. Pub. Health, 1984, Recognition of Svc. award Hypertension program, 1979-80. Office: East Tenn State U James Quillen Coll Medicine PO Box 70 622 Johnson City TN 37614-0622

MEIER, ENGE, preschool educator; b. N.Y.C., Jan. 17; d. Rudolf and Kate (Furstenow) Pietschyck; children: Kenneth Randolph, Philip Alan. BBA, Western States U., 1987, MBA, 1989. Tchr. nursery sch. Neu Ulm, Fed. Republic Germany, 1963-64; sec. Brewster (N.Y.) Mid. Sch., 1969-72; teaching asst. Brewster Elem. Sch., 1972-73; office asst. Bd. Coop. Edn., Yorktown Heights, N.Y., 1973-76; sec. Am. Can. Co., Greenwich, Conn., 1976-77, adminstrv. sec., 1977-79, exec. sec., 1979-84; adminstrv. asst. U. Tex., Austin, 1984-85, 88-90, adminstrv. assoc., 1985-86, sr. adminstrv. assoc., 1986-88; exec. asst. DTM Corp., Austin, 1990; funds asst. mgr. Tex. Assn. Sch. Bds., Austin, 1991-92; nursery sch. tchr. Westlake Presbyn. Sch., Austin, 1992-95; tchr. Grace Covenant Christian Sch., 1995—. Docent LBJ Libr. and Mus., Austin, 1984—; mem. Women's Polit. Caucus, 1988—; bd. dirs. Leadership, Edn. and Devel., 1991. Mem. Women in Mgmt., Bus. and Profl. Women (pres. 1989, bd. dirs. Austin chpt. 1987—), Women's C. of C. Presbyterian. Office: Westlake Hills Presbyn Presch 7127 Bee Caves Rd Austin TX 78746-4102

MEIER, GERRY HOLDEN, judge; b. Gainesville, Tex., Jan. 5, 1949; d. Louis Lee and Patsy Darlene (Sullivant) Holden; m. Todd Charles Meier, May 26, 1978; children: Brennan Holden, Mackenzie Alexandra. BS, Tex. Tech. U., 1972, JD, 1975. Bar: Tex. 1975. Asst. dist. atty. Dallas County, Dallas, 1975-81; criminal dist. judge State of Tex., Dallas, 1981—; mem. faculty New Judges Sch., State of Tex., 1985-90. Dir. Dallas Rep. Club, 1985. Fellow Tex. State Bar Assn. (past chmn. criminal justice sect.); mem. Dallas Bar Assn. Office: 291st Jud Dist Ct 133 N Industrial Blvd Dallas TX 75207-4399

MEIER, WILBUR LEROY, JR., industrial engineer, educator, former university chancellor; b. Elgin, Tex., Jan. 3, 1939; s. Wilbur Leroy and Ruby (Hall) M.; m. Judy Lee Longbotham, Aug. 30, 1958; children: Melynn, Marla, Melissa. BS, U. Tex., 1962, MS, 1964, PhD, 1967. Planning engr. Tex. Water Devel. Bd., Austin, 1962-66, cons., 1967-72; research engr. U. Tex., Austin, 1966; asst. prof. indsl. engring. Tex. A&M U., College Station, 1967-68; assoc prof. Tex. A&M U., 1968-70, prof., 1970-73, asst. head dept. indsl. engring., 1972-73; prof., chmn. dept. indsl. engring. Iowa State U., Ames, 1973-74; prof., head sch. of indsl. engring. Purdue U., West Lafayette, Ind., 1974-81; dean Coll. Engring., Pa. State U., University Park, 1981-87; chancellor U. Houston System, 1987-89; prof. indsl. engring. Pa. State U., University Park, 1989-91; dir. div. engring. infrastructure devel. NSF, Washington, 1989-91; dean Coll. Engring. N.C. State U., 1991-93, prof. indsl. engring., 1991—; mem. bd. visitors Air Force Inst. Technology; cons. Ohio Bd. Regents, 1990, U. Arizona, 1989, Indsl. Rsch. Inst., St. Louis, 1979, Environments for Tomorrow, Inc., Washington, 1970-81, Water Resources Engrs., Inc., Walnut Creek, Calif., 1969-70, Computer Graphics, Inc., Bryan, Tex., 1969-70, Kaiser Engrs., Oakland, Calif., 1971, Tracor, Inc., Austin, 1966-68, div. planning coordination Tex. Gov.'s Office, 1969, Office of Tech. Assessment, 1982-86, Southeast Ctr. for Elec. Engring. Edn., 1978—; mem. rev. team Naval Rsch. Adv. Com. Editor: Marcel Dekker Pub. Co., 1978—; Contbr. articles to profl. jours. Recipient Bliss medal Soc. Am. Mil. Engrs., 1986, Am. Spirit award USAF, 1984; named Outstanding Young Engr. of Yr. Tex. Soc. Profl. Engrs., 1966, Disting. Grad. Coll. Engring., U. Tex. at Austin, 1987; USPHS fellow, 1966. Fellow AAAS, Am. Soc. Engring. Edn. (chmn. indsl. engring. divsn. 1978-83), Inst. Indsl. Engrs. (dir. ops. rsch. div. 1975, pres. Ind. chpt. 1976, program chmn. 1973-75, editorial bd. Trans., publ. chmn., newsletter editor engring. economy div. 1972-73, v.p. region VIII 1977-79, exec. v.p. chpt. ops. 1981-83, pres. 1985-86), mem. Ops. Rsch. Soc. Am., Inst. Mgmt. Scis. (v.p. S.W. chpt. 1971-72), ASCE (sec.-treas. Austin br. 1965-66, chmn. rsch. com., tech. coun. water resources planning and mgmt. 1972-74), Am. Assn. Engring. Socs. (bd. govs. 1984-86), Nat. Assn. State Univ. and Land Grant Colls. (mem. engring. legis. task force 1983-87), Assn. Engring. Colls. Pa. (pres. 1985-86, treas. 1981-87), Air Force Assn. (advisor sci. and tech. com. 1984-87), Nat. Soc. Profl. Engrs., Profl. Engrs. in Edn. (vice chmn. N.E. region 1985-87, bd. govs. 1983-85), Sigma Xi, Tau Beta Pi, Alpha Pi Mu (asso. editor Cogwheel 1970-75, regional dir. 1976-77, exec. v.p. 1977-80, pres. 1980-82), Phi Kappa Phi, Chi Epsilon. Lodge: Rotary. Home: 7504 Grist Mill Rd Raleigh NC 27615-5411*

MEILMAN, PHILIP WARREN, psychologist, education educator; b. N.Y.C., Jan. 9, 1951; s. Sidney and Hilda (Cohen) M.; m. Alice Dixon Wheeler, May 17, 1980; children: Anna, Laura. BA, Harvard U., 1973; PhD, U. N.C., 1977. Lic. clin. psychologist, Va. Staff psychologist counseling ctr. Coll. William and Mary, Williamsburg, Va., 1977-80, dir. counseling ctr., 1990—; asst. prof. U. Nebr. Med. Ctr., Omaha, 1980-85; asst. dir. counseling ctr. Dartmouth Coll., Hanover, N.H., 1986-90; dir. counseling and psychol. svcs. Cornell U., Ithaca, N.Y., 1996—; com. mem. drug prevention program, survey instrument com. U.S. Dept. Edn., Washington, 1987—; co-dir. Core Inst. So. Ill. U., 1990—. Contbr. articles to profl. jours. Drug Abuse Prevention grantee U.S. Dept. Edn., 1987, 90-92, 94. Office: Cornell U Counseling and Psychol Svcs Gannett Health Ctr Ithaca NY 14853

MEINDL, JAMES DONALD, electrical engineering educator, administrator; b. Pitts., Apr. 20, 1933; s. Louis M. and Elizabeth F. (Steinhauser) M.; m. Frederica Ziegler, May 21, 1961; children: Peter James, Candace Ann. B.S., Carnegie Mellon U., 1955, M.S., 1956, Ph.D., 1958. Engr. Autonetics Co., Downey, Calif., 1957, Westinghouse Co., Pitts., 1958-59; head sect. microelectronics U.S. Army Electronics Command, Ft. Monmouth, N.J., 1959-62; chief br. semicondr. and microelectronics U.S. Army Electronics Command, 1962-65, dir. div. integrated electronics, 1965-67; assoc. prof. elec. engring. Stanford U., 1967-70, prof., 1970-84, John M. Fluke prof. elec. engring., 1984-86, assoc. dean research, 1984-86, dir. integrated circuits lab., 1969-84; co-founder Telesensory Systems Inc., 1971-84; dir. Electronics Labs., Stanford U., 1972-86, dir. Ctr. Integrated Systems, 1981-86; v.p. acad. affairs, provost Rensselaer Poly. Inst., Troy, N.Y., 1986-88, prof. sci. and engring., 1986-93, sr. v.p. acad. affairs, provost, 1988-93; Joseph M. Pettit Chair prof. microelectronics Ga. Inst. Tech., Atlanta, 1993—; cons. to govt., industry. Author: Micropower Circuits, 1969; editor: Brief Lessons in High Technology, 1989; patentee integrated cir. field; contbr. numerous articles to profl. publs. Served to 1st lt. AUS, 1959-61. Recipient Arthur S. Flemming Commn. award Washington Jr. C. of C., 1967; J.J. Ebers award IEEE Electron Devices Soc., 1980. Fellow IEEE (Solid State Circuits Coun. editor jour. 1966-71, Internat. Outstanding Paper ann. awards 1970, 75-78, Beatrice K. Winner award Internat. conf. 1988, solid State Circuits medal, 1989, Edn. medal 1990), AAAS, Am. Acad. Arts and Scis.; mem. AAUP, NAE, Am. Soc. Engr. Edn. (Benjamin Garver Lamme edal 1991), Electrochem. Soc., Biomed. Engring. Soc. (co-editor Annals of Biomed. Engring. 1976-80), Sigma Xi, Tau Beta Pi, Eta Kappa Nu, Phi Kappa Phi.

MEINDL, MAX J., III, environmental consultant, professional inspector; b. Buffalo, N.Y., June 21, 1951; s. Max John Jr. and Doris Elisabeth (Wessel) M.; m. Rachel Pratt, Apr. 23, 1983; 1 child, Elisabeth Bancroft Wessel Meindl. Student, U. St. Thomas, 1973-75, U. Houston, 1983-84, Tex. A & M U., 1989-91. Lic. profl. insp.; lic. asbestos cons.; lic. underground storage tank contractor. Prin. E. Daughter & Co., Houston, 1976-91, Texan Inspection & Environ. Svcs., Houston, 1980-89; program mgr. real estate svcs. TSP Inc., Houston, 1989-91; prin. MJM Cons., Houston, 1991—; catastrophe adjuster Crawford & Co., 1995—; cons. Resolution Trust Corp., Houston, 1991, Bridas Oil Co., Argentina; Compaq Computer Corp. facility engr.; coord. Spartan Internat. Project, 1993-95; project mgr., estimator Evans Am. Corp., Disaster Restoration; constrn. insp. Ft. Bend Ind. Sch. Dist., Tex., 1996—. Mem. disaster relief ARC, Houston; disaster insp. Fed. Emergency Mgmt. Agy.; tech. specialist Bechtel/Sonatrach Algerian Pipeline Project, Algeria, 1995; disaster restoration project mgr. Evans Am. Corp., 1996; constrn. insp. Ft. Bend (Tex.) Ind. Sch. Dist., 1996—. Mem. Nat. Assn. Environ. Profls., Am. Assn. Energy and Environ. Engrs., Nat. Asbestos Coun., Nat. Environ. Health Assn., Mensa. Office: MJM Cons PO Box 1464 Houston TX 77251-1464

MEINERS, ROGER EVERT, university administrator, researcher; b. Walla Walla, Wash., Dec. 28, 1948; s. Eugene Evert and Mary Jane (Ganguet) M.; m. Cary O'Keefe Brown, Nov. 28, 1981; children: Callie O'Keefe, William Evert, Alix Joseph, Mary Taylor. BA, Wash. State U., 1970; MA, U. Ariz., 1972; PhD, Va. Tech. U., 1977; JD, U. Miami, 1978. Asst. prof. Tex. A&M U., College Station, 1978-81; prof. Emory U., Atlanta, 1981-82, U. Miami, 1982-83; regional dir. FTC, Atlanta, 1983-85; prof. Clemson (S.C.) U., 1985-

93; prof. law/econs. and spl. asst. to pres. U. Tex., Arlington, 1993-95; Commr. S.C. Ins. Commn., Columbia, 1989-91; acad. advisor Polit. Economy Rsch. Ctr., 1992—; bd. dirs. Roe Found., Greenville, S.C., 1987—. Author of 11 books including: Taking the Environment Seriously, 1993 (with Bruce Yardle). Trustee Consumer Alert, Washington, 1990—. Home: 2615 Jane Ln Arlington TX 76017-5521

MEISINGER, HENRY PETER, electronics engineer; b. N.Y., Mar. 24, 1921; s. Henry Paul and Sophie (Denenberg) M.; m. Jeanne Alma Van Horn, June 1940 (dec. Aug. 1961); children: Shannon Peter, Daniel Claude, Mark Colin; m. Catherine C. Stephenson, Oct. 1962; 1 child, Mary Cover; m. Susan Barney Cushing, June 25, 1969. Registered profl. engr., D.C. Chief engr. U.S. Recording Co., Washington, 1940-41; engr. radio station WINX, Washington, 1940-42; engr. Recording Lab. Libr. Congress, Washington, 1941-42; engr. in charge Radio Sect. Dept. Interior, Washington, 1942-47; chief engr. U.S. Recording Co., Washington, 1947-54; dir. engr. Lab. Elec. Engring., Washington, 1954-58; pres. Versitron Inc., Washington, 1958-85; pres. elec. group Keene Corp., N.Y.C., 1982-85; cons. engr. Vienna, Va., 1985—; dir. NationsBank D.C., 1984-94; adv. Nat. Security Agy., Ft. Meade. Contbr articles to profl. jours. Pres. Cen. H.S. Alumni Assn., 1976-77. Capt. USMC, 1943-46, PTO, 1950-52, Korea. Fellow Audio Engring. Soc. (chmn. 1974-76); mem. Inst. Radio Engrs. (chmn. 1952-54, Disting. Svc. award 1962, sr.), Wash. Audio Soc. (pres. 1949-50), Ind. Telephone Pioneers (pres. 1973-74). Home and Office: 8618 Wolftrap Rd Vienna VA 22182-5025

MEISNER, JENNIFER LEE, secondary school educator; b. Metairie, La., Feb. 9, 1971; d. Ernest Frank II and Jacquelyn Ann (Lubrano) M. BA, La. State U., 1993. Bus. tchr. Archbishop Chapelle H.S., Metairie, 1994—. Mem. Am. Vocat. Assn., Nat. Bus. Edn. Assn., Sigma Alpha Agrl. Soc. (alumni, sec. 1992-93). Roman Catholic. Home: 649 Grove Ave Harahan LA 70123

MEITIN, DEBORAH DORSKY, health care executive; b. Cleve., July 25, 1951; d. Irving and Rosalind (Lewis) D.; m. Samuel R. Meitin, Dec. 6, 1987. BS, Mich. State U., 1973; M Health Adminstrn., Ohio State U., 1981. Cert. med. technologist. Med. technologist U. Hosps., Cleve., 1974-79; adminstrv. dir. surgery and anesthesiology Cleve. Met. Gen. Hosp., 1981-86; sr. cons. Ernst & Whinney, Chgo., 1986-87; sr. v.p. Diversified Health Search, Maitland, Fla., 1988-89; pres. Health Search Cons., Altamonte Springs, Fla., 1989-91; pres. Greater Fla. Devel. Co., Altamonte Springs, 1988—; sr. cons. Ernst & Young, Orlando, 1991-92, mgr., 1992-94; sys. analyst Fla. Hosp., Orlando, 1995—. Mem. bd. profl. women's group Jewish Fedn., Chgo., 1986-87; mem. coms. Jewish Cmty. Ctr., Chgo., 1986-87, Orlando, Fla., 1990—, v.p., 1991-94; bd. dirs. Michael Reese Hosp.-Jr. Med. Rsch. Coun., Chgo., 1986-87, Temple Israel, Orlando, 1989—. Fellow Am. Coll. Healthcare Execs.; mem. Ctrl. Fla. Healthcare Exec. Group (pres. 1995-96), Ohio State U. Grad. Program in Health Adminstrn. Alumni Assn. (bd. dirs. 1982-84), Phi Kappa Phi, Beta Beta Beta. Democrat. Home: 268 Buttercup Cir Altamonte Springs FL 32714-5844 Office: 601 E Rollins St Orlando FL 32803-1248

MEJIA, PAUL ROMAN, choreographer, dancer; b. Lima, Peru, Oct. 29, 1947; s. Pablo Enrique and Romana (Kryzanowska) M.; m. Suzanne Farrell, Feb. 21, 1969. Student, Sch. Am. Ballet, 1959. Dancer N.Y.C. Ballet, 1965-70; dancer Ballet of the XX Century, Belgium, 1970-75; guest dir. Stars of Am. Ballet, Ballet Guatemala, 1977-79; assoc. artistic dir., dancer, choreographer Chgo. City Ballet, 1981-87; dir., artistic dir. Ft. Worth Ballet, 1987—; dir. Cedar Islands Ballet Summer Camp, 1980—. Office: Ft Worth Ballet 6845 Green Oaks Rd Fort Worth TX 76116-1713*

MELAMED, RICHARD, lawyer; b. Houston, Dec. 22, 1952; s. Gerald Sylvan and Elaine (Rubenstein) M.; m. Ann Roosth, Sept. 17, 1978; children: Faith Elizabeth, Tina Cecile, Tanya Grace. BA, U. Tex., 1975; JD, S. Tex. U., 1978. Bar: Tex. 1978, U.S. Dist. Ct. (so. dist.) Tex. 1979, U.S. Ct. Claims 1981, U.S. Tax Ct. 1981, U.S. Ct. customs and Patent Appeals 1981, U.S. Ct. Appeals (5th cir.) 1981, U.S. Supreme Ct. 1981. Assoc. Evans & Birnberg, Houston, 1978-80; counsel Stewart Title Co., Houston, 1980-83; sole practice Houston, 1984-85; ptnr. Jacobus & Melamed, Houston, 1986-88, Jacobus and Melamed, Houston, 1986—; assoc. prof. Houston Community Coll., continuing edn. U. Houston. Mem. ATLA, ABA, Fed. Bar Assn., State Bar Tex. (broker-lawyer joint com.). Home: 5403 Queensloch Dr Houston TX 77096-4027 Office: Jacobus & Melamed Ste 450 Three Riverway Houston TX 77056

MELANÇON, TUCKER LEE, judge; b. 1946. BS, La. State U., 1968; JD, Tulane U., 1973. Atty. Knoll & Knoll, 1973-75; pvt. practice Marksville, La., 1975-83; prin. Melancon & Rabalais, Marksville, 1984-94; judge U.S. Dist. Ct. (we. dist.) La., Monroe, 1994—; Mem. adv. bd. Catalyst Old River Hydroelectric Partnership, Vidalia, La., 1989-92, La. Workers Compensation, 1990-91; mem. com. Study Backlog in Cts. of Appeal, 1st and 3d Cirs., 1991; bd. dirs. Catalyst Vidalia Corp., N.Y.C., 1993-94. Active La. Pub. Broadcasting. Mem. Am. Judicature Soc., Am. Inns of Ct., La. State Bar Assn., Bar Assn. 5th Fed. Cir., New Orleans Track Club. Office: US Dist Ct 705 Jefferson St Lafayette LA 70501*

MELCHER, ARCHIBALD LOUIS, III, neurologist; b. New Orleans, La., Sept. 17, 1962; s. Archibald Louis and Doris Mae (Hallberg) M.; m. Carolyn Jeanne Rodgers; children: Archibald IV, Andrew. MD, La. State Univ., 1988. Neurologist Metairie, La. Mem. Am. Acad. Neurology. Office: 4224 Houma Blvd Metairie LA 70006

MELGAR, JULIO, retired mechanical engineer; b. Bklyn., July 4, 1922; s. Lorenzo and Maria (Lopez) M.; BME, U. Detroit, 1952. Mech. engr. Chance Vought Aircraft, Dallas, 1952-53, Wyatt C. Hedrick Architects and Engrs., Dallas, 1953, Zumwalt & Vinther, Cons. Engrs., Dallas, 1953-54, Joe Hoppe, Inc., Dallas, 1954-55, A.J. Boynton & Co., Dallas, 1956-57, Wyatt Metal and Boiler Works, Dallas, 1958, Tinker AFB, Okla., 1958-60; mech. engr. FAA, Ft. Worth, 1960-85, ret., 1985. Mem. Metroplex Recreation Coun., 1975—; mem. Am. Mus. Natural History, Ft. Worth Opera Guild, Dallas Opera Guild, Goodwill Industries; bd. dirs. Ft. Worth Opera Assn., Humane Soc. North Tex., Common Cause Disabled Am. Vets., Animal Protection Inst. With USMCR, 1943-45. Mem. ASME, Nat. Soc. Profl. Engrs., Am. Soc. Heating, Refrigerating and Air Conditioning Engrs., Profl. Soc. Protective Design, Fed. Bus. Assn., Amateur Athletic Union. Roman Catholic. Home: 6108 Menger Ave Dallas TX 75227-6228

MELHUISH, KIRK THOMAS, meteorologist, journalist; b. Chgo., Mar. 13, 1962; s. Jack Leroy and Shirley Louise Ann (Rapp) M. BA, Valparaiso U., 1984; EMS Geosci., Miss. State U., 1992. Cert. meteorologist. Meteorologist WAKE-AM/WLJE-FM, Vaplaraiso, Ind., 1980-83; news, anchor/reporter, meteorologist WVUR-FM, Vaplaraiso, Ind., 1980-84, news dir., 1983-84; meterorolgist Vidette Messenger, Vaplaraiso, Ind., 1982-84; meteorologist WWJY-FM, Crown Point, Ind., 1983, WZVN-FM, Lowell, Ind., 1981-84, Torch Newspaper, Valparaiso, Ind., 1982-84; meteorologist, floor dir, camera-operator TV-4 News, Valparaiso, Ind., 1983-84; meterologist, producer, environ. reporter WILL-AM/FM/TV, Urbana, Ill., 1984-87; meteorologist, personality and sci. reporter NEWS/TALK Radio AM 750 WSB, Atlanta, 1987—; weather columns and cons. Gwinnett Daily News/N.Y. Times Co., Atlanta, 1991-93. Contbg. author: Pascal Al Algorithms: Introduction to Programming, 1988, History of Weather Casting, 1991, Travel Visitors Guide to Atlanta, 1994. Recipient NWA Spl. Coverage award for Hurricane Hugo, Green Eyeshade Excellence in Journalism award, NWA Meteorologist of Yr., Best Weathercaster in Atlanta, Atlanta Mag., Most Accurate Forecaster award Peachtree Mag., AP-Radio/TV Outstanding Spl. Coverage award, Best Newscast Ga.-AP, yearly 1987-93; profiled in History of TV Weathercasting. Mem. Am. Meteorological Soc., Nat. Weather Assn., Soc. Profl. Journalists, Sigma Delta Chi, Union Concerned Scientists, Nat. Assn. Weathercasters. Home: 4273 Glenlake Dr Kennesaw GA 30144-7106 Office: Sta WSB Radio 1601 W Peachtree St NE Atlanta GA 30309-2641

MELLISH, GORDON HARTLEY, economist, educator; b. Toronto, May 3, 1940; came to U.S., 1958; s. Gordon Day and Catherine (Hartley) M.; m. Nancy Bernice Newsll (div. Nov. 1972); m. Diane Evelyn Bostow, Jan. 1, 1978; children: Jennie Bostow, Luke Bostow. BA, Rockford (Ill.) Coll., 1962; PhD, U. Va., 1965. Econs. educator U. South Fla., Tampa, 1965-89; pvt. practice Tampa, Fla., 1966—; vis. prof. U. Va., 1969, Hillsborough Jr. Coll., 1968; vis. lectr. U. Tampa, 1965, 74. Contbr. articles to profl. jours. Mem. Tampa Club, Tampa Country Club, Leadership Tampa Alumni. Mem. Tampa Yacht and Country Club, Tampa Club, Leadership Tampa Alumni. Democrat. Home: 2510 W Shell Point Pl Tampa FL 33611-5033

MELLON, WILLIAM DANIEL, communications executive; b. Darby, Pa., June 22, 1951; s. William and Eleanor M.; m. Nikki Dersin, July 15, 1978; children: William D. III, Logan, Megan. BA in Broadcast Journalism, St. Louis U., 1972, MA in Pub. Rels. and Advt., 1974. Various positions, including regional dir. pub. rels. Boeing Comml. Airplane Co., Seattle, 1978-85; dir. corp. communications Beech Aircraft Corp., Wichita, 1985-87; dir. news and info. Rockwell Internat., Seal Beach, Calif., 1987-92, dir. pub. rels., 1992-94; dir. internat. comms. and pub. affairs Rockwell Internat., Arlington, Va., 1994—. Capt. USAF, 1973-78; Lt. Col. USAFR, 1978-95. Mem. Aerospace Industries Assn. (mem. comm. coun.), Pub. Rels. Soc. Am., Internat. Assn. Bus. Communicators, Internat. Pub. Rels. Dirs. Roundtable, Coun. Communication Mgmt., Nat. Investor Rels. Inst., Am. Mktg. Assn., Global Pub. Affairs Inst. (bd. dirs.), Electronic Industries Assn. (comm. coun.), Nat. Press Club, L.A. Press Club, Mfrs. Alliance (pub. affairs coun.). Office: Rockwell Internat Corp 1745 Jefferson Davis Hwy Arlington VA 22202-3402

MELLOR, GAIL MCGOWAN, author; b. Louisville, July 8, 1942; d. William Bringhurst and Virginia Williams (McGowan) M.; m. Jorge Alfredo Tarafa, Aug., 1963 (div. Nov. 1971); 1. child, Jorge Daniel; m. Steven Anthony Friend Weller, March 13, 1988; children: William Seth, Laura Linellen. BA cum laude, Newcomb Coll., New Orleans, 1964; postgrad., Tulane U., New Orleans, 1968; teaching degree, Manhattanville Coll., Purchase, N.Y., 1971. Coordinator Paedeia Exptl. Sch., Armonk, N.Y., 1971-73; adminstr., coordinator Lakewood Community Sch., Dallas, 1973-74; prof. English Postgrad. Sch. Edn., Toluca, Mexico, 1974-75; asst. planetarium dir. John Young Planetarium, Orlando, Fla., 1976-77; freelance med. journalist Orlando Sentinel Star and mags., 1978-79; sr. editor Louisville Today, 1980-81; contbg. editor Beaux Arts mag., Louisville, 1981-83; rsch. cons. Am. Coll. Emergency Physicians, 1985; med. writing cons. NKC Inc. and Louisville Hand Surgery, 1986-92; pres. Writer's Inc., Louisville, 1980-95; v.p. bd. dirs. Windsor Systems Inc., Louisville, 1980-95; chmn. bd. dirs. WM, Inc., 1985—; lectr. Bellarmine Coll.; pres. Earth Scis./Writer's Inc., 1996—; panelist radio, TV discussions, Internet confs. Author: The First Hundred Years, 1988, Kosair Children's Hosp., 1992; also articles in profl. jours. and newspapers. Mem. state com. Health Care Rationing, LWV, Ky., 1985, mem. health panels, 1992; area coord. Brown presdl. campaign, 1992; del. 1st Internat. Conf. on Women's Health, Beijing, 1993; co-host Peace Conf., WELL, 1994; website architect BRAD; active various other civic orgns. Recipient First Pl. award Greater Orlando Press Club, 1979, Presdl. Commendation Pres. of Mexico, 1973, awards Ad. Coun. Louisville, 1982, 84, Excellence in Writing award Ky. Hosp. Assn., 1989, Internat. award for Excellence Internat. Tech. Communicators Conf., 1990. Mem. AAAS, APHA, Soc. for Tech. Communicators (bd. dirs. local chpt., Disting. Tech. Comm. award 1990), Soc. Profl. Journalists, Am. Med. Writers Assn., Physicians for Nat. Health Program, Mensa.

MELLOR, JAMES ROBB, electronics executive; b. Detroit, May 3, 1930; s. Clifford and Gladys (Robb) M.; m. Suzanne Stykos, June 8, 1953; children: James Robb, Diane Elyse, Deborah Lynn. BS in Elec. Engring. and Math., U. Mich., 1952, MS, 1953. Mem. tech. staff Hughes Aircraft Co., Fullerton, Calif., 1955-58; pres. Data Systems divsn. Litton Industries, Van Nuys, Calif., after 1958; exec. v.p. Litton Industries, Inc., Beverly Hills, Calif.; pres., COO AM Internat., Inc., L.A., to 1981; exec. v.p., dir. Gen. Dynamics Corp., Falls Church, Va., 1981-90, pres., 1990—, COO, 1990-93, CEO, 1993-94, chmn., CEO, 1994—; bd. dirs. Bergen Brunswig Corp., Kerr, Computer Scis. Corp. Patentee in fields of storage tubes and display systems; contbr. articles to profl. publs. 1st lt., Signal Corps, AUS, 1953-55. Mem. IEEE, Am. Mgmt. Assn., Armed Forces Comm. and Electronics Assn. (bd. dirs.), Computer and Bus. Equipment Mfrs. Assn. (former chmn.), L.A. Country Club, Calif. Club, Eldorado Club, Congl. Country Club, Burning Tree Club, Sigma Xi, Tau Beta Pi, Eta Kappa Nu. Home: 7901 Sandalfoot Dr Potomac MD 20854-5449 Office: Gen Dynamics Corp 3190 Fairview Park Dr Falls Church VA 22042-4524

MELNICK, JOSEPH L., virologist, educator; b. Boston, Oct. 9, 1914; s. Samuel and Esther (Melny) M.; m. Matilda Benyesh, 1958; 1 child, Nancy. AB, Wesleyan U., 1936; PhD, Yale U., 1939; DSc, Wesleyan U., 1971; MD (hon.), Charles U., Prague, Czech Republic, 1993. Asst. in physiol. chemistry Sch. Medicine Yale U., New Haven, 1937-39; Asst. in physiol. chemistry, Finney-Howell Research Found. fellow, 1939-41, NRC fellow in med. scis., 1941-42, rsch. asst. in preventive medicine with rank of instr., 1942-44, asst. prof., 1944-48, rsch. assoc., 1948-49, assoc. prof. microbiology, 1949-54, prof. epidemiology, 1954-57; chief virus labs. divsn. biologics stds. NIH, USPHS, 1957-58; prof., chmn. virology and epidemiology Coll. Medicine Baylor U., Houston, 1958-68; Disting. Svc. prof. Coll. Medicine Baylor U., 1974—, dean grad. scis., 1968-91, dean emeritus, 1992—; mem. com. on viral diseases WHO, 1957—, mem. internat. task force on hepatitis B immunization, 1992—, dir. Internat. Ctr. Enteroviruses, 1963-93, mem. cons. group on poliomyelitis vaccine, 1973—, dir. Collaborating Ctr. for Virus Reference and Rsch., 1970—; mem. com. on live poliovirus vaccines USPHS, 1958-61; mem. virus reference bd. NIH, 1962-70, mem. dir. adv. com. on DNA recombinants, 1976, mem. evaluation com. divsn. rsch. resources, 1975-76, mem. nat. adv. cancer coun., 1965-69; mem. human cancer virus task force Nat. Cancer Inst., NIH, USPHS, 1962-67; sec.-gen. Internat. Congresses Virology, Helsinki and Budapest, 1968-71; chmn. Internat. Conf. on Viruses in Water, Mexico City, 1974; mem. rsch. coun. Am. Cancer Soc., 1971-75; mem. com. on hepatitis NAS/NRC, 1972-77; lectr., cons. Chinese Acad. Med. Scis., 1978, 79, 93; mem. adv. com. Comparative Virology Orgn., 1978-86; chmn. adv. com. on viral hepatitis Ctr. fo Disease Control, 1989, 95, mem. adv. com. on respiratory and enteric viruses, 1991, mem. adv. com. on evaluation of U.S. polio cases, 1963-75, 76-84; cons. devel. program for health manpower and svcs. of Palestinian people UN, 1981-83. Author: Textbook of Medical Microbiology; editor: Progress in Medical Virology and Monographs in Virology, also over 1000 rsch. papers in virology; editor-in-chief ofcl. jour. virology Intervirology, Internat. Union Microbiol. Socs., 1972-85. Bd. dirs. Houston Acad. Medicine-Tex. Med. Ctr. Libr., 1967-90, chmn., 1988-89; trustee Albert B. Sabin Vaccine Found., 1994—; chmn. U.S. Commn. on Polio Eradication, 1994—. Univ. scholar Yale U., 1939; co-recipient Internat. medal for rsch. in immunity to poliolyelitis Argentinian Found. Against Infantile Paralysis, 1949, Indsl. Rsch.-100 award, 1971, 74; recipient Humanitarian award Jewish Inst. Med. Rsch., 1964, Modern Medicine Disting. Achievement award, 1965, Eleanor Roosevelt Humanities award, 1965, Inventor of Yr. award Houston Patent Law Assn., 1972, Gold medal South African Poliomyelitis Rsch. Found., 1979, Maimonides award State of Israel, 1980, Raymond E. Baldwin medal for Disting. Svc., Wesleyan U., 1986; named to Nat. Found.'s Polio Hall of Fame, 1958. Fellow AAAS, APHA, N.Y. Acad. Scis. (Freedom Found. award for rsch. in virology 1973), Am. Acad. Microbiology; mem. Am. Soc. Microbiology, Am. Soc. Virology, Soc. Exptl. Biology and Medicine (mem. coun. 1965-69), Am. Assn. Immunologists, Am. Epidemiol. soc., Am. Assn. Cancer Rsch. (pres. S.W. sect. 1968), Internat. Assn. Microbiol. Socs. (life, chmn. sect. on virology 1970-75, mem. exec. com. 1976-79, mem. internat. commn. on microbiol. ecology 1972-87, mem. internat. com. on taxonomy of viruses 1966—, Albert Sabin medal for work in polio vaccines 1996), Microbiol. Soc. Israel (hon.), Microbiol. Soc. Argentina (hon.), USSR Soc. Microbiologists and Epidemiologists (hon.), Chinese Soc. Med. Virology (hon.), Med. Soc. Bulgaria (hon.), Phi Beta Kappa, Sigma Xi.

MELNYKOVYCH, ANDREW O., journalist; b. Mpls., Aug. 23, 1952; s. George and Oksana (Demianchuk) M.; m. Debra Denise Mamigonian, May 24, 1986; children: Alexander Vartan, Anna Emilia. BS in Biology, Yale U., 1975, M in Forest Sci., 1977; postgrad., U. Wyo., 1978-82. Lab. instr. dept. biochemistry U. Wyo., Laramie, 1982-83; corr. Casper (Wyo.) Star-Tribune, 1982-83, environ. writer, 1983-86, Washington reporter, 1986-90; environ. writer Louisville Courier-Jour., 1990—; contbg. writer High Country News, Paonia, Colo., 1987-90, The Post-Register, Idaho Falls, Idaho, 1989-90. Recipient George S. Polk award L.I. U., N.Y., 1989, 2d pl. Barnet Nover award Standing Com. of Corrs., Washington, 1989. Mem. Soc. Environ. Journalists. Office: Louisville Courier-Jour 525 W Broadway St Louisville KY 40202-2206*

MELOSI, MARTIN VICTOR, history educator, researcher, writer; b. San Jose, Calif., Apr. 27, 1947; s. Elmo Victor and Nancy Corinne (Rossi) M.; m. Carolyn Ann Ronchetto, June 19, 1971; children: Gina Michelle, Adria Marie. BA, U. Mont., 1969, MA, 1971; PhD, U. Tex., 1975. From instr. to prof. Tex. A&M U., College Station, 1975-84; prof. U. Houston, 1984—; pres. Pub. Works Hist. Soc., Chgo., 1988-89, Am. Soc. for Environ. History, 1993-95, Nat. Coun. Pub. History, 1992-93. Author: Pollution and Reform in American Cities, 1980, Garbage in the Cities, 1981, Coping With Abundance, 1985, Thomas A. Edison and the Modernization of America, 1990, Urban Public Policy, 1993. Mem. adv. bd. Houston Corp. Recycling Coun., 1994—; mem. Harris County Hist. Commn., 1987-88. Postdoctoral fellow Nat. Humanities Ctr., 1982-83, Rockefeller Found., 1976-77; rsch. grantee NEH, 1988-92; vis. scholar Smithsonian Instn., 1991. Mem. Hist. Rsch. Assocs. (bd. dirs. 1994—), Am. Hist. Assn., Orgn. of Am. Historians, Soc. for History of Tech., Urban History Assn. (bd. dirs. 1991-93). Office: U Houston Dept History Houston TX 77204-3785

MELTON, ELAINE WALLACE, small business owner; b. Rock Hill, S.C., June 14, 1948; d. David Dewitt Wallace and Myrtle Mae (Johnson) Threatt; m. John H. Melton, July 21, 1966 (div. 1979); children: John David, Rodney Dwayne. BS in Bus. Mgmt., Wingate Coll., 1987. Sec. Monroe (N.C.) City Schs., 1969-73; supr. Comar Mfg., Monroe, 1974-78; with Mut. Industries, Monroe, 1978—; owner, operator Melton's Acctg., Secretarial and Tax Svc., Monroe, 1978—. Walk coord. March of Dimes, Monroe, 1988—. Recipient Spl. Svcs. award March of Dimes, 1988—. Mem. Am. Inst. Profl. Bookkeepers, Federated Tax Svc., NAFE, Am. Soc. for Notary Pub., Monroe Bus. Assn. Home: PO Box 1272 Monroe NC 28111-1272

MELTON, G. KEMP, mayor; b. Charleston, W.Va., Nov. 19, 1929; m. Corena Mae Melton; 4 children. BS in Bus., W.Va. U. Sheriff, treas. Kanawha County, W.Va., 1965-68, 73-80, assessor, 1981-95; mayor City of Charleston, W.Va., 1995—. 1st lt. U.S. Army, 1953-55, Korea. Presbyterian. Office: Office of Mayor 1203 Hunters Ridge Rd Charleston WV 25314

MELTON, HOWELL WEBSTER, SR., federal judge; b. Atlanta, Dec. 15, 1923; s. Holmes and Alma (Combee) M.; m. Margaret Catherine Wolfe, Mar. 4, 1950; children—Howell Webster, Carol Anne. J.D., U. Fla., 1948. Bar: Fla. 1948. Mem. firm Upchurch, Melton & Upchurch, St. Augustine, 1948-61; judge 7th Jud. Circuit of Fla., St. Augustine, 1961-77, U.S. Dist. Ct. (mid. dist.) Fla., Jacksonville, 1977—; past chmn. Fla. Conf. Cir. Judges, 1974; past chmn. coun. bar pres.'s Fla. Bar. Trustee Flagler Coll., St. Augustine. Served with U.S. Army, 1943-46. Recipient Disting. Service award St. Augustine Jaycees, 1953. Mem. ABA, St. Johns County Bar Assn., Jacksonville Bar Assn., Fed. Bar Assn., Fla. Blue Key, Phi Delta Theta, Phi Delta Phi. Methodist (past chmn. bd. trustees). Clubs: Ponce de Leon Country (St. Augustine), Marsh Creek Country (St. Augustine Beach), St. Augustine Fla. Officer's. Lodges: Masons, Kiwanis (past pres.). Office: US Dist Ct PO Box 52957 Jacksonville FL 32201-2957

MELTON, JUDY PIEROTTI, university official; b. Atlanta, Nov. 26, 1945; d. Julius Vincent and Sara Frances (Harris) Pierotti; m. Martin LeCroy Melton III, May 30, 1968; 1 child, Rachel Victoria. BA, Ga. State U., 1968; JD, Tulane U., 1986, MBA, 1992. Bar: La. 1986. Adminstrv. asst. Emory U. Med. Sch., Atlanta, 1966-78; adminstrv. asst. Med. Sch., Tulane U., New Orleans, 1978-80, asst. dean for CLE, Law Sch., 1980—. Mem. Assn. for CLE (bd. dirs.-at-large 1992, sec.-treas. exec. com. 1992-94, pres.-elect, pres. 1994-96), Assn. Am. Law Schs. (exec. com. CLE sect. 1990). Office: Tulane U Law Sch Ste 300 8200 Hampson St New Orleans LA 70118

MELTON, MICHAEL ERIC, lawyer, engineer; b. Dallas, Sept. 14, 1958. BSEE, U. Mo., 1981, JD, 1984. Bar: Mo. 1984, Tex. 1992, U.S. Dist Ct. (ea. dist.) Mo. 1984, U.S. Ct. Appeals (fed. and 8th cirs.) 1984, U.S. Dist. Ct. (no. dist.) Tex. 1991, U.S. Patent and Trademark Office 1986. Patent advisor Office of Naval Rsch. U.S. Dept. Navy, Washington, 1984-86; assoc. Haverstock, Garrett and Roberts, St. Louis, 1986-87, Spensley, Horn, Jubas and Lubitz, Washington, 1987-88; license counsel Tex. Instruments, Inc., Dallas, 1988-92; European counsel Tex. Instruments, Inc., Nice, France, 1993-95; corp. sec. Texas Instruments Info. Engring. Internat., Inc., 1993-96; corp. patent counsel mgr. legis. affairs intellectual property, 1995-96; assoc. tech. counsel, chief patent counsel MCI Comms. Corp., Washington, 1996—; mem. U.S. Naval Rsch. Lab., EEOC, 1985-86; lectr. continuing legal edn. Mound City Bar Assn., St. Louis, 1986-87. Editl. assoc. Insight into Cts. newsletter, 1989-92, Jour. Cts., Health Sci. and the Law, 1989-92. Statewide officer Mo. Young Dems., 1986-87; vol. lectr. Mo. and Tex. Pub. Sch. Dists., 1986-96, others; bd. govs. Dallas Symphony Assn., 1991-94, mem. mktg. com., 1992, cmty. affairs com., 1992. Fellow Dallas Bar Found.; mem. ABA, Nat. Bar Assn., J.L. Turner Legal Assn. (v.p. 1991, bd. dirs. 1992, co-chair polit. action com. 1996), Dallas Bar Assn., Fed. Bar Assn., Nat. Soc. Black Engrs. (Region V adv. bd. 1991-92), Am. Inn of Ct., Coll. State Bar of Tex. Roman Catholic. Home: PO Box 33816 Washington DC 20033-0816 Office: MCI Comms Corp 1133 19th St NW Washington DC 20036

MELTON, NANCY KERLEY, medical/surgical and oncological nurse; b. Lamesa, Tex., Nov. 13, 1949; d. Ralph Burton Sr. and Edna Dale (Bearden) K.; 1 child, Stacey Dale Kent. LVN, Paris (Tex.) Jr. Coll., 1987, ADN, 1990. RN; ACLS. PRN McCuistion Regional Med. Ctr., Paris, 1996; team leader St. Joseph's Hosp., Paris, 1996—.

MELTON, TERRY RAYMOND, artist; b. Gooding, Idaho, Nov. 20, 1934; s. Omar D. and Loyce (Lue) M.; m. Glenda Smith, 1961 (div. Dec. 1974); children: Robert W., Susan N. BA, Idaho State U., 1959; MFA, U. Oreg., 1964. Dir. Yellowstone Art Ctr., Billings, Mont., 1964-67, C.M. Russell Mus., Gt. Falls, Mont., 1967-70; exec. dir. Oreg. Arts Commn., Salem, 1970-75; regional rep. Nat. Endowment for Arts, Seattle, 1975-84; exec. dir. Western States Art Fedn., Santa Fe, 1984-90, chmn. artist com. Santa Fe Inst. Fine Arts, 1986. One-man shows and group exhbns., 1959-82; contbr. poetry to various publs. Chmn. Capitol Planning Commn., Salem, 1973-75; bd. overseers Lewis and Clark Coll., Portland, Oreg., 1975-80; mem. adv. com. Santa Fe Mus. Fine Arts, 1987-88; vice chmn. Santa Fe Arts Commn., 1988--. Recipient Luther A. Richman award Mont. Arts Coun., 1970, Gov.'s Arts award Mont., 1991; Ina McLung scholar, 1963. Mem. Western Assn. Art Mus. (v.p. 1971-73, bd. dirs. 1971-78), Western States Arts Fedn. (bd. dirs. 1984--), Am. Assn. Mus. Home: 1100 Bluebird Ave Mcallen TX 78504-4121

MELTON, WAYNE CHARLES, real estate executive; b. Oak Ridge, Aug. 30, 1954; s. Charles Estel and Una Faye (Hull) M.; m. Carol Susan Carson, Mar. 21, 1975 (div.); 1 child, April Suzanne; m. Terri Marlene Deal, Oct. 2, 1983; 1 child, Bonnie Elizabeth. AB in European Intellectual History, U. Ga., 1975. Br. rep. Household Internat. Consumer Fin. Co., Athens, Ga., 1975-76; asst. mgr. Athens and Hickory, N.C., Doraville, Ga., 1976-77; pres., ceo Impact Realty-Melton & Assocs. Inc., Athens, 1987—; cons. Ga. Furniture, Charlotte (N.C.) Realty, 1987—. Trustee Mu, Inc., Page, Ga. Ho. of Reps., 1968; chmn. Madison County Reps., 1973-74. Mem. Zeta Beta Tau. Office: 855 Sunset Dr Bldg 5A Athens GA 30606-2285

MELTZER, MORTON, physician; b. N.Y.C., Oct. 5, 1939; s. Abraham Samuel and Fannie Ruth (Nydick) M.; m. Rosaly Marcia Gaynor, Jan. 8, 1967; children: Marcus Jacob, Neri Janis. BA, U. Mich., 1961; MD, N.Y. Med. Coll., 1965. Emergency physician, dir. emergency dept. Wake Med. Ctr., Raleigh, N.C., 1991-93, 95-96, chmn. dept. psychiatry, 1991-93; pres. Cameron (N.C.) Med. Assocs., 1974—; emergency physician Cape Fear Valley Med. Ctr., Fayetteville, N.C., 1978-80, dir. emergency dept., 1980-84; owner, ptnr. Cary Family Med. and Ambulatory Care Ctr., Cary, N.C., 1978-81; owner Dr.'s Urgent Care Ctr. Fayetteville P.A., 1981-85, med. dir., 1982-84, 92, 1995—; owner, pres. Cameron Family Practice P.A., 1985-90; batallion surgeon USAR, Raleigh, N.C., 1990-95; maj., brigade surgeon 13FA NC ARNG, Greensboro, 1996—; chmn. dept. psychiatry Wake Med. Ctr., Raleigh, 1996—; dir. med. svcs. N.C. Dept. Correction, Raleigh, 1970-72; consulting psychiatrist Wake County Mental Health, 1972—, dir. forensic program, 1990—; pres. Sondcrest Out Patient Svcs., P.A., Cameron, 1980-86. Fellow Am. Acad. Family Physicians; mem. AMA, APA, AAEP,

N.C. Med. Soc., Wake County Med. Soc., Cumb County Med. Soc., Kiwania Club. Home and Office: 448 Horse N Carriage Ln Cameron NC 28326-7848

MELVIN, MARGARET, nurse, consultant; b. Thomasville, Ga., July 13, 1927; d. Robert and Lorene Elizabeth (Barrett) M. BS in Nursing Edn., Duke U., 1953. Cert. Occupational Health Cons. Head nurse Duke U. Med. Ctr., Durham, N.C., 1947-54; charge nurse med. clinic U. Mich. Med. Ctr., Ann Arbor, 1955-59; occupational health nurse State Farm Ins. Co., Jacksonville, Fl., 1960-65; dir. ins. edn. Baptist Hosp. Med. Ctr., Jacksonville, 1965-68; various positions Wausau Ins. Co., Orlando, Fla., 1968-80; sr. cert. occupational health cons. Wausau Ins. Co., Orlando, 1980—; lectr. various hosps. and orgns. Developed, created nat. teaching program for back problems, 1976, program for emergency care industry, 1974. Am. Cancer Soc. grantee, 1968. Mem. ANA, Am. Assn. Occupational Health Nurses, Fla. State Assn. Occupational Health Nurses (chmn. 1982, conf. sec. 1980-84), Am. Bd Occupational Health Nurses. Republican. Home: 610 Cranes Way Apt 301 Altamonte Springs FL 32701-7781

MELVIN, R. DOUGLAS, professional sports team executive; b. Aug. 8, 1952; m. Ellen Melvin; children: Ashley, Cory. Pitcher Pittsburgh Pirates orgn., 1972-73; pitcher N.Y. Yankees orgn., 1975-78, coord. advance scouting reports, 1979-85, scouting dir., 1985-86; spl. asst. to club owner and gen. mgr. Baltimore Orioles, 1986-87, dir. player pers. minor league ops., 1987-88, asst. gen. mgr., 1988-94; v.p., gen. mgr. Texas Rangers, Arlington, 1994—. Office: Texas Rangers Baseball Club PO Box 90111 Arlington TX 76004-3111

MELVIN C., HIGH, protective services official. Police chief Norfolk, Va. Office: 100 Brook Ave Norfolk VA 23510

MENCHACA, ROBERT, elementary education educator; b. Del Rio, Tex., Jan. 24, 1952; s. Antonio and Alicia (Espinoza) M.; m. Estella Calzada; children: Roberto Jr., Antonio, Rosalva, Mariza, Daniel. BS in Edn., Sul Ross State U., 1973; MEd, East Tex. State U., 1980. Bilingual kindergarten tchr. San Felipe-Del Rio I.S.D., 1974-77, Dallas I.S.D., 1978-84, Seguin I.S.D., 1984-90; bilingual kindergarten tchr. North East I.S.D., 1990-92, tchr. 4th grade, 1992—; speaker, presenter in field. Author: Fue David, 1992, Una noche inolvidable, 1992, Daniel y el dia de la pesca, 1992, (with E. Menchaca) Daniel Goes Fishing, 1992. Nominated Tchr. of Yr. Tex. Assn. Bilingual Edn., 1992. Mem. Tex. State Reading Assn. (v.p.-elect Tex. coun. reading and bilingual child group, Tchr. Excellence award 1991), Internat. Reading Assn., Nat. Assn. Bilingual Edn., Tex. Assn. Bilingual Edn. (Bilingual Tchr. of Yr. award 1992), San Antonio Area Assn. Bilingual Edn. (recognized for teaching excellence 1992, Tchr. of Yr. award 1992), Alamo Reading Coun. (bd. dirs., co-chair San Antonio libr. found., treas. 1992-93, Tex. State Tchrs. Assn. Indiv. award for Human and Civil Rights 1995, Excellence in Teaching award 1991). Office: Olmos Elementary School 1103 Allena Dr San Antonio TX 78213-4107*

MENDEL, MAURICE, audiologist, educator; b. Colorado Springs, Colo., Oct. 6, 1942; married; 3 children. BA, U. Colo., 1965; MS, Washington U., 1967; PhD in Audiology, U. Wis., 1970. Asst. prof. audiology U. Iowa Hosp., 1970-74, assoc. rsch. scientist, 1975-76; assoc. prof. U. Calif., Santa Barbara, 1976-84, prof. audiology, 1984-88; chmn. dept. audiology and speech pathology Memphis State U., 1988-92; dean Sch. Audiology and Speech-Lang. Pathology U. Memphis, 1993—; program dir. speech and hearing sci. U. Calif., Santa Barbara, 1980-82. Fellow Am. Speech-Lang.-Hearing Assn., Soc. Ear Nose and Throat Advance in Children; mem. Am. Acad. Audiology, Internat. Elec. Response Audiology Study Group, Internat. Soc. Audiology, Tenn. Assn. Audiology and Speech-Lang. Pathologists, Sigma Xi. Office: U Memphis CRISCI 807 Jefferson Ave Memphis TN 38105-5042

MENDELL, JAY STANLEY, humanities educator; b. N.Y.C., Mar. 13, 1936; s. Emanuel and Lillian (Danenbaum) M.; m. Joan Wilma Brightman, Dec. 17, 1961; children: Risa Sue Mendell Silverman, Eden Sharon Mendell Thomas. BS, Rensselaer Polytech. Inst., Troy, N.Y., 1956; MA, Vanderbilt U., 1958; PhD, Rensselaer Polytech. Inst., 1964. Engr. Pratt & Whitney, East Hartford, Conn., 1963-73; assoc. prof. Fla. Internat. U., Miami, 1973-76; prof. Fla. Atlantic U., Boca Raton, 1976—. Editor: Non-extrapolative Forecasting in Business, 1985; mem. editl. bd. Public Voices, Newark, N.J., 1994-96, Futurist, Bethesda, 1968-96, Futures Quarterly, Bethesda, 1986-96. Jewish. Home: 11295 NW 38th St Coral Springs FL 33065 Office: Fla Atlantic U 220 SE 2nd Ave Fort Lauderdale FL 33301-1905

MENDELSOHN, LOUIS BENJAMIN, financial analyst; b. Providence, R.I., Mar. 26, 1948; s. Alvin Harold and Frances (Leitner) M.; m. Illyce Deborah Greenspan, Aug. 29, 1976; children: Lane Jeffrey, Ean Graham, Forrest Lee. BS, Carnegie Mellon U., 1969; MSW, SUNY, Buffalo, 1973; MBA with hons., Boston U., 1977. Rsch. asst. Mass. Gen. Hosp., Boston, 1969-71; regional health planner Comprehensive Health Planning Coun., Buffalo, 1973-74; adminstv. resident New Eng. Hosp., Boston, 1976; mgmt. specialist Humana Hosp. Bennett, Ft. Lauderdale, Fla., 1977-78; asst. exec. dir. Humana Women's Hosp., Tampa, Fla., 1978-80; pres. Mendelsohn Enterprises, Inc., Wesley Chapel, Fla., 1979—, Mendelsohn Trading Corp., Wesley Chapel, 1989—. Contbg. rschr.: The Encyclopedia of Technical Market Indicators, 1988; contbg. author: High Performance Futures Trading, 1990, Virtual Trading, 1995, Artificial Intelligence in the Capital Markets, 1995; editor newsletter Neural-Financial News, 1991; developer investment software ProfitTaker, 1980—, VantagePoint, 1988—. USPHS fellow, 1975-77. Mem. Market Technicians Assn., Beta Gamma Sigma. Office: Mendelsohn Enterprises Inc 25941 Apple Blossom Ln Wesley Chapel FL 33544-5108

MENDELSOHN, STUART, management consultant, environmental engineer, lawyer; b. Jersey City, Aug. 8, 1952; s. Norman and Florence (Dubin) M.; m. Laura Dick, May 30, 1987; children: Michelle Leigh, Sarah Anne. BS in Ocean Engring., Fla. Inst. Tech., 1974, MS in Environ. Engring., 1975; JD, George Mason U., 1984. Bar: Va. 1986, D.C. 1988, U.S. Bankruptcy Ct. (ea. dist.) Va. 1989. Project engr. Naval Facilities Engring. Command, Washington, 1975-80; project mgr. Analysis and Tech., Inc., Arlington, Va., 1980-81, mgmt. cons., 1981-83, dept. mgr., 1983-85, divsn. mgr., 1985-87, mgmt. cons., 1987-88; elected supr. Dranesville Dist. Fairfax County Bd. Suprs., 1996-99. Bd. mentor Spl. Olympics Internat. Va. Spl. Olympics, 1981-87; bd. dirs. Va. Spl. Olympics, 1981-87, v.p., 1982-84, pres., 1984-86, area coun., 1980-83, workshop leader, 1983-89; bd. dirs. Colonies Condominium Assn., 1979-81; founding bd. dirs. Hugs Are Better Than Drugs, Alexandria, 1986-89; mem. adv. com. on Gifted/Talented Students, 1989-90, Fairfax County 4-H Assn., 1989-90, Fairfax Com. 100, 1988—, v.p., 1990-92, pres., 1992-93; active Leadership Fairfax, Referenda, Citizens Adv. Task Force on Redistricting, 1991; mem. Fairfax County Rep. Com., 1991—; vice chair Fairfax County Sch. Bd., 1993-95; chair WJLA-TV Fairfax County Edn. Roundtable, 1992-93. Recipient Gold medal Va. Spl. Olympics, 1986, Spirit of Spl. Olympics award, 1987. Mem. ABA, Am. Mgmt. Assn., Va. State Bar, Fairfax Bar Assn., Internat. Platform Assn., Presdl. Classroom for Young Ams., Alumni Assn. (vol. 1976-80, bd. dirs. 1976-80, pres. 1976-77), Fairfax County C. of C. (chair edn. com. 1987-91, mem. supt. adv. com. on performance evaluation 1988-91, bd. dirs. 1991—, exec. com. 1992-95), No. Va. Pvt. Industry Coun. (v.p. 1991, chmn. 1992-93). Republican. Methodist. Lodge: Kiwanis (life, gov. dist. chair 1984-90, key club adminstr. 1985-87, lt. gov. 1983-84, gov.-elect 1990-91, gov. 1991-92, div. chair 1977-85, pres. 1980-81, Disting. Pres. 1982, George F. Hixon fellow 1986, from Capital Dist. Disting. Mem. 1987-90, Govs. award 1985, Key of Honor 1987, cert. trainer 1988, Kiwanian of Yr. 1988-89). Office: Mendelsohn & Ishee PC 10480 Armstrong St # A Fairfax VA 22030-3648

MENDEZ, ERWIN PETER, elementary and secondary education educator; b. N.Y.C., Mar. 9, 1956; s. Francisco I. and Arcelia (Torres) M. BA in Elem. Edn., Inter-Am. Univ., Ft. Buchanan, Puerto Rico, 1987. Cert. elem. tchr., Tex. Tchr. Colegia Muslet, Bayamon, Puerto Rico, 1987; tutor Eng. Colegia Tecnologie S.J., Huto Rey, Puerto Rico, 1988; bilingual tchr. Waukegan (Ill.) Pub. Schs., 1988-89; health sci. tchr. ESL Lurgren C.C., Lewiltown, Puerto Rico, 1989-90; owner, ednl. cons., tutor EPM Ednl. Cons. and Tchg. Svcs., Dallas, 1995—; chmn. grade level Mt. Auburn Elem., Dallas, 1993-95; tchr. Spanish, Cornerstoen Sch., Dallas, 1996—, Northbook Elem. Sch. Vol., tchr. Dallas Can Acad.-Tex. Can, 1991;. Recipient Mgr. of Yr. award Jr. Achievement, 1972; U.S. Achievement Acad. scholar, 1987. Mem. Toastmasters, Dallas Singles Toastmasters (competent toastmaster, 1995, Most Accomplished 1994). Home: 2124 Turnberry Dr Orviedo FL 32765

MENDEZ, JESUS, history educator, education administrator; b. Havana, Cuba, Oct. 3, 1951; came to U.S., 1960; s. Jesus Mendez and Maria (del Carmen) Gonzalez. BS, U. Miami, 1972, MA, 1974; PhD, U. Tex., 1980. Teaching asst. U. Tex., Austin, 1974-80; lectr. SUNY, Binghamton, 1981; asst. prof. history Barry U., Miami Shores, Fla., 1981-87, assoc. prof. history, 1987—, dept. chmn., 1989-93, asst. dean, 1993—; textbook cons. Glencoe Pub., Westerville, Ohio, 1991-92, 95-96. Contbr. articles to profl. jours. Bd. dirs. Dade Heritage Trust, Dade County, Miami, 1993-95, Fulbright Assn., Washington, 1995—. Recipient Travel Rsch. grant NEH, 1988, Rsch. grant Rockefeller Archive Ctr., 1984, Fulbright Rsch. grant USIA, 1983, Disserta- tion Rsch. grant Orgn. Am. States, 1977-78. Mem. Am. Hist. Assn., Am. Cath. Hist. Assn., Southeastern Coun. Latin Am. Studies, Fla. Hist. Assn., Nat. Collegiate Honors Coun., Fulbright Assn. (pres. south Fla. chpt.). Home: 720 Minorca Ave Coral Gables FL 33134-3759 Office: Barry Univ 11300 NE 2nd Ave Miami FL 33161-6628

MENDIOLA, ANNA MARIA G., mathematics educator; b. Laredo, Tex., Dec. 21, 1948; d. Alberto and Aurora (Benavides) Gonzalez; m. Alfonso Mendiola Jr., Aug. 11, 1973; children: Alfonso, Alberto. AA, Laredo C.C., Tex., 1967; BA, Tex. Woman's U., 1969, MS, 1974. Tchr. math. Laredo Ind. Sch. Dist., 1969-81; math instr. Laredo C.C., 1981—, organizer Jaime Escalante program, 1991-92; tech. prep. com. mem., 1991-92; ednl. coun., sec. Christen Mid. Campus, 1992-94; mem. site based campus com. Martin H.S., 1994—; vis. instr. St. Augustine Sch., Laredo, 1987-88; evaluator So. Assn., Corpus Christi, 1981, So. Assn. Colls. and Schs., United H.S., 1991; juror Higher Edn. Coord. Bd. Report, San Antonio, 1989; mem. quality improvement coun. Laredo C.C., 1993-94, mem. instrn. coun., 1995-96; participant SC3 Calculus Reform Inst., NSF, 1996. Producer slide promo, Mathematics at LCC, 1983. V.p., bd. dirs. Our Lady of Guadalupe Sch., Laredo, 1988-91; sec. Laredo C.C. Faculty Senate, 1986-87, v.p., 1995-96, pres., 1996—; active Boy Scouts Am., 1985-86. Recipient Teaching Excellence award NISOD, 1993. Mem. AAUW (pres. 1979-81, v.p. 1987-89, scholarship chair 1993-94, membership chair 1994—), Am. Math. Assn. Two-Yr. Colls., Math. Assn. Am., Tex. State Tchrs. Assn., Tex. C.C. Tchrs. Assn., Tex. Woman's U. Alumnae Assn., Blessed Sacrament Altar Soc., Tex. Assn. Ch. Higher Edn., Delta Kappa Gamma (membership chair 1993—). Democrat. Roman Catholic. Office: Laredo CC West End Washington St Laredo TX 78040

MENDOZA, JOANN AUDILET, nurse; b. Beaumont, Tex., Sept. 15, 1943; d. Jack Ernest and Ottie (Craig) Audilet; m. M.A. Mendoza, June 2, 1971; children: Danny Russell Myers, Shawna Laurene Rosco. BSN magna cum laude, Lamar U., Beaumont, 1989. RN, Tex.; CEN; cert. ACLS, advanced burn life support, BTLS instr.-coord., instr. truama nurses core course, PALS instr.-coord., emergency nurse pediatric course coord., ACLS course dir. Vocat. nurse Stat Care Inc., Beaumont; lic. vocat. nurse Jefferson County Jail Infirmary, Beaumont, Bapt. Hosp., Beaumont; emergency rm. charge nurse Columbia Beaumont Med. Ctr., Beaumont; Mem. Coun. Workplace Issues Dist. and State. Mem. ANA, Tex. Nurses Assn. (pres. Dist. 12), Lamar U. Student Nurse Assn. (sec.), Internat. Honor Soc. Nurses, Emergency Nurses Assn., Sigma Theta Tau (program com.), Phi Kappa Phi. Baptist. Home: RR 5 Box 23 Beaumont TX 77713-9673 Office: Beaumont Regional Med Ctr 3680 College St Beaumont TX 77701-4616

MENDOZA, MARILYN L., nurse practitioner; b. Batac Ilocos Norte, The Philippines, Nov. 11, 1956; d. Galo Francisco and Consuelo (Lactaoen) Luzod; m. Uldarico Jr. Mendoza, July 15, 1982; children: Easterlyn, Mary-Grace. BSN, Manila Central U., The Philippines, 1978; diploma in advanced nursing, Fla. Internat. U., 1988, M in Nursing, 1994. RN, Calif., Fla. Nurse Mariano Marcos Meml. Hosp., Batac, Ilocos Norte, Miami (Fla.) Gen. Hosp.; nurse surgical ICU Mt. Sinai Med. Ctr., Miami Beach, Fla.; nurse critical care unit Miami Heart Inst.; advanced nurse practitioner Jackson Meml. Hosp., Miami. Tanchoco. Meml. scholar. Mem. Fla. Nurses Assn., Manila Central U. Alumni (pres. class 1978).

MENDOZA, SHARON RUTH, customer service manager; b. Lake Charles, La., June 16, 1963; d. John Richard and Clara Joycelyn (Daigle) Ogea; m. Guadalupe Mendoza, Jul. 25, 1992; 1 child, Justin. BS in mktg., McNeese State U., 1984, MBA, 1988. Accounting instr. Massey Bus. Coll., Houston, 1989-90; acct. svcs. coord. Tabs Direct, Stafford, Tex., 1990-91, sr. acct. svcs. coord., 1991-93, acct. svcs. mgr., 1993—. Mem. Internat. Customer Svc. Assn., Am. Mktg. Assn., Houston Direct Mail Assn., Houston Advt. Fedn., Phi Chi Theta, Ft. Bend Zeta, Tau Alpha Alumni, Zeta Tau Alpha (sec. 1981-82). Home: 16803 Winnstream Ln Sugar Land TX 77478 Office: Tabs Direct 1002 Texas Pkwy Stafford TX 77477

MENEFEE, SAMUEL PYEATT, lawyer, anthropologist; b. Denver, June 8, 1950; s. George Hardiman and Martha Elizabeth (Pyeatt) M. BA in Anthropology and Scholar of Ho. summa cum laude, Yale U., 1972; diploma in Social Anthropology, Oxford (Eng.) U., 1973, BLitt, 1975; JD, Harvard U., 1981; LLM in Oceans, U. Va., 1982, SJD, 1993; MPhil in Internat. Rels., U. Cambridge, Eng., 1995. Bar: Ga. 1981, U.S. Ct. Appeals (11th cir.) 1982, Va. 1983, La. 1983, U.S. Ct. Mil. Appeals 1983, U.S. Ct. Internat. Trade 1983, U.S. Ct. Claims 1983, U.S. Ct. Appeals (10th cir.) 1983, (fed., 1st, 3d, 4th, 5th, 6th, 7th, 8th and 9th cirs.) 1984, D.C. 1985, Nebr. 1985, Fla. 1985, U.S. Supreme Ct. 1985, U.S. Ct. Appeals (D.C. cir.) 1986, Maine 1986, Pa. 1986. Assoc. Phelps, Dunbar, Marks, Claverie & Sims, New Orleans, 1983-85; of counsel Barham & Churchill PC, New Orleans, 1985-88; sr. assoc. Ctr. for Nat. Security Law U. Va. Sch. Law, 1985—; lectr. U. Cape Town, 1987; vis. asst. prof. U. Mo.-Kansas City, 1990; law clk. Hon. Pasco M. Bowman, U.S. Ct. Appeals (8th cir.), 1994-95; vis. prof. Regent U., 1996; lectr. various nat. and internat. orgns.; mem. ICC Consultive Task Force on Comml. Crime, 1996. Author: Wives for Sale: An Ethnographic Study of British Popular Divorce, 1981, Contemporary Piracy and International Law, 1995; co-editor: Materials on Ocean Law, 1982; contbr. numerous articles to profl. jours. Recipient Katharine Briggs prize Folklore Soc., 1992; Bates traveling fellow Yale U., 1971, Ctr. for Oceans Law and Policy fellow Law Sch. U. Va., 1982-83, sr. fellow, 1985-89, Maury fellow, 1989—, Cosmos fellow Sch. Scottish Studies U. Edinburgh, 1991-92, IMB fellow, ICC Internat. Maritime Bur., 1991—, Regional Piracy Ctr. fellow, Kuala Lumpur, 1993—; Rhodes scholar, 1972. Fellow Royal Anthrop. Inst., Am. Anthrop. Assn., Royal Asiatic Soc., Royal Soc. Antiquaries of Ireland, Soc. Antiquaries (Scotland), Royal Geog. Soc., Soc. Antiquaries; mem. ABA (vice-chmn. marine resources com. 1987-90, chmn. law of the sea com. subcom. naval warfare, maritime terrorism and piracy 1989—, mem. working group on terrorism), Southeastern Admiralty Law Inst. (com. mem.), Maritime Law Assn. (proctor, com. mem., chmn. subcom. law of the sea 1988-91, vice chmn. com. internat. law of the sea 1991— , chair working group piracy 1992—), Marine Tech. Soc. (co-chmn. marine security com. 1991-95, chmn. 1995—), Selden Soc., Am. Soc. Internat. Law Internat. Law Assn. (com. mem., rapporteur Am. br. com. EEZ 1988-90, rapporteur Am. br. com. Maritime Neutrality 1992, observer UN conv. on Law of the Sea meeting of States Parties 1996, chmn. Am. br. com. on Law of the Sea 1996), Am. Soc. Indsl. Security (com. mem.), U.S. Naval Inst., USN League, Folklore Soc., Royal Celtic Soc., Internat. Studies Assn., Royal Scottish Geog. Soc., Royal African Soc., Egypt Exploration Soc., Arctic Inst. N.Am., Internat. Studies Assn., Am. Hist. Soc., Internat. Assn. Rsch. on Peasant Diaries, Nat. Eagle Scout Assn., Raven Soc., Jefferson Soc., Fence Club, Mory's Assn., Elizabethan Club, Yale Polit. Union, Leander Club, Cambridge Union, United Oxford and Cambridge Univ. Club, Yale Club (N.Y.C.), Paul Morphy Chess Club, Pendennis Club, Round Table Club (New Orleans), Phi Beta Kappa, Omicron Delta Kappa. Republican. Episcopalian. Office: U Va Ctr Nat Sec Law 580 Massie Rd Charlottesville VA 22903-1789

MENEFEE-GREENE, LAURA S., psychiatric nurse; b. Owensboro, Ky., June 4, 1953; d. Robert Gordon and Maxine Opal (Wooten) Menefee; m. David H. Greene. BSN, Berea Coll., 1976; MSN, U. Tenn., 1986. RN, Ky., Tenn. Clinic nurse Mountain Maternal Health League, Berea, Ky., 1976-79; instr. Job Corps, Knoxville, Tenn., 1980-84; staff nurse Upjohn Health Care, Knoxville, 1980-86; leader, supr. hospice team St. Mary's Med. Ctr., Knoxville, 1990-92, gero-psychiat. clin. case mgr., 1992-93, clin. case mgr., 1993-94, adult psychiat. nurse, 1994-95, psychiat. case mgr., 1995—; cons. in field. Author: Hospice: History, Philosophy and Care Service, 1990; creator Life Cards. Instr., vol. ARC, Knoxville, 1980—. Mem. NAFE, APHA, Nat. Hospice Assn., Hospice Nurses Assn., Berea Coll. Alumni Country Dancers (pres. 1984-91), Sigma Theta Tau. Office: St Mary's Med Ctr Oak Hill Ave Knoxville TN 37917

MENG, QING CHENG, chemistry educator; b. Qiqihari, Peoples Republic of China, Nov. 1, 1947; came to the U.S., 1985; s. Xian Zhong and Huaiqing (Yin) M.; m. Bao Guang Zhao. BS in Polymer Chemistry, Nankai U., Tianjing, China, 1975; PhD in Analytical and Polymer Chemistry, Academia Sinica, Beijing, 1983. Rsch. assoc. Inst. Chemistry, Academia Sinica, 1975-85; vis. scholar U. Tenn., Knoxville, 1985-86; asst. prof. U. Ala., Birmingham, 1986—. Contbr. articles to profl. jours.; patentee in field. Recipient award Commendation of Sci. and Tech., China, 1979, Disting. Sci. Achievement award, Beijing, 1983, fellowship Coun. for High Blood Pressure Rsch., Am. Heart Assn., 1993; named Outstanding Vis. scholar U. Ala., 1993. Mem. Am. Chem. Soc. Home: 1611 9th Ave S Apt 8 Birmingham AL 35205-3616 Office: Univ Ala Birmingham 1011 Zeigler Rsch Bldg Birmingham AL 35294

MENNELL, MILES HORNER, professional association executive; b. Richmond, Va., Nov. 24, 1943; d. Lawson Clifton Jr. and Mary LaRue (Miles) Horner; m. Thomas Andrew Mennell, Feb. 24, 1968 (div. Aug. 1982); children: Mathes Horner, Mollie LaRue. BA in English, U. Colo., 1966; postgrad., U. N.D., 1968-70. Editorial asst. Am. Petroleum Inst., N.Y.C., 1966-67; rsch. assoc., editor publs. Project Head Start Yeshiva U., N.Y.C., 1967-68; grad. fellow U. N.D., Grand Forks, 1968-70; assoc. editor Outdoor People Newspapers Inc., Canonsburg, Pa., 1970-71; pub. rels. dir., cons. U. Pitts. (Pa.) Sch. Medicine, Divsn. Continuing Edn., 1971-76; coord. newspapers in edn. Bristol (Va.) Newspapers, Inc., 1983-84; dir. creative svcs. Quality Printers, Bristol, 1984-86; pub. rels. cons. Miles Mennell & Assocs., Bristol, Tenn., 1986—; dir. tourism and pub. info. Abingdon (Va.) Conv. and Visitors Bur., 1993-95; exec. dir. Assn. Tenn. Valley Govts., Nashville, 1995—. Vice pres. bd. dirs. S.W. Va. travel divsn. Va. Hospitality and Travel Industry Assn., 1994-95; charter mem., founding dir., bd. dirs. Hands On! Mus.; founding mem., bd. dirs. Bristol Main Street; past mem. bd. dirs. Theatre Bristol, Girls, Inc., Bristol Leadership Tomorrow, Bristol Arts Coun., Keep Bristol Beautiful; past mem. bd. trustees Sullins Acad. Recipient 1st place award for comm. program, nat. award of merit Keep Am. Beautiful, 1984, 85, gov.'s award of excellence Keep Va. Beautiful, 1985, achievement award for excellence and innovation in comm. Va. Mcpl. League, 1995. Mem. Pub. Rels. Soc. Am., Assn. Profl. Brochure Distbrs. (best brochure award 1993), Bristol C. of C. (bd. dirs., v.p. quality of life, Pres.'s award 1985), Bristol Morning Rotary Club (bd. dirs.). Episcopalian. Home: 42 Compton Rd Bristol TN 37620-2904 Office: Assn Tenn Valley Govts PO Box 24473 Nashville TN 37202-4473

MENO, LIONEL R., state agency administrator. Commr. edn. Tex. Edn Agy., Austin; dist. supt. Board of Corp. Education Services, Angola, NY. Office: Board of Corp Education Svcs 8685 Erie Rd Angola NY 14004

MENSCHER, BARNET GARY, steel company executive; b. Laurelton, N.Y., Sept. 5, 1940; s. Samuel and Louise (Zaimont) M.; student Centenary Coll., 1958-59; B.B.A., U. Tex., 1963; m. Diane Elaine Gachman, June 12, 1966; children—Melissa Denise, Corey Lane, Scott Jay. Vice pres. mktg. Ella Gant Mfg., Shreveport, La., 1964-66; warehouse mgr., dir. material control Gachman Steel Co., Fort Worth, 1966-68, gen. mgr., Houston, 1968-70, v.p., sales mgr. Gulf Coast, 1971-76; pres. Menko Steel Service, Inc., Houston, 1979—; v.p., treas. Gachman Metal Co.; investment cons. D & L Enterprises, 1966—. Mem. solicitation com. United Fund, 1969-76; mem. Nat. Alliance of Businessmen Jobs Program, 1969—. Served with AUS, 1963-65. Mem. Tex. Assn. Steel Importers, Purchasing Agts. Assn. Houston, Credit Assn. Houston, Am. Mgmt. Assn., Assn. Steel Distbrs., Nat. Assn. Elevator Contractors, Phi Sigma Delta, Alpha Phi Omega. Home: 314 Tealwood Dr Houston TX 77024-6113 Office: PO Box 40296 Houston TX 77240-0296

MENTER, M(ARTIN) ALAN, dermatologist; b. Doncaster, Eng., Oct. 30, 1941; came to U.S., 1975; s. Harry Menter and Esme (Green) Behr; m. Pamela Mary Williams, Dec. 4, 1966; children: Keith, Colin, Kerith. MB Bch, U. Witwatersrand, 1966; MMed in Dermatology, U. Pretoria, 1971. Diplomate Am. Bd. Dermatology. Intern dept. medicine then dept. surgery Johannesburg (Republic South Africa) Gen. Hosp., 1967, sr. intern medicine and dermatology, 1968; resident in dermatology U. Pretoria and Pretoria Gen. Hosp., 1968-71; sr. resident in dermatology Guy's Hosp., London, 1972; sr. resident, tutor in dermatology St. John's Hosp. for Disease of Skin, London, 1972-73; cons. dermatologist Pretoria Gen. Hosp., 1973-75; dermatologist Baylor U. Med. Ctr., Dallas, 1975—; chmn. div. dermatology Baylor U. Med. Ctr., 1992—; med. dir. Nat. Psoriasis Found. Tissue Bank, Dallas, 1993—; clin. prof. dermatology U. Tex. Southwestern Med. Sch., 1996—; fellow dept. dermatology U. Tex. Southwestern Med. Sch., Dallas, 1977-79, assoc. clin. prof. dermatology, 1977-95; med. dir. Psoriasis Ctr., Baylor U. Med. Ctr., Dallas, 1979—; clin. assoc. prof. dept. periodontics Baylor Coll. Dentistry, Dallas, 1985—; presenter local, state and nat. dermatol. orgns. and teaching programs. Editorial bd. Jour. Am. Acad. Dermatology, 1993—; contbr. numerous articles to profl. jours., chpts. to books. Coach Rugby football team U. Pretoria, 1974; represented S. Africa Nat. Rugby football team, 1968; coach, commr. Boys Under 12 Classic League Soccer, Dallas, 1978-82; active various local civic organizations and coms. Recipient Clin. Rsch. award Imperial Chem. Industries, 1972-73. Mem. AMA, Acad. Dermatology (com. on psoriasis 1988-93, chmn. 1990-93, com. on stds. care for psoriasis 1988-92, chmn. 1989-92, dir. Psoriasis Symposium 1990-93, bd. dirs. 1995—), Am. Acad. Dermatol. Surgery, Brit. Assn. Dermatology, Dallas County Med. Soc. (med. student rels. com. 1989-94), Dallas Dermatol. Soc. (sec.-treas. 1979, pres. 1980, rep. to adv. coun. Am. Acad. Dermatology 1987-89), Dermatol. Therapy Assn. (pres. 1985), Tex. Dermatol. Soc. (program coord. 1987-93, pres. 1995-96), Tex. Med. Assn. (subcom. on joint sponsorship 1992-95). Home: 5230 Royal Ln Dallas TX 75229 Office: Tex Dermatology Assocs Tullhill Office Park W 5310 Harvest Hill Ste 260 Dallas TX 75230

MENTZ, HENRY ALVAN, JR., federal judge; b. New Orleans, Nov. 10, 1920; s. Henry Alvan and Lulla (Bridewell) M.; m. Ann Lamantia, June 23, 1956; children—Ann, Carli, Hal, Frederick, George. B.A., Tulane U., 1941; J.D., La. State U., 1943. Bar: La. 1943, U.S. Dist. Ct. (ea. dist.) La. 1944. With legal dept. Shell Oil, New Orleans, 1947-48; pvt. practice Hammond, 1948-82; judge U.S. Dist. Ct. (ea. dist.) La., 1982—, sr. judge, 1992—. Editor: Combined Gospels, 1976. Pres. La. Soc. Music and Performing Arts, 1994—, L.A. Civil Service League, 1979-81; bd. dirs. Southeastern La. U. Found., Salvation Army; chmn. Tulane U. 50th Anniversary Reunion for 1991. Decorated 2 Battle Stars, Bronze Star; recipient Disting. Svc. award AMVETS, 1950. Mem. SAR, Royal Soc. St. George (pres.), Boston Club New Orleans, Delta Tau Delta. Republican. Episcopalian. Home: 2105 State St New Orleans LA 70118-6255 Office: US Dist Ct C-114 US Courthouse 500 Camp St New Orleans LA 70130-3313*

MENZIE, DONALD E., petroleum engineer, educator; b. DuBois, Pa., Apr. 4, 1922; s. James Freeman and Helga Josephine (Johnson) M.; m. Jane Cameron Redsecker, Nov. 6, 1946; children: Donald, William Lee, John Peter, Thomas Freeman. B.S in Petroleum and Natural Gas Engring., Pa. State U., 1942, M.S, 1948, Ph.D., 1962. Marine engr. Phila. Navy Yard, 1943-46; rsch. asst. air-gas dr. recovery Pa. State U., 1946-48, instr. petroleum and natural gas engring., 1948-51; asst. prof. petroleum engring. U. Okla., Norman, 1951-55, assoc. prof., 1955-64, prof., 1964-91, Kerr-McGee Centennial prof. Petroleum and Geol. Engring., 1991—, Halliburton Disting lectr., 1982-84; disting. lectr. Okla. U., 1986-87; dir. Sch. Petroleum and Geol. Engring U. Okla., Norman, 1963-72, petroleum engr. rsch. info. systems program, 1979-88, assoc. exec. dir. Energy Resources Ctr., 1988; assoc. exec. dir. Microbial Enhanced Oil Recovery Rsch. Project, Norman, 1982-; microbial enhanced oil recovery rsch. project U. Okla., 1982—; pres., owner Petroleum Engring. Educators, Norman, 1971—; cons. in field. Author: Reservoir Mechanics, 1954, Waterflooding for Engineers, 1968, Applied Reservoir Engineering for Geologists, 1971, New Recovery Techniques, 1975, Microbial Enhanced Oil Recovery, 1987, Dispersivity As An Oil Reservoir Rock Characteristic, 1989; contbr. articles to profl. jours. Mem. enhanced oil com. Interstate Oil and Gas Compact Commn., 1982-; commr., scoutmaster Last Frontier Coun. Boy Scouts Am., 1951-81; mem. adminstrv. bd. McFarlin United Meth. Ch., Norman, also sunday sch. tchr., pres. fellowship class, treas.; pres. Jackson PTA, Norman, 1962-68; treas. Cleveland County Rep. Com.; mem. Norman Park Commn., 1974-80; co-chmn., dir. Norman Parks Found., 1983-; mem. Cen. Com. U. Okla., 1987-. Mem. AIME, Am. Assn. Petroleum Geologists, Okla. Soc. Profl. Engrs., Nat. Soc. Profl. Engrs., Am. Soc. Engring. Edn., Soc. Petroleum Engrs., Am. Petroleum Inst., AAAS, Okla. Engring. and Tech. Guidance Coun., Okla. Anthropol. Soc., Soc. Petroleum Engrs. (recipient Nat. Disting. Achievement award for petroleum engring. faculty 1989), Sigma Xi, Pi Epsilon Tau, Alpha Chi Sigma, Phi Lamda Upsilon, Phi Kappa Phi. Clubs: Sportsmen of Cleve. County, Sooner Swim (dir. 1966-78). Lodge: Masons. Home: 1503 Melrose Dr Norman OK 73069-5366 Office: U Okla F314 The Energy Ctr Norman OK 73019

MERCADANTE, ANTHONY JOSEPH, special education educator; b. Newark, N.J., Mar. 10, 1951; s. Anthony Joseph Jr. and Anna Rose (Cocuzzo) M.; m. Barbara Ferrari, May 27, 1979; children: Anthony, Lisa, David. BS in Edn., Seton Hall U., 1973; MA in Audiology and Communication Sci., Kean Coll., 1978; cert. in adminstrn. and supervision, U. S. Fla., 1987. Cert. audiologist, adminstr./supr., tchr. bus. edn., tchr. hearing impaired. Acctg. clerk supply div. U.S. Steel Corp., Newark, 1973-75; acctg. and bookkeeping instr. Sch. Data Programming, Union, N.J., 1976-78; bus. adminstrn. instr., curriculum coord. Roberts-Walsh Bus. Sch., Union, 1978-83; clin. audiologist Ea. Speech, Lang. and Hearing Ctr., Woodbridge, N.J., 1980-83; ednl. audiologist exceptional student edn. dept. Polk County Pub. Schs., Bartow, Fla., 1983—; advisor Fla. Audiologists in Edn., Orlando, 1987—; mem. multidisciplinary team Polk County Pub. Schs., 1983—; mem. planning com. Project Healthy Start, Polk County Pub. Schs., Bartow, 1994—. Baseball coach S. Lakeland Babe Ruth Baseball League, Lakeland, Fla., 1993, baseball mgr., 1994. Mem. Am. Speech, Lang. and Hearing Assn., Nat. Youth Sports Coaches Assn., Fla. Speech, Lang. and Hearing Assn., Scott Lake Elem. PTA. Home: 6122 Donegal E Lakeland FL 33813-3713 Office: Polk Life and Learning Ctr 1310 S Floral Ave Bartow FL 33830-6309

MERCANDINO, SHARON ANN, small business owner; b. Connecticut, N.J., Oct. 28, 1963; d. Joseph and Margaret (Culligan) Yiachos; m. Allen R. Mercandino, May 10, 1986. BS, Adelphi U., 1984. Pres., owner Innovative Med. Data Mgmt., Highland Lakes, N.J., 1986-94, Merc's Mdse. Madness Wholesalers, Highland Lakes, N.J., 1991-94; co-pres., adminstr. Shar-Al, Inc. Constrn. & Devel., Highland Lakes, 1986-94; co-owner Sunset Dive Ctr, New Port Richey, Fla., 1996—. Office: 2525 Almond Dr Holiday FL 34691-3102

MERCER, WILLIAM EDWARD, II, chemical research technician; b. Neubrücke, Fed. Republic Germany, Dec. 28, 1956; (parents Am. citizens); s. William Edward and Julia (Didio) M.; m. Debra Lynn Mokry, Nov. 3, 1979; children: Crystal Nichole, Lacey Lynn, Dustin Edward. Student, Tex. A&M U., 1974-75, 76-77, Del Mar Coll., Corpus Christi, Tex., 1975-76, 78-79. Asst. mgr., then dist. supr. Kwik Pantry Food Stores, Bryan and Beaumont, Tex., 1977-78; frozen foods mgr. H.E.B. Food Stores, Rockport, Tex., 1978-79; rsch. aide Tex. div. Dow Chem. Co., Freeport, 1979-81, rsch. aide II Tex. div., 1981-83, sr. chem. asst. researcher, 1983-87, chem. technician, 1987-90, sr. chem. technician, 1990—; treas. Am. Chem. Soc. - Brazosport Technicians Group, 1996—. Contbr. articles to profl. jours.; author scientific paper; patentee in field. Pres. Clute Girls Softball Assn., 1993-94. Named Technician of Yr., Am. Chem. Soc.-Brazosport Technicians Group, 1994. Mem. South Brazoria County Bowling Assn. (bd. dirs. 1991-93, exec. dir. 1994-97, Dir. of Yr. 1992-93). Republican. Baptist. Home: 136 Cannon St Clute TX 77531-3612 Office: Dow Chem Co LJRC-212 Freeport TX 77541

MERCK, GERRY ELIZABETH, counselor; b. Rutherfordton, N.C., July 10, 1951; d. Charles Hedrick Stanley and Elizabeth Ann (Lovelace) Cash; 1 adopted child, Joshua Jordan Matheson. BS in Psychology, BS in Art, Western Carolina U., 1974; postgrad., U. N.C., Charlotte, 1990—. Dir. activities Rutherford County Convalescent Ctr., Rutherfordton, 1974-82, Meadowbrook Manor, Cherryville, N.C., 1982-85; coord. adult svcs. Child Abuse Prevention Svcs. Cleveland County, Shelby, N.C., 1985-89; therapeutic foster parent Lifegains, Inc., Morganton, N.C., 1982—; program cons. Cleveland Vocat. Industries, Lawndale, N.C., 1988—. Writer songs. Recipient gov.'s vol. award State of N.C., 1982. Mem. ACA, Assn. for Multicultural Counseling Devel., N.C. Counseling Assn., Am. Mensa, Psi Chi, Phi Kappa Phi, Chi Sigma Iota. Democrat. Presbyterian. Home: 108 Spiral Ln Shelby NC 28152-6244

MERDINGER, EMANUEL, retired chemistry educator; b. Suczawa, Austria, Mar. 29, 1906; came to U.S., 1947; s. Josef and Rosa (Stanger) M.; m. Raidie Poole, Mar. 23, 1953. M of Pharmacology and Pharmacy, German U., Prague, 1931; D of Pharmacy, Ferrara (Italy) State U., 1934, D of Chemistry, 1935, D of Natural Scis., 1939. Assoc. prof. Ferrara State U., 1936-38, 45-47; prof. Roosevelt U., Chgo., 1947-72; rsch. assoc. U. Chgo., 1954-56; Disting. Lectr. Loyola U. Med. Sch., Maywood, Ill., 1972-76; sr. chemist rsch. Chem. & Bacteriological Lab., Gainesville, Fla., 1976-77; researcher U.S. Agrl. Lab., Gainesville, 1977-82; disting. prof. Dept. Entomol. Biochem. and Lang. Dept. U. Fla., Gainesville, 1978-91, U. Fla., 1980—; NAS exch. scientist to Romania, Bulgaria and Germany, 1971, 74, personal amb. to Romania; pres. Ill. State Acad. Sci., 1972-73, hon. mem.; head biochemistry sect. Roosevelt U. Mem. Am. Chem. Soc. (emeritus), Soc. Med. Balkanique (hon.), Union de Socs. (hon.), Med. Rumania (hon.). Home: 4908 NW 16th Pl Gainesville FL 32605-3412

MEREDITH, DONALD LLOYD, librarian; b. Batesville, Miss., Sept. 11, 1941; s. Duward Lee and Julia Mae (Ferguson) M.; m. Evelyn Charlene Rickett, Aug. 15, 1964; Christopher Todd, Tracey Hope. BA, Harding U., 1964; MTh, Harding Grad. Sch., 1967; MS in Libr. Sci., U. N.C., 1968. Asst. libr. Harding Grad. Sch. Religion, Memphis, 1968-70, assoc. libr., 1970-83, libr., 1983—. Mem. Am. Theol. Libr. Assn., Tenn. Theol. Libr. Assn. (pres. 1981-82), Memphis Libr. Coun. (chmn. 1982-83, treas. 1994—). Home: 4897 Welchshire Ave Memphis TN 38117-5646 Office: Harding Grad Sch Libr 1000 Cherry Rd Memphis TN 38117-5424

MEREDITH, HOWARD LYNN, American Indian studies educator; b. Galveston, Tex., May 25, 1938; s. Howard and Lillian (Pitts) M.; m. Mary Ellen Meredith; m. Lynn, Lee. BS, U. Tex., 1961; MA, Stephen F. Austin State U., 1963; PhD, U. Okla., 1970. Asst. prof. history Ky. Wesleyan Coll., Owensboro, 1967-71; exec. Indian work Exec. Coun. Episcopal Ch., N.Y.C., 1971-75; dir., hist. pres. Okla. Hist. Soc., Oklahoma City, 1975-79; adminstr., editor Eco. Co., Ginn, C. Merrill & Bacone, Oklahoma City, 1979-85; assoc. prof. Am. Indian studies U. Sci. and Arts of Okla., Chickasha, 1985—. Author: Bartley Milam: Principal Chief, 1985, Hasinai, 1988 (award 1989), Modern American Indian Tribal Government, 1993-94, Dancing on Common Ground, 1995. Bd. mem., sec. Red Earth, Oklahoma City, 1988-94; bd. mem. Nat. Indian Hall of Fame, Anadarko, 1990—. Recipient Muriel Wright award Okla. Hist. Soc., Oklahoma City, 1980, Co-Founders Book award Westerners Internat., Tucson, 1989, McCasland award Okla. Heritage Assn., Oklahoma City, 1994. Episcopalian. Office: U Sci and Arts Okla Am Indian Studies Chickasha OK 73105

MEREDITH, KAREN ANN, accountant, financial executive; b. San Antonio, Sept. 30, 1954; d. Carroll J. and Doris J. (Calvin) Keller; m. William F. Meredith, July 6, 1974; children: Brian, Matthew. BBA in Acctg., U. North Tex., 1979. CPA, Tex.; CFP. Sr. acct. Deloitte Haskins & Sells, Dallas, 1979-82; CFO, sr. v.p. Commerce Savs. Assn., Dallas, 1982-86; exec. dir., chmn. bd. Am. Assn. Boomers, Irving, Tex., 1989-95; mng. ptnr. Meredith & Assocs., Irving, 1986—. Author various ednl. programs, 1991. Bd. dirs. Generations Found., N.Y.C., 1992. Recipient Fin. Edn. and Awareness award H.D. Vest Fin. Svcs., 1990. Mem. AICPA, Tex. Soc. CPAs (mem. Dallas chpt.), Internat. Assn. CFPs. Office: Meredith & Assocs 2621 W Airport Fwy Ste 101 Irving TX 75062-6069

MEREDITH, OWEN NICHOLS, public relations executive, genealogist; b. Etowah, Tenn., Mar. 27, 1924; s. Owen Habner and Ora (Nichols) M.; m. Mary Virginia Wright, July 19, 1980. BA, U. Va., 1946; MA, Syracuse U., 1952. Sub-features editor Together mag.-Meth. Pub. House, Nashville and Chgo., 1953-57; pub. info. dir. Nashville-Davidson County ARC, 1957-70; exec. dir. Tenn. State Mus., Nashville, 1970-72; owner, mgr. Gazetteer Typesetters, Nashville, 1973-74; pub. relations dir. Tenn. ARC, Nashville, 1974-89; pvt. practice Nashville, 1989—. Author: The Parish Activities Handbook, 1996, (with R. McBride) The Hedden Family of North Georgia, 1957, The Nichols Family of North Georgia, 1960, (with Lee Seitz) A History of the American Red Cross in Nashville, Tennessee, 1982; editor: (with McBride and M. Rothrock) Eastin Morris' 1834 Tennessee Gazetteer, 2d edit., 1971; contbr. articles, photographs and book revs. to hist. jours. Mem. ARC Disaster Res., 1989—; vol. archivist Diocese of Nashville, 1992—. Mem. Pub. Rels. Soc. Am. (cert.), Tenn. Soc. Health Care Pub. Rels., Internat. Assn. Bus. Communicators, Confederate Meml. Lit. Soc. (Tenn regent 1972-80), Tenn. Exec. Residence Preservation Found., 1983—), Conf. for Pastoral Planning and Coun. Devel. Office: 410 Lancaster Ave Nashville TN 37212-4013

MEREDITH, RUBY FRANCES, radiation oncologist, researcher, educator; b. Sedalia, Mo., Feb. 6, 1948; d. Russell R. and Eunice (Curry) M.; m. Michael Pfaff. BA, U. Mo., 1969; MA, Ind. U., 1971, PhD, 1974; MD, Ohio State U., 1983. Diplomate in therapeutic radiology Am. Bd. Radiology. Intern, resident Med. Coll. Va., 1983-87; assoc. scientist Allegheny-Singer Rsch. Corp., Pitts., 1978; asst. prof. U. Ala. Sch. Medicine, Birmingham, 1987-92, assoc. prof., 1992—; audio reviewer Ednl. Revs., Inc., Birmingham, 1992—. Mem. edn. com. Cancer Supporters, Birmingham, 1990; bd. dirs. Leukemia Soc. Am., Pitts., 1979. Recipient Harold C. Bold rsch. award Am. Inst. Biol. Scientists, 1974; HSF Health Rsch. award United Way/Health Svcs., Pitts. Office: U Ala Birmingham Dept Radiation Oncology 619 19th St S Birmingham AL 35233-1924

MEREDITH, THOMAS C., academic administrator. Vice chancellor exec. affairs U. Miss., until 1988; pres. Western Ky. U., Bowling Green, 1988—. Office: Western Ky U Office of President Bowling Green KY 42101

MERHIGE, ROBERT REYNOLD, JR., federal judge; b. N.Y.C., Feb. 5, 1919; s. Robert Reynold and Eleanor (Donovan) M.; m. Shirley Galleher, Apr. 24, 1957; children: Robert Reynold III, Mark Reynold. LLB, U. Richmond, 1942, LLD (hon.), 1976; LLM, U. Va., 1982; LLD (hon.), Washington and Lee U., 1990, Wake Forest U., 1994. Bar: Va. 1942. Ptnr. Bremner Merhige Montgomery & Baber, Richmond, 1945-67; judge U.S. Dist. Ct., Richmond, 1967—; guest lectr. trial tactics Law Sch. U. Va., Ewald disting. prof. law, 1987-88; adj. prof. Law Sch. U. Richmond, 1973-87; appeal agt. Henrico County Draft Bd., 1954-67; mem. NCAA spl. com. on discipline rules; profl.-in-residence, Zambia, Africa, 1994. Co-author: Virginia Jury Instructions. Mem. Richmond Citizens Assn. Served with USAAF, World War II. Decorated Air medal with four oak leaf clusters; recipient Amara Civic Club award, 1968, Spl. award City of Richmond, 1967; named Citizen of the Yr., 3d Dist. Omega Psi Phi, 1972, Citizen of the Yr., Richmond Urban League, 1977, Richmonder of Yr. Style mag., 1984, 87, Citizen of Yr., 1986; recipient Disting. Alumni award U. Richmond, 1979, Disting. Svc. award Nat. Alumni Coun., U. Richmond, 1979, Herbert T. Harley award Am. Judicature Soc., 1982, Athenian Citizen medal, 1979, Torch of Liberty award Anti-Defamation League of B'nai Brith, 1982, T.C. Williams Sch. of Law Disting. Svc. award, 1983, Pres.'s award Old Dominion Bar Assn., 1986, William J. Brennan award, 1986, Merit Citation award NCCJ, 1987, William B. Green award for professionalism U. Richmond, 1989, Marshall-Wythe medallion (William & Mary Faculty award), 1989. Fellow Va. Law Found.; mem. Va. Bar Assn., Richmond Bar Assn. (pres. 1963-64, multi-dist. litigation panel 1990—, Hill-Tucker award 1991), Am. Law Inst. (faculty), Va. Trial Lawyers Assn. (chmn. membership com. 1964-65, Disting. Svc. award 1977), Jud. Conf. U.S., John Marshall Inns of Ct. (founding mem.), Omicron Delta Kappa. Office: Lewis F Powell Jr Courthouse Bldg Ste 307 1000 E Main St Richmond VA 23219-3525

MERILH, MARIETTA PAULA, critical care nurse; b. New Orleans; d. Edmond Louis Sr. and Lillian Marie Jung (Stanton) M. BSN, U. Tenn., 1978, MA in Speech Pathology, 1988. Nurse CRU and cardiac care unit U. Tenn. Med. Ctr., Knoxville; nurse ICU, speech lang. pathologist St. Mary's Med. Ctr./Oak Ridge Speech Ctr., Knoxville and Oak Ridge, Tenn. Mem. AACN, Am. Speech-Lang.-Hearing Assn., Tenn. Speech & Hearing Assn., Phi Kappa Phi, Pi Delta Phi.

MERIN, ROBERT GILLESPIE, anesthesiology educator; b. Glens Falls, N.Y., June 16, 1933; s. Joseph Harold and Jessie Louisa (Gillespie) M.; m. Barbara R. Rothe, Mar. 1, 1958; children: Michael, Jan, Sarah. BA, Swarthmore Coll., 1954; MD, Cornell U., 1958. Diplomate Nat. Bd. Med. Examiners, Am. Bd. Anesthesiology. From asst. prof. to prof. anesthesiology U. Rochester (N.Y.) Med. Ctr., 1966-81; prof. anesthesiology U. Tex. Health Sci. Ctr., Houston, 1981-92; prof Anesthesiology Med. Coll. Ga., Augusta, 1992—; mem. anesthetic life support drug com. FDA, Washington, 1982-87, spl. cons., 1987—; Murray Mendolsohn Meml. lectr. U. Toronto Sch. Medicine, 1976, Harry M. Shields Meml. lectr., 1988; Litchfield lectr. Oxford U., 1977, William and Austin Friend Meml. vis. prof. Queens U., 1981, Joseph F. Artusio endowed lectr. Cornell U. Med. Coll., N.Y.C., 1991, and others. Editorial bd. Anesthesiology, 1977-86; contbr. articles to Anesthesiology, Jour. Pharmacology and Exptl. Therapeutics. Capt. U.S. Army, 1961-63. Recipient Rsch. Career Devel. award NIH, 1972-77. Mem. Assn. Univ. Anesthesiologists (pres. 1987-88), Am. Soc. Pharmacology and Exptl. Therapeutics. Office: Med Coll Ga Dept Anesthesiology 1120 15th St Augusta GA 30901-3157

MERITT, YVONNE EDELL, public health nurse; b. Enid, Okla., Apr. 28, 1954; d. Raymon Alfred and Jewell Frances (Lancaster/Turner) Haymaker; m. Kay Lee Meritt, Aug. 31, 1973; children: Kristen, Nickolas (dec.). Diploma, St. Anthony's Hosp., 1976; BSN, So. Nazarene U., 1994. Cert. cmty. health nurse, ANA. Staff nurse Bapt. Med. Ctr., Oklahoma City, 1976-78; supr. Bethany (Okla.) Gen. Hosp., 1978-85; staff nurse South Comty. Hosp., Oklahoma City, 1986-88, Mercy Med. Ctr., Oklahoma City, 1985-88; pub. health nurse Canadian County Health Dept., Yukon, Okla., 1988-94; dist. nursing supr. Okla. Dept. Health, Oklahoma City, 1994—; mem. adv. bd. Canadian Valley Vocat. Tech., El Reno, Okla., 1990, Okla. State U. Extension, El Reno, 1992. Mem. Nat. Assn. Pediat. Nurse Assocs. and Practitioners (cert. pediat. nurse), Okla. Nurses Assn. (nominating com. 1994), Okla. Grange (state sec. 1993—), St. Anthony's Sch. Nursing Alumni Assn. (treas. 1993-95, dir. 1995—). Roman Catholic. Home: Rt 1 Box 254-D Union City OK 73090 Office: Okla Dept Health PO Box 53551 1000 NE 10th St Oklahoma City OK 73152

MERIWETHER, WILLIAM CRAWFORD, personnel executive; b. Tampa, Fla., Dec. 12, 1944; s. William G. and Topsy (Huggins) M.; m. Sigrid Lee Tapperson, June 11, 1966; children: William G., Bonnie Lee, Nicholas. Student, Andrew Jr. Coll., cuthbert, Ga., 1963-65, LaGrange (Ga.) Coll., 1965-66, U. Fla., Hillsborough C.C., U. Colo., Erwin Vocat. Sch. From teller to auditor First Nat. Bank, Plant City, Fla., 1966-81; br. mgr. People's Bank of Hillsborough County, Plant City, 1981-84; dir. ctrl. govt. depository Clk. of Cir. Ct., Tampa, Fla., 1985-88; pers. adminstr. Hillsborough County Property Appraiser, Tampa, 1989—. Commr. Hillsborough County Planning Commn., 1993—; bd. dirs. Hist. Soc., 1995—; mem. Teddy Roosevelt's 1st U.S. Vol. Cavalry Rough Riders; mayor pro-tem/commr. City Commn. City of Plant City, 1978-93; dir. congl. dist. 9 Fla. League of Cities; pres.-elect Suncoast League of Cities, 1993; mem. Tampa Bay Region Planning Coun., Met. Planning Commn., mem. statewide adv. com., vice chmn.; mem. Hillsborough County Planning Commn., 1978; mem. industry adv. com. Erwin tech.; bd. dirs. DACCO, 1978-84; past dir. Bank adminstrv. Inst., Plant City Mental Health Bd.; mem. Criminal Justice Bd., State of Fla., 1978-84; mem. fin., adminstrn. and intergovtl. rels. coms. Nat. League Cities, also small cities com.; mem. East Hillsborough County Law Enforcement Appreciation Com.; mem. Hillsborough County Sheriff's Aux., 1968-84; mem. parade com. Fla. Strawberry festival, 1976, 77; past treas. East Hillsborough County United Fund, numerous others. Recipient Outstanding Young Man award Plant City Jaycees, 1977, Good Govt. award, 1980. Mem. Internat. Pers. Mgrs. Assn., Fla. Pub. Pers. Assn., Soc. Human Resource Mgmt., Greater C. of C. (beautification com., transp. com., Pride in Plant City com.), Kiwanis (past pres. Noon Club), Rotary (Daybreak chpt.). Methodist. Office: Hillsborough County Property Appraiser 16th Fl County Ctr 601 E Kennedy Blvd Tampa FL 33602-4932

MERKEL, CHARLES MICHAEL, lawyer; b. Nashville, Nov. 2, 1941; s. Charles M. and Lila K. Merkel; m. Donna White, Jan. 7, 1967; children: Kimberly Dale, Charles M. III. BA, U. Miss., 1964, JD, 1966; LLM in Taxation, Georgetown U., 1969. Bar: Miss. 1966. Trial atty. U.S. Dept. Justice, Washington, 1966-70; ptnr. Dunbar & Merkel, Clarksdale, Miss., 1970-73, Holcomb Dunbar Connell & Merkel, Clarksdale, 1973-82, Merkel & Cocke, Clarksdale, 1982—; pres. Miss. chpt. Am. Bd. Trial Advs., 1989. Bd. dirs. Lula Rich Edn. Found., Clarksdale, 1983-89. Carrier scholar U. Miss. 1959-63. Fellow Miss. State Bar Found.; mem. ATLA, Am. Bd. Trial Advocates, Am. Coll. Trial Lawyers, Miss. Trial Lawyers Assn. (sec. 1985-87). Episcopalian. Home: 101 Cypress Ave Clarksdale MS 38614-2603 Office: PO Box 1388 30 Delta Ave Clarksdale MS 38614-2718

MERKIN, DONALD H., internist; b. Bronx, N.Y., Nov. 12, 1945; s. Eugene and Hortense Ruth (Erdrich) M.; m. Carol Ann Williams, July 22, 1967; children: Daniel Hansen, Andrew David. BA, Parsons Coll., 1968; MS, Colo. State U., 1972; PhD, Cornell U., 1974; MD, U. Autonoma de Ciudad, Juarez, Mexico, 1978. Asst. prof. U. So. Colo., Pueblo, 1973-74, Bethel Sch. of Nursing, Colorado Springs, 1973-74, U. Colo., Colorado Springs, 1973-74, So. Ill. U. Sch. Medicine, Springfield, Ill., 1975-76; internist Westside Med. Assocs., Bradenton, Fla., 1982-84, pvt. practice, Sarasota, Fla., 1984-88, Superior (Wis.) Clinic, Ltd., 1989-91; internist Gulf Coast Ortho. Ctr.- Inst. for Spl. Surgery, Hudson, Fla., 1991-94, dir. orthopedic medicine, 1992-94; pvt. practice Internal Medicine Assocs. of Pasco County, Hudson, Fla., 1995—; dir. Orthopedic Medicine Clinic, 1992-94. Author: Pregnancy as a Disease, 1976. Officer candidate USMC, 1969. Nat. Inst. Child Health and Human Devel. fellow Cornell U., 1970-73; Fulbright fellow Nat. Assn. Colls. for Tchr. Edn., India, 1974. Mem. AMA, Fla. Med. Soc., Pasco County Med. Soc., Am. Soc. Internal Medicine, Fla. Soc. Internal Medicine. Lutheran. Office: Internal Medicine Assocs Pasco County 13906 Lakeshore Blvd Ste 330 Hudson FL 34667-1481

MERMELSTEIN, ISABEL MAE ROSENBERG, financial consultant; b. Houston, Aug. 20, 1934; d. Joe Hyman and Sylvia (Lincove) Rosenberg; m. Robert Jay Mermelstein, Sept. 6, 1953 (div. July 1975); children: William, Linda, Jody. Student U. Ariz., 1952, Mich. State U., 1974, Lansing (Mich.) C.C., 1975. Exec. dir. Shiawassee County YWCA, Owosso, Mich., 1975-78; real estate developer F&S Devel. Corp., Lansing, Mich., 1978-79, Corum Devel. Corp., Houston, 1979-81; adminstrv. fin. planner, sr. citizen cons. Investec Asset Mgmt. Group, Inc.; owner Ins. Filing Svcs. Sr. Citizens, 1985-96; guardian VA, 1990—. Author: For You! I Killed the Chicken, 1972. Mem. Older Women's League, Houston, 1st Ecumenical Council of Lansing, Nat. Mus. Women in Arts, Judaica Mus., Houston, Mus. Fine Arts, Houston, Mus. Natural Sci., Houston; docent Holocaust Mus., Houston; mem. African-Jewish Dialogue Group, Houston. Recipient State of Mich. Flag, 1972, Key to City, City of Lansing, 1972-73. Mem. Nat. Assn. Claims Assistance Profls., Afro-Am. Jewish Dialogue Group, Internat. Women's Pilot Orgn. (The 99's), Jewish Geneal. Soc., Internat. Directorate Disting. Leadership. Republican. Jewish. Lodges: Zonta, Licoma, B'nai B'rith, Hadassah, Nat. Fedn. Temple Sisterhoods. Flew All Women's Transcontinental Air Race (Powder Puff Derby), 1972, 73. Avocations: flying, gourmet cooking, needlepoint, knitting, skiing. Home: 4030 Newshire Dr Houston TX 77025-3921

MERRELL, DAVID BOLES, educator, university administrator; b. Akron, Ohio, June 24, 1942; s. Ralph John and Audrey Dale (Boles) M.; m. Martha Ann Page Gaines, Aug. 21, 1971; children—Jocelyn Leigh, Phylliese Ann, Flynt Page Gaines, Dezarae Gaines. B.A., Abilene Christian U., 1964; M.A., U. Ark., 1966; Ph.D., Tex. A&M U., 1979. English tchr. Abilene Christian U., Tex., 1966-69, 70-72, 75—; v.p. Cascade Fashions Akron, Ohio, 1969-70; English instr. Tex. A&M U., College Station, 1972-75; golf coach Abilene Christian U., 1976-78, chmn. English dept., 1981-85, dean Coll. Liberal and Fine Arts, 1985-93, faculty athletics rep., 1988—, dir. Curriculum and Advising, 1993-95, dir. Curriculum and Advising, registrar, 1995—; councillor Conf. Coll. Tchrs. English, Tex., 1983-86. Coordinator: (book) Good Writing, 1974. Recipient Tchr. of Yr. award Abilene Christian U., 1984. Mem. Am. Assn. Advancement Core Cirriculum, Am. Assn. Collegiate Registrars and Admissions Officers, Nat. Academic Advising Assn., Conf. on Christianity and Lit., Sports Lit. Assn., South Cen. Modern Lang. Assn., Tex. Assn. Deans Liberal Arts and Scis. (bd. dirs. 1990-93, v.p. 1993-94, pres. 1994-95), Conf. Coll. Tchrs. English Tex., Tex. Acad. Advising Network, Tex. Assn. Collegiate Registrars and Admissions Officers, Tex. Humanities Alliance, Tex. Coll. English. Assn. Mem. Ch. of Christ. Avocations: photography, physical fitness, music, drama, woodworking. Home: 833 Harrison Ave Abilene TX 79601-4605

MERRICK, RAYMOND DANIEL, internist, educator; b. Somerset, Ky., Oct. 4, 1955; s. Leland and Wanza Elizabeth (Combest) M.; m. Marla Jane Scherrer, Dec. 29, 1979; children: Nathan Daniel, John Jacob, Leah Elizabeth, Paul Christian. BS, Eastern Ky. U., 1978; MS, U. Ky., 1981; MD, U. Ky. Coll. Medicine, 1985. Resident in internal medicine East Tenn. State U., Johnson City, 1985-88, assoc. prof. medicine, 1993—; lab. dir. Med. Edn. Assistance Corp., Johnson City, 1992—, clinic coord., 1991—. Bd. dirs. Access to Cmty. Svcs., Johnson City. Fellow Am. Coll. Physicians; mem. Soc. Gen. Internal Medicine. Republican. Baptist. Office: Univ Physicians Practice 325 N State of Franklin Rd Johnson City TN 37604

MERRILL, CHERYL SINGER, editor; b. Akron, Ohio, Oct. 13, 1947; d. Robert Russell and Mary Elizabeth (McClain) Singer; m. John Philip Merrill, Feb. 14, 1970; 1 child, Philip Patrick. BA, U. Calif. Santa Barbara, 1969. Editl. asst. The Antioch Rev., Yellow Springs, Ohio, 1974-75; editor News and Views Nat. Assn. Biology Tchrs., Reston, Va., 1987—. Editor: Bitten By the Biology Bug, 1991. Mem. Ednl. Press. Assn. Am., Alpha Phi. Lutheran. Office: Nat Assn Biology Tchrs 11250 Roger Bacon Dr Ste 19 Reston VA 22090

MERRILL, RICHARD AUSTIN, lawyer; b. Logan, Utah, May 20, 1937; s. Milton Rees and Bessie (Austin) M.; m. Elizabeth Duvall, Aug. 26, 1961; children—Patricia, John. AB, Columbia U., 1959, LLB, 1964; BA (Rhodes scholar), Oxford (Eng.) U., 1961, MA, 1965. Bar: N.Y. 1964, D.C. 1965, Va. 1980. Law clk. to Hon. Carl McGowan, U.S. Ct. Appeals for D.C., 1964-65, Va. bar, 1980; assoc. firm Covington & Burling, Washington, 1965-69, spl. counsel, 1991—; assoc. prof. law U. Va., 1969-72, prof., 1972-75, Daniel Caplin prof. law, 1977—, Arnold Leon prof., 1985-88, dean sch. law, 1980-88, Albert C. Tate Jr. rsch. prof., 1989-91; gen. counsel FDA, Washington, 1975-77; cons. in field. Mem. Inst. Medicine (council) 1985-88, Nat. Acad. Scis., 1977—, Bd. on Toxicology and Environ. Health Hazards, 1979-85; bd. dirs. Immunex Corp. Author: (with Jerry L. Mashaw and Peter Shane) American Administrative Law, 2d edit., 1985, (with Peter B. Hutt) Food and Drug Law, 1980. Bd. trustees Thomas Jefferson Meml. Found. Mem. Am. Bar Found., Va. Bar Found., Am. Law Inst., Food and Drug Inst. (trustee). Office: U Va Sch Law 580 Massie Rd Charlottesville VA 22903-1789*

MERRIMAN, GLEN D., fundraising executive; b. Wichita, Kans, Aug. 10, 1943; s. Dell and Mildred LaVerne (Seiner) M.; m. Sharon Gayle Swearengin, July 2, 1967; children: Matthew Chad, Donald Anthony. BA in Religious Edn. and Sociology, Okla. Bapt. U., 1969; M of Religious Edn., Midwestern Theol. Sem., 1972; attended, Coll. William & Mary, U. Mo. Cert. estate planner. Min. edn. and youth Armour Heights Bapt. Ch., Kansas City, 1970-72, Mayridge Bapt. Ch., Oklahoma City, 1972-74; min. edn. Winnwood Bapt. Ch., Kansas City, 1974-76; min. edn. and outreach Clarkston (Ga.) Bapt. Ch., 1977-79, Dalewood Bapt. Ch., Nashville, 1980-81; min. edn. and adminstrn. Ctrl. Bapt. Ch., Knoxville, Tenn., 1981-84, Birchwood Bapt. Ch., Independence, Mo., 1984-87; devel. officer Missouri Bapt. Children's Home, Bridgeton, Mo., 1987-91; asst. v.p. planned giving Hardin-Simmons U., Abilene, Tex., 1991—; adj. prof. in supervised ednl. ministry Midwestern Bapt. Theol. Sem., Kansas City, 1974-76. Vol. activities 1st Bapt. Ch., Abilene, Tex., 1991—, Head Start Program, Abilene, 1991—; bd. dirs. Rolling Plains Tech. Found., Sweetwater, Tex., 1994. Mem. Nat. Soc. Fund Raising Execs. (cert., bd. dirs., treas. 1991—), Mo. Bapt. Devel. Office Assn. (v.p., pres.-elect 1990-91), Tex. Bapt. Devel. Office Assn., Kiwanis. Office: Hardin-Simmons U PO Box 16100 Abilene TX 79698

MERRIOTT, VICKI ANN, elementary and secondary education teacher; b. Tulsa, Okla., July 25, 1952; d. Robert Lee and Mary Irene (Henry) M. BS, U. Okla., 1974; M of Learning Disability, U. Ctrl. Okla., 1989. Cert. elementary tchr., Okla. Receptionist, legis. asst. U.S. Ho. of Reps., Washington, 1974-76; social worker Dept. Human Svcs., Oklahoma City, 1977-83; youth counselor High Pointe Residential Psych. Unit, Oklahoma City, 1983-84; tchr. Oklahoma City Pub. Schs., 1984-89, Edmond (Okla.) Pub. Schs., 1989—; tchr., cons. in discipline Ida Freeman Elem. Sch., 1995. Author: Super Stars, 1995. Campaign worker Risenhoover for U.S. Ho. of Reps., Muskogee, Okla., 1976; campaign coord. Gene Howard for U.S. Senate, Oklahoma City, 1980. Mem. Okla. Edn. Assn., Kappa Delta Pi. Democrat. Presbyterian. Office: Ida Freeman Elem Sch 501 W Hurd Edmond OK 73003

MERRITT, GILBERT STROUD, federal judge; b. Nashville, Tenn., Jan. 17, 1936; s. Gilbert Stroud and Angie Fields (Cantrell) M.; m. Louise Clark Fort, July 10, 1964 (dec.); children: Stroud, Louise Clark, Eli. BA, Yale U., 1957; LLB, Vanderbilt U., 1960; LLM, Harvard U., 1962. Bar: Tenn. 1960. Asst. dean Vanderbilt U. Law Sch., 1960-61, lectr., 1963-69, 71-75, assoc. prof. law, 1969-70; assoc. Boult Hunt Cummings & Conners, Nashville, 1962-63; city atty. City of Nashville, 1963-66; U.S. Dist. atty. for (mid. dist.) Tenn., 1966-69; ptnr. Gullett, Steele, Sanford, Robinson & Merritt, Nashville, 1970-77; judge U.S. Ct. Appeals (6th cir.), Nashville, 1977—; chief judge U.S. Ct. Appeals (6th cir.), 1989—; exec. sec. Tenn. Code Commn., 1977. Mng. editor: Vanderbilt Law Rev, 1959-60; contbr. articles to law jours. Del. Tenn. Constl. Conv., 1965; chmn. bd. trustees Vanderbilt Inst. Pub. Policy Studies. Mem. ABA, Fed. Bar Assn., Tenn. Bar Assn., Nashville Bar Assn., Vanderbilt Law Alumni Assn. (pres. 1979-80), Am. Law Inst., Order of Coif. Episcopalian. Office: US Ct Appeals 303 Customs House Nashville TN 37203*

MERRITT, JEAN, consulting firm executive; b. N.Y.C., Oct. 29, 1952; d. Harry and Ruth (Happel) Packman; m. Richard L. Kashinsky, Aug. 2, 1976 (div.); m. Richard L. Merritt, May 5, 1985; children: Courtney Morgan, Melissa Morgan. Grad. high sch., Bayside, N.Y. Contr. Kaswol Corp., Richmond Hill, N.Y., 1973, jr. v.p., 1974-75, v.p., sec., treas., 1975-85; Corp. exec. Federated Cons. Svc., Inc., Bayside, N.Y.; sr. v.p., CFO Federated Cons. Svc., Inc., Jupiter, Fla., 1985—. Coach Queens Spl. Olympics, 1985. Mem. Nat. Trust for Hist. Preservation, Nat. Fedn. Wildlife, Ctr. for Environ. Edn., Defenders of Wildlife, Nat. Resource Def. Coun., Humane Soc. of U.S. Presbyterian. Home: 20 E 76th St New York NY 10021-2688 Also: 120 Cypress Cv Jupiter FL 33458-8156 Office: Federated Cons Svc Inc 1016 Clemmons St Jupiter FL 33477-3301

MERRITT, JOE FRANK, industrial supply executive; b. Paris, Tex., Dec. 9, 1947; s. Henry Grady and Margaret Leon (Murrell) M.; m. Barbara Jean Sands (div. May 1973); 1 child, Daniel Joe; m. Bonnie Louise McLure, Feb. 1, 1975; 1 stepchild, David Wright Dwyer. BA in Govt., U. Tex., Arlington, 1970. Cert. contractor Dept. Def. USA and Can. With purchasing A.F. Holman Boiler Works Inc., Dallas, 1970-77; supply salesman Stanco Indsl. Supply, Dallas, 1977-79, Tool Specialty Indsl. Supply, Dallas, 1979-80, Briggs-Weaver Indsl. Supply, Dallas, 1980-81; owner, pres. Joe F. Merritt & Co., Inc., Carrollton, Tex., 1981; v.p., gen. mgr. Abrasives & Buffs Co., Dallas, 1981-83; owner, pres. Buff, Polish & Grind Indsl. Supply Co., Inc., Argyle, Tex., 1984—; cons. The Broadway Collection, OLathe Kans., 1990, Ofenhauser Co., Houston, 1993, 94; Innovation Industries, Russellville, Ark., 1994; instr. buff, polish and grind methods quality control dept. Rsch. Facility, Peterbilt Motors Co., 1994. Creator State of the Art Rsch. and Tchg. Facility, 1984, 100% Virgin Lambswool Buffing Belt, 1987, spl. extra wide spindle buffers to be manufactured by Baldor Electric, Ft. Smith, Ark., 1995; contbr. article to profl. jour. Recipient Cert. of Appreciation, City of Carrollton, Tex., 1981. Mem. Soc. Mfg. Engrs. Republican. Methodist. Office: Buff Polish & Grind Indsl Supply 1907 Fm 407 E Argyle TX 76226-9447

MERRITT, WILLIAM DORRIS, electronics company executive; b. Searcy, Ark., Dec. 15, 1935; s. Taylor Wilson and Inez Edna (Beard) M.; m. Carolyn Lee Askew, Oct. 13, 1962; children: Kathryn Inez, Lee Ann. BS, Ark. State U., Jonesboro, 1957; MA, U. Ctrl. Mich., 1974. Commd. 2nd lt. U.S. Army, 1957, advanced through grades to col., 1977; ret., 1979; sr. asst. program devel. Hughes Aircraft Co., Washington, 1979-81; dir. govt. programs Hughes Aircraft Co., Alexandria, Va., 1981-85; v.p. bus. devel. Hughes Aircraft Co., Fullerton, Calif., 1985-89; v.p., U.S. bus. exec. Hughes Aircraft Co., Alexandria, 1989-94; corp. v.p. Hughes Electronics, Arlington, Va., 1994—. Mem. Rep. Senate Roundtable, Washington, 1990-95, Pres.'s Coun. on Competitiveness, Washington, 1993-96. Decorated Legion of Merit, Bronze Star medal, Meritorious Svc. medal, Air medal with cluster, Army Commendation medal, Vietnam medal of honor. Mem. Officers of the First Divsn. (chmn. 1990-94), United Svcs. Orgn. (vice chmn. 1994-96), Electronic Ind. Assn. (dir. 1992-96), Am. Def. Preparedness Assn. (dir. 1993-96), Burning Tree Club. Methodist. Home: 3009 Nathaniels Green Williamsburg VA 23185

MERRON, JEFFREY L., editor, educator; b. Phila., Nov. 9, 1961; s. Alfred E.B. and Myrna (Weisman) M.; m. Jacqueline L. Quay, Nov. 20, 1994. BA in Polit. sci., Bennington (Vt.) Coll., 1983; MA in Journalism and Mass. Comm., U. Wis., 1985; PhD in Mass Comm. Rsch., U. N.C., 1991. Sports editor Princeton (N.J.) Packet, 1981; assoc. news editor BYTE Mag., Peterborough, N.H., 1987-88; asst. prof. comm. Elon Coll., N.C., 1991-95; corp. comm. editor IBM, Raleigh, N.C., 1995—. Contbr.: (book) Dictionary of American History, 1996; author: (monograph) Journalism Mongraphs, 1988. Fellow Gannett Found., 1988-89, 89-90, Vilas Found., 1986; Outward Bound scholar, 1994. Mem. Assn. for Exptl. Edn., Sierra Club. Democrat. Home: 2420 Timber Oak Dr Hillsborough NC 27278

MERRYDAY, STEVEN D., federal judge; b. 1950. BA, U. Fla., 1972, JD, 1975. With Holland & Knight, Tampa, 1975-83; ptnr. Glenn, Rasmussen, Fogarty, Merryday & Russo, Tampa, 1983-91; federal judge U.S. Dist. Ct. (mid. dist.), Fla., 1992—. Mem. Fed. Bar Assn., The Fla. Bar, Hillsborough County Bar Assn. Office: US Courthouse 611 N Florida Ave Ste 310 Tampa FL 33602-4500*

MERSON, CHARLES SAMUEL, anesthesiologist; b. N.Y.C., May 20, 1954; s. Lawrence Nelson and Elizabeth Rachel Merson; m. Robin Hillary Gingold-Merson, Nov. 26, 1988; children: Andrew James, Sara Beth. BA in Psychology, SUNY, Buffalo, 1975; MD, Autonomous U. Guadalajara, Mex., 1983, Albert Einstein Coll., 1984. Intern in internal medicine Flushing Hosp., Queens, N.Y., 1985-86; resident in anesthesiology N.Y. Med. Coll., Valhalla, 1987-90; v.p., ptnr. Plantation-Tamarac Anesthesiology, PA, Lauderhill, Fla., 1990—. N.Y. State regent's scholar, 1971. Mem. AMA, Am. Soc. Anesthesiologists, Internat. Anesthesia Rsch. Soc. Office: Plantation-Tamarac Anesthesiology 4979 N University Dr Fort Lauderdale FL 33351-4508

MERTEN, DAVID FISCHER, radiologist, pediatrician and educator; b. Cin., Feb. 7, 1930; s. Harold Adams and Adele (Fischer) M.; m. Barbara Ann Bush, June 26, 1954; children: Melissa, John, Peter, Katherine, Elizabeth. BS, U. Cin., 1952, MD, 1956. Diplomate Am. Bd. Radiology. Intern Med. Coll. Va., Richmond, 1956-57; resident in pediatrics Children's Hosp., Cin., 1957-59; resident in radiology U. Calif., San Francisco, 1968-71; pvt. practice San Rafael (Calif.) Med. Group, 1961-68; asst. prof. pediatrics U. Calif., San Francisco, 1962-68, asst. prof. radiology, 1971; asst. prof. radiology U. Calif., Davis, 1974-77; fellow pediatric radiology Tex. Children's Hosp., Houston, 1971-72; attending pediatric radiologist Wm. Beaumont Hosp., Royal Oak, Mich., 1972-74; assoc. prof. radiology and pediatrics Duke U. Med. Ctr., Durham, N.C., 1977-87; prof. radiology and pediatrics U. N.C., Chapel Hill, 1987-96, prof. emeritus, 1996—; cons. USAF, Travis AFB, Calif., 1974-77, med. radiation adv. bd. FDA, Washington, 1985-87, radiol. devices panel, 1987—; mem. WHO Expert Adv. Panel on Radiation, Geneva, 1990—. Capt. USAF, 1959-61. Recipient award for distinction in reviewing Radiology, 1991-93. Fellow Am. Coll. Radiology (devel. award 1988); mem. Am. Roentgen Ray Soc., Am. Acad. Pediatrics (chmn. radiology 1979-81), So. Pediatric Radiology Soc. (pres. 1985-87), Soc. for Pediatric Radiology. Office: Univ N C Sch Medicine Radiology CB # 7510 Chapel Hill NC 27599-7510

MERTENS, DAVID GERHARD, financial executive; b. Muncie, Ind., May 29, 1960; s. Thomas Robert and Beatrice Janet (Abair) M.; m. Jill Marie Hedrich, June 1, 1985; children: Meredith Leigh, Jack Robert Thomas. BS, Ball State U., 1982; CLU, Am. Coll., 1989. Registered rep. Nat. Assn. Securities Dealers. Pension specialist Am. United Life, Indpls., 1982-83, Atlanta, 1983-86; regional pension sales dir. State Mut. Life Assurance Co. of Am., Atlanta, 1986-92, State Mut. 1844 Soc., Atlanta; regional v.p. INVESCO Funds Group, Atlanta, 1992—. Loaned exec. United Way of Greater Indpls., 1982. Mem. Internat. Assn. Fin. Planning, So. Employee Benefit Conf., Am. Soc. CLUs, Alpha Romeo Owners, Simga Alpha Epsilon. Republican. Episcopalian. Home: 1351 Valley Reserve Dr Kennesaw GA 30144-4850 Office: INVESCO Funds Group 1355 Peachtree St NE Ste 250 Atlanta GA 30309-3269

MERTZ, SUSAN JEANNE, small business owner, writer; b. Toms River, N.J., May 15, 1953; d. Norman Patrick and Jeanne Barbara (Seibel) Trepiccione; m. Kenneth Alexander Mertz, Jr., Aug. 3, 1975; 1 child, Kenneth Alexander III. BS, Hood Coll., Frederick, Md., 1975; MA in Teaching, George Washington U., 1987. Freelance edn. specialist, Washington, Md., Va., 1983-88; dir. Sandy Spring (Md.) Mus., 1987-88; assoc. dir. devel. San Diego Space and Sci. Found., 1988-91; owner, mgr., writer IMPACT! Innovative Mus Programs and Creative Teaching, San Diego, 1991-92; owner, mgr. IMPACT! Innovative Mus Programs and Creative Teaching, Charleston, S.C., 1992—; cons. Fukutake Pub. Co., Ltd., Torrance, Calif., 1991, Nat. Coun. for History Edn., Ohio, 1992, Gibbes Mus. Art, Charleston, Midway Environ. Trust, Charleston, U.S. Dept. Natural Resources, Charleston. Author curriculum materials Recycle Team. Mem. Jr. League San Diego, 1990—. Mem. Am. Assn. Mus., Am. Assn. for State and Local History, Mus. Edn. Round Table. Republican. Home: 141 Scalybark Rd Summerville SC 29485-6025 Office: IMPACT! Summerville SC 29485

MERVES, MARLENE, elementary school educator; b. Lorain, Ohio; d. Solomon and Mary Merves; 1 child, Yosi. BS in Elem. Edn., Ohio State U., 1972, MA in Elem. Edn., 1978. Cert. tchr. Fla., N.Y., Ohio, Tenn. Tchr. 2d grade, coord. student coun. Columbus (Obio) Pub. Schs., 1972-79; telephone solicitor Arthritis Found., Memphis, 1980; tchr. grades 1 and 2 Fayette County Schs., Somerville, Tenn., 1980-81; docent Children's Mus., S.I., N.Y., 1983-84; substitute tchr. N.Y.C. Pub. Schs., 1983-84, Memphis City Schs., 1981-82, Dade County pub. and pvt. schs., Miami, Fla., 1992-94, 95-96; tchr. Bright Horizons Student-Patient Resource Ctr., Miami, 1994-95; Educator substitute and tutor Teacher's Global Insts. of Lang. and Culture Inc.,; pvt. tutor, 1984-92. Youth group advisor Nat. Coun. Synagugue Youth, Memphis, 1982-83; Life Blood chairperson Anshei Sphard Beth El Emeth Congregation, Memphis, 1981-83; v.p. fund-raising Sisterhood Arshei Sphard Beth El Eneth, 1981-83, pub. and media chairperson, 1981-83; cmty.r els. chairperson Orgn. for rehab. Through Tng., Memphis, 1982-83. Bland L. Stradley scholar, 1968-72, Samuel Melton scholar, 1969-70. Mem. Alpha Lambda Delta. Home: 3625 N Country Club Dr #203 Miami FL 33180

MERY, LAURA ROSE BASHARD, microbiologist, educator; b. Austin, July 4, 1959; d. Joseph Christopher and Myrtle Frances (Lamme) Bashara; married, Mar. 25, 1983; four children. BA with high honors, U. Tex., 1980; postgrad., U. Tex., San Antonio, 1993—. Lab technician Shoal Creek Hosp., Austin, 1977, U. Tex., Austin, 1979; rsch. asst. U. Tex. Health Sci. Ctr., San Antonio, 1983-84, tchg. asst., 1994—; microbiologist Tex. Dept. Health, Austin, 1980-82. Mem. Bd. Young Adult Ministry, San Antonio, 1990-91; served on charity com. Lawyers Guild, San Antonio, 1993; parliamentarian Ameleb, San Antonio, 1994. Mem. Am. Soc. Cell Biologists, Internat. Behavioral Soc. Neurosci., Soc. Neurosci. (Alama chpt.), Phi Beta Kappa, Phi Kappa Phi. Office: U Tex Divsn Life Scis 4900 North Loop 1604 W San Antonio TX 78249

MERZBACHER, EUGEN, physicist, educator; b. Berlin, Germany, Apr. 9, 1921; came to U.S., 1947, naturalized, 1953; s. Siegfried and Lilli (Wilmersdoerffer) M.; m. Ann Townsend Reid, July 11, 1952; children: Celia, Charles, Matthew, Mary. Licentiate, U. Istanbul, 1943; A.M., Harvard U., 1948, Ph.D., 1950; DSc (hon.), U. N.C., Chapel Hill, 1993. High sch. tchr. Ankara, Turkey, 1943-47; mem. Inst. Advanced Study, Princeton, N.J., 1950-51; vis. asst. prof. Duke U., 1951-52; mem. faculty U. N.C., Chapel Hill, 1952—; prof. U. N.C., 1961—, acting chmn. physics dept., 1965-67, 71-72, Kenan prof. physics, 1969-91, Kenan prof. physics emeritus, 1991—, chmn. dept., 1977-82; vis. prof. U. Wash., 1967-68, U. Edinburgh, Scotland, 1986; Arnold Bernhard vis. prof. physics Williams Coll., 1993; vis. rsch. fellow Sci. and Engring. Rsch. Coun., U. Stirling, 1986; chair Internat. Conf. on Physics of Electronic and Atomic Collisions, 1987-89, chair APS task force on jour. growth, 1994-95. Author: Quantum Mechanics, 2d edit, 1970; also articles. NSF Sci. Faculty fellow U. Copenhagen, Denmark, 1959-60; recipient Thomas Jefferson award U. N.C., 1972; Humboldt sr. scientist award U. Frankfurt, Germany, 1976-77. Fellow Am. Phys. Soc. (pres. 1990); mem. AAUP, Am. Assn. Physics Tchrs. (Oersted medal 1992), Sigma Xi. Home: 1396 Halifax Rd Chapel Hill NC 27514-2724

MESCHAN, ISADORE, radiologist, educator; b. Cleve., May 30, 1914; s. Julius and Anna (Gordon) M.; m. Rachel Farrer, Sept. 3, 1943; children: David Farrer, Eleanor Jane Meschan Foy, Rosalind Weir, Joyce Meschan Lawrence. BA, Western Res. U., 1935, MA, 1937, MD, 1939; ScD (hon.), U. Ark., 1983. Instr. Western Res. U., 1946-47; prof., head dept. radiology U. Ark., Little Rock, 1947-55; prof., dir. dept. radiology Bowman Gray Sch. Medicine, Wake Forest U., Winston-Salem, N.C., 1955-77; now prof. emeritus Bowman Gray Sch. Medicine, Wake Forest U. Author: Atlas of Normal Radiographic Anatomy, 1951, Roentgen Signs in Clinical Diagnosis, 1956, (with R. Meschan) Synopsis of Roentgen Signs, 1962, Roentgen Signs in Clinical Practice, 1966, Radiographic Positioning Related Anatomy, 1969, 2d edit., 1978, Analysis of Roentgen Signs, 3 vols, 1972, Atlas of Anatomy Basic to Radiology, 1975, Synopsis of Analysis of Roentgen Signs, 1976, Synopsis of Radiographic Anatomy, 1978, 2d rev. edit., 1980, (with B.W. Wolfman) Basic Atlas of Sectional Anatomy, 2d edit.; co-author: Atlas of Cross-Sectional Anatomy, 1980, Roentgen Signs in Diagnostic Imaging, vol. 1, 1984, vol. 2, 1985, vol. 3, 1986, vol. 4, 1987; editor: The Radiologic Clinics of North America, 1965; contbr. articles to profl. jours. Recipient Disting. Alumnus award Case-Western Res. U. Sch. Medicine, 1984, Disting. Faculty Svc. Alumni award Wake Forest U. Bowman Gray Sch. Medicine, 1989. Fellow Am. Coll. Radiology (com. chmn., Gold medal 1978, Living Legends of Radiology 1986); mem. Am. Roentgen Ray Soc., AMA, Radiology Soc. N.Am., N.C. Radiol. Soc., So. Med. Assn., Soc. Nuclear Medicine, Assn. U. Radiologists, Phi Beta Kappa, Sigma Xi, Alpha Omega Alpha. Home: 305 Weatherfield Ln Kernersville NC 27284-8337

MESCHAN, RACHEL FARRER (MRS. ISADORE MESCHAN), obstetrics and gynecology educator; b. Sydney, Australia, May 21, 1915; came to U.S., 1946, naturalized, 1950; d. John H. and Gertrude (Powell) Farrer; m. Isadore Meschan, Sept. 3, 1943; children: David Farrer-Meschan, Jane Meschan Foy, Rosalind Meschan Weir, Joyce Meschan Lawrence. MB, BS, U. Melbourne (Australia), 1940; MD, Wake Forest U., 1957. Intern Royal Melbourne Hosp., 1942; resident Women's Hosp., Melbourne, 1942-43, Bowman-Gray Sch. Medicine, Wake Forest U., Winston-Salem, N.C., 1957-73, asst. clin. prof. dept. ob-gyn, 1973—; also marriage counselor. Co-author (with I. Meschan): Atlas of Radiographic Anatomy, 1951, rev., 1959; Roentgen Signs in Clinical Diagnosis, 1956; Synopsis of Roentgen Signs, 1962; Roentgen Signs in Clinical Practice, 1966; Radiographic Positioning and Related Anatomy, 1968; Analysis of Roentgen Signs in General Radiology, 1973; Roentgen Signs in Diagnostic Imaging, Vol. III, 1986, Vol. IV, 1987. Home: 305 Weatherfield Ln Kernersville NC 27284-8337

MESCHKE, DEBRA JOANN, polymer chemist; b. Elyria, Ohio, Oct. 22, 1952; d. Loren Willis and JoAnne Elizabeth (Meyer) M. BS, U. Cin., 1974; MS, Case Western Res. U., 1976, PhD, 1979. Sr. chemist Union Carbide Corp., South Charleston, W.Va., 1979-82, project scientist, 1982-85, chair research and devel. Exempt Women's Group, 1980-81, chair research and devel. Ctr. Safety Team, 1981-82, coordinator Polymer Methods Course, 1982-83; project scientist Union Carbide Corp., Tarrytown, N.Y., 1985-86; sr. prin. research chemist Air Products and Chems. Inc., Allentown, Pa., 1986-88, chmn. waste disposal com., 1986-88; rsch. scientist Union Carbide Corp., South Charleston, W.Va., 1988-95, sr. rsch. scientist, 1995—. Author chpts. in textbooks; patentee in field. Bd. dirs. Overbrook Home Owners Assn., Macungie, Pa., 1987. Case Western Res. U. grad. fellow, 1974-79. Mem. AAAS, Am. Chem. Soc. (Polymer div.), Iota Sigma Pi. Home: 2022 Parkwood Rd Charleston WV 25314-2244

MESCO, EDWARD CHARLES PATRICK, accountant, consultant; b. Chgo., Aug. 15, 1962; s. Victor Francis and May E. (Bachman) M.; m. Diane C. Sandquist (div. Dec. 1995). BS in Acctg., Denver U., 1984; postgrad, DePaul U. CPA, Ill., Fla. Asst. auditor Blue Cross and Blue Shield of Ill., Chgo., 1984-85, auditor, 1985-86, sr. auditor, 1986-88; healthcare fin. cons. United Reimbursement-Strategic Reimbursement, Chgo. and Phoenix, 1988-93; mgr. Ernst & Young LLP, Miami, Fla., 1993-94; sr. mgr. Ernst & Young LLP, West Palm Beach, Fla., 1994-96, Tampa, Fla., 1996—. Mem. Am. Coll. Healthcare Execs. (assoc.), Healthcare Fin. Mgmt. Assn., Ill. CPA Soc. (mem. hosp. com. 1988-89), Fla. Hosp. Soc. Office: Ernst & Young LLP 100 N Tampa St Ste 2200 Tampa FL 33602

MESIC, HARRIET LEE BEY, medical support group administrator; b. Norfolk, Va., Aug. 4, 1937; d. Daniel Douglas and Bessie Lee (Wrenn) Bey; m. Harry Randolph Mesic, Mar. 18, 1956; children: Catherine Denise Mesic Stringer, Daniel Douglas Mesic. AA, Trident Tech. Coll., Charleston, S.C., 1981, 1984. Editor L.E. Beacon, Lupus Erythematosus Support Group, Charleston, S.C., 1984-88, exec. dir., 1988—. Contbr. articles to profl. jours. Leader Girl Scouts Am., Isle of Palms, S.C., 1968-79; svc. unit chmn. Carolina Low Country Girl Scouts, E. Cooper, S.C., 1972-79. Recipient Friendship award, Carolina Low Country Girl Scouts, 1978. Lutheran. Office: LE Support Group 8039 Nova Ct Charleston SC 29420

MESSER, BILLY FREEMAN, JR., critical care nurse; b. Dothan, Ala., Feb. 13, 1968; s. Billy Freeman and Sharlene (Williams) M. ADN, Wallace Community Coll., Dothan, 1989; BSN, U. Ala., Tuscaloosa, 1993; postgrad., Xavier U., 1995—. RN, Ala. Staff nurse DCH Regional Med. Ctr., Tuscaloosa, 1989-92, U. Ala. at Birmingham Hosp., 1992-93, Grady Meml. Hosp., Atlanta, 1993-94; nursing legal cons., Ala., 1992. Author profl. papers. Mem. AACN (cert. CCRN), Am. Assn. Nurse Anesthetists, Wallace Assn. Nursing Students. Republican. Home: Apt D231 3901 N I 10 Service Rd W Metairie LA 70002-6836 Office: Med Ctr La at New Orleans 1532 Tulane Ave New Orleans LA 70140-1004

MESSER, MITCHEL ANTHONY, educational consultant, electrical engineer; b. Bronx, N.Y., July 9, 1964; s. Paul Basil and Sandra Ann (Banks) M.; m. S. Monique Baldwin, Sept. 18, 1993. BSEE, MIT, 1985; MS in Computer Sci., U. So. Calif., 1988. Engring. intern AT&T Bell Labs., Lincroft, N.J., 1981-85, design engr., 1985-91; systems engr. AT&T Bell Labs., Holmdel, N.J., 1991-92, Atlanta, 1992-93; mng. ptnr. Messer, Baldwin & Assocs., Marietta, Ga., 1993—. Editor Coll. Money Digest newsletter, 1992—; mng. dir. The Academia Group, 1994—. Amb. MIT Alumni Assn., Cambridge, 1992—; mentor Wheeler High Sch., Marietta, 1993—. Mem. Atlanta C. of C. (amb.). Office: Academia Group 1117 Perimeter Ctr W Atlanta GA 30338-5417

MESSER, TRYMON, religious organization executive. Gen. dir. Bd. of Home Missions of the Nat. Assn. Free Will Baptists. Address: PO Box 5002 Antioch TN 37011

MESSERSMITH, HARRY LEE, museum director, sculptor; b. Buckhannon, W.Va., Aug. 7, 1958; s. Fred Lawrence and Jane Elizabeth (Paryzek) M.; m. Lisa Deloise Sumner, Mar. 25, 1988. BA, Stetson U., 1981; MFA, U. Fla., 1983. Instr. art Stetson U., DeLand, Fla., 1983-86, Crealde, Winter Park, Fla., 1986; tchr. art Volusia County Pub. Schs., DeLand, 1986-89; exec. dir. DeLand Mus. Art, 1989-95, Lighthouse Gallery and Sch. Art, Tequesta, Fla., 1995-96; Bd. dirs. 1st St. Gallery, Sanford, Fla., 1993-94. Prin. works include life size bronze statue Don Iverson, bronze portrait bust Dr. Richard Morland, Dr. Vernon Moore, Warren Cowell, Carl Johnson; pub. commns. include The House Next Door Family Counseling Ctr., DeLand, 1995. Mem. fin. com. Arts Coun. Volusia County, 1992-93; mem. adv. coun. Coun. on Aging, Volusia County, 1992, Very Spl. Arts, Volusia County, 1993-94; mem. com. Volusia Vision/Cultural Task Force, Volusia County, 1993-95. Artist in Edn. grantee Fla. Arts Coun., 1986-89. Mem. Fla. Art Mus. Dirs. Assn., Fla. Soc. Goldsmiths (founding mem., bd. dirs. N.E. chpt. 1992-95), Fla. Pyrotechnic Arts Guild, Kawa Bonsai Soc., Internat. Sculpture Soc. Office: Lighthouse Gallery Sch Art 373 Tequeota Dr Tequesta FL 33469-3027

MESSERSMITH, WILLIAM DALE, retired corrections official; b. Taylorville, Ill., Oct. 11, 1937; s. Willian Laverne and Elizabeth Alma (Dillehunt) M.; m. Barbara Ann Spinner, Sep. 10, 1960; children: Susan, Eileen, Jacqueline, Gina, Deanne. BS in Psychology, U. Ill., 1960; MA in Correctional Adminstrn., Denver U., 1961. Parole officer Fed. Correctional Inst. Dept. of Justice, U.S. Bur. of Prisons, Englewood, Colo., 1959-62; asst. dir., dir. Pre-release Guidance Ctr. Dept. of Justice, U.S. Bur. of Prisons, Los Angeles, 1962-70; dir. residential facilities Dept. of Justice, U.S. Bur. of Prisons, Washington, 1970-72; regional dir. cmty. svcs. Dept. of Justice, U.S. Bur. of Prisons, Chgo., 1972-74, assoc. warden Met. Correctional Ctr., 1974-82; exec. asst. to warden Fed. Correctional Inst. Dept. of Justice, U.S. Bur. of Prisons, El Paso, 1982-87; ret., 1987; v.p., sec., treas., Internat. Halfway House Assn., Los Angeles, 1965-67. Active Discover El Paso (spl. cmty. svc. award, 1994). Recipient Outstanding Young Man in the Cmty. award, Jaycee of the Yr. award Temple City (Calif.) Jaycees, 1966, 68. Mem. El Paso County Hist. Soc., El Paso Genealogical Soc. Roman Catholic.

MESSIER, WILLIAM PAUL, computer science educator, software developer; b. Youngstown, Ohio, Sept. 28, 1949; s. Robert Lucien and Helen Luciel Messier. BA in Comm., Barry U., 1988, MS in Computer Edn., 1990; EdD in Instrnl. Tech., Nova U., 1993. cons. on application of instrn. tech. Polish Govt., 1993—, German Govt., 1994-95; cons. computer scis. Barry U., 1993—, Broward C.C., 1993—; developer/marketer instrnl. techs. to assist educators and minorities; developer/owner interactive video data svcs. FCC Bandwidth, 1996—. Lectr., instr. Fla. Internat. U., 1980-85; pres. ednl. software div. Air & Sea Software Co., North Miami Beach, Fla., 1986—; asst. prof. computer sci. Fla. Meml. Coll., 1990-91, coord. instrnl. tech. rev., 1992—; assoc. prof. computer sci. Brevard C.C., 1993-94, adj. prof., 1994—; adj. prof. Miami Dade C.C., 1994—; computer lab. mgr., trainer graphic design computer programs U. Miami, 1995-96; tech. lab. mgr. Internat. Fine Arts Coll., 1996—; cons. on application of instrn. tech. Polish Govt., 1993—, German Govt., 1994-95; cons. on computer scis. Barry U., 1993—, Broward C.C., 1993—; computer tech. lab mgr. Internat. Fine Arts Coll., 1996—; developer/marketer instrl. technologies to assist educators and minorities. Author (software) COGLE, 1990, The Atlantian Chronicles; contbr. numerous articles to profl. jours. Mem. postsecondary task force Adv. Coun. on Math./Sci. Tech., Miami, 1990—. Bush grantee, 1990-92, Apple Crossroads 3 grantee, 1992-93. Mem. Apple Programmers and Developers Assn., Fla. Assn. for Computers in Edn.

MESSMORE, DAVID WILLIAM, construction executive, former psychologist; b. Indpls.; s. Max J. and Betty G. (Miller) M.; m. Sondra Renée Bastian, Aug. 22, 1981; children: Kristen Nicole, Eric Christian William David. AB in Social Sci., Calif. State Coll., Long Beach, 1968; PhD in Student Devel., Counseling and Clin. Psychology, Mich. State U., 1972. Lic. class A gen. contractor, Tex., Va.; lic. psychologist, Calif., Mich.; lic. sch. psychologist, Calif. Counselor Okemas (Mich.) Pub. Sch., 1970-72; psychologist Frederick Ctr. Day Hosp., Grand Rapids, Mich., 1972-73, Newport-Mesa Schs., Newport Beach, Calif., 1973-80; commr. Bd. Med. Quality Assurance, State of Calif. Psychol. com., Sacramento, 1980-82; pres. Bridgewater Constrn., Inc., Chesapeake, Va., 1987—; psychol. counselor Camp Highfields Residential Sch., Onondago, Mich., 1971; cons. The Open Door, Lansing, Mich., 1971-72, Juv. and Domestic Rels. Ct. the Family Ct., State of Va., Chesapeake, 1989-91; pres. Bridgewater Consultation Svcs., Chesapeake, 1989-91; intern Counseling Ctr., Calif. State U., Long Beach, asst. prof. ednl. psychology, 1981; instr. Golden West Coll., Huntington Beach, Calif., 1977-78; advisor, counselor dean of students Mich. State U., 1969-71. Author: (manual) The Impact of Divorce on Families, 1989; designer sch. crest Long Beach City Coll., 1965. Active Gt. Bridge Conf. Com., Chesapeake, 1987-91; treas. Paint Your Heart Out, Chesapeake, 1993, Hampton Rds. Rep. Alliance, 1996—; coach parks and recreation, commr. transp. and safety City of Chesapeake, 1994—, vice-chmn., 1995-96; fin. com. city com. Rep. Party of Chesapeake, vice-chmn., 1996—; vice-chmn. Citizens for a Better Chesapeake, 1996—. Served with USMC, 1959-63. Recipient Cert. of Appreciation Chesapeake Vols. in Youth Svcs., Inc., 1989, Outstanding Svc. award, 1990, Gov.'s award State of Va., 1990. Mem. Rotary Internat. (bd. dirs. Chesapeake club 1990-94, co-chmn. programs 1996—, Disting. Svc. award 1990), Nat. Youth Sports Coaches Assn., Delta Tau Delta.

MESTEPEY, JOHN THOMAS, executive search consultant; b. San Diego, Mar. 15, 1943; s. John Benjamin and Mary Beatrice (McGuire) M.; m. Wendy Katherine Sullivan; children: Todd William, Brian Sullivan, Meghan Katherine. BS, Loyola U., Los Angeles, 1964. V.p., mng. ptnr. Fleming Assocs., Miami, Fla., 1978-87, A.T. Kearney, Inc., Miami, 1987—; also bd. dirs. Kearney: Exec. Search. Trustee Ransom-Everglades Sch.; bd. dirs. The Beacon Coun. Served to 1st lt. USMC, 1968-71, Vietnam. Decorated Purple Heart; Cross of Gallantry (Vietnam). Mem. Assn. Exec. Search Cons., Inc. Republican. Roman Catholic. Club: City (Miami). Office: A T Kearney Miami Ctr 201 S Biscayne Blvd Ste 3180 Miami FL 33131-4331

METCALF, CORWIN MOORE (MICKEY), business educator, businessman, consultant; b. Port Arthur, Tex., May 25, 1940; s. Richard Jackson and Loreah Alpha (Davis) M.; m. Pauline W. Ferry, May 10, 1960 (div. Jan. 1965); 1 child, Richard Louis; m. Patricia Ann Crout, June 15, 1967 (div. May 1991); children: Allison Ann, James Moore; m. Janice Ann Frye, May 24, 1991. BA, Oglethorpe U., 1963; MBA, U. S.C., 1965; JD, Wake Forest U., 1988. Staff mktg., supply and distrbn. Gulf Oil Corp., Atlanta, Houston, 1966-70; v.p., div. mgr. Bank of S.W., Houston, 1970-75; v.p., mgr., comml. loan officer Merc. Nat. Bank, Dallas, 1975-78; exec. v.p., COO, Mid Continent Systems, Inc., West Memphis, Ark., 1978-80; pres., CEO, Automated Fleet Svcs., Greensboro, N.C., 1980-84, Silverscreen Mgmt. Co., Greensboro, 1987-93; pres., CEO Video Co. Inc., Greensboro, 1987-90; CEO, CFO, SCM Mktg. Ltd., Winston-Salem, N.C., 1990-91; assoc. prof. Elon Coll., N.C., 1993—, prin. TMG, 1993—. Capt. CAP, Greensboro, 1985-87. Mem. Fin. Execs. Inst., Airplane Owners and Pilots Assn., The Turnaround Mgmt. Assn., Am. Arbitration Assn., Phi Alpha Delta, Beta Sigma Phi. Home: 112 Georgetown Dr Elon College NC 27244-9267 Office: Elon Coll Campus Box 2278 Elon College NC 27244-2020

METCALF, ETHEL EDGERTON, elementary school educator; b. Rutherfordton, N.C.; d. John Harris and Estelle Caroline (Weeks) Edgerton; m. John Samuel Metcalf, June 3, 1954; children: Anne, Caroline. AA, Gardner-Webb Coll., 1951; BS, Limestone Coll., 1953. Cert. secondary and elem. tchr. Tchr. Harris (N.C.) High Sch., 1953-57, Glenwood (N.C.) High Sch., 1958-59, Paris High Sch., Greenville, S.C., 1959-60, Nebo (N.C.) High Sch., 1961-62; tchr. spl. edn. Forest City (N.C.) Elem. Sch., 1962-64; tchr. Mt. Vernon Elem. Sch., Forest City, 1965-68, North Belmont (N.C.) Elem. Sch., 1969-70, Ruth Elem. Sch., Rutherfordton, 1970-92; cheerleader advisor, Ruth Sch., 1975-80, chair sci. fair, 1980-88, organizer, advisor Just Say No club, 1985-92. Mem. NEA, N.C. Assn. Educators (sch. rep. 1980-85). Democrat. Baptist. Home: RR 2 Box 186 Rutherfordton NC 28139-9447

METCALF, LYNNETTE CAROL, naval officer, journalist, educator, gemologist; b. Van Nuys, Calif., June 22, 1955; d. William Edward and Carol Annette (Keith) M.; m. Scott Edward Hruska, May 16, 1987. BA in Comm. and Media, Our Lady of Lake, 1978; MA in Human Rels., U. Okla., 1980; MA in Mktg. Webster U., 1986; cert. diamond grading, gem identification and colored stone grading Gemology Inst. Am., 1991, diploma, grad. gemologist, 1992. Enlisted USAF, 1973, advanced through grades to sgt., 1975; intelligence analyst, Taiwan, Italy and Tex., 1973-76; historian, journalist, San Antonio, 1976-78; commd. officer USN, 1978, advanced through ranks to lt. comdr., 1988; pub. rels. officer, Rep. of Panama, 1979-81; mgr. system program, London, 1981-82; ops. plans/tng., McMurdo Sta., Antarctica, 1982-84; exec. officer transient pers. unit Naval Tng. Ctr., Great Lakes, Ill., 1984-86, comdg. officer transient pers. unit, 1986-87; asst. prof. naval sci. U. Notre Dame NROTC, 1987-89; nat. curriculum, 1987-89; staff comm. plans U.S. Naval Forces Japan, 1989-91, network transp. officer pers. support activity Japan, 1991-92, Far East, 1992-93, adminstrv. mgr., automated Data processing and mgmt. rev. dir. pers. support activity, 1992-93; ret., 1993; freelance writer, desktop pub.; anchorwoman USN-TV CONTACT, 1986-87; adj. prof. Far East divsn. Chapman U., 1990-93; founder Profl. Gemological Cons., Japan, 1991, Far East Fed. Sales Group, Inc., 1993; founder. Profl. Gemol. Svc., Japan 1992, Far East Trading Co., Dolphin Comms., 1993, Desk Top Publishing, 1993. Author: Winter's Summer, 1983, A Walter Mitty Romance, 1995, Retired List, 1996; editor Naval Station Anchorline, 1979-81, WOPN Caryatides, 1985-86, Lollipop Landing Lantern; contbr. articles to profl. jours. Sec. San Vito Dei Normanni theatre group, Italy, 1975-76; coord. Magic Box Theater, Zion, Ill., 1984-86; dir. Too Bashful for Broadway variety show, Naval Tng. Ctr., 1986-87; treas. Yokosuka Little Theatre Group, 1990-91. Mem. Women Officers' Prof. Network (communications chair 1985-86, programs chair 1986-87), Am. Legion, Disabled Am. Vets., Ret. Officers Assn., Romance Writers of Am., Internat. Soc. Appraisers, Corp. Sponsor Tokyo Internat. Players, JHF Theater Soc. (co-founder 1990-93), McMurdo Club, Soc. of South Pole, Gemological Inst. Am. Alumni. Avocations: gardening, gemology, research, snorkeling, theatre. Home: 9120 Mint Ave Frankston TX 75763

METCALF, MARGARET LOUISE FABER, infosystems specialist, small business owner, consultant; b. Washington, Jan. 1, 1943; d. Marshall Lee and Martha Noreen (Mogan) Faber; m. George Taft Metcalf, June 1, 1968. BA in Math., U. Denver, 1966; JD, South Tex. Coll. of Law, 1974. Mathematician Falcon Research and Devel., Denver, 1965-67; systems analyst Chrysler Space Div., Slidell, La., 1967-68, Philco Ford, Houston, 1968-69, Lockheed Corp., Houston, 1969-70; sr. programmer Celanese Chem. Corp., Bayport, Tex., 1970-72; ch. adminstr. Epis. Ch. of the Redeemer, Houston, 1974-85; dir. Altar Guild, Houston, 1974-84; owner Celebration Designs, Houston, 1983—; cons. GTM Tech., Houston, 1986—, assoc. systems analyst, 1987—; corp. sec. Eastwood Ltd., Inc., Houston, 1982-83. Mem. Div. of World Missions, Bd. of Missions, Episc. Diocese of Tex., 1981—; pres. Redeemer's Episc. Ch. Women, 1989-92; judge local area sci. fair, 1991-93; lay adminstr. Santa Cruz Episcopal Ch., 1993-96; coord. diocesan bd. ECW, 1993-94, del. diocesan coun., 1993-94, comms. chair, 1996—; mem. Cmty. of Hope St. Luke's Hosp. Lay Chaplain Corps, 1996—; comms. chair Diocesan ECW Bd. Team, 1996—. Recipient Zonta award, 1960, Amelia Earheart award. Mem. Soc. Women Engrs. (assoc.), IEEE, Assn. for Computing Machinery (local treas. 1967-72), South Tex. Coll. of Law Alumni Assn., U. Denver Alumni Assn. Club: Episcopal Ch. Women. Home and Office: 4609 University Oaks Blvd Houston TX 77004-6705

METCALF, ROBERT JOHN ELMER, industrial consultant; b. Glen Ellyn, Ill., June 27, 1919; s. Elmer Simpson and Vida Marie Metcalf; B.S.M.E., U. Pitts., 1947; m. Rosemarie Rusch, Sept. 11, 1947; children: Kathleen, Karen, Patti, Pamela. Asst. staff supr. Westinghouse Electric Co., Buffalo, 1949-52, assoc. engr., 1952-54; assoc. Gemar Assocs., Inc., Greenwich, Conn., 1954-66. v.p., 1966-83; cons., 1983-92 . Served with U.S. Army, 1943-46. Mem. Inst. Mgmt. Cons. (founding). Roman Catholic. Home and Office: 300 Woodette Dr Apt 201 Dunedin FL 34698-1762

METTINGER, KARL LENNART, neurologist; b. Helsingborg, Sweden, Nov. 1, 1943; came to the U.S., 1989; s. Nils Allan and Anna Katarina (Hallberg) M.; m. Chesne Maree Ryman, Jan. 27, 1979. MD, U. Lund, 1973; PhD, Karolinska Inst., 1982. Intern Stockholm Hosps., 1973-74; resident Karolinska Hosp., Stockholm, 1974-77, clin. neurologist, 1977-85; med. dir. Kabi Hematology, Stockholm, 1985-87; dep. gen. mgr. Kabi Cardiovascular, Stockholm, 1987-89; med. dir. Ivax/Baker Norton Pharms., Miami, Fla., 1989-93, sr. clin. rsch. dir., 1993—; assoc. prof. Karolinska Inst., Stockholm, 1983-91; cons. neurologist Odenplan Med. Ctr., Stockholm, 1984-89. Author: Cerebral Thromboembolism, 1982, Refaat—Myths and Billions in Biotech, 1987; editor: Coronary Thrombolysis: Current Answers to Critical Questions, 1988, Controversies in Coronary Thrombolysis, 1989. Lt. Swedish Army, 1979. Recipient Silver award Spanish Health Ministry, 1989, Classical Langs. award King Gustav V Found., 1963. Mem. Swedish Stroke Soc. (bd. dirs. 1979-89, pres. 1984-86), Swedish Med. Soc., Swedish Christian Med. Soc. (bd. dirs. 1972-88, pres. 1983-88), Am. Heart Assn., N.Y. Acad. Scis., Nat. Found. for Advancement of Arts, Internat. Assn. Christian Physicians (exec. com. 1975-86). Home: 5401 Collins Ave Apt 1022 Miami FL 33140-2535 Office: IVAX 4400 Biscayne Blvd Miami FL 33137-3212

METZ, LARRY EDWARD, lawyer; b. Phila., Mar. 20, 1955; s. Harry Franz and Joan (Nye) M.; m. Mariko Tomisato, Mar. 26, 1980; children: Marla Jo, Christina Jill. BA, U. Fla., 1976; JD with high honors, Fla. State U., 1983. Bar: Fla. 1983, U.S. Dist. Ct. (so., mid. and no. dists.) Fla. 1984, U.S. Ct. Appeals (11th cir.) 1984, U.S. Supreme Ct. 1987. Assoc. Fleming, O'Bryan & Fleming, Ft. Lauderdale, Fla., 1983-86; atty. Westinghouse Electric Corp., Coral Springs, Fla., 1986-88; pvt. practice Ft. Lauderdale, 1988-91, Coral Springs, 1991-93; assoc. Herzfeld & Rubin, Miami, 1993-96, ptnr., 1996—. Area leader, sign co-chmn., spkr. George Bush for Pres. Broward County (Fla.) Victory Com., 1988; pres. Broward County Regional Rep. Club, 1991, 95; mem. exec. com. Broward County Reps., 1988-91, 93-96; Rep. nominee U.S. Ho. Reps. 19th dist. Fla., 1992. Mem. ABA, Broward Lawyers Care (pro bono project), Fla. Guardian Ad Litem Program, Order of the Coif. Home: 11143 SW 1st St Coral Springs FL 33071-8144 Office: Herzfeld & Rubin Ste 1501 801 Brickell Ave Miami FL 33131

METZ, ROBERT EDWARD, quality assurance executive; b. Hamilton, Ohio, Nov. 24, 1945; s. Edward Frank and Elizabeth Catherine (Kling) M.; m. Michelle Schlemmer, Aug. 3, 1968. A.Chem. Engring., Ohio Coll. Applied Sci., Cin., 1965; BS, U. Cin., 1978; MBA, U. Ala., Birmingham, 1984. With IBM, Lexington, Ky., 1966-67, Philip Carey Corp., Cin., 1967-72; research tech. Panacon Corp., Cin., 1972; research chemist Jim Walter Research Corp., Cin., 1972-76; quality control supr. Celotex Corp., Cin., 1976-82; mgr. cen. quality control Celotex Corp., Birmingham, 1982-88; dir. quality assurance Celotex Corp., 1988—. Pres. parish coun. St. Aloysius, Bessemer, Ala., 1984-93, 94—; pres. Harrison High Boosters Athletic Club, Ohio, 1970; chmn. ch. rebldg. steering com., 1990-93. Mem. ASTM (D8 roofing com. 1984—), Am. Soc. Quality Control (program chmn. 1986-88), Asphalt Roofing Mfrs. Assn. (co. rep. 1984—, chmn. rsch. com. 1993—). Roman Catholic. Office: Celotex Corp 1327 Erie St Birmingham AL 35224-2305

METZFIELD, WILLIAM, supply company executive. Pres. Gannett Supply Corp. Office: Gannett Com Inc 1100 Wilson Blvd Arlington VA 22209-2297*

METZGER, JAMES EDWARD, economics consultant, educator; b. Ft. Wayne, Ind., Feb. 15, 1950; s. Cletus Victor and Beatrice Ann (Grothouse) M.; m. Deborah Jo Baldwin, Apr. 1, 1974; children: Kirsten Anne, Anisa Marie. BA in Polit. Sci., U. Notre Dame, 1971; MA in Social Sci., U. Chgo., 1975. Staff economist U.S. Dept. Labor, Chgo., 1975-76; asst. economist Argonne (Ill.) Nat. Lab., 1976-78; economist Mountain West Rsch., Tempe, Ariz., 1978-80; pres. Histecon Assocs., Inc., Little Rock, 1980—; lectr. Ariz. State U., Tempe, 1979-80, U. Ark., Little Rock, 1986—; instr. Webster U., Little Rock, 1981—. Founder Ark.-Bavaria Youth Exchange, Little Rock, 1984—; pres. Friends of Stas. KLRE-KUAR, Little Rock, 1989-90. Exch. program grantee USIA, Washington and Munich, 1985-86. Mem. Am. Econ. Assn., Western Regional Sci. Assn., Assn. Comparative Econ. Studies. Home: 1418 Kavanaugh Blvd Little Rock AR 72205-4324 Office: Histecon Assocs Inc 2821 Kavanaugh Blvd Little Rock AR 72205-3868

METZGER, JEFFREY PAUL, lawyer; b. St. Louis, Oct. 13, 1950; s. John E. and Ellen J. M.; m. Stephanie Ann Stahr, Dec. 27, 1977. BA magna cum laude, Amherst Coll., 1973; JD, Georgetown U., 1976. Bar: D.C., 1977. Legis. asst. to U.S. Senator Joseph Biden, Jr. of Del., 1973; assoc. Collier, Shannon, Rill and Scott, Washington, 1976-79, Cole and Groner, P.C., Washington, 1979-82; trial atty. comml. litigation br. civil div. U.S. Dept. Justice, Washington, 1982-85; mem. profl. staff Pres.'s Blue Ribbon Commn. on Def. Mgmt., 1985-86; asst. gen. counsel Unisys Corp., McLean, Va., 1986-88, v.p., assoc. gen. counsel, 1989—. Mem. ABA.

METZGER, LEWIS ALBERT, brokerage house executive, financial consultant; b. Mobile, Ala., Sept. 24, 1952; s. Albert A. and Carolyn (Simon) M.; m. Peggy Brooks, Aug. 24, 1985; children: Michelle, Austin. BS in Commerce and Business, U. Ala., 1974, MBA, 1976. Registered securities broker, N.Y. Stock Exch., Am. Stock Exch., N.Am. Securities Dealers; commodities and commodities options broker Chgo. Mercantile Exch., Chgo. Bd. Trade, N.Y. Futures Exch.; real estate and life ins. broker, Tex.; debt instruments options, fgn. currency options broker. Mdse. mgr. Electrotex, Houston, 1976-79; 1st v.p. Drexel Burnham Lambert, Inc., Houston, 1979-89; sr. v.p. Smith Barney Inc., Houston, 1989—. Active Houston Big. Bros., 1979; apptd. to Ala. Citizen's Task Force on Higher Edn., 1974; bd. dirs. Gulf Coast Conservatin Assn., 1988-92, Bus. Rorrorrow Conf., 1973, St. Francis Episcopal Children's Ctr., 1988-92. Mem. U. Ala. Nat. Alumni Assn. (pres. and bd. dirs. Houston chpt., dist. v.p. 1982-86), Commerce Exec. Soc. U. Ala., Jaycees (mem. various coms.), Houston Options Soc., Zeta Beta Tau Fraternity (bd. trustees 1974-78), Omicron Delta Kappa, Alpha Kappa Psi. Home: 10327 Holly Springs Dr Houston TX 77042-1529 Office: Smith Barney Inc 5065 Westheimer Rd Ste 1200 Houston TX 77056-5605

METZGER, MARIAN, retired management consultant; b. Bklyn., Mar. 19, 1931; d. William David and Marian (Kemmet) Averell; m. Lester W. Metzger, June 17, 1951 (div. Nov. 1965); children: Edward L., Leslie I. Bowden; m. Robert L. Hirsh, June 16, 1973. Grad. high sch., Bellmore, N.Y., 1948. Administrv. asst., office mgr. Profl. Mgmt. Corp., Bayshore, N.Y., 1958-65, v.p., 1965-83; exec. v.p. R.L. Hirsh Assocs., Ltd., Bayshore, N.Y., 1972-85, R. L. Hirsh Assocs., Inc., Key Largo, Fla., 1985-95; co-editor, cons. Ophstart (program for eye surgeons); lectr. and instr. in field. Edit. advisor Types of Med. Practice, 1982; edit. cons. Physicians Management mag., 1974-93, New Practice Planning mag., 1980-93, Physicians Marketing mag., 1985-88; contbr. articles to profl. jours. Mem. Med.-Dental Hosp. Burs. Am. (pres. 1986-87), Soc. Profl. Bus. Cons. (sec., treas. 1979-82), Profl. Secs. Internat. (pres. 1966-67, Sec. of Yr. award 1969). Republican. Jewish.

METZGER, MARIE CRUZ, chemist; b. Beeville, Tex., May 27, 1959; d. Eladio Francisco and Maria Lourdes (Ocampo) Cruz; m. Steven Michael Buck, July 24, 1982 (div. Jan. 1991); 1 child, Stephanie Marie; m. David Francis Metzger, Jan. 27, 1995. BS in Chemistry, Coll. William and Mary, 1981. Spl. assignments chemist BASF Corp., Freeport, Tex., 1981-82, process devel. chemist, 1982-83, prodn. chemist, 1983-89, quality assurance leader, 1989-94; lab. svcs. mgr. Freeport site, 1994-95, procurement mgr. Freeport site, 1995—. Advisor Jr. Achievment, Lake Jackson, Tex., 1982; mem. Rep. Party Inner Circle, Washington, 1992; asst. troop leader Girl Scouts U.S.A., 1993-95; bd. dirs. Friends of the Lake Jackson Libr. Mem. AAAS, Am. Chem. Soc. (budget and fin. com. 1991—, editor younger chemists com. newsletter 1989-91, treas. local sect. 1987, Notable Women's Chemist honors 1992), Am. Soc. Quality Control, Corp. Assocs., Bus. and Profl. Women's Club of Angleton (2d v.p. 1988, Young Career Woman region III 1988). Office: BASF Corp 602 Copper Rd Freeport TX 77541-3001

METZGER, W. JAMES, JR., physician, researcher, educator; b. Pitts., Oct. 30, 1945; s. Walter James Sr. and Marion Smith (Vine) M.; m. Carol Louise Hughes, Sept. 14, 1968; children: James Andrew, Joel Robert, Anne Elizabeth. BA, Stanford U., 1967; MD, Northwestern U., Chgo., 1971. Intern, resident Northwestern U. Sch. of Medicine, Chgo., 1971-74, rsch. fellow, 1974-76; asst. prof. medicine U. Iowa Coll. of Medicine, Iowa City, 1978-84; assoc. prof., sect. head East Carolina U. Sch. of Medicine, Greenville, N.C., 1984-90, prof., sect. head, 1990—, vice chmn medicine for rsch., 1993—; chmn. med. rsch. com. med. rsch. com., 1989-95; mem. study sect. merit rev. Nat. VA Rsch. Com., 1991-94. Co-editor: Drugs and the Lung, 1994; mem editl. Allergy Procs., 1989-93; contbr. chpts. to books, papers to med. jours. Forum leader Jarvis Meml. United Meth. Ch., Greenville, 1985-95. NIH grantee, Bethesda, Md., 1988-92. Fellow ACP, Am. Coll. Chest Physicians; mem. Am. Acad. Allergy Rsch. Coun. (vice chair 1988-92, 93-95, chair 1995—), Am. Acad. Allergy Asthma (chair bronchoalveolar lavage com. 1994-95), Rhinitis, Respiratory Diseases (chair interest sect. 1991-92), Chilean Lung Soc. (hon.). Office: East Carolina U Sch Medicine Brody Bldg Rm 3E-129 Greenville NC 27834

METZLER, JERRY DON, nursing administrator; b. Mishawaka, Ind., Mar. 6, 1935; s. Gerald Donald and Cleota Christabell (Dowell) M.; m. Dorothy J. Masters, Aug. 18, 1962. BS, Ariz. State U., 1962, MEd, 1967; BSN, San Diego State U., 1973; MS, U. Ariz., Tucson, 1980. Sci. tchr. Washington Sch., Sanger, Calif., 1963-68; tchr. biology San Jacinto (Calif.) High Sch., 1968-70; staff nurse Maricopa County Hosp., Phoenix, 1973-76; staff nurse St. Luke's Hosp., Phoenix, 1976-77; nursing instr., dept. head Gila Pueblo Coll., Globe, Ariz., 1977-78; nurse educator, asst. dir. nursing USPHS Indian Hosp., Tuba City, Ariz., 1980-84; asst. nursing svc. mgr. Phoenix Indian Med. Ctr., 1984-85; pub. health educator Phoenix Indian Med. Ctr., 1985-88; dir. nursing USPHS Indian Hosp., Owyhee, Nev., 1988-90; sr. project officer USPHS, Dallas, 1990—. With USN, 1956-60, USPHS, 1980—. Mem. Res. Officers Assn., Am. Nurses Assn., Commd. Officers Assn. of USPHS, Masons, Sigma Theta Tau. Republican. Methodist. Home: 420 Shockley Ave De Soto TX 75115-3229 Office: PHS ROVI 1200 Main St Dallas TX 75202-4348

METZNER, DAVID MARK, plastic and reconstructive surgeon; b. Cleve., Jan. 16, 1939; children: Damon Hires, Rowan Aliya von Zanthier. AB, U. Mich., 1960; MD, Case Western Res. U., 1964. Diplomate Am. Bd. Otolaryngology, Am. Bd. Plastic Surgery, Nat. Bd. Med. Examiners; lic. MD, Ohio, Calif., Mass., La. Internship Mt. Sinai Hosp., Cleve., 1964-65, residency in gen. surgery, 1965-66; residency in otolaryngology Harvard Med. Sch., Boston, 1966-69; chief of otolaryngology The Cambridge (Mass.) Hosp., 1971-74; residency in plastic and reconstructive surgery La. State U., New Orleans, 1975-76; active staff Lakeside Hosp., Metairie, La., 1977—, Highland Pk. Hosp., Covington, La., 1977—, Prytania Surgery Ctr., New Orleans, 1986—; pvt. plastic surgery New Orleans & Covington, 1977—; active, courtest staff So. Bapt. Hosp., New Orleans, 1977—; courtesy staff St. Tammany Parish Hosp., Covington, 1977—; clin. instr. Harvard Med. Sch., 1971-75; vis. prof. Nassau County, N.Y. Med. Ctr., 1988, Med. Coll. Wis., 1992; vis. lectr. U. Calif. San Diego, 1991; clin. asst. prof. La. State U., 1994—. Recipient AMA Physician's Recognition award, 1981, 84, 87, 90, Walter Scott Brown award Am. Soc. for Aesthetic Plastic Surgery, 1989, Appreciation award North Am. Med./Dental Assn. Mem. Am. Soc. Plastic and Reconstructive Surgeons, Inc., The Am. Soc. for Aesthetic Plastic Surgery, Inc., Southeastern Soc. Plastic and Reconstructive Surgeons, Inc., Am. Acad. Facial Plastic and Reconstructive Surgery, Inc., Am. Acad. Otolaryngology-Head and Neck Surgery, Inc., La. Soc. Plastic and Reconstructive Surgeons, The Double Boarded Soc. Office: Lakeside Hosp Med Staff Office Bldg 4720 S I 10 Service Rd W Metairie LA 70001-1242 also: 106 Park Pl Covington LA 70433

MEUTER, MARIA COOLMAN, lawyer; b. New Albany, Ind., July 17, 1915; d. William Edmund and Hundley Love (Wells) Coolman; m. Walter Frederick Meuter, Jan. 9, 1942; children: Stephen, Craig Frederick. Student, New Albany Bus. Coll., 1933; LLB, Jefferson Sch. Law, 1939; JD, U. Louisville, 1971. Bar: Ky. 1939, U.S. Ct. Internat. Trade, 1980. Clk. Fed. Land Bank of Louisville, 1933-41; exec. dir. Louisville Bar Assn., 1952-70; trial judge County Ct., Jefferson County, Louisville, 1962-70; assoc. dir. Law Alumni Affairs, U. Louisville, 1970—; exec. dir. Continuing Legal Edn., U. Louisville, 1978-83; pvt. practice, Louisville, 1970—; life trustee Law Alumni Found. Vice pres. Beechmont Civic Club, Louisville, 1987-91. Named Disting. Alumnae, U. Louisville Sch. Law, 1976, Ky. col., 1968, Master of Steamboat Flotilla of Jefferson County, 1968. Mem. Ky. Bar Assn. (rec. sec. ho. of dels. 1964-68), Louisville Bar Assn., Jefferson County Women Lawyers (pres.), Nat. Assn. Bar Execs. (rec. sec. 1969-70), DAR (com. chmn. John Marshall chpt. 1991), Daus. Am. Colonists, Colonial Dames, Law Alumni Assn. U. Louisville (treas., sec. 1970-75), South Park Country Club. Republican. Episcopalian. Home: 1313 Marret Pl Louisville KY 40215-2368 also: 2855 Gulf Shore Blvd N Naples FL 33940-4339

MEWS, SIEGFRIED, German language educator; b. Berlin; came to U.S., 1961; MA, So. Ill. U., Carbondale, 1963; PhD, U. Ill., 1967. From asst. prof. to prof. German U. N.C., Chapel Hill, 1967—. Author: Ulrich Plenzdorf, 1984; editor: Critical Essays on B. Brecht, 1989; co-editor: Nineteenth-Century German Writers, 2 vols., 1993; editor South Atlantic Rev., 1983-89. Mem. South Atlantic MLA (exec. dir. 1983-89). Office: Univ NC CBH 3160 4389 Dey Hall Chapel Hill NC 27599-3160

MEWS, SIEGFRIED ERNST, language educator; b. Berlin, Sept. 28, 1933. Grad., U. Hamburg, 1961; MA, So. Ill. U., 1963; PhD, U. Ill., 1967. Asst. prof. of German U. N.C., Chapel Hill, 1967-71, assoc. prof. of German, 1971-77, prof. of German, 1977—, chmn. dept., 1990-94. Author: Carl Zuckmayer, 1981, Ulrich Plenzdorf, 1984; editor: Critical Essays on Bertolt Brecht, 1989, South Atlantic Rev. jour. 1983-89, U.N.C. Studies in the Germanic Langs. and Lits., 1968-80. Recipient Friendship award Fed. Republic of Germany, 1989. Mem. South Atlantic Modern Lang. Assn. (exec. dir. 1983-89, pres. 1991-92), other orgns. Office: University N C Dept Germanic Langs CB # 3160 438 Dey Hall Chapel Hill NC 27699-3160

MEYER, ANNETTE COLE, real estate company executive; b. Rockmart, Ga., Nov. 21, 1942; d. Charles Floyd and Marie G. Cole; m. Bobby E. Shirah, June 20, 1960 (div. 1974); children: Nathan, Stanton. Lic. real estate broker, Atlanta. Dir. leasing Taylor & Mathis, Atlanta, 1970-84; v.p. Franklin Property Co., Atlanta, 1984-86, Rostland, Atlanta, 1986-87, Skanska Real Estate, Atlanta, 1988—; pres. Comml. Real Estate Women, Atlanta, 1995-96. Mem. bd. Women's Resource Ctr., Decatur, Ga., 1995-96. Recipient Million Dollar Club award, Natl. Assn. of Indsl. and Office Properties, Atlanta, 1993, 94, 95. Mem. Nat. Assn. Indsl. and Office Properties, Urban Land Inst., Atlanta Bot. Soc., Atlanta Symphony. Presbyterian.

MEYER, B. FRED, small business executive, home designer and builder, product designer; b. Long Island, N.Y., Jan. 6, 1918; s. Barthold Fred and Edna May (Clark) M.; m. Mary E. Carman, July 18, 1951; children: Patricia Meyer Sauer, Susan Meyer Sachs. Student, Pratt Inst., 1935-39, Johns Hopkins U., 1946-48, Wayne State U., 1954-55. Registered builder, Fla. Project engr. Lear, Inc., Grand Rapids, Mich., 1948-51; engring. exec. GM Corp., Warren, Mich., 1951-75; pres. BFM Assocs., Inc. (name Fred Meyer, Inc. 1990), Sarasota, Fla., 1975—. Patentee on pendulum type seat belt retractor, power window switch, power window actuator, 6-way seat switch, 6-way seat actuator, rear trunk pull-down mechanism, numerous others. Capt. USAAF, 1942-46, ETO. Mem. Oaks Country Club (Osprey, Fla.). Home and Office: 4131 Boca Pointe Dr Sarasota FL 34238

MEYER, BILLIE JEAN, special education educator; b. Kansas City, Mo., July 27, 1943; d. Charles William and Dorothy Ellen (Alt) Emerson; m. Kenneth Lee Morris, Aug. 24, 1963 (div. Oct. 1985); 1 child, Darla Michelle Morris Stewart; m. Gordon Frederick Meyer, June 1, 1986 (dec. May 1994); stepchildren: Ardith Helmer, Susan Stanford, Gary, Geneace, Patti Draughon, Shari Mohr. BS in Edn., Northeastern State U., 1965, M in Tchg., 1968. Cert. tchr., Okla.; cert. visually impaired, Braille. Substitute tchr. Muskogee (Okla.) Pub. Schs., 1965; elem. tchr. Okla. Sch. for the Blind, Muskogee, 1965-67, elem. tchr., computer tchr., 1969—; adj. lectr. Northeastern State U., Tahlequah, summers 1990-92, 94, 95-96; on-site team mem. Nat. Accreditation Coun., 1987; mem. com. revision cert. stds., State of Okla., 1982. Author: A Sequential Math Program for Beginning Abacus Students, 1979. Mem. Assn. of Edn. and Rehab. of the Blind and Visually Impaired, Okla. Assn. of Ednl. Rehab. of the Blind and Visually Impaired (pres.-elect 1985-86, pres. 1986-87, sec. 1993-96), Computer Using Educators, Epsilon Sigma Alpha (state pres. 1981-82, Girl of Yr. 1971). Office: Okla Sch for the Blind 3300 Gibson St Muskogee OK 74403-2811

MEYER, CAROL FRANCES, pediatrician, allergist; b. Berea, Ky., June 2, 1936; d. Harvey Kessler and Jessie Irene (Hamm) Meyer; m. Daniel Baker Cox, June 5, 1955 (div. Apr. 1962). AA, U. Fla., 1955; BA, Duke U., 1957; MD, Med. Coll. Ga., 1967. Diplomate Am. Bd. Pediatrics, Am. Bd. Allergy and Immunology. Intern in pediatrics Med. Coll. Ga., Augusta, 1967-68; resident in pediatrics Gorgas Hosp., Canal Zone, 1968-69; fellow in pediatric respiratory disease Med. Coll. Ga., 1969-71, instr. pediat., 1971-72; med. officer pediatrics Canal Zone Govt., 1972-79; med. officer pediatrics Dept. of Army, Panama, 1979-82, med. officer allergy, 1982-89, physician in charge allergy clinic, 1984-89; asst. prof. pediatrics and medicine Med. Coll. Ga., Augusta, 1990—; mem. Bd. of Canal Zone Merit System Examiners, 1976-79. Contbr. articles to profl. jours. Mem. First Bapt. Ch. Orch., 1992—; founding mem., violoncello Curundu Chamber Ensemble, 1979-89. Recipient U.S. Army Exceptional Performance awards, 1985, 86, 89, Merck award Med. Coll. Ga.,, 1967; U. Fla. J. Hillis Miller scholar, 1954. Mem.

AAAS, Am. Coll. Rheumatology, Allergy and Immunology Soc. Ga., Hispanic-Am. Allergy and Immunology Assn., Ga. Pediatric Soc., Pan Am. Med. Assn., Soc. Leukocyte Biology, Am. Coll. Allergy, Asthma and Immunology, Am. Acad. Allergy, Asthma and Immunology, Am. Acad. Pediat., Am. Med. Women's Assn., Panama Canal Soc. Fla., Ga. Ornithol. Soc., Ga. Thoracic Soc., Am. Lung Assn. (Ga. East Ctrl. br. exec. bd.), Am. Assn. Ret. Persons, Nature Conservancy, Royal Soc. for Preservation Birds, Nat. Assn. Ret. Fed. Employees, Nat. Audubon Soc., Panama Audubon Soc., Willow Run Homeowner's Soc. (pres.), Alpha Omega Alpha. Office: Med Coll Ga BG 232 1120 15th St Augusta GA 30912

MEYER, CHERYL LYNN, secondary school educator; b. Sayre, Okla., May 29, 1953; d. Virgil Dale and Amo Jean (Bohannon) Addis; m. Gary Allen Meyer, July 22, 1973; children: Jerremy, Nathan, Dale. BS in Biology and English, West Tex. A—M, 1975, postgrad., 1976-77. Libr. asst. Frank Phillips Coll., Borger, Tex., 1971-73; salesperson menswear Woolco Dept. Store, Amarillo, Tex., summer 1973; salesperson material Hancock Fabrics, Amarillo, 1973-75; tchr. sci. Hereford (Tex.) Ind. Sch. Dist., 1975-76; tchr. sci., English, tennis coach White Deer (Tex.) Sch. Dist., 1977-79, substitute tchr., 1980-89; tchr. phys. sci. West Tex. H.S., Stinnett, 1990; tchr. St. Vincent de Paul Sch., Pampa, Tex., 1990-92; substitute tchr. Borger (Tex.) Ind. Sch. Dist., 1992-95, tchr. chemistry, 1995-96, Alternative Edn. Program tchr., 1996—. Baptist. Home: PO Box 33 Skellytown TX 79080 Office: Borger High School Borger TX 79007

MEYER, EDGAR F., crystallographer; b. El Campo, Tex., July 19, 1935; s. Edgar F. and Lydia (Lowke) M.; m. Catarina Pestalozzi, Apr. 30, 1965; children: Erik, Claudia, Felix. BS, N. Tex. St. U., 1959; PhD, U. Tex., 1963. Post doctoral fellow Swiss Federal Inst. Tech., Zurich, Switzerland, 1963-65, Mass. Inst. Tech., Cambridge, Mass., 1965-67; from asst. prof. to prof. Tex. A&M U., College Station, Tex., 1967--. Office: Tex A&M U Biochemistry Dept College Station TX 77843

MEYER, FRANCES MARGARET ANTHONY, elementary and secondary school educator, health education specialist; b. Stella, Va., Nov. 15, 1947; d. Arthur Abner Jr. and Emmie Adeline (Murray) Anthony; m. Stephen Leroy Meyer, Aug. 2, 1975. BS, Longwood Coll., 1970; MS, Va. Commonwealth U., 1982, PhD, 1996. Cert. tchr., Va. Health, phys. edn., and dance tchr. Fredericksburg (Va.) City Pub. Schs., 1970-89; AIDS edn. coord. Va. Dept. Edn., Richmond, 1989-90, health edn. specialist, 1990-94, comprehensive sch. health program specialist, 1994—. Author: (with others) Elementary Physical Education: Growing through Movement--A Curriculum Guide, 1982; health editor Va. Jour., 1994—; contbr. articles to profl. jours. Mem. pub. edn. coun., comprehensive sch. health edn. team Va. affiliate, Am. Cancer Soc., Richmond, 1990—; dir. Va. Children's Dance Festival, Hist. Fredericksburg Found., Inc., 1981—; vol. ARC, Fredericksburg, 1976-84. Mem. AAUW (com. 1989-90), ASCD, NEA, AAPHERD (past v.p., chmn. divsn. 1970—, mem. Nat. Mid. Sch. Assn., So. Dist. Honor award 1995), Va. Edn. Assn., Va. Mid. Sch. Assn., Va. Alliance for Arts Edn., Internat. Coun. for Health, Phys. Edn., Recreation, Sport and Dance (internat. commns. for health edn. and commn. for dance and dance edn.), Va. Health Promotion and Edn. Coun. (bd. dirs. 1990—), Soc. State Dirs. Health, Phys. Edn. and Recreation (legis. affairs com. 1994—), Longwood Coll. Alumni Coun. (bd. dirs. 1987-90), Nat. Network for Youth Svcs. (rev. panel, adv. bd. 1994—), Am. Coll. Health Assn. (curriculum and tng. rev. panel 1992-94), Va. Alliance for Arts Edn. (adv. bd. 1980-83, 89-90, 95—), Va. Assn. for Health, Phys. Edn., Recreation and Dance (past pres., various coms. 1970—, Tchr. of Yr. 1983), Delta Kappa Gamma (pres. Beta Eta chpt. 1988-90), Nat. Dance Assn. (bd. dirs. 1996—). Baptist.

MEYER, GEORGE WILBUR, internist, health facility administrator; b. Cleve., Apr. 30, 1941; s. George Wilbur and Emily Fuller (Campbell) M.; m. Carolyn Edwards Garrett, Apr. 8, 1967; children: Robert James, Elizabeth Jackson, Dobro Goodale. BS, MIT, 1962; MD, Tulane Med. Sch., 1966. Intern So. Pacific Hosps. Inc., San Francisco, 1966-67; resident Pacific Presbyn. Med. Ctr., San Francisco, 1969-72; commd. 1st lt. USAF, advanced through grades to col., 1980; fellow in gastroenterology David Grant USAF Med. Ctr., Travis AFB, Calif., 1974-76; asst. chair dept. medicine USAF Med. Ctr., Keesler AFB, Miss., 1976-78; asst. prof. dept. medicine Uniformed Svcs. Univ., Bethesda, Md., 1978-80; chair dept. medicine Wright Patterson AFB, Dayton, Ohio, 1980-82; chief of medicine Wilford Hall USAF Med. Ctr., Lackland AFB, Tex., 1982-86; chief clin. svcs. USAF Acad., Colo., 1986-88; comdr. 1st Med. Groups, Langley AFB, Va., Germany, 1988-89, 86th Med. Group, Ramstein AFB, Germany, 1989-92; program dir. internal medicine Ga. Bapt. Med. Ctr., Atlanta, 1993—; cons. Walter Reed Army Med. Ctr., Washington, 1978-80, Nat. Naval Med. Ctr., Bethesda, 1978-80; assoc. prof. Wright State U. Sch. Medicine, Dayton, 1980-82; cons. Dayton VA Med. Ctr., 1980-82; clin. assoc. prof. medicine U. Tex. Health Sci. Ctr., San Antonio, 1982-86, Med. Coll. Ga., Augusta, 1993—. Mem. editl. bd. Gastrointestinal Endoscopy, 1993—; contbr. articles and revs. to profl. jours. and chpts. to books. Mem. leadership com. Am. Cancer Soc., Ramstein AFB, 1989-93, bd. dirs. Atlanta City Unit, 1995—, Ga. divsn. 1996—, El Paso Teller Unit, Colorado Springs, 1986-88, Bexar Metro Unit, San Antonio, 1984-86; mem. adv. com. United Health Svcs., Dayton, 1980-82. Fellow ACP, Am. Coll. Gastroenterology; mem. Am. Soc. for Gastro Endoscopy, Am. Gastrointestinal Assn., Am. Assn. for Study of Liver Diseases. Office: Ga Bapt Med Ctr 303 Parkway Dr NE Atlanta GA 30312-1212

MEYER, HARVEY KESSLER, II, retired academic administrator; b. Carlisle, Pa., Feb. 6, 1914; s. Harvey Kessler and Frances May (Shultz) M.; m. Jessie Irene Hamm, Feb. 22, 1935; children: Carol Frances, Harvey Kessler III, Howard Madison. BA, Berea (Ky.) Coll., 1936; MA, Eastern Ky. U., 1942; D Edn., U. Fla., Gainesville, 1951. Surveyor Wash. State Hwy. Engrs., 1932; furniture designer Berea Woodwork, 1932-36; lic. contractor Bailey Constrn. Co., Seattle, Wash., 1935, Alachua County, Fla., 1948-50.; instr. U. Fla., Ocala, 1936-37; supr. Nat. Youth Adminstrn., Jacksonville, Fla., 1937-38; vocat. tchr. Richmond (Ky.) City Schs., 1938-40; asst. prof. Eastern Ky. U., Richmond, 1940-43; tchr. P.K.Yonge Lab. Sch., Gainesville, Fla., 1946-47, prin., 1947-48; assoc. prof. U. Fla., Gainesville, 1948-51, prof., 1951-65; assoc. dean acad. affairs Fla. Atlantic U., Boca Raton, 1965-68, grad. prof., 1968-73; dir. Indsl. Arts and Vocat. Edn., Managua, Nicaragua, 1955-57; founder Instituto Nacional Educacion Vocacional, Nicaragua; dir., trustee Moravian Theol. Sem., Bethlehem, Pa., 1976; dean radio and TV Fla. Inst. for Continuing Univ. Studies, 1962-65; adminstrv. cons. Brit.-Am. Investment Fund, Luxembourg City, Europe, 1969-71; owner, design Plantation Glen, Alachua County, 1948-77, Hacienda Ocotlan, Clay County, N.C., 1975-78. Author: Technical Eduction in Nicaragua, 1958, Historical Dictionary Nicaragua, 1972, Historical Dictionary Honduras, 1976, rev. edit., 1994. Pres. Fla. dist. Moravian Ch., 1970-73, Melrose (Fla.) Library Assn., 1983—, pres., 1984-90, 92—; trustee Moravian Coll. and Sem., 1966-78. Comdr. USNR, ret.; naval aviation observer. Named Disting. Alumnus Berea Coll., 1986. Mem. Berea Coll. Alumni Assn. (pres. 1990-91), Rotary, Phi Kappa Phi, Phi Delta Kappa, Epsilon Pi Tau (trustee 1950—). Democrat. Home: Quinta la Maya Atlán 2805 NW 83d St #405C Gainesville FL 32606-6288

MEYER, JOHN STIRLING, neurologist, educator; b. London, Feb. 24, 1924; came to U.S., 1940; s. William Charles and Alice Elizabeth (Stirling) M.; m. Wendy Haskell, July 20, 1947 (dec. 1986); children: Jane, Anne, Elizabeth, Helen, Margaret; m. Katharine Sumner, Aug. 2, 1987; m. Cora Bess Parks, Apr. 6, 1996. BSc, Trinity Coll., Hartford, Conn., 1944; MD, CM, McGill U., Montreal, Que., 1948, MSc, 1949. Diplomate Am. Bd. Neurology and Psychiatry. Intern Yale-New Haven Hosp., 1948-49, resident immunology, 1949-50; resident neurology Boston City Hosp., 1950-52, resident neurophysiology, 1952-53, fellow neurophysiology, 1954-55; instr. rsch. assoc. Harvard Med. Sch., Boston, 1955-57; resident neurophysiology Harvard Med. Sch., 1952-53; prof., chair dept. Wayne State U., Detroit, 1957-69; prof., chair dept. Baylor Coll. Medicine, Houston, 1969-75, prof. neurology, 1976—; demonstrator neuropathology and teaching fellow neurology Harvard U. Med. Sch., 1950-52; sr. rsch. fellow USPHS, 1952-54; instr. medicine Harvard U. Med. Sch., 1954-56; assoc. vis. physician neurology Boston City Hosp., 1956-57; cons. and lectr. neurology U.S. Naval Hosp., Chelsea, Mass., 1957; prof. neurology and chmn. dept. sch. medicine Wayne State U., 1957-69, chmn. dept., 1969-76; prof. neurology, dir. stroke lab. Baylor Coll. Medicine, Houston, 1976—; with VA Med. cTr., Houston; chair stroke panel Pres.' Commn. on Heart Disease Cancer & Stroke, Washington, 1964-65; mem. nat. adv. coun. Nat. Inst. Neurol. Diseases & Stroke, Bethesda, Md., 1965-69. Author 28 books; contbr. 768 articles to profl. jours. Mem. jury Albert Lasker Med. Rsch. Awards, N.Y.C., 1965-69. Lt. (s.g.) Med. Corps USN, 1953-55, Korea. Recipient Harold G. Woff award, Am. Assn. for Study of Head Ache, 1977, 79, Baylor Coll. Medicine award, Houston, 1980, 85, 90, Mihara award Mihara Found., Tokyo, 1987, Bertha Lecture award Salzburg Conf., Washington, 1992. Mem. Am. Heart Assn. (bd. dirs. 1968-70, chair coun. on stroke 1968-70). Republican. Episcopalian. Office: VA Med Ctr Rm 225 2002 Holcombe Blvd Bldg 110 Houston TX 77030-4211*

MEYER, LINDA CORRINE SMITH, employment and training operations executive; b. Monroe, Mich., June 5, 1949; d. William Lambert and Marion Adelia (Hopkins) S.; m. Rodney William Meyer, Sept. 7, 1969 (div. Nov. 1979); children: Jason William, Megan Kathleen. BS in Mgmt., U. South Fla., 1992. Cert. employment and tng. adminstr. Ambulance attendant, unit mgr. emergency room Jackson Meml. Hosp., Dade City, Fla., 1967-69; unit mgr. ob-gyn. Glens Falls (N.Y.) Hosp., 1969-71; unit mgr. phys. occupational speech therapy Mass. Gen. Hosp., Boston, 1971-74; grant coord. Boston U., 1971-74; unit adminstr. ob./infirtility Mass. Gen. Hosp., 1974-77; divsn. mgr. Pasco County Bd. County Commrs., Dade City, 1977-83; divsn. mgr. greater N.Y.C. comm. consulting Henkels & McCoy, Inc., Blue Bell, Pa., 1983-87; v.p. client svcs. and tng., ops. mgr. Withlacoochee Pvt. Industry Coun., Ocala, Fla., 1992-94; mgmt. cons. Fla. Dept. Labor and Employment Security, Tallahassee, Fla., 1994—; mem. vocat. edn. coord. com. Dist. Sch. Bd. Pasco County, Fla.; mem. edn. coord. com. Pasco-Hernando C.C., Fla. Editor Henkels & McCoy Tng. Svcs. Newsletter. Mem. legis. com. vocat. rehab. coun. and chairing coun. State of Fla.; mktg. mgr. USF Univ. Singers; vol. counselor San Antonio Boys Village; instr. LDS Ch., choruster women's orgn., ch. choruster, ch. choir dir., homemaking counselor, homemaking leader, pres. relief soc., sec. stake relief soc., sec. sunday sch.; active community dinner theatre, Broomall, Pa. Mgmt. scholar USF Coll. Bus. Adminstrn., 1992. Mem. Am. Soc. Tng. and Devel., Nat. Assn. Female Execs., Nat. Assn. Counties, Nat. Assn. County Employment and Tng. Adminstrs (legis./issues com., chmn. recipient population subcom.). Southeastern Employment & Tng. Assn. (pres. Fla. chpt., ad hoc com., keynote speaker fall conf.), Fla. Tng. Inst. (sec. exec. com., bd. dirs.), Fla. Employment and Tng. Assn., Inc. (life, pres., incorporating officer 1983), Bay Area Consortium for Women (founding mem., charter sec.), East Pasco Bus. and Profl. Women (charter, past pres.), Women in Cable, Phila. Cable Club, Gold Key Nat. Honor Soc. Independent. Office: Fla Dept Labor and Employment Security 1320 Executive Center Dr Tallahassee FL 32399-6511

MEYER, LOUIS B., superior court judge, retired state supreme court justice; b. Marion, N.C., July 15, 1933; s. Louis B. and Beulah (Smith) M.; m. Evelyn Spradlin, Dec. 29, 1956; children: Louis B. III, Patricia Shannon, Adam Burden. B.A., Wake Forest U., 1955, J.D., 1960; LLM, U. Va., 1992. Bar: N.C. 1960, U.S. Dist. (ea. dist.) N.C. 1960, U.S. Ct. Appeals (4th cir.) 1960, U.S. Supreme Ct. 1962. Law clk. Supreme Ct. N.C., Raleigh, 1960; spl. agent FBI, 1961-62; atty. Lucas, Rand, Rose, Meyer, Jones & Orcutt P.A., Wilson, N.C., 1962-81; assoc. justice Supreme Ct. N.C., Raleigh, 1981-95, ret., 1995; spl. judge Superior Ct., 1995—. Former county chmn. Wilson County Dems., N.C.; former mem. N.C. State Exec. Com. Dem. Party. Served to 1st lt. U.S. Army, 1955-57. Mem. Wilson County Bar Assn. (former pres.), 7th Jud. Dist. Bar Assn. (former pres.), N.C. Bar Assn. (former v.p.), Masons. Baptist.

MEYER, MARION M., editorial consultant; b. Sheboygan, Wis., July 14, 1923; d. Herman O. and Viola A. (Hoch) M. BA, Lakeland Coll., 1950; MA, NYU, 1957. Payroll clk. Am. Chair Co., Sheboygan, 1941-46; tchr. English and religion, dir. athletics Am. Sch. for Girls, Baghdad, Iraq, 1950-56; mem. edn. and publ. staff United Ch. Bd. for Homeland Ministries, United Ch. Press/Pilgrim Press, 1958-64, sr. editor, 1965-88, ret., 1988; cons. to individuals and orgns. on editorial matters and copyrights. Editor Penney Retirement Cmty. Newsletter, 1990—; contbr. articles to various publs.; writer hymns Look to God, Be Radiant, 1989, Be Still, 1990, Come, God, Creator, 1992, Something New! (extended work), 1993, Our Home is PRC, 1996. Incorporating mem. Contact Phila., Inc., 1972, bd. dirs., 1972-75, v.p., chmn. com. to organize community adv. bd., chmn. auditing com., editor newsletter, 1972-74, pres., 1974-75, assoc. mem., 1977—; mem. ofcl. bd. Old First Reformed Ch., Phila., 1984-89; deacon United Ch. Christ, 1984—, Mid.-East Com. of Pa. SE Conf. United Ch. Christ, 1986-88. Honored as role model United Ch. of Christ, 1982, 85. Mem. AAUW, NOW, Nat. Mus. Women in the Arts (charter mem.), Nat. Trust for Hist. Preservation. Home: PO Box 656 Penney Farms FL 32079-0656

MEYER, PATRICIA HANES, psychiatric social worker; b. Champaign, Ill., Feb. 10, 1947; d. Walter Ernest and Mary Kathryn (Kemp) Hanes; B.A., Carroll Coll., Waukesha, Wis., 1969; M.S.W., Cath. U. Am., 1976; m. Scott Kimbrough Meyer, June 15, 1969; children—Jennifer Suzanne, Claire Catherine, John Andrew. Dir. family therapy program Fairfax County Juvenile Ct., Fairfax, Va., 1970-77; clin. instr. Georgetown U. Med. Sch., Washington, 1976-84; pvt. practice family therapy, 1976—. Mem. Am. Orthopsychiat. Assn., Am. Family Therapy Assn., Nat. Assn. Social Workers. Adv. editor The Family, 1977-84. Home: 13042 Thompson Rd Fairfax VA 22033-1501 Office: Ste 440 11800 Sunrise Valley Dr Reston VA 22091-5302

MEYER, PHILIP EDWARD, journalism educator; b. Deshler, Nebr., Oct. 27, 1930; s. Elmer Edward and Hilda Grace (Morrison) M.; m. Sue Quail, Aug. 5, 1956; children: Caroline, Katherine, Melissa, Sarah. BS, Kans. State U., 1952; MA, U. N.C., 1963. Asst. state editor Topeka (Kans.) Daily Capital, 1954-56; reporter Miami (Fla.) Herald, 1958-62; Washington corr. Akron Beacon Jour., 1962-66; nat. corr. Knight-Ridder, Inc., Washington, 1967-78; dir. news research Knight-Ridder, Inc., Miami, 1978-81; William Rand Kenan Jr. prof. journalism U. N.C., Chapel Hill, 1981-93; Knight prof., 1993—. Author: Precision Journalism, 1973 (Sigma Delta Chi Disting. Service award 1974), The Newspaper Survival Book, 1985, Ethical Journalism, 1987, The New Precision Journalism, 1991; co-author: To Keep the Republic, 1975. Project dir. Russell Sage Found., N.Y.C., 1969-70. Served with USNR, 1952-54. Recipient Disting. Contbns. to Journalism award Nat. Press Found., 1994, Disting. Contbns. to Media and Media Studies award Freedom Forum Media Studies Ctr., 1995; Nieman fellow Harvard U., 1966-67, fellow Freedom Forum Ctr. for Media Studies, 1985. Mem. Am. Assn. for Pub. Opinion Rsch. (pres. 1989-90), World Assn. for Pub. Opinion Rsch. (pres. 1994-95), Assn. for Edn. in Journalism and Mass Comm., Nat. Press Club (Washington). Democrat. Episcopalian. Home: 610 Croom Ct Chapel Hill NC 27514-6706 Office: UNC Sch Journalism & Mass Comm Howell Hall CB3365 Chapel Hill NC 27599

MEYER-ARENDT, KLAUS JOHN, geography educator; b. Hamburg, Germany, Nov. 6, 1950; s. Jurgen R. and Erica A. (Suck) M.-A.; m. Michele M. DeRouen, May 23, 1981; children: Camille, Greta, Nicolas. BA in Geography, Portland (Oreg.) State U., 1975; MA in Geography, La. State U., 1979, PhD in Geography, 1987. Teaching asst. La. State U., Baton Rouge, 1976-78, 83-85; rsch. assoc. Coastal Environments Inc., Baton Rouge, 1978-83; instr. Southeastern La. U., Hammond, 1986-87, La. State U., Baton Rouge, 1987; asst. prof. Geography Miss. State U., Starkville, 1987-92, assoc. prof. Geography, 1992—. Mem. edit. bd. Jour. of Cultural Geography, 1990—; editor: Recreation, Tourism & Sport newsletter, 1991-93; co-editor: Jour. of Cultural Geography, 1990, 92. Regional coord. Miss. Geog. Alliance, Starkville, 1989—; mem. Tenn.-Tom Tourism Coun., Columbus, Miss., 1990—; faculty advisor Students Concerns About Protecting the Environment, 1989—; pres. Morrill Rd. Water Assn., Starkville, 1993—. Miss. Office of Geology rsch. grantee, 1991—, Miss./Ala. SeaGrant grantee, 1992; Fulbright scholar, 1994. Mem. Assn. Am. Geographers (Miss. rep. S.E. chpt. 1990-94), Miss. Acad. Scis. (div. chair 1989-90), Conf. of Latin Americanist Geographers (bd. dirs. 1990-93), The Coastal Soc. Office: Miss State U Dept Geoscis PO Box 5448 Mississippi State MS 39762-5167

MEYERS, CAROL LYONS, religion, history and archaeology educator; b. Wilkes Barre, Pa., Nov. 26, 1942; d. Harry J. and Irene R. (Winkler) Lyons; m. Eric Mark Meyers, June 25, 1964; children: Julie Kaete, Dina Elisa. AB with honors, Wellesley Coll., 1964; MA in Near Ea. and Judaic Studies, Brandeis U., 1966, PhD, 1975. Area supr. Joint Expdn. to Tell Gezer, Israel, 1964-67; editorial asst., asst. to registrar Ashdod Excavation Project, Israel, 1963, 64-65; quadrangle dir. Brandeis U., Waltham, Mass., 1965-67; teaching asst. Boston Area Seminar Internat. Students, 1965; area supr., lect. Joint Expdn. to Khirbet Shema, Israel, 1970-71, area supr., 1971, field supr., 1972; assoc. dir. Joint Expdn. to Meiron, Israel, 1978; co-dir. Joint Sepphoris Project, Israel, 1985—, Sepphoris Regional Project, Israel, 1993—; instr. Bible Acad. Jewish Studies without Walls, N.Y.C., 1974-78; instr. Ctr. Continuing Edn., Duke U., Durham., N.C., 1978-79; asst. prof. religion Duke U., Durham., N.C., 1977-84, assoc. prof., 1984-90, assoc. dir. women's studies, 1985—, prof., 1990—, acting dir. women's studies, 1992. Author: The Tabernacle Menorah, 1976, Excavations at Ancient Meiron, Upper Galilee, Israel, 1971-72, 74-75, 77, The Word of the Lord Shall Go Forth, 1983, Haggai, Zechariah 1-8, 1987, Discovering Eve: Ancient Israelite Women in Context, 1988, Sepphoris, 1991, Zechariah 9-14, 1993, Ethics and Politics in the Hebrew Bible, 1995; contbr. articles to profl. jours. Bd. dirs. Bethel Community, Durham, 1980. Wellesley Coll. scholar, 1962-64, Brandeis U. fellow, 1967-69, Thayer fellow Albright Inst. Archaeol. Rsch., Jerusalem, 1975-76, NEH Fellow 1982-83, 90-91, Oxford Ctr. for Postgrad. Hebrew Studies fellow, 1982-83, Queen Elizabeth House fellow, U. Oxford, 1982-83, Howard Found. fellow, 1984-85, Ctr. Theol. Inquiry fellow, 1990-91, rsch. assoc. Fachbereich Evangelische Universität, U. Frankfort, 1995, Duke Rsch. Coun. 1983-84, 85-86, 87-88, 90-91, 92-93, 93-94; grantee Ednl. Found. Girls, 1963, 64, Brandeis U., 1966, Undergrad. Tchg. Coun. Duke U., 1978-79, Coop. Program in Judaic Studies, 1981. Mem. Jewish Fedn., Am. Acad. Religion, Am. Sch. Oriental Rsch. (fellowship com. 1979-82, editl. com. 1978—), Archaeol. Inst. Am. (v.p. 1976, sec. treas. 1984-85), Assn. Jewish Studies, Brit. Sch. Archaeology Jerusalem, Cath. Bibl. Assn., Albright Inst. Archaeol. Rsch. (v.p. 1982-94, program com. 1995—), Israel Exploration Soc., Soc. Bibl. Lit. (steering com. seminar on monarchy 1982), chmn. seminar 1981), Nat. Women's Studies Assn., Soc. for Values Higher Edn., Hadassah (edn. chmn. 1970-71). Mem. Jewish Reconstructionist Ch. Home: 3202 Waterbury Dr Durham NC 27707-2416 Office: Duke U Dept Religion PO Box 90064 Durham NC 27708-0964

MEYERS, CHARLES LOUIS, occupational physician, consultant; b. Oakland, Calif., Mar. 9, 1930; s. Charles Louis Sr. and Effie Rowella (Hudson) M.; m. Janice Fay Schley, Sept. 1, 1951; children: Stephen A., Karen E., Janina L., David C., Daniel L. BS in Engring., U. Calif., Berkeley, 1951; MS in Metallurgical Engring., Stanford U., 1960; MSE in Elec. Engring., So. Meth. U., 1974; DO, Tex. Coll. Osteo. Medicine, 1977; MPH, Med. Coll. Wis., 1989. Registered profl. metallurgical engr., Calif.; cert. safety exec., safety mgr., safety specialist. Rsch. fellow in engring. So. Meth. U., Dallas, 1970-73; resident in phys. medicine and rehab. VA Hosp., Martinez, Calif., 1977-78; occupational physician Idaho, Wis. and Tex., 1978-79, 83-93; cons. in occupational medicine Amarillo, Tex., 1993—. Contbr. articles to profl. jours. Active Ch. of Jesus Christ of Latter Day Saints, 1957—. Lt. USNR, 1951-55. Recipient scholarship USPHS, 1975-76; Spl. fellow U.S. NIH, 1971-73. Fellow Am. Coll. Occupational and Environ. Medicine; mem. Am. Pub. Health Assn., Am. Osteo. Assn. Home and Office: 3503 Brennan Gardens Amarillo TX 79121-9999

MEYERS, ERIC MARK, religion educator; b. Norwich, Conn., June 5, 1940; s. Karl D. and Shirlee M. (Meyer) M.; m. Carol Lyons, June 25, 1964; children: Julie Kaete, Dina Elisa. AB, Dartmouth Coll., 1962; MA, Brandeis U., 1964; PhD, Harvard U., 1969. Prof. religion, archeology, biblical studies, ancient hist. Duke U., Durham, N.C., 1969—; dir. Annenberg Inst., Phila., 1991-92; pres. Am. Schs. of Oriental Rsch., Balt., 1990-96. Author 9 books; editor-in-chief The Oxford Encyclopedia of Archaeology in the Near East, 5 vols., 1997; contbr. over 250 articles to profl. jours. Jewish. Home: 3202 Waterbury Dr Durham NC 27707-2416 Office: Duke U PO Box 90964 Bldg Durham NC 27708-0964

MEYERS, JAMES FRANK, electronics engineer; b. Binghamton, N.Y., Sept. 9, 1946; s. Edwin Fox and Louise (Okrepkie) M.; B.E.E., U. Louisville, 1969, M.E., 1972; postgrad. George Washington U. Instr. elec. engring lab. U. Louisville, 1968-69; engring coop. technician Langley Research Center, NASA, Hampton, Va., 1966-69, aerospace technologist, 1969—. Mem. IEEE (sect. chmn. 1975), Turnberry Two Owners Assn. (pres., dir. 1979-82), Sports Car Club Am. (div. rallye exec. 1982-86), Eta Kappa Nu, Tau Beta Pi, Sigma Tau. Contbr. articles to profl. jours.; patentee in field. Office: NASA Langley Rsch Ctr M S # 235A Hampton VA 23681-0001

MEYERSON, STANLEY PHILLIP, lawyer; b. Spartanburg, S.C., Apr. 13, 1916; s. Louis A. and Ella Meyerson; m. Sharon Maxwell Train, Nov. 30, 1996; children—Marianne Martin, Camilla Meyerson, Margot Ellis, Stanley P. A.B., Duke U., 1937, J.D., 1939. Bar: S.C. 1939, N.Y. 1940, Ga. 1945. Ptnr. Johnson Hatcher & Meyerson, Atlanta, 1945-55, Hatcher, Meyerson, Oxford & Irvin, Atlanta, 1955-78, Westmoreland, Hall, McGee, Oxford & Meyerson, Atlanta, 1978—; former adj. prof. Ga. State U.; dir., officer various corps. Co-founder West Paces Ferry Hosp., Atlanta, Annandale at Suwanee for the handicapped; trustee Hudson Libr., Inc., Highlands, N.C.; del. Moscow Conf. Law and Bilateral Econ. Rels., 1990. Contbr. legal jours. Served to lt. cmdr. USNR, 1941-45. Mem. Duke Alumni Assn. (former pres. Atlanta chpt.).

MEYNIG, ANITA RAE, artist; b. O'Donnel, Tex., Apr. 29, 1928; d. August William and Carrie Elizabeth (Hilliard) M.; m. Robert Dean Hill, Aug. 22, 1959. BA in Comml. Art, Tex. Tech U., 1951; grad., Famous Artists Sch., Rockport, Maine, 1956. Draftsman Humble Oil Co., Midland, Tex., 1952-59; pvt. art tchr. Farmington, N.Mex., 1959-62; art tchr. Mann-Meynig Studies, Hobbs, N.Mex., 1962-65; art tchr. Meynig Studio, Roswell, N.Mex., 1965-70, Dallas, 1970-82; in art prodn. Meynig Design Studio, Dallas, 1982—. Exhibited in shows, including Breckenridge (Tex.) Fine Arts Internat., 1992, 93 , 94, 95, 96 (Juror's Choice award 1996), N.W. Watercolor Soc., Kirkland, Wash., 1992, 94, We. Colo. Watercolor Soc. Nat., Grand Junction, 1992, 94, Allied Artists Am., 1991, 92, 94, 95, State U., Baton Rouge, 1993, La. Watercolor Soc., New Orleans, 1993, 94 (Juror's Choice award 1994), State of the Art '93 Invitational, Boston, Evergreen Artists Guild 1st Ann. Nat., Vancouver, Wash., 1993, 95, . Art Workshops Nat., Tulsa, 1993, Nat. Watercolor Soc., L.A., 1993, Salmagundi Non-Members, N.Y.C., 1992, 93, 94, 95, So. Watercolor Soc., Nashville, 1994, 95, 96 (Juror's award); contbr. articles to various vols. Recipient Trudy Duff award N.E. Watercolor Soc., 1990, Bronze award Women Artists of the West, 1991, Spl. Recognition award Ariz. Aqueous VIII, 1993, award of excellence Okla. Art Workshops, Tulsa, 1993, Cert., Salmagundi, N.Y., 1995, Merit award Arts Experiment Sta., N.C., 1995, Grand Exhbn. Ohio '95, Par award, MS, 1995, others. Mem. Southwestern Watercolor Soc. (pres. 1981-82, Merit award 1990), Allied Artists of Am., Am. Watercolor Soc., Watercolor Soc. Ala., Hawaii Watercolor Soc., Western Colo. Watercolor Soc. Republican. Baptist. Home and Office: 6335 Brookshire Dr Dallas TX 75230-4017

MEYTHALER, JAY MERLIN, physician, researcher, educator; b. Monroe, Wis., Dec. 23, 1953; s. Merlin Jacob and Dorothy L. Meythaler; m. DeAnn Rae Meythaler, Aug. 20, 1979; children: Nicholas, Andrew. BA with honors in History and Geology, U. Wis., Madison, 1976; JD, So. Meth. U., 1980; MD, Med. Coll. Wis., 1983. Diplomate Am. Bd. Electrodiagnostic Medicine, Am. Bd. Phys. Medicine and Rehab., Nat. Bd. Med. Examiners; grant reviewer Nat. Inst. Disability and Rehab. Rsch., 1990, 92, 93. Intern then resident dept. phys. medicine and rehab. Med. Coll. Wis., 1983-86; asst. prof. U. Va., Charlottesville, 1986-92; assoc. prof. U. Ala., Birmingham, 1992—, dir. head injury program Spain Rehab. Ctr., 1992—, dir. dept. rehab. medicine electrodiagnosis lab., 1992—; cons. physician Woodrow Wilson Rehab. Ctr., Fishersville, Va., 1987-92; lectr., researcher, participant numerous mtgs. and confs. in field. Contbr. articles and abstracts to profl. and med. publs.; Reviewer Archives Phys. Medicine and Rehab., 1987-93, alt. editor, 1992—; reviewer Am. Jour. Phys. Medicine and Rehab., 1991. Recipient award Ill. Soc. Phys. Medicine and Rehab., 1985; grants include Ctrs. for Disease Control, 1993; Dept. Edn., 1992, Medtronics Corp., 1989, 91, Nat. Inst. on Disability and Rehab. Rsch., 1987, 88, 90. Fellow Am. Acad. Phys. Medicine and Rehab. (reviewer sci. presentations 1990-93, many coms.), Am. Assn. Electrodiagnostic Medicine; mem. AMA (Physician's Recognition award 1988-91), Am. Congress Rehab. Medicine (chmn. task force AIDS 1988—), Ala. Soc. Phys. Medicine and Rehab., Ala. Head Injury Found., Am. Rheumatism Assn. (clin.), Am. Spinal Cord Injury Assn., Assn. Acad. Physiatrists, Internat. Med. Soc. Paraplegia, Am. Paraplegic Soc., Internat. Assn. for Study of Traumatic Brain Injury, Phi Alpha Delta,

Phi Eta Sigma. Home: 4700 Seminole Cir Birmingham AL 35243-3040 Office: U Ala-Birmingham Spain Rehab Ctr Birmingham AL 35233*

MEZEY, JUDITH PAUL, social worker; b. N.Y.C., Nov. 14, 1946; d. Chester Eugene and Shirley (Bagley) Paul; m. Robert Joseph Mezey, Apr. 6, 1968; children: Jennifer Robin, Barry Paul. BS, Boston U., 1968; EdM, Columbia U., 1972; MSW, Barry U., 1990. Lic. social worker; RN. Pediatric staff nurse Albert Einstein Coll., N.Y.C., 1967-69; clin. instr. Morrisania-Montefiore Hosp., N.Y.C., 1969-71; grad. student nursing Tchrs. Coll., Columbia U., N.Y.C., 1971-72; clin. instr. Pace U., N.Y.C., 1972-74, U. Miami, 1976-77, Fla. Internat. U., Miami, 1978-79; clin. instr. Barry U., Miami, 1979-86, social work grad. student, 1987-90; psychotherapist A&A Profl. Assocs., South Miami, 1991-93; pvt. practice Miami, Fla., 1993—; facilitator support group Bapt. Hosp., Miami, 1991—. Bd. dirs. Dave and Mary Alper Jewish Cmty. Ctr., Miami, 1986—, chmn. spl. needs com., Miami, 1988—; founding chairperson Spl. Needs Program, 1988. Recipient Fed. Nurse Traineeship grant U.S. Govt., 1970. Mem. NASW. Democrat. Jewish. Home: 6740 SW 99th Ter Miami FL 33156-3240 Office: 9260 Sunset Dr Ste 203 Miami FL 33173-3255

MEZZATESTA, MICHAEL PHILIP, art museum director. BA, Columbia Coll., 1970; mus. teaching cert., Inst. Fine Arts/Met. Mus. Art, 1976; MA, NYU, 1974, PhD, 1980. Curator European art Kimbell Art Mus., Ft. Worth, 1980-86; dir. Duke U. Mus. Art, Durham, N.C., 1987—; adj. prof. dept. art and art history Duke U.; visitor Inst. Advanced Study, Princeton, N.J., 1986; orginator, coord. Kimbell Art Mus. theatre program; lectr. various museums and univs. Contbr. articles to profl. jours. Inst. Fine Arts NYU fellow, 1973-74, Ford Found. fellow, 1974-77, Am. Acad. in Rome fellow, 1977-79, John J. McCloy fellow Am. Coun. on Germany, 1982.

MIAH, ABDUL MALEK, electrical engineer, educator; b. Dhaka, Bangladesh, Feb. 14, 1948; came to U.S., 1985; s. Abdur Rahim Miah and Monjuman Begum; m. Meherunnesa Begum, Dec. 11, 1972; children: Tanveer Ahmed, Rudia Begum. BSEE, Bangladesh U. Engring. & Tech., 1969, MSEE, 1981; PhD in Elec. Engring., Wayne State U., 1992. Asst. works mgr. Bangladesh Ordnance Factories, Ghazipur, 1972-76; asst. prof. Bangladesh U. Engring. and Tech., Dhaka, 1976-82; elec. engr. SWS Engring., Inc., Birmingham, Mich., 1989; asst. prof. S.C. State U., Orangeburg, 1990-95, assoc. prof., 1995—. Mem. IEEE.

MICA, JOHN L., congressman; b. Binghamton, N.Y., Jan. 27, 1943; s. John and Adeline Resciniti M.; m. Patricia Szymanek, 1972; children: D'anne, Clark. AA, Miami (Fla.)-Dade C.C., 1965; BA, U. Fla., 1967. Chief of staff U.S. Senate; v.p. Winter Park (Fla.) Antique Mall; pres. M.K. Devel. Corp., Winter Park, Fla.; mem. Fla. Ho. of Reps., 1976-80; mem. appropriations com., mem. ethics com., mem. elections com., mem. community affairs com.; mem. transp. and infrastructre com., govt. reform and oversight com., chmn. civil svc. com. 103d Congress from 7th Fla. Dist., 1993—. Author: Factor affecting local government reorganization efforts in Florida, Urban and Environmental Issues. Active Beth Johnson Mental Health Bd., PTA Bd., Zora Neale Hurston Meml. Com. Recipient Outstanding Svc. award Fla. Conservative Union, Outstanding Svc. award Fla. Cancer Soc., Outstanding Svc. award Sertoma, Outstanding Young Men of Am. award; named as one of five outstanding Young Men in Fla. Mem. C. of C., Kiwanis, Winter Park Jaycees (Good Govt. award 1972), Fla. Jaycees Statewide (Good Govt. award 1973), Tiger Bay, Crime Line Bd. Republican. Episcopal. Office: PO Box 756 Winter Park FL 32790-0756 Office: US House of Reps 336 Cannon Washington DC 20515*

MICHAEL, CAROLINE MARSHALL, religious organization administrator; b. Bangor, Maine, Oct. 30, 1923; d. Walter S. and Hazel Elizabeth (Day) Marshall; m. Forrest L. Michael, Sept. 10, 1947; children: Janet Elizabeth, David Gregory. BS, Aurora U., 1946; MS in Edn., U. So. Maine, 1974. Cert. travel agent. Instr. Aurora (Ill.) U., 1945-49, U. Maine, Farmington, 1969-77; travel agt. Day's Travel, Waterville, Maine, 1979-81; dir. women's ministries Advent Christian Denomination, Charlotte, N.C., 1981-92. Author, editor: Advent Christian Witness, 1981-92; editor newsletter for AAUW, 1974-75; author, editor numerous seminars. Mem. Rep. Women's Club, Farmington, 1970-80; violinist Symphony and Civic Orchs., Bangor and Farmington, Maine, Aurora, and Alliance, Ohio, 1940-80; mem. N.Am. Women's Track of AD2000 & Beyond, 1992-95; mem. steering com. Praying Women, 1994—. Recipient Violin Playing award Rubinoff, 1940; scholar Husson Coll., 1941-42, Aurora U., 1942-46. Mem. Nat. Assn. Evangs. (chmn. women's commn. 1989-92, mem. exec. com. 1993-96). Home: 10402 Meadow Hollow Dr Charlotte NC 28227-5431

MICHAEL, DOUGLAS CHARLES, law educator; b. Omaha, Dec. 8, 1957; s. B.B. and Arleen M. (Heinz) M.; m. Susan Lindsey, Jan. 11, 1986; children: Stuart Douglas, Amanda Lindsey. AB, Stanford U., 1979; MBA, U. Calif., Berkeley, 1982, JD, 1983. Bar: Calif. 1984, D.C. 1988. Staff atty. SEC, Washington, 1983-85, commr.'s counsel, 1985-87; assoc. Arnold and Porter, Washington, 1987-89; asst. prof. U. Ky. Coll. Law, Lexington, 1989-93, assoc. prof., 1993—. Contbr. articles to legal jours. Mem. ABA, Order of Coif. Home: 4625 Hickory Creek Dr Lexington KY 40515-1509 Office: U Ky Coll Law Lexington KY 40506-0048

MICHAEL, JAMES HARRY, JR., federal judge; b. Charlottesville, Va., Oct. 17, 1918; s. James Harry and Reuben (Shelton) m. Barbara E. Puryear, Dec. 18, 1946; children: Jarrett Michael Stephens, Victoria von der Au. BS, U. Va., 1940, LLB, 1942. Bar: Va. 1942. Sole practice Charlottesville; ptnr. Michael & Musselman, 1946-54, J.H. Michael, Jr., 1954-59, Michael & Dent, 1959-72, Michael, Dent & Brooks Ltd., 1972-74, Michael & Dent, Ltd., 1974-80; assoc. judge Juvenile and Domestic Rels. Ct., Charlottesville, 1954-68; judge U.S. Dist. Ct., Charlottesville, 1980-95, sr. judge, 1996—; mem. Va. Senate, 1968-80; exec. dir. Inst. Pub. Affairs, U. Va., 1952; chmn. Council State Govts., 1975-76, also mem. exec. com.; chmn. So. Legis. Conf., 1974-75. Mem. Charlottesville Sch. Bd., 1951-62; bd. govs. St. Anne-Belfield Sch., 1952-76. Served with USNR, 1942-46; comdr. Res. ret. Wilton Park fellow Wilton Park Conf., Sussex, Eng., 1971. Fellow Am. Bar Found.; mem. ABA, Va. Bar Assn. (v.p. 1956-57), Charlottesville-Albermarle Bar Assn. (pres. 1966-67), Am. Judicature Soc., 4th Jud. Conf., Va. Trial Lawyers Assn. (Va. disting. svc. award 1993), Assn. Trial Lawyers Am., Raven Soc., Sigma Nu Phi, Omicron Delta Kappa. Episcopalian (lay reader). Office: US Dist Ct 255 W Main St Rm 320 Charlottesville VA 22902-5058*

MICHAEL, M. BLANE, federal judge; b. Charleston, S.C., Feb. 17, 1943. AB, W.Va. U., 1965; JD, NYU, 1968. Bar: N.Y. 1968, U.S. Dist. Ct. (so. and ea. dists.) N.Y. 1968, W.Va. 1973, U.S. Ct. Appeals (4th cir.) 1974, U.S. Dist. Ct. (no. dist.) W.Va. 1975, U.S. Dist. Ct. (so. dist.) W.Va. 1981. Counsel to Gov. W.Va. John D. Rockefeller IV, 1977-80; atty. Jackson & Kelly, Charleston, W.Va., 1981-93; fed. judge U.S. Ct. Appeals (4th cir.), Charleston, W.Va., 1993—; active 4th Jud. Conf. Mem. ABA, W.Va. Bar Assn., Kanawha County Bar Assn., Phi Beta Kappa. *

MICHAEL, MAX, III, internist; b. Atlanta, Mar. 14, 1946; s. Max, Jr., and Barbara Elizabeth (Seigel) M.; m. Marilyn Anne Losco, June 22, 1970 (dec. Nov. 1991); children—David Max, Sara Adrienne; m. Ellen Alexander, May 14, 1994. B.A. cum laude with honors in Biology, Vanderbilt U., 1968; M.D., Harvard U., 1972. Diplomate Am. Bd. Internal Medicine. Med. resident Med. Ctr., U. Ala., Birmingham, 1972-74; Robert Wood Johnson clin. scholar, Chapel Hill, N.C., 1974-76; staff physician Cooper Green Hosp., Birmingham, 1977—, dir. outpatient services, 1977-92, chief staff, 1982-86, 91-92, chmn. dept. medicine, 1983-92, CEO, med. dir., 1992—; assoc. prof. U. Ala. Birmingham; med. dir. Birmingham Health Care for the Homeless Coalition. Recipient Advanced Achievement Internal Medicine award Am. Bd. Internal Medicine, 1987. Fellow ACP; mem. Am. Pub. Health Assn., Jefferson County Med. Soc. Democrat. Jewish. Contbr. articles to sci. jours. Home: 4316 Glenwood Ave Birmingham AL 35222-4303 Office: 1515 6th Ave S Birmingham AL 35233-1601

MICHAELS, AGNES ISABELLE, education educator; b. Cooperstown, N.Y., Feb. 3, 1912; d. Howard Nehemiah and Edna Isabelle (Potter) M. BS, SUNY, Cortland, 1936; MA, NYU, 1948; EdD, U. Buffalo, 1954. Tchr. Montour Falls (N.Y.) Pub. Schs., 1936-38; supr. phys. edn. North Tonawanda (N.Y.) Pub. Schs., 1938-41; tchr. phys. edn. Bethlehem Cen. Schs., Delmar, N.Y., 1941-44; club dir. ARC, CBI Theater, 1944-46; dir. phys. edn. St. Mary's Hall, San Antonio, 1946-47; asst. prof. Okla. State U., 1947-48; assoc. prof. dir. women's physical edn., health SUNY, Fredonia, 1948-73, assoc. prof. emeritus, 1973—; mem. curriculum com. SUNY, Fredonia, 1948-73; mem. Village of Fredonia Parks Commn. 1959-61. Contbr. articles to profl. jours. Recipient Life Sav. medal ARC, 1929, Presidential citation for meritorius svc., World War II, 1946. Mem. AAUW, Eastern Assn. Phys. Edn. for Coll. Women (emeritus), Vero Beach Art Club, Kappa Delta Pi, Pi Lambda Theta. Methodist. Home: 7000 20th St Lot 874 Vero Beach FL 32966-8877

MICHAELS, ALAN J., safety, occupational health and security executive; b. Stowe, Pa., Nov. 29, 1946; s. Joseph and Helen (Arena) Pavelish; m. SherriLea Amy Gering, Dec. 1, 1967; children: Catherine Michaels Stokes, Victoria Anne Desireé. AA with high honors, Mesa Community Coll., 1967; BA with high honors, Ariz. State U., 1970; MS with highest honors, Colo. State U., 1979. Cert. safety profl. Tchr. Phoenix Area Pub. Schs., 1970-78; supr. safety and tng. Amax Inc., Greenwich, Conn., 1980-84; supr. employee rels. and safety Colowyo Coal Co., Meeker, Colo., 1984-86; corp. dir. safety and tng. Echo Bay Mgmt. Corp., Reno, 1986-88; mgr. safety and human resources various locations Occidental Chem. Corp., 1979-80, 86-94; dir. safety, fire protection, indsl. hygiene, security Rayon divsn. Courtaulds Fibers Inc., Axis, Ala., 1994—; mem. exec. bd. Copper Devel. Assn., N.Y., 1980-82; mem. exec. safety com. Fla. Phosphate Coun., Orlando, 1989-90; mem. exec. com safety and health Tex. Chem. Coun., 1990-91. Contbr. articles to profl. jours. Mem. steering com. Drug Free Mobile Coalition, 1993-94; mem. Mobile Area Tng. and Edn. Symposium, 1992—; mem. adv. coun. Dsit. Magnet Sch., 1994; pres. Alhambra Sch. Dist. of Classroom Tchrs., 1973-74; mem. LeMoyne Cmty. Adv. Panel, 1994—. Recipient Medallion of Merit, Ariz. State U., 1967; NIOSH fellow, 1978-79. Mem. Am. Soc. Safety Engrs. (prof., Pres. Cir. 1990, Mobile chpt. sec. 1995—), Bus. Coun. Ala., Indsl. Pers. Assn. Mobile, Chickasaw C. of C. (pres. 1994). Home: 406 Saint John Pl Mobile AL 36609-2433 Office: Courtaulds Fibers Inc PO Box 141 Axis AL 36505-0141

MICHAELS, CINDY WHITFILL (CYNTHIA G. MICHAELS), educational consultant; b. Plainview, Tex., Aug. 31, 1951; d. Glenn Tierce and Ruby Jewell (Nichols) Whitfill; m. Terre Joe Michaels, July 16, 1977. BS, W. Tex. State U., 1972; MS, U. Tex., Dallas, 1976; postgrad. cert., E. Tex. State U., 1982. Registered profl. ednl. diagnostician, Tex.; cert. supr. (gen. and spl. edn.), elem. edn. tchr., K-8 English tchr., spl. edn. tchr. (generic and mental retardation), Tex. Gen. and spl. edn. tchr. Plano (Tex.) Ind. Sch. Dist., 1972-76; dependents' sch. tchr. U.S. Dept. Def., Office of Overseas Edn., Schweinfurt, West Germany, 1976-77; asst. dir. edn. dept. spl. edn. Univ. Affiliated Ctr., U. Tex., Dallas, 1977-80; asst. to acting dir. edn., dept. pediatrics, Southwestern Med. Sch. Univ. Affiliated Ctr., U. Tex. Health Sci. Ctr., Dallas, 1980-82; dir. Collin County Spl. Edn. Coop., Wylie, Tex., 1982-89; dir. spl. svcs. Terrell (Tex.) Ind. Sch. Dist., 1989-92; cons. for at-risk svcs. instrnl. svcs. dept. Region 10 Edn. Svc. Ctr., Richardson, Tex., 1992-93, cons. for staff devel., 1993-95; cons. Title I Svcs., 1995-96; ind. rep. Am. Communications Network, 1995—; owner Strategic Out-Source Svcs., Garland, Tex., 1996—; self-employed ednl. cons. Strategic Outsource Svcs., 1996—; regional cons. presenter and speaker Region 10 Adminstrs. Spl. Edn., Dallas, 1982-92; state conf. presenter and speaker Tex. Assn. Bus. Sch. Bds., Houston, 1991, Tex. Edn. Agy., Austin, 1992, grant reveiwer, 1984; cons. S.W. regional tng. program educators U. So. Miss., 1992-93; regional coord. H.S. mock trial competition State Bar Tex., 1993; regional liaison Tex. Elem. Mentor Network, 1993-96; state presenter Tex. Vocat. Educators Conf., 1994. Active Dance-A-Thon for United Cerebral Palsy, Dallas, 1986; area marcher March of Dimes, Dallas, 1990, Park Cities Walkathon for Multiple Sclerosis, 1994, 95. Grantee Job Tng. & Partnership Act, 1991, Carl Perkins Vocat. Program, 1991, Tex. Edn. Agy., 1990, 91, 92; named Outstanding Young Woman in Am., Outstanding Young Women in Am., 1981. Mem. AAUW, Assn. Compensatory Educators of Tex. (state conf. com. 1996), Tex. Assn. for Improvement of Reading, Tex. Assn. Sect. 504 Coords. and Hearing Officers, Nat. Coun. Adminstrs. Spl. Edn., Coun. Exceptional Children (chpt. pres. 1973-74), Tex. Assn. Supervision & Curriculum Devel. (mem. leadership team Project Pathways 1992-93), Tex. Coun. Adminstrs. Spl. Edn. (region 10 chairperson 1985-87, state conf. presenter 1989, 92), Tex. Ednl. Diagnosticians Assn. (Dal-Metro v.p., state conf. program chair 1982-83, state conf. presenter 1983), Internat. Reading Assn., Nat. Assn. Supervision and Curriculum Devel., Alpha Delta Pi (Richardson alumnae, philanthropy chair 1988, v.p. 1989, 90, 91, v.p./sec. 1993-94, v.p. 1994-95, 95-96, 96-97). Home and Office: 2613 Oak Point Dr Garland TX 75044-7809 also: 232 Broadmoor Alto NM 88312

MICHAELS, JOHN PATRICK, JR., investment banker, media broker; b. Orlando, Fla., May 28, 1944; s. John Patrick and Mary Elizabeth (Slemons) M.; m. Igeborg D. Theimer, May 2, 1970; 1 child, Kimberly Lynn. Grad. Jamaica Coll., Kingston, 1961; BA magna cum laude, Tulane U., 1966; MA in Communications (ABC fellow), U. Pa., 1968; student London Sch. Econs., U. London, 1964. With Times Mirror Co., 1968-72, v.p. mktg. and devel. TM Communications Co., 1968-72; v.p. Cable Funding, N.Y.C., 1973; founder, chmn. Communications Equity Assocs., cable TV investment bankers, 1973—. Tulane scholar, 1962-66; Tulane fellow, 1963-66. Fellow Inst. Dirs. (London); mem. Master of Fox Hounds, Nat. Cable TV Assn., Univ. Club, Phi Beta Kappa, Phi Eta Sigma. Home: 3024 W Villa Rosa Park Tampa FL 33611-2840 Office: 101 E Kennedy Blvd Ste 3300 Tampa FL 33602-5151

MICHAELS, KEVIN RICHARD, lawyer; b. Buffalo, Feb. 9, 1960; s. Richard Ronald and Marlene Constance (Mnich) M.; m. Beatrice Mary Szeliga, Jan. 15, 1983; 1 child, Jaena René. BS in Govt., U. Houston, 1987; JD, South Tex. Coll. Law, 1992. Bar: Tex. 1992, U.S. Dist. Ct. (so. dist.) Tex. 1996. Ct. coord. Harris County Dist. Clk., Houston, 1985-88; paralegal O'Quinn, Kerensky, McAninch & Laminack, Houston, 1988-92, atty., 1992—. Mem. Assn. Trial Lawyers Am. (Tex. gov. New Lawyers div. 1994—). Office: O'Quinn Kerensky McAninch and Laminack 440 Louisiana St Ste 2300 Houston TX 77002-1636

MICHAELS, MICHAEL MAGED, urologist; b. Alexandria, Egypt, July 7, 1945; came to U.S., 1969; s. Aziz and Angele (Grais) Mikhail; m. Debra Ann Bortz, May 5, 1973; children: Kimberley Anne, Bradley Scott. MB, ChB, Alexandria U., 1968. Diplomate Am. Bd. Urology. Intern Princeton (N.J.) Hosp., 1969-70; resident in gen. surgery Coll. Medicine and Dentistry N.J., Newark, 1970-71; resident in urology Geisinger Med. Ctr., Danville, Va., 1971-74; pvt. practice, Palatka, Fla., 1974—; staff urologist Hosp. Corp. Am.-Putnam Community Hosp., Palatka, 1974—, trustee, 1991-92. Contbr. articles to med. jours. Recipient physicians recognition award AMA, 1972—. Fellow ACS; mem. Am. Urol. Assn., Southeastern Sect. Am. Urol. Assn., Fla. Urol. Soc., Fla. Med. Assn. Office: 700 Zeagler Dr Ste 4 Palatka FL 32177-3826

MICHALOWICZ, KAREN DEE, secondary education educator; b. Garrett, Ind., Nov. 7, 1942; d. Perry Linsey and Irene Veronica (Viers) Shuman; children: Joleen, Michael. AB, Cath. U., 1964; MA in Ednl. Psychology, U. Va., 1990. Tchr. St. Anthony Sch., Falls Church, Va.; math. coord., tchr. Queen of Apostles Sch., Alexandria, Va.; chair math. dept., tchr. Langley Upper Sch., McLean, Va.; adj. prof. George Mason U.; leader, spkr. numerous workshops; VQUEST lead tchr./trainer. Contbr. articles to profl. jours. Named AAUW Tchr. of the Yr., 1994, Presdl. Award in Math., 1994; Woodrow Wilson fellow, 1991, SCIMAT/NSF, 1992; Yale U. scholar, summer 1987. Mem. ASCD, Nat. Coun. Tchrs. Math., Va. Coun. Tchrs. Math. (Va. Outstanding Math. Tchr. 1992), Math. Assn. Am., Va. Assn. for Supervision and Curriculum Devel., Va. Mid. Sch. Assn., Va. Assn. Ind. Schs. Office: The Langley Sch 1411 Balls Hill Rd Mc Lean VA 22101-3415

MICHALSKI, JEANNE ANN, human resources professional; b. Tampa, Fla., Nov. 7, 1958; d. Enrique and Mary Ellen (Bandi) Escarraz; m. Michael John Michalski, Nov. 24, 1984. BA in Psychology, U. South Fla., 1979, MA in Indsl. Psychology, 1983, PhD in Indsl. Psychology, 1990. Human resource coord. GTE Data Svcs., Tampa, 1984-86, mgmt. cons., 1986-87, mgr. human resource planning, employment office, 1987-88, mgr. human resource, 1988-89; mgr. testing and performance mgmt. GTE Telephone Ops., Irving, Tex., 1989-90, mgr. continuity planning and performance mgmt., 1990-94; asst. v.p. human resources planning Burlington No., Fort Worth, 1994-95; asst. v.p. staffing and devel. Burlington No. Santa Fe, Fort Worth, 1995—; cons. Herb Meyer Assocs./TECO, Tampa, 1983-84, Mail Prescriptions, Tampa, 1989-90. Campaign worker Dem. state legislator election, St. Petersburg, Fla., 1980; mem. Polit. Action Com., Irving, 1989-90. Grad. fellowship scholar U. South Fla., 1979. Mem. APA, Soc. for Indsl./Orgnl. Psychologists, Dallas/Ft. Worth Indsl. Orgn. Psychologist Group, Human Resource Planning Soc. Roman Catholic. Home: 505 Woodland Trl Keller TX 76248-2634 Office: Burlington No 3000 Continental Plz Fort Worth TX 76161

MICHAUX, HENRY GASTON, art educator; b. Morganton, N.C., Jan. 19, 1934; s. Fred D., Sr. and Mary Annie (Phillips) M.; m. Hazel A. Scott, Aug. 6, 1977 (div. Dec. 1982). BFA, Tex. So. U., 1959; EdM, Pa. State U., 1960, EdD, 1971; postgrad., Rochester Inst. Technology, 1962. Art instr. Va. State Coll., Petersburg, 1960-62; art prof. So. Univ. in New Orleans, 1962-67, Cen. State U., Wilberforce, Ohio, 1967-68, Coll. of the Virgin Islands, St. Thomas, 1971, Appalachian State U., Boone, N.C., 1972-76, N.C. Cen. U., Durham, 1977-78, S.C. State U., Orangeburg, 1978-96. One-man show Henri Studio Galleries, 1964 (winner 1964); represented in pvt. collections. 1st pres. Caldwell Arts Coun., Lenoir, N.C., 1975; chmn. Lenoir Community Adv. Com., 1975-76; appointee Lenoir Planning Bd., 1976; bd. dirs. Tri-County Citizens Against Sexual Assault, Orangeburg, S.C., 1988; planner Indoor/Outdoor Sculpture Competition, Lenoir, 1986; mem. S.C. Acquisitions Com., Columbia, 1982-84. Recipient Jesse Jones Fine Arts Scholarship Tex. So. U., 1956-59, Purchase award J.B. Speed Art Mus., 1988. Mem. Nat. Art Edn. Assn., Am. Crafts Coun., Nat. Black Child Devel. Inst., Inc., Sculputre Internat., Nat. Coun. for Edn. of Ceramic Arts, African Am. Mus. Assn., N.C. Cultural Arts Coalition, Nat. Assn. Schs. of Art and Design. Methodist. Home: 310 Mulungu Pl NW Lenoir NC 28645

MICHEL, DANIEL JOHN, broadcast educator, writer, photographer, artist; b. New Orleans, June 18, 1949; s. Nolan Joseph and Evelyn Marie (Breaux) M. Diploma, Sta. WKG-TV, 1986; BA in Mktg. Mgmt., Kensington U., 1989; cert. diploma photography, Media West, 1990; cert., Art Instrn. Schs. Inc., 1991, Brit.-Am. Sch. of Writing, 1991. Instr. English East Baton Rouge Sch. Bd., 1982-84; instr. broadcast prodn. Sta. WKG-TV, Baton Rouge, 1986—; freelance writer Baton Rouge, 1987—; announcer Nat. Sports Festival, Baton Rouge, 1985. Writer song lyrics including I've Sat So Long, Now I Became Lonely, stage plays, works in Libr. of Congress, 1982—. Camera dir. La. Pub. Broadcasting Fund Raising, Baton Rouge, 1986—; instr. TV broadcasting Boy Scouts Am., Baton Rouge, 1986—. Mem. Lafayette Art Assn. (2d v.p. 1994). Roman Catholic.

MICHEL, STEPHEN LEWIS, physician; b. Chgo., Aug. 16, 1938. MD, U. Chgo.-Pritzker Sch. Med., 1962. Intern UCLA Med. Ctr., 1962-63; resident gen. surgery Cedars-Sinai Med. Ctr., L.A., 1963-67, fellow oncology, 1966-67, assoc. dir. surgery, 1976-90; assoc. clin. prof. surgery UCLA. Office: Surg Assts Fla Inc PO Box 811027 Boca Raton FL 33481

MICHELINI, SYLVIA HAMILTON, auditor; b. Decatur, Ala., May 16, 1946; d. George Borum and Dorothy Rose (Swatzell) Hamilton; m. H. Stewart Michelini, June 4, 1964; children: Stewart Anthony, Cynthia Leigh. BSBA summa cum laude, U. Ala., Huntsville, 1987. CPA, Ala.; cert. govt. fin. mgr. Acct. Ray McCay, CPA, Huntsville, 1987-88; auditor Def. Contract Audit Agy., Huntsville, 1989-92; auditor-office of inspector general George C. Marshall Space Flight, Center, Ala., 1992—. Mem. exec. bd. Decatur City PTA, 1976-78; pres., v.p. Elem. Sch. PTA, Decatur, 1977-79; leader Girl Scouts U.S. and Cub Scouts, Decatur, 1972-77; active local ARC, 1973-77. Mem. AAUW (chpt. treas. 1988-90), Nat. Assn. Accts. (dir. community svc. 1987-88, v.p. adminstrn. and fin. 1988-89, pres. 1989-90, nat. com. on ethics 1990-91), Am. Inst. CPAs, Am. Soc. Women Accts. (chpt. treas. 1989-90, dir. chpt. devel. 1989-90), Assn. Govt. Accts. (sec. 1992-93, chmn. pub. rels. 1993-94), Ala. Soc. CPAs (profl. ethics com. 1993-94), Inst. Internal Auditors (dir. awards and recongnition 1996-97), Inst. Mgmt. Accts. (v.p. communications, dir. program book 1991—, Dixie coun. dir. newsletters 1992-93, dir. ednl. programs 1992-93, 93-94, nat. com. ethics, 1990—), Ala. Soc. CPAs (govtl. acctg. and auditing com. 1994—), Inst. Mgmt. Accts. (nat. bd. dirs. 1994—), Phi Kappa Phi. Baptist. Home: 2801 Sylvia Dr SE Decatur AL 35603-9381 Office: NASA Office Inspector Gen M-DI Marshall Space Flight Ctr Huntsville AL 35812

MICHELSON, GAIL IDA, lawyer; b. N.Y.C., Sept. 19, 1952; d. Max and Virginia (Seames) M. BA, Columbia U., 1984; JD, W.Va. U., 1993. Bar: W.Va. 1993, U.S. Dist. Ct. (so. dist.) W.Va. Assoc. Kopelman & Assocs., Charleston, W.Va., 1994; asst. atty. gen. Atty. Gen. State of W.Va., Charleston, 1995—. Actor: (soap operas) Another World, Guiding Light, All My Children, 1976-79; contbg writer W.Va. Quar. Dir./staff Am. Theatre of Actors, N.Y.C., 1985-90; mem. policy bd. Mental Health Assn. Mem. ABA, W.Va. Bar Assn., W.Va. Trial Lawyers Assn., ACLU. Home: 300 Park Ave Charleston WV 25302 Office: Atty Gen State of W Va Capitol Complex Charleston WV 25305

MICHELSON, ROBERT CARROLL, electronics engineer, educator; b. Washington, Apr. 24, 1951; s. Carroll Edward and Evelyn Othea (Jonas) M.; m. Denise Dodson, Dec. 1973; children: Christian, Stuart. BSEE, Va. Polytech. U., 1973; MSEE, Ga. Inst. Tech., 1974. Rsch. engr. U.S. Naval Rsch. Lab., 1971-73; rsch. engr. I, 1975-77, rsch. engr. II, 1977-81; sr. rsch. engr. Ga. Tech. Rsch. Inst., 1981-92; prin. rsch. engr. Ga. Inst. of Tech., 1992—, br. head instrumentatin tech. br. radar/instrumentation lab., 1985-90, tech. area. mgr., battlefield robotics and unmanned systems, 1990—, assoc. prof. Sch.of Aerospace Engring. Contbr. articles to profl. jours. Mem. IEEE (sr. mem.), Scientific Rsch. Soc. of N.Am., Assn. for Unmanned Vehicle Systems (pres. Atlanta chpt., pres., past mem. bd. dirs. internat. orgn.), sigma Xi. Office: Ga Inst of Tech GTRI-AERO-CCRF Atlanta GA 30332

MICHIE, JOSEPH ALLEN, English language educator; b. Little Rock, Nov. 4, 1963; s. Joe Allen and Juliana (Hawkins) M.; m. Stacey Cone, June 6, 1993. BA, U. N.C., 1986; MA, Oxford (Eng.) U., 1988; PhD, Emory U., 1993. Vis. asst. prof. English Emory U., Atlanta, 1993-94; asst. prof. English Coastal Carolina U., Conway, S.C., 1994—. Contbr. articles to profl. jours. Vol. Atlanta Project, 1993-94. TATTO fellow Emory U., 1992-93, dissertation fellow, 1991; recipient Douglas Sladen Essay prize Trinity Coll., Oxford, 1988. Mem. MLA, Am. Soc. for Eighteenth-Century Studies, Carolinas Symposium on Brit. Studies, Phi Beta Kappa. Office: Coastal Carolina University PO Box 1954 Conway SC 29526

MICHNIAK-MIKOLAJCZAK, BOZENA BERNADETA, pharmaceutical educator; b. Leicester, Eng., Sept. 18, 1955; came to U.S., 1986; m. Adam Mikolajczak. BS in Pharmacy with honors, Leicester Poly., 1977; PhD in Pharmacology, Coun. for Nat. Acad. Awards, Eng., 1980. Intern Derbyshire Area Health Auth. Hosps., 1980-81; locum tenens pharmacist Chesterfield (Eng.) Royal Hosp., 1981; clin. pharmacist in profl. unit CCU Leicester Gen. Hosp., 1981; postdoctoral rsch. fellow U. Fla. Coll. Pharmacy, 1981-83; sr. postdoctoral rsch. fellow U. Bradford, 1984-86; asst. prof. basic pharm. scis. U. S.C. Coll. Pharmacy, Columbia, 1986-93, assoc. prof. basic pharm. scis., 1993—; lectr. in physiology, pharmacology Leicester Poly. Sch. Pharmacy, 1977-80; lectr. in pharmaceutics U. Fla. Coll. Pharmacy, 1982-83; vis. asst. prof. basic pharm. scis. U. S.C. Coll. Pharmacy, Columbia, 1986-87; adj. assoc. prof. bioengring. Clemson (S.C.) U. Coll. Engring., 1993—; lectr. pharmaceutics and microbiology U. Bradford, 1984-86; presenter in field. Contbr. articles to profl. jours. Grantee Hoffman-La Roche, 1989-94; Rsch. and Productive scholar, 1988-89; recipient Best Publ. prize Internat. Jour. Cosmetic Sci., 1981. Mem. AAAS, Royal Pharm. Soc. Gt. Britain, Am. Assn. Colls. Pharmacy, Am. Assn. Pharm. Scientists, Controlled Release Soc., Am. Chem. Soc., Leicester Pharmacy Students Assn. (hon. mem.), Women in Biomed. Sci. Group, Sigma Xi, Rho Chi, Kappa Epsilon. Office: Univ SC Coll Pharmacy 700 Sumter St Columbia SC 29208

MICKEY, BOB, association executive. Exec. v.p. Tex. Med. Assn., Austin. Office: Tex Med Assn 401 W 15th St Austin TX 78701

MICKEY, BRUCE EDWARD, neurosurgeon; b. New Orleans, Sept. 5, 1952; m. Barbara Ann Schultz, Jan. 23, 1988. AB, Harvard U., 1974; MD, U. Tex. Southwestern Med. Sch., 1978. Diplomate Am. Bd. Neurol. Surgery. Intern U. Tex. Southwestern Med. Sch., Dallas, 1978-79, resident in neurol. surgery, 1979-84, asst. prof., 1984-90, assoc. prof., 1990—. Mem. Am. Assn. Neurol. Surgeons, Congress Neurol. Surgeons, North Am. Skull Base Soc. Office: U Tex Southwestern Med Sch 5323 Harry Hines Dallas TX 75235-8855

MICKLOW, CRAIG WOODWARD, marketing and financial executive; b. Greensburg, Pa., Feb. 9, 1947; s. John Edward and Magdalen Mary (McClaren) M.; m. Judy Anne Fate, Aug. 27, 1976. BS, Pa. State U., 1969; M Mgmt., Northwestern U., 1983. Project cost acct. Westinghouse Corp., Swissvale, Pa., 1969-73; sr. internal auditor H.K. Porter Co., Inc., Pitts., 1973-74, Lykes div. Youngstown (Ohio) Sheet & Tube Steel Co.), 1974-78; chief internal auditor Tool Group Hdqrs., Dresser Industries, Chgo., 1978-83; inside mktg. mgr. gen. abrasive div. Dresser Industries, Niagara Falls, N.Y., 1983-84; regional mktg. mgr. GTE Directories, Irving, Tex., 1984-86; mgr. strategic mktg. CRISA Corp. (Vitro S.A.), Plano, Tex., 1986-87; mktg. mgr. Computer Lang. Rsch., Addison, Tex., 1987-88; bus. mgr., cons. Adelglass, MDPA, Irving, 1988-89; dir. mktg. Tidel Systems, Inc., Carrollton, Tex., 1990-91; chief fin. officer The Gammon Group, Carrollton, 1991—. Mem. Am. Mgmt. Assn., Nat. Mgmt. Assn., Am. Mktg. Assn., Inst. Cost Analysts (cert.), Northwestern U. Alumni Assn., Metrocrest C. of C., Pa. State U. Alumni Club North Tex. (pres.. 1990—), Rotary, Moose. Home and Office: 913 San Saba Dr Grapevine TX 76092-8832

MIDDAUGH, JACK KENDALL, II, management educator; b. Springfield, Ill., Oct. 8, 1949; s. Jack Kendall and Mildred Viola (Davis) M.; m. Maureen Ann Tewey, Aug. 7, 1976; children: Cheryl Lynn, Allison Helen. BBA in Acctg., George Washington U., 1973, MBA, 1975; PhD in Acctg., Ohio State U., 1981. Instr. Ohio State U., Columbus, 1975-80; asst. prof. U. Va., Charlottesville, 1980-87; assoc. prof. Wake Forest U., Winston-Salem, N.C., 1987—; cons. IBM, Armonk, N.Y., 1981—, Amtrak, Washington, 1982-85, U.S. Postal Svc., Washington, 1984-85, Ernst & Whinney, Cleve., 1985-87, U.S. Civil Svc. Commn., 1973-76, Digital Equipment Corp., 1985, Armstrong World Industries, 1989—; dir. 1st Soviet-Am. Mgmt. Devel. Program, 1989; lectr. selected Soviet cities, 1989. Contbr. articles to profl. jours. Dir. Ptnrs. in Edn., 1990-91. Recipient commendation Ohio Ho. of Reps., 1978, Sara Lee award for excellence, 1990; named Outstanding Tchr. of Yr., Pacesetters of Ohio State U., 1977, 78. Mem. Am. Acctg. Assn., Decision Sci. Inst., Beta Gamma Sigma. Home: 8016 Kilcash Ct Clemmons NC 27012-8666 Office: Wake Forest U Babcock Grad Sch Mgmt 7659 Reynolds Sta Winston Salem NC 27109

MIDDAUGH, RICHARD, information systems analyst, researcher; b. Tampa, Fla., Dec. 18, 1951; s. Donald Blair and Leona (Johnson) M.; m. Brenda M. Mitchell, June 10, 1990; 1 child, Richard W. Jr.; 1 stepchild, Nathan Wade Mitchell. AA with honors, Hillsborough C.C., 1973; BA in Psychology, U. South Fla., 1975, MA in Edn., 1979. Psychometrist Divsn. Student Svcs. Hillsborough C.C., Tampa, 1975-79, rsch. analyst Office Instl. Rsch. and Computer Svcs., 1979-82, coord. Office Instl. Rsch. and Computer Svcs., 1982-84; sys. cons. Sweda Internat. div. Litton Industries, Miami, Fla., 1984-87; assoc. dir. Office Instl. Rsch. and Planning U. South Ala., Mobile, 1987-90; dir. Office Instl. Rsch. Sam Houston State U., Huntsville, Tex., 1990—, presenter workshop for dept. chairs and dirs., 1991-92; workshop presenter City Cultural Planning Coun., 1992; cons. City of Huntsville, 1992, Huntsville-Walker County Tourism Coun., 1991, Stephen F. Austin State U., 1993, Trinity Valley C.C., 1993; panelist Tex. Assn. Instnl. Rsch., 1993, presenter, 1994; presenter Assn. for Instnl. Rsch. Ann. Forums, 1994. Editor: Resource Director for Texas Higher Education, 1994-95. Bd. dirs. Huntsville Leadership Inst., 1992-94, chmn., 1993; bd. dirs. Huntsville-Walker County United Way, v.p., 1992-93, campaign chmn. U. South Ala., 1908-89. Mem. Huntsville-Walker C. of C., Ala. Assn. Instnl. Rsch. (sec.-treas. 1990), Lions (bd. dirs. Huntsville chpt. 1991-93, v.p., pres.-elect 1991-92). Democrat. Office: Sam Houston State U Office Instnl Rsch Huntsville TX 77341

MIDDENDORF, MICHAEL PAUL, clergyman educator; b. St. Paul, Apr. 27, 1959; s. Marvin Luther and Melba Catherine (Eckert) M.; m. Lana Lee Kinunen, July 20, 1985. BA, Concordia Coll., St. Paul, 1981; MDiv, Concordia Sem., St. Louis, 1987, STM, 1989, ThD, 1990. Admissions counselor Concordia Coll., St. Paul, 1980-83, guest instr., 1982-83; guest instr. Concordia Coll., River Forest, Ill., 1989, Concordia Sem., St. Louis, 1990, 92, 94; pastor Concordia Luth. Ch., Jamestown, N.D., 1990-92; prof. Concordia U., Austin, Tex., 1992—; vicar Bethlehem Luth. Ch., Lakewood, Colo., 1985-86. Walther faculty devel. fellow Concordia Sem., St. Louis, 1988-90. Mem. Soc. Bibl. Lit. Lutheran. Home: 4504 Abelia Dr Austin TX 78727-5865 Office: Concordia Univ 3400 I-35 North Austin TX 78707

MIDDLEDITCH, BRIAN STANLEY, biochemistry educator; b. Bury St. Edmunds, Suffolk, Eng., July 15, 1945; came to U.S., 1971; s. Stanley Stafford and Dorothy (Harker) M.; m. Patricia Rosalind Nair, July 18, 1970; 1 child, Courtney Lauren. BSc, U. London, 1966; MSc, U. Essex, 1967; PhD U. Glasgow, 1971. Rsch. asst. U. Glasgow, Scotland, 1967-71; vis. asst. prof. Baylor Coll. Medicine, Houston, 1971-75; asst. prof. U. Houston, 1975-80, assoc. prof., 1980-89, prof., 1989—; hon. prof. Eurotechnical Rsch. U. Author: Mass Spectrometry of Priority Pollutants, 1981, Analytical Artifacts, 1989, Kuwaiti Plants, 1991; editor: Practical Mass Spectrometry, 1979, Environmental Effects of Offshore Oil Production, 1981. Grantee Nat. Marine Fisheries Service 1976-80, Sea Grant Program, 1977-81, NASA, 1980-90, IBM, 1985-88, NIH, 1988—, Tex. Advanced Rsch. Program, 1988—, Nat. Dairy Coun., 1991—. Mem. Am. Chem. Soc., Am. Soc. Mass Spectrometry, World Mariculture Soc. Home: 4101 Emory St Houston TX 77005-1920 Office: U Houston Dept Biochemistry Houston TX 77204

MIDDLETON, CHARLENE, retired medical and surgical nurse, educator; b. Ennis, Tex., Sept. 13, 1922; d. Charles Silvester and Harriet Eugenia (Ford) M. Diploma, Scott and White Hosp., Temple, Tex., 1945; AA, Temple Jr. Coll., 1947; BA, U. Tex., Austin, 1956. Nurse coord., ambulatory care svcs. Naval Regional Med. Ctr., Long Beach, Calif.; instr. nursing arts Scott and White Hosp., evening supr.; now ret. Lt. comdr. U.S. Navy, 1957-77. Mem. Scott and White Alumni Assn. (past pres. Dist. 7).

MIDDLETON, DAVID ANDREW, radio announcer, printer; b. Augusta, Ga., Jan. 22, 1966; s. David Eugene and Lillian Myrtle (Dye) M. BS in BA, U. S.C., Aiken, 1993. Sports, appliance salesman Sky City, Augusta, 1983-84; automatic printer operator foreman Qualex of Augusta, 1984-94; radio announcer WJES/WKSX Radio, Johnston, S.C., 1989—; pres., freelancer A&M Features, North Augusta, S.C., 1987—; sr. caseworker Dept. Family and Children Svcs., Augusta, Ga., 1995—. Author puzzle features, Searchtime, 1987. Baptist. Office: 316 Sycamore Dr North Augusta SC 29841-4030

MIDDLETON, GEORGE, JR., clinical child psychologist; b. Houston, Feb. 26, 1923; s. George and Bettie (McCrary) M.; m. Margaret MacLean, Nov. 17, 1953. BA in Psychology, Birmingham-Southern Coll., 1948; MA in Psychology, U. Ala., Tuscaloosa, 1951; PhD in Clin. Psychology, Pa. State U., 1958. Lic. psychologist, La.; diplomate Am. Bd. Examiners, Am. Bd. Forensic Examiners. Asst. clin. psychology Med. Coll. Ala., Birmingham, 1950-52; dir. dept. psychology Bryce Hosp., Tuscaloosa, 1952-54; instr. counseling Coll. Bus. Adminstrn. Pa. State U., 1956-58; asst. prof. spl. edn. McNeese State U., 1962-65, assoc. prof. spl. edn., 1962-65; dir. La. Gov.'s Program for Gifted Children, 1963—; prof. spl. edn. McNeese State U., 1965-73, prof. psychology, 1973-74; pvt. practice clin. psychology and neuropsychology, 1974—; cons. psychologist Calcasieu Parish Sch. Bd., 1975—; cons. Charter Hosp. Adolescent Psychiat. Unit, dir. psychol. svcs., 1990-95. Mem. Am. Psychol. Assn., Nat. Acad. Neuropsychology, Internat. Neuropsychol. Soc., La. Psychol. Assn. (pres. 1973-74), La. Sch. Psychol. Assn., S.W. La. Psychol. Assn. (pres. 1965, 73, 84), La. State Bd. Examiners Psychologists (chmn. 1977-78), Coun. for Exceptional Children, Am. Coll. Forensic Examiners, Assn. for the Gifted. Episcopalian. Home and Office: 2001 Southwood Dr Ste A Lake Charles LA 70605-4139

MIDDLETON, KENT R., communications educator; b. Worcester, Mass., May 19, 1944; s. John Slater and Frances Janet (Hamilton) M.; m. children: Margaret, Hillary, Arthur. BA, Mich. State U., 1966, MA, 1971; PhD, U. Minn., 1977. Asst. prof. U. Tex., Austin, 1976-80; assoc. prof., prof. U. Ga., Athens, 1980—. Co-author: (textbook) Law of Public Communication, 3d edit., 1993; contbr. articles to profl. jours. Office: Coll Journalism and Comm Univ Ga Athens GA 30602

MIDDLETON, NORMAN GRAHAM, social worker, psychotherapist; b. Jacksonville, Fla., Jan. 21, 1935; s. Norman Graham and Betty (Quina) M.; m. Judy Stephens, Aug. 1, 1968; stepchildren: Monty Stokes, Toni Stokes. BA, U. Miami (Fla.), 1960; MSW, Fla. State U., 1962. Casework counselor Family Svc., Miami, 1962-64; psychiat. social worker assoc. firm Drs. Warson, Steele, Wiener, Sarasota, Fla., 1964-66; psychotherapist, Sarasota, 1966—. Instr. Manatee Jr. Coll., Bradenton, Fla., 1973-76. Author: The Caverns of My Mind, 1985, Imaginative Healing, 1993. Pres. Coun. on Epilepsy, Sarasota, 1969-70. Served with USAF, 1954-58. Fellow Fla. Soc. Clin. Social Work (pres. 1978-80); mem. Am. Group Psychotherapy Assn., Am. Assn. Sex Educators and Counselors (cert. sex educator). Democrat. Episcopalian. Home: 16626 Winburn Dr Sarasota FL 34240-9221 Office: 1257 S Tamiami Trl Sarasota FL 34239-2219

MIDDLETON, SILVIA GILBERT, dean, engineering educator; b. Florence, S.C., Nov. 3, 1953; d. Silvanus Taco II and Jewell Virginia (Saylor) Gilbert; m. John Richard Middleton II, May 21, 1988; children: Lindsey Grace, John III. BS, Clemson U., 1975, MS, 1976, PhD, 1984. Jr. engr. Union Carbide Corp.-Linde Div., Florence, 1974; grad. rsch. asst. Clemson U., S.C., 1975-76, instr. elec. & computer engring., 1976-81, grad. rsch. asst., 1981-84; asst. prof. U. N.C., Charlotte, 1984-90, asst. dean engring., 1990—; pres. Thinking Success; mem. N.C. state subcom. for engring. transfer, 1994—. Co-inventor remote control for heliarc welders. Adult Edn. Coord. First Presbyn. Church, Concord, 1989-90. Mem. IEEE (sec. 1987, 2d vice chmn. 1988, 1st vice chmn. 1989, chmn. 1990, awards and nominations com. 1991-93, treas. N.C. coun. chpt. 1992-93, sec. 1994-95, vice chair 1996—, gen. chmn. ann. southeastern region conf. 1993), Soc. Women Engrs. (pres. Western Carolina chpt. 1981), Am. Soc. for Engring. Edn., Charlotte Engrs. Club (bd. dirs. 1993-95, v.p. 1995-96, pres. 1996—), Women in Engring. Programs Advocates Network (chmn. AGRED 1996-98, ex-officio bd. mem.). Presbyterian. Home: PO Box 520 Newell NC 28126-0520 Office: U NC Charlotte William States Lee Coll Engring Charlotte NC 28223

MIDKIFF, KIMBERLY ANN, paralegal; b. Kingsport, Tenn., Nov. 27, 1958; d. Harold Douglas and Mary Lou (Carden) M. Student, U. Tenn., 1976-80. Cert. legal asst. Nat. Assn. Legal Assts. Legal sec. Gilreath & Rowland, Knoxville, Tenn., 1981-83, Tenn. State Atty. Gen.'s Office, Knoxville, 1983-84, Bond, Carpenter & O'Connor, Knoxville, 1984; paralegal Gilreath & Assocs., Knoxville, 1984-89, Lewis, King, Krieg, Waldrop & Catron, P.C., Knoxville, 1989—. Mem. Nat. Assn. Legal Assts., Tenn. Paralegal Assn., Knoxville Paralegal Assn., Delta Gamma Alumnae Assn. Democrat. Presbyterian. Office: Lewis King Krieg Waldrop & Catron PC 1 Century Ct Knoxville TN 37919-4104

MIELE, ANGELO, engineering educator, researcher, consultant, author; b. Formia, Italy, Aug. 21, 1922; came to U.S., 1952, naturalized, 1985; s. Salvatore and Elena (Marino) M. D.Civil Engring., U. Rome, Italy, 1944, D.Aero. Engring., 1946; DSc (hon.), Inst. Tech., Technion, Israel, 1992. Asst. prof. Poly. Inst. Bklyn., 1952- 55; prof. Purdue U., 1955-59; dir. astrodynamics Boeing Sci. Research Labs., 1959-64; prof. aerospace scis., math. scis. Rice U., Houston, 1964-88, Foyt Family prof. engring., 1988-93, Foyt prof. emeritus engring., aerospace scis., math. scis., 1993—; cons. Douglas Aircraft Co., 1956-58, Allison divsn. GM Corp., 1956-58, U.S. Aviation Underwriters, 1987, Boeing Comml. Airplane Co., 1989; Breakwell Meml. lecturership Internat. Astron. Fedn., 1994. Author: Flight Mechanics, 1962; editor: Theory of Optimum Aerodynamic Shapes, 1965, Math. Concepts and Methods in Science and Engineering, 1994; editor-in-chief Jour. Optimization Theory and Applications, 1966—; assoc. editor Jour. Astronautical Scis., 1964-93, Applied Math. and Computation, 1975—, Optimal Control Applications and Methods, 1979—; mem. editl. bd. RAIRO-Ops. Rsch., 1990—; mem. adv. bd. AIAA Edn. Series, 1991—; contbr. numerous articles on aerospace engring., windshear problems, hypervelocity flight, math. programming, optimal control theory and computing methods to sci. jours. Pres. Italy in Am. Assn., 1966-68. Decorated knight comdr. Order Merit Italy, 1972; recipient Levy medal Franklin Inst. of Phila., 1974, Brouwer award AAS, 1980, Schuck award Am. Automatic Control Coun., 1988. Fellow AIAA (Pendray award 1982, Mechanics and Control of Flight award 1982), Am. Astronautical Soc., Franklin Inst.; mem. NAE, Russian Acad. Scis. (fgn.), Internat. Acad. Astronautics, Acad. Scis. Turin (corr.). Home: 3106 Kettering Dr Houston TX 77027-5504 Office: Rice Univ MS-322 Aero-Astronautics Group PO Box 1892 Houston TX 77251-1892

MIELKE, HOWARD WALTER, environmental toxicologist, educator, researcher; b. St. Paul, Feb. 7, 1941. BA in Biology, Macalester Coll., 1963; MS in Biology, U. Mich., 1967, PhD in Geography, 1972. U.S. Peace Corps vol., tchr. Likuni Boys Secondary Sch., Lilongwe, Malawi, Africa, 1963-65; secondary sch. tchr. biology Anatolia Coll., Thessaloniki, Greece, 1966; adj. asst. prof. geography UCLA, 1971-73; asst. prof. geography, biogeography, climatology U. Md. of Balt. County, Balt., 1973-78; sr. rschr. waste mgmt. lab. Md. Environ. Svc./USDA, Beltsville, 1979; asst. prof. geography and environ. studies Macalester Coll., St. Paul, 1979-85, vis. rsch. scientist, 1985-86; rsch. assoc. with Ctr. for Urban and Regional Affairs Hubert H. Humphrey Ctr., U. Minn., Mpls., 1986-88; assoc. prof. Coll. of Pharmacy Xavier U. of La., New Orleans, 1988—; summer faculty fellow Earth Resources Divsn., NASA Goddard Space Flight Ctr., Greenbelt, Md., 1975-76; adj. assoc. prof. Dept. Environ. Health Scis., Sch. Pub. Health and Tropical Medicine, Tulane U. Med. Ctr., New Orleans, 1991—. Author: Patterns of Life, 1989; co-author: (monograph) Environmental Lead Risk in the Twin Cities, 1989, The Environment: Global Issues, Local Solutions, 1994, Lead in Soil Guidelines, 1994; co-producer film Earth: An Interplanetary Perspective, 1975; contbr. numerous articles to profl. jours., chpts. to books. Grantee NSF, 1985, St. Paul Found., 1984-88, City of St. Paul, 1986, Legis. Commn. on Minn. Resources, 1988, La. Edn. Quality Support Fund, 1989-92, DOE, 1990, Chgo., N.Y., L.A. and N-Viro Inc., 1992-94, ATSDR, 1992-96, NIEHS, 1992-94. Mem. APHA, AAAS, Soc. for Environ. Geochemistry and Health, Soc. Environ. Toxicology and Chemistry, Sigma Xi. Home: 3233 Desoto St New Orleans LA 70119-3231 Office: Xavier U of La Coll of Pharmacy 7325 Palmetto St New Orleans LA 70125-1056

MIERDIERKS, KENNETH A., controller. BS in Bus., Jacksonville U. Fin. exec. various cos., Jacksonville, Fla.; project controller Riverside Golf Group Inc, Jacksonville, Fla., 1990. Office: Riverside Golf Group Inc 111 Riverside Ave Ste 330 Jacksonville FL 32202-4929

MIERNYK, WILLIAN HENRY, economics educator; b. Durango, Colo., Jan. 4, 1918; s. Andrew Taber and Elizabeth (Sopko) M.; m. Mary Lorraine Davis, Oct. 4, 1942; children: Jan, Judith, Jeanne, James. BA, U. Colo., 1946, MA, 1947; MA, Harvard U., 1952, PhD. in Econs., 1953. Asst. prof. econ. Northeastern U., Boston, 1953-62, dir. bur. bus. and econ., 1954-62; vis. prof. econ. MIT, Cambridge, 1957-58; prof. econ., dir. bur. econ. rsch. U. Colo., 1962-65; dir. regional rsch. inst. W. Va. U., Morgantown, 1965-83, C.W. Benedum prof. econ., 1965-83; vis. prof. econ. Harvard U., Cambridge, 1969-70; L.J. Buchan dist. vis. prof. W. Va. Inst. of Tech., Montgomery, 1989-90; Benedum prof. econ. emeritus W. Va. U., 1987—. Author: Inter-industry Labor Mobility, 1955, Illusions of Conventional Economics, 1982; author or co-author of ten books, 1962-82; contbg. author of 37 books, 1960-89. Fellow South Regional Sci. Assn., Washington, 1981; disting. scholar Internat. Regional Sci. Assn., Pitts., 1982, Order of Vandalia, W. Va. U., 1989.

MIESSE, MARY ELIZABETH (BETH MIESSE), special education educator; b. Amarillo, Tex. BA, BS, MEd in Guidance and Counseling, MA, West Tex. State U., Canyon, 1952, MBA, 1960; M in Pers. Svc., U. Colo., Boulder, 1954. Cert. in spl. edn. supr., spl. edn. counselor, ednl. diagnostician, spl. edn. (lang. and/or learning disabled, mentally retarded) tchr., profl. counselor, profl. tchr., supt., prin., Tex. With various bus. firms and radio stas., 1940-47; prof. Amarillo Coll., 1947-63; tchr. pvt. and pub. schs., also TV work, 1963-78; spl. edn. cons., 1978—; freelance writer-prodr. in radio/TV, 1978—. Former editor Tex. Jr. Coll. Tchrs. Assn. Mag. Pioneered in ednl. TV in West Tex.; recipient various lit. awards, awards in ednl. TV. Mem. AAUP, AAUW, APA, ASCAP, NEA, Nat. Fedn. State Poetry Socs., Poetry Soc. Tex., Tex. State Tchrs. Assn., Bus. Profl. Womens Club, Am. Bus. Women's Assn. (named one of Top Ten Women of Yr.), North Plains Assn. for Children with Learning Disabilities, Panhandle Profl. Writers, ASCA Writers, High Plains Poetry Soc., Inspirational Writers, Alive!, Cowboy Poets Assn., Toastmistress Internat. Home and Office: PO Box 3133 Valle De Oro TX 79010-3133

MIGALA, ALEXANDRE FREDERYK, physician, osteopath; b. Balt., July 15, 1965; s. Marian Lechoslaw and Anna Iréne (Makowski) M. AA, U. Md. Munich Campus, 1983; BA, U. Tex., Arlington, 1987; DO, Tex. Coll. Osteo Medicine, Fort Worth, 1993. Grad. teaching, rsch. asst. U. Tex., Arlington, 1988-89; teaching asst. manipulative medicine Tex. Coll. Osteo. Medicine, Fort Worth, 1990-91, student (peer) tutor surgery, 1990-91; intern internal medicine Wm. Beaumont Army Med. Ctr. U.S. Army Med. Corps, El Paso, Tex., 1993—. Assoc. editor: The E.C. Barksdale Student Lectures, 1987-88. advisor, counselor youth group, Holy Spirit Cath. Ch., Duncanville, Tex., 1987-89, religious edn. instr., 1987-89. Recipient Non-Commd. Officers Assn. award for heroism, 1994. Mem. Am. Osteo. Assn., Tex. Osteo. Med. Assn., Assn. Mil. Osteo. Physicians and Surgeons, Soc. U.S. Army Flight Surgeons (life), Am. Coll. Gen. Practitioners and Surgeons, Am. Acad. Osteopathy (undergrad. local v.p. nat. sec. 1990-91). Office: HHC 1/1o SFG (A) CMR 445 APO AE 09046 Address: ODC 1/10 SFG (A) CMR 445-679 APO AE 09046

MIGGINS, MICHAEL DENIS, retired career officer, arms control analyst; b. White Plains, N.Y., Aug. 8, 1944; s. Michael Joseph Miggins and M. Gabrielle (Daly) O'Neill; m. Kathleen Ann Isherwood, Oct. 22, 1966; children: Kristin D., Michael C. BA in Polit. Sci., Providence Coll., 1966; MA in Internat. Rels., St. John's U., 1972. Commd. lt. U.S. Army, 1966, advanced through grades to col., 1989; company comdr. and platoon leader 2nd Battalion, 325th Inf., 82nd Airborne Div., Ft. Bragg, N.C., 1966-68; dist. sr. advisor An Xuyen Province, Ca Mau, Vietnam, 1968-69; instr. ROTC St. John's U., Jamaica, N.Y., 1969-72; with joint security area Armistice Affairs div. UN Forces, Pan Mun Jom, Korea, 1973-74; ops. officer, company comdr., intelligence officer 4th Battalion, 6th Inf., Berlin (Germany) Brigade, 1974-77; sec. gen. staff Army Combined Arms Test Activity, Ft. Hood, Tex., 1978-80; staff officer ODCSOPS Army Staff, Washington, 1980-84; br. chief priorities, programs and budget br. Army Staff, 1984-85; exec. officer 1st brigade (armored) 1st Cavalry Divsn. U.S. Army, Ft. Hood, Tex., 1985-86, chief exercise divsn. III Corps., 1986-87; mem. joint staff, internat. negotiations divsn. Washington, 1987-91; U.S. del. mutual and balanced force reduction negotiations mandate talks Conventional Armed Forces in Europe Negotiation, Vienna, Austria, 1987-89; mil. advisor to U.S. rep. High Level Task Force NATO, Brussels, 1988-90; rep. to interagy. conventional arms control Joint Staff, Washington, 1990-91; sr. advisor to chmn. verification coord. com., internat. staff, polit. affairs divsn. NATO, Brussels, 1991-93; mgr. conventional arms ctrl. and open skies projects Ctr. Verification Rsch. Sci. Applications Internat. Corp., Newington, Va., 1994—. Decorated Silver Star, Bronze Star, Legion of Merit, Def. Superior Svc. medal, Meritorious Svc. medal, Army Commendation medal. Mem. Assn. U.S. Army, Army and Navy Club. Republican. Roman Catholic. Home: 9352 Braymore Cir Fairfax Station VA 22039-3124 Office: Ctr for Verification Rsch Cinder Bed Rd Newington VA 22122

MIGL, DONALD RAYMOND, therapeutic optometrist, pharmacist; b. Houston, Tex., Sept. 18, 1947; s. Ervin Lawrence and Adele Marie (Boenisch) M.; m. Karen S. Coale, Mar. 23, 1974; children: Christopher Brian, Derek Drew, Monica Michelle. BS in Pharmacy, U. Houston, 1970, BS, 1978, OD, 1980, cert., 1992; postgrad., U. Ala. Med. Ctr., Birmingham, 1974-76, Stephen F. Austin State U., Nacogdoches, Tex., 1987-88. Registered pharmacist; cert. Nat. Bds. Examiners Optometry, Treatment & Mgmt. Ocular Disease; cert. therapeutic optometrist. Pharmacist Tex. Med. Ctr., Houston, 1967-69, St. Luke's and Tex. Childrens Hosp., 1967-69, Meml. Hosp., 1969-70, Ben Taub (Harris County) Hosp., 1970-71, Shades Mountain Pharmacy, Birmingham, 1974-76, Westbury Hosp., Houston, 1976-81; instr. pharmacology lab. Coll. Optometry U. Houston, 1980; pvt. practice, Nacogdoches, Tex., 1981—; mem. interdisciplinary health teams, 1977; charter advisor publ. Contact, CIBA Vision Corp., 1988-89. Judge health sci. div. Houston Area Sci. Fair, 1970. Recipient svc. award Houston Community Interdisciplinary Health Screening Programs, 1977, Spl. Academic Achievement award in pharmacy and optometry U. Houston, 1980. Mem. Am. Optometric Assn. (Optometric recognition award 1985-97), Tex. Optometric Assn. (recognition cert. 1979), Piney Woods Optometric Soc. (pres. 1984), Am. Pharm. Assn. (recognition cert. 1970), Tex. Pharm. Assn., Am. Soc. Hosp. Pharmacists, U.S. Jaycees, Gold Key, Omicron Delta Kappa. Methodist. Lodge: Rotary (Paul Harris Fellow 1987, Pres. award Outstanding Svc., 1991-92). Home: 4122 Ridgebrook Dr Nacogdoches TX 75961 Office: Eagle Eye 20/20 Plus Vision PO Box 632730 Nacogdoches TX 75963-2730

MIGL, SANDRA MITCHELL, secondary education educator; b. Corsicana, Tex., Mar. 26, 1950; d. J. Wayne and Yvonne Louise (Hutzler) Mitchell; m. Dennis George Migl, June 14, 1975; 1 child, Chesney. Student, Navarro Jr. Coll., Corsicana, 1968-70; BA, East Tex. State Univ., 1972; MA, Univ. Tex., 1978. Tchr. N.E. Sch. Dist., San Antonio, 1972-84, Judson Sch. Dist., Live Oak, Tex., 1990-94, Floresville, Tex., 1994—. Tchr. St. John Newmans, San Antonio, St. Monica's, Selma, Tex., Our Lady Perpetual Hope, Convese, TEx., 1977-94; pres. St. Anthony Altar Soc., Elmendorf, Tex. 1994-95. Mem. Kappa Kappa Iota (various offices), Delta Kappa Gamma. Roman Catholic. Home: 214 Eagle Ridge Floresville TX 78114

MIHAL, SANDRA POWELL, computer systems educator; b. Balt., Dec. 15, 1941; d. Sanford William and Mary Louise (Barry) Powell; m. James George Anderson, June 15, 1963; children: Robin Marie, James Brian, Melissa Lee, Derek Claire; m. Charles Turner Barber, Apr. 18, 1978; stepchildren: Gretchen Jayco, Katrina Hope; m. Ladislaw Paul Mihal, May 25, 1991; stepchildren: Alexander Paul, Suzie May, Natasha Elizabeth, Rudy Darius. BA, Mt. St. Agnes Coll., 1963; MA, N.Mex. State U., 1970, Purdue U., 1975; EdD, Vanderbilt U., 1990. Cert. tchr., Md. Tchr. Ridgely-Dulaney Jr. H.S., Towson, Md., 1964; grad. asst. N.Mex. State U., Las Cruces, 1967-69; acad. advisor, instr. polit. sci. Purdue U., West Lafayette, Ind., 1974-78; prof., acad. sys. analyst U. So. Ind., Evansville, 1978-82; assoc. prof., chair dept. computer info. sys. Henderson (Ky.) C.C., 1982-88; prof. computer tech., divsn. chair Anne Arundel C.C., Arnold, Md., 1988-91; computer sys. analyst Immigration & Naturalization Svc., Dept. of Justice, Washington, 1991-92, Glynco, Ga., 1995—; bd. dirs. Ind. Polit. Sci. Assn., Muncie, 1984-88, Internat. Studies Assn.-Midwest, Chgo., 86-88; pres. Ky. Acad. Computer Users' Group, Lexington, 1985-86; mem. telecom. adv. bd. C.C. Sys., Annapolis, Md., 1990-91; computer syst. network analyst CLARC Svcs., Pt. Charlotte, Fla., 92-95; adj. prof. history and polit. sci. Edison C.C., Punta Gorda, Fla., 1993-95. Author: Learning By Doing BASIC, 1983, Computers Learning By Doing, 1984; contbr. to several profl jours. 1980-90; author, spkr. series Faculty/Staff Edison CC 94, Ednl. Tech. Nova U., 1995. Block coord. several neighborhood assns.; mem. Henderson County Sch. Computer Adv. Bd. 1982-88; chmn. Newburgh (Ind.) Youth Orgn., 78-86; judge Sci. Fair, Annapolis, 1988-90; mem. nomination bd. Ky. Higher Edn. Assn., 1989-91; mem. Charlotte Chorale, Port Charlotte, 1992-94, Peace River Power Squadron, Port Charlotte, 1994-96. Md. State Tchr. Bd. Edn. scholar, 1960-63; fellow Sloan Found., 1973-75, U. Ky., 1984. Mem, Soc. Applied Learning Tech., Am. Legion, Assn. Computing Machinery (v.p. 1985—), Pi Gamma Mu. Democrat. Roman Catholic. Home: 112 Oak Ridge Rd Brunswick GA 31525 Office: USINS Distance Learning Ctr FIETC Bldg 64 Glynco GA 31524

MIHAS, ANASTASIOS ATHANASIOS, gastroenterologist; b. Athens, Greece, Feb. 26, 1943; came to U.S., 1971; s. Athanasios A. and Penelope (Gikas) M.; m. Catherine A. Mastotis, Apr. 26, 1969; children: Thanos, George, Penelope. MD, Athens U., 1967, PhD, 1971. Diplomate Greek Bd. Internal Medicine. Intern Beekman Hosp., N.Y.C., 1971-72; resident Sinai Hosp., Balt., 1972-73; rsch. fellow Harvard Med. Sch., Cambridge, Mass., 1973-74; clin. fellow Boston City Hosp., 1973-74; fellow U. Ala., Birmingham, 1974-75, instr. medicine, 1975-76, asst. prof. medicine, 1976-78, staff gastroenterologist, 1975-78; chief gastroenterology Hellemic Cancer Inst., Athens, 1979-88; staff physician VA Med. Ctr., Jackson, Miss., 1988-

92, chief gastroenterology, 1992—; cons. USAF Gen. Hosp., Athens, 1979-88; clin. prof. medicine Athens U., 1988—; assoc. prof. medicine U. Miss., Jackson, 1988-93, prof. medicine, 1993—. Contbr. over 200 articles to profl. jours. Lt. Greek Air Force, 1967-70. Fulbright scholar, 1971. Fellow ACP, Am. Coll. Gastroenterology; mem. AMA (Physician Recognition award 1975, 77, 80, 89, 90, 91, 92), Am. Gastroenterol. Assn., Am. Fedn. Clin. Rsch., Sigma Xi. Greek Orthodox. Home: 1309 Woodfield Dr Jackson MS 39211-2027 Office: VA Med Ctr 111A 1500 E Woodrow Wilson Ave # 111A Jackson MS 39216-5116

MIHM, JOHN CLIFFORD, chemical engineer; b. Austin, Tex., July 28, 1942; s. Clifford Henry and Adeline (Cleary) M.; m. Janet Elanor Skales, May 29, 1964; 1 child, Mary Lynn. AA, Frank Phillips Coll., 1962; BSChemE, Tex. Tech. Engring., 1964. Registered profl. engr., Tex. With Phillips Petroleum Co., 1964—; v.p. corp. engring. Phillips Petroleum Co., Bartlesville, Okla., 1987-92, v.p. R & D, 1992-93, sr. v.p. corp. technology, 1993—; engr. mgr. E & P Phillips Petroleum Co., Stavanger, Norway, 1977-82; adv. bd. Tex. Tech. Engring., Lubbock, Tex., 1985—. Bd. dirs. Boy Scouts Am., Bartlesville, 1986—. Mem. ASME (ind. adv. bd. 1989—), NSPE, AIChE (ECC divsn., bd. dirs. 1989-93, chmn. 1992-93), Okla. Soc. Profl. Engrs. (Outstanding Engr. in Mgmt. award 1991), Soc. Profl. Engrs., Okla. Engring. Found. (bd. dirs., pres. 1993—). Republican. Roman Catholic. Office: Phillips Petroleum Co 4th and Keeler Sts Bartlesville OK 74004

MIILLER, SUSAN DIANE, artist; b. N.Y.C., June 10, 1953; d. Elwood Charles and Alyce Mary (Gebhardt) Knapp; m. Denis Miiller, May 22, 1982. MA, Queens Coll., 1980; BFA, SUNY, 1988; MFA, U. North Tex., 1992. Palynologist Phillips Petroleum Co., Bartleville, Okla., 1980-85; scenic designer Forestburgh (N.Y.) Playhouse, 1989; rsch. asst. Lamont-Doherty Geol. Observatory, Palisades, N.Y., 1990; adj. prof. Tex. Christian U., Ft. Worth, 1992-94; lectr. U. Tex., Dallas, 1995—; lectr. U. Tex., Dallas, 1995-96; treas. mem. 500X Gallery, Dallas, 1991-92. One-woman shows include Western Tex. Coll., 1993, Brazos Gallery, Richland Coll., 1993, Women & Their Work Gallery, 1995 (Gallery Artists Series award 1995), A.I.R. Gallery, 1996, Milagros Contemporary Art, 1996, Peutimenti Gallery, Pa., 1996. Recipient 4th Nat. Biennial Exhbns., Grand Purchase award, 1991, Mus. Abilene award, 1992, Lubbock Art Festival Merit award, 1992, 2d pl. award Matrix Gallery, 1995, Hon. Mention award 3d Biennial Gulf of Mex. Exhbn., 1995, 1st place award Soho Gallery, 1996. Mem. Tex. Fin Arts Assn., Dallas Mus. Art, Coll. Art Assn., Dallas Visual Art Ctr., Art Initiatives. Home: 449 Harris St # J102 Coppell TX 75019-3224 Studio: 3309 Elm St # 3E Dallas TX 75226-1637

MIKA, WALTER VALENTINE, nurse, nursing administrator, quality assurance professional; b. Chgo., May 9, 1939; s. Walter V. Mika and Helene Marie (Kozial) Troccoli; m. Carol Ann Rice, May 17, 1966; children: Paul, Rosemary, Suzanne, Timothy. Diploma in Nursing, Mt. Sinai Hosp., Chgo., 1961; BSN, U. Tex., San Antonio, 1975, MSN, 1979. RN, Tex. Commd. 1st lt. U.S. Army, 1966, advanced through grades to col., 1993; chief nurse Vaihingen (Germany) Health Clinic, 1980-81; supr. outpatient clinics 5th Gen. Hosp., Stuttgart, Germany, 1981-82, asst. chief nurse, 1982-83; chief nursing edn. and tng. William Beaumont Army Med. Ctr., Ft. Bliss, Tex., 1983-85; asst. chief nurse Silas B. Hayes Army Cmty. Hosp., Ft. Ord, Calif., 1985-88, DON, 1988-91; DON Frankfurt (Germany) Army Med. Ctr., 1991-93, Ctrl. Tex. Home Health, San Antonio, 1993-95; supervising nurse Am. Home Health Svcs., San Antonio, 1995—; nurse cons. Ctrl. Home Care Svcs., Largo, Fla., 1995; quality assurance nurse Ctrl. Okla. Care at Home, Oklahoma City, 1995; dep. dir. for hosp. mgmt. Frankfurt Med. Ctr., 1991-93. Decorated Legion of Merit. Mem. Taunus Med. Soc., San Antonio Choral Soc. (v.p. 1995—), Army of USA. Roman Catholic. Home: 2355 Pendant Pass San Antonio TX 78232 Office: Am Home Health Svcs Inc 5372 Fredericksburg Rd San Antonio TX 78229

MIKAN, KATHLEEN JOYCE KEHRER, medical/surgical nurse, educator; b. Galion, Ohio. BSN cum laude, Ohio State U., Columbus, 1961; MSN, U. Colo., Denver, 1963; PhD, Mich. State U., East Lansing, 1972; postdoctoral, U. Utah, Salt Lake City, 1991. Staff nurse Ohio State U. U. Hosp., Columbus, 1961; asst. instr. Ohio State U., Columbus, 1961-62, instr. med.-surg. nursing, team nursing and fundamentals of nursing, 1963-65; asst. prof. Mich. State U., East Lansing, 1965-67, co-dir. multi-media project, 1967-69; asst. prof. Case Western Res. U., Cleve., 1970-72, assoc. in nursing, 1970-74, program dir. Health Sci. Communications Ctr., 1971-74, ednl. specialist primary health practitioner program, 1972-74, assoc. prof., 1972-74, adminstrv. officer, 1973-74; dir. learning resources U. Ala., Birmingham, 1974-91, prof., 1974—, mem. faculty post master fellowship program in oncology nursing edn., 1980-83, media dir., 1984-87, 1985-89, project faculty, cost mgmt. edn. for nurses contract, 1986-88, media expert, 1988-91, prof., 1974—; nurse Camp Taconic, Pittsfield, Mass., summers, 1961, 62; mem. planning com. 5th Nat. Learning Resources Conf. U. Tex., San Antonio, 1994; SCAMC referee for paper selection Ann. Symposium on Computer Applications in Med. Care, 1985—; out of state expert rsch. proposal reviewer La. Edn. Quality Support Fund State of La. Bd. Regents, 1990; cons. expansion of learning resource capacity and computer utilization to various schs. nursing; mem. spl. project review panel divsn. of Nursing HEW, 1989—; mem. adv. bd. dirs. The Soc. Nursing Profls., 1991—; speaker, presenter in field; cons. WHO, Indonesia, 1995; sec. Univ. Ala. Birmingham Faculty Senate, 1995—. Manuscript reviewer FOCUS, 1984—; author (with Eula Aiken) In Computer Applications in Nursing Education and Practice, 1992; contbr. articles to profl. jours. Mem. Lung Resource Ctr. Com. Ala. Lung Assn., 1980-90, community health and program support com., 1990—. Recipient Red Ribbon award Am. Film Festival Case Western Res. U., 1972, Bronze award Internat. Film and TV Festival Case Western Res. U., 1972. Fellow Am. Acad. Nursing (Svc. cert. 1990); mem. ANA (coun. on computer applications in nursing), Assn. for Ednl. Communications and Tech., Nat. League for Nursing (nat. forum on computers in health care and nursing, coun. on nursing informatics), Ala. Instrl. Media Assn., Ala. Lung Assn., Ala. State Nurses Assn., Am. Acad. of Nursing (pub. rels. com. 1987-90), Ohio State U. Nursing Alumnae Assn., U. Colo. Alumni Assn., U. Colo. Sch. of Nursing Alumni, Lambda Alpha Delta, Sigma Theta Tau (Internat. Officer award 1985-91, heritage com. 1985-91, sec. 1985-91, publ. com. 1987-91, Internat. Heritage award, chair 1991, co-chair resolutions com. biennial conv. 1991, co-chair voting com. biennial conv. 1991, libr. sci. com. 1991—, evaluation visitor 1991, installing officer 1992), Phi Kappa Phi, Am. Nurses Found. Century Club.

MIKELS, J(AMES) RONALD, bank executive; b. Knoxville, Tenn., Nov. 21, 1937; s. Jesse R. and Virginia L. (Walters) M.; m. Norma Jean Weatherly, Jan. 8, 1966; 1 child, J. Richard. M in Graphoanalysis, Internat. Graphoanalysis Soc., Chgo., 1961; BS, U. Tenn., 1980; MRE, Bethany Theol. Sem., 1993. Cert. human resources profl. Electronic data processing auditor Park Nat. Bank, Knoxville, 1956-78; retirement specialist U. Tenn., Knoxville, 1979-80; dir. pers. Home Fed. Bank, Knoxville, 1980—; instr. U. Tenn., Knoxville, 1972-77; mem. adv. com. Pellissippi State Coll., Knoxville, 1986-88; ct. handwriting expert, 1968—. Contbr. articles to mags. and jours. Campaign coord. United Way, Knoxville, 1985-96; cons. Jr. Achievement, Knoxville, 1990, 92, 93, 94. Mem. Full Gospel Businessmen's Fellowship Internat., Tenn. League Savs. Instns. (bd. dirs. 1989). Wesleyan Methodist. Office: Home Fed Bank 515 Market St Knoxville TN 37902-2145

MIKKELSON, DEAN HAROLD, geological engineer; b. Devils Lake, N.D., July 25, 1922; s. John Harold and Theodora (Eklund) M.; m. Delphene Doss, May 30, 1946; 1 child, Lynn Dee Hoffman. Student, N.D. State Coll., 1940-41; midshipman, U.S. Naval Acad., 1942-45; BS in Geological Engring., U. N.D., 1956. Registered profl. engr., Okla. 2d officer U.S. Lines, Quaker Lines-States Lines, Portland, Oreg., 1945-48; ptnr. J.I. Case Farm Machinery & Packard Automobile Franchises, Devils Lake, N.D., 1948-52; oil and gas lease broker Devils Lake, N.D., 1952-54; geologist Sohio Petroleum Co., Oklahoma City, 1956-58; geol. engr. Petrobras, Belem do Para, Brazil, 1958-60; pvt. practice Oklahoma City, 1961-78; pres., owner Dogwatch Petroleum, Inc., Oklahoma City, 1978—; agrl. pilot, N.D., Mont., Tex., N.Mex., summers, 1952-56. Author: (as Dee Geo) Danny; contbr. articles to profl. jours. Candidate Okla. Rep. State Legislature, Oklahoma City, 1958; del. various county and state conv., N.D. and Okla., 1948-68. With N.D. N.G., 1938-40, U.S. Army Air Corps., 1942. Mem. Oklahoma City Geol. Soc., Masons, Shriners, Jesters, Am. Legion, Sportsmans Country Club. Republican. Office: Dogwatch Petroleum Inc Ste H 4430 NW 50 St Ste H Oklahoma City OK 73112-2295

MIKSA, RONALD W., mechanical engineer; b. Aurora, Ill., Jan. 12, 1968; s. Ronald L. and Sherry R. (Mitchell) M. BSME, No. Ill. U., 1990. Lic. engr.-in-tng., Ark.; cert. mfg. technologist. Surveyor's asst. Fermi Nat. Accelerator Lab., Batavia, Ill., 1986, Compass Ltd., Naperville, Ill., 1987-90; intern GE, DeKalb, Ill., 1990-91; mfg. engr. Cloos Internat., Inc., Elgin, Ill., 1991-92; liaison engr. S-B Power Tools, Walnut Ridge, Ark., 1992-94; product design engr. Colson Caster Corp., Jonesboro, Ark., 1994—. Mem. ASME (assoc.), Soc. Mfg. Engrs. (chpt. chmn.). Home: 3412 Turtle Creek Dr Jonesboro AR 72401-7773 Office: Colson Caster Corp 3700 Airport Rd Jonesboro AR 72401-4464

MILAM, JUNE MATTHEWS, life insurance agent; b. Preston, Ga., Mar. 27, 1931; d. Curtis J. and Mary (Doster) Matthews; m. James Cage Lowry, Dec. 20, 1952 (dec.); m. Walker Hinton Milam, Jr., June 15, 1957; children: James L., Melinda K., Lisa W., Matthew W. BA, La. State U., 1952. Agt. N.Y. Life Ins. Co., Metairie, La., 1966—; alderman City of Harahan, La., 1980-86; mayor pro-tem City of Harahan, 1982-84; guest spkr. to industry in 26 states, 1968—; charter leader N.Y. Life Ins. Women's Network, N.Y.C., 1981-83. Contbr. articles to profl. and trade jours. Mem. adv. bd. Battered Women's Program, New Orleans, 1978-86, Jefferson Parish Econ. Devel. Coun., 1988-92, sec., 1990; bd. dirs. Abused Children's Advocacy Ctr., 1990—; bd. dirs. Extra Mile, Inc., 1995—, sec., 1995-96, pres., 1996—; co-founder, charter pres. Jefferson 25 Women's Polit. Orgn., 1991-92; chairperson JEDCO Citizen's Adv. Group, 1993; mem. East Jefferson Gen. Hosp. Found. Planned Giving Com., 1994—. Named Boss of Yr. Am. Bus. Women's Assn., Metairie, 1976, Man of Yr. New Orleans Assn. Life Underwriters, La. State Assn. Life Underwriters, 1976; recipient Natt. Quality award 25 yrs.; Quality of Life grantee, 1990. Mem. Nat. Assn. Life Underwriters, La. Assn. Life Underwriters, New Orleans Assn. Life Underwriters, Womens Bus. Owners Assn. (adv. bd. 1984-88), Million Dollar Round Table, New Orleans Top Twenty Study Group. Republican. Presbyterian. Office: NY Life Ins Co 3333 W Napoleon Ave Ste 200 Metairie LA 70001-2882

MILANO, CECELIA MANCHOR, mental health nurse; b. Pitts., Apr. 19, 1924; d. Joseph and Anna (Plisowski) Manchor; m. Louis J. Milano, Aug. 12, 1946. BSN, Duquesne U., 1945; MS in Adult Psychiat. Nursing, Boston U., 1961; cert. in family therapy, Cambridge Family Inst., 1977; postgrad., Boston U., 1978; cert. in Advanced Grad. Study Spl. Edn., Nova U., 1991, D. in Public Admistrn., 1991. RN, Calif., Pa., Fla., Mass. Head nurse med.-surg. unit various hosps., Akron, Ohio, 1945-47; adminstrv. supr. med.-surg. unit Presbyn.-Univ. Hosp., Pitts., 1949-50; asst. prof. psychiat. nursing U. Miami, Fla., 1955-66, U. Pitts., 1966-67, Duquesne U., 1967-68; asst. prof. grad. psychiat. nursing Boston U., 1970-74; nurse psychiat. emergency svcs. Jackson Meml. Hosp., Miami, 1979—; presenter workshops; speaker at seminars. Rep. Pres. Carter's Freedom Forces, spring 1995, Moscow. Fellow Orthopsychiat. Assn.; mem. Alpha Tau Delta. Office: 1611 NW 12th Ave Miami FL 33136-1005

MILASKI, JOHN JOSEPH, business transformation industry consultant; b. Johnson City, N.Y., Sept. 16, 1959; s. John Walter and Nellie Joan (Panaro) M.; m. Ann Mildred Caldwell, Jan. 22, 1994. AAS, Broome Community Coll., 1979; BSEE, Rochester Inst. Tech., 1984; MBA, Syracuse U., 1991. Registered engr., N.Y.; cert. bus. transformation cons. Design engr. IBM, Endicott, N.Y., 1979-84; systems engr. IBM, Endicott, 1984-85, mktg. cons., 1985-91, cons. Cons. & Sys. Integration Svcs. upstate N.Y., 1992-94; cons. Worldwide Document Mgmt. Solutions Group IBM, 1995-96, con. Worldwide Cons. Svcs., 1996—. Inventor. Vol. IBM Olympic Force Team 1996 Summer Olympics; trust mgr. Nat. Trust for Historical Preservation; charter mem. Statue of Liberty-Ellis Island Found., Inc. Recipient Utilities Industry Mktg. Excellence award IBM Systems Engring. Symposium, 1989, 91. Mem. IEEE (sr.), ASME (sr.), Am. Mgmt. Assn., Am. Prodn. and Inventory Control Soc. (sr.), Internat. Platform Assn., Computer and Automated Sys. Assn., N.Y. State Sheriff's Assn., U.S. Holocaust Meml. Mus. (charter mem.), IBM 100 Percent Club, U.S. C. of C., Internt. Directory of Disting. Leadership, Nat. Mus. of the Am. Indian (charter mem.). Republican. Roman Catholic. Home: 6170 Song Breeze Trce Duluth GA 30155

MILBRATH, SUSAN, museum curator, art historian; b. Annapolis, Md., July 19, 1945; d. Robert Henry and Margaret (Ripperger) M.; m. Jorge Lopez Pelliza, June 20, 1971 (div. 1976); 1 child, Mariano Lopez Pelliza; m. Mark Brenner, Nov. 16, 1989. BA in Art History, Columbia U., 1970, MPhil in Primitive and Pre-Columbian Art, 1973, PhD in Art History, Archaeology, 1975. Adj. instr. pre-Columbian art dept. art Hunter Coll., 1974; adj. curatorial asst. Lowie Mus. Anthropology, Berkeley, Calif., 1976; asst. prof. art history dept. art U. Fla., Gainesville, 1977-79; Tinker postdoctoral fellow Yale U., 1979-80; rsch. assoc. Mus. Am. Indian, N.Y.C., 1980-81, guest curator, 1981-83; adj. assoc. curator dept. anthropology Fla. State Mus., Gainesville, 1983-85, vis. assoc. curator dept. anthropology, 1985-86; vis. curator pre-Columbian art Mint Mus., Charlotte, N.C., 1986-87; asst. curator dept. interpretation Fla. Mus. Natural History, Gainesville, 1987-92, assoc. curator, dept. of interpretation, 1992—; lectr. in field. Prodr. PBS, Sta. WUFT Channel 5 Arts Update, 1985; prodr., screenwriter various art and anthropology video prodns., 1985—; contbr. articles to profl. jours. Grantee NEH, 1981-82, 85-86, 87-89, Tinker Field, 1990, Fla. Dept. State Hist. Mus., 1991, 92-93, 96-97, U. Fla., 1990. Mem. Am. Anthropol. Assn., Am. Assn. Mus., Archaeol. Inst. Am., Assn. Latin Am. Art, Coun. Mus. Anthropology, Nat. Mus. Am. Indian (charter), Phi Beta Kappa. Office: Fla Mus Natural History Museum Rd Gainesville FL 32611

MILBURN, HERBERT THEODORE, federal judge; b. Cleveland, Tenn., May 26, 1931; s. J.E. and Hazel (Shanks) M.; m. Elaine Dillow, Aug. 23, 1957; children: Blair Douglas, Elizabeth Elaine. Student, U. Chattanooga, 1949-50, Boston U., 1950-51; BS, East Tenn. State U., 1953; JD, U. Tenn., 1959. Bar: Tenn. 1959, U.S. Supreme Ct. 1971. Assoc. Folts, Bishop, Thomas, Leitner & Mann, Chattanooga, 1959-63; ptnr. Bishop, Thomas, Leitner, Mann & Milburn, Chattanooga, 1963-73; judge Hamilton County Cir. Ct., Chattanooga, 1973-83, U.S. Dist. Ct. (ea. dist.) Tenn., Chattanooga, 1983-84; judge U.S. Ct. Appeals (6th cir.), Chattanooga, 1984—, sr. judge; mem. faculty Nat. Jud. Coll. U. Nev., Reno, 1980, Tenn. Jud. Acad., Vanderbilt U., Nashville, 1982. Pres. Hamilton County Young Reps., Chattanooga, 1965; mem. Chancellor's Roundtable U. Tenn., Chattanooga, 1983-86; pres. Lakeside Kiwanis, 1964. With U.S. Army Security Agy., 1953-56. Recipient award Chattanooga Bd. Realtors, 1987, Outstanding Alumnus award East Tenn. State U., 1988; named Outstanding Young Rep., Hamilton County Young Reps., 1965. Mem. ABA, Tenn. Bar Assn. (commr. 1971-73, mem. profl. ethics and grienvance com.), Chattanooga Bar Assn. (sec.-treas. 1967), Fed. Bar Assn. (chairperson U.S. jud. conf. com. on adminstrv. office of U.S. cts. 1994—), Am. Legion, East Tenn. State U. Found., Signal Mountain Golf and Country Club, Univ. Club Cin., Kiwanis. Republican. Episcopalian. Office: US Ct Appeals PO Box 750 Chattanooga TN 37401-0750

MILDREN, JACK, legal services company executive, former state official; b. Kingsville, Tex., Oct. 10, 1949; s. Larry J. and Mary Glynne (Lamont) M.; m. Janis Susan Butler, Jan. 14, 1972; children: Leigh, Lauren, Drew. BBA, U. Okla., 1972. Cert. petroleum landman. Mem. Balt. Colts Football Club, 1972-73, New England Patriots Football Club, 1974; v.p. Saxon Oil Co., 1972-79; co-founder, pres. Regency Exploration Inc., 1977-88; ind. oil oper., 1988-90; lt. gov. State of Okla., Oklahoma City, 1990-95; pres., CEO Pre-Paid Legal Svcs. Inc., Ada, OK, 1995. Bd. dirs. Children's Med. Rsch. Found., Arts Coun. Oklahoma City, Nat. Football League Players Found. and Hall of Fame, State Ctr. Com., Jim Thorpe Club; mem. Leadership Okla., Leadership Oklahoma City; mem. Com. to Devel. Biotech. Industry in Okla. Named All-Am. Football Player, 1971, Acad. All-Am., 1971, NAt. Football Found. Hall Fame, 1971, Most Valuable Player Sugar Bowl, 1972. numerous other athletic awards. Mem. Beta Gamma Sigma, Phi Delta Theta (past pres., bd. dirs.). Meth. Home: 1701 Guilford Oklahoma City OK 73120 Office: Pre-Paid Legal Svcs Inc 321 E Main St Ada OK 74820

MILES, BRUCE WILLIAM, academic administrator; b. Middletown, N.Y., Sept. 19, 1947; s. Donald Willis and Gertrude Estelle (Piatt) M.; m. Elizabeth Skydel, Apr. 30, 1976 (div. 1993); children: Shana, Tova.; m. Kim Ina Miller, Dec. 10, 1993. AA, Suffolk County C.C., Selden, N.Y., 1973; BA in Anthropology, SUNY, Stony Brook, 1975; MS in Counseling, C.W. Post Coll., 1981; PhD in Ednl. Adminstrn., Mellen U., 1996. Staff devel. specialist Kings Park (N.Y.) Psychol. Ctr., 1968-83; tng. dir. Uniforce Temporary Svcs., New Hyde Park, N.Y., 1983-85; mgr. franchise mktg. Success Motivation Internat., Inc., Waco, Tex., 1985-86; tng. dir. Dunhill Pers. Sys., Inc., Carle Place, N.Y., 1986-87; owner, tng. cons. Mobius Co., Greensboro, N.C., 1987-88; tng. specialist Ris Paper Co., Garden City, N.Y., 1988-90; admissions rep. Webster Coll., New Port Richey, Fla., 1991; dean acad. affairs Tampa (Fla.) Coll., 1991-95; dept. chair B.S.E.T. Tampa Tech. Inst., 1995-96, edn. dir., 1996—. With U.S. Army, 1965-68. Jewish. Home: 3015 Whispering Ln Zephyrhills FL 33543 Office: Tampa Tech Inst 2410 E Busch Blvd Tampa FL 33612-8410

MILES, HELEN, oncological nurse; b. Pitts., Dec. 17, 1936; d. John Michael and Mary (Kurtz) Sharak; m. James Robert Miles, June 3, 1956 (div. 1974); children: Ron, Dave, Kevin, Susan, Tina. Grad., Allegheny C.C., 1976; LPN, Connelly Skill Learning Ctr., 1981. Sec. Bd. Edn., Pitts., 1970-80; staff nurse oncology Mercy Hosp., Pitts., 1981-85; pvt. duty nurse Quality Care, Pitts., 1985; staff nurse oncology Naples (Fla.) Cmty. Hosp., 1986-96; pvt. practice oncol. nurse Naples, 1996—; notary pub., Pa., 1975-83; counseling asst. Tom Connelly Med. CAP, Pitts., Naples, 1984-86; assoc. producer, co-host TC Prodns., Pitts., 1984-85; preceptor oncology unit, Naples Hosp., 1990—, mem. adv. bds., 1986—. Author: (poetry) Walk Through Paradise, 1995; (with others) The Voice Within, Where Dawn Lingers, 1996. Vol. Naples Hotline, 1987-88; environ. def. mem. Nat. Trust for Historic Preservation. Recipient Clin. Excellence award, 1995, cert. appreciation Project Hotline, 1993, Nat. Humane Edn. Soc., 1995, Cmmdrs. Club Bronze Leader award DAV, 1996. Mem. Nat. Parks Conservation Assn., Ctr. for Marine Conservation, Smithsonian Assn., Internat. Soc. Poets (Internat. Poet of Merit award 1995, Editor's Choice award 1995, 96), The Conservancy, Nat. Geographic Soc., Swarovski Crystal Soc. Republican. Home: Royal Pk Villas #6 Hackney Ln Naples FL 34112

MILES, JAMES L(ARRY), JR., environmental and safety consultant; b. Savannah, Ga., July 9, 1958; s. James Larry Sr. and Elizabeth (Dasher) M.; m. Kathleen Ann Campbell, Oct. 22, 1983; children: Kathryn Elizabeth, Alexander Campbell. BS in Criminal Justice, Armstrong State U., 1981; MS in Safety Mgmt., W.Va. U., 1983. Safety insp. Morton-Thiokol, Shreveport, La., 1983-85; safety engr. Gulfstream Aerospace, Savannah, 1985-87; mgr. safety and security Intermarine U.S.A., Savannah, 1987—, indsl. rels. mgr., 1990-91; pvt. practice bus. cons. Ga., 1991—. Lt. comdr. USNR, 1984—. Mem. Am. Soc. Safety Engrs., Nat. Fire Protection Assn., Internat. Assn. Narcotic Enforcement Officers. Republican. Home: 622 Rose Dhu Rd Savannah GA 31419-3324

MILES, JIM, state official. Prof. of law Greenville Tech. Coll.; sec. of state S.C. Mem. Soc. Internat. Bus. Office: Sec of State PO Box 11350 Columbia SC 29211-1350*

MILES, MINNIE CADDELL, retired business educator; b. Glen Allen, Ala., Mar. 4, 1910; d. Thomas Elias and Bertha Eveline (Griggs) Caddell; m. Murphie Alton Miles, Mar. 4, 1928 (dec. 1979). BS, Mary Hardin-Baylor, 1936; MBA, Northwestern U., 1941; PhD, Purdue U., 1951; LLD (hon.), Mary Hardin-Baylor, 1965; D Humanities (hon.), U. Ala., 1987. Tchr. rural schs. Ala. Sch. System, 1926-32; collector student loans Mary Hardin-Baylor, Belton, Tex., 1934-41; exec. sec. Northwestern U., Evanston, Ill., 1941-42; bus. tchr. U. Ala., Tuscaloosa, 1942-78; dir. indsl. rels. Olan Mills, Chattanooga, 1945-47; Fulbright prof. Pusan (Republic of Korea) Nat. U., 1969, Victoria U., Wellington, New Zealand, 1977-78; vis. prof. Purdue U., Lafayette, Ind., 1951; cons. Druid City Hosp., Tuscaloosa, 1954-55, TVA, Knoxville, Tenn., 1972, U.S. Civil Svc. Commn., Washington, 1973-77; field assoc. Fry Assocs., Consultants, Chgo., 1957-73. Contbr. articles to profl. jours. Chmn. Ala. Status of Women Commn., Montgomery, 1964-70; mem., chmn. Def. Adv. Com. on Women in Svc., Washington, 1965-67; specialist Latin Am. program U.S. Dept. State, 1963; bd. dirs. U.S. Bus. and Profl. Women's Found., Washington, 1957-64; nat. trainer Widowed Persons Svc. Rsch. grantee U. Ala., Tuscaloosa, 1954; named to Faculty hall of Fame/Coll. of Bus., U. Ala., Tuscaloosa, 1990, Women Committed to Excellence Girl Scouts U.S., 1989, Inducted Ala. Women's Acad. of Honor, 1992, Civitan Citizens of Yr., 1993; established Professorship Grad. scholar U. Ala., Coll. Bus. Adminstrn. Mem. U.S. Fedn. Bus. and Profl. Women (pres. 1962-63), Ala. Fedn. Bus. and Profl. Women (pres. 1955-57), Ala. Bus. and Profl. Women's Found. (life mem. bd. dirs., chmn. bd. dirs. 1981-88), ASTD (life), APA, Tuscaloosa Club Altrusa Internat. (pres. 1952-53). Democrat. Methodist. Home: 27 Beech Hls Tuscaloosa AL 35404-4959 Office: U Ala Tuscaloosa AL 35487-0122

MILES, OSCAR LANDON, III, engineering company executive; b. Monroe, La., Apr. 5, 1920; s. Oscar Landon II and Gladys (Skinner) M.; m. Virginia Vaughan, Dec. 9, 1944; children: Margaret M. Miles McInnis, Michael Landon. BS, La. Tech. U., 1940. Mgr. payrolls Constrn. Quarter Master, Alexandria, La., 1940-41; acct. Ford, Bacon & Davis, Jackson, Miss., 1941-42; chief project acct. Ford, Bacon & Davis, Monroe, 1946-61, mgr., v.p. sealants dept., 1961-69, v.p. bus. devel., 1969-78, corp. v.p., corp. mktg., 1978-80, sr. v.p., 1980-91; pres., dir. Sealants Internat., West Chester, Pa., 1979-91; cons. Monroe, 1991—. Chmn. sustaining membership enrollment Boy Scouts Am., Monroe, 1985-92; pres. Lotus Club, Monroe, 1969-70; spkr. United Way, Monroe, 1971-74; sponsor Jr. Achievement, Monroe, 1967-69. Lt. comdr. USN, 1942-46. Decorated 5 Battle Stars; O.L. Miles Day named in his honor City of Monroe, 1991. Mem. Am. Gas Assn., Monroe Gas Assn. (bd. dirs.), New Eng. Gas Assn., Mystic Shrine, Knight's Templar, Masons (32 degree), Bayou DeSiard Country Club. Republican. Episcopalian. Office: OL Miles Cons 130 DeSiard St # 513 Monroe LA 71201

MILES, ROBERT HENRY, management consultant, educator; b. Norfolk, Va., Mar. 10, 1944; s. Henry Bateman and Mildred Verda (Cuthrell) M.; m. Jane Irving Calfee, Aug. 27, 1966; children: Alexander Bateman, Holen Irving. BS, U. Va., 1967; MBA, Old Dominion U., 1969; PhD, U. N.C., 1974. Ops. analyst Ford Motor Co., Norfolk, 1968; project mgr. Advanced Rsch. Projects Agy. Office Sec. Def., Washington, 1970-71; asst. prof., co-founder Inst. Pub. Welfare Mgmt., U. Ala. Grad. Sch. Bus., Tuscaloosa, 1974-75; asst. prof. Sch. Orgn. and Mgmt. Yale U., New Haven, 1975-78; assoc. prof. Harvard Bus. Sch., Boston, 1978-85; vis. prof. Stanford Exec. Inst., 1987-95; Isaac Stiles Hopkins prof. orgn. & mgmt. Goizzneta Bus. Sch. Emory U., Atlanta, 1987—; dept. dean Emory U. Bus. Sch., Atlanta, 1989-91, dean of faculty, 1991-93, Hopkins fellow, 1995—; mem. sec.'s adv. bd. U.S. Dept. Energy, Washington, 1993—; mem. adv. bd. orgn. effectiveness programs The Conf. Bd., N.Y.C., 1994—; mem. adv. bd. McIntire Sch. Commerce, U. Va., Charlottesville, 1987-95. Author: Macro-Organizational Behavior, 1980, (with J.R. Kimberly) The Organizatoinal Life Cycle: Issues in the Creation, Transformation, and Decline of Organizations, 1980, Managing the Corporate Social Environment: A Grounded theory, 1987, Corporate Comeback: The Renewal and Transformation of National Semiconductor, 1996; (in collaboration with K.S. Cameron) Coffin Nails and Corporate Strategies, 1982, (with A. Bhambri) The Regulatory Executives, 1983, (with W.A. Randolph) The Organization Game: A Simulation, 1979, 83, 93; mem. edit. bd. Adminstrv. Sci. Quar., 1978-86, Mgmt. Sci., 1979-82. 1st lt. U.S. Army, 1969-71. Recipient Disting. Svc. award Emory U., 1993. Mem. APA, Acad. Mgmt. (chmn. orgn. and mgmt. theory divsn. 1984-85), Strategic Mgmt. Soc., Harvard Club (Boston), Commerce Club (Atlanta), Cherokee Town Club (Atlanta), Beta Gamma Sigma. Unitarian Universalist. Home and Office: 3414 Habersham Rd NW Atlanta GA 30305 Home (summer): 3414 Habersham Rd NW Atlanta GA 30305-1157

MILES, THOMAS CASWELL, aerospace engineer; b. Atlanta, Mar. 21, 1952; s. Franklin Caswell and Eugenia Frances (Newsom) M.; m. Linda Susan Duggleby, Aug. 10, 1980. BMET, So. Tech. Inst., 1977; postgrad., Troy State U., 1978-80. Assoc. engr. aircraft design Lockheed Martin Aero. Sys., Marietta, Ga., 1980-82, engr., aircraft design, 1982-85, sr. engr., aircraft design, 1985-89, group engr., 1989-90, specialist engr., 1990—; mem. SAE-A-6 Mil. Aircraft & Helicopter Panel, 1987-91, SAE-A-10 Aircraft Oxygen Equipment Com., 1996—. Mem. AIAA (sr.), ASME, ASTM, Nat. Mgmt. Assn., Lockheed Ga. Mgmt. Assn. (bd. dirs. 1996), Soc. Automotive Engrs.

(SAE co. rep., SAE Atlanta sect. vice chmn. aircraft), Oxygen Standardization Coord. Group Assn. Fraternity Advisors (affiliate), Wick's Lake Homeowners Assn. (pres. 1995, v.p. 1996), Tau Kappa Epsilon (dist. pres. 1987-88, dist. v.p. 1984—, chpt. advisor 1980-87, key leader 1985, 90, So. Order of Honor 1989). Home: 1926 Wicks Ridge Ln Marietta GA 30062-6777 Office: Lockheed Martin Aero Sys Dept 73-05 cc-34 Marietta GA 30063-0199

MILES, WILLIAM TRICE, state legislator; b. Fulton, Miss., Jan. 6, 1938; s. Ira Matison and Ellen Ozema (Webb) M.; m. Patricia Ann Reed, May 16, 1957; William T. Jr., Pattie Miles Cox. BA, U. Miss., 1959. Journalist Itawamba Times, Fulton, Miss., 1954-56; pub. rels. exec. Miss. State U., Starkville, Miss., 1958-59; journalist Tupelo (Miss.) Jour., 1959-63; journalism instr. Itawamba C.C., Fulton, 1959-69; CEO Bill Miles Assocs., Inc., Tupelo, 1963-95; editor, publisher, owner The Amory (Miss.) Advertiser, 1972-80, The Nettleton (Miss.) News, 1975-80; rep. 21st dist. Miss Ho. of Reps., Jackson, Miss., 1996—. Author: (manual) How to Gain and Maintain Public Confidence for Police Organizations, 1968. Mem. Cmty. Devel. Found., Tupelo, Miss., 1983—, Itawamba County Devel. Coun., Fulton, Miss., 1985—; bd. trustees Magnolia Bible Coll., Kosciusko, Miss., 1989—; bd. dirs. Sunnybrook Children's Home, 1990-96; pres. Sunnybrook Estates Ret. Ctrs., 1996. Mem. Sigma Delta Chi. Democrat. Mem. Ch. of Christ. Home: PO Box 246 Fulton MS 38843

MILEY, NINA M., law librarian; b. Blakely, Ga., Mar. 9, 1945; d. Vadie L. and Pearl (Regan) McG.; m. James D. Miley, Jan. 31, 1963 (div. 1982); children: Thorin, Katy. BA magna cum laude, U. N. Ala., 1965; JD, Washburn Law, 1990; MLS, U. Ill., 1991. Bar: Kans. 1990, U.S. Dist. Ct. Kans. Secondary English instr., art instr. Alcie Fortier Sr. H.S., New Orleans, 1966-69; owner, mgr. Nina Miley Advtsg., Manhattan, Kans., 1975-87; reference libr. U. Okla. Law Libr., Norman, 1991-93, interim dir., 1993-94, assoc. dir., 1994—. Author: (postcard series) Kansas Women's Historical Postcard Series, 1982; contbr. article to profl. jour. Mem. Manhattan, Kans. Downtown Redevel. Adv. Bd., 1980-82; Dem. nominee Kans. Ho. of Reps. Riley County Dems., Manhattan, 1984. Named Outstanding Svc. to City of Manhattan, Kans. City of Manhattan, 1985, Outstanding Woman Graduate Assn. Women Lawyers, 1990, 91. Mem. ABA, Am. Assn. Law Librs., Mid-Am. Assn. Law Librs., Order of Barristers. Democrat. Presbyterian. Office: U Okla Law Libr 300 Timberdell Rd Norman OK 73019

MILKEREIT, JOHN EUGENE, public relations and marketing executive, consultant; b. Dayton, Ohio, May 23, 1937; s. Richard David and Clara Rowena (Fellers) M.; m. Martha Joanne Benham, June 17, 1961; children: John Richard, David Allen, William Fellers. BS, Purdue U., 1960; MA, U. Chgo., 1977. Univ. editor U. Akron, 1965-67, dir. News Bur., 1967-70; assoc. dir. pub. info. U. Chgo., 1970-72; dir. med. ctr. pub. affairs U. Chgo. Med. Ctr., 1972-80; dir. pub. relations Med. U. S.C., Charleston, 1980-90; owner Milkereit Pub. Rels. and Mktg., Charleston, 1990—; cons. health care and gen. bus. pub. rels. Bd. dirs. Charleston Symphony, 1984-90. Served to capt. USAR, 1961-69. Mem. Pub. Rels. Soc. Am. (pres. S.C. chpt. 1982-83, accredited 1972), Rotary (Charleston downtown bd. dirs. 1996), Harbour Club. Office: PO Box 22068 Charleston SC 29413-2068

MILL, MICHAEL ROBERT, cardiothoracic surgeon, educator; b. Denver, Mar. 20, 1954; s. Walter Clark and Jeanne (Grigg) M.; m. Elizabeth Trousdale Sherwood, May 30, 1980; children: Isabella Sherwood, Cassandra Darrah. BA, The Colo. Coll., Colorado Springs, 1976; MD, U. Colo., 1980. Asst. prof. surgery U. N.C., Chapel Hill, 1988-93, assoc. prof. surgery, 1993—. Contbr. profl. publs. Pres. bd. dirs. Carolina Organ Procurement Agy., Greenville, 1992—. Fellow Am. Coll. Surgeons, Am. Coll. Cardiology, Am. Coll. Chest Physicians; mem. AMA, Internat. Soc. Heart and Lung Transplantation. Office: U NC Sch Medicine 108 Burnett-Womack Bldg Chapel Hill NC 27599-7065

MILLAR, DORINE MARIE AGNES, real estate agent, artist; b. Pos, Td'ad, West Indies, Apr. 20, 1924; d. Victor and Elsie (Dumoret) Sellier. Lic. real estate agt., Fla. Artist Millar Agencies Inc., Ft. Lauderdale, Fla., 1964—; real estate agt. Ft. Lauderdale, Fla., 1970—. Recipient 1st pl. award Hollywood Art Guild Ann. Mem. Show, 1993, 2d pla. prize Palm Beach Water Color Soc., 1990, 3rd pl. prize Coral Springs Art Guild, 1990. Mem. Gold Coast Watercolor Soc., Palm Beach Watercolor Soc., Fla. Watercolor Soc., Broward Art Guild.

MILLARD, JAMES KEMPER, marketing executive; b. Lexington, Ky., Oct. 28, 1948; s. Lyman Clifford and Cora (Carrick) M.; m. Madelyn Hooper, Nov. 26, 1983; children: Lyman Clifford III, Sean Duffy, James Kemper Jr., Caroline Carrick. BA, Transylvania U., Lexington, Ky., 1971. Writer AP, Lexington, 1970-71; asst. news. dir. Sta. WLEX-TV, FM, Lexington, 1971-76; producer Ky. Dept. Pub. Info., Frankfort, 1973; dir. univ. rels. Transylvania U., Lexington, 1973-79; acct. supr. Abbott Advt., Inc., Lexington, 1979-85; mktg. dir. Steak N' Shake, Inc., Indpls., 1985; field mktg. mgr. Blue Bell, Pa., 1985-86; field mktg. dir. Nutri/System Inc., Blue Bell, Pa., 1986-88, v.p. communications, 1988-90, sr. v.p. mktg., 1990-91; pres. Mktg. Comm. Overview, Inc., Exton, Pa., 1991-93, Waterwild Mktg., Lexington, Ky., 1993-94; dir. New Projects Devel. Sta. WKYT-TV, Lexington, Ky., 1994—; mem. acad. adv. com. Ea. Ky. U., Richmond, 1983-87; treas. Bluegrass Integrated Pest Mgmt., Lexington, 1983-85; case study spkr. Radio Advertisers Bur., 1989, 90. Author: C&O Streamliners, 1994. Bd. dirs. Chesapeake and Ohio Ry. Hist. Soc., Clifton Forge, Va., 1983—, v.p., 1994—; mem. Comdr.-in-Chief Leadership Circle, 1990—; pres. Swan Kitchen Car Co., 1990—; mem. Am. Assn. pvt. R.R. Car Owners, 1990—, R.R. Passenger Car Alliance, 1990—, Hon. Order Ky. Cols., 1976—; deacon Ctrl. Christian Ch., Lexington, 1984-86, 94—; cons. Jr. Achievement; bd. dirs. Found. for Affordable Housing, 1995—; mem. campaign cabinet United Way of the Bluegrass, 1995; pres. Delta Sigma Phi U. Ky. Corp. Bd., 1994—. Recipient Great Menu award Nat. Restaurant Assn., 1982, Key Man award Jerrico Inc., 1981, Silver and Bronze ADDY Awards Lexington Advt. Club, 1982, Gold Award Fla. Restaurant Assn., 1984, Innovative Idea award Ky. Broadcasters Assn., 1995. Mem. Rotary Internat., Delta Sigma Phi (pres. U. Ky. corp. bd. 1994—). Democrat. Mem. Disciples of Christ. Address: Waterwild Farm PO Box 12012 Lexington KY 40579

MILLAY-FULLENLOVE, CARMEN (KIT MILLAY-FULLENLOVE), newspaper editor; b. Louisville, Aug. 27, 1959; d. Joseph Claude and Erma Louise (Fleischmann) Millay; m. William Burnley Wolfe, Oct. 10, 1981 (div. 1986); m. James Martin Fullenlove, Sr., Sept. 12, 1987; 1 child, Rachel Renee. BS in journalism and polit. sci., Murray State U., 1980. Reporter, photographer Leisure Scene, Benton, Ky., 1979; editor The Murray (Ky.) State News, 1979-80; reporter, photographer The Mt. Vernon (Ind.) Democrat, 1980-81, city editor, 1981-82; editor Cobb County Softball Watch, Marietta, Ga., 1982; lead sales Ellman's, Smyrna, Ga., 1982-83; reporter, photographer The Sentinel News, Shelbyville, Ky., 1983-84; editor The Oldham Era, LaGrange, Ky., 1984—. Mem. Oldham C. of C., LaGrange, 1990—; bd. mem. March of Dimes, LaGrange, 1992-95; campaign cabinet United Way, LaGrange, 1995—. Recipient first place column writing Ky. Press Assn., editl. writing first place Landmark Cmty. Newspapers, 1995. Mem. Soc. of Profl. Journalists (past pres., mem. chair 1995—), Honorable Order of Ky. Colonels (Ky. Colonel 1992—). Office: The Oldham Era 204 S First La Grange KY 40031

MILLER, ALBERT LEON, county official; b. Kinston, N.C., Dec. 30, 1953; s. Albert and Gertrude (Wiggins) M.; m. Consuella Mae Gibson Chavis, Feb. 14, 1987; children: Sterling Avery Chavis, Jr., Yohanna Meatta Chavis. BA in Sociology, Fayetteville State U., 1975; M of Regional Planning, U. N.C., 1977. Cert. in interaction mgmt. Regional planner I Centralina Council Govts., Charlotte, N.C., 1977-79; regional planner II Centralina Coun. Govts., Charlotte, N.C., 1979-83, job tng. adminstr., 1983-90; dir. minority affairs Mecklenburg County Govt., Charlotte, 1990—; mem. Mecklenberg County Pers. Commn., 1990. Contbr. articles to newspapers and Sphinx mag. Fellow Leadership Charlotte , 1986, Focus on Leadership, Charlotte, 1988; bd. dirs. Charlotte Civic League, 1981—; mem. Charlotte Mecklenburg Adv. Energy Com., Charlotte, 1983-86, Am. Inst. Planners, Washington, 1977-78; team chmn. Mecklenburg County chpt. Ams. with Disabilities, 1992—; mem. Mecklenburg County Employee Suggestion Program, 1990—, Charlotte Chamber Cmty. Leadership Sch., 1992; v.p., bd. dirs. Mecklenburg Ministries, 1990—; bd. dirs. African-Am. Coalition on Edn., 1991—, Charlotte-Mecklenburg Schs. Com. Twenty-Five, 1992—; mentor Project Motivation and Inspiration, 1990—; bd. dirs. HopeSpring, 1991—; 2d v.p. Nat. Forum Black Pub. Adminstrs., 1992-93, 1st v.p., 1994-96, pres. 1996—; active Coalition for Improvement of African Am. Student Enviornment, 1991—, USS Charlotte Commissioning Com., 1991—, Task Force on Needs of Internationals, 1992—, Mayor's Internat. Cabinet, 1992—; mem. nominating com. Hornets' Nest coun. Girl Scouts U.S., 1992—; bd. dirs. The Bros. Found., chmn. search com., 1992—. Named to Outstanding Young Men of Am., 1979, 87, Dr. Martin L. King Jr. Keepers of the Dream Honor Roll, 1991; recipient cert. of appreciation Women's Commn., 1990. Mem. NAACP, N.C. Job Tng. Adminstrs. Assn. (v.p. 1985-86, pres. 1986-87, Leadership award 1987), Am. Soc. Pub. Administrs., N.C. Employment and Tng. Assn., Southeastern Employment and Tng. Assn., The Partnership for Tng. and Employment Careers (charter mem.), Nat. Assn. Counties Employment and Tng. Profls. (bd. dirs. 1988-89), N.C. Inst. Govt. Mcpl. Adminstrs. Cert., Am. Planning Assn. (charter mem.), Nat. Gov.'s Assn. (trainer 1984), N.C. Job Tng. Adminstrs. Assn. (charter, pres. 1987), Charlotte-Mecklenburg Black Polit. Caucus, Internat. City Mgmt. Assn. (trainee 1979-80), Nat. Urban League, Alpha Phi Alpha (life, pres. N.C. chpt. 1984-86, Alumni Brother of Yr. 1987-89, Man of Merit 1989, state parliamentarian 1985—), others. Democrat. Baptist. Home: 9733 Harris Glen Dr Charlotte NC 28269-0328 Office: Office of Minority Affairs 600 E 4th St Charlotte NC 28202-2870

MILLER, ANNETTE YAFFEY, elementary school educator; b. Norfolk, Va., Nov. 30, 1930; d. Benjamin Edward and Gladys Elizabeth (Hansen) Yaffey; m. William A. Miller, Nov. 18, 1950 (dec. 1987); children: William A. Jr., Sharon, Kimberly. AA with honors, Coll. William and Mary, 1951; BS summa cum laude, Fla. Atlantic U., 1966, MEd, 1975. Asst. buyer Paul H. Rose Dept. Store, Norfolk, 1940-51; tchr. asst. Holy Spirit Episc. Day Sch., West Palm Beach, Fla., 1952-59; tchr. Palm Beach County Sch. System, 1963-94, ret., 1994. Treas. Juno Beach Civic Assn.; active Marinelife Ctr., Juno Beach, Fla. Recipient Disting. Alumni award Fla. Atlantic U., 1992, William T. Dwyer award for excellence in teaching Econ. Coun. Palm Beach County, 1991, I Make a Difference Tchr. award Palm Beach Post and WPEC-TV, 1991; scholar Va. Chem. Co., 1949. Mem. Classroom Tchrs. Assn. (chair retirement com. 1988-91), Fla. Tchrs. Assn., NEA, Nature Conservancy, Audubon Soc., Internat. Platform Assn., Phi Delta Kappa. Democrat. Home: 204 Sea Oats Dr Apt A Juno Beach FL 33408-1417

MILLER, APRIL D., special education educator; b. McKeesport, Pa., Apr. 11, 1961; d. Albert L. and Mary M. Roney; m. Craig A. Miller, Aug. 11, 1984. BS, Ohio State U., 1983, MA, 1988, PhD, 1992. Cert. tchr. K-12 reading, K-12 spl. edn., supervision, Ohio. Mem. adj. faculty Ashland U., Columbus, Ohio, 1989-92, Wright State U., Dayton, Ohio, 1991-92, Ohio Dominican Coll., Columbus, 1991-92; asst. prof. U. So. Miss., Hattiesburg, 1992-96; assoc. prof., chair dept. spl. edn. U. So. Miss., 1996—; presenter convs. various nat. profl. orgns.; ednl. cons. local edn. agys., 1992-96. Contbr. articles to profl. jours. Faculty senator U. So. Miss., 1995-96; mem. coun. U. So. Miss. Tchr. Edn. Coun., 1994—; vol. Assn. for Retarded Citizens, Very Spl. Arts Festival, Spl. Olympics, 1992—. Mem. Coun. for Exceptional Children (nominee Susan Phillips Gorin award 1996, faculty advisor 1992—), Assn. for Behavioral Analysis (Outstanding Svcs. award 1994, com. chair profl. devel. 1995—, coord. internat. sci. and engring. fair initiative 1993—), Phi Delta Kappa (conf. planner U. So. Miss. 1996, v.p. programs chpt. 75 1994-95, pres. 1995-96). Home: 115 N 23d Ave Hattiesburg MS 39401 Office: U So Miss PO Box 5115 Hattiesburg MS 39406

MILLER, BARRY M., human services administrator; b. Balt., Sept. 14, 1952; s. Charles M. and Sonia F. (Weiner) M.; BA in Sociology, U. Md., 1975; MS in Child Devel., W.Va. U., 1978; m. Lynn D. Sears, Aug. 23, 1975. With Am. Rsch. Bur., Beltsville, Md., 1973-77; dir. child devel. Scotts Run Settlement House, Osage, W.Va., 1978-84; dir. children's svcs. Child Care Connection, Ft. Lauderdale, 1985—; cons. in field. Mem. Fla. Forum (chmn. family day care div.), Nat. Assn. Edn. of Young Children, Nat. Assn. Family Child Care Credential (validator), Child and Adult Care Sponsors Assn. (state rep.), So. Assn. Children Under Six, Broward Assn. for Edn. Young Children, Broward County Family Day Care Assn. (founder), Phi Upsilon Omicron. Democrat. Jewish. Home: 11180 Royal Palm Blvd Pompano Beach FL 33065-6828 Office: Child Care Connection 840 SW 81st Ave North Lauderdale FL 33068-2001

MILLER, BONNIE SEWELL, marketing professional; b. Junction City, Ky., July 24, 1932; d. William Andrew and Lillian Irene (McCowan) Sewell; m. William Gustave Tournade Jr., Nov. 5, 1950 (div. 1974); children: Bonnie Sue Tournade Zaner, William Gustave III, Sharon Irene Tournade Leach; m. Bruce George Miller, Nov. 15, 1981. BA, U. South Fla., 1968, MA, 1973. Cert. tchr., Fla. Chair dept. English Tampa (Fla.) Cath. High Sch., 1972-78; tchr. Clearwater (Fla.) High Sch., 1978-80; mgr. prodn. svcs. Paradyne Corp., Largo, Fla., 1980-83; freelance writer, cons. Tampa, 1983-84; mgr. product documentation PPS, Inc., Largo, 1984-86; mgr. mktg. communications PPS, Inc., 1986-87; writer Nixdorf Computer Corp., Tampa, 1988-89; mktg. dir. Suncoast Schs. Fed. Credit Union, Tampa, 1989—; instr. English, Hillsborough C.C., Tampa, 1975-87; adj. instr. profl. writing U. South Fla., 1993; cons. bus. writing Coronet Instrnl. Media Writing Project, Tampa, 1976, Nat. Mgmt. Assn., Tampa, 1981-87. Contbr. tech. articles to various publs. Bd. dirs. SERVE, Tampa, Credit Union Mktg. Assn. Coun., Sing Parent Displaced Homemakers Group; legis. chair Tampa PTA, 1965; judge speech contest Am. Legion, Tampa, 1976; vol. North Tampa Vol. Libr., 1988. NEH fellow, 1975. Mem. NAFE, Internat. Assn. Bus. Communicators, Soc. Tech. Communicators, Am. Assn. Bus. Women, Internat. Platform Assn., Toastmasters Internat., Kappa Delta Pi,Credit Union Natl. Assn. Democrat. Baptist. Home: 4014 Hudson Ter Tampa FL 33624-5349 Office: Suncoast Schs Fed Credit Union 6801 E Hillsborough Ave Tampa FL 33610-4110

MILLER, BRIAN KENT, auditor; b. Gulfport, Miss., June 16, 1954; s. Carl Maynard and Elsie Darleen (Nēufeld) M.; m. Cynthia Gayle Fore, Nov. 5, 1977. BSBA, U. So. Miss., 1975. CPA, Miss. Acct. Moore & Powell, CPA, Biloxi, Miss., 1975-81; auditor spl. contracts Gulf Oil Corp., Houston, 1981-85; auditor, fin. Chevron Corp., Concord, Calif., 1985-87; auditor ops. Chevron Corp., New Orleans, 1987—. Mem. AICPA, Inst. Mgmt. Accts., Inst. Internal Auditors, Miss. Soc. CPA. Mennonite. Office: Chevron USA Inc 935 Gravier St New Orleans LA 70112

MILLER, BRYANE KATHERINE, artist, writer; b. Front Royal, Va., Dec. 26, 1949; d. Carl Bryan and Gertrude (Erbe) M. AA, Marymount U., 1970; BA, Lynchburg Coll., 1972. Dir. arts City of Lynchburg (Va.), 1972-73; adminstrv. asst. to dir. Va. State Water Control Bd., Richmond, 1973-76; tchr. art St. Mary's Sch., Richmond, 1974-76; mgr., buyers asst. Hecht's (formerly Miller and Rhoad's Corp.), 1976-77, divsn. store mgr., 1976-79; mgr. Dunhill Temps., Inc., Richmond, 1979-84; freelance artist, 1984—; publicity cons. Trinity Hist. House Tour, Little Washington, Va., 1992%; mem. Christmas Decorating com. Belle Grove Plantation, Middletowqn, Va., 1992; lectr. in field, pub. speaker. Author: Dignified Departure, 1993; exhibited in group show Shenandoah Valley Va., Richmond. Bd. dirs. Richmond Urban League, 1980-84, Lynchburg Pub. Works, 1973; bd. dirs. Am. Heart Assn., Gochland County, Va., 1990-91, cmty. chmn. Manakin Sabot, Va., 1987-90; vol. radio broadcaster weekly program for blind The Va. Voice, 1980-87; history chmn. Rep. Women's Club, Gochland County, 1989-90, 3d v.p., 1987-89; arts coun. del. Cath. Parochial Schs., Richmond, 1974-77; v.p. Blue Ridge Arts Coun., 1994—, bd. dirs., 1993—. Mem. Shenandoah Valley Artists Assn., Shenandoah Valley Writer's Guild, Front Royal C. of C., Bus. and Profl. Women, Women of Washington (charter), Older Women's League (del. to White House), Garden Club Warren County (corr. sec., flower chmn. Hist. Garden Week in Va.), Thomas Jefferson Garden Club (bd. dirs. 1989-91), Ibebana (1st v.p. 1990-91, 2d v.p. 1989-90, bd. dirs. 1989-91, planning bd. 1987-90). Home and Office: PO Box 1171 Front Royal VA 22630-1171

MILLER, CARL CHET, business educator; b. Richmond, Va., June 23, 1961; s. Carl Chester and Nancy Ellis (Peters) M.; m. Laura Bridget Cardinal, Dec. 28, 1982. BA summa cum laude, U. Tex., 1982, PhD, 1990. Shift mgr. Frontier Enterprises, Austin, Tex., 1983; instr. Ind. U., Bloomington, 1983-84; tchg. asst. U. Tex., Austin, 1984-85, instr., 1985, rsch. assoc., 1985-89; asst. prof. bus. Baylor U., Waco, Tex., 1989-95, assoc. prof. bus., 1995—; mem. faculty senate, 1996-99; reviewer Acad. of Mgmt. Jour., Briarcliff Manor, N.Y., 1991—, Mgmt. Sci., Providence, 1987, 88, 93—, Orgn. Sci., Providence, 1990, 94, 95. Contbr. articles to profl. jours., chpts. to books; author numerous conf. papers; liaison Tex. Conf. on Orgns., Austin, 1989—. Bd. dirs. Windridge Home Owners Assn., Dallas, 1993—; pres. Assn. Mgmt., Austin, 1985-87; bd. advs. Cin. Glory Drum and Bugle Corps, 1995—. Grantee Hankamer Sch. Bus., 1990, 91, 92, 94, 95, 96, Grad. Sch. Bus., U. Tex. Bonham Meml. Rsch. Fund, 1985, 89. Mem. Acad. Mgmt. (divsnl. regional liaison 1994-96, reviewer ann. meeting 1987, 88, 93—), Inst. Mgmt. Scis., Phi Beta Kappa (chpt. scholarship chair 1992-94), Phi Kappa Phi. Office: Baylor U Hankamer Sch Bus PO Box 98006 Waco TX 76798

MILLER, CAROL LYNN, librarian; b. Kingsville, Tex., Mar. 31, 1961; d. Walter Edward Jr. and Emma Lee (Nelson) M. BS in Early Childhood Edn., So. Nazerene U., 1985; M in Early Childhood Edn., Ala. A & M U., 1987; MLS, U. Ala., 1993. Office worker Salvation Army, Huntsville, 1979-83; libr. Madison (Ala.) Branch Library, 1985; sub. tchr. Huntsville (Ala) City and Madison County Sch. System, 1986-87; br. head Madison Br. Libr., 1987-92, Madison Square Mall Br. Libr., Huntsville, 1992—. Mem. Asbury Meth. Ch., Upbeat Vol. Program. Mem. ALA. Office: Huntsville Madison City Library Madison Square M 5901 University Dr NW Huntsville AL 35806

MILLER, CHARLES EDMOND, library administrator; b. Bridgeport, Conn., Aug. 3, 1938; s. Edmond and Irene Ovelia (Boudreaux) M.; m. Alice Ann Phillips, June 2, 1962; children—Alison, Charles Edmond, Catherine, Susan. Student, U. Hawaii, 1957-58; B.A., McNeese State U., 1964; M.S. in L.S, La. State U., 1966. Tchr. Lake Charles (La.) High Sch., 1964-65; mem. staff La. State U. Library, Baton Rouge, 1966-69; asso. dir. Tulane U. Library New Orleans, 1969-73; dir. Fla. State U. Library, Tallahassee, 1973—; vis. coms. So. Assn. Colls. and Schs.; bd. dirs. SOLINET, 1979-81, 85-86, corp. v.p., vice chmn., 1980-81; cons. in field; adv. com. State Libr. Fla.; bd. dirs. Ctr. for Rsch. Librs., 1976-77, 91-97, sec., 1993-96; mem. policy bd. Fla. Libr. Network; pres. Assn. Southeastern Rsch. Librs., 1982-84; mem. rsch. libr. adv. com. Online Computer Libr. Ctr., Inc., Dublin, Ohio, 1993—. Asst. editor: La. Library Assn. Bull, 1967; contbr. articles to library sci. jours.; book revs. to Southeastern Librarian. Served with USMCR, 1956-59. Mem. ALA, Fla. Libr. Assn. (dir. 1979-81), Southeastern Libr. Assn., Assn. Coll. and Rsch. Librs., Assn. Rsch. Librs. (bd. dirs. 1985-90, v.p., pres.-elect 1987-88, pres. 1988-89), Fla. Ctr. Libr. Automation (chmn. bd. dirs. 1985-96), Rsch. Librs. Group (exec. com. 1988-90, bd. dirs. 1991-94), Phi Kappa Phi, Beta Phi Mu, Sigma Tau Delta.

MILLER, CHARLES GREGORY, biomedical researcher; b. Raleigh, N.C., May 14, 1960; s. Thurman Greene and Sally Lou (Everhart) M.; m. Kimberly Michelle Trivette, Aug. 14, 1982; 1 child, Charles Parker Trivette Miller. BS in Marine Biology, U. N.C. at Wilmington, 1983, MS in Biology, 1993. Rsch. asst. Inst. for Marine Biomedical Rsch., Wilmington, 1979-83; rsch. technician Ctr. for Marine Sci. Rsch., Wilmington, 1983-90; rsch. assoc. Duke U., Durham, N.C., 1990; rsch. scientist Burroughs Wellcome Co., Research Triangle Park, N.C., 1990-95, Glaxo Wellcome Inc., Research Triangle Park, 1995—. Author several publs., 1984-96. Counselor Boy Scouts Am., Hampstead, N.C., 1988-90; adminstrv. bd. mem. St. Andrews United Meth. Ch., Garner, N.C. Mem. Outstanding Young Men of Am., Sigma Xi. Democrat. Methodist. Home: 5021 Theys Rd Raleigh NC 27606-8916 Office: Glaxo Wellcome Inc 5 Moore Dr Research Triangle Park NC 27709

MILLER, CHARLES MURPHY, city official; b. Pineville, La., Nov. 24, 1939; s. Julius Murell and Amy (Amoynd) M.; m. Joji David, Nov. 12, 1956; children: Christopher, Joyce, Abigail, Allyson, Anatte. Engring. Technician, La. State U., 1980. Commd. USMC, 1956, advanced through grades to master sgt., 1975, ret., 1977; engring. technician Daigre Engring., Alexandria, La., 1979-82, Willis Engring., Alexandria, 1982-84; water prodn. and distbn. supt. City of Alexandria, 1984—. Author: Consolidated Complex Alexandria, 1995; co-author: Water at Your Service, 1995. Recipient Environ. Excellence award EPA, 1991, 94. Mem. Am. Water Wks. Assn. (S.W. sect. program chmn. 1992-93), Ctrl. Region Water Assn. (chmn. 1985-92, sec. 1984-85), La. Conf. Water (time and place chmn. 1989-93). Home: 300 Pleasant Dr Alexandria LA 71303 Office: City of Alexandria 2021 Industrial Rd Alexandria LA 71302

MILLER, CHARLES RICKIE, thermal/fluid systems analyst, engineering manager; b. New Albany, Ind., Oct. 4, 1946; s. Marshall Christian and Thelma Virginia (Martin) M.; m. Janel Howell, Nov. 24, 1968; children: Kimberly, Brian, Audrey, Rachel. BA in Physics, DePauw U., 1969; postgrad., Rice U., 1969-70, U. Houston, 1972-76. Tech. editor ITT/Fed. Electric Corp., Houston, 1970-71, LTV/Svc. Tech. Corp., Houston, 1971; sys. safety engr. Boeing Aerospace Corp., Houston, 1971-76; thermal analyst space sys. divsn. Rockwell Internat. Corp., Houston, 1976-89; mgr. thermal and fluid sys. for space shuttle payloads Space Shuttle Program-Office NASA/L.B. Johnson Space Ctr., Houston, 1989—; mem. edtl. team Apollo 14, 15 preliminary sci. reports, 1971-72; mem. sys. integration negotiating team for Space Shuttle to Mir Space Sta. rendezvous and docking missions, 1993—, chmn. negotiating team for Space Shuttle to Mir Space Sta. water preparation and transfer, 1994—, space shuttle program co-chmn. for shuttle/internat. space sta. program joint tech. working groups for thermal control, environ. control and life support sys., 1996—. Bd. dirs. Space City Aquatic Team, Houston, 1990-91. Rector scholar DePauw U., 1964-68; Rice fellow Rice U., 1969-70. Mem. AIAA, ASME, Nat. Space Soc., Air Force Assn., Am. Inst. Physics, Sigma Pi Sigma. Home: 806 Walbrook Dr Houston TX 77062 Office: Nat Aeronautic & Space Admn L B Johnson Space Ctr Houston TX 77058

MILLER, CHRISTINE MARIE, marketing executive; b. Williamsport, Pa., Dec. 7, 1950; d. Frederick James and Mary (Wurster) M.; m. Robert M. Ancell, Mar. 30, 1985. BA, U. Kans., 1972; MA, Northwewstern U., 1978, PhD, 1982. Pub. rels. asst. Bedford County Commr., Bedford, Pa., 1972-73; teaching asst. Northwestern U., Evanston, Ill., 1977-80; asst. prof. U. Ala., Tuscaloosa, 1980-82, Loyola U., New Orleans, 1982-85; vis. prof. Ind. U. Sch. Journalism, Bloomington, 1985-86; mktg. dir. Nat. Inst. Fitness & Sport, Indpls., 1986-88; program dir. Nat. Entrepreneurship Acad., Bloomington, 1986-88; mgmt. assoc. community and media rels. Subaru-Isuzu Automotive, Inc., Lafayette, Ind., 1988-91; dir. pub. rels. Giddings & Lewis, Fond Du Lac, Wis., 1991-93; v.p. comm. and enrollment mgmt. Milton Hershey (Pa.) Sch., 1993-94, dir. adminstrn., 1994-95; mktg. comms. mgr. MCI Govt. Markets, McLean, Va., 1995—. Co-author: The Biographical Dictionary of World War II General and Flag Officers, 1996; contbr. articles to profl. jours. Bd. dirs. Indpls. Entrepreneurship Acad., 1988-91, Area IV Agy., Greater Lafayette Mus. Art, 1989-91. With USN, 1973-77, comdr. USNR, 1977—. Mem. Pub. Rels. Soc. Am., Naval Order of the U.S. (nat. pub. affairs com.), Naval Res. Assn. (v.p. pub. affairs), Res. Officers Assn. Presbyterian. Home: 7406 Salford Ct Alexandria VA 22315 Office: MCI Govt Markets 6th Fl 8200 Greensboro Ave Mc Lean VA 22102

MILLER, CLEVE ARTHUR, auctioneer; b. Hutchinson, Kans., Nov. 7, 1940; s. Lawrence Noble and Ruby Lee (Cramer) M. ; m. Norma Charlene Miller. May 30, 1959 (div. June 1, 1960); 1 child, Charles Alhom; m. Alison Renee Miller, Mar. 17, 1986; stepchildren: Roy Kelly Whitfill, Gina Renee Whitfill. Diploma, Mo. Auction Sch. Owner, auctioneer H-M Auction Co., Wichita, Kans., 1983-85, Auction Am., Liberal, Kans., 1985-87; owner Sparkling Crystal of Ark., Bauxite, Ark., 1987-94, Keep-Cool, Bauxite, 1994—; owner, tchr. Midwest Auction Sch., Wichita, Kans., 1984-87. Author: (poetry book) Oh America, 1994 (Golden Poet 1989). Mem. Internat. Order Odd Fellows (Guardin Wichita 1983). Office: Keep Cool PO Box 189 Bauxite AR 72011

MILLER, CLINT, technology company executive. Pres. Maxim Tech., Inc., Dallas. Office: Maxim Tech Inc 2342 Fabens Dallas TX 75229

MILLER, DAN, congressman; b. Mich., 1943; m. Glenda Darsey; children: Daniel, Kathryn. Grad., U. Fla., 1964; MBA, Emory U.; PhD, La. State U. Ptnr. Miller Enterprises, Bradenton, Fla.; restaurant owner Memorial Pier, Fla., 1977—; instr. Ga. State U., U. South Fla., Sarasota; mem. 103d-104th Congresses from 13th Fla. Dist., 1993—; mem. appropriations com., mem. budget com. Active Rep. Leader's Task Force on Health. Mem. Manatee

C. of C. Episcopalian. Office: US Ho of Reps 117 Cannon HOB Washington DC 20515-0913*

MILLER, DANNY LESTER, English language educator; b. Vallscreek, W.Va., July 9, 1949; s. Howard Lester and Mary Leona (Jones) M. BA, Berea Coll., 1971; MA, Ea. Ky. U., 1975; PhD, U. Cin., 1985. From asst. prof. to assoc. prof. English Northern Ky.U., Highland Heights, 1986—. Editor: Friend of Animals, 1995; editor Jour. Ky. Studies, 1989—i. Bd. dirs. Appalachian Cmty. Devel. Assn., Cin., 1985—, Jesse Stuart Found., Ashland, Ky., 1993—, Brighton Ctr., Newport, Ky., 1985-92. Mem. MLA, Ky. Philol. Assn., Appalachian Studies Assn. (sec.). Home: 21 W Charlton St Cincinnati OH 45219

MILLER, DARWIN LEON, healthcare administrator; b. Post, Tex., Oct. 1, 1933; s. Thomas Jefferson and Orbie Penelope (Landmon) M.; m. JoAnn Moreman, Nov. 2, 1956; children: J. Scott, G. Tim, L. David. Student, Tex. Tech. U., 1951-53, 55-56, Grand Canyon Coll., 1971-72, U. Ala., 1972-74; cert. health adminstr., Trinity U. Grad. Sch., 1976. Performance supr. U.S. Dept. Agriculture, Post, 1956-60; dist. scout exec. Boy Scouts Am., Midland/Lubbock, Tex., 1960-68; adminstrv. asst., chief of staff U.S. VA, Phoenix, Birmingham,, Dallas, 1968-89; clin. adminstr. U.S. Dept. Vet. Affairs, Ft. Worth, 1989—. Active Ft. Worth Med. Dist., 1990-95; bd. dirs. Dallas-Ft. Worth Fed. Exec. Bd., 1991-95, chmn. vet. affairs com., 1992-93; bd. dirs. Southside Med. Dist., Ft. Worth, 1993, 95. Recipient Outstanding Svc. award State of Tex., 1992. Mem. Rotary. Home: 1109 Briarcliff Dr Arlington TX 76012-5320

MILLER, DONALD LANE, publishing executive; b. Pitts., May 14, 1918; s. Donald Edwin and Arvilla (Lane) M.; A.B., Kenyon Coll., 1940; Russian interpreter cert. U. Colo., 1946; postgrad. U. Pitts., 1947-48; m. Norma Reno, Feb. 2, 1951. Reporter, Pitts. Sun-Telegraph, 1940-42, Washington Post, 1946; with pub. rels. dept. Westinghouse Electric Corp., Pitts., 1947-51; reporter Billboard and Tide, 1953; pub. rels. dir. Nat. Agrl. Chem. Assn., Washington, 1954-58; sec. Donald Larch & Co., Washington, 1958-61; pres. Asso. Pub. Rels. Counselors, Washington, 1961-77; chmn. bd. Braddock Comm., Inc., Washington; chmn. bd. Children's Aid Internat.; exec. dir. All Am. Conf., Washington, 1962-75. Editor, GOP Nationalities News, Rep. Nat. Com., 1960; pub. rels. nationalities div. Rep. Nat. Com., 1964; coord. life underwriters sect. Citizens for Nixon-Agnew, 1968. Served from ensign to lt., USNR, 1942-46; from lt. to lt. comdr., 1951-53. Decorated Knight of Europe. Mem. English Speaking Union, SAR, Phi Beta Kappa, Delta Tau Delta. Clubs: Nat. Press. Author: Strategy for Conquest, 1966, George to George: 200 Years of Presidential Quotations, 1989, Call of the Northern Neck, 1992. Home: Fleets Bay Rd PO Box 1978 Kilmarnock VA 22482-1978 Office: 11501 Sunset Hills Rd Ste 200 Reston VA 22090-4704

MILLER, DORIS ANNE, English language educator; b. El Paso, Sept. 15, 1949; d. Fredric and Victoria (Cotton) M. BS in Edn., U. Tex., 1969; MA in Psychology, U. No. Colo., 1978; MA in English, Colo. State U., 1979; PhD in English, U. Tex. at Austin, 1984. Sci. tchr. Ysleta Ind. Sch. Dist., El Paso, 1969-70; commd. 2d lt. USAF, 1970, advanced through grades to maj., space systems ops. officer, 1970-78; English instr., prof. USAF Acad., Colo., 1978-90; ret. USAF Acad., 1990; writing cons. Nat. Edn. Found., Inc., Colorado Springs, 1991-92; English lectr. U. So. Colo., Pueblo, 1992-93; English prof. McMurry U., Abilene, Tex., 1993—; adj. English instr. Pikes Peak C.C., Colorado Springs, 1991-92. Chair worship com. St. Paul United Meth. Ch., Abilene, 1995. Mem. West Tex. Hist. Assn., Nat. Coun. of Tchrs. of English, Phi Kappa Phi. Office: Dept of English McM Sta Box 608 Abilene TX 79697

MILLER, E. HITE, banker, holding company executive. Pres. First Citizens Bancorp of S.C., Columbia, First Citizens Bank TR of S.C., Columbia; chmn., CEO First Citizens Bank of S.C. (now First Citizens Bancorporation), Columbia. Office: First Citizens Bank & Trust of SC 1230 Main St Columbia SC 29201-3213*

MILLER, EDGAR HUDSON, JR., newspaper editor, journalism educator; b. Jellico, Tenn., Oct. 17, 1934; s. Edgar Hudson Sr. and Mabel (Baird) M.; m. Ghislaine Myriam da Costa Ribeiro, Oct. 24, 1958; children: John M., Thomas, Jacqueline Miller Laurito, Richard, Edgar B. BS, U. Tenn., Knoxville, 1992, MS, 1994. Corr. AP, Sao Paulo and San Juan, 1970-75; bur. chief/fgn. AP, Rio de Janeiro, 1975-78; mng. editor Chattanooga Times, 1979-83; exec. editor Carroll Pub. Co., Washington, 1983-86; dep. fgn. editor UPI, Washington, 1986-87, asst. mng. editor/news, 1989-91; editor The Oak Ridger, Oak Ridge, Tenn., 1987-89; founding editor East Tenn. Cath., Knoxville, 1991—; pres. Fgn. Corrs. Club. Brazil, Rio de Janeiro, 1975-78. Translator: A Hidden Life, 1968, My Sweet Orange Tree, 1969. Pulitzer Prize juror, 1980-81; press sec. U.S. Senator Howard Baker, Washignton, 1967-68. With U.S. Army, 1956-59, Germany. Mem. Knoxville Choral Soc. (sec.), Crazy Quilt Friendship Ctr. (bd. dirs.). Roman Catholic. Home: 3636 Taliluna Ave # 504 Knoxville TN 37919 Office: Diocese of Knoxville 805 Northshore Dr Knoxville TN 37919

MILLER, EDWARD GODFREY, JR., biomedical sciences educator, researcher; b. Pitts., Feb. 16, 1941; s. Edward G. and Helen J. (Yuhas) M.; m. Brenda Dianne Halyard, Sept. 5, 1964; 1 child, Elizabeth Venia. BS in Chemistry, U. Tex., 1963, PhD in Biochemistry, 1969. Postdoctoral U. Wis., Madison, 1969-72; asst. prof. dept. biochemistry Baylor Coll. Dentistry, Dallas, 1972-75, assoc. prof. dept. biochemistry, 1975-88, prof., chair dept. biochemistry, 1988-92, prof. dept. biomed. scis., 1992—. Contbg. author: ADP-Ribosylation of Proteins, 1985, ADP-Ribose Transfer Reactions. Mechanisms and Biological Significance, 1989, 14th International Scientific Colloquium on Coffee, 1992, 15th International Scientific Colloquium on Coffee, 1993, Food Phytochemicals for Cancer Prevention I. Fruits and Vegetables, 1994. Precinct chair Dem. Party, Richardson, Tex., 1978-82. Mem. Am. Inst. Nutrition, Am. Soc. Cell Biology, Am. Chem. Soc., Am. Assn. Dental Rsch., Soc. Exptl. Biology and Medicine, Sigma Xi, Phi Beta Kappa, Phi Lambda Upsilon. Presbyterian. Home: 1820 Blake Dr Richardson TX 75081-2656 Office: Baylor Coll Dentistry 3302 Gaston Ave Dallas TX 75246-2013

MILLER, EDWARD MCCARTHY, economics educator; b. Richmond, Va., Sept. 2, 1944; s. Edward M. B.S. in Econs. and Mech. Engring., MIT, 1965, Ph.D. in Econs., 1970. Staff mem. White House, Washington, 1973-74, various govt. positions, 1974-79; staff v.p. Am. Productivity Ctr., Houston, 1979-80; Tsanoff prof. pub. affairs Rice U., Houston, 1981-84; prof. econs. and fin. U. New Orleans, 1984—, research prof., 1987—. Contbr. articles to profl. jours. Presbyterian. Home: 500 Lake Marina Dr Apt 421 New Orleans LA 70124-1609 Office: Dept Econs and Fin U New Orleans New Orleans LA 70148

MILLER, ERICA T(ILLINGHAST), aesthetician, skincare and cosmetics company executive, writer; b. Laramie, Wyo., Oct. 17, 1950; d. Walter McNab and Martha (Brown) M. Student Sophia U., Tokyo, 1969-72, U. Md., Tokyo, 1969-72, Simultaneous Interpreting Acad. Tokyo, 1974; cert. Christian Shaw Sch. Beauty, London, 1973, Kanebo Total Beauty Acad., 1974; internat. diploma CIDESCO, 1977. Instr., Nakano Am. English Ctr., Tokyo, 1969-72; instr., researcher Kanebo Cosmetics Inc., Tokyo, 1973-76, internat. cons., 1976—; dir. edn. Aestheticians Internat., Dallas, 1976-79; pres. Correlations Inc., Dallas, 1979—; dir. skin care sect. Esthetics Am., 1986-88; instr. Purdue U., 1989; cons. Nieman Marcus Greenhouse, Arlington, Tex., 1981—. Mem. adv. bd. San Jacinto Coll., Houston, 1989—, Skyline High Sch., Dallas, 1989—. Assoc. pub., editor Aesthetics World Mag., 1980-85; contbr. articles to various publs.; translator tech. film. Mem. Aestheticians Internat. (dir. edn. 1976-79), Am. Inst. Esthetics (lectr.), Am. Beauty Assn. (bd. dirs. esthetic mfg. and distbrs. alliance 1995-96, v.p. 1996—), Nat. Hairdressers and Cosmetology Assn. (dir. skin care sect. aesthetics com.), Dallas C. of C., North Dallas C. of C. Republican. Avocations: tennis, English riding, swimming, care and training of animals. Office: Correlations Inc 4803 W Lovers Ln Dallas TX 75209-3137

MILLER, FREDERICK ROBERT, sorghum breeder, agronomist; b. Brownwood, Tex., Sept. 3, 1937; s. Albert Frederick and Lois Elizabeth (Oliver) M.; m. Carol Jean Sparks, Aug. 24, 1958; children: Charles Frederick, Robert Lance. BS, A&M Coll. Tex., 1963; MSc, Tex. A&M U., 1965, PhD in Plant Breeding, 1974. Rsch. assoc. Tex. Agrl. Expt. Sta., College Station, 1963-65, 70-74; rsch. geneticist USDA/ARS, Mayaguez, P.R., 1965-70; asst. prof. dept. soil and crop sci. Tex. A&M U., College Station, 1974-78, assoc. prof., 1978-84, prof., 1984-94, prof. emeritus, 1994—; cons. sorghum breeding and prodn. to more than 23 nat. govts. including Argentina, Brazil, Honduras, Mex., Australia, China, India, Ethiopia, Tanzania, Mali and South Africa; lectr., seminar facilitator. Author 14 book chpts., more than 90 jour. articles. Recipient Disting. Faculty Rsch. award Tex. A&M U., 1988, NCCPB Genetics and Plant Breeding award Am. Seed Trade, 1991, Sci. award Nat. Agri-Mktg. Assn., 1994. Fellow Am. Soc. Agronomy, Crop Sci. Soc. Am. Methodist. Home: 6417 Zak Rd Bryan TX 77808

MILLER, GARY DONALD, physician; b. Johnstown, N.Y., July 2, 1939; s. Theron Arthur and Vivian (Swift) M.; m. Katherine Ann Walker, May 30, 1965; children: Taunja Lea, Christopher Todd. BA, U. Rochester, N.Y., 1961; MD, Union U., Albany, N.Y., 1965. Diplomat Am. Bd. Family Practice. Intern gen. medicine D.C. Gen. Hosp., Washington, 1965-66, resident in medicine, 1966-67; staff mem. pediatrics Albany Med. Ctr. Hosp., N.Y., 1967-68, staff mem. surgery, obstetrics, gynecology, othopedics, 1968-69; chief of medicine USAF, Fla., 1969-72, Turkey, 1969-72; pvt. practice Family Med. Ctr., Orlando, Fla., 1972-87, Orlando, Fla., 1987—; active staff Orlando Regional Med. Ctr., 1972—; solo family practice, 1987—; team physician Lake Highland Preparatory Sch.; preceptor P.A. program Shands Hosp., Gainesville, Fla.; preceptor for med. students, Syracuse, N.Y.; active staff, past chmn. family practice Orlando Regional Med. Ctr.; past chmn. family practice, bd. trustees, vice chief of staff Lucerne Med. Ctr.; active Fla. Hosp., Humana Care Plus Physician Adv. Bd. and Utilization Rev. Bd., Metlife Physician Adv. Bd. Coach Downtown Orlando Soccer Club; referee Ctrl. Fla. Youth Soccer League. Maj. M.C., USAF, 1969-72. Fellow Am. Acad. Family Medicine; mem. AMA, Fla. Med. Assn., Orange County Med. Soc. (past treas., sec.), Am. Coll. Sports Medicine. Office: 101 E Miller St Orlando FL 32806-2123

MILLER, GENE EDWARD, newspaper reporter and editor; b. Evansville, Ind., Sept. 16, 1928; m. Electra Sonia Yphantis, Apr. 13, 1952 (dec. May 1993); children: Janet Irene, Theresa Jean, Thomas Raphael, Roberta Lynn. A.B. in Journalism, Ind. U., 1950, LL.D. (hon.), 1977; Nieman fellow, Harvard U., 1967-68. Reporter Jour.-Gazette, Ft. Wayne, Ind., 1950-51, Washington Bur. Wall St. Jour., 1953-54, Richmond (Va.) News Leader, 1954-57, Miami (Fla.) Herald, 1957—. Author: Invitation To A Lynching, 83 Hours Till Dawn. Served with AUS, 1951-53. Recipient Pulitzer prize for local reporting, 1967, 76. Office: 1 Herald Plz Miami FL 33132-1609

MILLER, GEORGE HENRY, journalist; b. Manville near Madison, Ind., Jan. 5, 1915; s. Silas Jacob and Georgia Renetta (Haumesser) M.; m. June Nelore Reynolds, Jan. 24, 1940; 1 child, Jacob Lee. B in Journalism, U. Mo., 1940; M in Journalism, U. Ill., 1948; postgrad., U. Fla., 1957-62. Sports editor The Mexico (Mo.) Ledger, 1940-41; feature writer The Evansville (Ind.) Courier-Press, 1941-42; proof dir. Army's Jefferson Proving Ground, Madison, Ind., 1942-44; copy editor The Louisville Courier Jour., 1946; sports editor The Peru (Ind.) Tribune, 1947; tchg. asst. U. Ill., Urbana, 1947-48; asst. prof. journalism Butler U., Indpls., 1948-51; editor Louisville Mag., Louisville C. of C., 1951-53; pub. rels. dir. Tampa (Fla.) C. of C., 1953-56; pub. rels. worker various orgns., Madison, 1956-57; asst. prof. journalism U. Fla., Gainesville, 1957-60; asst. prof. journalism U. South Fla., Tampa, 1960-62, dir. coop. edn., 1961-72, dir. S.E. Ctr. for Coop. Edn., 1972-80; columnist Madison Courier and The Weekly Herald, 1964-95. Contbr. chpts. to books. Lt. comdr. USN, 1944-46, USNR, 1946-72. Mem. Ret. Officers Assn. (life), Soc. for Profl. Journalists (50 Yr. award 1989), Can. Coop. Edn. Assn. (hon. life), U.S. Coop. Edn. Assn. (hon. life). Democrat. Congregationalist. Home: Apt I-114 4000 E Fletcher Ave Tampa FL 33613-4819

MILLER, GEORGE WILLIAM, III, career officer, financial banking executive; b. Phila., Sept. 17, 1930; s. George William Jr. and Dorothy (Hartwig) M.; divorced. BA, Harvard U., 1952, MBA, 1954. Commd. 2d lt. USAF, 1952, advanced through grades to maj. gen., 1979; assoc. Loeb Rhodes Investment Bankers, N.Y.C., 1959-63; v.p., gen. mgr. Citicorp, N.Y.C., 1963-75; v.p. Provident Nat. Bank, Phila., 1975-83; pres. Provident Internat. Corp., Phila., 1975-83, John L. Loeb Jr. Assocs., Alexandria, Va., 1982-85; exec. v.p. Nazareth (Pa.) Nat. Bank, 1983-85; advisor Dept. Def., Washington, 1985—; pres. Armed Forces Benefit Assn. Bank, Alexandria, Va., 1991—, also bd. dirs.; bd. dirs. Metallic Ceramic Inc., Bridgeport, Pa., Robbins Gioia Inc., Armed Forces Benefit Svcs. Nat. Def. U. Found., Washington; lectr. USAF Acad., Colorado Springs, Colo., 1988—, Indsl. Coll. Armed Forces, Air Force Retirement Officers Cmty.; trustee Res. Officers Assn. Investment Trust. Decorated D.S.M. Mem. Am. Soc. Mil. Comptrollers, Nat. Contract Mgmt., Assn. Mil. Banks Am. (bd. dirs.). Episcopal. Home: PO Box 325 58 Hunters Ln Devon PA 19333-1252

MILLER, GERALD CECIL, immunologist, laboratory administrator, educator; b. Wichita, Kans., Dec. 20, 1944; s. Cecil William and Mildred Ester (Carlisle) M.; m. Josephine Buller, June 1, 1968; children: Nathan Gerald, Natalie Buller. BA, Emporia (Kans.) State U., 1967, MS, 1969; PhD, Kans. State U., 1972. Diplomate Am. Bd. Med. Lab. Immunology. Rsch. fellow Mayo Med. Sch. and Mayo Found., Rochester, Minn., 1972-75; sr. scientist Health Cen. Rsch. Found., Mpls., 1975-77; grad. teaching and rsch. asst. Emporia State U., 1967-69; grad. teaching and rsch. asst. Kans. State U., Manhattan, 1969-70, NIH predoctoral fellow, 1970-72; ast. prof. microbiology and immunology Oral Roberts U. Sch. Medicine, Tulsa, 1977-82; owner, dir. Immuno-Diagnostics Lab. Inc., Tulsa, 1982-94; adj. assoc. prof. Oral Roberts U. Sch. Medicine, Tulsa, 1986-90; mem. ancillary med. staff Children's Med. Ctr., Tulsa, 1979—; chief immunology, microbiology and flow cytometry Regional Med. Lab., Tulsa, 1994—; clin. lab. immunologist Pathology Lab. Assocs., Tulsa, 1994—; adj. asst. prof. U. Okla. Med. Coll., Tulsa, 1986—. Mem. editl. bd. Jour. Clin. Lab. Analysis; contbr. articles and abstracts to sci. jours. Trustee 1st United Meth. Ch., 1994—, mem. adminstrv. bd., 1978—; bd. dirs. Brush Creek Boys Ranch, 1996—; cert. ofcl. USA Track and Field, 1986—. Named Outstanding Faculty Mem., Oral Roberts U. Sch. Medicine, 1982. Mem. AAAS, Am. Soc. Microbiology, Assn. Med. Lab. Immunologists (treas.-elect), Clin. Immunology Soc., N.Y. Acad. Scis., Sigma Xi. Office: Regional Med Lab 1923 S Utica Ave Tulsa OK 74104-6520

MILLER, HELEN, history educator; b. Bronx, N.Y., Jan. 15, 1955; d. Jack and Frieda (Ringelheim) Greenberg; m. Mark Steven Miller, Sept. 17, 1978; children: Matthew, Adam. BA in History summa cum laude, Lehman Coll., 1976; AM in History, Harvard U., 1978. With Jewish Chautauqua Soc., N.Y.C., 1977-80, Conceptual Planning, Inc., N.Y.C., 1980-81; with dept. pers. mgmt. Dept. Employment City of N.Y., 1981-83; with dept. material scis. & engring. MIT, Cambridge, Mass., 1984-86; adj. instr. history Frederick (Md.) C.C., 1988-90; adj. instr. history arts & scis. divsn. Pellissippi State Tech. C.C., Knoxville, Tenn., 1992-95, instr. history dept. humanities, 1995—. Mem. bd. edn. Heska Amuna Cong., Knoxville, 1993-95. Mem. AAUP, AAUW, U.S. Holocaust Meml. Mus., Phi Beta Kappa. Office: Pellissippi State Tech CC 10915 Hardin Valley Rd Knoxville TN 37932-1412

MILLER, HERBERT DELL, petroleum engineer; b. Oklahoma City, Sept. 29, 1919; s. Merrill Dell and Susan (Green) M.; BS in Petroleum Engring., Okla. U., 1941; m. Rosalind Rebecca Moore, Nov. 23, 1947; children: Rebecca Miller Friedman, Robert Rexford. Field engr. Amerada Petroleum Corp., Houston, 1948-49, Hobbs, N.Mex., 1947-48, dist. engr., Longview, Tex., 1949-57, sr. engr., Tulsa, 1957-62; petroleum engr. Moore & Miller Oil Co., Oklahoma City, 1962-78; owner Herbert D. Miller Co., Oklahoma City, 1978—. Maj., F.A., AUS, 1941-47; ETO. Decorated Bronze Star with oak leaf cluster, Purple Heart (U.S.); Croix de Guerre (France). Registered profl. engr., Okla., Tex. Mem. AIME. Republican. Episcopalian (pres. Men's Club 1973). Clubs: Oklahoma City Golf, Country. Home and Office: 6708 NW Grand Blvd Oklahoma City OK 73116-6016

MILLER, J. DOUGLAS, business owner; b. Rome, N.Y., Apr. 19, 1943. BA in Chemistry, Dartmouth Coll., 1965; MEd, U. Buffalo, 1967. Sales mgr. NCR, Washington, 1969-73; v.p. sales Atlantic Tel., Rockville, Md., 1973-81; v.p. mid-Atlantic L.M. Ericsson, Balt., 1981-84; v.p. sales and mktg. TDX Systems, Vienna, Va., 1984-85; exec. v.p. Sonitrol, Alexandria, Va., 1985-87; pres., owner CDR of Washington, Vienna, 1987—. Office: CDR of Washington 2011 Madrillon Springs Ct Vienna VA 22182-3763

MILLER, JACK EVERETT, retired lawyer; b. Monroe, La., Dec. 10, 1921; s. Herman M. and Sybil (Harrison) M.; m. Vivian G., May 13, 1945; m. 2d, Kathryn G., Dec. 23, 1970; children—Jack Everett, John A. Attended Ga. Inst. Tech., Gilbert Johnson Law Sch. Bar: U.S. Ct. Claims, U.S. Tax Ct., U.S. Ct. Mil. Appeals, U.S. Supreme Ct. Assoc. Lewis & Sullivan, Savannah, Ga., 1948-52; ptnr. Glass & Miller, Savannah, 1954-57; ptnr. Duffy, Miller & Duffy, Savannah, 1957-69; sole practice, Savannah, 1969-89. Served with JAGC, USAF, 1952-54. Decorated Meritorious Service medal. Mem. Am. Bus. Clubs (pres. 1959, dist. gov. 1964), Nat. Bus. Clubs. Home: 2 S Stillwood Ct Savannah GA 31419-2737

MILLER, JAMES ALFRED LOCKE, JR., aircraft maintenance technician; b. Freeport, N.Y., June 6, 1943; s. James Alfred Locke and Leila James (Wootten) M. AA in Paralegal Tech., Ctrl. Carolina Tech. Inst., 1976; AA in Aviation Maintenance, Wayne C.C., 1981; BS in Aviation Mgmt., So. Ill. U., Carbondale, 1989. Lic. aircraft mech. FAA. Ramp serviceman Eastern Air Lines, Raleigh-Durham, N.C., 1965-71; U.S. Customs warehouse officer R.J. Reynolds Tobacco Co., Winston-Salem, N.C.; seaman/helmsman USNS Mizar T-Agor 11, 1972; mech. Naval Air Depot, Cherry Point, N.C., 1981-87, Piedmont Airlines, Winston-Salem, 1987; FAA/FCC tech. USAir, Winston-Salem, 1987—. Mem. Assn. Former Intelligence Officers, Profl. Aviation Maintenance Assn., Internat. Asn. Machinist and Aerospace Workers, Soc. Indsl. Archaeology, U.S. Horse Cavalry Assn., Lower Cape Fear Hist. Soc., Sons Am. Revolution. Republican. Episcopalian. Home: 2810-K Carriage Dr Winston Salem NC 27106 Office: USAir Smith Reynolds Airport 4001 N Liberty St Winston Salem NC 27105

MILLER, JAMES MONROE, lawyer; b. Owensboro, Ky., Apr. 20, 1948; s. James Rufus and Tommie (Melton) M.; m. Patricia Kirkpatrick, Nov. 28, 1975; children: Marian Elizabeth, James Graham. Student, George Washington U., 1966-67; BE, U. Ky., 1970, JD, 1973. Bar: Ky. 1973, U.S. Dist. Ct. Ky. 1973, U.S. Ct. Appeals (6th cir.) 1976, U.S. Supreme Ct. 1976. Law clk. to chief judge U.S. Dist. Ct. (we. dist.) Ky., Louisville and Owensboro, 1973-74; ptnr. Sullivan, Mountjoy, Stainback & Miller, P.S.C., Owensboro, 1974—. Mem. Leadership Ky., 1988, Leadership Owensboro, 1986; bd. dirs. Wendell Foster Ctr. Endowment Found., Inc., Owensboro; sec., trustee Owensboro-Daviess County Pub. Library, Owensboro; chmn. subcom. on sch. system merger Strategies for Tomorrow, Owensboro; v.p. legal Owensboro-Daviess County C. of C.; bd. dirs., sec. Owensboro-Daviess County Indsl. Found., Inc. Mem. ABA, Ky. Bar Assn. (chmn. Law Day/Spkrs. Bur. com. 1989-91), Daviess County Bar Assn., Ky. Coun. on Higher Edn. (chmn. programs com. 1991-93, chmn. 1993-96), Gov.'s Higher Edn. Rev. Commn. (chmn. 1993), Gov.'s Task Force on Tchr. Edn. Democrat. Methodist. Home: 1920 Sheridan Pl Owensboro KY 42301-4525 Office: Sullivan Mountjoy et al PO Box 727 100 Saint Ann St Owensboro KY 42303-4144

MILLER, JANE ANDREWS, accountant; b. Nashville, Aug. 14, 1952; d. Joseph Raymond Andrews and Allison (Bartlett) Fang; m. Thomas C. Heselton, June 22, 1970 (div. 1978); 1 child, Elizabeth Lyn; m. Keith Evan Miller, Apr. 14, 1984. Degree in Bus. Typing and Computers, Fairfax (Va.) Bus. Sch., 1974. Cert. notary public. Adminstrv. asst. T.J. Fannon & Sons, Alexandria, Va., 1973-79; distbn. clk., adminstrv. asst. U.S. Post Office, Merrifield, Va., 1980-83; acct., sec., treas. Aux. Electric Power Co., Fairfax, 1983—; pvt. practice, investment counselor, Fairfax; sec., treas. AEPCO, Inc., K & J, Inc., 1990—. Mem. Friends of Calypso; assoc. mem. Smithsonian Instn.; v.p. Grand Masters Bowling League, 1994-95; founder Millers Doubles League, 1995, sec., 1995-96, Millers Doubles, 1996-97. Mem. Grand Masters League (v.p.), Millers Doubles (sec. 1996-97). Republican.

MILLER, JANEL HOWELL, psychologist; b. Boone, N.C., May 18, 1947; d. John Estle and Grace Louise (Hemberger) Howell; BA, DePauw U., 1969; postgrad. Rice U., 1969; MA, U. Houston, 1972; PhD, Tex. A&M U., 1979; m. C. Rick Miller, Nov. 24, 1968; children: Kimberly, Brian, Audrey, Rachel. Asso. sch. psychologist Houston Ind. Sch. Dist., 1971-74; research psychologist VA Hosp., Houston, 1972; asso. sch. psychologist Clear Creek Ind. Sch. Dist., Tex., 1974-76; instr. psychology, counseling psychology intern Tex. A. and M. U., 1976-77; clin. psychology intern VA Hosp., Houston, 1977-78; coordinator psychol. services Clear Creek Ind. Sch. Dist., 1978-81, assoc. dir. psychol. services, 1981-82; pvt. practice, Houston, 1982—; faculty U. Houston-Clear Lake, 1984—; adolescent suicide cons., 1984—. DePauw U. Alumni scholar, 1965-69; NIMH fellow U. Houston, 1970-71; lic. clin. psychologist, sch. psychologist, Tex. Mem. APA, Tex. Psychol. Assn., Houston Psychol. Assn. (media rep. 1984-85), Am. Assn. Marriage and Family Therapists, Tex. Assn. Marriage and Family Therapists, Houston Assn. Marriage and Family Therapists, Soc. for Personality Assessment. Home: 806 Walbrook Dr Houston TX 77062-4030 Office: Southpoint Psychol Svcs 11550 Fuqua St Ste 450 Houston TX 77034-4537

MILLER, JANICE LYNNE, medical/surgical nurse; b. Lubbock, Tex., May 5, 1954; d. George T. and Anita J. (Marr) Storrs; m. Kenneth W. Miller, Jan. 7, 1972; children: Georginna, Sarah, Jennifer. BSN, Tex. Tech U., 1985. Cert. CNN Am. Nephrology Nurses, med./surg. ACLS instr. ANA. Staff nurse Univ. Med. Ctr., Lubbock, Tex., 1985, hemodialysis nurse, 1986, transplant team leader, 1987, charge nurse, 1987-89, nurse mgr., 1990-93, charge nurse med./surg. transplant unit, 1993-96, utilization rev. coord. RN, 1996—. Mem. Sigma Theta Tau.

MILLER, JEROME M., civic worker; b. New Brunswick, N.J., Mar. 16, 1917; s. Edward I. and Beatrice (Kalisch) M.; m. Dorothy Tishler, Apr. 29, 1921; children: David G., Eliot K. Student, Pa. State U., 1935-37, Rutgers U., 1935-39. With E.I. DuPolnt De Nemours & Co., N.J. Dept. Transp., N.Y. Shipbuilding; agt. Equitable Life Assurance Soc.; owner Sally's Steak House, Highland park, N.J., 1952-73; adv. bd. Pan-Am Bank, 1980-84, Broward Fed. Savs. and Loan, Lauderdale, Fla., 1984-89. Chmn. Planning and Zoning Bd., City of Lauderhill, Fla., 1987—; bd. dirs. Garden Lakes of Inverrary Condominium Assn., 1978-81, pres., 1980; bd. dirs. Ornada of South Fla.; pres. Inverrary Assn., 1980—; mem. Fla. State Dem. Exec. Com.; founder Highland Park (N.J.) Lions Club, pres., 1960, past zone chmn., dep. dist. gov.; active Down's Syndrome Program, N.J., 1968-71; mem. exec. bd. Inverrary Tournament, LPGA, Ed Kranpoll Am. Diabetes Assn. Golf Tournament; chmn. Urban Forestry Com., Lauderhill. Sgt. U.S. Army, 1942-46. Recipient Community Service award, Inverrary Assn., 1988, others. Mem. B'nai B'rith, Jewish War Vets. Democrat. Jewish. Home: The Hills of Inverrary 5625 Hammock Ln Lauderhill FL 33319-5112 Office: 3310 Inverrary Blvd Fort Lauderdale FL 33319-4520

MILLER, JERRY ELKIN, JR., minister; b. Batesville, Ark., Aug. 20, 1963; s. Jerry Earick and Elisabeth (Mayer) M.; m. Adrienne Lynn Hart, June 23, 1990. BA, Ouachita Bapt. U., 1985; MDiv, GOlden Gate Bspt. Theol. Sem., 1988. Ordained to ministry Bapt. Ch. English pastor East Bay Korean Bapt. Ch., Oakland, Calif., 1986-88; chaplain intern Bapt. Med. Ctr., Little Rock, Ark., 1988-89; min. of youth Ruddell Hill Bapt. Ch., Batesville, Ark., 1989-90; English pastor Korean 1st Bapt. Ch., Cary, N.C., 1990—; assoc. dir. Share His Light Ministries, 1993—. Home: 5900 Timber Creek Ln Apt 1001 Raleigh NC 27612-6209 Office: Korean 1st Bapt Ch 8905 Ray Rd Raleigh NC 27613

MILLER, JO CAROLYN DENDY, family and marriage counselor, educator; b. Gorman, Tex., Sept. 16, 1942; d. Leonard Lee and Vera Vertie (Robison) Dendy; m. Douglas Terry Barnes, June 1, 1963 (div. June 1975); children: Douglas Alan, Bradley Jason; m. Walton Sansom Miller, Sept. 19, 1982. BA, Tarleton State U., 1964; MEd, U. North State, 1977; PhD, Tex. Women's U., 1993. Tchr., Mineral Wells (Tex.) High Sch., 1964-65, Weatherford (Tex.) Middle Sch., 1969-74; counselor, instr. psychology Tarrant County Jr. Coll., Hurst, Tex., 1977-82; pvt. practice family and marriage counseling, Dallas, 1982—. Author: (with Velma Walker, Jeannene Ward) Becoming: A Human Relations Workbook, 1981. Mem. ACA, Tex. State Bd. Examiners Profl. Counselors, Tex. State Bd. Marriage and Family Therapists, Tex. Counseling Assn., Am. Mental Health Counselors Assn., North Ctrl. Tex. Counseling Assn., Dallas Symphony Orch. League, Nat. Coun. Family Rels., Tex. Mental Health Counselors Assn., Internat. Assn. for

Marriage & Family Counselors. Methodist. Office: Counseling & Consulting of North Dallas 8222 Douglas Ave Ste 777 Dallas TX 75225-5938

MILLER, JOHN EDDIE, lawyer; b. Wayne, Mich., Nov. 14, 1945; s. George Hayden and Georgia Irene (Stevenson) M.; m. Nancy Carol Sanders, Jan. 7, 1968; children: Andrea Christine, Matthew Kit. BA, Baylor U., 1967; JD, U. Memphis, 1973; LLM, U. Mo., 1980. Bar: Mo. 1974, U.S. Dist. Ct. (we. dist.) Mo. 1974, Tex. 1982. Asst. prof. Central Mo. State U., Warrensburg, 1973-74; sole practice, Sedalia, Mo., 1974-79; sr. contract adminstr. Midwest Research Inst., Kansas City, Mo., 1979-81; sr. contract adminstr Tracor Inc., Austin, Tex., 1981-84; contract negotiator Tex. Instruments, Austin, 1984-86; sr. contract adminstr., Tracor Aerospace Inc., Austin, 1986-87, Radian Corp., Austin, 1987-96; asst. co. sec., Radian Internat. LLC, Austin 1996—, Radian Corp., Austin, 1987-96; corp. sec. Radian Southeast Asia (SEA) Ltd., Bangkok, 1995—, dir. Radian Southeast Asia (SEA) Ltd., Bangkok, 1996—, Radian Sys. Corp., Austin, 1995—; corp. sec. Radian Internat. Overseas Mgmt. Co., 1996—; instr. bus. law State Fair Community Coll., Sedalia, 1974-79, Austin Community Coll., 1983-84. Bd. dirs. Legal Aid Western Mo., 1977-79, Boy's Club, Sedalia, 1974-79, Austin Lawyers Care, 1987—. Served with U.S. Army, 1968-71. Mem. Mo. Bar Assn. (mem. internat. law com., mem. computer law com.), Tex. Bar Assn. (intellectual property law sec., internat. law sect., corp. sec.), Coll. of State Bar of Tex., Nat. Contract Mgmt. Assn., Travis County Bar Assn., U.S. Tennis Assn., AM Tennis Club, Phi Alpha Delta. Baptist. Office: Radian International LLC 8501 North Mo-Pac Blvd PO Box 201088 Austin TX 78720-1088

MILLER, JOHN HARRIS, JR., physics educator; b. Norfolk, Va., Nov. 28, 1957; s. John Harris and Judy Helen (Dorrance) M.; m. Karen Sue Henk, Sept. 7, 1985; children: John Harris III, Michael Hamilton. BSEE in Computer Sci., Northwestern U., 1980; MSEE, U. Ill., 1983, PhD in Elec. Engring., 1985. Elec. engr. Eastman Kodak, Rochester, N.Y., 1977-80; electronic design engr. Magnavox Govt. and Indsl. Divsn., Ft. Wayne, Ind., summer 1980; rsch. asst. dept. elec. engring. U. Ill., Urbana-Champaign, 1980-85, IBM postdoctoral fellow, 1985-86; asst. prof. physics, adj. asst. prof. applied sci. U. N.C., Chapel Hill, 1986-89; asst. prof. dept. physics Tex. Ctr. for Superconductivity, U. Houston, Tex., 1989-95; assoc. prof. dept. physics Tex. Ctr. for Superconductivity, U. Houston, 1995—; resident visitor Bell Comm. Rsch., Red Bank, N.J., summer 1988; co-organizer Internat. Symposium on High Temperature Superconducting Materials, U. N.C., Chapel Hill, 1987; presenter in field. Editor: High-Temperature Superconducting Materials, 1988; contbr. articles to profl. jours.; patentee in field. Recipient GE Found. Predoctoral fellowship, 1982-83, AT&T Bell Labs. Predoctoral scholarship, 1984-85, IBM Postdoctoral fellowship, 1985-86, Alfred P. Sloan Rsch. fellowship, 1987-92; grantee Inst. Space Systems Ops., U. Houston, 1992, Energy Lab., U. Houston, 1992, U.S. Army Rsch. Office, 1992-93, Presdl. Rsch. and Scholarship Fund, U. Houston, 1992-93, Robert A. Welch Found., 1992—, Tex. Advaned Tech. Program-Rsch., 1994—, Tex. Advanced Tech. Program, 1994—, others. Mem. Am. Phys. Soc., Materials Rsch. Soc., Houston Soc. for Engring. in Medicine and Biology, Phi Kappa Phi, Tau Beta Pi. Episcopalian. Home: 5622 Briarbend Dr Houston TX 77096-4913 Office: U Houston Dept Physics 4800 Calhoun Rd Houston TX 77204-5506

MILLER, JOHN PENDLETON, publishing company executive; b. Middletown, Ohio, Sept. 11, 1931; s. John William and Helena Bernice (Pendleton) M.; m. Barbara Elaine Stutsman, Jan. 19, 1952; children: Stacy Lynn, John Dewey, Tamara Leigh, Mark Douglas, Matthew Scott, Delano Mitchell. BS in Civil Engring., Wash. State U., Pullman, 1958. Sales engr. Armco Steel Corp., Middletown, Ohio, 1958-64; v.p., dir. mktg. Mes-Tex, Houston, 1964-67, Kirby Bldg. Sys., Houston, 1967-69; pres. Group Comm., Inc., Houston, 1969-81; chmn. bd. dirs. Group Comm., Inc., 1981—; lectr. in field; condr. seminars in field. Author: Selling Building Systems, 1970, Profitable Management Techniques for Contractors, 1973, A Professional Approach to Marketing for the Construction Industry, 1977, Human Stress ... How to Turn It Into Success, 1978, The Jack Miller Reports, 1985, Rules You Should Know About Investing, 1988, 16 Opportunities in Build/Lease, 1988, Rules You Should Know About Motivation, 1988, Rules You Should Know to be a Better Manager, 1988, The Important Steps that Take You to Health, Wealth and Happiness, 1992, Rules You Should Know Before You Build Your Important Project, 1993, Total Quality Management for the Construction Industry, 1993. Elder Grace Presbyn. Ch., Houston, 1977—. With USAF, 1950-54. Mem. ASCE, Associated Builders and Contractors, Associated Gen. Contractors, Am. Soc. for Quality Control, Tau Beta Pi, Phi Kappa Phi. Republican. Presbyterian. Office: Group Comm 10417 Rockley Rd Houston TX 77099-3525

MILLER, JOHN ULMAN, minister, author; b. N.Y.C., Dec. 9, 1914; s. Clarence James and Edythe Gladys (Shaffer) M.; m. Marcella E. Hubner, June 12, 1937; children: John U., Mark C. (dec.), Mary Kay (Mrs. Charles Bolin, dec.), Gretchen (Mrs. Ernest Micka). BA cum laude, Taylor U., 1937; MA, Butler U., 1942; DD, Geneva (Wis.) Theol. Coll., 1968. Ordained to ministry Bapt. Ch., 1937; pastor First Bapt. Ch., Bluffton, Ind., 1946-49, Boston, 1949-56; pastor Tabernacle Ch., Utica, N.Y., 1956-63, United Ch. of Christ, Hagerstown, Ind., 1963-66, St. John's Evang. Ch., Louisville, 1967-77; Participant Churchmen Weigh News, WNAC, Boston, 1953-56; preacher Meml. Chapel; instr. religion N.Y. Masonic Home, Utica, 1957-62; broadcast weekly services WKBV, Richmond, Ind., 1965-66; preacher Fellowship Chapel WHAS, Louisville, 1967-77; maintains 24 hour Dial-A-Prayer, Louisville, 1968-77; minister Royal Poinciana Chapel, Palm Beach, Fla., 1978-84; ret., 1984. Author: Only to the Curious, The Voice of St. John, Providence on Pilgrimage, Two Wonders I Confess, Stop! Look! Listen!, He Opened the Book, Christian Ethic in the Sermon on the Mount, Windows on the Agony, Prayers Under Pressure, 1989. Chmn. Campaigns Crippled Children, Tb, U.S.O., 1946-49. Capt. USAAF, 1942-45, PTO. Named Community Leader Am. News Pub. Co., 1969. Mem. Ind.-Ky. Conf. United Ch. of Christ, Bach Soc. Louisville. Home: 4409 Green Pine Dr Louisville KY 40220-1542

MILLER, JOSEPH ALFRED, printing executive; b. Richmond, Va., Feb. 23, 1907; s. Ernest Hutchinson and Caroline (Lipscombe) M.; m. Berenice K. Moss, Sept. 5, 1929 (dec.); 1 child, James Alfred. Student, U. N.C.-Chapel Hill, 1953-54. Pres., Miller Printing Co., Asheville, N.C., 1930-71, Millco, Inc., Asheville, 1972—; hon. dir. First Union Nat. Bank, Asheville. Trustee, U. N.C., Asheville, 1958-63, Montreat-Anderson Coll., Montreat, N.C., 1961-65; chmn. Asheville Redevel. Commn., 1961-70; chmn. bd. deacons Presbyterian Ch., 1954. Recipient Spl. award City of Asheville, 1970, Chancellor's Medallion U. N.C., 1990. Mem. Printing Industry of the Carolinas (pres. 1955, hon.), Blue Ridge Pkwy. Assn. (pres. 1963-64), Asheville C. of C. (dir. 1957-62, spl. award 1959). Democrat. Clubs: Am. Bus. (pres. Asheville 1938), Rotary, Country Club of Asheville (pres. 1949-50). Home: Givens estates 100 Wesley Dr #710 Asheville NC 28803 Office: Millco Inc PO Box 760 Skyland NC 28776-0760

MILLER, JUDITH ANN, retired financial executive; b. Chgo., Sept. 8, 1941; d. Frank G. and Kathryn M. (Stocklin) Bell; m. William J. Shrum, Aug. 3, 1958 (div. 1976); children: Steven W., Vickie L. White, Lisa A. Rhodes, Mark A., Brian D.; m. William L. Miller Jr., Nov. 28, 1976. Student, Ind. Cen. Coll., 1959-60, DePaw U., 1964-65. Lic. minister Christian Ch. (Disciples of Christ). Office cashier, mgr. G.C. Murphy Co., Indpls., 1967-70; asst. treas., office mgr. Missions Blvd. Fed. Credit Union, Indpls., 1970-72; treas., office mgr. Bd. Higher Edn., Christian Ch. (Disciples of Christ), Indpls. and St. Louis, 1972-77; dir. fin. Mt. Olive United Meth. Ch., Arlington, Va., 1978-79; exec. dir. Interfaith Forum on Religion, Art and Architecture, Washington, 1979-82; devel. assoc. Nat. Benevolent Assn., Des Moines, Iowa, 1982-85; adminstrv. asst. Davis, Hockenberg, Wine, Brown, Koehn & Shors, Des Moines, 1985-88; fin. officer Episcopal Diocese of Iowa, Des Moines, 1988-93; ret., 1993; owner Cakes by Judy, Manteo, N.C., 1994—. Mem. citizen adv. coun. Parkway Schs., St. Louis, 1976-77; county rep., mem. Fairfax County Sch. Bd. adv. coun., Springfield, Va., 1979-81; treas. congl. campaign Des Moines, 1983-85; mem. exec. St. Louis Children's Home, 1976-78; v.p., treas. Emmaus Fellowship Project on Aging, Washington, 1980-82; bd. dirs. Urban Mission Coun., Des Moines, 1983-86, Pre-Trial Release Prog., Des Moines, 1984-87; mem. steering com. Iowa Interfaith Network on AIDS, Des Moines, 1989-94; chmn. Cancer Awareness Sunday, Am. Cancer Soc., 1990; mem. pub. rels com. Dare County Librs., 1996—. Named Vol. of Yr., Iowa Victorian Soc., 1985, Our Community Kitchen, 1986. Mem. NAFE, Nat. Soc. Fund Raising Execs. (chpt. sec. 1985-87), Nat. Assn. Ch. Bus. Adminstrs. Dare County Libr. Assn. Democrat. Mem. Christian Ch. (Disciples of Christ). Home: PO Box 194 Manteo NC 27954-0194

MILLER, KENNETH TURNER, JR., surgeon; b. Waterloo, Iowa, Nov. 22, 1942; s. Kenneth Turner and Wilma Marie (Kurth) M.; m. Laura Mae Harrison, Dec. 9, 1972; children: Tinsley Elizabeth, Kristin Devere. BA, Baylor U., 1965; MD, U. Tex., 1969. Diplomate Am. Bd. Surgery. Intern in surgery U. Ala. Hosps., Birmingham, 1969-70, resident physician in surgery, 1970-72, 74-77; staff surgeon, pvt. practice Meth. Med. Ctr., Oak Ridge, Tenn., 1977—. Maj. U.S. Army, 1972-74. Fellow ACS (cancer liaison physician 1989—), Southeastern Surg. Congress. Republican. Baptist. Office: Mitchell Weight & Miller PC 988 Oak Ridge Tpke Ste 245 Oak Ridge TN 37830-6919

MILLER, LEWIS NELSON, JR., banker; b. 1944. BA, Washington and Lee U., 1966; postgrad., U. Va., 1972. With 1st & Mchts. Nat. Bank, 1969-70; planning mgr. Cen. Fidelity Bank N.A., Richmond, Va., 1972-73, planning officer, then asst. v.p., 1973-75, v.p., 1975-76, sr. v.p., mgr. fin. group, 1976-78, chief fin. officer, 1978-79, exec. v.p., 1979-82, exec. v.p., chief adminstrv. officer, from 1982; with Cen. Fidelity Banks Inc., Richmond, 1972—, sr. v.p., 1980-82, corp. exec. officer, 1982-83; exec. v.p. Cen. Fidelity Banks Inc., Richmond, Va., 1983-84; pres., later also treas., bd. dirs. Cen. Fidelity Banks Inc., Richmond, from 1984; now chmn., pres., chief exec. officer Cen. Fidelity Banks, Richmond. Lt. USN, 1966-69. Office: Cen Fidelity Banks Inc PO Box 27602 1021 E Cary St Richmond VA 23219-4000*

MILLER, LISA MICHELLE, newspaper editor; b. Regensburg, West Germany, Apr. 7, 1971; d. John Douglas and Sandy Lee (Blizzard) (dec.) M. B in Journalism, Okla. State U., 1993. Composition worker Edmond (Okla.) Evening Sun Newspaper, 1987-90; staff writer Daily O'Collegian, Stillwater, Okla., 1991; reporter Stillwater NewsPress, 1991-93, South Oklahoma City Leader, 1993; departmental editor Stillwater NewsPress, 1993—; news writing lab. instr. Okla. State U., 1994-95, 96—; participant Gov.'s State Media Tour, 1992; contest judge Okla. Collegiate Press Assn., 1994-95. Vol. Stillwater Christmas Store, 1992; participant LWV, Stillwater, 1994; local fundraisers and benefits, Stillwater, 1993—; sec. Payne County Rep. Party, 1995—. Recipient AP Writing awards, 1993-95, writing award Soc. Profl. Journalists, 1995, journalism awards Nat. Newspaper Assn., 1994-96; Don W. Reynolds Journalism scholar Reynolds Com., 1991-93, Bailey Meml. scholar Okla. State U., 1993. Mem. Nat. Fedn. Rep. Women (sec. 1996—), Altrusa Internat., Okla. Press Assn., Okla. State U. Alumni Assn., Clan Irwin Assn., Phi Kappa Phi, Phi Eta Sigma. Office: Stillwater NewsPress 211 W 9th Ave Stillwater OK 74074-4406

MILLER, LYNNE MARIE, environmental company executive; b. N.Y.C., Aug. 4, 1951; d. David Jr. and Evelyn (Gulbransen) M. AB, Wellesley Coll., 1973; MS, Rutgers U., 1976. Analyst Franklin Inst., Phila., 1976-78; dir. hazardous waste div. Clement Assocs., Washington, 1978-81; pres. Risk Sci. Internat., Washington, 1981-86, Environ. Strategies Corp., Reston, Va., 1986—. Editor: Insurance Claims for Environmental Damages, 1989, editor-in-chief Environ. Claims Jour.; contbr. chpts. to books. Named Ins. Woman of Yr. Assn. Profl. Ins. Women, 1983. Mem. AAAS, Am. Cons. Engrs. Coun., N.Y. Acad. Sci., Washington Wellesley Club, Wellesley Bus. Leadership Coun. Office: Environ Strategies Corp 11911 Freedom Dr Ste 900 Reston VA 22090-5602

MILLER, MARGARET ALISON, chief state academic officer; b. L.A., Dec. 17, 1944; d. Richard Crump and Virginia Margaret (Dudley) M.; m. Spencer Hall, Aug. 21, 1967 (div. 1977); 1 child, Justin Robinson; m. Alan Blair Howard, Oct. 7, 1990. BA, UCLA, 1966; postgrad., Stanford U., 1966-67; PhD, U. Va., 1971. English instr. U. Va., Charlottesville, 1971-72; prof. English U. Mass., North Dartmouth, 1972-86, co-dir. women's studies program, 1981-83, asst. to dean arts and scis., 1983-85, asst. to pres., 1985-86; acad. affairs coord. State Coun. Higher Edn. for Va., Richmond, 1986-87, assoc. dir. for acad. affairs, 1987—; cons. Coun. Rectors, Budapest, 1993, Minn. State U. System, Mpls., 1992, U.S. Dept. Edn., Washington, 1990-94, S.C. Higher Edn. Commn., 1989-90, Edn. Commn. States, Denver, 1994. Contbr. articles to profl. jours. Mem. Am. Assn. Higher Edn. (leadership coun.), Am. Coun. on Edn. (exec. com. identification program in Va. 1988—, participant nat. identification program's 41st nat. forum for women leaders in higher edn. 1989). Home: 2176 Lindsay Rd Gordonsville VA 22942-1620 Office: State Coun Higher Edn 101 N 14th St Fl 9 Richmond VA 23219-3684

MILLER, MARGARET ANN, physician, military officer; b. New Orleans, Oct. 1, 1952; d. W. Charles and Marjorie Therese (Kister) M. BS, Tulane U., 1973, MD, 1981, MPH, 1987. Diplomate Am. Bd. Psychiatry. Intern Tulane U., New Orleans, 1981-82, psychiatry resident, 1981-85; staff psychiatrist VA Hosp., New Orleans, 1985-86; maj. med. corps U.S. Army, Rhineland-Pfalz, Federal Republic Germany, 1987—. Mem. AMA, Am. Psychiatric Assn., Am. Soc. for Microbiology, Phi Beta Kappa. Roman Catholic.

MILLER, MARK STEVEN, pharmacologist, educator; b. Bronx, N.Y., May 28, 1956; s. Meyer and Marion (Schiff) M.; m. Helen Greenberg, Sept. 17, 1978; children: Matthew Alan, Adam Michael. BS in Biol. Scis. cum laude, Fordham U., 1977; MA in Pharmacology, Columbia U., 1978, MPhil, 1980, PhD, 1983. Grad. rsch. fellow dept. pharmacology Columbia U., N.Y.C., 1977-83; postdoctoral fellow dept. applied biol. scis. MIT, Cambridge, 1983-86; sr. staff fellow perinatal carcinogenesis sect. Nat. Cancer Inst. Frederick (Md.) Cancer R&D Ctr., 1986-90; asst. prof. dept. pathology U. Tenn., Knoxville, 1990-95; asst. prof. dept. cancer biology Bowman Gray Sch. Medicine, Wake Forest U., Winston-Salem, N.C., 1996—; adj. faculty scis. and techs. divsn. Frederick C.C., 1989-90. Contbr. articles and revs. to profl. jours. Grantee NIH, 1990-93, 92-95, 94—, USDA, 1992-94. Mem. AAAS, Am. Assn. for Cancer Rsch., Am. Soc. for Biochemistry and Molecular Biology, Soc. Toxicology (sec.-treas. Molecular Biology Specialty sect. 1996-97). Office: Wake Forest Univ Dept of Cancer Biology Medical Center Blvd Winston Salem NC 27157

MILLER, MARTHA LAFOLLETTE, foreign languages and literature educator; b. Albuquerque, Sept. 12, 1944; d. Robert Hoath and Martha Rutledge (Pugh) LaFollette; m. James Victor Miller, May 27, 1967 (div. 1975); 1 child, Matthew LaFollette. BA magna cum laude, Smith Coll., 1965; MA, U. Wis., 1967; PhD, Washington U., St. Louis, 1972. Acting asst. instr. Yale U., New Haven, 1973; instr. Ohio State U., Columbus, 1975-76; asst. prof. U. N.C., Charlotte, 1976-80, assoc. prof., 1980-89, prof., 1989—; cons., lectr. in field. Author: Politics and Verbal Play: The Ludic Poetry of Ángel González, 1995; contbr. chpts. to books, articles, revs. to profl. jours. Fellow U. Wis., 1965-67, Washington U., 1967-69, NEH, 1978, 92, U. Calif.-Irvine, 1979; travel grantee U. N.C., 1977, U. N.Mex., 1985, Internat. Congress of Rosalia de Castro-U. Santiago de Compostela, Spain, 1985, So. Regional Ednl. Bd., 1986. Mem. MLA, Am. Assn. Tchrs. Spanish and Portuguese, 20th Century Spanish Assn. Am., Feministas Unidas, Asociacion de Literatura Femenina Hispanica, Philol. Assn. Carolinas (del.-at-large 1988-90, 2d v.p. and program chair fgn. langs. 1990-91, 1st v.p. and program chair 1991-92, pres. 1992-93), Asociacion Internacional de Hispanistas, Asociacion Internacional de Valleinclanistas, Asociacion de Estudios Galegos. Office: U NC Fgn Langs Dept Charlotte NC 28223

MILLER, MARTIN EUGENE, school system administrator, negotiator; b. Decatur, Ill., May 14, 1945; s. Floyd Homer and Vivian LaVerne (Gould) M.; m. Sherry Kay Bandy, May 25, 1968; children: Liane, Laura. BS, U. Ill., 1968; MEd, U. North Fla., 1974. Cert. math. tchr.; cert. ednl. adminstrn. and supervision. Tchr. Decatur (Ill.) Pub. Schs., 1968, Clay County Sch. Bd., Orange Park, Fla., 1970-74; coordinator cert. personnel Clay County Sch. Bd., Green Cove Springs, Fla., 1974-77, dir. instructional personnel, 1977-78, dir. personnel services, 1978-81, asst. supt. for human resources and labor rels., 1981-93, dir. cmty. and govtl. rels., 1993—; past mem. Edn. Stds. Commn., Tallahassee, 1985-93, vice chmn., 1988-92; past mem. Blue Cross-Blue Shield Adv. Coun., Jacksonville, Fla.; past mem. Fla. Ednl. Leaders Forum. Served as staff sgt. USAF, 1968-70. Mem. Am. Assn. Sch. Pers. Adminstrs. (chmn. constn. and bylaws com. 1984-85), Fla. Assn. Sch. Pers. Adminstrs. (v.p. 1980-83, pres. 1983-85, bd. dirs. 198-90), Am. Assn. Sch. Adminstrs., Fla. Assn. Sch. Adminstrs., Fla. Pub. Employer Labor Rels. Assn., Fla. Edn. Negotiators, Fla. Ednl. Legis. Liaisons, Phi Delta Kappa. Democrat. Presbyterian. Home: 1612 Bay Cir W Orange Park FL 32073-4746 Office: Clay County Sch Bd 530 Stiles Ave Orange Park FL 32073-4000

MILLER, MARY JEANNETTE, office management specialist; b. Washington, Sept. 24, 1912; d. John William and David Evengeline (Hill) Sims; m. Cecil Miller, June 17, 1934 (dec.); children: Sylvenia Delores Doby, Ferdi A., Cecil Jr. (dec.). Student, Howard U., 1929-30, U. Ill., 1940-42, Dept. Agr. Grad. Sch., 1957-59, U. Md., 1975; cert. in Vocat. Photography, Prince George's C.C., 1986. Chief mail processing unit Bur. Reclamation, Washington, 1940-57; records supr. AID, Manila, Korea, Mali, Guyana, Dominican Republic, Indonesia, Laos, 1957-71; office engr. Bechtel Assocs., Washington, 1976-79; real estate assoc; tchr. English as 2d lang. Ministry of Edn., Seoul, Korea, 1960-61, Ministry of Fin., Laos, 1968-70; cons. to Ministry of Fin. Royal Lao Govt., 1971-74; cons. AID missions to Yemen, Sudan, Somalia, 1982; records mgmt. cons. AID, Monrovia, Liberia, 1980-81, Sri Lanka, 1984; docent Mus. African Art Smithsonian Inst., Washington, 1986-89; circulation asst. Prince George County Meml. Libr. System, Hyattsville, Md., 1987-91, ret.; mem. Friends of Internat. Edn. Com., 1985-92; sec./treas., bd. dirs. Miller Transitional, Inc.Author handbooks on office mgmt. Mem. AARP, NAFE, Mayor's Internat. Adv. Coun. Mem. Soc. Am. Archivists, Am. Mgmt. Assn., Montgomery County Bd. Realtors, Am. Fgn. Svc. Assn., Nat. Trust Hist. Preservation, Assn. Am. Fgn. Svc. Women's Writer Group, Consumer Mail Panel, Zeta Phi Beta. Roman Catholic. Home: 14200 Pimberton Dr Hudson FL 34667-8542

MILLER, MICHAEL T., education educator; b. Omaha; s. Harry G. and Mary F. (Shugrue) M. BA, So. Ill. U., 1986, MS, 1988; EdD, U. Nebr., 1991. Asst. dir., dir. ann. giving So. Ill. U., Carbondale, 1986-88; dir. R&D unit U. Nebr., Lincoln, 1991-94; asst. prof. edn. U. Ala., Tuscaloosa, 1994—; mem. steering com. Coun. Acad. Programs Studying Higher Edn., 1995—; mem. coordinating com. Ctr. for Study of Higher Edn., U. Nebr.; bd. dirs. Mid-State Industry and Edn. Consortium. Author 9 books/monographs; contbr. more than 100 articles to profl. jours. Recipient Outstanding Svc. to Vocat. Edn. award Omicron Tau Theta, 1992, Cert. of Recognition, Univ. Coun. for Vocat. Edn., 1992, Am. Coll. Pers. Assn., 1995. Mem. Assn. for Study of Higher Edn., Popular Culture Assn., Nat. Assn. Student Pers. Adminstrn. Office: U Ala 206 Wilson Hall Tuscaloosa AL 35487

MILLER, MILDRED JENKINS, local historian, genealogist; b. Statesville, N.C., Mar. 13, 1932; d. Carroll Lee and Pernia Cornelia (Sharpe) Jenkins; m. John Jackson Miller, Mar. 3, 1955; children: David Clarence, Sandra Leigh Miller Blevins. Grad., Scotts (N.C.) H.S.; cert. rsch. and creative writing, Mitchell Coll. Continuing Edn., Statesville, N.C. Historian Iredell Hist. Properties Commn., Statesville, N.C., 1977—; chmn. Iredell Hist. Properties Commn., Statesville, 1990—; editor Iredell County Tracks Genealog. Soc. of Iredell County, States, 1991—. Author: (books) Carolina Summers, 1980 (N.C. Soc. Local Historians award 1981), From Sterling to Sterling, 1990 (N.C. Local Historians award 1991); co-author: (Book) Time Is, Time Was, 1990, (N.C. Soc. Local Historians award 1991), also newspaper articles. Mem. Genealog. Soc. Iredell County (v.p. 1977, pres. 1981). Democrat. Presbyterian. Home: 112 Katy Ben Ln Stony Point NC 38678

MILLER, PAMELA GUNDERSEN, city official; b. Cambridge, Mass., Sept. 7, 1938; d. Sven M. and Harriet Adams Gundersen; A.B. magna cum laude, Smith Coll., 1960; m. Ralph E. Miller, July 7, 1962; children—Alexander, Erik, Karen. Feature writer Congressional Quar., Washington, 1962-65; dir. cable TV franchizing Storer Broadcasting Co., Louisville, Bowling Green, Lexington, and Covington, Ky., 1978-80, 81-82; mem. 4th Dist. Lexington, Fayette County Urban Council, 1973-77, councilwoman-at-large, 1982-93, vice-mayor, 1984-86, 89-93, mayor, 1993—; dep. commr. Ky. Dept. Local Govt., Frankfort, 1980-81; pres. Pam Miller, Inc., 1984—, Community Ventures Corp., 1985—. Mem. Fayette County Bd. Health, 1975-77, Downtown Devel. Commn., 1975-77; alt. del. Dem. Nat. Conv., 1976; bd. dirs. YMCA, Lexington, 1975-77, 85-90, Fund for the Arts, 1984-93, Council of Arts, 1978-80, Sister Cities, 1978-80; treas. Prichard Com. for Acad. Excellence, 1983—. Named Woman of Achievement YWCA, 1984, Outstanding Woman of Blue Grass, AAUW, 1984. Mem. LWV (dir. 1970-73), Profl. Women's Forum, NOW, Land and Nature Trust of the Bluegrass. Home: 140 Cherokee Park Lexington KY 40503-1304 Office: 200 E Main St Lexington KY 40507-1315

MILLER, PATRICIA ANNE, speech and language pathologist; b. Lamesa, Tex., Aug. 19, 1957; d. Warren Layton and Evelyn Joyce (Pearson) Oliver; m. John Ernest Roberts, May 25, 1979 (div.); 1 child, Jason Aaron; m. Michael David Miller, Nov. 30, 1984; children: Jennifer Anne, Catherine Denise. BS, Howard Payne Coll., 1979; postgrad., Baylor U., 1983. Cert. tchr., Tex.; lic. speech-lang. pathologist, Tex. Speech therapist Crosbyton (Tex.) Cen. Ind. Sch. Dist., 1980-81; speech therapist Hillsboro (Tex.) Spl. Edn. Coop., 1981, speech therapy cons., 1982-83; speech therapist Cleburne (Tex.) Ind. Sch. Dist., 1987-89, Levelland (Tex.) Ind. Sch. Dist. Coop., 1989; speech therapist Speech, Lang. and Hearing Ctr. Lamesa Ind. Sch. Dist., Lubbock, Tex., 1990-95; speech-lang. pathologist Sundance Rehab. Corp., Lamesa, Tex., 1995—. Mem. Tex. Speech and Hearing Assn. Baptist. Office: 703 S 1st St Lamesa TX 79331-6249

MILLER, PAUL ALLEN, literature educator; b. Kansas City, Nov. 7, 1959; s. Melvin Joe and Mary Ellen (Testerman) M.; m. Ann Louise Poling, Aug. 15, 1958. BA summa cum laude, Washington U., 1982; MA, U. Tex., 1985, PhD, 1989. Asst. prof. Drury Coll., Springfield, Mo., 1989-91; asst. prof. Tex. Tech U., Lubbock, 1991-96, assoc. prof., 1996—; dir. comparative lit., 1995—; beta tester Perseus Project, Cambridge, Mass., 1990-94; vis. prof. Hamilton Coll., Clinton, N.Y., 1996. Author: (poetry) Lyric Texts and Lyric Consciousness, 1994; editor Intertexts; contbr. articles to profl. jours. Recipient Honorable Mention award U. Paris, 1986; grantee Tex. Tech. U., Lubbock, Tex., 1992. Mem. MLA, Renaissance Soc., Am. Philol. Assn., Classical Assn. of Mid. West and South. Office: Tex Tech U Dept Classical Modern Lang & Lit Lubbock TX 79409

MILLER, PAULA, government employee; b. Warwick, Va., Oct. 31, 1955; d. Alton Roscoe and Verna Mae (Simpson) M. BSBA, Charleston So. U., 1995. Purchasing agt. Naval Electronic Systems Engring. Ct., N. Charleston, S.C., 1984-87; logistics mgmt. specialist Navy Logistics Career Intern Program, Washington, 1987-90; logistic support mgr. ISE East Coast div. Naval Command Control and Ocean Surveillance Ctr., North Charleston, S.C., 1990-95. Mem. Soc. Logistics Engrs., Am. Def. Preparedness Assn. Republican. Baptist. Office: NISE East 4600 Marriott Dr North Charleston SC 29406-6556

MILLER, PAULETTE E., community health nurse, critical care nurse; b. Hazlehurst, Miss., Feb. 21, 1957; d. Charles and Corrine (Moore) M. BS, U. So. Miss., 1979, MS, 1988. Cert. critical care nurse; cert. diabetic foot specialist. Home care, pvt. duty nurse Quality Care, Jackson, Miss.; nursing supr., DON Albermarle Health Care Ctr., Jackson; staff nurse, preceptor med./surgical Miss. Bapt. Med. Ctr., Jackson; staff nurse, acting head nurse MICU Va. Med. Ctr., Jackson. Sponsor blood pressure screening, Hazlehurst Youth Ctr. and Hazlehurst High Sch.; active RN coun. and rsch. com. Recipient Cert. of Appreciation, Delta State U., Spl. Contbrn. award VA mission. Mem. ANA, AACN, Miss. Nurses Assn., Eliza Pillars RN State Assn., Golden Key./. Home: 138 Simmons St Hazlehurst MS 39083-3519

MILLER, PHILLIP EDWARD, environmental scientist; b. Waterloo, Iowa, May 29, 1935; s. Joe Monroe and Katherine Elva (Groom) M.; m. Cathy Ann Love, Sept. 15, 1962; children: Eric Anthony, Bryan Edward, Stefan Patrick, Gregory Joseph. BA in Sci. Edn., U. No. Iowa, 1961; MA in Sci. Edn., U. Iowa, 1964; postgrad., U. Wis., 1966-68. Physics and chemistry tchr. Millersburg (Iowa) Community High Sch., 1961-62; supervising tchr. NSF Insvc. Inst. U. Iowa, Iowa City, 1962-64; instr. biology, area coord. Office Equal Opportunity Western Ky. U., Bowling Green, 1964-66; sci. editor, journalism instr.-sci. and tech. Mich. State U., East Lansing, 1968-74; asst. prof. agr., forestry and home econs. U. Minn., St. Paul, 1974-77; sr. editor atomic energy div. E.I. du Pont de Nemours and Co., Aiken, S.C., 1977-89; sr. scientist environ. protection dept. Westinghouse Savannah River

Co., Aiken, 1989—; pres. Agy. for Book Authors, Collectors and Understanding of Sci., Aiken, 1994—; panelist 26th Internat. Tech. Comm. Conf., L.A., 1979; participant Dept. Energy/Westinghouse Sch. for Environ. Excellence, Cin., 1991; invited contbr. to proceedings of the 1st Tatarstan Symposium on Energy, Environment and Econs., Kazan, Tatarstan, Russia, 1992. Mem. publs. com. Cen. Assn. Sci. and Math. Tchrs., Iowa City, 1969-72; editor Nat. Task Force on Agrl. Energy R&D, Washington, 1976; editor, contbr. Minn. Sci. Mag., 1974-77; contbr. several hundred med., sci. and engring. articles including to Procs. of Iowa Acad. Sci., Sch. Sci. and Math., Am. Biology Tchrs., Procs. of Internat. Communication Conf., and Procs. of Westinghouse Computer Symposium. Pres. Savannah River Rifle & Pistol Club, Aiken, 1981-82, Aiken Toastmasters, 1984; judge speech contests Optimist and 4-H Club Contests, Aiken, 1985-86. Sgt. U.S. Army, 1955-58. Decorated Disting. Marksman Badge gold medal; recipient 1st place sci. writing Argonne Labs. Assn., 1973, Profl. Achievement Permanent Profl. cert. Iowa State Bd. of Pub. Instrn., 1974, Blue Ribbon, Am. Assn. Agrl. Coll. Editors, Tex. A&M, 1976. Mem. AAAS, N.Y. Acad. Scis., Am. Chem. Soc., Phi Delta Kappa, Sigma Xi. Office: Westinghouse Savannah River Co Environ Protection Dept Aiken SC 29801

MILLER, RANDEL KENNETH, rheumatologist; b. Lancaster, Pa., Mar. 4, 1951; s. Kenneth Wickersham Miller and Doris (Furnival) Mahoney; m. Susan Teresa Siepietowski, June 22, 1974; children: Tamara E., Shaun R., Ashley D. BA, Lehigh U., 1972; MD, U. Pitts., 1977. Cert. in internal medicine and rheumatology Am. Bd. Internal Medicine. Intern and resident in internal medicine U. Pitts. Health Ctr., 1977-80; fellow and instr. in clin. immunology and rheumatology U. Ala., Birmingham, 1980-82; rheumatologist Watson Clinic, Lakeland, Fla., 1982—; mem. exec. com. Watson Clinic, Lakeland, 1985, spokesperson for rheumatology, 1989-95; chmn. credentials com. Lakeland Regional Med. Ctr., 1995-96. Contbr. articles to profl. jours. Youth soccer coach Highlands Youth Soccer Assn., Lakeland, 1992-96; youth baseball coach Lakeland Little League, 1993-95. Recipient Sr. Rheumatology award Am. Rheumatism Assn., 1982. Fellow Am. Coll. Rheumatology, Am. Coll. Physicians; mem. Am. Coll. Sports Medicine, Am. Soc. Internal Medicine, Fla. Soc. Rheumatology, Lakeland Yacht and Country Club. Republican. Home: 1605 Inverness Dr Lakeland FL 33813 Office: Watson Clinic 1600 Lakeland Hills Blvd Lakeland FL 33805-3019

MILLER, RAYMOND VINCENT, JR., lawyer; b. Providence, July 1, 1954; s. Raymond Vincent and Mary Eunice (Mullen) M.; m. Elizabeth Ann White, May 31, 1980; children: Travis, Charles. BA, U. R.I., 1976; JD, U. Miami, 1981. Bar: Fla. 1981, U.S. Dist. Ct. (so. dist.) Fla. 1981, U.S. Ct. Appeals (11th cir.) 1986, U.S. Dist. Ct. (mid. dist.) Fla. 1987. Area supr. job devel. and tng. div. R.I. Dept. Econ. Devel., Providence, 1977-78; assoc. Thornton & Herndon, Miami, Fla., 1981-83, Britton, Cohen et al, Miami, 1983-85, Edward A. Kaufman, P.A., Miami, 1985-88; ptnr. Kaufman, Miller, Dickstein & Grunspan, Miami, 1988—. Mem. ABA, Fla. Bar Assn., Nat Order Barristers, Soc. Bar and Gavel, Acad. Fla. Trial Lawyers (chair comml. law sect. 1993-95). Home: 6805 SW 98th St Miami FL 33156-3044 Office: Kaufman Miller Dickstein & Grunspan PA 200 S Biscayne Blvd Ste 4650 Miami FL 33131-2310

MILLER, RICHARD JOSEPH, lawyer; b. San Diego, Jan. 20, 1941; s. Daniel Preston and June (Beissel) M.; divorced, 1972; 1 child, Shelli Renee; m. Paula Anne English, May 29, 1982. BA, U. Tex., Arlington, 1970; M of Pub. Adminstrn., So. Meth. U., Dallas, 1974; JD, Baylor U., 1983. Bar: U.S. Dist. Ct. (we. dist.) Tex. 1988. Officer, supr. Dallas Police Dept., 1963-75; program coord. Tex. Organized Crime Prevention Council, Austin, 1975-76; chief of police Killeen (Tex.) Police Dept., 1976-79; tng. cons. Tex. Commn. on Law Enforcement Officer Standards and Edn., Austin, 1979-80; chief of police Denton (Tex.) Police Dept., 1980; sole practice Killeen, 1983-88; ptnr. Kleff, Lewis, Miller & Assocs., Killeen, 1989; pvt. practice Killeen, Tex., 1989-92; elected county atty. Bell County (Tex.), Bell County, 1993—. Author: The Train Robbing Bunch, 1981, Texas Firemen's and Policemen's Civil Service Law, 1987, Bounty Hunter, 1988, Bloody Bill Longley, 1996. Vice chmn. Leon Valley dist. Boy Scouts Am., 1987-88; bd. dirs. Killeen Crimestoppers, Inc., 1986-91, Killeen Literacy Coun., 1987-90; mem. Bell County Hist. Commn., 1988-91. With U.S. Army, 1958-61. Fellow Tex. Bar Found.; mem. Bell-Lampassas-Mills Counties Bar Assn., Tex. Dist. and County Attys. Assn., Nat. Assn. Outlaw and Lawman History (bd. dirs. 1986—), Rotary. Home: 1201 Holly Ct Harker Hts TX 76548-1538 Office: PO Box 1127 Belton TX 76513-5127

MILLER, RITA GAYLE, respiratory therapist, biofeedback specialist; b. Springfield, Mo., May 27, 1953; d. William Clifford and LaVelle Berniece (Tuttle) Boyd; m. Robert Douglas McKemie, Sept. 10, 1971 (div. 1976); 1 child, Marjorie; m. William F. Miller, Jan. 2, 1980; children: Leslie Herd, Karla Henderson, Chris, Lisa Hearn, Katy Merriman, Mary Frances, Franklin. AS, El Centro Coll., 1975; BA in Psychology, U. Tex., Dallas, 1990; BS in Gerontol. Counseling, U. Tex. S.W. Med. Ctr., 1993. Cert. and registered in respiratory care Nat. Bd. Respiratory Care; cert. biofeedback therapist, respiratory technician; registered respiratory therapist. Supr. respiratory therapy Meth. Hosps. Dallas, 1974-76; instr. respiratory tech. program Tarrant County Jr. Coll., 1976-77; tech. dir. pulmonary rehab., respiratory therapy svcs., biofeedback therapist. Meth. Hosps. Dallas, 1977-80; instr. Tex. Inst. Respiratory Therapy, 1978-80; chief technician, physician's asst. Respiratory Care Ctr., Dallas, 1980-81; researcher pulmonary rsch. div. Meth. Hosps. Dallas, 1981-86; instr. respiratory therapy Dallas County Community Coll., 1981-83; dir. edn. and rehab. pulmonary svcs. Med. City Dallas Hosp., 1983-86; cons. biofeedback program Dallas Rehab. Inst., 1985-86; rsch. asst. to pvt. practice physician Dallas, 1986—. Author: (manuals) Progressive Respiratory Care, 1979, (with William F. Miller) Home Respiratory Care, 1979, Ventilator Dependent Patient Care, 1985; contbr. articles to profl. jours. Bd. adv. El Centro Coll., Respiratory Therapy Program, 1983-86. Mem. Applied Assn. Advancement Behavioral Therapy, Biofeedback Soc. Tex., Assn. Applied Psychophysiology, Am. Assn. Respiratory Care, Tex. Soc. Respiratory Care, North Tex. Region Respiratory Care, Am. Lung Assn. (Dallas area).

MILLER, ROBERT JAMES, lawyer; b. Dunn, N.C., Jan. 14, 1933; s. Robert James and Edith (Crockett) M.; m. Patricia L. Shaw, Sept. 29, 1984; children: Patricia Ann, Susan Ballantine, Nancy Crockett. B.S., N.C. State U., 1956; M.F., Yale U., 1962, M.S., 1965, Ph.D., 1967; J.D., N.C. Central U., 1984. Registered land surveyor. Forester W.Va. Pulp & Paper Co., 1956-59, Tilghman Lumber Co., 1959-61; asst. in instrn. and research Yale U., New Haven, 1962-65; assoc. prof. biology Radford (Va.) Coll., 1965-67, prof., chmn. biology dept., 1967-68, dean div. natural scis., 1968-71, v.p. for acad. affairs, 1971-73; prof. law, dean of coll. St. Mary's Coll., Raleigh, N.C., 1973-85; atty. Patton, Boggs & Blow, Raleigh, N.C., 1985-89; pvt. practice, 1989—; mediator N.C. Gen. Ct. of Justice; ecol. cons.; arbitrator Am. Arbitration Assn., Better Bus. Bur.; lectr. comml. law Tomsk (Russia) State U. Author: The Assimilation of Nitrogen Compounds by Tree Seedlings, 1967, Some Ecological Aspects of Dry Matter Production, 1962, Liberal Arts and the Individual, 1972, Liberal Arts: An Educational Philosophy, 1973, Laboratory Notebook: General Biology, 1976, Educational Malpractice, 1984, Issues in International Commercial Mediation, 1995. Mem. Am. Soc. Plant Physiologists, Ecol. Soc. Am., ABA, Am. Immigration Lawyers Assn., N.C. Acad. Trial Lawyers, N.C. Bar Assn., Sigma Xi, Phi Kappa Phi, Xi Sigma Pi. Episcopalian. Lodges: Masons; Shriners. Home: 3404 Lake Boone Trl Raleigh NC 27607-6756

MILLER, ROBERT ORAN, bishop. Bishop Episcopal Diocese of Ala., Birmingham, Ala., 1988—. Office: Episcopal Diocese of Ala 521 20th St N Birmingham AL 35203-2611

MILLER, RONALD BAXTER, English language educator, author; b. Rocky Mount, N.C., Oct. 11, 1948; s. Marcellus Cornelius and Elsie (Bryant) M.; m. Jessica Garris, June 5, 1971; 1 child, Akin Dasan. BA magna cum laude, N.C. Ctrl. U., 1970; AM, Brown U., 1972, PhD, 1974. Asst. prof. English Haverford Coll., Haverford, Pa., 1974-76; assoc. prof. English, dir. Black lit. program U. Tenn., Knoxville, 1977-81, prof. English, dir. Black lit. program, 1982-92, Lindsay Young prof. liberal arts and English, 1986-87; prof. English, dir. Inst. for African Am. Studies U. Ga., Athens, 1992—; instr. summer sch. Roger Williams Coll., Bristol, R.I., 1973; lectr. SUNY, 1974; Mellon prof. Xavier Univ., New Orleans, 1988; Irvine Found. visiting scholar Univ. San Francisco, 1991. Author: (reference guide) Langston Hughes and Gwendolyn Brooks, 1978, The Art and Imagination of Langston Hughes, 1989 (Am. Book award, 1991), (monograph) Southern Trace in Black Critical Theory: Redemption of Time, 1991; editor, contbr.: Black American Literature and Humanism, 1981, Black American Poets Between Worlds, 1940-60, 1986; co-editor: Call and Response The Riverside Anthology of African American Literary Experience, 1996; mem. editl. bd. Tenn. Studies in Lit., 1991-93, Black Fiction Project (Yale-Cornell-Duke-Harvard), 1985—, U. Ga. Press, 1994—; contbr. numerous articles and revs. to profl. jours. Recipient award Am. Coun. of Learned Socs., 1978, Golden Key Faculty award Nat. Golden Key, 1990, 95, Alpha award for disting. svc. U. Ga. Athens, 1993; Lilly Sr. Teaching fellow U. Ga. Athens, 1994, Nat. Rsch. Coun. sr. fellow, 1986-87, NDEA fellow, 1970-72, Ford Found. fellow, 1972-73, NEH fellow, 1975; Nat. Fellowships Fund dissertation grantee, 1973-74, others. Mem. MLA (exec. com. Afro-Am. Lit. Discussion Group 1980-83, chair 1982-83, mem. del. assembly 1984-86, com. on langs. and lits. of Am. 1993—, chair 1996), Langston Hughes Soc. (pres. 1984-90). Office: U Ga Inst African Am Studies Athens GA 30602

MILLER, RUSSELL EDMUND, lay worker, energy investment banker; b. Schenectady, N.Y., Mar. 23, 1942; s. L. Russell and Arline (Wooden) M.; m. Nancy Steeble, June 6, 1964; children: Laura, Ted, Sarah, Andrew. AB, Bowdoin Coll., 1964; MBA, Columbia U., 1966. Met. chmn. Christian Bus. Men's Com., Balt., 1976-84; deacon Timonium Presbyn Ch., Balt., 1978-83; dir. Balt. Billy Graham Crusade, 1982; trustee Washington Bible Coll., Lanham, Md., 1982-90, chmn., 1987-90; trustee Arlington Bapt. Ch., Balt., 1985-89; dir. Balt. Logos Com. of Operation Mobilization, 1987, Ch. Disciples Ministry Coun. Navigators, Colorado Springs, Colo., 1989—; v.p. Alex Brown & Sons Inc., Balt., 1981-90; pres. Miller & Co., Balt., 1991—. Chmn. Energy Conservation Com., Balt., 1983-85. 1st lt. U.S. Army, 1967-74. Republican. Home and Office: 702 Edwards Rd Apt D-80 Greenville SC 29615-1206

MILLER, SAMMY JOE, historian, writer, editor; b. Memphis, Feb. 2, 1968; s. Clarence Eugene Jr. and Barbara Dean (Gosnell) M. Grad. h.s., 1986. Hist. cons. Pomegranate Publs., Rohnert Park, Calif., 1993—, author, interviewer, 1994—, editor, 1995—. Author (calendars) Blackball: Negro Baseball Leagues, 1995, 96; author, editor (calendar) Blackball: Negro Baseball Leagues, 1997. Mem. Soc. for Am. Baseball Rsch., Soc. for Am. Baseball Rsch.'s Negro Leagues Com. Republican. Home: 3916 Archer Ct Florence KY 41042

MILLER, SANDRA PERRY, middle school educator; b. Nashville, Aug. 3, 1951; d. James Ralph and Pauline (Williams) Perry; m. William Kerley Miller, June 22, 1974. BS, David Lipscomb U., 1973; MEd, Tenn. State U., 1983, cert. in spl. edn., reading splty., 1986. Cert. tchr., Tenn. Tchr. Clyde Riggs Elem. Sch., Portland, Tenn., 1973-86; tchr. social studies Portland Mid. Sch., 1986—; adv. bd. tech. and comm. in edn. Sumner County Sch. Bd., Gallatin, Tenn., 1990—; co-dir., cons. Tenn. Students-at-Risk, Nashville, 1991—; assoc. edn. cons. Edn. Fgn. Inst. Cultural Exch., 1991-92; fellow World History Inst., Princeton (N.J.) U., 1992—; awards com. Tenn. Dept. Edn., Nashville, 1992; U.S. edn. amb. E.F. Ednl. Tours, Eng., France, Germany, Belgium, Holland, 1991; ednl. cons. HoughtonMifflin Co., Boston; apptd. Tenn. Mini-Grants award com., Tenn. 21st Century Tech. Com.; mem. Tenn. Textbook Com., 1995, Think-Tank on 21st Century Edn., Tenn. and Milliken Nat. Educator Found.; apptd. to Gov.'s Task Force Commn. on 21st Schs., Gov.'s Task Force for Anti-Drug and Alcohol Abuse Among Teens; mem. nat. com. for instnl. tech. devel. Milken Family Found. Nat. Edn. Conf., 1996; apptd. to Instrnl. Tech. Devel.-Project Strand, 1996 Milken Family Found., Nat. Edn. Conf. Author curriculum materials; presenter creative crafts segment local TV sta., 1990-93; producer, dir. documentary on edn. PBS, Corona, Calif., 1990. Performer Nashville Symphony Orch., 1970-73; leader Sumner County 4-H Club, 1976-86; mem. Woodrow Wilson Nat. Fellowship Found. on Am. History, Princeton U., 1994; nat. com. Instructional Tech. Devel. Project Strand of the 1996 Milken Family Found. Nat. Edn. Conf., L.A., 1996. Recipient Excellence in Teaching award U. Tenn., 1991-92, 92-93, award for Outstanding Teaching in Humanities Tenn. Humanities Coun., 1994; named Tchr. of Yr. Upper Cumberland dist. Tenn. Dept. Edn., 1991-92, 92-93, Mid. Tenn. Educator of Yr. Tenn. Assn. Mid. Schs., 1991, Tenn. Tchr. of Yr. Tenn. Dept. Edn., 1992, Nat. Educator of Yr. Milken Family Found., 1992; recipient grant Tenn. Dept. Edn. for Devel. of Model Drop Out Prevention Program, 1996. Mem. NEA, ASCD, Sumner County Edn. Assn. (sch. rep. 1973—, Disting. Tchr. of Yr. 1992), Tenn. Edn. Assn. (rep. 1973—), Nat. Geographic Tenn. Alliance (rep. 1990—, grantee 1990), Tenn. Humanities Coun. (rep. 1990—), Nat. Coun. Social Studies. Baptist. Office: Portland Mid Sch 922 S Broadway Portland TN 37148-1624

MILLER, SCOTT ANDREW, geotechnical engineer; b. Pitts., May 24, 1959; s. Carl Ludwig and Arlene M. (Morrissey) M.; m. Edna Marie Kunkel, July 17, 1981 (div. Dec. 1986); 1 child, Clay Michael; m. Kelly Ruth Haynes, Feb. 14, 1989 (div. Mar. 1996); 1 child, Lydia Sioux. BSCE, Carnegie-Mellon U., 1981, MSCE, 1983. Registered profl. engr., Tenn., Ala., Ark., Fla., Ga., Miss., N.C., Va., Md., Pa., N.Y., Ohio, Ky., Ill., Ind., Mo., Tex., N.Mex., Ariz., La., Minn., Iowa. Engr. Ogden Svcs., Nashville, 1983-91; constrn. svcs. mgr. Bhate Engring. Corp., Birmingham, Ala., 1991-92; sr. geotech. engr., v.p. Anderson Engring. Cons., Inc., Little Rock, 1992—. Mem. ASCE (pres. Ark. sect. 1996), NSPE, Am. Concrete Inst. (sec.-treas. mid-Tenn. chpt. 1987-91, bd. dirs. Ark. chpt. 1993-96). Republican. Roman Catholic. Home: 2001 Reservoir Rd #46 Little Rock AR 72227 Office: Anderson Engring Cons Inc 10205 W Rockwood Rd Little Rock AR 72204-8138

MILLER, SCOTT DOUGLAS, college president; b. Phila., Mar. 24, 1959; s. Rudolph Peter Jr. and Iris Lorraine (Troutman) M.; m. Andrea Jo Cook, Feb. 26, 1983; children: Katelyn, Ashlee. BA, Wesleyan Coll., Buckhannon, W.Va., 1980; MS, U. Dayton, 1984; EdS, Vanderbilt U., 1987; PhD, Union Grad. Sch., Cin., 1990. Reporter The Edinboro (Pa.) Independent, 1976-77; weekend editor, govt. reporter The Buckhannon Record, 1977-81; dir. coll. rels. U. Rio Grande, Ohio, 1981-84; v.p. devel. Lincoln Meml. U., Harrogate, Tenn., 1984-88, exec. v.p., 1988-91, pres., 1991—. Author: Seven Faces of Lincoln, 1988, McMurtry on Lincoln, 1989, Courage in Mission, 1990; pub. jour. The Lincoln Herald, 1984—. Bd. dirs. United Way, 1989—, Wesley Found., 1988—, Frank White Acad., 1989—, The Lincoln Mus., 1984—. Pew Charitable Trusts fellow, 1985-90. Mem. Kiwanis, Lions. Mem. United Meth. Ch. Office: Lincoln Meml Univ Cumberland Gap Pky Harrogate TN 37752-2001

MILLER, STEPHEN LAURENCE, responsive services executive; b. Vernon, Tex., Jan. 11, 1951; s. Laurence Odell and Patricia Ann (Pearson) M. Student, Tex. Tech. U., 1969-76. Salesman Lubbock (Tex.) Sun Times, 1974-75; sales mgr. A-1 Awards, Inc., Lubbock, 1975-76; v.p. sales Internat. Awards, Inc., Lubbock, 1977-78, pres., chief exec. officer, 1979-82; pres., chief exec. officer Responsive Svcs. Internat., Lubbock, 1983—, also bd. dirs.; mem. adv. bd. dept. computer sci. Tex. Tech. U., Lubbock, 1982-85, inst. studies of organizational automation, 1990-93; cons. Knlau, Inc., Vernon, Tex., 1990-91. Ways and means dir. Lubbock Jaycees, 1980; program dir. S.W. Optimists, Lubbock, 1981; campaign aide Delwin Jones Re-election Campaign, Lubbock, 1990. Mem. Lubbock T.T.A. (pres. 1988-91). Office: Responsive Svcs Internat 1220 Broadway St Ste 909 Lubbock TX 79401-3202

MILLER, STEVEN ARTHUR, academic administrator; b. Winston-Salem, N.C., July 18, 1952; s. Irving Joshua and Nell Bernice (Joyce) M.; m. Patricia Sue Craddock, Apr. 6, 1985; 1 child, Heather. BS, Wake Forest U., 1974; MBA, U. Ga., 1975; EdD in Higher Edn. Adminstrn., U. N.C., Greensboro, 1985. Instr. Winsalm Coll., Winston-Salem, 1975-78; instr. Davidson (N.C.) C.C., Lexington, 1978-89, chmn. bus div., 1989—; adj. faculty Highpoint Coll., 1987-89. Author: The Legal Aspects of Academic Freedom and Tenure in Community Colleges, 1986. Mem. budget allocation com. LExington Area United Way, 1989-92; precinct sec. Forsyth County Reps., 1988—. Mem. N.S. Assn. Bus. Chmn. & Dept. HEads (v.p.), N.C. Assn. C.C. Instructional Adminstrs., Inland Sea Sailing Assn., Deacon Club Wake Forest U. Republican. Baptist. Home: 3019 Cambridge Rd Winston Salem NC 27104-4001 Office: Davidson CC PO Box 1287 Lexington NC 27293-1287

MILLER, STEVEN DOUGLAS, federal agency executive; b. Chateauroux, France, Jan. 30, 1960; came to U.S., 1960; s. Frank Lee and Athalee Evelyn (Bailey) M. BA, Evergreen State Coll., Olympia, Wash., 1981; MPA, U. Tex., 1987. Budget analyst IRS, Washington, 1987-90; budget examiner Dept. of Treasury, Washington, 1990-92; budget officer Bur. of the Pub. Debt, Parkersburg, W.Va., 1992-96; acting dir. divsnl. fin. mgmt. Bur. of the Pub. Debt, Parkersburg, 1996—. Delegation mem. Citizen Amb. Program (Russia), Spokane, Wash., 1994; bd. dirs. Family Crisis Intervention Ctr., Parkersburg, 1993-94, pres. bd. dirs., 1995—. Mem. Am. Assn. for Budget and Program Analysis, Am. Soc. for Pub. Adminstrn., Evergreen State Coll. Alumni Assn. (bd. dirs. 1983-84). Democrat. Roman Catholic. Home: 1511 Park Ave Parkersburg WV 26101 Office: Bureau of the Public Debt Rm 201 200 Third St Parkersburg WV 26102

MILLER, THOMAS EUGENE, lawyer, writer; b. Bryan, Tex., Jan. 4, 1929; s. Eugene Adam and Ella Lucille (Schroeder) M. BA, BS Tex. A&M U., 1950; MA, U. Tex., 1956, JD, 1966; postgrad. U. Houston, 1956-58, U Calif., 1983. Bar: Tex. 1966. Rsch. technician M.D. Anderson Hosp., Houston, 1956-58; claims examiner trainee Soc. Security Adminstrn., New Orleans, 1964; trademark examiner U.S. Patent and Trademark Office, Washington, 1966; editor Bancroft-Whitney Co., San Francisco, 1966-92. Author book under pseudonym, 1984. Contbg. mem. Dem. Nat. Com., 1981-96; mem. Celebrate Bryan Com. Mem. World Lit. Assn., World Inst. of Achievement, United Writers Assn. India; mem. ABA, Nat. Trust for Hist. Preservation, Tex. Bar Assn., Brazos County Bar Assn., African Wildlife Found., World Wildlife Fund, Internat. Platform Assn., Nat. Writers Assn., Scribes, Press Club, Commonwealth Club, Rotary Club, Tex. A&M U. Faculty Club, Phi Kappa Phi, Psi Chi, Phi Eta Sigma. Methodist. Home: 101 N Haswell Dr Bryan TX 77803-4848

MILLER, TRAVIS MILTON, association executive, accountant; b. Jasper, Tex., May 18, 1946; s. Clinton E. and Estelleen (Odom) M.; m. Mary E. Griffin, May 24, 1970; children: Tamera, Christianne. BS in Edn., Tex. A&M U., 1970; MS in Accountancy, U. Houston, 1976. CPA, Tex. Contr., then regional contr. Stewart Title Co., Houston, 1975-81; v.p. Griffin's Jewelers, Longview, Tex., 1981-89; contr. Hydrolex, Inc., Longview, 1989-91; pvt. practice, acctg., Arlington, Tex., 1991-94; exec. dir. Nat. Assn. of Women in Constrn. Edn. Found., Ft. Worth, 1994—. 1st lt. U.S. Army, 1970-74. Mem. Am. Soc. Assn. Execs. Methodist. Home: 744 Glenhaven Dr Hurst TX 76054 Office: NAWIC Edn Found 327 S Adams St Fort Worth TX 76104

MILLER, W. DENISE SAUNDERS, community health nurse; b. Camden, N.J., Feb. 28, 1954; d. John Francis and Mary Lou (Decker) Saunders; m. John R. Boharsik, Feb. 9, 1974 (div. 1984); m. Irvin Miller, Aug. 29, 1987. Diploma, Del. Valley Acad., 1973; AAS, Mercer County Community Coll., 1978; BSN, SUNY, Albany, 1984. Nurse clinician III Deborah Heart & Lung Ctr., Browns Mills, N.J., 1978-81; charge nurse CCU Zurbrugg Meml. Hosp., Riverside, N.J., 1981-82; clin. coord. ICU/CCU Zurbrugg Meml. Hosp., Willingboro, N.J., 1982-84; asst. head nurse MICU Fawcett Meml. Hosp., Port Charlotte, Fla., 1984-86; part-time staff nurse ICU Venice (Fla.) Hosp., 1986-89; paramed. ins. nurse examiner Port Charlotte, 1987-92; home care and nursing svcs. clin. dir. Nursefinders, Port Charlotte, 1992-94; dir. staff edn. Housecall Home Health, Sarasota, Fla., 1994-95; dir. staff devel. and tng. Housecall Home Health, Port Charlotte, Ft. Myers, Fla., 1995-96, clin. care mgr., 1996—; instr. intravenous therapy Deborah Heart & Lung Ctr., 1980; instr. BCLS Zurbrugg Meml. Hosp., 1981-84; ACLS provider Am. Heart Assn., Burlington County, N.J., 1979-84, BCLS instr., 1980-84; citizen advisor Sta. WBBH-TV, Fort Myers, Fla., 1987-89; pres. Charlotte County Home Health Network, 1993-94. Pres. S.W. Lupus Found. of Fla., Port Charlotte, 1992; active Arthritis Found., Juvenile Diabetes Found.; edn. chairperson Charlotte County Home Health Network, 1995-96; membership chairperson Charlotte Elder Affairs Network, 1993. Mem. ANA, Fla. Nurses Assn., VFW Aux., Am. Legion Aux., 42d Rainbow Divsn. Aux. Republican. Methodist. Home: 2411 Whisperlow St Port Charlotte FL 33948 Office: Housecall Home Health 2765 Tamiami Trail Port Charlotte FL 33952

MILLER, W. SCHUYLER, chemistry; b. East Orange, N.J., Mar. 15, 1910; s. William Benjamin and Anna Sabina (Hartman) M.; m. Margaret Louise Reeve, Sept. 7, 1935; children: Marnie Sabina Miller-Gutsell, W. Schuyler Miller, Jr. BS in Chemistry with hon., Lehigh U., 1930, MS, 1932; PhD, Syracuse U., 1936; DSc, Randolph-Macon Coll., 1990. Instr. in chemistry Bethany (W.Va.) Coll., 1936-40; asst. prof. to prof. Randolph-Macon Coll., Ashland, Va., 1940-75, prof. geology, 1940-92, chmn. Divsn. of Scis., 1947-74, head chem. dept., 1963-75, prof. emeritus of chemistry, 1975—; vis. prof. chemistry U. Richmond, Va., 1944-45, vis. prof. geology Mary Washington Coll. Fredericksburg, Va., 1956-59, vis. sr. rsch. assoc. Pa. State U., State College, 1962-63; chmn. chemistry sect. Va. Acad. Scis., 1951; dir. Va. Sci. Talent Search, 1956-58. Contbr. articles to profl. publs. Mem. Am. Chem. Soc. (trustee Va. sect. 1970-72, mem.-at-large exec. com. 1968-70), Torch Club of Richmond (pres. 1954-55), Sigma Xi, Phi Beta Kappa.

MILLER, WALTER EDWARD, physical scientist, researcher; b. St. Johns, Ariz., Oct. 15, 1936; s. Walter Edward and Geraldine Marie (Sides) M.; m. Emma Lee Nelson, June 10, 1960; children: Carol Lynn, Brenda Kay Miller Flowers, Melissa Joy Johnson Williams. BS in Natural Sci. magna cum laude, Bethany Nazarene Coll., 1958; postgrad., Vanderbilt U., 1958-59, U. Ala., 1964-69. Cert. math. tchr., Tenn. Aviator, flight leader USMC, 1959-64; math. tchr. Trevecca High Sch., Nashville, 1958-59; physicist Electromagnetics Lab U.S. Army Missile Command, Redstone Arsenal, Ala., 1964-68; rsch. physicist RD & E Ctr. Army Missile Command, Redstone Arsenal, Ala., 1968-90, supr., phys. scientist, 1991—; quality control chemist S.W. Fertilizer Mfg., Bethany, Okla., 1957-58; tech. cons. D-7 panel NATO, Brussels, 1972, 4 power working group, Paris, 1983; test dir. Joint U.S.-German Laser Expt., Graffenwoehr, 1979; prin. investigator Hypervelocity Missile/LOSAT, Advanced Sensors, U.S. Army Missile Command, Redstone Arsenal, 1984-94; mem. Tri-Svc. Working Group U.S. Experts on optical guidance, 1986—; mem. long term sci. study on combat ID, panel 1 NATO Def. Rsch. Group, 1994-95. Contbr. numerous articles to scholarly and profl. jours.; patentee 32 U.S. and 3 fgn. patents, 9 patents pending. Speaker, mem. Gideons Internat., 1980—; mem. governing bd. Mastin Lake Nazarene Ch., 1975—. Capt. USMC, 1960-64, Cuba. Recipient Svc. award Mastin Lake Nazarene Ch., 1985, Army-wide R & D award, 1968, 74, 83. Mem. Phi Delta Lambda. Office: US Army Missile Command AMSMI-RD-MG-OL Redstone Arsenal AL 35898

MILLER, WILLIAM FREDERICK, lawyer; b. Washington, July 18, 1946; s. Benjamin and Mary Frances (Zarbock) M.; m. Suzanne Lee Christmas, Dec. 21, 1975; children: Christopher McKenzie, Lindsay Noelle. BA, Coll. William & Mary, 1968, JD, 1974. Bar: Va. 1974, U.S. Dist. Ct. (ea. dist.) Va. 1974, U.S. Ct. Appeals (4th cir.) 1982. Ptnr. Loring & Miller, Williamsburg, Va., 1974-76, Rideout & Miller, Williamsburg, 1976-1990; sole practice William F. Miller, P.C., Williamsburg, 1990—; spl. justice 9th Jud. Dist., Williamsburg, 1976—; commr. in chancery Cir. Ct., Williamsburg, 1983—. Pres. Williamsburg unit Am. Cancer Soc., 1977; state pres. Va. JCI Senate, 1984-85; chpt. pres., state officer Va. Jaycees, 1972-82; trustee Coll. William & Mary Athletic Ednl. Found., 1986-90; trustee U.S. JCI Found., 1986, pres., 1989-90. Served to maj. U.S. Army, 1968-71. Decorated Bronze Star. Mem. ABA, Va. Bar Assn., Phi Delta Phi, Omicron Delta Kappa. Lutheran. Home: 417 Hempstead Ln Williamsburg VA 23188-1526 Office: 210 Parkway Dr Williamsburg VA 23185-4534

MILLER, WILLIAM LEE, JR., minister; b. Mammoth Spring, Ark., Dec. 27, 1926; s. William L. and Janie Katherine (Murrell) M.; m. Marion Evelyn O'Neal, Mar. 23, 1947 (div. 1976); children: Georgia Katherine Miller Beach, William Lee III; m. Judith Ann Bell, Nov. 28, 1977. AB, Phillips U., 1950, LittD, 1968; postgrad., U. Ark., 1951-52, Tex. Christian U., 1958, U. Ky., 1961; BD, Lexington Theol. Sem., 1961. Ordained to ministry Christian Ch. (Disciples of Christ), 1950. Pastor 1st Christian Ch., Rogers, Ark., 1952-59, Rogers Heights Christian Ch., Tulsa, 1961-62; v.p. Bd. Higher Edn., Indpls., 1962-68; pres. Bd. Higher Edn. Christian Ch. (Disciples of Christ), 1968-77; v.p. devel. Nat. City Christian Ch. Corp., Washington, 1977-82; upper Midwest regional min., pres. Christian Ch. (Disciples of Christ), Des Moines, 1982-93; pres. Miller Devel. Assocs.; dir. Christian Ch. Found., Indpls., 1968-77, 84-93; trustee Bethany Coll., W.Va., 1972-85, Culver Stockton

Coll., 1970-77, 82—, Tougaloo Coll., Jackson, Miss., 1970-76, Christian Theol. Sem., Indpls., 1987-94. Precinct committeeman Dem. Party, Indpls., 1968-72; mem. Reagan First Inaugural Religious Com.; bd. dris. St. Louis Christian Home, 1956-59; chmn. Coop. Coll. Registry, Washington, 1963-70; mem. Disciples of Christ Ch., Disciples Soc. for Faith & Reason; bd. dirs., exec. com. Christian Ch. D.C., N.C., 1995—. Mem. Disciples of Christ Hist. Soc., Coun. Christian Unity (exec. com. 1968-77), Nat. Evangelitic Assn. (bd. dirs. 1983-86), Am. Assn. Higher Edn., Masons, KT, Sigma Chi. Disciples of Christ and Presbyterian. Home: 113 Kellam Ct Manteo NC 27954 Office: Miller Devel Assocs PO Box 194 Manteo NC 27954-0194

MILLER, WILLIAM Q., airlines executive. V.p. inflight Southwest Airlines Co., Dallas. Office: SW Airlines Co Love Field Dr Dallas TX 75235

MILLER, ZELL BRYAN, governor; b. Young Harris, Ga., Feb. 24, 1932; s. Stephen Grady and Birdie (Bryan) M.; m. Shirley Carver, Jan. 14, 1954; children: Murphy Carver, Matthew Stephen. Student, Young Harris Coll.; AB, MA, U. Ga. Dir. Ga. Bd. Probation, 1965-66; dep. dir. Ga. Dept. Corrections, 1967-68; exec. sec. to gov. Ga., 1968-71; mem. State Bd. Pardons and Paroles, Atlanta, 1973-75; lt. gov. State of Ga., 1975-90, gov., 1990—; prof. polit. sci. and history U. Ga., Young Harris Coll., 1959-64. Author: The Mountains Within Me, Great Georgians, They Heard Georgia Singing. Mem. Ga. Senate, 1960-64; mayor Young Harris, 1959; exec. dir. Democratic Com. Ga., 1971-72; pres. Coun. State Govts., 1991—; vice chmn. So. Gov.'s Assn., 1991—; bd. dirs. Towns County Hosp. Authority. Served with USMC, 1953-56. Mem. Ga. Sch. Food Services Assn. (life), Ga. Peace Officers Assn. (life), Gridiron Soc. U. Ga., Blue Key, Lions Club. Methodist. Office: Office of Governor State Capitol Rm 203 Atlanta GA 30334

MILLERO, FRANK JOSEPH, JR., marine and physical chemistry educator; b. Greenville, Pa., Mar. 16, 1939; s. Frank Joseph and Jennie Elizabeth (Marta) M.; m. Judith Ann Busang, Oct. 2, 1965; children: Marta, Frank, Anthony. BS, Ohio State U., 1961; MS, Carnegie-Mellon U., 1964, PhD, 1965. Chemist, Nat. Bur. Standards, 1961; teaching and research asst. Carnegie-Tech., 1961-65; research chemist ESSO Research and Engring. Co., Linden, N.J., 1965-66; chemist Research Sci. U. Miami, 1966-68, asst. prof., 1968-69, prof. marine and phys. chemistry, 1969—, assoc. dean grad. studies, Rosenstiel Sch. Marine and Atmospheric Studies, 1987—, assoc. dean rsch., 1995—; vis. prof. U. Kiel, W.Ger., 1975, Water Research Inst., Rome, 1979-80, U. Goteborg, Sweden, 1986; mem. UNESCO Panel for Ocean Standards, 1976—, NSF Panel, 1973-75, 82, Ocean Sci. Bd., 1981-83; chmn. Gordon Conf., 1983; cons. in field. Coach Little League, Miami, Fla. Recipient Gold medal for Contbns. to Marine Chemistry U. Zagreb, Croatia, 1990, Gold medal award for Sci. Achievements Fla. Acad. Sci., 1992, Disting. Faculty Scholar award U. Miami, 1996. Mem. AAAS, Am. Chem. Soc., N.Y. Acad. Sci., Geochem. Soc., Omicron Delta Kappa, Sigma Xi (Prof. Yr. 1989). Democrat. Roman Catholic. Lodge: K.C. Contbr. numerous articles to profl. jours. Home: 7720 SW 90th Ave Miami FL 33173-3482 Office: Rosenstiel Sch Marine and Atmospheric Studies U Miami Miami FL 33149

MILLETT, RALPH LINWOOD, JR., retired newspaper editor; b. Memphis, Oct. 30, 1919; s. Ralph Linwood and Alice (Campbell) M.; m. Mary Virgina Smith, Dec. 10, 1944; children—Mary Jo, Alice Virginia, Jan Vasco, Ralph Linwood III. Student, U. Wyo., 1938-40; B.J., U. Mo., 1942. Copy reader, copy desk chief, news editor Knoxville (Tenn.) News-Sentinel, 1947-66, editor, 1967-84; ret., 1984. Served to lt. USNR, 1942-45. Mem. Am. Soc. Newspaper Editors, Sigma Chi, Sigma Delta Chi, Kappa Tau Alpha. Presbyterian. Club: Cherokee.

MILLIFF, KAREN CHAMPAGNE, secondary education educator; b. Pt. Arthur, Tex., July 18, 1951; d. Arthur J., Sr. and Dorothy M. (Richard) C.; m. Michael A. Milliff, Sr., July 4, 1975; children: Sean Michael, Ryan Montgomery, Mike Jr., Matt, Laura, Paul, Jeff. BA, Lamar Univ., Beaumont, Tex., 1973; MEd, Prairie View (Tex.), 1978. Tchr. Conroe (Tex.) Ind. Sch. Dist., 1973—. Mem. Tex. State Tchrs. Assn. (rep.). Roman Catholic. Office: Conroe HS Annex 3200 West Davis Conroe TX 77303

MILLIGAN, BRYCE, author, arts administrator; b. Dallas, Jan. 18, 1953; s. Joseph Bryce and Maxine (Carey)M.; m. Mary Guerrero, May 24, 1975; children: Michael, Brigid. BA, North Tex. State U., 1977; MA, U. Tex., 1980. Founding editor Pax: A Jour. for Peace, San Antonio, 1983-86, Vortex: A Critical Rev., San Antonio, 1986-90; book critic San Antonio Express News, 1983-87, San Antonio Light Newspaper, 1987-90; artist-in-residence San Antonio Ind. Sch. Dist., 1990-93; dir. lit. program Guadalupe Cultural Arts Ctr., San Antonio, 1986, 94—, adv., cons., 1987-91; pub., editor Wings Poetry Press, 1995—. Editor: (anthology) Daughters of the Fifth Sun, 1995; author: (book of poetry) Working the Stone, 1994, (novel) With the Wind Kevin Dolan, 1987, 2d edit. 1992; author over 1500 articles, 3 poetry collections, 5 plays, 3 novels, 1 short story collection. Ancient Order of Hibernians fellow, 1984; City of San Antonio Lit. grantee, 1994. Mem. PEN/Am. Ctr., Nat. Book Critics Cir. Democrat. Roman Catholic. Home: 627 E Guenther San Antonio TX 78210 Office: Guadalupe Cultural Arts Ctr 1300 Guadalupe St San Antonio TX 78207

MILLIGAN, JOHN MICHAEL, visual communication educator; b. Phila., Sept. 29, 1941; s. John C. and Ada (Yarnell) M.; m. Nancy W. Milligan, Jan. 25, 1964; children: Michael, Patrick, Sean. BS, U. Bridgeport, 1963; MS, Ill. Inst. of Tech., 1965. Graphic designer Corning (N.Y.) Glass Works, 1966-68; sr. designer IBM, White Plains, N.Y., 1968-73; dir. design Polaroid Corp., Cambridge, Mass., 1973-77; prin. John Milligan Design, St. Petersburg, Fla., 1977—; prof. visual comm. Syracuse (N.Y.) U., 1989—. Art dir. print manual competition, 1982-94, N.Am. Corp. Design Rev., 1994, Graphics Anns. Recipient Cert. of Excellence Comm. Arts, 1971-81, AICA, 1971-78; named Best of Last 25 Yrs. IDEA Mag., 1980. Mem. AAUP, Art Dir. Club of N.Y. (Cert. of Excellence 1974-84), Type Dirs. Club of N.Y.

MILLIGAN, ROBERT F., state agency administrator; b. Teaneck, N.J., Dec. 27, 1932; m. June; 4 children. BS in Engring., U.S. Naval Acad.; MBA, U. Rochester; postgrad., U. Md. Commd. USMC, advanced through grades to lt. gen.; comdr. pre-positioning ATO, ETO; comdr. U.S. Forces in Caribbean; comdg. gen. Fleet Marine Forces, Hawaii; ret., 1991; comptr. State of Fla., Tallahassee, 1994—; mem. Fla. Cabinet. Republican. Office: Office of Comptr Dept Banking and Fin Plaza Level Place, Capitol Bldg Tallahassee FL 32399*

MILLIKAN, CHARLES REAGAN, pastor; b. Houston, Feb. 8, 1946; s. Herman Charles and Eva Geraldine (Isbell) M.; m. Laura Nan Jackson, Aug. 7, 1970; children: Kevin, Kristin, Katy. BA, Southwestern U., 1968; ThM, So. Meth. U., 1971; D of Ministry, Drew U., 1984. Youth min. Marvin United Meth. Ch., Tyler, Tex., 1968-70; pastor Winona (Tex.) United Meth. Ch., 1970-72, Friendship United Meth., Porter, Tex., 1972-76, Wesley United Meth. Ch., Tyler, 1976-81; sr. pastor St. Peters United Meth. Ch., Katy, Tex., 1981-85, Seabrook (Tex.) United Meth. Ch., 1985-88, Pollard Meml. United Meth. Ch., Tyler, 1988-93, Moody Meml. 1st United Meth. Ch., Galveston Island, Tex., 1993—; bd. trustees Tex. Wesleyan U., Ft. Worth, 1992—, Southwestern U., Georgetown, Tex., 1995—, Permanent Endowment Fund-Moody Meml. 1st United Meth. Ch., Galveston Island, 1993—; bd. dirs. Meth. Retirement Cmtys., The Woodlands, Tex. Recipient David Knox Porter award Southwestern U., 1968, Bishops award Tex. Ann. Conf., 1995. Mem. Rotary, Galveston Country Club, Toastmasters (Outstanding Club Pres. dist. 25 1977, Disting. Toastmaster 1981). Office: Moody Meml 1st United Meth Ch 2803 53d St Galveston TX 77551

MILLIKAN, JAMES ROLENS, cleaning service executive, musician, composer; b. Beaumont, Tex., Jan. 15, 1950; s. George Lee and Gertrude Louise (Mann) M.; m. Dorothy Jane Albright, Apr. 22, 1989. BFA, U. Houston, 1968; MFA, Juilliard Sch., 1971. Mgr., ptnr. Edward, Bankers & Co., Houston, 1971-73; prop. gen. Max M. Kaplan Properties, San Antonio, 1973-75; gen. bldg. mgr. Property Mgmt. Systems, Atlanta, 1975-79; dir. real estate Sun Life Group Am., Atlanta, 1979-81; prin. The Millikan Cos., Atlanta, 1981-85, J.R. & Co., Atlanta, 1985-87; sr. v.p., gen. mgr. east coast Nat. Cleaning Contractors, Inc., Atlanta, 1987-93; prin., pres. Master Bldg. Cleaners Inc., Atlanta, 1993—; cons., Sun Life Group Am., 1982-84, McFaddin Ventures, Houston, 1983-84. Composer: Crystal Blue Persuasion (gold record 1969), Crimson & Clover (gold record 1969), Mony Mony (gold record 1969), I Love You More Today than Yesterday (gold record 1970), 1900 Yesterday (gold record 1971), others; instrumentalist for orchs. of Duke Ellington, Count Basie, Buddy Rich, Woody Herman and Glenn Miller, 1965-68; drummer, arranger, conductor for recording artist Petula Clark, 1968-71, leader J.R. and Co., Jazz Ensemble. Founder, pres., St. Luke's Econ. Devel. Corp., Atlanta, 1979, bd. dirs.; bd. dirs. St. Jude's House, Atlanta, 1984, Am. Suicide Found., chmn. Southeastern Divsn. Nat. Bd. Mem. Am. Suicide Found.; mem. Home Bldg. with Habitat for Humanity. With U.S. Army, 1970-76. Mem. Bldg. Owners and Mgrs. Atlanta, Am. Mktg. Assn., Am. Suicide Found. (bd. dirs.), Bldg. Svc. Contractors Assn. Internat. Democrat. Episcopalian. Home: 4600 Runnemede Rd NW Atlanta GA 30327-3461 Office: Master Bldg Cleaners Inc 4600 Runnemede Rd NW Atlanta GA 30327-3461

MILLIKAN, MARSHALL ROBERT, software engineer; b. Columbia, Mo., June 20, 1962; s. Larry Edward and Jeanine Dorothy (Johnson) M.; m. Pamela Kay Howington, May 25, 1991; children: Mattie Alyssa, Ryan Robert. BS in Computer Sci., Tulane U., 1987; MBA, U. Ala., Birmingham, 1995. Asst. staff mgr. South Cen. Bell Tel. Co., New Orleans, 1987-90; software engr. BellSouth Info. Systems, Birmingham, 1990-93; software engr., staff analyst BellSouth Telecomm. Inc., 1993-96; project leader NCR Corp., Duluth, Ga., 1996—. Mem. IEEE, Project Mgmt. Inst. Home: 51 Grand Ave Suwanee GA 30174 Office: NCR Corp 2651 Satellite Blvd Duluth GA 30136

MILLIKEN, ROGER, textile company executive; b. N.Y.C., Oct. 24, 1915; s. Gerrish and Agnes (Gayley) M.; m. Justine V. R. Hooper, June 5, 1948; children: Justine, Nancy, Roger, David, Weston. Student, Groton Sch., 1929-33; A.B., Yale U., 1937; LL.D. (hon.), Wofford Coll., Rose-Hulman Inst. Tech., Phila. Coll. Textiles and Sci., Brenau Coll., The Citadel; D. Textile Industry (hon.), Clemson U.; D.H.L. (hon.), Converse Coll. CEO Milliken & Co., N.Y.C., 1947-83, chmn., chief exec. officer, 1983—; bd. dirs. Merc. Stores Co.; chmn. bd. Inst. Textile Tech., 1948—; bd. dirs. Am. Textile Mfrs. Inst., S.C. Textile Mfrs. Assn. Chmn. Greenville-Spartanburg Airport Commn.; trustee Wofford Coll., S.C. Found. Ind. Coll. Mem. Bus. Council, Textile Inst. (Eng.) (companion mem.). Clubs: Union League, Links, Augusta Nat. Golf, Yeamans Hall. Office: Milliken & Co PO Box 3167 Spartanburg SC 29304

MILLMAN, BARRY A., editor-in-chief; b. N.Y.C., July 16, 1957; s. Joseph and Shirley Millman; m. Deborah Robbins, 1992. Editor-in-chief Good Times Mag., N.Y.C., 1979-84; journalist Greenville (S.C.) News, 1984-87, Tampa (Fla.) Tribune, 1987-90, Bristol (Conn.) Press, 1990-91; editor-in-chief The Chronicle, Sarasota, Fla., 1991—. Contbr. articles to profl. and popular publs. Recipient Best Newspaper award Coun. Jewish Fedns. Mem. Am. Jewish Press Assn. (Best Comty. Spl. Sect.), Nat. Newspaper Assn., Nat. Press Club.

MILLNER, THOMAS, manufacturing and holding company executive. P-res. The Pilliod Cabinet Co., High Point, N.C., Pilliod Holding Co., Swanton, Ohio, Remington Arms Co., Madison, WI. Office: Remington Arms Co. 870 Remington Dr PO Box 700 Madison NC 27025-0700*

MILLS, AGNES EUNICE KARLIN, artist, printmaker, sculptor; b. N.Y.C., Apr. 2, 1915; d. Herman Karlin and Celia (Ducoffe) Karlin; m. Saul Mills, May 10, 1910 (dec. Nov. 1993); children: Karen, Marghe Mills Thysen. Grad., Cooper Union Art Sch., N.Y.C., 1938; BFA, Pratt Inst., 1975; student, NYU. One-woman shows include Carus Gallery, N.Y.C., Unitarian Soc., Manhasset, N.Y., Harbor Gallery, Cold Spring Harbor, N.Y., North Truro Art Gallery, Cape Cod, Mass., Alfredo Valente Gallery, N.Y.C., Robbins Gallery, East Orange, N.J., Nuance Galleries, Tampa, Friends of Tampa Ballet, Graphic Eye Coop Gallery, Pt. Washington, N.Y., City Ctr. Gallery, N.Y.C., Lincoln Ctr. Art Gallery, N.Y.C., North Shore Cmty. Arts Ctr., Great Neck, N.Y., Delray Beach Works in Progress Gallery, Boca Raton Cmty. Ctr., Palm Beach Pub. Libr.; exhibited in group shows at Alfredo Valente Gallery, N.Y.C., Audubon Soc., N.Y.C., Bowdoin Coll. Mus. Art, Brunswick, Maine, Brandeis U., Waltham, Mass., Bklyn. Mus. Art, Brown U., Providence, Butler Inst. Am. Art, Youngstown, Ohio, Colgate U. Libr., Hamilton, N.Y., Cornell U., Ithaca, N.Y., East Hampton (N.Y.) Guild Artists, Gallery K, Woodstock, N.Y., Graphic Eye Coop Gallery, Port Washington, N.Y., Heckscher Mus., Huntington, N.Y., Hunterdon County Mus., Clinton, N.J., Joan Avnet Gallery, Great Neck, N.Y., Lincoln Ctr. Libr. Performing Arts, N.Y.C., Madison Gallery, N.Y.C., Boca Raton City Hall, Boca Raton Cmty. Ctr., Boca Raton Libr.; represented in permanent collections at Boca Raton Mus. Art, Nat. Women in the Arts Mus. Home: Ste L 9 144 8903 Glades Rd Boca Raton FL 33434-4019 Studio: 9763 Majorca Pl Boca Raton FL 33434-3713

MILLS, ANDY RAY, computer programmer; b. Lebanon, Mo., Mar. 2, 1967; s. Willard and Patsie Marie (Ford) M. BS, U. Mo.-Rolla, 1989. Sr. assoc. programmer IBM, Austin, Tex., 1989—. Mem. IEEE-Computer Sci., Assn. Computing Machinery. Home: PO Box 81363 Austin TX 78708-1363

MILLS, BELEN COLLANTES, early childhood education educator; s. Ricardo and Epifania (Tomines) C.; children: Belinda Mills Keiser, Roger A. BSE, Leyte Normal Coll., Tacloban, Leyte, Philippines, 1954; MS in Edn., Ind. U., 1955, EdD, 1967. Prof. early childhood edn. Fla. State U., Tallahassee; early childhood cons. to ednl. agys. and orgns. Author books on early childhood edn. and acad. readiness computer programs; contbr. articles to profl.jours. Smith-Mundt Fulbright scholar. Mem. Nat. Assn. for the Edn. of Young Children, Nat. Assn. of Early Childhood Tchr. Edn., World Coun. for Curriculum and Instruction, Assn. of Childhood Edn. Internat. Home: PO Box 20023 Tallahassee FL 32316-0023

MILLS, BOBBY EUGENE, sociologist, educator; b. Spartanburg, S.C., Mar. 7, 1941; s. Clarence and Gladys (Brewton) M.; m. Larnita B. Mills, Jan. 15, 1977; children: Daryl, Karen, Kelly. BS in Edn., Barber-Scotia Coll., 1963; BD in Theology, Colgate-Rochester Div., 1966; MA in Sociology, U. Rochester, 1968; PhD in Sociology, Syracuse U., 1975. Dean of instrn. Monroe C.C. Urban Ctr., Rochester, 1968-69; instr. Syracuse (N.Y.) U., 1969-72; prof. Govs. State U., University Park, Ill., 1972-77; assoc. prof. Tex. So. U., Houston, 1977-79, rsch. assoc. inst. rsch., 1988-93, asst. dir. inst. rsch., 1993—; exec. dir. Minority Rep. Ctr., Houston, 1979-88. Mem. Am. Sociol. Assn., Tex. Assn. Inst. Rsch., So. Assn. Inst. Rsch. Baptist. Home: 2206 Ashmont Ct Missouri City TX 77489 Office: Tex So Univ 3100 Cleburne St Houston TX 77004

MILLS, BRUCE RANDALL, infosystems and micro computer specialist; b. Warren, Ark., Nov. 2, 1963; s. Fred Adam and Meta Lanette (Calvert) M.; m. Betty Ann Marshall, May 23, 1985; children: Anita, Timothy, Yovonnie, Donovan. BBA, So. Ark. U., 1985. Programmer Jack Tyler Engring. Co., Little Rock, Ark., 1986-88, Blue Cross/ Blue Shield, Little Rock, 1988—; auditor Holiday Inns Am., 1985; cons. in field. V.p. Young Reps., 1983. Office: Blue Cross/Blue Shield 6th And Gaines St Little Rock AR 72203

MILLS, CANDY, magazine publisher; b. Schenectady, N.Y., Apr. 26, 1964; d. Earl T. and Delois Mills; m. Gabe Grosz, July 27, 1982; children: Gabriela, Laszlo. BS in Econs., Union Coll., 1991. Pub./editor Interrace Publs., Atlanta, 1989—. Editor, author: (mag.) Black Child, Child of Colors, and Interrace Mags., 1989—. Office: Interrace Publs 2870 Peachtree Rd # 264 Atlanta GA 30305

MILLS, CAROL ELAINE, sales representative; b. Mt. Pleasant, Iowa, Oct. 15, 1942; d. David Thomas and Grace Zella (Clark) Williams; m. Robert Loten Mills, June 16, 1963; children: Jeffrey Todd, Timothy Robert. Cert., Am. Inst. Bus., 1963. Legal asst. Gartin Law Office, Mt. Pleasant, 1973-78; sales rep. Woline Realtors, Mt. Pleasant, 1978-81; sec. Gen. Homes, Houston, 1981-82; sales rep. Henry S. Miller Realtors, Houston, 1982-85; customer svc. rep. 3M, Houston, 1985-90, sales rep., 1990—. Vol. Houston Livestock Show and Rodeo, 1989—, lifetime mem.; ladies patron com. Consular Ball, Houston, 1991-92; pub. rels. com. Houston Interam. C. of C., 1991-92; bus. rels. com. Greater Houston Partnership, 1991-92, mem. trade missions subcom., world trade divsn., 1992-93; mem. Houston/Grampian Assn., 1993—, bd. dirs., 1996—. Mem. Soc. of Profl. Women in Petroleum. Republican. Methodist. Home: 1767 Roanwood Ct Houston TX 77090 Office: 3M Co 2525 North Loop W Ste 100 Houston TX 77008-1038

MILLS, CHARLES G., photography company executive; b. 1935; married. Grad., Auburn U., 1960. With Olan Mills, Inc., Chattanooga, Tenn., 1962—, now vice chmn., also bd. dirs. Served with U.S. Army, 1962-63. Office: Olan Mills Inc 4325 Amnicola Hwy Chattanooga TN 37406-1014 also: PO Box 23456 Chattanooga TN 37422

MILLS, DAVID REEVE, insurance agent, commissioner; b. Lincoln, Nebr., Aug. 27, 1938; s. James Forrest and Dorothy (Reeve) M.; m. Patricia Kay Mahoney, June 11, 1960; children: Craig, Scott. BA, Nebr. Wesleyan U., 1961; MEd, U. Nebr., 1964. Tchr. York (Nebr.) Pub. Schs., 1960-63; sales rep. IBM, Lincoln, 1964-70; mktg. mgr. IBM, St. Paul, 1970-73; broker, owner Woodbury (Minn.) Realty Co., 1973-83; dist. rep. Aid Assn. for Lutherans, Sarasota, Fla., 1983-87; dist. mgr. Aid Assn. for Lutherans in So. Fla., Sarasota, 1985-87; prin. David R. Mills Ins. Agy., Sarasota, 1987—. County commr. Sarasota Bd. County Commr., 1990—; chmn. Sarasota County Econ. Devel. Bd., 1991—, Sarasota County Tourist Development Coun., 1991—, Met. Planning Orgn., 1991—, Sarasota County Transp. Disadvantaged Coord. Bd., 1992—; com. mem. Rep. Exec. Com., Sarasota, 1994; exec. com. Suncoast Offshore Grand Prix; task force Sarasota Bradenton Airport Air Svc.; bd. dirs. Sarasota Cmty. Blood Bank, Sarasota French Film Festival; active Big Brothers/Big Sisters; past chmn. Boy Scouts Am.; ambassador Sahib Shrine Temple. With USNG, 1957-63. Mem. Fla. Assn. Counties (bd. dirs. 1992—), Sarasota Sister Cities Assn., Downtown Assn., Elks, Rotary (bd. dirs.). Republican. Presbyterian. Office: Bd County Commrs 1660 Ringling Blvd Sarasota FL 34236

MILLS, EDWARD WARREN, corporation executive, lawyer; b. N.Y.C., Apr. 7, 1941; m. Maria Parascandolo, Sept. 19, 1971; children: Edward Warren, Foy Fitzhugh, Joseph V.O. BS, Washington and Lee U., 1962; MBA, Hofstra U., 1974; JD, N.Y. Law Sch., 1977. Bar: N.Y. 1978. Acct., Wasserman & Taten, N.Y.C., 1962-69; exec. v.p. L.H. Keller, Inc. and Hugo P. Keller, Inc., N.Y.C., 1969-74; pres. Gen. Ruby & Sapphire Co., 1974-94, Qualistar Corp., 1974-94, EWM Gen. Corp., 1993—; sole practice, N.Y.C., 1978—. Mem. ABA, N.Y. State Bar Assn., D.C. Bar Assn. Home: 10748 Melba Ct New Port Richey FL 34654-5231 Office: 60 E 42nd St New York NY 10165

MILLS, ELIZABETH SHOWN, genealogical editor; b. Cleve., Miss., Dec. 29, 1944; d. Floyd Finley Shown and Elizabeth Thulmar (Jeffcoat) Carver; m. Gary Bernard Mills, Apr. 15, 1963; children: Clayton Bernard, Donna Rachal, Daniel Garland. BA, U. Ala., 1980. Cert. genealogist. Profl. geneal., writer, 1972-86; editor Nat. Geneal. Soc., Arlington, Va., 1987—; faculty Samford U. Inst. of Genealogy and Hist. Rsch., Birmingham, Ala., 1980-96, trustee Assn. for Promotion of Scholarship in Genealogy, N.Y., 1984-90, contract dir., cons. U. Ala., 1985-92, faculty Nat. Inst. of Geneal. Rsch., 1985-96. Author, editor, translator Cane River Creole Series, 6 vols.; contbr. articles to profl. jours. Mem. adv. bd. Assn. for Preservation of Historic Natchitoches, La., 1972-80, bd. mem. Friends of La. State Archives, Baton Rouge, 1976-77, Tuscaloosa (Ala.) Preservation Soc., 1984-85, chair Hist. Records Task Force Ala. State Archives, Montgomery, 1984-85; trustee Nat. Bd. Certification Genealogists, 1984-89, v.p., 1989-94, pres., 1994—. Named Outstanding Young Women of Am. Jaycees, Gadsden, 1976, Outstanding Alumna award U. Ala. New Coll., Tuscaloosa, 1990. Fellow Am. Soc. of Geneal. (sec. 1992-95, v.p. 1995—), Nat. Geneal. Soc., Utah Geneal. Assn.; mem. Assn. of Profl. Geneal. (Smallwood Svc. award, 1989),. Republican. Roman Catholic. Home: 1732 Ridgedale Dr Tuscaloosa AL 35406-1942 Office: Nat Geneal Soc 4527 17th St N Arlington VA 22207-2399

MILLS, GORDON CANDEE, biochemist educator; b. Fallon, Nev., Feb. 13, 1924; s. Percy Edward and Ruth Eliza (Candee) M.; m. Mary Jane Medlin, June 13, 1947; children: David Gordon, John Steven, Melinda Jane. BS in Chemistry, U. Nev., Reno, 1946; MS, U. Mich., 1948, PhD, 1951. Rsch. assoc. U. Tenn. Med. Sch., Memphis, 1950-55; asst. prof., assoc. prof. U. Tex., Galveston, 1955-68, prof., 1968—. Contbr. numerous articles to profl. jours. Fellow Am. Sci. Affiliation; mem. Am. Soc. Biochemistry and Molecular Biology, Am. Chem. Soc., Christian Med. and Dental Soc., Sigma Xi (pres. 1972-73, John Sinclair award 1987). Presbyterian. Home: 118 Barracuda Ave Galveston TX 77550-3221 Office: Univ Tex Med Br Galveston TX 77555

MILLS, JERRY WOODROW, lawyer; b. Springfield, Mo., July 17, 1940; s. Woodrow Wilson and Billie Louise M.; m. Marion Cargile, Mar. 27, 1964; children: Eric E., Brendon W. BSEE, Tex. A&M U., 1963; JD, Georgetown U., 1967. Bar: Tex. 1967, U.S. Patent Office 1967. Ptnr. Richards, Harris & Hubbard, Dallas, 1970-82, Baker, Mills & Glast, Dallas, 1982-90; sr. ptnr. Baker & Botts, Dallas, 1990—; adj. prof. So. Meth. U. Law Sch., 1994—. Bd. dirs. Dallas Legal Svcs. Project, 1972-75. Fellow Tex. Bar, Dallas Bar; mem. ABA, Tex. State Jr. Bar Assn. (treas. 1975, dir.), Dallas Jr. Bar Assn. (pres. 1971, Outstanding Young Lawyer award 1975), Dallas Bar Assn. (bd. dirs. 1983-85). Methodist. Home: 5316 Montrose Dr Dallas TX 75209 Office: Baker & Botts 800 Trammell Crow Ctr 2001 Ross Ave Dallas TX 75201-8001

MILLS, KATHRYN OLIVER, French language educator; b. San Francisco, Aug. 6, 1962; d. Raymond Davies and Mary Ann (McPherson) O.; m. Wilmer Hastings Mills, Dec. 30, 1995. BA, U. Va., 1984; BA, MA, Oxford (Eng.) U., 1987; PhD, Yale U., 1995. Lectr. U. Tex.-Pan Am., McAllen, 1994-95, Belmont U., Nashville, 1995; vis. asst. prof. Vanderbilt U., Nashville, 1996; asst. to editor Yale French Studies, New Haven, 1989-91; v.p. McAllen French Club, 1994-95. Author of poetry. Vol. Soup Kitchen, New Haven, 1990-93; tutor Literary Vols., New Haven, 1993-94. Mem. Phi Beta Kappa. Episcopalian. Home: PO Box 657 Sewanee TN 37375

MILLS, OLAN, II, photography company executive; b. 1930; married. G-rad., Princeton U., 1952. With Olan Mills, Inc., Chattanooga, 1950—, now chmn., sec., also bd. dirs. Office: Olan Mills Inc PO Box 23456 Chattanooga TN 37422 also: 4325 Amnicola Hwy Chattanooga TN 37406-1014

MILLS, ROBERT THEO, denominational executive minister; b. Miami, June 23, 1949; s. James Theo and Dorothy Elizabeth (Sands) M.; m. Lynne Marlene Davis, April 27, 1984; children: Emily Elizabeth Mills, Brittney Lynne Mills, Jordan Wayne Mills. BA, William Carey Coll., Hattiesburg, Miss., 1971; MDiv, Midwestern Baptist Theological Seminary, Kansas City, Mo., 1974, DMin, 1980. Coord. of weekday ministries Home Mission Bd., Kansas City, Mo., 1971-72, 1972-74; coord. of weekday ministries Kansas City (Kans.) Baptist Assn., 1974-76, dir. Christian Social Ministries, 1976-79; pastor First Baptist Church of Bethel, Kansas City, 1978-81; asst. dir. Mission Svc. Corps. Home Mission Bd., Atlanta, 1981-87, dir. Mission Svc. Corps., 1987—; coord. supervision tng. Home Mission Bd., Atlanta, 1982-96, coord. supervision tng. and leadership devel., 1995—. Author: Christian Social Ministries Interns, Volunteers A Strategy for the 21st Century. Mem. bd. dirs. Mid-America Health Systems Agy., Kansas City, Mo., 1977-79; cmty. cons. Wyanootte County Juvenile Court, Kansas City, Kans., 1976-81; supervisor festival entertainment Olympic Village Atlanta Com. on the Olympic Games, 1996—. Mem. ASTD, Am. Mgmt. Assn., Am. Acad. of Crisis Interveners, Religious Conf. Mgmt. Assn. So. Baptist Convention. Home: 1838 American Way Lawrenceville GA 30243 Office: Home Mission Bd 4200 North Point Parkway Alpharetta GA 30202

MILLS, ROGER MARION, cardiologist; b. Athens, Ohio, Jan. 23, 1943; s. Roger Marion Sr. and Adrienne Ellen (McGuire) M.; m. Susan Brownell (div. Sept. 1987); children: David McGuire, Andrew Loomis; m. Diane Evans, Dec. 19, 1987. BA, Amherst (Mass.) Coll., 1964; MD, U. Pa., 1968. Diplomate Am. Bd. Internal Medicine; lic. pilot. Intern, then resident in internal medicine Hosp. U. of Pa., Phila., 1968-71; rsch. fellow in cardiology Harvard Med. Sch. Peter Bent Brigham Hosp., Boston, 1973-75; cardiologist, dir. coronary care unit Worcester (Mass.) Meml. Hosp., 1975-87, dir. catherization lab., acting chief of cardiology, 1985-87; assoc. prof. U. Mass. Med. Sch., Worcester, 1975-87; dir. clin. cardiology, assoc. prof. medicine Boston U. Hosp., 1987-90; med. dir. cardiac transplant program, dir. clin. cardiology Shands Hosp. at U. Fla., Gainesville, 1990—, co-chair Transplant Ctr.,

1992—; assoc. prof. Coll. Medicine U. Fla., Gainesville, 1990-95, prof., 1995—; treas. med. staff Worcester Meml. Hosp., 1978-82; pres. med. staff U. Mass. Med. Ctr., Worcester, 1983-84; contbr. articles to profl. jours. Bd. dirs. Home for Aged Women, Worcester, 1980-87. Lt. comdr. USNR, 1971-73. Fellow ACP, Am. Coll. Cardiology, Coun. on Clin. Cardiology, Am. Heart Assn. (bd. dirs. Fla. affiliate), Soc. for Cardiac Angiography and Intervention. Republican. Episcopalian. Office: U Fla Coll Medicine Box 100277 JHMHSC 1600 SW Archer Rd Gainesville FL 32610

MILLS, ROGER WAYNE, nurse administrator; b. Crawfordsville, Ind., Oct. 28, 1947; s. Frederick Wilson and Etta-Marie (Hightower) M. ASN, Fla. Jr. Coll., 1972. RN, Fla. Nursing supervisor Meth. Hosp., Jacksonville, Fla., 1972-78; nursing home adminstr. Beverly Enterprises, Fla., Ga., 1978-84; nursing supervisor Grady Meml. Hosp., Atlanta, 1984-86; ER, operating room staff nurse Lower Keys Health Sys., Key West, Fla., 1986-95; adminstr. Island Healthcare, Key West, Fla., 1995-96; adj. faculty EMT program Fla. Keys C.C.; home health nurse Island Health Care, Key West, 1994-95, adminstr.; adv. bd. Fla. Jr. Coll., Jacksonville, 1980-81. Served in USN, 1965-69, Vietnam. Recipient 2 Purple Hearts USN, 1967, Cross of Gallantry Govt. S. Vietnam, 1967. Mem. Fla. Nurses Assn. Democrat. Home: 724 Simonton St Key West FL 33040

MILLS, SAMUEL DAVIS, JR., professional football player; b. Neptune, N.J., June 3, 1959. Student, Montclair State U. With Cleve. Browns, 1981, Toronto Argonauts, CFL, 1982, Phila. Stars, USFL, 1982; linebacker New Orleans Saints, 1986-95, Carolina Panthers, 1995—. Named USFL All-Star Team Inside Linebacker by Sporting News, 1983, 85, NFL All-Pro Team Inside Linebacker by Sporting News, 1991-92. Office: Carolina Panthers 800 S Mint St Charlotte NC 28202-1502*

MILLS, SOPHIE JANE VICTORIA, classics educator; b. London, June 20, 1964; came to U.S., 1994; d. Roger Edwin Stuart and Kathleen Barbara (Hayward) M. BA, Oxford U., 1987, MA, 1991, PhD, 1993. Lectr. in classics Oxford U., England, 1990-94; asst. prof. classics U. N.C., Asheville, 1994—; chmn. classics dept. U. N.C., 1995—. Author: Theseus, Tragedy, The Athenian Empire, 1997. Mem. Am. Philol. Assn., Soc. for Promotion of Hellenic Studies. Home: 14 Cedarwood Dr Asheville NC 28803 Office: U NC 1 Univ Heights Asheville NC 28804-3299

MILLS, STEPHEN NATHANIEL, computer software company executive; b. Boston, Apr. 18, 1942; s. Nathaniel and Alice Mary (Lerner) M.; m. Lorraine Hill Ransom, Mar. 27, 1966 (div. Apr. 1993); children: Nathaniel Stephen, George Robert, Beman Ransom (dec.), Priscilla Alden; m. Patricia Punch Meadows, Mar. 5, 1994 (div. Dec. 1995); stepchildren: James Christopher, Katherine Alexandra. Student, MIT, 1959-61; BS, Regents Coll., 1989. Programmer analyst Cambridge (Mass.) Computer Assocs., 1966-68; sr. programmer, analyst Computer Fulfillment, Winchester, Mass., 1968-69; pres. Software Engring., Inc., Norton, Mass., 1969-73; product devel. mgr. Pecan Software Corp., Roswell, Ga., 1987-88; pres. Software Eclectics, Inc., Alpharetta, Ga., 1988—; cons. in field; mem. Lang. Test Mgmt. Coun., Inst. Cert. Computer Profls., Des Plaines, Ill., 1994—; adj. faculty Gwinnett Tech. Inst., Lawrenceville, Ga., 1992, Chattahoochee Tech. Inst., Marietta, Ga., 1992. Sgt. USAR, 1964-70. Mem. IEEE Computer Soc., Southeastern Software Assn., Data Processing Mgmt. Assn. (Atlanta bd. dirs. 1992-93), Assn. Computing Machinery, Mensa (Boston chpt. pres. 1967-68, Little Rock newsletter editor 1978). Office: Software Eclectics Inc Ste 401 10945 State Bridge Rd Alpharetta GA 30202-5676

MILLS, WILLIAM OLIVER, III, international tax accountant, consultant; b. Del Rio, Tex., Oct. 24, 1951; s. William Oliver M. Jr. and Betty Lou Winslow; m. Susan Elizabeth Miller, Sept. 6, 1986. BBA, U. Tex., 1975; postgrad., Am. U. CPA, Tex. Pres. Children of the Ams., Dallas, 1973-82; CEO W.O. Mills III P.C., Dallas, 1982—. Fin. chmn. Wilkinson Ctr., Dallas, Dumbarton Ch., Washington. Mem. AICPA, Tex. Soc. CPAs. Methodist. Office: W O Mills III PC PO Box 140165 Dallas TX 75214

MILNES, HAROLD WILLIS, mathematician, physicist; b. Detroit, June 9, 1925; s. Godfrey Milnes and Lottie Victoria Middlebrook. MA, Wayne State U., 1952, PhD, 1955. Rsch. scientist A GM Corp., Detroit, 1956-61; chief tech. staff Land-Air Inc., Oxnard, Calif., 1962-63; sect. leader Burroughs Corp., Detroit, 1963-64; group leader Boeing Corp., Seattle, 1964-67; chief scientist Lockheed Electronics, Houston, 1967; prof. maths. Tex. Tech. U., Lubbock, 1967-73; self employed, 1973-85. Editor: Industrial Mathematics, Detroit, 1957-59, Toth-Maatian Rev., Lubbock, 1981-94; contbr. articles to profl. jours.; translator (book by W. Hauff) A Heart of Stone. Recipient Top award Assn. for Gravitational Rsch., 1987. Libertarian. Mem. Soc. of Friends. Home: 3101 20th St Lubbock TX 79410

MILOY, LEATHA FAYE, university program director; b. Marlin, Tex., Mar. 12, 1936; d. J. D. and Leola Hazel (Rhudy) Hill; m. John Miloy, June 20, 1960; children: Tyler Hill, David Reed, Nancy Lee. BA, Sam Houston State U., 1957; MS, Tex. A&M U., 1967, PhD, 1978. Dir. pub. affairs Gulf Univs. Rsch. Corp., College Station, Tex., 1966-69; asst. dir. Ctr. for Marine Resources Tex. A&M U., College Station, 1974-76, dir. edn. svcs., 1974-78; dir. info. and spl. svcs. Tex. Woman's U., Denton, 1978-79; asst. v.p. univ. advancement S.W. Tex. State U., San Marcos, 1979-83, asst. to pres., 1983-84, v.p. student and instl. rels., 1984-90, v.p. univ. advancement, 1990-93, dir. capital campaign, 1993—; vis. lectr. humanities and sea U. Va., 1972-73; cons. Office Tech. Assessment, Washington, 1976-86, Tex. A&M U., Galveston, 1979-82, Bemidji State U., Glassboro State Coll., 1984; mem. Task Force on Edn. and Pub. Interest, 1987-88. Editor: The Ocean From Space, 1969; author, editor Sea Grant 70's, 1970-79 (Sea Grant award 1973-74); contbr. articles to profl. jours. Ad hoc mem. Marine Resources Coun. Tex., Austin, 1971-72, Tex. Energy Adv. Coun., 19174-75; chmn. United Way, Bryan, Tex., 1976; com. mem. various local elections, 1974-78. NSF grantee, 1970-78; recipient Marine Resources Info. award NSF, 1969-71, Tex. Energy Info. award Gov.'s Office, 1974-75, Tex. Water Info. award Dept. Interior, 1977-79. Mem. Nat. Soc. Fundraising Execs., Coun. for the Advancement and Support Edn. (bd. dirs. 1979-81), Coun. Student Svcs. (v.p. Tex. 1988-90). Home: PO Box 712 Buchanan Dam TX 78609-0712 Office: SW Tex State U 601 University Dr San Marcos TX 78666-4684

MILTNER, REBECCA SUZANNE, women's health nurse, pediatrics nurse; b. Memphis, May 1, 1958; d. V. Patrick and Peggy Sue (Lamb) Ellis; m. Kristopher F. Miltner, June 19, 1982; children: Mary Frances, Kathleen Elizabeth, Daniel Patrick. BSN summa cum laude, Med. Coll. Ga., 1982; MS in Nursing, U. Wis., 1990; postgrad., U. Md., Balt., 1996—. Army officer ICU nursery U.S. Army Corps, El Paso, Tex.; staff nurse obstetrics Ft. Atkinson (Wis.) Meml. Hosp.; staff nurse labor and delivery Sinai Samaritan Med. Ctr., Milw., U. Kans. Med. Ctr., Kansas City, Kans., 1992; staff nurse neonatal ICU Humana Hosp., Overland Park, Kans., 1991-92; maternal-child clin. nurse specialist Ga. Bapt. Med. Ctr., Atlanta, 1992, L&D/perinatal nurse mgr., 1992-96. Capt. U.S. Army, 1982-88. Mem. AWHONN (cert., coord. Atlanta chpt. 1995-96), Sigma Theta Tau.

MILTON, MARCIA E., critical care nurse; b. Waycross, Ga., Mar. 8, 1949; d. Charles and Mary Margaret Milton. Diploma, St. Vincent's Hosp. Sch. Nsg., 1971; BS in Nursing, U. Fla., 1976; MSN, Valdosta State U., 1996. RN, Ga. Staff nurse operating room St. Vincent's Med. Ctr., Jacksonville, Fla.; instr. practical nursing Waycross (Ga.)-Ware Area Vo-Tech Sch.; staff nurse ICU Satilla Regional Med. Ctr., Waycross, nurse mgr. med.-surg. nursing. Mem. Acad. Med.-Surg. Nursing, Sigma Theta Tau.

MIMS, M. DOUGLAS, banker; b. 1932; married;. Pres. City Bank of Childersburg, Ala., 1954-81; chmn. bd. dirs., CEO Troy (Ala.) Bank & Trust Co., 1982—. Office: Troy Bank & Trust Co PO Box 967 Troy AL 36081

MIMS, NANCY GRIFFIN, English language educator; b. Chgo., Mar. 11, 1943; d. Walter Thomas and Mary Elizabeth (Lax) Griffin; m. Kenneth Lee Mims, May 5, 1962; children: Erron Scott, Garrett Todd. BA, Fla. Atlantic U., 1978, MEd, 1981, EdS, 1984, EdD, 1988. English educator Cardinal Neman H.S., West Palm Beach, Fla., 1977-81; dept. head Pope John Paul II H.S., Boca Raton, Fla., 1981-87; summer sch. prin. H.D. Henderson Lab. Sch., Boca Raton, Fla., 1984-87; clin. educator/trainer Fla. State Beginning Tchg. Program, Ft. Lauderdale, 1987-89; assoc. prof. State U. W. Ga., Carrollton, 1989—; vis. asst. prof. Fla. State U., Tallahassee, 1988-89; evaluator Ga. State Dept. Edn., 1992-95; grad. faculty U. Ga., Athens, 1994-96. Author: Readings, Skills and Activities for Teacher Support Programs, 1990; guest editor Ga. Elem. Prin., 1993. Asst. dist. dir. Boy Scouts Am., Carroll County, Ga., 1993-95. Grantee Fulbright Found., 1996. Mem. Ga. Assn. Curriculum and Staff Devel. (dist. dir. 1995—), Ga. Asssn. Tchr. Educators (state editor newsletter 1992-96), DAR (regent Estahakee chpt. 1974-76, Abraham Baldwin 1993-96), Nat. Staff Devel. Coun., Phi Kappa Phi (pres. 1994-96), Phi Delta Kappa, Delta Kappa GAmma, Order Ea. Star (past matron 1969). Roman Catholic. Home: 17 Hickory Trail Villa Rica GA 30180 Office: State U W Ga Edn Ctr Carrollton GA 30118-5160

MIMS, PAULA CAIN, secondary education educator; b. Dothan, Ala., Dec. 5, 1954; d. Bennie E. and Bobbie (Casey) Cain; m. Tom Wesley Mims Jr., Sept. 20, 1975; children: Casey Leigh, Ashley Elizabeth. AA in Bus. Adminstrn., Wallace State C.C., Dothan, 1975; BS in Bus. Edn., Troy State U., 1981; postgrad. in Bus. Edn., Auburn U. Vocat. cert. Auburn U., 1982. With Bank of the South, Abbeville, Ala., 1976-78; instr. bus. edn. dept. Eufaula (Ala.) H.S., 1981—; Mem. supt. adv. com. Eufaula City Schs., 1993-94. Advisor, sponsor Future Bus. Leaders of Am., Eufaula, 1991—; active Esther Sunday Sch. First Bapt. Ch. of Abbeville; active women's com. ALFA Ins. Co., Henry County, Ala., 1990—. Scholar tech. program for Ala. tchrs. State Dept. of Edn., 1995-97. Mem. NEA, Nat. Bus. Edn. Assn., Ala. Edn. Assn., Ala. Bus. Edn. Assn., Ala. Vocat. Assn., Eufaula Tchrs. Assn., Delta Kappa Gamma. Home: Rt 4 Box 458 Abbeville AL 36310 Office: Eufaula HS 530 Lake Dr Eufaula AL 36027-9564

MIN, HOKEY, business educator; b. Seoul, South Korea, June 28, 1954; s. Byungjoo and Hangwon (Seo) M. BA, Hankuk U. of Fgn. Studies, Seoul, South Korea, 1978; MBA, Yonsei U., Seoul, South Korea, 1980, U. S.C., 1982; PhD, Ohio State U., 1987. Freelance writer Chas. E. Merrill Pub. Co., Columbus, Ohio, 1983; teaching assoc. Ohio State U., Columbus, 1983-87; asst. prof. U. New Orleans, 1987-89, Northeastern U., Boston, 1989-92, Auburn U., 1992—; cons. Shoe Corp. Am., Columbus, 1983-84, Nationwide Ins. Co., 1984. Contbr. articles to profl. jours. Recipient Most Outstanding Rsch. award Coll. Bus. at Auburn U., 1993. Mem. Decision Scis. Inst., Inst. Mgmt. Scis., Ops. Rsch. Soc. Am., Am. Prodn. and Inventory Soc., Coun. of Logistics Mgmt., Southeastern Decision Scis. Inst. (Hon. Mention 1986), Southeastern TIMS (Best Student Paper 1986). Republican. Office: Auburn U Dept Bus Adminstrn Auburn AL 36849

MINARDI, RAYMOND ANTHONY, librarian; b. Omaha, Dec. 11, 1957; s. James Joseph and Bernadette Janice (Klaes) M.; m. Martha Jean Wooddy, Aug. 23, 1986; 1 child, Kyle Anthony. BS in Edn., U. Ga., 1981; MA in Christian Edn., So. Bapt. Theol. Sem., 1986. Missionary Home Mission Bd. of So. Bapt. Conv., Atlanta, 1981-83; editor Bapt. Sunday Sch. Bd., Nashville, 1986-89, 92-93, archivist, 1989-92, rsch. libr., 1993—; Sunday sch. growth clinician Bapt. Sunday Sch. Bd., 1989-90. Author: God is In Charge, 1993; editor curriculum periodicals Exploring 2, 1993, Preschoolers at Ch., 1993. Ch. media libr. dir. Crievewood Bapt. Ch., Nashville, 1994-95. Named one of Outstanding Young Men of Am., 1984. Mem. Tenn. Theol. Libr. Assn. (v.p. 1994-96, pres. 1996), So. Bapt. Libr. Assn. (chairperson local arrangements 1991-92). Home: 4800 Trousdale Dr Nashville TN 37220 Office: Bapt Sunday Sch Bd 127 9th Ave N Nashville TN 37203-3601

MINCH, VIRGIL ADELBERT, civil and sanitary engineer; b. Cleve., Dec. 24, 1924; s. Henry Joseph and Mary (Terlaak) M.; m. Elma Queen, Jan. 6, 1947 (dec. July 1989); children: David (dec.), Philip; m. Priscilla Faust, July 6, 1991. BS, N.D. State U., 1946; SM in San. Engring., MIT, 1948. Research assoc. Mass. Inst. Tech., 1948-49; sr. san. engr. USPHS, Cin., 1949-53; staff engr. Mead Corp., Chillicothe, Ohio, 1953-55, group leader, 1956-59, mgr. pollution control activities, 1960-65, assoc. dir. tech. services, 1966-68, corp. coörd. environmental resources, Dayton, Ohio, 1969-73; v.p., dir. Assoc. Water and Air Resources Engrs., Nashville, 1972-74; project mgr. Stanley Cons., Muscatine, Iowa, 1974, v.p., 1974-77; v.p. John J. Harte Assocs., Inc., Atlanta, 1977-78; SE regional mktg. mgr. Environ. Research and Tech., Atlanta, 1978-80; engr., design mgr. Fluor Daniel, Inc., Greenville, S.C., 1980-83, project mgr., 1983-86; pres. VAMCO Engring. Group Exec. Search Firm, 1986—; engr. dir., capt. USPHS Res., 1980—. Recipient Indsl. liaison service award Ohio River Valley Water Sanitation Commn., 1959. Registered profl. engr. Ga., N.J. Mem. Scioto Conservancy dist. (v.p., dir. 1959—), Am. Meteorol. Soc., Am. Water Works Assn., Water Pollution Control Fedn., Air Pollution Control Assn., TAPPI, Ga. Pulp and Paper Assn. (sec. 1955-65), Nat. Council Air and Stream Improvement (chmn. S. Central region 1963-69), Nat. Rivers and Harbors Congress (chmn. S.E. Ohio sect. 1968-72), Sigma Xi, Tau Beta Pi, Sigma Phi Delta. Contbr. articles profl. jours. Patentee plastic film trickling filter. Home: 3146 Smoke Creek Ct NE Atlanta GA 30345-1539 also: 249 Kimberly Ave Asheville NC 28804-3510 Office: 3000 Langford Rd Ste 700 Norcross GA 30071-1521

MINCHEW, HARRISON GRAY, director golf course architecture. BS in Landscape Arch., U. Ga., 1979. Various golf course arch. positions Various orgns.; v.p., sr. golf cours architect Palmer Course Design Co., Ponte Vedra Beach, Fla., 1982—. Contbr. to design of over 60 golf courses in U.S. and internationally, including The Bog, Saukville, Wis., Cherokee Run, Conyers, Ga., Northview Golf and Country Club, Surrey, B.C., Can., Kildare Hotel and Country Club, Straffan, County Kildare, Ireland. Mem. Am. Soc. Golf Course Architects, Am. Soc. Landscape Architects, Urban Land Inst. Office: Palmer Course Design Co 572 Ponte Vedra PO Box 1639 Ponte Vedra Beach FL 32082

MINCHEW, JOHN RANDALL, lawyer; b. Washington, July 31, 1957; s. John Richard and Lucile Elizabeth (Shaw) M. AB, Duke U., 1980; JD, Washington & Lee U., 1984; Cert. in Jurisprudence, Oxford U., 1982. Bar: Va. 1984, U.S. Dist. Ct. (ea. dist.) Va. 1985, U.S. Ct. Appeals (4th cir.) 1985. Jud. clk. Supreme Ct. Va., 1984-85; ptnr. Hazel & Thomas, P.C., Fairfax, Falls Church, Leesburg, Va., 1985—; v.p., dir. devel. The Minchew Corp., Fairfax, Va., 1985—; gen. counsel Fairfax C. of C., 1987-88; asst. gen. counsel No. Va. Bldg. Industry Assn., Fairfax, 1987-89; pres. Va. Shelter Corp. Adminstrv. editor: Washington & Lee Law Rev., 1984. Pro bono caseworker Legal Aid Soc. Roanoke Valley, Lexington, Va., 1982-84. Mem. ABA, Va. State Bar (mem. Commn. on Unauthorized Practice of Law 1994-96), Fairfax Bar Assn., Loudoun Bar Assn. (pres. 1995-96), Rotary, Phi Delta Phi. Home: 330 W Market St Leesburg VA 22075-2601 Office: Hazel & Thomas PC 44084 Riverside Pky # 300 Leesburg VA 22075-5102

MINCKLEY, BARBARA B., nurse, educator, retired; b. Boston, Feb. 25, 1925; d. Kenneth Cotton and Dorothy (Riley) Brown; children: Alison, Barbara, Carrie, Gregory. BSN, Stanford U., 1960; MSN, U. Calif., San Francisco, 1967, D Nursing Sci., 1972; cert. adult nurse practitioner, Stanford U., 1975. Assoc. dean grad. divsn. U. Utah Coll. Nursing, Salt Lake City, 1975-78; project dir. nursing rsch. div. U. Ill. Coll. Nursing, Chgo., 1978-80; exec. dir. Midwest Alliance in Nursing, Indpls., 1980-85; project coord. nursing rsch. Ariz. State U. Coll. Nursing, Tempe; dir. dept. nursing Calif. State U., Long Beach, 1988-93; lectr. in field. Contbr. articles to profl. publs. Fellow Am. Acad. Nursing, Sigma Xi, Sigma Theta Tau. Home: 22 Ocean Woods Dr W Saint Augustine FL 32084

MINEAR, ALANA WILFONG, alumni affairs director; b. Elkins, W.Va., Aug. 25, 1947; d. Dewey Lyle and Gail Ruth (Ours) Wilfong; m. Larry Wayne Minear, May 26, 1973 (dec. Oct. 1993); 1 child, Stacey Elizabeth. BA, Fairmont (W.Va.) State Coll., 1970; postgrad., Davis & Elkins Coll., W.Va.; MA, W.Va. U., 1996. Lic. social worker, W.Va. Alcoholism and drug abuse counselor Appalachian Mental Health Ctr., Elkins, W.Va., 1970-73; teller Union Fed. Savs. & Loan, Elkins, W.Va., 1973-75; salesperson Fletcher Real Estate, Elkins, W.Va., 1975-79; dir. Tucker County Sr. Citizens Program, Elkins, 1980-86; adminstr., dir. alumni rels. Davis & Elkins Coll., Elkins, 1986-96; salesperson Archer Real Estate, Elkins, 1996—; visual-artist-in-residence Tucker County Visual Artist Program. Pres. Tucker County Planning Commn., Parsons, W.Va., 1982-86; v.p. St. George Med. Clinic Bd., St. George, 1982-86; mem. Randolph County Bi-Centennial Com., Elkins, 1989-90; mem. Elkins state adv. coun. Pub. Transp., Charleston, W.Va., 1984-86; bd. dirs. Am. Heart Assn., 1991—; mem. Woman's Club; campaign chmn., bd. dir. United Way; bd. dirs. Elkins Main St.; bd. dir., chair Adult Christian Edn. Named Pub. Employee of the Yr., C. of C. Tucker County, 1985, Outstanding Leader, Adminstrn. on Aging, 1985. Mem. Nat. Soc. Fund Raising Execs., Coun. for Advancement and Support of Edn., Randolph County C. of C. Republican. Baptist. Home: 115 Westview Dr Elkins WV 26241-3246 Office: Archer Real Estate Harrison Ave Elkins WV 26241-3971

MINEHART, JEAN BESSE, tax accountant; b. Cleve., Nov. 8, 1937; d. Ralph Moore and Augusta (Mitchell) Besse; m. Ralph Conrad Minehart, Aug. 28, 1959; children: Patricia Minehart Miron, Deborah, Elizabeth, Stephen. BA, Mass. Wellesley Coll., 1959; MEd, U. Va., 1971. Rsch. assoc. Age Ctr. of New Eng., Boston, 1959-61; substitute tchr. Charlottesville (Va.) Sch. System, 1976-81; tax acct. H&R Block, Charlottesville, 1982-94, Huey & Bjorn, Charlottesville, 1994—. Past pres. Ephitha Village Housing for the Deaf, Charlottesville, 1984-87; bd. dirs. Tues. Evening Concert Series, Charlottesville, 1990-94; sec., bd. dirs. Family Svc., Inc., Charlottesville, 1987-91; elder Westminster Presbyn. Ch., 1979-81, 94-96. Mem. LWV (v.p., treas. 1991-95) Blue Ridge Wellesley Club (pres. Charlottesvillechpt. 1989-91). Home: 1714 Yorktown Dr Charlottesville VA 22901-3034 Office: Huey & Bjorn 408 E Market St Apt 207B Charlottesville VA 22902-5252

MINER, MARY ELIZABETH HUBERT, secondary school educator; b. Provident City, Tex., Mar. 25, 1921; d. Fred Edward and Charlotte Alice (Haynes) Hubert; m. Daniel Bowen Miner, Jan. 29, 1945 (dec. Aug. 1979); children: Charlotte Martelia Miner Williams, Daniel Bowen Jr., Mary Elizabeth Miner Martinez, Joseph Frederick, William McKinley. BA, Rice U., 1942; postgrad., U. Houston, East Tenn. State U., 1959, U. Tenn., 1961. Cert. tchr. math., English, French, history, Tex., 8th grade, math., English, French, Am. history grades 9-12. Math. tchr. Crosby (Tex.) H.S., 1942-43; office mgr. Uvalde Rock Asphalt, Houston, 1943-44; tchr. math., English, health Rogersville (Tenn.) H.S., 1947-49, 55-78; tchr. math., English, French Ch. Hill. (Tenn.) H.S., 1949-51, 53-55; tchr. 8th grade Rogersville (Tenn.) City Schs., 1951-53; tchr. math. Cherokee Comprehensive H.S., Rogersville, 1978-84; chmn. math. and sci. planning com., Hawkins County, Tenn., 1977-79; pvt. tutor, Rogersville. Tchr. ladies Bible class Rogersville United Meth. Ch., 1952—, mem. choir, 1979—, sec., 1967-96, sec. adminstr. bd. dirs.; blood donor ARC, Rogersville, 1974-75. Lt. Women's Corps USNR, 1944-47. Recipient Apple award Sta. WKGB, 1956. Mem. NEA (life), Tenn. Edn. Assn. (life), Rogersville Bus. and Profl. Women (pres. 1953-55, treas. 1948-53), Am. Legion Aux. (pres.), Delta Kappa Gamma (Alpha Iota chpt. pres.). Republican.

MINES, RICHARD OLIVER, JR., civil and environmental engineer; b. Hot Springs, Va., July 23, 1953; s. Richard Oliver and Dreama Irene (Blankenship) M. BSCE, Va. Mil. Inst., 1975; ME in Civil Engring., U. Va., 1977; PhD, Va. Poly. Inst., 1983. Instr. Va. Mil. Inst., Lexington, 1977-79; project engr. William Matotan & Assocs., Albuquerque, 1979; grad. asst. Va. Poly. U., Blacksburg, 1980-83; asst. prof. U. South Fla., Tampa, 1983-85, Va. Mil. Inst., 1985-86; project engr. CH2M Hill, Gainesville, Fla., 1986-90; sr. process engr. Black & Veatch, Tampa, 1990-92; asst. prof. U. South Fla., Tampa, 1992—; adj. prof. Santa Fe Community Coll., Gainesville, 1989, U. South Fla., 1990—. Contbr. chpt. to book, articles to profl. jours. Capt. USAF, 1977. Engring. Found. grantee, 1985. Mem. ASCE (Student chpt. prof. of the yr. award 1995), Water Environ. Fedn., Am. Water Works Assn., Chi Epsilon, Alpha Kappa. Baptist. Office: U South Fla ENB118 4202 E Fowler Ave Tampa FL 33620-9900

MINETTE, DENNIS JEROME, financial computing consultant; b. Columbus, Nebr., May 18, 1937; s. Lawrence Edward and Angela Ellen (Kelley) M.; B.S. in Elec. Engring., U. Nebr., 1970; M.B.A., Babson Coll., 1978; m. Virginia Rae Jordan, Oct. 27, 1961; children—Jordan Edward, Lawrence Edward II. Brokerage systems designer Honeywell Info. Systems, Mpls. and Wellesly, Mass., 1970-75; devel. mgr. Investment Info., Inc., Cambridge, Mass., 1975-77; product support mgr. Small Bus. Systems div. Data Gen. Corp., Westboro, Mass., 1977-81; pres. Minette Data Systems, Inc., Sarasota, Fla., 1981—. Capital improvement programs committeeman Town of Medway (Mass.), 1978-79, mem. town fin. com., 1979-80. With USN, 1956-60, 61-67, served to lt. commdr. res., 1967-87. Mem. IEEE, IEEE Computer Soc., Data Processing Mgmt. Assn. (cert.), Naval Res. Assn. (life), Res. Officers Assn., Am. Legion, U. Nebr. Alumni Assn. (life), Eta Kappa Nu, Sigma Tau. Republican. Roman Catholic. Office: Minette Data Systems Inc PO Box 15435 Sarasota FL 34277-1435

MINGO, JOE LOUIS, elementary school educator; b. Kershaw, S.C., Nov. 14; s. John L. and Ella (Wilson) M. BA in Elem. Edn., U. S.C., 1980, MEd, 1982, postgrad., 1994—. Cert. tchr. elem. edn., early childhood edn. Singer operator Springs Industries, Lancaster, S.C., 1972-79; with BJH Realty, Columbia, S.C., 1980-81, Carabo Inc., Columbia, 1980-85; tchr. 3d grade Sumter County (S.C.) Sch. Dist. #2, 1982-86, tchr. 4th grade, 1986-94, tchr. math, 1994—; lead tchr. math Shaw Heights Elem. Sch., Shaw AFB, S.C., 1993—; Author poetry in New Voices in Am. Poetry, 1986, 88. With USAF, 1984—, Desert Storm. Office: Shaw Heights Elem Sch 5121 Frierson Rd Shaw AFB SC 29152

MINISI, ANTHONY JOSEPH, cardiologist, educator; b. Phila., May 9, 1954; m. Margaret Joan Conroy, May 23, 1980; children: John Anthony, Karen Margaret. BA cum laude, U. Pa., 1976, MD, 1980. Diplomate Am. Bd. Internal Medicine, Am. Bd. Cardiovascular Disease, Nat. Bd. Med. Examiners. Intern in internal medicine Med. Coll. Va., Richmond, 1980-81, resident, 1981-83, clin. fellow cardiology div., 1984-86, clin. instr. dept. medicine, 1983-84, instr., 1987-88, asst. prof., 1989—; mem. clin. attending staff cardiology div. McGuire VA Med. Ctr., Richmond, 1986-87, clin. attending in cardiology-Cardiac Catheterization Lab., 1987-88, attending staff, 1988-90, assoc. dir. Cardiac Catheterization Lab., 1989-93; dir. Cardiac Catheterization Lab., Richmond, 1993—. Co-author: (with others) Reflex Control of the Circulation, 1991, Cardiovascular Reflex Control in Health and Disease, 1993, Cardiovascular Reflex Control in Health and Disease, 1993; contbr. articles to profl. jours. Tng. grantee NIH, 1986. Fellow Am. Coll. Cardiology; mem. Am. Fedn. Clin. Rsch., Am. Heart Assn. Home: 7609 Dell Dr Richmond VA 23235-6303 Office: McGuire VA Med Ctr Div Cardiology Box 111J-1 1201 Broad Rock Blvd Richmond VA 23249-0001

MINNICK, BRUCE ALEXANDER, lawyer; b. New London, Conn., Apr. 16, 1943; s. Robert Wood Minnick and Nedra Louise (Alexander) Wiesman; m. Judith Anita Saxon, Sept. 23, 1967 (div. 1981); children: Audra Anne, Lisa Michelle; m. Charlotte Ann Springfield, Apr. 10, 1983 (div. 1991); 1 child, Matthew Alexander. AA, Broward Community Coll., 1970; BS with honors, Fla. State U., 1971, JD, 1977. BarL Fla. 1978, U.S. Dist. Ct. (no. dist.) Fla. 1979, U.S. Dist. Ct. (mid. and so. dists.) Fla. 1982, U.S. Supreme Ct. 1981, U.S. Ct. Appeals (11th cir.) 1982, U.S. Tax Ct. 1983, U.S. Ct. Claims 1983, U.S. Dist. Ct. (ea. dist.) Mich. 1990. Staff dir., counsel rules com. Fla. Ho. Reps., Tallahassee, 1976-78; v.p., gen. counsel Fla. Credit Union League, Tallahassee, 1978-80; asst. atty. gen. dept. legal affairs State of Fla., Tallahassee, 1981-86; ptnr. Mang, Rett & Collette, P.A., Tallahassee, 1986-93, Mang, Rett & Minnick PA, Tallahassee, 1994-95; pvt. practice Tallahassee, 1995—; lectr. state agys., 1982—, Fla. Bar, 1986—. Mem. Leon County Dist. Adv. Com., 1980-82, 92-94; mem. exec. com. Leon County Dems., 1984—. Mem. ABA (labor sect., local govt. and law sect.), Fla. Bar Assn. (chmn. com. labor sect. 1987-91, mem. exec. coun. labor sect. 1989-93, founding chmn. Fed. Ct. practice com. 1990-92, del. to 11th Cir. Jud. Conf. 1990-92, com. chmn. govt. lawyer sect. 1991—, rep. mem. pub. rels. com. 1991-93), Tallahassee Bar Assn., Fla. Govt. Bar Assn., Fla. Women Lawyers Assn., Fed. Bar Assn. (pres.-elect Tallahassee chpt. 1995, pres. 1996), Govs. Club, Phi Alpha Delta. Christian Scientist. Home: 9002 Eagles Ridge Dr Tallahassee FL 32312-4045 Office: 2810 Remington Green Cir PO Box 15588 Tallahassee FL 32317-5588

MINNIGH, BRICE MARTIN, journalist, researcher; b. Ft. Belvoir, Va., June 26, 1970; s. George Edward and Janet Lee (Smarr) M. BA in Journalism, Belmont U., Nashville, 1992. Features intern The Tennessean, Nashville, 1991; editor-in-chief Belmont Vision, Nashville, 1991-92; gen. assignment reporter Nashville Banner, 1992, 94; news intern NBC News, Moscow, Russia, 1993; copy editor Bus. World, Moscow, 1993, China Daily, Beijing, 1994-95; Fulbright fellow/rschr. U.S. Fulbright Program, Vilnius, Lithuania, 1995-96; freelance journalist The Moscow Guardian, 1993, Pacific Rim News Svc., Seattle, 1995, The Baltic Times, Vilnius, 1996. Recipient First Amendment Freedom award Belmont U., 1991-92; named Coll. Journalist of the Yr., S.E. Journalism Conf., 1991-92; Moscow State U.

Journalism scholar, 1993. Mem. Soc. Profl. Journalists, Blue Key, Gamma Beta Phi, Alpha Chi, Phi Sigma Tau.

MINOCHA, ANIL, physician, educator, researcher; b. India, Feb. 4, 1957; Came to U.S., 1982; s. Ram Saroop and Kamla Devi M. Pre-med. diploma, Punjab U., India, 1974; MD, Med. Coll., Rohtak, India, 1980; postgrad. studies in pharmacology, Baylor Coll. Medicine, 1982-84. Diplomate Am. Bd. Internal Medicine, Am. Bd. Gastroenterology, Am. Bd. Forensic Medicine, Am. Bd. Geriatric Medicine. House officer depts. ophthalmology and dermatology Med. Coll. Hosp., Rohtak, India, 1980-81; med. officer State Health Svcs. Govts. of Punjab and Haryana, India, 1981-82; rsch. asst. Baylor Coll. Med., Houston, 1982-84; fellow clin. pharmacology U. Va., Charlottesville, 1984-86; resident physician Franklin Square Hosp., Balt., 1986-89; fellow gastroenterology Mich. State U., East Lansing, 1989-91; asst. prof. U. Louisville, 1991-95; assoc. prof. medicine U. Okla., Oklahoma City, 1995—; instr. dept. medicine Mich. State U., 1989-91; staff physician dept. medicine VAA Med. Ctr., Louisville, 1991-95; mem. credentials com. Humana Hosp., U. Louisville, 1992, other coms., 1992-94; mem. R&D com. VA Hosp., 1992-95; presenter in field. Contbr. numerous articles to profl. jours. Prin. investigator Gulf Biosystems, Charlottesville, 1985; biomed. rsch. grantee Mich. State U., 1990; sch. medicine rsch. grantee U. Louisville, 1993. Fellow ACP, Am. Coll. Gastroenterology, Am. Coll. Forensic Examiners; mem. Am. Gastroenterol. Assn., Am. Assn. for Study of Liver Disease.

MINOR, EDWARD COLQUITT, lawyer; b. Balt., Dec. 1, 1942; s. Edward Essau and Mary Newell (Schultz) M.; m. Joan Slade, Aug. 29, 1964; 1 child, Elizabeth Colquitt. AB in Econ., Western Md. Coll., 1964; LLB cum Laude, Boston U., 1967. Bar: Md. 1967, Ga. 1972, Va. 1974, U.S. Supreme Ct. Assoc. Semmes Bowen & Semmes, Balt., 1967-68; judge adv. U.S. Army, Savannah and Vietnam, 1968-72; assoc. Connerat Dunn & Hunter, Savannah, 1972-74; sr. atty. Kraft Paper div. Union Camp Corp., Savannah, 1974; asst. gen. counsel, asst. sec. Fine Paper div. Union Camp Corp., Franklin, Va., 1974-85; assoc. gen. counsel, asst. sec. Fine Paper div. Union Camp Corp., Franklin, 1985—; mgr. Fine Paper div. Union Camp Corp., Franklin, Va., 1988-95, divsn. procurement mgr. purchasing, 1995—; mem. citizens adv. bd. Va. Dept. Environ. Quality. Bd. dirs. Tidewater Heart Assn., Norfolk, Va., 1980-86, Future of Hampton Roads, Inc., Rawles Mus. Arts, 1992-93; mem. Va. Gov.'s Commn. on Efficiency, 1988; chmn. Franklin Constl. Bicentennial Commn.; chmn. bd. dirs. Southampton Acad., Courtland, Va., 1985-88; dep. mem. Va. Bus. Coun.; chmn. citizens adv. bd. Va. Dept. Air Pollution Control, 1992, mem., 1993-96; mem. exec. bd. Diocese of S.E. Va., Episcopal Ch., 1985-89; vestryman Emmanuel Episcopal Ch., Franklin, 1985, 87, 91; mem. Roundtable on Environ. Standing, 1991. Decorated Bronze Star. Fellow Royal Soc. Encouragement Arts; mem. Va. State Bar (chmn. environ. sect. 1990-91, Va. Bar Assn. (co-chmn. corp. counsel sect. 1990-92, bd. govs. adminstrv. law sect.), Md. Bar Assn., Ga. Bar Assn., Va. Bus. Coun., Va. Mfrs. Assn. (bd. dirs. 1994-95, chmn. environ. affairs com.), Norfolk Yacht Club, Town Point Club (founding), Rotary (pres. Franklin 1992-93). Home: 23456 Thomas Cir Courtland VA 23837-1336 Office: Union Camp Corp RR 58 Franklin VA 23851

MINOR, GEORGE GILMER, III, drug and hospital supply company executive; b. 1940; married. BA, Va. Mil. Inst., 1963; MBA, U. Va., 1966. With Owens & Minor, Inc., Richmond, Va., 1963—, mgr. sales Acme Candy Co. div., 1966-68, mgr. retail mktg., 1968-73, div. mgr. wholesale drug br., 1973-77, v.p., 1977-80, exec. v.p., 1980-81, pres., chmn., CEO, 1981—, also bd. dirs. Office: Owens & Minor Med Inc 4800 Cox Rd Richmond VA 23060*

MINOR, KEVIN ISAAC, criminology educator; b. Jasper, Ind., Sept. 19, 1959; s. Moses P. and Muriel M. (Eisenhut) M.; m. Marsha A. Whitehead, June 25, 1988; 1 child, Kevin Nicholas. BS, Ind. State U., 1982; MS, Emporia State U., 1984; PhD, Western Mich. U., 1988. Asst. prof. criminology S.W. Mo. State U., 1988-92; assoc. prof. Ea. Ky. U., Richmond, 1992—; cons. Dept. Corrections, State of Mo., 1988-92, Dept. Social Svcs., 1989-92, Ho. of Reps. 1991, Ky. Corrections Cabinet, 1992—. Editor: Prisons Around The World: Studies in International Penology, 1992; contbr. articles to profl. publs. Mem. Am. Soc. Criminology, Acad. Criminal Justice Scis., So. Criminal Justice Assn. Office: Ea Ky Univ Dept Correctional Svcs Richmond KY 40475

MINOR, LISA GRAVES, English language educator; b. Florence, Ala., Sept. 14, 1959; d. Arthur Davis and Jean A. (Long) Graves; m. Julian Ondell Minor, Jr., Aug. 17, 1985; 1 child, Leslie J. BS, U. North Ala., 1980; MA, Vanderbilt U., 1982, PhD, 1990. Dept. bibliographer Vanderbilt U., Nashville, 1981-82, tchg. fellow, 1982-85; asst. prof. Ala. A&M U., Normal, 1985-88; assoc. prof. U. North Ala., Florence, 1988—. Mem. MLA, Nat. Coun. Tchrs. English, Ala. Coun. Tchrs. English, Delta Sigma Theta. Democrat. Mem. Ch. of Christ. Office: U North Ala Box 5197 Florence AL 35632-0001

MINOR, MARK WILLIAM, allergist; b. Steubenville, Ohio, May 19, 1956; s. Garland Edgar Minor and Norma Jean McKenzie Shidock; m. Rachael Anne Hatfield, Aug. 15, 1987; children: Megan, Emily. BS in Biology magna cum laude, U. Miami, 1978; MD, W.Va. U., 1982. Resident in internal medicine W.Va. U., Charleston; fellow in allergy/immunology U. So. Fla., Tampa; staff physician Holmes Regional Hosp., Melbourne, Fla.; clin. asst., prof. medicine U. South Fla.; physician Brevard Allergy Assocs., Melbourne, Fla., 1987—. Contbr. articles, referee Jour. Allergy and Clin. Immunology, So. Med. Jour. Fellow Am. Coll. Allergy and Immunology, Am. Coll. Physicians; mem. Am. Acad. Allergy and Immunology, Alpha Omega Alpha. Office: Brevard Allergy Assocs 1515 Airport Blvd Melbourne FL 32901-2946

MINOR, MARY ELLEN, civilian military employee; b. Konawa, Okla., Jan. 11, 1947; d. Tom Loye and Barbara Anna (Wheeler) Bounds; 1 child, Rose Mary Minor Wright. BS in Math., East Ctrl. State U., Ada, Okla., 1968; MS in Math., U. Ark., 1970; postgrad., U. Utah, 1970-72. Ops. rsch. analyst U.S. Army Comm. Command, Ft. Huachuca, Ariz., 1974-78; mathematician U.S. Dept. Treasury, Washington, 1978-79; ops. rsch. analyst U.S. Army Concepts Analysis AG., Bethesda, Md., 1979-80, Office Chief of Staff of Army, Washington, 1980-82; program integration specialist U.S. Army Materiel Command, Alexandria, Va., 1982-88, supervisory ops. rsch. analyst, 1988-93; supervisory ops. rsch. analyst U.S. Army Logistics Integration Agy., Alexandria, 1993—. Parent sponsor Girl Scouts U.S., Annandale, Va., 1981-84. Mem. Am. Def. Preparedness Assn. Home: 20583 Snowshoe Sq Apt 302 Ashburn VA 22011-3964 Office: US Army Logistics Integration Agy 5001 Eisenhower Ave Alexandria VA 22333

MINTER, PATRICIA HAGLER, history educator; b. Pasadena, Calif., Oct. 1, 1964; d. James Edgar and Jean (Ziegler) Hagler; m. Michael Andrew Minter, June 25, 1988. BA in History, U. Tenn., 1986; MA in History, U. Va., 1988, PhD in History, 1994. Asst. prof. history Western Ky. U., Bowling Green, 1993—. Mem. Am. Hist. Assn. (Littleton-Griswold fellow 1990-91), Am. Soc. Legal History, Orgn. Am. Historians, So. Hist. Assn., Landmark Home Assn., Zeta Tau Alpha. Home: 1262 Chestnut St Bowling Green KY 42101 Office: Western Ky U Dept History Bowling Green KY 42101

MINTICH, MARY R., art educator, sculptor; b. Detroit; d. Clayton Harris and Mary Inez (Barber) Ringelberg; m. George Mintich, Mar. 9, 1954; children: Barbara, Mark. MFA, U. N.C., Greensboro, 1971. Tchr. Charlotte(N.C.)-Mecklenburg Schs., 1961-66, Sacred Heart Coll., Belmont, N.C., 1967-72; prof. Winthrop U., Rock Hill, S.C., 1973—. One and two artist shows include Greenville County Mus. Art, Mint Mus. Art, Southeastern Ctr. Contemporary Art, Asheville Mus. Art, St. John's Mus., Clemson U. Recipient Ferro Purchase award Everson Mus., Purchase awards Mint Mus., S.C. State Art Collection, Nations Bank, St. Johns Mus., Capitol Ctr., Raleigh, N.C. Mem. Coll. Art Assn., Piedmont Craftsmen Inc. (bd. dirs.), Tri-State Sculptors, Soc. N. Am. Goldsmiths. Home: 515 Dogwood Ln Belmont NC 28012 Office: Winthrop U Oakland Ave Rock Hill SC 29733

MINTON, JOHN WILLIAM, management educator; b. Alexandria, Va., May 22, 1946; s. John William and Irma Christie (Hay) M.; m. Nancy Elizabeth Niles, Dec. 19, 1970. MA in Social Sci., U. No. Colo., 1975; MBA, MS in Mgmt., Memphis State U., 1983; PhD in Bus. Adminstrn., Duke U., 1988. Dir. community devel. CIty of Asheboro, N.C., 1973-77; circuit-riding mgr. Mid-East Commn., Washington, N.C., 1977; exec. dir. office community devel. County of Columbus, Chadbourn, N.C., 1977-78; mgr. Town of Carolina Beach, N.C., 1978-80; adminstr. City of Germantown, Tenn., 1980-81; asst. prof. dept. mgmt. Appalachian State U., Boone, N.C., 1986-88, assoc. prof., 1993—; vis. asst. prof. Duke U., 1988-93; profl. edn. rsch. fellow Nat. Inst. for Dispute Resolution, 1985-86. Author: (with others) Negotiation, 2d edit., 1994, Negotiation: Readings, Exercises and Cases, 2d edit., 1993, Organizational Justice: The Search for Fairness in the Workplace, 1992; contbr. articles to profl. jours.; ad hoc reviewer Mgmt. Sci., Organization Sci. V.p. bd. Blue Ridge Dispute Settlement Ctr.; mem., arbitrator N.C. Dept. Labor Arbitration Coun.; vol. arbitrator Better Bus. Bur. Mem. ASTD, Acad. Mgmt. Democrat. Office: Appalachian State U Dept Management Wcob Boone NC 28608

MINTON, KATHY DICKERSON, rehabilitation administrator; b. Peru, Ind., Sept. 22, 1952; d. Paul Eugene and Mary Magdeline (Flamm) Dickerson; m. Roger Owen Minton, Aug. 25, 1973; children: Heather Caryn, Leslie Frances. BS in Nursing, Murray State U., 1974; MBA, Jacksonville State U., 1989. RN Ky., Tex. Staff nurse West Paces Ferry Hosp., Atlanta, 1975-76; nurse mgr. Doctor's Hosp., Tucker, Ga., 1976-78; dir. nursing Body Nursing Ctr., Woodstock, Ga., 1978-80, The Jewish Home, Atlanta, 1980-82; cons. Nat. Healthcare Linen Svc., St. Louis, 1983-86; chmn. of vols. ARC, Ft. McClellan, Ala., 1987-89; nurse mgr. Warm Springs Rehab. Hosp., San Antonio, Tex., 1990-92; dir. nursing Warm Springs Rehab. Hosp., San Antonio, 1992-94, dir. patient care svcs., 1994-95, asst. adminstr. patient care svcs., 1995—; mem. S.W. Tex. Regional Adv. Coun., San Antonio, 1994—. Author: (3 day rev. course) An Overview of Rehab Concepts: Preparation for the CRRN Exam, 1994. 1st v.p. Army Pers. Ctr. Officers' Wives Club, St. Louis, 1985, Ft. McClellan Officers Wives Club, 1986; Ft. McClellan rep. Army Family Action Planning Conf, Washington, 1986; program chmn. Ga. Assn. Nurses in Long Term Care, Atlanta, 1981-82. Recipient ARC Nurse Pin, 1989. Mem. Assn. Rehab. Nurses (cert., bd. dirs. 1993—), Alamo Area Nurse Execs. (sec.-treas. 1994-95, pres. 1996—). Office: Warm Springs & Bapt Rehab Network 5101 Med Dr San Antonio TX 78229

MINTON, MELANIE SUE, neuroscience nurse; b. Cin., Apr. 3, 1950; d. Lester L. and Wanda (Harman) M. Diploma, The Christ Hosp. Sch. Nursing, 1971; BS in Nursing, Prairie View U. A&M, 1982; MBA in Health Care Mgmt., Our Lady of Lake U., Houston, 1995. RN, Tex.; CNRN, ACLS instr., BCLS instr., bd. cert. neurosci. Staff, charge nurse The Christ Hosp., Cin., 1971-72, Barnes Hosp, St. Louis, 1972; asst. head nurse The Christ Hosp., Cin., 1972-74; relief nurse supr. The Meth. Hosp., Houston, 1975-87, clin. educator, 1989; trauma rehab. nurse Inst. for Rehab. & Rsch., Houston, 1987-89; nurse specialist neurosurg., neurol. and otolaryn. ICUs Meth. Hosp., Houston, 1989—; presenter, speaker in field. Mem. Am. Assn. Neurosci. Nurses, S.E. Tex. Chpt. Am. Assn. Neurosci. Nurses, World Fedn. Neurosci. Nurses, Soc. Otolaryngology & Head & Neck Nurses. Home: 2021 Spenwick Dr Apt 210 Houston TX 77055-1546

MINTZ, DANIEL GORDON, technical company executive; b. Washington, July 8, 1948; s. Nathan Louis and Rose Betty (Gordon) M.; m. Ellen Sue Elow, Feb. 15, 1981; children: Miriam Chana, Tamar Elisheva. BS in Info. Systems Mgmt., U. Md., 1971. Pvt. cons., 1968-76; systems analyst Computer Data Systems, Inc., Rockville, Md., 1976-78; pres. Bus. Info. Assocs., Inc., Bethesda, Md., 1978-83; dir. ops. PC Telemart, Inc., Fairfax, Va., 1983-84, Centel Info. Systems, Reston, Va., 1984-88; program mgr. Lockheed, Fairfax, 1988-90; v.p. bus. devel., program mgr. WJ Culver Consulting, Inc., Vienna, Va., 1990-95; program mgr. Sun Microsystems Inc., Vienna, Va., 1995—; rep. Info. Tech. Assn. Am. Editor newsletter Insights; developer Dynasty League Computer Baseball; contbr. articles to profl. jours. Republican. Jewish. Home: 6449 Windermere Circle North Bethesda MD 20852-3538 Office: Sun Microsystems Inc Ste A110 7900 Westpark Dr Mc Lean VA 22102

MINTZ, DANIEL HARVEY, diabetologist, educator, academic administrator; b. N.Y.C., Sept. 16, 1930; s. Jacob A. and Fannie M.; m. Dawn E. Hynes, Jan. 15, 1961 (dec.); children: David, Denise, Debra; m. Marge K Peiman, Nov. 30, 1996. B.S. cum laude, St. Bonaventure Coll., 1951; M.D., N.Y. Med. Coll., 1956. Diplomate: Am. Bd. Internal Medicine. Intern Henry Ford Hosp., Detroit, 1956-57; resident Georgetown med. div. D.C. Gen. Hosp., Washington, 1957-59, Georgetown U. Hosp., Washington, 1958-59; fellow medicine Nat. Inst. Arthritis and Metabolic Diseases, 1959-60, Am. Diabetes Assn., 1960-61; practice medicine, specializing in internal medicine Miami, Fla.; asst. prof. medicine Georgetown U. Sch. Medicine, 1963-64; assoc. prof. medicine U. Pitts. Sch. Medicine, 1964-69; prof. medicine U. Miami Sch. Medicine, 1969—, Mary Lou Held prof. medicine, 1981—, chief div. endocrinology and metabolism, dept. medicine, 1969-80, Sci. dir. Diabetes Research Inst., 1980—; chief of service Georgetown U. Med. div. D.C. Gen. Hosp., Washington, 1963-64; chief of medicine Magee-Women's Hosp., Pitts., 1964-69; guest prof. U. Geneva, 1976-77. Contbr. articles to profl. jours. Fellow ACP; mem. Endocrine Soc., Am. Diabetes Assn. (program dir. 1972), Am. Fedn. Clin. Research, Am. Soc. Clin. Investigation, Central Soc. Clin. Investigation, So. Soc. Clin. Investigation., Am. Assn. Physicians. Office: U Miami Diabetes Rsch Inst PO Box 016960 R-134 Miami FL 33101-6960

MINTZ, JOEL ALAN, law educator; b. N.Y.C., July 24, 1949; s. Samuel Isaiah and Eleanor (Streichler) M.; m. Meri-Jane Rochelson, Aug. 25, 1975; children: Daniel Rochelson, Robert Eli. BA, Columbia U., 1970, LLM, 1982, JSD, 1989; JD, NYU, 1974. Bar: N.Y. 1975, U.S. Dist. Ct. (so. and ea. dists.) N.Y. 1982, U.S. Ct. Appeals (2d cir.) 1982. Atty. enforcement div. EPA, Chgo., 1975-76, chief atty. case devel. unit, 1977-78, policy advisor to regional adminstr., 1979; sr. litigation atty. Office Enforcement, EPA, Washington, 1980-81; asst. prof. environ. law Nova U. Law Ctr., Ft. Lauderdale, Fla., 1982-85, assoc. prof., 1985-87, prof., 1987—. Author 2 books; contbr. articles to legal jours. and treatises. Mem. ABA, Environ. Law Inst. Assocs., Fla. Bar (assoc.), Internat. Coun. Environ. Law, Assn. Am. Law Schs. (exec. com., state and local govt. law sect.), Phi Alpha Delta. Home: 1985 NE 208th Ter Miami FL 33179-2264 Office: Nova U Law Ctr 3305 College Ave Fort Lauderdale FL 33314-7721

MINTZ, PAUL DAVID, pathologist; b. N.Y.C., Sept. 17, 1948; s. Bernard Jacod and Alene Paula (Lowenstein) M.; m. Susan Joyce Levy, June 3, 1973; children: Jeremy, Emily. AB in Philosophy with high distinction, U. Rochester, 1970, MD with honors, 1974. Lic. physician, N.Y., Pa., Va., Nat. Bd. Med. Examiners. Summer oncology fellow Boston U. Sch. Medicine, 1972; resident clin. pathology SUNY, Upstate Med. Ctr., Syracuse, 1974-77, chief resident, 1976-77; fellow clin. coagulation U. N.C. Sch. Medicine, Chapel Hill, 1977-78; fellow Specialized Ctr. Thrombosis Rsch. Temple U. Health Scis. Ctr., 1978-79; asst. prof. pathology U. Va. Sch. Medicine, Charlottesville, 1979-85, assoc. prof., 1985-88, assoc. prof. pathology and internal medicine, 1988-94; prof. pathology and internal medicine, 1994—; assoc. dir. Blood Bank and Transfusion Svcs. U. Va. Med. Ctr., Charlottesville, 1979-82, dir., 1982—; cons. lab. svc. VA Hosp., Salem, Va., 1979—; chmn. continuing med. edn. com. Transfusion Medicine Acad. Awardees, 1986-88; mem. planning com. Nat. Blood Resources Edn. Program, Nat. Heart, Lung and Blood Inst., 1987, spl. grant rev. com. transfusion medicine acad. award, 1991; mem. blood svcs. com. Red Cross Blood Svcs., Charlottesville chpt., Washington region; mem. hosp. transfusion com. Health Scis. Ctr., 1979—, faculty grievance com. Sch. Medicine, 1992—, continuing med. edn. com., 1993—. Mem. editl. bd. Am. Jour. Clin. Pathology, 1991—; contbr. articles to profl. jours. Bd. dirs. ARC, Ctrl. Va. chpt., 1984-90, Hillel Found., U. Va., 1986-88, Va. Discovery Mus. Recipient Charles E. Walter Meml. award Mid-Atlantic Assn. Blood Banks, 1992; grantee NIH, 1978-79, Ciba-Geigy Corp., 1979-82, Nat. Heart, Lung and Blood Inst., 1985-90, Am. Assn. Blood Banks Found., 1986-88, IVAC Corp., 1986, 88, 89, 91, 93, Baxter Healthcare Corp., 1990, ARC Jerome Holland Rsch. Lab., 1991, IBG Corp., 1991, Cobe Labs., 1991, 92, Va. Blood Svcs., 1992. Mem. Am. Assn. Blood Banks (chair subcom. on immunohematology com. on stds. 1989-93, transfusion quality assurance com. 1992—), Mid-Atlantic Blood Banks (pres. 1986-87, chair awards com. 1992—), Internat. Soc. Blood Transfusion, Assn. Clin. Scientists (coun. on immunohematology 1983—), Am. Soc. Apheresis, Acad. Clin. Lab. Physicians and Scientists, Internat. Soc. Hematotherapy and Gene Engineering, B'nai B'rith (pres. Thomas Jefferson Lodge 1985-86). Office: U Va Health Scis Ctr PO Box 286 Charlottesville VA 22902-0286

MINTZ, STUART ALAN, insurance company executive, consultant; b. L.A., Jan. 7, 1956; s. Robert Meyer and Sondra Ruth (Handler) M.; m. Joanna Ruth Toombs, May 20, 1977 (div. Jan. 1985); children: Daniel Isaac, Jacob Aaron; m. Paula Mae Nevlin, Nov. 25, 1987. AA, Orange Coast Coll., 1975; BA, U. Calif., Irvine, 1976; A in Claims, Ins. Inst. Am., 1990. Claims mgr. Farmers Ins., L.A., 1979-88, deVries and Co., Glendale, Calif., 1988-91, Blaker, Monk and Elliston, Glendale, 1991-94; asst. v.p. Maxson-Young Assoc., Inc., Houston, 1994—; access control supr. L.A. Olympic Organizing Com., 1984. Mem. Calif. Fraud Investigators, So. Calif. Fraud Investigators, No. Calif. Investigators, L.A. Adjusters Assn., Orange County Adjusters Assn., Villa Sestri Ho (treas. 1990—), Blue Goose Internat, Eagle Scout. Office: Maxson Young Assoc Inc 550 Westcott # 360 Houston TX 77007-5043

MINTZ, SUSAN ASHINOFF, menswear manufacturing company executive; b. N.Y.C., Dec. 7, 1949; d. Lawrence Lloyd and Thelma B. (Rubens) A.; m. Robert Beier Mintz, June 18, 1983; children: Geoffrey Harrison, Tyler Edward Richard. BA, Finch Coll., 1971; MPA, NYU, 1977. Menswear advt. asst. New Yorker Mag., N.Y.C., 1971-72; assoc. Staub, Warmbold & Assocs., Inc., exec. search co., N.Y.C., 1972-80; exec. v.p. Muhammad Ali Sportswear, Ltd., N.Y.C., 1980-81; pres. Forum Sportswear, Ltd., N.Y.C. and Portsmouth, Va., 1981—; group v.p. Coronet Casuals, Inc., Portsmouth, 1985—, also bd. dirs. Trustee Dean Jr. Coll. Named to Outstanding Young Women Am., U.S. Jaycees, 1980. Mem. Nat. Assn. Men's Sportswear Buyers, Men's Apparel Guild Calif., Beacon Hill Club. Office: 2615 Elmhurst Ln Portsmouth VA 23701-2736

MINTZ, SUSANNAH BETH, English language educator; b. Morristown, N.J., Jan. 9, 1965; d. Jim and Beth (MacKenzie) M. BA, U. Calif., Berkeley, 1986; MFA, Columbia U., 1992; PhD, Rice U., 1996. Instr. Columbia U., N.Y.C., 1990-92, Rice U., Houston, 1994-95; asst. prof. English Wittenberg U., Springfield, Ohio, 1996—. Contbr. articles to profl. jours. Jacob K. Javits Ednl. fellow Dept. Edn., 1994-96. Mem. MLA, John Donne Soc., Soc. for Study of Early Modern Women. Office: Wittenberg University Dept English Box 720 Ward St at N Wittenberg Ave Springfield OH 45501

MINYARD, LIZ, food products executive. BBA, Tex. Christian U., 1975. CEO Minyard Food Stores, Coppell, Tex., 1976—; dir. consumer affairs Minyard Food Stores Inc., Coppell, Tex., v.p. consumer affairs, 1980, v.p. corp. rels., 1983, also vice-chmn. bd. dirs., also co-chmn. bd. dirs. Chmn. United Way Dallas and Tarrant Counties, 1978, 83-95, Tarrant County sect. chmn., 1983-84, merchants divsn. chmn. Dallas County, 1987, Dallas County bd. dirs., 1995; bd. mem. Goodwill Industries of Dallas, Inc., 1981-94, mem. exec. com., 1987-88, 93-95, vice-chmn., 1992-94, chmn., 1995; mem. YWCA Dallas campaign drive spring 1982, chmn. campaign, 1983-85, co-chmn. of capital campaign, 1995, mayor's summer youth employment commn. co-chmn., 1994, chmn., 1995, bd. dirs., 1995; v.p. Dallas Urban League, 1989-91, bd. dirs., 1985-95, chmn. bd. dirs., 1992-93, bldg. com. chmn., 1995; mem. Dallas Citizens Coun., 1988-94, bd. dirs. exec. com., 1992-95; bd. dirs. Leukemia Assn. of North Ctrl. Tex., 1988-95; mem. Dallas Assembly, 1989-95; bd. dirs. Baylor Hosp. Found., 1989-95; mem. Dallas Summit, 1992-95, Dallas Together Forum, 1993-95, Dallas Women's Forum, 1994-95; bd. dirs. Zale Lipshy Hosp., 1993-95, Am. Heart Assn., 1991-94; chmn. City of Dallas Bond Program, 1995; nat. trustee Boys and Girls clubs of Am., 1995, and numerous others. Recipient Dallas/Ft. Worth Dist. Women in Bus. Advocate of Yr. award U.S. Small Bus. Adminstrn., 1995, Tex. Family Bus. of Yr.-Cmty. Involvement award Tex. Inst. Family Bus., 1995, Bus. award for Cmty. Involvement Martin Luther King, Jr. Cmty. Ctr., 1995, Contbrs. award Black State Employees Assn. of Tex., 1995, Art of Achievement award Nat. Fedn. of Women Bus. Owners, 1995. Mem. Food Mktg. Inst. (mem. consumer coun. 1977-88, mem. steering com. 1982, mem. pub. affairs com. 1989-90, bd. dirs. 1991-95), Tex. Food Mktg. Assn. (v.p. 1981-82, pres. 1982-84), North Tex. Food Bank (founding bd. mem., sec. 1981-83, bd. mem. 1982-95, pres. 1984, v.p. devel. 1987, chmn. hunger link program 1989-90), Second Harvest (Chgo., bd. dirs. 1992-95), CIES The Food Bus. Forum (ann. congress com. mem. 1996), North Tex. Commn. (bd. dirs. 1992-95), Greater Dallas C. of C. (mem. leadership program 1982-83, bd. dirs. 1994-95, bd. dirs. 1987-90, mem. women's bus. issues exec. com. 1994-95, women's convenant diamond cutters award 1995). Home: PO Box 518 Coppell TX 75019 Office: Minyard Food Stores Inc PO Box 518 Coppell TX 75019-0518*

MIRA, JOAQUIN GOMEZ, JR., oncologist, educator; b. Madrid, Apr. 21, 1941; came to U.S., 1967; s. Joaquin Gomez Mira, Sr. and Juana (Garcia) Gobantes; m. Sheila Martin, Jan. 21, 1975; children: Jean=Marc, Christina, Gregory. MD, U. Madrid, Spain, 1965. Diplomate Am. Bd. Radiology, Am. Bd. Therapeutic Radiology; lic. radiologist, Spain, N.Y., Calif., Tex. Resident in internal medicine Jimenez Diaz Inst. for Clin. Rsch., Madrid, 1965-67; rotating intern Providence Hosp., Seattle, 1967-68; resident in gen. surgery St. Vincent Hosp., Portland, Oreg., 1968-69; resident in therapeutic radiology Penrose Cancer Ctr., Colorado Springs, Colo., 1969-72; fellow in therapeutic radiology Meml. Hosp. Sloan-Kettering Ctr., N.Y.C., 1972-73; staff radiotherapist Meth. Hosp., Houston, 1974-75, VA Hosp., Houston, 1974-75; asst. prof. radiology Baylor Coll. Medicine, Houston, 1974-75; staff radiotherapist Cancer Therapy and Rsch. Found. South Tex., San Antonio, 1976—; acting. chief divsn. radiation oncology dept. radiology U. Tex. Health Sci. Ctr., San Antonio, 1976, asst. prof. radiology, dep. chief divsn. radiation oncology dept radiology, 1976-82, clin. assoc. prof. radiology, 1982—, dir. residency program, 1991—; staff radiotherapist Meth. Hosp., San Antonio, 1983—, Nix. Hosp., San Antonio, 1983—; pvt. practice radiotherapist San Antonio, 1983—; mem. numerous coms. Tex. Health Sci. Ctr., Audie Murphy VA Hosp., Cancer Therapy and Rsch. Ctr., Meth. Hosp., San Antonio, Santa Rosa Hosp.; cons. radiotherapist Med. Ctr. Hosp., San Antonio, 1976—, Audie L. Murphy VA Hosp., San Antonio, 1976—, State Chest Hosp., San Antonio, 1976—, St. Luke's Hosp., San Antonio, 1983—; mem. sci. adv. coun. Cancer Therapy and Rsch. Ctr. South Tex., 1976—; invited lectr. and presenter in field. Contbr. over 61 papers and abstracts to profl. jours., chpts. to books. Bd. dirs. San Antonio Symphony Orch., 1990—. Recipient Vis. Prof. dimploma Panama Soc. Oncology; grantee NIH, 1978—. Mem. AMA, Am. Coll. Radiology, Am. Coll. Therapeutic Radiologists, Am. Soc. Clin. Oncology, Radiol. Soc. N.Am., Nat. Surg. Adjuvant Breast Project, S.W. Oncology Group (quality control com. 1980—), Tex. Med. Assn., Tex. Radiol. Soc., Harris County Med. Soc., Bexar County Med. Soc., Coll. Physicians Madrid, Internat. Assn. for Study Lung Cancer, Sociedad Hispano Americano de Tex. en San Antonio., Circulo de Radioterapeutas Ibero Latino Americano (coord. lung session 4th congress 1983, sec. lung seminar 5th congress 1985). Home: 200 Bluff Knoll Dr San Antonio TX 78216-1915 Office: Cancer Therapy and Rsch Ctr 4450 Medical Dr San Antonio TX 78229-3710

MIRACLE, JAMES FRANKLIN, hospitality company executive; b. Duluth, Ky., Nov. 30, 1938; s. Carl James and Jessie (Hayes) M.; m. Iris Mae Cole, Dec. 31, 1958 (div. Apr. 1988); children: Gregory Lynn, Stuart Douglas, Kevin Carl. BS in Bus. Adminstrn., Berea (Ky.) Coll., 1962. Mgmt. trainee to gen. mgr. ITT Sheraton Corp., Boston, 1962-74; v.p., gen. mgr. Sheraton Gibson Hotel, Cin., 1969-71; gen. mgr. Sheraton Cleve. Hotel, 1971-72, Sheraton Chgo. Hotel, 1972-74, Ambassador Hotel, L.A., 1974-75; v.p. Hertz Skycenter Inc., Huntsville, Ala., 1975-80; pres. Miracle Inc., Huntsville, N. Wilkesboro, N.C., 1980—, Miracle Hostels Am., North Wilkesboro, 1988—; mem. adv. bd. Huntsville Conf. and Visitors Bur., 1976-80; instr. Wilkes C.C., Wilkesboro, N.C., 1986—, also mem. adv. com.; bd. dirs. John A. Walker Events Inc. Pres. North Ala. Arthritis Found., Huntsville, 1981; chmn. Madison County Tourism Bd., Huntsville, 1979-81, Miss World Am. Pageant, 1979. Mem. Ala. Hotel-Motel Assn. (state pres. 1979-80), North Ala. Lodging and Hospitality Assn. (pres. 1978-79). Republican.

MIRANDA, CARLOS SA, food products company executive; b. Fall River, Mass., Nov. 16, 1929; s. Carlos Sa and Annette (Pratt) M.; m. Natalie Cardoso, Jan. 5, 1949; children—Carla, Lucy, John. B.S. in Mech. Engring., Marquette U., 1956. With internat. div. Kellogg Co., Battle Creek, Mich., 1964-65, gen. mgr., Brazil, 1965-80, gen. mgr. Kellogg's Spain, 1983-84, v.p.

Kellogg Internat., Battle Creek, 1980-89, country dir. internat. exec. svc. corps., Costa Rica, 1990-91; mediator Fla. County Cts., 1994—. Recipient Pero Vaz Caminha award, Brazil, 1976; conferred title Comdr. of Legion of Honor of Marshal Rondon, Brazil, 1971. Mem. ASME. Republican. Roman Catholic. Home: Apt 614 988 Boulevard Of The Arts Sarasota FL 34236-4840

MIRANDA, CECILIA, librarian, consultant; b. Juarez, Chihuahua, Mex., Jan. 14, 1945; came to U.S., 1962; d. Carlos and Carmen (Rueda) M.; m. Jorge Chavez, Oct. 7, 1967 (div. Jan. 1976); 1 child, Jorge; m. Charles Cummings, Jan. 31, 1987 (div. Nov. 1995). BS in Secondary Edn., U. Tex., El Paso, 1977; MLS, U. Wis., 1979. Tech. libr. Sacramento Peak Obs., Sunspot, N.Mex., 1979-81; tech. svcs. libr. Midland (Tex.) Coll., 1981-92, automation and tech. svcs. libr., 1992—; cons. Midland Meml. Hosp. and Med. Ctr., 1986—; book reviewer Nat. Libr., 1985. Contbr. articles to profl. jours. Bd. dirs. Midland Need to Read, 1984-87. Recipient scholarship Tex. Libr. Assn., 1978; fellow U. Wis., Madison, 1978-79. Mem. ALA. Office: Midland Coll 3600 N Garfield St Midland TX 79705-6329

MIREE, KATHRYN WALLER, brokerage house executive; b. Ft. Rucker, Ala., Apr. 13, 1953; d. Bogue Maultsby Waller and Joy (Purifoy) Drum; m. Benjamin Kyser Miree, Nov. 17, 1984; children: Christopher Kyser, Harrison Moore. BA in History, Emory U., 1975; JD, U. Ala., 1978. Cert. fin. svcs. counselor. Mgr. estate adminstrn. Amsouth Bank, Birmingham, Ala., 1983-86, mgr. charitable trust adminstrn., 1986-90, mgr. personal trust adminstrn., 1990-93, mgr. personal trust dept., sr. v.p. and trust officer, 1993-94; pres., CEO The Trust Co. of Sterne, Agee & Leach, Inc., 1994-96; mng. dir. Sterne Agee's Leach Group, Inc., Birmingham, 1996—; bd. dirs. Ala. Planned Giving Coun., 1991-96, pres. 1991-92; pres. Estate Planning Coun. Birmingham, Inc., 1993; pres. Nat. Com. Planned Giving, 1995. Mem. editl. adv. bd. Planned Giving Today, 1994-96. Mem. pres.'s coun. U. Ala., Birmingham, 1996, mem. leadership coun., 1990-95; bd. dirs. Capstone Found., 1993-96; mem. adv. bd. Boy Scouts Am., Birmingham, 1993-96; pres. Traveler's Aid Soc., 1992-94; bd. deacons Ind. Presbyn. Ch., 1991-93; mem. Children's Hosp. Found. Coun. on Planned Giving, 1991-94, Birmingham So. Coll. Ctr. for Leadership Studies Coun., 1992-94, steering com. libr. U. Ala. Capital Campaign, 1992-94; bd. dirs. Jr. League Birmingham, 1986-88, editor Newsheet, 1987-88; bd. dirs. United Way Ctrl. Ala., 1996. Mem. Ala. Bankers Assn. (trust div. sec. com., sec./treas. 1992, pres. 1993-94), Ala. Bar Assn. (vice chmn. task force legal edn. 1992-94), Birmingham Bar Assn. Office: 1901 6th Ave N Ste 2100 Birmingham AL 35203-2618

MIRSKY, JEFFREY, science foundation administrator. Pres., COO Nat. Diagnostics, Inc. Address: 305 Patton Dr Atlanta GA 30336

MISHRA, NAWIN CHANDRA, genetics educator; b. Bhagalpur, Bihar, India, Feb. 2, 1935; came to U.S., 1967, naturalized, 1979; s. Trilochan and Jimeshwari (Choudhary) M.; m. Purnima, June 1, 1958; children: Prakash, Rashmi, Kiron. BS, Patna U., 1956, MS, 1958; PhD, McMaster U., 1967. Rsch. assoc. Rockefeller U., N.Y.C., 1969-73; assoc. prof. U. S.C., Columbia, 1973-84; prof. U. S.C., 1984—; Jane Coffin Child Meml. Fund for med. rsch. fellow Rockefeller U., N.Y.C., 1967-69; fellow Max Planck Inst., Heidelberg, Germany, 1980; cons. to UN, 1990-93, Novo Nordisk, Denmark, 1993; mem. rev. panel human genome project U.S. Dept. Energy, 1988—. NSF grantee, 1973-75; NIH grantee, 1974-77, 80-84. Fellow AAAS; mem. Gen. Soc. Am. (chair program com. 1977-79, orgn. com. 46th ann. mtg. 1978), Am. Soc. Cell Biology (congl. liaison com. 1993—). Office: U SC Dept Biol Scis 700 Sumter St Columbia SC 29201

MISIEK, DALE JOSEPH, oral and maxillofacial surgeon; b. Hartford, Conn., Dec. 10, 1952; s. Joseph John and Jadwiga Magdelena (Wojtowicz) M.; m. Patricia Ann Munson, June 28, 1975; children: Matthew Bryan, Stacy Lynne, Michael Stephen. BA magna cum laude, U. Conn., Storrs, 1974; DMD, U. Conn., Farmington, 1978; cert. advanced tng. oral and maxillofacial surgery, La. State U., 1982. Diplomate Am. Bd. Oral and Maxillofacial Surgery. Resident oral surgery Charity Hosp. of La., New Orleans, 1978-82, mem. clin. surgery com., 1984-86, mem. surgery com., 1986—, mem. credentials com., 1988—; asst. prof. dept. oral and maxillofacial surgery Sch. Dentistry, La. State U., New Orleans, 1984-87, assoc. prof., 1987-94; prof. dept. oral and maxillofacial surgery Sch. Dentistry La. State U., New Orleans, 1994—; also mem. various coms. Sch. Dentistry, La. State U., New Orleans; practice dentistry specializing in oral surgery New Orleans, 1982-84; mem. staff Ear, Eye, Nose and Throat Hosp., New Orleans, 1982—, chmn. dental dept., also mem. exec. com., credentials com. and instrument com., 1983-84; mem. staff East Jefferson Gen. Hosp., Metairie, 1982, chmn. dental dept., 1990-94, med. records com., 1983-85, credentials com., 1994—; mem. staff Univ. Hosp., New Orleans, 1982—; courtesy staff Children's Hosp., New Orleans, 1982—, Mercy Hosp., New Orleans, 1982—, So. Bapt. Hosp., New Orleans, 1983—, Our Lady of the Lake Regional Med. Ctr., Baton Rouge, 1985, Kenner (La.) Regional Med. Ctr., 1986—, Dr.'s Hosp., Metairie, 1986—; cons. VA Med. Ctr., New Orleans, 1984—; lectr. in field. Contbr. articles and abstracts to profl. jours. Recipient C.V. Mosby Book award. Fellow Am. Assn. Oral and Maxillofacial Surgeons (mem. spl. com. for devel. stds. and criteria for care 1986—, spl. com. on oral and maxillofacial surgery self-assessment program 1990), Am. Coll. Oral and Maxillofacial Surgeons; mem. ADA (cons. commn. on dental accreditation 1986—), Am. Bd. Oral and Maxillofacial Surgery (adv. com. 1990-95), La. Dental Assn., New Orleans Dental Assn. (mem. sci. program com. 1983-84), La. Soc. Oral and Maxillofacial Surgeons (mem. anesthesia com. 1983-85, mem. advanced cardiac life support com. 1986-88, sec./treas. 1991-95, v.p. 1996—), Internat. Assn. Oral and Maxillofacial Surgery, Acad. Osseointegration, Internat. Assn. Dental Rsch., Am. Assn. Dental Rsch., Orleans Parish Med. Soc., Am. Heart Assn. (instr.), Phi Beta Kappa, Phi Kappa Phi, Omicron Kappa Upsilon. Republican. Roman Catholic. Office: La State U Med Ctr Sch Dentistry Dept Oral Surgery 1100 Florida Ave # 220 New Orleans LA 70119-2714

MISRA, JAYADEV, computer science educator; b. Cuttack, Orissa, India, Oct. 17, 1947; s. Sashibhusan and Shanty (Kar) M.; m. Mamata Das, Nov. 30, 1972; children: Amitav, Anuj. B Tech, Indian Inst. Tech., Kanpur, 1969; PhD, Johns Hopkins U., 1972. Staff scientist IBM, Gaithersburg, Md., 1973-74; from asst. prof. to prof. computer sci. U. Tex., Austin, 1974—, Regents chair in computer sci., 1992—; vis. prof. Stanford (Calif.) U., 1983-84; cons. on software and hardware design. Contbr. articles to profl. jours. Guggenheim fellow, 1988-89. Fellow IEEE, Assn. Computing Machinery (Samuel N. Alexander Meml. award 1970). Office: Univ Tex Dept Computer Sci Austin TX 78712-1188

MITCHAM, JULIUS JEROME, accountant; b. Pine Bluff, Ark., Jan. 2, 1941; s. James Vernon and Bertha Lee (Robertson) M.; m. Janet Claire Berry, Mar. 31, 1970 (div. Sept. 1981); m. Marsha Lee Henderson, Oct. 22, 1983; 1 child, Timothy John. BBA, U. Cen. Ark., 1971. CPA, Ark.; cert. healthcare fin. mgr. Br. mgr. Comml. Nat. Bank, Little Rock, 1961-66; auditor, acctg. supr. Ark. Blue Cross and Blue Shield, Little Rock, 1971-77; controller Riverview Hosp., Little Rock, 1977-81; pvt. practice acctg. Little Rock, 1981-82; controller Henryetta (Okla.) Med. Ctr., 1982-83; fin. report supr. Am. Med. Internat., Inc., Houston, 1983; dir. corp. acctg. Ft. Myers (Fla.) Community Hosp., 1984-86; controller Med. Ctr. of Southeast Okla., Durant, 1986-87; chief fin. officer Gulf Coast Community Hosp./Qualicare of Miss., Inc., 1987-88; asst. adminstr. fin. S.W. Gen. Hosp., San Antonio, 1988-89; pvt. practice San Antonio, 1989-90; chief fin. officer Bapt. Meml. Hosps. of Mississippi County, Blytheville, Ark., 1991-94; CFO Med. Arts Hosp., Texarkana, Tex., 1994-96. Served with USN, 1959-61. Mem. AICPA, Ark. Soc. CPAs, Healthcare Fin. Mgmt. Assn. (cert. fellow), Lions (sec. 1985-86, 2d v.p. 1995-96), Masons. Republican. Baptist. Office: 7122 John Sealy Annex 301 University Blvd Texarkana TX 77555-0518

MITCHELHILL, JAMES MOFFAT, civil engineer; b. St. Joseph, Mo., Aug. 11, 1912; s. William and Jeannette (Ambrose) M.; BS, Northwestern U., 1934, CE, 1935; m. Maurine Hutchason, Jan. 9, 1937 (div. 1962); children: Janis Maurine Mitchelhill Leas, Jeri Ann Mitchelhill Riney; m. 2d, Alicia Beuchat, 1982; registered profl. engr., Mont., P.R., Tex.; Engring. dept. C., M., St. P. & P.R.R. Co., Chgo. and Miles City, Mont., 1935-45; asst. mgr. Ponce & Guayama R.R. Co., Aguirre, P.R., 1945-51, v.p., gen. mgr., 1969-70; mgr. Cen. Cortada, Santa Isabel, P.R., 1951-54; r.r. supt. Braden Copper Co., Rancagua, Chile, 1954-63; staff engr. Coverdale & Colpitts, N.Y.C., 1963-64; asst. to exec. v.p. Central Aguirre Sugar Co., 1964-67; v.p., gen. mgr. Coddea, Inc., Dominican Republic, 1967-68; asst. to gen. mgr. Land Adminstrn. of P.R., La Nueva Central Aguirre, 1970-71, for Centrals Aguirre Lafayette and Mercedita, 1971-72; asst. to gen. mgr. Corporacion Azucarera de P.R., 1973-76, asst. to exec. dir., 1977-79, asst. exec. dir. for environ., 1979-82; engring. cons., 1982-92; Kendall County engr., 1985-96. Fellow ASCE; mem. Am. Ry. Engring. Assn., Colegio de Ingenieros y Agrimensores de P.R., Explorers Club, Circumnavigators Club, Travellers Century Club, Sigma Xi, Tau Beta Pi. Home: PO Box 506 Boerne TX 78006-0506 Office: 12 Staudt St Boerne TX 78006-1820

MITCHELL, ADELE DICKINSON, health facility administrator; b. Va., Sept. 29, 1952; d. William A. Dickinson and Nancy (McGowen) Ring; m. William L. Mitchell, May 23, 1977. BSN cum laude, U. Va., 1977. RN, Va.; cert. CPR and spl. care cons. Staff nurse emergency rm. Trauma I Ctr. Care U. Va., Charlottesville, 1976-78; coronary intensive care specialist Cmty. Hosp. Roanoke (Va.) Valley, 1978-85; adminstr. nursing/clin. nursing, clin. dir. protocol, dir. rsch. Clinician Svcs., Roanoke, 1984-92; vol. free clinics for the working poor, 1978-85; vol. tchr. adult edn. classes, 1978-85; vol. tchr. natural childbirth, 1978-85; bd. dirs. rsch. muscle tissue regeneration in field. Author: The Anesthesia Syndrome; designer templates to patent in field. Named Profl. Woman of Yr., Internat. Pilot Orgn., 1991, Nat. Competition Pilot Clubs Internat., 1991.

MITCHELL, ALLAN EDWIN, lawyer; b. Okemah, Okla., May 13, 1944; m. Neva G. Ream; children: Brian, Amy. BA in Mass. Comm., Northwestern Okla. State U., Alva, 1991; JD, U. Okla., 1994. Bar: Okla. 1994, U.S. dist. ct. (we. and no. dists.) 1994. Asst. state mgr. Oklahomans for Right to Work, Oklahoma City, 1967-68; exec. dir. London Sq. Village, Oklahoma City, 1968-73; dist. mgr. Farmland Ins. Svc., Oklahoma City, 1974-80, Nat. Farmers Union, Oklahoma City, 1980-85; dist. agt. Prudential Ins., Cherokee, Okla., 1985-89; atty. Hughes & Grant, Oklahoma City, 1994—. Mem. Cherokee Bd. Edn., 1985-90; mem. fin. com. Rep. Party of Okla., 1995; scoutmaster, 1981-86; adult advisor Girl Scouts Am.; pres. United Way Cherokee, 1984; mem. Okla. Sch. Bd. Mems. Legis. Network, 1985-90. Mem. Ch. of the Nazarene.

MITCHELL, BELINDA KAYE, oncology nurse; b. Poplarville, Miss., Oct. 24, 1955; d. Joyce Marie (Davis) Hariel; m. Michael P. Mitchell. ADN, Pearl River Jr. Coll., Poplarville, 1978; BSN, U. So. Miss., Long Beach, 1984; MSN, U. South Ala., Mobile, 1992. RN, Miss. Head nurse Meml. Hosp. Gulfport, Miss., 1982-84, staff nurse outpatient chemotherapy, 1988—. Mem. ANA, Oncology Nursing Soc. Home: 868 Barth Rd Poplarville MS 39470-3447 Office: Meml Hosp at Gulfport 4500 13th St Gulfport MS 39501

MITCHELL, BURLEY BAYARD, JR., state supreme court chief justice; b. Oxford, N.C., Dec. 15, 1940; s. Burley Bayard and Dorothy Ford (Champion) M.; m. Mary Lou Willett, Aug. 3, 1962; children: David Bayard, Catherine Morris. BA with honors, N.C. State U., 1966, DHL (hon.), 1995; JD, U. N.C., 1969. Bar: N.C. 1969, U.S. Ct. Appeals (4th cir.) 1970, U.S. Supreme Ct. 1972. Asst. atty. gen. State of N.C., Raleigh, 1969-72, dist. atty., 1973-77, judge Ct. Appeals, 1977-79, sec. crime control, 1979-82; justice Supreme Ct. N.C., Raleigh, 1982-94; chief justice Supreme Ct. of N.C., Raleigh, 1995—. Served with USN, 1958-62, Asia. Recipient N.C. Nat. Guard Citizen Commendation award, 1982. Mem. ABA, VFW, N.C. Bar Assn., Mensa, Am. Legion. Democrat. Methodist. Home: 820 Glen Eden Dr Raleigh NC 27612-5038 Office: Supreme Ct NC PO Box 1841 Raleigh NC 27602-1841

MITCHELL, CAROLYN COCHRAN, college official; b. Atlanta, Dec. 27, 1943; d. Clemern Covell and Agnes Emily (Veal) Cochran; m. W. Alan Mitchell, Aug. 30, 1964; 1 child, Teri Marie. AB magna cum laude, Mercer U., 1965, M in Svc. Mgmt., 1989. Caseworker Ga. Dept. Family & Children Svcs., Macon, 1965-67, Covington, 1967-69; presch. dir. Southwestern Theol. Sem., Ft. Worth, 1969-70; presch. tchr., dir. Noah's Ark Day Care, Bowden, Ga., 1970-72, First Bapt. Ch., Bremen, Ga., 1972-75, Roebuck Park Bapt. Ch., Birmingham, Ala., 1975-79; freelance office mgr. and bookkeeper Macon, 1979-84; asst. to pres. Ga. Wesleyan Coll., Macon, 1984—; exec. dir. Ga. Women of Achievement, 1991-95; dir. Macon Arts Alliance, 1987-91; mem. Cultural Plan Oversight Com., 1989-90. Mem. Get Out the Vote Task Force, Macon, 1981—, Macon Symphony Guild, 1986-91; dep. registrar Bibb County Bd. Elections, Macon, 1981-95. Mem. AAUW (bd. dirs. Ga. chpt., v.p. 1991-93, chair coll.-univ. rels. com. 1993-94, bylaws com. 1991-92, state ednl. found. chair 1996—, v.p., treas., historian, Macon chpt., Named Gift Honoree 1988), NAFE, NOW, Women's Network for Change, Am. Mgmt. Assn., Presdl. Assts. in Higher Edn., Religious Coalition for Reproductive Choice, The Interfaith Alliance, Women's Polit. Orgn. Macon, Sigma Mu. Democrat. Unitarian. Office: Ga Wesleyan Coll 4760 Forsyth Rd Macon GA 31210-4407

MITCHELL, EDDIE, writer, activist, health issues educator; b. Stuttgart, Germany, Nov. 4, 1964; s. Carl Bernard and Carolyn Marie (Campbell) M. BA in Spanish, Berea Coll., 1987. Family worker Vols. of Am., Louisville, 1988-90, resident mgr., 1990; caseworker Cabinet for Human Resources, Louisville, 1990-93; freelance writer Louisville, 1993—; refugee caseworker Cabinet for Human Resources, Louisville, 1991-93; edn. programs coord. Comty. Health Trust, 1995—. Author of poems. Vol. project coord. Fairness Campaign, Louisville, 1991—; vol. coord. Gay and Lesbian Hotline, 1994; mem. North Cen. Ky. HIV Prevention Comty. Planning Group, 1994—. Mem. Honesty Louisville (programming com.), March for Justice (treas. 1993—, co-chair 1994-96), Gays and Lesbians United for Equality (sec. 1990-92, pres. 1994-96, Man of Yr. 1994). Democrat. Baptist. Home: PO Box 2543 Louisville KY 40201-2543

MITCHELL, ELIZABETH MARELLE, nursing educator, medical, surgical nurse; b. Bemis, Tenn., Dec. 2, 1937; d. William Columbus and Ruth Marelle (Wadley) Latham; m. Thomas Alton McNatt, June 20, 1953 (dec. Mar. 1984); children: Glenn McNatt, Craig McNatt, Chris McNatt; m. Charles Leon Mitchell, Sept. 7, 1985; stepchildren: Melanie Campbell, Mike, Allyson Flanagan. AA in Nursing, Union U., 1965; BSN, U. Tenn., Martin, 1994; MSN, FNP, U. Tenn., Memphis, 1996. RN, Tenn.; CNOR; cert. BCLS, BCLS instr., BCLS instr. trainer, ACLS, ACLS instr. Staff nurse med.-surg. units Jackson (Tenn.)-Madison County Gen. Hosp., 1965-66; physician 1st asst. Jackson Clinic Surgeons, 1966-74; nursing instr. Jackson Area Vo-Tech Sch., 1974-78, nursing instr. supr., 1978-81; supr. oper. rm. Jackson Splty. Hosp. (acquired by Jackson-Madison County Gen. Hosp. 1983), 1981-85; instr. nurse edn. Jackson-Madison County Gen. Hosp., 1985—; mem. nursing adv. bd. Jackson Area Vo-Tech Sch., 1987—; mem. task force nursing asst. curriculum devel. State of Tenn., Nashville, 1992; clin. skills judge Health Occupations Student Assn. Tenn. State Competition, Nashville, 1992. Tchr. Sunday sch. Malesus (Tenn.) Bapt. Ch., 1975-86. Mem. Assn. Oper. Rm. Nurses (del. to congress 1992, mem. program com. 1993, 94), Am. Soc. Healthcare Edn. and Tng. (svc. rep. West Tenn. 1988, Outstanding Regional Rep. Tenn. chpt. 1988), West Tenn. Healthcare Edn. and Tng. Conf. Group (pres. 1987, regional rep. 1988, sec. 1994), U. Tenn. Martin Nursing Honor Soc., Phi Theta Kappa. Home: RR 3 Box 378 Linden TN 37096-9544 Office: Jackson-Madison County Gen Hosp 708 W Forest Ave Jackson TN 38301-3901

MITCHELL, GUY PATRICK, manufacturing executive; b. Jonesboro, Ark., Mar. 15, 1937; s. Joseph Francis and Artie (Cook) M.; student LaSalle U., 1961, Wharton Sch., 1977; m. Patricia Ann Thurber, July 18, 1964; children: Jennifer and Juliana (twins), Richard Dale, Larry Guy, Elizabeth Ann, Alan Dane. Engring. technician Phillips Petroleum Co., Bartlesville, Okla., 1956-69; sales engr. Ameron Inc., Houston, 1969-70; gen. sales mgr. Porter Paint Co., Louisville, 1970-78; v.p. Sigma Coatings, Inc. subs. Am. Petrofina, New Orleans, 1978-83; dir. Sigma Internat. Marine/Protective Coatings, Amsterdam, 1978-83; exec. v.p. Hempel's Indsl. Coatings Inc., 1983-87; exec. v.p., gen. mgr. Internat. Paint U.S.A., Houston, 1987-88; gen. mgr. Cook Paint & Varnish Co., Houston, 1988—, v.p. Cook Paint & Varnish Co.; pres. Sunark Inc., Kingwood, Tex., 1988—, Natasco Svcs., Inc., Kingwood, Tex., 1993—; chmn. Environ. Tech. Group, Inc., Houston, 1994—; bd. dirs., sec. Crown Paint Ltd., Montego Bay, Jamaica; chmn. Protection Plus Systems Inc., Dallas. Named hon. Ky. col. Mem. Am. Mgmt. Assn., Nat. Assn. Corrosion Engrs., Soc. Naval Architects and Marine Engrs., Inst. Certification Engring. Technicians, Officers Assn. (mem. car dept.). Republican. Mem. Ch. of Christ.

MITCHELL, JACKIE WILLIAMS, state agency administrator, consultant; b. Madison, Miss., June 22, 1964; d. Fillmore and Annie Mae Williams; m. Johnny Lee Mitchell, Dec. 6, 1986. BS in Computer Sci., Jackson State U., 1986, MS in Ednl. Adminstrn. and Supervision, 1991, postgrad., 1992—; grad., Inst. Cmty. Devel., U. Ctrl. Ark. Cert. profl. cmty. developer. Computer sci. instr. Phillips Jr. Coll., Jackson, Miss., 1991-92; cmty. assistance specialist Miss. Dept. of Econ. and Cmty. Devel., Jackson, Miss., 1993—; del. White House Cmty. Empowerment Conf., 1996. Dir. cmty. events The Arts Alliance of Jackson & Hinds County, Jackson, 1987-93. Grantee Miss. Arts Commn., Jackson, 1992. Mem. ASPA (Miss. state coun. mem. 1995—), Cmty. Devel Soc. (Milw.), Toastmasters, Order Eastern Star (Prince Hall Affiliated). Home: 2503 Rutledge Ave Jackson MS 39213 Office: Miss Dept Econ & Cmty Devel PO Box 849 Jackson MS 39205

MITCHELL, JEFFREY THOMAS, health science facility administrator; b. Columbus, Ohio, Aug. 9, 1946; s. Roger Lyman and Virginia Claire (Sands); children: Lauren Claire, Spencer Thomas. BS, Wright State U., 1976; Masters in Hosp. Adminstr, Xavier U., 1978. Asst. v.p. Grandview Hosp., Dayton, Ohio, 1977-81; v.p. Wyandotte (Mich.) Gen. Hosp., 1981-85; assoc. prof. Mercy Coll. Detroit, 1981-85; v.p. Aultman Hosp., Canton, Ohio, 1985-91; adminstr., chief exec. officer The Shriner's Children's Hosp., Lexington, Ky., 1992-93; v.p. Innovative Med. Svcs., Inc., Bradenton, Fla., 1994—; bd. dirs. Erie Shores Health Services Inc., Monroe, mem. ambulatory surgery S. Mich. Program Afford. Health, 1980-85, adminstrv. mem. S. Detroit Ongoing Med. System Council, 1981-85, ambulatory task force mem. Miami Valley Health Systems Agy., Dayton 1977-81; instr. grad. program health adminstrn. Cen. Mich. U., Mt. Clemens. Mem. United Arts Found. Stark County, Stark County Cancer Com. Mem. Am. Coll. Health Care Execs. Republican. Episcopalian. Home: 7001 20th Ave W Bradenton FL 34209 Office: Innovative Med Svcs Inc 1235 Talleunst Rd Sarasota FL 34243

MITCHELL, JERE HOLLOWAY, physiologist, researcher, medical educator; b. Longview, Tex., Oct. 17, 1928; s. William Holloway and Dorothea (Turner) M.; m. Pamela Battey, Oct. 1, 1960; children: Wendy Mitchell O'Sullivan, Laurie Mitchell Woods, Amy Mitchell Poeppel. BS with honors, Va. Mil. Inst., 1950; MD, Southwestern Med. Sch., 1954. Intern Parkland Meml. Hosp., Dallas, 1954-55, resident in internal medicine, 1955-56; asst. prof. medicine and physiology U. Tex. Southwestern Med. Ctr., Dallas, 1962-66, dir. Weinberger Lab. for Cardiopulmonary Research, 1966—, assoc. prof., 1966-69, prof., 1969—, dir. Harry S. Moss Heart Ctr., 1976—, holder Frank M. Ryburn Jr. chair in heart research, 1982—; holder Carolyn P. and S. Roger Horchow Chair in Cardiac Rsch., 1989—; Pfizer vis. profl. Pa. State U., 1990; Percy Russo lectr. U. Sydney, Cumberland Coll., 1991. Established Investigator, Am. Heart Assn., 1962-67. Recipient Career Devel. award USPHS, 1968-73; Donald W. Seldin Research award U. Tex. Southwestern, 1978; recipient Carl J. Wiggers award Am. Physiology Soc. 1992. Attending physician Parkland Meml. Hosp., 1963—, St. Paul Med. Ctr., 1966—, VA Med. Ctr. Dallas, 1969—; mem. courtesy staff Zale-Lipshy U. Hosp., 1990—. Mem. Internat. Union Physiol. Soc. (commn. on cardiovascular physiology 1977—), Applied Physiol. Orthopedics Study Sect., NIH, 1979-81; Respirat. Appl. Physiol. Study Sect., NIH, 1981-82; Council of Cardiac Rehab. of Internat. Soc. & Fed. Cardiol., 1981—; Sci. Adv. Bd., USAF, 1986-90; mem. cardiology adv. com. NHLBI, 1988-92, rsch. review com. A-NHLBI, 1992—; Med. Sci. Com. AAAS, 1988—. Mem. editorial bd. Am. Jour. Physiology, 1972-76, Circulation, 1978-81, 93—, Am. Jour. Cardiology, 1965-74, 82-84, Cardiovascular Research, 1979-87, Jour. Cardiopulmonary Rehab., 1981—, Clin. Physiology, 1981—, Experimental Physiology, 1993—, Jour. Applied Physiology, 1978-82, 84-89, assoc. editor, 1990-93. Fellow Am. Coll. Cardiology (Young Investigator award 1961), Am. Coll. Sports Medicine (Citation award 1983, Honor award 1988, Joseph B. Wolffe lectr. 1989); mem. Am. Heart Assn. (Award of Merit 1984, pres. Dallas div. 1977-78, pres. Tex. affiliate 1983-84, nat. v.p. 1990-91), Am. Fedn. Clin. Research (emeritus), Am. Soc. Clin. Investigation (emeritus), Assn. Am. Physicians, Am. Physiol. Soc. (cardiovascular sect.), Assn. Univ. Cardiologists, Alpha Omega Alpha. Office: U Tex Southwestern Med Ctr Harry S Moss Heart Ctr 5323 Harry Hines Blvd Dallas TX 75235-9034

MITCHELL, JERRY CALVIN, environmental company executive; b. Shubuta, Miss., Feb. 27, 1938; s. Joe Calvin and Elizabeth (Hudson) M.; s. Thelma Baker Becker, 1957; children: Jerry Jr., Charles Joseph, Stephen Thomas. BS in Chem. Engring., Miss. State U., 1960. Chem. engr. U.S. Gypsum Co., Greenville, Miss., 1960-61, quality engr., 1963-67; quality supt. U.S. Gypsum Co., Danville, Va., 1967-71; plant mgr. waste water treatment, City of Greenville, 1971-77; v.p. McCullough Environ., Murfreesboro, Tenn., 1977-83, pres., 1983-91; pres. Mitchell Tech. Svcs., Murfreesboro, 1991—; bd. dirs. Barton ATC. Charter organizer Sertoma Club, Greenville, 1972; pres. Rutherford County Assn. for Retarded Citizens, Murfreesboro, 1985-86; mem. Rutherford County Spl. Olmpics, Murfreesboro, 1986. Served to 2d lt. U.S. Army, 1961-62, 1st lt. Miss. Army Nat. Guard, 1962-67. Mem. Water Environment Fedn., Miss. Water and Wastewater Operators Assn., Miss. Water Environment Assn. (pres., v.p. 1974-76), Okla. Water and Pollution Control, Ky.-Tenn. Water Pollution Control Assn., Tenn. Water and Wastewater Operators Assn. Methodist. Office: Mitchell Tech Svcs Inc 325 W Mcknight Dr Murfreesboro TN 37129-2450

MITCHELL, JO KATHRYN, hospital technical supervisor; b. Clarksville, Ark., Dec. 1, 1934; d. Vintris Franklin and Melissa Lucile (Edwards) Clark; m. James M. Mitchell, June 4, 1955 (dec. Feb. 1973); children: James, Karen Ann, Leslie Kay, Vicki Lynn. Student, U. Ark., Fayetteville, 1952-53; student, Coll. Ozarks, 1953-54, U. Ark., 1954-55, Little Rock U., 1958. Technologist clin. chemistry U. Hosp., Little Rock, 1956-57, asst. supr., 1957-59, rsch. technologist, 1960-62, asst. supr. clin. chemistry, 1979-82, supr. clin. chemistry, 1982—; technologist Conway County Hosp., Morrilton, Ark., 1959; office mgr., co-owner Medic Pharmacy, Little Rock, 1962-71; owner The Cheese Shop, Little Rock, 1977-80. Adult advisor Order Rainbow Girls local, Little Rock, 1970-84, state, Ark., 1977-84. Mem. Pharmacy Aux. (pres. 1967-69), Order Eastern Star. Methodist. Home: 6908 Lucerne Dr Little Rock AR 72205-5029

MITCHELL, JOHN DIETRICH, theatre arts institute executive; b. Rockford, Ill., Nov. 3, 1917; s. John Dennis Royce and Dora Marie (Schroeder) M.; m. Miriam Pitcairn, Aug. 25, 1956; children: John Daniel, Lorenzo Theodore, Barbarina Mitchell Heyerdahl. BSS, Northwestern U., 1939, MA, 1941; EdD, Columbia U., 1956; HHD (hon.), Northwood U., 1986. Dir., producer Am. Broadcasting Co., N.Y.C., 1942-46; assoc. editor Samuel French, Publ., N.Y.C., 1946-48; assoc. prof. Manhattan Coll., N.Y.C., 1948-58; pres. Inst. for Advanced Studies in the Theatre Arts, N.Y.C., 1958—; founder, pres. Eaton St. Press, Key West, Fla., 1994; bd. dirs. Beneficia Found., Jenkintown, Pa. Author: Staging Chekhov, 1990, Actors Talk, 1991, Gift of Apollo, 1992, Staging Japanese Theatre: Noh and Kabuki, 1995, Men Stand on Shoulders, 1996; author: (aka Jack Royce) The Train Stopped at Domodossola, 1993, Murder at the Kabuki, 1994, Dressed to Murder, Way to the Towers of Silence, 1996. Trustee Northwood U., Midland, Mich., 1972-91; patron Met. Opera, N.Y.C.; mem. Cmty. Ch. Key West. Named Hon. conch Key West (Fla.) Commrs., 1994. Mem. Met. Mus., Key West Arts and Hist. Soc., Tennessee Williams Fine Arts Ctr. (founder), Key West Literary Seminar (emeritus), Nippon Club N.Y.C., N.Y. Athletic Club. Home: 703 Eaton St Key West FL 33040-6843 also: Eaton Street Press 524 Eaton St # 30 Key West FL 33040-6881 Office: Inst Advanc Studies Theater 703 Eaton St Key West FL 33040-6843

MITCHELL, KIMBERLY JEAN, human resources director; b. St. Augustine, Fla., Aug. 2, 1961; d. Robert Edward and Barbara Jean Mitchell. Student, Nashville State Tech. Coll. Asst. buyer Svc. Mdse., Brentwood, Tenn., 1976-85; store mgr. Koenig Art Emporium, Goodlettsville, Tenn., 1985-88; store mgr., new store opening coord. Cracker Barrel and Country Store, Lebanon, Tenn., 1988-91; store mgr. Old Time Pottery, Madison, Tenn., 1991-93; dir. human resources A Home Care, Inc., Brentwood, 1993—; policy and procedure com. A Home Care, Inc., 1994-96; muscular dystrophy-regional coord. Svc. Mdse., Brentwood, Nashville,

1976-82. Mem. C. of C. Office: A Home Care Inc 116 Wilson Pike Ste 202 Brentwood TN 37027-3930

MITCHELL, KOSSUTH MAYER, business educator; b. Thomasville, Ala., Aug. 10, 1942; s. Zadock and Carrie Bell (Harvel) M.; m. Sandra Shafer Mitchell; children: Sherry Roy, Kossuth II, Lenore Pollard, Christie Snyder, Maribeth. AA, Monterey Peninsula Coll., 1975; BBA, James Madison U., 1982, MBA, 1984; D in Bus. Adminstrn., Nova Southea. U., 1993. Enlisted U.S. Army, 1960, advanced through grades to sgt. maj., ret., 1983; prof. bus. adminstrn., bus. program coord. Alice Lloyd Coll., Pippa Passes, Ky., 1984—; dir. Ctry. for Econ. Edn., Alice Lloyd Coll., 1988-92, founder Students in Free Enterprise team, 1988, faculty sponsor Bapt. Student Union, 1985-88, guest spkr., 1985—, workshop leader Mission Project, spring 1993; presenter ednl., profl., civic and ch. orgns. Bd. dirs. Our Lady of the Way Hosp., Martin, Ky., 1993—; mem. adv. bd. Caney Creek Mental Rehab. Complex, Pippa Passes, 1994—; active Gideons, 1995—. Decorated Bronze Star with two bronze oak leaf clusters; Kossuth M. Mitchell scholarship endowed in his name Alice Lloyd Coll., 1996. Mem. Acad. Mgmt., Midwest Acad. Mgmt., Ky. Bus. Soc., Acad. Fin. Mgmt., Noncommd. Officers Assn. (life), Am. Fedn. Police (Am. Patriotism award 1996), VFW (life), DAV (life), Kiwanis (lt. gov. divsn. 8 Ky.-Tenn. dist. 1993-94, pres. Knott County club 1991-92, club sec., treas. 1990-91, 94-95), Ky. Cols., Alpha Chi (v.p. region V 1990-92, pres. 1992-94, inaugurator Ky. Eta chpt Alice Lloyd Coll. 1988, inaugurator Caney Creek Cmty. Ctr. alumni chpt. 1993), Phi Beta Lambda (founder, primary advisor Omega Alpha Tau chpt. 1986-88, asst. advisor 1988—, advisor Alice Lloyd Coll. bus. club 1984-86). Baptist. Home and Office: Alice Lloyd Coll 100 Purpose Rd # 28 Pippa Passes KY 41844

MITCHELL, LANSING LEROY, federal judge; b. Sun, La., Jan. 17, 1914; s. Leroy A. and Eliza Jane (Richardson) M.; m. Virginia Jumonville, Apr. 18, 1938; children—Diane Mitchell (Mrs. Donald Lee Parker), Lansing Leroy. B.A., La. State U., 1934, LL.B., 1937. Bar: La. 1937. Pvt. practice Pontchatoula, 1937-38; spl. agt. FBI, 1938-41; atty. SEC, 1941-42; asst. U.S. atty. Eastern Dist. La., 1946-53; also engaged in pvt practice; ptnr. Deutsch, Kerrigan & Stiles., New Orleans, 1953-66; U.S. dist. judge Eastern Dist. La., 1966—. Chmn. nat. security com. New Orleans C. of C., 1963-66; vice chmn. New Orleans Armed Forces Day, 1964, 65, New Orleans Heart Fund campaign, 1959-60; mem. New Orleans Municipal Auditorium Adv. Com., 1957-61, New Orleans Municipal Com. Finance, 1955-67, Small Bus. Adv. Council La., 1963-66; pres. Camp Fire Girls Greater New Orleans, 1965-67; La. chmn. Lawyers for Kennedy-Johnson, 1960. Served to lt. col. AUS, 1942-46; col. Res. (ret.). Decorated Royal Order St. George Royal Order Scotland. Mem. ABA, Inter-Am. Bar Assn., La. Bar Assn., New Orleans Bar Assn., Maritime Law Assn. U.S., Judge Adv. Assn., Soc. Former Spl. Agts. FBI, Am. Legion, Mil. Order World Wars, V.F.W., Navy League, Assn. U.S. Army (pres. La. 1964-65, pres. New Orleans 1961-64, v.p. 4th Army region 1963-66), Soc. Mayflower Descendants in State of La. (assoc.), Scabbard and Blade, SAR, S.R., Soc. War 1812 La., Pi Kappa Alpha, Phi Delta Phi, Theta Nu Epsilon. Clubs: Mason (33 degree, New Orleans) (Shriner), Press (New Orleans), Paul Morphy Chess (New Orleans), Southern Yacht (New Orleans), Bienville, Pendennis (New Orleans); Tchefuncta Country (Covington, La.). Office: US Dist Ct C-508 US Courthouse 500 Camp St New Orleans LA 70130-3313*

MITCHELL, LAURA ANNE GILBERT, critical care nurse; b. Anniston, Ala., Oct. 13, 1957; d. Leonard A. and Betty Joyce (Wilkinson) Gilbert; m. Lee H. Mitchell, June 20, 1981; 1 child, Joseph L. ADN, DeKalb Coll., 1987; BSN magna cum laude, Med. Coll. Ga., 1993. CCRN. Staff nurse, preceptor ICU and CCU Gwinnett Med. Ctr., Lawrenceville, Ga., 1987-89, charge nurse cardiac catheterization lab., 1989—. Mem. AACN, Phi Theta Kappa (internat.), Sigma Theta Tau. Home: 435 Clark Lake Estate Dr Grayson GA 30221-1234

MITCHELL, MALINDA JANE, writer; b. Heflin, Ala., May 21, 1949; d. Thomas Jackson Fields and Malinda Audine (Carter) Brown; m. Michael Lee Stephenson, Oct. 13 (div. 1981); children: Michael Shane, Kristilee, David Wayne, Kasey Lynn; m. Alton Mitchell, Jan. 31, 1986. Author juvenile books: Cindy and Tommy Enjoys Their Life, 1967, The Chicken and the Weed, 1993, D.A.W.D. (Do Away With Drugs), 1994, Chicken Continues to Teach, 1995. Home: 43 Fred Ellzey Rd Soso MS 39480-5112

MITCHELL, MICHELLE B., protective services official. Sheriff City of Richmond, Va. Office: City of Richmond Sheriff's Office 1701 Fairfield Way Richmond VA 23223

MITCHELL, MOZELLA GORDON, English language educator, minister; b. Starkville, Miss., Aug. 14, 1936; d. John Thomas and Odena Mae (Graham) Gordon; m. Edrick R. Woodson, Mar. 20, 1951 (div. 1974); children: Cynthia LaVern, Marcia Delores Woodson Miller. AB, LeMoyne Coll., 1959; MA in English, U. Mich., 1963; MA in Religious Studies, Colgate-Rochester Divinity Sch., 1973; PhD, Emory U., 1980. Instr. in English and Speech Alcorn A&M Coll., Lorman, Miss., 1960-61; instr. English, chmn. dept. Owen Jr. Coll., Memphis, 1961-65; asst. prof. English and religion Norfolk State Coll., U. Norfolk, Va., 1965-81; assoc. prof. U. South Fla., Tampa, 1981-93, prof., 1993—; pastor Mount Sinai AME Zion Ch., Tampa, 1982-89; presiding elder Tampa dist. AME Zion Ch., 1988—; vis. assoc. prof. Hood Theol. Sem., Salisbury, N.C., 1979-80, St. Louis U., 1992-93; vis. asst. lectr. U. Rochester, N.Y., 1972-73; co-dir. Ghent VISTA Project, Norfolk, 1969-71; cons. Black Women and Ministry Interdenominational Theol. Ctr; lectr. Fla. Humanities Coun., 1994-95. Author: Spiritual Dynamics of Howard Thurman's Theology, 1985, Howard Thurman and the Quest for Freedom, Proc. 2d Ann. Howard Thurman Convocation (Peter Lang), 1992, African American Religious History in Tampa Bay, 1992;, New Africa in America: The Blending of African and American Religious and Social Traditions Among Black People in Meridian, Mississippi and Surrounding Counties (Peter Lang), 1994, also articles, essays in field; editor: Martin Luther King Meml. Series in Religion, Culture and Social Devel.; editorial bd. Cornucipia Reprint Series. Mem. connectional coun. A.M.E. Zion Ch., Charlotte, 1984—, staff writer Sunday sch. lit., 1981—, mem. jud. coun.; mem. Tampa-Hillsborough County Human Rels. Coun., 1987—; pres. Fla. Coun. Chs., Orlando, 1988-90; del. 7th assembly World Coun. Chs., Canberra, Australia, 1991, 17th World Meth. Coun., Rio de Janiero, 1996; founder Women at the Well, Inc. Recipient ecumenical leadership citation Fla. Coun. Chs., 1990, Inaugural lectr. award Geddes Hanson Black Cultural Ctr. Princeton Theol. Sem., 1993; fellow Nat. Doctoral Fund, 1978-80; grantee NEH, 1981, Fla. Endowment for Humanities, 1990—, U. South Fla. Rsch. Coun., 1990—. Mem. Coll. Theology Soc., Am. Acad. Religion, Soc. for the Study of Black Religion (pres. 1992-96), Joint Ctr. for Polit. Studies, Black Women in Ch. and Soc., Alpha Kappa Alpha. Phi Kappa Phi. Democrat. Methodist. Office: U South Fla 301 CPR Religious Studies Dept Tampa FL 33620

MITCHELL, PAULA RAE, nursing educator; b. Independence, Mo., Jan. 10, 1951; d. Millard Henry and E. Lorene (Denton) Gates; m. Ralph William Mitchell, May 24, 1975. BS in Nursing, Graceland Coll., 1973; MS in Nursing, U. Tex., 1976; EdD in Ednl. Adminstrn., N.Mex. State U., 1996. RN, Tex., Mo.; cert. childbirth educator. Commd. capt. U.S. Army, 1972; ob-gyn. nurse practitioner U.S. Army, Seoul, Korea, 1977-78; resigned, 1978; instr. nursing El Paso (Tex.) C.C., 1979-85, dir. nursing, 1985—, acting div. chmn. health occupations, 1985-86, div. chmn., 1986—, curriculum facilitator, 1984-86; ob-gyn. nurse practitioner Planned Parenthood, El Paso, 1981-86, mem. med. com., 1986—; cons. in field. Author: (with Grippando) Nursing Perspectives and Issues, 1989, 93; contbr. articles to profl. jours. Founder, bd. dirs. Health-C.R.E.S.T., El Paso, 1981-85; mem. pub. edn. com. Am. Cancer Soc., El Paso, 1983-84, mem. profl. activities com., 1992-93; mem. El Paso City-County Bd. Health, 1989-91; mem. Govt. Applications Rev. Com., Rio Grande Coun. Govts., 1989-91; mem. collaborative coun. El Paso Magnet H.S. for Health Care Professions, 1992-94. Decorated Army Commendation medal, Meritorious Svc. medal. Mem. Nat. League Nursing (mem. resolutions com. Assocs. Degree coun. 1987-89, accreditation site visitor, AD coun. 1990—, mem. Tex. edn. com. 1991-92, Tex. 3rd v.p. 1992-93), Am. Soc. Psychoprophylaxis Obstetrics, Nurses Assn. Am. Coll. Obstetricians & Gynecologists (cert. in ambulatory women's health care; chpt. coord. 1979-83, nat. program rev. com. 1984-86, corr. 1987-89), Advanced Nurse Practitioner Group El Paso (coord. 1980-83 legis. committee 1984), Am. Phys. Therapist Assn. (commn. on accreditation, site visitor for phys. therapist assistant programs 1991—), Orgn. Assoc. Degree Nursing (Tex. membership chmn. 1985-89, chmn. goals com. 1989—, mem nat. by-laws com., 1990—), Am. Vocat. Assn., Am. Assn. Women Community & Jr. Colls., Tex. Orgn. Nurse Execs., Nat. Coun. Occupational Edn. (mem. articulation task force 1986-89, program standards task force 1991-93), Nat. Coun. Instructional Adminstrs., Tex. Soc. Allied Health Profls., Tex. Nurses Assn., Nat. Soc. Allied Health Profls. (mem. edn. com. 1993—), Sigma Theta Tau, Phi Kappa Phi. Mem. Christian Ch. (Disciples of Christ). Home: 4616 Cupid Dr El Paso TX 79924-1726 Office: El Paso C C PO Box 20500 El Paso TX 79998-0500

MITCHELL, ROBERT EDGAR, JR., gastroenterologist; b. Oct. 20, 1919; s. Robert Edgar and Julia Gardner (Carlton) M.; m. Mary Elizabeth Hiester, June 26, 1954; children: Robert Edgar III, Clark Carlton, Richard Gardner. AB, Hampden-Sydney Coll., 1940; MD, U.Va., 1950. Instr. in medicine Tulane U. Med. Sch., New Orleans, 1953-54; resident gastroenterology svc. of Dr. Bockus Univ. Pa. Grad. Hosp., Phila., ., 1954-55; chief gastroenterology sect. McGuire VA Hsop., Richmond, Va., 1955-56; clin. prof. medicine Med. Coll. Va. Commonwealth U., Richmond, 1956—; past pres., chmn. bd. Richmond Acad. Medicine, 1976-79. chief of staff Henrico Doctors' Hosp., Richmond, 1982; chief of medicine Henrico Doctors' Hosp., Richmond Meml. Hosp., Sheltering Arms Hosp. Lt. USNR, 1942-46; capt. Res. ret. Fellow Am. Coll. Physicians; mem. Am. Coll. Gastroenterology, Med. Soc. Va. (chmn. ethics com. 1990-91, assoc. editor quarterly med. jour.), Bockus Alumni Internat. Soc. Gastroenterology, N.Y. Acad. Sci., Am. Fedn. for Clin. Rsch., Sigma Xi. Office: 7605 Forest Ave Ste 211 Richmond VA 23229

MITCHELL, RONNIE MONROE, lawyer; b. Clinton, N.C., Nov. 10, 1952; s. Ondus Corneilius and Margaret Ronie (Johnson) M.; m. Martha Cheryl Coble, May 25, 1975; children: Grant Stephen, Mitchell, Meredith Elizabeth Mitchell. BA, Wake Forest U., 1975, JD, 1978. Bar: N.C. 1978, U.S. Dist. Ct. (ea. dist.) N.C. 1978, U.S. Ct. Appeals (4th cir.) 1983, U.S. Supreme Ct. 1984. Assoc. atty. Brown, Fox & Deaver, Fayetteville, N.C., 1978-81; ptnr. Harris, Sweeny & Mitchell, Fayetteville, 1981-91, now Harris, Mitchell & Hancox, 1991—; adj. prof. law Norman Adrian Wiggins Sch. of Law, Campbell U; bd. dirs. Mace, Inc. Contbr. chpts. to books. Chmn. Cumberland County Bd. Adjustment, 1985—, Cumberland County Rescue Squad, 1986-93; bd. dirs. Cumberland County Rescue Squad, Fayetteville, 1983-91. Recipient U.S. Law Week award Bur. Nat. Affairs, 1978. Mem. ABA, ATLA, Twelfth Judicial Dist. Bar Assn. (pres. 1988-89), N.C. Bar Assn. (councillor Young Lawyers divsn. 1982-85), N.C. Legis. Rsch. Commn. (family law com. 1994), Cumberland County Bar Assn. (mem. family law com., N.C. State Bar Bd. legal specialization), N.C. Acad. Trial Lawyers, Fayetteville Ind. Light Infantry Club, Dem. Men's Club (pres. 1993-94), Moose, Masons. Home: RR 23 Box 108C Fayetteville NC 28301-9125 Office: Harris Mitchell & Hancox 308 Person St Fayetteville NC 28301-5736

MITCHELL, RUSSELL HARRY, dermatologist; b. Erie, N.D., Oct. 19, 1925; s. William John and Anna Lillian (Sögge) M.; B.S., B.A., U. Minn., Mpls., 1947, B.M., M.D., 1951; postgrad. U. Pa. Med. Sch., 1968-69; m. Judith Lawes Douvarjo, May 24, 1968; children: Kathy Ellen, Gregory Alan, Jill Elaine, Crystal Anne. Intern, Gorgas Hosp., C.Z., 1951-52; resident in dermatology U.S. Naval Hosp., Phila., 1967-70; asst. chief out-patient dept. Gorgas Hosp., 1955-64; chief med. and surg. wards Ariz. State Hosp., Phoenix, 1965; commd. lt. (j.g.) M.C., U.S. Navy, 1953, advanced through grades to capt., 1968; svc. in Vietnam; ret., 1981; pvt. practice specializing in dermatology, Leesburg, Va., 1978—; mem. staff Loudoun Meml. Hosp., 1975—; dermatologist Nat. Naval Med. Center, Bethesda, Md., 1973-81; asst. prof. Georgetown U. Med. Sch., 1975-85. Pres. Archaeol. Soc. Panama, 1962-64. Decorated Bronze Star with combat V; Vietnam Gallantry Cross with palm and clasp; Condecoratión Vasco Nuñez de Balboa in orden de Caballero (Panama); diplomate Am. Bd. Dermatology. Fellow Am. Acad. Dermatology, Am. Acad. Physicians, Explorers Club; mem. AMA, Assn. Mil. Surgeons, Assn. Mil. Dermatologists (life), Am. Soc. Contemporary Medicine and Surgery, Soc. Am. Archaeology, Royal Soc. Medicine, Pan Am. Med. Assn., Loudoun County Med. Soc., Dermatology Found., Marine's Meml. Club (assoc.), Internat. Platform Soc., Phi Chi. Contbr. articles to med. and archaeol. publs. Home: 18685 Woodburn Rd Leesburg VA 20175-9008 Office: 823J S King St Leesburg VA 20175-3910

MITCHELL, RUTH ELLEN (BUNNY MITCHELL), advertising executive; b. Mpls., Jan 2, 1940; d. Burt and Helen (Bolnick) Horwitz; div.; children: Cathy Ann, Thomas Charles, Andrew Robert. Student UCLA, 1957, U. Minn., 1960. Substitute tchr. Holy Innocents' Sch., Atlanta, 1972-76; mem. staff Issues Dept., Carter-Mondale, Atlanta, 1976; office mgr. Atlanta Area Family Psychiatry Clinic, 1976-79; account exec. Am. Advt. Distributors, Atlanta, 1979-81, Brown's Guide Ltd., Atlanta, 1981-82; account mgr. Billian Pub., Atlanta, 1983-85; regional sales dir. Am. Hosp. Pub., Inc., Chgo., 1985—; cons. G.C.C., Inc., Atlanta, 1982-83. Bd. dirs. Nat. Council Jewish Women, Mpls., 1963-70, Temple Israel Sch., Mpls., 1964-68, Minn. Symphony Assn., Mpls., 1963-71; The Temple Sisterhood, Atlanta, 1972-77, Holy Innocents' Sch., Atlanta, 1973-77; vol. fundraiser KTCA-TV Pub. Broadcasting Svc., Mpls., 1968-71, WETV-TV, Atlanta, 1976-80; vol. Northside Hosp., Atlanta, 1971-77, Arts Festival of Atlanta, 1971-80, Holy Innocents' ch. summer program, 1974-76, Buckhead Mental Health Clinic, Atlanta, 1975-77. Mem. Nat. Assn. Profl. Saleswomen, Bus./Profl. Advt. Assn., Am. Advt. Fedn., Atlanta Advt. Club, Mag. Advt. Reps. of the South (sec. 1982-83, v.p. 1983-84, 88-89), High Mus. Art., Atlanta Symphony Orch., Found. for Hosp. Art Assn. (spl. events coord. 1987-88, bd. trustees 1988—), Atlanta Ballet, Southeastern Hosp. Conf. (mem. exhibits com. 1988, 89, 90), Ravinia Club. Home: 7155 Roswell Rd NE # 57 Atlanta GA 30328-5419 Office: 3150 Holcomb Bridge Rd #310 Norcross GA 30071

MITCHELL, SHARON STANLEY, supply analyst; b. Roanoke, Va., July 29, 1953; d. Jack Dempsey and Juanita Jeannette (Reed) Stanley; m. Jack W. Hobbs, July 20, 1980 (div. 1987); 1 child, Sarah Whitney; m. R. Edward Mitchell, Jr., Feb. 12, 1993. Acctg., Va. Western Coll., 1971-73, 80-81. Lic. realtor, Va. Accounts receivable Am. Motor Inns, Inc., Roanoke, Va., 1973-76; cost acct. VA Med. Ctr., Salem, Va., 1976-90, supply analyst, 1990—; assoc. editor Valley Views, VA Med. Ctr.; v.p. Rose Motors, Ltd., Roanoke, 1982-81; real estate salesperson Peery & Flora, Ltd., 1988—. Contbr. articles to profl. jours. Chmn. edn. Fed. Women's Program, Salem, Va., 1984-87; co-chmn. hist. com. Grandin Ct. Bapt. Ch., Roanoke, Va., 1986—; admission com. North Cross Sch., 1988—; mem. Jr. League of Roanoke, fin. advisor, 1996; mem. Hist. Mus. Com., Dept. Va. Med. Cntr., Salem; vol. Mill Mountain Theatre, Mus. of Theatre History at Ctr. in the Sq., Roanoke, Va.; loaned exec. Combined Fed. Campaign/United Way, 1994-95, 96. Recipient Equal Employment Opportunity award Fed. Women's Program Wk., 1984, Star award VA Med. Ctr., 1990. Mem. Va. Assn. Realtors, Nat. Assn. Realtors, Porsche Club Am. (bd. dirs. Blue Ridge region 1992—), Roanoke Symphony Assn. (season ticket com., polo com.), Aircraft Owners and Pilots Assn. Home: 4938 Mount Holland Dr SW Roanoke VA 24018-1630

MITCHELL, STEPHEN MILTON, manufacturing executive; b. Atlanta, Oct. 23, 1943; s. Judge Stephenson and Elizabeth Ruth (Morgan) M.; m. Carolyn Docia Goss, June 29, 1968; children: William Stephenson, Scott Milton, Gregory Stephen. B of Indsl. Engring. with honors, Ga. Inst. Tech., 1965, MS in Indsl. Engring., 1966. Registered profl. engr., Ga. Sr. engr. Lochkeed-Ga. Corp., Marietta, 1966-70; mgr. material control Snapper Power Equipment, McDonough, Ga., 1970-73; pres. Atlanta Processing Co., Conley, Ga., 1973-86; sr. v.p., gen. mgr. Norcom, Inc., Norcross, Ga., 1986-93; chmn., CEO Atlanta Processing B, Inc., Tucker, Ga., 1993-94; CEO Internat. Processing Corp., Atlanta, 1994; CEO Sertec Corp., Atlanta, 1995—, also bd. dirs.; bd. dirs. Atlanta Processing Co., Conley, Ga., Norcom, Inc., Norcross, APB Inc., Tucker, Ga., IPC, Atlanta; mem. exec. com., chmn., bd. dirs. Clairmont Oaks, Inc., 1988—. Bd. dirs., treas. Common Cause, Ga., 1989—; active First Bapt. Ch. of Decatur, Ga., 1968—, chmn. bd. deacons, 1993, 95. Mem. Young Presidents Orgn., World Presidents Orgn., Ga. Tech. Alumni Assn. (trustee 1981-87). Republican. Home: 5268 Browning Way SW Lilburn GA 30247-7029 Office: Sertec Corp Ste 200 2100 Powers Ferry Rd Atlanta GA 30339-5014

MITCHELL, STEVE HAROLD, behavior specialist; b. Madison, Tenn., Nov. 28, 1954; s. Ralph O. Sr. and Doris C. (Quillen) M. BS, Tenn. Tech U., 1977; MS, U. Ala., 1978; PhD, Ohio State U., 1983. Program dir. North Side Child Devel. Ctr., Columbus, Ohio, 1978-82; assoc. prof. dept. edn. Cumberland Coll., Williamsburg, Ky., 1986-92; asst. prof. Ball State U., Muncie, Ind., 1983-85; behavior specialist, 1989—. Contbr. articles to profl. jours. Mem. Coun. for Exceptional Children, Coun. Children with Behavior Disorders, Soc. for Rsch. in Child Devel. Home: PO Box 60 Bronston KY 42518-0060

MITCHELL, TEDDY LEE, physician; b. Columbia, La., Feb. 24, 1962; s. Oliver Clayton nad Mary Elizabeth (Johnston) M.; m. Janet Luisa Tornelli, Apr. 9, 1988; children: Mary Katherine, Oliver Charles. BS in Biology, Stephen F. Austin State U., 1983; MD, U. Tex. Med. Br., 1987. Diplomate Am. Bd. Internal Medicine, Cert. of Added Qualification-Sports Medicine. Intern U. Tex. Med. Br., Galveston, 1987-88, resident, 1988-90, 90-91; staff physician Cooper Aerobics Ctr., Dallas, 1991—, med. dir. wellness program, 1991—. Mem. Rep. Sen. Inner Cir., Washington, 1993, Heritage Found., Washington, 1993. Capt. U.S. Army Res. Med. Corps, 1988-96. Mem. AMA, Am. Coll. Sports Medicine, Am. Coll. Physicians (cert Merit 1990), Tex. Med. Assn., Dallas County Med. Soc. Methodist. Home: 3224 Lovers Ln Dallas TX 75225-7626

MITCHELL, WILLIAM ALLEN, air force officer, political geography educator; b. Waco, Tex., Apr. 21, 1940; m. Joan Mary Woodill, May 31, 1958; children: Bill, Jim, John, Brian. BS in Geography and Bus., East Tex. State U., 1965; MA in Geography, UCLA, 1969; PhD in Geography, U. Ill., 1974. Commd. 2d lt. USAF, 1965, advanced through grades to col., 1986, ret., 1991; dir. intercultural edn. USAF Acad., 1980-83, prof., head geography, 1985-86, prof. nat. security affairs, 1986-88; seminar dir. Am. War Coll., 1987, Air War Coll.; assoc. prof. Baylor U., Waco, Tex., 1993; adj. faculty U. Md., 1970, U. Colo., Colorado Springs, 1975-80, Troy State U., Montgomery, 1979-80. Author: (with John Kolars) The Euphrates River and The Southeast Anatolia Development Project, 1991; contbr. articles to profl. jours. Decorated U.S. Legion of Merit, Bronze Star, Humanitarian award for Kurdish Relief Effort, Humanitarian award for Turkish relief effort, Orgn. Excellence award, Vietnam Cross of Gallantry with bronze palm, Humanitarian award for Armenian earthquake relief, Spl. Rsch. award for intercultural edn. Dept. Air Force; named one of Outstanding Young Men of Am., 1976; recipient rsch. and travel grants NSF Quick Response to Earthquakes, 1978, 80, 84, 92, 95, Inst. Turkish Studies, 1985, Atlantic Coun. of the U.S.-NATO Discussion Series Assoc. to Brussels, 1988, German Marshall fund grant to Turkey, 1988, others. Mem. Phi Kappa Phi. Baptist. Home: 501 Brint Ln Waco TX 76706-6207 Office: Baylor Univ PO Box 97276 Waco TX 76798-7276

MITCHELL, WILLIAM AVERY, JR., orthodontist; b. Greenville, S.C., Apr. 26, 1933; s. William Avery and Eva (Rigdon) M.; m. Patricia Ann Scott, June 26, 1965; 1 child, William Avery III. BS, Furman U., 1955; DDS, Emory U., 1959; MS in Dentistry, 1967. Diplomate Am. Bd. Orthodontics. Pvt. practice Decatur, Ga., 1963-67, Greenville, 1967—; instr. Emory U. Dental Sch., Atlanta, 1965-66, instr. dept. orthodontics, 1966-68; guest lectr. Greenville Tech. Coll., 1979—; councilor Coll. Diplomates of Am. Bd. Orthodontics, 1988-91, treas., 1991-92, sec., 1992-93, pres.-elect, 1993-94, pres., 1994-95, pres. CDABO Found., 1995-96. Bd. dirs. United Speech and Hearing, Greenville, 1972-75; chmn. dental divsn. United Way, Greenville, 1983, 84, 96; fund raiser Roper Mt. Sci. Ctr., 1985; mem. adv. bd. Greenville Tech. Coll., 1985-88; pres. Booster Club Christ Ch. Episc. Ch., 1987-88, mem. bd. visitors, 1990—; deacon 1st Bapt. Ch. Lt., capt. U.S. Army, 1959-61. Recipient Emil Eisenberg Scholarship, Ga. Dental Assn., Atlanta, 1958-59. Fellow Am. Coll. Dentists, Internat. Coll. Dentists; mem. ADA, Am. Assn. Orthodontists (del. 1985-91, 93—), S.C. Dental Assn. (gen. chmn. ann. meeting, 1996, George P. Hoffmann Outstanding Dentist award 1996), So. Assn. Orthodontists (pres. 1993-94, trustee 1983, 84, 85, sr. dir. 1989-92), S.C. Orthodontic Assn. (pres. 1978), Piedmont Dist. Dental Soc. (bd. dirs. 1972, Greenville County Dental Soc. (pres. 1972, Outstanding Svc. award 1994), S.C. Acad. Dental Practice Adminstrn., Emory Orthodontoc Assn. (pres. 1972), Furman Paladin Club (bd. dirs. 1980-84), Commerce Club (bd. dirs. Greenville chpt. 1983—), Rotary, Greenville Country Club. Office: 10 Cleveland Ct Greenville SC 29607-2414

MITCHUM, DONALD C., advertising executive. Pres., CEO BBDO Atlanta. Office: BBDO Atlanta 3414 Peachtree Rd NE, STE 1600 Atlanta GA 30326-1113*

MITLIN, LAURANCE ROBERT, university dean, educator; b. Bklyn., Feb. 8, 1947; s. Norman and Luceille (Liston) M.; m. Debbie Sue Molycheck, Jan. 3, 1976; 1 child, Frank M. BA, Miss. State U., 1969; MSLS, U. N.C., 1971. Documents libr. Winthrop Coll., Rock Hill, S.C., 1971-76, asst. coll. libr., 1976-81, asst. dean libr. svcs., 1981-90; assoc. dean libr. svcs., prof. Winthrop U., Rock Hill, 1990—; mem. S.C. Higher Edn. Libr. Network Task Force, Columbia, 1994; chair S.C. Interlibr. Loan Code Com., Columbia, 1989-90. Editor S.C. Libr., 1977-85; contbr. articles to profl. jours. Bd. dirs. Consolidated Area Transp. Authority, Rock Hill, 1986-90. Mem. ALA, AAUP, S.C. Libr. Assn. (editor 1971-85, exec. bd. 1977-85, Svc. award 1985), Metrolina Libr. Assn., Southeastern Libr. Network (bd. dirs. 1991-94). Home: 1477 Farrow Dr Rock Hill SC 29732 Office: Winthrop University Dacus Library Rock Hill SC 29733

MITLIN, NORMAN, physiologist, consultant; b. Bklyn., Feb. 13, 1918; s. Joseph and Rachel Fannie (Goldfein) M.; m. Luceille Liston; 1 child, Laurance R. BS, NYU, 1945; postgrad., U. Md., 1958-59, Oak Ridge Inst. Nuclear Study, 1957, USDA Grad. Sch., Washington, 1950-60. Ptnr. Shaff Labs., Bklyn., 1945-48; entomologist USDA, Beltsville, Md., 1949-54, insect physiologist, 1954-61; insect physiologist USDA Boll Weevil Rsch. Lab. Miss. State U., Mississippi State Univ., 1961-78; physiologist Miss. State U., 1978-79; adj. prof. biology Winthrop U., Rock Hill, S.C., 1980—. Contbr. chpts. to books, more than 100 articles to profl. jours. Sgt. USAAF, 1942-43. Mem. AAAS, Entomol. Soc. Am., S.C. Entomol. Soc., Sigma Xi, Gamma Sigma Delta. Democrat. Jewish. Home: 1830 Huntington Pl Rock Hill SC 29732-1029

MITMAN, GREGG ALDEN, history of science educator; b. Bethlehem, Pa., Oct. 9, 1960. BS in Biology, Dalhousie U., 1981; MA in History of Sci., U. Wis., 1984, PhD in History of Sci., 1988. Rockefeller fellow in humanities dept. history of sci. U. Okla., Norman, 1988-89, asst. prof. dept. history of sci., 1991-95; assoc. prof., 1995—; vis. asst. prof. dept. history of sci. U. Wis., Madison, 1989-90; vis. asst. prof. program in history of sci. and tech. U. Minn., 1990-91; co-organizer Dibner Seminar in History of Biology, Marine Biol. Lab., Woods Hole, Mass., 1992; dir. Mellon postdoctoral fellow in history of Sci. U. Okla., 1994—; presenter in field. Author: The State of Nature: Ecology, Community and American Social Thought, 1900-1950, 1992; contbr. articles and revs. to profl. publs.; mem. bookshelf bd. Jour. of History of Biology. Scholar Dalhousie U., 1980-81; travel fellow U. Wis., 1986-87, Charlotte W. Newcombe fellow Woodrow Wilson Nat. Fellowship Found., 1986-87, WARF fellow U. Wis., 1987-88, jr. faculty summer rsch. fellow U. Okla., 1992; NSF doctoral dissertation rsch. grantee, 1986-87, NSF rsch. grantee, 1990-93, 93—, NEH/NSF/FIPSE grantee, 1994—. Mem. History of Sci. Soc., Internat. Soc. for History, Philosophy, and Social Studies of Biology, Soc. for Lit. and Sci. Office: U Okla 601 Elm Ave Norman OK 73069-8802

MITROVGENIS, JAMES WILLIAM, JR., journalist; b. McAlester, Okla., Feb. 15, 1950; s. James William Sr. and Kula (Karrant) M.; m. Sharon Turnbo, July 21, 1973 (div. Mar. 1981); m. Brenda Martin, June 4, 1988 (div. Dec. 1995). Student, U. Okla., 1969-72. Reporter McAlester Daily Dem., 1973-76; news editor Muskogee (Okla.) Phoenix, 1976-81; night copy editor Daily Okla., Oklahoma City, 1981-86, night news editor, 1986-91, day copy editor, 1991—. Mem. NRA, AP Okla. News Execs. (bd. dirs. 1987-89, 1st pl. page one layout award 1987, 2d pl. gen. excellence award 1987, 3d pl. page one layout award 1987, 2d pl. gen. excellence award 1986). Greek Orthodox. Office: Daily Okla 9000 N Broadway Ext Oklahoma City OK 73114-3708

MITTEL, JOHN J., economist, corporate executive; b. L.I., N.Y.; s. John and Mary (Leidolf) M.; 1 child, James C. B.B.A., CUNY. Researcher econs.

dept. McGraw Hill & Co., N.Y.C.; mgr., asst. to pres. Indsl. Commodity Corp., J. Carvel Lange Inc. and J. Carvel Lange Internat., Inc., 1956-64, corp. sec., 1958-86, v.p., 1964-80, exec. v.p., 1980-86; pres. I.C. Investors Corp., 1972—, I.C. Pension Adv., Inc., 1977—; bd. dir. several corps.; plan adminstr., trustee Combined Indsl. Commodity Corp. and J. Carvel Lange Inc. Pension Plan, 1962-86, J. Carvel Lange Internat. Inc. Profit Sharing Trust, 1969-86, Combined Indsl. Commodity Corp. and J. Carvel Lange Inc. Employees Profit Sharing Plan, 1977-86. Mem. grad. adv. bd. Bernard M. Baruch Coll., CUNY, 1971-72. Mem. Conf. Bd., Am. Statis. Assn., Newcomen Soc. N.Am. Club: Union League (N.Y.C.). Co-author: How Good A Sales Profit Are You, 1961, The Role of the Economic Consulting Firm. Office: 10633 Saint Andrews Rd Boynton Beach FL 33436-4714

MIXON, DEBORAH LYNN BURTON, elementary school educator; b. Charleston, S.C., Mar. 26, 1956; d. Harold Boyd and Peggy Wynell (Seagraves) Burton; m. Steven Douglas Schmidt (div. Mar. 1982); 1 child, Julie Ann Schmidt; m. Timothy Lamar Mixon, Oct. 11, 1982; children: Phillip Lamar, Catherine Elizabeth. BS in Edn., U. Ga., 1994. Cert. early childhood educator, Ga. Office coord. Morrison's Cafeteria, Athens, Ga., 1974-76; cashier Winn-Dixie, Athens, 1976-78; data entry clk. Athens Tech. Data Ctr., 1978-79; adminstrv. sec. U. Ga., Athens, 1980-86; sec. to plant mgr. Certain Teed Corp., Athens, 1986-87; s. adminstrv. sec. U. Ga., Athens, 1987-93; tchr. 4th grade Hall County Sch. Sys., Gainesville, Ga., 1994—. Leader Cub Scouts den Boy Scouts Am., 1993-94; troop vol. Girl Scouts U.S., 1992—; vol. leader 4-H Clarke County, Athens, 1992-94. Presdl. scholar U. Ga., 1993-94. Mem. Assn. for Childhood Edn. Internat., Profl. Assn. Ga. Educators, Golden Key, Kappa Delta Epsilon (perfect scholar 1994). Home: 171 Scottwood Dr Athens GA 30607-1338

MIYAMOTO, MICHAEL DWIGHT, neuroscience educator, researcher; b. Honolulu, Apr. 22, 1945; s. Donald Masanobu and Chisako (Moriwaki) M.; m. Janis Ways Chin, June 16, 1973; children: Julie Lynn, Scott Michael. BA, Northwestern U., 1966, PhD, 1971. Instr. Rutgers Med. Sch., Piscataway, N.J., 1970-72; asst. prof. U. Conn. Health Ctr., Farmington, 1972-78; assoc. prof. East Tenn. State U., Johnson City, 1978-87, prof., 1987—. Contbr. articles to Jour. Theoretical Biology, Jour. Physiology, Pharmacol. Revs. Grantee Pharm. Mfg. Assn. Found., 1975, Epilepsy Found. Am., 1976, NIH, 1975, 78, 88, 92, 94. Mem. Am. Soc. for Pharmacology and Exptl. Therapeutics, Soc. Neurosci. (Appalachian chpt.). Presbyterian. Home: 318 Baron Dr Johnson City TN 37601-3934 Office: East Tenn State U Dept Pharmacology PO Box 70577 Johnson City TN 37614-0577

MIZE, B. DIANNE, artist; b. Carnesville, Ga., Mar. 11, 1942; d. William Thomas and Willie J. (Cole) M. AA, Young Harris (Ga.) Coll., 1962; BA, Newberry (S.C.) Coll., 1964; BFA, U. Ga., 1968; MFA, Goddard Coll., Plainfield, Vt., 1974. Art tchr. various pub. schs., Hart, Franklin Counties, Ga., 1964-69; art tchr. Gov. Honors Program, Macon, Ga., 1968, 69; art tchr., chair Gov. Honors Program, 1970-73; gifted resource tchr. pub. schs., Walker, Stephens Counties, Ga., 1970-72; art dept. chmn. Piedmont Coll., Demorest, Ga., 1974-83; dir., instr. Dianne Mize Studio, Inc., Clarkesville, Ga., 1984—; also bd. dirs., pres. Dianne Mize Studio, Inc.; evaluator So. Assn. of Colls. and Secondary Schs., 1976, 78; chmn. curriculum com. Franklin County schs., 1964-69. Artist 600 paintings, 30 sculptures, 1960—. Cons. Clarkesville nursing homes, 1985—; critique cons. to individuals, art contest cons. various orgns., annual exhibits various sponsorships, sponsor student shows, 1984—. Recipient Ga. Teaching scholarship, 1968, Rotary Exch. Sch., 1970, Continued Study grant Goddard Coll., 1973. Episcopalian. Office: Dianne Mize Studio Inc 191 Walls Complex Cir Clarkesville GA 30523-9723

MIZE, JOHNNY EDWIN, risk management information systems company executive; b. Big Spring, Tex., Sept. 27, 1960; s. Alvin Clayton and Billie Yvonne (Norris) M.; m. Jill Dunnam, Mar. 5, 1983; children: Justin Brett, Jenna Brooke. BBA in Fin. magna cum laude, Tex. Tech. U., 1982. Systems mgr. western region Corporate Systems, Amarillo, Tex., 1983-84, account exec. western, 1984-85, eastern regional mgr., 1985, western regional mgr., 1985-88, v.p. customer svc., 1985-92, pres., CEO, 1992—; bd. mem. Corporate Systems Corp. Gen. Ptnr., Inc., Amarillo, 1988—, Corporate Systems User Assn., Amarillo, 1985—; mem., corp. mentor adv. com. West Tex. State U., Canyon, 1990—. Bd. dirs. High Plains Food Bank, Amarillo, 1990-91, Ch. of the Nazarene, Amarillo, 1989-91; participant Leadership Amarillo, 1990—; pacesetter United Way, Amarillo, 1989-90. Mem. Christian Bus. Mens Club, Toastmasters Risky Bus. Republican. Office: Corp Systems 1212 Ross St Amarillo TX 79102-4410

MIZELL, ANDREW HOOPER, III, concrete company executive; b. Franklin, Tenn., Sept. 26, 1926; s. Andrew Hooper, Jr. and Jennie McEwen (Fleming) M.; B.A., Vanderbilt U., 1950; m. Julia Yolanda Mattei, Dec. 20, 1947; children—Andrew Hooper, Julia Fleming. Supt., Wescon Construction Co., Nashville, 1950-52; accountant McIntyre & Asso., Nashville, 1952-55; credit mgr. Ingram Oil Co., Nashville, 1955-56, v.p. and dir., 1956-62; v.p., dir. Comml. Sign & Advt. Co., Nashville, 1957-59; v.p. and dir. Gen. Properties Co., New Orleans, 1957-62; v.p. and dir. Minn. Barge & Terminal Co., St. Paul, 1957-62; mgr. real estate and devel. Murphy Corp., El Dorado, Ark., 1962-63, mgr. retail sales, 1962-63; pres. and chmn. bd. Transit Ready Mix, Inc., Nashville, 1963—; pres., Conco, Inc., Apollo Concrete Products, Inc.; ptnr. Mizell Riggs Enterprises. Active United Givers Fund, 1965-66; chmn. Concrete div. Office Emergency Planning, 1965—; mem. Nat. UN Day Com., 1978. Served with USNR, 1944-46. Named Ark. Traveler, 1966, Ky. Col., 1969. Mem. Nat. Ready Mix Concrete Assn. (chmn. membership com. Tenn. sect. 1971—, chmn. marketing com. Tenn. chpt. 1973—), Assn. Gen. Contractors, Tenn. Bldg. Material Assn., Nat. Fedn. Ind. Businessmen, Portland Cement Assn., Nat. Area Bus. and Edn. Radio, Asso. Builders and Contractors, Spl. Indsl. Radio Service Industry, Tenn. Road Builders, Boat Owners Assn. U.S., Nashville C. of C., U.S. C. of C., Am. Concrete Inst. Clubs: Nashville Yacht, Nashville City, Belle Meade Country, The Honors Course, Commodore Yacht (past commodore). Home: 4340 Beekman Dr Nashville TN 37215-4504

MIZRAHI, EDWARD ALAN, allergist; b. Tyler, Tex., Aug. 24, 1945. BS in Econs., U. Pa., 1967; MD, U. Fla., 1972. Diplomate Am. Bd. Internal Medicine, Am. Bd. Allergy and Immunology. Intern Med. Coll. Ga., Augusta, 1972-73, resident, 1973-75; fellow Nat. Jewish Hosp., U. Colo., Denver, 1975-77; pvt. practice Jacksonville, Fla., 1977—; physician Bapt. Med. Ctr., Jacksonville, Meml. Med. Ctr., Jacksonville, St. Luke's Med. Ctr., Jacksonville, St. Vincent's Med. Ctr., Jacksonville, Meth. Hosp., Jacksonville, Orange Park (Fla.) Med. Ctr. Mem. Am. Coll. Allergy, Asthma and Immunology, Am. Acad. Allergy, Asthma and Immunology, Fla. Med. Assn., Fla. Allergy and Immunology Soc., Duval County Med. Soc., Southeastern Allergy Assn. Office: 3636 University Blvd S Ste B2 Jacksonville FL 32216-4223

MIZRAHI, ELI M., neurologist, pediatrician, educator; b. N.Y.C., Apr. 26, 1949. BA in Psychology, Emory U., 1971; MD, U. Miami, 1975. Diplomate Am. Bd. Pediats., Am. Bd. Psychiatry and Neurology with spl. qualification in child neurology, and added qualification in clin. and neurophysiology; Am. Bd. Clin. Neurophysiology, Nat. Bd. Med. Examiners. Intern and resident in pediatrics Albert Einstein Coll. Medicine, Bronx Mcpl. Hosp. Ctr., 1975-78; resident in neurology Stanford (Calif.) U. Med. Ctr., 1978-81; postdoctoral fellow in clin. neurophysiology Baylor Coll. Medicine, Houston, 1981-82, asst. prof. neurology and pediatrics, 1982-89, assoc. prof. neurology and pediatrics, 1989—; faculty Epilepsy Rsch. Ctr., The Meth. Hosp. and Baylor Coll. Medicine, 1982—; attending physician The Meth. Hosp., Tex. Children's Hosp., St. Luke's Episcopal Hosp., Harris County Hosp. Dist., Ben Taub Gen. Hosp., 1982—; dir. Clin. Rsch. Ctr. for Neonatal Seizures, The Meth. Hosp. in assn. with Tex. Children's Hosp. and Baylor Coll. Medicine, 1991—; cons., presenter in field. Recipient Tchr.-Investigator Devel. award Nat. Inst. Neurol. and Communicative Disorders and Stroke, NIH, 1984, The Michael prize Stiftung Michael Found., Bonn, Germany, 1988, Am. Epilepsy Soc. Rsch. award Clin. Investigator, 1992. Mem. Am. Acad. Neurology, Child Neurology Soc. (sci. selection com. 1987-88, awards com. 1994—, others), Am. Epilepsy Soc. (childhood epilepsy com. 1992—, ad hoc rsch. adv. com. 1992—, others), Am. Acad. Pediat. (cons.), Epileptic Assn. Houston and Gulf Coast (chmn. profl. adv. bd. 1994, others), Am. EEG Soc. (coun. 1991), Epilepsy Found. Am. (bd. dirs. 1994—, profl. adv. bd. 1989—), Internat. League Against Epilepsy (cons.). Office: Baylor Coll Medicine Sect Neurophysiol Dept Neur One Baylor Plaza Houston TX 77030

MJOR, IVAR ANDREAS, dental educator; b. Norderhov, Norway, Sept. 18, 1933; came to U.S., 1992; s. Peter Sigvart and Thora (Elnaes) M.; m. Birgit E. Gron, Dec. 26, 1959; children: Per I., Siri E., Thor A. BDS, U. St. Andrews, Dundee, Scotland, 1957; MS in Dentistry, U. Ala., 1960, MS in Anatomy, 1961, D in Odontology, 1967; D in Odontology, U. Umeå, Sweden, 1983, U. Turku, 1986, U. Copenhagen, Greece, 1991, U. Lund, 1993; LLD, U. Dundee, 1987; D Dentistry, U. Athens, Greece, 1995. Postdoctoral fellow U. Ala., Birmingham, 1959-61; rsch. assoc. Norwegian Inst. Dental Rsch., Oslo, 1961-67; assoc. prof. U. Oslo, 1968-70, prof., 1970-73; dir. NIOM Scandinavian Inst. Dental Materials, Oslo, 1973-93; prof., eminent scholar U. Fla., Gainesville, 1993—. Author, co-editor: Histology of the Human Tooth, 1973, Human Oral Embryology and Histology, 1986, Modern Concepts in Operative Dentistry, 1988; author, editor: Reaction Patterns in Human Teeth, 1983, Dental Materials: Biological Properties and Clinical Evaluation, 1985; editor-in-chief Acta Odontologica Scandinavica, 1977-81; sect. editor Quintessence Internat., 1989—. Lt. Dental Corps Norwegian armed forces, 1957-59. Mem. ADA (hon.), FDI World Dental Fedn. (mem. coun. 1992—, chmn. commn. 1992—), Acad. Operative Dentistry, Internat. Assn. for Dental Rsch. (pres. 1988, sci. award 1987), Finnish Dental Assn. (hon.), Danish Dental Assn. (hon.), Accademia Italians de Conservativa (hon.). Office: U Fla Coll Dentistry 1600 SW Archer Rd Gainesville FL 32610

MOAK, ELIZABETH, critical care and operating room nurse; b. Augusta, Ga., Nov. 13, 1950; d. James Seymour and Audrey Beth (Morris) M.; children: Jason William, James Jeffrey. ADN, Augusta Coll., 1977. CNOR. Charge nurse-clinic Med. Coll. Ga., Augusta; staff nurse oper. rm., coord. and preceptor insvc. edn. VA Med. Ctr., Augusta, coord. CQI and laparoscopic surgery, 1981—. Mem. Assn. Oper. Rm. Nurses (sec.), Augusta Coll. Alumni Assn., Ga. Freelance Writers Assn.

MOBLEY, J. DAVID, environmental engineer; b. Winterville, N.C., June 27, 1948; s. James Hughie and Bessie Christine (Allen) M.; m. Peggy Smith, July 12, 1970; children: Diane Christine, Sarah Catherine, Paul David. BS in Mech. Engring., N.C. State U., 1970. Cert. profl. engr., Va. Environ. engr. EPA, Ann Arbor, Mich., 1970-73, City of Richmond, Va., 1973-76; leader, emission factor and inventory group EPA, Rsch. Triangle Pk., N.C., 1976—. Named Fed. Engr. of the Yr., U.S. Govt., Washington, 1993; recipient Five Star award Pollution Engring. Mag., Washington, 1983. Mem. ASME (sect. chmn. 1984), Air and Waste Mgmt. Assn. (conf. chmn. 1991-95). Baptist. Home: 909 Thoreau Dr Raleigh NC 27609 Office: EPA Mail Drop 14 Durham NC 27711

MOBLEY, JOHN HOMER, II, lawyer; b. Shreveport, La., Apr. 21, 1930; s. John Hinson and Beulah (Wilson) M.; m. Sue Lawton, Aug. 9, 1958; children: John Lawton, Anne Davant. AB, U. Ga., 1951, JD, 1953. Bar: Ga. 1952, U.S. Dist. Ct., D.C. Ptnr. Kelley & Mobley, Atlanta, 1956-63, Gambrell & Mobley, 1963-83; sr. ptnr., Sutherland, Asbill & Brennan, 1983—. Chmn. Cities in Schs. of Ga.; dir. Cities in Schs. Capt. JAGC, USAF, 1953-55. Mem. ABA, D.C. Bar, State Bar Ga., Atlanta Bar Assn., Am. Judicature Soc., Atlanta Lawyers Club, Phi Delta Phi. Clubs: Atlanta Athletic, Atlanta Country, Commerce, Piedmont Driving, Georgian (Atlanta), N.Y. Athletic, Metropolitan (Washington). Home: 4348 Sentinel Post Rd NW Atlanta GA 30327-3910 Office: Sutherland Asbill & Brennan 999 Peachtree St NE Atlanta GA 30309-3996

MOBLEY, PAUL RAY, retired engineering technician, writer; b. Paintlick, Ky., Jan. 15, 1931; s. Lucious Herbert and Lola (Blount) M.; m. Shirley Ann Fey; children: Michael Ray, Paul Ray Jr., Herbert Allen, Danita Colleen Mobley Combs. Student, U. Cin., 1954-58; cert., Am. Soc. for Metals, 1962, Writer's Digest Course, 1988. Engring. technician GE Co., Evendale, Ohio, 1955-60; engring. specialist GE Co., Evendale, 1960-75; supr. shop svcs. Ladish Co. Ky. Divsn., Cynthiana, Ky., 1980-82; instr. company courses GE Co., Evendale, Ohio. Inventor: 6 patents metallic alloys, 1962-70; poet World of Poetry, Golden awards 1985, 86, Silver awards 1990, 91; columnist Bourbon County Citizen; contbr. articles to newspapers, tech. jours. Jr. Achievement advisor Ladco IV, Cynthiana, Ky. 1978-79, Jr. Achievement instr. St.. Edward's Middle Sch., Cynthiana, 1995. With USAF, 1950-53, Thule. Named Ky. Col., Governor Wallace Wilkinson, Frankfort, Ky., 1991; recipient United Way Solicitor award, Frankfort, Ky. Democrat. Home: Route # 3 Box 410 Cynthiana KY 41031

MOBLEY, WILLIAM HODGES, management educator, researcher; b. Akron, Ohio, Nov. 15, 1941. BA, Denison U., 1963; PhD, U. Md., 1971. Mgr. employee relations research PPG Industries, Pitts., 1971-73; prof. U. S.C., Columbia, 1973-80; head dept. of mgmt. Tex. A&M U., College Station, 1980-83, dean. coll. of bus. adminstrn., 1983-86, exec. dep. chancellor, 1986-88, pres., 1988-93; chancellor Tex. A&M U. Sys., College Station, 1993-94; prof. mgmt. Tex. A&M U., College Station, 1994-97; pres. PDI Global Rsch. Consortium, Ltd., Hong Kong, Dallas, 1996—; pres. PDI Global Rsch. Ltd., Dallas, Hong Kong, 1996—; bd. dirs. So. Region Inst. for Internat. Edn., Pool Energy Svc., Medichi Sci. Co.; vis. fellow Cornell U., 1994, vis. prof. Hong Kong U. Sci. and Tech., 1995-96. Author: Employee Turnover, 1982. Bd. dirs. Amma Found., 1991—, Internat. Food and Agrl. Devel. and Econ. Coop., U.S. Agy. Internat. Devel., 1992-94; mem. trilateral task force on N.Am. Higher Edn. Coop., USIA, 1993-95; mem. Pres. Bush's Commn. on Minority Bus. Devel., 1990-92, U.S. com. of the Pacific Econ. Coop. Coun., 1995—. Fulbright scholar Found. for Scholarly Exchange, Republic China, 1978-79; recipient DAAD, Rep. Germany, 1984; Fellow NDEA U.S. Dept. of Edn., 1968-71. Fellow APA, Am. Psychol. Soc. Home: 4317 Famin Dr Irving TX 75038 Office: PDI Global Rsch Ltd 600 E Las Colinas Blvd Ste Irving TX 75039

MOCK, DAVID BENJAMIN, history educator; b. Eustis, Fla., June 8, 1951; s. Benjamin Franklin and Margarette Ellen (Stearnes) M.; m. Marie Annette Bisignano, Dec. 28, 1974; children: Kimberly Elizabeth, Scott Michael. AA, Lake-Sumter C.C., Leesburg, Fla., 1971; BA, Fla. State U., 1973, MA, 1978, PhD, 1983; MA, Pepperdine U., 1975. Rsch. assoc. Ctr. for Needs Assessment and Planning Fla. State U., Tallahassee, 1980-84; history instr. Edison C.C., Ft. Myers, Fla., 1984-90, Tallahassee C.C., 1990—; vis. assoc. prof. history Fla. State U., Tallahassee, 1993—. Coauthor: Book, Educating Hand and Mind: A History of Vocational Education in Florida, 1986, 2d edit., 1987, (brief) Supershell II Tutorial for Civilizations of the West, 1993; editor: History and Public Policy, 1991, Legacy of the West, 1995; co-editor: Dictionary of Obituaries of Modern British Radicals, 1989; contbr. articles to profl. jours. 1st lt. U.S. Army, 1974-76. Mem. Fla. Coll. Tchrs. History (v.p. 1988, pres. 1989-90), Am. Hist. Assn., Nat. Coun. Pub. History (state of Fla. membership chair 1990—), Fla. Conf. Historians, Fla. Founds. Edn. and Policy Studies Soc., Politics of Edn. Assn., N.Am. Conf. Brit. Studies, 16th Century Studies Soc., Carolina Symposium on Brit. Studies, Phi Theta Kappa, Phi Alpha Theta, Kappa Delta Phi, Scabbard and Blade, Phi Delta Kappa. Republican. Baptist. Home: 1697 Copperfield Cir Tallahassee FL 32312-3755 Office: Tallahassee CC Divsn Social Scis 444 Appleyard Dr Tallahassee FL 32304-2815

MOCK, FRANK MACKENZIE, lawyer; b. South Bend, Ind., May 17, 1944; s. Frank Carlton and Julia (Baughmann) M.; m. Virginia Johns, Dec. 31, 1974 (div. Feb. 1991); children: Shannon, John, Bridget. BA, Duke U., 1966, JD, 1969. Bar: Fla. 1969. Assoc. Mahoney, Adams, Criser, Jacksonville, Fla., 1969-74, ptnr., 1977-92; gen. counsel Builders Investment Group, Valley Forge, Pa., 1974-77; ptnr. Baker & Hostetler, Orlando, Fla., 1992—. Mem. ABA, Duval County Bar Assn., Orange County Bar Assn., Dade County Bar Assn., Palm Beach County Bar Assn., Turnaround Mgmt. Assn. Republican. Episcopalian. Home: 2147 Santa Antilles Rd Orlando FL 32806-1533 Office: Baker & Hostetler 200 S Orange Ave Orlando FL 32801-3410

MOCK, LARRY JOHN, elementary education educator; b. Quincy, Ill., Jan. 13, 1950; s. Frank Paul and Elizabeth Katherine (Hugenberg) M. BS, Quincy U., 1972; MEd, Ga. State U., 1985, specialist in edn., 1989, postgrad., 1993—. Cert. tchr. grades 1-8, Ga. Tchr. grade 4 Cmty. Dist. #3, Clayton, Ill., 1972-74; tchr. adult edn. Atlanta (Ga.) Pub. Schs., 1975-91, tchr. grade 5, 1991-94, tchr. grade 3, 1994-95; asst. prin. Atlanta Pub. Schs. Author: Daily Living Lab Manual, 1978. Chairperson Ho. Dist. 68 Dekalb County Dem. Party, Atlanta, 1993-94; active Butler St. YMCA, Scottie Club of Greater Atlanta. Mem. NEA (Atlanta chpt.), ASCD, Am. Rsch. Assn., Am. Parkinson Disease Assn., Ga. Coun. for Social Studies, East Atlanta Cmty. Assn. (treas., sec., v.p. 1980-93), Capitol View PTA, Phi Kappa Phi (Alumnus chpt.). Home: 1213 Gracewood Ave SE Atlanta GA 30316-2665

MOCK, LAWRENCE EDWARD, JR., venture capitalist; b. Louisville, Apr. 21, 1946; s. Lawrence Edward and Mary Ann (McCoy) M.; m. Beth Grace Butler, Sept 12, 1983; children: Mary Grace, Katherine Lawrence. BA, Harvard U., 1968; MS, Fla. State U., 1973; postgrad., London Sch. Econs., 1974. Assoc. Booz Allen & Hamilton, Atlanta, 1975-78; ops. mgr. Fuqua Industries, Atlanta, 1978-80; exec. v.p. Hangar One, Inc., Atlanta, 1980-83; pres., CEO, gen. ptnr. River Capital, Inc., Atlanta, 1983-93; pres., CEO Mellon Ventures, Inc., Pitts., 1995—; bd. dirs. Winston Furniture, Inc., Birmingham, chmn. 1985-88, Internat. Bus. Fellows, also pres.; chmn. Romanoff Internat., 1989-91. Bd. dirs. Atlanta Internat. Sch., 1990-96, Rebel chpt. YPO, 1990-91. Served as capt. USMC, 1968-71. Home: 56 Beaver St Sewickley PA 15143 Office: One Mellon Bank Ctr Rm 3200 Pittsburgh PA 15258-0001

MOCK, MARILYN RHOADS, university administrator; b. Ft. Worth, Sept. 5, 1947; d. William R. and Frieda (Williams) M.; 1 child, Elizabeth. BA in English and Speech, U. North Tex., 1970; MA in Mgmt., Goddard Coll., 1978; postgrad. Inst. Ednl. Mgmt., Harvard U., 1987. Instr. comm. Cinnaminson (N.J.) Pub. Schs., 1970-72; coord. pub. rels. Venture Farm, Moorestown, N.J., 1972-73; mgr. internal ops., conv. sales Advt. and Promotion Commn., Little Rock, 1973-74; dir. advt. and promotion Northcross Mall, Austin, Tex., 1974-75; instr. English Austin Ind. Sch. Dist., 1975-76; grant writer, adminstr. Piedmont Tech. Coll., Greenwood, S.C., 1976-77, dir. coop. edn., 1977-78; dir. alumni rels., annual giving Southwestern U., Georgetown, Tex., 1978-82, dir. devel., 1980, dir. univ. rels., 1982-85, v.p. univ. rels., 1985—. State bd. dirs. Tex. Fine Arts Assn., 1986—. Mem. Coun. Advancement and Support Edn. (bd. dirs. 1984-85, nat. com. instl. rels. 1987-89, nat. commn. mgmt. rsch. 1990-93, nat. commn. comm. 1993-96). Office: Southwestern U University at Maple Georgetown TX 78628

MOCKLIN, KEVIN ETIENNE, physician, medical educator; b. New Orleans, May 14, 1951; s. Stephen Gilbert and Shirley Ann (Bartchy) M.; m. Cynthia Jean Scott, May 19, 1978; children: Christine, Kathleen. BS in Pharmacy, U. Miss., 1974; MD, La. State U., 1978. Diplomate Am. Coll. Physicians. Intern dept. medicine U. Miss., Jackson, 1978-79; resident dept. medicine La. State U., New Orleans, 1979-81, chief resident dept. medicine, 1981-82, clin. instr. medicine, 1982-84, clin. asst. prof. medicine, 1984—; ptnr. Internal Medicine Clinic of Lake Charles, La., 1982—. Home and Office: 2770 3d Ave Ste 350 Lake Charles LA 70601

MODANO, MICHAEL, professional hockey player; b. Livonia, Mich., June 7, 1970. Right wing/center Minn. North Stars, 1988-93, Dallas Stars, 1993—; player World Hockey League East All-Star Game, 1988-89, NHL All-Rookie Game, 1989-90, NHL All-Star Game, 1993. *

MODER, JOHN JOSEPH, academic administrator, priest; b. St. Louis, Apr. 9, 1948; s. Helen (Freihaut) M. BA in English and Philosophy, St. Mary's U., San Antonio, 1970; MA in Philosophy, Fordham U., 1972, PhD in Philosophy, 1977; M Div, U. St. Michael's, 1979. Joined Soc. of Mary, ordained priest Roman Cath. Ch., 1979. Mem. faculty Assumption High Sch., East St. Louis, Ill., 1973-75, Vianney High Sch., St. Louis, 1975-77; faculty mem. Irish Christian Bros. Sch., Mono Mills, Ont., Can., 1977-79; asst. prof. philosophy St. Mary's U., San Antonio, 1979-86, assoc. prof. philosophy, trustee, co-chmn. peace commn., 1986-88, pres., 1988—. Bd. advisors Communities-in-Schs., San Antonio, 1988—. Mem. Am. Cath. Philos. Assn., Am. Cancer Soc., Hispanic Assn. Colls., World Affairs Coun., Greater San Antonio C. of C., Rotary Club of San Antonio. Office: St Mary's U Office of Pres 1 Camino Santa Maria St San Antonio TX 78228-8572

MODY, BHARAT GANGADAS, engineer; b. Bombay, India, Sept. 11, 1948; arrived in U.S., 1968; s. Gangadas H. and Taralaxmi (Desai) M.; m. Prafulata B. Desai, Mar. 10, 1974; children: Seema, Priti. BSc in Chemistry/Physics, U. Bombay, 1968; BSc in Petroleum Engring., U. Pitts., 1971, MSChemE, 1973. Registered profl. engr., Tex. Engr. Halliburton Svcs., Duncan, Okla., 1974-80; tech. advisor Halliburton Svcs., Midland, Tex., 1980-86; v.p. Profile Control Svc., Midland, 1986-89; pres. Oil Water Ration Control, Midland, 1989—; cons. Improved Petroleum Recovery, Dallas, 1986-89; expert witness C.F. Lawrence, Midland, 1986, Dale Rittenhouse, Midland, 1992. Contbr. articles to profl. jours. Treas. HAWT, 1993. Mem. AIME, Soc. Petroleum Engrs. Home: 1202 Mcdonald St Midland TX 79703-4918 Office: Oil Water Ration Control 1200 W Front Midland TX 79701-6620

MOELLER, HANS-BERNHARD, Germanic languages, literature and film educator; b. Hannover, Germany, June 26, 1935; came to U.S., 1959; s. Bernhard and Gertrud (Machens) M.; m. Nancy Hodgson, Dec. 22, 1962 (div. 1979); 1 child, Nicole K.; m. Sheila K. Johnson, May 5, 1987. Student, Oberhausen (Germany)-Kolleg, 1957, U. Hamburg, Germany, 1957, U. Tübingen, Germany, 1957-59; BA in Sociology, Knox Coll., 1960; MA in German, U. So. Calif., 1962, PhD in German, 1964; postgrad., Inst. de Estudios Norteamericanos, U. de Barcelona, 1966-68. Teaching asst., lectr. U. So. Calif., L.A., 1960-62; instr. Northwestern U., Evanston, Ill., 1962-64; asst. prof. U. Md., College Park, 1964-66; with Instituto Aleman de Cultura (Goethe-Inst.), Barcelona, 1966-68; asst. prof. Hofstra U., Hempstead, N.Y., 1969-70; assoc. prof. Germanic langs. and lit. U. Tex., Austin, 1970—; vis. prof. U. So. Calif., 1974-75, Philipps U., Marburg, Germany, 1988. Author: Latin America and the Literature of Exile: A Comparative View of 20th Century Refugee Writers in the New World, 1983. Fulbright grantee 1959-60, Inst. Latin Am. Studies summer rsch. grantee, 1977, German Acad. Exch. Svc. summer study grantee, Thyssen rsch. grantee, 1982; Clune fellow, 1961-62, Andrew Mellon postdoctoral fellow, 1968-69. Mem. MLA (organizer and discussion leader spl. session 1977), AAUP, Am. Assn. Tchrs. German, S. Ctrl. MLA (sec. comparative lit. sect. 1974, chair, 1975), Rocky Mountain MLA (sec. sect. on film theory 1988, chair, 1989, sec. sect. German lit. since 1900, 1989, chair, 1990, organizer and chair German spl. session 1990), German Studies Assn., Internat. Vereinigung Germanische Sprach und Literaturwissenschaft, Tex. Assn. Coll. Tchrs., Delta Phi Alpha. Home: 393 S Sycamore Ave New Braunfels TX 78130-5848 Office: U Tex Dept Germanic Langs E P Schoch H 3.102 Austin TX 78712

MOELLER, HELEN HERGENRODER, ceramic engineer; b. Buffalo, Apr. 30, 1954; d. Ralph Joseph and Barbara C. (Anetzberger) Hergenroder; m. Robert Emil Moeller, May 29, 1976; 1 child, Robert E. Jr. BS in Ceramic Engring., Alfred U., 1976; MS in Engring. Adminstrn., George Washington U., 1980. Rsch. engr. Babcock & Wilcox Co., Lynchburg, Va., 1976-84; sect. mgr. Babcock & Wilcox Co., 1984—. Patentee in field; contbr. to profl. publs. Master gardener Va. Extension Svc., Lynchburg, 1987—. Mem. ASTM (sec. 1984-90), Am. Ceramic Soc., Soc. for Advancement of Material and Process Engring. Office: Babcock & Wilcox Lynchburg Rsch Ctr PO Box 11165 Lynchburg VA 24506-1165

MOESER, JOHN VICTOR, urban studies and planning educator; b. Colorado City, Tex., Nov. 3, 1942; s. Charles Victor and Virginia Alice (James) M.; m. Sharon Ann Gary, June 11, 1966; children: Jeremy Mark, Charles David. BA, Tex. Tech U., 1965; MA, U. Colo., 1967; PhD, George Washington U., 1975. Asst. prof. urban studies and planning Va. Commonwealth U., Richmond, 1971-77, assoc. prof., 1977-85, prof., 1985—, chair dept. urban studies and planning, 1992-95. Author: (with Rutledge M. Dennis) The Politics of Annexation: Oligarchic Power in a Southern City, 1982, (with Christopher Silver) The Separate City: Black Communities in the Urban South, 1940-1968, 1995; editor: A Virginia Profile, 1960-2000: Assessing Current Trends and Problems, 1981. Bd. dirs. Housing Opportunities Made Equal, James River Assn., Met. Interfaith Assembly; mem. governing bd. Va. Interfaith Ctr. for Pub. Policy; mem. governing coun. Richmond Urban Inst.; mem. steering com. Hope In the Cities; vice chair Downtown

Coop. Ministry; mem. magnet sch. task force Richmond Pub. Schs.; mem. cen. Va. citizens adv. bd. Va. Power Co.; mem. exec. com. Caucus for the Future of Cen. Va.; chair Richmond Commn. on Human Rels.; chair adv. coun. Metro Teen Program; elder 2d Presbyn. Ch.; trustee Presbyn. Sch. Christian Edn. Democrat. Presbyterian. Home: 1400 Brookland Pky Richmond VA 23227-4706 Office: Va Commonwealth U VCV Box 842008 Richmond VA 23284-2008

MOESSNER, HAROLD FREDERIC, allergist; b. Lincoln, Nebr., Mar. 29, 1945; s. Samuel Frederick and Helen Lucy (Larson) M.; m. Linda McLeod, Apr. 30, 1972; children: Annie Larson, John Christopher, Sarah Elizabeth. BS with distinction, U. Nebr., 1967; MD, U. Minn., 1971. Diplomate Am. Bd. Pediatrics, Am. Bd. Allergy and Immunology. Intern VA Hosp., Dallas, 1971-72; resident in pediatrics Children's Med. Ctr., Dallas, 1972-74; commd. 2d lt. U.S. Army, 1974-78, advanced through the grades to col., 1980-87; pediatrician Fort Ritchie, Md., 1974-75, U.S. Army Hosp, Augsburg, Germany, 1975-78; fellow in adolescent medicine U. Tex. Health and Sci. Ctr., Dallas, 1978-79; asst. prof. pediatrics Uniformed Svcs., U. Health Scis., Bethesda, Md., 1980-83; fellow allergy and immunology Walter Reed Army Med. Ctr., Washington, 1983-85; chief allergy immunology svc., chief dept. medicine Blanchfield Army Hosp., Fort Campbell, Ky., 1985-87; pvt. practice Nashville, 1987—; staff hosp. courtesy appointment Williamson Med. Ctr., Franklin, Tenn., Maury Regional Hosp., Columbia, Tenn. Contbr. to profl. jours. Fellow Am. Bd. Pediats., Am. Bd. Allergy and Immunology; mem. Am. Acad. Allergy and Immunology, Montgomery County Med. Soc., Tenn. Soc. Allergy, Tenn. State Med. Assn., Nashville Allergy Soc., Phi Beta Kappa. Home: 5304 Otter Creek Ct Brentwood TN 37027-4126 Office: 1909 Mallory Ln Ste 308 Franklin TN 37067 also: 1754 Madison St Ste 2 Clarksville TN 37043-4913

MOFFAT, FREDERICK LARKIN, JR., surgeon, surgical oncologist; b. Port Colborne, Ont., Can., Aug. 2, 1952; came to U.S., 1984; s. Frederick Larkin Sr. and Molly McKinley (Foskett) M.; m. Jennyfer Louise Simpson, Sept. 17. 1983; children: Frederick Larkin III, Schuyler McKinley. MD, Queens U., 1977. Diplomate Am. Bd. Surgery. Attending surgeon Toronto (Ont., Can.) Gen. Hosp., 1986-87; cons. surgeon Princess Margaret Hosp., Toronto, 1986-87; lectr. surgery U. Toronto, 1987; asst. prof. clin. surgery U. Miami, Fla., 1988-89, asst. prof. surgery, 1989-93, assoc. prof., 1993—; attending surgeon Jackson Meml. Hosp., Miami, 1988—, U. Miami Hosp. & Clinic, Sylvester Comprehensive Cancer, Miami, 1988—, VA Med. Ctr., Miami, 1988—. Author: Locoregional Treatment Considerations in Early Breast Cancer, 1994; assoc. editor Cancer Investigation jour., N.Y., 1991—; contbr. numerous articles to med. jours. Rsch. fellow Med. Rsch. Coun. Can., Toronto, 1983-84, Regular Clin. fellow Am. Cancer Soc., Miami, 1984-86; recipient Clin. Oncology Career Devel. award Am. Cancer Soc., 1990-93. Fellow ACS, Royal Coll. Surgeons Can.; mem. Soc. Head and Neck Surgeons, Soc. Surg. Oncology, Assn. Acad. Surgery, Am. Assn. Cancer Rsch., Am. Radium Soc., Am. Soc. Clin. Oncology, Soc. Am. Gastrointestinal Endoscopic Surgeons, Soc. Pelvic Surgeons, Surg. Biology Club III. Episcopalian. Office: U Miami Sch Medicine Sylvester Comprehensive Ctr 1475 NW 12th Ave Rm 3550 Miami FL 33136-1002

MOFFAT, MARYBETH, automotive company executive; b. Pitts., July 25, 1951; d. Herbert Franklin and Florence Grafe (Knerem) M.; m. Brian Francis Soulier, Nov. 30, 1974 (div.). BA, Carroll Coll., 1973. Indsl. engring. technician Wis. Centrifugal Co., Waukesha, Wis., 1976-77; indsl. engr. Utility Products, Inc., Milw., 1977-79; mgr. indsl. engring. Bear Automotive (div. SPX Corp.), Bangor, Pa., 1980-90; program mgr. Toyota Johnson Controls, Inc. Automotive Systems Group, 1990—. Group home house parent Headwaters Regional Achievement Ctr., Lake Tomahawk, Wis., 1974. Mem. Am. Inst. Indsl. Engrs., MTM Assn. for Standards Rsch., Indsl. Mgmt. Soc., Alpha Gamma Delta (standards chmn. 1971-72). Republican. Methodist. Avocations: skiing, horseback riding, swimming, reading. Office: Johnson Controls Inc Automotive Systems Group One Quality Drive Georgetown KY 40324-2011

MOFFAT, ROBERT CHARLES LINCOLN, law educator; b. Mar. 22, 1937; m. Janette C.M. Moffat (dec. Jan. 1994); children: Kaaren, Iain. BA, So. Meth. U., 1958, MA in Govt., 1962, LLB, 1962; LLM, U. Sydney, 1966; postgrad., Harvard Law Sch., 1965-66. Bar: Tex. 1962. Asst. prof., assoc. prof. law U. Fla., Gainesville, 1966-71, prof. law, 1971—; fellow Social Sci. Methods in Legal Edn. Inst. U. Denver, 1968; fellow NEH Seminar on Legal and Polit. Theory, Harvard U. 1978; Russell Sage resident in law and social sci. U. Calif., Berkeley, 1972-73; vis. prof. U. Ga., 1974-75, Monash U., Melbourne, Australia, 1983; vis. scholar Swarthmore Coll., 1982, Oxford U., 1978-79. Co-editor: Ethics and Law in the Scientific Age, 1991, Perspectives on the Family, 1990; contbr. chpts. in books and articles to profl. jours. Mem. Internat. Assn. Philosophy of Law and Social Philosophy (Am. sect., exec. dir., 1987—, exec. com.), Am. Soc. Polit. and Legal Philosophy, Law and Soc. Assn. (life), Am. Soc. Ethics, State Bar Tex., Fla. Philos. Conf. Office: Dept Law Univ Fla Gainesville FL 32611-7625

MOFFATT, JOYCE ANNE, performing arts executive; b. Grand Rapids, Mich., Jan. 3, 1936; d. John Barnard and Ruth Lillian (Pellow) M. BA in Lit., U. Mich., 1957, MA in Theatre, 1960; HHD (hon.), Sch. Psychology, San Francisco, 1991. Stage mgr., lighting designer Off-Broadway plays, costume, lighting and set designer, stage mgr. stock cos., 1954-62; nat. subscription mgr. Theatre Guild/Am. Theatre Soc., N.Y.C., 1965-67; subscription mgr. Theatre, Inc.-Phoenix Theatre, N.Y.C., 1963-67; cons. N.Y.C. Ballet and N.Y.C. Opera, 1967-70; asst. house mgr. N.Y. State Theater, 1970-72; dir. ticket sales City Ctr. of Music and Drama, Inc., N.Y.C., 1970-72; prodn. mgr. San Antonio's Symphony/Opera, 1973-75; gen. mgr. San Antonio Symphony/Opera, 1975-76, 55th St. Dance Theater Found., Inc., N.Y.C., 1976-77, Ballet Theatre Found., Inc./Am. Ballet Theatre, N.Y.C., 1977-81; v.p. prodn. Radio City Music Hall Prodns., Inc., N.Y.C., 1981-83; artist-in-residence CCNY, 1981—; propr. mgmt. cons. firm for performing arts N.Y.C., 1983—; exec. dir. San Francisco Ballet Assn., 1987-93; mng. dir. Houston Ballet Assoc., 1993-95; gen. mgr. Chgo. Music and Dance Theater, Inc., 1995—; cons. Ford Found., N.Y. State Coun. on Arts, Kennedy Ctr. for Performing Arts.; mem. dance panels N.Y. State Coun. on Arts, 1979-81; mem. panels for Support to Prominent Orgns. and Dance, Calif. Arts Coun., 1988-92. Appointee San Francisco Cultural Affairs Task Force, 1991; chmn. bd. Tex. Inst. for Arts in Edn., 1994—; trustee of I.A.T.S.E. Local 16 Pension and Welfare Fund, 1991-94. Mem. Assn. Theatrical Press Agts. and Mgrs., Actors Equity Assn., United Scenic Artists Local 829, San Francisco Visitors and Conv. Bur. (bd. dirs.). Club: Argyle (San Antonio). Office: Chicago Music & Dance Theater Mezz Level 203 No LaSalle Chicago IL 60601

MOFFATT-BLEY, LAURA L., critical care nurse; b. Ocala, Fla., July 6, 1961; d. Don Lee Moffatt and Joan Louise (Recard) Glorius; m. Volker Fritz Bley, Sept. 27, 1985. AS, Cen. Fla. Community Coll., 1983, AA, 1989; BSN, U. Fla., 1992, postgrad., 1993—. RN, Fla.; cert. critical care nurse, post anesthesia nurse, ACLS, BCLS. Nursing asst. Munroe Regional Med. Ctr., Ocala, staff nurse surg., staff nurse surg. ICU, staff nurse post anesthesia care. Mem. AACN, ANA, Fla. Nurses Assn., Nat. League Nursing, Am. Soc. Post Anesthesia Nurses, Fla. Soc. Post Anesthesia Nurses. Home: 2104 SE Lake Weir Rd Ocala FL 34471-5437

MOFFETT, JAMES ROBERT, oil and gas company executive; b. Houma, La., Aug. 16, 1938; s. Robert E. and Mary G. (Pollack) M.; m. Louise C. Hohmann, June 5, 1960; children: Crystal Louise, James R. B.S., U. Tex., 1961; M.S., Tulane U., 1963. Cons. geologist oil and gas industry New Orleans, 1964-69; v.p. founding ptnr. McMoRan Exploration Co., New Orleans, 1969-74; pres., chief exec. officer McMoRan Oil & Gas Co., New Orleans, 1974-81, 81-85; chmn., chief exec. officer McMoRan Oil & Gas Co., from 1985; dir. McMoRan Oil & Gas Co., New Orleans, from 1974; vice-chmn. Freeport McMoRan Inc., New Orleans, 1981-85, chmn., chief exec. officer, 1985—, dir., 1981—. Mem. Nat. Petroleum Council, Washington, 1979, Commn. on the Future of South, 1986; bd. dirs. La. Energy Nat. PAC, Metairie, La., 1979, World Trade Ctr., New Orleans, Am. Cancer Soc. Greater New Orleans, Bus. Task Force Edn., Inc.; chmn. bd. La. Coun. Fiscal Reform; chmn. bus. coun. New Orleans and River Region, 1985-87. 2nd lt. U.S. Army, 1961-68, capt. Res. ret. Recipient T award Ex Students Assn. U. Tex., 1960, Hornblower Yr. award Pub. Relations Soc. Am., 1986, Vol. Yr. award Urban League Greater New Orleans, 1987; Minnie Stevens Piper Found. scholar U. Tex., 1960, Jacques E. Yenni, S.J. award Loyola U. of New Orleans for Outstanding Community Svc., Jr. Achievement Bus. Hall of Fame award, 1987, Loyola U. of New Orleans' Integritas Vitae award, 1988; named One of Ten Outstanding Persons of 1985 Inst. for Human Understanding, New Orleans. Mem. All Am. Wildcatters, New Orleans Geol. Soc., Petroleum Club New Orleans, Greater New Orleans Mktg. Com. (exec. com. 1987), Geology Found U. Tex. (adv. council 1972-85), Devel. bd. U. Tex., La. Ind. producers Royalty Owners Assn.. South La. Mid-Continent Oil Gas Assn. (v.p.), Dinner Steering Com. (Disting. Citizen award 1983, 85 Boy Scouts Am. New Orleans div.), Green Wave Club. Republican. Office: Freeport-McMoRan Copper & Gold 1615 Poydras St New Orleans LA 70112-1254*

MOFFETT, KENWORTH W., art museum director; b. Newark, Nov. 26, 1934. BA with honors, Columbia U., 1958; MA, Harvard U., 1962, PhD, 1968; postgrad. studies, Mus. Mgmt. Inst., Getty Found, Berkeley, Calif., 1990. Tchg. fellow Harvard U., Cambridge, Mass., 1962; from instr. to prof. art history Wellesley Coll., Wellesley, Mass., 1968-79; curator of Contemporary Art Mus. Fine Arts, Boston, 1971-78, curator of twentieth century art, 1978-84; curator in charge of Mus. of Fine Arts, Faneuil Hall, Boston, 1979-81; curator of Mus. of Fine Arts/Hines Contemporary Collection Universty Place, Cambridge, Mass., 1984; exec. dir. Mus. of Art, Fort Lauderdale, Fla., 1989—. Author 8 books; contbr. 32 articles to profl. jours,; books include: New, New Painting, 1982, Odd Nerdrum, 1994. Harvard U. fellow, 1960, 63, Traveling fellow, 1964-65, Sheldon Traveling fellow, 1963-64, Fritz Thyssen Stiftung fellow, 1965-67; Ford Found. grantee, 1970; recipient Ann. award for Art Criticism, NEA. Mem. Phi Beta Kappa. Office: Mus of Art Inc 1 E Las Olas Blvd Fort Lauderdale FL 33301-1807

MOFFETT, T(ERRILL) K(AY), lawyer; b. Becker, Miss., July 11, 1949; s. Elmer C. and Mary Ethel (Meek) M.; m. Rita C. Millsaps, Mar. 11, 1972; 1 child, Tara Leigh. BS, U.S. Mil. Acad., 1971; MA in Polit. Sci., U. Hawaii, 1974; JD, U. Miss., 1979, Fellow, Harvard U., 1995-96. Bar: Miss. 1979. Grad. tchr. Am. govt. U. Miss., Oxford, 1977-80; ptnr. Moffett and Thorne, Tupelo, Miss., 1980-88; owner Moffett Law Firm, Tupelo, 1988—; pros. atty, City of Tupelo, 1989—. Republican candidate for U.S. Congress 1st Miss. Dist., 1978, 80; 1st dist. coord. Reagan for Pres., 1980; co-chmn. Lee County George Bush for Pres. Com., 1988, 92; mem. Lee County Rep. Exec. Com., 1980—; chmn. Tupelo Rep. Exec. Com., 1988—; active 1st Baptist Ch., Tupelo; bd. dirs. Sav-A-Life Tupelo, Inc. Capt. U.S. Army, 1971-76; col. Miss. Army N.G., 1996. Harvard fellow, 1995-96. Mem. Miss. State Bar Assn., Lee County Bar Assn., Civitan, Masons, Habitat for Humanity, Corinth, Phi Sigma Alpha. Avocations: music, hunting, tennis, travel. Home: 5 N Parc Cir Tupelo MS 38801-9764 Office: PO Drawer 1707 330 N Broadway St Tupelo MS 38802

MOFFITT, DERRICK L., political science educator; b. Athens, Ga., May 20, 1970; s. James E. and Elizabeth (Chenault) M. BA in Polit. Sci., Newberry Coll., 1992; MA, Ga. So. U., 1995. Instr. polit. sci. Ga. Mil. Coll., Milledgeville, 1994—; cons. elder hostel program Ga. Coll., 1994—. Mem. Am. Polit. Sci. Assn. Office: Ga Mil Coll 201 E Green St Milledgeville GA 31061-3519

MOFFITT, SUSAN RAYE, critical care nurse; b. Mt. Carmel, Ill., July 22, 1964; d. Merle E. and Donna R. (Moore) Holsen; m. Tony Lee Moffitt, June 4, 1991; children: Sarah Ann, Alexander Lee. AASN, Kankakee (Ill.) Community Coll., 1984. Cert. critical care nurse, ACLS provider and instr., PALS. Staff nurse med./surg. emergency rm. Lawrence County Meml. Hosp., Lawrenceville, Ill., 1984-87; staff nurse CCU, charge nurse Welborn Bapt. Hosp., Evansville, Ind., 1987-89; charge nurse CCU Lakeland (Fla.) Regional Med. Ctr., 1989—; staff nurse Cardiac Interventional Unit Lakeland Regional Med. Ctr., 1996—; preceptor Lakeland Regional Med. Ctr., Welborn Bapt. Hosp.

MOFFITT, TONY LEE, emergency nurse; b. Vincennes, Ind., Nov. 7, 1961; s. Larry Richard Moffitt and Bonita Jean (Burrell) Shidler; m. Susan Raye Holsen, June 4, 1991; children: Sarah Ann, Alexander Lee. ADN, Olney Coll., 1987. RN, Fla.; cert. ACLS provider, emergency nurse, pediatric emergency nurse, PALS. Staff nurse Lawrence County Meml., Lawrenceville, Ill., 1987; staff nurse Lakeland (Fla.) Regional Med. Ctr., 1987-90, mem. recruitment and retention, 1988-90, asst. charge nurse, 1990-93; emergency nurse South Fla. Bapt., Plant City, 1991—, charge nurse, 1993-94; team leader Cardiac Interventional Unit, 1994-95. Emergency med. tech. and paramedic clin. instr. Polk Community Coll., Lakeland, 1990-92. Republican. Home: 1522 Sherwood Lakes Blvd Lakeland FL 33809-6800 Office: Lakeland Regional Med Ctr Lakeland Hills Blvd Lakeland FL 33802

MOGGE, HARRIET MORGAN, educational association executive; b. Cleve.; d. Russell VanDyke and Grace (Wells) Morgan; m. Robert Arthur Mogge, Aug. 17, 1948 (div. 1977); 1 child, Linda Jean. BME, Northwestern U., 1959; postgrad., Ill. State U., 1969. Instr. piano, Evanston, Ill., 1954-58; instr. elem. music pub. schs., Evanston, 1959; editorial asst. archivist Summy-Birchard Co., Evanston, 1964-66, asst. to editor-in-chief, 1966-67, cons., 1968-69, ednl. dir., 1969-74, also historian, 1973-74; supr. vocal music jr. high sch., Watseka, Ill., 1967-68; asst. dir. profl. programs Music Educators Nat. Conf., Reston, Va., 1974-84, dir. meetings and convs., 1984-94, mgr. direct mktg. svc., 1981-89; sr. cons. Convention Consulting Svc., 1993—. Mng. editor Am. Suzuki jour., 1972-74, Gen. Music Today, 1987-91; mgr. diplay advt. Model T Times, 1971—; vice chair editorial bd. Exposition Mgmt., 1991-93; Active various community drives. Mem. Music Educators Nat. Conf., Am. Choral Dirs. Assn., In and About Chgo., Music Educators Assn. (bd. dirs.), Suzuki Assn. Ams. (exec. sec. 1972-74), Disting. Svc. award, Suzuki Assn. Am., 1996, Internat. Assn. Expn. Mgmt. (cert.; mem. edn. com. 1979-88, chmn. edn. com. 1985-87, bd. liaison edn. com. 1987-88, bd. dirs. Washington chpt. 1983-85, nat. bd. dirs. 1986-91, del. to conv. liaison coun. 1989-90, nat. v.p. 1989, nat. pres. 1990, nat. past pres. 1991), Mu Phi Epsilon, Kappa Delta (province pres. 1960-66, 72-76, regional chpts. dir. 1976-78, nat. dir. scholarship 1981-84). Republican. Presbyterian. Clubs: Bus. and Profl. Women's (Watseka) (bd. dirs. 1968-70); Antique Automobile (registrar ann. meeting 1961-86), Model T Ford Internat. (v.p. 1971-72, 76-77, pres. 1981, treas. 1983-87, bd. dirs. 1971-87). Home: 1919A Villaridge Dr Reston VA 20191-4824 Office: PO Box 3362 Reston VA 20195-1362

MOGHIS, CHERIE LYNN, elementary school educator, marketing professional; b. Lawton, Okla., May 10, 1959; d. Noel Charles And Gayle Elizabeth (Jones) Allen; m. Moe Moghis, Oct. 5, 1985; children: Matthew, Sara. BS in Bus. Adminstrn., U. S. La., 1982. Pharmacy technician Lourdes Hosp., Lafayette, La., 1980-82; adminstrv. asst., sales Tandy Corp., Mataire, La., 1982-85; mktg., sales Telecomms./Sales, New Orleans, Nat. Edn. Ctr., New Orleans, 1990-92; tchr. Jefferson Parish Schs., Harvey, La., 1992-96. Mem. Phi Delta Kappa, Alpha Theta Epsilon. Home: 4332 Colorado Ave Kenner LA 70065-1324

MOGIELNICKI, JOHN WAYNE, journalist; b. Glen Ridge, N.J., Sept. 9, 1951; s. John Anthony and Catherine (Bubenas) M.; m. Marguerite Kathleen Beck, Apr. 23, 1983. BA in journalism, Rutgers Univ., 1973; MA in journalism, Univ. Tex., 1980. Reporter The News Tribune, Woodbridge, N.J., 1973-77; section editor The Home News, New Brunswick, N.J., 1980-82, sunday editor, 1982-85, editorial page editor, 1985-86; copy/layout editor Philadelphia Inquirer, Phila., 1986-91; mng. editor The Daily Progress, Charlottesville, Va., 1991-92, editor, 1992—. Bd. dirs. Blue Ridge Area Food Bank, Verona, Va., 1996—. Mem. Va. Associated Press Editors. Office: The Daily Progress PO Box 9030 Charlottesville VA 22906

MOGY, CATHERINE WADDELL, nurse anesthetist, critical care nurse; b. Florence, S.C., Mar. 13, 1964; d. Harold Dean and Sarah Margaret (Windham) Waddell; m. Richard A. Mogy, Sept. 13, 1986; children: Austin Waddell, Sarah Catherine. ADN, Florence-Darlington Tech Ctr., 1985; BSN, Med. U. S.C., Florence, 1989; cert., Richland Meml. Sch. Anesthesia, 1991. RN, S.C.; cert. advanced cardiac life supports, nurse anesthetist. Staff nurse McLeod Regional Med. Ctr., Florence, S.C., 1985-86; staff nurse ICU Bruce Hosp., Florence, 1986-89; nurse anesthetist Carolina's Hosp. System, 1991—. Recipient Francis Marion almuni scholarship. Mem. Am. Assn. Nurse Anesthetists, ANA, Sigma Theta Tau.

MOHAIDEEN, A. HASSAN, surgeon, healthcare executive; b. Ramanathapuram, India, Aug. 14, 1940; s. Abdul and Mariam (Pitchai) Kader; m. Zarina M. Meera, May 30, 1965 (dec. July 1986); children: Ahamed, Mariam, Najeeba, Azeema; m. Laurie J. Kucich, June 23, 1989; children: Yasmin Sara, Leila Jahan. MD, U. Madras, India, 1965; MBA, Wagner Coll., 1996. Diplomate Am. Bd. Surgery, Am. Bd. Quality Assurance and Utilization. Intern Govt. Stanley Hosp., Madras, 1965-66, Good Samaritan Hosp., West Islip, N.Y., 1967-68; resident in gen. and vascular surgery L.I. Coll. Hosp., Bklyn., 1968-73, asst. attending surgeon, 1973-76, assoc. attending surgeon, 1976-78, attending surgeon, 1978—, chief divsn. vascular surgery, 1980-93, dir. vascular lab., 1981-93; sr. v.p., managed care and exec. vice-chmn. dept. surgery The Bklyn.-Caledonian Hosp. Ctr. (affiliate of NYU), 1995-96; sr. v.p. Bklyn.-Caledonian Hosp. Ctr. (affiliate of NYU), 1995-96; asst. surgeon G.H.Q. Hosp., Ramnad, India, 1966-67; assoc. attending surgeon Meth. Hosp., Bklyn., 1982-90, attending surgeon, 1991; asst. attending surgeon Bklyn. Caledonian Med. Ctr., 1973-85, mem. courtesy staff, 1985-94, attending surgeon, 1994—; attending physician Victory Meml. Hosp., Bklyn., 1982-95; vs. physician Kings County Hosp. Ctr., Bklyn., 1973—; clin. instr. in surgery Downstate Med. Ctr., SUNY, Bklyn., 1973-78, clin. asst. prof. surgery, 1978—; mem. exec. com. of med. staff L.I. Coll. Hosp., Bklyn., 1979-93, treas. med. staff, 1982-85, pres., 1985-87, med. chmn. Guild Ball com., 1981, mem. quality assurance com. dept. surgery, 1988-94, chmn. credentials com., 1990-93, quality assurance and risk mgmt. com., 1990-93; bd. dirs. Aetna Health Plans of N.Y., AIDS adv. com., 1987—, stds. com., 1986-94, quality assurance com.; mem. credentials com. Prucare, 1988-92; sr. v.p. managed care Bklyn. Hosp., 1995-96; mem. quality mgmt. com. Oxford Health Plans, 1995—; mem. quality improvement com. Chubb Health, N.Y., 1994—. Contbr. articles to med. jours. Fellow ACS (com. on Long Island dist. applicants, 1988—), Royal Coll. Physicians and Surgeons Can. (cert.), Internat. Coll. Surgeons; mem. AMA (Physician's Recognition award), AAAS, Am. Coll. Physician Execs., Med. Soc. of State of N.Y., N.Y. State Soc. of Surgeons, N.Y. Acad. of Scis., Med. Soc. of County of Kings (mediation com., 1979-85), Bklyn. Surg. Soc., Soc. for Non-Invasive Vascular Technicians, Kings Physicians I.P.A. (pres./med. dir., 1985-95), Bklyn. Physicians I.P.A. (v.p., 1985-96, pres.). Office: 705 86th St Brooklyn NY 11228-3219

MOHALLEY, PATRICIA JOANN, library media specialist; b. Lafayette, Ind., Aug. 24, 1951; d. Robert Dean and Alta Mae (Hancock) Clerget; m. Jeremiah J. Mohalley, Mar. 17, 1979; Sarah Frances and Jeremiah J. Jr. BA in Edn., Purdue U., 1973, MS in Edn., 1978. Cert. edn.-libr. media specialist, Ind., Tex. Tchr. grade 5 Crown Point (Ind.) Sch. Corp., 1973-74; tchr. grades 5 and 6 South Newton Sch. Corp., Kentland, Ind., 1974-77; dir. elem. librs. Community Sch. Corp. of Ea. Hancock County, Wilkinson, Ind., 1977-80; libr. media specialist Met. Sch. Dist. of Lawrence Twp., Indpls., 1980-81, Spring Br. Ind. Sch. Dist., Houston, 1981-89, Klein (Tex.) Ind. Sch. Dist., 1989—. Active Cypress Creek Friends Libr., Spring, Tex., 1988—; life mem. Tex. PTA, 1989—. Mem. ALA, Tex. Libr. Assn. Home: 7814 Springberry Ct Spring TX 77379-4084

MOHAMED, DONNA FAHIMAH, counselor; b. Chapel Hill, N.C., Oct. 19, 1959; d. Thomas Lloyd and Helen Eleanor (Helms) Pendergraft; m. Dilip Gandhi, Aug. 19, 1978; 1 child, Sundeep; m. Mustafa Hussein Al-Bar, Apr. 15, 1991; 1 child, Maidah Nasreen. BA in Religious Studies with high honors and distinction, U. N.C., 1994. Rehab. therapist John Umstead Hosp. Continuing Treatment, Butner, N.C., 1985-86; immigration paralegal Law Offices of Douglas Holmes, Durham, N.C., 1986-87; immigration specialist Law Offices of Manlin Chee, Greensboro, N.C., 1987-92; program dir., accredited counselor Immigration & Minority Assistance Network, Durham, 1992—; pro bono project rep. Lawyers Com. for Human Rights, Fredericksburg, Va., 1987-88; minority devel. counselor, Ibad Ar-Rahman Sch., Durham, 1990-91; immigration cons. to bd. dirs. Jamaat Ibad Ar-Rahman, Inc., Durham, 1990-94; dir. cmty. counseling IMAN, Durham, 1991—; speaker N.Am. Coun. for Muslim Women, Chgo., 1994; panelist on cultural awareness, Dept. Edn. and Counseling, U. N.C., Chapel Hill, 1994; organizer, presenter ann. workshops Coll. Bound Program for Youth, Chapel Hill, 1992—. Recipient 1st prize ann. cooking contest Triangle Muslim Women's Group, 1992. Mem. Am. Muslim Coun., Am. Immigration Lawyers Assn. (pro bono affiliation), Muslim Women's Orgn. (pres. Chapel Hill, N.C. chpt. 1991-93), Muslim Student's Assn. (exec. dir. Chapel Hill chpt. 1992-93), Islamic Soc. N.Am., Social Scientists Am., Golden Key Nat. Honor Soc. Democrat.

MOHAN, TUNGESH NATH, television and film producer, film educator; b. Lucknow, India, Oct. 30, 1949; came to U.S., 1979; s. Bhola Shambu and Saraswati P. (Devi) Nath; m. Annette Gonsalves; 1 child, Lathika. BS, Kampur (India) U., 1969; diploma in Cinema, Film and TV Inst. India, Poona, 1972; MA, Andrews U., 1980. Producer Bombay TV, 1972-75, 77-79; asst. prof. Film and TV Inst. India, Poona, 1975-77; TV producer 700 Club, Virginia Beach, Va., 1980-82; producer spl. projects Christian Broadcasting Network, Virginia Beach, 1982-86, Christian Broadcasting Network Cable Prodns., Inc., Virginia Beach, 1986-87; dir. Internat. CBN Producers Group, 1987-89, Internat. NorthStar Entertainment Group, L.A., 1989-92; mgr. Adventist Comm. Network, Silver Springs, Md., 1992-93; pres. Tri-Angel Media Corp., Thousand Oaks, Calif., 1992—; adj. prof. Film and TV Inst. India, Poona, 1975-79, Spicer Coll., Poona, 1975-79, Hampton (Va.) U., 1980-92; pres. Producers Unit-One, Virginia Beach, 1982—, L.I.F.E. Inc., 1993—; cons. Global Comm. Assocs., Virginia Beach, 1987-88, Global TV Syndication, 1996—. Prodr., dir. (films) Even So, 1972, Dishantar (cert. Proficiency 1975), Raktajeevee (Golden Lion award 1977), (documentary) Afghanistan: Under the Iron Claw, 1982; prodr., dir., writer (film) U-Turn (Garima award 1973); exec. prodr. Stand at Ease, 1989-90; co-exec. prodr. Rin Tin Tin K-9 Cop, 1988-89; prodr. Touching the Supernatural, 1992, Midnight Cry, 1994, Master Control, 1994, The Way We Were, 1995, Bought at a Price, 1996, Hanged on a Twisted Cross, 1996 (Chris award for script Columbus Internat. Film Festival 1996), Inn-Keeper, 1996. Mem. NATAS, Writers Guild Am., Dirs. Guild Am., Lions. Mem. Seventh-Day Adventists. Home: 920 Amherst Ln Virginia Beach VA 23464-3703 Office: Creative Cir Box 64175 Virginia Beach VA 23467-4175

MOHD ZAIN, A. ZAIDY, academic administrator; b. Kelantan, Malaysia, Jan. 24, 1956; came to U.S., 1979; s. Mohd Zain Abd Rahmman and Siti Katijah Kechik;m. Tracey A. West; Children Andrew, Jasmine, 1 foster child, Andrew Nault. BBA, Western Mich. U., 1980; MPA, Sangamon State U., 1983, MA in Counseling, 1989; PhD.in Counseling Edn. and Supervision, Kent State U., 1995—. Bank exec. Bank of Commerce BHD, Kuala Lumpur, Malaysia, 1983-85; dir. Sasquatch Group Cos., Kuala Lumpur, 1985-86; therapist Kemmerer Village Children's Home, Assumption, Ill., 1988-89; mental health counselor Community Resource Ctr., Centralia, Ill., 1989-90; part time lectr. Mara Inst. Tech., Kuala Lumpur, 1984-85. Mem. Am. Counseling Assn., Internat. Assn for Marriage and Family Counselors, Assn. for Counselor Edn. and Supervision, Chi Sigma Iota. Home: 1313 West Sunflower Rd #112 Cleveland MS 38732-2401 Office: Divsn of Behavioral Scis Delta State U 310 White Hall Kent State Cleveland MS 38733-3142

MOHLER, RICHARD ALBERT, JR., academic administrator, theologian; b. Lakeland, Fla., Oct. 9, 1959; s. Richard Albert Sr. and Janet Rae (Johnson) M.; m. Mary Ann Kahler, July 16, 1983; children: Mary Katherine, Christopher Albert. BA magna cum laude, Samford U., 1980; MDiv, So. Bapt. Theol. Sem., Louisville, 1983, PhD, 1989; postgrad., St. Meinrad Sch. Theology, 1985, Oxford (Eng.) U., 1986. Ordained min. So. Bapt. Ch. Pastor Union Grove Bapt. Ch., Bedford, Ky., 1982-87; asst. to pres., coord. found. support, dir. capital funding So. Bapt. Theol. Sem., Louisville, 1983-89, pres., 1993—; editor The Christian Index, Atlanta, 1989-93; prof. christian theology, 1996—; assoc. dir. The So. Sem. Found., 1983-89; lectr. in field. Assoc. editor Preaching, 1985-93, contbg. editor, 1993—; gen. editor: The Gods of the Age of the God of the Ages?, 1993; contbr. articles to profl. jours. Named one of 40 Rising Evangelical Leaders, Christianity Today, 1996, One of 96 Southerners to Watch, Atlanta Jour. and Constitution, 1996. Mem. Am. Acad. Religion, Soc. Biblical Lit., Evangelical Theol. Soc., So. Bapt. Hist. Soc., Bapt. Pub. Rels. Assn., So. Bapt. Press Assn., Evangelical Press Assn., Nat. Assn. Evangelicals, Ga. Bapt. Hist. Soc., Rotary Internat., Phi Kappa Phi, Omicron Delta Kappa. Office: So Bapt Theol Sem 2825 Lexington Rd Louisville KY 40280-0001

MOHNER, CARL MARTIN RUDOLF, movie actor, artist; b. Vienna, Austria, Aug. 11, 1921; came to U.S., 1978; s. Karl and Maria (Budiner) m.; m. Ina Maria Fox (div.); children: Gernot, Gunther; m. Therese Marie Windsor-Brown (div.); m. Wilma Marie Langhamer, Dec. 9, 1978. Ed., Neuber-Gaudernak Theater Sch., Graz, Austria. Appeared in over 60 films, including Cleopatra, Sink the Bismark, Rififi, 1953, The Last Bridge, 1953 (Gold Palm award Cannes Film Festival 1954); one-man shows include Galerie d'Arte Zanini, Rome, 1962, also in Stuttgart, Munich, Vienna, Belgrade, Milan, Graz, Zurich, Titograd; one man retrospective exhbn. McAllen (Tex.) Internat. Mus., 1979, The Art Mus. S. Tex., Corpus Christi, 1996; exhibited in group shows at Dallas, Houston, Corpus Christi, 1991-92; works represented in collections at Albertina in Vienna, also Smithsonian Instn. Served in World War II. Recipient Gold medal IX Premio Internationale de Pittura San Vitto Romano, 1963, 1st place award Summerfair, Cin., Wichita (Kans.) Art Mus. Art Fair, 1992, 93. Home and Office: Orange Hill Studio RR 1 Box 322 Mission TX 78572-9773

MOHNEY, NELL WEBB, religion educator, speaker, author; b. Shelby, N.C., Oct. 31, 1921; d. John Wonnie and Maude (Ferree) Webb; m. Ralph Wilson Mohney, Dec. 31, 1948; children: Richard Bentley, Ralph Wilson Jr. BA, Greensboro Coll., 1943; LHD (hon.), Tenn. Wesleyan Coll., 1982. Dir. youth work Western N.C. Conf., Salisbury, 1945-48; dir. Christian edn. 1st United Meth. Ch., Lenoir, N.C., 1943-45, Washington Pike United Meth. Ch., Knoxville, Tenn., 1952-56; dir. adult ministries 1st Centenary United Meth. Ch., Chattanooga, 1967-73, dir. membership devel., 1973-81; dir. membership devel. 1st Broad St. United Meth. Ch., Kingsport, Tenn., 1981-87; speaker, seminar leader for bus., profl., religious orgns. S.E. U.S., 1960—; spkr. Internat. Women's Conf., Crystal Cathedral, 1991; adj. staff Bd. Discipleship Sect. on Evangelism, Nashville, 1987-96. Author: Inside Story, 1979, Don't Put a Period Where God Put a Comma, 1993; co-author: Parable Churches, 1989, Churches of Vision, 1990; contbr. weekly article Chattanooga Free Press, 1977—, Kingsport Times, 1981—. Recipient Freedom Founds. award for writing, Valley Forge, Pa., 1973, for speaking, 1974, Key to City of Chattanooga, 1979; named Disting. Alumnae Greensboro Coll., 1988, Woman of Distinction in Chattanooga, 1992, Woman of Distinction Hall of Fame, 1993. Republican. Home: 1004 Northbridge Ln Chattanooga TN 37405-4214

MOHR, JEFFREY MICHAEL, real estate and insurance executive; b. Baton Rouge, Sept. 20, 1960; s. Lewis Thompson Sr. and Josephine (Agosta) M.; m. Lisa Juneau, Mar. 9, 1961; children: Jeffrey Michael Jr., Brittany Danielle. BS in Mgmt. Adminstrn., La. State U., 1982. CPCU; cert. assoc. in risk mgmt. Ins. agt., producer Lewis Mohr Real Estate and Ins. Agy., Inc., Baton Rouge, 1983-84, pres., 1984—. Mem. La. Edn. Adv. Coun., 1994—. Mem. Ind. Ins. Agts. Am. (edn. com.), Ind. Ins. Agts. La. (chmn. editorial adv. bd. 1994—, chmn. personal lines tech. com.), Ind. Ins. Agts. Baton Rouge (pres. 1994), Baton Rouge C. of C., Exch. Club (bd. dirs. 1985-88), Capitol Area Tigers Club (sec. 1986-90, v.p. 1990-92, bd. dirs. 1992—), Soc. CPCU (Bayou chpt. bd. dirs. 1995), Delta Tau Delta (v.p. house corp. 1988-91, pres. 1992—, pres. so. divsn. house corp. 1994). Republican. Roman Catholic. Office: Lewis Mohr Real Estate & Ins 8281 Goodwood Blvd Ste C Baton Rouge LA 70806-7742

MOHR, LAWRENCE CHARLES, physician; b. S.I., N.Y., July 8, 1947; s. Lawrence Charles Sr. and Mary Estelle (Dawsey) M.; m. Linda Johnson, June 14, 1970; 1 child, Andrea Marie. AB, U. N.C., 1975, MD, 1979. Diplomate Am. Bd. Internal Medicine. Commd. 2d lt. U.S. Army, 1967, advanced through grades to col., 1989; med. intern Walter Reed Army Med. Ctr., Washington, 1979-80, resident in medicine, 1980-82, chief resident, 1982-83, attending physician, 1984-86, pulmonary fellow, 1986-87; command surgeon 9th Inf. Div., Ft. Lewis, Wash., 1983-84; med. cons. Madigan Army Med. Ctr., Tacoma, 1983-84; White House physician Washington, 1987-93; asst. prof. medicine Uniformed Svcs. U. of the Health Scis., Bethesda, Md., 1984-91; assoc. prof. medicine Uniformed Svcs. U. Health Scis., Bethesda, Md., 1991-94; assoc. clin. prof. medicine George Washington U., Washington, 1990-94; prof. medicine Med. U. S.C., Charleston, 1994—, dir. environ. hazards assessment program, 1995—; mem. Working Group on Disability in U.S. Presidents, 1995—. Bd. dirs. Internat. Lung Found., Washington; mem. adv. bd. Nat. Mus. Health and Medicine, Washington. Decorated Silver Star, Bronze Star with 2 V devices and 3 oak leaf clusters, Purple Heart, Meritorious Svc. medal with oak leaf cluster, Air medal, Army Commendation medal with oak leaf cluster; recipient Erskine award Walter Reed Army Med. Ctr., 1982; named Outstanding Med. Resident, 1982. Fellow ACP, Am. Coll. Chest Physicians; mem. AMA, Army and Navy Club, Order Mil. Med. Merit, Harbour Club, Phi Beta Kappa. Episcopalian. Home: Ste 11-R 310 Broad St Charleston SC 29401 Office: Med U S C Environ Hazards Assess Prgm 171 Ashley Ave Charleston SC 29425

MOINET, ERIC EMIL, accountant, controller, cost accountant, inventory control and internal systems specialist, traffic safety administrator; b. Paris, Mar. 17, 1952; s. Emil and Marguerite (Baccon) M.; m. Glynis Carol Moinet, May 6, 1980; children: Danielle Louise, Nicolette Anne. Assoc. in Applied Sci., Queensborough C.C., 1982; BBA, Baruch Coll., 1988. Jr. acct. Jason & Berman, CPA's, N.Y.C., 1982-84; sr. asst. internat. tax specialist KPMG, Peat, Marwick, Main & Co., CPAs, N.Y.C., 1984-88; tax specialist KPMG, Peat, Marwick, Main & Co., CPAs, Raleigh, N.C., 1988-89; cost acct., inventory control/internal systems specialist, traffic safety adminstr., environ., safety and emergency coord. Dixie Forming & Bldg. Specialties, Inc., Raleigh, N.C., 1989-93, asst. controller, 1993-95; acct. II Healthsourse N.C., Inc., 1995-96; billing and purchasing adminstr. Strategic Techs., Inc., 1996—. Mem. Am. Soc. Safety Engrs., N.C. Assn. CPAs (assoc. Triangle chpt.), Inst. Mgmt. Accts. (assoc., dir. edn. and profl. devel. com., team capt. adminstrn. 1990-93), N.Y. State Assn. CPA Candidates (chmn. pub. rels. com., recruiting and career coms. 1985-87, bd. dirs. 1985-87, v.p. 1986-87), Fin. and Econ. Soc. (rec. sec.), Club for Accts. Seeking Heights (pres., advisor, founding mem.), Queensborough C.C. Acctg. Soc., Queensborough C.C. Alumni Assn., Baruch Coll. Acctg. Soc., Baruch Coll. Alumni Assn., KC (Father Price coun.). Republican. Roman Catholic.

MOJTABAI, ANN GRACE, author, educator; b. N.Y.C., June 8, 1937; d. Robert and Naomi (Friedman) Alpher; m. Fathollah Mojtabai, Apr. 27, 1960 (div. 1966); children: Chitra, Ramin. B.A. in Philosophy, Antioch Coll., 1958; M.A. in Philosophy, Columbia U., 1968, M.S. in L.S., 1970. Lectr. philosophy Hunter Coll., CUNY, 1966-68; librarian CCNY, 1970-76; fellow Radcliffe Inst. Ind. Study, Cambridge, Mass., 1976-78; Briggs-Copeland lectr. in English Harvard U., 1978-83; writer-in-residence U. Tulsa, 1983—, Yaddo Found., Saratoga, N.Y., 1975, 76. Author: Mundome, 1974, The 400 Eels of Sigmund Freud, 1976, A Stopping Place, 1979, Autumn, 1982, Blessed Assurance, 1986, Ordinary Time, 1989, Called Out, 1994. Recipient Richard and Hinda Rosenthal award Am. Acad. and Inst. Arts and Letters, 1983, Lillian Smith award So. Regional Council, 1986, Lit. Acad. award AAAL, 1993; Guggenheim fellow, 1981-82. Mem. PEN, Mark Twain Soc., Tex. Inst. Letters, Phi Beta Kappa. Home: 2102 S Hughes St Amarillo TX 79109-2212 Office: U Tulsa Dept English 600 S College Ave Tulsa OK 74104-3189

MOKHA, SUKHBIR SINGH, physiology educator, researcher; b. Poona, India, Feb. 7, 1952; came to U.S., 1988; s. Sarwan S. and Nasib K. (Chohan) M.; m. Dilraj Kaur, June 1, 1990. BSc, Punjab State Med. Coll., Amritsar, India, 1974; MSc, U. Southampton, Eng., 1977; PhD, U. Edinburgh, U.K., 1981. Postdoctoral fellow U. Edinburgh, 1980-83; rsch. scientist Nat. Inst. Med. Rsch., Mill Hill, Eng., 1984-87; asst. prof. Meharry Med. Coll., Nashville, 1988-95, assoc. prof., 1995—; adj. asst. prof. Vanderbilt U., Nashville, 1992-95, adj. assoc. prof., 1995—. Contbr. articles to profl. jours. Rsch. fellow Univ. Coll. London, 1988; State Merit scholar Punjab State, 1969, Rsch. scholar U. Edinburgh, 1977-80, Birrell Gray Travelling scholar, U. Edinburgh and U. London, 1979. Mem. Brit. Physiol. Soc., Brit. Pharm. Soc., Internat. Assn. Study Pain, Internat. Assn. Dental Rsch., Soc. Neuroscience. Office: Meharry Med Coll Dept Anatomy and Physiology 1005 D B Todd Blvd Nashville TN 37208

MOKHTARZADEH, AHMAD AGHA, agronomist, consultant; b. Fassa, Fars, Iran, Oct. 23, 1933; came to U.S., 1989; s. Mohamad Hassan and Assieh (Kadivar) M.; m. Brigitte Becker, Nov. 12, 1980; 1 child, Mitra. BSc, BA, U. Tehran, Iran, 1956; MSc, U. Md., 1960; PhD, U. Paris, France, 1964. Assoc. prof. Shiraz U., Iran, 1964-80; cons. S. Pacifc regions Somalia, Vietnam, Namibia Food and Agrl. Orgn. U.N., Rome, 1981-89; cons. pvt. practice Leesburg, Va., 1990—; mem. Pres. Program Com. Shiraz U., Iran, 1977-79; advisor German Remote Sensing in Agrl., Somalia, 1984; officer-in-charge Food Agrl. Orgn., U.N., Western Samoa, 1985. Co-author: Bibliography of Natural History of Iran, 1965; contbr. articles to profl. jours. including Crop Sci., Der Züchter, Nematologia Mediterranea. Recipient 4-yr. scholarship Govt. of Iran, 1958-62, 2-yr. scholarship Govt. of France, 1962-64, Fulbright fellowship N.D. State U., 1968-69, Rsch. fellowship, Energy Rsch. and Devel., Oak Ridge, Tenn., 1976-77. Mem. Am. Soc. Agronomy, Sigma Xi. Home and Office: 141 Davis Ave SW Leesburg VA 20175-3405

MOLAND, KATHRYN JOHNETTA, computer scientist, software engineer; b. Tallahassee, Nov. 5, 1961; d. John and Kathryn Vastavia (Gadson) M. BS in Sociology, Fla. A&M U., 1982; MS in Computer Sci., Southern U., 1987; PhD in Info. Systems, Nova U., 1996. Programmer, summer intern IBM, Lexington, 1985; mem. tech. staff Bell Communications Rsch., Piscataway, N.J., 1986; programmer Logos Corp., Mount Arlington, N.J., 1987-88, Telecommunications Inds., Vienna, Va., 1988; systems analyst Advanced Tech., Inc., Reston, Va., 1988; project leader Advanced Tech., Inc., Aiken, S.C., 1989-90; sr. systems analyst, project leader Westinghouse Savannah River Co., Aiken, S.C., 1990-94; devel. mgr. SCT Utility Systems, Inc., Columbia, S.C., 1994—; tech. mem. Occurrence Reporting Spl. Interest Group, Oak Ridge, Tenn., 1991-94. Bd. govs. Am. Biog. Inst. Rsch. Assn. Mem. IEEE (treas. 1991-92, vice chair 1992-93, chair 1993-94, mem. tech. coun. software engrng.), NAFE, Nat. Mgmt. Assn., Project Mgmt. Inst., Assn. Computing Machinery. Home: PO Box 981 Irmo SC 29063 Office: SCT Utility Systems Inc 9 Science Ct Columbia SC 29203

MOLINAR, LUPE RODRIQUEZ, librarian, library director; b. Marathon, Tex., June 6, 1942; d. Luciano and Ignacia (Ramirez) Rodriquez; m. Victor O. Molinar, July 29, 1961; 1 child, Lynn Molinar Boutwell. AA, N.Mex. Jr. Coll., 1989. Cert. libr., Tex. Store clk., waitress Big Bend (Tex.) Nat. Pk., 1960-64; cafeteria worker Sul Ross State U., Alpine, Tex., 1964-65; nurse's aide Twilight Acres, Seminole, Tex., 1969-75; circulating clk. Gaines Co. Libr., Seminole, Tex., 1975-76, processing clk., 1976-91, libr., 1991—. Vol. Voters Registration, Seminole, 1980—; chair St. James Fall Festival, Seminole, 1994; bd. trustees Seminole Ind. Sch. Dist., 1994—. Mem. Tex. Libr. Assn., Guadalupanas Soc. (pres. 1988-89). Democrat. Roman Catholic. Home: 400 NW H Seminole TX 79360 Office: Gaines County Libr 704 Hobbs Hwy Seminole TX 79360-3402

MOLINO, MICHAEL ANTHONY, trade association executive; b. Bklyn., June 25, 1940; s. Angelo T. and Jean (Tepedino) M.; m. Barbara Ann Melzarek, Mar. 20, 1971; children: Michael Richard, Timothy A. BS in History, St. Peter's Coll., Jersey City, 1961; MA in History, U. Mo., Kansas City, 1973. Commd. 2d lt. U.S. Army, 1961, advanced through grades to col., 1983; ops. planner U.S. Army, Long Binh, Vietnam, 1967-68; instr. U.S. Army Command Gen. Staff Coll., Ft. Leavenworth, Kans., 1969-73; tng. coord. U.S. Army in Europe, Erlangen, Fed. Republic Germany, 1973-77; dep. community comdr. U.S. Army in Europe, Nurenberg, Fed. Republic Germany, 1983-86; dean students Def. Fgn. Lang. Ctr., Monterey, Calif., 1977-79; dean students and adminstrn. Indsl. Coll. Armed Forces, Washington, 1986-88; ret., 1988; asst. exec. v.p. Recreation Vehicle Dealers Assn., Fairfax, Va., 1988-91, v.p., 1991-96; pres., 1996—. Contbr. articles to various publs. Chmn. schs. adv. coun. Dept. Def. Dependent Schs., Nurenberg, 1983-86; v.p. Mid. Franconian Men's Club, Fuerth, Fed. Republic Germany, 1985-86; dir. Springfield (Va.) Babe Ruth Baseball League, 1986-90, pres., 1987-89. Decorated Bronze Star, Legion of Merit; named Knight Order of St. George, U.S. Armor Assn., 1988. Mem. Am. Soc. Assn. Execs. (mem. com. 1991-92), Greater Wash. Soc. Assn. Execs. (career cons 1989, edn. com. 1990-91, vice chmn. edn. com. 1991-92), Ret. Officers Assn., VFW. Roman Catholic. Home: 7405 Carath Ct Springfield VA 22153-1605 Office: Recreation Vehicle Dealers Assn 3930 University Dr # 100 Fairfax VA 22030-2515

MOLL, DAVID CARTER, civil engineer; b. Ames, Iowa, Aug. 5, 1948; s. Dale Curtis and Virginia (Carter) M.; m. Margaret E. Newman (div. 1989); 1 child, Megahn Elizabeth. BSCE, Iowa State U., 1971; cert. advanced study, Am. Grad. Sch. Internat. Mgmt., 1983; MBA with distinction, U. Mich., 1984. Engr. in tng. Iowa; field engr. Chgo. Bridge & Iron Co., 1971; subcontract supr., field engr. Morrison-Knudsen Internat. Co., Inc., Surinam and Panama, 1976; site supt. engrng., asst. supt. constrn. Fluor Corp., Saudi Arabia, 1977-82; group mgr. Cummins Engine Co., Columbus, Ind., 1984-85; mgr. spl. projects Kerr-McGee Coal Corp., Oklahoma City, 1985-88; project mgr. Kerr-McGee Corp., Oklahoma City, 1989, U.K., 1989-90, Saudi Arabia, 1990-92; Oklahoma City, 1993—. Lt. USN, 1971-75. Mem. ASCE, Civil Engr. Corps (Meritorious Svc. medal), Am. Soc. Quality Control (constrn. tech. com.), N.Y. Acad. Scis., Am. Legion, Order of the Knoll (Pres.' Cir.), Marston Club, Project Mgmt. Inst., Chi Epsilon.

MOLLEN, EDWARD LEIGH, pediatrician, allergist and immunologist; b. Richmond, Va., May 13, 1946; s. Irving Roth and Ruth (Damsky) M.; m. Mary Viola Jeffrey, Dec. 14, 1975; children: Shawn, Michael, Eric, Christopher. BS in Chemistry, Coll. William and Mary, 1968; MD, Med. Coll. Va., 1972. Diplomate Am. Bd. Pediatrics, Am. Bd. Allergy and Immunology. Resident in pediatrics Med. Coll. Va., Richmond, 1972-75, fellow in allergy and immunology, 1975-77; practice allergy and pediatric allergy and clin. immunology Allergy Assocs. of Richmond, 1977-85; pvt. practice allergy/pediatric allergy and clin. immunology Richmond, 1985—. Fellow Am. Acad. Allergy and Immunology, Am. Acad. Pediatrics; mem. Med. Soc. Va., Richmond Acad. Medicine, Am. Thoracic Soc., Va. Allergy Soc. Office: 5855 Bremo Rd Ste 702 Richmond VA 23226-1926

MOLLITT, DANIEL LAWRENCE, pediatric surgeon; b. Cin., Oct. 23, 1948; m. Barbara Yount, 1978; children: Todd Yount, Meredith Ann, Erin Elizabeth, Seth Yount. BS, St. Joseph's Coll., 1970; MD, St. Louis U., 1974. Diplomate Nat. Bd. Med. Examiners, Am. Bd. Surgery, Am. Bd. Surgery in Pediatric Surgery; cert. advanced trauma life support, advanced trauma life support instr., advanced pediatric life support, pediatric advanced life support. Intern in surgery Ind. U., Indianapolis, 1974-75, resident in surgery, 1975-78; resident in pediatric surgery Babies Hosp., Columbia-Presbyn. Med. Ctr., N.Y.C., 1979-81; inst. surgery Ind. U., Indianapolis, 1978-79; asst. prof. surgery U. Ark. Med. Scis., 1981-85, asst. prof. pediatrics, 1982-85; assoc. prof. surgery U. Fla. Coll. Medicine, 1985-92, prof. surgery, 1992—, prof. pediatrics, 1992—; dir. surg. rsch. U. Fla. Health Sci. Ctr., Jacksonville, 1994; chief childrens surg. svcs., Wolfson childrens Hosp., Jacksonville; lectr. in field. Author books and chpts. in books; contbr. over 70 articles to profl. jours. Recipient rsch. grants Am. Cancer Soc., 1978-79, U. Ark. Instl. Biomed. Rsch. Support, 1984, Groh Trust, 1987-88, 88-89, Dean's Intramural, 1989, Nemours Found., 1990, 92. Fellow ACS (Ensminger award 1977, Gatch award 1978), Am. Acad. Pediatrics; mem. Am. Assn. Surgery of Trauma, Am. Pediatric Surg. Assn., Assn. Acad. Surgery, Brit. Assn. Pediatric Surgeons, Duval County Med. Soc. (John A. Beals award 1988), Ea. Assn. Surgery of Trauma, Fla. Assn. Pediatric Surgeons (sec.-treas. 1992—), Fla. Med. Assn., Internat. Assn. Surgery of Trauma and Surg. Intensive Care, Internat. Soc. Surgery, So. Med. Assn., So. Soc. Pediatric Rsch., Southwestern Surg. Congress, N.E. Fla. Pediatric Soc., Pediatric Oncology Group, Shock Soc., Soc. Critical Care Medicine, Surg. Infection Soc. Home: 9229 Beauclerc Cir W Jacksonville FL 32257-4917 Office: Univ Fla Health Sci Ctr 655 W 8th St Jacksonville FL 32209-6511

MOLLOHAN, ALAN B., congressman, lawyer; b. Fairmont, W.Va., May 14, 1943; s. Robert H. and Helen (Holt) M.; m. Barbara Whiting, Aug. 7, 1976; children: Alan, Robert, Andrew, Karl, Mary Kathryn. AB in Polit. Sci., Coll. William and Mary, 1966; JD, W.Va. U., 1970. Assoc. law firm, 1970-82; mem. 98th-104th Congresses from 1st W.Va. dist., 1983—; mem. appropriations com., budget com. Mem. ABA, W.Va. Bar, Moose, Elks. Baptist. Office: US Ho of Reps Office of Postmaster 2427 Rayburn Ho Office Bldg Washington DC 20515

MOLLOY, MICHAEL JOHN, public relations professional; b. Phila., July 19, 1939; s. William John and Florence Hope (Buckley) M.; m. Johnise Josette Retossa, June 26, 1965; children: Johnise Michelle, Michael John Jr. BA, Coll. William and Mary, Williamsburg, Va., 1962. Reporter The Daily Press, Gloucester, Va., 1962-66; state news editor The Daily Press, Newport News, Va., 1967-68; asst. editor New Dominion mag., Newport News, Va., 1966-67; editor publs. Newport News Shipbldg. and Dry Dock Co., 1968-70; with Va. Power, 1970-94; staff project adminstr. Va. Power, Fairfax, 1989-94. Mem. County Planning Commn., Warrenton, Va., 1987-94, chmnm., 1989, 94. Mem. Pub. Rels. Soc. Am., Soc. Profl. Journalists, Warrenton-Fauquier C. of C. (pres. 1984), John Marshall Club (pres. 1990), Fauquier Springs Country Club. Home: 7907 Sir Topas Dr Warrenton VA 22186-8613

MOLOFF, ALAN LAWRENCE, army officer, physician; b. Bklyn., Sept. 29, 1954; s. Louis Rubin and Muriel (Trabeck) M. BS, U. Vt., 1976; DO, U. N.J., 1983; MPH, Harvard U., 1988; student, U.S. Army Command/Gen. Staff Course, 1994-95. Diplomate Am. Bd. Preventive Medicine; bd. cert. aerospace medicine, undersea medicine. Commd. platoon leader U.S. Army, 1976, advanced through grades to lt. col., 1993; intern Fitzsimons Army Med. Ctr., Aurora, Colo., 1983-84; med. officer 1st Battalion 10th Spl. Forces Group, Bad Tolz, Fed. Republic of Germany, 1984-87; resident in aerospace medicine Harvard U., Boston, 1987-89; chief spl. ops. forces divsn. Acad. Health Scis., San Antonio, 1989-92; command surgeon Spl. Forces Command, Ft. Bragg, N.C., 1992-93, dep. surgeon, 1993-94; with command and gen. staff coll. U.S. Army, 1994-95; dep. surgeon 30th Med. Brigade, Heidelberg, Germany, 1995-96; dep. forward surgeon, surgeon V corps. U.S. Army Europe, Heidelberg, Germany, 1996—; lectr. advanced trauma life support NOAA, Aerospace Med. Assn. Contbr. articles to profl. jours. Active in civic activities. Decorated Meritorious Svc. medal with 2 oak leaf clusters, Joint Svc. Commendation medal, S.W. Asian Svc. medal, Army Commendation medal with oak leaf cluster, Armed Forces Svc. medal, NATO medal, German Paratrooper badge, Pathfinder badge, Expert Field Med. badge, Order of Mil. Med. Merit, Master Parachutist award. Fellow Am. Coll. Preventive Medicine, Aerospace Med. Assn. (assoc.); mem. Am. Osteo. Assn., Aerospace Med. Assn., Assn. Mil. Surgeons of U.S., Assn. Mil. Osteo Physicians and Surgeons, Soc. U.S. Army Flight Surgeons (life). Home: 67 Im Emmertsgrund, Emmertsgrund Germany Office: HHC 30th Med BDE Dep Surgeon Unit 29218 Box 246 APO AE 09102

MOLONEY, MICHAEL CHARLES, career officer, pilot; b. Louisville, Ky., July 1, 1959; s. Daniel Aloysius and Hattie Margaret (Hall) M.; m. Joy Regina Kellner, Aug. 24, 1991; 1 child, Justina Joy. BA in Secondary Edn., U. Ky., 1982, postgrad., 1994-95. Commd. U.S. Army, advanced through ranks to capt., 1994—; platoon leader HHC task force 23 U.S. Army, Germany, 1987-90; tng. officer HHC 15th MI Bn. U.S. Army, Giebelstadt, Germany, 1990-91; budget officer HHC 15th MI bn. U.S. Army, Ft. Hood, Tex., 1991-92, asst. HHC S3 15th MI bn., 1992-93, bn. S4. HHC 15th MI bn., 1993-94, co. comdr. HHC 15th MI bn., 1994-95; tng. officer U.S. Army, Korea, 1994-96, airfield comdr., 1996—. Mem. Assn. U.S. Army, Army Aviation Assn., U. Ky. Alumni Assn., Sigma Pi. Republican. Roman Catholic. Home: 5739B Dalton St Fort Knox KY 40121 Office: HHC 19th TAACOM, Box 2520, APO 96218, Korea

MOLONY, MICHAEL JANSSENS, JR., lawyer; b. New Orleans, Sept. 2, 1922; s. Michael Janssens and Marie (Perret) M.; m. Jane Leslie Waguespack, Oct. 21, 1951; children: Michael Janssens III (dec.), Leslie, Megan, Kevin, Sara, Brian, Ian, Duncan. JD, Tulane U., 1950. Bar: La. 1950, D.C. 1979, U.S. Dist. Ct. (ea. and mid. dists.) La. 1951, U.S. Ct. Appeals (5th cir.) 1953, U.S. Supreme Ct. 1972, U.S. Dist. Ct. (we. dist.) La. 1978, U.S. Ct. Appeals (11th and D.C. cirs.) 1981. Ptnr., Molony & Baldwin, New Orleans, 1950; assoc. Jones, Flanders, Waechter & Walker, 1951-56; ptnr. Jones, Walker, Waechter, Poitevent, Carrere & Denegre, 1956-75, Milling, Benson, Woodward, Hillyer, Pierson & Miller, 1975-91, Chaffe, McCall, Phillips, Toler & Sarpy, 1991-92, Sessions & Fishman, 1993—; instr., lectr. Med. Sch. and Univ. Coll. Tulane U., 1953-59; mem. Eisenhower Legal Com., 1952. Bd. commrs. Port of New Orleans, 1976-81, pres., 1978; mem. bd. rev. Associated Br. Pilots, 1990-96; bd. dirs. La. World Expn. Inc., 1974-84; bd. dirs., exec. com. New Orleans Tourist and Conv. Commn., 1971-74, 78, chmn.; family attractions com. 1973-75; chmn. La. Gov.'s Task Force on Space Industry, 1971-73; chmn. La. Gov.'s Citizens' Adv. Com. Met. New Orleans Transp. and Planning Program, 1971-77; mem. La. Gov.'s Task Force Natural Gas Requirements, 1971-72; mem. La. Gov.'s Proaction Commn. for Higher Edn., 1995; mem. Goals Found. Coun. and ex-officio mem. Goals Found., Met. New Orleans Goals Program, 1969-72, vice chmn. ad hoc planning com. Goals Met. New Orleans, 1969-73; vice chmn. Port of New Orleans Operation Impact, 1969-70, mem. Met. Area Com., New Orleans, 1970-84; trustee, Pub. Affairs Rsch. Coun. La., 1970-73, mem. exec. com. Bus./Higher Edn. Coun., U. New Orleans, 1980-94, bd. dirs., 1980—, v.p. 1986-88, pres., 1988-90, chmn. Task Force on Pub. Higher Edn. Funding, 1990-95, chmn. governmental affairs, 1995—, Task Force on Edn./Econ. Devel. Alliances, 1993-95; mem. Mayor's Coun. on Internat. Trade and Econ. Devel., 1978; mem. Mayor's Transition Task Force Econ. Devel., 1994; bd. dirs. La. Partnership for Tech. and Innovation, 1989—; bd. dirs. Acad. Sacred Heart, 1975-77, Internat. House, 1985-86, adv. coun. 1985—; bd. dirs. U. New Orleans Found., 1991—; mem. vis. com. Loyola Sch. Bus. Adminstrn., Loyola U., New Orleans, 1981—, trustee Loyola U., 1985-91, vice chmn. bd. trustees, 1990-91; mem. Dean's Coun. Tulane U. Law Sch., 1988-96, vice chmn. building com., 1991-95; bd. dirs., mem. exec. com. Internat. Trade Mart, chmn. internat. bus. com., 1983-85; World Trade Ctr.-New Orleans (bd. dirs. 1983—, mem. Port Activity com. 1985-91, transp. com. 1991-95, govt. affairs com. 1996—); chmn. Task Force on Internat. Banking, 1982; mem. Mayor's Task Force on Drug Abuse, 1989-90. Capt. JAGDR, USAAF, 1942-46, PTO, Recipient Leadership award AIAA, 1971, Yenni award Loyola U., New Orleans, 1979, New Orleans Times Picayune Loving Cup, 1986, First Citizen of the Learning Soc. Dean's award UNO Met. Coll, 1992; also various civic contbn. awards; co-recipient Silver Anvil award Pub. Rels. Soc. Am., 1991. Mem. ABA (labor and employment law and litigation sects., com. equal opportunity law, chmn. regional com. liaison with equal opportunity commn., office of fed. contract compliance programs), D.C. Bar Assn., Fed. Bar Assn., La. Bar Assn. (past sec.-treas., bd. govs. 1957-60, editor jour. 1957-59, sec. spl. supreme ct. com. on drafting code jud. ethics), New Orleans Bar Assn. (dir. legal aid bur. 1954, chmn. standing com. legis. 1968, vice chmn. standing com. pub. rels. 1970-71), Am. Judicature Soc., La. Law Inst. (asst. sec.-treas. 1958-70), Am. Arbitration Assn. (bd. dirs., 1995—, chmn. reg. adv. coun., chmn. reg. adv. coun. employment law cases, mem. spl. panel large complex arbitration/mediation cases, Whitney North Seymour Sr. award 1991), So. Inst. Mgmt. (founder), AIM, U.S. C. of C. (urban and regional affairs com. 1970-73), La. C. of C. (bd. dirs. 1963-66), New Orleans and River Region C. of C. (v.p. met. devel. and urban affairs 1969, past chmn. labor rels. coun., bd. dirs. 1970-78, pres.-elect 1970, pres. 1971, dir., exec. com. 1972, ex officio mem., bd. dirs. 1979—), Bienville Club, City Club, English Turn Golf and Country Club, Pickwick Club, Plimsoll Club, Serra Club, So. Yacht Club, Sigma Chi (pres. alumni chpt. 1956). Roman Catholic. Home: 3039 Hudson Pl New Orleans LA 70131-5337 Office: Sessions & Fishman 201 Saint Charles Ave New Orleans LA 70170-1000

MOLPUS, DICK H., resource management company executive; b. Philadelphia, Miss., Sept. 7, 1949; s. Richard and Frances (Blount) M.; m. Sally Nash, May 27, 1971; children—Helen Nash, Richard Gregory. BBA, U. Miss., 1971. V.p. mfg. Molpus Co., Phila., 1971-80; exec. dir. Gov's Office Fed.-State Programs, Jackson, Miss., 1980-83; sec. of state State of Miss., Jackson, 1984-96; pres. Molpus Co. and Woodlands Resource Mgmt. Group, Phila., 1996—; dir. Citizens Bank and Trust Co. Vice pres. Miss. Agr. and Forestry Mus., 1979; campaign dir., chmn. bd. United Givers Fund, Neshoba County, Miss., 1979-80; bd. dirs. Miss. PTA, 1980—; founder Parents for Pub. Schs. orgn., 1989. Recipient Friends of Children award Miss. Assn. Elem. Sch. Adminstrs., 1984, Pub. Ofcl. of Yr. award Miss. chpt. Am. Soc. for Pub. Adminstrn., 1985. Mem. Miss. Forestry Assn. (bd. dirs. 1980-87), Nat. Assn. Secs. of State (pres. 1992), Nature Conservancy (bd. dirs. Miss. chpt.), Sigma Chi, Omicron Delta Kappa, Pi Sigma Alpha (Theta Beta chpt.). Office: PO Box 59 Philadelphia MS 39350-0059

MOLTZAU, HUGHITT GREGORY, retired management training specialist; b. Strum, Wis., Aug. 9, 1914; s. Herman Alfred and Goldie (Knudtson) M.; m. Orvetta Nellie Braker, Dec. 30, 1940; children: Paula Lou Moltzau Lepak, Ann Marie Moltzau Bosworth. BS in Edn., U. Wis., Stout, 1936; MS in Edn., Wayne State U., 1941. Tchr. Grosse Pointe Country Day Sch., Grosse Pointe Farms, Mich., 1938-41; tng. supr. Chrysler Corp., Detroit, 1941-46; tng. dir. Kaiser-Frazer Corp., Willow Run, Mich., 1946-49, Parke-Davis/Warner Lambert, Detroit, 1949-79; mgmt. cons. Warner Lambert,

Morris Plains, N.J., 1979-89; ret., 1989; conducted seminars in field. Author tng. materials. Pres. bd. dirs. Adult Psychiat. Clinic, Detroit, 1961-62; vice chmn. edn. com. Detroit Bd. Commerce, 1966-67. Mem. Am. Soc. Tng. and Devel. (pres. Greater Detroit chpt. 1962-63), Am. Mgmt. Assn., Epsilon Pi Tau, Phi Delta Kappa. Congregationalist.

MOLZ, FRED JOHN, III, hydrologist, educator; b. Mays Landing, N.J., Aug. 13, 1943; s. Fred John Jr. and Viola Violet (MacDonald) M.; m. Mary Lee Clark, Dec. 17, 1966; children: Fred John IV, Stephen Joseph. BS in Physics, Drexel U., 1966, MCE, 1968; PhD in Hydrology, Stanford U., 1970. Hydraulic engr. U.S. Geol. Survey, Menlo Park, Calif., 1970; asst. prof. Auburn (Ala.) U., 1970-74, alumni asst. prof., 1974-76, alumni assoc. prof., 1976-80, asst. dean research, 1979-84, dir. Eng. exptl. sta., 1981-84, prof., 1980-84, Feagin prof., 1984-89, Huff eminent scholar, 1990-95; Dept. Energy disting. scientist Clemson U., 1995—; cons. Battelle N.W., Richland, Wash., 1982-83, 84-85, Argonne (Ill.) Nat. Labs., 1983-85, Electric Power Rsch. Inst., Menlo Park, Calif., 1984-85, U.S. NRC, 1991—. Author: (with others) Numerical Methods in Hydrology, 1971, Modeling Wastewater Renovation, 1981; contbr. articles to profl. jours. Recipient Disting. Faculty award Auburn U. Alumni Assn., 1987; grantee EPA, 1983, 86, 90, U.S. Dept. Edn., 1991, NSF, 1992, 94. Mem. Am. Geophys. Union (Horton award 1992), Am. Soc. Agronomy, Nat. Ground Water Assn., Am. Inst. Hydrology. Home: 213 Amethyst Way Seneca SC 29672 Office: Clemson U Dept of Environ Sys Engring 342 Computer Ct Anderson SC 29625

MOMOH, PAUL J., educator, insurance underwriter; b. Kailahun, Sierra Leone, June 25, 1955; came to U.S., 1977; s. Kdevei and Abie (Lahai) M.; married; children: Victoria Grace, Paul Marvin. BBA, Tex. So. U., 1980. Rep. Bankers Life Ins., Houston, 1981-84; mktg. dir. Pro-Maxx Products, Houston, 1984-88; sales coord. Chuck Navis Chevy, Houston, 1988-90; individual practice fin. planning Houston, 1980-83; educator Northforest Ind. Sch. Dist., Houston, 1984—. Fellow Nat. Assn. Life Underwriters, Pasadena Life Assn. (bd. dirs., v.p. 1986). Roman Catholic. Home: 7233 Miley St Houston TX 77028 Office: Momoh Fin Svcs PO Box 710282 Houston TX 77271

MONAHAN, JOHN T., law educator, psychologist; b. N.Y.C., Nov. 1, 1946; s. John Joseph and Dorothy (King) M.; m. Linda Costa, Aug. 24, 1969; children: Katherine, John. BA, SUNY, 1968; PhD, Ind. U., 1972. Asst. prof. U. Calif., Irvine, 1972-80; prof. U. Va., Charlottesville, 1980-84, Doherty prof., 1985—; dir. mental health law MacArthur Found., Chgo., 1988—. Author: Predicting Violent Behavior, 1981 (Guttmacher award 1981), Social Science in Law, 1994. Recipient Disting. Contbn. Pub. Policy award APA, Washington, 1990. Mem. APA (Isaac Ray award 1996). Home: 939 Rosser Ln Charlottesville VA 22903-1645 Office: U Va Sch Law 580 Massie Rd Charlottesville VA 22903-1789

MONAHAN, THOMAS PAUL, accountant; b. Pitts., Feb. 27, 1951; s. Thomas Andrew and Patricia (Tompkins) M.; m. Ellen McKeithan Easterby, Aug. 2, 1975; children: Kelley Kathleen, Thomas Patrick, Kyle Easterby, Tessa Elizabeth. BS in Acctg., U. S.C., 1973. CPA, S.C. Staff acct. Rogers, Brigman, Peterson & Co., Columbia, S.C., 1972-75, ptnr., 1975-82; treas., prin. GMK Assocs., Columbia, 1982—; bd. dirs., treas. Devel. Properties Inc.; trustee Town Theater Trust; lectr., cons. Mem. Com. of 100. Mem. bus. coun. S.C. Dems., 1986—. Mem. AICPA, S.C. Assn. CPAs, Columbia Stage Soc. (trustee, bd. dirs.), Spring Valley Country Club, Faculty House Club, Capital City Club, Sertoma, Zeta Beta Tau (trustee emeritus). Home: 1117 Adger Rd Columbia SC 29205-1942 Office: GMK Assoc 1333 Main St Ste 400 Columbia SC 29201-3201

MONAS, SIDNEY, retired history educator; b. N.Y.C., Sept. 15, 1924; s. David Joseph and Eva (Kiener) M.; m. Carolyn Babcock Munro, Sept. 5, 1948 (dec. Dec. 1985); children: Erica Beecher Monas Raved, Deborah Gardner Monas Werdmuller, Stephen Sidney; m. Claire Anderson, Nov. 1, 1987. A.B., Princeton U., 1948; A.M., Harvard U., 1951, Ph.D., 1955. Instr. history Amherst (Mass.) Coll., 1955-57; asst. prof. history Smith Coll., 1957-62; prof. history and lit., dir. Russian Studies Ctr., U. Rochester, N.Y., 1962-69; prof. Slavic lang. and history U. Tex., Austin, 1969-93; chmn. dept. Slavic langs. U. Tex., 1969-75; prof. emeritus, 1993—; Fulbright prof. Russian history Hebrew U., Jerusalem, 1966-67; sr. assoc. St. Antony's Coll., Oxford, 1984-85. Author: The Third Section, 1961; editor: Selected Works of N. Gumilev, 1972, Complete Poems of Osip Mandelstam, 1973; editorial bd. Jour. Modern History, 1967-70, Soviet Studies in Literature, from 1968, Am. Hist. Rev, 1980-83, PMLA, 1980-83; editor Slavic Rev., 1985-91; translator: Scenes from the Bathhouse, 1961, Crime and Punishment, 1968; editor, translator: Selected Essays of Osip Mandelstam, 1977. With AUS, 1943-45. Ford fellow, 1954-55, NEH fellow, 1973-74, fellow Humanities Rsch. Centre Australian Nat. U., 1977, Nat. Inst. Humanities U. Chgo., 1977-78, Rockefeller Humanities fellow, 1984-85. Mem. MLA, Am. Hist. Assn., Am. Assn. Advancement Slavic Studies.

MONCK, HARRY NELSON, IV, lawyer; b. Wilmington, Del., May 27, 1958; s. Harry Nelson III and Flora (DeCecco) M.; m. Pamela Adele Gee, Sept. 27, 1986; children: Harry Nelson V, Margaret Alice. BS, U. Del., 1980; JD, U. Houston, 1984. Bar: Tex. 1984, U.S. Dist. Ct. (so. dist.) Tex. 1984, U.S. Dist. Ct. (no. dist.), Tex. 1985, U.S. Ct. Appeals (5th cir.) 1986; U.S. Supreme Ct. 1992; cert. family law, 1989. Assoc. Scott Ramsey & Assocs., Houston, 1984-90, Ronald J. Waska, P.C., Houston, 1990—. Roman Catholic. Office: Ronald J Waska PC 952 Echo Ln Ste 180 Houston TX 77024-2757

MONCRIEF, JAMES E., petroleum geologist; b. Vivian, La., Dec. 22, 1930; s. Joseph Miller and Dorothy Edna (Barnett) M.; m. Barbara Lawton, Sept. 10, 1950; children: Jo Lynn, Jane Lawton M., James Robert, Janice Michelle, Jefferson Miller. BS, La. State U., 1952, MS, 1954. Exploration geologist Tidewater Associated Oil Co., Lafayette, La., 1954-55, Austral Oil Co., Houston, Lafayette, Tex., La., 1955-59; exec. officer Moncrief Oil and Gas, Inc., Lafayette, 1959-62; cons. Lafayette, 1962-69; pres., CEO Cyclops Oil and Gas, Inc., Lafayette, 1969-75; cons. Lafayette, 1975—. Mem. Am. Assn. Petroleum Geologists (cert.), Am. Petroleum Inst., Geol. and Mining Soc. (pres. 1949-50), Lafayette Geol. Soc. Office: Moncrief and Assocs PO Box 52062 Lafayette LA 70505-2062

MONCURE, THOMAS MCCARTY, JR., state agency adminstrator; b. Fredericksburg, Va., 1951; m. Margaret Clay Morris; children: Kathryn Louise, Anne Mason. BA, Va. Military Inst., 1973; MA, George Mason U., 1990. Bar: Va., 1979, U.S. Ct. Appeals (4th dist.), U.S. Dist. Ct. (ea. dist.), 1980, U.S. Ct. Military Appeals, 1983, U.S. Supreme Ct; cert. firearms and firearms safety instr. Mem. Gen. Assembly Va., 1982-88; clerk of circut ct. Stafford, 1991—. Co-author: The Story of Aquia Church, 1987; contbr. articles to mags. Active Stafford Rep. Com., St. George's Episcopal Ch.; bd. visitors VMI. With U.S. Army Res., Military Police Corps. Decorated Meritorious Svc. medal, Army Commendation medal; named Outstanding Young Men in Am. Mem. Stafford Am. Legion, Law Enforcement Alliance of Am., Stafford County Hist. Soc., Va. Hist. Soc., Mil. Police Regimental Assn., Va. State Bar, Phi Alpha Theta. Home: 301 Greenwood Dr Falmouth VA 22405-3129 Office: PO Box 5254 Fredericksburg VA 22403-0254

MONEY, JOY ANN FUENTES, healthcare administrator; b. Jacksonville, Fla., Nov. 27, 1957; d. Jorge G. and Gloria Faye (Schafer) Fuentes; m. James E. Money Jr., Oct. 3, 1987; children: Jennilyn Estell, Kimberly Kristin. ASN, Cen. Fla. Community Coll., Ocala, 1978; BSN, Fla. So. Coll., 1984; postgrad., U. South Fla. RN, Fla.; CNOR. Perioperative clin. nurse H. Lee Moffitt Cancer Ctr. and Rsch. Inst., Tampa, coord. otolayngology svc., outpatient and operating rm. svcs., patient edn. com., outpatient surgery task force and quality assurance, various others, 1990-95; clin. project mgr., Allegiance Healthcare Corp., 1995—. Mem. Asns. Oper. Rm. Nurses (rsch. liaison Tampa Bay chpt. 1988-91, congress del. 1989), Fla. Coun. Oper. Rm. Nurses. Home: 1705 Cobbler Dr Lutz FL 33549-3316

MONEY, MAX LEE, nursing educator, medical, surgical nurse; b. Pineville, Ky., Apr. 17, 1949; s. Arthur Lee and Laura (Hendrickson) M. ASN, Lincoln Meml. U., 1991, BSN, 1993. RN, Ky., Tenn. Staff nurse ICU Pineville Cmty. Hosp., 1991-93, med.-surg. flr. supr., 1993-94, staff nurse med.-surg., 1994—; instr. sch. nursing Lincoln Meml. U., Harrogate, Tenn., 1994—; mem. profl. adv. bd. Comprehensive Home Health, Middlesboro, Ky., 1994; in-svc. educator Pineville Cmty. Hosp., 1994. Agent coll. fair Lincoln Meml. U., 1994, organizer breast cancer awareness seminar Schenck ctr., 1994; tchr. Sunday sch. Harmony Bapt. Ch., Pineville, 1994. Recipient Bronze Good Citizenship award Nat. Soc. of Sons of Am. Revolution, 1991, Nursing Leadership award Tenn. Nurses Assn., 1991. Mem. ANA, Nat. League Nursing (adv. 1992—), Ky. Nurses Assn. (pres. satellite 6B). Home: RR 1 Box 53 Pineville KY 40977-9706 Office: Lincoln Meml U Sch Nursing Schenck Health Scis Ctr Harrogate TN 37752

MONG, ROBERT WILLIAM, JR., publisher; b. Fremont, Ohio, Jan. 22, 1949; s. Robert William and Betty (Dwyer) M.; m. Carla Beth Sweet, July 25, 1975 (div. 1979); m. Diane Elizabeth Reischel, Jan. 23, 1988; children: Eric Robert, Elizabeth Diana. BA, Haverford (Pa.) Coll., 1971. Reporter Cin. Post, 1973-75, Capital Times, Madison, Wis., 1975-77; city editor Madison Press Connection, 1977-79; asst. city editor Dallas Morning News, 1979-80, bus. editor, 1980-81, projects editor, 1981-83, asst. mng. editor, 1983-88, dep. mng. editor, 1988-90, mng. editor, 1990-96; pub. Owensboro Messenger-Inquirer, 1996—. Mem. Am. Soc. Newspaper Editors, Newspaper Assn. Am. Office: Messenger-Inquirer PO Box 1480 1401 Frederica St Owensboro KY 42302-1480

MONHOLLON, LELAND, lawyer; b. Corbin, Ky., Nov. 8, 1925; s. Lewis Tom and Thelma (Prewitt) M.; m. Gawinna Owens, 1946 (div. 1969); 1 child, Patricia Lynn; m. Alice Faye Burden, July 3, 1970. JD, U. Ky., 1952. Bar: Ky. 1952. Supervising adjustor Travelers Ins. Co., Louisville, 1955-69; pvt. practice law Madisonville, Ky., 1969—. With USN, 1943-46, PTO, USNR, 1963-69. Mem. Ky. Bar Assn., Hopkins County Bar Assn., Am. Legion, VFW. Republican. Baptist. Home: 185 Threadneedle Dr Madisonville KY 42431-6439 Office: 111 S Main St Madisonville KY 42431-2555

MONK, KATHY JO, secondary education educator; b. Ft. Worth, Oct. 10, 1968; d. Roy Edward and Frances Dolores (Roberson) Kirk; m. Jeffrey Lee Monk, Jan. 1, 1994; 1 child, Nikole Shaye. BS in Secondary Edn. and Math., Southwestern Adventist Coll., 1991. Tex. tchg. cert. for math., biology and spl. edn. Tchr. Rio Vista (Tex.) Middle Sch., 1991—; cosponsor Student Coun., Rio Vista, 1993-96. Mem. Assn. Tchrs. and Profl. Educators. Baptist. Home: 623 Johnathon Ct Joshua TX 76058 Office: Rio Vista Middle Sch 100 Capps PO Box 369 Rio Vista TX 76093

MONK, RICHARD HUNLEY, JR., textile company executive; b. Anniston, Ala., Aug. 25, 1939; s. Richard Hunley and Marjorie Louise (Schneider) M.; m. H. Ann McDougald, June 24, 1961; children: Jennifer L. Borden, Richard H. III. AB, Emory U., 1961, LLB, 1963. Pvt. legal practice Atlanta, 1963-65; legal counsel WestPoint Pepperell, West Point, Ga., 1965-74, asst. sec., 1967-70, sec., 1970-83, v.p., 1973-90, gen. counsel, 1977-83, pres. internat. div., 1983-90; exec. v.p. Avondale Mills, Inc., Sylacauga, Ala., 1990, pres., COO, 1990-94, pres., 1990-95, bd. dirs., 1990-95, chief adminstrv. officer, sec., 1994-95; former mem. bd. dirs. First Nat. Bank and First Nat. Bankshares, West Point, Lantor Internat., Manchester, Eng., chmn. Arthur Sanderson & Sons Ltd., Uxbridge, Eng., 1985-90; sec. West Point-Pepperell Found., 1971-83, vice chmn., 1976-83. Bd. dirs. Chattahoochee-Lee Jr. Achievement, Lanett, Ala., 1978-82; commr. West Point Housing Authority, 1968-74; trustee Chattahoochee Valley Ednl. Found., 1969-86, v.p., 1980-81, pres., 1981-83; past pres. Chattahoochee Valley Hist. Soc.,West Point; mem. exec. bd. G.H. Lanier coun. Boy Scouts Am., 1981-88, fin. chmn., 1981-83, v.p., 1982-83, pres., 1983-85; Chmn. Sylacauga Remembers Committee(World War II 50th Anniversary Commemoration) 1992-95; mem. bd. visitors Presbyn. coll., Clinton, S.C., 1981-84, vice chmn. bd. visitors, 1982-83, chmn. bd. visitors, 1983-84; trustee Presbyn. Coll., 1987—; bd. dirs. Valley United Fund, West Point, 1967-73, 76-81, v.p., 1977-78, pres., 1978-79; Sylacauga City Sch. Fedn., 1992—, Coosa Valley Med. Ctr. Fedn., 1992—; chmn. Sylacauga Remembers com., 1992-95; fin. chmn. Troup County YMCA of Ga., 1983-90. Mem. ABA, Ga. Textile Mfrs. Assn. (bd. dirs. 1977-80, 81-83, 86-88, treas. 1983-84, v.p. 1984-85, pres. 1985-86), Am. Textile Mfrs. Inst., Soc. Internat. Bus. Fellows, State Bar Ga. (sec. antitrust sect. 1970-72, vice chmn. 1972-73, chmn. 1973-74, cochmn. corp. counsel com. 1981-82, ex-officio dir. 1988—), Sylacauga C. of C. (bd. dirs. 1995—), Am. Yarn Spinners Assn. (2nd v.p. 1991-92, 1st. v.p. 1992-93, pres. 1993-94, bd. dirs. 1991-94), Coosa Valley Country Club (Sylacauga, Ala.).

MONKS, REGINA See WATKISS, REGINA

MONROE, CARL DEAN, III, lawyer; b. Birmingham, Ala., Sept. 15, 1960; s. Carl D. and Martha Jo M. BA, Birmingham-So. Coll., 1982; JD, Georgetown U., 1985. Bar: Ala. 1986, U.S. Ct. Appeals (11th cir.) 1988. Scheduler Siegelman for Atty. Gen., Montgomery, 1986; legal rsch. aide Office of Sec. of State State of Ala., Montgomery, 1986; asst. atty. gen., adminstrv. asst. Office of Atty. Gen., Montgomery, 1987-89; atty.-advisor Office Gen. Counsel, U.S. Dept. Energy, Washington, 1989—; mem. panel of judges Georgetown Law Ctr. Moot Ct., 1991, 92, CIA Environ. Roundtable. Mem. panel of judges Ala. YMCA Youth Legislature, Montgomery, 1979, 87, 88, 89; office coord. blood dr. ARC, Montgomery, 1987, 88; com. mem. Georgetown Alumni Admissions, Washington, 1986-91; mem. Nat. Trust for Hist. Preservation. Mem. ABA (author environ. law sect. newsletter Looking Ahead), Acad. Polit. Sci., Ala. Bar Assn., Birmingham-So. Alumni (alumni leader 1986—), Smithsonian Assocs., Phi Beta Kappa. Democrat. Presbyterian. Home: 1200 N Nash St Apt 264 Arlington VA 22209-3620

MONROE, EDWARD LEE, political campaign consultant; b. Newport News, Va., June 25, 1961; s. Harry Jr. and Rosemary (Ryan) M.; m. Lisa K. Schwarz, Dec. 3, 1994. BA in Govt., William and Mary Coll., 1983. Dep. regional polit. dir. Rep. Nat. Com., Washington, 1989-92; exec. dir. Rep. Party of Fla., Tallahassee, 1992-94; campaign mgr. Mortham For Sec. of State, Tallahassee, 1994; polit. dir. Re-Elect Senator Warner, Alexandria, Va., 1995—. Roman Catholic. Home: 7417 Park Terrace Dr Alexandria VA 22307

MONROE, FREDERICK LEROY, chemist; b. Redmond, Oreg., Oct. 13, 1942; s. Herman Sylvan Monroe and Mary Roberta (Grant) Monroe Emery; B.S. in Chemistry, Oreg. State U., 1964; M.S. in Environ. Engring., Wash. State U., 1974. Control specialist Air Pollution Control Authority, Centralia, Wash., 1969-70; asst. chemist Wash. State U., 1970-74; environ. engr. Ore-Ida Foods, Inc., Idaho, 1974-77; cons., Idaho, 1977-78; applications engr. AFL Industries, Riviera Beach, Fla., 1979-80; mgr. chem. control PCA Internat., Matthews, N.C., 1980-85; quality assurance mgr. Stork Screens Am., Charlotte, N.C., 1985-93, environ. mgr., 1993—, grade IV N.C. wastewater treatment operator. Pres. Unity Ch., 1982-84. Served with USAF, 1964-68, maj. Res. ret.; served with N.G., 1973-78. Decorated Air Force Commendation medal; recipient Blue Thumb award Charlotte-Mecklenburg Utility Dist., 1993. Fellow Am. Inst. Chemists; mem. Am. Chem. Soc. Republican. Achievements include approved international shipment of hazardous wastes for recycling. Home: 1008 Autumnwood Ln Charlotte NC 28213-5722 Office: Stork Screens Am Service Rd 3001 N Interstate 85 Charlotte NC 28269-4493

MONROE, HELEN LEOLA, nurse, consultant, educator; b. Alma, Ga., Jan. 30, 1931; d. Silas Leo Monroe and Thelma (Fussell) Smith; 1 child, Reavena M. M. Oliver. BS, Fla. A&M U., 1954; MS, St. John's U., L.I., N.Y., 1959. Staff nurse Vis. Nurse Assn. Duval County, Jacksonville, Fla., 1954-55; instr. sch. nursing Fla. A&M U., Tallahassee, 1955-57, asst. prof., 1959-64; dir. nursing edn. Mississippi Valley State Coll., Itta Bena, Miss., 1964-67; asst. prof. Norfolk State Coll. Va., 1967-68; asst. prof., dir. nursing edn. Lincoln U., Jefferson City, Mo., 1968-80; pvt. practice nursing Jefferson City, 1981-85; pvt. practice achievement cons. Jacksonville, 1987—; cons. Jacksonville, 1987—; cons. nursing William Woods Coll., Fulton, Mo., 1972-73; established first ednl. program for nonwhites to become RNs in Miss. Sec. Jefferson City chpt. NAACP, 1971-73; chmn. edn. com. Cancer Soc. Cole County, Jefferson City, 1972-74; v.p. Cole County Mental Health Assn., 1973; mem. fin. com. United Way Cole County, 1975. Recipient Outstanding Achievement award Citizens' Com. of Jefferson City, 1970, Woman of Achievement award AAUW, 1974, Permanent Royal Patronage from Principality of the Hutt River Province, 1994. Home: 5436 Mays Dr Jacksonville FL 32209-2926

MONROE, PAULA RUTH, psychologist; b. Worcester, Mass., Dec. 23, 1951; d. Dudley Benson and Gladys Elinor (Norbery) Sherry; m. David Michael Monroe, Feb. 19, 1977; 1 child, Allison. BA, U. North Tex., 1974; MA, U. Tulsa, 1980, PhD, 1990. Lic. psychologist, Okla. Asst. dean Coll. Arts and Scis. U. Tulsa, 1983-85; staff psychologist, mgr. psychol. testing ctr. Children's Med. Ctr., Tulsa, 1990-95; pvt. practice Psychosocial Enhancement Svcs., Inc., Tulsa, 1995—. Contbr. articles to profl. jours. Mem. APA.

MONROE, ROBIN PRINCE, writer, educator; b. Tampa, Fla., July 27, 1956; d. Frank Ramos Prince and Shirley Ann (Van Eyck) Granger; m. Merlin Eugene Monroe, July 9, 1977; children: J. Caleb, Anna Elizabeth (dec.), Daniel Aaron, Lydia Grace. BA in Elem. Edn. magna cum laude, Mercer U., 1977. Cert. tchr., S.C. Sign lang. tchr. Furman U., Greenville, S.C., 1983-92; author, writer Greenville, S.C., 1989—; spkr., workshop leader, Greenville, 1994—. Author: In This Very Hour/Loss of a Loved One, 1994, In This Very Hour/Loss of a Dream, 1994; staff writer Visions mag., 1995-96. Vol. Greenville Jr. League, 1994-96. Recipient Best Work award in children's category Fla. Christian Writer's Conf., 1995. Mem. nat. League of Am. Pen Women. Home and Office: 27 Richwood Dr Greenville SC 29607

MONSALVE, MARTHA EUGENIA, pharmacist; b. Bogotá, Colombia, Sept. 27, 1968; came to U.S., 1985; d. Oscar and Martha Lucia (Vidal) M.; m. Dale James Morphonios, Dec. 16, 1989. AA, Miami-Dade Community Coll., 1989; BS in Pharmacy, Southeastern U., 1993. Lab. asst. William Harvey Co., Bogotá, 1981-82; purchasing agt. FEPARVI, Ltd., Miami, 1985-93; pharmacy asst. Galloway Pharmacy, Miami, Fla., 1988; pharmacy intern Bapt. Hosp., Miami, 1992; pharmacist Eckerd Drugs, Miami, 1993-94, Walgreens, Miami, Fla., 1994-96. Vol. Bapt. Hosp., Miami, 1988. Mem. Am. Soc. Hosp. Pharmacists, Fla. Soc. Hosp. Pharmacists. Roman Catholic. Home: 8640 SW 84th Ave Miami FL 33143-6912 Office: 29601 S Dixie Hwy Homestead FL 33033-3320

MONSIVAIS, DIANE B., surgical nurse, writer; b. White Plains, N.Y., Feb. 9, 1951; d. C. Neilson and Evelyn Thoben (Goerke) Burn; m. Jose J Monsivais, Jun. 26, 1983; children: Daniel, Sharon, Suzanne. BSN, Duke U., 1972; MSN, U. Tex., El. Paso, 1988. Cert. RN. Staff nurse, head nurse adminstrn. U.S. Army Nurse Corps., 1972-81; clin. nurse mgr., pubs. mgr. Hand & Microsurgery Ctr. of El Paso, Tex., 1988—. Contbr. to profl. jours. Mem. Tex. Nurses Assn. (bd. dirs. 1993-94, v.p. 1995-96, pres. dist. I 1996—), Am. Med. Writers Assn. (cert. in writing/editing), Assn. Hand Care Profls. (program chair 1994-95, edn. chair 1995-96, pres.-elect 1996—), Coun. Biology Editors (cert. editor life scis.). Home: 716 Twin Hills Dr El Paso TX 79912-3412 Office: Hand & Microsurgery Ctr El Paso 10525 Vista del Sol #200 El Paso TX 79925

MONTAÑEZ, CARMEN LYDIA, Spanish language educator, literature researcher, lawyer; b. Santurce, P.R., Dec. 17, 1944; d. Pablo and Amalia (Falcón) Cotto; m. Carmelo Montanez, Nov. 14, 1965; children: Carmen Aracelis, Carlos, Juan-Carlos. BA magna cum laude, U. Turabo, P.R., 1979; JD, Interam. U., P.R., 1983; MA in Spanish Lit., U. Louisville, 1987; PhD, U. Ky., 1995. Assoc. instr. Ind. U., Bloomington, 1987; lectr. U. Louisville, 1985-89; assoc. instr. Ind. U. S.E., New Albany, 1987-89; mem. adj. faculty Troy U., Montgomery, Ala., 1990-91; grad. teaching asst. U. Ky., Lexington, 1991-93; vis. asst. prof. U. Louisville, 1993-94; asst. prof. Ind. State U., Terre Haute, 1994—. Contbr. essays to profl. jours.; author: El personaje femenino en la cuentistica de varias escritoras puertorriquenas: Subversion y creatividad, 1997. Mem. MLA (exec. com. discussion group on Puerto Rican lit. and culture 1994—), Am. Assn. Tchrs. Spanish and Portuguese, SIGSA, Asociació de Literature Femenina Hispánica, Instituto Hispanoamericano, Sigma Delta Pi, Phi Kappa Phi. Mem. MLA (exec. com. discussion group on Puerto Rican lit. and culture 1994—), Am. Assn. Tchrs. Spanish and Portuguese, SIGSA, Sigma Delta Pi, Phi Kappa Phi. Office: Ind State Univ Dept Foreign Langs and Lit Terre Haute IN 47809

MONTEITH, LARRY KING, university chancellor; b. Bryson City, N.C., Aug. 17, 1933; s. Earl and Essie (King) M.; m. Nancy Alexander, Apr. 19, 1952; children: Larry, Carol, Steve. BSEE, N.C. State U., 1960; MSEE, Duke U., 1962, PhDEE, 1965. Registered profl. engr., N.C. Mem. tech. staff Bell Telephone Labs., Burlington, N.C., 1960-62; mem. tech. staff Resch. Triangle Inst., Raleigh, 1962-66, group leader rsch. sect., 1966-68; adj. asst. prof. elec. engring. N.C. State U., Raleigh, 1965-68, assoc. prof., 1968-72, prof., 1972—, head dept. elec. engring., 1974-78, dean of engring., 1978-89, interim chancellor, 1989-90, chancellor, 1990—; bd. dirs. Microelectronics Ctr. N.C., Rsch. Triangle Inst. Contbr. articles to profl. jours. Trustee Nat. Tech. Univ., Triangle Univ. Ctr. Advanced Studies, Inc.; corp. mem. Underwriters Labs., Inc.; bd. visitors Air U. With USN, 1952-55. Recipient Disting. Engring. Alumnus award Duke U., 1984, Outstanding Engring. Achievement award N.C. Soc. Engrs., 1990. Fellow IEEE, Am. Soc. for Engring. Edn.; mem. NSPE (edn. adv. group), Raleigh C. of C. (bd. dirs.), Rotary Internat. (Paul Harris fellow Rotary Found. 1991), Phi Beta Kappa, Sigma Xi, Sigma Iota Rho, Phi Kappa Phi, Eta Kappa Nu, Tau Beta Pi, Sigma Beta Delta. Home: 1903 Hillsborough St Raleigh NC 27607-7348 Office: NC State U Chancellor's Office Pullen Rd Raleigh NC 27695

MONTEITH, MARYANN, critical care nurse, nursing educator; b. Oshkosh, Wis.; d. Joseph William and Dorothy Mae (Karow) M. BS in Nursing, U. Md., 1976; MS in Nursing, Marquette U., Milw., 1987. Cert. critical care nurse. Commd. 1st lt. U.S. Army, 1976, advanced through grades to lt. col., 1993; from staff nurse thoracic ICU to sr. clin. nurse critical care Walter Reed Army Med. Ctr., Washington, 1979-82; head nurse CCU Brooke Army Med. Ctr., San Antonio, 1985-88, dep. dir. critical care nursing course, 1988-89; chief nursing edn. and staff devel. Ireland Army Community Hosp., Ft. Knox, Ky., 1990-93; chief nurse Second Region (ROTC), 1993—. Mem. ANA, AACN, N.Am. Nursing Diagnosis Assn., Sigma Theta Tau.

MONTEMAYOR, CARLOS R., advertising executive; b. San Antonio, Nov. 21, 1945; s. Raul Martin and Mary (Lyall) M.; m. Marina Cara Cook, Sep. 21, 1967 (div. Dec. 1978); m. Barbara Kay Volmer, Dec. 23, 1979; 1 child, Justin Norman. BBA in Mktg., U. Tex., 1967; MS in Journalism, Northwestern U., 1968. Account exec. Campbell-Ewald Co., Detroit and Cin., 1968-72, Ross Roy Inc., Detroit, 1972-74, Pitluk Group, San Antonio, 1974-76; v.p. GSD&M Advt., San Antonio, 1976-78; mktg. mgr. Church's Fried Chicken, San Antonio, 1978-81; v.p. Ed Yardang & Assocs., San Antonio, 1981-83; pres. Montemayor y Asociados, San Antonio, 1983—; bd. dirs. USAA Fed. Savs. Bank, Witte Mus., San Antonio Zoo; sec. Fiesta San Antonio Commn. 2d lt. USAR, 1968-74. Mem. S.W. Found. Biomed. Rsch. (bd. govs.), Friends of McNay Club (bd. dirs.), Art Inst. San Antonio, Club Giraud, Argyle Club. Republican. Roman Catholic. Home: 563 Elizabeth Rd San Antonio TX 78209-6132 Office: Montemayor Y Asociados Inc Ste 500 70 NE Loop 410 San Antonio TX 78216-5843

MONTENYOHL, ERIC LAWRENCE, English language educator, folklorist; b. Wilmington, Del., Mar. 16, 1951; s. Victor Irl Jr. and Joan Abercrombie (Hill) M.; m. Margaret Elizabeth McGrath, Jan. 3, 1981; children: Elizabeth Laurence, Andrew Christopher. BA in English, U. N.C., 1971, MS in English/Folklore, 1975; PhD in Folklore/English, Ind. U., 1986. Instr. English dept. Aiken Tech. Edn. Ctr., 1975-76, instr. to dept. head remedial English, 1976-79; instr. English dept. U. S.C., Aiken, 1977-80, Augusta Coll., 1979-80; assoc. instr. folklore dept. Ind. U., Bloomington, 1981-83, instr., 1983, assoc. instr. math. dept., 1983-84; adj. asst. prof. English dept. U. Southwestern La., Lafayette, 1986-87, asst. prof., 1987-94, mem. grad. faculty, 1987-94; mem. exec. com. La. Folklife Festival Bd., Baton Rouge, 1989-93; archivist folklore archives Ind. U., 1980-81; asst. archivist Archives of Acadian and Creole Folklore, U. Southwestern La., 1991-94; co-curator Celebrating the Seasons, Lafayette Natural History Mus., 1990; grant evaluator, cons. State of La. Divsn. Arts, Folklife, Arts in Edn., La. Folklore Soc. Staff Folklore Forum, 1981-84, asst. editor, 1982-83, book rev. editor, 1983-84;; book rev. editor Victorian Studies, 1984-85; contbr. MLA Internat. Bibliography, 1987-88; assoc. editor La. Folklore Miscellany, 1990-93; book rev. editor So. Folklore, 1991-95; reader Folklore Forum, Victorian Studies, Jour. Folklore Rsch., Pub.-MLA; contbr. articles to profl. jours. Grantee L.J. and Mary C. Skaggs Found., 1986, 87, NEH

Summer Seminar, 1989, La. Ednl. Quality Support Fund, 1991. Mem. MLA, South Ctrl. MLA, Am. Folklore Soc. (sect. chair 1993, Richard Reuss prize on history of folkloristics), La. Folklore Soc. (exec. com. 1987-93, pres. 1989-90), Internat. Soc. Contemporary Legend Rsch., Am. Studies Assn., La. Folklife Soc., Calif. Folklore Soc., Hoosier Folklore Soc., Phi Kappa Phi.

MONTESI, JOHN W., JR., mortgage banking executive; b. Memphis, Feb. 11, 1950; m. Blanche R. Butler; children: Sydney, Blanche. BA, Vanderbilt U., Nashville, 1972; MBA, So. Meth. U., Dallas, 1974. Pres. Fin. Fed. Savings Bank, Memphis, 1986—. Trustee The Hutchison Sch., Memphis, 1990-93, Christian Bros. U., Memphis; bd. dirs. Memphis Botanic Garden Found., Neighborhood Christian Ctr., Memphis. Office: Fin Fed Savings Bank 1755 Kirby Pkwy Ste 150 Memphis TN 38120-4399

MONTGOMERY, ANNA FRANCES, elementary school educator; b. Spokane, Wash., Nov. 5, 1945; d. Carl Jacob and Edna Frances (Evans) Kuipers; m. William Lee Montgomery Jr., Oct. 7, 1989. AA, Mid. Ga. Coll., 1965; BS in Elem. Edn., Woman's Coll. of Ga., 1966; MEd, Ga. Coll., 1969, specialist in edn., 1973. Cert. elem. tchr., Ga. Classroom tchr. Muscogee County Sch. Dist., Columbus, Ga., 1966—, reading tchr. Title 1 tutorial program, summer 1975, instr. staff devel. program, 1977-80; social sci. lead tchr. Wesley Heights Elem. Sch., Columbus, 1992—; tennis and athletic instr. Camp Tegawitha, Tobyhanna, Pa., summer 1970; presenter workshop Chattahoochee Valley Coun. for Social Studies, 1977; mem. social studies textbook adoption com. Muscogee County Sch. Dist., 1977-78, 82-83, sick leave com., 1993-95; judge Columbus Regional Social Sci. Fair, 1977, 93-96. Treas. Wesley Heights PTA, 1983-86; vol. Med. Ctr. Aux., Columbus, 1975-79; pres. pastor's Bible study class St. Luke United Meth. Ch., 1993-94, 96, mem. Sarah cir., cir. #11, sec., 1969-71, 78-80, co-chmn., 1976-78; mem. Bessie Howard Ward Handbells Choir; devel. chmn. Ga. state divsn. Centennial/fellowships com. AAUW, 1974-76. Recipient Valley Forge Tchrs. medal Freedoms Found. at Valley Forge, 1975, Outstanding Tchr. of Yr. award Wesley Hts. Elem. Sch., 1975, Muscogee County Sch. Dist., 1979; named Very Important Lady award Girl Scouts Am., Columbus, 1976, Outstanding Young Woman Am., 1982. Mem. AAUW (chmn. centennial fellowship com. Columbus br. 1973-75), Ga. PTA (hon. life), Profl. Assn. Ga. Educators (bldg. rep. Muscogee County chpt. 1983—, sec. 1992-94, treas. 1994—), Nat. Coun. Social Studies (mem. hostess and registration coms. ann. meeting 1975), Ga. Coun. for Social Studies, Ga. Sci. Tchrs. Assn., Valley Area Sci. Tchrs. (corr. sec. 1996-97), Ga. Coll. Alumni Assn., Mid. Ga. Coll. Alumni Assn., Order of Amaranth (charity com. 1991-93, 95, assoc. conductress 1996), Scottish Rite Ladies Aux., Alpha Delta Kappa (Rho chpt., sec. 1975-76, pres.-elect 1976-78, pres. 1978-80), chaplin, 1996— Delta Kappa Gamma (Beta Xi chpt., pres. 1980-82, chmn. pubs. and publicity 1976-78, chmn. profl. affairs 1978-80, nominations com. chair 1980-82, chmn. world fellowship and fund raising 1984-86, chmn. fin. 1990-92, chmn. membership 1994-96), Wesley Heights Elem. Sch. PTA. Home: 5134 Stone Gate Dr Columbus GA 31909-5573

MONTGOMERY, DAVID EMERSON, library director; b. Brownsville, Pa., Apr. 5, 1952; s. Emerson Ulysses and Ada Leslie (Fulton) M. BA, Westminster Coll., New Wilmington, Pa., 1974; MA, Slippery Rock State U., 1977; MS, U. Ill., 1983. Cert. libr., Iowa; cert. tchr., Pa. Treasury officer U.S. Treasury Dept., Camden, N.J., 1975-76; instr. history U. Ill., Urbana, 1978-80; rsch. asst. Ill. Hist. Survey, Urbana, 1980-83; archivist Ill. Geol. Survey, Urbana, 1985; city archivist, libr. City of Davenport, Iowa, 1985-88; mgr. Tyrrell Hist. Libr., Beaumont, Tex., 1988—; pres. 222 Franklin Inc., 1995—; archives cons. Scott County, Iowa, Davenport, 1987; chmn., treas. Beaumont (Tex.) History Conf., 1991—; treas. Assn. Records Mgrs. and Adminstrs.-Iowa-Ill., Moline, 1986-87. Compiler: Davenport History - A Select Bibliography, 1986. Internat. Studies Inst. fellow, New Wilmington, 1976; grantee Nat. Hist. Publs. and Records Commn., U.S. Govt., Washington, 1985-87, Tex. Com. for Humanities, Austin, 1991. Mem. Am. Hist. Assn., Soc. Am. Archivists, Soc. S.W. Archivists, Tyrrell Hist. Libr. Assn. (bd. mem. 1988—). Democrat. Presbyterian. Home: 6915 Killarney Dr Beaumont TX 77706-4115 Office: Tyrrell Hist Libr 695 Pearl St Beaumont TX 77701

MONTGOMERY, DOUGLAS MORRISON, perinatologist, obstetrician-gynecologist; b. Birmingham, Ala., Aug. 28, 1959; s. Donald Russel and Delores Ruth (Whissler) M.; m. Carrie May Kelley, Oct. 10, 1992; children: Michael, Christina, Mitchell, Kaitlyn. BA in Biology, U. New Orleans, 1982; MD, La. State U., 1986. Bd. cert. ob-gyn., maternal fetal medicine. Intern. Ochsner Found. Hosp., New Orleans, 1986; resident in ob-gyn. Ochsner Hosp., New Orleans, 1986-90; fellow in perinatology U. Calif., Irvine, 1990-92; staff perinatologist Ochsner Clinic, New Orleans, 1992—; chmn. perinatal adv. Ochsner Hosp., 1993-95; dir. divsn. maternal fetal medicine Ochsner Clinic, 1996—, dir. network devel. ob-gyn., 1994—; med. dir. Elmwood Fitness in Pregnancy, New Orleans, 1993—; dir. women's health in pregnancy Elmwood Fitness Ctr., Harahan, La., 1996; cons. Am. Jour. Ob-Gyn., 1995; guest cons. Ctrl. Assn. Obstetricians and Gynecologists, 1995. Contbr. articles to med. publs. Fellow ACOG (course coord. dist 7 meeting 1996); mem. Soc. Perinatal Obstetricians. Republican. Roman Catholic. Office: Ochsner Clinic 1516 Jefferson Hwy New Orleans LA 70121

MONTGOMERY, GILLESPIE V. (SONNY MONTGOMERY), congressman; b. Meridian, Miss., Aug. 5, 1920; s. Gillespie M. and Emily (Jones) M. B.S., Miss. State U. Mem. Miss. Senate, 1956-66, 90th-104th Congresses from 3rd Miss. Dist., 1967-96; chmn. vets. affairs com., 1981-94; mem. vets. affairs com., chmn. spl. com. on S.E. Asia 90th-102d Congresses, 1978-96; ranking minority mem., 1994-96; mem. armed services. com. 90th-103d Congresses, chmn. select com. on missing persons in southeast Asia, 1975-96; mem. vets. affairs com.; mem. Woodcock Commn., 1977. Pres. Miss. N.G. Assn., 1959; pres. Miss. Heart Assn., 1967-68. Served with AUS, World War II, Korea, ret. maj. gen. Miss N.G. Decorated Bronze Star medal, Combat Inf. Badge; recipient Miss. Magnolia award, 1966, Lifetime Achievement award Mil. Educators & Counselors Assn., 1992. Mem. VFW, Am. Legion 40 and 8, Congl. Prayer Breakfast Group (pres. 1970). Episcopalian. Lodges: Masons; Shriners; Scottish Rite. Office: US Ho Reps Office of Postmaster Washington DC 20510*

MONTGOMERY, HUBERT THERON, JR., physician, health care administrator; b. Birmingham, Ala., July 29, 1935; s. Hubert Theron and Edna M. (Morrison) M.; m. Sarah Diane Bryans, Sept. 19, 1969; children: Alfred Peter, Melanie Anne, Laurel Elaine, Amy Diane. AB, Birmingham So. Coll., 1957; MD, Tulane U., 1961. Diplomate Am. Bd. Surgery, Am. Bd. Plastic Surgery. Rotating intern St. Vincent Hosp., Birmingham, 1961-62; resident surgery Lloyd Noland Hosp., Fairfield, Ala., 1964-68; pvt. practice Montgomery, Ala., 1968-73, 75—; resident plastic surgery U. Tenn., Memphis, 1974-75; pres., chief exec. officer Med One Inc., Montgomery, 1983—; exec. v.p., chief exec. officer Central Ala. Preferred Provider, Inc., Montgomery, 1984—; sec.-treas. Montgomery Surg. Ctr., Inc., 1984-85; sect. chief plastic surgery Bapt. Med. Ctr., Montgomery, 1976-78, St. Margaret's Hosp., Montgomery, 1987—. Sec.-treas. Ala. Soc. Plastic Surgeons, 1990-92, pres. 1994-96; mem. Hitchcock Award Com., Montgomery, 1985. Maj. U.S. Army, 1963-69. Named New Bus. of Yr., Ala. Bus. Rev., Montgomery, 1985. Fellow ACS; mem. Capitol City Kiwanis (dir. 1987-88), Montgomery Country Club, Wynn Lakes Country Club, Newcomen Soc. N.Am. Baptist.

MONTGOMERY, JAMES EDWARD, JR., lawyer; b. Champaign, Ill., Feb. 8, 1953; s. James Edward Sr and Vivian M.; m. Linda C.; children: James III, Anne. AB Polit. Sci., Duke U., 1975; JD, So. Meth. U., 1978. Bar: Tex., 1978, Md., 1994; U.S. Dist. Ct. (ea. dist.) Tex. 1978, U.S. Dist. Ct. (we. dist.) Tex., 1985, U.S. Dist. Ct. (so. dist.) Tex. 1986, U.S. Dist. Ct. (no. dist.) Tex. 1987, U.S. Dist. Md., 1994; U.S. Ct. Appeals (5th cir.) 1979; U.S. Supreme Ct., 1993. Assoc. Strong, Pipkin, Nelson & Parker, Beaumont, Tex., 1978-81; owner Sibley & Montgomery, Beaumont, 1981-85; assoc. Law Offices of Gilbert Adams, Beaumont, 1985; prin. James E. Montgomery, Beaumont, 1985-88; ptnr. Montgomery & Kontiuszcy, Beaumont, 1988-89; assoc. Sawtelle, Goode, Davidson & Troilo, San Antonio, Tex., 1989-91; shareholder Davidson & Troilo, San Antonio, 1991-94; pres. Montgomery & Assocs., San Antonio, 1994—. Editor: Fifth Cir. Reporter, 1983-86. Bd. dirs. Boys and Girls Clubs of San Antonio, 1995—; dist. chmn. Boy Scouts, San Antonio, 1994. Mem. ABA, State Bar of Tex., San Antonio Bar Assn., Rotary (pres.-elect Alamo Hts. chpt. 1997-98), 5th Cir. Bar Assn. (bd. dirs. 1983-86), Jefferson County Bar Assn. (treas. 1986). Office: Montgomery & Assocs P C Ste 620 613 NW Loop 410 San Antonio TX 78216

MONTGOMERY, JOSEPH WILLIAM, investment broker; b. Wytheville, Va., Dec. 23, 1951; s. Ivan Martin and Evelyn Powell (Delp) M; m. Linda Gail Winebarger, Aug. 30, 1980. BBA, William and Mary Coll., 1974. cert. fin. planner. With Wheat First Butcher Singer, Lynchburg and Williamsburg, Va., 1975—; v.p., investment officer Wheat, First Securities, Inc., Williamsburg, 1981-82, sr. v.p., investment officer, 1982-90, mng. dir., 1990; bd. dirs. William and Mary Soc. of Alumni, pres., various offices, steering com., nat. campaing, 1992-93, tercentenary commn., 1992-93, mem. Pres.'s Coun.; bd. visitors Coll. William & Mary, 1995—, chair fin. affairs com., 1996—. Bd. dirs. Peninsula chpt. NCCJ, 1986-90; mem. planning com. Kingsmill Cmty. Svcs. Assn., Williamsburg, 1981-82; bd. dirs. Future of Hampton Roads, 1996—; mem. Sports Opportunity Group, Norfolk, Va., 1984-90, adv. coun. Peninsula White Sox, 1986; treas. William and Mary Athletic Found., Williamsburg, 1980-81, v.p., 1981-83, 1st v.p., 1983-85, pres., 1985-87; fin. planning com. Williamsburg United Meth. Ch., 1985-87; bd. dirs. Williamsburg Cmty. Hosp., mem. fin. com., 1988, personnel com., 1986-88, bylaws com., 1990, exec. compensation com., 1990. Named one of Outstanding Young Men Am., 1982-83, one of Outstanding Coll. Athletes Am., 1973, 74, Outstanding Broker of 1984, Registered Rep. mag., 1985, one of Ten Best Brokers in Am., Fin. Planning on Wall St., 1995; named to William and Mary Athletic Hall of Fame, 1986, Broker Hall of Fame, Rsch., 1996; recipient Alumni medallion Soc. Alumni William and Mary, 1996. Mem. Internat. Assn. Fin. Planning, Inst. Cert. Planners, Registery Fin. Planning Practitioners, William and Mary Williamsburg Alumni Chpt., Williamsburg German Club (v.p. 1985-86, pres. 1986-87), Williamsburg Sports Club (pres. 1981-82), Rotary. Methodist. Office: Wheat First Butcher Singer PO Box W Williamsburg VA 23187-3646

MONTGOMERY, JUDY G(LASS), child care executive; b. Jacksonville, Fla., July 19, 1945; d. Paul H. and Pearle V. (Greene) Glass; m. Jack T. Montgomery, Jan. 4, 1970; 1 child, Sean Christopher. BS in Math., La. State U., 1967. Group chief operator South Central Bell Telephone Co., Baton Rouge, 1967-69; systems analyst Sperry Univac, Baton Rouge, 1969-70; pres. M & M Playland Inc., Baton Rouge, 1973-87, L'Ecole, Inc., Baton Rouge, 1976-87, Child Care Info., Baton Rouge, 1984—; cons. in field. Author: Door To Learning, 1983; contbg. author and mem. adv. bd. for tng. manuals Day Care Directions, 1984. Chairperson La. Women's Conf. on Day Care, Baton Rouge, 1977; day care rep. Senator Thomas Hudson, Baton Rouge, 1977; mem. Gov.'s Council on Children, La., 1980; lobbyist children's services Baton Rouge, 1976—; bd. dirs. Baton Rouge Vocat. Tech. Sch., 1980-85; mem. Govs. Task Force on Child Care Block Grant, 1991, Lt. Gov.'s Task Force on Child Care, 1991—. Mem. La. Fedn. Child Devel. Ctrs. (lobbyist 1976-81, pres. 1978-81), Baton Rouge C. of C. (edn. com. 1980), Internat. Platform Spkrs. Assn. Avocations: reading, sewing. Office: Child Care Info Inc PO Box 45212 # 223 Baton Rouge LA 70895-4212

MONTGOMERY, LYNA LEE, English language educator; b. Granby, Mo., Oct. 18, 1925. BA summa cum laude, S.W. Mo. State U., 1964; MA, U. Ark., 1964, PhD, 1967. Asst. prof. U. Ark., Fayetteville, 1966-71, assoc. prof., 1971-75, prof., 1975—; dir. undergrad. studies, 1983—, assoc. chair, 1995—; asst. in dept. adminstr. U. Ark., Fayetteville, 1966-82, M.A. exams. com., 1967-82, pers. com., 1972-75, coll. cabinet, 1974, univ. tenure com., 1976-78, campus coun., 1976, univ. grievance panel, 1981-83, Laura Yeater scholarship com., 1982-90, dir. undergrad. studies, 1983—, ad hoc search com. for faculty positions, 1983-84, 95-96. Author: (with Nancy Ellen Talburt) A Mystery Reader, 1975; contbr. numerous papers to profl. publs. Recipient Cardinal Key award for excellence in tchg., 1981; NDEA fellow, Univ. rsch. grantee, 1981. Office: U Ark Dept English 333 Kimpel Hall Fayetteville AR 72701

MONTGOMERY, MARVIN, musical producer. Mem. band Light Crust Doughboys, 1935—; prodr., leader Light Crust Doughboys, mus. orgn., Mesquite, Tex., 1948—; mem. touring act. State of Tex. Commn. on Arts. Originator western swing music. Named to Tex. Western Swing Hall of Fame; named ofcl. music amb. Tex. Ho. of Reps. Office: Light Crust Doughboys 105 Broad St Mesquite TX 75149

MONTGOMERY, MARY KATHRYN KEENER, special education educator; b. Selma, Ala., Aug. 2, 1956; d. Garlin Preston and Mary Ellouise (Friday) Keener; m. Robert Keith Montgomery, June 23, 1984. BS, Auburn (Ala.) U., 1978, MEd, 1981; postgrad., St. Leo (Fla.) Coll., 1986-87. Cert. tchr., Ala., Fla. Tchr. 1st thru 9th grades Hazen-Harrell Jr. High Sch., Marion Junction, Ala., 1978-84; recreation tchr. Bailey's Elem. Sch., Falls Church, Va., 1984-85; tchr. Belleview (Fla.) Elem. Sch., 1985-88; tchr. self contained mentally handicapped Ward-Highlands Elem. Sch., Ocala, Fla., 1988—; tchr. learning disabilities Oakcrest Elem. Sch., Ocala, summer 1988; sch. sponsor Spl. Olympics, Marion Junction, 1978-84, Ocala, 1988—; outreach chmn. Marion County Spl. Olympics, Ocala, 1989-91, steering com., 1991—. Mem. Ala. Edn. Assn., Selma, 1978-84. Named Tchr. of Yr., Belleview Elem. Sch., 1987, Ward-Highlands Elem. Sch., 1991. Mem. Coun. for Exceptional Children (v.p. 1988-89, sec. 1989-91), Marion Edn. Assn. (bldg. rep. Ocala chpt. 1986-91), Marion Edn. Assn. (bldg. rep. Ocala chpt. 1986-91, membership com. 1988-91), Alpha Delta Kappa, Kappa Delta Pi. Baptist. Home: 2516 NE 34th St Ocala FL 34479-3072 Office: Ward Highlands Elem Sch 537 SE 36th Ave Ocala FL 34471-3013

MONTGOMERY, PHILIP O'BRYAN, JR., pathologist; b. Dallas, Aug. 16, 1921. BS, So. Meth. U., 1942; MD, Columbia U., 1945. Diplomate Am. Bd. Pathology, Am. Bd. Clin. Pathology and Forensic Pathology. Intern Mary Imogene Bassett Hosp., Cooperstown, N.Y., 1945-46; fellow in pathology Southwestern Med. Sch., Dallas, 1950-51, asst. prof. pathology, 1953-55, assoc. prof., 1955-61, prof., 1961—, assoc. dean, 1968-70, Ashbel Smith prof. pathology, 1991—; rsch. asst. pathology and cancer rsch. Cancer Rsch. Inst. New Eng. Deaconess Hosp., Boston, 1951-52; spl. asst. to chancellor U. Tex. System, 1971-75; exec. dir. Cancer Ctr. U. Tex. Health Sci. Ctr. Dallas, 1975-89; pathologist Parkland Meml. Hosp., Dallas, 1952—, Dallas City Zoo, 1955-68; med. examiner DallasCounty, 1955-58; cons. Navarro County Meml. Hosp., Corsicana, Tex., 1952-53, McKinney (Tex.) Vets. Hosp., 1952-65, Lisbons Vets. Hosp., Dallas, 1953—, St. Paul Hosp., Dallas, 1958—, Flow Meml. Hosp., Denton, Tex., 1958-65; pathologist Tex. Children's Hosp., Dallas, 1954-55. Contbr. numerous articles to profl. jours., sci. abstracts, jours. Bd. dirs. Planned Parenthood of Dallas, 1958-63, pres., 1958-60; trustee St. Mark's Sch. Tex., 1958—, v.p., chmn. exec. com. bd. trustee, 1966-68, v.p., 1968-69, pres. 1974-76; trustee Lamplighter Sch., 1967-70; chmn. Dallas Area Libr. Planning Coun., 1970-72, Goals for Dallas Health Task Force com., 1975-76, Fleet Adm. Nimitz Mus. commn., 1979-81; mem. adv. bd. Dallas Citizens coun., chmn. health com. 1988-89; bd. dirs. Met. YMCA, 1960-63, Dallas Coun. on World Affairs, 1962-65; pres., bd. dirs. Damon Runyon, Walter Winchell Cancer Fund, 1974-79; cord. Dallas Arts Dist., 1982-95. Fellow Am. Soc. Clin. Pathologists; mem. Am. Assn. Pathologists and Bacteriologists, Am. Assn. Cancer Rsch., Internat. Acad. Pathology, Am. Acad. Forensic Scis., Soc. Exptl. Biology and Medicine, Internat. Soc. Cell Biology, Biophys. Soc., Am. Soc. Cell Biology, Am. soc. Exptl. Pathology, Tissue Culture Assn., Internat. Fedn. Med. Electronics, Profl. Group Med. Electronics of Inst. Radio Engrs., AAAS, Optical Soc. Tex. (founding), Pan-Am. Med. Assn., AMA, So. Med. Assn., Tex. Med. Assn., AAUP.

MONTGOMERY, ROBERT MOREL, JR., lawyer; b. Birmingham, Ala., June 9, 1930; s. Robert Morel and Ella Bernice (Smith) M.; m. Mary Lemerle McKenzie, Mar. 6, 1953; 1 child, Courtnay Elizabeth. B.S., U. Ala., 1952; LL.B., U. Fla., 1957. Bar: Fla. 1957; diplomate Acad. Fla. Trial Lawyers. With Howell & Kirby Attys at Law, Jacksonville, Fla., 1957-59; ptnr. Howell, Kirby, Montgomery, Sands & D'Aiuto, Jacksonville, Fla., 1959-66, Howell, Kirby, Montgomery, D'Aiuto, Dean & Hallowes, West Palm Beach, Fla., 1966-75, Montgomery, Lytal, Reiter, Denny & Searcy, West Palm Beach, Fla., 1976-85, Montgomery Searcy & Denny, West Palm Beach, Fla., 1986-89; sr. ptnr. Montgomery & Larmoyeux, West Palm Beach, Fla., 1989—; civil trial adv. Nat. Bd. Trial Advocacy. Chmn. Palm Beach Opera; vice chmn. Kravis Ctr., Palm Beach Cultural Coun. 1st lt. AUS, 1952-54. Mem. ABA, Fla. Bar Assn. (lectr. continuing edn.), Palm Beach County Bar Assn., Trial Lawyers Assn. Am., Inner Circle Advs. Home: 1800 S Ocean Blvd Palm Beach FL 33480-5104 Office: PO Box 3086 West Palm Beach FL 33402-3086

MONTGOMERY, WILLARD WAYNE, physicist; b. Gamaliel, Ky., May 26, 1949; s. Willard Osborne Montgomery and Mildred Lucille (Parkhurst) Morse; m. Brenda Kaye Winberg, Aug. 3, 1973. BS, Mid. Tenn. State U., 1973; MS, Purdue U., 1975; PhD, The U. Tenn., 1980. Staff scientist Lockheed Missiles & Space Co., Huntsville, Ala., 1978—. Contbr. articles to profl. jours. Mem. Optical Soc. Am., Sigma Xi. Republican. Office: Lockheed Missiles & Space PO Box 70017 Huntsville AL 35807-7017

MONTGOMERY-DAVIS, JOSEPH, osteopathic physician; b. Annapolis, Md., Aug. 27, 1940; s. John and Flonila Alice (Sutphin) Swontek. Student, U. Wis., Milw., 1967-70; DO, Chgo. Coll. Osteo. Medicine, 1974. Diplomate Nat. Bd. Examiners for Osteo. Physicians and Surgeons. Chief technologist nuclear medicine dept. Columbia Hosp., Milw., 1964-70; intern Richmond Heights (Ohio) Gen. Hosp., 1974-75; pvt. practice Raymondville, Tex., 1975—; med. care adv. com. Tex. Dept. Human Svcs., Austin, 1983-86, 90-94, physician payment adv. com., 1991—; cons. health care issues Tex. Osteo. Med. Assn., 1991—; health officer Willacy County Bd., Raymondville, 1984—. Contbr. articles to profl. jours. With USAF, 1959-63. Mem. Am. Osteo. Assn., Am. Coll. Osteo. Family Physiaicns (spl. Recognition award 1995), Tex. Soc. Am. Coll. Osteo. Family Physicians (pres. 1985-86, Physician of Yr. award 1989), Tex. Med. Found., Tex. Osteo. Med. Assn. (pres. 1989-90), Tex. Coll. Osteo. Medicine Alumni Assn., Phi Eta Sigma, Sigma Sigma Phi. Office: Raymondville Med Clinic 525 S 10th St Raymondville TX 78580

MONTICELLO, CHRISTINE DARLEA, health and physical education educator; b. Endicott, N.Y., Feb. 13, 1971; d. Joseph Anthony and Anne Teresa (Darlea) M. Degree, Valdosta (Ga.) State U., 1994. Tchr. Humpty Dumpty Playsch., Valdosta, 1983—. Mem. AAHPERD, Ga. Traditional Country Western Dance Assn., Alpha Lambda Delta. Roman Catholic. Home: 420 Connell Rd Apt 37D Valdosta GA 31602

MONTIJO, RALPH ELIAS, JR., engineering executive; b. Tucson, Oct. 26, 1947; m. Guillermina Paredes, Dec., 1947; children: Rafael (dec.), Suzanne, Felice. BSEE, U. Ariz., 1952; postgrad. in digital computer engring., U. Pa., 1953-57; postgrad. in mgmt., U. Calif., Los Angeles, 1958-60; DSc (hon.), London Inst. for Applied Rsch., 1993. Registered profl. engr., Tex. With RCA Corp., 1952-67; design and devel. engr. RCA Corp., Camden, N.J., 1952-55; mgr. West Coast EDP engring. RCA Corp., L.A., 1960-61, mgr. EDP systems engring., 1961-64; mgr. special systems and equipment planning, product planning divsn. RCA Corp., Cherry Hill, N.J., 1964-65; mgr. Calif. Dept. of Motor Vehicles program RCA Corp., Sacramento, 1965-66; mgr. spl. EDP programs RCA Corp., 1966-67; with Planning Rsch. Corp., 1967-72; dep. div. mgr. Eastern and European ops., computer systems div. Planning Rsch. Corp., Washington, 1968; dep. div. mgr. advanced systems planning, reservations systems, computer systems div. Planning Rsch. Corp., Moorestown, N.J., 1968-69; v.p., gen mgr. Internat. Reservations Corp. div. Planning Rsch. Corp., L.A., 1969-70, exec. v.p., 1970-71, pres., 1971-72, also bd. dirs.; v.p. Systems Sci. Devel. Corp. subs. Planning Rsch. Corp., L.A., 1972—; CEO Omniplan Corp., Culver City, Calif. and Houston, 1972—. Contbr. 37 articles to profl. jours.; patentee in field. Recipient Alumni Achievement award U. Ariz., 1985, Centennial medal U. Ariz., 1989. Mem. IEEE, NSPE, Am. Mgmt. Assn., Assn. Computing Machinery, U. Ariz. Alumni Assn. (pres. So. Calif. chpt. 1980-81, centennial medallion award 1989, alumni achievement award 1985, pres. Houston chpt. 1992-93, officer nat. bd. dirs.). Republican. Roman Catholic. Home: 2222 Gemini Ave Houston TX 77058-2049

MONTLE, VICKI LEMP, library director; b. Peoria, Ill., Sept. 16, 1956; d. John Frederick and Barbara Ellen (King) Lemp; m. John Michael McDonald, Dec. 27, 1980 (div. Dec. 1990); m. Robert Ellwyn Montle, Nov. 19, 1994; 1 child, Robert Thomas. BA in Theatre Arts, U. Va., 1978; MLS, Ind. U., 1988; postgrad., U. Minn., 1979-80. Reference libr. N.Y. Libr. for Performing Arts at Lincoln Ctr., N.Y.C., 1988-90; dir. reference svcs. Mus. TV and Radio, N.Y.C., 1990-92; dir. Semans Libr., N.C. Sch. of Arts, Winston-Salem, 1992—; mem. Univ. Libr. Adv. Coun., Chapel Hill, N.C., 1992—; com. mem. Forsyth County Free-Net Project, Winston-Salem, 1993—. Mem. chorus Piedmont Chamber Singers, Winston-Salem, 1992—. Mem. ALA, Theatre Libr. Assn., Phi Beta Kappa, Phi Kappa Phi, Beta Phi Mu. Lutheran. Office: Semans Libr NC Sch Arts PO Box 12189 200 Waughtown St Winston Salem NC 27117

MONTONE, LIBER JOSEPH, engineering consultant; b. Apr. 21, 1919; s. Vito and Philomena (Carnicelli) M.; m. Clara Elisabeth Edwards, June 1, 1945; 1 child, Gregory Edwards. MS, Temple U., 1961; PhD (hon.), 1994. Registered profl. engr., Pa. Quality control supr. Haskell Electronic and Tool Corp., Homer, N.Y., 1950-53; researcher IBM Airborne Computer Lab., Vestal, N.Y., 1954-56; devel. engr. Western Electric Co. and Bell Labs., Laureldale, Pa., 1956-61; sr. devel. engr. Western Electric Co. Inc., Reading, Pa., 1961-65, sr. staff engr. R&D, 1965-82; cons. Naples, Fla., Fenwick Island, Del., 1983—; biomed. engr., cancer rsch. projects pathology and clin. lab. St. Joseph's Hosp., Reading, 1961-80; tech. cons. Reading Hosp., 1961-78. Contbr. articles to profl. jours. including The Engr., Am. Assn. Clin. Scientists Symposium. Capt. USAAF, 1942-45, ETO. Recipient Outstanding Paper award Engring. Rsch. Ctr., Princeton, N.J., 1963. Mem. NSPE, Fla. Engring. Soc., Res. Officer's Assn. (life). Office: 4242 Vanderbilt Dr Naples FL 33963

MONTS, ELIZABETH ROSE, insurance company executive; b. LaPorte, Ind., June 13, 1955; d. William David and Marguerite Elizabeth (Burge) Miller; m. James Edwin Monts, May 26, 1978 (div. Aug. 1982); 1 child, Katherine Elizabeth. AA with highest honors, Coll. of Mainland, 1984; BS magna cum laude, U. Houston, Clear Lake, 1989. CPA. Credit adjustment asst. Jaymar-Ruby, Inc., Michigan City, Ind., 1974-79; acctg. clk. Am. Indemnity Co., Galveston, Tex., 1979-80, staff acct., 1980-81, adminstrv. acct., 1981-85, asst. treas., 1985-86, asst. treas., asst. dept. mgr., 1986-87, sec., asst. dept. mgr., 1987-91, asst. v.p., asst. dept. mgr., 1991—. V.I.P. escort Rep. Nat. Conv., Houston, 1992. Mem. AICPA, Nat. Assn. for Female Execs., Fedn. Ins. Women Tex. (regional dir. 1992-94), Tex. Soc. CPA's, Ins. Women Galveston County (pres. 1987-88, 90-91), Beta Gamma Sigma, Phi Kappa Phi, Alpha Chi. Republican. Methodist. Office: Am Indemnity Co PO Box 1259 Galveston TX 77553-1259

MONZINGO, AGNES YVONNE, veterinary technician; b. Mangum, Okla., July 16, 1942; d. Ira Lee and Opal Alice (McAlexander) Mayfield; m. Monty Brent Monzingo, Dec. 19, 1959; children: Tara, Dawn, Michael, Kermit. AS, San Antonio Coll., 1969. Mgr. Tupperware Corp., Wichita Falls, Tex., 1966-69; with La Louisiane, San Antonio, 1974-79; counselor Diet Ctr., Duncanville, Tex., 1984-87; vet. technician DeSoto (Tex.) Animal Hosp., 1985—. Author: (weekly column) Happy Tracks, 1981. Pres. Dallas Stake Primary, 1983-88; commr. Boy Scouts Am., 1988-93. Recipient Wood badge Boy Scouts Am., 1987, Wisdom Trail Dist. award of merit, 1990, Silver Beaver award Boy Scouts Am., 1993. Mem. Tex. Assn. Registered Vet. Technicians (v.p. 1991), Tex. Assn. Animal Technicians (pres. 1988, com. chair 1990-92), Tex. Assn. Registered Technicians (pres. 1992), Am. Boxer Club, Dallas Boxers Club (sec. 1982-92), Metroplex Vet. Hosp. Mgrs. Assn. Mem. LDS Ch.

MOODY, CHARLES EMORY, information systems analyst; b. Hazlehurst, Ga.; s. Alwyn Otho and Elise (McKinney) M.; m. Sandra Lee Martin, June 5, 1969; 1 child, Tamara Elise Moody Benbow. BS in Math., Ga. So. Coll., 1974. Sr. MIS analyst Ga. Power Co., Wayneboro, 1974—. Mem. gallery control staff Masters Golf Tournament, Augusta, Ga., 1981-86, computer scorer, 1986—; driver U.S. Olympics, Atlanta, 1995. With U.S. Army, 1968-68. Mem. Ga. State Golf Assn. (golf course rating team 1994—). Republican. Baptist. Home: 4428 Goshen Lake Dr S Augusta GA 30906 Office: Ga Power-Plant Vogtle River Rd Waynesboro GA

MOODY, CHERYL ANNE, social services administrator, social worker, educator; b. Winston-Salem, N.C., July 31, 1953; d. Fred Bertram and Mary Edna (Weekley) M. BSW with honors, Va. Commonwealth U., 1975; MSW, U. Mich., 1979. Social worker Family Svcs., Inc., Winston-Salem, 1974-77;

sch. social work intern Huron Valley Jr. H.S., Milford, Mich., 1977-78; children's social work intern Downriver Child Guidance Clinic, Allen Park, Mich., 1978-79; children's svcs. specialist Calhoun County Dept. Social Svcs., Battle Creek, Mich., 1979-81; children's psychiat. social worker Eastern Maine Med. Ctr., Bangor, 1981-82, sr. med. social worker, 1982-85; clin. social worker Ctr. for Family Svcs. in Palm Beach County, Inc., West Palm Beach, Fla., 1988-89, Jupiter, Fla., 1989-91; dir. children's programs Children's Home Soc. of Fla., West Palm Beach, 1985—; asst. prof. social work Fla. Atlantic U., Boca Raton, 1993—. Vol. group leader Lupus Found., Boca Raton, 1994—. Mem. NASW, Acad. Cert. Social Workers. Democrat. Methodist. Home: 6212 62nd Way West Palm Beach FL 33409-7130 Office: Children's Home Soc of Fla 3600 Broadway West Palm Beach FL 33407-4844

MOODY, DONALD ERNEST, rescue mission administrator; b. Green Cove Springs, Fla., Sept. 5, 1939; s. Ernest T. and Doris B. (Wingo) M.; m. Patricia Lee Halstead, May 1, 1961; children: LeeDawn Terese Moody Carpenter, LeeTrisha Dawn Moody Koepsell. Grad. in Theology, Tenn. Temple, Chattanooga, 1962. Staff Union Mission, Charleston, W.Va., 1963-64; dir. City Rescue Mission, Jacksonville, Fla., 1964-72, Huntington (W.Va.) City Mission, 1972-78; exec. dir. Orlando (Fla.) Union Rescue Mission, 1978—. Mem. Internat. Union of Gospel Missions (southeastern dist. pres. 1993). Office: Orlando Rescue Mission 1521 W Washington St Orlando FL 32805-1739

MOODY, EDWARD BRIDGES, physician, biomedical engineer; b. Omaha, Apr. 2, 1954; s. Edson Bridges and Sara Jane (Sears) M.; m. Virginia Jane Welch, Mar. 18, 1978; 1 child, Alexander. BA in Chemistry, Knox Coll., 1976; MD, Rush Med. Coll., 1980; MS, Rutgers U., 1987. Diplomate Am. Bd. Nuclear Medicine. Intern in diagnostic radiology W.Va. U. Med. Ctr., Morgantown, 1980-81; rsch. fellow in neurophysiology Lyons (N.J.) VA Med. Ctr., 1987-89; resident physician in nuclear medicine Vanderbilt U. Med. Ctr., Nashville, 1989-92; asst. prof. diagnostic radiology U. Ky. Coll. Medicine, Lexington, 1992—. Contbr. articles to profl. jours. Capt. U.S. Army, 1980-83. Mem. IEEE, Soc. Nuclear Medicine, Am. Coll. Nuclear Physicians. Office: Univ Ky Med Ctr Nuclear Medicine Rm N-3 800 Rose St Lexington KY 40536

MOODY, EVELYN WILIE, consulting geologist; b. Waco, Tex.; d. William Braden and Enid Eva (Holt) Wilie; children: John D., Melissa L., Jennifer A. Student, Baylor U., 1934-35; BA with honors in Geology and Edn. U. Tex., 1938, MA with honors in geology, 1940. Cert. profl. geologist; cert. permanent tchr., Tex. Geologist Ark. Fuel Oil Co., Shreveport, La., New Orleans and Houston, 1942-45; teaching asst. Colo. Sch. Mines, Golden, 1946-47; exploration cons. geologist Gen. Crude Oil Co., Houston, 1975-77; ind. cons. geologist, Houston, 1977—; exploration cons. geologist Shell Oil Co., Houston, 1979-81; faculty dept. continuing edn. Rice U., Houston, 1978. Contbr. articles to profl. jours.; editor: The Manual for Independents, 1983, The Business of Being a Petroleum Independent (A Road Map for the Self Employed), 1987; co-author: How (to Try) To Find An Oil Field, 1981. Mem. Am. Assn. Petroleum Geologists (del. Houston chpt. 1986-89, 89-91, 91-94, 94—), Soc. Ind. Profl. Earth Scientists (hon. Houston chpt., sec. 1978-79, vice chmn. 1979-80, chpt. chmn. 1980-81, nat. dir. 1982-85, chpt. award for Outstanding Svc. 1986, editor SIPES Bull., 1983-85, treas. SIPES Found. 1984, pres. 1985, Nat. award for Outstanding Svc. 1988, SIPES Found. award 1994, hon. mem. in SIPES Houston chpt., 1994), Geol. Soc. Am., Watercolor Soc. Houston, Art Students League N.Y.C., Art Assn., Am. Inst. Profl. Geologists, Houston Geol. Soc. (chmn. libr. com. 1978—), Soc. Econ. Paleontologists and Mineralogists, Pi Beta Phi (nat. officer 1958-60, 66-68), Pi Lambda Theta. Republican. Presbyterian.

MOODY, GENE BYRON, engineering executive, small business owner; b. Calhoun, Ga., Aug. 29, 1933; s. Denzel Elwood and Mary Edna (Hughes) M.; m. Willie Earline Chauncey, Sept. 1, 1955; children: Byron Eugene, Iva Marie Levy. BSCE, U. Tenn., 1956. Registered profl. engr., Ala., Ark., Ga., La., Miss., Tex. V.p. S.I.P. Engring. Corp., Baton Rouge, 1968-70; project engr. S.I.P., Inc., Houston, 1970-73; dir. of engring. Jacus Assoc., Mpls., 1972-73; dir. of civil engring. Barnard & Burk, Baton Rouge, 1973-79; project mgr. Process Svcs., Baton Rouge, 1979-80, Salmon & Assoc., Baton Rouge, 1980-81; chief engr. Minton & Assoc., Lafayette, La., 1982; mgr. Assoc. Engr. Cons., Baton Rouge, 1982-86; owner Gene B. Moody, P.E., Baton Rouge, 1986—. Author: Good Homemakers, 1988, Deliverance Manual, 1989; contbr. articles to profl. jours. Deacon South Side Bapt. Ch., Baton Rouge, 1974; tchr. Hamilton Bible Camp, Hot Springs, Ark., 1981-91; trustee Manna Bapt. Ch., Baton Rouge, 1989-91. With U.S. Army, 1957. U. Chattanooga scholar, 1951, U. Tenn. scholar, 1953. Fellow ASCE; mem. Am. Soc. Safety Engrs., La. Soc. Profl. Surveyors, Soc. Automotive Engrs., Inst. Transp. Engrs., La. Engring. Soc., Transp. Res. Rsch. Bd. Mem. Christian Ch. (minister). Home and Office: 9852 Hillyard Ave Baton Rouge LA 70809-3109

MOODY, GEORGE WALTER, aviation executive; b. London, Mar. 15, 1943; s. George Walter and Margaret (Foster) M.; m. Carol Ann Pettiford, July 11, 1964 (div. 1972); m. Eva Leopoldine Kotek, Jan. 9, 1973; children: Robert Spencer George, Michael David, Stuart Armstrong. Degrees in Elec. and Mech. Engring., Luton (Eng.) Coll., 1964. Chartered engr. Sr. design engr. Brit. Aircraft Corp., Herts, Eng., 1963-68; program mgr., chief engr., gen. mgr. mktg. Redifon Simulation, Sussex, Eng., 1968-75; founder, chmn., pres. George W. Moody Ltd, Sussex, 1975-85, George Moody Inc., Tulsa, 1979-85, Aviation Resources, Inc., Tulsa, 1985—, Aviation Resources Ltd., Sussex, 1985—, George W. Moody Investments, Inc., 1985—, Simulator Mgmt. Corp., 1991—, Aviation Investments, Inc., 1992—. Fellow Inst. Elec. Engrs. (chartered engr.). Home: 2465 E 73rd Pl Tulsa OK 74136-5520 Office: Aviation Resources Inc PO Box 307 Broken Arrow OK 74013-0307

MOODY, LAMON LAMAR, JR., retired civil engineer; b. Bogalusa, La., Nov. 8, 1924; s. Lamar Lamon and Vida (Seal) M.; BS in Civil Engring., U. Southwestern La., 1951; m. Eve Thibodeaux, Sept. 22, 1954 (div. 1991); children: Lamon Lamar III, Jennifer Eve, Jeffrey Matthew. Engr., Tex. Co., N.Y.C., 1951-52; project engr. African Petroleum Terminals, West Africa, 1952-56; chief engr. Kaiser Aluminum & Chem. Corp., Baton Rouge, 1956-63; pres., owner Dyer & Moody, Inc., Cons. Engrs., Baker, La., 1963-94, also chmn. bd., dir.; ret., 1994. Chmn., Baker Planning Commn., 1961-63. Trustee La. Coun. on Econ. Edn., 1987-93. Served with USMCR, 1943-46. Decorated Purple Heart; registered profl. engr., La., Ark., Miss., Tex.; registered profl. land surveyor, La., Tex. Fellow ASCE, Am. Congress Surveying and Mapping (award for excellence 1972); mem. La. Engring. Soc. (dir., v.p. 1980-81, pres. 1982-83, Charles M. Kerr award for public relations 1971, A.B. Patterson medal 1981, Odom award for disting. svc. to engring. profession, 1986), Profl. Engrs. in Pvt. Practice (state chmn. 1969-70), La. Land Surveyors Assn. (pres. 1968-69, Land Surveyor of Yr. award 1975), Cons. Engrs. Coun., Pub. Affairs Rsch. Coun. of La. (exec. com., trustee 1983—), Good Roads and Transp. Assn. (bd. dirs. 1984—), Baker C. of C. (pres. 1977, Bus. Leader of Yr. award 1975), NSPE (nat. dir. 1982-83), Blue Key. Republican. Baptist. Clubs: Masons (32 deg., K.C.C.H. 1986), Kiwanis (dir. 1964-65). Home: 451 Ray Weiland Dr Baker LA 70714-3353 Office: 2845 Ray Weiland Dr Baker LA 70714-3247

MOODY, MAXWELL, JR., retired physician; b. Tuscaloosa, Ala., Aug. 7, 1921; s. Maxwell and Jean Kilroy (Lahey) M.; m. Betty Alice Morrissey, May 10, 1946 (dec. Feb. 1994); children: Maxwell III, Susan, Elizabeth Sims; m. Barbara Loftis, Mar. 4, 1995. BA, U. Ala., 1941; MD, U. Pa., 1944. Diplomate Am. Bd. Internal Medicine. Intern Gorgas Hosp., Ancon, C.Z., 1944-45, Ancon, 1944-45; resident Grad. Sch. Medicine, U. Pa., Phila., 1947-48, Univ. Hosp., Birmingham, Ala., 1948-50; jr. and sr. resident in medicine U. Ala. Hosp., Birmingham, 1948-50; pvt. practice Tuscaloosa, 1950-87, ret., 1987; pres. Tuscaloosa County Med. Soc., Ala. Soc. Internal Medicine; pres., chn. bd. Ala. Heart Assn. Former state chmn., nat. trustee Ducks Unltd. Capt. U.S. Army, 1945-47. Fellow Am. Coll. Physicians. Republican. Episcopalian. Home: 7604 Mountbatten Rd NE Tuscaloosa AL 35406-1110

MOODY, ROBERT LEE, insurance company executive; b. 1936. Chmn., chief exec. officer Nat. Western Life Ins. Co., Austin, Tex., also bd. dirs.; chmn. Am. Nat. Ins. Co., Galveston, Tex., also bd. dirs.; also pres. Moody Bankshares, Inc., Galveston; pres. Moody Investments, Galveston. Office: Am Nat Ins Co 1 Moody Plz Galveston TX 77550-7999*

MOODY, WILLARD JAMES, SR., lawyer; b. Franklin, Va., June 16, 1924; s. Willie James and Mary (Bryant) M.; m. Betty Glenn Covert, Aug. 2, 1948; children: Sharon Paige Moody Edwards, Willard J. Jr., Paul Glenn. AB, Old Dominion U., 1946; LLB, U. Richmond, 1952. Bar: Va. 1952. Pres. Moody, Strople & Kloeppel Ltd., Portsmouth, Va., 1952—; commr. Chancery, Portsmouth, 1960—, Accounts, 1960—. Del. Va. Ho. of Reps., Portsmouth, 1956-68; senator State of Va., 1968-83; chmn. Portsmouth Dems., 1983—. Recipient Friend of Edn. award Portsmouth Edn. Assn., 1981. Mem. ABA, Va. Bar Assn., Portsmouth Bar Assn. (pres. 1960-61, lectr. seminars), Va. Trial Lawyers Assn. (pres. 1968-69), Hampton Roads C. of C. (bd. dirs. 1983-86), Portsmouth C. of C. (bd. dirs. 1960-61), Inner Circle Advs., VFW, Cosmopolitan Club, Moose. Home: 120 River Point Cres Portsmouth VA 23707-1028 Office: Moody Strople & Kloeppel Ltd 500 Crawford St Portsmouth VA 23704-3844

MOOERS, CHRISTOPHER NORTHRUP KENNARD, physical oceanographer, educator; b. Hagerstown, Md., Nov. 11, 1935; s. Frank Burt and Helen (Miner) M.; m. Elizabeth Eva Fauntleroy, June 11, 1960; children: Blaine Hanson MacFee, Randall Walden Lincoln. BS, U.S. Naval Acad., 1957; MS, U. Conn., 1964; PhD, Oreg. State U., 1969. Postdoctoral fellow U. Liverpool (Eng.), 1969-70; asst. prof. U. Miami (Fla.), 1970-72, assoc. prof., 1972-76; assoc. prof. U. Del., Newark, 1976-78, prof., 1978-79; prof., chmn. dept. oceanography Naval Postgrad. Sch., Monterey, Calif., 1979-86; dir. Inst. Naval Oceanography, Stennis Space Ctr., Miss., 1986-89; sci. advisor to dir. Inst. for Naval Oceanography, 1989; rsch. prof. U. N.H., Durham, 1989-91; prof., chmn. div. applied marine physics U. Miami, Fla., 1991-93, dir. Ocean Pollution Rsch. Ctr., 1992—; coord. Coastal Ocean Scis. Program, 1991—. Editor Jour. Phys. Oceanography, 1991-96; mng. editor Coastal and Estuarine Studies, 1978—. Served with USN, 1957-64. NSF fellow, 1964-67; NATO fellow, 1969-70; Sr. Queen Elizabeth fellow, 1980. Mem. AAAS, The Oceanography Soc. (interim councilor 1987-88), Am. Geophys. Union (pres. ocean sci. sect. 1982-84), Eastern Pacific Oceanic Conf. (chmn. 1979-86), U.S. Nat. Com. Internat. Union Geodesy and Geophysics (chmn. 1996—), U. Nat. Oceanographic Lab. Sys./Fleet Improvement Com. (chair 1994-97), Am. Meteorol. Soc. (chmn. sci. and tech. activities com. on the meteorology and oceanography of the Coastal Zone 1996—), Marine Tech. Soc., Sigma Xi. Home: 2521 Inagua Ave Coconut Grove FL 33133-3811 Office: U Miami Div Applied Marine Physics RSMAS 4600 Rickenbacker Causeway Miami FL 33149-1098

MOON, BILLY G., electrical engineer; b. Louisville, Oct. 22, 1961; m. Catherine Alice Haunz, May 26, 1984; children: William Victor, Timothy David. BSEE, U. Louisville, 1984. Elec. engr. coop. GTE of Ky., Lexington, 1981-82, Louisville (Ky.) Gas and Elec., 1982-83; elec. engr. II Motorola, Inc., Ft. Lauderdale, Fla., 1984-85, elec. engr. I, 1985-87; engring. sect. mgr. Americom Corp., Atlanta, 1987-89, advanced product planning mgr., 1989-90, dir. tech., 1990-91; v.p. engring. Uniden Am. Corp., Ft. Worth, 1992-95; mgr. new concepts Ericsson, Inc., Research Triangle Park, 1995—; owner Moonsoft, Inc., Ft. Lauderdale, 1984-87. Deacon Duluth (Ga.) Seventh Day Adventist ch., 1989-92. Recipient 2nd place award elec. engring. design competition, U. Louisville, 1982. Mem. Nat. Honor Soc., Beta Club. Republican. Home: 305 Parkbranch Ln Apex NC 27502 Office: Ericsson Inc 1 Triangle Dr Research Triangle Park NC 27709

MOON, DOUG, director of development; b. Hendersonville, N.C., Sept. 17, 1954; s. Grady Collie and Lila (Dalton) M.; m. Karen Gayle Corn, Sept. 20, 1980; children: Tyler, Colby. BS, N.C. State U., 1977. Cert. non-profit mgmt. Recreation dir. Fairfield Mountains, Lake Lure, N.C., 1977-79; atheletic dir. Henderson (N.C.) County, 1979-83, dir. parks and recreation, 1983-93; dir. devel. Hospice of Henderson County, 1993—. Contbr. articles to profl. jours. Chairperson, bd. dirs. Gov's. Youth Adv. Coun., Raleigh, N.C., 1989-91, N.C. Apple Festival, Hendersonville, 1993—; sec., bd. dirs. Ret. Sr. Vol. Program, Asheville, N.C., 1990—; dep. state commr. N.C. Amatuer Softball Assn., Winston-Salem, N.C., 1979—. Recipient Cert. of Appreciation, Gov. Jim Martin, 1991; named Outstanding Youth Svc., Nat. Assn. of Counties, 1991. Mem. Nat. Recreation and Park Assn. (cert. leisure profl.), Nat. Hospice Orgn. (cert. hospice profl.), N.C. Recreation and Park Soc., Fellowship Christian Athletes, West N.C. Funding and Devel. Assn., Elks, Kiwanis (pres. Hendersonville chpt. 1989—, lt. gov. Carolinas Dist. 1995). Republican. Baptist. Home: 108 Amelia Dr Hendersonville NC 29792 Office: Hospice of Henderson County 802 Old Spartanburg Highway Hendersonville NC 29792

MOON, JOHN HENRY, SR., banker; b. Van Buren, Ark., Aug. 19, 1937; s. B.R. and Alma (Witte) M.; m. Agnes Rose Dickens, Aug. 16, 1958; children: John Henry, Randall Allen. AA, Delmar Coll., Corpus Christi, 1956; BBA cum laude, Tex. A&M Univ., Kingsville, 1958. Sr. acct. Tex. Eastern Transp. Co. and subs., 1958-63; exec. v.p., dir. Houston Research Inst., 1963-68; sr. v.p., asst. to chmn. bd., dir. Main Bank, 1968; vice chmn. bd., dir. N.E. Bank, 1969; CEO, chmn. bd., dir. Pasadena (Tex.) Nat. Bank, 1970-81; gen. ptnr. Moon and Assocs., Ltd., 1977—; chmn. bd., pres. Interservice Life Ins. Corp., Phoenix, Cmty. Bank, Houston, 1975-81, Interstate Bank, Houston, 1977-81; chmn. bd., pres. Cmty. Capital Corp., Pasadena, 1975—, Peoples Bank, Houston, 1983-93; chmn. bd. Cmty. Nat. Bank, Friendswood, Tex., 1981-93; chmn. bd. Peoples Nat. Bank, Pasadena, Tex., 1984-93; dir. San Jacinto River Authority, 1991-93; chmn., pres. Sam Houston Pky. Transp. Corp., 1991—; bd. dirs. Harris County Indsl. Devel. Corp., 1996—, Pro Technologies, Inc., 1987-96. Past bd. dirs. Pasadena Heart Assn., Salvation Army, Tex. Assn. Prevention of Blindness; past chmn. City of Pasadena Bd. Devel.; past chmn. adv. bd. Pasadena Civic Ctr.; past dir. S.E. Econ. Devel., Inc. Named Outstanding Young Man of Yr., Pasadena Jr. C. of C., 1973; named to Pasadena Hall of Fame, 1988. Mem. AICPA, Pasadena C. of C. (bd. dirs. S.E. Econ. Devel., Citizen of Yr. 1994), Tex. Soc. CPAs, Tex. Bankers Assn., Rotary. Home: 3914 Peru Cir Pasadena TX 77504-2320 Office: PO Box 910 Pasadena TX 77501-0910

MOON, TESSIE JO, mechanical engineering educator; b. Butler, Pa., Dec. 7, 1961; d. Edward Vincent and Verda Viola Moon; m. Glenn Y. Masada; 1 child, Kendall M. Masada. BS, Grove City Coll., 1983; MS, U. Ill., 1986, PhD, 1989. Jr. engr. AMP Inc., Harrisburg, Pa., 1982; devel. engr. AMP Inc., Winston-Salem, N.C., 1983-84; grad. teaching asst. U. Ill., Urbana-Champaign, 1984-86, grad. rsch. asst., 1986-89; postdoctoral rsch. assoc. Office Naval Rsch.-U. Rsch. Inst. Nat. Ctr. for Composite Materials Rsch., Urbana-Champaign, 1989; asst. prof. U. Tex., Austin, 1989-95, assoc. prof., 1995—; faculty fellow Naval Surface Warfare Ctr. Carderock Divsn., Annapolis, Md., 1991. Editor: Mechanics in Materials Processing and Manufacturing, 1994. Recipient Young Investigator award NSF, 1992-97; initiation grantee Engring. Found., 1992-93, rsch. grantee Office of Naval Rsch., 1992—. Mem. ASME (mem. heat transfer divsn. tech. com. on heat transfer materials processing and mfg. 1991—, vice chmn. applied mechanics divsn. tech. com. on mechanics of materials processing and mfg. 1992—, contbr. articles to jours.), AAUP, AAUW, Am. Acad. Mechanics, Am. Soc. Engring. Edn. (Outstanding New Mechanics award 1992-93), Am. Soc. Materials, The Minerals, Metals and Materials Soc. of AIME, Soc. for the Advancement of Material and Processing Engring. Republican. Office: U Tex Mech Engring Dept ETC 5 160 Austin TX 78712-1063

MOONEY, CHRISTOPHER ZIMMER, political science educator; b. Kewanee, Ill., June 20, 1958; s. Harris C. and Mary Lou Mooney; m. Laura Ann Zimmer, June 11, 1983; children: Allison Carmichael, Charles Zimmer. BA with honors, U. Wis., Milw., 1982; MPA, U. Wis., Madison, 1985, MA, 1987, PhD, 1990. Pres. Mootown Records, Madison, 1982-85; policy analyst Dept. Devel., State of Wis., Madison, 1985-86; instr. U. Wis., Milw., 1988-89, Madison, 1989-90; asst. prof. polit. sci. W.Va. U., Morgantown, 1990-96, assoc. prof., 1996—; vis. lectr. U. Essex, Colchester, Eng., 1993-95. Co-author: Bootstrapping: . . ., 1993, West Virginia Politics and Government, 1996; mem. editorial bd. Am. Jour. Polit. Sci., 1994—; contbr. articles to profl. jours. Mem. Internat. Polit. Sci. Assn., So. Polit. Sci. Assn., Midwest Polit. Sci. Assn., Am. Polit. Sci. Assn. Office: WVa U Box 6317 Morgantown WV 26506-6317

MOONEY, EUGENE C., food company executive; b. 1944. With Fla. Ho. of Reps., Tallahassee, 1968-76, Citrus Cen., Orlando, Fla., 1977-84, L. D. Plant Inc., Oviedo, Fla., 1985-89, Silver Springs Citrus Coop., Ocoee, Fla., 1989-92, Winter Garden (Fla.) Citrus Coop., 1992; pres. Orange Co. Inc. Office: Orange Co Inc 2020 Us Highway 17 S Bartow FL 33830-7525

MOONEY, JAMES HUGH, newspaper editor; b. Pitts., Aug. 18, 1929; s. James H. and Kathryn A. (Hall) M.; m. Eileen Jane Casey, July 30, 1960; children: Mark Hall, Sean Francis, Annina Marie, James Matthew, Lorelei Jane, Paul Adam, Kathryn Celeste. B.A. in Journalism, Duquesne U., Pitts., 1957. With advt. dept., then editorial dept. Pitts. Post-Gazette, 1953-61; writer-editor Nat. Observer, 1961-77, Nat. Geographic, 1977-79; editor Found. News mag., Washington, 1979-81; press sec. Congressman Mickey Edwards of Okla., Washington, 1982; asst. nat. editor Washington Times, 1982-83; editor Status Report, 1983-92; dir. info. resources Ins. Inst. for Hwy. Safety, 1992-93; editor Western Pa. Medicine, Johnstown, 1993-95, Embassy Flash, Aspen Hill, Md., 1995—. Mem. editorial adv. bd. Nat. Study Ctr. Trauma and Emergency Med. Systems. Served with AUS, 1951-53. Mem. European Assn. Sci. Editors, Washington Automotive Press Assn., Nat. Press Club. Home: 13820 N Gate Dr Silver Spring MD 20906-2215

MOONEY, JOHN BRADFORD, JR., oceanographer, engineer, consultant; b. Portsmouth, N.H., Mar. 26, 1931; s. John Bradford and Margaret Theodora (Akers) M.; m. Martha Ann Huntley, Dec. 25, 1953 (dec. May 1990); children: Melinda Jean, Pamela Ann, Jennifer Joan; m. Jennie Marie Duca, Nov. 24, 1990. BS, U.S. Naval Acad., 1953; postgrad., George Washington U., 1970, 71, 76; grad. nat. and internat. security program, Harvard U., 1980. Commd. ens. USN, 1953, advanced through grades to rear adm., 1979; chief staff officer Submarine Devel. Group 1, 1971-73; commdr. Bathyscaphe Trieste II, 1964-66, Submarine Menhaden, 1966-68; comdg. officer Naval Sta., Charleston, S.C., 1973-75; dep. dir. Deep Submergence Systems Div., Office Chief Naval Ops., Washington, 1975-77; comdr. Naval Tng. Ctr., Orlando, Fla., 1977-78; dir. Total Force Planning Div., Office Chief Naval Ops., Washington, 1978-81; oceanographer USN, 1981-83, chief naval rsch., 1983-87, ret., 1987; pres. Harbor Br. Oceanographic Instn., Inc., Ft. Pierce, Fla., 1989-92, marine bd., 1991-94; bd. dirs. Coltec Industries, 1992—; mem. marine programs adv. coun. U. R.I., Narragansett, 1989—; chmn. study panel on undersea vehicles and nat. needs NRC, 1993—, mem. adv. com. for postdoctoral and sr. rsch. associateship programs, 1995—; mem. panel to visit the former Soviet Union to evaluate undersea tech. for U.S. govt., 1993, chair, 1995. At controls of Trieste II when hull of Thresher was found on floor of Atlantic, 1964; coordinated deep search and recovery of hydrogen bomb lost off coast of Spain, 1966; condr. recovery operation from depth of 16,400 feet in Mid-Pacific, 1972. Decorated Legion of Merit with 1 gold star; recipient spl. citation Armed Forces Recreation Assn., 1975, Dist. Eagle Scout award, 1986. Fellow NAE, Marine Tech. Soc. (pres. 1991-93), Explorers Club; mem. U.S. Naval Inst., Nat. Geog. Soc., Smithsonian Assocs., Masons, Shriners, Order of DeMolay, Tau Beta Pi. Avocations: racquetball, sailing. Home and Office: 2111 Jeff Davis Hwy #1009S Arlington VA 22202

MOONEY, ROBBI GAIL, operations officer; b. Hobbs, N.Mex., Dec. 11, 1955; d. Wilson Henry and Geneva Ann (Ober) Teague; divorced; children: Daymond, Ginger; m. Timothy G. Mooney, Oct. 18, 1991. Student, Ark. Valley Vocat.-Tech. Sch., 1977. Exec. sec. Jacuzzi, Inc., Little Rock, 1977-80; chief exec. officer Mid South Roller Co., Clarksville, Ark., 1981—. Mem. adv. coun. Ark. Valley Vocat. Sch., Ozark, 1990—. Mem. Am. Bus. Women (pres. 1986-89, Woman of Yr. award 1987), Rubber Roller Group, Clarksville C. of C., Rotary. Home: PO Box 1072 Clarksville AR 72830-1072 Office: Mid South Roller Co PO Box 130 Clarksville AR 72830-0130

MOONEY, ROBERT THURSTON, health care educator; b. Bryan, Tex., Jan. 5, 1935; s. Archie T. and Eda Belle (Arrington) M.; m. Jean Russell, June 24, 1955; children: Cynthia Mooney Conyers, Sandra Mooney Cook. BS, Tex. A&M U., College Station, 1958, MEd, 1963. Cert. trainer. Tchr. Navasota (Tex.) Ind. Sch. Dist., 1958-61; tchr. Bay City (Tex.) Ind. Sch. Dist., 1961-65, dir. audio-visual instrn., 1965-66; ednl. media specialist Ednl. Media Labs., Austin, Tex., 1967-68; dir. edn. and tng. Bexar County Hosp. Dist., San Antonio, 1968-75; asst. prof. Southwest Tex. State U., San Marcos, 1974-80, assoc. prof., 1980—, chmn. allied health scis., 1976-81, dir. health svcs. mgmt., 1988-90, dir. Health Resource Ctr., 1981-82; mayor pro tem City of San Marcos, 1995-96; dir. Sch. Paramed. Tng., Bexar County Hosp. Dist., San Antonio, 1970-72; cons. pvt. contractor, San Marcos, 1975—; mem. community/environ. task force Cen. Tex. Health Systems Agy., 1977; mem. health occupations edn. adv. com. Tex. Edn. Agy., 1989-91; mem. summer games organizing com. Tex. Spl. Olympics, 1990-91, security chmn., 1990; mem. health occupations projects adv. com. U. Tex., Austin, 1990-91. Author: Overhead Projection, 1968; (with Sister Rene Fisher and Beth Knox) Guidelines for the Development of a Hospital-Wide Education Service, 1979; contbr. articles to profl. jours. Chmn. disaster svc. Hays County Red Cross, San Marcos, 1988-89, bd. dirs., 1986-89; res. comdr. San Marcos Police Res., 1984-85; treas. Hays/Caldwell Counties Alcohol and Drug Abuse Coun., 1984-85, exec. bd. mem., 1984-85; res. dep. Hays County Sheriffs Dept., 1985-86, San Marcos Police Dept., 1986-87; zoning commr. City of San Marcos, 1991-93, city councilman, 1993-96; bd. dirs. Hays County Ctrl. Appraiser Dist., 1994—; bd. pres. San Marcos/Hays County EMS. Mem. ASTD, Am. Coll. Healthcare Execs., Soc. Human Resource Mgmt., Am. Soc. Healthcare Edn. and Tng. (bd. mem. 1971-72), Am. Hosp. Assn., Tex. Soc. Healthcare Educators (pres. 1971-72, pres. 1991-92, disting. svc. and achievement award 1989), Bay City Classroom Tchrs. Assn. (pres.), Navasota Classroom Tchrs. Assn. (pres.), Alamo Tng. and Insvc. Coun. Hosp. and Allied Health Educators (pres. 1969-71), Internat. Personnel Mgmt. Assn. (publs. adv. bd. 1988), Tex. Hosp. Assn., Assn. of Univ. Programs in Health Adminstrn., Soc. for Human Resource Mgmt. (reviewer HR magazine 1990—), Kiwanis. Home: 133 E Sierra Cir San Marcos TX 78666-2533 Office: Southwest Tex State U San Marcos TX 78666

MOONEYHAN, MARK EARNEST, secondary school educator, administrator, coach; b. Marion, Ind., June 30, 1959; s. Earnest Ray and Linda Sue (Montgomery) M.; m. Jo Michelle, Dec. 12, 1981; children: Nathaniel Ross, Corbett Ray. BS in Edn., Ball State U., 1981; postgrad., Valdosta State U., 1989—. Tchr. substitute Muncie (Ind.) Cmty. Schs., 1981-82; tchr. jr. high sch. Howe Mil. Acad., 1982-83; tchr. Ctr. Jr. High Sch., Waycross, Ga., 1983-94, asst. jr. high football coach, 1983-88, head jr. high girls basketball coach, 1983-94, head jr. high football coach, 1988—, jr. high athletic dir., 1988-94, asst. jr. high track coach, 1987-94; tchr. Ware Middle Sch., Waycross, 1994—, asst. h.s. football coach, 1994—, asst. jr. high wrestling coach, 1994—, head jr. high baseball coach, 1994—, asst. jr. high golf coach, 1994—; dir. Polynation Middle Sch. Summer Enrichment Program, 1992—; regional dir. Youth Sci. and Tech. Ctr., Okefenokee, Ga., 1994—; cons. and presenter in field; tchr. Confetti Summer Enrichment Program, 1985-92. Author: Frog Dissection Guide For The Middle School Student, 1990. Sports coach Y.M.C.A., Waycross; pres. Okefenokee Radio/Control Club. Recipient Ctr. Jr. High Tchr. of Month award, Waycross (Ga.) City Sch.'s Tchr. of Yr. award, 1985, Ga. Mid. Sch. Sci. Tchr. of Yr. award, 1991, Dist. 10 Sci. Tchr. of Yr. award, 1990, Katherine E. Foss Excellence in Edn. award, 1992, Presdl. award for Sci. and Math. Nomination, 1993; named Math and Sci. Roundtable honoree, 1990, System/Area Star Tchr., 1992, On-site Exemplary Tchr., 1992. Home: 1779 Meadowood Dr Waycross GA 31503-4514

MOOR, ANNE DELL, education director; b. Atlanta, Mar. 29, 1947; d. Kenneth Orman and Lida Louise (Springer) Dupree; m. Philip Ellsworth Moor, June 6, 1970; children: Andrew, Laura. BA, La Grange Coll., 1968. Cert. elem. edn. tchr., Tenn. Tchr. DeKalb County Bd. Edn., Atlanta, 1968-71, Briarcliff Bapt. Presch., Atlanta, 1972-73, Tates Sch., Knoxville, 1973-76; dir. after sch. care Cedar Springs Presbyn., Knoxville, 1993—. Discussion leader Bible Study Fellowship, Knoxville, 1980-93. Mem. Assn. for Childhood Edn. Internat., Tenn. Assn. for Young Children, Knoxville Area Assn. for Young Children. Presbyterian. Office: Cedar Springs Presbyn Ch 9132 Kingston Pike Knoxville TN 37923-5227

MOORE, ALICE CRAVENS, secondary school educator; b. Ridgely, Tenn., Dec. 14, 1947; d. Ezell and Rosa May (Stem) Ivy; m. Robert J. Cravens (dec. 1987); children: Christina Gann, Robert J. Cravens II, Casey Cravens; m. Mark Allen Moore, 1991; stepchildren: Kristina, Hailey. BS in Edn., U. Tenn., Martin, 1968; MEd, U. Memphis, 1976; postgrad., Freed-Hardemann U., 1988-91, Cumberland U., 1990-91. Cert. tchr., Tenn. Classroom tchr. Lake County Schs., Ridgely, 1968-69, Humboldt (Tenn.) City Schs., 1969—; motivational and inspirational speaker to ladies' groups and religious groups; interactive video tchr. Gibson County Schs., Humboldt, 1990—. Author: A New Song, 1988, Ways Which Be in Christ, 1990, Comforted of God, 1990; contbr. articles to profl. jours. Bd. dirs. Humboldt Pub. Libr., 1994—. Named Outstanding Young Educator Humboldt Exch. Club, 1976, Tchr. of Yr. Humboldt C. of C., 1994, Outstanding Tchr. Using Emerging Technologies South Ctrl. Bell, 1994, 95. Mem. Humboldt Edn. Assn., Tenn. Edn. Assn., NEA. Home: 3122 Northwood Humboldt TN 38343 Office: Humboldt Jr High Sch 1811 Ferrell St Humboldt TN 38343-2556

MOORE, CARL SANFORD, SR., management analyst local government; b. San Bernardino, Calif., Apr. 24, 1953; s. Wesley A. and Emily (Lawton) M.; m. Susan Johnson, Apr. 15, 1978; children: Josh, Carl Jr., Antoinet, Octavia. BA in Polit. Sci., U. S.C., 1975, MA in Pub. Adminstrn., 1976; cert. mgmt. analyst, Reneslarville Inst., Pa. Tax officer County of Charleston, Charleston, S.C., 1977-78; acct. clk. County of Charleston, Charleston, 1978-80, fixed assets mgr., 1980-83, buyer, 1983-85, sr. buyer, 1985-88, sr. mgt. analyst, 1988-96. Exec. com., panel leader Trident Unied Way-Allocations, Charleston, S.C., 1987-95; chmn. fin. com. Charleston County Human Svcs. Commn., 1991-94; commr. CoastalCarolina Softball League, 1991-94; sec. James Island (S.C.) Park Commn., 1992-96; mem. exec. bd., fin. chmn. Honeyhill Neighborhood Assn., 1992-95; exec. com. Boy Scouts Am., Charleston, 1993-96. Mem. Am. Soc. Pub. Adminstrn. (exec. com. local chpt.), S.C. Purchasing Assn., Assn. Mgmt. Analysts, Soc. Property Adminstrs. Republican. Methodist. Home: 1415 Fort Johnson Rd Charleston SC 29412 Office: 2 Court House Sq 6th Fl Charleston SC 29412

MOORE, CHARLES GERALD, educational administrator; b. Spartanburg, S.C., Oct. 29, 1949; s. Charles Edward and Betty Louise (Jarrett) M.; m. Carolyn Lancaster, June 15, 1977. BS, Clemson U., 1971, MA in Edn., 1983, postgrad., 1987—. Cert. vocat. dir., secondary supr., supt., prin. Agriculture tchr. Dorman High Sch., Spartanburg, 1977-87, asst. prin., 9th grade prin., 1987-90, asst. prin. 11th grade, 1990, vice prin. adminstrn., 1990-93; dir. technology edn. Spartanburg County Sch. Dist. 6, 1990-93; prin. Boiling Springs H.S., Spartanburg Dist. 2, 1993-96, Dorman H.S., Spartanburg, 1996—; mem. steering com. Upstate Tech. Prep. Consortium, 1990-93. Maj. USAFR, 1971—. Named S.C. Honor Roll Tchr., Dist. Tchr. of Yr. Mem. NEA, ASCD, Am. Assn. Sch. Adminstrs., Nat. Assn. Secondary Sch. Prins., S.C. Edn. Assn., Am. Vocat. Assn., S.C. Assn. Sch. Adminstrs., S.C. Assn. Secondary Sch. Prins. Home: 141 Waite Ave Spartanburg SC 29302-3089

MOORE, CHRISTOPHER BARRY, industrial engineer; b. Deal, Kent, Eng., Feb. 25, 1938; s. Ernest Stanley and Millicent Lillian (Harris) M.; diploma mgmt. studies Barking Regional Coll. Tech., Eng., 1966; m. Jill Irene Porter, July 6, 1963; came to U.S., 1977; children—Andrew, Stephen, Jeremy, Jennifer. Prodn. unit mgr. Plessey Co. Ltd., Ilford, Eng., 1968-70, productivity mgr., Upminster, 1970-72, regional indsl. engr., Ilford, 1972-74; mgr. mfg. devel. Northern Telecom Ltd., Montreal, Que., Can., 1974-77, dir. mfg. engring., Nashville, 1977-88; dir. mfg. devel. No. Telecom Inc., Atlanta, 1988—. Served with RAF, 1956-59. Mem. Am. Inst. Indsl. Engrs. (sr.), Inst. Electrical Engrs., Inst. Mgmt., Soc. Mfg. Engrs. (sr.), Ravinia Club. Home: 5167 Killingsworth Trace Norcross GA 30092-1739

MOORE, CHRISTOPHER ROBERTSON KINLEY, petroleum geologist; b. Manchester, England, Sept. 28, 1954; came to U.S., 1989; s. James Robertson Kinley and Irene (Mason) M.; m. Marian Isabel Pope, Sept. 3, 1977; children: Andrew Christopher, Scott David. BA, U. Cambridge, 1975, MA, 1979. Geologist Brit. Petroleum Co., Scotland, England, Tunisia, 1975-80; sr. geologist Tricentrol Oil Corp., London, 1980-88; planning mgr. ARCO Brit. Ltd., London, 1988-89; from exploration planning advisor to dir. exploration ARCO Internat. Oil & Gas Co., Plano, Tex., 1989—. Fellow Geol. Soc. London; mem. Am. Assn. Petroleum Geologists, Soc. Petroleum Engrs., Geol. Soc. Am. Home: 2133 Country Club Dr Plano TX 75074 Office: Arco Internat Oil & Gas Co 2300 W Plano Pkwy Plano TX 75075

MOORE, CLEMMIE ARCHER, elementary school educator; b. Ahoskie, N.C., Dec. 3, 1949; d. Everette Warren and Mary (Daniels) Archer; m. Bernard Moore, Nov. 23, 1972; children: Marlo Oweita, Amber Crystal. BS, Elizabeth City State U., 1971; MA in Edn., E. Carolina U., 1987. Cert. elem. edn. mentor. Tchr. 2d grade, instrnl. specialist Hertford County Bd. Edn., Winton, N.C., 1971—; mem. N.C. Teaching Excellence and Math. Project. Mem. N.C. Coun. Tchrs. Math., N.C. Assn. Educators. Home: PO Box Y Winton NC 27986-0325 Office: Hertford County Bd Edn 200 Talmadge Ave Ahoskie NC 27910-2500

MOORE, DAVID BRUCE, social service administrator, psychotherapist; b. Spring Valley, N.Y., Dec. 20, 1956; s. Benjamin Peter and Mary Elizabeth (Pitt) M.; m. Belinda Lee Ellis, May 14, 1978 (div. May 1987); 1 child, Katrina Lee; m. Neva Dawn Gilliatt, Dec. 31, 1992. BA, Carson-Newman Coll., 1978; MDiv, So. Bapt. Theol. Sem., Louisville, 1983; MSW, U. Louisville, 1984; PhD in Social Work, Pacific Western Univ., 1991. Diplomate Internat. Conf. for Advancement of Pvt. Practice Clin. Social Work. Social worker DHS, Kingsport and Rutledge, Tenn., 1978-80; psychiat. social worker Our Lady of Peace Hosp., Louisville, 1984-86; dir. social services Ky. Med. Inc. Med. Ctr., Louisville, 1986-88; outpatient dir. Ten Broeck Outpatient Ctr., Shelbyville, Ky., 1988-9; exec. dir., founder Family Life Ctr., Shelbyville, Ky., 1989—; lectr. U. Louisville, 1983-86; adj. lectr. Ind. U., New Albany, 1984; counselor Peace Counseling Referral Ctr., Louisville, 1985-86; cons. Home Mission Bd. So. Bapts., Louisville, 1984-86; social work cons. pvt. practice, Louisville, 1983-87; pvt. psychotherapist Wood & Assocs., Louisville, 1987—; outpatient coord. Ky. Med. Inc. Outpatient Ctr., Louisville, 1987-88; pastor So. Bapt. Ch., 1979-80; admissions coord., clin. social worker post-traumatic stress disorder program Dept. VA, Louisville, 1992—. Author: All Stressed Up and No Place to Go, 1990; editor: (guidebook) Ministers' Guide to Community Resources, 1985, (workbook) Stress Management, 1986; syndicated columnist on Family Relationships through So. Media Group, Inc. Cons. Wayside Christian Mission, Louisville, 1987; bd. dirs. Family Counseling Ctr., Louisville, 1986-89; diplomate Internat. Conf. for Advancement Pvt. Practice of Clin. Social Work; clin. cons. Coalition for the Homeless, Louisville, 1994—. Recipient Clyde T. Francisco Preaching award, 1983. Mem. NASW (diplomate clin. social work), Am. Assn. Sex Educators, Counselors and Therapists, Nat. Acad. Counselors and Family Therapists, Ky. Soc. Clin. Social Workers, Am. Acad. Cert. Social Workers (cert.), Am. Assn. Marriage and Family Therapists, Am. Group Therapy Assn., Internat. Conf. for Advancement of Pvt. Practice of Clin. Social Work (cert. psychoanalytic psychotherapy). Office: Family Life Ctr 720 Hospital Dr # 986 Shelbyville KY 40065-1685

MOORE, EDWARD RAYMOND, JR., pastor, chaplain, campaign consultant; b. Coos Bay, Oreg., Sept. 1, 1943; s. Edward Raymond Sr. and Daisy (Burnette) M.; m. Gail Pinckney, Aug. 23, 1969; children: E. Ray III, Richard P., Dorothy L., William R. BA in Polit. Sci., The Citadel, 1965; postgrad., Dallas Theol. Sem., 1965-68; MDiv cum laude, Grace Theol. Sem., 1974, ThM, 1979. Campus pastor at Purdue U. Trinity Fellowship, West Lafayette, Ind., 1977-85; so. regional dir. Freedom Coun., Virginia Beach, Va., 1985-86; state coord. Americans for Robertson (presdl. campaign), Columbia, S.C., 1986-88; v.p. for devel., pub. rels. Internat. Friendship Ministries, Columbia, 1988-89; pres. Frontline Ministries, Columbia, 1993—; chaplain USAR, Columbia, 1980—. Lt. Col., USAR, 1969-96, Persian Gulf. Decorated Bronze Star. Republican. Home: 4700 Norwood Dr Columbia SC 29206-1113

MOORE, EMMA SIMS, executive secretary; b. Branford, Fla., Oct. 27, 1937; d. Lawton Edward and Annie Ruth (Hewitt) Sims; m. H. Dean Moore, Sr., Sept. 30, 1961; 1 child, H. Dean Jr. Secretarial sci., Jones Coll., 1955; B., Butler U., 1984; MS, Ind. Wesleyan U., 1989; MA, The Fielding Inst., 1995, EdD, 1996. Cert. profl. sec.; cert. adminstrv. mgr. Sec. to svc. mgr. Buick Motor div. GM, Jacksonville, Fla., 1956-72, Charlotte, N.C., 1972-74; sec. to br. mgr. Motors Holding div. GM, Washington, 1974-78, Phila., 1978-82; exec. sec. to dir. product support Allison Gas Turbine div. GM, Indpls., 1982-92; ret., 1992; mem. faculty Ind.- Wesleyan U., 1993-94, Southern Wesleyan Univ. Central, S.C., 1995—. Mem. exec. com. Boy Scouts Am., West Chester, Pa., 1981-82. Mem. AAUW, NAFE (profl. secs. internat. goodwill people to people del. to People's Republic of China, Singapore, Thailand, Indonesia and Hong Kong), Profl. Secs. Internat. (v.p. 1986-87, pres. 1987-89, 500 chpt., Sec. of Yr. 1986 500 chpt., 1989 Ind. divs.), CPS Acad., Inst. Certification. Wesleyan. Home: 107 Catawbah Rd Clemson SC 29631-2826

MOORE, FAY LINDA, software quality engineer; b. Houston, Apr. 7, 1942; d. Charlie Louis and Esther Mable (Banks) Moore; m. Noel Patrick Walker, Jan. 5, 1963 (div. 1967); 1 child, Trina Nicole Moore. Student, Prairie View Agrl. and Mech. Coll., 1960-61, Tex. So. U., 1961, Our Lady Lake U., 1993, Thomas Edison State Coll., 1995-96; capability maturity model assessor tng. Software Engring. Inst., 1995. Cert. ISO 9000 Internal Auditor, 1994—. Instr. Internat. Bus. Coll., Houston, 1965; keypunch operator IBM Corp., Houston, 1965-67, sr. keypunch operator, 1967-70, programmer technician, 1970-72, asst. programmer, 1972-73, assoc. programmer, 1973-84, sr. assoc. programmer, 1984-87, staff programmer, 1987-94, staff systems analyst, 1994—; sr. software quality engineer Loral Space Info. Systems, Houston, 1994-96; owner, pres. AFT Co., Houston, 1993—; sr. software quality engr. Lockheed Martin Corp., Houston, 1996—; mem. space shuttle flight support team IBM, 1985-92; mem. space sta. team IBM, 1992-93. Recipient Apollo Achievement award NASA, 1969, Quality and Productivity award NASA, 1986, 1992. Mem. NAFE, Soc. Software Quality, Booker T. Washington Alumni Assn., Ms. Found. for Women, Inc. Democrat. Roman Catholic. Avocations: personal computing, board games. Office: Lockheed Martin Corp Mail Stop F6M1A 1322 Space Park Dr Houston TX 77058-3410

MOORE, FAYE HALFORD, jewelry manufacturer; b. Granville, Tenn., Oct. 16, 1941; d. Benton Mack and Dora Mai (Carter) Halfacre; m. Travis Edward Halford, Jan. 2, 1965 (div. 1989); children: Kristi Faye, Trent Edward; m. Charles Harold Moore, Jan. 23, 1989. BSBA, Tenn. Technol. U., 1963. Exec. sec. E.I. du Pont de Nemours, Old Hickory, Tenn., 1963-65, Amoco, New Orleans, 1965-66; adminstrv. asst. Thompson & Moss, Atlanta, 1967-72; founder, owner Strictly Natural, Ltd., Atlanta, 1975—, Elegant Accessories, Internat., Atlanta, 1980—. Pres. Sandy Springs Arts and Heritage Soc., Atlanta, 1986; founding dir. Leadership Sandy Springs, 1987; bd. dirs. Lindsey-Wilson Coll., Columbia, Ky., 1989, Cardinal Hill Hosp., Lexington, 1989, Ky. Ednl. TV Authority (vice chmn. 1992), Ky. Literacy Commn., Ky. Literacy Found., chmn. 1991; bd. dirs. Lexington Philharmonic Found., 1989, chmn. 1991—. Named Citizen of Yr. Sandy Springs Jr. Women's Club, 1976. Mem. Women Bus. Owners, Assn. Women Entrepreneurs (founder), Women's Commerce Club, Kiwanis. Democrat. Methodist. Home: 5900 Russell Cave Rd Lexington KY 40511-8441 Office: Strictly Natural Ltd 1845 The Exchange NW Atlanta GA 30339-2019

MOORE, GEORGE ELLIOTT, management consultant; b. Pilot, N.C., Nov. 20, 1935; s. Woodrow Wilson and Kate Nell Moore; m. Barbara Jean Spivey, Aug. 29, 1958; children: Sharon Lynne, Todd Elliott. BA, U. N.C., 1962. Exec. dir. Sci. and Humanities Symposium, Duke U., Durham, N.C., 1962-66; dir. fed. programs Roanoke (Va.) City Schs., 1966-68; dir. devel. Hollins (Va.) Coll., 1968-80; assoc. vice chancellor N.C. State U., Raleigh, 1980-83; exec. v.p., chief exec. officer N.C. Med. Soc., Raleigh, 1983-93; sr. cons. Mgmt. Concepts, Inc., Raleigh, 1994—; treas. Carolina Drs. Care, Inc., Raleigh, 1987-93, also bd. dirs.; bd. dirs. Med. Soc. Svcs., Inc., Raleigh, State Med. Jour. Advt. Bur., Inc., Chgo.; trustee, officer N.C. Med. Soc. Found., Inc., 1988-93. Contbg. author: Corporate Foundation Support for Public Institutions, 1985, Multiple Foundations: Advantages and Problems, 1986. Mem. adv. bd. Kate B. Reynolds Health Care Trust, Winston-Salem, N.C., 1983-93; committeeman N.C. Citizens for Bus. and Industry, Raleigh, 1984-94; bd. dirs. N.C. Forum for Rsch. and Econ. Edn., Raleigh, 1988-93; sec. bd. trustees Hollins Coll., 1968-80. Sgt. USMC, 1954-58. Recipient Grand award Alumni Programs, U.S. Steel Found., Pitts., 1978, Award for Excellence in Publs., Time Inc., N.Y.C., 1979, 80. Mem. Am. Soc. Assn. Execs., Am. Assn. Med. Soc. Execs., N.C. Inst. Medicine, Assn. Execs. N.C. (bd. dirs. 1983-93), Capital City Club, Raleigh Country Club, Pine Valley Country Club.

MOORE, G(EORGE) PAUL, speech pathologist, educator; b. Everson, W. Va., Nov. 2, 1907; s. George B. and Emma (Ayers) M.; m. Gertrude H. Conley, June 10, 1929 (dec.); children—Anne Gertrude Moore Dooley, Paul David; m. 2d, Grace MacLellan Murphey, Mar. 1, 1981. A.B., W. Va. U., 1929, D.Sc. (hon.), 1974; M.A., Northwestern U., 1930, Ph.D., 1936. Faculty dept. communicative disorders, Sch. Speech, Northwestern U., 1930-62, dir. voice research lab., 1940-62, dir. voice clinic, 1950-62; lectr. in otolaryngology Northwestern Med. Sch., 1953-62, dir. research lab. Inst. Laryngology and Voice Disorders, Chgo., 1957-62; prof. speech U. Fla., Gainesville, 1962-77, chmn. dept. speech, 1962-73, dir. communicative scis. lab., 1962-68, disting. service prof., 1977, acting chmn. dept. speech, 1977-78, disting. service prof. emeritus, 1980, adj. prof. elec. engring., 1981—; vis. faculty U. Colo., summer 1948, 51, 67, U. Minn., 1963, U. Witwatersrand, Johannesburg, S.Africa, summer 1971; co-chmn. Internat. Voice Conf., 1957; mem. communicative scis. study sect. NIH, 1959-63; mem. speech pathology and audiology adv. panel, Vocat. Rehab. Adminstrn., HEW, 1962, 64; mem. rev. panel speech and hearing, Neurol. and Sensory Disease Service Program, Bur. State Services, HEW, 1963-66, adv. com., 1964-67; mem. communicative disorders research tng. com. Nat. Inst. Neurol. Diseases and Blindness, NIH, 1964-68; mem. communicative disorders program project rev. com. Nat. Inst. Neurol. diseases and Stroke, 1969-73, chmn. 1971-72, mem. nat. adv. neurol. and communicative disorders and stroke council, 1973-77; mem. Am. Bd. Examiners in Speech Pathology and Audiology, 1965-67. Recipient merit award Am. Acad. Ophthalmology and Otolaryngology, 1962; Gould award William and Harriet Gould Found., 1962; Barraquer Meml. award Smith, Miller and Patch, 1969; Disting. Faculty award Fla. Blue Key, 1975; Tchr. Scholar award U. Fla., 1976; honors Ill. Speech, Lang. and Hearing Assn., 1979; Fellow Am. Speech-Lang.-Hearing Assn. (pres. 1961; Honors of Assn. award 1966); mem. Fla. Speech and Hearing Assn. (honor award 1977), So. Speech Assn., Speech Communication Assn. (Golden Anniversary award for scholarship 1969), Internat. Coll. Exptl. Phonology, Internat. Assn. Logopedics and Phoniatrics, Am. Assn. Phonetic Scis., AMA (spl. affiliate), Sigma Xi. Republican. Presbyterian. Club: Kiwanis. Author: Organic Voice Disorders, 1971; patentee laryngoscope, 1975; contbr. chpts. to books, articles to profl. jours. Home: 2234 NW 6th Pl Gainesville FL 32603-1409 Office: U Fla 63 Dauer Hall Gainesville FL 32611-2005

MOORE, HARRY RUSSELL, retired lawyer, consultant; b. Cumberland, Ohio, Dec. 28, 1921; s. Harry Alvin and Blanche Edith (Blackstone) M.; m. Marcella Virginia Williams, Jan. 12, 1946. Student, Ohio State U., 1940-41, U. Notre Dame, 1944-45, Naval War Coll., 1962-63; AB, George Washington U., 1964, AM in Internat. Affairs, 1965; JD, Internat. Sch. Law, Washington, 1977, George Mason U., 1982. Bar: Va. 1977, U.S. Dist. Ct. (we. dist.) Va. 1980, U.S. Ct. Appeals (4th cir.) 1982, U.S. Supreme Ct. 1990. Enlisted man USN, 1942, commd. ensign, 1945, advanced through grades to capt., 1967; combat svc. in South Pacific, 1943-44; in Vietnam, 1969; sea commands in Atlantic, U.S.S. Hawk (AMS-17), 1948-49, Mine Divsn. 85, 1960-62, U.S.S. Hugh Purvis (DD-709), 1965-67; U.S. naval attache, naval attache for air Am. Embassy, Karachi, Pakistan, 1967-68; sea command in Pacific, Mine Flotilla Three, 1968-69; ret. USN, 1972; pvt. practice law Moneta, Va., 1977-92; pvt. atty. Legal Aid Soc. Roanoke Valley (Va.), 1983-92; prof. nav. sci. Coll. of Holy Cross, Mass., 1970-72. Author: A Navigation Compendium, 1953, 2d edit., 1966, 3d edit., 1972. Decorated legion and merit. Mem. Va. State Bar (ret. status 1992), Bedford County Bar Assn. (ret. status 1992), Ret. Officers Assn., Am. Legion, Piedmont Beekeepers Assn., N.C. State Beekeepers Assn., Va. State Beekeepers Assn., Ea. Apicultural Soc., Internat. Bee Rsch. Assn. Anglican Catholic. Home: Honeymede Rte 4 Box 760 Moneta VA 24121

MOORE, HENDERSON ALFRED, JR., retired savings and loan executive; b. Hattiesburg, Miss., May 28, 1912; s. Henderson Alfred and Lucy Alice (Currie) M.; m. Mary Cleo Barnes, June 16, 1946 (dec. Dec. 1976); children: Betty Barnes Moore McKenzie, H.A., Lucy Currie Moore Pledger (dec.); m. 2d, Dot Marie R. Evans, Oct. 24, 1979. BA, U. Miss., 1934, LLB, 1936, JD, 1968. Bar: Miss. 1936. Mem. Moore and Jones, Hattiesburg, 1961-77, of counsel, 1977—; exec. v.p. Magnolia Fed. Bank for Savs. (formerly First Magnolia Fed. Savs. and Loan Assn., and formerly First Fed. Savs. and Loan Assn. of Hattiesburg), Hattiesburg, 1961-68, pres., 1968-77, chmn. bd., chief exec. officer, 1977-84, chmn. emeritus, 1984—; city pros. atty., 1938-41, 47-49; city judge, 1941-42, city atty., 1949-53. Mem. Forrest County Indsl. Bd., 1965-77; mem. Hattiesburg Redevel. Authority, 1981-87, vice chmn., 1984, chmn., 1985. Miss. Econ. Council, 1960-84. Lt. USN, 1942-46. Mem. Inst. Fin. Edn., Miss. Bar Found., ABA, South Central Bar Assn., Miss. State Bar, Newcomen Soc. N.Am., Miss. Econ. Council (dir. 1960-84), U.S. League of Savs. Assn. (dir. 1968-71, 74-77), Fed. Home Loan Bank (dir. 1973-74), Miss. Savs. and Loan League (past pres.), Southwestern Savs. and Loan Conf. (dir. 1965-67), Miss. Folklore Soc., Hattiesburg Civic Assn., Soc. War of 1812, SAR, Miss. Hist. Soc., Hattiesburg C. of C., U. So. Miss. Found., U. So. Miss. Alumni Assn. (Alumni Hall of Fame 1995), U. Miss. Alumni Assn., Pi Kappa Alpha, Phi Alpha Delta, Phi Kappa Phi, Hattiesburg Country Club, Elks. Home: 2312 Carriage Rd Hattiesburg MS 39402-2526 Office: 100 W Front St Hattiesburg MS 39401-3460

MOORE, HERFF LEO, JR., management educator; b. San Antonio, Jan. 24, 1937; s. Herff Leo Moore Sr. and Constance (Benesh) Wold; m. Helen Lucille Weidert, Nov. 1991; children by previous marriage: Terri Lynne, Christopher Scott, Kimberly Anne. BSBA, The Ohio State U., 1964; MBA, U. Tex., 1968; MS in Community Svcs., U. Rochester, 1976; PhD, U. Tex. at Arlington, 1980. Cert. sr. profl. in human resources. Prodn. mgmt., quality assurance officer Sacramento (Calif.) Air Logistics Ctr. USAF, 1964-67; personnel mgmt., adminstrv. cons. Aero. Systems Div. Wright-Patterson AFB, Dayton, Ohio, 1968-73; pers. mgmt. and quality assurance cons. Defense Contract Adminstrv. Svcs. Dist. Hdqrs., Rochester, N.Y., 1973-76; lectr. in mgmt. and doctoral student The Univ. of Tex. at Arlington, 1976-79; asst. prof. bus. adminstrn. Ea. Ky. U., Richmond, 1979-81; assoc. prof. mgmt. East Tex. State U. at Texarkana, 1981-83, Saint John Fisher Coll., Rochester, 1983-85, U. Cen. Ark., Conway, 1985—; pres. H.M.C.C. Mgmt. Group, Conway, 1988—; participant Leadership Texarkana Leadership Tng., 1981-82; mgmt. cons., Calif., N.Y., Ark., Ohio, N.J., Fla., Ga., Tex., 1964—. Author: (with others) Language, Customs and Protocol: A Guidebook for International Students and Employees, 1992; contbr. numerous articles to profl. jours. Capt. USAF, 1964-76. Recipient Significant Performance Contbr. award Def. Supply Agy., 1975; Nat. scholar Phi Kappa Phi, 1968; named Honor Grad. USAF Officers Tng. Sch., 1964. Mem. Soc. for Human Resource Mgmt. (tng. and devel. com. 1989-94, select panel on edn. 1989-91, coll. rels. com. 1989-92, bd. dirs. area IV 1987-91, sec., treas. Ark. coun. 1986-87), Ark. Human Resources Assn. (pres. 1991-92, bd. dirs. 1991-93), Acad. Mgmt., Soc. Human Resources Mgmt. (superior merit awards student chpt. U. Ctrl. Ark. 1985-90, 93), Alpha Kappa Psi, Phi Kappa Phi, Sigma Iota Epsilon. Methodist. Home: 15 Smoking Oak Rd Conway AR 72032-3617 Office: U Ctrl Ark Dept Mktg and Mgmt UCA Box 4983 Conway AR 72035

MOORE, HUGH JACOB, JR., lawyer; b. Norfolk, Va., June 29, 1944; s. Hugh Jacob and Ina Ruth (Hall) M.; B.A., Vanderbilt U., 1966; LL.B., Yale, 1969; m. Jean Garnett, June 10, 1972; children: Lela Miller, Sarah Garnett. Bar: Tenn. 1970, U.S. Dist. Ct. (mid. dist.) Tenn. 1970, U.S. Supreme Ct., 1973, U.S. Ct. Appeals (6th cir.), 1973, U.S. Dist. Ct. (ea. dist.) Tenn. 1973, U.S. Dist. Ct. (we. dist.) Tenn. 1982, U.S. Ct. Claims. 1993. Law clk. U.S. Dist. Court (mid. dist.) Tenn., Nashville, 1969-70; trial atty. civil rights div. U.S. Dept. Justice, Washington, 1970-73; asst. U.S. atty., Eastern Dist. of Tenn., Chattanooga, 1973-76; assoc. Witt, Gaither & Whitaker, P.C., Chattanooga, 1976-77, shareholder, 1977—, also bd. dirs.; mem. Commn. Women and Minorities Profession Law; mem. mediation panel U.S. Dist. Ct. (ea. dist.) Tenn.; cert. arbitrator Nat. Assn. Securities Dealers, N.Y. Stock Exch.; mem. adv. commn. on rules of civil and appellate procedure Tenn Supreme Ct. Mem. bd. dirs. Adult Edn. Council, Chattanooga, 1976-81, pres., 1977-79; bd. dirs. Chattanooga Symphony and Opera Assn., 1981-87, Riverbend Festival, 1983-85, 91—, pres., 1995—, Landmarks Chattanooga, 1983-84, Cornerstones, 1995—. Mem. alumni coun. McCallie Sch., 1980-85; trustee St. Nicholas Sch. 1983-89, chmn. 1986-88. Contbr. articles to profl. jours. Fellow Am. Coll. Trial Lawyers, Tenn. Bar Found., Chattanooga Bar Found.; mem. ABA (mem. bd. editors jour. Litigation News 1983-90), Tenn. Bar Assn., Chattanooga Bar Assn. (mem. bd. govs. 1985-87), Mountain City Club, Rotary. Methodist. Home: 101 Ridgeside Rd Chattanooga TN 37411-1830 Office: Witt Gaither & Whitaker 1100 Albany St Chattanooga TN 37405-2905

MOORE, JAMES E., state supreme court justice; b. Laurens, S.C., Mar. 13, 1936; s. Roy Ernest and Marie (Hill) M.; m. Mary Alicia Deadwyler, Jan. 27, 1963; children—Erin Alicia, Travis Warren. B.A., Duke U., 1958, J.D., 1961. Bar: S.C. 1961, U.S. Dist. Ct. S.C. 1961. pvt. practice, Greenwood, S.C., 1961-76; cir. judge 8th Jud. Cir. S.C., Greenwood, 1976-1991; Assoc. Justice S.C. Supreme Ct., 1992—; Mem. S.C. Ho. of Reps., Columbia, 1968-76. Mem. S.C. Bar Assn., ABA, Am. Judicature Soc. Baptist. Home: 148 Amherst Dr Greenwood SC 29649-8901 Office: PO Box 277 Greenwood SC 29648-0277

MOORE, JAMES TICE, history educator; b. Greenville, S.C., Aug. 8, 1945; s. William Furman and Aileen Sylvester (Pinion) M.; m. Jessie Louise Roberts, 1965; children: Leslie Anne, Evan Christopher, Sharon Elizabeth. BA in History, U. S.C., 1966; MA in History, U. Va., 1968, PhD in History, 1972. Instr. history Va. Commonwealth U., Richmond, 1970-72, asst. prof. history, 1972-78, assoc. prof. history, 1978-84, acting chmn. dept. history, 1981-82, chmn. dept. history, 1982-86, prof. history, 1984—; mem. editorial adv. bd. Jour. Southern History, Houston, 1982-85, Va. Mag. History & Biography, Richmond, 1988-91; bd. dirs. Univ. Press of Va., Charlottesville, 1986-89. Co-editor: The Governors of Virginia, 1860-1978, 1982; contbr. articles to books, profl. jours. & encys.; contbr. book revs. to various publs. Apptd. mem. Patrick Henry Meml. State Commn., Richmond, 1985-87. Danforth-Va. tchg. fellow, 1966-67; summer rsch. grantee Va. Commonwealth U., 1977, 92. Mem. Raven Soc. U. Va., Phi Beta Kappa, Phi Kappa Phi. Methodist. Home: 1703 Lauderdale Dr Richmond VA 23233-4007 Office: Va Commonwealth U Dept History Box 2001 Richmond VA 23284

MOORE, JEAN MOORE, secondary education educator; b. Selma, Ala., Oct. 30, 1945; d. James Freeman and Millie Jane (Bean) Moore; m. Herman Moore, Jr., June 27, 1975; stepchildren: Kevin, Kelvin. Diploma, Selma U., 1965; BS in English and History, Ala. State U., 1967, MEd in Secondary Edn., 1973. Cert. secondary tchr., Ala. Tchr. Keith High Sch., Orrville, Ala., 1967-75, 95—. Asst. sec. matron's div. Ala. Women's Bapt. State Conv., 1985—. Named Tchr. of Yr., Dallas County High Sch., 1983, 85; Selma U. Bus. and Profl. Womens scholar, 1964. Mem. NEA, Nat. Council Tchrs. English, Ala. Edn. Assn., Academic and Curriculum Devel. Assn., Dallas County Profl. Tchrs. (sec. 1984-85), Elks (Elk of Yr. award, Selma 1983), Order Eastern Star. Democrat. Home: 2712 Prospect Ln Selma AL 36703-1432

MOORE, JEANNE, arts educator and administrator; b. L.A., Aug. 28, 1932; d. George E. and Ellen Kearny (Patrick) M. AA, Pasadena (Calif.) City Coll., 1952; BA with honors, UCLA, 1954; MM, U. So. Calif., 1965, DMA, 1970. Music tchr. Arvin (Calif.) H.S., 1955-60, Santa Maria (Calif.) H.S., 1960-65, Arroyo H.S., El Monte, Calif., 1965-66; asst. prof. edn. U. Victoria, B.C., Can., 1968-70; asst. prof. music edn. Bowling Green (Ohio) State Coll., 1970-71; prof. music West Chester (Pa.) State Coll., 1971-72; lectr. music San Jose (Calif.) State U., 1972-73; asst. prof. music Madison Coll., Harrisonburg, Va., 1974-76; coord. fine arts W.Va. Dept. Edn., Charleston, 1977—; choral dir. Santa Maria Choral Soc., 1963-64, Silver Lake Presbyn. Ch., L.A., 1966-67, Wesley United Meth. Ch., San Jose, 1972-74; contbr./cons. Nat. Study of Sch. Evaluation, Falls Church, Va., 1983-85, 89. Author, editor more than 40 books/monographs; editor, project coord.: (6 books, audio and video) West Virginia Music Test Item Bank, K-4, 1989, (2 books, slides and video) West Virginia Museum Resources for Teaching Art, 1991; co-author: Beyond the Classroom: Informing Others, 1987. Staff mem. Gov.'s Task Force on Arts Edn., W.Va., 1990-94. Nat. Endowment for Arts grantee, 1989-90, 91-92. Mem. Nat. Art Edn. Assn., Nat. Coun. State Suprs. Music (pres. 1984-86), Music Educators Nat. Conf., W.Va. Music Educators Assn. (bd. dirs. 1977—, Presdl. award 1990), W.Va. Art Edn. Assn. (bd. dirs. 1986—, Outstanding Adminstr. award 1991, 92, 93), Phi Delta Kappa, Pi Kappa Lambda, Mu Phi Epsilon. Episcopalian. Home: 102 Brammer Dr Charleston WV 25311-1738 Office: WVa Dept Edn 1900 Kanawha Blvd E Rm B-330 Charleston WV 25305-0002

MOORE, JOANNA ELIZABETH, real estate professional; b. Hot Springs, Ark., Dec. 2, 1937; d. Herbert A. and Jewel (Mosier) Casey; m. Merlin Richard Moore, July 13, 1956; children: Melanie Moore Sevcik, Rick Moore, Michelle Moore Folks. Student, Bethany Nazarene Coll., 1956-57, Houston C.C., 1978, U. St. Thomas, 1987-88, 90—. Cert. residential specialist, Residential Sales Coun. of Realtors Nat. Mktg. Inst. Realtor Red Carpet Realtors, Temple, Tex., 1979-80, Century 21, Temple, 1981-85; broker-owner RE/MAX Realtors, Temple, 1986—; speaker Homebuilders Assn. seminars, 1985-88, 92. Fund chairwoman Bluebonnet coun. Girl Scouts U.S., 1987, mem. exec. bd., 1989; fund chairwoman March of Dimes, Temple, 1988; pres. Cen. Tex. chpt. Rep. Women's Club, 1983-84. Named Woman of Distinction, Girl Scouts U.S., 1992. Mem. Nat. Assn. Realtors, Tex. Assn. Realtors (mem. Polit. Action com. 1983-92), Temple-Belton Realtors (social chairwoman 1986, legis. chairwoman 1987, edn. chairwoman 1989), Temple Area Homebuilders (builder-realtor com. 1991, Realtor of Yr. 1993-95), Temple C. of C. (mem. govt. com. 1988, visitation com. 1989, tourist com. 1990, awards com., govt. affairs com. 1992). Home: 7112 Boutwell Dr Temple TX 76502-4204 Office: RE/MAX Realtors 4016 S 31st St Ste 200 Temple TX 76502-3348

MOORE, JOHN HENRY, II, federal judge; b. Atlantic City, Aug. 5, 1929; s. Harry Cordery and Gertrude (Wasleski) M.; m. Joan Claire Kraft, Dec. 29, 1951; children—Deborah Joan, Katherine Louise. Student, Cornell U., 1947; BS, Syracuse U., 1952; JD, U. Fla., 1961. Bar: Fla. 1961. Assoc. Fisher & Phillips, Atlanta, 1961; ptnr. Flemming O'Bryan & Fleming, Fort Lauderdale, Fla., 1961-67, Turner, Shaw & Moore, Fort Lauderdale, Fla., 1967; judge 17th Jud. Circuit, Fort Lauderdale, Fla., 1967-77, U.S. Dist. Ct. Appeals for 4th Cir., West Palm Beach, Fla., 1977-81; judge U.S. Dist. for Mid. Dist. Fla., Jacksonville, 1981-92, chief judge, 1992—; mem. Fla. Constitution Revision Com., 1977-78; chmn. Fla. Jud. Qualifications Commn., 1977-81. Bd. dirs. Community Service Council, Fort Lauderdale, 1970-75; pres. Broward County Assn. for Retarded Children, Fort Lauderdale, 1962; hon. bd. trustees Broward Community Coll., Fort Lauderdale, 1970. Served to comdr. USNR, 1948-71, Korea. Named hon. Alumnus Nova U., 1977; recipient cert. of good govt. Gov. of Fla., 1967. Mem. ABA, Fla. Bar Assn., Fed. Bar Assn., Jacksonville Bar Assn., Fla. Conf. Circuit Judages (chmn.-elect 1977), Fla. Blue Key (hon.), U.S. Navy League, Naval Res. Assn., Ret. Officers Assn. Republican. Presbyterian. Clubs: Timuquana Country, Jacksonville Quarterback, Seminole (Jacksonville). Lodge: Rotary. Office: US Dist Ct PO Box 53137 Jacksonville FL 32201-3137*

MOORE, JOHN REES, retired language educator, editor; b. Washington, Oct. 15, 1918; s. John Brooks and Florence Dubois (Rees) M.; m. Betty Lucille Drawbaugh, July 16, 1954; children: Steven Abel, Sarah Brooks. BA, Reed Coll., 1940; MA, Harvard U., 1942; PhD, Columbia U., 1957. Instr. U. Ga., Athens, 1946; asst. prof. Carnegie Tech., Pitts., 1946-47, Lehigh U., Bethlehem, Pa., 1947-50; instr. Columbia U., N.Y.C., 1954-57; prof. Hollins (Va.) Coll., 1957-85, prof. emeritus, 1985; v.p., pres. Am. Com. Irish Studies, 1965-71. Author: Masks of Love and Death: A Study of W.B. Yeats' Drama, 1970; co-author: The Idea of the American Novel, 1961; editor Hollins Critic, 1964-96; contbr. article to profl. jour. Sgt. USAF, 1942-45, England. Danforth grant Yeats Summer Sch., Sligo, Ireland, 1969, grantee Ford Found., 1973. Home: 7038 Goff Rd Hollins VA 24019

MOORE, JOHN STERLING, JR., minister; b. Memphis, Aug. 25, 1918; s. John Sterling and Lorena (Bounds) M.; m. Martha Louise Paulette, July 6, 1944; children: Sterling Hale, John Marshall, Carolyn Paulette. Student, Auburn U., 1936-37; AB, Samford U., 1940; ThM, So. Bapt. Theol. Sem., 1944. Ordained to ministry So. Bapt. Conv., 1942. Pastor chs. Pamplin, Va., 1944-48, Amherst, Va., 1949-57; pastor Manly Meml. Bapt. Ch., Lexington, Va., 1957-84, pastor emeritus, 1984—; mem. Hist. Commn., So. Bapt. Conv., 1968-75; pres. Va. Bapt. Pastor's Conf., 1963. Author: History of Broad Run Baptist Church, 1762-1987, 1987; co-author: Meaningful Moments in Virginia Baptist Life, 1715-1972, 1973; editor Va. Bapt. Register, 1972—; contbr. articles to profl. jours. Chmn. Lexington Mayor's Com. on Race Rels., 1962-65; bd. dirs. Stonewall Jackson Hosp., 1967-72, pres., 1969-71; treas. Rockbridge Mental Health Clinic, 1971-84. Recipient Disting. Svc. award Hist. Commn., So. Bapt. Conv., 1988. Mem. Am. Soc. Ch. History, So. Bapt. Hist. Soc. (bd. dirs. 1972-91, pres. 1975-76, sec. 1977-85), Va. Bapt. Hist. Soc. (exec. com. 1963—, pres. 1984-85), Va. Hist. Soc., Masons. Home: 8709 Gayton Rd Richmond VA 23229-6331

MOORE, KEVIN MICHAEL, federal judge; b. 1951. BA, Fla. State U.; JD, Fordham U. Bar: Fla. 1976. U.S. atty. no. dist. State of Fla., Tallahassee, 1987-89; dir. U.S. Marshals Svc., Arlington, Va., 1989-92; judge US. Dist. Ct. So. Dist. Fla., Miami, 1992—. Office: US Dist Ct Federal Justice Bldg 99 NE 4th St Rm 1168 Miami FL 33132-2139*

MOORE, LAWRENCE WILLIAM, law educator; b. Kansas City, Mo., July 17, 1946; s. James Andrew and Frances Claire (Kennedy) M. AB, St. Louis U., 1970, MA, 1972; MDiv, Jesuit Sch. Theology, 1977; JD, U. Mo., 1981; LLM, NYU, 1982. Bar: Mo. 1981; joined Soc. of Jesus, Roman Cath. Ch., 1964. Asst. prof. law Loyola U., New Orleans, 1982-85, assoc. prof. law, 1985-91, sec., treas., 1990—, prof. law, 1991—; bd. dirs. Loyola U., New Orleans. Support person Jesuit Vol. Corp., New Orleans, 1984-86. Mem. ABA. Roman Catholic. Home: 6363 Saint Charles Ave New Orleans LA 70118-6143 Office: Loyola U Sch of Law 7214 Saint Charles Ave New Orleans LA 70118-3538

MOORE, LINDA KATHLEEN, personnel agency executive; b. San Antonio, Tex., Feb. 18, 1944; d. Frank Edward and Louise Marie (Powell) Horton; m. Mack B. Taplin, May 25, 1963 (div. Feb. 1967); 1 child, Mack B.; m. William J. Moore, Mar. 8, 1967 (div. Nov. 1973). Student, Tex. A&I Coll., 1962-63. Co-owner S.R.O. Internat., Dallas, 1967-70; mgr. Exec. Girls Pers. & Modeling Svcs., Dallas, 1970-72, Gen. Employment Enterprises, Atlanta, 1972-88; owner, mgr. More Pers. Svcs., Inc., Atlanta, 1988-94, pres., chmn. bd., 1994—; Contbr. short story to Writer's Digest. Mem. NAFE, Nat. Fedn. Bus. and Profl. Women, Am. Soc. Profl. and Exec. Women, Women Bus. Owners, Nat. Assn. Women Cons., Nat. Assn. Personnel Svcs., Ga. Assn. Personnel Svcs., Women's Clubs, Atlanta C. of C. (speaker's bur.), Better Bus. Bur., Cobb County C. of C. Office: More Pers Svcs Inc Ste A-1190 4501 Circle 75 Pkwy Atlanta GA 30339

MOORE, LISA LYNNE, literary critic, English educator; b. Calgary, Alta., Can., Jan. 12, 1964; came to the U.S., 1986; d. Donald William and Nellie Joyce (Dick) M.; m. Lila Paige Warren, Jan. 11, 1997. BA with honors, Queen's U., Kingston, Can., 1986; MA, Cornell U., 1989, PhD, 1991. Asst. prof. U. Tex., Austin, 1991—. Mentor Austin (Tex.) Ind. Sch. Dist., 1994—. Social Scis. and Humanities Rsch. Coun. of Can. Doctoral fellow, Govt. Can., 1987-89. Mem. MLA, Am. Soc. for 18th Century Studies. Office: Dept English Univ Tex Austin Austin TX 78712-1164

MOORE, LOIS JEAN, health science facility administrator; married; 1 child. Grad., Prairie View (Tex.) Sch. Nursing, 1957; BS in Nursing, Tex. Woman's U., 1970; MS in Edn., Tex. So. U., 1974. Nurse Harris County (Tex.) Hosp. Dist., 1957—; pres., chief exec. officer Harris County Hosp.; adminstr. Jefferson Davis Hosp., Houston, 1977-88, exec. v.p., chief ops. officer, 1988—; Mem. adv. bd. Tex. Pub. Hosp. Assn. Contbr. articles to profl. jours. Mem. Mental Health Needs Council Houston and Harris County, Congressman Mickey Leland's Infant Mortality Task Force, Houston Crack-down Com., Gov.'s task force on health care policy, 1991; chairperson Tex. Assn. Pub. and Nonprofit Hosps., 1991, subcom. of Gov.'s task force to identify essential health care svc., 1992; bd. dirs. ARC, 1991—, Greater Houston Hosp. Coun., March of Dimes, United Way. Recipient Pacesetter award North-East C. of C., 1991; named Nurse of Yr. Houston Area League Nursing, 1976-77, Outstanding Black Achiever YMCA Century Club, 1974, Outstanding Women in Medicine YWCA, 1989. Mem. Am. Coll. Hosp. Adminstrs., Tex. Hosp. Assn. (chmn. pub. hosp. com.), Young Hosp. Adminstrs., Nat. Assn. Pub. Hosps. (bd. dirs., mem. exec. com. Tex. assn.), License Vocat. Nurses Assn., sigma Theta Tau. Home: 3837 Wichita St Houston TX 77004-6536 Office: Harris County Hosp Dist PO Box 66769 Houston TX 77266-6769

MOORE, MARCUS LAMAR, environmental engineer, consultant; b. Chattanooga, Mar. 6, 1965; s. Homer Douglas Jr. and Pansy Ann (Smith) M.; m. Deena Lee, May 20, 1989; children: Luke Copeland, Sarah Beth. BSME, U. Tenn., 1988. Registered prof. engr., Tenn. Mech. engr. David Talor R & D, Annapolis, Md., 1984-85, Acco-Cast, Inc., Chattanooga, 1985-86, Norton Chem., Soddy Daisy, Tenn., 1987-88, E.I. DuPont, Aiken, S.C., 1988-89; project engr. Nuclear Fuel Svcs., Erwin, Tenn., 1989-90; project and facility engr. Lockheed Martin Energy Systems, Oak Ridge, Tenn., 1990—; mem. Nuclear Crticality Safety Div., Knoxville, Tenn., 1989—, fin. com. Knox County Solid Waste Bd., 1993; judge Chattanooga Regional Engring. Fair, 1990-91. Contbr. articles to profl. jours. Leader Bapt. Assn., Johnson City, Tenn., 1990. Recipient DOE HQ award of excellence for hazardous waste shipment startup. Mem. ASME, Am. Nuclear Soc., Chattanooga Engr. Club, Phi Eta Sigma. Home: 9300 Camrose Ln Knoxville TN 37931-1523 Office: Lockheed Martin Energy Systems MS 8222 Bldg 9624 Oak Ridge TN 37830

MOORE, MARGARET BEAR, American literature educator; b. Zhenjiang, China, Mar. 14, 1925; came to U.S., 1929; d. James Edwin Jr. and Margaret Irvine (White) Bear; m. Rayburn S. Moore, Aug. 30, 1947; children: Margaret Elizabeth Moore Kopcinski, Robert Rayburn. BA, Agnes Scott Coll., 1946; MA, U. Ga., 1973. Book rev. editor East Ark. Record, Helena, Ark., 1948-50; bibliographer Perkins Libr. Duke U., Durham, N.C., 1950-52; instr. in English Hendrix Coll., Conway, Ark., 1955-56, U. Ctrl. Ark., Conway, 1958-59; editor Inst. Cmty. & Area Devel. U. Ga., Athens, 1974-79; tchr. Latin Athens Acad., 1980-81; ind. scholar Athens, 1981—. Author (book revs.) Am. Lit., 1989, 94, Nathaniel Hawthorne Rev., 1992; contbr. articles to profl. jours. Tchr. Presbyn. Ch., Va., Ark., N.C. and Ga., 1945—; deacon, elder First Presbyn. Ch., Athens, 1974—. Mem. MLA, Am. Lit. Assn., Philol. Assn. Carolinas, Soc. for Study So. Lit., South Atlantic MLA, Nathaniel Hawthorne Soc. (exec. com. 1987-90), William Gilmore Simms Soc., Peabody Essex Mus., House of Seven Gables, Va. Hist. Soc., Mortar Bd., Phi Beta Kappa, Phi Kappa Phi. Home: 106 Saint James Dr Athens GA 30606-3926

MOORE, MARILYN PATRICIA, community counselor; b. Nashville, Jan. 16, 1950; m. Roy Allen Moore; children: Christopher Manuel, Christina Marilyn, Catrina Marilyn. Merchandising cert., Bauder Coll., 1969; BS, Tenn. Wesleyan Coll., 1975; MEd., Tenn. Tech., 1979, EdS, 1981. Lic. profl. adminstr. and tchr., Tenn. Head resident/counselor Tenn. Wesleyan Coll., Athens, 1974-75; tchr. Rhea County Dept. Edn., Dayton, Tenn., 1975-81; prin. Rhea County Dept. Edn., 1981, 84-86; adj. coll. instr. Tenn. Tech. U., Cookeville, 1981—; coord. off campus program Tenn. Tech. U., 1981-86; tchr. Rhea County Dept. Edn., Dayton, 1982-83; prin. Rhea County Dept. Edn., 1983-86, supt. schs., 1986-90; evaluator, community intervention counselor Behavioral Health Svcs., Kingsport, Tenn., 1992-94, cmty. intervention counselor, 1994—; voting mem. Rhea County Purchase and Fin., Dayton, 1986—; adj. faculty East Tenn. State U., 1991, Holston Svcs., 1991. Chairperson Polit. Action Com. for Edn., Dayton, 1978-81; bd. dirs. Battered Women, Inc., Crossville, Tenn., 1987—; chairperson allocations United Way, Dayton, 1987-88; mem. Tenn. Sheriff's Assn., Nashville, 1988—; aide-de-camp Rep. Shirley Duer, Nashville, 1987; life mem. Presdl. Task Force, 1991—. Recipient Cert. Appreciation, Am. Legion, 1988, Cert. Participation, Very Spl. Arts, 1989, Am. Fedn. of Police Edgar Hoover award, 1991, John Edgar Hoover Meml. Gold medal, 1991; named Hon. Mem. Staff, Senator Anna Belle O'Brien, Nashville, 1987. Mem. NEA (past del.), Tenn. Edn. Assn., Tenn. Orgn. Sch. Supts., Alliance for a Drug Free Tenn. (chairperson 1987-91), Women Hwy. Safety Leaders Tenn. (county leader 1989—), USAF Aux. Aerospace (capt. 1987—), Tenn. Assn. Sch. Bus. Officials, Dayton C. of C., Nat. Police Assn. (Am. Patriotism award 1993). Republican. Methodist. Home: 205 Santa Fe Dr Bristol TN 37620-6441 Office: Behavioral Health Scis 425 E Stone Dr Kingsport TN 37660-4058 also: Family Healthcare Med Ctr 441 Clay St Kingsport TN 37662

MOORE, MARJORIE W., artist; b. Akron, Ohio, Mar. 17, 1944; d. Simon Louis and Louise (Jessup) Wansky; m. Steven A. Moore, Aug. 21, 1966; children: Ian, Jenny Hannah. BFA, Syracuse U., 1966. Graphic artist Syracuse (N.Y.) War on Poverty, 1966-67; tchr. U.S. Peace Corps, Sanandaj, Iran, 1967-69; craft-artist self-employed, Rumford Point, Maine, 1970-77; artist, painter self-employed, Brunswick, Maine, 1977—; artist, tchr. pvt. practice, Tex., 1993—. One-women shows include Barridof Galleries, 1986, Yezerski Gallery, Boston, 1988, 91, Portland Mus. Art, 1990, Weekend Gallery, Houston, 1996, Maj's Stuff Gallery 68, Belfast, Maine, 1993; exhibited in group shows Amarillo Mus. Art, 1995, Close to the Border N.Mex. State U., 1996, Intimate Observations, Baxter Gallery Maine Coll. Art, Portland, 1993, New Eng. Now, 1987-89. Recipient awards in visual arts, 1984, 86; fellow New Forms Fellowship, 1991, Regional Fellowship, 1992, NEFA, Earthwatch Artists Fellowship, 1993, Creative Artist Fellowshop Cultural Arts Coun. Houston, 1996; grantee Maine Arts Inc., 1986, Nat. Endowment for Arts and Rockeller Found., 1987, New Eng. Found. for Arts, 1991; fellow MacDowell Colony, 1989. Mem. Union of Maine Visual Artists. Democrat. Home: 1821 Nueces Dr College Station TX 77840

MOORE, MARKITA ALBERTA, charitable trust program officer; b. Trenton, N.J., Dec. 12, 1958; d. George Azel Jr. and Katherine (Easley) M. BA, Dartmouth Coll., 1980; BS in Pub. Health, U. N.C., 1982, MPH, 1983, DPH, 1990. Nutritionist I West Midlands health dist. S.C. Dept. Health and Environ. Control, West Columbia, 1984-85; rsch. asst. bieenial survey pub. health nutrition programs U. N.C., Chapel Hill, 1986-89, acting nutrition sect. head Clin. Ctr. for Study of Devel. and Learning, 1987-88; exec. dir. S.C. Maternal, Infant and Child Health Coun. Office of the Gov., Columbia, 1990; exec. mgr. Office of the Exec. Dir. S.C. Kids Count, S.C. Budget and Control Bd., Columbia, 1991—; program officer Kate B. Reynolds Charitable Trust, Winston-Salem, N.C., 1994—. U. N.C. fellow, Chapel Hill, 1982-83, 86-90; USPHS grantee, 1985-86; traineeship Boling Ctr., Child Devel. Ctr., U. Tenn., Memphis, 1989; recipient Outstanding Young Woman of Yr. award Jaycees, Columbia, S.C., 1993. Mem. Continental Socs., Inc., Jr. League of Winston-Salem, N.C., Delta Sigma Theta. Home: 819 Braehill Blvd Winston Salem NC 27104-5391 Office: Kate B Reynolds Charitable Trust 128 Reynolda Village Winston Salem NC 27106

MOORE, MARY ELLEN, community health, hospice nurse; b. New Milford, Conn., May 16, 1949; d. Robert J. and Josephine (Parylak) Moore; divorced. BSN, Russell Sage Coll., 1971; postgrad., Boston U. Head nurse Faulkner Hosp., Jamaica Plain, Mass., Hebrew Rehab. Ctr., Roslindale, Mass.; nurse Hospice of Wilkes Inc./Wilkes Regional Med. Ctr., North Wilkesboro, N.C., 1982-90; charge nurse inpatient unit Caldwell County Hospice, Lenoir, N.C., 1990-94; cons., insvc. instr. Home Care Mgmt. Corp., 1994-95; supr. health svcs. Home Care Mgmt. Corp., Lenoir, N.C., 1995—; mem. ethics com. Wilkes Regional Med. Ctr., 1990-92; mem. profl. adv. bd. Hospice of Wilkes, Inc. Sec. 1st Responders of Boomer; treas., bd. dirs. Ctr. for Awakening; active United Way, other cmty. projects; head class agt. Russell Sage Alumnae Assn., 1996. Boston U. scholar. Home: PO Box 3204 Lenoir NC 28645-3204 Office: Ste 100 506 Wilkesboro Blvd SE Lenoir NC 28645

MOORE, MICHAEL T., lawyer; b. Mullins, S.C., Feb. 21, 1948; s. Claude Richard and Melinda Doris (Stone) M.; m. Leslie Jean Lott, Nov. 12, 1978; children: Michael T. Jr., Emmett Russell Lott. BA, U. Fla., 1970, JD, 1974. Assoc. Burlingham, Underwood & Lord, N.Y.C., 1974-77, Hassan, Mahassni, Burlington, Underwood & Lord, Jeddah, Saudi Arabia, 1977-79; ptnr. Holland & Knight, Miami, Fla., 1982—; bd. dirs. Holland & Knight, Miami, 1986—, exec. ptnr. Miami office, 1993—; bd. dirs. Marine Arbitration Bd., Inc., Miami, 1985—; pres. The Marine Coun., 1989-90. Editor-in-chief Southern District Digest, 1980-82; contbr. articles to profl. jours. Mem. Orange Bowl Com.; bd. dirs. United Way Greater Miami, 1994—, U.S. Sailing Ctr., YMCA; chmn. Alexis de Tocqueville Soc.; mem. Miami River Coordinating Com.; trustee St. Stephens Sch.; mem. Coral Gables (Fla.) Youth Adv. Bd. Mem. ABA, Maritime Law Assn. U.S., Fla. Bar Assn., Dade County Bar Assn. (bd. dirs. 1981—, Outstanding Young Lawyer award 1982). Republican. Home: 3515 Anderson Rd Miami FL 33134-7050 Office: Holland & Knight 701 Brickell Ave PO Box 15441 Miami FL 33101

MOORE, MIKE, state attorney general; m. Tisha Moore; 1 child, Kyle. Grad., Jackson County Jr. Coll., 1972; BA, U. Miss., 1974, JD, 1976. Asst. dist. atty. State of Miss., 1977-78, dist. atty., 1979, atty. gen., 1988—. Mem. ABA, Miss. State Bar Assn. Office: Office of Atty Gen PO Box 220 Jackson MS 39205-0220*

MOORE, REBECCA ANN RUCKER, speech-hearing and language therapist; b. Little Rock, Aug. 29, 1952; d. Thurman K. and Wilibel (Hester) Rucker; m. Thomas Daniel Moore, Oct. 2, 1976 (div. July 1985); 1 child, Lauren Elizabeth. BA in Speech-Hearing and Lang. Pathology, Baylor U., 1974, postgrad., 1976; postgrad., Henderson State U., 1988. Lic. speech-hearing-lang. pathologist, Tex., Ark. Speech therapist Dripping Springs Kindergarten, Waco, Tex., 1974-76, Oakwood Early Childhood, Waco, 1976-80, Gurley Elem. Sch., Waco, 1981-82, Connelly Northcrest Elem. Sch., Waco, 1982-83, Connelly High Sch., Waco, 1982-83; dir. curriculum First Bapt. Ch., Waco, 1984-86; coord. early childhood edn. First Bapt. Ch., Arkadelphia, Ark., 1986-89; speech therapist Gurdon (Ark.) Ind. Schs., 1989-92, Popham Elem., Del Valle, Tex., 1992-95; pvt. bus. owner, 1995—; vis. lectr. Weekday Early Edn. Conv., Little Rock, 1987, 88, 89. Mem. steering com. weekday early edn. program So. Bapt. Conv., Little Rock, 1986-88; mem. pre-sch. coordinating com. Dawson Ednl. Corp., Arkadelphia, 1988-89. Home: 7212 Chimney Cors Austin TX 78731-2147

MOORE, RICK ALAN, insurance adjuster; b. Muskogee, Okla., July 14, 1968; s. Donald Lee and Betty Lois (Barney) M. BBA, Northeastern State U., Tahlequah, Okla., 1992; A in Claims, Ins. Inst. Am., Malvern, Pa., 1995. Real estate sales assoc. Lancaster Agy., Wagoner, Okla., 1991-95; sr. claim rep. State Farm Fire & Casualty, Tulsa, 1993—; mem. spl. disaster team State Farm Fire & Casualty, Muskogee, Okla., 1993-95; mem. Mental Health Planning and Coordination Bd., 0kla., 1995. N.E. bur. chief quar. newspaper The Okla. Constn., 1991—. Del. Okla. State Rep. Conv., Oklahoma City, 1993, 95; precinct chair Wagoner County Rep. Party, 1993, 94; co-founder, bd. dirs. Eternity Fraternity Ministry of Faith for Youth, 1995. Recipient Blue Key award Okla. Rep. Party, 1993, 95; named to Outstanding Young Men of Am., 1992. Mem. Internat. Assn. Arson Investigators, SCV (adj./treas. 1993—), The Conservative Forum, Pi Kappa Alpha. Republican. Baptist.

MOORE, ROBERT BLAINE, biochemistry and cell biology educator, researcher; b. Toronto, Ont., Can., July 27, 1949; came to U.S., 1978; s. Kenneth Wayne and Dorothy Mary (Camamile) M.; m. Elizabeth Gizella Köszegi, Aug. 4, 1973; children: Nicole Elizabeth, Paul Kery. BSc, U. Toronto, 1972, MSc, 1974, PhD, 1978. Postdoctoral fellow in neurology Baylor Coll. Medicine, Houston, 1978-82; asst. prof. biochemistry dept. pediatrics U. South Ala., Mobile, 1982-90, assoc. prof., 1990—, assoc. dir. Sickle Cell Ctr., 1989-92, interim dir., 1992-93, mem. exec. com. faculty senate, 1989-93; trainee NIH, Bethesda, Md., 1980-82; hematology rschr. Co-editor: Sickle Cell Disease: Pathophysiology, Diagnosis and Management, 1993. Scholar U. Toronto, 1971; fellow Muscular Dystrophy Assn. Can., 1978-80; grantee NIH, 1983-86. Fellow Am. Inst. Chemists; mem. AAAS, Am. Soc. Biochemistry and Molecular Biology, Am. Soc. Hematology, N.Y. Acad. Scis., Order of Grape (coord. Mobile 1983—). Methodist. Home: 6508 Sugar Creek Dr N Mobile AL 36695-2733 Office: U So Ala Med Ctr Dept Pediatrics 2451 Fillingim St Mobile AL 36617-2238

MOORE, ROBERT PAUL, elementary school educator; b. Houston, July 1, 1968; s. Robert Vance and Joyce Mae (Mikulenka) M. A in Behavioral Scis., San Jacinto Jr. Coll., Pasadena, Tex., 1988; BS in Edn. cum laude, U. Houston, 1991. Cert. tchr., Tex. Tchr. 5th grade math., sci. and social studies W. A. Carpenter Elem. Sch., Deer Park, Tex., 1992—, adv. com. campus improvement com., 1992-94, rep. dist. improvement com., 1996-97, campus tech. support leader, 1996-97; chmn. yearbook com., 1992-95, sponsor student coun., 1992-93, 93-94, mem. inclusion com., 1993-94, portfolio assessment com., 1993-94, hall monitor supr., 1995—; mem. social studies essential elements clarification team, 1995-97. Mem. ASCD, NEA, Nat. Coun. Tchrs. Math., Assn. Tex. Profl. Educators, Tomorrow's Tchrs. Club, Phi Delta Kappa, Kappa Delta Pi. Roman Catholic.

MOORE, RONALD QUENTIN, minister; b. Langley, S.C., Aug. 12, 1939; s. George Quentin and Jennie Evelyn (Workman) M.; m. Doris Lorene Jones, July 5, 1959; children: David Quentin, Timothy Ray, Phillip Edward. BTh, Holmes Theol. Sem., Greenville, S.C., 1960; BA, Central (S.C.) Wesleyan Coll., 1969; MEd, Clemson U., 1975; postgrad., Columbia (S.C.) Bible Sem., Fuller Theol. Sem.; DD (hon.), Holmes Coll. of the Bible, Greenville, S.C., 1991; M. in Min., Southwestern Coll. of Christian Min. Ordained to ministry Pentecostal Holiness Ch., 1959. Founder, pastor Pentecostal Holiness Ch., Belvedere, S.C., 1961-64; pastor Pentecostal Holiness Ch., Easley, S.C., 1965-70, Taylor Meml. Pentecostal Holiness Ch., Anderson, S.C., 1970-75; asst. dir. world missions dept. Pentecostal Holiness Ch., Okla., 1975-90; pres. Southwestern Coll. Christian Ministries, Oklahoma City, 1990—; chmn. Pastoral Care Dept. Internat. Pentecostal Holiness Ch., Oklahoma City, 1989—. Assoc. editor (mag.) Worldorama, 1975-90; exec. editor INSIGHT, Southwestern Alumni Assn., 1990—; contbr. articles to Advocate Pentecostal Holiness Ch. Office: Southwestern Coll Christian Ministries 7210 NW 39th Expy Bethany OK 73008-2321

MOORE, SHERYL STANSIL, medical nurse; b. Birmingham, Ala., May 17, 1963; d. Willie Caesar and Irene (Fisher) Stansil; m. Kyle R. Moore, Aug. 5, 1994; children: Tyler Christina Lowe, Danladi, William. BSN, Dillard U., 1987; MSN in Trauma Nursing, U. Ala. in Birmingham, 1992. Staff nurse Nursefinders, Colorado Springs, Colo., 1994—, Progressive Care Ctr., Terrace Gardens, Colo., 1995—; instr. clin. nursing Beth-El Coll. Nursing, 1995; past instr. clin. nursing Beth-El Coll. Nursing; beauty cons. Mary Kay Cosmetics, 1996—. Named one of Outstanding Young Women of Am., 1988. Mem. ANA, AACN, State Nurses Assn., AMSN. Home: 1985 Mittenwald Dr #102 Colorado Springs CO 80918

MOORE, STANLEY RAY, lawyer; b. Dallas, July 20, 1946; s. Elzey and Heloise (Dillon) M.; children—Natalie, William. B.S.M.E., So. Meth. U., 1969, J.D., 1973. Bar: Tex. 1973; U.S. Dist. Ct. (no. dist.) Tex. 1974. Assoc. Clegg, Cantrell, Crisman, Dallas, 1973-75; ptnr. Crisman & Moore, Dallas, 1975-80, Schley Cantrell & Moore, Dallas, 1980-83, Schley, Cantrell, Kice & Moore, Dallas, 1983-87, Johnson & Wortley, P.C., 1987-94, Jenkews & Gilchrist, 1995—. Patentee in field. Foster parent Hope Cottage, Dallas, 1982-90; fund raiser Am. Heart Assn., Republican Party. Recipient Outstanding Leadership commendation ASME, 1969. Mem. Dallas Bar Assn., ABA, Am. Patent Law Assn. Baptist. Home: 1 Victoria Cir Rowlett TX 75088-6059 Office: Jenkews & Gilchrist 1445 Ross Ave Ste 3200 Dallas TX 75202-2770*

MOORE, STEPHEN TIMOTHY, artist, museum registration technician; b. Memphis, Sept. 17, 1947. Student, Memphis Acad. Arts, summer 1968; BFA in Painting, Memphis State U., 1969; MFA in Painting, U. Fla., 1971. Grad. tchg. asst. dept. art U. Fla., Gainesville, 1969-71, illustrator II Coll. Dentistry and Learning Resources Ctr., 1972-76; instr. art Shenandoah Coll. and Conservatory of Music, Winchester, Va., 1976-79; lectr. art No. Va. C.C., Sterling, 1978-79; asst. dir. Gallery K, Washington, 1980-81; instr. art Corcoran Sch. Art, Washington, 1981-84; adj. instr. art Corcoran Sch. Art, 1988-89; preparator Corcoran Gallery of Art, Washington, 1982; exhibit specialist Nat. Mus. Art and The Renwick Gallery Smithsonian Instn., Washington, 1984, 85-86; mus. registration technician Hirshhorn Mus. and Sculpture Garden Smithsonian Instn., Washington, 1991—; co-founder HMB Art Transfer, Washington, 1984-85; art svcs. technician Nat. Gallery of Art, Washington, 1986-88; instr. art The New Black Mountain (N.C.) Coll., 1989; vis. artist, lectr. Memphis State U., 1981, Tunxis C.C., Farmington, Conn., 1981, 85, Colo. Coll., Colorado Springs, 1983, Tulane U., New Orleans, U. Miss., Oxford, Prince George's C.C., Largo, Md., Conn. Coll., New London, 1987, The Penland (N.C.) Sch., U. N.C., Asheville, 1989, Valencia C.C., Orlando, Fla., 1995; juror juried art competition, Maitland (Fla.) Art Ctr., 1996. One-man shows include Shenandoah Coll. and Conservatory of Music, Winchester, Va., 1976, Fraser's Stable Gallery, Washington, 1977, Eric Schindler Gallery, Richmond, Va., 1979, Addison/Ripley Gallery, Washington, 1983, Foxley/Leach Gallery, Washington, 1986, 88, Conn. Coll., New London, 1987, Arnold & Porter, 1993; exhibited in group shows at Jack Rasmussen Gallery, Washington, 1980, Allan Stone Gallery, N.Y.C., 1980, Still/Zinsel Gallery, New Orleans, 1988, David Adamson Gallery, Washington, 1989, 90, 92, Vanderbilt U., Nashville, 1990, Tartt Gallery, Washington, 1991, Sylvia Schmidt Gallery, New Orleans, 1991, Franco-Norwegian Cultural Exch., Stavanger, Norway, 1991, Corcoran Gallery of Art, Washington, 1992, Franz Bader Gallery, Washington, 1992, Collector Gallery, Washington, 1993, Southside Gallery, Oxford, Miss., 1994, Internat. Gallery, Ripley Ctr., Smithsonian Inst., 1996—, numerous others; represented in permanent collections of Susquehanna Art Mus., Harrisburg, Pa., Mus. Contemporary Art, Chamalieres, France, Fine Arts Mus. of the South, Mobile, Ala., The Artery Corp., Bethesda, Md., Washington Post Co., E.F. Hutton & Co., N.Y.C., Lerner Corp., Rockville, Md., Valley Nat. Bank, Phoenix, Shenandoah Coll. and Conservatory of Music, E.H. Little Gallery Memphis State U. Dept. Art, Office of Mayor City of Orlando, Fla., Harn Mus. Art, U. Fla., Gainesville, Corcoran Gallery Art, Washington (collections) Mus. Fine Art, Fla. State U., Tallahassee; represented in numero us private collections. Visual artist grantee D.C. Commn. on Arts and Humanities, 1987-88. Office: Registrar's Office Hirshhorn Mus and Sculpture Washington DC 20560

MOORE, TERESA ANN, middle school mathematics educator; b. Houston, June 16, 1953; d. Leodis Fredrick and Annie V. (Daughtry) Barnes; m. Alton Earl Moore, Sr., June 29, 1974 (div.); children: Alton E. II, Erik Renard, Tiffany Nacole. BS in Math., Prairie View A&M U., 1974. Math. tchr. Sam Houston High Sch. Houston Ind. Sch. Dist., 1975-78, math. tchr. Kashmere Sr. High Sch., 1979-84, math. tchr. T. H. Rogers Mid. Sch., 1989—; math. tchr. Forest Brook High Sch. North Forest Ind. Sch. Dist., Houston, 1986-89; math. tchr. Houston Community Coll. Systems, 1982-86, Tex. So. Upward Bound Prog., Houston, 1986-88; chpt. 1 coord. Bonham Elem. Sch., Houston, 1994—; title 1 specialist Houston Ind. Sch. Dist., 1995—; curriculum writer/math. North Forest Ind. Sch. Dist., 1988, gifted and talented/math. Houston Ind. Sch. Dist., 1991, master tchr. math., 1993, Rice U., 1993; spkr. for ednl. seminars Houston Ind. Sch. Dist. and Region IV. Adminstrv. sec. Northeast Nursing Bd. Dirs., 1987—; bd. dirs. LaPorte (Tex.) Apothecary, 1985—; mem. Shepherd Park Terrace Civic Club, Houston, 1976—. Named Coll. Woman of Yr., Prairie View (Tex.) A&M U., 1973, Outstanding Black Educator, Lydia Brew's Ednl. Soc., 1992-93, Tchr. of Yr., Houston Coun. Tchrs. Math., 1992-93, HISD Tchr. of Yr., 1992-93; recipient MathCounts 1st Place Coach regionals award Tex. Soc. Profl. Engrs., 1991, 2d Place region, 1990; Collins Hall scholar, 1973, 74. Mem. Tex. Coun. Tchrs. Maths., Nat. Coun. Tchrs. Math., Houston Area Alliance of Black Sch. Educators (Tchr. of Yr. 1992-93), Nat. Alliance Black Sch. Educators, Afro-Am. Assn. Math. Educators, Alpha Kappa Alpha. Republican. Home: 5422 Sue Marie Ln Houston TX 77091-5640 Office: T H Rogers Sch 5840 San Felipe St Houston TX 77057

MOORE, THOMAS ALVA, information services director; b. Walnut Ridge, Ark., Sept. 29, 1951; M. Darlene; 1 child, Matthew. BS in Journalism, Ark. State U., 1973, MPA, 1991. Staff writer, photographer The Jonesboro (Ark.) Sun, 1973-76; staff writer, photographer The Times Dispatch, Walnut Ridge, 1976-77, editor, 1977-85; dir. news and info. svcs. office instnl. advancement Ark. State U., Jonesboro, 1985—; mem. Coun. Advancement and Support of Edn., 1985—; lectr., concert com. Ark. State U. Presenter in field. Named Outstanding Alumnus, Lambda Chi Alpha, 1985; Ark. Endowment for Humanities grantee, 1982-83. Mem. Soc. Profl. Journalists, Ark. Press Assn. (assoc., In-depth Reporting award Weeklies Divsn. 1983, News Photography award 1977, 78, 80), Ark. Broadcasters Assn. (assoc.), Lawrence County Hist. Soc. (pres. 1981-84, bd. dirs. 1989-92, 95—, Sesquicentennial Project Commendation award 1986), Kiwanis Club of Walnut Ridge (pres. 1984, v.p. 1981-83), C. of C. (Walnut Ridge pres. 1982, v.p. 1981, bd. dirs. 1980). Democrat. Baptist. Home: 415 Eastwood Cir Walnut Ridge AR 72476-2027 Office: Ark State U News and Info Svcs PO Box 1990 State University AR 72467-1990

MOORE, THOMAS KAIL, chief judge; b. Idaho Falls, Idaho, Jan. 15, 1938; s. Burton L. and Clara E. (Kail) Moore; m. Judith Diane Gilman, July 30, 1966; children: David T., Jonathan G. AB in Phys. Scis., Harvard U., 1961; JD, Georgetown U., 1967. Bar: D.C., V.I., Va. Law clk. to Hon. John A. Danaher U.S. Ct. Appeals (D.C. Cir.), 1967-68; staff atty. Office Gen. Coun., Office Sec. Dept. Transp., Washington, 1968-69; assoc. Stanford, Reed & Gelenian, Washington, 1969-70; asst. U.S. Atty. U.S. Attys. Office, Washington, 1970-71; asst. U.S. Atty. U.S. Attys. Office (ea. dist.), Va., 1971-76, prin. asst. Alexandria office, 1974-76; asst. U.S. Atty. U.S. Attys. Office (V.I. dist.), 1976-78; pvt. practive St. Thomas, V.I., 1978-81; shareholder Hoffman & Moore, P.C., St. Thomas, 1981-87; ptnr. Grunert, Stout, Moore & Bruch, St. Thomas, 1987-92; chief judge U.S. Dist. Ct. (V.I. dist.), 1992—. Editor-in-chief Georgetown Law Journal, 1966-67. Scoutmaster Antilles Sch. Troop; trustee V.I. Montessori Sch. Capt. USAF, 1961-64, USAFR. Mem. ABA, V.I. Bar Assn. (judicial), V.I. C. of C., St. Thomas Yacht Club. Office: Dist Ct of VI 5500 Veterans Dr Ste 310 Charlotte Amalie VI 00802-6424

MOORE, THURSTON ROACH, lawyer; b. Memphis, Dec. 10, 1946; s. Richard Charlton Moore and Halcyon Hall (Roach) Lynn; m. Grace Branch, Nov. 8, 1969. BA with distinction, U. Va., 1968, JD, 1974. Bar: Va. 1974. Rsch. analyst Scudder, Stevens & Clark, N.Y.C., 1968-71; ptnr. Hunton & Williams, Richmond, Va., 1974—; bd. dirs. Exec. Info. Sys., Inc., Darien, Conn., Met. Advantage Corp., Richmond. Bd. dirs. Met. Bus. Found., Richmond, Mary Morton Parsons Found., Charlottesville, Va., The Nature Conservancy, Charlottesville, vice chmn. Va. chpt.; trustee Va. Aerospace Bus. Roundtable, Hampton, 1989—, Va. Ea. Shore Sustainable Devel. Corp., 1995—. Mem. ABA (bus. law sect., chmn. ptnrs. com., mem. fed. regulation security com.), Va. Bar Assn., Va. State Bar. Office: Hunton & Williams 951 E Byrd St Richmond VA 23219-4040*

MOORE, TRESI LEA, lawyer; b. Brownwood, Tex., Dec. 3, 1961; d. Dean Moore and Patsy Ruth (Evans) Adams. BA in Fgn. Svc., BA in French, Baylor U., 1984, JD, 1987. Bar: Tex. 1987, U.S. Dist. Ct. (no. dist.) Tex. 1988, U.S. Ct. Appeals (5th cir.) 1989. Atty. Richard Jackson & Assocs., Dallas, 1987-91, Amis & Moore (and predecessor firm), Arlington, Tex., 1992—. Vol. Legal Svcs. of North Tex., Dallas, 1988—, Dallas Com. for Fgn. Visitors, 1989-92; bd. dirs. Plano Internat. Presch., 1995-96. Recipient Pro Bono Svc. award Legal Svcs. of North Tex., 1989, 90, 91. Mem. AAUW (pub. policy dir. Plano, Tex. br. 1992, 93-94, v.p. 1994-95), ABA, State Bar Tex. (mem. mentor program for lawyers com. 1994—, mem. local bar svcs. com. 1994-96), Dallas Bar Assn., Tarrant County Bar Assn., Dallas Women Lawyers Assn. (bd. dirs. 1989-90, v.p. 1992, pres. 1993). Office: Amis Moore & Davis 2301 E Lamar Blvd Ste 250 Arlington TX 76006-7416

MOORE, WALTER D., JR., pathologist; b. Houston, Sept. 29, 1924; s. Walter D. and Mary Nellie (Kincaid) M.; m. Barbara Jane Farrar; children—Diane Elizabeth, Michelle Louise, Michael Andrew. Student U. Tex., 1946-48; M.D., Baylor Coll., 1952. Diplomate Am. Bd. Pathology, Am. Bd. Nuclear Medicine. Intern, Cleve. City Hosp., 1952-53; resident VA Hosp., Houston, 1953-54; Albany Hosp., N.Y., 1954-55, U. Tex. Med. Br.-Galveston, 1955-59; pathologist Wilson N. Jones Hosp., Sherman, Tex., 1959-65, Fox Hosp., Oneonta, N.Y., 1965-76, St. Mary's Hosp., Galveston, 1976—, ret., 1981; mem. chancellors council U. Tex. Served with U.S. Army, 1943-46. Fellow Coll. Am. Pathologists, Am. Soc. Clin. Pathology; mem. Am. Coll. Nuclear Physicians, Am. Coll. Radiology, Soc. Nuclear Medicine, Pres.'s Assocs. U. Tex. (life), Alpha Epsilon Delta, Phi Sigma Kappa, Alpha Kappa Kappa. Roman Catholic. Avocation: jogging. Office: PO Box 730 League City TX 77574-0730

MOORE, WANDA C., college administrator; b. Greer, S.C., Apr. 19, 1969; d. Timmy Douglas and Carolyn (Beason) Moore. BA in Psychology, Converse Coll., 1991. Admissions cons. Converse Coll., Spartanburg, S.C., 1991-93, asst. dean admissions, 1993-94, acting dean admissions, 1994-95, dir. admissions, 1995—. Mem. Leadership Spartanburg, 1994, bd. regents, 1995—; mem. Jr. League of Spartanburg, 1993—. Home: 23 Sweetbriar Ln Spartanburg SC 29301 Office: Converse Coll 580 E Main St Spartanburg SC 29302

MOORE, WILLIAM BLACK, JR., retired aluminum company executive; b. Jackson, Miss., Sept. 18, 1924; s. William Black and May Isom (Whitten) M.; m. Lillian Wells, Sept. 14, 1946; children—Kathryn Ramsey Moore Dannels, William Black III, Bethany Moore Richmond. B.S. in Chem. Engring., U. Louisville, 1945, M.S. in Chem. Engring., 1947. Registered profl. engr., Ky. Chem. engr. U. Louisville Research Inst., 1947-49; mktg. mgr. Reynolds Metals, Louisville, 1949-58, dir. mktg., Richmond, Va., 1958-61, regional gen. mgr., St. Louis, 1961-69, v.p., Richmond, 1969-80, ret. Author: Letters to Rebecca; contbr. articles to profl. jours. Pres. bd. dirs. Rappahannock Found. Served to lt. USNR, 1943-47. Mem. AIA (hon.). Baptist. Clubs: Indian Creek (Kilmarnock, Va.); Country of Va. (Richmond). Avocations: fishing, farming, genealogy. Home: PO Box 1300 Kilmarnock VA 22482-1300

MOORE, WILLIAM CAREY, librarian, editor, writer; b. Nashville, May 31, 1933; s. LeRoy and Lala (Mullins) M.; m. Linda Ann Banks, June 23, 1962 (div. May 1984); children: Jonathan Edward, James Michael, Stephanie Joy, Kathryn Elizabeth; m. Pamela Rosewell, Sept. 13, 1986. BS in Journalism, So. Meth. U., 1950-54; MDiv, Southwestern Bapt. Theol. Sem., Ft. Worth, 1963; postgrad., U. North Tex., 1994—. Pastor Olivet So. Bapt. Ch., Lancaster, Calif., 1963-64; asst. editor United Evang. Action Nat. Assn. Evangs., Wheaton, Ill., 1964-67; asst. editor Harvest Publs., Chgo., 1968-69; asst. editor Decision Billy Graham Evangelistic Assn., Mpls., 1969-72; dir. editl. dept. Wycliffe Bible Translators, Huntington Beach, Calif., 1972-76; editor Logos Jour. Logos Internat., Plainfield, N.J., 1976-78; book editor Doubleday & Co., N.Y.C., 1979-80; editor acad. books Fleming H. Revell, Old Tappan, N.J., 1981-85; sr. editor acad. books WORD, Inc., Waco and Dallas, Tex., 1985-91; serials libr. Dallas Bapt. U., 1993—; judge Evang. Press Assn., Kansas City, Mo., 1974-78; tchr. writing class N.Y. Sch. of Bible, N.Y.C., 1984; spkr. in field. Co-author: (with Pamela Moore) If Two Shall Agree, 1992; author, editor: Evang. Sunday Sch. Tchrs. Guide, 1982-83, 83-84, 84-85. Trustee Internat. Mus. Cultures, Dallas, 1993—, trustee, 1994—. 1st lt. USAF, 1954-57. Mem. AARP, Evangs. for Social Action, Wycliffe Assocs., Tex. Libr. Assn. Home: 3330 Willouby Dr Grand Prairie TX 75052 Office: Dallas Bapt U 3000 Mountain Creek Pkwy Dallas TX 75211

MOORE, WILLIAM GROVER, JR., consultant, former air freight executive, former air force officer; b. Waco, Tex., May 18; s. William Grover and Annie Elizabeth (Pickens) M.; student Kilgore (Tex.) Coll., 1937-39, Sacramento State Coll., 1951, George Washington U., 1962; grad. Air War Coll., Air U., 1957, Nat. War Coll., 1962; m. Marjorie Y. Gardella, Jan. 18, 1943; 1 dau., Allyson. Enlisted U.S. Army Air Force, 1940, commd. 2d lt., 1941, advanced through grades to gen., 1977; comdr. 777th Squadron, 15th AF, Italy, 1944-45, 3535th Maintenance and Supply Group, Mather AFB, Calif., 1951, 3d Bomb Group, Korea, 1952; chief bases and units div. Hdqrs. USAF, 1952-56; asst. dep. chief of staff ops. Hdqrs. USAF Europe, 1957-61; comdr. 314th Troop Carrier Wing, Sewart AFB, Tenn., 1962-63, 839th Air Div., 1963-65; asst. J3 U.S. Strike Command, 1965-66; comdr. 834th Air Div., Vietnam, 1966-67; dir. operational requirements Hdqrs, USAF, 1967-70; comdr. 22d AF, 1970-73, 13th AF, 1973; chief of staff Pacific Command, 1973-76; asst. vice chief of staff Hdqrs. USAF, 1976-77; comdr. in chief Mil. Air Lift Command, 1977-79; ret., 1979; pres., chief operating officer Emery Air Freight Corp., Wilton, Conn., 1981-83; bus. cons., 1983—; pres. Met. Nashville Airport Authority, 1984—. Decorated Def. D.S.M., Air Force D.S.M. with 2 oak leaf clusters, Legion of Merit with 4 oak leaf clusters, Silver Star, D.F.C. with oak leaf cluster, Air medal with 9 oak leaf clusters, AF Commendation medal with 10 oak leaf clusters (U.S.); Croix de Guerre with palm (France); Armed Forces Honor medal 1st class (Vietnam); Republic of China Cloud and Banner; Legion of Honor (Republic of Philippines); recipient L. Mendel Rivers award of excellence; Jimmy Doolittle fellow in aerospace edn., 1978; named to Minuteman Hall of Fame, 1979. Mem. Air Force Assn., Nat. Def. Transp. Assn., Am. Ordnance Assn. Home: 932 W Main St Franklin TN 37064-2730 Office: Nashville Internat Airport 1 Terminal Dr Ste 501 Nashville TN 37214-4110

MOORE, WILLIAM JASON, museum director; b. Asheboro, N.C., Aug. 4, 1938; s. Lonnie James and Pauline (Hamilton) M.; m. Jane Beane, Dec. 16, 1962; 1 son, William David. B.B.A., High Point Coll., 1960. Asst. to archeologist Town Creek Indian Mound, Mt. Gilead, N.C., 1959; dir. Greensboro Mus., (N.C.), 1963—; assessor Am. Assn. Mus., Washington, 1976—. Mem. N.C. Mus. Council (award 1976; pres. 1973-74), Am. Assn. Mus., Am. Assn. State and Local History. Episcopalian. Lodge: Rotary.

MOORE, WILLIAM THOMAS, psychiatrist, educator; b. Houston, Dec. 21, 1925; s. Lloyd Edwin and Gertrude and Theresa (Nordlund) M.; m. Bernice Marie Doucet, June 5, 1952 (div. Jan. 1968); children: William Thomas Jr., Nanette Moore Gonzales, Ceceile Moore Dutka, Guy M.; m. Sarah C. Barnett, Feb. 8, 1969; 1 child, John T.E. Student, U. Houston, 1943-44; BA, MA, U. Tex., Austin, 1949; MD, U. Tex., Galveston, 1953. Diplomate Am. Bd. Psychiatry and Neurology; lic. marriage and family therapist, Tex. Intern King's Daus. Hosp., Temple, Tex., 1953-54; resident in psychiatry LaRue Carter Hosp.-Ind. U. Med. Ctr., Indpls., 1954-56; resident fellow Parkland Meml. Hosp.-U. Tex. Southwestern Med. Sch., Dallas, 1956-57, instr., 1957-59, asst. prof., 1959-63, clin. asst. prof., 1964-80, clin. assoc. prof., 1980—, also supervisory psychiatrist psychiatry residency program, sr. attending; pvt. practice, Dallas, 1964—; lectr. occupational therapy dept. Tex. Women's' U., 1960, cons. Sch. Nursing, 1958-63; cons. Terrell State Hosp., 1964-70; med. dir. Woodlawn Hosp., Dallas, 1960-63; cons. staff Baylor U. Med. Ctr., Dallas; co-founder, bd. dirs. S.W. Family Inst., 1979-83; bd. dirs. Isthmus Inst., Reverchon Press Inc., Sabrook Press Inc. Co-author: Environmental Encounter, 1979; also articles. With AUS, 1945-46. Fellow Am. Psychiat. Assn. (life); mem. AMA, Tex. Med. Assn., Dallas County Med. Soc., So. Med. Assn., Am. Assn. Marital and Family Therapists, Tex. Soc. Psychiat. Physicians (numerous coms.), North Tex. Soc. Psychiat. Physicians (past pres., numerous coms.). Home: 10333 Marsh Ln Dallas TX 75229-6013 Office: 3613 Cedar Springs Rd Dallas TX 75219-4945

MOORE-BERRY, NORMA JEAN, secondary school educator; b. Hampton, Ark., Jan. 7, 1949; d. James E. and Alma Lee (McRae) Moore, Sr.; children: Rhemona Moore, Nerissa Moore. BA in English Edn., U. Ark., Pine Bluff, 1971; MA in Reading Edn., So. Ark. U., 1985; postgrad., Henderson State U., 1986, U. Ark., 1989-90. Cert. mid. and secondary English tchr., adult edn., all levels reading. Tchr. English Chidester (Ark.) Sch. Dist., 1971-73; tchr. English, adult edn. instr. Lewisville (Ark.) Sch. Dist., 1973-92, secondary tchr., 1973-93, reading tutor, 1991—; instr. adult edn. Texarkana (Ark.) Pub. Sch. Dist., 1984-91; tchr. English Ctrl. High Sch., 1984-93, Hall Sr. High Sch., Little Rock, 1987-90; chmn. English dept. Lewisville Sch. Dist.; instr. English Ctrl. High Sch., summer 1992; tchr. Ctrl. High Sch. Summer Sch., Little Rock Sch. Dist., summer 1994; English and reading secondary instr., 1994-95. Sponsor sr. class; active sch. charity fundraising; organizer, sponsor Lewisville Reading Club, Lewisville English Club; mem. bible study group Bethel CME Ch., Stamps, Ark., sponsor, sec. ceo com. Ethnic Club Lewisville High Sch. Named Tchr. Yr., 1984, Lewisville Mid. Sch. Reading/English Tchr., Woman of Yr. ABI, 1993-94. Mem. ASCD, Nat. Coun. Tchrs. English, Ark. Edn. Assn., Ark. Tchr. Retirement Assn., Ark. Reading Coun. Assn. (lit. coun.), Lewisville Edn. Assn. (treas. 1993-94), Phi Delta Kappa. Home: 507 Hope Rd Stamps AR 71860-2017

MOOREFIELD, JENNIFER MARY, legislative staff member; b. Danville, Va., Nov. 10, 1950; d. Folger Lester and Mildred (Cox) M. BA in Psychology, Averett Coll., 1972; A in Applied Sci., Danville C.C., 1986; postgrad., Longwood Coll., 1995—. Social worker Henry County Social Svcs., Collinsville, Va., 1972-75, sr. social worker, 1975-80; clk. inventory control Dan River, Inc., Danville, Va., 1981-83; staff asst. U.S. Congressman Dan Daniel, Danville, 1984-88; staff asst. U.S. Congressman L.F. Payne, Danville, 1988-91, casework supr., 1991—; office mgr. U.S. Congressman L.F. Payne, Danville, 1991—. Bd. recording sec. Danville Speech & Hearing Ctr., 1988; Sunday Sch. tchr. Emmanuel Wesleyan Ch., Danville, 1975—; dir. Wesleyan Kids for Missions, Danville, 1993—, Ch. Vacation Bible Sch., Danville, 1993. Mem. Luncheon Pilot Club of Danville, Inc. (recording sec. 1988-89, pres.- elect 1989-90, pres. 1990-91), Va. Dist.- Pilot Internat. (area fundraising leader 1990-91, dist. chaplain 1993-94). Home: 136 Brookview Rd Danville VA 24540-3408 Office: Office of Congressman LF Payne 700 Main St Ste 301 Danville VA 24541-1819

MOORES, ANITA JEAN YOUNG, computer consultant; b. Poplar Bluff, Mo., Oct. 11, 1944; d. Joseph Samuel and Irene Anita (Sollars) Young; m. James Stephen Moores, June 5, 1965 (div. Jan. 1979); 1 child, Carolyn Terra. BS in Edn., So. Ill. U., 1972, MS in Edn., 1979. Cons. edn. and bus., sales Forsythe Computers, St. Louis, 1979-81; floor sales mgr., bus. cons., sales Computerland of Southwest Houston-Westheimer, 1981-82; bus. cons., sales Bus. Computer Systems and Software, Houston, 1982-83, MicroTask Computers, 1983-84; adminstrv. asst., tech. support Computerland-Techtron, 1984-85; distributer sales Cyber/Source, Houston, 1985; southwest regional sales mgr. Professions Info. Network, Houston, 1987; adminstrv. asst., computer specialist Human Affairs Internat. Inc., Houston; owner Moores' Consulting, Houston, 1986—. Author: (manuals) Choosing a Business Computer, 1983, Career Management, 1984, Training Manual-Computer, 1989; editor: Hounix Newsletter, 1988-89; artist oil paintings. Cons., trainer Meml. Luth. Ch., Houston, 1980-85; adminstr. Olympic Devel.-Soccer, Houston, 1988-89. So. Ill. U. Grad. fellow, 1975-76; named Outstanding Young Women Athlete, So. Ill. U., 1972.

MOORMAN, ROBERT LAWSON, real estate appraiser; b. Waco, Tex., Sept. 2, 1951; s. George Robertson and Gladys Lee Billie (Scoggin) M.; m. Rebecca Ann Averitt, Sept. 9, 1983; children: Jason, Benjamin, Kate, William, Bethany. BBA, So. Meth. U., 1973; MS in Fin., Tex. A&M U., 1990; postgrad., Hawthorne U. CFP; cert. real estate appraiser; registered investment adviser; lic. real estate broker. Self-employed musician Austin, N.Mex., 1973-83; asst. v.p. Brenham (Tex.) Nat. Bank, 1983-85, First Nat. Bank, Navasota, Tex., 1985-87, First Savs. Assn., Brenham, 1987-89; asst. lectr. fin. Tex. A&M U., College Station, 1990-93; pres. RLM Fin. Group, Inc., Brenham, 1990—. Editor: (book) Goals for Washington County, 1984. Dir. Brenham Opportunity Ctr., 1983-85; mem. Downtown Parking Com., Brenham, 1985; chmn. Parks Adv. Bd., Brenham, 1988-93; pres. Washington County Coalition, Brenham, 1993. Recipient Bookman Peters Banking fellowship Tex. A&M Grad. Sch. Bus., 1989, 90. Mem. Nat. Assn. Ind. Fee Appraisers (IFAS 1993—), Brenham Rotary Club, Nat. Assn. of Realtors Appraisal Divsn. (GAA 1995—), Am. Soc. Appraisers, Appraisal Inst. (assoc.), Soc. of Tex. A&M Real Estate Profls., Inst. of CFP, Internat. Assn. Fin. Planners, SAR. Office: The RLM Fin Group Inc 114 S Park St Brenham TX 77833-3645

MOORMAN, ROSE DRUNELL, county administrator, systems analyst; b. Miami, Fla., May 13, 1945; d. Willie and Claudia (Fluker) M. BA in Mathematics, Fisk U., 1967; MSE in Computer and Info. Scis., U. Pa., 1976. Computer programmer GE, Valley Forge, Pa., 1967-70; programmer/analyst Price Waterhouse Co., Phila., 1970-72; sr. programmer/analyst Inst. Environ. Medicine U. Pa., Phila., 1972-77; systems analyst Honeywell, Ft. Washington, Pa., 1977-78; dir. tech. svcs. Gill Assocs., Inc., Washington, 1978-83; owner, CEO Computer and Info. Mgmt., Inc., Miami, 1983-88; mgr. tech. support City of Miami, 1988-94, coord. diversity, 1994-95; exec. adminstr. to county commr. Metro-Dade County, 1996—; facilitator Women in Info. Processing, Washington, 1979-83; computer edn. adv. panel Dade County Pub. Schs., 1984-88. Editor: (newsletter) Bits and Bytes, 1979-82; co-editor: (newsletter) Ebenezer Speaks, 1992—. Active Ebenezer United Meth. Ch., Miami, 1954—, treas., chair fin. com., 1992—, Family Christian Assn., 1989-94; troop leader Girl Scouts Am., 1990—; pres. Loran Park Sch. PTA, Miami, 1991-93; treas., bd. dirs. Overtown Comty. Health Clinic, Miami, 1992—, New Miami Group, Inc., 1994—; mem. Dade Heritage Trust, Miami, 1994—; mem. Dade County Hist. Preservation Bd., 1996—. Recipient Leadership award ARC, 1957, 63, Bronze medallion for Community Svc. NCCJ, 1963, Svc. Excellence award Delta Sigma Theta, 1986. Meritorious Svc. award Fisk U., 1992. Mem. NAACP, Nat. Forum Black Pub. Adminstrs. (bd. dirs., 2d v.p. 1993—), Nat. Coun. Negro Women. Republican. Home: 820 NW 172nd Ter Miami FL 33169-5305 Office: Metropolitan Dade County 111 NW 1st St Ste 220 Miami FL 33128-1903

MOORMAN, STEVE THOMAS, systems analyst; b. Lynchburg, Va., Apr. 4, 1959; s. Lloyd Woodie and Parke (English) M. AA in Computer Sci., Nat. Bus. Coll., 1984; postgrad., Liberty U., 1995—. Machine operator Burlington Industries, Altavista, Va., 1980-82; owner, mgr. Moorman's Body Shop & Garage, Gladys, Va., 1985-86; computer operator Lynchburg (Va.) Gen. Hosp., 1986-88; computer operator City of Lynchburg, 1988-89, computer programmer, 1989-91, systems analyst, 1991—. Republican. Methodist. Office: City of Lynchburg PO Box 60 Lynchburg VA 24505-0060

MOORMAN, WILLIAM JACOB, agronomist, consultant; b. Nickerson, Kans., Jan. 15, 1923; s. Elmer O. and Abbie L. (Mood) M.; m. Mildred L. Morris, Nov. 1, 1947; children: David Morris, Margaret Jane. Student in Chem. Engring., Kans. U., 1941-43; student in Agronomy, Kans. State U., 1946-47. Pres., mgr. Moorman Feed & Seed Co., Inc., Nickerson, Kans., 1947-61; ter. sales mgr. Northrup King Co., Nickerson, Kans., 1961-65; regional sales mgr. Northrup King Co., Columbia, Mo., 1965-68; div. sales promotion, agronomic svcs. Northrup King Co., Richardson, Tex., 1968-73; br. mgr. Northrup King Co., St. Joseph, Mo., 1973-74; div. mktg. mgr. Northrup King Co., Columbus, Miss., 1974-82, sales agronomist, 1982-85; mktg. specialist Northrup King Co., Fredericksburg, Va., 1985-88; owner, mgr. Moorman Enterprises, Fredericksburg, Va., 1988—; agri-bus. cons. Contbr. articles to profl. jours. Committeeman Rep. Party, Kans., 1948-61, Lions Club, 1948-62; active United Meth. Ch., 1948—; mem. Vols. in Overseas Coop. Assistance (VOCA), Bulgaria, 1994, 96 as agri-business cons. With U.S. Army, 1942-46. Mem. Nat. Agri-Mktg. Assn., Svc. Corps Ret. Execs. (adv. com. Fredericksburg chpt. 1991—). Home: 1127 James Madison Cir Fredericksburg VA 22405-1632 Office: Moorman Enterprises PO Box 885 Fredericksburg VA 22404-0885

MOORMANN, DAVID LAWRENCE, sportswriter, journalist; b. Cin., Sept. 1, 1953; s. Ambrose Francis and Susan Jane (Guckes) M.; m. Carol Fontenot; 1 child, Chelsea. BA in Mass Communications, U. South Fla., 1975. County reporter Naples (Fla.) Daily News, 1975; sportswriter St. Petersburg (Fla.) Times, 1975-77; sportswriter Jackson (Miss.) Clarion-Ledger, 1977-79, sports deskman, 1980; sports editor Monroe (La.) News-Star, 1979-80; sportswriter Baton Rouge Morning Adv., 1980—. Recipient Sports Columnist award La. Press Assn., 1988. Mem. La. Sports Writers Assn. (co-sweepstakes winner 1986, sweepstakes winner 1988). Roman Catholic. Home: 7536 Lew Hoad Ave Baton Rouge LA 70810-1741

MOOS, VERNA VIVIAN, special education educator; b. Jamestown, N.D., July 1, 1951; d. Philip and Violena (Schweitzer) M. BS in Edn., Valley City State U., 1973; MEd, U. So. Miss., 1983, EdS, 1988; AA, Minot State U., 1987; postgrad., East Tex. State U., U. Tex., N.D. State U., U. N.D., Kans. State U., McGill U. Supr. recreation Valley City (N.D.) Recreation Dept., 1969-73; tchr. Harvey (N.D.) Pub. Schs., 1973-75; tchr. spl. edn. Belfield (N.D.) Pub. Schs., 1975-77; edn. therapist N.D. Elks Assn., Dawson, 1976-77; tchr. spl. edn. Dickinson (N.D.) pub. Schs., 1977-87; ednl. technician ABLE, Inc., Dickinson, 1984-87; tchr. spl. edn. Pewitt Ind. Sch. Dist., Omaha and Naples, Tex., 1987—; tchr. adult edn. N.E. Tex. C.C., Mt. Pleasant, 1989—. Local and area dir. Tex. Spl. Olympics, Austin, 1988—; local, regional and state dir. N.D. Spl. Olympics, 1972-87; local coord. Very Spl. Arts Festival; mem. Am. Heart Assn., 1979-87, N.D. Heart Assn., 1979-87; mem. adminstrv. bd. First United Meth. Ch., Naples, Tex., 1994—. Named Dickinson Jaycees Outstanding Young Educator, 1979, Dickinson C. of C. Tchr. of Yr., 1985, Dallas area Coach of Yr., Tex. Spl. Olympics, 1993, Dir. of Yr., N.D. Spl. Olympics, 1985. Mem. NEA, Coun. Exceptional Children, Naples C. of C., Delta Kappa Gamma (scholar), Phi Delta Kappa, Kappa Delta Pi. Home: PO Box 788 Omaha TX 75571-0788 Office: Pewitt CISD PO Box 1106 Omaha TX 75571-1106

MOOSE, TALMADGE BOWERS, artist, illustrator, portrait artist; b. Albemarle, N.C., June 4, 1933; s. Cecil Hahn and Flora (Bowers) M.; m. Miriam Ruth Morris, June 17, 1956; children: Lyle Morris, Barry Neal. BFA, Va. Commonwealth U., 1955. Staff artist Porter, Hargis, Inc., Winston-Salem, N.C., 1958-59; art dir. Arts Engraving Co., Inc., Charlotte, N.C., 1959-64; pvt. practice artist, designer, illustrator, Charlotte, 1964-72; art instr. Stanly C.C., Albemarle, N.C., 1972-77; pvt. practice artist, tchr., Albemarle, 1977—; project dir. Artists/Writers Dialogue, Albemarle, 1975; bd. mem. Stanly County Arts Council, 1974-76, N.C., Cultural Adv. Com., Raleigh, 1980-84. Works include drawing: Rain, 1970 (1st prize 1971), paintings and drawings; illustrator: Exploring the Piedmont, 1985. Named Artist of Month, sta. WBTV, Charlotte, 1978; recipient Cert. of Recognition, Stanly County C. of C., 1976, Sam Ragan Fine Arts award, 1996; winner over 30 awards for works. Mem. N.C. Watercolor Soc. (advisor 1978), Uwharrie Artists (pres. Albemarle 1974-76). Republican. Presbyterian. Home: 810 Lauras Ln Albemarle NC 28001-3004 Office: Funtime Playgrounds Inc 1915 E Main St Albemarle NC 28001-5333

MOO YOUNG, CATHY RHEA, industrial engineer; b. Knoxville, Apr. 11, 1959; d. Jimmie Rhea and Imogene (Beeler) Knisley; 1 child, Kayann Rhea Moo Young. BS in Indsl. Engring., U. Tenn., 1981, MS in Indsl. Engring., 1983; PhD in Indsl. Engring., U. Ctrl. Fla., 1995. Project scheduler Martin

Marietta, Oak Ridge, Tenn., 1981-84, sr. indsl. engr., 1984-88, prodn. ops. engr., 1988-95; sr. staff prodn. ops. systems Lockheed Martin, Orlando, 1996—. Mem. Tau Beta Pi. Office: Lockheed Martin 5600 Sand Lake Rd # 345 Orlando FL 32819-8907

MORA, DAVID SAUL, optometrist; b. Laredo, Tex., Jan. 6, 1956; s. Salvador Saul and Sally (Cotilla) M.; m. Cynthia Jan Hunter, June 20, 1987; children: Ian Saul, Katherine Isabella. BS, U. Houston, 1979, OD, 1983; PhD, Columbia Pacific U., San Rafael, Calif., 1991. Optometrist in pvt. practice Laredo, 1983—. Major Biomed. Sci. Officer, USAFR. Mem. APHA, Am. Optometric Assn. (also Multide Assn., Contact Lens Assn., Sports Vision Assn.), Tex. Optometric Assn., Coll. of Syntonic Optometry, Armed Forces Optometric Assn., N.Y. Acad. Scis., Orton Dyslexia Soc., Am. Acad. Optometry, Nat. Eye Rsch. Found., Coll. Optometrists in Vision Devel., Psychophysiology and Applied Biofeedback, Soc. Light Treatment and Biological Rhythms. Roman Catholic. Office: 1601 Corpus Christi St Laredo TX 78043-3302

MORADI, AHMAD F., software company executive, consultant; b. Tehran, Persia, Mar. 21, 1955; came to U.S., 1973; s. Akbar and Afsar (Mokaram) M.; m. Lourdes Pernas; 1 child, Aimee. AS, Broward Community Coll., 1978; BA, Fla. Atlantic U., 1980, MBA, 1982; Phd, LaSalle U., 1987. Advisor restaurant industries Miami, Fla., 1974-78; pres. Octa-8, Inc., Ft. Lauderdale, Fla., 1980-82; mgmt. cons. MGI-MCG, Boca Raton, Fla., 1982-83; dir. ops. Datamation, Hollywood, Fla., 1983-85; pres. Software Intelligence Corp., Ft. Lauderdale, 1985—; with ARM Financial Corp., 1987-89; MIS dir., CIO Churchill Tech., Inc., Davie, Fla., 1992—; CEO Westmack Group Holding Co., Delray Beach, 1995—; prin. G4, Inc., Ft. Lauderdale, 1992—; lectr. South Fla. Bus. Jour., 1984-85, Victoria Hosp., Miami, Fla., 1985, Mt. Sinai Hosp., Miami, Fla., 1985, U. Miami, Fla., 1986, Chiropractic Today, 1989; cons., bus., mktg., internat. mktg. and telemarketing mgmt. Software Intelligence Corp., 1985—; systems analyst Softway, Inc., Ft. Lauderdale, 1986—. Mem. Data Processing Mgmt. Assn., Small Bus. Inst.

MORAITIS, KAREN KARL, real estate broker; b. Orange, Tex., Sept. 28, 1943; d. Richard Louis and Betty (Crandall) Karl; m. George Reynold Moraitis, Aug. 14, 1965; children: George Reynold Jr., Alexandra. BS in Advt., U. Fla., 1965; MEd, Fla. Atlantic U., 1968, EdS, 1974. Cert. real estate broker. Welfare worker State of Fla., Ft. Lauderdale, 1967; guidance counselor Broward County Pub. Schs., Ft. Lauderdale, 1968-70; adj. faculty Fla. Atlantic U., Boca Raton, 1971-74; real estate assoc. Blackwell Realty, Ft. Lauderdale, 1976-77; real estate broker Karen Moraitis Realty, Inc., Ft. Lauderdale, 1978—. Editor: Official Florida Publications, 1966. Mem. Pres.'s Council U. Fla., 1980—, scholarship ptnr. Gator Boosters, 1983—; pres. Harborside at Hillsboro Beach (Fla.) Condominium Assn., 1982, Parent Tchr. Student Orgn. Ft. Lauderdale High Sch., 1985-91. pres., 1986-88, Parent Tchr. Student Assn. Sunrise Middle Sch., Ft. Lauderdale, 1981-87. pres., 1982-84; v.p. PTA Bayview Elem. Sch., Ft. Lauderdale, 1980; chmn. Winter Cotillion, Ft. Lauderdale, 1986-88; bd. dirs. Sunrise Intracoastal Homeowners Assn., 1977, 96—, Broward County Zoning Bd., 1980-81, Imperial Village Condominium Assn., Ft. Lauderdale, 1983; ambassador edn. City of Ft. Lauderdale, 1986-88. Served with USN, 1965. Mem. Nat. Assn. Realtors, Fla. Assn. Realtors, Ft. Lauderdale Bd. Realtors, Humane Soc. Broward County (life), Navy League (life), Ft. Lauderdale H.S. Boosters (pres. 1984-85, 87-88), Broward County Athletic Assn. (waiver rev. com. 1992-96), Nat. Football Found. and Coll. Hall of Fame (bd. dirs. Brian Piccolo chpt. 1992-96). Democrat. Office: Karen Moraitis Realty Inc 915 Middle River Dr Ste 506 Fort Lauderdale FL 33304-3561

MORALES, CARLOS F., physician, military officer; b. Munich, Germany, Aug. 23, 1957. BS in Biology, U. Puerto Rico, 1980, MD, 1984. Cert. Nat. Bd. Med. Examiners, Am. Bd. Internal Medicine (pulmonary and critical care medicine). Intern dept. medicine Wilford Hall USAF Med. Ctr., Lackland AFB, Tex., 1984-85; resident dept. medicine Wilford Hall USAF Med. Ctr., Lackland AFB, 1985-87; asst. chief dept. internal medicine 23D Med. Group, England AFB LA, 1987-89, asst. chief hosp. svcs., 1989; staff internist human immunodeficiency virus unit Wilford Hall USAF Med. Ctr., Lackland AFB, 1989, pulmonary/critical care fellowship, 1990-93, staff pulmonologist, pulmonary/critical care medicine dept., 1993—, assoc. med. dir. medicine ICU, 1993—; tng. officer pulmonary/critical care fellowship USAF/USAF Med. Ctr., Lackland AFB, Tex., 1994—; aerospace medicine primary class USAF Sch. Aerospace Medicine, Brooks AFB, Tex., 1988. Contbr. articles to profl. jours. Mem. ACP, Am. Coll. Chest Physicians, Soc. Air Force Physicians, Am. Thoracic Soc. Office: Wilford Hall Med Ctr Lackland AFB/PSMP 2200 Bergquist Dr San Antonio TX 78236-5302

MORALES, CARLOTA ELOISA, principal; b. Havana, Cuba, Oct. 18, 1946; came to U.S., 1961; d. Jose Ramon and Rosa (Paradela) M. AA, Miami Dade Jr. Coll., 1964; BEd in Secondary Edn. Adminstrn., U. Miami, 1966, MEd, 1969, EdD in Adminstrn., 1984. Cert. Math. and langs. tchr., Fla. Tchr. Spanish Acad. of the Assumption, Miami, Fla., 1967-68; tchr. 6th grade Sts. Peter and Paul Sch., Miami, 1968-71, tchr. math., 1971-81, asst. prin., 1981-90; lectr. in Spanish Barry U., Miami Shores, Fla., 1981-82; prin. St. Agatha Sch., Miami, 1990—; judge literary contest Patronato de Cultura Pro-Cuba, Miami, 1973; judge Dade County Youth Fair, Miami, 1985-86; curriculum writer Archdiocese of Miami, 1983—; mem. vis. team Fla. Cath. Conf., Tallahassee, 1982—. Chairperson Sts. Peter and Paul Ann. Festival, Miami, 1971—. Mem. Assn. for Supervision and Curriculum Devel., Phi Delta Kappa. Roman Catholic. Home: 1400 SW 14th Ave Miami FL 33145-1541 Office: Saint Agatha Sch 1111 SW 107th Ave Miami FL 33174-2506

MORALES, DAN, state attorney general. Grad. with honors, Trinity U., 1978; JD, Harvard U., 1981. Asst. dist. atty. Bexar County, 1983-85; former mem. Ho. of Reps. Tex.; atty. gen. State of Tex., Austin, 1991—. Bd. dirs. NCCJ, World Affairs Coun.; trustee So. Meth. U., Schreiner Coll., Kerrville; elder First Presbyn. Ch. Named one of Seven Best Legislators Dallas Morning News, Politician of Yr. San Antonio Express News; recipient Outstanding Svc. award Ind. Colls. and Univs., Outstanding Leadership award Texan's War on Drugs,. Mem. Tex. Lyceum Assn. Office: Office of Atty Gen PO Box 12548 Austin TX 78711-2548*

MORALES, PEDRO ALLISON (PETE), accountant, consultant, writer; b. Hurley, N.Mex., July 22, 1944; s. Jose T. and Dora (Allison) M.; m. Priscilla Melendrez, Aug., 6, 1966; children: Lawrence David, Anna Martina, Eddye Lynn. BA in Bus. Adminstrn., Western N.Mex. U., 1967. Acctg. supr. GTE, Inc., El Paso, 1967-72, Santa Monica, Calif., 1975-78; acct., auditor Elmer Fox and Co., El Paso, Tex., 1972-73; asst. contr. Blue Bell Inc., El Paso, 1973-75; divsn. contr. Ind. Gen., El Paso, 1978-82; plant contr. Allen Bradley Co., Juarez, Mex., 1982-84; contr. Ceramic Tile Internat., El Paso, 1984-86; cons., owner Twin Plant Consultants, El Paso, 1986-96; plant contr. Georgia-Pacific Corp., El Paso, 1994—. Author: The Plant, 1995; contbr. articles to profl. jours.; inventor automobile carpet shampooer, 1991. Fin. advisor Christo Rey Cath. Ch., El Paso, 1986-88. Mem. AICPA. Democrat. Roman Catholic. Home: 1508 Randy Wolff Pl El Paso TX 79935

MORALES-HENDRY, MARIA HOLGUIN, real estate agent, poet; b. Bogota, Apr. 19, 1948; came to U.S., 1949; d. Alfredo Lazaro H. and Beatrice (Murray) Cayzer; m. Ricardo Morales-Hendry, July 26, 1969 (div. Feb. 28, 1992); children: Vanessa Isobel, Veronica Alexandra. AS, Palm Beach Jr. Coll., 1968; student, Pratt Inst., 1971-72, U. de los Andes, Bogota, 1980-81. Computer programmer Banco de Colombia, Bogota, 1968, Estudios Tecnicos, Bogota, 1968-69, Pratt Inst., Bklyn., 1969-71, PMI, N.Y.C., 1971-73; real estate agent Inmobiliarias Asociadas, Bogota, 1978-83; art salesperson Jean Lavigne Art Gallery, Palm Beach, Fla., 1983-84; real estate agent VIP Realty, Wellington, Fla., 1984-89, Linda Schumacher Realty, Palm Beach, Fla., 1989-92, Prestige Property, Wellington, Fla., 1992—. Author: (poem) Reflections, 1989 (hon. mention World of Poetry 1989), (poem) Tonight is Forever. 1990 (hon. mention World of Poetry 1990), (book) La Joya del Verso, 1992, (poem) Dream of Love, 1994, (Editor's Choice award Nat. Libr. Poetry 1994), (poem) Treasure My Love, 1996 (Editor's Choice award Nat. Libr. Poetry 1996). Mem. Nat. Assn. Realtors, Fla. Assn. Realtors. Republican. Roman Catholic. Home: 675 Spinnaker Ct Wellington FL 33414

MORAN, CHRISTA ILSE MERKEL, investor, linguist; b. Leipzig, Saxony, German Dem. Republic, Jan. 5, 1946; came to U.S., 1968; d. Erich Harry and Ilse Dora (Waehnert) Merkel; m. William Joseph Moran, May 5, 1967 (dec. Mar. 4, 1979); children: Leslie Paige, Linda Christa. BA, U. Tuebingen, 1968; postgrad. U. Alaska, 1968-69. Cert. in German linguistics. Clk. Anchorage Westward Hotel, 1969-71; sales mgr. Windsor Park Hotel, Washington, 1971-75; linguist, instr. Def. Lang. Inst., Dept. Def., Washington, 1975-79; investor in real estate, sports cars, Atlanta, 1979—; cons. Dept. Def., 1976-79; real estate agt., Northside Realty Co., Atlanta, 1992—. Author: Die Mille Miglia, 1969; Der Nuerburgring, 1975; German Culture, 1977. Chairperson For a United Germany Com., Washington, Atlanta, Leipzig chpts.; fundraiser UNICEF. Named Sportswriter of Yr., ADAC of Germany, 1977. Democrat. Home: PO Box 34165 Pensacola FL 32507-4165 Office: Buckhead Brokers 5395 Roswell Rd NE Atlanta GA 30342-1976 Address: PO Box 34165 Pensacola FL 32507-4165

MORAN, JAMES D., III, child development educator; b. Bklyn., Mar. 2, 1951; s. James D. and Monica (Scherzinger) M.; m. Laurette Virginia Miller, Aug. 11, 1973; children: Ryan, Mollie. BA magna cum laude, Duke U., 1973; MS, U. Okla., 1975; PhD, Okla. State U., 1978. Asst. prof. U. Okla., Norman, 1978-80; asst. prof. Va. Poly. Inst. and State U., Blacksburg, 1980-83, assoc. prof., asst. head dept. family and child devel., 1983-85; prof., head dept. family rels. and child devel. Okla. State U., Stillwater, 1985-89; assoc. dean coll. human ecology U. Tenn., 1989—. Editorial bd. Home Econs. Research Jour., 1983-85, Family Relations, 1985-91, Creativity Research Jour., 1988-90, Home Econs. Forum, 1990-91, Jour. Family and Consumer Scis., 1993-95. Recipient Outstanding Research award Va. Home Econs. Assn., 1982. Mem. Am. Home Econs. Assn. (vice chmn. family relations and child devel. sect. 1985-86, chmn. nominating com., 1987, chair coun. for accreditation, 1989, 91, chair, strategic planning com., 1989, named among New Faces to Watch 1984, Leadership award 1986), Nat. Assn. for Edn. Young Children, Soc. for Research in Child Devel. Democrat. Roman Catholic. Avocation: golf. Home: 824 Andover Blvd Knoxville TN 37922-1532 Office: U Tenn Coll Human Ecology Knoxville TN 37996

MORAN, JAMES PATRICK, JR., congressman, stockbroker; b. Buffalo, N.Y., May 16, 1945; s. James Patrick and Dorothy (Dwyer) M.; m. Mary Craig, Dec. 27, 1967 (div. 1974); children: Jimmy, Mary; m. Mary Howard; children: Michael, Patrick, Dorothy. BA in Econs., Coll. of Holy Cross, Worcester, Mass., 1967; postgrad., CUNY, 1967-68; MA in Pub. Adminstrn., U. Pitts., 1970. Budget analyst HEW, Washington, 1969-74; budget and fiscal policy specialist, Congl. rsch. Libr. of Congress, Washington, 1974-76; sr. staff appropriations com. U.S. Senate, Washington, 1976-79; city councilman Alexandria, Va., 1979-91, vice-mayor, 1982-84, mayor, 1985-91; investment broker A.G. Edwards & Sons, Alexandria, Va., 1979—; mem. 102nd-103rd Congresses from 8th Va. dist., Washington, D.C., 1991—; mem. govt. reform & oversight coms.; ranking minority mem. civil svcs. subcom.; mem. internat. rels. on internat. ops. & human rights coms. Councilman, City of Alexandria, 1979-82, vice-mayor, 1982-84, mayor, 1985—; chmn. No. Va. Transportation Bd., 1988—, United Way, 1977-79; vice chmn. Mental Health Retard and Substance Abuse Bd., 1976-78, vice chmn. D.E.O., 1976-78;dir., Met. Area Council Govts., dir. No. Va. Transp. Commn., 1985—. Recipient Outstanding Citizenship award YMCA, 1983. Mem. C. of C. (dir. 1985-86). Democrat. Roman Catholic. Home: 205 Uhler Ter Alexandria VA 22301-1551 Office: US Ho of Reps 405 Cannon HOB Washington DC 20515-4608*

MORAN, PATRICIA GENEVIEVE, corporate executive; b. Evanston, Ill., July 26, 1945; d. James M.; children: Christine Coyle, Thomas Beddia, Donald Beddia. Attended, Marquette U. Pers. mgr. Sesco, 1983-84, dir. corp. transp., assoc. rels. dir., 1984-85, v.p. assoc. rels., 1985-88; group v.p. sales Southeast Toyota, Deerfield Beach, Fla., 1988-89, ceo., 1989-94; v.p. H.R. JM Family Enterprises, Inc., Deerfield Beach, pres., 1989-94. Dir. Beacon Coun., Miami, Fla., 1992—, Broward Econ. Devel., Ft. Lauderdale, Fla., 1991—, Youth Automotive Tng. Ctr., Hollywood, Fla., 1985—. Named Top 50 Working Women by Working Woman's Mag. Mem. Ft. Lauderdale C. of C. (dir. 1991—), Tower Club, The Haven (adv. bd. 1994-95). Office: JM Family Enterprises 100 NW 12th Ave Deerfield Beach FL 33442-1702*

MORAN, SAMUEL JOSEPH, public relations executive; b. Chgo., Oct. 4, 1929; s. Samuel Joseph and Lillian Rose (Burns) M.; m. Colette Catherine Murphy, June 18, 1955; children: Mindy, Mark, Monica, Melissa, Joe, Michael. BA, U. Iowa, 1955; postgrad., Milw. Sch. of Engring., 1970. Reporter Telegraph-Herold, Dubuque, Iowa, 1955-56, Register-Republic, Rockford, Ill., 1956-59; asst. pub. rels. dir. Nat. Lock Co., Rockford, 1959-60; account exec. E.R. HOllingsworth & Assoc., Rockford, 1960-62; sr. account exec. Burson Marsteller, Chgo., 1962-67; v.p. Aaron D. Cushman & Assoc., Chgo., 1967-69, Hoffman York & Compton, Milw., 1969-95; founder S. Joseph Moran & Assocs., Naples, Fla., 1995—. Contbr. articles to profl. jours. Bd. dirs. United Arts Coun., Collier County, Fla., 1993—. Mem. PRSA (pres. 1983, counselor acad. 1974—, tech. sect., 1989—, exec. com., chair tech. sect. 1990—), Nat.

MORAN, WILLIAM EDWARD, academic administrator; b. White Plains, N.Y., May 28, 1932; s. Frank Joseph and Margaret Mary (Farrell) M.; m. Barbara Carol Baillet, Apr. 20, 1963; children: Kathryn, Kevin, Colin, Christian. A.B., Princeton U., 1954; M.B.A., Harvard U., 1959; Ph.D., U. Mich., 1967. Mgmt. cons. Booz, Allen & Hamilton, N.Y.C., 1959-61; mem. adminstrv. staff Harvard U., Boston, 1961-63; asst. exec. v.p. SUNY-Stony Brook, 1966-71; chancellor Flint Campus U. Mich., 1971-79, U. N.C., Greensboro, 1979-94; sr. v.p. Connors Investor Svcs., Inc., 1994—; dir. J.P. Money Market Fund, Jefferson Pilot Money Market Fund, Greensboro, N.C. Connors Investor Services, Reading, Pa. Contbr. articles to profl. jours. Pres. So. Univ. Conf., 1987. Served with USN, 1954-57. Mem. N.C. Assn. Colls. and Univs. (pres. 1992), Princeton Club (N.Y.), Rotary. Home: 5206 Barnfield Rd Greensboro NC 27455 Office: Connors Investor Svcs Inc 1100 Berkshire Blvd Wyomissing PA 19610

MORAN, WILLIAM MADISON, fundraising executive; b. Albany, Ky., Apr. 15, 1948; s. Marvin Madison and Eula Pickens (Duvall) M.; m. Mary Ruth Shanks, June 5, 1971; 1 child, Alice Janette. Student, U. Ky., 1966-68; BS, Tenn. Technol. U., 1971. Field rep. March of Dimes, Nashville, 1972-77; state dir. Nat. Found. March of Dimes, Nashville, 1977; dir. devel. East Tenn. Children's Hosp., Knoxville, 1977-84; exec. dir. St. Vincent's Found. Ala., Birmingham, 1984—; founding participant, Children's Miracle Network Telethon, 1982-84. Co-founder, bd. dirs. Ronald McDonald House, Knoxville, 1982-84; bd. dirs. Tanasi coun. Girl Scouts U.S.A., Knoxville, 1981-84, Cahaba coun. Girl Scouts U.S.A., Birmingham, 1986-94; bd. dirs. Cath. Housing Authority, Birmingham, 1989—, Seton Inst. for Internat. Devel., 1994—. Recipient Thanks badge Girl Scouts Am., 1992, 94. Fellow Assn. Healthcare Philanthropy (regional dir. 1986-88, bd. dirs. 1987-88, chmn. 1992 internat. conf.); mem. Soc. Fundraising Execs. (advanced cert., pres. Tenn. chpt. 1983, pres. Ala. chpt. 1989, 1990, bd. dirs. 1989-94, asst. treas. 1990, exec. com. 1990-94, chmn. fin. com. 1991, 92, 93, treas. 1992, 93, vice chair 1994, Outstanding Fundraising Exec. Ala. 1988), Optimists (Knoxville), Kiwanis (Birmingham), Phi Delta Theta. Methodist. Home: 3712 Spring Valley Rd Birmingham AL 35223-1526 Office: Saint Vincent's Found 2800 Eight Ave S Ste 304 Birmingham AL 35233

MORANDI, JOHN ARTHUR, JR., nursing administrator, educator, nurse; b. Mass., Feb. 26, 1952; s. John Arthur and Mary Elizabeth (DiPersio) M. AAS in Nursing, No. Va. Community Coll., 1974; BSN, DePaul U., 1984, MS in Nursing, 1988; postgrad. in edn., Va. Poly. Inst. and State U., 1990. RN, Va., D.C. Nursing supr., staff nurse Alexandria (Va.) Hosp.; part-time faculty mem. Marymount U., Arlington, Cath. U. Am., Washington. Mem. AACN, DePaul U. Nursing Alumni Assn., Sigma Theta Tau (scholar).

MORD, IRVING CONRAD, II, lawyer; b. Kentwood, La., Mar. 22, 1950; s. Irving Conrad and Lillie Viva (Chapman) M.; m. Julia Ann Russell, Aug. 22, 1970 (div. Apr. 22, 1980); children: Russell Conrad, Emily Ann; m. Kay E. McDaniel, Aug. 31, 1985; children: Kurt August, Clayton Troy. BS, Miss. State U., 1972; JD, U. Miss., 1974. Bar: Miss. 1974, U.S. Dist. Ct. (no. dist.) Miss. 1974, U.S. Dist. Ct. (so. dist.) Miss. 1984. Counsel to bd. suprs. Noxubee County, Miss., 1976-80, Walthall County, Miss. 1980—, Bd. Educ., Walthall County, 1980—. Trustee, Walthall County Gen. Hosp., 1982—; county pros. atty. Noxubee County, Miss., Macon, 1974-80, Walthall County, Tylertown, 1982-88, 91-96. Bd. dirs. East Miss. Coun., Meridian, 1978-80, Trustmark Nat. Bank, Tylertown, 1986—; v.p. Macon counc. Boy Scouts Am., 1978, mem. coun., 1979; county crusade chmn. Am. Cancer Soc., Macon, 1976-78, county pres., 1979; chmn. fund drive fine arts complex Miss. State U., Macon, 1979. Recipient Youth Leadership award Miss. Econ. Coun., 1976; Walthall County family master, 1996—, Walthall County Youth referee, 1996—. Mem. ATLA, Miss. Prosecutors Assn., Miss. Assn. Board Attys. (v.p. 1985, pres. 1986), Miss. Assn. Sch. Bd. Attys., Miss. State Bar, Am. Judicature Soc. (Torts award 1972), Miss. Criminal Justice Planning Commn., Nat. Fed. Ind. Bus., Miss. State U. Alumni Assn., Macon-Noxubee County C. of C., Phi Kappa Tau (bd. govs. 1976-80, grad. coun., 1972—, pres. grad. coun. 1977-80, pres. house corp. 1977-80, Alumnus of Yr. Alpha Chi chpt. 1979), Phi Delta Phi. Republican. Methodist. Lodge: Rotary (sec. treas. 1977, v.p. 1978, pres. Macon 1979, pres. Tylertown club 1986—). Office: 816 Morse Ave Tylertown MS 39667-2130

MOREHOUSE, JEFFREY, mechanical engineering educator; b. San Diego, May 1, 1943; s. Harold Julian and Jetty Grace (DeLong) M.; m. Sherry Lynn Ragan, May 27, 1967 (div. July 1988); 1 child, Katherine DeLong Morehouse; m. Candace Diane Coombs Bartman, May 7, 1990. BSME, Rutgers U., 1965; MSME, Rice U., 1967; PhDME, Auburn U., 1976. Registered profl. engr., Ala. Assoc. prodn. engr. IBM Office Products Divsn., Austin, 1967-68; sr. scientist Sci. Applications Internat. Corp., McLean, Va., 1978-84, divsn. mgr., 1980-84; asst. prof. mech. engring. dept. Tex. A&M U., 1976-78; asst. chmn., grad. coord. U. S.C., 1985-89, assoc. prof. mech. engring. dept. 1984—; cons. ICC Internat., Bethesda, Md., 1995—, S.C. Electric and Gas, Columbia, 1996, Monsanto Co., Greenwood, S.C., 1990-92, TPI, Inc., Bethesda, Md., 1988-90, Solar Energy Rsch. Inst., Golden, Co., 1985-88, Sci. Applications Internat. Corp., McLean, 1984-88; curriculum and courses com. U. S.C., 1988-91, new courses/program subcom to grad. coun., 1987-90, rsch. and productive scholarship com., 1985-89, grad. com., 1986-89, scholastic stds. and petitions com., 1989—, student orgn. advisor Pi Tau Sigma, 1988—, SAE, 1993—. Recipient S.C. Energy Achievement award S.C. Govs. Office, 1987, Nat. award U.S. Dept. Energy, 1987. Mem. ASHRAE (student orgn. advisor 1988—), ASME (assoc. editor Jour. Solar Energy Engring. 1989-95, solar energy divsn. tech. com. chmn. 1984-90, solar energy divsn. newsletter editor 1984-89, exec. com. solar energy divsn. 1995—, coun. on engring. energy com. 1986—, chmn. 1990-96), Internat. Solar Energy Soc. (reviewer for solar energy 1986-96), Internat. Hydrogen Energy Soc. Home: 309 Newridge Rd Lexington SC 29072-7947 Office: Mech Engring Dept U SC Columbia SC 29208

MOREL, EUGENE ALLEN, entrepreneur; b. Amarillo, Tex., Dec. 6, 1956; s. Wilbur Adolph and Alma (Allen) M.; 1 child, Andrea Jean. Student, Stephen F. Austin State U., 1979-82; BBA, Tulane U., 1988. Lic. real estate broker, Tex. Onwer Morel Import & Investments Ltd., Austin, Tex., 1979—, Morel Real Estate Investment, Austin, Tex., 1979-93, Morel Imports, Austin, Tex., 1984-93; co-owner Heart Break Cafe, New Orleans, 1987-91; owner Quarter Time Photography, New Orleans, 1987-90, South of the Border Imports, New Orleans, 1987—, Mad Dog Spice Co., Rockport, Tex., 1990—, Rod and Reel Motel and Guide Svc., Rockport, Tex., 1993—; cons. Morel Import & Investments, Dallas, 1975-79. V.p. Abbott Terrace Homeowners Assn., Dallas, 1990—; mem. New Orleans Mus. of Art, 1988—. Republican. Episcopalian. Home: 1105 E Market St Rockport TX 78382-2539 Office: Morel Import & Investments 1105 E Market Rockport TX 78382

MORELAN, PAULA KAY, choreographer; b. Lafayette, Ind., Nov. 24, 1949; d. Dickie Booth and Marian Maxine (Fetterhoff) M.; m. Kerim Sayan, Aug. 10, 1974. Student U. Utah, 1968-69; BFA, Tex. Christian U., 1972; postgrad., El Centro Coll., 1969-70. Tchr., Rosello Sch. Ballet, Dallas, 1972-74; mgr., tchr. Ballet Arts Ctr., Dallas, 1974-76; owner, tchr. Ballet Classique, Garland, Tex., 1976-87, Garland Ballet Acad., 1977-87; asst. to Mythra Rosello, Tex. Civic Ballet, Dallas, 1972-74; assoc. artistic dir. Dance Repertory Theatre Dallas, 1974-75; artistic dir. Dance Repertory Theatre Dallas, 1975-76, Garland (Tex.) Ballet Assn., 1977-90, Classical Ballet Acad., Performing Arts Sch., 1987-90; resident choreographer Garland Civic Theatre, 1988—; nominee Leon Rabin award for Best Choreography, 1996.

MORELAND, DONALD EDWIN, plant physiologist; b. Enfield, Conn., Oct. 12, 1919; s. Albert Sinclair and Ruth (Cowan) M.; m. Verdie Brown Stallings, Nov. 6, 1954; 1 child, Donna Faye; stepchildren: Frank C., Paul Ziglar. BS in Forestry, N.C. State U., 1949, MS in Plant Physiology, 1950, PhD in Plant Physiology, 1953. Plant physiologist SUNY Coll. Forestry, Syracuse, 1952-53; plant physiologist USDA-Agrl. Rsch. Svc., Raleigh, N.C., 1953-71, rsch. leader, 1972-78, sr. exec., 1979—; asst. prof. to prof. N.C. State U., Raleigh, 1953—; mem. toxicology study sect. NIH, USPHS, Bethesda, Md., 1963-67. Editor: Biochemical Responses Induced by Herbicides, 1982; mem. editorial bd. Pesticide Biochemistry and Physiology, 1971—, Pesticide Sci., 1987—; contbr. articles to profl. jours. 1st lt. U.S. Army, 1941-46. AEC predoctoral fellow, 1950-52. Fellow AAAS, Weed Sci. Soc. Am. (outstanding rsch. award 1973); mem. Am. Chem. Soc., Plant Growth Regulator Soc. Am., Am. Soc. Plant Physiologists, So. Weed Sci. Soc., Sigma Xi. Home: 1508 Pineview Dr Raleigh NC 27606-2562 Office: USDA-Agrl Rsch Svc NC State U Crop Sci Dept 4123 Williams Hall Raleigh NC 27695

MORELAND-BEY, TERRI LYNN, elementary school educator; b. Oklahoma City, Okla., Mar. 20, 1965; d. Harold Lee and Mary Ann (Fannin) Moreland; m. Emanuel Atega Martin-Bey, Aug. 19, 1989 (div. June 1996); children: Malik El-Hajj, Nandi Lolita Bey. BA, Savannah State U., 1988; postgrad., Kennesaw State U., 1994—. Tchr. Atlanta Pub. Schs., 1988—. Vol. AID Atlanta, 1995—, Spl. Olympics, Atlanta, 1996. Mem. Kennesaw Assn. of Student Educators, Profl. Assn. of Ga. Educators, Nat. Assn. of Black Journalist, Alpha Kappa Alpha. Democrat. Home: 3200 Stone Rd S-9 Atlanta GA 30331

MORENO, FEDERICO ANTONIO, federal judge; b. Caracas, Venezuela, Apr. 10, 1952; came to U.S., 1963; s. Francisco Jose and Rejane Genevieve (Nogues) M.; m. M. Cristina M. Morales-Gomez, May 31, 1977; children: Cristi, Ricky, Victoria. AB cum laude, U. Notre Dame, 1974; JD, U. Miami, 1974. Bar: Fla. 1978, U.S. Dist. Ct. (so. dist.) Fla. 1978, U.S. Ct. Appeals (5th cir.) 1979, U.S. Ct. Appeals (11th cir.) 1981, U.S. Supreme Ct. 1981, U.S. Dist. Ct. (mid. dist.) Fla. 1986. Ptnr. Thornton, Rothman & Moreno, Miami, 1982-86; judge Dade County Cir. Ct., Miami, 1986-90; dist. judge U.S. Dist. Ct. (so. dist.) Fla., Miami, 1990—. Recipient People Helping People award United Way, 1980, Pro Bono award Pub. Interest Law Bank, 1985. Mem. ABA, FBA, Fla. Bar Assn., Dade County Bar Assn., Trial Lawyer's Assn. Roman Catholic. Office: US Courthouse 301 N Miami Ave Miami FL 33128-7702

MORENO, JOSEPH FLORENCIO, nurse; b. Sinton, Tex., Apr. 16, 1964; s. Florencio Gonzales and Ramona Torres (Rodriguez) M. AAS in Nursing, Del Mar Coll., Corpus Christi, Tex., 1987. RN. Lic. vocat. nurse Coastal Bend Hosp., Aransas Pass, Tex., 1985-87, nurse spl. care unit, 1992-94; nurse med. ICU Spohn Hosp., Corpus Christi, Tex., 1987-90, charge nurse 23 hour observation, 1990; travel nurse Preferred Med. Placement, Inc., Olathe, Kans., 1990—; mem. staff utilization mgmt. dept. Columbia North Bay Hosp., 1994-96, interim DRG codes, 1996—. Named one of Outstanding Young Men Am., 1985. Mem. AACN. Democrat. Roman Catholic. Home: 214 N 8th St Aransas Pass TX 78336-4104

MORENO, SUSAN ELIZABETH, Spanish language educator; b. Boston, Nov. 22, 1943; d. Francis Egar and Jeanne Pauline (Kenney) Kinne; m. Leopold Segismundo Moreno, May 27, 1972; children: Francis Leopold, Susan Cecilia. BA in Spanish, Creighton U., 1967; postgrad., Old Dominion U. Cert. tchr. Nebr., Va. Tchr. Omaha Pub. Schs., summer 1967; tchr. Spanish and French Lake Taylor H.S., Norfolk, Va., 1968-75, Norfolk Collegiate Sch., 1975-76, Rosemont Jr. H.S., Norfolk, 1976-80; tchr. Spanish Granby H.S., Norfolk, 1980—. Sponsor Granby H.S. Spanish Club, 1980—; den mother Cub Scouts/Boy Scouts Am., Talbet Pk., Norfolk, 1984-85; parent vol. Bay Youth Orchs., Norfolk, 1991. Mem. Circulo Medico Latino (bd. dirs. 1993—), Fgn. Lang. Assn. Va., Club Hispanoamericano Tidewater (rec. sec. 1970-80). Roman Catholic. Home: 441 Hariton Ct Norfolk VA 23505 Office: Granby H S 7101 Granby St Norfolk VA 23505

MORETON, THOMAS HUGH, minister; b. Shanghai, China, Dec. 2, 1917; came to U.S., 1946; s. Hugh and Tsuru M; m. Olive Mae Rives, Apr. 1, 1947 (dec. Apr. 1986); children: Ann Rives Moreton Smith, Andrew Hugh, Margaret Evelyn Moreton Hamar; m. Selma Littig, June 7, 1986. LLB, 1939, BD, 1942, PhD, 1946; ThD, Trinity Sem., 1948; LittD, 1949. Ordained to ministry Bapt. Ch., Glasgow, Scotland, 1942. Min. various chs., also tchr. Seaford Coll. Eng., 1945-46; tchr. coll. and sem. level. div. courses various schs., Atlanta, Oklahoma City, 1946-51; founder Tokyo Gospel Mission, Inc., House of Hope, Inc., Tokyo, 1951—; also World Gospel Fellowship, Inc., Norman, Okla., 1967—; pastor chs., Moore, Okla., Shawnee, Okla., Ada., Okla., Del City, Okla., Tahlequah, Okla. and Oklahoma City, 1968—; preacher numerous fgn. countries; internat. tour dir., radio broadcaster. Contbr. articles to religious jours. Charter mem. Am.-Japan Com. for Assisting Japanese-Am. Orphans. Chaplain AUS, 1952-63. Recipient various awards Japanese govt. Fellow Royal Geog. Soc., Philos. Soc.; mem. Royal Soc. Lit., Am.-Japan Soc., Israel-Japan Soc.

MORETTO, JANE ANN, nurse, public health officer; b. Belgium, Ill., Apr. 9, 1934; d. Bernard James and Mildred Bertha (Sutton) Moretto; RN, Mercy Hosp. Sch. Nursing, Urbana, Ill., 1955; B.S. in Nursing, St. Joseph Coll., Emmitsburg, Md., 1969. Relief head nurse, staff nurse Mercy Hosp., Urbana, Ill., 1955-57; staff nurse in psychiatry VA Hosp., Danville, Ill., 1957-59; staff nurse pulmonary disease VA Hosp., Long Beach, Calif., 1959-60, staff nurse surg. unit, L.A., 1960-61, staff nurse oper. rm., 1961-64; commd. lt. comdr. USPHS, 1969, advanced through grades to capt., 1975—; staff nurse USPHS Hosp., Galveston, Tex., 1964-66, staff nurse tumor ICU, Balt., 1967, asst. oper. rm. supr., New Orleans, 1969-71, oper. rm. supr., Brighton, Mass., 1971-78, dep. dir. nursing, dir. insvc. edn. Carville, La., 1978-80, dir. nurses Gillis W. Long Hansen's Disease Ctr., 1980-91, clin. nurse cons. lower extremity amputation prevention program Carville Diabetic Foot Program, 1991-95; cons. in field; lectr. in field. Inventor teaching foot model. Recipient Superior Performance award, USPHS Hosp., Galveston, 1966, Outstanding Svc. medal for exemplary performance of duty Dept. Health Human Svcs.-Pub. Health Svc., 1986 (citation, 1990, Unit Commendation award USPHS, 1981, Isolated Hardship award USPHS, 1981, Hazardous Duty award USPHS, 1992, Commendation medal USPHS, 1993); named Nurse of Yr., Baton Rouge Dist. Nurses Assn., 1991. Mem. Am. Nurses Assn., La. Nurses Assn., La. Hosp. Assn., La. Soc. Nursing Svc. Adminstrs., Nat. Assn. for Uniformed Svcs., Assn. Mil. Surgeons of U.S., Assn. Oper. Rm. Nurses, Alumnae Assn. of Schlarman High Sch., Alumnae Assn. of St. Joseph Coll., Commd. Officers Assn. USPHS. Roman Catholic. Home: 1741 Cobble Ln Mount Dora FL 32757

MOREY, MARK HOWARD, museum educator; b. Southbridge, Mass., Mar. 20, 1947; s. Howard Ralph and Barbara Virginia (Cypher) M.; m. Susan Lynn Burnette, June 2, 1984; children: Barbara Elizabeth, Marianne McGrady. BFA, U. Tulsa, 1977, MFA, 1985. Mus. edn. intern Dallas Mus. Art, 1980-81; curator of edn. Amarillo (Tex.) Mus. of Art, 1981—; instr. painting Amarillo Coll., 1983—, instr. in art history, 1993-94. Author exhbn. brochures, 1982-93; designer exhibit brochure Spiritual Eye, 1986 (M. Wilder design award Tex. Assn. Mus.). Bd. dirs. Planned Parenthood, Amarillo, 1989-92; deacon 1st Presbyn. Ch., Amarillo, 1990-93. Sgt. USAF, 1966-70. Grantee Tex. Com. for Humanities, 1982—, Tex. Commn. on Arts, 1982—. Mem. ACLU (bd. dirs. 1989—), Am. Assn. Mus., Tex. Assn. Mus. (bd. dirs. educators' com. 1988-90). Democrat. Office: Amarillo Mus of Art PO Box 447 Amarillo TX 79178-0001

MOREY, PHILIP STOCKTON, JR., mathematics educator; b. Houston, July 11, 1937; s. Philip Stockton and Helen Holmes (Wolcott) M.; m. Jeri Lynn Snyder, Sept. 5, 1964; children: William Philip, Christopher Jerome. BA, U. Tex., 1959, Ma, 1961, PhD, 1967. Asst. prof. math. U. Nebr., Omaha, 1967-68; assoc. prof. Tex. A&I U., Kingsville, 1968-76; prof. Tex. A&M U., Kingsville, 1976—; lectr. U. Tokyo, 1976, U. Hokkaido, 1977, 88. Contbr. articles to Tensor N.S., Internat. Jour. Engring. Sci, Tex. Jour. Sci. Recipient Researcher of Yr. awrd Tex. A&I Alumni Assn., 1985. Mem. Tex. Acad. Sci. (chmn. math. sect. 1982, '85), Am. Math. Soc., Tensor Soc., (Japan). Home: 1514 Lackey St Kingsville TX 78363-3199 Office: Tex A&M Univ Dept Math Kingsville TX 78362

MORFESIS, FLORIAS ANDREW, surgeon; b. Lancaster, Pa., Aug. 12, 1952; s. Andrew and Helen (Tsidonis) M.; m. Gail Ann Fahnestock, Apr. 12, 1980; children: Francesca Nicole, Alicia Claire. BS in Math. and Chemistry, Antioch Coll., 1975; MD, Pa. State U., Hershey, 1979. Diplomate Am. Bd. Surgery. Surgery resident U. Md. Hosp., Balt., 1979-81, Lankenau Hosp., Phila., 1981-84; attending surgeon Noyes Meml. Hosp., Dansville, N.Y., 1984-87, Daniel Boone Clinic, Harlan, Ky., 1988—, Harlan Appalachian Regional Hosp., 1988—; trauma surgeon emergency rm. St. Mary's Hosp., Rochester, N.Y., 1987-88; cons. Groveland State Prison, Sonyea, N.Y., 1984-89, Craig Devel. Ctr., 1985-89; flight examiner Fed. Aviation Adminstrn., Harlan, 1988—. Mem. SAGES, Soc. Laparoendoscopic Surgeons. Mem. Ea. Orthodox Ch. Office: Daniel Boone Clinic Harlan KY 40831

MORGAN, ALAN H., oil company executive; b. Dayton, Ohio, Apr. 11, 1954; s. Irvin M. and Eleanor (Freeman) M.; m. Betsy Jan Hoff, Nov. 18, 1979; children: Bonnie, Cara, Jeremy. BA in Govt., U. Tex. at Austin, 1975, BBA in Petroleum Land Mgmt., 1977. Cert. profl. landman. Landman Texaco Inc., Bellaire, Tex., 1978-80, Border Exploration Co., Houston, 1980-81, Mesa Petroleum Co., Houston, 1981-85; sr. landman Internat. Oil & Gas Corp., Houston, 1985-86; pres. Remora Oil Co., Houston, 1986—. Responsible for Tex. House Bill 520 becoming law. Outstanding landman Houston Assn. Petroleum Landmen, 1988; recipient Edn. award Am. Assn. Petroleum Landmen. Mem. Houston Assn. Profl. Landmen (pres. 1990-91), Am. Assn. Profl. Landmen (dir. 1992-94, com. chmn. 1993, 2d v.p. 1995-96), Houston Producers' Forum, Houston Geol. Soc. (assoc.). Office: Remora Oil Co PO Box 710914 Houston TX 77271-0914

MORGAN, ALLEN B., JR., securities executive; b. 1942. BA, U. N.C., 1965. Branch mgr. Courts & Co., Memphis, Tenn., 1965-69; founder Morgan Keegan & Co., Inc., Memphis, 1969; now chmn. bd. dirs. Morgan Keegan & Co., Inc. Office: Morgan Keegan & Co Inc Morgan Keegan Tower 50 N Front St Memphis TN 38103-2126*

MORGAN, BEVERLY HAMMERSLEY, middle school educator, artist; b. Wichita Falls, Tex.; d. Vernon C. and Melba Marie (Whited) Hammersley; m. Robert Lewis Morgan, Sept. 21, 1957 (div. 1972); children: Janet Claire, Robert David. BA, So. Meth. U.; MA, U. Ala., 1980, AA certification, 1982; postgrad., U. Tex., 1991—. Cert. art tchr., Tex., Ala.; cert. elem. tchr., Ala. Art tchr. Ft. Worth Pub. Schs., 1955-60; English tchr. Lincoln County Schs., Fayetteville, Tenn., 1961-62; 6th grade tchr. Huntsville (Ala.) Pub. Schs., 1960-61, 62-68, art tchr., 1972-92, 93-94. One man shows include U. Ala., 1980, Huntsville Art League, 1981. Mem. Huntsville-Madison County Art Tchrs., Huntsville Mus. Art, Internat. Platform Assn. Republican. Home: 12027 Chicamauga Trl SE Huntsville AL 35803-1544

MORGAN, CATHERINE MARIE, psychologist, writer; b. Duluth, Minn., Mar. 27, 1947; 1 child, Andrew. BS, U. Nebr., 1968; MEd, U. Okla., 1973; PhD Okla. State U., 1987; postgrad., Menninger Found. Psychotherapy Tng. Program, 1987-89. Child devel. specialist Southwest Guidance Ctr., Wheatland, Okla., 1973-74; pvt. practice Family Counseling Assocs., San Antonio, 1974-75; psychol. asst. Edmond Guidance Ctr., Okla., 1975-82; psychol. asst. supr. Southeast Guidance Ctr., Del City, Okla., 1982-86; psychol. intern Cleve. County Health Dept., Moore, Okla., 1986-87; psychologist Cen. State Hosp., Norman, Okla., 1987-89; pvt. practice assocs. in psychology, Edmond, Okla.; v.p. Behavior Mgmt. Specialists, Oklahoma City, 1983—; pres. Assocs. in Psychology, 1988—. Mem. AAUW, APA, Okla. Psychol. Assn., Southwestern Psychol. Assn., Am. Pers. and Guidance Assn., Am. Bus. Women's Assn., P.E.O., Kappa Delta Pi. Avocations: writing, reading, knitting, racquetball. Office: 5400 NW Grand Blvd Oklahoma City OK 73112

MORGAN, CHARLES DONALD, JR., manufacturing executive; b. Ft. Smith, Ark., Feb. 4, 1943; s. Charles Donald Sr. and Betty (Speer) M; m. Jane Dills Morgan, Aug. 20, 1966; children: Caroline Speer, Charles Robert. ME, U. Ark., 1966. Systems engr. IBM, Little Rock, Ark., 1966-71; v.p. Acxiom Corp. (formerly CCX Network, Inc.), Conway, Ark., 1972-75; pres. CCX, Conway, Ark., 1976-82, chief exec. officer, 1983—, also chmn. bd. dirs.; bd. dirs. First State Bank & Trust, Conway. Trustee Hendrix Coll., Conway, 1985—; chmn. bd. dirs. Jobs for Ark. Future, 1986-87, mem. commn. 1988—; mem. Southern Growth Policies Bd., N.C., 1986, Ark. Bus. Council, 1987—. Mem. Third Class Mailers Assn., Pub. Chief Exec. Officers Council. Episcopalian. Office: Acxiom Corp 301 Industrial Blvd Conway AR 72032-7168*

MORGAN, CONSTANCE LOUISE, real estate executive; b. Denver, July 24, 1941; d. Willis Stephen and Evelyn (Rutar) Claus; m. Robert M. Morgan, Jan. 3, 1963; children: Stephen, Melayne. BS, U. N. Mex., 1963. Lic. real estate broker; master gardener, Fla., 1996. Realtor, assoc. Investors Realty, Tallahassee, 1980-82, br. mgr., 1982-83; pres., broker Connie Morgan Realty, Inc., Tallahassee, 1983-96, Constance L. Morgan, Broker, Tallahassee, 1996—; founder Network for Ind. Brokers, 1989-93. Chmn. docents Fla. Gov.'s Mansion, Tallahassee, 1979-80; pres. Newcomers-Univ. Women, Tallahassee, 1968; bd. dirs. Tallahassee Symphony Orch., 1990-96; bd. dirs. Rotary Youth Camp, Inc., 1995—, Tallahassee United Way. Mem. Nat. Assn. Realtors, Fla. Assn. Realtors, Tallahassee Bd. Realtors (chmn. Multiple Listing Svc. 1984, 94), Tallahassee Cmty. Realty Group, Tallahassee C. of C. (bd. dirs. 1984-86, 89-92), Rotary, Chi Omega (treas. 1962), Phi Gamma Nu (pres. 1962). Home: 3322 Remington Run Tallahassee FL 32312-1462 Office: 2810 Remington Green Cir Tallahassee FL 32308-3762

MORGAN, DAHLIA, museum director. BA, McGill U., Montreal, 1958; postgrad., Sir George Williams U., Montreal, 1968-69, U. Miami, Fla., 1974. Lectr. Mus. of Fine Arts, Montreal, 1965-70; lectr./rschr. Sir George Williams U., Montreal, 1968-70; grad. asst. dept. art and art history U. Miami, Fla., 1971-74; adj. prof. visual arts dept. Fla. Internat. U., Miami, 1975-77, vis. rof. visual arts dept., 1978-79, faculty visual arts dept., 1979—, dir. Art in State Bldgs. Program, 1984—, dir. Art Mus., 1980—; lectr. in field; curator numerous exhbns.; panelist NEA Mus. Grants, 1993, Cultural Advancement Grants, 1992, 90; cons. Fed. Gen. Svcs. Adminstrn., 1992, Metro-Dade Art in Pub. Places Program, 1992. Prodr. numerous catalogues to exhbns. Juror South Miami Art Fair Photo Group; bd. dirs. Nat. Found. for Advancement in the Arts, 1984—; founder Friends of the Art Mus. Support Group at Fla. Internat. U., 1984—; chmn. State of Fla. Art in Bldgs., 1984—; chmn. Art in Pub. Places, Dade County, Fla., 1980-84. Recipient 3d Ann. MAXIE award Miami Arts Exchange, 1990; grantee Fla. Endowment for Humanities, 1986, Metro Dade County Cultural Affairs Coun., 1986, Fla. Internat. U., 1990, 91; U. Miami-Coral Gables merit scholar, fed. scholar. Mem. Assn. Coll. and Univ. Mus. and Galleries, Am. Assn. Mus., Coll. Art Assn. Am., Fla. Mus. Dirs. Assn., Fla. Higher Edn. Arts Network, Internat. Coun. Mus. (fine arts com.), Miami Cultural execs. Coun., Southeastern Mus. Assn., Fla. Cultural Action Alliance, Phi Kappa Phi. Office: Art Mus at Fla Internat U University Park Pc # 110 Miami FL 33199

MORGAN, ETHEL BRANMAN, accountant; b. N.Y.C., Jan. 16, 1914; d. Morris and Dina Branman; BS, U. Ala., 1964; m. Donald Arol Morgan, Mar. 14, 1936; children: Margaret Voelkel, Barbara Weeks, John T., Janet Katich, Ethel Lynn. Mathematician, Army Missile Command, Redstone Arsenal, Ala., 1964-67, computer specialist, 1967-71, lead engr. air def. system command control software, 1971-73; pvt. practice tax acctg., fin. cons., Huntsville, Ala., 1974—. Pres., Huntsville-Madison County Council on Aging, 1980-82; vice chmn. Citizens Adv. Com. to Small Claims Ct., 1980-83; bd. dirs. Madison County Sr. Center, 1979-83; bd. dirs. Madison County Council on Aging, 1978-82. Mem. AAUW, Nat. Soc. Pub. Accts., Nat. Assn. Enrolled Agts. Ala. Soc. Public Accts., Ala. Soc. Enrolled Agts. (treas. 1983-89), Phi Beta Kappa. Office: PO Box 4312 Huntsville AL 35815-4312

MORGAN, EVAN, chemist; b. Spokane, Wash., Feb. 26, 1930; s. Evan and Emma Anne (Klobucher) M.; m. Johnnie Lu Dickson, Feb. 14, 1959; 1 child, James. BS, Gonzaga U., 1952; MS, U. Wash., 1954, PhD, 1956. Staff chemist IBM Corp., Poughkeepsie, N.Y., 1956-60; group supr. Olin Mathieson Co., New Haven, 1960-64; assoc. prof. chemistry High Point (N.C.) Coll., 1964-65; sr. rsch. chemist Reynolds Metals Co., Richmond, Va., 1965-72; chemist Babcock & Wilcox, Lynchburg, Va., 1972-95, Lynchburg Tree Steward, Lynchburg, 1995—. Mem. Am. Chem. Soc. Home: 5128 Wedgewood Rd Lynchburg VA 24503-4208

MORGAN, EVELYN BUCK, nursing educator; b. Phila., Nov. 3, 1931; d. Kenneth Edward and Evelyn Louise (Rhineberg) Buck; m. John Allen McGeary, Aug. 15, 1958 (div. 1964); children—John Andrew, Jacquelyn Ann McGeary Keplinger; m. Kenneth Dean Morgan, June 26, 1965 (dec. 1975). R.N., Muhlenberg Hosp. Sch. Nursing, 1955; B.S. in Nursing summa cum laude, Ohio State U., 1972, M.S., 1973; Ed.D., Nova. U., 1978. R.N., N.J., Ohio, Fla., Calif.; cert. clin. specialist Am. Nurses Assn. Psychiat.-Mental Health Clin. Specialists; advanced R.N. practitioner Fla. Bd. Nursing. Staff nurse Muhlenburg Hosp., Plainfield, N.J., 1955-57; indsl. nurse Western Electric Co., Columbus, Ohio, 1957-59; supr. Mt. Carmel Hosp., Columbus, 1960-65; instr. Grant Hosp. Sch. Nursing, 1965-72; cons. Ohio Dept. Health, 1972-74; prof. nursing Miami (Fla.)-Dade Community Coll., 1974-96, ret., 1996; family therapist Hollywood Pavilion Hosp., 1977-82; pvt. practice family therapy, Ft. Lauderdale, Fla., 1982—. Sustaining mem. Democratic Nat. Com., 1975—. Mem. ANA (cert. clin. specialist Fla.), Fla. Council Psychiat.-Mental Health Clin. Specialists, Nat. Guild Hypnotists, Am. Nurses Found., Am. Holistic Nurses Assn., Sigma Theta Tau. Democrat. Roman Catholic.

MORGAN, FRANK T., business educator, consultant; b. Shamokin, Pa., July 8, 1944; s. Burgess Sherman and Marion Regina (Lewis) M.; m. Nancy Ida Bishop, May 30, 1970; children: Elizabeth Marion, Douglas Bishop. AB, Princeton U., 1966; MS, Pa. State U., 1967; postgrad., Stevens Inst. Tech., Hoboken, N.J., 1976-79; PhD, Calif. Coast U., 1983. Cert. sr. profl. in human resources. Plant pers. mgr. Gen. Foods, Jacksonville, Fla., 1967-69; assoc. placement mgr. Gen. Foods, White Plains, N.Y., 1969-70; mgr. sales devel. Gen. Foods, 1970-71; mgr. orgn. devel. Berol Corp., Daubury, Conn., 1971-73; v.p. human resources Berol Corp., 1973-78, group v.p., 1978-87; dir. exec. edn. U. Va. Grad. Sch. Bus., Charlottesville, 1987-94, U. N.C., Chapel Hill, 1994—; bd. dirs. Danbury Med. Ctr., 1977-85; chmn. Danbury Edn. Adv. Coun., 1978-86; pres. Morgan Assocs., Charlottesville, 1987—. Contbr. articles to publs. Mem. Am. Psychol. Assn., Am. Soc. for Tng. and Devel., Am. Soc. for Pers. Adminstrn., Consortium for Exec. Edn. Republican. Episcopalian. Office: U NC CB 3445 Kenan Center Chapel Hill NC 27599-3445

MORGAN, G. KENNETH, association executive; b. Farmville, Va., Dec. 2, 1947; s. Raymond Henry and Evelyn (Healy) M.; m. Winnie Williams, Mar. 17, 1989; 1 child, Rebecca. BA, U. Richmond, 1974; MEd, Va. Commonwealth U., 1978. Cert. fundraising exec.; cert. assn. exec. Program dir. Va. affiliate Am. Heart Assn., Richmond, 1970-79; mgmt. cons. nat. office Am. Heart Assn., Dallas, 1979-82; exec. v.p. N.C. Am. Heart Assn., Chapel Hill, 1982-93; nonprofit cons. Morgan & Assocs., Chapel Hill, 1993—; mem. bd. advisors U. N.C. Sch. Pub. Health, Chapel Hill, 1984-93. Vol. Orange County chpt. ARC; bd. dirs. Orange County United Way. Mem. Nat. Health Agy. (pres. 1989-90), Am. Soc. Assn. Execs., Va. Assn. Rescue Squads (life, past pres.), Rotary (Service Above Self award). Presbyterian. Home: PO Box 16067 Chapel Hill NC 27516-6067 Office: Morgan and Assocs PO Box 16067 Chapel Hill NC 27516-6067

MORGAN, GEORGE EMIR, III, financial economics educator; b. Carmel, Calif., Jan. 2, 1953; s. George Emir Jr. and Dolores (Prydzial) M.; m. Donna Batts Vail, Dec. 31, 1977; 1 child, Abbie Vail. BS in Math., Georgetown U., 1973; MS in Stats., U. N.C., 1975, PhD in Fin., 1977. Sr. fin. economist Office of the Compt. of the Currency, Washington, 1978-79; asst. prof. U. Tex., Austin, 1979-84; assoc. prof. Va. Poly. Inst., Blacksburg, 1984-89, dir. PhD program, 1985-89, prof., 1989—, head dept. fin., 1995-96, Crestar prof. fin., 1995—; assoc. dir. bus. rsch. Ctr. Comml. Space Comms., 1990-94; assoc. dir. Ctr. for Wireless Telecomms. Ctr. Comml. Space Comm., 1994—; exec. dir. Ctrl. Comml. Space Comm., 1994—; cons. Investment Co. Inst., Washington, 1982-83. Editor (newsletter) 90 Day Notes, 1986-90. Mem. Am. Econ. Assn., Am. Fin. Assn., Am. Statis. Assn., So. Fin. Assn., Fin. Mgmt. Assn., Macintosh Blacksburg Users Group (faculty advisor 1989—), Beta Gamma Sigma. Office: Va Poly Inst Dept Fin 1016 Pamplin Hall Blacksburg VA 24061

MORGAN, GEORGE PIDCOCK, minister; b. Charleston, W.Va., Oct. 5, 1923; s. F. Bruce and Helen (Pidcock) M.; m. Helen Elizabeth Reiter Shoemaker, June 23, 1945 (div. 1983); children: Beth Ann Morgan Adcock, Melody Sue Morgan Srygley; m. Clara McMahon, Oct. 8, 1983; children: David Christopher, Sean Jarrett. BA, Lafayette Coll., 1943; BD, Princeton (N.J.) Sem., 1945; PhD, U. Edinburgh, Scotland, 1958. Ordained to ministry Presbyn. Ch., 1945. Pastor Freehold Presbyn. Ch., Charlton, N.Y., 1945-48, Cmty. Ch., Peru, N.Y., 1948-56; resident chaplain Rensselaer Poly. Inst., Troy, N.Y., 1956-63; campus ministry coord. Presbyn. North Coastal Area, San Francisco, 1963-65; exec. presbyter Presbytery of Albany, Watervliet, N.Y., 1965-75; synod exec. Synod of the Covenant, Columbus, Ohio, 1975-91; rehab. chaplain ServiceMaster Rehab. L.P., St. Augustine, Fla., 1993—. Editor Chapel and Coll. jour. Bd. dirs. N.Y./Ohio/Mich./Ky. Coun. Chs., 1957-91, Nat. Coun. Chs., 1982-85, Nat. Ch. Residences, Columbus, 1982-91; mem. faith and order commn. Consultation on Ch. Union, Princeton, 1981-89; del. World Coun. Chs., Vancouver, B.C., Can., 1983; moderator Champlain Presbytery, Plattsburgh, N.Y., 1955-56, Albany Presbytery, 1961-62; sec.-treas. N.E. Career Devel. Ctr., Princeton, 1959-65; mem. Tampa Bay Presbytery; assoc. admissions rep. Lafayette Coll., 1991—. Fulbright fellow, 1952-53, 53-54. Mem. Witherspoon Soc., Presbyn. Health Edn. and Welfare Assn. Democrat. Home and Office: 4818 Harbor Woods Dr Palm Harbor FL 34683

MORGAN, GEORGE WILLIAM, trade association administrator, consultant; b. Amityville, N.Y., July 4, 1935; s. George Howard and Ethel Elizabeth (Ferington) M.; m. Mary Petro, July 2, 1954 (div. Apr. 1979); children: George Anthony, Mary Elizabeth; m. Lillian White, Aug. 12, 1981. AA, Chabot Coll., 1966; BA, U. Md., 1975; MA, Cen. Mich. U., 1976; PhD, Columbia Pacific U., 1987. Registered profl. engr., Calif. Fire protection specialist Goddard Space Flight Ctr., Greenbelt, Md., 1968-73; chief fire and safety NASA, Washington, 1973-77; dir. fire protection div. USAF, Panama City, Fla., 1977-79, tech. dir. fire programs, civil airports Kingdom of Saudi Arabia, 1979-81; sr. fire protection engr. hdqrs. USAF, Washington, 1982-85; pres. Fire Safety Internat., Panama City, 1982—; gen. mgr. Sun Belt Fire & Safety Supply, Panama City, 1988—; cons. Western Hemisphere Sales, Clearwater, Fla., 1988—, Earli Gard Safety Products, Clearwater, 1988—, Pioneer Mfg., Inc., Pinellas, Fla., 1988—. Bd. dirs. Odenton (Md.) Fire Dept., 1968-77. With USN, 1953-58. Recipient Life Sav. award Am. Heart Assn., 1985, Space Ship Earth award NASA. Mem. Am. Soc. Safety Engrs., Soc. Fire Protection Engrs., Nat. Fire Protection Assn., Internat. Assn. Fire Chiefs, Fla. Engring. Soc. (sec. Gulf Coast chpt. 1988-89). Home: 1500 Dover Rd Panama City FL 32404-7313

MORGAN, GLENDA ANDERSON, municipal government official, educator; b. Liberty, Tex., July 19, 1944; d. Edgar Lloyd and Verley Lanell (Barnes) Anderson; m. Howard Lamont Morgan. AA, Copiah-Lincoln Jr. Coll., 1964; BA, Miss. State Coll. for Women, 1966; MRE, New Orleans Bapt. Theol. Sem., 1968; postgrad., U. South Ala., 1971—. Cert. mcpl. pers. adminstr., Ala., cert. mcpl. clk. Youth dir. Woodmont Bapt. Ch., Mobile, Ala., 1968; sec. Daupin Way Bapt. Ch., Mobile, 1968-70; tchr., guidance counselor 1st Ind. Meth. Ch. Sch., Mobile, 1970-76; personnel officer Mobile Pub. Library, 1976-85; tchr. 20th Century Coll., Mobile, 1980-85, U. South Ala., Mobile, 1984—; asst. city clk. City of Mobile, 1985-94, city clk., 1994—; owner, operator Frames & Things, Mobile, 1969-94; tchr. Ala. Christian Coll., Mobile, 1975-76, Bishop State Jr. Coll., Mobile, 1984-85. Sec. Daupin Way Bapt. Ch., Mobile, 1968-70; v.p. Mobile County Merit System Employee Assn., 1979-80, pres., 1980-84. Mem. Ala. Assn. Personnel Adminstrs., Ala. Assn. Mcpl. Clks. and Adminstrs., Ala. City Mgmt. Assn., Mobile Personnel Assn., Internat. Inst. Mcpl. Clks., Phi Theta Kappa. Baptist. Home: 1906 Navco Rd Mobile AL 36605-2810 Office: City of Mobile 205 Government St Mobile AL 36602-2613

MORGAN, HENRY COKE, JR., judge; b. Norfolk, Va., Feb. 8, 1935; s. Henry Coke and Dorothy Lea (Pebworth) M.; m. Margaret John McGrail, Aug. 18, 1965; 1 stepchild, A. Robertson Hanckel Jr.; children: Catherine Morgan Stockwell, Coke Morgan Stewart. BS, Washington and Lee U., 1957, JD, 1960. Bar: Va. 1960, U.S. Dist. Ct. (ea. dist.) Va. 1961, U.S. Ct. Appeals (4th cir.) 1964. Asst. city atty. City of Norfolk (Va.), 1960-63; ptnr., chief exec. officer Pender & Coward, Virginia Beach, Va., 1963-92; vice chmn., gen. counsel Princess Anne Bank, 1986-92; judge U.S. Dist. Ct. (ea. dist.) Va. 1992—. Served with U.S. Army, 1958-59. Episcopalian. Office: US Dist Ct, Eastern Disrtict of VA Walter E Hoffman US Courthouse 600 Granby St Norfolk VA 23510-1915*

MORGAN, LARRY RONALD, minister; b. Springhill, La., Mar. 12, 1936; s. Woodrow Wilson Morgan and Alma Elizabeth (Dunn) Burch; m. Elizabeth Dianne Baker, May 24, 1958; children: Elizabeth Denise Morgan Davis, Dennis Kevin. ADiv, Bapt. Missionary Assn. Theol. Sem., Jacksonville, Tex., 1990. Ordained to ministry Bapt. Ch., 1971. Clk., carrier U.S. P.O., Springhill, La., 1956-71; assoc. pastor Webb Chapel Bapt. Ch., Dallas, 1971-72, pastor, 1972—; clk., trustee Bapt. Missionary Assn. Sem., Jacksonville, 1983-86; chmn. bd. trustees Bapt. Progress, Dallas, 1984-87. Pres. PTA Browning Elem. Sch., Springhill, 1969-70. With USAR, 1959-66. Mem. Bapt. Missionary Assn. Am. (v.p. hdqrs. Little Rock 1985-86, pres. 1986-88, v.p. Am. 1996-97), Dallas County Bapt. Assn. (moderator 1982-84). Home: 14517 Heartside Dr Dallas TX 75234-2152

MORGAN, LINDA RICE, secondary education educator; b. Troy, Ohio, Feb. 14, 1949; d. George William and Eileen Dolores (Sines) R.; m. Thomas Buford Morgan, Nov. 25, 1978; 1 child, Malory Sue. BA, Marshall U., 1971, MS, 1974. Cert. profl. tchr., W.Va. Tchr. Marshall U. Community Coll., Huntington, W.Va., part-time 1977-79, Fairfield Sch., Cabell County Pub. Schs., Huntington, 1971-80; tchr. bus. edn. Huntington High Sch., 1980—, chmn. dept. bus., 1989—. Bd. dirs. Tri-State Montessori Pre-Sch., 1988-89. Mem. NEA, W.Va. Edn. Assn., Nat. Bus. Edn. Assn., Cabell County Edn. Assn., Phi Delta Kappa. Democrat. Home: 2224 Pleasant Valley Dr Huntington WV 25701-9304

MORGAN, LONA SCAGGS, speech professional educator; b. Chillicothe, Ohio, Oct. 2, 1949; d. Drewey P. and Ruth A. (McCloskey) Scaggs; m. Terry A. Morgan, Dec. 23, 1972; 1 child, Zachary Drew Morgan. BS in Hearing and Speech Sci., Ohio U., 1971; MEd in Adminstrn., Supervision, U. South Fla., 1983. Cert. speech and hearing sci., ednl. adminstrn. Speech pathologist Ross County Soc. for Crippled Children and Adults, Chillicothe, 1971; speech pathologist Zanesville (Ohio) City Schs., 1971-72, Hernando County Schs., Brooksville, Fla., 1973-74, Pasco County Sch. Dist., New Port Richey, Fla., 1974—; speech pathologist, speech mentor Pasco County Sch. Dist., 1994—. Recipient Pasco Pub. Schs. Found. grant, 1993. Mem. Fla. Speech and Hearing Assn., West Paco Jr. Woman's Club, Phi Delta Kappa. Methodist. Home: 7011 Tanglewood Dr New Port Richey FL 34654-5721 Office: Pasco County School Board Calusa Elem School 5720 Orchid Lake Dr New Port Richey FL 34654

MORGAN, LOU ANN, physical education educator; b. Andrews, N.C., Apr. 26, 1949; d. Jerry Myditt and Alice Josephine (O'Dell) Long; m. Frederick Wayne Morgan, July 9, 1972; children: Mandi Marie, Chad William. BS, Mars Hill Coll., 1971. Tchr. Farmer (N.C.) Elem. Sch., 1971-74, Flat Rock (N.C.) Jr. High Sch., 1974-81; craft dir. Camp Windy Wood, Tuxedo, N.C., 1981-84; tchr. weekday early edn. 1st Bapt. Ch., Hendersonville, N.C., 1983-84; phys. edn. specialist Dana (N.C.) Elem. Sch., 1984—. Co-author: (video) Outdoor Education ... Success for Everyon, 1993. Mem. scholarship com. 1st Bapt. Ch., Hendersonville, 1993—, mem. weekday early edn. com., 1985-86, mem. recreation/activities com., 1993-94. Named Outstanding Spring Vol. Henderson County Parks and Recreation, 1992; recipient Gov.'s Award for Fitness N.C. Gov.'s Coun. on Phys. Fitness and Health, 1994. Mem. AAHPERD, N.C. Assn. Health, Phys. Edn., Recreation and Dance (phys. edn. Western regional rep. 1994-95, Phys. Edn. Leadership Tng. steering com. 1989, 93, presider, presenter 1991, 94, Norm Leafe State Phys. Edn. Tchr. of Yr. 1990). Republican. Baptist. Home: 447 Sunset Dr Hendersonville NC 28791 Office: Dana Elem Sch PO Box 37 Dana NC 28724-0037

MORGAN, LUCY W., journalist; b. Memphis, Oct. 11, 1940; d. Thomas Allin and Lucile (Sanders) Keen; m. Alton F. Ware, June 26, 1958 (div. Sept. 1967); children—Mary Kathleen, Andrew Allin; m. Richard Alan Morgan, Aug. 9, 1968; children—Lynn Elwell, Kent Morgan. A.A., Pasco Hernando Community Coll., New Port Richey, Fla., 1975; student, U. South Fla., 1976-80. Reporter Ocala Star Banner, Fla., 1965-68; reporter St. Petersburg Times, Fla., 1967-86, capitol bur. chief, 1986—; assoc. editor and bd. dirs. Times Pub. Co. Recipient Paul Hansel award Fla. Soc. Newspaper Editors, 1981, First in Pub. Service award Fla. Soc. Newspaper Editors, 1982, First Place award in pub. service Fla. Press Club, 1982, Pulitzer award for investigative reporting Columbia U., 1985, First Place award in investigative reporting Sigma Delta Chi, 1985; named to Kappa Tau Alpha Hall of Fame, 1992. Home: 1727 Brookside Blvd Tallahassee FL 32301-6769 Office: Saint Petersburg Times 336 E College Ave Tallahassee FL 32301-1551

MORGAN, MARIANNE, corporate professional; b. Muncie, Ind., Oct. 13, 1940; d. Clarence Wilson and Mary Estle (Shafer) M. BA, Calif. State U., Long Beach, 1962; MS, U. So. Calif., 1968. Lic. real estate salesperson, Fla. Lab. technician Ball Meml. Hosp. Pathology Lab, Muncie, 1956-61; sr. libr. asst. Anaheim (Calif.) Pub. Libr., 1963-68; coll. libr. Orange Coast Coll., Costa Mesa, Calif., 1968-73; exec. v.p. Brady Products, Inc., Clearwater, Fla., 1973—; bd. dirs. Brady Products, Inc., Clearwater, Suncoast Fluid Power, Inc., Clearwater. Fiction book reviewer, Libr. Jour., 1969-73; photography pub. in Irvine mag., 1973. Named Alice Miriam Kitselman Scholar, Kitselman Estate, Muncie, 1958. Mem. Nat. Water Well Assn., Boat Owners of the U.S., U.S. Tennis Assn., Eastlake Woodlands CountryClub, Sea Ray Boat Owners Club. Republican.

MORGAN, MICHAEL JOHN, international consultant; b. Casablanca, Morocco, Nov. 7, 1958; s. Bruce Ray and Bette Jeanne (Moore) M.; m. Kathleen Marie Kren, Sept. 29, 1984; children: Julianne Nicole, Jeffrey Daniel. BA, U. S.C., 1980; MPA, Am. U., 1983. Mgmt. analyst Saudi Basic Industries Corp., Riyadh, Saudi Arabia, 1982; mktg. rep. Mastercard Middle East, Dubai, United Arab Emirates, 1983-84; co-op edn. coord. Am. U., Washington, 1984-87; program evaluator U.S. Gen. Acctg. Office, Washington, 1987-88, dep. project mgr., 1988-90; dir. planning and new ventures Bruce Morgan Assocs., Inc., Arlington, Va., 1991-95, v.p. ops., 1995—; facilitator for a "Table Talk" on Internat. Coop. Edn., Co-op Conf., Williamsburg, Va., 1986; cons. Inst. for Planned Change, Inc., 1982. Recipient Outstanding Achievement award U.S. GAO, 1988, Spl. Commendation award, 1988; selected Woodrow Wilson fellow, 1985. Mem. Am. Mktg. Assn., Am. Mgmt. Assn. Office: Bruce Morgan Assocs Inc 1010 N Glebe Rd Ste 500 Arlington VA 22201-4749

MORGAN, MICHAEL JOSEPH, consultant; b. Canton, Ohio, Nov. 28, 1953; s. Edward A. and Mary Arlene (Maier) M.; m. Deborah Mae Beach, Mar. 2, 1979 (div. Sept. 1986). BSBA, Old Dominion U., 1982, MBA, 1989. Lic. journeyman, aircraft mechanic. Aircraft mechanic Naval Air Rework Facility, Norfolk, Va., 1976-82; resource analyst Newport News (Va.) Shipbuilding, 1982-84; sr. planner Bendix Electronic Controls Div., Newport News, 1984-85; program mgr. Superior Engring., Norfolk, 1985-88; dept. mgr. CACI, Virginia Beach, Va., 1988-94; pres. The Acquisition Group, Inc., Hampton, Va., 1994—. With USN, 1971-75. Mem. Am. Prodn. and Inventory Control Soc. Republican. Roman Catholic. Home: 512 Concord Dr Hampton VA 23666-2205 Office: The Acquisition Group Inc Hampton VA 23666

MORGAN, PHILLIS PIERCE, English language educator; b. Tupelo, Miss., July 3, 1951; d. Milford Doris and Elsie Flora (Hogue) Magers; m. David Wayne Morgan, Dec. 22, 1983; 1 child, Jonathan David. AA, Southeastern Bapt. Coll., 1971; BA, William Carey Coll., 1973, MA, 1978. Tchr. George County H.S., Lucedale, Miss., 1973-75, 76-80, East Ctrl. H.S., Hurley, Miss., 1981—. Mem. Nat. Coun. Tchrs. English. Baptist. Home: 109 Romania Tanner Rd Lucedale MS 39452 Office: East Central H S PO Box 13 Hurley MS 39555

MORGAN, RALPH REXFORD, manufacturing company executive; b. Denver, Nov. 5, 1944; s. William and Norma Elaine (Bowery) Skow; 1 child, Andrew. BA, U. Omaha, 1967; MA, U. Nebr., 1969. Cert. reliability engr.; cert. quality engr. Dir. spl. projects Oklahoma City Housing Authority, 1975-77; dir. of ops. Behavior Mgmt., Inc., Oklahoma City, 1977-79; sr. statis. engr. Firestone Tire & Rubber Co., Oklahoma City, 1979-87; statistician Control Data Corp., Oklahoma City, 1987-89; dir. quality assurance York Internat. Corp., Norman, Okla., 1989-93, quality mgr., 1993—; v.p. Morgan, Morgan & Assocs., Edmond, Okla., 1983-89. Capt. USAF, 1969-75. Mem. Am. Soc. for Quality Control. Home: 2129 NW 113th St Oklahoma City OK 73120-7617

MORGAN, ROBERT GEORGE, accounting educator, researcher; b. Sanford, Maine, Feb. 20, 1941; s. George Andrew and Katherine (Gray) M.; children: Robert George, Katherine Neva. BA, Piedmont Coll., Demorest, Ga., 1969; MAcctg, U. Ga., 1971, PhD, 1974. CPA, N.C.; cert. mgmt. acctg. Asst. prof. acctg. U. Wyo., Laramie, 1974-76, Drexel U., Phila., 1976-80; assoc. prof. acctg. U. N.C.-Greensboro, 1980-83; prof. acctg. Loyola Coll., Balt., 1983-85; chmn. dept. acctg. East Tenn. State U., Johnson City, 1985-92; prof. acctg., 1985—. Editor jour. The Mgmt. Rev., 1983-85; contbr. articles to profl. jours. Treas. Running Brook PTA, Columbia, Md., 1984-85. Mem. AICPA, Inst. Mgmt. Accts. (pres. East Tenn. chpt. 1995-96), Am. Acctg. Assn., Acad. Acctg. Historians, Tenn. Soc. Acctg. Educators (pres. 1986-87), Beta Gamma Sigma, Beta Alpha Psi. Methodist. Avocation: golf. Home: 757 Hamilton Trl Piney Flats TN 37686-3925 Office: E Tenn State U Dept Acctg PO Box 70710 Johnson City TN 37614-0710

MORGAN, ROBERT STEVE, mechanical engineer; b. Oklahoma City, Oct. 10, 1945; s. Chester Steve and Madelein Ruth (Stowers) M.; m. Margaret Ann Groves, June 7, 1971; children: Jerri Dianna, Jamie Deann. Diploma, S.W. Tech. Inst., 1967. Chief draftsman R.L. Gilstrap Inc., Oklahoma City, 1966-67; mgr. print dept. Phelps-Spitz-Ammerman-Thomas Inc., Oklahoma City, 1967-68; sr. drafter GE, Oklahoma City, 1968-70; mech. designer Honeywell Inc., Oklahoma City, 1970-75; pvt. practice Oklahoma City, 1970—; sr. designer Control Data Corp., Oklahoma City, 1970-75; sr. designer, drafting coord., cad adminstr. BancTec Inc., Oklahoma City, 1984-96; design engr. Climate Master, Oklahoma City, 1996, Texas Instruments, Dallas, 1996—. Patentee overlap document detector, double document detector, ribbon cartridge. Voter organizer Rep. Party, Oklahoma City, 1967; asst. leader Girl Scouts of Am., Yukon, Okla., 1984. Mem. Confederate Air Force (col.). Republican. Home: 704 Victoria Dr Yukon OK 73099-5341

MORGAN, RUTH PROUSE, academic administrator, educator; b. Berkeley, Calif., Mar. 30, 1934; d. Ervin Joseph and Thelma Ruth (Prcesang) Prouse; m. Vernon Edward Morgan, June 3, 1956; children: Glenn Edward, Renée Ruth. BA summa cum laude, U. Tex., 1956; MA, La. State U., 1961, PhD, 1966. Asst. prof. Am. govt., politics and theory So. Meth. U., Dallas, 1966-70, assoc. prof., 1970-74, prof., 1974-95; prof. emeritus, 1995—; asst. provost So. Meth. U., Dallas, 1978-82, assoc. provost, 1982-86, provost ad interim, 1986-87, provost, 1987-93, provost emerita, 1993—; pres. RPM Assocs., 1993—; v.p. ABATECH, Inc., 1995—; Tex. state polit. analyst ABC, N.Y.C., 1972-84. Author: The President and Civil Rights, 1970; mem. editorial bd. Jour. of Politics, 1975-82, Presdl. Studies Quar., 1980—; contbr. articles to profl. jours. Active Internat. Women's Forum, 1987—; trustee Hockaday Sch., 1988-94; trustee The Kilby Awards Found., 1993-95; bd. dirs. United Way, Met. Dallas, 1993—; mem. adv. com. U.S. Army Command and Gen. Staff. Coll., 1994—; chmn. adv. com. Archives of Women of the Southwest, 1995—. Mem. Am. Polit. Sci. Assn., So. Polit. Sci. Assn. (mem. exec. coun. 1979-84), Southwestern Polit. Sci. Assn. (pres. 1982-83, mem. exec. coun. 1981-84), The Dallas Forum of Internat. Women's Forum (pres. 1996-98), Charter 100 Club (pres. 1991-92), Dallas Summit Club (pres. 1992-93), Phi Beta Kappa, Pi Sigma Alpha, Phi Kappa Phi, Theta Sigma Phi.

MORGAN, SYLVIA DENISE (MRS. HAROLD MORGAN), school administrator; b. Rome, Ga., Sept. 1, 1952; d. Herman Hamilton and Garnette Lucille (Strickland) Haynes; m. Harold Morgan, Feb. 22, 1980; 1 child, Amber. BS in English, Knoxville Coll., 1974; MEd, Ga. State U., 1977; EdS, Jacksonville State U., 1989. Tchr. Ga. Sch. for the Deaf, Cave Spring, 1974-80, reading lab. coord., 1980-82, curriculum dir., 1982-90, vocat. supr., 1990-94, case mgmt./mgr. coord., 1994-96, ednl. supr., 1996—. Mem. NAACP, Nat. Edn. Assn., Ga. Assn. Educators, Ga. Educators for the Hearing Impaired, Alpha Kappa Alpha. Home: 8 Tasso Cir Rome GA 30161-5776

MORGAN, TIM DALE, physical education educator; b. Covington, Ky., Jan. 8, 1964; s. Thomas Benjamin and Audrey (Crider) M.; m. Shirley Mae Oliver, Nov. 9, 1992; children: Joshua David-Thomas, Andrew Jacob. BS in Phys. Edn., Ch. Recreation, Campbellsville Coll., 1991; MS in Phys. Edn., Ea. Ky. U., 1992, MS in Recreation and Park Adminstrn., 1993; diploma in fitness and nutrition, Internat. Corr. Schs., 1992. Cert. in real estate, Ky. Asst. facility coord. Bapt. Student Union No. Ky. U., Highland Heights, 1986-88, supr. health ctr., 1986-87; dept. asst. Campbellsville (Ky.) Coll., 1988-91; mem. staff dept. phys. edn. Ea. Ky. U., Richmond, 1991-92, intramurals facility coord., 1992-93, phys. edn. instr., 1993—; survey coord. Champions Against Drugs, Campbellsville, 1990-91; adminstr. phys. testing Ky. State Police, Ea. Ky. U., Richmond, 1992. Fellowship dir. Bapt. Student Union, 1987-88, commuter coord., 1989, dir., adminstr. recreation, 1992; summer missionary So. Bapt. Conv. Home Mission Bd., Atlanta, 1987-89; vol. Christian Life Ctr., Campbellsville Bapt. Ch., 1990-91; music dir., tchr. coll. Sunday sch. Acton (Ky.) Bapt. Ch., 1990. Lance Cpl. USMC, 1982-88. Mem. AAHPERD. Democrat. Home and Office: Ea Ky U 136 Oakland Ave Richmond KY 40475-1958

MORGAN, TIMI SUE, lawyer; b. Parsons, Kans., June 16, 1953; d. James Daniel and Iris Mae (Wilson) Baumgardner; m. Rex Michael Morgan, Oct. 28, 1983; children: Tessa Anne, Camma Elizabeth. BS, U. Kans., 1974; JD, So. Meth. U., 1977. Bar: Tex. 1977, U.S. Dist. Ct. (no. dist.) Tex. 1978, U.S. Ct. Appeals (5th cir.) 1979, U.S. Tax Ct. 1980; cert. tax law specialist. Assoc. Gardere & Wynne, Dallas, 1977-79; assoc. Akin, Gump, Strauss, Hauer & Feld, Dallas, 1979-83, ptnr., 1984-86; of counsel Stinson, Mag & Fizzell, Dallas, 1986-88; sole practice Dallas, 1988—; adj. lectr. law So. Meth. U., 1989-90, '92—. Bd. dirs. Dallas Urban League Inc., 1987-91. Mem. ABA (mem. taxation sect.), State Bar Tex. (mem. taxation sect.), Dallas Bar Assn., So. Meth. U. Law Alumni Coun. (sec. 1985-86), Order of Coif, Beta Gamma Sigma. Republican. Episcopalian. Home: 3719 Euclid Ave Dallas TX 75205

MORGAN, VICTOR HALL, clergyman; b. Jacksonville, Fl., Dec. 14, 1956; s. Clifton Hall and Evelyn Virginia (Sandidge) M. BA, Miss. Coll., 1979; cert., St. Joseph Angelican Coll., 1985. Asst. to episc. chaplain U. Ala. Trinity Episc., Tuscaloosa, Ala., 1986-87; founding rector St. Luke's Episc. Ch., Blue Ridge, Ga., 1987—; mem. standing com. Episc. Diocese Miss. South, Monteagle, Tenn., 1993—; mem. bd. dirs. N. Ga. Crisis Network, Blue Ridge. Editor: The News Observer, Blue Ridge, Ga., 1987—. Episcopalian. Home: 141 Forest Crescent Blue Ridge GA 30513 Office: Saint Luke Episc Ch Jones at Ewing St Blue Ridge GA 30513

MORGAN, VIRGINIA DEAPO, business owner; b. Syracuse, N.Y., Oct. 28, 1934; d. William John and Mary (Sojewicz) Deapo; m. Robert Lee Morgan Jr., Sept. 1, 1962; 1 child, Robert Lee III. BS, SUNY, Cortland, 1956, MS, 1961; EdD, Nova U., 1979. Tchr. math. Camillus (N.Y.) Sch. Dist. # 1, 1956-61, Dept. Def. Dependent Sch., Clark AFB, The Philippines, 1961-63, Charles County Bd. Edn., La Plata, Md., 1966-68; asst. prof. math. Charles Community Coll., La Plata, 1968-72; instr. Anson Tech. Coll., Ansonville, N.C., 1972-74, dean students, 1974-79; prin. Southview Acad., Wadesboro, N.C., 1979-82; funeral dir. Morgan & Son. Funeral Home, Marshville, N.C., 1982—; dept. chair gen. edn., math. instrn. Montgomery Community Coll., Troy, N.C., 1985—; part time instr. Gardner-Webb Coll., Boiling Springs, N.C., 1988—. Chmn. Union County Bd. Edn., Monroe, N.C., 1977-85. Mem. Am. Math. Assn. Two Yr. Colls., N.C. Assn. Tchrs., N.C. Funeral Dirs. Assn., Women Adminstrs. N.C. Higher Edn., N.C. State Sch. Bd. Assn. (bd. dirs. 1981-85). Office: Montgomery C C PO Box 787 Troy NC 27371-0787

MORGAN, WANDA BUSBY, health care executive, educator; b. Cromwell, Okla., Aug. 27, 1930; d. Charles C. and Gladys J. (Beaty) Busby; m. James O. Morgan, Oct. 23, 1954; children: Terri, Kathleen, Martha. BA, Lincoln (Ill.) Christian Coll., 1954; MA, Kans. State U., 1973; postgrad., Cen. State U., Edmond, Okla., 1977-79, U. Okla., 1980-84, Purdue U., 1983. Prof. Manhattan (Kans.) Christian Coll., Manhattan, 1970-74; instr. Seminole (Okla.) Jr. Coll., 1978-80; prof. Bethany (Okla.) Nazarene Coll., 1980-84; instr. Moravian Coll., Bethlehem, Pa., 1984-85, Allentown Coll., Center Valley, Pa., 1985-88; edn. coordinator Sacred Heart HealthCare System, Allentown, Pa., 1985-87; v.p. Sacred Heart Health Care System, Allentown, Pa., 1987-95; instr. Ctrl. Ala. C.C., Alexander City, Ala., 1995-96; dir. investor rels. Guilford Capital Corp., Montgomery, Ala., 1996—; cons. Communication Arts, Ltd., Allentown, 1978-95; advisor Okla. Dept. Edn., Oklahoma City, 1981; tchr., cons. U. Okla. Dept. Edn., Norman, 1980-84, Okla. Writing Project, 1980-84; instr. Lehigh County Cmty. Coll., 1989-91. Author: Bridging the English Gap, 1983; co-author: Grammar, Ltd., 1983. Mem. adv. bd. Lehigh County (Pa.) Human Svcs. Dept., 1986-89, chmn., 1988-89; mem. Lehigh Valley Action Com. United Way, 1992-94, Children's Coalition Lehigh Valley, 1993-94. Fellow U. Okla., 1980. Mem. Am. Soc. Healthcare Mktg. and Pub. Rels., Okla. Coun. Tchrs. English (vice chair coll. sect. 1983-84), Rotary. Democrat. Presbyterian.

MORGANTE, JOHN-PAUL, state government training administrator; b. Yonkers, N.Y., June 26, 1962; s. Enzo and Teresa (DellaToffola) M.; m. Ellen Rothberger, May 26, 1984; children: Camden Anne, Bethany Nicole, Hailee Marie. BA, U. So. Calif., L.A., 1984. Ordained to ministry Christian Ch., 1987; cert. profl. in human resources. Adminstrv. dir. MCM Internat., Lomita, Calif., 1984-91; exec. dir. Champions for Christ, Austin, Tex., 1991-93; pres. Annimar Assocs., Austin, 1994; tng. specialist Tex. Dept. Health, Austin, 1994—. Mem. ctrl. com. Orange County (Calif.) Reps., 1988-89; intern U.S. Rep. Robert Badham, Washington, 1983, campaign worker, 1984; intern Assemblyman Curt Pringle, Garden Grove, Calif., 1988; campaign worker U.S. Senator Chic Hecht, 1982, U.S. Rep. Robert Dornan, 1984, Reagan-Bush, 1984, Tex. State rep. Terry Keel, Austin, 1996; mem. solicitation bd. City of Austin, 1996—; del. Dist. 14 Rep. Conv., Austin, 1996; mem. nat. nominating com. Outstanding Young Ams., 1996—. Recipient Rep. Presdl. Legion of Merit, Presdl. Commemorative Honor Roll, 1991, Staff Mem. of Yr., 1987; commd. Hon. Texan by Gov. George Bush, 1995. Mem. ASTD, Soc. for Human Resource Mgmt., Internat. Platform Assn. Office: Tex Dept Health 1100 W 49th St Austin TX 78756

MORIN, RICHARD, professional society administrator. Exec. v.p. Nat. Assn. Temple Educators, Nashville. Office: Nat Assn Temple Educators 707 Summerly Dr Nashville TN 37209-4218*

MORIN, THOMAS H., food distribution executive; b. Blue Island, Ill., Oct. 31, 1952; s. Richard Harold and Lillian Marie (Hickey) M.; m. Wendy Louise Psomas, Apr. 4, 1981; children: Timothy, Michael, Shannon, Douglas. BBA, U. Wis., Whitewater, Wis., 1973. Food technologist Nat. Portion Control, Chgo., 1974-75; dir. quality assurance Federated Foods, Pk. Ridge, Ill., 1976-82; v.p. quality assurance Nifda, Atlanta, 1982-88; v.p. quality assurance/logistics ComSource, Atlanta, 1988—; chmn. tech. stds. com. Internat. Foodsvc. Distbrs. Assn., Falls Church, Va., 1993-96. Author: Canned Goods Specification Manual, 1983, Frozen Food Specification Manual, 1985. Asst. cubmaster Pack 1776 Boy Scouts of Am., Marietta, Ga., 1990-92, cubmaster, 1993—, asst. scoutmaster, 1995—, commr. Cobb Dist. Roundtable, 1996—; mem. family mass liturgy com. Cath. Ch. of St. Ann's, Marietta, 1994—. Recipient Disting. Svc. award Internat. Foodsvc. Distbrs. Assn., 1996, Bronze Pelican award Cath. Com. Scouting, 1996. Mem. KC (3d degree), Inst. Food Technologists. Roman Catholic.

MORONEY, LINDA L. S., lawyer, educator; b. Washington, May 27, 1943; d. Robert Emmet and Jessie (Robinson) M.; m. Clarence Renshaw II, Mar. 28, 1967 (div. 1977); children: Robert Milnor, Justin W.R. BA, Randolph-Macon Woman's Coll., 1965; JD cum laude, U. Houston, 1982. Bar: Tex. 1982, U.S. Ct. Appeals (5th cir.) 1982, U.S. Dist. Ct. (so. dist.) Tex. 1982, U.S. Supreme Ct. 1988. Law clk. to assoc. justice 14th Ct. Appeals, Houston, 1982-83; assoc. Pannill and Reynolds, Houston, 1983-85, Gilpin, Pohl & Bennett, Houston, 1985-89, Vinson & Elkins, Houston, 1989-96; adj. prof. law U. Houston, 1989-91, dir. legal rsch. and writing, 1992-96. Fellow Houston Bar Found.; mem. ABA, State Bar Tex., Houston Bar Assn., Assn. of Women Attys., Order of the Barons, Phi Delta Phi. Episcopalian. Home and Office: 3730 Overbrook Ln Houston TX 77027-4036

MOROSANI, GEORGE WARRINGTON, real estate developer, realtor; b. Cin., July 20, 1941; s. Remy Edmond and Virginia Caroline (Warrington) M.; m. Judith Clontz, July 3, 1980; children by previous marriage: Katherine Carmichael, Elizabeth Warrington. BA, Rollins Coll., 1964, MBA, 1965. Fin. mgr. Lunar Orbitor and Minuteman Programs, Boeing Co., Cape Canaveral, Fla., 1965-68; controller Equitable Leasing Co., Asheville, N.C., 1968-69; founder, pres., treas. Western Carolina Warehousing Co., Asheville, 1969-87; co-founder, pres. Asheville Jaycee Housing, Inc., 1971-77; founder, pres., treas. A Mini Storage Co. (dba George's Stor-Mor), Asheville, N.C., 1976—; co-founder, treas. Accent on Living Co., Asheville, 1978-81; founder, pres., treas. G.M. Leasing, Asheville, N.C. 1986—, The Kingswood Co., Fletcher, N.C., 1986—; gen. partner Pine Needle Apts., Arden, N.C., 1978—, Pine Ridge Apts., Skyland, N.C., 1980—, Morganton Heights Apts., Morganton, N.C., 1981—, Maiden (N.C.) Apts., 1981—, Valley View Shopping Ctr., Candler, N.C., 1982-86, Meadow Garden Apts., Hendersonville, N.C., 1983—, Drexel Apts., N.C., 1983—, Heritage Hill Apts., Marion, N.C., 1983—, Cavalier Arms Apts., Waynesville, N.C., 1986—, Gwenmont Arms Apts., Murphy, N.C., 1986—, Nicol Arms Apts., Sylva, N.C., 1986—, Meadowwood Arms Apts., Gray, Tenn., 1986—, 4 Seasons Apts., Erwin, Tenn., 1986—, M. Realty LP, Asheville, 1986—, Woods Edge Apts., North Wilksboro, N.C., 1987—, Pond and Assocs., Asheville, 1992-94, Deer Park Apts., Cleve., N.C., 1987—; ptnr. Laurel Ridge Realty, Litchfield, Conn., 1973—, Laurel Properties, Rochester, Vt., 1978-94, Ashland Assocs., Asheville, N.C., 1985-88, Airport Assocs., Asheville, 1986-87; founder, owner George W. Morosani & Assocs., Asheville, 1981—, George's Rent-All, Asheville, N.C., 1988—; mgr. FI Realty I LLC, 1993—, Western Realty LLC, Asheville, 1994—, M Realty I LLC, 1994—, Sweeten Creek Realty LLC, 1994—, FI Realty I, LLC, 1994—, Patton Ave, LLC, 1995—, 3M Realty, LLC, 1995—. Bd. dirs. Jr. Achievement Greater Asheville Area, 1977—; mem. Regional Housing Adv. Com., 1981-86, Land-of-Sky Regional Coun., 1981-86, bd. dirs, 1990—; mem. Council Rural Housing and Devel., 1982-86, N.C. Real Estate Licensing Bd., S.C. Real Estate Commn., Tenn. Real Estate Commn., Ga. Real Estate Licensing Bd., Asheville Multiple Listing Svc., Hendersonville Multiple Listing Svc.; co-founder, treas. N.C. Council Rural Rental Housing, 1985—, sec., 1986-91; mem. Buncombe County Bd. Adjustment, 1988—, vice chmn., 1991—. Named Man of Yr., Asheville Jaycees, 1976. Mem. Sales and Mktg. Execs. Asheville (dir. 1974-76, 1982-84, chmn. membership com. 1976-77), Asheville Bd. Realtors, Hendersonville Bd. Realtors, Nat. Assn. Realtors, N.C. Assn. Realtors (property mgmt. div.). Mem. Asheville Comml. and Investment Realty Assn. (v.p. programs 1986-87, sec.-treas. 1987-92, 94—, pres., 1993), Nat. Mini-Storage Inst., W.N.C. Exchangers, Greater Asheville Apt. Assn. (chmn. membership com. 1988-89), Council Ind. Bus. Owners, Better Bus. Bur. Asheville/Western N.C. (dir. 1987—, second vice chmn. 1990, first vice chmn. 1991, chmn., 1992, chmn. nominating com., 1993), Econ. Devel. Assn. Western N.C., Self-Service Storage Assn., Asheville Area C. of C. (chmn. indsl. relations 1978-79), Hendersonville C. of C., Buncombe County Bd. of Adjustment (bd. dirs. 1988—, vice chmn. 1991—). Episcopalian. Clubs: Biltmore Forest Country, Asheville Downtown City. Lodge: Civitan (dir. 1975-77). Office: 932 Hendersonville Rd Asheville NC 28803-1761

MORREAU, JAMES EARL, JR., lawyer, entrepreneur; b. Richmond, Ky., Mar. 23, 1955; s. James E. and Betty Ann (Willoughby) M.; m. Jane Cecil, Apr. 11, 1981; children: Jacqueline Mary, Gregory James. BA, U. Louisville, 1977, JD, 1980. Bar: Ky. 1980, U.S. Dist. Ct. (we. dist.) Ky. 1984, U.S. Dist. Ct. (we. dist.) Tenn. 1985, U.S. Ct. Appeals (6th cir.) 1987, U.S. Supreme Ct. 1988, U.S. Ct. Appeals (9th cir.) 1995. Assoc. Taustine, Post et al, Louisville, 1980-87; co-owner, v.p., gen. counsel Investment Properties Assocs., Louisville, 1987—; pres., chief counsel Morreau Law Offices, P.S.C., Louisville, 1991; chief litigation ptnr. Kruger, Schwartz & Morreau, 1992—; gen. counsel MKS Enterprises, Memphis, 1987-93; owner, operator Mother & Child, Louisville, 1988-91. Mem. ABA, ATLA, Ky. Assn. Trial Lawyers, Ky. Bar Assn., Louisville Bar Assn., Internat. Platform Assn., Louisville Entrepreneur Soc. Republican. Roman Catholic. Home: 8108 Limehouse Ln Louisville KY 40220-3831 Office: 2 Paragon Ctr Ste 220 Louisville KY 40205

MORREIM, E. HAAVI, medical ethics educator; b. Austin, Minn., July 21, 1950; d. Paul Eugene and Florence Adeline (Haavik) M. BA in Philosophy, St. Olaf Coll., 1972; MA in Philosophy, U. Va., 1976, PhD, 1980. Med. philosopher program in human biology and soc. U. Va. Sch. Medicine, Charlottesville, 1980-82, asst. prof. philosophy in medicine, 1982-84; from asst. to assoc. prof. dept. human values and ethics U. Tenn. Coll. Medicine, Memphis, 1984-93, prof. dept. human values and ethics, 1993—; adj. prof. philosophy Va. Commonwealth U., Richmond, 1980; vis. prof. philosophy St. Olaf Coll., Northfield, Minn., 1982; Andrew Mellon vis. asst. prof. humanities and medicine Georgetown U. Sch. Medicine, Washington, 1983; sr. vis. rsch. scholar Kennedy Inst. Ethics, Georgetown U., 1983; manuscript reviewer; presenter and lectr. in field. Author: Balancing Act: The New Medical Ethics of Medicine's New Economics, 1991: mem. editorial bd. Theoretical Medicine, Jour. Medicine and Philosophy, Jour. Law, Medicine and Ethics; author articles. Active Hastings Ctr. Mem. Nat. Health Lawyers Assn., Am. Soc. Law, Medicine and Ethics, Soc. for Bioethics Consultation (bd. dirs. 1993—), Soc. for Health and Human Values (exec. coun. 1992-95), Phi Beta Kappa. Home: 2032 Harbert Ave Memphis TN 38104-5331 Office: Univ Tenn Coll Medicine 956 Court Ave Ste B328 Memphis TN 38103-2814

MORRILL, RICHARD LESLIE, university administrator; b. Weymouth, Mass., June 4, 1939; s. Duncan Russel and Violet Erma (Gibson) M.; m. Martha Leahy, June 24, 1964; children: Katie, Amy. A.B. in History magna cum laude, Brown U., 1961; B.D. in Religious Thought, Yale U., 1964; Ph.D. in Religion, Duke U., 1968. Instr. Wells Coll., Aurora, N.Y., 1967-68; asst. prof. Chatham Coll., Pitts., 1968-74, assoc. prof., 1974-77, assoc. provost and asst. to pres., 1973-77; assoc. provost Pa. State U., University Park, 1977-79; pres. Salem Coll. and Acad., Winston-Salem, N.C., 1979-82, Centre Coll., Danville, Ky., 1982-88, U. Richmond, Va., 1988—; bd. dirs. Ctrl. Fidelity Banks, Inc.; v.p. So. Univ. Conf., 1993—; chmn. Assoc. Colls. of the South, 1993-94; v.p. So. Univ. Conf., 1993—; mem. governing coun. Wye Faculty Seminar, 1994—; mem. presdl. adv. com. KPMG Peat Marwick, 1989—; cons. edn. divsn. Lilly Endowment, 1990—. Author: Teaching Values in College, 1980; contbr. articles to profl. jours. Bd. dirs., mem. program com. Teagle Found., 1989—; mem. nat. bd. visitors Ind. U. Ctr. on Philanthropy, 1991—; mem. commn. on leadership devel. Am. Coun. on Edn., 1992-94; trustee Williamsburg Investment Trust, 1993—; mem. Richmond Symphony Coun., 1995—; mem. Va. Coun. for Internat. Edn., 1995-96; bd. dirs. Assn. Am. Colls. and Univs., 1996—. Woodrow Wilson fellow, 1961-62; James B. Duke fellow Duke U., 1964-67. Mem. Soc. for Values in Higher Edn. (dir. 1981-84), Am. Acad. Religion, Am. Soc. for Christian Ethics, Am. Assn. Higher Edn., So. Assn. Colls. and Schs. (commr. 1985—), Coll. Athletic Conf. (chmn. 1985-87), Council Ind. Ky. Colls. and Univs. (sec. 1984-86, v.p. 1986-88, exec. com. 1984-86), Assn. Presbyn. Colls. and Univs. (exec. com. 1984-86), Phi Beta Kappa. Club: University. Lodge: Rotary. Home: 7000 River Rd Richmond VA 23229-8532 Office: U Richmond Pres Office Richmond VA 23173-1903*

MORRIN, VIRGINIA WHITE, retired college educator; b. Escondido, Calif., May 16, 1913; d. Harry Parmalee and Ethel Norine (Nutting) Rising; BS, Oreg. State Coll., 1952; MEd, Oreg. State U., 1957; m. Raymond Bennett White, 1933 (dec. 1953); children: Katherine Anne, Marjorie Virginia, William Raymond; m. 2d, Laurence Morrin, 1959 (dec. 1972). Social caseworker Los Angeles County, Los Angeles, 1934-40, 61-64; acctg. clk. War Dept., Ft. MacArthur, Calif., 1940-42; prin. clk. USAAF, Las Vegas, Nev., 1942-44; high sch. tchr., North Bend-Coos Bay, Oreg., 1952-56, Mojave, Calif., 1957-60; instr. electric bus. machines Antelope Valley Coll., Lancaster, Calif., 1961-73; ret., 1974. Treas., Humane Soc. Antelope Valley, Inc., 1968—. Mem. Nat. Aero. Assn., Calif. State Sheriffs' Assn. (charter assoc.), Oreg. State U. Alumni Assn. (life).

MORRIS, ANNA ROCHELLE, retail and wholesale executive; b. Lubbock, Tex., Dec. 31, 1957; d. Raphael and JoAnn (Davis) Gillespie; m. Gary Dean Rosselle (div.); m. Randall C. Fraelich (div.); m. Aaron Myles Morris, Nov.

15, 1988. Photographer Miami Seaquarium, Key Biscayne, Fla., 1975-77, Trader Publs., Clearwater, Fla., 1978; salesperson Rex Art Co., Miami, 1979-81, customer svc. rep., 1981-84, asst. purchaser, 1984-87, exec. asst., 1987—. Mem. hospitality com. Miami Film Festival, 1985-86; sec. Freddick Bratcher & Co., South Miami, Fla., 1986—. Democrat. Jewish. Office: Rex Art Co 2263 SW 37th Ave Miami FL 33145-3009

MORRIS, DAVID HARGETT, broadcast executive, rancher; b. Paris, Tex., Mar. 28, 1920; s. Eugene F. and Elizabeth (Hargett) M.; m. June Burton, Oct. 23, 1942; children: Elizabeth Anne, David H. II. Student, U Tex., 1938-41. Salesman Sta. KTBC, Austin, Tex., 1946-47; sales mgr. Sta. KTBS, Shreveport, La., 1947-48; pres. Sta. K-NUZ and K-QUE, Houston, 1948—; bd. dirs. Radio Adv. Bur., N.Y.C., Bank Houston; prin. Morris Lazy K Ranch. Past pres. Tex. Assn. Broadcasters, 1957-59.; bd. dirs. Tex. Prevention of Blindness, Houston, 1982—. Capt. USAF, 1942-45. Decorated DFC, 4 Bronze Battle stars. 5 Air medals; named Industry Leader of Industry Am. Women Radio-TV, 1981, Herford Booster of Yr., Tex. Herford Assn., 1983, Region of Merritt Show, Am. Hereford Assn., 1984. Mem. 100 Club of Harris County (pres. 1984-87, chair 1987-90), Farm and Ranch Club (pres. 1980-85), Houston Hereford Club (chmn. bd. dirs. 1980—), Optimist (pres. Downtown Houston club 1957, pres. Prevention of Blindness 1991-94). Republican. Presbyterian. Home: 11706 Monica St Houston TX 77024-6407 Office: KNUZ-AM/K-QUE FM 4701 Caroline St Houston TX 77004-5024

MORRIS, DEWEY BLANTON, lawyer; b. Richmond, Va., Sept. 15, 1938; s. Thomas Cecil and Mary Katherine (Rowlett) M.; m. Nancy Edmunds, Aug. 27, 1960; children: Sally Pendleton, Katherine Archer. BA, U. Va., 1960, LLB, 1965. Bar: Md. 1965, Va. 1968, D.C. 1991, U.S. Dist. Ct. Md. 1965, U.S. Dist. Ct. (ea. dist.) Va. 1968, U.S. Ct. Appeals (4th cir.) 1966. Assoc. Piper & Marbury, Balt., 1965-67; ptnr. Hunton & Williams, Richmond, 1967—. Served to 1st lt., USMC, 1960-62. Mem. ABA (bus. law sect.), Va. Bar Assn. (bus. law sect.), Richmond Bar Assn., Raven Soc., Commonwealth Club, Country Club Va. (Richmond), Army & Navy Club (Washington), Kiwanis, Phi Alpha Delta, Omicron Delta Kappa. Presbyterian. Clubs: Commonwealth, Country Club Va. (Richmond). Lodge: Kiwanis. Home: 302 Locke Ln S Richmond VA 23226-1714 Office: Hunton & Williams Riverfront Plaza East Tower 951 E Byrd St Richmond VA 23219-4040

MORRIS, DONALD R(OBERT), publisher, journalist; b. Frankfurt, Germany, Nov. 11, 1924; came to U.S., 1924; s. S. Fred and Vera (Dreyfuss) M.; m. Sylvia Stallings, 1953 (div. 1974); children: Sarah, Michael, Julia, Margaret (dec.); m. Karen Friman, 1977 (dec. 1986). BSEE, U.S. Naval Acad., 1948. Cert. comml. pilot, flight instr. Enlisted USN, 1942, advanced through grades to lt. commdr., active duty, 1942-56; with CIA, 1956-72, Berlin, 1958-62, Paris, 1965-67, Kinshasa, Zaire, 1969-70, Saigon, Vietnam, 1970-72; op-ed page columnist, news analyst Houston Post, 1972-89; pres., writer Trident Syndicate, Houston, 1989—; tchr. Rice U., U. Houston; lectr. in field. Author: China Station, 1951, Warm Bodies, 1957, The Washing of the Spears, 1965, 2nd edit., 1986; contbr. Atlantic Monthly, Am. Heritage, Ency. Britannica, others. Mem. Mensa. Home and Office: PO Box 271667 Houston TX 77277-1667

MORRIS, ELSIE COLEMAN, allergist, immunologist, pediatrician; b. Norfolk, Va., 1947. MD, Howard U., 1975. Diplomate Am. Bd. Allergy & Immunology, Am. Bd. Pediatrics. Intern Childrens Hosp. Mich., Detroit, 1975-76; resident D.C. Gen. Hosp., Washington, 1976-78; fellow allergy and immunology Howard U., Washington, 1978-80; with Henrietta Egleston Hosp., Atlanta; asst. prof. Emory U. Office: Morehouse Sch Medicine 487 Winn Way Ste 206 Decatur GA 30030*

MORRIS, FLORENCE HENDERSON, auditor; b. Mobile, Ala., Sept. 8, 1964; d. Thomas Gordan Henderson and Joanne Elizabeth (Pfleger) Martin; m. Fred S. Morris, July 28, 1995. BS in Fin., U. Ala., 1986. Payment and receipt rep. SouthTrust Bank of Mobile, 1988-89; internal bank auditor SouthTrust Corp., Birmingham, 1989-90, compliance audit officer, 1990-92; prin. compliance auditor, asst. v.p. SouthTrust Corp. and SouthTrust Bank of Ga., Atlanta, 1992-95; compliance audit supr., v.p. SouthTrust Corp., Birmingham, 1995—. Mem. Inst. Internal Auditors, Bankers Adminstrn. Inst. (cert. bank compliance officer), Am. Bankers Assn., Ala. Fin. Assn., U. Ala. Alumna, Delta Sigma Pi. Office: SouthTrust Corp Audit Dept PO Box 2554 Birmingham AL 35290

MORRIS, GEORGE THOMAS ARNOLD, internist; b. Raleigh, N.C., Mar. 29, 1934; s. George T. and Jessie M. (Arnold) M.; m. Mary Lide, Mar. 17, 1956; children: G. Thomas, Robert W., Francis L., David S. BS, Wake Forest U., 1955; MD, Bowman Gray Sch. Medicine, 1959. Diplomate Am. Bd. Internal Medicine. Resident N.C. Bapt. Hosp., Winston-Salem, 1963-66; physician Alamance Health Svcs., Burlington, N.C., 1966—. Capt. M.C., U.S. Army, 1960-63. Mem. AMA, ACP, Am. Soc. Internal Medicine. Republican. Baptist. Home: 25 Brookside Plr Durham NC 27705 Office: 711 Hermitage Rd Burlington NC 27215-3511

MORRIS, GORDON JAMES, financial company executive, financial consultant; b. Mt. Vernon, Ohio, Oct. 6, 1942; s. R. Hugh and Betty Jane (Roberts) M.; m. Janet Ann Swanson, Aug. 28, 1965 (div. 1971); m. Nancy Joan Meyfarth, July 26, 1975; 1 child, Lawrence Hugh; stepchildren: Richard, Gregory. Student, Ohio State U., 1960-61; BA, Otterbein Coll., 1966; postgrad. in law, Capital U., Bexley, Ohio, 1967-68; postgrad., Coll. Fin. Planning, Denver, 1983-90, Am. Coll., Bryn Mawr, Pa., 1990—, Inst. Cert. Fund Specialists, 1991. Registered investment adviser; cert. fin. planner, fund specialist. lic. loving trust advisor. Asst. to pres. Jaeger Machine Co., Columbus, Ohio, 1968-73; rep. Equitable Fin. Svcs., Sarasota, Fla., 1974-81; pres. Morris & Assocs. P.A., Sarasota, 1981—; pres., Beacon Wealth Mgmt. Inc., Sarasota, Fla., 1994—; co-gen. ptnr. Beacon Bridge Loan Pool, Ltd., 1994—; chmn. bd. dirs. MAP Fin. Group, Inc., Sarasota, 1985-89; co-owner U.S.I.S.L. West Fla. Fury Soccer Team, 1996—; bd. dirs. Soccer Resource Group, Sarasota. Past chmn. West Coast chpt. March of Dimes, Bradenton, Fla., bd. dirs., 1986-88; pres. Epilepsy Found. Southwest Fla., Inc., 1986-87. Mem. Million Dollar Roundtable, Nat. Assn. Realtors, Soccer Players Club Inc. (bd. dirs. 1994). Republican. Methodist. Lodge: Sertoma (pres. local club 1979-80). Office: Beacon Group Cos Inc 1343 Main St Ste 501 Sarasota FL 34236-5630

MORRIS, HOWARD EUGENE, construction company executive; b. Nashville, May 2, 1934; s. Harry Howard and Mary Sue (Biggers) M.; m. Martha Lou Hayes, June 28, 1952; chldren: Sadricia Anne Morris Wilson, Karen Dyanne Morris Leupold. Student, U. Ala., 1959-61, Ga. State U., 1973, Chattanooga State Tech. U., 1980. Mem. design devel. staff Monsanto Chem. Co., Decatur, Ala., 1954-62; project engr. Brown Engring. Co., Inc., Huntsville, Ala., 1962-70; chief exec. officer, bd. dirs. Tech. Svcs., Inc., Florence, Ala., 1970—. Patentee electro-mechanical devices. Chmn. bd. dirs. Internat. Bible Coll., Florence, 1980-82; panelist Nat. Housing for the Elderly Conf. Mem. Nat. Mgmt. Assn., So. Bldg. Code Conf., Ala. Inventors Assn., Shoals C. of C. Republican. Mem. Ch. of Christ. Office: Tech Svcs Inc 1949 Florence Blvd Florence AL 35630-2729

MORRIS, JAMES BRUCE, internist; b. Rochester, N.Y., May 13, 1943; s. Max G. and Beatrice Ruth (Becker) M.; B.A., U. Rochester, 1964; M.D., Yale U., 1968; m. Susan Carol Shencup, July 31, 1966; children: Carrie, Douglas, Deborah, Rebecca. Intern, SUNY, Buffalo, 1968-69, resident, 1969-70, 72-73, chief resident, 1973; fellow U. Miami, 1974; pvt. practice medicine specializing in internal medicine and infectious diseases, Plantation, Fla., 1974—; chmn. infection control com. Lauderdale Lakes Gen. Hosp., 1974-76; chmn. infection control com. Plantation Gen. Hosp., 1976-80, 83-85, chmn. pharmacy com., 1980-81, chmn. tissue com., 1982; sec., program chmn. dept. medicine Bennett Community Hosp., 1978-80, chmn. dept. medicine, 1980-81, vice chief staff, 1981-83; chmn. infection control com. Fla. Med. Center, 1980-82; chief staff Humana Hosp. Bennett, 1983-85, trustee, 1983-88, chmn. infection control com., 1985-87 ; clin. assoc. prof. U. Miami Med. Sch., 1975—. Served with USAR, 1970-72. Diplomate Am. Bd. Internal Medicine, Am. Bd. Infectious Diseases. Fellow ACP; mem. AMA, Am. Soc. Microbiology, Infectious Diseases Soc. Am., Am. Soc. Internal Medicine, Fla. Med. Assn., Broward County Med. Assn. Office: Sachs Morris & Sklaver 7353 NW 4th St Fort Lauderdale FL 33317-2202

MORRIS, JAMES MALACHY, lawyer; b. Champaign, Ill., June 5, 1952; s. Walter Michael and Ellen Frances (Solon) M.; m. Mary Delilah Baker, Oct. 17, 1987; children: James Malachy Jr., Elliot Rice Baker, Walter Michael. Student, Oxford U. (Eng.), 1972; BA, Brown U., 1974; JD, U. Pa., 1977. Bar: N.Y. 1978, U.S. Dist. Ct. (so. and ea. dists.) N.Y. 1978, Ill. 1980, U.S. Tax Ct. 1982, U.S. Supreme Ct. 1983; admitted to Barristers Chambers, Manchester, Eng., 1987. Assoc. Reid & Priest, N.Y.C., 1977-80; sr. law clk. Supreme Ct. Ill., Springfield, 1980-81; assoc. Carter, Ledyard & Milburn, N.Y.C., 1981-83; sole practice N.Y.C., 1983-87; counsel FCA, Washington, 1987—; acting sec., gen. counsel FCS Ins. Corp., McLean, Va., 1990—; cons. Internat. Awards Found., Zurich, 1981—, Pritzker Architecture Prize Found., N.Y.C., 1981—, Herbert Oppenheimer, Nathan & VanDyck, London, 1985—. Contbr. articles to profl. jours. Mem. ABA, Ill. Bar Assn., N.Y. State Bar Assn., N.Y. County Lawyers Assn., Assn. Bar City N.Y., Brit. Inst. Internat. and Comparative Law, Lansdowne Club (London), Decatur (Ill.) Club. Office: PO Box 1407 Mc Lean VA 22101-1407

MORRIS, JENNIFER KELLY, early childhood specialist; b. Winter Haven, Fla., Dec. 4, 1972; d. James Elton Morris and Madaline Jett (Mcguire) Brantley. AA in Elem. Edn., Polk C.C., Winter Haven, 1993; BS in Early Childhood, U. So. Fla., 1996. Edn. employee First Bapt. Ch., Winter Haven, 1990-94, Mus. Sci. Industry, Tampa, Fla., 1995—; kindergarten tchr. Hillsborough County Pub. Schs.; tchr. Bldg. Block, Lake Alfred, Fla., 1991-93; mem. steering com. Sun Coast Area Tchr. Tng., Tampa, 1994. Mem. Assn. Childhood Edn. Internat., Nat. Assn. Edn. Young Children, Kappa Delta Pi, Golden Key. Democrat. Baptist. Home: 3801 Stanley Rd Plant City FL 33565

MORRIS, JERRY DEAN, academic administrator; b. Gassville, Ark., May 11, 1935; s. James Henry and Maud Idella (Taylor) M.; m. Marilyn Jo Pitman, June 11, 1955; children: Joseph, Neil, Laura, Kara. BS, U. Ark., 1960, MEd, 1964, EdD, 1971. Cert. sch. adminstr., Ark. High sch. tchr. Cotter (Ark.) Pub. Schs., 1959-60, high sch. prin., 1960-63; jr. high prin. Mountain Home (Ark.) Pub. Schs., 1963-66, high sch. prin., 1966-67, asst. supt., 1967-69; editor Ark. Sch. Bds. Newsletter, U. Ark., Fayetteville, 1969-70; dir. placement services Tex. A&M U.-Commerce (formerly East Tex. State U.), 1970-71, dean admissions & records, 1971-73, dean grad. sch., 1973-81, v.p. acad. affairs, 1982-86, pres., 1987—; cons. Ark. Basic Edn., 1970, U. Cen. Ark., Conway, 1972, coordinating bd. Tex. Colls. & Univs., Austin, 1981. Pres. Commerce C. of C., 1975; bd. dirs. Commerce Lions Club, 1977; chmn. Commerce United Way, 1978; mem. Commerce Indsl. Devel. Assn., 1974—. Named an Outstanding Young Man in Edn., Ark. Jaycees, 1966, Outstanding Young Man in Am., 1967. Mem. Tex. Assn. Coll. Tchrs., Assn. Tex. Grad. Schs. (pres. 1978-79), Coun. of So. Grad. Schs. (bd. dirs. 1976-79), Coun. of Grad. Schs. in U.S., Coun. of Pub. U. Pres. and Chancellors (exec. com. 1989-90, 1996-97), Assn. of Tex. Colls. and Univs. (exec. com. 1989-90), Tex. Internat. Edn. Consortium (exec. com. 1990—), Alliance for Higher Edn. (bd. dirs. 1986—), Phi Delta Kappa. Methodist. Home: ET Sta PO Box 3001 Commerce TX 75429-3001 Office: Tex A&M U-Commerce ET Station Commerce TX 75429

MORRIS, JOHN ALLEN, JR., state government administrator, educator; b. Charleston, S.C., Nov. 22, 1946; s. John Allen and Margaret Mary (Kelly) M.; m. Jennie Farquhar Holmes, Nov. 11, 1972; children: Daniel Holmes, Paul McCarrel. BA, St. Mary's Seminary and Univ., Balt., 1968; MSW, Washington U., St. Louis, 1978. Lic. ind. social worker. Child welfare caseworker Fulton County Dept. Family and Children Svcs., Atlanta, 1968-69; psychiat. nursing asst. S.C. State Hosp. S.C. Dept. Mental Health, Columbia, 1969-71, family svcs. coord. div. alcohol and drug addiction svcs., 1971-72, group therapy coord. div. alcohol and drug addiction svcs., 1972-76, dir. spl. programs office div. alcohol and drug addiction svcs., 1978-86, dir. child and adolescent svc. S.C. State Hosp., 1986; dir. ancillary svcs. William S. Hall Psychiat. Inst. child and adolescent svcs. S.C. State Hosp., Columbia, 1986-88; exec. asst. to state commr. S.C. Dept. Mental Health, Columbia, 1988-90, dep. dir., 1990—; interim state dir. mental health S.C. Dept. Mental Health, 1995—; clin. prof. dept. neuropsychiatry and behavioral sci. U. S.C. Sch. Medicine, 1988-94, clin. assoc. prof., 1994—; vis. assoc. prof. George Warren Brown Sch. Social Work, Washington U., St. Louis; mem. vis. faculty U. S.C., 1972-76, 80, 82, 91; dir. youth substance abuse treatment unit St. Louis State Hosp., 1977-78; chair treatment resources subcom. Gov. Children's Coordinating Cabinet, 1985; mentor Nat. Assn. State Mental Health Program Dirs. Rsch. Inst., 1993—; mem., chair subcom. S.C. Pub. Acad. Mental Health Consortium, 1991—; mem. state adv. coun. S.C. Prochild, 1989-91; mem. spl. grant review panels, 1987-89; regional clin. supr. S.C. Alcohol and Drug Abuse Commn., 1986-87; mem. steering com. Children's Advocacy Ctr., 1987; vis. lectr. mental health policy Washington U., St. Louis, 1991—; cons. in field. Author: (chpt.) Managing Finances, Personnel and Information in Human Services, 1985; contbr. articles to profl. jours. Vol. counselor Camp Kemo, 1987—, chmn. programs coun., 1989—; mem. steering com. Columbia Youth-The Year 2000, 1986-88; chartered orgn. rep. Post 295 Boy Scouts Am.; v.p. Columbia Choral Soc., 1987-88, sec., 1986-87; mem. Palmetto Leadershi Soc. Recipient Outstanding Vol. award Mental Health Assn. Mid-Carolina, 1988, Pres.'s award S.C. Youth Worker's Assn., 1986, Disting. Alumnus award Washington U., 1996. Fellow Am. Coll. Mental Health Adminstrn.; mem. Am. Coll. Healthcare Execs. (diplomate), Mental Health Assn. Mid-Carolina (co-chair, chair 1986-88, steering com. parent support project 1988), Rock Hill Alliance for Mentally Ill, S.C. State Employees Assn., Washington U. Alumni Assn. Home: 1001 Barton St Columbia SC 29203-4207 Office: SC Dept Mental Health 2414 Bull St Columbia SC 29201-1906

MORRIS, JOHN CHARLES, sales executive; b. Cleve., Oct. 27, 1949; s. David John and Janet Louise (Ecker) M.; m. Susan Ruth Tate, Aug. 7, 1970; children: John Charles, David tate, Annie, Luke, William. BFA, Valdosta (Ga.) State Coll., 1972. Sports reporter USAV-TV, Savannah, Ga., 1972-74; sales rep. Merico Inc., Atlanta, 1975-78, sales mgr., 1978-85; sales mgr. Quaker Oats Co., Tampa, Fla., 1985-92; regional sales mgr. Cole's Quality Foods, Tampa, 1992—. Mem. Fla. Family Coun., Tampa, 1985—, PTA, Bloomingdale H.S., Tampa, 1985—. Mem. Fla. Frozen Food Assn., Ga. Frozen Food Assn. Republican. Home: 2107 Dillon Ct Valrico FL 33594

MORRIS, JOHN SCOTT, textile company executive; b. Atlanta, Nov. 13, 1955; s. John Stewart and Marion Jeanette (Cowan) M.; m. Cathy Dixon Hensley, Aug. 16, 1975 (div.); chldren: Jeffrey Scott, Justin Walter; m. Brenda Gail Standard, Apr. 22, 1988; 1 child, John Spencer. BS in Agr., U. Ga., 1977. Asst. mgr. Pikes Nurseries, Atlanta, 1977; meter reader Ga. Power Co., Atlanta, 1977-79; owner Green Jeans Landscaping, Lithonia, Ga., 1979-80; customer service rep. Southeastern Die Co. Inc., Decatur, Ga., 1980-83, adminstrv. mgr., 1983-85, v.p, contr., 1985-86, v.p., gen. mgr., 1986—, exec. v.p., 1990—. Office: Southeastern Die Co Inc 5205 Snapfinger Woods Dr Decatur GA 30035-4024

MORRIS, JULIE ANN ROSE, poet, foundation executive; b. Milw., Apr. 12, 1955; d. Donald and Mary Rose Jambretz; m. Sam Morris (div. Dec. 1988); children: Tammy Lynn, Samantha. Student in Mass Media Tech., Okla. C.C., 1985, student in Computer Tech., 1989. Owner, mgr. Morris Kennels, Yukon, Okla., 1980-88; printer, copy technician Oklahoma City C.C., 1985-91; pres., caretaker Hart's for Christ Found., Yukon, 1991—; dir. adminstrn. Hart's for Christ Found., 1995—; spkr. Head Start programs, Yukon, 1996, (TV) Fields of Harvest, Oklahoma City, 1996; cons. in field, 1995—. Author: Hearts of Light, Souls of Christ, 1996; poet: The Best Poet Ever Encountered, 1995, The Best Poets Ever Encountered, 1996; poet (newspaper) Poet Answers Her Call Through Poetry, 1996. Named to Internat. Poets Hall of Fame, 1996. Mem. Harry S. Truman Soc. (grant 1986, hon., life), Internat. Soc. Poets (Disting. award 1995, 96). Home and Office: Harts for Christ 418 S Seventh St Yukon OK 73099

MORRIS, KENNETH EARL, sociology educator, writer; b. Balt., Mar. 19, 1955; s. Earl William and Audrey Jane (Schreiber) M.; 1 child, Halie Francesca. BS, Ind. U., 1976; AM, Stanford U., 1977; PhD, U. Ga., 1983. Prof. U. Ga., Athens, 1984—; reader Dept. of Edn., Washington, 1988. Author: Bonhoeffer's Ethic of Discipleship, 1986, Jimmy Carter: American Moralist, 1996; writer Athens Mag., 1991-92; editorial contbr. Athens Observer, 1989—; contbr. articles to profl. jours. Mem. Clarke County Dem. Com., Athens, Ga., 1991—. NEH fellow, 1987, 94. Mem. Am. Studies Assn., Am. Sociol. Assn. (grant 1982), Athens-Clark Safe Cycling Assn. (pres. 1992). Home: 187 Chattooga Ave Athens GA 30601-1805

MORRIS, LOIS LAWSON, education educator; b. Antoine, Ark., Nov. 27, 1914; d. Oscar Moran and Dona Alice (Ward) Lawson; m. William D. Morris, July 2, 1932 (dec.); 1 child, Lavonne Morris Howell. B.A., Henderson U., 1948; M.S., U. Ark., 1951, M.A., 1966; postgrad. U. Colo., 1954, Am. U., 1958, U. N.C., 1968. History tchr. Delight High Sch., Ark., 1942-47; counselor Huntsville Vocat. Sch., 1947-48; guidance dir. Russellville Pub. Sch. System, Ark., 1948-55; asst. prof. edn. U. Ark., Fayetteville, 1955-82, prof. emeritus, 1982—; ednl. cons. Ark. Pub. Schs., 1965-78. Mem. Commn. on Needs for Women, 1976-78, Hist. Preservation Alliance Ark.; pres. Washington County Hist. Soc., 1983-85; pres. Pope County Hist. Assn.; mem. Ark. Symphony Guild; charter mem. Nat. Mus. in Arts; bd. dirs. Potts Inn Mus. Found. Named Ark. Coll. Tchr. of Year, 1972; recipient Plaque for outstanding svcs. to Washington County Hist. Soc., 1984. Contbr. articles to jours. Mem. LWV, AAUW, Ark. Coun. Social Studies (sec.-treas.), Washington County Hist. Soc. (exec. bd. 1977-80), NEA, Nat. Coun. Social Studies, Ark. Edn. Assn., Ark. Hist. Assn., Pope County Hist. Assn. (pres. 1991-92), The So. Hist. Assn., U. Ark. Alumni Assn., Sierra Club, Nature Conservancy, So. Hist. Assn., Ark. River Valley Arts Assn., Phi Delta Kappa, Kappa Delta Pi, Phi Alpha Theta. Democrat. Episcopalian. Address: 1601 W 3rd St Russellville AR 72801-4725

MORRIS, MAX KING, foundation executive, former naval officer; b. Springfield, Mo., Oct. 23, 1924; s. Lee Howard and Aldyth (King) M.; m. Mary Jane Bull, June 19, 1952; children: Jane, William, Mary. B.S., U.S. Naval Acad., 1947; M.A. in Internat. Law, Tufts U., 1960, M.A. in Internat. Econs., 1961, Ph.D., 1967. Commd. ensign U.S. Navy, 1947, advanced through grades to rear adm., 1972; carrier pilot with combat duty in Korea and Vietnam, 1947-71, comdr. jet squadron U.S.S. America, 1965-67, maj. command at sea, 1969-70, comdt. U.S. Naval Acad., 1971-73, Joint Chiefs of Staff rep. UN Law of Sea Conf., 1973-77, ret., 1977; pres. Thalassa Rsch. Co., Jacksonville, Fla., 1977—; trustee Arthur Vining Davis Founds., Fla. Author: Politico-Military Coordination in the Armed Forces, 1968; Contbr. numerous articles to naval and legal jours. Served with arty. U.S. Army, 1942-44. Decorated D.S.M., Legion of Merit (2), Air medal (5). Mem. Internat. Inst. Strategic Studies (London), Council on Fgn. Relations, Middle East Inst., U.S. Naval Inst. Clubs: N.Y. Yacht, Fla. Yacht; Belfry (London); Ponte Vedra (Fla.). Home: 4990 Vandiveer Rd Jacksonville FL 32210-8314

MORRIS, MICHELE DIAN, secondary education educator; b. Oklahoma City, Sept. 18, 1971; d. Ronald Rex and Diana Kae (Robinson) Reneau; m. Jason Glen Morris, June 7, 1991; 1 child, Jessica Michele. BA in Edn., Southwestern Okla. State U., 1993. Cert. K-888 tchr. with lang. arts and math. endorsements, Okla. Tchr. Sallisaw (Okla.) Mid. Sch., 1994—. Named Tchr. of Today, Masons, 1996. Republican. Mem. Assembly of God. Home: 1910 N Spillman St Sallisaw OK 74955 Office: Sallisaw Mid Sch 211 S Main St Sallisaw OK 74955

MORRIS, NANCY GARNETT, biology educator, administrator; b. Hopkinsville, Ky., June 29, 1953; d. Thomas Whitlock and Ruth Miller (Oliver) Garnett; m. Michael E. Morris, Aug. 6, 1977; 1 child, Daniel Eugene. BS in Chemistry/Biology, Austin Peay State U., Clarksville, Tenn., 1975; MS in Biology, Vanderbilt U., 1976, postgrad., 1995. NSF intern scholar Peabody/Met. Nashville Pub. Schs., 1975-76; life sci. educator Sumnar County Sch. System, Gallatin, Tenn., 1976-80; assoc. prof., curriculum coord. biology, chmn. depts. sci. Vol. State C.C., Gallatin, 1980—; leader Nat. Inst. Leadership Devel., Eugene, Oreg., 1991; local organizer Nat. Assn. Biology Tchrs. Two Yr. Sect. Meeting, Nashville, 1991; faculty Sub-Coun. to Coun. of Pres.; NILD Righting the Std. conf., Phoenix, 1996facilitator state planning com. Am. Coun. on Edn. Identification Program, 1992-94, state planning exec. com., 1991—; vis. com. evaluator So. Assn. Colls. and Schs. Commn. on Colls., 1992; mem. U. Tenn. Inst. Leadership Effectiveness, 1993; dir. HS/CC Collaboratives in Math. and Sci., Vol. State C.C., 1996; sci. olympiad coach for two gold metalists, Tenn., 1995; keynoter Tenn. Chpt. Am. Assn. Women in C.C., apring 1996. Contbg. editor: Proceedings Annual Women's Conference- Higher Edn. Adminstrn. in Tenn., 1995—. Local coord. Room in the Inn Program, Nashville, 1990-91; foster parent Dept. Human Svcs., Omni Visions, Inc., Nashville, 1987-94; ecumenical amb. to Renosa, Mex., 1989; promoter Amnesty Internat.; elder Second Presbyn. Ch.; del. Southeastern Partnership for Environ. Tech., 1995. Recipient Outstanding Faculty award, Vol. State C.C., 1991. Mem. AAUP, Am. Assn. Women in C.C.s (Tenn. exec. com. 1990—, instl. rep. 1989-90), Tenn. Assn. Sci. Dept. Chairs Affiliated, Tenn. Acad. Sci. (exec. com.), Tenn. Math. Tchrs. Assn., Women in Higher Edn. in Tenn. Office: Vol State CC Nashville Pike Gallatin TN 37066

MORRIS, PETER DELANEY, epidemiologist; b. Ft. Worth, Dec. 22, 1954; s. Horace Conde and Betty Lou (Whitehurst) M.; m. Katherine Alice Koepp, Dec. 31, 1976 (div. 1981); m. Ellen Patti Ruben; children: Austen Isaac, Elijah Edward. BA in Biology, U. North Tex., 1977; MD, U. Tex., 1981; MPH, U. Wash., 1984. Bd. cert. Fedn. State Licensing Bds., Am. Bd. Family Practice for Family Practice, Am. Bd. Preventive Medicine for Gen. Preventive Medicine/Pub. Health. Resident internal medicine Good Samaritan Hosp. and Med. Ctr., Portland, Oreg., 1981-82; resident preventive medicine U. Wash. Sch. Pub. Health and Community Medicine, Seattle, 1982-84; resident family practice U. Tex. Health Sci. Ctr., San Antonio, 1984-86; family practice physician North Dist. Health Clinic, Seattle King County Pub. Health, Seattle, 1983-84, Health Am., San Antonio, 1986, Family Physician Care, San Antonio, 1986-87; pub. health physician San Antonio (Tex.) Met. Health Dist., 1987; epidemic intelligence svc. officer Ctrs. for Disease Control, Atlanta, 1987-89; med. epidemiologist environ. epidemiology sect. N.C. Dept. Environment, Health & Natural Resources, Raleigh, 1989—; presenter in field. Contbr. articles to profl. jours. Recipient Pub. Health Nat. Rsch. Svc. award Nat. Cancer Inst., 1982-84. Fellow Am. Coll. Preventive Medicine; mem. APHA, Soc. for Epidemiologic Rsch., Am. Coll. Epidemiology, Coun. of State and Territorial Epidemiologists. Home: 112 Vicksburg Dr Cary NC 27513-4813

MORRIS, ROBERT RENLY, minister, clinical pastoral education supervisor; b. Jacksonville, Fla., Feb. 15, 1938; s. Joseph Renly and Sybil (Stephens) M.; m. Lenda Smith, Dec. 7, 1963; children: Christopher Renly, Jennifer Kelly. BA, U. Fla., 1959; MDiv, Columbia Theol. Sem., Atlanta, 1962, ThM, 1967, D Ministry, 1990. Ordained to ministry Presbyn. Ch. (U.S.A.), 1962. Min. to students Ga. State Coll., Atlanta, 1959-60; asst. min. Trinity Presbyn. Ch., Atlanta, 1960-62; min. Clanton (Ala.) Presbyn. Ch., 1963-65, Kelly Presbyn. Ch., McDonough, Ga., 1965-67; pastoral counselor Ga. Assn. for Pastoral Care, Atlanta, 1966-68; coord. pastoral svcs. Winter Haven (Fla.) Hosp. and Community Health Ctr., 1969-79; min. Presbytery of Greater Atlanta, mem. div. pastoral care, 1984-86; dir. clin. pastoral edn. Emory Ct. for Pastoral Svcs., Atlanta, 1979—; adj. faculty Candler Sch. Theology, 1979-88. Contbr. book chpts., articles to profl. jours. Mem. AIDS Task Force, Atlanta, 1988-95, Task Force on Chem. Dependency, 1988. Mem. Am. Assn. Pastoral Counselors, Coll. Chaplains, Am. Assn. Marriage and Family Therapists (clin.), Assn. for Clin. Pastoral Edn. (cert. supr., gen. assembly nominating com. 1984, chmn. 1985, coord. ann. conf. 1986, long range planning com. of C com., standards com. S.E. region 1990-93), Beta Theta Pi. Democrat. Home: 542 Cross Creek Pt Stone Mountain GA 30087-5328 Office: Emory U Hosp Dept Pastoral Svcs 1364 Clifton Rd NE Atlanta GA 30322-1059

MORRIS, ROGER DALE, bank officer, artist; b. Huntington, W.Va., Feb. 23, 1947; s. Guy Robert and Corena Ellen (Irby) M. Student, art instrn. schs., Mpls. Teller Gary (Ind.) Nat. Bank, 1965-70; treas. City of Carrsville, Ky., 1980-89; asst. cashier The Peoples Bank, Marion, Ky., 1971—. Exhibited in group shows Libr. of Archives, Ky., 1983, Pen and Brush Gallery, N.Y.C., 1986, Pastel Soc. Am., N.Y.C., 1987, High Mus., Atlanta, 1994. Recipient Northlight award Pen and Brush Gallery, 1986, Marie Devor Meml. award Pastel Soc. Am., 1987; Major Castner Lewis award Ctrl. South Art Exhibit, Nashville, 1989, Dow Corning award, 1990. Home: 1007 1st St Carrsville KY 42081-9427 Office: The Peoples Bank 116 S Main St Marion KY 42064-1508

MORRIS, ROY ALLEN, publishing executive; b. Sumter, S.C., Dec. 27, 1946; s. Roy E. and Margaret (Morris) Marklin; m. Thelma Avillano, Dec. 25, 1986; children: Beverly, Francis, Christopher. DD, Ch. Gospel Ministry, 1982. Pub., owner Morris Pub. Co., Cayce, S.C., 1963—; CEO, owner, Morris Cinema/Xanadu Studio, Cayce, 1991—. Editor Telling The Story, 1963-91, The Supernatural Mag., 1991-96, The Children's Jour., 1994, The Family Jour. Pastor, presiding bishop Ch. Gospel Ministry, Sumter, 1963-91. Recipient Movers and Shakers award WLTX & Milk Daires, Columbia, S.C., 1992. Mem. K. of C. Roman Catholic. Home & Office: 1415 Hemlock St Cayce SC 29033

MORRIS, SHARON LOUISE STEWART, former day care provider; b. Washington, Feb. 9, 1956; d. George Arthur Jr. and Shirley Ann (Dickinson) S.; m. Brian Stanley Morris, Feb. 9, 1979; children: Jessica Kristin, Krystle Maria. BS, Atlantic Christian Coll., Wilson, N.C., 1978. Cert. tchr. elem. edn. and math., N.C., EMT. Cashier Safeway Fin., Wilson, 1980-81, Provident Fin., Wilson, 1981-85; mktg. svc. mgr. Beneficial of N.C. Inc., Wilson, 1985-91; ind. carrier Wilson Daily Times, 1991-94; care provider Crestview Day Sch., Wilson, 1994-95; EMT Wilson Meml. Hosp., Elm City, N.C., 1996—; agt. Cen. Nat. Life Ins., Wilson, 1988-91, Olde Republic, 1990; EMT Elm City Emergency Svcs., 1990—. Notary pub. State of N.C., 1986—. Democrat. Methodist. Home: 1201 Herring Ave NE Wilson NC 27893-3319

MORRIS, SUSAN STEERS, service executive; b. Detroit, Dec. 24, 1929; d. Philip John and Lucille (Garvie) Steers; divorced; children: Steven C., Sandra L., Scott W., Bradley A., Vivian G. BS, Tex. Christian U., 1950. Cert. personal cons. Pres. The Idea House, Inc., Baton Rouge, 1966-76; sales rep. Bekins Van Lines, Baton Rouge, 1977-80; pres. Career Cons., Inc., Baton Rouge, 1980—, So. Comfort Bed and Breakfast Reservation Svc., Baton Rouge, 1982-92; exec. dir. Bed and Breakfast Reservation Services Worldwide, Inc. Trade Assn., Baton Rouge, 1985—; pres. Bed & Breakfast Cons., Baton Rouge, 1990—; cons. Bed and Breakfast Industry, La. Dept. Tourism, others; pres. Person to Person Travel Prodns., Inc., Baton Rouge, 1985—; organized first Mardi Gras Krewe of Phoenix, 1987. Recipient Order of the Pelican, La. Dept. Tourism, 1987. Mem. NAFE, Nat. Assn. Profl. Organizers (membership rep. for La., Miss. and Ala., referral rep. for La., Miss., Ala.), Orgn. Personified (pres. 1993—). Republican. Methodist. Office: B&B Reservation Svcs Worldwide PO Box 14841 Baton Rouge LA 70898

MORRIS, TERRY LEE, ergonomist, management educator; b. Eastland, Tex., July 20, 1947; s. Melvin Gene Morris and Billie Faye Mitchell; m. Sarah E. Hetherly, July 17, 1970 (div. Nov. 1987); children: Allen, Kristopher, Mechelle. AA, SUNY, Albany, 1975; BS in Psychology, Tex. A&M U., 1977, MS in Psychology, 1979, PhD in Indsl. Engring., 1984. Cert. profl. ergonomist. Staff aide to chief naval personnel USN, Washington, 1974-77; rsch. scientist USAF Sch. Aerospace Medicine, Brooks AFB, Tex., 1982-84, NRC postdoctoral fellow, 1984-85; prodn. coord. Unicor Textiles, Dallas, 1986-90; v.p. Advanced Ergonomics Inc., Dallas, 1990—; adj. prof. Amber U., Garland, Tex., 1991—. Contbr. numerous articles to tech. and profl. publs. Lt. comdr. USN, 1967-77. Recipient Amoco Found. award for Disting. Svc. to Students, Chgo., 1982. Mem. Human Factors and Ergonomics Soc., Am. Inst. Indsl. Engrs., N.Y. Acad. Scis., Am. Psychol. Assn. Office: Advanced Ergonomics Inc Ste 350 5550 Lyndon B Johnson Fwy Dallas TX 75240-6219

MORRIS, THERESA LOUISE, clinical pharmacist; b. Tacoma, Wash., Feb. 1, 1956; d. Marvin Eugene and Annette Helen (Selinger) M. PharmD, U. of Pacific, 1979. Registered pharmacist; bd. cert. nutritional support pharmacist. Pharmacy resident Holy Cross Hosp., Ft. Lauderdale, Fla., 1979-80, staff pharmacist, 1980-81; clin. pharmacist Meml. Hosp., Hollywood, Fla., 1981-87; patient care unit pharmacist N.C. Meml. Hosp., Chapel Hill, 1988-89; clin. pharmacy coord. Rex Hosp., Raleigh, N.C., 1989—; pharmacy counselor Fla. Assn. Nutritional Support, 1983-86; test writer Bd. Pharm. Specialties, Washington, 1992; cons. clin. resource group Med Econ Svcs., Inc., Louisville, 1992—. Vol. pharmacist Open Door Clinic, Raleigh, 1993—. Mem. Am. Soc. Microbiology, Am. Soc. Parenteral and Enteral Nutrition (mem. practice interest group on drug nutrient interactions 1991—), Am. Soc. Hosp. Pharmacists, N.C. Soc. Hosp. Pharmacists (mem. adv. com. spl. interest group on pharmacotherapy), Mid-Atlantic Soc. Parenteral and Enteral Nutrition, Christian Pharmacists Fellowship Internat. (mem. profl. rels. com. 1991-92, mem. edn. com. 1993—), Wake County Pharm. Assn. Baptist. Office: Rex Hosp 4420 Lake Boone Trl Raleigh NC 27607-7505

MORRIS, WILLIAM SHIVERS, III, newspaper executive; b. Augusta, Ga., Oct. 3, 1934; s. William Shivers Jr. and Florence (Hill) M.; m. Mary Sue Ellis, Jan. 18, 1958; children: William Shivers IV, John Tyler, Susie Blackmar. A.B. in Journalism, U. Ga., 1956. Asst. to pres., pub. Southeastern Newspapers and Augusta Newspapers, 1956-60; v.p., dir. Savannah Newspapers, Inc. and Savannah News-Press, Inc., Ga., 1960-63; v.p., dir. Southeastern Newspapers Corp., 1963-65, chmn. bd., chief exec. officer; chmn. bd., chief exec. officer Banner-Herald Pub. Co., Athens, Ga., 1965, Morris Communications Corp., Augusta, Southwestern Newspapers Corp., N. Am. Publs., Inc., Fla. Pub. Co., Jacksonville; chmn. bd., chief exec. officer, pub. Augusta Chronicle, Athens Star, and Augusta Herald, Ga., 1966-94, Augusta Chronicle and Athens Star, Ga., 1966—; pub. Juneau Empire; dir. Ga. Power Co., Atlanta, So. Co., Atlanta, Associated Press. Trustee Augusta Coll. Found.; bd. regents Univ. System Ga., 1967-73. Served to capt. USAF, 1956-58. Hon. mem. Golden Quill Soc., 1960. Mem. Am. Newspaper Pubs. Assn., Southeastern Newspaper Pubs. Assn. (dir. 1966—), So. Newspaper Pubs. Assn., Internat. Press Inst. Presbyterian (elder). Clubs: Pinnacle (Augusta) (pres.); University (N.Y.C.); Oglethorpe (Savannah); Commerce (Atlanta). Office: Morris Communications Corp PO Box 936 Augusta GA 30903-0936 also: Amarillo Globe-News Div PO Box 2091 Amarillo TX 79166-0001

MORRISEY, MARENA GRANT, art museum administrator; b. Newport News, Va., May 28, 1945. BFA in Interior Design, Va. Commonwealth U., 1967, MA Art History, 1970. With Orlando (Fla.) Mus. Art, 1970—, exec. dir., 1976—; former v.p., chmn. mus. svcs. com., mem. ad hoc com. on collections sharing and long range planning com., past chmn. exhbns. and edn. com. Am. Fedn. Arts; former mem. nat. adv. coun. George Washington U. Clearinghouse on Mus. Edn.; former mem. accreditation com. Nat. Found. for Interior Design Edn. Rsch. Former mem. strategic planning adv. coun. Orange County Sch. Dist.; former mem. advt. rev. bd. BBB; former mem. Orlando Pub. Art Adv. Bd., Orlando Leadership Coun., Orlando Hist. Bldg. Commn.; former chmn. art selection com. Orlando Internat. Airport; former mem. bd. dirs. Sta. WMFE-TV. Named Orlando's Outstanding Woman of Yr. in Field of Art; recipient Fla. State of Arts award. Mem. Am. Assn. Mus. (former mem. governing bd., accreditation commn., profl. stds. and practices com., internat. com. on mus.), Assn. Art Mus. Dirs., Southeastern Mus. Conf. (past pres.), Fla. Art Mus. Dirs. Assn. (past pres.), Fla. Assn. Mus. (former bd. dirs.), Greater Orlando C. of C. (past mem. steering com. Leadership Orlando, former mem. Project 2000), Jr. League Orland-Winter Park, Rotary Club Orlando (program com. Orlando, membership com., chmn. found. com., Paul Harris fellow). Office: Orlando Museum of Art 2416 N Mills Ave Orlando FL 32803-1426

MORRISEY, MICHAEL A., health economics educator; b. Crookston, Minn., Mar. 20, 1952; s. Charles Arthur and Eleanor E. (LaFleur) M.; m. Elaine M. Mardian, Aug. 26, 1972; children: Michelle Ann, David Michael. BA, No. State U., Aberdeen, S.D., 1974; MA in Econs., U. Wash., 1975, PhD in Econs., 1979. Rsch. asst., specialist Battelle HARC, Seattle, 1976-79; sr. economist Am. Hosp. Assn., Chgo., 1979-85; sr. economist, asst. dir. Hosp. Rsch. & Ednl. Trust, Chgo., 1983-85; vis. scholar Northwestern U., Evanston, Ill., 1984-85; assoc. prof. U. Ala., Birmingham, 1985-88, prof., 1988—; acting dir. Lister Hill Ctr. for Health Policy, Birmingham, 1990-93, dir., 1993—; dep. editor Med. Care, Cleve., 1987-96; mem. Pa. Mandates Benefits Rev. Panel, Harrisburg, 1987—; mem. Ala. Task Force on Rural Health Care Crisis, 1989; cons. NIH, VA, U.S. HHS, Washington, 1980—, also pvt. industry; mem. health svcs. devel. grants rev. com. Agy for Health Care Policy and Rsch., Rockville, Md., 1992-96. Author: Price Sensitivity in Health Care, 1992, Cost Shifting in Health Care, 1994; contbr. over 90 articles to profl. jours. Recipient John D. Thompson prize in health svc. rsch. Assn. Univ. Programs in Health Adminstrn., 1991; grantee Nat. Ctr. Health Svcs. Rsch., NIH, Agy. for Health Care Policy & Rsch., Robert Wood Johnson Found. Mem. APHA (com. chmn. 1987-90), Am. Econ. Assn., Assn. Health Svcs. Rsch., Internat. Health Econs. Assn. (treas. 1994—). Republican. Roman Catholic. Office: U Ala Sch Pub Health Birmingham AL 35294-2010

MORRISH, THOMAS JAY, golf course architect; b. Grand Junction, Colo., July 6, 1936; s. Wilbur Merle and Margaret Beula (Cronk) M.; m. Louise Ann Dunn, Apr. 2, 1965; children: Carter J., Kimberly L. Coder. AA, Mesa Coll., Grand Junction, 1956; BS in Landscape and Nursery Mgmt., Colo. State U., 1964. Golf course arch. Robert Trent Jones, Montclaire, N.J., 1964-67, George Fazio, Jupiter, Fla., 1967-69, Desmond Muirhead, Newport Beach, Calif., 1969-72, Jack Nicklaus, North Palm Beach, Fla., 1972-83; prin. Jay Morrish & Assocs. Ltd., Flower Mound, Tex., 1983—. Prin. golf course designs include: Troon Golf & Country Club, Scottsdale, Ariz., Las Colinas Sports Club, Irving, Tex., Mira Vista, Ft. Worth, Foothills Golf Course, Phoenix, Forest Highlands, Flagstaff, Ariz. (One of 100 Top Golf Courses in World, Golf mag., Golf Digest), Bentwater on Lake Conroe, Houston, Shadow Glen Golf Club, Olathe, Kans. (Best New Private Course, Golf Digest 1989), Troon North Golf & Country Club, Scottsdale (One of 100 Top Courses in U.S., Golf mag.), Harbor Club on Lake Oconee, Greensboro, Ga., Loch Lomond, Scotland, The Country Club of St. Albans, Mo., Broken Top, Bend, Oreg., Dauble Eagle Club, Galena, Ohio (one of Top 100 Courses in World, Golf Mag.), Buffalo Creek Golf Course, Rockwall, Tex., La Cantera, San Antonio (Best New Pub. Course of 1995, Golf Digest Mag.), numerous others. Edn. grantee State of Colo., 1961-64; Trans-Miss. golf scholar, 1962-64. Mem. Am. Soc. Golf Course Archs., Nat. Golf Found., Safari Club Internat., Dallas Safari Club. Republican. Office: 3700 Forums Dr Ste 207 Flower Mound TX 75028-1840

MORRISON, BARBARA HANEY, educational administrator; b. Ft. Campbell, Ky., June 27, 1953; d. Charles L. and Rosemary (Blakeman) Haney; m. J.D. Morrison; 1 child, Carol Marie. BA, U. Ala., 1978; MS, Troy State U., 1985. Dir. quality improvement and edn. Charter Med. Corp., Dothan, Ala., 1992—, dir. edn., 1987—, student assistance program dir.; classroom tchr. Ozark, Ala.; dir. Westgate Learning Ctr., Albany, Ga., 1993—; mem. drug adv. bd. Houston County Schs. Mem. ASCD, NEA, Ala. Edn. Assn., Coun. for Children with Behaviour Disorders, Assn. for Healthcare Quality, Dothan-Houstan C. of C. (edn. com.), Alpha Delta Kappa. Office: Charter Med Corp PO Box 6138 Dothan AL 36302-6138

MORRISON, EDGAR CARROLL (JED), JR., lawyer; b. Teaneck, N.J., Apr. 27, 1953; s. Edgar Carroll and Eileen (Brady) M.; m. Jane Barron Clark, Feb. 6, 1982; children: Ashby, David, Brady. BA in Econs., U. Okla., 1975, JD, 1979. Bar: Tex., Va. Legis. analyst Legis. Digest, Washington, 1980; Rep. counsel U.S. House of Reps. Com. on the Budget, Washington, 1981-85; atty. Office of Gen. Counsel U.S. Dept. HHS, Washington, 1985-87; atty. Brite & Drought, San Antonio, 1988-90; ptnr. Cauthorn & Tobin, San Antonio, 1990-94, Jackson & Walker LLP, San Antonio, 1994—. Contbr. articles to profl. jours. Bd. dirs. S.W. Mental Health Ctr., San Antonio, 1988-96, chmn. bd., 1994; coach Little League. Recipient Sec.'s citation U.S. Dept. HHS, 1987. Mem. Nat. Health Lawyers Assn., Am. Acad. Healthcare Attys., Healthcare Fin. Mgrs. Assn. Republican. Episcopalian. Office: Jackson & Walker LLP 112 E Pecan St S-1200 San Antonio TX 78205

MORRISON, GARY BRENT, hospital administrator; b. Anamosa, Iowa, Aug. 30, 1952; s. Kenneth Dale and Norma Elizabeth (Higgens) M.; children: Daniel, Lindsay. BA Polit. Sci., U. Mich., Dearborn, 1975; M Health Svc. Adminstrn., U. Mich., 1978. With Univ. Hosp. Univ. Mich., Ann Arbor, 1975-78, Robert Packer Hosp., Sayre, Pa., 1978-88; assoc. adminstr. St. Mary's Hosp., Rochester, Minn., 1988-90, adminstr., 1990-93; exec. v.p., COO Scott & White Meml. Hosp., Temple, Tex., 1993—. Dir. Tex. State Tech. Coll.; mem. Airport Adv. Bd.; bd. dirs. Better Bus. Bur., Temple Free Clinic, Temple Edn. Found. Mem. Am. Coll. Healthcare Execs. (diplomate), Tex. Assn. Pub. and Not-for-Profit Hosps. (bd. dirs.). Office: Scott & White Meml Hosp 2401 S 31st St Temple TX 76508-0001

MORRISON, GRACE BLANCH SIMPSON, auditor, accountant, government official; b. Waterloo, Iowa, Dec. 18, 1933; d. Lyle Meredith and Grace Luella Blanch Simpson; m. Glenn Harry Murphree, July 2, 1955 (dec.); children: Gregory Alan, Gina Grace; m. Henry Joseph Morrison, Jr., July 23, 1974. B.S., So. Meth. U., 1956; M.Ed., U. Houston, 1973. CPA, Tex. Tchr. math., Mesquite (Tex.) Ind. Sch. Dist., 1957-58, Clear Creek Ind. Sch. Dist., Seabrook, Tex., 1967-73, Richardson (Tex.) Ind. Sch. Dist., 1973-74; equal opportunity asst. Office for Civil Rights, HEW, Dallas, 1974-75; govt. relations specialist, consumer affairs officer Region VI, Dept. Energy, Dallas, 1975-81; audit acctg. aide IRS, Dallas, 1981-82, revenue agt., 1982-85; sr. auditor Def. Contract Audit Agy., Dallas, 1985—. Mem. AICPA, Assn. Cert. Fraud Examiners (cert.), Lone Star Puppet Guild, Puppeteers Am., Nat. Assn. Parliamentarians, Assn. Govt. Accts., Mensa. Unitarian. Home: 118 Glen Knoll Dr Wylie TX 75098-5053

MORRISON, GREGG SCOTT, minister; b. Rome, Ga., Mar. 9, 1964; s. Glen Warren and Joyce (Lannom) M.; m. Laura Edge, Jan. 21, 1995. BS in Acctg., U. Ala., 1986; MDiv, Beeson Div. Sch./Samford U., 1996. Tax assoc. Coopers & Lybrand, Atlanta, 1986, tax specialist, 1987-88; tax supr. Coopers & Lybrand, Birmingham, Ala., 1988-89, sr. tax assoc., 1990-91, tax mgr., 1991-93; min. outreach Shades Mountain Bapt. Ch., 1993-96; dir. external rels. Beeson Div. Sch. Samford U., Birmingham, Ala., 1996—. Active United Way Ctrl. Ala., Inc., Birmingham, 1989; pres. Beeson Div. Sch. of Samford U., 1995-96; bd. dirs. Ctr. for Urban Missions, Inc., Birmingham, chmn. fin. com., 1991-94, 96—; bd. dirs. Univ. Cmty. Coop., Inc., Tuscaloosa; treas. Martin Luther King Unity Breakfast Planning Com.; southside campaign capt. Boy Scouts Am.; mem. planned giving adv. group Bapt. Hosp. Found., Inc.; deacon Shades Mt. Bapt. Ch., 1992-94, 96—, chmn. Innercity Ministry Partnership Task Force, 1996—; deacon Shades Mountain Bapt. Ch. Mem. Nat. Health Lawyers Assn., Health Care Fin. Mgmt. Assn., Birmingham Hist. Soc. (planning com. 1990-91), PGA Fin. Com., Young Bus. Leaders Birmingham, Vestavia Country Club, Theta Chi (treas. Alpha Phi house corp. 1992-94). Republican. Bapt. Home: 1844 Laurel Rd Birmingham AL 35216-1404 Office: Samford Univ Beeson Div Sch 800 Lakeshore Dr Birmingham AL 35229-2252

MORRISON, H. ROBERT, writer, editor, politician; b. Pitts., Apr. 7, 1938; s. Hugh and Gertrude Mary (Gehenio) M.; m. Meredith Wollenberg, Dec. 8, 1979; children: Hugh Robert Jr., Justin William, Elizabeth Jeanne. BA in English, Howard U., 1969. Cert. govtl. treas. Writer Nat. Geog. Soc., Washington, 1969-73, editor ednl. filmstrips, 1973-77, sr. writer, 1977-88, mng. editor nat. geography bee, 1988-89; elected treas. City of Falls Church, Va., 1993—; bd. dirs. Falls Church Cable Access Corp., pres. 1990-93, Treas. Assn. Va. Contbg. author to numerous books including America's Seashore Wonderlands, 1985, America's Wild Woodlands, 1985, Exploring America's Valleys, 1984, America's Hidden Corners, 1983, America's Magnificent Mountains, 1980, America's Majestic Canyons, 1979, Mysteries of the Ancient World, 1979, The Ocean Realm, 1978, As We Live and Breathe, 1971; co-author: America's Atlantic Isles, 1981. Vice chmn. Falls Church (Va.) Dem. Com., 1988-89; treas. City of Falls Church, 1994—. With U.S. Army, 1961-64. Mem. Mcpl. Treas.' Assn. U.S. and Can., Treas.' Assn. Va. (bd. dirs. 1996—), Clan Morrison N.Am. (life), St. Andrew's Soc. Washington. Home: Bonnie Briar 502 Walden Ct Falls Church VA 22046-2628 Office: City Hall 300 Park Ave Falls Church VA 22046-3351

MORRISON, HARVEY LEE, JR., lawyer; b. Hattiesburg, Miss., June 7, 1947; s. Harvey Lee Sr. and Tommye (Walker) M.; m. Norma Hairston, Aug. 21, 1976; 1 child, Harvey Lee III. BBA, U. Miss., 1970, JD, 1972. Bar: Miss. 1972, U.S. Dist. Ct. (no. dist.) Miss. 1982, U.S. Ct. Appeals (5th cir.) 1982. Ptnr. Tubb, Stevens & Morrison, West Point, Miss., 1972—. Mem. ABA, Miss. State Bar Assn., Miss. Def. Lawyers Assn., Clay County Bar Assn. (pres. 1986—). Presbyterian. Lodge: Rotary (sec. 1975, v.p. 1976, pres. 1977, dist. gov. Miss. and Tenn. 1984-85, Paul Harris fellow 1985). Home: PO Box 1131 West Point MS 39773-1131 Office: Tubb Stevens & Morrison PO Box 324 West Point MS 39773-0324

MORRISON, HELENA GRACE, guidance counselor; b. Neillsville, Wis., Aug. 20, 1957; d. Harold Allen and Nettie Stella (Schafer) Freedlund; m. William James Morrison, Sept. 11, 1981; 1 child, Meghan Marie. BS, U. Wis., Stevens Point, 1980; MEd, Nat. Louis U., Evanston, Ill., 1990; cert., Western Ky. U., 1994, postgrad. Cert. guidance counselor; cert. tchr. Tchr. grades 2 through 3 Pittsville (Wis.) Elem. Sch., 1980-82; tchr. grade 2 Vernon Parish Schs., Leesville, La., 1987-88; tchr. grade 3 Dept. Def. Dependant Schs., Vogelweh, Germany, 1989-92; student svcs. specialist, tchr. gifted edn. LaRue County Schs., Hodgenville, Ky., 1993—, gifted coord., 1995—; leader grade 3 team Vogelweh Elem. Sch., 1990-92; editor Hodgenville Elem. Sch. Yearbook, editor HES News, 1993—. Statistician Kaiserslantern Softball, Vogelweh, 1991; coach girls softball LaRue County Softball, Hodgenville, 1994. Mem. ASCD, Nat. Geog. Soc., Ky. Assn. for Gifted Edn., Ky. Counseling Assn. Home: 3220 Dangerfield Rd Hodgenville KY 42748-9223 Office: Hodgenville Elem Sch 208 College St Hodgenville KY 42748-1404

MORRISON, IAN ALASTAIR, foundation executive; b. Glasgow, Scotland, Apr. 22, 1924; came to U.S., 1932, naturalized, 1937; s. William John and Alexandrina (Smith) M.; m. Naida Brown, Apr. 19, 1946; children: Craig William, Sheila Elise. BA, Wagner Coll., S.I., N.Y., 1948, LHD, 1968; MA, Columbia U., 1950, MS, 1958, EdD, 1961; LHD, Bard Coll., 1968. Assoc. prof. history, dean students Wagner Coll., 1949-56; exec. Inter Royal Corp., N.Y.C., 1956-57; exec. sec. Greer Sch., Millbrook, N.Y., 1958-61; exec. dir. Greer Sch., Millbrook, 1961-72; pres. Greer-Woodycrest Children's Found., N.Y.C., 1972-89, The Greer Inst. of Group Care Cons., 1979-90; pres. Greer Crest retirement community, N.Y.C., 1984-89, pres. emeritus, 1989-95. Author: Higher Education in World War II, 1950, American Political Parties, Political Science Handbook, 1953, Foster Care in the United States, 1975; editor NAHC Pub. Affairs Bull., 1975-87, Continuing Care Retirement Communities: Social, Political and Financial Issues; pub. Resdl. Group Care quar.; contbr. articles to profl. jurs.; author pub. affairs newsletter. Pres. Eastchester (N.Y.) Bd. Edn., 1962-66, Unionvale (N.Y.) Bd. Edn., 1969-87; mem. adv. coun. Dutchess C.C.; mem. long-range com. Columbia U. Divsn. Geriatrics and Gerontology; trustee emeritus St. Francis Hosp., Poughkeepsie, N.Y., 1981-90, chmn., 1990; bd. dirs. Palma Sola Bot. Park, Bradenton, Fla., 1994, Anna Maria Island Orch. and Chorus. With AUS, WWII, ETO, POW, Germany. Decorated Purple Heart with oak leaf cluster, Prisoner of War medal, Bronze Star; Grad. fellow 1948 Wagner Coll., 1948. Mem. N.Y. State Assn. Child Care Agencies (pres. 1969), N.Y. State Assn. Children's Inst. (chmn. edn. com. 1961-68, pres. 1968), Nat. Assn. Homes for Children (hon. life mem., dir. 1975-89, pres. 1977-79, chmn. pub. affairs com. 1975-87, bd. dir. 1975-87, author code of ethics, 1976), Nat. Assn. Sr. Living Industry (founding mem.), Child Welfare League Am., Fgn. Policy Assn., St. Andrews Soc., Caledonia Soc. (bd. dirs. Sarasota), Nat. Assn. Homes for Children, Am. Assn. Homes for Aged, Nat. Assn. Fundraising Execs., Union League Club (N.Y.C.), Milbrook (N.Y.) Golf and Tennis Club, Columbia U. Club (N.Y.C.), Bradenton Country Club.

MORRISON, K. JAYDENE, education counseling firm executive; b. Cherokee, Okla., Aug. 22, 1933; d. Jay Frank and Kathryn D. (Johnson) Walker; m. Michael H. Morrison, Aug. 11, 1955; children: Jay, Mac. B.S., Okla. State U., 1955, M.S., 1957; postgrad. U. Colo., 1965, Central State U., Okla., 1968-70, 84, U. Denver, 1981-82. Lic. coun., Okla.; lic. marriage and family therapist; cert. sch. psycologist; cert. counselor. Psychologist, Okla. Tchr., Cushing Pub. Schs., Okla., 1955-57, Indpls. Pub. Schs., 1958-59; counselor, tchr. spl. edn. Helena-Goltry Pub. Schs., Okla., 1965-73; psychometrist Okla. State Title III Program, Alva, 1974-75; sch. psychologist Okla. State Dept. Edn., Enid, 1977-85; pres., dir. Ventures in Learning, Inc., Helena, 1984—, career counselor, Oklahoma City, 1985-86, rural specialist Okla. Conf. Chs. AG LINK, 1986-88, v.p., sec./treas. Okla. Made, Inc., Oklahoma City, 1988-89; sch. psychologist Okla. City Pub. Schs., 1988-93, therapist and pub. sch. liaison Chisholm Trail Counseling Svc., 1993-95; coord. Statewide Farm Stress Program, 1994-95; therapist Greenleaf Drug/Alcohol Rehab., 1988-89; sec., treas. Okla. Pure; part-time counselor Clayton Clinic, 1987-89; cons. Okla. Family Inst., 1990-93; with Dept. of Edn. Behavior Mgmt. Ctrl. Dist., Hawaii, 1995—. Author: Coping with ADD/ADHD, 1995; co-author: Coping With a Learning Disability, 1992. Chmn., Alfalfa County Excise and Equalization Bd., Cherokee, 1979-83; asst. state coord. Okla. Am. Agr. Movement, Oklahoma City, 1982-83; counselor, United Meth. Counseling Ctr., 1987-88; co-chmn. Alfalfa County Democratic party, Cherokee, 1976-83, sec.-treas. 6th Dist. Okla. Dem. State Exec. Bd., 1983-87. Recipient Tchr. of Yr. award Helena Masonic Lodge, 1967, Spl. award Okla. Women for Agr., 1979; named Citizen of Yr., Okla. chpt. Nat. Assn. Social Workers, 1988. Mem. Biofeedback Soc. Am., Okla. Soc. for Advancement Biofeedback, Nat. Assn. Sch. Psychologists, Okla. Sch. Psychologists Assn., Garfield County Interagy. Task Force, Okla. Assn. Learning Disabilities, Delta Kappa Gamma, Chi Omega Alumni. Elder Christian Ch. Office: 2943 Kalakaua Ave Apt 407 Honolulu HI 96815-4607

MORRISON, LINDA MARIE, dietitian; b. Lewistown, Pa., Dec. 16, 1950; d. John Benner and Lucille Marie Hostetler; m. Arna Glenn Morrison, May 17, 1986; 1 child, Amy Louise. BS in Home Econs. Edn., Ind. U. Pa., 1972; BS in Dietetics, U. Vt., 1982; postgrad., James Madison U. Registered dietitian; cert. health fitness instr. Am. Coll. Sports Medicine. Home econs. tchr. West Shore Sch. Dist., Lemoyne, Pa., 1972-73, 74-76; tchr. aide Laconia (N.H.) State Sch., 1976-77; home econs. tchr. Tilton (N.H.) Middle Sch., 1977-81; grad. asst. U. Vt., Burlington, 1981-82; registered dietitian Rockingham Meml. Hosp., Harrisonburg, Va., 1983-87; dietitian RMH Nutritional Svcs., Harrisonburg, Va., 1995—; cons. Leaner Weigh Program, 1994—; vol. dietitian nutrition com. Am. Heart Assn., Harrisonburg, 1994—. Mem. nutrition com. Am. Heart Assn., Harrisonburg, 1994—. Mem. Blue Ridge Dietetics Assn., Am. Dietetics Assn. Lutheran. Office: RMH Nutritional Svcs 741 S Main St Harrisonburg VA 22801-9660

MORRISON, RAYMOND EARL, JR., engineering executive; b. Latham, N.Y., Dec. 3, 1941; s. Raymond Earl, Sr., and Mary Ellen (Doran) M.; m. Christine Marie Owocki, Oct. 22, 1982; children—Arianne, Michael, Janine. A.A.S., Hudson Valley Community Coll., 1967; B.S., SUNY-Oswego, 1964; M.S., Syracuse U., 1970; Ph.D., U. Mo., 1975. Tng. mgr. Los Alamos Nat. Lab., N.Mex., 1975-80, sr. budget, fiscal analyst, 1980-83; exec. dir. High Tech. Adv. Council, Atlanta, 1983-87; exec. dir. Assn. Media Based Continuing Edn. for Engrs. Inc., Atlanta, 1987-89; cabinet mem. Indsl./Tech. Edn. State of Ark., 1989-91; editor The Evolution of Engring. Tech. in the Field of Engring. Edn., 1990-92; cons. Morrison & Assocs., Los Alamos, 1970-75, State Dept. Edn., Atlanta, 1983-84, William T. Grant Found., 1991; internal cons. U. Calif., Los Alamos, 1980-83, Los Alamos Tech. Assn., 1979-81. Contbr. articles to profl. jours. Mem. bd. reviewers Los Alamos Schs. Credit Union, 1979-81; mem. exec. com. Private Industry Council, Santa Fe, N.M., 1980-82. Recipient Outstanding Contbn. to Engring. Tech. Edn. in State of Ga., 1987, Cert. of Recognition Ark. Assn. for Continuing and Adult Edn., 1991. Mem. Nat. Soc. Profl. Engrs., Soc. Automotive Engrs. (sec. 1968-69), Am. Soc. Engring. Edn. (dir. 1979-82, S.I.G. chmn. 1980), Am. Psychol. Assn., AAAS, Soc. Mfg. Engrs., Rotary Internat. Home: 3051 Woodlake Ct Marietta GA 30062-5451 Office: Lockheed Martin Aeronautical Systems D/90-21 Z/0311 86 S Cobb Dr Marietta GA 30063

MORRISON, RICHARD PEARCE, microbiologist; b. Great Falls, Mont., Aug. 17, 1954. BS, Mont. State U., 1976, MS, 1978; PhD, U. Okla., 1982. Staff fellow NIH, NIAID, Rocky Mountain Labs., Hamilton, Mont., 1982-86, sr. staff fellow, 1986-90, rsch. microbiologist, 1990-94; assoc. prof. medicine U. Ala., Birmingham, 1994—. Contbr. articles and revs. to profl. jours.; patentee in field. Grantee Edna McConnell Clark Found., 1986, 88, NIH, 1996. Fellow Am. Acad. Microbiology; mem. Am. Soc. Microbiology (chmn. divsn. gen. med. microbiology 1994-95), Am. Soc. Clin. Pathologists, Sigma Xi. Office: U Ala Dept Medicine Tinsley Harrison Tower 1900 University Blvd Rm 229 Birmingham AL 35233-2008

MORRISON, SHIRLEY MARIE, nursing educator; b. Stuttgart, Ark., June 13, 1927; d. Jack Vade Wimberly and Mabel Claire (Dennison) George; m. Dana Jennings Morrison, Mar. 12, 1951 (dec. Dec. 1995); children: Stephen Leslie, Dana Randall, William Lee, Martha Ann Morrison Carson. Diploma, Bapt. Hosp. Sch. Nursing, Nashville, 1949; BSN, Calif. U., Fullerton, 1977; MSN, Calif. U., L.A., 1980; EdD, Nova Southeastern U., 1987. RN, Tex., Calif.; cert. pub. health nurse, Calif.; cert. secondary tchr., Calif. Staff nurse perinatal svcs. Martin Luther Hosp., Anaheim, Calif.,

1960-77, relief 11-7 house supr., 1960-77; dir. vocat. nursing program Inst. Med. Studies, 1978-81; mem. faculty BSN program Abilene (Tex.) Intercollegiate Sch. Nursing, 1981-92, dir. ADN program, 1992—; mem. profl. adv. bd. Nurse Care, Inc., Abilene, 1988—. Mem. adv. bd. parent edn. program Abilene Ind. Sch. Dist., 1985—; active Mar. Dimes, Abilene, 1990—, Ednl. Coalition for Bob Hunter, Abilene, 1994; bd. dirs. Hospice Big Country, Abilene, 1987—. Grantee NIH, 1992. Mem. Nat. Orgn. Assn. Degree Nurses (mem. program com. 10th anniversary nat. conv.), Tex. Orgn. Assoc. Degree Nurses, So. Nursing Rsch. Soc. (rsch. presenter), Health Edn. Resource Network Abilene (founding mem., pres. elect, pres. 1995-96). Democrat. Methodist. Home: PO Box 2583 Abilene TX 79604 Office: Abilene Intercollegiate Sch Nursing 2149 Hickory St Abilene TX 79601-2339

MORRISON, WALTON STEPHEN, lawyer; b. Big Spring, Tex., June 16, 1907; s. Matthew Harmon and Ethel (Jackson) M.; m. Mary Lyon Bell, Dec. 19, 1932. Student Tex. A&M U., 1926-28; J.D., U. Tex., 1932. Bar: Tex. 1932. Asso., Morrison & Morrison, Big Spring, 1932-36, ptnr., 1939, 46; atty. County of Howard, 1937-39, judge, 1941-42, 47-48; atty. City of Big Spring, 1949-58; sole practice, Big Spring, 1953—; lectr. Am. Inst. Banking. Served with USAF, 1942-46. Fellow Tex. Bar Found., Am. Coll. Probate Counsel; mem. Tex. City Attys. Assn. (pres. 1955-56), Am. Judicature Soc., Tex. Bar Assn., ABA. Baptist. Clubs: Rotary (pres. 1949), Masons, Shriner. Home: 1501 E 11th Pl Big Spring TX 79720-4903 Office: PO Box 792 113 E 2nd St Big Spring TX 79720-2502

MORRISON-CARBONE, DAWN ELIZABETH, communications director; b. Dallas, May 6, 1965; d. Donald Gene and Barbara Ann Morrison; m. John Nicholas Carbone, Oct. 29, 1988; children: Cameron Alexander, Ryan Anthony. BA in Journalism/Mktg., Baylor U., 1987. Assoc. news editor Bowling Proprietors' Assn. of Am., Arlington, Tex., 1987-89; editor Windsor Comms., Dallas, 1989-91; comms. dir. Dallas Bar Assn., 1991—; mem. adv. coun. journalism dept. Baylor U. Mem. Nat. Assn. of Bar Execs., Soc. of Profl. Journalists. Roman Catholic. Office: Dallas Bar Assn 2101 Ross Ave Dallas TX 75021

MORROW, A. LESLIE, neuropharmacology, neurobiology and toxicology educator; b. Balt., Jan. 22, 1955; m. Michael C. Lish; children: James Carbery, Matthew Rowland. BS in Psychobiology, U. Calif., Davis, 1977; PhD in Neurosci., U. Calif., San Diego, 1985. Pharmacology rsch. assoc. Lab. Molecular Pharmacology NIMH, Bethesda, Md., 1985-88, sr. rsch. assoc. Lab. Molecular Pharmacology, 1988-90; asst. prof. dept. psychiatry, Ctr. for Alcohol Studies U. N.C. Sch. Medicine, Chapel Hill, 1990-95, assoc. prof. dept. psychiatry and pharmacology, 1991-96, neurobiology curriculum, 1993-96; assoc. prof. toxicology Ctr. for Alcohol Studies U. N.C. Sch. Medicine, Chapel Hill, 1996—. Referee Molecular Pharmacology Jour., Jour Neurosci., Jour. Neurochemistry, Jour. Pharmacol. Exp. Therapy, Psychopharm. Jour., Pharmacology, Biochemistry and Behavior Jour., Brain Rsch. Jour.; ad hoc reviewer NSF, VA; contbr. more than 50 articles to profl. jours. NAS-NRC rsch. assoc., 1988-90; recipient Travel award Am. Coll. Neuropsychopharmacology, 1989, Pharm. Mfrs. Assn. Found. Rsch. Starter award, 1992-93; Alice Hohn Fee scholar U. Calif., San Diego, 1980-81, Earle C. Anthony Fee scholar U. Calif., San Diego, 1981-82; NIMH fellow, 1982-84, 84-85, Pharmacology Rsch. Assn. fellow NIH, 1986-88, NAS rsch. fellow. Mem. NIAAA (spl. study sect.), AAAS, Soc. Neurosci. Rsch. Soc. Alcoholism (membership com.). Office: U NC Sch Medicine Alcohol Studies CB 7178 Dept Psychiatry Chapel Hill NC 27599

MORROW, BRUCE WILLIAM, educational administrator, business executive, consultant; b. Rochester, Minn., May 20, 1946; s. J. Robert and Frances P. Morrow; m. Jenny Lea Morrow. BA, U. Notre Dame, 1968, MBA with honors in Mgmt., 1974, MA in Comparative Lit., 1975; grad. U.S. Army Command and Gen. Staff Coll., 1979. Co-mg. Wendy's Old Fashioned Hamburgers, South Bend, Ind., 1976-77; adminstrn. mgr. Eastern States Devel. Corp., Richmond, Va., 1977; v.p. JDB Assos., Inc., Alexandria, Va., 1976-78; owner Aardvark Prodns., Alexandria, 1978-80, Servital Foods, Alexandria, Va., 1980-82; sr. cons. Data Base Mgmt., Inc., Springfield, Va., 1979-80; systems analyst/staff officer Hdqrs., Dept. Army, Washington, 1980-84; chmn. bd. Commonwealth Dominion Corp., Sierra Vista, Ariz., 1982—; co-founder Southwest Bus. Group, Tucson, 1995—; pres. Sierra Vista Golf, Inc., Ariz., 1994-95; dir. continuing edn. Southside Va. C.C., Alberta, Va., 1989-91; Cochise County team leader Ariz. Coun. Econ. Conversion, 1994-95; mem. com. Ariz. Small Bus. Initiative, 1994—. Author: (radio series) Survival in the Computer Jungle, 1986; (classroom text) Introduction to Computers, 1988, Defense Conversion Handbook, 1995; contbg. columnist Notre Dame mag., 1974-86; composer songs. Active Boy Scouts Am., 1960-69; chmn. elem. German, U. Notre Dame, 1973-75; mem. Roanoke Wildwood Vol. Fire Dept., 1991-93. Lt. col. USAR, ret. Decorated Bronze Star, Army Commendation medals, Army Achievement medal, Meritorious Svc. medals, Parachutist's badge. Mem. VFW (life), Nat. Eagle Scout Assn., Lake Gaston C. of C. (bd. dirs.), Am. Legion, Sierra Vista Area C. of C., Lions (v.p. local club), Beta Gamma Sigma, Delta Phi Alpha. Clubs: Friends Internat. (Am. v.p. 1969-71, Boeblingen, Germany), Order of DeMolay. Office: Commonwealth Dominion Corp 2160 E Fry Blvd Ste 400 Sierra Vista AZ 85635-2736

MORROW, FRANK SPURGEON, JR., alternative views television program producer; b. Bartlesville, Okla., May 17, 1933; s. Frank Spurgeon and Mary Ethel (Goodfellow) M.; m. Ann Lee Welch, Mar. 31, 1956 (Mar. 1966); children: Frank Spurgeon III, Mitchell Stewart, Michael Parker. BA, U. Tulsa, 1955, MA, 1968; PhD, U. Tex., 1984. Radio announcer, newsman, disk jockey KAKC, KTUL, KRMG, KFMJ, Tulsa, 1951-57; commd. ensign U.S. Navy, 1957, advanced through grades to capt., 1965; ops. officer Naval Sec. Grp. Activity, Winter Harbor, Maine, 1968-69; naval sec. grp. res. coord. 3d Naval Dist., N.Y.C., 1969-72; dep. dept. head Nat. Security Agy., Ft. Meade, Md., 1972-73; ret. U.S. Navy, 1973; originator, producer, performer Alternative Views, Austin, Tex., 1978—; bd. dirs. Austin Cmty. TV, 1982-85; pres. Alternative Info. Network, Austin, 1979—. Prodr. Alternative Views, 1978—. Decorated Navy Commendation medal. Mem. Alliance for Cmty. Media, Navy Cryptologic Vets. Assn., Gray Panthers. Home: 8703-B Pineridge Dr Austin TX 78729

MORROW, JASON DREW, medical and pharmacology educator; b. St. Louis, Mar. 30, 1957; s. Ralph Ernest and Vera Rowena (Cummings) M.; m. Lisa Lee Hyman, Mar. 26, 1983; children: Jeremy Nash, Stephanie Rose. BA magna cum laude, Vanderbilt U., 1979; MD, Washington U., St. Louis, 1983. Diplomate Am. Bd. Internal Medicine, Am. Bd. Infectious Diseases. Med. intern, resident Vanderbilt U. Hosp., Nashville, 1983-86, Hugh J. Morgan chief med. resident, 1987-88, rsch. fellow in clin. pharmacology, 1988-91; sr. rsch. fellow dept. pharmacology Vanderbilt U., Sch. Medicine, Nashville, 1991-94, asst. prof. pharmacology and medicine, 1994-95; assoc. prof. Vanderbilt U., Nashville, 1995—, dir. Eicosanoid Core Lab. dept. pharmacology, 1992—; clin. fellow in infectious diseases Barnes Hosp./Washington U., 1986-87; staff physician in medicine and infectious diseases VA Med. Ctr., Nashville, 1991—; mem. internat. adv. com. 9th Internat. Conf. on Prostglandins and RElated Compounds, Florence, Italy, 1994, 10th Conf., Vienna, Austria, 1996. Ad hoc reviewer Jour. Biol. Chemistry, Prostglandins, numerous other sci. publs.; contbr. over 140 articles, abstracts, revs. and papers to sci. jours., chpt. to book. Physician Nashville Union Rescue Mission, 1988—. Recipient Physician-Scientist award NIH, 1990-91, grantee; recipient Rsch. Found. Devel. award Internat. Life Scis. Inst., 1992—; Centennial Clin. Pharmacology fellow Boehringer-Ingelheim, 1990-91, Howard Hughes Med. Inst. Physician rsch. fellow, 1991-94. Mem. AMA, ACP, AAAS, Am. Fedn. Clin. Rsch., So. Soc. Clin. Investigation, Infectious Diseases Soc. Am., Am. Soc. Pharmacology Exptl. Therapeutics, Phi Beta Kappa. Home: 6129 Montcrest Dr Nashville TN 37215-5621 Office: Vanderbilt U Dept Pharmacology 23rd and Pierce Aves Nashville TN 37232-6602

MORROW, WILLIAM CLARENCE, lawyer, mediator, investor; b. Austin, Tex., Aug. 9, 1935; s. Theodore Faulkner and Gladys Lee (Ames) M.; 1 stepchild, Shana Lynn Barbee; m. Sandra Jean Scott, Jan. 19, 1959 (div. Feb. 1971); m. Sheila Beth Pfost, June 29, 1973. children: Scott Fitzgerald Morrow, Elizabeth Ann Rettig. BA, Baylor U., 1957; JD, So. Meth. U., 1962. Bar: Tex., 1962. Trial atty. SEC, Ft. Worth, 1963-65; former ptnr. Cotton, Bledsoe, Tighe, Morrow & Dawson, Lynch, Chappell, Alsup & Midland; exec. v.p. Magnatex Corp., Midland, 1980-86; v.p., gen. counsel and sec. Elcor Corp., Midland, 1986-88. Mem. Midland City Coun., 1992-95, mayor pro tem, 1994-95; former vice chmn. Tex. Rehab. Commn.; pres. Found. Mental Health and Mental Retardation Permian Basin; pres. United Way of Midland, 1985, Indsl. Found. Midland, 1987; trustee Midland Community Theatre, 1980—, chmn. 1995—; elder 1st Presbyn. Ch., Midland. Mem. Tex. Bar Assn., Midland County Bar Assn., Midland C. of C. (past v.p.), Petroleum Club of Midland (past bd. dirs.), Phi Delta Phi. Home: 3110 Gulf Ave Midland TX 79705-8205 Office: 2500 N Big Spring Midland TX 79705

MORSE, F. D., JR., dentist; b. Glen Lyn, Va., Apr. 5, 1928; s. Frank D. and Ida Estell (Davis) M.; B.S., Concord Coll., 1951; DDS, Med. Coll. Va., 1955; m. Patsy Lee Apple, Feb. 4, 1967; 1 child, Fortis Davis; m. Nancy Zink: 1 child, Pamela Marie. Free lance photographer, 1950-56; practice dentistry, Pearisburg, Va., 1958—; mem. staff Giles Hosp., Pearisburg, 1958-86. Served from asst. dental surgeon to sr. asst. dental surgeon USPHS, 1955-57; assigned to USCG, 1957-58. Mem. Am., S.W. Va. dental assns., Assn. Mil. Surgeons, AAAS Nat. Assn. Advancement Sci., Fedn. Dentaire Internat., Internat. Platform Assn., W.Va. Collegiate Acad. Sci., Beta Phi. Kiwanian. Achievements include research in dental ceramics and roof coatings. Home: Bicuspid Acr Pearisburg VA 24134 Office: Giles Profl Bldg Pearisburg VA 24134

MORSE, M. PATRICIA, biology educator; b. Hyannis, Mass., Aug. 29, 1938; d. Charles Verannus and Elizabeth M. BS, Bates Coll., 1960; MS, U. N.H., 1962, PhD, 1966; DSc, Plymouth State Coll. From instr. biology to prof. biology Northeastern U., Boston, 1964—; vis. investigator U. Reading, England, 1972; Fulbright-Hays rsch. fellow U. South Pacific, Fiji, 1978-79; NSF vis. prof. zoology U. Wash., Seattle, 1992-93; program dir. NSF, Alexandria, Va., 1994—. Trustee Bates Coll., 1976—. Mem. Am. Soc. Zoologists, Sigma Xi (past pres.). Office: NSF Rm 885 ESIE 4201 Wilson Blvd Arlington VA 22230

MORSE, MARTIN A., surgeon; b. Louisville, June 25, 1957; s. Marvin Henry and Betty Anne (Hess) M. BS in Zoology with distinction, Duke U., 1979, MD, 1983. Diplomate Nat. Bd. Med. Examiners. Intern, jr. resident dept. surgery Barnes Hosp./Washington U., St. Louis, 1983-85; rsch. fellow dept. pediatric surgery Children's Hosp./Harvard Med. Sch., Boston, 1985-87; sr. resident dept. of surgery U. Rochester, N.Y., 1987-89, chief resident, 1989-90; rsch./clin. fellow in transplantation dept. pediatric surg. Children's Hosp. Med. Ctr., Cin., 1990-92; clin. fellow hand and upper extremity surgery dept. orthopedic surgery U. Pitts. Med. Ctr., 1992-93; fellow in plastic and reconstructive surgery, dept. surgery U. Fla. Coll. Medicine, Gainesville, 1993-95; clin. staff Georgetown U., Washington, 1995—; pvt. practice plastic and reconstructive surgery McLean, Va., 1995—; lab. investigator Lab. Exptl. Pathology div. cancer cause and prevention Nat. Cancer Inst./NIH, Rockville, Md., summers 1974-80; invited prof. dept. grad. nursing Simmons Coll., Boston, 1986-87; NASA flight surgeon. Contbr. articles to profl. jours. Vol. Cystic Fibrosis, Am. Cancer Soc., Am. Heart Assn., March of Dimes, Am. Lung Soc.; founding mem. Statue of Liberty/Ellis Isle Found., N.Y.C., 1985, JFK Libr. Found., Boston, 1987, Challenger Ctr. for Space Sci. Edn., Washington, 1987, U.S. Naval Meml. Found., Washington, 1990; active Friends Nat. Libr. Medicine, Col. Williamsburg Found., Met. Mus. Art, Boston Mus. Fine Arts, Carnegie Mellon Mus.; patron The John F. Kennedy Ctr. for the Performing Arts, Friends of the Nat. Zoo, Nat. Audobon Soc., World Wildlife Fund. Farley Found. fellow Children's Hosp., Harvard Med. Sch., 1986; recipient Outstanding Svc. award Nat. Cancer Inst., NIH, 1977, Nat. Def. medal. Fellow ACS (assoc.); mem. AMA, AAAS, Soc. Laparoendoscopic Surgeons, Am. Soc. Artificial Internal Organs, Am. Trauma Soc., Fla. State Med. Soc., Assn. for Acad. Surgery, Surg. Infection Soc., Aerospace Med. Assn., Assn. Mil. Surgeons U.S., Am. Soc. Cell Biology and Tissue Culture Assn., So. Med. Assn., Physicians for Social Responsibility, Rochester Surg. Soc., N.Y. Acad. Scis., Fairfax County Med. Soc., Fla. State Med. Soc., Fla. Hand Soc., Va. State Med. Soc., Am. Legion, Naval Res. Assn., Res. Officers Assn., Phi Beta Kappa, Alpha Omega Alpha, Phi Lambda Epsilon.

MORSE, RICHARD VAN TUYL, manufacturing executive, consultant; b. N.Y.C., May 7, 1931; s. Norvell V. and Julie M. (Lamisha) M.; m. Florence Denby, June 21, 1953 (div. June 1983); children: Stuart V., Andrew D.; m. Emilie Atolli, Sept. 14, 1983. BS in Econs., U. Pa., 1953; MBA, NYU, 1958. Account supr. various advt. agys., N.Y.C., 1956-66; v.p., account supr. Wells, Rich, Greene, Inc., N.Y.C., 1960-70, Norman, Craig & Kummell, Inc., N.Y.C., 1970-74; sr. v.p., mgmt. supr. William Free & Co., N.Y.C., 1974-80; v.p. mktg. Canada Dry, Inc., N.Y.C., 1980-87; v.p. mktg. comm. Lithonia Lighting, Conyers, Ga., 1987—; dir. Pop Warner Football, N.Y.C., 1967-69. Contbr. articles to profl. jours. Elected Rep. rep. Union County, N.J., 1970-76. Capt. USAR. Mem. Am. Mktg. Assn., Nat. Lighting Bur. (bd. chmn.), Bus. and Profl. Advt. and Mktg. Assn. Republican. Episcopalian. Home: 7155 Roswell Rd NE # 53 Atlanta GA 30328-5419 Office: Lithonia Lighting PO Box A Conyers GA 30207-0067

MORSE, STEPHEN ALLEN, microbiologist, researcher; b. L.A., Apr. 11, 1942; s. Norman and Sallie (Mozur) M.; m. Ruth Rose Logan, Apr. 1, 1967 (div. 1973); 1 child, Nicole; m. Rhona Ellen Wolfe, Aug. 6, 1974 (div. 1980); 1 child, Nathaniel; m. Brenda Rae Smith, June 19, 1988. BA in Microbiology, Calif. State U., San Jose, 1964; MS in Pub. Health, U. N.C., 1966, PhD in Microbiology, 1969; postdoctoral in Microbiology, U. Ga. Postdoctoral rsch. asst. dept. microbiology U. Ga., Athens, 1969-70; asst. prof. dept. biology Southeastern Mass. U., North Dartmouth, 1970-71; rsch. assoc. dept. microbiology Harvard Sch. Pub. Health, Boston, 1971-72, asst. prof. dept. microbiology, sr. inst. clin. bacteriology, 1972-74; asst. prof. dept. microbiology and immunology Oreg. Health Sci. U., Portland, 1974-75, assoc. prof. dept. microbiology and immunology, 1975-82, prof. dept. microbiology and immunology, 1982-84, adj. prof. dept. microbiology and immunology, 1984—; adj. prof. dept. microbiology and immunology Emory U. Sch. Medicine, Atlanta, 1985—; adj. prof. dept. microbiology U. Ala., Birmingham, 1995—; dir. div. sexually transmitted diseases lab. rsch. Nat. Ctrs. for Disease Control and Prevention, Atlanta, 1994-95; assoc. dir. sci. divsn. AIDS, sexually transmitted diseases and TB lab rsch. Ctrs. for Disease Control and Prevention, Atlanta, 1995—; vis. lectr. Sch. Pub. Health, UCLA, 1972, dept. microbiology Meharry Med. Sch., Nashville, 1976; vis. prof. dept. microbiology U. Birmingham, Eng., 1978, dept. infectious diseases Johns Hopkins Sch. Medicine, 1982, dept. medicine UCLA, 1982, dept. pathobiology U. Wash. Sch. Medicine and Infectious Diseases Div., Pacific Med. Ctr., Seattle, 1983-84; affiliate scientist STD program project U. Wash., 1976-84, Oreg. Regional Primate Rsch. Ctr., Beaverton, 1981-84; speaker in field. Ad hoc reviewer numerous jours. and grants; contbr. over 190 articles to profl. jours. Recipient Milton Fund grant Harvard U., 1971-72, grant U.S. Army Med. R&D Command, 1973-74, 74-75, EPA grant, 1972-74, grant Med. Rsch. Found. Oreg., 1975, 75-76, 80-81, grant NIAID, 1976-84, 76-80, 76-81, grant Miles Labs., 1976-80 and numerous others. Fellow Infectious Diseases Soc. Am. (editorial bd. 1982-84); mem. Am. Soc. Microbiology (Behring diagnostics award com. 1987-90, fin. com. 1986-88, coun. policy com. 1985-88, coun. 1985-88, div. lectr. 1984, found. lectr. 1981-82, 91-92, chmn. med. microbiology sect. 1978, 95, chmn. elect med. microbiology sect. 1977, 94, election com. med. microbiology sect. 1975, editorial bd. 1978-95), Am. Acad. Microbiology (chmn. com. to review accreditation and cert. nominating com. 1988-89), Soc. Gen. Microbiology, Soc. Experimental Biology and Medicine, Am. Sexually Transmitted Diseases Assn. (mem. bd. dirs. 1978-79, 88-91, sec., treas. 1997—, mem. com. 1977-78, program chmn. 1978-79, election com. 1975-76, awards com. chmn. 1988-94, publications com. chmn. 1989-90, editorial bd. 1977-82, 90—). Office: Ctrs for Disease Control 1600 Clifton Rd Atlanta GA 30333

MORSON, PHILIP HULL, III, psychiatrist, osteopath; b. Tupelo, Miss., Oct. 1, 1948; s. Philip Hull and Jane Allen (McGee) M.; m. Brenda Lott, Aug. 28, 1970 (div. July 1986); children: Andrew Eugene, Benjamin Terrell; m. Katherine Ann Smith, Dec. 12, 1992; children: Bobbie Nichole, Samantha Grace. BA, Miss. State U., 1970; M of Combined Scis., U. Miss., Jackson, 1973; DO, U. Health Scis., Kansas City, Mo., 1978. Diplomate Nat. Bd. Osteo. Med. Examiners; cert. forensic physician. Brigade surgeon U.S. Army, Fort Stewart, Ga., 1979-81; ranger bn. surgeon 1st Bn, 75th inf. U.S. Army, Savannah, Ga., 1981; chief outpatient clinic Winn Army Hosp., Ft. Stewart, Ga., 1981-82; chief emergency med. svcs. Winn Army Hosp., Ft. Stewart, 1982-83; pvt. practice Cleveland, Tenn., 1983-89, Bristol, Tenn., 1989-91; staff physician Western Mental Health Inst., Bolivar, Tenn., 1991—; chmn. treatment rev. com. Western Mental Helath Inst., 1991—, vice chmn. pharmacy and therapeutics com., 1993-94, mem. exec. med. staff, 1994—. Sponsor troop Girl Scouts Am., Bolivar, Tenn., 1992-94; mem. PTA, Bolivar, 1992-94. Mem. Am. Osteo. Assn., Western Tenn. Osteo. Assn., Tenn. State Employees Assn. (treas. S.W. chpt. 1994-95, legis. com. 1994-95), Mensa, NRA. Republican. Unitarian. Home: 1915 Levy Ln Bolivar TN 38008 Office: Western Mental Health Inst 11000 Hwy 64 W Bolivar TN 38008

MORTEL, KARL FREDERICK, neuropsychologist; b. Chgo., June 26, 1945; s. Emil M. and Faye (Fortess) M.; m. Tami M. Martin, Sept. 22, 1984. BA in Psychology, Calif. State Coll., 1970; MA in Psychology, U. Houston, 1974, PhD in Psychology, 1981. Lic. psychologist, Tex. Computer technician dept. of info. engring. U. Ill., Chgo., 1965-66; teaching asst. dept. psychology Calif. State Coll., L.A., 1966-68, rsch. asst. dept. psychology, 1968-71; rsch. asst. div. rsch. in med. edn. U. So. Calif. Med. Sch., L.A., 1970-71; rsch. fellow dept. otolaryngology Baylor Coll. Medicine, Houston, 1971-73, rsch. assoc. dept. neurology, 1978-82; rsch. fellow dept. neuropharmacology Tex. Rsch. Inst. Mental Scis., Houston, 1973-74; teaching fellow dept. psychology U. Houston, 1974-76; rsch. assoc. Cerebral Blood Flow Lab. VA Med. Ctr., Houston, 1978-83; instr. dept. psychology Houston Community Coll., 1981-82; assoc. dir. Cerebral Blood Flow Lab. VA Med. Ctr. and Baylor Coll. Medicine, Houston, 1983—; adj. clin. asst. prof. dept. psychology U. Houston, 1988—; mem. neuropsychology tng. com. and neuropsychology grad. student selection com. dept. psychology U. Houston; mem. radionuclide use subcom., neurobehavioral subcom, R&D com. Vets. Affairs Med. Ctr., Houston. Contbr. articles to profl. jours. Grantee VA, 1987-89, 91-93, Miles, Inc., 1988-91, McNeil Consumer Products Co., 1989, Hoechst-Roussel Pharms., Inc., 1990-91, 96, Abuse Prevention Group, 1995—. Fellow Am. Coll. Angiology; mem. AAAS, Internat. Stroke Soc., Internat. Neuropsychol. Soc., Internat. Soc. Neuropathology, Soc. Exptl. Neuropathology, Am. Psychol. Assn., Houston Neuropsychol. Soc. Home: 2031 Sheridan St Houston TX 77030-2105 Office: VA Med Ctr Cerebral Blood Flow Lab 2002 Holcombe Blvd Houston TX 77030-4211

MORTENSON, THOMAS CARL, property and business developer; b. Racine, Wis., Nov. 21, 1947; s. Thomas and Dolores Charlotte (Lojeski) M.; m. Pamela Jean Bliss, Aug. 5, 1967; children: Shawn Lea, Thomas Carl II, Todd Robert. BA in Polit. Sci., History, Carthage Coll., 1970; MPA, Golden Gate U., 1981; grad., Army Command Gen. Staff Coll., 1989; MA, U. South Fla., 1991; grad., U. Command and Gen. Staff Coll., 1991; grad. in Def. Strategy, Army War Coll., 1993; postgrad., Naval War Coll. Cert. elec. journeyman/contractor; cert. bldg. ofcl. Elec. journeyman Mortenson Electric, Racine, 1969-75; v.p. Electrically Yours, Racine, 1975-77; sales mgr., ad cons. Telecable/Teleprompter, Racine and Tampa, 1977-79; territory mgr. S.C. Johnson & Son, Inc., Racine, 1979-84; dir. community devel. City of Temple Terrace, Fla., 1984-87; pub. info. officer Office of Sec. Def./Army, Washington, 1987-88; mgr. maintenance supply Unisource, Tampa, Fla., 1988-93; dist. mgr. ABC Compounding, Atlanta, 1994-95; owner MPG, Tampa, 1995—. Pres. city coun. City of Racine, 1971, mem. city planning commn.; mem. tech. adv. com. Unified Sch. Dist., Racine, 1976-77; mem. Hillsborough County Governance Com., Tampa, 1991; mem. coun. adv. com. City of Temple Terrace, 1991; chmn. troop 84 Boy Scouts Am., 1991—, mem. eagle scout com. Gulf Ridge coun., 1992—. Maj. U.S. Army; ops. officer Fla. N.G. Recipient Mil. Achievement award The Milw. Jour., 1974, 76; named one of Outstanding Young Men of Am., Jaycees, 1971, 74, 75; honored by Boy Scouts Am., 1992, 93, 94. Mem. N.G. Officers Assn. (Lowry award 1988), Better Govt. Assn. (pres. 1993—, Excellence award 1993), Fla. Assn. Vol. Agys. Caribbean Action, Kiwanis (past pres., bd. dirs.). Republican. Lutheran. Home: 6612 Peachtree Dr Tampa FL 33617-2516 Office: MPG PO Box 16047 Tampa FL 33687

MORTHAM, SANDRA BARRINGER, state official; b. Erie, Pa., Jan. 4, 1951; d. Norman Lyell and Ruth (Harer) Barringer; m. Allen Mortham, Aug. 21, 1950; children: Allen Jr., Jeffrey. AS, St. Petersburg Jr. Coll., 1971; BA, Eckerd Coll. Cons. Capital Formation Counselors, Inc., Bellair Bluffs, Fla., 1972—; commr. City of Largo, Fla., 1982-86, vice mayor, 1985-86; mem. Fla. Ho. of Reps., 1986-94, Rep. leader pro tempore, 1990-92, minority leader, 1992-94; Sec. of State State of Fla., 1995—. Bd. dirs. Performing Arts Ctr. & Theatre, Clearwater, Fla.; exec. com. Pinellas County Rep. Com., Rep. Nat. Com. Named Citizen of Yr., 1990; recipient Tax Watch Competitive Govt. award, 1994, Bus. and Profl. Women "Break the Glass Ceiling" award, 1995, Fla. League of Cities Quality Floridian award, 1995, also numerous outstanding legislator awards, achievement among women awards from civic and profl. orgns. Mem. Am. Legis. Exch. Coun., Nat. Rep. Legislators Assn., Largo C. of C. (bd. dirs. 1987—, pres.), Largo Jr. Woman's Club (pres., Woman of Yr. award 1979), Suncoast Community Woman's Club (pres., Outstanding Svc. award 1981, Woman of Yr. award 1986), Suncoast Tiger Bay, Greater Largo Rep., Belleair Rep. Woman's, Clearwater Rep. Woman's. Presbyterian. Home: 6675 Weeping Willow Dr Tallahassee FL 32311 Office: Secretary of State The Capitol, PL-02 Tallahassee FL 32399-0250

MORTIMER, RORY DIXON, lawyer; b. Flint, Mich., Jan. 6, 1950; s. Kenneth N. and Phyllis (Rouleau) M.; m. Patricia Ann Amstadt, Sept. 18, 1971; children: Melissa Marie, Ryan Douglas. BA, Mich. State U., 1972, JD, 1978. Bar: S.C. 1978, Mich. 1979, U.S. Ct. Appeals (4th cir.) U.S. Tax Ct., U.S. Supreme Ct. 1979. Trust officer C&S Nat. Bank, Charleston, S.C., 1978-79; pvt. practice law Summerville, S.C., 1979-80; ptnr. Chellis & Mortimer, Summerville, 1980-85, Chellis, Mortimer & Frampton, Summerville, 1985-95; sr. ptnr. Mortimer, Leiendecker & Rose, Summerville, 1995—; gen. counsel Commr. of Pub. Wks., Summerville, 1982-96. Atty., Dorchester County Human Devel. Bd., 1987—. Mem. ATLA, S.C. Bar Assn., S.C. Trial Lawyers Assn., Mich. Bar Assn., Am. Soc. CLUs and ChFC (pres. 1989). Republican. Roman Catholic. Home: 105 Old Postern Rd Summerville SC 29483-3770 Office: Mortimer Leiendecker & Rose 1810 Trolley Rd Summerville SC 29485-8282

MORTON, JAMES CARNES, JR., public relations executive; b. Duncan, Okla., May 8, 1945; s. James Carnes and Syble Lyda (Looney) M.; m. Susan Phillips, May 25, 1968; children: James III, Terrissa Anne, Scott Thomas. BA, Westminster Coll., 1967; JD, U. Mo., 1972. Bar: Mo. 1972, S.C., 1991. Tax acct. Arthur Andersen Co., St. Louis, 1972-74; tax atty. Gen. Dynamics Corp., St. Louis, 1974-76; asst. gen. counsel Michelin Tire Corp., Greenville, S.C., 1976-86; gen. counsel Michelin Tire Corp. and Michelin Tires (Can.) Ltd., Greenville, S.C., 1990-92; dir. pub. rels. and govt. affairs Michelin Tire Corp., Greenville, S.C., 1986-92; exec. dir. external rels. Michelin N.Am., Greenville, S.C., 1992-96; v.p. pub. rels. and govt. rels. Michelin N.Am., Inc., 1996—. Bd. dirs. Ednl. Resources Found., 1992—, Greenville Symphony Orch., 1986-89, United Way Greenville, 1987-88, Greenville YMCA, 1988-89, Ednl. Resource Found.; trustee S.C. Gov.'s Sch. for Sci. and Math.; mem. S.C. State Reorgn. Commn., 1987—; mem. bd. visitors and fin. com. Christ Church Episcopal Sch., Greenville, 1991—. Capt. U.S. Army, 1967-72, Vietnam. Mem. ABA, Rubber Mfrs. Assn. (bd. dirs. 1995—, govt. affairs com., tire mgmt. com.), Mo. Bar Assn. (nonresident), S.C. C. of C. (bd. dirs., pres. 1993-94, chmn. 1994-95, exec. com. 1981-84, 86-95, Svc. Recognition award 1982), Greater Greenville C. of C. (chmn. govt. affairs com. 1990, chmn. legis. affairs com. 1996, bd. dirs. 1990-93), Greenville Country Club, Greenville City Club, Commerce Club, Faculty House Club (U.S.C.). Presbyterian. Office: Michelin NAm PO Box 19001 Greenville SC 29602-9001

MORTON, JANICE KENEFAKE, nurse administrator; b. Mt. Carmel, Ill., Nov. 2, 1951; d. Francis William and Kathleen Helen (Stanley) Kenefake; m. Danny Joe Morton, Feb. 19, 1979; children: Melissa Ann, Michael Jonothan, Jonothan Edward. ADN, Henderson (Ky.) Community Coll., 1971; BSN, U. Evansville, 1978, MA, 1989. Cert. Nurse Adminstr. Advanced, 1991. Staff nurse Community Meth. Hosp., Henderson, 1971, Vanderbilt U., Nashville, 1971-72, Deaconess Hosp., Evansville, Ind., 1972-73; dir. nursing MEDCO Nursing Home, Henderson, 1973; home health coord. Henderson County Health Dept., 1973-74; staff nurse Fayette County Home Health Agy., Lexington, Ky., 1974-75; staff RN Ft. Logan Hosp., Stanford, Ky., 1975-77; staff nurse Community Methodist Hosp., 1977-79; asst. dir. nursing Community Meth. Hosp., Henderson, 1979-89; Healthtrust chief nursing officer Meadowview Regional Hosp., Maysville, Ky., 1989-94; chief nursing officer Colleton Regional Hosp., Walterboro, S.C., 1994-95; v.p. clin. svcs. Nat. Hosp. Med. Ctr., Arlington, Va., 1995—, chief nursing exec., 1995—; corneal eye tech. U. Ky., Lexington, 1988-94, U. Louisville, 1988-94; mem. adv. com./nursing Morehead (Ky.) State U., 1990-94; adv. bd. nursing Maysville C.C., 1990-94; mem. curriculum adv. com. NOVA, 1996. Bd. dirs. United Way, Maysville, 1991-94. Named Embassador to Ky. Pk. System Gov. Julian Carrol, 1976. Mem. Am. Orgn. Nursing Execs. Home: 10743 Burr Oak Way Burke VA 22015 Office: Nat Hosp Med Ctr 2455 Army Navy Dr Arlington VA 22206

MORTON, JEROME HOLDREN, school psychologist; b. Duluth, Minn., July 30, 1942; s. Jerome Raefield and Svea (Holdren) M.; m. Anna Mary Moore, June 9, 1964; children: Scot, Jeanette. BA, Centre Coll., 1964; MS, Miami U., Oxford, Ohio, 1966; PhD, U. Tenn., 1973. Psychologist Pinellas County Sch. System, Clearwater, Fla., 1969-71; dir. psychol. and spl. edn. svcs. Little Tenn. Valley Ednl. Coop., Lenoir City, Tenn., 1973-76, exec. dir., 1977—; pres. and bd. dirs. Psychol. and Ednl. Cons., P.C., Knoxville, Tenn., 1985—; dir. Knoxville Alternative Ct. for Learning, 1985-91; rsch. assoc. spl. svcs. dept. Coll. Edn. U. Tenn., Knoxville, 1991-93; due process hearing officer State Tenn. Dept. Edn., Nashville, 1974-85; hon. asst. prof. psychology dept. U. Tenn., Knoxville, 1978—; mem. bd. advisors Big South Fork Regional Assn., Outdoor Adventure and Rsch. Ctr., 1991-93; bd. dirs. Mental Health Assn. Knox County, 1990-92, v.p. pub. policy, 1991-92; bd. dirs. East Tenn. Spl. Tech. Access Ctr, 1989-96, chmn. bd. dirs., 1993-95. Co-author: Students at risk and intervention strategies, 1989; contbr. author Dropouts: Who Drops Out and Why-And The Recommended Action, 1990; contbr. articles to profl. jours. Co-chmn. East Tenn. Coalition for Children, 1983-84, chmn., 1984-85. Served with U.S. Army, 1966-69. Recipient Best Principal/Best School award Knoxville C. of C., 1989. Mem. APA, Tenn. Assn. Psychology in Schs. (pres. 1976-77), Tenn. Psychol. Assn. (v.p. 1976-77), Nat. Assn. Sch. Psychology, Internat. Speakers Network, Inc. Office: 1432 E Lee Hwy Loudon TN 37774-6440

MORTON, LINDA P., journalism educator; b. Nashville, Ark., Oct. 3, 1946; d. Clerence Augustus and Wanda Low (Greenleigh) King; m. Truman F. Patterson, Aug. 14, 1964; m. Gail Morton, Feb. 14, 1976; children: Jene C., John D. BA in English Edn., Northeastern State U., Tahlequah, Okla., 1971; MA in English, Ark. State U., 1972; EdD in Higher Edn., Okla. State U., 1984. Asst. prof. lang. arts Bacone Coll., Muskogee, Okla., 1972-76; dir. pub. rels. Inst. Journalism, Carl Albert Jr. Coll., Poteau, Okla., 1976-80; pub. info. officer Coll. Bus. Adminstrn., Okla. State U., Stillwater, 1980-83; asst. prof. pub. rels./advt. N.E. Mo. State U., Kirksville, 1983-84; coord. and lang. arts instr. Inst. Journalism, Carl Albert Jr. Coll. Extension Office, Sallisaw, Okla., 1985-88; dir. pub. rels., assoc. prof. pub. rels. Miss. U. for Women, Columbus, 1988-90; asst. prof. journalism U. So. Miss., Hattiesburg, 1990-92, U. Okla., Norman, 1992—; lectr. in field. Mem. rev. bd. Pub. Rels. Rev., 1994—; contbr. articles to scholarly and profl. jours. Recipient Grad award for comm. programs CASE, 1983, Silver Addy for vision poster Ctrl. Miss. Advt. Assn., 1989. Mem. Pub. Rels. Soc. Am. (accredited, dir. ednl. sect. 1993-94, dir. at large ednl. sect. 1994-95, sec.-treas. ednl. sect. 1995, ednl. affairs com. 1995—, editor ednl. sect. newsletter 1996), Okla. Coll. Pub. Rels. Assn. (pres. 1980-81), Assn. for Educators in Schs. of Journalism and Mass Comm. Baptist. Home: 2401 Larkhaven St Norman OK 73071-4326 Office: U Okla Sch Journalism 860 Van Vleet Oval Norman OK 73019-2050

MORTON, LUIS JAC-REMELG M., manufacturing executive, educator; b. Odessa, Tex., Dec. 12, 1957; s. Luis Meza Morton and Mari (Marin) Meyer; m. Sharla Gay Spence, Aug. 14, 1982; children: Mallorie Lou, Spence Currie. A of Gen. Studies, Cen. Tex. Coll., Killeen, 1978; BS, Am. Tech. U., Killeen, 1979, MS, 1980; MEd, East Tex. State U., 1984, PhD, 1991. Sr. bookkeeper First Nat. Bank, Killeen, 1974-77; intern to pres. Union State Bank, Florence, Tex., 1978-79; liaison East Tex. State U., Commerce, 1979-81; dean coll. ctrs. Navarro Coll., Corsicana, Tex., 1981-85; chief fin. officer, mgr. N-CYCLE Engine Co., Ennis, Tex., 1982—; CEO Stillhouse Devel. Co., Killeen, 1977—; mgr., chief info. officer Double O Resources, Boulder City, Nev., 1986; ITV coord./developer Panhandle State U., Panhandle Shar-Ed Video Network. Served to 2d lt. USNG, 1980-86. Mem. Killeen C. of C. (mil. affairs div. 1979), Assn. of U.S. Army, (bd. govs. 1975), Phi Delta Kappa. Club: ATU-MBA (Killeen) (pres. 1978-80). Lodge: Kiwanis (v.p. Ennis chpt. 1983-85). Home: Okla Panhandle State U PO Box 126 Goodwell OK 73939 Office: Box 126 Goodwell OK 73939

MORTON, MARILYN MILLER, genealogy and history educator, lecturer, researcher, travel executive, director; b. Water Valley, Miss., Dec. 2, 1929; d. Julius Brunner and Irma Faye (Magee) Miller; m. Perry Wilkes Morton Jr., July 2, 1958; children: Dent Miller Morton, Nancy Marilyn Morton Driggers, E. Perian Morton Dyar. BA in English, Miss. U. for Women, 1952; MS in History, Miss. State U., 1955. Cert. secondary tchr. Tchr. English, speech and history Starkville (Miss.) H.S., 1952-58; part-time instr. Miss. State U., 1953-55; mem. spl. collection staff Samford U. Libr., Birmingham, Ala., 1984-92; lectr. genealogy and history, instr. Inst. Genealogy & Hist. Rsch., Samford U., Birmingham, 1985-93, assoc. dir., 1985-88, exec. dir., 1988-93; founding dir. SU British and Irish Inst. Genealogy & Hist. Rsch. Samford U., Birmingham and British Isles, 1986-93; owner, dir. Marilyn Miller Morton Brit-Ire-U.S. Genealogy, Birmingham, also British Isles, 1994—; instr. genealogy classes Samford U. Metro Coll., 1989-94; lectr. nat. conf. Fedn. of Geneal. Socs. Contbr. articles and book revs. to profl. jours. Active Birmingham chpt. Salvation Army Aux., 1982—. Inducted into Miss. U. for Women Hall of Fame, 1952. Fellow Irish Geneal. Rsch. Soc. London; mem. Internat. Soc. Brit. Genealogy and Family History, Nat. Geneal. Soc. (mem. nat. program com. 1988—, lectr. nat. mtgs.), Assn. Profl. Genealogists, Soc. Genealogists London, Antiquarian Soc. Birmingham (sec., 2d v.p. 1982-84), DAR (regent Cheaha chpt. 1977-78), Daus. Am. Colonists (regent Edward Waters chpt. 1978-79), Nat. League of Am. Penwomen, Phi Kappa Phi (charter mem. Samford U. chpt. 1972). Home and Office: 3508 Clayton Pl Birmingham AL 35216-3810

MORTON, MARK EDWARD, accountant, clothing store executive; b. Charleston, W.Va., July 20, 1956; s. Edward Roy and Loretta Vay (White) M. BSBA cum laude, W.Va. State Coll., 1978. CPA, W.Va. Salesman Kelley's Mens Shop, Inc., Charleston, 1975-82, contr., 1982-84, treas., 1984—, also corp. sc., bd. dirs. Bd. dirs., treas. Gift of Love Com. Inc., South Charleston, W.Va., 1986-96; asst. treas. Cen. Ch., 1983-92, chmn. coun. of ministries, 1990. Mem. W.Va. Soc. CPA's. Office: Kelley's Men's Shop Inc 108 W Washington St Charleston WV 25302

MORTON, MICHAEL RAY, retail company executive; b. Memphis, Nov. 10, 1952; s. James Ray and Margaret Regina (Stevens) M.; m. Mary Elizabeth Harkness; children: Mary Harkness, Margaret Jeanne, Molly Ray. BBA, U. Miss., 1973; MBA, U. Denver, 1975. Cost acct. Dover Corp., Memphis, 1975-76; internal auditor W.R. Grace and Co., Memphis, 1976-78; sr. fin. analyst W.R. Grace and Co., N.Y.C., 1979-80; v.p. Handy Dan div. W.R. Grace and Co., San Antonio, 1981-82; chief fin. officer, sec., treas. Home Ctrs. Am., San Antonio, 1983; sr. v.p. Builders Square K-Mart Corp., San Antonio, 1984-89; pres. Orion Strategic Solutions, Inc., 1989—; bd. dirs. Builders Design Inc., Dania, Fla., 1989-91, treas., 1985-87; bd. dirs., v.p. Tex. Ind. Newspapers, Inc., San Antonio; mem. exec. com. Home Ctr. Industry Conf. Mem. San Antonio C. of C. (amb. 1981), Home Ctr. Leadership Coun. Republican. Roman Catholic. Home: 8060 Pimlico Ln Boerne TX 78006-4705

MORTON, THEODORE ROOSEVELT, JR., clergyman; b. Wilson, N.C., June 18, 1931; s. Theodore Roosevelt and Katherine (Morton) M.; m. Henrietta Mayo Rosson, Aug. 20, 1954; children: Kenneth Patterson, Theodora Rosson Miles, William Spencer II. BA in English and History, Wofford Coll., Spartanburg, S.C., 1953, DD (hon.), 1981; MDiv in Theology, Duke U. Div. Sch., 1956. Ordained deacon United Meth. Ch., 1955, elder, 1956. Assoc. pastor Shandon United Meth. Ch., Columbia, S.C., 1961-64; pastor Bethel and Wesley Chapel United Meth. Chs., Jackson, S.C., 1964-68; pres., CEO Greenwood (S.C.) Meth. Home, 1968-94, assoc. in devel., 1994-95; ret., 1995; del. Gen. Conf. United Meth. Ch., 1980, 84; sec. S.C. Conf. United Meth. Ch., 1975-84, ex-officio mem. conf. bd. health and welfare ministries, 1968-94, ex-officio mem. conf. nominating com., com. on the conf. jour. and the conf. Commn. on Archives and History, 1978-84, other positions in past; trustee S.C. United Meth. Advocate, 1975-82, S.C. United Meth. Found., 1996—. Trustee The Self Found., Greenwood, 1983-87; organizer, pres. Greenwood County Coun. on Aging, 1970-76; past bd. dirs. Greenwood County chpt. ARC, Greenwood United Way. Lt. col. USAR, 1956-67, 71-91. Decorated Army Commendation medal, Meritorious Svc. medal; Paul Harris fellow, 1982. Mem. Greater Carolina Assn. Non-Profit Homes (pres. 1975-77), S.C. Assn. Non-Profit Homes for Aging (pres. 1982-84), Am. Assn. Homes for Aging (mem. ho. dels. 1990-94)), Greenwood C. of C. (bd. dirs., com. chair 1972-78), Ret. Officers Assn. (v.p. Star Fort chpt.), Rotary (past pres. and treas., Cmty. Svc. award 1976). Home: Forest Hills Forest Hills 167 Rutledge Rd Greenwood SC 29649-8992

MOSCATELLO, SALVATORE ANTHONY, gastroenterologist; b. Jersey City, Nov. 15, 1958; s. Salvatore Alfred and Theresa Rose (Damato) M.; m. Julie Ann Blades, Sept. 14, 1985; children: Nicholas Joseph, Matthew Frederick. BA, Cornell U., 1980; DO, Phila. Coll., 1985. Diplomate Am. Bd. Internal Medicine, Am. Bd. Gastroenterology. Physician Trident Gastroenterology Assn., N. Charleston, S.C, 1993—. Fellow ACP, Am. Coll. of Osteopathic Internists; mem. Am. Coll. of Gastroenterology, Am. Soc. for Gastro-intestinal Endoscopy. Office: Trident Gastroenterology 9267 Medical Plaza Dr North Charleston SC 29406

MOSCHELLA, RALPH, physician; b. Naples, Italy, July 2, 1914; came to U.S., 1920; s. Frank Stanislaus and Maria Grazia (Ippariello) M.; m. Helen Irene Homesley, Apr. 8, 1940; 1 child, Pamela. MD, Coll. Physicians & Surgeons, Boston, 1938. Intern St. Francis Hosp., Poughkeepsie, N.Y., 1937; resident in anesthesiology Berkshire Med. Ctr., 1962-64; fellow in anesthesiology Georgetown Hosp., 1969; physician. Mem. AMA, Va. Med. Soc., Mass. Med. Soc. Home: 7116 Park Terrace Dr Alexandria VA 22307

MOSELEY, JAMES FRANCIS, lawyer; b. Charleston, S.C., Dec. 6, 1936; s. John Olin and Kathryn (Moran) M.; m. Anne McGehee, June 10, 1961; children: James Francis Jr., John McGehee. AB, The Citadel, 1958; JD, U. Fla., 1961. Bar: Fla. 1961, U.S. Supreme Ct. 1970. Pres. Moseley, Warren, Prichard & Parrish, Jacksonville, Fla., 1963—; chmn. jud. nominating com. 4th Jud. Cir., 1978-80. Assoc. editor: American Maritime Cases; contbr. articles on admiralty, transp. and ins. law to legal jours. Pres. Jacksonville United Way, 1979; chmn. bd. dirs. United Way Fla., 1992-93, S.E. regional coun. United Way, 1992-96; trustee Jacksonville Cmty. Found.; chmn. bd. trustees Jacksonville Pub. Libr.; trustee Libr. Found., sec., 1987-91; trustee CMI Am. Found.; chmn. Jacksonville Human Svcs. Coun., 1989-91; chmn. bd. trustees United Way N.E. Fla., 1995—; bd. govs. United Way Am., 1996—. Fellow Am. Coll. Trial Lawyers, Am. Bar Found.; mem. Jacksonville Bar Assn. (pres. 1975), Fla. Coun. Bar Pres. (chmn. 1979), Maritime Law Assn. U.S. (exec. com. 1978-81, chmn. navigation com. 1981-88, v.p. 1992-96, pres. 1996—), Comm. Maritime Internat. (titulary), Com. on Collision (Lisbon Rules), Fed. Ins. Corp. Counsel (chmn. maritime law sect.), Internat. Assn. Def. Counsel (chmn. maritime com. 1989-91), Am. Inns of Ct. (master of bench), Assn. of Citadel Men (bd. mem. 1989-93, exec. com. 1994, Man Yr. award 1992), Citadel Inn of Ct. (sr. bencher), Deerwood Club, River Club, Downtown Athletic Club (N.Y.C.), India House (N.Y.C.), Army Navy Club (Washington), St. John's Dinner Club (pres. 1988). Home: 7780 Hollyridge Rd Jacksonville FL 32256-7134 Office: Moseley Warren Prichard Parrish 1887 Bldg 501 W Bay St Jacksonville FL 32202

MOSELEY, JOHN MARSHALL, nurseryman; b. New Canton, Va., Aug. 8, 1911; s. John Marshall and May Baxter (Staehlin) M.; m. Edith Batchelor Hancock, Dec. 31, 1942 (div. Jan. 1966); children: John Marshall, James Hancock, William Rogers. BS, U. Richmond, Va., 1930. Analytical chemist Va. State Dept. Hwys, Richmond, 1930-31; chemist Am. Tobacco Co., Richmond, 1931-56, asst. to dir. rsch., 1956-59, from asst. to dir. rsch. to asst. to v.p., 1959-64; dir. agrl. rsch. Am. Tobacco Co., Hopewell, Va., 1964-69, mgr. basic materials rsch., 1969-71, leaf svcs. mgr., 1971-72; farmer Dillwyn, Va., 1973-78; English boxwood nurseryman Dillwyn, 1978—; mem. industry adv. com. tobacco divsn. Agrl. Stabilization and Conservation Svc., mem. industry adv. com. tobacco divsn. Agrl. Rsch. Svc., USDA, 1955-72; mem. state adv. com. Sch. Agriculture, Va. Poly. Inst. and State U., Blacksburg, 1955-72. Contbr. articles to profl. jours. Mem. Agrl. Rsch. Inst., Nat. Acad. of Scis. Washington, 1955-72, Am. Chem. Soc., 1935-72, Va. Acad. Sci., 1939-72; mem. Fishing Bay Yacht Club, 1939-72, commodore, 1947-48. Capt. USAAF, 1942-46, PTO. Recipient Citation, Am. Men of Sci., 1961, 66, Tobacco Sci., 1967, Am. Men & Women of Sci., 1972, The Daily Progress, 1991. Mem. Va. Farm Bur., Richmond Nursery Assn., Am. Tree Farm System, Buckingham Ruritan (sec. 1989-91, v.p. 1993), Theta Chi. Baptist. Home: RR 4 Box 1210 Dillwyn VA 23936-9525

MOSELEY, KAREN FRANCES F., school system administrator, educator; b. Oneonta, N.Y., Sept. 18, 1944; d. Albert Francis and Dorothy (Brown) Flanigan; m. David Michael McLaud, Sept. 8, 1962 (div. Dec. 1966); m. Harry R. Lasalle, Dec. 24, 1976 (dec. Feb. 1990); 1 child, Christopher Michael; m. Kel Moseley, Jan. 22, 1994. BA, SUNY, Oneonta, 1969, MS, 1970. Cert. secondary edn. tchr., Fla., Mass., N.Y. Tchr. Hanover (Mass.) Pub. Schs., 1970-80; lobbyist Mass. Fed. Nursing Homes, Boston, 1980-84; tchr., dept. chair Palm Beach County Schs., Jupiter, Fla., 1985-95; chair of accredidation Jupiter H.S., 1990-91; Fulbright tchr., Denmark, 1994-95. Author: How to Teach About King, 1978, 10 Year Study, 1991. Del. Dem. Conv., Mass., 1976-84; campaign mgr. Kennedy for Senate, N.Y., 1966, Tsongas for Senate, Boston, 1978; dir. Plymouth County Dems., Marshfield, Mass., 1978-84; Sch. Accountability Com., 1991-95; polit. cons. Paul Tsongas U.S. Senate, Boston, 1978-84, Michael Dukakis for Gov., Boston, 1978-84. Mem. AAUW, NEA (lifetime mem.), Nat. Honor Soc. Polit. Scientists, Classroom Tchrs. Assn., Mass. Coun. Social Studies (bd. dirs. Boston chpt. 1970-80), Mass. Tchrs. Assn. (chair human rels. com. Boston chpt. 1976-80), Plymouth County Social Studies (bd. dirs. 1970-80), Mass. Hosp. Assn. (bd. dirs. Boston chpt. 1980-84), Nat. Coun. for Social Studies, Fulbright Alumni Assn. Roman Catholic. Home: 369 River Edge Rd Jupiter FL 33477-9350

MOSELEY, MARC ROBARDS, sales executive; b. L.A., July 14, 1954; s. Thomas Robards and Doris Cecile (Tye) M. Student, U. Ky., 1972-74, U. Ga., 1977-78; BA, La. Tech. U., 1985; postgrad., Western Mich. U., 1986. Svc. rep. Ky. Mortgage Co., Lexington, 1973; loan rep. Termplan Fin. Co., Atlanta, 1975-77; sr. cons. Co-Ordinated Planning Assocs., Atlanta, 1979-80; sales rep. Nat. Starch & Chem. Corp., Monroe, La., 1980-84; v.p. sales Ednl. Funding Svc., Monroe, 1984-85; tech. sales rep. Polymer div. Ralston Purina, St. Louis, 1985-87, account mgr. Protein Techs. Internat. Polymer Group subs., 1988-90, sr. account mgr. Protein Tech. Internat. Polymer Group subs., 1990—, area dir. market ops. Protein Tech. Internat. Polymer Group, 1992—, dir. Industry Mgmt. Protein Tech. Internat. Polymer Group, 1996; v.p. sales and mktg. RANA Enterprises, Inc., Atlanta, 1991—, dir. industry mgmt. and bus. devel., 1996; dir. Radiant Chem., Atlanta; v.p., dir. Bishop Pharm. Co., Inc., West Monroe, La., 1994-96. Mem. TAPPI Greater Atlanta, U. Ky. Alumni Assn. (bd. dirs. 1991—, exec. v.p. Ga. sect. 1992-94). Home: 7455 Princeton Ter NE Atlanta GA 30328-1045 Office: Protein Tech Internat Inc Checkerboard Square Saint Louis MO 63164

MOSELEY, MARY PRUDENCE, elementary school educator; b. Ft. Worth, Dec. 31, 1922; d. Alexander Thomas and Clara (Strong) M. BA, So. Meth. U., 1943; MS, State U. Iowa, 1945. Cert. lifetime profl. tchr., Tex. Supr. Penn Mutual Life Ins. Co., Phila., 1945-47; instr. math. So. Meth. U., Dallas, 1949-50; tchr. math. Corpus Christi (Tex.) Ind. Sch. Dist., 1950-54; mgr. office H. Raymond Strong and Assocs., Consulting Actuaries, Dallas, 1958-60; computer programmer Southwestern Life Ins. Co., Dallas, 1960-63, Republic Nat. Life Ins. Co., Dallas, 1964-66; actuarial technician Arthur Stedry Hansen Cons. Actuaries, Dallas, 1967; tchr. math. Carrollton-Farmers Branch (Tex.) Ind. Sch. Dist., 1967-69; clk. policy svc. Conn. Mutual Life Ins. Co., Dallas, 1970-75; policyholder svc. Peerless Life Ins. Co., Dallas, 1975-79; pers. asst. Allan McDonnell Found., Waco, 1980-86; tchr. substitute Waco (Tex.) Ind. Sch. Dist., 1986—. Mem. AAAS, Am. Assn. Ret. Persons, Sigma Xi (assoc.). Baha'i Faith. Home: 4018 Homan Ave Waco TX 76707-1650

MOSELEY, WILLIAM LATIMER TIM, psychotherapist; b. Birmingham, Ala., Dec. 14, 1936; s. William Jones and Alice (Latimer) M. BA in Econs., Rhodes Coll., 1958; MA in Family Therapy, U. Houston, 1983. Lic. profl. counselor, Miss.; lic. marriage and family therapist, Tex. Owner Southland Homes, Inc., Memphis, 1965-80, W.L. Moseley Antiques, Memphis, 1970-85; psychotherapist Belle Pk. Hosp., Houston, 1983-86, Houston Internat. Hosp., 1986, Healthful Living Ctr., Houston, 1987-90; pvt. counseling practice Houston, 1990-92, Pass Christian, Miss., 1992—. Lt. (j.g.) USNR, 1958-61. Mem. Am. Assn. Marriage and Family Therapists (clin.), Nat. Assn. Drug and Alcohol Abuse Counselors, Miss. Assn. Counseling and Devel. Democrat. Home: 220 Henderson Ave Pass Christian MS 39571-4310 Office: 307 Ulman Ave Bay Saint Louis MS 39520-4634

MOSES, HAMILTON, III, neurology educator, hospital executive, management consultant; b. Chgo., Apr. 29, 1950; s. Hamilton Jr. and Betty Anne (Theurer) M.; m. Elizabeth Lawrence Hormel, 1977 (dec. 1988); m. Alexandra McCullough Gibson, 1992. BA in Psychology, U. Pa., 1972; MD, Rush Med. Coll., Chgo., 1975. Intern in medicine Johns Hopkins Hosp., Balt., 1976-77, resident in neurology, 1977-79, chief resident, 1979-80, assoc. prof. neurology, 1986-94, vice chmn. neurology and neurosurgery, 1980-86, v.p., 1988-94, dir. Parkinson's Ctr., 1984-94; dir. neurol. inst., prof. neurology and neurosurgery and mgmt. U. Va., Charlottesville, 1994—; sr. advisor Boston Cons. Group, 1995—; founder several tech. bus. Editor, major author: Principles of Medicine, 1985-96; editor newsletter Johns Hopkins Health, 1988—; contbr. numerous articles to med. jours. Mem. com. on med. ministries Episcopal Diocese Md., Balt., 1987; bd. dirs. Valleys Planning Ctr. Mem. Am. Acad. Neurology (sec. 1989-91), Am. Neurol. Assn., Md. Neurol. Soc. (pres. 1984-86), Movement Disorders Soc., Md. Club, Green Spring Valley Hunt Club (Garrison, Md.). Republican. Office: PO Box 150 North Garden VA 22959

MOSES, HENRY ARCHIE, biochemistry educator; b. Gaston City, N.C., Sept. 8, 1939; widowed. BS, Livingston Coll., 1959; MS in Biochemsitry, Purdue U., 1962, PhD in Biochemistry, 1964. Teaching asst. Livingstone Coll., Salisbury, N.C., 1957-58; rsch. asst. Purdue U., Lafayette, Ind., 1959-64; asst. prof. biochemistry Meharry Med. Coll., Nashville, 1964-69; prof. biochemistry Fisk U., Nashville, 1966—; assoc. prof. biochemistry and nutrition C.W. Hubbard Hosp., Meharry Med. Coll., Nashville, 1969-81; provost internal affairs Meharry Med. Coll., Nashville, 1976-83, dir. continuing edn., 1981—, prof. biochemistry, 1981—, asst. v.p. acad. support, 1983-95; assoc. v.p. coll. rels. and life long learning Area Health Edn. Ctrs., 1995—, Meharry Med. Coll., Nashville, 1995—; vis. prof. Fisk U., 1982—; vis. lectr. Tenn. State U., Nashville, 1966-70, Purdue U., 1988, The Groton (Mass.) Sch., 1989; cons. in field. Contbr. articles to profl. jours. Bd. dirs. 18th Ave. Community Ctr., 1970-83, North Nashville Br. YMCA, 1968-76, Isaiah House, The Alzheimer's Assn., 1991—; mem. adminstrv. bd. McKendre United Meth. Ch., 1987—; bd. trustees Blakemore United Meth. Ch., 1985-87, Clark Meml. United Meth. Ch., 1974-84, chmn. bd. trustees, 1982-84; sustaining mem. Boy Scouts Am., 1969—charter chpt. advisor Meharry chpt. NAACP, 1983. Recipient Golden Apple award, 1968, Harold D. West award, 1972, Kaiser-Permanente award, 1976, Meritorious Svc. award Meharry Med. Coll. Alumni Assn., 1985, 20th Martin Luther King Jr. award, 1987. Mem. AAAS, AAUP, Am. Chem. Soc., Tenn. Acad. Sci. (chmn. med. scis. sect. 1971), Alpha Omega Alpha, Alpha Chi Sigma, Beta Kappa Chi. Office: Meharry Med Coll Biochemistry Dept Nashville TN 37208

MOSES, JEFFREY MICHAEL, customer services executive; b. Nov. 16, 1945; s. George John and Mildred (Kronz) M.; m. Barbrae Danowsky, Apr. 24, 1976; children: Apryl Richelle, Heather Lorien. AA, Eckel's Coll., Phila. Sales supr. Internat. Tariff Svcs., Inc., Washington, 1970-71; transp. analyst to mgr. of tariff pub. Charles Donley & Assocs., Pitts., 1973-81; transp. mgr. Texas Aromatics, Houston, 1981-83; dir. customer svcs. ChemCoast, Inc., LaPorte, Tex., 1983-91, v.p., 1991-96; pres. Compliance Packaging & Svcs., 1996—; mem. adv. bd. Tex. Workers' Compensation Ins. Fund. Mem. Internat. Hazardous Materials Inst. (chmn. bd. 1993, 94, cert. master transp. specialist), Am. Assn. Inspection and Lab. Cos. (chmn.).

MOSHER, EDWARD BLAKE, investment company executive, consultant; b. San Antonio, Apr. 9, 1969; s. Stephen Edward and Suzanne (Wolters) M. BA, U. Tex., 1992. Intern Jenswold, King and Assocs., Houston, summer 1989, Merrill Lynch, Austin, spring 1990; pvt. practice investor Houston, 1992-93; CEO Mosher Internat., Inc., Houston, 1993—; bd. advisors Mars Hill Prodns., Houston, 1989—, Mosher Inst. for Internat. Policy Studies, College Station, Tex., 1991—, Ctr. for Internat. Studies, U. St. Thomas, Houston, 1994—; bd. trustees Francis A. Schaeffer Found., Briar Cliff Manor, N.Y., 1992—; bd. dirs. U.S. Baltic Found., Camp RedCloud, Inc., 1994—. Editorial columnist: The Daily Texan, 1991; editor-in-chief: (quarterly publs.) Footnotes, 1992—. Youth leader Bethel Ind. Presbyn. Ch., Houston, 1992—. Mem. Am. Enterprise Inst. (sponsor), The Wilson Ctr. (assoc.), Univ. Club Houston. Office: Mosher Internat Inc 1990 Post Oak Blvd Ste 1630 Houston TX 77056-3813

MOSHIER, DAVID IRWIN, church administrator; b. Roanoke, Va., Sept. 14, 1954; s. Emery Irwin (dec.) and Evelyn Mae (Kunkel) M.; m. Bonnie Sharon Dailey, Feb. 13, 1982. STD, Am. Bible Inst., 1991. Ordained to ministry Am. Evang. Christian Chs., 1992, Reformed Presbyn. Ch., 1995. Rsch. asst. mktg. dept. Clarendon Bank & Trust, Arlington, 1974; collection agt., installment loan dept. Clarendon Bank & Trust, Arlington, Va., 1974-75; loan collection officer George Washington U., Washington, 1975-77, sr. loan collection officer, 1977-79; student loan collection coord. Hahnemann Med. Coll. and Hosp., Phila., 1979-80; prin. account clk. George Washington U., Washington, 1980-83; pastor The Wesleyan Ch., Waldorf, Md., 1983-86; asst. pastor Floor Meml. Wesleyan Ch., Arlington, 1986-89; pastor First Wesleyan Ch., Alexandria, Va., 1989-91; dir. govt. rels. Am. Evang. Christian Chs., Alexandria, 1992-93, moderator Mid-Atlantic region, 1992-95, nat. exec. dir., 1993; pastor Fredericksburg (Va.) Area Reformed Presbyn. Mission, 1995; stated clk. Reformed Presbyn. Ch., Hanover, 1996—; coord. Conf. Confessing Presbyn. Chs., 1996—; bd. dirs. TransAmericas Transp. Info. Svcs., Inc., Falls Church, Va.; sec. ext. and evangelism Capital Dist. Wesleyan Ch., Great Falls, Va., 1986-88; spl. asst. Office Army Chief of Chaplains, Arlington, 1987-90, cemetery rep., 1996—; alumni coun. Flint Hill Sch., Oakton, Va., 1991—; supply pastor Cmty. Ch./Am. Rescue Workers, Capitol Heights, Md., 1992; ch. resls. cons. WABS Radio, Arlington, 1992-94; mem. adv. bd. Covered Bridge Ministries, Morristown, Ind., 1993—, others. Contbr. articles to profl. jours. Officer of election Electoral Bd., Alexandria, 1991-92, Arlington, 1992-93. Recipient Cert. of Commendation, Army Chief of Chaplains, Washington, 1988, 89, 90, Cert. of Civil Svc., Desert Shield-Storm/Hqrs. U.S. Army, Washington, 1992. Mem. George Washington U. Gen. Alumni Assn. Republican. Home: Apt 102 5928H Cloverdale Way Arlington VA 22310-5412 Office: Westminster Chapel Arlington Nat Cemetery Arlington VA 22211-5003

MOSIER, EDWARD BERT, minister; b. Clinton, Okla., July 25, 1947; s. Bert E. and Martha V. (Fike) M.; m. Martha Louise Blocker, Dec. 21, 1979; children: Bennett Ryan, Katie Elizabeth. BS, Abilene (Tex.) Christian U., 1969; MS, Sam Houston State U., 1975. Ordained to ministry Ch. of Christ, 1969. Singles minister Westbury Ch. of Christ, Houston, 1976-79; youth minister Edmond (Okla.) Ch. of Christ, 1979-81; minister of youth/family life Highland Oaks Ch. of Christ, Dallas, 1981-89; family minister Meadowlark Ch. of Christ, Ft. Collins, Colo., 1989-91; assoc. minister Park Pla. Ch. of Christ, Tulsa, 1991—; adv. bd. York Coll., 1987—; pres. Nurturing the Seed Family Seminars, Tulsa, 1990. Editor: Brick by Brick Teen Discipleship, 1987; author youth curriculum: Teen Study of James, 1988, Teen Study of 1, 2, 3 John, 1988. Mem. adv. bd. Tex. Distributive Edn. Clubs Am., Austin, 1976-78. Named among outstanding young men in Am., Abilene Christian U. Alumni, 1982. Mem. Christian Edn. Assn. Home: 1802 S Aster Ct Broken Arrow OK 74012-5958 Office: Park Pla Ch of Christ 5925 E 51st St Tulsa OK 74135-7703

MOSIER, STEPHEN RUSSELL, college program director, physicist; b. San Rafael, Calif., Nov. 14, 1942; s. Russell Glenn and Marjorie Jean (Carhart) M.; m. Catherine Priscilla Spindle, June 14, 1964; children: Catherine Priscilla, Roger Carhart. BS, Coll. William & Mary, 1964; PhD, U. Iowa, 1970. Rsch. scientist NASA/Goddard Space Flight Ctr., Greenbelt, Md., 1971-78; dir. U.S.-Japan programs NSF, Washington, 1978-81, dir. U.S.-France program, 1981-83; assoc. v.p. internat. affairs U. Houston System, 1983-86; dir. rsch. svcs. U. N.C., Greensboro, 1986—; vice chmn., bd. dirs. N.C. Assn. for Biomed. Rsch., Raleigh, 1989—; bd. dirs. Ctr. for Applied Tech., Houston, 1984-86; rsch. cons. various univs. Contbr. articles to Jour. Geophys. Rsch., Solar Physics, Nature, Transactions (IEEE). Mem. exec. bd. Old North State Coun. Boy Scouts Am., Greensboro, 1987—; Scout leader, Washington, Houston, Greensboro, 1970—. Mem. AAAS, Am. Geophys. Union, Soc. Rsch. Adminstrs., Sigma Xi. Methodist. Office: U NC at Greensboro Rm 100 McIver Bldg Greensboro NC 27412

MOSKOP, JOHN CHARLES, bioethics educator; b. Blue Island, Ill., Oct. 19, 1951; s. Charles L. and Cornelia Catherine (DeBoer) M.; m. Ruth Marie Walker, June, 1977; children: Daniel Jacob, Megan Ruth. BA, U. Notre Dame, 1973; PhD, U. Tex., 1979. Vis. asst. prof. U. Calgary, Alta., Can., 1979; asst. prof. East Carolina U., Greenville, N.C., 1979-84; assoc. prof. East Carolina U., Greenville, 1984-89, prof., 1989—; vis. prof. U. Mont., Missoula, 1988, Med. Coll. Wis., Milw., 1994; dir. Bioethics Ctr. Univ. Med. Ctr. East Carolina, Greenville, 1995—; chair faculty East Carolina U., 1991-93. Author: Divine Omniscience and Human Freedom, 1984; co-editor: Ethics and Mental Retardation, 1984, Ethics and Critical Care Medicine, 1985, Children and Health Care: Moral and Social Issues, 1989; editor book revs. Theoretical Medicine, Dordrecht, The Netherlands, 1981-94. Mem., faculty advisor Physicians for Social Responsibility East Carolina U. Sch. Medicine, 1983—; co-dir. conf. grants N.C. Humanities Coun., 1981, 83, 86; co-dir. bioethics ctr. grant Pitt County Meml. Hosp., Greenville, 1995. Fellow Soc. Health and Human Values; mem. Am. Philos. Assn., Internat. Assn. Bioethics, Phi Beta Kappa, Phi Kappa Phi. Home: 201 Poplar Dr Greenville NC 27834 Office: Dept Med Humanities E Carolina Sch Medicine Greenville NC 27858

MOSKOW, JOHN BRUCE, emergency physician; b. L.A., Nov. 1, 1952; s. C.M. and Sheiala (Ratner) M.; m. Elaine Courtney, July 17, 1994; children: Michael Andrew, Juliana Michelle, Joshua Adam Greller. BA in Biol. Scis., Rutgers U., 1974; MD, U. Tex. Med. Br., 1979; JD, U. Tex., 1983. Bar: Tex. 1983; ACLS, ATLS, PALS; diplomate Am. Bd. Utilization Rev. and Quality Assurance. Intern U. Louisville Hosp., 1979-80; pvt. practice as emergency physician Tex., 1980-83; staff physician dept. emergency svcs. Seton Med. Ctr., Austin, Tex., 1983-88, asst. dir. emergency svcs., 1988-91; med. dir. emergency svcs., med. exec. com., staff physician Seton N.W. Hosp., Austin, 1991—, mem. quality improvement com., 1991—; founding ptnr., v.p. Third Coast Emergency Physicians, P.A., 1988—; speaker in field. Contbr. articles to profl. jours.; contbr. chpt.: Manual of Medical Toxicology, 1989. Fellow Am. Coll. Emergency Physicians (liability com. Tex. chpt. 1989-92, reimbursement com. 1985—, legis. com. 1994—), Am. Acad. Emergency Physicians; mem. Tex. Med. Assn., Tex. State Bd. Med. Examiners (physician reviewer), Travis County Med. Soc., Austin Area Emergency Physicians (sec. 1986-87, chmn. 1987-89). Office: Third Coast Emergency Physi 4412 Burnet Rd Austin TX 78756

MOSS, BETTY SMITH, social worker; b. Fairfield, Ala., Dec. 8, 1931; d. James William Clarke and Helen Sarah (McKelduff) Smith; m. Cameron Gresham, Nov. 1, 1952; children: James Michael, David Patrick, Catherine Alice Moss Hodges, Nancy Carol Moss Weaks. BSSW, U. Ala., Birmingham, 1983. Lic. social worker, Ala.; cert. AIDS counselor, Fla. Staff Cooper Green Hosp., Birmingham, Ala., 1983-86; vol. Medicare, Medicaid Advocacy prog. counselor AARP, Panama City, Fla., 1987; vol. chmn. of hosp. vols. ARC, Tyndall AFB, Panama City, Fla., 1987-88; case mgr. Bay County Coun. on Aging, 1988; discharge planner Bay Med. Ctr., Panama City, Fla., 1988-94; ret., 1994. Bd. dirs. Western Mental Health Clinic; com. mem. AIDS Task Force, Birmingham, 1985-86. Mem. Nat. Assn. Social Workers, Acad. of Cert. Baccalarate Social Workers, Omicron Delta Kappa, Phi Kappa Phi, Alpha Lambda Delta. Home: 3007 Whispering Pines Ln Fultondale AL 35068

MOSS, BILL RALPH, lawyer, publisher; b. Amarillo, Tex., Sept. 27, 1950; s. Ralph Voniver and Virginia May (Atkins) M.; m. Marsha Kelman, Mar. 2, 1985; 1 child, Brandon Price. BS with spl. honors, West Tex. State U., 1972, MA, 1974; JD, Baylor U., 1976; cert. regulatory studies program, Mich. State U., 1981. Bar: Tex. 1976, U.S. Dist. Ct. (no. dist.) 1976, U.S. Tax Ct. 1979, U.S. Ct. Appeals (5th cir.) 1983. Briefing atty. Ct. Appeals 7th Supreme Jud. Dist. Tex., Amarillo, 1976-77; assoc. Culton, Morgan, Britain & White, Amarillo, 1977-80; hearings examiner Pub. Utility Commn. Tex., Austin, 1981-83; asst. gen. counsel State Bar Tex., Austin, 1983-87; founder, owner Price & Co. Publs., Austin, 1987—; instr., lectr. West Tex. State U., Canyon, Ea. N.Mex. U., Portales, 1977-80. Active All Saints' Episcopal Ch. Mem. ABA, Tex. Bar Assn. (speaker profl. devel. programs 1983—), Nat. Orgn. Bar Counsel, Internat. Platform Assn., Alpha Chi, Lambda Chi Alpha, Omicron Delta Epsilon, Phi Alpha Delta, Sigma Tau Delta, Pi Gamma Mu. Home and Office: 2719 Mountain Laurel Ln Austin TX 78703-1142 Office: PO Box 164002 506 Explorer Dr Austin TX 78716-4002

MOSS, DAN, JR., stockbroker; b. Greensboro, N.C., Aug. 11, 1948; s. Dan and Caroline (Callaway) M.; m. Gail Summers, Sept. 11, 1976; 1 child, Morgan Callaway. BA, U. N.C., 1970. Mgr. Edison Bros. Stores, Syracuse, N.Y., 1970-72; acct. exec. duPont Walston, Atlanta, 1972-74; v.p. E.F. Hutton & Co., Atlanta, 1974-88; 1st v.p. Prudential Securities, Inc., Atlanta, 1988—; adj. instr. Emory U., Atlanta, 1975—. Bd. dirs. Lady Tara Golf Classic, Atlanta, 1981-82. Mem. Internat. Assn. Fin. Planners (cert.), Rotary (local pres. 1981-82, pres. Altanta Coun. of Club Pres. 1981-82). Home: 251 W Paces Ferry Rd NW Atlanta GA 30305-1163 Office: Prudential Securities 14 Piedmont Ctr NE Ste 200 Atlanta GA 30305-4603

MOSS, DAVID NEAL, administrative assistant; b. Houston, July 22, 1970; s. Daryl Neal and Brenda Juanita (Robinson) M.; m. Elise Ann Reinhart, Nov. 11, 1995. BS in Pub. Adminstrn., Stephen F. Austin State U., 1992; MA in Pub. Adminstrn., U. Houston, 1994. Adminstrv. intern City of Lufkin, Tex., 1992; urban planner intern Houston Cmty. Devel. Agy., 1992-94; adminstrv. asst. City of Houston Fire Dept., 1994—; mem. Houston Galveston Area Coun. Govt. Criminal Justice Adv. Com., Houston, 1995—. Mem. Tex. City Mgmt. Assn. Democrat. Baptist. Home: 13907 Bay Tree Dr Sugar Land TX 77478

MOSS, JOE ALBAUGH, lawyer; b. Waco, Tex., July 26, 1925; s. Robert Edwin and Winnie (Hughes) M.; m. Anna Lee Reese, 1947; 1 child, Joe David. B.B.A., U. Tex., 1948, J.D., 1950. Bar: Tex. 1949, Supreme Ct. U.S. 1960, U.S. Dist. Ct. (we. dist.) Tex. 1956, U.S. Dist. Ct. (no. dist.) Tex. 1980. Ptnr. firm Moss & Prewett, Austin, Tex., 1950; atty. State of Tex., Abilene, 1952; sec., asst. gen. counsel Cosden Petroleum Corp., Big Spring, Tex., 1952-63, v.p., sec., gen. counsel Cosden Oil & Chem. Co., Big Spring, 1963-85; v.p., gen. counsel Am. Petrofina, Inc., Dallas, 1971-91, sec., 1984-91; of counsel Vinson & Elkins, L.L.P., 1991-93; counsel Nimir Petroleum Co. U.S.A., Inc., 1993—. V.p., dir. Trust P/L Co., 1957-90, River P/L Co., 1958-90, Fina Oil and Chem. Co., 1971-91, Petrofina Delaware, Inc. 1979-91; sec., dir. Cos-Mar, Inc., 1968-90; v.p. Am. Petrofina Exploration Co., 1971-91, v.p. Am. Petrofina Co. Norway, 1971-91. Trustee, pres. Big Spring Ind. Sch. Dist., 1961-71; trustee Siblings Found., Permian Basin Petroleum Mus. Served with USNR, 1942-46, 50-52; PTO. Recipient Spl. Merit award Big Spring Ind. Sch. Dist., 1971. Fellow Tex. Bar Found. (life), Dallas Bar Found. (life); mem. ABA, Dallas County Bar Assn., State Bar Tex., Ind. Petroleum Assn. Am. (dir. 1972-85), Tex. Mfrs. Assn. (dir. 1971-72), Am. Petroleum Inst., Tex. Mid-Continent Oil and Gas Assn. Presbyn. Mason. Club: Petroleum. Home: 5230 Royal Crest Dr Dallas TX 75229-5539

MOSS, NANCY EVANS, nurse midwife, women's health nurse; b. Louisville, Sept. 20, 1944; d. Howard Heath and Emily Trimble (Muir) Evans; m. Edward Jewell Moss Jr., Dec. 21, 1984; children: Catherine Howard Rehm, Keith Hayes Rehm. Diploma, Norton Meml. Infirmary, Louisville, 1967; BSN, U. Pitts., 1973; MS in Nursing, U. Ky., 1975; PhD in Health Edn., U. Utah, 1991. Cert. Am. Coll. Nurse Midwives. Mem. clin. faculty dept. ob-gyn. U. Utah Coll. Medicine, Salt Lake City; asst. prof. U. Ky. Coll. Nursing, Lexington; asst. prof., dir. nurse midwifery ednl. program East Carolina U., Greenville, N.C. Mem. Sigma Theta Tau.

MOSS, ROBERT WILLIAMS, real estate developer; b. Balt., May 16, 1942; s. Ambler Holmes and Dorothea (Williams) M.; m. Marguerite McKee, Jan. 30, 1971; children: Dorothy Williams, Lucile Aycock. BA, MCP, Yale U., 1967. V.p. Howard R&D Corp. subs. The Rouse Co., Balt., 1967-73; dir. devel. Flower Mound New Town Raymond D. Nasher Co., Dallas, 1973-76; regional dir. Campaign for Yale Yale U., Dallas, 1976-78; dir. devel. Tecon Realty (Murchison Interests), Dallas, 1978-85; exec. v.p. Cityplace Devel. Corp. subs. The Southland Corp., Dallas, 1985-91; prin. Moss & Assocs., Dallas, 1991—; exec. v.p. PEALE Housing Corp.; dir. Historic Landmarks, Inc. Mem. Urban Land Inst., Yale Club Dallas (pres. 1984-86). Episcopalian. Home: 4319 Allencrest Ln Dallas TX 75244-7406 Office: Moss & Assocs 4106 Office Pky Dallas TX 75204-3693

MOSS, SANDRA HUGHES, law firm administrator; b. Atlanta, Dec. 24, 1945; d. Harold Melvin and Velma Aileen (Norton) H.; m. Marshall L. Moss, May 1, 1965; children: Tara Celise, Justin Hughes. Student West Ga. Coll., 1964-65, Ga. State U. Legal sec. Smith, Cohen, Ringel, Kohler & Martin, Atlanta, 1965-78; real estate salesman Century 21-Phoenix, College Park, Ga., 1978-80; office mgr./pers. dir. Smith, Cohen, Ringel, Kohler & Martin, Atlanta, 1980-85; dir. adminstrn. Smith, Gambrell & Russell, Atlanta, 1985—. Bd. dirs., sec. North Clayton Athletic Assn., Riverdale, Ga., 1981-83; sec. E.W. Oliver PTA, Riverdale, 1981; exec. com. E.W. Oliver and N. Clayton Jr. PTA, Riverdale, 1980, 81, 82; den leader Cub Scouts, Pack 959, Riverdale, 1984. Mem. Soc. Human Resource Mgmt., Assn. Legal Adminstrs. (sec. Atlanta chpt. 1988, v.p., pres. 1990-91, regional meetings officer 1992, 93). Home: 200 Deer Forest Trl Fayetteville GA 30214-4016 Office: Smith Gambrell & Russell 1230 Peachtree St NE Ste 3100 Atlanta GA 30309-3575

MOSS, SIDNEY LOUISE GILL, county official; b. Tampa, Fla., June 29, 1943; d. Fred Bertram and Marth Louise (Braswell) Gill; m. Lewis C. Moss; 1 child, leLainya. BA in Elem. Edn., U. South Fla., 1964. Tchr. elem. Hillsborough, Palm Beach, Alachua Counties, Fla., 1964-69; job placement counselor, sr. cmty. worker Hosp. Welfare Bd. Welfare Cmty. Action Agy., Hillsborough County, Fla., 1969-75; field supr. Cmty. Act. Agy., Hillsborough County, 1977-80; mgr. Ruskin Cmty. Svc. Ctr. Social Svcs. Dept., Hillsborough County, 1980-82; asst. project dir. svcs. dept. Homemaker Svcs. Aging, Hillsborough County, 1982-84; resource program developer Health and Social Svcs. Dept., Hillsborough County, 1984-86, dir. social svcs. divsn., 1986—. Commr. Commn. for Transp. Disadvantaged, Fla., 1992-95. Mem. Fla. Assn. for Coordinated Transp. Sys. (v.p. 1992), Keystone Civic Assn. Democrat. Methodist. Home: 12834 Olive Jones Rd Tampa FL 33625 Office: Hillsborough County Govt Dept Social Svcs 601 E Kennedy Blvd Fl 24 Tampa FL 33602-4932

MOSS, SIMON CHARLES, physics educator; b. Woodmere, N.Y., July 31, 1934; divorced; 4 children. SB, Mass. Inst. Tech., 1956, SM, 1959, ScD in Metallurgy, 1962. Mem. rsch. staff metallurgy Raytheon Mfg. Co., 1956-57; from asst. to assoc. prof. Mass. Inst. Tech., 1962-70; dir. sci. dept. Energy Conversion Devices, Inc., 1970-72; prof. physics U. Houston, 1972—; M.D. Anderson chair of physics, 1991—. Ford Engring. fellow Mass. Inst. Tech., 1962-64, Guggenheim fellow, 1968-69; Alexander von Humboldt Sr. Scientist grantee U. Munich, 1979; Recipient David Adler Lectureship award Am. Physical Soc., 1993, Max Planck award Alexander von Humboldt Soc., 1993. Fellow Am. Physical Soc. Office: U Houston Dept Physics 4800 Calhoun Houston TX 77204-5506

MOSS, STEPHANIE ELLEN, drama educator, actress, theater manager; b. St. Paul, Minn., Feb. 29, 1944; d. Arthur and Alice Sylvia (Litman) M.; m. Victor J. Meyrich, Apr. 12, 1982 (div. Sept., 1993) 1 child, Hart Moss. BA, UCLA, 1993; MA, U. So. Fla., 1995. Actress Milw., 1966-67, N.Y.C., 1967-69; actress Asolo Theatre, Sarasota, Fla., 1969-70; mgr. Asolo Theater, Sarasota, 1972-90; instr. Eckerd Coll., St. Petersburg, 1993-94, U. S. Fla., Sarasota, Tampa, Fla., 1991—; cons. Coaxial Cable programs Columbus, Ohio, Sarasota, 1971-77. Contbr. articles, story to mags. Mem. MLA, Lora Ruthven Soc., Marlowe Soc., 16th Century Assn., Internat. Alliance of the Fantastic, Shakespeare Assn. Democrat. Jewish. Office: U S Fla English Dept 4202 E Fowler Ave Tampa FL 33620-9900

MOSS, STEPHEN B., lawyer; b. Jacksonville, Fla., July 14, 1943; s. Rudy and Betty (Sobel) M.; m. Rhoda Goodman, Nov. 24, 1984; children: Kurt, Shannon. BA, Tulane U., 1964; JD, Samford U., 1968. Bar: Fla. 1968, U.S. Dist. Ct. (so. dist.) Fla., U.S. Tax Ct. From assoc. to ptnr. Heiman & Crary, Miami, Fla., 1971-74; pvt. practice law So. Miami, Fla., 1974-75; ptnr. Glass, Schultz, Weinstein & Moss P.A., Coral Gables, Fla., 1975-78, Ft. Lauderdale, Fla., 1978-80; ptnr. Holland & Knight, Ft. Lauderdale, 1980—; gen. counsel Greater Ft. Lauderdale C. of C., 1991-92. Capt. U.S. Army, 1968-70, Vietnam. Named Outstanding Kiwanian, Miami, 1974; Olympic torchbearer, 1996. Fellow ABA, Fla. Bar Found.; mem. Fla. Bar Assn., Greater Ft. Lauderdale C. of C. (chmn. bd. dirs., bd. govs. 1995, Chmn.'s award 1991), Tower Club, Tower Forum (pres. 1993-94). Democrat. Jewish. Office: Holland & Knight Fl 13 1 E Broward Blvd Fort Lauderdale FL 33301-1804

MOSS, THOMAS WARREN, JR., state legislator, speaker of the house; b. Norfolk, Va., Oct. 3, 1928; s. Thomas Warren Moss and Laura Burckard Moss; m. Lorna Payne; three c.: Elizabeth Ann, Susan Bruce, Thomas Warren, III. BS, Va. Poly. Inst.; LLB, U. Richmond. Mem. Ho. of Dels., Richmond, Va., 1966—, majority leader, 1980—, speaker of the house, 1991—. Mem. lay adv. bd. DePaul Hosp.; former chmn. Am. Cancer Soc.; bd. dirs. Va. chpt. Cystic Fibrosis Assn.; former mem. Tidewater Vocat. Ctr.; bd. trustees Jamestown-Yorktown Found., Va. Mus. Fine Arts; ex-officer chmn. Commn. on Militia and Police, Commn. on Gen. Laws, Commn. on Corps., Ins. and Banking; del. Dem. Nat. Conv., 1980; active Commn. on Preservation of Capitol, Jud. Coun. Va. Recipient Disting. Svc. to Humanity award VA Assn. Optometrists, 1983, Disting. Svc. award Alumni U. Richmond, Class '56, 1984, VA Crime Prevention Assn. award, 1986, VA State Sheriffs' Assn. award, 1987, Svc. award Med. Coll. Hampton Roads, 1988, Disting. Svc. award Louise W. Eggleston Ctr., 1988, Spl. Legis. award Edn. Assn. Norfolk, 1989; named Legis. of Yr., VA Assn. Locally Elected Constitutional Leaders, 1989. Mem. ABA, Va. Trial Lawyers Assn., Norfolk-Portsmouth Bar Assn., Va. Bar Assn., Va. Poly. Inst. Alumni Assn. (Tidewater chpt. former pres., bd. dirs.), Sertoma Club of Norfolk, Mason (32 degree). Lutheran. Home: 425 W Princess Anne Rd Norfolk VA 23517-2104 Office: Va Ho of Dels State Capital Richmond VA 23219*

MOSSBARGER, DAVID LEE, career officer; b. Oak Hill, Ohio, Sept. 15, 1954; s. William Gerald and Margaret Elenora (Smith) M.; children: Alisa Ann, David Scott, Laura Elizabeth. BS, U.S. Mil. Acad., 1976; MA in Polit. Sci., Ball State U., 1984; MBA, Ind. U., 1988. From tng. mgr. to asst. v.p. recruiting policy U.S. Army, 1976-95, lt. col., asst. v.p. human resources planning, 1995-96, ret., 1996; mil. advisor Venture Prodns., Miami, 1996—. Recipient George Washington Honor medal Freedom Foun. at Valley Forge, 1977. Mem. Assn. U.S. Army, Assn. Grads. U.S. Mil. Acad., D.C. Road Runners Club, Ski Club Washington. Home: 2342 McKinley St Hollywood FL 33020 Office: Venture Prodns 16505 NW 13th Ave Miami FL 33169

MOSTOFF, ALLAN SAMUEL, lawyer, consultant; b. N.Y.C., Oct. 19, 1932; s. Morris and Ida (Goldman) M.; m. Alice Tamara Popelowsky, July 31, 1955; children: Peter Alexander, Nina Valerie. BS, Cornell U., 1953; MBA, N.Y.U., 1954; LLB, N.Y. Law Sch., 1957. Bar: N.Y. 1958, D.C. 1964. Assoc. Olwine Connelly Chase O'Donnell & Weyher, N.Y.C., 1958-61; atty. SEC, Washington, 1962-66, asst. dir. 1966-69, assoc. dir. 1969-72, dir. div. investment mgmt. regulation, 1972-76; ptnr. Dechert Price & Rhoads, Washington, 1976—; adj. prof. Georgetown U. Law Ctr., 1972-82; mem. Fin. Acctg. Standards Adv. Bd., 1982-86; mem. adv. bd. Investment Lawyer. Mem. ABA (chmn. internat. devel. sub-com., com. on devels. in investment svcs.), Assn. of Bar of City of N.Y., Fed. Bar Assn. (chmn. exec. coun. securities regulation com. 1990-92), Am. Law Inst. Home: 6417 Waterway Dr Falls Church VA 22044-1325 Office: Dechert Price & Rhoads 1500 K St NW Washington DC 20005-1209

MOTE, MARIE THERESE, reference librarian; b. Madisonville, Ky., May 5, 1948; d. John H. and Mary Cecelia (Sullivan) M. BA, Lincoln Meml. U., 1973; MLS, Vanderbilt U., 1974. Children's libr. Harris County Libr. System, Houston, 1975-76; learning resource ctr. coord. Aldine Sch. Dist., Houston, 1976-81; reference libr. Bellaire (Tex.) City Libr., 1983—; poetry columnist Tazewell-New Tazewell Observer, 1969-74. Mem. ALA (social responsibility roundtable, intellectual freedom roundtable), Pub. Libr. Assn., Tex. Libr. Assn., Cherokee Cultural Soc., Alpha Chi, Phi Alpha Theta. Home: PO Box 1752 Bellaire TX 77402 Office: Bellaire City Libr 5111 Jessamine Bellaire TX 77401

MOTE, VICTOR LEE, political science educator; b. Corpus Christi, Tex., Nov. 2, 1941; s. Ershal Lee and Annie Laura (Lewis) M.; children: Vicki Lynn, Eliot Dean. BA, U. Denver, 1964, MA, 1969; PhD, U. Washington, 1971. From asst. prof. polit. sci. to assoc. prof. U. Houston, 1971—; vis. asst. prof. U. Denver, 1976; vis. sr. rschr. Slavic Rsch. Ctr., Hokkaido (Japan) U., 1988-89; adj. prof. U. St. Thomas, Houston, 1978—; rsch. assoc. Wharton Econometric Assn., Washington, 1982-83, Plan Econ., Washington, 1985; cons. Nat. Geog. Soc., Washington, 1990-93, Booz Allen and Hamilton, 1992—, Vinson & Elkins, Houston, 1992; cons. and dir. post Soviet activities Indsl. Info. Resources, Houston, 1992—. Co-author: Gateway to Siberian Resources, 1976 (Outstanding Rsch. award 1977); contbr. articles to profl. geog. jours. Capt. US Marine Corps, 1964-67, Vietnam. Fellow Royal Canadian Geog. Soc.; mem. Assn. of Am. Geographers, Am. Assn. for Advancement of Slavic Studies, Am. Polit. Sci. Assn., Acad. Polit. Sci., Wilson Ctr. (assoc.), Golden Key, Phi Beta Kappa, Omicron Delta Kappa, Gamma Theta Upsilon, Sigma Xi, Pi Sigma Alpha. Home: 4347 Bugle Rd Houston TX 77072-1823 Office: U Houston Dept Polit Sci Univ Park Houston TX 77006

MOTES, JOSEPH MARK, cruise and convention promotion company executive; b. Leesburg, Fla., Oct. 12, 1948; s. Lewis Jackson and Yolanda (Fernandez) M. AA in Computer Sci., Miami-Dade Community Coll., 1976. Promoter Trekruise & Seatrek, 1975—; conv. promoter Trekon & Vulkon, Fla., 1977—; v.p. Seatrek Ent., Inc., Cooper City, Fla.; pres. Genesis Prodns., Inc., 1992—. Sgt. USMC, 1967-74, Vietnam. Mem. SAR, SCV. Republican. Roman Catholic. Home and Office: 12237 SW 50th St Fort Lauderdale FL 33330-5406 also: 8306 Mills Dr Miami FL 33183-4838

MOTSETT, CHARLES BOURKE, sales and marketing executive; b. Peoria, Ill., Jan. 13, 1949; s. William James and Matilda (Robb) M.; m. Mary T. Werner, Aug. 26, 1972; children: Jon Bourke, Jill Suzanne, Brian Werner. BA in Polit. Sci., U. So. Fla., 1984. Product support mktg. analyst Caterpillar Tractor Co., 1974-75; parts and service sales rep. Caterpillar Ams. Co., Mexico City, 1976-79; product support rep. Caterpillar Tractor Co., Vancouver, B.C., Can., 1979-80; leadman remanufactured products Caterpillar Tractor Co., Peoria, 1981-84; mgr. parts and service sales Caterpillar Tractor Co., Jacksonville, Fla., 1984-85; v.p. sales and mktg. Multi Media Productions of Am., Inc., Jacksonville, 1985-86; v.p. sales and mktg. Consol. Indsl. Skills Corp., Jacksonville, 1987—, corp. officer, 1988-92; v.p., gen. mgr. Ogden CISCO Inc., Jacksonville, 1992-94; v.p. sales and mktg. CompuTown Technologies Corp., Miami, 1994—. Shred All, 1995; pres. Bus. Solutions, Inc., Jacksonville, 1996—; pres. Bus. Solutions Internat., Jacksonville. Author: If It Wasn't For The People...This Job Would Be Fun (Coaching For Buy-in and Results), 1996; contbr. articles to profl. jours. Vice pres. PTO, Dunlap, Ill., 1981-82; vice chmn. St. Anthony's Ch., Vancouver, 1979-80; chmn. St. Jude Ch., Dunlap, 1982-83, Bishop Kenny High Sch. PTO Polit. Action Com., 1989; mem. adv. coun. Sch. Bd. Vocat. Edn., 1991-92. Capt. U.S. Army, 1967-70, prisoner of war, Vietnam. Decorated Silver Star, Bronze Star with V device, Purple Heart, Air medal with V device., Combat Infantryman's Badge, Underwater Ops. Badge, Vietnamese Jump Wings, Commendation medal, Good Conduct medal. Mem. Soc. Automotive Engrs., Am. Soc. Naval Engrs., Soc. Naval Architects and Marine Engrs., Am. Inst. Plant Engrs. (bd. dirs., conf. presenter), Am. Nuclear Soc., Propellor Club. Republican. Roman Catholic. Home: 4457 Barrington Oaks Dr Jacksonville FL 32257-5092

MOTSINGER, JOHN KINGS, lawyer; b. Winston-Salem, N.C., Aug. 13, 1947; s. Madison Eugene and Margaret Mary (Kings) M.; m. Elisabeth Sykes, June 18, 1989; children: Christian Sykes, Lissa Sykes, John, Jr. BA, Washington & Lee U., 1970; MS, Georgetown U., 1972; JD, Wake Forest U., 1983. Bar: N.C. 1983, U.S. Dist. Ct. (mid. dist.) N.C. 1984. Consumer affairs assoc. U.S Postal Svc., Washington, 1972-73; pres., gen. mgr. Sta. WIPS-Radio, Ticonderoga, N.Y., 1973-79; staff atty. United Guaranty Corp., Greensboro, N.C., 1983-86, Republic Mortgage Ins. Co., Winston-Salem, 1986-91; v.p. law RMIC Corp., Winston-Salem, 1988-91; exec. dir. Carolina Concilation Svcs. Corp., 1992—. Pres.-elect Unitarian-Universalist Fellowship of Winston-Salem, 1993-94. Mem. ABA, N.C. Bar Assn. (corp. counsel sect. councilor 1989-93), N.C. State Bar, Acad. of Family Mediators. Democrat. Unitarian-Universalist. Home: 204 W Cascade Ave Winston Salem NC 27127-2029 Office: Carolina Conciliation Svcs Corp 1001 S Marshall St Ste 65 Winston Salem NC 27101-5858

MOTT, MICHAEL CHARLES ALSTON, writer; b. London, Dec. 8, 1930; came to U.S., 1966; s. Eric Alston and Margaret Bart (Berger) M; m. Margaret Ann Watt, May 6, 1961 (dec. 1990); children: Sophie Jane and Amanda Margaret (twins); m. Emma Lou Powers, Nov. 16, 1992. BA with honors, London U., 1970; PhD, St. Mary's Coll., Notre Dame U., 1983. Asst. editor Adam Internat. Rev., London, 1956-66; editor Thames & Hudson Publishers, London, 1961-64; asst. editor The Geog. Mag., London, 1964-66; vis. prof. Kenyon Coll., Gambier, Ohio, 1966-70; writer-in-residence Emory U., Atlanta, 1970-77, College William and Mary, Williamsburg, Va., 1978-79, 85-86; prof. English Bowling Green (Ohio) State U., 1980-92. Author: (novels) The Notebooks of Susan Berry, 1963, Helmet and Wasps, 1966, Master Entrick, 1966, The Blind Cross, 1969, (biography) The Seven Mountains of Thomas Merton, 1984; chief poetry collections: Absence of Unicorns, Presence of Lions, 1976, Counting the Grasses, 1980, Corday, 1986, 95; editor poetry The Kenyon Rev., 1967-70. 2d lt. inf. Brit. Army, 1949-50. Recipient Gov.'s award in Fine Arts, Ga., 1974; Guggenheim fellow, 1979-80. Fellow Royal Geog. Soc.; mem. Geog. Club, Brit. Lichen Soc., Kilvert Soc., Amnesty Internat., Phi Beta Kappa. Episcopalian. Home: 122 The Colony Williamsburg VA 23185-3157

MOUCHATY, GEORGES, accelerator physicist; b. Aleppo, Syria, June 9, 1950; came to U.S., 1980; s. Elias and Jeanette (Dib) M.; m. Suzette Dural, Mar. 23, 1994. Advanced studies diploma, U. Paris VI, 1975, doctorate, 1977. Rsch. assoc. Tex. A&M U., College Station, 1980-84, accelerator physicist, 1985—; devel. engr. Schlumberger, Houston, 1984-85. Contbr. articles to profl. jours. Lt. Mil. Acad., 1977-80, Aleppo. French Govt. scholar Acad. of Paris, 1974-77. Mem. Am. Phys. Soc., Am. Chem. Soc., Tex. Acad. Sci. Office: Tex A&M Univ The Cyclotron Inst College Station TX 77843

MOULDER, WILTON ARLYN, financial management consultant; b. Atlanta, July 1, 1931; s. Ottis Arrell and Eula Mae (Whitlock) M.; m. Margie Nell Harrington, Mar. 12, 1955; children: W. Arlyn Jr., Carol Elaine. Student, Ga. Inst. Tech., Atlanta, 1949-50; BA, Emory U., Atlanta, 1953, MDiv, 1956, D Ministry, 1977. Ordained to ministry Meth. Ch. as deacon, 1954, as elder, 1956; cert. fin. planner, cert. fund raising exec. Pastor St. Luke Meth. Ch., Atlanta, 1956-57, St. Matthew Meth. Ch., East Point, Ga., 1957-62; assoc. pastor Druid Hills Meth. Ch., Atlanta, 1962-64; pastor Duluth (Ga.) United Meth. Ch., 1964-69; devel. dir. United Meth. Children's Home, Decatur, Ga., 1969-95; self-employed cons.; trustee United Meth. Found., Atlanta, 1984—; del. Jurisdictional Conf., Lake Junaluska, N.C., 1984; sect. chmn. United Meth. Assn. Health and Welfare Ministries Pub. Rels. and Devel., 1978-80. Author: Financial Planning for Clergy Families, 1987. Judge Ga. Occupational Award of Leadership Program, Decatur, 1985—; bd. dirs. DeKalb Coll. Found., Decatur, 1990—. Mem. Inst. Cert. Fin. Planners, Nat. Soc. Fund Raising Execs., Internat. Assn. Fin. Planning, Rotary (bd. dirs. Decatur club 1988-90). Home and Office: 4104 Warrior Trl Stone Mountain GA 30083-3129

MOULTON, JAMES ROGER, small business owner; b. Washington, Dec. 9, 1950; s. Roger Daniels and Vivian (Marshall) M.; m. Lynne Fellman, Feb. 5, 1977 (div. Aug. 12, 1984); m. Diane Marthe Allard, Jan. 6, 1986; children: Melissa Jane, Justin Roger. BS in Computer Sci., N.C. State U., 1972; MS in Computer Sci, U. Md., 1981. Computer specialist U.S. Naval Acad., Annapolis, Md., 1973-75; mem. tech. staff Computer Scis. Corp., Arlington, Va., 1975-78; sytem developer System Devel. Corp., McLean, Va., 1978-81; computer specialist Nat. Bur. of Standards, Gaithersburg, Md., 1981-86; dist. mgrg. Bell Comm. Rsch. Inc., Red Bank, N.J., 1989-90; pres. Open Network Solutions, Inc., Sterling, Va., 1981—; cons. Protocol Stds. and Comm., Ottawa, Can., 1986-88, ORS Assocs., McLean, Va., 1989-93, Open Network Solutions, Inc., Sterling, Va. Co-author (with others) Internat. Computer Standards, 1980-88; contbr. numerous articles to profl. jours. Recipient Dept. of Commerce Bronze medal, 1981. Democrat. Office: Open Network Solutions Inc PO Box 669 Sterling VA 20167-0669

MOULY, EILEEN LOUISE, financial planner; b. Milw., Apr. 18, 1955; d. George Joseph and Gertrude Mary (DuBois) M. BBA in Acctg. summa cum laude, U. Miami, Coral Gables, Fla., 1977, MBA, 1978. CPA, Fla.; cert. fin. planner. Acct. Main Hurdman, CPA's, Miami, Fla., 1979-82, Coopers & Lybrand, CPA's, West Palm Beach, Fla., 1982-83, Pannell Kerr Forster CPA's, Miami, 1983-84; cert. fin. planner Consortium Group, Miami, 1984-86; ptnr., fin. planner Evensky & Brown, Miami, 1986-91; pres. Eileen L. Mouly & Assocs. Inc. Fin. Advisors, Miami, 1991—; instr. U. Miami, 1987-90, Fla. Internat. U., 1987-90; speaker in field. Active Am. Cancer Soc. Mem. AICPA, Fla. Inst. CPAs (bd. dirs. 1991—, sec. South Dade chpt. 1993-94, treas. 1994-95, v.p. 1995-96, pres.-elect 1996-97), Internat. Assn. Fin. Planning, Registry Fin. Planning Practitioners, Inst. CFPs (cert., v.p. greater Miami chpt. 1987-91), Leadership South Dade. Office: Eileen L Mouly & Assocs Inc 290 NW 165th St Ste Ph2 Miami FL 33169-6457

MOUNTAIN, CLIFTON FLETCHER, surgeon, educator; b. Toledo, Apr. 15, 1924; s. Ira Fletcher and Mary (Stone) M.; children: Karen Lockerby, Clifton Fletcher, Jeffrey Richardson. AB, Harvard U., 1947; MD, Boston U., 1954. Diplomate Am. Bd. Surgery. Dir. dept. statis. rsch. Boston U., 1947-50; cons. rsch. analyst Mass. Dept. Pub. Health, 1951-53; intern U. Chgo. Clinics, 1954, resident, 1955-58, instr. surgery, 1958-59; sr. fellow thoracic surgery Houston, 1959; mem. staff M.D. Anderson Hosp. and Tumor Rsch. Inst.; asst. prof. thoracic surgery U. Tex., 1960-63, assoc. prof surgery, 1973-76, prof., 1976-94, prof. emeritus, 1995—, prof. surgery Sch. Medicine, 1987—, chief sect. thoracic surgery, 1970-79, chmn. thoracic oncology, 1979-84, chmn. dept. thoracic surgery, 1980-85, chmn. program in biomath. and computer sci., 1962-64, Mike Hogg vis. lectr. in S.Am., 1967; prof. surgery U. Calif., San Diego, 1996—; mem. sci. mission on cancer USSR, 1970-78, and Japan, 1976-84; mem. com. health, rsch. and edn. facilities Houston Cmty. Coun., 1964-78; cons. Am. Joint Com. on Cancer Staging and End Result Reporting, 1964-74, Tex. Heart Inst., 1994-96; mem. Am. Joint Com. on Cancer, 1974-86, chmn. lung and esophagus task force; mem. working party on lung cancer and chmn. com. on surgery Nat. Clin. Trials Lung Cancer Study Group, NIH, 1971-76; mem. plans and scope com. cancer therapy Nat. Cancer Inst., 1972-75, mem. lung cancer study group, 1977-89, chmn. steering com., 1973-75, mem. bd. sci. counselors divsn. cancer treatment, 1972-75; hon. cons. Shanghai Chest Hosp. and Lung Cancer Ctr., Nat. Cancer Inst. of Brazil; sr. cons. Houston Thorax Inst., 1994-96. Editor The New Physician, 1955-59; mem. editorial bd. Yearbook of Cancer, 1960-88, Internat. Trends in Gen. Thoracic Surgery, 1984-91; contbr. articles to profl. jours., chpts. to textbooks. Chmn. profl. adv. com. Harris County Mental Health Assn.; bd. dirs. Harris County chpt. Am. Cancer Soc. Lt. USNR, 1942-46. Recipient award Soviet Acad. Sci., 1977, Garcia Meml. medal Philippine Coll. Surgeons, 1982, Disting. Alumni award Boston U., 1988, Disting. Achievement U. Tex. M.D. Anderson Cancer Ctr., 1990, Disting. Svc. award Internat. Assn. for the Study of Lung Cancer, 1991, Disting. Alumnus award Boston U. Sch. of Medicine, 1992. Fellow ACS, Am. Coll. Chest Physicians (chmn. com. cancer 1967-75), Am. Assn. Thoracic Surgery, Inst. Environ. Scis., N.Y. Acad. Sci., Assn. Thoracic and Cardiovascular Surgeons of Asia (hon.), Hellenic Cancer Soc. (hon.), Chilean Soc. Respiratory Diseases (hon., hon. pres. 1982); mem. AAAS, Am. Assn. Carcer Rsch., AMA, So. Med. Assn., Am. Thoracic Soc., Soc. Thoracic Surgeons, Soc. Biomed. Computing, Am. Fedn. Clin. Rsch., Internat. Assn. Study Lung Cancer (pres. 1976-78), Am. Radium Soc., Pan-Am. Med. Assn., Houston Surg. Soc., Soc. Surg. Oncology, James Ewing Soc., Sigma Xi.

MOUNTCASTLE, MARY BABCOCK, social services administrator; b. Winston-Salem, N.C., Nov. 17, 1953; d. Kenneth Franklin and Mary Katharine (Babcock) M.; m. James Stanton Overton, May 27, 1990; 1 child, Katharine Overton Mountcastle. BA in Am. Civilization cum laude, Williams Coll., 1976; M in Pub. and Pvt. Mgmt., Yale U., 1983. Staff asst. Office of Congressional Liaison The White House, Washington, 1977; staff asst. dept. sci. and tech. Ho. of Reps., Washington, 1977-78; legis. aide Bd. Suprs., San Francisco, 1979-81; project mgr. Fin. Svcs. Corp. N.Y.C., 1983-85; dir. social investment program Met. Life Ins. Co., N.Y.C., 1985-88; v.p. econ. devel. MDC Inc., Chapel Hill, N.C., 1988-92; asst. dir. Ctr. Community Self-Help, Durham, N.C., 1993—; trustee Tides Found., San Francisco, 1983—, Z. Smith Reynolds Found., Winston-Salem, N.C., 1984—, pres., 1992; bd. dirs. Ctr. Community Change, Washington, 1986—, Devel. Tng. Inst., Balt., 1989—, Boggs Rural Life Ctr., Keysville, Ga., 1992—; trustee Mary Reynolds Babcock Found., N.C., 1991—. Recipient Robert W. Scrivner award Coun. on Founds., 1992; Pub. Affairs fellow Coro Found., 1978-79.

MOUNTZ, WADE, retired health service management executive; b. Winona, Ohio, Nov. 19, 1924; s. Lowell J. and Ethel M. (Coppock) M.; m. Betty G. Wilson, June 3, 1946; children: David John, Timothy Wilson. BA, Baldwin-Wallace Coll., 1948; MHA, U. Minn., 1951; LHD (hon.), Ky. Wesleyan Coll., 1991. With Norton Meml. Infirmary, Louisville, 1951-69; adminstr. Norton Meml. Infirmary, 1958-69; pres. Norton-Children's Hosps., Inc., Louisville, 1969-81, NKC, Inc., Louisville, 1981-85; vice chmn. NKC, Inc., 1985-87, pres. emeritus, 1987—. Vice chmn. Comprehensive Health Planning Council Ky., 1968-73, chmn., 1973-79; bd. dirs. Louisville chpt. ARC, 1961-74; trustee Blue Cross Hosp. Plan, 1959-72; trustee Am. Hosp. Assn., 1971-76, chmn. bd., 1975. Served with A.C., USNR, 1943-45. Recipient Disting. Service award Ky. Hosp. Assn.; Disting. Layman award Ky. Med. Assn. Fellow Am. Coll. Hosp. Healthcare Execs. (gold medal), Masons. Home: 9 Muirfield Pl Louisville KY 40222-5074 Office: 4350 Brownsboro Rd Ste 110 Louisville KY 40207-1681

MOURSUND, ALBERT WADEL, III, lawyer, rancher; b. Johnson City, Tex., May 23, 1919; s. Albert Wadel and Mary Frances (Stribling) M., Jr.; m. Mary Allen Moore, May 8, 1941; children: Will Stribling, Mary Moore Moursund. LLB, U. Tex., 1941. Bar: Tex. 1941, U.S. Ct. Appeals (5th cir.) 1964, U.S. Dist. Ct. (so. dist.) Tex. 1964, U.S. Dist. Ct. (we. dist.) Tex. 1964, U.S. Tax Ct. 1972. Pvt. practice law, Johnson City, 1946-63; mem. Moursund & Moursund Johnson City, Round Mountain and Llano, Tex., 1963-80; ptnr. Moursund, Moursund, Moursund & Moursund, 1980—, county judge Blanco County, Tex., 1953-59; chmn. bd. Arrowhead Bank, 1963—, Cattleman's Nat. Bank, Round Mountain; bd. dirs., pres. Arrowhead Co., Arrowhead West, Inc., Tex. Am. Moursund Corp., S.W. Moursund Corp., Ranchlander Corp. Mem. Parks and Wildlife Commn., 1963-67, Tex. Ho. reps., 1948-52. With USAAF, 1942-46. Mem. ABA, Tex. Bar Assn., Hill County Bar Assn. (past pres.), Blanco Country Hist. Soc. (charter), Masons, Woodmen of World. Office: Moursund Moursund Moursund & Moursund PO Box 1 Round Mountain TX 78663-0001

MOURSUND, KENNETH CARROLL, grocery chain executive; b. Austin, Tex., Oct. 21, 1937; s. Leif Erickson and Ethel Alberta (Aiken) M.; BBA, U. Tex., Austin, 1963; m. Claudia Frances Reifel, Dec. 21, 1963; 1 son, Kenneth Carroll. Mgmt. trainee Am. Warehouses, Inc., 1963-64; with Kroger Co., Houston, 1964—, transp. supr., 1964, distbn. mgr. charge all warehousing and transp. Houston div., 1969-83, dir. distbn. Houston, S. Tex. and S. La., 1983-86; dir. distbn. Tex., 1986—; profl. baseball player N.Y. Yankees and Detroit Tigers, 1957-61; vestryman Trinity Episcopal Ch., 1977-79, jr. warden, 1978, sr. warden 1979, mem. endowment bd, 1980-82; bd. dirs. Bill Williams Ann. Capon Charity Dinner, Inc. Served with USAR, 1960-66. Mem. Delta Nu Alpha (life mem.), Ex-Student Assn. U. Tex., Nat. Rifle Assn., Tex. Long Horn Breeders Assn., Cattlemen's Tex. Longhorn Registry, Houston Livestock and Rodeo Assn. (life, bd. dirs., chmn. group ticket com., v.p. 1996—). Club: U. Tex. Century. Office: PO Box 1309 Houston TX 77251-1309

MOUSER, GRANT EARL, III, retired foreign service officer; b. Marion, Ohio, July 11, 1923; s. Grant Earl M. and Hilda Kenyon (Gorham) Crenshaw; m. Lena Little, Feb. 12, 1955; 1 son, Grant Earl IV. B.A., Washington and Lee U., 1943, J.D., 1948; student, Mannix Walker Sch. Fgn. Service, 1949-50, U.S. Naval War Coll., 1966, Fed. Exec. Inst., 1973. Vice consul Am. consulate gen., Hamburg, W. Ger., 1950-53; econ., comml. officer Am. embassy, Tehran, Iran, 1953-56; Iranian desk officer Dept. State, Washington, 1957-60; polit. officer Am. embassy, Bonn, W. Ger., 1960-65; Indian desk officer Dept. State, 1966-70; polit. officer Am. embassy, New Delhi, India, 1970-73; fgn. service insp. Dept. State, worldwide, 1973-76; State Dept. rep. Armed Forces Staff Coll., Norfolk, Va., 1977-80; cons. gen. Am. consulate gen., Hamburg, W. Ger., 1980-85; exchange officer Dept. Def., Washington, 1966-68; ret., 1985; diplomat in residence Old Dominion U., Norfolk, Va., 1985—; vis. prof. Allegheny Coll., Meadville, Pa., 1976-77; lecturer Old Dominion U., Norfolk, 1985-86, William and Mary, Williamsburg, Va., 1986-93. Bd. dirs. World Affairs Council, Norfolk, 1977-80; vice chmn. James City County Rep. com., 1991; layman Bruton Parish Ch., 1985-93. Served to lt. USNR, 1943-46. Recipient Superior Service award Dept. State, 1977; recipient Meritorious Honor award Dept. State, 1980, Joint Service Commendation medal Dept. Def., 1978. Mem. SAR (pres. 1992), Am. Fgn. Service Assn., U.S. Naval Inst., Phi Gamma Delta, Rotary. Republican. Epicopalian. Home: 104 Clara Croker Williamsburg VA 23185-6504

MOUSSEAU, TIMOTHY ALEXANDER, biology educator; b. Marville, France, Oct. 10, 1958; came to U.S., 1988; m. Heather S. Preston; children: Preston Alexander, Campbell Bruce. BSc, U. Ottawa, 1980; MSc, U. Toronto, 1983; PhD, McGill U., 1988. Postdoctoral fellow U. Calif., Davis, 1988-90; asst. prof. biology U. S.C., Columbia, 1991—. Mem. Soc. for Study of Evolution, Am. Soc. Naturalists, Entomological Soc. Am., Sigma Xi. Office: U SC Dept Biol Scis Columbia SC 29208

MOUTON, FRANCIS EDWARD, III, academic administrator; b. New Orleans, Mar. 29, 1957; s. Francis Edward Mouton Jr. and Lynne Marie Moore; Sherry Lynn Storbakken-Thomas, Aug. 14, 1993; children: Rebecca Lynne, Camille Marie. AA, Delgado C.C., 1991; BA, U. of New Orleans, 1993; JD, La. State U. Law Ctr., Baton Rouge, 1996. Adminstrv. asst. U. New Orleans, 1991-93, campus rep. internat. programs, 1993-95; charter mem. Liberal Arts Coun. U. New Orleans, 1992. Mem. ABA, Phi Alpha Delta, Golden Key, Phi Theta Kappa, Kiwanis. Republican. Roman Catholic.

MOVAHED, ASSAD, cardiologist; b. Shooshtar, Iran, July 22, 1950; m. Azita Movahed; 1 child, Kimia Olivia. MD, Jondi ShaPour Med. Sch., Ahwaz, Iran, 1975. Diplomate Am. Bd. Internal Medicine, subspecialty cardiovascualr disease. Resident medicine Reza Pahlavi Med. Ctr., Tehran, Iran, 1975-77, Wayne State U., Detroit, 1977-80; fellow cardiology Cleve. Met. Gen. Hosp., 1980-82; fellow nuclear cardiology Johns Hopkins Med. Instn., Balt., 1982-83; asst. prof. medicine dept. medicine Eastern Va. Med. Sch., Norfolk, 1983-86; assoc. prof. medicine sect. cardiology dept. medicine East Carolina U. Sch. Medicine, Greenville, N.C., 1986-90, prof. medicine sect. cardiology dept. medicine, 1990—, prof. radiology dept. radiology, 1992—; dir. coronary care unit U. Med. Ctr. Eastern Carolina Pitt County, Greenville, 1986-90; dir. nuclear cardiology Pitt County Meml. Hosp., East Carolina U. Sch. Medicine, Greenville, 1986—; staff cardiologist, dir. cardiac radionulcear imaging and exercise physiology lab. VA Med. Ctr., Hampton, Va., 1983-85; contbr. Am. Bd. Internal Medicine; cons. cardiology Doctors' Diagnostic Svcs., Virginia Beach, Va., 1985-86, Humana Bayside Hosp., Virginia Beach, 1985-86, Virginia Beach Gen. Hosp., 1985-86, Med. Ctr. Hosps., Norfolk, 1985-86; mem. adv. com. nuclear medicine radiologic scis. dept. Pitt C.C., Greenville, 1992—; vis. prof. cardiac imaging Nat. Heart & Chest Hosps., London, 1988. Reviewer Am. Family Physician, Am. Jour. Cardiology, Annals Internal Medicine, Chest, Current Surgery, So. Med. Jour.; Author: Diagnostic Ultrasound, 1975; contbr. articles to profl. jours. Grantee Am. Heart Assn., N.C. chpt., 1987, Eli Lilly and Co., 1988, East Carolina U., 1990, DuPont Merck Pharm. Co., 1992, Soc. Nuclear Medicine, 1993; recipient Physician's Recognition award AMA, 1984. Fellow ACP, Am. Coll. Cardiology, Am. Coll. Chest Physicians (coun. cardiovascular disease, coun. critical care), Am. Heart Assn. (coun. clin. cardiology, coun. cardiovascular radiology); mem. Soc. Nuclear Medicine, Am. Soc. Hypertension, N.C. Med. Soc., N.C. Soc. Nuclear Medicine (coun. cardiovascular imaging), Am. Soc. Nuclear Cardiology, Pitt County Med. Soc. Office: East Carolina U Sch Med Dept Nuclear Cardiology Greenville NC 27858-4354

MOWELL, JOHN BYARD, investment management executive, technology company executive; b. Washington, Pa., Oct. 21, 1934; s. Donald H. and Mabel V. (Burdick) M.; m. Sara Sandra Moore, June 15, 1957; children: John Byard Jr., Sarah Anne Mowell Reinhard. BS in Econs., U. Pa., 1956. Asst. v.p. Florindin Co., Tallahassee, 1960-62; ofcl. State of Fla., Tallahassee, 1962-65; owner, mgr. Mowell & Assocs., Tallahassee, 1965-75; v.p. so. ops. Carret & Co., Inc., N.Y.C., 1975-80; pres. Mowell Fin. Group Inc., Tallahassee, 1980—; bd. dirs. Electromagnetic Scis., Inc., Atlanta, Capital City 1st Nat. Bank, Tallahassee, LXE, Inc., Norcross, Ga., 1991—, CAL Corp., Ottawa, Ont., Can., Netcast Comm. Corp., N.Y.C., Netcast, Inc., N.Y.C., Novicon, Washington. Chmn. investment adv. coun. Fla. Bd. Adminstrn., 1991—. Mem. Fla. Econs. Club (bd. dirs., chmn. emeritus), Fla. Gov.'s Club, Rotary. Republican. Methodist. Office: Mowell Fin Group Inc 407 E 6th Ave Tallahassee FL 32303-6301

MOWERY, ANNA RENSHAW, state legislator; b. Decatur, Tex., Jan. 4, 1931; d. Lafayette William and Early Virginia (Bobo) Renshaw; m. Wesley Harold Mowery, June 2, 1951; children: Jeanette Mowery Hefferman, Mark William, Timothy Dean, Marianne Mowery Fichera. BA, Baylor U., 1951; MA, Ctrl. State U., 1967. Tchr. Ft. Hood (Tex.) Pub. Schs., 1951-52; petroleum landman Ft. Worth, 1979-82; dist. dir. U.S. Congl. Dist. 6 Joe Barton, Ft. Worth, 1985-86; polit. cons., pres. Trinity Assocs., Ft. Worth, 1987-88; state rep. Tex. House Reps., Ft. Worth, 1988—. Chmn. Tarrant County (Tex.) Rep. Party, 1975-77; mem. Tex. Rep. Exec. Com., Ft. Worth, 1980-84, Greater Ft. Worth Literacy Coun., 1990—; mem. adv. bd. Sr. Citizen Svcs./Tarrant County, Ft. Worth, 1988—. Recipient 4-H Clubs Am. Alumni award, 1990; nominee Newsmaker of Yr., Ft. Worth Press Club, 1974, 76. Mem. Southwest Rep. Club, Tex. Women's Alliance, Ft. Worth Rep. Women (v.p. 1991-92), Women's Policy Forum. Baptist. Home: 4108 Hildring Dr W Fort Worth TX 76109-4722 District Office: Ste 534 Twr II 4100 International Plz Fort Worth TX 76109-4820 Office: Tex House of Reps State Capitol Austin TX 78768-2910

MOWREY, TIMOTHY JAMES, management and financial consultant; b. Lewiston, N.Y., Oct. 18, 1958; s. William Ronald and Joan (Cupp) M.; children: Christin R., Andrea M., Ryan T. B of Profl. Studies in Mgmt., Empire State Coll., Buffalo, 1982. Registered investment advisor SEC. Rsch. technician Carborundum Co., Niagara Falls, N.Y., 1978-79; programmer KVS Info. Sys., Kenmore, N.Y., 1979-80; sys. analyst Moore Bus. Forms Inc., Niagara Falls, 1980-83; coord. telecom. project Marine Midland Bank, N.A., Buffalo, 1983-85; pres., owner Micro-Tec, Niagara Falls, 1982-86; telecom. specialist Electronic Data Sys., Lockport, N.Y., 1985-86; from mng. cons. to practice dir. mgmt. cons. Computer Task Group Inc., Buffalo, 1986-93; owner Mowrey Investment Mgmt., 1992—; pres. The Odysseus Group, 1993—. Scholar N.Y. State Bd. of Regents, 1976. Mem. Soc. Mfg. Engrs., John Locke Soc. Roman Catholic. Office: Mowrey Investment Mgmt 3333 Clandon Park Dr Raleigh NC 27613-8841

MOYA, OLGA LYDIA, law educator; b. Weslaco, Tex., Dec. 27, 1959; d. Leonel V. and Genoveva (Tamez) M.; m. James Troutman Byrd, Aug. 24, 1985; children: Leanessa Geneva Byrd, Taylor Moya Byrd. BA, U. Tex., 1981, JD, 1984. Bar: Tex. 1984. Legis. atty. Tex. Ho. of Reps., Austin, 1985; atty. Tex. Dept. Agr., Austin, 1985-90; asst. regional counsel U.S. EPA, Dallas, 1990-91; asst. prof. law South Tex. Coll. of Law, Houston, 1992-95, assoc. prof. law, 1995—. Author: (with Andrew L. Fono) The User's Guide to Federal Environmental Law, 1996. Bd. dirs. Hermann Children's Hosp., Houston, 1993—; mem. Leadership Tex., Austin, 1991—; bd. dirs. Tex. Clean Water Coun., Austin, 1992; U.S. del. to UN Conf. on the Environ. for Latin Am. and the Caribbean, San Juan, P.R., 1995. Recipient Vol. of Yr. award George H. Hermann Soc., 1995, Hispanic Law Prof. of Yr. Hispanic Nat. Bar Assn., 1995. Mem. ABA (environ. law sect.), Hispanic Bar Assn. (bd. dirs. 1992—, Excellence award 1995, 96), Mex.-Am. Bar Assn. Office: South Tex Coll of Law 1303 San Jacinto St Houston TX 77002

MOYÉ, ERIC VAUGHN, district court judge, lawyer; b. N.Y.C., Aug. 22, 1954; s. Lemuel Alexander and Florence (Miller) M.; 1 child, Amy Michelle. BA in Polit. Sci. with distinction, So. Meth. U., 1976; JD, Harvard U., 1979. Bar: Tex. 1979, U.S. Dist. Ct. (no. dist.) Tex. 1980, U.S. Ct. Appeals (5th cir.) 1980, N.Y. 1985, U.S. Supreme Ct. 1985, U.S. Dist. Ct. (no. dist.) Calif. 1986, U.S. Ct. Claims 1986. With Office Gen. Counsel CIA, McLean, Va., 1978; assoc. Akin, Gump, Strauss, Hauer & Feld, Dallas, 1979-83; prin. Law Office of Eric V. Moyé & Assocs., Dallas, 1983-89; ptnr. Lannen & Moyé, Dallas, 1990-92; judge 101st Jud. Dist. Ct. of Tex., Dallas, 1992—; adj. prof. history So. Meth. U. Mem. Permit and License Appeals Bd., 1984-88, Dallas Bail Bond Bd., 1988—; chmn. Mayor's Task Force on Housing and Econ. Devel., Dallas, 1983-85; bd. dirs. Dispute Mediation Service, Dallas, 1980-89, Dallas Urban League, 1980-84, Pub. Utility Counsel Adv. Bd., 1984-85; barrister, Dallas Inn of Ct., 1988; gov. Dallas Symphony Assn. Named one of Outstanding Young Men in Am., 1982, 83. Fellow Tex. Bar Found.; mem. Assn. of Bar of City of N.Y., Nat. Bar Assn., Dallas Bar Assn. (chmn. membership com. 1990), State Bar Tex. (com. on admissions dist. 6, liaison with fed. judiciary com. 1990—), Tex. Assn. Young Lawyers, Am. Arbitration Assn. (arbitrator), Mayor's Commn. on Race Rels. (Dallas Together), Dallas Assembly, Dallas Alliance. Democrat. Methodist. Home: 4656 Christopher Pl Dallas TX 75204

MOYÉ, LINDA EVERETT, mediator; b. Franklin, Va.; d. Langston L. and Susie C. (Chavis) Everett; m. Donald B. Moyé; children: Sidney, Michelle, Bryan, Sheryl. BS in Psychology, Va. State U., Petersburg, 1976; JD, St. Mary's U., San Antonio, 1996. Cert. mediator Bexar County Dispute Resolution Ctr., Tex. Pers. mgmt. specialist Norfolk (Va.) Naval Shipyard, 1975-78; employee devel. specialist IRS, Austin, Tex., 1978-85; employee rels. specialist Kelly AFB, San Antonio, 1985-93; owner Litigation Alternatives, San Antonio, 1996—. Author: (poetry) From a Delta's Heart, 1995, Best Poetry of the 90's, 1995, Best Poetry of 1995, 1995, Best Poetry of 1996, 1996. Class mem. Leadership Tex., Austin, 1996; bd. dirs. San Antonio Food Bank, 1996—, Miss Fiesta Scholarship Pageant, 1993-96, Arts! San Antonio, 1996—. Recipient Editor's Choice award Nat. Libr. Poetry, 1995, 96. Mem. Alamo Area Mediation Assn., Delta Sigma Theta (life). Office: Litigation Alternatives PO Box 700333 San Antonio TX 78270-0333

MOYER, JERRY MILLS, financial services company executive; b. Oklahoma City, Mar. 19, 1940; s. Charles and Dorothy Moyer; m. Cecilia L. Clark, Aug. 28, 1960; children: Jerry, James. BS, Okla. State U., 1962. Salesman Jamco, Inc., 1965, Procter & Gamble, 1966; from salesman to credit mgr. B.F. Goodrich Co., 1967-71; with UCC-Communications Systems, Inc., Dallas, 1971-73; mgr. funds control Dr. Pepper Co., Dallas, 1973-80; pres. Cash Cons., Inc., Dallas, 1985—; v.p. InterFirst Svcs. Corp., Houston, 1981-85; v.p. fin. Med. Acceptance Corp., Houston, 1986; pres. Cash Cons. Co., 1986-87; internat. treas. Yemen Hunt Oil Co., 1987-90. Contbr. articles to profl. jours. Active United Fund, InterFirst Polit. Action Com. Served with U.S. Army, 1962-65. Decorated Air medal (26), Purple Heart; various profl. awards. Mem. Tex. Cash Mgmt. Assn. (founder, past pres.), Nat. Corp. Cash Mgmt. Assn. (co-founder), Masons, Shriners. Baptist.

MOYER, RONALD PETER, allergist, immunologist, pediatrician; b. Columbus, Ohio, Mar. 18, 1943. MD, Ind. U. Sch. Med., 1968. Diplomate Am. Bd. Allergy and Immunology, Am. Bd. Pediatrics. Intern Riley Hosp., 1968-69; resident in pediatrics Kansas Med. Ctr., 1971-72; fellow in allergy Kans. Med. Ctr., 1972-74; staff mem. Kosair Children's Hosp., Louisville. Mem. AMA, Am. Acad. Allergy and Immunology. Office: 9822 3rd St RD #203 Louisville KY 40272

MOYERS, ERNEST EVERETT S., retired missile research scientist; b. Gadsden, Ala., Sept. 4, 1933; s. Ernest Everett S. Moyers and Lena Mae (Goode) Grigsby; m. Mary Violet Roden, Oct. 25, 1952; children: Mary N., Ernest E.S. III, Nora E., Karl H., Barton V., Troy W. BS, Midwestern U., 1954; MS, U. Miss., 1957; PhD, Rice U., 1963, Pacific West U., 1988. Mathematician various cos., 1963-76; rsch. scientist other def. contractors, Huntsville, Ala., 1976-82; missile scientist Delta Rsch., Inc., Huntsville, 1982—, v.p., 1989—; dir. Evangel Christian Sch., Huntsville, 1977-80. Designer anti-tank missile system, 1985; contbr. articles to tech. publs. Pastor Grace Bapt. Ch., Huntsville, 1977-79, Parkview Bapt. Ch., Ardmore, Ala., 1984-89. Mem. Math. Assn. Am., Soc. Computer Simulation (chmn. 1983-94), Soc. for Indsl. and Applied Math., Am. Math. Soc., Toastmasters (founder High Noon club). Republican.

MOYERS, ROBERT CHARLES, systems analyst, state official, microcomputer consultant; b. San Angelo, Tex., Mar. 15, 1951; s. Robert Eugene and Florence (Sprinkles) M.; m. V. Jean Wiggermann, June 30, 1984. BA, U. Tex., 1975. Cons. programming Xerox Ctr. Health Care Research, Houston, 1973-74; systems analyst, mgr. software support Baylor U. Coll. Medicine, Houston, 1974-79; systems analyst Tex. Dept. Transp., Austin, 1980-87, dir. ADP systems, 1987-94; client/server cons., 1994—; cons. microcomputer, 1986—; freelance writer, 1987—. Creator computer programs Loan Analyzer, 1987, BASIC Line Number Generator, 1987, Capital Gains Calculator, 1987, Loan Officer, 1988, PARD Office Program, 1990, Round Rock PARD System, 1992, PARDner, 1994; contbr. articles to profl. jours. Mem. Assn. Systems Mgmt. Roman Catholic. Home: 1605 Drop Tine Dr Cedar Park TX 78613 Office: RFD & Assocs 1210 W 5th St Austin TX 78703

MOYERS, SYLVIA DEAN, retired medical record librarian; b. Independence, W.Va., Oct. 22, 1936; d. Wilkie Russell and Ina Laura (Watkins) Collins; m. Paul Franklin Moyers, June 29, 1957; children: Tammy Jeanne, Thomas Paul, Tara Sue. Student, Am. Med. Record Assn., 1977-79. Sec., Teets Lumber Co., Terra Alta, W.Va., 1954-58, Preston County News, Terra Alta, 1958-60; med. record clk. med. record dept. Hopemont (W.Va.) Hosp., 1960-75, dir., 1975-88; sec. The Terra Alta Bank, W.Va., 1990-95; ret., 1995. Charter mem., past mother advisor Terra Alta Assembly No. 26, Order of Rainbow for Girls, past grand editor Mountain Echoes. Republican. Methodist. Home: RR 2 Box 273-e Albright WV 26519-9753

MOYNE, YVES M., water treatment executive; b. Jallieu, Isere, France, May 23, 1955; came to U.S., 1994; PhD, Hautes Etudes Commerciales, Paris, 1980; M in Econs., U. La Sorbonne, Paris, 1980. Sr. KPMG Peat Marwick, Paris, 1980-83; fin. controller Lyonnaise Des Eaux, Paris, 1983-86, mgr. orgn., 1986-88; group dir. for Hong Kong, China, Macau Lyonnaise Des Eaux, Hong Kong, 1988-91; exec. dir. The Macau Water Supply Co., 1988-91; v.p., fin. and adminstr. Degremont, Rueil, France, 1991-94; chmn., pres., CEO INFILCO Degremont, Inc., Richmond, Va., 1994—; v.p. JOUD, Crolles, France, 1994; dir. French-Am. C. of C., Washington; advisor to French Govt. for Fgn. Trade, 1995—; dir. Great Richmont Devel. Coun.; prof. U. Paris IV, Creteil, 1981; lectr. pub. utility mgmt., S.E. Asia, and China. Author survey: For a Better Knowledge of The Consumers' Habits, 1978. With French Air Force, 1976-77, Istres, France. Mem. French Am. C. of C. (bd. dirs. 1996—). Office: INFILCO Degremont Inc 2924 Emerywood Pky Richmond VA 23294-3746

MOYNIHAN, GARY PETER, industrial engineering educator; b. Little Falls, N.Y., Mar. 5, 1956; s. Peter H. and Frances S. (Ferjanec) M.; m. Eleanor T. McCusker, Mar. 10, 1984; children: Andrew Ross, Keith Patrick. BS in Chemistry, Rensselaer Polytech. Inst., 1978, MBA in Opsl. Mgmt., 1980; PhD in Indsl. Engring., U. Ctrl. Fla., 1990. Prodn. supr. Am. Cyanamid, Bound Brook, N.J., 1978-79, Nat. Micronetics, Kingston, N.Y., 1980-81; assoc. mfg. engr. Martin Marietta Aerospace, Orlando, Fla., 1981-82, indsl. engr., 1982-85, sr. indsl. engr., 1985-87, group indsl. engr., 1987-90; asst. prof. indsl. engring. U. Ala., Tuscaloosa, 1990-96, assoc. prof., 1996—; cons. in field. Contbr. articles to profl. jours. Regents scholarship N.Y. State Bd. of Regents, 1974-78; rsch. fellow NASA, 1992-93; rsch. grant BellSouth Telecomm., 1994—; recipient Outstanding Tchg. award AMOCO Found., 1993-94. Mem. IEEE, Inst. of Indsl. Engrs. (sr. mem., chpt. dir. 1991-95, v.p. fin. and adminstrn. Aerospace & Def. Soc. 1994—). Office: U Ala Dept Indsl Engring Tuscaloosa AL 35487

MOYNIHAN, JOHN BIGNELL, lawyer; b. N.Y.C., July 25, 1933; s. Jerome J. and Stephanie (Bignell) M.; m. Odilia Marie Jacques, Nov. 13, 1965; children—Blair, Dana. B.S., Fordham U., 1955; J.D., St. John's U., N.Y.C., 1958. Bar: Tex. 1961, U.S. Supreme Ct. 1965, U.S. Dist. Ct. (we. dist.) Tex. 1968, U.S. Ct. Apls. (5th cir.) 1973. Sole practice Brownsville, Tex., 1961-62; asst. city atty. City of San Antonio, 1962-63; sole practice, San Antonio, 1963-65; estate tax atty. IRS, San Antonio, 1965-73; dist. counsel EEOC, San Antonio, 1973-79; asst. U.S. atty. Office U.S. Atty., San Antonio, 1980-87, sr. litigation counsel, 1987-94; sole practice, San Antonio, 1995—. Served with U.S. Army, 1958-60; lt. col. USAFR (ret.), 1986. Mem. San Antonio Bar Assn. (chmn. state and nat. legis. com. 1972-73, Meritorious Service award 1968), Fed. Bar Assn. (bd. dirs. San Antonio chpt. 1983—, pres. elect 1986, pres. 1987). Chmn. reform and renewal com. San Antonio Roman Catholic Archdiocese, 1968. Lodge: K.C. (pres. 1967). Home and Office: 11011 Whispering Wind St San Antonio TX 78230-3746

MOZDAB, LAILA, osteopath; b. Ahwaz, Iran, July 3, 1960; came to U.S., 1979; d. Majid and Shahrbano (Vafazadeh) M. BS in Biology, U. South Fla., 1984, BA in Chemistry, 1984, MS in Microbiology, 1986; DO, Southeastern U. Health Scis., 1992. Teaching asst. U. South Fla., Tampa, 1984-86; microbiologist Nat. Health Labs., Tampa, 1986-87, Town and Country Hosp., Tampa, 1987-88; rsch. asst. Southeastern U. Health Scis., North Miami Beach, Fla., 1989-90; resident in internal medicine U. Ala., Montgomery, 1992-94; resident in anesthesiology Vanderbilt U., Nashville, 1994—. Contbr. articles to profl. jours. Vol. Camilus House Clinic for Homeless, Miami, 1990-92. Mem. AMA, Am. Osteo. Assn., Student Osteo. Med. Assn., Am. Soc. Microbiology. Office: Vanderbilt U Dept Anesthesiology Nashville TN 37232-2125

MRAZIK, TINA MARIA, writer; b. North Miami, Fla., Apr. 15, 1963; d. Matthew George and Berutha (Listowich) M. Sales cons. Alliance Entertainment, Miami, 1990—. Author: C.H.R.I.S.T., 1995, When Heart and Mind Collide, 1996; author (music mag.) Intune, 1992-94; author poems and short stories. Recipient Marvin Curry Meml. Poetry award John F. Kennedy Jr. H.S., 1976. Democrat. Office: Alliance Entertainment 4250 Coral Ridge Dr Coral Springs FL

MROCHEK, MICHAEL J., physician; b. Ames, Iowa, Mar. 3, 1960; m. Diana Jo Ayoub, June 27, 1987; 1 child, Justin. BA in Chemistry, U. Tenn., 1982; MD, U. Tenn., Memphis, 1986. Diplomate Am. Bd. Phys. Medicine and Rehab., Am. Bd. Electrodiagnostic Medicine. Commd. 2d lt. U.S. Army, 1986, advanced through grades to maj., 1992; intern William Beaumont Army Med. Ctr., 1986-87; resident Walter Reed Army Med. Ctr., 1988-91; chief phys. medicine and rehab. William Beaumont Army Med. Ctr., El Paso, Tex., 1992-94; outpatient med. dir. Rio Vista Rehab. Hosp., El Paso, 1994—. Fellow Am. Acad. Phys. Medicine and Rehab., Am. Assn. Electrodiagnostic Medicine; mem. AMA, Tex. Med. Assn., El Paso County Med. Soc. Office: 1700 Murchison Dr El Paso TX 79902

MUCCIANO, STEPHANIE LYONS, hospitality, tourism, markting, and association management executive; b. Pitts., Jan. 8; m. Richard Francis Mucciano (dec.); 1 child, Stephanie Lynn. Student St. Petersburg Jr. Coll., 1963-64, Alamogordo Bus. Coll., 1970-71. Sales mgr. Bahama Cruise Line, Tampa, Fla., 1980-82; dir. mktg./sales AAA Holidays/St. Petersburg Motor Club, Fla., 1982-84; dir. mktg./sales Travel and Tourism Resources, Inc., St. Petersburg, 1986, prin., pres., 1986-90; dir. mktg./sales Island Harbor Resort, Cape Haze, Fla., 1984-86; mgr. Radisson-Pan-Am. Ocean Hotel, Miami Beach, Fla., 1986-90; sr. dir. Fla. Restaurant Assn., 1990-95; v.p. Europa Tours, 1989—; pres., mng. ptnr. Mucciano, Reyes & Assocs., Inc., 1995—; mktg. cons., bd. dirs., adv. bd. Travel Marketplace, Royal Fiesta Cruises, Clearwater; mem. adv. bd. Culinary Inst., Ft. Lauderdale Art Inst., Acad. Travel and Tourism, Dade County Magnet Schs., Fla.; seminar leader, internat. industry speaker, guest lectr. and tchr. Mem. Fla. Gulf Coast Symphony Guild, St. Petersburg, 1975-86, All Childrens Hosp. Guild, 1975-86, Infinity League to Aid Abused Children, 1981-86, Pinellas Assn. for Retarded Adults, 1975-86, St. Petersburg Internat. Folk Fair Soc., Host Com. Super Bowl XXVIIII; pres. Tampa Bay Mag. Leaders on the Move, 1982, Pinellas County Leaders Move Recipient Cert. of Recognition, George Greer County Commr., Pinellas, 1986; panelist Broward Cultural Arts Coun., Broward City, Fla., 1992-93; state bd. dirs. Am. Heart Assn., 1992-95, v.p. So. Broward chpt., mem. Pub. Affairs Com. State Bd.; bd. dirs. South Fla. Friends of Jazz City of Hollywood, Fla., 1992-94. Mem. Nat. Assn. Female Execs., Women in Food Svc., Internat. Platform Assn., Pacific Area Travel Assn. (dir.), Sun Coast Travel Industry Assn., Sales and Mktg. Execs. Internat., Travel and Tourism Research Assn., C. of C. (tourism com., chmn. econ. devel. coun., Super Bowl Hoat com. 1995, co-chair restaurant com. for Super Bowl, 1995), Women Execs. in Travel, Fla. Assn. Sales Execs., Hotel Sales and Mktg. Assn., Fla. Women's Network, Am. Mktg. Assn., Italian-Am. Club, St. Petersburg Internat. Folk Fair Soc., Assn. Internat. Des Skal Clubs. Avocations: reading, volunteer work. Office: Europa Tours Mucciano Reyes & Assocs 20533 Biscayne Blvd Ste 423 Aventura FL 33180 also: Europa Tours PO Box 592 Hollywood FL 33020

MUCK, TERRY CHARLES, religious publisher and educator; b. Batavia, N.Y., June 24, 1947; s. Webster Charles and Oaklie Mae (Floyd) M.; m. Judith Lee Keim, Sept. 15, 1970; children: David, Paul, Joseph. BA, Bethel Coll., St. Paul, 1969; MDiv, Bethel Theol. Seminary, St. Paul, 1973; PhD, Northwestern U., 1977. Editor Leadership Jour., Wheaton, Ill., 1980-85, Christianity Today Mag., Wheaton, 1985-90; prof. religion Wheaton Coll., 1986-90; prof. comparative religion Austin (Tex.) Presbyn. Theol. Sem., 1990—. Author: Liberating Leader's Prayer Life, 1984, When to Take A Risk, 1986, Alien Gods on American Turfs, 1990, Those Other Religions in Your Neighborhood, 1992, The Mysterious Beyond: A Basic Guide to Studying Religion, 1993; author, editor: Sins of the Body, 1988. Fulbright Hayes rsch. grantee, 1976-77. Mem. Soc. for Buddhist-Christian Studies (bd. dirs. 1989—), Pali Text Soc., Am. Acad. Religion, Evang. Theol. Soc., Soc. for Scientific Study Religion. Home: 4305 Bamford Dr Austin TX 78731-1205 Office: Austin Presbyn Theol Sem 100 E 27th St Austin TX 78705-5711

MUDD, JOHN PHILIP, lawyer; b. Washington, Aug. 22, 1932; s. Thomas Paul and Frances Mary (Finotti) M.; m. Barbara Eve Sweeney, Aug. 10, 1957; children: Laura, Ellen, Philip, Clare, David. BSS, Georgetown U., 1954; JD, Georgetown Law Center, 1956. Bar: Md. 1956, D.C. 1963, Fla. 1964, Calif. 1973. Pvt. practice Upper Marlboro, Md., 1956-66; v.p., sec., gen. counsel Deltona Corp., Miami, Fla., 1966-72; sec., gen. counsel Nat. Community Builders, San Diego, 1972-73; gen. counsel Continental Advisers (adviser to Continental Mortgage Investors), 1973-75, sr. v.p., gen. counsel, 1975-80; sr. v.p., gen. counsel Am. Hosp. Mgmt. Corp., Miami, 1980-89; legal coord. Amerifirst Bank, Miami, 1989-92; v.p., legal counsel Cartaret Savs. Bank, Morristown, N.J., 1991-93, cons., 1991-92; gen. counsel Golden Glades Hosp., Miami, 1992-93, Bank of N.Am., Miami, 1994—; gen. counsel Golden Glades Hosp., Miami, 1992-93; cons. FSLIC, 1988-89, J.E. Robert Cos., Alexandria, Va., 1988-89, Real Estate Recovery, Inc., Boca Raton, Fla., 1991-92, Bank N.Am., Ft. Lauderdale, Fla., 1992; dir. Unitower Mortgage Corp., Miami, Fla.; dir. Unitower Mortgage Corp., Miami; pres. Marquette Realty Corp., Miami. Former mem. Land Devel. Adv. Com. N.Y. State; chmn. student interview com. Georgetown U.; bd. dirs. Lasalle High Sch., Miami; corp. counsel Com. of Dade County, Fla.; trustee Golden Glades Gen. Hosp., Miami, Fla., 1992—, gen. counsel, 1991—, Bank of North Am., Miami, 1992—. Mem. Fla. Bar Assn., Calif. Bar Assn., Md. Bar Assn., D.C. Bar Assn., Fla. State Bar (exec. com. on corp. counsel com.). Democrat. Roman Catholic. Home: 411 Alhambra Cir Miami FL 33134-4901 Office: Bank of North Am Golden Glades Med Plz 8701 SW 137th Ave Ste 301 Miami FL 33183-4498

MUDD, MARY MOLLIE B., editor; b. Balt., Sept. 22, 1971; d. John Francis and Mary B. (Moreland) M. BA, U. Notre Dame, 1993. Reporter, day editor The Observer Newspaper, Notre Dame, Ind., 1992; campus life editor Scholastic Mag., Notre Dame, 1992-93; editor Found. Philanthropy The Taft Group, Rockville, Md., 1993-96; editor Capitol Publs. Inc., Alexandria, Va., 1996—. Editor: National Directory of Nonprofit Organizations, 1995, Foundation Reporter, 1997; newsletter editor Found. and Corp. Grants Alert. Mem. Notre Dame Alumni Assn., Washington D.C. Notre Dame Club. Roman Catholic. Office: 1101 King St Ste 444 Alexandria VA 22314

MUDD, SHERYL KAY, secondary school educator, guidance counselor; b. Ft. Thomas, Ky., July 14, 1960; d. Robert Leslie and Marvel Maxine (Youtsey) M.; m. Jackie Elaine Nichols, Lawrence Robert, Gerald Leslie, Randy Kent, Ronald Lee, Rhonda Dee, Michael Todd. BA, Transylvania U., 1982; MEd in Guidance Counseling, Xavier U., Cin., 1988. Cert. elem. tchr., K-12 phys. edn. tchr., Ky. Substitute tchr. Pendleton County Schs., Falmouth, Ky., 1982-84, Campbell County Schs., Alexandria, Ky., 1982-84; tchr. No. Elem. Sch., Butler, Ky., 1984-86; tchr. math. Pendleton Mid. Sch., Falmouth, 1986-88, tchr. reading, 1988-89, tchr. health and phys. edn., 1989-92; tchr. 7th and 8th grades Risk Youth, 1992—. Named to Honorable Order of Ky. Colonels, Commonwealth of Ky., 1979, Tchr. of Yr., Pendleton Mid. Sch., 1989, 93, 94, 95. Mem. ASCD, AAHPERD, Assn. for Advancement Health and Phys. Edn., AACD, Ky. Assn. for Gifted Assn., Ky. Mid. Sch. Assn., No. Ky. Assn. Counseling and Devel. Democrat. Roman Catholic. Home: Tammy Ln Lot 17 Box 166 RR 2 Butler KY 41006-0166 Office: Pendleton County Mid Sch 500 Chapel St Falmouth KY 41040-1410

MUELLER, AGNES C., German language educator; b. Rosenfeld, Germany, Apr. 3, 1968. MA, Munich U., 1993; postgrad., Vanderbilt U., 1994—. With McDonald's Inc., Munich, 1987-91; pub. rels. rep. Virgin Records Inc., Munich, 1991-93; freelance writer BMG Ariola Munich, 1993-95; instr. German, Vanderbilt U., Nashville, 1994—; conf. presenter in field. Mem. MLA, Am. Assn. Tchrs. German, South Atlantic MLA. Home: 2104 Ashwood Ave Nashville TN 37212 Office: Vanderbilt U Dept German Box 1567 Sta B Nashville TN 37235

MUELLER, JAMES R., religious studies educator; b. Memphis, July 16, 1951; s. Raymond J. and Hazel (Jones) M.; m. Scarlott Kimball, July 19, 1980; 1 child, Andrew Paul. BA, Duke U., 1973, MDiv, 1977, MA, 1984, PhD, 1986. Vis. instr. N.C. State U., Raleigh, 1982-86, Duke U., Durham, N.C., 1986-87; vis. asst. prof. U. N.C., Chapel Hill, 1987-88; asst. prof. U. Fla., Gainesville, 1988-95, assoc. prof., 1995—. Author: The Five Fragments of the Apocryphon of Ezekiel, 1994; co-editor: The Oxford Study Bible, 1992; editor Jour. for the Study of the Pseudepigrapha, 1992—. Rsch. grantee Sassoon Internat. Ctr. for Study of Anti-Semitism, 1995. Mem. Am. Acad. Religion, Soc. Biblical Lit., Am. Schs. Oriental Rsch., Cath. Biblical Assn. Office: U Fla Dept Religion 125 Dauer Hall Gainesville FL 32611

MUELLER, LOIS M., psychologist; b. Milw., Nov. 30, 1943; d. Herman Gregor and Ora Emma (Dettmann) M.; BS, U. Wis.-Milw., 1965; MA, U. Tex., 1966, PhD, 1969. Cert. family mediator. Postdoctoral intern VA Hosp., Wood, Wis., 1969-71; counselor, asst. prof. So. Ill. U. Counseling Center and dept. psychology, Carbondale, 1971-72, coordinator personal counseling, asst. prof., 1972-74, counselor, asst. prof., 1974-76; individual practice clin. psychology, Carbondale, 1972-76, Clearwater, Fla., 1977-90, Port Richey, Fla., 1990—; family mediator, 1995—; mem. profl. adv. com. Mental Health Assn. Pinellas County, 1978, Alt. Human Services, 1979-80; cons. Face Learning Center, Hotline Crisis Phone Service, 1977-87; advice columnist Clearwater Sun newspaper, 1983-90; pub. speaker local TV and radio stas., 1978, 79; talk show host WPLP Radio Sta., Clearwater, 1980-83, WTKN Radio Sta., Tampa Bay, 1988-89, WPSO Radio Sta., New Port Richey, 1991. Campaign worker for Sen. George McGovern presdl. race, 1972. Lic. psychologist, Ill., Fla. Mem. Am., Fla., Ill., Pinellas (founder, pres. 1978) psychol. assns., Am. Soc. Clin. Hypnosis, Fla. Soc. Clin. Hypnosis, West Pasco C. of C., Calusa Bus. & Profl. Women. Contbr. articles to profl. jours. Office: 9501 US Highway 19 Ste 212 Port Richey FL 34668-4641

MUELLER, MICHAEL LEE, editor; b. Mt. Vernon, Ill., May 28, 1959; s. James E. Sr. and Nancy L. (Hart) M.; m. Denise A. Smith, Mar. 9, 1985; 1 stepchild, Zachariah Smith. BS in Journalism, U. Ill., 1983. Freelance writer/photographer various publs., 1983—; editor, mng. editor various automotive mags. Dobbs Pub. Group, Lakeland, Fla., 1987-91; feature editor Classic Pub., Atlanta, 1988—; assoc. editor Automobile Quar., Kutztown, Pa., 1991, contbg. editor, photographer, 1992—. Mem. Internat. Motor Press Assn., Soc. Automotive Historians, Soc. Am. Baseball Rsch. Home and Office: 4943 Hidden Hills Dr Lakeland FL 33813

MUELLER, O. THOMAS, molecular geneticist, pediatrics educator; b. Berlin, Germany, Aug. 17, 1950; arrived in U.S., 1955; s. Heinz Carl and Gertrud (Jung) M.; m. Mary Gail Craig, April 24, 1976; children: Cara Lynne, Kyle Thomas, Eric Andreas. BA, Lehigh U., 1972; PhD in biol. chemistry, Pa. State U., 1978. Diplomate: Am. Bd. Med. Genetics in Molecular and Biochemical Genetics. Postdoctoral fellow U. Colo. Med. Ctr., Denver, 1978-80; rsch. asst. Roswell Park Meml. Inst., Buffalo, N.Y., 1980-84, rsch. affiliate, 1984-87; assoc. prof. pediats. U. So. Fla., Tampa, 1987—; dir. molecular genetics All Children's Hosp., St. Petersburg, Fla., 1994—. Contbr. numerous articles to scientific jours. including Human Genetics, Am. Jour. Med. Genetics, Am. Jour. Human Genetics, Jour. Biol. Chemistry, and others. Home: 207 Halton Cir Seffner FL 33584-4158 Office: Dept Pathology All Children's Hosp 801 6th St S Saint Petersburg FL 33701-4816

MUELLER, PATRICIA WESTBROOK, research chemist; b. Atlanta, Sept. 1, 1948; d. James Arthur and Winifred (Andrews) Westbrook; m. Heinz Juergen Mueller, Mar. 24, 1968; children: Christina Marie, Stefanie Elizabeth. BS in Chemistry, U. Tenn., 1970; PhD in Biochemistry, Ga. Inst. Tech., 1981. Postdoctoral fellow Ga. Inst. Tech., Atlanta, 1981-83; chief health effects lab. Ctrs. for Disease Control, Atlanta, 1983—; mem. exec. com. Nutrition and Health Scis. Grad. Program, Grad. Div. Biol. and Biomed. Scis. Emory U., Atlanta, 1991—, adj. prof. Biochemistry. Contbr. articles to Jour. Biol. Chemistry, Biochemistry, Jour. Toxicological Environ. Health Clin. Chemistry, Archives of Environ. Contaminant Toxicology, Nephron, Am. Jour. Hypertension, others. Rhenium scholar U. Tenn., 1969. Mem. Am. Assn. Clin. Chemistry, Am. Chem. Soc., N.Y. Acad. Scis., Sigma Xi (Outstanding Doctoral Rsch. in Sci. award 1981). Office: Ctrs for Disease Control Mailstop F50 4770 Buford Hwy NE Atlanta GA 30341-3724

MUELLER, PEGGY JEAN, dance educator, choreographer, rancher; b. Austin, Tex., June 14, 1952; d. Rudolph George Jr. and Margaret Jean (Locke) M.; m. John Yerby Tarlton, June 24, 1972 (div. June 1983). BS in Home Econs., Child Devel., U. Tex., Austin, 1974. Dance tchr. Shirley McPhail Sch. Dance, Austin, 1972-75; dance tchr. Jean Tarlton Sch. Dance, Alpine, Tex., 1975-77, College Station, Tex., 1977-80; dance tchr. Sul Ross State U., Alpine, 1975-77, Tex. A&M U., College Station, 1977-80, A&M Consol. Community Edn., Coll. Station, 1977-78, Jean Mueller Sch. Dance, Austin, 1980—, U. Tex., Austin, 1980—; dancer, contest judge Gt. Tex. Dance-Off, Austin, 1985-86; mem. equestrian com. Austin-Travis County Livestock Show and Rodeo, 1980-92, chmn. trail ride, 1986—; trail boss, pres. Austin Founders Trail Ride, 1986—; trail boss Bandera Longhorn Cattle Drive and Trail Ride, 1990, 91; choreographer, head cheerleader Austin Texans Pro Football Team, 1981; dance tchr. Austin Ballroom Dancers, 1988; dancer, agt. George Strait/Bud Light Comml. Auditions, 1990; head contest judge Am.'s Ultimate Dance Contest, Austin, 1994; contest judge Two-Stepping Across Am., Austin, 1994; speaker in field. Dancer Oklahoma, Austin, 1969, Kiss Me Kate, Austin, 1970; choreographer, lead role Cabaret, Alpine, 1976. Active Women's Symphony League Austin, 1972—, Settlement Club, Austin, 1987—; recreation chmn. St. Martin's Evang. Luth. Ch., Austin, 1972—; hon. trail boss St. Jude Children's Rsch. Hosp. Trail Ride, Austin and Kyle, Tex., 1991. Recipient Outstanding Trail Rider of Yr. award Wild Horse Trail Ride, Okla., 1984; named Tex. First Lady Trail Boss, Gov. Mark White, Mayor Frank Cooksey, Austin City Coun., 1986, Judge Bill Aleshire, Travis County Commrs., 1989, Outstanding Intramural Sports Team Mgr.-Player, Tex. A&M U., 1978-79. Mem. Tex Assn. Tchrs. of Dancing, Inc., U.S. Twirling and Gymnastics Assn., Univ. Tex. Ex-Students Assn., Tex. Execs. in Home Econs., Am. Vet. Med. Assn. Aux. (v.p. 1978-79, pres. 1979-80), Am. Horse Shows Assn., Internat. Arabian Horse Assn., Austin Women's Tennis Assn. (v.p. 1985-86, pres. 1986-90, spl. events chmn. 1990-92, advisor 1990—, winner 2d ann. Harriet Crosson Outstanding Player & Community Svc. award), Women's Team Tennis of Austin Assn. (pres.-elect 1992-93, pres. 1993-94), Capital Area Tennis Assn. (membership com. 1991, 92), Houston Salt Grass Trail Ride Assn., San Antonio Alamo Trail Ride Assn., Ft. Worth Chisholm Trail Ride Assn., U. Tex. Longhorn Alumni Band, Austin C. of C., Am. Bus. Women's Assn., Austin Alumnae Panhellenic Assn. (1st v.p. 1989-90, rush forum chmn. 1990, pres. 1990-91, parliamentarian 1991-92), Omicron Nu (v.p. 1973-74), Jr. Austin Woman's Club (historian 1990-91), Austin Country Club (team tennis captain 1994—), Zeta Tau Alpha (Austin Alumnae Chpt., alumnae photographer, social advisor 1982-87, treas. 1987-89, publicity chmn. 1989, Easter Seals fundraiser, Honor Cup winner 1990, pres. 1991-92, internat. convention official del. 1988, 92, nominating chmn. 1992-93, mem. yearbook com. 1992-94, 2d v.p. 1993-94). Republican. Clubs: Cen. Tex. Arabian Horse, Capitol Area Quarter Horse Assn., Jr. Austin Woman's, Austin Country. Home and Office: PO Box 14762 Austin TX 78761-4762

MUELLER, ROY CLEMENT, graphic arts company and direct mail executive; b. Weehawken, N.J., Aug. 15, 1930; s. Adam and Bertha (Le Blanc) M.; m. Patricia Robinson, Sept. 3, 1970; children: Eric, Janet, Deborah, Gregory. Student Rochester Inst. Tech., 1976. Mgr. estimating/billing dept. Editors Press, Hyattsville, Md., 1962-66; v.p., gen. mgr. Peninsula Press div. A.S. Abell Corp., Salisbury, Md., 1967-70; owner, mgr. Crown Decal & Display, Co., Bristol, Tenn., 1972—; pres. chief exec. officer Bristol Screen, Inc., 1977—, CEO Decor-Pak. Recipient Ad award Tri-City Advt. Fedn., 1975. Mem. Printing Industry Am., Am. Philatelic Soc. Republican. Lutheran. Office: 200 Delaware Ave Bristol TN 37620-5004

MUELLER, WERNER HEINRICH, organic chemist, technology administrator; b. Aldersbach, Germany, Apr. 7, 1939; came to U.S., 1984; s. August and Rosina (Schned) M.; m. Janice Williams, Aug. 14, 1968; children: Carolyn, Alexander. BS, Tech. U. Munich, 1963, MS in Organic Chemistry, 1965, PhD in Organic Chemistry, 1967; postgrad., Temple U., 1967-68. Rsch. specialist Monsanto Co., Pensacola, Fla., 1968-72; group leader spl. chemistry Hoechst AG, Frankfurt, Germany, 1972-80, asst. to mem. bd., 1980-83; rsch. specialist div. electronic products Hoechst AG, Wiesbaden, Germany, 1983-84; asst. ops. mgr. Knapsack Works Hoechst AG, 1984-85; mgr. indsl. chemistry Am. Hoechst Corp., Coventry, R.I., 1985-88; assoc. dir. R&D adv. tech. group Hoechst Celanese, Corpus Christi, Tex., 1988-89, tech. dir. chems. group, 1989-93; dir. tech. devel. group engring., spl. chems. group Hoechst Celanese, Charlotte, N.C., 1993—; mem. indsl. vis. com. dept. chemistry and biochem. U. Tex., Austin, 1990-93. Contbr. articles to profl. jours. Mem. AAAS, Am. Chem. Soc., N.Y. Acad. Scis., Indsl. Rsch. Inst., Inc., Coun. for Chem. Rsch. Roman Catholic. Office: Hoechst Celanese Corp Bldg 5200 77 Center Dr Charlotte NC 28217

MUELLER-HEUBACH, EBERHARD AUGUST, obstetrician gynecologist, medical researcher; b. Berlin, Feb. 24, 1942; came to U.S., 1968; s. Heinrich Gustav and Elisabeth (Heubach) M.; m. Cornelia Rosemarie Uffmann, Feb. 6, 1968; 1 child, Oliver Maximilian. MD, U. Cologne, 1966. Diplomate Am. Bd. Ob-Gyn. Intern U. Cologne, Germany, 1967-68, Middlesex Gen. Hosp., New Brunswick, N.J., 1968-69; rsch. fellow reproductive physiology Columbia U., N.Y.C., 1969-71; resident ob-gyn. Columbia-Presbyn. Med. Ctr., N.Y.C., 1971-74, chief resident ob-gyn., 1974-75; asst. prof. ob-gyn. U. Pitts., 1975-81, assoc. prof. ob-gyn., 1981-89; prof., chmn. dept. ob-gyn. Wake Forest U., Winston-Salem, N.C., 1989—; oral examiner Am. Bd. Ob-gyn., Dallas, 1984—. reviewer Am. Jour. Ob-gyn., Ob-gyn., Biology Reproduction. Fellow Am. Coll. Ob-gyn. (Hoechst award 1972); mem. Soc. Gynecol. Investigation, Am. Gynecol. Obstet. Soc., Perinatal Rsch. Soc., Coun. Univ. Chairs Ob-gyn. (pres.-elect), Soc. Perinatal Obstetricians. Office: Bowman Gray Sch Medicine Med Ctr Blvd Winston Salem NC 27157

MUENCH, KARL H., clinical geneticist; b. St. Louis, May 3, 1934. MD, Wash. U., St. Louis, 1960. Diplomate Am. Bd. Med. Genetics, Am. Bd. Clin. Genetics. Intern Barnes Hosp., St. Louis, 1960-61; fellow in biological chemistry Stanford U. Sch. Medicine, 1961-65; staff mem. Jackson Meml. Hosp., Miami, Fla.; prof. medicine U. Miami Sch. Medicine. Mem. AMA, Am. Chemistry Soc., Am. Coll. Med. Genetics, Am. Coll. Physicians. Office: U Miami Sch Med Div Genetic Med PO Box 16960 Miami FL 33101-6960

MUENZLER, KENDELL DEAN, purchasing manager, city government administrator; b. San Antonio, Dec. 28, 1940; s. Arlie Paul and Alyce Marie (Raeke) M.; m. Janet McCarver, 1965 (div. 1974); 1 child, Kaye Lynne; m. Carol Debish, 1991 (div. 1996). BBA, U. Tex., 1962. Mgmt. trainee Western Union, N.Y.C., 1962; staff asst. to pres. White Instruments, Austin, Tex., 1962-63; purchasing and prodn. control specialist Anderson Clayton Foods, Dallas, 1963-70; purchasing mgr. Wortz Co., Dallas, 1970-71; mgr. prodn. control, customer svc. ITT Grinnell Corp., Temple, Tex., 1971-73; materials control mgr. City of Austin, 1973-79, purchasing mgr., 1982—; purchasing mgr. FrosTex Foods, Inc., Austin, 1979-80; contract adminstr. Tracor Aerospace, Austin, 1980-82; instr. in purchasing Austin C.C., 1996—. Precinct chmn. Rep. Party, Austin, 1988—. Named Purchasing Mgr. of Yr., Tex. Assn. Pub. Purchasers, 1991. Mem. Nat. Inst. Govtl. Purchasing (cert. pub. purchasing officer, cert. NIGP instr. pres. Austin chpt.), Nat. Assn. Purchasing Mgmt. (cert. purchasing mgr.), Am. Prodn. and Inventory Control Soc. (cert. in prodn. inventory mgmt., cert. integrated resource mgmt.), Nat. Contracts Mgmt. Assn., Mensa. Baptist. Home: 3326 Linda Kay Dr San Antonio TX 78222 Office: City of Austin Purchasing Office PO Box 1088 Austin TX 78767

MUHLENFELD, ELISABETH S., college president, educator, author; b. Washington, Nov. 12, 1944; d. Merle Roberts and Cornelia Elizabeth (Herring) Showalter; m. Edward F. Muhlenfeld, Sept. 10, 1966 (div. 1975); children: Allison Elisabeth, David Edward; m. Laurin A. Wollan, Jr., June 5, 1982; stepchildren: Ann Louise Wollan, Laurin A. Wollan III. BA in Philosophy, Goucher Coll., 1966; MA in English, U. Tex., Arlington, 1973; PhD, U. S.C., 1978. Rsch. asst., adminstrv. asst. So. Studies program U. S.C., Columbia, 1975-78; asst. prof. English Fla. State U., Tallahassee, 1978-82, assoc. prof., 1982-87, dir. undergrad and grad. studies, assoc. chmn. dept. English, 1987-96, prof. English, 1987-96, dean undergrad. studies, 1984-86; pres. Sweet Briar (Va.) Coll., 1996—; mem. ABA Commn. on Coll. and Univ. Legal Studies, 1991-94. Author: Mary Boykin Chesnut: A Biography, 1981; editor: William Faulkner's Absolom, Absolom: A Critical Casebook, 1984, The Private Mary Chesnut: The Unpublished Civil War Diaries, 1984. Mem. Capital Women's Network. NEH Dir.'s grantee, 1983-84. Mem. MLA, St. George Tucker Soc. (charter fellow), So. Assn. Women Historians, William Faulkner Soc. (charter mem; sec.-treas. 1991-94), Phi Kappa Phi (exec. bd., pres. 1992-93). Office: Sweet Briar Coll Pres's Office Box C Sweet Briar VA 24595

MUHLERT, JAN KEENE, art museum director; b. Oak Park, Ill., Oct. 4, 1942; d. William Henry and Isabel Janette (Cole) Keene; m. Christopher Layton Muhlert, Jan. 1, 1966; 1 son, Michael Keene. B.A. in Art and French, Albion (Mich.) Coll., 1964; M.A. in Art History, Oberlin (Ohio) Coll., 1967; student, Neuchatel (Switzerland) U., Inst. European Studies, Paris, Inst. de Phonetique, Acad. Grande Chaumiere. Asst. curator Allen Meml. Art Mus., Oberlin, 1967-68; asst. curator 20th Century painting and sculpture Nat. Collection Fine Arts, Smithsonian Instn., Washington, 1968-73; assoc. curator Nat. Collection Fine Arts, Smithsonian Instn., 1974-75; dir. U. Iowa Mus. Art, 1975-79, Amon Carter Mus., Ft. Worth, 1980-95, Palmer Museum of Art, University Park, Pa., 1996—. Author museum brochures, catalogues. Mem. Nat. Mus. Act Adv. Council, 1980-83, vis. com. Allen Meml. Art Mus. of Oberlin (Ohio) Coll., 1987—. Grantee Nat. Endowment Arts-Donner Found., 1979; recipient Friend of Art Edn. award Tex. Art Edn. Assn., 1994. Mem. Assn. Art Mus. Dirs. (trustee 1981-82, 84-86, 92-93, chmn. govt. and art com. 1982-84, chmn. profl. practices com. 1990-92), Western Assn. Art Mus. (regional rep. 1978-79), Am. Assn. Mus. (commn. for new century 1981-84, gen. co-chair 1993 ann. meeting), Am. Arts Alliance (dir. 1980-86, vice-chmn. 1982-84). Office: Palmer Museum of Art Penn State University Park State College PA 16802-2507

MUIR, HELEN, journalist, author; b. Yonkers, N.Y., Feb. 9, 1911; d. Emmet A. and Helen T. (Flaherty) Lennehan; student public schs.; m. William Whalley Muir, Jan. 23, 1936; children: Mary Muir Burrell, William Torbert. With Yonkers Herald Statesman, 1929-30, 31-33, N.Y. Evening Post, 1930-31, N.Y. Evening Jour., 1933-34, Carl Byoir & Assos., N.Y.C., and Miami, Fla., 1934-35; syndicated columnist Universal Svc., Miami, 1935-38; columnist Miami Herald, 1941-42; children's book editor, 1949-56; women's editor Miami Daily News, 1943-44; freelance mag. writer, numerous nat. mags., 1944—; drama critic Miami News, 1960-65. Trustee Coconut Grove Libr. Assn., Friends U. Miami Libr., Friends Miami-Dade Pub. Libr.; vis. com. U. Miami Librs.; bd. dirs. Miami-Dade County Pub. Libr. System; past chmn., mem. State Libr. Adv. Coun., 1979-91, past chmn. Recipient award Delta Kappa Gamma, 1960; Fla. Libr. Assn. Trustees and Friends award, 1973, Coun. Fla. Librs. award, 1990; trustee citation ALA, 1984, Spirit of Excellence award, 1988; named to Fla. Women's Hall of Fame, 1984, Miami Centennial '96 Women's Hall of Fame. Mem. Women in Communications (Cmty. Headliner award 1973), Soc. Women Geographers (Meritorious Svc. award 1996), Author's Guild. Clubs: Florida Women's Press (award 1963); Cosmopolitan (N.Y.C.); Biscayne Bay Yacht. Author: Miami, U.S.A., 1953, 3d rev. edit., 1990, Biltmore: Beacon for Miami, 1987,

2d rev. edit., 1993, Frost In Florida: A Memoir, 1995. Home: 3855 Stewart Ave Miami FL 33133-6734

MUIR, J. DAPRAY, lawyer; b. Washington, Nov. 9, 1936; s. Brockett and Helen Cassin (Dapray) M.; m. Louise Rutherfurd Pierrepont, July 16, 1966. A.B., Williams Coll., 1958; J.D., U. Va., 1964. Bar: Md., Va., D.C. 1964, U.S. Supreme Ct. 1967. Asst. legal advisor for econ. and bus. affairs U.S. Dept. State, 1971-73; pvt. practice law, 1974—; mem. U.S. del. to Joint U.S./USSR Comml. Commn., 1972; chmn. D.C. Securities Adv. Com., 1981-84, mem. 1985-88. Bd. editors Va. Law Rev, 1963-64; contbr. articles to profl. jours. Mem. bd. adv. G.W. Jour. Internat. Law & Econs., 1976-. Lt. (j.g.) USNR, 1958-61. Mem. D.C. Bar (chmn. internat. law div. 1977-78, chmn. environ., energy and natural resources div. 1982-83, Met. Club (Washington), Chevy Chase (Md.) Club. Home: 3104 Q St NW Washington DC 20007-3027 Office: Ste 200 1025 Connecticut Ave Ste 20 Washington DC 20036-5405

MUIR, MALCOLM, JR., history educator; b. Williamsport, Pa., Apr. 24, 1943; s. Malcolm and Alma May (Brohard) M.; m. Carol Quay Thornton, June 16, 1965; children: T. Thornton, Thomas C. BA, Emory U., Atlanta, 1965; MA, Fla. State U., 1966; PhD, OHio State U, 1976. Asst. prof. Middle Ga. Coll., Cochran, 1967-72; asst. prof. to prof. history Austin Peay State U., Clarksville, Tenn., 1977-90, chair dept. history, 1990—; Secnav rsch. fellow USN, Naval Hist. Ctr., Washington, 1987-88; vis. prof. U.S. Mil. Acad., West Point, N.Y., 1988-90, Air War Coll., Maxwell AFB, Ala., 1996-97. Author: The Iowa Class Battleships, 1987, Black Shoes and Blue Water: Surface Warfare in the United States Navy, 1945-1975, 1996; contbr. articles to profl. jours. Trustee Soc. for Mil. History, Washington, 1989—. Mem. Assn. for Preservation Civil War Sites, Confederate Hist. Inst., Internat. Naval Rsch. Orgn., Nat. Assn. Scholars, Naval Hist. Found., Surface Warfare Assn., Assn. U.S. Army, Phi Alpha Theta, Phi Kappa Phi. Office: Dept History Austin Peay State U Clarksville TN 37044

MUJICA, MARY BERNADETTE, mechanical engineer; b. Red Bank, N.J., Feb. 2, 1963; d. Patrick Peter and Linda Jean (Mohler) McCall; m. Frank Elias Mujica, Apr. 16, 1988; children: Keith Alan, Shannon Yvette, Angela Andrea, Kasey Alan. BSME summa cum laude, Bucknell U., 1985. Asst. to corp. maintenance mgr. Air Products & Chems., Allentown, Pa., 1985-86; plant maintenance engr. Air Products & Chems., Pasadena, Tex., 1986-87; prodn./quality engr. Air Products & Chems., Pasadena, 1987-88; chem. plant engr., project engr. Shell Oil/Chem., Deer Park, Tex., 1988-90, chem. plant and refinery effluent engr., 1990-92, safety/process safety mgmt. engr., 1992-93, asst. maintenance mgr., reliability engr., 1993—. Asst. leader Jr. Achievement, Allentown, 1985-86; industry sponsor Soc. Women Engrs., Allentown, 1985-86; mem. fin. com. Heritage Park Bapt. Ch., Webster, Tex., 1990-92; firefighter, mem. rescue squad Shell Emergency Response, 1990-94. Kodak scholar, 1982-85. Mem. Tau Beta Pi (sec. 1984). Home: 1001 Glenshannon Ave Friendswood TX 77546-5339 Office: Shell Oil Co PO Box 100 Deer Park TX 77536-0100

MUKAMAL, DAVID SAMIER, sign manufacturing company executive; b. Baghdad, Iraq, Oct. 6, 1944; came to U.S., 1950; s. Abraham Sassoon and Mary (Murad) M.; m. Anitamarie Costa, July 31, 1970; children—Adam Scott, Rebecca Kate. B.B.A. in Econs. with honors, Bryant Coll., 1970; M.B.A. in Fin. Mgmt., Iona Coll., 1975. Budget analyst USV Pharm./Revlon, Inc., Tuckahoe, N.Y., 1970-72; sr. budget officer Met. Transp. Authority, N.Y.C., 1972-74; sr. fin. analyst Am. Airlines, Inc., Dallas, 1974-82; pres. All State Signs, Richardson, Tex., 1982—, Framed Image Enterprises, Inc., Irving, Tex., 1995—. Served with USN, 1965-66. Recipient Jeremiah Clarke Barber award Bryant Coll., 1970. Mem. Dallas Apt. Assn., Tex. Sign Mfrs. Assn., Omicron Delta Epsilon. Republican. Jewish.

MULDOON, THOMAS LYMAN, writer; b. Sioux Falls, S.D., Apr. 23, 1945; s. Lyman Thomas and Margaret Mary (Wallace) M.; m. Kathryn Lee Harmon, June 30, 1973; m. Kathryn Muldoon. B in Polit. Sci., Merrimack Coll., 1967; MS in Mass. Comm., Fla. State U., 1973, MA in English, 1994. Bur. chief Palm Beach Post, 1970; gen. reporter Daytona Beach News-Jour., 1973; contract editor Frankfurt, Germany, 1973-74; reporter North Dade County bur. Miami Herald, 1977-78; journalist Nat. Enquirer, 1978-89; travel editor Petite Mag., 1992; tchr. journalism, TV journalism, cinema, TV prodn. Fla. State U., 1971-73. Contract writer: Football Little Big Leaguers, 1990, More Baseball Little Big Leagues, 1991; freelance writer newspapers and mags.; appearances on local TV shows; interviewee nat. programs; producer TV programs for local ednl. TV; scriptwriter Future Shock; screenwriter 4 movie scripts. Polit. press sec. Mayor Kevin White, Boston, 1974-75; pub. affairs dir. Boston Community Schs., 1975; campaign pres sec. State Rep. Joseph Timilty, 1975; pub. affairs dir. Barry U., Miami, 1976-77; sports info. dir. Quantico Marines football and basketball programs, 1968. With USMC, 1968-70, Vietnam.

MULHOLLAN, PAIGE ELLIOTT, academic administrator emeritus; b. Ft. Smith, Ark., Dec. 10, 1934; s. Paige Elwood and Ruth Dickinson (Berry) M.; m. Mary Bess Flack, July 8, 1956; children: Paige E. Jr., Kelly V. BBA, U. Ark., 1956, MA in History, 1962; PhD in History, U. Tex., 1966. From asst. to assoc. prof. history U. Ark., Fayetteville, 1963-70; assoc. dean arts and scis. Kans. State U., Manhattan, 1970-73; dean arts and scis. U. Okla., Norman, 1973-78; provost, v.p. acad. affairs Ariz. State U., Tempe, 1978-81, exec. v.p., 1981-85; pres. Wright State U., Dayton, Ohio, 1985-94; ret., 1994; cons. examiner North Ctrl. Assn., Chgo., 1972-94; chair Interuniv. Coun. Ohio, 1993-94. Mem. Okla. Humanities Com., 1974-77, chmn., 1975-77; bd. dirs. Pub. Sta. WPTD-TV, Dayton Art Inst., Miami Valley Rsch. Found., Coastal Discovery Mus., Hilton Head Island, 1995—; mem. adv. com. Air Force ROTC, 1989-93. 1st lt. U.S. Army, 1956-57. Mem. nat. Assn. State Univs. and Land Grant Colls. (commn. on arts and scis. 1973-78, chmn. 1974-76), Am. Assn. State Colls. and Univs. (bd. dirs. 1991-92), Coun. Colls. Arts and Scis. (bd. dirs. 1976-78, sec.-treas. 1977-78), Dayton Area C. of C., Ohio Coll. Assn. (pres. 1989), Rotary (Hilton Head bd. dirs. 1996—). Home: 24 Big Woods Dr Hilton Head Island SC 29926

MULHOLLAND, ANGELA BROADWAY, lawyer; b. Charleston, S.C., Sept. 22, 1957; d. Reid Archie and Althea (Sineath) Broadway; m. R. Mark Mulholland, June 25, 1989; children: Kristina Lucille, Robert Reid. BS, Med. U. S.C., 1980; JD, U. S.C., 1983. Bar: S.C. 1983. Law clk. Law Office Donald Rothwell, Columbia, part-time, 1981-82; assoc. Law Office Wheeler M. Tillman, Charleston, S.C., 1983-86, Tillman & McConnell, 1987-88; ptnr. McConnell & Mulholland, 1988—. Mem. ABA, S.C. Bar Assn., Charleston County Bar Assn., S.C. Hist. Soc., Phi Delta Phi. Avocations: photography, travel, sailing. Office: McConnell & Mulholland 1535 Sam Rittenberg Blvd Ste A Charleston SC 29407

MULKEY, CARROLE ANNE, marketing communications professional; b. Orlando, Fla., Nov. 18, 1947; d. Thomas Wayne and Florence Elizabeth (Boone) M.; m. Robert Lewis Altemus, Jan. 22, 1968 (div. June 1977); children: Jennifer Kent, Adria Leigh; m. John Gregory Ange, Dec. 31, 1988. Student, Phila. Coll. of Art, 1968-69, Md. Sch. of Art, 1970-71, U. of New Orleans, 1980-83; cert., East Carolina U., 1986. Prodn. artist Montgomery County Bill, Gaithersburg, Md., 1972-73; asst. art dir. Altemus Studio, Washington, 1973-79; assoc. art dir. Sta. WYES-TV, New Orleans, 1979-80; owner, creative dir. CAM Graphics, New Orleans, 1980-84; art dept. mgr. Morgan Printers, Greenville, N.C., 1984-89; mktg. mgr. Kircher & Assocs., Greenville, 1989-90; mktg. comms. mgr. Teledyne Thermatics, Elm City, N.C., 1990-92, Linpac Plastics, Wilson, N.C., 1993—. Designer: (poster) Nutcracker New Orleans Ballet, 1982, (booklet) A Guide to Greenville Mus. of Art, 1985 (1st place award 1986), (materials) United Way Regional Campaign, 1986 (Bronze Addy award 1987). Apptd. mem. Women's Commn. of Pitt County, Greenville, 1988-92; community edn. chair Pitt County Family Violence Program, Greenville, 1986-90; task force spkr., presenter N.C. Gov.'s Commn. on Crime, Greenville, 1986; co-publicity chair So. Flue-Cured Tobacco Festival, Greenville, 1985-87; judge Blue Pencil awards Nat. Assn. Govt. Communicators, Washington, 1978; vice chair for bus. of Small Entrepreneurs, Pitt County C. of C., 1990; chrmn. of bd. Keep Am. Beautiful for Wilson County, 1996-97; chairperson 25th Anniversary Earth Day, Wilson, N.C. 1994—; mem. formation com. for devel. of women's commission of Wilson Co. sponsored by NCCounc. for Women, 1996. Recipient Silver Addy award Advt. Fedn., Greenville, 1990, Bronze Addy award, 1987, 88, 90, Certs. of Merit, Internat. Broadcast Assn., 1980, Art Dirs. Club, Washington, 1975. Mem. Am. Mktg. Assn., Am. Bus. Womens Assn., Meeting Planners Internat. Episcopalian. Office: Linpac Plastics P O Box 3611 1901 S Tarboro St Wilson NC 27895-3611

MULKEY, CHARLES ERIC, environmental engineer; b. Sweetwater, Tenn., Jan. 27, 1955; s. Charles Franklin and Margaret Elizabeth (Autry) M. BA in Natural Scis., Johns Hopkins U., 1976; MS in Environ. Engring., U. Del., 1978. Registered profl. engr., Tenn.; cert. hazardous materials mgr.; diplomate Am. Acad. Environ. Engrs. Environ. engr. II TVA Water Quality Dept., Chattanooga, 1978-79, environ. engr. III, 1979-81, environ. engr. IV, 1981-87; environ. engr. IV TVA Watts Bar Nuclear Plant, Spring City, Tenn., 1987-88; sr. environ. engr. Watts Bar Nuclear Plant TVA Water Quality Dept., Spring City, Tenn., 1988-90; sr. environ. engr. PAI Corp., Oak Ridge, Tenn., 1990, Oak Ridge Nat. Lab., 1990—. Author tech. reports in field; contbr. articles to profl. jours. Publicity chmn. Chattanooga Engrs. Week, 1983-87. Maj. USAFR, 1994—. Recipient Davis fellowship U. Del., Newark, 1976-77, state scholarship, State of Md., Annapolis, 1972-76. Fellow ASCE; mem. NSPE (Nat. Publicity award 1984), Tenn. Soc. Profl. Engrs. (state dir. 1990-91, pres. Chattanooga chpt. 1989-90, v.p. 1988-89, sec. 1987-88, treas. 1986-87, young engrs. chmn. 1984-86), Water Environ. Fedn., Am. Acad. Hazardous Materials Mgrs., Res. Officers Assn. (life), Air Force Assn. (life), Chattanooga Engrs. Club, U.S. Triathlon Fedn., U.S. Masters Swimming, Masons. Republican. Presbyterian. Office: Oak Ridge Nat Lab MS 6049 Bldg 2001 Oak Ridge TN 37831-6049

MULKEY, JACK CLARENDON, library director; b. Shreveport, La., Oct. 31, 1939; s. Jack Youmans and Hilda Lillian (Beatty) M.; m. Mary Lynn Shepherd, Jan. 30, 1971; 1 child, Mary Clarendon. B.A., Centenary Coll., 1961; postgrad. (Rotary scholar), U. Dijon, France, 1961-62, Duke U. Law Sch., 1962-63; M.S., La. State U., 1969. Jr. exec. Lykes Bros. S.S. Co., 1964-66; asst. dir. admissions Centenary Coll. of La., 1966-67; head reference services and acquisitions Shreveport Pub. Library, 1968-71; dir. Green Gold Library System of N.W. La., 1971-73; mgmt. cons. Miss. Library Commn., 1973-74, asst. dir., 1974-76, dir., 1976-78; dir. Jackson Met. Library System, 1978-85; assoc. dir. Ark. State Library, 1986—; adj. prof. U. So. Miss. Grad. Sch. Library Sci., 1979—; treas., bd. dirs. Southeastern Library Network (SOLINET), 1985-86; cons. in field; mem. White House Conf. Taskforce on Libraries and Info. Services, 1980—. Chmn. Miss. Govs. Conf. on Libraries, 1979; chmn. Miss. delegation White House Conf. on Libraries, 1979; hon. del. White House Conf. on Librs., 1991. Served with USAF, 1963-64. Mem. ALA (chmn. state libr. agy. sect. 1995-97), Southeastern Libr. Assn., Miss. Libr. Assn. (pres. 1981-82), Ark. Libr. Assn. (exec. bd. dirs. 1994-96), Chief Officers of State Libr. Agys., Phi Alpha Delta, Beta Phi Mu, Omicron Delta Kappa, Phi Kappa Phi. Episcopalian. Home: 1805 Martha Dr Little Rock AR 72212-3840 Office: 1 Capitol Mall Little Rock AR 72201

MULLANAX, MILTON GREG, lawyer; b. Galveston, Tex., Mar. 16, 1962; s. Milton Gayle and Sharon Kay (Sanders) M.; m. Susan Lynn Griebe, Apr. 19, 1986; 1 child, Adrienne Irene. BA in History, U. Tex., Arlington, 1987; JD, U. Pacific, 1991. Bar: Calif., 1991, Nev., 1992, Tex., 1993, Colo., 1993, Minn., 1994, D.C., 1993; U.S. Dist. Ct. (ea. dist.) Calif. 1991, U.S. Dist. Ct. Nev., 1993. Congrl. intern U.S. Rep. Richard K. Armey, Arlington, Tex., 1985; senate aide U.S. Sen. Phil Gramm, Dallas, 1985-86; legis. aide State Rep. Kent Grusendorf, Austin, Tex., 1987; law clk. Criminal Divsn. U.S. Atty., Sacramento, 1989-90; legal researcher Nev. Atty. Gen., Carson City, 1991-92, dep. atty. gen., 1992-94; pvt. practice Fort Worth, Tex., 1995—. Vol. Reagan/Bush 1984, Dallas/Ft. Worth, 1984, Rep. Nat. Conv., Dallas, 1984, Armey for Congress, Arlington, 1984, Vol. Lawyers of Washoe County, Reno, Nev., 1993-94. Mem. ABA, ATLA, Tarrant County Bar Assn. Office: 111 N Houston St Ste 205 Fort Worth TX 76102

MULLE, GEORGE ERNEST, petroleum geologist; b. Collingswood, N.J., Dec. 21, 1919; s. George Melvin and Eleanor (Matilda) (Clevenger) M.; m. Molly Elizabeth Jones, Nov. 17, 1950; children: Alan Russell, David George, William Ernest. Student Rutgers U., 1942-44; A.B. in Earth Scis., U. Pa., 1948. Cert. petroleum geologist, Tex. Geologist, Tide Water Oil Co., Houston and Corpus Christi, 1948-51; dist. geologist La Gloria Oil & Gas Co., Corpus Christi, Tex., 1952-60; ptnr. Santa Rosa Gas Co., 1960-62; pvt. practice geology, Corpus Christi, 1962-73, 75-80, 83—; v.p. Corpus Christi Mgmt. Co., 1973-75; exploration mgr. So. Tex., Mormac Energy Corp., 1980-82. Pres. Palm Harbor Property Owners Assn., Rockport, Tex., 1984, 90, 91, 92, Bahia Log Libr., Corpus Christi, 1980, Santa Fe Log Libr., Corpus Christi, 1981; sec.-treas. The Villas of Harbor Oaks Owners Assn., 1985-88, v.p., 1992-96; del. People-to-People Petroleum Tech., People's Republic China, 1983. Served with USN, 1944-46. Author, spec. editor AAPG symposium natural gases N.Am., 1968. Mem. Corpus Christi Geol. Soc. (author book 1967), Soc. Ind. Profl. Earth Scientists (chmn. Corpus Christi chpt. 1995). Republican. Baptist. Avocation: photography. Home: 121 Ocean Dr Rockport TX 78382-9405

MULLEN, ANDREW JUDSON, physician; b. Selma, Ala., June 23, 1923; s. Andrew J. and Helen (Johnson) M.; A.B., Vanderbilt U., 1948; M.D., Jefferson Med. Coll., 1952; children: J. Thomas, Debbie, Gail, Andrea, Shawn, Connie, Beth. Intern, U.S. Marine Hosp., Galveston, Tex., 1952-53; resident Tex. Med. Center, Houston, 1954-57; chief neurology and psychiatry service VA Hosp., Jackson, Miss., 1957; dir. Mobile (Ala.) Mental Health Center, 1957-58; practice medicine, specializing in psychiatry and neurology, Shreveport, La., 1958—; chief female service Confederate Meml. Med. Center, 1959-63, bd. dirs., chmn. pub. rels. com., 1964-72; med. dir. Shreveport Child Guidance Center, 1961-64; mem. med. adv. bd. Humana Corp.; cons. psychiatry and neurology Barksdale AFB, VA Hosp.; chief staff Brentwood Neuro-Psychiat. Hosp., Shreveport, 1970-73; clin. prof. psychiatry La. State U. Sch. Medicine, 1975—. Dep. coroner, cons., Caddo Parish, La., 1964; chmn. mental health com. Community Council, 1964—; chmn. bd. dirs. Brentwood Hosp., Shreveport, 1982-84, chief med. staff, 1985-86; bd. dirs. Humana, Brentwood hosps., 1986—; psychiat. dir. Charter Outreach Program, Shreveport, 1987—; chief of staff, med. dir. Charter Forest Hosp, 1988—, Caddo Oaks Hosp., 1993—; charter Forest Hosp. 1988-94. With RCAF, 1941-42, Sgt. AUS, 1942-45. Decorated Purple Heart with oak leaf cluster, Bronze Star. Diplomate Am. Bd. Psychiatry and Neurology (asso. examiner). Fellow Am., So. psychiat. assns., Am. Coll. Psychiatrists; mem. AMA, So. Med. Assn., Shreveport Med. Soc. (dir. 1971-72), Am. Soc. Psychol Analytical Physicians, Flying Physicians Assn., Alpha Tau Omega, Nu Sigma Nu. Episcopalian. Home: 241 Symphony Ln Shreveport LA 71105-4143 Office: 745 Olive St Ste 203 Shreveport LA 71104-2246

MULLEN, CORAZON ALIP, librarian; b. Manila, Philippines, Sept. 6, 1932; came to U.S., 1956; d. Edmigio Melo Alip and Paquita (Bernarte) Mendoza; m. John Paul Mullen, Feb. 20, 1956; children: Gregory P., Cynthia P. Barker, David P., Myra P. BS, U. Philippines, 1955; MLS, Fla. State U., 1972. Reference libr. Pensacola (Fla.) Naval Air Base, 1963-64; cataloger Pensacola Pub. Libr., 1964-65; cataloger Jacksonville (Fla.) Pub. Libr., 1965-69, reference libr., 1969-71, mgr. Westbrook br., 1972, sr. mgr. Northside br., 1973-86, dept. mgr. Mandarin br., 1986—. Mem. Jacksonville Suprs. Assn. (bd. dirs. 1988—), Duval County Libr. Assn. (pres.), U. of Philippines Alumni Assn. Am. (pres. Fla. chpt. 1992-94), Beta Phi Mu. Democrat. Mem. Ch. of Christ. Home: 3756 Julington Creek Rd Jacksonville FL 32223-3715 Office: Mandarin Br Jacksonville Pub Libr 3330 Kori Rd Jacksonville FL 32257-5454

MULLEN, GRAHAM C., federal judge; b. 1940. BA, Duke U., 1962, JD, 1969. Bar: N.C. 1969. Ptnr. Mullen, Holland, Cooper, Morrow, Wilder & Sumner, 1969-90; judge U.S. Dist. Ct. (we. dist.) N.C., Charlotte, 1990—. Lt. USN, 1962-66. Mem. N.C. Bar Assn. (bd. govs. 1983-88), Mecklenburg County Bar Assn. Office: US Courthouse 401 W Trade St Charlotte NC 28202-1619

MULLEN, PHILIP EDWARD, artist, educator; b. Akron, Ohio, Oct. 10, 1942; s. Philip Edward and Margaret Virginia (Williams) M.; children: Vanessa Jay, Dana Rachel. BA, U. Minn., 1964; MA, U. N.D., 1966; PhD, Ohio U., 1970. Prof. U. S.C., Columbia, 1969—. One man shows include Hunter Mus. Art, Chattanooga, 1972, 85, Franz Bader Gallery, Washington, 1974, Heath Gallery, Atlanta, 1974, 77, David Findlay Galleries, N.Y.C., 1976, 78, 80, 82, 83, 85, 95, 96, A.D.I. Gallery, San Francisco, 1979, Dubins Gallery, L.A., 1979, 80, 82, 83, 85, 86, 88, 89, 91, Suzanne Brown Gallery, Scottsdale, 1981, Traveling Mus. Exhbn., Columbia Mus. of Art, 1984-85, Schmidt Bingham Gallery, N.Y., 1987, Malton Galler, Cin., 1981, 84, 89, Carol Saunders Gallery, Columbia, 1992, 95, Koger Ctr. Performing Arts, Columbia, 1990, 94-96, Eva Cohon Gallery, Highland Park, 1986, 88, 89, 91, Chgo., 1988, 89, 91; exhibited in group shows at Whitney Mus., N.Y., Bklyn. Mus., Smithsonian Traveling Show, San Francisco Mus. Art, Randolph Macon Women's Coll., U.S. Info. Agy. Travel Show, Japan; represented in permanent collections Solomon R. Guggenheim Mus., N.Y., Bklyn. Mus., Palm Springs (Calif.) Desert Mus., Denver Art Mus., Byer Mus. Arts, Evanston, Ill., Sonje Mus. Contemporary Art, Korea, Hunter Mus. Art, Chattanooga, Neiman Marcus, Dallas, Terra Mus. Am. Art, Evanston, Atlantic Richfield Co., L.A., Columbia Pictures TV, Calif., Hallmark, N.Y., Sheraton Plz. Hotel, Palm Springs, Price Waterhouse & Co., L.A., Chase Manhattan Bank, N.Y., Bank Am., San Francisco, Am. Telephone & Telegraph Co., N.Y., Am. Express, N.J., Crown Prince Fadio Abdulaziz of Saudia Arabia, Neil & Marcia Diamond, L.A., Lincoln Properties, Atlanta, Gen. Electric, N.Y., Vincent Price Gallery, L.A.; illustrator (book covers): Learning and Memory, 1989, Teaching Exceptional Students in Your Classroom, 1989, Foundations of Education, 1995. Home and Office: 5926 Marthas Glen Rd Columbia SC 29209-1345

MULLEN, RUTH GONZÁLEZ, artist, secondary school educator; b. Havana, Cuba, Feb. 11, 1939; came to U.S., 1953; d. Romualdo Eduardo González-Agüeros and Naomi (Diaz-Alvarez) de González; m. Harold Mullen, Aug. 29, 1959; children: Ruth Mabel Forrest, Mark Edward. BA in Art magna cum laude, Auburn U., 1961; MFA, Tulane U., 1969. Grad. fellow Tulane U., New Orleans, 1969; tchr. art Trinity Episcopal Sch., New Orleans, 1970-80; tchr. painting and drawing Isidore Newman Sch., New Orleans, 1980—. One-woman shows include Orleans Gallery, New Orleans, World Trade Ctr.; exhibited in group shows at Studio 8, New Orleans, Mobile (Ala.) Art Gallery (1st prize, Betty McGowin award), Capitol Bldg., Baton Rouge, St. Tammamy Parrish, Covington, La., Contemporary Arts Ctr., New Orleans, 1994, Bienville Gallery, New Orleans, 1995, Latina, 1996, Delgado Coll. Invited participant Met. Area Com.; head aid to victims of hurricane Hugo Operation New Orleans-Viegues, P.R.; past mem. Hispanic coun. Episcopal Ch. Recipient Deposit Guaranty award Cottonlandia Collection, Greenwood, Miss., Applause 1996 award for visual arts (bilingual newspaper) Aqui. Mem. Nat. Assn. Women Artists (N.Y.C.), Cuban Profl. Club (pres. 1980-81), Mortar Bd., Phi Kappa Phi, Alpha Lambda delta. Democrat. Home: 51 Nerón Pl New Orleans LA 70118 Office: Isidore Newman Sch 1903 Jefferson Ave New Orleans LA 70115

MULLENIX, KATHY ANN, relocation company executive; b. Goodland, Ind., Mar. 8, 1955; d. Boyd Dale and Edith Marie Hoaks; 1 child, Joseph F. Hamburg IV. Diploma, South Newton Jr./Sr. H.S., Goodland, Ind., 1973. Asst. to pres. Planes Moving, Cin., 1981-88; sales mgr. Tru-Pak Moving, Greenville, S.C., 1988-89; account exec. Armstrong Relocation, Atlanta, 1989—. Den leader Cub Scouts, Blue Ash, Ohio, 1982-86; coach's asst. Soccer Assn., Mason, Ohio, 1985-88; treas. PTA Mason Mid. Sch., 1988; tutor Gwinnette Co. Adult Literacy, Lawrenceville, Ga., 1994. Mem. NAFE. Office: Armstrong Relocation 6950 Business Ct Atlanta GA 30340-1429

MULLER, FRANK MAIR, III, industrial engineer; b. Ft. Belvoir, Va., June 24, 1966; s. Frank Mair Jr. and Patricia Ann (Felter) M.; m. Lisa Lynn Supercinski, June 30, 1990; 1 child, Whitney Rebekah. BS in Indsl. Engring., Tex. A&M U., 1988. Project mgr., engr. Conoco, Inc., 1988-92; vessel inspection program mgr. Industrial NDT Co., Inc., Tex., 1992-93; dist. rep. Nalco Chem. Co., Sugarland, Tex., 1993—. Pres. Meml. Student Ctr. Coun.; v.p. ops. Meml. Student Ctr. Coun.; co-chmn. TAMU Fish Camp. Recipient Chmn.'s award for Leadership, Buck Weirus Spirit/Leadership award. Home: 16343 Rainbow Lake Houston TX 77095

MULLER, FREDERICA DANIELA, psychology educator; d. Leopold and Elena; m. Dr. L. Muller; children: Daniela, Adrian. Grad., Med. Inst. Radiology, Romania, 1962, PsyD in Clin. Psychology, 1965, M in Internat. Law and Bus., 1966; specialization courses in Psychodrama, Moreno Inst., Vienna, 1969; grad., Inst. Rsch. in Aging, Rome, 1970, Miami Inst. Psychology, 1987. Diplomate Am. Bd. Forensic Medicine, Am. Bd. Forensic Examiners; lic. psychologist, Pa.; lic. psychotherapist, Fla.; cert. family mediator, Fla. Supreme Ct. continuing edn. units provider psych. Prof. Sch. Continuing Edn. Barry U., North Miami, Fla.; instr. advanced courses in psychology, psychodrama, med. ethics, social manners; guest speaker Colloque Internat., Bucharest, Romania, 1989-93; guest lectr. U. Arboga, Sweden 1968-72; founder Internat. Studies for Biopsychosocial Issues, 1991; cons. dept. of marriage, family and child devel. systemic studies, Nova U., 1992; founder Euro Am. Exch. Co., 1980; with Santé Internat., Switzerland, 1982-85; dir. Ctr. Biopsychosocial Medicine, 1995. Conducted rsch. on stress and aging with Dr. Anna Aslan, world renowned author; developed 45 minute stress reduction program for use in the work place. Author: The Management of Occupational Stress and Its Linkage to Social Pressures; contbr. articles to profl. jours. Mem. APA, Medicins du Monde (hon.), Am. Soc. Group Psychotherapy and Psychodrama, Soc. Psychol., Studies Social of Issues, World Fedn. for Mental Health.

MULLER, JULIUS FREDERICK, chemist, business administrator; b. Bklyn., Sept. 5, 1900; s. Edward Jefferson and Julia (Lang) M.; m. Ethel Mae Johnson, June 18, 1927; children: Richard J., J. Edward, James H. BS, Rutgers U., 1922, MSc, 1928, PhD, 1930. Mgr. Princewick Farm, Franklin Park, N.J., 1922-26; rsch. fellow Walker-Gordon Labs., Plainsboro, N.J., 1930-32; bacteriologist Nat. Oil Products Co., Harrison, N.J., 1932-35; owner, mgr. Muller Labs., Balt., 1935-41; div. mgr. Borden, Inc., N.Y.C., 1941-65; cons. Borden, Inc., N.Y.C., 1965-68. Contbr. articles to profl. jours. Fellow Am. Inst. Chemists, mem. Am. Chem. Soc. (emeritus), Alpha Zeta, Sigma Xi. Republican. Presbyterian. Home: # 313 5700 Williamsburg Landing Dr Williamsburg VA 23185-3779

MULLER, LLOYD HOLDEN, logistics and education consultant; b. Flint, Mich., Sept. 4, 1939; s. Lloyd Ernest and Margaret Jane (Holden) M.; m. Sigrid Anna Hasenknopf, June 20, 1964; children: Heidi Catherine Muller Torre, Stephanie Ann Muller. BA, Denison U., 1964; MS, U. So. Calif., L.A., 1969; EdD, George Washington U., 1982. Commd. 2d lt. USAF, 1964, advanced through grades to col., 1988, ret., 1991; ctr. dir., adj. asst. prof. Embry-Riddle Aero U., Daytona Beach, Fla., 1991-93; cons. Muller Enterprises, Alexandria, Va., 1991—. Mem. Soc. of Logistics Engrs. (D.C. chpt. edn. chmn. 1993—), Profl. Ski Instrs. of Am. Home and Office: 6260 Chaucer Ln Alexandria VA 22304

MULLER, MAX PAUL, artist, educator; b. Dover, N.J., Sept. 26, 1935; s. Max Paul Sr. and Elsie (Drexel) M.; m. Dolores Maria Johnson, Sept. 24, 1961; children: Jeffrey, Mark. BA, W.Va. Wesleyan U., Buckhannon, 1957. In lettering and layout design O'Mealia Advt., Dover, 1959-61; advt. and art dept. pres. Aristo Aluminum, Lake Hopatcong, N.J., 1961-88; pres., curator art gallery M.P. Muller Showcase of Fine Art, Sarasota, Fla., 1988-91; exec. dir. Sarasota Visual Art Ctr., 1991-96; pres. Muller Art Studios, Sarasota, 1996—; pres. Art Uptown Galleries, Sarasota, 1992-95. Exhibited in shows at Fla. Watercolor Soc., Fla. So. U., S.W. Fla. All Media Exhbn., Longboat Key, W.Va. Wesleyan Coll., Charlotte County Art Guild, Mcht. Marine Acad., Hunts Point, N.Y., Walt Disney World/EPCOT Invitational, numerous others; represented in collections at Sarasota Yacht Club, Sarasota Opera, Inc., Grumbacher Corp. Hdqrs., numerous pvt. collections. With U.S. Army, 1957-59, Germany. Recipinet awards for art. Mem. Am. Watercolor Soc. (assoc.), So. Watercolor Soc., Fla. Watercolor Soc. (signature mem., v.p. 1995), Internat. Soc. Marine Painters (signature mem.), Fla. Artists Group (signature mem.), Sarasota Art Assn. Home: 6902 Stetson St Cir Sarasota FL 34243

MULLER, PATRICIA ANN, nursing administrator, educator; b. N.Y.C., July 22, 1943; d. Joseph H. and Rosanne (Bautz) Felter; m. David G. Smith, Mar. 19, 1988; children: Frank M. Muller III, Kimberly M. Muller. BSN, Georgetown U., 1965; MA, U. Tulsa, 1978, EdD, 1983. RN. Staff devel. coord. St. Francis Hosp., Tulsa, 1978-79, asst. dir. for nursing svc., nursing edn., 1979-82, dir. dept. edn., 1982—; presenter various confs. and convs., 1978—. Contbr. articles to profl. jours. Mem. Leadership Tulsa, 1991. Mem. ANA, Nat. League for Nursing, Am. Soc. for Nursing Svc. Administrs., Am. Soc. for Health Manpower Edn. and Tng., Okla. Nurses

Assn., Okla. Orgn. of Nurse Execs. (pres. 1992-93), Sigma Theta Tau. Office: Saint Francis Hosp 6161 S Yale Ave Tulsa OK 74136-1902

MULLER, ROBERT JOSEPH, gynecologist; b. New Orleans, Dec. 5, 1946; s. Robert Harry and Camille (Eckert) M.; m. Susan Philipsen, Aug. 22, 1974; children: Ryan, Matt. BS, St. Louis U., 1968; BS, MSc, Emory U., 1976; MD, La. State U., New Orleans, 1981. Intern Charity Hosp., New Orleans, 1981-82; resident La. State U. Affiliate Hosp., 1982-85; resident staff physician La. State U. Med. Ctr., New Orleans, 1981-85; pvt. practice Camellia Women's Ctr., Slidell, La., 1985—; staff physician Tulane Med. Ctr., New Orleans, 1986—; med. dir. Northshore Regional Med. Ctr., Slidell, 1987—, New Orleans Police Dept., 1981-95, S.W. La. Search and Rescue, Covington, La., 1986—, St. Tammany Parish Sheriff Dept., Covington, 1989—, commdr., 1990—, Camellia City Classic, Slidell, 1989—, Crawfishman Triathalon, Mandeville, La., 1988—, Res-Q-Med Laser Team, 1984—. Contbr. articles to profl. jours. Recipient Commendation Medal New Orleans Police Dept., 1986, 87, 89, Medal Valor St. Tammany Parish Sheriff Office, Covington, 1990, Cert. Valor S.E. La. Search and Rescue, Mandeville, 1990; named one of Outstanding Young Men of Am., 1984. Mem. Am. Coll. Ob-Gyn., La. State Med. Soc., Profl. Assn. Diving Instrs. (divemaster 1991, asst. instr. 1995), So. Offshore Racing Assn. (med. dir. 1982—), Offshore Profl. Racing Tour (med. dir. staff 1990—), Am. Power Boat Assn. (med. staff 1984-89). Roman Catholic. Home: 128 Golden Pheasant Dr Slidell LA 70461-3007 Office: Camellia Womens Ctr 105 Smart Pl Slidell LA 70458-2039

MULLER, WILLIAM ALBERT, III, library director; b. Savannah, Ga., Jan. 1, 1943; s. William Albert Jr. and Julia Catherine (Cleary) M.; m. Claudya Barbara Burkett, Dec. 12, 1965 (div. 1986); 1 child, Martha Genevieve; m. Pamala Qualls, Apr. 9, 1988; 1 child, Tabitha Rodgers. BA, Ga. So. Coll., 1966; MLS, Emory U., 1969. Dir. War Woman Regional Libr., Elberton, Ga., 1969-73; rsch. libr. City of Savannah, 1973-75; dir. Mason County Pub. Libr., Point Pleasant, W.Va., 1976-78; pub. rels. cons. Eastern Shore Regional Libr., Salisbury, Md., 1978-81; dir. Brooke County Pub. Libr., Wellsburg, W.Va., 1982-84, McDowell Pub. Libr., Welch, W.Va., 1984-88, Bristol (Va.) Pub. Libr., 1988—; sec. So. W.Va. Libr. Automation Corp., Beckley, 1984-87, pres. 1987-88, S.W. Info. Network Group, Abingdon, Va., 1990-91, treas. (swing) 1993—. Fundraiser Paramount Found., Bristol, 1989; acct. exec. United Way of Bristol, 1991; bd. dirs. Mid-Atlantic Chamber Orch., Bristol, 1988-92, treas., 1992; bd. dirs. Bristol Preservation Soc., 1988—, Nat. Ctr. for Quality, 1992, Main St. Bristol, 1991-95, treas., 1994. Mem. ALA, Southeastern Libr. Assn., Va. Libr. Assn., Rotary Internat. (club pres. 1980-81). Democrat. Home: 706 Piedmont Ave Bristol VA 24201-3446 Office: Bristol Pub Libr 701 Goode St Bristol VA 24201-4155

MULLER, YVONNE, artist; b. Ann Arbor, Mich., June 8, 1943; d. Jerome and Elizabeth Conn; 1 child, Nicole Claudia Muller. BFA, Syracuse U., 1971; MFA, Bard Coll., 1996. guest cinematographer Wells Coll., Aurora, N.Y., 1967; vis. artist Duke U., 1983-84, 85-86. One woman shows include Tibor de Nagy Gallery, N.Y.C., 1975, 78, 80, 85, Duke U. Mus. Art, Durham, N.C., 1983, 85, Gina Farahnick Fine Art, N.Y.C., 1988, La Galerie Les z'Arts, Les Cerqueux Sous Passavant, France, 1994; exhibited in group shows at SUNY, Cortland, N.Y., 1974, Herbert F. Johnson Mus. Art, Cornell U., Ithaca, N.Y., 1974, 82, Everson Mus. Art, Syracuse, N.Y., 1976, 80, Tibor de Nagy Gallery, N.Y.C., 1976-86, Armstrong Gallery, N.Y.C., 1986, Matrix Gallery, Austin, Tex., 1989, N.C. Mus. Art, Raleigh, 1990; represented in permanent collections AT&T, N.Y.C., Duke Univ. Medical Ctr., Durham, N.C., Edmonton Art Gallery, Alta., Can., Agnes Etherington Art Ctr. Queens U., Kingston, Ont., Can., Herbert F. Johnson Mus. Art, Cornell U., Ithaca, N.Y., Lloyds Bank, Calif.; commd. by New Performing Dance Co., Durham, 1985, 86; cinematographer Tales of Hoffman, 1966, Wells May Well Be, 1967, Solitaire, 1968. CAPS grant for painting, N.Y., 1973. Home: 4100 Five Oaks Dr # 40 Durham NC 27707 also: Old Chelsea Sta PO Box 1096 New York NY 10113-1096

MULLIKIN, KENT ROBERTS, academic administrator; b. Washington, Mar. 13, 1942; s. Kent Roberts and Winifred (Cary) M.; m. Miriam Murchie, Sept. 22, 1973; children: Anna Hilary, Sarah Winifred. BA, Princeton U., 1964; MLitt, Trinity Coll., Dublin, Ireland, 1968; PhD, U. N.C., 1976. Asst. dir. Nat. Humanities Ctr., Rsch. Triangle Pk., N.C., 1980-88, acting dir., 1988-89, assoc. dir., 1989-93, dep. dir., 1993-96, v.p., dep. dir., 1996—. Episcopalian. Home: 101 Windsor Place Chapel Hill NC 27516 Office: National Humanities Center 7 Alexander Dr Durham NC 27711

MULLIKIN, THOMAS WILSON, mathematics educator; b. Flintville, Tenn., Jan. 9, 1928; s. Houston Yost and Daisy (Copeland) M.; m. Mildred Virginia Sugg, June 14, 1952; children—Sarah Virginia, Thomas Wilson, James Copeland. Student, U. South, 1946-47; A.B., U. Tenn., 1950; post-grad., Iowa State U., 1952-53; A.M., Harvard, 1954, Ph.D., 1958. Mathematician Rand Corp., Santa Monica, Calif., 1957-64; prof. math. Purdue U., 1964-93, interim v.p., dean grad. sch., 1991-93, dean grad. sch., prof. math emeritus, 1993—. Served with USNR, 1950-52. Mem. Am. Math. Soc., Soc. for Indsl. and Applied Math., AASS, Sigma Xi. Home: Cape Carteret 104 Club Ct Swansboro NC 28584-9736

MULLIN, PATRICK JOSEPH, librarian; b. Kansas City, Mo., Mar. 31, 1948; s. Michael Edward and Rosalee (Jarvies) M.; m. Ann Frances Greenwell, Jan. 29, 1972. BA, U. Notre Dame, 1970; MA, Purdue U., 1972; MS in Libr. Sci., U. Ky., 1973. Spl. collection libr. Marietta (Ohio) Coll., 1973-77; mktg. rep. OCLC Online Computer Libr. Ctr., Dublin, Ohio, 1977-87; acting dir. Triangle Rsch. Librs. Network, Chapel Hill, N.C., 1988-91; systems libr. U. N.C., Chapel Hill, 1987-90, asst. univ. libr., 1990-94, assoc. univ. libr. for access svcs. and systems, 1994—. Author: Ohio Census Population Schedules, 1977, (with others) AACR2 and it's Impact on Libraries, 1980; contbr. articles to profl. jours. Home: 513 Farmington Wood Dr Cary NC 27511-5647 Office: Univ NC at Chapel Hill CB #3900 Davis Libr Chapel Hill NC 27514-8890

MULLINGS, ARNOLD R., engineering manager; b. Staten Island, N.Y., Aug. 10, 1932. BSMe, Tri-State U., Angola, Ind., 1964; MBA, Wayne State U., 1978. Engineering mgr. Uni Royal, Detroit, 1967-71, Atlas Copco, Sterling Heights, Mich., 1971-91, AFS, Sterling Heights, 1991. Petty officer 1st class U.S. Navy, 1951-55. Home: 3053 Brandy Ln Sanford NC 27330-7421

MULLINS, DON ELROY, economics educator; b. Sherman, Tex., Nov. 27, 1939; s. Byron Elroy and Virgie Frances (Pratt) M.; m. Marsha Lorene Carpenter, Oct. 6, 1962 (div. June 1977); 1 child, Reade Alan. BA in Fine Arts, U. North Tex., Denton, 1963; MS in Econs./Ind. Mgmt., U. N.D., 1971; postgrad., U. Tex. at Dallas, Plano, 1989—. Commd. 2d lt. USAF, 1963, advanced through grades to maj., 1973, ret., 1983; prof. econs. Grayson County Coll., Denison, Tex., 1986—; advisor and tutor in econs. and bus. Sherman (Tex.) H.S., 1990-95. Mem. Republican Presdl. Task Force, Washington, 1986. Decorated Bronze Star medal. Mem. Air Force Assn. (life), Assn. Air Force Missilers, Tex. Jr. Coll. Tchrs. Assn. Republican. Office: Grayson County Coll 6101 Grayson Dr Denison TX 75020

MULLINS, WAYMAN C., psychologist, educator, consultant; b. Little Rock, Nov. 10, 1951; s. William Wayman and Mary Anna (Beall) M.; m. Louise C. Casey, Aug. 2, 1976; children: Ruth, Rachael. BA, U. Ark., 1978, MA, 1979, PhD in Psychology, 1983. Diplomate in police psychology. Teaching and rsch. asst. U. Ark., Fayetteville, 1977-82; asst. prof. psychology Hofstra U., Hempstead, N.Y., 1982-84; asst. prof. criminal justice S.W. Tex. State U., San Marcos, 1984-87, assoc. prof., 1987-93, prof., 1993—; cons. San Antonio Police Dept., 1984—, U.S. Govt., 1987—. Author: Terrorist Organizations in the U.S., 1988, 1942: Issue in Doubt, 1994, Crisis Management, 1996; editor Jour. Police and Criminal Psychology, 1984-95; contbr. articles to profl. jours. and books. Pres. N.W. Ark. Vets. Assn., Fayetteville, 1975-77, San Marcos Little League, 1989-94; mem. exec. coun. San Marcos Explorer Post, 1988-93; advisor Criminal Justice Explorer Post #120; res. police officer San Marcos Police Dept., 1987-95; res. deputy with Hays County Sheriff's Dept. Recipient grants. Mem. Soc. Police and Criminal Psychology (pres. 1984-85), Acad. Criminal Justice Scis., Am. Psychol. Assn., Human Factors Soc., Internat. Assn. Chiefs of Police, N.Y. Acad. Scis., Internat. Narcotic Enforcement Officers Assn. Office: SW Tex State U Dept Criminal Justice San Marcos TX 78666

MULVANEY, MARY FREDERICA, systems analyst; b. N.Y., Nov. 27, 1945; d. Michael Joseph and Mary Catherine (Clapper) M. BA, Marymount Coll., 1967; MA, U. Va., 1968. Cert. data processor Inst. Certification of Computer Profls., Ill. Computer systems analyst Dept. of Def., Ft. Meade, Md., 1968-74; sr. programmer analyst Planning Rsch. Corp., McLean, Va., 1974-83; mem. tech. staff Fed. Systems Group TRW Inc., Fairfax, Va., 1983-90; sr. mem. tech. staff GTE Govt. Systems Corp., Rockville, Md., 1990-94; engr., sci. TRW, Inc., Fairfax, Va., 1994—. Mem. IEEE, Data Processing Mgmt. Assn., Computer Measurement Group, Cath. Assn. of Scientists and Engrs. Roman Catholic. Office: TRW Sys Integration Group One Federal Systems Park Dr Fairfax VA 22033

MULVEY, DENNIS MICHAEL, chemist; b. Lockport, N.Y., Nov. 17, 1938; s. James William and Ruth Elizabeth (Hamilton) M.; m. Diane Holdermiller, Aug. 23, 1963 (div. Nov. 1982); children: Kim, Colleen; m. Beverly June Butler, May 21, 1983; stepchildren: Kenneth Hicks, Karen Hicks, Ronald Hicks. AB in Chemistry, U. Pa., 1960; PhD in Organic Chemistry, SUNY, Buffalo, 1964. NIH postdoctoral rsch. assoc. Columbia U., N.Y.C., 1964-65; sr. rsch. chemist Merck, Sharp and Dohme Rsch. Labs., Rahway, N.J., 1965-70, rsch. fellow, 1970-77; group leader Ortho Pharm. Corp., Raritan, N.J., 1977-80, rsch. mgr., 1980-85; tech. support mgr. Molecular Design Ltd., San Leandro, Calif., 1985-86; polymer design mgr. Pennwalt Corp., King of Prussia, Pa., 1986-88; gen. mgr. fine chems. Vega Biotechs., Inc., Tucson, 1988-89; mgr. peptide mfg. ProCyte Corp., Kirkland, Wash., 1989-92; dir. process scis. ISIS Pharms., Carlsbad, Calif., 1992-93; dir. mfg. and process devel. Triplex Pharm. Corp. (now Aronex Pharms., Inc.), The Woodlands, Tex., 1993—; adj. prof. dept. chemistry and biotech. Montgomery County C.C., Conroe, Tex., 1995—; cons. in field. Contbr. articles to profl. publs.; patentee in field. Bd. dirs. Hunt. County Office of Alcoholism, Flemington, 1979-81; vol. fire and rescue squad Oldwick (N.J.) and Milford (N.J.) Squads, 1967-79; v.p. Oak-Tree/Menlo Lions Club, Edison, N.J., 1965-75; v.p. Forest Hills (Tex.) Homeowners Assn., 1994-95, pres., 1996—. Home: 110 Glenmora Ct Conroe TX 77385-9104 Office: Aronex Pharm 9391 Grogans Mill Rd The Woodlands TX 77380-3627

MULVEY, JOHN THOMAS, JR., financial consultant; b. N.Y.C., Mar. 13, 1941; s. John T. and Jeanette (Fox) M.; m. Ruth I. Dieicks, May 5, 1962 (div. June 1982); m. Elaine R. Anderson, Oct. 6, 1984; children: Deborah, Karen, Laura. BA, Westminster Coll., Fulton, Mo., 1972. Corp. trust rsch. clk. Chem. Bank N.Y. Trust Co., 1959-60; asst. dir. personnel Fedn. Bank and Trust Co., 1960-62; personnel rep. Meadow Brook Nat. Bank, 1962-65; controller Reevesound Co., 1965-69; cost control mgr. Veco Instruments, Inc., 1972-74; supr. corp. income tax Mo. Dept. Revenue, 1974-80; asst. treas., controller Sangamon Co., 1980-82; mgr. Ford and Co. CPA, 1982-84; asst. controller Meml. Hosp., 1984-88; fin. cons. Pompano Beach, Fla.; pres. Ardus Real Estate, Inc., Pompano Beach, Fla., Ardus, Inc., Pompano Beach; pres., CEO Atlantic Mgmt. Svcs., Inc., Pompano Beach, Fla. Republican. Episcopalian. Home: 1800 S Ocean Blvd Apt 107 Pompano Beach FL 33062-7915 also: Ardus Inc PO Box 1178 Pompano Beach FL 33061-1178

MUMERT, TOMMY LEE, news bureau director; b. Mammoth Spring, Ark., Oct. 13, 1955; s. Glen Arthur and Susan Frances (Golden) M.; m. Suzanne Linke, Jan. 8, 1982; 1 child, Jeffery Paul. BS, Ark. State U., 1978, MS, 1986. Reporter Stone County Leader, Mountain View, Ark., 1978-79, Newport (Ark.) Ind., 1980-81, Jonesboro (Ark.) Sun, 1981-85; instr. Ark. State U., Jonesboro, 1985-86; editor Stuttgart (Ark.) Daily Leader, 1986-89; news bur. dir. Ark. Tech. U., Russellville, 1989—. Publicity co-chair River Valley United Way, Russellville, 1990-91; publicity com. mem. Boys and Girls Club of River Valley, Russellville, 1991. Recipient 3d Pl. feature photos Ark. Press Assn., 1990, 3d Pl. column writing, 1989. Home: 1309 Ridgewood Dr Russellville AR 72801-2480 Office: Ark Tech U Bryan Hall Russellville AR 72801

MUMFORD, STEPHEN DOUGLAS, population growth control research scientist; b. Louisville, Aug. 28, 1942; s. Adrian Leroy and Mildred Margaret (Cardwell) M.; m. Judy Sheng-Ju Lee, Dec. 26, 1966; children: Christopher Lee, Sonia Lea. BS in Agr., U. Ky., 1966; MPH in Internat. Health/Population Study, U. Tex., Houston, 1971, DrPH in Health Svcs. Adminstrn., 1975. Indsl. hygienist Ky. State Dept. Health, Frankfort, 1966-67; rsch. asst. dept. ob.-gyn. Baylor Coll. Medicine, Houston, 1973-75; rsch. statis. aide population studies U. Tex., Houston, 1971-75, rsch. asst. dept. reproductive biology/endocrinology, 1971-76; dir. rsch., sr. vasectomy counselor Planned Parenthood of Houston, 1972-76; adminstr. Nat. Swine Flu Immunization Program/Houston/Harris County, Tex., 1976-77; from sect. leader design/analysis divsn. to scientist Internat. Fertility Rsch. Program, Research Triangle Park, N.C., 1977-83; pres. Ctr. for Rsch. on Population and Security, Research Triangle Park, N.C., 1984—; bd. dirs. The Churchman Assocs., Inc., St. Petersburg, Fla. Author: The Pope and the New Apocalypse: The Holy War Against Family Planning, 1986, American Democracy and the Vatican: Population Growth and National Security, 1984, Population Growth Control: The Next Move is America's, 1977, The Decision-Making Process that Leads to Vasectomy: A Guide for Promoters, 1977, Vasectomy Counseling, 1977, The Life and Death of NSSM 200: How the Destruction of Political Will Doomed a U.S. Population Policy, 1994; contbr. numerous articles to profl. jours., chpts. to books; contbr. editor The Churchman, 1991—. Mem. Alan Guttmacher Inst., Assn. for Vol. Sterilization, Environ. Def. Fund, Fund for Feminist Majority, Nat. Abortion Rights Action League, Population Action Coun., Population Ref. Bur., Religious Coalition for Abortion Rights. Capt. U.S. Army, 1966-70. Recipient Cert. of Appreciation for Outstanding Contbns. to Advancing the Cause of Reproductive Rights, Feminist Caucus of Am. Humanist Assn., 1986, Humanist Disting. Svc. award, 1981, Margaret Mead Leadership prize in population and ecology, 1981, Award for Outstanding Single Project in Area of Human Rels., U.S. Jaycees, 1974-75, Award for Outstanding Chmn. of a Single Project in Area of Human Rels., 1974-75. Mem. Am. Humanist Assn., Am. Pub. Health Assn. (population sect.), Ams. for Immigration Control, Ams. for Religious Liberty, Fedn. for Am. Immigration Reform, Internat. Epidemiol. Assn., Nat. Coun. Internat. Health, Negative Population Growth, Res. Officers assn. of U.S., Soc. for Epidemiologic Rsch., World Future Soc., World Population Soc., Zero Population Growth, NOW. Home: 322 Azalea Dr Chapel Hill NC 27514-9120 Office: Ctr Rsch Population PO Box 13067 Research Triangle Park NC 27709-3067

MUNCEY, JAMES ARTHUR, JR., architect; b. Dallas, July 9, 1933; s. James Arthur and Thelma (Bush) M.; m. Virginia Diers, Aug. 12, 1955; children: James G., Leah V., Laura E. BArch, Tex. A & M U., 1956. Registered architect, Tex. Design assoc. Wright Rich Assoc. Architects, Dallas, 1958-70; ptnr. Manos & Muncey Architects, Dallas, 1970-80; pres. James A. Muncey Inc., Dallas, 1980—; pres. 4th Generation Inc. Dallas, 1980-87; dir. Mickey Finns Inc. Dallas, 1984-87. 1st Lt. U.S. Army, 1956-58. Mem. AIA, Tex. Soc. Architects. Republican. Episcopalian.

MUNCH-KEEN, MARY VIRGINIA, primary education educator; b. Lake City, Fla., Jan. 24, 1968; d. Oscar Harry Jr. and Revia Yvonne (Coward) M.; m. Richard James Keen, Dec. 10, 1994. AA, Lake City C.C., 1988; BS, Fla. State U., 1991. State FHA/HERO asst. Dept. of Edn., Tallahassee, 1990-91; family and consumer scis. tchr. Dunnellon (Fla.) Mid. Sch., 1991-92, Lake City Mid. Sch., 1992—; FHA advisor, 1991—; family and consumer scis. adv. bd. Coop. Extension, Lake City, 1996—; bd. dirs. Fla. Family and Consumer Scis. Unity Coalition, 1996—. Vol. Guardian Ad Litem. Mem. NEA, Fla. Assn. of Family and Consumer Scis. (state officer, state sec. 1995-97), Am. Assn. of Family and Consumer Scis., Am. Vocat. Assn., Fla. Vocat. Assn., Kappa Omicron Nu. Democrat. Baptist. Office: Lake City Middle Sch Route 18 Box 230 Lake City FL 32025

MUNCY, ESTLE PERSHING, physician; b. Tazewell, Tenn., Apr. 9, 1918; s. William Loyd and Flora Media (Monday) M.; m. Dorothy Davis, Dec. 31, 1946 (div. Apr. 1980); children: Robert H., Teresa A., Dorothy J., Estle II, James; m. Jean Marie Hayter, Mar. 19, 1985. AB, Lincoln Meml. U., 1939; MD, U. Tenn., 1943. Resident Dallas Meth. Hosp., 1948; tchg. resident Tufts Med. Sch., Boston, 1949-50; physician Jefferson City, Tenn., 1950-96. Author: The Muncys in the New World, 1988, People and Places in Jefferson County, Tennessee, 1994. Alderman Jefferson City, 1974-77; chmn. Jefferson City Planning Comm., 1976-79. Capt. M.C., U.S. Army, 1944-46. Mem. Tenn. Heart Assn. (pres. 1966-67), Hamblen County Med. Soc. (pres. 1960-61), Jefferson County Hist. Soc. (pres. 1993-94, historian 1995—). Republican. Baptist. Home: 1428 Russell Ave Jefferson City TN 37760-2529

MUNDAY, JOHN CLINGMAN, JR., science policy educator, remote sensing researcher; b. Plainfield, N.J., June 10, 1940; s. John Clingman and Anna (Fegley) M.; m. Judith Berrien, Jan. 29, 1965; children: Brandon, Sarah, Sherrod. A.B., Cornell U., 1962; Ph.D., U. Ill., 1968. Postdoctoral fellow Holloman AFB, Alamogordo, N.Mex., 1968-69; asst. prof. geography U. Toronto, Can., 1971-75; assoc. prof., prof. marine sci. Coll. William and Mary, Gloucester Point, Va., 1975-84, mem. assoc. faculty, 1984-86; prof. natural scis. sch. govt. Regent U., Virginia Beach, Va., 1983—, asst. dean, 1985-87, assoc. dean, 1987-93, interim dean, 1993-96, assoc. dean acad. affairs, 1996—; cons. Commonwealth Data Base, Commonwealth of Va., 1978-83. Contbr. articles to profl. jours. and chpt. to tech. book. Va. edn. coordinator Freedom Council, 1984-86; mem. Chesapeake, Va. Wetlands Bd., Va. Pesticide Control Bd. Mem. AAAS, Am. Soc. Photogrammetry (chmn. hydrospheric scis. com. 1981), Am. Sci. Affiliation, Assn. Am. Geographers, Internat. Assn. Energy Econs., Sigma Xi. Republican. Avocations: music performance and composition, ragtime piano; folk music. Home: 1204 Murray Dr Chesapeake VA 23322-1833 Office: Regent U Sch Govt Virginia Beach VA 23464

MUNDY, GARDNER MARSHALL, lawyer; b. Roanoke, Va., July 19, 1934; s. Gardner Adams and Betty (Marshall) M.; m. Jean Stephens, Nov. 13, 1956 (div. 1979); children: Stephens M., Liza I.; m. Jenice Hamrick, June 21, 1980; children: G. Marshall Jr., Natalie J. BA, Va. Mil. Inst., 1956; LLB, U. Va., 1962. Bar: Va. 1962, U.S. Dist. Ct. (we. dist.) Va. 1962, U.S. Ct. Appeals (4th cir.) 1962. Ptnr. Woods, Rogers & Hazlegrove, Roanoke, 1962-71, Mundy & Garrison, Roanoke, 1973-76, Mundy & Strickland, Roanoke, 1976-82; pvt. practice Roanoke, 1982-86; ptnr. Mundy, Rogers & Frith, Roanoke, 1986—. 1st lt. U.S. Army, 1957-59. Fellow Am. Coll. Trial Lawyers, Am. Bd. Trial Advocates (pres. Western Va. chpt. 1990-91), Am. Bar Found., Va. Bar Found.; mem. ABA, Va. State Bar Assn. (chmn. bd. govs. litig. sect. 1985-86), Roanoke Bar Assn. (bd. dirs. 1986-90, pres. 1990-91), Shenandoah Club, Roanoke Country Club, Coral Beach and Tennis Club (Bermuda). Presbyterian. Home: 1542 Electric Rd Roanoke VA 24018-1106 Office: Mundy Rogers & Frith 1328 3rd St SW Roanoke VA 24016-5219

MUNDY, LAURIE JO, radio news director, producer; b. Mobile, Ala., May 27, 1970; d. Michael J. and Jo (Shipman) M. BA, U. Ala., 1992. Dance instr. Acad. of Ballet, Tuscaloosa, Ala., 1983-89; anchor, reporter, producer WVUA-TV U. Ala., Tuscaloosa, Ala., 1992; news intern WCFT-TV Channel 33, Tuscaloosa, Ala., 1993; asst. news dir. WTXT-FM, Tuscaloosa, Ala., 1993-94, news dir., 1994—, news dir., prodr., 1996—; bd. dirs. Ala. AP. Mem. Ala. Dem. Party, Tuscaloosa, 1994—. Mem. Soc. Profl. Journalists, Ala. Assoc. Press (bd. dirs., Press award 1995), Radio and TV News Dirs. Assn., Phi Mu (pub. rels. stds. 1990-92). Democrat. Episcopalian. Home: 1631 2d Ave Tuscaloosa AL 35401 Office: WTXT-FM 1848 Mcfarland Blvd # 35476 Northport AL 35476-3273

MUNFORD, ROBERT SIMS, III, internist, researcher, educator; b. Orlando, Fla., Nov. 5, 1942; m. Barbara A. Brown, July 22, 1983. BA, Vanderbilt U., 1964; BA, MA, Oxford U., 1967; MD, Harvard U., 1970. Resident Parkland Meml. Hosp., Dallas, 1970-72, Epidemic Intelligence Svc., CDC, Atlanta, 1972-74; postdoctoral rsch. fellow Rockefeller U., N.Y.C., 1974-76; fellow in infectious disease Mass. Genl. Hosp., Boston, 1976-77; asst. prof. internal medicine and microbiology U. Tex.-Southwestern Med. Ctr., Dallas, 1977-82, assoc. prof., 1982-88, prof., 1988—, Jan and Henri Bromberg prof., 1994—. Patentee in field; contbr. numerous articles to profl. jours. Office: U Tex SW Med Sch 5323 Harry Hines Blvd Dallas TX 75235-9113

MUNGER, JAMES GUY, protective services executive; b. Elyria, Ohio, Aug. 9, 1951; s. William James and Patricia Ann (Mederith) M.; m. Karen Ann Johnson, Oct. 30, 1971; 1 child, Jennifer Lisa. AAS in Fire Sci., Wallace State Community Coll.; BS in Fire Sci., Memphis State U.; postgrad., U. Ala., Birmingham; MS in Fire Sci. and Safety, Western States U. Cert. Fire Fighter I, Instr. I, Fire Prevention/Investigation Officer I, Fire Prevention Officer II, III, Fire Investigation Officer II, III, Ala. Fire Fighters' Personnel Standards & Tng. Commn., Fire Protection Specialist, Fire Protection Certification Bd., Pa. Plant maintenance supr. Challenger Homes, Columbia, Tenn., 1972-74; pvt. practice Cullman (Ala.) Appliance & Refrigeration, 1972-79; fireman City of Cullman, 1980-85; dep. state fire marshal State of Ala., Montgomery, 1980-85; pvt. practice Cullman, 1985—; bd. dirs. Soc. Nat. Fire Acad. Instrs., Ala.; adj. faculty Fed. Emergency Mgmt. Agy. Nat. Fire Acad., Emmitsburg, Md., Ala. State Fire Coll., Tuscaloosa, Ala.; expert on fire protection and investigation state and fed. cts. Fire commr. Cullman City Coun., 1992-96, City of Cullman, 1992-96. Mem. Soc. Fire Protection Engrs., Am. Fire Sprinkler Assn., Assn. Fire Protection Designers, C. of C. (pub. safety com.), Nat. Fire Protection Agy., Architects, Engrs. and Bldg. Ofcls. Sect., Fire Marshals Assn. No. Am., Internat. Assn. Elec. Insps., So. Std. Bldg. Code Congress Internat., Inc., Internat. Conf. Bldg. Ofcls., Bldg. Ofcls. and Code Adminstrs. Internat., Inc. Republican. Presbyterian. Office: PO Box 1773 Cullman AL 35056-1773

MUNGER, PAUL DAVID, educational administrator; b. Selma, Ala., Oct. 12, 1945; s. Paul Francis and Arlene Lorraine (McFillen) M.; m. Paula Jean Dominici, May 30, 1969; children: Kimberley Beth, Christopher David. AB in Philosophy, Kenyon Coll., 1967; MA in Govt., Ind. U., 1969. Commd. 2d lt. USAF, 1969, advanced through grades to capt., resigned, 1972; asst. dir. faculty devel. Ind. U., Bloomington, 1974-77; from asst. dean to dean continuing studies Am. U., Washington, 1980-83, asst. provost acad. devel., 1983-84; dir. Commn. on Future Acad. Leadership, Washington, 1984-86; v.p. Acad. Strategies, Washington, 1986-88; pres. Strategic Edn. Svcs. Inc., Sterling, Va., 1988—. Bd. advisors Madeira Sch., McLean, Va., 1993-96; treas. Bus.-Higher Edn. Fedn., Washington, 1992—; asst. scoutmaster Boy Scouts Am., 1991-93, scoutmaster, 1994—. Mem. Am. Soc. Tng. & Devel. (chmn. strategic planning com. 1993-95, continuing profl. edn. electronic forum coord. 1995—), Assn. Continuing Higher Edn., Am. Soc. Curriculum Devel. Office: Strategic Education Services Inc 624 W Church Rd Sterling VA 20164-4608

MUNHOLLON, SAMUEL CLIFFORD, investment brokerage house executive; b. Harlan, Iowa, Jan. 12, 1948; s. Clifford Ferrell and Juanita Rosalie (Smith) M.; m. Tommie Verlene Gist, Mar. 16, 1973 (div. May 1977); m. Rosalie Jane Sholtes, May 21, 1981; stepchildren: Charles Randall Oglesby, Richard Martin Oglesby, Ronald Nelson Oglesby, Janelle Marie Oglesby Skelton, Robert Steven Oglesby. BS, Okla. State Univ., 1970; postgrad., So. Meth. Univ., 1970-71. Cert. fgn. currency, index options, gen. securities prin., options prin.; registered rep. life-health-accident ins.; registered investment advisor; cert. estate planning specialist, retirement planning specialist. Auditor Ernst & Ernst, Dallas, 1970-71; sr. analyst Champlin Petroleum Corp., Enid, Okla., 1971-72; chief acct., controller Basin Petroleum Corp., Oklahoma City, 1972-75; account exec. A.G. Edwards & Sons, Inc., Oklahoma City, 1975-78; prin. ptnr. Adams, James, Foor Inc., Oklahoma City, 1978-79; v.p., branch mgr. Stix & Co. Inc., Oklahoma City, 1979-81; v.p. Smith Barney Harris Upham, Oklahoma City, 1981-82, Paine Webber Jackson Curtis, Oklahoma City, 1982-84, Stifel Nicolaus & Co. Inc., Oklahoma City, 1984-87, Dean Witter Reynolds Inc., Oklahoma City, 1987—; mem. C.Am. task force U.S. Def. Commerce, 1985—. Mem. Okla. Heritage Assn., Oklahoma City, 1988, Nat. Congl. Club, Raleigh, N.C., 1986—, Second Amendment Found., Bellevue, Wash., 1968—, Young Reps. Oklahoma City, 1968-88, Okla. Rep. Party, Oklahoma City, 1968—, Rep. Nat. Com., Washington, 1978—, Gun Owners Am., Falls Church, Va., 1979—, Okla. Coun. on Campaigning Compliance and Ethical Standards, Oklahoma City, 1988, Rep. Sen. Inner Circle, Washington, 1988, Rep. Eagles, 1980-81, Citizens Com. for Right to Keep & Bear Arms, 1988—; bd. dirs. Okla. Shooting Sports, Inc., 1990—, Okla. Found. for Disabled, 1990-92, Northside YMCA, 1994—, Okla. Wildlife Fedn., 1994—; mem. Gov.'s Interstate Indian Affairs Coun., 1996, Lt. Gov.'s Grand Nat. Invitational Turkey Hunt Com. Named Citizen of Yr., Presdl. Task Force, 1980, Citizen of Yr., Citizens Com. for Right To Keep and Bear Arms, 1993, 93; recipient award Am. Def. Inst., 1986. Mem. NRA (life), Nat. Assn. Investment Brokers, Internat. Assn. Registered Reps. (state chair 1981-82), World Affairs Coun. Ctrl. Okla., Nat. Assn. Registered Reps., Security Industry Assn. (govt. rels. com. 1982-85), Stifel Nicolaus Club (pres. 1986, chmn. 1985, 87), Dean Witter Reynolds Dirs. Club, Paine Webber Jackson Curtis Pace Setters Club, Nat. Wild Turkey Fed., Grand Nat. Quail Assn., N.Am. Found. Big Game, Ducks Unlimited, Quail Unlimited, N.Am. Hunt Club, Okla. State U. Alumni Assn., Sons Confederate Vets., Safari Club Internat. (region 9 rep. 1995-96), Rotary (bd. dirs., sec. 1991, v.p. 1992, pres.-elect 1993, pres. 1994, 95, program chmn. N.W. chpt. 1989—, pres. 1994), Safari Club Internat. (chpt. bd. 1991—, dirs., chpt. v.p. 1991, pres.-elect 1992, pres. 1993-94, 94-95, membership com., ethics com., internat. bd. dirs. 1993—), Sierra Club, Oklahoma City Gun Club, Tau Kappa Epsilon Alumni Assn. Republican. Home: 10830 N Bryant Oklahoma City OK 73131-5017 Office: Dean Witter Reynolds 6305 Waterford Blvd Ste 240 Oklahoma City OK 73118-1116

MUNIZ, CARLOS ENRIQUE, psychiatry educator; b. Havana, Cuba, Aug. 26, 1924; came to U.S., 1961; s. Manuel and Marie (Del Valle) M.; m. Sara A. Rojas, Aug. 17, 1952; children: Sara, Carlos A., Albert, Ana. MD, Havana U., 1948. Diplomate Am. Bd. Psychiatry and Neurology. Intern Sacred Heart Hosp., Havana, 1949-61; resident in psychiatry U. Mo. Med. Sch., Columbia, 1965-66, asst. prof. psychiatry, 1967-69; asst. prof. psychiatry U. Fla., Gainesville, 1969-75, assoc. prof. psychiatry, 1975-82, prof. psychiatry, 1982-84; chief of psychiatry VA Med. Ctr., Gainesville, 1982—, cons., 1990—. Contbr. articles to profl. jours. Mem. Am. Psychiat. Assn. (life). Roman Catholic. Home: 2271 NW 21st Ave Gainesville FL 32605-3937 Office: Shands Teaching Hosp Archer Rd Gainesville FL 32610

MUNK, ZEV MOSHE, allergist, researcher; b. Stockholm, July 14, 1950; m. Susan Deitcher; 4 children. BS, McGill U., 1972; MD, C.M., 1974. Licentiate Med. Council Can.; diplomate Am. Bd. Internal Medicine, Am. Bd. Allergy and Clin. Immunology. Intern Royal Victoria Hosp., Montreal, 1974-75, resident, 1975-76; resident in clin. immunology and allergy Montreal Gen. Hosp., 1976-78; practice medicine specializing in allergy and clin. immunology, Houston, 1978—; mem. staff Meml. City Med. Ctr., Meml. S.W., Meth., Spring Branch Meml., West Houston Med. Ctr, Cy-Fair hosps. (all Houston); clin. instr. allergy and clin. immunology Baylor Coll. Medicine, 1979—, U. Tex.-Houston, 1979—; pres. Breco Rsch., Pharm-Olam Internat. Clin. Rsch. Orgn., 1994—. Pres. Young Israel Synagogue of Houston, 1994-96; founder Allergy Ctr., Inc., Houston, Clin. Rsch. Ctr., Houston. McGill U. scholar, 1968-74. Fellow Am. Acad. Allergy, Am. Coll. Allergy and Immunology, Royal Coll. Physicians (Can.); mem. ACP, Tex. Med. Assn., Que. Med. Assn., Am. Fedn. Clin. Research, Am. Acad. Allergy, Tex. Allergy Soc., Harris County Med. Soc., Houston Allergy Soc. Contbr. articles to med. jours. Office: 902 Frostwood Dr Ste 222 Houston TX 77024-2402

MUNN, JOHN WILLIAM, telecommunications executive; b. Lubbock, Tex., Mar. 11, 1947; s. N. Harold and Martha Margaret (Collier) M.; m. Ann Louise Elliott, Apr. 10, 1971; children: Jeffrey, Eric, Lisa. BSBA, Tex. Tech. U., 1969; MPA, Southern Methodist U., 1972; PHD, U. Tex., 1992. Cert. emergency mgr. Nat. Coord. Coun. Emergency Mgmt. Asst. dir. aviation City of Dallas, 1969-83; dir. properties Southwest Airlines, Dallas, 1983-84; dir. facilities U.S. Sprint (formerly U.S. Telecom), Dallas, Westwood, Kans., 1984-85; exec. dir. Tarrant County 911 Dist., Ft. Worth, 1985—; appt. adv. com. Tex. Emergency Commn., Austin, 1987—, chmn. addressing com., 1991—; access to care com. Nat. Heart Attack Alert Program, Washington, 1993—; pres. NENA Inst., 1996-97. Precinct chair Dallas County Rep. Party, 1991—. Mem. Nat. Emergency Number Assn. (v.p. 1995—, Gulf Coast regional 1992-95, nat. issues chmn. 1992-94, cert. com. chmn. 1994—, pres. Inst. 1995—). Methodist. Office: Tarrant County 911 Dist 100 E 15th St LB 123 Fort Worth TX 76102

MUNOZ, CELIA ALVAREZ, artist; b. El Paso, Tex., Aug. 15, 1937; d. Frank P. and Enriqueta (Limon) Alvarez; m. Andres Munoz, July 27, 1965; children: Anna Celia, Andres III. BA, U. Tex., 1964; MFA, U. North Tex., 1982. Fashion illustrator White House Dept. Store, El Paso, Tex., 1961; art instr. El Paso Pub. Schs., 1964-74, Bauder Fashion Coll., Arlington, Tex., 1984-88; lectr. U. Tex., Arlington, 1984-89; adv. bd. Arlington Mus. Art, 1993—; design team cons. Sky Harbor Internat. Airport, 1993, N.Y. for Art, P.S. 8, Henry B. Gonzalez Convention Ctr. Expansion Project, 1995-96; chartered artist The Contemporary Art Ctr. of Fort Worth, 1996. Author: If Walls Could Speak, 1991, Biennial Whitney Mus. of Am. Art. NEA fellow, 1988, 91. Mem. Tex. Fine Arts Assn. (adv. bd. 1993—). Home: 5815 Arbor Valley Dr Arlington TX 76016

MUÑOZ, MARIO ARCADIO, social services administrator; b. Laredo, Tex., Jan. 18, 1954; s. A. F. and Aminta Muñoz; children: Rene M., Rebecca E. BA in Liberal Arts, S.W. Tex. State U., 1976; MS in Counseling, Corpus Christi State U., 1990. Lic. master social worker, advanced practitioner. Admissions coord. Corpus Christi (Tex.) State Sch., 1980-90; program dir. County Mental Health Mental Retardation, Corpus Christi, 1990; social svcs. cons. Tex. Dept. of Health, Corpus Christi, 1990-92; social worker Westwood, Sinton Manor, Riveridge, Corpus Christi, 1992—; residential dir. Ada Wilson, Corpus Christi, 1992-96; HCS program mgr. Am. Habilitation Svcs., Corpus Christi, 1996—; social svcs. cons. Tejas Mgmt., Corpus Christi, 1990-91; mem. County Mental Retardation Adv. Coun., Corpus Christi, 1992—, Spl. Edn. Parent Adv. Coun., Corpus Christi ISD, 1992—. Mem. South Tex. Med. Soc. for Social Workers. Roman Catholic. Home: 2606 Persimmon Corpus Christi TX 78415

MUNOZ, STEVEN MICHAEL, physician associate; b. Dallas, Aug. 7, 1952; s. Joseph Paul and Connie Rae (Coffman) M.; m. Paula Lou Marchant, Dec. 12, 1974 (div. 1983); 1 child, Kimberly Rene; m. Maureen Geneva Flowers, Aug. 12, 1984; children: Danielle Geneva, Sean Michael. B Med. Sci., Emory U., 1977. Physician assoc. Med. Ctr. Cen. Ga., Macon, 1977-79, William B. Martin M.D., P.C., Loganville, Ga., 1979-80, Howell Indsl. Clinic, Atlanta, 1980-81, Stanley Fineman M.D., P.C., Marietta, Ga., 1981-82; physician assoc., dir. sales and adminstrn. Family Practice Ctr./ Atlanta Occupational Medicine, 1982-85; physician assoc., dir. mktg. Gwinnette Ctr. med. Clinic, Norcross, Ga., 1985-89; physician assoc. So. Orthopedic Clinic, Atlanta, 1989-90, North Fulton Health Care Assoc., Roswell, Ga., 1990-96; physician assoc. adult & pediatric care Kaiser Permanente Internal Medicine Clinic, Atlanta, 1996—; asst. clin. prof. Emory U. Sch. Medicine, Atlanta, 1981—; dir. patient edn. com. Ga. Lung Assn., 1981-82; med. adviser ARC, Atlanta, 1980-83, Ga. Statewide Hypertension Task Force, 1981-82. With U.S. Army, 1972-75, Res., 1975-94. Mem. Am. Acad. Physician Assts., Ga. Assn. Physician Assts. (bd. dirs., pub. edn. com. chair 1984), Soc. Army Physician Assts. Republican. Home: 5785 Stonehaven Dr Kennesaw GA 80152-3759 Office: Kaiser Permanente 20 Glenlake Pky Atlanta GA 30328

MUNRO, CINDY LOUISE, nursing educator; b. Syracuse, N.Y., Nov. 23, 1955; d. John Squire and Joan Louise (Hohl) M.; m. Brett William Stevenson, May 27, 1989; 1 child, Joseph Munro; 1 child, by previous marriage, Jessie Ann Louise Myers. Diploma profl. nursing, York Hosp. Sch. Nursing, 1976; BSN, Millersville U. Pa., 1983; MS, U. Del., 1984; PhD, Va. Commonwealth U., 1992. RN, Va. Staff nurse Columbia (Pa.) Hosp., 1976; vol. ARC, Naval Regional Med. Ctr., Charleston, S.C., 1976-79; office nurse Office of J.D. Weinberg, MD, Columbia, 1979-81; staff nurse Lancaster (Pa.) Gen. Hosp., 1981-82; critical care charge nurse Meml. Hosp., York, Pa., 1982-84; asst. prof. nursing Lynchburg (Va.) Coll., 1985-88; rsch. assoc. Va. Commonwealth U., Richmond, 1992, asst. prof. nursing, 1992—; Grad. trainee U. Del., 1983-84. Contbr. articles to profl. jours. A.D. Williams scholar Med. Coll. Va., Va. Commonwealth U., 1988-89; recipient Doris B. Yingling Rsch. award Nursing Svcs., Med. Coll. Va. Hosps., 1993, 95. Mem. ANA, AACN, Am. Soc. Microbiology, Sigma Theta Tau, Phi Kappa Phi, Gold Key.

MUNRO, CRISTINA STIRLING, artistic director; b. London, May 22, 1940; came to U.S., 1977; m. Richard Munro (div. 1986); children: Alexandra, Nicholas. Attended various artistic schs., London. Mem. ballet corps Sadlers Wells Opera Ballet, London, 1960-62, Het Nederlands Ballet, The Hague, Holland, 1962-63; soloist London Festival Ballet, 1963-72; prin. soloist Eliot Feld Ballet, N.Y.C., 1972-75; prin. dancer, artistic dir. Old Dominion U., Norfolk, Va., 1975; artistic dir. Louisville Ballet Co., 1975-79; ballet mistress Houston Ballet, 1979-85; dir. Munro Ballet Studies, Corpus Christi, Tex., 1985—; artistic dir. Corpus Christi Ballet, 1985—; guest artist and choreographer numerous cos. in U.S. Recipient Giovanni Martini award Louisville, 1978. Mem. Imperial Soc. Tchrs. of Dance, Royal Acad. Dancing, Brit. Actors Equity Assn., Am. Guild Mus. Artists. Office: Munro Ballet Studios Corpus Christi Ballet 5610 Everhart Rd Corpus Christi TX 78411-4905

MUNSELL, ELSIE LOUISE, lawyer; b. N.Y.C., Feb. 15, 1939; d. Elmer Stanley and Eleanor Harriet (Dickinson) M.; m. George P. Williams, July 14, 1979. AB, Marietta Coll., 1960; JD, Marshall-Wythe Coll. William and Mary, 1972. Bar: Va. 1972, U.S. Dist. Ct. (ea. dist.) Va. 1974, U.S. Ct. Appeals (4th cir.) 1976, U.S. Supreme Ct. 1980. Tchr. Norview High Sch., Norfolk, Va., 1964-69; asst. Commonwealth atty. Commonwealth Atty.'s Office, Alexandria, Va., 1972-73; asst. U.S. atty. Alexandria, 1974-79; U.S. magistrate U.S. Dist. Ct. (ea. dist.) Va., Alexandria, 1979-81; U.S. atty. Dept. Justice, Alexandria, 1981-86; sr. trial atty. Office of Gen. Counsel, Dept. Navy, Washington, 1986-89, asst. gen. counsel installations and environ. law, 1989-91; dep. asst. environ. and safety Sec. Navy, 1991—. Active Va. Commn. on Status of Women, 1966-74; bd. vistors Coll. William and Mary, 1972-76; active Atty. Gen.'s Adv. Com. U.S. Attys., 1981-83; bd. dirs. Carpenter's Shelter, Inc., 1990-93. Mem. Environ. Law Inst. (assoc.), Sr. Execs. Assn. Episcopalian. Office: Dept Navy 1000 Navy Pentagon Washington DC 20350-1000

MUNSON, ERIC BRUCE, hospital administrator; b. Elmhurst, Ill., Mar. 11, 1943; married. B, Wabash Coll., 1965; MHA, U. Chgo., 1967. Asst. to adminstr. Swedish Covenant Hosp., Chgo., 1966-67; asst. dir. U. Chgo. Hosps., 1970-73; assoc. adminstr. U. Hosp., Denver, 1973-77, adminstr., 1977-80; exec. dir. U. N.C. Hosp., Chapel Hill, 1980—. Home: 119 Black Oak Pl Chapel Hill NC 27514-6502 Office: Univ N C Hosps 101 Manning Dr Chapel Hill NC 27514-4220*

MUNTZ, CHARLES EDWARD, school system administrator; b. Cynthiana, Ky., May 26, 1944; s. Charles Edward and Hedy Wright (Shaw) M.; m. Betty Jean Dance, June 7, 1986; children: Susan Lynn Lanter, Christopher, Laura Cox. AB, Ea. Ky. U., 1967, MA, 1968. Social sci. tchr. Harrison County Schs., Cynthiana, Ky., 1967, Georgetown (Ky.) Ind. Schs., 1968-69; spl. edn. tchr. Harrison County Schs., Cynthiana, 1969-76; dir. spl. edn. Franklin County Schs., Frankfort, Ky., 1976-94; instr. U. Ky.; spl. edn. cons., presenter in field. Chairperson issues com. Ky. Coalition for the Handicapped, 1988. Named Outstanding Spl. Edn. Adminstr. of Yr., 1991. Mem. Coun. for Exceptional Children (past pres.), Ky. Coalition for People with Handicaps, Ky. Coun. Adminstrs. of Spl. Edn. (past pres.), Phi Delta Kappa.

MURAI, NORIMOTO, plant molecular biologist, educator; b. Sapporo, Japan, Mar. 4, 1944; came to U.S., 1968; s. Nobuo and Hideko (Odagiri) M.; m. Andreana Lisca, Nov. 14, 1977; 1 child, Naoki. BS, Hokkaido U., 1966, MS, 1968; PhD, U. Wis., 1973. Rsch. assoc. dept. botany U. Wis., Madison, 1974-78, project assoc. dept. bacteriology, 1979, postdoctoral fellow dept. plant pathology, 1980-82; lab. head dept. molecular biology Nat. Inst. Agrobiol. Resources, Tsukuba, Japan, 1983-84; assoc. prof. plant pathology and crop physiology La. State U., Baton Rouge, 1985-92, prof., 1992—; adj. prof. biochemistry, full mem. grad. faculty and interdept. studies in plant physiology and genetics La. State U.; mem. study sect. on minority biomed. rsch. support program NIH, 1993; grant reviewer USDA, NSF, NIH. Reviewer manuscripts Genome, Protein Engring., Plant Cell, Plant Physiol., Planta, Plant Molecular Biology, Plant Cell Report, Australia Jour. Plant Physiol. Named Honors Rschr., Phi Delta Kappa, 1989; grantee Fulbright Found., 1968, Sci. and Tech. Agy., Tokyo, 1984, La. Edn. Quality Support Fund, 1988, 89, 91, 94, 95, Monsanto Co. Fund, 1992, 93, U.S. Dept. Agr., 1995. Mem. AAAS, Am. Soc. Plant Physiologists, Internat. Soc. Plant Molecular Biology, Japan Molecular Biology Assn., Crop Sci. Soc. Am., Fulbright Assn., Sigma Xi, Gamma Sigma Delta, Phi Delta Kappa. Office: La State U Dept Plant Path Crop P Baton Rouge LA 70803

MURAI, RENE VICENTE, lawyer; b. Havana, Cuba, Mar. 11, 1945; came to the U.S., 1960; s. Andres and Silvia (Muñiz) M.; m. Luisa Botifoll, June 12, 1970; 1 child, Elisa. BA, Brown U., 1966; JD cum laude, Columbia U., 1969. Bar: Fla. 1970, N.Y. 1972, U.S. Supreme Ct. 1977. Atty. Reginald Heber Smith Fellow Legal Svcs. Greater Miami, Fla., 1969-71; assoc. Willkie, Farr & Gallagher, N.Y.C., 1971-73; ptnr. Paul, Landy & Beiley, Miami, 1973-79; shareholder Murai, Wald, Biondo & Moreno, Miami, 1979—; bd. dirs. PanAm. Bank, Miami; dir. Cuban Am. Bar Assn., 1982-96, pres., 1985; vice chmn., lectr. Internat. Conf. for Lawyers of the Ams., 1982, chmn. and lectr., 1984; mem. panel grievance com. Fla. Bar, 1983-86. Mng. editor Columbia Law Rev., 1967-69. Bd. dirs., sec. Archtl. Club of Miami, 1978-86; bd. dirs. Dade Heritage Trust, 1979-82, Facts About Cuban Exiles, Inc., 1982—, pres., 1989, Legal Svcs. of Greater Miami, Inc., 1980-90, pres. 1986-88, ARC, 1984-90, exec. com., 1988-90, Mercy Hosp. Found., 1985-91, United Way, 1986-89, chmn. voluntary sector trust, Dade Cmty. Found., 1988-93, chair grants com., 1991-93; mem. adminstrn. of justice com. Fla. Bar Found., 1989—, bd. dirs., 1991—, chmn. audit and fin. com., 1993—; mem. task force leadership Dade County Ptnrs. for Safe Neighborhoods, 1994—, Code Enforcement Bd. City of Coral Gables, 1982-86, Bd. Adjustment, 1987-89, city mgr. selection com., 1987, charter rev. commn., 1980; trustee U. Miami, 1994-96. Mem. ABA, Cuban-Am. Bar Assn., Dade County Bar Assn. (dir. 1987-88), Greater Miami C. of C., Spain-U.S. C. of C. Democrat. Roman Catholic. Home: 3833 Alhambra Ct Coral Gables FL 33134 Office: Murai Wald Biondo & Moreno PA 25 SE 2nd Ave Ste 900 Miami FL 33131-1600

MURCHISON, BRADLEY DUNCAN, lawyer; b. Washington, Jan. 5, 1957; s. David Claudius and June Margaret (Guilfoyle) M.; m. Anita Lynne Cadieu, Oct. 14, 1957; children: Grace Guilfoyle, Meredith Lynne. AB in Polit. Sci., U. N.C., 1979; JD, George Washington U., 1982. Bar: N.C. 1983, U.S. Dist. Ct. (we. dist.) N.C. 1983, U.S. Tax Ct. 1983. Assoc. Thigpen and Hines, P.A., Charlotte, N.C., 1982-85; assoc. Moore & Van Allen, Charlotte, 1985-87, ptnr., 1988; assoc. gen. counsel Collins & Aikman Corp., Charlotte, 1988-89; asst. gen. counsel Collins & Aikman Products Co., Charlotte, 1989—. Active Lincoln Forum, N.C., 1995. Mem. N.C. Bar Assn., Am. Corp. Counsel Assn., Mecklenburg County Bar Assn. Republican. Roman Catholic. Office: Collins & Aikman Products C 701 Mccullough Dr Charlotte NC 28262-3318

MURCHISON, DAVID RODERICK, lawyer; b. Washington, May 28, 1948; s. David Claudius and June Margaret (Guilfoyle) M.; m. Kathy Ann Kohn, Mar. 15, 1981; children: David Christopher, Benjamin Michael. BA cum laude, Princeton U., 1970; JD, Georgetown U., 1975. Bar: D.C. 1975, Fla. 1993. Legal asst. to vice chmn. CAB, Washington, 1975-76, enforcement atty., 1976-77; sr. atty. Air Transport Assn., Washington, 1977-80, asst. v.p., sec., 1981-85; sr. assoc. Zuckert, Scoutt and Rasenberger, Washington, 1980-81; v.p., asst. gen. counsel Piedmont Aviation, Inc., Winston-Salem, N.C., 1985-88; v.p., gen. counsel, sec. Braniff, Inc., Dallas, 1988-89; chief exec. officer Braniff, Inc., Orlando, 1990-94; fed. adminstrv. law judge Office of Hearings and Appeals, Charleston, W.Va., 1994-96; chief adminstrv. law judge Office of Hearings and Appeals, Mobile, Ala., 1996—; lectr. continuing legal edn. program Wake Forest U., Winston-Salem, 1988. Contbr. articles to legal jours. Lt. USNR, 1970-72. Mem. ABA, Met. Club Washington. Republican. Roman Catholic. Office: Office Hearings and Appeals 3605 Springhill Bus Park Mobile AL 36608

MURDOCH-KITT, NORMA HOOD, clinical psychologist; b. Clinton, S.C., May 16, 1947; d. Bernard Constantine and Martha Grace (Hood) Murdoch; m. Jonathan Michael Murdoch-Kitt, Mar. 23, 1974; children: Kelly Michelle, Mark Jason, Sabrina Brittany, Laura Kristina. BA, Wake Forest U., 1969; MS, U. Pitts., 1971, PhD, 1975 . Psychology intern Eastern Pa. Psychiat. Inst., 1972-73; asst. prof., therapist campus counseling center Coll. William and Mary, Williamsburg, Va., 1973-74; staff psychologist child psychiatry dept. Med. Coll. Va., 1974-75; pvt. practice individual psychotherapy and family and marital therapy, Richmond, Va., 1975—; clin. prof. psychiatry Med. Coll. Va., 1995—. Mem. Richmond Dem. Com., 1976-79, 82-85, 88-89, 91—; v.p. govtl. relations com. Ginter Park Residents Assn., 1987, pres., 1988, 89; mem. Richmond Human Rels. Adv. Commn., 1976-80, Richmond Mayor's Com. on Concerns of Women, 1987—, chair, 1989-93; mem. Richmond Citizens Crime Commn., 1985-88, co-chair police chief sect. com. 1994-95; founder, 1st state chmn. polit. action com. ERA, 1977-78; chief lobbyist ERA Ratification Council, 1977-79; mem. long range planning com. Bapt. Theol. Sch., Richmond, 1993—; long range planning com. Bapt. Theol. Seminary, Richmond, 1993-96; v.p. The Women's Ctr., Inc. 1996—. USPHS fellow, 1969-72. Mem. APA (steering com. State Leadership Conf. 1986-91, chair 1991, Richmond area chair Red Cross/Am. Psychol. Assn. Disaster Mental Health Network 1993—), Va. Psychol. Assn. (state legis. lobbyist 1978-79, chmn. legis. com. 1981-83, bd. profl. affairs 1981-85, pres. 1986), Va. Acad. Clin. Psychologists (chmn. profl. affairs com. 1982-84), Va. Breast Cancer Found. (rsch. chair 1992-96), Richmond Area Psychol. Assn. (pres. elect 1994, pres. 1995), Chronic Fatigue Assn. (Va chpt.), Internat. Soc. for Study Multiple Personality and Dissociation, LWV, ACLU. Presbyterian. Club: Richmond First (chmn. edn. com. 1979-80, dir. 1980-81). Office: Murdoch-Kitt Profl Bldg 3217 Chamberlayne Ave Richmond VA 23227-4806

MURILLO, JOSÉ-LUIS, Spanish language educator; b. Cabra, Spain, Oct. 9, 1951; came to U.S., 1978; s. Francisco and Carmen (Amo) M. BA in Spanish, U. New Orleans, 1983; Masters, U. Tulane, 1987, PhD, 1992. Tchg. asst. U. Tulane, New Orleans, 1984-89, vis. instr., lectr., 1990-94; assoc. prof. U. Mobile, Ala., 1995—; rep. grad. student U. Tulane, 1987-89; internat. rels. com. U. Mobile, 1994-95, rsch. com., 1995—. Editor: Spain: Myth and Reality in Contemporary Spanish Song, 1995; contbr. articles to profl. jours. Mem. internat. com. Tricentia, Mobile, 1995—. Recipient grant Spanish Govt., 1995. Home: 560 Mohawk St Mobile AL 36606 Office: Univ Mobile PO Box 13220 Mobile AL 36663

MURKETT, PHILIP TILLOTSON, human resource executive; b. Chattanooga, Apr. 3, 1931; s. Philip Tillotson and Dorothy (Ingram) M.; m. Mary Jane Brewer, Dec. 10, 1960; children: Emmette, Mary Jane Easter, Leanne. BA, Duke U., 1954; MBA, U. Pa., 1957; postgrad., Warnboro Coll., Oxford, England, 1980. Methods engr. Westinghouse Elec. Co., Staunton, Va., 1957-60; adminstrv. mgr. Vulcan Materials Co., Birmingham, Ala., 1960-68; human resources mgr. Blount, Inc., Montgomery, Ala., 1968-74; pres. Murkett Enterprises Inc., Montgomery, 1974—; with internat. affairs Yonok Coll., Lampang, Thailand; search cons. Murkett Assocs., Montgomery, 1974—. Author: Use & Value of References, 1957; editor (newsletter) H.R. Quar., 1983. Pres. Montgomery Mus. Fine Art, 1982, Community Concert Assn., Montgomery, 1982, Montgomery Symphony Assn., 1987; pres. Am.-Thai Edn. Devel. Found. Inc., 1991, bd. dirs. 1990; jr. warden Episcopal Ch. of Ascension, 1972. Recipient Gov.'s Arts award Ala. Arts Coun., 1983, commendation from crown princess of Thailand, 1992. Mem. Montgomery C. of C. (task chair 1983), Montgomery Country Club, Capitol City Club, Kiwanis (bd. dirs. 1972), Delta Tau Delta (chpt. v.p. 1953). Office: PO Box 527 Montgomery AL 36101-0527

MURKISON, EUGENE COX, business educator; b. Donalsonville, Ga., July 2, 1936; s. Jeff and Ollie Mae (Shores) M.; m. Marilyn Louise Adams, July 3, 1965; children: James, David, Jennifer. Grad., U.S. Army JFK Spl. Warfare Sc., 1967, U.S. Naval War Coll., 1972, U.S. Army Command/Staff Coll., 1974; BSA, U. Ga., 1959; MBA, U. Rochester, 1970; PhD, U. Mo., 1986. Surveyor USDA, Donalsonville, Ga., 1956-59; commd. 2d lt. U.S. Army, 1959, advanced through grades to lt. col., 1974; inf. bn. leader U.S. Army, Vietnam, 1967-68; mechanized comdr. (G-3), ops. officer Brigade Exec. Officer, Korea, Europe and U.S., 1968-70; prof. leadership & psychology West Point, N.Y., 1970-73; ops. officer (J-3) Office of Chmn. Joint Chiefs of Staff, Washington, 1974-77; prof. mil. sci. and leadership Kemper Mil. Coll., 1977-81; ret. U.S. Army, 1981; instr. U. Mo., Columbia, 1981-84; asst. prof. Ga. So. U., Stateboro, 1984-89, assoc. prof., 1989-94, prof., 1995—; vis. prof. mgmt. and bus. U. Tirgoviste, Romania, 1994, 95, 96; vis. prof. human resource mgmt. Tech. U. Romania, Cluj-Napoca, 1995, 96. Contbr. numerous articles to profl. jours., chpts. to books in field. V.p. Optimist Club, 1993-94, dir., 1993, v.p., 1994-95; trustee Pittman Pk. Meth. Ch., Statesboro, 1992—, chmn., trustee, 1995—. Recipient Bronze Star medal with oak leaf cluster, Devel. award Ga. So. U., 1990, Teaching award U. Mo., 1983, Albert Burke Rsch. award, 1992; grantee IREX, 1994, SOROS, 1995, 96. Mem. VFW, Inst. Mgmt. Sci., So. Mgmt. Assn., Inst. for Info. and Mgmt. Sci., Internat. Acad. Bus. (program chair 1994, 95), Acad. Mgmt., Bus. History Conf., Newcomen Soc., Blue Key, Scabbard & Blade, Beta Gamma Sigma, Alpha Zeta. Republican. Office: Ga So U Coll Bus Adminstrn Statesboro GA 30460-8152

MURPHREE, KENNETH DEWEY, elementary school educator; b. Memphis, July 28, 1953; s. Dewey and Garneita (Bryant) M.; m. Beverly Ann Hurt, Sept. 7, 1974. AE, N.W. Miss. Jr. Coll., Senatobia, 1973; BSE, Delta State U., 1975, ME, 1976, Ednl. Specialist degree in adminstrn. and supervision, 1992. Grad. asst. dept. elem. edn. Delta State U., 1975-76; elem. tchr. Helena (Ark.) West - Helena Pub. Schs., 1976-81; prin. Woodruff Elem. Sch., West Helena, 1981-93, Westside Elem. Sch., West Helena, 1993—. Mem. NAESP, ASCD, Ark. Assn. Ednl. Adminstrs., Ark. Assn. Elem. Sch. Prins., East Ark. Schoolmasters Assn., Lions (pres., past pres., 1st v.p., bd. dirs. tail twister West Helena), Phi Theta Kappa (past pres. Theta Sigma chpt.), Kappa Delta Pi, Phi Delta Kappa. Office: Westside Elem Sch 339 S Ashlar St West Helena AR 72390-3401

MURPHREE, SHARON ANN, lawyer; b. Maryville, Tenn., June 14, 1949; d. R.L. and Alice (Pierick) M. BS, U. Tenn., 1970; JD, South Tex. Coll. Law, 1987. Bar: Tex. 1988. Pvt. practice law Houston, 1988—; negotiations trainee Harvard Negotiation Project, 1990; advanced negotiator Harvard Negotion Project, 1991; founding chair Cmty. Mediation Ctr., 1994-95; tchr. mediation clinic U. Tenn. Coll. Law, 1993-95; gen. sessions mediator, trainer and mentor; mediator Dept. Justice Americans with Disabilities Act. Conbtr. articles to profl. jours. Mem. Foley's Women's Adv. Bd., Houston, 1988; bd. dirs. Ind. Living Ctr., 1996; mem. Domestic Abuse Task Force, 1995-96. Mem. Knoxville Bar Assn., Mediation Assn. Tenn. (sec. 1994-96, v.p. Knoxville chpt. 1994), Soc. Profls. in Disbute Resolution, Citizens' Police Acad. Alumni Assn., Phi Delta Phi. Democrat. Roman Catholic. Office: 1074 Scenic Dr Knoxville TN 37919-7640

MURPHY, ARTHUR ELLERY, safety manager; b. Providence, Nov. 15, 1948; s. Arthur Ellery and Esther (Caldarone) M. BS in Mgmt. Sci., Fla. Inst. Tech., 1973. Spl. hazards system designer Grinnell Fire Protection, Providence, 1974-76; loss control rep. St. Paul (Minn.) Cos., 1976-80, Am. Internat. Group Cons., Inc., N.Y.C., 1980-85; safety dir. Taylor Concrete and Supply, Inc., Green Cove Springs, Fla., 1985-88; no. regional safety mgr. Tarmac Fla., Inc., Deerfield Beach, 1989—; adj. faculty U. North Fla., Jacksonville, 1986. Mem. Am. Soc. Safety Engrs. (sec. north Fla. chpt. 1984-85, prs. 1985-86, 86-87, v.p. region VIII 1990-94, asst. regional v.p. region VIII 1987-88, pub. affairs com. 1988-89, 89-90, Safety Profl. of Yr. 1994), Fla. Affiliation Ins. Safety Com., Nat. Ready Mix Concrete Assn. (safety com.), Nat. Fire Protection Assn., Fla. Fedn. for Safety, Fla. Inst. Tech. Alumni Assn., Theta Xi. Roman Catholic. Home: 3412 Country Manor Dr Daytona Beach FL 32119-3163 Office: Tarmac Fla Inc 405 Madison Ave Daytona Beach FL 32114-2009

MURPHY, BEN CARROLL, engineering company executive; b. Rome, Miss., Aug. 21, 1931; s. Benjamin Franklin and Effie (Lett) M.; BS, Delta State U., 1969, MBA, 1974; grad. United Electronic Inst., 1972; m. Vivian Inez Hancock, Mar. 3, 1950; children: Lanny Carroll, Debra Kay Murphy Snead, Kathy M. Murphy David, Gregory Lynn, Jon Patrick. With U.S. Gypsum Co., Greenville, Miss., 1951-54, 55-56, Atlantic & Pacific Tea Co., Greenville, 1954-55; cost acct. Baxter Labs., Cleveland, Miss., 1966-69; project engr. mfg. U.S. Gypsum Co., Danville, Va., 1969-72; plant personnel and safety mgr. Cook Industries, Inc., Memphis, 1972-73, div. safety dir., plant personnel mgr., 1973-75, corp. compensation sr. analyst, 1976, div. indsl. relations and personnel mgr., 1975-76, corp. compensation mgr., 1976-79; div. asst. personnel mgr. Mitchell Engring. Co., Columbus, Miss., 1979-80, structural supt., 1980-82, mgr. prodn. control systems, 1982-92, divsn. prodn. control, schedule mgr., 1992—. night instr. bus. and econs. N.W. Jr. Coll., Southaven, Miss., 1975-79, Golden Tri-Angle Vo-Tec, 1980—; cons. in compensation S.E. Memphis Mental Health Center, 1978-82. Mem. Mid-South Compensation and Benefits Assn. (dir. 1977-80, mem. organizing team 1976), Univ. for Women (adv. com. for extended studies of Miss. U.), Am. Compensation Soc., Soc. Mfg. Engrs. (sr., 3d v.p. chpt.), Miss. Mfg. Assn., Am. Mgmt. Compensation Soc. Baptist. Lodge: Masons (32 degree). Home:

Rt 2 Box 96 Vaiden MS 39176-9606 Office: PO Box 911 Columbus MS 39703-0911

MURPHY, CHARLES HAYWOOD, JR., retired petroleum company executive; b. El Dorado, Ark., Mar. 6, 1920; s. Charles Haywood and Bertie (Wilson) M.; m. Johnie Walker, Oct. 14, 1939; children: Michael Walker, Martha, Charles Haywood, III, Robert Madison. Ed. pub. schs., Ark.; LLD (hon.), U. Ark., 1966. Ind. oil producer, 1939-50; ret. chmn., also bd. dirs. Murphy Oil Corp., El Dorado, Ark., 1972—; chmn. exec. com. 1st Comml. Corp., Little Rock. Bd. govs. Oschner Med. Found.; bd. adminstrs. Tulane U.; mem. nat. adv. bd. Smithsonian Instn.; past mem. Ark. Bd. Higher Edn. Served as infantryman World War II. Recipient citation for outstanding individual service in natural resource mgmt. Nat. Wildlife Fedn. Mem. Am. Petroleum Inst. (past exec. com., hon. bd. dirs.), Nat. Petroleum Council (past chmn.), 25 Yr. Club Petroleum Industry (past pres.).

MURPHY, DAVID FRANK, mechanical engineering executive; b. Cape Girardeau, Mo., Nov. 30, 1946; s. Joe R. and Edna F. (Irvin) M.; m. Sharon R. Prince, Sept. 24, 1965; children: David Scott, Chris A. Student, Ark. State U., 1964-66, U.S. Army Engring. Sch., 1971; BS in Mech. Engring., Memphis State U., 1974. Registered profl. engr., Tenn. Engr. CBI Nuclear, Memphis, 1969-74; project engr. FMC, Inc., Jonesboro, Ark., 1974-79; sr. project engr. Dempster Dumpster Systems, Inc., Knoxville, Tenn., 1979-80; engring. mgr. Wyite Engring., Inc., Knoxville, 1980-83, Daniel, Mann, Johnson and Mendenhall, Oak Ridge, Tenn., 1983-86; div. dir. Automated Scis. Group, Inc., Oak Ridge, 1986-90, v.p., 1990-92; sr. v.p., 1992—. Baseball coach Cedar Bluff Farragut Optimist/West Hills Baseball League, Knoxville, 1979-84; scout leader Cub Scouts, Paragould, Ark., Knoxville, 1978-80; active Knoxville Zool. Soc., 1989—; deacon Gallaher Meml. Bapt. Ch., Knoxville, 1986—; min. Parkway Bapt. Ch., Knoxville, 1979. Mem. Nat. Contract Mgmt. Assn., Waste Mgmt. Assn., Am. Soc. Quality Control. Republican. Home: 9500 Bolivar Cir Knoxville TN 37922-3514

MURPHY, DEBORAH HILL, school nurse, psychotherapist; b. Seminole, Okla., Nov. 10, 1952; d. Bob R. and Claudia Mae (Duvall) Hill; m. Daniel Charles Murphy, July 30, 1982 (div.); children: Tiffeani Anne, Daniel Charles III. Diploma, St. Anthony Hosp. Sch. Nursing, 1982; cert. in minister of health, Iowa Luth. Hosp., 1990; BS in Health Arts, Coll. of St. Francis, Joliet, Ill., 1990; MS in Counseling Psychology, So. Nazarene U., Bethany, Okla., 1994. RN, Iowa, Okla. Dir. clin. anf profl. svcs. Kimberly Quality Care, Des Moines; nurse cons. Blue Cross/Blue Shield, Des Moines; ministr of health Inner City Coop. Parish, Des Moines; pastoral care minister in health ministry Holy Trinity Cath. Ch., Des Moines; pvt. practice psychotherapist Oklahoma City; school nurse Oklahoma City Pub. Schs. John Pearson scholar. Mem. Nat. Health Ministries Assn. (charter), Am. Holistic Nurse Assn., Iowa Minister of Health Assn., Nat. Assn. Sch. Nurses, Okla. Sch. Nurse Assn. Home: 3247 Castle Rock Rd Oklahoma City OK 73120-1859

MURPHY, DEBORAH JUNE, lawyer; b. Clinton, Tenn., Dec. 19, 1955; d. Robert Carlton and Mary Ruth (Melton) M.; m. Charles L. Beach, Dec. 9, 1987. BS, U. Tenn., 1977; postgrad. Vanderbilt U., 1983; JD, Nashville YMCA Law Sch., 1987. Bar: Tenn. 1987. Tax auditor State of Tenn., Knoxville, 1977-82, Nashville, 1983-85, legal advisor, 1985-86; with office legal services Tenn. Gen. Assembly, Nashville, 1986-87; atty. U.S. Dept. Treasury, 1987—; Mem. ABA, ATLA, Tenn. Trial Lawyers Assn., Anderson County Bar Assn., Lawyers Assn. for Women. Democrat. Methodist. Avocation: travel. Home: PO Box 510 Clinton TN 37717 Office: 710 Locust St Fl 4 Knoxville TN 37902-2540

MURPHY, EDWARD THOMAS, engineering executive; b. Boston, Nov. 20, 1947; s. Edward William and Eleanor Catherine (Brown) M.; m. Marianne Scheid, May 1, 1976; children: Edward Robert, Cynthia Kathrine. BS, Calif. Inst. Tech., 1969; MS in Nuclear Sci. and Engring., Carnegie Mellon U., 1971. Registered profl. engr., Pa., Md. Containment system engr. Westinghouse Electric Corp., Monroeville, Pa., 1969-74, fuel projects engr., 1974-80; mgr. licensing ops. Westinghouse Electric Corp., Bethesda, Md., 1980-84; acting regulatory com. supr. Westinghouse Electric Corp., Avila Beach, Calif., 1984-85; mgr. control system analysis and support Westinghouse Electric Corp., Monroeville, 1985-88; spl. project mgr. reactor restart div. Westinghouse Savannah River Co., Aiken, S.C., 1989-92, site configuration mgmt. regulatory affairs/startup projects mgr. Engring. & Projects Divsn., 1992-94; facilities configuration mgmt. support mgr. Westinghouse Savannah River Co., Aiken, 1994-96; acting mgr. safety svcs., 1996—. Mem. Am. Nuclear Soc. Roman Catholic. Office: Westinghouse Savannah River Co Savannah River Site Aiken SC 29808

MURPHY, GRETA WERWATH, retired college official; b. Milw., Aug. 24, 1910; d. Oscar and Johanna (Seelhorst) Werwath; m. John Heery Murphy, Sept. 18, 1941. Ed. Ohio State U., 1943-45; PhD in Comms. (hon.) Milw. Sch. Engring., 1993 . With Milw. Sch. Engring., 1928—, head admissions dept., 1931-42, dir. pub. rels, 1945-66, v.p. pub. rels. and devel., 1966-77, v.p., cons., 1978—, regent emeritus, 1985—. Mem. Milw. County Planning Commn., 1966—, vice chmn., 1974-75, chmn., 1976-77. Fellow Pub. Rels. Soc. Am. (founder, past pres. Wis. chpt.); mem. Am. Coll. Pub. Rels. Assn. (past dir., sec., trustee), Women's Advt. Club (pres.). Club: Womans of Wis. Home: 1032 Malaga Ave Miami FL 33134-6319 also: 5562 Cedar Beach S Belgium WI 53004-9646

MURPHY, HAROLD LOYD, federal judge; b. Haralson County, Ga., Mar. 31, 1927; s. James Loyd and Georgia Gladys (McBrayer) M.; m. Jacqueline Marie Ferri, Dec. 20, 1958; children: Mark Harold, Paul Bailey. Student, West Ga. Coll., 1944-45, U. Miss., 1945-46; LL.B., U. Ga., 1949. Bar: Ga. 1949. Pvt. practice Buchanan, Ga., from 1949; ptnr. Howe & Murphy, Buchanan and Tallapoosa, Ga., 1958-71; judge Superior Cts., Tallapoosa Circuit, 1971-77; U.S. dist. judge No. Dist. of Ga., Rome, 1977—; rep. Gen. Assembly of Ga., 1951-61; asst. solicitor gen. Tallapoosa Jud. Circuit, 1956; mem. Jud. Qualifications Commn., State of Ga., 1977. With USNR, 1945-46. Fellow Am. Bar Found.; mem. ABA, Ga. Bar Assn., Dist. Judges Assn. for 11th Cir. Bar Assn., Am. Judicature Soc., Tallapoosa Cir. Bar Assn., Old War Horse Lawyers Club, Am. Inns Ct. (past pres. Joseph Henry Lumpkin sect.), Fed. Judges Assn. (exec. com.). Methodist. Home: 321 Georgia Highway 120 Tallapoosa GA 30176-3114 Office: US Dist Ct PO Box 53 Rome GA 30162-0053

MURPHY, JAMES J., electronics executive; b. Kenosha, Wis., Nov. 4, 1954; s. Eugene C. and Thelma M. (Jensen) M.; m. Susan M. Larson, June 10, 1978. BA in Bus. Mgmt. and Labor Econs. with honors, U. Wis., 1976. Sales rep. Inland Steel, Chgo., 1976-77, product analyst, 1977; sales rep. Joerndt & Ventura, Inc., Kenosha, 1977-78; field sales rep. Applied Power Corp., New Berlin, Wis., 1978-79; Magnavox regional mgr. Philips Consumer Electronics Co., Knoxville, Tenn., 1979-87, zone mgr., 1987-89, div. field sales mgr., 1989-91, natl. account dir., 1991-95, gen. mgr., 1995—, v.p. merchandising, 1996—. Mem. Lincoln Continental Owners Club (treas. 1991), Vintage Radio-Phonograph Soc. Home: 709 Foxfield Ln Knoxville TN 37922-5242 Office: Philips Consumer Electronics Co One Philips Dr Knoxville TN 37914

MURPHY, JEFFREY LAWRENCE, digital imagemaker, photographer, educator; b. Dayton, Ohio, July 21, 1965; s. Roger Lawrence and Charlene Mary Murphy. BFA, Ohio State U., 1989; MFA, U. Fla. Staff photographer Creative Concepts, Dayton, 1989-90; instr. Sinclair C.C., Dayton, 1991-92; freelance artist Dayton, 1989-92; lectr. Cerro Coso Coll., Ridgecrest, Calif., 1990, Ariz. State U., Tempe, 1991, rschr., 1991. One-man shows include Silver Image Gallery, Columbus, Ohio, 1989, Maxwell Gallery, Columbus, 1989, Cerro Coso C.C., 1990, Time Gallery, Columbus, 1990, U. Colo., Boulder, 1991, Tex. Tech U., Lubbock, 1991, Doo-Wac Gallery, Columbus, 1992, Mich. State U. Lightfantastic Gallery, East Lansing, 1992, So. Oreg. State U., Ashland, 1992; exhibited in group shows at Ohio Citizens Bank, Toledo, 1987, Concoursce Gallery, Columbus, 1988, Silver Image Gallery, 1989, U. Cairo, Egypt, 1989, Ohio State U., Columbus, 1989, First Ave. Office Ctr., Columbus, 1990, John Michael Kohler Arts Ctr., Sheboygan, Wis., 1990, U. Tex., San Antonio, 1990, Trumbull Gallery, Warren, Ohio, 1991, Wiseman Gallery, Grants Pass, Oreg., 1991, Chandler (Ariz.) Ctr. for Arts, 1991, Jazzberry's Uptown Gallery, Rochester, N.Y., 1991, Taste of the Arts Gallery, Syracuse, N.Y., 1992, Dayton Visual Arts Ctr., 1992, Wayne County Arts Gallery, Lyons, N.Y., Doo-Wac Gallery, 1992; represented in permanent collections Kresge Mus. of Art, East Lansing, Advanced Computing Ctr. for Art and Design; contbr. cover photographs to Camera and Darkroom Photography, 1991, Spook; contbr. photographs to Exploring Color Photography, and profl. jours. Recipient Best Art Shows '89 award Columbus Dispatch, 1989, Firestone Project grant, 1989, Ohio Understanding award Ohio News Photographers. Mem. Phi Kappa Phi. Office: U Fla Dept Art 302 FAC Gainesville FL 32611

MURPHY, JIMMY DEAN, consulting company executive; b. Lohman, Mo., Aug. 17, 1932; s. Edward Anderson and Emma Lou (Walters) M.; m. Betty Elaine Peucker, Oct. 16, 1954. BA in Econs., U. Nebr., Omaha, 1970. Enlisted USAF, 1954; advanced through grades to master sgt., 1964; resigned USAF, 1966; systems engr. Bunker-Ramo Corp., St. Louis, 1966-67; program mgr. Planning Rsch. Corp., Omaha, 1967-71, USDA, Washington, 1971-72; program dir. Europe Planning Rsch. Corp., McLean, Va., 1972-74; dep. asst. adminstr. Fgn. Agrl. Svcs., Washington, 1974-81; divn. pres. Planning Rsch. Corp., McLean, 1981-85; sr. exec. CIA, Washington, 1985-92; cons. Murphy Adv. Svcs., Orange Park, Fla., 1992—. Contbr. articles to profl. jours.; speaker in field. Mem. Assn. for Computing Machinery, Masonic Lodge, Scottish Rite, Shriners, Am. Legion. Republican. Home and Office: Murphy Adv Svc 2236 Salt Myrtle Ln Orange Park FL 32073-7076

MURPHY, JOHN CARTER, economics educator; b. Ft. Worth, July 17, 1921; s. Joe Preston and Rachel Elsie (Carter) M.; m. Dorothy Elise Haldi, May 1, 1949; children: Douglas C., Barbara E. Student, Tex. Christian U., 1939-41; BA, North Tex. State U., 1943, BS, 1946; AM, U. Chgo., 1949, PhD, 1955; postgrad., U. Copenhagen, 1952-53. Instr. Ill. Inst. Tech., 1947-50; instr. to assoc. prof. Washington U., St. Louis, 1950-62; vis. prof. So. Meth. U., Dallas, 1961, prof., 1962-90, prof. emeritus, 1990—, dir. grad. studies in econs., 1963-68, chmn. dept., 1968-71, faculty summer program in Oxford, 1982-91, dir., 1991, pres. faculty senate, 1988-89, co-dir. Insts. on Internat. Fin., 1982-87; vis. prof. Bologna (Italy) Ctr., Sch. Advanced Internat. Studies, Johns Hopkins U., 1961-62; UN tech. assistance expert, Egypt, 1964; vis. prof., spl. field staff Rockefeller Found., Thammasat U., Bangkok, 1966-67; sr. staff economist Coun. Econ. Advisers, 1971-72, U.S. dels. econ. policy com. and working party III OECD, 1971-72, U.S. del. 8th meeting Joint U.S.-Japan Econ. Com., 1971; cons. Washington U. Internat. Econs. Rsch. Project, 1950-53, U.S. Treasury, 1972, Fed. Res. Bank Dallas, 1994—; referee NSF; witness and referee congl. coms.; lectr. USIA Program, Germany, 1961-62, 84, Philippines, South Viet Nam, Thailand, 1972, France, Belgium, 1984; lectr. Southwestern and Midwestern Grad. Sch. Banking; adj. scholar Am. Enterprise Inst. for Pub. Policy Rsch., 1976—. Author: The International Monetary System: Beyond the First Stage of Reform, 1979; (with R.R. Rubottom) Spain and the U.S.: Since World War II, 1984; editor: Money in the International Order, 1964; contbr. articles to profl. books and jours. Chmn. rsch. com. on internat. conflict and peace Washington U., 1959-61; lectr. mgmt. tng. programs Southwestern Bell Telephone Co., 1961-66, St. Louis Coun. on Econ. Edn., 1958-61; mem. regional selection com. H.S. Truman Fellowships, 1976-89; pres. Dallas Economists, 1981, Town and Gown of Dallas, 1980-81; mem. Dallas Com. on Fgn. Rels. Lt. USNR, 1943-46. Decorated Silver Star; Fulbright scholar to Denmark, 1952-53; Ford Found. Faculty Research fellow, 1957-58; U.S.-Spanish Joint Com. for Cultural Affairs fellow, 1981; Sr. Fulbright lectr. Italy, 1961-62. Mem. Am. Econ. Assn., So. Econ. Assn. (bd. editors Jour. 1969-71), Midwest Econ. Assn., Am. Fin. Assn., Soc. Internat. Devel., Peace Rsch. Soc., Southwestern Social Sci. Assn. (pres. econs. sect. 1971-72), AAUP (chpt. pres. 1964-65). Home: 10530 Somerton Dr Dallas TX 75229-5323 Office: So Meth Univ Dept Econs Dallas TX 75275

MURPHY, JOHN JOSEPH, manufacturing company executive; b. Olean, N.Y., Nov. 24, 1931; s. John Joseph and Mary M.; m. Louise John; children: Kathleen A. Murphy Bell, Karen L. Murphy Rochelli, Patricia L. Murphy Smith, Michael J. AAS in Mech. Engring., Rochester Inst. Tech., 1952; MBA, So. Meth. U. Engr. Clark div. Dresser Industries, Olean, 1952-67; gen. mgr. roots blower div. Dresser Industries, Connersville, Ind., 1967-69; pres. crane, hoist and tower div. Dresser Industries, Muskegon, Mich., 1969-70; pres. machinery group Dresser Industries, Houston, 1970-75; sr. v.p. ops. Dresser Industries, Dallas, 1980, exec. v.p., 1982, pres., 1982-92, CEO, 1983-95; chmn. bd., 1983—; bd. dirs. PepsiCo, Inc., NationsBank Corp., Kerr-McGee Corp.; mem. Bus. Roundtable, Bus. Coun.; bd. dirs. U.S.-Russia Bus. Coun.; chmn. Citizens Democracy Corps. Trustee St. Bonaventure (N.Y.) U., So. Meth. U. With U.S. Army, 1954-56. Office: Dresser Industries Inc PO Box 718 2001 Ross Ave Dallas TX 75201-2911

MURPHY, JUSTIN DUANE, history educator; b. Idabel, Okla., Oct. 14, 1964; s. Hurchel Joe Murphy and Shirley L. White; m. Jessica Yvonne Rooks, Sept. 7, 1983; children: Jonathan Andrew, Jason Alexander. BA in History and Polit. Sci., Southeastern Okla. State U., 1987; MA in History, Tex. Christian U., 1989, postgrad. Grad. asst. Tex. Christian U., Ft. Worth, 1987-89, tchg. asst., 1989-91; adj. instr. history Tarrant County Jr. Coll., Ft. Worth, 1989-91; instr. history Howard Payne U., Brownwood, Tex., 1991-94, asst. prof., 1994—; asst. dir. Douglas MacArthur Acad. Freedom Honors Program Howard Payne U., 1993-95, acting brand resident chair of free enterprise and pub. policy, 1995—. Author: Wheelock Female Seminary, 1842-1861, Chronicles of Oklahoma, 1991; assoc. editor: The European Powers in the First World War: An Encyclopedia; contbr. numerous articles to profl. jours. Pres. scholar Southeastern Okla. State U., 1982-87, Brown scholar, 1986-87, William P. Willis scholar, 1986-87. Mem. Soc. Historians of Early Am. Republic, S.W. Social Scis. Assn., Okla. Hist. Soc., Soc. French Hist. Studies, Kiwanis Internat., Phi Alpha Theta (v.p. 1988-89), Pi Sigma Alpha, Alpha Chi. Office: Howard Payne U 1000 Fisk Ave Brownwood TX 76801-2715

MURPHY, KATHLEEN JANE, psychologist, educator; b. Worcester, Mass., Nov. 9, 1962; d. Frederick George and Dorothy Jane (McGuiness) M.; m. Gary Lee Tatum, July 3, 1991. BA cum laude, Holy Cross Coll., 1984; MA, Assumption Coll., 1987; PhD, Tex. A&M U., 1991. Lic. profl. counselor, marriage and family therapist. Counselor Tex. Rehab. Commn., College Station, 1988-89, psychometrician, 1989; intern clin. psychology Worcester (Mass.) State Hosp., 1989-90; psychotherapist Sandstone Ctr., College Station, 1991-92, Luth. Social Svc., Bryan, Tex., 1992-93; instr. Blinn Coll., College Station, Tex., 1993—. Mem. APA, Nat. Register Health Svc. Providers in Psychology, Phi Beta Kappa, Psi Chi, Phi Kappa Phi. Democrat. Roman Catholic. Home: 614 Abbey Ln College Station TX 77845-8141

MURPHY, KEVIN GEORGE, novelist; b. Albany, N.Y., Feb. 29, 1952; s. Matthew George and Kathleen Mary (Dvorak) M.; m. Cathy Ann Clampett, July 14, 1973 (div. 1975); m. Judith Marion Chester, Jan. 9, 1987. Student, Empire State Coll., 1972-74. Novelist Scott Meredith Literary Agy., N.Y.C., 1984—, Barbara Bauer Lit. Agy., N.J., 1990. Author: The Dawn Run, 1986, Let Freedom Ring, 1986, In Someone Else's World, 1987, The Small Adventures of a Quiet Man, 1989, Humanform 2891, 1990, The Short Stories of Kevin George Murphy, 1991, Laura and the Abyss, 1991, Emergence, 1991, Angels, 1992, Alexandre and Philomena, 1993-94, others; (poetry) Though Villages May Sleep, 1989, Her Hands Untied the Sun, 1991, Judy in the Rain, 1992; contbr. to mags. and jours. Participant anti-nuclear marches, N.Y., Washington, 1977, anti-Klan march, Albany, 1991. Mem. Mental Health Assn. (plaque 1986), Amnesty Internat. Democrat. Mem. Soc. of Friends. Home and Office: 125 Brittany C/Kingspoint Delray Beach FL 33446

MURPHY, KRISTINE LYNN, librarian. MusB, Lawrence U., 1978; MLS, SUNY, Geneseo, 1979. Grad. asst. SUNY, 1978-79; acad. sales rep. The Baker & Taylor Co., Momence, Ill., 1980-83; assoc. libr. Brookhaven Coll., Dallas, 1983-84; local systems mktg. specialist AMIGOS Bibliog. Coun., Dallas, 1985-86; head acquisitions So. Meth. U., Dallas, 1986—, chmn. acquisitions task force, 1987-92; rep. acquisitions subcom. Alliance for Higher Edn., Richardson, Tex., 1986—, mem. vendor evaluation task force, 1986-92; participant state and nat. libr. confs., 1986—; chair libr. enrichment and devel. com. So. Meth. U., Dallas, 1993—, fine arts. libr. search com., 1995, mem. univ. choir, 1994—, mem. music, theater, dance search com., 1996. Contbg. author: AHE Vendor Directory for Acquisitions Librarians, 1988; contbr. articles to profl. jours. Mem. ALA, (assn. for libr. collections and technical svcs. acquisitions sect. publs. com., 1995-97, intern serials sect. acquisitions com. 1995-97), Tex. Libr. Assn. (sec.-treas. coll. and univ. libr. divsn. 1990, mem. membership com. 1993—, contg. edn. com. 1996-99, sec. acquisitions and collection devel. roundtable 1995-96, vice chair/chair-elect acquisitions and collection devel. roundtable 1996—), Tall Texans Leadership Inst., NASIG, Pi Kappa Lambda. Office: So Meth U Fondren Libr Box 750135 Dallas TX 75275-0135

MURPHY, LESTER F(ULLER), lawyer; b. East Chicago, Ind., Nov. 28, 1936; s. Lester Fuller Sr. and Angelique (Molloy) M.; divorced; children: John Justin, Angelique, Lester Fuller III, Christopher, Colleen, Bridget, Erika, Shannon. AB, U. Notre Dame, 1959, JD, 1960. Bar: Ind. 1960, U.S. Dist. Ct. (no. and so. dists.) Ind. 1960, U.S. Ct. Appeals (7th cir.) 1961, U.S. Supreme Ct. 1963, Ill. 1976, U.S. Dist. Ct. (no. dist.) Ill. 1983, U.S. Ct. Appeals (8th cir.) 1985, Fla. 1987, U.S. Dist. Ct. (mid. dist.) Fla. 1989. Assoc. Riley, Reed, Murphy & McAtee, East Chgo., Ind., 1960-64, ptnr., 1964-65; ptnr. Murphy, McAtee & Murphy, East Chgo., 1965-68, Murphy, McAtee, Murphy & Costanza, East Chgo., 1968-87, Burke, Murphy, Costanza & Cuppy, East Chgo., 1988-90; adj. prof. Stetson Law Sch., St. Petersburg, Fla.; mem. faculty NITA. Author: Indiana Medical Malpractice, 1988 (with annual supplements); contbr. articles to profl. jours. Mem. ABA, Ind. Bar Assn., Fla. Bar Assn., Clearwater Bar Assn. (lectr.), Ind. Bar Found., Ind. CLE Found. (lectr.), Fla. Acad. Trial Lawyers, Nat. Bd. Trial Advocacy (cert.), Innisbrook Club (Tarpon Springs). Roman Catholic. Office: Burke Murphy Costanza & Cuppy 33920 Us Hwy N Ste 280 Palm Harbor FL 34684

MURPHY, MARILYN, artist, educator; b. Tulsa, Okla., Sept. 22, 1950; d. John Joseph and Hattie Teresa (Reneski) M.; m. Wayne Roland Brown, Sept. 19, 1992. BFA, Okla. State U., 1972; MFA, U. Okla., 1978. Instr. art U. Okla., Norman, 1978-80; asst. prof. fine arts Vanderbilt U., Nashville, 1980-86, assoc. prof., 1986—; geophys., geol. and archtl. drafter The Drafting Rm., Oklahoma City, 1974-76; geol. drafter John A. Taylor Petroleum Exploration, Oklahoma City, 1976-77; tech. asst. screen print for SW Theatre Assn., Oklahoma City, 1978, for Okla. Mental Health Assn., Oklahoma City, 1978; asst. instr. silkscreen workshop Okla. Arts Inst., Quartz Mountain, 1977-80 ; print demonstration Tenn. State Mus., Nashville, 1981; instr. silkscreen workshop Cheekwood Fine Arts Ctr., Nashville, 1982; guest lectr. Cheekwood Fine Arts Ctr., 1983, 84, 87, 93; lectr. and presenter Nat. Assn. Campus Activities, Opryland, Nashville, 1984, Southeast Coll. Art Assoc., New Orleans, 1994; curated 25 exhibitions. One-woman shows include Baldwin (N.Y.) Pub. Libr., 1975, E. Ctrl. U., Ada, Okla., 1978 (2 Purchase awards), Sarratt Gallery, Vanderbilt U., Nashville, 1980, Cumberland Gallery, Nashville, 1984, 91, 94, Smith Coll., Northhampton, Mass., 1986, Townsville (Australia) Coll. Art, 1990, Gallery 210, U. Mo. St., Louis, 1990, Sch. Art, U. Okla., Norman, 1992, Queensland (Australia) Coll. Art, Brisbane, 1992, U. Ala., Huntsville, 1994, numerous others; two-woman shows The Arts Place, Oklahoma City, 1977, Jan Cicero Gallery, Chgo., 1987, others; exhibited in group shows at Okla. Art Ctr., Oklahoma City, 1977, Amarillo (Tex.) Art Ctr., 1977, 79, U. Kans. Gallery, Lawrence, 1979, Ogden (Utah) State U. Gallery, 1981, Met. Arts Commn., Nashville, 1983, 87, 91, Martha White Gallery, Louisville, 1983, Tins-Damman, Al-Khobar, Saudi Arabia, 1983, Lee Hall Gallery, Clemson (S.C.) U., 1983 (hon. mention), 200 E. Gallery, Knoxville, 1985, Jan Cicero Gallery, Chgo., 1985, 87, 89, Ewing Gallery, U. Tenn., 1987, The Drawing Ctr., N.Y., 1988, Evansville (Ind.) Mus. Art, 1989, 91, 96, Purchase award 1991), Tenn. Arts Commn. Gallery, Nashville, 1989, Bradley U., Peoria, Ill., 1989, Montclair (N.J.) Art Mus., Upper Montclair, 1991, Atlanta Coll. Art, Atlanta, 1991, Brooks Mus., Memphis, 1992, Cheekwood Fine Arts Ctr., 1993-95, Amos Eno Gallery, N.Y., 1993, Comus Gallery, Portland, Oreg., 1993, Laguna Gloria Art Mus., Austin, Tex., 1993, San Diego Art Inst., Calif., 1994, NW Art Ctr. Minot, N.D., 1995, Parkside Nat. U. Wisc., Nat. Acad. of Design, N.Y.C., 1996, Delta Nat., Ark. State U., 1996, numerous others; represented in numerous permanent collections; works published in book Art in Embassies, 25 Years at the U.S. Department of State 1964-1989, 1989; portfolio of work in various mags.; subject numerous articles in newspapers, mags. and jours.; TV appearances: Sta. WDCN, 1982, WTVF-5 and WPLN Pub. Radio, 1983. Featured artist and designer poster for action auction Sta. WDCN TV, 1984; juried exhbn. U. Ala., Birmingham, 1995; guest spkr. Elam Sch. Art U. Auckland, New Zealand, 1995, James Cook U. North Queensland, Cairns, Australia, 1996, Okla. State U., Stillwater, 1996; guest artist and seminar James Cook U., Townsville, Queensland, Australia, 1994; visual arts planning bd. Summer Lights art festival Met. Arts Commn., 1983-90; bd. dirs. Sinking Creek Film Festival, 1989—, v.p., 1990-94; mem. fellowship rev. panel Arts Midwest, 1994. Recipient Purchase award Okla. Arts and Humanities for State, 1976, SUNY, Potsdam, 1984, hon. mention S.E. Ctr. Contemporary Art, Winston-Salem, N.C., 1984, Merit award Evansville Mus. Art, 1988, Laguna Gloria Mus., 1993, 1st Place award Huntsville Mus. Art, 1991, purchase award Evansville Mus. Art, 1991, purchase award U. Wis., Parkside, 1995, top purchase award Cheekwood Mus. Art, 1995; Tenn. Arts Commn. fellow, 1988, So. Arts Fedn. fellow, 1990. Office: Vanderbilt U Dept Fine Arts PO Box 1801 Nashville TN 37235-1801

MURPHY, MARY KATHLEEN, nursing educator; b. Elkins, W.Va., Jan. 27, 1953; d. Wyatt W. and Emma Loretta (Bohan) M.; children: Bridget Allyn, Kelley M. Poling. Diploma, Upshur County Sch. Nursing, Buckhannon, W.Va., 1982; ADN, Davis and Elkins Coll., 1984, BSN magna cum laude, 1986; MSN, W.Va. U. Cert. correctional health profl., substitute vocat. tchr. practical nursing, W.Va. Nurse, asst head nurse in ob-gyn. Meml. Gen. Hosp., Elkins, W.Va.; staff nurse, resource pool in ob-gyn. W.Va. U., Morgantown; DON Correctional Med. Systems, Huttonsville, W.Va.; instr. in nursing Davis and Elkins Coll.; nurse mgr. Elkins Mountain Sch. Randolph County Bd. Edn. Reviewer nursing texts Lippincott-Raven Pub. Mem. ANA, W.Va. Nursing Assn. (reviewer approval unit com. edn., dist. 7 bd. dirs., chairperson legislative com.), Inst. Noetic Scis., So. States Correctional Assn., Alpha Chi, Sigma Theta Tau.

MURPHY, MARY KATHLEEN CONNORS, college administrator, writer; b. Pueblo, Colo.; d. Joseph Charles and Eileen E. (McDermott) Connors; m. Michael C. Murphy, June 6, 1959; children: Holly Ann, Emily Louise, Patricia Marie. AB, Loretto Heights Coll., 1960; MEd, Emory U., 1968; PhD, Ga. State U., 1980. Tchr. English pub. schs., Moultrie, Ga., 1959, Sacramento, 1960, Marietta, Ga., 1960-65, DeKalb County, Ga., 1966; tech. writer Ga. Dept. Edn., 1966-69; editorial asst. So. Regional Edn. Bd., Atlanta, 1969-71; dir. alumni affairs The Lovett Sch., Atlanta, 1972-75, dir. publs. and info. svc., 1975-77; coord. summer series in aging Ga. State U., 1979; dir. devel. found. rels. Ga. Inst. Tech., 1980-87, dir. devel., 1987-89; asst. dir. devel. for spl. gifts U Ga., 1989-91; assoc. v.p. for devel. Oglethorpe U., 1991—; state coord. for Ga., Am. Coun. on Edn. nat. identification program for women in higher edn. administrn., 1983-85; presenter profl. confs.; freelance edn. writer, 1968—; co-author: Fitting in as a New Service Wife, 1966; contbr. and contbg. editor numerous articles on teaching, secondary edn., higher edn., and fund raising to profl. publs.; columnist Daily Jour., Marietta, 1963-67, The Atlanta Constn., 1963-68; editor: Cultivating Found. Support for Edn., 1989, Building Bridges: Fund Raising for Deans, Faculty, and Development Officers, 1992. Bd. advisors Bridge Family Counseling Ctr., 1981-86, Northside Sch. Arts, 1981-83; bd. dirs. Atlanta Women's Network, 1982-84, v.p., 1983-84; prin., bd. dirs. Sch. Religion, Cathedral of Christ the King, 1979-84; mem. devel. com. Archdiocese of Atlanta, 1991-94; publicity chmn. Phoenix Soc. Atlanta, 1981-91, adv. bd., 1988-91; mem. allocations com., exec. com. United Way Met. Atlanta, 1983; bd. counseling Fulton Svc. Ctr., Met. Atlanta chpt. ARC, 1982-83; mem. Leadership Atlanta, class of 1983-84; group facilitator, 1984-85, co-chmn. edn. program, 1987; co-chair bldg. fund com. Mary Our Queen Ch., 1996—. NDEA fellow, 1965-66; Adminstrn. of Aging fellow, 1977-79; recipient Image Maker award Atlanta Profl. Women's Directory, Inc. 1984. Mem. Coun. for Advancement and Support of Edn. (publs. com., alumni adv. com., 1974-76, dist. III bd., 1981-95, chmn. corp. and found. support conf., N.Y.C., 1985, maj. rsch. conf., Atlanta, 1986, matching gift conf., Tampa, 1989, dist. III conf. chmn. 1986, chair elect 1989-91, chair dist. III bd., 1991-93, past chair and nonminations com. chair, 1993-95, membership svcs. com. 1989-93, Washington bd. dirs. 1992-96, exec. com., trusteeship com., dist. svcs. and governance com., Alice Beeman Writing award, 1994), Ga. Coun. on Planned Giving (bd. dir., chair edn. com. planned giving com., 1995—), Nat. Assn. Ind. Schs. (publs. com. 1974-76), Edn. Writers Assn., Nat. Soc. Fund Raising Execs. (v.p. Ga. chpt. 1985, pres. 1986-87, mem.-at-large nat.

bd. 1985-89, chmn. pub. rels. com. 1985-87, asst. treas., chair audit com., mem. exec. com. 1988-90), Kiwanis (co-chair membership com. Atlanta club 1990-91, chair program com. 1991-96, dir. 1993-94, asst. sec. 1994-95, v.p. 1995-96, pres. elect. 1996—), Phi Delta Kappa, Kappa Delta Pi (pres. 1980-81).

MURPHY, MICHAEL GORDON, investment consultant; b. Dallas, Jan. 26, 1939; s. Elbert Gordon and Mary Emma (Ford) M.; m. Charlotte Head, July 30, 1965; children: Shannon, Marshall. BBA, So. Meth. U., 1960; JD, U. Tex., 1963. Bar: Tex. 1963, U.S. Dist. Ct. (no. and so. dist.) Tex. 1964. Lawyer Tenneco, Inc., Houston, 1963-66; lawyer self-employed Houston, 1966-73; chmn. bd., CEO Tex. Commerce Bank-Chem., Houston, 1973-84; pres., CEO Houston Nat. Bank, 1984-86; chmn., CEO South Main Bank, 1986-92; dir. devel. So. Va. Coll. for Women, Buena Vista, 1992-93; pres. Atlantic Mgmt. Assocs., Inc., Lexington, Va., 1993—. Mem. devel. coun. U. Tex. Health Sci. Ctr., Houston, 1990-92; bd. dirs., treas. Rockbridge unit Am. Cancer Soc. Mem. Ind. Bankers of Tex., Tex. Bankers Assn., Brit.-Am. C. of C., Lexington Golf and Country Club, Rotary. Presbyterian. Office: Murphy Mgmt 407 Jackson Ave Lexington VA 24450-1905

MURPHY, PATRICK FRANCIS, printing company executive; b. Jacksonville, Fla., Sept. 9, 1958; s. Stanley Wilford and Sarajane (Leonard) M.; m. Kelly Pyatt, Mar. 23, 1991; children: Patrick Francis Jr., Laura Elizabeth, Richard Austin, Zane Davis. Sales and prodn. Sir Speedy Printing, Jacksonville, 1974-79; salesman A.B. Dick Co., Jacksonville, 1980-81; spl. agt. Northwestern Mut. Life, Jacksonville, 1981-82; v.p. Stan Murphy Co., Jacksonville, 1982-89, pres., 1989-92, also bd. dirs.; pres., CEO Classic Motor Carriages Inc., Miami, 1992—, Am. Graphic Comms., 1992—. Active Doug Milne for Mayor Campaign, Jacksonville, 1986-87; mem. adminstrv. bd. 1st United Meth. Ch., Jacksonville, 1984-86; pres. United Meth. Ch. Men, 1989; mem. pub. info. com. Am. Cancer Soc., Jacksonville, 1984-86. Mem. Exec. Women Internat. (exec. sponsor 1986-92), Jacksonville C. of C. (amb. 1986-89, Cornerstone sponsor 1991—), Belle Meade Hunt Club, Univ. Craftsmen's Club, Traffic Club. Republican. Office: The Murphy Co's 3030 Powers Ave # 104 Jacksonville FL 32207-8012

MURPHY, RAMON BIRKETT, financial services company executive; b. Jamaica, Sept. 7, 1935; s. Vincent Hubert and Ruby Mae (Earle) M.; m. Ouida Vivienne Bair, Aug. 18, 1962; children: Juliet A., Donna M., Gordon R., Angela V. Student, U. Toronto, 1968, Coll. Fin. Planning, 1985. Chartered life underwriter, cert. fin. planner. Sales rep. N.Am. Life Assn. Can., Jamaica, 1963-68, tng. mgr., 1968-70; tng. dir. Life of Jamaica, 1970-73, dir. agys., 1973-75, v.p. mktg., 1975-76, sr. v.p. agy., bd. dirs., 1976-78; v.p. sales Lincoln Nat. Miami Fin. Svcs., Fla., 1983—; v.p., sec., bd. dirs. Advanced Fin. Planning, Miami, 1984—. Fundraiser Miami Children's Hosp., 1986—, March of Dimes, 1980—, Assn. Devel. Exceptional, Miami, 1980—. Mem. Internat. Assn. Fin. Planners, Internat. Bd. Fin. Planners, Inst. Cert. Fin. Planners, Nat. Assn. Life Underwriters, Fla. Assn. Life Underwriters (co-chmn. edn. 1987-88), Miami Assn. Life Underwriters (pres. 1986-87), Million Dollar Roundtable (life). Republican. Club: Country (Miami). Home: 6329 NW 175th Ter Hialeah FL 33015-4438 Office: Ray Murphy & Assocs Inc PO Box 170867 Hialeah FL 33017-0867

MURPHY, RANDALL KENT, consultant; b. Laramie, Wyo., Nov. 8, 1943; s. Robert Joseph and Sally (McConnell) M.; student U. Wyo., 1961-65; MBA, So. Meth. U., 1983; m. Cynthia Laura Hillhouse, Dec. 29, 1978; children: Caroline, Scott, Emily. Dir. mktg. Wycoa, Inc., Denver, 1967-70; dir. Communications Resource Inst., Dallas, 1971-72; account exec. Xerox Learning Systems, Dallas, 1973-74; regional mgr. Systema Corp., Dallas, 1975; pres. Performance Assocs.; pres., dir. Acclivus Corp., Dallas, 1976—; founder, chmn. Acclivus Inst., 1982—. Active, Dallas Mus. Fine Arts, Dallas Hist. Soc., Dallas Symphony Assn.; vice chmn. bd. trustees The Winston Sch., 1994—; mem. adv. bd. The Women's Ctr. of Dallas, 1995—. Served with AUS, 1966. Mem. Am. Soc. Tng. and Devel., Sales and Mktg. Execs. Internat., Inst. Mgmt. Scis., Soc. Applied Learning Tech., Nat. Soc. Performance and Instrn., , Assn. Mgmt. Cons., Am. Assn. Higher Edn., World Future Soc., Soc. for Intercultural Edn., Tng. and Rsch., Internat. Fedn. Tng. and Devel. Orgns., Inst. Noetic Scis., Nat. Peace Inst., Amnesty Internat. The Acad. Pol. Sci., The Nature Conservancy, Children's Arts & Ideas Found., So. Meth. U. Alumni Assn. U. Wyo. Alumni Assn. Roman Catholic. Author: Performance Management of the Selling Process, 1979; Coaching and Counseling for Performance, 1980; Managing Development and Performance, 1982; Acclivus Performance Planning System, 1983; (with others) BASE for Sales Performance, 1983, Acclivus Coaching, 1984, Acclivus Sales Negotiation, 1985; BASE for Effective Presentations, 1987, BASE for Strategic Sales Presentations, 1988, The New BASE for Sales Excellence, 1988, Major Account Planning and Strategy, 1989, Strategic Management of the Selling Process, 1989, Building on the BASE, 1992, Negotiation Mastery, 1995; co-inventor The Randy-Band, multi-purpose apparel accessory, 1968. Home: 6540 Crestpoint Dr Dallas TX 75240-8615

MURPHY, RICHARD PATRICK, lawyer; b. Elizabeth, N.J., Dec. 13, 1954; s. Richard Francis and Marie (Conlon) M.; m. Ana Alvarez. AB with distinction, Cornell U., 1976; JD cum laude, AM, U. Mich., 1980. Bar: D.C. 1980, U.S. Dist. Ct. (D.C.) 1981, U.S. Ct. Appeals (D.C. cir.) 1981, U.S. Supreme Ct. 1984, Calif. 1987, U.S. Dist. Ct. (so. dist.) Calif. 1987, U.S. Dist. Ct. (cen. dist.) Calif. 1992, Ga. 1993, U.S. Dist. Ct. (no. dist.) Ga. 1993, U.S. Ct. Appeals (11th cir.) 1993. Assoc. Bergson, Borkland, Margolis & Adler, Washington, 1980-82; atty. enforcement div. SEC, Washington, 1982-84, br. chief enforcement div., 1984-87; assoc. Gray, Cary, Ames & Frye, San Diego, 1987-92; sr. trial counsel SEC, Atlanta, 1993—. Mem. ABA, D.C. Bar Assn., Calif. Bar Assn., Ga. Bar Assn. Office: SEC 3475 Lenox Rd NE Ste 1000 Atlanta GA 30326-1232

MURPHY, RICKY KEITH, elementary school principal; b. Carrollton, Ga., Jan. 30, 1965; s. Billy Joe and Linda Elaine (Daniel) M.; m. Paula Sue Brown, July 1, 1989; children: Riley, Reed. BS, U. Ala., 1987; MS, Jacksonville State U., 1992. Cert. tchr., adminstr., elem., secondary levels, Ala. Tchr., coach Wadley (Ala.) H.S., 1987-88, Cleburne County H.S., Heflin, Ala., 1988-92; tchr. Randolph-Roanoke Area Vocat. Ctr., Wedowee, Ala., 1992-94; tchr., coach Woodland (Ala.) H.S., 1994-95; prin. Fruithurst (Ala.) Elem. Sch., 1995—. Preacher Ch. of Christ, Woodland, Ala., 1985—. Mem. Ala. Edn. Assn., Ala. Coun. Sch. Adminstrs. and Prins. Republican. Home: Rte 1 Box 341 Fruithurst AL 36262 Office: Fruithurst Elem Sch 101 School St Fruithurst AL 36262-3712

MURPHY, RUSSELL ELLIOTT, literature educator; b. Providence, May 15, 1944; s. Joseph Ignatius and Virginia Marie (Stavolone) M.; m. Susan Katherine Finkle , June 10, 1967 (div. June 1976); children: Sean Stephen, Matthew Edward; m. Teressa Rose Ezell, May 10, 1980; children: Michael Joseph, Sara Flannery, Gabriel James, Raphael Russell Umberto, Anna Mary Rose, John Francis DeAngelis. BA, U. Mass., 1966, MA, 1972, PhD, 1975. Instr. English U. Ark., Little Rock, 1972-74, asst. prof., 1974-78, assoc. prof., 1978-93, prof., 1993—; pub. Milestone Press, Little Rock, 1992—. Editor: (anthologies) Structure and Meaning, 1976, 2nd edit., 1983; author: (novel) Spent, 1981; editor: Yeats Eliot Review, 1987. Mem. Am. Conf. Irish Studies. Roman Catholic. Home: 8524 Asher Ave Little Rock AR 72204 Office: U Ark Little Rock Dept English 2801 S University Little Rock AR 72204

MURPHY, THOMAS BAILEY, state legislator; b. Bremen, GA, Mar. 10, 1924; s. W.H. and Leita (Jones) M.; m. Agnes Bennett, July 22, 1946; children: Michael L., Martha L., Marjorie Lynn, Mary June. Grad., N.Ga. Coll., 1943; LL.B., U. Ga., 1949. Bar: Ga. bar 1949. Since practiced in Bremen as partner firm Murphy & Murphy; mem. Ga. Ho. of Reps., 1961—, adminstrv. floor leader for gov., 1969-70, speaker pro tem, 1971-74, speaker, 1974—. Mem. Ga. Bar Assn., Am. Legion, VFW, Gridiron Secret Soc.; hon. life mem. Ga. Peace Officers Assn.; hon. mem. Ga. Fraternal Order Police, Ga. Sheriffs Assn. Democrat. Baptist. Club: Moose. Office: Ho of Reps State Capitol SW Rm 332 Atlanta GA 30334-1160

MURPHY, WILMA LOUISE BRYANT, critical care nurse; b. Ogden, Utah, Dec. 31, 1947; d. Bernard W. and Wilhelmena C. (Barenberg) Bryant; m. William J. Murphy, Nov. 24, 1972 (dec.); children: Carol Sue, Michael Douglas, Catherine Elizabeth. Diploma, Presbyn. Med. Ctr. Denver, 1969. RN, cert. emergency med. technician, burn specialist, cert. emergency nurse, trauma nurse, cert. emergency pediatric care provider. Dir. insvc. edn., burn unit Shriners Hosp. for Crippled Children, Galveston, Tex.; head nurse, burn unit U. Tex. Med. Br., Galveston; staff nurse Danforth Hosp., Texas City, Tex.; critical care staff nurse Norrell Health Care, Indpls., Midwest Med. Ctr., Indpls.; dir. nursing Miller's Merry Manor, Tipton, Ind.; emergency room staff nurse Westview Hosp., Indpls., 1994-95; critical care staff nurse BonSecarus St. Josephs Hosp., Port Charlotte, Fla., 1995—; post anesthesia care unit nurse Fla. Regional Hosp., 1995—. Contbr. articles to profl. jours. Mem. Emergency Room Nurses Assn. Home: 2860 Bardahl Ct Deltona FL 32738

MURRAH, DAVID J., archivist, historian; b. Shattuck, Okla., Sept. 13, 1941; s. G. Leroy and M. Leila (Montgomery) M.; m. Sherry Edwards, Mar. 2, 1962 (div. 1966); 1 child, Jerel; m. Ann Lynskey, Dec. 29, 1973; children: Donna, Elaine, Gene. BA, Hardin-Simmons U., 1964; MA, Tex. Tech. U., 1970, PhD, 1979. Pub. sch. tchr. Springtown (Tex.) I.S.D., 1966-67, Morton (Tex.) I.S.D., 1967-71; asst. archivist S.W. Collection Tex. Tech U., Lubbock, 1971-76, asst. dir. S.W. Collection, 1976-77, dir. S.W. Collection, 1977-83, assoc. dir. librs., dir. S.W. Collection, 1983—; bd. dirs. Centercorp, Inc., Lubbock, 1990—. Author: C.C. Slaughter: Rancher, Banker, Baptist, 1981, Pitchfork Land and Cattle Co., 1983, Oil, Taxes and Cats, 1994; co-author: Lubbock & The South Plains, 1989, 2d edit., 1995. Bd. dirs. Broadway Festivals, Inc., Lubbock, 1990—. Recipient Disting. Svc. award Soc. Southwest Archivists, 1988. Mem. Soc. Am. Archivists, Tex. State Hist. Assn., West Tex. Hist. Assn. (pres. 1991-92). Democrat. Baptist. Office: Southwest Collection Tex Tech U PO Box 41041 Lubbock TX 79409-1041

MURRAY, ALAN L., construction executive; b. Syracuse, N.Y., Jan. 8, 1959; m. Alexandra J. Murray, June 1, 1985. BS in Civil Engring. with honors, U. Ky., 1983. Exec. v.p. ops. James N. Gray Construction, Lexington, Ky., 1983-94; exec. v.p. sales & mktg. The Facility Group, San Francisco, 1995; pres. ConstructionNet, Lexington, 1995—. Lead analyst Gov.'s Commn. on Quality and Efficiency of Govt., 1993-94. Mem. Assn. Builders and Contractors (Design-Build Project of Yr. 1993), Assn. Gen. Contractors (Project of Yr. 1994), Ready Mix Mfg. Assn. (Project of Yr. 1990). Office: ConstructionNet Ste 23 141 Prosperous Place Lexington KY 40509

MURRAY, ALLEN EDWARD, retired oil company executive; b. N.Y.C., Mar. 5, 1929; s. Allen and Carla (Jones) M.; m. Patricia Ryan, July 28, 1951; children: Allen, Marilyn, Ellen, Eileen, Allison. B.S. in Bus. Adminstrn, NYU, 1956. Trainee Pub. Nat. Bank & Trust Co., N.Y.C., 1948-49; acct. Gulf Oil Corp., 1949-52; various fin. positions Socony-Vacuum Overseas Supply Co. (Mobil), 1952-56; with Mobil Oil Corp. (subs. Mobil Corp.), 1956-94, v.p. planning N.Am. div., 1968-69, v.p. planning, supply and transp. N.Am. div., 1969-74, exec. v.p. N.Am. div., 1974, pres. U.S. mktg. and refining div., exec. v.p., 1975-82, pres. worldwide mktg. and refining, 1979-82, corp. pres., 1983-84, COO, 1984-86, CEO, COO, chmn. exec. com., 1986—, chmn. bd., 1986—, also dir., 1976—; pres., chief operating officer Mobil Corp., N.Y.C., 1984-86, chmn., pres., chief exec. officer, 1986—, dir., 1977—; dir. Met. Life Ins. Co., 3M Co., Lockheed Martin Corp., Morgan Stanley Group Inc., St. Francis Hosp. Hon. trustee NYU. Served with USNR, 1946-48. Mem. Am. Petroleum Inst. (dir.), Coun. Fgn. Rels., Bus. Coun., Bus. Roundtable, Tri Lateral Commn. Club: Huntington Country. Office: Mobil Corp PO Box 2072 New York NY 10163-2072

MURRAY, ARTHUR JOSEPH, business executive, lecturer; b. Portsmouth, Va., Jan. 12, 1954; s. Arthur Patrick and Regina Agneta (Lescavage) M.; m. Deborah Marie Moyer, Sept. 6, 1975; children: Arthur III, Andrew. BSEE, Lehigh U., 1975; MEA, George Washington U., 1982, DSc, 1989. Electronics engr. USN Ordnance Sta., Indian Head, Md., 1975-81; rsch. engr. Inst. for Artificial Intelligence, Washington, 1985-87; sr. tech. staff The Titan Corp., Vienna, Va., 1982-89; professorial lectr. Sch. Engring. and Applied Sci., The George Washington U., Washington, 1985—; mgr. advanced technology McDonnell Douglas Electronic Systems Co., McLean, Va., 1989-91; sr. tech. cons. Gemini Industries, Inc., Vienna, Va., 1991-93; pres. Telart Techs., Arlington, Va., 1993—; conf. com. AI Systems in Govt. Conf., Washington, 1986, 90, Am. Soc. Info. Sci., Atlanta, 1988; referee Interfaces, 1993—. Named First Titan fellow Titan Systems, Inc., 1985. Mem. IEEE, Am. Assn. for Artificial Intelligence, Nat. Bus. Incubation Assn., Agility Forum, Am. Soc. for Performance Improvement (bd. dirs. 1978-79), Lambda Chi Alpha. Republican. Roman Catholic. Home: 203 S Fillmore St Arlington VA 22204-2079 Office: Telart Techs 203 S Fillmore St Arlington VA 22204-2079

MURRAY, BARRY WAYNE, economics educator; b. Dublin, Ga., June 1, 1946; s. Archie Guy and Helen Avis (Smith) M.; m. Laurie Lee Yoder, Sept. 11, 1976; children: Elisabeth Hope, Jonathan Guy, Caitlin Anna. BS in Econs., Auburn U., 1968; MEd in Econs. Edn., West Ga. Coll., 1978, EdS in Econs. Edn., 1980. Tchr. social studies Cobb County Bd. Edn., Marietta, Ga., 1968-85; dir. gifted program Osborne H.S., Marietta, 1985—, tchr. econs., 1989—; coach, advisor stock market game Ga. Coun. Econ. Edn., Atlanta, 1987—, advisor 4th State Stock Market Game Championship, 1994; coord. gov.'s honors selection Gov.'s Honors Program, Atlanta, 1985—. Author: (periodical) Level of Economic Understandng of Teachers, 1980 (Student Rsch. award 1980). Active Citizenship Coun. Cobb County, Marietta, 1985-86, Ga. Coun. Econ. Edn., Atlanta, 1987—. Mem. Ga. Acad. Team Assn., Ga. Assn. Educators. Office: Osborne HS 2451 Favor Rd Marietta GA 30060-7338

MURRAY, DALE NORRIS, engineering scientist, researcher; b. Cleveland County, N.C., Sept. 8, 1945; s. Walter Griffin and Iva Muriel (White) M.; m. Barbara Jean Bridges, June 6, 1965 (div. July 1977); children: Laura Nicole, Kimberly Michelle; m. Lynda Sue Bonds, May 16, 1981 (div. Nov. 1985); m. Alma D. Vigueria, Aug. 29, 1994. BS, Clemson (S.C.) U., 1967; MS in Info. and Computer Sci., Ga. Inst. Tech., 1983. With U.S. Civil Service, 1967-84; electronic engr. U.S. Army Missile Command, Huntsville, Ala., 1967-78, gen. engr., 1978-80; sr. project officer U.S. Army Inst. Rsch. in Mgmt. Info. and Computer Sci., Atlanta, 1980-84; sr. staff engr. TRW, Inc. Huntsville Ops., 1984-86; sr. engr./scientist Gen. Rsch. Corp., Huntsville, 1986-91; sr. systems analyst Hughes Aircraft Co., Huntsville, 1991—; mem. program com. Conf. Local Computer Networs, Mpls., 1980-86, tech. program chmn., 1985; mem. program com. Symposium Simulation Computer Networks, Colorado Springs, Colo., 1987; mem. rev. com. Nat. Computer Conf., 1983-86; mem. attendance com. Southcon Show and Conf., Atlanta, 1983-86. Contbr. articles to profl. jours. Mem. IEEE (sr.), Assn. for Computing Machinery, Armed Forces Comm. and Electronics Assn., Huntsville Soaring Club, Soaring Soc. Am. Home: 4907 Middleton Ln NW Huntsville AL 35816-1439 Office: Hughes Aircraft Co 670 Discovery Dr NW Huntsville AL 35806-2802

MURRAY, ELEANOR F., educator, freelance writer; b. Omaha, Nov. 30, 1916; d. Fred Blatchford and Calista June (Reynolds) Greusel; m. Jack Earl Buckley, June 15, 1970 (dec. Nov. 1977); m. Hubert Larkin Murray; children: Thomas M. B. Hicks, Mary E. Sharp, Barbara R. Wilke. BS in Edn., U. Nebr., 1939. Cert. tchr. of English. Newswriter Etowah Observer, Alabama City, Ala., 1939-40; feature writer Stars 'n Stripes, Tokyo, 1947-51; columnist Japan Times, Tokyo, 1949-51; in pub. relations Am. Internat. Underwriters, Tokyo, 1948-51; writer news and features Paterson (N.J.) Evening News, 1952-54; tchr. Riverdale (N.J.) Sch., 1954-55, Panama Canal Zone Schs., 1955-60, Skokie (Ill.) Schs., 1961-66; freelance writer Sebring, Fla., 1980—. Author: (non-fiction) Bend Like the Bamboo, 1982, Growing Up In Aunt Molly's Omaha, 1990; (poetry) Cherokee County Summer, 1981, God's Green Valley, 1983; author articles. Democrat. Presbyterian. Home: 1418 NE Lakeview Dr Sebring FL 33870-2700

MURRAY, ESTHER ELAINE, occupational health nurse; b. Bklyn., Oct. 19, 1957; d. Harold Albert and Lydia Freida (Schirmer) Herzog; m. David Keith Murray, June 17, 1978; 1 child, Victoria. Diploma, Burge Sch. of Nursing, 1978. Cert. occupational health nurse. Tng. specialist Med. Networks, Inc., Houston, 1984-86; relief occupational nurse NALCO, Sugarland, Tex., 1987-89; occupational nurse Mobay Chem., Baytown, Tex., 1988-89; with EXXON Chem., Baytown, Tex., 1989, Shell DPMC, Deer Park, Tex., 1986-92; employee health nurse St. Joseph Hosp., Bryan, Tex., 1990-93; mgr. occupational health Bapt. Hosp., Beaumont, Tex., 1993-95; with Park-Med Occupational Health Svcs., Knoxville, Tenn., 1995—. Chairperson Am. Cancer Soc., 1990-92, pub. edn. com. BCS chpt.; instr. ARC, 1986—, Am. Heart Assn., 1991—. Recipient Patient Svcs. award Bryan-Coll. Sta. C. of C., 1991. Mem. Am. Assn. of Occupational Health Nurses, Nat. Assn. Occpl. Health Profls. Office: Park Med Occup Health Svcs Bapt Hosp of SE Tex PO Box 30698 Knoxville TN 37930

MURRAY, GAYLON EUGENE, mass communication educator; b. Eddyville, Ky., Nov. 5, 1945; s. Gathon Emmett and Julia (Lovell) M.; m. Leslye Marion Mercer, Nov. 23, 1966 (div. Aug. 1977); children: Michael, Shannon; m. Susan Jane Schneider, Mar. 12, 1983; 1 child, Alexa Jane. BS, Murray State U., 1967; MS, Ohio U., 1968; PhD, Tex. A&M U., 1991. Reporter, editor various newspapers, 1963-95; asst. prof. journalism, assoc. dir. pub. info. Morehead (Ky.) State U., 1968-79; asst. prof. journalism Trinity U., San Antonio, 1979-80; commd. 2d lt. U.S. Army, 1967, advanced through grades to lt. col., 1988; pub. affairs officer U.S. Army, San Antonio, Chgo., Ft. C, Ark., 1980-92; instr. English Westark C.C., Ft. Smith, Ark., 1991; asst. prof. mass comm. Grambling (La.) State U., 1992—; res. pub. affairs officer 100th Tng. Divsn., Louisville, 1975-79; v.p. pub. rels. Assn. of U.S. Army, San Antonio, 1986-89. Contbr. articles to book and profl. jours. Sec.-treas. Optimist Club, Morehead, 1977-79. With U.S. Army Res., 1967-94. Recipient Minority Educator internship Am. Press Inst., 1993, Editing fellowship Dow Jones Newspaper Fund, 1994, Prof.-in-residence award Pioneer Press newspaper, 1995. Mem. Assn. for Edn. in Mass Comm. and Journalism, Soc. Profl. Journalists (chpt. advisor 1994—), Text and Acad. Authors Assn. Home: 2508 Cedar Creek Dr Ruston LA 71270 Office: Grambling State U Dept Mass Comm PO Box 45 Grambling LA 71245

MURRAY, J. ALEC G., manufacturing executive; b. 1936. With Coopers and Lybrand, Eng., 1957-69; with Standard Comml. Corp., London, 1969—, chmn. bd. dirs. Office: Standard Comml Co 2201 Miller Rd S Wilson NC 27893-6860*

MURRAY, JOHN WILLIAM, JR., legal investigator, writer; b. Apr. 8, 1934; s. John William and Frances (Bryan) M.; m. Norma Sousa, Oct. 30, 1959 (div. Apr. 1989); children: John William III, James Patrick, Jeffrey Dean, Jerome Bryan, Jay Joseph. BS, U. Hartford, 1968; MBA, U. Conn., 1971. Legal investigator Dallas, 1974—. 1st lt. USMC, 1957-60. Author: Accident Investigation in the Private Sector, 1994 (best new investigative book of yr.), Forensic Photography in the Private Sector, 1995, Sex Crimes, 1995. Mem. Nat. Assn. Legal Investigators (cert., chmn. nat. cert. 1987-89, nat. chmn. editor-pub. awards com. 1992-96, Editor-Pub. award Legal Investigator mag. 1989, 91), Evidence Photographers Internat. Coun., Nat. Assn. Investigative Specialists (cert. expert in investigative photography, expert in accident investigation, Outstanding Spkr. of Yr. award 1995, Lifetime Achievement award 1996), Nat. Acad. for Continuing Edn. (co-founder). Office: 3942 Rochelle Dr Dallas TX 75220

MURRAY, JOSEPH JAMES, JR., zoologist; b. Lexington, Va., Mar. 13, 1930; s. Joseph James and Jane Dickson (Vardell) M.; m. Elizabeth Hickson, Aug. 24, 1957; children—Joseph James III, Alison Joan, William Lister. B.S., Davidson Coll., 1951; B.A., Oxford U., Eng., 1954, M.A., 1957, D.Phil., 1962. Instr. biology Washington & Lee U., Lexington, Va., 1956-58; asst. prof. biology U. Va., Charlottesville, 1962-67, assoc. prof., 1967-73, prof., 1973-77, Samuel Miller prof. biology, 1977—, chmn. dept. biology, 1984-87; co-dir. Mountain Lake Biol. Sta., Pembroke, Va., 1963-91. Author: Genetic Diversity and Natural Selection, 1972; contbr. articles to profl. jours. Served with U.S. Army, 1955-56. Rhodes scholar, 1951-54. Fellow AAAS, Va. Acad. Sci.; mem. Am. Soc. Naturalists, Genetics Soc. Am., Soc. Study Evolution, Am. Soc. Ichthyologists and Herpetologists, Va. Acad. Sci. (pres. 1986-87), Va. Soc. Ornithology (pres. 1976-79). Office: U Va Dept Biology Gilmer Hall Charlottesville VA 22901

MURRAY, PETER WILLIAM, airline executive, educator, college administrator; b. Boston, Mar. 24, 1942; s. William Andrew Murray and Carlotta Catherine (Cenedella) Catusi; m. Carolyn Pfaff, Feb. 23, 1967; children: Eric, Trevor. AB, U. Notre Dame, South Bend, Ind., 1964; MBA, U. Pa., 1966. Analyst Delta Airlines, Atlanta, 1966-67; mgr. So. Airways, Atlanta, 1969-72; sr. analyst Eastern Airlines, N.Y.C., 1968-69; mgr. Eastern Airlines, Miami, Fla., 1972-89; dir. Discovery Airways, Honolulu, 1989-90; dean sch. bus. Chaminade U. Honolulu, 1990-94, dir. MS in Japanese bus. studies, 1990-93; assoc. prof. mgmt., dir. grad. adminstrn. Winthrop U., Rock Hill, S.C., 1995-96; dir. divsn. of lifelong learning Johnson C. Smith U., 1996—; adj. prof. U. Miami, Fla. Internat. U., Barry U., U. Hawaii, Pfeiffer U., Embry-Riddle Aero. U., 1975—. Mem. Wharton Grad. Alumni Club, Notre Dame Alumni Club, Am. Mktg. Assn. Democrat. Home: 4307 Cantey Pl Charlotte NC 28211-0404 Office: Johnson C Smith U Divsn of Lifelon Learning MBA/EMBA Office Charlotte NC 28216

MURRAY, RAYMOND LE ROY, nuclear engineering educator; b. Lincoln, Nebr., Feb. 14, 1920; s. Ray Annis and Bertha (Mann) M.; m. Ilah Mae Rengler, June 16, 1941; children: Stephen, Maureen, Marshall; m. Quin Meyer, June 3, 1967; 1 stepdau., Tucker; m. Elizabeth Reid, May 12, 1979; stepchildren: Michael, Nancy, James. B.S., U. Nebr., 1940, M.S., 1941; Ph.D., U. Tenn., 1950; postgrad., U. Calif., Berkeley, 1941-43. Physicist U. Calif. Radiation Lab., Berkeley, 1942-43; asst. dept. supt. Tenn. Eastman Corp., Oak Ridge, 1943-47; research physicist Carbide & Carbon Chem. Co., Oak Ridge, 1947-50; prof. physics N.C. State U., 1950-57, Burlington prof. physics, 1957-80, prof. emeritus, 1980—, head dept. physics, 1960-63, head dept. nuclear engring., 1963-74; acting dir. Nuclear Reactor Project, 1956-57; cons. Oak Ridge Nat. Lab., 1950-68, Los Alamos Nat. Lab., 1988-92, also to industry and govt. Author: Introduction to Nuclear Engineering, 1954, 2d edit., 1961, Nuclear Reactor Physics, 1957, Physics: Concepts and Consequences, 1970, Nuclear Energy, 1975, 4th edit., 1993, Understanding Radioactive Waste, 1982, 4th edit., 1994; mem. edit. adv. bd., U.S. exec. editor Jour. Nuclear Energy, 1963-73; adv. editor Annals Nuclear Energy, 1973—; contbr. numerous articles to profl. jours. and encys. Mem. adv. com. on radiation N.C. Bd. Health, 1958-59; mem. Gov.'s Tech. Adv. Com. on Low Level Radioactive Waste, 1980-87; mem. N.C. Radiation Protection Commn., 1979-87, chmn., 1980-82; mem., vice chmn., chmn. N.C. Low Level Radioactive Waste Mgmt. Authority, 1987-93. Recipient O. Max Gardner award U. N.C., 1965; Arthur H. Compton award, 1970, Donald G. Fink award IEEE, 1988, Eugene P. Wigner Reactor Physicist award, 1994. Fellow Am. Phys. Soc., Am. Nuclear Soc. (chmn. edn. div. 1966-67, chmn. Eastern Carolinas sect. 1976-77, mem. nominating com. 1989); mem. Am. Soc. Engring. Edn. (chmn. com. on relationships with AEC 1967-68, chmn. nuclear engring. div. 1970-71, Glenn Murphy award 1976), N.C. Soc. Engrs. (Outstanding Engring. Achievement award 1975), Atomic Indsl. Forum (edn. coun. 1970-73), Inst. Nuclear Power Ops. (adv. coun. 1985-87, 89-94), Phi Beta Kappa, Sigma Xi, Pi Mu Epsilon, Phi Kappa Phi. Home: 8701 Murray Hill Drive Raleigh NC 27615

MURRAY, RUSSELL, II, aeronautical engineer, defense analyst, consultant; b. Woodmere, N.Y., Dec. 5, 1925; s. Herman Stump and Susanne Elizabeth (Warren) M.; m. Sally Tingue Gardiner, May 22, 1954; children: Ann Tingue, Prudence Warren, Alexandria Gardiner. BS in Aero. Engring, MIT, 1949, MS, 1950. Guided missile flight test engr. Grumman Aircraft Engring. Corp., Bethpage, N.Y., 1950-53, asst. chief operations analysis, 1953-62; prin. dep. asst. sec. of def. for systems analysis The Pentagon, Washington, 1962-69; dir. long range planning Pfizer Internat., N.Y.C., 1969-73; dir. review Center for Naval Analyses, Arlington, Va., 1973-77; asst. sec. of def. for program analysis and evaluation Dept. of Def., The Pentagon, Washington, 1977-81; prin. Systems Research & Applications Corp., Arlington, Va., 1981-85; spl. counsellor Com. on Armed Services U.S. Ho. of Reps., 1985-89, nat. security cons., 1989—. Served with USAAF, 1944-45. Recipient Sec. of Def. Medal for meritorious civilian service, 1968; Disting. Public Service medal Dept. Def., 1981. Home: 210 Wilkes St Alexandria VA 22314-3839

MURRAY, TIMOTHY DOUGLAS, art educator; b. Reading, Eng., Oct. 28, 1938; naturalized citizen, 1976; Student, Mars Hill Coll., 1957-59; BA, U. N.C., 1961, MA, 1966. Prof. art Brevard (N.C.) Coll., dir. Sims Art Ctr.; art cons. Queens Coll., Charlotte, N.C., 1987;. Exhibited works in numerous shows including Western Carolina U., Cullowhee, N.C., 1989, Broadway Arts, Asheville, N.C., 1991, Arts Coun., Spartanburg, 1991, Friedholm Gallery, Asheville, 1991, New Lincolnton (N.C.) Performing Arts Ctr., 1991, Lander U., Greenwood, S.C., 1993, Studio Gallery B., Lancaster, Ohio, 1993,

N.C. Mus. Art, Greensboro, 1993, Vrevard Coll., 1994, 95, Mars Hill Coll., 1995, Images Friedman Gallery, Louisville, 1995, Zone on Gallery, Asheville, 1996; executed commns. for Sacred Heart Cath. Ch., Brevard, 1989, also pieces for pvt. homes. Mem. Smokey Art Consortium, 1988—; trustee Asheville Art Mus., 1989-95; mem. Arts Coun., Brevard, 1990-96. Office: Sims Art Ctr Brevard Coll Brevard NC 28712

MURRAY, TOM REED, II, program manager, engineer; b. McKinney, Tex., Feb. 3, 1939; s. Tom Reed and Ione Edna (McBee) McC.; m. Karen Marie Noteboom, May 17, 1986; children: Kelly Murray Oakeley, Tom Reed III. BS in Naval Engring., U.S. Naval Acad., 1961. Commd. ens. USN, 1961, advanced through grades to capt.; head ship systems Office Chief Naval Ops., The Pentagon, 1970-73; exec. officer USN, Newport News, Va., 1973-77; commanding officer USS Lapon, Norfolk, Va., 1977-81; head cruise missile sect. Office of Chief of Naval Ops., 1981-83; dir. fast attack submarine performance USN, Arlington, Va., 1983-85; chief navy sect. Joint U.S. Mil. Mission for Aid to Turkey, Ankara, 1985-87; ret. USN, 1987; advanced tech. analyst Systems Planning Corp., Arlington, Va., 1988-89; program mgr. Decision-Sci. Applications, Inc., Arlington, 1989-92, CAE-Link Corp., Silver Spring, Md., 1992-94; gen. mgr. Decision Sys. Technologies, Inc., Greenbelt, Md., 1994-95. Author reports in field. Pres. Rep. Bd. Dirs., Arlington, 1990; mem. Tidewater Civic Assn., Hampton, Va., 1971-73. Decorated DSM, 1987. Mem. Am. Soc. Naval Engrs., Am. Turkish Friendship Coun., Am. Nuclear Soc., U.S. Naval Submarine League, U.S. Naval Inst., Nat. Security Indsl. Assn. (anti-submarine warfare com.). Episcopalian. Home: Ste 1207 1101 S Arlington Ridge Rd Arlington VA 22202

MURRAY, WILLIAM JAMES, anesthesiology educator, clinical pharmacologist; b. Janesville, Wis., July 20, 1933; s. James Arthur and Mary Helen (De Porter) M.; m. Therese Rose Dooley, June 25, 1955; children: Michael, James, Anne. BS, U. Wis., 1955, PhD, 1959; MD, U. N.C., 1962. Diplomate Am. Bd. Anesthesiology. Rsch. asst. U. Wis., Madison, 1955-59; instr. pharmacology U. N.C., Chapel Hill, 1959-62, resident and fellow in surgery (anesthesiology), 1962-64, instr., 1964-65, asst. prof., 1965-68; asst. to dir. for drug availability FDA, Washington, 1968-69; assoc. prof. pharmacology, clin. pharmacology and anesthesiology U. Mich., Ann Arbor, 1969-72; assoc. prof. anesthesiology Duke U., Durham, N.C., 1972-81, prof., 1981—; assoc. dir. Upjohn Ctr. for Clin. Pharmacology, Ann Arbor, 1969-72. Mem. AMA, Am. Soc. Anesthesiologists, Internat. Anesthesia Rsch. Soc., Soc. for Ambulatory Anesthesia, Am. Pharm Assn., N.Y. Acad. of Sci., N. C. Soc. Anesthesiologists, Am. Soc. Hosp. Pharmacists, U.S. Pharmacopeial Conv., Am. Coll. Clin. Pharmacology, Am. Soc. for Clin. and Therapeutic Pharmacology, Am. Soc. Pharmacology and Exptl. Therapeutics, N.C. Soc. Hosp. Pharmacists, So. Med. Assn., The Annals of Pharmacotherapy. Republican. Roman Catholic. Home: 135 Pinecrest Rd Durham NC 27705 Office: Duke U Med Ctr Dept Anesthesiology Box 3094 Durham NC 27710

MURRELL, CARLOS DEVONNE, poet, Spanish language educator, translator; b. Raleigh, N.C., Dec. 3, 1966; s. Robert James Murrell and Hilda Jo Seberry; m. LaShonda Jones, June 15, 1985 (div. July 1991); 1 child, Carlos Devonne II. Diploma, Def. Lang. Inst., Monterey, Calif., 1988; AA, City Colls. Chgo., Ramstein, Germany, 1990; BA, SUNY, Albany, 1993; MA, U. N.C., Greensboro, 1995. Cert. K-12 tchr., N.C. Curriculum specialist Wake County Pub. Schs., Raleigh, 1993, 95-96; asst. editor Internat. Poetry Rev., Greensboro, 1993-94; instr. Spanish, U. N.C., 1994-95; adj. lectr. Spanish, N.C. Ctrl. U., Durham, 1995—. Mem. editl. bd. Nat. Assn. Black and White Men Together Jour., 1995—; publs. include poetry in Am. Collegiate Poets Anthology, 1993, NABWMT Jour., VII, 1995, The Ebbing Tide, 1996. Sgt. U.S. Army, 1987-91; mem. USAR, 1992-95. Recipient Dual award N.Am. Open Poetry Contest, 1996; LaRochelle scholar, 1994-95. Mem. MLA, Coll. Lang. Assn., Fgn. Lang. Assn. N.C., Am. Translators Assn., Carolina Assn. Transl. and Interpreters, Sigma Delta Pi. Democrat. Episcopalian. Office: NC Ctrl U Dept Modern Fgn Langs Durham NC 27707

MURRELL, IRVIN HENRY, JR., librarian, minister; b. Charlotte, N.C., July 25, 1945; s. Irvin Henry and Lula Maie (Sullivan) M; m. Phoebe Maria Moore, June 15, 1974; 1 child, Irvin Henry III. BS, N.C. State U., 1967; MRE, Southeastern Bapt. Theol. Sem., 1973; M of Ch. Music, Southwestern Bapt. Theol. Sem., 1978, MusM, 1980; DMA, New Orleans Bapt. Theol. Sem., 1984; MLS, La. State U., 1986. Ordained to ministry Bapt. Ch., 1974. Math. tchr. Coulwood Jr. High Sch., Charlotte, 1967-71; min. music Fieldcrest Bapt. Ch., Durham, N.C., 1972-73, Immanuel Bapt. Ch., Ft. Worth, 1975-80; min. music/edn. Five Points Bapt. Ch., Wilson, N.C., 1973-75; reference/circulation libr. New Orleans Bapt. Theol. Sem., 1980-85; dir. Montgomery Libr. Campbellsville (Ky.) Coll., 1986-89; dir. McMillan Libr. Fla. Bapt. Theol. Coll., Graceville, Fla., 1989—; part-time math. tchr. Sem. South Assembly of God Day Sch., Ft. Worth, 1979-80; interim min. music Meadville (Miss.) Bapt. Ch., 1980-81, Christ Bapt. Ch., Houma, La., 1982-83, Bethlehem Bapt. Ch., Springfield, Ky., 1986, 1st Bapt. Ch., Lacombe, La., 1983-85, Edmonton (Ky.) Bapt. Ch., 1986-89, 1st Bapt. Ch., Shellman, Ga., 1989-93, Providence Bapt. Ch., Grand Ridge, Fla., 1993-94, 1st Bapt. Ch., Colquitt, Ga., 1994—; contract tchr. Div. Ch., Music Ministries, New Orleans Bapt. Theol. Sem., 1984-85. Contbr. articles to profl. jours. Mem. Hymn Soc. Am., So. Bapt. Libr. Assn. (pres. 1987-88), So. Bapt. Ch. Music Conf., Optimists. Republican. Home: PO Box 284 5396 O B Knight Dr Graceville FL 32440-1900 Office: Fla Bapt Theol Coll 1306 College Dr Graceville FL 32440-1898

MURRELL, KENNETH LYNN, management educator; b. Topeka, Nov. 6, 1945; s. John Milton and Sarah Ellen (Randolph) M.; m. Catherine Marie Garner, Apr. 28, 1984; children: Kenyan John, Kyra Alexandra, Jackson Randolph. Student, Washburn U., 1968; student, Am. U., 1972, George Washington U., 1977. Registered orgn. devel. cons. Rsch. asst. Environ. Rsch. Found., Topeka, 1967-68; cons. Washington, 1972—; orgn. devel. cons. G.D. Searle, Inc., Chgo., 1977-78; assoc. prof. St. Bonaventure (N.Y.) U., 1980-82, U. West Fla., Pensacola, 1982—; adj. and vis. prof. Am. U., George Washington U., Washington, 1975—; vis. prof. Am. U. in Cairo, 1978-80; internat. devel. cons. UNDP, U.S. AID, World Bank, several fgn. govts., 1988—; orgn. devel. cons. numerous businesses and social agys., U.S., 1972—; mgmt. expert World Bank, Washington, 1982-83; founder, sr. assoc. Devel. Mgmt. Assocs., Pensacola, 1988—; pres. Empowerment Leadership Systems, cons. to Motorola, Honeywell, Toyota, UN and fgn. govts. Coauthor: Organization Development, 1976, Management Infrastructure, 1986, Empowerment, 1990; contbr. articles to profl. jours.; editor several publs. Exec. com. Devel. Mgmt. Network, Washington, 1985-90; selection com. Senator Graham's West Point Selection Com., Tallahassee, 1988-90; bd. mem. County Alcohol and Drug Coun., Olean, N.Y., 1981, Favor House-Spouse Abuse Ctr., Pensacola, 1983. 1st lt. U.S. Army, 1968-71, Vietnam. Mem. Acad. Mgmt., Internat. Orgn. Devel. Network, Orgn. Devel. Inst., Devel. Mgmt. Network (planning com.), Coun. on Aging. Home: 3149 Deep Water Cir Milton FL 32583-2936 Office: U West Fla 11000 University Pky Pensacola FL 32514-5732

MURRELL, SUSAN DEBRECHT, librarian; b. St. Louis, Aug. 10, 1951; d. Edward August and Edith (Keeney) DeB.; m. Harry Thornton Murrell, Oct. 18, 1974; children: Brian, Katherine. BA in History, U. Ky., 1973; MLS, U. Mo., 1976. Children's libr. Louisville Free Pub. Libr., 1974-76, talking book libr. head, 1976-83; lower/mid. sch. libr. Ky. Country Day Sch., Louisville, 1983-84; children's libr. Emmet O'Neal Libr., Mountain Brook, Ala., 1984-86, asst. dir., 1986-89, dir., 1989—. Bd. dirs. Mountain Brook Libr. Found., 1993—; active Jefferson County Pub. Libr., mem. publicity com., 1989-92; mem. allocations com. United Way. Mem. Ala. Libr. Assn. (mem. publicity com. 1992-93, pub. libr. chair 1995-96), Rotary Internat. Roman Catholic. Office: Emmet O'Neal Libr 50 Oak St Birmingham AL 35213-4219

MURRELL, WILLIAM IVAN, accountant; b. Bessemer, Ala., Dec. 28, 1923; s. Virgil Stewart Murrell and Mae (Rutledge) Ferguson; m. Virginia Byrd Reynolds, May 27, 1944; children: Melinda Ann, Barbara Kay, Shirley Sue. Student, Walton Sch. Commerce, 1941-46, Tex. Christian U., 1947-48, So. Meth. U., 1949-50. CPA. Bookkeeper Continental Oil Co., Ft. Worth, 1942-43; staff acct. Patterson & Leatherwood, Ft. Worth, 1946-48; sr. acct. Coopers & Lybrand, Dallas, 1949-51; sr. ptnr. Parish, Murrell & Co., Dallas, 1951-85; cons. Dallas, 1986—; bd. dirs. Rancho Oil Co., Dallas, Nat. Industries Corp., Dallas, Warehouse Properties Corp., Dallas. Author: World War II Love Letters, 1993, This Is It, Men, 1991, Murder for Profit or Loss, 1992. With U.S. Army, 1943-46. Mem. AICPA (life), Accts. Computer Users (Devoted Svc. award 1971), Tex. Soc. CPA (life, pres. 1968-69), Horatio Alger Soc. (Rags to Riches award 1990). Baptist. Home: 4321 W Lawther Dr Dallas TX 75214-2921

MURTAGH, FREDERICK REED, neuroradiologist, educator; b. Phila., Nov. 20, 1944; s. Frederick and Mary (Shaner) M.; (div.); children: Ryan David, Kevin Reed; m. Dorothy Rossi. BA, William and Mary Coll., 1966; MD, Temple U., 1971. Prof., dir. neuroradiology U. S. Fla., Tampa, 1978—. Author: Imaging Anatomy of Head & Spine, 1991. Lt. USNR, 1972-74. Mem. Am. Coll. Radiology (cert. added qualification in neuroradiology 1995), Assn. Univ. Radiologists, Am. Soc. Neuroradiology (sr. mem.), Radiol. Soc. N.Am., Southeastern Neuroradiology Soc. Office: U South Fla 3301 Alumni Dr Tampa FL 33612-9413

MURTAGH, JOHN EDWARD, alcohol production consultant; b. Wallington, Surrey, Eng., Sept. 12, 1936; came to U.S., 1982; s. Thomas Henry and Elsie (Kershaw Paterson) M.; m. Eithne Anne Fawsitt, July 18, 1959; children: Catherine, Rhoda, Sean, Aidan, Doreen. BSc, U. Wales, 1959, MSc, 1970, PhD, 1972. Rsch. coord. House of Seagram, Long Pond, Jamaica, 1959-63; whisky distillery mgr. House of Seagram, Beaupre, Que., Can., 1963-65; rum distillery mgr. House of Seagram, Richibucto, N.B., Can., 1965-68; rsch. mgr. House of Seagram, Montreal, Que., 1968-70; alcohol prodn. cons. Murtagh & Assocs., Buttevant, Ireland, 1972-77, 79-82, Winchester, Va., 1982—; vodka distillery mgr. Iran Beverages, Tehran, 1977-79; ethanol tech. cons., adv. bd. Info. Resources, Inc., Washington, 1988—; lectr. Alltech Ann. Alcohol Sch., Lexington, Ky., 1982—. Author: Glossary of Fuel-Ethanol Terms, 1990; co-author, editor: The Alcohol Textbook, 1995; editor: Worldwide Directory of Distilleries, 1996; contbr. articles to profl. jours. Adv. bd. Byrd Sch. Bus., Shenandoah U., Winchester, Va., 1989—. Recipient Millers Mutual prize, U. Wales, 1959. Fellow Am. Inst. Chemists, Inst. Chemistry of Ireland, Inst. Food Sci. and Tech. of Ireland; mem. Royal Soc. Chemistry (chartered), Am. Arbitration Assn. (arbitrator nat. comml. panel 1990—). Home and Office: 160 Bay Ct Winchester VA 22602-4700

MURTHY, KRIS, computer services executive; b. Gorakpur, India, Oct. 25, 1952; s. Bala and Jaya (Iyer) Subramanian. BS, Indian Inst. Tech., 1974; MS, U. Wis., 1976. Cert. pilot, FAA. Quality assurance mgr. Porex Corp., Atlanta, 1976-78; indsl. engr. IBM Corp., Rochester, Minn., 1979-81; cons. IBM Corp., Boca Raton, Fla., 1981-86; mktg. mgr. IBM Corp., St. Louis, 1986-91; engagement mgr. IBM Corp., Atlanta, 1991—. Home: 4739 Adams Rd Dunwoody GA 30338

MURTHY, VANUKURI RADHA KRISHNA, civil engineer; b. Hyderabad, India, June 20, 1928; came to U.S., 1963; s. Rama Vannkuri and Sita (Dittakavi) Rao; m. Lakshmi Gruha Gadiraju, Mar. 12, 1952; children: Siva, Prabha, Jyothy, Lata. BE in Civil, Osmania U., 1949; MS in Engring., U. Fla., 1964; PhD, U. Pa., 1967. Registered profl. engr., Tex. Engr. Govt. of Andhra Pradesh, Hyderabad, 1949-62; grad. rsch. asst. U. Fla., Gainesville, 1963-64, U. Del., Newark, 1964-67; grad. rsch. asst. U. Pa., Phila., 1964-67, instr., 1967-68; hydrologist Tex. Water Rights Commn., Austin, 1968-71, head hydraulics design sect., 1972-77; head basin modeling Tex. Water Commn., Austin, 1978-90; chief engr. Tex. Water Commn., 1990-91; cons. water resources, 1991—; engr. advisor to commr. Pecos River Compact Commn., Austin, 1987-91, chmn. engring. adv. com., 1987-91; prin. expert witness in interstate law suit for Tex. against N.Mex., 1977-90. Author: Allocation of Pecos River Basin Water, 1991; also articles. Travel grantee NSF, 1975. Mem. ASCE (life, editor Jour. Pipeline Div. 1969-74), Internat. Water Resources Assn., Sigma Xi. Home: 5910 Mountain Villa Dr Austin TX 78731-3753 Office: 600 W 28th St Austin TX 78705-3708

MURTY, KOMANDURI SRINIVASA, criminal justice educator; b. Rajahundry, India, July 1, 1956; came to U.S., 1981; s. Komanduri Krishna and Komanduri Andalamma (Eyani) M.; m. Andal Komanduri, Aug. 23, 1986; children: Vandana, Chandana. BS, Andhra U., Waltair, India, 1975, MA, 1977; diploma, Internat. Inst. for Population, Bombay, India, 1979; PhD, Miss. State U., 1984. Rsch. officer Population Rsch. Ctr., Waltair, 1979-81; grad. rsch. asst. sociology dept. Miss. State U., 1981-84; resident counselor, adj. prof. Atlanta U., 1984-85, asst. prof., 1985-89; assoc. prof., acting dept. chair Clark Atlanta U., 1989-90, assoc. prof., dept. chair, 1990—; dir. Criminal Justice Inst., Clark Atlanta U., 1990—; cons. Acad. Computer Ctr., Atlanta, 1990—, U. Community Devel. Corp., Atlanta, 1991—, Nat. Conf. Black Mayors, Atlanta, 1993. Author: (with others) Intimate Violence: Interdisciplinary Perspectives, 1992, Studies in Symbolic Interactions, 1993; author: The Place of Black Histori-Colleges & Universities, 1993; assoc. editor: Internat. Jour. Comparative & Applied Criminal Justice, 1985—; contbr. to Ency. of Am. Prisons, 1996, Southern Subculture of Drinking and Driving, 1996. Grantee Fulton County (Ga.) Govt., 1985—, Gov.'s Office of Hwy. Safety, Atlanta, 1989, Ga. Dept. of Children & Youth Svcs., 1993-94, Fulton County Govt. Security and Tng. Program, 1994, Fulton County Govt./DEFACS, 1990, Dept. Human Resources, Atlanta, 1991. Mem. Internat. Assn. for Study of Organized Crime, Am. Statis. Assn., Am. Soc. Criminology, Mid-South Soc. Assn. Hindu. Office: Clark Atlanta U James P Brawley St Atlanta GA 30314

MUSACCHIO, MARILYN JEAN, nurse midwife, educator; b. Louisville, Dec. 7, 1938; d. Robert William and Loretta C. (Liebert) Poulter; m. David Edward Musacchio, May 13, 1961; children: Richard Peter, Michelle Marie. BSN cum laude, Spalding Coll., 1968; MSN, U. Ky., 1972, degree in Nurse-Midwifery, 1976; PhD, Case Western Res U., 1993. RN; cert. nurse-midwife; advanced registered nurse practitioner; registered nurse-midwife. Staff nurse gynecol. unit St. Joseph Infirmary, Louisville, 1959-60, staff nurse male gen. surgery unit, 1960; instr. St. Joseph Infirmary Sch. Nursing, Louisville, 1960-71; from asst. prof. to assoc. prof., dir. dept. nursing edn. Ky. State U., Frankfort, 1972-75; asst. prof. U. Ky. Coll. Nursing, Lexington, 1976-79, assoc. prof., coord., 1979-92, acting coordinator nurse-midwifery, 1982-84, coordinator for nurse-midwifery, 1987-92; assoc. prof., dir. nurse-midwifery U. Ala., Birmingham, 1992—; cons. in field. Mem. editorial bd. Jour. Obstet., Gynecol. and Neonatal Nursing, 1976-82; author pamphlet; contbr. articles to profl. jours. Active St. James Parish Coun., chmn., 1980-81; mem. Louisville Fire Prevention Coun., 1973-80, Louisville Safety Coun., 1973-80. Brig. Gen. Army Nurse Corps, USAR, 1992-95. Recipient Disting. Citizen award City of Louisville, 1977, Jefferson Cup award Jefferson County, Ky., 1991; named Outstanding Alumna, Mercy Acad., 1993; named to Hall of Disting. Alumni, U. Ky., 1995; recipient scholarships and fellowships, other awards. Fellow Am. Acad. Nursing; mem. AWHONN, NAFE, Am. Nurses Assn. (nurse rschr. coun. 1985—, maternal child coun. 1985—), Nurse Assn. Am. Coll. Ob-Gyn. (charter; nat. sec. 1970-72, chmn. dist. V 1969), Am. Coll. Nurse-Midwives, Internat. Childbirth Edn. Assn., Am. Soc. Psychoprophylaxis in Obstetrics, Nat. Assn. Parents and Profls. for Safe Alternatives in Childbirth, Res. Officers Assn., Assn. Mil. Surgeons U.S., Sr. Army Res. Commdr. Assn., Assn. U.S. Army, Retired Army Nurse Corps. Assn., Army War Coll. Alumni Assn. Roman Catholic. Home: 1318 Springs Ave Birmingham AL 35242-4862

MUSE, WILLIAM VAN, academic administrator; b. Marks, Miss., Apr. 7, 1939; s. Mose Lee and Mary Elizabeth (Hisaw) M.; m. Anna Marlene Munden, Aug. 22, 1964; children: Amy Marlene, Ellen Elizabeth, William Van. B.S. (T.H. Harris scholar), Northwestern La. State U., 1960; M.B.A. (Nat. Def. Grad. fellow), U. Ark., 1961, Ph.D. (Nat. Def. Grad. fellow), 1966. Instr. U. Ark., 1962-63; field supr. Tau Kappa Epsilon Fraternity, 1963-64; asst. prof. Ga. Tech., 1964-65; assoc. prof., chmn., dir. rsch. Ohio U., 1965-70; dean Coll. Bus. Appalachian State U., Boone, N.C., 1970-73; dean Coll. Bus. Adminstrn. U. Nebr., Omaha, 1973-79; dean Coll. Bus. Adminstrn. Tex. A&M U., College Station, 1979-82, vice chancellor, 1983-84; former pres. U. Akron, Ohio, 1984-92; now pres. Auburn U., Ala., 1992—. Author: Business and Economic Problems in Appalachia, 1969, Management Practices in Fraternities, 1965; Contbr. articles to profl. jours. Found. for Econ. Edn. fellow, 1967. Mem. Blue Key, Omicron Delta Kappa, Phi Kappa Phi, Delta Sigma Pi, Beta Gamma Sigma, Pi Omega Pi, Tau Kappa Epsilon. Club: Rotarian. Office: Auburn U Office of Pres 107 Sanford Hall Auburn AL 36849*

MUSGROVE, RONNIE, state official; b. July 29, 1956; m. Melanie Ballard; children: Jordan, Carmen Rae. Grad., Northwest Miss. Jr. Coll., U. Miss.; JD, U. Miss. Ptnr. Smith, Musgrove & McCord, Batesville, Miss.; lt. gov. State of Miss., Jackson, 1996—. Fellow Miss. Bar Found.; mem. Am. Inns Ct., Miss. State Bar (bd. bar commrs. 1990), Miss. Bar Assn., Miss. Young Lawyers Assn. (bd. dirs.), Panola County Bar Assn. (v.p., pres.), Tri-County Bar Assn. (pres.), Phi Beta Lambda. Office: Office of Lt Governor New Capitol Rm 316 Jackson MS 39215

MUSIELAK, ZDZISLAW EDWARD, physicist, educator; b. Piwonice, Kalisz, Poland, Feb. 13, 1950; came to U.S., 1983; s. Edward and Irena (Bak) M.; m. Grazyna Roszkiewicz, Aug. 23, 1975; 1 child, Agnieszka Maria. MS in Physics, A. Mickiewicz U., 1976; PhD in Physics, U. Gdansk, 1980, hon. scholar, 1990. Cert. tchr., Poland, 1976. Teaching asst. A. Mickiewicz Univ., Poznan, Poland, 1976-77; rsch. asst. U. Gdansk, Poland, 1977-80, instr., 1980-82; vis. scientist U. Heidelberg, Fed. Republic Germany, 1982-83; rsch. staff MIT, Cambridge, 1983-86; NAS/NRC fellow NASA Marshall Space Flight Ctr., Huntsville, Ala., 1986-89; prof. U. Ala., Huntsville, 1989—; vis. scientist Harvard-Smithsonian Ctr. for Astrophy., Cambridge, 1985; cons. Univ. Chgo., Ill., 1988—; vis. prof. Univ. Heidelberg, 1990. Contbr. articles to Acta Astron., Astron. & Astrophys. Jour., Astrophys. Jour., Jour. Plasma Phys. Mem. Solidarity, Gdansk, 1980-83, deputy, 1980; mem. Nat. Geographic Soc., Washington, 1984. Recipient Sonnenforschungsbereich award U. Heidelberg, 1985, NAS/NRC award U.S. Nat. Acad. Scis., Huntsville, 1986, Rsch. award Smithsonian Obs., Cambridge, 1987, NASA theory grant NASA Marshall Space Flight Ctr., Huntsville, 1989, NASA Astrophysics Theory Program grant, 1995; named Rosat Guest Observer, NASA, German Space Agy., Wsahignton, 1990; NSF grantee, 1991, 92. Mem. AIAA, Am. Astron. Soc., Internat. Astron. Union (grants 1982, 88), Am. Geophys. Soc., Polish Astron. Soc. (travel grant 1979, 80). Office: U Ala Eb # 117H Huntsville AL 35899

MUSSELMAN, NORMAN BURKEY, retired editor; b. Arkansas City, Kans., Mar. 21, 1929; s. Norman Beachy and E. Ruth (Burkey) M.; m. Elizabeth Temple Henry, Oct. 26, 1957; children: Elizabeth Temple Whitson, Norman Henry, Robert Beachy. BA, U. Okla., 1951, MA, 1954. Columnist McGraw Hill Pub. Co., Washington, 1954-67; editor Nat. Assn. Electric Cos., Washington, 1967-80; dir. govt. com. Edison Electric Inst., Washington, 1980-94; retired, 1994. Pres. Okla. U. Alumni Club, Washington, 1957-58; pres. men of ch. Presbyn. Meeting House, Alexandria, Va., 1962-63, clk. of session, 1980-82; elder 1st Presbyn. Ch., Glenwood Springs; precinct capt. Rep. Party, 1968-69; cubmaster, pack chmn., scout com. Boy Scouts, Alexandria, 1970-73, 78-82. 1st lt. U.S. Army, 1951-53. Mem. Soc. for the Preservation and Enhancement of Barber Shop Singing in Am., Nat. Press Club, Sigma Delta Chi (pres. Okla. U. chpt. 1953-54). Home: 700 Silver Oak Dr Glenwood Springs CO 81601-2804

MUSSELMAN, ROBERT METCALFE, lawyer, accountant; b. N.Y.C., June 12, 1914; s. Joseph Franklin and Susan (Metcalfe) M.; m. Lucie Carolyn Clarke, Sept. 6, 1958; 1 child, Susan Carole. BS, U. Va., 1934, MA in Polit. Sci., 1940, LLB, 1945. Bar: Va. 1945, U.S. Dist. Cts. (ea. dist.) Va. 1948, U.S. Dist. Ct. (we. dist.) Va. 1951, U.S. Dist. Ct. (cen. dist.) Ill. 1994, U.S. Ct. Appeals (4th cir.) 1953, U.S. Ct. Appeals (11th cir.) 1987, U.S. Ct. Appeals (fed. cir.) 1988, U.S. Ct. Appeals (7th cir.) 1994, U.S. Claims Ct. 1986, U.S. Tax Ct. 1948, U.S. Supreme Ct. 1964. Instr., lectr. U. Va., Charlottesville, 1936-59, chief acct., 1943-46; law clk. to judge U.S. Ct. Appeals (4th cir.), 1945-46; ptnr. Michael and Musselman, Charlottesville, 1946-53, Musselman and Drysdale, Charlottesville, 1953-56; sole practice, Charlottesville, 1956—; lectr. in field. Pres. Charlottesville-Albemarle Young Democratic Club, 1940-43; mem. Albemarle County Dem. Com., 1978—. Mem. 4th Cir. Jud. Conf., Am. Assn. Atty.-C.P.A.s (charter mem., bd. dirs.), ABA, Va. Bar Assn., Charlottesville-Albemarle Bar Assn., AICPAs, Va. Soc. CPAs (bd. dirs.), Phi Sigma Kappa. Democrat. Episcopalian. Editor-in-Chief: Alexander's Fed. Tax Handbook, 1955-61; bd. editors Jour. Taxation, 1954-73. Home: 306 Carrsbrook Dr Charlottesville VA 22901-1006 Office: 413 7th St NE PO Box 254 Charlottesville VA 22902-0254

MUSSENDEN, GERALD, psychologist; b. N.Y.C., June 1, 1941; s. Geraldo and Adele (Gimenez) M.; m. Iris Manuela Prado, Aug. 11, 1967; children: Gerald, Ricardo-Antonio, Gina. BA, Tarkio Coll., 1968; MS, Brigham Young U., 1971, PhD, 1974. Diplomate Am. Bd. Profl. Disability Cons., Am. Bd. Forensic Examiners. Dir. child program Albert Einstein Coll. Medicine, N.Y.C., 1974-76; psychologist Mental Health Ctr., Bartow, Fla., 1976-77, Norside Community Mentala Health Ctr., Tampa, Fla., 1977-80; pvt. practice Brandon (Fla.) Counseling Ctr., 1980—; criminal ct. psychologist Fla. Cts., Hillsborough, Fla., 1978—; with children's svcs. State Rehab., Hillsborough, 1977—; rehab. psychologist Vocat. Rehab., Hillsborough; psychologist Div. Blind Svcs., Hillsborough. Fellow Ford Found., 1972-73. Mem. APA, Fla. Psychol. Assn., Bay Area Psychol. Assn., Soc. Personality Assessment. Home: 317 Cactus Rd Seffner FL 33584-6105 Office: Brandon Counseling Ctr 134 N Moon Ave Brandon FL 33510-4420

MUSSER, DALE ROY, software engineer, instructional designer, educator; b. Ephrata, Pa., Oct. 29, 1964; s. Elmer Gehman and Emma Mae (Mohler) M. BSEd, Shippensburg U. Pa., 1982; MA, Ohio State U., 1989, PhD, 1992. Developer software and hardware Temple U., Phila., 1984; physics tutor Shippensburg U. Pa., 1985-86; tchr. physics Hanover (Pa.) High Sch., 1986-88; grad. teaching assoc. Ohio State U., Columbus, 1988-90, grad. rsch. assoc., 1990-91; cons., developer Dale Musser Consulting, Columbus, 1991; intern IBM, Atlanta, 1990, edn. instrn. specialist, 1990-92, programmer/analyst, team leader, 1993—; asst. prof. ednl. tech. U. Mo., Columbia, 1994—; dir. Ctr. for Tech. Innovations in Edn., Columbia, 1996—; multimedia software developer, 1990—; contingent expdn. leader to Krakatau, Ohio State U., 1989. Editor PILOT SIG Newsletter, ADCIS, Bellingham, Wash., 1989-90. Recipient Sallie Mae Outstanding First Yr. Tchr. award Sallie Mae, 1987. Mem. IEEE, Nat. Sci. Tchrs. Assn., Internat. Soc. Tech. in Edn., Nat. Coun. Tchrs. Math., Am. Ednl. Rsch. Assn. Home: 1030 Southpark # 1A Columbia MO 65201 Office: U Mo Columbia 111 London Hall Columbia MO 65211

MUSSETT, RICHARD EARL, city official; b. Erie, Pa., June 24, 1948; s. Clarence Harold and Elva (Brueckner) M.; m. Alaine Kathleen Rau, Aug. 14, 1971; children: Matthew, Mark. BPA, U. N.D., 1974; M of Urban Planning, U. Mich., 1975. Chief planner City of Largo, Fla., 1976-77; chief long-range planning Pinellas County Planning Dept., Clearwater, Fla., 1977-80; planning dir. City of St. Petersburg, Fla., 1980-85, dep. city mgr., adminstr., 1987—; adminstr. community devel. City of Bloomington (Minn.), 1985-87; chmn. Pinellas County Planners Adv. Com., 1982. Alternate del. N.D. Dem. Conv., 1972; mem. Tampa Bay Study Commn., 1984-85; mem. environ. quality com. Fla. League of Cities, 1984-85, devel. strategies legis. policy com., 1986. Served with USAF, 1967-71. Rackham grantee, 1975. Mem. Am. Inst. Cert. Planners (charter), Am. Planning Assn. (chmn. Suncoast sect. 1984, mem. legis. policy com. Fla. chpt. 1984-85, editor Suncoast sect. newsletter 1985). Lutheran. Office: City of St Petersburg 175 5th St N Saint Petersburg FL 33701-3708

MUSTIFUL, CURTIS JAMES, education educator; b. Mansfield, La., Apr. 21, 1944; s. David and Jannie R. (Johnson) M.; m. Sally Larvadain, Aug. 9, 1969; children: TaShawn L., Adrienne M. BS in Math., Southern U., 1966; MS in Edn., Syracuse U., 1970, PhD, 1972. Cartographic trainee Aeronautical Chart Ctr., St. Louis, 1966; film shipping clk. Lookout Mountain AFS, L.A., 1968-69; asst. prof. Grambling (La.) State U., 1972-76; tech. info. specialist U. Calif.-Lawrence Livermore Lab., summer 1980; assoc. prof. Southern U., Baton Rouge, La., 1976—. Mem. Assn. for Ednl. Comm. and Tech. Home: PO Box 1291 Zachary LA 70791-1291

MUTH, WILLIAM HENRY HARRISON, JR., medical/surgical nurse; b. Allentown, Pa., May 28, 1953; s. William Henry Harrison Sr. and Katie (Martin) M. BA in Psychology, Wheaton (Ill.) Coll., 1979, BA in German, 1979; MDiv, Luth. Theol. Sem., 1987; BSN, Cath. U. of Am., 1990. Cert. med.-surg. nurse; Cert. RNC, ACLS, BCLS, PALS, NRP, EMT. Vicar, pastor, chaplain Evangelical Luth. Ch. of Am., Allentown, Pa., 1985-87; neuro med-surg. nurse VA, Washington, 1990-91; commd. USAF, 1991-95; with Washington Hosp. Ctr., 1996—; med.-surg. staff nurse 7th Med. Group, Dyess AFB, Tex., 1991-93, staff nurse-staff devel., 1993, obstetric staff nurse, 1993-94, med-surg. staff nurse, 1994—. AIDS edn. vol. Dyess

AFB and Local Schs., Abilene, Tex., 1993—; clin. pastoral educator Lehigh Valley Hosp., Allentown, 1986. Health profl. scholarship program VA, 1989-90. Mem. Officers Christian Fellowship, Sigma Theta Tau Internat. (Kappa chpt.). Republican. Lutheran. Home: 1003 Newton St NE Washington DC 20017-1763

MUTTERS, DAVID RAY, real estate broker; b. Ashland, Ky., Apr. 2, 1949; s. Frank R. and Ruth Evelyn (Duncan) M. AB, U. Ashland, 1974. Lic. real estate broker, Fla. Mil. police sgt. U.S. Army, 1968-70; painter Ashland (Ky.) Oil Inc., 1970-73; asst. purchaser Ky. Road Oiling Inc., Ashland, 1973-77; v.p. Anderson Radio Inc., Bluefield, W.Va., 1977-80; pres., owner Advanced Comm. Inc., Bluefield, 1980-82; broker, salesman Douglas Realty Inc., Cape Coral, Fla., 1982-91; pres., broker David R. Mutters Realty Group, Inc., Cape Coral, Fla., 1991—. Mem. Cape Coral Bd. Realtors, Nat. Assn. Realtors, Cape Coral C. of C., Naples C. of C., Rush Lodge, Araba Temple, Cape Coral Shrine. Republican. Methodist. Home: 1409 El Dorado Pky W Cape Coral FL 33914-8032 Office: Coldwell Banker McFadden and Sprouts 3301 Del Prado Blvd Cape Coral FL 33904-8545

MUZYKA, JENNIFER LOUISE, chemist, educator; b. Fredericksburg, Va., Nov. 9, 1963; d. Kie Muzyka and Jo Anne (Martin) Cepeda; m. Mark Stephan Meier, June 4, 1994. BS in Chemistry, U. Dallas, 1985; PhD in Orcanic Chemistry, U. Tex., 1990. Asst. prof. Roanoke Coll., Salem, Va., 1990-94, Centre Coll., Danville, Ky., 1994—; Petroleum Rsch. Fund summer faculty fellow U. Ky., 1992. Contbr. articles to profl. jours. Rsch. grantee Ky. NSF EPSCOR, 1995, rsch. grantee Petroleum Rsch. Fund, 1992; Engrs. Club Dallas scholar, 1981-82. Mem. AAUP, Am. Chem. Soc. (chair-elect Lexington sect. 1995-96, chair 1996—, sec. Va. Blue Ridge sect. 1993-94), Ky. Acad. Sci. (Marcia Athey Rsch. grantee 1995), Coun. Undergrad. Rsch., Sigma Xi, Iota Sigma Pi (sec. Argentum chpt. 1993-94). Office: Centre Coll Chemistry Dept 600 W Walnut St Danville KY 40422-1309

MYATT, SUE HENSHAW, nursing home administrator; b. Little Rock, Aug. 16, 1956; d. Bobby Eugene and Janett Lanell (Ahart) Henshaw; m. Tommy Wayne Myatt; children: James Andrew, Thomas Ryan. BS in Psychology, Old Dominion U., 1978, MS in Ednl. Counseling, 1982. Cert. activity cons. Nat. Cert. Coun. of Activity Profls., gerontol. activity therapy cons., Va. Dir. activity Manning Convalescent, Portsmouth, Va., 1983-84, Camelot Hall, Norfolk, Va., 1984-86; coord. activities Beverly Manor, Portsmouth, 1986-87, Gerogian Manor Assisted Living Facility, 1989-90; dir. activities Huntington Convalescent Ctr., Newsport News, Va., 1990-91; nursing home adminstr.-in-tng. Bayview Healthcare Ctr., Newport News, 1991-92; adminstr. Evangeline of Gates, Gatesville, N.C., 1992-95, Mary Washington Health Ctr., Colonial Beach, Va., 1993-95, Brian Ctr. Health & Rehab., Lawrenceville, Va., 1995—; instr. Tidewater Community Coll., 1990. Mem. Nat. Assn. Activity Profl. (cert. legis. com.), Va. Assn. Activity Profl. (v.p. 1986-87, creator logo), Hampton Roads Activity Profls. Assn. (sec. 1985-86, pres. 1986-87, v.p. 1987-88). Home: 518 Tanglewood Dr Bracey VA 23919

MYER, JERRY O'BRIEN, manufacturing technologist, computer programmer; b. San Antonio, Oct. 14, 1954; s. Jerry Windham Myer and Patricia Caroline (O'Brien) Tenenbaum; m. Roberta Kim Menzel, Jan. 30, 1982. BS in Indsl. Tech., Tex. A&M U., 1976; postgrad., St. Phillips Coll., 1982, U. Tex., San Antonio, 1996—. Molder, foundry engr., mgr. quality control Alamo Iron Works, San Antonio, 1978-81; mech. engring. technician U.S. Dept. Def., Kelly AFB, Tex., 1983—; owner, mgr. Axis Unltd., San Antonio, 1990—; mem. tech. com. on numerical control programming lang. Am. Nat. Standards Inst., 1992—. Author software programs calculating optimum machining parameters for most common machine shop ops., software utilities converting geometric entities between standard formats (IGES, ANSI) for mfg. purposes. Scoutleader Boy Scouts Am., San Antonio, 1982, 90; counsellor Melchizedek priesthood quorum LDS Ch., San Antonio, 1990-94, chmn. temple and family history, 1993-94, pres. 2d ward, 1996—. Scholar Foundry Ednl. Found., 1975; recipient Outstanding Engring. Technician award San Antonio-Air Logistics Command, 1993. Republican. Office: Axis Unltd 654 Shadywood Ln San Antonio TX 78216-6816

MYER, JOHN DANIEL, II, restaurant executive; b. Columbus, Ohio, Apr. 25, 1950; s. John Daniel and Virginia Lee (Julian) M.; m. Mary Lynn Ivy Vickerman, Oct. 9, 1976; children: J. Daniel, Carolyn Ivy. BA, Ohio State U., 1973. Underwriter Continental Ins. Co., Columbus and Detroit, 1973-78; regional underwriting mgr. Universal Underwriters Inc., Columbus, 1978-80; prin., owner Julian-Myer Ins. Agy., Columbus, 1980-85; v.p., owner-operator Lynn Enterprises Inc., Asheville, N.C., 1985—. Founder, chmn. Buncombe County Young Reps., Asheville, 1988-90; cons., bd. dirs. Jr. Achievement, Asheville, 1989—, chmn. 1993-94; chmn. bd. Buncombe County Am. Heart Assn., Western N.C., 1990-94; bd. dirs. Leadership Asheville IX, 1990-91; v.p. leadership Asheville Found., 1992-94; pres. Buncombe County Rep. Men's club, 1994-95. Named Agt. of Month, Ind. Ins. Agts., 1983, Golden Ladle award Little Caesars, 1990. Mem. Ohio Jaycees (govt. affairs program mgt. 1983-85, Outstanding Program Mgr. award 1984, Seiji Horiuchi award 1984), Asheville C. of C., Young Bus. Club (show dir. 1982-84), Highlands Sportscar Club. Home: 30 Glen Cove Dr Arden NC 28704-3219 Office: Lynn Enterprises Inc 1278 Hendersonville Rd Asheville NC 28803-1905

MYERS, BERTINA SATTERFIELD, secondary education business educator, administrator; b. Muskogee, Okla., Apr. 17, 1936; d. Bert and Vera Louise (Lowrimore) Satterfield; m. Don E. Thompson, Aug. 17, 1957 (div. Nov. 1985); children: Curtis Lynn, Patrick Kevin; m. C.K. Myers, Mar. 21, 1992. BSEdn., Northeastern State Coll., Tahlequah, Okla., 1958, M in Teaching, 1967; postgrad., U. Mo., 1970, U. North Fla., 1972. Cert. jr. high, jr. coll. bus. edn. tchr., Okla., Mo., Fla. Bookkeeper Phoenix Fed. Savs. & Loan, Muskogee, 1956-60, Home Savs. & Loan, Bartlesville, Okla., 1960; clk. in bus. office Northeastern State Coll., Tahlequah, 1964-67; tchr. Shidler (Okla.) Sch. Dist., 1961-64, R-7 Sch. Dist., Webb City, Mo., 1967-71, Clay County (Fla.) Schs., 1971—; head of bus. dept. Orange Pk. (Fla.) High Sch., 1980—; adj. prof. Fla. C.C., Jacksonville, 1987-96; test bank coore Dept. Edn., Tallahassee, 1985-87; chmn. text book evaluation com. Clay County, 1983, 85, 87; coord. computer workshops for bus., 1983, 85, 88; coord. bus. edn. workshop Clay County Sch. Secs., 1990; coord. data processing workshop Orange Park High Sch. Tchrs., 1990. Sunday sch. coord. Orange Pk. United Meth. Ch., 1988-91, sec. council on min., 1995—; bd. dirs. Am. Cancer Soc., Orange Pk., 1984. Named Tchr. of Yr., Orange Park High Sch., 1981, 91, Tchr. of Month, 1985; recipient Excellence in Edn. award Clay County, 1989. Mem. Future Bus. Leaders Am. (profl. adviser 1977—), So. Assn. Colls. and Schs. (steering com. Orange Park High Sch. 1979, 90-91), Fla. Bus. Edn. Assn. (city chmn.), Am. Vocat. Assn., Fla. Vocat. Assn., Northeastern State Coll. Alumni Assn., Delta Pi Epsilon, Sigma Sigma Sigma. Republican. Home: 1633 Bay Cir W Orange Park FL 32073-4747 Office: Orange Pk High Sch 2300 Kingsley Ave Orange Park FL 32073-5125

MYERS, CHARLES EDWIN, science foundation administrator; b. Phila., Dec. 15, 1940; s. Charles Miller and Helen Rebecca (Axenfeld) M.; m. Sandra Goldberg, Aug. 4, 1963; children: Eric, Jason, Susan. BS, Pa. State U., 1962; MS, U. Md., 1965, postgrad., 1971; postgrad., Drexel U., 1968. Rsch. engr. U.S. Dept. Interior, College Park, Md., 1965-67, Sybron Corp., Princeton, N.J., 1967-69; engr. Fed. Water Quality Adminstrn., Arlington, Va., 1969-71; program mgr. U.S. EPA, Washington, 1971-74; program mgr., dir. NSF, Washington, 1974-91; head Arctic interagy. staff NSF, Arlington, 1991—; adj. prof. Montgomery Coll., Takoma Park, Md., 1984. Editor-in-chief Arctic Rsch. of the U.S., 1991—; contbr. articles to profl. jours. Office: Nat Sci Found (OPP) 4201 Wilson Blvd Arlington VA 22230

MYERS, CHARLES LAWRENCE, anesthesiologist; b. Houston, June 17, 1954; s. Charles Robert and Betty June (Simpson) M.; m. Deborah Louise Remont, Dec. 20, 1976; children: James, Brian, William. BS, La. State U., Baton Rouge, 1975; MD, La. State U., Shreveport, 1979. Diplomate Am. Bd. Anesthesiology. Intern La. State U. Med. Ctr., Shreveport, 1979-80; resident Parkland Meml. Hosp., Dallas, 1980-82; anesthesiologist Anesthesiology Assocs., Shreveport, 1982-85, Alexandria (La.) Anesthesia Svc., 1985-93, Profl. Anesthesiology Cons., Alexandria, 1993—. Home: 4914 Windermere Blvd Alexandria LA 71303-2458

MYERS, CLIFFORD ALEXANDER, chemist; b. St. Louis, Oct. 15, 1953; children: Nicole Renée, Jason Andrew, Rebekah Annette. BS in Chemistry, Old Dominion U., 1976. Supr. quality asurance lab. ITT Gwaltney, Smithfield, Va., 1976-78; phys. sci. technician, chemist Norfolk Naval Shipyard, Portsmouth, Va., 1978-80; chemist U.S. Army Gen. Material and Petroleum Activity, New Cumberland, Pa., 1980-82, San Antonio Air Logistics Ctr., Kelly AFB, Tex., 1982-85, Def. Supply Ctr., Richmond, Va., 1985—. Comdr. Awana Club Gill Grove Bapt. Ch., Chesterfield, Va., 1990—. Recipient Eagle Scout award Boy Scouts Am., 1969; recipient Closing the Circle award, Environ. award White House, 1996. Mem. Armed Forces Pest Mgmt. Bd. Home: PO Box 1105 Chesterfield VA 23832 Office: Def Supply Ctr Richmond 8000 Jefferson Davis Hwy Richmond VA 23297-5810

MYERS, DANE JACOB, lawyer, podiatrist; b. Murray, Utah, June 20, 1948; s. Lorin LaVar Myers and Irma Lee (Bell) Willette; m. Mary Jo Jackson, June 22, 1970; children: Troy, Chad, Melissa, Apryll, Tristan, Remington. DPM, Pa. Coll. Podiatric Medicine, 1977; BA, U. Utah, 1983; JD, U. Ark., 1986. Bar: Ark. 1986. Pres. Tooele (Utah) Foot Clinic, 1977-83; owner N.W. Ark. Foot Clinic, Rogers, Ark., 1983—; pvt. practice law Fayetteville, 1986—. Mem. ABA, APHA, Am. Coll. Foot and Ankle Surgeons (assoc.), Am. Diabetes Assn., Ark. Bar Assn., Am. Soc. Law and Medicine, Am. Podiatric Med. Assn., Ark. Podiatric Med. Assn., Delta Theta Phi. Republican. Mormon. Home: 106 Woodcliff Rd Springdale AR 72764-3691 Office: NW Ark Foot Clinic 1001 W Walnut Ste 6 Rogers AR 72756

MYERS, DAVID GERSHOM, English language educator, writer; b. Crawfordsville, Ind., Feb. 27, 1952; s. Donald Wayne and Jessie Lee (Harrel) M.; m. Beth Diane Deutsch, Feb. 14, 1982 (div. Sept. 1987). BA, U. Calif., Santa Cruz, 1974; AM, Washington U., St. Louis, 1977; PhD, Northwestern U., Evanston, Ill., 1989. Reporter, 1977-84; asst. prof. English Tex. A&M U., College Station, 1989-95, assoc. prof., 1995—. Author: Elephants Teach: Creative Writing Since 1880, 1996; founder/mem. editl. bd. Philosophy and Literature. Home: 1209A Baker Ave Bryan TX 77803-4726 Office: Tex A&M Univ Dept English College Station TX 77840

MYERS, DONALD ALLEN, university dean; b. Nebraska City, Nebr., Dec. 17, 1932; s. Merle D. and Ruth Irene (Potter) M.; m. Dixie Lois Ashton, Aug. 10, 1957; 1 son, Eric; m. Lilian Rose Bautista, Apr. 18, 1966; children: Sherri, Johnny, David; m. Alice L. Twining, July 15. 1990; 1 child, Aaron. B.A., Mcpl. U. Omaha, 1956; M.A., U. Chgo., 1957, Ph.D., 1962. Asst. supt. Sch. Dist. Riverview Gardens, Mo., 1962-65; research assoc. NEA, Washington, 1965-66; curriculum and research specialist Inst. for Devel. of Ednl. Activities, Los Angeles, 1966-70; assoc. prof. SUNY, Albany, 1970-73; head dept. curriculum and instrn. Olka. State U., Stillwater, 1973-79; dean Coll. Edn., U. Nebr., Omaha, 1979-85; dean Sch. Edn. Old Dominion U., Norfolk, Va., 1985—. Author: Teacher Power, 1973, Open Education Reexamined, 1973; contbr. articles, chpts. to profl. jours., books. Washington intern in edn. Ford Found., 1965-66. Democrat. Home: 1272 Belvoir Ln Virginia Beach VA 23464-6746 Office: Coll Edn Old Dominion Univ Norfolk VA 23508-1506

MYERS, EUGENE EKANDER, art consultant; b. Grand Forks, N.D., May 5, 1914; s. John Q. and Hattye Jane (Ekander) M.; m. Florence Hutchinson Ritchie, Sept. 9, 1974. BS in Edn., U. N.D., 1936, MS in Edn., 1938; postgrad., U. Oreg., 1937; MA, Northwestern U., 1940, Columbia U., 1947; grad., Advanced Mgmt. Program, Harvard U., 1953; cert., Cambridge (Eng.) U., 1958; postgrad., U. Md., 1958-61, Oxford (Eng.) U., 1964; diploma, various mil. schs. Student asst. U. N.D., 1935-36, instr. summer sessions, 1936, 37, asst., 1936-37; prof., head dept. N.D. Tchrs. Coll., 1938-40; instr. Columbia U. Tchrs. Coll., 1940-41; vis. prof. U. Vt., summers, 1941, 42; commd. 1st lt. USAAF, 1942, advanced through grades to col., 1951; dir. personnel plans and tng. Hdqrs. Air Force Systems Command Washington, 1959-60; dir. personnel research and long-range plans Hdqrs. Air Force Systems Command, 1960-62; head dept. internat. relations Air War Coll., Air U. Maxwell AFB, Ala., 1962-63; dir. curriculum, dean (Air War Coll., Air U.), 1963-65; dir. res. affairs Hdqrs. Air Res. Personnel Center Denver, 1965-66; ret., 1966; dean Corcoran Sch. Art, Washington, 1966-70; founder Corcoran Sch. Art Abroad, Leeds, Eng., 1967; v.p. mgmt. Corcoran Gallery Art, Washington, 1970-72; vis. art dir. Washington, also Palm Beach, Fla.; art cons., 1972—; adv. Washington chpt. Nat. Soc. Arts and Letters.; bd. assos. Artists Equity. Author: (with Paul E. Barr) Creative Lettering, 1938, (with others) The Subject Fields in General Education, 1939, Applied Psychology, 1940; contbr. articles, reports to mags. and profl. publs. bd. dirs. Columbia (Md.) Inst. Art, World Arts Found., N.Y., Court Art Center, Montgomery, Ala. and Palm Beach, Fla., Order of Lafayette, Boston, English-Speaking Union, Palm Beach; mem. Hamilton St. Vol. Fire Dept. and Lit. Soc., Balt., Pundits, Palm Beach. Recipient Sioux award U. N.D., 1978. Mem. Internat. Communication Assn. (hon.), U. N.D. Alumni Assn. (pres. Washington chpt. 1959), Mil. Classics Soc., Titanic Soc., Mil. Order Carabao, Order of St. John of Jerusalem, Knightly Assn. St. George the Martyr, Co. Mil. Historians, Mil. Order World Wars, Ancient Order United Workmen, Saint Andrews Soc., Clan Donnachaidh (Perthshire, Scotland), Soc. Friends St. Andrews (Scotland) U., Delta Omicron Epsilon, Lambda Chi Alpha, Delta Phi Delta, Phi Delta Kappa, Phi Alpha Theta. Republican. Presbyterian. Clubs: Union (Manchester, Eng.) (hon.); Royal Scottish Automobile (Glasgow, Scotland); Royal Overseas (London); New (Edinburgh, Scotland) (assoc.); Army and Navy (Washington), Nat. Aviation (Washington), City Tavern (Washington), Harvard Business School (Washington); Army and Navy Country (Arlington, Va.); Metropolitan (N.Y.C.), Wings (N.Y.C.), Explorers (N.Y.C.) (fellow), Harvard (N.Y.C.); Minneapolis; Everglades (Palm Beach, Fla.), Beach (Palm Beach, Fla.), Sailfish of Fla. (Palm Beach, Fla.); Liitle (Gulf Stream, Fla.); Fairmont (W.Va.) Field Country, Lions. Home: 1 Royal Palm Way Palm Beach FL 33480 also: 3320 Volta Pl NW Washington DC 20007-2733 also: 721 Mount Vernon Ave Fairmont WV 26554-2522

MYERS, FRANKLIN, lawyer, oil service company executive; b. Pensacola, Fla., Nov. 2, 1952; s. T.F. Sr. and D. Bernice (Brewer) M.; m. Melinda Munson, Aug. 9, 1974; children: Amanda C., Adam F., Anne Marie M. BS, Miss. State U., 1974; JD, U. Miss., 1977. Bar: Miss. 1977, Tex. 1978. Ptnr. Fulbright and Jaworski, Houston, 1978-88; sr. v.p., gen. counsel Baker Hughes Inc., Houston, 1988-95; sr. v.p., gen. counsel, corp. sec. Cooper Cameron Corp., Houston, 1995—; adj. prof. U. Tex. Sch. Law, 1990; bd. dirs. Convest Energy, Reunion Industries, Inc., Totalnet Comms. Bd. dirs. U. St. Thomas, Houston. Fellow Houston Bar Found., Tex. Bar Assn., Miss. Bar Assn., Houston Bar Assn. Baptist. Office: Cooper Cameron Corp 515 Post Oak Blvd Ste 1200 Houston TX 77027

MYERS, JOHN WILLIAM, academic administrator; b. Cleve., Apr. 12, 1944; s. William M. and Virginia A. (Shartzer) M.; m. Janet A. Dangel, Sep. 20, 1969; children: John W. II, Jennifer A. BA in Eng., U. Akron, 1966, MA in Eng., 1968, PhD in Secondary Edn., 1977. Commd. 2d lt. U.S. Army, 1966, advanced through ranks to lt. col., 1986; tchr. Eng. North Canton (Ohio) City Schs., 1972-75; asst. prof. Tenn. Tech. U., Cookeville, 1978-85; acad. dean Father Ryan H.S., Nashville, 1985-90; chair dept. middle grades, secondary edn. State U. of West Ga., Carrollton, 1990—; lectr., spkr. in field. Author (monograph) Writing to Learn Across the Curriculum, 1984, Involving Families in Middle Schools, 1994, Making Sense of Whole Language, 1994; editor Current Issues in Mid Level Edn., 1991—. Permanent deacon Cath. Archdiocese, Nashville, 1985-90, Newnan, 1990—. Mem. Nat. Middle Sch. Assn., Nat. Coun. Tchrs. Eng., Phi Delta Kappa (v.p. 1994-95, pres. 1995-96). Roman Catholic. Office: State U of West Ga Carrollton GA 30118

MYERS, KAREN SANDS, social services administrator; b. Phila., Mar. 7, 1950; d. John Robert and Carol Marie (Dietrich) Sands; m. James Palmer Myers, Oct. 30, 1971; 1 child, Drew Garland. Student, Johns Hopkins U., Balt., 1970-71; BS in Psychology, Lynchburg (Va.) Coll., 1972, MA in Tchg. Early Childhood, 1974. Psychol. asst. Lynchburg Tng. Ctr., 1972-73; elem. sch. tchr. Perrymont Elem. Sch., Lynchburg, 1974; nurse's aide Kluge Children's Rehab., Charlottesville, Va., 1975-76; team leader Lynchburg Tng. Ctr., 1976-78; dir. YWCA Infant Care Ctr., Lynchburg, 1979-80; dining rm. mgr. Mountain Lake (Va.) Resort, 1980-86; estate mgr. Don Johnson, Miami Beach, Fla., 1986-87; program mgr. Ctrl. Va. Cmty. Svcs., Lynchburg, 1990—; mem. adv. bd. Kareline, Lynchburg, 1990—; mem. task force Va.-Children Action Network, Richmond, 1993—, Partnership for Prevention of Substance Abuse, Lynchburg, 1992—, Early Learning Task Force, Lynchburg, 1993—. Sunday sch. tchr. Peakland United Meth. Ch., Lynchburg, 1988-91; vol. Dem. Party, Lynchburg, 1993, Fine Arts Ctr., Lynchburg, 1988—. Recipient Specialkare award Coun. on Child Care, Richmond, 1993, 94. Home: 1905 McGuffey Ln Lynchburg VA 24503 Office: Ctrl Va Cmty Svcs Project Daniel 2235 Landover Pl Lynchburg VA 24501

MYERS, KENNETH M., lawyer; b. Miami, Fla., Mar. 11, 1933; s. Stanley C. and Martha (Scheinberg) M.; div. 1973. AB, U. N.C., 1954; JD, U. Fla., 1957. Bar: Sept. 1957, Colo. 1986, N.Y. 1987. Ptnr. Myers, Kenin Levinson & Richards, Miami, 1957-87, Shea & Gould, N.Y.C., 1987-88, Squire, Sanders & Dempsey, Miami, 1988—; mem. Fla. Ho. Reps., 1965-69, mem. Fla. Senate, 1969-80. Trustee U. Miami, 1985—. Mem. ABA, Fla. Bar Assn., Colo. Bar Assn., N.Y. State Bar Assn., Am. Law Inst., Nat. Assn. Bond Lawyers, Dade County Bar Assn., Greater Miami C. of C. (bd. govs.). Democrat. Jewish. Office: Squire Sanders & Dempsey 2900 Miami Ctr 201 S Biscayne Blvd Miami FL 33131-4332

MYERS, MARK EDEN, chemical sales executive; b. Louisville, Feb. 18, 1953; s. Larry Holton and Anne (Dennison) M.; m. Trudy Lynette Cecil (div.); children: Corey, Shawn. BS in Zoology, U. Louisville, 1981. With Westinghouse, Louisville, 1977-78; sales rep. Terminix Internat., Louisville, 1982-83, svc. mgr., 1983-87, tech. specialist for Ky. region, 1987-94, svc. mgr., 1994-95; sales rep. Oldham Chem. Co., Inc., Memphis, 1995—; speaker in field. Designer, builder lab. apparatus, models and displays in field. Cub master Boy Scouts Am., asst. scoutmaster. Named to Honorable Order of Ky. Colonels. Mem. Ky. Pest Control Assn. (bd. dirs. 1991-93), Ky. Karate Club. Democrat. Roman Catholic. Office: Oldham Chem Co Inc 4340 Sanita Ct Ste J Louisville KY 40213-1829

MYERS, MILLER FRANKLIN, finance company executive, retail executive; b. Aberdeen, S.D., Sept. 26, 1929; s. Burton Franklin and Virginia (Miller) M.; m. Janet Arlene Rylander, June 16, 1951; children: Leslie Ann, Burton F., Claudia Ann, Georgianna. Student, Grinnell Coll., 1947-49; BA, U. Minn., 1951-53, LLD, 1953. From v.p. to pres. Internat. Dairy Queen, Mpls., 1961-65, Dairy Queen of Can., Hamilton, Ont., 1953-70; chmn., chief exec. officer Internat. Dairy Queen, Mpls., 1970-74; pres. Econo-Therm Energy Systems, Mpls., 1975-84; chmn., chief exec. officer Aero Drapery Corp., Mpls., 1984-94, Franklin Investments, Inc., Mpls., 1984-93; pres., chmn. Dairy Queen Nat. Devel. Corp., St. Louis, 1960-64, Bayview Capital Corp., 1980-95; bd. dirs. Northwestern Nat. Bank, Mpls., 1965-69, Northwestern Teleprodns., Mpls., 1969-77, Keller Grad. Sch. Mgmt., 1974—. Del. Rep. Conv., St. Paul, 1968; student organizer Stassen for Pres., 1948. Mem. Young Pres. Orgn., 1966-82, World Bus. Counsel, Minn. Execs. Orgn., Mpls. Club, Minikahda Club, Wilderness Country Club, Lafayette Club. Republican.

MYERS, NORMAN ALLAN, marketing professional; b. Beeville, Tex., Dec. 10, 1935; s. Floyd Charles and Ruby (Lee) Myers; m. Suzanne Carlile, Oct. 11, 1935; children: Lisa Leigh Myers Nowlin, Matthew Scott. BS in Banking and Fin., Okla. State U., 1958. Salesman Jones and Laughlin Steel Corp., Houston, 1958-64; agt. Acacia Mutual Life Ins., Houston, 1964-69; with Browning-Ferris Industries, Houston, 1969—, exec. v.p., 1976-81, chief mktg. officer, 1981—, vice chmn., 1982—; also bd. dirs. Bd. dirs. My Friends-A Neuenschwander Found. for Children in Crisis. 2d lt. U.S. Army, 1958-59. Named to Okla. State Univ. Coll. of Bus. Adminstrn. Hall of Fame, 1996. Mem. Lakeside Country Club, Hills of Lakeway Club, Barton Creek Lakeside Country Club, Shriners, Holland. Republican. Office: Browning-Ferris Ind Inc 757 N Eldridge Pky Houston TX 77079-4435

MYERS, STEPHEN HAWLEY, lawyer; b. Washington, Mar. 28, 1953; s. Robert Holt and Antoinette (Hawley) M.; children: Stephen, Hampton, Brielle; m. Laura Lee Fuller, Dec. 1, 1989. BA in Polit. Sci. with honors, Union Coll., 1976; JD, Loyola U., 1979. Bar: D.C. 1979, La. 1979, U.S. Dist. Ct. D.C. 1980, U.S. Tax Ct. 1980, U.S. Ct. Claims 1980, U.S. Ct. Appeals (fed. and D.C. cirs.) 1980, U.S. Ct. Appeals (5th cir.) 1985, U.S. Dist. Ct. (we. and ea. dists.) La. 1985, U.S. Supreme Ct. 1989. Atty. advisor to hon. judge Edward S. Smith U.S. Ct. Appeals (Fed. cir.), Washington, 1979-80; assoc. Duncan Allen & Mitchell, Washington, 1980-82; atty. advisor to Judge Jules G. Körner U.S. Tax Ct., Washington, 1982-84; assoc. Davidson Meaux Sonnier & McElligott, Lafayette, La., 1984-85; ptnr. Roy Forrest, Lopresto, DeCourt & Myers and predecessor firms, Lafayette, 1985—; lectr. for continuing legal edn. seminars on corp., sales tax and personal injury litigation. Vice chmn., bd. dirs. La. Coun. for Fiscal Reform, New Orleans, 1986—; bd. dirs., treas. Acadiana Youth, Inc., Lafayette, 1986-94. Mem. ABA, Am. Platform Assn., Lafayette Bar Assn., La. Counsel Def. Attys., La. Trial Lawyer's Assn., Phi Delta Phi. Avocations: writing, photography. Home: 100 Old Settlement Rd Lafayette LA 70508-7030 Office: Roy Forrest Lopresto DeCourt & Myers 301 E Kaliste Saloom Rd Lafayette LA 70508-3288 also: 301 French St New Iberia LA 70560-4465

MYERS, SUE BARTLEY, artist; b. Norfolk, Va., Aug. 22, 1930; d. Louis and Rena M. Bartley; m. Bertram J. Myers, Nov. 24, 1949; children: Beth R., Mark F., Alyson S. Student, Stephens Coll., Va. Wesleyan. V.p. Jamson Realty Inc., Myers Realty Inc.; ltd. ptnr. Downtown Plaza Shopping Ctr., Warwick Village Shopping Ctr., Suburban Park Assocs. Solo shows at Village Gallery, Newport News, 1988, Artist at Work Gallery, Virginia Beach, Va., 1991, Va. Wesleyan U., Virginia Beach, 1991, 92, Will Richardson Gallery, Norfolk, Va., 1993, 94, Ctrl. Fidelity Bank, Norfolk, Va., 1995. Pres. adv. coun. Va. Wesleyan U., 1982-94; mayor's del. Sister Cities, Norwich, Eng., 1984, Kidikushu, Japan, 1982, Edinburgh, Scotland, 1991, Toulon, France, 1992; mem. entertainment com. Azalea Festival Norfolk, 1984; founder art scholarship Va. Wesleyan; bd. dirs. corp. campaign Va. Zool. Soc., 1996. Mem. Tidewater Artists Assn., Art Odyssey. Jewish. Home: 7338 Barberry Ln Norfolk VA 23505-3001

MYERS, TERRY LEWIS, clinical geneticist, educator; b. Jackson, Miss., Apr. 14, 1941; s. Gordon Harry and Leta Wanda (Smith) M.; m. Marian Kathryn Solowy; children: Wesley, Terry Jr. BS, Mich. State U., 1963; PhD, Fla. State U., 1969; MD, U. Va., 1973. Diplomate Am. Bd. Med. Genetics. Instr. pediats. U. Va., Charlottesville, 1970-73; assoc. prof. pediats. Creighton U., Omaha, Neb., 1973-78; prof. pediats. East Tenn. State U., Johnson City, Tenn., 1978-88, Tex. Tech U., Lubbock, 1988—; assoc. dean Sch. Medicine Tex. Tech U., Amarillo, 1995—; bd. dirs. Texgene. Fellow Am. Coll. Med. Genetics, Am. Acad. Pediats. Home: 6 Cloister Pkwy Amarillo TX 79121 Office: Tex Tech U Health Sci Ctr 1400 Wallace Blvd Amarillo TX 79106

MYETTE, JERÉ CURRY, nursing administrator; b. Liberty, N.Y., July 19, 1955; d. James Specht Sr. and Jean (Swarthout) Curry; m. Thomas C. Myette, Oct. 11, 1980; children: Thomas A., Jamie J. AS, Nassau Community Coll., Garden City, N.Y., 1980; BSE, SUNY, Cortland, 1977; M Health Svcs. Adminstrn., New Sch. for Social Rsch., N.Y.C., 1992. Charge nurse Cen. Gen. Hosp., Plainview, N.Y., 1981-84; home care nurse Vis. Nurse Svc., Huntington, N.Y., 1987-92; adminstr., dir. nursing Health Power, East Meadow, N.Y., 1992-93; dir. patient svcs. Good Samaritan Home Health, Babylon, N.Y., 1992-93; dir. prof. svcs. Columbia Home Care West, Bradenton, Fla., 1993—. Home: 1103 79th St NW Bradenton FL 34209-9762

MYNATT, CECIL FERRELL, psychiatrist; b. Knoxville, Tenn., May 10, 1995; s. Cecil Ferrell and Ethel (May) Mynatt; m. Minnie Lee Rouser, Dec. 8, 1945 (div. Nov. 1988); children: Matthew, Cecilia, Melissa, Martha, Richard; m. Yong Cha Lee, Oct. 10, 1990; children: Katherine, John. BS, U. Tenn., 1950, MD, 1951. Pvt. practice in gen. medicine Morristown, Tenn., 1952-61; resident Menninger Sch. Psychiatry, 1961-65; suprt. Ea. State Hosp., Knoxville, 1965-67; pvt. practice Wright Ferry Hosp., Knoxville, 1967-68; pvt. practice, co-owner Pvt. Hosp., Knoxville, 1968-73, Las Vegas, 1973-84; dir. Taliferro Mental Health Ctr., Lawton, Okla., 1984-89; supt. Western State Hosp., Woodword, Okla., 1989-91; med. dir. Rolling Hills Psychiat. Hosp., Ada, Okla., 1991—; CEO Sun Enterprises, Inc., Ada, 1987—; cons. Pononotoc County Mental Health Assn., Ada, 1992—, Valley View Meml. Hosp., Ada, 1992—. Editor, pub. Voice of Experience, 1993—;

contbr. articles to profl. jours. Maj. OSS, 1941-45. Decorated Silver star, Bronze star, (2) Purple Hearts. Mem. VFW, AMA, Okla. Med. Assn., Pononotoc County Med. Assn. Republican. Baptist. Home: 126 Kings' Rd Ada OK 74820 Office: Rolling Hills Psychiat Hosp 1000 Rolling Hills Ada OK 74820

MYRICK, JOHN PAUL, librarian, library building consultant; b. Birmngham, Ala., Sept. 14, 1967; s. William Casey and Dorothy Elna (Nichols) M. BA, U. Ala., Birmingham, 1990; MA, U. Ala., Tuscaloosa, 1991. Reference libr. Tuscaloosa (Ala.) Pub. Libr., 1990; archival intern Birmingham (Ala.) Pub. Libr., 1990; adult svcs. libr. Memphis-Shelby County Libr., Memphis, 1991-92; dir. librs. Cullman (Ala.) County Libr., 1992—; mem. adv. bd. Correctional Libr. State of Ala., Montgomery, 1992-94; sr. vol. adv. bd. Tri-County Cmty. Action, Decatur, Ala., 1993; libr. cons. LIS Assocs. Cullman, 1994—. Info. officer Cullman County Emergency Mgmt., 1994-96, state sec. Ala. Young Dems., Montgomery, 1994-96; treas. Cullman County Young Dems., 1994-96. Recipient Profl Tng. scholarship Ala. Pub. Libr. Svc., Montgomery, 1990-91. Mem. Am. Libr. Assn., Pub. Libr. Assn. Ala. Libr. Assn. (co-chair standards com. 1993—), Southeastern Libr. Assn., Cullman Area C. of C., Cullman Kiwanis Club. Democrat. Episcopalian. Office: Cullman County Pub Libr System 200 Clark St NE Cullman AL 35055-2913

MYRICK, SUE, congresswoman, former mayor; b. Tiffin, Ohio, Aug. 1, 1941; d. William Henry and Margaret Ellen (Roby) Wilkins; m. Jim Forest (div.); children: Greg, Dan; m. Wilbur Edward Myrick Jr., Sept. 11, 1977. Student, Heidelberg Coll., 1959-60, HHD (hon.), 1995. Exec. sec. to mayor and city mgr. City of Alliance, Ohio, 1962-63; dir. br. office Stark County Ct. of Juvenile and Domestic Rels., Alliance, 1963-65; pres. Myrick Agy., Charlotte, N.C., 1971-95; mayor of Charlotte, 1987-91; mem. 104th Congress from 9th N.C. District, Washington, D.C., 1995—; candidate for U.S. Senate from N.C., 1992; active Heart Fund, Multiple Sclerosis, March of Dimes, Arts and Scis. Coun. Fund Dr.; past mem. adv. bd. Uptown Shelter, Uptown Homeless Task Force, bd. dirs. N.C. Inst. Politics; v.p. Sister Cities Internat.; mem. Pres. Bush's Affordable Housing Commn.; founder, coord. Charlotte vol. tornado relief effort; former bd. dirs. Learning How; former mem. adv. bd. U.S. Conf. Mayors; mem.-at-large Charlotte City Coun., 1983-85, Strengthening Am. Commn.; lay leader, Sunday sch. tchr. 1st United Meth. Ch.; treas. Mecklenburg Ministries; former trustee U.S. Conf. of Mayors. Recipient Woman of Yr. award Harrisonburg, Va., 1968; named one of Outstanding Young Women of Am., 1968. Mem. Women's Polit. Caucus, Beta Sigma Phi. Republican. Home: 310 W 8th St Charlotte NC 28202-1704 Office: US House Reps 509 Cannon House Office Bldg Washington DC 20515-3309 also: Myrick Enterprises 505 N Poplar St Charlotte NC 28202-1729

MYRMO, ERIK, computer company executive. V.p. engring. Computone Corp. Address: 1100 N Meadow Pkwy Roswell GA 30076

NA, (TERRY) TSUNG SHUN, Chinese studies educator, writer; b. Beijing, Nov. 3, 1932; came to U.S., 1964; s. Chi-L and Hui (Hu) N.; m. Yen Yen Chao, 1964. BA, Taiwan Normal U., 1956; MA, U. B.C., 1970; PhD, U. Minn., 1978. Assoc. prof. Taipei Normal Coll., Taiwan, Republic of China, 1956-64; vis. lectr. Ind. U., Bloomington, 1964-66; asst. prof. U. Minn., Mpls., 1970-80; vis. prof. Sun Yat-sen U., Taiwan, 1981-84; prof., dir. Am. Inst. Chinese Studies, Charles Town, W.Va., 1985—. Author: (English books) A Linguistic Study of P'i-pa Chi, 1969, Studies on Dream of the Red Chamber: A Selected and Classified Bibliography, 1979, Supplement, 1981, Taiwan Studies on Dream of the Red Chamber: A Selected and Classified Bibliography, 1983, Chinese Studies in English: A Selected Bibliography, 1991, (Chinese) Mandarin Pronunciation, 1966, Teaching Chinese in the U.S.A., 1983, Studies on Chinese Classical Novels, 1985, A Collection of Short Stories, 1987; contbr. numerous articles, short stories, and research essays to jours. and newspapers in U.S., Taiwan, ROC, and China. Mem. MLA, Assn. Asian Studies. Office: Am Inst Chinese Studies PO Box 453 Charles Town WV 25414-0453

NAALBANDIAN, ARSHAM, neurologist; b. Aleppo, Syria, May 14, 1949; came to U.S., 1976; s. Nishan and Alice (Kevork) N.; m. Jilberte Kayal, July 26, 1975; 1 child, Christopher. BS, Aleppo U., 1972, MD, 1975. Intern Framingham (Mass.) Union Hosp., Boston U., 1976-78; resident in neurology SUNY, Syracuse, 1978-81; staff neurologist Rapid Regional Med. Ctr., Alexandria, La., 1981—. Fellow Am. Acad. Neurology. Office: Alexandria Neurology Ctr 301 4th St Alexandria LA 71301-8423

NABHAN, LOU ANNE JONES, public relations executive; b. Anderson, Ind., Jan. 6, 1955; d. Lewis E. and Anne Theresa (Jacobsen) Jones; m. Douglas Michael Nabhan, May 12, 1979. BA, Purdue U., 1977. Corp. communications specialist Internat. Paper Co., N.Y.C., 1977-78; pub. rels. rep. Reynolds Metals Co., Richmond, Va., 1978-79, pub. rels. mgr., 1979-83, dir. corp. communications, 1983-90, dir. pub. rels. div., 1990-92, dir. corp. info., 1992—. Mem. Pub. Rels. Soc. Am. (pres. Richmond chpt. 1987, dist. officer 1991—). Office: Reynolds Metals Co 6601 W Broad St Richmond VA 23230-1701*

NACHIMSON, HAROLD IRWIN, physician, mediator; b. N.Y.C., June 30, 1928; s. Abraham and Yetta (Greenberg) N.; m. Esther E. Thurman; children: David, Joel, Beverly. BS, Long Island U., 1952; MA, Rice U., 1955; MD, Southwestern Med. Coll., Dallas, 1963; JD, Kensington Law Sch., 1993. Diplomate Am. Bd. Family Practice. Intern John Peter Smith Hosp., 1963-64; pvt. pracice Irving, Tex., 1964-93; physician Primacare, Dallas, 1993—. Lt. USNR, 1955-63. Fellow Am. Acad. Family Practicioners. Republican. Jewish. Home: 612 Sonora Ct Irving TX 75062-6545 Office: 11888 Marsh Ln Ste 104 Dallas TX 75234-8060

NACHMAN, RONALD JAMES, research chemist; b. Takoma Park, Md., Feb. 1, 1954; s. Joseph Frank and Rosemary (Anderson) N.; m. Lita Rose Wilson, Dec. 18, 1976 (div. 1987); m. Isidora Austria Panis, May 6, 1989. BS in Chemistry, U. Calif., San Diego, 1976; PhD in Organic Chemistry, Stanford U., 1981. Rsch. asst. Scripps Inst. Oceanography, La Jolla, Calif., 1974-76; chemist Western Regional Rsch. Ctr., USDA, Berkeley, Calif., 1981-89, Vet. Toxicology and Entomology Rsch. Lab., College Station, Tex., 1989—; vis. scientist dept. molecular biology The Salk Inst., La Jolla, 1985, Scripps Rsch. Inst., La Jolla, 1988-89. Contbr. sci. articles to profl. jours. Recipient USDA Cert. of Merit, 1988, 91, Arthur S. Flemming award for sci. achievement, 1994. Fellow Sci. and Humanities Symposia; mem. AAAS, Am. Chem. Soc., N.Y. Acad. Scis., Sigma Xi. Home: 14891 Pollux Willis TX 77378-0014 Office: USDA Vet Toxicology Entomology Rsch Lab 2881 F and B Rd College Station TX 77845-9594

NACHWALTER, MICHAEL, lawyer; b. N.Y.C., Aug. 31, 1940; s. Samuel J. Nachwalter; m. Irene, Aug. 15, 1965; children: Helynn, Robert. BS, Bucknell U., 1962; MS, L.I. U., 1967; JD cum laude, U. Miami, 1967; LLM, Yale U., 1968. Bar: Fla. 1967, D.C. 1979, U.S. Dist. Ct. (so. dist.) Fla. 1967, U.S. Dist. Ct. (mid. dist.) Fla. 1982, U.S. Ct. Appeals (5th and 11th cirs.) 1967, U.S. Supreme Ct. 1975. Law clk. to judge U.S. Dist. Ct. (so. dist.) Fla.; shareholder Kelly, Black, Black & Kenny; now shareholder Kenny Nachwalter Seymour Arnold Critchlow & Spector, P.A., Miami; lectr. Law Sch. U. Miami. Fellow Am. Coll. Trial Lawyers; mem. Judicial Qualifications Commn.; mem. ABA, Am. Bd. Trial Advocates, Fla. Bar Assn. (bd. govs. 1982-90), Fed. Bar Assn., Internat. Soc. Barristers, Dade County Bar Assn., Omicron Delta Kappa, Phi Kappa Phi, Phi Delta Phi, Iron Arrow, Soc. Wig and Robe. Editor-in-chief U. Miami Law Rev., 1966-67. Office: Kenny Nachwalter Seymour Arnold Critchlow & Spector PA 201 S Biscayne Blvd Ste 1100 Miami FL 33131-4327

NACOL, MAE, lawyer; b. Beaumont, Tex., June 15, 1944; d. William Samuel and Ethel (Bowman) N.; children: Shawn Alexander Nacol, Catherine Regina Nacol. BA, Rice U., 1965; postgrad., S. Tex. Coll. Law, 1966-68. Bar: Tex. 1969, U.S. Dist. Ct. (so. dist.) Tex. 1969. Diamond buyer/appraiser Nacol's Jewelry, Houston, 1961—; pvt. practice law, Houston, 1969—. Author, editor ednl. materials on multiple sclerosis, 1981-85. Nat. dir. A.R.M.S. of Am. Ltd., Houston, 1984-85. Recipient Mayor's Recognition award City of Houston, 1972; Ford Found. fellow So. Tex. Coll. Law, Houston, 1964. Mem. Houston Bar Assn. (chmn. candidate com. 1970, chmn. membership com. 1971, chmn. lawyers referral com. 1972), Assn. Trial Lawyers Am., Tex. Trial Lawyers Assn., Am. Judicature Soc. (sustaining), Houston Fin. Coun. Women, Houston Trial Lawyers Assn. Presbyterian. Office: 600 Jefferson St Ste 850 Houston TX 77002-7326

NADEAU, JOSEPH EUGENE, health care management consultant, information systems consultant; b. Portland, Maine, Sept. 23, 1937; s. Edwin Tustin and Beatrice Margaret (Spiller) N.; m. Mary Lou Prendible, Dec. 2, 1961; children—Laura, Keith, Michael. B.S. in Math., Boston Coll., 1960. Dir. systems devel. Mass. Hosp. Assn., Burlington, 1967-72; S.E. regional mgr. Automatic Data Processing, Miami, Fla., 1972-73; S.E. regional mktg. mgr. Space Age Computer Systems, Louisville, 1973-74; prin. COMPUTERx Cons., Miami, 1974—. Asst. scoutmaster South Fla. council Boy Scouts Am., 1972-81. Served to 1st lt. U.S. Army, 1960-64; Germany. Mem. Am. Hosp. Assn., Soc. Computer Medicine, Data Processing Mgmt. Assn., Hosp. Mgmt Systems Soc., Assn. Systems Mgmt. (pres. 1971-72), Hosp. Fin. Mgmt. Assn. (chmn. data processing com. 1967-84), Am. Arbitration Assn. (arbitrator 1980—). Cert. Computer profl. Home: 7750 SW 118th St Miami FL 33156-4433 Office: COMPUTERx Consulting 9719 S Dixie Hwy # 1 Miami FL 33156-2806

NADEAU, ROBERT LEE, English language educator, inventor, entrepreneur; b. Jan. 21, 1944. BA, U. of the South, 1966; MA, U. Fla., 1967, PhD, 1970. Asst. prof. Mary Washington Coll., Fredericksburg, Va., 1970-75; asst. prof. George Mason U., 1975-79, assoc. prof., 1979-91, prof., 1991—, dir. Am. studies program, 1975-80, gen. culture coord. D of Arts in Edn., 1983-84; cons. Toyota Motor Co., 1992; co-founder Linus Corp., 1988; co-inventor electronic checkbook, 1993; co-founder Electric Paper Co., 1992. Author: Readings From the New Book on Nature, 1981, Nature Talks Back, 1984, Mind, Machines and Human Consciousness: Are There Limits to Artificial Intelligence?, 1991, (with Minas Kafatos) The Conscious Universe: Part and Whole in Modern Physical Theory, 1990, The S/he Brain: Science, Sexual Politics and the Myths of Feminism, 1996; contbr. articles to profl. jours. Univ. fellowship U. of the So., 1962-66, NDEA fellowship U. Fla., 1966-70; fellowship Aix-en-Province, 1964-65. Univ. fellowship U. of the South, 1962-66, NDEA fellowship U. Fla., 1966-70; fellowship Aix-en-Province, 1964-65. Home: 10310 Cleveland St Fairfax VA 22030-3502 Office: Dept English George Mason Univ Fairfax VA 22030

NADER, SHAHLA, endocrinologist educator; b. Tehran, Iran, Feb. 19, 1946; came to U.S., 1981; d. Hassan and Forough (Moktari) N.; m. Farzin Eftekhari, Sept. 26, 1976; children: Shiva, Kian. BS in Physiology, U. Leeds, 1967, MD, 1970. Registrar in endocrinology Royal Postgrad. Med. Sch., London, 1974-75; asst. prof. U. Tehran, 1975-78; pvt. practice Tehran Clinic, 1978-81; instr. ob-gyn. U. Tex. Med. Sch., Houston, 1982-84, asst. prof., 1984-89, assoc. prof., 1989-96, prof., 1996—. Contbr. articles to med. jours., chpts. to books. Recipient Women's Fund for Edn. and Rsch. award, Tex., 1992. Mem. Endocrine Soc., Am. Diabetes Assn., Am. Fertiligy Soc., Am. Assn. Clin. Endocrinologists (pres. 1993—), Soc. for Gynecologic Investigation. Islamic. Home: 3027 Robinhood St Houston TX 77005-2343 Office: U Tex Med Sch 6431 Fannin St # 3204 Houston TX 77030-1501

NADERI, JAMIE BENEDICT, hazardous waste services brokerage executive; b. New Castle, Pa., Aug. 6, 1951; d. Harold James and June Marilyn (Sipe) Benedict; children: Robert Brian, Eric James. Student, New Castle Bus. Coll., 1967-69, Truckee Meadows Community Coll., 1979-82; M in Govt. Contracting, George Washington U., 1992. Owner, pres. Moheat Inc., Houston. Mem. Nat. Assn. Female Execs., Nat. Contract Mgmt. Assn., Tex. Hazardous Waste Mgmt. Soc., Women in Waste. Presbyterian. Office: Moheat Inc 15915 Katy Frwy Ste 170 Houston TX 77094

NADIJCKA HANSON, MARY DIANE, biologist, consultant; b. Gloucester, Eng., Aug. 1, 1945; d. Stephen Stanley and Marjorie Joyce (Clements) N.; m. Victor Arthur Hason, Sept. 13, 1985. BA, Holy Family Coll., 1967; MA, Temple U., 1971, PhD, 1975. Rsch. assoc. Temple U., Phila., 1975-80; rsch. biologist Veteran's Adminstrn. Med. Ctr., Wilmington, Del., 1980-87, rsch. lab. dir., 1983-87; assoc. dir., rsch. dir. Nat. Disease Rsch. Interchange, Phila., 1987-89; head sci. dept. Atlanta Internat. Sch., 1992-96; biomed. cons. Pike Creek Enterprises, Inc., Atlanta, 1989—; chairperson rsch. and devel. com. Vet. Adminstrn. Med. Ctr., Wilmington, Del., 1983-84, internal rev. bd., chemical and waste control com., 1985-87. Contbr. articles to profl. jours. Grantee Vet.'s Adminstrn., 1983-84, FDA, 1988. Mem. AAAS, AAUW, Nat. Sci. Tchr.'s Assn., Tissue Culture Assn. (lab. materials and biosafety com.). Home: 3875 W Nancy Creek Ct Atlanta GA 30319

NADLER, RONALD DAVID, psychologist, educator; b. Newark, N.J., Jan. 19, 1936; s. Samuel and Blanche (Knobler) N.; m. Judith Faye Baskin, June 21, 1959 (div. Feb. 1976); children: T. Scott, Sari Jennifer; m. Elizabeth White, Aug. 24, 1991. BA, UCLA, 1960, MA, 1963, PhD, 1965. Asst. prof. Downstate Med. Ctr. SUNY, Bklyn., 1966-71; assoc. rsch. prof. Yerkes Regional Primate Rsch. Ctr., Atlanta, 1971-82, rsch. prof., 1982-96, prof. emeritus, 1996—; vis. prof. Karisoke Rsch. Ctr., Rwanda, 1981, Ctr. Internat. Rsch. Med. Franceville, Gabon, 1982-85; sci. adv. bd. Digit Fund, Englewood, Colo., 1986-91; cons. in field. Contbr. articles to Jour. Comparative Psychology, Sci., Jour. Comparative Physiol. Psychology, Jour. Physiology, Brain Behavior Evolution, Physiol. Behavior, Am. Jour. Phys. Anthropology, Neuroendocrinology, Primates, Jour. Human Evolution, Zoo News, Med. Sexology, Transitions N.Y. Acad. Scis., Brain Behavior Evolution, Internat. Jour. Primatology, Am. Jour. Primatology, Primates, others. With U.S. Army, 1955-58. USPHS fellow, 1961-67, Population Coun. fellow, 1965-66, faculty fellow U. Oxford, 1965-66; grantee Rsch. Opportunity Fund, 1964, 65, Rsch. Found., 1968-70, USPHS, 1969-72, NSF, 1969-83, 87-94, Emory U., 1975, 78, 79, Ctr. Internat. Recherches Medicales de Franceville, 1982-85, NIH, 1984-87. Mem. Am. Soc. Primatologists, Internat. Acad. Sex Rsch., Internat. Primatological Soc., Sigma Xi. Home: 2008 Lavista Rd NE Atlanta GA 30329-3914 Office: Emory U Yerkes Reg Primate Rsch Ctr Atlanta GA 30322

NAGDA, DURGA SHANKER, environmental engineer, researcher; b. Udaipur, India, Dec. 25, 1941; came to U.S., 1977; m. Amba Nagda, May 28, 1958; children: Yugal, Pushpa, Krish, Dimple. Grad., Instn. Engrs. India, 1966; MPhil, U. Leeds, Eng., 1973. Registered profl. engr., Ky. Instr. U. Jodhpur, India, 1964-70, 74-75; rsch. asst. U. Leeds, 1972-73; mine engr. Hindustan Zinc Ltd., Udaipur, 1974; lectr. Indian Sch. Mines, Dhanbad, 1975-77; instr., advisor Belmont Tech. Coll., St. Clairsville, Ohio, 1978-79; asst. prof. Hazard (Ky.) C.C., 1980-86; cons. engr. Day Engring., Hazard, Ky., 1982-86; rsch. and design engr. Hellard & Whitaker Engring., Hazard, 1986-87; chief engr. Whitaker Coal Corp., Hazard, 1987-88; environ. engr. Ky. Dept. Environ. Protection, Frankfort, 1988—. Mem. NSPE, Inst. Explosive Engrs. (assoc.), Soc. Mining Engrs., Am. Inst. Mining, Metall., and Petroleum Engrs. Home: 433 Pasadena Dr Lexington KY 40503-2255 Office: Dept Environ Protection 14 Reilly Rd Frankfort KY 40601-1139

NAGEL, JAMES EDWARD, English literature educator; b. St. Paul, May 20, 1940; s. Ray and Mae Lillian (Fjeldseth) N.; m. Gwen Marie Lindberg, Sept. 9, 1967. BS, Moorhead State U., 1962; MA, Pa. State U., 1964, PhD, 1971. Instr. Moorhead State U., 1965-68; asst. prof. Northeastern U., 1971-75; Fulbright prof. New Zealand, 1977; assoc. prof. Northeastern U., 1975-80, prof. English, 1980-90, Disting. Prof., 1990-93, Stanton W. and Elisabeth K. Davis disting. prof. Am. lit., 1990-93; J.O. Eidson disting prof. U. Ga., Athens, 1991—. Author: Critical Essays on Catch-22, 1974, American Fiction: Historical and Critical Essays, 1977, Sarah Orne Jewett: A Reference Guide, 1978, Stephen Crane and Literary Impressionism, 1981, American Literature: The New England Heritage, 1981, Critical Essays on Hamlin Garland, 1982, Ernest Hemingway: The Writer in Context, 1984, Critical Essays on Joseph Heller, 1984, Hemingway in Love and War, 1989, Bibliography of American Fiction 1866-1918, 1993, Ernest Hemingway: The Oak Park Legacy, 1996, many others. Mem. Am. Lit. Assn. (exec. coord. 1988—), South Atlantic Modern Lang. Assn., Modern Lang. Assn., Hemmingway Soc. (pres. 1983-86), Phi Kappa Phi. Independent. Home: 168 Red Fox Run Athens GA 30605-4405 Office: U Ga Dept English Athens GA 30602

NAGEL, JOACHIM HANS, biomedical engineer, educator; b. Haustadt, Saarland, Feb. 22, 1948; came to U.S., 1986; s. Emil and Margarethe Nagel; m. Monika Behrens. MS, U. Saarbruecken, Fed. Republic Germany, 1973; DSc, U. Erlangen, Fed. Republic Germany, 1979. Rsch. assoc., lectr., instr. U. Saarbruecken, 1973-74; rsch. assoc., lectr., instr. Dept. Biomed. Engring., U. Erlangen-Nuernberg, 1974-75, asst. prof., 1975-79, dir. med. electronics and computer div., 1976-85, assoc. prof., 1980-86; assoc. prof. radiology Med. Sch. U. Miami, Coral Gables, Fla., 1990-91, assoc. prof. psychology Sch. Arts and Scis., 1988-91, assoc. prof. biomed. engring. Coll. Engring., 1986-91, prof. biomed. engring, radiology and psychology, 1991-96; dir. Inst. Biomed. Engring. U. Stuttgart, 1996—; adj. prof. biomed. engring. U. Miami, 1996—. Editor Annals of Biomedical Engineering, Section Instrumentation, 1989-94, Inst. of Physics Physiological Measurement, 1994—; contbr. articles numerous articles to profl. jours. NIH grantee since 1986. Mem. IEEE (sr.), IEEE/Engring. in Medicine and Biology Soc. (chmn. Internat. Conf. 1991, chmn. Internat. Progr. Com. Conf. 1989, 90, 92), IEEE/Acoustics, Speech, and Signal Processing Soc., Biomed. Engring. Soc. (sr.), N.Y. Acad. Scis., Internat. Soc. Optical Engring., Romanian Soc. for Clin. Engring. and Med. Computing (hon.), Sigma Xi. Roman Catholic. Office: U Stuttgart, Seidenstrasse 36, D-70174 Stuttgart Germany

NAGEL, LEROY F., manufacturing and supply company executive; b. 1939. BSME, U. Tex., 1960. With Nagel Mfg. & Supply Co., Austin, Tex., 1960—, chmn. bd. Office: Nagel Mfg & Supply Co 9100 United Dr Austin TX 78758

NAGIN, STEPHEN E., lawyer, educator; b. Phila., Nov. 7, 1946; s. Harry S. and Dorothy R. (Pearlman) N.; m. Marjorie Riley. BBA, U. Miami, 1969, JD, 1974. Bar: Fla. 1974, D.C. 1976, U.S. Supreme Ct. 1978. Asst. atty. gen. State of Fla., Miami, 1974-75; atty., FTC, 1975-80; spl. asst. U.S. atty. D.C., 1980-81; ptnr. Litchford, Christopher, Nagin & Figueredo, 1996—; adj. prof. St. Thomas U. Sch. Law, 1984-94; instr. Nat. Inst. Trial Advocacy, 1992—. Mem. Fla. Correctional Med. Authority, 1990-91. Mem. ABA, Fed. Bar Assn., D.C. Bar Assn., Fla. Bar Assn. (editor, trial lawyers sect. 1983-84; mem. spl. antitrust task force 1983—, chmn. editorial bd., 1982-83, chmn. antitrust com. 1996—), Coral Gables Bar Assn. (bd. dirs. 1983-87), Assn. Trial Lawyers Am., Am. Arbitration Assn., Nat. Health Lawyers Assn. Office: 3580 First Union Fin Ctr Miami FL 33131

NAGLEE, ELFRIEDE KURZ, retired medical nurse; b. Phila., Mar. 13, 1932; d. Emil and Frida (Keppler) Kurz; m. David I. Naglee, Sept. 6, 1952; children: Joy, Miriam, Deborah, Joanna, David. Grad., Phila. Gen. Hosp., 1952. RN, Ga. Dir. nursing City County Hosp., LaGrange, Ga.; house supr. West Ga. Med. Ctr., LaGrange, from 1967; staff nurse med. fl. West Ga. Med. Ctr., LaGange, to 1995; ret., 1995. Mem. Ga. Nursing Assn. Home: 804 Piney Woods Dr Lagrange GA 30240

NAGLIERI, EILEEN SHERIDAN, special education educator; b. Queens, N.Y., Oct. 3, 1962; d. Raymond J. and Julia C. (Giusani) Sheridan; m. Raymond M. Naglieri, May 2, 1987. BA, St. Joseph's Coll., 1984; MS in Edn., St. John's U., 1987; postgrad., U. Cen. Fla., 1988—. Cert. elem. tchr., reading, mentally handicapped. Tchr. 1st grade Incarnation Sch., Queens Village, N.Y., 1984-87; tchr. exceptional students Denn John Mid. Sch., Kissimmee, Fla., 1987-91; resource compliance specialist Denn John Mid. Sch. and Ventura Elem. Sch., Kissimmee, 1991-93; resource compliance specialist, program specialist emotionally handicapped Lakeview Elem. Sch., Kissimmee, 1993—; instr. adult basic edn. Vocat., Adult and Community Edn. Osceola County, Kissimmee, 1988-91. Vol. spl. religious edn. program Our Lady Lourdes, Queens, 1976-85, Queens Children's Psychiat. Ctr., 1979-80; vol. counselor autism and devel. delays, Queens, 1984-86. Blanche A. Knauth scholar, 1980. Mem. NEA, Coun. Exceptional Children, Delta Epsilon Sigma. Roman Catholic.

NAGY, ALBERT N., entrepreneur, consultant; b. Fairfield, Conn., Apr. 29, 1929; s. Frank J. Nagy and Elizabeth (Fekete) Ferrucci; m. Embeth Stumpf (div. 1990); 1 child, Laura Elizabeth Bedard; m. Mary Margaret Evans, 1996. BA, Colby Coll., 1956; MBA, Northeastern U., Boston, 1969. Lic. real estate broker, Fla., Mass., N.H.; lic. mortgage broker, Fla.; cert., mediator Supreme Ct. Fla. Co-chmn. Ford Found. Challenge, Santa Barbara, Calif., 1965; chmn. Pierre Salinger for Sen. campaign, Santa Barbara, 1967-68; bd. dirs. Samaritans Merrimack Valley, Lawrence, Mass., 1985-87, Samaritans U.S.A., Boston, 1986, Samaritans U.S.A., Boston, 1986, Samaritans Manchester, N.H., 1986-87; jr. comdt. Marine Corps League, 1992-94; mediator Fla. Supreme Ct. 5th Jud. Cir. Ct.; bd. dirs. S.W. Dem. Club, 1996; mem. Citrus County Dem. Exec. Com. Democrat. Roman Catholic. Home: 7885 W Inn Ln Homosassa FL 34446-1201

NAHAI, FOAD, plastic surgery educator; b. Teheran, Iran, Sept. 23, 1943; came to U.S., 1970; m. Shannaz Mossanen, Aug. 4, 1969; children: Farzad R., Fariba R. BSc with honors, U. Bristol, Eng., 1966, MB ChB, 1969. Diplomate Am. Bd. Surgery, Am. Bd. Plastic Surgery. Med. and surg. intern United Bristol Hosps., 1969-70; intern in surgery Balt. City Hosps., 1970-71; resident in surgery Johns Hopkins Hosp., Balt., 1971-72; resident in gen. surgery Emory U. Affiliated Hosps., Atlanta, 1972-74, chief resident, 1974-75, fellow in hand surgery and microsurgery, 1975-76, resident in plastic surgery, 1976-77; instr. in surgery Emory U., Atlanta, 1975-76, 78, from asst. to assoc. prof., 1978-91, prof., 1991—. Author: (with S.J. Mathes) Clinical Atlas of Muscle and Musculocutaneous Flaps, 1979, Clinical Applications for Muscle and Musculocutaneous Flaps, 1982, (with others) Microvascular Surgery in Reconstruction of the Head and Neck, 1989, Plastic and Reconstructive Breast Surgery, 1990, Grabb's Encyclopedia of Flaps, 1990, (with Boswick Jill Eaves) Encyclopedia of Plastic Surgery, 1994, others; mem. editl. bd. Annals Plastic Surgery, 1984, Outlook Plastic Surgery, 1988; contbr. articles to profl. jours.; co-prodr. (movies) Breast Reconstruction After a Radical Mastectomy with Latissimus Dorsi Musculocutaneous Flap, 1978, The Tensor Fascia Lata Free Flap, 1979; prodr. (videotapes) TFL Neurosensory Flap for Coverage of Greater Trochanteric and Ischium, Rectus Abdominis Flap for Sternal Coverage, Gastrocnemius Muscle Flap for Coverage of Tibia, others. Recipient Gold Medal Paper Presentation, Southeastern Surg. Conf., 1976, Best Paper award Atlanta Clin. Soc., 1980, award Am. Med. Writers Assn., 1983. Fellow ACS (3d Ann. Residents Competition award Ga. chpt. 1977); mem. AMA, Am. Assn. Plastic Surgeons (James Barrett Brown award 1982), Am. Soc. Aesthetic Plastic Surgery, Am. Soc. Surgery Hand, Am. Soc. Plastic and Reconstructive Surgeons (rsch. grantee ednl. found.), Brit. Med. Assn., Ga. Soc. Plastic Surgeons, Med. Assn. Ga., Ga. Surg. Soc., Med. Assn. Atlanta, So. Med. Assn., Southeastern Soc. Plastic and Reconstructive Surgeons (Outstanding Resident award 1977), Internat. Assn. Univ. Plastic Surgeons, Internat. Soc. Reconstructive Microsurgery, Plastic Surgery Rsch. Coun. (program chmn. 1988, chmn. 1989); corr. mem. Brazilian Coll. Surgeons, Brazilian Soc. Plastic Surgeons, italian Soc. Plastic, Reconstructive and Aesthetic Surgery; hon. mem. Soc. Residents and Ex Residents of Inst. Reconstructive Surgery, Sociedad Jaime Planas de Cirurgia Plastica. Office: Emory Clinic Ste B2100 1365 Clifton Rd NE Atlanta GA 30322

NAHMIAS, BRIGITTE BUCHMANN, physician, radiologist; b. Kiel, Schleswig-Holstein, Germany, June 30, 1932; came to U.S., 1947; d. Erich H. and Klara (Fueting) Buchmann; m. Andre J. Nahmias, June 9, 1956 (div. 1986); children: Cynthia, David, Edward; m. Donald B. Norton, Feb. 19, 1994. BA, George Washington U., 1954, MD, 1957. Diplomate Am. Bd. Internal Medicine. Rotating intern USPHS Hosp., S.I., N.Y., 1957-58; rsch. fellow pulmonary function and diseases Grady Meml. Hosp., Atlanta, 1958-60; jr. asst. resident in medicine Boston City Hosp., 1960-61, sr. asst. resident in medicine, 1962-63; fellow in cardio-pulmonary function and disease Boston U. Sch. Medicine/Mass. Meml. Hosp., 1961-62; emergency room physician DeKalb Gen. Hosp., Decatur, Ga., 1963-65; dir. Albert Steiner Meml. Emphysema Clinic St. Joseph's Infirmary, Atlanta, 1965-75; clinician, radiologist Tb control divsn. Fulton County Dept. Health, Atlanta, 1967-93; clin. asst. prof. medicine sch. medicine Emory U., Atlanta, 1968-85, med. dir. and editor med. TV network sch. medicine, 1982-85; pres. Med. Video Prodns., 1986—; vis. faculty Sch. Allied Health Scis., Ga. State U., 1973-76; vis. attending physician St. Elizabeth's Hosp., Perth, Australia, 1976; cons. Interactive Health Network, 1993—. Prodr., writer, editor (videotapes) Herpes and Pregnancy: Implications for Parents, Newborns and Personnel, 1984, Life or Death in the Terminal Patient: Whose Decision is It?, 1984, Herpes in Schools, 1985, Osteoporosis: Can We Prevent It?, 1985, Osteoporosis: How Can We Treat It?, 1985, Skin Peeling Therapy: Medium Depth Chemical Peel, 1985, Reach for Excellence: Reproductive Health Management, 1985, AIDS Carriers in MY Practice, 1987, Health Effects of Asbestos Exposure, 1988, AIDS in Your Life, 1989, A Closer Look, 1990, also comms.; contbr. articles to med. jours. Chair Cliff Valley Pre-Sch., 1966-67; tchr. Sunday Sch., singer choir; active Peace Network; pres. Briar Vista Sch. PTA, 1981-83. Fellow ACP; mem. AMA, Am. Med. Writers Assn., Nat. Bd. Med. Examiners (lic.), Internat. TV Assn., Med. Women's Assn., Physicians for Social Responsibility, Ga. State Bd. Med. Examiners (lic.), Med. Assn. Ga., Med. Assn. Atlanta (health edn. com. 1989-90), Atlanta Prodrs. Assn., Mason Mill Civic Club. Home and Office: 859 Vistavia Cir Decatur GA 30033-3409

NAIDE, ADAM MICHAEL, sales executive; b. Silver Spring, Md., Nov. 3, 1966; s. Elliot and Marlene Rubin N.; m. Karen Leslie Schneiderman, May 17, 1992. BBA in Fin., Emory U., 1988; MBA, U. Ga., 1991. Internal review analyst U.S. Mint, Washington, 1987-87; sr. advt. rep. Emory Wheel, Atlanta, 1987-88; sales rep. Xerox Corp., Atlanta, 1988-90; nat. acctount mgr. USA Today, Arlington, Va., 1991—. Mktg. advisor Fairlington Arts Ctr., Arlington, Va., 1992—; vol. United Way, Boys Clubs, 1982-90. Mem. Am. Mgmt. Assn. (pres. 1991), Nat. Assn. Parterships in Edn. (adv. coun., pres. 1991), Delta Tau Delta (chpt. advisor 1991—, chpt. advisor award 1992). Office: USA Today 1000 Wilson Blvd Arlington VA 22209-3901

NAIL, JASPER MONROE, electrical engineer; b. Grenada, Miss., July 25, 1939; s. William Lamar and Nannie Beatrice (Lott) N.; m. Shirley Ann Carpenter, June 21, 1960; children: John, Rebecca. BSEE, Miss. State U., 1963; MS in Physics, U. So. Miss., 1971. Cert. fin. planner. Lab. engr. Am. Bosch Arma, Columbus, Miss., 1962-63; elec. design engr. Saturn I program Space Div. Chrysler Corp., New Orleans, 1963-65; lead engr. Apollo Space div. N.Am. Rockwell, Miss. Test Facility, Miss., 1965-71; project engr. Gen. Electric, Miss. Test Facility, 1971-73; lead test engr. Rocketdyne div. Rockwell Internat., Nat. Space Technology Lab, Miss., 1973-78; instrumentation mgr. Rocketdyne div. Rockwell Internat., Stennis Spacecenter, Miss., 1978—; investment advisor Structure Key Fin. Planning and Svcs., 1990-93; cons in field. Patentee in field. Lt. gov. Civitan Internat., Gulf Coast Dist., Miss., 1975. Recipient Dir.'s award North Am. Rockwell, 1968, Pres.'s Achievement award Rockwell Internat., 1982; named Civitan of the Year Picayune Civitan Club, 1972. Mem. Miss. Profl. Engrs., Civitan Internat. (club v.p. 1972-73, pres. 1973-74), Sigma Pi Sigma. Home: RR 2 Box 501E Carriere MS 39426-2602 Office: Rocketdyne Bldg 4110 Stennis Space Center MS 39529

NAILOR, RICHARD ANTHONY, SR., research company executive; b. New Haven, July 27, 1935; s. Earl Edward and Theresa Mary (Massaro) N.; m. Sandra Louise Grace, Jan. 16, 1960; children: Richard, Michele, Keith. Student, Fairfield U., 1952-54; AA, USN Elect. Officers, 1964. Enlisted, terrier MSL fire control technician USMC, Egypt, Lebanon and Cuba, 1954-62; radar maintenance officer 9th MEB USMC, Vietnam, 1965, 69-70; project officer Hdqs. USMC, 1966-74; logistics analyst Potomac Rsch., Inc., Alexandria, Va., 1974-79, head publs. br., 1978-80, dir. ILS dept., 1980-82, dir. ILS div., 1982-83, v.p. OPS, 1983-86; sr. v.p. OPS Potomac Rsch. Internat., Alexandria, 1986-94, exev. v.p., COO, 1994-96, pres., CEO, 1996—. Troop leader Boy Scouts Council, Woodbridge, Va., 1968-69; pres. Woodbridge Parks Assn., 1978-81; park authority rep. Pr. William County (Va.) Park Authority, 1982-86. Mem. VFW, Ret. Officers Assn., Marine Corps Mustang Assn. (charter), Soc. Logistics Engrs., 1st Marine Aircraft Wing Assn. Republican. Roman Catholic. Home: 12307 Beaver Lodge Rd Stafford VA 22554-3427 Office: Potomac Rsch Internat 11320 Random Hills Rd Ste 300 Fairfax VA 22030-6001

NAIR, RAMACHANDRAN P.K., agroforestry educator, researcher; b. Trivandrum, Kerala, India, Mar. 12, 1942; came to U.S., 1987.; s. Krishna Kittu Pillai and Parukutty Amma; m. Vimala Devi Pillai, Aug. 29, 1973; children: Bindu, Deepa, Rekha. BS in Agr., Kerala Agrl. U., 1961, MS in Agr., 1968; PhD, Pantnagar U., India, 1971; Dr. Sci. Agr., U. Goettingen, W. Germany, 1978. Research asst. Kerala Agrl. U., 1961-66, lectr. in agronomy, 1966; post-doctoral fellow Rothamsted Experimental Sta., Harpenden, Eng., 1971-72; agronomist ICAR (CPCRI), Kasaragod, Kerala, 1972-76; Humboldt fellow U. Goettingen, 1976-78; prin. sci. Internat. Centre for Rsch. in Agroforestry, Nairobi, Kenya, 1978-87; prof. agroforestry U. Fla., Gainesville, 1987—; cons., rschr. numerous orgns. Author: Intensive Multiple Cropping with Coconuts in India, 1979, Agroforestry Species: A Crop Sheets Manual, 1980, Soil Productivity Aspects of Agroforestry, 1984, An Introduction to Agroforestry, 1993; co-editor: Agroforestry: A Decade of Developments, 1987; editor: Agroforestry Systems in the Tropics, 1989, Agroforestry Systems, 1982—, chief editor, 1994. Mem. Internat. Soil Sci. Soc., Internat. Soc. Tropical Foresters, Am. Soc. Agronomy (chair divsn. A-6 internat. agronomy 1995-96), Soc. Am. Foresters. Office: U Fla 118 Newins Ziegler Hall Gainesville FL 32611-0410

NAIZER, KENNETH C., electrical engineer; b. Pt. Arthur, Tex., Oct. 2, 1946; s. William J. and Mary A. (Zurovetz) N.; m. Jon Carole Dubose, Aug. 13, 1977; children: Lindsey Marie, Lorrie Nicole. BSEE, Lamar Coll. Tech., 1968; MBA, Lamar U., 1978. Registered profl. elec. engr. Elec. engr. Texaco Inc., Port Arthur, 1968; infantry officer USMC, 1968-72; from sr. elec. engr. to supervising engr. Texaco Inc., 1975-91; staff engr. Star Enterprise, Port Arthur, 1981—. Patentee in field. Advisor Girl Scouts Am., Beamont, Tex., 1988-91; bd. dirs. West End Little League, Beaumont, 1993-95. Mem. Instrument Soc. Am. (Kates award 1989), Marine Corps League, Marine Corps Res. Officers Assn., Res. Officers Assn., Am. Legion. Home: 1310 Sheridan Ln Beaumont TX 77706 Office: Star Enterprise N End Houston Ave Port Arthur TX 77640

NAKARAI, CHARLES FREDERICK TOYOZO, music educator, adjudicator; b. Indpls., Apr. 25, 1936; s. Toyozo Wada and Frances Aileen N.; B.A. cum laude, Butler U., 1958, Mus.M., 1967; postgrad. U. N.C., 1967-70. Organist, dir. choirs Northwood Christian ch., Indpls., 1954-57; minister music Broad Ripple Christian Ch., Indpls., 1957-58; asst. prof. music Milligan Coll., Tenn., 1970-72; pvt. instrn. organ, piano, Durham, 1972—; adjudicator N.C. Fedn. Music Clubs, Raleigh Music Tchrs. Assn. Served with USAF, 1958-64. Mem. Am. Musicol. Soc., Coll. Music Soc., Am. Guild Organists, Music Tchrs. Nat. Assn., Music Library Assn., N.C. Music Tchrs. Assn. (chair student activities), Organ Hist. Soc., Durham Music Tchrs. Assn. Composer: Three Movements for Chorus, 1971, Bluesy, 1979. Address: 3520 Mayfair St Apt 205 Durham NC 27707-2673

NALAND, JOHN KIDDOO, diplomat; b. Wichita, Kans., Mar. 25, 1957; s. Willard Hugh and Carol Lea (Kiddoo) N.; m. Barbara Reioux, Dec. 31, 1994. BA in History, Tulane U., 1979, BS in Anthropology, 1980. Apptd. as fgn. svc. officer U.S. Dept. State, Washington, 1986; 3d sec., vice consul Am. Embassy Bogotá, Colombia, 1986-88; 2d sec., adminstv. officer Am. Embassy San José, Costa Rica, 1988-90; staff asst. Sec. State's Policy Planning Staff, Washington, 1990-91; watch officer State Dept. Ops. Ctr., Washington, 1991-92; duty officer Nat. Security Coun.'s White House Situation Rm., Washington, 1992-93; econ. officer U.S. Dept. State, Washington, 1993-95, Am. Embassy, Managua, Nicaragua, 1995—. Candidate Orleans Parish Sch. Bd., New Orleans, 1976; alt. del. Rep. Nat. Com., Kansas City, Mo., 1976, Detroit, 1980; La. Coll. coord. Pres. Ford Com., La., 1976. 1st lt. U.S. Army, 1981-84. Decorated Army Achievement medal U.S. Army, 1983, Army Commendation medal U.S. Army, 1984, Meritorious Honor award U.S. Dept. State, 1988. Mem. Am. Fgn. Svc. Assn. Office: US Dept State 2201 C St NW Washington DC 20520-0001

NALL, LAWANDA CAROL, nursing administrator; b. Monroeville, Ala., July 19, 1964; d. Charles Edward and Willie Earline (Brantley) N. AA, Pensacola Jr. Coll., 1983, AS, 1984; BS, MS, Columbia Pacific U., 1986; DSc, London Inst. Applied Rsch., 1991. Cert. advanced cardiac life support, basic trauma life support, nursing adminstr. Nursing asst. W.D. McMillan Hosp., Brewton, Ala., 1982; nursing asst. Sacred Heart Hosp., Pensacola, Fla., 1982-83, unit sec., 1984; nursing supr. Columbia Regional Med. Ctr., Andalusia, Ala., 1984-85, dir. edn., 1984-85; nursing dir. Perry Community Hosp., Marion, Ala., 1985; nursing instr. S.W. Va. Community Coll., Logan, 1986; clin. dir. nursing Med. Ctr. Baton Rouge, 1987-88; asst. adminstr. for nursing Terrell (Tex.) Community Hosp., 1988, clin. rsch. assoc. Drug Rsch. and Analysis, 1988-90; nursing adminstr. Copper Basin Med. Ctr., Copperhill, Tenn., 1990-92, Atmore Nursing Care Ctr., 1992-93, Atmore Community Hosp., 1992-93; dir. patient care svcs. Man Appalachian Regional Hosp., Man, W.Va., 1993-95; DON Sports Medicine Hosp., Riyadh, Saudi Arabia, 1995—. Author: Manual of Inservice Education, 1985, Manual of Effective Communication and Managament Techniques for Nursing Adminstrators, 1986, others. Mem. AACN, NAFE, ANA (cert. nursing adminstr. advanced 1988), Emergency Nurses Assn., Am. Heart Assn. (cert. BCLS, ACLS, basic trauma life support).

NALL, LUCIA LYNN, controller; b. Jackson, Miss., Nov. 22, 1954; d. Aldert S. and Jean (Eaves) Nall. BA in History, Belhaven Coll., 1975, BS in Acctg., 1981; MBA, Miss. Coll., 1994. Acct. Miss. State Bd. Health, Jackson, 1979-85; asst. contr. Miller-Wills Aviation, Jackson, 1985-87; contr. Alston, Rutherford, Tardy & Van Slyke, Jackson, 1987-96; owner Freight Brokers, Brandon, Miss., 1996—. Mem. NAFE, Inst. Mgmt. Accts. Home: 930 N Livingston Rd Jackson MS 39213-9207 Office: Freight Brokers 108 Office Park Dr Brandon MS 39042-2404

NALL, SANDRA LILLIAN, securities company official; b. Waverly, N.Y., Apr. 5, 1943; d. Harvey Moyer and Mildred Helen (Raw) Foster; m. Douglas Clay Ogden, Nov. 30, 1961 (div. Nov. 1974); 1 child, James Douglas; m. Ralph Gene Nall, Nov. 24, 1984. Student, U. Louisville, 1963-65, U. Ky., 1975-76. Cert. profl. sec., fin. and ops. prin., Ky. Sec. Louisville Water Co., 1964-66; exec. sec. Bank of Lexington (Ky.), 1966-69; office mgr. Dupree & Co., Inc., Lexington, 1969-73; adminstrv. asst. Jerrico, Inc., Lexington, 1973-79; adminstrv. sec. Coun. State Govts., Lexington, 1979-81; personnel asst. U. Ky., Lexington, 1981-82; v.p. fin. and ops. 1st Ky. Securities Corp., Frankfort, 1982—, sec.-treas., 1986, also bd. dirs. Mem. budget panel agy. affairs com. United Way Bluegrass, Lexington, 1976-79; mem. Plaza Pops Picnic Com., Frankfort, 1986-88. Mem. Nat. Soc. Compliance Profls., Am. Inst. Profl. Bookkeepers, NAFE. Republican. Office: 1st Ky Securities Corp State Nat Bank Bldg Ste 400 Frankfort KY 40601

NALLEY, ELIZABETH ANN, chemistry educator; b. Catron, Mo., July 8, 1942; d. Arthur E. and Thelma L. (King) Frazier; m. Robert L. Mullican, Jan. 2, 1986; 1 child, George L. BS, Northeastern Okla. State U., 1965; MS, Okla. State U., 1969; PhD, Tex. Woman's U., 1975. High sch. tchr. Muskogee (Okla.) Ctrl. High Sch., 1964-65; instr. Cameron U., Lawton, Okla., 1969-72; asst. prof. Cameron U., Lawton, 1972-75, assoc. prof., 1975-78, prof., 1978—. Contbr. articles to profl. jours. Recipient Disting. Svc. award Cameron U., 1995. mem. AAAS, Assn. for Advancement of Computers in Edn., Am. Chem. Soc. (councilor 1980—, sec. div. profl. rels. 1987—, sec. divsn. profl. rel. 1987-96, chair-elect divsn. profl. rels. 1996, Okla. Chemist award 1992, divsn. profl. rels. Henry Hill award, 1996), Am. Inst. Chemists (nat. bd. dirs.), Phi Kappa Phi (regent 1981-89, nat. v.p. 1989-92, nat. pres.-elect 1992-95, nat. pres. 1995—, Disting. Faculty award 1978), Sigma Xi, Sigma Pi Sigma, Iota Sigma Pi. Home: RR 3 Box 176-1 Chickasha OK 73018-9544 Office: Cameron U Dept of Chemistry 2800 W Gore Blvd Lawton OK 73505-6320

NANCE, BETTY LOVE, librarian; b. Nashville, Oct. 29, 1923; d. Granville Scott and Clara (Mills) Nance. BA in English magna cum laude, Trinity U., 1957; AM in Library Sci., U. Mich., 1958. Head dept. acquisitions Stephen F. Austin U. Library, Nacogdoches, Tex., 1958-59; librarian 1st Nat. Bank, Fort Worth, 1959-61; head catalog dept. Trinity U., San Antonio, 1961-63; head tech. processes U. Tex. Law Library, Austin, 1963-66; head catalog dept. Tex. A&M U. Library, College Station, 1966-69; chief bibliographic services Washington U. Library, St. Louis, 1970; head dept. acquisitions Va. Commonwealth U. Library, Richmond, 1971-73; head tech. processes Howard Payne U. Library, Brownwood, Tex., 1974-79; library dir. Edinburg (Tex.) Pub. Library, 1980-91; pres. Edinburg Com. for Salvation Army. Mem. ALA, Pub. Library Assn., Tex. Library Assn., Hidalgo County Library Assn. (v.p. 1980-81, pres. 1981-82), Pan Am. Round Table of Edinburg (corr. sec. 1986-88, assoc. dir. 1989-90), Edinburg Bus. and Profl. Womens Club (founding bd. dirs., pres. 1986-87, bd. dirs. 1987-88), Alpha Lambda Delta, Alpha Chi. Methodist. Club: Zonta Club of San Antonio (bd. dirs. 1996—). Home: 5359 Fredericksburg Rd Apt 806 San Antonio TX 78229-3549

NANCE, MARTHA MCGHEE, rehabilitation nurse; b. Huntington, W.Va., Jan. 24, 1944; d. Orme Winford and Sadie Mae (Dudley) McGhee; m. John Edgar Nance, Mar. 17, 1990; children: Laura Beckner, Suzie Brickey. RN, St. Mary's Sch. Nursing, Huntington, W.Va., 1980; student, Marshall U., Huntington, W.Va., 1978-88. Cert. rehab. nurse, cert. case mgr. Surg. head nurse Huntington Hosp. Inc., nursing supr.; quality assurance dir. Am. Hosp. for Rehab., Huntington, 1988-89, DON, 1989-90; rehab. charge nurse Am. Putnam Nursing and Rehab. Ctr., Hurricane, W.Va., 1990—; mgr. health svcs. Mountain State Blue Cross/Blue Shield, Charleston, W.Va., 1995—, mgr. precert., case mgmt. and med. rev., 1995—. Mem. Assn. for Practitioners in Infection Control. Home: RR 4 Box 100 Hurricane WV 25526-9351

NANCE, MARY JOE, secondary education educator; b. Carthage, Tex., Aug. 7, 1921; d. F. F. and Mary Elizabeth (Knight) Born; m. Earl C. Nance, July 12, 1946; 1 child, David Earl. BBA, North Tex. State U., 1953; postgrad., Northwestern State U. La., 1974; ME, Antioch U., 1978. Tchr., Port Isabel (Tex.) Ind. Sch. Dist., 1953-79; tchr. English, Tex., 1965, Splendora (Tex.) High Sch., 1979-80, McLeod, Tex., 1980-81, Bremond, Tex., 1981-84. Vol. tchr. for Indian students, 1964-65, 79. Served with WAAC, 1942-43, WAC 1945. Recipient Image Maker award Carthage C. of C., 1984; cert. bus. educator. Mem. ASCD, NEA, Nat. Bus. Edn. Assn., Tex. Tchrs. Assn., Tex. Bus. Tchrs. Assn. (cert. of appreciation 1978), Nat. Women's Army Corps Vets. Assn., Air Force Assn. (life), Gwinnett Hist. Soc., Hist. Soc. Panola County, Panola County Hist. & Geneal. Assn., Coun. for Basic Edn., Nat. Hist. Soc., Tex. Coun. English Tchrs. Baptist.

NANCE, RETHA HARDISON, reading specialist; b. Athens, Ala., July 18, 1952; d. Roy King and Bertie Mae (Pettus) McLemore; m. Amos Wayne Hardison, July 23, 1971 (dec. Mar. 1983); children: Genoa, Karol, Nancy; m. Robert Arthur Nance, May 30, 1984. BS in Edn., U. Ctrl. Okla., 1987, MEd summa cum laude, 1988. Cert. tchr. reading, Okla. Reading specialist Moore (Okla.) Pub. Schs., 1987—; officer Moore Sch. Dist. Profl. Devel. Com., 1990—; mem. Moore Pub. Schs. Supts. Adv. Com., 1996—; participant Ann. Monticello-Stratford Hall Summer Seminar for Tchrs., U. Va., Charlottesville, 1994. Co-founder We the People Living Memls., Oklahoma City, 1987—. Recipient Liberty award Downtown Oklahoma City, 1990. Mem. Internat. Reading Assn., Okla. Reading Assn., Ctrl. Okla. Reading Coun. (pres. 1992), Christian Educators Assn. Internat. Home: PO Box 405 Wheatland OK 73097-0405

NANDA, CHITTA RANJAN, industrial hygienist, metallurgical engineer; b. Puri, Orissa, India; s. Janardan and Sulakhyana (Rath) N.; m. Gita Rani Devi, Mar. 13, 1970; children: Nellie, Tusar Kanti. BS, Banaras Hindu U., Varanasi, India, 1964; MS, U. Ill., 1966; PhD, U. Wis., 1969. Cert. indsl. hygienist, safety profl. Asst. prof. U. Roorkee, India, 1969-71, Rourkela (India) Engring. Coll., 1972-76; resident in phys. sci. Touro Infirmary, New Orleans, 1977-78; rsch. assoc. La. State U., New Orleans, 1978-79; adj. faculty Sch. of Engring. & APP Sci., Portland, Oreg., 1980-81; indsl. hygienist VA Med. Ctr., Saginaw, Mich., 1986-87; chief safety & indsl. hygiene VA Med. Ctr., Danville, Ill., 1987-91; regional indsl. hygienist Dept. Vet. Affairs, Ann Arbor, Mich., 1991-92, Grand Prairie, Tex., 1992—. Contbr. articles to Jour. Am. Inst. of Metall. Engring., Metall. Transaction, The Eastern Metals Rev. and other profl. jours. Mem. Am. Indsl. Hygiene Assn., Am. Soc. Safety Engrs., Am. Conf. Govt. Indsl. Hygienists, Sigma Xi. Republican. Home: 3102 Voltaire Blvd Mc Kinney TX 75070-4248

NANGLE, CLINT, investment company executive, writer; b. Marblehead, Mass., July 4, 1930; s. John and Jane (Potter) N.; children: Dana, John, Gene, Rod. AB, Harvard U., 1952. Gen. ptnr. Fla. Shopping Ctr. Devel. Co., Boca Raton, 1970-85; chmn. bd. Gulfstream Equity Mgmt., Inc., Boca Raton, 1985—. Author: Some Things Harvard Never Taught Me, 1993. With USAF, 1952-54. Mem. U.S. Polo Assn. (gov. 1990—). Office: Gulfstream Equity Mgmt Inc 397 NW 35th Pl Boca Raton FL 33431-5847

NANK, LOIS RAE, financial executive; b. Racine, Wis., Jan. 6; d. Walter William August and Lanora Elizabeth (Freymuth) N. BS in Econs., U. Wis., 1962; postgrad. in profl. mgmt., Fla. Inst. Tech., 1977. Contract specialist U.S. Naval Ordnance Sta., Forest Park, Ill., 1963-66, U.S. Army Munitions Command, Joliet, Ill., 1966-72; plans/program specialist U.S. Army Munitions Command, Joliet, 1972-73, U.S. Army Armament Command, Rock Island, Ill., 1973-77; chief budget office U.S. Army Auto Log Mgmt. System Act, St. Louis, 1977-81; sr. budget analyst U.S. Army Materiel Command, Alexandria, Va., 1981-87; sr. fin. mgr. Def. Mapping Agy., Reston, Va., 1987-93; cons. Springfield, Va, 1993-96, Leesburg, Fla., 1996—. Coun. mem. chairperson bldg. com. Bread of Life Luth. Ch., Springfield, Va., 1986-90, Christ Luth. Ch., Fairfax, Va., 1990—; bd. dirs. Cedar Wood Homeowners' Assn., Bettendorf, Iowa, 1975-77, Oak Homeowners' Assn., Chesterfield, Mo., 1980-81. Mem. NAFE, Am. Soc. Mil. Comptrollers, Va. Assn. Female Execs., Order of Ea. Star.

NANTS, BRUCE ARLINGTON, lawyer; b. Orlando, Fla., Oct. 26, 1953; s. Jack Arlington and Louise (Hulme) N. BA, U. Fla., 1974, JD, 1977. Bar: Fla. 1977. Asst. state's atty. State Atty.'s Office, Orlando, 1977-78; pvt. practice, Orlando, 1979—. Columnist The Law and You, 1979-80. Auctioneer pub. TV sta., 1979; campaign coord. cen. Fla. steering com. Bob Dole for Pres., 1988; bd. dirs. Cystic Fibrosis Found. Mem. Acad. Fla. Trial Lawyers, Am. Arbitration Assn., Fellowship Christian Athletes (past bd. dirs. Cen. Fla.), Tiger Bay Club Cen. Fla., Orlando Touchdown Club, Fla. Blue Key, Omicron Delta Kappa, Phi Beta Kappa, Phi Delta Theta. Democrat. Baptist. Home: 1112 Country Ln Orlando FL 32804-6934 Office: PO Box 547871 Orlando FL 32854-7871

NAPIER, DOUGLAS WILLIAM, lawyer; b. Alexandria, Va., Sept. 11, 1951; s. William Wilson and Leo Elizabeth (Moore) N.; m. Kathy Gwen Talbert, Aug. 24, 1974; children: Brian Douglas, Adam Scott, Brooke Elizabeth. B.S., Va. Poly. Inst. and State U., 1973; J.D., Wake Forest U., 1976. Bar: Va. 1976, U.S. Ct. (ea. and we. dist.) Va. 1978, U.S. Ct. Appeals (4th cir.) 1983. Assoc., Ambrogi, Mote & Ritter, Winchester, Va., 1976-77; ptnr. Napier & Napier, Front Royal, Va., 1977—; county atty. Warren County (Va.), 1978—; atty. Chem. Abuse Task Force, 1983—. Author: The Cross, 1982. Mem. staff, contbr. Wake Forest Law Rev., 1976. Bd. dirs. United Way, Front Royal, 1978; parliamentarian Warren County Rep. Com., 1981; cons. Council Domestic Violence, 1984; del. People to People Citizen Amb. Program's Legal Del. to China, 1987; active Rep. Nat. Com. Mem. Warren County Bar Assn. (v.p., pres.), Va. Bar Assn., Va. Trial Lawyers Assn., ABA, Nature Conservancy, Front Royal C. of C. (bd. dirs., v.p. 1986-88, pres. 88-89), Blue Ridge Arts Coun. (bd. dirs. 1992—), Rotary Internat., Front Royal Rotary Club, Internat. Platform Assn., Warren Workshop (bd. dirs. 1992—). Baptist. Clubs: Optimist Internat. (sec. 1980-81, Achievement award 1980), Isaac Walton League. Home: 195 Park Ridge Ct Front Royal VA 22650

NAPIER, JOHN HAWKINS, III, historian; b. Berkeley, Calif., Feb. 6, 1925; s. John Hawkins and Lena Mae (Tate) N.; m. Harriet Elizabeth McGehee (dec.), m. Cameron Mayson Freeman, Sept. 11, 1964. BA, U. Miss., 1949; MA, Auburn U., 1967; postgrad. Georgetown U., 1971. Journalist, tchr. Picayune (Miss.) H.S., 1946; commd. 2d lt. U.S. Air Force, 1949, advanced through grades to lt. col., 1966, ret., 1977; staff dir. Congressional Com. on S.E. Asia, 1970; faculty Air War Coll., 1971-74; Air U. Command historian, 1974-77; asst. to exec. dir. Ala. Commn. on Higher Edn., Montgomery, 1977-78; adj. history faculty Auburn U., Montgomery, 1980-85; columnist Montgomery Advertiser, 1980-87; lectr. in field. Pres., Montgomery Opera Guild, 1974-75, Montgomery Community Concert Assn., 1974-76, Old S. Hist. Soc., 1977-78. Served with USMC, 1943-46, Col. Ala. State Defense Force, 1991—. Decorated Legion of Merit, Lord of Cloghroe, also others; recipient award of Merit, Ala. Hist. Commn., 1976, Order of St. John of Jerusalem, Niadh Nask, Order of St. Stanislas, Milit. and Hospitaller Order of St. Lazarus of Jerusalem, Sovereign Mil. Order of Temple of Jerusalem; Merit award English-Speaking Union U.S., 1983; Taylor Medal and grad. fellow U. Miss., 1949; Storrs scholar Pomona Coll., 1942-43. Fellow Soc. Antiquaries Scotland. Mem. English-Speaking Union (pres. 1978-87, nat. dir. 1980-86, 87-90, 91-94), Royal Order Scotland, Ala. Hist. Assn. (pres. 1979-80), Soc. Pioneers Montgomery (pres. 1980-81), Soc. Colonial Wars, SCV (vice comdr. Ala. 1979-80), Soc. War of 1812 (pres. Ala. 1980-82), St. Andrews Soc., S.R., SAR (pres. 1974-75), Clan Napier in N.Am. (lt. to chief 1985—), Order 1st Families Va., Gov. Ala. Soc. Order Founders & Patriots Am., Noble Soc. Celts., Jamestowne Soc., Sigma Chi, Phi Kappa Phi, Omicron Delta Kappa, Phi Alpha Theta, Pi Sigma Alpha, Scabbard and Blade. Democrat. Episcopalian. Clubs: Montgomery Country, Aztec 1847, Mil. Order Carabao, St. John House (London). Author: Lower Pearl River's Piney Woods: Its Land and People, 1985; The Air Force Officers Guide, 30th edit., 1995, Dr. Patrick Napier: His Ancestors and Some Descendants, 1991; contbr. articles to profl. jours. Home: Kilmahew RR 2 Box 614 Ramer AL 36069-9245

NAPIER, WILLIAM JAMES, JR., marine oil and gas construction consultant; b. Dallas, July 19, 1952; s. William James and Frankie (Hanchey) N.; m. Christine Ann Douget, June 18, 1977; children: Jay, Stephanie, George, Catherine. BS in Marine Biology, U. So. Miss., 1974; BS in Civil Engring., La. Tech. U., 1976. Project engr., field engr. inland svcs. divsn. McDermott Internat. Inc., Harvey, La., 1976-80; project coord. McDermott Internat. Inc., New Orleans and Houston, 1982-86; sr. project coord./project coord. worldwide bus. devel. McDermott Internat. Inc., New Orleans, 1986-89; project engr. McDermott Nigeria, Ltd., Warri, 1980-82; mgr. marine sales/dir. marine sales, nat. accounts mgr. Bailey Controls Co., New Orleans, 1989-92; pres. COO Balehi Marine, Inc., Lacombe, La., 1992-94; pres., owner Fairwinds Internat. Inc., Mandeville, La., 1994—. Elder Lakeview Christian Ctr., New Orleans, 1985-92. Mem. Soc. Naval Architects and Marine Engrs., Franco's Athletic Club. Republican. Presbyterian. Home and Office: Fairwinds Internat Inc 913 Beau Chene Dr Mandeville LA 70471-1505

NAPLES, JEAN MARIE, physician; b. Suffern, N.Y., Apr. 27, 1955; d. Ralph Peter and Antoinette (Toscano) N. BS in Med. Tech., Phila. Coll. Pharmacy and Sci., 1977; MPH, U. Calif., Berkeley, 1981; MD, U. Md., 1989; PhD in Tropical Medicine, Johns Hopkins U., 1989. Diplomate Am. Bd. Family Physicians. Lab. dir. Peace Corps USA, Wouakchott, Mauritania, West Africa, 1977-79; lab. tech., food ctr. dir. Med. Vols. Internat., Somalia, 1980-81; med. lab. tech. Church-Home-Hosp., Balt., 1982-89; family medicine resident La. State U. Med. Ctr., Shreveport, 1989-92; high-risk obstetrics fellow Tacoma (Wash.) Family Medicine, 1992-93; resident gen. surgery La. State U. Med. Ctr., Shreveport, 1993—; med. lab. tech. Johns Hopkins Infectious Disease Lab., Balt., 1984-85. Patentee in field. Blood donor ARC, Shreveport, 1989-94; mem. Physician Com. for Responsible Medicine, Washington, 1993. Mem. Am. Med. Women's Assn., Am. Acad. Family Practice, Am. Soc. Clin. Pathologists, Alpha Omega Alpha, Alpha Delta Theta (v.p. 1976-77). Democrat. Roman Catholic. Office: La State Univ Med Ctr 1501 Kings Hwy Shreveport LA 71103-4228

NAPSKY, MARTIN BEN, insurance executive; b. Miami, Fla., June 17, 1938; s. Samuel Ben and Dorothy May N.; m. Carol Ann Rella, Sept. 26, 1978; children: David, Kimberly, Victoria, Bradley, Jason, Keith. BA, Houston (Tex.) U., 1957-61; LLB, Atlanta (Ga.) Law Sch., 1971-74. Ins. agent Continental Casualty Co., Chgo., 1961-70; v.p. Eastern Reg Brokerage, Miami, 1974-88, Western Reg Brokerage, San Diego, 1988—; pres. Fla. Bldg. Contractors, Miami, 1978—. Contbg. editor Wings mag., 1984. Chancellor Nu Beta Epsilon, Atlanta, 1973; mem. George Bush Inner Circle, Washington, 1992, Naders Raiders, Atlanta, 1973-74. Mem. Nat. Assn. Health Underwriters (Health Ins. Quality award 1983), Miami Assn. Health Underwriters, Millionaires Club, Presidents Inner Circle (pres. 1983-84). Republican. Jewish. Home: 1060 Papaya St Hollywood FL 33019

NAQUIN, PATRICIA ELIZABETH, employee assistance consultant; b. Houston, Jan. 28, 1943; d. Louie Dee and Etha Beatrice (English) Price; m. Hollis James Naquin, Mar. 23, 1961; children: Price Naquin, Holli Campbell. BS, U. Houston, 1969, MS, 1982; PhD, Tex. Woman's U., 1988. Lic. profl. counselor; lic. chem. dependency counselor; nat. cert. counselor; cert. chem. dependency specialist; cert. employee assistance profl. Purchasing agt. Internat. Affairs U. Houston, 1966-68; elem. sch. tchr. Pasadena (Tex.) Ind. Sch. Dist., 1969-82; spl. edn. counselor Alvin (Tex.) Ind. Sch. Dist., 1982-85, drug-free schs. coord., 1988-92; marriage and family therapist Lifespan Counseling, Pasadena, 1985-92; employee assistance cons. DuPont, LaPorte, Tex., 1992—; adv. com. mem. Sam Houston U., Huntsville, Tex., 1983; trainer and instr. Bay Area Coun. on Drugs and Alcohol, Houston, 1988-92; cons. Alvin Ind. Sch. Dist., 1989-92, DuPont Valuing People Core Team, 1993—; supr. State Bd. of Profl. Counselors, Houston, 1988—. Co-author: Life is for Everyone Manual, 1990. Com. co-chair Alvin S.A.P. Task Force, 1988-92; com. mem. Tri-Dist. Task Force, Alvin, 1990-91; com. chmn. Alvin Bus./Edn. Partnership, 1992; bd. dirs. Brazoria (Tex.) County Coun. Drugs and Alcohol, 1991. Mem. Am. Assn. Marriage and Family Therapists, Tex. Assn. Counselors of Alcohol and Drug Abuse, Am. Counseling Assn., Employee Assistance Program Assn., Nat. Disting. Svc. Registry/Libr. of Congress, Phi Delta Kappa. Republican. Methodist.

NASH, CHARLES D., investment banker; b. Atlanta, Feb. 8, 1943; s. Floyd Johnson and Ida Lee (Camp) N.; m. Linda K. Nash; 1 child, Paren J. BBA in Fin., Ga. State U., 1968. V.p. Courts & Co., Atlanta, 1961-70, The Dornbush Co., Atlanta, 1970-76; pres., chief exec. officer So. Turf Nurseries, Inc., Tifton, Ga., 1976-83, Neville & Gladstone, Inc., Atlanta, 1984-86; sr. v.p. Wheat First Securities, Atlanta, 1987-91, Interstate/Johnson Lane, Atlanta, 1991—. Mem. Ansley Golf club. Republican. Episcopalian. Office: Interstate/Johnson Lane 2300 Resurgens Plaza Atlanta GA 30326

NASH, JOHN GROVER, journalist, photographer; b. Sherburne, N.Y., Oct. 7, 1927; s. Dudley Owen and Gladys (Grover) N.; m. Mary Claudine Norton, Aug. 26, 1958 (dec. June 1988); children: Debra Lee, Mary Norton, John Grover Jr. BSEE, U. Colo., 1959; MS in R&D System Mgmt., U. So. Calif., 1968. Marine engr. U.S. Army Transp. Corp., 1945-47; commd. 2d lt. USAF, 1953, advanced through grades to col., 1973, ret., 1983; freelance journalist, photographer, 1976—. sr. U.S. govt. rep. to Govt. of Seychelles, 1970-72. Mem. Beta Gamma Sigma. Republican. Home and Office: 25 Wild Olive Ct Homosassa FL 34446

NASH, JOHNNY COLLIN, real estate broker and appraiser; b. Ithaca, N.Y., June 22, 1949; s. John Thomas and Kathleen (Mulvihill) N. BS, U. S.C., 1972; MA in Bus., U. Tenn., 1974. Lic. real estate broker, S.C., N.C. Sales mgr. Hyatt Regency Hotel, Hilton Head, S.C., 1976-80; dir. mktg. Playboy Resort Gt. Gorge, McAfee, N.J., 1980-82; v.p. hotel devel. Atlantic Shores Corp., Hilton Head, 1982-86; broker in charge Royal Real Estate, Hilton Head, 1986-89; owner, pres. Harbour Town Rentals & Real Estate, Sea Pines Plantation, Hilton Head, 1989—; mem. honor bd. S.C. Assn. Realtors, 1988-89; mem. edn. com. Hilton Head Bd. Realtors, 1988-90. Dir. pub. relations Amvets, Hilton Head, 1989—. With U.S. Navy, 1969-70. Republican. Roman Catholic. Home: PO Box 6352 2011 Sea Loft Villas Hilton Head Island SC 29928-4342 Office: Harbour Town Rentals 2011 Sea Loft Villas Hilton Head Island SC 29928-4342

NASH, MARY HARRIET, artist, lecturer; b. Washington, May 8, 1951; d. Richard Harvey and Janet Rose (Nivinski) N. BA, George Washington U., 1973; MFA, Washington State U., 1976. Guest lectr. Mus. Art, Wash. State U., Pullman., 1976, 2d St. Gallery, Charlottesville, Va., 1980, U. Ala., Tuscaloosa, 1981, SEWSA Conf., Charlottesville, 1983; artist-in-residence Va. Mus. Fine Arts, Richmond, 1984—; guest juror Twinbrook Art Show, Fairfax, Va., 1978; tchg. asst. Wash. State U., 1975-76 vis. artist, lectr. Johnson (Vt.) State Coll., 1995; guest lectr. Julian Scott Meml. Gallery Johnson State Coll., Vt., 1995. Author art show catalogue: Personal Paintings, 1978, artist's book: Skulls Are Forever, 1986; contbr. articles to profl. jours. Recipient Cert. Outstanding Achievement, Women in Design International, 1983; MacDowell Colony fellow, 1977; recipient 3 gubernatorial citations Gev. George Allen, Richmond, 1995-96; nominee Cultural Olympiad, Atlanta, 1995. Mem. Southeastern Ctr. for Contemporary Art (hon. mention 1979), Phi Kappa Phi.

NASH, WARREN LESLIE, banker; b. Jackson, Miss., Aug. 26, 1955; s. Henry Warren and Frances Lora (Venters) N.; m. Valerie Ann Roberts, Nov. 22, 1980; children: John Wilson, Warren Graham. Student, U.S. Naval Acad., 1973-75; BS in Banking and Fin., Miss. State U., Starkville, 1978; MBA, U. Ala., Birmingham, 1982; profl. cert., Stonier Grad. Sch. Banking, Newark, Del., 1987. Asst. br. mgr. 1st Nat. Bank of Birmingham, Ala., 1978-80, br. officer, 1980-81, asst. v.p., 1981-84; v.p. AmSouth Bank, N.A., Birmingham, 1984-86; v.p., regional retail banking mgr. AmSouth Bank, N.A., Montgomery, Ala., 1986-89; sr. v.p. AmSouth Bank, Montgomery, 1989-91; sr. v.p. consumer banking AmSouth Bank, N.A., Birmingham, 1991-93; v.p. productivity AmSouth Bank, Birmingham, 1993-94, sr. v.p. tech., 1994-95, sr. v.p. retail delivery, 1995—; instr. fin. Samford U., Birmingham, 1982-84; v.p., Ala. Automated Clearing house, 1983-84. Counselor Jr. Achievement, Birmingham, 1980-82; loaned exec. United Way, Birmingham, 1980; com. chmn. Birmingham Festival Arts, 1985-86. Named one of Outstanding Young Men of Am., 1984, 85, 86. Mem. Am. Mktg. Assn. (bd. dirs. 1983-84), Am. Inst. Banking, Birmingham C. of C. (dept. coord. 1985), Newcomen Soc., Young Montgomerians Bus. Club, Summit Club, Kiwanis (local pres. 1985-86), Alpha Kappa Psi, Beta Gamma Sigma. Republican. Methodist. Home: 3772 Rockhill Rd Birmingham AL 35223-1520 Office: AmSouth Bank NA PO Box 11007 Birmingham AL 35288

NASH, WILLIAM WRAY, JR., retired city planning educator; b. N.Y.C., Nov. 25, 1928; s. William Wray and Janet Caroline (Fobes) N.; m. Dorothy Elaine Westerberg, Dec. 23, 1950; children: Meryl Elaine, Wendy Wray, Janet Amanda, Joseph Adamson. BA, Harvard U., 1950; M City Planning, U. Pa., 1956, PhD, 1961. Rsch. analyst Am. Coun. To Improve Our Neighborhood, Phila., 1956-58; mem. faculty Harvard U., Cambridge, Mass., 1958-71, chmn. dept. city planning, 1964-69; advisor on urban affairs Office of Gov., State of Ga., Atlanta, 1970-74; mem. faculty Ga. State U., Atlanta, 1971-90, dean Coll. Urban Life, 1976-81, Regents prof., 1983; ret., 1990; prin. Nash-Vigier, Inc., Cambridge, 1962-71; advisor UN Tech. Assistance Bd., Bandung, Indonesia, 1961-62; traveling lectr. USIA, Japan, 1980. Author: Residential Rehabilitation, 1959, (with B. Frieden) Shaping an Urban America, 1969; contbg. author: Taming the Metropolis, 1967, Four Days: Forty Hours, 1970. Mem. Atlanta Mayor's Com. To Reorganize City Govt., 1973, Atlanta Zoning Rev. Bd., 1974-75, Atlanta 2000, 1982; pres. Ga. Planning Assn., Atlanta, 1973-74; chmn. Atlanta Regional Forum, 1976; vestryman Ch. of Incarnation, 1973-76, 83-85, sr. warden, 1986-88; mem. Atlanta Multiple Sclerosis Support Group, 1986. With U.S. Army, 1950-53. Decorated Bronze Star. Mem. Am. Inst. Planners, Am. Inst. Cert. Planners, Sigma Xi, Tau Sigma Delta, Phi Kappa Phi. Democrat. Episcopalian. Home: 3086 Cascade Rd SW Atlanta GA 30311-3630

NASHMAN, ALVIN ELI, computer company executive; b. N.Y.C., Dec. 16, 1926; s. Joseph and Fay (Portnoy) N.; m. Honey Weinstein, May 29, 1960; children—Jessica Rachel, Pamela Wynne, Stephanie Paige. B.E.E., CUNY, 1948; M.E.E., NYU, 1951; Sc.D. (hon.), Pacific U., 1968, George Washington U., 1986. With Ketay Mfg. Corp., N.Y.C., 1951-52; sr. project engr., exec. engr., assoc. lab. dir., lab. dir. ITT Fed. Labs., Nutley, N.J., 1952-62; dir. ops. ITT Intelcom, Inc., Falls Church, Va., 1962-65; pres. System Scis. Corp., Falls Church, 1965-67; with Communications & Systems, Inc., Falls Church, 1967-69; pres. Systems div., corp. v.p. Computer Scis. Corp., Falls Church, 1969-77; pres. Systems Group, corp. v.p., 1977-91, also dir. Patentee in field; contbr. articles to profl. jours. Trustee Fairfax Hosp. System Found. With USN, 1944-46. Fellow IEEE; mem. Armed Forces Communications and Electronics Assn. (dir., internat. v.p. 1976-79, chpt. pres. 1979-80, exec. com. 1980-84, chmn. bd. 1984-86), AIAA, Nat. Space Club, Nat. Security Indsl. Assn., Tau Beta Pi, Eta Kappa Nu. Republican. Jewish. Home: 3609 Ridgeway Ter Falls Church VA 22044-1308 also: Computer Scis Corp 2100 E Grand Ave El Segundo CA 90245-5024

NASSER, JOSEPH YOUSEF, public safety administrator, consultant; b. Welch, W.Va., Mar. 19, 1943; s. Joseph H. and Betty Anne (Caldwell) N.; divorced; children: Robert, Eric, Melanie, Matthew, Michelle. BS, Pacific Western U., 1989, PhD, 1991. Patrolman, firefighter, emergency med. technician Mich. Dept. Pub. Safety, Oak Park, 1962-75; patrolman Daytona Beach (Fla.) Police Dept., 1975-76; lt., capt., dir. Volusia County (Fla.) Sheriff's Dept., 1976-90; pres., founder, owner Ctr. for Pub. Safety Studies, Ormond Beach, Fla., 1990—; Pres. Associated Pub. Safety Comm. Officer, Inc., 1987-88, Land Mobile Comm. Coun., Washington, 1988-89; chmn. Nat. Pub. Safety Planning Com./F.C.C., 1987-88; life mem. APCO, Inc. Past chmn. Fla. State Standards and Telecommunicator Cert. Com., Fla. State Emergency Mgmt. 9-1-1 Com.; past mem. exec. coun. Volusia County Emergency Med. Found.; past chmn. Volusia County Emergency Med. Svcs. Trust Fund Adv. Bd. Recipient Dayton Beach Cooper-Taylor Pub. Safety Achievement award, 1985, Nat. Achievement award Pub. Safety Comm. Coun., 1987, FCC Recognition award, 1987, APCO Life Mem. award, 1988, Emergency Mgmt. Recognition award State of Fla., 1989, Appreciation award Emergency Med. Found., 1990, Disting. Svc. award Volusia County Sheriff's Dept., 1990. Fellow Radio Club of Am.; mem. Associated Pub. Safety Comms. Ofcls. Internat. (life), Internat. Mcpl. Signal Assn. (sustaining, Journalistic Excellence award 1991). Democrat. Methodist. Home: Eagle's Nest Ranch Ormond Beach FL 32174 Office: Ctr for Pub Safety Studies 595 N Nova Rd Ste 207 Ormond Beach FL 32174-4425

NASSER, MOES ROSHANALI, optometrist; b. Sumve, Mwanza, Tanzania, Jan. 20, 1956; came to U.S., 1976; s. Roshanali Hassanali and Rehmat (Kara) N.; m. Anar Hemnani, Dec. 20, 1979; children: Faria, Sarah. BS in Optometry, U. Houston, 1980, OD, 1982. Cons., mgr. optometric practice Houston, 1984—; mem. adv. bd. Houston Eye Assocs.; cons. in field. Vol. Agakhan Ch., Tanzania, 1966-71; sec. Agakhan Ch. health com., 1976-82, mem. ch. coun., Houston, 1981-82, mem. coun. for S.W., 1987-90, chmn. edn. bd. for Southwest, 1987-90, Agakhan Found.; hon. sec. Shia Imami Ismaili Tarigah and Religious Edn. Bd. U.S., 1990-93, chmn. Southwestern U.S., 1996—; convenor S.W. U.S.A. for Inst. of Ismaili Studies, London. Mem. Harris County Optometric Soc., Tex. Optometric Assn., Tex. Assn. for Optometrists, Am. Optometric Assn., Alta. Optometric Assn., Can. Assn. Optometrists. Office: 1524 Willowbrook Mall Houston TX 77070-5715

NATALE, LAUREL A., nursing case manager; b. N.Y.C., Apr. 25, 1945; d. Laurence C. and Grace O. (McIntyre) Armitage; m. Carmen J. Natale, Feb. 13, 1964; children: Julia Ann Gerson, Christine Cartwright, Kathryn Natale. Diploma, Charity Hosp. Sch. Nursing, New Orleans, 1978; BSN, U. Tex., Galveston, 1984; MSN, U. Tex., Houston, 1990. RN, Tex. Staff nurse SICU trauma Hermann Hosp., Houston, asst. head nurse renal transpant intensive care unit; patient care supr. hospice Vis. Nurse Assn., Houston; instr. clin. nursing U. Tex. Health Sci. Ctr.-Houston Sch. Nursing, Houston; staff nurse emergency dept. Meml. Hosp. System, Houston; case mgr. Worklink, 1994-95; supr. case mgmt., 1996—; divsn. case mgr. Nat. Convenience Stores, 1995-96.

NATALICIO, DIANA SIEDHOFF, academic administrator; b. St. Louis, Aug. 25, 1939; d. William and Eleanor J. (Biermann) Siedhoff. BS in Spanish summa cum laude, St. Louis U., 1961; MA in Portuguese lang., U. Tex., 1964, PhD in Linguistics, 1969. Chmn. dept. modern langs. U. Tex., El Paso, 1973-77, assoc. dean liberal arts, 1977-79; acting dean liberal arts, 1979-80; dean Coll. Liberal Arts U. Tex., El Paso, 1980-84, v.p. acad. affairs, 1984-88, pres., 1988—; bd. dirs. El Paso br. Fed. Res. Bd. Dallas, chmn., 1989; mem. Presdl. Adv. Commn. on Ednl. Excellence for Hispanic Ams., 1991; bd. dirs. Sandia Corp., Enserch Corp.; bd. dirs. Nat. Action Coun. for Minorities in Engring., 1993-96; mem. Nat. Sci. Bd. 1994-2000; mem. NASA Adv. Coun., 1994-96; bd. mem. Fund for Improvement of Post-Secondary Edn., 1993-97; bd. dirs. Fogarty Internat. Ctr. of NIH, 1993-96; bd. chair Am. Assn. Higher Edn., 1995-96; bd. dirs. U.S.-Mexico Commn. for Ednl. and Cultural Exch., 1994-96. Co-author: Sounds of Children, 1977; contbr. articles to profl. jours. Bd. dirs. United Way El Paso, 1990-93, chmn. needs survey com., 1990-91, chmn. edn. divsn., 1989; chmn. Quality Edn. for Minorities Network in Math. Sci. and Engring., 1991-92; chairperson Leadership El Paso, Class 12, 1989-90, mem. adv. coun., 1987-90, participant, 1980-81; mem. Historically Black Colls. and Univs./Minority Instns. Consortium on Environ. Tech. chairperson, 1991-93. Recipient Torch of Liberty award Anti-Defamation League B'nai B'rith, 1991, Conquistador award City of El Paso, 1990, Humanitarian award Nat. Coun. Christians and Jews, El Paso chpt., 1990; mem. El Paso Women's Hall of Fame, 1990. Mem. Philos. Soc. Tex. Home: 711 Cincinnati Ave El Paso TX 79902-2616 Office: U Tex at El Paso Office of the President El Paso TX 79968-0500

NATARAJAN, T. RAJ, communications executive, electrical engineer; b. Chidambaram, India, Oct. 25, 1948; came to U.S., 1971; s. P.T.K. and Vasantha (Ayyasamy) Thillaigovindan; m. Santhi Swamivelu, June 30, 1976; children: Karthik, Dhevi. BE, Annamalai U., India, 1970; MSEE, Kans. State U., 1972, PhD in Elec. Engring., 1976. Mem. tech. staff Tex. Instruments, Dallas, 1976-80; sr. engr. Mead Office Systems, Richardson, Tex., 1980-82; sr. rsch. engr. Atlantic Richfield Co., Plano, Tex., 1982-85; v.p. engring. DSP Tech., Carrollton, Tex., 1985-90; v.p. Forum Communication Systems, Richardson, 1991—. Co-author: Discrete-time Systems, 1983; patentee in field. Mem. IEEE. Home: 2136 Argyle Dr Plano TX 75023-5229 Office: Forum Communication Systems 1223 N Glenville Dr Richardson TX 75081-2412

NATHAN, DANIEL EVERETT, retired surgeon; b. Tifton, Ga., May 18, 1916; s. Max and Edith (Lease) N.; m. Muriel Halprin, 1942; children: David Harris, Sherrie Halprin Nathan Schrage. BS, U. Ga., 1937, MD, 1940. Diplomate Am. Bd. Family Practice. Intern St. Elizabeth Hosp., Elizabeth, N.J., 1940-41; intern City Hosp., N.Y.C., 1941-42, resident, 1945; pvt. practice medicine & surgery Fort Valley, Ga., 1946—; chief of staff Peach County Hosp., 1962, 71-72, 76-78; dir. Citzens Bank Fort Valley; pres. Westview Devel. Corp.; v.p., dir. Fort Valley Nursing Home, 1967-92, pres., 1972-92; instr. family practice & cmty. medicine Mercer U., 1978-88, prof. cmty. medicine, 1986—. Dir. Am. Camellia Soc., 1971—. With USAFMC, 1942-45, col. Res. ret. Home: 405 Westview Dr Fort Valley GA 31030

NATHAN, DAVID AARON, retired cardiologist; b. Cin., Jan. 19, 1912; s. Nathan and Frieda N.; m. Doris Silver (dec. June 5, 1984); m. Sonia Duke, 1988; children: Nancy Nathan Goldstein, Robert Alan. BS, U. Cin., 1933, MD, 1936. Diplomate Am. Bd. Internal Medicine. Intern Cin. Gen. Hosp., 1935-36, resident in pathology, 1936-37; resident in chest disease Dunham Hosp., Cin., 1937-39; attendant Nat. Children's Cardiac Hosp., Miami, 1945-60; from asst. prof. medicine to assoc. prof. medicine U. Miami Sch. Medicine, 1955-71. Developer synchronous pacemaker. Maj. U.S. Army, 1942-45. Fellow Am. Coll. Cardiology, Am. Coll. Physicians, Coun. Clin. Cardiology, Am. Coll. Chest Physicians; mem. AMA, So. Med. Assn., Fla. Med. Assn., Dade County Med. Assn., Am. Heart Assn., Fla. Heart Assn., Am. Thoracic Soc., Internat. Soc. Internal Medicine, Pan Am. Med. Assn. Home: 10155 Collins Ave #206 Bal Harbour FL 33154

NATHAN, JAMES A., political science educator; b. Chgo., May 1, 1942; s. Samuel and Dorothy (Goldsmith) N.; m. Lisa Harry; children: Michael, Alexander. AB with honors, Ind. U., 1960; MA, Johns Hopkins U., 1966, PhD, 1972. With U.S. Fgn. Svc., 1966-70; asst. prof. U. Del., Newark, 1972-75, assoc. prof., 1976-78, prof. polit. sci., 1978-90; prof. polit. sci. Auburn U., Montgomery, Ala., 1991—; vis. prof. Am. U., Washington, 1979, U. Adelaide, 1982, Army War Coll., 1982-85, Johns Hopkins U., 1986; rsch. assoc. Columbia U., 1980-83; Fulbright prof. U. New South Wales, 1987, Curtin U., Perth, Australia, 1987. Author: (with others) The Future of United States Naval Power, 1979 (Furness prize 1979), The United States Foreign Policy and World Order, 1976, 2d edit., 1981, 3d edit., 1985, 4th edit., 1989, Foreign Policy Making and the American Political System, 1983, 2d edit., 1987, 3rd edit., 1994; editor: The Cuban Missile Crisis Revisited, 1992; contbr. numerous articles to profl. jours. Exec. dir. Ala. World Affairs Coun., 1991—. Faculty scholar Naval War Coll., 1979, Johns Hopkins U., 1979, Khaled bin Sultan Eminent scholar, 1991—, NDEA fellow, Melville Locker fellow, Sch. Advanced Internat. Studies, 1964-66, 68-72, Arms Control and Disarmament Agy. fellow, 1969-71, Spencer fellow, 1973-75, Naval War Coll. fellow, 1973-76, Fulbright-Hays fellow, 1976, NATO fellow, 1982-85, Dept. Def. fellow, 1983-86; grantee U. Del., 1972-82, 87, 94. Home: 616 Thorn Pl Montgomery AL 36106-1851

NATION, PHILIP DAVID, financial planner; b. London, May 31, 1962; came to U.S., 1965; s. John A. and Sally G. (Leeds) N.; m. Cynthia Anne Bateman, Apr. 19, 1986. BA in Econs., Cornell U., 1984; M in Estate Planning, Coll. Fin. Planning, 1993. CFP. Sr. fin. advisor Am. Express Fin. Advisors, Raleigh, N.C., 1987—. Mem. Internat. Platform Assn., Cornell Alumni Club. Home: 4724 Worchester Pl Raleigh NC 27604-4700 Office: Am Express Fin Advisors Inc 3720 Benson Dr Raleigh NC 27609

NATTIER, FRANK EMILE, JR., lawyer, educator; b. St. Joseph, Mo., Sept. 2, 1915; s. Frank Emile Sr. and Irene Ellen (Acre) N.; m. Rosario Manuela Pereyó, Dec. 17, 1939; children: Albert Emile (dec.), Michele Irene. BS in FS, Georgetown U., 1937, LLB, 1940; LLM, NYU, 1952. Bar: D.C. 1941, U.S. Ct. Appeals D.C. 1945, N.Y. 1946, U.S. Dist. Ct. (so. dist.) N.Y. 1948, U.S. Supreme Ct. 1962, Tex. 1984. Asst. special rep. Brazil U.S. Coord. Inter-Am. Affairs, Rio de Janeiro, Brazil, 1941-45; assoc. Breed, Abbott & Morgan, N.Y.C., 1946-55; ptnr. O'Gorman, Nattier & Anderson, N.Y.C., 1955-63; pvt. practice, N.Y.C., 1963-69; internat. counsel Quantum Chem. Corp., N.Y.C., 1970-80; adj. prof. U. Tex. Law Sch., Austin, 1981-85; pvt. practice, Austin, 1984—; vis. law prof. U. Chile, Santiago, 1981; counsel Braziliam Consulate Gen., N.Y. C., 1950-70. Contbr. book chpts., lectures, law revs. on Latin Am. bus. law and arbitration. Pres. Austin chpt. Internat. Good Neighbor Coun., 1995—. Mem. ABA, Assn. Bar City N.Y. (chmn. inter-Am. affairs com. 1972-74), Inter-Am. Bar Assn. (coun. and exec. com.), Am. Fgn. Law Assn. (pres. 1976-78), Am. Arbitration Assn. (nat. panel arbitrators), State Bar Tex. Democrat. Roman Catholic. Office: 1815 Richwood Dr Austin TX 78757-7816

NAU, DOUGLAS SCOTT, psychotherapist; b. Perth Amboy, N.J., Aug. 18, 1952; s. Charles Mathiasen and Ruth June (Agesen) N.; m. Jane Elizabeth Zimmerman; 1 child, Adam Henry. BA, Thiel Coll., 1974; MDiv, Princeton (N.J.) Theol. Sem., 1977; PhD, Nova Southeastern U., 1996. Cert. med. hypnotherapist. Chaplain The Peddie Sch., Hightstown, N.J., 1977-81; dir. guidance Roland Park County Sch., Balt., 1981-82; assoc. pastor Second Presbyn. Ch., Balt., 1981-89; dir. pastoral svcs. Charter Glade Hosp., Ft. Myers, Fla., 1989-92; pvt. practice Ft. Myers, Fla., 1989-92; staff therapist Family Therapy Assocs., Ft. Lauderdale, 1993; mental health therapist MCC Behavioral Care, Ft. Lauderdale, 1993-95, West Palm Beach, Fla., 1993-95; therapist All Care Wellness and Rehab., Ft. Lauderdale, 1996; pres. Springdale Behavioral Health, Inc., York, Pa., 1996—; adj. faculty Bradley Acad. for Visual Arts, 1996—. Author: The New CR.I.S. Case Studies, 1982, C.R.I.S. Case Studies for the 90's, 1994; contbr. articles to profl. jours. Pres. bd. dirs. Chesapeake Habitat for Humanity, Balt., 1987-88. Recipient Bravo award MCC Behavioral Care, 1994, Doris B. Harold award Nova Southeastern U., 1996. Mem. Am. Assn. for Marriage and Family Therapy (clin. mem.), Fla. Assn. for Marriage and Family Therapy, Scientific Hypnosis Soc., Pa. Assn. for Marriage and Family Therapy, Peace River Presbytery. Home: 930 Arlington Rd York PA 17403

NAUMANN, WILLIAM CARL, consumer products company executive; b. Peoria, Ill., Mar. 25, 1938; s. William Louis and Emma (Bottin) N.; m. Polly Roby, May 20, 1962 (div. 1980); children: Jeff, Heather, Derek; m. Patricia Gallagher, Sept. 9, 1993. BSCE, Purdue U., 1960; MBA, U. Chgo., 1975. With Inland Steel Products Co., Chgo., 1960-74, N.Y. dist. mgr., 1968-70, div. gen. mgr., 1971-74; group v.p., bd. dirs. Inryco, Melrose Park, Ill., 1974-81; asst. chief engr. Inland Steel Co., Chgo., 1981-82, asst. gen. mgr. corp. planning, 1982-83, asst. gen. mgr. sales, 1983-85, gen. mgr. sales and mktg., 1985-87; exec. v.p. internat. ops. Hussmann Corp., Bridgeton, Mo., 1987; exec. v.p. sales and mktg. Hussmann Corp., Bridgeton, 1987; pres. Hussmann Food Svc. Co., Bridgeton, 1987-89; corp. v.p., chief quality officer Whitman Corp., Chgo., 1989-91; CEO Ranger Industries, 1992; sr. v.p., COO Pexco Holdings, Inc., Tulsa, 1993-96; chmn. bd. dirs. Sports Holdings Corp., Montreal, Can., 1997—. Mem. U. Chgo. Exec. Program Club (past pres.), Cedar Ridge Country Club (Tulsa), U. Chgo. Alumni Assn. (past pres., bd. govs. 1986-95), Beta Gamma Sigma. Home: 5146 E 107th Pl Tulsa OK 74137 Office: 7130 S Lewis Ave Ste 850 Tulsa OK 74136-5490

NAUTA, FRANS, operations research analyst; b. Amsterdam, The Netherlands, Mar. 12, 1937; came to U.S., 1966; s. Doede and Jeltje (Sytsma) N.; m. Janet C. Westbrook, Dec. 26, 1969; 1 child, Jennifer A. BS in Math., Tech. U., Delft, The Netherlands, 1957, MS in Aero. Engring., 1963, diploma in aero. engring., 1965. Ops. rsch. intern KLM Royal Dutch Airlines and Fokker N.V., The Netherlands, 1964-65; mgmt. cons. Coun. for Econ. and Indsl. Rsch., Inc., The Hague and Bethesda, Md., 1965-67; assoc. Decision Systems Assocs., Inc., Rockville, Md., 1967-77; rsch. fellow Logistics Mgmt. Inst., Bethesda, 1977-94; sr. logistician JAYCOR, Vienna, Va., 1995—. Contbr. book revs. to profl. publs. Mem. AIAA, Inst. Mgmt. Scis., Am. Def. Preparedness Assn. Democrat. Presbyterian. Office: JAYCOR 1608 Spring Hill Rd Vienna VA 22182

NAVAS, LUIS RAMON, family physician; b. Guatemala, Guatemala, June 14, 1963; came to U.S., 1991; s. Raul and Dora Maria (Padilla) N.; m. Deborah Ann Jordan; 1 child, Jordan Tatiana. BS, U. Francisco Marroquin, Guatemala, 1986; MD, U. Francisco Marroquin, 1990. Diplomate Bd. Guatemala; lic., Ala., N.C. Physician in charge Angel Care, Guatemala, 1991; resident in family practice U. South Ala., Mobile, Ala., 1992-95; fellow in geriatrics Duke U., Durham, N.C., 1995—; asst. prof. gross anatomy U. Francisco Morroquin, Guatemala, 1990-92; chief resident U.S.A. Family Practice, 1994-95. Mem. AMA, Am. Acad. Family Physicians, Am. Geriatric Soc., The Gerontol. Soc. of Am. Methodist. Office: VA Med Ctr/Duke U GRECC 182 508 Fulton St Durham NC 27705

NAWROCKI, H(ENRY) FRANZ, propulsion technology scientist; b. Pueblo, Colo., Dec. 10, 1931; s. Henry Vincent and Verna Ella (Weyand) N.; m. Marlene Charlotte Kryak, Sept. 1, 1973. BS Aero. Engring., U. Colo., 1953; MS Aerospace Engring., U. So. Calif., 1968. Group supr. for RJ43 qualification Marquardt, Van Nuys, Calif., 1953-64; flight test analyst engr. for L-1011 cert. Lockheed, Palmdale, Calif., 1964-72; flight test program coord. for B-1 qualification Rockwell Internat., El Segundo, Calif., 1972-77; propulsion group supr. for CL600 cert. Canadair Ltd., Montreal, Que., Can., 1977-80; design mgr. for LF2000 devel. Lear Fan Ltd., Reno, 1980-82; staff scientist Gulfstream Aerospace Corp., Savannah, Ga., 1982—. Mem. Aerospace Industries Assn. (mem. propulsion com., mem. inclement weather cubcom.), Soc. Automotive Engrs. (alternate mem. propulsion com.), Engine Harmonizing Working Group (ad hoc mem.), Aviation Rulemaking Adv. Com. Power Plant Installation Harmonization Working Group (ad hoc mem.). Home: 18 Landon Ln Savannah GA 31410-3830

NAYLOR, OLEN CLYDE, JR., pharmacist; b. Washington, N.C., Nov. 13, 1958; s. Olen Clyde Sr. and Ruth (Spruill) N. BS in Pharmacy, U. N.C., 1982. Registered pharmacist. Owner. Pharm. Cons., Greenville, N.C., 1984-89; pres. Apple Nursing Svc. Inc., Greenville, 1986-91; staff pharmacist Pitt County Meml. Hosp., Greenville, 1982—; realtor Boswell & Co., Greenville, RE/MAX Preferred, Greenville, 1993-96; pharmacist Nayco Enterprises, Greenville, 1996—. V.p. Greenville Jaycees, 1988-89, pres., 1989-90. Mem. Am. Pharm. Assn., Am. Soc. Hosp. Pharmacists, N.C. Pharm. Assn., N.C. Soc. Hosp. Pharmacists, Greenville Area Preservation Assn., Pitt-Greenville C. of C. (com. chair 1987-88), Pitt-Greenville Bd. Realtors. Democrat. Home: PO Box 30313 Greenville NC 27833-0313 Office: Nayco Enterprises 313 St Andrews Dr Greenville NC 27834

NDIMBA, CORNELIUS GHANE, language educator; b. Ngeptang-din, Cameroon, Sept. 5, 1953; came to the U.S., 1981; s. Dominic Kimah and Sabina (Meilo) N.; 1 child, Melvynne Meilo. BS in Econs. and Mgmt., S.E. Okla. State U., 1984, M in Adminstrv. Studies, 1989; postgrad., Tex. Woman's U. Cert. tchr. bus. adminstrn. and mgmt., Tex. Customer svc. rep. Internat. Bank of West Africa, Cameroon, 1979-81; storeroom clk. S.E. Okla. State U., Durant, 1981-84, student counselor, 1989-90; purchasing asst. Las Colinas Sports Club, Irving, Tex., 1985-88; assembler GM Corp., Arlington, Tex., 1988; admissions rep. ATI Career Tng., Dallas, 1991-92; ESL tchr. Dallas Ind. Sch. Dist., 1992—; sales cons. Am. Foods, Irving, 1989-94. Mem. com. Boy Scouts Am., Dallas, 1992, Cmty. Adv. Com., East Dallas, 1994. Mem. Internat. Reading Assn., Parent-Tchr. Assn., Sasse Old Boys Assn. (pres. 1989—). Republican. Roman Catholic. Home: 3113 W Northgate Dr Apt 1045 Irving TX 75062-3104 Office: 4800 Ross Ave Dallas TX 75204

NEAL, FRANK ALLEN, JR., city planner; b. Augusta, Ga., Sept. 7, 1968; s. Frank Allen and Sarah Ann (McCarthy) N. BA in Polit. Sci., U. Ga., 1991; MPA, Ga. So. U., 1993; M.City and Regional Planning, U. Memphis, 1994. Rsch. adminstr. Bur. Pub. Affairs, Statesboro, Ga., 1992-93; asst. to city adminstr., dir. planning/code enforcement City of Tybee Island, Ga., 1993-94; regional planner Regional Econ. Devel. Ctr., Memphis, Ga., 1994; cmty. planner VISTA/the H.E.A.D. Corp., Beren, Ky., 1994-95; planner City of Statesboro, 1995—. Contbr. articles to profl. jours. Bd. dirs., treas. Tybee Island Marine Sci. Found., 1992-93; ex-officio mem. Statesboro Tree Bd., 1995-96; vol. VISTA, Beren, 1994-95, Save the Children, Clay County, Ky., 1995, Tybee Island Marine Sci. Ctr., 1993-94, Keep America Beautiful, 1995-96. Grad. assistantship Ga. So. U., 1992, U. Memphis, 1994; Shorter

Coll. tennis scholar, 1986. Mem. ASPA, Am. Planning Assn., Ga. Planning Assn., Internat. City Mgrs. Assn., Ga. City Mgrs. Assn., Ga. Assn. zoning Adminstrs. Home: 29A Pate Pl Statesboro GA 30458 Office: City of Statesboro Statesboro GA 30459

NEAL, JERRY HAROLD, protective services official; b. Wanette, Okla., Mar. 10, 1943; s. William Odus and Anna (Way) N.; m. Ellen Teresa Robertson; children: Jamee Lynn, Jerry Harold Jr., Jordan Kent, Natalie Ellen. AA, Okla. State U., 1972, BS, 1973, MS, 1977. Patrolman, sgt., lt., capt. Norman Police Dept., Okla., 1968-78, maj. of police, 1978-81; chief of police Amarillo Police Dept., Tex., 1981—; bd. mem. State Police Pension System, Okla., 1980-81; regional dir. Tex. Police Chiefs Assn., 1981-83; tng. adv. bd. Tex. Commn. Law Enforcement, Austin, 1982-84. Bd. dirs. Maverick Boys Club, Amarillo, 1985, Rape Crisis, Domestic Crisis Violence, Amarillo, 1981-84, Amarillo Council Alcoholism, 1981-84; exec. bd. Llayno council Boy Scouts Am., 1985. Served to Sgt. E-5 U.S. Army, 1965-68. Mem. Tex. Police Chiefs Assn. (v.p.), Tex. Police Assn. (pres.), Fed. Bur. Investigation Nat. Assocs., Rotary. Democrat. Avocations: golf, softball. Home: 1 Barber Pl Amarillo TX 79124-1701 Office: Amarillo Police Dept 200 E 3rd Ave Amarillo TX 79101-1500 also: Office of Police Chief City Hall PO Box 1971 Amarillo TX 79186-0001

NEAL, MARGARET SHERRILL, writer; b. Memphis, Apr. 13, 1950; d. Wilburn Franklin and Merle Aileen (Willis) N. BA, Memphis State U., 1972, postgrad., 1973; MS, Columbia Pacific U., 1984. Air traffic controller FAA, Memphis, 1974-76, New Bern, N.C., 1976-81, Vero Beach, Fla., 1981-83; detection systems specialist U.S. Customs Service, Miami, 1983-87, intelligence rsch. specialist, 1987-89; ret., 1989. Mem. NOW, Smithsonian Instn., Mensa, Nat. Trust Hist. Preservation, Greenpeace, Clan Macneil Soc., Nature Conservancy, Save the Manatee Club. Republican. Presbyterian.

NEAL, MARK LEE, quality assurance manager; b. Victoria, Tex., July 23, 1957; s. Jerry Lee and Barbara (Hoover) N.; m. Cheryl Ann Kalem, June 10, 1989. BS in Nuclear Engring., Tex. A&M U., 1980. Radioactive device technician Gamma Industries, Houston, 1980; mgr. software quality assurance Tex. Instruments, Dallas, 1983-90; dir. quality assurance NAC, Inc., Richardson, Tex., 1990-91; mgr. software process Mentor Graphics, Wilsonville, Oreg., 1991-92; mgr. software product assurance Abbott Diagnostics Divsn., Irving, Tex., 1992—; software process assessor Tex. Instruments, Dallas, 1987-90, Mentor Graphics, Wilsonville, Oreg., 1991-92; software process assessor Abbott Labs., Abbott Park, Ill., 1992-93, ISO 9000 auditor, 1993-94; speaker in field. Contbr. articles to profl. jours. 1st lt. U.S. Army, 1980-83. Mem. Am. Soc. Quality Control, Dallas/Ft. Worth Assn. for Software Engring. Excellence (founding mem., chmn. 1987—, programs chmn.). Office: Abbott Diagnostics Divsn PO Box 152020 MS2-8 Irving TX 75015

NEAL, PATRICIA ANNE, English language educator; b. Kansas City, Mo.; d. Frank H. and Serra A. Maggard; m. Charles O. Neal; children: Christopher, Kathleen, Charles, Michael, Danny. BA in Eng., Avila Coll.; MA in Eng., San Jose State U., 1962; postgrad., Defense Lang. Inst.; PhD in English, U. Tex., 1986. Lectr. Trinity U., San Antonio, 1979-80; art critic, reviewer San Antonio Light, 1980-83; vis. asst. prof. St. Mary's U., San Antonio, 1987-89; assoc. prof. Eng. dept. Spring Hill Coll., Mobile, 1989—; lectr. Spring Hill Coll., 1992, Christus Theol. Inst., 1992, McNay Art Mus., San Antonio, 1978-79, 81, 84, 86-87, edn. dir. docent program, 1979-80, AAUW, San Antonio, 1987, San Antonio Mus. Art, 1987, San Antonio Coll., 1987, San Antonio Art League, 1987; resident art critic, prodr., editor, writer TV sta. KLRN-TV, San Antonio, 1979-83; presenter and art reviewer in field. Arts and cultural adv. com. mem. City of San Antonio, 1987-90, vice-chair, 1988-89; peer panel Multi-Disciplinary Arts Com., San Antonio, 1986-87, chair, 1987; chair student publ. bd. Spring Hill Coll., 1990-94; active Brit. Embassy Playreading Group, Bonn, Germany, 1968-71. NEH grantee, 1990, 92, 94, 95. Mem. MLA, Ruskin Assn., Dickens Assn., So. Assn. MLA, Friends Fine Arts Mus. of the South Mobile. Office: Spring Hill College Mobile AL 36608

NEALE, WALTER CASTLE, retired economics educator; b. N.Y.C., Aug. 9, 1925; m. Anne Mayhew, Nov. 7, 1967. AB in Pub./Internat. Affairs with honors, Princeton U., 1947; MA in Econs., Columbia U., 1948; PhD, U. London, 1953. Instr. U. N.C., 1948-50; instr. econs. Yale U., New Haven, 1953-58; field rsch. assoc. India Project MIT, Maharashtra and Punjab, 1955-56; asst. prof. U. Tex., Austin, 1958-62, assoc. prof., 1962-64, prof. econs., 1964-68; prof. econs. U. Tenn., 1968-91; ret.; sr. Fulbright lectr. Panjab U., India, 1960-61; vis. lectr. Rice U., 1962-63; vis. fellow U. Exeter, U.K., 1985; reader/reviewer various yrs. for NSF, Princeton U. Press, U. Calif., Econ. Devel. and Cultural Change, Jour. Econ. History, Jour. Asian Studies, Jour. of Developing Areas, Woodrow Wilson Ctr. Editl. bd. Jour. Econ. Issues, 1987-89; author: Economic Change in Rural India: Land Tenure and Reform in Uttar Pradesh, 1800-1955, 1962, 2d edit., 1973, India: The Search for Unity, Democracy and Progress, 1965, (co-author John Adams), 2d edit., 1976, Monies in Societies, 1976, Developing Rural India: Policies, Politics and Progress, 1990; contbr. numerous articles to profl. jours., chpts. to books. Fulbright-Hays Faculty Rsch. fellow, 1964-65, Ford Found. Faculty Rsch. fellow, 1967-68; William B. Stokely scholar U. Tenn., 1989-90. Mem. Assn. for Evolutionary Econs. (v.p. 1980, pres. 1981, Veblen-Commons award 1989), Soc. for Econ. Anthropology (pres. 1984-85, bd. dirs. 1980-86, local arrangements chair ann. meeting 1988), Tenn. Consortium for Asian Studies (pres. 1982-83), Assn. for Asian Studies (pres. S.E. conf. 1985-86, exec. com. 1984-87, local arrangements chair 1995-96). Home: 2307 Laurel Ave Knoxville TN 37916 Office: Univ of Tennessee Dept Econs Knoxville TN 37996-0550

NEAS, JOHN THEODORE, petroleum company executive; b. Tulsa, May 1, 1940; s. George and Lillian J. (Kaspar) N.; BS, Okla. State U., 1967, MS, 1968; m. Sally Jane McPherson, June 10, 1966; children: Stephen, Gregory, Matthew. CPA, Okla. With acctg. dept. Rockwell Internat., 1965; with controller's dept. Amoco Prodn. Co., 1966-67; mem. audit and tax staff Deloitte, Haskins & Sells, 1968-75; pres. Nat. Petroleum Sales, Inc., Tulsa, 1975—, John Neas Tank Lines, Inc., 1986—; pres. McPherson Fuels & Asphalts, Inc., 1981-88, sec., 1989—; mem. NPS/Hallmark LLC, 1994—; mem. Bailey Ranch Estates LLC, 1994—; asst. instr. U. Tulsa, 1974; former mem., bd. dirs. Waterways Bd. Okla. Dept. Transp. and Okla. Dept. of Commerce. Mem. AICPA, Inst. Mgmt. Accts. (v.p. membership 1976-77), Okla. Soc. CPAs, Am. Petroleum Inst., McClellan-Kerr Arkansas River Navigation System Hist. Soc., Okla. Heritage Assn., Okla. State U. Pres.'s Club, Okla. State U. Coll. Bus. Adminstrn. Assocs. (v.p. memberships 1989-91, Hall of Fame 1991, Acctg. Dept. Hall of Fame, 1993), Oaks Country Club, The Golf Club Okla. Republican. Lutheran. Home: 2943 E 69th St Tulsa OK 74136-4541 Office: Nat Petroleum Sales Inc 5401 S Harvard Ave Ste 200 Tulsa OK 74135-3861

NEASE, JUDITH ALLGOOD, marriage and family therapist; b. Arlington, Mass., Nov. 15, 1930; d. Dwight Maurice Allgood and Sophie (Wolf) Allgood Morris; student Rockford Coll., 1949-50; BA, NYU, 1953, MA, 1954; MS, Columbia U. Sch. Social Work, 1956; m. Theron Stanford Nease, Sept. 1, 1962; children: Susan Elizabeth, Alison Allgood. Social worker, psychiatric social worker Bellevue Psychiat. Hosp., N.Y.C., 1956-59; psychiat. social worker St. Luke's Hosp., N.Y.C., 1959-62; asst. psychiat. social work supr. N.J. Neuropsychiat. Inst., Princeton, 1962-64; group co-leader Ctr. for Advancement of Personal and Social Growth, Atlanta, 1973-76, asst. dir., social work supr., group co-leader Druid Hills Counseling Ctr., Columbia Theol. Sem., 1973-82; marriage and family therapist Cath. Social Svcs., Atlanta, 1978-87; chief Cmty. Mental Health Svc., Ft. McPherson, Atlanta, Ga., 1987-92; master's level clinician Ctr. for Psychiatry, Smyrna, Ga., 1990-92; pvt. practice marriage and family therapy. Mem. NASW, Acad. Cert. Social Workers, Am. Assn. Marriage and Family Therapy, Am. Group Psychotherapy Assn. Republican. Episcopalian. Home and Office: 1557 Bennett Road Grayson GA 30221

NEATHERY, PATRICIA SUE, dietitian, consultant; b. Dothan, Ala., Apr. 18, 1934; d. John Joseph and Sue (Latil) Astleford; m. Thornton Lee Neathery, Aug. 25, 1956; children: Susan, David, Leanne. BS, U. Ala., 1956, grad., 1970-73. Dietitian Bryce Hosp., Tuscaloosa, Ala., 1963-65; pvt. practice cons. West Ala., 1970-86; dietitian Brewer-Porch Children's Ctr. U. Ala., Tuscaloosa, 1982—. Am. Heart Assn. scholar, 1964. Mem. AAUW (1st v.p. 1980-82), Am. Dietetic Assn., Ala. Dietetic Assn., Tuscaloosa Dietetic Assn. (chmn. legis. com. 1979, pres. 1990-91), Ala. Home Econs. Assn. (treas. 1974, pres. 1990-91), Civitan Internat. (bd. mem.), Alpha Delta Pi (alumnae pres. 1986-87). Republican. Episcopalian. Home: 3032 Firethorn Dr Tuscaloosa AL 35405-2747 Office: U Ala Dept Psychology Brewer-Porch Children's Ctr PO Box 870156 Tuscaloosa AL 35487-0156

NEBEL, WILLIAM ARTHUR, obstetrician, gynecologist; b. Charlotte, N.C., Dec. 23, 1936; s. Arthur Ernest and Marie (Hunter) N.; m. Ann Elizabeth Bonner, June 20, 1959; children: Ann Marie Nebel, William Arthur Jr. AB in History, U. N.C., 1958, MD, 1962. Diplomate Am. Bd. Ob-Gyn. Intern Duke Univ. Med. Ctr., Durham, N.C., 1962-63; asst. clin. prof. ob-gyn Duke Univ. Med. Ctr., Durham, 1973—; resident in ob-gyn U. N.C., Chapel Hill, 1963-67, clin. instr. Sch. Med., 1969-70, clin. prof., 1989—; pvt. practice medicine specializing in ob-gyn Chapel Hill, 1970—; chmn. ob-gyn dept. Durham County Gen. Hosp., 1978-80, pres. med. staff, 1988-89, cons. staff, 1992—; mem. Steering Com. Chapel Hill Health Maintenance Orgn. Planning Project, 1973; mem. Orange County Health Bd., 1977, 80; mem. Birth, Neonatal Task Force, State of N.C. Dept. Human Resources, 1985; mem. organizing com. Coordinated Med. Svcs. N.C., 1985; bd. dirs. N.C. Blue Cross/Blue Shield, 1985-87; bd. dirs. Cen. Carolina Physicians Health, Village Bank, chmn. bd. 1987-89. Contbr. numerous articles to profl. jours.; author numerous presentations to profl. assns. Chmn. troop com. Boy Scouts Am., Troop 39, 1975-78; basketball coach Chapel Hill Recreation Dept., 1975-79; mem. Orange County Com. of N.C. 2000; bd. dirs. U. N.C. Ednl. Found.; vestryman Ch. of the Holy Family, 1973-76; pres. orange County unit Am. Cancer Soc., 1975-76, N.C. divsn. bd. dirs. 1977-78; bd. dirs. N.C. Blue CrossBlue Shield Personal Care Plan, 1985, Ctrl. Carolina Physicians Health, 1985-88, Found. for Better Health of Durham, 1988-89. Recognized by Am. Acad. Family Physicians, 1976-80; named Chapel Hill-Carrboro Father of Yr., 1977; United Cerebral Palsy Med. student fellow, 1960-61, Am. Cancer Soc. fellow, 1965-66. Mem. Internat. Corr. Soc. of Obstetricians and Gynocologists, Am. Fertility Soc., Am. Cancer Soc., S. Cen. Ob-Gyn. Soc. (pres. 1984-85), N.C. Med. Soc. (sect. chmn. 1983-84), N.C. Ob-Gyn. Soc. (pres. 1982-83), Piedmont Ob-Gyn. Soc., Durham-Orange County Med. Soc., Robert A. Ross Ob-Gyn. Soc. (pres. 1976), Village Med. Soc. (pres. 1970-80), Def. Orientation Conf. Assn., Chaime des Potisseurs, Rotary (past pres., Paul Harris fellow), Alpha Omega Alpha, Phi Alpha Theta, Phi Chi, Pi Kappa Alpha. Democrat. Episcopalian. Office: Chapel Hill Ob-Gyn PO Box 3317 Chapel Hill NC 27515-3317

NEBERGALL, ROBERT WILLIAM, orthopedic surgeon, educator; b. Des Moines, Dec. 31, 1954; s. Donald Charles and Shirley (Williams) N.; m. Teresa Rae Fawell, May 27, 1978; children: Nathaniel Robert Baird, Bartholomew William Campbell. BS in Biology, Luther Coll., 1977; DO, U. Osteo. Health Scis., 1981. Intern Des Moines Gen. Hosp., 1981-82; resident orthopedic surgery Tulsa Regional Med. Ctr., 1982-86; trauma fellow Assn. Osteosynthesis/Assn. Study of Internal Fixation Fellowship Program, Stuttgart and Mainz, West Germany, 1986; sports medicine fellow U. Oreg. Orthopedic and Fracture Clinic, Eugene, 1986; orthopedic surgeon Tulsa Orthopedic Surgeons, 1987—; team physician Tulsa Ballet Theatre, 1987—, Internat. Pro Rodeo Assn., Oklahoma City, 1987—, Nathan Hale H.S. Football, 1992—, Ctrl. H.S., 1993—, Tulsa Roughnecks Soccer, 1993—, Okla. All State Games, 1994—; clin. asst. prof. surgery Okla. State U. Coll. Osteo. Medicine; chmn. dept. orthopedic surgery Tulsa Regional Med. Ctr.; pres. Green Country Ind. Practice Assn. Mem. Okla. Found. for Peer Rev., Oklahoma City, 1988—; past pres. Culver (Ind.) Summer Sch. Alumni Assn., 1991; trustee Culver Ednl. Found. of Culver Mil. Acad., 1991-93. Recipient Vol. award Tulsa Ballet Theatre, 1990, Physicians Recognition award AMA, 1990; named Outstanding Young Man in Am., U.S. Jaycees, 1983. Mem. Am. Osteo. Acad. Orthopedics, Am. Coll. Sports Medicine, Am. Osteo. Orthopedic Soc. Sports Medicine (past pres.), N.Y. Acad. Scis., Assn. Osteosynthesis Fellowship Alumni Orgn., Sigma Sigma Phi. Methodist. Home: 2116 S Detroit Ave Tulsa OK 74114-1208 Office: Tulsa Orthopedic Surgeons 802 S Jackson Ave Ste 130 Tulsa OK 74127-9010

NEBLOCK, CARL SCOTT, chemical engineering educator; b. New Braunfels, Tex., Feb. 12, 1953; s. Rosemary McQueen Neblock; m. Michele L. Lehr; 1 child, Carl Eric. BA in Chemistry, So. Ill. U., Edwardsville, 1984; MBA in Govt. Contracts, U. Dallas, Irving, 1991; EdD, Tex. Tech. U., 1996. Draftsman Sverdrup & Parcel, St. Louis, 1974-76, Edison brother Shoe Co., St. Louis, 1976, A.G. McKee Engrs., St. Louis, 1976-78; sr. draftsman/designer Fruco Engrs., St. Louis, 1978-81; sr. engr. Gen. Dynamics, Ft. Worth, Tex., 1984-91. Chair exploring coun. South Plains coun. Boy Scouts Am., Lubbock, 1993-96, dist. commr., 1996, scouting outreach chair, 1992-96. Recipient Dist. Award of Merit, South Plains coun. Boy Scouts Am., 1994, Silver Beaver, Nat. coun., 1996. Mem. ASCD, Math. Assn. Am., Am. Edn. Fin. Assn., South Edn. Rsch. assn., Am. Edn. Rsch. Assn., Golden Key, Sigma Iota Epsilon. Home: 6115 Louisville Dr Lubbock TX 79413

NECCO, E(DNA) JOANNE, school psychologist; b. Klamath Falls, Oreg., June 23, 1941; d. Joseph Rogers and Lillian Laura (Owings) Painter; m. Jon F. Furyear, Aug. 25, 1963 (div. Oct. 1987); children: Laura L., Douglas F.; m. A. David Necco, July 1, 1989. BS, Cen. State U., 1978, MEd, 1985; PhD in Applied Behavioral Studies, Okla. State U., 1993. Med.-surg. asst. Oklahoma City Clinic, 1961-68; spl. edn. tchr. Oklahoma City Pub. Schs., 1978-79, Edmond (Okla.) Pub. Schs., 1979-83; co-founder, owner Learning Devel. Clinic, Edmond, 1983-93; asst. prof. profl. tchr. edn. U. Ctrl. Okla., Edmond, 1993—; adj. instr. Ctrl. State U., Edmond, 1989-93, Oklahoma City U., 1991-93; mem. rsch. group Okla. State U., Stillwater, 1991-93; presenter in field. Contbr. articles to profl. jours. Com. mem. Boy Scouts of Am., SCUBA Post 604, Oklahoma City, 1981-86; mem. Edmond Task Force for Youth, 1983-87, Edmond C. of C., 1984-87; presenter internat. conf. Okla. Ctr. for Neurosci., 1996; evaluator for Even Start Literacy Program, 1994-96, presenter internat. conf., Singapore, 1996. Mem. Assn. Supervision and Curriculum Devel., Nat. Assn. for Sch. Psychologists, Am. Bus Women's Assn., Coun. for Exceptional Children, Learning Disabilities Assn., Am. Assn. for Gifted Underachieving Students, Okla. Learning Disabilities Assn., Okla. Assn. for Counseling and Devel., Golden Key Nat. Honor Soc., Internat. Soc. for Scientific Study of Subjectivity, Am. Coun. on Rural Spl. Edn., Ctrl State U. (Okla., life), Phi Delta Kappa. Republican. Home: 17509 Woodsorrel Rd Edmond OK 73003-6951 Office: U Ctrl Okla Coll Edn 100 N University Dr Edmond OK 73034

NEEB, BARBARA JEAN, women's health and geriatric nurse; b. Shelbyville, Ind., Jan. 27, 1952; d. Robert Dale and N. Jean (Banker) N. BA in Edn., Hobe Sound (Fla.) Bible Coll., 1974; LPN, Palm Beach Prac. Nursing Sch., Fla., 1980; ADN, Marian Coll., Indpls., 1988. RN, Ind., Ala.; lic. practical nurse; ordained min. Nat. Assn. Holiness Chs., 1976. Lic. practical nurse Palm Beach, Martin County Hosp., Jupiter, Fla., 1981; missionary Fla. Evangelistic Assn., Grand Bahamas Islands, 1974-79; missionary, nurse God's Missionary Ch., Port Au Prince, Haiti, 1981-85; charge nurse Druid City Hosp., Tuscaloosa, Ala., 1990-91; head staff devel., unit mgr. Park Manor Nursing Home, Northport, Ala., 1990-92, assoc. DON, 1992; DON Park Manor Nursing Home, 1992-94; unit mgr. Glen Haven Nursing Home, Northport, 1994—; chaplain Hobe Sound (Fla.) Bible Coll. Mem. Nat. Assn. Practical Nurses Edn. Soc. Home: 10904 W Manor Dr Cottondale AL 35453-6737

NEEDEL, STEPHEN PAUL, marketing research executive; b. Boston, Nov. 8, 1955; s. Edward Charles and Ruth (Stein) N.; m. Diane Marie Cullis, Feb. 18, 1977 (div. 1982); m. Antoinette Maria Popescu, Apr. 8, 1984; children: Nicolas Mikhail, Lucas Enric. BA in Psychology, Am. U., 1976; MA in Psychology, U. Conn., 1979, PhD in Social Psychology, 1980. Rsch. analyst Quaker Oats, Chgo., 1980-81, sr. rsch. analyst, 1981-82; dir. analytical svcs. Burke Mktg. Rsch., Cin., 1982-84, Chgo., 1984-86; dir. analytical svcs. Info. Resources, Inc., Chgo., 1986-88; dir. applications devel. Nielsen Mktg. Rsch., Northbrook, Ill., 1988; v.p. analytical svcs. Nielsen Mktg. Rsch., Atlanta, 1988-90; v.p. product devel. Nielsen Mktg. Rsch., Northbrook, Ill., 1990-93; dir. Simulation Svcs. Marketware Corp., Norcross, Ga., 1993-94; pres. Simulation Rsch. Inc., Marietta, Ga., 1994—. Mem. APA, Am. Mktg. Assn., Soc. for Consumer Psychology. Jewish. Home: 4272 Revere Cir Marietta GA 30062-5767 Office: Simulation Research Inc 2265 Roswell Rd Marietta GA 30062

NEEDHAM, MAUREEN, dance educator; b. Washington, June 11, 1938; d. Maurice d'Arlan and Thyria (Hughart) Needham; children: Terri, Jon, Sarah. BA, Harvard U., 1960; MA, U. Ill., 1972; PhD, NYU, 1989. Dancer New Orleans Opera Assn., 1952-56; choreographer, tchr. Harand Theatre Arts, Lake Elkhart, Wis., 1957-59; choreographer Hasty Pudding Theatricals, Cambridge, Mass., 1959; tchr. Jewish Found. Sch., Staten Island, 1961-62, Dwight Sch. for Girls, Englewood, N.J., 1962-63, Tenafly (N.J.) Pub. Schs., 1963-65; dance therapist Adler Zone Ctr., Champaign, Ill., 1971-75; asst. prof. U. Ill., Champaign, 1975-77; assoc. prof. Vanderbilt U., Nashville, 1984—; cons. day care ctrs. for handicapped, Ill., 1974; advisor U.S. Rsch. Internat. Music, 1987—. Editor: Therapy in Motion, 1978; contbr. articles to profl. jours., chpts. to books and encys., dance revs. The Nashville Scene, 1996—; editor Channels newsletter, Am. World Dance Alliance. Sen. Vanderbilt Faculty Senate, 1985-89, 96-97; bd. dirs. Nashville City Ballet, 1986-88; active Mayor's Task Force on Arts, Nashville, 1988-90, 94; bd. dirs. Coun. Cmty. Svcs., Nashville, 1995—, Ctr. Health Coalition, Nashville, 1995—; mem. grants allocations com. Metro Arts Coun., 1980; chair faculty adv. coun., Blair Sch. Music, 1991—. Edmund James scholar U. Ill., 1972; Tenn. Endowment for Humanities grantee, 1987; NEH summer rsch. fellow, 1993. Mem. Soc. Dance History Scholars (bd. dirs. 1991-95), World Dance Alliance (North/South Am. rep. 1990—, co-editor calendar 1990-93), Woman's Faculty Orgn. (chair 1991—). Office: Vanderbilt U Blair Sch Music 3400 Blakemore Ave Nashville TN 37212-3499

NEELEY, DELMAR GEORGE, human resources consultant; b. Charleston, Ill., June 4, 1937; s. Glenn Truman and Gladys Bernice (Dittman) N.; m. Yvonne Tamara Penrod, Mar. 2, 1957 (div. Feb. 1969); children: Timothy Del, Kimberly Yvonne, Terry; m. Terry Anne Barbour, Aug. 28, 1971; children: Robert James, Stephen Edward. BA in Philosophy, Olivet Nazarene U., 1965, MA in Lit., 1969; EdD, U. Sarasota, 1996. Cert. mediator and arbitrator, Fla. Mgr. mgmt. devel. Rauland Divsn. Zenith Corp., Chgo., 1967-70; sr. personnel cons. Mid. West Svc. Co., Chgo., 1971-73; dir. human resources Nichols-Homeshield Inc., West Chicago, Ill., 1974-76, Gould Inc./Ind. Battery Divsn., Langhorne, Pa., 1976-81; pres., owner Barbour-Neeley Inc., Sarasota, Fla., 1982-91; Stephen Ministries leader. Recipient Meritorious Svc. award Chgo. Boys Club, 1970, Svc. award Chgo. Jaycees, 1967-71. Mem. ACA, Ctr. for Study of Presidency, The Century Club (life), Libr. of Congress Assocs., Coll. of Chaplains, Fla. Acad. Profl. Mediators. Independent. Methodist. Home: 5161 Cedar Hammock Dr Sarasota FL 34232-2243

NEELY, ALAN PRESTON, religious studies educator; b. Little Rock, Nov. 3, 1928; s. Arthur Preston and Effie Mae (Sargent) N.; m. Virginia Emma Garrett; children: Jennifer Alane, Elizabeth Anne, Roger Alan. BA, Baylor U., 1950; ThD, Southwestern Bapt. Theol. Sem., 1960; PhD, Am. U., 1977. Pastor Clariette (Tex.) Bapt. Ch., 1950-53, First Bapt. Ch., Detroit, Tex., 1953-55, Rosalind Hills Bapt. Ch., Roanoke, Va., 1956-61, Broadway Bapt. Ch., Boulder, Colo., 1961-63; prof. Internat. Baptist Theol. Sem., Cali, Colombia, 1963-76, Southeastern Bapt. Sem., Wake Forest, N.C., 1976-88, Princeton (N.J.) Theol. Sem., 1988—. Author: Being Baptist Means Freedom, 1988, Christian Missions: A Case Study Approach, 1995; translator: A History of the Church in Latin America, 1981; contbr. articles to profl. jours. Co-founder, bd. dirs. Habitat for Humanity, Raleigh, N.C., 1984-88. Mem. Assn. Profs. Mission, Am. Soc. Missiology (pres. 1988-89). Democrat. Home: 2209 Middlefield Ct Raleigh NC 27615-4427 Office: Princeton Theol Sem PO Box 821 Princeton NJ 08540

NEELY, RICHARD, lawyer; b. Aug. 2, 1941; s. John Champ and Elinore (Forlani) N.; m. Carolyn Elaine Elmore, 1979; children: John Champ, Charles Whittaker. AB, Dartmouth Coll., 1964; LLB, Yale U., 1967. Bar: W.Va. 1967. Practiced in Fairmont, W.Va., 1969-73; chmn. Marion County Bd. Pub. Health, 1971-72; mem. W.Va. Ho. of Dels., 1971-73; justice, chief justice W.Va. Supreme Ct. of Appeals, Charleston, 1973-95; ptnr. Neely & Hunter, Charleston, 1995—; chmn. bd. Kane & Keyser Co., Belington, W.Va., 1970-88. Author: How Courts Govern America, 1980, Why Courts Don't Work, 1983, The Divorce Decision, 1984, Judicial Jeopardy: When Business Collides with the Courts, 1986, The Product Liability Mess: How Business Can Be Rescued from State Court Politics, 1988, Take Back Your Neighborhood: A Case for Modern-Day Vigilantism, 1990, Tragedies of our Own Making: How Private Choices have Created Public Bankruptcy, 1994; contbr. articles to nat. mags. Capt. U.S. Army, 1967-69. Decorated Bronze Star, Vietnam Honor medal 1st Class. Mem. Am. Econ. Assn., W.Va. Bar Assn., Fourth Cir. Jud. Conf. (life), Internat. Brotherhood Elec. Workers, VFW, Am. Legion, Moose, Phi Delta Phi, Phi Sigma Kappa. Episcopalian. Office: Neely & Hunter 159 Summers St Charleston WV 25301

NEELY, ROBERT ALLEN, ophthalmologist; b. Temple, Tex., Mar. 1, 1921; s. Jubal A. and Almeida (Fordtran) N.; BA, U. Tex., 1942, MD, 1944; postgrad. Washington U., 1951-52; m. Eleanor V. Stein, June 29, 1944 (dec.); m. Joy S. Brown, Aug. 24, 1990; children: Byron D., Warren F. Intern, also resident Hermann Hosp., Houston, 1944-45, 55-57; gen. practice medicine, 1946-51, specializing in ophthalmology, Bellville, Tex., 1955—, ret.1992; trustee, staff mem. Bellville Hosp., Inc.; pres. Mid-Tex. Nursing Homes, Inc.; ret., 1992; chmn. bd. dirs. 1st Nat. Bank of Bellville. Mem. Bellville Ind. Sch. Dist. Sch. Bd., 1948-53; past pres. Bellville Area United Fund; adv. bd. mem. Sam Houston Area coun. Boy Scouts Am., past mem. nat. council; mem. chancellor's coun. U. Tex. System. Served with USNR, 1943-46, 53-55. Recipient Silver Beaver award Boy Scouts Am. Fellow Am. Acad. Ophthalmology; mem. AMA, Austin-Grimes-Waller Counties (past pres.), Ninth Dist. (past pres.) med. soc., Tex. Med. Assn., Tex. Ophthal. Assn., Tex. Soc. Opthalmology and Otolaryngology, Bellville C. of C., VFW (life), Bellville Golf Club (past pres.), Doctors Club, Lions (past pres.). Republican. Lutheran. Home: 105 E Hacienda St Bellville TX 77418-3103

NEELY, VICKI ADELE, legal assistant, poet; b. Dallas, Nov. 29, 1962; d. Robert Theodore and Linda Carolyn (Vogtsberger) Kissel; 1 child, Travis Wade. Student, Richland Coll., 1981-82, Austin C.C., 1983, San Antonio Coll., 1983, Am. Coll. Real Estate, 1983. Asst. mgr., leasing cons. Nash Phillips/Copus, Inc., 1983-85; loan processor Univ. Nat. Bank, 1985-87; co-owner Reels on Wheels, 1987; loan sec. Tex. Am. Bank/Richardson, N.A., 1987-88; legal sec., paralegal Clements, Allen & Warren, 1988-89; legal sec. Jackson & Walker, A Profl. Corp., 1989-90, Robins, Kaplan, Miller & Ciresi, 1990-91; freelance litigation sec. Smith & Underwood, 1991-92, legal asst., 1992-94; legal asst. Collins, Norman & Basinger, P.C., Dallas, 1994, Law Offices of Arlen D. (Spider) Bynum, 1995; sole practice Richardson, Tex., 1996—. Author: (poems) Animal Love, Believe, 1993; co-author: Texas Rent-A-Bank, 1993. Methodist. Home: 1911 Eastfield Dr Richardson TX 75081-5435 Office: Hampton Ct 1911 Eastfield Richardson TX 75081

NEER, CHARLES SUMNER, II, orthopedic surgeon, educator; b. Vinita, Okla., Nov. 10, 1917; s. Charles Sumner and Pearl Victoria (Brooke) N.; m. Eileen Meyer, June 12, 1990; children: Charlotte Marguerite, Sydney Victoria, Charles Henry. BA, Dartmouth Coll., 1939; MD, U. Pa., 1942. Diplomate Am. Bd. Orthopaedic Surgery (bd. dirs. 1970-75). Intern U. Pa. Hosp., Phila., 1942-43; asso. in surgery N.Y. Orthopedic-Columbia-Presbyn. Med. Center, N.Y.C., 1943-44; instr. in surgery Coll. Physicians and Surgeons, Columbia U., N.Y.C., 1946-47; instr. orthopaedic surgery Coll. Physicians and Surgeons, Columbia U., 1947-57, asst. prof. clin. orthopaedic surgery, 1957-64, asso. prof., 1964-68, prof. clin. orthopaedic surgery, 1968-90, prof. clin. orthopaedic surgery emeritus, spl. lectr. orthopaedic surgery, 1990—; attending orthopaedic surgeon Columbia-Presbyn. Med. Ctr., N.Y.C.; chief adult reconstructive svc. N.Y. Orthopaedic Hosp.; chief shoulder and elbow clinic Presbyn. Hosp.; cons. orthopaedic surgeon emeritus N.Y. Orthopaedic-Columbia-Presbyn. Med. Ctr., 1991—; chmn. 4th Internat. Congress Shoulder Surgeons; chmn. Internat. Bd. Shoulder Surgery, 1992—. Founder, chmn. bd. trustees Jour. Shoulder and Elbow Surgery, 1990—; contbr. articles to books, tech. films, sound slides. Served with U.S. Army, 1944-46. Recipient Disting. Svc. award Am. Bd. Orthopaedic Surgeons 1975. Fellow ACS (sr. mem. nat. com. on trauma), Am. Acad. Orthop. Surgeons (com. on upper extremity, shoulder com.); mem. AMA, ACS (mem. com. trauma), Am. Bd. Orthop. Surgeons (bd. dirs. 1970-75, Disting. Svc. award 1975), Am. Shoulder and Elbow Surgeons (inaugural pres.), Am. Assn. Surgery Trauma, Am. Orthop. Assn., Mid-Am. Orthop. Assn. (hon.), N.Y. Acad. Medicine, Allen O. Whipple Surg. Soc., N.Y. State Med. Soc., N.Y. County Med. Soc., Pan Am. Med. Assn., Am. Trauma Soc., Soc. Latino Am. Orthop. y Traumatology, Internat. Soc. Orthop. Surgery and Traumatology, Va. Orthop. Soc. (hon.), Carolina Orthop. Alumni Assn. (hon.), Conn. Orthop. Club (hon.), Houston Orthop. Assn. (hon.), Soc. Française de Chirurgie Orthop. et Traumatology (hon.), Soc. Italiana Orthop. Etravmatologia; patron, Shoulder and Elbow Soc. Australia, South African Shoulder Soc., Giraffe Club, Internat. Bd. Shoulder Surgery (chmn. 1992—), Alpha Omega Alpha, Phi Chi. Home and Office: 231 S Miller St Vinita OK 74301-3625

NEESE, HELEN DUVALL, healthcare practice management executive; b. Excelsior Springs, Mo., July 24, 1947; d. Lonnie Thomas and Myrtle (Hunnicutt) Duvall. BS, N.W. Mo. U., 1968, MS, 1970. Dir. lang. arts St. Joseph (Mo.) Sch. Dist., 1968-74; owner Katherine's Distinctive Gifts, St. Joseph, 1974-78; mgmt. cons. Alexander Proudfoot, Chgo., 1978-79; project mgr., v.p. Sci. Mgmt. Corp., Basking Ridge, N.J., 1979-83, v.p., 1983-88; dir. Brooks Internat., West Palm Beach, Fla., 1988-91; v.p. PhyCor, Nashville, 1991—. Republican. Presbyterian. Office: PhyCor 30 Burton Hills Blvd Ste 500 Nashville TN 37215-6140

NEFF, CECIL LEWIS, JR., real estate appraiser, author; b. Columbus, Ohio, Dec. 7, 1937; s. Cecil Lewis and Jessie Marie (Franklin) N.; children: Guy Alan, Edward Yancy, Shelley Mari. BS, Miami (Fla.) Christian Coll., 1992. Pres. Cecil L. Neff & Assocs., Plantation, Fla., 1973—; v.p. Amerifirst Appraisal, Plantation, Fla., 1985-86; mem. Am. Inst. Real Estate Appraisers, Chgo., Soc. Real Estate Appraisers, Chgo. Author: Timbre: the Quest, 1979, U.R.P. Excuse Me!, 1980, Timbre Tarnished Brass, 1989, Drink From My Cup, 1990, Poems and Promises, 1975-92, Beth, 1994, Sundown, 1994, Copper Casino, 1996, Broken Promises, 1996. With U.S. Army 1960-62. Mem. MAI, SRA, RM, SRPA, Appraisal Inst. Methodist. Home and Office: 7420 NW 16th St Plantation FL 33313

NEFF, DIANE IRENE, naval officer; b. Cedar Rapids, Iowa, Apr. 26, 1954; d. Robert Mariner and Adeline Emma (Zach) N. BA in Psychology and Home Econs., U. Iowa, 1976; MA in Sociology, U. Mo., 1978; MEd in Ednl. Leadership, U. West Fla., 1990. Contract compliance officer, dir. EEO, City of Cedar Rapids, 1979-81; commd. ensign USN, 1981, advanced through grades to lt. comdr.; asst. legal officer Naval Comm. Area Master Sta., Guam, 1982-83; comm. security plans and requirements officer Comdr.-in-Chief US Naval Forces in Europe, London, 1983-85; dir. standards and evaluation dept. Recruit Tng. Command, Orlando, Fla., 1985-89; rsch. and analysis officer Naval Res. Officers Tng. Corps Office Chief Naval Edn. and Tng., Pensacola, Fla., 1989-91; tech. tng. officer Recruit Tng. Command, Great Lakes, Ill., 1991-92, mil. tng. officer, 1992-93, dir. apprentice tng., 1993-95; coord. ednl. and tng. programs U. Ctrl. Fla., Orlando, 1995—. Founding mem. Unity of Gulf Breeze, Fla., 1990; performer various benefits for chs., mus., others, Orlando, 1988, 91, 95, 96. Fellow Adminstrn. on Aging, 1977. Unitarian.

NEFF, RAY QUINN, electric power educator, consultant; b. Houston, Apr. 29, 1928; s. Noah Grant and Alma Ray (Smith) N.; m. Elizabeth McDougald, Sept. 4, 1982. Degree in Steam Engring., Houston Vocat. Tech., 1957; BSME, Kennedy Western U., 1986. Various positions Houston Lighting & Power Co., 1945-60, plant supr., 1960-70, plant supt. asst., 1970-80, tech. supr., 1980-85, tng. supr., 1985-87; owner, operator Neff Enterprises, Bedias, Tex., 1987—; tng. supr. Tex. A&M U., 1991—; cons. Houston Industries, 1987-89. Author: Power Plant Operation, 1975, Power Operator Training, 1985, Power Foreman Training, 1986. Judge Internat. Sci. and Engring. Fair, Houston, 1982, Sci. Engring. Fair Houston, 1987. Mem. ASME, Assn. Chief Operating Engrs., Masons. Republican. Methodist. Home: Hwy 90 Rte 2t Box 193-A Bedias TX 77831 Office: Tex A&M U Power Plant College Station TX 77843

NEGRON-GARCIA, ANTONIO S., state supreme court justice; b. Rio Piedras, P.R., Dec. 31, 1940; s. Luis Negron-Fernandez and Rosa M. Garcia-Saldana; m. Gloria Villardefrancos-Vergara, May 26, 1962; 1 son, Antonio Rogelio. B.A., U. P.R., 1962, LL.B., 1964. Bar: P.R. bar 1964. Law aide and lawyer legal div. Water Resources Authority, 1962-64; judge Dist. Ct., 1964-69, Superior Ct., 1969-74; justice P.R. Supreme Ct., San Juan, 1974—; administrating judge, 1969-71; exec. officer Constl. Bd. for Revision Senatorial and Rep. Dists., 1971-72; mem. Jud. Conf., 1974; first exec. sec. Council for Reform of System of Justice in P.R., 1973-74; chmn. Gov.'s Advisory Com. for Jud. Appointments, 1973-74; lectr. U. P.R. Law Sch., 1973-74. Mem. P.R. Bar Assn., Am. Judicature Soc. Roman Catholic.

NEIDICH, GEORGE ARTHUR, lawyer; b. N.Y.C., Feb. 22, 1950; s. Hyman and Rosalyn (Eisenberg) N.; m. Alene Wendrow, Jan. 10, 1982. BA, SUNY, Binghamton, 1971; JD magna cum laude, SUNY, Buffalo, 1974; MLT, Georgetown U., 1981. Bar: N.Y. 1975, D.C. 1979, U.S. Ct. Appeals (2d cir.) 1975, U.S. Dist. Ct. (we. dist.) N.Y. 1975, U.S. Tax Ct. 1976, Conn. 1990. Assoc. Runfola & Birzon, Buffalo, 1973-75, Duke, Holzman, Yaeger, & Radlin, Buffalo, 1975-77; gen. counsel subcom. on capital, investments and bus. opportunity, com. on small bus. U.S. Ho. of Reps., Washington, 1977-79, subcom. on gen. oversight, 1979-80; sr. legal advisor Task Force Product Liability and Accident Compensation, Office of Gen. Counsel, Dept. Commerce, Washington, 1980-81; assoc. Steptoe & Johnson, Washington, 1981-86, of counsel, 1986-89; gen. counsel, sr. v.p. Preferred Health Care, Ltd., Wilton, Conn. (now Value Behavioral Health, Inc.), 1989-93, COO, 1993-95; cons., 1995—; adj. prof. Georgetown U. Law Ctr., 1985-87. Author: Report on Product Liability, 1980. Contbr. articles to profl. jours. Mem. N.Y. State Bar Assn. Home: 9301 Morison Ln Great Falls VA 22066-4153 Office: PO Box 536 Great Falls VA 22066

NEIDIGK, DIANNE, management consultant; b. Monette, Ark., June 28, 1945; d. William Thomas and Thelma Elizabeth (Wells) Wilkerson; m. Lester Dale Neidigk, Feb. 28, 1964; children: Tami Elizabeth, Scott Alan, Lance Dale, Byron Ross. Student, Sam Houston State U., 1963-65, U. Houston, 1969-70. Sub. tchr. Tomball Ind. Sch. Dist., Tex., 1970-74; owner Total Image & Assocs., Houston, 1980—; dir. Colorific, Houston, 1983-85; v.p. L.D. Neidigk Inc., Magnolia, 1978—; dir. pub. relations, corp accounts Travel Depot, Tomball, 1987-88; bd. dirs. The Discovery Fields, 1987; pres. Excel Tng. Dynamics, 1987-94; CEO Am. Inst. Learning and Productivity, 1994—. Author: Scarves: How to Tie One On, 1987, 1987; (newspaper) Total Image, 1984; Total Image, 1986. Mem. ASTD, NAFE, Exec. Women's Network, Assn. Image Cons., Tomball Bus. and Profl. Women, Tomball C. of C., Fedn. Profl. Women, Internat. Platform Assn. (bd. dirs.), PALS of Tex. (bd. dirs. 1996), Houston Women's Bus. Coun. (bd. dirs. 1996), Beta Sigma Phi. Republican. Club: Study (Tomball). Avocations: private pilot; tennis; sewing; reading. Home: 1543 Virgie Magnolia TX 77355 Office: 363 N Sam Houston Pky Houston TX 77060

NEIHEISEL, STEVEN RICHARD, educator; b. Cin., Feb. 10, 1959; s. Vincent John and Mary Jane (Haverkos) N.; m. Margaret Helen DePiore, June 14, 1984; children: Jane, Steven Jr., Emily. BA, Xavier U., 1982, MBA, 1990; PhD, Washington U., 1991. Assoc. prof. St. Mary's U., San Antonio, 1990—. Author: Corporate Strategy and the Policies of Goodwill, 1994. Pres. bd. Downtown Youth Ctr., San Antonio, 1994-96; bd. dirs. Hospice San Antonio, 1995-96; leadership San Antonio Greater C. of C., 1994. Mem. Am. Soc. Pub. Adminstrn. (chpt. pres. 1992—), Tex. City Mgmt. Assn., Internat. City Mgmt. Assn. Roman Catholic. Office: St Mary's U One Camino Santa Maria San Antonio TX 78228

NEILL, RITA J., elementary school educator; b. Lincolnton, N.C., Oct. 20, 1950; d. George William and Mozelle (Boyles) Jarrett; m. Randy William Neill, Nov. 27, 1970; children: Jennifer Neill Huffman, Julie Neill Foster. AB, Lenoir Rhyne Coll., 1972; MA, Gardner Webb, 1987. Presch. tchr. Wayside Elem., Statesville (N.C.)/Iredell County Schs. Mem. ASCD, Assn. Edn. Young Children (treas. Iredell County 1994-96, membership chmn. 1996—), N.C. Assn. Edn. (sec. 1986-88). Home: 308 Wiggins Rd Mooresville NC 28115-9393

NEILL, ROLFE, newspaper executive; b. Mount Airy, N.C., Dec. 4, 1932; s. Kenneth A. and Carmen (Goforth) N.; m. Rosemary Clifford Boney, July 20, 1952 (div.); children: Clifford Randolph, Sabrina Ashley, Dana Catlin, Jessica Rosemary Ingrid, Quentin Roark Robinson; m. Ann Marshall Snider, Sept. 24, 1988. A.B. in History, U. N.C., 1954. Reporter Franklin (N.C.) Press, 1956-57; reporter Charlotte (N.C.) Observer, 1957-58, bus. editor, 1958-61; editor, pub. Coral Gables (Fla.) Times and The Guide, 1961-63, Miami Beach (Fla.) Daily Sun, 1963-65; asst. to pub. N.Y. Daily News, 1965-67, suburban editor, 1967-68, asst. mng. editor, 1968-70; editor Phila. Daily News, 1970-75; v.p., dir. Phila. Newspapers Inc., 1970-75; chmn., pub. Charlotte (N.C.) Observer, 1975—. Served with AUS, 1954-56. Office: Knight Pub Co 600 S Tryon St PO Box 32188 Charlotte NC 28232

NEILSEN, CRAIG H., business executive; b. 1942. Prse. Cactus Pete, Inc., Jackpot, Nev., 1984—, Ameristar Casino Vicksburg, Miss., 1993—. Office: Ameristar Casino Vicksburg 4116 S Washington St Vicksburg MS 39180

NEIMAN, NORMAN, aerospace business and marketing executive; b. Phila., May 23, 1935; s. Harry and Clara (Schuller) N.; m. Sandra Elaine Berk (dec. 1989); children: Nadene Lori Eisaman, Andrea Neiman-Pearce, David Michael; m. Bonnie Gail McCoy, Sept. 5, 1990. BSME, U. Miami, 1957; postgrad., Alexander Hamilton Inst., N.Y.C., 1959; postgrad. real estate law, Brevard C.C., Cocoa, Fla., 1973. Lic. real estate broker, Fla.; lic. fed. firearms dealer. Engr. Sperry Gyroscope Corp., Gt. Neck, N.Y., 1957-59; lead mech. engr. Convair Aerospace Co., Cape Canaveral, Fla., 1959-62; engring. scientist Douglas Aircraft Corp., Cape Canaveral, 1962-65; chief support engr. Grumman Aerospace Corp., Kennedy Space Center, Fla., 1965-73; mgr. Cocoa Beach (Fla.) ops. Grumman Aerospace Corp., 1973-74, mgr. Orlando (Fla.) ops., 1974-79; pres. Neiman and Co., Inc., Orlando, 1980—; pres. Sunshine State Realty, Inc., Cocoa Beach, 1972-76; v.p. Vitality Workshop, Inc., Orlando, 1978-80, Reconnaissance Techs., Arlington, Va., 1985-89; U.S. Govt. sales agt. Calico Light Weapon Systems, 1989-91; dir. program devel. NYMA Inc., Cocoa Beach, 1990—. Patentee waveguide disconnect. Mem. NRA, AIAA, Tech. Mktg. Soc., Range, Missile and Space Pioneers (life), Am. Meteorol. Soc., Am. Numismatic Assn., Air Force Assn., Mensa, Intertel. Republican. Jewish. Office: Neiman and Co Inc PO Box 140094 Orlando FL 32814-0094

NEINER, A(NDREW) JOSEPH, corporate executive; b. Ft. Scott, Kans., Feb. 15, 1950; s. Andrew W. and Celeste H. (Beck) N.; m. Linda M. Koenig, Aug. 21, 1969; children: Carrie L., Christine M., Joseph M., Elizabeth A. BSBA, U. Mo., St. Louis, 1972; MBA, St. Louis U., 1976; postgrad. in advanced mgmt. program, Harvard U., 1990. Fin. analyst Chrysler Corp., Fenton, Mo., 1972-75; fin. mgr. Gen. Cable Corp., St. Louis, 1975-79; contr. Consol. Aluminum Corp., St. Louis, 1979, group contr., 1980-84, corp. contr., 1983-85, dir. corp. planning, 1985-86, v.p., chief fin. officer, 1986-91, dir., 1987; exec. v.p. strategic planning Alusuisse-Lonza Am., 1991-94; exec. v.p. fin. and planning Clarke Am., Inc., San Antonio, 1994—; also bd. dirs.; v.p., CFO Specialty Painting Group Inc., 1995—; conducted fin. workshops Alusuisse Lonza (Holding) Ltd., Interlaken Switzerland, 1985, St. Gallen, Switzerland, 1992, Morschach and Wegis, Switzerland, 1993; instr. St. Louis Jr. Coll., 1978-80, U. Mo., St. Louis, 1977; bd. dirs. Electro Savs. Credit Union, 1988-90, 93-94. Recipient Disting. Leadership award Am. Biog. Inst., 1987-88, Disting. Am., 1987, 90, 91; counseling recognition certs. SBA, 1975, 76. Mem. Am. Mgmt. Assn., Fin. Execs. Inst., Assn. for Corp. Growth (v.p., officer, dir. 1993-94), Strategic Mgmt. Soc., The Planning Forum. Roman Catholic. Home: 23 Inwood Autumn San Antonio TX 78248-1679

NEITZEL, GEORGE PAUL, engineer, educator; b. Atlanta, Nov. 28, 1947; s. George Paul Sr. and Bettymae Irene (Chapman) N.; m. Evelyn Kathleen Heaps; children: Erik Paul, Jason Ward, Michael Brent, Timothy Jacob. BS, Rollins Coll., 1969; MS, Johns Hopkins U., 1974, PhD, 1979. Mathematician, engr. U.S. Army Ballistic Research Lab., Aberdeen Proving Ground, Md., 1969-79; asst. to full prof. engring. Ariz. State U., Tempe, 1979-90; prof. mech. engring. Ga. Inst. Tech., Atlanta, 1990—; cons. Monsanto Corp., St. Peters, Mo., 1984-86, Rockwell Internat., Thousand Oaks, Calif., 1987; vis. prof. U. Karlsruhe, Fed. Republic Germany, 1985-86, Imperial Coll., London, 1986, U. d'Aix-Marseille II, 1995. Contbr. articles to sci. jours. Repcipient Presdl. Young Investigator award NSF, 1984; Alexander Von Humboldt fellow, 1985. Fellow Am. Phys. Soc.; assoc. fellow AIAA; mem. ASME, Sigma Xi. Democrat. Unitarian. Home: 8165 Grogans Ferry Rd Atlanta GA 30350-3107 Office: Ga Inst Tech George Woodruff Sch Mech Engring Atlanta GA 30332-0405

NEITZKE, ERIC KARL, lawyer; b. Mobile, Ala., Dec. 10, 1955; s. Howard and Otti S. Neitzke; m. Geri Fabricatore, Nov. 5, 1983; children: Kyle, Blake, Blaire. BA, U. Fla., 1979, JD, 1982. Bar: Fla. 1982, U.S. Dist. Ct. (mid. dist.) Fla. 1987. Asst. state atty. 7th Jud. Cir., State Atty., Daytona Beach, Fla., 1982; atty. Dunn, Smith & Withers, Daytona Beach, 1982-88, Monaco, Smith, Hood and Perkins, Daytona Beach, 1988—; adj. faculty family law and criminal law Daytona Community Coll. Contbr. articles to profl. jours. Mem. Fla. Acad. Trial Lawyers, Assn. Trial Lawyers Am., Volusia Bar Assn., Fla. Assn. Criminal Def. Lawyers, Phi Beta Kappa. Home: 19 Lost Creek Ln Ormond Beach FL 32174-4840 Office: Eric K Neitzke PA 444 Seabreeze Blvd Ste 900 Daytona Beach FL 32118-3953

NEKRITZ, LEAH KALISH, dean, college administrator; b. N.Y.C., Apr. 6, 1932; d. Jacob Joseph and Anna (Feldman) Kalish; m. Richard Nekritz. BA, Bklyn. Coll., 1953; MLS, Cath. U. Am., 1963. Libr. Prince George's C.C., Largo, Md., 1961-67, dir. libr. svcs., 1967-71, dir. learning resources, 1971-77, assoc. dean for learning resources, 1977-90, dean of learning resources, 1991-95, ret., 1995; mem. adv. com. State Libr. Resource Ctr., Md., 1976; mem. Met. Washington Coun. of Govts. Libr. Coun., 1976-77, 79-81; mem. bd. advisors Libr. System Coop. in Mid Atlantic, Washington, 1985-88; exec. dir. Md. Congress Acad. Libr. Dirs., 1989-90. mem. adv. com. State Libr. Resource Ctr., Md., 1976; mem. libr. coun. Met. Washington Coun. Govts., 1976-77, 79-81; mem. bd. advisors Libr. Sys. Coop. in Mid Atlantic, Washington, 1985-88; exec. dir. Md. Congress Acad. Libr. Dirs., 1989-90; mem. acad. librs. adv. bd. U. Md. CLIS, 1994. Mem. AAUP, ALA (sec. cmty. and jr. coll. sect. 1974), Md. Libr. Assn., Assn. for Ednl. Comm. and Tech. (treas. 1974, chmn. post-secondary guide 1981). Home: 417 N Fairfax St Alexandria VA 22314-2321

NELSEN, MARTIN CLAUDE, management services professional; b. Kankakee, Ill., Nov. 12, 1942; s. Claude Brink and Mildred Pauline (Paraday) N.; m. Darlene Marie Buckardt, Mar. 31, 1962; children: Dawn Therese (dec.), Deena Marie Nelsen Hyatt, Martin Arthur. AS, Waubonsee C.C., Sugar Grove, Ill., 1973; B in Mgmt., Elmhurst Coll., 1983; cert. gen. mgr., Planty Sr. Seminar. Cert. laundry/linen mgr. Nat. Assn. Instnl. Linen Mgmt., advanced devel. program for mgrs. Prodn. control mgr. Lyon Metal Products, Aurora, Ill., 1969-72; plant mgr. Lyon Metal Products, Aurora, 1972-80, dir. mfg., 1980-85; gen. mgr. Marriott Mgmt. Svcs., Opa Locka, Fla., 1985—. Contbr. articles to profl. jours. and in-house news periodicals. Active Mens Rep. Club Boca Raton, Fla., 1986-94. Named Laundry Mgr. of Yr., Nat. Assn. Instl. Linen Mgmt. South Fla. Chpt., 1987, 92, 95. Mem. Am. Soc. ASHES, South Fla. Healthcare Exec. Forum, South Fla. Chpt. Nat. Assn. Instnl. Linen Mgmt. (pres. 3 terms, sec.-treas. 5 terms), Elks, Moose. Lutheran. Office: Marriott/Combined Svcs 2358 NW 151st St Opa Locka FL 33054-2712

NELSON, ALAN REX, editor; b. Arkadelphia, Ark., Sept. 2, 1959; s. Robert and Carolyn (Caskey) N.; m. Melissa Garcia, Oct. 14, 1989; 1 child, Austin Robert. BA in Communications, Ouachita U., 1981. Washington bur. chief Ark. Dem., Washington, 1986-89; communications dir. U.S. Rep. Tommy Robinson, Washington, 1989-91; editor Ark. Bus., Little Rock, 1991-92; polit. editor Ark. Dem.-Gazette, Little Rock, 1992-96; dir. policy and comms. Ark. Gov., Little Rock, 1996—. Author: The Hillary Factor, 1993. Press sec. Petty for Congress, Little Rock, 1984; communications dir. Robinson for Gov., Little Rock, 1990. Mem. Soc. Profl. Journalists (pres. Ark. chpt. 1994-95). Baptist.

NELSON, BARBARA KAY, insurance agent, financial services consultant; b. Dayton, Ohio, May 20, 1947; d. Orville James and Catherine Ann (Pentenburg) Weber; m. Theodore Joseph Nelson II, Nov. 8, 1969 (div. Nov. 1990); children: Theodore Joseph III, Jason Michael. BA, U. Dayton, 1969; MA, Webster U., 1985. CLU. TV co-host Sta. WHIO-TV, Dayton, 1969; dept. mgr. Elder-Beerman, Dayton, 1969-70; customer service rep. Ohio Bell Telephone, Dayton, 1970; adminstrv. coordinator AmeriSource, San Antonio, 1984-86; agt. N.Y. Life Ins., 1986-89; sales mgr. John Hancock Fin. Svcs., 1989-93; dir. tng. San Antonio regional mktg. office Lincoln Nat., 1993-96, long term care specialist, 1995-96, USAA, 1996—; chair bd. San Antonio Women's C. of C. Tex., 1988-91; sec. bd. dirs. Network Power Tex., 1987-90. Mem. exec. bd. Oak Grove Elementary Sch. PTA, San Antonio, 1981-83; mem. San Antonio Life Underwriters, San Antonio C. of C., local govt. com., 1991—; mem. religious edn. com. St. Mark's Ch., San Antonio, 1983-84; mem. North San Antonio Chamber/Pub. Art, 1984-85. Mem. NAFE, Women Life Underwriters Confederation (pres. 1992—). Club: FLW Officers Wives (pres. 1980-81). Avocations: art; jogging; bicycling; racquetball; reading.

NELSON, BERNARD P., publishing executive, writer; b. San Angelo, Tex., Mar. 27, 1936; s. Bernard and Artina (Long) N.; children: Bernie, Kathy. Student, Trinity U., 1956-57. Owner Bernard P. Nelson and Assoc., Ins., San Antonio, Tex., 1968-79, Nelson Agy. Ins., Del Rio, Tex., 1979—, Lightword Pub. Co., Del Rio, 1995—; field investigator trainee Mut. UFO Network, 1994—. Author: Mind Control Wars, 1995. Named Ky. Col., Gov. Martha Layne Collins, 1984, Hon. Tar Heel, State of N.C. Gov.'s Office, 1984, Hon. Lt. Col. Aide-de-Camp, Gov. George C. Wallace, Ala., 1984. Mem. San Antonio Assn. of Life Underwriters, Nat. Assn. of Life Underwriters. Office: Nelson Agy Lightword Pub Co 525 S Main Ste 308 Del Rio TX 78840-5814

NELSON, BILL, state official; b. Miami, Fla., Sept. 29, 1942; s. C.W. and Nannie (Merle) N.; m. Grace H. Cavert, Feb. 19, 1972; children: C. William, Nan Ellen. B.A., Yale U., 1965; J.D., U. Va., 1968. Bar: Fla. 1968. Practice law Melbourne, Fla., 1970-78; mem. Fla. Ho. of Reps., 1972-78, U.S. Congress, 1979-91; astronaut 34th Flight og Space Shuttle, 1986; treas. State of Fla., Tallahassee, 1991—. Served to capt. USAR, 1965-75, with U.S. Army, 1968-70. Office: Office of the Treas PL-11 The Capital Tallahassee FL 32399

NELSON, CHRIS, fisheries company executive. V.p. R&D Bon Secour (Ala.) Fisheries, Inc. Address: 17449 County Rd 49S Bon Secour AL 36511

NELSON, CLARA SINGLETON, aerospace company executive; b. Union Ridge, Tenn., Apr. 10, 1935; d. Ernest Caldwell and Willie Emma (Hord) Singleton; m. Joe Edward Nelson, July 26, 1953; children: Drexel Edward, Dorissia Lynett. Student Tenn. State U., 1961-62, Middle Tenn. State U., 1984; AS, Motlow Coll., 1978; BS in Edn. with highest honors U. Tenn., Knoxville, 1991. Cert. personnel specialist. Sec., adminstrv. asst. Bedford County Sch., Shelbyville, Tenn., 1957-64; sec., personnel asst. Aro, Inc., Arnold Air Force Sta., Tenn., 1964-71; mem. pub. relations staff, job interviewer Employment Security, Shelbyville, 1971-81; mgr. employment EE Calspan Corp., Arnold Air Force Sta., 1981-94; with Micro Craft Tech, 1994-95; employment & recruiting mgr. Sverdrup Tech., 1995—; mem. adv. bd. Tenn. Area Vocat. Sch., Shelbyville, 1979—, Bedford Moore Vocat. Ctr., Shelbyville, 1979—; cons., dir. Career Devel. Workshops, Shelbyville. Chmn. adv. commn. Equal Employment Opportunity, 1983—, chmn. employer com. Tullahoma Job Service, Tenn., 1985—; former mem. Patrons Council Argie Cooper Libr., Shelbyville; Bus. Adv. Group Motlow State Coll., Tullahoma; trustee Motlow Coll. Found.; mem. Shelbyville Regional Planning Commn. Recipient cert. of appreciation ARC, 1985. Mem. Am. Mgmt. Assn., Highland Rim Human Resource Mgmt. Assn. (treas. 1983-84, 87, sec. 1988, 94, chair program com. 1989, 1994—), Nat. Assn. Female Execs. (network dir. 1985, charter), Nat. Mgmt. Assn., Nat. Assn. Bus. and Profl. Women's Clubs, Inc. (chair membership 1991-93), Am. Assn. Affirmative Action, Tenn. State U. Cluster (chmn. com. 1984—), Better Homes and Gardens Shelbyville Club. Methodist. Avocations: reading, gardening. Home: 118 Scotland Hts Shelbyville TN 37160-2912 Office: Sverdrup Tech 877 Ave E Arnold AFB TN 37389-5051

NELSON, CYNTHIA KAYE, training professional; b. Kearney, Nebr., May 8, 1949; d. LeRoy J. and W. Eileen (Schmidt) Wacker; m. James C. Nelson (div. 1987); children: Alexis Ann, Whitney Eileen. BA, U. No. Iowa, 1971; postgrad., No. Ill. U., 1973. Cert. tchr., Ill., Mo. Tchr. Dixon (Ill.) Pub. Schs., 1972-74, Maplewood (Mo.)-Richmond Heights Sch. Dist., 1974-75; counselor Mo. Bus. Men's Clearing House, St. Louis, 1975-76; dir. edn. Deltex Co., Naperville, Ill., 1982-84; trainer Electronic Data Systems Co., LaGrange, Ill., 1985-86; learning technologist Bellcore Tng. and Edn. Ctr., Lisle, Ill., 1988-90; sr. tech. tng. engr. Fujitsu Network Comm., Raleigh, N.C., 1990—. Mem. ASTD, AAUW, Internat. Soc. of Performance and Improvement, Alpha Chi Omega, Beta Sigma Phi. Republican. Lutheran. Office: 4403 Bland Rd Raleigh NC 27609

NELSON, DEBRA JEAN, journalist, public relations executive, consultant; b. Birmingham, Ala., Nov. 12, 1957. BA, U. Ala., Tuscaloosa, 1980. Dir. pub. afffairs Sta. WSGN Radio, Birmingham, 1980-84, news anchor, reporter, 1982-84; dir. community affairs Sta. WBRC-TV, Birmingham, 1984-88, producer, anchor, 1986-88; instr. spl. studies U. Ala., Birmingham, 1988—; dir. media rels. U. Ala. System, Tuscaloosa, 1991-94; adminstr. external affairs Mercedes-Benz U.S. Internat., Inc., Tuscaloosa, 1994—. Pub. affairs prodr./host Sta. WUAL-FM/WQPR, Tuscaloosa, 1991—. Pres.-elect Found. Women's Health in Ala., Inc., 1993—; mem. U.S. libr. lieracy rev. panel Dept. Edn., Washington, 1987-92; mem. Leadership Birmingham, 1991-92; bd. dirs., mem. exec. com. Ala. affiliate Am. Heart Assn., 1986-91; mem. U.S. Mil. Rev. Panel for 6th Congl. Dist., 1987; mem. gen. campaign com. Ala. campaign United Negro Coll. Fund, 1992. Recipient award of distinction Internat. Assn. Bus. Communicators, 1985, Disting. Leadership award United Negro Coll. Fund, 1985, 87, 88, Outstanding Achievement award Delta Sigma Theta, 1986, Outstanding Vol. Svc. award ARC, Birmingham, 1987, Woman of Distinction award Iota Phi Lambda, 1987, Human Rights award So. Christian Leadership Conf. Mem. Assn. Black Women in Higher Edn. (bd. dirs. 1993—, chair com. on pub. rels.), Am.-Japan Soc., Coun. for Advancement and Support of Edn. Home: 1129 Amberley Woods Dr Helena AL 35080 Office: Mercedes-Benz US Int Inc PO Box 100 Tuscaloosa AL 35403

NELSON, EDITH ELLEN, dietitian; b. Vicksburg, Mich., Sept. 26, 1940; d. Edward Kenneth and Anna (McManus) Rolffs; m. Douglas Keith Nelson; children: Daniel Lee, Jennifer Lynn. BS, Mich. State U., 1962; MEd in Applied Nutrition, U. Cin., 1979. Lic. dietitian, Fla. Clin. dietitian Macon (Ga.) Gen. Hosp., Blodgett Meml. Hosp., Grand Rapids, Mich.; grad. teaching asst. U. Cin., 1978-79; dir. nutrition svcs. Dialysis Clinic, Inc., Cin., 1979-88; cons. dietitian Panama City Devel. Ctr., Ft. Walton Beach Devel. Ctr., Fla., 1988-94, N.W. Fla. Community Hosp., Chipley, Fla., 1993-94, Beverly Enterprises, Panama City Beach, 1994—; renal dietitian Dialysis Svcs. Fla., Ft. Walton Beach, 1989-92. Mich. Edn. Assn. scholar, 1958; Nat. Kidney Found. grantee, 1986. Mem. Am. Dietetic Assn., Fla. Dietetic Assn., Panhandle Dist. Dietetic Assn., Nat. Kidney Found. (coun. on renal nutrition, Fla. coun. on renal nutrition), Omicron Nu. Home: 150 Grand Lagoon Shores Dr Panama City FL 32408

NELSON, EDWIN L., federal judge; b. 1940. Student, U. Ala., 1962-63, Samford U., 1965-66; LLB, Samford U., 1969. Mem. firm French & Nelson, Ft. Payne, Ala., 1969-73; pvt. practice Ft. Payne, Ala., 1974—; magistrate U.S. Dist. Ct. (no. dist.) Ala., Birmingham, 1974-90, judge, 1990—. With USN, 1958-62. Mem. Ala. Bar Assn., Birmingham Bar Assn., 11th Cir. Assn. U.S. Magistrates, Nat. Coun. Magistrates, Phi Alpha Delta. Office: US Dist Ct Hugo L Black Courthouse 1729 5th Ave N Fl 7 Birmingham AL 35203-2000

NELSON, FREDERICK HERBERT, lawyer; b. Ft. Bragg, N.C., Sept. 19, 1960; s. Grant H. II Nelson and Sandra J. (Dexter) Bergen. BA magna cum laude, Toccoa Falls (Ga.) Coll., 1989; JD, Stetson U., 1993. Bar: Fla. 1993, U.S. Dist. Ct. (ea. dist.) Wis. 1993, U.S. Ct. Appeals (11th cir.) 1993, U.S. Dist. Ct. (mid. dist.) Fla. 1994, U.S. Ct. Appeals (D.C., 6th, 7th, 9th, 10th cirs.) 1994, U.S. Dist. Ct. (no. and so. dists.) Fla. 1995, U.S. Ct. Appeals (2d, 3d, 4th, 5th, 8th cirs.) 1995. Rsch. asst. Stetson U. Coll. Law, St. Petersburg, Fla., 1992-93; exec. counsel Liberty Counsel, Orlando, Fla., 1993—; pres., gen. counsel Am. Liberties Inst., Orlando, 1994—. Contbg. editor: The International Sale of Goods, 1994; contbr. articles to profl. jours. Bd. dirs. Cmty. Issues Forum, Orlando, 1994—, Ctrl. Fla. CLS, Orlando, 1994—. Mem. ABA (mem. bd. dirs.), ATLA (Fla. bar appellate practice & advocacy sect., Fla. bar fed. appellate practice com.), Phi Delta Phi. Home: 528 Terraceview Cove Altamonte Springs FL 32714 Office: Liberty Counsel 1900 Summit Tower Blvd Ste 560 Orlando FL 32810-5912

NELSON, GEORGE HUMPHRY, biochemist, physician, researcher; b. Charleston, S.C., Nov. 24, 1930; s. Leroy and Rose May (Humphry) N.; m. Harriet Anne McCraw, June 9, 1956; children: Martha Nelson Robinson, Elizabeth Nelson Walpert, Rose Nelson Stephens, Caroline Nelson Werber. AB, Coll. of Charleston, 1951; MS, Med. Coll. S.C., 1953, PhD, 1955; MD, W.Va. U., 1962. Instr. dept. chemistry Tex. Western Coll., El Paso, 1955; USPHS postdoctoral fellow Med. Coll. S.C., Charleston, 1955-56; asst. prof. biochemistry U. S.D., Vermillion, 1956-58; instr. W.Va. U., Morgantown, 1958-62; asst. prof. Med. Coll. Ga., Augusta, 1962-68; intern Talmadge Meml. Hosp., Augusta, Ga., 1962-64; assoc. prof. Med. Coll. Ga., Augusta, 1968-71, assoc. prof. dept. ob.-gyn., 1968-74, prof., 1974-86, prof. emeritus, 1986—; rsch. prof. dept. ob-gyn. U. S.C., Columbia, 1989-95; assoc. chief of staff Talmadge Meml. Hosp., Augusta, 1982-86; chief sect. ob-gyn. labs. Med. Coll. Ga., 1978-86, chmn. faculty, 1980; chief sect. clin. rsch. U. S.C., 1989-95. Editor: Pulmonary Development, 1985; contbr. articles, revs. and abstracts to profl. jours. and chpts. to books. Grantee numerous orgns.; recipient Svc. Recognition award U. Saigon, 1973. Mem. AMA, AAAS, Internat. Soc. Reproductive Medicine, S.C. Med. Assn., Soc. for Gynecologic Investigation, SO. Med. Assn., Elks, Alpha Omega Alpha, Sigma Xi. Unitarian. Home: 1305 15 Mile Landing Rd Awendaw SC 29429-5990

NELSON, GLENDA KAY, special education educator; b. Crosby, Miss., Oct. 11, 1942; d. John and Nellie (McDonald) Jackson; m. Ralph Gordon Nelson, Nov. 26, 1964; children: Karl Christian, Andrew Jon. BS, U. Houston, 1964; MEd, Incarnate Word Coll., San Antonio, 1985. Cert. sch. counselor; lic. profl. counselor. Tchr. history Houston Ind. Sch. Dist., 1964-70; tchr. spl. edn. San Antonio Ind. Sch. Dist., 1985—. Vol. counselor Bexar County Women's Ctr.; coach Spl. Olympics, 1987-92; mem. San Antonio Conservation Soc., 1983—. Mem. AAUW, UDC, Delta Kappa Gamma. Home: 13403 Southwalk San Antonio TX 78232

NELSON, GORDON LEIGH, chemist, educator; b. Palo Alto, Calif., May 27, 1943; s. Nels Folke and Alice Virginia (Fredrickson) N. BS in Chemistry, U. Nev., 1965; MS, Yale U., 1967, PhD, 1970; DSc (hon.), William Carey Coll., 1988. Staff research chemist corp. research and devel. Gen. Electric Co., Schenectady, N.Y., 1970-74; mgr. combustibility tech. plastics div. Gen. Electric Co., Pittsfield, Mass., 1974-79, mgr. environ. protection plastics div., 1979-82; v.p. materials sci. and tech. Springborn Labs. Inc., Enfield, Conn., 1982-83; prof., chmn. dept. polymer sci. U. So. Miss., Hattiesburg, 1983-89; dean Coll. Sci. and Liberal Arts, prof. chemistry Fla. Inst. Tech., Melbourne, 1989—, mem. coun. sci., soc. pres., sec., 1989-90, chair-elect, 1991, chair, 1992; cons. in field. Author: Carbon-13 Nuclear Magnetic Resonance for Organic Chemists, 1972, 2d edit., 1980; co-author: Polymeric Materials--Chemistry for the Future, 1989,Carbon Monxide and Human Lethality, 1993; editor: Fire and Polymers--Hazard Identification and Prevention, 1990; editor: Fire and Polymers II-Materials and Tests for Hazard Prevention, 1995; editor books on coating sci. tech.; contbr. articles to profl. jours. Mem. ASTM (E5 cert. of appreciation 1985), Am. Inst. Chemists (Mems. and Fellows Lectr. award 1989), Soc. Plastics Engrs., Am. Chem. Soc. (pres. 1988, bd. dirs. 1977-85, 87-89, 92-94, Henry Hill award 1986), Info. Tech. Industry coun. (chmn. plastics task group), Ctr. Sci., Tech. and the Media (bd. dirs. 1991-94), So. Soc. for Coatings Tech., Internat. Electrotech. Commn. (U.S. tech. adv. group on info. processing equipment), Soc. of Plastics Industry (structural plastics divsn., Man of Yr. 1979), Coun. Colls. Arts and Scis., Yale Chemists Assn. (pres. 1981—), Nev. Hist. Soc., Sigma Xi. Republican. Presbyterian. Office: Fla Inst Tech Coll Sci & Liberal Arts 150 W University Blvd Melbourne FL 32901-6982

NELSON, JOHN PETER, JR., biology educator; b. Mt. Holly, N.J., Apr. 9, 1955; s. John Peter Sr. and Virginia Margaret (Meissner) N.; m. Elizabeth Ann Jones, Aug. 12, 1978 (div. Aug. 1989); children: Katherine Leigh, Andrew John. BA in Biology, Lycoming Coll., 1977; MS in Biology, U. N.D., 1981; PhD in Biology, U. Memphis, 1996. Lab. technician Upjohn Labs., King of Prussia, Pa., 1977-78; mus. technician Fla. Mus. of Nat. History, Gainesville, Fla., 1982-83; instr. biology Bethel Coll., McKenzie, Tenn., 1990-95; asst. prof. biology Bethel Coll., McKenzie, 1995—; dir., instr. firefighter tng. West Tenn. Emergency Svcs. Edn. Ctr., 1995—. Firefighter McKenzie Fire Dept., 1990—. Mem. AAAS, Soc. for Conservation Biology, Tenn. Acad. of Sci., The Wildlife Soc., Am. Soc. Mammalogists. Office: Biology Dept Bethel Coll Mc Kenzie TN 38201

NELSON, JOSEPH LEE, JR., religion educator; b. Norfolk, Va., Oct. 3, 1923; s. Joseph Lee and Margaret Randolph (East) N.; m. Margaret Angela Miller, June 26, 1948; children: Joseph L. III, John Randolph, Milton Miller, Margaret Angela, Thomas East, David Francis. BS, Hampden-Sydney Coll., 1945, AB summa cum laude, 1947; BD cum laude, Union Theol. Sem., 1950, PhD, 1969; ThM, Harvard U., 1961. Instr. math. Hampden-Sydney (Va.) Coll., 1946-47; asst. prof. history, social sci., assoc. prof. religion Lynchburg (Va.) Coll., 1952-69, prof. religious studies and Greek, 1969-94; chmn. Divsn. Humanities; disting. prof. Humanities John Franklin East; pastor Gilboa & Salem Christian Chs., Louisa County, Va., 1951-53; interim pastor Va., W.Va., N.C., Mass., 1953—. With USMC, 1943-46. Mem. AAUP, Am. Acad. Religion, Soc. Bibl. Lit. Home: 2808 Link Rd Lynchburg VA 24503

NELSON, LAURENCE CLYDE, pastoral psychotherapist; b. Milford, Del., Feb. 5, 1947; s. Leon Clare and Myrtle Wing Nelson; m. Nancy Jane Demory, July, 4, 1986; 1 child, Ryan Brooks. BA in Biol. Rsch., Ottawa (Kans.) U., 1970; MDiv Pastoral Counseling, Cen. Bapt. Theol. Sem., 1972; D Ministry, Eden Theol. Sem., 1979. Lic. prof. counselor, Okla.; lic. marital and family therapist. Min. christian edn. 1st Bapt. Ch., Springfield, Ill., 1972-73; assoc. min. of youth and counseling 1st Bapt. Ch., Columbia, Mo., 1973-76; assoc. min. Webster Groves (Mo.) Presbyn. Ch., 1976-79; pastoral psychotherapist Care and Counseling, St. Louis, 1976-79; dir. Triborough Counseling, Worcester, Mass., 1979-81; dir. dept. counseling Presbyn. Hosp., Oklahoma City, 1981-85; exec. dir. Assocs. in Psychotherapy and Religion, Inc., Edmond, Okla., 1985—; cons. Infant Crisis Ctr., Oklahoma City, 1986-89, Redlands Girls Scouts, 1984-85, Welway Coun., 1989—; crisis intervention counselor and debriefer for Edmond postal killings; mem. critical incident debriefing team for Oklahoma City Fed. bldg. bombing, 1995. Specialized min. Am. Bapt. Chs., 1972—, Christian Ch., 1987—. Fellow Am. Assn. Patroral Counseling (ctrs. and tng.-nominating chair 1986-91); mem. Am. Assn. Christian Counselors (charter), Am. Assn. Marriage and Family Therapists (clin. mem.), Am. Assn. Marriage and Family Therapists (supr.-in-tng.), Lic. Profl Counselors, Okla. Assn. Alcohol and Drug Abuse, Crisis Mgmt. Internat., Inc., Okla. Corvette Club. Home: 1909 Walking Sky Rd Edmond OK 73013-6839 Office: Assocs in Psychotherapy & Religion Inc 2500 S Broadway St Ste 134 Edmond OK 73013-4038

NELSON, LINDA CAROL, corporate chief executive; b. Knoxville, Tenn., Feb. 18, 1954; d. Solon Morris and Dorothy Thelma (Randles) Woods. BA in Polit. Sci. and Psychology magna cum laude, U. Tenn., 1975; BS in Acctg. summa cum laude, Ga. State U., 1978. Cert. of mgmt. acct.; enrolled agt. Pvt. investigator Hanover Security Systems, Knoxville, 1968-74; office mgr. Dale Carnegie Inst., Knoxville, 1969-75; instr. Dale Carnegie course and profl. devel. series Dale Carnegie Inst., Atlanta, 1980-88; legal asst. office of regional atty. H.E.W., Atlanta, 1975; tech. support staff Dist. Conf. U.S. Treasury Dept., Atlanta, 1976, instr., tng. analyst continuing profl. edn., 1976-88, recruiter, 1979-86, team coord. large case exam, 1980-85, resident lead instr. S.E. Region, 1984, fed. racketeering investigator, 1985-86, coord. Joint Com. Taxation in Congress, 1986-87; internal revenue agt., tax technician of exam. div. IRS, Atlanta, 1976-79; consolidations tax dept. staff mgr. Bellsouth, Atlanta, 1984-85; ind. mgmt. cons. Ga., 1980-86; pres., CEO Exec. Svcs. Inc., Atlanta, 1988—; active Speakers' Bur., Atlanta, 1993—. Hospitality com. mem. Atlanta Women's Network, 1990-92; vol. worker Eagles Boy's Ranch, Atlanta, 1986—; River of Life Family Ch.; vol. counselor Atlanta Home for Abused Children, 1980-83; Sunday sch. tchr., choir, nursery, various chs., 1975—; fundraiser Atlanta Symphony Orch., 1985-86; cons. adopt-a-student program, 1985-86; vol. missions program 1st Bapt. Ch., Atlanta, 1986; key person United Way Atlanta Combined Fed. Campaign, 1978-84; calling com. Norcross (Ga.) United Meth. Ch., 1983-84; coord. blood drive ARC, Atlanta, 1984; vol. counselor Helen Ross McNabb Ctr., Knoxville, 1970-72; campaign com. mem. Senator Paul Coverdell. Recipient citation U.S. Sec. Labor Brennan, Superior Instr. award Dale Carnegie, 1988; named one of Outstanding Young Women of Am., 1984. Mem. ASTD (vol. placement com. 1988-92), NAFE, Inst. Mgmt. Accts. (program speaker Atlanta chpt., bd. dirs. 1989), High Mus. Art Young Career Mems. Guild, Young Women of the Arts, Nat. Assn. Enrolled Agts., Nat. Soc. Tax Profls., Profl. Info. Network (mem. spkr.'s bur.), Gwinnett County Leads Network (founder), Women's Life Underwriters' Assn. (program spkr.), Altanta C. of C., Ga. State U. Alumni Assn., U. Tenn. Alumni Assn., Golden Key Nat. Honor Soc., Mortar Bd., U.S. Tennis Assn., Atlanta Lawn Tennis Assn., So. Bicycle League, Sierra Club, Phi Beta Kappa, Beta Alpha Psi, Pi Sigma Alpha, Pi Kappa Phi, Alpha Lambda Delta, Delta Gamma (social chair), Chi Phi Little Sisters (pres.). Home: 6001 Meadowbrook Dr Norcross GA 30093-3729 Office: Exec Svcs Inc PO Box 450822 Atlanta GA 31145-0822

NELSON, LOREN DOUGLAS, surgeon, educator, critical care intensivist; b. Des Moines, Dec. 26, 1947; s. Lester A. and Mildred (Holme) N.; m. Nancy R. St. Clair, June 2, 1984. BS in Biology Edn., U. Iowa, 1970, MD, 1976. Diplomate Am. Bd. Surgery. Rsch. asst. in internal medicine and cardiology U. Iowa, Iowa City, 1971-72, fellow in cardiology, 1973; gen. surgery resident U. Utah, Salt Lake City, 1976-78, rsch. fellow in surgery, 1978-79; asst. prof. surgery and anesthesiology U. Miami, Fla., 1982-87, assoc. prof. surgery, 1987; assoc. prof. surgery Vanderbilt U., Nashville, 1987-89, assoc. prof. surgery and anesthesiology, 1989-95; dir. surg. ICU Vanderbilt U. Hosp., 1987-95, dir. critical fellowship program, 1991-95; dir. surg. crit. care, assoc. dir. med. edn. Orlando (Fla.) Regional Med. Ctr., 1995—; mem. coun. on respiratory care Bd. Med. Examiners, Nashville, 1992-95. N.Am. editor Clin. Intensive Care, 1989-95; mem. editl. bd. Critical Care Medicine, 1991-96; contbg. editor newsletter Critical Care Alerts, 1993-95. With USAR, 1967-73. Named Jr. Faculty Mem. of Yr. surg. chief residents U. Miami, 1987; recipient surg. ICU staff appreciation award Jackson Meml. Hosp., Miami, 1987, Thomas E. Brittingham clin. teaching award Vanderbilt U., 1991. Fellow ACS, Am. Coll. Chest Physicians, Am. Coll. Critical Care Medicine (regent 1989-96); mem. Soc. Critical Care Medicine (sec., pres. S.E. regional chpt. 1992-94, pres.-elect), Am. Assn. for Surgery of Trauma, Internat. Assn. for Trauma and Critical Care. Office: Orlando Regional Med Ctr 1414 Kuhl Ave # 100 Orlando FL 32806-2008

NELSON, MICHAEL JAMES, distribution executive; b. Cin., July 15, 1951; s. Sidney William and Ada Mae (Howard) N.; m. Deborah Maxine Wilbanks, July 19, 1975 (div. 1986); children: Michael, James II, Courtney Elizabeth, Allyson Leigh; m. Linda Lee Funke, Dec. 12, 1987. Student, U. Cin., 1969-71, Wright State U., Dayton, Ohio, 1971-73; grad., Southwestern Grad. Sch. Banking, 1985. V.p. Econs. Corp., Winter Park, Fla., 1976-80, First Nat. Bank Orlando, Winter Park, 1980-86; bus. adminstr. Dick Gephardt for Pres., Washington, 1987-88; pres., chmn. Elec. Motor Svcs., Inc., Orlando, Fla., 1989-93; also bd. dirs. Elec. Motor Svcs., Inc.; chmn., pres. Am. Generator Co., Maitland, Fla., 1993—. Mem. fin. com. Bill Nelson for Gov. campaign, Orlando, 1990; mentor Rollins Coll. Mentor Program, Winter Park, 1985-86; bd. dirs. Fla. Symphony Orch., Orlando, 1984-86; mem. Econ. Devel. Commn. of Mid-Fla., 1991. Recipient Hon. Citizen award Jewish Community Ctr., 1983. Mem. Elec. Apparatus Svc. Assn., Christian C. of C. (founding dir. 1996), Citrus Club of Orlando. Episcopalian. Office: Am Generator Co 240 Circle Dr Maitland FL 32751-6457

NELSON, NORMAN CROOKS, surgeon, academic administrator, educator; b. Hibbing, Minn., July 24, 1929; s. Sander Noble and Lillian Olive (Olsen) N.; m. Annie Lee Pitre, June 25, 1955; children—Norman, Charles, Jennifer. B.S., Tulane U., 1951, M.D., 1954. Diplomate: Am. Bd. Surgery. Intern Charity Hosp. La., New Orleans, 1954-55; resident Charity Hosp. La., 1958-62; USPHS fellow Nat. Inst. Arthritis and Metabolic Diseases, Harvard and Mass. Gen. Hosp., 1962-63; pvt. practice Houston, 1955-56; instr. surgery, Sch. Medicine La. State U., New Orleans, 1963-65; asst. prof., Sch. Medicine La. State U., 1965-68, assoc. prof., Sch. Medicine, 1968-71, prof., assoc. dean Sch. Medicine, 1969-71, dean Sch. Medicine, 1971-73; vice chancellor health affairs, dean Sch. Medicine, prof. surgery U. Miss. Med. Ctr., Jackson, 1973-94, vice chancellor health affairs emeritus, prof. surgery emeritus, 1993-94. Capt. AUS, 1956-58. John and Mary Markle scholar in acad. medicine, 1965-70; recipient Outstanding Alumnus award Tulane U. Sch. Medicine, 1989, laureate Miss. Bus. Hall of Fame, 1995; named to U. Miss. Alumni Hall of Fame, 1994. Fellow ACS, Southeastern Surg. Congress; mem. AAAS, AMA, Assn. Acad. Surgery, Assn. Am. Med. Colls., Central Med. Soc. Miss., Endocrine Soc., James D. Rives Surg. Soc. (founders group), Miss. Acad. Scis., Miss. Med. Assn., Miss. Hosp. Assn. (hon.), New Orleans Surg. Soc., N.Y. Acad. Scis., Soc. Exptl. Biology and Medicine, Soc. Head and Neck Surgeons, Soc. Univ. Surgeons, Am. Surg. Assn., So. Surg. Assn., Soc. Internationale de Chirurge, Surg. Assn. La. (pres. 1973), Allen O. Whipple Surg. Soc., Univ. Club (Jackson), Sigma Xi, Alpha Omega Alpha, Phi Kappa Phi, Omicron Delta Kappa, Omicron Kappa Upsilon (hon.), Alpha Eta Soc. Home: 109 Cardinal Cir Brandon MS 39042-6418

NELSON, RALPH ERWIN, investment company executive, coin dealer; b. Chgo., July 30, 1946; s. Vernon Leslie and Astrid Lorene (Seagren) N.; BS, McPherson Coll., 1971; MBA, U. Sarasota, 1980, MFM, 1981; MHS, U. Sarasota, 1983; PhD, Columbia Pacific U., 1984; m. Elarie Marie Fletcher, Oct. 14, 1967; 1 child, Anne Marie. Chief planning dept. Roberts & Zoller Inc., Bradenton, Fla., 1971-76; v.p., supr. planning div. Dan Zoller Engring. Inc., Bradenton, 1976-78; pres. Ralph Nelson & Assocs., Inc., Landscape Architects, Planners, Architects and Engrs., Bradenton, 1978-88, Nelson Investments, Inc., 1981—. Baptist. Address: PO Box 301 Bradenton Beach FL 34217-0301

NELSON, RICHARD M., lawyer; b. Newark, N.J., July 19, 1961; m. Jackie Orth, Feb. 28, 1996; children: J.C., Erika, Michael, Daniel, Sean. BA, U. Fla., 1983; JD, Nova Law Sch., 1986. Bar: Fla. 1986, U.S. Dist. Ct. (so. dist.) Fla. 1987. Assoc. Bunnel & Woulfe, Fort Lauderdale, Fla., 1986-88, Barnett & Clark, Miami, Fla., 1988-92; ptnr. Clark, Sparkman, Robb, Nelson and Mason, Miami, Fla., 1992-95, mng. ptnr., 1995—. Review editor: Nova Law Review, 1984, editor, 1985, 86. Recipient Goodwin Rsch. fellow Nova Law, 1984, 85, 86. Office: Sparkman Robb & Nelson 19 W Flagler St Ste 1003 Miami FL 33130-4410

NELSON, RUTH NAOMI, marketing professional; b. Beaumont, Calif., Oct. 11, 1948; d. Ashel LeRoy and Hazel J. (Cain) N. BA in Phys. Edn. and Psychology, U. No. Colo., 1970; MS in Phys. Edn., George Williams Coll., 1973; postgrad., Concordia Coll., Montreal, Can., 1978. Head women's volleyball coach, head men's tennis coach, instr. phys. edn. George Williams Coll., Downers Grove, Ill., 1970-72; mem. U.S. Nat. Volleyball Team, 1972, 75; head women's tennis coach U. Houston, 1974-76, head women's volleyball coach, instr. phys. edn., supr. student tchrs., advisor men's volleyball club team, 1974-81; pres., dir. jr. devel. program, camps, clinics, and coaches devel. program Houston Stars Volleyball Club, 1977-81; head women's volleyball coach, advisor to men's volleyball club team, instr. phys. edn., supv. student tchrs. La. State U., Baton Rouge, 1981-85; volleyball dir. Spl. Olympics Internat., Washington, 1985-91, sport mktg. mgr., 1991-92, 94—, sports mktg. dir., 1992-93, corp. mktg. dir., 1993-94; dir. nonprofit and sports mktg. Intellicall, Inc., 1995—; head volleyball coach Dallas Belles women's profl. team Major League Volleyball, Dallas, 1987; head women's vollyball coach, instr. phys. edn., advisor to men's volleyball club team U. Iowa, 1989-91; dir. nonprofit & sports mktg. Intellicall, Inc., Dallas, 1995-96; dir. nonprofit and sports mktg. Global Affinity Group, Dallas, 1996—; coach top 3 Olympic players Flo Hyman, Rita Crockett, Rose Magers, 1974-81; asst. coach U.S. Women's Nat. Volleyball Team, 1977; mem. adv. bd. Volleyball Enterprises, 1978; head coach U.S. World Univ. Games Team, 1979, South and Midwest Sports Festival Teams, 1979, Houston Stars Volleyball AAU Jr. Olympic Team, 1979, U.S. Jr. Nat. Volleyball Team, 1984; volleyball dir. La. Spl. Olympics, 1982, 83, 84, 85, volleyball advisor, 1986, 87, 88; pres. sales, mktg., cons. on weight tng., dir. for players' and coaches' clinics Baton Rouge Volleyball Club, 1981—; pres. not-for-profit La. Volleyball Club, 1986—; tech. expert U.S. Women's Nat. Team, 1983; volleyball rules chairperson Spl. Olympics Internat., 1984-91, volleyball dir., 1985-91, dir. model chpt. programs, 1989, volleyball advisor, 1991-94; cons. sales and mktg. for splty. advt. and promotional programs Acadian Advt., 1985-89, cons. mktg., promotion and sales, 1989—; cons. advanced jump tng. and rehab. Plyometric Inc., 1989-90; instr. volleyball for coaches cert. U.S. Volleyball Assn., 1990-91; volleyball color analyst Iowa Pub. TV, Des Moines, 1985, 86, 87, 88; dir. placement U.S. men's and women's profl. volleyball players in Europe Internat. Players Promotion, Mulhouse, France, 1989; cons. disability players in France and Switzerland Inst. Internat. Sports, Kingston, R.I.; head coach jrs. Springfield Jr. Volleyball Club, 1989; mem. adv. bd. Women's Sports Found., 1992-95; dir. Hawkeye Challenge Jr. Volleyball Clinic, U. Iowa, 1990, U. Iowa Overnight Camp, 1991; bd. dirs. Wallyball, Inc., 1992—; numerous others; presenter in field; cons. in field. Contbr. articles to profl. publs. Sponsor West Germany vs. Houston Stars, 1978; co-sponsor Volleyball Enterprises-Japan vs. U.S. Women's Olympic Team, 1979, USA vs. Japan Olympic Team, 1982, Aspri Sports-USA vs. Korean Olympic Team, 1983, Audubon Ford-USA vs. Japan Olympic Team, 1984, United Cos., Piccadilly and Episcopal H.S., Pelican State Games, 1985-86; cons. Iowa Spl. Olympics Tng. Sch., 1989-91. Recipient Tachikara Victory Club award for 500 wins, 1985, U.S.A. Volleyball Meritorious Svc. award Spl. Olympics Internat. Volleyball, 1994; named one of Outstanding Young Women of Am., 1980, 84; named Outstanding Prof., U. Houston, 1981. Mem. AAHPERD, AAUP, USTA, Nat. Assn. Phys. Edn. Coll. Women, Assn. Intercollegiate Athletics for Women (nat. volleyball chair 1979-80), U.S. Volleyball Assn. Delta Region (jr. volleyball devel. dir. 1986), Collegiate Volleyball Coaches Assn. (nat. seedling com. 1981-84), Am. Volleyball Coaches Assn. (profl. mem.), Am. Mktg. Assn. (profl. mem.), So. Assn. Phys. Edn. Coll. Women, Women's Sports Found. (mem. adv. bd. 1991—), La. Volleyball Coaches Assn. (co-founder, bd. dirs. 1983-87), Tex. Assn. Intercollegiate Athletics for Women (mem. sending com., Tex. state volleyball sports dir. 1979-80), S.W. Assn. Intercollegiate Athletics for Women (mem. regional sending com., mem. region 4 volleyball rep. 1978-80), Assn. Intercollegiate Athletics for Women (nat. volleyball chairperson 1979-80), Tex. Assn. for Health, Phys. Edn. and Recreation, La. Volleyball Club (pres. 1985—), Baton Rouge Volleyball Club, 1981—. Home: PO Box 829 Merrifield VA 22116-2829

NELSON, SCOTT RUSSELL, osteopath; b. Luverne, Minn., Jan. 28, 1954; s. John Eugene and Phyllis Adeline (Bauer) N.; m. Donna Marie McGorty, June 2, 1979; children: Jennifer Elizabeth, Melissa Rachael, Shawn Michael Thomas, Erik Daniel Thomas, Breanna Ariel Nelson. BS magna cum laude, Tex. A&M U., 1978; DO, North Tex. State U., 1982. Cert. advanced cardiac/trauma life support. Intern Dallas-Ft. Worth Med. Ctr., 1983; osteo. physician, dir. Theodosia (Mo.) Med. Clinic, 1983-84; emergency osteo. physician Ozarks Med. Ctr., West Plains, Mo., 1984—, cons. osteo. physician, 1986—; dir. osteo. biomechanical evaluation and treatment service Ozarks Med. Ctr., West Plains, 1987; staff osteo. physician Baxter County Regional Hosp., Mountain Home, Ark., 1984-87; emergency physician Amarillo Emergency Receiving Ctr. N.W. Tex. Hosp., Amarillo, Tex., 1987—; assoc. clin. prof. dept. surgery and internal medicine Tex. Tech. U. Health Scis. Ctr. Sch. Medicine; staff physician Seton Med. Ctr., Austin, Tex., 1991—, Bapt. Meml. Hosp. System, San Antonio, 1991-92; mng. ptnr. Amarillo Emergency Physicians. Deacon Emmanuel Ch., Mountain Home, 1986. Fellow Am. Coll. Emergency Physicians; mem. Beta Beta Beta, Phi Kappa Phi, Sigma Sigma Phi. Republican. Office: NW Tex Hosp Amarillo Emergency Receiving Ctr 1501 Coulter Dr Amarillo TX 79106-1770

NELSON, STUART JAMES, internist, health facility administrator; b. Santa Monica, Calif., Apr. 25, 1947; s. Clair Edmund and Ruth (Gibson) N.; m. Linda K. F. Mui, June 18, 1978; children: Victoria, Mark, Elizabeth. AB in Math., U. Calif., Berkeley, 1970; MD, SUNY, Bklyn., 1975. Diplomate Nat. Bd. Med. Examiners, Am. Bd. Internal Medicine. Intern Phila. Gen. Hosp., 1975-76; resident Met. Hosp., N.Y.C., 1976-78; instr. medicine SUNY, Stony Brook, 1978-82, asst. prof. clin. medicine, 1982-86, clin. assoc. prof. medicine, preventive medicine, 1986-91; assoc. prof. medicine Med. Coll. Ga., Augusta, 1991-96; head med. subject headings Nat. Libr. Medicine, Bethesda, Md., 1996—; assoc. head divsn. gen. internal medicine SUNY, Stony Brook, 1985-90; reviewer for profl. jours. Contbr. articles to profl. jours. Fellow Am. Coll. Physicians; mem. AAAS, Am. Med. Informatics Assn., Soc. Gen. Internal Medicine, Med. Libr. Assn. Presbyterian. Office: Nat Libr Medicine Bldg 38A Rm B 2 E17 Bethesda MD 20894

NELSON, SUSAN BRANON, coordinator comprehensive system personnel development; b. Milan, Tenn., Sept. 3, 1946; d. Howard Brooks and Mary Louise (Black) Branon; divorced; 1 child, Eric Dean. BS in Elem. Edn., Lambuth U., 1968; MA in Spl. Edn., Memphis State U., 1974; postgrad., Nat. Coll. of Edn., 1977-80, U. Louisville, 1982, Old Dominion U., 1985, Coll. William and Mary, 1987. Elem. edn. tchr. Orlando, Fla., 1968-70; tchr. learning disabilities Memphis City Sch. System, 1970-74; resource and learning disabilities tchr. Am. Dependent Schs., Fed. Republic Germany, 1974-77; team leader learning disability North Suburban Spl. Edn. Dist., 1977-80; elem. and high sch. tchr. learning disabilities Ft. Knox Ind. Sch. System, 1981-83; learning disabilities developer Norge Elem. Sch., Williamsburg, Va., 1984; learning disability resource and itinerant tchr. Williamsburg James City County Schs., 1984-86; learning disabilities resource tchr., ednl. diagnostician Matthew Whaley Elem. Sch., 1984-87; area supr. spl. edn. sect. Ark. Dept. Edn., Little Rock, 1988-94, coord. comprehensive sys. personnel devel. spl. edn., 1994—; asst. in planning state and nat. confs. and insvc. workshops; asst. in developing state program for indirect svc. model; coop. cons. for spl. edn. dept.; program chmn. State Edn. Conf., 1992, 94; state arranger for Nat. Assn. State Dirs. of Spl. Edn. ann. meeting, 1993, asst. to developing program ann. meeting, 1995; presenter Nat. Paraprofessions Conf., Snowbird, Utah, 1996. Vol. adv. Ft. Monroe's Family Mem. of the Handicapped; v.p. United Cerebral Palsy Aux., pres.; bd. dirs. Indian Hill Condo Assn.; mem. edn. com. Sunday sch. class. Mem. CEC (symposium presenter 1990, 96, sec. divsn. for learning disability Va. chpt.). Home: 1917 Dakota St North Little Rock AR 72116-4481 Office: Ark Dept Spl Edn 4 State Capitol Little Rock AR 72201-1011

NELSON, TOZA, elementary school educator; b. Beaumont, Tex., Feb. 25, 1948; d. Silas Bailey and Mary Eula (Prudhomme) Estes; m. Don W. Nelson, Oct. 26, 1974; 1 child, Bryan Alan Jones. BS, West Tex. State U., 1972; MEd, Tex. Tech U., 1975. Cert. elem. tchr., reading specialist, supr., Tex. Elem. tchr. Lubbock (Tex.) Ind. Sch. Dist., 1972-78, elem. demonstration tchr., 1978-83, coord. elem. reading and lang. arts., 1983-93, elem. prin., 1993—; mem. staff devel. adv. team Lubbock Ind. Sch. Dist. Mem. Tex. Assn. for Improvement Reading (state treas., area v.p.), Internat. Reading Assn. (Caprock coun.), Coalition of Reading and English Suprs. Tex., Lubbock Elem. Prins. and Suprs. Assn., Alpha Chi, Kappa Delta Pi, Delta Kappa Gamma, Phi Delta Kappa. Office: Lubbock Ind Sch Dist Maedgen Elem 4401 Nashville Ave Lubbock TX 79413-3313

NELSON, WARREN LOUIS, newspaper editor, writer; b. Abington, Pa., Dec. 29, 1940; s. Harry Lloyd and Gertrude Linda (Zaun) N.; m. Susan Keeny Eberly, July 1, 1972. BA, Fla. State U., 1962. MA in Internat. Rels., Am. U., Washington, 1967. Pentagon corr. UPI, 1969-75; sr. aide Rep. Les Aspin, 1975-90; staff dir. investigations subcom. House Armed Svcs., 1990-95; ind. writer, 1996—. editor Iran Times Internat. weekly newspaper, 1973—. Democrat. Home and Office: 1609 N Fillmore St Arlington VA 22201-3947

NELSON, WESLEY JOSEPH, librarian; b. Beloit, Wis., Aug. 13, 1935; s. Joseph Oliver and Grace Helen (Wheeler) N.; m. Jeannette Clara Conrad, Aug. 29, 1959 (div. June 1966); children: Deborah Ruth, Eugene Joseph; m. Annita Marie Palmer, Nov. 28, 1968; 1 child, Michael Lee. BA, Beloit Coll., 1957; ThM, So. Meth. U., 1962; MLS, George Peabody Coll. Tchrs., Nashville, 1967. Pastor United Meth. Ch., Johnson Creek, Wis., 1962-63, Monona, Wis., 1963-66; catalog librn. Joint Univ. Librs., Nashville, 1966-70; assoc. librn. tech. svcs. Stanley Libr. Ferrum (Va.) Coll., 1970—. Bd. dirs. Franklin County United Way, Franklin County Red Cross; 1st lt. Ferrum Rescue Squad, 1987—; sec., treas. Ferrum Vol. Fire Dept., 1977—. Recipient Cooper Cmty. Svc. award Franklin County C. of C., 1989. Mem. Lions (pres., sec., treas. 1970—, Melvin Jones award 1994). Home: Rte 3 Box 25D Ferrum VA 24088 Office: Ferrum Coll Stanley Libr Ferrum VA 24088

NELSON, WILLIAM, state insurance commissioner. Commissioner Dept. Ins. State of Fla., Tallahassee. Office: State of Fla Dept Ins State Capital Pla Level 11 Tallahassee FL 32399

NELSON, WILLIAM HOYT, accountant; b. Texas City, Tex., June 3, 1966; s. Robert William and Elizabeth Kathryn (Hanson) N.; m. Carol Lynn Hansen, June 25, 1988; children: Emily Elizabeth, Robert William. BS in Acctg., U. Houston, 1988. CPA, Tex. Acct., CPA Shelby, Rucksdashel &

Jones CPA, Houston, 1988-91; CPA Coopers & Lybrand, Houston, 1991-93; CPA, asst. controller TEAM, Inc., Alvin, Tex., 1993—. City councilman Alvin City Coun., 1994—. Mem. AICPA, Tex. Soc. CPAs, Houston Chpt. CPAs, Rotary Club Alvin (dir. cmty. svc. 1995—, dir. club svc. 1996—). Roman Catholic. Office: City of Alvin 216 W Sealy St Alvin TX 77511-2341

NELSON, WILLIAM NEAL, academic librarian, Latin American culture specialist; b. Bastrop, La., Dec. 26, 1941; s. Noble William and Nova Helen (Jenkins) N.; m. Julia Elizabeth Carden, Jan. 28, 1968; children: Beth Ann, Christopher William. BA in English, Centenary Coll., Shreveport, La., 1963, BA in History, 1964; MA, La. State U.-Baton Rouge, 1973, MLS, 1974, PhD, 1981. Vol., U.S. Peace Corps, Brazil, 1964-66; library dir. Mobile Coll. (Ala.), 1974-82; library dir. Carson-Newman Coll., Jefferson City, Tenn., 1982-85; Univ. librarian Samford U., Birmingham, Ala., 1985-93; curator Ala. Bapt. Hist. Collection, 1985-93; dir. Inst. Genealogy and Hist. Research, 1985-93; libr. dir. Augusta State U., 1993—; curator Richmond County Hist. Soc., 1994—. Author: Status and Prestige as a Factor in Brazilian Foreign Policy 1905-1908, 1981; editor: Faculty Status for Librarians, Trends and Issues, 1989; contbr. articles to profl. jours. Deacon, So. Baptist Conv., 1973; eagle scout, 1958. Served to lt. U.S. Navy, 1966-71; capt. USNR, 1989, commdg. officer, 1992-94. Recipient Robertson/Farmer scholarship So. Bapt. Conv., 1978. Mem. ALA, Southeastern Library Assn., Tenn. Library Assn. (speaker 1984), Ala. Library Assn. (chmn. CUS div. 1990, 2d v.p. 1991), Ga. Libr. Assn., Conf. Latin Am. History, South Eastern Council on Latin Am. Studies, Ctrl. Savannah River Area Libr. Assn. (v.p. 1994-95, pres. 1995-96, 96-97), Fellowship Christian Librs. and Info. Specialists (mem. nat. bd. 1994—), Phi Alpha Theta, Beta Phi Mu (pres. Ala. ch. 1989, treas. 1991-93). Office: Augusta Coll Reese Libr 2500 Walton Way Augusta GA 30904-2200

NELSON-COLLINS, ELLA M., foundation administrator, consultant; b. Carthage, Tex., Aug. 25, 1950; d. Anthony and Nellie (Delaney) Collins; divorced; children: Makeba Collins, Brittany Collins. BSc, Tex. Coll., 1971; postgrad., U. Houston, 1978-80, Tex. Women U., 1989. Tchr. biology, earth and life sci. Lamar Fleming Jr. High Sch. Houston Ind. Sch. Dist., 1975-86, coord. sci. dept., 1975-86; drug edn. specialist Tarrant Coun. Alcoholism and Drug Abuse, Ft. Worth, 1987-89; drug coord. Ft. Worth Housing Authority, 1987-91; regional coord. Texans' War Drugs, Ft. Worth, 1991-93; pres./CEO Neighborhoods Organized Substance Abuse Prevention, Inc., Ft. Worth, 1993—; coach girl's basketball Lamar Fleming Jr. High Sch., Houston Ind. Sch. Dist., 1975-86. Pres. Matilda Tolbert Perkins Delaney Found.; mem. North Tex. inter-alumni coun. United Negro Coll. Fund; mem. citizen's crime commn. Tarrant County Gangs Task Force. Recipient Valuable Svc. to Assn. award Houston Tex. Coll. Alumni Assn., 1986, Human Svcs. award Phi Beta Sigma, 1989, Region VI Housing and Urban Devel. award, 1990, Gov.'s award Gov. Bill Clements, 1990, Leadership award United Negro Coll. Fund, 1992, U.S. HUD award, 1992. Mem. NAFE, Tex. Coll. Alumni (pres.), Ft. Worth Lions Club, Zeta Phi Beta (pres.). Home: 1524 Hollowbrook Ct Fort Worth TX 76103-1735

NEMEC, MICHAEL LEE, lawyer; b. Tulsa, Aug. 1, 1949; s. Milton L. and Betty D. (Lawrence) N.; m. Vivian Strobel, Dec. 26, 1970; children: Adam, Jennifer, David. BA in Polit. Sci., U. Tulsa, 1971, JD, 1976. Bar: Okla. 1976. Pvt. practice law Tulsa, 1976-78; dir. deferred giving Okla. State U. Found., Stillwater, 1978-80; asst. v.p., trust officer Bank Okla. N.A., Tulsa, 1980; v.p., trust officer Bank Commerce & Trust Co., Tulsa, 1980-85; pvt. practice law Tulsa, 1985-89; assoc. Hall, Estill, Hardwick, Gable, Golden & Nelson P.C., Tulsa, 1989-93, shareholder, 1993—. Mem. fin. com. Monte Cassino Sch., Inc., Tulsa, 1987; vol. Boy Scouts Am., Tulsa, 1984-86; participant U.S. Naval Acad. Fgn. Affairs Conf., 1971. Named Family of Yr., LDS Ch., Tulsa, 1985. Mem. ABA, Okla. Bar Assn., Tulsa County Bar Assn. (sec. tax sect. 1988), Tulsa Title and Probate Lawyers, Tulsa Estate Planning Forum, Tulsa Tax Forum (pres. 1994, 95), Thomas Gilcrease Mus. Assn., Nature Conservancy. Roman Catholic. Office: Hall Estill Hardwick Et Al 320 S Boston Ste 400 Tulsa OK 74103

NEMETH, BONNIE KEITH, dance educator, choreographer, writer, publisher; b. Springfield, Ill., Dec. 31, 1949; d. Byron Keith Croxton and Eva Darlene (Ridings) Christian; m. Ludwig Wolfgang Nemeth, Apr. 19, 1969; children: Matthew, Elisabeth, Lucas, Mischa. BFA, U. Ill., 1973. Cert. tchr., Ill. Co-owner, co-founder Sunshine Imports, 1972-77; dir., owner, tchr. Woodbury (Tenn.) Dance Studio, 1987—; artistic dir. Children's Dance Co., Woodbury, Tenn., 1989—; dir., owner, tchr. Smithville (Tenn.) Dance Studio, 1989—; CEO, founder Dance Innovators Pub. Co., Auburntown, Tenn., 1995—; cons., instr. Dry Creek Cmty. Sch., Dowelltown, Tenn., 1977-80. Author: Timeless Tap series, 1994; choreographer: over 50 modern dances for children and young adults, 1989-95, over 100 ballet dances for children and young adults, 1989-95, over 100 tap dances for children and adults, 1993-95. Mem. Profl. Dance Tchrs. Assn., Tenn. Assn. Dance, Internat. Tap Assn. Home: 20106 Hwy 96 Auburntown TN 37016

NEPOMUCENO, CECIL SANTOS, physician; b. The Philippines, Feb. 1, 1936; came to U.S. 1967; s. Dominador and Augustina (Santos) N.; m. Edna Manacsa, Dec. 4, 1963; children: Joy, Regina, Celeste. MD, U. Santo Tomas, Manila, The Philippines, 1962. Diplomate Am. Bd. Physical Medicine and Rehab. Intern St. Francis Hosp., Wichita, Kans., 1963; resident Baylor U. Med. Ctr., Dallas, 1967-70; med. dir. orthopedic svcs. Lakeshore Rehab. Hosp., Birmingham, Ala., 1994—; cons. Social Security Adminstrn.; oral bd. examiner Am. Acad. Physical Medicine and Rehab. Lt. col. USAMR, 1982—. Mem. So. Soc. Phys. Medicine and Rehab. (past pres.), Ala. Soc. Phys. Medicine and Rehab. (past pres.), Am. Acad. Preventive Medicine and Rehab., Am. Assn. Electrodiagnostic Medicine, Ala. Med. Assn., Nat. Assn. Disability Evaluating Profls. Catholic. Home: 1070 Country Club Cir Birmingham AL 35244-1478 Office: Lakeshore Hosp. 3800 Ridgeway Dr Birmingham AL 35209-5506

NERO, SHIRLEY MAE, real estate executive; b. Marietta, Ga., Apr. 26, 1936; d. Harvey Herbert and Ruby Lois (Waldrop) Dooley; m. Buford Sammy Freeze, May 10, 1954 (dec. Feb. 1973); children: Peggy Eisenhauer, Michael Freeze, Melodie Freeze Hudson, Jeffery Freeze; m. Curt Turner Clark, Nov. 3, 1973 (div. Apr. 1984); m. Robert J. Nero, Apr. 2, 1988. Student, Sch. Mortgage Banking, Chgo., 1965-66. Lic. real estate broker, Ga.; cert. gen. real estate appraiser, real estate agt., Fla. Bookkeeper, payroll clk. Marietta Hosiery Co., 1954-61; bookkeeper, mortgage loan servicing adminstr. The McNeal Cos., Smyrna, Ga., 1961-68; bookkeeper, office mgr. Pulte Homes of Ga. Corp., Marietta, 1968-71, Personality Homes, Inc., Smyrna, 1971-77; real estate agt. Jack W. Boone & Co., Smyrna, 1978-79; bookkeeper Devin Mgmt. Co., College Park, Ga., 1979-80; co-owner, corp. treas. Tube Analysis, Inc., Mableton, Ga., 1979-84; owner, mgr. S.C. Properties, Lithia Springs, Ga., 1984-86; ptnr., appraiser Clark & Assocs., Acworth, Ga., 1986-88; appraiser W.H. Benson & Co., Melbourne, Fla., 1988—. Pres. Parents Without Ptnrs., Douglasville, Ga., 1985-86, treas. Peach St. Regional Council, 1987, conf. chmn. 1987. Named Mem. of Yr., Douglas County Parents Without Ptnrs., 1986. Mem. Appraisal Inst. Home: 2237 Granville St NE Melbourne FL 32907-2608 Office: WH Benson & Co 4031 Dixie Hwy Melbourne FL 32905

NESBIT, PHYLLIS SCHNEIDER, judge; b. Newkirk, Okla., Sept. 21, 1919; d. Vernon Lee and Irma Mae (Biddle) Schneider; m. Peter Nicholas Nesbit, Sept. 14, 1939. BS in Chemistry, U. Ala., 1948, BS in Law, 1958, JD, 1969. Bar: Ala. 1958. Ptnr. Wilters, Brantley and Nesbit, Robertsdale, Ala., 1958-74; pvt. practice, Robertsdale, 1974-76; dist. judge Baldwin County Juvenile Ct., 1977-88; supernumerary dist. judge and juvenile ct. judge Baldwin County, 1989—. Bd. dirs. Baldwin Youth Services; bd. dirs., v.p. women's activities So. Ala. chpt. Nat. Safety Council, 1978-83; chmn. quality assurance com. The Homestead Retirement Vill., 1992-95. Mem. Nat. Assn. Women Lawyers, Nat. Assn. Women Judges, N.Am. Judges Assn., Ala. Dist. Judges Assn., Ala. Council Juvenile Judges, Am. Judicature Soc., Baldwin County Bar Assn., Baldwin Sr. Travelers (sec. 1994—), Spanish Fort, Fairhope Bus. and Profl. Women's, Phi Alpha Delta. Democrat. Methodist.

NESBITT, DEETTE DUPREE, small business owner, investor; b. Houston, May 5, 1941; d. Raymond Benjamin DuPree and Alice Lula (Cade) Foster; children: Alice L., Charles S. Massey Nesbitt; m. Ernest V. Nesbitt, Aug. 20, 1971. Student, Sam Houston State U., 1960-61, U. Houston, 1961-62, 81-83. Lic. real estate, Tex. Co-owner K & N Perforators, Inc., Houston. Contbr. articles to various publs. Former bd. trustees Pace Soc. Am., Inc., Ladies Oriental Shrine N.Am., Inc.; bd. dirs. Evergreen Friends, Inc., 1991—; dir., sec. competitive swim team Dad's Club YMCA, Houston, 1981-83; vol. adminstrv. asst. numerous orgns., Houston. Recipient Varina Howell Davis medal Mil. Order Stars and Bars, 1992, Silver Good Citizenship medal SAR, 1992, Honor award Tex. Sons of Confederate Veterans, 1992; featured on Eyes of Texas, NBC, 1992. Mem. Nat. Soc. DAR, Huguenot Soc., S.C. Soc. Descendants of the Colonial Clergy, Nat. Soc. Magna Charta Dames (historian Houston Colony 1992-95), Plantagenet Soc., Col. Order of the Crown, The Sovereign Colonial Soc. Am. Royal Descent, Nat. Jamestown Soc. (mem. coun. 1993-95, auditor gen. 1995—), First Tex. Co. Jamestowne Soc. (lt. gov., gov. 1985-93, hon. gov. life), Soc. First Families of Ga. 1733-1797 (v.p. gen. Tex. State Soc. 1987—), Soc. First Families of S.C. 1670-1700 (life), Order of First Families of Va. 1607-1624/5 (life), Order of First Families of Miss. 1699-1817 (life), Daus. Rep. Tex. (Tex. Star chpt., Appreciation award 1996), Colonial Dames Am. (pres. chpt. VIII 1995—), United Daus. Confederacy (Jefferson Davis chpt., Confederate Ball com. 1985-95, co-chmn. ball 1988, advisor to chmn. 1989, 90, Jefferson Davis Hist. award, Winnie Davis medal, Spl. Recognition award, honorary chmn. Houston's Confederate Ball 1995), Sons and Daus. of Pilgrims (mem. nat. com. 1993-97), Freedoms Found. Valley Forge (George Washington Honor medal 1994), Harris County Hist. Commn., Petroleum Club Houston, Galveston Yacht Club. Republican. Episcopalian. Home: 15411 Old Stone Trl Houston TX 77079-4206

NESBITT, FRANK WILBUR, lawyer; b. Miami, Okla., Dec. 26, 1916; s. Frank Wilbur and Nelle M. (Grayson) N.; m. Delores M. Shaw, 1950 (div. 1978); children: Kathleen Marie Smith; m. Mary Louise Turner Gardner, Aug. 22, 1982. AB, Okla. U., 1937; JD, U. Tex., 1939. Bar: Tex. 1939, U.S. Dist. Ct. (so. dist.) Tex. 1939, U.S. Ct. Appeals (5th cir.). Sole practice, Corpus Christi, Tex., 1939-41; asst. city atty. Corpus Christi, 1941-42; ptnr. King & Nesbitt, Corpus Christi, 1946-54, Wood & Burney (name now Wood, Burney, Cohn & Viles), Corpus Christi, 1954—. Capt. AUS, 1942-46. Mem. ABA, State Bar Tex., Nueces County Bar Assn., Am. Coll. Trial Lawyers, Tex. Bar Found. Democrat. Presbyterian. Office: Wood & Burney Cohn & Viles 1100 Frost Bank Bldg 802 S Carancahua St Corpus Christi TX 78401-3465

NESBITT, JIMMIE A., elementary school educator; b. Scott City, Kans., July 2, 1942; s. Fletcher and Estelle N.; m. Beatrice, Nov. 15, 1980; children: Stephanie, Michelle. BA in English, Fort Hays State U., 1992; MS in Edn., Baylor U., 1994. Contract compliance analyst Panhandle Eastern Corp., Liberal, Kans., 1967-72; contract analyst, supr. Coastal Corp., Houston, 1973-80; contract adminstr. Occidental Petroleum Corp., Tulsa, 1984-85; home sch. tchr. Nesbitt Children's Home Sch., Waco, Tex., 1993-94; pvt. fin. cons. Waco, 1993-94; divsn. sales rep. Electrolux Corp., Longview, Tex., 1996—. Bd. dirs. City of Garden City, Kans., 1988-89. With Kans. Army Nat. Guard, 1965-72. Mem. Nat. Coun. Tchrs. English, Am. Vocat. Assn., Fort Hays State U. Alumni Assn., Baylor U. Alumni Assn. Home: 103 W Hughes St Daingerfield TX 75638-1317

NESBITT, LENORE CARRERO, federal judge; m. Joseph Nesbitt; 2 children: Sarah, Thomas. A.A., Stephens Coll., 1952; BS, Northwestern U., 1954; student U. Fla. Law Sch., 1954-55; LLB, U. Miami, 1957. Rsch. asst. Dist. Ct. Appeal, 1957-59, Dade County Cir. Ct., 1963-65; pvt. practice Nesbitt & Nesbitt, 1960-63; spl. asst. attorney gen., 1961-63; with Law Offices of John Robert Terry, 1969-73; counsel, Fla. State Bd. Med. Examiners, 1970-71; with Petersen, McGowan & Feder, 1973-75; judge Fla. Cir. Ct., 1975-82, U.S. Dist. Ct. (so. dist.) Fla., Miami, 1983—. Bd. trustees U. Miami; bd. dirs. Miami Children's Hosp. Mem. FBA, Fla. Bar Assn., U.S. Jud. Conf. Com. on Criminal Law and Probation Adminstrn. Office: US Dist Ct 301 N Miami Ave Miami FL 33128-7702

NESBITT, ROBERT EDWARD LEE, JR., physician, educator, scientific researcher; b. Albany, Ga., Aug. 21, 1924; s. Robert E.L. and Anne Louise (Hill) N.; m. Ellen Therese Morrissey. B.A., Vanderbilt U., 1944, M.D., 1947. Diplomate: Am. Bd. Ob-Gyn (asso. examiner). Asst. prof. Johns Hopkins U., 1954-56, chief obstetric pathology lab., acting chief obstetrics, 1955-56; prof., chmn. dept. ob-gyn Albany (N.Y.) Med. Coll., Union U., 1956-61; prof., chmn. dept. ob-gyn SUNY Health Sci. Ctr., Syracuse, 1961-81, dir. gen. gynecology service, 1982-84, prof. and chmn. emeritus dept. ob-gyn; obstetrician-gynecologist-in-chief Albany Hosp., 1956-61; obstetrician, gynecologist-in-chief Syracuse Meml. Hosp., 1961-65; obstetrician-gynecologist-in-chief Crouse-Irving Hosp., 1963-70, attending staff, 1970-84; prof. surgery U. South Fla., Tampa, 1988-92, prof. ob.-gyn., 1988-92; chief ob-gyn State U. Hosp., 1964-81, chmn. med. staff and med. bd., 1964-66; attending staff St. Joseph's Hosp.; cons., chief gynecology sect. surg. service Syracuse VA Hosp., 1984-88; chief gynecology sect., asst. chief surgery, dir. urogynecology VA Med. Ctr., Bay Pines, Fla., 1988-92, acting chief of staff, 1990, interim chief surgery, 1991-92, chmn. O.R. com. surg. svc., 1988-92, chmn. patient care evaluation com., 1989-90, chmn. clin. exec. bd., 1990, chmn. drug usage evaluation com., 1990-91, chmn. profl. standards bd., 1990; cons. Syracuse Psychiat. Inst.; mem. cancer tng. grants and edn. com. Nat. Cancer Insts.; mem. adv. com. Bur. Maternal and Child Health, N.Y. State Dept. Health, 1957-61; nat. adviser to Children, publ. of Children's Bur., HEW, 1959-63; cons. Children's Bur., 1959-62; mem. prenatal care guide subcom. Am. Pub. Health Assn., 1962-64; cons. to regional adviser in maternal and child health Pan Am. San. Bur., WHO, 1963-65; numerous guest professorships including univs. in Mex., Chile, Uruguay, Colombia, St. Vincent (W.I.), Venezuela, People's Republic of China; numerous guest professorships including univs. in others. Author: Perinatal Loss in Modern Obstetrics, 1957; sect. on ob-gyn in Rypin's Med. Licensure Exams; also chpts. in numerous anthologies; co-author: Infant, Perinatal, Maternal and Childhood Mortality in U.S, 1968; editor: sect. on obstetrics and gynecology Stedman's Medical Dictionary, 1958-64; sect. on fetus Funk and Wagnalls Universal Standard Ency, 1959; 1st guest editor: sect. on fetus Clinics in Perinatology, 1974; 1st editor: sect. on fetus Clinical Diagnosis Quiz for Obstetrics and Gynecology, 1976, Clini-Pearls in Obstetrics and Gynecology, 1977; contbr. to: sect. on fetus Attorneys' Textbook of Medicine. Capt. M.C., U.S. Army, 1952-54. Named One of Ten Outstanding Young Men in Am., U.S. Jr. C. of C., 1957; Robert E.L. Nesbitt Jr. scholarship, Sr. Resident in Ob-Gyn, and Robert E.L. Nesbitt Jr. student scholarship established in his honor, SUNY Health Sci. Ctr. at Syracuse, 1987. Fellow Am. Assn. Maternal and Child Health, Am. Coll. Obstetricians and Gynecologists (chmn. com. mental retardation and perinatal health 1966), A.C.S. (com. forum fundamental surg. problems 1962-67), Venezuelan Obstetrics-Gynecol. Soc. (hon.), N.Y. Acad. Scis.; mem. AMA, Soc. for Gynecol. Investigations (council), Pan Am. Med. Assn. (med. ambassador goodwill, life mem. sect. on cancer), Med. Soc. N.Y. State (regional obstetrics chmn., subcom. Maternal and Child Welfare), Onondaga County Med. Soc., Am. Soc. Cytology, Pub. Health Council N.Y. State, Alpha Omega Alpha; hon. mem. Southwest, Fla. obstet. and gynecol. socs., others. Home: 11639 Grove St North Seminole FL 33772-7137

NESBITT, VANCE GORDON, computer software company executive; b. Apr. 27, 1959. Student in computer sci., U. Tex., 1977-82. Operator Seismic Data Ctr. Tex. Instruments, Austin, 1983-84; facilities and tech. svcs. assoc. Microelectronics & Computer Tech. Corp., Austin, 1984-85; v.p. product devel. Kent * Marsh Ltd., Houston, 1985-90; chmn., CEO Kent & Marsh Ltd., Houston, 1990—. Author: (comml software) MacSafe, 1990, FolderBolt, 1992, Cryptomatic, 1993, WinShield, 1995. Mem. IEEE Computer Soc., Computer Security Inst., Nat. Computer Security Assn., Assn. Computing Machinery, Electronic Frontier Found., Computer Profls. for Social Responsibility, Info. Systems Security Assn., South Tex. Info. Systems Security, Houston Area Apple Users Group, Houston Area League of PC Users, Boston Computer Soc., Apple Programmers and Developers Assn., Assn. Corp. Computing Tech. Profls., Data Processing Mgmt. Assn., Optimist Club, Alpha Phi Omega. Office: Kent & Marsh Ltd 3260 Sul Ross St Houston TX 77098-1930

NESHYBA, VICTOR PETER, retired aerophysics engineer; b. New Ulm, Tex., Oct. 8, 1922; s. Peter and Anna (Zietz) N.; m. Mary Cecilia Gwazdacz, Jan. 6, 1945; children: Victor Jr., Ronald, Janice, Mary Lee, Valiant, Michele, Dolores, Keith, David. BSEE, U. Calif., 1949; diploma, Mass. Inst. Tech., 1968, Naval Intelligence Sch., 1950. Registered profl. engr., Tex. Commd. 2d lt. USMC, 1942-47, advance through grades to col., 1970; Aerophysics engr. Gen. Dynamics, Ft. Worth, Tex., 1957-62; mgr., project off NASA, Houston, 1962-73; pres. Ener-G-Eco, Inc., Dickinson, Tex., 1974-80; owner, gen. mgr. Star Square Ranches, Wilson, Galveston, Colorado counties, Tex., 1980—; dir. Rabbit Hill Sch. Charity Found. Precinct chmn. Rep. Party, Galveston, Tex., 1974-76; sch. bd. Cath. Diocesan Schs., 1968. Decorated Medal of Honor by Shah of Iran, 1952; recipient Mgmt. award U.S. pres., 1970. Mem. Profl. Engrs. of Tex., Marine Corps. Res. Officers Assn., Rep. Senatorial Club, VFW, Knights of Columbus (4th degree). Roman Catholic.

NESSMITH, H(ERBERT) ALVA, dentist; b. Miami, Fla., Nov. 27, 1935; s. William Boyd and Florence Editha (Lowe) N.; m. Paula Ann Fox, Oct. 1, 1960 (div. 1984); children: Amy Susan, Lynn Margaret, Mark Alva. Student, U. Miami, Fla., 1953-56; DDS, Northwestern U., 1960. Gen. practice dentistry Tequesta, Fla., 1963—; dental cons. Palm Beach-Martin County Med. Ctr., Jupiter, Fla., 1970—. Mem. advminstrv. bd. United Meth. Ch. Tequesta, Jupiter, 1970—, chmn., 1988-90; pres. Meth. Men, 1982; chmn. Coun. on Ministries, 1992-94; pres. Jupiter Elem. PTO, 1972; clarinetist Symphonic Band of Palm Beaches, Fla. Concert Band; pianist and clarinetist United Meth. Ch.; mem. adminstrv. com. Christian Dental Soc., 1994—; active Village of Tequesta Hist. Commn., 1992—, Jupiter (Fla.) Cmty. Resource Ctr., 1994—; mem. adminstrv. bd. Christian Dental Soc., 1994—. Mem. ADA, North Palm Beach County Dental Soc., Fla. Dental Assn., Jupiter-Tequesta-Juno Beach C. of C. Democrat. Lodge: Kiwanis (pres. Jupiter/Tequesta chpt. 1980-81). Home: 196 River Dr Tequesta FL 33469-1934 Office: Inlet Profl Bldg 175 Tequesta Dr Jupiter FL 33469-2733

NESTER, GEORGE WALTER, management consultant; b. Roanoke, Va., Nov. 16, 1950; s. George Roy and Elizabeth (Harris) N.; m. Janet Overstreet, Jan. 14, 1951; 1 child, Lara Fay. AS in Edn., Bluefield (Va.) Coll., 1972; BA in Polit. Sci., Va. Poly. Inst. and State U., 1974; MS in Pub. Mgmt., LaSalle U., 1991, PhD in Mgmt., 1992. Cert. prof. mgr. Town mgr. Town of Ashland, Va., 1978-80; city mgr. City of Covington, Va., 1980-83; town mgr. Town of Vinton, Va., 1983-90; v.p. Mattern & Craig, Roanoke, 1990-93; pres. CTG&B Inc., Vinton, 1993—; gen. mgr. Va.'s Explore Park, Roanoke, 1994-95; exec. dir. Maury Water & Sewer Authority, Lexington, 1994—; v.p. NWS Developers, LLC, 1995—. Pres. Vinton Dist. Sports Assn., 1994—; exec. bd. Regional Econ. Devel. Partnership, Roanoke Valley, 1993—; vice chmn. Va. Recreational Facilities Authority, Roanoke, 1986-90, Roanoke Valley Solid Waste Mgmt. Bd., 1987-90. Mem. Am. Inst. Cert. Planners. Methodist. Home: 1115 Jeanette Ave Vinton VA 24179 Office: Cons to Govt & Bus 228 S Pollard St Vinton VA 24179

NESTVOLD, ELWOOD OLAF, telecommunications industry executive; b. Minot, N.D., Mar. 19, 1932; came to Netherlands 1979; s. Ole Enevold and Ragnhilda (Quanbeck) N.; m. Simone Chriqui, Dec. 6, 1955 (dec. Jan. 1990); children: Rebecca Lynn, Paul Stephen; m. Jeannette Garvin, Mar. 23, 1991; stepchildren: Michele Marie, Jennifer Ann, Michael Dennis. BA, Augsburg Coll., Mpls., 1952; postgrad., U. Wash., 1952-53; MS, U. Minn., 1959, PhD, 1962. Physics instr. U. Minn., Mpls., 1956-61; physicist and section leader Shell EP Rsch. Lab., Houston, 1962-68, mgr. geophysics rsch., 1968-71; mgr. geophysics Shell Western Div., Denver, Houston, 1971-74, Pecten Internat., Houston, 1974-77; chief geophysicst Woodside Petroleum, Perth, Australia, 1977-78; mgr. EP processing ctr. Shell EP Rsch. Lab., Rijswijk, Netherlands, 1979-81; chief geophysicst Shell Internat. Petroleum, The Hague, 1981-86, dir. geophysics and topography, 1986-92; chief geophysicist Geco-Prakla div. Schlumberger Ltd., Paris, 1992-94, v.p. mktg. Geco-Prakla div., 1993-94; sr. geophysics cons. Schlumberger Oilfield Svcs., Houston, 1994-95; exploration and prodn. sector exec. IBM Corp., Houston, 1995—; cons. Lighting and Transients Rsch. Inst., Mpls., 1957-61; lectr. Australian Petroleum Exploration Assn, 1991, Internat. Assn. Geophysical Contractors, 1992, European Assn. Exploration Geophysicists, 1994 and others. Presenter keynote addresses; contbr. articles to profl. and trade jours. 1st lt. USAF, 1952-56. Recipient award of appreciation Internat. Assn. Geophys. Contractors, 1992. Mem. IEEE, Am. Assn. Petroleum Geologists (Disting. lectr. 1993-94), Am. Assn. Physics Tchrs., European Assn. Petroleum Geoscientists, European Assn. Exploration Geophysicists, Soc. Exploration Geophysicists, N.Y. Acad. Scis., Soc. Petroleum Engrs. (Disting. lectr. 1994-95), Sigma Xi. Home: 9059 Briar Forest Houston TX 77024 Office: 2 Riverway Houston TX 77056

NETTERVILLE, GEORGE BRONSON, minister; b. McComb, Miss., Dec. 31, 1929; s. George Irving and Eula Hazel (Bronson) N.; m. Mary Elbridge Bogie, Mar. 15, 1957. BA with honors, Southeastern La. U., 1951; BD, Lexington Theol. Sem., 1957, ThM, 1958; PhD, Sussex Coll. (Eng.), 1971. Ordained to ministry Christian Ch. (Disciples of Christ), 1952. Minister various chs. in Miss. and Ky., 1953-59; minister 1st Christian Ch., Clarksdale, Miss., 1959-64, Univ. Christian Ch., Starkville, Miss., 1964-68; assoc. regional minister Christian Ch. in Tenn., Nashville, 1968-80; regional minister, pres., 1980-90; ret.; sr. min. emeritus East Ridge Christian Ch., Chattanooga, 1992; min. First United Ch., Nashville, 1993-94; regional min. Christian Ch. in Ala.- Northwest Fla., Birmingham, Ala., 1995-96; bd. dirs. Christmount Christian Assembly, Black Mountain, N.C., 1975-90; mem. gen. bd. Christian Ch., Indpls., 1980-90, 95; pres. Tenn. Assn. Chs., Nashville, 1982-84; bd. dirs. Ch. Fin. Council, Indpls., 1986-90; treas. So. Christian Services, Macon, Ga., 1986-88. Served as cpl. U.S. Army, 1951-53; Korea. Mem. Conf. Regional Ministers, Am. Acad. Religion, Soc. Bibl. Lit., Am. Schs. of Oriental Research, Council of Ministers of Christian Ch., Masons.

NETTLES, JOSEPH LEE, dentist; b. Fairhope, Ala., Jan. 11, 1954; s. Arthur and Gladys (Fore) N.; m. Dana Renea Samuels, July 11, 1981; children: Joseph Jr., Nicholas, Kimberly. Cert., Meharry Med. Coll., 1973-75, Brookhaven Nat. Lab., 1975; BS, Jarvis Christian Coll., 1976; DMD, U. Ala., 1981. Asst. dental officer, lt. USNR, San Diego, 1981-83, Subic Bay, Philippines, 1983-85, Orlando, Fla., 1985-87; dental officer, lt. comdr. USNR, Mobile, Ala., 1987-89, Individual Ready Reserves, New Orleans, 1989—; gen. dentist pvt. practice Mobile, 1987—. Active PTA and elem. sch. couns. Recipient Award for Patriotism, USN, 1986-89, Plaque of Appreciation, 1982, Cert. of Appreciation, Baker Elem. Sch., 1989, 90, 91, Cert. Appreciation for Career Day, O'Rourke Elem. Sch., 1994; Navy scholar, 1976. Mem. ADA, Ala. Dental Assn., 1st Dist. Dental Soc., Am. Fund for Dental Health, Republic of Philippines Dental Assn., Tri-Svc. Dental Soc. Japan, NAACP, Nat. Parks Assn., Gulf Coast Conservation Assn., Internat. Platform Assn., Am. Legion, Alpha Kappa Mu, Beta Kappa Chi. Home and Office: 103 Holly St Mobile AL 36608-4512

NETZER, AHARON, environmental consultant; b. Tel Aviv, Israel, May 11, 1941; came to U.S., 1977; s. Menashe and Chaya N.; m. Shulamit Avraham, May 6, 1969; children: Giora, Karen. BSc, Hebrew U., 1964, MSc, 1965, PhD, 1989. Post doctorate fellow McMaster U., Hamilton, Ontario, Can., 1969-71; rsch. assoc. McMaster U., Hamilton, 1971-72; head rsch. project Can. Ctr. for Inland Waters, Burlington, Ontario, 1972-75; head phys.-chem. processes rsch. Can. Ctr. for Inland Waters, Burlington, 1975-77; prof. environ. scis. U. Tex., Dallas, 1977-89; prin., pres. Netzer Environ. Consulting, Dallas, 1989—. Author: Over 70 articles and books in various aspects of environ. scis. Office: Netzer Environ Consulting 16950 Dallas Pky Ste 120 Dallas TX 75248-1925

NEU, JOYCE, linguist educator; b. Aug. 27, 1950; d. Ernest Lugwig and Janet (Levy) N. BA in English and French, U. Colo., Boulder, 1972; MA in Linguistics, U. So. Calif., 1980, PhD in Linguistics, 1985. Vol. Peace Corps, Senegal, West Africa, 1972-74; teaching fellow summer program for fgn. students Harvard U., 1983; asst. lectr. Am. Lang. Inst. U. So. Calif., L.A., 1978-83, lectr., comm. cons. bus. comm. dept. Sch. Bus. Adminstrn., 1983-85; vis. lectr. program in linguistics and ESL U. Calif., Irvine, 1985-86; asst. prof. Ctr. ESL, dept. speech comm. Pa. State U., University Park, 1986-91; assoc. dir. conflict resolution program Carter Ctr., Emory U., Atlanta, 1992—; acting dir. Emory U., Atlanta, 1993-94, adj. assoc. prof. anthropology, 1993—; acad. specialist USIA, Poznan, Poland, 1990; invited speaker throughout U.S., 1985—. Editor: (with Susan Gass) Speech Acts Across Cultures, 1996; reviewer TESOL Qaur., The ESP Jour., Mgmt. Comm. Quar.; contbr. articles to profl. jours., chpts. to books. Mem. TESOL (mem. rsch. task force 1991, chair applied linguistics interest sect. 1990-91, assoc. chair 1989-90), Am. Assn. Applied Linguistics (nominating com. 1993-94),

Internat. Studies Assn., Linguistic Soc. Am. Office: Carter Ctr of Emory U Conflict Resolution Program 1 Copenhill Ave NE Atlanta GA 30307-1400

NEU, WAYNE LAWRENCE, ocean engineering educator; b. Buffalo, Oct. 1, 1955; s. Lawrence William and Pauline Susanne (Jewett) N. BS in Engring. Sci., SUNY, Buffalo, 1977, MS in Engring. Sci., 1981, PhD in Engring. Sci., 1981. Asst. prof. dept. aerospace and ocean engring. Va. Poly. Inst. and State U., Blacksburg, 1981-87, assoc. prof. dept. aerospace and ocean engring., 1987—; presenter, rschr. in field of phys. oceanography and marine meteorology; cons. Monsanto Chem. Intermediates Co., Amoco Chems. Corp., ETS, Inc. Contbr. articles to profl. jours. Mem. Am. Soc. Engring. Edn. (mem. exec. com. ocean and marine engring. divsn. 1984-87), Am. Geophys. Union, Soc. Naval Architects and Marine Engrs. (mem. exec. com., advisor student chpt. Chesapeake sect. 1988—, mem. edn. com. 1995—), Sigma Xi. Office: Va Poly Inst and State U Aerospace & Ocean Engring Blacksburg VA 24061

NEUBAUER, HUGO DUANE, JR., software engineer; b. Mankato, Minn., Oct. 31, 1959; s. Hugo Duane and Joan Marie (Habinger) N.; m. Susan A. May, July 7, 1990. Student, U. Miami, 1978-80; AA, U. Fla., 1981; AS, Santa Fe C.C., 1984; student, U. Fla., 1984—. Aquaculture specialist, technician Aqualife Rsch. Inc., 1979-80; automotive dept. K-Mart, 1981-82; electronic technician Synergetics, Inc., 1983-84; water resources equipment technician Environ. Sci. and Engring., Inc., Gainesville, Fla., 1984-89; tech. ops. equipment mgr. Environ. Sci. and Engring., Inc., Gainesville, 1990-91, geosciences divsn. equipment mgr., 1992-93, Ctr. 3 equipment mgr., 1994-95; mgr. rental and sales Kech Instruments Inc., 1996—; founder, owner ICIS, 1996—; ind. cons. in field; owner, founder Innovative Computer and Instrument Svcs., Dances with Hooves Horse Farm. Mem. IEEE, IEEE Computer Soc., Assn. for Computing Machinery. Home: PO Box 1270 14108 NW 195th St Alachua FL 32615 Office: ICIS PO Box 1270 Alachua FL 32616-1270 also: Kech Instruments Inc Kech South 404 SW 140th Terr Bldg 100 Newburg FL 32669

NEUFELDER, ANN MARIE, software consulting company executive, consultant; b. Swedesboro, N.J., Nov. 19, 1960; d. George Leone and Mary Judith (Keese) Leone; m. Thomas Joesph Neufelder, July 20, 1991; 1 child, Rachel Lynn. BS in Indsl. and Systems Engring., Ga. Tech., 1983. Assoc. engr. Computer Scis. Corp., Atlanta, 1983-84; engr. Unisys, Atlanta, 1984-86; sr. engr. Westinghouse Electric, Balt., 1986-91; quality engr. Entek Scientific, Cin., 1991—; owner SoftRel, Hebron, Ky., 1992—; cons. Reliability Analysis Ctr., Rome, N.Y., 1991—, George Washington U., Washington, 1989-91; cons. U. Md., College Park, 1988-91, instr., 1990; editor-at-large Marcel Dekker, N.Y.C., 1992—. Author: Ensuring Software Reliability, 1993; contbr. numerous articles to tech. publs.; patent pending for PStiMate. Vol. Rep. Nat. Com., Hebron, Ky., 1989—. Recipient Burroughs Excellence award, 1984. Mem. IEEE (assoc. editor Reliability Transactions 1988-90), Am. Soc. Quality Control (past sec. software quality tech. com.). Republican. Roman Catholic. Home: 1518 Jolee Dr Hebron KY 41048-9514 Office: Soft Rel PO Box 453 Hebron KY 41048-0453

NEUMANN, ANDREW CONRAD, geological oceanography educator; b. Oak Bluffs, Mass., Dec. 21, 1933; s. Andrew Conrad Neumann and Faye Watson (Gilmore) Gilmour; m. Jane Spaeth, July 7, 1962; children: Jennifer, Christopher, Jonathan. BS in Geology, Bklyn. Coll., 1955; MS in Oceanography, Tex. A&M U., 1958; PhD in Geology, Lehigh U., 1963. Asst. prof. marine geology Lehigh U., Bethlehem, Pa., 1963-65; asst. prof. marine sci. U. Miami, Fla., 1965-69, assoc. prof. marine sci., 1969-72; prof. marine sci. U. N.C., Chapel Hill, 1972-85, Bowman and Gordon Gray prof. geol. oceanography, 1985—; program dir. NSF, Washington, 1969-70; Kenan prof. U. Edinburgh, Scotland, 1978; summer vis. investigator U.S. Geol. Survey, Woods Hole, Mass., 1981—, Woods Hole Oceanographic Inst., 1981—; vis. prof. U. Naples, Italy, 1984, 92, 95, Eötvös U., Budapest, Hungary, 1991. Contbr. articles to profl. jours. Trustee Bermuda Biol. Sta. for Research Inc., 1972-76. Recipient Disting. Alumni award Bklyn. Coll., 1987. Fellow Geol. Soc. Am.; mem. Soc. Econ. Paleontologists and Mineralogists, N.C. Acad. Sci. Office: U NC Dept Marine Scis 1205 Venable Hall 045a Chapel Hill NC 27599-3300

NEUMANN, THOMAS WILLIAM, archaeologist; b. Cin., Aug. 30, 1951; s. William Henry and Virginia Marie (Walz) N.; m. Mary Louise Spink, Sept. 3, 1988. BA in Anthropology, U. Ky., 1973; PhD in Anthropology, U. Minn., 1979. Instr. U. Minn., Mpls., 1977-79; asst. prof. Syracuse U., 1979-86, dir. archaeology field program, 1979-86; sr. ptnr. Neumann & Sanford Cultural Resource Assessments, Syracuse, 1985-87; sr. scientist R. Christopher Goodwin & Assocs., Inc., Frederick, Md., 1987-92; rsch. assoc. Terrestrial Environ. Specialists, Phoenix, N.Y., 1980-83, SUNY Rsch. Found., Potsdam, 1985-87; external reviewer NSF, Washington, 1982-85; dir. Ctr. for Archaeol. Rsch. and Edn., Houston, Minn., 1982-84; vis. assoc. prof. Emory U., 1991-93, 96; ind. cons., 1991—. Author, co-author more than 70 monographs including 2 winners of the Anne Arundell County Hist. Preservation award; asst. editor Amanuensis, 1972-73; contbr. more than 30 articles to profl. jours. Nat. Trust Historic Preservation honor award. Grantee, Am. Philos. Soc., 1981, Appleby-Mosher Found., 1983, Landmarks Assn. Cen. N.Y., 1984; recipient Oswald award, U. Ky., 1973. Mem. AAAS, N.Y. Acad. Sci., Soc. for Am. Archaeology, Ea. States Archaeol. Fedn., Mid. Atlantic Archaeol. Conf., Phi Beta Kappa. Roman Catholic. Home: 3859 Wentworth Ln SW Lilburn GA 30247-2260 Office: Ind Archeol Cons 3859 Wentworth Ln SW Lilburn GA 30247-2260

NEUPERT, LARRY DOUGLAS, nurse anesthetist, naval officer; b. Syracuse, N.Y., Mar. 30, 1950; s. Harry Douglas and Hazel Marie (Bort) N.; m. Christina Ann Kennedy, May 17, 1970 (div. March 1986); 1 child, Mark Douglas; m. Patricia Denise Wickham, April 5, 1986; 1 child, Tyler Douglas. ADN in Nursing, Sinclair Community Coll., Dayton, Ohio, 1975; BSN in Nursing, Univ. State N.Y., Albany, 1986; MS in Nurse Anesthesia, St. Joseph U., Phila., 1992. RN, Ohio, Pa; Cert. CCRN, CRNA Am. Assn. Nurse Anesthetists. Staff nurse, charge nurse, surgical and pediatric Reid Meml. Hosp., Richmond, Ind., 1975-76; staff nurse, charge nurse St. Elizabeth Med. Ctr., Dayton, Ohio, 1976-90; staff nurse, charge nurse, ICU pediatric and newborn Western Med. Nurses, Dayton, Ohio, 1980-83, Kimberly Nurses, Dayton, 1981-83; staff nurse, charge nurse, ICU Greene Meml. Hosp., Xenia, Ohio, 1983-84, Southview Hosp., Dayton, 1984-88; officer Res. Nurse Corps, U.S. Navy, 1988; advanced through the grades to lt. Naval Hosp., Charleston, S.C., 1988—; instr. ACLS and CPR U.S. Navy. Deacon Metro North Presbyn. Ch., Goose Creek, S.C., 1994—. Officer U.S. Navy Nurse Corps Res. Mem. Navy Anesthesia Soc., Naval Inst., Am. Nurses Assn., Am. Assn. Critical Care Nurses. Home: 104 S Pembroke Dr Goose Creek SC 29445-7046

NEUSAENGER, JOHN MICHAEL, financial company executive; b. Orlando, Fla., Nov. 8, 1958; s. John D. and Dorothy J. (Robertson) N.; m. Donna Jean Boyd, Oct. 10, 1981 (div. Oct. 9, 1987); m. Mary Jane Gonzalez, May 14, 1988; children: Morzan Jane, John Adam, Michael James. BA in History, Rollins Coll., 1980, MBA, 1997. Cert. credit union exec. Credit Union Nat. Assn. Wage analyst Sears Roebuck & Co., Winter Park, Fla., 1979-85; di. ops. ORMC Fed. Credit Union, Orlando, Fla., 1985-87; v.p. CFHC Fed. Credit Union, Orlando, 1987-88; exec. v.p. Orlando Fed. Credit Union, 1988-91, pres., CEO, 1991—; instr. Nat. Credit Union Inst., Orlando, 1986-88. Cons. Jr. Achievement, Orlando, 1989—; coach SAY Little League, 1991—; pres. of the bd. Gatlin Place Homeowners' Assn., Orlando, 1993—. Credit Union Mgmt. award Fla. Credit Union Mgmt. Inst., Fla. State U., 1989. Democrat. Presbyterian. Office: Orlando Fed Credit Union 1117 S Westmoreland Dr Orlando FL 32805-3866

NEVAREZ, MIGUEL A., university president. Pres. U. Tex.-Pan Am., Edinburg, Tex. Office: The U Tex-Pan Am 1201 W University Dr Edinburg TX 78539-2909*

NEVELS, CHARLES THOMAS, psychiatrist; b. Greenville, Miss., July 3, 1949; s. Frederick Bruce and Jennie Mae (Daniel) N.; m. Janet S. Herr, Aug. 26, 1981 (div. July 1986); 1 child, Eric C.; m. Linda Jo Foree, Aug. 28, 1991. BS in Biology, Emory U., 1971; MD, Med. Coll. Ga., 1975. Diplomate Am. Bd. Psychiatry and Neurology, Nat. Bd. Med. Examiners; lic. physician, Kans.; cert. adminstrv. psychiatrist. Resident in psychiatry Menninger Sch. Psychiatry, Topeka, 1978; with U.S. Indian Health Svc., 1978; pvt. practice Topeka, 1978-80; staff psychiatrist Tuscaloosa (Ala.) VA Med. Ctr., 1981—, acting chief psychiatry, 1982-84, chief psychiat. svc., 1984-91, clin. dir. post-traumatic stress disorder program, 1991—; clin. assoc. prof. psychiatry Coll. Cmty. Health Scis. U. Ala., 1981—; mem. dist. 10 planning bd. VA, 1982-90, mem. region 3 planning bd., 1987-90, mem. clin. exec. bd., 1981-91, mem. profl. standards bd., 1982—, chmn. mental health coun., 1982-91, active coms.; mem. joint coms. U. Ala. and VA, 1981—; mem. family practice curriculum com. Coll. Cmty. Health U. Ala., 1987—; bd. dirs. Tuscaloosa Rsch., Inc.; cons. Kans. Reception and Diagnostic Ctr., 1977-79, I Care-Indian Ctr., 1978-80, Shawnee County Combined Ct. Svcs., 1977-80, Ala. Disabilities Advocacy Program; presenter profl. confs. Contbr. articles to profl. publs. Recipient Physician's Recognition award, 1992, Sci. Writing award, 1977-78; Sealy fellow in psychiatry, 1977-78. Mem. AMA, Am. Psychiat. Assn., Am. Assn. Psychiat. Adminstrns., Ala. Psychiat. Soc. (pres. 1991-92, mem. exec. bd. 1991—, chmn. pub. psychiatry com. 1992—, mem. ethics com. 1982-84), Tuscaloosa Soc. Psychiatry and Neurology (pres. 1984-85), Rotary (Paul Harris fellow Tuscaloosa chpt. 1993), Quarterback Club. Home: PO Box 40204 Tuscaloosa AL 35404-0204 Office: Tuscaloosa VA Med Ctr Psychiatry Svc Loop Rd # 116A Tuscaloosa AL 35404

NEVES, KERRY LANE, lawyer; b. San Angelo, Tex., Dec. 19, 1950; s. Herman Walter and Geraldine (Ball) N.; m. Sharon Lynn Briggs, July 28, 1973; 1 child, Erin Lesli. BBA, U. Tex., 1975, JD, 1978. Bar: Tex. 1978, U.S. Dist. Ct. (so. and ea. dists.) Tex. 1979, U.S. Ct. Appeals (5th cir.) 1979, U.S. Dist. Ct. (we. dist.) 1980; cert. personal injury trial law, Tex. Bd. Legal Specialization, 1994. Ptnr. Mills, Shirley, Eckel & Bassett, Galveston, Tex., 1978-93, Neves & Crowther, Galveston, Tex., 1993—. Vice-chmn. Bldg. Stnds. Commn., Dickinson, Tex., 1991—. Sgt. USMC, 1969-72. Fellow Tex. Bar Found.; mem. ABA, State Bar Tex. (grievance com. 1989-92, disciplinary rules profl. conduct com. 1990-92), Galveston County Bar Assn. (pres. 1989-90), U. Tex. Law Alumni Assn. (pres. 1991-92). Home: RR 2 Box 95 Dickinson TX 77539-9204 Office: Neves & Crowther 1802 Broadway St Ste 206 Galveston TX 77550-4953

NEVIDJON, BRENDA MARION, nursing administrator; b. Norwalk, Conn., Dec. 22, 1950; d. Carl James and Rosemary (Bibby) N.; m. Benjamin C. Staples, Feb. 28, 1983; 1 child, Jameson. BSN magna cum laude, Duke U., 1972; MSN, U. N.C., 1978. Staff nurse Duke U. Med. Ctr., Durham, N.C., 1972-73, 77-78, nurse clinician, 1973-75; staff nurse Kantonsspital, Basel, Switzerland, 1975-76; head nurse Duke U. Med. Ctr., 1978-81; clin. nurse specialist Cancer Control Agy British Columbia, Vancouver, Can., 1981-83, dir. nursing, 1983-85; mgr. cancer program Providence Med. Ctr., Seattle, 1985-88; clin. dir. cancer ctr. U. Wash. Med. Ctr., Seattle, 1988-89; clin. nurse specialist Virginia MAson Med. Ctr., Seattle, 1989-91; dir. nursing medicine/oncology Duke U. Med. Ctr., 1991-94, sr. assoc. chief oper. officer patient care svcs., 1994—; clin. assoc. Duke U. Sch. Nursing, 1992—; clin. instr. U. Wash. Sch. Nursing, Seattle, 1987-91; asst. prof. U. B.C. Sch. Nursing, 1983-84; clin. instr. Duke U. Sch. Nursing, 1980-91. Editor, ONS News, 1989—; contbr. chpts. to books, articles to profl. jours. Vol., bd. dirs. Am. Cancer Soc., Seattle, 1985-88, ARC, Durham, 1991—. Mem. Am. Orgn. Nurse Execs., N.C. Orgn. Nurse Execs., Oncology Nursing Soc., Internat. Assn. Nurse Editors, Sigma Theta Tau. Democrat. Episcopalian. Office: Duke U Med Ctr PO Box 3543 Durham NC 27702-3543

NEVILLE, THOMAS LEE, food service company executive; b. Columbus, Ind., Jan. 1, 1947; s. Frank Thomas and Esquline Coons (Davis) N.; m. Shavona Rose Lagneau, Aug. 10, 1966; children: Timothy David, Sherry Lynn. AAS, Austin Peay State U., Clarksville, Tenn., 1994. Cert. exec. chef. Enlisted U.S. Army, 1966, apptd. WO1, 1976, commd. CW3, 1986; food advisor Army Food Rsch., Devel. and Engring. Ctr., Natick, Mass.; ret. U.S. Army, 1990; regional mgr. KCA Corp., Hopkinsville, Ky., 1990—; mem. Warrant Officers Assn., 1976-90. Mem. Ret. Officers Assn., Am. Soc. Quality Control, Am. Culinary Fedn., Am. Mgmt. Assn., Masons. Home: 1728 Clara Ct Clarksville TN 37040-7823 Office: KCA Corp PO Box 641 Hopkinsville KY 42241-0641

NEVILLE, TINA MARIE, associate university librarian; b. Madison, Ohio, Sept. 28, 1957. BA in Zoology, Ohio Wesleyan U., 1980; MA in Libr. Sci., U. South Fla., 1989. Instr., libr. U. South Fla., St. Petersburg, 1990-92, asst. univ. libr., 1992-95, acting asst. libr. dir., 1994, assoc. univ. libr., 1995—. Book reviewer Libr. Jour., 1994—. Mem. ALA, Assn. of Coll. and Rsch. Librs., Fla. Libr. Assn., Suncoast Info. Specialists (v.p. 1991-92, pres. 1992-93), Phi Kappa Phi. Office: Univ of South Fla Libr 140 Seventh Ave S Saint Petersburg FL 33701

NEVIN, JAMES EDMONSON, III, surgeon; b. Cleve., Aug. 19, 1931; s. James Edmonson and Charlotte (Clary) N.; m. Tommi Kay Tomlinson; children: James, Cynthia, Jenifer, John. BA, Bowdoin; MD, Tufts U. Intern surgery Case Western Res. Hosp., Cleve., 1957-58, surg. resident, 1958-59, 61-65; pvt. practice surgeon Danville, Va., 1965—; asst. prof. surgery Med. Coll. of Va., Richmond, 1972-76, assoc. prof. surgery, 1976—; chmn. dept. surgery Danville (Va.) Regional Med. Ctr., 1968-72, 78-82; bd. dirs. Regional Med. Program, Va., 1978-82. Bd. dirs. Gateway Health Alliance Inc., 1995—; pres. Danville Mus. Fine Arts and History; mem. Va. divsn. Am. Cancer Soc. Mem. Med. Soc. Va. (bd. dirs. 1972—, del. 1982—), Va. Profl. Standard Rev. Orgn. (bd. dirs. 1975—). Home: 339 Hawthorne Dr Danville VA 24541-3515 Office: 990 Main St Danville VA 24541-1828

NEVINS, JANICE RUTH, management consultant; b. Houston, Dec. 24, 1947; d. George Arthur and Vivian Lucille (Roy) Derr; m. William James Nevins, Apr. 29, 1978 (div. Apr. 1993); 1 child, George Eric. BS in Bus. Tech., U. Houston, 1976. Employment recruiter Mitchell Energy and Devel., Houston, 1973-76; employment mgr. Pace Industries, Houston, 1976-77; regional personnel dir. Health Industries, Inc., Atlanta, 1980-81; personnel dir. Miller/Zell, Inc., Atlanta, 1981-82; personnel svcs. dir. Rollins, Inc., Atlanta, 1983-85; personnel dir. Gwinnett County Govt., Lawrenceville, Ga., 1985-87; exec. v.p. Slavin, Nevins & Assoc., Inc., Atlanta, 1987-95; mgmt. cons. William M. Mercer Inc., Houston, 1995—; presenter in field. Music dir. Prince of Peace Ch., Buford, Ga., 1989-92; mem. Houston Humane Assn., 1992-94, Gwinnett Arts Coun., Lawrenceville, Ga., 1987-93; fundraiser Gwinnett Mental Health Mental Retardation, Lawrenceville, 1986-87; sustainer Jr. League of Gwinnett/No. Fuhon County, Atlanta, 1988-93, Houston Jr. League, 1994—. Mem. Internat. City/County Mgmt. Assn., Soc. Human Resource Mgmt. (cert. sr. profl. human resources, life, chair com. 1975-94), Am. Compensation Assn., Internat. Personnel Mgmt. Assn., Leadership Gwinnett (bd. dirs. 1988—, alumni chair 1991). Republican. Roman Catholic. Home: 2219 Round Lake Dr Houston TX 77077-6128 Office: William M Mercer Inc 1331 Lamar Ave Ste 1250 Houston TX 77010

NEW, CLAUDIA MOSS, hospice social worker; b. Mexia, Tex., Oct. 17, 1941; d. William Thomas and Viola (Reynolds) Moss; m. Noah Edward New Jr., Sept. 22, 1963; 1 child, Courtney Page. AA, Coll. of the Mainland, 1969; BS in Psychology, U. Md., 1984; MS in Social Svc. Work, U. Tex., Arlington, 1991. Lic. master social worker, Tex. Vol. caseworker ARC, Seoul, Korea, 1984-85; exec. dir. DeSoto (Tex.) Community Outreach, 1987-90. Mem. NASW, Assn. for Applied Psyhophysiology and Biofeedback North Tex., Bus. and Profl. Women (pres.), DeSoto Jr. Svc. League, LaMarque Jaycee-ettes (pres.), Pilot Club, Alpha Delta Mu. Democrat. Methodist. Home: 136 Highridge Dr De Soto TX 75115-6222 Office: Vis Nurse Assn 211 W Mulberry St Kaufman TX 75142-1940

NEW, PAMELA ZYMAN, neurologist; b. Chgo., Jan. 24, 1953; d. HIllard Anthony and Virginia Lillian (Drechsler) Zyman; m. Joseph Keith New, Sept. 12, 1982; children: Matthew, Anneliese, Theresa. BS in Medicine, Northwestern U., 1973, MD, 1976. Resident in internal medicine Baylor Affiliated Hosps., Houston, 1977-80, resident in neurology, 1983-85; mem. staff dept. medicine VA Hosp., Houston, 1980-81; resident in gen. surgery N.Y. Hosp., Cornell Med. Ctr., N.Y.C., 1981, resident in neurosurgery, 1981-83; fellow neuro-oncology M.D. Anderson Hosp. and Tumor Inst., Houston, 1985-87; asst. prof. divsn. neurology dept. medicine U. Tex. Health Sci. Ctr., San Antonio, 1987—; staff physician Audie L. Murphy Meml. VA Hosp., San Antonio, 1987—; lectr., researcher in field. Contbr. articles to profl. publs., chpts. to books. Mem. ACP, S.W. Oncology Group, Assn. VA Investigators and Rsch. Adminstrs., Am. Acad. Neurology, Am. Parkinson's Disease Assn. (co-dir. Parkinson's Disease Info. Referral Ctr.), Movement Disorders Soc., Soc. of Neuro-Oncology. Roman Catholic. Office: U Tex Health Sci Ctr 7703 Floyd Curl Dr San Antonio TX 78284-6200

NEWBERN, DAVID, state supreme court justice. Justice Ark. Supreme Ct., Little Rock. Office: Justice Bldg 625 Marshall Little Rock AR 72201

NEWBERN, LAURA LYNN, forestry association executive, editor; b. Valdosta, Ga., Feb. 25, 1954; d. Jefferson Lamar Jr. and Laura Helen (Downs) N. BA in Art History, Emory U., 1977. Adminstrv. asst. Ga. Forestry Assn., Norcross, 1977—, editor TOPS, Ga. Forestry Assn. News, 1987—; state coord. Project Learning Tree, Norcross, 1988—; officer, bd. dirs. Turn In Poachers, Inc., Atlanta, 1987—. Recipient Natl. Outstanding Program award Project Learning Tree, Washington, 1988, Outstanding Svc. award Ga. Tree Farm Com., 1987, Outstanding Tree Farm Svc. award Am. Forest Coun., Atlanta, 1988, Nat. Outstanding New Program award Project Learning Tree, Washington, 1988, Outstanding Svc. award Coalition for Green Ga., Macon, 1989, Friend of Ga. Wildlife award Turn In Poachers, Inc., 1990, Miracle Maker award Children's Miracle Network, 1994; named Outstanding Facilitator of Yr., Ga. Project Learning Tree, 1988, Outstanding Educator of Yr., Ga. Urban Forest Coun., 1992, Outstanding State Coord. award Ga. Project Learning Tree, 1994.

NEWBERN, WILLIAM DAVID, state supreme court justice; b. Oklahoma City, May 28, 1937; s. Charles Banks and Mary Frances (Harding) N.; m. Barbara Lee Rigsby, Aug. 19, 1961 (div. 1968); 1 child, Laura Harding; m. Carolyn Lewis, July 30, 1970; 1 child, Alistair Elizabeth. B.A., U. Ark., 1959, J.D., 1961; LL.M., George Washington U., 1963; M.A., Tufts U., 1967. Bar: Ark. 1961, U.S. Dist. Ct. (we. dist.) Ark. 1961, U.S. Supreme Ct. 1968, U.S. Ct. Appeals (8th cir.) 1983. Commd. 1st lt. advanced to maj. U.S. Army JAGC, 1961-70; Prof. law U. Ark., Fayetteville, 1970-84; adminstr. Ozark Folk Ctr., Mountain View, Ark., 1973; judge Ark. Ct. Appeals, Little Rock, 1979-80; assoc. justice Ark. Supreme Ct., Little Rock, 1985—; mem. faculty sr. appellate judges seminar NYU, 1987-91. Editor Ark. Law Rev., 1961; author: Arkansas Civil Practice and Procedure, 1985, 2d edit., 1993. Mem. Fayetteville Bd. Adjustment, 1972-79; bd. dirs. decision Point, INc., Springdale, Ark., 1980-85, Little Rock Wind Symphony, 1993, pres. 1993-95. Fellow Ark. Bar Found.; mem. Am. Judicature Soc. (bd. dirs. 1985-89), Washington County Bar Assn., Inst. Jud. Adminstrn., Ark. IOLTA Found. (bd. dirs. 1985-87). Democrat. Office: Ark Supreme Ct 625 Marshall St Little Rock AR 72201-1020

NEWBERRY, TRUDELL MCCLELLAND, retired dean; b. Junction City, Ark., Jan. 30, 1939; d. Roosevelt and Margaret (Knighten) McClelland; div.; children: FeLesia Michelle, Thomas W. III. BA, U. Ark., 1962; MA, Roosevelt U., 1980; postgrad., Gov.'s State U., Arlington Heights, Ill., 1982-84, No. Ill. U., 1988-89. Cert. tchr., Ark., Ill. Tchr. Almyra (Ark.) Pub. Schs., 1962-65; social worker Franklin-Wright Settlement, Detroit, 1965-69; tchr. North Chicago (Ill.) Sch. Dist. #64, 1970—; dean of students North Chgo. Community High Sch., Unit Dist. 187, 1990-93; retired, 1993; sec. com. of ten. Unification of North Chgo. Sch. System, 1988. Recreational supr. Foss Park Dist., North Chicago, 1982-83; mem. North Chicago Library Bd., 1982-86; North Chicago Alderperson, 1983-87; mem. North Chicago High Sch. PTO, Booster Club, 1984—. Mem. North Chgo. Tchrs. Assn. (bldg. rep. 1986-87, rep. to Lake County Fedn. Tchrs. Local 504 1987-89, pres. coun. 1987-89), Am. Fedn. Tchrs. (adv.), Lake County Fedn. Tchrs. (exec. bd.), Ill. Fedn. Tchrs., AFL-CIO. Democrat. Baptist. Lodge: Eureka Temple.

NEWBOLD, BENJAMIN MILLARD, JR., library manager, education consultant; b. La Grange, Ga., June 20, 1941; s. Benjamin Millard and Zeppa (Dasher) N.; married, 1968 (div. 1977); 2 children. BA in Sociology, Roger Williams Coll., 1970; MEd in Spl. Edn., Mid. Tenn. State U., 1975; MLS, U. So. Fla., 1985. Cert. tchr., Tenn., Fla., Ga., S.C., La. Tchr. psychotic, emotionally disturbed, mentally retarded Montanari Clin. Sch., Hialeah, Fla., 1970-72, 76-77; tchr. educatable mentally retarded Colleton County Bd. Edn., Walterboro, S.C., 1972-73, John Coleman Sch., Smyrna, Tenn., 1973-76, Hahnville H.S., Boutte, La., 1978-79, Gulf Comprehensive H.S., New Port Richie, Fla., 1979-80; tchr. severely mentally retarded, psychology supr. Sunniland Tng. Ctr., Ft. Myers, Fla., 1983-84; grad. asst. U. So. Fla., Tampa, 1984-85; adult reference libr. Houston Pub. Libr., 1986-89, libr. br. mgr., 1989-94, collection devel. mgr. Scenic Woods Regional Cluster, 1994; geneal. researcher Clayton Libr./Ctr. for Geneal. Rsch., 1994—; pilot project tchr. Garrison Environ. Model, Rutherford County Bd. Edn., Murfreesboro, 1973-76; county coord. Spl. Edn. Grad. Credit, Murfreesboro, 1973-76; supr., adminstr., cons. pub. schs., pub. and pvt. facilities, librs.; active community pub. rels. P.T.A., sch. dists., librs.; ind. distbr. Enviro-tech Internat. Vol. tchr. ESL Houston Pub. Libr., 1996—; active CONNECTEXAS, Austin, Fonwood P.T.A., Houston, Fontaine-Scenic Woods Civic Club, Houston, positive interaction program Houston Police Dept.; past mem. exec. bd. Houston Pub. Libr. Staff Assn. Recipient Spirit award Wall St.-The Club, 1991. Republican. Home: 401 S Bender Ave Apt 1109 Humble TX 77338-7706 Office: Clayton Libr Ctr Gen Rsch 5300 Caroline Houston TX 77004-6896

NEWBURY, DON, university administrator. Pres. Howard Payne U., Brownwood, Tex. Office: Howard Payne U Office of President Brownwood TX 76801

NEWBY, STEVEN RAY, headmaster; b. Warsaw, Ind., Apr. 2, 1952; s. Raymond Everett and Virginia Dean (Loftice) N.; m. Sherry Diane Fischer, Aug. 17, 1973; children: CLifford Raymond, Melissa Joy, Russell Steven. BA in Edn., East Tex. State U., 1974, MEd, 1977. Cert. tchr., Tex. Jr. h.s. English tchr. Aba-Golden (Tex.) Ind. Sch. Dist., Haagard Mid. Sch., Plano, Tex.; secondary English tchr. Vines H.S., Plano, Tex., libr.; prin., min. Christian edn. Bethany Christian Sch., Plano, Tex.; prin. Grace Acad. Dallas; elem. prin. Pantego Christian Acad., Arlington, headmaster, elem. prin., headmaster, secondary prin. Mem. Plano VIP planning com., 1988. Mem. ASCD, Assn. Christian Schs. Internat. (sec./treas. 1989-90, asst. to conv. dir. 1990—). Republican. Home: 1907 Camden Ct Arlington TX 76013 Office: Pantego Christian Acad 2201 W Park Row Arlington TX 76013

NEWCOM, SAMUEL RALPH, physician; b. Bastrop, Tex., June 14, 1943; s. Samuel George and Grethel Joy (Conklin) N.; m. Janis Sue Williams, June 14, 1969; children: Samuel Joshua, Cassandra Lynn, Seth Emerson. MD, U. So. Calif., 1969. Diplomate Am. Bd. Internal Medicine. Intern, USPHS, S.I., N.Y., 1969-70; resident U. So. Calif., 1970-72; fellow U. Calif., San Francisco, 1972-74, chief med. oncology clinic, 1975-79; instr. medicine U. Oreg., Portland, 1974-75; head med. oncology Oreg. Health Sci. U., Portland, 1979-84; assoc. prof. medicine Emory U., Altanta, 1984—; chief Lymphoma Leukemia Svc., Grady Meml. Hosp., chief hematology/oncology svc., Atlanta Vet. Affairs Hosp.; presenter to local, nat. and internat. sci. organizations. Editor: Supplemental 5 Blood, 1977; Hematologic Malignancies, 1979; asst. editor Am. Jour. Med. Sci., 1995. Contbr. articles to profl. jours. Served with USPHS, 1969-70. Am. Cancer Soc. fellow, 1980-83; grantee Am. Cancer Soc., 1980, NIH, 1981, 84, 90, M.J. Murdock Trust, 1981. Fellow Am. Coll. of Physicians; mem. Am. Soc. Clin. Oncology, Am. Assn. Cancer Research, Am. Soc. Hematology, Am. Fedn. Clin. Research, So. Soc. Clin. Investigation, AAAS. Democrat. Methodist. Office: Emory U 69 Butler St Atlanta GA 30307-1018

NEWCOMB, MARGUERITE E., paralegal, educator; b. Austin, Tex., Feb. 1, 1961; d. Lon H. and Mary June (Hardy) Cantrell; 1 child. BA in English Lit. magna cum laude, St. Edward's U., Austin, 1996; postgrad., Tex. Tech U., 1996—. Cert. paralegal. Teaching intern St. Edward's U., 1994—; Editor: Freshman Studies Handbook, 1996. Cub Scout leader Boy Scouts Am., 1991-93, Webelos leader, 1993-94. Mem. Kappa Gamma Pi, Alpha Sigma Lambda. Democrat. Methodist.

NEWCOMB, ROBERT CARL, real estate broker; b. Woburn, Mass., Apr. 14, 1926; s. Horace Irving and Hester Elizabeth (Fuller) N.; m. Elizabeth Canaday, Oct. 12, 1952; children: Janet E., Glenn R., Mark H., Carl A. BA, Tufts Coll., 1947; cert., Grad. Realtors Inst. Commd. ensign USN, 1947, advanced through grades to capt., 1968, comdg. officer USS Pigeon, 1954-55, comdg. officer USS Nicholas, 1964-65, ret., 1973; realtor Merkli-McGuire Realty, Alexandria, Va., 1973-80; broker, owner Parkway Realty, Inc.,

Alexandria, 1980—; assoc. broker Century 21 Quality Homes Realty, Inc., Alexandria, 1991—. Pres. Gunston Manor Property Owners Assn., Lorton, Va., 1975. Decorated Bronze Star; Newcomb Bay named in his honor, Antarctica, 1955. Mem. Nat. Assn. Realtors, U.S. Naval Inst. (life), Antarctican Soc., Masons, Ruritans. Republican. Methodist.

NEWELL, HAROLD JOE, quality assurance engineer; b. Fernbank, Ala., Dec. 31, 1945; s. Homer Isaiah and Beulah Mae (Tomlin) N.; m. Brenda Kay Guin, Sept. 24, 1966 (div. Jan. 1993); m. Kathy Lane Vaughn, Oct. 2, 1995; children: Tyrena Kay, Wesley Joe. Student, E. Miss. Jr. Coll., 1976, Miss. U. for Women, 1984, 86, U. Ala., 1990—. lic. rep. Franklin Life Ins. Co. Lineman Four-County Elec. Power Assn., 1964-65; tool and die apprentice Quality Tooling, Fayette, Ala., 1965-66; quality assurance engr., quality control supr. United Techs. Motor Sys., Columbus, Miss., 1966-95. Pastor S.C. Bapt. Ch., Vernon, Ala., Mt. Olive Bapt. ch., Millport, Ala.; conducts weekly radio program Sta. WVSA, Vernon; mgr. five mem. band, 1968-73. Recipient award of excellence in photography Photographer's Forum Mag., Santa Barbara, Calif., 1984, 87. Mem. Am. Soc. Quality Control (sr. mem., pub. rels. com.). Republican. Home: 6215 Hwy 18 W Vernon AL 35592

NEWELL, JAMES ROBERT, telephone company executive; b. Portsmouth, Va., June 29, 1941; s. James Melvin and Hazel (Coltrain) N.; m. Judith Kabo, Nov. 3, 1963; children: Ashlyn, James. BS, N.C. State U., 1966. Jr. engr. Carolina Tel. Co., Tarboro, N.C., 1966-67; mfg. mgmt. trainee GE, Ind. and S.C., 1967-69; mgr. engring. Mid-South Cons. Engrs., Charlotte, N.C., 1969-76; gen. mgr. Citizens Telephone Coop., Floyd, Va., 1976—, gen. mgr. Citizens Cellular, Inc. subs., 1990—; pres., bd. dirs. Citizens Comm. Corp.; bd. dirs. Svc. Mgmt. Corp. subs. Nat. Telephone Coop. Assn. Officer, bd. dirs. New River C.C., Dublin, Va., 1980-81. Mem. Va. Telephone Assn. (bd. dirs., pres. 1985-86). Home: PO Box 425 Floyd VA 24091-0425 Office: Citizens Tel Coop PO Box 137 Floyd VA 24091-0137

NEWELL, SILVIA ANNA, accountant; b. Fulda, Fed. Republic of Germany, July 20, 1953; came to U.S., 1953; d. Tommie Lee and Maria Justina Anna (Rupple) Combs; m. Jerry W. Smith, Apr. 27, 1973 (div. Feb. 1982); children: Elizabeth Ann, Jenny Marie; m. Thomas E. Newell Jr., May 5, 1984. BBA in Acctg., Columbus Coll., 1977. CPA, Ga. Supr. acctg. dept. BC/BS, Columbus, Ga., 1973-81; sr. fin. analyst Am. Family Life, Columbus, 1981-84; asst. fin. report officer New England Life, Boston, 1984-85; bus. analyst Consol. Group, Framingham, Mass., 1985-86; founding ptnr. Newell & Newell CPAs, Columbus, 1986—. Mem. Am. Inst. CPAs, Ga. Soc. CPAs. Baptist. Office: Newell & Newell CPAs 3575 Macon Rd Ste 5 Columbus GA 31907-8225

NEWELL, STEVEN YOUNG, research microbial ecologist; b. Cleve., Jan. 20, 1945; s. William H.B. and Elizabeth E. Newell; m. Becky McCranie, Apr. 9, 1966. BS in Biology magna cum laude, U. Miami, 1967, MS in Biol. Oceanography, 1969, PhD in Biol. Oceanography, 1974. Postdoctoral rsch. assoc. U. Miami (Fla.) Rosenstiel Sch. Marine and Atmospheric Sci., 1972-75, rsch. assoc., 1976-79; rsch. assoc. U. Ga. Marine Inst., Sapelo Island, 1979-80, asst. marine scientist, 1981-82, assoc. rsch. scientist, 1982-87, sr. rsch. scientist, 1987—, chmn. vis. scientist program, 1986—, radiation safety officer, 1988, 90—, acting dir., 1982, 84, 86, 87, 90; adj. prof. dept. marine scis. U. Ga., Athens, 1981-92; adj. assoc. prof. Ga. State U., Atlanta, 1982-87; presenter in field at symposia and seminars, 1971—; mem. proposal-rev. panel for Estuarine habitat resotration program Nat. Sea Grant Coll. Program, Silver Springs, Md., 1990; cons. Biomarine Rsch., Inc., 1972, Fla. Power and Light Co., 1975, Bioindustries Devel. Co., 1976, ERDA, 1977, EPA, 1979, Waterways Expt. Sta., C.E., Dept. Army, 1986, U. Iowa, 1988, U. P.R., 1990—. also others. Mem. editorial bd. Microbial Ecology, 1986—, Marine Ecology Progress Series, 1985—, Scientia Marina, 1993—, Mycological Rsch., 1996—, Aquatic Microbial Ecology, 1996—; contbr. articles to profl. jours., chpts. to books. Grantee Coca-Cola Export Corp., 1973-74, Office Sea Grant, 1974-75, 79-81, 86-88, Denius Found., 1974, NSF, 1976-78, 83-95, 96—, U. Ga. Sea Grant Program, 1980, Sapelo Island Rsch. Found., 1980-82; Grad. fellow NSF, 1967-71; Recipient creative rsch. medal U. Ga., 1990. Mem. INTECOL, Mycol. Soc. Am., Am. Soc. Limnology and OCeanography, Brit. Mycol. Soc., Am. Soc. for Microbiology, Ecol. Soc. Am., Phi Kappa Phi. Home and Office: U Ga Marine Inst Sapelo Island GA 31327

NEWELL, THOMAS DAVID, pediatric/family nurse practitioner; b. Waterloo, Iowa, Jan. 22, 1951; s. William Francis and Virginia Clare (Winginger) N.; m. Diane Carol Gordon, Aug. 21, 1976; children: Brian, Jeffrey. ADN, Galveston Coll., 1974; BSN, U. Tex., Galveston, 1982; MSN, U. Tex., Arlington, 1983; Nursing Doctorate, Rush U., 1992. RN, Tex.; cert. pediatric nurse practitioner, family nurse practitioner. Staff nurse U. Tex. Med. Br., Galveston, 1972-78, pediatric nurse practitioner, 1978-82; family nurse practitioner Parkland Meml. Hosp., Dallas, 1983-85, Anchor Family Practice, Chgo., 1991-92; pediatric nurse practitioner Pediatric Assocs. Denton, Tex., 1986-92; pediatric nurse practitioner in pvt. practice Denton, Tex., 1992—. With U.S. Army, 1969-72, Vietnam. Fellow Nat. Assn. Pediatric Nurse Practitioners; mem. Tex. Nurse Practitioners Assn., Dallas Area Nurse Practitioners Group. Home: 6852 Myrtle Beach Dr Plano TX 75093-6325 Office: 1160 N Bonnie Brae St Denton TX 76201-2421

NEWFIELD, NANCY LANG, naturalist, writer; b. New Orleans, Feb. 19, 1945; d. Thomas J. and Lorraine (Jacquet) Lang; m. Paul C. Newfield III, Nov. 26, 1966; children: Charlotte, Aimée. Freelance naturalist, 1979—; news columnist Nature Soc., 1986—; article writer LivingBird; Bird Watcher's Digest, Birder's World & L.O.S. News. Co-author: Hummingbird Gardens, 1996; contbr. articles to profl. jours. Mem. Am. Ornithologists Union, Wilson Ornithol. Soc. (Margaret Morse Nice award 1980), Cooper Ornithol. Soc., La. Ornithol. Soc. (pres. 1989-91), Tex. Ornithol. Soc. Home and Office: Casa Colibrí 3016 45th St Metairie LA 70001

NEWILL, JAMES WAGNER, accounting executive; b. Greensburg, Pa., Dec. 22, 1934; s. James Meyers and Ruth Elizabeth (Wagner) N.; m. Helene Margaret Dolibois, Feb. 18, 1957; 1 child, J. Eric. BBA, St. Vincent Coll., Latrobe, Pa., 1962. CPA, Pa., Ohio, Fla. Staff acct. George Conti & Co., CPA, Greensburg, 1962-65; internal auditor Duquesne Light Co., Pitts., 1965-67; supr. accounts payable and gen. ledger Kennametal, Inc., Latrobe, 1967-71; asst. controller Glosser Stores, Inc., Johnstown, Pa., 1971-73; controller, asst. treas. Meridian Plastics, Inc., Byesville, Ohio, 1973-76; regional controller Friendly Ice Cream Corp., Wilbraham, Mass., 1976-79; pres. J.W. Newill Co., Troy, Ohio, 1979-92; pvt. practice Fla., 1993—; bd. dirs. Southwest Nat. Bank, Greensburg. v.p., bd. dirs. Troy-Hayner Cultural Ctr., 1982-85. Served to staff sgt. USAF, 1954-58. Mem. AICPA, Pa. Inst. CPAs, Ohio Soc. CPAs, Fla. Inst. CPAs, Nat. Assn. Accts., Masons, Scottish Rite, Rotary (chmn. com., Paul Harris fellow), Shrine, Elks. Republican. Presbyterian.

NEWITT, JOHN GARWOOD, JR., lawyer; b. Charlotte, N.C., Apr. 9, 1941; s. John Garwood and Sarah Elizabeth (Stratford) N.; m. Catherine Elizabeth Hubbard, Aug. 28, 1965; children: Catherine Stratford, Elizabeth Blake. BA, Wake Forest U., 1963, JD, 1965; postgrad., U. Va., 1966-68. Bar: N.C. 1965, U.S. Ct. Mil. Appeals 1965, U.S. Dist. Ct. (we. dist.) N.C. 1968, U.S. Ct. Claims 1968, U.S. Tax. Ct. 1968, U.S. Ct. Appeals (4th cir.) 1984. Ptnr. Newitt & Newitt, Charlotte, 1968-73; sr. ptnr. Newitt & Bruny, Charlotte, 1973—; lectr. The Judge Advocate Gen.'s Sch., 1965-68, United Way Vol. Leadership Devel. Program, 1986-93. Contbr. articles to law revs. Chmn. Bd. Zoning Adjustment, 1971-77; bd. dirs. Carolina Group Homes, 1992-95. Mem. ASCAP (awards), N.C. Acad. Trial Lawyers, N.C. Bar Assn., Mecklenburg County Bar Assn. (chmn. arbitration subcom.), Internat. Assn. Fin. Planning, Internat. Platform Assn., N.C. Coll. Advocacy (cert. competency), Myers Park Country Club (pres., bd. dirs.), Selwyn Men's Fellowship (pres.), Good Fellows, Phi Delta Phi (past sec.). Republican. Presbyterian. Home: 3216 Ferncliff Rd Charlotte NC 28211-3259 Office: Newitt & Bruny 417 East Blvd Ste 104 Charlotte NC 28203-5163

NEWKIRK, TRIXIE DARNELL, critical care nurse; b. Sault St. Marie, Mich., July 22, 1964; d. Mitchell and Lois I. (Johnston) Darnell; m. Shane P. Newkirk, July 19, 1986. BSN, Southwestern Okla. State U., 1986; MS, Tex. Woman's U., 1994. RN., Okla., Tex.; cert. instr. BCLS, ACLS, CCRN. Staff nurse St. Francis Hosp., Tulsa; asst. nurse mgr. CCU Humana MCD Hosp., Dallas; staff nurse Baylor U. Med. Ctr., Dallas, supr. nurse educator critical care unit, 1991-95; clin. nurse specialist for cardiovasc. svcs., 1995—. Mem. AACN, T.N.P., Sigma Theta Tau. Home: 6505 Rosebud Dr Rowlett TX 75088-6773

NEWLAND, HILLARY REID, pathologist; b. Wilmington, N.C., July 3, 1940; s. Hillery Reid and Annie Mae (Bowden) N.; m. Eleanor Milner, Aug. 25, 1963; children: Benjamin Reid, Sarah O'Beirne, Emily Cobb. BS, Davidson (N.C.) Coll., 1962; MD, Med. Coll. Ga., 1968. Diplomate Am. Bd. Pathology. Intern in internal medicine New Eng. Med. Ctr. Hosps., Boston, 1968-69; resident in pathology Med. Coll. Ga. Hosps., Augusta, 1969-70, Madigan Army Med. Ctr., Tacoma, 1970-72; asst. prof. medicine U. Alta., Edmonton, Can., 1974-75; clin. instr. U. Vt. Med. Sch., Burlington, 1975-77; pathologist diagnostic svcs. Lancaster, N.H., 1975-77; pathologist Athens (Ga.) Regional Med. Ctr., 1977-78, 79—, Wentworth-Douglass Hosp., Dover, N.H., 1978-79; pres. Athens Rsch. and Tech., Inc., 1985—; adj. faculty mem. dept. cell biology U. Ga., Athens, 1988—. Contbr. articles to profl. publs. Maj. USAR, 1970-74. Fellow ACP, Coll. Am. Pathologists, Am. Soc. Clin. Pathologists, Am. Coll. Quality Assurance Physicians; mem. Athens C. of C. (bd. dirs. 1990-92), Med. Assn. Ga. (chmn. continuing med. edn. 1989). Democrat. Office: Athens Regional Med Ctr 1199 Prince Ave Athens GA 30606-2767

NEWLAND, JAMES LEROY, banker; b. Washington, Ga., Dec. 8, 1942; s. Hillery Reid and Annie Mae (Bowden) N.; m. Dorothy Greve Sams, Mar. 19, 1966; children: Harriet Greve, James L. Jr. BBA in Fin., U. Ga., 1966. Trainee First Nat. Bank of Athens (Ga.), 1966-69; trainee The Citizens and So. Nat. Bank (now Nations Bank), Athens, 1969-70, asst. trust officer, 1970-75, trust officer, 1975-80, asst. v.p., 1980-87, v.p., 1987-92; v.p., trust officer Athens 1st Bank & Trust Co., 1992-95; v.p. Commercial Banking, 1995—; instr. Am. Inst. Banking, Athens, 1981-82. Treas. N.E. Ga. United Way, Athens, 1974-80; mem. CSC, Athens, 1974-76; trustee Ga. Banking Schs. of Ga. Banking Assn., 1986-89; mem. constn. com. Boys Clubs Am., 1986-88, nat. bd. trustees, 1987—, vice chmn. nat. area coun. com., 1987—; mem. mission bd. Gen. Assemlby, Presbyn. Ch., co-chmn. churchwide campaign, 1984-88; pres., bd. dirs. Jeannette Rankin Found., 1991-92; pres., trustee Athens Neighborhood Health Ctr., 1990-92; mem. Athens Regional Med. Ctr. Hosp. Authority, 1992—. Recipient medallion Boys Club Am., 1980, Southeastern Pacemaker award, 1984, Bronze Keystone award, 1990. Mem. Rotary Internat. Democrat.

NEWLAND, JANE LOU, nursing educator; b. Toledo, July 18, 1931; d. Clarence Charles Meinen and Bernice Isabell (Floyd) Scott; m. Byron Merle Newland, Aug. 4, 1962; children: Jeffrey Bruce, Brian James. Diploma in nursing, Lima (Ohio) Meml. Hosp., 1952; BSN, Ohio State U., 1959; M Vocat. Edn., U. South Fla., 1983, EdS in Vocat. Edn., 1989. RN, Ohio, Fla.; cert. tchr., Fla. Stewardess nurse Balt. & Ohio R.R., Cin., 1953-56; dir. nursing Lima State Hosp., 1960-67, dir. nursing edn., 1967-72; renal nurse children's svc. Health and Rehabilitative Svcs. Fla., Ft. Myers, 1975-78; practical nursing instr. Lee High-Tech. Ctr. Ctrl., Ft. Myers, 1979—; mem. adv. bd. Practical Nurse Assn., Lima, 1966-71. Mem., sec. St. James City Civic Assn., 1973-76; den leader Boy Scouts Am., St. James City, 1970-76; treas. PTA Pine Island Elem. Sch., Pine Island Center, Fla., 1973-75. Recipient Assoc. Master Tchr. award Fla. State Bd. Edn., 1986. Mem. Assn. Practical Nurse Educators Fla., Nat. Assn. health Occupations Tchrs., Lee County Vocat. Assn. (Outstanding Health Occupation Tchr. award 1985, Outstanding Vocat. Edn. Tchr. award 1990), Fla. Vocat. Assn., Health Occupation Educators Assn. Fla., Ladies Aux. VFW, Ladies Oriental Shrine, Order Ea. Star, Niobians of Cape Coral (Fla.), Kappa Delta (v.p. 1983-85, pres. 1993—), Phi Kappa Phi. Lutheran. Home: 2261 Carambola Ln Saint James City FL 33956 Office: Lee County High Tech Ctr 3800 Michigan Ave Fort Myers FL 33916-2204

NEWLIN, KIMREY DAYTON, personal computer analyst; b. Greensboro, N.C., Jan. 27, 1944; s. Dayton Gilbert and Pearl (Kimrey) N.; m. Beverly Jane Agnew, Mar. 9, 1968; children: Kim, Jr., Stephanie, Laurie. BS in Physics, Guilford Coll., 1966; MS in Agrl. Econs., Clemson U., 1969; MEd in Indls. Engring., Texas A&M U., 1970. Cert. Prof. Logistician, Cost Analyst, Profl. Estimator. Gen. engr., lifetime staff and faculty mem. Army Logistics Mgmt. Ctr./Darcom/Dept. of Def., Ft. Lee, Va., 1968-71; economist Army Procurement Rsch. Office/Army Logistics Mgmt. Ctr./Darcom/Dept. of Def., Ft. Lee, 1971-75, operations rsch. analyst, 1975-78; statistician S.E. Fisheries Ctr./Nat. Marines Fisheries Svc./Nat. Oceanographic Atmospheric Adminstrn./Dept. Commerce, Miami, 1978—. Author: Treatment of Textile Waste, 1971, How to Run Successful Projects, 1976-90, Handbook for Chapter Plan Guide, 1976-90, DT LCC, Logistics Spectru, 1978; contbr. numerous articles to profl. jours. Logistics chmn. U.S. JCI Senate, 1992; chief of staff Coconut Grove (Fla.) Jaycees, 1979-90; adminstrv. v.p., treas. Fla. JCI Senate, Lakeland, 1988-90, lifetime mem., 1983—; presdl. advisor Fla. Jaycees Act Team, 1983-89, Fla. Jaycees Lakeland, 1985-86; sec. Friendship JCS, 1990—; v.p. Va. Jaycees, Roanoke, 1978-79, commonity devel., life mem., 1977—; lifetime col. Fla. Gator Corps, 1993—; ctr. rep. SEFSC Miami Fed. Exec. Bd., 1986—. Recipient Outstanding Svc. Plaque as Adminstr. V.P. Fla. JCI Senate, 1990, Coconut Grove Jaycees Palm award for Outstanding Svc. for Last 10 Yrs., 1989, Hommer Shepard Meml. award Fla. JCI Senate, 1989, Presdl. award of Honor Plaque for Outstanding Svc. Cocnut Grove Jaycees, 1981-87, Cert. Appreciation for Inter City Marine Program Performance Dade County Pub. Schs., 1987-88, Henry Colona award Fla. Jaycees, 1986, 82, Expo 87 Career & Job Fair award Greater Miami C. of C., 1987, Logistics Cert. Miami Fed. Volunteerism Cert. Exec. Bd., 1991, Adminstrvt. Spt. Cert., Exec. Bd., 1992, Get Up Off That Thing Plaque, Coconut Grove JCS, 1993, Cert. Resource Com, Roster Update Chmn. Cert., Fla. JCI Senate, 1995. Fellow Soc. Logistics Engrs. (life, corp.), Nat. Estimating Soc. Republican. Presbyterian. Home: 755 Allendale Rd Miami FL 33149-2402

NEWMAN, BETTY LOUISE, accountant; b. Llano, Tex., Dec. 1, 1946; d. Travis Alger and Edith Lucile (Tate) N.; m. Vernon George Mangold (div. July 1981); 1 child, Ian Keith. Student, San Antonio Jr. Coll., 1965-66; BBA, U. Tex., San Antonio, 1985. Data claims analyst Blue Cross/Blue Shield, San Antonio, 1980-82; regional sec., acct. BioMed. Applications, San Antonio, 1982-83; with acctg. dept. Comprehensive Bus. Svcs., Boerne, Tex., 1983-84; acct. Cadwallader Ins. Agy., San Antonio, 1986, Data Processing Support, Inc., San Antonio, 1986-87, Archive Retrieval Sys., Inc., San Antonio, 1986-87; pvt. practice acctg. San Antonio, 1987—; acct. atty., 1989-92; acct. Night in Old San Antonio, 1996. Vol. Boy Scouts Am., San Antonio, 1978-89, unit commr., 1989; bd. dirs. San Antonio Met. Ministries, 1987-90. Scholar Women in Bus., 1983. Mem. NAFE, Nat. Assn. Accts. (assoc. bd. dirs. 1988-90), Inst. Mgmt. Accts., Leon Springs Bus. Assn., Am. Luth. Women. Home and Office: 25403 Brewer Dr San Antonio TX 78257-1139

NEWMAN, BRUCE ALLAN, political science educator; b. Wilmington, Del., Aug. 30, 1960; s. Thomas Allan and Ethel Mae (Stayton) N. BA, U. Del., 1986; MA, U. Dallas, 1990, ABD, 1993. Instr. in polit. sci. Western Okla. State Coll., Altus, 1991—. With U.S. Army, 1980-83. Earhart Found. fellow, 1987-88, 88-89. Mem. Am. Polit. Sci. Assn., Acad. Polit. Sci., Okla. Polit. Sci. Assn., Nat. Assn. Scholars. Republican. Home: 421 E Tamarack Rd B-21 Altus OK 73521 Office: Western Okla State Coll 2801 S Main St Altus OK 73521

NEWMAN, CHARLES FORREST, lawyer; b. Grenada, Miss., Jan. 15, 1937; s. Wiley Clifford and Lurene (Westbrook) N.; m. Jeannette Kay Bailey, May 26, 1973. BA magna cum laude, Yale U., 1959, JD, 1963; postgrad., U. Bonn, Fed. Republic Germany, 1959-60. Bar: Tenn. 1964, U.S. Supreme Ct. 1981. Law clk. U.S. Dist. Judge Bailey Brown, Western Dist. Tenn., 1963-64; mem. firm Burch Porter & Johnson, Attys., Memphis, 1965—, ptnr., 1966—; bd. dirs. Metro. Interfaith Assn., Memphis Coll. Art, Nat. Civil Rights Mus.; mem. exec. com. Yale U. Law Sch. Assn., 1984-88, Pres.'s Coun. Rhodes Coll., chair; commr. Memphis Landmarks commn., 1983-87; mem. class coun. Class of '59, Yale Coll., 1980-90; assoc. Environ. Law Inst.; former bd. trustees Lemoyne-Owen Coll., Nature Conservancy. Adenauer fellow U. Bonn, 1959-60; recipient 1990 Disting. Svc. medal Rhodes Coll. Fellow Am. Bar Found., Tenn. Bar Found.; mem. ABA, Tenn. Bar Assn., Memphis Bar Assn. (bd. dirs. 1990—, pres. 1996), Am. Judicature Soc., Am. Inns Ct. (master of bench), Tenn. Bar Assn., Tenn. Club, Memphis Rotary Club (bd. dirs. 1996—), Econ. Club of Memphis, Yale Club of Memphis (past pres.), Rotary, Phi Beta Kappa. Home: 3880 Poplar Ave Memphis TN 38111-7614 Office: Burch Porter & Johnson 130 Court Ave Memphis TN 38103-2217

NEWMAN, CHARLES JUDSON, financial planner, employee benefits consultant; b. Knoxville, Tenn., Nov. 29, 1950; s. Hugh Wallace and Agnes Turbyville Newman; m. Rosemary Harris, Apr. 7, 1983. BBA, Cumberland U., 1988. Lic. rep. gen. securities series 7 Nat. Assn. Securities Dealers. Registered rep. Paine Webber, Jackson & Curtis, L.A., 1976-78; muni bond trader Henderson Few & Co., Knoxville, Tenn., 1978-79; investment exec. J.C. Bradford Co., Knoxville, 1979-81; CEO Newman Agy., Knoxville, 1981-92; pres. Benefit Plan Solutions, Inc., 1992—. Capt. USAR, 1969-76. Republican. Episcopalian. Home: 5029 Mountain Crest Dr Knoxville TN 37918-4427

NEWMAN, DOROTHY ANNE, secondary school educator; b. Minden, La., Jan. 25, 1947; d. George Malcolm and Neva Estelle (Reeder) Temple. AA, Kilgore Coll., 1967; BA summa cum laude, East Tex. Bapt. Coll., 1972; MA, Stephen F. Austin State U., 1979. Cert. tchr., Tex. Tchr. social studies Marshall (Tex.) Ind. Sch. Dist., 1974—, sponsor student council, 1975—; bd. dirs. Tex. Energy Edn. Day Project, Austin, 1982—. Mem. regional planning com. Youth Alcohol and Treatment Conf., Austin, 1983. Recipient awards for energy edn. day project, nat. student safety program, alcohol edn. project, Excellence award for U. Tex., Austin, 1988, Outstanding Alumni award East Tex. Bapt. U., 1991; named Outstanding High Sch. Tchr., So. Meth. U., 1988; Tex. Edn. Agy. Energy and Environ. Edn. award, Tex. Humanities Outstanding Tchr. award, 1990. Mem. Tex. Classroom Tchrs. Assn. (membership chmn. 1981-82), Nat. Coun. for Social Studies, Tex. Coun. for Social Studies (curriculum coun. 1990—), East Tex. Coun. on Social Studies, Nat. Assn. Workshop Dirs., Tex. Assn. Student Couns. (state sec. 1981-82, 88-89, parliamentarian 1983-84), Phi Alpha Theta, Alpha Chi. Republican. Methodist. Office: Marshall High Sch 1900 Maverick Dr Marshall TX 75670-6352

NEWMAN, FRANCIS A., executive medical device company; b. 1947. Sr. v.p. merchandising F.W. Woolworth, 1980-84, exec. v.p. household merchandising, 1984-85; pres., CEO, dir. F&M Distributors, Inc., 1986-93; pres., COO Eckerd Fleet, Inc., Largo, Fla., 1993—. Office: Eckerd Fleet Inc 8333 Bryan Dairy Rd Largo FL 33777-1230

NEWMAN, JAY RICHARD, archaeologist; b. Chgo., Mar. 26, 1954; s. Sidney and Patricia Estelle Elias N.; m. Margaret Grigor, Sept. 22, 1995. AA, Triton Coll., River Grove, Ill., 1974; BA, Grinnell Coll., 1976; MA, So. Meth. U., 1984; PhD, 1996. Archaeologist, rsch. assoc. Ft. Burgwin Rsch. Ctr., Ranchos de Taos, N.Mex., 1978-79, asst. archaeol. field dir., 1979-81; teaching asst. stats./computers So. Meth. U., Dallas, 1980-81, asst. curator collections dept. anthropology, 1981-85, archaeology field dir., 1985-86; archaeology survey dir. U. North Tex., Denton, 1986-87; acting supervisory archaeologist U.S. Army C.E., Ft. Worth, 1991-92, archaeologist, 1987-91, 92—; archaeol. cons. Air Combat Command, Langley AFB, 1993—, Joint Task Force 6, Dept. Def., Ft. Bliss, Tex., 1988—, USMC, Camp Pendleton, Calif., 1995—, USN, Corpus Christi Naval Air Sta., 1992-93, U.S. Army, Ft. Bliss, 1994—. Author: Historic Preservation Plans for Four Navy Bases in Texas and Louisiana, 1988; contbr. articles to profl. jours. Recipient Cert. of Appreciation, Dept. of Def., 1990, U.S. Army Achievement medal for Civilian Svc., 1990. Mem. Soc. for Am. Archaeology, Soc. of Profl. Archaeologists, Tex. Archaeol. Soc., Coun. Tex. Archaeologists, Dallas Archaeol. Soc., Tarrant County Archaeol. Soc. Office: US Army Corps of Engrs CESWF-PL-RC PO Box 17300 819 Taylor St Fort Worth TX 76102-0300

NEWMAN, JOHN WILBURN, oil company executive; b. Ashland, Ky., Dec. 11, 1937; s. Clarence Matthew and Theresa Eudora (Tate) N.; m. Faye Louise Taylor (wid.); 1 child, Karen Lynne. Chem. Engr., U. Cin. Various positions to v.p. Carbon Fibers Divsn. Ashland Petroleum Co. divsn. Ashland, Inc., 1956—; pres. MotorCarbon, LLC; presenter papers in field; mem. materials tech. adv. com. U.S. Dept. Commerce. Co-patentee in field; co-editor Petroleum-Derived Carbons, 1986. Adv. bd. Ctr. for Applied Energy Rsch. of U. Ky., Ky. State U; bd. dirs. Southwest Chpt. Software Valley of W.Va., Boyd County Ky. Hist. Soc. Mem. Am. Carbon Soc. (mem. advisory com.), other tech. orgns. Episcopalian. Home: 2740 Jackson Ave Ashland KY 41102-6032 Office: Ashland Petroleum Co PO Box 391 Ashland KY 41105-0391

NEWMAN, MARY THOMAS, communications educator, management consultant; b. Howell, Mo., Oct. 15, 1933; d. Austin Hill and Doris (McQueen) Thomas; m. Grover Travis Newman, Aug. 22, 1952 (div. 1967); 1 child, Leah Newman Lane; m. Rodney Charles Westlund, July 18, 1981. BS, S.F. Austin State U., 1965; MA, U. Houston, 1956; PhD, Pa. State U., 1980. Cert. permanent tchr., Tex. Instr. communications South Tex. Coll., Houston, 1965-70; assoc. prof. communications Burlington County Coll., Pemberton, N.J., 1970-72; teaching asst. in communications Pa. State U., University Park, 1972-73; asst. prof. Ogontz Campus Pa. State U., Abington, 1973-80; lectr. mgmt. and communications U. Md., Europe and Asia, 1980-83; mem. vis. faculty dept. communications U. Tenn., Knoxville, 1984-85; asst. prof. human factors U. So. Calif., L.A., 1985-88; assoc. prof. human factors, dir. profl. devel. U. Denver Coll. Systems Sci., 1988-92; assoc. prof. USC, Berlin, Germany, 1992-93; assoc. prof., assoc. dir. Whitworth Coll., Spokane, Wash., 1993-95; assoc. prof. comms. Houston Baptist U., 1995—; pres. Human Resource Communications Group, Easton, Md., 1984—; lectr. Bus. Rsch. Inst., Toyo U., Tokyo, 1983, Saitama Med. U., Japan, 1983; scholar in residence U.S. Marine Corps., Quantico, Va., 1990-92; mem. final phase faculty USC MSSM Troop Draw Down, Berlin, Germany, 1992-93; team mem. Spokane Inter-Collegiate Rsch. & Tech. Inst., 1993-95; dir. Women's Leadership Conf., Moses Lake, Wash., 1993; mem. world svcs. com. YWCA, Spokane; Lilly fellow 1996. Author: Introduction to Basic Speech Communication, 1969; contbr. articles to profl. jours. Program developer U.S. Army Hdqrs. Sch. Age Latch Key Program, Alexandria, Va., 1987; mem. Govt. of Guam Women's Issues Task Force, 1985. Lilly fellow in humanities and arts, summer 1996. Mem. Human Factors Soc., Speech Communication Assn. (legis. coun. 1970-73, editl. bd. jour. 1970-76), Ea. Communication Assn. (editl. bd. jours. 1975-80), Univ. Film Assn. (publicity dir. 1978-80), Indsl. Comm. Coun., Chesapeake Women's Network, Easton Bus. and Profl. Women, Alpha Chi, Alpha Psi Omega, Pi Kappa Delta, Delta Kappa Gamma. Office: Houston Baptist U Dept Comms 7502 Fondren Houston TX 77074

NEWMAN, MAXINE PLACKER, insurance consultant; b. Haslem, Tex., Nov. 21, 1922; d. L. H. and Beatrice Rosetta (Stuart) Placker: B.S., Stephen F. Austin State U., 1943; m. Robert Wayne Newman, May 23, 1975; 1 son, Stephen Randall Hillin (by previous marriage). Acct., Lamar U., Beaumont, Tex., 1953-55; office mgr. Williamson Ins. Agy., Beaumont, 1955-72; v.p. Alexander & Alexander, Dallas, 1972-79; cons. Bellefonte Ins. Co., Cin., 1979—; v.p., office mgr., treas. Ralph K. Kemp & Assocs., Inc., Dallas,1979-92; ret. Mem. Am. Bus. Women Assn. (Woman of Yr. 1979), Nat. Assn. Ins. Women, Dallas Assn. Ins. Women, Beta Sigma Phi (Woman of Yr. 1966). Republican. Baptist. Clubs: Trophy, Women's, Beaumont Country, Trophy Ladies Golf Assn. Address: 6654 Marshall Pl Beaumont TX 77706

NEWMAN, SAMUEL MARK, animator; b. Kerrville, Tex., Sept. 25, 1957; s. Ellis William and Maxleen June (Ersch) N.; m. Sherri Lynn Bell, May 8, 1982; 1 child, Jackson Ellis. BFA, Southwest Tex. State U., 1980. Retail and promotions artist San Angelo (Tex.) Standard-Times, 1981; audio visual assoc. Gen. Telephone of Southwest, San Angelo, 1981-82; staff artist San Antonio Express-News, 1982-83; sr. computer graphics illustrator Datapoint Corp., San Antonio, 1983-85; computer graphics design dir. Third Coast Video, Austin, Tex., 1986; art dir. Match Frame Computer Graphics, San Antonio, 1986-89; animation designer Avid Prodns., Houston, 1990-92; owner Digital Canvas, Kerrville, Tex., 1992—; art instr. Southwest Tex. State U., San Marcos, 1987-92; animation dir. ARS Interactive, Chattanooga, 1996—. Recipient Best of Show award Brazos Valley Arts Coun. Computer Graphics Competition, 1991, 1st place Fine Art Still Image AT&T Graphic Software labs. Internat. Competition, 1991, 2d place Corporate Still Image, 1992, 1st place Graphic Design Animation, 1991, Addy awards, 1982, 83, 88; Runner-Up in Crystal Graphics Art and Design Contest, 1994; named to Outstanding Young Men of Am., 1985. Mem. Assn. for Computing Machinery Siggraph. Democrat. Home and Office: Digital Canvas 409 Mississippi Ave Signal Mountain TN 37377

NEWMAN, SHARON LYNN, elementary education educator; b. Lewisburg, Tenn., Jan. 9, 1946; d. Hermit Taft and Martha Elizabeth (Pardue) Simmons; m. George Wynne Newman Sr., June 11, 1967; 1 child, George Wynne Jr. BS in Edn., Athens State Coll., 1979. Substitute tchr. Giles County Bd. Edn., Pulaski, Tenn., 1979-81; chpt. 1 reading tchr. Giles County Bd. Edn., Pulaski, 1981-91, chpt. 1 math. tchr., 1991—; chpt. 1 coord. Elkton (Tenn.) Elem. Sch., 1989—, mem. steering com., 1989—, chair math. dept., 1993-95, chpt. title I com., 1995—, mem. disaster preparedness team. Ch. libr. Elkton (Tenn.) Bapt. Ch., 1992—; vol. Giles County Hist. Soc. Libr. and Mus., 1995—. Mem. NEA, Nat. Coun. Tchrs. Math., Giles County Edn. Assn. (rsch. chairperson 1993-95). Home: 1758 Old Stage Rd Ardmore TN 38449 Office: Elkton Elem Sch Elkton TN 38455

NEWMAN, STUART, lawyer; b. Hackensack, N.J., June 7, 1947; s. Joseph and Rose (Wilenski) N.; m. Tina Gilson; children: Leslie, Dara, Mindy, Robert. BA, SUNY, Cortland, 1971; JD cum laude, Albany Law Sch., 1974. Bar: N.Y. 1975, Ga. 1978. Assoc. Dewey, Ballantine, Bushby, Palmer & Wood, N.Y.C., 1974-76; from assoc. to ptnr. Jackson, Lewis, Schnitzler & Krupman, Atlanta, 1976—; lectr. U. Ala., Tuscaloosa, 1980-84, Auburn U., 1986—. Dir. Ruth Mitchell Dance Co. of Atlanta, 1986-88. Mem. ABA, Atlanta Bar Assn., Ga. Bar Assn., Shakerag Hounds, Inc., Midlands Fox Hounds, Inc., Live Oak Hounds, Ansley Golf Club. Office: Jackson Lewis Schnitzler & Krupman 2400 Peachtree Ctr Harris Tower 233 Peachtree St NE Atlanta GA 30303

NEWMAN, TERRIE LYNNE, advertising and marketing executive; b. Boston; d. Joseph and Clara (Bistry) N.; m. Fredric Aron Kerstein, June 18, 1978. BA in English, U. Mass., Boston, 1973. Copywriter Vanda Beauty Counselor, Inc., N.Y.C., 1973-75; creative dir. Vanda Beauty Counselor, Inc., 1975-76; sr. writer Avon Products, Inc., N.Y.C., 1976-79; copywriter Hume, Smith, Mickelberry Advt., Inc., Miami, Fla., 1979-80, Beber, Silverstein & Ptnrs., Advt., Miami, 1980-81; pres., creative dir. Terrie Lynne Newman, Inc., Miami, 1981-92, Terrie Newman Communs., Miami, 1992—. Recipient Internat. Gold Echo award Direct Mktg. Assn., 1987, 88, Internat. Bronze Echo award, 1987, Gold Award for Excellence in Mktg., Gold Coast chpt. Am. Mktg. Assn., 1987, First Place Gold medallion Broadcast Promotion & Mktg. Execs., 1986, Clio award, 1981, Emmy award, 1981, others. Home: 6970 SW 125th St Miami FL 33156-6240

NEWMAN, THOMAS WALTER GOLDBERG, therapist, consultant; b. N.Y.C., May 25, 1955; s. Edward Gunther and Marga Irene (Kirschbaum N.; m. Cindy Goldberg, July 12, 1981; children: Robert Goldberg, Elliot Goldberg. BA in Psychology, San Francisco State U., 1977; MA in Psychology, Humboldt State U., 1982. Therapist Parent & Child Study Ctr., West Palm Beach, Fla., 1982-83; residential therapist ACT Corp., Deland, Fla., 1983-84; outpatient therapist ACT Corp., Daytona Beach, Fla., 1984-86; pvt. practice marriage and family therapist Newman Counseling Alternatives, P.A., Daytona Beach, 1986—; dir. Domestic Abusers Program, Daytona Beach; psychol. cons., lectr. in field, Daytona Beach, 1986—; family therapy columnist Volusia Kids mag., 1990—; mem. Commn. Minimum Stds. for Batterers' Treatment, Fla., 1994. Mem. Volusia County Child Abuse Task Force, Daytona Beach, 1986-88, chairperson, 1987-88; mem. Volusia County Constituency for Children, Daytona Beach, 1987—, legis. chairperson, 1988-90; bd. trustees Temple Beth-El, Ormond Beach, Fla., 1986-91. Mem. Am. Assn. Marriage and Family Therapists (clin. mem.), Employee Assistance Profls. Assn. (assoc.), Fla. Alcohol and Drug Abuse Assn., Nat. Assn. Underwater Instrs. Democrat. Jewish. Office: 533 Seabreeze Blvd Ste 300 Daytona Beach FL 32118-3977

NEWMAN, TILLMAN EUGENE, JR., food company executive; b. Greenwood, Ark., Feb. 13, 1938; s. Tillman Eugene and Theresa Christine (Simmons) N.; m. Linda Gail Childers, Feb. 13, 1983; children: James Barton Langley, Robert, John, Michael, Kristen Newman. BS in Chem. Engring., U. Ark., 1963. Registered profl. engr., Ark., Iowa, Mo. Plant mgr. Ralston Purina, St. Louis, 1963-67, project mgr., 1967-71; v.p. Huxtable-Hammond, Kansas City, Mo., 1971-79; dir. engring. Tyson Foods, Russellville, Ark., 1979-95; v.p. sales and engring. Burrough Brasuell Corp., Van Buren, Ark., 1995—; bd. dirs. Mech. Controllers of Iowa, 1976-78; mem. Ark. Allied Industries, Little Rock, 1980—. Bd. dirs. Ark. Fedn. Water and Air, 1984—. Served to sgt. USNG, 1956-65. Mem. Nat. Soc. Profl. Engrs., Am. Inst. Chem. Engrs., Am. Soc. Mech. Engrs., Russellville C. of C. Baptist. Avocations: fishing; boating.

NEWMARK, HOWARD, surgeon, entrepreneur; b. Perth Amboy, N.J., Mar. 12, 1944; s. Carl and Ruth (Kestenbaum) N.; m. Mary Ella Adkins, Feb. 19, 1989; 1 child, Alexander Joseph. BA, Duke U., 1966; MD, Meharry Med. Coll., 1970; MBA, Ohio U., 1988. Diplomate Am. Bd. Abdominal Surgery. Intern Cook County Hosp., Chgo., 1971; resident in surgery Med. Coll. of Ohio, Toledo, 1975; resident in thoracic surgery U. Louisville, 1979; CEO, pres. Summa Med. Systems, Ashland, Ky., Ironton, Ohio, Huntington, W.Va., 1987—; pvt. practice surgeon Portsmouth, Ohio, 1979-81, Ashland, 1981-83, Ironton, 1983—, Huntington, 1990; surgeon Lawrence County Med. Ctr., Ironton, Cabell-Huntington Hosp., Huntington; med. dir. dept. of emergency medicine Vets. Meml. Hosp., Pomeroy, Ohio, 1996—. Maj. USAF, 1975-77. Named Eagle Scout Boy Scouts Am. Fellow Am. Soc. Phlebology, Am. Soc. Abdominal Surgeons, Am. Coll. Angiology, Internat. Coll. Angiology, Internat. Coll. Surgeons; mem. AMA, ASPCA, PETA, Am. Thoracic Soc., N.Am. Soc. Pacing and Electrophysiology, Soc. Vascular Tech., Internat. Endovascular Soc., Am. Coll. Chest Physicians, Am. Coll. Physicians Execs. (alt. del.), Ohio State Med. Assn. (pres.), Lawrence County Med. Assn., Am. Mgmt. Assn., Pres.'s Assn., Greenpeace, Costeau Soc. Democrat. Jewish. Office: 207 S 7th St Ironton OH 45638-1621 also: 1631 Offnere St Portsmouth OH 45662-3537

NEWMARK, MICHAEL EDE, neurologist; b. San Antonio, June 9, 1947; married; 3 children. AB, Columbia Coll., 1968; MD, Columbia U., 1972. Diplomate Am. Bd. Psychiatry and Neurology, Am. Bd. Qualification in Electroencephalography; lic. physician, N.Y., Va., Washington, Tex. Intern internal medicine Harlem Hosp., Columbia U., N.Y.C., 1972-73; resident neurology Columbia U. Program Neurol. Inst. Presbyn. Hosp. and Harlem Hosp., N.Y.C., 1973-76; pub. health officer Va., 1978-81; clin. asst. prof. Georgetown U., Washington, 1978-81; neurologist epilepsy br. NINCDS, NIH, 1979-81; attending physician neurology D.C. Gen. Hosp., 1979-81; assoc. prof. U. Louisville Sch. Medicine; chief neurology svc. VA Med. Ctr., Louisville, 1981-83; neurologist Kelsey-Seybold Clinic, Houston, 1983—; mem. exec. bd. Kelsey-Seybold Clinic, Houston, 1992—, chmn. hosp. task force, 1993—, chmn. rsch. and edn. com., 1993—, chmn. new shareholder com., 1992—; clin. assoc. prof. neurology U. Tex. Health Sci. Ctr., Houston, 1983; clin. assoc. prof. Baylor Coll. Medicine, Houston, 1993—; mem. profl. adv. bd. Epilepsy Found. Am., Gulf Coast chpt., Houston, 1982—, chmn., 1990-92; lectr. various symposia. Contbr. articles to profl. jours. With USPHS, 1976-79. Grantee Bob and Vivian Smith Found., 1988-94, Compaq Computer Corp., 1989-90. Fellow Am. Acad. Neurology, Am. EEG Soc.; mem. Am. Epilepsy Soc. Home: 2222 Goldsmith St Houston TX 77030-1119 Office: Kelsey-Seybold Clinic 6624 Fannin St Ste 1900 Houston TX 77030-2331

NEWPORT, CAROL WIMMLER, special education educator; b. Sheboygan, Wis., Mar. 20, 1946; d. Edward Louis and Emma (Richter) Wimmler; m. Archie Lindsley Newport, Feb. 18, 1984. BS in Elem. Edn., Lakeland Coll., 1968; MA in Curriculum and Instrn., U. No. Colo., 1975. Elem. tchr. Mapledale Elem. Sch., Sheboygan, 1968-69, Malley Dr. Elem. Sch., Denver, 1969-70; elem. tchr., team tchr. Comstock Elem. Sch., Miami, Fla., 1970-75; tchr. spl. assignment Dade County Schs., Miami, 1975-77; 2d grade team tchr. Pine Lake Elem. Sch., Miami, 1977-78, compensatory edn. tchr., 1978-82, specific learning disabilities tchr., 1982-84; specific learning disabilities tchr. North Miami Elem. Sch., 1984-91; learning disabilities tchr. Meadowlane Elem. Sch., 1991—; instr. math. Fla. Internat. U., Miami, 1977; summer curriculum writer Dade County Schs., 1979, 82, career awareness basic skills facilitator, 1983-89; mem. Fulbright Exch. Program, 1983; alt. rep. United Tchrs. Dade County, North Miami Elem. Sch., 1988-91. Author poetry Fla. Adult Edn. Newsletter, Fla. Adult Edn. Anthology, Fla. Poetry Anthology, Whispers of Dark, Nat. Poetry Anthology. Mem. greater Miami Opera Assn., 1981-91, Miami City Ballet, 1991, Bass Mus., Lowe Mus., Hist. Mus., Miami, 1984-91; bd. dirs. Ring Theater, U. Miami, 1990-94. Mini grantee Citicorp. Found., Miami, 1987. Mem. AAUW, Coun. Exceptional Children (mem. chmn. 1989-90, sec. 1990-91, Rookie Tchr. of Yr. 1983), Am. Bus. Women's Assn. (pres. 1989-90, Woman of Yr. Alhambra chpt. 1990), Nat. Notary Assn., Fla. Coun. Tchrs. Math. (Tchr. of Yr. 1996), Fla. State Poet's Assn., Dade County Coun. Tchrs. Math., Delta Kappa Gamma (state mem. Indian project com. 1989-91), Alpha Delta Kappa (pres. Dade County 1990-92). Republican. Home: 10775 N Bayshore Dr Miami FL 33161-7447

NEWSOM, BARRY DOUGLAS, cardiovascular and thoracic surgeon; b. Tucson, Ariz., Sept. 27, 1953; s. Douglas Lee and Annie Laura (Tribble) N.; m. Nancy Macfarlan Irby, Feb. 11, 1978; children: Lori Anne, Julia Caroline, Ellen Brown, Jonathan David. MD, U. Miss., Jackson, 1978. Diplomate Am. Bd. Surgery, Am. Bd. Thoracic Surgery. Intern in gen. surgery U. Miss., 1978-79, resident in gen. surgery, 1979-83, fellow in vascular surgery, 1983-84, resident thoracic surgery, 1984-86; pvt. practice, Tuscaloosa, Ala., 1986—. Contbr. articles to profl. jours. Fellow ACS; mem. AMA, Soc. Thoracic Surgeons, So. Thoracic Surg. Assn., Alpha Omega Alpha. Office: Thoracic and Cv Assocs 701 University Blvd E Tuscaloosa AL 35401-2086

NEWSOM, DOUGLAS ANN JOHNSON, author, journalism educator; b. Dallas, Jan. 16, 1934; d. J. Douglas and R. Grace (Dickson) Johnson; m. L. Mack Newsom, Jr., Oct. 27, 1956 (dec.); children: Michael Douglas, Kevin Jackson, Nancy Elizabeth, William Macklemore; m. Bob J. Carrell, 1993. BJ cum laude, U. Tex., 1954, BFA summa cum laude, 1955, M in Journalism 1956, PhD, 1978. Gen. publicity State Fair Tex., 1955; advt. and promotion Newsom's Women's Wear, 1956-57; publicist Auto Market Show, 1961; lab. instr. radio-tv news-writing course U. Tex., 1961-62; local publicist Tex. Boys Choir, 1964-69, nat. publicist, 1967-69; pub. rels. dir. Gt. S.W. Boat Show Dallas, 1966-72, Family Fun Show, 1970-71, Horace Ainsworth Co., Dallas, 1966-76; pres. Profl. Devel. Cons., Inc., 1976-89; faculty Tex. Christian U., Ft. Worth, 1969—, prof. dept. journalism, chmn. dept., 1979-86, adviser yearbook and mag., 1969-79; dir. ONEOK Inc., diversified energy co., 1980—; Fulbright lectr. in India, 1988. Author: (with Alan Scott) This is PR, 1976, 3d edit., 1984, (with Alan Scott and Judy Van Slyke Turk) 4th edit., 1989, 6th edit., 1995, (with Judy Van Slyke Turk and Dean Kruckeberg), 1996, (with Bob Carrell) Writing for Public Relations Practice, 4th edit., 1994, (with Jim Wollert) Media Writing, 1984, 2d edit., 1988; editor (with Carrell) Silent Voices, 1995; mem. editorial bd. Pub. Rels. Rev., 1978—. Sec.-treas. Pub. Rels. Found. Tex., 1979-80, also trustee; pub. rels. chmn. local Am. Heart Assn., 1973-76, state pub. rels. com. 1974-82, chmn., 1980-82; trustee Inst. for Pub. Rels. Rsch. and Edn., 1985-89; mem. Gas Rsch. Adv. Coun., 1981—. Fellow Pub. Rels. Soc. Am. (chmn. Coll. Fellows 1992, nat. edn. com. 1975, chmn. 1978, nat. faculty adviser, chmn. edn. sect.); mem. Assn. Edn. in Journalism and Mass Communication (pres. pub. rels. div. 1974-75, nat. pres. 1984-85), Women in Communications (nat. conv. treas. 1967, nat. pub. rels. chmn. 1969-71), Tex. Pub. Rels. Assn. (dir. 1976-84, v.p. 1980-82, pres. 1982-83), Mortar Bd. Alumnae (adviser Tex. Christian U. 1974-75), Phi Kappa Phi, Kappa Tau Alpha, Phi Beta Delta. Episcopalian. Home: 4237 Shannon Dr Fort Worth TX 76116-8043 Office: Tex Christian U Dept Journalism PO Box 298060 Fort Worth TX 76129

NEWSOME, GEORGE MARVIN, lawyer; b. Phenix City, Ala., June 30, 1919; s. Thomas L. and Mary E. (Spivey) N.; m. Norma Elizabeth Hollomon, Aug. 19, 1941; children—Keith, Glenn, Carol. AA, George Washington U., LLB, 1948. Bar: D.C. Dist. Ct. 1949, Va. 1990. With IBM 1945-83, office adminstrn., Washington, 1945-49, atty., N.Y.C., 1949-51, plant counsel, Poughkeepsie, Kingston, N.Y., 1951-59, div. counsel, White Plains, N.Y., 1959-68, staff counsel, Armonk, N.Y., 1968-79, staff counsel, Washington, 1979-83; pvt. practice law, Washington, 1983-89, Fairfax, Va., 1989—. Pres., United Way No. Westchester, 1974-79, v.p., 1977-79. Sgt. USAF, 1942-45; 1st lt. (JAG) Res., 1951-56. Recipient Marshall award United Way No. Westchester, 1977. Mem. ABA, Fairfax Bar Assn., D.C. Bar Assn., Va. Bar Assn., Nat. Security Indsl. Assn. Home: 10520 Wickens Rd Vienna VA 22181-3032 Office: 10623 Jones St Ste 301-B Fairfax VA 22030-5116

NEWTON, ALEXANDER WORTHY, lawyer; b. Birmingham, Ala., June 19, 1930; s. Jeff H. and Annis Lillian (Kelly) N.; m. Sue Aldridge, Dec. 22, 1952; children: Lamar Aldridge Newton, Kelly McClure Newton Hammond, Jane Worthy Newton, Robins Jeffry Newton. B.S., U. Ala., 1952, J.D., 1957. Bar: Ala. 1957. Pvt. practice law Birmingham; assoc. Hare, Wynn & Newell, Birmingham, 1957; ptnr. Hare, Wynn, Newell & Newton, Birmingham, 1961—; del. U.S. Ct. Appeals (11th cir.) Jud. Conf., 1988, 89, 90, 91; mem. Jefferson County Jud. Nominating Com., 1983-89; mem. Birmingham Airport Authority, 1991—. Vice chmn. Birmingham Racing Commn., 1984-87; v.p. U. Ala. Law Sch. Found., 1978-79, pres., 1980-82. Served to capt. inf. U.S. Army, 1952-54. Recipient Disting. Alumnus award Farrah Law Soc. U. Ala., 1982. Fellow Am. Coll. Trial Lawyers (state chmn. 1983-84, regents' nominatin com. 1984-85), Internat. Soc. Barristers (bd. dirs. 1974-75, sec.-treas. 1976-77, v.p. 1977-78, pres. 1979-80), Internat. Acad. Trial Lawyers; mem. ABA, Am. Bar Found., Ala. State Bar (chmn. practices and procedures subsect. 1965, governance com. and pres.'s task force 1984-86, pres.'s com. 1987-88), Birmingham Bar Assn. (exec. com. 1967), Ala. Trial Lawyers Assn. (sec.-treas. 1958-65), Assn. Trial Lawyers Am., Am. Judicature Soc., 11th Cir. His. Soc. (trustee 1988—), Sigma Chi. Democrat. Presbyterian. Clubs: Shoal Creek, Birmingham Country (Birmingham); Capital City (Atlanta); Garden of the God (Colorado Springs, Colo.); University Club (New York). Home: 2837 Canoe Brook Ln Birmingham AL 35243-5908 Office: Hare Wynn Newell & Newton 800 Massey Bldg 290 21st St N Birmingham AL 35203-3702

NEWTON, CLARENCE JONATHAN, physicist; b. Decatur, Nebr., Feb. 25, 1923; s. Clarence E. and Bertha B. (McKee) N. BA, U. Tex., 1944, MA, 1947, PhD, 1952. Physicist Naval Rsch. Lab., Washington, 1944-45; teaching fellow dept. Physics U. Tex., Austin, 1945-51, instr. Physics, 1951-52; physicist Nat. Bur. Standards, Gaithersburg, Md., 1952-70; phys. metallurgist lab. Naval Ordnance Sta., Louisville, 1976-77, lab. Corpus Christi (Tex.) Army Depot, 1980-83; ind. acad. cons. Edinburg, Tex., 1985—. Contbr. 16 articles to profl. jours. Mem. Phi Beta Kappa, Sigma Xi, Sigma Pi Sigma. Home: 1504 S 2nd Ave Edinburg TX 78539-5412

NEWTON, DON ALLEN, chamber of commerce executive; b. Laurel, Miss., Oct. 19, 1934; s. Wilfred L. and Mary (McMullan) N.; m. Coleta Farrell, Oct. 11, 1958; children: Don Jr., Coleta Midge Rast. AA, Meridian C.C., 1954; BA in Journalism, U. Ala., 1956; postgrad. bus. mgmt., U. N.C.; postgrad., U. Okla. Asst. mgr. Meridian C. of C., Miss., 1956; mgr. Winston County C. of C., Louisville, Miss., 1960-61; asst. dir. Delta Council Indsl. and Community Devel. Bd., Stoneville, Miss., 1961-62; dir. Delta Coun. Indsl. and Cmty. Devel. Bd., Stoneville, Miss., 1963-70; exec. v.p. Met. Devel. Bd., Birmingham, Ala., 1970-74; exec v.p. Birmingham Area C. of C., 1974-88, pres., 1988—; pres. Birmingham Area C. of C. Found., Inc., 1988—; pub. Birmingham Mag., Birmingham Bus. Mag. Contbr. articles to profl. jours., newspapers. Appointee Ala. Export Coun.; bd. dirs. Birmingham Met. Devel. Bd., Ala. Sports Found., Birmingham Festival Arts. Lt. USNR, 1957-60. Named Ala. Mktg. Man of Yr., 1972. Mem. Ala. C. of C. Execs., Econ. Devel. Assn. Ala., Am. C. of C. Execs., U. Ala. Commerce Execs. Soc., Sigma Chi. Home: 2541 Canterbury Rd Birmingham AL 35223-1909 Office: Birmingham Area C of C PO Box 10127 2027 First Ave N Birmingham AL 35202-0127

NEWTON, HOWARD EDWIN, retired minister; b. Readsboro, Vt., Mar. 1, 1929; s. William Alfred and Florence Leslie (Walden) N.; m. Frances Margaret Perry, June 26, 1954; children: Bruce John, Wayne Stuart, Lisa Carol Newton. BA, Hope Coll., 1951; MDiv, New Brunswick Theol. Sem., 1954; STM magna cum laude, Union Theol. Sem., 1959; postgrad., Columbia U., 1960-63. Ordained to ministry Ref. Ch. in Am., 1954; transferred to United Meth. Ch., 1971. Assoc. min. First Reformed Ch., Scotia, N.Y., 1954-57; min. Reformed Ch., Middletown, N.J., 1958-60, First Reformed Ch., Long Island City, N.Y., 1960-64, Christ Community Reformed Ch., Stony Brook, N.Y., 1964-71, Christ United Meth. Ch., Staten Island, N.Y., 1971-78, United Meth. Chs., Hobart and Township, N.Y., 1978-84, Mary Taylor Meml. United Meth. Ch., Milford, Conn., 1984-94; ret., 1994; sec. N.Y./Conn. Found. United Meth. Ch., White Plains, N.Y., 1988-94; mem. com. on min. supv. candidates for min. Conn. Ctrl. Dist. United Meth. Ch., Hamden, 1986-94. Bd. dirs. human resources devel. City of Milford, Conn., 1990-94; mem. evaluation of agys. com. United Way, Milford, 1989-94; bd. dirs. YMCA. Mem. Blue Key, Rotary (bd. dirs.), Masons (grand chaplain Grand Lodge of Conn. 1993-94), Phi Alpha Theta. Home: 911 Silver Leaf Pl Port Orange FL 32127-7779

NEWTON, MICHAEL DAVID, lawyer; b. Dearborn, Mich., Feb. 1, 1967; s. Nicholas and Dorothy Marlene (Falk) N. BS, Birmingham-So. Coll., 1989; JD, U. Memphis, 1992. Bar: Tenn. 1992, U.S. Dist. Ct. (ea. dist.) Tenn. 1993. Assoc. J. Troy Wolfe & Assoc., Chattanooga, 1992-93; pvt. practice Chattanooga, 1993—; staff atty. Tenn. Mediation Group, Inc., Chattanooga, 1994—; guest lectr. U. Tenn., Chattanooga. Mem. sponsorship com. March of Dimes, Chattanooga, 1994. Mem. ABA, ATLA, Tenn. Bar Assn., Tenn. Trial Lawyers, Chattanooga Bar Assn. Home: 2035 Rock Bluff Rd Hixson TN 37343 Office: University Tower Ste 401 851 E 4th St Chattanooga TN 37403

NEWTON, RHONWEN LEONARD, writer, microcomputer consultant; b. Lexington, N.C., Nov. 13, 1940; d. Jacob Calvin and Mary Louise (Moffitt) Leonard; children: Blair Armistead, Newton Jones, Allison Page, William Brockenbrough III. AB, Duke U., 1962; MS in Edn., Old Dominion U., 1968. French tchr. Hampton (Va.) Pub. Schs., 1962-65, Va. Beach (Va.) Pub. Schs., 1965-66; instr. foreign lang. various colls. and univs., 1967-75; foreign lang. cons. Portsmouth (Va.) Pub. Schs., 1973-75; dir. The Computer Inst., Inc., Columbia, S.C., 1983; pres., founder The Computer Experience, Inc., Columbia, 1983-88, RN Enterprises, Columbia, 1991—. Author: WordPerfect, 1988, All About Computers, 1989, Microsoft Excel for the Mac, 1989, Introduction to the Mac, 1989, Introduction to DOS, 1989, Introduction to Lotus 1-2-3, 1989, Advanced Lotus 1-2-3, 1989, Introduction to WordPerfect, 1989, Advanced WordPerfect, 1989, Introduction to Display/Write 4, 1989, WordPerfect for the Mac, 1989, Introduction to Microsoft Works for the Mac, 1990, Accountant, Inc for the Mac, 1992, Introduction to Filemaker Pro, 1992, Quicken for the MAC, 1993, Quicken for Windows, 1993, WordPerfect for Windows, 1993, Advanced WordPerfect for Windows, 1993, Lotus 1-2-3 for Windows, 1993, Introduction to Quick Books, 1994, Quick Book for Windows, 1994, Introduction to Word for Windows, 1995. Mem. Columbia Planning Commn., 1980-87; bd. dirs. United Way Midlands, Columbia, 1983-86; bd. dirs. Assn. Jr. Leagues, N.Y.C., 1980-82; trustee Heathwood Hall Episcopal Sch., Columbia, 1979-85. Mem. The Investment, Inc. (pres. 1994-96). Republican. Episcopalian. Home and Office: 1635 Kathwood Dr Columbia SC 29206-4509

NEWTON-WARD, CHARLES MICHAEL, public health program consultant; b. Morganton, N.C., Mar. 27, 1956; s. Charles Walker and Bertha Sue (Oxford) Newton; m. Janie Ward, Sept. 12, 1992. BA in Religion and Psychology, U. N.C., 1978, MSW, 1984, MPH in Maternal and Child Health, 1986. Co-dir., counselor Human Sexuality Info. and Counseling Svc. U. N.C., Chapel Hill, 1979-82; health care technician Child Psychiat. Inst., John Umstead Hosp., Butner, N.C., 1978-80; trainer, group facilitator The Fleming Ctr., Inc., Raleigh, 1979-82; psychodiagnostic test technician divsn. med. psychology Duke U. Med. Ctr., Durham, N.C., 1980-82; contraceptive health educator student health svcs. U. N.C., Chapel Hill, 1980-85; social work intern Chatham County Mental Health Ctr., Pittsboro, N.C., 1982-83, Durham County Mental Health Ctr., Durham, N.C., 1983-84; rsch. asst. Gov.'s Advocacy Coun. on Children and Youth, Raleigh, 1985-86; tng. cons. child mental health tng. unit N.C. Divsn. Mental Health Mental Retardation Substance Abuse, Raleigh, 1986-88; pub. health program cons. women's preventive health br. N.C. Dept. Environ., Health, and Natural Resources, Raleigh, 1988—; mem. pub. health film libr. adv. com. N.C. Dept. Environment, Health and Natural Resources, 1988-94, pub. health social work steering com., 1990-94, local health dept. forms mgmt. com., 1991-92, chair cmty. devel. adv. com. health generations infant mortality reduction project, divsn. maternal and child health, 1989-92; field edn. adv. com. U. N.C. Sch. Social Work, 1989-92, 95—, field edn. instr., 1989—, adj. instr., 1994—; pub. affairs com., internat. com. Nat. Family Planning and Reproductive Health Assn., 1993-94. Contbr. articles to profl. jours. Mem. Wake Coun. on Adolescent Pregnancy, Raleigh, 1990-92. Grantee U.S. HHS, 1990-93. Mem. APHA, Nat. Family Planning and Reproductive Health Assn. Democrat. Episcopalian. Office: NC Dept Health & Natural Resources PO Box 27687 Raleigh NC 27611-7687

NEYLAN, JOHN FRANCIS, III, nephrologist, educator; b. Chgo., Feb. 20, 1953; s. John Francis and Mary Alice (Coogan) N.; m. Cynthia Barnes, May 17, 1980; children: John Francis IV, Elizabeth Marie. BS, Duke U., 1975; MD, Rush Med. Coll., Chgo., 1979. Intern in medicine Vanderbilt U., Nashville, 1979-80, resident, 1980-82; fellow in nephrology Brigham and Women's Hosp., Boston, 1983-84; fellow in immunogenetics Harvard U. Med. Sch., Boston, 1984-86, clin. preceptor, 1986; asst. prof. medicine U. Calif., Davis, 1986-88; asst. prof. medicine Emory U., Atlanta, 1988-93, assoc. prof., 1993—, med. dir. renal transplantation, 1988—; vis. cons. Wanless Hosp., Miraj, India, 1982-83; assoc. med. dir. Lifelink of Ga. Organ Procurement Orgn., Atlanta, 1989—; bd. govs. Lifelink Found., Tampa, Fla., 1988—. Editor: American Society of Transplant Physicians Newsletter, 1994—; contbr. articles and abstracts to med. jours., chpts. to books. Vol. Nat. Kidney Found., N.Y.C., 1990—, ARC, Atlanta, 1991, Spl. Olympics, Atlanta, 1991—, Habitat for Humanity, 1993—; chmn. Nat. Kidney Found. Coun. on Transplantation, 1995—. Recipient Physician's Recognition award AMA, 1989. Mem. ACP, Am. Fedn. Clin. Rsch. (councillor 1988), Am. Soc. Transplant Physicians (co-chmn. patient care com. 1988-90, chmn. 1991-93, councillor-at-large exec. coun. 1993-96, sec.-treas. 1996—, newsletter editor), Am. Soc. Nephrology, Internat. Soc. Nephrology, Transplantation Soc., United Network for Organ Sharing, Circumnavigator Club, Alpha Omega Alpha. Office: Emory U Hosp D240 1364 Clifton Rd NE Atlanta GA 30322

NG, KWOK-WAI, physics educator; b. Hong Kong, Aug. 15, 1958; came to U.S., 1981; s. Wan-Fu and Kam-Har (Sin) N.; m. Grace Mun Yan, Dec. 28, 1987; 1 child, Nelson Eukai. BSc, U. Hong Kong, 1981; PhD, Iowa State U., 1986. Postdoctoral fellow U. Tex., Austin, 1986-88; asst. prof. U. Ky., Lexington, 1988-94, assoc. prof., 1994—. Contbr. articles to Phys. Rev. Letter, Phys. Rev. B, Japanese Jour. Applied Physics. Mem. IEEE, Am. Phys. Soc., Phi Kappa Phi. Office: Univ Ky Dept Physics Astronomy Lexington KY 40506

NG, LILY KA-PO, hotel hospitality consultant; b. Hong Kong, May 18, 1967; came to U.S., 1985; d. Kok-Kong and Chi-Nor (Fan) N. BS, U. Houston, 1989; postgrad., Harvard U., 1993. Coord. on-site meetings and confs. Deloite and Touche, 1988-89; with Hilton Hotels Corp., 1989-93, corp. trainee, 1988-90; corp. policies & projects coord. hotels divsn., pres. office Hilton Hotels Corp., Beverly Hills, Calif., 1989-90, corp. recruitment coord. hotels divsn. recruitment dept., 1991-92; asst. dir. front office Anaheim (Calif.) Hilton and Towers, Beverly Hills, Calif., 1992; corp. human resources adminstr. Conrad Internat. divsn., 1992-93; assoc. PKF Consulting/Hospitality Adv. Svcs., Houston, 1994—; pres., bd. dirs. Nuestros Ninos Inc. Sponsor, vol. The L.A. Mission; vol. Armand Hammer Mus., L.A.; child sponsor World Vision Internat.; active Houston World Affairs Coun. Recipient Outstanding Mem. award Par Excellence, 1988, 89, Salute of Excellence award Nat. Restaurant Assn., 1989. Mem. Hilton Coll. of Alumni Assn. (Medallion of Appreciation), Hong Kong Students Assn. (pres.), Asian-Am. Hotel and Motel Owners Assn., Forum Club, Omega Delta Kappa (com. chair). Office: PKF Cons/Hosp Adv Svcs 5 Post Oak Park Ste 1940 Houston TX 77027-3415

NG, PAK C., banker; b. Canton, China; m. teresa L. Ng; 1 child, Abrahan S. PhD, U. Louisville, 1988. Mktg. rsch. analyst Maritz Rsch., Toledo, 1989-91; ops. rsch. analyst Philip Morris USA, Richmond, Va., 1991-93; v.p. Signet Banking Corp., Richmond, 1993—. Mem. APA, Am. Statis. Assn., Am. Mktg. Assn. Office: Signet Bank 101 gateway Pkwy 3d Fl Richmond VA 23112

NGUYEN, AN DUC, industrial development, consultant; b. Hai-Hung, Vietnam, Feb. 27, 1930; came to U.S., 1983; s. Giat Duc and Bien Thi (Pham) N.; m. Thuoc Thi Bui, Dec. 21, 1948; children: Tuan, Khoi, Thang, Phuong Nguyen Khanh Nguyen, Long Nguyen Kein Nguyen. BA, U.

Hanoi, Vietnam, 1952. Custom officer Directorate of Vietnam Customs, Haiphong, Saigon, Vietnam, 1952-63; dist. mgr. Royal Dutch Shell, Saigon, Vietnam, 1964-75; pres. Windeco World Industrial Devel., Inc., Houston, Hanoi, 1990—. Pres. Lion Internat., Saigon, 1970-71; coord. United Medical Found., 1992. Decorated Economic medal Minister of Econ., Saigon, 1974. Office: Windeco Inc 1010 Lamar St Ste 1150 Houston TX 77002-6314

NGUYEN, CAM VAN, electrical engineer, researcher; b. Quang Ngai, Vietnam, July 14, 1954; s. Suong Xuan and Huong (Le) N.; m. Diep Ngoc Tran, Sept. 1, 1979; children: An,Christine. BS in Physics, U. Saigon, Vietnam, 1975; BSEE, Calif. State Poly. U., Pomona, 1980; MSEE, Calif. State U., Northridge, 1983; PhD, U. Ctrl. Fla., 1990. Design engr. ITT Gilfillan, Van Nuys, Calif., 1979-82; mem. tech. staff Hughes Aircraft Co., Torrance, Calif., 1982-83, TRW, Redondo Beach, Calif., 1983-86; tech. specialist Aerojet ElectroSystems, Azusa, Calif., 1986-87; mem. profl. staff Martin Marietta Co., Orlando, Fla., 1987-89; sr. staff engr. TRW, Redondo Beach, Calif., 1989-90; assoc. prof. Tex. A&M U., College Sta., Tex., 1990—. Contbr. over 85 tech. papers to profl. jours., chpt. to book. Mem. IEEE (sr.). Office: Tex A&M U Dept Electrical Engring College Station TX 77843-3128

NGUYEN, DUY THAI, research scientist; b. Saigon, South Vietnam, Nov. 14, 1961; came to U.S., 1975; s. Doa Tu and Dung Kim Nguyen. B-SChemE, La. State U., 1983; PhD in Colloid/Surface Chemistry, U. Mo., Rolla, 1987. Rsch. scientist IRECO, Inc., Salt Lake City, 1988-89; postdoctoral fellow U. Pierre and Marie Curie, Paris, 1989; rsch. scientist Betz PaperChem, Inc., Jacksonville, Fla., 1989-92, sr. rsch. scientist, 1992—. Patentee in field, U.S., Autralia, New Zealand; contbr. articles to profl. jours. V.p. Vietnamese Jacksonville Community, 1992—. CSSR fellow, 1989. Mem. Am. Chem. Soc., Sigma Xi, Tau Beta Pi. Office: Betz PaperChem Inc 7510 Baymeadows Way Jacksonville FL 32256-7524

NGUYEN, HOA NGOC, gynecology researcher; b. Ho Chi Minh City, Vietnam, Aug. 25, 1957; came to U.S., 1975; s. Sang Ngoc and An Thi (Bui) N.; m. Mai Hoang Pham, may 6, 1983; children: Michelle Lan Anh, Mindy Mai Anh. BS in Chemistry magna cum laude, Millersville State U., 1979; MD, Albert Einstein Coll. Medicine, 1983; postgrad. Biochemistry/ Molecular Biology, U. Miami (Fla.), 1989—. Diplomate Am. Bd. Ob-gyn., Nat. Bd. Med. Examiners; bd. cert. gyn. oncology. Intern, resident in ob-gyn. Womens Hosp. U. So. Calif. Med. Ctr., L.A., 1983-87; fellow in Gynecol. Oncology Jackson Meml. Med. Ctr. U. Miami, Miami, 1989-92, rsch. fellow in Gynecol. Oncology, 1992—; head sect. gyn. oncology Cleveland Clinic Fla., Ft. Lauderdale. Reviewer: Gynecol. Oncology: An Internat. Jour., 1992—, Jour. of Cancer, 1992—, Internat. Jour. Cancer, 1993—; contbr. articles to profl. jours. Am. Cancer Soc. Startup grantee, 1989, Am. Cancer Soc. Instnl. grantee for Young Investigators, 1989; recipient Upjohn award, 1990, The Sylvester Comprehensive Cancer Ctr. Instnl. Rsch. award, 1992-93. Fellow Am. Coll. Ob-gyn.; mem. AAAS, Soc. Surg. Oncologists, Soc. Gynecol. Oncologists, Am. Assn. Cancer Rsch., Am. Soc. Clin. Oncology, Alpha Omega Alpha. Office: Cleveland Clinic Fla 3000 W Cypress Creek Rd Fort Lauderdale FL 33309-1710

NGUYEN, TRUC CHINH, analytical chemist; b. Saigon, Vietnam, Apr. 21, 1960; came to the U.S., 1981; s. Duc Huu Nguyen and Cam Thi Doan. BS, U. Tex., 1987. Rsch. asst. Univ. Tex., San Antonio, 1984-87; assoc. scientist Radian Corp., Austin, Tex., 1987-88; scientist Radian Corp., Austin, 1988-90, staff scientist, project dir., 1991—; assistance dir. Southeast Asia Internat. Trade Assocs., Inc., 1992-93; pres. L'Expression Internat., Austin, 1993—. Contbr. articles to profl. jours. Pres. Young Vietnamese-Am. Assn., Tex., 1990-94; bd. dirs. Vietnam TV, Austin, 1988-90. Recipient Minority Biomed. Rsch. Support grant NIH, 1984-87. Mem. Am. Chem. Soc. (analytical chemistry div.), Internat. Platform Assn. Home: 11914 Snow Finch Rd Austin TX 78758-3008 Office: L'Expression Internat 8760-A Rsch Blvd Ste 293 Austin TX 78758

NGUYEN-DINH, THANH, internist, geriatrician; b. Saigon, Vietnam; s. Bam and Chanh Thi (Duong) Nguyen-Dinh; m. Kim-Chi Nguyen-Dinh; children: Trung, Kim-Trang, Kim-Trinh, Trong. MD, Free U. Brussels, 1974; Tropical MD, Antwerp Tropical Med. Inst., 1975. Diplomate Am. Bd. Internal Medicine, Am. Bd. Geriatric Medicine. Asst. prof. medicine Howard Med. Svc., Washington, 1981-93; physician dir. St. Elizabeth Unit, D.C. Gen. Hosp., Washington, 1983-94; co-dir. Howard U. Md. Clinics, D.C. Gen. Hosp., 1990-96. Contbr. articles to profl. jours. Fellow ACP. Office: 611 S Carlin Springs Rd Ste 21 Arlington VA 22204-1061

NIBLACK, NANCY LEE PARHAM, insurance agent, financial consultant; b. Martin, Tenn., Jan. 24, 1941; d. Thomas Anderson Jr. and Helen Rose (Hilliard) Parham; m. John Cumming Watkins Jr., Sept. 26, 1964 (div. Oct. 1971); 1 child, Scott Christopher Watkins Niblack; m. James Frederick Niblack, June 7, 1981 (div. Oct. 1990). AA, St. Johns River Jr. Coll., 1961; BA, U. Fla., 1963; MSW, U. Ala., 1969. CLU, ChFC. Psychiat. social worker Bryce Hosp., Tuscaloosa, Ala., 1965-69; asst. prof. Inst. Contemporary Corrections & Behavioral Sci. Sam Houston State Univ., Huntsville, Ala., 1969-70; clin. social worker Comprehensive Care Ctr., Lexington, Ky., 1971-79, Mental Health Svcs., Inc., Gainesville, Fla., 1979-80; spl. agt. Prudential Preferred Fin. Svcs., Gainesville, 1980-96; life specialist Allstate Life, Gainesville, 1996—; part time lectr. Univ. Ky., Lexington, 1971-79. Elder, treas. Grace Presbyn. Ch., 1987-90; pres., meet coord. Buchholz High Sch. Swim Team. Fellow Life Underwriting Tng. Coun.; mem. NASW, Acad. Cert. Social Workers, Am. Soc. CLUs and ChFCs, Gainesville Assn. Life Underwriters (pres. 1988-89, Key Man award 1988, Agt. of Yr. award 1992), Estate Planning Coun. Gainesville, Gainesville Area Investment Network (pres. 1989), Gainesville Sports Organizing Com., Hon. Order Ky. Cols. (treas. Gator chpt. 1988-94), Kiwanis, Alpha Omicron Pi (corp. treas. 1986-95). Democrat. Office: Allstate PO Box 14404 Gainesville FL 32604-2404

NIBLOCK, WALTER RAYMOND, lawyer; b. Little Rock, Nov. 19, 1927; s. Freeman John and Nellie (Wolfe) N.; m. Marjorie Lee Hammond, Oct. 17, 1953; children: Fred William, George Hammond, Walter Lester, Raymond Lee. Student, Tex. A&M Coll., 1945, Little Rock Jr. Coll., 1947; B.S., U. Ark., 1951, J.D., 1953. Bar: Ark. 1953. Field dir. ARC, 1953-59; asst. gen. mgr., dir. Industria de Pollos (S.A.), Cali, Colombia, 1959-61; practice in Fayetteville, 1961—; now sr. ptnr. Niblock Law Firm; exec. sec. Ark. Judiciary Commn., 1963-65; U.S. commr. Fayetteville div. U.S. Dist. Ct., Western Dist. Ark.; part-time mem. U.S. Magistrate, 1965-79; mem. Jud. Ethics Com. State Ark., 1978-83, Supreme Ct. Com. on Profl. Conduct, 1979-86, chmn., 1981; mem. com. U.S.-Soviet Rels., 1992—. Bd. dirs. Washington County chpt. ARC.; mem. Pub. Employees Retirement Study Commn., 1983-85; trustee Iolta Found., 1989—. Served with AUS, 1945-47. Recipient Meritorious Service award ARC, 1963. Fellow Ark. Bar Found. (sec.-treas. 1973-74, chmn. 1976-77), Roscoe Pound Found.; mem. ABA, ATLA (bd. govs. 1978-90, home office and budget com. 1987-88, chair, key person com. 1987-88, chair ATLA PAC taskforce com. 1988-89, co-chair membership com. 1989-90, co-chair state fund devel. com. 1989-90, mem. exec. com. 1989-90, bd. dirs. ATLA assurance 1991—, PAC trustee 1993—, chair Group Ins. Trust 1994—), Am. Bd. Trial Advocates, So. Trial Lawyers Assn. (gov. 1988—, War Horse award 1992, parliamentarian 1995-96, sec. 1996-97), Ark. Trial Lawyers Assn. (pres. 1974-76), Ark. Bar Assn. (pres. 1977-78), Washington County Bar Assn. (v.p. 1973-74, pres. 1974-75), N.Y. Trial Lawyers Assn., Am. Inns. Ct. (master 1989), William B. Putnam Inn, Delta Theta Phi. Democrat. Home: 265 Holly St Fayetteville AR 72703-1814 Office: Niblock Bldg 20 E Mountain St Fayetteville AR 72701-6050

NICANDROS, CONSTANTINE STAVROS, business consultant, retired oil company executive; b. Port Said, Egypt, Aug. 2, 1933; came to U.S., 1955, naturalized, 1963; s. Stavros Constantine and Helen (Lianakis) N.; m. Tassie Boozalis, May 24, 1959; children: Steve Constantine, Vicky Ellen. Diploma, HEC Ecole des Hautes Etudes Commerciales, 1954; lic. en droit, Law Sch. U. Paris, 1954, doctorate in econ. sci., 1955; MBA, Harvard U., 1957. With planning dept. Conoco Inc., Houston, 1957-61; with planning dept. Conoco Inc., N.Y.C., 1961-64, with land acquisition internat. exploration-prodn. dept., 1964-66, dir. planning ea. hemisphere, 1966-71, gen. mgr., then v.p. supply and transp. ea. hemisphere, 1971-74, exec. v.p. ea. hemisphere refining, mktg., supply, transp., 1974-75; exec. v.p. worldwide supply and transp. Conoco Inc., Stamford, Conn., 1975-78; group exec. v.p. petroleum products Conoco Inc., Houston, 1978-83, pres. petroleum ops., 1983-87, pres., CEO, 1987-96; vice chmn. E.I. duPont deNemours (parent co. of Conoco), 1991-96, bd. dirs., mem. strategic direction co., 1996—; chmn. CNS and Co., 1996—; bd. dirs. strategic direction com. E.I. duPont de Nemours & Co., 1983-96; bd. dirs. Tex. Commerce Bank, Cooper Industries, Inc., Mitchell Energy and Devel., Keystone Internat.; active mem. adv. bd. Tex. Ctr. for Superconductivity, U. Houston, 1989-91. Bd. dirs., chmn. Houston Symphony; bd. dirs. Greater Houston Partnership, 1989-95; bd. dirs. Tex. Gulf Coast affiliate United Way, 1986-91, campaign chmn., 1988; trustee Mus. Fine Arts, Houston, 1987-94, 95—, Houston Ballet Found., Baylor Coll. Medicine, Rice U.; sr. chmn. bd. trustees Houston Grand Opera; chmn. Tex. chpt. Am. Com. on French Revolution Bicentennial, 1989. Mem. Am. Petroleum Inst. (bd. dirs.), The Houston Forum (mem. bd. govs.), Nat. Petroleum Coun. Greek Orthodox. Office: CSN and Co 10000 Memorial Dr Houston TX 77024

NICASSIO, ANTHONY ROBERT, economist, lecturer, consultant; b. L.A., May 9, 1938; s. Trifone Joseph and Frances (Eros) N.; m. Susan Kathryn Vandiver, Oct. 7, 1961; 1 child, Alexander Raymond. BS in Econs., La. State U., 1985, MPA in Econs., 1988; postgrad., U. Bologna, Italy, 1986-87. Various positions Dublin, 1971-81; mgr., ptnr. Computer Shop, Dublin, 1976-81; adj. prof. econs. Alamance C.C., Haw River, N.C., 1989-91, Jefferson State Coll., Birmingham, Ala., 1991—; bd. dirs. Techno Bar Inc., Birmingham; cons. Big Boy Toyz Inc., Graham, N.C., 1989-90, St. Laurence Ctr., Dublin, 1971-72. Served to capt. USAF, 1957-67. Resident Am. Acad. in Rome, 1993-94. Mem. Soc. Pub. Adminstrn., Exptl. Aircraft Assn., B-52 Stratofortress Assn., Ret. Officers Assn., KC (4 deg.), Omicron Delta Epsilon. Democrat. Roman Catholic. Home: 2117 Grayson Valley Dr Birmingham AL 35235-2029

NICASSIO, SUSAN VANDIVER, history and humanities educator; b. Muskogee, Okla., Mar. 25, 1941; d. Clarence Raymond and Sari Frances (Chase) Vandiver; m. Anthony Robert Nicassio, Oct. 7, 1961; 1 child, Alexander Raymond. BA, La. State U., 1981, MA, 1985, PhD, 1989. Asst. prof. history Elon (N.C.) Coll., 1989-91; asst. prof. U. Ala., Birmingham, 1991-96; assoc. prof. history and interdisciplinary humanities U. Southwestern La., Lafayette, 1996—; Am. Soc. for 18th-Century Studies fellow Newberry Libr., Chgo., 1990; fellow Am. Acad. in Rome, 1993-94. Fulbright fellow, 1986-87. Roman Catholic. Office: Univ SW La Dept History and Geography PO Box 42531 Lafayette LA 70504-2531

NICASTRO, DAVID HARLAN, forensic engineer, consultant, author; b. L.A., Mar. 12, 1961; s. Leo and Ruth Elizabeth (Moody) N. BA, Pomona Coll., 1983; MS, U. Tex., 1985. Registered profl. engr., Tex. Staff engr. Law Engring. Inc., Houston, 1985-86, project engr., 1986-90, sr. engr., 1990-91; prin. engr., 1992-94; pres. Engring. Diagnostics, Inc., 1994—. Contbr. articles to profl. jours. Recipient Tileston prize Pomona Coll., 1983. Mem. ASCE (chmn. materials divsn. Houston chpt. 1989, tech. coun. for forensic engring., chmn. com. on dissemination of failure info., 1991—), ASTM (vice chmn. com. C24). Democrat. Mem. Christian Ch. Office: Engring Diagnostics Inc 3200 Southwest Fwy Ste 3300 Houston TX 77027-7526

NICHOLAS, JONATHAN DAVID, realtor; b. Muskogee, Okla., Nov. 16, 1966; s. Franklin D. and Mary Ellen (Norman) N.; m. Dee Ann Miller, Oct. 5, 1989; 1 child, Montgomery Bradford. Cert. resdl. specialist NAR. Relocation dir., property mgr. Century 21, Tulsa, 1985-88; owner/broker J. Nicholas & Assoc., Inc., Tulsa, 1988-93, Property Shoppe Realtors, Tulsa, 1993-95; realtor/broker assoc. Keller Williams Realty, Tulsa, 1995—; state supervisor Resolution Trust Corp., Austin, Tex., 1993-94. Sponsor, mentor DECA Clubs, Tulsa Pub. Schs., 1985—; instr., vol. Jr. Achievement, Tulsa, 1994—; vol. Young Republicans, Tulsa, 1993—. Named vol. of month Tulsa C. of C., 1993. Mem. NAR, Okla. Assn. Realtors, Greater Tulsa Assn. Realtors (focus group 1994—). Office: Keller Williams Realty 5555 E 71st #9102 Tulsa OK 74136

NICHOLAS, LAWRENCE BRUCE, import company executive; b. Dallas, Nov. 9, 1945; s. J. W. and Helen Elouise (Whiteacre) N.; m. Virginia Pearl Farmer, Aug. 5, 1967; children: Helen Brooke, John Lawrence, Alexis Bradlee. BBA, So. Meth. U., 1968. Mem. sales staff Nicholas Machinery Co., Dallas, 1963-69; sales mgr. Indsl. and Comml. Research Corp., Dallas, 1969-74; v.p. Precision Concepts Corp., Dallas, 1974-76, gen. mgr., 1976-78, pres., Addison, Tex., 1978-86, dir., 1974-86 ; pres. INCOR Inc., Addison, 1974—, dir., 1972—; pres. INCOR Internat., Dallas, 1981—; pres., dir. Multiple Axis Machine Corp., 1981—, Investment Svcs. Corp., 1991-93; mem. adv. bd. Consultores Patrimoniales, Mex. City, 1992—; pres. Equity Capital Interests, Inc., San Antonio, Tex., 1993—; chmn. bd. dirs. Cross Securities Internat. Corp., San Antonio, 1993-94; pres. Worldwide Exec. Aviation, 1996—. Served as officer Ordnance Corps, U.S. Army, 1968, N.G., 1968-74. Mem. Soc. Mfg. Engrs., Nat. Rifle Assn., Nat. Shooting Sports Found., , Safari Club Internat, Game Conservation Internat., Dallas Council on World Affairs (dir.), Internat. Trade Assn. of Dallas. Club: Bent Tree Country.

NICHOLAS, NICKIE LEE, retired industrial hygienist; b. Lake Charles, La., Jan. 19, 1938; d. Clyde Lee and Jessie Mae (Lyons) N.; B.S., U. Houston, 1960, M.S., 1966. Tchr. sci. Pasadena (Tex.) Ind. Sch. Dist., 1960-61; chemist FDA, Dallas, 1961-62, VA Hosp., Houston, 1962-66; chief biochemist Baylor U. Coll. Medicine, 1966-68; chemist NASA, Johnson Spacecraft Center, 1968-73; analytical chemist TVA, Muscle Shoals, Ala., 1973-75; indsl. hygienist, compliance officer OSHA, Dept. Labor, Houston, 1975-79, area dir., Tulsa, 1979-82, mgr., Austin, 1982-96; mem. faculty VA Sch. Med. Tech., Houston, 1963-66. Recipient award for outstanding achievement German embassy, 1958, Suggestion award VA, 1963, Group Achievement award Skylab Med. Team, NASA, 1974, Personal Achievement award Dept. Labor Fed. Women's Program, 1984, Career Achievement award Federally Employed Women, Inc., 1988, Meritorious Performance award DOL-OSHA, 1990, Disting. Career Svc. award Dept. Labor, 1991, Sec.'s Exceptional Achievement award Dept. Labor, 1991, Cert. Appreciation, OSHA, 1991, Asst. Sec.'s Leadership award DOL-OSHA, 1992, 96. Mem. Am. Chem. Soc. (dir. analytical group Southeastern Tex. and Brazosport sects. 1971, chmn. elect 1973), Am. Assn. Clin. Chemists, Am. Conf. Govtl. Indsl. Hygenists, Am. Ind. Hygiene Assn., Am. Soc. Safety Engrs., Am. Harp Soc., Fed. Exec. Assn. (pres. 1984-85), Kappa Epsilon. Home: 1002 Sundance Ridge Rd Dripping Springs TX 78620-9501

NICHOLAS, TIMOTHY ALAN, journalist; b. Atlanta, Nov. 14, 1947; s. Thomas Albert and Mildred Geneva (Gunn) N.; 1 child, Lacey Nicholas. BS in Journalism, Ga. State U., 1971; MA in Comm., U. So. Miss., 1984, PhD, 1996. Photo feature editor So. Bapt. Home Mission Bd., Atlanta, 1972-76; assoc. editor Miss. Bapt. Record, Jackson, 1976-90; dir. comm. Miss. Bapt. Conv. Bd., Jackson, 1990—. Author: More Than Just Talk, 1979. With USAF, 1969-71. Mem. Bapt. Pub. Rels. Assn. (pres. 1986), Soc. Profl. Journalists.

NICHOLLS, RICHARD AURELIUS, obstetrician, gynecologist; b. Norfolk, Va., Aug. 12, 1941; s. Richard Beddoe and Aurelia (Gill) N.; m. Geri Bowden, Feb. 24, 1986. BS in Biology, Stetson U., 1963; MD, Med. Coll. Va., 1967. Diplomate Am. Bd. Ob-Gyn. Intern, Charity Hosp., Tulane div., New Orleans, 1967-68, resident in ob-gyn, 1968-71; asst. prof. ob-gyn Tulane Med. Sch., New Orleans, 1973-74, clin. asst. prof., 1974-83; practice medicine specializing in ob-gyn, Pascagoula, Miss., 1974-89; pvt. practice medicine, Ocean Spring, Miss., 1989—; mem. staff Singing River Hosp., chmn. surg. and ob-gyn depts., 1979-80, chmn. Ob-Gyn Dept., 1984, mem. staff Ocean Springs Hosp., laser com., pharmacy com., and theraputics com., chmn. OB-Gyn dept., mem. exec. bd., 1990-91; sec., treas. staff Ocean Springs Hosp., 1991-92, exec. bd., 1991-92, chief of staff elect, 1992-93, chief of staff, 1993-94; bd. dirs. Singing River Hosp. System, 1993-94. Bd. dirs. Miss. Racing Assn. Maj. US. Army, 1971-73. Fellow Am. Coll. Ob-Gyn, ACS; mem. Miss. State Med. Soc., Singing River Med. Soc., Am. Fertility Soc., Am. Assn. Gynecol. Laparoscopists, Am. Med. Soc., So. Med. Soc., New Orleans Grad. Med. Assembly, New Orleans Ob-Gyn Soc., Gulf Coast Ob-Gyn Soc., Conrad Collins Ob-Gyn Soc., Am. Venereal Disease Soc., Am. Cancer Soc. (bd. dirs Jackson County Br.). Contbr. articles to med. jours.

NICHOLS, BRENDA SUE, nursing educator; b. Henderson, Ky., Dec. 6, 1950; d. Marvin Elam and Cleona Jane (Bentley) Ashby; m. Harry David Nichols, Nov. 13, 1967; children: David Allen, Christopher Lynn, Thomas Andrew. AS in Nursing, U. Evansville, 1972, BSN, 1976, MA, 1978; DSc in Nursing, Ind. U., 1983. Staff nurse Community Meth. Hosp., Henderson, 1972-76, 81, 83; sch. nurse Evansville (Ind.)-Vandeburg Sch. Corp., 1977-78; nursing instr. Ky. Wesleyan Coll., Owensboro, 1978; asst. prof. U. Evansville, Ind., 1978-84; assoc. prof., dir. rsch. U. So. Miss., Hattiesburg, 1984-87; prof. nursing, dean sch. health sci. U. New Eng., N.Rivers, Lismore, Australia, 1987-90; assoc. prof., chair sch. nursing Old Dominion U., Norfolk, Va., 1990—; statis. cons. Dr. James Crumbaugh and R. Henrion, Biloxi, Miss., 1984-85; cons. Gold Coast Coll., Queensland, Australia, 1988-89, Mitchell Coll., Bathurst, Australia, 1988, Children's Hosp. of the Kings Daus., 1990-94; WHO cons. to U. Indonesia, 1995. Author: Nursing Theories, 1989; contbr. chpts. to book, articles to profl. jours.; NCLEX item writer, 1993—. Vol. Am. Cancer Soc., 1983—, Drug and Alcohol Prevention, Virginia Beach, Va., 1990-92. Fellow Am. Pain Soc., Royal Coll. Nursing; mem. ANA, Nat. League for Nursing (program evaluator 1991—), Va. Assn. Colls. Nursing (sec. 1991), Va. League for Nursing (bd. dirs. 1996—). Democrat. Episcopalian. Home: 4620 Schooner Blvd Suffolk VA 23435 Office: Old Dominion U Sch Nursing Norfolk VA 23529-0500

NICHOLS, EUGENE DOUGLAS, mathematics educator; b. Rovno, Poland, Feb. 6, 1923; came to U.S., 1946, naturalized, 1951; s. Alex and Anna (Radchuk) Nichiporuk; m. Alice Bissell, Mar. 31, 1951. BS, U. Chgo., 1949, postgrad., 1949-51; MEd, U. Ill., 1953, MA, 1954, PhD, 1956. Instr. math. Roberts Wesleyan Coll., North Chili, N.Y., 1950-51, U. Ill., 1951-56; assoc. prof. math. edn. Fla. State U., 1956-61, prof., head dept., 1961-73; dir. Project for Mathematical Devel. of Children, 1973-77; dir. math program NSF, 1958-61; dir. Math. Inst. Elem. Tchrs., 1961-70; pres. Nichols Schwartz Pub., 1992—; prof. math. edn. Fla. State U., 1974-90; Chmn. U. Ill. Com. on Sch. Math., 1954-55; cons. editor math McGraw-Hill Book Co., summer 1956. Co-author: Modern Elementary Algebra, 1961, Introduction to Sets, 1962, Arithmetic of Directed Numbers, 1962, Introduction to Equations and Inequalities, 1963, Introduction to Coordinate Geometry, 1963, Introduction to Exponents, 1964, Understanding Arithmetic, 1965, Elementary Mathematics Patterns and Structure, 1966, Algebra, 1966, Modern Geometry, 1968, Modern Trigonometry, 1968, Modern Intermediate Algebra, 1969, Analytic Geometry, 1973, Holt Algebra 1, 1974, 78, 82, 86, 92, Holt Algebra 2, 1974, 78, 82, 86, 92, Holt Geometry, 1974, 78, 82, 86, Holt School Mathematics, 1974, 78, 81, Holt Pre-Algebra Mathematics, 1980, 86, Holt Mathematics, 1981, 85, Elementary School Mathematics and How to Teach It, 1982, Geometry, 1991, Holt Pre-Algebra, 1992, Mathematics Dictionary and Handbook, 1993, 95; author: Pre-Algebra Mathematics, 1970, Introductory Algebra for College Students, 1971, Mathematics for the Elementary School Teacher, 1971, College Mathematics, 1975, College Mathematics for General Education, rev. edit., 1975. Named Fla. State U. Disting. Prof., 1968-69; recipient Disting. Alumni award U. Ill. Coll. Edn., 1970. Mem. Am. Math. Soc., Math. Assn. Am., Sch. Sci. and Math. Assn., Nat. Coun. Tchrs. Math., Coun. Basic Edn., Text and Acad. Authors Assn., Pi Mu Epsilon, Phi Delta Kappa. Home: 3386 W Lakeshore Dr Tallahassee FL 32312-1305

NICHOLS, HORACE ELMO, state justice; b. Elkmont, Ala., July 16, 1912; s. William Henry and Lou Ella (Bates) N.; m. Edith Bowers, Oct. 20, 1945; children: Nancy (Mrs. Lewis Glenn), Carol (Mrs. Scott Henwood), Horace Elmo Jr. Mus.B., Columbia U., 1933, postgrad. in constnl. law, 1937-38; LL.B., Cumberland Law Sch., 1936. Bar: Ga. 1935. Practice in Canton, Ga., 1938-40, Rome, Ga., 1940-48; judge Superior Ct., Rome, 1948-54; mem. Ct. Appeals Ga., 1954-66; justice Supreme Ct. Ga., Atlanta, 1966-80; chief justice Supreme Ct. Ga., 1975-80. Vocal soloist, World's Fair, Chgo., 1933. Mem. Sigma Alpha Epsilon, Blue Key. Democrat. Presbyterian. Clubs: Coosa Country (Rome); Piedmont Driving (Atlanta), Capitol City (Atlanta), Atlanta City (Atlanta). Lodge: Elks (Rome). Home: 13 Virginia Cir Rome GA 30161-4473 Office: 28 Jud Bldg Atlanta GA 30334

NICHOLS, JACK BRITT, lawyer; b. Tampa, Fla., Mar. 14, 1936; s. Robert Jack and Dora Virginia (Knight) N.; m. Janice Magill, Apr. 4, 1958; children: Sara Lynn, Douglas Britt. BS in Bus. Adminstrn., U. Fla., 1958, JD, 1965. Bar: Fla. 1966. Assoc. Gurney & Skolfield, Winter Park, Fla., 1966-68, Gurney, Skolfield & Frey, 1968-69, officer Skolfield, Gilman, Cooper, Nichols, Tatich & Adams, 1969-71, v.p. Skolfield, Nichols & Tatich, 1971-73, pres. Nichols & Tatich, 1973-75, Jack B. Nichols, P.A., Orlando, Fla., 1975—. Chmn., Maitland (Fla.) Arts Festival, 1979; mem. Pres.'s Council, U. Fla., 1973—. Served to maj. AUS, 1958-63. Decorated Army Commendation medal; recipient Disting. Service award Winter Park Jaycees, 1972. Mem. Acad. Fla. Trial Lawyers (diplomate), Nat. Bd. Trial Advocacy (cert. civil trial adv. cert. civil trial lawyer), Assn. Trial Lawyers Am. (sustaining), Fla. Bar, Orange County Bar Assn. (exec. council 1973-75), Fla. Blue Key, Rotary (pres. Maitland 1978, Paul Harris fellow), Delta Tau Delta. Methodist. Home: 20 Maitland Grove Rd Maitland FL 32751-4819 Office: PO Box 33 Orlando FL 32802-0033

NICHOLS, JOSEPH J., SR., surgeon; b. Atlanta, July 16, 1929. MD, Med. Coll. Ga., 1958. Diplomate Am. Bd. Surgery, Am. Bd. Colon & Rectal Surgery. Intern Ga. Bapt. Hosp., Atlanta, 1958-59, resident, 1959-61, 65-67; fellow Precept Drs. Boling-Finch, 1967-69; with Piedmont Hosp., Atlanta; asst. clin. prof. surgery Med. Coll. Ga.; clin. asst. prof. surgery Emory U. Sch. Med. Mem. AMA, ACS, Am. Soc. Colon and Rectal Surgery, Southern Med. Assn., Southeastern Surg. Congress. Office: 2001 Peachtree Rd NE Ste 540 Atlanta GA 30309-1476

NICHOLS, LARANDA C., newspaper reporter; b. Summerville, Ga., July 8, 1949; d. Edward and Betty Jane (Chitwood) Carroll; m. Nick G. Nichols, Jan. 21, 1975; 1 child, Jonathan Alan. BA, U. Ala., 1971. Reporter The Sand Mountain Reporter, Albertville, Ala., 1971-72; news editor The Leader Dispatch, Boaz, Ala., 1972-74; reporter The Huntsville (Ala.) Times, 1974—. Mem. Soc. Profl. Journalists, Press Club of Marshall County (sec.-treas. 1986-96). Office: The Huntsville Times PO Box 55 Guntersville AL 35976

NICHOLS, PADGETT SINGLETON, publishing executive; b. Florence, S.C., Nov. 12, 1968; d. Sidney Earl and Jaywan (Hardee) Singleton; m. Christopher Bryan N., Mar. 21, 1992. BJ, U. S.C., 1990. Stringer Lexington Dispatch News, 1989-90; asst. to exec. dir./office mgr. S.C. Press Assn., 1988-91; news asst. The State, 1990-91; acct. exec./dir. of publs. Hendricks and Co., 1991-93; publs. mgr. S.C. Bar, Columbia, 1993-94, comms. dir., 1994—. Mem. pub. rels. fundraising com. Ronald McDonald House. Recipient SCSAE Best in the Business award The S.C. Appraiser, 1993, Rookie of the Year award, S.C. Chpt. of Public Relations Soc. of Am., 1991, Best of the Best Gold (top honor) The S.C. Appraiser, 1992, Against All Odds award comms./pub. rels. sect. NABE, 1993, Best in the Bus. Cert. of Merit for S.C. Lawyer, SCSAE, Cert. of Merit for S.C. Lawyer, SCPRSA; scholar S.C. Scholastic Press Assn., USC Coll. of Journalism. Mem. Nat. Assn. Bar Execs., S.C. Soc. Assn. Execs., Pub. Rels. Soc. Am. (S.C. chpt.), S.C. Press Assn., Alpha Delta Pi. Home: 3950 Live Oak St Columbia SC 29205 Office: South Carolina Bar PO Box 603 St Columbia SC 29202

NICHOLS, PATRICIA G., association administrator. Exec. sec. Am. Saddlebred Horse Assn., Lexington, Ky. Office: Am Saddlebred Horse Assn care Ky Horse Park 4093 Iron Works Pike Lexington KY 40511

NICHOLS, RICK, business executive; b. 1951. Asst. mgr. Spendthrift Farm, Lexington, Ky., 1979-85; gen. mgr. Shadwell Farm Inc., Lexington, Ky., 1985-88, pres., dir. ops., 1988—. Office: Shadwell Farm Inc 4600 Fort Springs Pinkard Rd Lexington KY 40513-9708

NICHOLS, RONALD LEE, surgeon, educator; b. Chgo., June 25, 1941; s. Peter Raymond and Jane Eleanor (Johnson) N.; m. Elsa Elaine Johnson, Dec. 4, 1964; children: Kimberly Jane, Matthew Bennett. MD, U. Ill., 1966, MS, 1970. Diplomate: Am. Bd. Surgery (assoc. cert. examiner, New Orleans, 1991), Nat. Bd. Med. Examiners. Intern U. Ill. Hosp., Chgo., 1966-67, resident in surgery, 1967-72, instr. surgery, 1970-72, asst. prof. surgery, 1972-74; assoc. prof. surgery U. Health Scis. Chgo. Med. Sch., 1975-77, dir. surg. edn., 1975-77; William Henderson prof. surgery Tulane U. Sch. Medicine, New Orleans, 1977—, vice chmn. dept. surgery, 1982-91, staff surgeon, 1977—, prof. microbiology, immunology and surgery, 1979—; cons. surgeon VA Hosp., Alexandria, La., 1978-93, Huey P. Long Hosp., Pineville, La., 1978—, Lallie Kemp Charity Hosp., Independence, La., 1977-85, Touro

Infirmary, New Orleans, Monmouth Med. Ctr., Long Branch, N.J., 1979-88; mem. VA Coop. Study Rev. Bd., 1978-81, VA Merit Rev. Bd. in Surgery, 1979-82; mem. sci. program com. 3d Internat. Conf. Nosocomial Infections, Ctr. Disease Control, mem. sci. program and fundraising com. 4th Internat. Conf.; bd. dirs. Nat. Found. Infectious Diseases, 1989—, v.p., 1994—; hon. fellow faculty Kasr El Aini Cairo U. Sch. Medicine, 1989; mem. adv. com. on infection control Ctrs. for Disease Control, 1991-95; disting. guest, vis. prof. Royal Coll. Surgeons Thailand 14th Ann. Clin. Congress, 1989, 17th Ann. Clin. Congress, 1992; mem. infectious diseases adv. bd. Roche Labs., 1988-95, Abbott Labs., 1990-92, Kimberly Clark Corp., 1990—, SmithKline Beecham Labs., 1990-95, Fujisawa Pharm., chmn., 1990—, Bayer Pharm., 1994—, Merck Sharpe Dohme, 1996, Depotech, 1996; mem. study group Prophylaxis Antibiotic Project La. Health Care Rev., Inc., 1995—; mem. adv. panel Gen. Drug Info. Divsn. of U.S. Pharmacopeia, 1995—. Author: (with Gorbach, Bartlett and Nichols) Manual of Surgical Infection, 1984; author, guest editor: (with Nichols, Hyslop Jr. and Bartlett) Decision Mking in Surgical Sepsis, 1991; guest editor, author: Surgical Sepsis and Beyond, 1993; mem. editl. bd. Current Surgery, 1977—, Hosp. Physician, 1980—, Infection Control, 1980-86, Guidelines to Antibiotic Therapy, 1976-81, Am. Jour. Infection Control, 1981—, Internat. Medicine, 1983—, Confronting Infection, 1983-86, Current Concepts in Clin. Surgery, 1984—, Fact Line, 1984-91, Host/Pathogen News, 1984—, Infectious Diseases in Clin. Practice, 1991—, surg. sect. editor, 1992—, Surg. Infections: Index and Revs., 1991—, So. Med. Jour., 1992—, ANAEROBE, 1994—; mem. adv. bd. Physician News Network, 1991-95; patentee (with S.G. schoenberger and W.R. Rank) Helical-Tipped Lesion Localization Needle Device. Elected faculty sponsor graduating class Tulane Med. Sch., 1979-80, 83, 85, 87, 88, 91-92. Served to major USAR, 1972-75. Recipient House Staff teaching award U. Ill. Coll. Medicine, 1973, Rsch. award Bd. Trustees U. Health Scis.-Chgo. Med. Sch., 1977, Owl Club Teaching award, 1980-86, 90; named Clin. Prof. of Yr. U. Health Scis., Chgo. Med. Sch., 1977, Clin. Prof. of Yr., Tulane U. Sch. Medicine, 1979; Douglas Stubbs Lectr. award Surg. Sect. Nat. Med. Assn., 1987, Prix d'Elegance award Men of Fashion, New Orleans, 1993. Fellow Infectious Disease Soc. Am. (mem. FDA subcom. to develop guidelines in surg. prophylaxis 1989-93, co-recipient Joseph Susman Meml. award 1990), Am. Acad. Microbiology, Internat. Soc. Univ. Colon and Rectal Surgeons, ACS (bd. dirs. 1978-80, vice chair 1980-81, chmn. operating room environment com. 1981-83, internat. relations com. 1987-93, sr. mem. 1983-87, 94—); mem. AMA, Nat. Found. for Infectious Diseases (bd. dirs. 1988—, v.p. 1994—), Joint Commn. on Accreditation of Health Care Orgn. (Infection Control adv. group, 1988—, sci. program com. 3d internat. conf. nosocomial infections CDC/Nat. Found. Infectious Diseases 1990, FDA Subcom. to Develop Guidelines in Surg. Prophylaxis, prophylactic antibiotic study group La. Health Care Rev. c. 1996—, AIDS commr. State of La. 1992-94), 5th Nat. Forum on AIDS (sci. program com.), U.S. Pharmacopeial Convention Inc. (adv. panel gen. drug info. divsn., surg. drugs and devices 1995—), Assn. Practitioners in Infection Control (physician adv. coun. 1991—), Internat. Soc. Anaerobic Bacteria, So. Med. Assn. (vice chmn. sect. surgery 1980-81, chmn. 1982-83), Assn. Acad. Surgery, N.Y. Acad. Sci., Warren H. Cole Soc. (pres.-elect 1988, pres. 1989-90), Assn. VA Surgeons, Soc. Surgery Alimentary Tract, Inst. Medicine Chgo., Midwest Surg. Assn., Cen. Surg. Assn., Ill. Surg. Soc., European Soc. Surg. Rsch., Collegium Internationale Chirugiae Digestivae, Chgo. Surg. Soc. (hon.), New Orleans Surg. Soc. (bd. dirs. 1983-87), Soc. Univ. Surgeons, Surg. Soc. La., Southeastern Surg. Soc., Phoenix Surg. Soc. (hon.), Hellenic Surg. Soc. (hon.), Cen. N.Y. Surg. Soc. (hon.), Tulane Surg. Soc., Alton Ochsner Surg. Soc., Am. Soc. Microbiology, Soc. Internat. de Chirugie, Surg. Infection Soc. (sci. study com. 1982-83, fellowship com. 1985-87, ad hoc sci. liaison com. 1986-89, program com. 1986-87, chmn. ad hoc com. rels. with industry 1990-93, mem. sci. liaison com. 1995-96), Soc. for Intestinal Microbial Ecology and Disease, Soc. Critical Care Medicine, Am. Surg. Assn., Kansas City Surg. Soc., Bay Surg. Soc. (hon.), Cuban Surg. Soc. (hon.), Panhellenic Surg. Soc. (hon.), Sigma Xi, Alpha Omega Alpha. Episcopalian. Home: 1521 7th St New Orleans LA 70115-3322 Office: 1430 Tulane Ave New Orleans LA 70112-2699

NICHOLS, SALLY JO, geriatrics nurse; b. Coldwater, Mich., Jan. 28, 1965; d. Leo Arnold and Charlotte (Ferguson) N. LPN, Pasco-Hernando C.C., 1985, AA, 1986, ASN, 1992; student, U. South Fla., 1990-91, 94—. RN, LPN, Fla. LPN All Cmty. Walk-In Clinic, Spring Hill, Fla., 1986; office mgr. Internat. Clerical Labs., Crystal River, Fla., 1986; LPN, charge nurse Eastbrooke Health Care Ctr., Brooksville, Fla., 1987-91; pvt. duty LPN Nursefinders, Inverness, Fla., 1991; med.-surg. LPN Oak Hill Hosp., Spring Hill, 1991; LPN charge nurse, then RN supr. Avante at Inverness, 1991—, resident assessment coord., care plan asst. coord., 1993-95, care plan coord., 1995-96, utilization rev./Medicare rev. coord., 1995-96, nurse mgr., 1996—. Relief ch. pianist Grace Tabernacle Ind. Bapt. Ch., Brooksville, 1983-91. Mem. ANA, Fla. Nurses Assn., Golden Key Honor Soc. Democrat. Home: 1225 W Highland Blvd Inverness FL 34452 Office: Avante of Inverness 304 N Citrus Ave Inverness FL 34450-4157

NICHOLS, SANDRA B., public health service officer; b. Little Rock, Mar. 27, 1958; m. Ronnie A. Nichols, 1985; 1 child, Marquise. BA in Chemistry, Columbia Coll., Mo., 1980; student, Meharry Med. Coll., 1979-80; MS in Biology, Tenn. State U., 1982; MD, U. Ark., 1988. With dept. physiology U. Ark. Med. Scis., Little Rock, 1984-85, with microbiology lab., 1985-88, resident dept. family and community medicine, 1988-91, chief resident dept. family and community medicine, 1990-91, fellow dept. family and community medicine, occupational and environ. medicine, 1991-92; dir. Ark. Dept. of Health, Little Rock, 1994—; physician Mid Delta Health Clinic, 1992—, interim med. dir., 1993-94; med. educator Delta Area Health Agy., U. Ark. Med. Scis., 1992—. Author: (with others) Family Practice textbook. Officer HHS, FDA; co-chair Pine Bluff Arsenal Citizen's Adv. Com.; mem. Gov.'s Partnership Coun. for Children and Families, Women Execs. in State Govt.; conf. participant Am. Swiss Found. Young Leaders Conf., 1995; mem. Ark. chpt. Internat. Women's Forum; mem. Ark. Arts Ctr.; spkr. Career Day, local schs.; vol. physician high schs. Recipient Nat. FBI Cmty. Leadership award, 1996; named one of Ark. Bus. Top 100 Women in Ark., 1996, Top 10 Women in Ark., 1995, one of Outstanding Young Women in Am., 1981; Nat. Med. fellow, 1984-85; Pub. Health Leadership Inst. scholar, 1996, scholar Columbia Coll., 1976-80. Office: Ark Dept of Health Ste 39 4815 Markham St Little Rock AR 72205-3867

NICHOLS, SANDRA LEE, community health nurse; b. Sanford, Maine, Mar. 5, 1949; d. Earl John and Lorraine (Beaulieu) Johnstone; m. Arland C. Nichols, May 5, 1978; 1 child, Anne Cathleen. Diploma, N.H. Hosp., 1970; BA, New Eng. Coll., 1975; MEd, Incarnate Word Coll., 1986. RN, Tex. Staff nurse psychiat. unit Santa Rose Hosp., San Antonio, 1977-78; staff nurse San Antonio State Sch. and Hosp., 1978-83; sch. nurse San Antonio Ind. Sch. Dist., 1983-86; infection control nurse, in-svc. edn. coord. Lubbock (Tex.) State Sch., 1986-88; sch. nurse Lubbock Ind. Sch. Dist., 1988—. Recipient award N.H. Dept. Health and Welfare Adv. Bd. Mem. NEA, Tex. State Tchrs. Assn., Lubbock Edn. Assn.

NICHOLSON, FRANKLIN N., interior designer; b. Dilley, Tex., Sept. 3, 1954; s. Harvey F. and Anne L. (Matthews) N.; m. Sharon Gail Lambert, July 10, 1974 (div. Aug. 1984); children: Harvey William, Danny Franklin; m. Nelda Jean Luna, Nov. 5, 1994. AA, Tex. State Tech. Inst., 1974. Gen. mgr. Nicholson Farms, Dilley, 1980—; owner/operator South tex. Pest Control, Dilley, 1980-86; ops. mgr. Lillie's Interior Landscape Inc., San Antonio, 1985-91, 93-94; owner/operator Planter Box Nursery, San Antonio, 1990-93; sales mgr. Tex. Tropicals, San Antonio, 1992-93; v.p., divsn. mgr. SRL Svcs., Inc., Houston, 1994-95, pres., gen. mgr., 1995—. Adv. bd. curriculum/scholastic devel. San Antonio C.C., 1988. Mem. San Antonio Interior Landscape Assn. (v.p. 1987-89). Republican. Methodist. Office: Geotech 1345 Campbell Rd Houston TX 77008

NICHOLSON, FREDA H., museum administrator. Pres., CEO, The Nature Mus., Charlotte, N.C. Office: The Nature Mus 1658 Sterling Rd Charlotte NC 28209

NICHOLSON, HENRY HALE, JR., surgeon; b. Statesville, N.C., June 22, 1922; s. Henry Hale and Haseltine Witherspoon (Miller) N.; m. Freda Hyams, Sept. 24, 1956; children: Henry Hale III, Thomas Dalton Miller, John Christie, Michael Witherspoon, Freda Amanda, W. Stuart, Cooper. BA in Chemistry, Duke U., 1944, MD, 1947. Diplomate Am. Bd. Gen. Surgery, Am. Bd. Colon and Rectal Surgery. Rotating intern U. Wis., Madison, 1948; resident in gen. surgery Med. Coll. Va., Richmond, 1949; resident in gen. surgery Alton Ochsner Hosp. and Clinic, New Orleans, 1949-51, 53-55, inaugeral resident in colon and rectal surgery, 1955-56; resident in gen. surgery Tulane U., La. Charity Hosp., New Orleans, 1949-51, 53-55; pvt. practice gen., colon and rectal surgery Charlotte, N.C., 1956—; mem. surg. staff Charlotte (N.C.) Presbyn. Hosp.; sr. surg. staff mem. Charlotte/Mecklenburg Med. Ctr., Mercy Hosp., Charlotte; sr. active staff Presbyn. Hosp., Charlotte; sr. active teaching staff Charlotte Med. Ctr., 1956-85, cons. staff, 1985—. Mem. adv. authority Charlotte/Douglas Internat. Airport, 1992—; mem. Com. of 100 Regional Transp. Study and Recommendations, 1993-94; sr. examiner FAA, 1952—; mem. athletic-med. bd. N.C. Shrine Bowl, 1980. With U.S. Army, 1943-46; flight surgeon USAF, 1951-53, Korea; col. USAFR, 1961-82; 1st air surgeon N.C. Air. NG, 1970-82. Fellow ACS, Am. Soc. Colon and Rectal Surgeons; mem. Mecklenburg County Med. Soc. (pres. 1972), Charlotte Surg. Soc. (pres. 1987), Shriners, Masons (32 degree), Jesters, Alton Ochsner Surg. Soc., Hazel Creek Trout Club, Robert Burns Soc., St. Andrews Soc. of Carolina, Hound Ears Club (Blowing Rock, N.C.), Charlotte Country Club, Alpha Tau Omega, Phi Chi, Omicron Delta Kappa. Methodist. Home: 635 Manning Dr Charlotte NC 28209-3441 Office: 1012 S Kings Dr Charlotte NC 28283-0001

NICHOLSON, JAMES RICHARD, real estate consultant; b. Morristown, Tenn., Feb. 7, 1945; s. Henry Monroe and Kathleen Elizabeth (Rhea) N.; m. Mary Adams Cheek; 1 child, Leslis Marie Helms. Economist, U.S. Bur. Labor Stats. Cert. property mgr., counsellor of real estate. Svc. rep. NCR, Charlotte, 1964-71; v.p. Percival's Inc., Charlotte, 1971-77; owner, pres. J.R. Nicholson & Co., Charlotte, 1977—. Chmn. bd. equalization Mecklenburg County, Charlotte, 1991-93. Cpl. USMCR, 1961-70. Mem. BOMA (sec.-treas. internat. chpt. 1989-91, bd. dirs. 1990—, Carolinas/Va. chpt. pres. 1983, so. conf. pres. 1992—), Soc. Real Estate Counsellors, Inst. Real Estate Mgmt., Comml. Listing Exchange (chmn. 1985).

NICHOLSON, JOHN CHRISTIE, internist; b. Charlotte, N.C., Aug. 19, 1963; s. Henry Hale and Freda Lewis (Hyams) N.; m. Pamela Eaton Bond, July 9, 1988; children: Jennifer Erin, Sara Lynn, Emily Nicole. BSBA, U. N.C., 1985; MD, Duke U., 1989. Resident U. Iowa, Iowa City, 1989-94, staff physician, 1994; physician vol. Janey Med. Clinic, Dominican Republic, 1994-95; pvt. practice Piedmont Health Care, Statesville, N.C., 1995—; bd. dirs. 5th St. Med. Bd., Statesville, N.C. Home: 138 N Mulberry St Statesville NC 28677

NICHOLSON, MYREEN MOORE, artist, researcher; b. Norfolk, Va., June 2, 1940; d. William Chester and Illeen (Fox) Moore; m. Roland Quarles Nicholson, Jan. 9, 1964 (dec. 1986); children: Andrea Joy, Ross (dec. 1965); m. Harold Wellington McKinney II, Jan. 18, 1981; 1 child, Cara Isadora. AA, William and Mary Coll., 1960; BA Old Dominion U., 1962; MLS, U. N.C., 1971; postgrad. Old Dominion U. 1962-64, 64-67, 75-85, 86-92, 94-96, The Citadel, 1968-69, Hastie Sch. Art, 1968, Chrysler Mus. Art Sch., 1964. English tchr., Chesapeake, Va., 1962-63; dept. head, Portsmouth (Va.) Bus. Coll., 1963-64; tech. writer City Planning/Art Commn., Norfolk, 1964-65; art tchr. Norfolk pub. schs., 1965-67; prof. lit., art Palmer Jr. Coll., Charleston, S.C., 1968; tchr. Penn Sch. John's Island, S.C., 1968; librarian Charleston Schs., 1968-69; asst. to asst. dir. City Library Norfolk, 1970-72, art and audio-visual librarian, 1972-75, rsch. librarian, 1975-83, librarian dept. fiction, 1983-90; dir. W. Ghent Arts Alliance, Norfolk, 1978—. Poet-in-schs., Virginia Beach, Va., 1987. Book reviewer Art Book Revs., Library Jour., 1973-76; editor, illustrator Acquisitions Bibliographies, 1970—, West Ghent newsletter, 1995—; juried exhibits various cities including Grand Hyatt, Mayflower, Washington, by Joan Mondale, Nohra Haime, curator of Freer Gallery, by sr. curator Nat. Mus. Am. Art, curator Phillips Collection, asst. curator, White House by curator of White House and by dir. of Nat. Portrait Gallery; group shows include Yorktown Small Works Show, 1996, Hampton Arts Commn. and Tidewater Artists Assn. Portfolio Show, 1996, Suffolk Artists and Writers Invitational Exhibit, 1996, Virginia Beach Resort and Conf. Ctr. Print Show, 1996, Peninsula Ann. Juried Art Exhibit, 1996, Hampton Bay Days Juried Art Exhibit, 1996; contbr. art and poetry to various publs. and anthologies. Mem. Virginia Beach Arts Ctr., 1978-93, Hampton Art League, 1990—, Suffolk Art League, 1990—; bd. dirs. W. Ghent Art/Lit. Festival, 1979; poetry reader Poetry Soc. Va., Va. Ctr. for Creative Arts, Sweetbriar, 1989, Walden Books, 1991, Christopher Newport U., 1994-95, Caberet Voltaire, 1994, J.M. Prince Books and Coffeehouse, 1995—, Statues St. Mark's Cath. Ch., 1991-92; graphics of hundreds of celebrities from life; curator Va. Winter Show Life Saving Mus., 1991-92; judge Bornstein art scholarship Chrysler Mus., 1992; mem. staff Mid-Atlantic Antiques Mag., 1993—. Recipient awards various art and poetry contests; Coll. William and Mary art scholar, 1958, Tricentenial award for Contbns. to the Arts in Va., 1993; recipient Cert. for Vol. Contbns. to Va. by Gov., 1994. Nat. Endowment Arts grantwriter, 1975; bd. dirs. Tidewater Literacy Coun., 1971-72; bd. dirs. West Ghent League. Mem. ALA (poster sessions rev. com. 1985-96, pub. relations judge, subcom. comm. 1988-90), Pub. Libr. Assn. (com. bylaws and orgns. 1988-90), Va. Libr. Assn. (pub. relations com. 1984-86, grievance and pay equity com. 1986-88, co-winner Paraprofl. Logo for Norfolk Pub. Libr., 1985, chair Pub. Documents Forum, 1992-93, sec. 1994), Southeastern Libr. Assn. (Rothrock award com. 1986-88, com. on coms. 1991-92), Poetry Soc. Va. (ea. pres. 1986-89, nominating com. 1989-90, state corr. sec., editor newsletter 1990-93, dir. publicity 1993-95, 70th Anniversary plaque for Wren Bldg.), Art Librs. Soc. N.Am., Tidewater Artists Assn. (bd. dirs. 1989—, chair grantwriting com. 1990—, pres. 1991-92), Southeastern Coll. Art Assn., Acad. Am. Poets, Irene Leache Soc., Internat. Platform Assn. (artists assn.), Old Dominion U. Alumni Assn. (artistic dir. Silver Reunion), Southeastern Soc. Archtl. Historians, Ikara (pres. 1989—), D'Art Ctr. (Dockside art rev., bd. dirs. 1991-92), Ex Libris Soc. (charter), Va. Writers Club (editor West Ghent newsletter). Home and Office: 1404 Gates Ave Norfolk VA 23507-1131

NICKELSEN, ERIC J., bank executive. With Citizens & Peoples Nat. Bank of Pensacola (Fla.), 1966-93; chmn. Barnett Bank of West Fla., Pensacola, 1993—, pres, CEO, 1994—. Office: Barnett Bank of West Fla 100 W Garden St Pensacola FL 32501

NICKELSON, KIM RENÉ, internist; b. Chgo., Feb. 13, 1956; d. Robert William and Carolynn Lucille (Marts) N.; m. Louis Peter Sguros; children: Brian Louis, Justin Robert Peter. BS in Chemistry, U. Ill., 1978; MD, Loyola U., Maywood, Ill., 1981. Diplomate Am. Bd. Internal Medicine. Intern and resident in internal medicine Luth. Gen. Hosp., Park Ridge, Ill., 1981-84; pvt. practice Oakbrook, Ill., 1984-87, Plantation, Fla., 1987—; adj. attending staff Rush-Presbyn. St. Luke's Med. Ctr., Chgo., 1984-87; assoc. attending staff Hinsdale (Ill.) Hosp., 1984-87, Westside Regional Med. Ctr., Plantation, Plantation Gen. Hosp., Fla. Med. Ctr. South, Plantation. Musician Elk Grove (Ill.) Community Band, 1978-87, Hollywood (Fla.) Symphony Orch., 1987—, Sunrise (Fla.) Pops Symphony, 1987—, Deerfield (Fla.) Community Band, 1987—. Mem. ACP, Internat. Horn Soc. Office: Internal Medicine Assocs 499 NW 70th Ave Ste 200 Plantation FL 33317-7573

NICKENS, HARRY CARL, academic administrator; b. Monterey, Tenn., June 25, 1944; s. Van B. and Martha (Winningham) N.; m. Alicia Beck, Aug. 26, 1967; children: Kimberly, Cassidee, Brad. BS, Tenn. Tech. U., 1966, MS, 1968; EdD, U. Tenn., 1972. Counselor Va. Western Community Coll., Roanoke, 1972-76, dir. student devel., 1977-78, dean students, 1979-84, exec. dir. community devel. and tng., 1985-89; pres. Coll. Health Scis., Roanoke, 1989—; chair Roanoke Valley Chamber's Sch., originator Grad, Ctr. Pres. Roanoke Valley Career Edn.; bd. dirs. Va. Cares, Adult Care Ctr., Am. Heart Assn., Va. Amateur Sports.; active mem. First Bapt. Ch.; sr. mem. Roanoke County Bd. Suprs. Mem. Kiwanis (pres. Roanoke chpt. 1990—). Home: 4179 Toddsbury Dr Vinton VA 24179-1113 Office: Coll Health Scis PO Box 13186 Roanoke VA 24031-3186

NICKS, ROY SULLIVAN, university president; b. Chapel Hill, Tenn., June 30, 1933; s. Richard D. and Cora (Sullivan) N.; m. Barbara Jean Love, Jan. 22, 1960; children: Beverly Jean, Richard Matthew. Student, Martin Coll., 1952-53; BS, Mid. Tenn. State U., 1955; MA, U. Tenn., 1957; EdD, Memphis State U., 1969. Personnel trainee State of Ala., 1955; instr., tng. officer Bur. Pub. Adminstrn., U. Tenn., 1956-57; sr. budget analyst dept. fin. and adminstrn. State of Tenn., 1959-60, chief of budget, 1961-63, dep. commr., 1963-65, commr. dept. welfare, 1963-65, asst. to gov., 1965-67; asst. to pres. Memphis State U., 1967-69; chancellor U. Tenn.-Nashville, 1970-75, State U. and C.C. System of Tenn., Nashville, 1975-92; pres. East Tenn. State U., Johnson City, 1992—; v.p. urban and pub. affairs U. Tenn. Sys., 1973-75. Pres. Tenn. Conf. Social Welfare, 1964-65; trustee United Givers Fund; bd. dirs. Frank G. Clement Found. Inc., BBB Nashville and Mid. Tenn. Served with AUS, 1957-58. Mem. Am. Pub. Welfare Assn. (pres. 1969-70), Nashville Area C. of C. (edn. com. 1970—, bd. govs. 1974—), Kappa Delta Pi. Democrat. Methodist. Contbr. articles to profl. jours. Office: East Tenn State U Office of President PO Box 70734 Johnson City TN 37614*

NICOL, JESSIE THOMPSON, librarian; b. Cleveland, Tenn., Dec. 26, 1931; d. Franklin Monroe and Lucile Geneva (Bagby) Thompson; m. Andrew Emerson Helms, July 30, 1953 (div. 1970); children: Diana Sue, Arthur William; m. William Kennedy Nicol, Jan. 1974 (dec. 1990). BFA, U. Houston, 1972; MLS, U. Tex., 1975; postgrad., U. Tenn., 1985-87. Cert. libr., Va. Libr., archivist Am. Nat. Ins. Co., Galveston, Tex., 1973-77; libr., head acquisitions U. Tenn., Chattanooga, 1977-87, Va. Poly. Inst. and State U., Blacksburg, 1987-91; libr., cons. Info. Emporium, Cleveland, 1991—; libr. Davis Conservation Libr., League City, Tex., 1972-73; substitute tchr. La Marque Ind. Sch. Dist., 1968-73; women's editor Tex. City Sun, 1962. Contbr. articles to profl. jours. Active La Marque PTA, 1957-68, Tex. City Art League, Boy Scouts Am., Little League Am.; vol. Galveston County Hosp. Aux.; asst. leader Girl Scouts Am. Mem. ALA (LAMA fiscal and bus. officers discussion group 1985-89), Southeastern Libr. Assn. (legis. com. 1987-88, 89-90, interstate cooperative com. 1987-88). Methodist. Home and Office: 471 Weatherly Switch Rd SE Cleveland TN 37323-9218

NICOLADIS, MICHAEL FRANK, engineering company executive; b. New Orleans, Aug. 15, 1960; s. Frank and Peggy (Yemelos) N. B Engring. magna cum laude, Vanderbilt U., 1982; MBA (Fuqua scholar, Conoco scholar), Duke U., 1984. Assoc. N-Y Assocs., Inc., Metairie, La., 1984-85, v.p., 1985—. Mem. Holy Trinity Greek Orthodox Cathedral, New Orleans. Mem. ASCE, Am. Cons. Engrs. Coun., Soc. Am. Mil. Engrs., Am. Pub. Works Assn., Tau Beta Pi, Chi Epsilon. Office: N Y Assocs Inc 2750 Lake Villa Dr Metairie LA 70002-6783

NICOLE, ROGER, theology educator; b. Charlottenburg, Germany, Dec. 10, 1915; s. Albert and Bertha C. (de Neufville) N.; m. Annette Marie Cyr, June 18, 1946. MA, U. Sorbonne, Paris, 1937; BD, Gordon Div. Sch., Boston, 1939, STM, 1940, ThD, 1943; PhD, Harvard U., 1967; DD, Wheaton Coll., 1978. Prof. theology Gordon Div. Sch., Boston, 1945-51, Wenham, Mass., 1951-70; prof. theology Gordon-Conwell Theol. Sem., South Hamilton, Mass., 1970-86; vis. prof. Reformed Theol. Sem., Orlando, Fla., 1989—; dir. libr. Gordon Div. Sch., Wenham, 1951-55, curator libr., 1955-59. Author: Moyse Amyraut, 1981; editor: Bibliography of B.B. Warfield, 1974, Inerrancy and Common Sense, 1980. Mem. Evang. Theol. Soc. (pres. 1956). Baptist. Home: 2103 Hidden Pine Ln Apopka FL 32712 Office: Reformed Theol Sem PO Box 945120 Maitland FL 32794

NICOSON, PATRICIA MCLAUGHLIN, transportation planner; b. N.Y.C., Oct. 6, 1942; d. James Matthew and May Clementine (Monte) McLaughlin; m. William Todd Fairbairn, Aug. 27, 1965 (div. 1978); children: William Todd, Mary Cameron; m. William Jarvie Nicoson, June 7, 1986. BA, U. Pa., 1964; MS, Pratt Inst., 1975. Community planner Yonkers (N.Y.) Devel. Orgn., 1972-73, D.C. Office of Planning, Washington, 1976-79; transp. planner Dept. Pub. Works, Washington, 1980-86; sr. transp. planner Dept. Pub. Works, Arlington, Va., 1986—; lectr. George Washington U., Washington, 1974-80; speaker numerous confs. for planners, developers, and preservationists. Contbr. articles to profl. jours. Pres. Chesapeake and Potomac Regional Alliance, 1993—; chmn. Reston (Va.) Transp. Com., Reston Environ. Edn. Found.; trustee Com. of 100 on Federal City. Mem. Am. Pub. Works Assn., Am. Planning Assn. (pres., bd. dirs. Nat. Capital Area chpt. 1988-90, co-chmn. regional steering com. Md., Nat. Capital Area and Va. chpts. 1991, svc. award 1988), Urban Land Inst., Lambda Alpha. Episcopalian. Home: 11302 Fairway Dr Reston VA 22090-4410

NIDIFFER, SHERI LYNN, medical/surgical nurse; b. Mohave Desert, Calif., July 29, 1964; d. Kenneth Eugene and Mary Emma (Walsh) N. BSN, Davis and Elkins Coll., 1987; postgrad., George Mason U., 1995. From aide to charge nurse Fairfax (Va.) Nursing Home, 1983-87; fl. nurse Fairfax Hosp., Falls Church, Va., 1987-88, asst. nursing coord., 1988-92, nurse trauma med.-surg. ICU, 1992—; HIV clin. specialist INOVA Home Infusion, 1994-95. Home: 8819 Aquary Ct Springfield VA 22153-1255 Office: 3300 Gallows Rd Fairfax VA 22030

NIEHOFF, FRED HAROLD, JR., mayor; b. Fairview Village, Ohio, Aug. 17, 1930; s. Fred Harold and Helen Marie (Champ) N.; m. Vivien Park, Sept. 10, 1949 (dec. Feb. 23, 1974); children: Margaret, Fred III; m. Caroline Wheeler Cooper, Apr. 1, 1975. B in Indsl. Engrin., GMI Inst. Mgmt., 1952; MA, Appalachian State U., 1973. Supervisor New Departure, Sandusky, Ohio, 1951-54; mgr. Colson Corp., Elyria, Ohio, 1954-57, Barden Corp., Danbury, Conn., 1957-70; chmn. engring. dept. Blue Ridge C.C., Hendersonville, N.C., 1970-84; plant mgr. Minute Man Anchors, Hendersonville, 1984-85; mayor City of Hendersonville, 1993—. Campaign chmn. United Way, Hendersonville, 1973; pres. YMCA, Hendersonville, 1974. Mem. Rotary Internat. (dist. gov. 1988-89), Hendersonville Country Club. Methodist. Home: 1351 Asheville Hwy Hendersonville NC 28739 Office: City of Hendersonville PO Box 1670 Hendersonville NC 28793

NIELSEN, KENNETH ANDREW, chemical engineer; b. Berwyn, Ill., Oct. 10, 1949; s. Howard Andrew and La Verne Alma (Wentzer) N.; m. Linda Kay Miller, Aug. 20, 1970; children: Annette Marie, Kirsten Viola. BS in Chem. Engring., Iowa State U., 1971, MS in Chem. Engring., 1974, PhD in Chem. Engring., 1977. Sr. engr. Union Carbide Corp., Charleston, W.Va., 1976-80, project scientist, 1980-87, rsch. scientist, 1987-94, sr. rsch. scientist, 1994—. Contbr. articles to profl. jours. Co-founder Forest Hills Asns., Charleston, 1981; advisor Boy Scout Explorer Post, Charleston, 1992. Recipient Fellowships NDEA Title IV, Procter and Gamble Co., Am. Oil Co., Elias Singer award Troy Chem. Co., 1990, Kirkpatrick Chem. Engring. Achievement award Chem. Engring. mag., 1991, Profl. Progress in Engring. award Coll. Engring. Iowa State U., 1992. Mem. Am. Inst. Chem. Engrs., Soc. Rheology, Inst. Liquid Atomization and Spraying Sys. Home: 108 Stratford Pl Charleston WV 25303-2819 Office: Union Carbide Corp PO Box 8361 South Charleston WV 25303

NIELSEN, LU ED, retired community health nurse; b. Oklahoma City, Sept. 23, 1933; d. Edwin F. and K. Louise (Ribb) Comiskey; m. Dean C. Nielsen, July 17, 1953; children: Cynthia, Catherine, Edwin, Donald. LPN, So. La. Vo-Tech, Houma, La., 1976; student, Nicholls State U., Thibodaux, La., 1974-75. Vol. program mgr. Rockcastle Emergency Assistance Program, Mt. Vernon, Ky.; br. mgr. ARC; program dir. Ashlee's House Homeless Shelter. Bd. dirs. Am. Cancer Soc., 1987-91, pres.; bd. dirs. ARC, instr., disaster coord., 1990—; bd. dirs. Literacy Coun., Mt. Vernon, 1987-92, Rockcastle Emergency Assistance Program, Mt. Vernon, Interagy. Coun., Mt. Vernon, K.I.D.S. Com., 1989—, Rockcastle County Cmty. Housing Bd., Forward in the 5th; mem. adv. bd. Home Ext. Rockcastle County; vol. LPN/office mgr. Hospice of Ky. River, 1990; mem. Sr. Citizens Adv. Coun., Mt. Vernon, 1989-93, others; mem. adv. bd. God's Pantry, Lexington, Ky.; adv. coun. mem. Legal Aid, 1994—; coun. mem. Ky. Cancer Program, 1993—. Recipient Vol. of Yr. award Ky. Dept. Edn., Lifesaver award Am. Cancer Soc., Disting. Svc. award ARC, 1991, Outstanding Vol. award, 1992, 20th Century Achievement award, 1995; named one of 2000 Notable Am. Women; commd. Ky. Col., 1995. Home: RR 3 Box 125 Mount Vernon KY 40456-8816

NIELSEN, MARCO KJAER, computer programmer; b. Almeria, Spain, Sept. 18, 1969; came to U.S., 1990; s. Kenneth Robert and Else Kjaer (Nielsen) Hansen. AA in Bus., Ikast Handelskostskole, Denmark, 1987; BS in Computer Sci., Vejle EDB Skole, 1990. Office asst. Bording Maskinfabrik, Denmark, 1984-87; analyst Expo-Team, Herning, Denmark, 1987-90; programmer/designer Logo Consult, Horsens, Denmark, 1990-92; analyst/programmer Gladstone's, Tampa, Fla., 1992-93; programmer

Bannex Corp., Tampa, 1993—. Mem. IEEE Computer Soc., Assn. Computing Machinery, Tampa Bay OS/2 User Group. Home: 14915 Greeley Dr Tampa FL 33625-1963 Office: Bannex Corp 5755 Hoover Blvd Tampa FL 33634-5340

NIELSEN, RALPH MARTIN, production designer, special effects expert, sound engineer; b. Miami, Fla., Mar. 22, 1941; s. Faris Martin Aston and Marguerite (Hand) Nielsen; m. Pat Sullivan (div.); 1 child, Martina Marie; m. Marci Lynn Gilbert, May 8, 1982. Student, Fla. State U., 1959, 60, U. Miami, 1961-65. Exhibit builder Mus. Sci., Miami, 1962-65; prodn. designer Walt Disney Imagineering, Glendale, Calif., 1969—, Spectra F/X, Camarillo, Calif., 1989—; owner, dir. Mountain Ear Prodns., Mountain City, Tenn., 1984—; audio engineer, archivist Nat. Assn. for Perpetuation of Profl. Storytellers, Jonesboro, Tenn., 1986—; concept engineer Miningtown Skunkworks, Mountain City, 1993—; freelance film/video camera operator BBC, CBS, NBC, ABC, Cablevision; freelance tech. dir., practical effects artist; tech. cons. various theme parks, 1969—; art dir., set dir., action props and spl. effects artist Rick Levine Prodns., Jenkins, Covington Prodns., Cooper, Dennis & Hirsch Prodns., Steve Horn Prodns., Whole Hog Prodns., Universal, Paramont, Burbank, CBS, Disney and TOHO Studios; guest instr. U. Miami, U. Ctrl. Fla. and Valencia C.C., 1988; tech. specialist Swan/Dolphin Hotels, Orlando, 1988-89, Pleasure Island Adult Entertainment Complex, Orlando, 1988-89, Typhoon Lagoon, Orlando, 1988-89, Euro-Disneyland, Paris, 1988-89. Prodr. (documentary series) How, What, Why?, 1982-83; tech. dir. (promotional video) Elk River Club, 1984, Realty World/Carolina Assn., 1984-85, High Country Realty, 1984-85; scenic prodn. artisan Julio Iglesias World Tour, 1986, Star Tours, Disneyland, 1986, Time Machine Sea World, Cleve., 1986; prodn. designer Norway Pavilion EPCOT Ctr., Orlando, Fla., 1986; field art dir. Submarine Ride Rehab Disneyland, 1986, tree and foliage prodn. and installation Norway Pavilion EPCOT Ctr., 1988-89, Tiki Rm. Que Area Rockwork Tokyo Disneyland, 1988-89, Down the Hatch Sandwich Bar, Gertie's Dinosaur Ice Cream Bar and Indiana Jones Stunt Spectacular Disney/MGM Studios Theme Park, 1988-89; tech. dir. Parting of Red Sea and Creature from the Black Lagoon Universal Studios Tour, 1987; tech. specialist Indiana Jones Stunt Spectacular, Catastrophe Canyon, Great Moments at the Movies, Honey, I Shrunk the Kids, Star Tours Preshow, Spl. Effects Shop Props, Spl. Effects Tank Model/Action Props, Acme Warehouse/Roger Rabbit Props and Back Lot Bone Yard, Disney/MGM Studios Theme Park, Orlando, 1988-89; prodn. designer Norway Pavilion EPCOT Ctr., 1986, Star Tours Disneyland, 1986, Indiana Jones Stunt Spectacular, Great Moments at the Movies, Honey, I Shrunk the Kids and Back Lot Bone Yard Disney/MGM Studios Theme Park, 1988-89; tech. rep., project mgr. giant grass fiberglass constrn. and installation Honey I Shrunk the Kids, 1990; design cons. giant grass prodn. Honey I Shrunk the Kids, 1990, EuroDisneyland, 1991, Splash Mountain Walt Disney World, 1991; field art dir. 20,000 Leagues Under the Sea Submarine Ride Rehab Walt Disney World, 1990, safety enhancements Honey I Shrunk the Kids, Muppets Area Devel., Ewok Village Queue Enhancements and Great Movie Ride safety enhancements Disney/MGM Studios Theme Park, 1991, Thatch Roofing R & D, Fantasyland Hub Planters, Adventureland Planters and Main Street Train Station Walt Disney World Magic Kingdom, 1991; art dir. Honey I Shrunk the Kids Wet Climber Enhancements Disney/MGM Studios Theme Park, 1992, Typhoon Lagoon and Splash Mountain Walt Disney World, 1992; tech. dir., cameraman (video) Angela, 1992; prop builder, prin. furniture (TV show) Christy, 1993; prop builder (TV motion picture) Bandit, 1993; prodr., dir. (TV spl.) Doc Watson, 1993; art dir. Ewok Village Disney/MGM Studios Theme Park, 1994, Sunset Blvd. and Tower of Terror, 1994, Toontown, Tokyo Disneyland, 1995; design cons. Opryland, Opryland Hotel Delta Expansion Project, 1995, 96; prop master (TV show) Unsolved Mysteries, 1995. Founding mem. Johnson County Comty. Theater, Johnson County Arts Coun., 1995. Mem. Tenn. Film and Tape Commn., Tenn. Arts Commn., N.E. Tenn. Film and Video Assn., 1995, Johnson County C. of C., Themed Entertainment Assn. (founding mem.). Office: Mountain Ear Prodns PO Box 77 Mountain City TN 37683-0077

NIEPORENT, RICHARD JOEL, physicist, consultant, educator; b. Bronx, N.Y., Oct. 24, 1943; s. Henry and Ida (Greenberg) N.; m. Enid Susan Nimetz, Jan. 28, 1967; children: David, Benjamin, Jeremy. AB, Columbia U., 1964; MS, Rutgers U., 1966, PhD, 1970. Rsch. asst. dept. physics Rutgers U., New Brunswick, N.J., 1966-70; dir. computer systems devel. Gen. Rsch. Corp., Dayton, Ohio, 1971-74; prin. mem. tech. staff Litton, AMECOM, College Park, Md., 1974-75; project mgr., proposal mgr. INCO, Inc., McLean, Va., 1975-78; with MITRE, various locations, 1978—; lead engr. Strategic and Theatre Army Systems div. MITRE, 1988-89, lead engr. C31 systems engring. Intelligence and CINC div., 1989-91; sr. prin. engr. Ctr. for Integrated Intelligence Systems Div. MITRE, McLean, Va., 1991—; sr. adj. faculty Grad. Sch. Engring., Johns Hopkins U., 1979—, head telecomms. concentration, 1992—; mem. computer sci. dept. program com. Continuing Profl. Programs div. Whiting Sch. Engring., 1986—; speaker in field. Contbr. articles to profl. jours. N.Y. State Regents Engring. scholar, 1960-64; Rutgers U. rsch. fellow, 1966-70. Mem. IEEE Comms. Soc., Am. Nat. Standards Inst. Office: MITRE Corp 7467 Ridge Rd Ste 140 Hanover MD 21076

NIERSTE, ROBERT WALTER, secondary school educator; b. Vincennes, Ind., Nov. 14, 1946; s. Norman R. and Ursulina M. (Ferree) N.; m. Patricia J. Nierste, July 28, 1983; children: Traeka, Keith, Jennifer. AS, Vincennes U., 1966; BA, Ind. State U., 1969, MS, 1974; postgrad., U. Tex., 1991—. Cert. tchr., Tex.; cert. supr., Tex.; cert. adminstr., Tex. Tchr. sci. Anderson (Ind.) Community Schs., 1971-76, Fayette County Schs., Connersville, Ind., 1976-84; head sci. dept. Raymondville (Tex.) Ind. Sch. Dist., 1984-86; chmn. dept. sci., coord. summer program for gifted Plano (Tex.) Ind. Sch. Dist., 1986—. Vol. Heard Mus. 4-H. Named Golf Coach of Yr. South Cen. Conf., 1984, Tex. Invent Am. Teach Yr., 1989. Mem. Am. Fedn. Tchrs., Assn. for Supervision and Curriculum Devel., Nat. Sci. Tchrs. Assn., Tex. Assn. Sci. Suprs., Classroom Assn. Sci. Tchrs., Hoosier Assn. Sci. Tchrs. Inc. Roman Catholic.

NIESWIADOMY, MICHAEL LOUIS, economics educator; b. Ft. Worth, Tex., Nov. 7, 1956; s. Benedict Louis and Rose Marie (Mieth) N. BA, U. Dallas, 1979; PhD, Tex. A&M U., 1983. Asst. prof. U. N. Tex., Denton, 1985-90, assoc. prof. eocnomics, 1990—; vis. asst. prof. U. Tex., Arlington, 1983-85; cons. U.S. Pres. Coun. Environ. Quality, 1987. Contbr. articles to profl. jours. Fellow H.B. Earhart Found., 1982-83; grantee AARP Andrus Found., 1990-91. Mem. Am. Econ. Assn., Am. Water Resources Assn., Am. Risk and Ins. Assn., Western Econ. Assn., Dallas Economist Club. Office: Univ N Tex Dept Econs Denton TX 76203

NIGHSWONGER, JAMES TODD, newspaper editor; b. Olathe, Kans., Oct. 18, 1963; s. James J. and Patricia G. (Moore) N.; m. Terri K. Baird, Jan. 3, 1987; 1 child, Brenden Neil. BS, Kans. State U., Manhattan, 1986; MA, Regent U., Virginia Beach, Va., 1994. Sports editor Marysville (Kans.) Advocate, 1987, Ardmore (Okla.) Daily Ardmorite, 1987-89; news editor, sports editor Arkansas City (Kans.) Traveler, 1989-92; bus. mgr. The Paper—Regent U., Virginia Beach, Va., 1993-94; editor Farragut (Tenn.) West Side Press Enterprise, 1994; gen. mgr. The Laker, Land O'Lakes, Fla., 1995; editor Paragould (Ark.) Daily Press, 1995—. Mem. Paragould Kiwanis Club. Republican. Office: Paragould Daily Press 1401 Hunt Paragould AR 72450

NIMMONS, M(AJOR) STUART, III, architect; b. Houston, May 17, 1940; s. Major S. Jr. and Lucille (Duff) N.; m. Carolyn Marie Melvin, Apr. 21, 1944; children: Parke Worthington, Brent Alexander. BArch, Tex. Tech U., 1965; postgrad., U. Houston, 1965-66. Cert. contract interior designer; lic. interior designer, Tex., Ga. Intern architect, interior designer Caudill Rowlett Scott, Houston, 1965-71; div. head Lloyd Morgan Jones, Houston, 1971-74; prin. Ufer Nimmons Barbaria, Houston, 1974-76; dir. design Planning Design Rsch., Houston, 1976-78, Lloyd Jones Brewer, Houston, 1978-81; sr. assoc. Pierce Goodwin Alexander, Houston, 1981-84; pres. Smallwood, Reynolds, Stewart, Stewart Interiors, Inc., Atlanta, 1984-87; dir. interior design John Portman & Assocs., Atlanta, 1988-90; project dir. Cooper Carry Studio, Ltd., Atlanta, 1990-91; asset mgmt./interior design cons. Atlanta, 1991—; owner Nimmons Consulting Group. Prin. works include interiors Zapata Corp. Hdqrs. and Shanghai Ctr., Embarcadero Ctr., Heritage Club, Capital Bank, Marathon Oil Tower, Metro Companies and Oxford Group (hon. award Am. Soc. of Interior Designers, 1988), Azalea Restaurant (hon. award Am. Soc. of Interior Designers, 1991). Usher Palmer Meml. Episc. Ch., Houston, 1979-83; head usher, fin. com. All Sts. Episc. Ch., Atlanta, 1987—; vol. Channel 8 Auction Pub. Broadcasting Sta., Houston, 1980-84; pres. North Riverside Homeowner's Assn. Mem. AIA (assoc., chmn. nat. task force 1983-85, apptd. nat. com. 1985-87, nat. com. 1970—, Outstanding Interior Arch. award, hon. award 1979, 80, 81, 84), Tex. Soc. Architects (chmn. com. 1979-81, Outstanding Interior Arch. award), Internat. Facility Mgrs. Assn., Inst. Bus. Designers (nat. exec. com., bd. dirs. Ga. chpt., nat. v.p. 1993-95, adv. bd. to U. of Ga. 1992-96), Internat. Interior Design Assn. (v.p. government affairs), Ga. Alliance Interior Design Profls. (pres.), Nat. Legis. Coalition for Interior Designers. Republican. Home and Office: 115 River North Ct NW Atlanta GA 30328-1108

NIMMONS, RALPH WILSON, JR., federal judge; b. Dallas, Sept. 14, 1938; s. Ralph Wilson and Dorothy (Tucker) N.; m. Doris Penelope Pickels, Jan. 30, 1960; children—Bradley, Paige, Bonnie. BA, U. Fla., 1960, JD, 1963. Bar: Fla. 1963, U.S. Dist. Ct. (mid. dist.) Fla. 1963, U.S. Ct. Appeals (5th cir.) 1969, U.S. Supreme Ct. 1970. Assoc. Ulmer, Murchison, Ashby & Ball, Jacksonville, Fla., 1963-65, ptnr., 1973-77; asst. pub. defender Pub. Defender's Office, Jacksonville, 1965-69; first asst. state atty. State Atty.'s Office, Jacksonville, 1969-71; chief asst. gen. counsel City of Jacksonville, 1971-73; judge 4th Jud. Cir. Ct., Jacksonville, 1977-83, First Dist. Ct. of Appeal Fla., Tallahassee, 1983-91; judge U.S. Dist. Ct. Mid. Dist. Fla., 1991—; mem. faculty Fla. Jud. Coll., Tallahassee, 1985, 86; mem. Fla. Bar Grievance Com., 1973-76, vice chmn., 1975-76; mem. Fla. Conf. Cir. Judges, 1977-83, mem. exec. com., 1980-83; mem. Met. Criminal Justice Adv. Council, 1977-79; mem. Fla. Gov.'s Task Force on Prison Overcrowding, 1983; mem. Trial Ct. Study Commn., 1987-88. Chmn. lay bd. Riverside Baptist Ch., Jacksonville, 1982; chmn. deacons First Bapt. Ch., Tallahassee, 1988—; trustee Jacksonville Wolfson Children's Hosp., 1973-83. Recipient Carroll award for Outstanding Mem. Judiciary Jacksonville Jr. C. of C., 1980, Disting. Svc. award Fla. Council on Crime and Delinquency, 1981; named Outstanding Judge in Duval County, Jacksonville Bar Assn. Young Lawyers Sect., 1981. Mem. Phi Alpha Delta (pres. chpt. 1962-63), Am. Inns of Ct. (master of bench), Delta Tau Delta (pres. chpt. 1959-60). Office: US Dist Ct 611 N Florida Ave Tampa FL 33602-4500

NIRSCHEL, ROY JOSEPH, academic administrator; b. Stamford, Conn., Apr. 5, 1952; s. Roy J. and and Catherine (Pelazza) N.; m. Paula Strouch, May 3, 1981; children: Christopher, Jane, Susan. BS, So. Conn. State U., New Haven, 1974; MA, U. Miami, Fla., 1994. Dir. devel. U. Hartford, West Hartford, Conn., 1982-86; asst. v.p. U. Pitts., 1986-90; v.p. U. Miami, 1991—; cons. America's Fund for Ind. Univs., Quito, Ecuador, 1992; dir. Gulliver Acad., Miami, 1994—. Chmn. United Way, U. Miami, 1994; Rep candidate Gen. Assembly, New Haven, 1974. Nat. Chengchi U. fellow, Taipei, Taiwan, 1972; recipient Grand Gold award CASE, Washington, 1990. Mem. Coun. for Advancement Support of Edn. Office: U Miami PO Box 248073 Coral Gables FL 33124-8073

NISBETT, DOROTHEA JO, nursing educator; b. Lodi, Tex., May 16, 1940; d. Cecil Robey and Lola Ruby (Pippin) Lovett; m. Leonce Paul Lanoux Jr., June 10, 1966 (div. July 1984); 1 child, Cecil Lance Lanoux; m. James Harris Nisbett, May 12, 1990. Diploma in nursing, Tex. Ea. Sch. Nursing, 1963; BSN, Tex. Christian U., 1965; MS, Tex. Woman's U., 1977. RN, Tex. Asst. charge nurse med./surg. unit Med. Ctr. Hosp., Tyler, Tex., 1963-64, asst. dir. nursing, 1967; instr. nursing Tex. Ea. Sch. Nursing, Tyler, 1965-66; head nurse med./surg. unit Providence Hosp., Waco, Tex., 1966-67; dir. nursing Laird Meml. Hosp., Kilgore, Tex., 1967-69; instr. nursing Kilgore Coll., 1969-73; instr. nursing McLennan C.C., Waco, 1973-96, ret., 1996; asst. prof. U. Tex. Health Sci. Ctr., San Antonio, 1996—. Charter sec. Am. Heart Assn., Kilgore, 1968-69; bd. dirs. Heart of Tex. Soccer Assn., Waco, 1982-85. Mem. Nat. Orgn. Assoc. Degree Nursing, Tex. Jr. Coll. Tchr. Assn., Assn. Profl. and Staff Devel., Beta Sigma Phi (Outstanding Young Woman of Yr. 1981, Sweetheart 1970, 82, 91, Woman of Yr. 1990, Order of the Rose 1980, Silver Cir. award 1990). Methodist. Office: Univ Tex Health Sci Ctr 7703 Floyd Curl Dr San Antonio TX 78284-7942

NISH, WILLIAM ANDERSON, allergist, pediatrician; b. Boise, Feb. 16, 1960; s. William Walter and Margaret Anderson (Newland) N. BS summa cum laude, Presbyn. Coll., 1982; MD, Med. Coll. Ga., 1986. Diplomate Am. Bd. Pediatrics, Am. Bd. Allergy and Immunology, Nat. Bd. Med. Examiners. Commd. 2d lt. USAF, 1986, advanced through grades to maj., 1002; pediatric intern USAF Med. Ctr. Keesler, Keesler AFB, Miss., 1986-87, pediatric resident, 1987-89; allergy-immunology fellowship Wilford Hall USAF Med. ctr., 1989-91; staff allergy-immunology svc. Keesler Med. Ctr., Keesler AFB, 1991-93; chief allergy-immunology svc. Keesler (AFB) Med. Ctr., 1993-94. Contbr. articles to profl. jours. Deacon First Prebyn. Ch., Gainesville, Ga.; co-chmn. judges for medicine and health Internat. Scis. and Engring. Fair, 1993. Fellow Am. Acad. Pediatrics, Am. Coll. Allergy, Asthma and Immunology, Am. Acad. Allergy, Asthma and Immunology; mem. AMA (USAF rep. to AMA-RPS 1987-89), Air Force Allergy Assn., Assn. Mil. Allergists, Hall County Med. Soc., Med. Assn. Ga., Allergy, Asthma and Immunology Soc. Ga. Office: Allergy & Asthma Clinic of NE Ga 520 Jesse Jewell Pkwy Gainesville GA 30501

NISHIOKA, KENJI, cancer researcher, educator, consultant; b. Yokohama, Japan, July 9, 1942; came to the U.S., 1966; s. Hitoshi and Masanoi (Komatsubara) N.; m. Jeanne Zona Heise, Jan. 26, 1985. BS in Pharmacy, Osaka U., 1966; PhD, Vanderbilt U., 1971; D in Med. Sci., Kyoto U., 1978. Postdoctoral rsch. assoc. Tufts U. Sch. Medicine, Boston, 1971-72; asst. biochemist U. Tex. M.D. Anderson Cancer Ctr., Houston, 1972-78, asst. prof. surgery (biochemistry), 1974-79, assoc. prof., 1979-83, prof. surg. oncology (biochemistry), 1983-95; grad. faculty mem. grad. sch. biomed. scis. U. Tex. Health Sci. Ctr., 1975-95. Patentee in field; contbr. articles and abstracts to profl. jours. Fulbright scholar, 1966-70; grantee NIH, founds. and pharm. cos., 1975—. Mem. Am. Assn. for Cancer Rsch., Japanese Cancer Assn., Am. Soc. for Biochemistry and Molecular Biology, Am. Soc. for Pharmacology and Exptl. Therapeutics, AAAS, Am. Peptide Soc. (charter).

NISLY, LORETTA LYNN, medical and surgical nurse, geriatrics nurse; b. Cheverly, Md., Jan. 26, 1967; d. Mart and Mary (Miller) Overholt; m. Timothy Daniel Nisly, July 18, 1987. AD, Germanna Community Coll., Locust Grove, Va., 1994; LPN, Piedmont Tech. Edn. Ctr., Culpeper, Va., 1989. LPN, RN, Va. Med.-surg. nurse Culpeper Meml. Hosp., 1989-90, 95—; charge nurse Mt. View Nursing Home, Aroda, Va., 1990-92, Orange County Nursing Home, Orange, Va., 1992-94. Recipient Florence Nightengale award Germanna Cmty. Coll., 1995. Mem. Brethren. Home: HC 5 Box 128 Aroda VA 22709-9540

NISWONGER, JEANNE DU CHATEAU, biologist, writer; b. Indpls.; d. Simon Nicholas and Portia (Reeves) Du Chateau; m. Joseph Niswonger; children: Kenneth Arnold, Laura Elaine, Nancy Jo. AB, Miami U., Oxford, Ohio; postgrad., Washington Sch. Psychiatry; MA, PhD, Calif. Western U. Rsch. assoc. HEW and W.Va. Dept. Health, Charleston; rsch. biologist Bio-Rsch. Inst., Fla. So. Coll., Lakeland, 1958-61; writer Tampa (Fla.) Tribune, 1960-70. Assoc. editor Fla. Medaux, 1963-65; editor Lake Region Naturalist, 1959-69, asst. editor Fla. Naturalist, 1964-70; editor Fla. Wilderness Calendar, 1964-67; author: That Doll Ginny, Troll Dolls, Ginny Doll Family. Mem. bd. dirs. Polk Pub. Mus.; dir. pub. rels. Polk County Coun. Parents and Tchrs.; pres. Fla. chpt. Nature Conservancy. Mem. Fla. Audubon Soc. (mem. adv. bd. 1960-72), Lake Region Audubon Soc. (pres. 1960-65), AAUW (br. sec. 1962-64), Wildlife Soc., Wilderness Soc., Am. Soc. Mammalogists, Am. Assn. Zool. Parks and Aquariums, Izaak Walton League, Fla. Wildlife Fedn. (dir. 1974—), Nat. Wildlife Fedn., Am. Mus. Natural History, Fla. Zool. Soc., Defenders of Wildlife, Nat. Parks and Conservation Assn., Nat. League Am. Pen Women (treas., pres. 1987—), United Fedn. Doll Clubs (bd. mgmt.), Ginny Doll Club (pres.), Modern Doll Club (pres.), Travelers Century Club. Home: 305 W Beacon Rd Lakeland FL 33803-7248

NIX, JOSEPH HANSON, JR., aviation instructor; b. Columbus, Ohio, Apr. 28, 1930; s. Joseph Hanson Nix Sr. and Ella (Conant) Riddle; m. Barbara Ann Davis, Oct. 7, 1950; children: Joseph Hanson III, John Howard. BS in Mgmt., Fla. State U., 1966; EdM in Psychology, Cen. State U., Edmond, Okla., 1979; EdD in Adult Edn., Okla. State U., 1983. Advanced through grades to sgt. maj., chief master sgt. USAF, 1948-74; psychology specialist Kelsey-Seybold, NASA, Houston, 1974-75; instr. aviation physiology FAA, Civil Aeromedical Inst., Oklahoma City, 1975-82; chief ednl. devel. USCG Inst., Oklahoma City, 1982-85; supr. ednl. support FAA Airway Facilities Tng., Oklahoma City, 1985-88; edn. tng. advisor USCG Aviation Tng. Ctr., Mobile, Ala., 1988—; mem. exec. com. Intersvc. Corr. Exch., 1983-85; assoc. Nat. Home Study Coun. Rsch. and Edn. Standards Com., 1984-85; instr. USAF, 1950-74, CAP Mem.s, 1964-71; supplemental faculty tchr. Rose State Coll., Midwest City, Okla., 1987-88; adj. prof. edn. Oklahoma City U., 1987-88. Contbr. various films and articles to USAF and profl. jours. Scoutmaster Tyndall AFB, Panama City, Fla., 1963, cubmaster, 1959-60; sec. Road Runners, Hadji Shrine Temple, 1971-74; sec., treas., capt. Con-V Patrol, India Shrine Temple, Oklahoma City, 1980-88; dist. tng. chmn. Boy Scouts Am., 1960-65; dir. Tyndall Fed. Credit Union, 1961-67, 72-74; pres. Beale AFB Fed. Credit Union, 1971; mem. York Rite Coll. Mem. Nat. Soc. Performance and Instrn. (pres.-elect Armed Forces chpt. 1995, pres. 1996), Fla. State U. Alumni Assn. (life), Mobile Coast Guard Fed. Credit Union (chmn. adv. com. pres. 1990-92, dir. 1994, treas., chmn. fin. com. 1995), York Rite Coll., Masons (Bay # 337 sec. Panama City, Fla. 1961-62, Altheston # 369 master Mobile 1994-95), Shriners Burns Ins. (bd. govs. Galveston, Tex. chpt. 1987-91, 94-95, treas. 1996), Abba Shrine Temple (Potentate 1993), Order of Quetzalcoatl (Bahi de Mobile # 369), Lamaxtli, Air Force Assn. (exec. com. sec. 1991-93, v.p. Mobile chpt. 1994-95, membership 1994, v.p. govt. affairs state of Ala. 1995-96), Alpha Kappa Psi (life), Phi Delta Kappa, Psi Chi. Episcopalian. Home: 6400 Pinehurst Run Mobile AL 36608-3856 Office: Tradiv Tng Adv USCG AVTRACEN Bates Field Mobile AL 36608

NIX, ROBERT LYNN, minister; b. Belleville, Ark., Nov. 24, 1940; s. Huey Watson and Edna Mae (Johnson) N.; m. Patricia Sue Palmer, Aug. 27, 1961; children: Kevin Lynn, Robert Keith, Jonathan Kyle, Kelly Eugene. Diploma, Jackson (Miss.) Coll. Ministries, 1965. Ordained to ministry United Pentecostal Ch. Internat., 1963. Prof. Pentecostal Bible Inst., Tupelo, Miss., 1965-66; missionary to Peru, United Pentecostal Ch. Internat., 1966-69; missionary supt. United Pentecostal Ch., Peru, 1966-85; pres. United Pentecostal Sem., Peru, 1969-85; missionary supt. United Pentecostal Ch., Costa Rica, Cen. Am.; pres. United Pentecostal Sem. United Pentecostal Ch., Costa Rica, Cen. Am., 1983-85; pastor United Pentecostal Spanish Ch., Hilsboro, Oreg., 1985-86, Christian Apostolic Ch., San Antonio, 1987—. Bd. dirs. Tex. Bible Coll., Houston, 1993—. Home and Office: 12016 White Birch St San Antonio TX 78245-3350

NIXON, ARLIE JAMES, gas and oil company executive; b. Ralston, Okla., May 22, 1914; s. James Gordon and Wella May (Platt) N.; BS, Okla. State U., 1935; m. Wylie Elizabeth Jones, Apr. 21, 1938 (div. May 1950); children: Cole Jay, Kathleen (Mrs. S. Brent Joyce); m. Lisa Marie Grant, Dec. 7, 1981 (div. June 1989). Airline capt. Trans World Airlines, N.Y.C., 1939-74; pres. Crystal Gas Co., Jennings, Okla., 1960—, Blackburn Gas Co., Jennings, 1964—, Blackberry Oil Co., Jennings, 1969—; represented U.S. in several ofcl. dels. to internat. aviation tech. meetings, also represented Internat. Fedn. Air Line Pilots Assns. at internat. confs. Lt. (j.g.) USN, 1935-63. Mem. Internat. Fedn. Air Line Pilots Assn. (regional v.p. 1972), Internat. Platform Assn., Wings Club. Democrat. Home: RR 2 Jennings OK 74038-9802 Office: PO Box 68 Jennings OK 74038-0068

NIXON, JAMES GREGORY, economic development consultant; b. Kansas City, Mo., Dec. 7, 1962; s. Gerald Glen and Jane Ardis (Mountain) N.; m. Carol Ann Lake, June 21, 1986; 1 child, Kathryn Grace. BBA, U. Okla., 1985; MBA, Okla. State U., 1992. Cert. econ. developer. Govt. rels. aide Pub. Svc. Okla., Oklahoma City, 1985-86; info. analyst Pub. Svc. Okla., Tulsa, 1986-87, econ. devel. cons., 1987—. Mem. Am. Econ. Devel. Coun., So. Indsl. Devel. Coun. (alt. dir. 1986—), Order of Arrow (Vigil honor mem.). Republican. Mem. Disciples of Christ. Office: Pub Svc Co Okla 212 E 6th St Tulsa OK 74119-1212

NIXON, JOHN TRICE, judge; b. New Orleans, La., Jan. 9, 1933; s. H. C. and Anne (Trice) N.; m. Betty Chiles, Aug. 5, 1960 (div. Nov. 1985); children: Mignon Elizabeth, Anne Trice. A.B. cum laude, Harvard Coll., 1955; LL.B., Vanderbilt U., 1960. Bar: Ala. bar 1960, Tenn. bar 1972. Individual practice law Anniston, Ala., 1960-62; city atty. Anniston, 1962-64; trial atty. Civil Rights Div., Dept. Justice, Washington, 1964-69; staff atty., comptroller of Treasury State of Tenn., 1971-76; pvt. practice law Nashville, 1976-77; cir. judge, 1977-78, gen. sessions judge, 1978-80; judge U.S. Dist. Ct. (mid. dist.) Tenn., Nashville, 1980—, now chief judge, 1980. Served with U.S. Army, 1958. Democrat. Methodist. Clubs: D.U. (Cambridge); Harvard-Radcliffe (Nashville). Office: US Dist Ct 825 US Courthouse Nashville TN 37203*

NIXON, SAM A., retired insurance company medical executive; b. Galveston, Tex., June 28, 1927; s. Sam A. and Margaret Emory (Sandel) N.; m. Elizabeth Hughes, June 22, 1950; children: Margaret Alice, Emilie Elizabeth Nixon Carrell, Janice Erin Nixon Mott, Dorothy Hughes Nixon Robinson. BS, Tex. A&M U., 1946; MD, U. Tex., Galveston, 1950. Diplomate Am. Bd. Family Practice. Intern Fordham Hosp., Bronx, N.Y., 1950-51; pvt. practice Nixon, Tex., 1954-62, Floresville, Tex., 1962-77; prof. dept. family practice and cmty. medicine U. Tex. Med. Sch., Houston, 1977; dir. continuing edn. U. Tex. Health Sci. Ctr., Houston, 1977-92; assoc. network med. dir. Blue Cross Blue Shield Tex., Houston, 1992-94. Author: AIDS: A Guide for Survival; med. editor: U. Tex. Lifetime Health Letter. Co-chmn. treatment and rsch. Houston Crackdown, 1990-94. Capt. M.C., U.S. Army, 1950-54, Japan, Korea. Recipient John P. McGovern award Tex. Sch. Health Assn., 1988, AIDS Educator of Yr. award Mayor Whitmire, Houston, 1988, Disting. Alumnus award Tex. A&M Assn. Former Students, 1990, U. Tex. Med. Br., Galveston, 1982. Mem. AMA (chmn. coun. on med. edn. 1991-93), Am. Social Health Assn. (bd. dirs.), State Med. Edn. Bd. (chmn.), Tex. Med. Assn. (pres. 1991-92, C. Frank Webber M.D. award 1990), Harris County Med. Soc. (pres. 1989). Republican. Methodist. Home: RR 1 Box 105 Nixon TX 78140-9707

NIXON, SARA JO, psychologist, educator; b. Chickasha, Okla., July 6, 1955; d. David O. and Jo Ann (Howard) N.; children: David Benjamin, Joshua. BS, Southwestern Okla. State U., 1976; MS, U. Okla., 1979, PhD, 1982. Asst. prof. Iowa State U., Ames, 1982-83; asst. dir. student devel. U. Okla., Norman, 1983-87; postdoctoral fellow U. Okla., Oklahoma City, 1987-90, asst. prof. rsch., 1990-93, assoc. prof., 1993—; chair Okla. State Epidemiol. Work Group, Oklahoma City, 1991-93; dir. Cognitive Studies Lab., Oklahoma City, 1991—; mem. NIH IRG (NIAAA), 1995-99; assoc. dir. Okla. Ctr. for Alcohol & Drug Related Studies; cons. in field. Editor: Alcohol-Induced Brain Damage, 1993, Neuropsychology in Clinical Practice: Etiology, Assessment and Treatment of Common Neurological Problems, 1996; mem. editl. bd. Alcoholism: Clinical & Experimental Research; contbr. articles to profl. jours. Instr aerobics Goodrich Meth. Ch., 1985—, trustee, 1993—; bd. dirs. Okla. Youth Symphony, Oklahoma City, 1992-93, New Destiny Treatment Facility; chair Rsch. Coun., Dept. Psychiatry and Behavioral Scis., Red Ribbon Com., Oklahoma City, 1993. Recipient Scientist Devel. award Nat. Inst. Alcohol Abuse and Alcoholism, 1990, grantee, 1989—. Mem. Southwestern Psychol. Assn., Rsch. Soc. Alcholism, Am. Psychol. Soc., Sigma Xi, Phi Kappa Phi. Methodist. Office: Okla Ctr Alcohol & Drug Related Studies Ste 410 800 NE 15th St Oklahoma City OK 73104-4602

NOAKES, BETTY L., retired elementary school educator; b. Oklahoma City, Okla., Aug. 28, 1938; d. Webster L. and Willie Ruth (Johnson) Hawkins; m. Richard E. Noakes, Apr. 22, 1962 (dec.); 1 child, Michele Monique. Student, Oklahoma City U., MEd, 1971; BS, Cen. State U., 1962; postgrad., Cen. State U., Okla. State U. Elem. tchr. Merced (Calif.) Pub. Schs., 1966-67, Oklahoma City Schs., 1971-73, Mid-Del Schs., Midwest City, Okla., 1973-95; founder, owner Noakes-I Care Day Care, 1995—. 2d v.p. PTA, Pleasant Hill, 1991, cert. recognition, 1992-93; active Nat. PTA, 1991-92; charter mem. Nat. Mus. of Am. Indian-Smithsonian Instn. Recipient Cert. Appreciation YMCA, 1992-93, Disting. Svc. award Mid-Del PTA, 1992. Mem. NEA, AAUW, NAACP, Nat. Therapeutic Recreation Assn., Nat. Ret. Educators Assn., Okla. Ret. Tchrs. Assn., Oklahoma County Ret. Tchrs. Assn., Smithsonian Instn., Oklahoma City U. Alumni Assn., United Meth. Women Assn., Cen. State U. Alumni Assn., Order Ea. Star, Phi Delta

Kappa (sgt.-at-arms), Zeta Phi Beta. Home: 5956 N Coltrane Rd Oklahoma City OK 73121-3409

NOAKES, DAVID RONALD, research scientist, educator; b. July 4, 1954; came to U.S., 1991; s. Thomas Edward and Eleanor Alice (Green) N.; m. Catherine Luena Windsor, June 5, 1976; children: Thomas Windsor, William Edward. BSc in Physics and Math., Brandon U., 1975; MSc in Physics, U. Alta., 1978; PhD in Physics, U. Chgo., 1983. Rsch. asst. physics dept. U. Chgo., 1979-80; rsch. asst. materials sci. and tech. divsn. Argonne (Ill.) Nat. Lab., 1981-83; postdoctoral fellow TRIUMF/physics dept. U. B.C., Vancouver, 1983-87; rsch. fellow neutron and solid state physics br. AECL Chalk River (Ont., Can.) Nuclear Labs., 1987-89; rsch. assoc. physics dept. U. Alta., Edmonton, 1989-90; vis. asst. prof. physics and astronomy dept. Brandon (Man., Can.) U., 1990-91; rsch. assoc. prof. superconducting materials rsch. program Va. State U., Petersburg, 1991—; teaching asst. physics dept. U. Alta., Edmonton, 1975-76, U. Chgo., 1978-79; tchr. U. B.C., 1985, U. Alta., 1989-90, Brandon U., 1990-91. Contbr. articles to profl. jours. Natural Scis. and Engring. Rsch. Coun. Can. scholar, 1976-81, Natural Scis. and Engring. Rsch. Coun. Can. postdoctoral fellow, 1983-85. Mem. Am. Phys. Soc., TRIUMF User Group, Can. Inst. Neutron Scattering. Office: Va State U Physics Dept Box 9325 Petersburg VA 23806

NOBIL, JAMES HOWARD, JR., real estate investor, developer, consultant, broker; b. Columbus, Ohio, Mar. 21, 1955; s. James Howard Nobil and Carol Mae (Wiesenberger) Greenbaum; m. Elizabeth Ann Corro, Apr. 16, 1983; children: Jonathan James Michael, Jennifer Carrie Lee. BA in Polit. Sci., Tufts U., 1973-75; postgrad., George Washington U., 1978-80. Lic. real estate broker Md., Va., D.C., W.Va., Fla.; lic. securities rep., NASD; cert. leasing specialist ICSC. Account exec. Riviere Securities Corp., Washington, 1977-78; v.p. ops. Fed. Realty Investment Trust, Bethesda, Md., 1978-83; mng. gen. ptnr. NRW Devel. Co., Vienna, Va., 1983-84; v.p. acquisitions Oxford Nat. Properties Corp., Bethesda, 1984-85; 1st v.p. Washington Real Estate Investment Trust, Bethesda, 1985-86; pres. Washington Comml. Properties, Inc., McLean, Va., 1986—, Rent Verification Svcs. (subs. of Washington Comml. Properties, Inc.), McLean, 1986—. Mem. Internat. Coun. Shopping Ctrs., Nat. Assn. Realtors, D.C. Assn. Realtors, Area Comml. Brokers Coun. Republican. Office: Washington Comml Properties Inc 6723 Whittier Ave Ste 303 Mc Lean VA 22101-4533

NOBLE, DOUGLAS ROSS, museum administrator; b. Sturgis, Ky., Jan. 19, 1945; s. Roscoe and Robbie Rae (Martin) N.; m. Catherine Ann Richardson, Nov. 3, 1973; children: Kate Faxon, Jennifer Martin. BS, Okla. State U., 1967; MSA, Ga. Coll., 1978; D of Pub. Adminstrn., U. Ga., 1987. Asst. to dir. Savannah Sci. Mus., Ga., 1971-73; exec. dir. Mus. of Arts and Scis., Macon, Ga., 1973-80; dir. of museums Memphis Mus. System, 1980—; mem. mus. assessment program Inst. of Mus. Services, Washington, 1982—, grant reviewer, 1983—; cons. Mus. Mgmt. Program, Sarasota, Fla., 1985. Contbr. articles to profl. jours. Grad. Leadership Memphis, 1984; bd. dirs. Memphis in May Internat. Festival. 1st lt. U.S. Army, 1968-70; Vietnam. Decorated Bronze Star. Mem. Natural Sci. for Youth Found. (trustee 1980-87), Naumburg award 1978), Am. Assn. Museums (S.E. rep. 1984-87, chmn. mus. assessment program adv. com. 1987-89, treas., v.p. fin. 1990-92), chmn. nature ctr. accreditation com. 1985), Southeastern Museums Conf. (pres. 1982-84), Memphis Museums Roundtable (co-founder). Episcopalian. Home: 330 Belhaven St Memphis TN 38117-1602 Office: Memphis Pink Palace Mus & Planetarium 3050 Central Ave Memphis TN 38111-3316

NOBLE, MICHAEL ANDREW, audit manager; b. Baton Rouge, La., May 26, 1953; s. Andrew Day and Elise (Prestridge) N.; m. Vickie Downs, Nov. 11, 1993; children: Andrew Joseph, Jill Mikelyn. BS in Acctg., Northwestern State U., 1975. CPA, La.; Cert. Fraud Examiner. Govtl. auditor II Legis. Auditor State of La., Baton Rouge, 1975-78, govtl. auditor III, 1978-79, sr. auditor I, 1979-82, sr. auditor II, auditor-in-charge, 1982-94; audit mgr. Shreveport, La., 1994—. Deacon Zoar Bapt. Ch., Baton Rouge, 1984—. Mem. AICPA, La. Soc. CPAs, Nat. Assn. Cert. Fraud Examiners, Govt. Fin. Officers Assn. La., Assn. Bass Profls., Assn. La. Bass Clubs, Bass Anglers Sportsmen Soc., Hassle Free Bass Club (sec.-treas. 1992-94). Office: Office Legis Auditor 820 Jordan St Ste 306 Shreveport LA 71101-4518

NOBLE, MICHAEL JAY, English language educator, poet; b. Lafayette, La., June 20, 1968; s. Jay P. and Nancy S. (McBride) N.; m. Tiffany Michelle Bunker, Feb. 5, 1994. BA, Brigham Young U., 1992, MA, 1994; postgrad., U. Southwestern La., 1995—. Reference asst. Brigham Young U. Libr., Provo, Utah, 1990-92; instr. Brigham Young U., Provo, 1992-94, Utah Valley State Coll., Orem, 1994; reference asst. Orem Pub. Libr., 1994-95; instr., fellow U. Southwestern La., Lafayette, 1995—. Recipient Voorhies Creative Writing award, Lafayette, 1996. Mem. MLA, Associated Writing Programs. Democrat. Office: U Southwestern La PO Box 40235 Lafayette LA 70504

NOBLE, RONALD MARK, sports medicine facility administrator; b. Atlanta, Dec. 28, 1950; s. Dexter Ron and Judy (Puckett) N.; m. Teresa Lowder, Sept. 20, 1975; children: Kimberly, Heather, James, Ashlee. AS, Ricks Coll., 1974; BS cum laude, Troy State U., 1976; MS, U. Tenn., 1977. Grad. asst. U. Tenn., Knoxville, 1976-77; lectr. Tex. A&M U., College Station, 1977-79; asst. prof. U.S. Mil. Acad., West Point, N.Y., 1979-80; dir. clin. phys. NASA Med. Ctr., MSFC, 1980-85; exec. dir. Total Wellness Ctr., Huntsville, Ala., 1986-90, Preventive and Rehab. Sports Medicine Assocs., Huntsville, 1990—; clin. advisor Huntsville Med. Sch., U. Ala., 1990—, exec. dir. preventive and clin. advisor, preceptor, 1992—; adj. prof. U. Ala., Huntsville, 1982-85; sports medicine cons. Mex. Olympic Com., San Luis Potosi, 1980, Duke U. Basketball, Durham, N.C., 1987—, U.S. Olympic Team, 1994—; coord. U.S. Olympic Com. Nat. Rehab. Network; cons. USAF Dept. Manned Space Flight Ops., L.A., 1983-84, athletic dept. Ala. A&M U., 1994—; asst. coach U.S. Olympic Com., Colorado Springs, 1979-83; spl. advisor Pres. Coun. on Phys. Fitness and Sports, Huntsville, 1991; clin. advisor, preceptor U. Ala. Huntsville Med. Sch. Developer computer software in field; contbr. articles to profl. jours., also to USAF manual. Campaign mgr. Brooks for State Legislature, Huntsville, 1992; bd. dirs. Huntsville Boys Club, 1988-89, Big Bros./Sisters of No. Ala., Huntsville, 1988-89, Ala. affiliate Am. Heart Assn., Huntsville, 1980-88; commr. Ala. Gov.'s Com. on Phys. Fitness, 1991-94; mem. U.S. Olympic Com. Spkrs. Bur., 1978-80; U.S. Olympic Com., Nat. Rehab. Network for Elite Athletes. With U.S. Army, 1970-73, Vietnam. Named Outstanding Leader Jaycees of Ala., 1983; Paul Harris fellow Huntsville Rotary Club, 1987—. Mem. Huntsville Rotary (Paul Harris fellow), Kappa Delta Pi. Mem. LDS Ch. Office: PRSM Assocs 1015 Airport Rd SW Ste 203 Huntsville AL 35802-1394

NOBLES, LEWIS J., JR., executive; b. 1919. Pres. Nobles-Collier, Immokalee, Fla., 1952—. Office: Nobles-Collier 212 Jerome Dr Immokalee FL 34142-3830

NOBLES, LORRAINE BIDDLE, dietitian; b. Washington, Apr. 27, 1926; d. Norton William and Lorraine Verna (Tabler) Biddle; m. Stevens Henry Nobles, Dec. 28, 1961 (dec. Apr. 1987). BS, Ohio U., 1952; MSHE, East Carolina U., 1973, MS, 1989. Asst. adminstr. dietitian Emergency Hosp., Washington, 1952-56; asst. supr. sch. lunch program Arlington (Va.) County, 1956-66; chief dietitian Pitt County Meml. Hosp., Greenville, N.C., 1966-91; adj. prof. East Carolina U., Greenville, 1969-91. Mem. Am. Dietetic Assn., N.C. Dietetic Assn. (chmn. ann. meeting 1982), Ea. N.C. Dist. Dietetic Assn. (pres. elect 1977-78, pres. 1978-79, sec. 1988-90), Am. and Mid-Atlantic Soc. Parenteral and Enteral Nutrition (2d Pl. Pearls session 1988), Tau Delta Epsilon, Phi Omicron Nu, Kappa Delta Pi. Republican. Episcopalian. Home: 205 Country Club Dr Ayden NC 28513-9545

NOBLES, ROBERT L., business executive; b. 1938. With S.E. Steel Corp., San Juan, P.R., 1959-76; pres. Nobles Marine, Leeburg, Fla., 1976—. Office: Nobles Marine 437 N Palmetto St Leesburg FL 34748

NOBLIN, CHARLES DONALD, clinical psychologist, educator; b. Jackson, Miss., Dec. 16, 1933; s. Charles Thomas and Margaret (Byrne) N.; m. Patsy Ann Beard, Aug. 12, 1989. BA, Miss. Coll., 1955; MS, Va. Commonwealth U., 1957; PhD, La. State U., 1962. Lic. psychologist, Miss., N.J., N.C. Instr. to asst. prof. La. State U., Baton Rouge, 1961-63; asst. to assoc. prof. U. N.C., Greensboro, 1963-66; assoc. prof. Rutgers Med. Sch., New Brunswick, N.J., 1966-69; dir. clin. training Va. Commonwealth U., Richmond, 1969-72; chmn. dept. psychology Va. Tech., Blacksburg, 1972-82; dir. clin. training U. So. Miss., Hattiesburg, 1982-85, chmn. dept. psychology, 1985-91, prof., 1991-93, dir. clin. tng., 1993—. Contbr. over 60 articles and presentations. Recipient Clin. Tng. grant NIMH, 1983-86, Victim Behavior & Personal Space rsch. grant U.S. Dept. Justice, 1970-71, Trubeck Found. Rsch. award, 1968-69. Baptist. Home: 7 Cane Ct Hattiesburg MS 39402-8716 also: PO Box 10036 Hattiesburg MS 39406-0036 Office: U So Miss Dept Psychology Hattiesburg MS 39406

NOBOA-STANTON, PATRICIA LYNN, corporate executive; b. Cin., Sept. 6, 1947; d. William Emile and Marie Virginia (Ballbach) Hakes; m. Donald R. Stanton, Nov. 10, 1987; children from previous marriage: Aric Israel, Rene Carlos. Diploma Presbyn.-St. Luke's Sch. Nursing, Chgo., 1967, Nat. Inst. Real Estate, 1989, No. Va. Community Coll., 190. Supr. patient care Alexandria Hosp., Va., 1976-78; pres. Renaissance Reprographics, Inc., Reston, Va., 1985-89; pres. Va. Leasing & Copying Inc., Reston, 1978-89; realtor Wellborn Comml., 1989-91; dir. ops., publ. and health cons. Atlantic Resources Corp., 1991-93, dir. ops. and adminstrn., 1991-93; exec. v.p. Mark Moseley's Travel, 1993-95; CEO Transitions 2000, 1995—. Pres. Reston Bd. Commerce, 1985, founding bd. dirs. 1982-85, v.p. 1984, sec. 1983; v.p. Planned Community Archives, Inc., 1985-88; mem. regional com. United Way, 1985-87; Dulles Area Regional Council steering com., 1985-88; pres. Myterra Home-owners Assn., 1990—; bd. dirs. N. Va. Local Devel. Corp., 1987—; bd. dirs. Fairfax Symphony, Reston Bd. Commerce, 1989. Named Reston Citizen of Yr., 1985; named Small Bus. Person of Yr. Fairfax County Commn. for Women, 1985-87. Mem. Northern Va. Assn. Realtors, Nat. Assn. Realtors, Va. Assn. Realtors, Nat. Assn. Quick Printers (bd. dirs. Capital chpt. 1984—, vice chair 1987—), Internat. Platform Assn., Fairfax County C. of C. (bd. dirs. 1985-86, 87—), Herndon C. of C., Washington-Dulles Task Force. Episcopalian. Lodge: Rotary. Avocations: computers, music, flying. Office: Transitions 2000 12401 Myterra Way Herndon VA 20171

NOE, RANDOLPH, lawyer; b. Indpls., Nov. 2, 1939; s. John H. and Bernice (Baker) Reiley; m. Anne Will, Mar. 2, 1968 (div.); children: J.H. Reiley, Anne Will, Randolph, Jonathan Baker. Student Franklin Coll. 1957-60; BS, Ind. State U., 1964; JD, Ind. U., 1967. Bar: Ind. 1968, Ky. 1970. Trust officer Citizens Fidelity Bank & Trust Co., Louisville, 1969-71; sole practice, Louisville, 1971-84; ptnr. Greenebaum, Treitz, Brown & Marshall, 1984—; asst. county atty. Jefferson County, 1979-84. Author: Kentucky Probate Methods, 1976, supplement, 1992; editor: Kentucky Law Summary, 1985—. Fellow Am. Coll. Probate Counsel; mem. ABA, Ind. Bar Assn., Ky. Bar Assn. Democrat. Clubs: Pendennis, Wranglers. Office: 1406 One Riverfront Plz Louisville KY 40202

NOEL, ROGER ARTHUR, French and German language educator; b. Wanne, Belgium, Nov. 22, 1942; came to U.S., 1970; s. Adolphe and Lucie (Hemroulle) N.; m. Alice E. Gubner, Mar. 28, 1969; children: Anouk Aileen, Nadine Valerie. Lic. in philosophy and letters, Liège, Belgium, 1965; MA in French Lit., U. Mo., 1966; PhD in French Lit., Washington U., St. Louis, 1984. Tchr. English SHAPE, Casteau, Belgium, 1967-68; lectr. English U. Liège, 1969-70; instr. French U. Mo., St. Louis, 1970-76, lectr. French, 1976-86, coord. elem. courses, 1976-86; asst. prof. French, Monmouth (Ill.) Coll., 1986-90, assoc. prof., chmn. dept., 1990-92; assoc. prof., chmn. dept. modern fgn. langs. Ga. Coll., Milledgeville, 1992—; asst. v.p. Internat. Edn., 1995-96. Author: Joufroi de Poitiers: Traduction Critique, 1987; co-author: An Introduction to an Academic Vocabulary, 1989, A Thesaurus of Word Roots of the English Language, 1992, A Thesaurus of Medical Word Roots, 1996; editor, translator French version ofcl. guide to Olympiad, 1988; co-editor Jour. Baltic Studies. With Belgian Army, 1968-69. Named chevalier Ordre des Palmes Académiques, 1991. Mem. MLA, AAUP, Am. Assn. Tchrs. French (pres. Ga.), Am. Assn. Tchrs. German, Ctr. for Belgian Culture We. Ill., Internat. Arthurian Soc., Ga. Classical Assn., So. Conf. on Lang. Tchg., Fgn. Lang. Assn. Ga., Am. Assn. French Acad. Palms, Soc. Prof. French and Francophones in Am., South Atlantic MLA. Democrat. Roman Catholic. Home: 3624 Sussex Dr NE Milledgeville GA 31061-9339 Office: Dept Modern Fgn Lang Ga Coll Campus Box 046 Milledgeville GA 31061

NOGUERAS, JUAN JOSE, surgeon; b. Rio Piedras, P.R., Apr. 23, 1956; s. Juan Jose and Agustina (Soroeta) N.; m. Michele LeMoal, Sept. 22, 1984; children: Nicole, John, Robert. AB in Biochemistry, Princeton U., 1978; MD, Jefferson Med. Coll., 1982. Diplomate Am. Bd. Surgery, Am. Bd. Colon and Rectal Surgery, Nat. Bd. Med. Examiners. Instr. surgery Wilford Hall Air Foce Med. Ctr., San Antonio, 1987-90; mem. staff dept. colorectal surgery Cleveland Clin. Fla., Ft. Lauderdale, 1991—; presenter in field. Contbg. author: Current Controversies in Breast Cancer, 1984, Pre-test Self Assessment and Review, 1987, Textbook and Atlas of Laparoscopic Colorectal Surgery, Intestinal Stomas, 1993; reviewer: Surgical Endoscopy, 1993—, So. Med. Jour., 1993—; contbr. articles to profl. jours. Major med. corps. U.S. Army, 1987-90. Recipient A.W. Martin Marino Sr. M.D. award N.Y. Soc. Colon and Rectal Surgeons, 1991; Fellow U. Minn., 1990-91. Fellow ACS (assoc.); mem. Am. Soc. Colon and Rectal Surgeons, Soc. Am. Gastrointestinal Endoscopic Surgeons, Crohn's and Colitis Found. Am. (chmn. med. adv. com. 1992—), Dominican Coll. Surgeons (hon.), Midwest Soc. Colon and Rectal Surgeons (pres. 1993-94), S.E. Med. Assn., S.E. Surg. Congress. Office: Cleveland Clin Dept Colorectal Surgery 3000 W Cypress Creek Rd Fort Lauderdale FL 33309-1710

NOHRNBERG, JAMES CARSON, English language educator; b. Berkeley, Calif., Mar. 19, 1941; s. Carson and Geneva Gertrude (Gibbs) N.; m. Stephanie Payson Lamport, June 14, 1964; children: Gabrielle L., Peter Carson L. Student, Kenyon Coll., 1958-60; BA, Harvard Coll., 1962, postgrad., 1965-68; PhD, U. Toronto, Ont., Can., 1970. Teaching fellow dept. English U. Coll., U. Toronto, 1963-64; jr. fellow Soc. of Fellows Harvard U., 1965-68; acting instr. dept. English Yale U., New Haven, 1968-69, lectr. dept. English, 1969-70, asst. prof. dept. English, 1970-75, assoc. prof., 1975; prof. English U. Va., Charlottesville, 1975—; adj. instr. English Harvard U., Cambridge, 1967; lectr. various univs., 1974-96; Gauss seminar in criticism lectr. Princeton U., 1987. Author: The Analogy of the Faerie Queene, 1976, 80, Like Unto Moses: The Constituting of an Interruption, 1995; mem. editl. bd. Spenser Ency., 1977-90; contbr. articles to profl. jours. and ed. vols. on Bible, Homer, Dante, Boiardo, Spenser, Milton, Thomas Pynchon, among others. Woodrow Wilson fellow, 1962, jr. fellow Harvard U., 1965-68, Morse fellow Yale U., 1974-75, U. Va. Ctr. for Advanced Studies fellow, 1975-78, Guggenheim fellow, 1981-82, Ind. U. Inst. for Advanced Studies fellow, 1991. Mem. MLA, Spenser Soc. Presbyterian. Home: 1874 Wayside Pl Charlottesville VA 22903-1631 Office: U Va Dept English Bryan Hall Charlottesville VA 22903

NOKES, MARY TRIPLETT, former university president, counselor, artist; b. Weatherford, Okla., Sept. 6, 1920; d. Ernest Carlton and Eva Hannah (Claridge) Triplett; m. George Willis Malcom Nokes, July 11, 1937; 1 child, William Careton. BA, Cen. State U., 1943; Masters Degree, U. Okla., 1949, Doctors Degree, 1969. Tchr., sec. Okla. Edn. Assn., Oklahoma City, 1943-83; advisor Nat. Honor Soc., Oklahoma City, 1955-83; 1st v.p. Internat. Porcelain Artist, 1966-68, pres., 1968-70, sec. bd., 1979-92; pres. Okla. State U., 1975-91; ret., 1991; legis. rep. for Okla. Edn. Assn., 1979-92; presenter seminars on china painting, 1991—. Sponsor Student Coun., 1955-83; pres. Okla. State China Painting Tchr., 1986-87; dir. Vacation Bible Sch., 1984-95, 96—; pres. Soccer Club, 1995-96, Sooner Art Club, 1996—. Named Vol. Woman of Yr. Salvation Army, Okla., 1992-93, Woman of Yr. Salvation Army, 1995-96, Personality of South, 1994-95, Cmty. Leader for Noteworthy Ams., 1994-95, Cmty. Leader Oklahoma City, 1994-95; recipient proclamation Mayor Oklahoma City, 1994-95, 95-96, named Amb. of Good Will by Governor of Okla. Mem. Internat. Porcelain Art Tchrs. (past v.p., past pres., regional chmn., sec. to internat. bd. dirs.), Intercontinental Biographical Assn., C. of C. (sec.), Les Lefeyetts Home Club (pres. 1941-43), Garden Club (pres.), Sooner Art Club (pres. 1991-97), Kermac Art Club, Alpha Phi Sigma, Kappa Delta Phi, Kappa Kappa Iota. Baptist. Home: 4125 NW 57th St Oklahoma City OK 73112-1505

NOLAN, CHARLES EDWARD, archivist, educator; b. Chgo., Apr. 6, 1935; s. Charles E. and Louise (Baldwin) N.; m. Patricia Gayle Kuehne, July 31, 1971; children: Bruce, Kathleen, Elizabeth. BA in Philosophy, St. Bonaventure U., 1958; STB in Theology, Lateran U., 1962; Licentiate in Eccles. History, Gregorian U., Rome, 1964, Doctorate in Eccles. History, 1977; MEd, Loyola U., New Orleans, 1981. Tchr., sch. adminstr. various schs., 1964-81; assoc. archivist Archdiocese of New Orleans, 1981-92, archivist, 1992—; adj. prof. U. New Orleans, 1984-94; lectr. edn., So. history, archives and records mgmt., 1978—. Author: A Southern Catholic Heritage, Vol. 1, The Colonial Period, 1704-1813, 1976, Bayou Carmel: The Sisters of Mount Carmel of Louisiana, 1833-1903, 1977, St. Maurice Parish of New Orleans, 1982, Mother Clare Coady: Her Life, Her Times and Her Sisters, 1983, St. Mary's of Natchez: The History of a Southern Catholic Congregation (1713-1988), 1992; co-author: The American Catholic Parish: A History from 1850 to the Present, 1987, Disaster Prevention and Recovery: A Planned Approach, 1988, Introduction to Christ: The Living Water, The Catholic Church in Mississippi, 1989; assoc. editor: Sacramental Records of the Roman Catholic Church of the Archdiocese of New Orleans (1718-1803), 11 vols., 1987-96, The Shiloh Diary of Edmond Enoul Livaudais, 1992; sect. editor, co-author: Cross, Crozer & Crucible, a Volume Celebrating the Establishment of a Catholic Diocese in Louisiana, 1993; editor: Sacramental Records of the Roman Catholic Church of the Archdiocese of New Orleans, 1804-1815, vols. 8-11, 1993-96. Active Am. Cath. Hist. Assn., La. Hist. Assn., Tex. Cath. Hist. Soc.; mem. La. gov.'s adv. com. Edn. of Handicapped Children, 1978-79; mem. La. Hist. Records Adv. Commn., 1989-91. Mem. Acad. Cert. Archivists (cert.), Inst. Cert. Records Mgr. (cert.), Assn. Records Mgrs. and Adminstrs. (pres. New Orleans chpt. 1983-84, co-chmn. host com. 1989, Internat. Conf. award of merit 1989), Assn. Cath. Diocesan Archivists (v.p. 1995-97). Roman Catholic. Office: Archdiocese of New Orleans 1100 Chartres St New Orleans LA 70116-2596

NOLAN, DAVID BRIAN, lawyer; b. Washington, Jan. 1, 1951; s. John Joseph and Mary Jane Nolan; m. Cheryl Ann Cottle, June 30, 1979; children: John Joseph II, David Brian II, Christopher Dalton. BA, Duke U., 1973; MPA, Am. U., 1975; JD, U. La Verne, 1978; postgrad., Georgetown U., 1981-89. Bar: Calif. 1978, U.S. Dist. Ct. (cen. dist.) Calif. 1979, U.S. Ct. Claims 1981, U.S. Tax Ct. 1981, U.S. Ct. Appeals (D.C. cir.) 1984. Intern Congressman Joel Broyhill, 1981; asst. dir. rsch. Younger-Curb Campaign, L.A., 1978; assoc. L. Rob Werner Law Offices, Encino, Calif., 1979-80; atty. conflicts Office of Pres. Elect, Washington, 1980-81; staff atty. Office of counsel to the Pres. White House, Washington, 1981; staff asst. office of sec. U.S. Dept. Treasury, Washington, 1981-85; spl. asst. office gen. counsel U.S. Dept. Energy, Washington, 1985-90, atty. advisor enforcement div. Office of Nuclear Safety, 1990-91, trial atty. adminstrv. litigation div. Econ. Regulatory Adminstrn., 1991-95, trial atty. Office of Gen. Counsel, 1995—; corp. dir., treas. Energy Fed. Credit Union. Assoc. editor New Guard Mag., 1983-85. Steering com. L.A. Reps., 1979-80, Reagan for Pres., L.A., 1980; chmn. 39th Assembly, Rep. Ctrl. Com., 1979-80; alt. del. 1972 Rep. Nat. Conv.; pres. N.C. Coll. Rep. Com., 1972-73; nat. treas., bd. dirs. Young Amers. for Freedom, Sterling, Va., 1983-85; corp. dir. Am. Sovereignty Task Force, Vienna, Va., 1984—, State Dept. Watch Ltd., Vienna, 1984—. Charles Edison Youth Found. scholar, 1971; named one of Outstanding Young Men in Am., Jaycees, 1976-86; recipient Mgr. of Yr. honor Dept. Energy Women's Adv. Coun., 1988, Achievement in Equal Opportunity Deptl. award, 1988. Mem. ABA, Fed. Bar Assn., Bar Assn. of D.C. (chmn. ethics com. young lawyers div. 1985-87), D.C. Bar, Calif. Bar, U.S. Supreme Ct. Soc., Federalist Soc., U.S. Justice Found. (co-founder, of counsel 1979—), Conservative Network Club. Home: 8310 Wagon Wheel Rd Alexandria VA 22309-2144 Office: US Dept Energy 1000 Independence Ave SW Washington DC 20585-0001

NOLAN, GERALD, career officer; b. San Francisco, Apr. 29, 1947; s. Edward Anthony Nolan and Esther (Regina) Foley; m. Mary Virginia Wieser. BS, U. San Francisco, 1970, MPA, 1984. Commd. 2d lt. U.S. Army, 1971, advanced through grades to lt. col., 1990. Decorated Joint Meritorious Svc. medal. Mem. Assn. of U.S. Army, Res. Officer Assn., Assn. Army Aviators, Dustoff Assn. Roman Catholic. Home: 107 Wyanoke Dr San Antonio TX 78209-6430 Office: Gt Plains Regional Med Ctr Fort Sam Houston San Antonio TX 78234-5000

NOLAN, LONE KIRSTEN, financial advisor; b. Copenhagen, Oct. 9, 1938; d. Johannes and Elizabeth (Zachariassen) Jansen; came to U.S., 1957, naturalized, 1964; m. Gene Nolan, Mar. 19, 1973; children—Glenn Muller, Erik Muller. Lic. securities broker; adminstrv. asst. Am. Nat. Bank and Trust, Morristown, N.J., 1967-72; asst. cashier First Nat. Iron Bank, 1972; comptroller and ops. officer Panama City Nat. Bank, 1973-74; asst. v.p. Lee County Bank, Ft. Myers, Fla., 1974-76; Priscilla Murphy Realty, Sanibel, Fla., 1976-77; pres. Century 21 Nolan Realty, Ft. Myers, 1977-80; pres. AAIM Realty Group, Ft. Myers, 1980-81; real estate investment counselor Merrill Lynch, Boca Raton, Fla., 1982-85; mgr. Merrill Lynch Realty, Palm Beach, Fla., 1984-85; mgr. J.W. Charles Realty, Inc., Boca Raton, 1985-89; investment advisor Dean Witter Reynolds, Ft. Lauderdale, Fla., 1990-96; fin. planner FFP Securities, 1996—. Mem. NAFE, Nat. Assn. Security Dealers, Stocks and Bonds Club. Address: 21380 Placida Ter Boca Raton FL 33433-2385 Office: FFP Securities Ste 355 One Park Pl 621 NW 53d St Boca Raton FL 33487

NOLAN, RICHARD THOMAS, clergyman, educator; b. Waltham, Mass., May 30, 1937; s. Thomas Michael and Elizabeth Louise (Leishman) N.; life ptnr. Robert C. Pingpank, Sept. 14, 1955. BA, Trinity Coll., 1960; cert. in clin. pastoral edn., Conn. Valley Hosp., 1962; diploma, Berkeley Divinity Sch., 1962; MDiv., Hartford Sem. Found., 1963; postgrad., Union Theol. Sem., N.Y.C., 1963; MA in Religion, Yale U., 1967; PhD, NYU, 1973; post doctoral, Harvard U., 1991. Ordained deacon Episcopal Ch., 1963, priest, 1965. Instr. Latin and English Watkinson (Conn.) Sch., 1961-62; instr. math. Choir Sch. of Cathedral of St. John the Divine, N.Y.C., 1962-64; instr. math. and religion, assoc. chaplain Cheshire (Conn.) Acad., 1965-67; instr. Hartford (Conn.) Sem. Found., 1967-68, asst. acad. dean, lectr. philosophy and edn., 1968-70; instr. Mattatuck C.C., Waterbury, Conn., 1969-70, asst. prof. philosophy and history, 1970-74, assoc. prof., 1974-78, prof. philosophy and social sci., 1978-92, prof. emeritus, 1992—; rsch. fellow in med. ethics Yale U., 1978, rsch. fellow in profl. and bus. ethics, 1987; vicar St. Paul's Parish, Bantam, Conn., 1974-88; pastor emeritus St. Paul's Parish, Bantam, 1988—; pres. Litchfield Inst., Conn. and Fla., 1984-96; mem. ethics com. Waterbury Hosp. Health Ctr., 1984-88; vis. and adj. prof. philosophy, theology and religious studies Trinity Coll., Conn., L.I. U., U. Miami, St. Joseph Coll., Conn., Pace U., Teikyo Post U., U. Conn., Hartford Grad. Ctr., Ctrl. Conn. State U., Barry U., Fla., Broward C.C., Fla., 1964-95; adj. assoc. in continuing edn. Berkeley Div. Sch. Yale U., 1987-89; Rabbi Harry Halpern Meml. lectr., Southbury, Conn., 1987; guest spkr. various chs. and orgns. including Cathedral of St. John the Divine, N.Y. and Trinity Cathedral, Miami; mem. faculty of consulting examiners Charter Oak State Coll., Conn., 1990-93; fellow Associated Fellows for Counseling and Psychotherapy, Inc., 1990-93; assoc. for edn. Christ Ch. Cathedral, Hartford, Conn., 1988-94, hon. canon, 1991—; cons. Dept. Def. Activity Non-Traditional Ednl. Support, Ednl. Testing Svcs., Princeton, 1990; vis. scholar Coll. Preachers Washington Nat. Cathedral, 1994; retired assisting priest Episcopal Ch. of Bethesda-by-the-Sea, Palm Beach, Fla., 1994—. Author: (with H. Titus and M. Smith) Living Issues in Philosophy, 7th edit., 1979, Indonesian edit., 1984, 8th edit., 1986, 9th edit., 1995, (with F. Kirkpatrick) Living Issues in Ethics, 1982; editor, contbr. Diaconate Now, 1968; host Conversations with ..., 1987-89. Founding mem. The Heritage Soc. of The Episcopal Ch. of Bethesda-by-the-Sea, Palm Beach. Mem. Am. Acad. Religion, Am. Philos. Assn., Authors Guild, Hemlock Soc., Boston Latin Sch. Alumni Assn., Tabor Acad. Alumni Assn., Cavalier King Charles Spaniel Club, Phi Delta Kappa. Home: 6342 Forest Hill Blvd # 350 West Palm Beach FL 33415-6158

NOLAND, ANNGINETTE ROBERTS, retired sales executive; b. Stillwater, Okla., Sept. 30, 1930; d. Cecil Andrew and Gladys Leah (Woods) Roberts; m. Thomas Vaughan Noland, June 11, 1949; children: Nanette Noland Crocker, Thomas Vaughan Noland, Bruce Andrew Noland. Student, Okla. State U., 1948-49; cert. in planning, U. Wis. Chpt. advisor Kappa Delta Sorority, Stillwater, 1953-54, Baton Rouge, 1956-59; province pres. Kappa Delta Sorority, Miss., 1970-77; chpt. dir. II Kappa Delta Sorority, 1977-84, nat. dir. scholarship program, 1984-87, past mem. evaluation com., chmn. conv. scholarship banquet com., 1985, chmn. fellowships evaluation com., 1984-87; accounts receivables clk. Sta. WLOX-TV, Biloxi, Miss., 1973-76, sales asst., 1976-82, nat. sales asst. and polit. sales, 1982-84, nat. sales supr., 1984-95. Recipient award Order of the Emerald

Kappa Delta Sorority, 1988. Mem. NAFE, DAR (treas. Biloxi chpt. 1983-89, corr. sec. 1989—), S.C. Geneal. Soc., Okla. Geneal. Soc., Colonial Dames XVII Century (corr. sec. local chpt. 1985-87, pres. 1987-89, 2d v.p. 1989-90, corr. sec. 1991—, state chair Colonial Heritage Week 1989-91, state chmn. yearbooks 1991-93, state organizing sec. 1993-95, corr. sec. 1993—, state insignia chair 1995—), Dau. Am. Colonists (charter mem. local chpt., 1st v.p. 1993—, state chair coll. Ozarks com. 1995—), UDC (1st v.p. local chpt. 1990-94, dist. dir., state conv. chair 1992, state fin. com. chair 1993-94, chpt. pres. 1994-96, state recorder crosses mil. svc. 1994—), Sons and Daus. Pilgrims (state recording sec. 1995—), U.S. Daus. of 1812, Magna Charta Dames, Biloxi Yacht Club (aux. corr. sec. 1986-88, sec. 1989-90). Republican. Episcopalian. Home: 2441 Old Bay Rd Biloxi MS 39531-2113

NOLEN, CYNTHIA ESTELLE, writer, poet; b. Port Acres, Tex., Mar. 3, 1962; d. Beverly Solon and Carrie Nell (Taylor) Guthrie; m. James Wayne Kelsey, Apr. 17, 1977 (div. Apr. 1989); children: Malisa Marie Kelsey Reeves, Jason August; m. Mark Eugene Nolen, Sept. 1, 1990. Student, Lamar U., Port Arthur and Beaumont, Tex., 1986-88. Sec. Tex. Rents Waterbed Gallery, Port Arthur, 1986-88; substitute tchr. Port Neches (Tex.) Ind. Sch. Dist., 1988-90; writer Lillian Books, Groves, Tex., 1990—; Author: Moving On, Pro Roll Sport Game, Exploring Tex. Cities, Exploring Arkansas Cities; contbr. poetry to anthologies. Spkr. on lit. Tex. schs., 1990—; actress Port Arthur Little Theatre, 1992. Recipeint Golden Poet award, 1988, 89, 90.; songwriter Hilltop Records, 1995—; albums include Musically Yours, America Together We Stand, There Is A Way To Stop the Pain. Democrat. Home: PO Box 971 Shepherd TX 77371 Office: Lillian Books 6340 32d St Groves TX 77619

NOLEN, ROY LEMUEL, lawyer; b. Montgomery, Ala., Nov. 29, 1937; s. Roy Lemuel Jr. and Elizabeth (Larkin) N.; m. Evelyn McNeill Thomas, Aug. 28, 1965; 1 child, Rives Rutledge. BArch, Rice U., 1961; LLB, Harvard U., 1967. Bar: Tex. 1968, U.S. Ct. Appeals (5th cir.) 1969. Law clk. to sr. judge U.S. Ct. Appeals (5th cir.), 1967-68; assoc. Baker & Botts, Houston, 1968-75, ptnr., 1976—; co-head Corp. Dept., 1985-90, mem. exec. com., 1988-91. Bd. dirs. Houston Ballet Found., 1980-92, Rice Design Alliance, 1995-96; exec. com. Contemporary Arts Mus., 1990-96; exec. com., gen. counsel Houston Symphony Soc., 1994—; sr. warden Christ Ch. Cathedral, 1991-92. 1st lt. USMC, 1961-64. Mem. ABA, State Bar of Tex., Houston Bar Assn., Coronado Club, Allegro, Paul Jones Club. Episcopalian. Office: Baker & Botts 3000 One Shell Plz 910 Louisiana St Houston TX 77002

NOLEN, WILLIAM LAWRENCE, JR., insurance agency owner, real estate investor; b. Austin, Tex., Oct. 3, 1922; s. William Lawrence Sr. and Mary Kate (Smith) N.; m. Joy I. Ingram, Aug. 28, 1946. Grad., Edinburg Jr. Coll., 1942; BBA, U. Tex., 1947. CLU. Active USN, South Pacific, 1942-46; office mgr. John B. Vaught Hardware Co., Austin, 1947-48; acct. Def. Rsch. Lab. U. Tex., Austin, 1948-51; gen. mgr. John B. Vaught Hardware Stores, Austin, 1951-56; agt. Southwestern Life Ins. Co., Austin, 1956-86; independent agt. William L. Nolen Jr. CLU & Assocs., Austin, 1986—; bd. dirs. Southwest AutoChlor Corp., Austin. Chair City of Austin Traffic Safety Commn., 1970-91, mem. Airport Adv. Commn., 1971-82; trustee Counseling and Pastoral Care Ctr., Austin, 1988-92; vestry mem., asst. treas. St. Matthew's Episc. Ch., Austin, 1965-68; bd. dirs. Better Bus. Bur. Austin, 1969-70, chmn., 1970, 71-72; U. Tex. Presidents Assn.; pres. Austin Community Found., 1989-90, treas., 1988-89. Lt. comdr. USNR, 1942-45, PTO. Named Boss of Yr. Am. Bus. Womens Assn., 1970, Assoc. of Yr., 1986. Mem. Nat. Sales Achievement award (charter), Tex. Leaders Round Table (life, Outstanding Achievement award 1969-70), Million Dollar Round Table (life), Tex. Assn. Life Underwriters (legis. v.p. 1963-74), Life Underwriters Polit. Action Com. (grandee), Austin Assn. Life Underwriters (past pres.), Austin Chpt. CLU Soc. (bd. dirs. 1986-88), Austin Steam Train Assn. (bd. dirs.), Advantage Austin, Austin C. of C. (bd. dirs. 1969-70, v.p. 1970), TIP Club, The Hundred Club, Headliners Club, Univ. Club (bd. dirs. 1992-94), Kiwanis (bd. dirs. 1960). Episcopalian. Home: 6405 Mesa Dr Austin TX 78731-2701 Office: William L Nolen CLU & Assoc 1304 San Antonio St Austin TX 78701-1650

NOLLY, ROBERT J., hospital administrator, pharmaceutical science educator; b. Amsterdam, N.Y., Jan. 8, 1947; m. Diera R. Lehtonen, June 21, 1969; children: Shelby Alexandra, Kirby Alycia, Kendall Alexis. BS in Pharmacy with honor, Albany Coll. Pharmacy, 1970; MSc in Hosp. Pharmacy, Ohio State U., 1979. Pharmacy extern Matt Pharmacy, Canajoharie, N.Y., 1967-70; pharmacy intern Park Row Drugs, Canajoharie, 1970-71, asst. mgr., 1971-72; staff pharmacist Mary Imogene Bassett Hosp., Cooperstown, N.Y., 1972-74, 75-77; med. svc. rep. Dista Products Co., Eli Lilly and Co., Indpls., 1974-75; resident hosp. pharmacy Grant Hosp., Columbus, Ohio, 1977-79; asst. dir. pharmacy svcs. City of Memphis Hosp., 1979-81; asst. dir. pharmacy svcs. U. Tenn. Bowld Hosp., Memphis, 1980-82, dir. pharmacy svcs. and materials mgmt., 1982-85, asst. adminstr. pharmacy svcs. and materials mgmt., 1985-91, adminstr., 1991—; asst. prof. dept. pharmacy practice Coll. Pharmacy U. Tenn., Memphis, 1979-83, asst. prof. dept. health sci. adminstrn. dept. pharmaceutics, 1983-92, assoc. prof. dept. clin. pharmacy divsn. pharmacy adminstrn., dept. pharm. scis., 1992—; attended confs., mgmt. tng. programs in field; lectr. Columbus Tech. Inst., 1978-79, City of Memphis Hosp., 1980-81; trustee Diversified Svcs., Inc., Tenn. Hosp. Assn., 1990-96, mem. pharmacy adv. com., 1990; bd. dirs. Ava Marie Nursing Home, chmn. nom. com., 1988, 89, mem. long-range planning com., 1989, 90, mem. constn. and by-laws com., 1990, mem. govtl. rels. com., 1991-93; presenter in field. Editor U. Tenn. Bowld Hosp. Pharmacy Newsletter, 1987-91; mem. editl. bd. Drug and Therapeutics Newsletter, U. Tenn. Coll. Pharmacy, 1989, 90. usher Ch. of Holy Spirit, 1988-96; mem. Am. Cancer Soc. Recipient Order of Sword award Am. Cancer Soc., 1992. Mem. Am. Soc. hosp. Pharmacists, Tenn. Soc. Hosp. Pharmacists (mem. com. 1980, constn. and by-laws com. 1985, 88, 89, 90, chmn. nominating com. 1989, orgn. and goals com. 1991, strategic planning com. 1992), Tenn. Pharmacists Assn. (pharmacy tech. task force 1988, 89, 90, ho. dels. 1988, 89, 90, 91, 92, 94, chmn. tech. curriculum com. 1991, tech. edn. accreditation com. 1991, 92, 94), Memphis Area Soc. Hosp. Pharmacists (pres.-elect 1984, pres. 1985, past pres. 1986, chmn. nominating com. 1991), Tenn. Hosp. Assn. (liaison Tenn. Med. Assn. com. 1991), Mid-South Healthcare Materials Mgmt. Assn. (co-chmn. founding orgnl. com. 1991), Kappa Psi, Rho Chi. Home: 2927 Mikeyair Dr Germantown TN 38138-7148 Office: UT Bowld Hosp 951 Court Ave Memphis TN 38103-2813

NONINI, DONALD MACON, anthropologist, educator; b. San Francisco, May 23, 1946; s. Lewis G. and Rose Carlyle (Miller) N.; m. Sandra Carol Smith, Oct. 16, 1993; 1 child, Roque. BA in Philosophy, Reed Coll., 1968; MA, Calif. State U., San Francisco, 1974; PhD, Stanford U., 1983. Asst. prof. anthropology New Sch. Social Rsch., 1983-87; asst. prof. anthropology U. N.C., Chapel Hill, 1987-94, assoc. prof. anthropology, 1994—; vis. scholar dept. anthropology U. Washington, 1985. Author: British Colonial Rule and the Resistance of the Malay Peasantry, 1900-1957, Yale Southeast Asia Monograph, 1992; editor: Ungrounded Empires: The Cultural Politics of Modern Chinese Transnationalism, 1996; assoc. editor Dialectical Anthropology, 1986-91, acting editor, 1991-92, 93. Doctoral Dissertation grantee NSF, 1978-80, U. Rsch. Coun. Rsch. grantee U. N.C., 1988-89, 89-90, 90-91, Course Devel. grantee Lupton Opportunities Fund, 1989, Luce Found. grantee, 1993, NSF sr. rsch. grantee in anthropology, 1996; Mellon fellow Am. Coun. Learned Socs./Social Sci. Rsch. Coun., 1985, Lurcy Faculty fellow Inst. Arts and Humanities, U. N.C., 1991. Fellow Am. Anthrop. Assn.; mem. Am. Ethnological Soc., Soc. Cultural Anthropology, Assn. Asian Studies, Soc. Econ. Anthropology, Assn. Black Anthropologists. Democratic Socialist. Home: 2030 Englewood Ave Durham NC 27705-4113 Office: U NC Dept Anthropology 301 Alumni Bldg CB # 3115 Chapel Hill NC 27599-3115

NOONAN, WILLIAM THOMAS, county administrator; b. Staten Island, N.Y., June 24, 1940; s. Edward Francis and Mary Elaine (Engleman) N.; m. Sandra Andrews, July 14, 1966; children: William Thomas Jr., James Edward, Mary Elisabeth, Laura Virginia. BA in Edn., Furman U., 1963; MA in Edn. Adminstrn., Appalachian State U., 1970; postgrad., U. S.C. Tchr., coach Greenville (S.C.) County Schs., 1963-65; tchr., coach, adminstr. Sumter (S.C.) Sch. Dist. 17, 1965-75; adminstr. Sumter Sch. Dist. 2, 1975-78; mgr. human resources Campbell Soup Co., Sumter, 1978-90; adminstr. Sumter County, S.C., 1990—. Trustee Sumter City Schs., 1984-90, Sumter County Career Ctr., 1984-90. Mem. Rotary. Home: 2511 Desmond Dr Sumter SC 29154 Office: Sumter County Govt 13 E Canal St Sumter SC 29150

NORAKO, VINCENT WALTER, SR., marketing executive; b. Bklyn., May 2, 1921; s. John and Josephine Madeline (Gregorewska) N.; m. Dorothy Belle Roland, Oct. 6, 1945; 1 child, Vincent W. Jr. BEE, Pratt Inst., 1949; MBA, U. Detroit, 1955. Product planner sales and application engring. to div. mgr. Westinghouse Electric Corp., Pitts. and Detroit, 1949-70; mgr. mktg., v.p. consumer products and internat. mktg. Pyrotronics, Cedar Knolls, N.J., 1970-83; v.p. mktg. Piezo Electric Products, Metuchen, N.J., 1983-85; pres. Internat. Mktg. Mgmt. Cons., Wilmington, N.C., 1986—. Col. USMC, 1942-78, PTO and Korea, World War II. Mem. VFW (comdr. 1968-69), Mil. Orde rof World Wars, Am. Legion, Ret. Officers Assn. (pres. Sencland chpt. 1990, 91), Kiwanis (chmn. coms. Wilmington chpt. 1986—). Republican. Roman Catholic. Office: Internat Mktg Mgmt Cons PO Box 3653 Wilmington NC 28406-0653

NORBY, RICHARD JAMES, plant physiologist; b. Chgo., Oct. 6, 1950; s. William C. and Camilla (Edbrooke) N.; m. Ellen D. Smith, Apr. 25, 1977; 1 child: Karl. BA, Carleton Coll., Northfield, Minn., 1972; PhD, U. Wis., 1981. Rsch. staff Oak Ridge (Tenn.) Nat. Lab., 1981—; adj. prof. U. Tenn., Knoxville, 1988—. Fellow AAAS; mem. Ecol. Soc. Am. Office: Oak Ridge Nat Lab PO Box 2008 Oak Ridge TN 37831-6422

NORDAN, ANTOINETTE SPANOS, curator; b. Birmingham, Ala., June 27, 1953; d. James Michael and Smaragdi (Hagefstration) Spanos. BA, U. Ala., Birmingham, 1975; MA, Vanderbilt U., 1985. Curator slides and photographs U. Ala., Birmingham, 1977-85, curator and administrative dir. Visual Arts Gallery, 1985—; cons. Birmingham Mus. Art, 1981, guest curator, 1986; guest curator Sloss Furnaces Nat. Hist. Landmark, Birmingham, 1988. Author: (exhbn. catalogues) Vision of the West: The Art of Will Crawford, 1986, Birmingham.Hitachi: An Exhibition of Birmingham Artists, 1989, Félix Vallotton: Prints and Preparatory Drawings, 1993, Ferrously Yours: Contemporary Cast Iron Art, 1994. Fellow Vanderbilt U., 1981-82. Office: UAB 900 13th St S Birmingham AL 35294-1260

NORDEN, ERNEST ELWOOD, foreign language educator; b. Chgo., July 11, 1938; s. Ernest and Jeleste Katherine (Diggle) N.; m. Janet Louise Burke, June 22, 1963; children: Brent C., Keith R. BS, Purdue U., 1961; MA, U. Oreg., 1963; PhD, U. Calif., Berkeley, 1974. Asst. prof. U. Colo., Boulder, 1969-71, Northeast La. U., Monroe, 1971-72, 73-75; assoc. prof. Baylor U., Waco, Tex., 1975-85; prof. Baylor U., Waco, 1985—. Contbr. articles to profl. jours. Vol. Dept. Pub. Health, Waco, 1993—. Jr. lectr. Fulbright Commn., 1972-73; fellow NEH, 1975, 87, Woodrow Wilson fellowship, 1961. Mem. Am. Assn. Tchrs. Spanish and Portuguese (v.p. Lone Star chpt. 1978-79, pres. 1979-80), Modern Lang. Assn. Am. (bibliographer Spanish sect. 1981—). Home: 1316 N 43rd St Apt C Waco TX 76710-4909 Office: Baylor Univ PO Box 97393 Waco TX 76798-7393

NORDGREN, RONALD PAUL, engineering educator, researcher; b. Munising, Mich., Apr. 3, 1936; s. Paul A. and Martha M. (Busse) N.; m. Joan E. McAfee, Sept 12, 1959; children: Sonia, Paul. BS in Engring., U. Mich., 1957, MS in Engring., 1958; PhD, U. Calif., Berkeley, 1962. Rsch. asst. U. Calif., Berkeley, 1959-62; mathematician Shell Devel. Co., Houston, 1963-68, staff rsch. engr., 1968-74, sr. staff rsch. engr., 1974-80, rsch. assoc., 1980-90; Brown prof. civil and mech. engring. Rice U., Houston, 1989—; mem. U.S. nat. com. on theoretical and applied mechanics NRC, 1984-86, U.S. nat. com. for rock mechanics, 1991-95. Contbr. tech. papers to profl. jours.; assoc. editor Jour. Applied Mechanics, 1972-76, 81-85; patentee in field. Fellow ASME; mem. NAE, ASCE, Soc. Industrial and Applied Math., Soc. Engring. Sci., Sigma Xi. Office: Rice U 6100 Main St Houston TX 77005-1892

NORDLUND, WILLIAM CHALMERS, lawyer; b. Chgo., Aug. 29, 1954; s. Donald E. and Jane H. (Houston) N.; m. Elizabeth Apell, Oct. 1, 1983; children: William Chalmers Jr., Scott Donald. BA, Vanderbilt U., 1976; JD, Duke U., 1979; MM, Northwestern U., 1990. Bar: Ill. 1979, Md. 1991, Mich. 1992. Assoc. Winston & Strawn, Chgo., 1979-87, ptnr., 1987-90; atty. Constellation Holdings, Inc., 1990-91; v.p., sec., gen. counsel The Oxford Energy Co., Dearborn, Mich., 1991-92, sr. v.p., sec., gen. counsel, 1992-93; gen. counsel Panda Energy Corp., Dallas, 1993-94, v.p. and gen. counsel, 1994-95; v.p., gen. counsel Panda Energy Internat., Inc., Dallas, 1995-96, sr. v.p., gen. counsel, 1996—. Bd. dirs. Orch. of Ill., Chgo., 1983-85; bd. dirs., sec. Literacy Vols. of Am.-Ill., Chgo., 1985-88, treas., 1988-90. Mem. Gleneagles C.C. Office: Panda Energy Internat Inc 4100 Spring Valley Rd Ste 1001 Dallas TX 75244-3646

NORICK, RONALD J., mayor; b. Oklahoma City, Aug. 5, 1941; m. Carolyn Marshall, July 28, 1961; children: Allyson, Lance. BS in Mgmt., Oklahoma City U., 1964, LHD (hon.), 1990. Pres. Norick Bros., Inc., 1981-92; mayor City of Oklahoma City, Oklahoma City, 1987—; gen. ptng. Norick Investment Inc.; former chmn. bd. Norick Software, Inc. Trustee Community Ch. of Redeener; mem. Ctrl. Okla. Transp. and Parking Authority, Oklahoma City Water Utilities Trust, Myriad Gardens Authority; bd. dirs. Okla. State Fair' mem. McGee Creek Authority; bd. dirs. Oklahoma City Philharm.; mem. exec. com. Oklahoma City U., Allied Arts Found. Mem. Nat. League Cities, U.S. Conf. Mayors, Okla. Mcpl. League, Oklahoma City C. of C. (bd. dirs.), South Oklahoma City C. of C. (bd. dirs.). Office: Office of Mayor City Hall 200 N Walker Ave Oklahoma City OK 73102-2247

NORIEGA, LAMAR JERNIGAN, political consultant; b. Jacksonville, Fla., Nov. 11, 1943; d. Joe Kennon and Nell Elizabeth (Tyson) Jernigan; m. William Louis Noriega, June 4, 1966 (div. 1984); children: Megan Tyson, William A., Joanna Kennon (dec). BA, Randolph-Macon Woman's Coll., 1965; MA, U. Miami, Fla., 1971. Investment adviser trainee Chase Manhattan Bank, N.Y.C., 1966; tchr. Dade County Pub. Schs., Miami, 1967-71; instr. math. Miami Dade Community Coll., 1971-73; assoc. producer documentary Miami the Magic City, 1978-80, hist. photograph editor for book, 1980-82; project dir. Gov.'s Challenge Conf., Fla., 1981; cons. Hist. Concepts, Bayside, Miami, 1986-87; adminstrv. coord. Congl. Campaign Com., Miami, 1982-94; treas. Congl. Campaign Com., 1987-94; pub. rels. Sch. Architecture U. Miami, 1995—; cons. Miami Dade C.C., 1984-85, Arva Parks & Co., Miami, 1986-87; lectr. U. Miami, 1994. Adviser, Youth Employment Program Greater Miami, 1981-82, Coral Gables Historic Preservation Bd., 1981-82; coord., Coral Gables Bus. Village Planning Coun., 1987-88. Mem. Vizcaya Guides (bd. dirs. 1980-83), Jr. League Miami (bd. dirs. 1980-83), Hist. Assn. South Fla. (trustee 1985-87), Dade County Cultural Affairs Coun. Home: 1001 Hardee Rd Coral Gables FL 33146-3329

NORIEGA, RUDY JORGE, hospital administrator; b. Havana, Cuba, Apr. 23, 1937; s. Rodolfo and Iris (Santini) N.; came to U.S., 1961; naturalized, 1966; BS, Masonic U., 1960; m. Rosa E. Del Castillo, Jan. 2, 1960; children: Rudy A., George. Acct., Continental Can Co., Havana, 1961, Am. Fgn. Ins. Assn., N.Y.C., 1961-62, North Miami Gen. Hosp., Miami, Fla., 1962-64; asst. controller Jackson Meml. Hosp., Miami, 1964-65; asst. adminstr. Plantation (Fla.) Gen. Hosp., 1965-72, adminstr., trustee, 1972-80; v.p., trustee Internat. Hosp., Miami, 1980-83; exec. v.p., COO Gen. Health L.P., Miami, 1983-93, 94-96; sr. v.p. Ornda So. Fla., 1993—; chmn. Golden Glades Gen. Hosp., 1991-94; mem. sch. bldg. com. U. Miami Law Sch., 1989—; bd. dirs. Kendall Hosp., 1989—; coord. health needs for Pope John Paul II's U.S. Visit, 1987. Mem. jud. nominating commn. 3rd dist. Ct. Appeals, Fla. Supreme Ct., 1992—. Mem. Am. Coll. Hosp. Adminstrs., So. Fla. Hosp. Assn. (pres. 1979-80), Broward County Hosp. Assn. (pres. 1978-79), Fla. League Hosps. (pres. 1974-75), Fedn. Am. Hosps. (dir. 1973-74), Hosp. Fin. Mgmt. Assn. (dir. 1971-72), Plantation C. of C. (pres. 1978-79), Kiwanis (v.p. 1978-79). Office: Gen Health LP 11880 Bend Rd Miami FL 33152

NORK, MARIANA, foundation administrator; b. Wilkes-Barre, Pa., May 7, 1962; d. Edward P. and Frances Anne (Pugliese) N. BA, Conn. Coll., 1984. Devel. asst. Dallas Opera Co., 1984-86; dir. membership and devel. Internat. Sculpture Ctr., Washington, 1986-88; exec. dir. Am. Soc. Landscape Architects Found., Washington, 1988-90; dir. devel. and corp. rels. Nat. Mus. of Women in Arts, Washington, 1990-92; v.p. club found. Club Mgrs. Assn. Am., Washington, 1992—; spkr. Assn. Found. Group, Washington, 1992—. Bd. dirs. Sutton Place Condo Assn., Washington, 1989-92, pres. 1990-92; bd. assocs. Nat. Rehab. Hosp., Washington, 1995—. Mem. Am. Soc. Assn. Execs. (spkr. bur.), Nat. Ctr. Non-Profit Bds., Univ. Club Washington (found. bd., membership com. chair, fitness comm.), Porsche Club Am. Republican. Roman Catholic. Office: The Club Found 1733 King St Alexandria VA 22314

NORMAN, ALBERT GEORGE, JR., lawyer; b. Birmingham, Ala., May 29, 1929; s. Albert G. and Ila Mae (Carroll) N.; m. Catherine Marshall DeShazo, Sept. 3, 1955; children: Catherine Marshall, Albert George III. BA, Auburn U., 1953; LLB, Emory U., 1958; MA, U. N.C., 1960. Bar: Ga. 1957. Assoc. Moise, Post & Gardner, Atlanta, 1958-60, ptnr., 1960-62; ptnr. Hansell & Post, Atlanta, 1962-86, Long, Aldridge & Norman, Atlanta, 1986—; dir. Atlanta Gas Light Co. Served with USAF, 1946-49. Mem. ABA, Ga. Bar Assn., Atlanta Bar Assn., Lawyers Club Atlanta (pres. 1973-74), Am. Law Inst., Am. Judicature Soc. (dir. 1975-78), Old War Horse Lawyers Club, (pres. 1991-92), Cherokee Town and Country Club. Episcopalian.

NORMAN, JAMES WILLIAM, JR., lawyer; b. Gainesville, Fla., Jan. 17, 1921; s. James William and Lucile (Pullen) N.; m. Nancy Rossetter, Mar. 3, 1945; children: Nancy, James III, Lucile, Martin. BA, U. Fla., 1941, JD, 1947; LLM, Harvard U., 1947. Bar: Fla., 1947. Asst. prof. Stetson Coll. of Law, De Land, Fla., 1947-49; mem. faculty Coll. of Law U. Fla., Gainesville, 1948; pvt. practice West Palm Beach, Fla., 1949; ptnr. Buck and Norman, Jacksonville, Fla., 1950; adminstrv. asst. to Charles E. Bennett, mem. U.S. Ho. of Reps., Washington, 1951-60; legis. asst. to U.S. Senator Spessard L. Holland, Washington, 1960-63; staff dir. spl. com. on aging. U.S. Senate, Washington, 1963-67, atty., 1967-69; legis. analyst U.S. Adminstrn. on Aging, Washington, 1969-86; tax law specialist Fla. Dept. Revenue, Tallahassee, 1986—. Lt. (s.g.) USNR, 1943-46. Named one of Five Outstanding Young Men of Fla., Fla. State Jaycees, 1954. Mem. Fla. Bar Assn. Democrat. Baptist. Home: 194 NE Villas Ct Tallahassee FL 32303-4855 Office: Fla Dept Revenue PO Box 7443 Tallahassee FL 32314-7443

NORMAN, LENA (SUTERA), drafting engineer, artist, poet; b. Bklyn., Nov. 27, 1924; d. Leonard and Emma Veronica (Baldassano) Sutera; m. Weston Kent Norman, Sr., Feb. 28, 1948 (div. Oct. 1966); children: Nancy Lynn, W. Kent Jr., Carl Thurman. Student, MIT, 1944-46. Drafting engr., cartographer U.S. Army Corps Engrs., Ft. Worth, Tex., 1948-49; drafting engr. Tex. Instruments, Dallas, 1956-57; drafting aeronautical engr. Volt Tech., Ft. Worth, 1966; drafting assoc. design engr. Gen. Dynamics, Ft. Worth, 1966-70; with Tex. Christian U., Ft. Worth, 1971-72, gallery asst., 1985; drafting engr. Watson Mfg., Ft. Worth, 1972-73; drafting design engr. Pressure Vessels, Inc., Ft. Worth, 1973-75, drafting design and checking engr., 1979-83; drafting cost analysis engr. Tex. Steel, Inc., Ft. Worth, 1975-79, Transit Bus. Co., Ft. Worth, 1984; drafting engr., cartographer Centel, Decatur, Tex., 1985; drafting weight calc. engr. Menasco Aerosys., Euless, Tex., 1985-90, ret., 1990; telephone salesperson Ft. Worth Star Telegram, 1985. Contbr. chpt. to book. Leader, troop cons. Girl Scouts Am., Ft. Worth, 1958-62; active Carter Found., 1996—. Recipient numerous art and literary awards. Mem. Composers, Authors and Artists Am. (corr. sec., art award, literary award), Poets of Tarrant County (tel. chmn.), Poetry Soc. Tex. (poetry award 1993), Habitat for Humanity. Democrat. Roman Catholic. Home: 473 Normandy Ln Saginaw TX 76179

NORMAN, ROSELLA, English language educator; b. Brevard, N.C., Jan. 28, 1943. BS, N.C. A&T State U., 1965; MA, U. D.C., 1990. Owner, mgr. Rose's Collected Poetry Cards, Pisgah Forest, N.C.; parenting instr. Henderson County Schs., Hendersonville, N.C.; adj. asst. prof. reading Blue Ridge C.C., Pisgah Forest; asst. prof. English composition Prince George's C.C., Largo, Md., instr. gen. edn.; English lab. instr. Bowie (Md.) State U.; instr. English D.C. Pub. Schs.; adj. asst. prof. English composition U. D.C.; lectr., writing instr. NCC U., Durham; tchr. English Charles County Schs., LaPlata, Md.; instr. English St. Pauls Coll., Lawrenceville, Va.; instr. English, Westmoreland County Schs., Montross, Va., Rutherford County Schs., Forest City, N.C. Author poetry various pubs.; author/pub. greeting cards. Recipient Golden Poet award World of Poetry, 1991, others. Mem. AAUP. Democrat. baptist.

NORMAN, WYATT THOMAS, III, landman, consultant; b. Austin, Tex., Dec. 30, 1952; s. Wyatt Thomas Jr. and Frances Claire (Bliss) N. BS in Agronomy, Tex. A&M U., 1975. Cert. profl. landman, environ. site assessor. Mgr. farm and ranch Bennett Bros., Inc., Pearsall, Tex., 1975-78; landman Corpus Christi, Tex., 1978—. Mem. Flour Bluff (Tex.) Vol. Fire Dept., 1984-90. Mem. Am. Assn. Profl. Landmen, Corpus Christi Assn. Profl. Landmen, Assn. Former Students, Century Club, Padre Isles Property Owners Assn., Internat. Game Fish Assn., Navy League, Corpus Christi Town Club. Republican. Presbyterian. Home: 15231 Cruiser St Corpus Christi TX 78418-6213 Office: 407 Oil Industries Bldg 723 N Upper Broadway St Corpus Christi TX 78401

NORRID, HENRY GAIL, osteopath, surgeon, researcher; b. Amarillo, Tex., June 4, 1940; s. Henry Horatio and Johnnie Belle (Combs, Cummins) N.; m. Andreia Maybeth Hudson, Jan. 29, 1966 (dec. 1988); children: Joshua Andrew, Noah Adam; m. Cheryll Diane Payne, Mar. 19, 1989; stepchildren: Kim Sheri Payne, Matthew Dominic Payne. AA, Amarillo Coll., 1963; BA, U. Tex., 1966; MS, West Tex. State U., 1967; DO, Kirksville Coll. Osteo. Medicine, 1973. Diplomate Bd. Osteo. Physicians and Surgeons, Nat. Bd. Examiners Osteo. Physicians and Surgeons; cert. basic sci. tchr. Iowa, Tex., Colo. Intern Interboro Gen. Hosp., Bklyn., 1973-74; attending physician dept. gen. practice Osteo. Hosp. and Clinic N.Y., N.Y.C., 1974-77; gen. practice medicine specializing in osteo., Amarillo, Tex., 1978—; emergency care physician Amarillo Emergency Receiving Ctr. Amarillo Hosp. Dist., Tex., 1978-79, Ready Care Emergency Center, Arlington and Bedford, Tex., 1990-92; emergency room physician St. Anthony Hosp., Amarillo, Tex., 1992; emeritus mem. consulting staff physician dept. family practice Northwest Tex. Hosp., Amarillo, 1995; emergency/trauma physician Tex. EM Care, 1995—; mem. mass casualty nat. disaster response team ARC, 1995; contract staff physician Tex. Tech Univ. Sch. Medicine and Health Scis. Ctr., med. dept. and infirmary Tex. Dept. Corrections, Tex. Dept. Criminal Justice; med. cons. rehab. medicine vocat. rehab. divsn Tex. Rehab. Commn., Plano; cattleman, ranch owner, Van Zandt County, Tex.; lectr. osteo. prins. and practice, The Osteo. Hosp. and Clinic N.Y., 1974-77, mem. credentials com., 1975-76; mem. exec. com. Southwest Osteo. Hosp., Amarillo, 1983-84, chief of staff, 1984-85; sec. dept. family practice Northwest Tex. Hosp., Amarillo, 1981-82, mem. credentials com., 1984-85, joint practice com. dept. family practice, 1986-87; mem. orgnl. com. for devel. of dept. osteo. prins. and practices, chmn. N.Y.C. group N.Y. Coll. Osteo. Med., 1977; mem. North Tex. Amputee Support Group, Dallas. Contbr. articles to Tex. Jour. Sci., other publs. Scout physician Llano Estecato council Boy Scouts Am., Texas, 1978-85. Served to E-4 U.S. Army, 1956-63. Recipient William M. Giltner Meml. Fund award 1972, Humanitarian award Am. Cath. Conf., 1979, Century award Boy Scouts Am., 1982; Maxwell D. Warmer Meml. scholar 1973; scholar Kirksville Coll. Osteo. Medicine, 1970, Tex. Legislature, 1969-73, Pfizer, 1973; named to Eminent Soc. Border Legionaires, 11th Armored Cavalry Regiment, Germany, 1958. Mem. Am. Coll. Gen. Practitioners, Tex. Osteo. Med. Assn. (pres. dist. I, mem. ho. of dels. 1981-82, 95), Sons of Am. Revolution, The Sons of Republic of Tex., Am. Congress Rehab. Medicine, Am. Osteo. Assn., World Future Soc. (profl.), Gen. Soc. War of 1812, Tex. & Southwest Cattle Raisers Assn., N.Y. Acad. Scis., Ex-Student's Assn. of The Univ. Tex. (life), 11th Armored Cavalry Regiment Assn., 36th (Tex.) Inf. Divsn. Assn. (life), Baron of the Magna Charta (Sommerset chpt. 1994—), Masons, Am. Legion, Trinity Fellowship, Beta Beta Beta, Sigma Sigma Phi (pres. 1972), Alpha Phi Omega, Psi Sigma Alpha, Theta Psi, Theta Psi Clowns (1969-73). Avocations: astronomy, short wave listening, camping, fishing, anthropology. Office: 1422 S Tyler St Ste 102 Amarillo TX 79101-4238

NORRIS, CYNTHIA JEANETTE, education educator; b. Chattanooga, July 7, 1937; d. David Leigh and Mary Juanita (Morgan) Hudson; m. Joseph Leon Norris, June 2, 1956 (div. Aug. 1984); children—Sherry Lynne Norris Hutsell, Dayna Karen. B.S., Tenn. Wesleyan U., 1967; M.S., U. Tenn., 1975, Ed.D., 1984. Tchr. Chattanooga City Schs., 1969-70; tchr. Athens City Schs.,

Tenn., 1964-74, spl. edn. dir., 1974-84, prin. Westside Sch., Athens, 1984-86; adj. prof. U. Tenn., Chattanooga, 1982-86; asst. prof. U. Houston, 1986-91, assoc. prof., 1992-96; sr. nat. lectr. Nova Southeastern U., 1995—; facilitator Danforth Prin. Preparation Program, 1989-95; exec. dir. Metro Houston Prin. Assessment Ctr (NASSP), 1986-94; cons. Tenn. elem. sch. com. So. Assn. Colls. and Schs., 1983-86; sr. lectr. Nova Southeastern U., Ft. Lauderdale, 1995-96. Mem. ASCD, Tenn. Assn. for Gifted (treas. 1978-80), Nat. Assn. Secondary Sch. Principles, Phi Delta Kappa (Knoxville chpt. outstanding research award 1984), Phi Kappa Phi. Avocations: music, dancing, poetry. Office: Univ Houston Dept Ednl Leadership Houston TX 77004

NORRIS, FRANKLIN GRAY, surgeon; b. Washington, June 30, 1923; s. Franklin Gray and Ellie Narcissus (Story) N.; m. Sara Kathryn Green, Aug. 12, 1945; children: Gloria Norris Sales, F. Gray III. BS, Duke U., 1947; MD, Harvard U., 1951. Resident, Peter Bent Brigham Hosp., Boston, 1951-54, Bowman Gray Sch. Medicine, 1954-57; practice medicine specializing in thoracic and cardiovascular surgery, 1957—; prof. anatomy and physiology, Valencia C.C., Orlando, Fla., 1995—; pres. Norris Assocs., Orlando, 1985—; mem. staff Brevard Meml. Hosp., Melbourne, Fla., Waterman Meml. Hosp., Eustis, Fla., West Orange Meml. Hosp., Winter Garden, Fla., Orlando Regional Med. Ctr., Fla. Hosp., Lucerne Hosp., Arnold Palmer Children Hosp., Princeton, Fla. Hosp. N.E. and South (all Orlando). Bd. dirs. Orange County Cancer Soc., 1958-64, Ctrl. Fla. Respiratory Disease Assn., 1958-65. Served to capt. USAAF, 1943-45. Decorated Air medal with 3 oak leaf clusters. Diplomate Am. Bd. Surgery, Am. Bd. Thoracic and Cardiovasc. Surgery, Am. Bd. Gen. Vascular Surgery. Mem. Fla. Heart Assn. (dir. 1958—), Orange County Med. Soc. (exec. com. 1964-75, pres. 1971-75), Cen. Fla. Hosp. Assn. (bd. dirs., 1980-85), ACS, Soc. Thoracic Surgeons, So. Thoracic Surg. Assn., Am. Coll. Chest Physicians, Fla. Soc. Thoracic Surgeons (pres. 1981-82), Am. Coll. Cardiology, So. Assn. Vascular Surgeons, Fla. Vascular Soc., Phi Kappa Psi. Presbyterian (elder). Clubs: Citrus, Orlando Country. Home: 1801 Bimini Dr Orlando FL 32806-1515 Office: Norris Assocs 1801 Bimini Dr Orlando FL 32806-1515

NORRIS, JOAN CLAFETTE HAGOOD, elementary school educator; b. Pelzer, S.C., June 26, 1951; d. William Emerson and Sarah (Thompson) Hagood; divorced; 1 child, Javiere Sajorah. BA in History and Secondary Edn., Spelman Coll., 1973; MA in Teaching in Edn., Northwestern U., 1974; MA in Adminstrn. and Supervision, Furman U., 1984. Cert. elem. edn. tchr., elem. prin., social studies tchr., elem. supr., S.C.; notary pub., S.C. Clk. typist Fiber Industry, Greenville, S.C., 1970, Spelman Coll. Alumni Office, Atlanta, 1970-73; tchr. Chgo. Bd. Edn., 1973-74, Greenville County Pub. Schs., Greenville, S.C., 1974—; tchr. Hollis Acad., Greenville, S.C., grade level chairperson sci. rep.; chair black history com. Armstrong Elem. Sch., Greenville, 1991, Am. edn. com., 1992; sch. acad. and student affairs com. St. Josephs H.S., 1995; steering com. N.W. area Greenville County Sch. Dist., 1994-95, chair elem. steering com., 1996, participant Curriculum Leadership I, 1996. Contbr. articles to profl. jour. Sec. Webette's Temple # 1312, Greenville, 1985, parliamentarian, 1986; active NAACP, Greenville, 1989-92. Alliance of Quality Edn. grantee, 1989-90; selected to Potential Adminstrs. Acad., Furman U., 1991; named Tchr. of the Yr., Armstrong Elem. Sch., 1981-82, 90-91. Mem. NEA, AAUW (Greenville br. exec. bd. cmty. rep. 1993-94, v.p. programs 1994-96, pres.-elect. 1996-97, nominating com., gift honoree), S.C. Alliance Black Educators, Spelman Alumni Assn., Northwestern Alumni Assn., Phi Kappa Delta (sec. chpt. 1993-94), Phi Delta Kappa (chpt. alt. del. 1992-93, v.p. membership 1996-97). Democrat. Baptist. Home: 219 Barrett Dr Mauldin SC 29662-2030 Office: Hollis Acad 14 Eight St Judson Greenville SC 29611

NORRIS, JOHN C., food products executive. Pres. Turner Foods Corp. Office: Turner Foods Corp 25450 Airport Rd Punta Gorda FL 33950-5746

NORRIS, JOHN MARTIN, theology educator; b. Albuquerque, N.Mex., Apr. 4, 1962; s. Michael Joseph and Catherine Mary (Wachtler) N. BA in Theology valedictorian, U. Dallas, 1984; PhD in Theology, Marquette U., 1990. Instr. Marquette U., Milw., 1990; visiting instr. U. Dallas, Irving, Tex., 1991-93; asst. prof. U. Dallas, 1993—; dir. of Rome Program U. Dallas, Rome, Italy, 1993-95. Mem. Rotaract (treas. 1991-92). Democrat. Catholic. Office: Univ of Dallas 1845 E Northgate Dr Irving TX 75062

NORRIS, KENNETH MICHAEL, lawyer; b. Ludlow, Mass., Jan. 22, 1952; s. Kenneth Richard and Santa (LiAntonio) N. BS in Nuclear Engring., USCG Acad., 1973; MSChemE, Purdue U., 1977; MBA, U. Md., 1979; JD, George Washington U., 1983. Bar: D.C. 1984, Tex. 1988, Calif. 1992; registered profl. engr., Tex. Marine engr. USCG, Seattle, 1973-75; chem. engr. USCG, Washington, 1977-82; del. Internat. Maritime Orgn., London, 1978-82, UN Com. on Trade and Devel., Geneva, 1979-82; resigned USCG, 1984; patent atty. Sandler & Greenblum, P.C., Arlington, Va., 1984-85; sr. cons. Booz, Allen & Hamilton, Inc., Washington, 1985-86; corp. counsel Resource Engring., Inc., Houston, 1986-88; environ. atty. Butler & Binion, Houston, 1988-90; ptnr., dir. environ. law dept. Norton & Blair, Houston, 1990-91; environ. atty. Morgan, Lewis & Bockius, L.A., 1991-93; sr. environ. counsel Chem. Waste Mgmt., Houston, 1993—; rep. Am. Nat. Standards Inst. Com. N-14 and Com. N-522; adj. prof. environ. law U. Houston Law Ctr., 1989—; mil. aide to Pres. Carter, Reagan, 1978-82. Contbr. articles to profl. publs. Treas. Westchester Found., Arlington, 1982-86; atty. Arlington Coun. on Fin., 1984; pres. Wroxton Owners Assn. With USCG, 1969-84, capt. USCGR, 1984—. Mem. ABA, AAAS, D.C. Bar, Tex. Bar, Calif. Bar, Am. Chem. Soc., Am. Nuclear Soc., Am. Soc. Nuclear Engrs., Houston Striker Rugby Club, West Potomac Rugby Club (Washington) (pres.), Masons. Republican. Home: 3627 Walnut Forest Ln Spring TX 77388-4503

NORRIS, MELANIE THOMAS, secndary education educator; b. Bellefonte, Pa., Aug. 3, 1943; d. Robert Kenneth and Ruth Evelyn (Mulbarger) Thomas; m. Charles C. Norris; BS, Lock Haven State U., 1965; M.A., Western Ky. U., 1974. Tchr., Elmira Heights (N.Y.) Sch. Dist., Thomas Edison High Sch., 1965-66, White Pines Sch. Dist., Ely, Nev., 1966-67, Poway (Calif.) Sch. Dist., 1967-69; tchr. English dept. Daviess County Sch. Dist., Owensboro, Ky., 1969-90; chmn. gifted com. Apollo High Sch., Owensboro, Ky., 1972-82; asst. prin. Daviess County H.S., 1990—; mem. steering com. Mid-Am. Conf. on Composition, 1980-85. Mem. Daviess County Republican Exec. Com., 1979-85; chair Daviess County Reps., 1980-83; sponsor Nat. Rep. Congl. Com., 1980—; mem. Ky. Rep. Com., Rep. Presdl. Task Force, Rep. Nat. Com., Am. Legis. Exchange Coun.; bd. dirs. Owensboro Area Spouse Abuse Ctr. Mem. Nat. Council Tchrs. English, AAUW, Nat. Mid. Sch. Assn., Nat. Assn. Secondary Sch. Prins., Assn. Supervision and Curriculum Devel., Ky. Coun. Tchrs. English, Alpha Delta Kappa. Presbyterian. Home: 2707 Hillbrooke Pkwy Owensboro KY 42303 Office: Daviess County H S 4255 New Hartford Rd Owensboro KY 42303-1802

NORRIS, SHERRIE LYNN KINCAID, clinical research and surgical intensive care unit nurse; b. Dallas, Aug. 14, 1959; d. Daryl B. and Betty J. (Mayo) Cordell; m. Walter Eric Norris; 1 child, John Christopher Riley. BS, Tex. Woman's U., 1983, MA, 1990. RN, Tex.; CCRN. Staff nurse Meth. Med. Ctr., Dallas, 1982-86; clinician Home Health Svcs. of Dallas, 1987; regional dir. Redicare Health Svcs. Co., Dallas, 1988; clin. dir. Home Health Svcs. II, Inc., Dallas, 1988-90; staff nurse II St. Paul Med. Ctr., Dallas, 1991-95; sr. rsch. nurse U. Tex. Southwestern Med. Ctr., Dallas, 1993—; ICU staff nurse Zale Lipshy U. Hosp., 1995—. Nurse, ARC. Mem. AACN, Am. Bus. Women's Assn. (past pres.), Tex. Woman's U. Alumnae Assn. Home: 431 Everest Cedar Hill TX 75104

NORRIS, WILLIAM RANDAL, psychologist; b. Lake City, Fla., Feb. 25, 1961; s. William Edgar and Katherine Irene (Brady) N.; m. Susan Ann Walter, Aug. 13, 1989; 1 child, William Christian. AA, Lake City Community Coll., Lake City, Fla., 1980; BS, U. Fla., 1984; MS, U. So. Miss., 1986, PhD, 1989. Lic. psychologist, Tex. Psychologist II Ellisville (Miss.) State Sch., 1988-90; clin. psychologist II Denton (Tex.) State Sch., 1990—, asst. chief psychologist, 1990—; mem. adj. faculty North Ctrl. Tex. Coll. Contbr. articles to profl. jours. Active with Trinity United Meth. Ch., Denton. Recipient U. So. Miss. grad. assistantship, 1986-88. Mem. Tex. Assn. for Behavior Analysis, Assn. for Behavior Analysis Internat., Psi Chi, Phi Theta Kappa. Home: 1908 Georgetown Dr Denton TX 76201-1737 Office: Denton State Sch State School Rd Denton TX 76205

NORRIS-TIRRELL, DOROTHY ANNE, public administration educator; b. Little Rock, Ark., Aug. 28, 1957; d. John Nathan Norris and Janice Reid (Hill) Coleman; m. Charles Gerard Tirrell, Dec. 6, 1980; children: Alexander John Norris Tirrell, Samantha Grace Norris Tirrell. BS in Social Work, Harding U., 1978; MSW, U. Ark., 1980; PhD in Pub. Adminstrn., Fla. Internat. U., 1992. Program dir. Ctrl. Orange County YWCA, Orange, Calif., 1980-82; casework supr. ARC, Tulsa, 1982; cons. Chador Assocs., Tulsa, 1982-85; coord. program promotion WPBT, Miami, 1985-88; rsch. assoc. Fla. Internat. U., Miami, 1988-92, vis. asst. prof., 1993; asst. prof. U. Memphis, 1993—. Author: Immigration and Its Impact on American Cities, 1996. Program svcs. com. Big Bros./Big Sisters, Memphis, 1995—; program com. March of Dimes Birth Defects Found., Memphis, 1994—; bd. dirs. LWV, Memphis, 1995—. Mem. AAUP, AAUW, Polity Studies Orgn., Assn. of Rschr. on Nonprofit Orgns. and Vol. Action, Acad. of Mgmt., Am. Soc. of Pub. Adminstrs. (program com. 1993—, nat. campaign for pub. svcs. 1995—), Ph Alpha Alpha. Home: 1852 Hunters Hill Dr Germantown TN 38138 Office: Univ of Memphis Dept Polit Sci Clement Hall 437 Memphis TN 38152

NORSTROM, CRAIG WILBUR, retired neurological surgeon; b. North Battleford, Can., Nov. 14, 1927; s. John Fredrick and Kathleen (Fitzgerald) N.; m. Jacqueline Darlene Lady, Feb. 22, 1958; children: Sandra, Pamela, Stacy, Jennifer. MS, U. Minn., 1961; MD, U. Alberta, 1955. Diplomate Am. Bd. Neurological Surgery. Clin. asst. prof. neurosurgery U. Tex. Med. Br., Galveston, 1970-95; Chief neurosurgery dept. Spohn Hosp., Corpus Christi, 1961-95. Served in Royal Can. Sea Cadet Corps, 1944-45. Recipient disting. alumni award Augustana U. Coll., 1995. Fellow Am. Coll. Surgeons; mem. AMA, Tex. Med. Assn., Tex. Assn. Neurol. Surgeons, Nueces County Med. Soc., Mayo Alumni Assn., Corpus Christi Country Club. Republican. Methodist. Home: 201 Cape Hatteras Dr Corpus Christi TX 78412

NORTH, ALEXA BRYANS, business educator; b. Dublin, Ga., Sept. 15, 1949; d. William B. and Trabue (Daley) Bryans; m. John Adna North, Jr., Mar. 20, 1976. BS in Edn., U. Ga., 1971, MEd, 1973; PhD, Ga. State U., 1981. Tchr. McDuffie H.S., Anderson, S.C., 1971-72; grad. rsch. asst. U. Ga., Athens, 1972-73; instr. Gordon Jr. Coll., Barnesville, Ga., 1973-76; adj. instr. DeKalb C.C., Ga., 1976-81; grad. tchg. asst. Ga. State U., Atlanta, 1978-81, asst. prof. bus. edn., 1984-94, acting area coord., 1986-87; asst. prof. bus. edn. dept. mgmt. and bus. sys. State U. of West Ga., Carrollton, 1994—; mem. bus. comm. adv. bd. Random House, 1985—. Sec. Ruth Mitchell Dance Adv. Bd., Atlanta, 1979—. Mem. Assn. for Bus. Comm. (mem. membership com.), Office Sys. Rsch. Assn., Am. Vocat. Assn., Nat. Bus. Edn. Assn., So. Bus. Edn. Assn., Ga. Bus. Edn. Assn., Delta Pi Epsilon (pres. 1980-81, faculty advisor 1987—), Phi Chi Theta, Kappa Delta. Anglican. Office: State Univ of West Ga Mgmt and Bus Sys Dept Carrollton GA 30118-3030

NORTH, HENRY, education educator, consultant; b. Houston, Aug. 21, 1949; s. Willie and Precious (Weir) N.; m. Alice N. North, July 1, 1972; children: Henry, Frank, Alise, Anson. BS, Tex. So. U., 1970, MA, 1972; MA, Tex. So. U., 1973; PhD, U. Colo., 1975. Prof. ednl. leadership and counseling Tex. So. U., Houston; tchr. Houston Ind. Sch. Dist.; instr. Houston Community Coll., U. Colo.; cons. to sch. systems and ednl. enterprises. Contbr. articles to profl. jours. Mem. AAUP, Tex. State Tchrs. Assn., Tex. Profs. of Ednl. Adminstrs., Nat. Bd. of Cert. Counselors, Phi Delta Kappa, Omega Psi Phi. Home: 1155 Lehman St Houston TX 77018-1347

NORTH, JOHN ADNA, JR., accountant, real estate appraiser; b. Atlanta, Oct. 20, 1944; s. John Adna and Julia Osborn (Napier) N.; m. Alexa Ruth Bryans, Mar. 20, 1976; 1 child, William Bryans. BA in Econs., U. Ga., 1966; M of Profl. Accountancy, Ga. State U., 1977, M of Taxation, 1980; JD, Woodrow Wilson Coll. Law, Atlanta, 1980. CPA, Ga.; cert. real estate appraiser. Trust adminstr. Trust Co. Bank, Atlanta, 1968-71; fin. produce sales exec. Dean Witter Reynolds Inc., Atlanta, 1971-73; with acctg. firm and in pvt. practice Atlanta, 1973-80; multi-state tax, staff, gen. tax counsel Texaco Inc., White Plains, N.Y., 1980-87; mgr. multi-state tax Price Waterhouse, Atlanta, 1987-88; dir. various corps. MacMillan Bloedel (USA) Inc., Wilmington, Del., 1988-91; pres. Cobb Svc. Assocs. Inc., Marietta, Ga., 1991—; chmn. supervisory com. Texaco Fed. Credit Union, Atlanta, 1980-88; bd. dirs., treas. Atlanta Credit Union League, 1986-87; v.p. The Planning Forum, Atlanta, 1984-85. Alumni trustee The Lovett Sch., Atlanta, 1985-89. Capt. U.S. Army, 1966-68. Mem. Ga. Soc. CPAs, Nat. Soc. Scabbard and Blade, Mil. Order of Stars and Bars, Beta Alpha Psi. Anglican. Home: 3242 Old Mill Trce Marietta GA 30067-5119

NORTH, KENNETH E(ARL), lawyer, educator; b. Chgo., Nov. 18, 1945; s. Earl and Marion (Temple) N.; m. Susan C. Gutzmer, June 6, 1970. AA with high honors, Coll. of DuPage, Glen Ellyn, Ill., 1970; BA with high honors, No. Ill. U., 1971; JD, Duke U., 1974. Bar: Ill. 1974, U.S. Dist. Ct. (no. dist.) Ill. 1974, U.S. Tax Ct., 1975, Guam 1978, U.S. Ct. Appeals (7th cir.), 1978, U.S. Supreme Ct., 1978, U.S. Ct. Internat. Trade 1978, U.S. Ct. Appeals (9th cir.) 1979. Div. chief DuPage County State's Attys. Office, Wheaton, 1976-78; spl. asst. U.S. atty. Terr. of Guam, Agana, 1978-79, atty. gen., 1979-80; prof. sch. law Regent U., Virginia Beach, Va., 1994—, dir. Ctr. for Leadership Studies, 1995—; assoc. counsel Am. Ctr. Law & Justice, 1995—; cons. Internet and Distance Edn., 1995—, Anglican Common Law, 1996—; pres., editor, North Pub. Co., 1986-92; adj. prof. law John Marshall Law Sch., Chgo., 1985-90, Keller Grad. Sch. Mgmt. Northwestern U.; instr. Northwestern U. Traffic Inst., 1985-92, Aurora U., 1989-93; cons. Terr. of Guam, 1980-81; lectr., cons. regarding computer-aided litigation support, 1985—; counsel to various internat. and domestic corps. and ins. carriers. Co-author: Criminal and Civil Tax Fraud, 1986, 2d edit., 1993; bd. editors Attorneys' Computer Report, 1986-92; articles editor The Tax Lawyer, 1990-93; contbr. articles to legal publs. Trustee, mem. adv. bd. Ams. for Effective Law Enforcement, 1986-91; v.p. Glen Ellyn Manor Civic Assn., 1981-84, pres., 1984-88; police commr. Village of Glen Ellyn, 1982-89; bd. dirs. YMCA Northeastern DuPage County, 1991-94, 1st v.p. 1994; mem., vestry St. Mark's Episcopal Ch., Glen Ellyn, Ill. Mem. ABA, Assn. Trial Lawyers Am. (sec. criminal sect. 1986-87, 2d vice chair 1987-88, 1st vice chmn. 1989-90, chmn. 1990-91, pres. adv. com. 1991—), Nat. Assn. Criminal Def. Lawyers (vice-chair white collar crimes com. 1992—), Ill. Bar Assn., Chgo. Duke Bar Assn. (pres. 1986-87), Computer Law Assn., Mensa. Republican. Episcopalian. Pioneer use of computer in ct. Office: Regent U Sch Law 1000 Regent Univ Dr Virginia Beach VA 23464

NORTHART, DEBRA LYNNE, history educator, social activist; b. Sioux City, Iowa, Feb. 26, 1956; d. Gerald Arthur and Gwennith Lynne (Kleinberg) Patterson; m. Mark Evan Northart, Aug. 15, 1974 (div. Nov. 1978); 1 child, Susannah Lynne. BA, U. Calif., Santa Barbara, 1981, MA, 1983; postgrad., U. Miss., University, to 1988. Inst. history U. Miss., University, 1987-91; instr. history and govt. N.W. Miss. C.C., Oxford, 1989—. Mem. NOW (Miss. pres. 1993-94, nat. bd. dirs. 1996—), Orgn. Am. Historians, So. Hist. Assn., Am. Hist. Assn. Democrat. Home: 14 Saint Georges Ln Oxford MS 38655-2836

NORTHCUTT, KATHRYN ANN, elementary school and gifted-talented educator, reading recovery educator; b. Ft. Worth, Nov. 11, 1953; d. Lawrence William and Eva Jo (McCormick) Lloyd; m. Frank E. Northcutt, Aug. 28, 1980; 1 child, Matthew Adam. Student, North Tex. State U., 1972-75; BS in Edn., U. Tex., Tyler, 1980, MEd, 1986. Cert. elem. educator, music educator, supr. K-8; cert. curriculum and instrn. supr. Tchr. grade 1 Longview (Tex.) Ind. Sch. Dist., Longview, 1980-87, tchr. gifted and talented reading, 1990-92, tchr. 3d grade, 1992-93, tchr. 4th grade, 1993-95, reading recovery tchr., 1995—; tchr. 1st grade Pine Tree Ind. Sch. Dist., 1987-90. Mem. Gregg County Hist. Soc., Longview Opera Guild (pres.). Mem. ASCD, Nat. Coun. Tchrs. Math., Assn. Tex. Profl. Educators, Reading Recovery Coun. N.Am., Jr. League of Longview (sustaining), Phi Beta Kappa, Sigma Alpha Iota. Home: 5 Latonia Ct Longview TX 75605-1537 Office: Longview Ind Sch Dist PO Box 3268 Longview TX 75606

NORTHEN, SHEILA STALLINGS, nursing educator, consultant; b. Sanford, N.C., July 7, 1950; d. Leighton Ray and Rebekah June (Patterson) Stallings; m. John Arlington Northen, May 20, 1972; children: Ashley Shannon, Lindsay Kathleen, Hadley Rebekah. BSN, U. N.C., 1972, MSN, 1991. Cert. ob-gyn. nurse practioner, N.C.; RN, N.C. Staff nurse ob-gyn. clinic U. N.C. Hosps., Chapel Hill, 1972-94, family nurse practitioner, ob-gyn nurse practitioner, 1991-95, mem. code team Ambulatory Care Ctr., 1993-94; cons. Dept. Women and Children, Chapel Hill, N.C., 1995—, Cmty. and Med. Health Sch. Nursing, 1995—; clin. asst. prof. UNC, Chapel Hill, 1995—; instr. CPR; presenter numerous workshops and seminars; founder, cons. med.-legal cons. svcs. Mem. ANA, Am. Acad. Nurse Practitioners, Am. Assn. Legal Nurse Cons., Assn. Women's Health, Obstetric and Neonatal Nurses, N.C. Coun. Primary Care Nurse Practitioners, N.C. Nurses Assn. (A Clin. Preceptor of Yr. award cabinet on edn. and resource devel. 1994), Am. Soc. Law, Medicine and Ethics. Democrat. Home: 704 Kensington Dr Chapel Hill NC 27514-6726

NORTHERN, JANE STRAUSS, association executive; b. Big Lake, Tex., Aug. 8, 1950; d. Joseph David and Helen (Schneemann) Strauss; m. John Perry Northern, Oct. 1972 (div. 1979); 1 child, Elizabeth Ann. BA, Tex. Christian U., 1972. Tchr. secondary schs. Ft. Worth Ind. Sch. Dist., 1972-77, 78-79; campaign mgr. Steve Stephens Campaign for State Legislator, San Angelo, Tex., 1984-85; owner, mgr. Jane Northern Ins., San Angelo, 1985-92; dir. membership Coun. for Affordable Health Ins., Alexandria, Va., 1992-95; mgr. registration svcs. Gifts In Kind Internat., Alexandria, 1995-96; ind. cons., 1996—. Bd. dirs., youth chmn. San Angelo Symphony, 1986-91; sec. bd. dirs. West Tex. Lighthouse for Blind, San Angelo, 1986-91; bd. dirs., pres. San Angelo Day Nursery, 1989-91; bd. dirs. San Angelo AIDS Found., 1990-91. Mem. Am. Soc. Assn. Execs., Delta Delta Delta (various offices).

NORTHINGTON, DAVID KNIGHT, III, research center director, botanist, educator. BA in Biology, U. Tex., 1967, PhD in Systematic Botany, 1971. Prof. Texas Tech U., 1971-84; exec. dir. Nat. Wildflower Rsch. Ctr., Austin, Tex., 1984—; vis. assoc. prof. Southwest Tex. State U., 1985—; adj prof. dept. botany U. Tex., 1984—; curator E.L. Reed Herbarium Tex. Tech. U.; dir. Tex. Tech. Ctr., Junction. Co-author 3 sci. books; contbr. numerous articles to profl. jours., mags., newspapers, newsletters. Mem. Am. Assn. Bot. Gardens and Arboreta, Am. Soc. Plant Taxonomists, Nature Conservancy. Office: Nat Wildflower Rsch Ctr 4801 La Crosse Ave Austin TX 78739

NORTHROP, GAYLORD MARVIN, dean, university official; b. Little Rock, Dec. 15, 1928; s. Guy Santee and Gladys Marie (Hilsmeyer) N.; m. Diane Joslyn Lake, Dec. 8, 1956 (div. 1980); children: Melanie Gay, Dana Rogers; m. Marjorie Joan Dyer, Aug. 8, 1981; stepchildren: Elizabeth, Sandra, Jonathan. BSEE, U. Ark., 1952; MA in Engring., Yale U., 1955, DEng, 1961. Rsch. specialist II N.Am. Aviation, Inc., L.A., 1952-53; engr. Sperry Gyroscope Co., Lake Success, N.Y., 1954; dep. dept. head Raytheon Missile System Div., Bedford, Mass., 1956-57; engr. Hughes Aircraft, Inc., Culver City, Calif., 1958, The RAND Corp., Santa Monica, Calif., 1960-67; v.p. Ctr. for Environment & Man, Inc., Hartford, Conn., 1967-82; assoc. prof. U. Bridgeport, Conn., 1982-86; assoc. prof. electronics and instrumentation dept. U. Ark., Little Rock, 1987-94, dir. Grad. Inst. Tech., 1988—, assoc. dean for rsch. Coll. Sci. and Engring. Tech., 1990—; dir. Ark. Space Grant Consortium, Little Rock, 1991—; dir. Ark./STRIVE Program, 1993—; mgr. NASA/EPSCoR Program, 1994—. Sgt. USMC, 1946-48. Mem. AIAA, IEEE, Data Processing Mgmt. Assn., Rotary Internat., Tau Beta Pi, Sigma Xi, Sigma Pi Sigma. Home: 9220 Sylvan Hills Hwy North Little Rock AR 72120-2938 Office: U Ark Grad Inst of Tech 2801 S University Ave Little Rock AR 72204-1000

NORTHROP, MARY RUTH, mental retardation nurse; b. Washington, June 5, 1919; d. William Arthur and Emma Aurelia (Kaech) N. Diploma in nursing, Georgetown U., 1951, BS in Nursing cum laude, 1952; MS, U. Md., 1958; MA in Anthropology, U. Va., 1970. RN, Va. Asst. dir. nursing U. Md. Hosp., Balt., 1958-60; dir. nursing Georgetown U. Hosp., Washington, 1961; nursing rep. ARC, Pa., 1962; regional dir. nursing ARC, New Eng. and N.Y., 1963-68; pediatric nursing cons. Va. Dept. Health, Richmond, 1971-84; clin. nursing specialist Va. Dept. Mental Health and Mental Retardation, Petersburg, Va., 1988—; adj. asst./assoc. prof. U. Md. Sch. Nursing, Balt., 1958-60. Nursing fellow rsch. HEW, Bethesda, U. Md., Bethesda, 1957-68, nursing fellow anthropology U. Va., 1968-70; recipient Recognition Georgetown U. Alumni Assn., Richmond, 1987. Mem. ANA, Va. Nursing Assn., DAR (chpt. regent 1983-86, dist. treas. 1992-95), Mensa, Sigma Theta Tau. Republican. Roman Catholic. Home: 300 W Franklin St # 401E Richmond VA 23220-4904 Office: Southside Va Tng Ctr PO Box 4110 Petersburg VA 23803-0110

NORTHRUP, TIMOTHY A., publisher; b. Parkersburg, W.Va., Jan. 1, 1953; s. Francis O'Donnell and Alice Ellsmore (Vall Spinosa) N.; m. Karen Ann Leitinger, July 23, 1977; children: Daniel Leitinger, Katherine Ellsmore, Frances Spinosa. BS in Econs., U. Pa., 1976. Sales rep. IBM, Fairfield, N.J., 1976-80; sales rep., gen. mgr. Northrup Equipment Co., Parkersburg, W. Va., 1981-88; publisher, owner Lightpoint Publ. Co., Parkersburg, 1989—. Author, editor: The Enthusiast, 1989, W&W Football Digest, 1989-96. Bd. dirs., pres. Boys Club of Parkersburg, 1985-88; bd. trustees, pres. Wood County Pub. Libr., 1986-96. W. Va. State Softball Squash Champion, 1994. Mem. Parkersburg Country Club, 1953. Republican. Home: 510 2d Ave Vienna WV 26105 Office: Lightpoint Publ Co 1600 Seventh St Parkersburg WV 26104

NORTON, CHARNETTE, foodservice management advisory company executive; b. Plattsburg, Mo., Nov. 17, 1941; d. Robert Rea and Helen Louise (Ditmars) N. BS in Food and Nutrition, U. Mo., Columbia, 1963, MS in Food Systems Mgmt., 1976; postgrad., U. Wis., Kenosha, 1975-76, U. Mo., Kansas City, 1978-81. Various food svc. mgmt. positions hospitality and health care orgns.; info. specialist U. Mo. Coll. Home Econs., Columbia; product mgr. Am. Hosp. Supply Corp., McGaw Park, Ill., 1974-76; dir. dietetics Bethany Med. Ctr., 1976-82; dir. food and nutrition svcs. U. Chgo. Med. Ctr., 1982-86; dir. nutrition and foodsvcs. U. Tex. M.D. Anderson Cancer Ctr., Houston, 1986-88; pres. The Norton Group, Missouri City, Tex., 1989—. Contbr. articles and abstracts to profl. jours. Col. USAR. Mem. Am. Dietetic Assn. (continuing edn. com., coun. on practice 1988-89, quality assurance com. 1989-91, chmn. div. mgmt. practice 1989-90, mem. nomination com. mems. with mgmt. responsibilities in health care delivery system 1992-93), Tex. Dietetic Assn., South Dietetic Assn., Am. Hosp. Food Svc. Adminstrs., Soc. for Food Svc. Mgmt., Nat. Assn. Coll. and Univ. Food Svcs., Health Care Foodsvc. Mgmt., Food Svc. Cons. Internat. (profl. designee), Roundtable for Women in Food Svc., Ft. Bend C. of C., Gamma Sigma Delta, Omicron Nu, Phi Epsilon Omicron. Home and Office: 919 Foxborrough Ln Missouri City TX 77489-3249

NORTON, DAVID C., federal judge; b. Washington, July 25, 1946; s. Charles Edward and Louise Helen (Le Feber) N.; m. Dee Holmes, June 16, 1973; children: Phoebe Elizabeth, Christine Baron. BA in History, U. of the South, 1968; JD, U. S.C., 1975. Assoc. Holmes & Thomson, Charleston, S.C., 1975-77, 80-82, ptnr., 1982-90; dep. solicitor 9th Jud. Ct., Charleston, 1977-80; U.S. Dist. judge Charleston, 1990—. With USN, 1969-72. Mem. Fed. Judges Assn., Charleston County Bar Assn. (sec.-treas. 1983-90), S.C. Def. Trial Attys. Assn. (exec. com. 1988-90), S.C. Bar Assn. (Ho. Dels. 1986-90). Episcopalian. Office: Hollings Judicial Ctr PO Box 835 Broad & Meeting Sts 3rd Fl Charleston SC 29402-0835

NORTON, HENRY W., JR., gas industry executive; b. Ardmore, Okla., July 17, 1946; s. Henry W. and Patty V. (Saxon) N.; m. Carol Anne Becker, Oct. 14, 1974; children: Stacey J., Brett A., Lindsey R., Jenna L., Kelsey A. BSME, U. Okla., 1969. Various engring. and mgmt. positions U.S., North Sea, Mid. East, 1969-88; mgr. gas processing Mobil Natural Gas Inc., Houston, 1988-90; projects mgr. P.T. Arun Lng Plant, Sumatra, Indonesia, 1990-92; v.p. transp. and mktg. ops. Mobil Natural Gas, Inc., 1993—. Author: (proceeding) Annual Proceeding of SPE, 1984. Soccer coach Kingwood Soccer Assn., 1989, 90, 92, Cherry Creek Soccer Assn., 1985-88; baseball coach Cherry Creek Baseball Assn., 1985-88. Mem. Nat. Gas Transp. Assn., Am. Mgmt. Assn., Gas. Processor's Assn., Assn. Computing Machinery, Soc. Petroleum Engrs. Office: Mobil Natural Gas Inc 12450 Greenspoint Dr Houston TX 77060-1905

NORTON, LARRY ALLAN, retailer; b. Laredo, Tex., May 19, 1947; s. Sam and Elizabeth Norton; m. Brenda D. Goodman, Sept. 5, 1971; children: Bradley, Mark. BS in Polit. Sci., Tex. A&M U., 1969. Retail mcht. Norton

Stores, Inc., Laredo, 1971—; bd. dirs. Commerce Bank, Laredo. Mem. Laredo Planning and Zoning Commn., 1983-88; bd. dirs. Laredo Devel. Found., 1987, Tex. A&M Hillel Found., 1984—. Capt. U.S. Army, 1970-71. Mem. State Bar Tex. (dist. grievance com. 1994—).

NORTON, PEGGY ANN POOLE, nurse; b. Sanford, N.C., July 1, 1938; d. Robert Bloom and Alma Ann (Luck) Poole; m. Jerry Lee Norton, June 14, 1958 (div. June 1968). Family Nurse Practitioner, Watts Sch. Nursing, 1973. Cert. adult nurse practitioner. Staff nurse Pitt County Meml. Hosp., Greenville, N.C., 1959-61; pediatric office nurse Greenville, 1961-63; staff nurse U. N.C. Infirmary, Chapel Hill, 1963-65; asst. dir. nurses Gravely Sanatorium for Tuberculosis, Chapel Hill, 1965-67; supr. Martha Jefferson Hosp., Charlottesville, Va., 1967-68; surg. office nurse Charlottesville, 1968-69; staff nurse Richmond (Va.) Meml. Hosp., 1969; supr. Cape Fear Valley Hosp., Fayetteville, N.C., 1970-72; staff nurse emerg. room N.C. Meml. Hosp., Chapel Hill, 1972; physician extender U. N.C. Student Health Svc., Chapel Hill, 1973—; mem. various coms. at U. N.C., including rape awareness com. 1986—, rape response plan com. 1990—, mem. task force on dating and relationship violence, 1994; lectr. in field. Contbr. articles to profl. jours. Past mem. South Orange Rescue Squad; bd. dirs. Planned Parenthood of Orange County, 1987-88, med. adv. bd., 1985-88; bd. dirs. Parkwood Homeowners Assn., 1985-86, Rape Crisis Ctr., 1991. Mem. N.C. Nurses Assn. (numerous offices including bd. dirs. 1981-83, dist. bd. dirs. 1978-82, chair commn. on practice 1981-83, chair various coms.), Nurse Practitioners in N.c. (vice chair and chair). Baptist. Home: 1522 Clermont Rd Durham NC 27713-2410 Office: U NC CH Student Health Cb 7470 # 469H Chapel Hill NC 27514

NORTON, RICHARD W., JR., art gallery director. CEO, pres. bd. control R.W. Norton Art Gallery. Office: The R W Norton Art Gallery 4747 Creswell Ave Shreveport LA 71106-1801

NORTON, ROBERT DILLARD, JR., marketing professional; b. Charlotte, N.C., Apr. 19, 1964; s. Robert Dillard and Ann Efird (Mason) N.; m. Penny Gay Beam, June 23, 1987; children: Celia Ann, Mia Chaas. BA, Duke U., 1986; MBA, Tulane U., 1990. Cert. mgmt. acct. Student mgr. Food Svcs. Duke U., Durham, N.C., 1982-86; mgr. trainee Roses Stores, Inc., Forest City, N.C., 1986-87; asst. mgr. Roses Stores, Inc., Blue Ridge, Ga., 1987, Fayetteville, N.C., 1987-88; sr. asst. mgr. Roses Stores, Inc., Wallace, N.C., 1988; machinist asst. Torrington, Inc., Forest City, 1988; rsch. asst. A.B. Freeman Sch. Bus. Tulane U., New Orleans, 1988, fellow, market analyst A.B. Freeman Sch. Bus., 1988-90; controller Escandell Assocs., Inc., Sulphur, La., 1990-91, asst. sec., controller, 1991-92, treas., controller, 1992-93; co-founder, pres. DataLore, Inc., Lake Charles, La., 1992-93; office mgr. Owensby & Kritikos, Inc., 1993; acct. Worknet Five Hundred Corp., Inc., 1993, mktg. dir., 1993—. Cubmaster Boy Scouts Am., Cub Scout Park 83, Sulphur, 1990-91. Recipient O.L. Putnam scholarship Tulane U., 1989-90. Mem. Inst. Mgmt. Accts. (cert. mgmt. acct.), Fin. Mgmt. Assn., Tulane U. Assn. Bus. Alumni (Outstanding Grad. award 1990), Lake Charles C. of C. (sml. bus. 1990-91, edn. com. 1990), Beta Gamma Sigma, Phi Delta Theta (rep. 1983-84). Office: Worknet 671 Whitney Ave # B Gretna LA 70056-2652

NORTON, ROBERT HOWARD, entertainer, musical arranger, author; b. N.Y.C., July 19, 1946; s. Howard R. and Lena (Triano) N.; m. Eileen Williams, Sept. 29, 1966 (div. 1976); children: Brian, Lelania. Student, Broward C.C., Ft. Lauderdale, Fla., 1970-75; community antenna TV engr. cert., Nat. Cable TV Inst., 1976. Rec. session artist Motown and various other recording labels, 1964—; entertainer various concerts, 1964—; systems technician Selkirk Communications, Ft. Lauderdale, Fla., 1979-81; cable TV engr. Gen. Instrument Corp., Hatboro, Pa., 1981-84; entertainer (with Leilani Chandler) The Sophisticats, Ft. Pierce, Fla., 1984—; owner, author, software writer Norton Music, Ft. Pierce, Fla., 1990—. Author: The Artist's and Entertainer's Tax Bible, 1990, Entertainer's Guide to Cruising, 1991—; writer mus. software 145 User Styles, 1991, Band-in-a-Box Supercharger, 1993, 3 Band-in-a-Box Fake Disks, 1994—, 5 Band-in-a-Box User Style Disks, 1993—; writer software 475+ Gen. MIDI Sequences, 1993—; composer numerous songs; arranger of more than 300 songs. Home and Office: Norton Music PO Box 13149 Fort Pierce FL 34979-3149

NORTON, SAUNDRA ELITHE, writer; b. Madison, Wis., July 14, 1967; s; d. Verland Wilson and Donna Elithe (Proue) N. BA, Tex. A&M U., 1990, MA, 1993; postgrad., U. S.C., 1993—. Rsch. asst. Tex. A & M U., Coll. Station, 1986-87, tchg. asst., 1987; classroom asst. Gifted and Talented Inst., Galveston, Tex., 1987, writing instr., 1991; writing instr., composition and rhetoric U. S.C., Columbia, 1993, composition and lit. instr., 1994; author Merrill-Prentice Hall, Columbus, 1995-96; cons. study abroad, Eng., Scotland Conoco-Tex. A & M U., Houston and College Station, 1987. Author: Instructor's Manual for Through the Eyes of a Child: An Introduction to Children's, 1995; co-author: Language Arts Activities for Children, 1993, Through the Eyes of a Child: An Introduction to Children's Literature, 1995; contbr. articles to profl. jours. Mgr. hosts and reception Opera and Performing Arts Soc., College Station, Tex., 1987-89, dir. opers., 1989-90. Recipient Poet of Merit award Internat. Soc. Poets, Libr. Congress, 1995. Mem. MLA, Phi Beta Delta, Phi Kappa Phi. Home: 125 Lee Ave College Station TX 77840

NORWOOD, CHARLES W., JR., congressman; b. Valdosta, Ga., July 27, 1942; m. Gloria Norwood; 2 children. BS, Ga. So. U., 1964; DDS, Georgetown U., 1967. Pvt. practice Augusta, Ga., 1969—; owner Norwood Tree Nursery, 1984—; mem. 104th Congress from 10th Ga. dist., 1995—, 105th Congress from 10th Ga. dist., 1996—. Capt. U.S. Army, 1967-69, Vietnam. Decorated Combat Medic badge, Bronze Star for Meritorious Svc., Bronze Star for Meritorious Achievement. Mem. Ga. Dental Assn. Republican. Methodist. Office: US Ho of Reps 1707 Longworth Washington DC 20515

NORWOOD, STEPHEN HARLAN, history educator; b. Washington, Jan. 20, 1951; s. Bernard and Janet (Lippe) N.; m. Eunice Gay Pollack, June 21, 1975. BA, Tufts U., 1972; MA in History, Columbia U., 1975, MPhil, 1978, PhD in History, 1984. Adj. prof. Manhattan Coll. and Queens Coll., N.Y.C., 1984; instr. Memphis State U., 1984-87; asst. prof. U. Okla., Norman, 1987-91, assoc. prof., 1991—; cons. in field for D.C. Heath and Co. and Houghton Mifflin Co. Author: Labor's Flaming Youth: Telephone Operators and Worker Militancy, 1878-1923, 1990 (Herbert G. Gutman award 1991); contbr. articles and book revs. to Jour. Social History, New Eng. Quar., Labor History, Revs. in Am. History, Jour. of the West, Jour. Women's History, Jour. So. History, others. Recipient Okla. Found. for Humanities award, 1993; Columbia U. Pres.'s fellow, 1976-77; grantee NEH, 1985, U. Okla. Rsch. Coun., 1988, 89, 90, 91, 93, 94; U. Okla. Jr. Faculty Summer Rsch. fellow, 1988, 89, 90. Mem. Am. Hist. Assn., Orgn. Am. Historians. Home: 529 NW 40th St Oklahoma City OK 73118-7041 Office: U Okla Dept of History 455 W Lindsey St Norman OK 73019-0535

NORWOOD, WILLIAM D., JR., English language educator; b. Greenville, Tex., Nov. 19, 1929; s. William D., Sr. and Bonibel (Young) W.; m. Mary Louise Simmons, July 4, 1959 (div. 1975); children: Tamara, John Simmons W.D., III; m. Nancy Frost Fogarty, Nov. 9, 1979. BA, Baylor U., 1950; MA, Lamar U., 1962; PhD, U. Tex., 1965. Instr. to asst. prof. Southwest Tex. State U., San Marcos, 1962-65; assoc. prof. Tex. Tec, Lubbock, 1965-68; prof., chmn. English dept. Angelo State U., San Angelo, Tex., 1968-69, U. So. Miss., Hattiesburg, 1969-72; dean New Coll. of Calif., Sausalito, 1972-74; prof. Tomball (Tex.) Coll., 1991—. Author: (book) The Judoka, 1973, 1974, John W. Thomason, Jr., 1969; contbr. articles to profl. jours., publs. Mem. Southwestern Philos. Soc., Tex. Assn. Depts. of English (pres. 1968-69). Democrat. Episcopalian. Home: 12703 Jones Rd # 604 Houston TX 77070 Office: Tomball Coll 30555 Tomball Pkwy Tomball TX 77375

NOSÉ, YUKIHIKO, surgeon, educator; b. Inamisawa, Hokkaido, Japan, May 7, 1932; came to U.S., 1962; s. Minoru and Haru (Murakami) N.; m. Bonnie Jean MacDonald, Mar. 15, 1965 (div. 1987); children: Kimi Wilhelmina, Ken Willem, Kevin Scott; m. Ako Funakoshi, May 5, 1990. MD, U. Hokkaido, Sapporo, Japan, 1957, PhD, 1962. Surgeon in charge sect. artificial organs U. Hokkaido Sch. Medicine, 1961-62; rsch. assoc. Maimonides Hosp., Bklyn., 1962-64; postgrad. fellow dept. artificial organs Cleve. Clinic Found., 1964-66; mem. staff dept. artificial organs Cleve. Clinic, 1966-67, chmn. dept. artificial organs, 1967-89, chmn. emeritus, 1989-90; prof. surgery Baylor Coll. Medicine, Houston, 1991—; v.p. Internat. Ctr. Artificial Organs and Transplantation, Cleve., 1979—; adj. prof. surgery Tokyo Med. Coll., Tsukuba (Japan) U., Keio (Japan) U.; cons., mem. surgery and bioengring. study sect. NIH, 1981-87; assoc. dean Asian region Internat. Faculty Artificial Organs, 1992—; prof. Bologna (Italy) U. Sch. Medicine, 1992—; congress pres. 1994 Houston Congress of World Apheresis Assn. Author: Manual on Artificial Organs: Volume I-The Artificial Kidney, 1969, Volume II-The Oxygenator, 1973, Cardia Engineering, 1970, Die Kunstliche Niere, 1974, Plasmapheresis, Historical Perspective, Therapeutic Applications and New Frontiers (with Kambic), 1983, Future Perspective for the Development of Artificial Organs (with Kolff), 1988; contbr. to numerous profl. publs. Fellow Am. Inst. Med. and Biol. Engring., N.Y. Acad. Sci.; mem. AMA, AAAS, Internat. Soc. Artificial Organs (trustee, past pres.), Am. Soc. Artificial Internal Organs (past pres., trustee), World Apheresis Assn. (congress pres. 1994), Am. Soc. Testing Materials (chair subcom. on cardiovascular prosthesis in med. and surg. materials and devices, Moses award 1979), Am. Heart Assn., Am. Soc. Apheresis, Am. Soc. Artificial Internal Organs (pres. 1992), Am. Soc. Biomaterials, Assn. Advancement Med. Instrumentation. Home: 1400 Hermann Dr Houston TX 77004-7142 Office: Baylor Coll Medicine Dept Surgery 1 Baylor Plz Houston TX 77030-3411

NOTCH, JAMES STEPHEN, structural engineering executive, consultant; b. Mpls., Aug. 24, 1950; s. Edwin Henry and Mary Adele (Heinz) N.; m. Sandra Jean Johnson, Apr. 28, 1973 (div. 1991); children: Kristin Rachelle, Ryan Christopher, Kelly Marie; m. Kay Ann Portner, May 1, 1992; 1 child, Chad Hix. BSCE summa cum laude with highest honors, Marquette U., 1973; MSCE with honors, Lehigh U., 1974; Murray Buxton diploma, Inst. Structural Engring., London, 1987. Registered profl. engr., Ala., Calif., Ind., Fla., Colo., La., Minn., Miss., Tex., Ky., Wis., N.Y., Ga., Mich., N.C., Okla., Pa., N.J., Ohio, Va., Md., Ariz., Mo., Mass., Conn. Mgr. constrn. project Rauenhorst (Opus) Corp., Mpls., 1970-73; project engr. Ellisor Engrs., Inc., Houston, 1974-76; project mgr. Ellisor & Tanner, Inc., Houston, 1976-81; v.p., dir. Ellisor & Tanner, Inc., Houston and Dallas, 1981-86; pres., mng. ptnr. Datum/Moore Partnership, Irving, Tex. and Washington, 1986-88; pres. Notch + Assocs., Arlington, Tex., 1988—; pres., chief exec. officer JSN Enterprises, Inc., Arlington, 1986—. Prin. works include (structural designs) Four Allen Ctr., Houston, Citicorp Ctr., LL&E Tower, New Orleans, NASA Mission Control Bldg., others; contbr. numerous articles to profl. jours. Chmn. Hurricane Alicia Code Rev. Commn. Constrn. Industry Coun., Houston, 1983; spokesman Sta. KPRC, Sta. KTRK, Houston, 1983; chmn. Dallas Com. on High Rise Bldgs. Lehigh U. research fellow, 1973-74; recipient Grand award Am. Consulting Engrs. Council, 1984; also others. Mem. ASCE (nat. chmn. tall bldgs. com., mem. various coms.), Am. Concrete Inst. (chmn. various coms.), Post-Tensioning Inst., Am. Inst. Steel Constrn., Rsch. Coun. Structural Connections of Engring. Found., Internat. Coun. Tall Bldgs. and Urban Habitat, Internat. Assn. Bridge and Structural Engrs., Structural Engrs. Assn. Tex. (pres.), Profl. Engrs. in Pvt. Practice, NSPE (chmn. edn. com., Houston Young Engr. of Yr. award San Jacinto chpt. 1984), Tex. Soc. Profl. Engrs. (Tex. Young Eng. of Yr. Roman Catholic. Office: 2603 Cypress Hills Ct Ste 200 Arlington TX 76006-4006

NOTHAFT, FRANK EMILE, economist; b. Jersey City, Apr. 10, 1956; s. Frank Emil and Rita Johanna (Laer) N.; m. Lisa Beth Greenfield, June 13, 1981; children: Frank Austin, Daniel Blake, John Paul. BA, N.Y.U., 1976; MA, Columbia U., 1977, MPhil, 1979, PhD, 1986. Economist Bd. Govs. Fed. Reserve System, Washington, 1983-86; sr. economist Freddie Mac, McLean, Va., 1986-88; dep. chief economist Freddie Mac, 1988-90, dir., office of chief economist, 1990—. Contbr. articles to profl. jours. Sec., bd. dirs. Falls Church Housing Corp., Va., 1988-91. Sloan Found. grantee, 1982; Columbia U. fellow, 1976-79; recipient Founders' Day award, N.Y.U., 1976. Mem. Am. Econ. Assn., Am. Real Estate Urban Econs. Assn. (bd. dirs. 1990-92), Fin. Mgmt. Assn. Office: Freddie Mac 8200 Jones Branch Dr Mc Lean VA 22102-3107

NOTHNICK, WARREN BEN, reproductive physiologist; b. Vineland, N.J., Jan. 18, 1965; W. Warren Carrey and Dominica Delores (Lombardi) N.; m. Giulia Anna Bonaminio, Aug. 8, 1992; children: Christopher Warren, Michael Anthony. BS, Ohio State U., 1987, MS, 1989; PhD, U. Ky., 1993. Postdoctoral rschr. Dept. of Ob-Gyn., U. Ky., Lexington, 1993—. Mem. AAAS, AAB, Soc. for the Study of Reproduction, Am. Soc. for Reproductive Medicine, Am. Andrology Soc. Office: Dept Ob-Gyn U Ky 800 Rose St Lexington KY 40536

NOTO, LUCIO R., gas and oil industry executive; b. Apr. 24, 1939. BS in Physics, U. Notre Dame; MBA, Cornell U.; Woodrow Wilson Fell., U. Notre Dame; Bache Fell., Cornell U. With Mobil Corp., 1962—; pres. Mobil Saudi Arabia, 1981-85, chmn., 1985-86; v.p. planning and econs. Mobil Corp./Mobil Oil Corp., 1986-88, CFO, 1989-93, pres., 1993—, chmn. bd., CEO, COO, 1994—. Internat. Business Machines Corp. (dir.), Amer. petroleum Inst. Public Policy Committee, The Business Council, The Council on Foreign Relations & Business Roundtable. Office: Mobil Corp 3225 Gallows Rd Fairfax VA 22037-0001*

NOTTINGHAM, JAMES (LEROY NOTTINGHAM), retired protective services official, professional society administrator; b. Ft. Myers, Fla., Sept. 6, 1937; s. George M. and Josephine E. (Holcomb) N.; m. Bonita Jean Hager, Sept. 2, 1957; children: James Jr., Mark, Dale, Valarie. Student, Fla. State Fire Coll., 1964—, St. Pete Jr. Coll., 1966—. Cert. firefighter, Fla., cert. EMT, cert. real estate agt., ins. salesman, notary; instr., Fla.; security lic.; bus. agt. permit, Fla. Firefighter, engr., capt. Ft. Myers Fire Dept., 1963-94; negotiator Ft. Myers Firefighters L. 1826, 1971—; instr. Fla. Standard Firefighters, Fla. State, 1973—, mem. and chmn., 1981-94; chmn. MDA, 12th Dist. IAFF, N.C., S.C., Ga., Fla., V.I., 1986—. Mem. Civil Svc. Bd. Ft. Myers City, 1968-71; pres. N. Ft. Myers Little League, 1971-76, N. Ft. Myers Pop Warner, 1973, Peace River Conf., 1974; head coach N. Ft. Myers Babe Ruth 16-18, 85-85, state champions, 1978, 81; fire commr. N. Ft. Myers Fire and Rescue, 1993. Named Firefighter of Yr., City of Ft. Myers, 1992, Fla. State Cabinet and Fla. Profl. Firefighters, 1993; recipient Good Neighbor award TV Sta. 20, NBC, Ft. Myers, 1993. Mem. Nat. Fire Protection Assn., Ft. Myers and S.W. Fla. Profl. Firefighters (pres. 1970—), Fla. Profl. Firefighters (lobbyist 1970—, dist. v.p. 1978—), Masons (32 deg.), Shriners. Democrat. Baptist. Home: 53 Victoria Dr Fort Myers FL 33917-4103 Office: SW Fla Profl Firefighters 1601 Lee St Fort Myers FL 33901-2933

NOVAK, ALAN LEE, retired pharmaceutical company executive; b. Chgo., Oct. 25, 1928; s. Samuel Adolph and Tina Lillian (Oris) N.; m. Delores Jane Tonkel, Dec. 17, 1950; children: Shaya Ray, G. Alexander, Cheryl Lynn. BS, Fla. So. Coll., 1951. Cert. purchasing mgr. Police officer Lakeland (Fla.) Police Dept., 1952-53; sales rep. Sinclair Refining Co., Tampa, Fla., 1954-58; prin. Novak's Texaco s/s and Fuel Co., Tampa, 1958-62; sales rep. Burroughs Wellcome Co., Columbus, Ohio, 1962-70; purchasing agt. Burroughs Wellcome Co., Research Triangle Park, N.C., 1970-74, dir. purchasing, 1974-94; bd. dirs. Eastern N.C. Better Bus. Bur., 1989-96. Mem. area contact Am. Israel Polit. Affairs Com., Raleigh, 1984-86; fin. sec. Temple Beth Or, Raleigh, 1975-77, treas., 1996—; mem. N.C. Coun. on the Holocaust, 1996—. With U.S. Army, 1946-47, Japan. Mem. Am. Legion Jewish War Vets. 1st Cav. Divsn. Assn., Drug, Chem., and Allied Trades Assn. (area rep. 1975-78, bd. dirs. 1978-84, treas. 1985, v.p. 1986, pres. 1987-88), Nat. Assn. Purchasing Mgmt., Purchasing Mgmt. Assn. Carolinas-Va., Triangle Purchasing Assn., Raleigh C. of C. Republican. Jewish. Lodge: B'nai B'rith (Double Chai award 1985-87), AMRAN Shrine Temple (charter).

NOVIS, ROBERTO AUGUSTO PASSOS, civil engineer; b. Salvador, Brazil, July 20, 1953; came to U.S., 1991; s. Jorge Augusto and Solange (Passos) N.; m. Maria Constancia Costa, Mar. 17, 1978; children: Maria Paula, Leticia, Roberta. BCE, Federal U. Brazil, Salvador, 1977. Registered profl. engr., Brazil. From trainee to engring. mgr. Construtora Norberto Oderbrecht S.A., Brazil, 1973-85; project engr. Construtora Norberto Oderbrecht S.A., Salvador, Brazil, 1988-91; engring. mgr. Oderbrecht Servicos No Exterior Ltd., Luanda, Malange, Angola, 1985-87; project mgr. Odebrecht Contractors of Fla., Inc., Miami, 1991—. Office: Odebrecht Contractors 201 Alhambra Cir Coral Gables FL 33134-5107

NOWAK, STEPHEN FRANCIS, medical equipment company sales executive; b. Toledo, Sept. 8, 1951; s. Francis Emery and Mildred Nettie (Wangrin) N.; m. Deborah Sue Hudson, Dec. 30, 1972 (div. 1989); children: Diana, Paul; m. Anne Marie Sternad, Oct. 14, 1989 (div. 1993). BBA, U. Toledo, 1980; MBA, U. Akron, 1991. Registered radiologic technologist. Sr. technologist Med. Coll. Ohio, Toledo, 1976-79; chief radiation technologist Mercy Hosp., Toledo, 1979-81; radiology adminstr. Barberton (Ohio) Citizens Hosp., 1981-85, asst. v.p., 1985-86; radiology adminstr. Univ. Hosp. of Cleve., 1986-88; mgr. applications Picker Internat., Inc., Highland Heights, Ohio, 1988-90, mgr. planning and ops., 1990-93, account exec., 1993—; cons. GE Med. Systems, Milw., 1976-82, Squibb Pharms., Stanford, N.J., 1986. Author: Getting the Most from Your Pocket Computer, 1984; editorial adviser, columnist Adminstrv. Radiology, 1982—; contbr. articles to profl. publs. Dir. Radio Amateur Civil Emergency Svcs., Cleve., 1992. Lt. USNR, 1990-91. Mem. Beta Gamma Sigma, Sigma Iota Epsilon.

NOWELL, MEDORA, medical/surgical nurse; b. Groom, Tex., July 14, 1935; d. Beryl Carroll and Edna Earl (Roach) Shaw; m. Calaph Benjiman Nowell, Apr. 21, 1971; children: D'Estaing, Beryl, Dysart and Derek Dobbins. ADN, Seminole (Okla.) Jr. Coll., 1974; BSN, U. Cen. Ark., 1977. Cert. ACLS. Charge nurse Valley View Hosp., Ada, Okla.; charge nurse, night supr. Conway (Ark.) Hosp.; charge nurse Doctors Hosp., Little Rock; evening supr. Meml. Hosp., Dumas, Tex., staff nurse Hospice. Home: 229 Plum Ave Dumas TX 79029-3439

NOWICKI, DENNIS, protective services official. Chief of police Mecklenburg County, Charlotte, N.C. Office: Police Dept 601 E Trade St Charlotte NC 28202

NOWLAND, JAMES FERRELL, lawyer; b. Talladega, Ala., Dec. 7, 1942; s. James Franklin and Wilma Delene (Dean) N.; m. Faye Roberts, Aug. 28, 1964; children: Angela Roschelle, James Ferrell II. BS, Jacksonville (Ala.) State U., 1967; BS in Med. Technology, U. Ark., 1972; grad., U. Ark. Med. Ctr., 1974; JD, Oglethorpe U., 1983. Bar: Ga. 1984, U.S. Dist. Ct. (no. dist.) Ga. 1984, U.S. Ct. Appeals (11th cir.) 1984, U.S. Supreme Ct. 1988. Chemist U.S. Army C.E., Marietta, Ga., 1972—; pvt. practice Cobb County, Ga., 1984—. Capt. USAF, 1967-72. Mem. ABA, Ga. Bar Assn., Cobb County Bar Assn. Home: 50 Mt Calvary Rd Marietta GA 30064-1918 Office: PO Box 1847 Marietta GA 30061-1847

NOWLIN, JAMES ROBERTSON, federal judge; b. San Antonio, Nov. 21, 1937; s. William Forney and Jeannette (Robertson) N. B.A., Trinity U., 1959, M.A., 1962; J.D., U. Tex., Austin, 1963. Bar: Tex. 1963, Colo. 1993, U.S. Dist. Ct. D.C. 1966, U.S. Ct. Claims 1969, U.S. Supreme Ct. 1969, U.S. Dist. Ct. (we. dist.) Tex. 1971. Assoc. Kelso, Locke, & King, San Antonio, 1963-65; assoc. Kelso, Locke & Lepick, San Antonio, 1966-69; legal counsel U.S. Senate, Washington, 1965-66; propr. Law Offices James R. Nowlin, San Antonio, 1969-81; mem. Tex. Ho. of Reps., Austin, 1967-71, 73-81; judge U.S. Dist. Ct. (we. dist.) Tex., Austin, 1981—; instr. Am. govt. and history San Antonio Coll., 1964-65, 71-73. Served to capt. U.S. Army, 1959-60, USAR, 1960-68. Life fellow State Bar Found; mem. ABA, Travis County Bar Assn., San Antonio Bar Assn. Republican. Presbyterian. Office: US Courthouse 200 W 8th St Austin TX 78701-2333

NOYES, RONALD TACIE, agricultural engineering educator; b. Leedey, Okla., Jan. 4, 1937; s. Johnnie Lyle and Anna Madeline (Allen) N.; m. Zona Gail McMillen, Apr. 16, 1960; children: Cynthia Gail, Ronald Scott, David Eric. BS in Agrl. Engring., Okla. State U., 1961, MS in Agrl. Engring., 1964; postgrad., Purdue U., 1966-68, U. Okla., 1988-96. Profl. engr., Ind., Okla. Asst. prof. Purdue U., West Lafayette, Ind., 1964-68; chief engr. Beard Industries, Inc., Frankfort, Ind., 1968-81, v.p. engring., 1981-85; assoc. prof. Okla. State U., Stillwater, 1985-88, prof., 1988—; cons. Ronald T. Noyes, Profl. Agrl. Engr., Stillwater, 1988—. Co-author: Designing Pesticide and Fertilizer Containment Facilities, 1991, revised edit., 1995; contbr. chpts. to books. 1st lt. U.S. Army, 1961-63. Recipient Disting. Svc. award U.S. Dept. Agr., 1992, Outstanding Ext. Faculty award Okla. State U., 1991. Fellow Am. Soc. Agrl. Engrs.; mem. Aircraft Owners & Pilots Assn., Nat. Agrl. Aviation Assn. (assoc.). Home: 1116 Westwood Dr Stillwater OK 74074-1116 Office: Oklahoma St Univ Biosyss & Agrl Engring Dept 224 Ag Hall Stillwater OK 74078-6041

NOZIGLIA, CARLA MILLER, forensic scientist; b. Erie, Pa., Oct. 11, 1941; d. Earnest Carl and Eileen (Murphy) Miller; m. Keith William Noziglia, Nov. 21, 1969; children: Pama Noziglia Cook, Kathryn Noziglia Volpi. BS, Villa Maria Coll., 1963; MS, Lindenwood Coll., 1984. Cert. med. technologist, Am. Soc. Clin. Pathologists. Med. technologist Monmouth (N.J.) Gen. Hosp., 1963-64; spl. chem. med. technologist Hamot Hosp. Med. Ctr., Erie, Pa., 1965-69; pathologist's assoc. Galion (Ohio) Comm. Hosp., 1969-75; dir. crime lab. Mansfield (Ohio) Police Dept., Richland County Crime Lab., 1978-81; crime lab. supr. St. Louis County Police, Clayton, Mo., 1981-84; dir. crime lab. Las Vegas (Nev.) Met. Police, 1984-88, dir. lab. svcs., 1988-93, dir., cons. forensic scis., 1993-95; lab. dir. Tulsa Police Dept., 1995—. Tech. abstracts editor Jour. Police Sci. and Adminstrn., 1983-91; editorial bd. Jour. Forensic Identification, 1988—; contbr. to (book) Journal of Police Science, 1989, Encyclopedia of Police Science, 1989. Mem. Gov.'s Com. on Testing for Intoxication, Las Vegas, 1984-93; mem. adv. bd. Nev. Bd. Pharmacy, 1988-93; recruiter United Blood Svcs., Las Vegas, 1986-93; bd. dirs., pres. Cmty. Action Against Rape, Las Vegas, 1987-94; co-founder So. Nev. Sexual Assault Protocol, 1986. Recipient award Ohio Ho. of Reps., 1981, Alumni of Yr. award Villa Maria Coll., 1981; named Outstanding Cath. Erie Diocese N.W. Pa., 1988, Woman of Achievement Las Vegas C. of C., 1989. Fellow Am. Acad. Forensic Sci. (bd. dirs. 1988-91, sec. Criminalistics sect. 1986, sect. chmn. 1987, Sect. award 1995); mem. Am. Soc. Crime Lab Dirs. (emeritus, bd. dirs. 1980-87, treas. 1981-82, 88-91, pres. 1986-87), Internat. Police Assn., Internat. Assn. for Identification (emeritus), S.W. Assn. Forensic Scientists, Am. Bus. Women's Assn. (Woman of Yr. 1988, one of Nat. Top Bus. Women 1993). Republican. Roman Catholic. Office: Tulsa Police Dept 600 Civic Ctr Tulsa OK 74103

NUCHIA, SAMUEL M., protective services official. Police chief Houston. Office: Police Chief 61 Riesner Houston TX 77002

NUCKOLS, FRANK JOSEPH, psychiatrist; b. Akron, Ohio, Apr. 7, 1926; s. William Alexander Jr. and Jean (Harrison) N.; m. Jane Fleetwood McIntosh, June 16, 1948; children: Claud Alexander, John Andrew. BA, U. Louisville, 1946; MD, U. Ala., 1951. Diplomate Am. Bd. Psychiatry and Neurology. Intern Holy Name Jesus Hosp., Gadsden, Ala., 1951; ward physician Ala. State Hosp., Tuscaloosa, 1951-52; resident U. Louisville, USPHS Hosp., Lexington, Ky., 1953-56; mem. faculty dept. psychiatry U. Ala. Med. Ctr., Birmingham, 1958-68, dir. tng. psychiat. residents, 1964-68, head div. community psychiatry, 1964-68, head continuing psychiat. edn. for physicians, 1964-68; chief psychiat. staff in-patient svc. U. Hosp., Birmingham, 1966-68; dir. tng. Hill Crest Hosp., Birmingham, 1975-79; pvt. practice Birmingham, 1968-93; cons. Ala. Div. Disability Determinations, Birmingham, 1993—; staff Med. Ctr. East Hosp., Birmingham, Bapt. Med. Ctr. Montclair, Birmingham; cons. staff St. Vincent's Hosp., Birmingham, Lloyd Noland Hosp., Birmingham, South Highland Hosp., Birmingham; vis. faculty, mem. interuniv. forum in cmty. psychiatry Harvard U., Boston, 1963-66; vis. faculty Baylor U. Med. Sch., Houston, 1967-71. Ensign USNR, 1941-43; sr. surgeon USPHS, 1956—. Fellow Am. Psychiat. Assn. (life), So. Psychiat. Assn.; mem. Med. Assn. Ala., So. Med. Assn., Jefferson County Mental Health Assn. (v.p. 1960), Jefferson County Med. Soc., Mental Health Assn. State Ala. (chmn. profl. adv. com. 1961), Nat. Assn. Disability Examiners, Phi Beta Pi, Tau Kappa Epsilon. Home and Office: 3741 River Oaks Cir Birmingham AL 35223-2117

NUESSLE, WILLIAM RAYMOND, surgeon; b. Bismarck, N.D., Sept. 17, 1951; s. Robert Frederick and Margaret Elizabeth (Bergeson) N.; m. Anna Maria Marlow, June 26, 1982; children: Aaron, Alexa, Matthew. BS, U. N.D., 1973, BS Medicine, 1975; MD, U. Ala., 1977. Diplomate Am. Bd. Surgery and Colon and Rectal Surgery. Resident gen. surgery Ochsner Found., New Orleans, 1977-1982; resident colon and rectal surgery U. La., Shreveport, 1982-83; colon and rectal surgeon Quain and Ramstat Clinic, Bismarck, N.D., 1983-90, Clinic for Colon & Rectal Surgery, Huntsville, Ala., 1990—, Huntsville (Ala.) Hosp., 1990—, Crestwood Hosp., Huntsville,

1990—. Fellow Am. Coll. Surgeons, Am. Soc. Colon and Rectal Surgeons; mem. SAGES. Office: Clinic for CRS 303 Williams Ave SW Ste 1011 Huntsville AL 35801-6001

NUGENT, GEORGE ROBERT, neurosurgeon; b. Yonkers, N.Y., Feb. 6, 1921; s. George Fitzsimmons and Alberta Belle (Wolven) N.; m. Virginia Ellen Hayes, July 3, 1947; children: Dana A., Robert W., Leslie Ellen, Barnes L., Courtney A. BA, Kenyon Coll., 1950; MD, U. Cinn., 1953. Diplomate Am. Bd. Neurol. Surgery. Resident Duke U. Med. Ctr., Durham, 1958, instr. of neurosurgery, 1957-58; asst. dir. Divsn. Neurosurgery U. Cinn. Coll. Medicine, 1958-61; asst. prof. neurosurgery to prof. neurosurgery W. Va. U. Med. Ctr., Morgantown, 1961—, chmn. dept. neurosurgery, 1970-85, prof. neurosurgery, 1985—; cons. VA Hosp., Clarksburg, W.Va., 1961-93, Pa. Trauma Found., Pittsburgh, 1991-92; participant seminars in field; guest prof. various univs. Exhibitor various sci. exhibits, 1973-79; contbr. articles to profl. jours. and publs. Team physician W. Va. U. Mountaineers, Morgantown, 1966-96. Lt. (j.g.) U.S. Maritime Svc., 1943-40. Fellow Am. Bd. Neurol. Surgery; mem. Am. Assn. Neurol. Surgeons, Congress Neurol. Surgeons, So. Neurosurg. Soc. (v.p. 1970-96), Soc. Neurol. Surgery. Democrat. Office: Robert Byrd Health Scis Ctr Morgantown WV 26506

NUHN, JOHN MARSHALL, editor; b. Bethesda, Md., Dec. 20, 1946; s. John Alfred and Margaret LeGrand (Fox) N.; m. Shirley Ann Namjestnik, Nov. 12, 1972. BA in Journalism, Marquette U., 1969. Asst. editor County Beautiful Corp., Milw., 1971-72, assoc. editor, 1972-74, mng. editor, 1974-79; photo editor Publs. Inc., Milw., 1979-82, Nat. Wildlife Fedn., Vienna, Va., 1982—; spkr., panelist, judge Maine Photography Workshop, Rockport, 1989-92, Roger Tory Peterson Inst., Jamestown, N.Y., 1993, Nature Photography Forum, Ft. Myers, Fla., 1995, San Diego, 1996; cons. and instr. in field. Editor: America's Natural Treasures, 1971, Splendor of the Seasons, 1973, Fires of America, 1973, The Great Lakes, 1974, Great Wilderness Days, 1975, Mountains of North America, 1976, Thoreau's Walden, 1976, Patterns In the Wild, 1992; (mags.) Outdoor World, 1971-74, Nat./Internat. Wildlife, 1979—. Lt. USNR, 1969-70, Vietnam. Recipient Best Use of Photographs in Mag. award U. Mo., 1983, 87, 88, 89, 90, 96, Photo Editing award, 1992. Mem. Am. Soc. Picture Profls. (chpt. v.p. 1984-85, pres. 1986-87, treas. 1988-92), N.Am. Nature Photography Assn. (founder, bd. dirs. 1994—), Nat. Press Photographers Assn., Soc. Profl. Journalists, Outdoor Writers Assn. Roman Catholic. Office: Nat Wildlife Fedn 8925 Leesburg Pike Vienna VA 22184-0001

NULK, RAYMOND HOWARD, army officer; b. San Francisco, Mar. 26, 1960; s. Robert Anthony and Carol Ann (Bocci) N.; m. Margaret Ann Zimmmerman, Feb. 29, 1992. BA in Natural Scis., Johns Hopkins U., 1982; MSBA, Boston U., 1985. Commd. 2d lt. U.S. Army, 1982, advanced through grades to maj., 1994; platoon leader, shop officer, co. comdr. 71st Ordnance Co., Hanau, Germany, 1983-87; project mgr. Rep-Europe MLRS Project, Heidelberg, Germany, 1989-92; dep. product mgr. Multiple Launch Rocket System Project, Redstone Arsenal, Ala., 1992-94; instr. U.S. Army Command and Gen. Staff Coll., Ft. Leavenworth, Kans., 1995—. Mem. Assn. U.S. Army, Ordnance Corps Assn., Johns Hopkins Alumni Assn., KC, Sigma Nu.

NUNES, MORRIS A., lawyer; b. Oceanside, N.Y., Apr. 9, 1949; s. Myron A. and Betty Ann (Ecoff) N.; m. Jane S. Chargar, Aug. 30, 1970; 2 children. BA, BS, U. Pa., 1970; JD, Georgetown U., 1975. Bar: Va. 1975, D.C. 1976. Auditor Arthur Young & Co. CPAs, Boston, 1970; controller Sanitary Group, Inc., West Haven, Conn., 1970-72; securities analyst Donatelli, Rudolph & Schoen, Washington, 1972-74; group controller Potomac Electric Power Co., Washington, 1974-77; sole practice Falls Church, Va., 1977—; bd. dirs. Editorial Experts, Inc., Alexandria, Va.; adj. prof. Cath. U. Law Sch.; arbitrator Am. Arbitration Assn., Washington, 1980—; bus. appraiser, pres. Net Worth, Inc., 1988—; hearing officer Va. Supreme Ct., 1996—. Author: Operational Cash Flow, 1982, Balance Sheet Mgmt., 1987, The Right Price for Your Business, 1988; co-author: Property Logbook, 1985, Basic Legal Forms for Business, 1989; producer, host TV show Gen. Counsel, 1985-87; contbr. articles to profl. jours. Appointed mem. Va. State Bd. Prof. & Occup. Regulation, 1995—; mem. Fairfax County Edn. Adv. Bd., Va., 1983-87; del. Rep. State Conv., 1993, 94. Mem. Va. State Bar Assn., D.C. Bar Assn., Am. Arbitration Assn., Washington Ind. Writers, Am. Soc. Appraisers, Alpha Lit. and Philosophy Soc., Sigma Chi. Republican. Office: 7247 Lee Hwy Falls Church VA 22046-3710

NUNIS, RICHARD A., amusement parks executive; b. Cedartown, Ga., May 30, 1932; s. Doyce Blackman and Winnie E. (Morris) N.; m. Mary Nunis; 1 child from previous marriage, Richard Dean. B.S. in Edn, U. So. Calif., 1954. With The Walt Disney Co., 1955—; dir. ops. Disneyland, Calif., 1961-68; chmn. park ops. com. Disneyland, 1968-74; corp. v.p. Disneyland Ops. (Disneyland, Walt Disney World, Tokyo Disneyland), 1968-91, Walt Disney World, Orlando, Fla., 1971—; exec. v.p., then pres. Walt Disney Attractions and Disneyland Internat., 1972-91; chmn. Walt Disney Attractions, 1991—; mem. Recreation Roundtable; bd. dirs. Suntrust, Orlando, Fla. Exec. adv. bd. dirs. Give the Kids the World; bd. dirs. Fla. Progress Bd., U. Ctrl. Fla. Found., Inc., Fla. Coun. of 100 Bd., United Arts of Ctrl. Fla., Enterprise Fla. Inc.; mem. adv. bd. In Roads/Ctrl. Fla. Inc. Named First Acad. All-Am. U. So. Calif., 1952, Richard L. McLaughlin Fla. Econ. Devel. Vol. of Yr., 1995. Mem. Fla. Isleworth Golf and Country Club. Republican. Office: Walt Disney Attractions Inc PO Box 10000 Lake Buena Vista FL 32830-1000

NUNLEY, MALINDA VAUGHN, retired elementary school educator; d. William D. and Callie (Ross) Vaughn; m. Harry H. Nunley, Dec. 24, 1940 (dec.); chidlren: Jerry Michael, Sally Coleen. BS in Edn., Mid. Tenn. State U., 1961; MEd in Psychology, Middle Tenn. State U., 1972; postgrad., U. Tenn., Chattanooga, 1974-80, Mid. Tenn. State U. Cert. art tchr., spl. edn. tchr., guidance counselor and cons., individual testing and diagnostics in spl. edn. Tenn. Tchr. Panama Canal Co, Balboa, Panama Canal Zone, 1954-56; adult tchr. U.S. Army, Ft. Davis, Panama Canal Zone, 1956-60; elem. tchr. Ancon Elem. Panama Canal Zone Sch., Tenn., 1961-64; tchr. South Pitts. High Sch., 1964-66, Normal Park Elem. Sch., Chattanooga, Tenn., 1966-71; spl. edn. tchr. Griffith Creek Elem. Sch., Tenn., 1971-83; ret. Tenn.; tutor, substitute tchr., speaker to groups, Tenn., 1994—; homebound tchr. for alcohol and drug abuse adolescents, 1989-90; spl. speaker to class groups 4th-7th, 1993-94. Mem. NEA, Tenn. Edn. Assn., Marion County Tchrs. Assn., Tenn. Ret. Tchrs. Assn., Chattanooga Edn. Assn. (past faculty rep.). Home: 6555 Highway 27 Chattanooga TN 37405-7288

NUNN, JENNY WREN, pharmacist; b. Atlanta, May 5, 1944; d. Joshua Hugh and Jenny Wren (Scott) N. Student, Gulf Park Coll.; BS, U. Tenn., 1967; AS, Dyersburg State Community Coll, 1975; BS in Law Enforcement, Samford U., 1980, BS in Pharmacy, 1981. Registered pharmacist, Tenn. Pvt. practice Ripley, Tenn., 1981—; planter, land owner Wren's Flight Plantation, Chestnut Bluff, Tenn., 1980—, Scottlawn Plantation, Ripley, 1980—; owner Whimzies Antiques, Scottlawn West, Ripley, Tenn., Corooda Electric, Memphis. Founder, bd. dirs. Mid South chpt. Greyhound Pets of Am., Memphis, 1985—; pres. Lauderdale County Humane Soc., bd. dirs. 1981—; bd. dirs. Nostalgia U.S.A. Fellow Internat. Inst. History of Pharmacy Assn.; mem. NRA (life), DAR, Am. Soc. Hosp. Pharmacists, Christian Med. Soc., Bus. and Profl. Women's Assn., Dames ofCt. of Honor, Am. Horse Protection Assn. (life), Ducks Unltd., Nat. Wild Turkey Fedn., Zeta Tau Alpha. Methodist. Home and Office: RR 1 Box 1 Scottlawn Plantation Ripley TN 38063-9709

NUNN, SAMUEL (SAM NUNN), senator; b. Perry, Ga., Sept. 8, 1938; s. Samuel Augustus and Elizabeth (Cannon) N.; m. Colleen O'Brien, Sept. 25, 1965; children: Michelle, Brian. Student, Ga. Tech. Coll., 1956-59; A.B., LL.B., Emory U., 1962. Bar: Ga. 1962. Legal counsel armed services com. U.S. Ho. Reps., 1963; mem. firm Nunn, Geiger & Rampey, Perry, Ga., 1964-73; mem. Ga. Ho. Reps., 1968-72; U.S. senator from Ga., 1972—; ranking Dem. mem. Armed Services Com.; mem. Govtl. Affairs Com., Small Bus. Com., Senate Dem. Steering and Coordination Com.; ranking Dem. Permanent Subcom. on Investigations of Govt. Affairs; farmer, Perry, 1964—. Office: US Senate 303 Dirksen Senate Bldg Washington DC 20510

NUNNALLY, DOLORES BURNS, retired physical education educator; b. Strong, Ark., Jan. 2, 1932; d. Marion Saunders Burns and Emma Jo (Burns) Baca; m. Curtis Jerome Nunnally, Apr. 16, 1954; 1 child, Jo Lynn Nunnally Blair. BSE, Ark. State Tchrs. Coll., 1953; MSE, State Coll. Ark., 1964; EdD, U. Sarasota, 1981. Phys. edn. tchr. El Dorado (Ark.) Pub. Schs., 1953-72; real estate salesman Continental Real Estate, Downers Grove, Ill., 1972-74; phys. edn. instr. Triton Coll., River Grove, Ill., 1973-74; substitute tchr. DuPage and Kane County Schs., Ill., 1972-74; phys. edn. tchr. Wheeling (Ill.) Sch. Dist. 21, 1974-91; tennis coach El Dorado Pub. Schs., 1953-73; tennis pro El Dorado Racquet Club, City of El Dorado, summers 1965-72. Contbr. articles to profl. jours. Pres. Ark. Sq. Dance Fedn., Little Rock, 1971-72, Progressive Sunday Sch., El Dorado, 1994—. Recipient All Star Coaches Clinic award Ark. H.S. Coaches Assn., 1971. Mem. NEA, AAHPERD (pres. 1969-70, State Honor award 1972), Ark. Assn. Health, Phys. Edn., Recreation and Dance (life), Ill. Assn. Health, Phys. Edn., Recreation and Dance (Quarter Century award 1981, Svc. award 1991), U.S. Tennis Assn., Order Eastern Star, Delta Phi Kappa. Methodist. Home: PO Box 641 1415 Huttig Hwy Strong AR 71765

NUNNELEE, JOHN ROGER, pharmaceutical marketing professional; b. Cape Girardeau, Mo., Aug. 6, 1938; s. John Fred and Myrtle May (Rogers) N.; m. Sharon Rae Hayward, Feb. 18, 1995; children: Angella Gaye Dylla, Beverly Sue, Lauri Michelle Gallegos. BA, Okla. Bapt. U., 1960; BA in Biology and Chemistry, U. Mo., 1960-61; postgrad., U. Houston, 1986. With Upjohn Co., Kalamazoo, 1966-94, dist. sales mgr., 1977-80, med. scis. liaison, 1980-93; v.p. mktg. Flemming Pharms., Inc., Houston, 1994-95; dist. mgr. MMD, Inc., N.Y.C., 1995—. Mem. St. Luke's United Meth. Ch., Houston, Houston Tidelanders Barbershop Chorus. Comdr. USNR, 1957-80. Mem. Naval Res. Officers Assn., Masons (Master Mason). Republican. Methodist. Home: 5600 Saint Moritz Bellaire TX 77401-2617

NUOTIO-ANTAR, VAPPU SINIKKA, physicist; b. Helsinki, May 17, 1940; came to U.S., 1976, naturalized, 1984; d. Martti Johannes and Aune Aili (Paavola) Nuotio; m. Basil Niman Antar, Dec. 20, 1974; children: Allie, Annie. BS, U. Helsinki, 1965, MS in Theoretical Physics, 1968, MS in Applied Math., 1969, PhD Theoretical Physics, 1970. Rsch. and teaching asst. U. Helsinki and Acad. Finland, 1966-76; asst. prof., physics U. Tenn. Space Inst., Tullahoma, 1976-88; sr. physicist USBI div. United Techs., Huntsville, Ala., 1988-92; Brown found. fellow U. South, Sewanee, Tenn., 1977-78; tchr. math. and French, Moore County High Sch., Lynchburg, Tenn., spring 1980; physicist space scis. lab. NASA Marshall Space Flight Ctr., Huntsville, 1985.; scientist Phys. Rsch., Inc., Huntsville, 1986-87. Co-author: (with Basil N. Antar) Fundamentals of Low Gravity Fluid Dynamics and Heat Transfer, 1993; contbr. articles to sci. jours. Choir soloist Trinity Luth. Ch., Tullahoma, 1976-84, Grace Luth. Ch., Huntsville, 1985—. ASLA-Fulbright fellow, 1970-71, Zonta Amelia Earhart fellow, 1971-72; Govt. of Denmark exchange scholar, 1972-73, Govt. of Fed. Republic Germany postdoctoral scholar, 1973, NATO scholar, 1984. Mem. Internat. Soc. for Optical Engring., Soc. Mfg. Engrs., Machine Vision Assn., AAUW, Sigma Xi. Home: 12021 Comanche Trl SE Huntsville AL 35803-2271

NUSSBAUM, HOWARD JAY, lawyer; b. N.Y.C., Dec. 17, 1951; s. Norman and Ruth (Rand) N.; children: Martin Garrett, Daniel Todd. BA, SUNY, Binghamton, 1972; JD, Boston Coll., 1976. Bar: Fla. 1977, U.S. Dist. Ct. (so. dist. trial and bankruptcy bar) Fla. 1977, U.S. Ct. Appeals (5th and 11th cirs.) 1981. Mng. atty. Legal Aid. Svc., Ft. Lauderdale, Fla., 1976-88; ptnr. Weinstein, Zimmerman & Nussbaum, P.A., Tamarac, Fla., 1988-92; pres. Howard J. Nussbaum, P.A., 1993—; chmn. Legal Aid com. North Broward Bar Assn., Pompano Beach, Fla., 1986-87; cons. Police Acad. of Broward County, Ft. Lauderdale, 1985-87. Author: Florida Landlord/Tenant Law and the Fair Housing Act, 1989. Legis. advisor Fla. Senate Majority Leader Peter Weinstein, Broward County, 1990—; gen. coun. Registered Apt. Mgrs. Assn. South Fla., 1993—, Wynmoor Cmty. Coun., 1993—, Skyline Properties, Inc., Ft. Lauderdale, 1994—, Kertz Security Sys., Inc., Ft. Lauderdale, Fla., 1996—, Accutrack Tracking Sys., Inc., 1996. Regents scholar N.Y. State, 1968-72, Presdl. scholar Boston Coll. Law Sch., 1973-76. Mem. ABA (litigation sect.), ATLA, Acad. Fla. Trial Lawyers, Broward Bar Assn., Justice Lodge J.C.C. Office: Howard J Nussbaum PA Ste 205 2400 E Commercial Blvd Fort Lauderdale FL 33308

NUSSBAUM, V. M., JR., former mayor; b. Ft. Wayne, Ind., June 25, 1919; m. Terry O'Hayer, 1943 (dec.); 9 children. Student, Holy Cross Coll., Univ. Pa., Harvard Univ. City councilman Greensboro, N.C., 1973-81; mayor City of Greensboro, Greensboro, 1987-93; founder, pres. So. Food Svc. Inc., 1954, So. Foods, 1960. Gen. chmn. united fund drive United Way, 1971, pres., 1972; former pres. United Arts Coun., Boy Scouts Am., Gen. Greene Coun. Lt. comdr. USN. Recipient Nat. Greene award Greensboro C. of C., 1983, Citizen of Yr. award, 1993; named N.C. Entrepreneur of Yr., 1995. Home: 9 Saint Augustine Sq Greensboro NC 27408-3834

NUSSBAUMER, MELANY HAMILTON, program director; b. Huntsville, Ala., Aug. 18, 1956; d. Douglas Wayne and Barbara (Reid) Hamilton; m. Bernard Joseph Nussbaumer, Jan. 26, 1980; children: Nicholas Lang, Elizabeth Reid. BS, Presbyn. Coll., Clinton, S.C., 1983; MA, U. S.C., 1989. Tchr. Bell Street Mid. Sch., Clinton, 1983-84, Saluda (S.C.) Elem. Sch., 1984-87, Riverside Mid. Sch., Saluda, 1987-94; dir. Upper Savannah Sci. and Math. Hub Lander U., Greenwood, S.C., 1994-95; curriculum dir., tchr. Salude (S.C.) H.S., 1995—; adj. prof. U. S.C., Columbia, 1990; cons. S.C. Dept. Edn., 1988-90; conf. presenter in field. Author: OceanSCope, 1989. Recipient Outstanding Earth-Sci. Tchr. award Nat. Assn. Geology Tchrs., 1992; grantee S.D. Dept. Edn., 1987-93. Mem. NSTA (Presdl. award for excellence in sci. and math 1991), S.C. Assn. for Children's Sci. (pres.-elect 1990-91), S.C. Sci. Coun., Marine Educators Assn. Roman Catholic. Home: 302 N Jefferson St Saluda SC 29138-1347 Office: Saluda Sch Dist 1 400 W Butler Ave Saluda SC 29138 Office: Saluda HS Saluda SC 29138

NUSYNOWITZ, MARTIN LAWRENCE, nuclear medicine physician; b. N.Y.C., July 21, 1933; s. Morris Nusynowitz and Esther Clara Pober; m. Harriet Rubinstein, Aug. 28, 1955; children: Murray Mark, Russell Neil, Leah Rachel. Student Fordham U. Coll. Pharmacy, 1951-53; BA, NYU, 1954; MD cum laude, SUNY-Syracuse, 1958. Cert. Nat. Bd. Med. Examiners; diplomate Am. Bd. Internal Medicine (Endocrinology and Metabolism), Am. Bd. Internal Medicine, Am. Bd. Nuclear Medicine. Intern Letterman Army Med. Ctr., San Francisco, 1958-59; resident in internal medicine Tripler Army Med. Ctr., Honolulu, 1959-62; commd. 2d lt. U.S. Army, advanced through grades to col., 1977; various med. assignments, 1962-65; chief med. R & D, nuclear medicine, endocrine services William Beaumont Army Med. Ctr., El Paso, Tex., 1965-77; ret., 1977; assoc. clin. prof. radiology George Washington U., Washington, 1974; clin. prof. medicine Tex. Tech U., Lubbock, 1974; chief nuclear medicine Bexar County Hosp., San Antonio, 1977-82; prof., head nuclear medicine U. Tex. Health Sci. Ctr., San Antonio, 1977-82, U. Tex. Med. Br., Galveston, 1982-92; cons. clin. nuclear medicine Surgeon Gen., U.S. Army, Washington, 1972-77, Audie Murphy Meml. VA Hosp., San Antonio, 1977-82; cons. in endocrinology and nuclear medicine Brooke Army Med. Ctr., San Antonio, 1978—. Contbr. articles to profl. jours., chpts. to textbooks. Bd. dirs., pres. El Paso Diabetes Assn., 1970-72; bd. dirs., mem. steering com. Gulf Coast Council on Fgn. Affairs, Galveston, 1982—. Decorated Legion of Merit; recipient Boss of Yr. award Am. Bus. Women's Assn., 1975. Fellow ACP, Am. Coll. Nuclear Physicians (pres.-elect 1996, pres. 1997), Am. Coll. Endocrinology; mem. Soc. Nuclear Medicine (sec.-treas. 1996—), Endocrine Soc., Southwestern Clin. Ligand Assay Soc. (pres. 1984-85, 91-93). Jewish. Avocations: dancing, sailing. Home: 15726 Brook Forest Dr Houston TX 77059-6402 Office: U Tex Med Br Sect Nuclear Medicine Galveston TX 77555-0793

NUTT, CRAIG LAURENCE, sculptor, furniture maker; b. Belmond, Iowa, Apr. 13, 1950; s. Richard Lawrence and Beverly Cora (Madsen) N.; m. Linda Marie Marsden, July 6, 1973. BA, U. Ala., 1972. Juror State of Ill. Craft Fellowship program, 1987, State of Ala. Artists Fellowship program, 1989, 91, State of W.Va. Crafts Fellowship program, 1993, Ctrl. Pa. Festival of Arts, 1988, 94, Am. Craft Enterprises, 1993; conf. coord. Am. Craft Coun. S.E. Region ann. conf., 1988; panelist Visual Arts and Design, Regional Designation Program, Atlanta Com. for Olympic Games Cultural Olympiad and So. Arts Fedn., 1993; lectr. in field. One-man shows include Great Am. Gallery, Atlanta, 1988, Huntsville (Ala.) Mus. Art, 1989, Maralyn Wilson Gallery, Birmingham, Ala., 1990, Meredith Gallery, Balt., 1993, The Art of the Toy, Scottsdale, Ariz., 1994, S.E. La. U., Hammond, 1994; exhibited in group shows at Sarratt Gallery, Vanderbilt U., Nashville, 1986, Huntsville Mus. Art, 1988, 90, The Dairy Barn, Athens, Ohio, 1989, Ark. Arts Ctr., Little Rock, 1989, John Michael Kohler Arts Ctr., Sheboygan, Wis., 1990, Port of History Mus., Phila., 1991, James A. Mitchener Mus., Doylestown, Pa., 1992, Smithsonian Inst., 1992, High Mus. Art Ga., 1992, U. Hawaii, 1982, 91, 94, Columbia (S.C.) Mus. Art, 1994, SECCA, Winston-Salem, N.C., 1995, Flagler Mus., Palm Beach, Fla., 1995, Huntsville (Ala.) Mus. Art, 1995, Mobile (Ala.) Mus. Art, 1995; represented in permanent collections including Birmingham Internat. Airport, Schering-Plough, Kenilworth, N.J., Huntsville Mus. Art, Mobile Mus. Art, Birmingham Mus. Art, High Mus. Art, Atlanta, Hartsfield Altanta Internat. Airport. Recipient Gov.'s Arts award, 1985, Harriet Murray award Birmingham Mus. Art, Druid Arts award Ala. Arts Coun., 1990; artists fellow Ala. State Coun. on Arts, 1988, 95, Nat. Endowment Arts - So. Arts Fedn., 1989. Mem. Am. Craft Coun. (S.E. regional assembly 1982-89, alternate 1989—), Kentuck Assn. Northport (bd. dirs. 1985-88), Magic City Art Connection (bd. dirs. 1985-89). Office: Craig Nutt Fine Wood Works 2014 5th St Northport AL 35476-5042

NUTTER, CAROL ANGELL, academic librarian; b. Hinton, W.Va., Aug. 13, 1948; d. Woodrow Wilson and Sadie Eileen (Yancey) Angell; m. David Henan Nutter, May 31, 1969; children: Jon David, Matthew Jay. MS in Libr. Sci., Univ. Ky., 1978; MA, Morehead State Univ., 1984. Interlibr. loan librarian Camden-Carroll Libr. Morehead State Univ., Morehead, Ky., 1976-78, coord. reg. libr. svcs., 1978-86, reference librarian, 1986-89, head, reference dept., 1989—. Mem. Am. Libr. Assn., Ky. Libr. Assn., Ky. Libr. Assn. Acad. Libr. Sect. (sec. 1994-95), Ky. Libr. Assn. Libr. Instruction Roundtable (chair 1991-92), Cen. Eastern Ky. Online Users Group, Am. Assn. Univ. Profs. Office: Camden Carroll Libr Morehead State Univ Morehead KY 40351

NUTTER, DANIEL LYON, librarian; b. Alcester, S.D., Jan. 16, 1932; s. Fayette Alonzo and Enolia (Lyon) N.; m. Elizabeth Jane Mohnkern, Dec. 21, 1964; children: Margaret Enolia, Charles Arthur. BA, Southeastern Okla. State U., 1956; MLS, U. North Tex., 1966. Libr. Buna (Tex.) Ind. Sch. Dist., 1956-61; dir. libr. Clarendon (Tex.) Coll., 1961-66; libr. Hamshire (Tex.)-Fannett Ind. Sch. Dist., 1966-67; dir. libr. East Tex. Bapt. Coll., Marshall, 1967-68, Southwestern Coll., Winfield, Kans., 1968-86; aquisitions libr. Southwestern Okla. State U., Weatherford, 1987-89; dir. libr. U. Tex., Brownsville, 1989-92; libr. III U. Tex. Brownsville/Tex. Southmost Coll., 1992—; mem. faculty senate U. Tex., Brownsville, 1995—. Editor (newsletter) EX LIBRIS, 1989-92; book reviewer Books of the Southwest, 1990—. Active Lions Internat., Buna, Tex. and Winfield, Kans., 1957-61, 72-82, Jaycees, Clarendon, Tex., 1961-66. Mem. Kans. Libr. Assn. (coun. mem., chmn. trustee sect., sec.-treas. coll. and univ. sect.), Pvt. Acad. Librs. (pres.). Democrat. Methodist. Home: 51 McFadden Hut Brownsville TX 78520 Office: Univ Tex Brownsville/Tex Southmost Coll 80 Fort Brown Brownsville TX 78520

NUTTING, PAUL JOHN, city official; b. Oswego, N.Y., July 6, 1952; s. Robert Truman and Joan Violet (Joyce) N. BA, SUNY, Oswego, 1974; MPA, SUNY, Albany, 1977. Adminstrv. asst. City of League City, Tex., 1978-79, acting city adminstr., 1979-80, 81, asst. city adminstr., 1980-81, exec. asst. to mayor, 1981-82, city adminstr., 1982-95; city mgr. City of Springfield, Tenn., 1995—; bd. dirs. Tenn. Natural Gas Acquisition Corp. Bd. dirs. League City Family Welfare Coun., 1978-89, United Way, Robertson County; mem. exec. bd. Mainland Communities United Way, Texas City, Tex., 1991-94; adv. dir. League City Mchts. and Bus. Assn., 1989-95, North Galveston County C. of C., Dickinson, Tex., 1989-95. Mem. Internat. City/County Mgmt. Assn., Tenn. City Mgmt. Assn., Texas City Mgmt. Assn., Am. Soc. for Pub. Adminstrn. (pres. Houston area chpt. 1991-93, dir. 1990-91, 93-95), Springfield-Robertson County C. of C., League City Rotary Club (pres. 1985-86, 93-94), Rotary Club of Springfield. Home: 130 Pepper Grove Cove Springfield TN 37172 Office: City of Springfield 405 N Main St Springfield TN 37172-2408

NUWER, HENRY JOSEPH (HANK NUWER), journalist, educator; b. Buffalo, N.Y., Aug. 19, 1946; s. Henry Robert and Teresa (Lysiak) N.; m. Alice May Cerniglia, Dec. 28, 1968 (div. Mar. 1980); 1 child, Henry Christian; m. Jenine Howard, Apr. 9, 1982; 1 child, Adam. BS in English, State Univ. Coll. N.Y., Buffalo, 1968; MA in English, N.Mex. Highlands U., 1971; Doctoral Equivalency, Ball State U., 1987. Freelance author, journalist, 1969—; asst. prof. Clemson (S.C.) U., 1982-83; assoc. prof. Ball State U., Muncie, Ind., 1985-89; sr. editor Rodale Press, Emmaus, Pa., 1990-91; editor in chief Arts Ind. Mag., Indpls., 1993-95; assoc. prof. journalism U. Richmond, Va., 1995—; pvt. practice Hazing expert-lectr., Richmond, 1990—; Hazing cons. NBC Movie-of-the-Week "Moment of Truth: Broken Pledges", Indpls., 1994. Author: Steroids, 1990, Broken Pledges: The Deadly Rite of Hazing, 1990, How to Write Like an Expert, 1995; contbr. articles to profl. publs. Grantee Nat. Endowment for the Arts, 1976, Idaho Humanities Coun., 1985, Gannett Found., 1988; named Mag. Adviser of Yr., Coll. Media Advisers, 1988. Mem. Soc. Profl. Journalists, Investigative Reporters and Editors. Democrat. Roman Catholic. Office: Univ Richmond Journalism Program Ryland Hall Richmond VA 23173

NWACHIE, JUDY FLAKES, government educator, consultant; b. New Ulm, Tex., Nov. 27, 1946; d. Roy M. Jones and Viola Flakes (Jones) Howard; m. Emeka Emmanuel Nwachie, Feb. 15, 1988. AA, Austin (Tex.) C.C., 1977; BA with high honors, U. Tex., 1979, MA, 1980, PhD, 1993. Mem. staff State Senator Chet Brooks Tex. Senate, Austin, 1973-77; mem. staff State Rep. Ron Wilson Tex. Ho. of Reps., Austin, 1977-84; prof. Austin C.C., 1982—; employment discrimination investigator Tex. Commn. on Human Rights, Austin, 1984-86; adj. prof. St. Edward's U., Austin, 1982—; ednl. cons., scorere Nat. Evaluation Systems, Inc., Austin, 1994—; textbook reviewer Houghton Mifflin Pub. Co., Boston, 1996—. Conf. moderator Cameroon Students Assn., Houston, 1996; vol. voter registrar Travis County Clk., Austin, 1995; cmty. vol. Am. Heart Assn., Austin, 1994. Fellow W.K. Kellogg Found., Washington, 1991; nominee Outstanding Tchr. award Phi Theta Kappa Student Honor Soc., Austin, 1990. Mem. AAUW (nat. com. 1994—), Tex. C.C. Women Educators Assn. (v.p. profl. devel. 1993-95), Tex. Jr. Coll. Tchrs. Assn., South African Assn. for R & D in Higher Edn. Home: 9804 Meadowheath Austin TX 78729

NYBERG, DONALD ARVID, oil company executive; b. Ridgewood, N.J., Aug. 23, 1951; s. Arvid H. and Rita T. (Tenwick) N.; m. Susan Radis, Feb. 16, 1985; children: Matthew D., Ryan T. BA, St. Lawrence U., 1973; MBA, Harvard U., 1975. Mgr. marine ops. Standard Oil, L.A., 1982-83; mgr. ops. planning Standard Oil, Cleve., 1984-85, dir. strategic studies, 1986; divsn. mgr. Brit. Petroleum, Ltd., London, 1987-88; v.p., gen. mgr. U.S. gas bus. BP Exploration, Houston, 1989, v.p., gen. mgr. tech., 1990; v.p. BP Exploration, Anchorage, 1991-94; pres., CEO BP Pipelines, Anchorage, 1991-94; pres. Marya Resources, 1994—; v.p. MAPCO, 1996—. Mem. adv. bd. Providence Hosp. Anchorage. Office: 5719 E 106th St Tulsa OK 74137

NYE, ERLE ALLEN, utilities executive, lawyer; b. Ft. Worth, June 23, 1937; s. Ira Benjamen N.; m. Alice Ann Grove, June 5, 1959; children: Elizabeth Nye Janzen, Pamela Nye Schneider, Erle Allen Jr., Edward Kyle, Johnson Scott. BEE, Tex. A&M U., 1959; JD, So. Meth. U., 1965. With Dallas Power & Light Co., 1960-75, v.p., 1975-80; exec. v.p. Tex. Utilities Co., Dallas, 1980-87, pres., 1987—, CEO, 1995—; pres. Chaco Energy Co., Dallas, 1994-96, CEO, 1996—; pres. Tex. Utilities Mining Co., Dallas, 1982-96, CEO, 1996—; CEO Tex. Utilities Svcs., Inc., Dallas, 1982—; chmn. bd., CEO Tex. Utilities Electric Co., Dallas, 1987—; CEO Basic Resources Inc., Dallas, 1994—, Chaco Energy Co., Dallas, 1994—, TU Svcs., 1982—, Tex. Utilities Commn., Dallas, 1995—; pres. Tex. Utilities Fuel Co., 1982—; chmn. Tex. Utilities Australia Pty., Ltd., 1996—. Bd. dirs. Dallas Bar Found., 1980-83, Dallas Cen. Bus. Plan Com., 1980-83, Inroads/Dallas-Ft. Worth Inc., 1984-88, trustee Baylor Dental Coll., Dallas, 1985-94; mem. Dallas Together Forum, 1989—, Dallas Com. Fgn. Rels., 1991—, Bd. of Boys & Girls Clubs of Am., 1991—; The Dallas Found., 1994—; The Science Pl., Dallas, 1995—; The Salvation Army's Dallas County Adv. Bd., 1995—. Mem. ABA, Dallas Bar Assn., Tex. State Bar Assn., Dallas C. of C. (bd. dirs. 1991-95, vice chmn. 1992-95). Methodist. Clubs: Engineers (pres. 1982-83), Northwood (Dallas). Home: 6924 Desco Dallas TX 75225-1716 Office: Texas Utilities Company 41st Floor 1601 Bryan Street Dallas TX 75201-3411

OAKES, HELEN MILLER, language educator; b. Teague, Tex., June 17, 1932; d. James Lawson and Ruby (Agnes) Miller; m. Kenneth Wayland Oakes, Aug. 18, 1961; children: Pamela Oakes Hancock, Deborah Oakes Evans, Michele Oakes Gonzales, Melinda Oakes Black. AS, McLennan Community Coll., Waco, Tex., 1983; BA, Baylor U., 1960. Cert. secondary and elem. ESL tchr., Tex. Tchr. 1st grade Spring Branch Ind. Sch. Dist., Houston, 1960-61; tchr. English and social studies Groesbeck Ind. (Tex.) Sch. Dist., 1964-66; tchr. remedial reading Groesbeck (Tex.) Ind. Sch. Dist., 1966-74; tchr. social studies and Spanish Teague Ind. Sch. Dist., 1974-76; tchr. bus. Leon Ind. Sch. Dist., Jewett, Tex., 1977-78; postmaster U.S. Postal Svc., Buffalo, Tex., 1980-95; tchr. Corsicana (Tex.) H.S., 1995-96; tchr. Spanish, English, ESL Star (Tex.), 1996—; postmaster trainer, 2d class newspaper auditor Postal Rev. Bd. Sec. Groesbeck Sch. PTA, 1969-70; active Operation Headstart. Mem. Nat. Assn. U.S. Postmasters, League of Postmasters, Order of Eastern Star, Groesbeck Study Club. Baptist. Home: RR 1 Box 61 Buffalo TX 75831-9708 Office: US Postal Svc Main & Center Buffalo TX 75831-9998

OAKES, MELVIN ERVIN LOUIS, physics educator; b. Vicksburg, Miss., May 11, 1936; married, 1963; three children. Student, Fla. State U., 1958-64, PhD in Plasma Physics, 1964. Physicist USAR Guided Missile Agy., Redstone Arsenal, 1960; asst. in physics Fla. State U., Tallahassee, 1958-60, 60-64; asst. prof. physics U. Ga., Athens, 1964, rsch. assoc., 1964-65, from asst. prof. to assoc. prof., 1965-70; prof. of physics U. Tex., Austin, 1975—. Mem. Am. Phys. Soc., Am. Assn. Physics Tchrs. Office: U Tex Dept Physics Austin TX 78712-1081

OAKES, THOMAS WYATT, environmental engineer; b. Danville, Va., June 14, 1950; s. Wyatt Johnson and Relia (Sceacre) O.; m. Terry Lynn Jenkins, June 15, 1974; 1 child, Travis Wyatt. BS in Nuclear Engring., Va. Polytechnic U., 1973, MS in Nuclear Engring., 1975; MS in Environ. Engring., U. Tenn., 1981. Ordained deacon Bapt. Ch., 1989. Health physics asst. Va. Polytechnic U., Blacksburg, 1972-74; radiation engr. Babcock and Wilcox Co., Lynchburg, Va., 1974-75; dept. mgr. Oak Ridge (Tenn.) Nat. Lab., 1975-78, environ. mgr., 1978-85; corp. environ. coord. Martin Marietta, Oak Ridge, 1985-87; asst. v.p. Sci. Applications Internat. Corp., Oak Ridge, 1987-90; environ. mmgr. Westinghouse Environ. and Geotech. Svcs., Knoxville, Tenn., 1990-91; mgr. S.E. region environ. svcs. ATEC & Assocs., Inc., Marietta, Ga., 1991-93; asst. v.p. environ. svcs. Scitek, Ft. Campbell, Ky., 1993—. Contbr. over 107 articles to scholarly and profl. jours. Recipient Spl. Recognition award Union Carbide Corp., 1980, Best Paper award Nat. Safety Coun., 1982, Tech. Publs. award Soc. Tech. Communications, 1987. Mem. AAAS, Am. Indsl. Hygiene Assn., N.Y. Acad. Scis., Health Physics Soc. (sec.-treas. environ. sect. 1984-85), Am. Naval Soc., Am. Soc. for Quality Control. Office: Scitek PO Box 527 Fort Campbell KY 42223

OAKLEY, CAROLYN COBB, library director, academic administrator; b. Wilson, N.C., Nov. 5, 1946; d. Raymond Earl and Edna Gay (Hardison) Cobb; m. Robert Carroll Oakley, Nov. 25, 1971 (div. Oct. 1988); 1 child, Robert Carroll Oakley, Jr. BS, E. Carolina U., 1969, MEd, 1970; postgrad., U. N.C., 1976-77, N.C. State U., 1986—. Cataloger N.C. Dept. C.C., Raleigh, 1969-70; libr. Vance-Granville C.C., Henderson, N.C., 1970-76, coord. library svcs., 1976-87; dir. Learning Resources Ctr., 1987-88; dept. chair for learning resources Wilson (N.C.) Tech. C.C., 1989-96; dir. Learning Resources Ctr. Cape Fear C.C., Wilmington, N.C., 1996—; cons. Rose's Stores, Henderson, 1986-87, Ark. Dept. of Higher Edn., Little Rock, Ark., 1994. Author: Index to Doctoral Theses, 1967-85 (N.C. State U.), 1987. Mem. ALA, N.C. Libr. Assn., Am. Assn. Women in Community Colls., SE Libr. Assn., N.C. Learning Resources Assn. Soc. Democrat. Baptist. Home: 1221 Buckingham Ave Wilmington NC 28401 Office: Cape Fear CC 411 N Front St Wilmington NC 28401

OAKLEY, RONALD E., business executive; b. 1945. Degree in acctg., Carson-Newman Coll. Exec. v.p., sec.-treas. Oakley Groves, Inc., Lake Wales, Fla., 1966—. Office: Oakley Groves Inc 101 Abc Rd Lake Wales FL 33853-6844

OAKLEY, THOMAS E., company executive; b. 1942. Student, U. South Fla. With Oakley Groves Inc., 1961—, pres.; with Oakley Bros. Inc., Lake Wales, Fla., 1973-90, Oakley Bros. Inc. merger Oakley Groves Inc., 1990—. Office: Oakley Groves Inc 101 Abc Rd Lake Wales FL 33853-6844

OAKLEY, WANDA FAYE, management consultant, educator; b. Durham, N.C., June 27, 1950; d. Joseph Napolian and Doris Gray (Thomas) O. BSBA, U. N.C., 1971, postgrad., 1972-73. CPA, N.C. Acct. Oakley Motors, Durham, 1965-73; controller Airheart Ins. Agy., Inc., Durham, 1973-75; controller, owner Quality Car Wash, Durham, 1974-83; acct. computer svcs. dept. William H. Mitchell, P.A. and CPAs, Durham, 1983-84; mgr. John Anderson & Assocs., Inc., Durham, 1984-85; v.p. CMS Svcs., Inc., York, S.C., 1985-86; adminstr. N.C. State U., Raleigh, 1986-89; pvt. practice bus. cons. Raleigh, 1989—; instr. Wake Tech. Community Coll., Raleigh, 1985—, Small Bus. Ctr., Johnston Community Coll, Smithfield, N.C., 1990—; proctor N.C. State Bd. CPA Examiners, Raleigh, 1986—; bus. cons. in field. Fellow N.C. Assn. CPAs, AICPA, ASWA; mem. NAFE, Exersafety Internat. (master's cert. 1984), U. N.C. Alumni Assn. (life). Home: PO Box 3257 Durham NC 27715-3257 Office: 453 Westcliffe Ct Raleigh NC 27606-2227

OATES, SHERRY CHARLENE, portraitist; b. Houston, Sept. 11, 1946; d. Charles Emil and Berniece Faye (Lohse) O. Student, North Tex. State U., 1965-66; student under Martin Kellogg; BA in English, Health and Phys. Edn., Houston Bapt. U., 1968. Cert. art tchr., Tex. Tchr. Jackson Jr. High Sch., Houston, 1968-69, Percy Priest Sch., Nashville, 1969-70, Franklin (Tenn.) High Sch., 1970-84; freelance illustrator Bapt. Sunday Sch. Bd., Nashville, 1978-85, United Meth. Pub. House, Nashville, 1980-85; portraitist in oils, owner Portraits, Ltd., Nashville, 1984—. Portraits include corp. leaders, educators, politicians, hist. and equestrian subjects, society figures and children; participated in various exhbns. at Bapt. Sunday Sch. Bd. and All State and Ctr. South Exhibits at the Parthenon. Recipient 3d place in graphics Ctrl. South Exhbn. at The Parthenon-Tenn. Art League, 1986. Mem. Tenn. Art League. Republican. Baptist. Studio: 816 Kirkwood Ave Nashville TN 37204-2602

O'BANNION, MINDY MARTHA MARTIN, nurse; b. Cushing, Okla., Aug. 19, 1953; d. John William and Martha Florence (Vineyard) Martin; student Okla. State U., 1971-73, Oscar Rose Jr. Coll., 1973; grad. St. Anthony Sch. Nursing, 1975; RN, Tex.; m. William Neal O'Bannion, Oct. 9, 1976; children: Mindi Martha Mae, William Neale Aaron. Med. clk. Martin Clinic, Cushing, Okla., 1968-72; nursing asst. Cushing Mcpl. Hosp., 1973-75, head nurse surg. fl., 1975-76, charge nurse med. unit, 1978-79, 82-83; staff nurse Met. Hosp., Dallas, 1985; staff nurse med. unit Mesquite (Tex.) Community Hosp., 1985-87; nurse post partum unit and discharge edn. post partum unit Trinity Med. Ctr., Carrollton, Tex., 1987—. ind. beauty cons. Mary Kay Cosmetics, Dallas, Tex., 1993—. Mem. social com. Royal Haven Bapt. Ch. Women's Missionary Union, Dallas, 1977-78; mem. extension dept. nursery First Bapt. Ch., Cushing, 1979-82, extension dept. presch., 1982-84; mem. extension dept presch. Royal Haven Bapt. Ch., Dallas, 1986-87; mem. Montgomery Elem. Sch. PTA, Farmers Branch, Tex., 1986-94, Vivian Field Jr. H.S. PTA, Farmers Branch, 1993—, R.L. Turner High Sch. PTA, Farmers Branch/Carrollton, 1995—; treas., mem. nominating com. Joyce Harms group Women's Missionary Union; clk., charter mem. Brookhaven Bapt. Ch., Farmers Br., 1989-92; mem. Valwood Park Baptist Ch., Farmers Br., 1994—. Mem. Am., Tex., Okla. State Nurses Assns., St. Anthony Hosp. Sch. Nursing Alumnae, Bluebonnet Shelties (founder), Tau Beta Sigma, Alpha Xi Delta (corr. sec. 1973). Baptist. Home: 13505 Onyx Ln Dallas TX 75234-4912

O'BANNON, DON TELLA, JR., lawyer; b. Ft. Eustous, Va., Feb. 16, 1957; s. Don T. and Doris (Salone) O'B.; children: Danielle, Dionne. BA, Dartmouth Coll., 1979; JD, U. Va., 1982. Bar: Tex. 1982, U.S. Dist. Ct. (so. dist.) 1984, (no. dist.) 1987, (we. dist.) 1989, (ea. dist.) 1992, U.S. Ct. Appeals (5th cir.) 1989. Law clk. to hon. Gabrielle K. McDonald, judge U.S. Dist. Ct. (so. dist.) Tex., Houston, 1982-84; assoc. Fulbright & Jaworski, Houston, 1984-87; sr. assoc. Bickel & Brewer, Dallas, 1987-88; ptnr. Arter & Hadden, Dallas, 1988-94; of counsel Robinson & West, Dallas, 1994—. Contbr. articles to profl. jours. Treas. Judge Victoria Welcome Re-election campaign, Dallas, 1989-90; bd. dirs. Dallas Park & Recreation, 1992-93; mem. Coun. on Child Abuse and Neglect Prevention, Austin, 1989-93; chmn. Moorland YMCA, 1990-94, Dallas Black Dance Theater, 1990—. Named Vol. of Yr. Moorland YMCA, 1989. Mem. Dallas Bar Assn., State Bar of Tex. Office: Robinson & West 400 S Zane Blve Ste 600 Dallas TX 75208

O'BANNON, JACQUELINE MICHELE, geriatrics and mental health nurse; b. Southampton, N.Y., Feb. 13, 1947; d. John Andrew Koval and Genevieve Cecelia Ryder; children: Christopher, Timothy. AAS in Nursing, SUNY, Farmingdale, 1967; student, Suffolk Community Coll., Brentwood, N.Y., 1990—, Stony Brook (N.Y.) U., 1990, St. Joseph's Sch., Patchogue, N.Y., 1991—. Cert. gerontol. nurse. Pvt. duty nurse Brightman Agy., East Islip, N.Y.; charge nurse Kings Park (N.Y.) Psychiat. Ctr.; admission acut unit Charter Hosp., Jackson, Miss.; mem. AIDS curriculum com., sexual abuse prevention com., 1987-91; mem. policy bd. Brentwood Tchr. Ctr., 1987-91; mem. evaluation and accountability com. Brentwood Dist., 1990. Mem. Madison chpt. Am. Cancer Soc., Madison County Ednl. Found. for Excellence. Mem. Nat. Sch. Bd. Assn., N.Y. Sch. Bd. Assn., Kings Park Nurses Assn., Suffolk County Orgn. Promotion Edn. Office: Charter Hosp of Jackson Acute Unit East Lakeland Dr Jackson MS 39216

O'BARR, BOBBY GENE, SR., lawyer; b. Houston, May 5, 1932; s. Walter Morris and Maggie (Whitt) O'B.; children: Morris Clayton, William Clinton, Candace Jean, Bobby G.; m. Jennifer Ryals, Dec. 5, 1984; 1 child, Richard. B.A., U. Miss., 1959, J.D., 1958. Bar: Miss. 1958, U.S. Dist. Ct. (no. dist.) Miss. 1958, U.S. Dist. Ct. (so. dist.) Miss. 1966, U.S. Ct. Apls. (5th cir.) 1970, U.S. Sup. Ct. 1971. Pvt. practice law, Houston, 1958-59; assoc. W.M. O'Barr, Jr., Okolona, Miss., 1959-60; adminstrv. judge Miss. Workmen's Compensation Commn., 1960-65; assoc. Cumbest, Cumbest, O'Barr and Shaddock, Pascagoula, Miss., 1965-68; assoc. Hurlbert & O'Barr, O'Barr, Hurlbert and O'Barr, O'Barr and Hurlbert, Biloxi, Miss., 1968-80; pvt. practice law, owner Bobby G. O'Barr, P.A., Biloxi, 1980—. Mem., pres. Biloxi Port Commn., 1975-90; mem. mgmt. coun. Gulf Mex. Fishery, 1979-82. With USAF, 1951-54. Mem. State Bar Found., Am. Judicuris Soc., Southeastern Admiralty Law Inst., Internat. Soc. Barristers, Miss. Trial Lawyers Assn., Am. Trial Lawyers Assn., VFW, Am. Legion. Masons, Shriners. Office: PO Box 541 185 Reynoir St Biloxi MS 39530

O'BARR, JEAN FOX, political science and women's studies educator; b. Chgo., Nov. 6, 1942. Student, Edinburgh (Scotland) U., 1962; BA in Polit. Sci. with honors, Ind. U., 1964; MA in Polit. Sci., Northwestern U., 1965, PhD in Polit. Sci., 1970. Lectr. Purdue U., 1964; rsch. asst., field researcher U. Dar es Salaam, Tanzania, 1967-68, 72, 81; vis. asst. prof. dept. polit. sci. U. N.C., Chapel Hill, 1970-72; lectr. in polit. sci. Duke U., Durham, N.C., 1969, 72, 78, adj. assoc. prof. dept. polit. sci., 1978-91, prof. practice of women's studies, adj. prof. polit. sci., 1991—, dir. continuing edn., 1971-83, dir. women's studies, 1983—; mem. teaching faculty Rockefeller Summer Inst. on Women's Studies, N.C. Coll. Tchrs., 1984, 85, Ford Curriculum Project, 1988; researcher, Kenya, 1982, 83. Author: Feminism in Action: Building Feminist Institutions and Community Through Women Studies, 1994; co-author: Shindano: Swahili Essays and Other Stories, 1971; editor: Perspectives on Power: Women in Africa, Asia and Latin America, 1982, Women and a New Academy: Gender and Cultural Contexts, 1989; co-editor: Language and Politics, 1976, Passbook Number # F 47927: Women and the Mau Mau in Kenya, 1985, Sex and Scientific Inquiry, 1987, Restructuring the Academy: Women's Education and Women's Studies, 1988, Feminist Theory in Practice and Process, 1989, Sisters and Workers in the Middle Ages, 1989, Black Women in America: Social Science Perspectives, 1990, Ties that Bind: Essays on Mothering and Patriarchy, 1990, Engaging Feminism, 1991, Talking Gender, 1996; editor: SIGNS: Jour. of Women in Culture and Soc., 1985-90; contbr. chpts. to books; contbr. articles, revs. to profl. jours. Chair adv. bd. Displaced Homers, 1979-81; program chair Gov.'s Conf. on Leadership Devel., 1979-80; mem. exec. com. Carolina Scientists and Engrs. Project, 1978-83; bd. dris. Carolina Friends Sch. Bd. Dirs., 1984-93, chair long range planning com., 1989-91, sec., 1991-93; mem. N.C. Humanities Com., 1978-82, exec. com., 81-82, vice chair, 1982-84; mem. exec. com. N.C. Adult Edn. Assn., 1979-80. Woodrow Wilson fellow, 1964, Univ. fellow Northwestern U., 1965; grantee Northwestern U., 1967, Wenner-Gren Found., 1970, Duke U., 1973, Carnegie Found., 1973, Mark Duke Biddle Found., 1975, 77, N.C. Humanities Com., 1976, 77, 82, Edna McConnell Clark Found., 1977, N.D. Bd. Sci. and Tech., 1979, U.S. Dept. Labor, 1980, D.H. Lawrence Conf., 1980, Ford Found., 1983, Ford Motor Co., 1988, 90, others. Mem. African Studies Assn., Am. Polit. Sci. Assn., Am. Assn. Higher Edn., Nat. Women's Studies Assn., Am. Coun. on Edn. (commn. on women 1977-79, chair 1979). Home: 713 Anderson St Durham NC 27706-2513 Office: Duke U Dept Women's Studies Durham NC 27708

OBEAR, FREDERICK WOODS, academic administrator; b. Malden, Mass., June 9, 1935; s. William Fred and Dorothea Louise (Woods) O.; m. Patricia A. Draper, Aug. 30, 1959 (dec. Dec. 1993); children: Jeffrey Allan, Deborah Anne, James Frederick. BS with high honors, U. Mass., Lowell, 1956, LHD, 1985; PhD, U. N.H., 1961. Mem. faculty dept. chemistry Oakland U., Rochester, Mich., 1960-81, prof., 1979-81, v.p. for acad. affairs, provost, 1970-81; chancellor U. Tenn., Chattanooga, 1981—; mem. nat. addv. panel Nat. Commn. on Higher Edn. Issues, 1981; mem. pres. commn. NCAA, 1991-94. Trustee Marygrove Coll., 1973-79. Am. Council Edn. fellow, 1967-68. Mem. AAAS, Am. Assn. State Colls. and Univs. (bd. dirs. 1992—, chair 1995), Am. Chem. Soc., Am. Assn. Higher Edn., Sigma Xi. Roman Catholic. Office: U Tenn Office of Chancellor 615 Mccallie Ave Chattanooga TN 37403-2504

OBERDIER, RONALD RAY, lawyer; b. Norwood, Mo., Nov. 11, 1945; s. Albert Jr. and Edith Louise (Vaughn) O.; children: James Myron, Steven Michael. Student, Ohio State U., 1963-64; A.A., SUNY-Albany, 1975; B.A., Mary Hardin-Baylor U., 1978; J.D., U. Tex., 1980. Bar: Fla. 1981, U.S. Dist. Ct. (no., so. and mid. dists.) Fla. 1981, U.S. Ct. Appeals (5th and 11th cir.) 1981. Enlisted U.S. Army, 1965, served as electronic intelligence specialist, 1965-77; assoc. Mahoney, Hadlow, Jacksonville, Fla., 1981-82, Coker, Myers & Schickel, Jacksonville, 1982-85; pvt. practice, Jacksonville, 1985-86; ptnr. Humphries & Oberdier, Jacksonville, 1987—. Mem. Fed. Bar Assn., Jacksonville Claims Assn., Jacksonville Bar Assn., Jacksonville Assn. Def. Counsel (pres. 1993), Am. Trial Lawyers Assn. (assoc.), Nat. Assn. R.R. Trial Lawyers, Fla. Def. Lawyers Assn. Club: Tex.-Exes (Austin). Office: 9550 Regency Square Blvd Jacksonville FL 32225-8170

OBERHAUSEN, JOYCE ANN WYNN, aircraft company executive, artist; b. Plain Dealing, La., Nov. 12, 1941; d. George Dewey and Jettie Cleo (Farrington) Wynn; m. James J. Oberhausen, Oct. 15, 1966; children: Georgann, Darla Renee Estein Oberhausen Christopher, Dale Henry Estein Oberhausen. Student Ayers Bus. Sch., Shreveport, 1962-63, U. Ala., 1964-65. Stenographer, sec. Lincoln Nat. Life Co., Shreveport, 1965-66; sec. Baifield Industries, Shreveport, 1975-86; internat. art tchr., Huntsville, Ala., 1974—; co-owner Precision Splty. Co., Huntsville, 1966—, Mil. Aircraft, Huntsville, 1979—; pres., owner Wynnson Enterprises, Huntsville, 1983—; owner, artist, designer Wynnson Galleries Pvt. Collections, Florist, Meridianville, 1987; owner North Ala. Wholesale Flowers, 1988—, Wynnson Enterprises Mil. Packaging Co., 1988—. Co-founder Nat. Mus. Women in Arts; active Nat. Mus. Women in Arts. Mem. NAFE, Internat. Porcelain Guild, People to People, Porcelain Portrait Soc., United Artists Assn., Am. Soc. of Profl. and Executive Women Hist. Soc., Nat. Trust Hist. Preservation, Internat. Platform Assn., Met. Mus. Art, Smithsonian Assn., Assn. Community Artists, Rep. Senatorial Inner Circle, Ala. Sheriffs Assn., C. of C., Better Bus. Bur., Huntsville Art League and Mus. Assocs., Avocations: oil painting, antiques, handcrafts, gourmet cooking, horseback riding. Home: 156 Spencer Dr Meridianville AL 35759-2023 Office: Wynnson Enterprises Inc 12043 Highway 231 431 N Meridianville AL 35759-1201

OBERMAN, STEVEN, lawyer; b. St. Louis, Sept. 21, 1955; s. Albert and Marian (Kleg) O.; m. Evelyn Ann Simpson, Aug. 27, 1977; children: Rachael Diane, Benjamin Scott. BA in Psychology, Auburn U., 1977; JD, U. Tenn., 1980. Bar: Tenn. 1980, Tenn. Supreme Ct. 1980, Tenn. Criminal Ct. Appeals 1980, U.S. Dist. Ct. (ea. dist.) Tenn. 1980, U.S. Ct. Appeals (4th cir.) 1981, U.S. Ct. Appeals (6th cir.) 1983, U.S. Supreme Ct. 1985. Law clk. Daniel, Duncan & Claiborne, Knoxville, Tenn., 1978-80; assoc. Daniel, Claiborne & Lewallen, Knoxville, Tenn., 1980-82; ptnr. Daniel, Claiborne, Oberman & Buuck, Knoxville, 1983-85, Daniel & Oberman, Knoxville, 1986—; pres., Project First Offender, Knoxville, 1983-86;bd. dirs. Fed. Defender Svcs. Eastern Tenn., Inc., v.p. 1994-96; guest instr. U. Tenn. 1988-96; guest lectr. U. Tenn. Law Sch., 1982-88; guest instr. U. Tenn. Grad. Sch. Criminal Justice Program, 1983, 84; guest speaker Ct. Clk's Meeting, Cambridge, Eng., 1984; instr. legal clinic , trial advocacy program U. Tenn., 1987-88; adj. prof. U. Tenn. Law Sch., 1993— (Forrest W. Lacey award for outstanding faculty contbn. to U. Tenn. Coll. Law Moot Ct. Program, 1993-94; coach U. Tenn. Law Sch. Nat. Trial Team, 1991—; spl. judge Criminal Divsn. Knox County Gen. Sessions Court; founding mem. Nat. Coll. for DUI Def.; speaker in field. Author: D.U.I.: The Crime and Consequences in Tennessee, 1991, supplemented annually; co-author: D.W.I. Means Defend With Ingenuity, 1987; contbr. legal articles on drunk driving to profl. jours. Bd. dirs. Knoxville Legal Aid Soc., Inc., 1986-88 (pres. 1990), Arnstein Jewish Community Ctr., 1987-91, pres. 1990; bd. dirs. Knoxville Racquet Club, 1991-93, pres. 1992-93. Col. Aide de Camp Tenn. Gov.'s Staff, 1983, Moot Ct. Bd. Spl. Svc. award, 1995-96. Mem. ABA, ATLA, Nat. Assn. Criminal Def. Lawyers (co-chair DUI advocacy com. 1995-96), Tenn. Assn. Criminal Def. Lawyers (bd. dirs. 1983-89), Knoxville Bar ASsn. Jewish. Office: Daniel & Oberman 550 W Main St Ste 950 Knoxville TN 37902-2567

OBERMAYER, HERMAN JOSEPH, newspaper publisher; b. Phila., Sept. 19, 1924; s. Leon J. and Julia (Sinsheimer) O.; student U. Geneva (Switzerland), 1946; AB cum laude, Dartmouth, 1948; m. Betty Nan Levy, June 28, 1955; children: Helen O. Levy-Myers, Veronica O. Atnipp, Adele O. Malpass, Elizabeth Rose. Reporter, L.I. Daily Press, Jamaica, N.Y., 1950-53; classified advt. mgr. New Orleans Item, 1953-55; asst. to pub. Standard-Times, New Bedford, Mass., 1955-57; editor, pub. Long Branch (N.J.) Daily Record, 1957-71, No. Va. Sun, Arlington, 1963-89; adj. prof. journalism U. Md., 1989-93; vis. lectr. U. West Indies, Jamaica, 1994-95; Pulitzer Prize juror, 1983, 84; publ. com. Commentary Mag., 1989—; chmn. fin. com. Washington Journalism Rev., 1990-91; lectr publs. mgmt. seminars, Warsaw, Budapest, Barbados, Jamaica, Vilnius, Lithuania, Riga, Latvia, Tallinn and Tartu, Estonia, Ljubljana, Slovenia, 1990-96, Ctr. Fgn. Journalists, 1992—. Bd. dirs. Monmouth Med. Center, 1958-71; mem. exec. coun. Monmouth Boy Scouts Am., 1958-71, mem. exec. com. Nat. Capital coun., 1971-79, v.p., 1974-77; mem. Va. Legis. Alcohol Beverage Control Study Commn., 1972-74; trustee Arlington (Va.) Bicentennial Commn., Am. Jewish Com. (Cmty. Svc. award 1986, nat. bd. govs., 1989-96, nat. coun. 1995—, v.p. Washington chpt.; trustee Inst. for Learning in Retirement, Marymount U., 1994-95. Served with AUS, 1943-46; ETO. Rhineland Campaign; Recipient Silver Beaver award Boy Scouts of Am., 1977, Knight Internat. Press fellow, 1994-95. Mem. Am. Soc. Newspaper Editors, So. Newspapers Pubs. Assn. (dir. 1981-84), Soc. Profl. Journalists, Sigma Chi. Jewish. Rotarian. Clubs: Nat. Press (Washington), Cosmos (Washington), Washington Golf and Country (Arlington, Va.), Dartmouth (N.Y.C.), Econ. (Washington). Contbr. articles to numerous mags. and newspapers. Home: 4114 N Ridgeview Rd Arlington VA 22207-4711

OBERMEYER, GERALD FREDERICK, industrial engineer; b. Port Jervis, N.Y., Sept. 15, 1922; s. Jacob Frances and Anna Olivia (Gumaer) O.; m. Mary Eileen Moran, Dec. 29, 1945; children: William Henry, Stephen Moran, Paul Richard. BS in Mech. Engring., U. Maine, 1949; postgrad. in bus. adminstrn., Am. Internat. Coll., 1968-71. Cert. profl. engr., Tex. Trainee in program Westinghouse, Bloomfield, N.J., 1950-51; indsl. engr. Gen. Inst., Chicopee, Mass., 1951-53; mgr. indsl. engring. Gen. Inst., Danielson, Conn., 1953-55, Kitchener, Ont., Can., 1955-57; indsl. engr. Gen. Inst., Chicopee, 1957-66; plant mgr. Gen. Inst., Lisbon, Portugal, 1967-70; plant mgr. Gen. Inst., Juarez, Mex., 1971-74, mgr. indsl. engring., 1975-90, sr. program mgr., mgr. facilities, 1990-95; sr. program mgr., mgr. facilities Pollak Co., El Paso, Tex., 1990-96. Sgt. U.S. Army Air Corps, 1940-45. Mem. KC, Am. Legion. Roman Catholic. Home: 1817 Tommy Aaron Dr El Paso TX 79936 Office: Pollak Trans Elect Divsn 11801 Miriam Dr El Paso TX 79936

OBERNE, SHARON BROWN, elementary education educator; b. Lakeland, Fla., Sept. 2, 1955; d. Morris C. and Amy (Beecroft) Brown; m. Ronald Allan Oberne, Mar. 29, 1980; children: Laura, Aaron, Kelley. AA in Pre-tchg., Hillsborough C.C., Tampa, Fla., 1975; BA in Elem. Edn., U. South Fla., 1976, cert., 1980, AA in Acctg., 1980. Cert. tchr. K-8. 3rd grade tchr. Zolfo Springs Elem., Wauchula, Fla., 1976-77, 2nd grade tchr., 1977-79; 1st grade tchr. Westgate Christian Sch., Tampa, Fla., 1979-80; 5th grade tchr. Pasoc Elem., Dade City, Fla., 1980-81; 3rd grade tchr. San Antonio Elem., Dade City, 1981-86; temporary reading tchr. Chesterfield Heights Elem., Norfolk, Va., 1986-87; 2nd grade tchr. Ocean View Elem., Norfolk, 1987—; dir. Ocean View Writing Club, Norfolk, 1992—. Author: Pink Monkey, 1994, Space Traveler, 1995, Daisy Dolphin (Spelling in Context). Pres. USS Guam's Wife's Club, Norfolk Naval Base, 1990-91; amb. of goodwill USS Guam, 1990-91; founder AmeriKids of Ocean View, Norfolk, 1991-93; liaison Adopt-A-Sch. Program, Norfolk, 1991—. Recipient Good Neighbor award NEA, 1994. Mem. Norfolk Reading Coun., Nat. Autism Soc., CHADD. Home: 8243 Briarwood Cir Norfolk VA 23518-2862

OBERST, PAUL, law educator; b. Owensboro, Ky., Apr. 22, 1914; m. Elizabeth Durfee; children—Paul, James, George, Mary, John. A.B., U. Evansville, 1936; J.D., U. Ky., 1939; LL.M., U. Mich., 1941. Bar: Ky. 1938, Mo. 1942. Assoc. firm Ryland, Stinson, Mag & Thomson, Kansas City, Mo., 1941-42; asst. prof. law Coll. of Law, U. Ky., Lexington, 1946-47; prof. Coll. of Law, U. Ky., 1947-82; acting dean, 1966-67; emeritus prof. Coll. of Law, U. Ky., 1982—; vis. prof. U. Chgo., 1954-55, Duke U., 1980; prof., dir. civil liberties program N.Y. U., 1959-61; mem. Nat. Commn. on Acad. Tenure, 1971-73. Contbr. articles to legal jours. Mem. Ky. Commn. on Corrections, 1961-65; mem. Ky. Commn. on Human Rights, 1962-66, 80-90, chmn., 1966-70, 73-76; trustee U. Ky., Lexington, 1963-69, 72-75; mem. Ky. state adv. com. U.S. Civil Rights Commn., 1979-92, chmn., 1982-86. Served to lt. USNR, 1942-46. Mem. Assn. Am. Law Schs. (exec. com. 1970-72), Am., Ky. bar assns., Am. Law Inst., Order of Coif, Phi Delta Phi. Home: 829 Sherwood Dr Lexington KY 40502-2919

OBIANWU-LAND, MARIAN MARIE, nurse; b. Ft. Hood, Tex., May 1; d. William Edward and Elena (Brisco) Land; children: DeFrederick Chrishane, La Tashea Ari, Roosevelt K.C. Grad. in Vocat. Nursing, Temple (Tex.) Jr. Coll., 1982; grad., U. Mary Hardin-Baylor, 1982; ASN, McClellan C.C., 1988. RN, Tex.; lic. voc. nurse; cert., lic. vocat. psychiat. and mental health nurse. Vocat. respiratory and neurology nurse Scott & White Hosp., Temple, Tex., 1982-86, staff nurse oncology, 1986-87; staff nurse psychiatry Scott & White Hosp., Temple, 1987-89, John Peter Smith Hosp., Ft. Worth, Tex., 1989-91; program mgr. adolescents John Peter Smith Hosp., Ft. Worth, 1991-94; RN adult partial hospitalization program Trinity Springs Pavilion, Ft. Worth, 1994—. Mem. NAFE, Nat. Alliance for Mentally Ill, Am. Assn. Univ. Women, Advocates of Adolescent and Child Psychiat. Nursing, Tex. Alliance for Mentally Ill. Baptist.

OBIORA, CHRIS SUNNY, architect; b. Lagos, Nigeria, Sept. 2, 1954; came to U.S., 1978; s. Patrick M. and Virginia E. Obiora. Diploma, Christ the King Coll., Onitsha, Anambra, 1974; student, Tex. A&M U., 1986, Coll. Profl. Mgmt., Lintas, Lagos, 1992. Accounts clk. Lintas, Ltd., Lagos, 1976-78, media accounts clk., 1977-78; with San Jacinto Jr. Coll., Houston, Tex., 1980-81; The Wacherhit Corp., Coral Gables, Fla., 1980-84; gen. merchant Joncod Overseas Ltd., Lagos, 1974—; world trade strategist Joncod Overseas Ltd., Houston, 1987—; retail trader Star Liquor Store, Hempstead, Tex., 1987—; owner, prin. Chris & Chris Assocs., 1989; coord. Jancod/Bexpharm, Houston, 1987-88; cost acct. Jancod Overseas Ltd., Houston, 1980—; founder, pres. Joncod Internat., Inc., 1987—; founder, com. group head Star Liquor Store, Hempstead, 1987—. Active ARC, 1967-70, PTO, also numerous charitable activities, Lagos, 1970-74. Recipient Professionalism Cert. AMA, 1994, Meritorious Svc. award AIA Students, 1985, Recognition award Nat. Fire Protection Assn., 1986. Fellow The Highlanders Club (svcs. prof. 1993—), Nat. Shrine, Oxford Club; mem. Internat. Assn. Fin. Planners, Am. Fin. Assn., Soc. Applied Learning Tech., Assn. Corp. Tech. Computer Profls., Instr. of Profl. Mgmt. and Adminstrn., Internat. Assn. of Account Practitioners, Constrn. Specs. Inst. Office: Joncod Overseas Ltd PO Box 87483 Houston TX 77287-7483

OBLIGACION, FREDDIE RABELAS, sociology educator, researcher; b. Legazpi City, Albay, The Philippines, July 20, 1959; came to U.S., 1988; s. Wilfredo and Lourdes Rances (Rabelas) O. BS magna cum laude, U. Philippines, Quezon City, 1980, MBA, 1981; MA, Ohio State U., 1990, PhD, 1995. Exec. asst. Concrete Aggregates, Quezon City, 1980-82; asst. prof. Bicol U., Legazpi City, 1982-88; rsch. asst. Ohio State U., Columbus, 1988-89, teaching asst., 1989-92; asst. prof. sociology SUNY Suffolk C.C., Selden, 1992-93; reviewer Academic Text Rev., Columbus, 1994—; asst. prof. sociology Moorhead (Minn.) State U., 1994-95; with faculty Wyo. Coll. Advanced Studies, 1996—. Contbr. essays and articles to profl. jours. Rsch. grantee Soc. for Psychol. Studies and Social Issues, U. Mich., 1992, Ohio State U. Grad. Sch., 1992. Mem. Am. Sociol. Assn., Internat. Inst. Sociology, Soc. for Applied Sociology (cons. 1992—), Soc. for Psychol. Study Social Issues, Assn. Humanist Sociol., Phi Kappa Phi, Phi Beta Delta.

O'BRIANT, MARY FRANCES PREVETTE, editor; b. Salisbury, N.C., July 1, 1939; d. James Keith and Olive (Bumgarner) Prevette; m. Walter Herbert O'Briant, June 17, 1962 children: Jennifer, Kathryn, Erin. BMus, Salem Coll., 1961; MS in Psychology, U. Ga., 1977, PhD in Psychology, 1984. Piano instr. Athens, Ga., 1969-72; psychology instr. Dept. of Psychology, U. Ga., Athens, 1973-83, temp. asst. prof. psychology, 1984, 91; copyeditor, project mgr. Athens, 1993—. Home: 198 Dearing St Athens GA 30605

O'BRIEN, CHARLES H., lawyer, retired state supreme court chief justice; b. Orange, N.J., July 30, 1920; s. Herbert Rodgers and Agnes Sidman (Montanya) O'B.; m. Anna Belle Clement, Nov. 9, 1966; children: Merry Diane, Steven Shawn (dec.), Heather Lynn. LLB, Cumberland U., 1947. Rep. Tenn. Legislature, Memphis, 1963-65, senator, 1965-67; assoc. judge Tenn. Ct. Criminal Appeals, Crossville, 1970-87; assoc. justice Tenn. Supreme Ct., 1987-94, chief justice, 1994-95; ret., 1995; pvt. practice, Crossville, 1995—. Bd. dirs. Lake Tansi Village Property Owners Assn., 1984-89, chmn., 1989. With U.S. Army, 1938-45, ETO, 1950, UN Command, Tokyo. Decorated Bronze Star, Purple Heart with oak leaf cluster. Fellow Tenn. Bar Found.; mem. ABA, Tenn. Bar Assn., Cumberland County Bar Assn., Am. Legion, Lake Tansi Village Chowder and Marching Soc. (pres.). Democrat.

O'BRIEN, DORIS J., librarian; b. Cheyenne, Wyo., Sept. 30, 1930; d. Asa Dell and Ethel Amy (Moore) Kilgore; m. John G. O'Brien, Feb. 16, 1952; children: Michael, Kathleen, Sean P. (dec.), Kevin P. Cert., Ctrl. Bus. Sch., Denver, 1949; AD Libr. Tech., Norwalk (Conn.) C.C., 1985. Unit sec. St. Joseph Hosp., Stamford, Conn., 1971-85; libr. asst. jud. sys. Conn. State Libr., Stamford, 1985-91; libr. asst. Timrod Libr., Summerville, S.C., 1991—; clk. Stamford Hosp., 1985-91; rschr. Blake & Blake, Fla., 1993—. Editor: The Kilgore Clan, The Preston Scoop. Republican. Home: 106 Mikel Ct Summerville SC 24985

O'BRIEN, GREGORY MICHAEL ST. LAWRENCE, university official; b. N.Y.C., Oct. 7, 1944; s. Henry Joseph and Mary Agnes (McGoldrick) O'B.; m. Mary K. McLaughlin, Dec. 28, 1968; children: Jennifer Jane, Meredith Kathleen. A.B. with honors, Lehigh U., 1966; A.M., Boston U., 1968, Ph.D., 1969. Assoc. in psychology Lab. Community Psychology, Harvard Med. Sch., Boston; dir. Human Svcs. Design Lab., Sch. Applied Social Scis., Case Western Res. U., Cleve., 1970-74; dean, prof. Sch. Social Welfare, U. Wis., Milw., 1974-78; provost, prof. psychology U. Mich.-Flint, 1978-80; prof. social work and psychology, v.p. acad. affairs U. South Fla., Tampa, 1980-83, provost, 1983-87, prof. mgmt., 1986-87; chancellor U. New Orleans, 1987—; evaluation research cons. Cambridge Dept. Health and Hosps. and USPHS, 1968. Contbr. chpts. to books, articles to profl. jours. NIMH fellow, 1968-69. Fellow Am. Coll. Mental Health Adminstrs. (founding fellow, pres. 1984-86); mem. NCAA (chair pres. commn. 1992-93), Nat. Assn. Social Workers, Nat. Conf. Social Welfare, Soc. Gen. Systems Research, Am. Psychol. Assn., Am. Public Health Assn., Metrovision Partnership Found. (1992-93), Council Social Work Edn. (presdl. task force on structure of assn.), Indsl. Relations Research Assn. Roman Catholic. Home: 2468 Lark St New Orleans LA 70122-4322 Office: U New Orleans Office of Chancellor New Orleans LA 70148

O'BRIEN, JAMES RANDALL, minister; b. McComb, Miss., Aug. 29, 1949; s. Donald Ray and Irene (Allred) O'B.; m. Patricia Kay Donahoe, Dec. 21, 1975; children: Alyson, Shannon, Christopher. BS, Miss. Coll., 1975; MDiv, ThD, New Orleans Bapt. Theol. Sem., 1977, 82; postdoctoral studies, Yale U., 1986, STM, 1987. Ordained to ministry So. Bapt. Conv., 1977. Assoc. missionary Home Mission Bd., New Orleans, 1976-78; pastor Red Bluff Bapt. Ch., Greensburg, La., 1978-80, DeGray Bapt. Ch., Arkadelphia, Ark., 1980-83; asst. prof. religion Ouachita Bapt. U., Arkadelphia, 1980-87; sr. pastor Calvary Bapt. Ch., Little Rock, 1987-91; assoc. prof. Baylor U., Waco, Tex., 1991—; nat. treas. New Orleans Bapt. Theol. Sem., 1990-91, bd. trustees, 1989-90. Author: The Mosaic Messiah, 1983, Who is Jesus?, 1993, I Feel Better All Over Than I Do Anywhere Else, 1996; editor: Journey in Faith, 1985; contbr. articles to profl. jours. Sgt. U.S. Army, 1970-71, Vietnam. Named Outstanding Faculty Mem. Ouachita Bapt. U., 1981-82, 84-85, Baylor U., 1993; Staley Disting. Christian scholar Miss. Coll., 1991, Carr P. Collins Outstanding Prof., Baylor U., 1995-96. Mem. Soc. Bibl. Lit., Am. Acad. Religion. Home: 8606 Green Branch Cir Waco TX 76712-2348 Office: Baylor U Dept Religion Waco TX 76798

O'BRIEN, JOHN MICHAEL, obstetrician/gynecologist; b. 29 Palms, Calif., Aug. 26, 1962; s. John Michael and Carol Lucille (Gratti) O'B.; m. Susan Thena O'Brien, Nov. 28, 1986; children: Jennifer, Michael, Matthew. BA in Biology with honors, Kalamazoo Coll., 1984; MD, Wayne State U., Detroit, 1988. Intern/resident Wayne State U. Affiliated Hosp., Detroit, 1988-92; fellow U. Tenn., Memphis, 1992-94; dir. perinatal diagnostics Ctrl. Bapt. Hosp., Lexington, Ky., 1994—, coord. neonatal clin. perinatology rsch. network, 1995—. Mem. AMA, ACOG, Soc. Perinatology (assoc.), Internat. Soc. Ultrasound in Medicine, Ky. Med. Assn., Fayette County Med. Soc., Lexington Ob-gyn. Soc. Republican. Roman Catholic. Office: Central Baptist Hospital Perinatal Diagnostic Ctr 1740 Nicholasville Rd Lexington KY 40503-1424

O'BRIEN, MARYANN ANTOINETTE, nursing educator; b. Keiser, Pa., Jan. 30, 1938; d. John James and Antoinette Phyllis (St. Mary) Rugalla; m. Vincent Dennis O'Brien, Nov. 15, 1958; children: Vincent, John, Therese, Joseph. Diploma, Temple U. Hosp., 1958; BA in Profl. Arts., St. Joseph's Coll., 1988; postgrad., Nova U., 1990—. Cert. emergency nurse; cert. BCLS; cert. ACLS. Vis. nurse Vis. Nurse Assn. of Jersey City, 1958-59; staff nurse Bayonne (N.J.) Hosp., 1961-66, Alexian Bros. Hosp., Elizabeth, N.J., 1966-76, Clearbrook Adult Community, Cranbury, N.J., 1976-78; asst. dir. nursing Cen. Jersey Jewish Home for the Aged, Somerville, N.J., 1978-79; surg. nurse S.W. Regional Med. Ctr., Fort Myers, Fla., 1980; staff, asst dir. nursing Cape Coral (Fla.) Hosp., 1980-89; assoc. exec. dir. nursing Humana McFarland Hosp., Lebanon, Tenn., 1989-90; nurse educator James Lorenzo Walker Vocat. Tech. Ctr., Naples, Fla., 1990—, mem. CISD team; mem. sch. adv. com., 1994-96, chair, 1996—. Reviewer, author: (with others) Practical Nurse Textbook, 1994, ECG Workbook, 1995; item writer NCLEX-PN, 1994, 96. Mem. NEA, Fla. Nurses Assn., Fla. Vocat. Assn., Fla. Teaching Profl. Assn., Collier County Vocat. Adult Assn., Assn. Practical Nurse Educators of Fla., Temple U. Alumni Assn.

O'BRIEN, PATRICK MICHAEL, library administrator; b. Newport, R.I., Mar. 17, 1943; s. Joseph Xavier and Loretta (DeCotis) O'B.; m. Roberta Luther, Nov. 27, 1977; children—Megan MacRae, Brendan Watters. B.A. in Eng. Lit., Merrimack Coll., North Andover, Mass., 1964; M.L.S., U. R.I., Kingston, 1965; M.B.A., Case Western Res. U., Cleve., 1983. Reference libr. Newsweek mag., N.Y.C., 1965-72; asst. dir. rsch. FIND/SVP, N.Y.C., 1972-74; head cen. libr., cultural ctr. Chgo. Pub. Libr., 1974-79; dir. Cuyahoga County Pub. Libr., Cleve., 1979-84; dir. librs. Dallas Pub. Libr., 1984-92; dir. Alexandria (Va.) Libr., 1992—. Mem. editorial bd. Handel's Nat. Directory for Performing Arts; contbr. articles to profl. jours. Participant, alumnus Leadership Dallas Program, 1984-85, Leadership Cleve. Program, 1981; mem. nat. adv. com. to Libr. of Congress; mem. adv. coun. Tex. State Libr., Libr. Svcs. and Constrn. Act, 1986-89; co-chair, del. selection com. Tex. Conf. on Librs. and Info. Svcs.; mem. com. Goals for Dallas, 1985; mem. exec. bd. univ. librs. So. Meth. U., 1985—; bd. dirs. Urban Community Sch., Cleve., 1982-84, Mus. African-Am. Life and Culture, 1985-86; mem. client data base com. Dallas Assn. Svcs. to Homeless, 1988-90; mem. Latchkey Children's Task Force, 1985-90. Recipient Servant as Leader award City of Dallas, 1989, Disting. Alumnus award U. R.I. Grad. Sch. Libr. and Info. Studies, 1990. Mem. ALA (coun. mem. 1987-95), Am. Libr. Trustee Assn. (bd. dirs.), Pub. Libr. Assn. (pres. 1985-86), Pub. Libr. Systems Sect (pres. 1983), Tex. Libr. Assn. (legis com. 1986-92), Tex. Women's Univ. Sch. Libr. and Info. Studies Vis. Com., Tex. Ctr. for Book Dallas Pub. Libr., Cleve. Area Met. Libr. Systems (pres. bd. 1980), Chgo. Libr. Club (pres. 1978), D.C. Libr. Assn., Va. Pub. Libr. Dirs. Assn. (bd. dirs. 1994—), Va. Libr. Assn., Online Computer Libr. Ctr. (bd. trustees 1992—), The White House Conf. on Librs. and Info. Svcs. (del. 1991), Pub. Lib. Adminstrs. N.Tex. (pres. 1990-91), Dallas 40, Rotary of Alexandria (bd. dirs. 1996—), Beta Gamma Sigma. Office: Alexandria Libr 717 Queen St Alexandria VA 22314-2420

O'BRIEN, ROBERT BROWNELL, JR., investment banker, consultant, yacht broker, opera company executive; b. N.Y.C., Sept. 6, 1934; s. Robert Brownell and Eloise (Boles) O'B.; m. Sarah Lager, Nov. 28, 1958; children: Robert Brownell III, William Stuart, Jennifer. BA, Lehigh U., 1957; postgrad., NYU, Am. Inst. Banking. Asst. treas., credit officer, br. locations officer Bankers Trust Co., N.Y.C., 1957-63; v.p., dir. bus. devel. George A. Murray Co., gen. contractors, N.Y.C., 1964; also v.p. Bowery Savs. Bank, 1964-69; dir., chief exec. officer Fed. Savs. & Loan Ins. Corp., Washington, 1969-71; chmn. exec. com. Fed. Home Loan Bank Bd., 1969-71; v.p. Bowery Savs. Bank, N.Y.C., 1972; exec. v.p. First Fed. Savs. & Loan Assn., N.Y.C., 1973-75; chmn., chief exec. officer Carteret Savs. Bank, Morristown, 1975-91, also bd. dirs.; mng. dir. Printon Kane Group Inc., Short Hills, N.J., 1991-94; dir., former chief exec. officer Govs. Bank Corp., West Palm Beach, 1992—; bd. dirs. Fed. Home Loan Bank N.Y., Govs. Bank Corp.; vice chmn. 1st Mortgage Capital Corp., Vero Beach, Fla.; chmn. Neighborhood Housing Svcs. Am., 1972-91; vice chmn., bd dirs. U.S. League Savs. Instns., Washington, O'Brien Yacht Sales. Contbr. articles to trade mags. Trustee Trinity Pawling Sch., Palm Beach County Housing Partnership, Lehigh U.; chmn. Housing Opportunities Found.; trustee, past chmn. Cmty. Found. of N.J., 1987—; vice chmn., bd. dirs. Dalt Found.; chmn. adv. bd. Palm Beach Maritime Mus., Peanut Island, Fla.; active Nat. Commn. on Neighborhoods; past chmn., exec. dir. N.J. State Opera. Mem. Nat. Coun. Savs. Instns. (past chmn.), Essex County Savs. and Loan League (past chmn.), N.J. Savs. League (past chmn.), N.J. Hist. Soc. (past chmn.), Greater Newark C. of C. (bd. dirs.), N.J. C. of C. (bd. dirs.), Union League Club, Delray Beach Yacht Club (past commodore), New York Yacht Club, Morris County Golf Club, Somerset Hills Golf Club, Palm Beach Yacht Club, Bay Head Yacht Club (past commodore). Republican. Episcopalian. Home: 12 Banyan Rd Gulf Stream FL 33483-7425 Office: 1400 Centrepark Blvd Ste 909 West Palm Beach FL 33401-7412

O'BRIEN, ROBERT JAMES, financial consultant, business owner; b. Waterbury, Conn., Nov. 22, 1940; s. Stephen Joseph and Ada Florence (Schiardli) O'B.; m. Janyce Leah Bruni, Sept. 24, 1966; children: Gayle Elizabeth O'Brien Blachura, Julie Maureen O'Brien Orlando. BA, U. Conn., 1964. Registered investment advisor SEC; CFP; registered fin. cons. Commd. ensign USN, 1964, advanced through grades to comdr., ret., 1984; fin. cons., CFP Davenport-Dukes Assocs., Virginia Beach, Va., 1984—; prin./ptnr. Davenport-Dukes Assocs., Virginia Beach, 1992—; adj. instr. Commonwealth Coll., Virginia Beach, 1988-91. Elder Kempsville Presbyn. Ch., Va. Beach, 1987—; bd. dirs. Edmarc Children's Hospice, Portsmouth, Va., 1988-92, pres. bd. dirs., 1992; bd. dirs. Bethany Christian Svcs., Va. Beach, Dec. 1995-96. Mem. Nat. Assn. Life Underwriters (Million Dollar Round Table 1994, 95), Internat. Assn. Registered Fin. Cons. Republican. Home: 4841 Kempsville Greens Pky Virginia Beach VA 23462 Office: Davenport-Dukes Assocs 448 Viking Dr Virginia Beach VA 23452

O'BRIEN, WILLIAM JAMES, software engineer; b. Boston, Jan. 7, 1954; s. Joseph Richard and Lillian (Queen) O'B.; m. Myrna Jean Grile, Oct. 31, 1981. BA in Psychology with honors, St. Leo (Fla.) Coll., 1980; student, Old Dominion U., 1981-83; BS in Info. Sci., Christopher Newport Coll., 1983; MS in Info. Systems, George Mason U., 1988. Systems analyst Calspan Command Support Div., Rosslyn, Va., 1983-84; software engr. Space Applications Corp., Vienna, Va., 1984-89; pres. Soft. Info. Inc. TRW, Fairfax, Va., 1991; chief exec. officer, pres. Soft Info. Inc., 1991—. Served with USAF, 1979-82. Mem. IEEE, Assn. for Computing Machinery. Republican. Roman Catholic. Office: Soft Info Inc 2751 Knollside Ln Vienna VA 22180-7005

O'BRIEN, WILLIAM JOSEPH, political scientist; b. Norwich, Conn., Feb. 13, 1961; s. Joseph Patrick and Louise Mary (Damos) O'B. BA, Loyola Coll., Balt., 1983; MA, U. Va., 1989, PhD, 1995. Chief-of-staff (rsch.) Sch. of Law U. Va., Charlottesville, 1987-90, project dir., sr. editor Ctr. for Pub. Svc., 1990-91, dir. rsch. Constitutionalism/Democracy, 1991-94; intelligence officer, rsch. analyst Nat. Security Agy. U.S. Dept. Def., Ft. George Meade, Md., 1985-86; spl. asst. U.S. Ho. Reps., 1983-84; news reporter, staff writer Howard County (Md.) News, 1980-81. Co-author: Democracy's Dawn, 1991, American Initiatives on Democracy, Constitutionalism and the Rule of Law in Central and Eastern Europe Vols. I and II, 1990; sr. editor: Jour. Law and Politics, 1988-93. Asst. Scoutmaster, merit badge counselor Boy Scouts Am., Balt., 1979—. Thomas Jefferson fellow U. Va., 1984; Eagle Scout, 1977; recipient degree of distinction Nat. Forensics League. Mem. Am. Polit. Sci. Assn., Am. Judicature Soc., Nat. Eagle Scouts Assn. Democrat. Roman Catholic. Office: U Va Govt & Fgn Affairs Dept Charlottesville VA 22904 Address: 17 Mourning Dove Ct Hackettstown NJ 07840-3200

O'BRIENT, DAVID WARREN, sales executive, consultant; b. Toledo, Oct. 2, 1927; s. Earl James and Jessie Carlton (Edwards) O'B.; m. Enid Jo Wynne O'Brient, Feb. 21, 1962 (div. Apr. 1978); 1 child, David Warren Jr. BS in Archtl. Engring., U. Tex., 1949. Registered profl. engr., Tex. Sales engr. Smith Engring. Co., Houston, 1949-53; dist. sales mgr. Dunham-Bush, Inc., Hartford, Conn., 1953-60; sales mgr. W.L. Lashley & Assoc., Houston, 1960-67; pres., owner OJ & C Co., Inc., Houston, 1967-78, exec. v.p., 1980-83; pres., owner O'Brient Engring. Co., Houston, 1983—. Mem., phone solicitor Rep. Party, Houston, 1962—; mem. adminstrv. bd. First United Meth. Ch., Houston, 1969—. With USN, 1945-46, 50-52, PTO, Korea. Mem. ASHRAE, Phi Eta Sigma, Tau Sigma Delta, Tau Beta Pi. Home and Office: 9550 Ella Lee Ln Apt 811 Houston TX 77063-1238

O'BRYAN, MARY LOUISE, nursing administrator, consultant; b. Louisville, Feb. 16, 1953; d. James B. Sr. and Helen (Jarboe) O'B. BSN, Spalding U., 1981, MSN, 1987. Charge nurse Sts. Mary & Elizabeth Hosp., Louisville; dir. nursing Georgetown Manor Nursing Home, Louisville; nurse adminstr., owner Health Care Promotions, Louisville. Mem. ANA, Ky. Nurse's Assn. Home: 6709 Manslick Rd Louisville KY 40214-1149

OCAMPO, ANGELA PATRICIA, real estate broker; b. Bogota, Colombia, Aug. 4, 1946; came to U.S., 1957; d. Enrique and Maria Teresa (Vargas) Ocampo-Berrio; married; 1 child, Gilberto Enrique Ocampo; m. Hector Castro, May 10, 1982 (div. Apr. 1986). Grad. high sch., North Plainfield, N.J. Bilingual sec. Metro-Goldwyn Mayer Inc., N.Y.C.; jr. analyst Chase Manhattan Bank, N.Y.C., 1966-68; sr. analyst Chase Manhattan Bank, San Juan, P.R., 1968-71; head analyst P.R. Sun Oil Co., San Juan, 1971-72; project leader Pueblo Supermarkets, San Juan, 1972-74; data processing mgr. Exxon Svcs. Venezuela, Inc., Caracas, 1974-82; owner, pres. Gilan Enterprises INc., Miami, Fla., 1982-86; real estate broker The Keyes Co., Miami, 1986—. Mem. com. Alliance Francaise D'Miami, 1986, 87, 88, 89. Mem. French-Am. C. of C. (bd. dirs. 1989-91), Spanish-Am. C. of C. (bd. dirs. 1991-92), Colombian-Am. C. of C. Roman Catholic. Office: The Keyes Co 634 Crandon Blvd Miami FL 33149-2008

O CARROLL, M. KEVIN, dentist, educator, radiologist; b. Galway, Ireland, May 2, 1945; came to U.S., 1976; s. Joseph and aAgnes Murphy O.; m. Eileen Lim Liao, June 5, 1971 (div. Nov., 1987); children: Christine, Katherine A., Madeleine A.; m. Marsha Elaine Anderson, Nov., 1987; 1 child, Michelle. B in Dental Surgery, Nat. U. of Ireland, Dublin, 1968; MS in Dentistry, Ind. U., Indpls., 1973. Diplomate Am. Bd. Oral and Maxillofacial Radiology. Dentist gen. practice Coleraine, Ireland, 1968, Dunstable, Eng., 1968-69; asst. prof. UCLA, 1971-73; radiologist Dublin (Ireland) Dental Hosp., 1973-76; asst. prof. dept. of dentistry U. Miss., Jackson, 1976-78, assoc. prof., 1979-94, prof. Sch. Dentistry, 1994—; vis. prof. U. Ill. Chgo., 1984; dir. ednl. programs U. Miss. Sch. of Dentistry, Jackson, 1986-87, dir. accreditation, self study 1986-88. Author: (with others) (book) Basic Principles of Oral Radiology; (book chpts.) Users Guide to the Problem-Oriented Dental Record, 1980, 3d revised edit., 1993, (ops. manual) Am. Acad. Oral and Maxillofacial Radiology, 1993; producer, author: videocassettes) Advanced Oral Radiographic Techniques Parts I and II; contbr. articles, reviews and abstracts to numerous profl. jours. Recipient Tchg. award Freshman Dental Class UCLA, 1972, Sophomore Dental Class, 1973, bronze medal Royal Acad. Medicine in Ireland, 1977. Fellow Am. Acad. Oral and Maxillofacial Radiology; mem. Am. Assn. Dental Schs., Farrar-Norgaard Soc., Internat. Assn. Dentomaxillofacial Radiology, Radiol. Soc. N. Am. Roman Catholic. Office: U Miss Sch Dentistry 2500 N State St Jackson MS 39216-4500

OCASIO-MELENDEZ, MARCIAL ENRIQUE, history educator; b. San Juan, P.R., Aug. 22, 1942; s. Manuel C. and Amparo (Melendez) Ocasio; m. Mimi Rivera, Apr. 15, 1973 (div. 1976). BA, U. P.R., 1964, MA, 1977; PhD, Mich. State U., 1988. Tchr. sci. P.R. Dept. Edn., San Juan, 1966-67; tchr. sci., history Nyack (N.Y.) Schs., 1967-71; tchr. sci. Robinson Prep. Sch., Condado, P.R., 1971-72; instr., asst. prof. P.R. Jr. Coll., Rio Piedras, 1972-80; teaching asst. Mich. State U., E. Lansing, 1979-83; instr. history Caribbean U., Bayamon, P.R., 1983-85; instr. Inter Am. U., Bayamon, 1985-87, U. P.R., Rio Piedras, 1983-87; vis. asst. prof. Mich. State U., E. Lansing, 1987-88; asst. prof. history U. Mich., Flint, 1988-91; assoc. prof. history U. P.R., Rio Piedras, 1991—, dir. grad. program history, 1991-93, assoc. dean acad. affairs Coll. Humanities, 1993-95, dir. internat. studies, 1995—; bd. dirs. Spanish Speaking Info. Ctr., Flint; lectr. Universidad del Valle, Cali, Universidad de Los Andes, Bogota, Universidad Pedagogica Nacional, Tunja, U. del Norte Barranquilla, Colombia; dir. Rockefeller Found. Caribbean 2000 Project, U. P.R., 1994-95, Urban Preservation Project of Rio Piedras, P.R., 1994-95; mem. editorial bd. Caribbean Review, 1994—. Author: Rio Piedras Notas, 1985. Geogratia e Historia Am. Latina, 1966; Fulbright scholar (Colombia) 1989, 90; NEH fellow, 1973, 78-79, 91. Mem. U.S. Nexus, Social Sci. Studies Assn., Coun. L.Am. History, Am. Hist. Assn., L.Am. Studies Assn., P.R. Assn. Historians (pres. 1995—), Joint Border Rsch. Inst., Assn. Caribeen Historians, Hispanic Coun. on Internat. Rels., Phi Alpha Theta. Office: Univ PR History Dept PO Box 23350 San Juan PR 00931-3350

OCHSNER, SEYMOUR FISKE, radiologist, editor; b. Chgo., Nov. 29, 1915; s. Albert Henry Ochsner and Fleda Fiske; m. Helen Keith, Sept. 8, 1945 (dec. Jan. 1976); children: Anne, Diana, Lida; m. Bobbie Sue Mercer, Dec. 31, 1981. AB, Dartmouth Coll., 1937; MD, U. Pa., Phila., 1947. Diplomate Am. Bd. Radiology, 1953. Intern Johnston-Willis Hosp., Richmond, Va., 1949-50; staff radiologist Ochsner Clinic, New Orleans, 1953-89, also chmn. dept., 1969-77; clin. prof. radiology Tulane Med. Sch., New Orleans, 1955-75; editor Orleans Parish Med. Bulletin, New Orleans, 1985-91. Contbr. articles to profl. jours. Pres. PTA, Metairie, La., 1964. Recipient Disting. Svc. medal So. Med. Assn., 1972, Disting. Svc. award AMA, 1993; fellow Acton Ochsner Med. Found., New Orleans, 1950-53. Mem. Radiol. Soc. La. (pres. 1965), So. Radiol. Conf. (pres. 1968), Am. Coll. Radiology (pres. 1972, Gold medal 1982), Am. Roentgen Ray Soc. (pres. 1975, Gold medal 1986), Rex Orgn., So. Yacht Club, Candlewood Club. Republican. Episcopalian. Home: 107 Holly Dr Metairie LA 70005-3915

O'CONNELL, ANTHONY J., bishop; b. Lisheen, County Clare, Ireland, May 10, 1938. Ed., Mt. St. Joseph Coll., Cork, Ireland; Mungret Coll., Mangret Coll., Limerick, Ireland; ed., Kenrick Sem., St. Louis. Ordained priest Roman Cath. Ch., 1963. Bishop Diocese of Knoxville, 1988—. Office: Bishop of Knoxville 805 Northshore Dr Knoxville TN 37919

O'CONNELL, JEFFREY, law educator; b. Worcester, Mass., Sept. 28, 1928; s. Thomas Joseph and Mary (Carroll) O'C.; m. Virginia Kearns, Nov. 26, 1960; children: Mara, Devin. Grad. cum laude, Phillips Exeter Acad., 1947; AB cum laude, Dartmouth Coll., 1951; JD, Harvard U., 1954. Bar: Mass. 1954, Conn. 1954, Va. 1983, hon. admittance to Ark. and Minn. bar. Instr. speech Tufts U., 1953-54; assoc. Sherburne, Powers & Needham, 1954-57, Hale & Dorr, Boston, 1958-59; asst. prof., then assoc. prof. law U. Iowa Coll. Law, 1959-62; assoc. dir. automobile claims study Harvard Law Sch., 1963-64; assoc. prof. law U. Ill. Coll. Law., 1964-65, prof., 1965-79; prof. law U. Va. Law Sch., 1980-83, John Allan Love prof., 1983-90, Samuel H. McCoy II prof., 1990—, Class of 1948 rsch. prof., 1994—; summer vis. prof. Northwestern U., 1963, U. Mich., 1966, 75, So. Meth. U., 1972, U. Tex., 1977, U. Wash., 1979; John Marshall Harlan vis. prof. N.Y. Law Sch., 1991; vis. fellow Centre for Socio-Legal Studies, Wolfson Coll., Oxford (Eng.) U., 1973, 79; Thomas Jefferson vis. fellow Downing Coll. Cambridge U., Eng., 1989; mem. U. Va. Ctr. for Advanced Study, 1980-83. Author: (with R.E. Keeton) Basic Protection for the Traffic Victim, 1965, After Cars Crash: The Need for Legal and Insurance Reform, 1967, (with Arthur Myers) Safety Last: An Indictment of the Auto Industry, 1966, (with R.E. Keeton, John McCord) Crisis in Car Insurance, 1968, (with Wallace Wilson) Car Insurance and Consumer Desires, 1969, The Injury Industry, 1971, (with Rita James Simon) Payment for Pain and Suffering, 1972, Ending Insult to Injury: No-Fault Insurance for Products and Services, 1975, (with Roger Henderson) Tort Law, No-Fault and Beyond, 1975, The Lawsuit Lottery: Only the Lawyers Win, 1979, (with C. Brian Kelly) The Blame Game: Injuries, Insurance and Injustice, 1986, (with Lester Brickman and Michael Horowitz) Rethinking Contingency Fees: A Proposal to Align the Contingency Fee System with its Policy Roots and Ethical Mandates, 1994; also chpts. in books. Mem. Nat. Hwy. Safety Adv. Com., 1967-70; ednl. adv. bd. John Simon Guggenheim Found., 1973-87; bd. dirs. Consumers Union, 1970-76; mem. com. on competitive safeguards and med. aspects of sports NCAA, 1985-87. Served as 1st lt. USAF, 1954-57. Recipient Robert B. McKay award for ins. scholarship Tort and Ins. Practice sect. ABA, 1992; Guggenheim fellow, 1972-73, 79-80. Mem. ABA, Va. Bar Assn., Casque and Gauntlet, Phi Beta Kappa, Phi Upsilon, Farmington Country Club. Democrat. Roman Catholic. Home: 4 Oak Cir Charlottesville VA 22901-3220 Office: U Va Sch Law 580 Massie Rd Charlottesville VA 22903-1738

O'CONNELL, JOHN BERNARD, JR., medical educator, chairman department of medicine; b. Chgo., July 27, 1949; s. John B. O'C; m. Mary Owens, Jan. 12, 1980; children: Jessica, Moira, Claire, Sheila, John. BS, U. Ill., Chgo., 1971; MD magna cum laude, Loyola U., Maywood, Ill., 1974. Diplomate Nat. Bd. Med. Examiners, Am. Bd. Internal Medicine, Am. Bd. Cardiovascular Disease. Intern Loyola U. Med. Ctr., Maywood, 1975-76, resident in internal medicine, 1976-78, chief resident in internal medicine, 1977-78, fellow in cardiology, 1978-80, staff physician emergency dept., 1979-81, attending cardiologist, 1980-86, med. dir. Cardiac Transplantation Program, 1984-86; clin. instr. in medicine Loyola U., Stritch Sch. Medicine, Maywood, 1977-80, asst. prof. medicine, 1980-85, assoc. prof. medicine, 1985-86; asst. chief med. svc. Hines VA Hosp., Maywood, 1981-83; attending cardiologist LDS Hosp., Salt Lake City, 1986-91, U. Utah Med. Ctr., Salt Lake City, 1986-91; assoc. prof. medicine Sch. Medicine, U. Utah, Salt Lake City, 1986-91, prof., 1991; attending physician Univ. Hosp., U. Miss. Med. Ctr., Jackson, 1991—; prof. medicine U. Miss. Med. Sch., Jackson, 1991—, chmn. dept. medicine, 1991—; cons. Salt Lake VA Med. Ctr., Salt Lake City, 1988-91, Primary Children's Med. Ctr., Salt Lake City, 1988-91; med. dir., chmn. exec. com. UTAH Cardiac Transplant Program, Salt Lake City, 1986-91; chmn. adv. bd. Exptl. Organ Transplantation Procedures, apptd. by Gov. of Ill., 1985-86; mem. working group on myocarditis Nat. Heart, Lung and Blood Inst., 1985; com. mem. Internat. Symposium Inflammatory Heart Disease, Snowmass, Colo., July, 1988; mem. sci. coun. Internat. Soc. and Fedn. Cardiology, 1990—; mem. spl. study sect. NIH , 1990; mem. sci. bd. Internat. Congress of Cardiology on Cardiovascular Pharmacotherapy and Cardiomyopathies, Greece, 1990; mem. adv. com. Miss. Health Scis. Info. Network, 1992-94; med. dir. Miss. Organ Procurement Agy., 1992-93; mem. sci. com. Internat. Workshop on the Cardiomyopathies, LaCoruna, Spain, 1993. Co-editor (monographs): Myocarditis: Precursor of Cardiomyopathy, 1983, Drug Therapy of Dilated Cardiomyopahty and Myocarditis, 1988, Intrathoracic Transplantation 2000, 1993; mem. editorial bd. Jour. Heart and Lung Transplantation, 1986—, Internat. Jour. Cardiology, 1992—, Transplantation, 1993—; manuscript cons. numerous publs.; contbr. articles to profl. jours. Recipient Norris L. Brookens Outstanding Resident award Ill. Soc. Internal Medicine, 1978, Robert Kark, M.D. Rsch. award Chgo. Soc. Internal Medicine, 1981, Outstanding Young Citizen award Chgo. Jr. Assocs. Commerce and Industry, 1985, Shinshu U. medal Matsumoto City, Nagano, Japan, 1992; grantee Earl M. Bane Charitable Trust, 1979-83, Fraternal Order Eagles, 1983-86, BRSG, 1983-84, NHLBI, 1986-91, Deseret Found., 1987-91, Bristol Myers Squibb, 1988-91, Burroughs Wellcome, 1992—, Otsuka Pharm., 1993—, Smith Kline Beecham Pharm., 1993—. Fellow ACP, Am. Coll. Chest Physicians, Am. Coll. Cardiology (cardiac transplantation com. 1991—, conf. steering com. 1991-92), Am. Coll. Angiology; mem. AMA, AAAS, Am. Soc. Transplant Physicians (mem. tng. and manpower com. 1990—, mem. pub. policy com. 1993—, numerous others), N.Y. Acad. Scis., Internat. Soc. Heart and Lung Transplant (mem. sci. program com. 1987, 89, 90, councilor 1989-91, pres.-elect 1991-92, pres. 1993-94, past pres. 1993-94, others), Transplantation Soc., Assn. Profs. Medicine, Rsch., Miss. (bd. dirs.), Jackson Acad. Medicine, So. Soc. Clin. Investigation, Am. Fedn. Clin. Rsch. (sen. midwest sect. 1983-86), So. Soc. Clin. Rsch., Ctrl. Soc. Clin. Rsch., Miss. State Med. Assn., Ctrl. Med. Soc., Am. Heart Assn. (bd. dirs. West Cook County 1982-86, v.p. 1985-86, chmn. 1990-92, numerous others), United Network for Organ Sharing (mem. coalition on organ doning 1991-92, mem. thoracic com. 1992—, mem. sci. adv. com. 1993—), Alpha Omega Alpha. Home: 8 Twelve Oaks Pl Madison MS 39110-9724 Office: Univ of Miss Med Ctr Dept of Medicine 2500 N State St Jackson MS 39216-4500

O'CONNELL, RICHARD (JAMES), English literature educator, poet; b. N.Y.C., Oct. 25, 1928; s. Richard James and Mary Ellen (Fallon) O'C.; BS, Temple U., 1956; MA, Johns Hopkins, 1957. Instr. English Temple U., Phila., 1957-61, asst. prof., 1961-69, asso. prof., 1969-86; sr. assoc. prof., 1986-93, assoc. prof. emeritus, 1993; guest lectr. poetry dept. writing seminars Johns Hopkins U., 1961-74; participant Poetry in Schs. Program, Pa. Council Arts, 1971-73; Fulbright lectr. Am. lit. U. Brazil, Rio de Janeiro, 1960, U. Navarre, Pamplona, Spain, 1962-63. Served with USN, 1948-52. Recipient prize Contemporary Poetry Press, 1972. Mem. PEN, MLA, Asso. Writing Programs, Walt Whitman Poetry Center (dir. 1975-84), Lit. Fellowship Phila. Author: From an Interior Silence, 1961, Cries of Flesh and Stone, 1962, New Poems and Translations, 1963; Brazilian Happenings, 1966, Terrane, 1967, Thirty Epigrams, 1971, Irish Monastic Poems (transl.), 1975, The Word in Time (selected transl. of Antonio Machado), 1975, Sappho (selected transl.), 1975, Lorca (selected transl.), 1976, Middle English Poems (transl.), 1976, More Irish Poems (transl.), 1976, Epigrams from Martial (transl.), 1976, One Hundred Epigrams from the Greek Anthology (trans.), 1977, Hudson's Fourth Voyage, 1978, The Epigrams of Luxorius (transl.), 1984, Temple Poems, 1985, Hanging Tough, 1986, Battle Poems, 1987, Selected Epigrams, 1990, Lives of The Poets, 1990, New Epigrams From Martial (transl.), 1991, The Caliban Poems, 1992, RetroWorlds, 1993 (translation) Simulations, 1993, Voyages, 1995; editor: Apollo's Day, 17th Century Songs, 1969; Atlantis Edits., 1962—, Poetry Newsletter, 1971-86. Home: 204 Ellesmere Dr Deerfield Beach FL 33442-3541

O'CONNOR, DENNIS, business executive; b. 1951. With Warehouse Foods, West Memphis, Ark., 1970-74, Memphis Cotton Sales, 1974-84; owner Flying O Nursery & Landscaping Inc., Millington, Tenn., 1985-89; ptnr. Phoenix Cotton Pickery, Phoenix, 1984—; owner Flying O Feed & Seed Co., Millington, 1984-88; pres. O'Flying Enterprises Inc., Millington, 1984—. Office: O Flying Enterprises Inc 8580 Us Highway 51 N Millington TN 38053-1515

O'CONNOR, DENNIS MICHAEL, physician; b. Stillwater, Okla., Apr. 11, 1948; s. Andrew Richard and Blanche Elizabeth (Freeman) O'C.; m. Stella Louise Huckstep, Mar. 24, 1973; children: David R., Richard A., Sarah L., Elizabeth A. BS in Biology, Va. Mil. Inst., 1970; MD, U. Va., 1974. Diplomate Nat. Bd. Med. Examiners, Am. Bd. Ob-Gyn., Am. Bd. Pathology. Commd. 2d lt. USMC, 1974, advanced through grades to col., 1994; intern, resident Tripler Army Med. Ctr., Honolulu, 1974-78; staff physician DeWitt Army Hosp., Ft. Belvoir, 1978-80, Walter Reed Army Med. Ctr., Washington, 1980-84; resident, fellowship in pathology Georgetown U., Washington, 1984-87; assoc. prof. Uniformed Svcs. Univ., Bethesda, Md., 1988-94; ret. USMC, 1994; assoc. prof. U. Louisville (Ky.) Sch. Medicine, 1994—; editl. cons. Internat. Jour. Gynecol. Pathology, 1990—, Am. Jour. Surgery, 1995—; mem. Cervical Cancer Prevention Task Force, Frankfort, Ky., 1994—. Author: (with others) Germ Cell Tumors, 1995, Mitotically Active Leiomyomas, 1994; contbr. articles to profl. jours. Mem Am. Coll. Ob-Gyn., Internat. Acad. Pathology, Internat. Soc. of Gyn. Pathologists, Am. Soc. of Colposcopist and Cervical Pathologists. Office: Dept Ob-Gyn 530 S Jackson St Louisville KY 40202-1675

O'CONNOR, EDWARD VINCENT, JR., lawyer; b. Yokosuka, Japan, Nov. 9, 1952; s. Edward Vincent and Margaret (Robertson) O'C.; m. Kathy J. Hunt, May 23, 1992. BA, Duke U., 1975; JD, N.Y. Law Sch., 1981. Bar: Va. 1982, D.C. 1983. Assoc. Lewis, Kinsey, Dack & Good, Washington, 1982-87; ptnr. Lewis, Dack, Paradiso & Good, Washington, 1988-89, Lewis, Dack, Paradiso, O'Connor & Good, Washington, 1994, The Lewis Law Firm, 1989-94, Byrd, Mische, Bevis, Bowen, Joseph & O'Connor, Fairfax, Va., 1995—; arbitrator D.C. Superior Ct.; neutral case evaluator Fairfax County Cir. Ct.; lectr. Va. Trial Lawyers Assn., Arlington County Bar Assn. Mem. Va. State Bar (lectr., spl. com. on access to legal svcs. 1994—), D.C. Bar, Fairfax County Bar Assn. (lectr., vice chair family law sect. 1995-96, continuing edn. com. 1988-95, chair 1995, mem. pub. svc. com. 1995, chair 1996—, mem. cir. ct. com. 1994-96).

O'CONNOR, JOHN JOSEPH, operations executive; b. Smyrna, Tenn., June 1, 1959; s. John O'Connor and Dolores Jane (Bell) Brem; m. Lea Ann Bradford, Sept. 6, 1986; 1 child, Colleen Michelle. BS, Tex. A&M U., 1981. Cert. marine engr. 3rd asst. engr. Marine Engrs. Beneficial Assn., Houston, 1981-84; asst. engr. Biehl Ship Mgmt., Houston, 1984; balance technician Hickham Industries, Inc., LaPorte, Tex., 1984-86, prodn. scheduler/Sulzer, 1986-87, project engr./Sulzer, 1987-88, engring. mgr./Sulzer, 1988-89; ops. mgr./Sulzer Hickham Industries, Inc., Huntington Beach, Calif., 1989-93; sr. engr., corp. mergers and acquisitions Hickham Industries, Inc., La Porte, Tex., 1993-94; tech. and field svc. mgr. Sulzer Turbosys. Internat., Houston, 1994—; guest speaker Tex. A&M U., Galveston, Tex., College Station, Tex., 1981-89, U. Houston, 1986-89; moderator Power Machinery and Compressor Conf., Houston, 1989. Prin. engr. inventions in field (Achievement awards 1989); author: Steam Turbine Overhaul and Repair Specifications. Bd. dirs. Cedar Lawn Assn. Recipient Outstanding Records in Engring., Gulf Oil Corp., Galveston, 1981. Mem. ASME (guest speaker convs.), Pacific Energy Assn. (guest speaker convs. 1990-92), Assn. of Former Students/Tex. A&M.

O'CONNOR, MICHAEL WAYNE, news editor; b. Midland, Tex., Aug. 25, 1952; s. Michael Francis and Mickey Frances (Kayler) O'C.; m. Sharon Kay Reagan, Aug. 16, 1975; children: Michelle, Aaron, Brandon. BA, Tex. Tech. U., 1974; MDiv, Asbury Theol. Sem., Wilmore, Ky., 1977; postgrad., Abilene Christian U., 1991-94. Ordained deacon, Meth. Ch., 1976, elder, 1978. Assoc. pastor First United Meth. Ch., Pampa, Tex., 1977-78; pastor Fritch (Tex.) United Meth. Ch., 1978-80, Lockney (Tex.) United Meth. Ch., 1980-84, Fairmont United Meth. Ch., Abilene, 1984-90, Wolfforth (Tex.) United Meth. Ch., 1990-91, Trent (Tex.) United Meth. Ch., 1991-93; night city editor/columnist Abilene Reporter-News, 1993—. Contbr. articles to profl. jours.; columnist Optimist, 1991-93. Named to Outstanding Young Men of Am., 1988. Mem. Soc. Profl. Journalists. Office: Abilene Reporter-News Box 30 100 Cypress Abilene TX 79604

O'CONNOR, RAYMOND VINCENT, JR., lawyer; b. N.Y.C., Feb. 27, 1951; s. Raymond Vincent and Rita Margaret (McCarthy) O'C.; m. Patricia Ellen Bliss, June 7, 1975 (div. 1980). AB in History, Georgetown U., 1973; JD, St. John's U., N.Y.C., 1976. Bar: N.Y. 1977, U.S. Ct. Mil. Appeals 1981. Labor relations specialist Def. Communications Agy., Washington, 1985—; dep. gen. counsel U.S. Army Audit Agy., Alexandria, Va., 1986—. Served to capt. JAGC, U.S. Army, 1977-83. Named one of Outstanding Young Men Am., 1985. Mem. ABA, Fed. Bar Assn. Roman Catholic. Home: 2500 N Van Dorn St Apt 1019 Alexandria VA 22302-1628 Office: US Army Audit Agy 3101 Park Center Dr Alexandria VA 22302-1500

O'CONNOR, TERENCE JAMES, roofing company executive; b. Nottingham, Eng., Mar. 25, 1948; came to U.S., 1987; s. Daniel Leslie and Dorothy Gertrude (James) O'C.; m. Catherine Claire O'Malley, Jan. 3, 1947; children: Emily Claire, Daniel Patrick. BS with honors, U. Newcastle-Upon-Tyne, Eng., 1969; MS, U. Waterloo, Ont., Can., 1971. Devel. chemist, lab. mgr. Iroquois Chems. Ltd., Cornwall, Ont., 1973-75; devel. chemist, mktg. mgr., market mgr.-scrim products Bayex Div., Bay Mills Ltd., St. Catharines, Ont., 1975—, bus. mgr. roofing div., 1987; mkt. devel. mgr. Baycomp Div., Bay Mills Ltd., Burlington, Ont., 1987; pres. Performance Bldg. Products, Inc., Kansas City, Kans., 1987-92; v.p. Performance Roof Systems, 1992-93; mgr. R & D Nord Bitumi U.S. Inc., Macon, Ga., 1993-96; mktg. mgr. Schuller Internat., Inc., Denver, 1996, Rubber Tech., Inc., Stockbridge, Ga., 1996—. Inventor roof fastener plate, 1992; patentee scrim/foil laminate, reinforcing composite. Recipient Citation, Jr. Achievement Niagara, 1985. Mem. ASTM, Nat. Roofing Contractors Assn., Midwest Roofing Contractors Assn., Western States Contractors Assn., Soc. Plastics Industry, Kansas City C. of C.

O'CONNOR, WILLIAM NOEL, pathologist; b. Cork, Ireland, Dec. 28, 1949; came to U.S., 1972, naturalized, 1981; s. William Francis and Marguerite (Constant) O'C. M.B.,B.Ch., Nat. U. Ireland, Cork, 1972. Lic. physician, Ireland, D.C., Ky. Rotating intern St. Mary's Hosp., Waterbury, Conn., 1972-73; resident in pathology Georgetown U. Hosp., Washington, 1973-75; instr. pathology Georgetown U., Washington, 1975-76; instr. pathology U. Ky., Lexington, 1976-77, asst. prof. dept. pathology, 1977-81, assoc. prof., 1982-94, prof., 1994—, assoc. prof. Grad. Ctr. for Toxicology, 1991—, dir. residency tng. program dept. pathology/lab. medicine, 1989—; mem. attending staff Georgetown U. Hosp., 1975-76; cons. dept. pathology VA Med. Ctr., Lexington, 1977—; mem. med. staff Univ. Hosp., Lexington, 1978—, St. Claire Med. Ctr., Morehead, Ky., 1978—; grant reviewer peer rev. com. Am. Heart Assn., Ky. affiliate, Louisville, 1980-92, rsch. com., 1993—; vis. prof. U. London, England, 1994—; lectr. in field; condr. workshops in field. Manuscript reviewer Histotechnology, 1978—, Stain Tech., 1978, Am. Jour. Cardiology, 1978—, Jour. Am. Coll. Cardiology, 1982—, Am. Jour. Pathology, 1993—; contbr. numerous articles and abstracts to profl. jours., chpts. to books. Grantee Am. Heart Assn., Ky. affiliate, 1978-79, 82-88, 90-91, BRSG, 1979-81, U. Ky. Dept. Pathology Acad. Enrichment Funds, 1980-82, Tobacco and Health Rsch. Inst. and NIH, 1985-88, NIH, 1988-91, 91—, Children Miracle Network Telethon Fund, 1991-92, 92-93. Fellow Am. Bd. Pathology, Coll. Am. Pathologists, Am. Coll. Cardiology; mem. AMA, Soc. for Cardiovascular Pathology, Ky. Med. Assn., Fayette County Med. Soc., Southeastern Pediatric Cardiology Soc., Ky. Soc. Pathologists, Irish and N.Am. Pathologists Soc., Irish and Am. Pediatric Soc., U.S.-Can. Acad. Pathology, Am. Soc. Clin. Pathologists, Am. Assn. Pathologists, Am. Heart Assn. (Ky. affiliate), Assn. Clin. Scientists, Children's Cancer Study Group, Brit. Heart Found., Alpha Omega Alpha. Democrat. Roman Catholic. Office: Univ of Kentucky Med Ctr Lab Medicine Dept Pathology 800 Rose St MS 141 Lexington KY 40536-0001

O'DAY, SHARON, marketing professional; b. Morristown, N.J., May 23, 1948; d. William Raymond and Jean Scott (Donaldson) O'D. Student, U. So. Calif., 1967-69, Fairfield (Conn.) U., 1977-79; MBA, U. Pa., 1981. Asst. mgr. pub. relations Carajás Iron Project Amazon, Rio de Janeiro, 1974-76; asst. to pres. Polycast Tech. Corp., Stamford, Conn., 1977-79; dir. mktg. Godiva Chocolatier S.A., Brussels, 1981-83; dir. internat. sales and mktg. Godiva Chocolatier Inc., N.Y.C., 1983; dir. mktg. Cognac Louis Royer, Jarnac, France, 1984-86; pres. Images de Marque, Inc., Miami, Fla., 1986—; cons. internat. mktg. to various European and L.Am. corps. on U.S. market entry investment, 1986—. Republican. Home: 7631 SW 53rd Ct Miami FL 33143-5826

ODELL, CHARLES ALEXANDER, health care facility administrator, consultant, substance abuse counselor; b. Charlotte, N.C., Jan. 15, 1955; s. Arthur Gould Jr. and Mary (Walker) O. Student, Rice U., 1973-75; BA in Human Svcs. magna cum laude, U. N.C., 1994. Cert. substance abuse counselor N.C. Substance Abuse Profl. Cert. Bd. Primary counselor Open House, Inc., Charlotte, 1984-85; ind. counselor Charlotte Treatment Ctr., 1985-86; ind. counselor, clin. supr., program dir. Rotary Adolescent Treatment Ctr., Gastonia, N.C., 1986-88; program dir. youth and young adult program Amethyst Charlotte Inc., 1988-91; substance abuse cons. Rehab. Ctr., Charlotte, 1991-94; employee assistance program profl. First Union Nat. Bank, Charlotte, 1993-94. Bd. dirs. 12 Step Svc., Inc., 1984-88, GOALS, Inc., 1991—. Mem. Nat. Adolescent Treatment Consortium (regional bd. dirs. 1989-91), Addiction Profls. of N.C., New Life Club Inc. (bd. dirs., treas. 1987-89). Democrat. Methodist. Home and Office: 301 Circle Ave Charlotte NC 28207-1403

ODELL, GEORGE HAMLEY, archaeology educator; b. Mpls., Apr. 17, 1942; s. Allan Gilbert and Grace (Evans) O.; m. Frieda Martina Vereecken, May 12, 1951. BA, Yale U., 1964, MA in Teaching, 1965; PhD, Harvard U., 1977. Tchr. Internat. Coll., Beirut, 1965-66; with Inst. Montana, Zug, Switzerland, 1966-68; tchr. Winchester High Sch., Winchester, Mass., 1968-70; vis. prof. U. B.C., Vancouver, Can., 1977-78, Brown U., Providence, 1978-79; dir. lithic analysis lab. Ctr. Am. Archeology, Kampsville, Ill, 1979-84; asst. prof. U. Tulsa, 1984-90, assoc. prof., 1990—; bd. dirs. Okla. Archaeological Survey, Norman; speaker for various orgns. Co-editor: Alternative Approaches to Lithic Analysis, 1989; editor: Stone Tools: Theoretical Insights into Human Prehistory, 1996; author: Stone Tools and Mobility in the Illinois Valley: from Hunter-Gatherer Camps to Agricultural Villages, 1996; editor Bull. Okla. Anthrop. Soc., 1986-95, Lithic Technology, 1993—; contbr. articles to profl. jours. Pres. bd. dirs. Canterbury Ctr. for United Ministry, U. Tulsa, 1989-90. Recipient Preservation award Okla. Hist. Preservation Office, 1992. Mem. Soc. Profl. Archaeologists, Am. Anthrop. Soc., Soc. for Am. Archaeology, Tulsa Archaeol. Soc. (pres. 1993-95), Sociètè Prèhistorique Française, Plains Anthrop. Soc., Ark. Archaeol. Soc., Southeastern Archaeol. Conf., Kans. Archaeol. Soc. Democrat. Unitarian. Office: U Tulsa Dept Anthropology Tulsa OK 74104

O'DELL, JOAN ELIZABETH, lawyer, business executive; b. East Dubuque, Ill., May 3, 1932; d. Peter Emerson and Olive (Bonnet) O'D.; children: Dominique R., Nicole L. BA cum laude, U. Miami, 1956, JD, 1958. Bar: Fla. 1958, U.S. Supreme Ct. 1972, D.C. 1974, Ill. 1978, Va. 1987; cert. mediator, 1994; lic. real estate broker Ill., Va., DC. Trial atty. U.S. SEC, Washington, 1959-60; asst. state atty. Office State Atty., Miami, Fla., 1960-64; asst. county atty. Dade County Atty.'s Office, Miami, 1964-70; county atty. Palm Beach County Atty.'s Office, West Palm Beach, Fla., 1970-71; regional gen. counsel. U.S. EPA, Region IV, Atlanta, 1971-73, assoc. gen. counsel, Washington, 1973-77; sr. counsel Nalco Chem. Co., Oakbrook, Ill., 1977-78; v.p., gen. counsel Angel Mining, Tenn. and Washington, 1979-96; pres. South West Land Investments, Miami, Fla., 1979-88; v.p., gen. counsel Events U.S.A., Washington, 1990—. Bd. dirs. Tucson Women's Found., 1982-84, U. Ariz. Bus. and Profl. Women's Club, Tucson, 1981-85; bd. dirs. LWV Tucson, 1981-85, pres., 1984-85; bd. dirs. LWV Ariz., 1984-85, chmn. nat. security study; bd. dirs. LWV, Palm Beach County, Fla., 1990-92; mem. Exec. Women's Council, Tucson, 1982-85. Mem. Fed. Bar Assn., Fla. Bar Assn., D.C. Bar Assn., Va. State Bar Assn. Avocations: camping, hiking, skiing.

ODEN, WILLIAM BRYANT, bishop, educator; b. McAllen, Tex., Aug. 3, 1935; s. Charles Alva and Evea (Bryant) O.; m. Marilyn Brown, July 12, 1957; children: Danna Lee Oden Bowen, William Dirk, Valerie Lyn, Charles Bryant. BA, Okla. State U., 1958; MDiv, Harvard U., 1961, postgrad., 1974; ThD, Boston U., 1964; DD (hon.), Oklahoma City U., 1980; LHD (hon.), Centenary Coll., 1990. Ordained to ministry Meth. Ch., 1961. Pastor Aldersgate United Meth. Ch., Oklahoma City, 1963-69, St. Stephen's United Meth. Ch., Norman, Okla., 1969-76, Crown Heights United Meth. Ch., Oklahoma City, 1976-83; prof. Phillips Grad. Sem., Enid, 1976-88; pastor 1st United Meth. Ch., Enid, 1983-88; bishop United Meth. Ch., Baton Rouge, 1988-96; bishop for the Dallas area United Meth. Ch., 1996—; assigned to La. area; pres. SCJ Coll. of Bishops, 1989-90; del. Gen. Conf., 1976, 80, 84, 88; chmn. Okla. Del. to Gen. and Jurisdictional Confs., 1984, 88; Jackson lectr. Perkins Sch. Theology, So. Meth. U., 1975, Wilson lectr. SCJ Bishop's Week, 1989; co-chair World Meth.-Anglican Dialogue, 1991—; bd. dirs. Wesley Works Project. Author: Oklahoma Methodism in the Twentieth Century, 1968, Liturgy as Life Journey, 1976, Wordeed: Evangelism in Biblical and Wesleyan Perspective, 1978; contbr.: Send Me: The Iteneracy in Crisis, 1991. Trustee Oklahoma City U., 1980-88, Southwestern U., Winfield, Kans., 1983-88, Centenary Coll., 1988—, Dillard U., 1988—. Mem. Am. Acad. Homiletics. Home: PO Box 8127 Dallas TX 75205-0127

ODLE, WESLEY PAUL, JR., museum director, pastor; b. Ina, Ill., Nov. 20, 1933; s. Wesley Paul Sr. and Edith Fern (Ligon) Odle; m. Carmaleta Juan Stubblefield; 1 child, Wesley Paul III. BS, MA, George Peabody Coll., Nashville, 1970, George Peabody Coll., Nashville, 1970. Lic. real estate broker, Ky. Ptnr. Slade Constrn. Co., Cedar Rapids, Iowa, 1959-60; asst. buyer Nat. Tea Co., Davenport, Iowa, 1960-67; pastor, founder Christ Gospel Ch., Nashville, 1967-70; owner Wes Odle Realty, Cave City, Ky., 1970—; pastor, pres. Panama City (Fla.) Christian Ctr., Inc., 1992—; founder, pres. Assessmbly of Christ, Inc., 1982—; pastor Christian Ctr. Ministries, Panama City, 1992—; pres. Lighthouse Worship Ctr. Inc., Youngstown, Fla., 1996—; adminstr. Christ Gospel Chs., Internat. Inc., Jeffersonville, Ind., 1970-76, Bible Coll., Jeffersonville, 1970-72; ptnr. Guntown Mountain Amusement Park, Cave City, 1979-80; owner Crystal Onyx Cave Park, Inc., 1980-84, Mammoth Cave Wax Mus., Cave City, 1984-92. Prin. River Falls Christian Acad., Jeffersonville, 1976; bd. dirs. Full Gospel Businessmen's Fellowship, Panama City Beach, Fla., 1986—; pres., founder Assemblies of Christ Internat., Inc., 1977—; mem. adv. bd. Advanced Home Health Care, Inc., Panama City, 1992—. Recipient Merit of Achievement Highland Neighborhood Soc., 1973. Mem. Ky. Real Estate Commn., Cave City C. of C., Tenn. Edn. Assn. (cert.), Assemblies of Christ, Internat. Inc. Republican. Home: 1929 W 24th St Panama City FL 32405-2221 Office: Assemblies of Christ Internat Inc 213 E 13th St Panama City FL 32401-2805

ODOM, FLOYD CLARK, surgeon; b. Cisco, Tex., 1946. MD, U. Tex., San Antonio, 1972. Diplomate Am. Bd. Colon & Rectal Surgery, Am. Bd. Surgery. Intern Bexar County Hosp., San Antonio, 1972-73, resident in gen. surgery, 1973-77; fellow in colon & rectal surgery Baylor Med. Ctr., Dallas, 1977-78; with Presbyn. Hosp., Dallas. Fellow ACS, Am. Soc. Colon and Rectal Surgeons. Office: 8220 Walnut Hill Ln Dallas TX 75231-4406

ODOM, JAMES VERNON, research psychologist; b. Laurinburg, N.C., Aug. 26, 1948; s. James Calvin Odom and Edna Elizabeth (Norton) Nichols; m. Monique J.J. Leys, July 21, 1990. BA in Psychology, Davidson Coll., 1970; PhD in Psychology, U. N.C., 1978. Rsch. assoc. Case Western Res. U., Dept. Psychology, Cleve., 1978-79; rsch. fellow U. Calif. Berkeley, Sch. Optometry, Berkeley, 1979-80; rsch. asst. prof. U. Fla., Dept. Ophthalmology, Gainesville, 1980-82; asst. prof. W.Va. U., Dept. Ophthalmology, Morgantown, 1982-88, assoc. prof., 1988—; adv. bd. Courts, Health Scis. and the Law, 1989-91. Mem. editorial bd. Documenta Ophthalmologica, 1988-92; contbr. 100 articles to profl. jours. Mem. Amnesty Internat., ACLU. NIH postdoctoral fellow, 1977, Netherlands Ophthalmic Rsch. Inst. rsch. fellow, 1989; grantee NEI, 1978, Knight's Templar, 1980, W.Va. Faculty Senate, 1984, 88, 92, USAF, 1994. Mem. AAAS, APA, IEEE/EMBS, Internat. Soc. for Clin. Electrophysiology of Vision (sec. for the Ams. 1990—), Am. Acad. Ophthalmology, Assn. for Rsch. in Vision and Ophthalmology, Optical Soc. Am., Soc. for Neurosci., Sigma Xi (chpt. pres. 1991). Democrat. Baptist. Office: W Va U Health Scis Ctr Dept Ophthalmology Morgantown WV 26506

O'DONNELL, EDWARD JOSEPH, bishop, former editor; b. St. Louis, July 4, 1931; s. Edward Joseph and Ruth Mary (Carr) O'D. Student, Cardinal Glennon Coll., 1949-53; postgrad., Kenrick Sem., 1953-57. Ordained priest Roman Cath. Ch., 1957, consecrated bishop, 1984; asso. pastor in 5 St. Louis parishes, 1957-77; pastor St. Peter's Ch., Kirkwood, Mo., 1977-81; assoc. dir. Archdiocesan Commn. on Human Rights, 1962-70; dir. Archdiocesan Radio-TV Office, 1966-68, Archdiocesan Vocation Council, 1965; editor St. Louis Rev., 1968-81; vicar-gen. Archdiocese of St. Louis, 1981-84, aux. bishop, 1984-94; bishop Diocese of Lafayette, Lafayette, LA, 1994—; bd. dirs. Nat. Cath. Conf. for Interracial Justice, 1980-85, NAACP, 1964-66, Urban League St. Louis, 1962-68; chmn. Interfaith Clergy Coun. Greater St. Louis, 1963-67. Named to Golden Dozen Internat. Soc. Weekly Newspaper Editors, 1970, 77. Mem. Cath. Press Assn., Nat. Assn. TV Arts and Scis. Office: PO Box 3387 Lafayette LA 70502-3387

O'DONNELL, JOSEPH MICHAEL, electronics executive; b. Rochester, N.Y., May 9, 1946; s. Robert Lawrance O'Donnell and Josephine Marie (Schickler) Vosper; m. Barbara Lee Hasselmann, Feb. 27, 1977; children: Shannon, Lindsey, Colleen. BS, U. Tenn., 1968, MBA, 1970. Sales mgr. telecommunications ITT, Chgo., 1973-75; dir. mktg. communication ITT, Hartford, Conn., 1975-77; dir. mktg. Gen. Instrument Corp., N.Y.C., 1977-81; gen. mgr. Gen. Instrument Corp., Post Falls, Idaho, 1981-84; v.p. Conrac Corp., Stamford, Conn., 1984-87; pres. OD & S Ventures, Stamford, 1987-88; v.p. Handy & Harman, N.Y.C., 1988-89; CEO, GO/DAN Industries, New Haven, 1990-92; pres., CEO Savin Corp., Stamford, Conn., 1993-94; pres., CEO, Computer Products Inc., Boca Raton, Fla., 1994—. Home: 3681 Carlton Pl Boca Raton FL 33496 Office: Computer Products Inc 7900 Glades Rd Boca Raton FL 33434-4167

O'DONNELL, LAWRENCE, III, lawyer; b. Houston, Dec. 14, 1957; s. Lawrence Jr. and Annell (Haggart) O'D.; m. Dare Boswell, May 22, 1981; children: Linley, Lawrence IV. BS in Archtl. Engring., U. Tex., 1980; JD cum laude, U. Houston, 1983. Bar: Tex. 1983. Assoc. Wood, Campbell, Moody & Gibbs, Houston, 1983-84; ptnr. Campbell & Riggs, Houston, 1984-91; dep. gen. counsel and corp. sec. Baker Hughes Inc., Houston, 1991-94; v.p., gen. counsel Baker Hughes Oilfield Ops., Houston, 1993-95; v.p., gen. counsel, corp. sec. Baker Hughes Inc., Houston, 1995—. Trustee Houston Police Activities League. Mem. ABA, Tex. State Bar (corp. law com. of bus. law), Houston Bar Assn., am. Corp. counsel Assn., Am. Soc. Corp. Sec., Tex. Bus. Law Found., Houston Bar Assn., Am. Soc. Civil Engrs., Order of Barons, Phi Delta Phi. Office: Baker Hughes Inc 3900 Essex Ln Ste 1200 Houston TX 77027-5112

O'DONNELL, MARY MURPHY, nurse epidemiologist, consultant; b. Lincoln, Ill., Feb. 21, 1918; d. Thomas Edward and Frances Ward (Hayes) Murphy; m. Maurice A. O'Donnell, Jan. 29, 1942. Diploma St. John's Sch. Nursing, Springfield, Ill., 1939. Registered nurse, Ill., Fla. Asst. to ear, nose and throat specialist, 1939-42; nurse U.S. Govt. Hosp., 1942-43; asst. to gen. practitioner, Springfield, 1943-55; staff nurse City Health Dept., Springfield, 1955-65; dir. tng. and edn. Springfield and Sangamon County Civil Def. Agy., 1965-66; exec., cons. in charge med. self-help Ill. Dept. Pub. Health, 1966-74; nurse epidemiologist St. Joseph Hosp., Port Charlotte, Fla., 1975-91, part-time epidemiologist, 1992-93, retired, 1993, cons. epidemiologist, 1993—. mem. Aids Task Force Charlotte County Dept. Pub. Health, Fla., pres. Charlotte County epidemiology group, 1991; instr. AIDS Program, 1987-93. V.p. S. Central area Ill. Women's Civil Def. Council; mem. Ill. Civil Def. Council; chmn. civil def. activities ARC; v.p., mem. health services adv. com. U.S. Civil Defense Council; ofcl. vol. rep. Am. Social Health Assn. Recipient Spl. award State Dept. of Am. Legion Aux., 1954, Cert. of Honor, hon. life membership U.S. Air Force Air Def. Team, 1959, Silver Wing Bracelet, Ground Observer Corps, 1959, Cert. of Honor, Mayor of City of Springfield, 1966, Pfizer award of merit U.S. Civil Def. Council, 1969, Presidential citation U.S. Civil Def. Council, 1972. Mem. Assn. for Practitioners in Infection Control, SW Regional Infection Control. Republican. Roman Catholic. Avocations: boating; swimming; clog dancing; golf; horses. Home: 819 Napoli Ln Punta Gorda FL 33950-6525

O'DONNELL, TIMOTHY SHAWN, graphic artist; b. Rockford, Ill., May 25, 1960; s. Gary Lee and Melba Susan (Manning) O'D. AA in Comms., Rock Valley C.C., 1987. Photo tech. crime lab. Winnebago County Sheriff's Dept., Rockford, 1987; editor Habitat World Habitat for Humanity, Americus, Ga., 1987-90; graphic artist, video editor, 1996—. Assoc. producer (short film) Underestimating Lisa, 1993; editor Valley Forge/Ecletic, Rockford, 1986-87; supr. short film Ladies Night, 1996; editor (short film) Window Pains, 1996, Can Do, 1996; sound mix (short film) Sheep, 1996. Active Habitat for Humanity Internat., Americus, Ga., 1987-90, Photographers and Friends United Against AIDS, N.Y.C., 1992—, Straight But Not Narrow, Atlanta, 1993—. Recipient 3M Data Preservation award, 1993, Photographer's Forum award, 1985-86, 92, Gwinnet Coun. Arts award, 1991. Home and Office: 41 Peachtree Ave NE Apt 12 Atlanta GA 30305-3035

ODUM, JEFFERY NEAL, mechanical engineer; b. Bristol, Tenn., Sept. 11, 1956; s. Herschel S. and Minnie Lee (Carrier) O.; m. Stacy Elaine Ferrell, mar. 18, 1989; 1 child, Charles Wesley Ferrell. BSME, Tenn. Technol. U., 1978; MS in Engring., U. Tenn., 1983. Sr. project engr. TVA, Knoxville,

1978-81; sr. constrn. engr. Stone & Webster Engring. Corp., Boston, 1981-84; div. engr. E.I. DuPont de Nemours & Co., Aiken, S.C., 1984-89; engring. mgr. Flour Daniel, Greenville, S.C., 1989-92; mgr. of projects, Pharmaceutical Bus. Group CRS Sirrine Engrs., Inc., Raleigh, N.C., 1992-93; sr. project mgr. Gilbane Bldg. Co., Raleigh, 1993-95; dir. engring. Gilbane Process Group, Raleigh, 1995—. Author: Sterile Product Facility Design and Project Management, 1996; contbr. articles to profl. jours. Vol. Spl. Olympics. Recipient DuPont Engring. Achievement award 1986, 88, 89, Nat. Svc. Alumni award Univ. Tenn. Mem. Parenteral Drug Assn., Soc. Mfg. Engrs., Internat. Soc. Pharm. Engrs. (bd. dirs., pres. Carolina chpt. 1996-97), U. Tenn. Nat. Alumni Assn. (pres. Augusta chpt. 1987-89), Order Engr., Kappa Sigma. Republican. Presbyterian. Office: Gilbane Bldg Co 400 Westchase Blv Ste 400 Raleigh NC 27607

ODUOLA, KAREN ANN, geriatrics nurse; b. Anna, Ill., Mar. 5, 1947; d. Edward Everett and Kathern Marie (Powell) Newton; m. Muyideen M. Oduola, May 11, 1988; children: Jonathon C. Newton, Shane L. Laminack, Christopher A. Oduola. Prac. Nurse Cert., Shawnee C.C., Ullin, Ill., 1978; BSN, OUHSC, Oklahoma City, 1993. Charge nurse, LPN Jonesboro (Ill.) Nursing Ctr., 1978-87, Carbondale (Ill.) Manor, 1987-88; flr. nurse, LPN Marion County Nursing Ctr., Indpls., 1988-89; charge nurse, LPN Cedar Crest Manor, Lawton, Okla., 1990-92; support svcs. coord., quality control coord., primary care coord. Okla. Christian Home, Edmond, 1992—; mem. CCRC accreditation com., Okla. Christian Home, 1994, quality assurance com., 1994-95, infection control com., 1994-95, pharmacy com., 1994-95. Mem. Sigma Theta Tau. Lutheran. Home: 1006 Swan Lake Ct Edmond OK 73003 Office: Oklahoma Christian Home 906 N Blvd Edmond OK 73034

OEHLER, RICHARD DALE, lawyer; b. Iowa City, Dec. 9, 1925; s. Harold Lawrence Oehler and Bernito Babb; m. Rosemary Heineman, July 11, 1952, (div.); m. Maria Luisa Holguin-Zea, June 11, 1962; children: Harold D., Richard L. BA in Med. Scis., U. Calif., Berkeley, 1951; JD, Loyola U., L.A., 1961. Bar: Calif. 1962, Fla. 1968. Sales rep. Abbott Labs., Pasadena, Calif., 1951-63; with claims dept. Allstate Ins., Tampa, 1963-70; pvt. practice Tampa, 1970—; instr. Dale Carnegie Courses West Fla. Inst., Tampa, Scott Hitchcock & Assocs., Tampa, 1969—. Pres. U. South Fla. Parents Assn., Tampa, 1986-87. Mem. Fla. Bar Assn., Hillsborough County Bar Assn., Acad. of Fla. Trial Lawyers, Assn. of Trial Lawyers of Am., Masons (32d degree), Shriners, Phi Beta Kappa. Republican. Presbyterian. Office: 200 N Pierce St Tampa FL 33602-5020

OEHLERT, WILLIAM HERBERT, JR., cardiologist, administrator, educator; b. Murphysboro, Ill., Sept. 11, 1942; s. William Herbert Sr. and Geneva Mae (Roberts) O.; m. L. Keith Brown, Mar. 14, 1976; children: Emily Jane, Amanda Elizabeth. BA, So. Ill. U., 1967; MD, Washington U., St. Louis, 1967. Diplomate Nat. Bd. Med. Examiners, Am. Bd. Internal Medicine, Am. Bd. Cardiovascular Disease, North Am. Soc. Pacing and Electrophysiology. Intern Union Meml. Hosp., Balt., 1967-68, resident, 1968-69; resident U. Iowa, Iowa City, 1969-70, cardiology fellow, 1970-72; asst. prof. medicine, dir. coronary care units U. Okla. Health Sci. Ctr., Oklahoma City, 1972-74, asst. clin. prof. medicine, 1974-82, assoc. clin. prof. medicine, 1982-88, clin. prof. medicine, 1988—; chmn. dept. cardiology Bapt. Med. Ctr., 1992-95; pvt. practice Oklahoma City, 1974—; med. dir. cardiovasc. svcs. Integris Bapt. Med. Ctr., 1993—; pres. Cardiovasc. Clinic, Oklahoma City, 1987-91, chmn. exec. com., 1987-91; pres., med. dir. Cardiovasc. Imaging Svcs. Corp., Oklahoma City, 1987-92; v.p. Plaza Med. Group, 1992-93; CEO W.H. Oehlert, MD, P.C., 1993—. Author: Arrhythmias, 1973, Cardiovascular Drugs, 1976; contbr. articles to profl. jours. Fellow Am. Heart Assn. (nat. program com. 1979-82, pres. Okla. affiliate 1985-86, bd. dirs. 1974-88, ACLS nat. affiliate faculty 1987-90), Am. Coll. Cardiology; mem. AMA, ACP, Nat. Assn. Residents and Interns, Am. Soc. Internal Medicine, Am. Coll. Physician Execs., Okla. County Med. Assn. (chmn. quality of care com. 1990-91), Okla. State Med. Assn., Okla. City Clin. Soc., Okla. Cardiac Soc. (pres. 1978-79), Osler Soc., Soc. Nuclear Medicine, Wilderness Med. Soc., Stewart Wolf Soc., Phi Eta Sigma, Phi Kappa Phi. Home and Office: 3017 Rock Ridge Pl Oklahoma City OK 73120-5713

OELBERG, DAVID GEORGE, neonatologist, educator, researcher; b. Waukon, Iowa, May 26, 1952; s. George Robert and Elizabeth Abigail (Kepler) O.; m. Debra Penuel, Aug. 4, 1979; 1 child, Benjamin George. BS with highest honors, Coll. William and Mary, 1974; MD, U. Md., 1978. Diplomate Am. Bd. Pediatrics, Am. Bd. Neonatal-Perinatal Medicine. Intern U. Tex. Med. Br., Galveston, 1978-79, resident, 1979-81, pediatric house staff, 1978-81; postdoctoral fellow in neonatal medicine U. Tex. Med. Sch., Houston, 1981-84, asst. prof. dept. pediatrics, 1984-90, assoc. prof., 1990-93; assoc. prof. dept. pediatrics, head perinatal rsch. Ctr. Pediatric Rsch., Ea. Va. Med. Sch., 1993—; mem. hosp. staff Hermann Hosp., Houston, 1983-93; physician Crippled Children's Services Program, Houston, 1985-93; mem. hosp. staff Lyndon B. Johnson County Hosp., 1990-93; visiting prof. Wyeth-Ayerst Labs., 1992; med. dir. Office Rsch. Children's Hosp. King's Daughter, Sentara Norfolk Gen. Hosp., 1993—. Mem. editorial adv. bd. jour. Neonatal Intensive Care; contbr. articles to profl. jours; ad hoc reviewer profl. jours.; patentee in field. Physician cons. Parents of Victims of Sudden Infant Death Syndrome, Houston, 1984. Recipient award in analytical chemistry Am. Chem. Soc., 1974, NIH Clin. Investigator award Nat. Heart, Lung and Blood Inst., 1989-94; rsch. grantee Am. Lung Assn., 1989-90, NIH, 1989-94. Fellow Am. Acad. Pediatrics, N.Y. Acad. Scis.; mem. AMA, NAS, Soc. Exptl. Biology and Medicine, So. Soc. Pediatric Rsch. (councilor), Soc. Pediatric Rsch. Achievements include a method for optical measurement of bilirubin in tissue. Avocations: sailing, gardening. Home: 1624 W Little Neck Rd Virginia Beach VA 23452-4720 Office: Ea Va Med Sch Ctr Pediatric Rsch 855 W Brambleton Ave Norfolk VA 23510-1005

OELRICH, PAUL RAYMOND, airline executive; b. Kalamazoo, Mich., Aug. 12, 1950; s. Carl Milton and Margaret Hazel (Malmborg) O.; m. Susan Selsted, Feb. 18, 1989. Student, Mt. San Antonio Jr. Coll., Walnut, Calif., 1968-70, San Jose State U., 1970-73; BS in Bus. Mgmt., Calif. Poly. U., Pomona, 1976. Lic. pvt. pilot, comml. and instrument pilot. Ops. agt. Am. Airlines, Ontario, Calif., 1974-78, acting supr. passenger svc., 1978-79; supr. ramp svcs. Am. Airlines, San Francisco, 1979-80, group supr., 1980-81; account exec. cargo Am. Airlines, L.A., 1981-83; gen. mgr. Air Cal, John Wayne, Orange County (Calif.) Airport, 1983-87; mgr. svcs. Am. Airlines, John Wayne/Orange County Airport, 1987-88; mgr. quality Am. Airlines Inc., Dallas, 1988-92; assoc. Exec. Devel. Systems, Inc., Dallas, 1991-92, v.p. mktg., 1992—; pres. Pro Enterprises, Dallas, 1994—; dir. No. Calif. Pilots Conf., 1968; speaker Internat. Customer Svc. Conf., Chgo., 1989. Mem. task force Am. Cancer Assn. Great Am. Smout Out, Orange County, 1985, 86. Mem. ASTD, Am. Assn. Quality Control, Am. Mgmt. Assn., Nat. Speakers Assn., Internat. Customer Svc. Assn., Aircraft Owners & Pilots Assn., Mercedes Benz Club N.Am., Brookhaven Country Club, Met. Soc. Clubs-Dallas. Republican. Office: Exec Devel Sys Inc 3818 Vinecrest Dr Dallas TX 75229-3931 also: Pro Enterprises 3479 Courtyard Cir Dallas TX 75234-3777

OESTERREICHER, JAMES E., department stores executive; b. 1941. B.S., Mich. State U., 1964. With J. C. Penney Co. Inc., 1964—; pres. Western Region J. C. Penney Co. Inc., 1987-88, exec. v.p., 1988-94; vice chm., CEO J.C. Penny Co. Inc., 1994—. Office: J C Penney Co Inc 6501 Legacy Dr Plano TX 75024-3612*

OFFUTT, ELIZABETH RHODES, education educator; b. Phoenix, Nov. 22, 1959; d. Marvin Ethmer and Lucienne M. (Ricaut) Rhodes; m. Charles Raymond Offutt, June 24, 1989. BA in Edn., Ariz. State U., 1981, MEd, 1983, PhD, 1990. Cert. tchr., Ariz. Music tchr. Isaac Sch. Dist., Phoenix, 1981-84, elem. tchr., 1984-86, 88-91; founder sch. for homeless children The Schoolhouse, Phoenix, 1987-88; asst. prof. Samford U., Homewood, Ala., 1991-96, assoc. prof., 1996—, dir. Ala. Gov.'s Sch., 1992—; presenter in field. Author: Teaching Science in a Multicultural World, 1996, (with Charles Offutt) Internet Without Fear: Practical Tips and Activities, 1996; contbr. articles to profl. publs. Advisor Kappa Delta Epsilon; mem. partnership Discovery 2000, SRI, Birmingham City Schs. and Samford U.; musician St. Francis Xavier Ch., Mountain Brook, Ala., 1991—. Mem. Ala. Acad. Sci., Assn. for Childhood Edn. Internat. (mem. minority devel. com.), Nat. Assn. Edn. Young Children, Valley of Sun Assn. Edn. of Young Children, Phi Delta Kappa. Democrat. Roman Catholic. Home: 4904 Great Oak Cir Birmingham AL 35223 Office: Samford U Sch Edn Homewood AL 35229

O'FLARITY, JAMES P., lawyer; b. Yazoo City, Miss., Oct. 15, 1923; s. James P. and Jessie E. (Marshall) O'F.; m. Betty Reichman, Apr. 9, 1955; children: Michael J., Deborah J. O'Flarity James, Steven M., Pamela G. BS, Millsaps Coll., 1950; postgrad., Miss. Coll. Sch. Law, 1948, 53-54; J.D., U. Fla., 1965. Bar: Miss. 1954, Fla. 1966, U.S. Dist. Ct. (so. dist.) Miss. 1954, U.S. Ct. Mil. Appeals 1957, U.S. Dist. Ct. (so. and mid. dists.) Fla. 1966, U.S. Dist. Ct. (no. dist.) Fla. 1967, U.S. Ct. Appeals (5th cir.) 1957, U.S. Ct. Appeals (11th cir.) 1981, U.S. Supreme Ct. 1957; state ct. cert. arbitrator. Assoc. law firm Cone, Owen, Wagner, Nugent & Johnson, West Palm Beach, Fla., 1966-69; sole practice law West Palm Beach, 1969—; mem. Supreme Ct. Matrimonial Law Commn. Fla., 1982-85; ABA observer family ct. proc. Nat. Jud. Coll., 1983; mem. U. Fla. Law Ctr. Coun., 1972—, mem. legal edn. com., 1973, chmn. membership and fin. com., 1977-78; lectr. on marital and family law; leader del. for legal exchange on family law to Ministry of Justice, Peoples Republic of China, 1984. Contbr. articles to profl. publs. Mem. U. Fla. Pres.'s Council; mem. U.S Rep. Senatorial Inner Circle, 1988—; col. La. Gov.'s Staff, 1982—. With USAAF, 1942-45. Decorated Air medal with five oak leaf clusters. Fellow Royal Geog. Soc. (life), Am. Bar Found. (life), Roscoe Pound-Am. Trial Lawyers Found. (life), Am. Acad. Matrimonial Lawyers (nat. pres. 1985-86, nat. bd. of govs. 1977-88, founding pres. Fla. chpt. 1976-80, bd. mgrs. Fla chpt. 1976—, hon. permanent pres. emeritus 1982—), Internat. Acad. Matrimonial Lawyers (convenor, founder), Trusler Soc., Fla. Bar Found. (life, exec. dir. screening com. 1976, chmn. projects com. 1976-77, asst. sec. 1973-79, dir. 1977-81); mem. Internat. Soc. Family Law, Internat. Bar Assn. (assoc.), Am. Law Inst. (consultative group law of family dissolution 1990—, Nat. Conf. Bar Pres'. 1991), ABA (chmn. coms. 1973-75, 78-81, 82-83, editor Family Law Newsletter 1975-77, mem. council family law sect. 1976-85, vice-chmn. sect. 1981-82, chmn. sect. 1983-84, mem. conf. sect. chairmen 1982-85, mem. adv. bd. jour. 1978-80), Assn. Trial Lawyers Am. (Fla. State committeeman 1973-75, 1st chmn. family law sect. 1971-72, 72-73), Fla. Supreme Ct. Hist. Soc., Fla. Council Bar Assn. Presidents (life mem.), U. Fla. Law Ctr. Assn. (life), Acad Fla. Trial Lawyers (dir. 1974-77, coll. diplomates 1977), Fla. Bar (exec. council 1973-84, sec.-treas. family law sect. 1973-74, chmn. family law sect. 1974-75, 75-76, guest editor spl. issue jour. 1978, chmn. jour. and news editorial bd. 1978-79, mem. bd. legal specialization and edn. 1982-91, 92-95, jud. nominating procedures com. 1992-93, Family Law Rules com. 1992-95), Palm Beach County Bar Assn. (cir. ct. civil adv. com. 1981, mem. cir. ct. juvenile domestic rels. adv. com. 1971-80, 81-83, adv. com. chmn. 1974-78), Solicitor's Family Law Assn. (Eng.), Gov.'s Club of Palm Beach (founder, life, gov's. coun.), Explorers Club (life, vice chmn. South Fla. chpt. 1990-95), Circumnavigators Club, Travelers Century Club (life), Phi Alpha Delta (life), Sigma Delta Kappa. Home: 908 Country Club Dr North Palm Beach FL 33408 Office: PO Box 14816 North Palm Beach FL 33408

OGANDO, ROGER MARLON, software engineer; b. Santo Domingo, Dominican Republic, Dec. 11, 1961; came to U.S., 1983; s. Roger B. and Flor F. (Nunez) O.; m. Olga Enid Rivera-Cruz, Mar. 14, 1992. BS in Indsl. Engring., Tech. Inst. Santo Domingo, 1981; MS in Computer Sci., U. Dayton, 1985; cert. mfg. systems engring., U. Fla., 1989, PhD in Computer Scis., 1991. Systems analyst Dept. Informatica Secretaria de Estado de Obras Publicas y Comm., Santo Domingo, 1982-83; rsch. asst. computer scis. dept. U. Dayton, Ohio, 1985; grad. teaching asst. computer and info. scis. dept. U. Fla., Gainesville, 1985-86, 90; grad. rsch. asst. Software Engring. Rsch. Ctr., U. Fla., Gainesville, 1987-91; prof. system engring. Tech. Inst. Santo Domingo Sch. Engring., 1992-93, dir. system engring. program, 1992-93; nat. cons., coord. informatics and computerization UN Devel. Programme, Banco Ctrl. Dominican Republic, Santo Domingo, 1992-93; systems analyst Info Tech, Inc., Gainesville, 1994—; mem. steering com. Interam. Congress Ednl. Informatics, Santo Domingo, 1992. Fulbright fellow; Latin Am. Scholarship Program of Am. Univs. fellow U. Dayton, 1983-85; OAS fellow U. Fla., 1987-88. Mem. Assn. Computing Machinery.

OGBONNAYA, CHUKS ALFRED, entomologist, agronomist, environmentalist; b. Akoli-Imenyi, Abia, Nigeria, June 30, 1953; came to U.S., 1975; s. Alfred Agbaeze and Christy (Agubuche) O.; m. Joyce Elizabeth Belgrave, Mar. 30, 1985; children: Latoya, Oluchi, Kelechi. BS, U. Nebr., 1979, PhD, 1985; MS, N.W. Mo. State U., 1981. Cert. profl. crop scientist, profl. agronomist. Lab. asst. U. Nebr., Lincoln, 1976-78, rsch. asst., 1978-80, 82-85, postdoctoral fellow, 1985; asst. prof., postdoctoral fellow Mountain Empire Coll., Big Stone Gap, Va., 1985-90, prof., 1990—, coord., prof. environ. sci. dept., 1986—; prof., 1995; Disting. scholar-in-residence Pa. State U., summer 1990, vis. prof., 1990. Soccer coach Parks and Recreation, Big Stone Gap, 1989; mem. Va. Water Resources Statewide Adv. Bd., govt.-mined land reclamation adv. bd. Recipient Times Teaching award, 1990, Chancellor's Profs. award Va., 1990; Fulbright scholar, 1993-94. Mem. Am. Soc. Agronomy, Crop Sci. Soc. Am., Entomol. Soc., Va. Acad. Sci., Va. Mining Assn. (Outstanding Contbn. to Comty. award 1993), Internat. Platform Assn., Phi Beta Kappa. Methodist. Home: 520 Bays View Rd Kingsport TN 37660-3202 Office: Mountain Empire Coll PO Box 700 Big Stone Gap VA 24219-0700

OGDEN, JOANNE, real estate executive; b. Cumming, Ga., Apr. 9, 1941; d. Crafton Kemp Sr. and Mary Evelyn (Willis) Brooks; m. William Rush Williams, Jan. 3, 1961 (div. 1966); 1 child, Paul Rush Williams; m. Cecil Leavern Ogden, Sr.; stepchildren: Cecil Laverne Jr., Michael Vann. Grad. high sch., Cumming. Prin. Ogden & Ogden, Milledgeville, Ga., 1966—. Candidate Baldwin County Commnr., Milledgeville, 1984. Mem. Nat. Geog. Soc., Better World Soc., Cousteau Soc., Audubon Soc., Smithsonian Inst., U.S. C. of C., 700 Club (Virginia Beach). Republican. Methodist. Home: 402 Allen Memorial Dr SW Milledgeville GA 31061-4608 Office: Ogden & Ogden 2600 Irwinton Rd Milledgeville GA 31061-9762

OGDEN, LOUANN MARIE, dietitian, consultant; b. Enid, Okla., Dec. 16, 1952; d. Raymond Michael Schiltz and Donna Mae Stuever; m. Wendell Edwin Ogden, Jan. 5, 1979; 1 child, Gregory Jacob Jeremiah. BS in Home Econs., Okla. State U., 1974, MS, 1977. Registered dietitian; lic. dietitian, Tex. Dietetic intern Ind. U. Med. Ctr., Indpls., 1974; therapeutic dietitian-clin. svcs. and trayline ops. Bapt. Med. Ctr. Okla., Oklahoma City, 1975-76; grad. teaching asst. lower and upper level food preparation Okla. State U., Stillwater, 1976-77, teaching assoc. lower and upper level food preparation, 1977; chief clin. dietitian adminstrv. and clin. coordination Borgess Hosp., Kalamazoo, 1978; dietary cons. nutrition program Iowa Commn. on Aging, Des Moines, 1979-80; asst. food svc. dir., adminstrv. dietitian Timberlawn Psych. Hosp., Dallas, 1980-92; rep. group one purchasing program, mem. student tng. program Zale Lipshy U. Hosp., Dallas, 1992-93, food svc. cons., 1993—. Mem. Am. Dietetic Assn., Am. Soc. Hosp. Food Svc. Adminstrn. (nat. nominating com. 1990-91, Disting. Health Care Food Svc. Adminstr. 1992, North ctrl. Tex. chpt.: corr. sec. 1985-86, comms. chair 1986-87, rec. sec. 1987-89, pres.-elect 1989-90, pres. 1990-91, nominating com. chair, health care food svc. week com. chair 1991-92, Outstanding Mem. award 1992), Tex. Dietetic Assn., Dallas Dietetic Assn. Democrat. Roman Catholic. Home and Office: 3302 Oxford Dr Rowlett TX 75088-5936

O'GEARY, DENNIS TRAYLOR, contracting and engineering company executive; b. Waverly, Va., Feb. 20, 1925; s. King William and Mary Virginia (Traylor) O'G.; m. Alice Stuart Baum, Aug. 3, 1947; children: Dennis Patrick, Mary Alice O'Geary Eisenbarth, Elizabeth Christina O'Geary Bernstorf. Surveing degree Tri-State U., 1943; BS in Civil Engring., Ill. Inst. of Tech., 1947. Resident engring. trainee Va. Hwy. Dept., Richmond, 1947-50; civil engring. supt. Wiley Jackson Co., Roanoke, Va., 1950-57; engr., asst. estimator, project mgr., v.p. and asst. to area mgr. S.J. Groves & Sons Co., Mpls. and Springfield, Ill., 1957-77, v.p., area mgr., 1978-82, v.p., asst. div. mgr., div. estimator, Atlanta, 1982-84; pres. Peabody S.W., Inc., Houston, 1984-85; v.p. Houston ops. J.D. Abrams, Inc., Austin, Tex., 1985—. Served with USNR, 1943-46. Mem. ASCE (life), Am. Concrete Inst., Soc. Am. Mil. Engrs., Nat. Maritime Hist. Soc., Cousteau Soc. (Friends of the Calypso). Methodist. Home: 15402 Cresent Oaks Ct Houston TX 77068-2079 Office: 111 Congress Ave Austin TX 78701-4043

OGILVIE, MARGARET PRUETT, educational counselor; b. McKinney, Tex., Jan. 8, 1922; d. William Walter and Ida Mae (Houk) Pruett; B.A., Baylor U., 1943; M.Ed., Hardin Simmons U., 1968; m. Frederick Henry Ogilvie, May 13, 1943; children: Ida Margaret, James William. Tchr. pub. and pvt. schs., Tex., Calif., Alaska, W.Ger., 1944, 53-65; guidance counselor Dentsville High Sch., Columbia, S.C., 1968-69, Northwest H.S., Clarksville, Tenn., 1970-72; personal and marital counselor, Fairfield Glade, Tenn., 1972—; co-owner F & M Gems & Jewelry. Treas. Officers' Wives Club, Ft. Irwin, Calif.; chmn. vols. ARC, Ft. Irwin, 1965; pres. Women's Golf Assn., Ft. Irwin, 1965-66; v.p. Ch. Women United, Crossville, Tenn., 1972-74; bd. dirs. Cumberland County Mental Health Assn., 1975-87; mem. legis. com. and pub. affairs com. Tenn. Mental Health Assn., 1976-81, mem. exec. bd., 1977-86; vol. Christian Svc. Corps, 1985—, Home Mission Bd. of So. Bapt. Conv., 1985-87; mem. Middle Tenn. com. Internat. Women's Yr., 1975; bd. dirs. Battered Women, Inc., Crossville, 1984-85. Mem. Am. Personnel and Guidance Assn., Nat. Ret. Tchrs. Assn., Bus. and Profl. Women's Club (chmn. 1973-75), DAR (parliamentarian Crab Orchard chpt. 1981), Pi Gamma Mu. Democrat. Baptist (choir dir., organist 1972—). Clubs: Fairfield Glade Women's (parliamentarian 1974-77), Fairfield Glade Ladies Club (chmn. scholarship com. 1989—), Fairfield Glade Women's Golf Assn. (pres. 1973, 2d v.p. 1986), Fairfield Glade Sq. Dance; Order Eastern Star (Amanda chpt. IV). Home: 509 Blackbird Dr Fayetteville NC 28314-5184

OGLESBY, BEVERLY CLAYTON, kindergarten educator; b. Jacksonville, Fla., Mar. 11, 1950; d. Willie Edward Clayton and Venetta (Preston) Singleton; m. Eugene Oglesby, June 23, 1974; children: Venetta, Erin. BS, Fla. Meml. Coll., 1971; MEd, U. North Fla., 1982. Cert. tchr., Fla. 3d grade tchr. S. Bryan Jennings Elem. Sch., Orange Park, Fla., 1971-75, kindergarten tchr., 1975-77, 83-90, 1993-94, 2d grade tchr., 1977-82, 1st grade tchr., 1982-83, devel. 1st grade tchr., 1990-92, devel. 2d grade tchr., 1992-93, devel. kindergarten tchr., 1994—; kindergarten team leader S. Bryan Jennings Elem. Sch. 1975-90; mem. instrnl. material coun. Clay County Schs., Green Cove Springs, Fla., 1989, devel. dist. com. 1990-92; presenter Clay County Whole Lang. Clay County Reading Coun., Orange Park, 1988-89, So. Early Childhood Assn. and Early Childhood Assn. of Fla. Confs. SACS com. mem. Forest Hill Elem. Sch., Jacksonville, 1973; SECA rep. State of Fla.; mem. PTA bd. Oceanway Jr. High Sch., Jacksonville, 1980. Named S. Bryan Jenning Elem. Sch. Tchr. of Yr., 1989-90. Mem. Early Childhood Assn. Fla. (past pres. 1973-91, pres. 1992-93, SECA rep. 1995—), So. Early Childhood Assn. (chair membership com. 1993-95, rep. to Early Childhood Assn. Fla., 1995—), Nat. Assn. for Edn. Young Children, Assn. Childhood Edn. Internat., North Fla. Assn. Young Children (pres. 1986-87), Phi Delta Kappa. Home: 215 Corona Dr Orange Park FL 32073

OGLESBY, THEODORE NATHANIEL, editor; b. Pine Grove, Ga., June 14, 1932; s. Theodore Nathaniel and Ruth (Moncrief) O.; m. Betty N. Mitchell, July 14, 1932; children: Reginald, Lydia. AB in Journalism, U. Ga., 1953, postgrad., 1956-59. News dir. Sta. WBGR, Jesup, Ga., 1953-54, Sta. WDUN, Gainesville, Ga., 1956-59; editor, pub. The Tribune, Gainesville, 1959-68; dir. U.S. Census, Ga. 9th Dist., Gainesville, 1970; with spl. assignments dept. The Times, Gainesville, 1970-77, assoc. editor, 1977-86, editorial page editor, 1986-95; chmn. SBA Adv. Coun., Atlanta, 1981-86; pres. WAVE Enterprises, Inc., Gainesville; radio talk show host Sta. WDVN, Gainesville; owner, dir. Ted's Travelers. Chmn. 9th dist. Rep. Party, Gainesville, 1970-72; bd. dirs. Boy's Club, Gainesville, 1959-62; chmn. com. on govtl. efficiency, 1977-78. With USAF, 1954-56, 68-70, col. USAFR, 1953-81. Mem. Gainesville Kiwanis Club (bd. dirs.), Res. Officers Assn., Blue Key Soc. Baptist. Office: The Times PO Box 663 Gainesville GA 30503

O'GRADY, ALBERT THOMAS, electrical engineer; b. Enid, Okla., July 2, 1945; s. Albert Joseph and Betty Lou (Honeywell) O'G.; m. Patricia L. Lunday, Dec. 27, 1969; children: John A., Chaseley S., Katherine E. BSEE, Okla. State U., 1972. Registered profl. engr., Okla. Elect. engr. Benham-Blair & Assoc., Oklahoma City, 1972-74; from staff engr. to sr. project engr. Conoco, Inc., Ponca City, Okla., 1974-84, project mgr., 1987-92; project engr. Conoco, Inc., Lake Charles, La., 1979-80; sr. project engr. Conoco, Inc., Humberside, U.K., 1984-87; supr., control engring. Caltex Petroleum Corp., Dallas, 1992-93; sr. instrument, elect. engr. Caltex Svcs. Corp., Muscat, Oman, 1993-94; supr. control engring. Caltex Svcs. Corp., Dallas, 1994—. Treas. Ponca Sailfish Swim Team, Ponca City, 1981-82, pres., 1991-92. With U.S. Army, 1966-69, Germany. Mem. Instrument Soc. Am. (sr. mem., treas. 1983-84, sec. 1989-90, v.p. 1990-91, sect. pres. 1991-92). Roman Catholic. Home: 6600 Carriage Dr Colleyville TX 76034 Office: Caltex Svcs Corp PO Box 619500 Dallas TX 75261-9500

OH, MYUNG-HI KIM, pediatrician, educator; b. Seoul, Republic of Korea, Aug. 4, 1938; d. Duck P. and Sang O. (Han) Kim; m. Shin J. Oh, July 30, 1966; children: David Younghee, Michael Moonhee. Pre-med. student, Yonsei U. Coll. Sci./Engring., Seoul, 1957-59; MD, Yonsei U. Coll. Medicine, Seoul, 1963. Fellow U. Louisville (Ky.), 1965-67, U. Minn., Mpls., 1968; instr., asst. prof. Pediatrics Meharry Med. Sch., Nashville, 1969-70; asst. prof. Pediatrics U. Ala., Birmingham, 1985-90, assoc. prof. Pediatrics, 1990—; med. dir. Jeff County Youth Detention Ctr., 1993—; dir. adolescent STD project, 1990—; cons. Jefferson County Dept. Health, Birmingham, 1987-90. Contbr. articles to profl. jours. Mem. adv. com. Young Mother's Club, Birmingham, 1989—, Perinatal Adv. Com., 1990-95, The Birmingham Compact, 1992-96; mem. aids and child welfare svc. com. Jefferson County Dept. Human Resources, 1990-91; mem. Jefferson County Juv. Justice Coord. Coun. Facilitating Com., 1995—. Fellow Am. Acad. Pediatrics; mem. AMA, APHA, Soc. for Adolescent Medicine, so. Soc. of Pediatric Rsch. Republican. Presbyterian. Office: Dept Pediatrics U Ala 1630 6th Ave S TCHA-CHOB Birmingham AL 35233-1711

O'HARA, FREDERICK M., JR., technical communications consultant, information specialist; b. Medford, Mass., Dec. 9, 1942; s. Frederick Michael and Mary Barbara (Gallagher) O'H.; m. Linda Maier, July 17, 1965; children: Laura, Michael, Eoin, Keiran. BS in Chemistry, Boston Coll., 1964; MS in Tech. Writing, Rensselaer Poly. Inst., 1967; PhD in Mass Comm., U. Ill., 1973. Tech. writer, editor, info. specialist, reference libr. Oak Ridge (Tenn.) Nat. Lab., 1964-70; mem. staff Inst. Comm. Rsch., U. Ill., Urbana, 1970-71; dir. Rensselaer Newman Found. Chapel and Cultural Ctr., Troy, N.Y., 1971-72; pvt. cons. in tech. comm. Oak Ridge, Tenn., 1972—; judge Internat. Tech. Publs. Competition; writer, presenter in field. Author: (with R.A. Sicignano) Handbook of U.S. Economic and Financial Indicators, 1986 (ALA Outstanding Bus. Book, 1986, Choice Mag. Outstanding Reference Book 1986); author chpts. to books; editor: Net Energy Analysis, 1989; editor CDIAC Comm., 1990—; prodn. editor ARM Outreach, 1992—; contbr. articles to profl. jours. Active Tenn. Adv. Coun. on Librs., Nashville, 1973-77, Oak Ridge (Tenn.) Beer Bd., 1981-83. NDEA fellow U. Ill., 1970-71; recipient Outstanding Libr. Rockroth award East Tenn. Libr. Assn., 1981, Best Socio-Econ. Presentation at WATTec '87 award, 1987, Merit award Internat. Tech. Pub. Competition, 1988, Achievement award, 1989, Francis E. McKinney Best of Show award, East Tenn. Tech. Pub. Competition, 1989. Fellow Soc. Tech. Comm. (internat. bd. dirs. 1988-91, mgr. nominating com. 1992-94, dep. mgr. profl. interest com. adv. com. 1992-94, former pres., former 1st v.p., former program chmn. East Tenn. chpt., mem. cons. and ind. contracting profl. interest com., mgr. environ., safety and health comm. profl. interest com.); mem. AAAS (mem. info., computing and comm. sect.), Am. Chem. Soc. (mem. divsn. chem. info.). Office: PO Box 4273 Oak Ridge TN 37831-4273

O'HARA, MARY ANN, pediatric ophthalmologists; b. N.Y.C., Jan. 14, 1953; d. John Kevin and Delia Agnes (Rafferty) O'H.; m. William Charles Lloyd, May 30, 1981; children: William, Maureen, Margaret Mary. BS, Fordham U., 1974; MD, U.S. Uniformed Health Scis. U., 1981. Diplomate Am. Bd. Ophthalmology. Staff ophthalmologist William Beaumont Army Med. Ctr., El Paso, Tex., 1985-86; asst. chief Martin Army Ctr. Hosp., Columbus, Ga., 1986-88; fellow Wills Eye Hosp., Phila., 1988-89; staff ophthalmologist Brooke Army Med. Ctr., San Antonio, 1989—; instr. dept. ophthalmology Emory U., Atlanta, 1987—; assoc. prof. U. Tex. Health Scis. Ctr., San Antonio, 1989—; asst. prof. Uniformed Svcs. U. Health Scis., Bethesda, Md., 1989—; asst. chief ophthalmology Brooke Army Med. Ctr., 1992—; commr. Joint Commn. on Allied Health Personnel in Ophthalmology, St. Paul, 1993—. V.p. St. Anthony's Catholic Sch. PTA, San Antonio, 1995—. Fellow Am. Acad. Ophthalmologists, Am. Coll.

Surgeons; mem. AMA (physician's recognition award 1994), Soc. Mil. Ophthalmology, Women in Ophthalmology, Uniformed Svcs. U. Health Scis. Alumni Assn., San Antonio Soc. Ophthalmology. Roman Catholic. Office: Brooke Army Med Ctr Ophthalmology Svc Fort Sam Houston TX 78234

O'HARA, ROBERT JAMES, evolutionary biologist; b. Arlington, Mass., Nov. 21, 1959. BA, U. Mass., 1981; PhD, Harvard U., 1989. Tutor Dudley House, Harvard Coll., Cambridge, 1983-89; fellow Smithsonian Instn., Washington, 1990-91, Ctr. for Critical Inquiry, U. N.C., Greensboro, 1992—; NSF fellow and adj. curator U. Wis., Madison, 1991-92; disting. vis. prof. Transylvania U., Lexington, Ky., 1992; adj. prof. biology U. N.C., Greensboro, 1993—, sr. tutor Cornelia Strong Coll., 1994—. Mem. Soc. of Systematic Biologists, Soc. for History of Natural History, Sigma Xi, Phi Beta Kappa. Office: U NC 100 Foust Bldg Greensboro NC 27412

O'HARE, CHRISTINE MARIE, critical care nurse; b. Chgo., Mar. 16, 1942; d. Albert Anthony and Dorothy Ann (Perry) Uebbing; m. Thomas Patrick O'Hare, Oct. 14, 1967; children: Brian, Carolyn, Michelle. Diploma in nursing, St. Elizabeth's Hosp., Chgo., 1963. CCRN. Staff nurse St. Elizabeth's Hosp., 1963-65, head nurse, 1965, instr. sch. nursing, 1966-68; tchr. Wheaton (Ill.)-Warrenville High Sch. Dist. 200, 1976-78; staff nurse Community Hosp., Geneva, Ill., 1978-85, Fairfax Hosp., Falls Church, Va., 1985—. Mem. AACN. Home: 4891 Oakcrest Dr Fairfax VA 22030-4568

OHL, RONALD EDWARD, academic administrator; b. Warren, Ohio, May 30, 1936; s. Howard Edward and Ella May (Van Auker) O.; m. Joan Ann Elizabeth Eschenbach, June 29, 1974. BA, Amherst Coll., 1958; MA, Columbia U., 1961; M in Divinity, Union Theol. Sem., N.Y.C., 1964; PhD, U. Pa., 1980. Ordained minister Congregationalist Ch., 1964. Counselor to grad. students Columbia U., N.Y.C., 1960-62; asst. dean students, asst. prof. history Elmhurst (Ill.) Coll., 1964-67; spl. asst. to dean of men Temple U., Phila., 1967-68; assoc. dean coll., dean student affairs, instr. in edn. Colo. Coll., Colorado Springs, 1968-74; with Fairleigh Dickinson U., Rutherford, N.J., 1975-83, successively acting v.p. for external relations, asst. to pres., acting chmn. and cons. relations div. univ. resources and pub. affairs; pres. Salem (W.Va.)-Teikyo U., 1983—, trustee, 1989—, also bd. dirs.; bd. dirs. One Valley Bank, Clarksburg. Contbr. articles to profl. jours. Bd. dirs. Sta. WNPB-TV, 1992—. Recipient Edward Poole Lay Traveling fellowship award Amherst Coll., 1958-59, Young Am. Artists' Dirs. award U.S. Embassy, Rome, 1959-60; Rockefeller Bros. Fund fellow, 1961-62; named Research Asst., U. Pa., 1967-68. Mem. W.Va. Assn. Ind. Colls. (pres. 1985-89), North Ctrl. Assn. Colls. and Schs. (cons.-evaluator 1987—), W.Va. Found. for Ind. Colls. (acad. vice chmn. 1992-94), Clarksburg C. of C. (bd. dirs. 1985-91, 93-96), Univ. Club, W.Va. Christopher Quincentenary Commn., Rotary. Home: 63 Terrace Ave Salem WV 26426-1124

OHNSMAN, DAVID ROBERT, insurance consultant; b. Pitts., July 8, 1943; s. Harry Leroy and Catherine Anna (Radcliffe) O.; m. Marilyn Alice Jameson, June 7, 1963; children: Laura Ohnsman, Kenneth R., Douglas J. BA, Grove City (Pa.) Coll., 1965; MBA, Jacksonville (Fla.) U., 1986. Underwriter Aetna Life & Casualty Co., Tampa, Fla., 1965-67; mktg. mgr. F.B. Hall, Inc., Jacksonville, 1968-70; sr. underwriter Home Ins. Co., Jacksonville, 1971-79, Aetna Ins. Co., Jacksonville, 1979-80; underwriting mgr. Mission Ins. Co., Jacksonville, 1980-84; cons. E.W. Siver & Assocs., Inc., St. Petersburg, Fla., 1984-85; v.p. Occidental/Peninsular Ins. Co., Jacksonville, 1985-87; pres. Peninsular Risk Mgmt., Inc., Jacksonville, 1987-90, Underwriting Svcs., Inc., Jacksonville, 1990—; instr. acctg. and mgmt. Jones Coll., Jacksonville, 1970-71, instr. ins. various local industry assns., Jacksonville, 1975-83; cert. instr. Nat. Safety Coun., 1988—; developed loss control and risk mgmt. programs for various clients. Mem. Colony Cove Civic Assn., Jacksonville, 1991—. Recipient Wall St. Jour. award Grove City Coll., 1965, Cert. of Appreciation, Ins. Women Jacksonville, 1980. Mem. Chartered Property and Casualty Underwriters Assn., Fla. Trucking Assn., Profl. Ins. Assn. (various offices), Ind. Ins. Agts. Jacksonville Fla. Assn. Ins. Agts., Univ. Country Club, Pi Gamma Mu. Republican. Presbyterian. Home: 3871 Colony Cove Trl Jacksonville FL 32277-2241 Office: PO Box 11452 Jacksonville FL 32239-1452

OHSFELDT, ROBERT LEE, health economist, educator; b. Houston, July 30, 1956; s. Ronald A. and Mildred A. (McInnis) O.; m. Peggy J. Moon, May 18, 1985; children: Erika K., Michael E. BS, U. Houston, 1977, PhD, 1983. Rsch. assoc. Southwest Ctr. for Urban Rsch., Houston, 1979-81; asst. prof. Ball State U., Muncie, Ind., 1982-86; rsch. economist Am. Med. Assn., Chgo., 1983-84; asst. prof. Ariz. State U., Tempe, 1986-89; assoc. prof. Sch. of Pub. Health U. Ala., Birmingham, 1989-96, scientist Injury Control Rsch. Ctr., 1989—, scholar Lister Hill Ctr. Health Policy, 1990—, prof. Sch. Pub. Health, 1996—; vis. asst. prof. La. Tech. U., Ruston, 1981-82; mem. rev. com. grant proposals Dept. Vet. Affairs, Agy. Health Care Policy and Rsch., 1992—; jour reviewer Am. Econ. Rev., Rev. Econs. and Statistics, Jour. Health Econs., JAMA, So. Econ. Jour., among others. Author numerous chpts. for books; co-editor: Socioeconomic Characteristics of Medical Practice, 1984; contbr. articles to profl. jours. Named Robert Wood Johnson Found. Faculty Fellow in Health Care Fin., Johns Hopkins U., Balt., 1987-88. Mem. Am. Econ. Assn., So. Econ. Assn., Am. Statis. Assn., Assn. Health Svcs. Rsch. Office: U Ala at Birmingham Sch Pub Health 1825 University Blvd Birmingham AL 35233-1913

OKA, KAZUHIRO, cell biologist, biochemist. BS in Chemistry, Nagoya Inst. Tech., 1977; MS in Biochemistry, Tokyo Inst. Tech., 1979, PhD, 1982. Rsch. fellow Inst. Comprehensive Med. Sci., Fujita-Gakuen Sch. Medicine, Japan, 1982; postdoctoral fellow Roche Inst. Molecular Biology, N.J., 1982-84; rsch. asst. prof. dept. medicine Mt. Sinai Sch. Medicine, N.Y.C., 1985-87; dir. Lab. Molecular Genetics Cholesterol Rsch. Ctr., Medlantic Rsch. Found., Washington, 1987-90; rsch. asst. prof. dept. cell biology Baylor Coll. Medicine, Houston, 1990-92, rsch. asst. prof. dept. cell biology and medicine, 1992-95; asst. prof. dept. cell biology and medicine, 1995—; adj. asst. prof. Fujita-Gakuen Sch. Medicine, 1985-88; adj. assoc. prof. Fujita Health U. Sch. Medicine, Japan, 1987—. Contbr. numerous articles to profl. jours. Mem. AAAS, Am. Soc. for Pharmacology and Exptl. Therapeutics, Am. Heart Assn. (arteriosclerosis com.), N.Y. Acad. Scis., Japanese Biochem. Soc. Office: Baylor Coll Medicine One Baylor Plaza Houston TX 77030

OKADA, ROBERT DEAN, cardiologist; b. Seattle, Sept. 18, 1947; m. Carolyn Okada. BA summa cum laude, U. Wash., 1969; MD, U. Pa., 1973. Intern U. Ariz. Health Scis. Ctr., Tucson, 1973-74, resident in internal medicine, 1974-76, clin. fellow in cardiology, 1976-78; clin. and rsch. fellow in medicine Mass. Gen. Hosp., Boston, 1978-79; fellow in medicine Harvard Med. Sch., Boston, 1978-79, instr., 1979-81, asst. prof., 1981-85; prof. U. Okla. Med. Sch., Tulsa, 1985—; staff cardiologist St. Francis Hosp., Tulsa, 1985—; asst. in medicine Mass. Gen. Hosp., 1982-86, cons. in nuclear medicine, 1981—, sr. staff cardiac catheterization lab., 1979-86, clin. asst. in medicine, 1979-82; established investigator Am. Heart Assn., 1982-87; clin. prof. Tulsa Med. Coll., 1985—. Contbr. articles to profl. jours. Recipient Am. Legion award U. Wash., 1966, Neisei Vets. award, 1966. Fellow Am. Coll. Cardiology, ACP, Am. Coll. Chest Physicians, N.Y. Acad. Scis.; mem. Am. Fedn. for Clin. Rsch., Paul Dudley White Soc., Soc. Nuclear Medicine, Am. Heart Assn. Coun. Clin. Cardiology, Soc. Magnetic Resonance in Medicine, AAAS, Mass. Med. Soc., Soc. for Magnetic Resonance Imaging, Suffolk County Med. Soc., Tulsa County Med. Soc., Okla. State Med. Soc., AMA, Am. Soc. Internal Medicine, AAUP, Phi Beta Kappa, Alpha Xi Sigma. Office: Cardiology of Tulsa Inc 6585 S Yale Ave Ste 800 Tulsa OK 74136-8321

O'KEEFE, JOSEPH KIRK, systems engineer; b. Paxton, Ill., Sept. 30, 1933; s. Richard Joseph and Ruth Louise (Shinn) O'K.; m. Mary Helen Waters, Oct. 4, 1958; children: Richard Kirk, Catherine Elizabeth. B Aero. Engring., Rensselaer Poly. Inst., 1955, MS in Mgmt., 1963. Aerodynamist N.Am. Aviation, Inglewood, Calif., 1955, McDonnell Aircraft Corp., St. Louis, 1957-59; systems analyst Lockheed Missiles & Space Co., Inc., Sunnyvale, Calif., 1959-61, program mgr., 1963-90; test engr. AVCO Rsch. & Advanced Devel., Wilmington, Mass., 1961-62; dir. ARGOSystems-Tex., Corinth, 1990-95; cons. sys. engring. and mgmt. Nacogdoches, Tex., 1995—; lectr. applied math. U. Santa Clara, Calif., 1963-65. Contbr. articles to profl. jours. Capt. USAF, 1955-57. Mem. Found. for N.Am. Wild Sheep, Safari Club Internat. Republican. Episcopalian. Home: 511 Fairway Dr Nacogdoches TX 75964-7807

O'KEEFE, RUTH RENEÉ, accountant, educator; b. Durham, N.C., Feb. 18, 1949; m. Daniel E. O'Keefe, 1971 (dec.); children: Patrick J., Christopher M. BBA, Stetson U., 1971; MBA, Old Dominion U., 1973; JD cum laude, SUNY, Buffalo, 1979. Bar: Fla.; CPA, Fla. Instr. acctg. Old Dominion U., Norfolk, Va., 1973; staff acct. Price Waterhouse, CPAs, Buffalo, N.Y., 1973-74; asst. prof., then adj. faculty acctg. Canisius Coll., Buffalo, 1974-79; instr. rsch. and writing Law Sch. SUNY, Buffalo, 1978; assoc. Moot, Sprague, Marcy, Landy, Fernbach and Smythe, Buffalo, 1979-81; pvt. practice law Jacksonville, Fla., 1981—; prof. acctg. Jacksonville U., 1982—; instr. Convisor-Duffy CPA rev. course, Jacksonville, 1990-93; mentor McNair Program, Jacksonville, 1991-94. Mem. Nat. Alliance for Mentally Ill, Fla. Alliance for Mentally Ill; v.p. Jacksonville Alliance for Mentally Ill, 1995—; pres. N.E. Fla. Hosp. Friends, 1996—. Recipient Nat. Alliance for Mentally Ill Wolf award, 1994; named Phi Beta Lambda Outstanding Bus. Prof. in N.E. Fla., Fla. C.C. at Jacksonville, 1995. Mem. AICPA, AAUP, Fla. Bar Assn., Fla. Inst. CPAs (bd. dirs. Jacksonville chpt., named Outstanding Acctg. Educator in Fla. 1995), Fla. Assn. Acctg. Educators, Rotary, Omicron Delta Kappa. Office: Jacksonville U 2800 University Blvd N Jacksonville FL 32211-3321

O'KEEFFE, HUGH WILLIAMS, oil industry executive; b. Ft. Smith, Ark., May 23, 1905; s. Patrick Francis and Elizabeth Ann (Williams) O'K.; m. Lucylle Davis Durkee, Mar. 27, 1949 (dec. Dec. 1965); m. Josephine Helen Loughmiller, June 10, 1969 (dec. May 1980); m. Grace H. Freeny, Sept. 3, 1983 (dec. Jan. 1990). BS with honors, U. Ark., 1928. Jr. geologist Phillips Petroleum of Okla., Tex., Kans. Colo. and, Okla., 1928-33; party chief on surface Phillips Petroleum of Okla., Shawnee, 1933, dist. geologist, 1934-37; div. geologist Phillips Petroleum of Okla., Bartlesville, 1937-40, asst. chief geologist, 1940-45; exploration mgr. Davon Oil Co., Oklahoma City, 1946-52; co-owner Davon Oil & Gas, Oklahoma City, 1952-55; pvt. practice cons. Oklahoma City, 1955-58; co-owner Wyant & O'Keeffe, Oklahoma City, 1930—. Mem. Am. Assn. Petroleum Geologists, Oklahome City Geol. Soc., Soc. Ind. Petroleum and Earth Scientists, Shawnee Geol. Soc. (v.p. 1936-37), Tulsa Geol. Soc., Petroleum Club of Oklahoma City (charter), Oklahoma City Golf and Country Club. Republican. Roman Catholic. Home: 6511 Avondale Dr Oklahoma City OK 73116-6405 Office: Wyant & O'Keeffe 222 NE 50th St Oklahoma City OK 73105-1812

O'KELLEY, WILLIAM CLARK, federal judge; b. Atlanta, Jan. 2, 1930; s. Ezra Clark and Theo (Johnson) O'K.; m. Ernestine Allen, Mar. 28, 1953; children: Virginia Leigh O'Kelley Wood, William Clark Jr. AB, Emory U., 1951, LLB, 1953. Bar: Ga. 1952. Pvt. practice Atlanta, 1957-59; asst. U.S. atty. No. Dist. Ga., 1959-61; partner law firm O'Kelley, Hopkins & Van Gerpen, Atlanta, 1961-70; U.S. dist. judge No. Dist. Ga., Atlanta, 1970—, chief judge, 1988-94; mem. com. on adminstrn. of criminal law Jud. Conf. U.S., 1979-82, exec. com., 1983-84, subcom. on jury trials in complex criminal cases, 1981-82, dist. judge rep. 11th cir., 1981-84, mem. adv. com. of fed. rules of criminal procedure, 1984-87; bd. dirs. Fed. Jud. Ctr., 1987-91, adv. com. history program, 1989-91, com. on orientation of newly appointed dist. judges, 1985-88; mem. Com. Jud. Resources, 1989-94; mem. Jud. Coun. 11th Cir., 1990-96, exec. com., 1990-96; mem. Fgn. Intelligence Surveillance Ct., 1980-87; corp. sec., dir. Gwinnett Bank & Trust Co., Norcross, Ga., 1967-70. Mem. exec. com., gen. counsel Ga. Republican Com., 1968-70; mem. fin. com. Northwest Ga. Girl Scout Coun., 1958-70; trustee Emory U., 1991—. Served as 1st lt. USAF, 1953-57; capt. USAFR. Mem. Ga. State Bar, Atlanta Bar Assn., Dist. Judges Assn. 5th Cir. (sec.-treas. 1976-77, v.p. 1977-78, pres. 1978-80), Lawyers Club Atlanta, Kiwanis (past pres.), Atlanta Athletic Club, Sigma Chi, Phi Delta Phi, Omicron Delta Kappa. Baptist. Home: 550 Ridgecrest Dr Norcross GA 30071-2158 Office: US Dist Ct 1942 US Courthouse 75 Spring St SW Atlanta GA 30303-3361

OKES, DUKE WAYNE, quality engineer, management consultant; b. Beckley, W.Va., Feb. 25, 1949; s. Karl J. and Virginia K. (Rawn) O.; m. Nancy L. Elliott, Feb. 2, 1974. AE in Indsl. Tech. and Electronics Tech., Tri Cities State Tech. Inst., 1976; BS in Bus. Adminstrn., Tusculum Coll., 1986. Quality technician TRW, Rogersville, Tenn., 1976-80, quality engr., 1980-84, mem. corp. electronics tech. transfer team, Cleve., 1983-85; project coord., 1984-85; owner, mgr., cons. APLOMET, Blountville, Tenn., 1985—. Served with U.S. Army, 1970-72. Mem. Am. Soc. for Quality Control (cert., dir. 1994—), Inst. of Mgmt. Cons. (cert.), Am. Soc. Tng. and Devel. Avocations: reading, photography, financial planning and investment. Office: APLOMET PO Box 471 Blountville TN 37617-0471

O'KON, JAMES ALEXANDER, engineering company executive; b. N.Y.C., Aug. 8, 1937; s. A.C. and Rita (McGaugh) O'K.; m. Carol Ann Smith, 1988; children: Sean Fitzgerald, Katherine Shannon. BCE, Ga. Inst. Tech., 1961; MCE, NYU, 1970. Registered profl. engr., Tenn., N.Y., Mo., Conn., Ill., Fla., Tex., Miss., Calif., Ga., Mass., La. N.J., S.C., Ala., Ky., Va., N.C., Kans., Colo. Hwy. engr. Ga. Hwy. Dept., Atlanta, 1960-62; structural engr. Robert & Co., Atlanta, 1962-64; project coord. So. Design, Spartanburg, S.C., 1964-67; project engr. Crawford-Russell, Stamford, Conn., 1967-68, Farkas Barron Ptnr., N.Y.C., 1968-69; v.p. Lev Zetlin Assocs., N.Y.C., Atlanta, 1969-77; pres. O'Kon and Co. (formerly Lev Zetlin Assocs.), Atlanta, 1977—; bd. dirs. Superior Demolition Co, Atlanta, Friends of Mexico; chmn. bd. Five Star Travel, Inc. Author: Floating Factory to Produce Precast Concrete Components, 1973, Energy Conservation Noise and Vibration Control in Construction of Offshore Power Plants, 1975, Guidelines for Failure Investigation, 1989, Methodology For The Life Prediction of Buildings, 1989. Author: Floating Factory to Produce Precast Concrete Components, 1973, Energy Conservation Noise and Vibration Control in Construction of Offshore Power Plants, 1975, Guidelines for Failure Investigation, 1989, Methodology for the Life Prediction of Buildings, 1989, Methods to Reduce Errors Due to Dependency on Computers, 1994, Bridge From the Past, 1995. Recipient Grand award Builder's Mag., 1983, Archtl. Excellence award Am. Inst. Steel Constructors, 1984, Engring. Excellence award Am. Consulting Engrs. Coun. Ga., 1983, 88, Grand Award for Engring. Excellence, 1988, 89, 91, 92, 93. Fellow Internat. Biog. Assn., World Lit. Acad.; mem. ASCE (chmn., com. to develop quidelines for failure investigation, vice-chmn. tech. coun. forensic engring.), Am. Inst. Archaeology, Ga. Tech. Bldg. Rsch. Ctr., Bldg. Futures Coun., Soc. Am. Mil. Engrs., Smithsonian Inst., Atlanta Preservation Soc. (mem. Preservation Profls. Group), Am. Arbitration Assn. (panel of arbitrators), Friends of Mex. (v.p.). Democrat. Roman Catholic. Home: 26104 Plantation Dr NE Atlanta GA 30324-2959 Office: O'Kon & Co Inc 1349 W Peachtree St # 1200 Atlanta GA 30309

OKPALA, COLUMBA CHRISTOPHER, art educator; b. Jos, Plateau, Nigeria, Apr. 29, 1962; s. Nathaniel and Cecilia (Onukah) O. BA (hon.), U. Nigeria, Nsukka, 1989; MS in Art Edn., Fla. Internat. U., 1994. Cert. tchr., Fla. Art tchr. Miami (Fla.) Carol City Sr. H.S., 1994—; visual comm. cons., printmaker, engraving artist Choice Graphics and Advt., Miami, 1994—; printing supr. Emman Ent. Inc., Miami, 1991-93. Prints commd. by many pvt. and pub. orgns. Mem. Bakehouse Art Ctr. (assoc., award monoprint exhbn. 1993). Home: 320 NW 139th St Miami FL 33168

OLAH, SUSAN MAY, secondary school educator, respiratory therapist; b. Washington, June 14, 1948; d. Clifford Daniel Jr. and Naoma Loretta (Smith) M.; m. Frank Donald Olah, Apr. 4, 1970; David Frank, Christine Marie. BS in Biology cum laude, Radford U., 1969; grad. respiratory therapy, Ctrl. Va. C.C., Lynchburg, 1981; MEd, Lynchburg Coll., 1993. Lab. specialist Va. Poly. Inst. and State U., 1970-72; sci. and math. tchr. Bertie Acad., Merry Hill, N.C., 1974-75; earth sci. tchr. William Campbell H.S., Naruna, Va., 1978-79; respiratory therapy technician Va. Bapt. Hosp., Lynchburg, 1981-83; respiratory therapy instr. Ctrl. Va. C.C., Lynchburg, 1982-85; biology tchr. Rustburg (Va.) H.S., 1987—. Vol. horse program 4-H, Campbell County, Va., 1987—; cert. scuba diver YMCA; mem. Ch. Ladies Aux.; vol. numerous sch. activities. Mem. Am. Quarter Horse Assn., Va. Quarter Horse Assn., Va. Horse Coun., Kappa Delta Pi, Phi Theta Kappa. Roman Catholic. Office: Rustburg HS PO Box 39 Rustburg VA 24588-0039

OLAJUWON, HAKEEM ABDUL, professional basketball player; b. Lagos, Nigeria, Jan. 21, 1963; s. Salaam and Abike O. Student, U. Houston, 1980-84. With Houston Rockets, 1984—. Named to Sporting News All-Am. First Team, 1984, NBA All-Rookie Team, 1985, All-Star team, 1985-90, 92-94, All-NBA First Team, 1987-89, 93-94, NBA All-Defensive First Team, 1987-88, 90, 93-94; named MVP 1993-94, NBA Defensive Player of Yr., 1993-94, mem. NBA championship team, 1994-95; named MVP NBA finals, 1994-95; recipient award IBM, 1993. Office: Houston Rockets The Summit Ten Greenway Pl E Houston TX 77046-3865*

OLANDER, RAY GUNNAR, retired lawyer; b. Buhl, Minn., May 15, 1926; s. Olof Gunnar and Margaret Esther (Meisner) O.; m. Audrey Joan Greenlaw, Aug. 1, 1959; children: Paul Robert, Mary Beth. BEE, U. Minn., 1949, BBA, 1949; JD cum laude, Harvard U., 1959. Bar: Minn. 1959, Wis. 1962, U.S. Patent Office 1968. Elec. engr. M. A. Hanna Co., Hibbing, Minn., 1950-56; assoc. Leonard, Street & Deinard, Mpls., 1959-61; comml. atty. Bucyrus Internat. Inc., South Milwaukee, Wis., 1961-70, dir. contracts, 1970-76, v.p. comml., 1976-88, gen. atty., 1978-80, corp. sec., 1978-88, gen. counsel, 1980-88, vice chmn., dir., 1988-92; ret. Bd. dirs. Ballet Found. Milw., Inc., 1978-92, Pub. Expenditure Rsch. Found., Inc., Madison, Wis., 1978-94, Pub. Expenditure Survey Wis., Madison, 1978-82. With USN, 1944-46. Mem. ABA, Wis. Bar Assn., Wis. Intellectual Property Law Assn., Am. Soc. Corp. Secs., Inc., Am. Corp. Counsel Assn., VFW, Harvard Club (N.Y.C.), Harvard of Wis. Club, Bonita Bay Club. Republican. Roman Catholic. Home: 3708 Woodlake Dr Bonita Springs FL 34134-8605

OLAR, TERRY THOMAS, health facilities administrator; b. Hammond, Ind., Mar. 1, 1947; s. Thomas and Gladys (Kaleta) O.; m. Sally Kaye Walker, Sept. 5, 1970 (div. 1983); 1 child, Kristin Rene; m. Cheryl Ann Renz, Feb. 10, 1990; children: Danielle Jade, Robert David, Brandon Michael. BS, Purdue U., 1973; MS, Wash. State U., 1975; PhD, Colo. State U., 1984. Tech. dir. Genetic Resources, San Marcos, Tex., 1984; lab. dir. High Plains Genetics, Rapid City, S.D., 1984-85, Swedish Med. Ctr., Denver, 1985-87; scientific dir. Fertility Inst. New Orleans, 1987—; asst. prof. Dept. Obstetrics and Gynecology Tulane U. Sch. Medicine, New Orleans, 1990—; cons. Northwest Fla. Fertility Inst., Gulf Breeze, 1988—, St. Francis Med. Ctr., Monroe, La., 1988—, Humana Hosp., Brazos Valley, Tex., 1989, Humana Hosp., Lake Charles, La., 1990. Contbr. articles to profl. jours. Bd. dirs. La. Wildlife Fedn., v.p., 1994—. Sgt. USAF, 1965-69. Grantee Am. Kennel Club, 1982, 83, Humana Hosp. Inc., 1988-92. Mem. AAAS, Am. Fertility Soc., Soc. for Study of Reproduction, Am. Soc. Andrology, Am. Assn. Tissue Banks, N.Y. Acad. Scis., Am. Assn. Bioanalysts, Am. Legion, VFW, KC. Republican. Roman Catholic. Home: 210 Chubasco Dr Slidell LA 70458-9156 Office: Fertility Inst New Orleans 6020 Bullard Ave New Orleans LA 70128-2813

OLDFIELD, RUSSELL MILLER, lawyer; b. Salem, Ohio, Aug. 18, 1946; s. Donald W. and Virginia Alice (Harold) O.; m. Mary Lou Kubrin, May 28, 1966; children: Lindsey Marie, Grant Russell. AB, Youngstown State U., 1971; JD, Ohio No. U., 1974. Bar: Ohio 1974, Tenn. 1984. Assoc. counsel Gulf. and Western Industries, Nashville, 1979-83; v.p., gen. counsel, sec. Rogers Group Inc., Nashville, 1983—. Served with U.S. Army, 1966-68. Mem. ABA, Nashville Bar Assn., Am. Corp. Counsel Assn. (pres. Tenn. chpt. 1994-95), Samaritan, Inc. (chmn. 1991-92), Indian Lake Swim and Tennis Club, Univ. Club. Episcopalian. Home: 101 Sioux Ct Hendersonville TN 37075-4634 Office: Rogers Group Inc PO Box 25250 Nashville TN 37202-5250

OLDHAM, DARIUS DUDLEY, lawyer; b. Beaumont, Tex., July 6, 1941; s. Darius Saran and Mary Francis (Carraway) O.; m. Judy J. White, Jan. 23, 1965; children: Steven, Michael. BA, U. Tex., Austin, 1964; JD, U. Tex., 1966. Bar: Tex. 1966, U.S. Dist. Ct. (so., no., ea. and we. dists.) Tex. 1966, U.S. Supreme Ct. 1974, U.S. Ct. Appeals (5th and 11th cirs.) 1968. Assoc. Fulbright & Jaworski, Houston, 1966-74, ptnr., 1974—, mem. policy com., 1980—; mem. faculty grad. litigation program U. Houston; lectr. on corp. def. ins. and product liability. Mem. bd. editors Aviation Litigation Reporter, Personal Injury Def. Reporter; country corr. Internat. Ins. Law Rev.; contbr. articles to profl. jours. Mem. Nat. Jud. Coll. Coun. for the Future; bd. dirs., former sec.-treas. FIC Found., 1979-87; past bd. dirs. Houston Pops Orch.; mem. liberal arts adv. coun. U. Tex. Fellow Am. Coll. Trial Lawyers (complex litigation com.), Tex. Bar Found. (life), Am. Bar Found. (life), Houston Bar Found. (life), Am. Bd. Trial Advs.; mem. ABA (vice chmn. aviation com. tips sect. 1980-82, chmn. aviation com. litigation sect. 1982-84, vice chmn. econs. law practice com. 1985-86, mem. coun. tort and ins. practice sect. 1988-91, vice chair 1991-92, chair-elect 1992-93, chmn. ann. meeting program com. 1987, chmn. professionalism com. 1990-91, fin. com. 1986-93, chmn. long range planning com. 1991-92, chair tort and ins. practice sect. 1994-95, presdl. emissary 1993-95), Tex. Bar Assn. (liaison law schs. and law students com. 1983-86, PEER com. 1979-82, chmn. liaison fed. jud. com. 1989-90, pattern jury charges Vol. IV com. 1988-92), Tex. Young Lawyers Assn. (bd. dirs., chmn.), Fed. Ins. and Corp. Counsel (exec. v.p., pres.-elect 1988-89, pres. 1989-90, chmn. bd. 1990-91, exec. com. 1988-91, coord. com. 1984-87, sec.-treas. 1987-88), Tex. Assn. Def. Counsel, Maritime Law Assn. U.S., Am. Counsel Assn. (bd. dirs. 1982-83, 89-94), Def. Rsch. Inst. (chmn. aerospace com. 1984-87, vice chmn. 1983-84, Presdl. Achievement award 1987, bd. dirs. 1989-92, exec. com. 1991-92), Lawyers for Civil Justice (bd. dirs. 1988-92, 95—, exec. com. 1990-92, 95—, pres. elect 1996, ores. 1996-97), River Oaks Country Club, Houston Ctr. Club, Sigma Chi, Phi Delta Phi. Office: Fulbright & Jaworski 1301 Mckinney St 51st Fl Houston TX 77010

OLDHAM, WILLIAM EDWARD, minister, accountant, educator; b. Delhi, La., Aug. 10, 1948; s. Edward Lincoln and Meriam Galdys (Boze) O.; m. Lucille Takkordai Telukdharrie, Aug. 25, 1971; children: Kenneth Ganash, Brian Rajpaul, Indra Anita. BA, Anderson U., 1973, postgrad., 1985-86; postgrad., Ind. Bus. Coll., 1975; ThM, Internat. Sem., 1991. Ordained to ministry Ch. of God (Anderson, Ind.), 1990; cert. tchr. Ind., Ala. Assoc. pastor East 10th St. Ch of God, Indpls., 1985-86; missionary Mercy Corp./Ch. of God, Honduras, 1986; sr. pastor Sheridan (Ind.) Ch. of God, 1987-88; sr. pastor First Ch. of God, Mobile, Ala., 1988-89, Shreveport, La., 1989—; pres. Right Hand Ministries, Inc., Indpls., 1986-94. Author: A Study in John's Gospel, 1991, 26 other books; developer bd. game Power, 1975. With USAF, 1969-70, Vietnam. Named Outstanding Coach Fall Creek Little League, Indpls., 1983, 84, 85, 86. Mem. Assn. Govt. Accts., Lions (pres. Fall Creek chpt. 1983-84, Pres.'s award 1984). Office: First Ch of God 107 Monterey Dr North Tazewell VA 24630

OLDWEILER, THOMAS PATRICK, lawyer; b. Lawrence, Kans., May 13, 1961; s. Harry Eldon and Jeanne Teresa (Boyle) O.; m. Laura Elise Busby, Dec. 31, 1988; children: T. Patrick Jr., Alexander B. AB, Duke U., 1983; JD, Vanderbilt U., 1986. Bar: Ala. 1986, Mo. 1987, Miss. 1987, U.S. Dist. Ct. (so. dist.) Miss. 1987. Assoc. Miller, Hamilton, Snider & Odom, Mobile, Ala., 1986-92, ptnr., 1993-94; ptnr. Zieman, Speegle, Oldweiler & Jackson, L.L.C., Mobile, 1994—; faculty mem. Ala. Bar Inst., Tuscaloosa, 1988—. Mem. ABA, Mobile Bar Assn., Athelstan Club. Office: Zieman Speegle Oldweiler & Jackson LLC 107 Saint Francis St #3200 Mobile AL 33602

OLEJAR, PAUL DUNCAN, former information science administrator; b. Hazelton, Pa., Sept. 13, 1906; s. George and Anna (Danco) O.; m. Ann Ruth Dillard, Jan. 6, 1933 (dec. Oct. 1978); 1 child, Peter; m. Martha S. Ross, Sept. 8, 1979. AB, Dickinson Coll., 1928. Dir. edn. W.Va. Conservation Commn., 1936-41; coordinator U.S. Fish and Wildlife Service, 1941-42; chief press and radio Bur. Reclamation, Dept. Interior, 1946-47; editor Plant Industry Sta. AGRI, 1948-51; chmn. spl. reports Agrl. Research Adminstrn., 1951-56; dir. tech. info. Edgewood Arsenal, Md., 1956-63; chief, tech. info. plans and programs Army Research Office, Washington, 1963-64; chmn. chem. info. unit NSF, Washington, 1965-70; dir. drug info. program Sch. Pharmacy, U. N.C., Chapel Hill, 1970-73, ret., 1973. Author: West Virginia Units in Conservation, 1939, Rockets in Early American Wars, 1946, A Taste of Red Onion, 1981, Sentinel at the Crossroads, 1991; editor: Computer-Based Information Systems in the Practice of Pharmacy, 1971; newspaper columnist, editor AP, Pa. and W.Va.; editor Hanover Record-Herald, Pa. Served with AUS, 1942-46. Decorated Army Commendation medal. Mem. Ravens Claw, Mil. Order of The World Wars (lt. col.), Masons (32 degree), Theta Chi, Omicron Delta Kappa. Methodist. Home: 407 Russell Ave # 111 Gaithersburg MD 20877 also: 724 Port Malabar Blvd NE Palm Bay FL 32905-4409

OLEN, MILTON WILLIAM, JR., marketing executive; b. Providence, Sept. 15, 1950; s. Milton William and Elizabeth Amanda (Goodrich) O.; m. Marsha Elizabeth Broughton, Mar. 15, 1971. Student, Fla. So. Coll., 1969-

72; BS in Behavioral Scis. magna cum laude, Nova U., 1978. Lic. comml. pilot, USCG capt.; lic. residential contractor, Fla. Mfr.'s rep. for Fla., The Siemens Corp., Ft. Lauderdale, Fla., 1972-77; product mgr., exec. salesman, sales mgr. The Ritter Dental Co., Romulus, Mich., 1977-85; gen. mgr., exec. salesman Olen Homes Internat. Inc., West Palm Beach, Fla., 1981—. Mem. Nat. Assn. Home Builders, C. of C. Miami Beach, Better Bus. Bur. Roman Catholic. Office: PO Box 70156 Fort Lauderdale FL 33307-0156

OLENDORF, WILLIAM CARR, JR., small business owner; b. Albany, N.Y., Oct. 3, 1945; s. William Carr Sr. and Mary Zilpha (Gillies) O.; m. Barbara Kay Cowan, Aug. 14, 1966; children: Mark, Julie, Jennifer. Student, Columbia Coll., 1964-65, So. Ill. U., 1965-66. Prodn. asst. Sta. WTTW-TV, Chgo., 1962-64; radio announcer Sta. WERX, Wyoming, Mich., 1967-68; sales rep. Sta. WCFL, Chgo., 1968-70, Sta. WJJD-AM & FM, Chgo., 1970-72; v.p. Promotion Network, Chgo., 1972-74; account exec. AVCO-TV, Chgo., 1974-76, Peters, Griffin & Woodward, Chgo., 1976-82, Petry TV, Chgo., 1982-83; owner, pres. Point South KOA Resort, Yemassee, S.C., 1983—. Commr. Point South Pub. Svc. Dist., 1987-88, Lowcountry & Resort Island Tourism Commn., 1994—; mem. tourism tax adv. bd. Jasper County, S.C., 1985; chmn. Jasper County Hist. Preservation Commn., S.C., 1994—; trusee S.C. Battleground Preservation Trust, Inc., 1994—. Mem. Nat. Campground Owners Assn. (campground nat. adv. bd. 1989-93, Take Pride in Am. award 1992), Kampground Owners Assn. (pres. 1994—, Award of Merit 1990), S.C. Campground Assn. (pres. 1987-88), Point South Mchts. Assn. (pres. 1990—), Jasper County Hist. Soc. Republican. Episcopalian. Home and Office: PO Box 1760 Yemassee SC 29945-1760

OLESON, RAY JEROME, computer service company executive; b. Windom, Minn., June 20, 1944; s. Ray Jerome and Evah Oleson; m. Kathleen Ruth Johnson, July 2, 1966; children: Michelle Dawn, Carrie Elisabeth. BS in Math., Mankato State U., 1966; MS in Applied Stats., Villanova U., 1970. Mgr., dir. Sperry Univac, Egan, Minn., 1966-77; v.p. Computer Scis. Corp., Moorestown, N.J., 1977-84; from v.p. mktg. to pres. Systems and Applied Scis. Corp., Vienna, Va., 1984-87; pres. systems devel. and implementation div. CACI, Inc., Arlington, Va., 1987-90; pres., COO CACI, Inc., Arlington, 1990—. Mem. Armed Forces Electronic and Comm. Assn. (pres. Phila. chpt. 1980-82), River Bend Country Club. Democrat. Lutheran. Home: 1312 Tulip Poplar Ln Vienna VA 22182-1340 Office: CACI 1100 N Glebe Rd Arlington VA 22201-4798

OLESZKIEWICZ, MALGORZATA, Latin American literature and culture educator; b. Warsaw, Poland; came to U.S., 1977; d. Eliquiusz and Kazimiera Oleszkiewicz. Magister in Iberian and L.Am. Studies, Warsaw U., 1981; MA, CUNY, 1981; MPhil in Latin Am. Lit., NYU, 1986, PhD, 1991. Lang. instr. CUNY, Flushing, 1979-81; instr. Spanish NYU, N.Y.C., 1981-87, 90-91; tchr. Spanish UN, N.Y.C., 1982; instr. Spanish CUNY, Bklyn., 1983-84, Rutgers U., Newark, 1987; lang. instr. SUNY, New Paltz, 1988; asst. prof. Bard Coll., Annandale-on-Hudson, N.Y., 1991-95, U. Tex., San Antonio, 1995—; lectr. Queens Coll., CUNY, N.Y.C., 1988, Bard Coll., N.Y., 1992; presenter XI Internat. Symposium Lit., Montevideo, Uruguay, 1993, II Internat. Conf. Ibero Am. and Argentine Theater, Buenos Aires, 1993; 48th Internat. Congress of Americanists, Stockholm, 1994; cultural meeting, The Birth of the Two Natures: The Creole and the Mestizo in Spanish America, Mérida, 1996, Afro-Latin Am. Rsch. Assn. Conf., Salvador, Brazil, 1996. Author: Teatro popular peruano: del precolombino al siglo XX, 1995; contbr. articles to profl. jours. Univ. fellow NYU, 1986-87, 89-90, Penfield fellow NYU, 1987-88, Dean's dissertation fellow NYU, 1988-89, Asher Edelman Released Time fellow Bard Coll., 1992; recipient CONCYTEC grant, Lima, 1988-89, Faculty Rsch. award U. Tex. San Antonio, 1995-96. Mem. MLA, LASA, Inst. Internat. Lit. Iberoamericana, Inst. Lit. Cultural Hispánico, Polish Inst. Arts and Scis. Home: 7667 Callaghan Rd #116 San Antonio TX 78229 Office: U Tex San Antonio Divsn Fgn Langs 6900 N Loop 1604 W San Antonio TX 78249

OLEXA, GEORGE RONALD, cellular telecommunication executive; b. West Chester, Pa., Sept. 14, 1955; s. George Paul and Marie Grace (Hanthorn) O.; 1 child, Danielle René. BSEE, Pa. State U., 1977. Cert. 1st class radiotelephone FCC. Cen. office engr. Conestoga Telephone and Telegraph Co., Birdsboro, Pa., 1977-82; chief engr. LIN Broadcasting, N.Y.C., 1982-86; v.p. engrng. L.A. Cellular Telephone Co., 1986-88; exec. dir. engrng. Pac Tel Cellular, Irvine, Calif., 1988-93; v.p. engrng. and ops. Dial Call Inc., Atlanta, 1993-96; CEO Superconducting Core Tech., Golden, Colo., 1996—. Home: 985 Manchester Pl NW Atlanta GA 30328-4848 Office: Superconducting Core Tech 720 Corporate Cir Golden CO 80401

OLI, MADAN KUMAR, wildlife ecologist; b. Pokhari, Terathum, Nepal, May 27, 1961; s. Bishnu P. and Laxmi K. (Thapaliya) O.; m. Monika Förstl, June 8, 1993; 1 child, Muna Oli. Diploma in sci., Tribhuvan U., Kathmandu, Nepal, 1983, MS, 1986; MPhil, U. Edinburgh, Scotland, 1992. Field biologist Red Panda Project, WWF-U.S., Nepal, 1987; co-investigator Nar-Phu Valley Project, WWF, Nepal, 1987; rsch. officer Annapurna CA Project, Nepal, 1988-92; prin. investigator Snow Leopard project WWF-U.S., Nepal, 1990-92; rsch. asst. Miss. State U., 1993-95; grad. asst. Auburn (Ala.) U., 1995—; rsch. dir. Wildland Rsch. Nepal program San Francisco State U., 1987. Contbr. articles to sci. jours. Recipient Young Scientist award UNESCO, South and Ctrl. Asia, 1988, 90, Tech. Coop. Tng. award Brit. Coun., Eng., 1989. Mem. Internat. Union for Conservation of Nature and Natural Resources (World Conservation Union, species survival commn., cat specialist group), Am. Soc. Mammalogists, Internat. Assn. Bear Rsch. & Mgmt., Internat. Snow Leopard Trust, Wildlife Soc., Smithsonian Assocs., Wildlife Conservation Soc., Sigma Xi. Home: 900 Linden Apt 6 Auburn AL 36830 Office: Dept Zoology and Wildlife Auburn U Auburn AL 36849-5414

OLILA, OSCAR GESTA, soil and water scientist; b. Cayang, Bogo, Cebu, The Philippines, Sept. 9, 1955; came to U.S., 1986; s. Escolastico Mangubat Olila and Gregoria (Jagdon) Gesta; m. Prima Carreon, July 11, 1987; children: Glen Charles, Eric James. BS in Agr., Cen. Mindanao U., Musuan, Bukidnon, The Philippines, 1977; MS in Soil Sci., U. Philippines, Los Baños, Laguna, 1983; postgrad., U. Mass., 1986-87; PhD, U. Fla., 1987-92. Instr. soil sci. Cen. Mindanao U., 1977-83, asst. prof., chmn. dept., 1984-86, head Soil and Plant Testing Lab., extension worker, 1985-86; grad. rsch. asst. U. Fla., Gainesville, 1987-92, post doctoral rsch. assoc., 1993—. Contbr. articles to profl. and sci. jours. Scholar Philippine Coun. for Agr. and Resources Rsch., 1979-81, Philippine Devel. scholar, 1983, Cen. Mindanao U. faculty scholar, 1986-89. Mem. AAAS, Soil Sci. Soc. Am., Am. Soc. Agronomy, Am. Soc. Limnology and Oceanography, Internat. Soc. Soil Sci., Cen. Mindano U. Alumni Assn. (v.p. 1985-86), Alpha Zeta, Gamma Sigma Delta. Roman Catholic. Office: U Fla Soil and Water Sci Dept 106 Newell Hall Gainesville FL 32611

OLIN, ROBERT FLOYD, mathematics educator and reseacher; b. Evanston, Ill., Oct. 8, 1948; s. Floyd Thomas and Anne Elanor (Knutson) O.; m. Linda Renee King, Aug. 23, 1969; children: Kristopher Robert, Susan Michelle. BSc, Ottawa U., 1970; PhD, Ind. U., 1975. Asst. prof. math. Va. Poly. Inst. and State U., Blacksburg, 1975-80, assoc. prof., 1980-87, prof., 1987—, dept. head, 1994—; vis. assoc. prof. Ind. U., Bloomington, 1985; rschr. NSF, 1975-94, grad. chmn., 1993-94; chmn. rsch. commn., 1993-94. Co-author: A Functional Calculus for Subnormal Operators II, 1977, Subnormal Operators, and Representations of Bounded Analytic Functions and Other Uniform Algebras, 1985. Pres. Southwestern Va. Soccer Assn., Blacksburg, 1989-90; tchr. Sunday Sch. Blacksburg Bapt. Ch., 1983—; treas. Margaret Beeks PTA, 1993-95; chmn. steering com. Southeastern Analysis Meeting, 1984—. Named Hon. Faculty Mem., Sichuan U., Chengdu, China, 1988; recipient cert. Math. Edn. Devel. Ctr., Ind. U., Bloomington, 1976. Mem. N.Y. Acad. Scis., Va. Acad. Scis., Am. Math. Soc., Math. Assn. Am., Nat. Coun. Tchrs. Math., Coun. Undergrad Rsch., Am. Assn. Higher Edn., Sigma Xi, Pi Mu Epsilon. Home: 707 Draper Rd SW Blacksburg VA 24060-4654 Office: Va Poly Inst and State U Math Dept Blacksburg VA 24061

OLINGER, SHEFF DANIEL, neurologist, educator; b. Olinger, Va., Oct. 23, 1930; s. Sheff Daniel and Ada Sue O.; m. Norma Lanier, June 25, 1953; children: Nancy, Sheff D. III, Amy. BS, Va. Mil. Inst., 1949; MD, U. Va., 1953. Diplomate Am. Bd. Psychiatry and Neurology. Intern Tripler Army Hosp., Honolulu, 1953-54; resident in neurology U. Mich., Ann Arbor, 1956-59, clin. instr., 1958-59; instr. Southwestern Med. Sch., Dallas, 1960-82, assoc. prof. neurology, 1982—; pvt. practice in neurology Dallas, 1959-72; dir. dept. neurology Baylor U. Med. Ctr., Dallas, 1972-90, dir. stroke unit and EEG dept., 1972-90; cons. Presbyn. Hosp., Dallas, 1960—, Parkland Hosp., Dallas, 1960—, Timberlawn Psychiatric Hosp., 1960-90, also U.S. Dept. Labor, Dallas Mil. Entrance Processing Sta. Contbr. articles to profl. jours. Fellow Am. Acad. Neurology; mem. AMA, Tex. Med. Assn., Tex. Neurol. Soc. (founding pres. 1975), Dallas County Med. Soc., Dallas So. Clin. Soc. Home: 3564 Colgate Ave Dallas TX 75225-5009

OLINS, ADA LEVY, cell biologist; b. Tel-Aviv, Mar. 5, 1938; came to U.S., 1946; d. Fred Simon and Hilda Pauline (Jacobson) Levy; m. Donald Edward olins, July 2, 1961; children: Joshua Daniel, Barak Levi. BS, CCNY, 1960; AM, Harvard U., 1961; PhD, NYU, 1965. Postdoctoral fellow Dartmouth Med. Sch., 1965-67; cons. biology divsn. Oak Ridge Nat. Lab., 1967-77; guest investigator, biophysics dept. King's Coll., London, 1970-71; rsch. assoc., lectr. U. Tenn.-Oak Ridge Grad. Sch. of Biomed. Scis., 1975-77, rsch. asst. prof., 1977-80, rsch. assoc. prof., 1980-82, rsch. prof., 1982—; Forscheimer vis. prof. Hebrew U., 1994; vis. prof. German Cancer Rsch. Ctr., Heidelberg, 1979-80; vis. scientist Pasteur Inst., Paris, 1987, max Planck Inst., Goettingen, 1987; hon. prof. N.E. Normal U., China, 1988; STEM adv. com. Brookhaven Nat. lab., 1995—; mem. adv. com. biol. microscopy and image reconstruction resource, Albany, 1996—; cell biology program rev. panel NSF, 1990-95, oversight com. divsn. of cellular bioscis., 1985; faculty senate U. Tenn. Co-editor European Jour. of Cell Biology, 1982-86, Molecular and Cellular Biochemistry, 1982-85. Recipient Chancellor's award for Rsch. and Creative Achievement, 1988, Theodor Boveri award U. Würzburg, 1987, Naito Found. award Lectrs. in Japan, 1982; predoctoral fellow USPHS, 1960-64, spl. fellow NIH, 1970-71, Eleanor Roosevelt Internat. Cancer fellow, 1987; Yamagiwa-Yoshida Meml. Internat. Cancer Studey grantee, 1994. Mem. Am. Soc. for Cell Biology (coun. 1984-86, constn. and bylaws com. 1983-86, chairperson 1985-86, minority affairs com. 1985-93, chairperson 1986, E.B. Wilson Award com.), Electron Microscop Soc. of Am. (program com. 1986). Office: Biology Divsn ORNL PO Box 2009 Oak Ridge TN 37831-8077

OLIPHANT, EDWARD DAVIS (DAVE OLIPHANT), editor; b. Ft. Worth, July 18, 1939; s. Mosby Davis and Dorothy Marie (Keetch) O.; m. Maria Isabel Jofré, Jan. 28, 1967; children: Dario Alejandro, Elisa. BA, Lamar U., Beaumont, Tex., 1963; MA, U. Tex., 1966; PhD, No. Ill. U., 1975. Tchr. English Hebbronville High Sch., 1963-64; faculty Am. lit. Cath. U. of Chile, 1966; instr. N.Mex. Jr. Coll., 1967-69, No. Ill. U., DeKalb, 1969-74; asst. prof. Voorhees Coll., Denmark, S.C., 1974-75; dir. creative writing program U. of Americas, Puebla, Mex., 1975-76; asst. prof. English U. Tex., Austin, 1976-78; part-time instr. Austin (Tex.) C.C., 1978—; editor The Libr. Chronicle quar. jour. Harry Ransom Humanities Rsch. Ctr., Austin, 1979—. Author: (poetry) Brands, 1972, Taking Stock, 1973, Lines and Mounds, 1976, Footprints, 1961-78, Austin, 1985, Maria's Poems, 1987; editor: The New Breed: An Anthology of Texas Poets, 1973, Washing the Cow's Skull: Texas Poetry in Translation, 1981, Six Women Poets at Tex., 1992, The Bebop Revolution in Words and Music, 1994; author: On a High Horse: Views Mostly of Latin American and Texan Poetry, 1983, Texan Jazz, 1996; poetry and translations in mags. and jours. Mem. Tex. Inst. Letters. Home: 1402 Mimosa Pass Cedar Park TX 78613-5505 Office: U Tex at Austin Harry Ransom Humanities Rsch Ctr Austin TX 78713

OLIVARES, ROSA MARIA GUAJARDO, bilingual educator; b. Laredo, Tamps, Mex., Oct. 5, 1940; came to U.S., 1952; d. Benjamin Cesar and Mercedes (Gonzalez) Guajardo; m. Ishmael Olivares, Sept. 3, 1967; children: Maria Rosa, Maeli Rebeca, Monica Raquel. BA, Andrews U., 1967; MLA, So. Meth. U., 1991; counselor cert., East Tex. State U., 1995. Bilingual endorsement, Mich., Tex. Tchr. Seventh-day Adventist Mich. Conf., Detroit, 1964-66, Benton Harbor (Mich.) Pub. Schs., 1967-69; tchr. bilingual edn. Berrien Springs (Mich.) Pub. Schs., 1969-84; legal translator Mich. Legal Assessor Project, Berrien Springs, 1980-84; tchr. bilingual edn. Dallas Ind. Sch. Dist., 1984-92, sch. counselor, 1992—; rschr. and evaluator Criterion Reference Testing, 1976-84. Proofreader: Bilingual Teacher, 1986. Youth leader Mesquite (Tex.) Seventh-day Adventist Ch., 1984-89, Garland (Tex.) Seventh-day Adventist Ch., 1989—. Grantee Am. Airlines, Dallas, 1989, scholar So. Meth. U., 1990. Mem. Bus. and Profl. Women's Club, Dallas, (sec. 1988-89, pres.-elect 1989-90). Office: Mount Auburn Elem Sch Dallas TX 75200

OLIVARIUS-IMLAH, MARYPAT, sales, advertising and marketing executive; b. Bklyn., Oct. 25, 1957; d. Kenneth William Joseph and Ann Marie (Beckley) Olivarius; m. Craig Alexander Olivarius-Imlah, Sept. 18, 1982; children: Christopher Edward, Jamison Robert, Meghan Patricia. BS in Mktg. and Communications, Ramapo State Coll. N.J., 1979; MBA in Mktg. and Mgmt., Fairleigh Dickinson U., 1985. Researcher, pub. rels. MacNeil/Lehrer Report, WNET-TV, N.Y.C., 1977; salesperson Terrace Realty, Montvale, N.J., 1977-79; direct mail advt. copywriter Prentice-Hall, Inc., Englewood Cliffs, N.J., 1979-81; editor, promotional designer Beauty & Barber Supply Inst., Englewood, N.J., 1981-83; nat. dir. advt. and pub. rels. Emerson Radio Corp., North Bergen, N.J., 1983-85; founder, pres. Imagery Print & Advt., Print Brokerage Design Agy.

OLIVAS, VALERIE SEGURA, legal assistant; b. Marfa, Tex., July 20, 1954; d. Joe D. and Vidala (Gonzalez) Segura; divorced; 1 child, Donny Rey Martinez. AAS, El Paso Community Coll., 1987. Grad. vocat. nurse Big Bend Meml. Hosp., Alpine, Tex., 1974-78; lic. cosmetologist styling salon J.C. Penney, Inc., El Paso, Tex., 1980-88; paralegal Donald L. Williams Law Office, El Paso, 1987-95; family law ct. coord. Hon. Donald L. Williams, San Antonio, 1995—. Mem. Tex. Assn. Ct. Adminstrs., El Paso Assn. Ct. Coord., El Paso Assn. Legal Assts. (v.p. continuing edn. and programs 1992-93, v.p. membership 1993-94, pres.-elect 1994-95, pres. 1995-96), El Paso Bar Assn. (assoc.). Democrat. Roman Catholic. Home: 11816 Jim Ryan Ln El Paso TX 79936-5781 Office: Family Law Ct 500 E San Antonio Rm 603 El Paso TX 79901

OLIVE, KENNETH EVERETT, internist, health facility administrator; b. Brewton, Ala., Mar. 11, 1956; s. John Gilbert and Lula Mae (Smith) O.; m. Diana Lynn Snodgrass, May 15, 1982; children: Elizabeth Emily, Susan Rachel. BS in Zoology magna cum laude, Duke U., 1977; MD, East Carolina U., 1982. Diplomate Nat. Bd. Med. Examiners, Am. Bd. Internal Medicine in internal medicine and geriatrics; lic. physician, Ohio, Tenn.; instr. ACLS, provider Advanced Trauma Life Support; cert. to perform flexible sigmoidoscopy. Internal medicine intern, resident USAF Med. Ctr., Wright-Patterson AFB, Ohio, 1982-85, chief med. resident, 1985-86, staff internist, 1986-89, chief gen. internal medicine, 1988-89; asst. clin. prof. medicine Wright State U., Dayton, Ohio, 1987-89; chmn. faculty adv. coun. James H. Quillen Coll. Medicine East Tenn. State U., Johnson City, 1992-93, asst. prof. internal medicine, 1989-94; assoc. prof. internal medicine James H. Quillen Coll. Medicine East Tenn. State U., Johnson City; attending physician Johnson City Med. Ctr. Hosp., 1989—, internal medicine residency program dir., 1991—, chmn. dept. medicine, 1992-93; bd. dirs. Washington County unit Am. Cancer Soc.,1990-93, chmn. profl. edn. com., 1990-92. Contbr. articles to profl. jours. Maj. USAF, 1982-89. Recipient Huffman award East Carolina U., 1979; named James H. Quillen Helath Care hero, 1994. Fellow ACP; mem. Soc. Gen. Internal Medicine, Alpha Omega Alpha. Office: East Tenn State U Dept Internal Medicine Johnson City TN 37614

OLIVE, STEWART BROADWELL, retired chemical engineer, management executive; b. Madison County, Miss., Sept. 23, 1923; s. Young Burt and Lillian Vesta (Broadwell) O.; m. Marian McCanne, Mar. 4, 1950; children: John MacKay, George Gilbert. BS in Chem. Engrng., La. State U., 1948. Reg. profl. engr. Chem. engr. Firestone Tire & Rubber, Lake Charles, La., 1948-56; chem. engr. Firestone Tire & Rubber, Orange, Tex., 1956-64, tech. mgr., 1964-66, prodn. mgr., 1966-82; ret. Mem. City of Orange planning and zoning com., 1963-69, city coun., 1992-93; Mayor Pro Tem, Orange, 1993-97. Ensign, USN, 1943-46, Pacific. Presbyterian. Home: 2003 Melwood Orange TX 77636

OLIVER, ANN BREEDING, fine arts education curator; b. Hollywood, Fla., Sept. 21, 1945; d. Harvey James and Ruth (Lige) Breeding; m. John Russell Kelso, July 22, 1972 (div. Feb. 1984); 1 child, Anna Liege; m. June 29, 1996. BA in Fgn. Lang., U. Ky., 1967; MA in History of Art, Ohio State U., 1971. Curatorial intern Lowe Art Mus., Coral Gables, Fla., 1972; adj. faculty Fla. Atlantic U., Boca Raton, Fla., 1972-73, 78; lectr. Miami (Fla.) Dade Community Coll., 1974, with art-music workshop, 1980-81; lectr.-cons., 1972—; adj. faculty music dept. Miami Dade (Fla.) Community Coll., 1991; curator of edn. Ctr. for the Fine Arts, Miami, 1987-92, High Mus. of Art, Atlanta, Ga., 1992-96; mem. Artists in Edn. Panel, Ga. Coun. for Arts, 1994; field reviewer Inst. Mus. Svcs., 1994; adj. faculty in art history Kennesaw State U., Marietta, Ga., 1996—. Contbg. editor African Art: An Essay for Teachers, 1993; project mgr. and contbg. author: Rings: Five Passions in World Art: Multicultural Curriculum Handbook, 1996. Recipient Nat. award for graphics Mead Paper Co., 1989, Gold Medal of Honor publication design S.E. Mus. Educators Publ. Design, 1994. Mem. Am. Assn. of Mus., Inst. Mus. Svcs., Nat. Art Edn. Assn., Fla. Art Edn. Assn. (dir. mus. divsn.), Ga. Art Edn. Assn. (dir. mus. divsn., Mus. Educator of Yr. 1993). Home: 2420 Mitchell Rd Marietta GA 30062-5321 Office: High Mus of Art Head Student/Family Prgms 1280 Peachtree St NE Atlanta GA 30309-3502

OLIVER, ARNOLD ROBERT, chancellor; b. Boston, July 18, 1945; s. Arnold D. and Barbara G. Oliver; m. Patricia Lea Johnson, Aug. 20, 1968; children: Arnold Jr., Daniel Geoff. AB, St. Michael's Coll., Winooski, Vt., 1967; MA, U. Idaho, 1969; PhD, So. Ill. U., 1972. Instr. Olney (Ill.) Cen. C.C., 1971-72; asst. div. chair No. Va. C.C., Annandale, 1972-74; div. chair No. Va. C.C., Manassas, 1974-79, acting provost, 1978-79; dean instrn. and student devel. Danville (Va.) C.C., 1980-86, pres., 1987-91; chancellor Va. C.C. System, Richmond, 1992—; mem. Southeastern Conf. for English. Contbr. articles to profl. jours. Mem. Va. Econ. Bridge Adv. Bd., Richmond, 1990—; bd. dirs. Downtown Danville Assocs., Hospice Danville/Pittsylvania County. Mem. Va. Coll. English Assn., N.C. Coll. English Assn., Va. Humanities Assn., Danville Arts and Humanities Assn. (bd. dirs., past pres. 1987-88), Pittsylvania County C. of C. (pres. Chatham chpt. 1991—), Riverview Rotary, Phi Theta Kappa. Roman Catholic. Office: Va Community Coll System 101 N 14th St Richmond VA 23219-3684

OLIVER, CLIFTON, JR., management educator; b. Amarillo, Tex., Dec. 3, 1915; s. Clifton and Laura Pearl (Hudson) O.; B.A., Tex. Tech U., 1935, M.A., 1936; postgrad. La. State U., 1937-38, U. Wis., 1938-39. Prof. mgmt. Tex. Christian U., Ft. Worth, 1939-43; prof. U. Fla., Gainesville, 1946-85, dir. Mgmt. Center, 1959-71; cons. in field; ednl. cons. State Farm Ins. Co., others. Served to lt., AUS, 1943-46. Recipient service award U. Fla. Athletic Assn., 1977, CADE award for service to track; elected to Fla. Track and Field Hall of Fame, 1979; track and field ofcl. 1984 Olympic Games; named hon. life mem. Fla. Sheriffs Boys Ranch and Assn. Mem. Acad. Mgmt., Am. Personnel Assn., Am. Soc. Tng. Dirs., Nat. Panel Am. Arbitration Assn., Mgmt. Assn. Gainesville (pres. 1969-86), Nat. Police Assn., Fla. Purchasing Assn. (life), Fla. Blue Key, Alpha Kappa Psi (Service award 1968), Alpha Tau Omega (trustee, Service award 1971), Alpha Chi, Pi Sigma Alpha, Pi Gamma Mu. Lodges: Elks, Kiwanis. Home: 3204 Ontario Dr Northport AL 35476-1948

OLIVER, ELOISE DOLORES (KITTY), ethnic diversity consultant, writer; b. Jacksonville, Fla., Dec. 16, 1947; d. Roy Hurschel and Terotha Elizabeth (Glover) Leeks; m. Richard Calvin Oliver, Jan. 26, 1968 (div. Sept. 1989); children: Kali Rita, Brian Kyle. BA in English, U. Fla., 1969; MFA in Creative Writing, Fla. Internat. U., 1994. Staff writer, columnist Miami Herald, Broward County, Fla., 1971-90; pres. Kitty O. Enterprises, Inc., Ft. Lauderdale, Fla., 1989—; asst. to pres. for diversity concerns Nova Southeastern U., Ft. Lauderdale, 1992-94; vis. instr., lectr. Fla. Internat. U., North Miami, Fla., 1994-96; vis. asst. prof. Fla. Atlantic U., Ft. Lauderdale, 1995—; cons., presenter ednl. video prodn. and workshops Broward County Sch. Sys., Nova U., Fla. Internat. U., Broward County Govt., 1989—. Author: Reflections of Broward: Ethnic Diversity, 1988, 2d edit., 1991, New Reflections: Ethnic Diversity, 1991; co-prodr., co-writer, co-dir. PBS documentary series Celebrate...The Cultural Connection, 1990-93. Founder Kitty Oliver Minority scholar award U. Fla., Gainesville, 1988, chair eng. adv. com., 1995-96; minority and youth chair for Leadership Broward programs Greater Ft. Lauderdale C. of C., 1989-90, 91-92. Named Woman of Yr. in Comms., Women in Comms., Inc., 1983; recipient 1st prize Nat. Edn. Writers Assn., 1982, Hon. Mention award New Letters Internat., 1994, Kurzweil Lit. award, 1994; Delores Auzenne fellow, 1992-93, Presdl. Rsch. fellow Nova Southeastern U., 1986. Mem. MLA, Associated Writing Programs, South Fla. Book Group. Office: Kitty O Enterprises Inc 1323 SE 17th St Ste 108 Fort Lauderdale FL 33316-1707

OLIVER, GARY LYNN, cartoonist; b. Beaumont, Tex., Feb. 27, 1947; s. Wade Ernest and Billy Jo (Eldridge) O. BA in English, U. Tex., 1970. Freelance cartoonist various mags., jours. and orgns.; staff cartoonist The Absolute Sound mag. Home and Office: Box 1174 Marfa TX 79843

OLIVER, JERRY A., protective services official; 2 children. BS in Criminal Justice, Ariz. State U., MS in Pub. Adminstrn.; postgrad., Police Exec. Rsch. Forum, Washington. From patrolman to supr. Phoenix Police Dept., from supr. to asst. chief of police, 1971-90; dir. drug policy Memphis Police Dept.; chief of police Pasadena (Calif.) Police Dept., Atty., Richmond (Va.) Police Dept., 1995—. Founder Spl. Friends Project, Richmond, 1988—. Inductee Ariz. State U. Coll. Pub. Programs Hall of Fame, 1989; recipient Phoenix chpt. Image award NAACP, 1990. Office: Police Dept Richmond 501 N 9th St Richmond VA 23219

OLIVER, JOHN PERCY, II, lawyer; b. Alexander City, Ala., Dec. 3, 1942; s. Samuel William and Sarah Pugh (Coker) D.; m. Melissa Vann, June 11, 1966; children: David M., Leslie E. AB, Birmingham (Ala.) So. Coll., 1964; JD, U. Ala., 1967. Bar: Ala. 1967, U.S. Dist. Ct. (mid. dist.) Ala. 1969, U.S. Supreme Ct. 1971, U.S. Ct. Appeals (5th cir.) 1975, U.S. Ct. Appeals (11th cir.) 1981, U.S. Dist. Ct. (mid. dist.) Ga. 1989. Assoc. Samuel W. Oliver, Atty., Dadeville, Ala., 1967; prin. John P. Oliver II, Atty., Dadeville, 1967-71; ptnr. Oliver & Sims, Attys., Dadeville, 1972-83, Oliver, Sims & Jones, Attys., Dadeville, 1984-85, Oliver & Sims, Attys., Dadeville, 1985—; dir. Bank of Dadeville. Mem. State Dem. Exec. Com., Tallapoosa County, Ala., 1986-94; judge Tallapoosa County Dist. Ct., Dadeville, 1973-76; mcpl. judge, Dadeville, 1976—; spl. probate judge Tallapoosa County Probate Ct., Dadeville, 1987-88. Sgt. USAFR, 1967-72. Mem. ABA, Ala. State Bar Assn. (law solicitation and advt. com. 1988-92; bd. bar commrs. 1992—), Ala. Trial Lawyers Assn. (exec. com. 1975-77), Tallapoosa County Bar Assn. (pres. 1990). Baptist. Office: Oliver & Sims 129 W Columbus St Dadeville AL 36853-1308

OLIVER, JOHN WILLIAM POSEGATE, minister; b. Vincennes, Ind., Apr. 9, 1935; s. Dwight L. and Elizabeth (Posegate) O.; m. Cristina Shepard Hope, Oct. 19, 1968; children: John William Posegate Jr., Sloan Christian Shepard. BA, Wheaton Coll., 1956; BD, Fuller Theol. Sem., 1959; ThM, So. Bapt. Theol. Sem., 1963; DD, Western Sem., 1996. Ordained to ministry Presbyn. Ch. in Am., 1962. Asst. pastor Covenant Presbyn. Ch., Hammond, Ind., 1964-66, Trinity Presbyn. Ch., Montgomery, Ala., 1966-69; pastor 1st Presbyn. Ch., Augusta, Ga., 1969—; moderator Cen. Ga. Presbytery, Presbyn. Ch. in Am., 1976. Founder, trustee Westminster Schs., Augusta, 1972—; chmn. clergy Augusta United Way Campaign, 1974; mem. exec. bd. clergy staff Univ. Hosp., Augusta, 1975-76; mem. bd. commrs. Augusta Housing Authority, vice-chmn., 1976-93; trustee, chmn. bd. Columbia Internat. U., 1978—; mem. ministerial adv. bd. Reformed Theol. Sem., 1978-85, 89-93; bd. dirs. Mission to the World, Presbyn. Ch. in Am., 1984-89, 92-96; dir. Bailey Manor Retirement Ctr., Clinton, S.C., 1992—. Mem. Evang. Theol. Soc., Nassau Club of Princeton, Augusta Country Club. Home: 3205 Huxley Dr Augusta GA 30909-3128 Office: 642 Telfair St Augusta GA 30901-2325

OLIVER, KATHERINE C., museum director. Office: Mid Ga Hist Soc Inc 935 High St Macon GA 31201-2034

OLIVER, WILLIAM LANGDON, brokerage office executive; b. Savannah, Ga., June 9, 1954; s. Robert Lee and Martha (Farr) O.; m. Mary Claudette McCord, Oct. 10, 1987. BS, Vanderbilt U., 1976; MBA, Emory U., 1978. CFA. Officer Ga. R.R. Bank & Trust Co., Augusta, 1978-82; asst. v.p. Barnett Bank of Jacksonville (Fla.) N.A., 1982-83; valuation cons. Valuation Counselors, Inc., Atlanta, 1983-87; v.p. Equitable Securities Corp., Nashville, Tenn., 1987-95; pres. Gulfstream Advisors LLC, Nashville, 1995—; dir. rsch. Edgar M. Norris & Co., Inc., Greenville, S.C., 1995—. Mem. Nashville Soc.

Fin. Analysts (sec.), Hillwood Country Club. Home: 2905 Polo Club Rd Nashville TN 37221-4346

OLIVIER, JASON THOMAS, lawyer; b. New Orleans, Sept. 8, 1961; s. Gerald L. and Beverly Marie (Beck) O.; m. Chellie M. Chitty, 1991. BS in Elec. Engring. Tech., Nicholls State U., Thibodaux, La., 1985; JD, Loyola U., New Orleans, 1990. Bar: La. 1990. Dir. music Sta. KNSU-FM, Thibodaux, 1984-85; prodn. dir. Sta. WTIX-AM, New Orleans, 1987, 89; owner, pres. Jason T. Olivier, A Profl. Law Corp., Metairie, La., 1990—; ptnr. Deas & Olivier, LLP, Metairie, La., 1992—; CEO, pres., gen. counsel Interstate Collection Bur., New Orleans, 1979—; host Hidden Talent Theatre TV Variety Show, Sta. WCOX, 1987; instr. Loyola Law Sch. Computer Ctr., 1988; extern U.S. Ct. Appeals (4th cir.) La. Author poetry; composer songs; vocal arranger, performer album Menagerie; mus. rev. columnist Rockaraound Mag., 1987-88. Mem. La. Bar Assn., Fed. Bar, Comm. Law Soc. (v.p.), The Federalist Soc. (sec. Loyola chpt., editor The Loyola Federalist, Leadership award Loyola chpt. 1990), Northlake Performing Arts Soc. Choir, Northlake Performing Arts Soc. Ensemble (soloist), Tau Kappa Epsilon (Outstanding Leadership award 1985). Republican. Roman Catholic. Office: 1515 Demosthenes St Metairie LA 70005-2701

OLMO, JAIME ALBERTO, physician; b. Barceloneta, P.R., Aug. 28, 1930; d. Juan and Emilia (Gonzalez) O.; m. Joaquina Rivas, June 24, 1954; children: Jaime A., Carlos A., Rosa I., Javier A., Ruth de Lourdes (dec.). BS, U. P.R., 1950; MD, Santiago de Compostela, Spain, 1956. Diplomate Am. Bd. Utilization Rev. Physicians. Intern Auxillo Mutuo Hosp., Hato Rey, P.R., 1956-57; med. dir. Mcpl. Hosp., Aibonito, P.R., 1957-58; resident Doctors Hosp., Santurce, P.R., 1958-59; practice family medicine Rio Piedras, P.R., 1959-88; dir. mktg. and utilization Cardiovascular Surgery of Tex., 1988-90; dir. mktg.-latin Am. St. Joseph Hosp., Houston, 1990—; mem. staff Doctors Hosp., Hosp. San Carlos, Auxilio Mutuo, Tchrs. Hosp., San Martin Hosp.; med. dir. Blue Cross P.R., 1977-88. Treas. Assn. Antituberculosa San Juan, 1958-68, v.p., 1968-69; mem. Instituto Cultura Hispanica, Madrid, 1963—, treas., 1972-78, pres. 1978-82; pres. dist. 2 Boy Scouts Am., 1971-75, mem. P.R. Council, 1965-75; pres. Consuelo Escalona Sch. PTA, Carolina, P.R., 1969-71, also bd. dirs. Decorated Knight Corpus Christi, Toledo, Spain, 1970; recipient Scouters Key, Boy Scouts Am., 1967, Pelican award, 1968, Guajataka award, 1969, 70, Silver Beaver award, 1971; awards Instituto de Cultura Hispanica in Madrid, 1963, 70; medalia al Merito Civil Govt. of Spain, 1977. Fellow Internat. Assn. Physicians and Surgeons, Royal Acad. Medicine (London), Royal Acad. Health (London); mem. AMA, Pan Am. Med. Assn. (sec. 1973-77), P.R. Med. Assn. (ho. of dels. 1958—61, 77, 83, pres. eastern dist. 1970, treas. 1969, vice speaker ho. of dels. 1973, pres. jud. coun., pres. med. services coun., pres. 1976, numerous awards, now dir.), Assn. Physicians and Surgeons, Assn. Profl. of P.r., Ateneo de P.R., Am. Acad. Family Medicine, Am. Assn. Med. Dirs., Asociacion Puertoriquena Graduados Universidades Españolas (pres. 1968, 87), Comandante Exch. Club (pres. 1962-64), P.R. Exch. Club (dir. 1964), Lions (v.p. Aibonito 1987). Roman Catholic. Home: 13410 Rosstown Ct Sugar Land TX 77478-6047

OLMSTEAD, PHYLLIS MELODY, computer specialist; b. Plant City, Fla., Sept. 15, 1960; d. George Donaldson and Shirley Ann (Buckler) Pirkle; m. Jeffery Wayne Olmstead, Aug. 1, 1983; stepchildren: Jeffery Wayne Jr., Jill Windee Olmstead Morales. AA, Hillsboro C.C., 1981; BSA, U. Fla., 1983; MEd, U. Ctrl. Fla., 1991, EdD, 1994. Cert. tchr., vocat. dir., jr. high math. tchr., Fla. H.S. tchr. Highlands County Schs., Lake Placid, Fla., 1983-84; computer specialist, mgr. Radio Shack-Tandy, Fla., 1985-86; floral designer Publix Supermarkets, Apopka and Orlando, Fla., 1986-88; mid. sch. tchr. Orange County Pub. Schs., Orlando, 1988-94, hosp./homebound distance educator, 1994-96; grant project dir., project asst. U. Ctrl. Fla., Orlando, 1992-93; academic computing specialist Nova Southeastern U., Ft. Lauderdale, Fla., 1996—; mem. exam. validation com. Fla. Dept. Edn., Orlando, 1991-92; ednl./tech. cons. Muslim Acad. of Ctrl. Fla., Orlando, 1992-95; testing supr. Ednl. Testing Svc., 1994-95. Co-author, co-editor: I Make a Difference: Making the Transition from Clinician to Educator, 1993; contbr. articles to profl. jours. Puppy raiser Canine Companions for Independence, Orlando, 1989-91; neighborhood watch coord. Forest Oaks Subdivsn., Ocoee, Fla., 1989-95; coord. Vial-of Life Program, Ocoee, 1992. Recipient Outstanding Additions Team Vol. Tchr., Orange County Additions, 1989-90; Tchrs. grantee Orange County Pub. Schs., 1990. Mem. NEA, Internat. Coun. for Distance Edn. (pres., chair women's internat. network 1992-95, presenter, author conf. 1992, 95, editor newsletter 1993-95), Fla. Tchr.'s Profl. Assn. Home: 6943 College Ct Davie FL 33317

OLSAN, LEA S. THOMPSON, English and foreign language educator; b. Monroe, La., Mar. 21, 1943; d. Lea S. and Eleanor Yvonne (McKenzie) Thompson; children: R. Charles, Adam Dale. BA, La. State U., 1965; PhD, Tulane U., 1973. Asst. prof. Latin Northeast La. U., Monroe, 1975-77, asst. prof. English and Fgn. Langs., 1977-87, assoc. prof. English and Fgn. Langs., 1988-93, prof. English and Fgn. Langs., 1993—; acting head dept. English, Northeast La. U., Monroe, 1991, head, 1991; teaching asst. Tulane U., New Orleans, 1968-69; spl. lectr. English, U. New Orleans, 1975; mem. numerous univ. coms. Contbr. articles to profl. jours. Coll. Arts and Scis. fellow La. State U., 1962-65, Woodrow Wilson fellow, 1965, NDEA fellow Tulane U., 1966-68; Vis. scholar U. Mich., 1973, NEH fellow U. Pa., 1976-77. Mem. MLA, Medieval Acad. of Am., La. Classical Assn., New Chaucer Soc.

OLSEN, JOHN RICHARD, education consultant; b. St. Paul, Aug. 6, 1930; s. Richard Lewis and Anita Marie (Cavanaugh) O.; m. Marlene Deloris Delaria, June 5, 1954; children: Mary Elizabeth Olsen Lavalley, Teresa Louise Olsen Preston. BS in Edn., U. St. Thomas, St. Paul, 1953; MEd, U. St. Thomas, 1959; PhD in Ednl. Tech., Cath. U. Am., 1969. Cert. tchr., Minn. Tchr. Minn. Pub. Schs., Holdingford, Minn., 1953-54; commd. 2d lt. USAF, 1954, advanced through grades to col., 1980; with res. USAFR; br. chief Ctr. for Disease Control, Atlanta, 1964-70; div. dir. FDA, Washington, 1970-72; dir. SAODAP, White House, Washington, 1972-74, Nat. Inst. on Drug Abuse, Washington, 1974-77; prin. advisor USN, Pensacola, Fla., 1977-79; pres. Tranex, Pensacola, 1979—; cons. Office Substance Abuse, Washington, 1985—, USN, Washington, 1986-89, CRS, Inc., 1989-92, Mantec Math., Washington, 1988-91. Author: Model Community Handbook, 1989; editor: Drug Abuse Evaluation, 1977; contbg. editor NSPI Jour., 1962—; contbr. articles to profl. jours. Chmn. Human Rights Adv. Com., Pensacola, 1987, Escambia Dem. Exec. Com., Pensacola, 1986—; bd. dirs. Avant Garde, Pensacola, 1991; mem. LEadership Pensacola, 1981. Decorated Meritorious Svc. medal; named Citizen of Yr., Fla. PTA, 1983, Profl. of Yr., Pensacola C. of C., 1984; recipient Disting. Svc. award Tng. Officers Conf., 1973. Mem. Nat. Soc. for Performance and Instrn. (life, treas. 1964, chpt. pres. 1965, 89), Fla. Alcohol and Drug Abuse Assn. (prevention chmn. 1984-89), Krewe of Neptune, Krewe of Lafitte. Roman Catholic.

OLSEN, MARTIN E., obstetrician/gynecologist; b. Morgantown, W.Va., Jan. 14, 1959; s. Elmer and Charlene Maria (Cole) O.; m. Natalie Maschmann, June 25, 1983; 1 child, Karen. BS, Muskingum Coll., 1981; MD, Med. Coll. Ohio, 1985. Diplomate Am. Bd. Family Practice, Am. Bd. Obstetrics & Gynecology. Resident in family practice Akron (Ohio) Gen. Med. Ctr., 1985-88; resident in ob/gyn U. Tenn., Chattanooga, 1989-91, instr., 1991-92; asst. prof., dir. residency program East Tenn. State U., Johnson City, 1992—. Fellow Am. Coll. Obstetrics and Gynecology; mem. N.Am. Soc. Pediatric & Adolescent Gynecology, So. Med. Assn., Tri-Cities Ob-Gyn Soc. Office: East Tenn State U Dept Ob/Gyn Johnson City TN 37686

OLSEN, MILES JEFFREY, religious educator, minister; b. Sidney, Nebr., Sept. 30, 1952; s. Harold Daniel and Genevieve Marie (Schwartz) O. BBE, Western Bible Coll., 1984; MA in Bib. Studies magna cum laude, Criswell Coll., 1989. Youth pastor intern Friendly Hills Bapt. Ch., Morrison, Colo., 1983-84; tchr. bible Derby Hill Bapt. Ch., Loveland, Colo., 1984-85; minister of youth and christian edn. First Bapt. Ch., North East, Pa., 1985-86; tchr. bible First Bapt. Ch., Dallas, 1986-91; pastor, tchr. Christ's Comty. Ch., Trinity Bapt. Ch., Ballinger, Tex., 1991-93; assoc. pastor, tchr. Trinity Bapt. Ch., Stamford, Tex., 1994-95; teaching fellow in pedagogy Western Bible Coll., 1983-84. With U.S. Army, 1973-76, ETO. Baptist.

OLSEN, NORMAN C., critical care nurse, educator; b. Worcester, Mass., May 27, 1955; s. Kenneth A. and Evelyn R. (Lapierre) O. AS in Mental Health, No. Essex Community Coll., Haverhill, Mass., 1975; BA in Psychology, U. North Fla., Jacksonville, 1978; ADN, DeKalb Coll., Clarkston, Ga., 1984. Cert. critical care nurse. Charge nurse burn unit Grady Hosp., Atlanta; ICU staff nurse, emergency rm. nurse Key West; skills lab. asst. Fla. Keys Community Coll. Sch. Nursing, Key West; dir. Home Health Agy., Key West; instr. ACLS, BLS, Critical Care, Key West. Mem. AACN, Fla. Nurses Assn. Home: 724 Simonton St Key West FL 33040-7475

OLSON, CARL ERIC, lawyer; b. Center Moriches, N.Y., May 19, 1914; s. August William and Sophie (Maiwald) O.; m. Ila Dudley Yeatts, May 31, 1945; children: Carl Eric, William Yeatts, Nancy Dudley. AB, Union Coll., 1936; JD, Yale, 1940. Bar: Conn. 1941, N.Y. 1947. Assoc. Clark, Hall & Peck, New Haven, 1940-41; assoc. Reid & Priest, N.Y.C., 1946-56, ptnr. 1956-80; pvt. practice, Palm Beach Gardens, Fla., 1981—. Maj. U.S. Army, 1941-45. Mem. Yale Club of the Palm Beaches, PGA Nat. Club. Republican. Congregationalist. Home and Office: 6 Surrey Rd Palm Beach Gardens FL 33418

OLSON, DAVID ALLEN, engineer; b. Rio de Janeiro, Mar. 6, 1953; s. Sherman Jerome and Edith Mary (Weskamp) O.; m. Betsey Good Appelbaum, Dec. 28, 1977; children: Daniel A., Rachel L. BS in Aircraft Maintenance Engring., Northrop Inst. Tech., Inglewood, Calif., 1974; MS in Industry and Tech., East Tex. State U., Commerce, 1984. Aircraft maintenance officer USAF, McClellan AFB, Calif., 1975-76; mem. tech. staff Rockwell Internat., El Segundo, Calif., 1976-77; assoc. engr. Hughes Aircraft Co., Fullerton, Calif., 1977-78; logistics specialist Gen. Dynamics, Ft. Worth, 1978-86, program devel. specialist, 1988-92; ILS program mgr. Lockheed-Ga. Co., Marietta, 1986-88; program mgr. GDE Systems, Inc., Ft. Worth, 1992—; maintenance officer USAF Res., Tinker AFB, Okla. and others, 1976—. Author, editor: F-16 Facilities Requirements and Design Criteria, 1985. 2d lt. USAF, 1974-76. Mem. Air Force Assn. (pres. Ft. Worth chpt. 1995—, Exceptional Svc. award 1994, 96, medal of merit 1990, 92, pres. Dobbins chpt.-Marietta, 1985-86). Republican. Roman Catholic. Office: GDE Systems Inc PO Box 122088 Ft Worth TX 76121-2088

OLSON, DENNIS OLIVER, lawyer; b. Seminole, Tex., Oct. 19, 1947; s. Edwin and Beulah Matilda (Strang) O.; m. Leonee Lynn Claud, Jan. 30, 1971; children: James Edwin, Stacy Rae. BA in English, U. Tex., 1969; JD, Tex. Tech U., 1974. Cert. consumer bankruptcy law, bus. bankruptcy law, bankruptcy law examiner, Tex. Bar: Tex. 1974, U.S. Ct. Mil. Appeals 1974, U.S. Dist. Ct. (no. dist.) Tex. 1978, U.S. Dist. Ct. (we. dist.) Tex. 1978, U.S. Ct. Appeals (5th cir.) 1984, U.S. Supreme Ct. 1985. Commd. USMC, 1969, advanced through grades to capt., 1973, infantry officer various locations including Vietnam, 1969-74, judge advocate, various locations, 1974-78, resigned, 1978; assoc. Carr, Evans, Fouts & Hunt, and predecessor, Lubbock, Tex., 1978-81, ptnr., 1981-85; sole practice, Dallas, 1985-88; shareholder, co-chmn. bankruptcy sect. Godwin & Carlton, P. C., Dallas, 1989-94; ptnr. Olson Gibbons Nicond Birne Sussman & Gueck, LLP, and predecessor, Dallas, 1994—. Bd. dirs. Presbyn. Ctr. Doctor's Clinic, Lubbock, 1983-85, United Campus Ministry, Tex. Tech U., Lubbock, 1984-85; elder Canyon Creek Presbyn. Ch., Richardson, Tex.; treas. bd. dirs. Lubbock chpt. ARC, 1981-82, v.p., bd. dirs. Quantico (Va.) chpt. ARC, 1975-77; vol. Lubbock United Way, 1978-80. Decorated Bronze Star; named Outstanding Young Man of Am., 1983. Fellow Tex. Bar Found.; mem. Dallas County Bar Assn., Lubbock County Bar Assn. (bd. dirs. 1983-85), Tex. Young Lawyers Assn. (bd. dirs. 1981-83), Judge Advocates Assn. (bd. dirs. 1976-78), Lubbock C. of C. (grad. Leadership Lubbock program 1981), Phi Delta Phi. Home: 407 Fall Creek Dr Richardson TX 75080-2508

OLSON, DONALD GEORGE, computer services administrator; b. Minot, N.D., May 16, 1941; s. George James and Ellen (Ranta) O.; BME, U. N.D., 1963; MME, N.D. State U., 1968; m. LuAnn Hiniker Olson; 1 son, Todd B. Analyst, programmer Bur. Reclamation, Denver, 1963-66; asst. dir. computer center N.D. State U., Fargo, 1966-69; data processing mgr. U. Calif. Sci. Lab., Los Alamos, 1969-74; dir. data processing nat. assessment ednl. progress Edn. Commn. States, Denver, 1974-77; staff mgr. Mountain Bell, Denver, 1977-80; dir. computer services Mankato (Minn.) State U., 1980-86, assoc. v.p. computer and info. services, 1986-96, interim dir. MSUS/PALS automated libr. system, 1993-96; chief info. officer Murray (Ky.) State U., 1996—; bd. dirs. Minn. Regional Network; cons. in field. Registered profl. engr., certified data processor. Mem. Assn. Computing Machinery, Rotary, Elks, Phi Delta Theta. Republican. Roman Catholic. Home: 1844 Douglas Rd Murray KY 42071 Office: Murray State U Info Syss Murray KY 42071

OLSON, GARY ANDREW, English language educator; b. Waterbury, Conn., Dec. 12, 1954; s. Joseph David and Charlotte (Anderson) O.; m. Marlyne Salitsky, June 3, 1978 (div. June 1993). BA, Kings Coll., 1976; MA, U. Conn., 1978; PhD, Indiana U. of Pa., 1980. Instr. U. Ala., Tuscaloosa, 1980-82; asst. prof. U. N.C., Wilmington, 1982-85; asst. prof. U. South Fla., Tampa, 1985-87, assoc. prof., 1987-92, prof. English, 1992—; mem. exec. com. Conf. on Coll. Composition and Comm., 1992—. Editor Journal Advanced Composition, 1985-95, Philosophy, Rhetoric, Literary Criticism: (Inter)Views, 1994, Writing Centers: Theory and Administration, 1984; co-editor: The Process Reader, 1985, Advanced Placement English, 1989, The Gender Reader, 1990, (Inter)Views: Cross Disciplinary Perspectives on Literacy, 1991, Composition Theory for the Postmodern Classroom, 1994; co-author: Style and Readability in Technical Writing. Founding pres. Southeastern Writing Ctr. Assn., 1981-83. Recipient Award for Outstanding Contbn. to English Tchrs. of N.C., 1983. Mem. MLA, Nat. Coun. Tchrs. English, Conf. on Coll. Composition and Comm., Assn. Tchrs. of Advanced Composition, Rhetoric Soc. Am. (bd. dirs. 1990-94), South Atlantic MLA. Democrat. Home: 3733 Murray Dale Dr Valrico FL 33594-6923 Office: U South Fla English Dept Tampa FL 33620

OLSON, JEAN KATHRYN, chemistry educator; b. Superior, Wis., May 1, 1944; d. John Raymond and Dolores Anna (Hanson) Lundberg; m. James I. Olson, Jan. 22, 1966; children: Jill Olson Scherrer, Rebecca Olson Cosford, Amanda. BS, U. Wis., Superior, 1966, MS, 1969; PhD, Fla. State U., 1993. Tchr. Duluth (Minn.) Pub. Schs., 1966-67; sch. psychologist Tucson (Ariz.) Pub. Schs., 1970-72; religious edn. dir. USAF, Homestead AFB, Fla., 1979-83; tchr. chemistry, dept. chair Rutherford H.S., Panama City, Fla., 1984—. Co-author Bay County Chemistry I Lab. Manual, 1987, Chemistry II Lab. Manual, 1988; contbr. articles to profl. jours. Safety trainer Bay Dist. Schs., Panama City, 1994—; sci. frameworks trainer Fla. Dept. Edn., Tallahassee, 1994—; chair Sch. Reform Com. Rutherford H.S., 1995-96. Mem. Nat. Sci. Tchrs. Assn., Am. Chem. Soc. Divsn. Chem. Edn., Fla Assn. Sci. Tchrs. (chair state conf. 1989, pres. 1990-91, editor newsletter 1994—), Alpha Delta Kappa (pres. Tau chpt. 1994-96). Republican. Presbyterian. Office: Rutherford HS 1000 School Ave Panama City FL 32401-5157

OLSON, JOHN KARL, lawyer; b. Springfield, Mass., Aug. 14, 1949; s. Harold Gunnar and Louise Theodora (Shukis) O.; m. Ann Catherine Sullivan, June 16, 1973; children: Elizabeth Ann, Katherine Louise. AB, Harvard Coll., 1971; JD, Boston Coll., 1975. Bar: Fla. 1975, U.S. Dist. Ct. (mid. and so. dists.) Fla. 1976, U.S. Ct. Appeals (5th cir.) 1979, U.S. Supreme Ct. 1979; U.S. Ct. Appeals (11th cir.) 1981. From assoc. to ptnr. Carlton, Fields, Ward et al., Tampa, Fla., 1975-86; exec. v.p., gen. counsel, dir. Jet Fla., Inc., Miami, 1986-88; ptnr. Stearns Weaver Miller Weissler Alhadeff & Sitterson P.A., Tampa, 1988—. Author: Creditors and Debtors Rights in Florida, 1979, 89, Collier Bankruptcy Practice Guide, 1986. Trustee Tampa Mus. Art, 1992—. Fellow U. Tampa, 1986—. Mem. ABA (vice-chmn. backruptcy com. 1984-86), Fla. Bar (chmn. bus. law sect. 1988-89), Harvard Club (pres. 1982-84), Turnaround Mgmt. Assn. (Ctrl. Fla. chpt. pres. 1995—). Home: 2632 W Prospect Rd Tampa FL 33629-5358 Office: Sun Trust Fin Ctr 401 E Jackson St Tampa FL 33602

OLSON, JUDITH ELAINE, education educator; b. Long Beach, Calif., July 11, 1945; d. Alma and Vivian (Reid) Mehr; m. James Stuart Olson, July 31, 1965; children: Susan Marie, Karin Elisa, Heather Kathleen, Bradley Asbjornsen. BA, Brigham Young U., 1967; MA, SUNY, Stony Brook, 1972; PhD, Tex. A&M U., 1991. Tchr. Rocky Point (N.Y.) Sch., 1968-69, Three Village Sch. Dist., Setauket, N.Y., 1969-72; tchr. continuing edn. Huntsville (Tex.) Ind. Sch. Dist., 1976-79; dir. Adult Edn. Ctr. Region VI Edn. Svc. Ctr., 1979-82; dir. ESL Ctr. Sam Houston State U., 1982-91, dir. Learning Assistance Ctr., faculty Coll. Edn., 1991—. Co-author: Cuban Americans, 1994. Mem. Walker County (Tex.) Housing Bd., 1988-90; mem. bd. mgrs. Walker County Hosp. Dist., 1993—. Fed. Title VII grantee for bilingual edn. Tex. A&M U., 1988-89. Democrat. Mem. LDS Ch. Office: Sam Houston State U Box 2074 Huntsville TX 77341

OLSON, MICHELE SCHARFF, kinesiology/physical education educator; b. McMinnville, Oreg., Nov. 29, 1960; d. Harold Alfred and Ellen Marcella Scharff; m. Brian Astor Olson, Dec. 22, 1986. BA, Huntingdon Coll., Montgomery, Ala., 1986; MEd, Auburn U., 1987, PhD, 1991. Grad. rsch. asst. Auburn U., Montgomery, 1986-87; dir. preventive cardiology Montgomery Cardiovascular Assocs., 1987-89; asst. prof. kinesiology Huntingdon Coll., Montgomery, 1990-95; assoc. prof. phys. edn. Auburn U., Montgomery, 1995—; founder, exec. dir. Aerobic Leadership Tng. and Seminars (ALTS), Montgomery, 1985—; cons. Studio Workout, Montgomery, 1987—, Montgomery Athletic Club, 1990—; continuing edn. provider Am. Coun. on Exercise, San Diego, 1989—, Aerobic and Fitness Assn. Am., 1989; lectr. in field. Author various rsch. studies; contbr. articles to profl. jours. Mem. Jr. League of Montgomery, 1992—. Auburn U. grantee, 1990. Mem. AAHPERD, Ala. Assn. Health, Phys. Edn., Recreation and Dance (rsch. pres. 1990, v.p. elect dance div. 1996—), Am. Coll. Sports Medicine, Assn. Fitness Excellence (hon. bd. 1990), Am. Heart Assn. (cert.), Women's Sports Found. Home: 2272 Rosemont Dr Montgomery AL 36111-1009

OLSON, NADINE FAYE, foreign language educator, consultant; b. Broken Bow, Nebr., Mar. 7, 1948; d. Warren Wendell and Lois Julia (Kolbo) O. BA in Edn., Ea. Wash. U., 1970; MA in Spanish, U. No. Iowa, 1981; PhD in Romance Langs., U. Ga., 1989. Tchr. English and Spanish Cen. Valley Sch. Dist., Spokane, Wash., 1970-82; instr. in Spanish U. of the South, Sewanee, Tenn., 1986-89; asst. prof. Spanish and fgn. lang. edn. Okla. State U., Stillwater, 1989-94, assoc. prof. Spanish and fgn. lang. edn., 1994—; freelance cons., Okla., 1989—; reader advanced placement Spanish exams. Ednl. Testing Svcs., Princeton, N.J., 1991—. Mem. Am. Coun. Tchg. of Fgn. Langs., Okla. Fgn. Lang. Tchrs. Assn. (exec. bd.), Am. Assn. Tchrs. Spanish and Portuguese, Delta Kappa Gamma (chpt. pres. 1979-81, 94-96), Phi Kappa Phi, Sigma Delta Pi (chpt. treas. 1983-84). Office: Okla State U 309 Gundersen Hall Stillwater OK 74078

OLSON, OSCAR JULIUS, international economist; b. Corpus Christi, Tex., Mar. 31, 1933; s. Oscar Julius and Kate (Arnold) O.; m. Patricia Kay Whipple, Nov. 12, 1955; children: Michael Alan, Kirsten Anne Olson Pruski, Kathleen Kay. BA, U. Tex., 1954; MA, Yale U., 1957; postgrad., Fletcher Sch. Law & Diplomacy, Medford, Mass., 1966-67. Fgn. svc. officer Dept. of State, Washington, 1957-84; exec. dir. U.S. Man & the Biosphere Program, Washington, 1976-80; counselor of embassy Am. Embassy, Quito, Ecuador, 1982-84; dir. Latin Am. BERI S.A., 1985—; cons. internat. office Smithsonian Instn., Washington, 1984-85, Dept. of State, Washington, 1985—. Bd. dirs. Civitan Club of Arlington, Va., 1991—. Mem. Am. Fgn. Svc. Assn., Diplomatic and Consular Officers, Retired, Soc. for Internat. Devel., World Affairs Coun. of Washington, D.C., Latin m. Studies Assn., Phi Beta Kappa. Methodist. Home: PO Box 106 Catlett VA 20119-0106 Office: Beri SA PO Box 513 Friday Harbor WA 98250

OLSON, PETER JOHN, business communication educator; b. New Haven, May 20, 1966; s. Vernon Gunnar and Ruth Anne (Walters) O.; m. Ethna Ann Murphy, Aug. 17, 1991. AA, Palm Beach C.C., Palm Beach Gardens, Fla., 1993; BA, Fla. Atlantic U., 1994, postgrad., 1995—. Profl. golfer, 1986-93, 94-95; golf profl. Yale U. Golf Course, New Haven, 1989-90; pro shop asst. mgr. Hilaman Park Golf Course, Tallahassee, 1990-92; grad. tchg. asst. Fla. Atlantic U., Boca Raton, 1995—. U. Oxford scholar English Speaking Union-Boca Raton, 1996. Mem. MLA, Grad. Student Assn.-Fla. Atlantic U. (treas.), English Grad. Student Soc.-Fla. Atlantic U., Sigma Tau Delta. Lutheran. Home: 1521 N 69th Way Hollywood FL 33024

OLSON, REX MELTON, oil and gas company executive; b. Alva, Okla., Mar. 6, 1940; s. Harrison and Zylpha Mable (Redgate) O.; m. Sandra Florence Barker, June 5, 1959; children: Brenda Carol Sikes, Brian Rex. Student, Abilene Christian U., 1958-60; BS, Okla. State U., 1963, DVM, 1965. Veterinarian Waynoka (Okla.) Animal Clinic, 1965-83; pres. Zoroco Petroleum, Inc., Waynoka, 1979-88, Santo Resources, Inc., Waynoka, 1982—; owner/operator ranch Waynoka, 1958—; co-founder Waynoka Mfg. Co., 1987; bd. dirs. First State Bank, Waynoka. Mem. Waynoka Airport Commn.; mem. Waynoka City Coun., Waynoka Indstrl. Authority; v.p. Woods County Indsl. Com.; bd. dirs. Waynoka Sch. Found., York Coll., Nebr., trustee, 1988—; pres. Waynoka Hist. Soc., 1992—. Mem. AVMA, Okla. Vet. Med. Assn. (past bd. dirs.), Okla. Mineral Owners Assn., Aircraft Owners and Pilots Assn., Waynoka C. of C. (pres. 1977, 87). Republican. Mem. Ch. of Christ. Home: RR 2 Box 36A Waynoka OK 73860-9706 Office: Santo Resources Inc 101 Missouri Waynoka OK 73860

OLSON, RICHARD E(UGENE), II, chiropractor, publisher, consultant; b. St. Joseph, Mo., July 21, 1954; s. Richard E. and Evelyn Joanne (Kerber) O.; m. Pamela J. Croft, Sept. 22, 1979; children: Stacey, Thomas, Kevin. D Chiropractic, Life Chiropractic Coll., 1979. Mem. faculty Life Chiropractic Coll., Marietta, Ga., 1979-83; pres. Data Mgmt. Ventures, Inc., Marietta, 1985—; practice chiropractic Southeastern Chiropractic Assocs., Inc., Atlanta, 1982-89. Author: Procedural/Utilization Facts, 1987, Chiropractic Services Program, 1988; editor: Fee Facts, 1985—. Active Heritage Found., Washington. Mem. Fla. Chiropractic Assn. Republican. Baptist. Office: Data Mgmt Ventures Inc Ste E-2 1335 Canton Rd Marietta GA 30066-6053

OLSON, SANDRA DITTMAN, medical and surgical nurse; b. Duluth, Minn., Mar. 27, 1953; d. Donald Gene and Evelyn Mae (Wilson) Dittman; m. Douglas Bruce Olson, Aug. 10, 1974; 1 child, Perryn Douglas. BSN, S.D. State U., 1974. Cert ACLS; cert. PALS. Staff nurse U.S. Army Hosp., Nurnberg, Fed. Republic Germany, 1975-79; dir. staff devel. Oak Ridge Care Ctr., Mpls., 1979-81; staff nurse med.-surg. Profl. Nursing, Metairie, La., 1982-83; staff nurse, weekend spl. Tulane Med. Ctr., New Orleans, 1982-83; charge nurse Meadowcrest Hosp., Gretna, La., 1983, house supr., 1983-95; utilization rev. and infection control nurse Advance Care Hosp., Marrero, La., 1995—; employee activity com. bd. mem. Pharmacy-Nursing Task Force; active numerous workshops on edn., staff devel., coronary and intensive care, infection control, long term care, mgmt. Bd. dirs., sec. Bon Temps Homeowners Assn.; chair ct. of honor Boy Scout Troop #378. Named Spink County Wheat Queen; recipient 1989 LA Great 100 Nurses award; S.D. Gov.'s scholar. Mem. Assn. of Women's Students (chmn. social-publicity), U. Women's Svc. Orgn. (Guidon historian), Sigma Theta Tau, Alpha Xi Delta (chmn. philathropy). Home: 2144 Lasalle Ave Terrytown LA 70056-4515

OLSON, TED (CHARLES STRONG), writer; b. Northampton, Mass., Nov. 16, 1960; s. Kenneth George and Claire Phoenix (Thomes) O. BA in English, U. Minn., 1982; MA in English, U. Ky., 1991; postgrad., U. Miss., 1991—. Tchr. Burgundy Ctr. for Wildlife Studies, Capon Bridge, W.Va., 1979-83; park ranger Nat. Pk. Svc., Blue Ridge Parkway, N.C., 1984-92; tchg. asst. U. Ky., Lexington, 1988-91; folklore instr. Haywood C.C., Clyde, N.C., 1990; grad. instr. U. Miss., Oxford, 1991-95; disc jockey WUMS/WOXD Radio, Oxford, 1994-95; tchr. Ctr. for English Lang. Learning, Maryville, Tenn., 1995—; adj. prof. Maryville (Tenn.) Coll., 1996; staff mem. Bluegrass Unltd. mag., 1993-96; proofreader Misnomer, Prestonsburg, Ky., 1992-94. Author: So Far: Poems, 1994; co-author: Hiking Trails of the Smokies, 1994; founding editor Cross Roads: A Jour. of So. Culture, 1992-96; co-editor: (textbook) Writing About Identity in the South, 1993-95; asst. editor: Mississippi Folklore Register, 1993; performer (rec.) Workin' on the New Railroad: Folk Songs, 1992; contbr. articles, essays, revs., interviews and poems to publs. Music cons., performer Miss. Modern Dance Co., University, 1992, So. Culture Celebration, Birmingham, Ala., 1996; organizer Waterrock Knob Folk Festival, Balsam, N.C., 1992; storyteller Oxford Storyteller Guild, 1993. Recipient first place traditional music performance High Country Mountain Fair, Boone, N.C., 1984, first place nat. student paper contest Fellows of the Am. Folklore Soc., 1992, first place Carl A. Ross student paper contest Appalachian Studies Assn., 1992, Fast Track award Nat. Pk. Svc.-S.E. Region, Atlanta, 1992, first place poetry chapbook contest Creeker Press, Oxford, 1994. Mem. MLA, Am. Studies Assn., Am. Folklore Soc., Assn. for the Study of Lit. and the Environment, Ctr. for

Appalachian Studies and Svcs., N.C. Writers' Network. Office: care Claire T Olson 5917 Grass Lake Ter Minneapolis MN 55419

OLSON, WILLIAM HENRY, neurology educator, administrator; b. Haxtun, Colo., Sept. 2, 1936; s. William Henry and Burdene (Anderson) O.; m. Shirley Gorden, July 24, 1967; children: Erik, Marnie. B.A., Wesleyan U., 1959; M.D., Harvard U., 1963. Diplomate: Am. Bd. Psychiatry and Neurology. Intern Beth Israel Hosp., Boston, 1963-65; resident Children's Hosp. Med. Ctr., Boston, 1965-67; staff assoc. NIH, Bethesda, Md., 1969-70; asst. prof. neurology and anatomy Vanderbilt U., Nashville, 1970-73, assoc. prof. neurology and anatomy, 1973-75; prof., chmn. dept. adult neurology U. N.D., Fargo, 1975-80; chmn., prof. dept. neurology U. Louisville, 1980—. Co-author: Practical Neurology and the Primary Care Physician, 1981, Symptom Oriented Neurology, 1994. Fulbright scholar Tubingen, Germany, 1958-59. Fellow Am. Acad. Neurology; mem. Phi Beta Kappa. Home: 331 Zorn Ave # 1 Louisville KY 40206-1542 Office: Univ Louisville Dept Neurology Louisville KY 40292

OLSON, WILLIAM JEFFREY, lawyer; b. Paterson, N.J., Oct. 23, 1949; s. Walter Justus and Viola Patricia (Trautvetter) O.; m. Janet Elaine Bollen, May 22, 1976; children: Robert J., Joanne C. AB, Brown U., 1971; JD, U. Richmond, 1976. Bar: Va. 1976, D.C. 1976, U.S. Ct. Claims 1976, U.S. Ct. Appeals (4th and D.C. cirs.) 1976, U.S. Supreme Ct. 1982. Assoc. Jackson & Campbell, Washington, 1976-79; ptnr. Gilman, Olson & Pangia, Washington, 1980-92; prin. William J. Olson PC, McLean, Va. and Washington, 1992—; sec., treas. bd. dirs. Victims Assistance Legal Orgn., Virginia Beach, Va., 1979—; presdl. transition team leader Legal Svcs. Corp., Washington, 1980; chmn. and bd. dirs. Nat. Legal Svcs. Corp., 1981-82; mem. Pres.'s Export Coun. Subcom. on Export Adminstrn., Washington, 1982-84; spl. counsel bd. govs. U.S. Postal Svc., Washington, 1984-86. Author: Tuition Tax Credits and Alternatives, 1978; co-author: Debating National Health Policy, 1977. Trustee Davis Meml. Goodwill Industries, Washington, 1980-86, 88-93; chmn. Fairfax County Rep. Com., Fairfax, Va., 1980-82; mem. Rep. State Ctrl. Com., Richmond, Va., 1982-86. Mem. Va. Bar Assn., Assn. Trial Lawyers Am., Va. Trial Lawyers Assn., Christian Legal Soc. Republican. Baptist. Office: 8180 Greensboro Dr Ste 1070 Mc Lean VA 22102-3823

OLSON-HAGAN, ARLENE, parochial school administrator; b. Bklyn., May 30, 1926; d. Carl Bernard and Helen Loretta (Segerdell) Olson; m. Raymond G. Hagan, Feb. 15, 1979; stepchildren: David, Clifford, Richard, Bruce. AB in English, Hofstra U., 1948; MS in Edn., SUNY, New Paltz, 1952; Cert. Adv. Study, Hofstra U., 1976. Tchr. Island Trees (N.Y.) Pub. Schs., 1950-55; tchr., dist. pubs. editor Garden City (N.Y.) Pub. Schs., 1955-82; pub. info. officer Amityville (N.Y.) Pub. Schs., 1982-84; dir. external affairs St. Edward's Sch., Vero Beach, Fla., 1986-93. Editor, layout and design newsletters, spl. brochures for schs. Mem. Nat. Sch. Pub. Rels. Assn., Fla. Pub. Rels. Assn., Ctr. for the Arts. Episcopalian.

OLSSON, JAMES EDWARD, otologist, neurotologist; b. Sheridan, Wyo., Sept. 17, 1941; s. Norton Elvern and Mary Frances (Crumpacker) Olsson; m. Sandra Marshall, Dec. 27, 1963; children: Kirsten Olsson Eastin, Ann Catherine Olsson Carrell, Nathan. Grad. order of merit, USAF Acad., 1959-63; MD, U. Colo., 1967. Bd. cert. Am. Bd. Otolaryngology. Intern Wilford Hall USAF Med. Ctr., Lackland AFB, Tex., 1967-68; resident otolaryngology Wilford Hall USAF Med. Ctr., Lackland AFB, 1969-73; chief Aerospace Med. Svcs., Holloman AFB, N.Mex., 1968-69; staff otolaryngologist USAF Hosp., Elmendorf AFB, Alaska, 1973-76; chief Aerospace Med. Svcs., Elmendorf AFB, 1974-76; fellow otology and neurotology U. So. Calif./L.A. Ear Med. Group, 1976-77; vice chmn. dept. otolaryngology Wilford Hall USAF Med. Ctr., Lackland AFB, 1977-81, chmn. dept. otolaryngology, 1981-84; pvt. practice Otologic Assocs., San Antonio, 1984—; tng. officer Otolaryngology Residency Tng. Program, Wilford Hall USAF Med. Ctr., Lackland AFB, 1977-81, dir., 1981-84; clin. asst. prof. Divsn. Otorhinolaryngology, U. Tex. Health Sci. Ctr., San Antonio, 1977-83, clin. assoc. prof., 1983-89, clin. prof., 1989—; spl. asst. Air Force Surgeon Gen. for Otolaryngology, 1981-84; pres. Tex. Neuroscis. Inst., 1990-95; bd. dirs. USAA Fed. Savs. Bank, San Antonio, 1984—, chmn. audit/fin. com., 1993—. Editorial bd. mem.: San Antonio Med. Digest, 1991—; contbr. articles to profl. jours. Mem. ACS, AMA, Am. Laryngol., Rhinol. and Otol. Soc., Am. Neurotologic Soc., Am. Otol. Soc., Inc., Barany Soc., Am. Acad. Otolaryngology-Head and Neck Surgery, Assn. for Rsch. in Otolaryngology, Am. Auditory Soc., William F. House Soc., Tex. Otolaryngol. Assn., Tex. Med. Assn., Am. Coun. Otolaryngology-Head and Neck Surgery, Bexar County Med. Soc., USAF Acad. Assn. Grads. (life), Soc. Air Force Clin. Surgeons, Soc. Mil. Otolaryngologists, Soc. Mil. Surgeons, Collegium Neuro-Otologicum. Office: Ear Medical Group Ste 550 4410 Medical Dr San Antonio TX 78229-3755

OLSSON, PETER ALAN, psychiatrist, psychoanalyst; b. Bklyn., June 26, 1941; s. John Berger and Doris Olsson; m. Sharon Maler, May 25, 1964 (div. June 1974); 1 child, Nathaniel J.; m. Pamela Nicholson, Oct. 27, 1975; 1 child, Andrew T. BS, Wheaton Coll., 1963; MD, Baylor Coll. Medicine, 1967. Diplomate Am. Bd. Psychiatry and Neurology. Intern U. Vt. Hosps., Burlington, 1967-68; resident in psychiatry Baylor Coll. Medicine, Houston, 1968-71; psychoanalytic tng. Houston-Galveston Psychoanalytic Inst., 1981; clin. faculty dept. psychiatry Baylor Coll. Medicine, Houston, 1973-94, U. Tex. Sch. Medicine, Houston, 1975-94; pvt. practice Houston, 1973-94; mem. adult adv. bd., edn. conf. com. MHMRA, 1979-80; co-instr. Houston-Galveston Psychoanalytic Inst. Ext. Sch., 1984; speaker B'nai B'rith Hillel Found., U. Houston Religion Ctr., 1985; lectr. in field. Contbr. poetry and articles to profl. jours. Mem. citizen review com. of internal affairs div. Houston Police Dept., 1990-92. Lt. comdr. USNR, 1971-73. Recipient William C. Menninger award Ctrl. Neuropsychiat. Assn., 1969, Judith Baskin Offer prize, 1979. Fellow Am. Psychiat. Assn.; mem. AMA, Tex. Psychiat. Assn., Am. Group Psychotherapy Assn., Houston Group Psychotherapy Soc. (Meritorious Contbns. award 1978), Tex. Med. Assn., Harris County Med. Soc., Am. Psychoanalytic Assn. (editl. assoc. jour. 1990-92), Houston-Galveston Psychoanalytic Soc., Houston Psychiat. Soc. (ethics com. 1978-79, chmn. ethics com. 1979-80, v.p. 1980-81, pres.-elect 1984-85, pres. 1986, past pres. 1987, pub. affairs com. 1988, exec. com. councilor 1990-93, assoc. editor newsletter Upstream 1981), Found. Houston Psychiat. Soc. (pres. and bd. dirs. 1987-89), Group for Advancement Psychiatry-Com. Internat. Affairs, Harris County Med. Soc. (cons. Houston Ind. Sch. Dist., substance abuse monitors program 1988—). Office: Peter A Olsson MD 14 Algonquin Dr Keene NH 03431-1809

OLUBADEWO, JOSEPH OLANREWAJU, pharmacologist, educator; b. Oroago, Kwara, Nigeria, Apr. 16, 1945; came to U.S., 1980; s. Solomon Akanbi and Leah Ifanike (Omodara) O.; m. Victoria Ibidunni Balogun, Aug. 20, 1972; children: Oludele, Oluseyi, Olubunmi, Oluwole. BSc with honors, Ahmadu Bello U., Zaria, Nigeria, 1970; PhD, Vanderbilt U., 1976. Asst. lectr. Ahmadu Bello U., 1970-75, lectr. II to lectr. I, 1975-80, sr. lectr., 1980; rsch. scientist U. Tenn. Ctr. Health Scis., Memphis, 1980-84, asst. prof., 1984-85; assoc. prof. Xavier U., New Orleans, 1985-91, prof., 1991—; spl. reviewer NIH, 1989-92. Mem. editorial bd. Jour. Nat. Pharm. Assn., 1989; reviewer Annals of Pharmacotherapy, Cellular and Molecular Biology; contbr. articles to profl. jours. Fellow African-American Inst. Grad. Program, 1971-75, Am. Heart Assn., 1983, 84, NIH, 1987, 88. Mem. AAUP, Am. Soc. for Pharmacology and Exptl. Therapeutics, Southeastern Pharmacology Soc. (life), Am. Assn. Colls. Pharmacy, N.Y. Acad. Scis. Baptist. Home: 13510 Dwyer Blvd New Orleans LA 70129-1530 Office: Xavier U La 7325 Palmetto St New Orleans LA 70125-1056

O'MALLEY, BERT WILLIAM, cell biologist, educator, physician; b. Pitts., Dec. 19, 1936; s. Bert Alloysius O'M.; m. Sally Ann Johnson; children: Sally Ann, Bert A., Rebecca, Erin K. BS, U. Pitts., 1959, MD summa cum laude, 1963; DSc (hon.), N.Y. Med. Coll., 1979, Nat. U. Ireland, 1985; MD (hon.), Karolinska Inst., Stockholm, 1984. Intern, resident Duke U., Durham, N.C., 1963-65; clin. assoc. Nat. Cancer Inst., NIH, Bethesda, Md., 1965-67, head molecular biology sect., endocrine br., 1967-69; Lucius Birch prof., dir. Reproductive Biology Ctr. Vanderbilt U. Sch. Medicine, Nashville, 1969-73; Tom Thompson prof., chmn. dept. cell biology Baylor Coll. Medicine, Houston, 1973—, Disting. Svc. prof., 1985, dir. Baylor Ctr. for Reproductive Biology, 1973—; mem. endocrine study sect., NIH, 1970-73, chmn., 1973-74; chmn. CETUS-UCLA Symposium on Gene Expression, 1982; con., mem. coun. rsch. and clin. investigation awards Am. Cancer Soc., 1985-87. Author: (with A.R. Means) Receptors for Reproductive Hormones, 1973, (with L. Birnbaumer) Hormone Action, vols. I and II, 1977, vol. III, 1978, (with A.M. Gotto) The Role of Receptors in Biology and Medicine, 1986; co-author: Methods in Enzymology: Hormone Action: Calmodulin and Calcium-Binding Proteins, 1983, Mechanism of Steriod Hormone Regulation of Gene Transcription, 1994; editor: Gene Regulation: UCLA Symposium on Molecular Cellular Biology, 1982; contbg. author to over 400 publs. Lt. comdr. USPHS, 1965-69. Recipient Ernst Oppenheimer award Am. Endocrine Soc., 1975, Gregory Pincus medal, 1975, Lila Gruber Cancer award, 1977, Disting. Achievement in Modern Medicine award, 1978, Borden award Assn. Am. Med. Colls., 1978, Dickson prize for Basic Med. Rsch., 1979, Philip S. Hench award U. Pitts., 1981, Axel Munthe Reproductive Biology award, Capri, Italy, 1982, Bicentennial Medallion of Distincton U. Pitts., 1987. Mem. AAAS, NAS, Inst. Med. NAS, Am. Soc. Biol. Chemists, Am. Acad. Arts and Scis., Endocrine Soc. (pres. 1985, Fred Conrad Koch medal 1988), Am. Soc. Clin. Investigation, Am. Inst. Chemists, Fedn. Clin. Rsch., Harvey Soc., Alpha Epsilon Delta, Phi Beta Kappa, Alpha Omega Alpha. Democrat. Roman Catholic. Office: Baylor Coll Medicine Dept Neuroscience One Baylor Pla Houston TX 77030-3411

OMOIKE, ISAAC IRABOR, chemist, publisher, author; b. Iruekpen, Nigeria, Apr. 29, 1957; came to U.S., 1976; s. Matthew Ighodalo and Rosaline Alice (Amiolemen) O.; m. Brenda Gail Roberts, Sept. 20, 1980 (div. Dec. 1993); children: Ann, Angel, Jeremey. BS in Biology and Chemistry, U. Southwestern La., 1980; MS in Food Sci. and Biochemistry, La. State U., 1986, Cert. Law Enforcement/Pvt. Investigation, 1995. Teaching asst. chemistry dept. La. State U., Baton Rouge, 1984, rsch. asst. food sci. dept., 1985-86; lab. analyst Fina Oil and Chem. Co., Caraville, La., 1987-88; chemist, supr. Bio-Now Lab. Inc., Amelia, La., 1989; lab. analyst Cibageigy corp., St. Gabriel, La., 1989-90; chemist West Paine Lab., Baton Rouge, 1991; dir. Isaac Omoike Books, Baton Rouge, 1990—; owner Family Pizza Lover Restaurant, Baton Rouge; pres. rsch. and investigations Baton Rouge, 1990—. Author: Genocide The Ultimate Threat of the Next milleniums, 1991, Insider America, 1993, Euthanasia Right or Wrong (Tell-Tale Signs of Murder), 1995. Mem. ALA, Am. Chem. Soc., U.S. Soccer Referees, Am. Civil Liberties Union, PUb. Mktg. Assn. Home: 1910 America St Baton Rouge LA 70806 Office: 8867 Highland Rd Ste 252 Baton Rouge LA 70808

O'NEAL, DENNIS LEE, mechanical engineering educator; b. Ft. Worth, Sept. 1, 1951; s. John Earl and Melba Pearl (Reed) O'N.; m. Sondra Kaye Walter, Jan. 11, 1975; children: Justin Earl, Stephen Walter, Sean Michael. BS, Tex. A&M U., 1973; MS, Okla. State U., 1977; PhD, Purdue U., 1982. Registered profl. engr., Tex. Project engr. Fluid Power Rsch. Ctr., Stillwater, Okla.; rsch. staff mem. Oak Ridge (Tenn.) Nat. Lab., 1977-80; rsch. asst. dept. mech. engring. Purdue U., West Lafayette, Ind., 1980-82; prof. dept. mech. engring. Tex. A&M U., College Station, 1983—, mem. energy com., 1985-87; cons. Lawrence Berkeley (Calif.) Lab., 1989-91, N.W. Power Planning Coun., Portland, 1991-92; mem. peer rev. group EPA, Research Triangle Park, N.C., 1992. Editor conf. procs. in field; contbr. articles to profl. publs. Mem. Energy Mgmt. Com., College Station, 1984-88. Exxon Ednl. Found. faculty asst. grantee, 1986; Tex. Engring. Exptl. Sta. rsch. fellow, 1991, 95. Mem. ASME, Am. Soc. Engring. Edn., Am. Soc. Heating, Ventilating and Air-Conditioning Engrs., Sigma Xi, Phi Kappa PHi. Office: Tex A&M U Dept Mech Engring College Station TX 77843

O'NEAL, EDWIN A., geologist, geophysicist, petroleum engineer; b. Gulfport, Miss., Jan. 5, 1929; s. Aurelius Pericles and Eula Lee (Walker) O'N.; m. Nelle Gray Fulton, Feb. 10, 1952 (dec. Dec. 25, 1994); children: David Edwin, Kerry Christian. BS in Petroleum Geology, Miss. State U., 1952; MS in Geology, Tulane U., 1973. Geophysicist Western Geophysical Co., Shreveport, La., 1954-56; asst. dist. geologist Ark. Fuel Oil Corp., Shreveport, 1956-59; mgr. exploration and prodn. Whitaker Oil Co., Carthage, Tex., 1959-64; geologist Internat. Helium Inc., Longview, Tex., 1964-66, Robbins Drilling Co., Longview, 1966-67; prof., dean engring. and indsl. tech. Delgado C.C., New Orleans, 1967-88; geologist, resource evaluation Minerals Mgmt. Svc., New Orleans, 1988-96. 1st lt. Army Artillery, 1952-54, Korea. Mem. Am. Assn. Petroleum Geologists, Soc. Petroleum Engrs. Home: 4942 Friar Tuck Dr New Orleans LA 70128

ONEAL, JOHN ROBERT, political science educator; b. Ft. Sill, Okla., May 8, 1946; s. Wilton Keith and Roberta Lea Oneal; m. Frances Hudson, Sept. 29, 1984; children: Mary Adelaide, Owen Michael. BS with distinction, U.S. Mil. Acad., 1968; AM, Stanford U., 1970, PhD, 1979. Asst. prof. dept. polit. sci. Vanderbilt U., Nashville, 1979-86, rsch. assoc. Inst. Pub. Policy Studies, 1986-88; asst. prof. dept. polit. sci. U. Ala., Tuscaloosa, 1988-91, assoc. prof., dir. internat. studies, 1991—; vis. asst. prof. dept. polit. sci. McGill U., Montreal, Can., 1987-88, Yale U., New Haven, Conn., 1996-97. Author: Foreign Policy Making in Times of Crisis, 1982; contbr. articles to profl. jours. Recipient Edgar S. Furniss Jr. award Mershon Ctr. of Ohio State U., 1979; internat. travel grantee Am. Coun. Learned Socs., 1989, rsch. grantee U. Ala., 1989, Collaborative rsch. grantee NATO Sci. Affairs Divsn., 1988, NSF grantee, 1996-97; nat. fellow Hoover Instn., 1989-90, fellow in fgn. policy studies Social Sci. Rsch. Coun., 1991-92; grad. summer scholar Woodrow Wilson Internat. Ctr. for Scholars, 1978. Mem. Internat. Studies Assn., Am. Polit. Sci. Assn. Office: Univ Ala Dept Polit Sci Tuscaloosa AL 35487

O'NEAL, KATHLEEN LEN, financial administrator; b. Ft. Riley, Kans., May 24, 1953; d. Leonard Arthur and Mary (Modlin) O'N. BS with honors, U. Mo., 1975; MBA, Calif. Coast U., Santa Ana, 1991. Cert. secondary tchr. Instr. math. Killian Sr. High Sch., Miami, Fla., 1975-78; mfg. supr. Western Electric Co., Lee's Summit, Mo., 1978-79; prodn. control supr. Western Electric Co., 1979-81; dept. mgr. Lee Wards Co., Independence, Mo., 1981-83; materials mgmt. specialist Northrup-Wilcox Electric, Kansas City, Mo., 1983-84; bus. resource planning mgr. AT&T, Lee's Summit, 1984-85; product mgr. AT&T, Berkeley Heights, N.J., 1985-87; fin. mgr. AT&T, Bedminster, N.J., 1987-89; info. sys. devel. mgr. AT&T, Piscataway, N.J., 1989-90; sr. fin. mgr. AT&T, Jacksonville, Fla., 1990-91, asst. treas., 1992-95, sr. procurement mgr., 1995-96, procurement system design dist. mgr., 1997—. Recipient Spl. Recognition award United Way, 1980. Mem. Am. Prodn. and Inventory Control Soc. (v.p. membership 1987-88, regional del. 1988-89, instr. inventory mgmt. 1987-88), NOW. Office: AT&T 8787 Baypine Rd Jacksonville FL 32256-8528

O'NEAL, NELL SELF, retired principal; b. Glenwood, Ark., Feb. 19, 1925; d. Jewell Calvin and Nannie May (Bankston) Self; m. Billie Kenneth O'Neal, Apr. 1, 1943 (div. Jan. 1976); children: Kenneth Dan O'Neal, Rikki Devin O'Neal, Teresa Lynn Severson. BA, Little Rock U., 1964; MS in Edn., Ark. State Tchrs. Coll., 1965. Cert. tchr. mentally retarded, blind; cert. elem. sch. prin. Spl. edn. tchr. Little Rock Pub. Schs., 1961-65; prin. exceptional unit Ark. Sch. for the Blind, Little Rock, 1965-95; retired, 1995. Mem. NOW, NEA, AAUW, Assn. for the Edn., and Rehab. of Blind and Visually Impaired (J. Max Woolly Superior Svc. award 1990), Ark. Edn. Assn., Sierra Club, Alpha Delta Kappa. Democrat. Methodist. Home: 6513 Cantrell Rd Little Rock AR 72207-4218

ONEAL, PATRICIA JEANNE, oil company executive; b. Sept. 18; d. Georre Daniel and Mary Ruth (Montgomery) Rigler; 1 child, David Diment. Pres. Oneal Drilling Co. Inc., Ft. Worth, Oley Distbg. Co. Inc., Ft. Worth; owner Oneal Oil Properties, Ft. Worth, P-J Ranches, Ft. Worth. Mem. Tex. Wholesale Beer Distbrs. (bd. dirs.), North Ft. Worth Bus. Assn. (b.p. 1993-94), C. of C. (bd. dirs. 1993-94), Rotary (v.p. 1993-94, pres. 1994—), others. Office: Oley Distbg Co Inc 920 N Main St Fort Worth TX 76106-9421

O'NEAL, SHAQUILLE RASHAUN, professional basketball player; b. Newark, Mar. 6, 1972; s. Philip A. Harrison and Lucille O'Neal. Student, La. State U. Center Orlando Magic, 1992-96, L.A. Lakers, 1996—. Appeared in movie Blue Chips, 1994, Kazaam, 1996. Named to Sporting News All-American first team, 1990-91; recipient Rookie of the Yr. award NBA, 1993; mem. NBA All-Star team, 1993, 94, Dream Team II, 1994; first pick overall, 1992 draft. Office: LA Lakers PO Box 10 Inglewood CA 90306*

O'NEIL, CHARLOTTE COOPER, environmental education administrator; b. Chgo., Sept. 21, 1949; d. Adolph H. and Charlotte Waters (Edman) Cooper; m. William Randolph O'Neil, Nov. 18, 1972; children: Sean, Megan. BA in Polit. Sci., Okla. State U., 1969; BS in Edn., U. Tenn., 1988. Cert. tchr., Tenn. Intern Senator Charles H. Percy, Washington, 1969; state treas., state hdqrs. office mgr. Jed Johnson for U.S. Senate, Okla., 1972; mem. acct. staff Pacific Architects & Engrs., Barrow, Alaska, 1973; tchr. social studies Jefferson Jr. High Sch., Oak Ridge, Tenn., 1988; edn. specialist Sci. Applications Internat. Corp., Oak Ridge, Tenn., 1988-94, mgr. environ. edn. and info. tech. sect., 1994-95, mgr. comm. edn. and pub. info. sect., 1995-96, mgr. pub. rels., edn. and multimedia/engring. design, 1996—; edn. strategies com. U.S. Dept. of Transp./FHWA/ITS Edn. 1995—. Author: Science, Society and America's Nuclear Waste, 1992, 2d edit., 1995, Technical Career Opportunities in High-Level Waste Management, 1993, The Environmental History of the Tonawanda Site, 1994, FAA Community Involvement Training: Better Decisions through Consensus, 1996; contbr. articles to profl. jours. Publicity chair, mem. steering com. Am. Mus. Sci. & Energy Tribute to Tech. Mem. ASCD, AAUW, Triangle Coalition, Tenn. Geography Alliance, Nat. Coun. for Social Studies (culture, sci. and tech. com., sci. and society com., sec.-treas. 1991—), Earthwatch, Internat. Alliance for High-Level Radioactive Waste Mgmt., Golden Key, Atomic City Aquatic Club (chair constl. rev. com. 1991—). Office: Sci Applications Internat PO Box 2502 Oak Ridge TN 37831-2502

O'NEIL, JOHN JOSEPH, artist, educator; b. N.Y.C., Apr. 20, 1932; s. John Joseph and Betty (Grady) O'N.; m. Iris Bird, Jan. 15, 1956 (dec. Aug. 1975); children: Virginia, John, Thomas; m. Robin Harmon, Dec. 3, 1977; 1 child, Robin Wade. Assoc. degree, SUNY, Bklyn., 1953; BS, SUNY, Buffalo, 1959; hon. degree, U. Florence, Italy, 1960; MA, Columbia U., 1965, EdD, 1972. Graphic designer Mutual Broadcasting, N.Y.C., 1951-52, Stanys Conliam Whitehead, N.Y.C., 1952, B. Altman, L.I., 1955, Givandan Advt., N.Y.C., 1955; tchr. art East Meadow (N.Y.) High Sch., 1950-63; prof. U. S.C., Columbia, 1963-66, assoc. head, 1966-73, chmn. art dept. Sloan Coll., 1973—; mem. presdl. bd. to evaluate and upgrade Fed. Graphics; chmn. southeastern region New Art Examiner, Washington. Exhibited in group shows at Florence Mus., S.C., Furman U., Chrysler Mus., Norfolk, Va., Gibbs Gallery, Charleston, S.C., Greenville Mus., Spartenson, S.C., St. Paul's Cathedral Gallery, N.Y.C.; represented by Aronsen Gallery, Atlanta. Bd. dirs. Columbia Mus. Art. With U.S. Army, 1952-55. Mem. Nat. Assn. Art Adminstrs., Guild S.C. Artists (bd. dirs.), S.C. Craftsmen (founder), Artist Guild Columbia (pres.), So. Graphic Coun. (pres.), Art Dirs. Club. Home: 1830 Greene St Columbia SC 29201-4017 Office: U SC Sloan Coll Art Dept Columbia SC 29208

O'NEIL, ROBERT MARCHANT, university administrator, law educator; b. Boston, Oct. 16, 1934; s. Walter George and Isabel Sophia (Marchant) O'N.; m. Karen Elizabeth Elson, June 18, 1967; children—Elizabeth, Peter, David, Benjamin. A.B., Harvard U., 1956, A.M., 1957, LL.B., 1961; LL.D., Beloit Coll., 1985, Ind. U., 1987. Bar: Mass. 1962. Law clk. to justice U.S. Supreme Ct., 1962-63; acting assoc. prof. law U. Calif.-Berkeley, 1963-66, prof., 1966-67, 1969-72; exec. asst. to pres., prof. law SUNY-Buffalo, 1967-69; provost, prof. law U. Cin., 1972-73, exec. v.p., prof. law, 1973-75; v.p., prof. law Ind. U., Bloomington, 1975-80; pres. U. Wis. System, 1980-85; prof. law U. Wis.-Madison, 1980-85; prof. law U. Va., Charlottesville, 1985—, pres., 1985-90; gen. counsel. AAUP, 1970-72, 91-92. Author: Civil Liberties: Case Studies and the Law, 1965, Free Speech: Responsible Communication Under Law, 2d edit., 1972, The Price of Dependency: Civil Liberties in the Welfare State, 1970, No Heroes, No Villians, 1972, The Courts, Government and Higher Education, 1972, Discriminating Against Discrimination, 1976, Handbook of the Law of Public Employment, 1978, 2d rev. edit., 1993, Classrooms in the Crossfire, 1981; co-author: A Guide to Debate, 1964, The Judiciary and vietnam, 1972, Civil Liberties Today, 1974. Trustee Tchrs. Ins. and Annuity Assn.; bd. dirs. Commonwealth Fund, James River Corp., Sta. WVPT Pub. TV. Home: 1839 Westview Rd Charlottesville VA 22903-1632 Office: Thomas Jefferson Ctr 400 Peter Jefferson Pl Charlottesville VA 22911-8691

O'NEILL, DONALD EDMUND, health science executive; b. Port Angeles, Wash., Feb. 10, 1926; s. Edward I. and Christine (Williamson) O'N.; m. Violet Elizabeth Oman, June 12, 1948; children: Shelly O'Neill Lane, Erin O'Neill Kennedy, Shawn O'Neill Hoffman. B.S., U. Wash., 1949. With G.D. Searle & Co., 1950-71, regional sales dir., 1962-64, dir. med. service, 1964-68, dir. mktg., 1968-71; with Warner-Lambert Co., 1971—, v.p., 1974-77, exec. v.p. pharm. group, 1977, exec. v.p.; chmn. Internat. profl. group, 1974-76; pres. Parke-Davis & Co., 1976-78; pres., exec. dir. Warner-Lambert/Parke Davis Research Div., 1978, pres. Health Care Group, 1978-81; pres. Parke-Davis Group, 1981, Health Techs. Group, 1982-86, Internat. Ops., 1986-89; exec v.p., chmn. internat. ops. Warner-Lambert Co, 1989-91; ret., 1991; bd. dirs. Fujisawa U.S.A., N.J. Resources, Alliance Pharm. Immunogen Co., Fuisz Techs., Cytogen, M.D.L. Info. Sys., Targeted Genetics. Served with USAF, 1944-46. Mem. John's Island and Bent Pine Golf Clubs, Morris County Golf Club, Elk River Country Club.

ONG, JOO LENG, biomaterials engineering educator; b. Singapore, Singapore, Mar. 13, 1962; s. Peck Ghee and Sue Geok (Tan) O.; m. Wee Gee Tio, May 20, 1988; children: Angee Peryinn, Kevin Perren. BS with distinction, U. Iowa, 1987; MS in Biomed. Engring., U. Ala., 1990, PhD, 1994. Rsch. asst. U. Ala., Birmingham, 1990-94; asst. prof. biomaterials engring. U. Tex. Health Sci. Ctr., San Antonio, 1994—. Contbr. chpt. to: Ceramics in Substitutive and Reconstructive Surgery, 1991, Encyclopedic Handbook of Biomaterials and Bioengineering, 1995, Medical Applications of Titanium and Its Alloys, 1996; contbr. articles on biomaterials to profl. publs. Mem. Am. Assn. Dental Rsch., Soc. for Biomaterials (sec. student sect. 1989-91), Biomed. Engring. Soc., Microbeam Analysis Soc. Office: Univ Tex Health Sci Ctr Dept Restor Dent, Biomat Dv 7703 Floyd Curl Dr San Antonio TX 78284-7890

ONGE, PAGE BURTON, architect; b. Elkhart, Ind., Oct. 21, 1954; s. Richard Charles and Mary Alice (Glace) Ong; m. Jeannine Marie Niemi, May 2, 1986; children: Joshua, Jason, Jaimé, Page Jr. (dec.). BArch, La. State U., 1981. Registered architect, La., Mich., Tenn., S.C.; cert. Nat. Coun. Archtl. Registration Bds. Architect A. Hays Town, Architect, Baton Rouge, 1982-87, U.P. Engrs. and Architects, Inc., Houghton, Mich., 1987-93, Earl Swensson Assocs., Inc., Nashville, 1993—. Prin. archtl. works include Baraga (Mich.) Lakeside Inn, 1988, Houghton Nat. Bank, Baraga, 1989, Agassiz Pk. Warming House, Calumet, Mich., St. Ignatius Loyola Ch. Rectory and Parish Offices, Hougton, Mich., 1992; co-inventor Telescoping Bathtub Assembly for Handicapped. Trustee Calumet (Mich.) Village Coun., 1989-92; bd. dirs. Copper Country Heritage Coun., Houghton, Mich., 1989-92; chmn. Calumet, Laurium, Calumet Twp. Historic Dist. Study Com., 1992-93; pres. Calumet, Laurium, Keweenaw (CLK) Foresight, Inc., 1992-93. Mem. AIA (treas. Upper Peninsula chpt. 1990-93, sec. 1991-93), Nat. Trust Hist. Preservation. Baptist. Home: PO Box 50856 Nashville TN 37205-0856

ONONYE, DANIEL CHUKA, social scientist; b. Aba, Mo., June 30, 1948; s. Daniel Okonai and Paulina N. (Ayuno) O.; m. Debbie S. Ononye, Sept. 3, 1977 (div. 1983); m. Kate Okonji Egoye, Dec. 6, 1984; 1 child, Ray E. BS, Huntington (Ind.) Coll., 1977; MA, Ball State U., 1979. Mgr. Huntington Meml. Hosp., 1978-79; sr. adminstrv. officer U. Portharcourt, Nigeria, 1979-82; personnel officer Anambra State Coll. Edn. Nigeria Registry Dept., Awka, 1983-85; pres. Super Nig Ltd., Portharcourt, 1985-87, Astros of St. Louis Internat. Inc., 1988—, Green Eagle Corp. of Dallas, Ft. Worth, 1991—. Mem. Nigerian Inst. Mgmt. (assoc.), Inst. Mgmt. Cons. (assoc.), Internat. Club (pres. 1975-76), Grand Lodge of Amroc.

ONUKWULI, FRANCIS OSITA, computer scientist, mathematics educator; b. Warri, Nigeria, Aug. 5, 1955; came to U.S., 1977; s. Chief Mathias Nwafor and Mercy (Okonowo) O.; m. Sandra Anthonia Mgbemena, Oct. 12, 1986; children: Francis Osita, Victor Chinedu, Anthony Tochukwu, Precious Chinenye. BS in Math., Physics, Philander Smith Coll., Little Rock, 1981; MS in Computer Sci., Atlanta U., 1983; EdD in Ednl. Leadership Higher Edn., Clark Atlanta U., 1990. Billing and credit supr. Standard Bank Nigeria Ltd., Benin, 1975-77; tutor, counselor Philander Smith Coll., 1978-81; math. rsch. asst. Atlanta U., 1982-83; instr. computer sci. Spelman Coll., Atlanta, 1983-86; asst. prof. computer sci., mgr. computer and info. sci. lab. Morris Brown Coll., Atlanta, 1986-96; chmn. computer sci. dept. Morris Brown Coll., 1991-92; cons. PBT Engring. Co., Atlanta, 1985-86; judge Ga.

Sci. Fair, 1989, 90, 93, 94, 95. Co-author: Computer Applicatons for the Twenty-First Century; author microcomputer materials for calculus students. Mem. NSF (co-chair proposal review panelist 1989-90), Math. Assn. Am., Assn. Computing Machinery, Am. Math. Soc., Internat. Devel. Edn. Coun. (sec. 1987), Igbo Union (pres. Atlanta chpt. 1986-91), Student Assn. Clark Atlanta U. (chmn. ednl. leadership 1989-90). Democrat. Roman Catholic. Home: 7544 Sedona Dr Jonesboro GA 30236-2740 Office: Morris Brown Coll 643 Martin Dr NE Atlanta GA 30314

OOMMEN, KALARICKAL JOSEPH, neurologist; b. Alleppey, Kerala, India, Apr. 5, 1947; came to U.S., 1975; s. Pallivathukkal Anthony and Poovathummannil (Chako) Joseph; m. Sept. 6, 1973; children: Joseph Anthony, Reena Elizabeth. BSc, S.D. Coll., Alleppey, Kereala, India, 1967; MBBS, Trivandrum Med. Coll., Trivandrum, Kerala, India, 1973. Diplomate Am. Board Psychiatry and Neurology, Am. Bd. Clin. Neurophysiology, Am. Bd. Electoencephalography. Resident dept neurology U. Ariz., Tucson, 1979-82, instr. dept. neurology, fellow in EEG, Epilepsy, and evoked, 1982-83; potentials dept neurology Med. Coll. Ga., Tucson, 1982-83; asst. prof. Med. Coll. Ga., Augusta, 1983-84; chief neurology svc. Kino Cmty. Hosp., Tucson, 1984-88; clin. asst. prof. U. Ariz. dept. neurology, Tucson, 1989-90; founding med. dir. Ariz. Comprehensive Epilepsy Program, Tucson, 1990-94; chmn. Continuing Edn. Program Coll. of medicine, U. Ariz., Tucson, 1991-94; assoc. prof. Neurology, U. Okla., 1994—. Contbr. articles to profl. jours., chpts to books. Nominated for Leadership award, Epilepsy Found., 1993; recipient Recognition of innovation in imoroving healthcare quality of mgmt. Am. Assn. Physician Execs., 1991-92, Creative Concepts award Univ. Med. Ctr., Tucson,. 1989. Fellow Am. Acad. Neurology; mem. AAAS, AMA, Am. Epilepsy Soc., Am. Electroencephalographic Soc., Alliance for Continuing Edn., Am. Psychiat. Assn., Assn. Kerala Med. Grads. (mem. ednl. com. 1985-89), Assn. Indian Neurologists in Am. Office: Dept Neurology OUHSC Oklahoma City OK 73104

OOSTEN, ROGER LESTER, medical manufacturing executive; b. Rock Valley, Iowa, Sept. 21, 1937; s. Henry and Martha (Kersbergen) O.; m. Patricia Nan Hanlon, Oct. 21, 1961; children: Kimberly Kay, Kurtis James, Jan Hendrik. BSEE, U. Iowa, 1967. Engr. Ball Bros. Research Corp., Boulder, Colo., 1967-73; pres. Mgmt. Bus. Machines, Inc., Denver, 1973-76; dir. research and devel. Neomed, Inc., Boulder, 1976-78; v.p. research and devel. Concept, Inc., Clearwater, Fla., 1978-81; v.p. surg. div. Birtcher Corp., El Monte, Calif., 1982-85; founder, pres. Bergen Mfg., Fla., 1985—. Patentee in field. Served with USN, 1956-60. Named Man of Yr., NASA, 1974. Home: 9345 Rookery Rd New Port Richey FL 34654-5546

OPALA, MARIAN P(ETER), state supreme court justice; b. Lódz, Poland, Jan. 20, 1921. BSB in Econs., Oklahoma City U., 1957, JD, 1953, LLD, 1981; LLM, NYU, 1968; HHD, Okla. Christian U. Sci. & Arts, 1981. Bar: Okla. 1953, U.S. Supreme Ct. 1970. Asst. county atty. Oklahoma County, 1953-56; practiced law Oklahoma City, 1956-60, 65-67; referee Okla. Supreme Ct., Oklahoma City, 1960-65; prof. law Oklahoma City U. Sch. Law, 1965-69; asst. to presiding justice Supreme Ct. Okla., 1967-68; adminstrv. dir. Cts. Okla., 1968-77; presiding judge Okla. State Indsl. Ct., 1977-78; judge Workers Compensation Ct., 1978; justice Okla. Supreme Ct., 1978—, chief justice, 1991-93; adj. prof. law Okla. City U., 1962—, U. Okla. Coll. Law, 1969—; prof. law U. Tulsa Law Sch., 1982—; mem. permanent faculty Am. Acad. Jud. Edn., 1970—; mem. NYU Inst. Jud. Adminstrn.; mem. faculty Nat. Jud. Coll., U. Nev., 1975—; chmn. Nat. Conf. State Ct. Adminstrs., 1976-77; mem. Nat. Conf. Commrs. on Uniform State Laws, 1982—. Co-author: Oklahoma Court Rules for Perfecting a Civil Appeal, 1969. Mem. Adminstrn. Conf. U.S., 1993-95. Recipient Herbert Harley award Am. Judicature Soc., 1977, Disting. Alumni award Oklahoma City U., 1979, Americanism medal Nat. Soc. DAR, 1984, ABA/Am. Law Inst. Harrison Tweed Spl. Merit award, 1987, Humanitarian award NCCJ, 1991, Jour. Record award, 1995, Constn. award Rogers U., 1996. Mem. AbA (edn. com. appellate judges conf. 1984-93), Okla. Bar Assn. (Earl Sneed Continuing Legal Edn. award 1988), Okla. County Bar Assn., Am. Soc. Legal History, Oklahoma City Title Lawyers Assn., Am. Judicature Soc. (bd. dirs. 1988-92), Am. Law Inst. (elected), Order of Coif, Phi Delta Phi (Oklahoma City Alumni award). Office: Okla Supreme Ct State Capitol Rm 238 Oklahoma City OK 73105

OPARA, EMMANUEL CHUKWUEMEKA, biochemistry educator; b. Lagos, Nigeria, July 4, 1951; came to U.S., 1984; s. Eugene Uba and Caroline (Adanma) O.; m. Clarice Adaku Njemanze, Mar. 28, 1980; children: Ogechi, Chiedu, Chukwuka, Ikenna. BS with honors, U. Nigeria, 1976; MS, U. Surrey, Eng., 1980; PhD, U. London, 1983. Assoc. Royal Coll. of Pathologists. Inspecting officer Food and Drug Adminstrn., Lagos, 1977-78; clin. biochemist Epsom (Eng.) Hosp. Labs., 1978-81; teaching asst. Chelsea Coll., London, 1981-83; rsch. fellow Mayo Clinic, Rochester, Minn., 1984-86; vis. fellow NIH, Bethesda, Md., 1986-88; rsch. assoc. Duke U. Med. Ctr., Durham, N.C., 1988-89; asst. prof. Duke U. Med. Ctr., 1989—. Contbr. articles to numerous scientific and med. jours. Com. chairperson Holy Cross Ch., Durham, 1992. WHO fellow, Geneva, 1984; Fogarty Internat. fellow, Bethesda, 1986; recipient Cystic Fibrosis Found. grant, 1990, Am. Diabetes Assn. grant, 1993. Mem. Am. Fedn. for Clin. Rsch., Am. Diabetes Assn., Am. Pancreatic Assn., Assn. Clin. Biochemists (U.K.), Biochemistry Soc. Democrat. Roman Catholic. Home: 2 Scarsdale Pl Durham NC 27707-5526 Office: Duke U Med Ctr Dept of Surgery PO Box 3065 Durham NC 27710

OPPENHEIM, JUSTIN SABLE, business executive; b. N.Y.C., Aug. 17, 1923; s. Ferdinand S. and Esther D. (Hirsch) O.; m. Joyce Marrits, June 26, 1949; children: Janet Wexler, Judith, Jeffrey, Ann Harrisburg. BS, NYU, 1943; postgrad., Cambridge U., Eng., 1945, New Sch. for Social Research, 1963. V.p. Consol. Mercantile Industries, N.Y.C., 1946-52; adminstrn. and mgmt. Norden div. United Aircraft Co., 1952-60; pres., gen. mgr. Potentiometer div. Litton Industries, 1960-68; pres. Office Products Ctrs. div., 1968-70; v.p. Litton Industries, 1970-84; chmn., pres. Joyce Internat., 1984-85, dir., 1985-89; chmn. Joyce Furniture (Can.), 1984-86; also v.p. Litton Bus. Systems, Inc., Litton Bus. Equipment Ltd., Can., Standard Desk Ltd., Can. to 1985; pres., dir. Streater Industries Ltd. 1968-85; lectr. on advt. NYU, CCNY, 1954-57. Contbr. articles to profl. jours. including the N.Y. Times. Mem. adv. com. N. Hempstead Housing Authority, 1956-59; mem. Nassau County Republican Com., 1961-73; founding mem. Ctr. Econ. Rsch., L.I. U.; hon. dep. sheriff Westchester County, 1967; mem. Hon. Legion Police Dept. City of N.Y., 1978; bd. dirs. Sephardic House, N.Y.C.; trustee Am. Jewish Hist. Soc., L.I. Stage, 1985-87, Friends of Touro Synagogue, 1989—, life mem. Served with AUS, 1943-45; Hon. Adm. Tex. Navy, 1969. Recipient citation Borough Pres. Manhattan, N.Y.C., 1980, key to Albert Lea, Minn., key to Selma, Ala. Mem. SAR, Actor's Fund (life), Am. Arbitration Assn., Mosaic (charter mem), So. Jewish Hist. Soc., Alpha Epsilon Pi. Jewish. Club: Lambs (N.Y.) (life). Lodge: Masons. Home: 6691 S Pine Ct West Palm Beach FL 33418-6960

O'QUINN, APRIL GALE, physician, educator; b. Columbia, Miss., Apr. 21, 1936; d. R.V. and Anna Pauline (Cook) O'Q.; diploma Scott and White Hosp. Sch. Nursing, 1965; A.A., Temple Jr. Coll., 1965; B.S. with honors, Baylor U., 1968; M.D., U. Tex. Med. Br., 1971. Intern, U. Tex. Med. Br., Galveston, 1971-72, resident ob-gyn., 1972-75; fellow in oncology M.D. Anderson Hosp., Houston, Tex., 1976-78; practice medicine specializing in ob-gyn., Galveston, 1978-81; asst. prof. dept. ob-gyn U. Tex. Med. Br., Galveston, 1975-81; practice medicine specializing in ob-gyn, New Orleans, 1981—; mem. staff John Sealy Hosp., St. Mary's Hosp., Galveston, Tulane Med. Center, New Orleans Charity Hosp., So. Baptist Hosp. and Touro Infirmary, New Orleans; assoc. prof., dir. div. gynecol. oncology dept. obgyn Tulane U. Sch. Medicine, New Orleans, 1981-85, prof., 1985-89, prof., chair dept. ob.-gyn., 1989—. Diplomate Am. Bd. Ob-Gyn. Fellow Willard R. Cooke Obstet. and Gynecol. Soc., Am. Coll. Ob-Gyn.; mem. AMA, Soc. Gynecologic Oncologists, Western Assn. Gynecol. Oncologists, Coun. Univ. Chmn. in Ob-Gyn., Assn. Profs. in Ob-Gyn., New Orleans Gynecol. and Obstet. Soc., La. Med. Assn., Galveston County Med. Soc., Felix Rutledge Soc. Orleans Parish. Republican. Baptist. Home: 5100 Bancroft Dr New Orleans LA 70122-1218 Office: Tulane U Sch Medicine Ob Gyn Dept New Orleans LA 70112

O'QUINN, NANCY DIANE, nurse, educator; b. Walton County, Ga., Nov. 22, 1944; d. L.C. Jr. and Eula Sandra (Hegwood) Kennedy; m. Charles Frank O'Quinn, Sept. 12, 1965; children: Robert, Spencer, Alan. Diploma, Ga. Bapt. Hosp., 1965; BSN, Valdosta State Coll., 1979, MEd, 1983; MSN, Valdosta State U., 1986; postgrad., Fla. State U., 1989—. Sr. nurse Tift County Health Dept., Tifton, Ga., 1979-80; instr. Abraham Baldwin Coll., Tifton, 1980-85, assoc. prof., 1992-94; asst. prof. Valdosta (Ga.) State Coll., 1985-94; asst. prof. nursing Albany (Ga.) State U., 1990-92, 94—. Lt. USNR, 1989—. Mem. Sigma Theta Tau, Alpha Chi.

ORDONEZ, NELSON GONZALO, pathologist; b. Bucaramanga, Santander, Colombia, July 20, 1944; came to U.S., 1972; s. Gonzalo and Itsmenia Ordonez; m. Miranda Lee Ferrell, Dec. 18, 1976 (div. June 1983); 1 child, Nelson Adrian; m. Catherine Marie Newton, Nov. 6, 1987; 1 child, Sara Catherine Itsmenia. BA and Sci., Instituto Daza Dangond, Bogota, Colombia, 1962; MD, Nat. U. Colombia, Bogota, 1970. Resident pathology U. N.C., Chapel Hill, 1972-73; resident pathology U. Chgo., 1974-76, asst. prof. pathology, 1977-78; asst. prof. pathology U. Tex. M.D. Anderson Cancer Ctr., Houston, 1978-82, assoc. prof., 1983-85, prof., 1985—, dir. immunocytochemistry sect., 1981—. Author: (with others) Renal Biopsy Pathology and Diagnostic and Therapeutic Implications, 1980, Tumors of the Lung, 1991; contbr. chpts. to books, numerous articles to med. jours. Nat. Kidney Found. fellow, 1977-78. Mem. AMA, Am. Assn. Pathologists, Internat. Acad. Pathology, Am. Soc. Clin. Pathologists, Am. Soc. Sytology, Am. Soc. Investigative Pathology, Internat. Acad. Cytology, Arthur Purdy Stout Soc. Surg. Pathologists, Latin-Am. Soc. Pathology. Office: U Tex MD Anderson Cancer Ctr 1515 Holcombe Blvd Houston TX 77030-4009

ORDOVER, ABRAHAM PHILIP, lawyer, mediator; b. Far Rockaway, N.Y., Jan. 18, 1937; s. Joseph and Bertha (Fromberg) O.; m. Carol M. Ordover, Mar. 23, 1961; children: Andrew Charles, Thomas Edward. BA magna cum laude, Syracuse U., 1958; JD, Yale U., 1961. Bar: N.Y. 1961, U.S. Dist. Ct. (so. and ea. dists.) N.Y., U.S. Ct. Appeals (2d cir.), U.S. Supreme Ct. Assoc. Cahill, Gordon & Reindel, N.Y.C., 1961-71; prof. law Hofstra U., Hempstead, N.Y., 1971-81; L.Q.C. Lamar prof. law Emory U., Atlanta, 1981-91; CEO Resolution Resources Corp., Atlanta, 1991—; mediator and arbitrator; vis. prof. Cornell U., Ithaca, N.Y., 1977; vis. lectr. Tel Aviv U., 1989, Am. Law Inst.; team leader nat. program Nat. Inst. Trial Advocacy, Boulder, Colo., 1980, 82, 84, 86, 89, tchr. program Cambridge, Mass., 1979-84, 88, adv. program Gainesville, Fla., 1978-79, northeast regional dir., 1977-81; team leader SE regional program, 1983; team leader Atlanta Bar Trial Tech. Program, 1981-91; lectr. in field. Author: Argument to the Jury, 1982, Problems and Cases in Trial Advocacy, 1983, Advanced Materials in Trial Advocacy, 1988, Alternatives to Litigation, 1993, Cases and Materials in Evidence, 1993, Art of Negotiation, 1994; producer ednl. films; contbr. articles to profl. jours. Bd. dirs. Atlanta Legal Aid Soc., 1984-91, 7 Stages Theatre, 1991—. Recipient Gumpert award Am. Coll. Trial Lawyers, 1984, 85, Jacobsen award Roscoe Pound Am. Trial Lawyer Found., 1986. Mem. ABA, N.Y. State Bar Assn., Assn. Am. Law Schs. (chair litigation sect.), Atlanta Lawyers Club, Am. Law Inst.

O'REAR, JACK, company executive. Pres. CMC Industries, Inc., Corinth, Miss. Office: CMC Industries Inc 1801 Fulton Dr Corinth MS 38834

O'REILLY, JOHN JOSEPH, engineer; b. Santa Cruz, Calif., May 12, 1959; s. Richard Carroll and Naydene Joyce (Hensley) O'R.; m. Michelle Marie Johnson, Sept. 27, 1986; 1 child, Shea Kathleen. BS in Mech. Engring., U. Nebr., 1982; MS in Engring. Mgmt., So. Meth. U., 1988. Registered profl. engr., Tex. Facilities engr. Texas Instruments, Dallas, 1982-85; internat. facilities engring. mgr. United Techs. MOSTEK, Carrollton, Tex., 1985; mech./contamination control engr. Henningson, Durham & Richardson, Dallas, 1985-86; with Digital Equipment Corp., Dallas and Austin, Tex., 1986-91; program mgr. reliability SEMATECH, Austin, 1988-91; equipment reliability engr. Motorola Advanced Products R&D Lab., Austin, Tex., 1991—; cons. Sematech's U. Nat. Lab. Program, 1990-91, Sandia Nat. Labs., Albuquerque. Contbr. articles to profl. jours. Charter mem. Diocesan Forum Cath. Profls., Austin, 1988-91; co-chair Diocesan ForuHomeless Com., 1989-92; vol. Our Lady's Youth Ctr., Austin, 1989-92; mem. Sematech Vol. Coun., 1990-91; bd. dirs., chair individual-giving subcom. Caritas Devel. Adv. Bd., 1991-92; bd. dirs. Sts. of Hope. Mem. Am. Soc. Quality Control, Inst. Environ. Scis. (newsletter editor 1985-86, annual tech. meeting facilities co-chair 1986, Achievement award 1986).

OREM, HENRY PHILIP, retired chemist, chemical engineer, consultant; b. Campbellsburg, Ky., Feb. 28, 1910; s. Mal Lee and Alice (Green) O.; m. Lydia C. Orem (dec. Feb. 1988). BS in Indsl. Chemistry, U. Ky., 1932, MS, 1934; postgrad., Pa. State U., 1934-36. Grad. asst. phys. chemistry U. Ky., 1933; grad. rsch. scholar Pa. State Coll., 1934-37; with rsch. dept. Calco Chem. Co. subs. Am. Cyanamid Co., Bound Brook, N.J., 1937-39; plant rschr./process developer Am. Cyanamid Co., Bound Brook, 1939-42; asst. chief chemist Azo Dye and Intermediate divsn. Am. Cyanamid Co., Bound Brook, N.J., 1942-46; departmental chemist Azo Dye and Intermediate divsn. Am. Cyanamid Co., Bound Brook, 1947, tech. supt., 1947-50; rsch. chemist Sloss Sheffield Steel and Iron Co. (now U.S. Pipe and Foundry Co. subs. Jim Walter Co.), Birmingham, Ala., 1950-52, rsch. ehcm. engr., 1952-65, group leader, 1965-75, ret., 1975; cons. Jim Walter Resources, Inc., Arichem, Inc. (now subs. Jim Walter Resources, Inc.). Contbr. articles to on black powder and ballistics to publs. Fellow Am. Inst. Chemists (profl. accredited chemist); mem. AIChE (life, 1st sec. N.J. sect. 1949-50, chmn. 1963, treas. Ala. sect. 1971, 72), Am. Chem. Soc. (emeritus life, sec.-treas. Raritan Valley group N.J. sect. 1948, chmn. 1950, sec. Ala. sect. 1956-57), NRA (life), Nat. Muzzle Loading Rifle Assn. (life, contbr. and reviewer articles Muzzle Blasts, technical advisor muzzle blasts, powder and ballistics), U.S. Revolver Assn. (life), Ala. Gun Collectors Assn. (life), Magic City Gun Club (life), Va. Gun Collectors Assn. (life), Kate Carpenter Muzzleloaders Inc., Stonewall Rifle and Pistol Club (Churchville, Va.), Shenandale Gun Club (Buffalo Gap, Va.), Homestead Shooting Club (Hot Springs, Va.), Va. Muzzle Loading Rifle Assn., Va. State Rifle and Revolver Assn., Ft. Lewis Hunting Club (life), Am. Def. Preparedness Assn., Sigma Xi. Home: HCR 02 Box 259 Warm Springs VA 24484-9508

ORENS, JOHN RICHARD, historian, educator; b. N.Y.C., Mar. 31, 1945; s. Sidney Ronald and Edith (Rothenberg) O.; m. Elizabeth Mills Pickering Allan, June 6, 1971; 1 child, Geoffrey Alexander. BS, U. Wis., 1965; MA, Columbia U., 1968, PhD, 1976. Lectr. in history Fairleigh-Dickinson U., Madison, N.J., 1974, Boston U., 1977-82; mem. faculty R.I. Sch. for Deacons, Pascoag, 1982-87; lectr. in history Georgetown U., Washington, 1988-89, Prince George's C.C., Largo, Md., 1989, Mary Washington Coll., Fredericksburg, Va., 1989-92; vis. assoc. prof. George Mason U., Fairfax, Va., 1987—; adj. asst. prof. Springfield (Mass.) Coll., 1983-86, Elms Coll., Chicopee, Mass., 1985-86. Co-author: F.D. Maurice: A Study, 1982, Conrad Noel and the Catholic Crusade, 1993; contbg. author: Mary, Mother of Socialism, 1995; contbr. to Essays Catholic and Radical, 1983; editor jour. Fellowship Papers, 1985—. Mem. Cath. Fellowship of Episcopal Ch. (nat. bd. dirs. 1983—, pres. 1985-86, 94-95), Affirming Anglican Catholicism (nat. steering com. 1995—), Hist. Soc. of Episcopal Ch. Democrat. Episcopalian. Home: 3511 Woodley Rd NW Washington DC 20016-5032 Office: George Mason U Dept History Fairfax VA 22030

ORENSTEIN, ROBERT, physician; b. Hartford, Conn., Nov. 21, 1959; m. Amy E. Foxx, May 30, 1987. BS, Trinity Coll., 1981; DO, Univ. Osteopat. Medicine, 1987. Diplomate Am. Bd. Infectious Diseases Am. Bd. Internal Medicine, Am. Bd. Osteopathic Examiners. Intern Botsford Gen. Hosp., Farmington Hills, Mich., 1987-88; resident Geisinger Med. Ctr., Danville, Pa., 1988-91; fellow Medical Coll. Va., Richmond, Va., 1991-93; staff physician McGuire VA Medical Ctr., Richmond, 1993—, dir. AIDS program, 1993—; cons. AIDS clinic Med. Coll. Va., 1993-95, adv. AIDS edn. program Va. Commonwealth, 1993-95; asst. prof. medicine Va. Commonwealth U./Med. Coll. Va., 1993-95. Contbr. articles to profl. jours. Mem. Richmond AIDS Consortium, 1993—. Mem. Infectious Diseases Soc. Am., Am. Soc. Microbiology, Am. Coll. Physicians, Am. Osteopathic Assn. Office: Hunter Holmes McGuire VA Med Ctr 1201 Broad Rock Blvd Richmond VA 23249

ORKAND, DONALD SAUL, management consultant; b. N.Y.C., Mar. 2, 1936; s. Harold and Sylvia (Wagner) O.; children: Dara Sue, Katarina Day. BS summa cum laude, NYU, 1956, MBA, 1957, PhD, 1963. Statistician, Western Electric Co., N.Y.C., 1956-58; group v.p. Ops. Rsch., Inc., Silver Spring, Md., 1960-69; pres. Ops. Rsch. Industries, Ltd., Ottawa, Ont., Can., 1968-69; pres., CEO The Orkand Corp., Tysons Corner, Va., 1970—; bd. dirs. U. Md. Found., Inc., College Park, 1993—. Contbr. articles to profl. jours. Bd. visitors coll. of bus. and mgmt. U. Md., College Park, 1985—; trustee Suburban Hosp., 1994—. 1st lt. Ordnance Corps, USAR, 1958-60. Mem. Am. Econs. Assn., Am. Statis. Assn., Ops. Rsch. Soc. Am. Republican. Jewish. Avocations: reading, theater, travel, exercise. Office: The Orkand Corp 7799 Leesburg Pike Ste 700N Falls Church VA 22043-2499

ORME, JOHN DAVID, political science educator; b. Portland, Oreg., June 1, 1952; s. Douglas W. and Iva Ruth (Curtis) O. BA in History and Gen. Social Sci., U. Oreg., 1974; MA in Govt., Harvard U., 1977, PhD in Govt., 1982. Asst. prof. Dickinson Coll., Carlisle, Pa., 1982-83; asst. prof. Oglethorpe U., Atlanta, 1983-89, assoc. prof., 1989-95, prof., 1995—; rsch. fellow Ctr. for Sci. and Internat. Affairs, Cambridge, Mass., 1990-92. Author: Political Instability and American Foreign Policy, 1989, Deterrence, Reputation and Cold War Cycles, 1992; contbr. articles to Internat. Security, Polit. Sci. Quar., Washington Quar., others. Recipient Golden Apple award, Kappa Alpha, 1987. Mem. Am. Polit. Sci. Assn., Phi Beta Kappa. Office: Oglethorpe Univ 4484 Peachtree Rd NE Atlanta GA 30319-2737

ORNOSKY, PAUL M., production engineer; b. Allentown, Pa., Aug. 29, 1961; s. Martin and Ethel R. (Fecko) O.; m. Amy L. Domer. BSChemE, U. Notre Dame, 1983; MBA, W.Va. U., 1990. Process engr. Avery Internat., Quakertown, Pa., 1983-87; prodn. engr. Amoco Performance Products, Inc., Marietta, Ohio, 1987-92; mgr. tech. ops. Aristech Chem. Co., Kenovia, W.Va., 1992—. Mem. Am. Inst. Chem. Engrs. Home: 435 Township Rd 1234 N Scott Dr Proctorville OH 45669 Office: Aristech Chemical Co PO Box 189 Kenova WV 25530-0189

OROFINO, THOMAS ALLAN, chemistry educator; b. Youngstown, Ohio, Nov. 12, 1930; s. Frank Anthony and Jeannette Louise (Peduzzi) O.; m. Dorothy Mae Janosik, Sept. 5, 1953 (dec.). BS in Chemistry, Kent State U., 1952; PhD in Phys. Chemistry, Cornell U., 1956; postgrad., Leiden U., 1956-57. Sr. chemist Rohm and Haas Co., 1957-58; group leader polymers Monsanto Co., Durham, N.C., 1964-68, rsch. mgr. membrane tech. polymers, 1968-74; rsch. mgr. optical fibers & instrumentation Monsanto Rsch. Corp., Dayton, Ohio, 1974-79; rsch. mgr. recreational products Monsanto Co., Dalton, Ga., 1979-85; adj. prof. chemistry, dir. William H. Wheeler Ctr. Odor Rsch U. Tenn., Chattanooga, 1985-90, adj. prof. chemistry, adv. bd., 1991—. Contbr. chtps. to books and over 50 articles to profl. jours.; patentee in field. Rsch. fellow Mellon Inst., Pitts., 1958-64. Mem. Am. Chem. Soc. (chmn. local sect. 1985, Outstanding Chemist's award 1987). Home: 2 Market St Apt 204 Chattanooga TN 37402-1015

O'ROURKE, TIMOTHY JOHN, internist, hematologist, health facility administrator, educator; b. Mpls., Aug. 1, 1950; s. Edward C. and Rita M. (Brosnan) O'R.; m. Debra D. Dickerson, May 19, 1979; children: Michael J., Jacob J. BS in Biochemistry, Mich. State U., 1971; MS in Biol. Chemistry, U. Mich., 1975, MD, 1976. Diplomate Am. Bd. Internal Medicine, Internal Medicine, Hematology, Med. Oncology, Geriatrics; lic. physician, Tex. Residency in internal medicine Madigan Army Med. Ctr., Tacoma, 1976-79; staff internist 5th Gen. Hosp., Bad Cannstatt, Germany, 1979-81, chief dept. medicine, 1981-82; fellowship in hematology/med. oncology Madigan Army Ctr., Tacoma, 1982-85; staff hematologist hematology/oncology svc., asst. chief Brooke Army Med. Ctr., Fort Sam Houston, Tex., 1985-87, 87-90, chief hematology/oncology svc., 1990—, program dir. hematology/oncology fellowship, 1990—, prin. investigator S.W. Oncology Group, 1988—; clin. instr., clin. asst. prof. dept. medicine U. Tex. Health Sci. Ctr., San Antonio, 1987-88, 88-89; clin. assoc. prof. dept. medicine U. Tex. Health Sci Ctr., San Antonio, 1989-95, clin. prof., 1995—; mem. clin. investigation com. Brooke, 1988—, instl. rev. bd., 1991—, hosp. edn. com., 1990—, chmn. cancer care com., 1990—. Contbr. articles to profl. jours. and chpts. to books. Fellow ACP; mem. AMA, Am. Soc. Hematology, Am. Soc. Clin. Oncology, Am. Assn. Cancer Rsch., S.W. Oncology Group (leukemia com., lymphoma com., myeloma com., devel. therapeutics com., bd. govs.). Office: Brooke Army Med Ctr Hematology/Oncology Svc Beach Pavilion Fort Sam Houston TX 78234-6200

ORR, BETSY, business education educator; b. Dermott, Ark., Nov. 24, 1954; d. Doy and Peggy (Johnson) Ogles; m. Gary Orr, July 10, 1976; children: Brent, Shane. BA, U. Ark., 1975, bus. edn. cert., 1978, MEd, 1987, EdD, 1994. Cert. tchr., Ark. Tchr. Springdale (Ark.) High Sch., 1978-89; instr. bus. edn. U. Ark., Fayetteville, 1989-94, asst. prof., 1994—. Mem. Nat. Bus. Edn. Assn., Ark. Bus. Edn. Assn. (editor 1989-92), AAUW, Delta Pi Epsilon (pres. 1992—), Phi Delta Kappa. Home: 1006 NW N St Bentonville AR 72712-4526 Office: U Ark Grad Edn 108 Fayetteville AR 72701

ORR, EMMA JANE, pharmacist, educator; b. Pennington, Va., Sept. 30, 1956; d. Clyde Wilson and Monnie Lee (Daugherty) O.; m. Allen Emerson Clark, Oct. 24, 1981; 1 child, Katherine Wilson. BS in Pharmacy, Med. Coll. Va., 1979; D of Pharmacy with highest hons., U. Ky., 1981. Registered pharmacist, Va., Ky., Tenn. Asst. dir. pharmacy St. Mary's Hosp., Norton, Va., 1980-84, Norton Community Hosp., 1984-90; clin. coord. Hoston Valley Hosp., Kingsport, Tenn., 1990—; adj. faculty Mountain Empire C.C., Big Stone Gap, Va., 1981—; asst. clin. prof. dept. pharmacy and pharmaceutics Med. Coll. Va., Richmond, 1982—. Tchr., children's spkr. Ch. United Meth. Ch., Duffield, Va., Mountain Empire Older Citizens, Wise, Va., 1983-85. Named Young Career Woman of Yr. Bus. and Profl. Women's Club, 1983. Mem. Am. Soc. Hosp. Pharmacists, Am. Pharm. Assn., Va. Soc. Hosp. Pharmacists. Methodist. Home: 100 Quillen Dr Duffield VA 24244

ORR, FRANK HOWARD, III, architect; b. Jasper, Ala., Sept. 4, 1932; s. Frank Howard Jr. and Lola Ruth (Lynch) O.; m. Nancy Gayle Gentry, Apr. 13, 1957; children: Mark Daniel, Steven Gentry, Karen Diann, Amy Ruth. B in Applied Art, Auburn U., 1961. Registered architect, Ala., Calif., Fla., Ga., Ky., N.C., Tenn., Va., Miss. Assoc. architect Edwin A. Keeble Assocs., Nashville, 1962-70, Bianculli & Tyler, Inc., Chattanooga, 1970; prin. Frank Orr Architects, Nashville, 1970-76; pres., prin. Orr/Houk & Assocs. Architects, Inc., Nashville, 1976—; adj. faculty O'More Sch. Design, Franklin, Tenn., 1972-77, Nashville State Tech. Inst., 1978-79; guest lectr. sch. architecture Victoria Univ., Wellington, New Zealand, 1987; exam grader Nat. Council Archtl. Registration Bds., Ft. Lauderdale, Fla., 1985. Author: Professional Practice in Architecture, 1982, Scale in Architecture, 1985; author (column) Urban Life, Nashville Bus. Jour., 1995; editor: Notable Nashville Architecture 1930-1980; contbr. articles to profl. jours.; prin. works include Woodmont Bapt. Ch. (design commendation 1979), Appalachian Ctr. for Crafts, Two Rivers Bapt. Ch. (design commendation 1979), 1st Bapt. Ch., Hendersonville, Tenn. (design award of merit 1992). Active Citizens com. Met. Nashville Gen. Plan, 1994. Mem. AIA (dir. Mid. Tenn. chpt. 1971-78, chmn. chpat. com. design awards 1985, com. environ. edn. 1972-76), Tenn. Soc. Architects (sec.-treas. 1977), Nashville C. of C. (regional transp. com. 1993-94). Baptist. Office: Orr Houk & Assocs Architects Inc 1905 21st Ave S Nashville TN 37212-3833

ORR, JOSEPH ALEXANDER, educational administrator; b. West Palm Beach, Fla., Nov. 20, 1929; s. Joseph Alexander and Eula (Terry) O.; m. Ardis W. Orr (div.); children: Eric, Pamela, Tracey; m. Linda F. Orr. BS, Fla. A&M U., 1951; MS, Mich. State U., 1953; MEd, Fla. Atlantic U., 1965; PhD, Fla. State U., 1972. Sci. tchr. Roosevelt Sr. H.S., West Palm Beach, Fla., 1953-68; counselor, coord. Adult Edn. Dept. Sch. Sys., Palm Beach County, Fla., 1960-72; dean of students Palm Beach H.S., West Palm Beach, 1968-70; asst. dean Fla. A&M U., Tallahassee, 1970-72; adj. prof. Ind. U., Bloomington, 1972-73; prin. Ctrl. Sr. H.S., Louisville, 1972-74, Jupiter (Fla.) H.S., 1974-78; adj. prof. Fla. Atlantic U., Boca Raton, 1978—; asst. supt. Palm Beach County (Fla.) Sch. Bd., 1978-84, assoc. supt., 1984-92; exec. dir. Palm Beach County Sch. Adminstrs. Assn., 1992—; bd. dirs. Sterling Savs. Bank, West Palm Beach; chair State Adv. Bd. for Severely Emotionally Disturbed. Contbr. articles to profl. jours. Bd. dirs. Children's Home Soc. of Fla., Palm Beach County Coun. of Arts; chair Health and Human Svcs. Bd., Palm Beach County, Fla., Inst. of New Dimensions, Palm Beach C.C., Assn. for Retarded Citizens, Inc., West Palm Beach; pres. Scholastic Achievement Found. Palm Beach County. Recipient Disting. Svc. award NEA, Pioneer award for excellence in pub. svc. Nat. Forum of Pub. Adminstrn., Outstanding Achievement award Fla. Assn. Cmty. Educators, Four

Seasons award Nat. Assn. for Year Round Edn. Mem. ASCD, Fla. Assn. Sch. Adminstrs., Am. Assn. Sch. Adminstrs., Nat. Assn. Secondary Sch. Prins., Nat. Cmty. Edn. Assn. (Sch. Leadership award), Kiwanis Internat. (bd. dirs. local club). Democrat. Episcopalian. Office: Palm Beach County Sch Adminstrs Assn PO Box 31511 Palm Beach Gardens FL 33420

ORR, JOSEPH NEWTON, recreational guide, outdoor educator; b. San Francisco, Oct. 25, 1954; s. James Neewah and Verna Louise (Butler) O. BA in Spanish, Sul Ross State U., 1981. Cert. swiftwater rescue technician; cert. wilderness first responder; cert. advanced open water SCUBA diver; cert. Utah river guide, Grand Canyon river guide. Instr. astronomy lab. Sul Ross State U., Alpine, Tex., 1972-75; svc. sta. attendent, store clerk Nat. Park Concessions, Big Bend Nat. Park, 1975-78; surveyor's aide Gila Nat. Forest U.S. Dept. Agriculture, N. Mex., 1979; instr. ESL Centro Universitario de Idiomas, Mexico City, 1981; English and Spanish tutor Ctr. Student Devel. Sul Ross State U., 1980-83, instr. ESL, Intensive Summer Lang. Tng. Inst., 1980-83; ednl. cons. Chihuahuan Desert Rsch. Inst., Alpine, Tex., 1983; editor The Skyline (student newspaper) Sul Ross State U., 1984; interpreter, translator, guide Dr. John M. Miller, Mexico, 1980-85; waiter Kangaroo Court Rest., San Antonio, 1981-82, 84-86; guide in U.S., Mex., Belize, Guatemala and Honduras for Far Flung Adventures, 1986-94, Remarkable Journeys, 1994—. Active Four Corners Sch. Outdoor Edn., Canyonlands Fld Inst., Crow Canyon Archeol. Ctr., Grand Canyon River Guides, Mus. No. Ariz., Friends of Lowell Obs., Grand Canyon Trust, others. Mem. Soc. for Am. Archaeology, Nat. Geog. Soc., Archaeol. Conservancy, Am. Rock Art Rsch. Assn., Astron. Soc. of Pacific, Planetary Soc., Internat. Dark Sky Assn., Sch. Am. Rsch., Beta Beta Beta. Democrat. Home: 223 N Guadalupe # 429 Santa Fe NM 87501-1850 Office: Remarkable Journeys PO Box 31855 Houston TX 77231-1855

ORR, LISA KAY, potter; b. Eastland, Tex., Sept. 7, 1960; d. Robert E. Lee Orr Jr. and Sandra Kay (Miller) Powell. BFA, U. Tex., 1983; MFA, Alfred U., 1992. Owner Lisa Orr Pottery, San Antonio, 1986-89, King William Pottery, San Antonio, 1995—; instr. ceramics Trinity U., San Antonio, 1995—, Southwest Craft Ctr., San Antonio, 1994-95, Carver Cultural Ctr., San Antonio, 1995; workshop leader Corcoran Gallery Sch., Washington, 1995. Work included in (book) The New Ceramics by Peter Dormer, 1994. Fellow NEA, 1995, Fulbright, 1993, grantee, 1993-94. Mem. Coll. Art Assn., San Antonio Potters Guild. Democrat. Home: 604 Mission St San Antonio TX 78210 Office: King William Pottery 712 A S Saint Mary's San Antonio TX 78205

ORR, ROBERT F., justice; b. Norfolk, Va., Oct. 11, 1946. AB, U. N.C., 1971, JD, 1975. Bar: N.C. 1975. News reporter, part-time photographer Sta. WSOC-TV, 1965-68, 71; pvt. practice Asheville, N.C., 1975-86; assoc. judge N.C. Ct. Appeals, 1986-94; assoc. justice N.C. Supreme Ct., Raleigh, 1994—; mem. N.C. Beverage Control Commn., 1985-86; adj. prof. appellate advocacy N.C. Ctrl. U. Sch. Law, 1989—. Mem. Asheville-Revitalization Commn., 1977-81, Asheville-Buncombe Hist. Resources Commn., 1980-81; bd. trustees Hist. Preservation Found. N.C., 1982-85; mem. Nat. Park Sys. Adv. Bd., 1990-95, chmn., 1992-93; mem. N.C. 2000, Com. for Excellence in Edn., Goal 6: Safe and Drug Free Schs. With U.S. Army, 1968-71. Mem. N.C. State Bar, 28th Jud. Dist., N.C. Bar Assn. Republican. Office: PO Box 1841 Raleigh NC 27607 also: 304 Justice Bldg 2 E Morgan St Raleigh NC 27601

ORR, T(HOMAS) J(EROME) (JERRY ORR), airport terminal executive; b. Charlotte, N.C., Feb. 25, 1941; m. Marcia Mincey; 3 children. BS in Civil Engring., N.C. State U., 1962. Registered profl. engr., N.C. Pvt. practice land surveyor Charlotte, 1962-75; with Charlotte/Douglas Internat. Airport, 1975—, asst. mgr. airport ops., until 1989, aviation dir., 1989—. Chmn. employes campaign United Way of Ctrl. Carolinas, 1990; active Neighborhood Task Force, Charlotte's Cities in Schs. Program. Recipient Outstanding Support award N.C. Air Nat. Guard, 1989, Spirit award Charlotte-MJecklenburg Spirit Sq. Ctr. for Arts, 1990. Mem. N.C. Airports Assn. (past pres.), Airport Operators Coun. Internat. Office: Charlotte/Douglas Internat Airport PO Box 19066 Charlotte NC 28219-9066

ORR-CAHALL, CHRISTINA, art gallery director, art historian; b. Wilkes-Barre, Pa., June 12, 1947; d. William R.A. and Anona (Snyder) Boben; m. Richard Cahall. BA magna cum laude, Mt. Holyoke Coll., 1969; MA, Yale U., 1974, MPhil, 1975, PhD, 1979. Curator of collections Norton Gallery Art, West Palm Beach, Fla., 1975-77; asst. prof. Calif. Poly. State U., San Luis Obispo, 1978-81, Disting. prof., 1981; dir. art div., chief curator Oakland (Calif.) Mus., 1981-88; chief exec. officer Corcoran Gallery Art, Washington, 1988-90; dir. Norton Mus. Art, West Palm Beach, 1990—. Author: Addison Mizner: Architect of Dreams and Realities, 1974, 2d printing, 1993, Gordon Cook, 1987, Claude Monet: Am Impression, 1993; editor: The Art of California, 1984, The American Collection at the Norton Museum of Art, 1995. Office: Norton Gallery of Art 1451 S Olive Ave West Palm Beach FL 33401-7162

ORSAK, CHARLIE GEORGE, community college administrator; b. Wichita Falls, Tex., May 18, 1945; s. Charlie George Sr. and Virginia Lorene (King) O.; m. Lana Beth Lawson; children: Clessa Ann, Erik Lawson, Charles Aaron. BA in English, Speech, Midwestern State U., 1968, MA in English, 1970; MEd in Adult and Continuing Edn., East Tex. State U., 1984, PhD in Secondary and Higher Edn., 1987. Instr. U. Md., Heidelberg, Fed. Republic Germany, 1972-73; curriculum devel. specialist project transition U.S. Army Europe Gen. Edn. Div., Worms, Fed. Republic Germany, 1972-74; dir. community coll. programs Cen. Tex. Coll., Wiesbaden, Fed. Republic Germany, 1974-76; dir. Far East programs Cen. Tex. Coll., Seoul, Republic of Korea, 1976; instr., dir. institutional devel. and effectiveness Navarro Coll., Corsicana, Tex., 1976-84; dean off-campus ctrs. Navarro Coll., Ellis County, Tex., 1985-86; fgn. expert Hefei (People's Republic China) U. Tech., 1986-87; acting dir. learning resource ctr. Navarro Coll., Corsicana, 1987-90; exec. dir. Superconducting Super Collider Tng. Project Navarro Coll./Dallas County C.C. Dist., Waxahachie, Tex., 1990-92, ESL instr., 1992-93; dir. rsch. and devel. Houston C.C. Sys., 1993—; dir. DOE Nat. Solar Manpower Needs Assessment and Task Analysis, Corsicana, 1976-77; curriculum devel. specialist TEA Energy Conservation Curriculum Project, Corsicana, 1977-78; prin. investigator NSF Solar Tech. Curriculum Project, Corsicana, 1978-82; cons. alcohol fuels curriculum Navarro Coll., Corsicana, 1982; cons. Title III Carl Perkins NSF, 1983-91; cons. grantsmanship, Cairo, Egypt, 1988; cons. Roboz-Katona Assoc., Budapest, Hungary, 1991. Contbr. articles to profl. jours. Mem. Navarro County Hist. Soc., Corsicana, 1980-91; mem. Navarro County Drug and Alcohol Abuse Com., Corsicana, 1987-91. 1st lt. U.S. Army, 1970-72. Mem. ASCD, Nat. Coun. Resource Devel., Am. Assn. Community Jr. Colls., Tex. Jr. Coll. Tchrs. Assn., Phi Delta Kappa (founding pres. Bluebonnet chpt. 1988-90). Home: 212 N 30th St Corsicana TX 75110-4219

ORSEE, JOE BROWN, library director; b. Fulton, Ky., Oct. 25, 1949; divorced; children: Amy, Matthew. BS in Libr. Sci., Murray State U., 1971, MS in Libr. Sci., 1972. Assoc. regional libr. Barren River Regional Libr., Russellville, Ky., 1972-73; dir. interlibr. cooperation Ky. Dept. Libr. and Archives, Frankfort, 1973-76; libr. cons. Miss. Libr. Commn., Jackson, 1976, asst. dir. adminstrn., 1976-78, dir., 1978-80; dir. pub. libr. svcs. Ga. Dept. Edn., Atlanta, 1980-95; dir. N.W. Ga. Regional Libr., Daton, Ga., 1995—; co-chmn. Gov.'s Conf. on Libr. and Info. Svcs.; past vice-chmn. White House Conf. Libr. and Info. Svcs. Task Force; del. 1st and 2d White House Confs. Libr. and Info. Scis. Contbr. articles to profl. jours., fed. and state docs.; guest spkr. in field. Mem. ALA, S.E. Libr. Assn. (pres.), Ga. Libr. Assn. Home: 214 Calhoun Ave Calhoun GA 30701 Office: NW Ga Regional Libr 310 Cappes St Dalton GA 30720

ORTEGA, RAFAEL CLEMENTE, English and Romance language educator; b. San Diego, Oct. 3, 1935; s. Rafael O. and Santos (Clemente) O.; m. Carol, Dec. 6, 1961 (div. 1969); children: Zelina, Rafael Rossano, Lance Sterling; m. Carol M., 1995. BA, San Diego State U., 1971, MA, 1972; ABD in Grad. Studies, U. So. Calif., L.A., 1977; EdD, Calif. Coast U., L.A., 1987. Head wrestling coach San Diego State U., 1971-74; asst. prof. Cerritos Coll., Norwalk, Calif., 1976-81; dir. Avco Saudi Arabia, Jeddah, 1981-86; asst. prof. Miramar Coll., San Diego, 1986-89; supr. USAIR, Charlotte, 1987—; lectr. English-as-second-lang. Winthrop U., Rock Hill, S.C., 1992-95; head Spanish Dept. Catawba Valley Cmty. Sch., Hickory, S.C., 1995—; tech. advisor Mexican Olympic Com., Mexico City, 1968. Author: Barrio Language, 1977, How to Win American Football, 1986, Anthology of Mexican-American Literature, 1993. With USN, 1953-55. Dept. Spanish and Portuguese, U. So. calif. grantee, 1975-77. Mem. Tchrs. of English as Second Land. Assn.

ORTEGO, GILDA BAEZA, librarian, information professional; b. El Paso, Tex., Mar. 29, 1952; d. Efren and Bertha (Singh) Baeza; m. Felipe de Ortego y Gasca, Dec. 21, 1986. BA, Tex. Woman's U., 1974, graduate, 1974-75; MLS, U. Tex., 1976, postgrad., 1990-93; cert., Hispanic Leadership Inst., 1988. Stack maintenance supr. El Paso Libr. U. Tex., 1974-75; pub. svcs. libr. El Paso Community Coll., 1976-77; ethnic studies libr. U. N.Mex., Albuquerque, 1977-81; br. head El Paso Pub. Libr., 1981-82; dep. head Mex.-Am. Svcs., El Paso Pub. Libr., 1982-84; libr. Mex.-Am. Studies U. Tex. Libr., Austin, 1984-87; libr. Phoenix Pub. Libr., 1987-89; assoc. libr., west campus Ariz. State U., Phoenix, 1989-90; Proyecto Leer libr. Tex. Woman's U., Denton, 1991-92; dir. div. learning resources Sul Ross State U., Alpine, Tex., 1992—; speaker and cons. in field. Founding editor jour. La Lista, 1983-84; founding indexer Chicano Periodical Index, 1981-86; reviewer jour. Voices of Youth Advocates, 1988-90; contbr. poetry and articles to books and jours. Mem. ALA (com. on standing of women in profession, com. on profl. edn.), MLA, Assn. for Libr. and Info. Sci. Edn., Tex. Libr. Assn., Ariz. State Libr. Assn. (pres. svcs. Spanish speaking Roundtable 1988-90), Reforma (pres. El Paso chpt. 1983, pres. Ariz. chpt. 1989-90, nat. v.p. 1993-94, pres. 1994-95), Unltd. Potential, Inc. (treas. 1988-89), Hispanic Leadership Inst. Alumni Assn.

ORTEGO Y GASCA, FELIPE DE, education educator; b. Blue Island, Ill., Aug. 23, 1926; s. Luis Darragh Ortego and Anita (Campos) Gasca; m. Gilda Baeza Ortego, Dec. 21, 1986. BA, Tex. Western Coll., 1959; MA, U. Tex., 1966; PhD, U. N.Mex., 1971; cert. mgmt. and planning studies, Columbia U., 1973. Asst. prof. of English N.Mex. State U., Las Cruces, 1964-70; dir. Chicano studies U. Tex., El Paso, 1970-72; asst. to pres. Met. State, Denver, 1972-74; vice chancellor, acad. devel. Hispanic U. of Am., Denver, 1974-78; dir. Inst. for Intercultural Studies and Rsch. Our Lady of the Lake U., San Antonio, Tex., 1978-82; chmn. bd. Hispanic Found., Washington, 1982-86; dean Hispanic Leadership Inst., prof. English Ariz. State U., Phoenix, 1986-90; prof. libr. and info. studies Tex. Woman's U., Denton, 1990-93; prof. of edn. Sul Ross State U., Alpine, Tex., 1993—, dir. Title III HSI, 1995—; bd. dirs. Ctr. for Big Bend Studies, Sul Ross State U.; pub. Nat. Hispanic Reporter, Washington, 1983-92; assoc. pub. La Luz mag., Denver, 1972-82; cons. info. mgmt. Exec. Office of Pres. of U.S., Washington, 1985-86. Author: Stamp of One Defect: Study of Hamlet, 1966, Backgrounds of Mexican American Literature, 1971, The Broken Arcs: Essays in the Quest for Human Dignity, 1989; editor: We Are Chicanos: Anthology of Mexican American Literature, 1973; editor The Hispanic Scholar; editor-in-chief Reforma Newsletter. Bd. dirs. Pub. TV, El Paso, 1970-72; del. White House Conf. on Libr. and Info. Svcs., Washington, 1991; chmn. Nat. Commn. on Status of Hispanics in DOD, Washington, 1984-85, Com. on Svc. to Hispanics, Am. Cancer Soc., N.Y., 1980-82. Recipient Presidio La Bahia award Sons of Rep. of Tex., Austin, 1980, NEA-Reader's Digest award for fiction, 1968; Lilly fellow for comty. leadership NACL, Indpls., 1990; Sr. Fulbright scholar Agy. for Internat. Edn., 1971. Mem. MLA, Am. Libr. Assn., Nat. Coun. Tchrs. of English, Tex. Libr. Assn., Tex. Assn. Chicanos in Higher Edn., Kiwanis (bd. dirs. 1993—). Methodist. Home: 503 Hendryx Dr Alpine TX 79830-2107 Office: Sul Ross State U PO Box 6031 Alpine TX 79832

ORTH, GEOFFREY CHARLES, modern languages educator; b. Phila., Feb. 12, 1947; s. Carl Stewart and Sara Louise (Zuber) O.; m. Kathryn Alice Owen, July 7, 1973; children: Andrew N., Timothy J. BA, Washington & Lee U., 1969; MA, U. Va., 1973, PhD, 1976. Instr. U. Va., Charlottesville, 1975-77; from instr. to prof. Longwood Coll., Farmville, Va., 1977—; mem. State Coun. Higher Edn. Task Force on Fgn. Langs., Richmond, Va., 1983-86; grant reviewer U.S. Dept. Edn., 1986. Vol. Farmville Area Cmty. Emergency Svcs., 1985—. Served to 1st lt. U.S. Army, 1969-71, Vietnam. Mem. MLA, Am. Assn. Tchrs. of German (exec. com. Va. chpt. 1979-91, newsletter editor 1980-86, testing chmn. 1986-91), South Atlantic Modern Lang. Assn., Fgn. Lang. Assn. Va., Delta Phi Alpha, Delta Upsilon. Episcopal. Office: Longwood Coll Dept Eng/Phil/Modern Langs Farmville VA 23909

ORTINAU, DAVID JOSEPH, marketing specialist, educator; b. Harvey, Ill., Dec. 14, 1948; s. Harold Raymond and Lois Agnice (Reich) O.; m. Shirley Keating, Aug. 15, 1975 (div. Nov. 1979); m. Renee Susan Hess, Apr. 30, 1983 (div. Aug. 1993). BS in Mgmt., So. Ill. U., 1970; MS in Bus. Adminstrn., Ill. State U., 1971; PhD in Mktg., La. State U., 1979. Sr. research analyst, dir. projects Rabin Research Co., Chgo., 1971-73; adminstrv. asst., instr. mktg. Coll. Bus. Ill. State U., Normal, 1973-76; grad. teaching assoc., instr. mktg. Coll. Bus. La. State U., Baton Rouge, 1976-79; from asst. prof. mktg. to assoc. prof. Coll. Bus. U. South Fla., Tampa, 1979-84, assoc. prof., 1984-95, prof., 1995—, coord. PhD program Dept. of Mktg., 1989-91; dir. mktg. and research Market Research Group, Tampa, 1980-83; v.p. mktg. Neaves, Neaves and Ortinau, Normal, 1974-77. Mem. editl. rev. bd. Jour. Acad. of Mktg. Sci., 1989-96 (Dist. Merit award for Outstanding Reviewer 1992-93); contbr. articles to Jour. Health Care Mktg., Jour. Mktg. Edn., Jour. Bus. Rsch., Jour. Svcs. Mktg., Jour. Acctg. Horizons, Jour. Retailing, others. Recipient Disting. Merit award Advt. Fedn. S.W. Fla., 1983, Coba Outstanding Rsch. award U. South Fla., 1987, Outstanding Tchg. award, 1980, 81, 82, 86, 90, 95. Mem. Am. Mktg. Assn. (doctoral consortium fellow 1978, reviewer 1982—), Assn. Consumer Rsch., So. Mktg. Assn. (reviewer 1975—, chmn. 1976—, sec. 1990-91, treas. 1992-95, pres. elect 1995-96, pres. 1996-97, chmn. Svcs. Mktg. Customer Satisfaction Track Program 1990-92, Outstanding Articles award 1981, 86, 87, 90, 92), Acad. Mktg. Sci. (reviewer 1988—, chmn. 1989, 92, Reviewer of Yr. 1992), Acad. Bus. Adminstrn. (track program chmn. 1993), Beta Gamma Sigma (pres. Fla. chpt. 1990-91). Home: 2305 Windsor Oaks Ave Lutz FL 33549-5880 Office: U South Fla Mktg Dept Tampa FL 33620

ORTIQUE, REVIUS OLIVER, JR., city official; b. New Orleans, June 14, 1924; s. Revius Oliver and Lillie Edith (Long) O.; m. Miriam Marie Victorianne, Dec. 29, 1947; children—Rhesa Marie (Mrs. Alden J. McDonald). AB, Dillard U., 1947; MA, Ind. U., 1949; JD, So. U., 1956; LLD (hon.), Campbell Coll., 1960; LHD (hon.), Ithaca Coll., 1971; LLD (hon.), Ind. U., 1983, Morris Brown Coll., 1992, Loyola U. South, 1993. Bar: La. 1956, U.S. Dist. Ct 1956, Eastern Dist. La 1956, U.S. Fifth Circuit Ct. of Appeals 1956, U.S. Supreme Ct 1956. Practiced in New Orleans, 1956-79; judge Civil Dist. Ct. for Orleans Parish, 1979-92; assoc. justice La. Supreme Ct., 1993-94; chmn. New Orleans Aviation Bd., 1994—; lectr. labor law Dillard U., 1950-52, U. West Indies, 1986-94; formerly assoc. gen. counsel Cmty. Improvement Agy.; gen. counsel 8th Dist. A.M.E. Ch.; mem. Fed. Hosp. Coun., 1966, Pres.'s Commn. on Campus Unrest, 1970, Bd. Legal Svcs. Corp., 1975-83; chief judge civil cts. Orleans Parish, 1986-87; spkr. in field. Contbr. articles to profl. jours. Former pres. Met. Area Com.; former mem. Bd. City Trusts, New Orleans, New Orleans Legal Assistance Corp. Bd., Ad Hoc Com. for Devel. of Ctrl. Bus. Dist. City of New Orleans; bd. dirs. Cmty. Rels. Coun., Am. Lung Assn.; trustee Antioch Coll. Law, New Orleans chpt. Operation PUSH, 1981—; pres. Louis A. Martinet Soc., 1959; active World's Fair, New Orelans, 1984, Civil Rights Movement, 1960-79; bd. dirs., mem. exec. com. Nat. Sr. Citizens Law Ctr., L.A., 1970-76, Criminal Justice Coordinating Com., UN Assn. New Orleans, 1980—; former mem. exec. bd. Nat. Bar Found.; mem. exec. com. econ. Devel. Coun. Greater New Orleans; past chmn. Health Edn. Authority of La.; trustee, mem. exec. com. Dillard U.; former mem. bd. mgmt. Flint Goodridge Hosp.; mem. adv. bd. League Women Voters Greater New Orleans; mem. men's adv. bd. YWCA; trustee AME Ch., aldo connectional trustee; chancellor N.O. Fedn. Chs.; bd. dirs. Nat. Legal Aid and Defender Assn.; bd. trustees Civil Justice Found.; served on over 50 bds., commns. 1st lt. AUS, 1943-47, PTO. Recipient Arthur von Briesen medal Disting. Svcs. Disadvantaged Ams. NLADA, 1971, Weiss award NCCJ, 1975, Brotherhood award NCCJ, 1976, Nat. Black Achievement award, 1979, Poor People's Banner award, 1979, William H. Hastie award, 1983, Outstanding Citizen award Kiwanis of Pontchartrain, 1986, Civil Justice award, 1989, Daniel E. Byrd award NAACP, 1991, A.P. Tureaud Meml. medal La. State NAACP, 1993; Revius O. Ortique Jr. Law Libr. named in his honor, Lafayette, La., 1988; named Outstanding Young Man Nat. Urban League, 1958, Outstanding Person in La. Inst. Human Understanding, 1976, Citizen of Yr. Shreveport, 1993. Mem. ABA (del., Legal Svcs. program, Nat. adv. coun., 1964-71, jud. divsn.), Nat. Bar Assn. (pres. 1965-66, exec. bd., Raymond Pace Alexander award, jud. coun. 1987, William Hastie award 1982, Gertrude E. Rush award 1991), La. State Bar Assn. (former mem. ho. of dels., Lifetime Achievement award 1986), Nat. Legal Aid and Defender Assn. (past pres., mem. exec. bd.), La. District Judges Assn., Am. Judicature Soc. (bd. dirs. 1975-79), Civil Justice Found. (trustee), Louis A. Martinet Legal Soc., World Peace Through Law (charter mem.), Blue Key Honor Soc., Phi Delta Kappa, Alpha Kappa Delta. Home: 10 Park Island Dr New Orleans LA 70122-1229 Office: New Orleans Aviation Bd PO Box 20007 New Orleans LA 70141-0007

ORTIZ, JAY RICHARD GENTRY, lawyer; b. Washington, Mar. 21, 1945; s. Charles and Catherine Gentry (Candlin) O.; m. Lois Wright Hatcher Greer, June 12, 1982. B.A., Yale U., 1967; postgrad. Stanford U. 1967-68; J.D., U. N.Mex., 1972. Bar: N.Mex. 1973, Mo. 1978, Tenn. 1982, Ga., 1991, U.S. Dist. Ct. N.Mex. 1973, U.S. Ct. Appeals (10th cir. 1973), U.S. Supreme Ct. 1977, U.S. Dist. Ct. (western dist.) Mo. 1978, U.S. Dist. Ct. (no. dist.) Ga. 1991, U.S. Ct. Appeals (8th cir.) 1978, U.S. Ct. Appeals (11th cir.) 1991. Assoc. Rodey, Dickason, Sloan, Akin & Robb, Albuquerque, 1972-75; ptnr. Knight, Sullivan, Villella, Skarsgard & Michael, Albuquerque, 1975-77; litigation atty. Monsanto Co., St. Louis, 1977-81; environ. atty. Eastman Kodak Co., Kingsport, Tenn., 1981-84; sr. atty. AT&T, Atlanta, 1984-91; gen. counsel AMS Group, Inc., 1991—, Consulta Solutions, Inc., 1994—; pres. VMS, Inc., 1994—. Precinct vice chmn. Dem. Party, Albuquerque, 1971-77. Served to lt. (j.g.), USN, 1969-70. Mem. ABA, Ga. Bar Assn., N.Mex. Bar Assn., Mo. Bar Assn., Tenn. Bar Assn., Order of Coif, Yale Club of Ga., English Speaking Union, Delta Theta Phi (tribune 1972-77). Episcopalian. Home: 1000 Buckingham Cir NW Atlanta GA 30327-2704 Office: VMS Inc Ste 300 3475 Lenox Rd Atlanta GA 30326

ORTIZ, LOIDA A., communications executive; b. Vega Baja, P.R.; d. Luis and Alicia Ortiz. AA in Computer Scis., U. P.R., 1979; BA in Comm., U. Sacred Heart, 1985. From field prodr. to news dir. Sta. WSJN-TV, Hato Rey, P.R., 1987-90; news editor Stas. WIPR-Radio and WKAQ-Radio, Hato Rey, 1989-90; announcer Sta. WMDO Radio Mundo, Tampa, Fla., 1990-91; media cons. Am. Region United Bible Socs., Miami, Fla., 1991—. Office: United Bible Socs 1989 NW 88th Ct Miami FL 33172-2641

ORTIZ-TAYLOR, SHEILA, English language educator; b. L.A., Sept. 25, 1939; d. John Santray and Juanita Loretta (Shrode) T.; m. John Leonard Clendenning, Aug. 27, 1958 (div. 1971); m. J.L. Lewis, Mar. 16, 1991; children: Andrea, Laura, Jessica, Will, Lynn. BA, Calif. State U., Northridge, 1963; MA, UCLA, 1964, PhD, 1973. Lectr. Calif. State U., Northridge, 1964-70; prof. English Fla. State U., Tallahassee, 1973—. Author: (novels) Faultline, 1982, Spring Forward/Fall Back, 1985, Southbound, 1990, (book of poetry) Slow Dancing at Miss Polly's, 1989 (memoir) Imaginary Parents, 1996. Recipient Fulbright fellowship Fulbright Assn., 1991. Democrat. Office: Fla State U Dept English Tallahassee FL 32306-1036

ORTLIP, MARY KRUEGER, artist; b. Scranton, Pa.; d. John A. and Ida Mae (Phillips) Smale; m. Emmanuel Krueger, June 1940 (dec. Nov. 1979); children: Diane, Keith; m. Paul D. Ortlip, June 26, 1981. Student, New Sch. Social Rsch., N.Y.C., 1957-59, Margarita Madrigal Langs., N.Y.C., Montclair (N.J.) Art Mus. Sch., 1978-79; Nomina Accademico Conferita, Accademia Italia, Italy, 1986; DFA (hon.), Houghton Coll., 1988. Dancer, dance instr. Fleischer Dance Studio, Scranton, Pa., 1934-38. One-woman shows include Curzon Gallery of Boca Raton, Fla. and London, 1986-93, Galerie Les Amis des Arts, Aix-en-Provence, France, 1987; group exhbns.: Salmagundi Club, N.Y.C., 1980, James Hunt Barker Galleries, Nantucket, Mass. and N.Y.C., 1983, Salon Internationale Musée Parc Rochteau à Revin, France, 1985, 90, Accademia Italia, Milan, 1986, many others in Europe and Am.; permanent collections Musée de parc Rocheteau, Revin, France, Pinacothèque Arduinna, Charleville-Meziéres, France. Named Invité d'Honneur, Le Salon des Nations a Retenu L'oeuvre, Paris, 1983, Artist of the Year, La Cote des Arts, France, 1986; recipient La Medaille d'Or, Du 13ème Salon Internationale al du Parc Rocheau au Revin, France, 1985, Medaille d' Honneur Ville de Marseille, France, 1987, Targo D'Oro, Accademia Italia Premio D'Italia, 1986; Trophy Arts Internationale Exposition de Peinture Marseille, Plaquette d' Honneur, Palais des Arts, 1987, Grand Prix Salon de Automne Club Internationale, 1987, Connaissance de Notre Europa Ardennes Eifel, Revin, France, 1990. Mem. Nat. Mus. Women in Arts, Accademia Italia (charter), Instituo D'Art Contemporanea Di Milano, Nat. Soc. Arts and Letters, Gov.'s Club, Salmagundi Club. Home (winter): 2917 S Ocean Blvd #703 Highland Beach FL 33487-1876 Home (summer): 588 Summit Ave Hackensack NJ 07601-1547 Office: The Curzon Gallery 501 E Camino Real Boca Raton FL 33432-6127

ORTLIP, PAUL DANIEL, artist; b. Englewood, N.J., May 21, 1926; s. Henry Willard and Aimee (Eschner) O.; m. Mary Louise Krueger, June 1981; children from previous marriage: Carol, Kathleen, Sharon (dec.), Danielle (dec.), Michelle. Diploma, Houghton Acad., 1944; student, Art Students League, 1947-49; diploma, Acad. la Grande Chaumiere, Paris, 1950; DFA (hon.), Houghton Coll., 1988. Tchr. Fairleigh Dickinson U., Teaneck, N.J., 1956-68; artist in residence, curator Fairleigh Dickinson U., Rutherford, N.J., 1968-72; official USN artist on assignment, Cuban missile crisis, Fla., 1963, Gemini 5 Recovery, Atlantic Ocean, 1965, Vietnam, 1967, Apollo 12 recovery, Pacific Ocean, 1969, Apollo 17 recovery, Pacific Ocean, 1972, Internat. Naval Rev., N.Y. harbor, 1976, USCG Sta., Key West, Fla., 1985; mem. USN Art Coop. and Liason Com. Exhbns. include Salonde L'Art Libre, Paris, 1950, Nat. Acad. Design, 1952, Allied Artists of Am., N.Y.C., Acad. Sci., Rundell Gallery, Rochester, N.Y., Monclair Art Mus., Hist. Mus, Lima, Ohio, Butler Art Inst., Youngstown, Ohio, Fine Arts Gallery, San Diego, State Capitol Bldg., Sacramento, Calif., Capitol Mus., Olympia, Wash., Mus. Gt. Plains, Lawton, Okla., Witte Meml. Mus., San Antonio, Nimitz Meml. Mus., Fredericksberg, Tex., Pentagon Collection of Fine Arts, James Hunt Barker Galleries, Palm Beach, Fla., Nantucket, Mass, N.Y.C., Smithsonian Inst., Gallerie Vollem Breuse, Biarritz, France, Galerie Mouffe, Paris, Guggenheim Gallery, London, Wickersham Gallery, N.Y.C., Soc. Illustrators, N.Y.C.; retrospective exhbn. Bergen Community Mus., Paramus, N.J. 1970, The Curzon Gallery, 1987, 88, 89, 93, Ardennes et de l'Eifel, Charleville Mézières, France, June-Sept. 1990; represented permanent collections including Salmagundi Club N.Y.C., Houghton (N.Y.) Coll., Portrait Meml. J.F. Kennedy Library, Fairleigh-Dickinson U., Nat. Air and Space Mus., Smithsonian Inst., Intrepid Sea-Air Space Mus., N.Y.C., Hist. Mural Visitors Ctr., Palisades Interstate Pk., Ft. Lee, N.J., Vets. Med. Ctr., East Orange, N.J., USN Exhbn. Ctr., Washington Navy Yard, Am. Coll. Clin. Pharmacology, N.Y.C., N.J. U. Dentistry & Medicine, Newark, Bergen County Ct. House, Hackensack, N.J., Dickinson Coll., Carlisle, Pa., George Washingtogn Meml Pk., Paramus, N.J., Marietta (Ohio) Coll., Mcpl. Bldg., Ft. Lee, N.J., Navy League U.S., Arlington, Va., Nat. Archives and Records Adminstrn., Washington, (mural) Pub. Libr., Fort Lee, N.J. Served to sgt. U.S. Army, 1944-47, ETO, PTO, 1946-47. Recipient 1st prize Am. Artists Profl. League State Exhibit N.J. chpt., Paramus, 1960, 1st prize U.S. Armed Forces Exhibit Far East, Seoul, Korea, Tokyo, 1946, Franklin Williams award, Salmagundi Club, N.Y., 1967, Outstanding Achievement award for oil painting, USN, 1968, Artist of Yr. award, Hudson Artists, Jersey City (N.J.) Mus., 1970, Statue of Victory World Culture prize, Academia Italia, Parma, 1982, Men of Achievement medal Cambridge, Eng., 1990, Connaissance de Notre Europe Gold medal Charleville-Mézières, France, 1990. Mem. Allied Artists Am. (art coop. and liaison com. with USN), Nat. Soc. Mural Painters, Nat. Soc. Arts and Letters, Bergen County Artists Guild (pres. 1960-62), Am. Portrait Soc., Artists Fellowship, Inc., U.S. Coast Guard Art Program, Art Students League N.Y. (life), Navy League U.S., VFW (life), Am. Legion. Clubs: Salmagundi (N.Y.C.) (art chmn. 1979-81); Gov.'s of the Palm Beaches (Fla.). Home: 588 Summit Ave Hackensack NJ 07601-1547 Office: care The Curzon Gallery 501 E Camino Real Boca Raton FL 33432-6127

ORTON, ROBERT DELL, military officer; b. Sioux City, Iowa, Oct. 12, 1939; s. Robert Adelbert and Olga (Jensen) O.; m. Sylvia Ann Spencer, May 25, 1985. BS in Chemistry, u. Tex., 1961; MS in Chemistry, Rensselaer Poly. Inst.; postgrad., U. Iowa. Commd. 2d lt. u.S. Army; advanced through grades to maj. gen., various battery command, bat. and bridge staff positions; chem. advisor 3d Vietnamese Corps; chem. officer, asst. to the chief of staff 3d Armored Divsn.; staff officer Mil. Pers. Ctr.; cheif chem. and NBC

Def. Divsn. Office of the Dep. Chief of Staff for Ops.; comdr. U.S. Army Chem. Activity Western Command; project mgr. binary munitions Office of the Program Exec. Officer for Chem./Nuclear; comdr. U.S. Army Chem. and Mil. Police Ctrs., Fort McClellan, 1992-94; dep. chief of staff base ops. support HQ U.S. Army Tng. and Doctrine Command, Fort Monroe, 1994-95; program mgr. Chem Cemil, Aberdeen Proving Ground, Md., 1995—. Decorated DSM, Legion of Merit with three oak leaf clusters, Bronze star medal, Air medal, Nat. def. medal, Vietnam Svc. medal with two oak leaf clusters, Disting. Svc. medal, Republic of Vietnam Tech. honor medal. Mem. Assn. of the U.S. Army, Rotary Internat., Am. Def. Preparedness Assn., Sigma Alpha Epsilon. Office: Chem Demil E4585 Hoadly Rd Aberdeen Proving Ground MD 21010

ORVIN, GEORGE HENRY, psychiatrist; b. Columbia, S.C., Aug. 6, 1922; s. Jesse Wright and Ruth Veril (Walton) O.; m. Rosalie Greer Salvo, Sept. 16, 1944; children: Candace, Jay Scott, Debra Anne, Nancy Lee. BS, The Citadel, 1943; MD, Med. U. S.C., Charleston, 1946; MD (hon.), The Citadel, 1996. Diplomate Am. Bd. Psychiatry. Pvt. practice Charleston, S.C., 1948-57; resident psychiatry Med. U. S.C., 1957-60; clin. asst. U. London, 1960-61; instr. Med. U.S.C., 1961; chief adolescent psychiatry Med. U. S.C., 1967-89, pres. faculty senate, 1977-79, prof. psychiatry, 1977-89, emeritus prof. psychiatry, 1993; founder, chmn. New Hope Treatment Ctrs., Inc., Charleston, 1984—. Author: Understanding the Adolescent, 1995; sr. editor Annals Adolescent Psychiatry, 1985; contbr. chpts. to books, articles to profl. jours. Vice-chmn. S.C. Com. Alcohol/Drug Abuse, 1973-89; mem. Gov.'s Cabinet for Children, 1984, Gov.'s Task Force Adolescent Pregnancies, 1985. Fellow Am. Psychiat. Assn. (life), Am. Soc. Adolescent Psychiatry (life), Royal Soc. Medicine, St. Andrews Soc., Citadel Brigadier Club (founder, pres. 1948-53). Episcopalian. Home: 126 Rutledge Ave Charleston SC 29401-1333 Office: New Hope Inc 225 Midland Pky Summerville SC 29485-8104

OSAGE, FRANK JOHN, university administrator; b. Omaha, Nebr., July 17, 1955; s. Frank J. and Mary T. (Cimino) O. BA, Creighton U., 1971, MA, 1976; PhD, Mich. State U., 1988. Resident dir. St. Mary's U. of Minn., Winona, 1978-85; v.p. student affairs Christian Bros. U., Memphis, 1988—. Recipient Bro. Finbar McMullan award, St. Mary's U., 1985. Mem. Nat. Assn. Student Pers. Adminstrs., Am. Coll. Pers. Assocs. (bd. dirs. 1990—). Office: Christian Bros Univ 650 E Parkway S Memphis TN 38104-5519

OSBORN, CHRISTOPHER RAYMOLN, JR., minister; b. Memphis, Aug. 13, 1950; s. Christopher Raymoln and Elsie Mae (Hatcher) O.; m. Judy Marie Moore, Oct. 5, 1968; children: Steven Ray, Richard Wayne, Brittany Anne. Assoc. Div., Mid-Atlantic Bible Inst., 1985; BA, Mid-Atlantic Bible Coll., 1987; M. Ministry, Mid-Atlantic Sem., 1987; D. Ministry cum laude, Covington Theol. Sem., 1988; student, Spartanburg Tech. Coll., 1974, DeVry Inst. Tech., 1968-69, Sem. Ext. So. Bapt. Conv., 1978-81, Isothermal C.C., 1990. Ordained to ministry So. Bapt. Conv., 1981. Pastor Bethel Meml. Bapt. Ch., Gaffney, S.C., 1981-87, Silver Creek Bapt. Ch., Mill Spring, N.C., 1987—. Foster parent Cherokee County DSS, Gaffney, S.C., 1981-87, Polk County DSS, Tryon, N.C., 1988-94, mem. foster care rev. bd., 1989—; mem. adv. bd. Cherokee Children's Home, Gaffney, 1986-87; bd. dirs. Thermal Belt Outreach Ministry, 1993-96, bd. dirs. Polk County chpt. ARC, 1992-94; chaplain Mill Spring Vol. Fire Dept., 1992—. Mem. Am. Assn. Christian Counselors (charter), Polk Bapt. Assn. (dir. evangelism 1990-93, dir. discipleship tng. 1987-90, vice moderator 1992-94, moderator 1994-96, pres. pastor's conf. 1993-94). Office: Silver Creek Bapt Ch 292 Silver Creek Rd Mill Spring NC 28756-8676

OSBORN, DAVID GUY, sales executive; b. Washington, Feb. 19, 1947; s. William G. and Christine E. (Thornhill) O.; m. Marilyn J. George, June 26, 1971; children: Jaime Michelle, Matthew David. BS, Stephen F. Austin State U., 1969; MBA, Tex. Christian U., 1975. Sales/mgmt. rep. AT&T, various locations, 1970-84; gen. mgr. Bramtel, Inc., Dallas, 1984-87; owner S.W. Telesis/Reliant Comms., Dallas, 1987-92; nat. account sales rep. Siemens Rolm Comms. Inc., Houston, 1992—. Author: Account Planning for High Technology Selling, 1981, Telecom Selling the Right Way, 1991. With USAFR, 1969-75. Republican. Presbyterian. Avocations: instructing and refereeing martial arts, golf, photography. Home: 19026 Owen Oak Dr Humble TX 77346-6070 Office: Siemens Rolm Comms Inc 13100 Northwest Fwy Ste 200 Houston TX 77040-6300

OSBORN, JACQUELINE ELIZABETH, water treatment systems company executive; b. Lexington, Nebr., Apr. 4, 1951; d. Samuel and Aurelie Bertha (D'orjo de Marchelovette) Janousek; 1 child, Aimee. Student, U. No. Colo. Asst. project mgr. Atascocita On Lake Houston, Houston, 1978-80; v.p. Walker Systems, Inc., Houston, 1980-86, DX Systems, Inc., Houston, 1986-90; owner Jacqueline E. Osborn & Assocs.; pres., prin., ind. cons. Dolphin Comml. Chem., Inc., Dallas, 1990-93, pres., owner, 1993—; guest lectr. Korea, 1993—, Japan, 1991—; lectr. CPO and AFO classes Tech. I and II Schs.; mem. Tex. Design Standards Com. for Swimming Pools, 1993—. Creator: (character and coloring book) Pat the Plat, The Platypus for Wagga Wagga, 1994. Guest lectr. ARC; mem. stewardship/fin. bd., mem. lay hosp. visitation team, mem. bldg. grounds com. LLUMC. Mem. NAFE, Nat. Spa and Pool Inst. (pres.-elect. 1991-92, 92-93), Nat. Swimming Pool Found., Nat. Assn. Women Bus. Owners, Tex. Recreation and Pks. Soc. (pres. comml. br. 1990-92), Nat. Spa and Pool Inst. (region III govt. rels. com. 1993—), Phi Beta Kappa. Republican. Methodist. Home: 3707 Northaven Rd Dallas TX 75229-2753

OSBORN, LA DONNA CAROL, clergywoman; b. Portland, Oreg., Mar. 13, 1947; d. T.L. and Daisy (Washburn) O.; m. Cory A. Nickerson, Dec. 11, 1981; children: Tommy O'Dell, LaVona Thomas, Daneesa Dolan, Donald O'Dell. Student, Assemblies of God Coll., 1963; BA, Okla. City U., 1994. Fgn. mission corr., purchaser, personnel agt. Osborn Found., Tulsa, 1969-75, exec. asst., 1975-76, internat. gen. mgr., 1976-81, internat. editor-in-chief, 1981-86, corp. pres., 1986-93; assoc. pastor Internat. Gospel Ctr., Tulsa, 1986-89, pastor, 1989-94, sr. pastor, overseer, 1994—; motivational speaker Nigeria, Kenya, Uganda, Colombia, Papua New Guinea, France, Russia, Belarus, Kazakhstan, Kyrgyzstan, Ukraine, U.S.; internat. spiritual advisor Christian Women's Fellowship Internat. Nigeria; founder Internat. Gospel Chs. and Mins., Believers' Network Internat. Author, editor Bible tng. courses. Republican. Office: Internat Gospel Ctr Box 700361 Tulsa OK 74170

OSBORN, LEN, business executive. Divsn. gen. mgr. JWK Internat. Corp., Annandale, Va. Office: JWK Internat Corp 7617 Little River Tpke Annandale VA 22003

OSBORN, MALCOLM EVERETT, lawyer; b. Bangor, Maine, Apr. 29, 1928; s. Lester Everett and Helen (Clark) O.; m. Claire Anne Franks, Aug. 30, 1953; children: Beverly, Lester, Malcolm, Ernest. BA, U. Maine, 1952; postgrad. Harvard U. 1952-54; JD Boston U. 1956, LLM, 1961. Bar: Maine 1956, Mass. 1956, U.S. Dist. Ct. Mass. 1961, U.S. Tax Ct. 1961, U.S. Claims 1961, N.C. 1965, U.S. Supreme Ct. 1979, U.S. Ct. Appeals (4th cir.) 1980, Va. 1991. Tax counsel State Mut. Life Assurance Co., Worcester, Mass., 1956-64; v.p., gen. tax counsel Integon Corp. and other group cos., Winston-Salem, N.C., 1964-81; ptnr. House, Blanco & Osborn, P.A., Winston-Salem, 1981-88, v.p., gen. counsel, dir. Settlers Life Ins. Co., Bristol, Va., 1984-89; prin. Malcolm E. Osborn, P.A., Winston-Salem, 1988—; lectr. The Booke Seminars, Life Ins. Co., 1985-87; adj. prof. Wake Forest U. Sch. of Law, Winston-Salem, 1974-82; Disting. guest lectr. Ga. State U., 1965; guest lectr. N.Y.U. Ann. Inst. Fed. Taxation, 1966, 68, 75, 80. Trustee N.C. Council Econ. Edn., 1968-76; bd. dirs. Christian Fellowship Home, 1972-80; co-founder Bereaved Parents Group Winston-Salem, 1978—. Mem. ABA (chmn. com. ins. cos. of taxation sect. 1980-82, chmn. subcom. on continuing legal edn. and publs. 1982-88), Am. Bus. Law Assn. (mem. com. fed. taxation 1968—, chmn. 1972-75), Assn. Life Ins. Counsel (com. on co. tax, tax sect. 1965—), N.C. Bar Assn. (com. taxation 1973-78), Fed. Bar Assn. (taxation com. 1973—), Maine State Bar Assn., Va. State Bar Assn., Internat. Bar Assn. (com. on taxes of bus. law sect. 1973—), AAUP, Southeastern Acad. Legal Studies in Bus. Club: Masons (Lincoln, Maine). Com. editor The Tax Lawyer, ABA, 1974-76; author numerous articles in field. Office: PO Box 5192 Winston Salem NC 27113-5192

OSBORN, RITA DEISENROTH, public relations executive; b. Louisville, Ky., Jan. 27, 1951; d. Lloyd Henry and Catherine Rita (Nicklies) Deisenroth; children: J. Matthew, Amy. BA in Communications cum laude, Bellarmine Coll., 1990. Office mgr. Most Blessed Sacrament & Ascension Schs., Louisville, 1980-88; program asst. Sta. WKPC-TV, Louisville, 1989; pub. rels. asst. Ky. Hosp. Assn., Louisville, 1990, Vis. Nurse Assn., Louisville, 1989-90; writer, researcher Writer's Inc., Louisville, 1990-91; pub. rels. coord. Archdiocesan Comm. Ctr. Archdiocese of Louisville, 1991-95; pub. rels. coord. Maryhurst, Louisville, 1995—; mem. exec. bd. Lupus Found. Kentuckiana, Inc., Louisville, 1989-91; v.p. communications Assn. Louisville Orch., 1990-91; exec. bd. Women in Communications Inc., Louisville, 1990— (Competitive scholar 1989). Vol. St. Matthew Area Ministries Intervention Svcs., Louisville, 1982-84, WKPC-TV Auction, Louisville, 1989—. Recipient 1st Place News Story, Ky. Intercollegiate Press Assn., 1990; Wilson Wyatt fellow Bellarmine Coll., 1990. Mem. Internat. Assn. of Bus. Communicators, Delta Epsilon Sigma. Democrat. Office: Maryhurst 1015 Dorsey Ln Louisville KY 40223-2612

OSBORNE, BARTLEY P., JR., aeronautical engineer; b. Akron, Ohio, Sept. 1, 1934; s. Bartley P. and Cordelia Inez (Sims) O.; m. Carol Ann Eubanks, Jan. 15, 1966; children: Roxane Elizabeth, Ashley Hamilton. BSME, Carnegie Mellon U., Pitts., 1956; MS in Aerospace Engring., U. So. Calif., 1962. Sr. stress analyst N. Am. Aviation, Columbus, Ohio, 1956-66; sr. design engr. Lockheed Aircraft, Burbank, Calif., 1966-70; project engr. Lockheed Aircraft, 1970-74; staff specialist aeronautics Office Sec. of Def., Washington, 1974-78; engring. prog. mgr. Lockheed Aircraft, 1978-82, chief adv. design engr., 1982-85, chief engr. ATF, 1985-87, dep. chief adv. design engr., 1987-89; prog. mgr. Lockheed Aero. Sys. Co., Burbank, 1989-90; v.p., engr. Lockheed Aero. Systems Co., Marietta, Ga., 1990-96; v.p. advanced concepts Lockheed Aero. Systems Co., Marietta, 1996—; chmn. NASA Aeronautics Adv. Com. Pres. Chesterfield Mews Homeowners Assn., Fairfax, Va., 1977-78; adv. bd. Mercer U.; engring. adv. bd. Ga. Inst. Tech. 1st lt. U.S. Army, 1956-58. Pa. State scholar, 1952. Fellow Royal Aero. Soc., AIAA (assoc.); mem. Am. Def. Preparedness Assn., L.A. Violin Cello Soc. Democrat. Home: 1395 Waterford Green Dr Marietta GA 30068-2927

OSBORNE, BURL, newspaper publisher, editor; b. Jenkins, Ky., June 25, 1937; s. Oliver and Juanita (Smallwood) O.; m. Betty S. Wilder, Feb. 14, 1974; 1 son, Burl Jonathan. Student, U. Ky., 1955-57; B.A. in Journalism, Marshall U., 1960; M.B.A., L.I. U. Sch. Bus., 1984; A.M.P., Harvard Bus. Sch., 1984. Reporter Ashland (Ky.) Daily Ind., 1957-58; reporter, editor Sta. WHTN-TV, Huntington, W.Va., 1958-60; corr. AP, Bluefield, W.Va., 1960-62; statehouse corr. AP, Charleston, W.Va., 1963-64; corr. AP, Spokane, Wash., 1964-67; news editor AP, Denver, 1967-70; chief of bur. AP, Ky., 1970-72, Ohio, 1972-74; asst. chief of bur. AP, Washington, 1974-76; mng. editor AP, N.Y.C., 1977-80; exec. editor Dallas Morning News, 1980-83, v.p., 1981, sr. v.p., editor, 1983-84, pres., editor, 1985-90, pub., editor, 1991—; bd. dirs., pres. publ. divsn. A.H. Belo Corp., bd. dirs. AP, Pulitzer Prize, 1986-95, co-chair, 1994-95; bd. mem. adv. com. Nieman Found., Harvard U.; mem. journalism adv. com. Knight Found.; bd. dirs. Newspaper Assn. Am. Named Newspaper Exec. of Yr., Nat. Press Found., 1992; inducted to Ky. Journalism Hall of Fame, 1994. Mem. Orgn. Profl. Journalists, Am. Soc. Newspaper Editors (bd. dirs. 1982-91, pres. 1990-91), Am. Press Inst. (chmn. 1988-93), Tex. Daily Newspaper Assn. (bd. dirs. 1982-92, pres. 1993), So. Newspaper Pub. Assn. (bd. dirs. 1995—). Home: 7609 Southwestern Blvd Dallas TX 75225-7927 Office: Dallas Morning News AH Belo Corp PO Box 655237 Dallas TX 75265-5237

OSBORNE, GAYLE ANN, manufacturing executive; b. Bossier City, La., Feb. 1, 1951; d. Walker Henry and Marjorie Evelyn (Cook) Pyle; m. Paul A. Huelsman, June 28, 1969 (div. Jan. 1976); children: Ginger, Paula; m. Luther L. Osborne, Sept. 10, 1976 (div. Aug. 1989). Sales assoc. Model City Real Estate, Midwest City, Okla., 1972-73; mgr. adminstrn. Equipment Renewal Co., Oklahoma City, 1973-76, Gulfco Industries, Inc., Casper, Wyo., 1976-77; with B&B Tool and Supply Co., Inc., Casper, 1977, 79, 81, v.p., 1983—, pres., 1990—; pres. BOP Repair & Machine, Inc., Casper, 1981—; owner Osborne Leasing Co. Mem. Casper Petroleum Club, Nat. Skeet Shoot Assn. (All Am. Skeet Team), Amateur Trapshooting Assn. Democrat.

OSBORNE, JAMES ALFRED, religious organization administrator; b. Toledo, July 3, 1927; s. Alfred James and Gladys Irene (Gaugh) O.; m. Ruth Glenrose Campbell, Nov. 26, 1945; 1 child, Constance Jean (Mrs. Donald William Canning). Grad., Salvation Army Coll., 1947; student, U. Chattanooga, 1954-55; D of Pub. Svc. (hon.), Gordon Coll., 1991. Corps officer Salvation Army, Magness, Nashville, 1947, Southside, Memphis, 1948, Owensboro, Ky., 1949-54; comdg. officer Salvation Army, Chattanooga, 1954-61; city comdr. Salvation Army, Miami, Fla., 1961-65; divisional sec. Ky.-Tenn. Div. Salvation Army, 1965-68, gen. sec. N.C. and S.C. Div., 1968-70, pub. rels. sec. 15 so. states, D.C. and Mex., 1970-71, divisional comdr. Md. and No. W.Va. Div., 1971-73; divisional comdr. Nat. Capital and Virginias Div. Salvation Army, Washington, 1973-78; divisional comdr. Fla. Div. Salvation Army, 1978-80, chief sec. Western Ter., 1980-84; nat. chief sec. Salvation Army, Verona, N.J., 1984-86; territorial comdr. so. states Salvation Army, Atlanta, 1986-89; nat. comdr., Republic of Marshall Islands, Guam, P.R., Virgin Islands Salvation Army USA, 1989-93; chmn. Salvation Army Nat. Planning and Devel. Commn., 1974-76, 84-86; exec. bd. Vision Interfaith Satellite Network, Nat. Assn. Evangelicals, Christian Children's Fund Inc.; chmn. bd. Christian Mgmt. Assn., 1993-94; exec. com. religious alliance Against Pornography; rep. Salvation Army to numerous orgns. Bd. dirs. Nat. Law Ctr. for Children and Families; sec. Tenn. Conf. on Social Welfare, 1959, v.p., 1960; pres. Fla. Conf. on Social Welfare, 1965; pres. Ky. Welfare Assn., 1970. Mem. Chattanooga Pastors Assn. (pres. 1958), Va. and W. Va. Welfare Confs., Rotary.

OSBORNE, LAUREN GARDNER, oncological nurse; b. Ft. Worth, Dec. 25, 1959; d. Lawrence Gale Gardner and Ann Bailey (Zehner) Reed; married. BA in Art History, Smith Coll., 1982; BSN, U. Tenn., 1987. RN, oncology cert. nurse. Patient care asst. Meth. Hosp., Memphis, 1986, staff nurse gyn. med.-surg., 1987-89; staff nurse gyn. oncology U. N.C. Hosps., Chapel Hill, N.C., 1989-90; nurse edn. clinician gyn. oncology U. N.C. Hosps., Chapel Hill, 1990-92, U. N.C., Chapel Hill, 1992—. Pres. Orange County chpt. Am. Cancer Soc., Durham, N.C., 1994-95. Mem. ANA, Soc. Gynecologic Nurse Oncologists, Oncology Nursing Soc. (bd. dirs., sect. N.C. Triangle chpt. 1992-94), Sigma Theta Tau. Office: U NC Dept Ob-Gyn Divsn Oncology 5017 Old Clinic Bldg Chapel Hill NC 27599

OSBORNE, MICHAEL JAMES, real estate executive, energy executive; b. Amarillo, Tex., Sept. 20, 1949; s. Jack Harold Osborne and Maxine Joan (Chambers) Novack; m. Dee Haws; children: Solomon, Hope; m. Layne Jackson, Dec. 22, 1991. Student, U. Tex., 1967-72. Owner Directions Co., Austin, Tex., 1971-74; mgr. Taylorvision, Taylor, Tex., 1974-76; owner/ptnr. Osborne Solar, Austin, 1977-94, Osborne Cos., Austin, 1988—, Catalina Investments and M&C Properties, Austin, 1984—, U.S. Renewables, Austin, 1991—, Virtual Conferencing, Austin, 1992—. Author: The Titanomachy, 1995; editor Spectra mag., 1981-83; inventor E.M.A.S.E.R., 1984, H.M.F. Power Plant, 1994. Trustee First Bapt. Ch., Elgin, 1980; bd. dirs. Kiwanis Club, Elgin, 1980; little league coach Optimist Club, Elgin, 1980; steering com. State of Tex. Energy Planning Partnership; chair Renewables; mem. Sustainable Energy Devel. Coun., State of Tex.; apptd. by Gov. Bush to Tex. Energy Coord. Coun., 1996. Recipient Disting. Svc. award Tex. Solar Energy Soc., 1985, Enlightened Leadership award Tex. Renewable Energy Industries Assn., 1993, Pres.'s award for Outstanding Contbns. in Renewable Energy, 1995. Mem. Tex. Renewable Energy Industries (pres. 1990-93), Solar Energy Soc., Internat. Solar Energy Soc., World Future Soc., Union of Concerned Scientists. Home: 909 W 23rd St Austin TX 78705-5007 Office: Osborne Energy PO Box 999 Elgin TX 78621-0999

OSBORNE, RICHARD JAY, electric utility company executive; b. N.Y.C., Feb. 16, 1951; s. Victor and Evelyn Celia (Sweetbaum) O. B.A., Tufts U., 1973; M.B.A., U. N.C., 1975. Fin. analyst Duke Power Co., Charlotte, N.C., 1975-78, sr. fin. analyst, 1978-80, mgr. fin. rels., 1980-81, mgr. treasury activities, 1981, treas., 1981-88, v.p. fin., CFO, 1988-94, sr. v.p., CFO, 1994—. Pres. Charlotte Jewish Fedn.; mem. bd. Found. for the sch. of Pub. Health, U. N.C., Chapel Hill. Mem. Fin. Execs. Inst., Edison Electric Inst. (fin. & regulatory sect.), Found. for the Carolinas (chmn. investment com.), N.C. Coun. Edn. (chair). Democrat. Jewish. Office: Duke Power Co 422 S Church St Charlotte NC 28242-0001

OSBORNE-POPP, GLENNA JEAN, health services administrator; b. East Rainelle, W.Va., Jan. 5, 1945; d. B.J. and Jean Ann (Haranac) Osborne; m. Thomas Joseph Ferrante Jr., June 11, 1966 (div. Nov. 1987); 1 child, Thomas Joseph Osborne; m. Brian Mark Popp, Aug. 13, 1988. BA cum laude, U. Tampa, 1966; MA, Fairleigh Dickinson U., 1982; cert., Kean Coll., 1983. Cert. English, speech, dramatic arts tchr., prin./supr.; cert. nursing child assessment feeding scale and nursing child assessment tchg. scale, 1996; cert. Deliver II, 1996, home trainer for assessments, 1996; cert. Denver II Assessment, 1996. Tchr. Raritan High Sch., Hazlet, N.J., 1966; tchr. Keyport (N.J.) Pub. Schs., 1968-86, coord. elem. reading and lang. arts, 1980-84, supr. curriculum and instrn., 1984-86; prin. Weston Sch., Manville, N.J., 1986-88, The Bartle Sch., Highland Park, N.J., 1988-91, Orange Ave. Sch., Cranford, N.J., 1991-92; dir. The Open Door Youth Shelter, Binghamton, N.Y., 1992-94; child protective investigator supr. Dept. Health and Rehab. Svcs., Orlando, Fla., 1994-95; program supr. Children's Home Soc., Sanford, Fla., 1995; clin. supr. Healthy Families-Orange, Orlando, Fla., 1995—; regional trainer Individualized Lang. Arts, Weehawken, N.J., 1976-86; cons. McDougal/Little Pubs., Evanston, Ill., 1982-83; chair adv. bd. women's residential program Ctr. for Drug Free Living, Orlando, 1996. Contbr. chpt.: A Resource Guide of Differentiated Learning Experiences for Gifted Elementary Students, 1981. Sunday sch. tchr. Reformed Ch., Keyport, 1975-80, supt. Sunday sch., 1982-84. Mem. Order Ea. Star (Tampa, Fla.), Phi Delta Kappa. Republican. Methodist. Office: Healthy Families 623 S Texas Ave Orlando FL 32805-3064

OSEN, GREGORY ALAN, water conditioning company executive; b. Beloit, Wis., Mar. 14, 1951; s. Vincent Darryl and Mavis Lucille (Lasher) O.; m. Deborah Ann Churchill Bladorn, Jan. 29, 1972 (div. Jan. 1987); m. Christine Adel Pulliam, Oct. 8, 1987; children: Leah Michelle, Felicia Ann. BA in Music Edn. with honors, Milton (Wis.) Coll., 1973; MBA, Cardinal Stritch Coll., 1985. Machinist, assembler Nat. Detroit, Rockford, Ill., 1973-78; sales tech. Ill. Water Treatment, Rockford, 1978-79, sales engr., 1979-80, dist. sales engr., 1980-85; sales mgr. Glegg Water Conditioning Inc., Guelph, Ont., Can., 1985—. Pres. Seekers, Strawbridge Meth. Ch., 1995-96, mem. adminstrv. bd., 1996, mem. choir, 1995-96; trumpeter Harris County Big Band, 1993-95. Mem. Am. Water Works Assn. Home: 6002 Boulder Lake Ct Kingwood TX 77345 Office: Glegg Water Conditioning, 29 Royal Rd, Guelph, ON Canada N1H 1G2

OSGOOD, CHRISTOPHER MYKEL, radio account executive; b. Northampton, Mass., Nov. 8, 1963; s. Robert Mansfield and Susanne (Mykel) O.; m. Rosie Chance; children: Randy, Brandon, Todd. BS, Cornell U., 1989. Media rsch. mktg. analyst Vitt Media Internat., N.Y.C., 1988-89; account exec. KAOI AM/FM Radio, Maui, Hawaii, 1989-91, KTXH-TV Paramount 20, Houston, 1991-92; dir. advt. Oilers News, Browns News Illustrated, 49ers Report, Cleve., 1992-93; account exec. KRBE-FM Radio, Houston, 1993-96, KLOL-FM Radio, Houston, 1996—. Coach Bear Creek Basketball League, Houston, 1993-94. Mem. Cornell Alumni Assn. of Greater Houston, Cornell Soc. Hotelmen. Office: Rock 101 KLOL Radio 510 Lovett Blvd Houston TX 77006

O'SHAUGHNESSY, ROSEMARIE ISABELLE, clinical nutritionist; b. N.Y.C., Sept. 25, 1940; d. John O. and Maria Wellmann (Larranaga) Rao; m. Louis L. Feldman, May 3, 1980; children: Michelle Marie, Chevonne Eileen, Melany Rose. BA, St. Mary's Coll., Notre Dame, Ind., 1961; MS, Donsbach U., 1978, PhD, 1979; postdoctoral, Union for Experimenting Colls. and Univs., Cin., 1987. Cert. clin. nutritionist. Pvt. practice clin. nutrition Orlando, Fla., 1979—; dir. Beauticontrol Cosmetics Inc., Orlando, 1992-94; expert witness for clin. nutritionists and nutritional cons. testimony before state legis. coms. State of Fla., Tallahassee, 1985-88; speaker in field. Interviewee numerous TV and radio programs. Fellow Am. Coun. Applied Clin. Nutrition; mem. Internat. and Am. Assn. Clin. Nutritionists (founder 1987, bd. dirs. 1987-91, co-founder Fla. chpt. 1983, bd. dirs. 1986-91, exec. dir. 1986-90, pres. 1991, founding dir. life), Internat. Acad. Nutrition and Preventive Medicine (bd. dirs. 1987-89), N.Am. Acad. Nutrition and Preventive Medicine. Republican. Roman Catholic. Home: 2219 Sylvan Ct Kissimmee FL 34746-3719

O'SHEA, CATHERINE LARGE, marketing and public relations consultant; b. Asheville, N.C., Feb. 27, 1944; d. Edwin Kirk Jr. and Mary Mitchell (Westall) Large; m. Roger Dean Lower, Dec. 19, 1970 (dec. Sept. 1977); children: Thaddeus Kirk Lower and David Alexander Lower (twins, dec.); m. Michael Joseph O'Shea, Dec. 29, 1980. BA in History magna cum laude, Emory U., 1966. Mktg. staff mem. Time Inc., N.Y.C., 1966-69; mktg. adminstr. Collier-Macmillan Internat., N.Y.C., 1970-71; circulation mgr. Coll. Entrance Exam. Bd., N.Y.C., 1971-73; spl. asst. to pres. Wayne Dressel Assocs. Exec. Search, N.Y.C., 1973-75; freelance writer, editor, pub. rels. Princeton, N.J., 1975-78; dir. constituency rels. Emory U., Atlanta, 1978-80; devel. assoc. U. Del., Newark, 1981-83; asst. to pres. Elizabethtown (Pa.) Coll., 1983-85; assoc. v.p. Beaver Coll., Glenside, Pa., 1985; cons. mktg. and pub. rels. Phila., S.C., 1985—. Co-author: 50 Secrets of Highly Successful Cats, 1994; editor Elizabethtown mag., 1983-85; contbr. articles to nat. mags. and profl. jours. Founder Helping Hands Internat.; trustee Large Found., Newberry Opera House Found. Mem. Pub. Rels. Soc. Am. (accredited), Mortar Bd., Phi Beta Kappa, Phi Mu.

O'SHEA, MICHAEL JOSEPH, humanities educator; b. Atlanta, June 13, 1955; s. Arthur Kevin and Lois Helen (McIntosh) O'S.; m. Catherine Alexander Large Lower, Dec. 29, 1980. BA in English & Music, Emory U., 1977; MA in English, U. Del., 1981, PhD in English, 1984. Asst. prof. humanities Drexel U., Phila., 1984-89, asst. head humanities, 1985-86, assoc. prof. humanities, 1989-91; prof., chair English Newberry (S.C.) Coll., 1992—; referee S.C. Arts Commn., Columbia S.C., 1993—. Author: James Joyce and Heraldry, 1986; co-author: 50 Secrets of Highly Successful Cats, 1994; editor (jour.) Studies in Short Fiction, 1990—. Mem. Vestry St. Luke's Episcopal Ch., Newberry, 1994-96. Travel grantee Am. Coun. Learned Soc., 1988, English-Speaking Union, London, 1986; Rsch. scholar Drexel U., 1987-88. Mem. Nat. Coun. Tchrs. English, Am. Conf. Irish Studies, James Joyce Found., Trustee (1996—), Heraldry Soc. Ireland (founding mem.), Modern Lang. Assn., Council of Editors and Learned Journals. Office: Newberry Coll 2100 College St Newberry SC 29108

OSHLO, ERIC LEE, oil company executive; b. Charleston, W.Va., Sept. 16, 1947; s. Frank Henry and Helene Elizabeth (Garst) O.; m. Pamela Gray Stevens, Sept. 4, 1971; children: Lisa Ann, Laura Michelle. BSEE, Tex. A&M U., 1970; cert. in exec. mgmt., Harvard U., 1979. Asst. to vice chmn. exploration and prodn. Conoco, Inc., Stamford, Conn., 1975-77; asst. mgr. Hobbs (N.Mex.) div. Conoco, Inc., 1977-78, asst. mgr. Lake Charles (La.) Prodn. div., 1978-79; project mgr. South Tex. tar sands Conoco, Inc., Corpus Christi, 1980-82; gen. mgr. Milne Point project Conoco, Inc., Houston, 1982-83, gen. mgr. adminstrn., exploration and prodn. N.Am., 1983-84, mgr. ras products, 1984-85, mgr. gas processing ops., 1985-87, gen. mgr. internat. natural gas, 1987-89; pres., gen. mgr. Conoco Indonesia, Jakarta, 1989-91; v.p., gen. mgr. exploration prodn. Conoco, Inc., Houston, 1991-92, v.p., gen. mgr. transp., 1992-93, v.p. crude oil supply trading, marine and materials svcs., 1993—. Pres. Walden Condominium Coun. Co-owners, Montgomery, Tex., 1985-87; bd. dirs. Walden Civic Improvement Assn., Montgomery, 1987-89, 94—. Mem. Soc. Petroleum Engrs. Republican. Methodist. Office: Conoco Inc PO Box 2197 Houston TX 77252-2197

OSIAS, RICHARD ALLEN, international financier, investor, real estate investment executive, corporate investor; b. N.Y.C., Nov. 13, 1938; s. Harry L. and Leah (Schenk) O.; m. Judy Delaine Bradford, Oct. 26, 1984; children: Kimberly, Alexandra Elizabeth. Grad., Columbia U., 1963; postgrad., David Lipscomb U., 1988—. Founder, chmn., CEO Osias Enterprises, Inc., numerous locations, 1953—; mem. bus. cabinet David Lipscomb U.; bd. dirs. Am. 21. Prin. works include city devel., residential and apt. units, founder City North Lauderdale, Fla., co-founder City of Lauderhill, Fla., complete residential housing communities, shopping centers, country clubs, golf courses, hotel chains, comprehensive housing communities; contributed Greystone Raquet and Tennis Club to Nolensville, Tenn.; owner, operator Coolsprings Exec. Plz., landmark office bldg., Internat. Common Market Shopping Complex and other office bldgs., shopping ctrs. in mid-southern region; co-author: South Florida Uniform Building Code. Mem. North Lauderdale City Coun., 1967—, mayor, 1968, pollice and fire commr., 1967—; mem. Gold Cir., Atlanta Ballet; benefactor Atlanta Symphony Soc.;

founder Boys Clubs Broward County, Tower coun. Pine Crest Prep. Sch., Ft. Lauderdale; mem. condr.'s cir. Nashville Symphony; mem. bd. advisors Williamson-Davidson County chpt. MADD, 1990; mem. univ. bus. adv. cabinet David Lipscomb U., Nashville, 1988—; bd. dirs. Rape, Nashville chpt. Cystic Fibrosis, Citizens Against Sexual Exploitation, N.Y.C., Queens County Assn. for Prevention Cruelty to Children, 1973—, Easter Seal Soc. Tenn.; bd. dirs. Tenn. Children's Home, mem. adv. coun., 1973; hon. police commr., N.Y.C.; mem. Children's Abuse and Sexual Exploitation; mem. Ft. Lauderdale Better Bus. Bur., N.Y.C. Better Bus. Bur., Nashville Better Bus. Bur. Recipient Best Am. House award Am. Home mag., 1962, Westinghouse award, 1968, Cert. of Merit for outstanding achievement and contbn. to City of Atlanta by Mayor Andrew Young, 1982; named Builder of Yr., Sunshine State Info. Bur., Fla. and Sunshine State Sr. Citizen, Fla., 1967-70, Builder of Month, Builder/Arch. Mag., 1992; profiles on nat. and internat. media, including CBS TV and Fuji Network. Mem. Ft. Lauderdale BBB, N.Y. BBB, Nashville BBB, Offshore Power Boat Racing Assn., Fraternal Order Police Assn. (pres.), U.S. C. of C., Fla. C. of C., Margate C. of C., Ft. Lauderdale C. of C., Smithsonian Instn., Soc. Founders U. Miami, Tower Coun., Columns Soc., Pinecrest Prep. Sch. (founder), Nat. Assn. Home Builders, Bankers Club (Miami, Fla.), Bankers Top of First Club, Quarter Deck Club (Galveston, Tex.), Boca Raton (Fla.) Yacht and Country Club, Maunalua Bay Club (Honolulu), Tryall Golf and Country Club (Jamaica), Top of the Home Club, Svc. Plus Club (France), Ensworth Red Gables Soc., Cannes Island Yacht Club, Canary Islands Yacht Club, Venitian Bay Yacht Club, The Club Pelican Bay, Collier's Reserve Country Club (Naples, Fla.), Grey Oaks Country Club (Naples). Home: Club Le Ciel #1401 3991 Gulf Shore Blvd N Naples FL 34103 also: The Hillsborough 505 Almonte Ct Nashville TN 37215

OSMAN, MARY ELLA WILLIAMS, journal editor; b. Honea Path, S.C.; d. Humphrey Bates and Jennie Louise (Williams) Williams; student Coll. William and Mary, Ga. State Coll. for Women; A.B., Presbyn. Coll., 1939; B.S. in L.S., U. N.C., 1944; m. John Osman, Oct. 22, 1936. Asst. libr. Presbyn. Coll., Clinton, S.C., 1936-38, Union Theol. Sem., Richmond, Va., 1938-44; sr. cataloger, asst. libr. Rhodes Coll., Memphis, 1944-52; asst. test cities project Ford Found. Fund for Adult Edn., N.Y.C., 1952-57, assoc. dir. office of info., 1957-61, exec. asst. to pres., sec. to bd. dirs., 1960-61; asst. libr. AIA, Washington, 1962-68, asst. editor AIA Jour., 1969-72, assoc. editor, 1972-77, sr. editor, 1978-87. Mem. AIA (hon.), Chi Delta Phi, Kappa Delta. Presbyn. Contbr. to various mags. Home: 3600 Chateau Dr Apt 244 Columbia SC 29204-3971

OSNES, PAMELA GRACE, special education educator; b. Burke, S.D., Sept. 10, 1955; d. John Ruben and Dortha Grace (Wilson) O.; children: Jocelyn Fern, Logan John. BS in Spl. Edn., U. S.D., 1977, BS in Elem. Edn., 1977; MA in Clin. Psychology, W.Va. U., 1981. Spl. edn. tchr. Sioux Falls (S.D.) Sch. Dist., 1977-79; instr. psychology dept. W.Va. U., Morgantown, 1982-85; dir. Carousel Preschool Program, Morgantown, 1982-85; assoc. prof. U. South Fla., Tampa, 1986-93, adminstrv. coord. advanced grad. programs dept. spl. edn., 1994—. Mem. Assn. for Behavior Analysis, Coun. for Exceptional Children (div. early childhood, div. rsch., tchr. edn. div.), Coun. Adminstrs. Spl. Edn., Coun. for Children with Behavior Disorders.

OSOWIEC, DARLENE ANN, clinical psychologist, educator, consultant; b. Chgo., Feb. 16, 1951; d. Stephen Raymond and Estelle Marie Osowiec; m. Barry A. Leska. BS, Loyola U., Chgo., 1973; MA with honors, Roosevelt U., 1980; postgrad. in psychology, Saybrook Inst., San Francisco, 1985-88; PhD in Clin. Psychology, Calif. Inst. Integral Studies, 1992. Lic. clin. psychologist, Mo., Ill. Mental health therapist Ridgeway Hosp., Chgo., 1978; mem. faculty psychology dept. Coll. Lake County, Grayslake, Ill., 1981; counselor, supr. MA-level interns, chmn. pub. rels. com. Integral Counseling Ctr., San Francisco, 1983-84; clin. psychology intern Chgo.-Read Mental Health Ctr. Ill. Dept. Mental Health, 1985-86; mem. faculty dept. psychology Moraine Valley C.C., Palos Hills, Ill., 1988-89; lectr. psychology Daley Coll., Chgo., 1988-90; cons. Gordon & Assocs., Oak Lawn, Ill., 1989—; adolescent, child and family therapist Orland Twp. Youth Svcs., Orland Park, Ill., 1993; psychology fellow Sch. Medicine, St. Louis U., 1994-95; clin. psychologist in pvt. practice Chgo., 1996—. Ill. State scholar, 1969-73; Calif. Inst. Integral Studies scholar, 1983. Mem. APA, Am. Psychol. Soc., Am. Women in Psychology, Am. Statis. Assn., Ill. Psychol. Assn., Calif. Psychol. Assn., Mo. Psychol. Assn., Gerontol. Soc. Am., Am. Soc. Clin. Hypnosis, Internat. Platform Assn., Chgo. Soc. Clin. Hypnosis, NOW (chair legal adv. corps, Chgo. 1974-76). Home: 6608 S Whipple St Chicago IL 60629-2916

OSSEWAARDE, ANNE WINKLER, real estate developer; b. Dallas, June 2, 1957; d. Lowell Graves and Ruth Lenore (Lind) Winkler; m. Kirk L Ossewaarde, Apr. 27, 1991. BBA in Fin. with honors, Emory U., 1979; MBA in Acctg. and Fin. with honors, U. Tex., 1983; MS in Real Estate Devel., MIT, 1988. Cert. comml. investment mem., Comml. Investment Real Estate Inst. Mgmt. trainee Citizens & So. Nat. Bank, Atlanta, 1979-81; banking assoc. Continental Ill. Nat. Bank, Chgo. and Dallas, 1983-85; asst. v.p., devel. assoc. Trammell Crow Residential, Dallas, 1985-87, Seattle, 1988-91; devel. mgr. Blackhawk Port Blakeley Cmtys., Seattle, 1991-93; real estate portfolio mgr. Aegon U.S.A. Realty, Atlanta, 1994—. Charles Harritt Jr. Presdl. scholar U. Tex., 1982, Alexander Grant scholar, 1982. Mem. Jr. League of Atlanta, Comml. Real Estate Women, MIT Ctr. for Real Estate Alumni Assn., Alpha Epsilon Upsilon. Methodist. Home: 5510 Mount Vernon Pky NW Atlanta GA 30327-4739

OSTEEN, PAUL ALLEN, construction executive; b. Fort Pierce, Fla., Aug. 6, 1960; s. Paul Loris Osteen Jr. and Joanne (Anderson) Woodcock; m. Theresa Ann Robinson, Mar. 2, 1991. BS in Mgmt., Tulane U., 1982. Div. sales mgr. Federated Dept. Stores, Houston, 1982-87; mdse. mgr. Stein Mart Stores, Jacksonville, Fla., 1987-89; v.p. East Coast Lumber and Supply Co., Fort Pierce, 1989-91, pres., 1992—. Pub., editor: Rotascope, 1991. Chmn. Fort Pierce Main St., Inc., 1991—; bd. dirs. Jr. Achievement, Fort Pierce, 1990-91, St. Lucie County (Fla.) Econ. Devel. Coun., 1991—; chmn. fin. Boy Scouts Am., Fort Pierce, 1990-91. Mem. Fla. Lumber & Bldg. Material Dealers Assn., Rotary (bd. dirs. Fort Pierce chpt. 1990—, pres. 1991—). Republican. Methodist. Home: 231 Riverway Dr Vero Beach FL 32963-2637 Office: East Coast Lumber Supply Co 308 Avenue A Fort Pierce FL 34950-4417

O'STEEN, RANDY A., nursing administrator; b. Oklahoma City, Sept. 14, 1954; s. Jim D. and June A. (Davis) O'S. AS, Oklahoma City Community Coll., 1981; BA in Mgmt., So. Nazarene U., Bethany, Okla., 1990. Charge nurse, post anesthesia care unit Bapt. Med. Ctr. of Okla., Oklahoma City, 1983-88, head nurse, post critical care unit, 1988-89, head nurse, nursing resource unit, 1989-91; dir. Nursing Systems, 1991-93; dir. systems and devel. Integris Health, Oklahoma City, 1993—. Editor newsletter Vital Signs, 1984-87. Mem. ANA, Am. Soc. Post Anesthesia Nurses, Okla. Nurses Assn., Okla. Soc. Post Anesthesia Nurses (pres. Oklahoma City chpt. 1983-86, chmn. publs. com. 1985-86), Am. Orgn. Nurse Execs., Okla. Orgn. Nurse Execs., Am. Med. Informatics Assn., Health Level Seven, Health Info. Mgmt. Sys. Soc. Home: 229 NW 33rd St Oklahoma City OK 73118-8613 Office: Integris Health Ste 200 5400 N Independence Ave Oklahoma City OK 73112-5300

OSTHEIM, PHILLIS QUINN, secondary education administrator; b. Goldsboro, N.C., Feb. 8, 1954; d. Aubrey D. and Peggy Jean (Roberts) Quinn; m. Mark Keith Ostheim, Dec. 22, 1973; children: Christel Joy, Amber Danielle, Garrett Keith. BS in Bus. Edn., Barton Coll., 1975; MA in Bus. Edn., East Carolina U., 1976, BS Edn./Mktg., 1988; EdD in Occupl. Edn., N.C. State U., 1995. Instr. part-time Wayne Cmty. Coll., Goldsboro, N.C., 1974-77; tchr. Brogden Jr. H.S., Dudley, N.C., 1975-86, Charles B. Aycock, Pikeville, N.C., 1986-90, So. Wayne H.S., Dudley, N.C., 1990-94; vocat. curriculum facilitator Wayne County Pub. Schs., Goldsboro, N.C., 1994-96; vocat. adminstr. Duplin County Schs., Kenansville, N.C., 1996—; chairperson S.E. Tchr. of Yr. Com., Wilmington, N.C., 1994-95; mem. S.E. Prin. of Yr. Selection Team, Goldsboro, 1994-95; spkr. in field. Grantee Learn and Serve Am., 1994; recipient S.E. Region Tchr. of Yr., 1993-94. Mem. Profl. Educators of N.C., Am. Vocat. Edn. Rsch. Assn., Am. Vocat. Assn., Mktg. Educators Assn. (regional rep. 1989), Mktg. Edn. Assn. (Gold Link award 1990). Republican. Presbyterian. Home: 790 Beautancus Rd Mount Olive NC 28365

OSTMO, DAVID CHARLES, broadcasting executive; b. Mason City, Iowa, Jan. 16, 1959; s. Gene Charles and Charlene Lucille (Evans) O.; m. Beverly M. Cannon, May 10, 1997. Diploma, Brown Inst., 1979. Maintenance engr. Sta. KJRH-TV, Tulsa, 1981-84; chief news editor Sta. KOTV, Tulsa, 1984-86; chief engr. Sta. KXON-TV/Rogers State Coll., Claremore, Okla., 1986-90; dir. engring. Fairview AFX, Tulsa, 1990-92, Sta. KABB-TV, San Antonio, 1992-95; dir. ops. KABB-TV, San Antonio, 1995—; columnist TV Tech., Falls Church, Va., 1988-90. Producer, dir. (TV show) Theodore Kirby Show, 1988; dir. (TV show) Zebra Sports Review, 1987, RSC Spotlight, 1987; writer mag. News From the Back Porch, 1988-90, Tulsa TV Tidbits, 1988-91. Named Eagle Scout Boy Scouts Am., 1974. Mem. Soc. Broadcast Engrs. (sr. broadcast engr., chmn. Tulsa chpt. 1989-90, chmn. San Antonio chpt. 1993-95). Lutheran. Home: 3500 Oakgate Dr Apt 2706 San Antonio TX 78230-3377 Office: Sta KABB-TV 4335 NW Loop 410 San Antonio TX 78229-5168

OSTRANDER, DIANE LORRAINE, counselor; b. Lansing, Mich., Feb. 28, 1952; d. William Eugene and Ardis Jean (Austin) Purvis; m. Charles Wesley Ostrander, July 14, 1973; children: Casendra Carmen, Rachel Jeanine, Tausha Reneé. BS, Colo. State U., 1975; MA, Ctrl. Mich. U., 1987; PhD, Okla. State U., 1991. Cert. family life educator. Day care provider St. Louis, Mich., 1983-86; teaching and rsch. asst. Ctrl. Mich. U., Mt. Pleasant, 1986-87; teaching and rsch. assoc. Okla. State U., Stillwater, 1988-91; asst. prof. S.D. State U., Brookings, 1991-96; intensive family specialist Southeast Colo. Family Guidance and Mental Health, Lamar, Colo., 1996—; family life and child cons., counselor Mental Health, Asheboro, N.C., 1995—; adj. faculty Davidson County C.C., Thomasville, N.C., 1995—; cons. family day care SMARTSTART, Thomasville, 1995—. Contbr. articles to profl. jours. Workshop speaker Communication in the Workplace, High Point Regional Hosp., High Point, N.C., 1996—, Teambuilding in the Work Place, SMARTSTART, Lexington, N.C., 1996, Soil and Crop Conf. S.D. State U., 1993, U. Week for Women, 1993, 94, Okla. Christian Edn. Assn., Del City, 1988, 89; children and youth program dir. various chs., Mich., Okla., S.D., Colo., 1974—. Named New Profl. of Yr. Okla. Coun. on Family Rels., 1991. Mem. Nat. Coun. on Family Rels., Am. Assn. Christian Counselors, N.C. Assn. Edn. Young Children, Phi Kappa Phi. Democrat. Mem. Ch. of God. Home: 735 Amb Thompson Blvd Las Animas CO 81054

OSTREICH, LEONARD L., obstetrician, gynecologist; b. Bklyn., June 7, 1922; s. Jacob and Annia (Leventhal) O.; m. Ellen S. Stein, Mar. 21, 1948; children: Marjorie Smith, Peter and Richard (twins), Steven. BS with high honors, Mich. State U., 1943; MD, Wayne State U., 1946. Diplomate Am. Bd. Obstetrics and Gynecology; F.A.C.S. Intern Queens Gen. Hosp., Jamaica, N.Y., 1946-47; resident in contagious diseases Kingston Ave. Hosp., Bklyn., 1947-48; fellow in ob-gyn. Lincoln Hosp., Bronx, 1948; resident in ob-gyn. Queens Gen. Hosp., Jamaica, 1950-53; pvt. practice, 1953—; instr. chemistry Mich. State U., Ann Arbor, 1942-43; assoc. clin. prof. ob-gyn. SUNY, Stonybrook, 1975-88, U. Miami/Jackson Meml. Hosp., 1988—; staff Boca Raton (Fla.) Community Hosp., 1987—, West Boca Med. Ctr., 1993—, Winthrop U. Hosp., Mineola, N.Y., chief of svc., 1957-87; full attending and cons. Nassau County Med. Ctr., East Meadow, N.Y., 1959-87, pres. med. staff, 1965; cons. ob-gyn. Mid-Island Hosp., Bethpage, N.Y., 1988; co-dir. ob-gyn. Ctrl. Gen. Hosp., Plainview, N.Y., 1961-87; full attending North Shore U. Hosp., Manhasset, N.Y., to 1988; attending Jackson Meml. Hosp., Miami, 1988—. Contbr. articles to profl. jours.; cons. editor Internat. Jour. Fertility, 1976—. Past pres. Nassau County Med. Ctr.; chmn. exec. com. Ctrl. Gen. Hosp., Plainview, N.Y.; former chmn. ob-gyn. sect. Nassau Acad. Medicine; bd. dirs., pres. U.S. Internat. Found. for Studies of Reprodn., 1980-92. Fellow Nassau Surg. Soc., Am. Soc. Sterility and Fertility (life); mem. Palm Beach County Med. Soc., Mil. Surgeons of U.S. Jewish. Home: 7204 Queenferry Cir Boca Raton FL 33496-5953 Office: 1500 NW 10th Ave Ste 203 Boca Raton FL 33486-1345

OTERO, ELIZABETH, allergist; b. Manhattan, N.Y., Dec. 5; d. Sergio and Luz Delia (Torres) O. B in Chemistry, U. P.R., 1981; MD, U. P.R. Sch. of Medicine, 1986. Diplomate Nat. Bd. Med. Examiners, Am. Bd. Internal Medicine, Am. Bd. Allergy & Immunology. Intern in internal medicine VA Hosp., Rio Pideras, P.R., 1986-87; resident in internal medicine Jewish Hosp., Washington U., St. Louis, 1987-89; fellowship Barnes Hosp., Washington U., St. Louis, 1989-91; allergist Allergy and Asthma Care of the Palm Beaches, Jupiter, Fla., 1992—. Mem. Am. Coll. Physicians, Am. Acad. Allergy & Immunology, Am. Coll. Allergy & Immunology. Home: 500 Ocean Trail Way Apt 607 Jupiter FL 33477 Office: Allergy & Asthma Care of the Palm Beaches 2141 Alternate A1A S Ste 220 Jupiter FL 33477-4063 Office: 3365 Burns Rd Ste 101 Palm Bch Gdns FL 33410-4302

OTHS, KATHRYN SUE, anthropology educator; b. Cin., Oct. 22, 1959; d. Joseph Anthony and Suzanne Elizabeth (Kronauge) Wells; m. William Wymer Dressler, June 28, 1992. BA in Human Biology, Stanford U., 1982; MA in Anthropology, Case Western Reserve U., 1985, PhD in Anthropology, 1991. Tchg. asst. Stanford U., 1978; substitute tchr. Wellston (Ohio) City Schs., 1982-83; teaching asst. Case Western Reserve U., 1985-86, instr., 1989-90; asst. prof. U. Ala., 1990—; vice chair Ala. Acad. Scis., 1992—; Campus Security and Safety com., 1993—; Grad. Faculty mem., 1993—; adjunct faculty Women's Studies, 1992—; adv. com. Women's Studies, 1992—. Contbr. articles to profl. jours. Recipient Departmental assistantship 1983-86, Grad. Alumni Fund award Case Western Reserve U., 1985, Pancoast Travel Fellowship award for Women Scholars, Case Western Reserve U., 1987, Rsch. Grants Com. award, U. Ala., 1992-93, First award Nat. Inst. Health and Human Devel., 1992-96; grantee Biomedical Rsch. Support, U. Ala., 1991, Inter.-Am. Found. Fellowship, 1988. mem. Am. Anthrop. Assn., Soc. Applied Anthropology, Soc. for Med. Anthropology, Ala. Acad. Scis., West Ala. Women's Health Forum, Survival Internat., Cultural Survival, Amnesty Internat. Office: Univ Alabama Dept Anthropology PO Box 870210 Tuscaloosa AL 35487-0210

OTIS, JOHN JAMES, civil engineer; b. Syracuse, N.Y., Aug. 5, 1922; s. John Joseph and Anna (Dey) O.; m. Dorothy Fuller Otis, June 21, 1958; children: Mary Eileen Dawn, John Leon. B of Chem. Engring., Syracuse U., 1943, MBA, 1950, postgrad., 1951-55. Registered profl. engr., Ala., Tex. Jr. process engr. GM, Syracuse, 1951-53, prodn. engr., 1954-58, process control engr., 1958-59, process engr., 1960-61; engr., writer GE, Syracuse, 1961-63; configuration control engr. GE, Phila., 1969; assoc. research engr. Boeing Co., Huntsville, Ala., 1963-65; assoc. Planning Rsch. Corp., Huntsville, 1965-67; prin. engr. Brown Engring. Co. subs. Teledyne Co., Huntsville, 1967-69; mech. designer Drever Co., Beth Ayres, Pa., 1970-71; civil engr. U.S. Army Corps Engrs., Mobile, Ala., 1971-74, Galveston, Tex., 1974—. Lector, lay minister Roman Cath. Ch. Served with USNR, 1944-50. Mem. Am. Inst. Indsl. Engrs. (past v.p. Syracuse and Huntsville chpts.), Tex. Soc. Profl. Engrs. (dir. Galveston County chpt. 1976-79, sec.-treas. 1979-80, v.p. 1980-81, pres. 1982-83), Am. Legion, Tau Beta Pi, Phi Kappa Tau, Alpha Chi Sigma, Chi Eta Sigma. Home: 2114 Yorktown Ct N League City TX 77573-5056 Office: US Army Corps Engrs Jadwin Bldg 2000 Fort Point Rd Galveston TX 77550-3038

OTIS, LEE LIBERMAN, lawyer, educator; b. N.Y.C., Aug. 19, 1956; d. James Benjamin and Deen (Freed) L.; m. William Graham Otis, Oct. 24, 1993. BA, Yale U., 1979; JD, U. Chgo., 1983. Bar: N.Y. 1985, D.C. 1994. Law clk. U.S. Ct. Appeals (D.C. cir.), Washington, 1983-84; spl. asst. to asst. atty. gen., civil div. U.S. Dept. Justice, Washington, 1984-86; dep. assoc. atty. gen. U.S. Dept. Justice, 1986, assoc. dep. atty. gen., 1986; law clk. to Justice Antonin Scalia U.S. Supreme Ct., Washington, 1986-87; asst. prof. law George Mason U., Arlington, Va., 1987-89; assoc. counsel to the Pres. Exec. Office of the Pres., Washington, 1989-92; assoc. Jones, Day, Reavis & Pogue, Washington, 1993-94; chief judiciary coun. U.S. Sen. Spence Abraham, 1995—; adj. prof. law Georgetown Law Sch., 1995, 96. Mem. Federalist Soc. for Law & Pub. Policy (founder, dir., nat. co-chmn.). Republican. Jewish.

O'TOOLE, FRANCIS J., lawyer; b. Dublin, Ireland, Feb. 10, 1944; came to U.S., 1960; s. Francis Herbert and Josephine (McCarthy) O'T.; m. Carole Ann Leland, Apr. 11, 1977; children: Kathleen, Kirra. AB, Harvard U., 1967; JD, U. Maine, 1970. Bar: Maine 1970, U.S. Supreme Ct. 1977, U.S. Dist. Ct. D.C., U.S. Dist. Ct. (ea. dist.) Va., U.S. Ct. Appeals (1st, 2d, 4th, 5th, 7th, 8th, 9th and 10th cirs.). Assoc. Fried, Frank, Harris, Shriver & Jacobsen, Washington, 1971-78, ptnr., 1978-92; ptnr. Sidley & Austin, Washington, 1992—. Editor-in-chief U. Maine Law Rev., 1969-70; contbr. articles to profl. jours. Reginald Heber Smith fellow Calif. Indian Legal Services, 1970-71. Mem. ABA. Home: 7700 Burford Dr Mc Lean VA 22102-1716 Office: Sidley & Austin 1722 I St NW Washington DC 20006-3705

OTT, DAVID ALAN, cardiac surgeon; b. North Adams, Mass., Nov. 5, 1946; s. Ellsworth and Marie Ott; m. Pamela Ferguson; children: Elizabeth, David A. Jr. MD, Baylor Coll. Medicine, 1972. Resident in gen. surgery Baylor Coll. Medicine, Houston, 1972-76; resident in thoracic and cardiovascular surgery Tex. Heart Inst., Houston, 1976-78, assoc. surgeon, 1978—. Contbr. numerous articles to profl. jours. Bd. dirs. Am. Heart Assn., Houston. With USNR. Mem. ACS, Am. Coll. Cardiology, Soc. Thoracic Surgeons, Am. Coll. Chest Physicians. Office: 1101 Bates PO Box 20345 Houston TX 77225-0345

OTT, DAVID JAMES, diagnostic radiologist; b. Toledo, Apr. 19, 1946; s. Jack Melvin and Betty June (Miller) O.; m. Susan Emily Becker, July 12, 1970; 1 child, Stephen Louis. BS, U. Mich., 1967, MD, 1971. Intern Bowman Gray Sch. Medicine, Winston-Salem, N.C., 1971-72, resident in radiology, 1972-75, from instr. to assoc. prof. radiology, 1977-86, prof., 1986. Author: (with Meschan) Introduction to Diagnostic Imaging, 1984, (with Fayez) Hystero-Salpingography, 1991, (with Chen, Zagoria, Gelfand) Radiology of the Small Bowel, 1992, (with Gelfand, Chen) Manual of Gastrointestinal Fluoroscopy, 1996; editor: (with Castell) Gastroesophageal Reflux Disease, 1985, Polypoid Disease of the Colon, 1986, (with Chen, Pope) Basic Radiology, 1996; contbr. articles to profl. jours. Served to maj. Med. Service Corps, U.S. Army, 1975-77. Recipient Quinn Teaching award Bowman Gray Sch. Medicine 1984. Fellow Am. Coll. Gastroenterology; mem. Am. Coll. Radiology, Radiol. Soc. N.Am., Am. Roentgen Ray Soc., Am. Gastroent. Soc., Soc. Gastrointestinal Radiologists. Unitarian. Office: Bowman Gray Sch Medicine Radiology Dept Winston Salem NC 27157

OTT, EDGAR ALTON, animal nutrition educator; b. Ft. Wayne, Ind., Jan. 10, 1938; s. Earl S. and Luella Fay (Keister) O.; m. Judith Charlene Smith, June 9, 1963; children: Gregory Mark, Ronda Fay Ott Banner. BS, Purdue U., 1959, MS, 1963, PhD, 1965. Rsch. assoc. Ralston Purina Co., St. Louis, 1965-70; assoc. prof. animal nutrition U. Fla., Gainesville, 1970-79, prof., 1979—. Co-author: Horse Production in Florida, 1979, Nutrient Requirements of Horses, 1989. Deacon 1st Bapt. Ch., Gainesville, 1980-88; elder Covenant Bapt. Ch., Gainesville, 1988-92. 1st lt. U.S. Army, 1959-61. Mem. Am. Soc. Animal Sci., Equine Nutrition and Physiology Soc. (past sec., past pres., past v.p.). Office: Univ Fla Dept Animal Sci Gainesville FL 32611-0910

OTTINGER, GUY EMEREL, accountant; b. Lakeland, Fla., Mar. 24, 1921; s. Isaac and Hattie Irene (Neas) O.; m. Vivian Hampton, Aug. 12, 1947; children: David J., Lois I. Ottinger Gonzalez. BSBA, U. Fla., 1942. CPA, Fla. With various acctg. firms, Lakeland, Fla., 1946-58; pvt. practice pub. acctg. Lakeland, Fla., 1959—. Mem. Salvation Army, 1967—, past adv. chmn.chmn. bd. and treas. Capt. U.S. Army, 1942-52, col. USAR, ret. 1975. Mem. AICPAs, Fla. Soc. CPAs, Lakeland Area C. of C., Kiwanis Club of Lakeland. Republican. Lutheran. Home: 4216 Forest Hills Dr Lakeland FL 33813-1713 Office: 720 S Missouri Ave Lakeland FL 33815-4738

OTTO, DONALD R., museum director; b. North Loup, Nebr., Oct. 7, 1943; s. Leonard R. and Lorraine E. (Lindsay) O.; B.A., Hastings (Nebr.) Coll., 1967; m. Sylvia D. Cook, Aug. 7, 1965; 1 dau., Allison Lindsay. With Kans.-Nebr. Natural Gas Co., Hastings, 1967-68; exhibits dir. Hastings Museum, 1968-72; asst. dir. Kans. State Hist. Soc., 1972-75; program dir. Ft. Worth Mus. Sci. and History, 1975-77, exec. dir., 1977—; pres. Kans. Mus. Assn., 1974, 75; officer Mountain Plains Mus. Conf., 1976-79, pres., 1977-78; spl. cons. mus. curriculum planning Coll. Liberal Studies, U. Okla., 1980. Mem. adminstrv. bd. 1st Meth. Ch., 1978-80, 81-83, 84-86; bd. dirs. Sci. Mus. Exhibit Collaborative, 1983—, Ft. Worth Conv. and Visitors Bur., 1986—, Internat. Space Theater Consortium, 1981—, pres. 1984-86, exec. com. 1991-92; mem. Ft. Worth Cultural Dist. Com., 1979—, Ft. Worth Air Power Coun., 1985—, Leadership Ft. Worth, 1988—, Forum Ft. Worth, 1989—; mem. grants com. Cultural Arts Coun. of Houston, 1988-89; mem. adv. coun. Ft. Worth Sr. Citizen Ctrs., 1986-88; trustee Big Bros.-Big Sisters, 1988-89; chmn. Ft. Worth Tourism Coun., 1983. Mem. Am. Assn. Mus. (accreditation on site com. 1974—), Mt. Plains Mus. Assoc. Bd., 1975-78, pres., 1977, Am. Assn. State and Local History, Am. Assn. Sci. and Tech. Ctrs. (bd. dirs. 1984-88), Assn. Sci. Mus. Dirs., Tex. Assn. Mus. (coun. 1980-82, v.p. 1983-84), Ft. Worth Aviation Heritage Soc. (bd. dirs. 1988—), Methodist. Clubs: Ridglea Country, Rotary (Ft. Worth). Office: Ft Worth Mus Sci & History 1501 Montgomery St Fort Worth TX 76107-3017

OTTO, INGOLF HELGI ELFRIED, banking institute fellow; b. Duesseldorf, Germany, May 7, 1920; s. Frederick C. and Josephine (Zisenis) O.; m. Carlyle Miller, 1943 (div. 1960); children: George Vincent Edward, Richard Arthur Frederick. A.B., U. Cin., 1941; M.A., George Washington U., 1950, Ph.D., 1959. CPCU. Assoc. prof. fin. NYU, N.Y.C., 1960-62; prof. fin. U. Nuevo Leon, Monterrey, Mexico, 1962-65, U. So. Miss., Hattiesburg, 1965-67, U. So. Ala., Mobile, 1967-81; sr. fellow Inst. Banking and Fin., Mexico City, 1981—. Contbr. articles on fin. to profl. jours. Served to col. U.S. Army, 1941-46. Decorated Legion of Merit, Meritorious Service medal, Purple Heart. Mem. Am. Econ. Assn., N.Am. Econ. and Fin. Assn.

OTTO, LUDWIG, publisher, educator; b. N.Y.C., Mar. 15, 1934; s. Ludwig and Anna V. (Messina) O.; m. Sara S. Sheffield, Apr. 18, 1966 (div. 1987); children: Molly, Ryan, Matthew, Katherine. LLB, Blackstone Sch., Chgo., 1958; BA, CUNY, 1975; MDiv, Southwestern Bapt. Sem., Ft. Worth, 1978, D of Ministry, 1980; PhD, Am. U., 1996. Ordained minister, Baptist Ch., 1975. Mgr. computer div. NCR, various locations, 1957-64, Honeywell, Houston, 1964-66; pres. U. Computer Scis., Houston, 1966-74; pastor, evangelist So. Bapt. Ch., Tex., 1974—; chmn., pub. Critical Thinking Cos. (formerly Am. Bus. Mgrs.), Bedford, Tex., 1982—; exec. dir. Nat. Ethics Inst., 1992—; mem. adj. faculty El Centro Coll., Collin County C.C., Northlake Coll., Irvine, Tex., U. Tex., Arlington; assoc. prof., chair divsn. arts and scis. Paul Quinn Coll., Dallas, 1994—. Author: Introduction to Computer Math, 1967, 69, Training Church Members, 1980, How to Protect Your Children, 1982, Critical Thinking Strategies, 1993, Reading for Speed and Comprehension, 1993. 2d lt. U.S. Army, 1950-53. Mem. North Tex. Alumni Assn. of CCNY (pres. 1993—), Sigma Tau Delta. Home and Office: Franklin Publ 2723 Steamboat Cir Arlington TX 76006

OTTS, JAMES MITCHELL, minister; b. Stutgartt, Fed. Republic Germany, May 24, 1968; s. James A. and Ruby Jean (Suddeth) O. Student, Campbell U., 1987-88. Youth minister Turner Meml. Bapt. Ch., Garner, N.C., 1988; pastoral assoc. Glacier Valley Bapt. Ch., Juneau, Alaska, 1990-91; music and youth min. Oak Grove Bapt. Ch., Jemison, Ala., 1991-92; youth min. Providence Bapt. Ch. #1, Jemison, Ala., 1993, 1st Bapt. Ch., Aldrich, Ala., 1995—; purchasing agt., svc. technician Primary Home Health Care, Inc., Birmingham, Ala., 1994—; outreach leader Campbell U. Bapt. Student Union, Buies Creek, N.C., 1988; mem. rd. crew Elishah Ministry, Erwin, N.C., 1988; disc jockey WCCE-FM sta. Campbell U., 1988. With USAR, 1985-90. Republican. Home and Office: 1st Bapt Ch Aldrich 14052 Couty Rd # 51 Jemison AL 35085

OUELLETTE, JANE LEE YOUNG, biology educator; b. Charlotte, N.C., Dec. 29, 1929; d. James Thomas and Nancy Isabel (Yarbrough) Young; m. Armand Roland Ouellette, Aug. 3, 1951 (dec. Oct. 1984); children—Elizabeth Anne, James Young, Emily Jane, Frances Lee. B.A., Winthrop Coll., 1950; M.A., Oberlin Coll., 1952; postgrad. Coll. Medicine, Baylor U., 1974, U. Tex.-Houston, 1976-83, Tex. Woman's U., 1980-82. Lic. tchr., Tex. Tchr. Maria Regina High Sch., Hartsdale, N.Y., 1969-70, Spring Ind. Sch. System, Tex., 1972-78; coordinator biology program, prof., North Harris County Coll., Houston, 1979—. Meadow's fellow Baylor Coll. Medicine, 1989. Mem. Internat. Assn. for Study of Pain, Internat. Pain Found., N.Y. Acad. Sci., AAAS, Internat. Chronobiol. Soc., People to People Internat. Democrat. Home: 1619 Big Horn Dr Houston TX 77090-1862 Office: North Harris County Coll 2700 W Thorne Dr Houston TX 77073-3426

OUIMET, JAMES MICHAEL, insurance company executive; b. Springfield, Mass., Feb. 4, 1947; s. Harold Peter and Mary Helen (Potasky) O.; m. Linda Ann Tassinari, June 17, 1972; children: Jason, Mary Megan. BA in Mgmt. Econs. cum laude, Dominican Coll., 1973; MBA in Mktg., U. Notre Dame, 1975. Dir. Met. Life Ins. Co., N.Y.C., 1976-89; v.p. Blue Cross & Blue Shield Ky., Louisville, 1989-90; sr. v.p., chief mktg. officer Ky. Home Mutual Life Ins. Co., Louisville, 1990-91, pres., CEO, 1991-94; pres., CEO The James Group, 1994—. Bd. dirs., former co-chmn. fund dr., mem. mktg. com. Jr. Achievement of Kentuckiana, Louisville, 1989—; bd. dirs., pres. Nat. Football Found., Louisville, 1989—; mem. promotion com. Louisville mag.; chmn., pres. Louisville IceHawks Booster Club, 1990-94; dir. emeritus Peter Stuyvesant Little League, N.Y.C., 1982-89. With USAR, 1968-74. Mem. Nat. Assn. Life Underwriters, Notre Dame Club Louisville, Jefferson Club Louisville, Pendennis Club Louisville, Oxmoor Golf & Steeplechase Club. Republican. Roman Catholic. Home: 1493 Sable Wing Cir Louisville KY 40223-6110 Office: The James Group 2010 Cherokee Pkwy Louisville KY 40204-2254

OUTLAND, MAX LYNN, school system administrator; b. Murray, Ky., Aug. 12, 1937; s. Milburn T. and Ola (McKinney) O.; m. Lorna Lee Alexander, May 26, 1961. BS, Murray State U., 1969, MS, 1970; postgrad., various univs. Cert. tchr. indsl. arts and bldg. trades, Fla.; cert. ednl. adminstr., Fla.; cert. dir. vocat. edn., Fla. Tchr. indsl. arts Charlotte County Sch. Bd., Punta Gorda, Fla., 1970-71, dean students, 1971-72, asst. prin. jr. high sch., 1972-79, asst. prin. sr. high sch., 1979-81, acting prin. sr. high sch., 1981, prin. vocat. ctr., 1981, dir. vocat. edn., 1982-85, dir. maintenance, 1985-93, coord. of risk mgmt., 1993—. With USAF, 1956-60. Mem. Nat. Assn. Secondary Sch. Adminstrs., Coun. Ednl. Facility Planners, Fla. Assn. Sch. Adminstrs., Rotary (bd. dirs. Port Charlotte, Fla. chpt. 1988). Republican. Baptist. Office: Charlotte County Sch Bd 1016 Education Ave Punta Gorda FL 33950-6259

OUTLAW, THOMAS WILLIAM, municipal agency executive; b. Houston, Dec. 21, 1941; s. James Archer and Willeb (Albright) O.; m. Sherry Breakiron, Dec. 31, 1967 (div. Jan. 1993); 1 child, Joel Thomas. BBA, U. Houston, 1970. Staff economist Lockwood, Andrews and Newman, Houston, 1970-79; owner Outlaw Landscaping, Houston, 1979-88; dep. asst. dir. City of Houston, 1988—. Scout Master Boy Scouts of Am., Houston, 1984-89. Staff Sgt. USAF, 1963-68. Office: City of Houston Trfc & Trn 2200 Patterson St Houston TX 77007-2327

OVERMAN, MARY REUT, reporter; b. Yonkers, N.Y., Aug. 7, 1950; d. Michael Konstintine and Mary (Krusko) Reut; m. Donald Thomas Overman, Jan. 17, 1969; children: Jennie, D.J., Tania. BA in English and Journalism, Sam Houston State U., 1995. Reporter Houstonian Newspaper, Huntsville, Tex., 1991-94, news editor, 1994-95; editor-in-chief Houstonian Mag., Huntsville, 1995; copy editor Bryan-College Station Eagle, Bryan, Tex., 1995-96; reporter Tomball (Tex.) Sun, 1996—. Pub. rels. chair Orwall Bd. Dirs., Oak Ridge-Woodlands area, Tex., 1984-86. Mem. Soc. Profl. Journalists, Sam Houston State U. Alumni Assn. Home: 210 W Stewart St Willis TX 77378 Office: The Tomball Sun 990 Village Square Dr Ste Q Tomball TX 77375

OVERSTREET, ROBIN MILES, parasitologist, researcher, educator; b. Eugene, Oreg., June 1, 1939; s. Robin M. and Laura (McGinty) O.; m. Kim Bunton, Mar. 31, 1964; children—Brian, Eric. B.A. in Gen. Biology, U. Oreg., 1963; M.S. in Marine Biology, U. Miami, 1966, Ph.D., in Marine Biology, 1968. NIH postdoctoral fellow in parasitology Tulane U. Med. Sch., New Orleans, 1968-69; head sect. parasitology Gulf Coast Rsch. Lab., Ocean Springs, Miss., 1969-92, sr. rsch. scientist, 1992—; adj. prof. U. So. Miss., U. Miss., La. State U., others; vis. prof. U. Queensland, 1984, 92, 95. Served with USN, 1956-62. Nat. Marine Fisheries Svc. grantee, 1969—, Miss.-Ala. Sea 1973-78, U.S.-Israel Binat. Sci. Found. 1974-75, Nat. Cancer Inst. 1982-88, USDA, 1985—, EPA 1990—, NSF, 1994—, others. Mem. Am. Soc. Parasitologists (editl. bd., assoc. editor 1979-95, v.p. 1991), Helminthological Soc. Washington (editl. bd. 1974—), Am. Micros. Soc. (bd. reviewers 1981-94), Am. Fish. Soc. (assoc. editor 1993—), Southeastern Soc. Parasitologists (v.p. 1991, pres. 1996), others. Author: Marine Maladies: Worms, Germs and Other Symbionts from the Northern Gulf of Mexico, 1978; contbr. numerous articles to profl. jours. Home: 13821 Paraiso Rd Ocean Springs MS 39564-2584 Office: Gulf Coast Rsch Lab Ocean Springs MS 39566-7000

OVERSTREET, SAMUEL A., English language educator; b. Agaña, Guam, June 26, 1957; s. A. Evan and Joanne (Harwell) O.; m. Marjorie Karen Eid, Aug. 19, 1978. BA, Yale U., 1978; PhD, Cornell U., 1985. Asst. prof. English Maryville (Tenn.) Coll., 1990-95, assoc. prof., 1995—. Contbr. articles to profl. jour. Mem. MLA, Soc. Early English and Norse Electronic Texts, Medieval Acad., Assn. Literary Scholars and Critics. Office: Maryville Coll 502 E Lamar Alexander Pkwy Maryville TN 37804-5907

OVERTON, BENJAMIN FREDERICK, state supreme court justice; b. Green Bay, Wis., Dec. 15, 1926; s. Benjamin H. and Esther M. (Wiese) O.; m. Marilyn Louise Smith, June 9, 1951; children: William Hunter, Robert Murray, Catherine Louise. B.S. in Bus. Adminstrn., U. Fla., 1951, J.D., 1952; LL.D. (hon.), Stetson U., 1975, Nova U., 1977; LL.M., U. Va., 1984. Bar: Fla. 1952. With Office Fla. Atty. Gen., 1952; with firms in St. Petersburg, Fla., 1952-64; city atty. St. Petersburg Beach, Fla., 1954-57; circuit judge 6th Jud. Circuit Fla., 1964-74, chief judge, 1968-71; chmn. Fla. Conf. Circuit Judges, 1973; justice Supreme Ct. Fla., Tallahassee, 1974—; chief justice Supreme Ct. Fla., 1976-78; past adj. faculty Stetson U. Coll., Law and Fla. St. U. Coll. Law; bd. dirs. Nat. Jud. Coll., 1976-87; mem. Fla. Car Continuing Legal Edn. Com., 1963-74, chmn., 1971-74; 1st chmn. Fla. Inst. Judiciary, 1972; mem. exec. com. Appellate Judges Conf.; chmn. Appellate Structure Commn., 1978-79, Article Rev. Commn., 1983-84, Matrimonial Law Commn., 1982-85; chmn. Jud. Coun. Fla., 1985-89.; chmn. adv. com. for LLM program for appellate judges U. Va., 1985-94. Contbr. legal publs. Past reader, vestryman, sr. warden St. Albans Episcopal Ch., St. Petersburg; chmn. U.S. Constn. Bicentennial Commn. Fla. 1987-91; ch. Family Ct. Commn., 1990-91; ch. Death Case Postconviction Relief Proceeding 1990-91. Fellow Am. Bar Found.; mem. ABA (chmn. criminal justice task force to rev. trial and discovery standards 1991—), Fla. Bar Assn., Am. Judicature Soc. (dir., sec.). Democrat. Lodge: Rotary. Office: Fla Supreme Ct Supreme Ct Bldg Tallahassee FL 32399

OWEN, CYNTHIA CAROL, sales executive; b. Ft. Worth, Oct. 16, 1943; d. Charlie Bounds and Bernice Vera (Nunley) Rhoads; m. Franklin Earl Owen, Oct. 20, 1961 (div. Jan. 1987); children: Jeffrey Wayne, Valeria Ann, Carol Darlena, Pamela Kay; m. John Edward White, Jan. 1, 1988 (div. Sept. 1991). Cert. Keypuncher, Comml. Coll., 1963; student, Tarrant County Jr. Coll., 1974-77; BBA in Mgmt., U. Tex., Arlington, 1981. Keypunch operator Can-Tex. Industries, Mineral-Wells, 1966-67; sec. Electro-Midland Corp., Mineral-Wells, 1967-68; exec. sec. to v.p. sales Pangburn Co., Inc., Ft. Worth, 1972-78; bookkeeper, sec. CB Svc., Ft. Worth, 1978-82; project mgr. Square D Co., Ft. Worth, 1982—. Mem. NAFE, NOW, AAUW. Baptist. Home: 816 Lee Dr Bedford TX 76022-7311 Office: Square D Co 860 Airport Fwy Ste 101 Hurst TX 76054-3262

OWEN, DAVID DALRYMPLE, transportation company executive; b. Louisville, Apr. 9, 1942; s. Douglas Henry and Leelia (Reynolds) O.; m. Hannah Bradford, Sept. 8, 1965; children: Leelia, Andrew, David. BA, Centre Coll., 1964. Asst. trust investment officer Citizens Fidelity Bank, Louisville, 1965-71; ltd. ptnr. Benjamin D. Bartlett & Co., Louisville, 1971-74; asst. sec. Louisville and Nashville RR, 1974-80; dir. fin. Seaboard System RR, Jacksonville, Fla., 1980-83; mng. dir. fin. CSX Corp., Richmond, Va., 1983—. Bd. dirs. Boy Scouts of Am., Richmond, Va., 1989. Sgt. USAF, 1964-65, 68-69. Mem. Assn. Am. RRs, Richmond C. of C. (bd. dirs. 1989—), Centre Coll. Alumni Bd. (bd. dirs. 1989—), Country Club of Va., Commonwealth Club (Richmond), Louisville Country Club. Republican. Episcopalian. Home: 4204 Sulgrave Rd Richmond VA 23221-3255 also: 3750 Blueberry Point Rd White Stone VA 22578 Office: CSX Corp One James Center Richmond VA 23219

OWEN, DIAN GRAVE, healthcare organization executive; b. 1940. Pres. Owen Healthcare, Houston, 1970—. Office: Owen Healthcare Inc 9800 Centre Pky Houston TX 77036-8223*

OWEN, DOROTHY, company executive. Pres., founder Owen Steel. Office: Owen Steel 801 Blossom St Columbia SC 29201-4101*

OWEN, KENNETH DALE, orthodontist; b. Charlotte, N.C., May 9, 1938; s. Olin Watson and Ruth (Watlington) O.; m. Lura Aven Carnes, Feb. 14, 1958; children: Kenneth Dale, Aven Anna. BS, Davidson Coll., 1959; DDS, U. N.C., 1963, MSc in Orthodontics, 1967. Diplomate Am. Bd. Orthodontics. Pvt. practice dentistry specializing in orthodontia, Charlotte, 1966—; asst. clin. prof. U. N.C. Sch. Dentistry, 1969-72. Bd. dirs. N.C. Dental Found., 1973-81, 89-90, exec. com., 1974-80, v.p. 1976-77, pres., 1978-79; bd. dirs. Holiday Dental Conf. Found., 1989—, v.p., 1990—, conf. chmn. 1990—. Adminstrv. bd. Myers Park United Meth. Ch., 1976-79, 93-95. Served with Dental Corps AUS, 1963-65. Fellow Internat. Coll. Dentists (dep. regent N.C. 1986, 87), Am. Coll. Dentists; mem. ADA (ho. of dels. 1981-92, 95, 16 trustee dist. caucus vice chmn. 1986-89, chmn. 1989-92, ADPAC bd. 1994—), Am. Assn. Orthodontists (ho. of dels. 1980-88, 90-93) So. Assn. Orthodontists (trustee 1983-85, dir. 1987-93, pres. 1991-92), N.C. Assn. Orthodontists (bd. dirs. 1976-88, sec.-treas. 1976-88, pres. 1979-80), N.C. Dental Soc. (ho. dels. 1969-77, 81-94, parlimentarian 1994-95, trustee 1980-91, sec. treas. 1987-88, pres. elect 1988-89, pres. 1989-90), 2d Dist. Dental Soc. (editor 1967-69, sec.-treas. 1971-74, pres. 1975-76, exec. coun. 1971-77, 80-87), Charlotte Dental Soc. (chmn. various coms., dir. 1978-79, v.p. 1980-81), Stanly County Dental Soc., Coll. Diplomates Am. Bd. Orthodontics, U. N.C. Orthodontic Alumni Assn. (sec.-treas. 1971, v.p. 1972-73, pres. 1974-75, exec. com. 1971-76), U. N.C. Gen. Alumni Assn. (life), U. N.C. Dental Alumni Assn., Orthovista Orthodontic Study Group, Delta Sigma Delta (life; pres. N.C. grad. chpt. 1970-71), Omicron Kappa Upsilon, Kappa Sigma, Alpha Epsilon Delta. Home: 3724 Pomfret Ln Charlotte NC 28211-3726 Office: 497 N Wendover Rd Charlotte NC 28211-1064 also: 119 Yadkin St Albemarle NC 28001-3437

OWEN, LARRY GENE, dean, educator, electronic and computer integrated manufacturing consultant; b. Pine Bluff, Ark., Oct. 2, 1932; s. Cecil Earl and Helen Marie (Jacks) O.; m. Ruth Myra Newton, Sept. 3, 1953; children: Deborah, Patricia, Larry Jr., Shea. BS in Physics and Math. U. So. Miss., 1967; postgrad. Inst. Tech., 1974-75; MS in Ops. Mgmt., U. Ark., 1987. Enlisted in U.S. Air Force, 1951, advanced through ranks to m. sgt., 1968; electronic technician, 1951-61; communications supt., 1961-71, retired, 1971; tchr. math. and physics Southwestern Tech. Inst., Camden, Ark., 1971-72, tchr. electronics, 1972-75; dean tech. engrng. So. Ark. U. Tech., Camden, 1978-88; dean, dir. tech. div. Computer Integrated Mfg. Ctr., 1988-89; So. Ark. U. Tech.; dean high tech. div., dir. Ctr. for Competitive Mfg., 1989-91, dean, 1991—, So. Ark. U. Tech, 1988—; project dir. Ark. Consortium for Mfg. Competitiveness So. Growth Policies Bd. Mem. Rep. Task Force; chair Atea Coll. Cons., 1991—; fin. dir. post # 45 Am. Legion. Contbr. articles to profl. jours. Mem. Instrumentation Soc. Am. (sr.); Am. Assn. Physics Tchrs., Am. Tech. Edn. Assn. (rep. Ark. 1989-91, 95-96, pres. so. region 1992-93, chair Coll. of Conss.), Soc. Mfg. Engrs. (sr., chmn. South Ark. chpt. 1991-92, South Ark. PIC coun. 1991-95, gov.'s mfg. network adv. coun.). Baptist. Home: 306 Lakeside Ave Camden AR 71701-3237 Office: So Ark U Tech Ctr for Competitive Mfg Camden AR 71701

OWEN, LARRY LESLI, management educator, retired military officer, small business owner; b. Dothan, Ala., Sept. 21, 1945; s. Lesley Homer and Doris (Teuten) O.; m. Betty Aldredge, Aug. 4, 1966; children: Kimberley, Larry Allen, Jonathan. BA in Human Resources, Pepperdine U., 1979; MS in Personnel Mgmt., Troy State U., Ala., 1986. Enlisted U.S. Army, 1963, advanced through grades to maj.; battlefield commn., commd. 2d lt. U.S. Army, Saigon, Socialist Republican of South Vietnam, 1970; inf. officer U.S. Army, 1970-85, ret., 1985; instr. mgmt. Chattahoochee Valley State Coll., Phenix City, Ala., 1987-90, Patrick Henry Jr. Coll., 1990-92; instr. tng. for bus. and industry program Ala. So. Coll. Sys., 1992-94, Wallace C.C.-Selma, 1994; cons. Mil. Profl. Resources, Inc.; mem. Boise Cascade Tng. Task Force, 1992, chmn. Mgr.'s Roundtable, 1992. Designer, developer interactive video disc Combat Decision-Making, 1986 (Designer of Yr. award 1986), Mortar Tactical Tng., 1987. Chmn. Ft. Mitchell Nat. Cemetery, Phenix City, 1986-87, trustee, 1988-90; chmn. Vietnam Wall Com., Columbus, Ga., 1986-87; trainer Econ. Improvement Project, Phenix City, 1987-90; chmn. Nat. Am. Flag Run Com., 1989; chmn. tourism com. Phenix City C. of C., 1989; mem. scholarship and recruitment com. Auburn U. Paper/Pulp Found. Named Instr. of Yr. U.S. Army, 1982. Mem. TAPPI (career devel. com. 1991—), ASTD, Soc. Human Resource Mgrs., Soc. Applied Learning Tech., Boise Tng. Devel. Task Force, Corp. Tng. Round Table (chmn.), Jackson C. of C. (pride com.), Phenix City/Russell County C. of C. (chmn. tourism com., bd. dirs.), 1st Cav. Assn. (Follow Me chpt., pres. 1985-87, 88-90), Chattahoochee Valley Vets. Coun. (co-chmn. 1986-90). Baptist. Home: 1634 Northpointe Dr Deatsville AL 36022-2557

OWEN, ROB, journalist; b. Fairfax, Va., Sept. 3, 1971; s. James Alan and Patricia May (Simpson) O. BS in Mag. Journalism and Mktg., Syracuse (N.Y.) U., 1993. Feature writer Richmond Times-Dispatch, 1993—. Office: Richmond Times-Dispatch 333 E Grace St Richmond VA 23219

OWEN, RODNEY DOYLE, real estate appraiser; b. Wichita Falls, Tex., Aug. 2, 1954; s. Estal Paul and Barbara Ann (Brown) O.; m. Linda Ray Miears, Nov. 9, 1979 (div. June 1992); 1 child, Ravanell. Student, Del Mar Jr. Coll., Corpus Christi, Tex., 1972-73. Cert. profl. appraiser, Tex. Ops. mgr. Serco Well Svc., Wichita Falls, 1978-82; dist. mgr. Mid-Con Gas Corp., Springtown, Tex., 1982-89; appraiser Parker County Ctrl. Tax Authority, Weatherford, Tex., 1989—. Mem. Tex. Assn. Assesing Officers, Kiwanis (Weatherford club, bd. dirs. 1990-92, treas. 1992-93, pres.-elect 1993-94). Office: Parker County Ctrl Tax Authority 118 W Columbia St Weatherford TX 76086-4312

OWEN, THOMAS CHARLES, history educator; b. Milw., Apr. 23, 1943; s. Cyril Maurice and Eunice (French) O.; m. Sue Ann Matthews, Aug. 29, 1964. BA with honors, U. Wis., 1964; AM, Harvard U., 1969, PhD, 1973. Vis. asst. prof. history U. Vt., Burlington, 1974; asst. prof. history La. State U., Baton Rouge, 1974-80, assoc. prof., 1980-90, prof., 1990—. Author: Capitalism and Politics in Russia. . .1855-1905, 1981, The Corporation under Russian Law, 1800-1917, 1991, Russian Corporate Capitalism from Peter the Great to Perestroika, 1995; contbr. articles to profl. jours. Served to lt. USN, 1964-67, Morocco. Internat. Rsch. and Exchs. Bd. travel grantee to Russia, 1971, 80, 92, 96; Russian Inst. sr. rsch. fellow Columbia U., 1981; NSF rsch. grantee, 1985-88, 91-93; Social Sci. Rsch. Coun. grantee, 1996-97, others. Mem. Phi Beta Kappa. Home: 2015 Gen Cleburne Ave Baton Rouge LA 70810-6824 Office: La State U Dept History Baton Rouge LA 70803

OWEN, WILEY C., librarian, consultant, retired; b. Buford, Ga., Nov. 17, 1929; s. William Clyde and Clara Lou (Stargel) O. BA in Journalism, U. Ga., 1956, BA in English, 1957; M Librarianship, Emory U., 1963. Cert. libr., Ga. Music libr. U. Ga., Athens, 1954-58; tchr., libr. West Rome High Sch., Rome, Ga., 1958-62; dir. Carnegie Libr., Rome, 1963-83; assoc. dir. Sara Hightower Regional Libr., Rome, 1983-95, retired, 1995; music cataloguer Shorter Coll., Rome, 1963-83, instr., 1970-83. Editor: Index to the History of Rome, 1976; joint editor: Rome and Floyd County; an illustrated history, 1985. Treas. Rome chpt. Nat. Found., 1967-77; pres. Rome Little Theatre, 1968-69; pres. Rome Community Concert Assn., 1974-75, treas., 1977-91; bd. dirs. Rome Area Heritage Found., 1974-77. Mem. ALA, Ga. Libr. Assn. (music cons. 1963-70, children's lit. cons. 1970-76), Southeastern Libr. Assn., Jane Austen Soc. (founding, treas. Atlanta chpt. 1988—), Ga. Hist. Soc., Rome C. of C. (chmn. fine arts com. 1964-65). Democrat. Episcopalian. Home: 216 E 10th St Rome GA 30161-6129

OWEN, WILLIAM REAGAN, cardiologist; b. Athens, Tex., Oct. 14, 1925; s. Charles Reagan and Gladys (Bishop) O.; m. Margaret Ellen Severin, Mar. 12, 1927; children: Claudia Owen Lummis, Susan Owen Dawson. MD, Harvard Med. Sch., 1949. Diplomate Am. Bd. Internal Medicine. Intern Mass. Gen. Hosp., Boston, 1949-50, resident in internal medicine, 1950-53; resident in cardiology Nat. Heart Inst., Bethesda, Md., 1953-55, sr. surgeon, 1953-55; pvt. practice Houston, 1955—; prof. clin. medicine U. Tex. Med. Sch., Houston, 1965—; assoc. prof. medicine Baylor Med. Sch., Houston, 1955—; bd. govs. Univ. Club, Houston, 1983-95. Sr. surgeon USPHS, NIH, 1952-55. Recipient Sr. Svc. award U.S. Tennis Assn., White Plains, N.Y., 1989. Fellow Am. Coll. Cardiology; mem. Tex. Tennis Assn. (pres. 1989-91, Caswell award 1992). Republican. Unitarian. Home: 1909 Olympia Dr Houston TX 77019-3025 Office: 3403 Marquart # 202 Houston TX 77027

OWENS, BOBBY, noncommissioned officer; b. Memphis, July 11, 1946; s. Ezekiel and Edna (Davis) O.; m. Dorothy V. Taylor, Apr. 30, 1976; children: Danny, Darrel, Orlando, Eric. AA, St. Leo Coll., 1979. Enlisted U.S. Army, 1965, advanced through grades to Commd. Sgt. Maj., 1986; chief instr. U.S. Army Sgts. Maj. Acad., Ft. Bliss, Tex., 1992—; pres., CEO Enlisted Leadership Lab., El Paso, Tex. Author: The Star and the Wreath, 1993, The Diamond, 1993, The Gray Area, 1993, Squad Leader, 1993, Platoon Sergeant, 1994; contbr. articles to profl. jours. Home: PO Box 8011 Fort Bliss TX 79908

OWENS, DORIS A., controller; b. Waukegan, Ill., June 8, 1950; d. Benjamin H. and Annie (Haisma) Bloede; m. Brian E. Owens, Aug. 28, 1971; children: Teresa, Kelly. BS in Acctg., So. Ill. U., 1972; MBA in Mgmt., Roosevelt U., 1979. Voucher audit VA Hosp., N. Chgo., 1972-74; cost acct. Kleinschmidt Div., Deerfield, Ill., 1974-79; sr. acct. Andes Candies, Delavan, Wis., 1980; acct. mgr. Andes Candies, Delavan; contr. Tobler Suchard, USA, Delavan; fin. mgr. Jacobs Suchard, USA, Delavan, contr.; contr. Egg Products, Inc., Muskego, Wis., 1987-88; chief fin. officer Monogram Chocolates, Palm Beach, Fla., 1988-89; contr. Michael Angelo's Gourmet Foods, Inc., Austin, Tex., 1989-96; cons Spectrum Software Svcs Group Inc, Austin, 1996—.

OWENS, DORIS JERKINS, insurance underwriter; b. Range, Ala., June 16, 1940; d. Arthur Charles and Jennie (Lee) Jerkins; m. Gilbert Landers Owens, Jan. 29, 1959; 1 child, Alan Dale. Student Massey Draughon Bus. Coll., 1958-59, Auburn U., Montgomery, 1980, 81, 82. Cert. ins. counselor, profl. ins. woman. Exec. sec. Henry C. Barnet, Gen. Agt., Montgomery, Ala., 1959-66; sr. underwriter personal lines So. Guaranty Ins. Co., Montgomery, 1966—. Author: Bike Safety, 1976. Instr. Coop. State Dept. Defensive Driver Instr., 1975, 78; instr. ins. classes; v.p. Montgomery Citizens Fire Safety, 1981; panelist Gov.'s Safety Conf., Montgomery, 1975—; mem., panelist Women Annual Hwy. Safety Leaders, Montgomery, 1976, 78, 80; apptd. mem. Alliance Against Drugs, 1989. Recipient Able Toastmaster award Dist. 48 Toastmasters, 1979, Outstanding Lt. Gov. award, 1981, Outstanding Area Gov. award, 1980; named Ins. Woman of Year, 1979. Mem. Ins. Women Montgomery (pres. 1961, 85-86), Internat. Platform Assn., Blue-Gray Civitan Club. Office: So Guaranty Ins Co 2545 Taylor Rd Montgomery AL 36117-4706

OWENS, FLORA CONCEPCION, critical care nurse; b. Manila, Nov. 23, 1949; d. Felix and Marieta (Obsuna) Concepcion; m. George Owens, Feb. 13, 1976. Grad., San Juan de Dios Sch. Nursing, Pasay City, The Philippines, 1970; BSN, Concordia Coll., Manila, 1971. RN, Ill., Ark.; cert. in ACLS; CCRN. Staff nurse San Juan de Dios Hosp., 1970-71, Jefferson Meml. Hosp., Mt. Vernon, Ill., 1972, Russellville (Ark.) Nursing Home Ctr., 1973-76; staff nurse, relief supr. St. Mary's Regional Med. Ctr., Russellville, 1972-74, head nurse med. fl., 1975-76, insvc. coord. and unit mgr. med.-surg. ICU, 1976-90, staff nurse, charge nurse med.-surg. ICU, 1990—; instr. basic coronary care class, 1979-90, basic arrythmia class, 1979-91, 94-96; adj. faculty ATW. Mem. AACN, CCRN, Ark. Tech. U. Nursing Honor Soc.

OWENS, GARLAND CHESTER, accounting educator; b. Wilson, N.C., Dec. 12, 1922; s. James F. and Leona (Owens) O.; m. Mary Elizabeth Wade, June 19, 1948; 1 dau., Lynn Carol. B.S., U. Richmond, 1947; M.S., Columbia U., 1948, Ph.D., 1956. C.P.A., N.Y. State. Acct. Arthur Young & Co. (C.P.A.s), N.Y.C., 1950-53; mem. faculty Columbia Grad. Sch. Bus., N.Y.C., 1956-86; prof. Columbia Grad. Sch. Bus., 1964-86, assoc. dean, 1962-70; prof. Mercer U. Sch. Bus., 1986-93; program dir. Mgmt. Devel. Center, Belo Horizonte Minas Gerais, Brazil, 1973-75; Controller Arctic Inst. N.Am., 1957-77. Author: Cost Basis in Business Combinations, 1956, (with James A. Cashin) Auditing, 1963; current reading editor: Jour. Accountancy. Mem. bd. edn. Union Free Sch. Dist. 5, Greenburgh, N.Y., 1964-69, v.p., 1965-68, pres., 1968-69; mem. N.E. Regional Postmaster Selection Bd., U.S. Postal Service, 1969-75. Served to capt. USAAF, 1942-45. Decorated D.F.C., Air medal. Mem. Am. Inst. C.P.A.s, N.Y. State Soc. C.P.A.s, Ga. State Soc. C.P.A.'s, Am. Acctg. Assn., Beta Gamma Sigma. Methodist. Home: 4923B Rivoli Dr Macon GA 31210-4107 Office: Mercer U Sch Bus and Econs 1400 Coleman Ave Macon GA 31207-1000

OWENS, HAROLD B., former state agency consultant; b. Knapp, Wis., Oct. 1, 1926; s. John Donald and Mabel Evelyn (Dunn) O.; m. Hazel Marie Allison, Aug. 23, 1927; children: Robert Bruce, Patrick Brian (dec.), Michael Shawn. Student, U. Mont., 1944, Rollins Coll., Winter Park, Fla., 1961-62, U. Hawaii, 1964-65. Field rep. Puget Sound Power & Light, Kirkland, Wash., 1946-48; machinist Boeing Co., Seattle, 1948; commd. officer and pilot USAF, 1949, advanced through grades to col., ret. 1979; exec. dir. Tex. Soc. Energy Auditors, College Station, 1979-80; v.p. ops. Entek Assocs., Inc., College Station, 1979-88; aviation cons. Tex. Aeronautics Commn., Austin, 1983-89; research assoc. Ctr. for Strategic Tech., Tex. A&M U. System, College Station, 1979-92; ret., 1992; aviation instr. Bryan, Tex., 1979—; ind. energy cons., 1988—. Contbr. articles to profl. jours. Commr. Bryan Hist. Landmark Commn., 1993—; assoc. SOCV, 1992—. With U.S. Army, 1944-46, ETO. Decorated Legion of Merit, Bronze Star, Air Medal (7). Mem. Nat. Soc. Historic Preservation, Tex. Hist. Found., Nat. R.R. Hist. Soc. (nat. dir. 1988—), Air Force Assn. (chpt. pres. 1980-82, charter mem.), Nat. Aeronautics Assn., Order of Daedalians, Tex. A&M Assn. Former Students, Century Club, Faculty Club, The Ret. Officers Assn., Aircraft Owner's and Pilots Assn., Sons of Confederate Vets. Republican. Home: 3207 Wilderness Rd Bryan TX 77807-3222

OWENS, HELEN DAWN, elementary school educator, reading consultant; b. Eastman, Ga., Oct. 9, 1949; d. Eli B. and Irene (Harrell) Branch; m. Bobby Lee Owens, Dec. 9, 1967; children: Leslie Owens-McDonald, Monica Dawn. AA, Miami (Fla.) Dade Jr. Coll., 1969; BS, Fla. Internat. U., 1978; MEd, Mercer U., 1986, EdS, 1991. Cert. presch.-12th grade, reading specialist, early childhood edn. specialist, Ga. Youth ctr. dir. Dept. Def., Clark AFB, Philippines, 1969-70; English lang. instr. Chinese Mil. Acad., Feng Shan, Taiwan, 1973-75; tchr., music instr. ABC Presch., Miami, 1976-78; kindergarten and music tchr. Berkshire Sch., Homestead, Fla., 1978-79; tchr., reading specialist Perdue Elem. Sch. Houston County Bd. Edn., Warner Robins, Ga., 1979—; mem. nominating com. mem. Ga. picture book of yr. U. Ga., Athens, 1990-91; reading cons. for schs., county edn. bds., regional reading ctrs., Ctrl. Ga., 1990—. Author: With Loving Hands and Tender Hearts, 1975. Exec. bd. dirs. Ladies Ministries, Ch. of God., Warner Robins, 1990-94; dir. Internat. City Girls' Club, Warner Robins, 1990—. Recipient 25-Yr. Bible Tchr. Svc. award Internat. City Ch. of God., 1991; named Fla. State Family Tng. Dir. of Yr., Fla. Ch. of God, 1979, Ga. Girls' Club Coord. of the Year, 1995. Mem. Internat. Reading Assn. (mem. Ga. coun. 1979-96, dir. mem. devel. 1993-96, v.p. 1996-97, past pres. HOPE coun. 1990-92), Profl. Assn. Ga. Edn. Republican. Home: 111 Crestwood Rd Warner Robins GA 31093-6803 Office: Perdue Elem Sch 856 Highway 96 Warner Robins GA 31088-2222

OWENS, JAMES M., human services administrator, consultant, artist; b. Amityville, N.Y., Nov. 14, 1953; d. James G. and Doris T. O. BS in Psychology, Biology, St. Bonaventure U., 1975; MA in Edn., NYU, 1979; PhD Interdisciplinary Studies, Grad. Sch. Am., 1996. Recreation therapist Columbia-Presbyn. Hosp., Neurol. Inst., N.Y.C., 1979-80; residential counselor children's counseling program Columbine Ctr. Battered Women, Denver, 1980-82; salesperson Denver Symphony Orch., 1981-82; Exec. dir. Ctr. Creative Arts Therapy, Denver, 1982-96. Home: 2452 Glenarm Pl Denver CO 80205

OWENS, JANA JAE, entertainer; b. Great Falls, Mont., Aug. 30, 1943; d. Jacob G. Meyer and Bette P. (Sprague) Hopper; m. Sidney Greif (div.); children: Matthew N., Sydni C.; m. Buck Owens. Student, Interlochen Music Camp, 1959, Internat. String Congress, 1960, Vienna (Austria) Acad. Music, 1963-64; BA magna cum laude, Colo. Womens Coll., 1965, MusB magna cum laude, 1965. Tchr. music Ontario (Oreg.) Pub. Schs., 1965-67, Redding (Calif.) Pub. Schs., 1969-74; entertainer Buck Owens Enterprises, Bakersfield, Calif., 1974-78, Tulsa, 1979—; concertmistress Boise (Idaho) Philharm., 1965-67, Shasta Symphony, Redding, 1969-74. Rec. artist (violinist, vocalist) Lark Records, 1978—. Office: Jana Jae Enterprises Lake Record Prodns Inc PO Box 35726 Tulsa OK 74153

OWENS, JOHN FRANKLIN, health care administrator, consultant, nurse; b. Slatington, Pa., May 19, 1935; s. William and Goldie Irene (Zerfass) O.; m. Shirley Ann Spade, June 15, 1957; children: Terri Ann Owens Albright, Rick Todd. Student, Orange County Community Coll., 1954-55; attended Sch. of Nursing, SUNY, 1954-57, student, 1954-57; student, Pa. State U., 1964, U. Pa., 1967. Pvt. practice, 1960-72, pvt. cons., 1961-72; nursing supr., instr. Easton (Pa.) Hosp., 1961-65, dir. in-svc. edn., 1963-65; dir. svcs. Northampton County Homemaker Svc., Bethlehem, Pa., 1965-67; exec. dir. Bucks County Homemaker-Home Health Aide Svc., Doylestown, Pa., 1967-72; zone mgr. UpJohn Healthcare Svcs., N.J., 1972-73; govt. adminstr. UpJohn Healthcare Svcs., 1973-79; zone mgr. UpJohn Healthcare Svcs., Fla., 1979-82; bus. mgr. UpJohn Healthcare Svcs., 1982-84, asst. to pres., 1984-85, regional mgr., 1985-88, govt. contracts nat. program mgr., 1989-90, dir. Nat. Govt. Affairs, 1990-91; pvt. cons. New Port Richey, Fla., 1991—; long term territory mgr. Kinetic Concepts, Inc., New Port richey, Fla., 1992-96; acct. exec. Kinetic Concepts, Inc., Hudson, Fla., 1994-96; ret., 1996. Author: PA Training Guide for Homemaker Home Health Aides, 1972, Government Contracting, 1990. Chmn. Bucks County Reps., Doylestown, 1972. With U.S. Army, 1953-54. Mem. Am. Pub. Health Assn., Am. Mgmt. Assn., Jr. Chamber Internat., Nat. Conf. on Aging, Jaycees (1st v.p. 1969-70, pres. 1970-71, chmn. bd. 1971-72). Republican.

OWENS, KELLY ANN, elementary education educator; b. Memphis, July 9, 1966; d. John Henry and Sally Lou (Emendorfer) O. Student, N.C. Sch. of the Arts, 1985-86; BS in Elem. Edn., U. Tenn., 1991, MEd in Curriculum, Instruction, 1996. Instr. Chattanooga Ballet, 1987-89; tchr. 1st grade The Senter Sch., Chattanooga, 1991-92; tchr.'s asst. Mayfield Elem. Sch., Cleveland, Tenn., 1986-89, tchr., 1992—. Recipient elem. teaching award U. Tenn.-Chattanooga Ctr. for econ. Edn. Mem. NEA, Tenn. Edn. Assn., Mortar Bd., Golden Key Soc., Kappa Delta Pi. Roman Catholic. Home: 1100 20th St NW Apt 5 Cleveland TN 37311-1203

OWENS, LINDSAY MEGGS, dentist; b. Tyler, TX, Feb. 9, 1952; s. W.B. and Sara Eden (Meggs) O.; m. Mersedeh Djafarihiri, Oct. 8, 1988. BS, Abilene Christian U., 1974; DDS, Baylor Coll. Dentistry-Dallas, 1983. Pvt. practice Dallas, 1983—. Active Heritage Found., Washington, 1987—; mem. health facilities bd. City of Dallas, 1993-95; two star donator Head Start Programs of Tex. Recipient Spl. Vol. of Yr. Dental Health Programs, Inc., 1992. Mem. ADA, Tex. Dental Assn. (jud. and ethics coun. 1994—), Dallas County Dental Soc. (jud. com. 1989-94, chmn. 1991-94). Mem. Ch. of Christ. Office: 6801 Snider Plz Ste 200 Dallas TX 75205-1374

OWENS, MERLE WAYNE, executive search consultant; b. Barnsdall, Okla., Mar. 30, 1933; s. Jesse Raymond and Beulah Juanita (Thompson) O.; m. Nettie Natalie Norris, June 6, 1953; children: Jesse Wayne, Jennifer Lee. BBA, U. Okla., 1955. Sales engr. Nat. Supply Co., Tulsa, 1956-60; underwriter Allstate Ins., Dallas, 1960-63; regional mgr. Blue Cross Blue Shield, Dallas, 1963-78; sr. v.p. Paul R. Ray & Co., Ft. worth, 1978-93; owner Merle Owens & Assocs., Ft. worth, 1993—. 1st lt. U.S. Army, 1955-56. Republican. Baptist. Home: 420 Blue Jay Ct Bedford TX 76021-3201 Office: Merle W Owens & Assocs Ste 1205 301 Commerce St Fort Worth TX 76102

OWENS, ROBIN SHANE, clergyman; b. Clinton, S.C., May 1, 1954; s. David Herbert Sr. and Doris Mabel (Wofford) O.; m. Susan Ann Modlin, Aug. 23, 1980; children: Wesley, Amy, Andrew. BA, Presbyn. Coll., 1975; MDiv, Columbia Sem., 1980, DMin, 1994. Ordained to ministry Presbyn. Ch., 1980. Pastor Wildwood Presbyn. Ch., Morehead City, N.C., 1980-84, Bixby Presbyn. Ch., Advance, N.C., 1984-87, Olney Presbyn. Ch., Gastonia, N.C., 1988—; moderator, evangelism com. Presbytery of Western N.C., Morganton, N.C., 1990-92; vice-moderator Evangelism Network, Synod of Mid-Atlantic, Richmond, 1991-92; mem. evangelism and ch. devel. min. unit com. Gen. Assembly, Presbyn. Ch. U.S.A., 1992-93. Home: 232 Olney Church Rd Gastonia NC 28056-6830 Office: Olney Presbyn Ch 251 Olney Church Rd Gastonia NC 28056-6853

OWENS, RODNEY JOE, lawyer; b. Dallas, Mar. 7, 1950; s. Hubert L. and Billie Jo (Foust) O.; m. Sherry Lyn Bailey, June 10, 1972; 1 child, Jonathan Rockwell. BBA, So. Meth. U., 1972, JD, 1975. Bar: Tex. 1975, U.S. Dist. Ct. (no. dist.) Tex. 1975, U.S. Tax Ct. 1975, U.S. Ct. Appeals (5th cir.) 1975. Assoc. Durant & Mankoff, Dallas, 1975-78, ptnr., 1978-83; ptnr. Meadows, Owens, Collier, Reed, Cousins & Blau, Dallas, 1983—. Contbr. articles to profl. jours. Baptist. Home: 6919 N Jan Mar Dr Dallas TX 75230-3111 Office: Meadows Owens Collier Reed 3700 Nations Bank Plz 901 Main St Dallas TX 75202-3714

OWENS, SANDRA NELL, nurse; b. Birmingham, Ala., Aug. 6, 1948; d. Willie Toney Jr. and Eleanor Johnson; children: Zondra Newson, Cassondra Bess, Kendra Owens, Marlon Riley II. BS in Chemistry and Math., Paine Coll., 1969; A in Bus. IBM/Clerical, So. Jr. Coll., Birmingham, 1971; AS in Nursing, Grayson County Jr. Coll., Denison, Tex., 1977; postgrad., LaSalle U. RN, Ala.; ordained to ministry Bapt. Ch., 1992, World Christian Ch., 1995. Tchr. Boggs Acad., Keysville, Ga., 1971-72; packaging engr. Johnson and Johnson, Sherman, Tex., 1972-74; teletype operator, train mover SLSF R.R., Sherman, 1974-75; tchr. Sch. of Open Learning, Sherman, 1975-76; insp. Oscar Mayer Corp., Sherman, 1976-77; nurse St. Vincent's Hosp., Birmingham, 1990—; worship team singer Internat. Nurses Conv., Birmingham, 1994; del. conf. on cancer prevention and detection in Black Ams., Oncology Nursing, Atlanta, 1991. Author (pamphlet) Let's Talk PMS, 1993; contbr. poems to lit. publs. (Internat. Soc. Poets awards 1994, 95). Mem. care of the poor com. St. Vincent's Hosp., 1992-93; instr. ARC, 1993—, Birmingham AIDS Outreach, 1994. Mem. Birmingham City C. of C. (active corp. leadership 1995-96). Home: 528 Ave T Birmingham AL 35214 Office: Saint Vincent's Hosp 833 Saint Vincent's Dr Birmingham AL 35205

OWENS, STEPHEN LEE, clinical psychologist, mental health administrator; b. Bonne Terre, Mo., Mar. 26, 1958; s. Harry Leeroy and Virginia Annelle (Birdwhistell) O.; m. Susan Marie Ramsey, 1988; children: Alyssa Marie, Claire Nicole. BS in Psychology, Milligan Coll., 1980; MA in Clin. Psychology, East Tenn. State U., 1985; D in Psychology, Wright State U., 1992. Lic. clin. psychologist, Tenn.; cert. forensic evaluator, cert. biofeedback technician Am. Bd. Clin. Biofeedback. Psychiat. technician Watauga Area Mental Health Ctr., Johnson City, Tenn., 1981-83, psychol. assessment technician, 1983-84, psychol. assessment asst., 1984-85; psychol. examiner divsn. psychol. svcs. Woodridge Hosp., Johnson City, 1985-87; psychol. examiner divsn. outpatient svcs. Erwin (Tenn.) Mental Health Ctr., 1987-89; psychology trainee outpatient svcs. Wright State U., U. Psychol. Svcs. Assn., Inc., Dayton, Ohio, 1989-90; psychology trainee The Duke E. Ellis Human Devel. Inst., Dayton, 1990-91; psychol. extender People Skills Assocs., Dayton, 1990-91; pre-doctoral intern Wright State U., Sch. Profl. Psychology, Dayton, 1991-92; lic. clin. psychologist Johnson City (Tenn.) Med. Ctr. Hosp., 1992-94; clin. dir. outpatient svcs., dir. psychol. assessment svcs., forensic coord. Watauga Mental Health Svcs., Inc., Johnson City, 1994—; dir. Fairview Assocs. Pres. Castle Hills Christian Ch. Youth Group, San Antonio, 1974-76; vol. Watauga Mental Health Ctr. Summer Camp, 1982-89; vol. counselor Supporting Emotional Needs of Gifted Conf., Wright State U., 1990-91. Mem. APA, Intermountain Psychol. Assn. (sec.-treas. 1988-89, pres. 1994, 96-98), Psi Chi (pres. 1985-86). Home: 328 Lynn Rd Johnson City TN 37604-2602 Office: Watauga Mental Health Svcs 109 W Watauga Ave PO Box 2226 Johnson City TN 37604-5621

OWENS, TYLER BENJAMIN, chemist; b. Norfolk, Va., Aug. 28, 1944; s. Arthur Samuel and Julia Tyler (Downs) O.; m. Brenda Anne Coates, Sept. 5, 1980; children: Brooks Downs, Elizabeth Tyler. BA in Chemistry, Campbell U., Buies Creek, N.C., 1967; postgrad., N.C. State U., 1967-69. Sanitarian State of Va. Health Dept., Manassas, Va., 1971-72; chief chemist Goodmark Foods, Raleigh, N.C., 1972-75; real estate broker Nadine Hodge Realty, Raleigh, 1976-77; sales engr. Hewlett Packard Co., Palo Alto, Calif., 1977-80; sales rep. Sperry Univac Corp., Blue Bell, Pa., 1980-81; sales engr. Spectra Physics Corp., San Jose, 1981-83; pres. Batchelor & Owens, Inc., Raleigh, 1983-88; territory mgr. Extrel Corp., Pitts., 1988-90; sales mgr. Delsi Nermag Instruments, Paris, 1990-91, Viking Instruments Corp., Reston, Va., 1989-93; account exec. Dean Witter, Raleigh, 1993—. Active YMCA, Raleigh, 1989—; bd. dirs. Stonebridge Homeowners Assn., Raleigh, 1990-93, pres., 1993; bd. govs. Friends of the Children, Wake Meml. Hosp., Raleigh, 1990-93; precinct del. Wake County Rep. Party, Raleigh, 1985; vestry Episcopal Ch. of the Nativity, Raleigh, 1988-90, sr. warden, 1988-89. Mem. Am. Soc. Mass Spectrometry, N.C. Real Estate Commn., Triangle Mass Spectrometer Discussion Group, Wake County Rep. Men's Club. Episcopalian. Home and Office: 1009 Carrington Dr Raleigh NC 27615-1212

OWENS, VIVIAN ANN, plant science educator, researcher; b. Conway, S.C., Sept. 2, 1948; d. Zack Jr. and Frances (Mishoe) O. BS, Howard U., 1971, MS, 1974; PhD, Cornell U., 1984. Assoc. prof. plant sci. Hampton (Va.) U., 1988-95; vis. prof. Purdue U., summer 1994; faculty fellow EPA, Washington, summer 1990. Contbr. articles to profl. jours. Mem. Bot. Soc. Am. Baptist. Office: Dept Biology Box 6625 Hampton VA 23668

OWENS, WILBUR DAWSON, JR., federal judge; b. Albany, Ga., Feb. 1, 1930; s. Wilbur Dawson and Estelle (McKenzie) O.; m. Mary Elizabeth Glenn, June 21, 1958; children: Lindsey, Wilbur Dawson III, Estelle, John. Student, Emory U., 1947-48; JD, U. Ga., 1952. Bar: Ga. 1952. Mem. firm Smith, Gardner & Owens, Albany, 1954-55; v.p., trust officer Bank of Albany, 1955-59; sec.-treas. Southeastern Mortgage Co., Albany, 1959-65; asst. U.S. atty. Middle Dist. Ga., Macon, 1962-65; assoc., then ptnr. Bloch, Hall, Hawkins & Owens, Macon, 1965-72; judge U.S. Dist. Ct. for Mid. Dist. Ga., Macon, 1972—, now sr. U.S. dist. judge. Served to 1st lt., JAG USAF, 1952-54. Mem. State Bar Ga., Macon Bar Assn., Am. Judicature Soc., Phi Delta Theta, Phi Delta Phi. Republican. Presbyterian. Clubs: Rotarian, Idle Hour Golf and Country. Office: US Dist Ct PO Box 65 Macon GA 31202-0065

OWENS, WILLIAM COUNCILMAN, JR., lawyer, accountant; b. Balt., May 6, 1946; s. William Councilman Sr. and Ella (Uhler) O. BS cum laude, Yale U., 1968; MBA with distinction, U. Mich., 1969, MA in Econ., 1970; JD magna cum laude, Harvard U., 1973. Bar: Calif. 1973, N.Y. 1975, Tex. 1977; CPA, Tex. Rsch. atty. Calif. Supreme Ct., San Francisco, 1973-74; assoc. atty. Milbank, Tweed, Hadley & McCloy, N.Y.C., 1974-77; atty. Am. Gen. Corp., Houston, 1977-80; sr. corp. atty. Tenneco Inc., Houston, 1980-92; fin. advisor Prudential Securities, Inc., Houston, 1992-93; atty.-CPA WCO Enterprises, San Antonio, 1993—; treas. Tenneco Employees Good Govt. Fund, Houston, 1980-82, counsel, 1980-92. Contbr. articles to profl. jours. Redistricting cons. Tex. State Legis., Houston, Austin, 1990, 91, 95; supporting mem. Arts Symposium of Houston, 1980—, Houston Symphony Profls. Group, 1980-86, Alley Theatre Guild, Houston, 1991-93. Fellow Life Ins. Mgmt. Inst. Houston (pres. 1980-82); mem. Am. Assn. Atty.-CPA's Inc. (pres. Tex. chpt. 1980—, Outstanding State leader 1988), Inst. Mgmt. Accts. (bd. dirs. 1995—), Houston Young Lawyers Assn. (chmn. program com. 1980-86), Houston Bar Assn. (corp. counsel sect., dir. 1980-82), Yale Club Houston (sr. v.p. 1978-93), Yale Club San Antonio, Harvard Club San Antonio (bd. dirs. 1995—), U. Mich. Club Houston (bd. dirs. 1985-91), Combined Schs. Alumni Club (program com. 1984-88), Phi Beta Kappa Alumni Assn. Office: WCO Enterprises PO Box 690445 San Antonio TX 78269-0445

OWENS, WILLIAM EDWARD, microbiologist; b. Homer, La., Dec. 14, 1953; s. William Claude and Edna Mae (McClung) O.; m. Denice Simmons, Dec. 31, 1972; children: William Drake, William Dane, William Devin, Afton Noel. BS in Microbiology, Northwestern State U., 1975, MS, 1977; PhD in Microbiology and Immunology, La. State U., 1980. Postdoctoral fellow UCLA, Wadsworth VA Med. Ctr., 1980, St. Lukes Episc. Hosp. Tex. Med. Ctr., Houston, 1982; microbiologist Highland Hosp., Shreveport, La., 1983, Bayou Labs., Monroe, La., 1984; asst. prof. microbiology La. State U. Agrl. Ctr., 1984-89, assoc. prof., 1989-95; prof., 1995—; cons. clin. microbiologist Homer Meml. Hosp., 1991—; adj. asst. prof., dir. anaerobic rsch. lab. UCLA, 1982. Reviewer: Jour Am. Vet. Medicine, Jour. Dairy Sci., Assn. Clin. MIcrobiology Revs.; contbr. articles to profl. jours. Sunday sch. tchr. 1st Bapt. Ch., Homer, 1983—, deacon, 1984—; active Ford Mus. Found., 1986—, Friends of Claiborne Parish Libr., 1986—, Homer Pub. Sch. Support Group, 1986—, pres., 1988-90, Claiborne Parish Farm Bur.; Tiger cub leader Cub Scouts, 1988-92, den leader, 1989—; coach Homer T-Ball Assn., 1988—, Homer Flag Football Assn., 1992; active Homer PTSA, 19926, v.p., 1993; sci. fair judge Homer Jr. High Sch., 1989, 90, Webster Jr. High Sch., 1991, others; With USAFR, 1972-78. Mem. Am. Soc. for Microbiology, Am. Dairy Sci. Assn., Nat. Mastitis Coun., Inc., Assn. Vet. Microbiologists, La. Dairy Fieldman's Assn., Mastitis Rsch. Workers, Beta Beta Beta, Blue Key, Sigma Xi, Gamma Delta Sigma. Baptist. Office: La State U Agrl Ctr Hill Farm Rsch Sta RR 1 Box 10 Homer LA 71040-9604

OXELL, LOIE GWENDOLYN, fashion and beauty educator, consultant, columnist; b. Sioux City, Iowa, Nov. 17, 1917; d. Lyman Stanley and Loie Erma (Crill) Barton; m. Eugene Edwin Eschenbrenner, Aug. 8, 1936 (dec. 1954); children: Patricia Gene, Eugene Edward (dec. Feb. 1994); m. Henry J. Oxell, Nov. 3, 1956 (dec. July 1994). AS in Fashion Merchandising, Broward C.C., Davie, Fla., 1978. Fashion rep. Crestmoor Suit & Coat Co., St. Louis, 1951-56; with "To the Ladies" weekly TV show KSD-TV, St. Louis, 1950's; cons./instr. Miami-Herald Newspaper Glamor Clinic, Miami, Fla., 1957-71; pres./owner Loie's (Loy's) Inc., Miami, Fla., 1958-71; owner West Coast East Talent Agy.; pres./owner W. Coast E. Talent Agy.; instr./lectr. Charron-Williams Coll., Miami, 1973-77; instr. Fashion Inst. Ft. Lauderdale, Fla., 1977-86; pres./owner Image Power Unltd., Plantation, Fla., 1992—; lectr. in field; columnist Sr. Life News, Fla., Sr. Beacon, Tex., 1995—, Sr. Life and Boomer Times, Fla., 1995—, others. Author: I'd Like You to Meet My Wife, 1964; appeared on weekly TV show To the Ladies, 1950s, Del Russo Beauty Show, 1960s, Red Skelton TV show, also fashion commentary, TV commls. Vol. The Work Force, lectr., instr. The AARP Sr. Cmty. Svc. Employment Program (SCSEP), Ft. Lauderdale, Hollywood, Fla., 1987—, SCSEP Product Dirs., Charlestown, S.C., 1986; life mem. women's com. Miami Children's Hosp.; faculty advisor Nu Tau Sigma sorority Charron Williams Coll., 1973-77; pres. Venice of Am. chpt. Am. Bus. Women's Assn., 1975-76. Recipient Cert. of Appreciation Dade County Welfare Dept. Youth Hall, Miami, 1966, Community TV Found., Miami, 1966, 71, Woman of the Yr. award Am. Bus. Women's Assn. (Venice of Am. chpt.), 1976-77, Award for Svc. AARP Sr. Community Svc. Program, 1993. Mem. The Fashion Group Internat. (life, womens com. Miami Childrens Hosp.). Office: Image Power Unltd 1859 N Pine Island Rd # 339 Plantation FL 33322-5224

OXENDINE, JOHN, state insurance commissioner, state official. Bar: Ga., D.C. Ptnr., prin. Oxendine and Assocs., Atlanta; chmn. pers. bd. State of Ga., Atlanta, commr. ins., fire safety, indsl. loan, comptroller gen. Mem. ABA, Gwinnett County Bar Assn., Atlanta Lawyers Club. Office: State of Ga Dept Ins Floyd Meml Bldg 704 W Tower Atlanta GA 30334

OXER, JOHN PAUL DANIELL, civil engineer; b. Atlanta, Sept. 7, 1950; s. Robert B. Sr. and Leila Marie (Hammond) O.; m. Catherine Ann Stevens, Jan. 8, 1977. BCE, Ga. Inst. Tech., 1973; postgrad., U. Tex., Arlington, 1982-83. Lic. profl. engr. Ala., Ark., Ariz., Calif., Colo., Conn., Fla., Ga., Hawaii, Idaho, Ill., Ind., Iowa, Kans., Ky., La., Maine, Mich., Minn., Miss., Mo., Mont., Nebr., Nev., N.H., N.J., N.Mex., N.C., N.D., Okla., Oreg., S.C., S.D., Tenn., Tex., Utah, Vt., Va., Wash., W.Va., Wis., Wyo.; diplomate Am. Acad. Environ. Engrs. Project engr. J.S. Ross & Assocs. Inc., Smyrna, Ga., 1973-75, Welker & Assocs. Inc., Marietta, Ga., 1976-78; sr. project. engr. Claude Terry & Assocs., Inc., Atlanta, 1978-79; chief environ. engr. Bernard Johnson Inc. (SE), Atlanta, 1979-80; chief civil engr. region VI Ecology & Environ., Inc., Dallas, 1981-84; S.E. regional mgr. Ecology & Environ., Inc., Tallahassee, Fla., 1984-88; dir. program devel. Ecology & Environ., Inc., Dallas, 1988-91, exec. asst. to the pres., 1991-92; exec. asst. to the pres. Ecology & Environ., Inc., Houston, 1992—; guest lectr. Fla. State U., U. Louisville, U. Houston, Fla. State U.; mem. Industry Functional Adv. Com. on Stds. for Trade Policy Matters, 1993—. Executive producer video documentary; writer, producer video documentary; co-author, dir. video prodn. Mem. indsl. bd. advisors Speed Sci. Sch. U. Louisville, 1991—. Named Young Engr. of Yr., Ga. Soc. Profl. Engrs., 1980. Mem. NSPE, ASCE, Am. Pub. Works Assn., Am. Soc. Landscape Archs., Am. Soc. Agrl. Engrs., Nat. Def. Exec. Res. (assigned to Fed. Emergency Mgmt. Agy.), Fla. Bar Assn. (assoc.), Masons. Republican. Office: Ecology & Environ Inc 4801 Woodway Dr # 280-w Houston TX 77056-1805 also: Ecology & Environ Inc 1999 Bryan St Ste 2000 Dallas TX 75201-6811

OXFORD, HUBERT, III, lawyer; b. Beaumont, Tex., Sept. 25, 1938; s. Hubert Burton and Virginia Mary (Cunningham) O.; m. Cynthia Lynn Culp, Apr. 25, 1987; children: Mary Francelia, Hubert IV, Mary Cunningham, Virginia Barrett, Alaina Danielle, Adriana Victoria, Gabriella Elizabeth. BSME, Tex. A&M U., 1960; JD, U. Tex., 1963. Bar: Tex., 1963, U.S. Ct. Appeals (5th cir.), 1967, (11th cir.) Tex., U.S. Dist. Ct. (ea., so., no, we. dists.) Tex., U.S. Supreme Ct., 1975, U.S. Dist. Ct. (we. dist.) Okla., Mont., 1996, Wyo., 1996, Okla., 1996. Briefing atty. to U.S. dist. judge Eastern Dist. Tex., Beaumont, 1966; asst. dist. atty. Jefferson County, Tex., 1967; mng. ptnr. firm Benckenstein & Oxford, L.L.P., Beaumont, 1966; gen. counsel Jefferson County Nav. Dist., Lower Neches Valley Authority; mem. Gov. Reorganization Commn. Tex. 70th. Legislature, 1987-88, Tex. Oil Spill Commn.; U.S. Commr. Ea. Dist. Tex., 1968-70; mem. Tex. Bd. Registration for Profl. Engrs. Assoc. editor Tex. Law Rev., 1962-63. Bd. dirs. Ducks Unltd., 1978-86, Gulf Coast Conservation Assn., 1978-86; sec. bd. regents Lamar U., 1978-84, gen. counsel, 1986; mem. Tex. Air Control Bd., 1984-90; chmn. Tex. Clean Air Study Com., 1989. Capt. JAGC, USAF, 1963-66. Fellow Tex. Bar Assn., Am. Bar Assn.; mem. ABA, ATLA, Southeastern Admiralty Law Inst., Internat. Assn. Def. Counsel, Tex. Assn. Def. Lawyers, Nat. Bd. Trial Advocacy, State Bar Tex. (chmn. CLE com. 1979-81, course dir. admiralty and maritime seminar 1991, 96, grievance com. Dist. 3A), Maritime Law Assn., Jefferson County Bar Assn. (pres. 1987-88, Outstanding Young Lawyer 1972), Def. Rsch. Inst., Beaumont C. of C. (dir. 1978-84), Phi Delta Theta, Tau Beta Pi, Phi Kappa Phi, Phi Delta Phi. Democrat. Roman Catholic. Office: Allied Bank Bldg 3535 Calder Ave PO Box 150 Beaumont TX 77704

OXHANDLER, MYRA, mental health nurse; b. Bklyn., June 14, 1948; d. Charles and Beatrice (Brown) Raye; m. David Oxhandler, Sept. 21, 1987; children: Bob, Seth. Cert. in Nursing, Cen. Fla. Community Coll., 1984; BS in Psychology, N.Y. External Regents, 1989. Cert. psychiat./mental health nurse, tech. effective aggression mgmt. instr. Former dir. clin. nursing Lake Sumter Psychiat. Hosp., Leesburg, Fla., 1988-89, staff devel. crisis stabilization nurse, inpatient counselor, 1990-91; mem. psychotic disorders team Shands Teaching Hosp./U. Fla., Gainesville, 1993—; preceptor RN program Lake Sumter C.C., 1987-89; preceptor psychiat. RN Shands Tchg. Hosp., U. Fla., 1995; regional program coord. for mental health svcs. ABC Home Health, Ocala, Fla., 1992. Author: Home Remedies—What Works, 1995. Mem. ANA (cert.), Alliance for the Mentally Ill, Am. Psychiat. Nurses Assn.

OXLEY, JAMES GRIEVE, mathematics educator; b. Sale, Victoria, Australia, Feb. 4, 1953; m. Judith Danute Surkevicius; children: Margaret Catherine, David Grieve. BSc, U. Tasmania, 1974; MSc, Australian Nat. U., 1975; PhD, U. Oxford, 1978. Lectr., rsch. fellow Australian Nat. U., 1978-82; asst. prof. La. State U., Baton Rouge, 1982-85; assoc. prof. La. State U., 1985-90, prof., 1990—; vis. instr. U. N.C., Chapel Hill, 1978. Author: Matroid Theory, 1992.; mem. editorial bd. Combinatorics, Probability and Computing; reviewer Mathematical Reviews, Zentralblatt für Mathematik; contbr. chpts. to books, articles to profl. jours. NSF grantee, 1985-87, 89-91, La. Edn. Quality Support Fund, 1987-91, 92-94, Nat. Security Agy. grantee, 1994—, others; Fulbright postdoctoral fellow U. N.C., 1980. Mem. Am. Math. Soc., London Math. Soc. Office: La State U Math Dept Baton Rouge LA 70803-4918

OXNER, GLENN RUCKMAN, financial executive; b. Greenville, S.C., July 10, 1938; s. G. Dewey and Frances O.; m. Kathleen Gallagher, 1992. Student Duke U., 1956-57; B.S., U.S.C., 1961. Trainee stock bd. broker Alester G. Furman Co., Greenville, S.C., 1961, v.p., 1964-67, exec. v.p., 1967-75; pres. S.C. Securities Co., 1975-77; sr. v.p. Interstate Securities, Charlotte, N.C., 1977-82, exec. v.p., 1982-85; chmn. First Tryon Securities, Charlotte, N.C., 1986-89; mng. dir. Nations Bank Investment Banking Co., Charlotte, 1989-92; chmn. Edgar M. Norris & Co., 1992—. Served with U.S. Army, 1957. Mem. Nat. Assn. Security Dealers (com. chmn. dist. 7 1974, gov. 1981-84), Security Industry Assn. (gov. 1974), Security Dealers Carolinas (pres. 1977). Home: 18 Woodland Way Cir Greenville SC 29601-3824 Office: Edgar M Norris & Co PO Box 247 Greenville SC 29602-0247

OZBOLT, JUDY G., nursing educator; b. Dothan, Ala., Nov. 16, 1944; d. Bernard R. and Cleo Grace (Whiddon) O.; m. Samuel R. Kaplan, July 14, 1981; children: Jay Y. Kaplan, Rebecca J. Kaplan, Ira D. Kaplan. BSN, Duke U., 1967; MS, U. Mich., 1974, PhD, 1976. Visiting prof. Institut Internat. de Formation des Cadres de Santé, Lyon, France; assoc. prof. U. Pitts., U. Mich., Ann Arbor; prof./dir. doctoral program U. Va., Charlottesville; chmn. priority expert panel nursing inf. systems, Nat. Ctr. Nursing Rsch. Author: (with Vandewal and Hannah) Decision Support Systems in Nursing, 1990; contbr. articles to profl. jours. Am. Acad. Nursing fellow, Am. Coll. Med. Info. fellow. Founding fellow Am. Inst. for Med. and Biol. Engrng.; mem. Am. Med. Informatics Assn. (bd. dirs., sec., co-chmn. profl. specialty group).

OZER, MARTHA ROSS, school psychologist; b. Richmond, Ky., Sept. 4, 1932; d. Robert Lee and Virginia Eudelle (Hurst) Ross; m. John Dudley Redden, Dec. 27, 1953 (dec. June 1969); children: Mary, Patricia, Robert, Mark; m. Mark N. Ozer, Aug. 12, 1979. BA in Elem. Edn., Georgetown Coll., 1954; MA in Counseling, Murray State U., 1966, MS in Psychology, 1968; EdD in Edn. Adminstrn., U. Ky., 1976; LLD (hon.), Georgetown Coll., 1995; postdoctoral cert. in infant and young child mental health program, Wash. Sch. Psychiatry, 1995—. Cert. sch. psychologist with automous functioning, Ky.; lic. sch. psychologist, Va. Elem. tchr. Jefferson County Pub. Schs., Louisville, 1954-58, Hickman County Pub. Schs., Campbellsburg, Ky., 1960-62; tchr. emotional disturbed, dir. psychol. svcs. Paducah (Ky.) Pub. Schs., 1965-70; psychologist, program dir. Louisville Pub. Schs., 1970-74; doctoral intern Bur. Edn. for Handicapped U.S. Dept. Edn., Washington, 1974-75; program dir. project sci. tech. and disability AAAS, Washington, 1975-86; postdoctoral intern NYU Brain Trauma Program NYU Med. Ctr., N.Y.C., 1986-87; program dir., adminstr., asst. prof. dept. rehab. medicine Med. Coll. Va., Richmond, 1987-89; psychologist MCV Pediatric Devel. Ctr., Richmond, 1989; sch. psychologist Fairfax (Va.) County Pub. Schs., 1989—; cons. Am. Coun. on Edn., Washington, 1976—; project coord. Higher Edn. and the Handicapped Am. Coun. on Edn., 1976-86; numerous other profl. and disability orgns. Authored more than 20 books and contbr. articles to profl. jours. on access for persons with disabilities to sci. edn. and careers, contbn. of sci./tech. to persons with disabilities. Advisor Disability Rights, 1975-86. Recipient U.S. Presdl. Pub. Sector award, award Am. Coalition Citizens with Disabilities, 1980, Alumni award Geotgetown Coll., 1985, Disting. Alumni award Murray St. U., 1996; grantee U.S. Dept. Edn., 1975-86, U.S. Dept. Civil Rights, 1975-90, Grant Found., 1975-77, Exxon Found., 1976, IBM, 1976, NSF, 1977-86, Nat. Inst. for Rehab. Rsch., 1978-84. Mem. NSTA (award), APA (bd. dirs. rehab. sect.), NASP (nat. cert.), Va. Psychol. Assn., Assn. Handicapped Student Svc. Programs in Post-Secondary Edn. (editor jour. 1988-91). Home: 3420 38th St NW Apt A-415 Washington DC 20016-3032

OZOLEK, JOHN ANTHONY, pediatrician, neonatologist; b. Dubois, Pa., Feb. 24, 1963; s. Anthony John and Ann Elaine (Castrilla) O.; m. Jamie Lynn McCombe, Oct. 29, 1994. BS in Biology, Case Western Res. U., 1985; MD, U. Pitts., 1989. Diplomate Am. Bd. Pediatrics. Intern in pediatrics Children's Hosp., Pitts., 1989-90, resident in pediatrics, 1990-92; fellow in neonatology Magee Women's Hosp., Pitts., 1992-95; physician rep. medication rev. com. neonatal ICU Magee Women's Hosp., Pitts., 1994—. Contbr. articles to profl. jours. Fellow Soc. Pediatric Rsch., Am. Acad. Pediat.; mem. AMA, Nat. Perinatal Assn. Roman Catholic. Home: 9501 Point Aux Chenes Ocean Springs MS 39564 Office: Dept Pediatrics Divsn Neonatology Keesler Med Ctr Biloxi MS 39534

PABON-PEREZ, HEIDI, physicist; b. San Juan, Oct. 6, 1939; d. José Antonio Pabon-Rivera and Tomasa D. (Pérez) Pabon. BS, U. Puerto Rico, 1960, MS, U. Rochester, 1961. Health physicist U. P.R. Nuclear Ctr., 1961-69, Dr. I. Gonzalez Martinez Hosp., San Juan, 1965-69; physicist State Dept. P.R., 1964-77; radiological physicist P.R. Med. Ctr., San Juan, 1969-77; instr. Radiological Scis. U. P.R., 1976-77; cons. Med. Physicist Caguas (P.R.) Nuclear Medicine Lab., 1977; lt. Med. Svc. Corps. USN, 1977-80;

acting program dir. U. P.R., 1981-84, asst. prof., 1980-84, 1980—; health physicist VA Med. Ctr., San Juan, 1984—. Mem., treas. P.R. YL Club, San Juan, 1977-96. Lt. USN, 1977-80. Home: Valle Arriba Heights BC9 Yagrumo Carolina PR 00983 Office: VA Medical Center One Veterans Pla San Juan PR 00927-5800

PACE, CAROLINA JOLLIFF, communications executive, commercial real estate investor; b. Dallas, Apr. 12, 1938; d. Lindsay Gafford and Carolina (Juden) Jolliff; student Holton-Arms Jr. Coll., 1956-57; BA in Comparative Lit., So. Meth. U., 1960; m. John McIver Pace, Oct. 7, 1961. Promotional advisor, dir. season ticket sales Dallas Theatre Ctr., 1960-61; exec. sec. Dallas Book and Author Luncheon, 1959-63; promotional and instl. cons. Henry Regnery-Reilly & Lee Pub. Co., Chgo., 1962-65; pub. trade rep. various cos., instl. rep. Don R. Phillips Co., Southeastern area, 1965-67; Southwestern rep. Ednl. Reading Svc., Inc.-Troll Assocs., Mahwah, N.J., 1967-72; v.p., dir. multimedia div. Melton Book Co., Dallas, 1972-79; v.p. mktg. Webster's Internat., Inc., Nashville, 1980-82; pres. Carolina Pace, Inc., 1982—; mem. adv. bd. Nat. Info. Ctr. of Spl. Edn. Materials; mem. materials rev. panel Nat. Media Ctr. for Materials of Severely-Profoundly Handicapped, 1981; mem. mktg. product rev. bd. LINC Resources, 1982, 83, 84, mktg. task force, 1983, adv. bd., 1987; reviewer spl. edn. U.S. Dept. Edn., 1975-79, 85; rev. cons. Health and Humas Svcs., 1982, 83, 84, 86; product rev. task force CEC, 1984, 85, 86; cons. Ednl. Cable Consortium, Summit, N.J., 1982-87. Mem. adv. coun. Grad. System Sch. Libr. and Info. Sci. Found., U. Tex., 1987—; co-vice chair Friends Highland Park Libr., 1989; mem. focus group City Dallas Growth Policy Plan; mem. art and design com. Downtown Ctrs.; active Dallas City Wide Parking Task Force, Ctrl. Transp. Forum Ctrl. Bus. Dist., Union Sta. Art & Design Com., Downtown Transfer Ctrs., Art and Design Com., West End Task Force, Ctrl. Bus. Dist. Task Force, Tex. Parking Assn.; co-founder Operation TexRec, 1990-91; bd. dirs. Transp. Mgmt. Assn., 1995—; chair Vanpool Use Study, 1995; budget chmn. Dallas County Sesquicentennial com., 1996; bd. mem. Friends of Old Red Courthouse, 1996—. Mem. Ctrl. Dallas Assn. (transportation com.), Dallas Plan (focus com.), Nat. Audio Visual Assn. (conf. panelist 1979), Internat. Comm. Industries Assn., Assn. Ednl. and Comm. Tech., Assn. Spl. Edn. Tech. (nat. dir., v.p. publicity 1980-82), Women's Nat. Book Assn, Women in Comm., Dallas Founders, Ctrl. Dallas Assn., Friends of the West End (pres. 1988—), West End Assn. Dallas (chmn. subcom. on traffic and parking 1986-87, com. demographic study 1987-88), Pub. Rels. Soc. Am., Coun. Exceptional Children (dir. exhibitors com., chmn. publ. com. 1979 conf., conf. speaker 1981), Downtown Transp. Mgmt. Assn. (adv. bd., chmn. vanpools subcom., 1995—), DAR (Jane Douglas chpt.), Dallas Zool. Soc., Dallas West End Hist. Dist. Assn., Dallas Mus. of Art, Dallas Southern Meml. Tex. Parking Assn., Kimball Art Mus., Alpha Delta Pi. Presbyterian. Producer ednl. videos; contbr. articles to profl. jours. Home: 4524 Lorraine Ave Dallas TX 75205-3613

PACE, HARRY RICHARD, retired obstetrician, gynecologist; b. N.Y.C., July 28, 1914; s. Sam and Ida Pace; m. Toby Lila Janvey, Jan. 11, 1942; 1 child, Randolph Kip. BA, NYU, 1934; MD, Royal Coll. Physicians & Surgs, Edinburgh, Scotland, 1939. Diplomate Am. Bd. Ob-Gyn. Intern Israel Zion Hosp., Bklyn., 1939-41, resident in ob-gyn., 1941-42, from clin. asst. to attending, 1943-79; cons. Maimonides Med. Ctr., Bklyn., 1979—; chief med. cons. N.Y. State Dept. Social Svcs., N.Y.C., 1978-88; ret., 1988; assoc. dir. gyn. Park East Hosp., N.Y.C., 1970-73; gyn. St. Luke's Hosp., N.Y.C., 1973-76; gyn. SUNY, Old Westbury, L.I., 1976-78; lectr. ob-gyn. SUNY, 1962—; regional med. dir. N.Y. State Drug Abuse Control Commn., 1973-74; sr. gyn. N.Y.C. Health and Hosp. Corp., 1974, med. dir. 1974-76. Fellow ACS, Am. Coll. Ob-Gyn. (founding), Bklyn. Gynecol. Soc. Republican.

PACE, JAMES ROBERT, art educator, painter, printmaker; b. Tahlequah, Okla., Feb. 19, 1958. BFA, U. Okla., 1981; MFA, Ariz. State U., 1984. Instr. Norman (Okla.) Parks & Recreation Dept., 1978-81; grad. teaching asst. Ariz. State U., 1981-84; instr. South Mountain C.C., Phoenix, 1985; instr. drawing and painting techniques Phoenix Inst. Tech., 1985; asst. prof. U. Tex., Tyler, 1985-90, assoc. prof., 1990—, chmn., 1993—; Liaison Okla. Summer Arts Inst., Okla. Arts and Humanities Coun., Quartz Mountain, 1976; asst. to dir./curator Yuma Fine Arts Ctr., 1985; vis. artist Ariz. Western Coll., Yuma, 1985; dir. exhbns. Univ. Gallery, U. Tex., Tyler, 1986-93, dir. spring portfolio, 1985-93, acting chmn. dept. art, summer 1990; curator Galveston Art Ctr., The Strand, 1989; panelist Mus. Art, Dallas, 1990, 500 X Gallery, Gallas, 1991; lectr. in field; juror various art exhbns. and symposiums. One-man shows include East Ctrl. State U., Ada. Okla., 1980, Gallery Milepost Nine, Ariz. Western Coll., 1984, 85, Harry Wood Gallery, Ariz. State U., 1984, Exposure Gallery, Dallas, 1984, Stoner Arts Ctr., Shreveport, 1987, Univ. Gallery, U. Tex., Tyler, 1988, Griffith Gallery, Stephen F. Austin State U., Nacogdoches, Tex., 1988, Fine Arts Gallery, Kilgore (Tex.) Coll., 1988, Fine Arts Gallery, Temple (Tex.) Jr. Coll., 1989, Dishman Art Gallery, Lamar U., Beaumont, Tex., 1989, U. Ark., Little Rock, 1990, Midwestern State U., Wichita Falls, Tex., 1991, Paris (Tex.) Jr. Coll., 1991, Forum Gallery Brookhaven Coll., Dallas, 1992, Bradley U., Peoria, Ill., 1992, Lon Morris Coll., Jacksonville, Tex., 1993, Local Color Gallery, Coll. Sta., Tex., 1994; group exhbns. include Cleve. Arts Inst., Okla. City, 1979, Syracuse (N.Y.) U., 1979, Wesleyan U., Macon, Ga., 1980, 83, Carson-Sapiro Gallery, Denver, 1981, Old Dominion U., Norfolk, Va., 1982, SW Tex. State U., San Marcos, 1984, 85, 87, U. Tex. at Tyler, 1985, 86, 87, 88, U. Fine Arts Gallery, Fla. State U., Tallahassee, 1985, 86, (Best of Show award 1989), 89, Rudolph E. Lee Gallery Clemson (S.C.) U., 1987, Minot (N.D.) State Coll., 1987, Foster Gallery U. Wis., Eau Claire, 1988, Beaumont (Tex.) Art League, 1988, 92, Del Mar Coll., Corpus Christi, Tex. (Haas Found. award), 1988, Laguna Gloria Art Mus., Tex. Fine Arts Assn., Austin (Grumbacher award, touring Citation award, Best of Show award), 1988, Ark. Art Ctr., Little Rock, 1989, Galveston (Tex.) Arts Ctr., 1989, SE Ark. Art & Sci. Ctr., Pine Bluff, 1989, U. Hamburg, W. Ger., traveling show, 1989, Brigham Young U., Provo, Utah, 1990, William Campbell Contemporary Art Gallery, Ft. Worth, Tex., 1990, Hill Country Arts Found., Ingram, Tex. (Merit award), 1990, Dallas Mus. Art, 1990, Fuller Art Ctr., Los Alamos, N.Mex., 1991, La. Tech. U., Ruston, 1991, Mid-Hudson Art Ctr., Poughkeepsie, N.Y., 1991, Gormley Gallery Coll. of Notre Dame, Balt., 1992, Nora Eccles Harrision Mus. of Art Utah State U., Logan, 1992, U. N.D., Grand Forks, 1993, Wichita Falls Mus. of Art, 1993, Arlington (Tex.) Mus. of Art, 1993, Lubbock (Tex.) Fine Arts Ctr., 1994, numerous others; represented in permanent collections Amoco Corp. Collections, Denver, Sette Pub. Co., Tempe, Ariz., St. John's Mus. Fine Art, Wilmington, N.C., Okla. State U., Wichita Falls Art Mus., Ariz. Western Coll., Tempe, Chattahoochee Valley Art Assn., Lamar Dodd Art Ctr., LaGrange, Ga. Faculty Rsch. Release grantee U. Tex., Tyler, 1987-88, Faculty Rsch. grantee, 1989-90, 93-94; Mid-Am. Arts Alliance/Nat. Endowments Arts fellow, 1992; recipient Best of Show award Tex. Fine Arts Assn., Laguna Gloria Art Mus., Austin, 1988, Univ. Gallery, Fla. State U., Tallahassee, 1989, Purchase award Okla. State Art Collection Competition, Oklahoma City, 1980, Gardiner Art Gallery, Okla. State U., Stillwater, 1989, Tex. Select Invitational Exhbn., Wichita Falls Art Mus., 1993, Merit award Hill Country Art Found., Ingram, 1990, 91, Juror's Choice award LaGuna Gloria Art Mus. Tex. Fine Arts Assn., 1989, Purchase award Wichita Falls Art Mus., 1993, Juror's Merit award Lagrange Nat., 1994, many others; MAAA/NEA fellow, 1992; named to Tamarind Inst., Albuquerque, 1994. Office: U Tex Tyler 3900 University Blvd Tyler TX 75799-0001

PACE, JOHN EDWARD, III, chemical engineer; b. Ridgeway, Va., Apr. 6, 1948; s. John Edward Jr. and Retta Jean Stanley Sheppard; m. Carolyn Ann Gray, Aug. 31, 1969; children: Brian Edward, Kimberly Carol. BSChemE, Va. Poly. Inst. and State U., 1971, MS in Chem. Engring., 1972. Registered profl. engr., W.Va. Summer engr. Exxon, Baytown, Tex., 1971; devel. engr. Dow Badische, Anderson, S.C., 1972-76; process devel. engr. Borg Warner, Parkersburg, W.Va., 1976-88, GE Plastics, Parkersburg, 1988—. Contbr. articles to profl. jours. Pres. Bethel Place Homeowners Assn., Washington, W.Va., 1984. Mem. AIChE, Elfuns. Republican. Baptist. Home: 51 Bethel Pl Washington WV 26181 Office: General Electric Plastics PO Box 68 Washington WV 26181

PACE, WAYNE H., communications executive. V.p. fin., CFO Turner Broadcasting Sys., Atlanta. Office: Turner Broadcasting Sys 1 CNN Ctr Box 105366 Atlanta GA 30348-5366

PACHECO, FELIPE RAMON, lawyer; b. Sagua la Grande, Las Villas, Cuba, Aug. 12, 1924; came to U.S., 1962; s. Felipe and Eugenia America (Rodriguez) P.; m. Maria Infiesta, Apr. 5, 1945; children: Carmen Pacheco Weber, Lilian C. Porter. D in philosophy and art, U. Havana, Cuba, 1947, D of laws, 1953; MS, Syracuse U., 1967; JD, U. Fla., 1975. Bar: Fla. 1975, U.S. Dist. Ct. (mid. dist.) Fla. 1976. Dir. librs. Ctrl. U. Las Villas, Santa Clara, Cuba, 1953-61; asst., assoc. catalog libr. Cornell U., Ithaca, N.Y., 1962-68, asst. law libr., 1969-70; law libr. Carlton, Fields, Tampa, Fla., 1971-75; pvt. practice Tampa, 1976—. Roman Catholic. Office: 4509 N Armenia Ave Tampa FL 33603-2703

PACHECO, MARGARET MARY, marketing executive; b. Waterville, Maine, June 9, 1962; d. Louis E. and Jeannine F. (Guguere) DeRosby; m. Joseph Pacheco III, Sept. 1, 1989; 1 child, Kathryn Reagan. BJ, U. Mo., 1984. Staff writer, photographer Gannett Newspapers Corp., Waterville, 1976-79; asst. news dir. Kennebec Broadcasting Co., Waterville, 1979-80; staff writer McClatchy Newspapers Corp., Sacramento, Calif., 1982-84; mktg. dir. Leatherby Mktg. Inc., Sacramento, 1984-85; sr. market rsch. analyst Electronic Data Systems, Dallas, 1985-90; dir. mktg. Power Computing Co., Dallas, 1990-93; pres. Daniel Group, Dallas, 1993-94, dir. corp. mktg. and comm., 1994—. Jacob Stein Meml. scholar U. Mo., 1984. Mem. Internat. Assn. Bus. Communicators, Soc. Competitive Intelligence Profls., Am. Mktg. Assn. Office: 14180 Dallas Pky Ste 600 Dallas TX 75240-4341

PACIOCCO, THOMAS, middle school educator; b. Alexandria, Va., May 15, 1954; s. Thomas and Merle (Dotson) P.; m. Mary Fredericks, Jan. 22, 1981; 1 child, Andrew Thomas. BA in Theatre Arts/Sociology, U. Richmond, 1976; MEd in Curriculum and Instrn., Lynchburg Coll., 1994. Project mgr. Accurate Inventory and Calculation Svc., Virginia Beach, Va., 1984-94; tchr. Amherst (Va.) County Pub. Schs., 1994—. Bd. dirs. Appomattox (Va.) Arts Coun., 1994—; mem. adv. bd. Lifenet Transplant Svcs., Richmond, Va., 1991—. Mem. ASCD. Democrat. Home: Rt 4 Box 462 Appomattox VA 24522 Office: Amherst Mid Sch PO Box 450 Amherst VA 24521

PACK, NANCY CLARA, librarian; b. Lonoke, Ark., Oct. 23, 1955; d. Robert Harvey and Beulah Catherine (Tedford) P.; m. Donald Dale Foos, Aug. 8, 1987. BS in Edn., U. Ark., 1978, MEd, 1984; MSLS, U. Tenn., 1981; PhD, Fla. State U., 1990. Cert. tchr., Fla., Ark. Kindergarten tchr. Lonoke County Sch. Sys., 1977-80; dir. William F. Laman Libr., North Little Rock, Ark., 1981-87; rsch. asst. Fla. State U., Tallahassee, 1987-90; cons. Fla. Bur. Libr. Svcs. for Blind and Physically Handicapped, Daytona Beach, 1989-92, S.W. Ga. Regional Libr., Bainbridge, 1992-93; asst. dir. pub. svc. Chattanooga-Hamilton County Bicentennial Libr., 1993—; lectr. libr. and info. sci. U. Ark., Little Rock, 1983-87; cons. on aging. Ctr. Libr. and Info. Sci. Edn. and Rsch., Little Rock, 1985-87. Co-editor, co-compiler: How Libraries Must Comply with the Americans With Disabilities Act, 1992; contbr. articles to profl. publs., chpt. to book; collection of materials on railroading included at Union Pacific Found., 1984-87. Alt. del. State of Fla. Gov.'s Conf. on Librs. and Info. Svcs., Tallahassee, 1990. Grantee Ark. Endowment for Humanities, 1983. Mem. ALA (life, mem. adv. com. White House conf. on libr. and info. svcs. for older adults 1994-95), Tenn. Libr. Assn., So. Conf. Librarians Serving Blind and Physically Handicapped, Clown Alley of Tallahassee (sec. exec. bd. 1988-89), Chattanooga Area Libr. Assn. (pres. 1995—). Methodist. Home: 211 N St Marks Ave Chattanooga TN 37411-3923 Office: Chattanooga-Hamilton County Bicentennial Libr 1001 Broad St Chattanooga TN 37402-2620

PACKARD, MILDRED RUTH, middle school educator; b. Boulder, Colo., Sept. 8, 1947; d. Peter L.M. and Jane G. Packard. BA, Lynchburg Coll., 1969; MS, Va. Poly. Inst. and State U., 1973. Cert. phys. edn. tchr., Va. Tchr., basketball, gymnastics and track coach Osbourn High Sch., Manassas, Va., 1969-73; tchr., coach girls softball, basketball and volleyball Rippon Mid. Sch., Woodbridge, Va., 1973-89, athletic dir., 1982-89; tchr., athletic dir., volleyball coach Lake Ridge Mid. Sch., Woodbridge, 1989—. Mem. NEA, AAHPERD, Va. Edn. Assn., Prince William Edn. Assn., Va. Assn. Health, Phys. Edn., and Recreation. Office: Lake Ridge Mid Sch 12350 Mohican Rd Woodbridge VA 22192-1757

PACKER, MARK NEIL, philosophy educator; b. N.Y.C., July 11, 1953. BA, SUNY, Brockport, 1975; MA, Northwestern U., 1977, PhD, 1979. Asst. prof. Vanderbilt U., Nashville, 1980-81, Dartmouth Coll., Hanover, N.H., 1981-84, Washington and Lee U., Lexington, Va., 1985-86; assoc. prof. philosophy Wofford Coll., Spartanburg, S.C., 1986—. Contbr. articles to profl. jours. Recipient Sears teaching award Sears-Roebuck and Wofford Coll., 1991. Jewish. Home: 185 Lakewood Dr Spartanburg SC 29302-4026 Office: Wofford Coll N Church St Spartanburg SC 29303

PACKERT, G. BETH, lawyer; b. Corpus Christi, Tex., Sept. 25, 1953; d. Gilbert Norris and Virginia Elizabeth (Pearce) P.; m. James Michael Hall, Jan. 1, 1974 (div. 1985); m. Richard Christopher Burke, July 18, 1987; children: Christopher Geoffrey Makepeace Burke Packert, Jeremy Eliot Marvell Packert Burke. BA, La. Tech. U., 1973; MA, U. Ark., 1976; postgrad., U. Ill., 1975-81, JD, 1985. Bar: Ill. 1985, U.S. Dist. Ct. (no. dist.) Ill. 1985, U.S. Ct. Appeals (7th cir.) 1987, Va. 1988, U.S. Dist. Ct. (we. dist.) Va. 1989. Assoc. Jenner & Block, Chgo., 1985-88; law clk. U.S. Dist. Ct. Va. (we. dist.), Danville, 1988-89; asst. commonwealth atty. Commonwealth of Va., Lynchburg, Va., 1989-95; pvt. practice Lynchburg, 1995—. Notes and comments editor U. Ill. Law Rev., 1984-85. Mem. ABA, Phi Beta Kappa. Home: 3900 Faculty Dr Lynchburg VA 24501-3110 Office: 725 Church St Ste 15B PO Box 529 Lynchburg VA 24505

PADGETT, DOUGLAS RALPH XAVIER, lawyer; b. Chgo., Mar. 19, 1942; s. Ralph Emerson and Agnes Mary (Loeb) P.; m. Rosemary Margaret Rowan, Sept. 8, 1970; children: Giselle Marie Elena, Claire Elise Marcella. BA, Fla. State U., 1967, JD, 1973. Bar: Fla. 1973, U.S. Dist. Ct. (so. dist.) Fla. 1973, Ga. 1977, U.S. Dist. Ct. (no. dist.) Ga. 1977. Asst. dist. atty. City of Tallahassee, Fla., 1973; assoc. Adams, George & Wood, Miami, Fla., 1973-74, Papy, Levy, Carruthers, Miami, 1974-75, Cobb & Blandford, Atlanta, 1977-80; sole practice Miami, 1975-77; pvt. practice Atlanta, 1980—; magistrate judge Dekalb County, Decatur, Ga., 1982-85. Coach local soccer and rugby orgns., Dekalb County, 1982-86; candidate for Justice of Peace, Dekalb County, 1980; candidate for Gen. Assembly, Dekalb County, 1988. With USN, 1960-66, PTO. Mem. Assn. Trial Lawyers Am., Fla. Bar Assn., Ga. Bar Assn., Ga. Trial Lawyers Assn., Dekalb Bar Assn., Masons. Democrat. Office: 3510 Clairmont Rd NE Atlanta GA 30319-3626

PADGETT, W. LEE, critical care nurse; b. Erwin, Tenn., Sept. 26, 1935; d. Richard Gilbert and Lillian Gertrude (Greenlee) Edwards; m. Glynn G. Padgett, Aug. 21, 1953; 1 child, Timothy. Diploma, Meml. Hosp. Sch. Nursing, Johnson City, Tenn., 1953; BSN magna cum laude, East Tenn. State U., 1973; postgrad., U. Tenn. Nursing supr., 1953-56, clin. nursing cons., 1956-74, asst. head nurse respiratory ICU, 1974-82, critical care nurse, 1982-90; ret. VA Med. Ctr., Bay Pines, Fla., 1990; free lance writer and ind. bus. owner. Mem. ANA, Am. Ca. Soc., Arthritis Health Profl. Assn., Assn. Women Bus. Owners, Fla. Assn. Realtors, Nat. Assn. Realtors, Sigma Theta Tau (Alpha Xi chpt.).

PADILLA, DON DIEGO, II, finance consultant; b. Paterson, N.J., Apr. 26, 1961; s. Diego and Laurinda M. (Teixeira) P.; m. Shari Josie Freeman, Apr. 10, 1984; children: Brooke, Amber, Brittany. Lic. real estate broker, N.J.; lic. insurance broker, Fla.; lic. securities agent NASD. Dir. sales & mktg. Nat. Am. Cos., Cautier, Miss., 1982-89; pres. Emerald Coast Cons., Valparaiso, Fla., 1989—. Chmn. One Nation Under God, Ft. Worth Beach, Fla., 1991-92; v.p. P.A.S.A., Ft. Worth Beach, 1992—. Mem. Nat. Assn. Realtors, Regional Leaders Corp., Pres. Club. Home: 7162 Siesta Rd Gulf Breeze FL 32566-8653 Office: Emerald Coast Cons PO Box 593 Mary Esther FL 32569-0593

PADRÓ, FERNANDO FRANCISCO, dean of students, history educator; b. San Juan, P.R., Mar. 9, 1957; s. Fernando Agustin and Helen Marie (Krabbe) P. BA, U. Ariz., 1977, MEd, 1981, PhD in History, Edn., 1988. Cert. Comty Coll. tchr. in History, Ariz., K-12 substitute tchr., Ariz. Instr. Resource Effectiveness Tng., Nogalez, Ariz., 1991-9; adj. faculty Prescott Coll., Tucson, Nogales, 1992; staff coord., mem. Crissman & Assocs., Houston, 1992—; dir. edn. programs Esmor Houston STISF, Houston, 1993-94; edn. mgr. NACE Internat., Houston, 1993-94; adjunct faculty Houston Comty Coll., 1994-95, N.E. Ariz. U., Flagstaff, Tucson, 1996—, Vt. Coll. of Norwich U., Burlington, Tucson, Vt., Ariz., 1996—; dean of students, adj. faculty Ariz. State Schs. for the Deaf and the Blind, Tucson, 1995—; chief adminstrv. officer, bd. dirs. USCI Adv. Group, Tucson, 1987-93; presenter Lee Hecht Harrison, Houston, Tucson, 1993—; 1st vice chair, bd. dirs. Tucson Residence Found., 1996—. Author: (in-svc. manuals) Esmore STISF Notes, 1993-94, ASDB Residence Notes, 1995-96; also articles. Co-chair candidate info. network, Pima County Rep. Party, Tucson, 1989-91, County chair cand. com. Tucson, 1991; interim chmn. Ariz. Hispanic Republican Assn., Pima County, Tucson, 1991-92; cons. Internat. Christian Inst., Houston, 1993-95. Office: Ariz State Schs for the Deaf & Blind PO Box 85000 Tucson AZ 85754

PAGANO, FILIPPO FRANK, financial broker, commercial loan consultant; b. East Paterson, N.J., Feb. 4, 1939; s. Frank and Katherine (Tavano) P.; m. Rose Ann Melisi, June 10, 1960 (div. Dec. 1972); children: Paul, Cynthia Pagano Grube, Stefanie; m. Darlene Ann Coryea, Mar. 1987. BS in Pharmacy, Rutgers U., 1960. Registered pharmacist, profl. ski instr.; lic. capt. master USCG. System analyst Parke-Davis & Co., Detroit, 1964-72; sr. mktg. analyst internat. Schering-Plough Pharm. Co., Kenilworth, N.J., 1972-73; v.p. Robert S. First, N.Y.C., 1973-74; pres. M-P Consultations Inc., N.Y.C., 1974-75; chief exec. officer Nordic Inn, Landgrove, Vt., 1975-83; sea capt. Bahamas, 1983-85; food and beverage dir. Meredith Guest House, Durham, 1985-86, gen. mgr., 1986-88; pres. Flagship Yachts, Durham, N.C., 1988—; gen. mgr. Inter-Global Capital, Raleigh, N.C., 1989—. Co-author: Nordic Inn Book of Soups, 1979; contbr. articles on skiing to newspapers and mags. Mem. Vt. Ski Touring Operators Assn. (pres. 1979-81), Beaufort Off-Shore Sailing Soc., Boss Club (Beaufort), Kappa Psi. Republican. Roman Catholic. Home and Office: 405 Hardscrabble Dr Hillsborough NC 27278-9766

PAGANO, JOSEPH STEPHEN, physician, researcher, educator; b. Rochester, N.Y., Dec. 29, 1931; s. Angelo Pagano and Marian (Vinci) Signorino; m. Anna Louise Reynolds, June 8, 1957; children: Stephen Reynolds, Christopher Joseph. A.B. with honors, U. Rochester, 1953; M.D., Yale U., 1957. Resident Peter Bent Brigham Hosp. Harvard U., Boston, 1960-61; fellow Karolinska Inst., Stockholm, 1961-62; mem. Wistar Inst., Phila., 1962-65; asst. prof., then assoc. prof. U. N.C., Chapel Hill, 1965-73, prof. medicine, 1974—, dir. div. infectious diseases, 1972-75; dir. U. N.C. Lineberger Comprehensive Cancer Ctr., Chapel Hill, 1974—; attending physician N.C. Meml. Hosp., Chapel Hill; vis. prof. Swiss Inst. Cancer Rsch., Lausanne, 1970-71, Lineberger prof. cancer rsch., 1986—; mem. virology study sect. NIH, Bethesda, Md., 1973-79; cons. Burroughs Wellcome Co., Research Triangle Park, N.C., 1978-95; mem. recombinant DNA adv. com. USPHS, 1986-90; mem. chancellor's adv. com. U. N.C., 1985-91, chair 1990-91; bd. dirs. Burroughs Wellcome Fund, 1993—; mem. adv. com. N.C. Cancer Coord. and Control, 1993—; mem. N.C. planning commn. for N.C. Inst. Medicine to Organize research! America, 1993; Mclaughlin vis. prof. U. Tex. Med. Br., 1996. Mem. editorial bd. Jour. Virology, 1974-90; bd. assoc. editors Cancer Rsch., 1976-80; assoc. editor Jour. Gen. Virology, 1979-84, Antimicrobial Agts. and Chemotherapy, 1984-93; contbr. numerous articles to profl. publs., chpts. to books. Bd. dirs. Am. Cancer Soc., N.C., 1980—; mem. Carolina Fedn. of Environtl. Programs, 1994-96. Recipient Sinsheimer award, 1966-68, USPHS Research Career award NIH, 1968-73; named Harry F. Dowling lecturer, 1991. Mem. AAAS (Newcomb Anderson prize selection com. 1984-88), AACI (bd. dirs. 1992-95, v.p. 1995, pres. 1996—), Infectious Disease Soc. Am., Am. Soc. Microbiology, Am. Soc. Clin. Investigation, Am. Soc. Virology, Am. Assn. Physicians, Internat. Assn. for Rsch. in Epstein-Barr Virus and Assocs. Diseases (pres. 1991-94, 1st Gertrude and Werner Henle lectr. on viral oncology 1990), Chapel Hill Tennis Club (pres. 1980-82), Carolina Club, Baldhead Island Club. Episcopalian. Home: 114 Laurel Hill Rd Chapel Hill NC 27514-4323 Office: U NC Lineberger Comp Cancer Ctr Chapel Hill NC 27599-7295

PAGE, EARL MICHAEL, management specialist; b. Providence, Sept. 5, 1950; s. Earl Gee and Joan V. (Moran) P.; m. Marilyn Martin Wagner, Nov. 30, 1984; children: Michael Page, Keri Wagner, Michael Wagner. BA, Boston Coll., 1972; MEd., Northea. U., 1977; MBA, Fla. Atlantic U., 1986. Program coord. Mass. Gen. Hosp., Boston, 1972-76; unit dir. Chandler St. Ctr., Worcester, Mass., 1977-80; pres. Page Three, Inc., North Palm Beach, Fla., 1981-83, Palm Beach Mgmt. Cons., Pompano Beach, Fla., 1983—; mgr. tng. and devel. AAA East Fla., Miami, 1986-87; v.p. adminstrn. and human resources City Furniture, Waterbed City, 1987—; prof. Coll. Bus. and Pub. Adminstrn. Fla. Atlantic U., Boca Raton, Fla. Mem. ASTD, Soc. Human Resource Mgmt., Phi Kappa Phi. Republican. Roman Catholic. Home: 8 SE 7th Ave Deerfield Beach FL 33441-4021 Office: 251 International Pky Fort Lauderdale FL 33325-6218

PAGE, JACK RANDALL, lawyer; b. Waco, Tex., Aug. 1, 1956; s. Jack Bennett and Mary Elizabeth (Cobbs) P.; m. Shirley Jean Hull, Aug. 5, 1978; children: Anna Christine, Sara Elaine. BBA magna cum laude, Baylor U., 1977, JD, 1980. Bar: Tex. 1980, U.S. Tax Ct. 1985, U.S. Dist. Ct. (we. dist.) Tex. 1987, U.S. Ct. Appeals (5th cir.) 1989; cert. in tax law Tex. Bd. Legal Specialization; CPA, Tex. Acct. Allie B. Gates Jr., CPA, Waco, 1975-78; assoc. Pakis, Giotes, Beard & Page, P.C., Waco, 1980-86, ptnr., 1986—. Chmn. exploring sales team Heart O' Tex. Coun. Boy Scouts Am., 1983, dist. chmn., 1984-85, v.p., 1986-88, coun. commr., 1989-91, coun. pres., 1991-94, asst. coun. commr., 1994—, v.p., 1995—; mem. adv. coun. dept. acctg. Baylor U., 1993—, faculty Philmont Tng. Ctr., 1991, summer youth program com., Waco-Mclennan County United Way, 1988; co-chair Scouting for Food, 1995—. Recipient Exploring Tng. award, Dist. Award of Merit Heart O' Tex. coun. Boy Scouts Am., 1985, Silver Beaver award 1993, Commrs. Key, 1994. Fellow Tex. Bar Found.; mem. ABA, AICPA, Tex. Bar Assn., Coll. of State Bar of Tex., Waco-McLennan County Bar Assn., Tex. Soc. CPAs, Waco Estate Planning Coun. (pres. 1983), Rotary, Order of Demolay (chevalier 1975). Roman Catholic. Office: Pakis Giotes Beard & Page PC 801 Washington Ave Ste 800 Waco TX 76701-1260

PAGE, OSCAR CLETICE, academic administrator; b. Bowling Green, Ky., Dec. 22, 1939; s. Elizabeth P.; m. Anna Laura Hood, June 12, 1965; children: Kristen, Matt. BA in Social Sci., Western Ky. U., 1962; MA in History, U. Ky., 1963, PhD in Early Modern European History, 1967. Instr. history Western Ky. U., Bowling Green, 1964; asst. prof., asst. chair history dept. U. Ga., Athens, 1967-71; dean Wesleyan Coll., Macon, Ga., 1971-78; v.p. acad. affairs Lander Coll., Greenwood, S.C., 1978-86, acting pres., 1985, provost, v.p. acad. affairs, 1986-88; pres. Austin Peay State U., Clarksville, Tenn., 1988-94, Austin Coll., Sherman, Tex., 1994—; mem. adv. com. Master of Mil. Art & Sci. Program, Leavenworth, Kans., 1994-96. Bd. dirs. United Way, Sherman, 1994—, Meml. Hosp., Clarksville, 1989-94, Nations Bank, Clarksville, 1988-94; mem. pres.'s commn. NCAA, 1990-94. Mem. Rotary, Sherman C. of C. Office: Austin Coll 900 N Grand Ave Sherman TX 75090-4440

PAGE, RICHARD LEIGHTON, cardiologist, medical educator, researcher; b. San Diego, Mar. 8, 1958; s. Ellis Batten and Elizabeth Latimer (Thaxton) P.; m. Jean Reynolds, Oct. 12, 1985; children: Franklin Reynolds, Gillian Grace, Edward Batten. BS in Zoology magna cum laude, Duke U., 1980, MD, 1984. Diplomate Nat. Bd. Med. Examiners, Am. Bd. Internal Medicine, subspecialties cardiovascular disease and clin. cardiac electrophysiology; lic. physician, Tex. Rsch. fellow in pharmacology Columbia Presbyn. Med. Ctr., 1982-83; intern dept. medicine Mass. Gen. Hosp., Boston, 1984-85, resident dept. medicine, 1985-87; cardiology fellow clin. electrophysiology Duke U. Med. Ctr., Durham, N.C., 1987-89, clin. cardiology fellow, 1989-90, lectr. medicine divsn. cardiology, 1989-90, assoc. in medicine, 1990, asst. prof., dir. sect. clin. electrophysiology lab., 1990-92; asst. prof. medicine U. Tex. Southwestern Med. Ctr., Dallas, 1992-95, assoc. prof., 1995—, dir. sect. clin. cardiac electrophysiology, 1992—; dir. sect. clin. electrophysiology U. Tex. Southwestern Med. Ctr., Dallas, 1992—; dir. clin. electrophysiology lab., arrhythmia and pacemaker vice, Parkland Meml. Hosp., Dallas, 1992—; dir. Stanley J. Sarnoff Endowment for Rsch. in Cardiovasc. Sci., Inc., Bethesda, Md., 1990-96, co-chmn., 1992. Mem. editl. bd. Cardiac Chronicle, 1993; author: (with others) Manual of Clinical

Problems in Cardiology, 5th edit., 1995; contbr. articles to profl. jours., chpt. to book. Sarnoff Endowment fellow, 1982, Sarnoff scholar, 1987. Fellow Stanley J. Sarnoff Soc., Am. Heart Assn., Am. Coll. Cardiology; mem. N.Am. Soc. Pacing and Electrophysiology, Tex. Med. Assn., Dallas County Med. Soc., North Tex. Electrophysiology Soc. (trustee), Sigma Xi, Alpha Omega Alpha. Episcopalian. Home: 1500 Ramsgate Cir Plano TX 75093-5044 Office: U Tex Southwestern Med Ctr 5323 Harry Hines Blvd Dallas TX 75235-9047

PAGE, WILLIS, conductor; b. Rochester, N.Y., Sept. 18, 1918. Grad. with distinction, Eastman Sch. Music, Rochester, 1939. Mem. Rochester Philharm., 1937-40, Rochester Civic, 1939-40; prof. conducting Eastman Sch. Music, 1967-69; prof. conducting, dir. orchestral activities Drake U., Des Moines, 1969-71; guest condr. Sony concerts, Chiba, Japan, 1992. Mem. Boston Symphony Orch., 1940-55; prin. bass Boston Pops, 1947-55; condr. Cecilia Soc. Boston, 1952-54, New Orchestral Soc. Boston; assoc. condr. Buffalo Philharm., 1955-59; music dir./condr. Nashville Symphony Orch., 1959-67; music dir. Linwood Music Sch., 1955-59; 1st condr. Yomiuri Nippon Symphony, Tokyo, 1962-63; condr. Des Moines Symphony, 1969-71, Jacksonville (Fla.) Symphony Orch., 1971-83; founder, condr. St. John's River City Band, 1985-86; guest condr. Boston Pops, Toronto, Rochester Civic, Eastman-Rochester, Denver, Muncie, Jerusalem, St. Louis, Colorado Springs, Memphis, Hartford orchs., Yomiuri Nippon Symphony, 1988; founding condr., exec. dir. First Coast Pops Orch., 1989; condr. all-state orchs. of N.Y., Iowa, Ky., Tenn., Fla., also regional festivals; condr. 13 L.P. recordings including Symphony of the Air (Roger Williams soloist), Boston Festival Orch., Cook Labs., Nashville Symphony. Sgt. 95th inf. divsn. U.S. Army, 1943-45. Decorated Bronze Star; recipient Ford Found. European travel award, 1967.

PAIGE, VIVIAN JO-ANN, accountant; b. Memphis, May 7, 1960; d. Charles Thomas and Mary Elizabeth (Manning) P. BS, Old Dominion U., 1981, MBA, 1994. CPA. With IRS, Norfolk, Va., 1980-85; pres. Individual Returns Svcs. Inc., Norfolk, 1991-95; prin. Vivian J. Paige, CPA, P.C., 1986—. Bd. dirs. St. Columba Ecumenical Ministries, Inc., 1989-93, v.p. bd. dirs., 1990-91, pres. bd. dirs., 1992-93. Served with USAR, 1979-81. Mem. AICPA, NAGE, AAUW, Nat. Fedn. Ind. Bus., Nat. Fedn. Ind. Bus., Va. Soc. CPAs. Office: Ste 203 5750 Chesapeake Blvd Norfolk VA 23513-5325

PAINE, JAMES CARRIGER, federal judge; b. Valdosta, Ga., May 20, 1924; s. Leon Alexander and Josie Carriger (Jones) P.; m. Ruth Ellen Bailey, Sept. 8, 1950; children: James Carriger, Jonathan Jones, JoEllen. B.S., Columbia U., 1947; LL.B., U. Va., 1950, J.D., 1970. Bar: Fla. 1950. Mem. firm Earnest, Lewis, Smith & Jones, West Palm Beach, Fla., 1950-54, Jones Adams Paine & Foster, 1954-60, Jones Paine & Foster, 1960-79; judge U.S. Dist. Ct. (so. dist.) Fla., West Palm Beach, 1979—. Bd. dirs., pres. Children's Home Soc. Fla., 1978-80; mem. bd. Episcopal Diocese S.E. Fla. Served to lt. USNR, 1943-47. Mem. Greater West Palm Beach C. of C. (pres. 1973-74), Palm Beach County Bar Assn. Democrat. Office: US Dist Ct 701 Clematis St West Palm Beach FL 33401-5101

PAINTER, THEOPHILUS SHICKEL, JR., physician; b. Austin, Tex., Apr. 29, 1924; s. Theophilus Shickel and Anna Mary (Thomas) P.; m. Dorothy Bulkley, July 11, 1957; children: Dana Parkey, Amy Hur, Theophilus III. BA, U. Tex., 1944, MD, 1947. Diplomate Am. Bd. Internal Medicine, Am. Bd. Allergy and Immunology. Rotating intern Univ. Hosp., U. Mich., Ann Arbor, 1947-48, resident in internal medicine, 1948-51, fellow, jr. clin. instr., 1956-58; pvt. practice Austin, Tex., 1958-65; physician Allergy Assocs., Austin, 1965-87, Allergy Assocs. of Austin Diagnostic Clinic, Austin, 1987—. Capt. USAF, 1951-53. Fellow ACP, Am. Coll. Allergy and Immunology, Am. Acad. Allergy and Immunology. Home: 2408 Mccall Rd Austin TX 78703-3026 Office: Allergy Assocs Austin Diagnostic Clinic 1510 W 34th St Austin TX 78703-1433

PAJUNEN, GRAZYNA ANNA, electrical engineer, educator; b. Warsaw, Poland, Dec. 15, 1951; d. Romuald and Danuta (Trzaskowska) Pyffel; m. Veikko J. Pajunen (div. 1990); children: Tony, Thomas, Sebastian. MSc, Warsaw Tech. U., 1975; PhD in Elec. Engring., Helsinki (Finland) U., 1984. Grad. engr. Oy Stromberg Ab, Helsinki, 1974; design engr. Oy Stromberg Ab, 1975-79; teaching/rsch. asst. Helsinki U. Tech., 1979-85; vis. asst. prof. dept. elec. and computer engring. Fla. Atlantic U., 1985-86, asst. prof. elec. and computer engring., 1986-90, assoc. prof. elec. engring., 1990—; vis. asst. prof. dept elec. engring. UCLA, 1988-89; cons. in field; lectr. in field. Author: Adaptive Systems - Identification and Control, 1986; contbr. articles to profl. jours. Grantee Found. Tech. in Finland, Ahlstrom Found., 1982, Wihuri Found., 1982, Found. Tech. in Finland, 1983, Acad. Finland, 1984, EIES Seed grantee, 1986, Finnish Ministry Edn., 1985, NSF, 1988-89, 93-94, State of Fla. High Tech. and Industry Coun., 1989. Mem. IEEE, Control Sys. Soc., N.Y. Acad. Sci., AAUW, SIAM, Control and Sys. Theory Group. Roman Catholic. Office: Florida Atlantic Univ Dept Elec Engring Boca Raton FL 33431

PAKES, STEVEN P., medical school administrator; b. St. Louis, Jan. 19, 1934; married; 4 children. BSc, Ohio State U., 1956, DVM, 1960, MSc, 1964, PhD in Vet. Pathology, 1972. Vet. pathologist U.S. Army, Ft. Detrick, Md., 1960-62; chief animal colonies Pine Bluff Arsenal, Ark., 1964-66; chief comparative pathology Naval Aerospace Med. Inst., 1966-69; dir. lab. animal medicine Coll. Vet. Medicine Ohio State U., 1969-72; assoc. prof. Southwestern Med. Sch. U. Tex. Southwestern Med. Ctr., Dallas, 1972-80, prof. comparative medicine, chmn. dept. Southwestern Med. Sch., 1980—; mem. exec. com. Inst. Lab. Animal Resources NAS-NRC; chmn. coun. accreditation Am. Assn. Accreditation Animal Care, 1974-76, treas., bd. trustees, 1983-90; adv. bd. Vet. Specialties, 1981-82, chmn., 1985; chmn. lab. guide rev. com. Inst. Lab. Animal Resources NAS, 1983-85; mem. Inst. Lab. Animal Resources Coun., 1985-93, chmn., 1987-93. Mem. AAAS, Internat. Coun. for Lab. Animal Scis. (sec.-gen. 1995—), Am. Assn. Lab. Animal Sci. (bd. trustees 1985-88), Am. Coll. Lab. Animal Medicine (pres. 1973, exam. com. 1968-69), Am. Vet. Medicine Assn., Am. Soc. Microbiology, Sigma Xi. Office: U Tex Southwestern Med Sch Dept Pathology 5323 Harry Hines Blvd Dallas TX 75235-7200

PALACIOS, CONNY, Spanish language educator, literary critic; b. Matagalpa, Nicaragua, Dec. 8, 1953; d. Abel Flores and Miriam Rayo; m. Edgar Palacios, May 1, 1971; children: Naraya, Edgar Joseé, Isaac.; Student, U. Nacional Autonoma Nicaragua, 1975-81; BA, St. Thomas U., Miami, Fla., 1984; PhD, U. Miami, 1995. Prof. Spanish Inst. Nacional Eliseo Picado, Matagalpa, Nicaragua, 1975-81, Colegio San Jose, Matagalpa, 1975-81; instr. of Spanish Barry U., Miami, Fla., 1990; tchg. asst. in Spanish U. Miami, Coral Gables, Fla., 1988-90. Inventor: En Carne Viva, 1994. Mem. Inst. Cultural Rubén Darío, Am. Assn. Tchrs. of Spanish and Portugese, Inc. Home: 1055 NE 135th St Miami FL 33161

PALACIOS, RONALD, immunologist; b. Sucre, Bolivia, Jan. 11, 1953; came to U.S., 1992; s. Enrique and Leddy (Castrillo) P.; m. Patricia Ibarra, June 4, 1977; children: Catherine, Patricia. B Humanities, Colegio Sagrado Corazon, Sucre, 1970; MD with distinction, U. Nat. Autonoma de Mex., Mexico City, 1976, degree in internal medicine splty., 1979. Cert. Mexican Bd. Internal Medicine. Instr. histology U. Nat. Mexico, Mexico City, 1973, asst. prof. introduction to medicine; fellow immunology Inst. Nat. Nutrition, Mexico City, 1979-80; mem. Basel (Switzerland) Inst. Immunology, 1982-92; prof., dep. chmn. dept. immunology U. Tex. M.D. Anderson Cancer Ctr., Houston, 1992—. Contbr. articles to profl. jours., chpts. to books. Fellow Swedish Inst., Stockholm, 1980-82, WHO, 1980-81. Fellow Mexican Bd. Internal Medicine; mem. AAAS, Am. Assn. Hematology, Assn. Medicos Internistas Mexico, Assn. Medicos Instituto Nat. Nutrition, Am. Assn. Immunology, Am. Assn. Microbiology, Scandinavian Soc. Immunology, U. Tex. M.D. Anderson Assocs., N.Y. Acad. Scis. Office: MD Anderson Cancer Ctr U Tex Dept Immunology 1515 Holcombe Blvd Houston TX 77030-4009

PALERMO, JUDY HANCOCK, elementary school educator; b. Longview, Tex., Sept. 7, 1938; d. Joseph Curtis and Bennie Lee (Deason) Hancock; m. Donald Charles Palermo, Apr. 1, 1961; 1 child, Donald Charles Jr. (dec.). BS in Secondary Edn., 1960. Cert. secondary and elem. edn. tchr., Tex. Art tchr. Dallas Ind. Sch. Dist., 1960-62, 65-67; asst. dir. freshmen orientation program North Tex. State U., Denton, summer 1969, dormitory dir. Oak St. Hall, 1968-71, tchr. part-time, 1970-77; substitute tchr. Denton Ind. Sch. Dist., 1975-78, tchr. 5th grade, 1979-87, art tchr., 1987—; tchr. kindergarten Kiddie Korral Pre-Sch., Denton, 1978-79; trained gifted tchr. Woodrow Wilson Elem. Sch., Denton, 1980, grade level chmn., 1980; grade level chmn. Eva S. Hodge Elem. Sch., Denton, 1988-89, 92-93; mem. rsch. bd. advisors Am. Biog. Inst., 1991—. Active Denton Humane Soc., 1982—, Denton Educators Polit. Action Com., 1984-85; Eva S. Hodge historian PTA, 1992—. Mem. NEA, NAFE, Tex. State Tchrs. Assn., Denton Classroom Tchrs. Assn. (faculty rep. 1984-85), Denton Edn. Assn., Denton Area Art Edn. Assn. (program chmn. 1990-91), Greater Denton Arts Coun., Numismatic Assn. (sec. Greater Denton chpt.), Denton Sq. Athletic Club, Denton Greater Univ. Dames Club (treas. 1970), Bus. and Profl. Women's Assn. (treas. 1990-91, chair audit com. 1992-93, chmn. 1993—), Delta Kappa Gamma (treas. 1986-88, comms. com. 1994—). Democrat. Home: 1523 Pickwick Ln Denton TX 76201-1290

PALIK, ROBERT RICHARD, mechanical engineer; b. Iowa City, Iowa, Mar. 10, 1923; s. Frank and Maria (Pavco) P.; m. Wanita Slaughter, Dec. 19, 1945; children: Andrea Denise, Stephen Brett, Robert Neil. BSME, State U. Iowa, 1949, MSME, 1950. Registered profl. engr. Va. Lab. tech. State U. Iowa Physics Dept., Iowa City, 1941-42; chief engr. Keokuk (Iowa) Steel Casting Co., 1950-54; mgr. rsch. engring. Reynolds Aluminuim Co., Richmond, Va., 1954-70; v.p. Crown Aluminium Inds., Roxboro, N.C., 1970-75; div. chief City of Richmond, 1975-79; gen. engr. U.S. Dept. Housing and Urban Devel., Richmond, 1979-94. Pres. West Wistar Civic Assn., Richmond, 1957; legis. chmn., treas. PTA, Richmond, 1957. Lt. Col. USAF, 1942-45. Fellow ASME; mem. Pi Tau Sigma. Home and Office: 9318 Westmoor Dr Richmond VA 23229-6247

PALINCHAK, ROBERT STEPHEN, academic administrator; b. Coaldale, Pa., Dec. 25, 1942; s. Michael and Susan (Karas) P.; m. Patricia Secara, July 4, 1967. BS in Physics and Math., East Stroudsburg U., 1964; postgrad., Lehigh U., Pa. State U., Temple U., Villa Nova U., U. Notre Dame, 1964-67; MA in Adminstrn., Supervision & Orgn., Loyola Coll., Balt., 1967; PhD in Higher Edn. Adminstrn., Syracuse U., 1969. Tchr. math. William Tennent Jr.-Sr. H.S., Bucks County, Pa., 1964-65; tchr. physics Wissahickon Sr. H.S., Montgomery County, Pa., 1965-66; prof., chairperson dept. physics Essex C.C., Baltimore County, Md., 1966-76; dean acad. svcs. Gloucester County Coll., Deptford Twp., N.J., 1976-80; pres. Lake Sumter C.C., Leesburg, Fla., 1980-88; ind. cons. higher edn. various locations, 1989-91; exec. asst. to pres., campus dean Milw. Area Tech. Coll., 1991-94; v.p. acad. affairs State Tech. Inst. Memphis, 1994—; adj. prof. Loyola Coll., Balt., 1967, Towson (Md.) State U., 1966-68, Rutgers U., Burlington County, N.J., 1977-78; cons. Va. State U., Petersburg, 1990-91; past participant Wingspread Conf., Wis. Author: Evolution of the Community College, 1973; editor newsletter Am. Cancer Soc., Md., 1975; contbr. articles to profl. publs. Bd. dirs. Lake-Sumter Mental Health Ctr./Hosp.; consumer arbitrator Better Bus. Bur., N.J. Mem. Am. Assn. Cmty. Colls. (mem. pres. acad. 1982), Phi Delta Kappa. Byzantine Catholic. Office: State Tech Inst Memphis Macon Cove Memphis TN 38134

PALKER, THOMAS JOSEPH, biologist, researcher; b. Torrington, Conn., Jan. 29, 1951; m. Nancy Elsa Brander, Aug. 12, 1978. BA in Biology, U. Conn., 1973, PhD in Immunology/Tumor Biology, 1982. Vol. Peace Corps, Grenada, 1973-75; postdoctoral fellow Duke U., Durham, N.C., 1982-84, asst. med. rsch. prof. dept. medicine, 1984-89, assoc. med. rsch. prof., 1989-96; rsch. fellow Merck & Co., Inc., Wes Point, Pa., 1996—; co-dir. Nat. Coop. Vaccine Devel. Group for HIV Vaccines, Duke U., 1994—; chmn. cancer biology and immunology contract rev. com. Nat. Cancer Inst., NIH, 1993-95, chmn. ad hoc contracts tech. rev. group, 1992, cons. on retroviral animal models and retroviral infection, 1988—; mem. sci. adv. com. Am. Found. for AIDS Rsch., 1990—; co-dir. basic scis. VA Hosp. Core Facility for AIDS Rsch., Durham, 1987-97. Contbr. articles to profl. jours.; patentee in field; ad hoc reviewer numerous scientific jours.; mem. editorial bd.: AIDS Rsch. and Human Retroviruses, 1990-93. Boys soccer coach YMCA, Durham, 1993, girls soccer coach, 1992; participant CROP Walk, Durham, 1988-92. Scholar Leukemia Soc. Am., 1989-94, spl. fellow, 1985-87. Mem. Am. Soc. for Microbiology, AAAS, Phi Kappa Phi. Home: 4776 Twinbrook Cir Doylestown PA 18901 Office: Merck & Co Inc Virus & Cell Biology WP16-107 Sumneytown Pike West Point PA 19486

PALKOVICH, DAVID ALLAN, mathematics educator; b. East Chicago, Ind., Jan. 21, 1950; s. Daniel and Margaret (Perevuznik) P. BS in Math., IIT, 1972; MLIR, Mich. State U., 1973; MS in Applied Math., U. Okla., 1986. Instr. mgmt. and econs. Calumet Coll., Whiting, Ind., 1981-82; grad. teaching asst. U. Okla., Norman, 1983-86; Title III math. instr. Spokane (Wash.) C.C., 1987-90; prof. math. Okla. City C.C., 1990—; adj. prof. math. Joliet (Ill.) Jr. Coll., 1995—; adj. math. instr. Prairie State Coll., Chicago Heights, Ill., 1981-83; adj. instr. mgmt. Purdue U., Hammond, Ind., 1981; mem. industry adv. bd. Calumet Coll., 1982; mem. small bus. adv. bd. Spokane C.C., 1988. Author: Using Mathematics in Nursing, 1988. Citizen scientific amb. to China People to People, Spokane, 1988. Mem. Math. Assn. Am., Soc. for Indsl. and Applied Math., Ops. Rsch. Soc. Am., Am. Math. Assn. Two-Yr. Colls. Office: Oklahoma City CC 7777 S May Oklahoma City OK 73159

PALLAS, CHRISTOPHER WILLIAM, cardiologist; b. Chattanooga, Mar. 27, 1956; s. William Charles and Katherine (Rigas) P. Student, Vanderbilt U., 1974-75; BA in Biology, U. Tenn., 1978; MD, Wake Forest U., 1982. Diplomate Am. Bd. Internal Medicine, Am. Bd. Cardiology. Intern Med. Coll. Ga., Augusta, 1982-83, resident, 1983-85, chief med. resident, 1985-86, clin. fellow cardiology, 1986-88, instr. in cardiology, 1988-89, attending physician, 1988—, asst. prof. cardiology, 1989—, researcher clin. and basic cardiology, 1989—; cons. cardiovascular diseases VA Med. Ctr., Dublin, Ga., 1988-89, dir. coronary care unit, Augusta, 1988—. Contbr. articles to profl. jours. Fellow Am. Coll. Chest Physicians, Am. Coll. Cardiology; mem. AMA, Med. Assn. Ga., Richmond County Med. Soc. Greek Orthodox. Home: Ste 1601 # 1 Seventh St Augusta GA 30901 Office: Med Coll Ga Cardiology BA-A535 1120 15th St Augusta GA 30901-3157

PALLOT, JOSEPH WEDELES, lawyer; b. Coral Gables, Fla., Dec. 23, 1959; s. Richard Allen Pallot and Rosalind Brown (Wedeles) Spak; m. Linda Fried, Oct. 12, 1956; children: Richard Allen, Maxwell Ross. BS, Jacksonville U., 1981; JD cum laude, U. Miami, Coral Gables, Fla., 1986. Bar: Fla. 1986. Comml. lending officer S.E. Bank, N.A., Miami, 1981-83; ptnr. Steel Hector & Davis, Miami, 1986—. Bd. dirs. MOSAIC: Jewish Mus. of Fla., Miami Beach, 1993—; gov. Fla. Philharm. Orch., Coral Gables, 1994—; dir. Fla. Grand Opera, 1996—. Mem. Miami City Club. Office: Steel Hector & Davis LLP 200 S Biscayne Blvd Miami FL 33131

PALLOTTA, GAIL CASSADY, writer; b. Charlotte, N.C., Jan. 7, 1942; d. Henry Gibbs and Evelyn (Mathis) Cassady; m. Frederick Vance Pallotta, Apr. 8, 1972; 1 child, Laurie Elizabeth. AB in Eng. and profl. writing, Western Carolina U., 1964. Asst. editor WRC Smith Publ. Co., Atlanta, 1964-65; editorial asst. Life Ins. Co. of Ga., Atlanta, 1965-67; editor Linefill Colonial Pipeline CO., Atlanta, 1967-68; copywriter Philip Denton Adv., Atlanta, 1968-70; freelance writer Marietta, Ga., 1972—; writing workshops PTA Sedalia Park Sch., Marietta, 1985-90, radio workshops PTA E. Cobb Mid. Sch., Marietta, 1992; career day PTA Wheeler H.S., Marietta, 1992; puppet shows county and pvt. schs., Cobb County, 1990—; pub. resl. com., Marietta Marlins Swim Team, Marietta, 1993—. Author: Linda And The Got Ya' Guest, 1989; contbr. to The Power of One, 1976, Anthology of American Poetry, 1983, Best New Poets of 1988, 1989; contbr. articles to profl. jours. Vol., mem. PTA, Sedalia Park and East Cobb., 1985-92; Sunday sch. tchr. First Presby. Ch., Marietta, 1985-91; mem. Parents Assn. of the Westminster Schs., 1993—. Home and Office: 251 Hunting Creek Dr Marietta GA 30068-3419

PALMER, ALLISON LEE, art history educator; b. Washington, Nov. 24, 1963; d. Melvin Delmar and Nancy Lee (Baugh) P. BA in Art History, Mount Holyoke Coll., 1985; MA in Art History, Rutgers U., 1987, PhD in Art History, 1994. Lectr. summer program Rutgers U., N.J., 1988, Urbino, Italy, 1989; adj. prof. art history Kean Coll., N.J., 1989-91; rsch. asst. Inst. for Advanced Study, Princeton, N.J., 1992-93; asst. prof. art history U. Okla., 1993—; spkr. museums, schs., univs. Contbr. articles to The International Dictionary of Architects and Architecture, 1993. Office: U Okla Sch of Art 520 Parrington Oval 202 Norman OK 73019

PALMER, BRUCE HARRISON, college director; b. Hartford, Conn., Apr. 13, 1955; s. David Alan and Marilyn Elaine (Shelburne) P. BA, Gordon Coll., 1977; MA, Gordon-Conwell Sem., 1979; MEd, Harvard U., 1982. Mng. publs. editor, asst. to fin. aid dir. Gordon-Conwell Sem., South Hamilton, Mass., 1979-81; dir. student fin. aid Roberts Wesleyan Coll., Rochester, N.Y., 1982-86; v.p. staff Roberts Wesleyan Coll., Rochester, 1983-84; assoc. dir. student fin. aid, coord. Info. and Data Svcs., lectr., gen. faculty U. Va., Charlottesville, 1986-94; dir. fin. aid Ea. Coll., St. Davids, Pa., 1994-95, Franklin Pierce Coll., Rindge, N.H., 1995—. Contbr. articles to newspapers. Program devel. Cmty. Outreach Park Street Ch., Boston, 1981; student pastor Park Street Bapt. Ch., Framingham, Mass., 1982; mem. Ivy Creek Found., Charlottesville, 1988—; vol. John Heinz Nat. Wildlife Refuge, Phila., 1994. Mem. Nat. Assn. Student Pers. Adminstrs., Nat. Assn. Student Fin. Aid Adminstrs. (editor jour.), Va. Assn. Student Fin. Aid Adminstrs. (tng. com., instr., automated svcs.), Phi Delta Kappa. Democrat. Home: RR 2 Box 459 Temple NH 03084-9759 Office: Franklin Pierce Coll College Rd Rindge NH 03461

PALMER, CHRISTINE (CLELIA ROSE VENDITTI), operatic singer, performer, pianist, vocal instructor; b. Hartford, Conn., Apr. 2; d. John Marion and Immacolata (Morcaldo) Venditti; m. Raymond Smith, Oct. 5, 1949 (div. June 1950); m. Arthur James Whitlock, Feb. 25, 1953. Student Mt. Holyoke Coll., 1937-38, student New Eng. Conservatory of Music, 1941-42, pvt. studies in Boston, Hartford, N.Y.C., Florence and Naples, Italy; RN with honors, Hartford Hosp. Sch. Nursing, 1941. Leading operatic soprano N.Y.C. Opera, Chgo., San Francisco, San Carlo, other cities, 1944-62; presented concert N.Y. Town Hall, 1951; soloist with symphony orchs. maj. U.S. cities, 1948-62; soloist Marble Collegiate Ch., Holy Trinity Ch.; coast-to-coast concert tour, 1948; numerous appearances including St. Louis Mcpl. Opera, Indpls. Starlight Theatre, Lambertville Music Circus; soloist Holiday on Ice, 1949-50; rec. artist; TV performer including Home Show on NBC, Telephone Hour on NBC, Holiday Hotel; performer at various supper clubs, N.Y.C., Atlanta, Bermuda, Catskills, others including Number One Fifth Avenue, The Embers, The Carriage Club, Viennese Lantern; artist-in-residence El Centro Coll., Dallas, 1966-71; pvt. vocal instr.-coach, specializing in vocal technique for opera, mus. comedy, supper club acts, auditions, Dallas, 1962-94; voice adjudicator San Francisco Opera Co., 1969-72, Tex. Music Tchrs. Assn., 1964-75, others; appearances with S.M. Chartocks' Gilbert and Sullivan Co.; now performing lecture/entertainment circuit. Hon. mem. women's bd. Dallas Opera Assn.; mem. adv. bd. Tex. Opera News; mem. Tex. Music Tchrs. Cert. Bd., Collegiate Chorale, Don Craig Singers, The Vikings; mem. women's bd. Dallas Bapt. Univ. Oliver Ditson scholar, 1942; recipient Phi Xi Delta prize in Italian, 1937; named Victor Herbert Girl, ASCAP; Spl. Recognition Gold book of Dallas Soc. Mem. Nat. Assn. Tchrs. of Singing (pres. Dallas chpt. 1972-74), Nat. Fedn. Music Clubs, Tex. Fedn. Music Clubs, Dallas Fedn. Music Clubs (pres. 1972-74), Dallas Symphony League, Dallas Music Tchrs. Assn. (pres. 1971-72, Tchr. of Yr. 1974), Thesaurus (pres. 1990-91), Friday Forum (Dallas, bd. dirs.), Dallas Women's C. of C., Eagle Forum, Pub. Affairs Luncheon Club, Dallas Fedn. Music Club, Pro Am., Tex. Fedn. Music Club, Wednesday Morning Choral Club, Dallas Knife and Fork Club, Prestoncrest Rep. Club. Presbyterian. Home: 6232 Pemberton Dr Dallas TX 75230-4036

PALMER, CURTIS DWAYNE, cardiopulmonary practitioner, microbiologist, researcher, builder; b. Leesville, La., Aug. 5, 1947; s. Curtis and Freda Elaine (Franklin) P.; m. Martha DeBlieux; children: Derrick Mitchell, Elizabeth Merritt. BSc, Northwestern U., Natchitoches, La., 1971; MSC, Northwestern U., 1972; cardiopulmonary diploma, U. Chgo., 1975. Registered respiratory therapist. From dir. pulmonary rsch. to rsch. assoc. La. State U., Shreveport, 1972-75, 79-81; pres., chmn. Pulmonary Care Assocs., Shreveport, 1975-79; med. student St. Lucia U., El Paso, Tex., 1981-83; supr. pulmonary svcs. Glenwood Reg. Med. Ctr., West Monroe, La., 1987-93; v.p. DeBlieux-Palmer Ltd., Natchitoches, La., 1994—; contract adminstr. Therapeutic Svcs., Shreveport, 1986-90; regional mgr. TriTek Industries, Inc., 1987-93; pres., chmn. Dwayne Palmer Realty Inc., Shreveport, 1974-80; faculty Inst. Microbiology and Pulmonary Rsch., La. Sch. Medicine, Shreveport, Northwestern U. Contbr. articles to profl. jours. Bd. dirs. March of Dimes, Shreveport, 1977; realtor Bd. Realtors, Shreveport, 1975-82, Natchitoches, 1995—; contractor La. Bd. Licensing Contractors, Shreveport, 1976-80, Natchitoches, 1995—. Mem. Nat. Bd. Respiratory Care, Am. Assn. Respiratory Care, Nat. Assn. Home Builders, La. Soc. Respiratory Care (chmn. judiciary bd. 1976), Soc. Critical Care Medicine, Nat. Bd. Realtors, Shreveport-Bossier Bd. Realtors, Kappa Sigma (Epsilon chpt.). Republican. Methodist. Home: 608 David Cir Natchitoches LA 71457

PALMER, DAISY ANN, marketing professional; b. Burkburnett, Tex.; d. Leroy Evans and Christine Cleo (Givens) Walker; children: Christy Ann Yazdi, Cyndi Ann Thornhill. Cert. in Human Rels., Oreg. Coll. Edn., 1976; BA, cum laude in Liberal Studies, Edwards U., Tex., 1983; MBA, Calif. Coast U., 1989, PhD, 1993. Cert. interpreter for hearing impaired, Tex. and U.S. Mgr., R.R. Realty/Ins., Wichita Falls, Tex., 1973-75; cons. state agys., 1975-85; asst. coord. Travis County Services for Deaf, Austin, 1979-81; adminstr. Tex. Assn. Deaf, Austin, 1981-85; promotion dir. McGregor Studios, Austin, 1981-92; mktg. coord. Tex. Mcpl. League, Austin, 1985—; sr. field svcs. rep.; interpreter, legis. communicator VISTA, 1981-82; mem. bd. dirs. Internat. Hospitality Coun., 1995—, Am. Fedn. Elderly Deaf, 1996—. Editor: Tex. Assn. Deaf Directory of Services, 1984; rschr. and author of statis. studies; interpreter for first Japan-U.S. Conf., 1985. Chmn. Gov.'s Communication Barriers Council, 1984; vice chair Austin St. Sch. Adv. Council, 1984-86. Recipient Golden Hand award Nat. Assn. Deaf, Toastmasters Internat. Communication Leadership award, 1976. Mem. Nat. Registry Interpreters, Tex. Assn. Deaf (Golden Hand award for legis. activities 1983), Austin Bus. League, Pub. Risk Ins. Mgmt. Assn., Risk Ins. Mgmt. Soc. Home: 7301 Ferndale Cv Austin TX 78745-6526 Office: Tex Mcpl League 1821 Rutherford Ln 1st Fl Austin TX 78754

PALMER, DEBORAH KAY, university administrator, educator, consultant; b. Waco, Tex., Aug. 16, 1953; d. Alva Odell and Eugenia (Allen) Ayres; m. Eric Carlton, Dec. 31, 1976; children: Erica Renée, Tasha Nicole. BA, Southwest Tex. State U., 1975; MA, U. North Tex., 1978. Cert. elem. educator, Tex., secondary cert. in speech and English, Tex. Instr. U. North Tex., Denton, 1975-76, editor, 1976-79; editor Tex. Tech. Div. Continuing Edn., Lubbock, 1979-84, program coord., 1984-89, asst. dir., 1989-92; dir. adult and continuing edn. Angelo State U., San Angelo, Tex., 1992—; cons. Met. Transit Authority, Houston, 1987—, Internat. Writing Inst., Cleve., 1987-93. Co-Author: Tex. Tech Style Manual, 1989; editor: Tex. Family Law, 1991; editorial bd. mem. Am. Assn. Paralegal Educators, N.Y.C. 1990—. Mem. adv. bd. Junior League San Angelo, 1992-94, adv. coun. Lubbock Cultural Affairs Coun., 1985-89; homecoming chmn. U. North Tex., Denton, 1988; mem. elem. curriculum com. Ramirez Sch., Lubbock, 1991-92; membership chmn. Meth. Women, St. Luke's United Meth. Ch., 1985-86; bd. dirs. Tex. Assn. Community Svc. and Continuing Edn., 1993—; mem. San Angelo Symphony Guild, 1993—, San Angelo Jr. League, 1994—. Recipient svc. award St. Luke's United Meth. Women, 1987, Friend of Counseling award N.Mex. Sch. Counselors Assn., 1988, spl. projects 1st place award Internat. In-Plant Printing Mgmt. Assn., 1990. Mem. Am. Bus. Women's Assn., Nat. Univ. Continuing Edn. Assn. (regional chmn. 1990-91, Disting. Mentor award 1990, Exemplary Activities award 1990), Women in Comm. (exec. bd. S.W. region 1988-89, pres. Lubbock 1989-90, President's award for excellence 1988, Leading Change award 1989), Private Industry Coun., Lubbock C. of C. (edn. com. 1988-91), San Angelo C. of C. (edn. com. 1993—), Kappa Delta Pi, Alpha Chi. Office: Angelo State U Divsn Adult and Continuing Edn PO Box 11022 San Angelo TX 76909

PALMER, DORA DEEN POPE, English and French language educator; b. Jackson, Miss., June 26, 1946; d. Melvin Sr. and Gladys (Wolfe) Pope; m. Carey Palmer Jr.; 1 child, Cawandra V. AA, Utica Jr. Coll., 1966; BS in Edn., Jackson State U., 1968, MA in Edn., 1976. Cert. English and French tchr. Tchr. English and French McCullough H. S., Monticello, Miss., 1968-69, Topeka-Tilton H.S., Monticello, 1969-70, Crystal Springs (Miss.) H.S., 1971-93; tchr. French Jackson (Miss.) Pub. Sch. Dist., 1993—; chair English Dept., Crystal Springs, 1983-93; lectr. Jackson State Upward Bound,

Jackson, 1984—; chair Crystal Springs H.S. steering and editing com. So. Assn. Colls. and Schs.; prodr., sponsor black history projects. Drama coach N.W. Mid. Sch., Jackson, 1993—; sponsor Beta Club, Crystal Springs, 1979; sec. Expo-Social & Civic Club, Jackson, 1988—; pianist Mount Wade Missionary Bapt. Ch., 1965-80, Terry Mission Missionary Bapt. Ch., 1979-87. Named Tchr. of Month, Tiger Pause newspaper, 1989, Star Tchr. Jackson State Upward Bound, 1992, Tchr. of Yr. Crystal Springs H.S., 1993; recipient Tchr. Appreciation award The Tiger ann., 1987, Outstanding Svc. award Terry Mission Bapt. Ch., 1983. Mem. ASCD, Nat. Assn. Edn., Miss. Assn. Edn. Democrat. Home: 316 S Denver St Jackson MS 39209-6303 Office: Jackson Pub Schs N W Jackson 7020 Hwy 49 N Jackson MS 39213

PALMER, EDDIE ALLEN, elementary education educator; b. Lexington, Ky., Sept. 20, 1954; s. Arthur and Jessie (Allen) P.; 1 child, Chris M. Stewart. B of Gen. Studies, U. Ky., 1979, BA, 1981; M of Elem. Edn., U. South Fla., 1993. Cert. elem. edn., mid. sch. sci. Typesetter Robin Typesetting, Lexington, 1973-80, MER Advt., Lexington, 1981-82, Crumbley & Assocs., Atlanta, 1983-84; owner Palmer Typesetting, Atlanta, 1984-89; desktop pub. Arthur Andersen & Co., Tampa, Fla., 1989-90, Carter Printing, Tampa, 1990-93; tchr. 5th grade Lewis Elem. Sch., Temple Terrace, Fla., 1994—. Author: The History of Forest Grove Christian Church, 1969. 2d v.p. Ky. Young Dems., Frankfort, 1973-74. Mem. Internat. Reading Assn., Nat. Coun. Tchrs. of Math. Democrat. Office: Lewis Elem Sch 6700 Whiteway Dr Temple Terrace FL 33617

PALMER, HUBERT BERNARD, dentist, retired military officer; b. San Antonio, Sept. 6, 1912; s. Hubert Victor and Rosemary (Garvey) P.; student St. Mary's U., 1931-34; D.D.S., Baylor U., 1938; postgrad. George Washington U., 1946-47, U. Md., 1950-53; m. Elizabeth Harriet McAlary, Aug. 16, 1945; children—Hubert Bernard II, Robert Leldon. Commd. 1st lt. USAAF, 1938, advanced through grades to col. USAF, 1971; chief dept. dental research U.S. Army, 1946-50; chief dept. exptl. dentistry, USAF, 1953-54, chief research dentistry div. 1954-56; command dental surgeon, 1958-59, 63-65, 65-68; dental staff officer, 1959-62, dir. dental services, 1968-71; dir. Eastside Dental Clinic San Antonio Met. Health Dist., 1972-81; dir. Mirasol Dental Clinic, 1982-83; clin. asst. prof. U. Tex. Dental Sch., San Antonio, 1973-76. Decorated Legion of Merit, Commendation medal First Oak Leaf Cluster, Meritorious Service medal. Fellow AAAS; mem. Am. Dental Assn., Internat. Assn. Dental Research, Soc. Gen. Microbiology, Am. Soc. Microbiology, Omicron Kappa Upsilon. Contbr. articles to profl. jours. Research reduction decalcification tooth enamel. Home: 6115 Forest Timber St San Antonio TX 78240

PALMER, JAMES DANIEL, information technology educator; b. Washington, Mar. 8, 1930; s. Martin Lyle and Sarah Elizabeth (Hall) P.; m. Margret Kupka, June 21, 1952; children: Stephen Robert, Daniel Lee, John Keith. AA, Fullerton Jr. Coll., 1953; BS (Alumni scholar), U. Calif., Berkeley, 1955, MS, 1957; PhD, U. Okla., 1963; DPS (hon.), Regis Coll., Denver, 1977. Chief engr. Motor vehicle and Illumination Lab. U. Calif., Berkeley, 1955-57; assoc. prof. U. Okla., Norman, 1957-63; prof. U. Okla., 1963-66, asst. to dir. Rsch. Inst., 1960-63, cons. Rsch. Inst., 1966-69, dir. Sch. Elec. Engring., 1963-66, dir. Systems Rsch. Center, 1964-66; dean sci. and engring., prof. elec. engring. Union Coll., Schenectady, 1966-71; pres. Met. State Coll., Denver, 1971-78; rsch. and spl. programs adminstr. Dept. Transp., Washington, 1978-79; v.p., gen. mgr. rsch. and devel. div. Mech. Tech., Inc., Latham, N.Y., 1979-82; exec. v.p. J.J. Henry Co., Inc., Moorestown, N.J., 1982-85; BDM internat. prof. info. tech. George Mason U., Fairfax, Va., 1985—; bd. dirs. J.J. Henry Co., Inc.; cons. Sym Mgmt. Co., Boston, Higher Edn. Exec. Assocs., Denver, PERI, Princeton; adj. prof. U. Colo. Co-author: (with A.P. Sage) Software Systems Engineering, (with Aseltine, Beam and Sage) Introduction to Computer Systems, Analysis, Design and Application. Bd. dirs., exec. v.p. adv. com. U.S.A. Vols. for Internat. Tech. Assistance, 1967-83, exec. v.p., 1970-71, chmn. exec. com.; trustee, vice chmn. Nat. Commn. on Coop. Edn.; mem. exec. policy bd. Alaska Natural Gas Pipeline, 1978-79; trustee Auraria Higher Edn. Program, Denver; mem. Fulbright fellow Selection Com., Colo.; bd. mgrs., mem. exec. com. Hudson-Mohawk Assn. Colls. and Univs., trustee, chmn. bd., 1970-71; adv. com. USCG Acad., 1972-82, chmn. adv. com., 1979-82; mem. Colo. Gov.'s Sci. and Tech. Adv. Council; pres. Denver Cath. Community Services Bd.; mem. Archdiocesan Catholic Charities and Community Services; mem. bd. U. Okla. Rsch. Inst.; mem. adv. com. Mile-Hi Red Cross. With USMC, 1950-51. Case-Western Res. Centennial scholar, 1981; recipient U.S. Coast Guard award and medal for meritorious pub. service, 1983. Fellow IEEE (exec. and adminstrv. coms., v.p. long-range planning and finance, chmn. com. on large scale systems, Joseph E. Wahl Outstanding Career Achievement award 1993); mem. Systems, Man and Cybernetics Soc. (pres., Outstanding Contbns. award 1987), alumni assns. U. Calif. and U. Okla., Inst. Internat. Edn. (bd. dir. Rocky Mt. sect.), Soc. Naval Architects and Marine Engrs., Am. Soc. Engring. Edn., Am. Mil. Engrs., N.Y. Acad. Sci., Navy League, Sigma Xi, Eta Kappa Nu, Pi Mu Epsilon, Alpha Gamma Sigma. Home: 860 Cashew Way Fremont CA 94536 Office: George Mason U Sch of Info Tech & Engring Fairfax VA 22030

PALMER, J.D. KEITH, rehabilitative medicine physician; b. Wales, June 1933; s. David James and Catherine (Thomas) P.; m. Yvonne Enright, Dec. 6, 1958; children: Vanessa, Pandora, Mark. MB, BS, U. London, 1948, MD, 1956, D in Physical Medicine, 1958; MA, Brown U., 1970. Diplomate Am. Bd. Internal Medicine. Asst. prof. Tufts U., Boston, 1966-67; assoc. prof. Boston U., 1967-71, Brown U., 1971-77; prof. Ea. Va. Med. Sch., 1979-82, 82-91; attending physician brain injury rehab. Tufts/New Eng. Med. Ctr., Boston, 1993—. Fellow Royal Coll. Physicians, ACP; mem. New Eng. Soc. Phys. Medicine (pres. 1969-71), Am. Congress Rehab. Medicine, Assn. Acad. Physiatrists, Br. Assn. Physical Medicine & Rheumatology, Can. Assn. Physical Medicine & Rehab., Internat. Congress of Physical Medicine, Am. Assn. Electromyography & Electrodiagnosis.

PALMER, JOYCE ARLINE CORNETTE, English language educator; b. Columbia, Tenn., Sept. 4, 1941; d. James Edward and Arline (Roberts) Cornette; m. Leslie Howard Palmer, Aug. 27, 1965; children: David Leslie, Rachel Joyce. BA, David Lipscomb U., Nashville, 1963; MA, U. Tenn., 1964, PhD, 1967. Prof. English Tex. Woman's U., Denton, 1967—; guest lectr. Denton Pub. Schs. Co-author: Modern Humanities Rsch. Assn.'s Annual Bibliography, 1973-80, Southwestern American Literature: A Bibliography, 1979, Dictionary of Anonymous and Pseudonymous Publications in the English Language, 1980; contbr. book revs. to newspapers and periodicals; presenter in field. Treas. Newton Rayzor PTA, 1978-79; mem. vis. com. Abilene Christian U. English Dept., 1991-96; mem. Native Plants Soc. Wildflower Prairie Restoration Project, 1995-96; mem. spl. com. to select novel all 5th graders would read Denton Ind. Sch. Dist.; mem., sec. Rhetoric Com. Fedn. North Tex. Area Univs., Denton; mem. conf. Coll. Tchrs. of English. Mem. MLA, Nat. Coun. Tchrs. of English, South Ctrl. Soc. for 18th Century Studies (charter mem., sect. chair), Modern Humanities Rsch. Assn., Denton Celtic Soc., The Rhetoric Soc., Phi Kappa Phi, Phi Delta Gamma. Office: Tex Woman's U Dept English Speech and Fgn Langs Denton TX 76204

PALMER, LESLIE HOWARD, literature educator; b. Memphis, Jan. 25, 1941; s. Milton Howard and Janie Lee (Weaver) P.; m. Joyce Arline Cornette, Aug. 27, 1965; children: David Leslie, Rachel Joyce. BA, Memphis State U., 1962; MA, U. Tenn., 1963, PhD, 1966. Instr. U. Tenn., Knoxville, 1966-67; prof. English U. North Tex., Denton, 1967—; mem. athletic coun. U. North Tex., 1975-82, scholarship com., 1988-94; presenter poetry readings and guest lectrs. in field. Author: (poetry books) A Red Sox Flag, 1983, Ode to a Frozen Dog: and Other Poems, 1992, Artemis' Bow, 1993, The Devil Sells Ice Cream, 1994; asst. editor: Studies in the Novel, 1973-86; contbr. articles to profl. jours. Faculty sponsor Amnesty Internat., U. North Tex., 1984-86, North Tex. Chess Club, Denton, 1978-90; sch. vol. Denton Ind. Sch. Dist., 1977—. Recipient Beaudoin Gemstone award, Memphis, 1963, 64, Mid-South Free Verse award, Memphis, 1965, Outstanding Poet mention Pushcart Press, 1981. Mem. MLA, Modern Humanities Rsch. Assn., PEN, Denton C. of C. (cons.), Mensa, Phi Kappa Phi. Office: Univ North Tex Denton TX 76203

PALMER, MARIANNE ELEANOR, real estate broker, educator; b. Glen Ridge, N.J., Jan. 28, 1945; d. Charles Norman and Eleanor Ednetta (Adamus) Zimmermann; m. Jack Garner Palmer, Nov. 25, 1975. Student, Cornell U., 1965; BA, Jacksonville U., 1967; postgrad., U. Cin., 1970-71, U. North Fla., 1981; grad., Real Estate Inst., 1987. Lic. real estate broker, Fla.; cert. site agt.; GRI; cert. elem. tchr., Fla. Kindergarten tchr. Pickett & Dinsmore Elem. Sch., Jacksonville, Fla., 1965-68, Lake Forest Elem. Sch., Jacksonville, 1968-69; 1st grade tchr. North Avondale Elem. Sch., Cin., 1969-70, Hilltop Sch., Wyoming, Ohio, 1970-72; 1st and 4th grade tchr. Jacksonville Country Day Sch., 1972-76; substitute tchr. Duval County Pub. Schs., Jacksonville, 1976-80; sch. prin. Christ Episcopal Day Sch., Ponte Vedra Beach, Fla., 1980-84; substitute tchr. Duval and St. John's County Pub. Schs., Jacksonville, 1984-90; kindergarten tchr. Ponte Vedra-Palm Valley Elementary Sch., 1990—; broker-salesman Watson Realty Corp., Ponte Vedra Beach, 1984—. Mem. Nat. Assn. Realtors, Fla. Assn. Realtors, Ponte Vedra Beach Bd. Realtors, N.E. Fla. Builders Assn. (sales and mktg. coun.), Nat. Assn. Tchrs., Fla. Assn. Children Under 6, Fla. Kindergarten Coun., Real Estate Inst. (GRI), Ponte Vedra Club, Multi-Million Dollar Club and Exec. Com., Delta Delta Delta. Episcopalian. Home: 65 San Juan Dr Ponte Vedra Beach FL 32082-1319 Office: Watson Realty Corp 615 Us Highway A1A N Ponte Vedra Beach FL 32082-2747 also: Ponte Vedra Palm Valley Elem Sch 630 Hwy AIA Ponte Vedra Beach FL 32082

PALMER, ROBERT LESLIE, lawyer; b. Porterville, Calif., Apr. 10, 1957; s. Harrison Rowe and Margaret Elizabeth (Witty) P.; m. Huisuk Kim, Feb. 1, 1986; 1 child, Aaron Rowe. BA, Tulane U., 1979; JD, Georgetown U., 1982. Bar: D.C. 1982, U.S. Ct. Mil. Appeals 1985, Tex. 1987, Ala. 1987, U.S. Dist. Ct. (no. dist.) Ala. 1987, U.S. Ct. Appeals (11th cir.) 1987. Assoc. Lewis Martin Burnett & Dunkle, P.C., Birmingham, Ala., 1987-89, Lewis and Martin, Birmingham, Ala., 1989-90; assoc. Martin, Drummond and Woosley, Birmingham, 1990-91, bd. dirs., 1991-92; bd. dirs. Martin, Drummond, Woosley and Palmer, Birmingham, 1992-95; atty. Environ. Litig. Group, P.C., Birmingham, Ala., 1995—; bd. dirs. AmKor Internat., Inc. Ala. del. 6th Joint Conf. between Korea and S.E. U.S., Kyongju, Republic of Korea, 1991, 7th Joint Conf., Atlanta, 1992. Capt. JAGC, U.S. Army, 1983-87, USAR, 1987-91. Recipient commendation Republic of Korea Ministry of Justice, 1984. Mem. ATLA, Christian Legal Soc., Phi Beta Kappa, Omicron Delta Kappa. Republican. Baptist. Home: 1408 E Whirlaway Helena AL 35080-9689 Office: Environ Litig Group PC 3529 7th Ave S Birmingham AL 35222-3210

PALMER, RONALD, police chief; b. St. Joseph, Mo., Feb. 5, 1950. BS, Avila Coll., Kansas City, Mo.; MS, Cen. Mo. State U.; grad., FBI Nat. Acad. Various positions, most recent rank of maj. Kansas City, Mo. Police Dept., 1971-90; chief of police Portsmouth, Va. Police Dept., 1990-92, Tulsa Police Dept., 1992—; bd. dirs. Motorcycle Tng. & Safety Ctr. Bd. dirs. Salvation Army. Named one of Outstanding Young Men of Am., 1989; recipient Centurion Leadership award Kansas City C. of C., 1990. Mem. Internat. Assn. Chiefs of Police, FBI Nat. Acad. Assocs., Am. Soc. for Indsl. Security, Okla. Assn. Chiefs of Police, Police Exec. Rsch. Forum, Phi Kappa Phi. Office: Rm 303 600 Civic Ctr Tulsa OK 74103

PALMER, SHERRY REGINA LEE, human resource specialist; b. Boone, N.C., Jan. 28, 1969; d. Clarence and Iva Lee (Phillips) P. AA, Lees-McRae Coll., Banner Elk, N.C., 1989; BA, Appalachian State, Boone, 1991; MPA, Appalachian State, 1993. Human resource rep. Palmer Trucking, Boone, 1992-95; supr., human resource specialist IH Svcs., Inc., Linwood, N.C., 1995. Home: 7502 Hwy 194 N Boone NC 28607

PALMER, TEKLA FREDSALL, retired dietitian, consultant; b. Harwinton, Conn., Sept. 1, 1918; d. Frank Albert and Bertha Elena (Weingart) Fredsall; m. Charles Peter Palmer, Apr. 13, 1946; children: Peter F., Karen F. BS, Pratt Inst., 1945; MA, Columbia U., 1947; postgrad., NYU, 1964, Syracuse U., 1968, U. Rochester, 1976. Instr. nutrition Pratt Inst., Bklyn., 1945-48; cons. dietitian Grace Clinic, Bklyn., 1952-55; instr. Skidmore Coll. U. Hosp., N.Y.C., 1955-56; chief clin. dietitian Beth Israel Hosp., N.Y.C., 1966; lectr. Keuka (N.Y.) Coll., 1970-71, Rochester (N.Y.) Inst. Tech., 1975; lectr. nutrition Roberts Wesleyan Coll., Rochester, 1975-81; cons. Buffalo Regional Health Dept., 1967-75. Author: (lab. manual) Nutrition, Diet Therapy and Foods, 1954; com. chmn. The Long Island Diet Manual, 1st edit., 1966. Pratt Inst. scholar, Bklyn., 1943-44; Gen. Foods grantee, 1944-45. Mem. Am. Dietetic Assn. (registered), Va. Dietetic Assn., Richmond Dietetic Assn. (legis. chair 1989), Genesee Dietetic Assn. (pres. 1970-71), L.I. Dietetic Assn. (chair diet therapy 1965-66), Oxford Civic Assn., Nat. Parks and Conservation Assn. Methodist. Home: 8033 Ammonett Dr Richmond VA 23235-3201

PALMER-HASS, LISA MICHELLE, state official; b. Nashville, Sept. 4, 1953; d. Raymond Alonzo Palmer and Anne Michelle (Jones) Davies; m. Joseph Monroe Hass, Jr. BSBA, Belmont Coll., 1975; AA in Interior Design, Internat. Fine Arts Coll., 1977; postgrad., Tenn. State U., 1991—. Interior designer Lisa Palmer Interior Designs, Nashville, 1977-84; sec. to pres. Hermitage Elect. Supply Corp., Nashville, 1981-83; sec. to dir. Tenn. Dept. Mental Health and Mental Retardation, Nashville, 1984-86; transp. planner Tenn. Dept. Transp., Nashville, 1986—. Mem. Nat. Arbor Day Found. Recipient cert. of appreciation Tenn. Dept. Mental Health and Mental Retardation, 1986; named Hon. Mem. Tenn. Ho. of Reps., 1990. Mem. NAFE, Nat. Wildlife Fedn., Profl. Secs. Internat. (cert.), Nashville Striders Club, The Music City Bop Club, Music City Bop Club Dance and Exhibn. Team, Mensa. Republican. Mem. Disciples of Christ Ch. Office: Tenn Dept Transp Environ Planning Office 505 Deaderick St Ste 900 Nashville TN 37219-1402

PALMON, LINDA C. See CALHOUN, LINDA PALMON

PALMORE, CAROL M., state official; b. Owensboro, Ky., Jan. 13, 1949; d. P.J. and Carrie Alice (Leonard) Pate; m. John Stanley Palmore Jr., Jan. 1, 1982. BS in History and Polit. Sci., Murray State U., 1971; JD, U. Ky., 1977. Social worker Dept. Human Resources, Frankfort, Ky., 1971-74; assoc. atty. Rummage, Kamuf, Yewell & Pace, Owensboro, 1977-81; hearing officer Ky. Bd. Claims, Frankfort, 1980-81; gen. counsel Ky. Labor Cabinet, Frankfort, 1982-83, dep. sec. labor, 1984, 1986-87, sec. labor, 1987-90, 91-94; ptnr. Palmore & Sheffer Attys., Henderson, Ky., 1984-86; dep. sec. Ky. Pers. Cabinet, Frankfort, 1996—; chmn. Ky. Safety & Health Stds. Bd., Frankfort, 1987-90, 91-94; co-chmn. Ky. Labor Mgmt. Adv. Coun., Frankfort, 1987-90, 91-94; bd. dirs. Ky. Workers' Comp Funding Commn., Frankfort, 1987-90, 91-94, Community Svc. Commn., Frankfort, 1993-94, Ky. Info. Resources Mgmt. Commn., Frankfort, 1994, Sch.-to-Work Partnership Coun., Frankfort, 1994; ex-officio bd. dirs. Pub. Employees Collective Bargaining Task Force, Frankfort, 1994, Ky. Workforce Partnership Coun., Frankfort, 1994. Labor liaison Jones for Gov., Lexington, 1990-91; del. Dem. Nat. Conv., N.Y.C., 1992; mem. inaugural class Ky. Women's Leadership Network, Frankfort, 1993; bd. dirs. Alliant Health Systems Adult Oper. Bd., Louisville, 1992-96, Ky. Commn. Homeless, Frankfort, 1993-94; candidate for Sec. State Commonwealth Ky., 1995; chair Dem. Women's Think Tank, 1995. Mem. Ky. Bar Assn. (del. ho. dels. 1985-86, chair law day/spkr. bur. 1985-86, mem. 1986-90), Ky. Bar Found. (bd. dirs. 1985-92, sec. 1986-89, pres. elect 1989-90, pres. 1990-91), Rotary (program chair Frankfort chpt. 1993-94). Episcopalian. Home: 2310 Peaks Mill Rd Frankfort KY 40601-9437 Office: Personnel Cabinet 200 Fair Oaks Ln Frankfort KY 40601-1134

PALMORE, JOHN STANLEY, JR., retired lawyer; b. Ancon, C.Z., Aug. 6, 1917; s. John Stanley and Antoinette Louise (Gonzalez) P.; m. Eleanor Anderson, July 31, 1938 (dec. 1980); 1 child, John Worsham (dec.); m. Carol Pate, Jan. 1, 1982. Student, Western Ky. State Coll., 1934-36; LL.B. cum laude, U. Louisville, 1939. Bar: Ky. 1938. Practice law Henderson, 1939-42, 47-59; judge Ct. Appeals Ky. (name changed to Supreme Ct. Ky. 1975), 1959-82, chief justice, 1966, 73, 77-82; practice law Frankfort, Ky., 1983-84; ptnr. Palmore & Sheffer, Henderson, 1984-86; sr. counsel Jackson & Kelly, Lexington, Ky., 1986-92; ret., 1992; city pros. atty., Henderson, 1949-53, city atty., 1953-55; commonwealth's atty. 5th Circuit Ct. Dist. Ky., 1955-59. Served to lt. USNR, 1942-46, 51-52. Mem. Ky. Bar Assn., Am. Legion, Ky. Hist. Soc., Frankfort Country Club, Lexington Club, Frankfort Rotary Club (pres. 1993-94), Masons, Shriners, Elks, Phi Alpha Delta. Episcopalian (past vestryman, sr. warden). Home: 2310 Peaks Mill Rd Frankfort KY 40601-9437

PALMS, JOHN MICHAEL, academic administrator, physicist; b. Rijswijk, The Netherlands, June 6, 1935; naturalized, 1956; s. Peter Joannes and Mimi Adele (DeYong) P.; m. Norma Lee Cannon, June 2, 1958; children: John Michael, Daniele Maria, Lee Cannon. BS in Physics, The Citadel, 1958, DSc (hon.), 1980; MS in Physics, Emory U., 1959; PhD, U. N.Mex., 1966. Commd. 2d lt. USAF, 1958, retired capt. Res., 1970; lectr. physics dept. U. N.Mex., 1959-62; instr. physics dept. USAF Acad., 1961-62; staff mem. Western Electric Sandia Lab., 1961-62, U. Calif. Los Alamos Sci. Lab., 1962-66, Oak Ridge Nat. Lab., 1966; asst. prof. Emory U., Atlanta, 1966-69; assoc. prof. Emory U., 1969-73, chmn., assoc. prof. dept. physics, assoc. prof. radiology dept. Med. Sch., 1973-74, prof., chmn. dept. physics, 1973-74, dean Coll. Arts. and Scis., 1974-80, acting chmn. dept. math. and computer sci., 1976-77, v.p. arts and scis., 1979-82, acting dean Emory Coll., 1979-80, acting dir. Emory U. Computing Ctr., 1980-82, v.p. acad. affairs, 1982-88, interim dean Grad. Sch., 1985-86, Charles Howard Candler prof. nuclear, radiation and environ. physics, 1988-90; pres., prof. physics Ga. State U., Atlanta, 1989-91, U. S.C., Columbia, 1991—; bd. dirs. Peco Energy Co., Fortis, Inc., N.Y.C., Carolina First, Greenville, S.C., Policy Mgmt. Sys. Corp., Columbia; adv. com. Oak Ridge Nat. Lab., 1984-89; mem. Nat. nuclear accredititng bd. Inst. Nuclear Power Ops., 1985-91, Inst., adv. coun., 1995; nat. adv. coun. Inst. Nuclear Power Ops.; mem. panel for semiconductor detectors NAS/NRC, 1963-74; cons. Acad. Natural Scis., Phila., EG&G, INc., Santa Barbara, Calif., Tennelec, Inc., radiology dept. U. So. Calif. Med. Sch., Three Mile Island Environ. Study, Phila. Health Funds, ORTEC, Inc., Oak Ridge, Allied-Gulf Nuclear Svcs., Barnwell, S.C., TRW Space Sys. Divsn., L.A., AEC, Harshaw Chem. Co., Canberra Industries, dept. radiol. health Ga. Dept. Human Resources, Nat. Cancer Inst.; mem. high tech. task force Atlanta C. of C. Contbr. articles on nuclear, atomic, med. and environ. physics to profl. jours. Mem. adv. be. The Citadel, Oak Ridge Nat. Lab.; mem. exec. bd. Atlanta Area Coun. Boy Scouts of Am., 1989-90; mem. cmty. rels. bd. U.S. Penitentiary, Atlanta; trustee Inst. Def. Analysses, Wesleyan Coll., 1984-89, Pace Acad., 1984-89, St. Joseph's Hosp., Atlanta, 1987-89, Ga. Rsch. Alliance, 1988-89; mem. S.C. Univs. Rsch. and Ednl. Found. Bd., S.C. Rsch. Authority Bd.; bd. dirs. Civic-Atlanta Partnership Bus. and Edn., Inc., 1988-90, United Way; chair Rhodes scholar selective com., 1989, S.C., 1995-96. Mem. AAAS, Am. Phys. Soc., Am. Assn. Physics Tchrs., IEEE (Nuclear Sci. Group), Am. Nuclear Soc., Am. Coun. Edn., Coun. Provosts and Acad. V.P.s, Am. Conf. Acad. Deans, Soc. Nuclear Medicine, Health Physics Soc., Columbia C. of C. (bd. dirs.), Rotary, Columbia C. of C., Phi Beta Kappa, Sigma Xi, Phi Kappa Phi, Omicron Delta Kappa, Sigma Pi Sigma. Home and Office: U SC House of the President Columbia SC 29208

PALOCZY, SUSAN THERESE, elementary school principal; b. Dayton, Ohio, Nov. 17, 1953; d. William Michael and Elfriede Meckel (Adkisson) P. BA, Our Lady of the Lake U., San Antonio, 1975, MA in Edn., 1978, cert. in mid-mgmt., 1979; postgrad., Tex. A&M U., 1991—. Cert. mid-mgmt. adminstr., supr., elem. and secondary tchr., Tex. Elem. acad. coord., tchr., summer sch. prin. Harlandale Ind. Sch. Dist., San Antonio, elem. prin. Mem. ASCD, Tex. Coun. Women Sch. Execs., Tex. Elem. Prins. and Suprs. Assn., Tex. Congress Parents and Tchrs., Kappa Delta Pi. Address: 623 Rockhill Dr San Antonio TX 78209-3148 Office: Wright Elem 115 E Huff Ave San Antonio TX 78214-2230

PALOR, JOHN, media group executive. Pres. Gannett News Media Group, Arlington, Va. Office: Gannett Co Inc 1100 Wilson Blvd Arlington VA 22234

PALOUMPIS, ANDREAS ATHANASIOS, academic administrator; b. Minonk, Ill., Sept. 30, 1925; s. Athanacious A. and Sophia (Christofilis) P.; m. Bessie Jolas, Sept. 3, 1950; children: Athanacious A. (Tom), Evan, Andrea (dec.). Student, U. Ill., 1946-49; BS, Ill. State U., 1950, MA, 1953; PhD, Iowa State U., 1956. Tchr. sci. Mason City (Ill.) High Sch., 1950-53; prof. zoology and fisheries Ill. State U., Normal, 1956-66; founding pres. Winston Churchill Coll., Pontiac, Ill., 1966-69; v.p. acad. affairs Ill. Cen. Coll., East Peoria, 1969-77; pres. Onondaga Community Coll., Syracuse, N.Y., 1977-83, Hillsborough Community Coll., Tampa, Fla., 1983—. Contbr. articles to profl. jours. Mem. NAACP, Greater Tampa C. of C. (bd. govs. 1987—, coun. high tech. 1986—). Greek Orthodox. Office: Hillsborough Community Coll PO Box 31127 Tampa FL 33631-3127

PALOVCIK, REINHARD ANTON, research neurophysiologist; b. Dornheim, Hessen, Germany, June 30, 1950; came to U.S. 1956; s. Anton and Elfriede (Lankus) P. BS, U. Mich., 1973; MA, Wayne State U., Detroit, 1979, PhD, 1982. Rsch. asst. E.B. Ford Inst. Med. Rsch., Detroit, 1973-78; teaching asst. Dept. Psychology, Wayne State U., Detroit, 1978-79, grad. trainee, 1979-81, grad. asst., 1981-82; postdoctoral assoc. dept. physiology U. Fla., Gainesville, 1982-86, postdoctoral assoc. dept. neurosci., 1986-89, postdoctoral assoc. dept. neurosurgery, 1989-90, postdoctoral assoc. neurology dept., 1991, rsch. cons.; rsch. health scientist rsch. svc. VA Med. Ctr., Gainesville, 1990-95, clin. rsch. cons., 1995—. U. Mich. Regents Alumni scholar, 1969; NIMH predoctoral tng. grantee, 1979; NIH Nat. Rsch. Svc. awardee, 1983; Epilepsy Rsch. Found. Fla. postdoctoral grantee, 1990. Mem. AAAS, IEEE, APA, Soc. for Neurosci., Am. Statis. Assn., Internat. Neural Network Soc. Home: 2209 NE 15th Ter Gainesville FL 32609-8918

PALS, DEAN CLIFFORD, insurance company executive; b. George, Iowa, Jan. 12, 1938; s. Clinton and Ellen (Cassens) P.; m. Blanche Peterson, June 1, 1963; 1 child, Sherri Lee. BA, Tenn. Temple U., 1963; BD, MDiv., Cen. Theol. Sem., Mpls., 1966; ThM, Westminster Sem., Phila., 1970. CLU, ChFC, Accredited Estate Planner. Sales rep. Met. Life Ins. Co., Chattanooga, 1972-74, sales mgr., 1975-82, branch mgr., 1983-86, fin. planner, 1987-91, account exec., 1992—. Mem. Am. Soc. CLU's and ChFC's (pres. Chattanooga chpt. 1989-90), Gen. Agts. and Mgrs. Assn. (pres. Chattanooga 1984-85, Tenn. 1985-86), Chattanooga Estate Planning Coun. (pres 1996-97), Nat. Assn. Estate Planners, Nat. Assn. Life Underwriters, Tenn. Assn. Life Underwriters. Republican. Baptist. Home: 8505 Creekstone Dr Chattanooga TN 37421-2739 Office: Met Life Ste 704 3727 Heritage Bus Ct Chattanooga TN 37422-2848

PALUMBO, DONALD EMANUEL, English language educator, department chair; b. Pitts., Jan. 17, 1949; s. Emanuel John and Florence Marie (Orlando) P.; m. Joan Reisman, Apr. 30, 1972 (div. 1976); m. Julie Marie Bell, Dec. 30, 1978 (div. 1990); children: Anthony D., David Vincent; m. Susan Elizabeth Conshue, May 8, 1992. AB, U. Chgo., 1970; MA, U. Mich., 1971, PhD, 1976. Teaching fellow U. Mich., Ann Arbor, 1971-75; instr. Lamar U., Beaumont, Tex., 1976-78; assoc. prof. No. Mich. U., Marquette, 1978-83; div. head Lorain County Community Coll., Elyria, Ohio, 1983-87; dept. chair Shippensburg (Pa.) U., 1987-92, East Carolina U., N.C., 1992—. Editor: Spectrum of the Fantastic, 1988, Eros in the Mind's Eye, 1986, Erotic Universe, 1986; series advisor Contbns. to the Study of Sci. Fiction and Fantasy, 1991—. Mem. Internat. Assn. for Fantastic in Arts (pres. 1989-92, treas. 1983-89), Popular Culture Assn. (film area chair 1991—, comics area chair 1980-91). Office: East Carolina Univ Greenville NC 27858

PALUMBO, JAMES FREDRICK, insurance company executive; b. Everett, Mass., Nov. 30, 1950; s. Bruno James and Lillian Elizabeth (Picardi) P.; m. Nancy Laurie Richards, July 24, 1976; children: Elizabeth Richards, Andrew Reid, Alexander Thomas. BA, Lake Forest Coll., 1973; MBA, Washington U., 1975. Market surveillance analyst Nat. Assn. of Securities Dealers, Washington, 1975-76, asst. treas., 1976-78; regional rep. Student Loan Mktg. Assn., Washington, 1978-79, mgr., 1979-81, dir., 1981-82, asst. v.p., 1982-83, v.p., 1983-87; sr. v.p. Connie Lee Mgmt. Svcs. Corp., Coll. Constrn. Loan Ins. Assn., Washington, 1987-95; with N.Y. Life Ins. Co., N.Y.C., 1995—; registered rep. N.Y. Life Securities Inc., N.Y.C., 1995—; participant Govt.-Univ.-Industry Rsch. Roundtable, Washington, 1986. Actor popular and children's theater, 1973-76. Chmn. sports announcers com. D.C. Spl. Olympics, Washington, 1986, 87, D.C. Regional Counsel, Lake Forest Coll., Washington, 1976-80; mem. Elliott Soc. membership com. Washington U., 1986-96, Great Falls (Va.) Hist. Soc.; bd. govs. Lake Forest Coll., 1978-82, trustee, 1993—. Mem. Nat. Fedn. Mcpl. Analysts, Soc. Coll. and Univ. Planners, So. Mcpl. Fin. Soc., Mcpl. Forum of N.Y., Great Falls Swim and Tennis Club (bd. dirs. 1988-91), Alpha Psi Omega. Office: 8075 Leesburg Pike Ste 200 Vienna VA 22182

PALUSZAK, NAOKO, artist; b. Iwamisawa, Hokkaido, Japan, Nov. 25, 1957; came to U.S., 1982; s. Masashi Omura and Keiko (Mito) Thayer; m. Stephen Paul Paluszak, June 27, 1982. Grad., Japan Designer Inst., Tokyo, 1979. Comml. artist Ad Pro. Co., Okinawa, Japan, 1979-81; freelance artist Ft. Myers, Fla., 1985—. Represented in collections Ariel Gallery, Artistes Ontarois-Organisme Arts Visuels et Musée, Ont., Can.; exhibited in group shows at Lancaster (Calif.) Mus./Art Gallery, 1988, Barrier Island Groups for Arts, 1989, Park Shore Gallery, 1989, Ariel Gallery, N.Y., 1990, Chautauqua Art Inst. Galleries, N.Y., 1991, Maska Internat., Seattle, 1991, Gallery Iris, Ont., 1991, Matsumoto Gallery, Fla., 1992, Eye of the Lizard Gallery, Fla., 1993, 94, Lahaina Galleries, Hawaii, 1996, others; also pvt. collections. Home and Office: 5236 SW 17th Pl Cape Coral FL 33914-6808

PAN, ELIZABETH LIM, information systems company executive; b. Manila, Dec. 6, 1941; came to U.S., 1961, naturalized, 1967; d. Lim Hu and Maria (Ramos) Lim; m. Jeff T. S. Pan, Jan. 17, 1962 (dec. 1978); children: Jeffrey, James. Student, U. Philippines, Quezon City, 1959-61; B.A., U. Ill., 1963, M.S., 1966; Ph.D., Rutgers U., 1974. Pres. Trulim, Inc., Inst. Info. Studies, Inc.; CEO PSI Internat. Editor: (with others) Collection Mgmt., 1977-80; editor: Annual Rev. Rehab., 1980-83; contbr. articles to profl. publs. Pres. Nat. Fedn. 8(a) Cos. (pres.). Home: 3220 Lake Edge Way Oakton VA 22124-2028 Office: 10306 Eaton Pl Fairfax VA 22030-2201*

PANDEY, RAGHVENDRA KUMAR, physicist, educator; b. Bath, India, Jan. 7, 1937; m. Christa U. Pandey, June 1, 1967. MS in Physics, Patna U., 1959; DSc in Physics, U. Cologne, 1967. Assoc. prof. elec. engring. Tex. A&M U., College Station, 1977-82, prof., 1982—, Halliburton prof. elec. engring., 1989-90, dir. ctr. for electronic materials, 1990—, Brockette prof., 1994—; founding dir. NSF Ctr. for Electronic Materials, Devices and Sys. Editor: (book) Crystal Growth of Electronic Materials; editor conf. procs.; contbr. 2 chpts. to books and numerous articles to sci. publs. Home: 1907 Amber Ridge Dr College Station TX 77845-5536 Office: Tex A&M U Elec Engring Dept College Station TX 77843-3128

PANETTA, CHARLES ANTHONY, chemistry educator; b. Albany, N.Y., Sept. 12, 1932; s. Domenic Pasquale and Mariantonia (Morreale) P.; m. Alicia Johanna Petruska, Aug. 22, 1959; children: Lawrence, John. BS in Biology, Manhattan Coll, 1954; PhD in Chemistry, Rensselaer Poly. Inst., 1961. Sr. chemist Bristol Labs., Syracuse, N.Y., 1960-64, project supr., 1964-65; postdoctoral rsch. assoc. MIT, 1965-67; asst. prof. chemistry U. Miss., University, 1967-70, assoc. prof., 1970-73, prof., 1973-87, 91—, Margaret McLean Coulter prof. chemistry, 1987-91; sr. rsch. fellow U.S. Army Chem. Rsch. and Devel. Ctr., Edgewood, Md., 1985; Navy-Am. Soc. Engring. Edn. disting. summer faculty rsch. fellow Naval Rsch. Lab., Washington, 1988; sr. resident rsch. assoc. NRC-U.S. Army Chem. Rsch., Devel. and Engring. Ctr., 1988-89; reviewer for proposals NSF and Petroleum Rsch. Fund; reviewer manuscripts Jour. Organic Chemistry and Jour. Medicinal Chemistry, Synthesis and Synlett. Contbr. articles to profl. jours.; patentee in field. Mem. Am. Chem. Soc., Sigma Xi. Office: U Miss Dept Chemistry University MS 38677

PANG, KAU CHAI, marketing professional; b. Labis Johore, Malaysia, Oct. 15, 1954; s. Hong and Cheong Liew Pang; m. Paige Elizabeth Ingle, Apr. 30, 1984; 1 child, Ian Kanzren Ingle Pang. BS, U. Ala., 1982, MBA, 1984. Mktg. analyst Auto Zone divsn. Malone and Hyde's, Memphis, 1984-86; sr. mktg. analyst Holiday Corp., Memphis, 1986-90; mktg. analyst, asst. to v.p. Meldisco, Mahwah, N.J., 1990-92; internat. mktg. mgr. Fed. Express Memphis, Singapore, 1992-94; adminstr. Contel CellularOne, Atlanta, 1994-95; product mgr. Bell South Wireless, Atlanta, 1995-96, VanStar, 1996—. Mem. Am. Bus. Assn. Baptist.

PANG, MAYBELINE MIUSZE (CHAN), software and systems engineer, analyst; b. Shanghai, China, Sept. 9, 1945; came to U.S. from Hong Kong, 1964; d. Yee Sun and Margaret H. (Kong) Chan; m. Patrick Yewwah Pang, Aug. 4, 1968 (div. 1987); children: Elaine Weikay, Irene Weisum, George Siu-On. BS in Physics/Math, Lincoln U., 1967; postgrad, U. Mo., 1967-68, U. Ariz., 1984-86. Application programmer Ariz. Health Sci. Ctr., Physiology Lab., Tucson, 1984-85; software engr. System and Software Engring. Dalmo Victor, Singer, Tucson, 1985-88, McDonnell Douglas Helicopter Co., Mesa, Ariz., 1988-90, Sperry Marine, Charlottesville, Va., 1990—; cons., worked with Air Force (F111 Weather Simulation), Army (Advanced Apache Helicopter), Navy (Seawolf weapons, ship control, CNO-Automatic Depth Finder) projects; comml. (Integrated Software Analysis Sys.; Sperry's docking sys., Guardian Star, SRD-500 SpeedLog) projects; familiar with sys. analysis and design; software devel. and testing; algorithms, pulse processing, sys. engr. and analyst for Marine Sensors; active in Sperry's New Tech. Group. Recipient Nat. Sci. Honor Soc. award, 1967, Teaching assistantship U. Mo., 1968. Home: 1517 Westfield Ct Charlottesville VA 22901-1602 Office: Sperry Marine Seminole Trail Charlottesville VA 22901

PANKEY, GEORGE EDWARD, former educator; b. Charlotte Court House, Va., Dec. 2, 1903; s. John Wesley and Cora Smith (Daniel) P.; B.A., U. Richmond, 1926; M.A., U. N.C., 1927; m. Annabel Atkinson, Mar. 6, 1931; 1 son, George Atkinson. Mem. faculty Ogden Coll. and Western Ky. State Tchrs. Coll., 1927-28, La. Poly. Inst., 1928-43; with land dept. Gulf Oil Corp., 1944-46; currently in research work. Mem. Huguenot Soc., S.A.R., Sons Am. Colonists, Sigma Tau Delta. Baptist. Mason. Author: John Pankey of Manakin Town, Virginia, and His Descendants, Vol. I, 1969, Vol. II, 1972, Vol. III, 1981; co-author: Five Thousand Useful Words, 1936; former editor La. Tech. Digest. Address: PO Box 84 Ruston LA 71273-0084

PANTER, RICHARD FRANKLIN, television documentary producer and director; b. Detroit, June 18, 1947; s. Bernard M. Pauter; m. Glynda Christian, June 25, 1988; 1 child, Juliet Christian Smith. BA with honor, Mich. State U., 1969; MEd, Springfield (Mass.) Coll., 1971. Tchg. fellow Boston U., 1972; assoc. prodr. Am. Univs. Field Staff, Eng., 1973-74; writer dir. Mich. State U., East Lansing, 1975-76; asst. dir. McCann Assocs., Boston, 1976-77; writer, prodr. Nat. Life Vt., Montpelier, 1978-80; news videographer KTUU-TV, Anchorage, 1981; videographer WCVB-TV, Boston, 1983, WBZ-TV, Boston, 1983-84; editor WGBH-TV, Boston, 1984-85; prodr., videographer Digital Equipment Corp., Bedford, Mass., 1985-87; writer, prodr. Sta. WGBY-TV, Springfield, 1987-89; prodr./dir. Veritech Prodns., East Longmeadow, Mass., 1989-90; prodr., dir. S.C. ETV, Columbia, 1990—. Prodr., dir. TV documentaries Fathers and Sons, 1989 (Tokyo prize 1989), The Tokyo Raiders, 1993 (award S.C. Film Fest 1994), The Snowbird Cherokes, 1995 (Best o Show award Am. Indian Film Fest 1995), Divining the Divine, 1996, In Siberia, 1995. Bd. dirs. Audubon Soc., Northampton, Mass., 1988. Fellow U. Hawaii, 1973. Mem. World Affairs Coun. Democrat. Unitarian. Office: SC ETV Drawer L 2712 Millwood Ave Columbia SC 29250

PAOLA, CAROL WESTERN, gifted education educator; b. Okmulgee, Okla., Nov. 24, 1944; d. Price Sydney and Frances Miriam (Moak) Western; m. Nathan Thomas Paola, Feb. 26, 1966; children: John David, Kimberly Michelle. BS in Elem. Edn., U. So. Miss., 1966, MEd in Elem. Edn., 1977, cert. gifted edn., 1980. Tchr. 3d grade Hancock North Ctrl. Elem. sch., 1966-67, St. John Elem. Sch., Gulfport, Miss., 1967-68; tchr. 2d grade Anniston Ave. Elem. Sch., Gulfport, 1968-72; tchr. 1st grade W.J. Quarles Elem. Sch., Long Beach, Miss., 1973-80; tchr. gifted W.J. Quarles Elem. Sch., Long Beach, 1980—; guest lectr. U. So. Miss., presenter parenting conf., 1993, 94, 95; guest lectr. William Carey Coll. gifted certification courses; staff devel. spkr. St. Thomas Cath. Sch., Long Beach, Orange Grove Elem. Sch., Gulfport, Picayune (Miss.) Elem. Sch.; dist. gifted contact person; chair dist. gifted dept., dist. gifted curriculum; mem. dist. assessment team for gifted screening. Mem. com. suggested outcomes for gifted programs State Dept. Edn., Process skills tng. guide for gifted programs; mem. sch. dist. strategic planning team; sponsor sch.-wide checkers competition, Quarles Week Celebration/Long Beach History, Ann. City-Wide 5th Grade Discovery Quiz Bowl Competition, confirmation classes 10th grade St. Thomas Cath. Ch., tchr. Sunday Sch.; coord. Quarles in-sch. clubs, Ann. 4th grade quiz bowl, Quarles Elem. KidVoting Program, on-going art exhibit Wm. J. Quarles Mus. Art; co-sponsor Quarles Yearbook Com.; co-chair Quarles Staff Condolence Com.; story teller history of Long Beach. Recipient Alan R. Barton Excellence in Tchg. award, 1994, Leo W. Seal Tchr. Recognition award Hancock Bank, 1995; named Educator of Month Long Beach Coast C. of C., 1993; grantee The Gulf Coast Traffic Club, 1995. Mem. Nat. Assn. Gifted Children (presenter nat. conv. 1993), Gulf Coast Assn. Tchr. of Gifted (presenter meetings, chair 1990-92, 92-93, 94-95, 95-96, co-chair 1991-92), Miss. Assn. Gifted Children (presenter state conf. 1990, 92, 93, 94, 95, chair pub. rels. 1992-93, v.p. 1993-94, pres.-elect 1994-95, pres. 1995-96), Miss. Profl. Educators, Alpha Delta Kappa. Roman Catholic. Home: 1513 Westward Dr Gulfport MS 39501 Office: WJ Quarles Elem Sch 111 Quarles St Long Beach MS 39560-2618

PAPADOPOULOS, PATRICIA MARIE, healthcare professional. AAS, No. Va. Community Coll., 1970; BS, George Mason U., 1988; MS, Va. Poly. Inst., 1992. RN, Va.; cert. nursing adminstr. Staff nurse ICU, PACU Jefferson Meml. Hosp., Alexandria, Va.; dept. dir. PACU Nat. Hosp. for Orthopedics and Rehab., Arlington, Va., 1977-82; dir. med. surg. dept. Nat. Hosp. for Orthopedics and Rehab., 1982-85, house supr., 1985-89; dir. nursing ops. Nat. Hosp. for Orthopedics and Rehab., Arlington, Va., 1989-92; asst. dir. emergency svcs. Potomac Hosp., Woodbridge, Va., 1992-95; dir. ICU Nat. Hosp. Med. Ctr., Arlington, Va., 1995; dir. nursing resources and ops. Nat. Hosp. Med. Ctr., 1995—. Mem. Emergency Nurses Assn. Office: 2455 Army Navy Dr Arlington VA 22206-2905

PAPAY, TWILA YATES, English language educator; b. Greensburg, Pa., Oct. 13, 1946; d. Ralph Yates and Mary (Emrick) Yates Hackett; m. Joseph Louis Papay, May 16, 1976. BA, Clarion U. Pa., 1968; MA in British Lit., Purdue U., 1969, PhD in 19th Century British Lit., 1976. Teaching asst. Purdue U., 1969-72, grad. instr., 1972-73; instr. Saint Peter's Coll., Jersey City, 1973-76; asst. prof. Saint Peter's Coll., 1976-78, Caldwell (N.J.) Coll., 1978-80, Hofstra U., Hempstead, N.Y., 1980-83; assoc. prof. Hofstra U., 1983-85, Rollins Coll., Winter Park, Fla., 1985-92; prof. Rollins Coll., 1992—; dir. writing programs and writing ctr. Rollins Coll., 1985—; dir. English composition program and writing ctr. Hofstra U., 1982-85; dir. English as a second lang. program Caldwell Coll., 1978-80, acad. cons. Am. English lang. studies program, 1978-80, coord. internat. assoc. program, 1978-79; dir. developmental English program Saint Peter's Coll., 1973-77, dir. writing lab., tutor trainer, 1974-76. Contbr. articles to profl. jours. Recipient tchg. excellence and campus leadership award Sears-Roebuck Found., 1991; Arthur Vining Davis Jr. fellow, 1988, also numerous local grants and awards. Mem. MLA, AAUP, Coll. English Assn., CUNY Writing Ctr. Assn., Coun. Writing Program Adminstrs., Conf. on Coll. Composition and Comm., Fla. Coll. English Assn., Fla. Coun. Tchrs. English, Gulf Coast Conf. on Tchg. Writing, Nat. Writing Ctrs. Assn., N.E. MLA, Popular Culture Assn., Southeastern Writing Ctr. Assn., Nat. Coun. Tchrs. English, Omicron Delta Kappa, Phi Kappa Phi. Democrat. Office: Rollins Coll Holt Ave Winter Park FL 32789

PAPERMASTER, BARRY A., marketing and sales executive; b. Mpls., Feb. 9, 1954; s. Theodore Capple and Dorothy P.; m. Cheryl Ann Buckles, Apr. 5, 1987; children: Benjamin, Ariel, Zacuary. BSEE, Yale U., 1972-76; MSEE, Stanford U., 1976-77; MBA, U. Chgo., 1979-81. Devel. engr. Honeywell, Mpls., 1977-79; ops. analyst in memory products II div. Mostek, Dallas, 1981-82; mgr. product mgmt. InteCom, Inc., Allen, Tex., 1982-84; dir. strategic planning Action Honeywell/Advanced Business Comms., Dallas, 1984-87; sr. mgr. Peat Marwick Mitchell, Dallas, 1987; dir. strategic sales and mktg. InteCom, Inc (sub. MAtra Comms.), Allen, 1987-91; v.p. mktg. and sales Internat. Power Machines, Garland, Tex., 1991-94; v.p. strategic devel. Avo Internat., Dallas, 1994—. Home: 1721 Riviera Dr Plano TX 75093-2911 Office: Avo Internat 4651 S Westmoreland Rd Dallas TX 75237-1017

PAPPACHRISTOU, JOYCE FLORES, dietitian, educator; b. Springfield, Mass., May 15, 1932; d. Hector and Henrietta (Hemerling) Flores; divorced; children: Dianne, Donna, Paul Jr., Gary. AA, Nassau Community Coll., 1970; BA in Math., Sci. and Home Econs. with honors, Queens Coll., 1973; MA, MS in dietetics/nutrition, NYU, 1976; postgrad., Nova U., 1989—. Cert. tchr., N.Y.C., N.Y., tchr. home econs., health edn., sci., Fla.; lic. dietitian, nutritionist Fla. Tchr. Roslyn High Sch., Elmont Meml. High Sch.; dietician L.I. (N.Y.) Jewish Hosp., St. Mary's Hosp.; instr. nutrition Cath. Med. Ctr. Nursing, 1974-76; chief dietician Jamaica (N.Y.) Hosp., 1976-80; tchr. Broward Coutny (Fla.) Bd. Educators, 1981—; adj. prof. Nassau Community Coll., Fla. Internat. U., 1976-80. Contbr. articles to profl. jours. Mem. Am. Dietetics Assn., Am. Home Econs. Assn. (cert.), Fla. Dietetics Assn., Fla. Assn. Computer Educators, Fla. Correctional Edn. Assn., Fla. Assn. Alternative Educators, Phi Beta Kappa, Kappa Delta Pi.

PAPPAS, JAMES MARCUS, petroleum engineer; b. Laredo, Tex., Mar. 30, 1956; s. Tino Santiago and Joann (Boyer) P.; m. Martha Imelda Lopez, Aug. 25, 1978; children: James Marcus Jr., George James. BA in Chemistry, U. Tex., Austin, 1979, BSChemE, 1979; MBA, U. Tex., Tyler, 1993. Registered profl. engr., Tex. Petroleum engr. Amoco Prodn. Co., Levelland, Tex., 1979-81; petroleum engr. S.G./petroleum engr. Amoco Prodn. Co., Houston, 1981-84; sr. engr., engr. IV Union Pacific Resources Co., Houston, 1984-89; sr. engr. adv., staff engr., sr. engr. Fina Oil and Chem. Co., Tyler, 1989-93; sr. engring. advisor Fina Oil and Chem. Co., Midland, Tex., 1993—. Contbr. articles to profl. jours. State alt. del., region del. Dem. Party, Houston, 1984, precinct chair, Laredo, Tex., 1974. Martin Luther King Jr. scholar U. Tex., Tyler, 1993. Mem. AIChE, Soc. Petroleum Engrs. (chmn. Gulf Coast sect. 1988-89, sec. Permian Basin sect. 1993—, bd. dirs. 1994-95), Am. Chem. Soc., Tex. Soc. Profl. Engrs., Tex. Alliance for Minority Engrs. Office: Fina Oil and Chem Co Ste 4400 6 Desta Dr Midland TX 79705

PAPPAS-SPEAIRS, NINA, financial planner, educator; b. Hazard, Ky.; d. Steve E. and Martha (Hicks) Kaifas; m. Harry J. Pappas (div.); children: John J., Nicholas S., Vivian E. Pappas Unger, Mark A., Carol A. Pappas Siegel; m. Mitchell F. Speairs. BS, U. Cin.; MA, Northwestern U.; PhD, U. Ill., 1978. Mem. faculty St. Mary's High Sch., Chgo., Sch. Dist. 102, LaGrange, Ill., U. Ill., Chgo., 1969-79, U. Tex., Arlington, 1979-82, Tex. Wesleyan Coll., Ft. Worth, 1982-83; realtor Merrill Lynch Realty, Ft. Worth, 1983-84; fin. planner Cigna Corp., Irving, Tex., 1984-90; organizer, condr. lst U.S. Olympic Acad., Chgo., 1977; collaborator Internat. Olympic Acad., Olympia, Greece, 1977, guest lectr., 1977, 78; chief of mission to Greece U.S. Olympic Com., 1977; guest lectr. Nat. Olympic Acad. Republic of China, 1982; mem. Sch. Bd. Lagrange, Ill. Dist. 107, 1971-74. Author: History and Development of the International Olympic Academy: 1927-1977, 1978; editor: Perspectives of the Olympic Games, 1979; also articles. Vice chair Edn. Coun. U.S. Olympic Com., 1977-85; pres. Opera Guild Ft. Worth, 1982. Recipient Silver Medal Internat. Olympic Acad., Olympia, Greece, 1981. Mem. Lecture Found. Ft. Worth, Ft. Worth Sister Cities Internat., Symphony League, Opera Guild, English Speaking Union, Woman's Club, River Crest Country Club, Ft. Worth Boat Club. Republican. Greek Orthodox. Home: 7705 Lake Highlands Dr Fort Worth TX 76179-2809

PAQUE, MICHEL JEAN, association executive director; b. Manitowoc, Wis., Dec. 2, 1947; s. Clarence Anselle and Jeanette Agnes (Helgeson) P.; m. Vicki Lee McKay, Jan. 21, 1977; children: Matthew, Joel. BS, U. Wis., Green Bay, 1969; MS, U. Wis., Milw., 1971. Cert. assoc. exec., planner. Planner Wis. Dept. Transp., Waukesha, 1969-76; prin. planner City of Oklahoma City, 1976-81; assoc. dir. Interstate Oil & Gas Compact Commn., Oklahoma City, 1981-84; exec. dir. Ground Water Protection Coun., Oklahoma City, 1984—. Traffic commr. Oklahoma City, 1982-86, planning commr., 1986—. Mem. Am. Soc. Assn. Execs., Am. Inst. Cert. Planners. Lutheran. Home: 4008 Apple Valley Dr Oklahoma City OK 73120-8531 Office: Groundwater Protection Coun 827 NW 63rd St Ste 103 Oklahoma City OK 73116-7639

PAQUIN, JEFFREY DEAN, lawyer; b. Milw., Dec. 7, 1960; s. James DeWayne and Helen Ann (Walter) P. BA, U. Wis., 1983; JD, U. Ky., 1986. Bar: Ga. 1986, U.S. Dist. Ct. (no. dist.) Ga. 1986, U.S. Ct. Appeals (11th cir.) 1986, U.S. Dist. Ct. (mid. dist.) Ga. 1987, D.C. 1989, U.S. Ct. Appeals (D.C. cir.) 1989, U.S. Supreme Ct. 1990. Assoc. Powell, Goldstein, Frazer & Murphy, Atlanta, 1986-94; litigation counsel United Parcel Svc., Atlanta, 1994—; v.p. Prodn. Values, Inc., Atlanta, 1987-88. Exec. editor U. Ky. Law Rev., 1985-86. Bd. dirs. Children's Motility Disorder Found., 1995—. Mem. ABA, ATLA (assoc.), Fed. Bar Assn., Nat. Inst. Dispute Resolution, Am. corp. Counsel Assn., D.C. Bar Assn., Ga. Bar Assn., Atlanta Bar Assn. (v.p., dir. alternative dispute resolution sect.), Mortar Board, Phi Delta Phi, Sigma Epsilon Sigma, Psi Chi. Roman Catholic. Home: 2100 Glenridge Ct Marietta GA 30062-1879 Office: United Parcel Svc 55 Glenlake Pky NE Atlanta GA 30328-3474

PARADICE, SAMMY IRWIN, real estate investor; b. Beaumont, Tex., May 26, 1952; s. Alfred E. and Timmia E. (Holder) P. Student, Lamar U., 1970, Okla. State U., 1970, U. Tulsa, 1971. Lic. real estate broker, Tex. Page U.S. House of Reps., Washington, 1969-70; owner Southwestern Mktg. Systems, Beaumont, 1972-75; owner, mgr. First Realty, Sam Paradice & Assocs., Vidor, Tex., 1976—; broker, owner Paradice Real Estate, Vidor, 1992—. Author: (books) Arab Money Hotline, 1985, Real Estate Counter-attack, 1984, Guerrilla Finance, 1992, (cassette study course), How to be a Business Tycoon; editor/pubr. The Money Source Newsletter, 1987—. Methodist. Office: PO Box 417 1765 Highway 12 Vidor TX 77662-3538

PARADIS, PHILIP, English language educator; b. New Britain, Conn., 1951; s. Norman and Claire (Boissonneau) P.; m. Marjorie Hull, May 27, 1978; 1 child, Bennett. BA in Eng., Ctrl. Conn. State Coll., 1976; MA in Eng., U. Utah, 1981; PhD in Eng., Okla. State U., 1984. Instr. Okla. State U., Stillwater, 1980-85; asst. prof. Iowa State U., Ames, 1985-87, We. Carolina U., Cullowhee, N.C., 1987-90; instr. Iowa State U., 1990-91; adj. instr. U. No. Iowa, Cedar Falls, 1992; asst. prof. No. Ky. U., Highland Hgts., 1992—. Author: (poems) Tornado Alley, 1986, From Gobbler's Knob, 1989, Something of Ourselves, 1933, Along the Path, 1996; poetry editor Midland Rev., 1985; contbg. editor Poet and Critic, 1985-87; book reviewer Prairie Schooner, Asheville Ctizen-Times, 1990—. Recipient 1st prize Poetry award Appalachian Writers Assn., 1989, Acad. Am. Poets prize, 1982. Mem. Assoc. Writing Programs, Acad. of Am. Poets, Nat. Coun. Tchrs. of English. Democrat. Office: No Ky Univ Dept of Literature Nunn Dr Highland Heights KY 41099

PARADISE, LOUIS VINCENT, educational psychology educator, university official; b. Scranton, Pa., Apr. 19, 1946; s. Louis Benjamin and Lucille (Bochicchio) P.; children: Christopher, Gabrielle,Victoria. BS, Pa. State U., 1968; MS, Bucknell U., 1974; PhD, U. Va., 1976. Lic. psychologist, profl. counselor; cert. sch. psychologist. Assoc. prof. Cath. U. Am., Washington, 1976-83; prof. edn., chmn. edn. leadership U. New Orleans, 1983-90, dean Coll. Edn., 1990-92, univ. exec. vice chancellor and provost, 1992-94, exec. vice chancellor for acad. affairs, 1994—. Author: Ethics in Counseling and Psychotherapy, 1979, Questioning: Skills for the Helping Process, 1979, Counseling in Community College, 1982. 1st lt. U.S. Army, 1968-72. DuPont scholar U. Va., 1974. Mem. APA, ACA (ethics com. 1986-89), Am. Edn. Rsch. Assn., So. Assn. Counselor Edn. (chmn. ethics com. 1988-89), Chi Sigma Iota (founding chpt. pres. 1985-87). Roman Catholic. Office: U New Orleans Office Acad Affairs New Orleans LA 70148

PARAISO, JOHNNA KAYE, elementary education educator; b. Wyandotte, Mich., Nov. 17, 1961; d. John Calvin and Ruth (Hughes) Underwood; m. Normandy Paraiso, Oct. 6, 1984; children: Sophia Elisabeth, Abigail Mahalia, Genevieve Christine. BS, Bob Jones U., 1983. Cert. ACSI, educator K-8 (all subjects). Tchr. fifth grade Temple Christian Sch., Redford, Mich., 1983-86; music tchr. Fairlane Christian Sch., Dearborn Heights, Mich., 1986-90; tchr. 2d grade Internat. Christian Sch., San Francisco, 1992-93, dept. head primary childhood edn., 1992-93; freelance musician children's concerts; leader Curriculum Selection Com.; initiator Elem. Music Program; dir. several dramatic prodns.; tchr. piano, guitar. Children's minister 1st Bapt. Ch., San Francisco, 1991-94. Mem. Pi Lambda Theta. Home: 2024 Stonebrook Rd Murfreesboro TN 37129

PARATORE-ZARZANA, MARY GAY, artist, art educator, lecturer; b. Galveston, Tex., Jan. 10, 1940; d. Owen Albert and Cora Louise (Hunter) Garrigan; m. Philip George Paratore Jr., Aug. 12, 1961 (div. Feb. 10, 1986); children: Philip G. III, Patrick Owen, Angela Gay, Amber Lynn Marie; m. Anthony Albert Zarzana, May 31, 1991. BA in Art, Sci., Edn., Sam Houston U., 1961; M in Art Edn., U. Houston, 1968; student, Art Students' League, 1985, 87, Nat. Acad. Design, 1987. Cert. all level art instr., Tex., Tex. State art cons. Med. illustrator U. Tex., Galveston, 1958, 60; elem. tchr. Stewart Elem., Hitchcock, Tex., 1961-64; art tchr. Ball H.S., Galveston, Tex., 1971-74; art instr. cont. edn. Alvin (Tex.) C.C., 1961-84, head art dept., 1974-75, art instr., 1990-92; sr. adult art instr. Coll. of the Mainland, Tex. City, Tex., 1985-93, art history instr., 1993; art tchr. Manuel (Tex.) Jr. H.S., 1993—; owner Paratore-Zarzana Studio and Gallery, Santa Fe, Galveston, Tex.; pvt. art instr. Hitchcock, Santa Fe, Manu, Tex.; demonstrator, lectr. Alvin, Santa Fe, Tex. City Art Leagues, 1961-96; workshop instr. Carrizo Lodge, Ruidoso, N.Mex., 1993; insvc. art cons. Tex. City Ind. Sch. Dist., 1974. One woman exhibns. include Tex. City (Tex.) Assn., 1974, U. Tex., Alvin, 1974, Alvin (Tex.) Pub. Libr., 1978, Tex. Med. Branch, Galveston, 1992; group exhibns. include Nat. Soc. Artists (Best of Show), Art Soc. Houston (First Place), Alvin (Tex.) Art League (First Place); featured in Le Review Moderne, 1968; staff artist Cedar Rock Press, 1979-85; designer (cover) poetry book by David C. Yates, 1983. Mem. sch. bd. Our Lady of Lourdes Parochial Sch., Hitchcock, Tex., 1969-73; pres. Santa Fe Friends of the Libr., 1979-81; chmn. spiritual devel. Our Lady of Lourdes Altar and Rosary Soc., 1967; liaison Nat. Soc. Artist and Galveston (Tex.) County Parks and Beach; mem. bd. restoration Alta Loma Cath. Ch., 1988-96. Recipient Dick Blick award, Tex. Art Supply award, Grumbacher award. Mem. Nat. Soc. Artists (founder, Best of Show, pres. 1985-87, 1991-94), Tex. Watercolor Soc. (signature mem.), Art League of the Mainland, Galveston Art Leageu, Tex. Middle Sch. Assn., Assn. Tex. Profl. Educators, Alpha Chi Omega (Delta Kappa chpt.),. Roman Catholic. Home: 2731-646 N Santa Fe TX 77510 Office: Paratore-Zarzana Gallery 3727 Avenue P Galveston TX 77550

PARDO MAZORRA, ANGEL ENRIQUE, poet, writer; b. Punta Brava, Cuba, Dec. 16, 1942; came to U.S., 1988; s. Angel Pardo and Dolores Mazorra; m. Emelina Nuñez, 1993; 1 child: Angel Enrique. Student, Masonic U., Havana, 1962, Miami-Dade C.C., 1993. Office mgr. Law Offices of Angel R. Pardo, Sr., 1961-64; political prisoner, 1964-88, poet, writer, journalist, 1988—; editorial asst. Scott, Foresman & Co., Glenview, Ill., 1988-89; mail clk. Northern Trust Bank of Fla., Miami, 1989—. Author: Cuba: Memoirs of a Political Prisoner, 1992; contbr. poems to jours. Recipient merit award Liceo of Punta Brava in Exile. Mem. Assn. Free Poets and Writers of Cuba, Masons of Cuba (merit award). Home: 4350 NW 8th Ter Apt 215 Miami FL 33126-3553

PARENT, DAVID HILL, investment company executive; b. Salem, Oreg., Apr. 13, 1940; s. Donald Allan and Pauline Louise (Lyons) P.; m. Christine Hedwige Marie Theérèse Wielezynski, Sept. 25, 1976; children: Marc Alexander Lair Thompson, Nathalie Jacqueline Marie Pauline. BS, U. Calif. Berkeley, 1963; Internat. fellow, Columbia U., 1963, MBA, 1965. Dir. mktg. Europe Vendo Internat., Brussels, 1965-69; exec. v.p. T.S.I., Hempstead, N.Y., 1969-70; v.p. mktg. Gateway-Globus, Forest Hills, N.Y., 1970-72; mgr. Ctrl. Africa, Leon Tempelsman & Son, N.Y.C., 1972-79; pres. The Parent Co., Plano, Tex., 1979—; advisor to pres. of Gabon, Libreville, 1976-79. Mem. Rockwall Citizens's Counc. (exec. com.), Rockwall C. of C., Plano C. of C. Republican. Roman Catholic. Home and Office: Lairgrove 3000 E Parker Rd Plano TX 75074

PARHAM, ANNETTE RELAFORD, librarian; b. Petersburg, Va., Dec. 13, 1954; d. William Rosley and Sarah Matthews (Pierce) Relaford; m. Keith Lionel Parham, June 14, 1975; children: Loretta Springfield, Alison Nicole. BSBA, Va. Union U., 1977. File clk. Va. Farm Bur. Mut. Ins., Richmond, Va., 1981-82, ins. rater, 1982-83; file clk. tech. svcs. dept. of libr. Colonial Williamsburg (Va.) Found., 1987-89, acquisitions libr., 1989—. Named to Outstanding Young Women of Am., 1981. Mem. Va. Libr. Assn., Ethnic Librs. Forum. Democrat. Baptist. Office: Colonial Williamsburg Found Dept of Libr 415 N Boundary St Williamsburg VA 23185-3614

PARHAM, BETTY ELY, credit bureau executive; b. Drumright, Okla., Aug. 14, 1928; d. Wayne Albert and Edith May (Ledgerwood) Bingamon; m. Richard D. Ely, Dec. 22, 1946 (dec. Jan. 1971); children: Richard Wayne, Stephen Wyatt; m. Billy S. Parham, Mar. 10, 1991. BS, East Cen. U., Ada, Okla., 1962, M Teaching, 1965. Office mgr. Louiis M. Long, Loans, Ada, 1946-78; owner Credit Bur. Ada, 1956—, mgr., 1978—. Mem. Soc. Cert. Credit Bur. Execs., Assoc. Credit Burs. Okla. (bd. dirs. 1980—, pres. 1990), AAUW (cert. of achievement 1989), Ada Bus. and Profl. Women (chmn. YC, Pres.'s award 1991), Toastmasters (pres. Ada 1984, Presdl. Excellence award 1984), Kiwanis (bd. dirs. Ada 1990-92). Democrat. Home: PO Box 506 Ada OK 74821-0506 Office: Credit Bur Ada 304 E 12th St Ada OK 74820-6510

PARHAM, IRIS ANN, gerontology educator; b. Orange, Tex., Nov. 14, 1948; d. George Kevlin and Nina Mabel Parham; m. Edward Swarbrick, Aug. 9, 1975; 1 child, Erin Elsbeth. BA, U. Tex., 1970; MS, W. Va. U., 1973; PhD, U. So. Calif., 1976. Asst. prof. gerontology Va. Commonwealth U., Richmond, 1976-81, assoc., 1981-91, prof., 1991—; exec. dir. Va. Geriatric Edn. Ctr. Co-editor: Modular Gerontology Curriculum, 1982, vol. II, 1984, Access, 1990, Resource Guides-Geriatrics, 1990, Gerontological Social Work, 1992, Alcoholism & Aging, 1995; Jour. Social Issues, 1980; spl. editor: Jour. Minority Aging, 1984. Grantee Adminstrn. on Aging, 1978-79, 79-82, 85-87—, Adjusting to Widowhood Va., 1978-79, Temple U., 1983-84, Health Resources and Svcs. Adminstrn., 1985-90, 91-94. Mem. APA, So. Gerontol. Soc. (treas. 1984-87), Assn. Gerontology in Higher Edn., Sigma Xi. Avocation: photography. Office: Va Commonwealth U Gerontology Dept Med Coll Va MCV Box 980228 Richmond VA 23298

PARIKH, ARVINDKUMAR MADHAVLAL, education educator, video producer; b. D.Baria, India, Aug. 8, 1925; came to U.S., 1954; s. Madhavlal C. and Maniben M. (Gandhi) P.; m. Amita C. Master, May, 15, 1960; children: Linken, Chinten. BA with honors, Elphinstone Coll., Bombay, 1949; MA, Ind. State U., 1955; EdD, Ind. U., 1958. Printer, pub. Usha Printery, Dohad, India, 1949-53; tchr. New Era Sch., Bombay, 1954, Bloomington (Ind.) High Sch., 1957-58; cons. Nat. Edn. Film Co., Bombay, 1959; instr. Dillard U., New Orleans, 1960-62, asst. prof., 1962-63; lectr. Regional Coll. Edn., Ajmer, India, 1963-65; assoc. prof. Dillard U., New Orleans, 1966-73, prof., 1973-89; v.p. New Orleans Video Access Corp., 1990-91; mem. State Review Bd. for Accreditation, La., 1979, State Bd. Edn., Rajasthan, India, 1964-65. Author: A Comparative Study of Western Theories of Literary Criticism, 1951, Lesson Planning in Indian Schools, 1967; editor: (with B. Rutherford) Parameters of Human Behavior, 1975; prodr. (video series) This Is India, 1988— (8 awards at Hometown U.S.A. video festival 1989-94); freelance writer Times Picayune, New Orleans, 1996—. V.p. Livingston Mid. Sch. PTA, 1975-76; chmn. parents' group New Orleans East Benjamin Franklin H.S.; bd. dirs. Indian Bus. Assn., 1989-91; founder, pres. Edn. India Found., 1989—. Recipient Outstanding Community Leadership award Cultural Heritage India, 1991, Personality of South award, 1971, Outstanding Educator of Am. award, 1972. Mem. India Assn. New Orleans (founder, pres. 1966-67, chmn. bd. trustees 1976-78, sec. 1978-87), Asian Pacific Am. Soc. (founder, v.p. 1979), Ednl. India Found. (founder, pres. 1988—). Home: 13111 Cherbourg St New Orleans LA 70129-1307 Office: Ednl India Found PO Box 29343 New Orleans LA 70189-0343

PARIS, CHARLES HENRY, JR., gastroenterologist; b. Memphis, Jan. 20, 1942; s. Charles H. Sr. and Volla (Deen) P.; m. Martha Virginia Hill, Dec. 11, 1965; children: Charles III, Elisabeth, Steven, Amy, Mary, Amanda. BS, Middle Tenn. State U., 1963; MD, U. Tenn., 1967. Intern John Gaston Hosp., U. Tenn., Memphis, 1967-68; resident internal medicine U. Tenn., Memphis, 1970-72, fellow gastroenterology, 1972-73; pvt. practice Cooper Clinic, Ft. Smith, Ark., 1973-80, 81—; fellow gastroenterology Royal North Shore Hosp., Sydney, Australia, 1980; staff St. Edward Mercy Hosp., Ft. Smith, Ark., 1973—. Served to lt. U.S. Navy, 1968-70. Fellow Am. Coll. Gastroenterology; mem. Am. Soc. Gastrointestinal Endoscopy, ACS. Office: Cooper Clin PO Box 3528 Fort Smith AR 72913-3528

PARIS, KAREN MARIE, nurse, educator; b. Bloomington, Ind., Oct. 15, 1952; d. Robert Ross and Theresa (Hessig) McEllininey; m. David J. Paris; 1 child, Stephanie. BS in Nursing, U. Evansville, 1975; M in Nursing Adminstrn., U. Tex.-Austin, 1989. RN, Ind., Tex.; cert. med.-surg. nurse. Commd. 1st lt. U.S. Army, 1973, advanced through grades to lt. col., 1990, ret. 1994; nurse instr. Acad. Health Scis., Ft. Sam Houston, Tex., 1978-79, phase 2 coord., 1979-80, tng. officer, 1980-81, dep. program dir. satellite TV, 1981-82; asst. head nurse Madigan Army Med. Ctr., Tacoma, Wash., 1983, nurse instr., 1983-85; head nurse surg. unit, 1986, exec. officer Spl. Assistance Team, Liberia, 1985; head nurse orthopedic unit Brooke Army Med. Ctr., Ft. Sam Houston, Tex., 1989-90; head nurse Consol. Troop Med. Clinic, 1990-94; nurse mgr. orthopedic dept. Bapt. Med. Ctr., 1994-95; resource nurse, healthcare finder Found. Health Fed. Svcs., San Antonio, 1996—. Prodr. 18 videotapes/live TV programs for health providers, 1981-82. Treas. Fox Glen Homeowners Assn., Tacoma, 1984; bd. dirs. Olympia Hills Neighborhood Assn., 1988-90; bd. dirs. Valhaven, Inc. Decorated Legion of Merit Army Commendation medal with 2 bronze oak leaf clusters, Humanitarian Svc. medal. Mem. AMSUS, Nat. Assn. Orthopaedic Nurses, Nat. League Nurses, Assn. Fed. Nurses (pres. 1984-85), Phi Kappa Phi, Sigma Theta Tau. Republican. Lodge: Order Eastern Star. Home: 8315 Athenian Dr Universal City TX 78148-2515 Office: Found Health Fed Svcs 7800 I10 Ste 300 San Antonio TX 78230-2025

PARIS, VIRGINIA HALL (GINGER PARIS), elementary school educator; b. Talladega, Ala., Sept. 25, 1962; d. Robert Dorch and Bonnie (Green) Hall; m. Walter Kevin Paris, June 8, 1985; children: Taylor Ray, Tyger Jean. AS, Jefferson State Jr. Coll., 1982; BS, Auburn U., 1984; MS, Jacksonville State U., 1991, U. Ala., Birmingham, 1994. Cert. ednl. leadership. Tchr. gifted program Talladega County Schs., 1984-85, tchr. learning disabled program, 1988-89; tchr. Big Bend C.C., Vicenza, Italy, 1986-87; tchr., dir. Villagio Child Devel. Ctr., Vicenza, 1987-88; tchr. social studies Dixon Mid. Sch., Talladega, 1989-91, tchr. sci., 1991—; insvc. edn. cons. U. Montevallo, 1994—; acad. pep squad sponsor, 1995—, sch. news reporter, 1989-93, 95—, ann. photographer, 1991-94, student coun. adv., 1989—, sponsor Trail Blazer/Ecology Club, 1992—, mem. staff devel. accreditation com. chairperson, comm. com. sec.; tchr. rep. spl. edn. screening com. Talladega City Schs., 1989-93; vis. com. So. Assn. Colls. and Schs., Montgomery, Ala., 1992. Vol. instr. ARC, Vicenza, 1986, Talladega, 1988; coord. Adopt-a-Grandparent program Talladega Health Care, 1991—; mem. Friends of Libr., Talladega, 1992; coord., sponsor March for Parks, Talladega, 1994, 95, 96; bd. dirs. Talladega Parks and Recreation, chairperson, 1995—; mem. planning com. Talladega 2000, mem. steering com., 1996. Recipient Tchr. of Yr. award Dixon Rep. Ala., 1991-92, Pilot Club Tchr. of Yr 1995, Tchr. of Yr. award Dixon Rep. Jacksonville State U., 1992-93; Tchr. of the Yr. Jaycees 1994-95. Mem. NEA, Ala. Edn. Assn., Nat. Sci. Tchrs. Assn., Talladega City Edn. Assn., Anniston Mus. Natural History, Ala. Cattlewomen's Assn., Environ. Edn. Assn., Nat. Pks. and Conservation Assn., Nat. Audubon Soc., Nat. Arbor Day Found., Nat. Wildlife Assn., Auburn U. Alumni Assn., Ala. Middle Sch. Assn. (program dir. region VI 1995—),S Kappa Delta Pi, Delta Zeta Alumni. Republican. Baptist. Home: 620 Cherry St Talladega AL 35160-2716 Office: Dixon Mid Sch 415 Elm St Talladega AL 35160-2704

PARK, BETH GUENZEL, public relation professional; b. Ft. Worth, Mar. 24, 1965; d. Edwin Louis and Mary Alice (Wilson) Guenzel; m. Douglas Natt Park, June 10, 1995. BS in Journalism, U. North Tex., 1987. Accredited in pub. rels. Part-time writer Ft. Worth Ind. Sch. Dist., 1987; cmty. rels. asst. Lena Pope Home, Inc., Ft. Worth, 1987-89, devel. assoc., 1989-91, dir. cmty. resources, 1991—; mem. mktg. com. North Tex. Behavioral Healthcare Network, Ft. Worth, 1995—. Recipient Addy award Advt. Club of Ft. Worth, 1995; Celebrity Breakfast scholar Women in Comm., 1985, 86, 87. Mem. Pub. Rels. Soc. of Am. (cert., sec. 1993—, bd. dirs. 1995), Women in Comm., Inc. (treas. 1985—, bd. dirs. 1995), Soc. of Profl. Journalists, Spl. Events Comm. Soc. Roman Catholic. Office: Lena Pope Home Inc 4701 W Rosedale Fort Worth TX 76107

PARK, CHERYL ANTOINETTE, women's health nurse, educator; b. Pitts., Mar. 4, 1945; d. Louis Joseph and Rose Gertrude (Rosenberger) Seethaler; m. Phocion Samuel Park Jr., Dec. 17, 1983; children: Louis Joseph, Phocion Samuel III. Diploma, St. Francis Med. Ctr., Pitts., 1974; BS in Edn., Carlow Coll., Pitts., 1971; MEd, U. Pitts., 1977; BSN magna cum laude, U. Tex., Houston, 1988. Cert. natural family planning practitioner, Am. Acad. Natural Family Planning. Primary therapist, staff nurse Western Psychiat. Inst. and Clinic/U. Pitts., 1975-76; dir., instr. psychiat. nursing edn. Ohio Valley Gen. Hosp. Sch. Nursing, McKees Rocks, Pa., 1976-78; charge nurse, clin. nurse St. Joseph Hosp., Houston, 1978-88; pres. N.W. Natural Family Planning Svcs., Houston. Contbr. articles to profl. jours. Charter mem. bd. dirs. Natural Family Planning Adv. Bd., Houston, 1982—. Mem. Assn. Christian Therapists, Med. Quality Found., Sigma Theta Tau. Home: 8114 Trail Side Dr Houston TX 77040-2655

PARK, FRANCES MIHEI, food products executive, author; b. Cambridge, Mass., Apr. 3, 1955; d. Sei-Young and Heisook Hong Park. BS in Psychology, Va. Poly. Inst. and State U., 1977. Supr. masters programs Sch. Govt. and Bus. Adminstrn. George Washington U., Washington, 1978-81; founder, co-owner Park Ltd. T/A Chocolate Chocolate, Washington, 1982—. Contbr. stories, poems to profl. publs. Bus. subject of various mag. and newspaper articles, including Washington Dossier, N.Y. Times, Victoria Mag., Washington Post, Gault Millau Guide, Washingtonian Mag., also featured on local, nat. and internat. cable TV, BBC and Nat. Pub. Radio; recipient Best Candy Store award Washingtonian Mag., 1986, 2d prize for fiction award Willow Rev., 1993, Rosebud Mag. award for contemporary writing for short story "Premonition", 1995. Office: Chocolate Chocolate 1050 Connecticut Ave NW Washington DC 20036-5303

PARK, PHOCION SAMUEL, JR., family and drug abuse therapist; b. Balt., Oct. 7, 1944; s. Phocion Samuel and Frances Jeanne (Schneider) P.; m. Cheryl Antoinette Seethaler, Dec. 17, 1983; adopted children: Louis Joseph, Phocion Samuel III. BA, U. St. Thomas, 1967; MA in Am. History, U. Houston, 1971; MDiv, U. St. Michael's Coll., 1973; Master of Applied Sci. in Human Rels. & Counseling Studies, U. Waterloo, 1975; postgrad., McMaster U., 1979-82. Lic. profl. counselor, Tex., lic. chem. dependency counselor, Tex., lic. marriage and family therapist, Tex.; cert. social work assoc., Tex. Social worker, family svc. Children's Aid Soc., Guelph, Ont., Can., 1974-79; team leader, family counseling unit Cath. Social Svc., Hamilton, Ont., 1979-82; family counselor, theology & hist. tchr. Diocese of Galveston-Houston, 1982-85; individual, marital, family therapist Houston Ctrs. for Christian Counseling, 1986-87; individual and group therapist, psychiat. and chem. dependency units Rapha, Houston, 1987—; pvt. practice Houston, 1987—; coord., inner healing teams Cathlolic Charismatic Ctr., Houston, 1982—; leader, word gifts ministry Bread of Life Community, Hamilton, 1979-82; liaison from diocese of Hamilton, Cath. Charismatic Svc. of Ont., 1977-79. Co-author: Creative Rosary Meditations, 1979; contbr. articles to profl. jours. Recipient Tex. Jr. Historian Writing Contest 2d Pl. award Tex. State Hist. Assn., 1962. Mem. Am. Assn. for Marriage and Family Therapy, Assn. of Christian Therapists, KC (chmn. pro-life com. 1987—). Roman Catholic. Home: 8114 Trail Side Dr Houston TX 77040-2655

PARK, W(ILLIAM) B(RYAN), cartoonist, writer, artist. BA in Design, U. Fla., 1959; postgrad., Sch. Visual Arts, 1960-61, Rollins Coll., 1977, 87. Creator, illustrator comic feature Off the Leash, 1985—; adj. instr. U. Ctrl. Fla.; lectr. in field. Author, illustrator children's books: The Pig in the Floppy Black Hat, 1974, Jonathan's Friends, 1977, Charlie-Bob's Fan, 1981, Bakery Business, 1983, The Costume Party, 1983, Who's Sick!, 1983, Off the Leash, 1987, Far Off the Leash, 1989; group shows include Nat. Fine Arts Mus., Budapest, Hungary, Time, Inc., N.Y.C., Internat. Biennial Humor and Satire in the Arts Show, Gabrovo, Bulgaria, N.Y. Soc. Illustrators Traveling Exhibition, 1993-94, others; illustrator: (books) American City, A Parade of Lines, Survival, others, (jours., mags., newspapers) Litigation, The New Yorker, The American Way, Smithsonian, Publishers Weekly, T.V. Guide, Travel & Leisure, The New York Times, The Washington Post, Look, Flying, Car & Driver, Intellectual Digest, St. Petersburg Times, America Illustrated, Topic; featured in various mags. including Communication Arts, Print, Today's Art and Denzu 08, Look; contbr. articles to profl. jours., mags. Recipient Silver Funnybone award N.Y. Soc. Illustrators, Reuben award 91 advt. illustration divsn. Nat. Cartoonist Soc., 1991, greeting cards illustration divsn., 1993, Orlandocon Lifetime Achievment award. Mem. N.Y. Soc. Illustrators, Nat. Cartoonists Soc. Studio: Park-Art Studio 110 S Park Ave Winter Park FL 32789-4315

PÁRKÁNYI, CYRIL, chemistry educator, research scientist; b. Prague, Czechoslovakia, Sept. 11, 1933; came to U.S., 1965; s. Ivan and Olga (Petrik) P.; m. Marie Hřebíček, Jan. 16, 1960; 1 child, Michael Peter. B.S. equivalent Charles U., Prague, 1954, M.S. with honors, 1956, Dr. rerum natur., 1966; Ph.D., Czechoslovak Acad. Scis., Prague, 1962. Phys. and analytical chemist Research and Control Inst. Food Industry, Prague, 1955-56; research scientist Inst. Phys. Chemistry, Czechoslovak Acad. Scis., Prague, 1960-65, sr. research scientist, 1967-68; assoc. prof. chemistry U. Tex.-El Paso, 1969-71, prof., 1971-88, chmn., 1982-88; prof., chmn. dept. chemistry Fla. Atlantic U., Boca Raton, 1989-94, prof., 1995—; vis. prof. Rijksuniversiteit te Leiden, Netherlands, 1965, Calif. Inst. Tech., Pasadena, 1965-67, 68-69, U. d'Aix-Marseille, France, 1974, 77, 86, 95, U. Kuwait, 1976, Rijksuniversiteit te Groningen, Netherlands, 1978, Univ. des Scis. et Techniques de Lille 1, Villeneuve d'Ascq, France, 1980, 81, 82, U. Denis Diderot-Paris 7, Paris, 1995; lectr. in field. Contbr. articles to profl. jours. Recipient Czechoslovak Acad. Scis. Rsch. award, 1963, Faculty Research award U. Tex.-El Paso, 1980, Disting. Achievement in Teaching award, 1982; Outstanding Tchr. award Amoco Found., 1982, Acad. Excellence award, 1985, medal U. Qatar, Doha, Qatar, 1993. Fellow AAAS, N.Y. Acad. Scis.; mem. Am. Chem. Soc., Fedn. Am. Scientists, Inter-Am. Photochem. Soc., Internat. Soc. Quantum Biology, Am. Soc. Photobiology, European Acad. Scis., Arts and Humanities (corr.), Sigma Xi, Phi Kappa Phi. Catholic (Byzantine rite). Achievements include research on physical properties of aromatic and heteroaromatic compounds. Home: 245 NW 69th St Boca Raton FL 33487-2390 Office: Fla Atlantic U Dept Chemistry & Biochemistry PO Box 3091 Boca Raton FL 33431-0991

PARKE, DAVID WILKIN, II, ophthalmologist, educator, healthcare executive; b. Columbus, Ohio, May 19, 1951; s. David William Parke and Eunice Joyce Erikson; m. Julie Diane Thorne, Sept. 15, 1975; children: David W. III, Laura Thorne, Lindsey Diane. AB, Stanford U., 1973; MD, Baylor U., 1977. Diplomate Am. Bd. Ophthalmology. Resident in internal medicine Baylor Coll. Medicine, Houston, 1977-78, resident in ophthalmology, 1978-81, fellow in med. retina, 1981-82, asst. prof., 1983-90, assoc. prof., 1990-92; fellow diseases and surgery of the retina and vitreous Med. Coll. of Wis., 1982-83; prof., chair dept. ophthalmology U. Okla., Oklahoma City, 1992—; pres., CEO McGee Eye Inst., Oklahoma City, 1992—. Active Okla. Econ. Devel. Found., 1992, Okla. Health Ctr. Found., 1992; trustee Presbyn. Health Found., 1995—; mng. dir. Stephenson Laser Ctr., 1996—; bd. mgrs. Okla. Health Alliance, 1995—. Fellow Am. Acad. Ophthalmology (assoc. sec. 1983-92, Honor award 1980); mem. Assn. Univ. Profs. Ophthalmology, Retina Soc., Vitreous Soc., Alpha Omega Alpha. Office: Dean A McGee Eye Institute 608 Stanton L Young Blvd Oklahoma City OK 73104-5014

PARKE, ROBERT LEON, communications executive; b. Jersey City, Aug. 28, 1940; s. Edwin Gager and Alice Elizabeth (Servis) P.; m. Geraldine R. Pavlick, Sept. 2, 1967; children: Cheryl Lynn, Tracy Ann, David Scott. Grad. high sch., Jersey City. Asst. bookkeeper Snow-Kist Frozen Foods, Jersey City, 1964-67; supr. accounts receivable Swift Line Transfer Co., Inc., North Bergen, N.J., 1967-69; contr. Imperial Cartage Co., Inc., Jersey City, 1969-79; supr. inventory mgmt. Vista United Telecommunications, Lake Buena Vista, Fla., 1980—; corp. sec. Imperial Warehouse Co., Inc., Jersey City, 1968-79, Arbe Transfer Co. Inc., 1968-79; v.p. Cole Foods, Inc., Jersey City, 1968-79;. Spl. min. of the eucharist Diocese Orlando, Fla., 1992; vol. Gave Kids The World, Kissimmee, Fla.; mem. Pemberton Twp. Zoning Bd., Browns Mills, N.J., 1977-79; trustee, bd. dirs. Browns Mills Improvement Assn., 1974-79; trustee Rebecca Worf Meml. Fund Browns Mills, N.J., Parke Soc., S.E. Milw.; hon. trustee Am. Indian Relief Coun. Recipient Cert. Appreciation Am. Indian Relief Coun., 1996, hon. trustee; recipient spl. recognition award masters degree program in Nat. Security Studies, Grad. Sch. of Georgetown U., 1996; Bob Parke day proclaimed by Twp. of Pemberton, 1979. Mem. Nat. Notary Assn., Fla. Notary Assn., Am. Soc. Notaries, Nat. Assn. Purchasing Mgmt. Ctrl. Fla. (named scholar), Nat. Assn. Purchasing Mgmt. (scholarship for continued edn., Ctrl. Fla. Most Supportive Mem. 1994), Fla. Sheriffs Assn. (life, hon.). Office: Vista United Telecommunications 3100 Bonnet Creek Rd Lake Buena Vista FL 32830

PARKER, BETTY MORRIS, association administrator retired; b. Gordonsville, Va., Feb. 28, 1933; d. Benjamin and Evie (Hall) Morris; m. James Clayton Parker, Feb. 28, 1958; children: Patricia, Paula, James Jr. BA, U. Ctrl. Fla., 1985. Cert. profl. health educator, smoking cessation trainer; accredited pub. rels. profl. Bookkeeper State Farm Ins., Richmond, Va., 1954-56, Daytona Beach, Fla., 1956-59; program adminstr. Am. Lung Assn., Daytona Beach, Fla., 1978-85, regional dir., 1985—; pres. Fla. Congress Lung Staff Devel., 1988-89; regional dir. Spaceport region Am. Lung Assn. of Fla., 1985-95. Mem. legis. com. Daytona Beach/Halifax Area C. of C., 1990—; charter mem., sec. U. Ctrl. Fla., Volusia/Flagler Alumni Assn., Daytona Beach, 1990; chairperson Volusia County Sch. Health Adv. Coun., 1991. Recipient Sci. Fair Judge award Sch. Bd. Brevard County, 1982. Mem. Fla. Pub. Rels. Assn., Pilot Club of Halifax Area (pub. rels. area leader 1995—), Brevard County Vol. Health Assn. (pres. 1984-85), Am. Assn. Univ. Women (scholarship com. chmn. 1995—), Mus. Arts & Sci., Daytona Beach, Art League of Daytona Beach. Baptist. Home: 2115 S Peninsula Dr Daytona Beach FL 32118-5235

PARKER, DAVID FORSTER, real estate development consultant; b. Sarnia, Ont., Can., July 4, 1934; s. George William and Bessie Havergal (Forster) P.; m. Marilynn Catherine McFadden, Oct. 15, 1960; children: John Christopher, Stephen, David, Daniel. Student, U. Toronto, Ont., Can., 1954-57; BS, Mich. State U., 1964, M in Urban Planning, 1965; D in Pub. Adminstrn., SUNY, Albany, 1980. Prin. Tricon Ltd. Builders, Sarnia, Ont., 1957-62; urban planner N.Y. State Dept. Transp., Albany, 1965-66; asst. to dir. N.Y. State Budget, Albany, 1967-69; pres. Audubon Devel. Corp., Buffalo, 1969-76; dep. dir. Sadat City, Cairo, Egypt, 1976-79; cons. Milton Keynes (Eng.), 1979-80; v.p. Bos Corp., Jacksonville, Fla., 1980-82; prin. Clark Parker Assocs., Jacksonville, 1982-90, Parker Assocs., Jacksonville, 1990—, Clark Parker Realty, Jacksonville, 1982-92; pres. Fla. Real Estate Clinic, Inc., 1991-94; real estate broker, 1992—; pres. PFE, Inc., 1994—. Author: Marketing New Homes, 1990 (recognition 1990), Selling New Homes, 1990 (recognition 1990); contbr. articles to profl. jours. Chmn. Albany Citizens Against Poverty, 1966-67, Ctrl. Jacksonville Residential Task Force, 1986-88, Mayor's Housing Com., Jacksonville, 1990—. Mem. Inst. Residential Mktg., Nat. Assn. Home Builders, Jacksonville C. of C., S.E. Resort Real Estate Coun., Urban Land Inst., Comty. Devel. Coun., Am. Inst. Cert. Planners, Soc. for Preservation and Encouragement of Barbershop Quartet Singing in America (greater Jacksonville chpt. pres. 1990-92, sunshine dist. dir. 1993—, v.p. 1995-97), Selva Marina Country Club, Phi Kappa Phi, Beta Alpha Sigma, Phi Sigma Alpha. Home: 1739 Live Oak Ln Jacksonville FL 32233-5605 Office: Parker Assocs 14500 Beach Blvd Jacksonville FL 32250-2302

PARKER, DONALD SAMUEL, lawyer; b. Jersey City, July 21, 1948; s. Raymond E. And Alice J. (Gilman) P.; m. Elizabeth F. Dalton, Aug. 11, 1978; children: Luke, Genevieve. AB, Wesleyan U., Middletown, Conn., 1970; JD, U. Chgo., 1973. Bar: N.Y. 1975, U.S. Dist. Ct. (so. dist.) N.Y. 1975, U.S. Ct. Appeals (2d cir.) 1975, U.S. Supreme Ct. 1976, Va. 1989. Assoc. Cahill Gordon & Reindel, N.Y.C., 1974-83; asst. gen. counsel Lever Bros. Co., N.Y.C., 1983-85; dep. gen. counsel Fairchild Industries, Inc., Chantilly, Va., 1985-89, v.p., gen. counsel, 1989-91; v.p., gen. counsel Sprint Internat., 1991-96; v.p. law, regulatory external affairs, gen. counsel Global One Telecomm., Inc., 1996—. Assoc. editor U. Chgo. Law Rev., 1972-73. Mem. ABA, Va. State Bar, N.Y. State Bar Assn., River Bend Country Club. Office: Global One Telecomm 12490 Sunrise Valley Dr Reston VA 22091-3470

PARKER, EDWARD FROST, retired surgeon; b. Charleston, S.C., Nov. 14, 1910; s. Edward Frost and Harriet (Horry) P.; m. Alice Cheatham Hodgson; 5 sons. BS, U. S.C., Columbia, 1931; MD, Duke U., 1933. Diplomate Nat. Bd. Med. Examiners, Am. Bd. Thoracic Surgery. Prof. surgery emeritus Med. U. S.C., Charleston, 1933-34; asst. resident in Surgery U. Va. Hosp., Charlottesville, 1935-36; intern in Surgery Vanderbilt U. Hosp., Nashville, 1934-35, asst. resident in Surgery, 1936-38, resident in Surgery, 1938-39; clin. assoc. in Surgery Med. U. S.C., Charleston, 1939-42, clin. asst. prof. Surgery, 1946-64, clin. assoc. prof. Thoracic Surgery, 1964-65, clin. prof. Thoracic Surgery, 1965-75; prof. Surgery emeritus VA Med. Ctr., Charleston, 1975—; instr. surgery Sch. Medicine Vanderbilt U. Hosp., Nashville, 1936-39, instr. surgery in absentia, 1942-46; pvt. practice, Charleston, 1939-42; cons. in thoracic surgery VA, Atlanta met. area, 1946-75. Contbr. 84 articles to profl. jours. Lt. Col. U.S. Army, 1942-45. Recipient Bronze Star for Meritorious Svc. U.S. Army, 1945, Golden Apple award Am. Med. Student Assn., 1978-79. Mem. AMA, ACS, Med. Soc. S.C., Am. Surg. Assn., Soc. Univ. Surgeons, Am. Trudeau Soc., Charleston County Med. Soc. (past pres.), Am. Heart Assn., So. Surg. Assn. (past pres.), So. Surgeons Club (past pres.), So. Thoracic Surg. Assn. (past pres.), S.C. Tuberculosis Assn. (past pres.), S.C. Surg. Soc. (past pres.), Excelsior Surg. Soc. (past pres.), S.C. Heart Assn., Nat. Lung Assn. (past rep. dir. S.C. chpt.), Alpha Tau Omega, Nu Sigma Nu, Alpha Omega Alpha.

PARKER, GEORGE PRIESTLEY, JR., lawyer; b. San Antonio, July 7, 1943; s. George P. Sr. and Imogene Irene (Challis) P.; m. Julie Beth Flatt; children: Laura Lee, George III. BA, U. Tex., 1965, JD, 1968. Bar: Calif. 1969, Tex. 1972, U.S. Supreme Ct., U.S. Dist. Ct. (no., we., ea. and so. dists.) Tex., U.S. Dist. Ct. (ctrl. dist.) Calif., U.S. Ct. Appeals (5th, 9th and 11th cirs.). Assoc. Kindel & Anderson, L.A., 1968-72; with Matthews & Branscomb, San Antonio, 1972-96, Wells Pinckney & McHugh, San Antonio, 1996—; lectr. in field. Contbr. chpt. to book. Pres. San Antonio Zool. Soc., 1988-91. Mem. ABA (labor and employment law sect., com. equal employment opportunity law 1974—), San Antonio Bar Assn. (chmn. fed. cts. com. 1984—), S.W. Legal Found. (labor law inst. planning com. 1984—), Tex. Assn. Bus. C. of C. (employment law subcom. 1985—, exec. com. S.W. chpt. 1984-95), Tex. Law Rev. Assn. (dir. 1987—). Office: Wells Pinckney & McHugh One Almo Ctr 106 S Saint Marys St San Antonio TX 78205-3601

PARKER, GERALD M., physician, researcher; b. Olean, N.Y., Nov. 20, 1943; s. Richard and Kathleen (Manwaring) P.; m. Linda Kay Stuart, Dec. 28, 1968; children: Kimberly, Gerald, Cassandra, Kevin. B.A., Western Wash. U., 1965; D.O., Kirksville Coll. Osteopathy & Surgery, 1969. Intern, Art Centre Hosp., Detroit, 1969-70; ptnr. Doctor's Clinic, Amarillo, Tex., 1969—; dir. Southwest Inst. Preventive Medicine, Amarillo, 1978—, Hyperbaric Oxygen Ctr., Amarillo, 1979—. Contbr. articles to profl. jours. Appeared on That's Incredible TV show, 1982. Pres., Southwest Amarillo Little Dribblers Assn., 1979—; coach Girls Nat. Champion Basketball Teams, 1981, 83, 84, 85, 86, 87, 89. Fellow Am. Acad. Med. Preventics; mem. Southwest Acad. Preventive Medicine (pres. 1980—), Am. Osteopathic Assn. Methodist. Avocation: athletics. Office: Doctors Clinic 4714 S Western St Amarillo TX 79109-5950 also: 9577 Osuna Rd NE Albuquerque NM 87111-2271

PARKER, GLENN RICHARD, political science educator; b. St. Paul, Mar. 5, 1946; s. Algernon Richardo and Grace (Raps) P.; m. Suzanne Lee Bore, Sept. 3, 1966; 1 child, Christopher Glenn. BA in Polit. Sci. with distinction, U. Ill., 1968; MA, U. Calif., Santa Barbara, 1970; PhD, U. Calif., 1973; postgrad., U. Mich., 1970, 71. Lectr. dept. polit. sci. U. Calif., Santa Barbara, 1972; from asst. to assoc. prof. dept. polit. sci. Miami U., Oxford, Ohio, 1973-79; assoc. prof. dept. polit. sci. Fla. State U., Tallahassee, 1979-82, prof. dept. polit. sci., 1982—; prof. Policy Scis. Ctr. Fla. State U., 1985—, disting. rsch. prof., 1992—; vis. asst. prof. dept. polit. sci. Earlham Coll., spring 1974; vis. assoc. prof. dept. polit. sci. U. Calif., Santa Barbara, summer 1978, 79; vis. rsch. assoc. Ctr. for Study of Pub. Choice, George Mason U., spring 1988; mem. standing com. on congl. election rsch. Nat. Election Studies, U. Mich., 1978; guest scholar The Brookings Instn., 1979-80; John Adams Prof. in Am. studies Fulbright Scholar Program, The Netherlands, 1993-94; participant and discussant various confs. and seminars in field. Author: Political Beliefs About the Structure of Govennment: Congress and the Presidency, 1974, Homeward Bound: Explaining Changes in Congressional Behavior, 1986, Characteristics of Congress: Patterns in Congressional Behavior, 1989, Institutional Change, Discretion, and the Making of Modern Congress: An Economic Interpretation, 1992, Congress and the Rent-Seeking Society, 1996, (with Suzanne Parker) Factions in House Committees, 1985; editor: Studies of Congress, 1985; contbr. chpts. to books; mem. editorial bd. Am. Politics Quar., 1981-87. Chmn. Senator Howard Metzenbaum's primary campaign, Oxford Twp., 1974; cons. govt. affairs tng. U.S. Civil Svc. Commn., 1974-75, mem. inter-agy. task force on pub. svc. briefing programs for polit. appointees, 1976, assoc. dir. govt. affairs tng., 1975-76; cons. commn. adminstrv. rev. U.S. Ho. Reps., summer 1977. Dissertation rsch. grantee U. Calif., 1971-72, faculty rsch. grantee, Miami U., 1975-76; developing scholar Fla. State U., 1981-82. Fellow Am. Polit. Sci. Assn. (congl., chmn. legis. studies sect. 1985-87, panel discussant/

chmn. ann. meetings, Congl. Quar. prize for best paper 1987); Western Polit. Sci. Assn. (panel discussant/chmn. ann. meetings), Am. Assn. for Pub. Opinion Rsch. (panel discussant/chmn. ann. meetings), Pub. Choice Soc. (co-chmn. local arrangements com. ann. meeting 1973, panel discussant), So. Polit. Sci. Assn. (panel discussant/chmn. ann. meetings), Midwest Polit. Sci. Assn. (panel discussant/chmn.). Office: Fla State U Policy Scis Ctr Bellamy Hall Tallahassee FL 32306-2018

PARKER, HARRY LEE, retired military officer, counselor; b. Birmingham, Ala., Feb. 20, 1944; s. Guy Milburn and Grace (Lee) P.; m. Sheri Lynn Pogue (div. Oct. 1973); children: John Lee, Suzanne Grace, Stephen Scott; m. Melanie Louise Cox, Apr. 20, 1979; 1 child, Christopher Robert. BA, Miss. State U., 1966; MS, Johns Hopkins U., 1980; postgrad., U.S. Army Command & Staff Coll, 1982. Commd. 2d lt. U.S. Army, 1966, advanced through grades to lt. col.; maintenance officer 85th Maintenance Bn., Hanau, Fed. Republic of Germany, 1967-69; commanding officer 143d Engr. Co. and A Co. 34th Engr. Bn., Long Binh, Vietnam, 1969-70; chief plans and ops. div. Dir. of Logistics, Ft. Rucker, Ala., 1971-73; supply and maintenance officer 97th Signal Bn. NATO, Mannehim, Fed. Republic of Germany, 1973-76; asst. materiel officer 8th Maintenance Battalion, Grossalheim, Fed. Republic Germany, 1977; tng. evaluator HQ 1st US Army, Ft. Meade, Md., 1978-81; logistics coord. Cuban Task Force, Ft. Indiantown Gap, Pa., 1980; project officer Dept. Def., Project Office, Mobile Electric Power, Washington, 1982-85; chief of maintenance U.S. Army South, Ft. Clayton, Panama, 1985-88; prof. mil. Sci. Army ROTC, Miss. State U., Starkville, Miss., 1988-90; ops. officer 101st area support group, Guardian City, Saudia Arabia, logistics officer, 1st Corps Support Command, XVIII Airborne Corps., Damman, Saudi Arabia (Desert Shield and Desert Storm), 1990-91; career/coop. edn. counselor Cen. Fla. C.C., Ocala, Fla., 1992-95. Presbyn. elder. Decorated 2 Bronze Stars, 3 Meritorious Svc. medals, 5 Army Commendation medals. Mem. Ret. Officers Asn., Am. Legion, Miss. State U. Alumni Assn., Sigma Chi (life). Home: 7514 NW 42nd Ave Gainesville FL 32606

PARKER, JACQUELYN SUSAN, military officer; b. Wilmington, Del., July 4, 1960; d. William Dale and Boots (Farthing) Parker. AA and BS, U. Cen. Fla., Orlando, 1978. Contr. space flight NASA, Houston, 1978-80; commd. 2d lt. USAF, 1980, advanced through grades to major, 1992; test pilot Wright Patterson AFB, Dayton, Ohio, 1989-92; major USAFR, 1993—, N.Y. Air Nat. Guard, 1993-96, Wash. State Air Nat. Guard, 1996—, F-16 fighter pilot. Emergency med. tech., Clearlake, Tex. Recipient Golden Eagle award Am. Acad. Achievement, 1979, Kitty Hawk award L.A. C. of C., 1980, Sands of Time award, 1989, Key to City of Dallas, 1980, Key to Success award, 1986-87; named Pathfinder of Yr., City of Lubbock, Tex., youngest grad of U. Ctrl. Fla. at age 17, 1st woman test pilot USAF, 1989, Ground Breaker award 1st Lady Hillary Clinton, 1994. Mem. Internat. Women's Air and Space Mus. (charter mem.), Mensa Internat., Order of Daedalians, VFW. Home: PO Box 1441 Titusville FL 32781-1441 Office: PO Box 246 Boone NC 28607

PARKER, JANICE MARIE, assistant principal, day camp director; b. Jackson, Ala., Mar. 17, 1956; d. Woodie and Annie Mae (Pugh) P. AA, U. Ala., Tuscaloosa, 1981, MA, 1979; BA, Stillman Coll., Tuscaloosa, 1978; EdS, U. Montevallo, Ala., 1997. Day camp coord./dir. Tuscaloosa County Park and Recreation Authority, Tuscaloosa, 1982—; tchr. Centreville (Ala.) Elem. Sch., Bibb County Bd. Edn., 1978-96, asst. prif., 1996—. Amsouth Bank grantee, 1993-94; Ala. Power Co. grantee, 1995-96; Bibb County Schs. Found. grantee, 1994-95, 95-96. Mem. Eastern Star, Phi Delta Kappa, Phi Theta Kappa, Alpha Kappa Mu, Zeta Phi Beta. Democrat. Baptist. Home: 1212 5th Ave E Tuscaloosa AL 35401 Office: Centreville Elem Sch 661 Montgomery Rd Centreville AL 35042

PARKER, JOHN GARRETT, lawyer; b. Roanoke Rapids, N.C., Mar. 6, 1947; s. Ben Thatch and Sarah Louise (Lessiter) P.; m. Helen Shell Nethercutt, Aug. 23, 1969; 1 child, Sarah Helen. BA in Econs., U. N.C., 1969, JD, 1976. Bar: Ga. 1976, U.S. Dist. Ct. (no. dist.) Ga. 1977, U.S. Ct. Appeals (5th and 11th cirs.) 1981, U.S. Ct. Appeals (9th cir.) 1986, U.S. Dist. Ct. (mid. dist.) Ga. 1989, U.S. Ct. Appeals (8th cir.) 1993. Assoc. atty. Hensell, Post, Brandon & Dorsey, Atlanta, 1976-83; ptnr. Hansell & Post, Atlanta, 1983-87, Paul, Hastings, Janofsky & Walker, Atlanta, 1987—. Co-chair Clark for Cong. com., Cobb County, Ga., 1992. Lt. U.S. Army, 1970-73. Mem. ABA, Atlanta Bar Assn., State Bar of Ga., Order of Coif. Republican. Episcopal. Home: 650 Mount Paran Rd Atlanta GA 30327 Office: Paul Hastings Janofsky & Walker 600 Peachtree St Ste 2400 Atlanta GA 30308

PARKER, JOHN HILL, lawyer; b. High Point, N.C., Feb. 1, 1944; s. George Edward and Tullia Virginia (Hill) P.; children from previous marriage: Alice Lindsey, Elizabeth Shelby (dec.); m. Lynette Becton Smith, July 7, 1977. BA, U. N.C., 1966; JD, U. Tenn., 1969. Bar: N.C. 1969, U.S. Dist. Ct. (ea dist.) N.C. 1970, U.S. Supreme Ct. Assoc. Sanford, Cannon, Adams & McCullough, Raleigh, N.C., 1969-73; pvt. practice Raleigh, 1974-76; judge N.C. Dist. Ct., Raleigh, 1976-82; ptnr. Cheshire & Parker, Raleigh, 1982—; instr. judges seminars Inst. Govt. Chapel Hill, N.C., 1977-82. Parlementarian Wake County Young Dems., 1971-73; mem. Raleigh Arts Commn., 1981-84, chmn. 1983. Fellow Am. Acad. Matrimonial Lawyers (ethics com. 1995-97); mem. ABA, N.C. Bar Assn. (editor family law sect. 1984-85, chmn. 1985-86, 96-97, continuing legal edn. for family law 1979, chmn. ethics com. 1989-90, chmn. gen. curriculum com. 1989-90), N.C. Acad. Trial Lawyers, Wake County Bar Assn. Episcopalian. Home: 1620 Park Dr Raleigh NC 27605-1609 Office: Cheshire & Parker PO Box 1029 133 Fayetteville St Mall Raleigh NC 27601-1356

PARKER, JOHN PATRICK, cardiologist; b. Chgo., May 19, 1948; s. Paul Patrick and Mary Eleanor (Metzgar) P.; m. Elizabeth Lane (div. 1976); m. Wendy Pocklington, Feb. 10, 1990; children: Paul Robert, Clare Allison. BA in Biology, Denison U., 1970; MD cum laude, Ohio State U., 1973. Diplomate Am. Bd. Internal Medicine, sub-bd. Cardiology; diplomate Nat. Bd. Med. Examiners; lic. physician, Ohio, N.C., Va. Resident in medicine Ohio State U., Columbus, 1973-76; fellow in cardiology Duke U. Med. Ctr., Durham, N.C., 1976-79; cardiologist Norfolk (Va.) Diagnostic Clinic, 1979-87, Cardiology Cons., Ltd., Norfolk, 1987—; active staff Sentara Norfolk Gen. Hosp., Sentara Leigh Hosp., DePaul Med. Ctr.; cons. staff Sentara Bayside Hosp., Southampton Meml. Hosp.; mem. bd. advisors Duke U. Heart Ctr. Fellow Am. Coll. Cardiology (allied health and edn. and accreditation com.); mem. IEEE, Am. Heart Assn. (coun. on clin. cardiology), Norfolk Acad. Medicine, Am. Med. Informatics Assn., Soc. for Med. Decision Making, Duke U. Cardiology Fellows Soc. (bd. dirs.). Home: 1220 Graydon Ave Norfolk VA 23507-1007 Office: Cardiology Cons Ltd 844 Kempsville Rd Ste 204 Norfolk VA 23502-3927

PARKER, JOHN R., physician, pathologist; b. Rochester, Minn., Apr. 29, 1967; s. Joseph Corbin and Patricia (Singleton) P. BA, MD, U. Mo., Kansas City. Rsch. asst. U. Tenn. Meml. Hosp., Knoxville, 1985; autopsy technician Truman Med. Ctr., Kansas City, 1990-93. Contbr. articles to Annals of Clin. and Lab. Sci., Archives of Pathology, Jour. Okla. State Med. Assn. Organizer 4-H Summer Scholars Med. Terminology, Lakewood Hosp., 1989-91; co-chmn. Impaired Med. Student Coun., 1990-91. Recipient Richardson K. Noback Clin. Excellence award, 1993, Gov.'s commendation State of Okla., 1995, cert. of appreciation Office of Chief Med. Examiner, State of Okla., 1995, U. Okla. Lloyd and Ruth Rader Trust Scholarship award, 1995-96; Pathology Student fellow Truman Med. Ctr., 1989-90. Mem. AMA, Okla. State Med. Assn., Coll. Am. Pathologists, Am. Soc. Clin. Pathologists, U.S. and Can. Acad. Pathology, Mortar Board, Golden Key, Alpha Omega Alpha, Omicron Delta Kappa. Democrat. Office: Office of Chief Med Examiner Ctrl Office 901 N Stonewall Oklahoma City OK 73117

PARKER, JOHN VICTOR, federal judge; b. Baton Rouge, La., Oct. 14, 1928; s. Fred Charles and LaVerne (Sessions) P.; m. Mary Elizabeth Fridge, Sept. 3, 1949; children: John Michael, Robert Fridge, Linda Anne. B.A., La. State U., 1949, J.D., 1952. Bar: La. 1952. Atty. Parker & Parker, Baton Rouge, 1954-66; asst. parish atty. City of Baton Rouge, Parish of East Baton Rouge, 1956-66; atty. Sanders, Downing, Kean & Cazedessus, Baton Rouge, 1966-79; chief judge U.S. Dist. Ct., Middle Dist. La., Baton Rouge, 1979—; vis. lectr. law La. State U. Law Sch. Served with Judge Adv. Gen.'s Corps U.S. Army, 1952-54. Mem. ABA, Am. Judicature Soc., Am. Arbitration Assn., La. State Bar Assn. (past mem. bd. govs.), Baton Rouge Bar Assn. (past pres.), Order of Coif, Phi Delta Phi. Democrat. Club: Baton Rouge Country. Lodges: Masons (32 deg.); Kiwanis (past pres.). Office: Russell B Long Fed Bldg & Courthouse 777 Florida St Ste 355 Baton Rouge LA 70801-1712

PARKER, JOSEPH MAYON, printing and publishing executive; b. Washington, N.C., Oct. 11, 1931; s. James Mayon and Mildred (Poe) P.; m. Lauretta Owen Dyer, Mar. 23, 1957; children: Katherine Suzanne, Joseph Wilbur. Student, Davidson Coll., 1949-51; BA, U. N.C., 1953, MPA, 1992; postgrad., Carnegie Inst. Tech., 1955-56. Mgr. print div. Parker Bros., Inc., Ahoskie, N.C., 1956-71, chief editorialist, 1961-77, gen. mgr., 1971-77, pres., chief exec. officer, 1977—; dir. Governor's Hwy. Safety Program, 1993—; treas. Chowan Graphic Arts Found., Murfreesboro, N.C., 1971-90, pres. 1990-92. Editor, columnist five community newspapers, N.C.; panelist: (TV talk show) North Carolina This Week, 1986-89. Mem. Ind. Devel. Commn., 1974-86; vice chmn. N.C. Goals and Policy Bd., Raleigh, 1977-84; trustee Pitt County Meml. Hosp., 1980-88; pres. Com. of 100, Winton, N.C., 1984-87; chmn. Northeastern N.C. Tomorrow, Elizabeth City, 1981-84, sec., 1984-90; del. Dem. Nat. Conv., N.Y.C., 1980, platform com., 1988; dist. chmn. N.C. Dem. Ctrl. Com., 1980-82. With U.S. Army, 1953-54, col. USAR, 1954-88. Mem. Soc. Profl. Journalists, East N.C. Press Assn. (past pres.), N.C. Press Assn., Nat. Newspaper Assn. (state chmn. 1976-83), Roanoke Island Hist. Assn. (vice-chmn. 1987-89), Ea. C. of C. (past chmn.), Rotary, Raleigh Exec. Club. Democrat. Methodist. Home: 4500 Connell Dr Raleigh NC 27612-5600 Office: 215 E Lane St Raleigh NC 27601-1035

PARKER, MARY ANN, lawyer; b. Pitts., Jan. 6, 1953; d. Harry N. Sr. and Mary (Sperl) P.; 1 child, Nickolas Parker Palacios. BS cum laude, SUNY, Buffalo, 1975; JD, U. Tenn., 1977. Bar: Tenn. 1978, U.S. Dist. Ct. (mid. dist.) Tenn. 1978, U.S. Ct. Appeals (5th cir.) 1980, U.S. Supreme Ct. 1982, U.S. Ct. Appeals (6th cir.) 1987. Asst. Dist. Atty. Gen., Ashland City, Tenn., 1977-78; sole practice Nashville, 1978—; instr. Nat. Trial Advocacy Coll., 1983-84. Cmty. svcs. vol. St. Henry's Women's Club, Nashville, 1984-90; mem. bldg. com. Holy Family, 1993-96; mem. Women's Polit. Caucus, Nashville, 1986—, Tenn. Dem. Polit. Com., 1988—, Tenn. Dem. Fin. Coun., 1991—; mem. Dem. Leadership Coun., 1991—, bd. dirs., 1992—. Mem. ABA, ATLA (del. 1983-86, sec. 1985-86, young lawyer's sect. sec. 1982-83, 2d vice chair 1983-84, 1st vice chair 1984-85, chair 1985-86, women's caucus sec. 1981-83, 1st vice chair 1983-84, chair motor vehicles, accidents, premises and govtl. liability sect. 1989-90, sec. torts sect. 1988-89, named Del. of Yr. 1986), Tenn. Trial Lawyers Assn. (bd. govs. 1978-86, chair consumer and victims coalition com. 1986-87), Trial Lawyers Pub. Justice (bd. govs. 1982—, treas. 1990-92, v.p. 1992-93, pres.-elect 1993-94, pres. 1994-95), Nashville Bar Assn. (ethics com. 1983—, chancery and cir. ct. com. 1993—), Tenn. Bar Assn., Pa. Trial Lawyers Assn. Roman Catholic. Home: 5113 Fountainhead Dr Brentwood TN 37027-5809 Office: Parker Allen & Crofford 209 10th Ave S Nashville TN 37203-4144

PARKER, MICHAEL (MIKE PARKER), congressman; b. Laurel, Miss., Oct. 31, 1949; m. Rosemary Prather; children: Adrian, Marisa, Thomas. BA, William Carey Coll., 1970. Operator various businesses; mem. vet. affairs com., textile caucus, sunbelt caucus, arts caucus 101st-104th Congresses from 4th Miss. dist., 1989—, mem. pub. works and transp. com., economic devel. subcom., water resources subcom., aviation subcom., 1989—. Presbyterian. Office: US Ho of Reps 2445 Rayburn Bldg Washington DC 20515-0004

PARKER, PATSY BOYD, academic counselor, educational consultant; b. Opelika, Ala., July 8, 1936; m. William A. Parker, Sr.; children: William A., Nancy Patriece. BS, Ala. State U., 1961; MEd, Auburn U., 1970. Counselor Opelika (Ala.) Parks and Recreation, 1952-53; adminstrn. sec. J.W. Darden H.S., Opelika, 1953-57; clk. stenographer VA Hosp., Tuskegee, Ala., 1960-61; chmn. English dept. J.W. Darden H.S., Opelika, 1961-67; counselor Opelika H.S., 1967-74, dir. guidance dept., 1974-91; counselor, student advisor So. Union State Jr. Coll., 1986—. Chmn. multicultural awareness coun., mem. sch. edn. adv. bd. Auburn U; mem. exec. bd. Ala. State Dem. Exec. Com.; vice chmn. Lee County Dem. Exec. Com., past chmn. Mem. NEA, Ala. Edn. Assn., Ala. Bus. and Profl. Womens Found., Ala Personnel and Guidance Assn., Opelika Edn. Assn., Ala. State U. Alumni Assn. (pres. Lee County chpt.), Phi Delta Kappa, Alpha Kappa Mu, Delta Sigma Theta. Office: ASU Bd Trustees 2504 Frederick Rd Opelika AL 36801-7234

PARKER, PAYUINA ERNEST, accountant, business consultant; b. Monrovia, Liberia, Sept. 28, 1959; s. Payuina Ernest and Johnet Claudia (Whitfield) P. BBA, U. Liberia, Monrovia, 1985; AA, Ricks Jr. Coll., 1980. CPA, Va. Mgr. Price Waterhouse, London and Monrovia, 1983-89, Nat. Bank of Washington, 1989-90, Gardiner, Kamya & Assoc., Washington, 1990-92; chmn., CEO Summit Fin. Ptnrs., Arlington, Va., 1993—; mng. ptnr. Parker Whitfield CPAs, Arlington, 1992—; mem. adv. bd. Summit Fin. Ptnrs., Arlington, 1994—. Author: (booklet) Strategies on Marketing to the Federal Government, 1993. Mem. Assn. Govt. Accts., Project Mgmt. Inst., Va. Bd. Accountancy. Presbyterian. Office: Parker Whitfield & Co Ste 205-A 1600 Wilson Blvd Arlington VA 22209-2405

PARKER, RICHARD LEO, journalist; b. Albuquerque, Feb. 17, 1964; s. James Robert and Josefina (Delgado) P.; m. Laurie Brooke Stowe, May 27, 1990; 1 child, Olivia. BA in Polit. Sci., Trinity U., 1985; MA in Polit. Sci., Tulane U., 1990. City hall reporter Gambit Weekly Newspaper, New Orleans, 1985-87; pres., sec. U.S. Ho. of Reps., Washington, 1987-88; contbg. editor Hispanic Mag., Washington, 1988-89; Washington corr., columnist Albuquerque Jour., 1989—; guest panelist C-SPAN, Washington, 1992. Contbr. to book: A Politics Reader, 1990, also to Playboy mag. Knight Ctr. for Specialized Journalism fellow, 1993. Mem. White House Correspondents Assn., Nat. Hispanic Journalists Assn., Soc. Profl. Journalists, Nat. Press Club.

PARKER, RICHARD MELVIN, librarian; b. Red Oak, Iowa, May 17, 1942; s. Melvin James and Marie (Cozad) P.; m. Charlotte Jean Bennett, July 9, 1964; children: Kyle, Danielle, Kevin. AA, Southwest Bapt. Coll., 1962; BS in edn., Southwest Mo. State U., 1964; MA in libr. sci., U. Mo., 1968. Tchr., sch. libr. Linn (Mo.) Pub. Schs., 1964-67; libr. dir. Boonslick Reg. Libr., Sedalia, Mo., 1968-77; asst. libr. dir. Tulsa (Okla.) City County Libr., 1977—; bd. dirs. Tulsa Literacy Coalition. Mem. Am. Libr. Assn., Pub. Libr. Assn., Okla. Libr. Assn., Libr. Administration and Mgmt. Assn., Literary Administration and Mgmt. Assn., Friends of Librs. USA, Friends of Librs. in Okla. Republican. Baptist. Home: 6720 S 255th East Ave Broken Arrow OK 74014 Office: Tulsa City County Libr 400 Civic Ctr Tulsa OK 74103

PARKER, RICHARD WILSON, lawyer; b. Cleve., June 14, 1943; s. Edgar Gael and Pauline (Wilson) P.; m. Carolyn Edith Kratt, Aug. 9, 1969 (dec. May 1995); children: Brian Jeffrey, Lauren Michelle, Lisa Christine. BA cum laude in Econs., U. Redlands, 1965; JD cum laude, Northwestern U., 1968. Bar: Ohio 1968, Va. 1974. Assoc. Arter & Hadden, Cleve., 1968-71; asst. gen. atty. Norfolk & Western Ry. Co., Cleve. and Roanoke, Va., 1971-74, asst. gen. solicitor, Roanoke, 1974-78, gen. atty., 1978-84; gen. atty. Norfolk So. Corp., 1984-88, sr. gen. atty., Norfolk, Va., 1988-93, asst. v.p. real estate, 1993—. Mem. ABA, Va. State Bar, Va. Bar Assn., Norfolk-Portsmouth Bar Assn. Presbyterian. Office: 3 Commercial Pl Norfolk VA 23510-2108

PARKER, ROBERT CURTIS, railway executive. BS in Bus. and Fin., Va. Poly. Inst., 1977. Mgmt. trainee RF&P Railroad, Potomac Yard, Alexandria, Va., 1979-80, svc. supr., 1980-81, transp. asst., 1981-83, asst. to trainmaster, 1983-87, from asst. trainmaster to trainmaster, 1987-91; transp. cons. Alexandria, 1991-93; mgr. ops. and analysis Rail Am., Alexandria, 1994—, gen. mgr. Delaware Valley Ry., 1994—; asst. gen. mgr. Saginaw Valley R.R., Alexandria, 1994—. Mem. Am. Assn. Railroad Supts., City of Alexandria Indsl. Devel. Authority (vice chmn.), West Potomac Trade Assn. (bd. dirs.), Old Town Civic Assn., Sigma Pi. Home: 524 S Court House Rd Apt 301 Arlington VA 22204-1957

PARKER, ROBERT M., federal judge; b. 1937. BBA, U. Tex., 1961, JD, 1964. Bar: Tex. 1964. Ptnr. Parish & Parker, Gilmer, Tex., 1964-65, Kenley & Boyland, Longview, Tex., 1965, Roberts, Smith & Parker, Longview, 1966-71, Rutledge & Parker, Ft. Worth, 1971-72, Nichols & Parker, Longview, 1972-79; judge U.S. Dist. Ct. (ea. dist.) Tex., 1979-94, chief judge, 1991-94; judge U.S. Ct. Appeals (5th Cir.), Tyler, Tex. Mem. Tex. Bar Assn. Office: 221 W Ferguson St Ste 400 Tyler TX 75702-7200

PARKER, ROBERT MICHAEL, toxicologist, anatomy educator; b. San Diego, Aug. 31, 1946; s. Thomas Jackson Parker and Sue Ellen (Randall) Muka; stepson Joseph Abbott Muka, Jr.; m. Karen May Green, Jan. 29, 1972; children: Jenifer May, Alexis Diane. BS, San Diego State Coll., 1970; MS, U. Calif.-Davis, 1975, PhD, 1980. Staff rsch. assoc. Calif. Primate Rsch. Ctr., Davis, 1976-80, postgrad. researcher, 1980-81; lectr. in biol. sci., Calif. State U., Sacramento, 1978; guest lectr. in embryology, Sch. Medicine U. Calif., Davis, 1980; lectr. in biology, Calif. State Coll., San Bernardino, 1982-84; asst. prof. anatomy Coll. Osteo. Medicine of the Pacific, Pomona, Calif., 1981-85; study dir., head reproductive and devel. toxicology Pathology Assocs., Inc., Nat. Ctr. for Toxicol. Rsch., Jefferson, Ark., 1985-91; mgr. toxicology TSI Redfield (Ark.) Labs., 1991-94; sr. scientist Argus Rsch. Labs., 1994—. Contbr. articles to profl. jours. Mem. Republican Presdl. Task Force, Washington, 1983-89, U.S. Senatorial Club, 1983-86, Jefferson County Rep. Cen. Com., 1985-86, coach Girls softball, 1985—; mem. sci. com. Southeast Ark. Arts and Sci. Ctr., 1985-86; vol. pub. schs., 1985—. Mem. AAAS, Teratology Soc., Soc. Toxicology, Sigma Phi Epsilon (alumni bd. 1975-78), Sigma Xi. Roman Catholic. Office: Argus Rsch Lab 905 Sheehy Dr Ste A Horsham PA 19044-1241

PARKER, SANDRA GAYLE, emergency room nurse; b. Nashville, Aug. 4, 1959; d. Dorothy Mae (Bush) P.; m. David Nando Jones, Aug. 15, 1992; children: Robin M., Barbara M., Ashton Drew. ADN, Tenn. State U., 1981. RN, Tenn.; cert. BLS, BLS trainer, PBLS instr. trainer, ACLS provider. Surg. staff nurse Miller Hosp., Nashville, 1982-85; triage nurse Miller Med. Group, Nashville, 1988-92; rehab. unit charge nurse Edgefield Hosp., Nashville, 1988-91, behavioral health unit charge nurse, 1988-93, emergency dept. charge nurse, 1985-91; emergency dept. charge nurse Nashville Rehab. Hosp., 1991—, night supr., 1994—, nursing educator, 1995—. Mem. Emergency Nurses Assn., Am. Trauma Soc. Republican. Baptist.

PARKER, THERESA ANN, special education educator; b. Spencer, W.Va., Jan. 16, 1947; d. Harry Clay and Betty Jean (Richards) Boggs; m. Larry Glen Parker, Apr. 29, 1967; children: Carey Ann, Jill Renee, Timothy Preston, Jeremy David, Leanna Michelle. AA in sec. studies, Glenville (W.Va.) State Coll., 1967, BA in music edn., 1970; MA in spl. edn., Coll. of Grad. Studies, 1991; EDS in ednl. leadership, W.Va. Grad. Coll., 1996. Cert. tchr. Pvt. practice piano teacher Spencer, 1967-95; sub. tchr. Roane County Schs., Spencer, 1970-71; tchr. spl. edn. Roane County Schs., 1987—, educator team mem.-parent/educator resource ctr., 1989—; sub. tchr. Marietta (Ohio) City Schs., 1986; administrator Sand Hill Day Care Ctr., Reno, Ohio, 1986-87; spl. edn. rep. W.Va. Dept. Edn., Charleston, 1995—; dir. Safetytown Roane County, Spencer, 1989-93. Author: (with others) Selected Teaching Models Integrated with West Virginia's Academic Model for Gifted Education, 1991. Chmn. Cub Scout Pack Boy Scouts Am., Reno, 1983-87, dist. trainer, Parkersburg, W.Va., 1986-87, chmn. Boy Scout Troop, Spencer, 1987-91; organizer First Bapt. Ch. Diabetes Sup. Group, 1995—. Safetytown grantee W.Va. Dept. Edn., Roane County, 1989, W.Va. Edn. Fund, Roane County, 1992; Dental Health grantee W.Va. Edn. Fund, Clover Sch., 1992; Diabetes Support Group grantee Benedium Found., Roane and Calhoun/Jackson Counties, 1995. Mem. Assn. for Supervision and Curriculum Develop., W.Va. Profl. Educators, Inc., Lions Club Internat. (program chmn.), Blue Grass Riding Club. Democrat. Baptist. Home: 749 Parkersburg Rd Spencer WV 25276 Office: Roane County Schs 102 Chapman Ave Spencer WV 25276

PARKER, WETONAH RICE, education educator, consultant; b. Indpls., July 11, 1948; s. William Carlton and Christine Anna (Mebane) Rice; divorced. BS, Ball State U., 1970; MEd, N.C. Ctrl. U., Durham, 1982; EdD, N.C. State U., Raleigh, 1994. Cert. in secondary sci., spl. edn., mid. grades, adminstrn. and supervision, curriculum, N.C. Tchr., chair dept. Wake County Pub. Schs., Raleigh, N.C., 1971-85; sci. edn. specialist Carolin Power & Light Co., Raleigh, 1985-89; ednl. cons. Ednl. Pers. Devel. Sys., Cary, N.C., 1989; instr., field supr. N.C. State U., Raleigh, 1990-93; asst. prof., dir. mid. and secondary student tchg. Meredith Coll., Raleigh, 1993—; adj. asst. prof. N.C. State U., 1994—; cons. editor Jour. Emotional and Behavioral Disorders, Austin, Tex., 1994—. Co-author: Best Bets: At Risk Programs That Work in North Carolina Middle Level Schools, 1992; author: (with others) Job Skills for the 21st Century, 1995. Mem. ASCD, Nat. Mid. Sch. Assn., Delta Sigma Theta, Phi Delta Kappa, Delta Kappa Gamma (parliamentarian 1994—). Presbyterian. Office: Meredith Coll 3800 Hillsborough St Raleigh NC 27607-5298

PARKER, WILLIAM DALE, management consultant, political adviser; b. Portsmouth, Va., Apr. 13, 1925; s. Otis Durie and Eva Estelle (Dempsey) P.; m. Frances Ross Jennings, Feb. 2, 1946 (dec.); children: Frances Lea, Elizabeth Dale, Kim Carolyn, Penny Jo Ann, Jacquelyn Susan; m. Boots Lee Farthing, 1968. Student Coll. William and Mary, 1946; grad. indsl. engring. Internat. Corr. Schs., 1956; student U. Del., 1959-60, Calif. Western U., 1961-62, U. Calif., 1964, Stetson U., 1969; D.Sc., James Balmes U., Saltillio, Mex., 1968; Ph.D. in Edn., Fla. Inst., 1970; Layout, process and prodn. engr. GM, Wilmington, Del., 1949-59, asst. dir. salaried personnel pub. relations, 1959-61; mfg. engr., lectr. Gen. Dynamics/Astronautic, San Diego, 1961-64; dir. Internat. Inst. Human Relations, LaJolla, Calif., 1964—; family and marriage counselor, Titusville, Fla., 1967-71; mgmt. cons., v.p. Multiple Services, Inc., Titusville and Boone, N.C., 1969—; bd. dir., v.p. ,Spangler TV, N.Y.C., 1969-73; chmn. bd. Travel Internat., Inc., Titusville, 1971-74; v.p. Pictorial Gravesite Creations, Inc., Boone, N.C., Titusville, Fla., 1989—. Author: Philosophy of Genius: American Values, Solutions to Family and Marriage Problems, Gutless America, 1973, God Knows I Want to Come Home, 1989, Prose and Poetry-9 to 90,, 1990, Geography 101, 1992, A Political Candidate Guide , 1995, A Selection of Writings, 1992-96, 1996, The Parker Family, 1616-1996, 1996; speaker in field; columnist Sentinal Newspapers, 1963-64; asst. editor Campers Illus. Mag., 1964-65, Star Adv., 1968. Insight, 1969-72, Challenge, 1970—, Mountain Times, 1981-84. Hon. mem. editorial adv. bd. Am. Biog. Inst., 1975—. Patentee Amy peanut dolls; inventor process to keep B/W and color pictures from aging in sunlight. Mem. Nat. Dem. Com., 1980—; ind. candidate for Gov. Fla., 1976; founder Monroe Park CD, 1951; mem. Wilmington council Boy Scouts Am., 1953-55; chmn. Varions Agy. Fund, 1954-60; co-chmn. Del. Dept. CD TV Shows, 1956-57; mem. Middle Atlantic States Conf. Correction, 1956-60; chmn., pres. Del. Md. Pa. Tri State Hosp. Com., 1957-59; mem. Wilmington Inner City Study Commn., 1957-60; chmn. Del. CD Evacuation Commn., 1958-59, Del. Hwy. Safety Campaign, 1959-60; active PTA; mem. Dem. Exec. Com., 1975-77; polit. cons. Congress, U.S. Pres., 1974—; traveler to Arctic Circle, Sept. 1990; bd. dirs. Boys and Girls Aid Soc. San Diego, 1962-64; bd. advisers Salvation Army. With USCGR, USN, World War II. Named Del. Outstanding Young Man of Yr., Wilmington/U.S. Jr. C. of C. 1957; recipient Silver award Del. Vol. Bur., 1957, ann. awards Va. Jr. Achievement, Inc., 1959; speech award U.S. Jr. C. of C., 1960, Gemini award NASA, 1967, Internat. Disting. Service to Humanity award 1969, Internat. Humanitarian award, 1971, Keys to City, Wilmington, 1959, 61, 72, Titusville, 1970, Miami, 1973; named Hon. Sheriff, Portsmouth, Va., 1973. Mem. Am. Legion (life), DAV (life), VFW (life), Am. Assn. Polit. Consultants, Wilmington Indsl. Mgmt. Club, Mensa (life), Monroe Park Civic Assn. (pres. 1952-53), Nat. Space Soc. (charter, life), Universal Space Assn. (co-founder 1992), vols. Speakers Bur. (San Diego), Coll. William and Mary Alumni Soc., S.A.R., Authors Guild, Authors League Am. Clubs: Royal Oak Golf and Country; Mexican Turf; S. Am. Turf (life). Lodges: Masons, Elks (life), Moose (life). First Family of Va. (1616 William Parker) Accamack, Va. Address: PO Box 246 Boone NC 28607 also: PO Box 1441 Titusville FL 32780

PARKER, WILLIAM THOMAS, insurance executive; b. Wilson, N.C., July 6, 1943; s. Mashariki Aisha, Sept. 14, 1975; children: Lisa, Jason, Gregory, Jefferson. BA, Shaw U., 1965; postgrad., Rochester Inst. Tech., 1976, Am. Coll., 1988. CLU, ChFC; lic. securities dealer, variable annuities dealer, ins. agt., Ga. Sales rep. Union Carbide Corp., N.Y.C., 1965-67; sales promotion mgr. Eastman Kodak Co., Rochester, N.Y., 1967-78; brand mgr. E & J Gallo Winery, Modesto, Calif., 1978-80; sr. v.p. Mktg. Forum, Inc., Atlanta, 1980-83; agt. Phoenix Home Life Ins. Co., Atlanta, 1983-87; pres. Assured

Benefits Group, Inc., Atlanta, 1987—; advisor to pres. Am. Coll., Bryn Mawr, Pa., 1992—; mem. agts. adv. com. State of Ga. Ins. Commn. Trustee The Galloway Sch., Atlanta, 1987-93; mem. Atlanta Estate Planning Coun. Recipient Nat. Quality award, 1988, 93, Nat. Sales Achievement award, 1983, 88, 92; named to Life Leaders of Ga., 1983-89. Mem. Nat. Assn. Life Underwriters (credentials com.), Atlanta Assn. Life Underwriters (pres. 1993-94), Am. Assn. Health Ins. Agts., Am. Soc.CLU and ChFC, Million Dollar Roundtable, Kappa Alpha Psi. Office: Assured Benefits Group Inc 1827 Powers Ferry Rd Ste 200 Atlanta GA 30339-5621

PARKERSON, HARDY MARTELL, lawyer; b. Longview, Tex., Aug. 22, 1942; s. Winifred Lenore (Robertson) P.; m. Janice Carol Johnson, Aug. 3, 1968; children: James Blaine Parkerson, Stanley Andrew Parkerson, Paul Hardy Parkerson. BA, McNeese State U., Lake Charles, La.; JD, Tulane U., 1966. Bar: La. 1966, U.S. Supreme Ct. 1971. Assoc. Rogers, McHale & St. Romain, Lake Charles, 1967-69; pvt. practice Lake Charles, 1969—; chmn. 7th Congl. Dist. Crime and Justice Task Force, La. Priorities for the Future, 1980; asst. prof. criminal justice La. State U., 1986. Bd. dirs. 1st Assembly of God Ch., Lake Charles, 1980—; bd. regents So. Christian U., Lake Charles, 1993—; mem. La. Dem. State Ctrl. Com., 1992—, Calcasieu Parish Dem. Com., 1988— (sec.-treas., exec. com., 1988—); former mem. Gulf Assistance Program, Lake Charles; 7th Congl. Dist. La. mem. Imports and Exports Trust Authority, Baton Rouge, 1984-88. Mem. Pi Kappa Housing Corp. of Lake Charles (bd. dirs., sec.-treas. 1985—), Optimists, Pi Kappa Phi (Beta Mu chpt.). Democrat. Mem. Assembly of God Ch. Home: 127 Greenway St Lake Charles LA 70605-6821 Office: The Parkerson Law Firm 807 Alamo St Lake Charles LA 70601-8665

PARKEY, ROBERT WAYNE, radiology and nuclear medicine educator, research radiologist; b. Dallas, July 17, 1938; s. Jack and Gloria Alfreda (Perry) P.; m. Nancy June Knox, Aug. 9, 1958; children: Wendell Wade, Robert Todd, Amy Elizabeth. BS in Physics, U. Tex., 1960; MD, S.W. Med. Sch., U. Tex., Dallas, 1965. Diplomate Am. Bd. Radiology, Am. Bd. Nuclear Medicine. Intern St. Paul Hosp., Dallas, 1965-66; resident in radiology U. Tex. Health Sci. Ctr., Dallas, 1966-69, asst. prof. radiology, 1970-74, assoc. prof., 1974-77, prof., chmn. dept. radiology, 1977—, Effie and Wofford Cain Disting. chair in diagnostic imaging, 1994—; chief nuc. medicine Parkland Meml. Hosp., Dallas, 1974-79, chief dept. radiology, 1977—. Contbr. numerous chpts., articles and abstracts to profl. publs. Served as capt. M.C., Army N.G., 1965-72. NIH fellow Nat. Inst. Gen. Med. Sci., U. Mo., Columbia, 1969-70; Nat. Acad. Scis.-NRC scholar in radiol. research James Picker Found., 1971-74. Fellow Am. Coll. Cardiology, Am. Coll. Radiology; mem. Am. Coll. Nuclear Physicians (charter, ho. of dels. 1974—), Council on Cardiovascular Radiology of Am. Heart Assn., AMA, Assn. Univ. Radiologists, Dallas County Med. Assn., Dallas Ft. Worth Radiol. Soc., Radiol. Soc. N.Am., Soc. Chairmen of Acad. Radiology Depts., Soc. Nuclear Medicine (acad. council), Tex. Med. Assn., Tex. Radiol. Soc., Sigma Xi, Alpha Omega Alpha. Avocations: gardening, golf, tennis. Academic research interests: nuclear cardiology, development of new imaging technologies, medical education. Office: U Tex Southwestern Med Ctr Dallas Dept Radiology 5323 Harry Hines Blvd Dallas TX 75235-8896

PARKO, JOSEPH EDWARD, JR., academic administrator; b. St. Louis, May 15, 1938; s. Joseph Edward Sr. and Florence Evelin (Graham) P.; m. Edith Margaret Jones, Apr. 16, 1966; 1 child, Kimberly Graham. BA, Stetson U., 1966; MBA, Ga. State U., 1972. Asst. to dean (Sch. Urban Life) Ga. State U., 1972-73, dir. (Urban Community Svc.), 1974-86, dir. (non-profit studies program), 1987—; cons. United Way, Atlanta, 1985-89, Met. Atlanta Rapid Transit Authority, 1986; trainer workshops non-profit and govt. orgns., 1974—; bd. dirs. Progressive Healthcare Providers, Inc., Urban Tng. Orgn. of Atlanta. Editor: Organizing for Action, 1976; editor Community Info. Clearinghouse newsletter, 1972-82; contbr. articles to profl. jours., mags. and newspapers. Mem. housing task force Atlanta Regional Commn., 1975, Human Svcs. Adv. Coun., Atlanta, 1976, Planning Zoning Commn., Avondale, Ga., 1984, Leadership Atlanta, 1980, Non-profit Mgmt. Assn.; bd. dirs. Nat. Assn. of Neighborhoods, D.C., 1977-80, Urban Life Assn., Atlanta, 1972-80; chmn. United Way Strategic Planning subcom., 1989. With USAF, 1957-61. Woodrow Wilson fellow, 1966; Higher Edn. Act grantee, 1973, 76; recipient Outstanding Atlantan award, 1975, Merit award Ga. Adult Edn. Assn., 1982. Mem. Ga. Assn. Vol. Adminstrn., Assn. Vol. Action Scholars, Amnesty Internat., ACLU, Greenpeace, Leadership Atlanta Alumni Assn., Am. Friends Svc. Com. Democrat. Quaker. Office: Ga State U Coll Pub and Urban Affairs University Ave SW Atlanta GA 30315-2205

PARKS, ANDREA MARROTTE, public relations executive; b. Charleston, S.C., Jan. 17, 1959; d. Paul Arthur and Lieta (Marchesi) M.; m. Theodore Benjamin Freeman, Dec. 19, 1981 (div. 1989); 1 child, Elizabeth; m. Scott Keller Parks, Sept. 18, 1989; 1 child, Cameron. BA, Wake Forest U., 1981. Gen. assignment reporter WXII-TV, Winston-Salem, N.C., 1981-82; asst. dir. instl. advancement Brevard (N.C.) Coll., 1983-85; asst. dir. media rels. U. S.C., Columbia, 1985-88; dir. media rels. Wake Forest U., Winston-Salem, N.C., 1988-90; v.p., mgr. PR and advt. Bank of Okla., Tulsa, 1991-92; mktg. dir. Doctor's Hosp., Tulsa, Okla., 1992—; bd. dirs. NCCJ, Palmer Drug Abuse Program; dir. preparations for visit of Pope John Paul II to U. S.C., 1987, for Bush/Dukakis presdl. debate, Wake Forest U., 1988. Recipient Award of Excellence, Grand award, TV News award , Radio Programming, CASE Dist. III, 1985, 86, Silver medal, TV PSA, Bronze medal, 1986, 88, National, Gold medal, Spl. Events, Silver medal, PR Program Improvement CASE, 1989, Tulsa Advt. Fedn., 1992. Mem. Pub. Rels. Soc. Am., Leadership Tulsa, Am. Mktg. Assn. Office: Doctor's Hospital 2323 S Harvard Ave Tulsa OK 74114-3301

PARKS, JAMES WILLIAM, II, public facilities executive, lawyer; b. Wabash, Ind., July 30, 1956; s. James William and Joyce Arlene (Lillibridge) P.; m. Neil Ann Armstrong, Aug. 21, 1982; children: Elizabeth Joyce, Helen Frances, James William III. BS, Ball State U., 1978; JD, U. Miami, 1981. Bar: La. 1981, Fla. 1982, U.S. Dist. Ct. (ea. dist.) La. 1981, U.S. Dist. Ct. (mid. dist.) La. 1982, U.S. Ct. Appeals (5th cir. and 11th cir.) 1981. Atty. Jones, Walker, Waechter, Poitevent, Carrere et al., New Orleans, 1981-83, Foley & Judell, New Orleans, 1983-88, McCollister & McCleary, pc, Baton Rouge, 1988-95; exec. dir. La. Pub. Facilities Authority, Baton Rouge, 1995—; adv. bd. Progressive Healthcare Providers, Inc., Atlanta, 1994—. Mem. AICPA, Nat. Assn. Bond Lawyers, La. State Bar Assn., Fla. Bar Assn., Assn. for Gifted and Talented Students, Baton Rouge (treas. 1994-96, pres.-elect 1996—), Soc. La. CPA (govt. acctg. and auditing com. 1994-95). Home: 5966 Tennyson Dr Baton Rouge LA 70817-2933 Office: La Pub Facilities Authority Ste 650 2237 S Acadian Thruway Baton Rouge LA 70808

PARKS, JANE DELOACH, law librarian, legal assistant; b. Atlanta, June 7, 1927; d. John Keller and Martha Lorena (Lee) deLoach; m. James Bennett Parks, Dec. 28, 1951 (dec. Sept. 1983); children: Carrie Anne Parks-Kirby, Susan Jane, Lora Beth Parks-Maury. BA magna cum laude, Vanderbilt U., 1949; postgrad., Emory U., 1950-51; tchr. cert., U. Chattanooga, 1954; postgrad., U. Tenn., Chattanooga, 1971-73. Med. rsch./writing dept. surgery Emory U., Atlanta, 1949-51; sec. to med. dir. Tenn. Tuberculosis Hosp., Chattanooga, 1951-53; tchr. Signal Mountain (Tenn.) Elem. Sch., 1954-55; tchr., dean jr. sch. Cleve. (Tenn.) Day Sch., 1963-70; law firm libr., legal asst. Stophel, Caldwell & Heggie, Chattanooga, 1972-85, Caldwell, Heggie & Helton, Chattanooga, 1985-93, Heiskell, Donelson, Bearman, Adams, Williams & Caldwell, Chattanooga, 1993-94, Baker, Donelson, Bearman & Caldwell, Chattanooga, 1994—; tchr. various seminars on legal rsch. and writing, organizing one-person librs. and ch. librs., Chattanooga Legal Secs. Assn., Chattanooga-Hamilton County Bicentennial Libr. Editor (mag.) The Gadfly, 1947-49; editorial asst.: Studio Collotype, 1988 and to profl. jours., 1949—. tchr. Chattanooga Area Literacy Movement, 1984-86; exec. coun. Friends of Chattanooga-Hamilton County Bicentennial Libr., 1989-94; del. Gov.'s Conf.-White House Conf. on Librs. and Info. Svcs., Nashville, 1990; libr. vol. Tenn. Aquarium. Environ. Learning Lab.; allocations com. United Way, 1994—. Mem. Tenn. Paralegal Assn., Chattanooga Area Libr. Assn. (2d v.p. 1989-90, sec. 1992-93), Non-Atty. Profl. Assn. (chmn. 1989-93), Phi Beta Kappa, Mortar Bd. Republican. Methodist. Office: Baker Donelson Bearman & Caldwell 1800 Republic Ctr 633 Chestnut St Chattanooga TN 37450-0002

PARKS, MADELYN N., nurse, retired army officer, university official; b. Jordan, Okla.. Diploma, Corpus Christi (Tex.) Sch. Nursing, 1943; B.S.N., Incarnate Word Coll., San Antonio, 1961; M.H.A. in Health Care Adminstrn, Baylor U., 1965. Commd. 2d lt. Army Nurse Corps, 1943, advanced through grades to brig. gen., 1975; basic tng. Fort Meade, Md., 1944; staff nurse eye ward Valley Forge (Pa.) Gen. Hosp., 1944; served in India, Iran, Italy, 1944-45; gen. duty staff nurse Fort Polk, La., 1951; nurse eye clinic Tripler Army Med. Center, Hawaii, 1951-54; staff nurse eye, ear, nose and throat ward Brooke Army Med. Center, San Antonio, 1954-57; ednl. coordinator Fort Dix, N.J., 1957-58; instr., supr. enlisted med. tng. U.S. Army Med. Tng. Center, Fort Sam Houston, Tex., 1959-61; chief nurse surg. field hosp. 62d Med. Group, Germany, 1961-62, sr. nurse coordinator, 1962-63; adminstrn. resident Letterman Gen. Hosp., San Francisco, 1964-65; dir. clin. specialist course Letterman Gen. Hosp., 1965-67; chief nurse 85th Evacuation Hosp., Qui Nhon, Vietnam, 1967-68; asst. chief nursing sci. div., asst. prof. Med. Field Service Sch., U.S. Army-Baylor U. Program in Health Care Adminstrn., 1968-72; chief nurse surgeons office Hdqrs. Continental Army Command, Fort Monroe, Va., 1972-73; chief dept. nursing Walter Reed Army Med. Center, Washington, 1973-75; chief Army Nurse Corps, Office of Surgeon Gen., Dept. Army, Washington, 1975-79; ret. Army Nurse Corps, Office of Surgeon Gen., Dept. Army, 1979; faculty assoc. adminstr. U. Md., 1974-78. Decorated D.S.M., Army Commendation medal with 2 oak leaf clusters, Legion of Merit, Meritorious Service medal; recipient Alumna of Distinction award Incarnate Word Coll., 1981. Mem. Ret. Officers Assn., AMEDD Mus. Found. Address: 5211 Metcalf San Antonio TX 78239-1933

PARLOS, ALEXANDER GEORGE, systems and control engineering educator; b. Istanbul, Turkey, July 12, 1961; came to U.S., 1980; s. George Alexander and Helen (Stavridis) P.; m. Dalila Marcia Vieira, Aug. 25, 1985. BS, Tex. A&M U., 1983; MS, MIT, 1985, DSc, 1986. Rsch. asst. Tex. A&M U., College Sta., 1982-83, MIT, Cambridge, Mass., 1984-86; sr. rsch. assoc. The U. N.Mex., Albuquerque, 1986-87; asst. prof. Tex. A&M U., College Sta., 1987-92, assoc. prof., 1993—; co-founder, pres. ANN Engring., Inc., 1992—; cons. engr. BDM Internat., Inc., McLean, Va., 1988—; sr. engring. assoc. API, Albuquerque, 1990—; cons. engr. Northrop-Grumman Corp., Bethpage, N.Y., 1994—; cons. engr. Kevin Kennedy & Assoc., Inc., Indpls., 1995—. Contbr. articles to Internat. Jour. Control, IEEE Trans. on Nuclear Sci., AIAA Jour. Guidance, Control and Dyamics, AIAA Jour. Propulsion and Power, Space Nucler Power Sys., Nuclear Tech., Nuclear Sci. Engring., IEEE Trans. on Neural Netwworks, IEEE Trans. Automatic Control, also others. Treas. S.W. Crossing Assn., College Sta., 1990-91; chair program planning Am. Nuclear Soc. Remote Systems Div., La Grange Pk., Ill., 1989-90; advisor Hellenic Student Assn., College Station, 1988-91. Grantee NASA, 1988—, Dept. Energy, 1989—, Lockheed Missile Co., 1989, Electric Power Rsch. Inst., 1988, Am. Pub. Power Assn., 1993—, Advanced Rsch. Projects Agy., 1993—, Tex. Advanced Tech. Program, 1995—. Mem. IEEE (sr., assoc. editor Trans. on Neural Networks 1994—), AIAA (sr.), ASME, Am. Nuclear Soc. (exec. com. human factors divsn. 1993—, chair tech. program com. human factors divsn. 1993—), Internat. Neural Networks Soc. (mem. conf. tech. program com. 1995—). Office: Tex A&M U 129 Zachry Bldg College Station TX 77843-3133

PARMAR, JITENDRA RAVJI, internist, gastroenterologist; b. Mombasa, Kenya, Feb. 2, 1954; came to U.S., 1980; s. Ravji Hirji and Jayagauri Parmar; m. Anjana P. Anand, Jan. 9, 1983; children: Nishaal J., Prashant J. MB, ChB, U. Nairobi, Kenya, 1978; MD, U. Ill., Chgo., 1985. Pvt. practice Eufaula, Okla., 1985—. Mem. AMA. Office: 1 Hospital Dr Eufaula OK 74432

PARMER, DAN GERALD, veterinarian; b. Wetumpka, Ala., July 3, 1926; s. James Lonnie and Virginia Gertrude (Guy) P.; 1 child by previous marriage, Linda Leigh; m. Donna Louise Kesler, June 7, 1980; 1 child, Dan Gerald. Student L.A. City Coll., 1945-46; DVM, Auburn U., 1950. Gen. practice vet. medicine, Galveston, Tex., 1950-54, Chgo., 1959-83; vet. in charge Chgo. Commn. Animal Care and Control, 1974-88; med. dir. food protection divsn. Chgo. Dept. Health, 1988-93; ret. 1993; chmn. Ill. Impaired Vets. Com.; tchr. Highlands U., 1959; humane officer Elmore County, 1994—; dir. sales for south, southeast and lower midwest Am. Vet. Identification Devices, Norco, Calif., 1993—. Pres. Elmore County Humane Soc. Served with USNR, 1943-45, PTO; served as staff vet. and 2d and 5th Air Force vet. chief USAF, 1954-59. Decorated 9 Battle Stars; recipient Vet. Appreciation award U. Ill., 1971, Commendation, Chgo. Commn. Animal Care and Control, 1987. Mem. VFW, AVMA (nat. com. for impaired vets., coun. pub. health and regulatory medicine 1990—), Ill. Vet. Medicine Assn. (chmn. civil def. and package disaster hosps. 1968-71, Pres.' award 1986), Chgo. Vet. Medicine Assn. (bd. govs. 1969-72, 74-81, pres. 1982), South Chgo. Vet. Medicine Assn. (pres. 1965-66), Am. Animal Hosp. Assn. (dir.), Ill. Acad. Vet. Practice (pres. 1993), Nat. Assn. of Professions, Am. Assn. Zoo Vets., Am. Assn. Zool. Parks and Aquariums, Elmore County Humane Soc. (pres. 1994-95), Midlothian Country Club, Valley Internat. Country Club, Masons, Shriners, Kiwanis. Democrat. Discoverer Bartonellosis in cattle in N.Am. and Western Hemisphere, 1951; co-developer bite-size high altitude in-flight feeding program USAF, 1954-56. Address: 6720 Post Oak Ln Montgomery AL 36117-2424 Office: Am Vet Identification Devices 3179 Hamner Ave Norco CA 91760-1983

PARMERLEE, MARK S., food service executive; b. Troy, Ohio, Feb. 17, 1955; s. Thomas Eugene and Patsy Jean (Bowers) P.; m. Diane Carol Petersen, May 23, 1981; children: Michael Peter, Matthew Steven. BS in Hotel, Restaurant Adminstrn., Cornell U., 1977. Chief oper. officer Gilliam Interests, Houston, 1982-85; pres. Golden Oper. Corp., Dallas, 1989—, Golden Franchising Corp./Golden Fried Chicken, Dallas, 1989—; adviser Meridian Ptnrs., N.Y.C., 1986-88. Mem. Rep. Com. Mem. Cornell Soc. Hotelmen, Tex. Restaurant Assn., Nat. Restaurant Assn., Rep. Nat. Com. Republican. Presbyterian. Office: Golden Franchising Corp 11488 Luna Rd Dallas TX 75234-9405

PARMLEY, ROBERT JAMES, lawyer, consultant; b. Madison, Wis., Oct. 23, 1950; s. Loren Francis and Dorothy Louise (Turner) P.; m. Debra Paliszewski, Dec. 23, 1982; children: Michelle Hope, Matthew Turner. B.A., U. Va., 1972; J.D., U. S.C., 1975. Bar: S.C. 1975, Tex. 1976, U.S. Dist. Ct. (so. dist.) Tex. 1976, U.S. Tax Ct. 1976, U.S. Ct. Appeals (5th cir.) 1978, U.S. Dist. Ct. (we. and no. dists.) Tex. 1980, U.S. Supreme Ct. 1980. Staff atty., VISTA vol., Tex. Rural Legal Aid, Inc., Alice, 1975-76, mng. atty., Kingsville, 1976-79, sr. staff atty., Kerrville, 1979-81; sole practice, Kerrville, 1981—. Mem. State Bar Tex., State Bar S.C., Kerr County Bar Assn. Episcopalian. Office: 222 Sidney Baker St S Ste 615 Kerrville TX 78028-5900

PARNES, EDMUND IRA, oral and maxillofacial surgeon; b. Pitts., Apr. 16, 1936; s. David E. and Sara (Engelberg) P.; m. Elizabeth Cameron, Nov. 27, 1977; children: Dana, Mara, Lauren. Student Vanderbilt U., 1954-55, U. Miami, 1955-56; DMD, U. Pitts., 1960, Diplomate Am. Bd. Oral and Maxillofacial Surgery. Oral surgery intern Jackson Meml. Hosp., 1960-61; resident, teaching fellow anesthesiology Presbyn. Univ. Hosp., Pitts., 1963-64; sr. resident oral surgery Ben Taub Gen. Hosp., Houston, 1964-65; pvt. practice oral and maxillofacial surgery, Miami, Fla., 1965—; interim assoc. chief oral surgery Jackson Meml. Hosp., Miami, 1970-72; clin. assoc. prof. U. Miami, 1975—; lectr. in field. Capt. U.S. Army, 1961-63. Fellow Am. Assn. Oral and Maxillofacial Surgeons (mem. com. legislation 1972-73, com. sci. sessions 1979-86, trustee 1991-94, pres.-elect 1994-95, pres. 1995-96); mem. ADA, Fla. Soc. Oral and Maxillofacial Surgeons (pres. 1974-75), Fla. Dental Assn. (ho. of dels., trustee 1982-95, v.p. 1996—), S.E. Soc. Oral Surgeons, East Coast Dist. Dental Soc. (chmn. coms. 1980-84, pres. 1981-82), North Dade Dental Soc. (pres. 1971-72), Am. Soc. Dental Anesthesiology (pres. Fla. chpt. 1970), Alpha Omega (pres. 1977-78, regent 1983). Jewish. Office: 8700 N Kendall Dr Ste 221 Miami FL 33176-2206

PARR, CHRISTOPHER ALAN, chemistry educator, university dean; b. Oakland, Calif., May 6, 1941; s. Melvin Fisher and Florence Marie (Farmer) P.; m. Patricia Ann Storck, Nov. 24, 1985. BS in Chemistry, U. Calif., Berkeley, 1962; PhD in Phys. Chemistry, Calif. Inst. Tech., 1969. Postdoctral fellow U. Calif., Irvine, 1968-69, U. Toronto, Ont., Can., 1969-71; asst. prof. U. Tex., Dallas, 1971-78, assoc. prof., 1978—, coll. master, 1980-87, assoc. dean, 1986-87, dean, 1987-94. Contbr. articles in reaction dynamics to profl. jours. Chmn. Found. Plano (Tex.) Pub. Librs., 1987-91; pres. Friends of Plano Pub. Libr., 1984-91. Mem. AAUP, Am. Chem. Soc., Fedn. Am. Scientists, Sigma Xi. Office: U Tex 2601 N Floyd Rd Richardson TX 75080-1407

PARR, EUGENE QUINCY, retired orthopaedic surgeon; b. Erlanger, Ky., Aug. 4, 1925; s. Benjamin Franklin and Sallie Frances (Wright) P.; m. Joan Lykins, June 9, 1951; children—Eugene Quincy Jr., Jeffrey Wright, Valerie. Student Berea Coll., Ky., 1944-45, 46-48; M.D., U. Louisville, 1952; fellow Mayo Grad. Sch. Medicine, 1956-60. Diplomate Am. Bd. Orthopaedic Surgery. Intern Baroness Erlanger Hosp., Chattanooga, 1952-53; resident in orthopaedic surgery Mayo Clinic, Rochester, Minn., 1956-60; practice medicine specializing in orthopaedic surgery, Lexington, Ky., 1960-96, ret.; adminstrv. trustee Central Baptist Hosp., Lexington, 1975-84. Trustee Berea Coll., 1966-72. Fellow Am. Acad. Orthopaedic Surgeons; mem. Am. Assn. Hip & Knee Surgeons, Am. Acad. Disability Evaluating Physicians, Christian Med. Soc., Doctors Mayo Soc. (founding), Mid-Am. Orthopaedic Assn., Lexington Orthopaedic Soc. (pres. 1964-66), Ky. Orthopaedic Soc. (pres. 1986), Clin. Orthopaedic Soc., Phi Kappa Phi. Home: Foxtale Farm 1825 Keene Rd Nicholasville KY 40356-9433

PARR, RICHARD ARNOLD, II, lawyer; b. Edmond, Okla., July 26, 1958; s. Jack Ramsey and Martha (Suttle) P.; m. Becky Fay Stapp, Feb. 28, 1987; 1 child, Victoria Martha. BA cum laude, Vanderbilt U., 1979; JD, Cornell U., 1982. Bar: Okla. 1982, Tex. 1983, U.S. Ct. Appeals (10th cir.) 1983, U.S. Supreme Ct. 1988, Tenn. 1993. Law clk. to chief judge U.S. Ct. Appeals for 10th Cir., Oklahoma City, 1982-83; assoc. Johnson & Swanson, Dallas, 1983-85, Gardner, Carton & Douglas, Dallas, 1986-88; sr. atty. Valero Energy Corp., San Antonio, 1988-89; pres., chief exec. officer Paragon Homecare Corp., San Antonio, 1989-91; assoc. gen. counsel OrNda HealthCorp (formerly Republic Health Corp.), Nashville, 1991-94, v.p., asst. gen. counsel, 1994-96; exec. v.p., gen. counsel OccuSystems, Inc., Dallas, 1996—. Sr. editor Cornell Law Rev., 1981-82, contbr., 1983. Mem. ABA, State Bar Tex., Okla. Bar Assn., Tenn. Bar Assn. Republican. Presbyterian. Home: 5224 Beckington Ln Dallas TX 75287 Office: OccuSystems Inc 3010 LBJ Fwy Ste 400 Dallas TX 75234

PARR, RICK VINCENT, rehabilitation services professional; b. Dyersburg, Tenn., Oct. 26, 1950; s. Dallas A. and Eloise (Carson) P.; m. Queen Ester Moore-Parr, Sept. 27, 1984; 1 child, Rickey Vincent Jr. BA, U. S.C., 1988. Cert. addictions counselor, 1988, mediator, 1994. Mgr. Greer, Parr & Parr, Inc., employment agy., Memphis, 1974-78; substance abuse counselor USMC, Parris Island, S.C., 1978-89, Charter Hosp., Savannah, Ga., 1989-91; profl. rels. mgr. Poplar Springs Hosp., Petersburg, Va., 1991—, customer svc. cons., 1994—; mem. substance abuse adv. bd. Savannah State Coll., 1989-91, Va. State U., Petersburg, 1992-95. Author: How to Thrive, Not Just Survive, 1995; writer, dir. docudrama Family in Crisis: The Intervention, 1993; author essays. Mem. Chesterfield County Youth Svcs. Bd., Chesterfield, Va., 1993-95; bd. dirs. Richmond (Va.) Urban League, 1994—; bd. dirs. Va. Assn. Alcohol and Drug Abuse Counselors, 1995—. Recipient gov.'s award for substance abuse edn. Commonwealth of Va., 1993. Mem. Nat. Assn. Alcohol and Drug Abuse Counselors, Va. Alliance for Mentally Ill (membership com. 1993—), Employees Assn. for Goodwill Leadership and Empowerment (pres. and founder). Home: 144 Crater Woods Ct Petersburg VA 23805 Office: Columbia/HCA Poplar Springs Hosp 350 Poplar Dr Petersburg VA 23805-9367

PARR, SANDRA HARDY, government affairs administrator; b. Atlanta, Dec. 30, 1952; d. Raymond William Hardy and Ruth (Berry) Yancey; m. James Parr Jr., Apr. 14, 1978; 1 child, James Andrew Parr III. Student, Lurleen B. Wallace Jr. Coll., 1972. Sales adminstr. Etec Corp., Hayward, Calif., 1976-77; adminstrv. sec. Cities Svc. Co., Atlanta, 1977-82; sales and planning coord. Intermodal Transp. Co., Norcross, Ga., 1982-83; freelance temp. sec. Atlanta met. area, 1983-86; freelance word processor, cons. Amoco Container Co., Norcross, 1986-88; psychiat. rev. asst. Am. Psychiat. Assn., Atlanta, 1988-89; support svcs. mgr. Parkside Health Mgmt. Corp., Atlanta, 1989-90; med. staff coord. C.P.C. Parkwood Hosp., Atlanta, 1991—; health svcs. asst. Ciba Vision Corp., 1991-93. Del. internat. nursing conf., citizen amb. program to People's Republic China, Seattle Washington People to People, Beijing, 1989; part-time exercise instr. Mem. NAFE. Home: 1301 Eugenia Ter Lawrenceville GA 30245-7437 Office: CPC Parkwood Hosp 1999 Cliff Valley Way NE Atlanta GA 30329-2420 Address: Philip Morris Mgmt Corp Govt Affairs 3 Ravinia Dr Ste 1560 Atlanta GA 30346-2118

PARRA, PAMELA ANN, physician, educator; b. New Orleans, La., Nov. 24, 1949; d. Morris Louis and Mary Elizabeth (Monaghan) P.; m. Garrett John Beadle, May 7, 1983; children: Erin Elizabeth, Ryan Garrett. BS, Loyola U., 1971; MD, Tulane U., 1975. Diplomate Am. Bd. Emergency Medicine. Emergency physician Lakewood Hosp., Morgan City, La., 1975-76, 81-86; resident Charity Hosp., New Orleans, 1976-79, staff physician, 1979-81; staff physician Baton Rouge (La.) Gen. Med. Ctr., 1986—; asst. prof. medicine La. State U., Med. Sch., New Orleans, 1989—. Fellow Am. Coll. Emergency Physicians (sec.-treas. La. chpt. 1993—); mem. La. State Med. Soc. Republican. Roman Catholic. Home: 1020 Pastureview Dr Baton Rouge LA 70810-4725 Office: Baton Rouge Gen Med Ctr 3600 Florida Blvd Baton Rouge LA 70806-3842

PARRADO, PETER JOSEPH, real estate executive; b. Tampa, Fla., July 7, 1953; s. Peter and Daisy M. (DeLaVina) P. AA, Hillsborough Community Coll., Tampa, 1972; BA in Design, U. Fla., 1976. Designated MAI, Appraisal Inst. Right of way agt. Dept. Transp., Mango, Fla., 1976-78; real estate appraiser Dept. Transp., Bartow, Fla., 1978-81; appraiser Buckley Appraisal Services, Inc., Tampa, 1981-82; appraiser, pres. Buckley-Parrado Appraisal Services, Tampa, 1982-83, Parrado Appraisal Services, Tampa, Fla., 1983—. Mem. planning assistance team City of Sarasota, Fla., 1985. Mem. Soc. Real Estate Appraiser (chmn. budget and fin. com. 1983-85, young adviser coun. 1987-88, bd. dirs. 1985-87, sec. 1987, instr., v.p. 1988-89, pres. 1989-90), Nat. Assn. Realtors, Urban Land Inst. (assoc.), Appraisal Inst. (mem. ethics and counseling panel 1992-94), Brandon C. of C. (legis. issues com. 1988). Democrat. Methodist. Home: 9105 Woodridge Run Dr Tampa FL 33647

PARREIRA, HELIO CORREA, physical chemist; b. Rio de Janeiro, Brazil, July 12, 1926, came to U.S., 1960, s. Francisco Correa and Maria Faria Parreira; m. Dulcinea M. Moreira, Jan. 2, 1953; children: Rogerio M., Regina M. BS in Chemistry, U. Brazil, Rio de Janeiro, 1949, tchrs. diploma, 1950; PhD, U. Cambridge, 1958. Asst. prof. U. Rio de Janeiro, 1950-52; phys. chemist Brazilian Atomic Commn., 1958-67; rsch. assoc. Columbia U., N.Y.C., 1960-62, dir. instrn. in chemistry Joint Program for Tech. Edn. N.S.F., 1960-64, asst. prof., 1963-65; group leader and prin. sci. Inmont Corp., Clifton, N.J., 1965-69; asst. dir. rsch. Johnson & Johnson, Brazil, 1969-70, exec. dir. rsch., mem. exec. com., 1970-72, sr. rsch. assoc., New Brunswick, N.J., 1972-84, sr. scientist, 1984-90; mem. bd. examiners Med. Sch. U. Brazil, 1953, 55, Faculdade Fluminense de Medicina, Niteroi R.J., Brazil, 1953. Contbr. articles to profl. jours.; contbg. editor Chemistry A to Z, 1964. Brit. Coun. scholar U. Cambridge , 1954; Oliver Gatty Scholar U. Cambridge, 1956-58. Mem. Am. Chem. Soc., Math. Assn. Am., Sigma Xi. Achievements include in surface and colloid science; transcutaneous drug delivery.

PARRISH, BENJAMIN EMMITT, II, insurance executive; b. Statesboro, Ga., Dec. 20, 1945; s. Benjamin E. and Ouida L. (Anderson) P.; m. Sandra Dianne Bragg, July 26, 1964; children: Michelle, Benjamin III, Sonya. Student, Atlanta Art Inst., 1963-65. Cert. ins. agt., Ga., Fla., S.C., N.C., Ala., Va. Art dir. Macy's, Atlanta, 1965-66; sales mgr. Clearbrook Realty, Atlanta, 1966-72; pres., comml. pilot, flight instr. Parrish Enterprises, Statesboro, 1972-77; v.p. Design Concepts, Statesboro, 1977-85; cons., pres. Parrish Assocs., Statesboro, 1985-87; ind. ins. agy. Statesboro, Ga., 1987—; dist. coord. Am. Family Life Assurance Corp., Ga., 1987-92, regional coord., 1993—. Author: Captive Management, 1972; writer/dir. (video) Tax Savings 125, 1991. Bd. dirs. Statesboro-Bulloch County C. of C., Chamber Connection, 1992-93; chmn. Statesboro Main Street Action Commn., 1993-94. Featured in Life & Health Ins. Sales mag., Apr. 1992. Republican. Baptist. Home: 5633 Ga Hwy 46 Statesboro GA 30458-8515 Office: Parrish and Assocs 18 S Main St Statesboro GA 30458-4933

PARRISH, BOBBY LEE, insurance executive; b. Randolph County, N.C., May 4, 1931; s. Lonnie Eugene and Lyda Effie (Kennedy) P.; m. Jo Arlene Bundy, June 13, 1953; children: Patricia Ann Parrish O'Connor, Pamela Jean Parrish Bye, Jill Marie Parrish Wilson. BSBA, High Point Coll., 1953. CLU, Chartered Fin. Cons. With Pilot Life Ins. Co., High Point, N.C., 1953-70; pres. Smith/Broadhurst, Inc., Greensboro, N.C., 1970—, Estate Analysis Svc., Inc., Greensboro, N.C., 1975—; v.p. Corp. Pension/Profit Sharing Cons. Svc., Inc., Greensboro, N.C., 1972—. Bd. dirs., chmn. High Point Salvation Army, 1990, High Point Urban Ministries, Youth Unltd., Alcoholic Homes, Inc.; bd. dirs. High Point Drug Action Coun., ARC, Inst. Ch. Renewal, Lay Renewal Ministries. Named Alumnus of Yr., High Point Coll. Mem. High Point Assn. Life Underwriters (pres.), High Point Estate Planning Coun. (pres.), Advance Assn. Life Underwriters, Am. Soc. CLUs and Chartered Fin. Cons., High Point Rotary, Million Dollar Roundtable (Top of the Table). Methodist. Home: 1317 Westminster Dr High Point NC 27262-7358 Office: Smith/Broadhurst Inc PO Box 10918 Greensboro NC 27404-0918

PARRISH, DAVID WALKER, JR., legal publishing company executive; b. Bristol, Tenn., Feb. 8, 1923. BA, Emory & Henry Coll., 1948, LLD, 1978; BS, U.S. Merchant Marine Acad., 1950; LLB, U. Va., 1951. Pres. The Michie Co., Charlottesville, Va., 1969-89, vice chmn., 1989-96; pub. cons., 1996—. Home: 114 Falcon Dr Charlottesville VA 22901-2013 Office: 300 Preston Ave Ste 103 Charlottesville VA 22902

PARRISH, EDWARD ALTON, JR., electrical and computer engineering educator, academic administrator; b. Newport News, Va., Jan. 7, 1937; s. Edward Alton and Molly Wren (Vaughan) P.; m. Shirley Maxine Johnson, Oct. 26, 1963; children: Troy Alton, Gregory Sinton. B.E.E., U. Va., 1964, M.E.E., 1966, D.Sc. in Elec. Engring., 1968. Registered profl. engr., Tenn., Va. Group leader Amerad Corp., Charlottesville, Va., 1961-64; asst. prof. elec. engring. U. Va., Charlottesville, 1968-71, assoc. prof. elec. engring., 1971-77, prof. elec. engring., 1977-86, chmn. dept. elec. engring., 1978-86; dean, centennial prof. electrical engring. Vanderbilt U., Nashville, 1987-95; pres., prof. elec. and computer engring. Worcester Poly. U., 1995—; cons. U.S. Army, Charlottesville, Va., 1971-77, ORS, Inc., Princeton, N.J., 1973-74, Sperry Marine Systems, Charlottesville, 1975-76, Hajime Industries Ltd., Tokyo, 1978-84. Contbr. numerous articles to profl. jours. Served with USAF, 1954-58. Recipient numerous grants, contracts from industry, govt. agys. Fellow IEEE (bd. dirs. 1990-91, v.p. ednl. activities 1992-93, mem. accreditation bd. engring. tech. commn. 1989—, exec. com. 1991—, officer 1993—, chair elect 1994-95, chair 1995-96, editor-in-chief IEEE Computer 1995—), IEEE Computer Soc. (sec. 1977, v.p. 1978-81, pres. 1988), Pattern Recognition Soc., Sigma Xi, Eta Kappa Nu, Tau Beta Pi. Baptist. Office: Office of Pres 100 Institute Rd Worcester MA 01609-2280

PARRISH, FLORENCE TUCKER, writer, retired government official; b. Greenville, Miss.; d. Victor Amos and Martha Buchannan (Binkley) Denslow; m. Joseph Nathaniel Tucker Jr., Nov. 9, 1946 (dec.); children: Joseph Nathaniel III, Frederick Steven, James Denslow; m. Noel Francis Parrish, June 25, 1983 (dec. Apr. 1987). Diploma piano, Ward-Belmont Coll., Nashville, 1945; studied piano with Michael Field, N.Y.C., 1945-46; B of Music Edn., Delta State U., Cleveland, Miss., 1960; MS in Counseling, U. So. Miss., 1971; EdD, George Washington U., 1983. Tchr. music Gulfport (Miss.) pub. schs., 1959-63; recreation therapist VA Hosp., Gulfport, 1964-70; edn. counselor USAF, Miss. and Japan, 1971-74, edn. svcs. officer, Republic of Korea, 1974-75, asst. dir. sr. tng. CAP nat. hdqrs., 1975-77; EEO officer D.C. Dept. Labor, 1977-80; bur. chief complaints processing and adjudication Office EEO, U.S. Geol. Survey, Reston, Va., 1980-82, mgr. human resources, Dept. Interior, 1982-84; internat. forum coord. Pres.'s Com. on Employment of Handicapped, 1985; commr. Alexandria Commn. on Aging, Va., 1985-88, chmn. edn. and cultural affairs com., 1985-88, sec., 1987-88; lead scholar pilot project Nat. Coun. on Aging; vis. prof. Kunsan Tchrs. Coll., Kunsan Jr. Coll., 1974-75; apptd. mem. del. People-to-People Internat. Amb. Program, Beijing, Peoples Republic China and Hong Kong, 1988; mem. steering com. Va. Home Care Alliance, 1990-92; mem. exec. bd. Washington Opera Guild, 1992-94; chmn. Night in Old Vienna benefit ball Embassy of Austria, Washington, 1993, co-chair, 1994; mem. adv. bd. Inst. Conflict Analysis and Resolution George Mason U., 1993—, vice chair 1995—, delegate to Arms Ctrl. Negotations in the Middle East, Athens, Greece, 1994; mem. ofcl. delegation 8th Internat. Helicopter Olympic Competition, Moscow, 1994; workshop leader, cons. and lectr. in field; bd. dirs. Wake Assocs., Ltd., Washington, 1980-84. Columnist on aging issues, Alexandria (Va.) Gazette-Packet, feature writer, 1986-92; contbr. articles to profl. jours. Organizer, pres. Gulfport chpt. Parents-Without-Ptnrs., 1962-64; charter mem. Westminster Presbyn. Ch., Gulfport, 1961; active Nat. Coun. on Aging, Military Classics Seminar; officer, bd. dirs. Stonehurst IV Homeowners Assn. Recipient Outstanding Vis. Prof. award Kunsan Tchrs. Coll., 1974, Kunsan Jr. Coll. award for promoting tchr. exchange program, also certs. of commendation, Brigadier Gen. Noel F. Parrish award The Nat. Tuskegee Airmen, Inc., commendation for organizing art show Alexandria Commn. on Aging. Mem. Women in Comm., Washington Opera Guild, USAF Assn. (v.p. for community programs Gen. Charles Gabriel chpt. 1991—, Woman of Distinction award Thomas Anthony chpt.), NATO Def. Coll. Anciens Assn., Am. Inst. Wine and Food, World Affairs Coun., Va. Assn. on Aging, Nat. Press Club (events and oral history coms., chmn. oral history com.), Miss. Soc. Washington, Ret. Officers Assn., Tex. Soc. Washington, Friends of Kennedy Ctr., Smithsonian Assocs., The Nat. Tuskegee Airmen Inc. Orgn. Home: Stonehurst 9302 Arlington Blvd Fairfax VA 22031-2503

PARRISH, JOHN WESLEY, JR., biology educator; b. Dennison, Ohio, Mar. 5, 1941; s. John Wesley Parrish Sr. and Dorothy Irene (Dickinson) Price; m. Paula Schmanke, July 9, 1966; children: Corinne Danelle, Wesley Allen. BS, Denison U., 1963; MA, Bowling Green (Ohio) State U., 1970, PhD, 1974. Tchr. sci. Northwood Jr. H.S., Norfolk, Va., spring 1967; vis. instr. dept. biology Kenyon Coll., Gambier, Ohio, 1973-74; postdoctoral fellow dept. zoology U. Tex., Austin, 1974-76; asst. prof. dept. biol. sci. Emporia (Kans.) State U., 1976-82, assoc. prof., 1982-88, assoc. chairperson dept. biol. sci., 1987-88; prof. Ga. So. U., Statesboro, 1988—, chairperson dept. biology, 1988-94; vis. rsch. assoc. prof. dept. physiology Cornell U., Ithaca, N.Y., fall 1986. Author: (with others) Field and Laboratory Biology, 1985; editor: Activities in the Environmental and Life Sciences, 1986; mem. editorial bd. Oriole, 1991—; contbr. numerous articles to profl. jours. Officer USNR, 1964-67. Josselyn Van Tyne Meml. Fund rsch. grantee, 1968; Faculty Rsch. Com. grantee Emporia State U., 1977-85, 87-88; NSF grantee, 1984; grantee Kans. Fish and Game Commn., 1985, Kans. Dept. Wildlife and Pks., 1987, Quail Unltd., 1988, Arcadia Wildlife Preserve, Inc., 1994, 95, 96, Ga. Dept. Nat. Resources, 1994, 95. Office: Ga So U Dept Biology LB 8042 Statesboro GA 30460

PARRISH, LINDA KRISTINE, data management consultant; b. Milw., Dec. 3, 1965; d. Leslie Urban Burgess and Karen Jean (Rauen) Gray; m. Peter Robert James, Feb. 13, 1988 (div. Sept. 1993); m. Gary Lane Parrish, July 31, 1994. BSN, Concordia U. Wis., Mequon, 1987. RN, Wis., N.C.; cert. ACLS, Am. Heart Assn. Staff nurse telemetry Trinity Meml. Hosp., Cudahy, Wis., 1987-88; staff nurse Olmsted Community Hosp., Rochester, Minn., 1988-89; packaging and shipping clk. Packaging Store, Rochester, 1989-90; payroll and pers. clk. U.S. Bur. of Census, Rochester, 1990; exec. case mgr. Safekeeping, Inc., South Milwaukee, Wis., 1986—; staff/charge nurse cardiac telemetry Durham (N.C.) Regional Hosp., 1986-94, chair primary nursing com. progressive care unit, 1992-93; case mgr. Alpha Omega Health Care Inc., Durham, 1994-95; ind. distbr. Rexall Showcase Internat., 1994; med. data coord. Manpower Tech./Clintrials Rsch., Inc., Morrisville, N.C., 1995-96; cons. data mgmt. Trilogy Cons. Corp., San Diego, 1996—. Vol. George Bush for Pres. campaign, Milw., 1988. Mem. Ofcl. Star Trek Fan Club. Lutheran. Office: Trilogy Cons Corp 3600 W Bayshore Rd Ste 100 Palo Alto CA 99305

PARRISH, PAUL AUSTIN, English language educator; b. Wichita, Kans., Oct. 26, 1944; s. Lee Marvin and Viola Vera (Rishel) P.; m. Linda Carol Hudson, June 9, 1967; children: Marc Hudson, Gavin Lee. Student, Friends U., Wichita, 1962-63; BA, Abilene Christian U., 1966; MA, U. Kans., 1968; PhD, Rice U., 1971. Vis. instr. Tex. So. U., Houston, 1969; asst. prof., dir. 1st yr. English, Ind. U., South Bend, 1971-74; asst. prof. English, Tex. A&M U., College Station, 1974-77, assoc. prof., 1977-82, prof., 1982—, coord. acad. affairs Coll. Liberal Arts, 1986-87, assoc. dean, 1987-94; vis. asst. prof. Tex. So. U., Houston, 1970; lectr. in field, 1973, including Internat. Milton Symposium, Vallombrosa and Florence, Italy, 1988, South-Ctrl. Renaissance Conf., 1991, Kazan (Russia) State U., 1991, U. Ams., Puebla, Mex., 1992. Author: Celebration: Introduction to Literature, 1977, Richard Crashw, 1980; contbr. articles and revs. to profl. jours., chpts. to books. Precinct chmn. Brazos County Dem. Com., 1985—; bd. dirs. Brazos Valley Arts Coun., 1990-94; mem. Tex. Humanities Alliance. Recipient Disting. Svc. award Tex. A&M U. Meml. Student Ctr., 1977. Mem. MLA, AAUP (pres. Tex. A&M U. chpt. 1978-79, sec. 1985-86, v.p. ctrl. region Tex. conf. 1980-82), South Ctrl. MLA (exec. dir. 1982-87, editor newsletter 1983-87), South-Ctrl. Renaissance Conf. (exec. bd. 1980-82, pres. 1984-85), Renaissance Soc. Am., Soc. for Lit. and Sci., Milton Soc. Am., John Donne Soc. (exec. com. 1990-92), Conf. Coll. Tchrs. English, Tex. Assn. Coll. Tchrs. (chpt. pres. 1982-83), Tex. Faculty Assn. (editorial bd. Symposium 1986-87), Phi Kappa Phi, Phi Beta Delta (pres. 1994—). Home: 2604 Faulkner Dr College Station TX 77845-5674 Office: Tex A&M U English Dept College Station TX 77843

PARRISH, RAMON OLENE, JR., gerontologist; b. Atlanta, June 2, 1955; s. Ramon Olene and Sue (Shelnutt) P.; married, 1978 (div. 1994); children: Christopher, Matthew, Daniel; m. Susan Marie Castle, June 17, 1995. AA, Oxford Coll., 1975; BS, Emory U., 1977, MD, 1981. Diplomate Am. Bd. Family Practice. Flt. surgeon 21st Tactical Air Support System, Shaw AFB, S.C., 1982-84; resident in family practice Eglin AFB Hosp., Fla., 1984-87; mem. family practice faculty Eglin AFB Hosp., 1987-88; sr. ptnr. Blue Ridge (Ga.) Med. Svcs., 1989—. Maj. USAF. Home: RR 4 Box 281 M 219 Shiloh Ln Ellijay GA 30540 Office: PO Box 1479 815 E Main St Blue Ridge GA 30513

PARRISH, SHERRY DYE, elementary school educator; b. Birmingham, Ala., Oct. 18, 1957; d. Charles Max and Peggy Gail (Doss) Dye; m. James Wiley Parrish, June 13, 1987; 1 child, Taylor Austin Shaw. BS in Elem. Edn., Samford U., 1979; MS in Elem. Edn., U. Ala., 1995. Cert. tchr. Rank I, Class A., Ala. Tchr. Franklin Acad., Birmingham, Ala., 1979-83, Shades Cahaba Elem. Sch., Homewood, Ala., 1986-94, Trace Crossings Sch., Hoover, Ala., 1994-95, South Shades Crest Sch., Hoover, Ala., 1995—; chairperson sci. fair Shades Cahaba Elem. Sch., Homewood, 1990-94; mem. accreditation team, Warrior (Ala.) Sch., 1990; presenter Homewood City Schs., 1988, Constructivist Conf., Birmingham, 1994, 95, co-presenter NCTM regional conf., 1995, presenter Mid-South Whole Lang. Conf., Birmingham, 1995. Rsch. participant (book) Theme Immersion: Inquiry Based Curriculum in Elementary and Middle Schools, 1994. Founder, tchr. Women in Transition, Shades Mt. Baptist Ch., Birmingham, 1993—; presenter Festival of Marriage, Ridgecrest N.C, 1994, Dayspring Women's Conf., Birmingham, 1994. Mem. Nat. Coun. Teachers of Math., Am. Edn. Rsch. Assn., Educator's Forum. Office: South Shades Crest Elem 3770 S Shades Crest Rd Hoover AL 35244-4123

PARROTT, JANICE MORTON, medical/surgical nurse, researcher; b. Atlanta, Apr. 27, 1954; d. James C. and Dorothy Fowler Morton; m. Danny J. Parrott, Feb. 16, 1980; children: Ashley, Olivia. Diploma, Grady Meml. Hosp. Sch. Nursing, Atlanta, 1978. Staff nurse Grady Meml. Hosp., 1978-89; rsch. nurse/cardiology Emory U. Sch. Medicine, Atlanta, 1989-91, researcher preventive medicine, 1991-93, project coord., 1993—; researcher in cardiology field. Home: 195 Trotters Walk Covington GA 30209 Office: Emory U Sch Medicine 69 Butler St SE Atlanta GA 30303-3033

PARROTT, NANCY SHARON, lawyer; b. Atoka, Okla., Jan. 11, 1944; d. Albert L. and Willie Jo (Parkhill) Furr. BA, Okla. U., 1967; MA, No. Tex. U., 1974; JD, Okla. City U., 1982. Bar: Okla. 1984, U.S. Supreme Ct. 1984. Ptnr. Chapman & Chapman, Oklahoma City, 1984-85; chief legal asst. marshal Okla. Supreme Ct., Oklahoma City, 1985—. Mem. Leadership Oklahoma, Leadership Oklahoma City; bd. dirs. Am. Cancer Soc. Mem. ABA, Okla. Bar Assn., Okla. County Bar Assn. Briefcase, Am. Adjudicature Soc., Okla. Bar Assn. (chmn. awards com.). Office: Okla Supreme Ct State Capital Bldg 245 Oklahoma City OK 73105

PARRY, JAMES THOMAS, management consultant; b. LaPorte, Ind., July 30, 1926; s. Edward Thomas and Ruth (Sweet) P.; m. Elsie Matovich, June, 1953 (dec. Aug. 1978); children: Barbara, Karen, Rochelle; m. Jeannette O. Whitworth, May 19, 1990. BA in Econs., Lake Forest (Ill.) Coll., 1950; MBA in Mktg., Ind. U., 1952. Mgr. mkt. rsch. Brunswick Corp., Chgo., 1952-55; account rsch. advisor Foote Cone & Belding, L.A., 1955-56; mgr. mkt. rsch. Hoffman Electronics, L.A., 1956-60; head mkt. rsch. Hughes Ground Sys., Fullerton, Calif., 1960-62; western regional sales mgr. TRW Computer Sys., Woodland Hills, Calif., 1962-65; dir. bus. devel. Gen. Precision, Glendale, Calif., 1965-68; mktg. dir. Datamate Computer, Big Spring, Tex., 1968-69; pres. Parry Assocs., Mission Viejo, Calif., 1969—, Leona, Tex., 1969—. With USN, 1945-46. Mem. Am. Mktg. Assn. (pres. 1961-62). Democrat. Methodist. Office: Perry Associates Rt 2 Box 280H Normangee TX 77871

PARRY, THOMAS HERBERT, JR., school system administrator, educational consultant; b. Detroit, June 28, 1928; s. Thomas Herbert Sr. and Isabel Constance (Brinsmead) P.; m. Frances Ellen Coley, Aug. 15, 1956; children: Virginia Gilkeson, William Thomas, Robert Brinsmead. BA in Edn., U. Fla., 1950; MEd, U. Va., 1958, EdD, 1967. Lic. profl. supr. of counselors; nat. cert. counselor. Tchr. Broward County Pub. Schs., Ft. Lauderdale, Fla., 1950-51, 54-62; instr. Mary Baldwin Coll., Staunton, Va., 1965-66; psychologist McGuffey Reading Ctr., Charlottesville, Va., 1966-67; prof. Clemson (S.C.) U., 1967-86; pres. Ednl. Horizons, Inc., Clemson, 1986-89, Poquoson, Va., 1989—; cons. Sch. Desegregation Ctr., Columbia, 1970; cons., counselor Advocacy Bd. S.C., 1980-82; exec. sec. S.C. Pers. and Guidance Assn., Columbia, 1980-81; founder S.C. Assn. Measurement and Evaluation in Guidance, 1974-75. Co-author: Beyond the Book: Activities to Correlate with the Virginia Young Readers, 1990-91, Developing a Leisure Learning Program, 1980; editor S.C. Pers. and Guidance Newsletter and Jour., 1969-74; founder, editor S.C. Pers. and Guidance Assn. Jour., 1972-74; contbr. articles to profl. jours. Recipient Svc. award S.C. Pers. and Guidance, 1968-81, Nat. Award for Excellence State Publs. and Guidance Assn., 1971, Meritorious Svc. award Am. Pers. and Guidance Assn., 1973, Award of Merit for Svc. to Youth Boy Scouts Am., 1975. Mem. APA, AACD, S.C. Assn. Counseling and Devel., Kiwanis (bd. dirs., chmn. community svc. com. 1991—), Ft. Benning Lodge # 579, Kappa Delta Pi, Phi Delta Kappa. Presbyterian. Home and Office: 1 Ebb Tide Lndg Poquoson VA 23662-1334

PARSLEY, JACQUE, visual artist, art gallery director; b. Memphis, Jan. 10, 1947; s. Jack Nelson and Bonnie Mae (Dinwiddie) Carter; m. William Millard Parsley, Aug. 2, 1969 (div. June 1979); children: Jessica Leigh, Molly Kristine; m. Thomas Donahue Henrion, Feb. 14, 1986. BFA, Louisville Sch. Art, 1980; MA, U. Louisville, 1990; MFA, U. Ky., 1994. Dir. WHAS Gallery, Louisville, 1979-80; dir. gallery Liberty Nat. Bank, Louisville, 1980—; adj. prof. U. Louisville, 1988-89; juror Nat. Scholastic Arts awards, Louisville, 1987, 90, 91; artist-in-residence Blackhawk (Colo.) Mountain Sch. of Art, 1984-85; juror for grant awards Ky. Found. for Women, 1995; interviewed pub. TV, Louisville, 1990, Cable TV Women in the Arts, Louisville, 1991; lectr. Artists Guild, Evansville Mus. Art, 1986, Speed Mus. Gallery, Louisville, 1985, Owensboro (Ky.) Art Guild, 1984, Visual Variety House, Water Tower Art Assn., 1984, 90, Bellarmine Coll., 1982, U. Ky., Lexington, 1985, 93; juror Artsplace, Lexington, 1989-90, Lincoln Days Celebration Art Show, Hodgensville, Ky., 1986, Nat. Scholastic Art Awards, N.Y.C., 1986, Capitol Arts Ctr., Bowling Green, Ky., 1985, Water Tower Art Assn., 1983. One person shows include Campbellsville (Ky.) Coll., 1981, Triangle Gallery, Lexington, Ky., 1989, Guild Gallery, Lexington, 1992; represented in permanent collections at Evansville Mus. Arts and Sci., Ala. Power and Light, Huntsville, Ala., U.S. Govt. Office Comptroller of Currency, Cin., Ky. Ctr. for the Arts, Louisville, Oxford Properties, Louisville, Rev. Alfred and Mary Shands, Louisville, Benefit Actuaries, Inc., Louisville, Hilliard Lyons, Louisville, Home of the Innocents, Louisville, Brown-Forman Cor., Louisville, Fetter Printing Co., Louisville, Pattco, Louisville, Lew Magram, N.Y.C., Prudential Life Ins., Louisville, Creative Alliance, Louisville, Owensboro (Ky.) Mus. Fine Art; exhibited in group shows at Speed Mus., Louisville, 1977, 85, Surface Design S.E. Visual Arts Gallery, Athens, Ga., 1977, Swearingen Gallery, Louisville, 1980, 84, Gary-Windsor Gallery, Richmond, Va., 1981, Art Ctr., Louisville, 1981, Gayle Willson Gallery, Southampton, N.Y., 1981, 82, 84, 85, 88, Arrowmont Sch. Arts and Crafts, Gatlinburg, Tenn., 1981, 84, Alexandria (La.) Mus., 1981, Gallery 106, Perrysburg, Ohio, 1982, Wadsworth Antheneum, Hartford, Conn., 1982, James Hunt Barker Galleries, N.Y.C., 1983, U. Ky., Lexington, 1983, Ky. Arts and Crafts Found., Louisville, 1984, 86, Washington Design Ctr., 1985, Longwood Coll., Farmville, Va., 1985, Berryhill Mansion, Frankfort, Ky., 1986, Craft and Folk Art Mus., L.A., 1988, Galeria Mesa, Ariz., 1988, 91, Evansville (Ind.) Mus. Arts and Sci., 1988, Morlan Gallery, Lexington, 1988, Louisville Visual Art Assn., 1989, 90, Contemporary Crafts Gallery, Louisville, 1989, New Harmony (Ind.) Gallery Contemporary Art, 1989, Owensboro (Ky.) Mus. Fine Art, 1989, Amos Eno Gallery, N.Y.C., 1989, 90, Allen R. Hite Art Inst. U. Louisville, 1989, 90, Headly-Whitney Mus., Lexington, 1989, 93, Ky. Art & Craft Gallery, Louisville, 1991, Sarratt Gallery, Nashville, 1991, Bellarine Coll., Louisville, 1992, Huntington (W.Va.) Mus. Art, 1992, Contemporary Crafts Assn., Portland, 1992, Yeiser Art Ctr., Paducah, Ky., 1993, Evansville Mus., 1993; contbr. articles to profl. jours. Auction donator Louisville Visual Art Assn., 1976—, Human Soc., Louisville, 1986, Louisville Zoo, 1991-94, Ronald McDonald House, 1987; mem. J. B. Speed Mus., 1976—. Recipient Mid-States Craft Exhbn. Purchase award Evansville (Ind.) Mus. Art, 1988, Finders Keepers merit award Galeria Mesa, 1991, 1st pl. Nat. Competition Amos Eno Gallery, 1989, Gamut mag., Cleve. State U., 1991. Mem. Am. Craft Coun. (Ky. rep. 1987-90, S.E. regional assembly alt. 1993-94, exhibit curator 1986, workshop leader S.E. Regional Conf.), Surface Design Assn. (Ky. rep. 1992—), Ky. Art and Craft Found. (bd. dirs. 1984-87), Ky. Guild Artists and Craftsmen, Ky. Watercolor Soc. (adv. bd.), Visual Art Network (pres. 1994—), Louisville Visual Art Assn. (past bd. dirs.). Office: Bank One Gallery Liberty 416 W Jefferson Louisville KY 40202-3202

PARSLEY, ROBERT CHARLES, minister; b. Tulsa, Aug. 11, 1956; s. Victor Bernard and Margery Sue (Mathews) P.; m. Carole Ellen McKenzie, Oct. 2, 1982; children: Robert McKenzie, Timothy James, Kelly Mathews. BA in Religion with high honors, Ouachita Bapt. U., 1978; MDiv, So. Bapt. Theol. Sem., 1982; D Ministry, Southwestern Bapt. Theol. Sem., 1990. Ordained to ministry Bapt. Ch., 1978. Youth minister First Bapt. Ch., Leithfield, Ky., 1979-80; chaplain Bapt. Med. Ctr., Little Rock, 1980-81; pastor Lula (Miss.) Bapt. Ch., 1982-84; pastor First Bapt. Ch., Prescott, Ark., 1984-88, Dardanelle, Ark., 1988-93; pastor Waialae Baptist Ch., Honolulu, 1993-95, First Baptist Ch., Smackover, Ark., 1995—. Mem. Ark. Alumni Soc. Bapt. Theol. Sem. (pres. 1986), ARVAC (bd. dirs. 1991-93), Rotary (club pres. 1992). Baptist. Home: 105 E 11th St Smackover AR 71762 Office: First Baptist Ch 201 W 7th St Smackover AR 71762

PARSONS, BRUCE ANDREW, biomedical engineer, scientist; b. Kingston, Jamaica, Mar. 13, 1960; came to U.S., 1961; s. Roy Dixon and Lupé Claudette (Bruce) P.; m. Jacquéline González, Dec. 19, 1987. BS in Elec. Engring., Fla. Atlantic U., 1983; MS in Biomed. Engring., U. Miami, 1985; PhD in Bioengring., Clemson U., 1990. Elec. engr. Trackmaster, Inc., Pompano, Fla., 1983-85, 90-91; bioengineer U. Miami (Fla.) Med. Sch., 1985-86; biol. and cardiology rschr. VA Med. Ctr., Charleston, S.C., 1987-90; sr. R&D engr. Becton Dickinson Vascular Access, Sandy, Utah, 1991-92; postdoctoral rschr. dept. cellular pharmacology U. Miami, Fla., 1992-96; indsl. fellow Coulter Corp., Hialeah, Fla., 1996—; R&D mgr. Biol. Components Corp., 1996—; sr. rsch. fellow W.M. Keck Ctr. for Molecular Electronics. Contbr. articles to Biomed. Sci. and Tech., Circulation. Tuition scholar State of Fla., 1984, Pre-doctoral scholar McKnight Found., 1986; NIH postdoctoral fellow, 1992, rsch. fellow Am. HEart Assn., 1993-96. Mem. IEEE Biomed. Engring. Soc. Home: 1951 NE 59th Pl Fort Lauderdale FL 33308-2113

PARSONS, DANIEL LANKESTER, pharmaceutics educator; b. Biscoe, N.C., Sept. 10, 1953; s. Solomon Lankester and Doris Eva (Bost) P. BS in Pharmacy, U. Ga., 1975, PhD, 1979. Asst. prof. pharmaceutics U. Ariz., Tucson, 1979-82; asst. prof. Auburn (Ala.) U., 1982-86, assoc. prof., 1986-91, prof., 1991—, chmn. divsn., 1990—; cons. Wyeth-Ayerst, Phila., 1989-93, Technomics, Ardsley, N.Y., 1990-93; presenter in field. Author: (with G.V. Betageri and S.A. Jenkins) Liposome Drug Delivery Systems, 1993. Named Disting. Alumni Sandhills Coll., 1990, Tchr. of Yr., Pharmacy Student Coun., 1987, Grad. Faculty Mem. of Yr., Grad. Student Orgn., 1994. Mem. Am. Pharm. Assn., Am. Assn. Pharm. Scientists, Am. Coll. Clin. Pharmacology (mem. coun. 1990-93), Phi Kappa Phi, Kappa Psi (advisor 1990-95, Svc. award 1990, 95, Advisor award 1992, nat. scholarship com. 1995). Office: Auburn U Sch Pharmacy Auburn AL 36849

PARSONS, EDMUND MORRIS, investment company executive; b. Houston, Oct. 19, 1936; s. Alfred Morris and Virgina (Hanna) P. AB, Harvard U., 1958; MBA, U. Pa., 1961; MS, MIT, 1970. Pres. Fredonia Enterprises, Inc., Houston, Tex., 1990—; fgn. service officer U.S. Dept. State, Washington, 1965-90; 1st sec. Am. Embassy, Mexico City, 1973-76; economist Fed. Res. Bank N.Y., N.Y.C., 1976-77; chief food aid div. U.S. Dept. State, Washington, 1977-80, dir. office devel., 1981-82, dir. office econ. policy, 1983-84; dep. chief mission U.S. Mission to FAO, Rome, 1985-86; dir. Office Ecology and Natural Resources U.S. Dept. State, Washington, 1986-88; dir. Office of Internat. Narcotics Control Programs, 1988-89; min.-counselor for econ. affairs Am. Embassy, Mexico City, 1989-90; pres. Fredonia Enterprises, Inc., Houston, 1990—; co-chmn. Tropical Forest Task Force, Washington, 1986-88; dep. U.S. rep. UN FAO, Rome, 1985-86; alt. U.S. rep. to environ. program U.S. Del. Nairobi, Kenya, 1987. Capt. USAF, 1962-72. Mem. Am. Fgn. Svc. Assn., Houston Restaurant Assn. (bd. dirs. 1992—), Houston World Affairs Coun. (bd. dirs. 1995—), Consular Corps of Houston (hon.), Houston Hispanic C. of C., Coun. Fgn. Rels. (Houston com.), Univ. Club (Houston). Republican. Methodist. Office: 2727 Fondren Rd Ste 2A Houston TX 77063

PARSONS, EILEEN CARLTON, science education educator; b. Lenoir, N.C., Aug. 17, 1967; d. Howard Lee and Ila Mae (Davenport) Carlton; m. Randolph Parsons, Dec. 21, 1992. BS, U. N.C., 1989; MS, Cornell U., 1991, PhD, 1994. Cert. sci. and math. tchr., N.C. Tutor, counselor, head counselor, program asst. U. N.C.-Chapel Hill's Summer Bridge Program, 1986-92; tech. conf. coord. U. N.C./N.C. Sci. and Math. Network, 1991-92; asst. JTPA-Caldwell County, Lenoir, N.C., summer 1992; sci. tchr. Catawba County Schs., Claremont, N.C., 1994-95; asst. prof. sci. edn. Lenoir Rhyne Coll., Hickory, N.C., 1995—; counselor project uplift, U. N.C., 1988-89, mem. adv. com. student svcs., 1985-87, counselor freshman camp, 1986-87. Recipient Century III Leader award Shell Oil Co., 1984 (Most Outstanding Student award 1984), N.C. Assn. Elks, 1985; Joseph E. Pogue scholar, 1985-89, N.Y. State fellow, 1989-91, 91-94, N.C. Bd. Govs. fellow, 1991-92. Mem. Am. Ednl. Rschr.'s Assn., nat. Sci. Tchr.'s Assn., nat. Assn. Rsch. on Sci. Tchg., Gamma Sigma Delta, Delta Sigma Theta, Phi Kappa, Phi. Home: 4986 Woodfield Dr Hickory NC 28602

PARSONS, HELGA LUND, writer; b. Seattle, Sept. 5, 1906; d. Gunnar and Marie Pauline (Vognild) Lund; m. Durwin David Algyer, June 6, 1937 (dec. 1971); children: Deanne Algyer Mathisen, Marilyn A. McIntosh; m. James Stewart Parsons, Sept. 30, 1972 (dec. 1988). Grad., Columbia Coll. Expression, Chgo., 1926. Lead actress Repertory Playhouse, Seattle, 1929-34; assoc. prof. drama U. Wash., 1931-32; dir. apprentice group Repertory Playhouse, Seattle 1932-34; writer, anchor radio programs Bon Marche Dept. Store, Seattle 1933-35; v.p. creative dir. Norwegian Am. Mus., Decorah, Iowa 1960-66. Author: Norway Travel Newspaper Series, Seattle, 1930, Concert Touring, Monodramas, 1936, (novelized version) Blondie and Dagwood King Features, 1946; script writer serials for WOR, CBS, NBC, N.Y.C.; appeared in Solid Gold Cadillac, I Remember Mama; editor Surfsedge Newsletter. Activities chmn. Glenview, Naples. Mem. Norwegian Am. Mus. (life), MIT (hon.). Republican.

PARSONS, ROBERT WILLIAM, JR., forensic chemist, consultant; b. Indpls., May 2, 1957; s. Robert William Sr. and Ann Grace (Arena) P.; m. Marion Louise Jacobs, Nov. 29, 1980. BS in Biology, Fla. Inst. Tech., 1980. Diplomate in Forensic Sci., Am. Bd. Criminalistics; diplomate, cert. profl. competency in criminalistics Calif. Assn. Criminalists; permit to conduct chem. analysis-blood alcohol testing State of Fla.; fellow forensic drug analysis Am. Bd. Criminalistics. Crime lab. technician Fla. Dept. Law Enforcement, Sanford, 1981-82; forensic chemist Regional Crime Lab. IRCC, Ft. Pierce, Fla., 1982—; pvt. practice forensic chemistry cons., Ft. Pierce, 1985—; part-time instr. criminal justice, biology, chemistry and physics Indian River C.C., Ft. Pierce, 1983—; mem. exam. com. Am. Bd. Criminalistics, Greenlawn, N.Y., 1990—, drug analysis coord., 1990—, vice chmn. exam com., 1994—; guest lectr. Fla. Nat. guard Mil. Acad., 1986, Fla. Corrections Acad., 1987. Contbr. articles to Electrolyte. Maj. U.S. Army N.G., 1981—. N.J. State scholar, 1975-79; recipient Young Ams. award N.J. Coun. Boy Scouts Am., 1975. Mem. Am. Acad. Forensic Scis., Forensic Sci. Soc. (contbr. commentary to jour.), So. Assn. Forensic Scientists, ASTM (com. E-30 on the forensic scis.), Nat. Honor Soc., N.G. Assn. U.S., Air Def. Artillery Assn., N.G. Officer's Assn. Fla. Roman Catholic. Office: Regional Crime Lab at IRCC 3209 Virginia Ave Fort Pierce FL 34981-5541

PARSONS, WAYNE DOUGLAS, air transportation risk specialist; b. Paintsville, Ky., Dec. 21, 1949; s. Dollberta Parsons; m. Debra Jean Dollar, July 25, 1981; children: Matthew Wayne, Sara Rene. Student, Ea. Mich. U., 1974-75, U. Tex., Arlington, 1985-86, Arlington Police Acad., Ins. Inst. of Am. Cert. constrn. safety specialist, accident reconstructionist; cert. in evacuation safety, occupational safety and health adminstrn., profl. safety; lic. ins. adjustor. Test driver Chrysler Corp., Chelsea, Mich., 1974-80; instr. Nat. Acad. for Profl. Driving, Dallas, 1980-82; asst. risk mgr., loss prevention mgr. City of Arlington, 1982-87; loss control cons. Alexander & Alexander, Richmond, Va., 1987-89; risk specialist Dallas/Ft. Worth Internat. Airport, 1990—; cons. 1989-90; sr. loss control cons. Wethe & Assocs. Author: Airport Risk Management and Loss Control, 1991, Emergency Driving for Aircraft/Fire Rescue Vehicle Training, 1991 (Risk Mgmt. Achievement award Pub. Risk Mgmt. Assn. 1992), Municipal Loss Control, 1991; co-author, developer: Firefighter Survival and Safety, 1984. With USAF, 1969-73. Recipient award of Honor, Tex. Safety Assn., Dallas, 1984. Mem. Am. Soc. Safety Engrs. Methodist. Home: 3202 Flintridge Ct Arlington TX 76017-2513 Office: Dallas/Ft Worth Internat Airport PO Box 619428 Dallas TX 75261-9428

PARTINGTON, JOHN EDWIN, retired psychologist; b. Union Springs, N.Y., Nov. 13, 1907; s. Eliezer and Flora (Hobson) P.; m. Gwen L. Gray, Aug. 18, 1938. AB, Earlham Coll., 1929; MA in Psychology, U. Ky., 1938; postgrad., U. Chgo., 1946, Purdue U., 1959-62. Diplomate in counseling Am. Bd. Profl. Psychology; cert. psychologist, Ind. Tchr. Ky. Houses of Reform, Lexington, 1930-35; asst. to rsch. psychologist USPHS Hosp., Lexington, 1935-40; psychologist USES, Washington, 1940-42; counsellor VA, Roanoke, Va., 1946-50; psychologist US. Naval Exam. Ctr., Great Lakes, Ill., 1950-58; chief test devel. U.S. Army Enlisted Evaluation Ctr., Ft. Harrison, Ind., 1958-70; chief of rsch. U.S. Army Enlisted Evaluation Ctr., Ft. Harrison, 1970-72. Author: Leiter-Partington Adult Performance Scale, 1950, Helpful Hints for Better Living, 1990, Vol. 2, 1996; contbr. articles to profl. jours. Chmn. adv. com. Ret. Sr. Vol. Program, 1973-88; chmn. ofcl. bd. Downtown Bapt. Ch., Lexington, Ky., 1989-91. Maj. AUS, 1942-46. Recipient Lt. Govs. Outstanding Kentuckian award, 1983. Mem. APA (Cert. Disting. Contbn. 1986), Ind. Psychol. Assn. Address: 3458 Flintridge Dr Lexington KY 40517-1119

PARTOYAN, GARO ARAKEL, lawyer; b. Toledo, Dec. 6, 1936; s. Garo and Vartoohi (Yessayan) P.; m. Kathleen D. Valencia, Apr. 1, 1981; children: Garo Linck, Elizabeth Margaret, Martin Joseph. BS in Chem. Engring., Northwestern U., 1959; JD, U. Mich., 1962; LLM, NYU, 1964. Bar: N.Y. 1963, U.S. Dist. Cts. (so. dist.) N.Y. 1964, U.S. Ct. Claims 1966, U.S. Ct. Appeals (2nd cir.) 1966, U.S. Dist. Ct. (ea. dist.) N.Y. 1968. Ptnr. Curtis, Morris & Safford, N.Y.C., 1962-76; gen. counsel mktg. and tech. Latin Am. Mars, Inc., Mc Lean, Va., 1976—. Mem. Dobbs Ferry (N.Y.) Bd. Edn., 1972-76, pres., 1975-76; chmn. Fairfax Citizens Group, Fairfax County, Va., 1988-90. Mem. ABA, Am. Intellectual Property Law Assn., N.Y. Intellectual Property Law Assn., Internat. Trademark Assn. (pres. 1990-91, bd. dirs. 1983—), Intellectual Property Owners (bd. dirs. 1992—). Home: 7008 Green Oak Dr Mc Lean VA 22101-1551 Office: Mars Inc 6885 Elm St Mc Lean VA 22101-3883

PARTRIDGE, BENJAMIN WARING, writer; b. Huntington, W.Va., Mar. 9, 1915; s. Benjamin Waring and May Garnet (Asbury) P.; m. Cora Cheney, Sept. 2, 1939; children: Benjamin Waring III, Irene Denny, Alan Cheney, Mary Denham. BS, U. Fla., 1937; MA, Am. U., 1962; JD, U. Miami, 1948. Bar: Fla., Vt. Field deputy State Ins. Dept., Miami, Fla., 1939-41; treas., lectr. Windham Coll., Putney, Vt., 1969-71; chmn. environ. bd., dir. state planning State of Vt., Montpelier, 1971-74; atty. pvt. practice, Vt., 1974-76; arctic planner Office of Gov. of Alaska, Juneau, 1976-77; planning cons. N. Slope Borough, Barrow, Alaska, 1978-85; city commr. City of St. Marks (Fla.), 1988-93; chmn. Wakulla County Plan/Zoning, Crawfordville, Fla., 1988-90; Co-author: Underseas, 1961, China Sea Roundup/Rendezvous in Singapore, 1965-66; Crown of the World, 1979, Florida's Family Album, 1993; author procs. and articles. Elected Justice of Peace, Windham, Vt., 1969-73. Capt. USN, 1941-68. Explorers Club fellow. Mem. Wakulla Rotary Club. Episcopalian.

PARYANI, SHYAM BHOJRAJ, radiologist; b. Bhavnagar, Gujarat, India, July 18, 1956; came to U.S., 1966; s. Bhojraj Thakurdas and Sarswati (Shewarkanani) P.; m. Sharon Dale Goldman, May 12, 1979; children: Lisa Ann, Jason Bhojraj, Gregory Shyam. BSEE, U. Fla., 1975, MSEE, 1979, MD, 1979. Diplomate Am. Bd. of Radiology. Intern U. Tex., M.D. Anderson Hosp., Houston, 1979-80; resident Stanford (Calif.) U. Hosp., 1980-83, chief resident, 1983; dir. Williams Cancer Ctr., Bapt. Med. Ctr., Jacksonville, Fla., 1983—, Fla. Cancer Ctr., Jacksonville, Fla., 1985—; bd. dirs. Bapt. Med. Ctr., Jacksonville, 1986—, Meml. Med. Ctr., Jacksonville, 1987—, Meth. Hosp., Jacksonville, 1988—. Contbr. articles to profl. jours. Pres. Am. Cancer Soc., Jacksonville, 1992; bd. dirs. Jacksonville C. of C., 1991; adv. bd. Boy Scouts, 1990—. Mem. Am. Cancer Soc. (pres. 1992), Rotary Club. Republican. Hindu. Office: Fla Cancer Ctr 3599 University Blvd S Ste 1500 Jacksonville FL 32216-7400

PASCHAL, DONALD EUGENE, JR., city manager; b. Dallas, Jan. 14, 1947; s. Donald Eugene and Ida Ruth (Smith) P.; m. Janice Lee Butt, May 31, 1968; children: Lori, Jeff. BBA, U. No. Tex., Denton, 1970, MPA, 1973. Adminstrv. asst. City Garland, Tex., 1968-72, community svcs. adminstr., 1973-78; city mgr. City McKinney, Tex., 1978—. Deacon First Baptist Ch., Mckinney 1978—, chmn. deacons, 1992, 97; bd. dirs. United Way Collin County, 1992—; mem. exec. bd. Bapt. Gen. Conv. Tex., 1996—. Recipient Excellence in Constrn. award Associated Gen. Contractors, 1985, Highest Honor award No. Ctrl. Tex. Reg. Am. Planning Assn., 1988, Nat. Merit award Nat. Inst. Parks and Grounds Maintenance, 1989, Reg. V Mgmt. Innovation award Tex. Recreation and Parks Soc., 1992. Mem. Internat. City Mgmt. Assn. (25 year svc. award), Tex. Mcpl. League, Tex. City Mgmt. Assn. (bd. dirs. 1992-94), No. Tex. City Mgmt. Assn. (pres. 1990, bd. dirs. 1992-94), No. Ctrl. Tex. Coun. Govts. (air transportation tech. adv. com. 1980—, chair 1987-94, reg. air carrier capacity study tech. adv. com. 1992—, local investment fund dir. 1989-94), U. No. Tex. Alumni (mem. adv. com.), Am. Soc. Pub. Adminstrn., Pi Alpha Alpha. Baptist. Office: City of McKinney 222 N Tennessee St Mc Kinney TX 75069-3937

PASCHAL, JAMES ALPHONSO, counselor, educator secondary school; b. Americus, Ga., Aug. 11, 1931; s. Bouie L. and Mary L. (Jackson) P.; widower Mar. 24, 1988; 1 child, Maret E. BA, Xavier U., New Orleans, 1957; MS, Ft. Valley State Coll., 1963; EdD, U. S.C., 1977. Cert. adminstr., tchr. counselor, social worker, S.C. Tchr. grade 5 East View Elem. Sch., Americus, Ga., 1957-59; libr., counselor Staley Jr. H.S., Americus, 1959-65; sch. social worker Americus City System, 1965-67; coord. student svcs. Augusta (Ga.) Tech., 1967-78; dir. student affairs Benedict Coll., Columbia, S.C., 1978-82; coord. facilities S.C. Commn. on Higher Edn., Columbia, 1982-89; counselor Swainsboro (Ga.) H.S., 1990-91, Monroe H.S., Albany, Ga., 1991—; vol. Caritas, New Orleans, 1953-57, Friendship House, New Orleans, 1955-56. With U.S. Army, 1951-53, Korea. Recipient scholarship Ft. Valley (Ga.) State Coll., 1948, grad. assistantship, Ft. Valley State Coll., 1962-63. Mem. NEA, ACA. Ga. Counseling Assn., Alpha Phi Alpha (v.p. 1972-74). Republican. Roman Catholic. Home: PO Box 5523 Albany GA 31706-5523

PASCO, HANSELL MERRILL, retired lawyer; b. Thomasville, Ga., Oct. 7, 1915; s. John and Katherine (Merrill) P.; m. Williamine Carrington Lancaster, June 28, 1941; children: Hansell Merrill, Dabney, Robert, Elizabeth, Carrington. B.A., Va. Mil. Inst., 1937; LL.B., U. Va., 1940. Bar: Va. bar 1939. Ptnr. Hunton & Williams, Richmond, Va., 1948-81, sr. counsel, 1981—; mng. partner Hunton & Williams, 1968-76. Chmn. State Counsel Higher Edn. for Va., 1978-80; trustee Protestant Episcopal Sem., Alexandria, Va., 1980-85. Served with U.S. Army, 1940-45. Office: Hunton & Williams Riverfront Plz E Tower 951 E Byrd St Richmond VA 23219-4040

PASCOE, CHARLES THOMAS, JR., computer systems company executive; b. Blacksburg, Va., July 21, 1941; s. Charles Thomas Sr. and Annie Pearl (Grubb) P.; m. Carole Ruth Kouse, Dec. 23, 1962 (div. 1991); children: Charlotte Ruth, Cheryl Anne, Carrie Marie, Charles John. BA in Music, Wittenberg U., 1964. Comm.-electronics officer USAF, Wright-Patterson AFB, Ohio, 1964-71; line control mgr. Gulf & Western's Assocs. Computer Svcs. Co. Inc., South Bend, Ind., 1971-74; telecom. group mgr. Continental Ill. Nat. Bank & Trust Co., Chgo., 1974-75; maj. acct. exec. COMTEN, Lombard, Ill., 1976-77; computer cons. Va., 1977-79; systems applications engr. ADT Sec. Systems, Fed. Mktg. Group, Alexandria, Va., 1979-82; cons. Wang Labs. Inc., Bethesda, Md., 1982-84; mktg. rep. Prime Computer Inc., Rockville, Md., 1984-86; telemktg. mgr. legal info. svcs. div. Sterling Software, Rockville, 1986-89; telesvcs. mgr. Internat. Telesystems Corp., Herndon, Va., 1989-91; sr. mgmt. analyst Software Control Internat., Inc., 1991-92; computer cons. Future Sys. Design, Fairfax, Va., 1992—; sr. cons. Data Procurement Corp., 1992-94, A Personnel Touch, Fairfax, 1993—. 1st lt. USAF, 1964-68, ret. Mem. DAV, Masons, Phi Mu Alpha Sinfonia, Alpha Tau chpt. Office: PO Box 2225 Merrifield VA 22116-2225

PASETTI, LOUIS OSCAR, dentist; b. Tampa, Fla., Dec. 27, 1916; s. Joseph G. and Carmen (Gonzalez) P.; m. Mary Mendez, Jan. 11, 1942; children: Louis M., Arleen Pasetti Shearer. BS, U. Fla., 1937; DDS, Emory U., 1941; postgrad., U. Pa., 1978. Capt. U.S. Army, 1942-46; dentist pvt. practice Tampa, Fla., 1947—. Past. pres. Tampa Civitan Club, 1953; past lt. gov. Civitan Clubs of Tampa, 1962; past dep. gov. Civitan Internat., Tampa, 1964; fin. officer Am. Legion Post 248. Named Fla. Dentist of the Yr., Fla. Acad. Gen. Dentistry, 1983; recipient meritorious Svc. award Fla. Acad. Gen. Dentistry, 1989, Disting. Svc. award, 1985. Fellow Acad. Gen. Dentistry, Am. Coll. Dentists, Internat. Coll. Dentists, Acad. Dentistry Internat.; mem. ADA, Fla. Dental Assn., Fla. Acad. Gen. Dentistry (pres. 1981, Lifetime Achievement award 1996), Tampa Bay Acad. Gen. Dentistry (pres. 1977-78), Elks, Round Table of Civic Clubs of Tampa (sec. 1953), Palma Ceia Golf and Country Club. Democrat. Roman Catholic. Home: 10023 Hampton Pl Tampa FL 33618-4227 Office: 220 E Madison St Ste 250 Tampa FL 33602-4826

PASHLEY, MARY MARTHA, corporate finance educator; b. Oak Ridge, Tenn., May 12, 1956; d. John Hamilton and Wilogene (Queener) P. BA, Vanderbilt U., 1976; MS, U. Tenn., 1978, MBA, 1985, PhD, 1986. Teaching asst. U. Tenn., Knoxville, 1978-82, rsch. asst., 1982-83, lectr., 1983-85; asst. prof. fin. Tenn. Tech. U., Cookeville, 1986-93, assoc. prof., 1993—, assoc. dir. honors program; textbook reviewer Scott, Foresman & Co., 1988; ad hoc referee Fin. Mgmt., 1988, Applied Fin. Econs., 1991—, Fin. Rev., 1988—. Treas Mastersingers Community Chorus, 1988-89. Walter Melville Bonham Meml. scholar U. Tenn., 1982-93. Mem. Am. Bus. Women's Assn. (charter v.p. Chilhowee Bandstand chpt. 1984), Fin. Mgmt. Assn. (faculty liaison 1986—, presenter 1980, 82, 87, 94), Nat. Collegiate Hons. Coun., Mensa proctor 1990-94, registrar 1992, 94, Mid Tenn.), Beta Gamma Sigma, (chpt. sec.-treas. 1987-88, pres. 1988-89), Phi Kappa Phi, Omicron Delta Kappa. Office: Tenn Tech U Dept Econs & Fin Cookeville TN 38505

PASKEY, MONICA ANNE, dietitian; b. Pasadena, Calif., Aug. 18, 1960; d. Harold Lloyd and Gloria Dolores (Swanson) Macomber; m. Dennis J. Paskey, Nov. 11, 1995; 1 child, Brittany Anne. Student, Mills Coll., 1978-80; BS cum laude, U. Conn., 1983. Registered dietitian. Clin. dietitian Marriott Corp., Washington, 1983-84; food svc. mgr. Marriott Corp., Virginia Beach, 1984-86; food svc. dir. Marriott Corp., Balt., 1987-88; oncology nutrition supr. Johns Hopkins U., Balt., 1988-89; cons. dietitian Beverly Enterprises, Balt., 1989-91; corp. menu mgr. Beverly Enterprises, Ft. Smith, Ark., 1991—; cons. dietitian, Virginia Beach, 1985-86. Author: (pamphlet) Campus Weekend Cooking Simplified, 1983; contbr. Beverly Enterprises Diet Manual, 1993, Thickened Liquids Manual, 1994. Recipient Spkr.'s award Eli Lilly, Inc., 1985. Mem. Am. Dietetic Assn., Va. Dietetic Assn., Tidewater Dist. Dietetic Assn. (treas. 1985-86), Md. Dietetic Assn. (job referral coord. 1987-89), Ark. Dietetic Assn. (media rep. 1996), Ark. Cons. Dietitians (health care facilities liaison 1992—, chair 1995-96). Roman Catholic. Office: Beverly Enterprises 5111 Rogers Ave Fort Smith AR 72919-3700

PASLIDIS, NICK (NICKOLAOS) JOHN, physician, scientist; b. Volos, Greece, June 12, 1959; arrived in U.S., 1975; s. Ioannis Nikolaos and Anna Theodora P.; m. Sarah Schelsier, Nov. 16, 1991; 1 child, Alexandra Nichol. BA in chemistry, Whitman Coll., 1981; MD, Ross Univ., 1988; PhD, Univ. Tex., 1991. Postdoctoral fellow M.D. Anderson Cancer Ctr., Houston, 1990-91; principal investigator Baylor Coll. Medicine, Houston, 1991-92; resident U Tex. Medical Sch., Houston, 1992-95; gastroenterology fellow Harvard Med. Sch./Brigham Young and Women's Hosp., 1995—; dir. Univ. Tex. Med. Sch. internal medicine resident's rsch. club, Houston, 1992-95; bd. dirs. Nat. Pub. Policy Com. Contbr. articles to profl. jours. Sec., treas. house staff coun. Univ. Tex. Medical Sch., 1993-94. Recipient N.A.T.O. Rsch. award, 1993, N.I.H. Rsch. Festival award, 1992, M.D. Anderson Assoc. award, 1988. Mem. Tex. Med. Assn. (council scientific affairs 1993-94, cancer com. 1993-94, del. to T.M.A.-R.P.S. 1993—), Tex. Soc. Internal Medicine (bd. dirs. 1995—), Am. Coll. Physicians (bd. dirs. 1995—). Home: 10120 Charterhouse Rd Little Rock AR 72227

PASOUR, ERNEST CALEB, JR., economics educator; b. Dallas, N.C., Sept. 12, 1932; s. Ernest Caleb and Hazel (Carpenter) P.; m. Adaline Armstrong, Dec. 17, 1967; children: Virginia Barton, Ernest Caleb III. BS, N.C. State U., 1954, MS, 1959; PhD, Mich. State U., 1963. Agrl. economist U.S. Dept. Agr., East Lansing, Mich., 1962-63; asst. prof. econs. N.C. State U., Raleigh, 1963-67, assoc. prof. econs., 1967-73, prof. econs., 1973—; acad. advisor John Locke Soc., Raleigh, 1989—. Author: Agriculture and the State, 1990; contbr. articles to profl. jours. With U.S. Army, 1954-56. Recipient Leavy award Freedoms Found., 1989; NSF faculty fellow U. Chgo., 1970-71. Mem. Am. Econ. Assn., Pub. Choice Soc. Lutheran. Home: 4215 Galax Dr Raleigh NC 27612-3713 Office: NC State U Dept Agr and Resource Econs Box 8109 Raleigh NC 27695

PASS, SUSAN JEANETTE, American history educator; b. Alameda, Calif., Sept. 30, 1944; d. Paul L. and Jeanette M. (Gardner) B.; m. Edward Henry Pass; children: Janette Pass Hendrix, Suzanne M., Michael Edward. BS, Georgetown U., 1966; MS, Western Ill. U., 1986; PhD, U. Houston. Cert. tchr., Tex. Tchr. Springfield (Ill.) Pub. Schs., 1982-86; lectr. U. Houston, 1994—; reader APUS History/ETS, San Antonio, 1994—; tchr. Bellaire (Tex.) H.S., 1986—; supervising tchr. U. Houston, Rice U., 1993—; cons. Coll. Bd., Princeton, N.J., 1996; vis. instr. Rice U., Houston, 1995-96; governing bd. Bellaire H.S., 1996, faculty concerns bd., 1995-96, pers. com., 1994—. Author: Economics for American History Classes, 1996; rev. editor The Social Studies, 1994—; author (TV documentary) The American Pagent, 1996. Lay min. St. Thomas More Ch., Houston, 1995-96, St. Mary's Ch., Annapolis, Md., 1974-81. Named Outstanding Educator Houston Bus. Cmty. for Ednl. Excellence, 1991, 92, 93, Outstanding Presenter Tex. Coun. for the Social Studies, 1996. Mem. Tex. Coun. for the Social Studies, Nat. Coun. for the Social Studies, Tex. Assn. for the Gifted and Talented, Am. Ednl. Rsch. Profls., Phi Delta Kappa. Democrat. Roman Catholic. Home: 5031 Lymbar St Houston TX 77096 Office: Bellaire High Sch 5100 Maple Bellaire TX 77401

PASTERNAK, JOANNA MURRAY, special education and gifted and talented educator; b. Houston, Feb. 9, 1953; d. Lee Roy and Evelyn Mary (Kirmss) Murray; children: Sheila Ann Tanner, Lawrence Ross Tanner IV; m. Allen Pasternak, Jan. 9, 1993. BA in Liberal Arts with honors, Our Lady of the Lake, San Antonio, 1990. Acctg. clk. Houston Post, 1981-85; owner, art cons. Tanner Fine Art, Houston, 1985-92; spl. edn. tchr. Houston Ind. Sch. Dist., 1991-94, dept. chmn., 1994—; art cons. Plz. Gallery, Houston, 1985; mem. benefits com. Houston Ind. Sch. Dist., 1992—; presenter Am. Fedn. Tchrs. Nat. Edn. Conf., 1994. Contrb. articles to profl. jours. Campaign worker Dem. party, 1996; mem. precinct and state del. Dem. Senate, 1994; vol. Nat. Health Care Campaign, legis. com. AFL-CIO; sec. Senatorial Conv., 1996; mem. nominations com. Dem. party, 1995; bd. dirs. PTA; participant At the Table White House Focus group on women's issues. Recipient Vick Driscoll award for outstanding tchr., 1996. Mem. Am. Assn. Children with Learning Disabilities, Tex. Fedn. Tchrs. (bd. dirs. quality ednl. stds. in tchg. 1993, legis. com., chairperson 1993—), Houston Fedn. Tchrs. (chair legis. liaison com. 1993—, v.p. 1992—), Westlawn Terr. Civic Club (pres.), Delta Mu Delta. Democrat. Home: 2141 Colquitt St Houston TX 77098-3310 Office: Houston Fedn Tchrs 3202 Weslayan St Ste 102 Houston TX 77027-5748

PASTIN, MARK JOSEPH, executive consultant, association executive; b. Ellwood City, Pa., July 6, 1949; s. Joseph and Patricia Jean (Camenite) P.; m. Joanne Marie Reagle, May 30, 1970 (div. Mar. 1982); m. Carrie Patricia Class, Dec. 22, 1984 (div. June 1990); m. Christina M. Brecto, June 15, 1991. BA summa cum laude, U. Pitts., 1970; MA, Harvard U., 1972, PhD, 1973. Asst. prof. Ind. U., Bloomington, 1973-78, assoc. prof., 1978-80; founder, bd. Compliance Resource Group, Inc., 1983—; chmn., CEO, pres. Coun. Ethical Orgns., Alexandria, Va., 1986—; prof. mgmt., dir. Ariz. State U., Tempe, 1988-92, prof. emeritus, 1996—; prof. emeritus, 1996—; chair Health Ethics Trust, 1995—; adv. bd. Aberdeen Holdings, San Diego, 1988-90; dir. Sandpiper Group, Inc., N.Y.C., 1987—, S.W. Projects, Inc., San Diego, 1988-90, Learned Nicholson, Ltd., 1990-91; bd. Japan Am. Soc. Phoenix, Found. for Ethical Orgns.; cons. GTE, Southwestern Bell, 1987-89, Tex. Instruments, MicroAge Computers, Med-Tronic, Blood Sys., Inc., Opus Corp., GTE, NyNex, Am. Express Bank, Kaiko Bussan Co., Japan, Arex Co., Japan, Century Audit Co., Japan, Scottsdale Meml. Hosp., Consanti Found., Lincoln Electric Co., Tenet Healthcare Corp., The Williams Co.; vis. faculty Harvard U., 1980; invited presenter Australian Inst. Mgmt., Nippon Tel. & Tel., Hong Kong Commn. Against Corruption, 1984, Young Pres.'s Orgn. Internat. U., 1990, Nat. Assn. Indsl. & Office Parks, 1990, ABA, 1991, Govt. of Brazil, 1991, Tzuzuki Edn. Sys., 1995. Author: Hard Problems of Management, 1986 (Book of Yr. award Armed Forces Mil. Comtrs. 1986, Japanese edit. 1994), Power by Association, 1991, The State of Ethics in Arizona, 1991, Planning Forum, 1992; editor: Public-Private Sector Ethics, 1979; columnist Bus. Jour. Founding bd. mem. Tempe Leadership, 1985-89; bd. mem. Ctr. for Behavioral Health, Phoenix, 1986-89, Tempe YMCA, 1986—, Valley Leadership Alumni Assn., 1989—; mem. Clean Air Com., Phoenix, 1987-90. Nat. Sci. Found. fellow, Cambridge, Mass., 1971-73; Nat. Endowment for the Humanities fellow, 1975; Exxon Edn. Found. grant, 1982-83. Mem. Strategic Mgmt. Soc. (invited presenter 1985), Am. Soc. Assn. Execs. (invited presenter 1987-95), Bus. Ethics Soc. (founding bd. dirs. 1983), Found. Ethical Orgns. (chmn. 1988, pres.), Pres.'s Assn., Am. Mgmt. Assn., Golden Key, Harvard Club, D.C. Club, Phi Beta Kappa. Home: 7206 Park Terrace Dr Alexandria VA 22307-2035 Office: 1216 King St Ste 300 Alexandria VA 22314-2825

PASTINE, MAUREEN DIANE, university librarian; b. Hays, Kans., Nov. 21, 1944; d. Gerhard Walter and Ada Marie (Hillman) Hillman; m. Jerry Joel Pastine, Feb. 5, 1966. AB, in English, Ft. Hays State U., 1967; MLS, Emporia State U., 1970. Reference librarian U. Nebr.-Omaha, 1971-77; undergrad. libr. U. Ill., Urbana, 1977-79; reference librarian, 1979-80; univ. libr. San Jose State U.-Calif., 1980-85; dir. librs. Wash. State U., Pullman, 1985-89; ctrl. univ. libr. So. Meth. U., 1989—; mem. adv. bd. Foothill Coll. Libr. 1983-85; leader ednl. del. librs. to People's Republic of China, 1985, Australia/New Zealand, 1986, Soviet Union, 1988, East & West Germany, Czechoslovakia, Hungary, Austria, 1991, Brazil, 1993. Co-author: Library and Library Related Publications: A Directory of Publishing Opportunities, 1973; asst. compiler: Women's Work and Women's Studies, 1973-74, 1975; compiler procs. Teaching Bibliographic Instruction in Graduate Schools of Library Science, 1981; editor: Integrating Library Use Skills into the General Education Curriculum, 1989, Collection Development: Present and Future in Collection Management, 1996; co-editor: In the Spirit of 1991: Access to Western European Libraries and Literature, 1992; contbr. articles to profl. publs. Recipient Disting. Alumni Grad. award Emporia State U., 1986, Dudley Bibliog. Instruction Libr. of Yr. award, 1989. Mem. ALA (chmn. World Book-ALA Goal awards jury 1984-85), Assn. Coll. and Rsch. Librs. (editorial adv. bd. BIS Think Tank 1982-85, chmn. bibliographic instrn. sect. 1983-84, editorial bd. Choice 1983-85, chmn. Miriam Dudley Bibliographic Instrn. Libr. of Yr. award com. 1984-85, mem. task force on librarians as instrs. 1986-88, chair task force internat. rels. 1987-89, BIS Libr. of Yr. 1989, rep. to AAAS/CAIP, 1989-94, chair internat. rels. com. 1990-94, ALA pay equity com. 1994—, chmn. rsch. libr. of yr. award's com. 1995-96, acad. status com. 1996—), Libr. Adminstrn. and Mgmt. Assn. (chmn. stats. sect. com. on devel., orgn., planning and programming 1982-83, sec. stats. sect. exec. com. 1982-83, mem. at large 1986-88), ALA Library Instrn. Round Table (long range planning com. 1986-94), ALA Libr. Rsch. Round Table, Wash. Libr. Assn., Assn. Libr. Collections & Tech. Svcs. Divsn., Libr. and Info. Tech. Assn., Assn. Specialized and Coop. Libr. Agencies (chair multilincs internat. networking discussion group 1990-92), Libr. Rsch. Roundtable, Women's Studies Sect., Eng. and Am. Lit. Studies Discussion Group, Tex. Libr. Assn. (mentor Tall Texans Leadership Inst., 1995-96), Pacific N.W. Libr. Assn., Phi Kappa Phi, Beta Phi Mu. Home: 8720 Hanford Dr Dallas TX 75243-6416 Office: So Meth U Cen Univ Librs PO Box 750135 Dallas TX 75275-0135

PASTORE, PETER NICHOLAS, JR., metal processing company executive; b. Richmond, Va., Oct. 5, 1950; s. Peter Nicholas and Julia Pastore; m. Ann Bray King, May 5, 1974; children: Emily, Ann Chandler, Peter III. BS in Space Scis. and Mech. Engring., Fla. Inst. Tech., 1972; MBA, U. Richmond, 1986. Rsch. asst. Med. Coll. Va., Richmond, 1973, sci. computer programmer, 1973-74; with Reynolds Metals Co., Richmond, 1974—, dir. employee fin. svcs., 1983-86, corp. dir. employee fin. svcs. and health care, 1986-89, flexible packaging div. subs. controller, 1990; adminstrn. and control mgr., 1991—; adj. faculty mem. Annual Inst., Georgetown Law Sch., Washington, 1985; pres., bd. dirs. Employer's Task Force on Unemployment Compensation, Washington, 1985-86; presenter in field. Lay min. St. Stephen's Ch., Richmond, 1985—, vestry mem., 1989-91, 94—; vice chmn. auction Pub. Broadcasting Sta., Richmond, 1987-88; vice chmn., trustee Ctrl. Va. chpt. Nat. Multiple Sclerosis Soc., 1991—, treas., 1994-96; v.p., bd. dirs. Richmond Areawide Regional Easter Seal Soc., 1993—; mem. MBA adv. bd. E. Clairborne Robins Sch. Bus., U. Richmond, 1994. Mem. Internat. Found. Employee Benefits Plans. Home: 5104 Riverside Dr Richmond VA 23225-3002 Office: Reynolds Metals Co 6603 W Broad St Richmond VA 23230-1701

PASTRICK, HAROLD LEE, aeronautical engineer; b. Ambridge, Pa., June 28, 1936; s. Samuel and Mary (Makara) P.; m. Vivienne Lee Nusser Heinricher, June 3, 1961; children: Tracy Lee, Gregory Harold, Michael Joseph Samuel. BSEE, Carnegie-Mellon U., 1958; postgrad., Rutgers U., 1959-61, CCNY, 1961-63, U. Ala. Huntsville, 1964-66, 68-73; student, MIT, summers 1961-63; MS in Aeronautics & Astronautics, Stanford U., 1967, engr. in Aeronautics & Astronautics, 1972; PhD in Engring., Calif. Western U., 1977. Registered prof. engr., Ala. Metallurgical engring. aide Jones & Laughlin Steel Corp., Aliquippa, Pa., 1955-56; asst. engr., designer Am. Bridge Divsn., U.S. Steel Corp., Ambridge, 1957; electronics engr. Avionics Divsn., U.S. Army Signal R&D Labs., Ft. Monmouth, N.J., 1958-63; aerospace engr., Inertial Systems Team Missile R&D Labs., Redstone Arsenal, Ala., 1963-64; tech. dir. Army Inertial Guidance & Tech. Ctr., Redstone Arsenal, 1964-66; project engr. Inertial Guidance Br., Redstone Arsenal, 1967-71; rsch. aerospace engr. Guidance & Control Br., Redstone Arsenal, 1971-73; group leader Terminal Homing Missile Analysis, Redstone Arsenal, 1973-79; staff specialist, asst. to dir., land warfare Office of Under Sec. Def., Rsch. and Engring., Washington, 1979-80; chief, guidance and control analysis U.S. Army Missile Command, Redstone Arsenal, Ala., 1980-81; v.p. engring. Control Dynamics Co., Huntsville, 1981-83; asst. v.p., engring. analysis divsn. Sci. Applications Internat. Corp., Huntsville, 1983-86; v.p. theater missile def. and system analysis operation, 1986-91; corp. v.p., gen. mgr. SRS Technologies, Huntsville, 1991—; lectr. Sch. of Sci. and Engring., U. Ala., Huntsville, 1967-83; lectr. dept. continuing edn. George Washington U., 1985-87; engring. seminar dir. Applied Tech. Inst., Frankfurt, Germany, 1984, Singapore, 1986; tech. tng. dir. Tech. Tng. Corp., Tel Aviv, 1988; lectr. Advanced Tech. Internat., Ltd., London, 1985; guidance and control cons. various labs Dept. of Def., Washington, 1971-93; lectr., rsch. advisor Southeastern Inst. Tech., Huntsville, 1978-84; lectr., seminar leader Guidance and Control Technologies, U.S., Europe, Asia, Mex., 1980-94. Contbr. over 120 articles to profl. jours. Chmn. combined fed. campaign ARDEC, United Way, Redstone Arsenal, 1976; mem. Huntsville Econ. Devel. Coun., 1994; chmn. indsl. contbns. C. of C., Armed Forces Week, Huntsville-Madison

County, 1993, 94, 96, vice chmn. mil. affairs com., 1994-95, chmn., 1996; program chmn. tech. and bus. exhbn. and symposium, Huntsville, 1994-95, gen. chmn., 1995-96; pres. Greek Orthodox Ch., 1967, 73, chmn. planning com., 1993—. Capt. U.S. Army, 1958-64. Fellow AIAA (assoc. missile tech. com. 1989-91, guest editor Jour. Guidance and Control 1981, vice-chmn. Huntsville chpt. 1979); mem. IEEE (sr., chpt. program chmn. 1972-73), Am. Def. Preparedness Assn. (vice-chmn. Huntsville chpt. 1974-75), Soc. for Computer Simulation, Assn. of U.S. Army, Inst. of Navigation, Ala. Acad. Sci. (vice chmn. 1978-79, engring. chmn. 1979-81), Rotary (dir. internat. svc. Greater Huntsville Club 1992-93, sec. 1994-95, pres.-elect 1995-96, pres. 1996—), Heritage Club (Huntsville), Greenwhyche Club (v.p. 1979), Redstone Golf Club. Home: 2624 Trailway Rd SE Huntsville AL 35801-1474 Office: SRS Technologies 500 Discovery Dr NW Huntsville AL 35806-2810

PASTUCH, BORIS MAX See MAX, BUDDY

PATARCA, ROBERTO, immunologist, molecular biologist, physician; b. Caracas, Venezuela, Feb. 12, 1958; came to U.S., 1981; s. Umberto Jose and Ivonne Noemi (Montero) P. MS, Ctrl. U. Venezuela, Caracas, 1981; PhD, Harvard U., 1987; MD, U. Miami, 1994. Cert. high-complexity clin. lab. dir., Am. Bd. Bioanalysis, cert. clin. cons., tech. cons. Computer programmer, systems analyst Centro Medico Docente La Trinidad, Caracas, 1978-81; rsch. fellow Mt. Sinai Sch. Medicine and Columbia U., N.Y.C., 1981-82, MIT-NASA Program, Boston, 1982; from rsch. fellow to asst. prof. pathology Harvard Med. Sch., Boston, 1982-90; asst. prof. medicine/immunology/microbiology U. Miami, Fla., Fla., 1994—; sci. dir. E.M. Papper lab. clin. immunology U. Miami, Fla., 1994—; teaching asst. Ctr. and Met. U., Caracas, 1977-80; lectr. and presenter in field. Co-editor Jour. Chronic Fatigue Syndrome and Critical Reviews in Oncogenesis/Clin. Mgmt. Chronic Fatigue Syndrome, 1994—; contbr. articles to profl. jours. Sub-guide Boy Scouts Am., Caracas, 1971-73; stake missionary Ch. of Jesus Christ of Latter Day Sts., Boston, 1985. Decorated Order of Merit (Venezuela); recipient Licha Lopez award Harvard Med. Sch., 1984, Richard A. Smith Rsch. award Dana-Farber Cancer Inst., 1989, Rsch. Distinction in Immunology U. Miami, 1994; Conicit and Gran Mariscal de Ayacucho Found. scholar, 1976-87, Am. Found. AIDS Rsch. scholar, 1990-93. Mem. AAAS, ACP, AMA, Fla. and Dade County Med. Assn., Clin. Immunology Soc., N.Y. Acad. Scis., Peruvian Soc. Immunology and Allergy, Alpha Omega Alpha. Home: 16445 Collins Ave Apt 328 Miami FL 33160-4562 Office: U Miami Sch Medicine PO Box 016960 Miami FL 33138

PATE, A. J., investment advisor; b. Palestine, Tex., Dec. 2, 1937; s. Harlen Jay Van and Nannie Faye (Hamilton) P.; divorced; children: John Harlen, Debra Darlene Pate Russo. BBA, Sam Houston State U., 1959. CPA, Tex. Auditor Arthur Andersen & Co., Houston, 1959-61; chief acct. Tenneco Inc., Houston, 1961-92; v.p. Omega Resource Group, Houston, 1992-94; v.p., CFO Career Visions, Inc., Houston, 1994-95; account exec. Lincoln Investment Planning, Inc., Houston, 1996—; redistricting cons. Tex. State Legislature, Houston/Austin, 1990-91, 95-96; treas., mem. exec. com. Tenneco Employees Good Govt. Fund, Houston, 1983-92. Contbr. poetry to anthologies. Treas. Texans for Edn., Austin, 1991-92, Pachyderm Club, Houston, 1989-92; del. Rep. Party, 1976-88. With U.S. Army, 1956. Named Outstanding Bus. Student, Wall St. Jour., 1959. Republican. Mem. Assembly of God. Home: 15118 Terrace Oaks Dr Houston TX 77068 Office: Lincoln Investment Planning Inc Ste 275 7670 Woodway Houston TX 77063

PATE, DAVID REGAN, healthcare executive, financial consultant; b. Lumberton, N.C., Oct. 26, 1955; s. James R. and Elizabeth (Regan) P.; m. Terry Joines, Aug. 30, 1985; children: Jessica, Laura, Caroline. BS in Bus. Adminstrn., U. N.C., 1978. CPA, N.C. Audit staff J.A. Grisette & Co., Morganton, N.C., 1979-82; audit sr. Coopers & Lybrand, Raleigh, N.C., 1982-85; contr. Teletec Corp., Raleigh, 1985-88; chief fin. officer EnviroScis., Inc., Raleigh, 1988-90, Carolina Doctors Care/Health Care Savs., Raleigh, 1990—. Mem. fin. com. Benson Meml. United Meth. Ch., Raleigh, 1992. Mem. AICPA, N.C. Assn. CPAs. Office: Carolina Doctors Care/Health Care Savs Inc PO Box 27987 Raleigh NC 27611-7987

PATE, DONALD WAYNE, academic administrator, educator; b. Bloomington, Ind., Jan. 3, 1939; s. William Edward and Edith Marie (Elliott) P.; m. Judith Ann Parham, May 11, 1961 (div.); children: Angela Marie Pate Springer, Donald Wayne; m. Valerie Ross Van Horn, May 4, 1991; children: Elliott Donald, Kyle Van Horn. BS, Moorhead State U., 1964, MS, 1965; PhD, U. Utah, 1972. Tchr., coach Fargo (N.D.) High Sch., 1964-67; prof., coach Wayne (Nebr.) State Coll., 1967-73; prof., adminstr. U. Richmond (Va.), 1973—; cons. drug edn. programs, 1983—; coord grad. program sport mgmt. U. Richmond, 1980—; exec. dir. Va. State Games, 1989-91; commr. Metro-Youth Football League, Richmond, 1977-79. Contbr. articles to profl. jours. Mem. Gov.'s Commn. on Phys. Fitness and Sport, Richmond, Va., 1990—. Named All Am. Nat. Assn. Intercollegiate Athletics, 1964, All Conf. Minn. Intercollegiate Athletic Assn., 1963, Coach of Yr. Va. State Coaches Assn., 1987, 89; named to Hall of Fame Moorhead State U., 1985. Mem. AAUP, AAHPERD, Va. Assn. Health, Phys. Edn. Recreation and Dance (v.p. 1993—). Republican. Home: 704 W Drive Cir Richmond VA 23229-6830

PATE, GARY RAY, minister; b. Ottawa, Ill., May 26, 1957; s. William Ray and Glena Ray (Blanchard) P.; m. Linda Sue Lane, July 2, 1976; chidlren: Tonika Rae, Megan Ellen, Jeffrey William. Student, Rend Lake Coll., 1975-77; Diploma in Christian Ministry, Boyce Bible Sch., 1988; BTh., Internat. Sem., 1991; MMin, So. Bapt. Sch., 1996. Lic. to ministry Bapt. Ch., 1984, ordained, 1988. Sr. adult minister Clifton Bapt. Ch., Louisville, 1986-87; assoc. pastor Ridgeview Bapt. Mission, Taylorsville, Ky., 1987; pastor Ridgeview Bapt. Mission, Taylorsville, 1988-89, Hurricane Bapt. Ch., Cadiz, Ky., 1989-93, New Salem Bapt. Ch., Nortonville, Ky., 1993—; camp pastor Land Between the Lakes Area Ministry, 1989-93; dir. family ministries Little River Bapt. Assn., Cadiz, 1989-93; evangelist Ky./Brazil Mission Link, Esperito Santos, Brazil, 1990, Ryzan, Russia, 1994. Mem. Trigg County Ministerial Alliance (pres. 1991-93), Hopkins County Ministerial Assn. (pres. 1993-95, treas. 1995—). Home: 71 New Salem Loop Nortonville KY 42442-9763 Office: New Salem Bapt Ch 69 New Salem Loop Nortonville KY 42442-9763

PATE, JACQUELINE HAIL, retired data processing company manager; b. Amarillo, Tex., Apr. 7, 1930; d. Ewen and Virginia Smith (Crosland) Hail; student Southwestern U., Georgetown, Tex., 1947-48; children: Charles (dec.), John Durst, Virginia Pate Edgecomb, Christopher. Exec. sec. Western Gear Corp., Houston, 1974-76; adminstr., treas., dir. Aberrant Behavior Ctr., Personality Profiles, Inc., Corp. Procedures, Inc., Dallas, 1976-79; mgr. regional site svcs programs Digital Equipment Corp., Dallas, 1979-92, ret. 1992; realtor Keller Williams Realty, Austin, Tex., 1996—; mem. Austin Bd. Realtors. Active PTA, Dallas, 1958-73. Mem. Daus. Republic Tex. (treas. French legation state com. 1996). Methodist. Home: 5505-B Buffalo Pass Austin TX 78745

PATE, JAMES LAVERT, lawyer; b. Shreveport, La., Feb. 16, 1952; s. Barney Fain and Mary Elizabeth (Stancil) P.; m. Andrea Carol Cofer, Nov. 7, 1975; children: Allison, Erin, Caitlin. BS, La. State U., 1975; JD, Loyola U., New Orleans, 1979. Bar: La. 1979, U.S. Dist. Ct. (ea., mid. and we. dists.) La. 1979. Assoc. Bailey & Leininger, New Orleans, 1979-80; ptnr. Onebane, Donohoe, Lafayette, La., 1982-87, Laborde & Neuner, Lafayette, 1987—; bd. mem. Acadiana Safety Assn., Lafayette, 1987—. Mem. ABA, Am. Arbitration Assn., La. Bar Assn., La. Assn. Def. Counsel, Def. Rsch. Inst. Republican. Episcopalian. Office: Laborde and Neuner 1 Petroleum Ctr 1001 W Pinhook Rd Ste 200 Lafayette LA 70503-2450

PATE, JAMES LEONARD, oil company executive; b. Mt. Sterling, Ill., Sept. 6, 1935; s. Virgil Leonard and Mammie Elizabeth (Taylor) P.; m. Donna Charlene Pate, Oct. 23, 1955; children: David Charles, Gary Leonard, Jennifer Elizabeth. Prof. econs. Monmouth (Ill.) Coll., 1965-68; sr. economist Fed. Res. Bank Cleve., 1968-72; chief economist B.F. Goodrich Co., Akron, Ohio, 1972-74; asst. sec. Dept. Commerce, Washington, Ohio, 1974-76, spl. adviser to White House, 1976, sr. v.p. fin., 1976; v.p. fin. Pennzoil Co., Houston, Ohio, 1976-89, exec. v.p., 1989, exec. v.p., chief oper. officer, 1990, pres., chief exec. officer, 1990—, also chmn. bd., 1994—. Contbr. articles to profl. jours. and text books. Bd. govs. Rice U.; mem. Senate Monmouth Coll.; bd. dirs. Am. Petroleum Inst., Nat. Petroleum Coun. Fellow Royal Econ. Soc.; mem. Pi Gamma Mu. Republican. Office: Pennzoil Co PO Box 2967 Houston TX 77252-2967

PATE, J'NELL LAVERNE, history and government educator; b. Jacksboro, Tex., July 31, 1938; d. Vernon Leon and Berta May (Riggs) Rogers; m. Kenneth Doyle Pate, June 3, 1960. BA, Tex Christian U., 1960, MA, 1964; PhD, U. North Tex., 1982. Cert. tchr., Tex. Tchr. Ft. Worth Ind. Sch. Dist., 1960-67; prof. Tarrant County Jr. Coll., Ft. Worth, 1968—. Author: Livestock Legacy, 1988, Ranald Slidell Mackenzie Brave Cavalry Colonel, 1994, North of the River, 1994, document Sets for Texas and the Southwest in U.S. History, 1991; contbr. articles to profl. jours. Sec. Azle (Tex.) Rep. Club, 1990—. Recipient Excellence in Teaching award, N.E. C. of C., 1986, Outstanding Educator award, 1991; named one of 100 Living Outstanding Grads., U. North Tex., 1990. Fellow Tex. State Hist. Assn. (Coral H. Tullis award 1989); mem. Western History Assn., North Ft. Worth Hist. Soc. (Joseph J. Ballard award), Azle Hist. Mus. Soc. (v.p. 1980-90), West Tex. Hist. Assn. (Mrs. Percy Jones award), Westerners Internat. (bd. dirs.), Phi Kappa Phi. Office: Tarrant County Jr Coll 828 W Harwood Rd Hurst TX 76054-3219

PATE, JOHN GILLIS, JR., financial consultant, accounting educator; b. Chattanooga, Jan. 27, 1928; s. John Gillis Pate and Iona Estelle (Bowman) Pate Ketchman; m. Daphne Mae Davis, Feb. 8, 1946; children: John Gillis III, Daphne Iona, Donna Gay. Student U. Tampa, 1947-48; AA with highest honors, U. Fla., 1950; BS cum laude, Fla. State U., 1953, MS, 1958; PhD, Columbia U., 1968. Cert. Cost Analyst, cert. Office Automation Profl., CPA. Mgr. Grocery Concession, Albany, Ga., 1944-45, Variety Store, Panama City, Fla., 1946-47; asst. to CPA Standard Brands, Inc., Birmingham, Ala., 1951-53, acctg. supervisory trainee, Birmingham, Ala., 1953-54; grad. asst. Fla. State U., Tallahassee, 1957-58; asst. to CPA, Pensacola, Fla., 1956-58; CPA, Pensacola, Fla., 1958; asst. prof. U. Ga., Athens, 1958-60; lectr. Columbia U., N.Y.C., 1961-64; asst. prof. Bernard M. Baruch Coll. of CUNY, 1963-69; prof. acctg. U. Tex.-El Paso, 1969-85, U. S.C., Spartanburg, 1988-93; cons., resource person Personnel Dept. City of El Paso, 1981-88; cons. resource person and human resources Charles Lea Ctr., Spartanburg, 1988—, dir. Internal Audit, 1994—. Co-author: Accounting Trends and Techniques, 1967-88, Index to Accounting and Auditing Services, 1971; Author: Index C.P.A. Exams and Unofficial Answers, 1974-81; contbr. articles to ann. profl. publs. Tither, Coronado Bapt. Ch., El Paso, 1969-86, Buck Creek Bapt. Ch., Spartanburg, 1987—; cons. Alderman of El Paso, 1982, County Councilman of Spartanburg, 1991—. Served as lt. j.g. USN, 1955-56. Columbia U. fellow, 1960; Earhart Found. fellow, 1960; Am. Acctg. Assn. fellow, 1960; recipient Haskins and Sells award, 1960; Ford Found. fellow, 1961-62. Mem. AICPAs (cons.), Am. Acctg. Assn., Inst. Cost Analysis, Office Automation Soc. Internat., Beta Alpha Psi, Beta Alpha Chi. Republican. Club: Sertoma. Lodges: Moose, Masons, Shriners. Home and Office: 106 Lori Cir Spartanburg SC 29303-5527

PATE, PATRICIA ANN, women's health nurse; b. Columbus, Ohio, Dec. 23, 1944; d. Wayne E. and Oneitta M. (Craig) Ballentine; m. Daniel B. Pate, July 1, 1989; children: Kimberly Ann Van Horn, Kellie Lynn Van Horn; stepchildren: Tracy Scott, Ronnie Pate, Richard Pate. BSN, Tex. Woman's U., 1979. Charge nurse post-anesthesia recovery rm. Green Park Surgery Ctr., Houston, 1987-88; nurse ob./gyn. office Dr. Mary Alice Cowan, Houston, 1983-87; nurse Bellaire Gen. Hosp., Houston, 1987-92; clin. rsch. coord. Rsch. for Health, Houston, 1988-89; nurse ob./gyn. dept. Dr. Ivor Safro, Houston, 1989-91; nurse Sam Houston Meml. Hosp., Houston, 1991-95, West Houston Surgicare, 1995—; mem. peer rev. com., 1991-93. Home: 10402 Shadow Wood Dr Houston TX 77043-2822

PATE, SHARON SHAMBURGER, secondary school educator; b. Kenosha, Wis., Mar. 30, 1954; d. Thomas Benjamin and Ruth (Penny) Shamburger; m. Johnny Lee Pate, July 23, 1976. BS, Miss. U. Women, 1975; MEd, Miss. State U., 1980; postgrad., Fla. State U., 1994—. Cert. tchr., Fla. Mgr. Cato Dept. Stores, West Point, Miss., 1975-76; area mgr. Wal-Mart Stores, West Point, 1976; tchr. home econs. South Sumter High Sch., Bushnell, Fla., 1977-78; instr. community edn. Riverdale (Fla.) High Sch., 1982-84; substitute tchr., asst. to dean North Ft. Myers (Fla.) High Sch., 1982-84, tchr. home econs., 1978-80, 84-92, instr. community edn., 1984-89; mktg. instr. Mosley High Sch., Panama City, Fla, 1992-94; interior design svcs. instr. Haney Tech. Ctr., Panama City, 1996—; mgmt. trainee J.C. Penney Co., Ft. Myers, 1980-81; sponsor Future Homemakers Am., Cypress Lake H.S., Ft. Myers, 1984-90, instr. cmty. edn., interior decorating; tchr. mktg. edn., fashion mktg. Mariner H.S., Cape Coral, 1989-92; adj. prof. fashion mktg. Gulf Coast C.C., Panama City, 1993-94. Recipient Grad. scholarship, 1996. Mem. Fla. Vocat. Assn., Fla. Assn. Mktg. Educators, Distributive Edn. Clubs Am. (advisor 1989-94), Elite Modeling Club (advisor 1990-92), Dauphin Allure Modeling (advisor 1993-94), Internat. Textile and Apparel Assn., Am. Family and Consumer Scis. (Grad. scholarship 1996), Fla. Family and Consumer Sci. Assn. Republican. Pentecostal. Home: 3515 Unit 7 19th St Panama City FL 32405

PATE, STEPHEN PATRICK, lawyer; b. Beaumont, Tex., May 6, 1958; s. Gordon Ralph and Shirley Jean (Riley) P.; m. Jean Janssen. BA, Vanderbilt U., 1980, JD, 1983. Bar: Tex. 1984, U.S. Dist. Ct. (ea. dist.) Tex. 1984, U.S. Dist. Ct. (so. dist.) Tex. 1985. Law clk. to judge Joe J. Fisher U.S. Dist. Ct. Tex., Beaumont, 1983-84; ptnr. Fulbright & Jaworski, Houston. Contbr. articles to profl. jours. Fellow Houston Bar Found., Tex. Bar Found.; mem. ABA (vice chmn. property ins. com. tort and ins. practice sect. 1994—), Tex. Bar Assn., Tex. Young Lawyers Assn. (bd. dirs. 1992-94), Houston Young Lawyers Assn. (bd. dirs. 1990-92, sec. 1992-93, chmn. professionalism com., mem. sunset rev. com. 1990—), Manitoba Master Angler Billfish Found. (Top Angler 1993). Republican. Roman Catholic. Home: 2740 Arbuckle St Houston TX 77005 Office: Fulbright & Jaworski 1301 Mckinney St Houston TX 77010

PATE, WILLIAM EARL, graphic services company executive, consultant; b. Gastonia, N.C., Jan. 21, 1953; m. Donna; children: Aaron, Hannah. Grad. high sch., York, S.C. Press asst. Carolina Newspaper, York, 1970-71; printer Progressive Printers, Davidson, N.C., 1975-76; plant mgr. Homelite-Textron, Charlotte, N.C., 1976-80; press repairman Progressive Sales, Concord, N.C., 1980-82; svc. mgr. Solna, Inc., Kansas City, Mo., 1982-85; gen. mgr. Rush Printing Co., Mobile, Ala., 1985-86; pres. Technigraphics, Inc., Mobile, 1986—. With USN, 1971-75, Vietnam. Republican. Baptist. Home: 1354 Spring Valley Ct Mobile AL 36693-4349 Office: Technigraphics Inc 5766 I-10 Indsl Pky Theodore AL 36582

PATE, WILLIAM PATRICK, city manager; b. Duplin County, N.C., July 30, 1962; s. William Atlas and Bonny Lou (O'Leary) P.; m. Sandra Martin, Aug. 17, 1985; children: William Glenn, Andrew Patrick. BA in Polit. Sci. and Religion, U. N.C., 1984, MPA, 1986. Budget and evaluation analyst intern City of Winston-Salem, N.C., 1985-86, budget and evaluation analyst, 1986-87, lead budget and evaluation analyst, 1987; budget and rsch. mgr. City of Greensboro, N.C., 1987-90, budget and evaluation dir., 1990—; Inst. of Govt. intern N.C. Office Coastal Mgmt., Raleigh, N.C., 1984; rsch. asst. U. N.C., Chapel Hill, 1984-85. Mem. Chmns. Soc. United Way of Greensboro, N.C., 1993, 94, 95; mem. Leadership Greensboro, 1993-96; elder, clk. session Faith Presbyn. Ch., Greensboro, 1992-94. Recipient Disting. Svc. award Alpha Phi Omega, 1984. Mem. Internat. City Mgrs. Assn., Am. Soc. Pub. Adminstrn. (pres. Piedmont Triad chpt. 1994), Gov. Fin. Officers Assn. (nat. com. on govtl. budgeting and mgmt. 1993—, Disting. Budget Presentation award reviewer, Disting. Budget Presentation award 1992, 93, 94, 95), N.C. Local Govt. Budget Assn. (bd. dirs. 1990-92, 95, 1st v.p. 1992-93, pres. 1993-94), U. N.C. MPA Alumni Assn. (program chmn. 1992, pres-elect 1993, pres. 1994, Scholarship award 1985), U. N.C. Gen. Alumni Assn. (bd. dirs. 1994-95). Presbyterian. Home: 1300 Wakefield Pl Greensboro NC 27410-3142 Office: City of Greensboro PO Box 3136 Greensboro NC 27402-3136

PATE-FULLER, DENISE, mathematics educator; b. Asheville, N.C., Feb. 4, 1967; d. Lawrence Veal and Imogene (Shope) P. BS in Mid. Grades Edn., Appalachian State U., 1990. Cert. statistical educator, N.C. 6th grade math tchr. C.D. Owen Mid. Sch., Swannanoa, N.C., 1990-95; prin. fellow Western Carolina U., Cullowhee, N.C., 1995—. Mem. ASCD, NASSP, NCAE (scholarship 1995), NCCTM. Methodist. Home: 323 Circle Ln Black Mountain NC 28711 Office: Buncombe County Schs 175 Brigham Rd Asheville NC 28806

PATEL, ASHVIN AMBALAL, psychiatrist; b. Meru, Kenya, Feb. 28, 1949; came to U.S., 1975; s. Ambalal A. and Maniben (Ambalal) P.; m. Taru Ashuin Patel, June 13, 1974; children: Akta, Aarti, Anooj. MS, B of Surgery, Baroda Med. Coll., India, 1972, B of Medicine, 1973. Diplomate Am. Bd. Psychiatry and Neurology. Resident in psychiat. medicine Bronx (N.Y.) Lebanon Hosp., 1975-78, attending physician, 1978-79, chief psychiat. emergency svc., 1979-83; assoc. clin. prof. psychiatry Albert Einstein Coll. Medicine, Bronx, 1981-83; assoc. clin. prof. Quillen Med. Sch. East Tenn. State U., Johnson City, 1983—; pvt. practice Bristol (Tenn.) Psychiatry, 1983—; med. dir. psychiat. unit Bristol Meml. Hosp., 1985—; cons. Bristol Mental Health Ctr., 1983—. Mem. Am. Psychiat. Assn. (sec. Bronx dist. 1982-83, sec. Upper East Tenn. br. 1988—). Democrat. Hindu. Home: 30 Kilmainhom Cir Bristol TN 37620-3061

PATEL, TARUN R., pharmaceutical scientist; b. Borsad, Gujarat, India, Feb. 18, 1952; s. Ramesh C. and Savitaben R.; m. Nilima T. Patel, Feb. 17, 1981; children: Vishal, Shalini, Neha. BS in Pharmacy, Tex. So. U., 1975; PhD in Pharmaceutics, U. Iowa, 1980. Registered pharmacist Tex., Ill., Ind. Scientist Ortho Pharm. Corp., Raritan, N.J., 1980-82; sr. scientist Ortho Pharm. Corp., Raritan, 1982; group leader, mfg. engr. Bristol Labs., Syracuse, N.Y., 1982-83; mgr. process engring. Bristol Labs., Syracuse, 1983-84, dir. process engring., 1984-86; assoc. dir. process engring. Bristol Myers-USPNG, Evansville, Ind., 1986-90; dir. pharm. devel. Schering-Plough Corp., Memphis, 1990-94, sr. dir. pharm. devel., 1994—; adj. prof. U. Tenn., Memphis, 1991—. Contbr. articles to profl. jours. Recipient Remington award Tex. So. Univ., 1975. Mem. Am. Assn. Pharm. Scientists, Am. Pharm. Assn. Office: Bayer Pharm Corp 400 Morgan Ln West Haven CT 06515-4175

PATEL, VINOD MOTIBHAI, accountant; b. Kilosha, Tanzania, Mar. 1, 1944; came to U.S., 1971; s. Motibhai R. and Lalitaben M. (Lalitaben C.) P.; m. Surekha J. Patel, Dec. 6, 1969; children: Chirag, Roshni. BComm, U. of Baroda, India, 1964. Chartered acct., India; CPA, Md. Acct. Dalal, Desai & Kumana, Bombay, India, 1964-70, Bellman, Atlas & Co., London, 1970-71, Garbelman, Winslow & Co., Upper Marlboro, Md., 1971-79; prin. Vinod M. Patel, CPA, Fairfax, Va., 1979—. Hon. auditor Shri Mangal Mandir, 1981—. Mem. AICPA, Md. Assn. CPA's, Inst. Chartered Accts. of India. Hindu. Home: 9644 Reach Rd Potomac MD 20854-2856 Office: 10829 Lee Hwy Fairfax VA 22030-4384

PATERSON, PAUL CHARLES, private investigator, security consultant; b. Bethlehem, Pa., Dec. 31, 1927; s. Thomas and Ida (Weiss) P.; m. Estelle Marie Nabors; children: Linda Ann, Thomas Scott, Terry Maurice Leard. Grad., Inst. Applied Sci., Chgo., 1950. Jr. credit analyst Bethlehem Steel Corp., Pa., 1947-50; inspector claim spec., claim dir., field supr. Equifax Svcs., Inc., Allentown, Pa., 1953-61; field claim supr. Equifax Svcs., Inc., St. Louis, 1961-63; regional claims mgr. Equifax Svcs., Inc., Phila., 1963-71; spl. claim sales, sales exec.-claims Equifax Svcs., Inc., Atlanta, 1971-89; pvt. investigator, pres. Paterson Investigations, Inc., Douglasville, Ga., 1989—. Editor CFE newsletter The Ga. Examiner, 1994-95. With U.S. Army, 1950-53. Mem. Life, Accident and Health Claims Assn. Phila. (pres. 1969-70), Mktg. Ins. Claims Assn. (life, v.p. 1985—, pres. 1989-90), So. Loss Assn., Atlanta Claims Assn., Am. Soc. Indsl. Security, Nat. Assn. Chiefs of Police, Internat. Narcotic Enforcement Officers Assn., Assn. Cert. Fraud Examiners (cert., past pres. Ga. chpt. 1990, 93, bd. dirs. 1991-92, faculty 1995-96, bd. regents 1996, Disting. Achievement award 1994, 95), Criminal Investigation Divsn. Agts. Assn. Inc., Ga. Assn. Chiefs of Police (profl.), Ga. Sheriffs' Assn., Ga. Claims Assn., Ga. Fire Investigators Assn., Ret. Mil. Police Assn., West Pines Golf Club. Republican. Home: 6703 Live Oak Ln Douglasville GA 30135-1625 Office: Paterson Investigations Inc PO Box 2037 Douglasville GA 30133-2037

PATIN, MICHAEL JAMES, oil company executive; b. Orange, Tex., Jan. 2, 1957; s. Lee Roy Julius and Theresa Estelle (Bonsall) P. BS in Petroleum Engring., U. Southwestern La., 1980. Registered profl. engr., Tex. Ops. engr. Getty Oil Co., Mobile, Ala., 1980-83; sr. petroleum engr. Kerr-McGee Corp., Calgary, Alta., Can., 1983-86; supr. joint ventures Kerr-McGee Corp., Oklahoma City, 1987-89; mgr. Dallas dist. Headington Oil Co., Dallas, 1990-92; pres. Michael J. Patin and Assocs., Houston, 1992—. Mem. Soc. Petroleum Engrs. (bd. dirs. Mobile/Pensacola chpt. 1981-83, Dallas chpt. 1983—), Am. Assn. Drilling Engrs., Soc. Petroleum Evaluation Engrs., Can. Joint Venture Assn., Toastmasters Internat. (regional spkrs. award 1989), Am. Assn. Profl. Landman, Stratford Pl. Home Owners Assn. (bd. dirs.1987-90, 92-95). Home: 301 Wilcrest Ste 7312 Houston TX 77042

PATMAN, PHILIP FRANKLIN, lawyer; b. Atlanta, Tex., Nov. 1, 1937; s. Elmer Franklin and Helen Lee (Miller) P.; m. Katherine Sellers, July 1, 1967; children: Philip Franklin, Katherine Lee. BA, U. Tex., 1959, LLB, 1964; MA, Princeton U., 1962. Bar: Tex. 1964, U.S. Dist. Ct. (we. dist.) Tex. 1975, U.S. Dist. Ct. (so. dist.) Tex. 1971, U.S. Supreme Ct. 1970. Atty. office of legal adviser Dept. State, Washington, 1964-67; dep. dir. office internat. affairs HUD, Washington, 1967-69; pvt. practice, Austin, Tex., 1969—. Ofcl. rep. of Gov. Tex. to Interstate Oil Compact Commn., 1973-83, 87-91. Woodrow Wilson fellow 1959. Fellow Tex. Bar Found.; mem. ABA, Tex. Bar Assn., Tex. Ind. Producers and Royalty Owners Assn., Tex. Mid-Continent Oil & Gas Assn., Tex. Law Review Assn., Phi Beta Kappa, Phi Delta Phi. Democrat. Episcopalian. Clubs: Austin, Headliners, Westwood Country. Contbr. articles to legal jours. Office: Patman & Osborn 515 Congress Ave Ste 1704 Austin TX 78701-3503

PATOSKI, MARGARET NANCY, historian, educator; b. Ellis County, Tex., Dec. 24, 1929; d. Bob Milton and Clara Clementine (Graham) Pearson; m. Victor Albert Patoski, July 22, 1960; children: Christina Victoria, Nicholas Joseph. BA magna cum laude, Tex. Christian U., 1968, MA, 1970, PhD, 1973. Asst. prof. history East Tex. State U., Commerce, 1973-77; asst. prof. history Tex. Wesleyan U., Ft. Worth, 1977-83, assoc. prof. history, 1983-89, prof. history, 1989—. Translator, annotator: Reminiscences of My Father, Peter A. Stolypin, 1970, The Career of a Tsarist Officer, 1975, Stolypin: Russia's Last Great Reformer, 1986, Boris Savinkov: Portrait of a Terrorist, 1987; contbr. numerous articles, revs. to profl. pubs. Dem. precinct chair Tarrant County, Ft. Worth, 1980-95; bd. dirs. Pleasant Valley Hist. Cemetery, Cedar Hill, Tex., 1983—, Humane Soc. North Tex., Ft. Worth, 1985-91. Mem. Am. Assn. Advancement of Slavic Studies, Am. History Assn., World History Assn., Western Social Sci. Assn. (pres. 1981-82, Outstanding Svc. award 1984), Rocky Mountain Slavic Studies Assn. (pres. 1980-81), Southwestern Slavic Studies Assn. (pres. 1978-79). Episcopalian. Home: 4325 Lovell Fort Worth TX 76107

PATRICIOS, NICHOLAS NAPOLEON, architectural educator, consultant; b. Johannesburg, Transvaal, South Africa, Jan. 8, 1938; came to U.S., 1978; s. Napoleon and Athena Patricios; m. Emily Venturas, Sept. 23, 1962; children: Leon, Lana. BArch, U. Witwatersrand, Johannesburg, 1962; diploma town and country planning, U. Manchester, Eng., 1965; PhD, U. Coll. London, 1970. Architect London County Coun., London, 1963; architect-planner Wilson & Womersley, London, 1965-67; group leader Borough of Southwark, London, 1968-70; prof., head dept. town and regional planning U. Witwatersrand, 1973-78; dir. program urban and regional planning U. Miami, Coral Gables, Fla., 1981-86, interim dean sch. architecture, 1983-84, master Stanford residential coll., 1987-90, assoc. dean sch. architecture, 1993-95, prof. architecture, 1995—; cons. in field, 1978—. Author: Building Marvelous Miami, 1994; editor: International Handbook on Planning, 1986; contbr. articles to profl. jours. Pres. St. Andrew Greek Orthodox Ch., Kendall, 1983, 93, 94; chmn. task force Area Agy. Aging, Dade and Monroe Counties, Fla., 1987-88, mem. exec. com., Miami, 1988; mem. Planning Com., Miami, 1992. Recipient Design for Elderly award Dept. Health, Edn. and Welfare, 1979, Architecture of Easter Island award Earthwatch, 1987; Fulbright fellow, 1990. Fellow Royal Town Planning Inst.; mem. Am. Planning Conf. (program chair Fla. chpt. 1985), Sigma Xi, Omicron Delta Kappa. Home: 9700 SW 73rd Ave Miami FL 33156-2921 Office: U Miami Sch Architecture Miami FL 33124

PATRICK, BRENDA JEAN, educational consultant; b. Dallas, Aug. 24, 1955; d. Gene Everett and Peggy Rose (Tanzy) P.; children: Michael Everett. BS in Elem. Edn., Tex. A&M U., Commerce, 1981, MS, 1984, postgrad., 1989—. Cert. profl. supr., mid-mgmt. adminstr. Tchr. Garland Ind. Sch. Dist., 1982-87, acad. coach, 1983-86; with Austin Acad. for Excellence, 1987-88; cons. Region 10 Edn. Svc. Ctr., 1988—; coord. Tchr. Expectation Student Achievement; trainer Devel. Capable People, Tex. A&M-Commerce/Profl. Devel. Ctr. Project; developer, presenter workshops and seminars in field; mem. adv. bd. Network for Effective Schs., Teh Effective Sch. Report. Bd. dirs. Dallas YWCA. Recipient Tex. History Tchr. award Daus. of Republic of Tex., Am. History Tchr. award Daus. of Am. Revolution. Mem. ASCD, Tex. PTA (hon. life), Tex. Staff Devel. Coun., Phi Delta Kappa.

PATRICK, EVA BERT, nurse; b. Pinehurst, N.C., July 25, 1953; d. John Patrick and Clara Elizabeth (Byrd) Pope; m. W. Ward Patrick, Mar. 29, 1986; children: Eric Quinn Bates, Scarlet Marie Bates, Ellen Elizabeth. Lic. practical nurse cert., Sandhills C.C., 1973, ADN in Nursing, 1983. RN, N.C. Charge nurse Sandhills Nursing Ctr., Pinehurst, 1977-78; mem. recovery room staff S.W. Miss. Regional Med. Ctr., McComb, 1978-80; head nurse Manor Care of Pinehurst, 1983-85; staff nurse emergency dept. Cen. Carolina Hosp., Sanford, N.C., 1985-86; home health nurse St. Joseph's Home Health Agy., Southern Pines, N.C., 1986-87, patient care coord., 1987; respite care coord. Dept. Aging Moore County, Carthage, N.C., 1986-87; staff nurse Moore Regional Hosp., Pinehurst, N.C., 1989-91; home care coord. St. Joseph Home Health Agy., Southern Pines, N.C., 1991-95, dir. resident svcs., 1995-96, dir. case mgmt., 1996—. Democrat. Baptist. Home: 702 Sunset Dr PO Box 1062 Carthage NC 28327 Office: Saint Josephs Home Health Agy 592 Central Dr Southern Pines NC 28387-2812

PATRICK, JAMES CARY, religious organization administrator; b. Atlanta, Feb. 28, 1948; s. James Henry Jr. and Alma Lee (Watkins) P.; m. Lisa Grace Peabody, Aug. 27, 1977. BA in History, Emory U., 1970; postgrad., U. N.C., 1970-71, Ga. State U., 1973-75. Pub. info. officer Ga. Dept. Transp., Atlanta, 1974-79; promotional writer news svcs. Emory U., Atlanta, 1979-81; promotional writer, editor Presbyn. Ch. U.S.A., Atlanta, 1982-88; freelance writer, editor Atlanta, 1988-90; dir. comm. Episcopal Diocese of Atlanta, 1990—; speaker in field. Editor: Go Therefore, 1987; editor newspaper DioLog, 1990—; contbr. photographs to nat. and regional mags. and newspapers (divsnl. award U.S. Dept. Transp.); producer video for Episcopal Diocese of Atlanta. Recipient Golden Flame hon. mention Internat. Assn. Bus. Communicators, 1993. Mem. Pub. Rels. Soc. Am. (accredited), Religious Pub. Rels. Coun., Episcopal Communicators (Polly Bond award 1993, 94). Democrat. Episcopalian. Home: 2141 Ector Ct NE Atlanta GA 30345-1901 Office: Episcopal Diocese Atlanta 2744 Peachtree Rd NW Atlanta GA 30363

PATRICK, JAMES DUVALL, JR., lawyer; b. Griffin, Ga., Dec. 28, 1947; s. James Duvall and Marion Wilson (Ragsdale) P.; m. Cynthia Hill, Jan. 19, 1991. BS in Indsl. Mgmt., Ga. Inst. Tech., 1970; JD, U. Ga., 1973. Bar: Ga. 1973, U.S. Dist. Ct. (mid. dist.) Ga. 1973, U.S. Dist. Ct. (so. dist.) Ga. 1983, U.S. Ct. Appeals (5th cir.) 1974, U.S. Supreme Ct., U.S. Ct. Appeals (11th Cir.) 1981, U.S. Tax Ct. 1985. Assoc. Cartledge, Cartledge & Posey, Columbus, Ga., 1973-74; ptnr. Falkenstrom, Hawkins & Patrick, Columbus, 1975, Falkenstrom & Patrick, Columbus, 1975-77; sole practice, Columbus, 1977—; instr. bus. law Chattahoochee Valley C.C., Phenix City, Ala., 1975-77; instr. paralegal course Columbus Coll., 1979, 84; del. U.S./China Joint Session on Trade, Investment, and Econ. Law, Beijing, 1987, Moscow Conf. on Law and Bilateral Econ. Rels., Moscow, 1990. Mem. Hist. Columbus Found., Mayor's Com. for the Handicapped, 1987-88; local organizer, worker Joe Frank Harris for Gov. Campaign, Columbus, 1982; bd. dirs. Columbus Symphony Orchestra, 1988-94. Mem. ATLA, ABA, State Bar Ga., Ga. Trial Lawyers Assn., Columbus Young Lawyers Club, Columbus Lawyers Club, Columbus Kappa Alpha Alumni Assn. (sec.), Phi Delta Phi, Kappa Alpha. Methodist. Clubs: Civitan (bd. dirs. 1975-77), Country of Columbus, Georgian (Atlanta), Buckhead. Office: 831 2nd Ave Columbus GA 31901-2703

PATRICK, JAMES NICHOLAS, SR., radio, television, newspaper commentator, consultant; b. Spokane, Wash., Oct. 5, 1950; s. Robert L. and Mamle R. (Canino) P.; m. Rita Irene Roelker, June 13, 1969; children: Stephanie, James Jr., Justin Tood. BA, U. Louisville, 1973. With GE Info. Svcs., Greensboro, N.C., 1975-85; asst. v.p. Am. Airlines, Dallas, 1986-88; v.p., gen. mgr. AMR Gen. Computing, Dallas, 1988-89; pres., profl. speaker, cons. James N. Patrick Group, Richardson, Tex., 1989—; chmn., chief exec. officer, pres. Millennium Prodns., Inc., Richardson, 1991—; analyst for maj. breaking bus. news; spokesperson for radio sports for Crest Cadillac, Plano, Tex. Founder Am. Airlines "Think Tanks", 1986; freelance corres. U.S., Europe for maj. radio and TV networks including #10 Downing St. Bombing, 1991, World Econ. Summit, 1990, Presdl. Election - Channel 5 Australia, 1992. Named Amb. of Goodwill City of Louiseville, 1969. Mem. Tex. Computing Industry Coun. (pres. 1988-89), Tex. Innovation Info. Network (bd. mem. 1988-89), El Centro Coll. Bus. Adv. Bd. (bd. mem. 1988-89), Commodore Lavon Yacht Club. Roman Catholic. Home: 423 Valley Cove Dr Richardson TX 75080-1844 Office: Millennium Prodns Inc PO Box 831830 Richardson TX 75083-1830

PATRICK, PAMELA ANN, secondary school educator, research analysis consultant; b. Mesquite, Tex., June 10, 1963; d. Gene Everett and Peggy Rose (Tanzy) P. AAS, Eastfield Coll., 1982; BA in English, East Tex. State U., 1987, MS in Edn., English, 1988. Tex. provisional cert. 1990. Sales clk. Sears, Mesquite, 1982-84; substitute tchr. various Ind. Sch. Dists., Tex., 1988—. Contbr. articles to profl. jours. Mem. UDC, DAR, Daus. Republic Tex., Daus. Union Vets. Civil War, Dallas County Heritage Soc., Dallas Geneal. Soc., Nat. Trust for Historic Preservation, Dallas Hist. Soc., Green County Hist. Geneal. Soc., Snyder Kennedy Cemetery Preservation Soc. (pres.), Robert Morris Hist. Soc. (pres.), Humane Soc. U.S., DAV Aux., Phi Delta Kappa, Sigma Tau Delta. Republican. Methodist. Home: 3531 Palm Dr Mesquite TX 75150-3432

PATSEL, E. RALPH, JR., registrar; b. Roanoke, Va., June 25, 1935; s. Elmer Ralph and Wynnie (Blosser) P.; m. Jane Neel Wells, Jan. 19, 1962; 1 child, Ralph Neel. AA, Bluefield (Va.) Coll., 1957; BA, Baylor U., 1959; MA, U. N.C., 1964; postgrad., U. Va., 1966-67. Dir. pub. rels. and devel. Bluefield Coll., 1961-65; dir. admissions King Coll., Bristol, Tenn., 1965-66; prof. history Bluefield Coll., 1966-72; registrar Bluefield State Coll., 1990—; asst. prof. history S.W. Va. Community Coll., Richlands, Va., 1972-75; computer software cons. Systems, Software & Svc., Bluefield, 1988-94; real estate agt. Ball Realty, Bluefield, 1983-96; owner, mgr. Neel's - The Fashion Pl., Bluefield, 1975-94; acting acad. dean Bluefield Coll., 1969-69, acting dean of students, 1995. Chmn. merchant com. Downtown Devel. Corp., Bluefield, 1976-85; councilman, vice mayor Town of Bluefield, 1974-78; vote/poll ofcl. Tazewell County, Va., 1982-91. Named Citizen of the Yr., Kiwanis of Bluefield, 1986, 79. Mem. Mercer County Realtors Assn., Phi Theta Kappa. Republican. Baptist. Office: Bluefield State Coll 219 Rock St Bluefield WV 24701-2100

PATT, RICHARD BERNARD, anesthesiologist; b. Balt., May 12, 1954; s. Howard H. and Shirley M. (Berman) P.; m. Cheryl A. Kelley, June 18, 1985 (div. 1993). BA in Philosophy, U. Md., 1977; MD, Am. Univ. Carribean, 1982. Diplomate Am. Bd. Anesthesiology. Intern dept. surgery St. Agnes Hosp., Balt., 1982-83; resident dept. anesthesiology Albert Einstein Coll. Medicine, Bronx, N.Y., 1983-85, fellow, 1985-86; sr. instr. anesthesiology Sch. Medicine and Dentistry, U. Rochester, N.Y., 1986-87, asst. prof., 1987-90, assoc. prof., 1990-93; dir. quality assurance com. Pain Treatment Ctr. Strong Meml. Hosp., Rochester, N.Y., 1986-87, acting med. dir., 1989-90, med. dir., 1990-93, founder, coord. Cancer Pain Initiative, 1986-93; med. dir. anesthesiology pain fellowship Anderson Cancer Ctr., U. Tex., Houston, 1993—, dir. anesthesia pain svc., 1993—, dep. chief sect. pain and sympton mgmt., 1993—; assoc. prof. anesthesiology Sch. Medicine, U. Tex., Houston, 1993—, assoc. prof. neuro-oncology, 1993—; rep. Univ. Risk Mgmt. Consortium, 1987-90; mem. faculty and med. adv. bd. Pain Mgmt. Info. Ctr., Ithaca, N.Y., 1990—; med. dir. Option Care Pharmacies, Rochester, N.Y., 1990-93; mem. profl. adv. com. Critical Care Pharmacy of Rochester, N.Y., 1990—; ad hoc con. Office Profl. Med. Conduct N.Y. State, 1992—, Upstate N.Y. Divsn. Medicare, 1992-93; mem. coun. hospice profls. Nat. Hospice Orgn., 1993—; rev. Agy. for Health Care Policy Rsch., 1993; mem. adv. coun. and faculty Pain Mgmt. Refined Janssen Parmaceutica, 1992—; mem. nat. med. adv. bd. Nat. Med. Care Home Care Divsn., 1992—; mem. pain mgmt. adv. bd. Wyeth Ayerst Co., 1993—; active Hospice Adv. Com., Genessee Region Home Care, 1989-93; vis. prof., lectr. in field. Author: (with W. Pfisterer) Keywords and Concepts for Anesthesia Boards, 1986, (with S. Lang) You Don't Have To Suffer: A Family's Guide to Cancer Pain Management, 1994; author chpts. in books; editor: Cancer Pain, 1993; assoc. editor Pain Mgmt., 1989-92, series editor, 1989-93; dept. editor Am. Pain Soc. Bull., 1993—; co-editor Dept. Anesthesiology Newsletter U. Rochester, 1990-92; chief editl. advisor Pain Relief Papers-Janssen Pharmaceutica, 1992—; mem. editl. bd. Pain Digest, 1993—, Jour. Pain and Sympton Mgmt., 1993—, Anesthesiology Rev., 1990—, Am. Jour. Hospice and Palliative Care, 1990—, Pain Mgmt., 1989-92, Jour. Occupational Rehab., 1992—, Anesthesiology News, 1991—, Sphere, 1990-93, Am. Pain Soc. Bull., 1993—, Lit. Scan in Anesthesiology, 1991-93, Anesthesiology News Video Jour., 1993—, Oncology, 1996—; rev. numerous profl. jours.; contbr. numerous articles to profl. jours. Recipient Disting. Physician of Yr. award Vis. Nurse Svc., 1992. Mem. AMA, Am. Soc. Anesthesiologists (del. to ho. of dels. 1989, mem. com. on cons. corner 1989-92, subcom. on local anesthesia and pain 1989-93, numerous others), Am. Soc. Regional Anesthesia, Am. Acad. Pain Mgmt., Am. Pain Soc. (dir.-at-large 1996-99), Internat. Anesthesia Rsch. Soc., Nat. Hospice Orgn., N.Y. State Med. Soc., N.Y. State Hospice Assn., N.Y. State Soc. Anesthesiologists (mem. speaker bur. 1987-93, chmn. pub. edn. and info. com. 1988-91, alt. dir. dist. 6 1991—, v.p. dir. sci. affairs 1988-89, pres.-elect dist. 6 1990-91, pres. dist. 6 1991-92, numerous others), Acad. Hospice Physicians (mem. publ. com. 1989-91), Monroe County Med. Soc., Soc. Behavioral Medicine, Soc. Practice Pain Mgmt., Anesthesia History Assn., Malignant Hyperthermia Assn. U.S., Soc. Anesthesiology in Developing Countries. Office: U Tex Anderson Cancer Ctr Dept Anesthesiology Box 42 1515 Holcombe Blvd Houston TX 77030-4009

PATTEN, ROBERT LOWRY, English language educator; b. Oklahoma City, Apr. 26, 1939; s. Charles H. and Helen (Lowry) P.; m. Faith L. Harris, June 12, 1960 (div. 1974); children: Jocelyn S., Christina S. BA, Swarthmore Coll., 1960; MA, Princeton U., 1963, PhD, 1965. Lectr. Bryn Mawr (Pa.) Coll., 1964-66, asst. prof. English, 1966-69; asst. prof. Rice U., Houston, 1969-71, assoc. prof., 1971-76, prof. English, 1976—, chair, dept. of English, 1991-92, master Grad. House, 1992-95; pres. PEN S.W., Houston, 1989-92. Author: Charles Dickens and His Publishers, 1978, George Cruikshank's Life, Times and Art, vol. 1, 1992, vol. 2, 1996; editor: (book by Charles Dickens) Pickwick Papers, 1972, George Cruikshank: A Revaluation, 1974, 2d edit., 1992, (with John O. Jordan) Literature in the Marketplace, 1995; editor SEL: Studies in English Lit., 1978-84, 90—. Bd. dirs. Cultural Arts Coun., Houston, 1979-80, Tex.Com. for the Humanities, 1979-80; pres., bd. dirs. Houston Ctr. for the Humanities, 1976-84. NEH fellow, 1968-69, 77-78, 87-88; Guggenheim fellow, 1980-81; Nat. Humanities Ctr. fellow, 1987-88; Nat. Gallery of Art Assoc., 1988-89. Mem. AAUP, MLA, PEN Am. Ctr., Dickens Fellowship, Dickens Soc., Phi Beta Kappa (pres. Beta chpt. Tex. 1991-94). Episcopalian. Office: Rice U Dept English MS 30 6100 Main St Houston TX 77005-1827

PATTEN, WILLIAM THOMAS, priest, consultant; b. Chattanooga, Aug. 7, 1924; s. George Holmes and Margaret (Thomas) P.; m. Mary Lynn Chapin, June 16, 1948; children: Mary, George, Thomas, Anne Elizabeth, Dorris. BA, Princeton U., 1949; MDiv, U. South, 1971; postgrad., U. Tenn., 1993. Ordained priest Episcopal Ch., 1971. V.p. sales Chattem Drug, Chattanooga, 1950-58; pres. Patten Motor Co., Chattanooga, 1958-68; vicar, then rector Grace Ch., Paris, Tenn., 1971-74, Ch. of the Nativity, Ft. Oglethorpe, Ga., 1974-80, St. Alban's Ch., Chattanooga, 1980-83; various ch. assignments, 1984-90; exec. dir. DuBose Conf. Ctr., Monteagle, Tenn., 1990-92; cons. (pro bono) various non-profits, Sewanee, Tenn., 1992—; bishop and coun. Diocese of Tenn., 1978-81; bd. dirs. Dandridge Trust, 1986-92; retreat leader and planner, 1972-91; treas. Cloud Forest Sch., Inc., Sewanee, Tenn., 1994—. Author: Episcopal Is Compelling, 1981, Fighting the Good Fight, 1992. Dist. chmn. Boy Scouts Am., Chattanooga, 1950s; campaign mgr. Hamilton County (Tenn.) Sheriff election, 1960s; treas. Friends of the South Cumberland State Park, Monteagle, Tenn., 1994—; sec.-treas. Ecol. Support, Inc., Sewanee, 1994—. With U.S. Army, 1943-46, Europe. Decorated Purple Heart, Combat Infantry Badge. Home and Office: 1441 Laurel Branch Trl Sewanee TN 37375-2863

PATTERSON, ANITA MATTIE, union administrator; b. Birmingham, Ala., Feb. 19, 1940; d. John Evans Patterson and Flora Ella (Paul) Patterson/Mitchell; m. LeRoy Harold Walden, Mar. 19, 1958 (dec. Apr. 1966); children: Christopher Ann, DeRoy, Chanita. Student, Wayne State U., 1968-72, 72-78, Wayne State U., 1976-79. Sr. counselor City of Detroit, 1965-79; area dir. AFSCME, Washington, 1979—; exec. bd. Coalition Labor Union Women, Washington, exec. dir., 1975-77; chair nat. women's com. Coalition Black Trade Unionists, Washington, 1985—; tchg. fellow AFL-CIO Organizing Inst., Washington, 1992—; ofcl. election observer South Africa Election, 1994. Active So. Regional Coun., Atlanta, 1992—; mem. social svcs. com. Salem Bapt. Ch., Atlanta, 1990—. Recipient Cmty. Svcs. award A. Philip Randolph Inst., 1990, Cmty. Svcs. award So. Christian Leadership Coun., 1991, Leadership award Ga. State Legislature Black Caucus, 1992, Disting. Recognition award City of Detroit, 1989, Sojourner Truth award Coalition of Black Trade Unionists, 1994, Labor award Operation PUSH, 1994; named Addie L. Wyatt Women of Yr., Coalition of Black Trade Unionists, 1990, Ga. Labor Hall of Fame, 1996. Mem. Nat. Coun. Negro Women (ad hoc labor com. 1986—, Recognition award 1989, Svc. award 1988), Marracci Ct. # 32. Democrat. Office: AFSCME Internat Area Office 1720 Peachtree St NW Ste 150B Atlanta GA 30309-2439

PATTERSON, AUBREY BURNS, JR., banker; b. Grenada, Miss., Sept. 25, 1942; s. Aubrey Burns and Elizabeth (Staten) P.; m. Ruby Kathryn Clegg, Dec. 12, 1964; children: Aubrey B. III, Clayton H., Jennifer L. BBA, U. Miss., 1964; MBA, Mich. State U., 1969; student, Grad. Sch. Banking, U. Wis. With Bank of Miss., Tupelo, 1972—, pres., 1983—, chmn., chief exec. officer, 1990—; chmn., CEO BancorpSouth, Inc.; bd. dirs. Vol. Bank, Jackson, Tenn. Former chmn. bd. dirs. Salvation Army, Tupelo, 1978—; bd. dirs. Cmty. Devel. Found., chmn. bd., 1994-95; bd. dirs. Columbia Theol. Sem., Decatur, Ga., U. Miss. Found., Miss. Univ. for Women Found., Presbyn. Ch. U.S.A. Found., Miss. Econ. Coun., Jackson, 1986—, chmn., 1994; bd. dirs. North Miss. Health Svcs. Inc., 1987—, also exec. com.; moderator St. Andrews Presbytery Presbyn. Ch. USA. Capt. USAF, 1965-72. Decorated Air Force Commendation medal, Meritorious Svc. medal. Mem. Am. Bankers Assn., Miss. Bankers Assn. (pres. 1995—), Robert Morris Assocs., Soc. Internat. Bus. Fellows, Tupelo Country Club, Univ. Club, Kiwanis (pres. Tupelo 1987), Beta Gamma Sigma, Beta Alpha Psi. Presbyterian. Home: 1 Overdale Dr Tupelo MS 38801 Office: Bancorp Miss PO Box 789 Tupelo MS 38802

PATTERSON, CHRISTOPHER NIDA, lawyer; b. Washington Courthouse, Ohio, Apr. 17, 1960; s. Donis Dean and JoAnne (Nida) O.; children: Travis, Kirsten. BA, Clemson U., 1982; JD, Nova U., 1985. Bar: Fla. 1985, U.S. Dist. Ct. (mid. dist.) Fla. 1985, U.S. Ct. Mil. Rev. 1986, U.S. Ct. Mil. Appeals 1987, U.S. Dist. Ct. (ea. dist.) Va. 1987, U.S. Supreme Ct. 1990, U.S. Ct. Appeals (11th cir.) 1992, U.S. Dist. Ct. (no. dist.) Fla. 1992, U.S. Dist. Ct. (so. dist.) Tex. 1995; cert. criminal trial lawyer Fla. Bar. and Nat. Bd. Trial Advocacy. Prosecutor Fla. State Attys. Office, Orlando, Fla., 1985; spl. asst. U.S. Atty. U.S. Dist. Ct. (ea. dist.) Va., 1987-90; ptnr. Patterson, Hauversburk and Cassidy, Panama City, Fla., 1992—; adj. prof. law Gulf Coast Coll. Author: Queen's Pawn, 1996. Capt. U.S. Army, 1986-92, Desert Storm. Mem. Nat. Assn. Criminal Def. Lawyers, Fla. Assn. Criminal Def. Lawyers, Acad. Fla. Trial Lawyers, Fla. Bar (criminal law sect., mil. law standing com., Pro Bono Svc. award), Bay County Bar Assn. Episcopalian. Office: PO Box 1368 303 Magnolia Ave Panama City FL 32401-3124

PATTERSON, COLEMAN E.P., management educator; b. Stamford, Conn., Aug. 31, 1966; s. Benton Rain and Patricia Jane (Roberts) P.; m. Tracy Lynne Potts, Aug. 1, 1992. BSBA in Fin., U. Fla., 1988, MEd, 1990; EdS, U. Ala., Tuscaloosa, 1995, PhD in Mgmt., 1996. Fin. aid officer U. Fla., Gainesville, 1990; fin. aid specialist Santa Fe C.C., Gainesville, Fla., 1988-90; acad. adviser Santa Fe C.C., Gainesville, 1990, assessment specialist, 1991; rsch. asst. U. Ala., Tuscaloosa, 1991-92, 94-95, teaching asst., 1992-94, 95—, ind. study instr., 1992—. Co-author mgmt. course. Mem. Acad. of Mgmt., So. Mgmt. Assn., S.W. Acad. Mgmt., Pinnacle Honor Soc. Baptist. Home: 315K Cedar Crest Sq Tuscaloosa AL 35401 Office: U Ala Mgmt/Mktg Dept Box 870225 Tuscaloosa AL 35487-0225

PATTERSON, DONALD EUGENE, research scientist; b. El Paso, Tex., Feb. 7, 1958; s. Donald M. Patterson and Beverly Lee (Viles) McElroy; m. Mary Jane Ingram, May 6, 1989. BS, U. Tex., 1982, MS, 1984; MA, Rice U., 1987, PhD, 1989. Rsch. scientist Rice U., Houston, 1989-91; sr. rsch. scientist Houston Advanced Rsch. Ctr., The Woodlands, Tex., 1989-93; sr. scientist SI Diamond Tech. Inc., Houston, 1991-95; sr. rsch. scientist TSA, Inc., The Woodlands, 1991-95; dir. R & D SI Diamond Tech. Inc., Houston, 1995—. Contbr. articles to profl. jours. Recipient Harry B. Wieser award Rice U., 1988; Rice U. Graduate fello, 1984; UTEP Grad. scholar, 1983, Davis and Bertha Green scholar, 1982, VFW Voice Democracy scholar, 1974. Mem. AAAS, Materials Rsch. Soc., Am. Chem. Soc., N.Y. Acad. Sci., Phi Kappa Phi, Sigma Xi. Home: 3622 Hansford Pl Pearland TX 77584 Office: SI Diamond Tech Inc 2435 North Blvd Houston TX 77098-5105

PATTERSON, DONALD ROSS, lawyer; b. Overton, Tex., Sept. 9, 1939; s. Sam Ashley and Marguerite (Robinson) P.; m. Peggy Ann Schulte, May 1, 1965; children: D. Ross, Jerome Ashley, Gretchen Anne. BS, Tex. Tech U., 1961; JD, U. Tex., 1964; LLM, So. Meth. U., 1972. Bar: Tex. 1964, U.S. Ct. Claims 1970, U.S. Ct. Customs and Patent Appeals 1970, U.S. Ct. Mil. Appeals 1970, U.S. Supreme Ct. 1970, U.S. Dist. Ct. (ea. dist.) Tex. 1982, U.S. Ct. Appeals (5th cir.) 1991, U.S. Ct. Appeals (D.C. cir.) 1994. Commd. lt. (j.g.) U.S. Navy, 1964, advanced through grades to lt. comdr., 1969; asst. officer in charge Naval Petroleum Res., Bakersfield, Calif., 1970-72; staff judge adv., Kenitra, Morocco, 1972-76; officer in charge Naval Legal Service Office, Whidbey Island, Washington, 1976-79; head Mil. Justice Div., Subic Bay, Philippines, 1979-81; ret., 1982; sole practice law, Tyler, Tex., 1982—; instr. U. Md., 1975, Chapman Coll., 1977-79, U. LaVerne, 1980-81, Tyler Jr. Coll., 1990—, Jarvis Christian Coll., 1990—, U. Tex., Tyler, 1993—. Mem. Tex. Bar Assn., Smith County Bar Assn., Am. Immigration Lawyers Assn., Masons, Rotary, Shriners, Phi Delta Phi. Republican. Baptist. Club: Toastmasters (Tyler) (past pres.). Home: 703 Wellington St Tyler TX 75703-4666 Office: 777 S Broadway Ave Ste 106 Tyler TX 75701-1648

PATTERSON, DONIS DEAN, bishop; b. Holmesville, Ohio, Apr. 27, 1930; s. Raymond J. and Louella Faye (Glasgo) P.; m. JoAnne Nida, Dec. 22, 1951; children: Christopher Nida, Andrew Joseph. BS, Ohio State U., 1952; STB, Episcopal Theol. Sch., 1957; M Div, Episcopal Divinity Sch., 1972; DD (hon.), Nashotah House Sem., 1984, U. of South, 1986. Rector St. Andrews Ch., Washington Court House, Ohio, 1957-63, St. Marks Ch., Venice, Fla., 1963-70, All Sts. Ch., Winter Park, Fla., 1970-83; bishop Episcopal Diocese Dallas, 1983-92; assisting bishop Episcopal Diocese of Ctrl. Gulf Coast, 1992-96; trustee Seabury Western Theol. Sem., Evanston, Ill., 1981-82, U. of South, 1983-92, Episcopal Theol. Sem. S.W., 1983-92. Chmn. Episcopal Ch. House of Bishops Armed Forces Com., 1989-93. Col., chaplain U.S. Army, 1952-54, Korea.

PATTERSON, DOUGLAS MACLENNAN, financial educator; b. Tallahassee, Jan. 16, 1945; s. Thomas and Ruth (MacLennan) P.; m. Sara Louise Lucas; children—Cara Beth, John Douglas. B.S.E.E., U. Wis., 1968, M.B.A., 1972, Ph.D., 1978. Elec. engr. Westinghouse Electric, Balt., 1968-71; asst. prof. U. Mich., Ann Arbor, 1976-80, Va. Tech., Blacksburg, 1980—, dir. PhD program in Fin., 1991—; vis. prof. U. Calif., Santa Barbara, 1989; vis. scholar U. Tex., Austin, 1994; presenter numerous seminars. Contbr. articles to profl. jours. Mem. ad hoc com. Detroit Area Hosp. Assn., 1978-79. Recipient Tchng. Excellence award Va. Tech., 1983; U. Mich. fellow, 1979; U.S. Navy grantee, 1984, 85, 90. Mem. Am. Finance Assn., Am. Economic Assn., Fin. Mgmt. Assn., Beta Gamma Sigma. Methodist. Home: 702 Crestwood Dr Blacksburg VA 24060-6006 Office: Va Poly Inst Dept Finance Blacksburg VA 24061

PATTERSON, EDWIN, minister; b. Andalusia, Ala., Sept. 6, 1921; s. Walter Levi and Kate Edline (Aughtman) P.; m. Margaret Alice Hall, May 14, 1966. Degree, Brennan Bus. Sch., 1940; postgrad., Samford U., 1950-57. Ordained to ministry So. Bapt. Conv., 1947. Pastor various chs. Ala., 1947—; including Hopwell, 1949-67, Harmony Bapt. Ch., Andalusia, 1967-80, Searight Bapt. Ch., Dozier, Ala., 1980—; acct. C.G. Tomberlin, M.D., Andalusia, 1985—. Mem. bd. regents Liberty U., Lynchburg, Va. Home: 407 Lakeview Dr Andalusia AL 36420-3542 Office: PO Box 486 Andalusia AL 36420-0486

PATTERSON, ELIZABETH JOHNSTON, former congresswoman; b. Columbia, SC, Nov. 18, 1939; d. Olin DeWitt and Gladys (Atkinson) Johnston; m. Dwight Fleming Patterson, Jr., Apr. 15, 1967; children: Dwight Fleming, Olin DeWitt, Catherine Leigh. BA, Columbia Coll., 1961; postgrad. in polit. sci., U. S.C., 1961, 62, 64; LLD (hon.), Columbia Coll., 1987; D Pub. Svc. (hon.), Converse Coll., 1989. Pub. affairs officer Peace Corps, Washington, 1962-64; postgrad. VISTA, OEO, Washington, 1965-66; D Pub. Svc. Head Start and VISTA, OEO, Columbia, 1966-67; tri-county dir. Head Start, Piedmont Community Actions, Spartanburg, S.C., 1967-68; mem. Spartanburg County Coun., 1975-76, S.C. State Senate, 1979-86, 100th-102nd Congresses from 4th S.C. dist., 1987-93. Trustee Wofford Coll., 1975-81; bd. dirs. Charles Lea Ctr., 1978-90, Spartanburg Coun. on Aging; pres. Spartanburg Dem. Women, 1968; v.p. Spartanburg County Dem. party, 1968-70, sec., 1970-75; trustee Columbia Coll., 1991—. Mem. Bus. and Profl. Women's Club, Alpha Kappa Gamma. Methodist. Office: PO Box 5564 Spartanburg SC 29304-5564

PATTERSON, EUGENE CORBETT, retired editor, publisher; b. Valdosta, Ga., Oct. 15, 1923; s. William C. and Annabel (Corbett) P.; m. Mary Sue Carter, Aug. 19, 1950; 1 child, Mary Patterson Fausch. Student, North Ga. Coll., Dahlonega, 1940-42; AB in Journalism, U. Ga., 1943; LL.D., Tusculum Coll., 1965, Harvard U., 1969, Duke U., 1978, Stetson U., 1984, Ind. U., 1990; Litt.D., Emory U., 1966, Oglethorpe Coll., 1966, Tuskegee U., 1966, Roanoke Coll., 1968, Mercer U., 1968, Eckerd Coll., 1977, U. South Fla., 1986, Dillard U., 1992; Colby Coll., 1994. Reporter Temple (Tex.) Daily Telegram and Macon (Ga.) Telegraph, 1947-48; mgr. for S.C. United Press, 1948-49; night bur. mgr. United Press, N.Y.C., 1949-53; mgr. London bur. United Press, also chief corr. U.K., 1953-56; v.p., exec. editor Atlanta Journal-Constitution, 1956-60; editor Atlanta Constitution, 1960-68; mng. editor Washington Post, 1968-71; prof. polit. sci. Duke U., 1971-72; editor, pres. St. Petersburg (Fla.) Times, 1972-84, chmn., chief exec. officer, 1978-88, editor emeritus, 1988—; editor, pres. Congl. Quar., Washington, 1972-86; chmn., chief exec. officer Congl. Quar., 1978-88; chmn. bd., chief exec. officer Fla. Trend mag., 1980-88, Ga. Trend mag., 1984-88, Ariz. Trend mag., 1986-88, Governing mag., 1987-88, Modern Graphic Arts, Inc., 1978-88, Poynter Inst. Media Studies, 1978-88, Poynter Fund, 1978-88. Vice chmn. U.S. Civil Rights Commn., 1964-68; mem. Pulitzer Prize Bd., 1973-84; trustee ASNE Found., 1981-84, U. Ga. Found., 1982-88, North Ga. Coll. Found., 1991-93, Am. Press Inst., Reston, Va., 1983-88, Duke U., 1988-94, Fla. Bar Found., 1992-93, LeRoy Collins Ctr. for Pub. Policy, 1990-93. Decorated Silver Star, Bronze Star with oak leaf cluster in 10th Armored Divsn., Gen. Patton's 3rd Army; recipient Pulitzer prize for editl. writing Columbia U., 1966, William Allen White Nat. Citation award U. Kans., 1980, Elijah Parish Lovejoy award Colby Coll., 1994. Fellow Soc. Profl. Journalists; mem. Am. Soc. Newspaper Editors (pres. 1977-78), St. Petersburg Yacht Club, Vinoy Club. Home: Snell Isle 1967 Brightwaters Blvd NE Saint Petersburg FL 33704-3007 Office: 535 Central Ave Saint Petersburg FL 33701-3703

PATTERSON, EVANGELINA G., nursing educator; b. Laredo, Tex., Sept. 11, 1932; d. Gildardo and Paula Gonzalez; m. Robert W. Patterson, June 4, 1956. RN, Parkland Hosp., Dallas, 1954; BSN, U. Ala., Huntsville, 1984; MSN, U. Ala., 1989. Cert. family nurse practitioner. Staff nurse Parkland Hosp., 1954-56, head nurse, 1956-61; case supr., epidemiologist City of Dallas, 1963-66; case supr. Galveston County Health Dept., 1974-75; charge nurse Crestwood Hosp., 1984-86; instr. nursing Wallace State Coll., Hanceville, Ala., 1985-90; nursing supr. Madison County Health Dept., Huntsville, Ala., 1990—. Mem. Am. Nurses Assn., Ala. Nurses Assn., Sigma Theta Tau.

PATTERSON, GRADY LESLIE, JR., financial advisor; b. Abbeville, S.C., Jan. 13, 1924; s. Grady Leslie and Claudia (McClain) P.; m. Marjorie Harrison Faucett, Dec. 22, 1951; children—Grady Leslie III, Steven G., M. Lynne, Laura A., Amy S., M. Beth. LLB, U. S.C., 1950, BS, 1975, LLD (hon.), 1980; LLD (hon.), The Citadel, 1985; HHD (hon.), Lander Coll., 1990; LLD (hon.), U. Charleston, S.C., 1992, Clemson U., 1992. Bar: S.C. 1950. County service officer Abbeville County, S.C., 1950; ops. officer S.C. Air N.G., Columbia, 1952-59; asst. atty. gen. State of S.C., Columbia, 1959-66, treas., 1967-94; fin. advisor, 1994—. Served with USAAF, 1943-46; maj. USAF, 1950-52, 61-61, ret. Maj. Gen. Decorated D.S.M. USAF. Mem. S.C. Bar Assn. Democrat. Presbyterian. Home: 3016 Petigru St Columbia SC 29204-3618

PATTERSON, GREGORY BROWNELL, reporter; b. Wilmington, Del., Mar. 5, 1972; s. Gary Buell and Elizabeth Patterson; m. Sarah Merle Wyatt, Aug. 17, 1996. BA in journalism, Washington and Lee U., 1994. Staff writer The Sumter (S.C.) Daily Item, 1994-96, The Augusta (Ga.) Chronicle, 1996—. Recipient Third Place Political Reporting Soc. of Profl. Journalists, S.C., 1995, Third Place Spot News Reporting S.C. Press Assn., 1996. Office: Augusta Chronicle S.C. Bur 123 Pendleton St NW Aiken SC 29801

PATTERSON, JAMES HARDY, entertainer, conductor, musician, educator, arranger, composer; b. Kingston, Ga., Oct. 12, 1935; s. Hardy and Laura (Cargile) P.; m. Lois Gartrell; children: Adonica Patterson Carson, Phillippa G. AB, Clark Coll., 1957; MusM, U. Mich., 1965; postgrad., Atlanta U., 1962, U. Wis., Lacrosse, 1978. Tchr., dept. chmn. (ret.) Fulton County Bd. Edn., Atlanta, 1957-84; instr. to asst. prof., dir. Jazz Orch. Clark Atlanta U., 1962—; entertainer Motown Band, Detroit, 1962-73; profl. condr. Freda Payne Show, Fairmont Hotel, Atlanta, 1975; musician Atlanta Pops Orch., 1970—; leader James Patterson Jazz Quartet, Atlanta and abroad, 1960—; profl. musician Lionel Hampton and Dizzy Gillespie Small Group, Duke Pearson's Big Band, Ringling Bros., Barnum and Bailey Circus, Ice Shows, Broadway mus. including Sophisticated Ladies, 1970; substitute, extra, soloist Atlanta Symphony, 1971; music panelist Ga. Coun. for the Arts, Atlanta, 1986—, Bur. Cultural Affairs, Atlanta, 1986—; cons. Fulton County Arts Coun., Atlanta, 1987. Composer music including Song for Mr. H.P., 1976, Reminiscence, 1986; author: Jazz And the Young Black Audience, 1982; asst. project dir. film In Search of Imporvision, The Essence of Virtuosity in Jazz, 1983; performer "Gillespiana" IAJE Conv., 1996; performed Montreux, Switzerland, Northsea, Den Hague, Holland, Grande Parade de Jazz, Nice, France, Kool Jazz Festivals, Avery Fisher, Lincoln Ctr., IAJE Convention, Atlanta. Served with 7th U.S. Army Band, 1958-60, Germany. Named one of Outstanding Young Men of Am., 1970; recipient Bronze Jubilee award Sta. WETV, 1983. Mem. AAUP, ASCAP, NARAS (nat. edn. com.), Nat. Flute Assn., Internat. Assn. Jazz Educators, N.Am. Saxophone Alliance World Saxophone Congress, Atlanta Fedn. Musicians (v.p. 1994—, bd. dirs. 1969—), Internat. Double Reed Soc., Internat. Clarinet Soc., Duke Ellington Soc., Optismits, YMCA, Alpha Phi Alpha. Democrat. Methodist. Home: 413 Fielding Ln SW Atlanta GA 30311-2020 Office: Clark Atlanta U James P Brawley Fair St SW Atlanta GA 30314

PATTERSON, JAMES THURSTON, marketing executive, consultant; b. El Paso, July 19, 1944; s. James Stephens and Lorraine (Gentry) P. BA, Abilene Christian U., 1966; MBA, Southwest U., 1987, PhD, 1989. Youth minister Ch. of Christ, Nashville, 1968-71; account exec. Sta. WTVF-TV, Nashville, 1971-78; v.p. mktg. and mgmt. MPII, Inc., Dallas, 1978-80; mktg. engr. Texas Instrument, Dallas, 1980-83; sales/mktg. mgr. Paragon Mktg., 1983—; account supr. Buntin Advt., Nashville, 1988—; mem. bd. Nashville Advt. Fedn., 1973-78. Youth editor Nashville Christian Jour., 1970; chmn. Com. Against Pornography, Nashville, 1971; chmn. pub. relations Am. Hearth Assn., Nashville, 1976; exec. bd. Lamb and Lion Ministries, Plano, Tex., 1980-84. Dep. sheriff reserve, Davidson City, Tenn. With USAFR. Named best speaker Toastmasters Internat., 1972, one of Outstanding Young Men of Am. Jaycees Internat., 1979, 80, Tenn. Squire, Tenn. Squires Assn., 1980, Adm. Tex. Navy, 1982, Ky. col., 1984. Office: 9 Music Sq S # 126 Nashville TN 37203-3211

PATTERSON, JEFFREY LYNN, police officer; b. Warren, Ohio, Nov. 17, 1958; s. Clarence and Doris Jean (Howell) P.; m. Deborah Lynn Ridzon, May 2, 1981 (div. Mar. 1989); m. Carolyn Sue Schmieder, Sept. 5, 1992. Student, Youngstown (Ohio) State U., 1977-83; BA, St. Leo (Fla.) Coll., 1991; MPA, U. So. Fla., 1991. Firefighter, EMT McKinley Heights Fire Dept., Niles, Ohio, 1976-79; safety and security officer Trumbull Meml. Hosp., Warren, Ohio, 1979; police officer Bazetta Township Police Dept., Cortland, Ohio, 1979-80, Columbiana (Ohio) Police Dept., 1980-83; police officer Clearwater (Fla.) Police Dept., 1983-88, detective, 1988-90, police sgt., 1990—. Contbr. articles to profl. jour. Named Police Officer of Yr., KC, 1987, 93; recipient Cert. of Appreciation award Mahonong Valley Police Chiefs, Youngstown, 1987. Mem. Am. Mensa, Fraternal Order of Police (v.p. Fla. lodge 4), Internat. Assn. Law Enforcement Planners (sec. Fla. chpt., Planner of Yr. 1990, 93), Clearwater Suprs. Union (pres.). Democrat. Home: 488 Mac Leod Ter Dunedin FL 34698-7311 Office: Clearwater Police Dept 644 Pierce St Clearwater FL 34616-5426

PATTERSON, JOHN BERNARD, lay worker, writer; b. Dayton, Ohio, May 15, 1923; s. John B. Sr. and Floy Belle (Van Marter) P.; children: Susan Eileen, Rebecca Louise. BA, U. Kans., 1950; BTh, United Theol. Sem., Dayton, Ohio, 1954. Freelance portrait artist, 1976-81. Author: The Christmas Star Theology of Ethics, 1984, rev. annually through 1988, The Theology of Jubilee Economics. Moderator Keys to the Kingdom Ch., 1984—. With U.S. Army, 1943-45, ETO. Decorated Bronze Star, Silver Star, Purple Heart. Home and Office: Keys to the Kingdom Ch 2521 Deer Run Saint Augustine FL 32095

PATTERSON, KAREN KAY, reference librarian; b. Pontotoc, Miss., Nov. 16, 1966; d. William Rex and Shirley Lou (Manning) P. BA, Blue Mtn. Coll., 1988; MLS, U. So. Miss., 1990. Children's libr., then reference libr. Washington County Library, Greenville, Miss., 1990—. Mem. Concerned Women for Am., Women on Mission, Blue Mtn. Coll. Alumnae Assn., U. So. Miss. Alumnae Assn. Republican. Southern Bapt.

PATTERSON, LOTSEE FRANCES, library and information studies educator; b. Apache, Okla.; d. James Earl and Merrell Fleta (Dietrich) P.; m. Don Gordon Smith, June 1, 1951 (div. 1966); children: Robin, Lisa, Karen, Kent, Kyle. BS, Okla. Coll. Women, 1959; MLS, U. Okla., 1969, PhD, 1979. Jr. high sch. tchr. Boone Sch., Apache, 1959-67; high sch. tchr. Riverside Indian Sch., Anadarko, Okla., 1967-68; libr. coord. Norman (Okla.) Pub. Schs., 1971-72; asst. prof. U. New Mex., Albuquerque, 1972-78; assoc. prof. Tex. Women's U., Denton, 1978-85; program dir. TRAILS U. Okla., Norman, 1985-87, assoc. prof., 1991—; assoc. prof. Northeastern State U., Tahlequah, Okla., 1987-89; dir. libr. media svcs. Okla. City Pub. Sch. Dist., 1989-91; cons. Nat. Commn. on Librs. & Info. Sci., Washington, 1989-92, Nat. Mus. of the Am. Indian, Smithsonian Institution, Washington, 1991. Author: Tribal Library Procedures Manual, 1992, Native American Resources, 1995-96; co-author: Indian Terms of the Americas, 1993; editor: Am. Indian Librs. Newsletter, 1991-96. Mem. ALA (coun. 1984-88), Am. Indian Libr. Assn. (v.p. 1991-95), Assn. Libr. and Info. Sci. Edn. Office: U Okla Sch of Libr and Info Studies 401 W Brooks St Norman OK 73019-6030

PATTERSON, MARK ROBERT, marine biology educator; b. North Tonawanda, N.Y., Apr. 3, 1957; s. Robert Carl and Marion Florence (Lister) P.; m. Sarah Laurie Sanderson, May 31, 1986. AB in Biology magna cum laude, Harvard Coll., 1979, AM in Biology, 1982, PhD in Biology, 1985. Asst. and assoc. prof. div. environ. studies U. Calif., Davis, 1986-92; assoc. prof. Coll. William and Mary Sch. Marine Sci., Gloucester Point, Va., 1992—; peer reviewer NSF, Washington, 1986—; peer reviewer, tech. cons. NOAA, Nat. Undersea Rsch. Program, Rockville, Md., 1987—; chief scientist/aquanaut in habitat Aquarius, NOAA, 1988, 95. Contbr. articles to profl. jours. Del. N.Y. state Nat. Youth Sci. Camp, W.Va., 1975; juror Yolo County Grand Jury, Woodland, Calif., 1990-91. NSF grad. fellow in ecology, 1979-82. Mem. AAAS, Am. Soc. Limnology and Oceanography, Soc. Integrative Comprehensive Biology (Best Paper in Invertebrate Zoology award 1982), Phi Beta Kappa (award for scholarship 1996), Sigma Xi. Office: Coll William and Mary Sch Marine Sci Va Inst Marine Sci Gloucester Point VA 23062

PATTERSON, NEIL, science publisher; b. Toronto, Ont., Can., Oct. 15, 1933; came to U.S., 1960; s. John and Anne (Atherley) P.; m. Noel Elizabeth Coe, June 10, 1959 (div. 1978); children: Tove Elizabeth, Julia Lee; m. Ippy Tarleton Gizzi, Jan. 29, 1979; 1 child, Grear Tarleton. BA, U. Toronto, 1954; postgrad., U. Paris, 1954-55. Mng. editor McGraw-Hill, Can., Toronto, 1955-60; v.p., editorial dir., co-founder Benjamin-Cummings formerly W.A. Benjamin, Inc., N.Y.C., 1960-66, Worth Pubs., Inc., N.Y.C., 1966-76; dir. coll. dept. W.W. Norton & Co., N.Y.C., 1976-80; pres. W.H. Freeman, San Francisco, N.Y.C., 1980-84; co-founder Sci. Am. Books, San Francisco, N.Y.C.; pres., co-founder Neil Patterson Pubs.-A Viacom/Paramount Co., Chapel Hill, N.C., 1984-95; founder, pres., CEO Harper Science-A Harper Collins Imprint, Chapel Hill, 1995—; bd. dirs. U. N.C. Pub. Inst. Bd. dirs. N.C. Bot. Garden, Chapel Hill. Mem. Biochem. Soc. (bd. dirs. 1991-94). Home: 3010 Arthur Minnis Hillsborough NC 27278 Office: Harper Science 101 B St Carrboro NC 27510

PATTERSON, OSCAR, III, communications educator, university official; b. Shelby, N.C., July 25, 1945; s. Oscar Jr. and Frances (Killian) P.; m. Julie A. Holmes, Dec. 28, 1990. BA, Pfeiffer Coll., 1967; MFA, U. Ga., 1973; PhD, U. Tenn., 1982. Asst. prof. theater Auburn (Ala.) U., 1973-75, Western Carolina U., Cullowhee, N.C., 1975-79; asst. prof. comm. Tex. Tech. U., Lubbock, 1982-83; prof. comm., dir. telecom. and gen. mgr. Sta. WNCP, U. N.C., Pembroke, 1984—; mem. adj. faculty Shaw U., N.C.; cons. Opelika (Ala.) Arts Assn., 1973-75, Cherokee (N.C.) Hist. Assn., 1979-81, Robeson Hist. Assn., Lumberton, N.C.; mem. nat. faculty Nat. Issues Forums Inst. Contbr. articles to Journalism Quar., Jour. Broadcasting and Electronic Media, So. Theater, Jour. Computing in Tchr. Edn., Social Sci. Quar., Am. Journalism. Capt. U.S. Army, 1968-75, Vietnam. Bickle fellow, 1979-82, Fulbright fellow, 1986. Mem. Broadcast Edn. Assn., Nat. Assn. Broadcasters, Pub. Rels. Soc. Am., Soc. Profl. Journalists, Am. Journalism Historians, N.C. Theater Conf., Southeastern Theater Conf. (chmn. auditions 1977-81), Officer's Candidate Sch. Assn., DAV, Am. Legion, Retired Officer's Assn., Alpha Psi Omega, Kappa Tau Alpha, Sigma Delta Chi, Phi Kappa Phi, Alpha Epsilon Rho. Republican. Methodist. Home: 3459 Brushy Hill Rd Fayetteville NC 28306-5662 Office: U NC PO Box 1510 Pembroke NC 28372-1510

PATTERSON, PATRICIA LYNN, applied mathematician, geophysicist, inventor; b. Kearny, N.J., Feb. 25, 1946; d. Clifford and Helen (Matthews) P. AA, St. Petersburg (Fla.) Jr. Coll., 1965; BA magna cum laude in Physics, U. South Fla., Tampa, 1966; MS in Geophys. Scis., Ga. Inst. Tech., Atlanta, 1976; PhD in Geophysics, Ga. Inst. Tech., 1980. Elec. engr. Burns & McDonnell Engring. Co., Miami, Fla., 1967-69; tchr. biology and physiology Orange County Bd. Edn., Orlando, Fla., 1969-70; acoustical cons. Bolt Beranek & Newman Inc., Downers Grove, Ill., 1971-72; geophysicist Exxon Co., U.S.A., New Orleans, 1976-77; comm. systems engr. E-Systems, St. Petersburg, Fla., 1980-85; pres. Solitonics (Rsch. & Cons.), Clearwater, Fla., 1985—; image-processing engr. E-Systems, Garland, Tex., 1991-93. Contbr. articles to profl. jours.; patentee in field. Recipient Sigma Xi research awards, 1977, 81, others. Mem. IEEE (reviewer tech. papers), Bioelectromagnetics Soc., Am. Geophys. Union.

PATTERSON, PATRICK O'BRIAN, criminology educator; b. McComb, Miss., Oct. 31, 1967; s. Frank Lee and Lena McCray P.; children: Patrick O'Neal, Cerena Donzart. BS in Criminal Justice, Grambling State U., 1990, MS in Criminal Justice, 1992. Security officer Grambling (La.) State U., 1988-89; security officer Pinkerton Security, Shreveport, La., 1989-93, Syracuse, N.Y., 1993-95; supr. Union U., Jackson, Tenn., 1996—. Participant Anti-Crime March, Jackson, 1996. Mem. Am. Soc. Indsl. Security.

PATTERSON, RICKEY LEE, clergyman; b. Indpls., Sept. 24, 1952; s. William Irving and Wanda Lou (Calbert) P.; BA, Ind. U., 1976; postgrad. U. Miami, 1976-80; ThM, Internat. Bible Inst. and Sem., 1983; ThD Christian Leadership U., 1995; m. Sharon Rose Leonard, May 4, 1974. Pres. Pat-Cat Enterprises, Inc., Miami, 1977—; pastor, 1972—; founder, pres. Jesus Students Fellowship, Inc., 1973—, pastor, 1979—, radio broadcast spkr., 1978—, dir. J.S.F. Cassette Ministries, 1978—; pres. Jesus Fellowship, Inc., 1981—; ordained to ministry Internat. Conv. Faith Chs. and Ministers, Inc., 1980; coll. unit dir. Northwestern Mut. Life Ins. Co., Milw., 1980-83; founder, supt. Jesus Fellowship Christian Sch., 1983—; CEO, pres., Magnetic Mktg. Group, Inc pres. Dade County Pvt. Sch. Sys., Inc., 1983—; instr. Bible, Ind. U., 1973-76; instr. Bible, U. Miami, 1976—, also guest lectr. dept. religion; pres. Miami Bible Inst., 1984—, pres., Christian Internet Radio; guest lectr. Miami North Community Correctional Center, Dade County Correctional Inst., Fed. Inst. Corrections; adv. Miami chpt. Women Aglow, 1980-82; campus minister Ind. U., U. Miami, Fla. Internat. U., Miami-Dade C.C., U. P.R.; exec. bd. mem. Internat. Congress of Local Chs., 1988—; dir. Christian Benefactor, 1990—. Charter mem. Rep. Presdl. Task Force; sustaining mem. Rep. Nat. Com.; bd. govs. Am. Coalition Traditional Values, 1984—; mem. exec. bd. Internat. Congress of Local Chs., 1989—. Mem. Bur. Bus. Practice, Nat. Audubon Soc., Am. Entrepreneurs Assn., Inst. Cert. Fin. Planners., Am. Security Council, U.S. Senatorial Club, Zool. Soc. Fla., Adult Congregate Living Facility (pres. Naples chpt. 1988—), Christian Booksellers Assn., Nat. Assn. Life Underwriters, Miami Assn. Life Underwriters, Am. Mktg. Assn., Full Gospel Businessmen's Fellowship Internat., Internat. Coalition of Local Chs. (mem. exec. bd. 1988—), Ind. U. Alumni Assn., Sigma Pi. Republican. Editor: Spirit of Life Mag., 1980-82; chief editor Miami Jour., 1984—, mem. bd. Internat Congress of Local Chs (mem. bd., 1988—). Home and Office: 9775 SW 87th Ave Miami FL 33176-2954

PATTERSON, ROBERT HOBSON, JR., lawyer; b. Richmond, Va., Jan. 30, 1927; s. Robert Hobson and Margaret S. (Sargent) P.; m. Luise Franklin Wyatt, June 15, 1952; children—India, Robert Hobson, Margaret. B.A., Va. Mil. Inst., 1949; LL.B., U. Va., 1952. Bar: Va. 1952, U.S. Ct. Appeals (4th cir.) 1953, U.S. Supreme Ct. 1955. Assoc. McGuire, Woods, Battle & Boothe, Richmond, 1952-56, ptnr., 1956—, sr. ptnr., chmn. exec. com., 1978-89, chmn., 1984-89. Pres. bd. visitors Va. Mil. Inst., 1975; pres. Va. Home for Boys, 1975. Served with USNR, 1945-46. Fellow Am. Coll. Trial Lawyers, Am. Bar Found., Va. Mil. Inst. Alumni Assn. (pres. 1963-65). Republican. Episcopalian. Clubs: Commonwealth, Country of Va. Office: McGuire Woods Battle & Boothe LLP 1 James Ctr 901 E Cary St Richmond VA 23219

PATTERSON, ROBERT HUDSON, library director; b. Alexandria, La., Dec. 11, 1936; s. Hubert Hudson and Beth (Jones) P.; 1 child, Jennifer Bookhart. B.A., Millsaps Coll., Jackson, Miss., 1958; M.A., Tulane U., 1963; M.L.S., U. Calif., Berkeley, 1965. Mem. profl. staff Tulane U. Libr., New Orleans, 1965-69, 73-76, asst. dir. collection devel., 1973-76; head spl. collections cataloging U. Tex., Austin, 1970-73; dir. librs. U. Wyo., Laramie, 1976-81, U. Tulsa, 1981—; chmn. exec. bd. Wyo. State Libr. Adv. Com., 1976-81; mem. bd. Okla. State Libr. Adv. Com., 1981-84; mem. adv. coun. Bibliog. Ctr. for Rsch., Denver, 1978-81; past mem. exec. bd. S.E. La. Libr. Network; bd. dirs. Amigos Bibliog. Coun., 1983-86; cons. NEH, Harry Ransom Humanities Rsch. Ctr., U. Tex., Austin. Editor Conservation Administrn. News, 1979-93; contbr. articles to profl. jours. Pres. Western Conservation Congress, 1981-82. Sr. fellow CLR/UCLA, 1989. Fellow Internat. Boswell Inst.; mem ALA (various offices), Okla. Libr. Assn. (various offices).

PATTERSON, STEVE, professional hockey team executive; b. Beaver Dam, Wis., Sept. 21, 1957. BBA with honors, U. Tex., 1980, JD, 1984. Bar: Tex. 1984. Gen. mgr., profl. basketball team counsel Houston Rockets, 1984-89, profl. basketball mktg. exec. group ticket sales, mgr., bus. ops. exec., gen. mgr., 1989-94; pres. profl. hockey team Houston Aeros, 1994—; pres. Arena Oper. Co., Houston, 1995—. Office: Houston Aeros 24 E Greenway Plz Ste 800 Houston TX 77046-2409

PATTERSON, STEVEN-MICHAEL, editor, literary translator; b. Long Branch, N.J., Dec. 17, 1961; s. Stephen Wayne and Judith Cathleen (Andrus-Boeker) P. Student, Montclair State Coll., 1980-82, Princeton U., 1982-83, Nat. U. Mexico, 1994. Bilingual advt. copywriter J.C. Penney Co., Inc., N.Y.C. and Dallas, 1985-89; fgn. lang. prodn. editor Harcourt Brace Pubs., Ft. Worth, 1990-92; founder, pres. Multii-Langue Editorial Svcs., San Antonio, 1992—; Spanish lang. tchr./tutor Peace Corps, San Antonio, 1993-94. Editor about 20 high sch./coll. texts in Spanish, French and Italian. AIDS educator Oak Lawn Community Svcs.-The Buddy Program, Dallas, 1988-90; patron San Antonio Pub. Libr. Found., San Antonio, 1994. Mem. Textbook Author's Assn. (ann. awards judge 1994), Soc. Children's Book Writers and Illustrators, Assn. Fgn. Lang. Editors (contbg. founder 1993). Democrat. Home and Office: 121 Broadway Ocean Grove NJ 07756-1275

PATTERSON, WILLIAM BROWN, university dean, history educator; b. Charlotte, N.C., Apr. 8, 1930; s. William Brown and Eleanor Selden (Miller) P.; m. Evelyn Byrd Hawkins, Nov. 27, 1959; children: William Brown, Evelyn Byrd, Lucy Miller, Emily Norvell. BA, U. South, 1952; MA, Harvard U., 1954, PhD, 1966, cert. ednl. mgmt., 1982; BA, Oxford (Eng.) U., 1955, MA, 1959; MDiv, Episc. Div. Sch., Cambridge, Mass., 1958. Ordained to ministry Episcopal Ch. as deacon, 1958, as priest, 1959. Asst. prof. history Davidson (N.C.) Coll., 1963-66, assoc. prof., 1966-76, prof. history, 1976-80; dean Coll. Arts and Scis. U. South, Sewanee, Tenn., 1980-91, prof. of history, 1980—. Author: (with others) Discord, Dialogue, and Concord, 1977; mem. bd. editors St. Luke's Jour. Theology, Sewanee, 1982-90; contbr. numerous articles to profl. jours. Trustee U. South, 1968-71; mem. internat. adv. com. U. Buckingham, Eng., 1977—; pres. So. Coll. and Univ. Union; organizer Associated Colls. of South, 1988-89. Danforth Found. grad. fellow, 1952, Mellon Appalachian fellow U. Va., 1992-93, rsch. fellow NEH, 1967, Folger Shakespeare Libr., Washington, 1975, Inst. for Rsch. in Humanities, U. Wis., Madison, 1976, Newberry Libr., Chgo., 1979; Rhodes scholar, 1953. Mem. Am. Hist. Assn., Am. Soc. Ch. History, N.Am. Conf. on Brit. Studies, Eccles. History Soc. Eng., Renaissance Soc. Am., So. Hist. Assn., Soc. for Values in Higher Edn., Episcopal Div. Sch. Alumni/ae Assn. (mem. exec. com. 1984-87), Phi Beta Kappa, Beta Theta Pi. Home: 195 North Carolina Ave Sewanee TN 37375 Office: U of the South Dept History Sewanee TN 37383-1000

PATTERSON, WILLIAM HENRY, regional planner, retired army officer; b. Indpls., July 2, 1927; s. William Henry and Pearl Mona (Larlee) P.; m. Joyce Ann Powell, Aug. 19, 1950; children: William H., Catherine E., Carol M., Patricia J., Christopher E., Michael T. BA in Polit. Sci., George Washington U., 1959; MA in Pub. Law and Govt., Columbia U., 1963. Commd. 2d lt. U.S. Army, 1946, advanced through grades to col., 1969; capital outlay com. Brevard County (Fla.) Sch. Dist., 1986-93; mem. Charter Com., Brevard County, 1993-94; chmn. Brevard County Planning and Zoning Bd. and Local Planning Agy., 1994; chmn. dept. Nat. and Internat. Security Studies, occupant Eisenhower chair U.S. Army War Coll., Carlisle Barracks, Pa., 1976-78. Chmn. Merritt Island (Fla.) Exec. Coun. Homeowner Assns., 1981-82; co-founder Civic Action Coun., Brevard County, 1983; dir. Washington-Moscow Presdn. Hot Line, 1962-63. Decorated Legion of Merit (4), Bronze Star, Air medal. Mem. Ret. Officers Assn., Mil. Order World Wars (chpt. comdr. 1995-96). Republican. Roman Catholic. Home: 455 Diana Blvd Merritt Island FL 32953-3038

PATTI, TONY J., retired electrical engineer; b. Phila., Dec. 29, 1919; s. Salvatore and Grace P. Patti; m. Doris Rossi, May 7, 1942 (dec. 1964); children: Antonia, Sandra G.; m. Doris H. Hess, Oct. 10, 1964. Student, Drexel U., 1946-47, SUNY, Binghamton, 1960-61. Devel. test engr. RCA, Camden, N.J., 1946-52, field engr., 1952-55; tchr. field engrs. IBM, Endicott, N.Y., 1955-57, devel. lab. engr., 1957-62, sr. engring. writer, 1962-75. Author: Photography For Fun, 1987, Photography: An Historical Account, 1992; contbr. articles to profl. jours; contbg. editor: PSA Jour., 1985—. Chmn. pub. info. Am. Cancer Soc., San Antonio, 1978-84. 1st lt. U.S. Army, 1943-46, ETO. Fellow Photographic Soc. Am. (pub. rels. v.p. 1985-91, svc. medal 1989, historian 1980—, sec. techniques divsn. 1980-84), India Internat. Photo Coun. (assoc.). Republican. Methodist. Home: 111 Austin Dr S Boerne TX 78006-8955

PATTILLO, WESLEY MOODY, JR., foundation executive; b. Mobile, Ala., Oct. 2, 1940; m. Zelma Mullins, Nov. 24, 1967; children: Laura, Stephen. AB, U. Ga., 1962; MA, Ohio State U., 1965; ATS-Lilly fellow, Columbia U., 1984. News reporter Daily Banner-Herald, Athens, Ga., 1958-59; announcer, newsman WGAU AM-FM/CBS, Athens, 1959-62; account exec. Forbes McKay Advt. Agy., Birmingham, Ala., 1962-63; advt. mgr. Ohio State U., Columbus, 1963-65; exec. asst. to pres. So. Bapt. Theol. Sem., Louisville, 1965-72, v.p. devel. and pub. rels., 1972-86; v.p. univ. rels. Samford U., Birmingham, 1986-94; pres., exec. dir. Nat. Found. for Youth, Clearwater, Fla., 1994-96; cons. Hong Kong Bapt. U., 1990-91, 96—. Contbr. articles to profl. jours. Bd. dirs. Birmingham Broadway Series, Inc.; active Leadership Louisville; chmn. promotion/devel. divsn. Bapt. World Alliance, McLean, Va., 1985-94; chmn. telecomm. com. Kentuckiana Metroversity, Louisville, 1980-83. Mem. Religious Pub. Rels. Coun. (nat. pres. 1990-92), Bapt. Pub. Rels. Assn. (nat. pres. 1974-75), Nat. Soc. Fund Raising Execs. (Exec. of Yr. in Ala. 1990, bd. dirs. Ala. chpt. 1988-92, cert.), Pub. Rels. Soc. Am. (pres. Bluegrass chpt. 1980-81, cert.), Ala. Ind. Colls. Devel./Pub. Rels. Adv. Bd. Home: 3821 Spring Valley Rd Birmingham AL 35223-1527

PATTISON, JON ALLEN, computer scientist, consultant; b. Sturgis, Mich., July 18, 1960; s. Jerome and Karen Pattison; m. Nandini Pattison, July 14, 1990; 1 child, Nisha Lynn. Student, Glen Oaks C.C., 1978-79, U. Tex., Arlington, 1987. Mgr. Magic City Hardware, 1978-79; engring. technician Quazon Corp., 1983-84, Sci. Machines Corp., 1984; design engr. Tex. Arrays, 1984-86, EMS Group, Inc., 1986-89; hardware project leader Vortech Data, 1990; systems engr. Computer Task Group, 1991; cons. Decision Cons. Inc., 1992; self-employed cons., 1989, 91-92, 93; cons. Oxford and Assocs., Inc., 1992-94, R.S. Internat., 1993-94; product mgr. Teknekron InfoSwitch, Fort Worth, 1994—. Author design papers and system design documents. Served to sgt. USMC, 1979-83.

PATTON, CARL VERNON, academic administrator, educator; b. Coral Gables, Fla., Oct. 22, 1944; s. Carl V. and Helen Eleanor (Benkert) P.; m. Gretchen West, July 29, 1967. BS in Community Planning, U. Cin., 1967; MS in Urban Planning U. Ill.-Urbana, 1969, MS in Pub. Adminstrn., 1970; MS in Pub. Policy, U. Calif.-Berkeley, 1975, PhD in Pub. Policy, 1976. Instr. to prof. U. Ill., 1968-83, dir. Bureau of Urban and Regional Planning Rsch., 1977-79, prof., chmn. dept., 1979-83; prof., dean Sch. Architecture and Urban Planning, U. Wis., Milw., 1983-89; v.p. acad. affairs, prof. polit. sci., geography and urban planning U. Toledo, 1989-92; pres. Ga. State U., Atlanta, 1992—. Author: Academia in Transition, 1979; (with others) The Metropolitan Midwest, 1985; (with David Sawicki) Basic Methods of Policy Analysis and Planning, 1986, rev. 2d edit., 1993; (with Kathleen Reed) Guide to Graduate Education in Urban and Regional Planning, 1986, 88; editor: Spontaneous Shelter: International Perspectives and Prospects, 1988, (with G. William Page) Quick Answers to Quantitative Problems: A Pocket Primer, 1991; assoc. editor Jour. of Planning Edn. and Rsch., 1983-87, mem. editl. bd., 1987-89; mem. editl. bd. Habitat International, 1993—, Atlanta International Magazine, 1993—; contbr. articles to profl. jours. Chmn. Community Devel. Commn., Urbana, 1978-82; mem. Civic Design Ctr., Milw., 1983-87; mem. City of Milw. Art Commn., 1988-89, ToledoVision, 1989-92, Toledo Art Ctr. Bd., 1989-92, City of Toledo Bd. Cmty. Rels., 1990-92; bd. dirs. The Atlanta Downtown Partnership, Ctrl. Atlanta Progress, Ga. Rsch. Alliance, Ctrl. Atlanta Hospitality Childcare, Inc., Atlanta Convention and Vis. Bur., Atlanta United Way, Woodruff Art Ctr., Fox Theatre; mem. exec. com. The Fairlie-Poplar Task Force, Grady Healthcare Inc., The Univ. Ctr. in Ga.; mem. Ga. Coun. on Econ. Edn., Atlanta Neighborhood Devel. Ptnrship. Fellow NIMH, 1973-75, U. Ill. Center for Advanced Studies, 1973-74. Mem. Am. Planning Assn., Am. Inst. Cert. Planners, Assn. Collegiate Schs of Planning (v.p. 1985-87, pres. 1989-91), Atlanta C. of C. Avocations: racquetball, photography, travel. Home: 3807 Tuxedo Rd NW Atlanta GA 30305-1042 Office: Ga State U Office of Pres University Plz Atlanta GA 30303-3083

PATTON, KEVIN JOEL, editor; b. Princeton, Ky., May 7, 1967; s. Gilford Hobson and Helen Joyce (Carner) P.; m. Katharine Doran, 1996. BS, Murray State U., 1989. Sports editor Fulton (Ky.) Daily Leader, 1989-90, Mayfield (Ky.) Messenger, 1990—. Recipient Best Sports Photograph award Ky. Press Assn., 1991, Best Sports Column award, 1992, 94. Mem. Soc. Profl. Journalists, Sigma Delta Chi (v.p. 1987-89). Baptist. Home: 177 Jeannie St Mayfield KY 42066-2226 Office: Mayfield Messenger 201 N 8th St Mayfield KY 42066-1825

PATTON, L(EWIS) K(AY), advertising agency executive, educator; b. Lima, Ohio, Nov. 18, 1932; s. Edgar Armon and Betty Eva (Oberdier) P. BA, U.

Cin., 1954; BFA, Conservatory Music, Cin., 1955; MEd, Xavier U., Cin., 1956, D (hon.), 1988. Notary pub., Ky. Pres. L.K. Patton Enterprises, Inc., Ft. Thomas, Ky., 1960—; tchr. comml. art and advt. Diamond Oaks Joint Vocat. Sch., Cin., 1979—; lectr. Civil War and Ky. history Thomas More Coll.; tchr. Wellman Sch.; owner, mgr. Vogue Coll. Hair Design, Cin., Las Vegas, Nev.; freelance radio and TV announcer; bd. dirs. No. Ky. Chiropractic Ctr., New Concepts, Inc., New Careers, Inc. Author: Kentucky Legends, 1963, Kentucky's Vanishing Landmarks, 1976, Kentucky's Timbered Tunnels, 1994; contbr. articles on history to profl. publs.; singer Cin. Symphony, Cin. Opera, nat. cos. Jesus Christ Superstar, Godspell; rec. album with Dave Brubeck. Mem. Ky. Gov.'s Adv. Coun. on Librs. Mem. AFTRA, Pub. Rels. Soc. Am., Ky. Hist. Soc., No. Ky. Hist. Soc. (past pres.), Christopher Gist Hist. Soc., Ky. Covered Bridge Assn. (founder, exec. dir. 1964—), Ky. Civil War Roundtable, No. Ky. Heritage League, Am. Assn. for State and Local History (Ky. Hist. Confedn. Merit award 1994), Am. Vocat. Assn., Ohio Vocat. Assn. (Ohio Tchr. of Yr. award 1988), Ind. Covered Bridge Assn., Ohio Covered Bridge Assn., So. Covered Bridge Assn., Internat. Platform Assn., Cin. Advertisers Club (bd. dirs.), Filson Club, Phi Delta Theta, Omicron Delta Kappa, Rho Tau Delta, Alpha Delta Sigma, Masons (32 degrees, past high priest, grand rep.), K.T., Shriners, Order of DeMolay (chevalier, legion of honor, past dep. for Ky.). Democrat. Home: 62 Miami Pky Fort Thomas KY 41075-1137

PATTON, PAUL E., governor; b. Fallsburg, KY. Grad. in mech. engring., U. Ky., 1959. With coal bus., until 1979, dep. sec. transp.; judge-exec. Pike County, 1981; lt. gov., sec. econ. devel., pres. senate State of KY, Frankfort, KY, 1991—; governor State of Kentucky, 1995—; served on Ky. Crime Commn., Ky. Tourism Commn., Task Force for Workplace Literacy; former mem. Prichard Com. for Acad. Excellence. Mem. bd. overseers Bellarmine Coll., bd. trustees Pikeville Coll.; chmn. Ky. Dems., 1981-83; del. Dem. Nat. Conv.; served numerous terms Pike County Dem. Exec. Com. Office: Office the Governor The Capitol 700 Capitol Ave Frankfort KY 40601-3410

PATTON, REBECCA JONES, community health nurse; b. Memphis, Mar. 4, 1950; d. Isaac W. Sr. and Carolyn (Crawford) Jones; m. George E. Patton, Feb. 19, 1983; 1 child, Martha Katherine. Diploma, Druid City Hosp., Tuscaloosa, Ala., 1971. Cert. in cmty. health, cert. in utilization rev. Epidemiology nurse N.W. Ala. Regional Health Dept., Sheffield, 1978-89; dir. utilization mgmt. dept. Med. City Shoals Hosp., Muscle Shoals, Ala., 1989-94; dir. utilization mgmt. Directions Mgmt. Svcs., Inc., Muscle Shoals, 1995-96; with Ala. Quality Assurance Found., Birmingham, 1996—. Mem. Ala. Nurses Assn. Home: 407 N High St Tuscumbia AL 35674-1342

PATTON, SUSAN OERTEL, clinical social worker, educator; b. Syracuse, N.Y., May 18, 1946; d. Robert William and Jane (VanWormer) Oertel; m. Joseph D. Patton, Jr., June 3, 1967; children: Jennifer, Joseph D. III. BA, SUNY, Geneseo, 1984; MSW, SUNY, Buffalo, 1987. Cert. social worker, N.Y.; lic. ind. social worker, S.C.; cert. employee assistance profl.; qualified clin. social worker; bd. cert. fellow in managed mental health care; diplomate in clin. social work. Counselor Profl. Counseling Svc., Gowanda, N.Y., 1987-88, Mental Health Mgmt., Rochester, N.Y., 1988-93; counselor The Health Assn., Rochester, 1988-89, sr. counselor, 1989-90, asst. dir. mktg. and tng., 1990-92; pvt. practice Rochester, 1988-93; employee assistance program dir. Recovery Ctr. EAP, Hilton Head, S.C., 1993-95; pres., dir. Employee Assistance Program, Inc., Hilton Head Island, S.C., 1995—; instr. Medaille Coll., Buffalo, 1990-93. Co-author: Treating Perpetrators of Sexual Abuse, 1990. Mem. NASW, Acad. Cert. Social Workers, Am. Bd. Cert. Managed Care Providers, S.C. Counselors Assn., Employee Assistance Profls. Assn. Office: Employee Assistance Program Carolina Bldg Ste 110 10 Office Park Rd Hilton Head Island SC 29928-7541

PATTON, TAMARA J., foreign language educator; b. Balt., Dec. 6, 1957; d. Martin Hobert Patton and Dixie J. Sult. BA in French, U. N.C., Greensboro, 1980, MA in French, 1987; PhD student, U. N.C., Chapel Hill, 1991—; cert. in Egyptian hieroglyphs, Arabic Lang. Inst., Cairo, 1991. Grad. French instr. U. N.C., Greensboro, 1981-84; mgr. Magic Travel, Greensboro, N.C., 1986-87; French tchr. South Florence (S.C.) High Sch., 1987; French, Persian, Arabic and ESL instr. High Point (N.C.) U., 1988—; French instr. U. N.C., Chapel Hill, 1993-94; Spanish instr. Guilford Tech. C.C., 1995; mem. Spanish study group U. N.C., summer 1995, moderator Ann. French Lit. Symposium, 1994; presenter, lectr. in field; resided with Berber tribe in Morocco, summer 1994. Illustrator, artist textbooks and portraits; fgn. corr. (Moroccan newspaper) La Tribune of Fez, 1994—; translator of articles. Officer Greensboro (N.C.) Com. for Relocation of Refugees, 1990; bd. dirs. UNA of USA, Winston-Salem, N.C., 1993—; active Greensboro Jaycees, 1991-92, Prince of Peace Luth. Ch., Greensboro, 1990-92; organizer comty. watch program Sedge Lake Garden, Kernersville, N.C., 1995—. French Embassy scholar, 1992. Mem. MLA, Fgn. Lang. Assn. N.C., UN Assn. Am. (bd. dirs. 1993—), Univ. Women Am., Archael. Inst. Am., Piedmont Indep. Coll. Assn., Pi Delta Phi (pres. 1982-83, hon.). Avocations: Egyptology, fgn. langs., rsch. in ancient documents, tennis. Home: 5045 Toucan Ln Kernersville NC 27284-7865 Office: High Point U Dept Fgn Langs Montlieu Ave Univ Sta High Point NC 27262

PATTON, WARREN ANDRE, non-commissioned officer, journalist; b. Chgo., Oct. 15, 1954; s. Willie Roosevelt and Adriana Ultima (Rhodes) P.; m. Annie Yolanda Thomas, Nov. 19, 1981 (div. May 1988); 1 child, Thomas; m. Olga Enid Ostalaza, July 31, 1993 (div. May 1996); children: Rafaela, Jennifer, Christopher, Michael. B in Criminal Justice, Chaminade U., 1986; MBA, Chadwick U., 1992; MPA, Troy State U., 1993. Enlisted USN, 1978, advanced through grades to chief, 1991; journalist USN, 1978—. Fundraiser Combined Fed. Campaign, Pensacola, Fla., 1991, Waterfront Mission, Pensacola, 1993. Mem. ASPA, Nat. Assn. Black Journalists, Conf. of Minority Pub. Adminstrs., Fleet Res. Assn., Hannibal Masonic Lodge No. 1. Office: US Naval Base San Francisco CA 94130-0411

PATTON, WESLEY ENNIS, III, marketing educator; b. Florence, Ala., Jan. 8, 1939; s. Wesley E. Jr. and Mary (Sammons) P.; m. Lynn Vickey Patton, Oct. 10, 1964. BS in Mktg., U. Ala., Tuscaloosa, 1961, MA in Mktg., 1973; PhD in Mktg., U. Colo., 1978. V.p., gen. mgr., sales mgr. Campbell Motors Inc., Florence, Ala., 1965-75; instr. mktg. U. Colo., Boulder, 1975-78; asst. prof. mktg. Walker Coll. Bus., Appalachian State U., Boone, N.C., 1978-80, assoc. prof. mktg., 1980-85, prof. mktg., 1985—; speaker and cons. in field. Mem. editorial bd. Jour. Mkgt. Edn.; reviewer jours.; contbr. numerous articles to profl. jours. Supr. mountain tourism project for Grandfather Mountain, N.C. Ctr. for Population and Urban-Rural Studies. Lt. USNR, 1961-65. Recipinet U. N.C. Bd. Govs. Teaching Excellence award, 1996; N.Am. Rockwell fellow, 1978, Am. Mktg. Assn. fellow, 1977, U. Ala. fellow, 1960-61. Mem. Am. Mktg. Assn., Acad. Mktg. Sci., So. Mktg. Assn. (name change task force 1982, track chmn. mktg. mgmt. 1982, v.p. 1985-86, trach chmn. mktg. rsch. 1990, Steven Shaw award 1981, 95), S.E. Decision Scis. Inst., Automobile Dealers Assn. Ala. (bd. dirs. 1968-75, exec. com. 1974-75, sec.-treas. 1974, v.p.-elect 1975), Pi Sigma Epsilon, Beta Gamma Sigma, Chi Alpha Phi. Home: 416 Center Ct Dr Boone NC 28607 Office: Appalachian State U Dept Mktg Raley Hall Boone NC 28608

PATUREAU, ARTHUR MITCHELL, chemical engineer, consultant; b. Beaumont, Tex., Nov. 22, 1913; s. Arthur M. Sr. and Gertrude Helen (Brammer) P.; m. Clara Davis, Dec. 24, 1934. BSChemE, U. Tex., 1943, postgrad.; postgrad., Pa. State U., 1946. Chief process engr. Gasoline Plant Constrn. Co., Corpus Christi, Tex., 1944-46, McCarthy Chem. Co., Houston, 1946-48; chief application engr. Fisher & Porter Co., Hatboro, Pa., 1948-50; cons. reactor coolant controls Nautilus nuc. submarine Westinghouse Atomic Power Divsn., Pitts., 1950-53; chief application engr. chem. industry Brown Instrument Divsn., Phila., 1953-55; western sales mgr. Barksdale Valves, L.A., 1955-56; western divisional mgr. Pa. Indsl. Chem. Co., L.A., 1956-73; divisional mgr. Hercules, Inc., L.A., 1973-75; cons. to chem. industry McQueeney, Tex., 1975—; pres. Artgraphics, Inc., 1975—. Editor: (tech. book) Resins in Rubber, 1975; contbg. author to Ency. Chem. Engring.; contbr. articles to profl. jours. mem. engring. found. adv. coun. U. Tex. Coll. Engring., 1970-75. Mem. AIChE, L.A. Rubber Group, River Art Group, Elks. Episcopalian. Home and Office: 4312 S 31st St Apt 55 Temple TX 76502-3359

PATURIS, E(MMANUEL) MICHAEL, lawyer; b. Akron, Ohio, July 12, 1933; s. Michael George and Sophia M. (Manos) P.; m. Mary Ann Paturis, Feb. 28, 1965; 1 child, Sophia E. Bruner. BS in Bus., U. N.C., 1954, JD with honors, 1959, postgrad. in Acctg., 1959-60. Bar: N.C. 1959, D.C. 1969, Va. 1973; CPA, N.C. With acctg. firms, Charlotte and Wilmington, N.C., 1960-63; assoc. Poyner, Geraghty, Hartsfield & Townsend, Raleigh, N.C., 1963-64; atty. Chief Counsel's Office, IRS, Richmond, Va. and Washington, 1964-69; ptnr. Reasoner, Davis & Vinson, Washington, 1969-78; pvt. practice, Alexandria, Va., 1978—; instr. bus. law, econs. and acctg. Bd. editors U. N.C. Law Rev. Served with U.S. Army, 1954-56. Recipient Block award U. N.C. Law Sch. Mem. Va. Soc. CPAs, Va. Bar Assn., Phi Beta Kappa, Beta Gamma Sigma. Republican. Greek Orthodox. Club: Washington Golf and Country (Arlington, Va.). Home: 6326 Stoneham Ln Mc Lean VA 22101-2345 Office: 431 N Lee St Alexandria VA 22314-2301

PAUL, ALIDA RUTH, arts and crafts educator; b. San Antonio, May 30, 1953; d. Richard Irving and Anne Louise (Holman) Paul. B.S. in Edn., Southwest Tex. State U., 1975; M.Ed., U. Houston, 1984. Cert. tchr., Tex. Tchr. art and crafts Houston Ind. Sch. Dist., 1975—. Republican. Episcopalian. Home: 16830 Grampin Dr Houston TX 77084-1945

PAUL, ANDREW ROBERT, trade association executive; b. N.Y.C., Aug. 14, 1938; s. Andrew B. and Maria (Filotas) P.; m. Britt-Marie Hagelbrant, Feb. 6, 1988. AB in French, Dartmouth Coll., 1960; MS in Fgn. Svc., Georgetown U., 1967. Dir. govt. rels. Motorola, Inc., Washington, 1968-75, Paramount Communications, Washington, 1975-90; sr. v.p. Satellite Broadcasting and Communications Assn., Alexandria, Va., 1990—; mem. Gatt adv. com. on Intellectual Property, Washington, 1988-94; advisor MS in Fgn. Svc. program Georgetown U., Washington, 1981—. Presdl. campaign advance man Rep. Nat. Com., 1964; pres. chpt. XI Spl. Forces Assn., Washington, 1981-82; chmn. Alternative House Crisis Intervention Ctr., Vienna, Va., 1983-84. Capt. U.S. Army, 1960-65. Roman Catholic. Home: 1013 Heather Hill Ct Mc Lean VA 22101-2024 Office: Satellite Broadcasting & Comm Assn 225 Reinekers Ln Alexandria VA 22314-2875

PAUL, EVELYN ROSE, critical care nurse; b. New Bern, N.C., May 10, 1953; d. Robert Austin and Sadie Marie (Simpson) P. BSN, U. N.C., 1975. Cert. critical care nurse, ACLS. Staff nurse Beaufort County Hosp., Washington, N.C., 1975-79; chief nurse, nurse clinician, staff nurse surg. ICU Med. U. S.C., Charleston, 1979-85; staff/charge nurse cardiac surgery Pitt County Meml. Hosp., Greenville, N.C., 1985-89, asst. nurse mgr. cardiac surgery, 1989-95, RN IV, 1995—. Mem. AACN (pres. elect Heart of the East chpt. 1991-92).

PAUL, GABRIEL (GABE PAUL), former professional baseball club executive; b. Rochester, N.Y., Jan. 4, 1910; s. Morris and Celia (Snyder) P.; m. Mary Frances Copps, Apr. 17, 1939; children: Gabriel, Warren, Michael, Jennie Lou, Henry. Ed. pub. schs., Rochester. Reporter Rochester Democrat and Chronicle, 1926-28; publicity mgr., ticket mgr. Rochester Baseball Club, 1928-34, traveling sec., dir., 1934-36; publicity dir. Cin. Reds Baseball Club, 1937, traveling sec., 1938-50, asst. to pres., 1948-49, v.p., 1949-60, gen. mgr., 1951-60, v.p., 1949-60; v.p., gen. mgr. Houston Astros Baseball Club, 1960-61; gen. mgr. Cleve. Indians Baseball Club, 1961-63, pres., treas., 1963-72, pres., 1978-84; pres. N.Y. Yankees, 1973-77, ret., 1984. Dir. or trustee various charitable instns. Served with inf. AUS, 1943-45. Named Major League Exec. of Yr. Sporting News, 1956, 74, Sports Exec. of Yr. Gen. Sports Time, 1956, Exec. of Yr., Braves 400 Club, 1974, Baseball Exec. Yr., Milw. Baseball Writers, 1976, Major League Exec. of Yr. UPI, 1976; recipient J. Lewis Comiskey Meml. award Chgo. chpt. Baseball Writers Assn. Am., 1961, Judge Emil Fuchs Meml. award Boston chpt., 1967, Bill Slocum award N.Y. chpt., 1975, Sports Torch of Learning award, 1976; named to Ohio Baseball Hall of Fame, 1980. Clubs: Palma Ceia Country (Tampa, Fla.), Centre Club (Tampa).

PAUL, JO ANN, management consultant; b. Great Falls, S.C., Jan. 8, 1947; d. John W. and Annie Laura (Knopf) Jones; m. Thomas Jay Paul, June 18, 1966; children: Andrea Alisa Paul Borer, Thomas Larry. BS, BA, Kennesaw State U., 1981; MBA, Brenau U., 1990. Bus. instr., placement counselor Branell Coll., Atlanta, 1979-85; acctg. supr. Sewell Plastics, Atlanta, 1983; dir. Accountants USA, Atlanta, 1985; software cons. Exec. Data, Atlanta, 1986-87; acctg./pers. mgr. Finish IT, Atlanta, 1987-88; dept. chair bus./acctg. Phillips Jr. Coll., Atlanta, 1988-90; bus. instr., personnel adminstr. Acctg. Benefits Chattahoochee Inst. Tech., Marietta, Ga., 1988-92; bus. adminstr. instr. Ala. So. Coll., Monroeville, 1992-93; cons., svc. auditor Acworth, Ga., 1995-96; internat. program officer Investment Tng. Inst.-Nash, Inc., Tucker, Ga., 1996—. Vol. WSB-Consumer Action Ctr., Atlanta, 1995; v.p. PTSA, Acworth, 1983-84; host family Youth for Understanding, Ga., 1983-84; acctg. adv. bd. mem. Chattahoochee Inst. Tech., 1990-92. Ala. So. Coll. fellow, 1993. Home: 3741 Laurel Dr Acworth GA 30101

PAUL, JOSEPH B., customer service administrator, desktop publisher; b. Bklyn., Jan. 21, 1961; s. Samuel and Ruth (Bassin) P.; m. Rose Jacklyn Futterman, Apr. 1, 1984. BS in Computer Sci., CUNY, S.I., 1983; MBA, Nova U., 1988. Computer programmer Office of Mgmt. and Budget, N.Y.C., 1981-83; programmer, analyst Harris Corp., Melbourne, Fla., 1983-84; sr. analyst AT&T, Maitland, Fla., 1984-85; project leader Fla. Power and Light, Miami, 1985-90; project mgr. S.E. Toyota Distbr., Deerfield Beach, Fla., 1990-93; dir. customer svcs. Data Net Corp., Miramar, Fla., 1993-95; v.p. PC support Citizens Fed. Bank, Ft. Lauderdale, Fla., 1995—; pres. S.E. Area Focus Users Group, Miami, 1986-89, Co-Log Users Group, Miramar, 1993-94. Mem. agy. rels. sub-com. United Way South Fla., Miami, 1988-90; pres. Archtl. Control Com., Sunrise, Fla., 1991-93. Mem. Am. Mgmt. Assn., Am. Mktg. Assn., Toastmasters, Tau Alpha Pi (pres. 1982-83). Republican. Jewish. Home: 13120 NW 11th Dr Sunrise FL 33323-2951 Office: Citizens Fed Bank 1100 W Mcnab Rd Fort Lauderdale FL 33309-1116

PAUL, THOMAS DANIEL, lawyer; b. Butte, Mont., June 10, 1948; s. Thomas Anthony and Helen (O'Brien) P.; m. Carolyn Hicks, Dec. 20, 1976; children: Thomas Richard, Jennifer Ann. AB, Carroll Coll., 1970; MS, Ind. U., 1975, PhD, 1977; JD, U. Houston, 1987. Diplomate Am. Bd. Med. Genetics. Asst. prof. SUNY, Buffalo, 1977-84; assoc. Fulbright & Jaworski, Houston, 1987-90, participating assoc., 1990-94, ptnr., 1994—; staff cons. N.Y. State Dept. Mental Hygeine, Perrysburg, 1978-84. Contbr. articles to profl. jours. Named to Order of Coif U. Houston, 1987. Mem. Am. Soc. Human Genetics, Tex. Bar Assn., Houston Bar Assn., Am. Intellectual Property Law Assn., Houston Intellectual Property Law Assn. Home: 11803 Fidelia Ct Houston TX 77024-7112 Office: Fulbright & Jaworski 1301 Mckinney St Ste 5100 Houston TX 77010

PAULEY, STANLEY FRANK, manufacturing company executive; b. Winnipeg, Man., Can., Sept. 19, 1927; came to U.S., 1954, naturalized, 1961; s. Daniel and Anna (Tache) P.; m. Dorothy Ann Ruppel, Aug. 21, 1949; children: Katharine Ann, Lorna Jane. B.E.E., U. Man., 1949. With Canadian Industries Ltd., Kingston, Ont., 1949-53; sr. engring. asst. Canadian Industries Ltd., 1952-53; controls designer Standard Machine and Tool Co. Ltd., Windsor, Ont., 1953-54; prodn. supt. E.R. Carpenter Co., Richmond, Va., 1954-57, pres., 1957-83, chmn., CEO, 1983-94; chmn., CEO, Carpenter Co. (formerly E.R. Carpenter Co.), Richmond, 1994—, also bd. dirs.; bd. dirs. Carpenter Co. of Can., Carpenter de Mexico, Carpenter Plc., Carpenter S.a., Am. Filtrona Corp., Carpenter Gmbh, Mentor Portfolio Fund. Trustee U. richmond, Hampden-Sydney Coll., Va. Mus. Found., Va. Mus. Fine Arts, Va. Higher Edn. Tuition Trust Fund. Mem. Commonwealth Club, Forum Club, Country Club of Va. Republican. Presbyterian. Home: 314 St Davids Ln Richmond VA 23221-3708 Office: Carpenter Co 5016 Monument Ave Richmond VA 23230-3620

PAU-LLOSA, RICARDO MANUEL, English language educator, poet, art critic, curator; b. Havana, Cuba, May 17, 1954; came to U.S., 1960; s. Ricardo Juan and Maria Clotilde (Llosa) Pau. BA in English, Fla. Internat. U., 1974; MA in English, Fla. Atlantic U., 1976; postgrad., U. Fla., 1978-83. Prof. English, Kendall Campus, Miami (Fla.)-Dade C.C., 1985—; lectr. art Art Inst. Chgo., High Mus. Art, Atlanta, Nat. Libr., Ottawa, Ont., Can., Centro Cultural La Recoleta, Buenos Aires, Mus. Contemporary Art de Caracas Sofia Imber, Cornell U., Bklyn. Mus., Meadows Mus., Dallas, U. Chgo., McGill U., Montreal, Que., Can., Nat. Libr. Buenos Aires, Fundacion Proscenio, Buenos Aires, Engleman-Ost Found., Montevideo, Uruguay, also others; numerous poetry readiings; past mem. internat. art jury, includng Mus. Modern Art, Rio de Janeiro, 1992. Author: (poetry) Sorting Metaphors, 1983 (1st Anhinga Poetry prize), Bread of the Imagined, 1992, Cuba, 1993, (art criticism) Dirube, 1979, Rogelio Polesello, 1984, (with Frank Trapp and Douglas Dreishpoon) Clarence Holbrook Carter, 1989 Humberto Calzada, 1991, (with Mario Vargas Llosa and Ana Maria Escallon) Fernando de Szyszlo, 1991; contbg. author: Dictionary of Art, 1996; sr. and contbg. editor Art Internat., Lugano Switzerland and Paris, 1983-91; co-editor (catalogue) Outside Cuba/Fuera de Cuba, 1989; contbr. poems to anthologies, fiction to mags. and anthologies, art criticism to numerous art mags. Office: Miami-Dade CC Dept English Kendall Campus 11011 SW 104th St Miami FL 33176-3330

PAULSEN, DARLYNE EVELYN, artist, interior decorator; b. Delaplaine, Ark., Feb. 16, 1936; d. Chacy Rudolph Sr. and Mary Edith (Rice) Eveland; m. Henry Stevens Paulsen, Feb. 22, 1960 (div. 1969); children: Sherry Lee, Pamela Fay; m. William Edgar Maddox Jr., 1989. BFA in Art, Ark. State U., 1968; BSE, U. Ark., Little Rock, 1970. Systems analyst, acct. Wurlitzer Co., DeKalb, Ill., 1954-63; acct. Eugene Stifani CPA, DeKalb, 1957; secondary art and drama instr. Westside High Sch., Jonesboro, Ark., 1968-69; secondary art instr. Poplar Bluff Pub. Schs., Poplar Bluff, Mo., 1969-70; owner, mgr. Paulsen Studios, N. Little Rock, Ark., 1970—; art supr. and instructional specialist Pulaski County Spl. Sch. Dist., Little Rock, 1970-79; office mgr., acct. Hardy L. Gage Co., Wichita Falls, Tex., 1980-84; computer acct. Gen. Properties, N. Little Rock, 1984-85; office mgr., acctg. supr. Carrier AR (br. UTC), Little Rock, 1985-86; guest lectr. U. Mex., Mexico City, 1973; producer, dir. 3 theatre prodn., WHS, Ark. State U., Jonesboro, Ark., 1968-69; mem. panel com. leading art educators in U.S., 1975; lectr. in field. Editor, co-author: Art in Secondary Schools Curriculum Guide for Pulaski County School District, 1977. Coord., hostess Ark. Annual Arts Patron's Christmas Ball, Little Rock, 1971-79; Ark. state com. chmn. Gifted and Talented Children, Little Rock, 1978-79; decorator Ark. Gov.'s Inaugural Ball, Little Rock, 1979; mem. Nat. Mus. for Women of the Art, Washington, 1988; affiliate Lahaima Art Gallery, Michael Angelo Gallery, Tex. Art Gallery, Roughton Galleries, Jay Hudson Gallery. Recipient cert. of recognition Gov. Clinton, Ark., 1989; NEA grantee, 1973. Mem. Ark. Art Edn. Assn. (treas. 1972-76), Nat. Art Edn. Assn. (v.p. Ark. chpt. 1969, workshop instr. 1973-75, Ark. voter rep. nat. level 1975), Ark. Alliance for the Arts. (chmn. constitution & legis.), Kappa Pi (sec. 1967-68), Beta Sigma Phi (Valentine Queen Wichita Falls, Tex. 1981). Home and Office: 3619 Lakeview Rd North Little Rock AR 72116-9022

PAULSEN, JAMES WALTER, law educator; b. Eau Claire, Wis., Feb. 17, 1954; s. Walter Henry and Doris Antoinette (Babington) P.; m. Robin Russell, Apr. 23, 1988. BFA, Tex. Christian U., 1976; JD, Baylor U., 1984.; LLM, Harvard U., 1992. Bar: Tex. 1984, U.S. Dist. Ct. (no. dist.) Tex. 1985, U.S. Dist. Ct. (so. dist.) Tex. 1986, U.S. Ct. Appeals (5th cir.) 1985. Asst. debate coach U. Utah, Salt Lake City, 1976-78; acting debate coach Brigham Young U., Provo, Utah, 1978-79; briefing atty. Supreme Ct. Tex., Austin, 1984-85; assoc. Liddell, Sapp, Zivley, Hill & LaBoon, Houston, 1985-91; assoc. prof. law South Tex. Coll. Law, Houston, 1992—. Editor-in-chief Baylor Law Rev., 1984; contbr. articles to legal jours. Mem. ABA, State Bar Tex. (vice chmn. legal svcs. com. 1987-88, 90-91), Tex. Bar Found., Tex. Assn. Bank Counsel (bd. dirs. 1990-93), Houston Bar Assn., Houston Vol. Lawyers Assn., Tex. State Hist. Assn., Nat. Order Barristers. Lutheran. Home: 2815 Wroxton Rd Houston TX 77005-4022

PAULSEN, SUSAN CAROL, health company executive; b. Hammond, Ind., Sept. 20, 1947; d. Thorwell Hoes and Margaret (Carroll) P.; children: Blake Barrett Denney, Wyatt Cole Denney. BSEd, U. Ga., 1969; BSN, U. Tex., Houston, 1981. RN, Tex., La.; cert. case mgr., cert. profl. in healthcare quality. Elem. tchr. Coweta County Bd. Edn., Houston, 1969-73; staff nurse St. Luke's Episcopal Hosp., Houston, 1981-87; head nurse orthopedics dept. U. Tex. Med. Sch., Houston, 1987-89; mgr. managed care Hermann Hosp., Houston, 1989-93; mgr. quality assurance Cigna Healthcare, Baton Rouge, 1993-95; dir. quality and risk mgmt. Gulf South Health Plans, Baton Rouge, 1995—. Mem. NAFE, Sigma Theta Tau. Republican. Presbyterian. Office: Gulf South Health Plans 5615 Corporate Dr Baton Rouge LA 70806

PAULY, THOMAS HOWARD, neonatologist; b. Covington, Ky., July 29, 1948; s. Howard Alfred and Marian (Frauxman) P.; m. Julie Kathleen Sullivan, Aug. 11, 1990; children: Allison, MacKenzie, Samuel Brown. BS in Chemistry, U. Ky., 1970, MD, 1974. Diplomate Am. Bd. Pediats., Nat. Bd. Med. Examiners, sub-bd. neonatal-perinatal medicine. Intern in pediatrics U. Ky. A.B. Chandler Med. Ctr., Lexington, 1974-75, resident, 1975-76, fellow in neonatal perinatal medicine, 1976-78; asst. clin. prof. U. Ky. Coll. Medicine, Lexington, 1978-84, asst. prof. pediatrics, 1986-91, assoc. prof., 1991—, chief divsn. neonatology, 1992—; assoc. clin. prof. W.Va. U. Coll. Medicine, Charleston, 1984-86; dir. neonatal intensive care svcs. U. Ky. Med. Ctr., 1992—, attending physician, 1986—; cons. staff Ctrl. Bapt. Hosp., Lexington, 1986—, Humana Hosp., Lexington, 1986—; dir. neonatal intensive care svcs. Charleston (W.Va.) Area Med. Ctr., 1985; dir. neonatal intensive care svcs. Ctrl. Bapt. Hosp., 1978-84, Good Samaritan Hosp., Lexington, 1978-84; pvt. pracitce, Lexington, 1978-84; mem. speakers bur. Burroughs-Wellcome Found., 1989—; dir. neonatal transport program U. Ky., 1986—. Reviewer: Pediatric Rsch., Am. Jour. Med. Scis.; contbr. articles to profl. jours. Bd. dirs. Lexington Dream Factory, 1988—; chmn. profl. adv. com. Bluegrass chpt. March of Dimes, 1987—. Grantee Commonwealth of Ky., 1993-94, Am. Heart Assn., 1990-91, 89-90, 88-89, Burroughs Wellcome Co., 1988—, Am. Lung Assn., 1987-88, others. Fellow Am. Acad. Pediatrics; mem. So. Soc. for Pediatric Rsch. (rsch. coun. 1990-92, instnl. rep. 1988—), Am. Heart Assn. (coun. on cardiovascular disease in the young), Ky. Pediatric Soc. (exec. com. 1989—), Ky. Perinatal Assn. (chmn. edn. com. 1988-91, v.p. 1988-91, pres. 1991-93), Nat. Perinatal Assn., Soc. for Pediatric Rsch., Am. Thoracic Soc., Phi Theta Kappa. Office: U Ky Med Ctr Dept Pediatric 800 Rose St # 472B Lexington KY 40536-0001

PAVEL, ELMER LEWIS, corporate executive, consultant; b. Bee, Nebr., Mar. 30, 1918; s. James Joseph and Mary Wilma (Barcal) P.; m. Georgia Marie Kolar, Jan. 30, 1946 (dec. Feb. 1993); children: Stephen Kent, Sharon Kay Pavel Conklin. Student, Barnes Sch. of Commerce, Denver, 1937-38, U. Denver, 1946-50. Asst. mgr. Denver Conv. and Visitors Bur., 1946-50; mgr. Ft. Wayne (Ind.) Conv. Bur., 1950-52; exec. sec., mgr. Des Moines Conv. Bur., 1952-57; mgr. conv. and visitors bur. Kansas City, Mo., 1957-66; exec. v.p., sec., treas. Conv. and Tourist Coun. Greater Kansas City, 1966-72; nat. conv. mgr. ANA, Kansas City, 1972-77; cons. Midwest Rsch. Inst., Kansas City, 1974-77; exec. dir. Orlando (Fla.) Conv. and Visitors Bur., 1977-79, Orlando/Orange County Conv. and Visitors Bur., 1977-81; pres., cons. Pavel & Assocs., Longwood, Fla., 1981—; instr. Nat. Inst. for Orgn. Mgmt., East Lansing, Mich., 1956-57. Mem. editl. adv. bd. Exhibits Mag., 1977-82; contbr. numerous articles to profl. jours. Mem. conv. planning com. Future Farmers Am., 1957-72; mem. Green-up Orlando com., 1985, 87—, Right-of-Way Beautification, 1985, 87—; sec. mcpl. auditorium adv. bd., Kansas City, 1957-72, organizer auditorium expansion com., 1986, expansion site com., 1968-70, expansion criteria com., 1969-71; mem. Orange County Tourist Devel. com., Orlando, 1977, adv. coun., 1977-82; vol. tourism cons. Internat. Exec. Svc., Keszthely, Hungary, 1991. Served to maj. USAAF, 1941-46, navigator, bombardier SWPA. Decorated Silver Star. Mem. Fla. Ctr. Resort Area Assn. (exec. dir. 1983-89), Am. Soc. Assn. Execs., Internat. Assn. Conv. Visitors Bur. (hon., pres. 1966-67), Air Force Assn., 38th Bomb Group Assn. (life, editor The Sunsetters), Mid Am. Soc. Health Execs. (organizer 1967), Rotary Internat. Office: Pavel & Assocs 5055 W Panther Creek Dr Spring TX 77381-3544

PAVLICK, CHARLES RALEIGH, architect, engineer, retired air force officer; b. Chgo., Mar. 28, 1918; s. Charles Harry and Myrtle Mildred (von Meyenberg) P.; m. Hilda Fay VanDeinse, Feb. 8, 1945; children: Ann, Charles, Elizabeth, James. Student, Deforrests Electronics Sch., Chgo. Art Inst., Chgo. Acad. Fine Arts, Air War Coll., Ohio State U. Joined USAAF, 1937; advanced through grades to col. USAF, 1968; served in WWII, Korea, Vietnam, USAAF and USAF; supervising arch.-engr. D.C. Dept. Pub. Works, Washington, 1968-93; owner, pres. Pavlick-Restordance, Alexandria, Va., 1993—; ret., 1968; cons. Met. Washington rea. Decorated Bronze Star, Air medal. mem. NRA, Mil. Order Purple Heart, Ret. Officers Assn., Navy Tailhood Assn., Air Force Assn., Am. Legion, Navy League, U.s. Naval Sailing Assn., Inst. Legis. Affairs, Naval Inst., USCG Aux., Brotherood of

St. Andrew. Republican. Episcopalian. Home and Office: 326 N Royal St Alexandria VA 22314

PAVLICK, PAMELA KAY, nurse, consultant; b. Topeka, Aug. 16, 1944; d. Cy Pavlick and June Lucille (Arnold) (dec.) Dull. Diploma nursing, St. Luke's Hosp., Kansas City, Mo., 1966; BA in Psychology magna cum laude, U. North Fla., 1982, MS in Health Adminstrn. summa cum laude, 1987. RN, Mo., Ill., Fla.; cert. ins. rehab. specialist; lic. rehab. providor, Fla. Clin. instr. St. Luke's Hosp., Kansas City, 1966-70; instr. lic. practical nursing Springfield (Ill.) Sch. Bd., 1970-72; nursing supr. Jacksonville Beach (Fla.) Hosp., 1972-74; pub. health nurse State of Fla., Ocala, 1974-76; dir. nursing Upjohn Health Care, Jacksonville, Fla., 1976-77, mem. adv. com.; med. rep. Travelers Ins. Co., Jacksonville, 1977-84; rehab. cons. Aetna Life & Casualty, Jacksonville, 1985—, rep. nurse cons. adv. coun., 1988-90. Mem. Am. Nurses Assn., Am. Assn. Rehab. Nurses, Nat. Assn. Rehab. Providers, Phi Kappa Phi. Republican. Episcopalian. Home: 14023 Tontine Rd Jacksonville FL 32225-2025 Office: Aetna Life & Casualty PO Box 2200 Jacksonville FL 32203-2200

PAWLYSHYN, WILLIAM JOHN, nurse; b. N.Y.C., Mar. 3, 1949; s. Methodius Joseph and Anne Pawlyshyn; m. Joyce Anne Cottle, May 1979. BSN, Old Dominion U., 1979; MS, Columbia Pacific U., 1992; M in Nursing, Mont. State U., 1994. RN; cert. BCLS instr.-trainer, ACLS provider. Staff nurse DePaul Hosp., Norfolk, Va., 1980-81, Chesapeake (Va.) Gen. Hosp., 1981-83; staff, acting clin. nurse supr. Chesapeake Health Dept., 1981-83; staff, asst. head nurse Brooke Army Med. Ctr., 1983-86; asst. head nurse 2d Gen. Hosp., 1986-89; LPN instr. Fitzsimons Army Med. Ctr., 1989-93; head nurse Coscom Med. Clinic, Ft. Bragg, 1994; head nurse Acute Care Ware Team ALPHA 5th Mobile Army Surg. Hosp., Ft. Bragg, N.C., 1994—; mem. internal rev. com. Nursing Edn. Svc. divsn. Womack Army Med. Ctr., Ft. Bragg, 1995—; mem. emergency cardiac care com. Chesapeake Gen. Hosp., 1982-83; refuge health care Chesapeake Health Dept., 1981-83; mem. quality assurance com. Brooke Army Med. Ctr., Ft. Sam Houston, Tex., 1983-86, mem. jour. rsch. com., 1984-86; mem. quality circle com. 2d Gen. Hosp., Landstuhl, Fed. Republic Germany, 1986-89. Dist. supr. Chesapeake Vol. Fire and REscue, 1982-83; jr. officers coun. 2d Gen. Hosp., U.S. Army, 1987-89; vol. ARC, Norfolk, 1981. With USN, 1969-75; maj. Nurse Corps, U.S. Army, 1983—. Mem. Am. Assn. Neurosci. Nurses, Assn. Mil. Surgeons of the U.S. Republican. Mem. Assembly of God.

PAXTON, J. WILLENE, retired university counseling director; b. Birmingham, Ala., Oct. 30, 1930; d. Will and Elizabeth (Davis) P. AB, Birmingham So. Coll., 1950; MA, Mich. State U., 1951; EdD, Ind. U., 1971. Nat. cert. counselor, lic. profl. counselor, Tenn. Dormitory dir. Tex. Tech U., Lubbock, 1951-53; counselor Mich. State U., East Lansing, summer 1951, 52; dir. univ. ctr. and housing SUNY, Fredonia, 1953-56, assoc. dean of students, 1956-57; asst. dean of women U. N.Mex., Albuquerque, 1957-63; dean of women East Tenn. State U., Johnson City, 1963-68, 70-78, dir. counseling ctr., 1978-92; ret., 1993. Sec. adminstrv. bd. Meth. Ch., 1983-86, vice chmn., 1993, chmn., 1994—, chmn. social concerns com., 1991-93, program chmn. Good Timers fellowship, 1994-95, pres. Sunday Sch. class, 1994, chmn. fin. campaign, 1995, chair promotion and publicity, bldg. com., 1996—, chair scholarship com., chair promotion and publicity sub-com. bldg. campaign, 1996—; tng. dir. Contact Teleministries, Inc., 1983-87, chmn., 1988, 95, vice chmn., 1993-95; bd. dirs. Asbury Cts., 1990—, policy com., 1991—, chmn. policy com., 1995-96, mem. fin. com., 1996. Mem. APA, AAUW (br. pres., mem. nominating com. 1993-96, fin. com. 1996), Am. Counseling Assn., Tenn. Psychol. Assn., Assn. Univ. and Coll. Counseling Ctr. Dirs. (conv. planning com. 1991), Am. Coll. Pers. Assn. (media bd., newsletter editor), Nat. Assn. Women Deans, Adminstrs. and Counselors, Tenn. Assn. Women Deans and Counselors (state pres., v.p., program chmn.), East Tenn. Edn. Assn. (chmn. guidance divsn.), East Tenn. State U. Retirees Assn. (bd. dirs. 1993—, program com. 1993—, chair program com. 1996, pres.-elect 1996), Gen. Federated Woman's Club (pres. 1980-81, 88-89, 95-96, 2d v.p. 1991-95), Univ. Women's Club (v.p. 1993-94, pres. 1994, 95), Delta Kappa Gamma (chpt. pres. 1974-76, state rec. sec. 1977-79, v.p. 1979-81, chmn. nominating com. 1981-83, internat. rsch. com. 1982-84, chmn. leadership devel. com. 1983-85, chmn. self-study com. 1985-87, com. to study exec. sec. 1987-89, state pres. 1989-91, parliamentarian 1991-93, internat. constn. com. 1992-94, awards com. 1993-95, chmn. internat. conv. meal functions com. 1994, state pers. com. 1995—, state achievement award 1987). Home: 1203 Lester Harris Rd Johnson City TN 37601-3335

PAXTON, JUANITA WILLENE, retired university official; b. Birmingham, Ala.; d. Will and Elizabeth (Davis) P. AB, Birmingham So. Coll., 1950; MA, Mich. State U., 1951; EdD, Ind. U., 1971; postgrad., U. Tex., summer 1965. Dormitory dir. Tex. Tech U., Lubbock, 1951-53; counselor Mich. State U., East Lansing, summer 1951; dir. univ. ctr. and housing SUNY, Fredonia, 1953-56, assoc. dean of students, 1956-57; asst. dean of women U. N.Mex., Albuquerque, 1957-63; dean of women East Tenn. State U., Johnson City, 1963-68, 70-78, dir. Counseling Ctr., 1978-93; tng. dir. CONTACT Teleministries, Tenn., 1984-92, chmn. bd. dirs., 1986, 95. Chmn. social concerns Munsey United Meth. Ch., 1989-92, sec. adminstrv. bd., 1980-84, vice chairperson, 1993, chair, 1994, mem. coun. on ministries, 1980-94, chair stewardship campaign, 1995, chair promotion and publicity subcom. building campaign, 1996—, chair scholarship com. U.S. Ednl. Profl. Devel. Act grantee, 1968-69. Mem. Am. Coll. Pers. Assn. (mem. media com. 1977-79, newsletter editor com. XVI 1977-79), Asbury Retirement Ctrs. Tenn. and Va. (bd. dirs. 1991-96, policy com. 1991-96, chair 1995-96, mem. fin. com. 1996, mem. nomination com. 1994-96), Univ. Women's Club (pres. 1994-96), Tenn. Coll. Pers. Assn. (legis. chair 1974), Tenn. Assn. Women Deans Counselors (pres. 1966-68), Monday Club Aux. (pres. 1980-81, 88-89, 95-96, v.p. 1993-95, corr. sec. 1979-80), Watauga Pers. and Guild Assn. (pres.-elect 1967-68, chair ETEA guidance divsn. 1968, pres. AAUW br. 1967), Delta Kappa Gamma Soc. Internat. (internat. chair rules com. 1992, mem. exec. bd. 1989-91, internat. rsch. com. 1982-84, constn. com. 1992-94, state rec. sec. 1975-77, v.p. 1977-79, state pres. 1989-91, chpt. pres. 1982-84, State Achievement award 1987, chair nominating com. 1983-85, chair ad hoc com. to study feasibility exec. sec. 1987-89, mem. pers. com. 1995-97), E. Tenn. State U. Retiree's Assn. (bd. dirs. 1993, program com. 1994-95, pres.-elect 1996, others).

PAXTON, RALPH, biochemist; b. Cin., Aug. 10, 1950; s. Herbert and Venice (Patrick) P.; m. Martha W. Wilder, Sept. 7, 1974; 1 child, Hannah K. BS, Miami U., Oxford, Ohio, 1972; PhD, U. Cin., 1980. Teaching asst. U. Cin., 1974-80; instr. No. Ky. State U., Highland, 1976-77; rsch. assoc. Ind. U. Sch. Medicine, Indpls., 1981-84; asst. prof. dept. biochemistry Ind. U., Indpls., 1984-86; asst. prof. dept. biol. sci. Tex. Tech U., Lubbock, 1986-88, assoc. prof., 1989; asst. prof. dept. biochemistry Tex. Tech U. Med. Sch., Lubbock, 1987-89; assoc. prof. dept. physiology & pharmacology Auburn (Ala.) U., 1989—; vis. scientist Free U., Brussels, Belgium, 1985. Assoc. editor: Jour. Experimental Zoology; scientific reviewer: Am. Jour. Vet. Rsch. Bd. dirs. Am. Heart Assn., Lubbock, 1988; mem. Cen. Rsch. Rev. Com., Tex., 1989, Ala., 1990; mem. adv. panel physiol. & behavior NSF; mem. adv. panel Res. Plan Grants & Career Adv. Awards for Women Scientists. With U.S. Army, 1972-74. Grantee Am. Diabetes Assn., 1985, NIH, 1987, Scott-Ritchey Found., 1990; recipient Grant-in-Aid, Am. Heart Assn., 1986; established investigator Am. Heart Assn. Mem. Am. Heart Assn., Am. Physiology Soc., Am. Soc. for Biochem. & Molecular Biology, Am. Soc. Zoologists, Sigma Xi. Home: 2087 Evergreen Dr Auburn AL 36830-6942 Office: Auburn U Coll Vet Medicine Dept Physiology Auburn AL 36849

PAYNE, ALMA JEANETTE, English language educator, author; b. Highland Park, Ill., Oct. 28, 1918; d. Frederick Hutton and Ruth Ann (Colle) P. BA, Wooster (Ohio) Coll., 1940; MA, Case Western Res. U., 1941, PhD, 1956. Tchr. English, history, Latin Ohio Pub. Schs., Bucyrus and Canton, 1941-46; from instr. to prof. English and Am. studies Bowling Green (Ohio) State U., 1946-79, dir. Am. studies program, 1957-79, chair Am. culture PhD program, 1978-79, prof. emerita English, Am. studies, 1979—; adj. prof. Am. studies U. South Fla., 1982—. Author: Critical Bibliography of Louisa May Alcott, 1980, Discovering the American Nations, 1981; contbr. articles to profl. jours.; editor Nat. Am. Studies Assn. Newsletter; contbr. articles to profl. jours. Nat. Coun. for Innovation in Edn. grantee, Norway, U.S. Embassy and Norwegian Dept. Ch. and State, 1978-79; recipient MAry Turpie award in Am. studies, 1996. Mem. AAUW (pres. 1982-84), Soc. Mayflower Descs in Fla. (state treas. 1985), Nat. Am. Studies Assn. (v.p. 1977-79), Zonta, Phi Beta Kappa, Phi Kappa Phi, Kappa Delta Pi, Alpha Lambda Delta. Republican. Presbyterian. Home and Office: 11077 Orangewood Dr Bonita Springs FL 34135-5720

PAYNE, CHRISTINE BABCOCK, career psychologist; b. Junction City, Kans., Jan. 14, 1943; d. David Edward and Dorothy (Viner) Babcock; m. James R. Payne, Oct. 16, 1982; children: Terrence Thomas, Melanie Payne Tate. AA, Stephens Coll., 1963; BA, Parsons Coll., 1966; MS, Calif. Coast U., 1993, postgrad., 1993—. Tchr. Page-Park Sch., St. Louis, 1966-68; assoc. buyer Famous-Barr Dept. Store, St. Louis, 1968-70; pers. asst. Gimbel's Dept. Store, N.Y.C., 1970-71; tng. dir. Gimbel's East, N.Y.C., 1971-72; employment mgr. Hosp. for Spl. Surgery, N.Y.C., 1972-73; pers. dir. J.B. Ivey & Co., Orlando, Fla., 1973-75; dir. employer rels. Okla. Employment Security Commn., Tulsa, 1980-84; pers. dir. Sanger-Harris Dept. Store, Tulsa, 1982; dir. career devel. Women's Ctr. U. Tulsa, 1988-93; pres., owner Transitions Counseling Ctr., Tulsa, 1992—; counseling dir. career and ednl. svcs. Resonance Ctr. for Women, Tulsa, 1993; coord. dislocated worker program Ctrl. Okla. Vo-Tech Sch., Drumright, 1984-86. Author: Tearing Down the Walls: An Adult Woman's Guide to Education and Financial Aid, 1993. Speech writer State Senator Ted V. Fisher, Okla., 1986; pres. Vol. Svc. Coun., St. Louis, 1975-79. Recipient Mayor's Pinnacle award for Outstanding Contbn. in Area of Edn., Mayor's Commn. on Status of Women, Tulsa, 1993. Mem. ACA, NAFE, Nat. Career Devel. Assn., Nat. Assn. Fin. Aid Adminstrs., Adult Career Devel. Network, Assn. for Measurement Evaluation in Counseling Devel. Office: Transitions Counseling Ctr 4853 S Sheridan Ste 606 Tulsa OK 74145

PAYNE, DAVID GORDON, marketing professional; b. Detroit, Dec. 10, 1951; s. William B. and Natalie (Sunday) P.; m. Lucia A. Biondo, Jul. 18, 1951; children: David G., Melissa A. BA in advt., Mich. State Univ., 1974. Sales rep. H.J. Heinz, Detroit, 1974-76; product mgr. Kendall Healthcare, Mansfield, Mass., 1977-90; v.p. mktg. EnvironMed Internat., Tampa, Fla., 1991-92; dir. mktg. Fashion Seal Uniforms, Seminola, Fla., 1993—. Inventor Barrier Challenge Device, 1996. Named Ky. Col., State of Ky. Mem. Am. Soc. Testing and Materials, Assn. Advancement of Medical Instrumentation. Office: Fashion Seal Uniforms 10099 Seminole Blvd Seminole FL 33772

PAYNE, EMILY MILLER, reading educator, literacy consultant; b. Alpine, Tex., May 5, 1948; d. Laurie Guthrie and Maribel (Wooley) Miller; m. Dennis Tilden, Jan. 11, 1975; 1 child, Spencer Reed Miller-Payne. BA in English, U. Tex., 1970; MAT in Reading, N.Mex. State U., 1978, EdD in Reading, 1984. Cert. K-12 tchr., Tex., N.Mex. Instr./tutor Project Hope Wayne C.C., Goldsboro, N.C., 1972-75; heavy equip. op. Amax Potash Mine, Carlsbad, N.Mex., summer 1975; learning assistance ctr. tutor N.Mex. State U., Las Cruces, 1978-79; instr. Austin (Tex.) C.C., 1980-82; reading specialist Austin Ind. Sch. Dist., 1982-85; edn. coord. State Property Tax Bd., Austin, 1985-88; asst. prof. S.W. Tex. State U., San Marcos, 1988—; cons. Adult Edn. Profl. Devel. and Curriculum Consortium, Tex., 1991—, Performance Measures Task Force in Literacy, Austin, 1994—; team mem. So. Assn. Evaluation, Lockhart, Tex., 1993. Mem. editl. bd. Tex. Rschr., 1991—; contbr. articles to profl. jours. Mem. Dem. Party, Tex., 1975—, Tex. Abortion Rights League, 1990—. Recipient Cert. of Recognition for contbns. in human resource and devel. U.S. Office of Personnel Mgmt., 1987. Mem. Internat. Reading Assn., Nat. Assn. Devel. Edn. Procs. (co-chair 1993, 94, rsch. adv. 1992—), Coll. Reading and Learning Assn., Phi Kappa Phi. Home: 11 Matador Cir Austin TX 78746 Office: SW Tex State Univ Edn Bldg 4004 San Marcos TX 78666

PAYNE, FOSTER PENNY, II, legislative staff member; b. Raleigh, N.C., Sept. 5, 1957; s. Foster P. and Sylvia E. (Walcott) P. BA in Polit. Sci. cum laude, Va. State U., 1979; MA in Mgmt., Webster U., 1981; postgrad., Command & Gen. Staff Coll., Leavenworth, Kans., 1991. From asst. ops. officer to military intelligence maj. assignment officer U.S. Army, 1983-93, lt. col. congl. liaison officer, 1993—; bd. dirs. Mentor Age Mag., Washington. Leadership Outreach Program mem. Rocks, Inc., Alexandria, Va., 1991—. Named Outstanding Young Man of Am., 1986. Mem. Ho. Legis. Assts. Assn., Omega Psi Phi (keeper of records and seal Omicron Pi chpt. 1984, pres. 1985-86, keeper of fin. Lambda Xi chpt 1988-90, Man of Yr. 1988). Home and Office: 7666 Wolford Way Lorton VA 22079 also: HHC 2ID Attn: G-2 Unit 15041 APO AP 02898 Office: B325 Rayburn House Office Bldg Washington DC 20515

PAYNE, FRED J., physician; b. Grand Forks, N.D., Oct. 14, 1922; s. Fred J. and Olive (Johnson) P.; m. Dorothy J. Peck, Dec. 20, 1948; children: Chris Ann Payne Graebner, Roy S., William F., Thomas A. Student U. N.D., 1940-42; BS, U. Pitts., 1948, MD, 1949; MPH, U. Calif., Berkeley, 1958. Diplomate Am. Bd. Preventive Medicine. Intern, St. Joseph's Hosp., Pitts., 1949-50; resident Charity Hosp., New Orleans, 1952-53; med. epidemiologist Ctr. Disease Control, Atlanta, 1953-60; prof. tropical medicine La. State U. Med. Ctr., New Orleans, 1961-66; dir. La. State U. Internat. Ctr. for Med. Rsch. and Tng., San Jose, Costa Rica, 1963-66; exec. sec. 3d Nat. Conf. on Pub. Health Tng., Washington, 1966-67; epidemiologist Nat. Nutrition Survey, Bethesda, Md., 1967-68; chief pub. health professions br. NIH, Bethesda, 1971-74, med. officer, sr. rsch. epidemiologist Nat. Inst. Allergy and Infectious Diseases, 1974-78; asst. health dir. Fairfax County (Va.) Health Dept., 1978-94, dir. HIV/AIDS case mgmt. program, 1988-94, cons. epidemiologist 1994—; med. advisor Ams. for Sound AIDS Policy, 1996—; clin. prof. La. State U., 1966-79; cons. NIH, 1979-81; leader WHO diarrheal disease adv. team, 1960. Contbr. articles to profl. jours. Served with AUS, 1942-46, 49-52. Decorated Combat Medic Badge. Fellow Am. Coll. Preventive Medicine, Am. Coll. Epidemiology; mem. AAAS, AMA, Am. Soc. Microbiology, Internat. Epidemiology Assn., Soc. Epidemiologic Rsch., USPHS Commd. Officers Assn., Sigma Xi. Home: 2945 Ft Lee St Herndon VA 22071-1813 Office: 102 Eldon St Herndon VA 22071

PAYNE, HARRY EUGENE, JR., state labor commissioner; b. Wilmington, Sept. 11, 1952; s. Harry E. and Margaret G. (Tucker) P.; m. Ruth Ann Sheehan, May 28, 1994; 1 child, Harry E., III. AB in Psychology and Polit. Sci., U. N.C., 1974; JD, Wake Forest U., 1977. Pvt. practice as lawyer; with Scott, Payne, Boyle & Swart, Wilmington; mem. N.C. Gen. Assembly, 1980-92; commr. labor N.C. Dept. Labor; co-chmn. adminstrv. rules rev. com. N.C. Gen. Assembly, 1983, chmn. mfrs. and labor com. 1985, chmn. constl. amendments com. 1987, chmn. rules, appointments and the calendar com. 1989, co-chmn. appropriations com. 1989, mem. subcom. edn. Active N.C. Small Bus. Adv. Coun.; mem. indsl. tech. adv. bd. East Carolina U.; mem. adv. bd. Z. Smith Reynolds Found., Shaw-Speaks Ctr.; chmn. credentials com. 7th dist. Dem. Conv., 1980; mem. State Dem. Exec. Com., 1993—, N.C. Commn. Indian Affairs, 1993—; chmn. literacy task force Gov.'s Commn.. Workforce Preparedness, 1993—; bd. dirs. N.C. Pub. Sch. Forum, Cmty. Penalties, N.C. Ctr. Pub. Policy Rsch. Recipient Right-To-Know award N.C. Occupl. Safety and Health, 1985, Award of Appreciation, Southeastern Sickle Cell Assn., 1985, Award of Appreciation, Wilmington C. of C., 1987, Friends of Labor award Am. Fedn. Labor-Congress Indsl. Orgns., 1987, Award of Appreciation, N.C. Speech & Hearing Assn., 1987-88, Cert. of Appreciation, Boys Club Am., 1988, Susan B. Anthony award New Hanover chpt. NOW, 1987, Legis. award N.C. chpt. Am. Planning Assn., 1988, Disting. Svc. award N.C. Pub. Health Assn., 1990; named Consumer Adv. of Yr., N.C. Consumer Coun., 1985, Outstanding Govt. Ofcl., Wilmington Jaycees, 1986, Boss of Yr. Battleship chpt. Am. Bus. Womens' Assn., 1988, Legislator of Yr., N.C. Acad. Trial Lawyers, 1989, Legislator of Yr., N.C. Assn. Deaf, 1989. Mem. Nat. Assn. Govtl. Labor Ofcls. (bd. dirs.), N.C. Bar Assn. (mem. dispute resolution com.), Southeastern Strategic Coun. Office: Labor Dept 4 W Edenton St Raleigh NC 27601-2805

PAYNE, JOHN HOWARD, university program director; b. Fukuoka, Japan, Aug. 13, 1951; came to U.S., 1951; s. John and Libby Lee (Small) P.; m. Elizabeth gigi Duis, Aug. 26, 1972; children: Nathan, Jessica. BS in Comm., U. No. Colo., 1974, MA in Ednl. Media, 1983. Audio/visual asst. U. No. Colo., Greeley, 1974-79, audio/visual dir., 1979-92; faculty AIMS C.C., Greeley, 1981-82; dir. ednl. and distance learning techs. U. Va., Charlottesville, 1993—; mem. adv. bd. Sta. WTJU-FM, Charlottesville. Writer, producer, dir. (video) Olgame, Olgame, 1991, Art and Community, 1989, The Turn of Our Century, 1989. Bd. dirs. Greeley Boys Club, 1974; loaned exec. Weld County United Way, Greeley, 1988; mktg. comm. Weld County United Way, Greeley, 1990; bd. dirs. United Way of Weld County, 1991, 92. Mem. Nat. Univ. Continuing Edn. Assn., Assn. Ednl. Comm. Technologists, Internat. TV Assn. (pres.-elect No. Colo. 1991-92, pres. No. Colo. 1992-93). Democrat. Home: 2822 Powell Creek Dr Charlottesville VA 22901-7401 Office: U Va 104 Midmont Ln Charlottesville VA 22903

PAYNE, LEWIS FRANKLIN, JR. (L.F. PAYNE), congressman; b. Amherst, Va., July 9, 1945; m. Susan King; children: Graham, Hunter, Sara, Anna. BA, Va. Mil. Inst., 1967; MBA, U. Va. Mem. 100th-104th Congresses from 5th Va. dist., Washington, 1988—. Democrat. Presbyterian. Office: US Ho of Reps 2412 Rayburn Washington DC 20515

PAYNE, LINDA CAROL, physiologist; b. Munford, Tenn., May 22, 1959; d. William Earl and Dorothy Ruth (Wynn) P.; 1 child, Lynette Lamb. BS in Biology, U. Tenn., Martin, 1981; PhD in Physiology and Biophysics, U. Tenn., Memphis, 1992. Seasonal data transcriber IRS, Memphis, 1981-82; technologist I Hoffman LaRoche Biomed. Lab., Southaven, Miss., 1982-87; sr. rsch. tech. U. Tenn., Memphis, 1985-87, grad. teaching asst., 1987-92; neuroimmunology postdoctoral fellow U. Ala., Birmingham, 1992-94; postdoctoral fellow St. Jude Children's Rsch. Hosp., Memphis, 1994-96; with LSE DuPont Splty. Chems., Memphis, 1996—. Contbr. articles, abstracts and revs. to profl. jours. Grantee NIH, 1988-92; named to Black Alumni Hall of Fame U. Tenn. at Martin, 1993. Mem. AAAS, Am. Physiol. Soc. (Proctor & Gamble Profl. Opportunity award 1992), Memphis Mid-South Sleep Soc., IMHOTEP Soc., Alpha Kappa Alpha (dean pledgees 1979—). Democrat. Baptist. Home: 174 Huffman Dr Brighton TN 38011

PAYNE, MARY LIBBY, judge; b. Gulfport, Miss., Mar. 27, 1932; d. Reece O. and Emily Augusta (Cook) Bickerstaff; m. Bobby R. Payne; children: Reece Allen, Glenn Russell. Student, Miss. Univ. Women, 1950-52; BA in Polit. Sci. with distinction, U. Miss., 1954, LLB, 1955. Bar: Miss. 1955. Ptnr. Bickerstaff & Bickerstaff, Gulfport, 1955-56; sec. Guaranty Title Co., Jackson, Miss., 1957; assoc. Henley, Jones, & Henley, Jackson, Miss., 1958-61; freelance rschr. Pearl, Miss., 1961-63; solo practitioner Brandon, Miss., 1963-68; exec. dir. Miss. Judiciary Commn., Jackson, 1968-70; chief drafting & rsch. Miss. Ho. Reps., Jackson, 1970-72; asst. atty. gen. State Atty. Gen. Office, Jackson, 1972-75; founding dean, assoc. prof. Sch. Law Miss. Coll., Jackson, 1975-78, prof., 1978-94; judge Miss. Ct. Appeals, Jackson, 1995—; adv. bd. Sarah Ison Ctr. Women Studies U. Miss., 1988-95; bd. disting. alumnae Miss. U. Women, 1988-95. Contbr. articles to profl. jours. Founder, bd. dirs. Christian Conciliation Svc., Jackson, 1983-93; counsel Christian Action Com. Rankin Bapt. Assn., Pearl, 1968-92. Recipient Book of Golden Deeds award Pearl Exch. Club, 1989, Excellence medallion Miss. U. Women, 1990; named Woman of Yr. Miss. Assn. Women Higher Edn., 1989. Fellow Am. Bar Found.; mem. Christian Legal Soc. (nat. bd. dirs., regional membership coord.). Baptist. Office: Ct Appeals PO Box 22847 Jackson MS 39225

PAYNE, NANCY SLOAN, visual arts educator; b. Johnstown, Pa., Aug. 5, 1937; d. Arthur J. and Esther Jenkins (Ashcom) Sloan; m. Randolph Allen Payne, Nov. 19, 1970; 1 child, Anna Sloan. BS in Art Edn., Pa. State U., 1959; MFA in Sculpture, George Washington U., 1981. Visual arts tchr. Alexandria (Va.) Schs., 1960-61; art tchr. sch. program Corcoran Gallery of Art, Washington, 1962; visual arts tchr. Montgomery County Schs., Rockville, Md., 1965-67; instr. No. Va. C.C., Alexandria, 1971-73, Mt. Vernon Coll., Washington, 1971-73; visual arts tchr. Arlington (Va.) County Schs., 1967-79; edn. coord. The Textile Mus., Washington, 1982-87; mid. sch. visual arts tchr., K-12 dept. chair St. Stephen's and St. Agnes Sch., Alexandria, 1988—; co-founder Fiber Art Study Group, Washington, 1988—; co-owner Art Gallery, Chincoteague Island, Va., 1989—. Exhibited in group shows at Craftsmen's Biennial Va. Commonwealth U. (Excellence in Textiles award), 1973, Va. Craftsmen Biennial The Va. Mus., 1980, Creative Crafts Coun. 15th Biennial, 1982, Alexandria's Sculpture Festival, 1983, 84, 13 Fiber Artists Exhbn. Foundry Gallery, Washington, 1985. Founding mem. Alexandria Soc. for Preservation Black Heritage, Alexandria, 1982—. Mem. Nat. Art Edn. Assn. Democrat. Home: 600 Johnston Pl Alexandria VA 22301-2512 Office: St Stephens and St Agnes Schs 4401 W Braddock Rd Alexandria VA 22304

PAYNE, ROBERT E., federal judge; b. 1941. BA in Polit. Sci., Washington and Lee U., 1963; LLB magna cum laude, Washington & Lee U., 1967. Assoc., ptnr. McGuire, Woods, Battle & Boothe, Richmond, Va., 1971-92; fed. judge U.S. Dist. Ct. (ea. dist.) Va., 1992—. Notes editor Wash. & Lee U. Law Rev. Capt. U.S. Army, 1967-71. Mem. ABA, Va. Bar Assn., Va. State Bar Assn., Va. Assn. Def. Attys. (chmn. comml. litigation sect. 1989-91), Richmond Bar Assn., Order of Coif. Episcopalian. Office: Lewis F Powell Jr US Courthouse 1000 E Main St Ste 334 Richmond VA 23219

PAYNE, ROSSER HAMILTON, urban planner, consultant; b. Washington, Oct. 6, 1925; s. Rosser Hansbrough and Frances Ker (Dashiell) P.; m. Mary Elizabeth Furr, Sept. 20, 1959; children: Anne Carter, Mary Frances, Martha Louise, Susan D., Courtney D., Melinda W. Student, George Washington U., Va. Poly. Inst., 1946-50; mgmt. cert., U. Chgo., 1962. Cert. city and county mgmt. Internat. City Mgrs. Assn. Civil and cartographic engr. Atlantic region U.S. Geol. Survey, Arlington, Va., 1950-52; planner Fairfax County Comprehensive Plan Project, 1952-54; dep. dir. planning, prin. planner County of Fairfax, Va., 1954-67; pvt. cons. urban planning and mgmt., 1967-96; spl. cons. Gov. of Va., 1965, Va. Outdoor Recreation Study Commn., 1965-66; mem. planning legis. com. Va. Adv. Legis. Coun., 1964-65, mem. air pollution legis. com., 1965, spl. cons. to task force soil and water conservation com., 1971, land use planning policies com., 1972-76; chmn., dir. Va. chpt. Am. Inst. Planners, 1965-66; prin. cons. County of Fairfax, 1958, County of Fauquier, 1967, City of Fredericksburg, Va., 1970, Town of Warrenton, Va., 1971, County of Albemarle, Va., 1971, Town of Leesburg, Va., 1974, County of Madison, Va., 1977; planning cons. County of Fairfax, 1965, County of Albemarle, 1967, County of Fauquier, 1968, County of Northumberland, Va., 1969, Town of Warrenton, 1971, Town of Leesburg, 1974, County of Madison, 1975, others; pvt. cons. U.S. Dept. Agriculture, 1974; spl. cons. County of Fauquier, 1974-75, 76-77; environ. cons. EPA, King George County, Va., 1977-78; vis. prof. city planning U. Va., Charlottesville, 1967, lectr., 1963-67; bd. dirs. Fauquier County Community Hosp., Fauquier County Indsl. Cert. Commn.; author Tax Policy Study, Va., 1965, Open Space Land Act, Va., 1966; expert witness Va. Cts. Contbg. author nat. planning publs. With USAF, 1942-45, ETO, PTO. Recipient Ann. award Va. Citizen's Planning Assn., 1965, Teaching Excellence citation Sch. Architecture U. Va., 1988. Mem. Am. Planning Assn., Am. Inst. Cert. Planners (charter), Fauquier County C. of C. (bd. dirs.), Fauquier Springs Country Club (bd. dirs. 1982-85).

PAYNE, RUBY KRABILL, educational director, publisher; b. Elkhart, Ind., Aug. 29, 1950; d. Murray Wayne and Alta Louise (Snyder) Krabill; m. Charles Franklin Paune, June 23, 1973; 1 child, Thomas Murray. BA in English Edn., Goshen Coll., 1972; MA in English, Western Mich. U., 1976; PhD in Ednl. Leadership, Loyola U., Chgo., 1994. Cert. tchr., adminstr., Ill., Tex. Tchr. h.s. Middlebury (Ind.) Ind. Sch. Dist., 1972-78; tchr., h.s. dept. chairperson Calallen Ind. Sch. Dist., Corpus Christi, Tex., 1979-82, secondary curriculum specialist, 1982-84; regional cons. Ednl. Svc. Ctr., Corpus Christi, 1984-86, Grayslake (Ill.) Ednl. Svc. Ctr., 1986-90; elem. prin. Barrington (Ill.) Ind. Sch. Dist., 1990-92; dir. profl. devel. Goose Creek Ind. Sch. Dist., Baytown, Tex., 1992-96; owner RFT Pub. Co., Baytown, 1996—; cons. numerous sch. dists., 1984—. Author: A Framework: Understanding and Working with Students and Adults from Poverty, 1995; reviewer Nat. Staff Devel. Jour., 1988-92; contbr. articles to various publs. Fellow Idea Kettering Found., 1990—. Mem. Am. Assn. Sch. Adminstrs., Nat. Staff Devel. Coun., Phi Delta Kappa, Delta Kappa Gamma. Office: RFT Pub Co 3411 Garth Rd Ste 229 Baytown TX 77521

PAYNE, R.W., JR., lawyer; b. Norfolk, Va., Mar. 16, 1936; s. Roland William and Margaret (Sawyer) P.; m. Gail Willingham, Sept. 16, 1961; children: Darrell, Preston, Darby, Clinton. BA in English, U. N.C., 1958, LLB, 1961; LLB, Stetson U., 1962. Bar: Fla. 1963, U.S. Dist. Ct. (so. dist.) 1964, U.S. Ct. Appeals (11th cir.) 1965, U.S. Supreme Ct. 1970. Assoc. Roney & Beach, St. Petersburg, Fla., 1963-64, Nichols, Giather, Beckham, Miami, Fla., 1964-67; ptnr. Spence, Payne, Masington, Miami, 1967-95, Payne, Leeds, Colby & Robinson, P.A., Miami, 1995—; presenter numerous profl. convs. and seminars. Contbr. articles to legal jours., legal edn. books.

Mem. Ottawa Roughriders, Can. Football League, fall 1958; capt. football team U. N.C., 1957, bd. dirs., v.p. alumni bd., 1984-92, bd. dirs. ednl. found., 1988-92; bd. dirs. Chem. Dependency Tng. Inst.; past pres. Coral Gables (Fla.) Sr. H.S. Athletic Boosters Club; past bd. dirs. Coral Gables War Meml. Youth Ctr., 1st United Meth. Ch. Coral Gables; past mem. gov.'s coun. on phys. fitness and sports, Fla.; past assoc. mem. Jr. Orange Bowl Com. With USMC, 1959. Fellow Am. Coll. Trial Lawyers, Internat. Acad. Trial Lawyers; mem. ABA, Fla. Bar Assn., Acad. Fla. Trial Lawyers (past mem. bd. govs.), Dade County Bar Assn. (past bd. dirs.), Dade County Trial Lawyers Assn. (founder, past pres.), Bankers Club, Miami Club, Univ. Club, Coral Reef Yacht Club, Order of Golden Fleece, Order of Old Well, Sigma Chi, Phi Delta Phi. Office: Payne Leeds Colby Robinson 2950 SW 27th Ave Ste 300 Miami FL 33133-3765

PAYNE, TIMOTHY E., management consultant; b. Valdosta, Ga., Oct. 12, 1948; s. Ernest Elbert and Lorraine (Tomlinson) P. BS, Valdosta State U., 1971. Profl. safety cert. Nat. Safety Coun.; cert. assoc. in risk mgmt. Ins. Inst. Am. Sr. cons. Kent Watkins & Assocs., Miami, Fla., 1975-80; mgmt. engrng. coord. U. Fla., Gainesville, 1980-86; adminstrv. sys. mgr. Amelia Island (Fla.) Co., 1986-89; CEO, pres. Payne & Assocs., Gainesville, Fla., 1989—; cons. Grace Com., Gainesville, 1991; teaching asst. La. State U., New Orleans, 1971. Author: Industrial Location Survey, 1971, (workbook) Bonus Calculation Procedures, 1977; contbr. articles to Indsl. Mgmt. Jour., Compete, Jour. Competitive Techs. Internat. Gov.'s intern State Ga., Atlanta, 1971. Mem. Am. Soc. Safety Engrs., Nat. Safety Mgmt. Soc. (state v.p. 1994-96).

PAYNE, VIRGINIA C., nurse educator; b. Greenville, N.C., July 23, 1949; d. Richard L. and Dora (Gurganus) Craft; m. Jim Payne, Nov. 27, 1969; 1 child, Joey. BS in Nursing, East Carolina U., Greenville, N.C., 1971, MSHE in Child Devel. and Family Rels., 1976, MS in Nursing, 1979. Mental health nurse II Wake County Mental Health Clinic, Raleigh, N.C., 1974; instr., asst. prof. East Carolina U., Greenville, 1974-79; asst. prof. Atlantic Christian Coll., Wilson, N.C., 1979-82; asst. prof., level II coord. U. N.C. at Wilmington Sch. Nursing, 1982-88; ednl. nurse specialist, coord. nursing edn. Pitt County Meml. Hosp., Greenville, 1988—; presenter seminars and workshops on mental health topics for nurses and other profls. in N.C., Va., Washington. Contbr. articles to profl. jours. Mem. Nat. League Nursing, Am. Nurses Assn., N.C. League Nursing (pres., pres.-elect, program chair), N.C. Nurses Assn. (psychiat.-mental health div. chair, commn. on practice, ad hoc task force on credentialing, vice-chair psychiat.-mental health div., dist. pres., nominating com. baccalaureate and higher degree forum), Sigma Theta Tau (chpt. sec.). Home: PO Box 4175 Greenville NC 27836-2175

PAYNE, WILLIAM SANFORD, insurance company executive; b. Lynchburg, Va., July 1, 1946; s. William Armistead Jr. and Katherine Christian (Marks) P.; m. Donna Faye McNutt, June 14, 1969; children: Cybill Katherine, Kyle Oniel. BA, Randolph-Macon Coll., 1968; M in Fin. Svcs., Am. Coll. of CLU, 1988. CLU, LUTCF. Dist. mgr. N.Am. Assurance Co., Richmond, Va., 1977-80; life brokerage cons. Comml. Union Life Ins. Co., Richmond, 1980-87; v.p., groups ins. mgr. Tabb, Brockenbrough & Ragland, Richmond, 1987—. Bd. dirs. Gayton Forest Assn., Richmond; coach Tuckahoe Little League, Richmond, 1988—; soccer referee Richmond Striker League, 1986-90; fund raiser Boy Scouts Am., Richmond, 1991. With U.S. Army Res., 1968-74. Mem. Va. Assn. Life Underwriters (bd. dirs.), Richmond Assn. Life Underwriters (bd. dirs.), Richmond chpt. CLU, Richmond Jaycees. Republican. Baptist. Home: 1905 Pump Rd Richmond VA 23233-3501 Office: Tabb Brockenbrough Ragland 4900 Augusta Ave Richmond VA 23230-3626

PAYNTER, VESTA LUCAS, pharmacist; b. Aiken County, S.C., May 29, 1922; d. James Redmond and Annie Lurline (Stroman) Lucas; m. Maurice Alden Paynter, Dec. 23, 1945 (dec. 1971); children: Sharon Lucinda, Maurice A. Jr., Doyle Gregg. BS in Pharmacy, U. S.C., 1943. Lic. pharmacist. Owner, pharmacist Cayce Drug Store, S.C., 1944-52, Dutch Fork Drug Store, Columbia, S.C., 1955-60, The Drug Ctr., Cayce, 1963-81; pharmacist Lane-Rexall, Columbia, 1952-55; dist. pharmacist S.C. Dept. Health and Environ. Control, Columbia, 1983-90, ret., 1990. Named Preceptor of Yr., Syntex Co., student body U. S.C., 1981. Fellow, 5th Dist. Pharm. Assn., S.C. Pharm. Assn., S.C. Pub. Health Assn., Alpha Epsilon Delta; mem. China, India, Burma VA Assn. (assoc.), 14th Air Force Assn. (assoc.). Baptist. Lodges: Order of Eastern Star, Order of Amaranth, Sinclair Lodge, White Shrine of Jerusalem, Columbia Shrine #6. Avocations: travel, tennis, golf, art. Home: 2351 Vine St Cayce SC 29033-3000

PAYSON, JOHN WHITNEY, art dealer; b. N.Y.C., Aug. 7, 1940; s. Charles Shipman and Joan (Whitney) P.; m. Nancy Lawler, Dec. 11, 1962 (div. Nov. 1983); children: Heather Lee, Charles Sherwood; m. Joanne D'Elia, June 1, 1985; 1 child, Joan Whitney. Student, Bowdoin Coll., 1959-61; BA in English Lit., Pepperdine U., 1966. V.p. sales House of Waldron, Inc., Portland, Maine, 1968-71; pres. Hobe Sound Galleries, Inc., Hobe Sound, Fla., 1971-91, Hobe Sound Galleries North Inc., Brunswick, Maine, 1982-91, Midtown Galleries, Inc., N.Y.C., 1985-91, Payson Enterprises, Inc., Hobe Sound, 1984-91, Midtown Payson Galleries, Inc., N.Y.C and Hobes Sound, Fla., 1991—. Author: (catalogue) Expressions from Maine, 1976. Trustee Maine Community Found., Ellsworth, 1988—, Skowhegan (Maine) Sch. Painting, 1981, chmn. bd. trustees, 1981-88; trustee, founder Joan Whitney and Charles Shipman Payson Charitable Maine Found., 1988—; founder, mem. adv. bd. Joan Whitney Payson Gallery, Westbrook Coll., Portland, 1977-91; trustee St. Garden's Meml., Cornish, N.H., 1983-91, Williamstown (Mass.) Regional Art Conservation Labs., 1990—, Portland Mus. of Art, 1991—; active Barn Gallery Assocs., Martin Coun. of Arts, Fla. Arts PAC. Recipient Maine Patron award, Skowhegan Sch. of Painting, 1977, spl. award, 1988. Mem. Salmagundi Club, N.Y. Yacht Club, Jupiter Island Club. Office: 11870 SE Dixie Hwy Hobe Sound FL 33455-5456

PAYTON, ANNIE MALESSIA, librarian; b. Kosciusko, Miss., Dec. 15, 1954; d. William Wright and Annie Ray Beatrice (Ross) Nash; children: Jonathan Ross, Christopher Jamal. BS, Tougaloo Coll., 1976; MLS, U. So. Miss., 1984. Head libr. Westwego (La.) Pub. Libr., 1984-85; libr. Orleans Parish Schs., New Orleans, 1985-89; head libr. Delta Jr. Coll., Gretna, La., 1989-92; libr. Boothville-Venice (La.) H.S., 1989-93; coord. reader svcs. Dillard U./Will W. Alexander Libr., New Orleans, 1993—. Youth counselor Fellowship M.B. Ch., New Orleans, 1988—; advisor Baptist Student Union Dillard U., 1994—; mem. People Housing Dev. Corp., Gretna, La., 1995; pres. Tougaloo Coll. New Orleans Alumni Assn., 1995—. Mem. Am. Libr. Assn., La. Libr. Assn., La. Assn. Educators. Democrat. Baptist. Home: 2456 Park Pl Dr Terrytown LA 70056 Office: Will W Alexander Libr 2601 Gentilly Blvd New Orleans LA 70122

PAYTON, CHRISTOPHER CHARLES, oil service company executive; b. London, June 24, 1957; s. Albert Alexander and Ermine Adelaide (Brown) P.; m. Fiona Lilias Fraser, Sept. 3, 1983. BA in Engrng. with honors, Cambridge U., Eng., 1978, MA in Engrng., 1984. Field engr. Dresser Atlas, Bremen, Fed. Republic Germany, 1978-81, tech. mgr., 1981-82; tech. mgr. Aberdeen, Scotland, 1982-84; area tech. mgr. Dresser Atlas Worldwide, London, 1984-85; gen. mgr. Dresser Atlas, Abu Dhabi, United Arab Emirates, 1985-87; mgr. U.K. Atlas Wireline Services, Aberdeen, 1987-89; gen. mgr. Asia/Pacific Atlas Wireline Svcs., Jakarta, Indonesia, 1990-92; mgr. internat. bus. devel. & mktg. Western Atlas Internat., Houston, 1992-94; mgr. rsch. Western Atlas Logging Svcs., Houston, 1994—. Mem. Soc. Profl. Well Log Analysts, Soc. Petroleum Engrs., Soc. Exploration Geophysicists. Office: Western Atlas International 10205 Westheimer Rd Houston TX 77042-3115

PAYTON, TONY, political consultant; b. Spearville, Kans., Aug. 31, 1940; s. Paul Winston and Betty (Wallingford) Sellers P.; m. Teresa Bell, Sept. 7, 1975; children: Zack, Claire. Newspaper reporter Ariz. Daily Star, Tucson, 1963-64, Orange Coast Daily Pilot, Costa Mesa, Calif., 1964-65; newspaper pub. The Record-Courier, Gardnerville, Nev., 1965-71, Lovelock Rev.-Miner, Nev., 1966-72; adminstrv. asst. Congressman David Towell, Washington, 1973-74; field dir. Rep. Nat. Com., Washington, 1974-76; adminstrv. asst. Senator Jack Schmitt, Washington, 1977; polit. con. Payton and Assocs., Washington, 1977—; chief of staff to Senator Conrad Burns, Washington, 1993-95. Republican. Methodist. Home: 2638 S Lynn St Arlington VA 22202-2264

PAZ, LUCIO R., management consultant; b. Santa Cruz, Bolivia, Nov. 19, 1928; s. Jorge J. and Margarita (Rivero) P.; m. Wilma Roca, Sept. 5, 1945; children: Lucio, Romy, Eduardo. MS, Rene Moreno Coll., Santa Cruz, 1955. Minister of agr. Govt. of Bolivia, La Paz, 1968-69; senator Bolivian Legis., La Paz, 1967-69; minister of planification Govt. Bolivia, La Paz, 1970, minister of economy, 1982, nat. sec. transport, 1994-95; exec. officer Interam. Devel. Bank, Washington, 1971-81, rep., 1985-90; cons. Teleconsult Co., Washington, 1983-84, 95—, CADEX, Santa Cruz, 1991-93; gen. consul Govt. El Salvador, Santa Cruz, 1991-95. Author: Integration agreements in the Americas, 1992. Knight of Malta, Chivalry of St. John of Jerusalem, Rhodes and Malta, Rome, 1991. Mem. Rotary (pres. 1993-94, Gold medal 1994). Home: 11440 SW 73 Ter Miami FL 33173

PAZANT, ROSALIE FRAZIER, retired English language educator; b. Beaufort, S.C., Nov. 19, 1916; d. William Bradford and Lauretta Lurene (Grayson) Frazier; m. Edward Theodore Pazant, Dec. 25, 1937 (dec. Nov. 1989); children: Lauretta, Edward, Alvin, DaRenne, Lolita, Charlotte, Reba. BS in English edn., Ga. State U., Savannah, 1938; MS in Edn., S.C. State U., Orangeburg, 1958; postgrad., U. S.C., Beaufort, 1960, N.C. A&T, 1963. English and music tchr. Jefferson County Sch., Louisville, Ga., 1938-41; English and music tchr. Robert Smalls High Sch., Beaufort, 1942-43, English dept. head, 1943-72; English dept. head Beaufort High Sch., 1972-74, Battery Creek High Sch., Beaufort, 1974-77; English coord. Savannah (Ga.) State Coll., 1977-83, assoc. prof., acting dir. devel. studies, 1983-85, ret., 1985; organist Mizpah chpt. # 4 Eastern Star, Beaufort, 1975-78; organist, dir. Tabernacle Gospel Choir, Beaufort, 1976—; reader Coll. Bd. English Competency Test, Princeton, N.J., 1977-82, 85-91; co-founder, pres. Gullah Festival S.C., Inc., Beaufort, 1986—; writing tutor U. S.C., Beaufort, 1993. Author: Never Too Late, 1993. Musician religious and civic orgns., Beaufort, 1938—; regional coord. African-Am. Consumer Edn. Orgn., Beaufort, 1990—. Named Tchr. of Yr. S.C. Am. Legion, 1973; recipient award for work with Gullah Festival, S.C. House of Reps., 1993. Mem. Delta Sigma Theta. Democrat. Baptist. Home: PO Box 83 Beaufort SC 29901-0083 Office: Gullah Festival of SC Inc Beaufort SC 29901

PAZMIÑO, PATRICIO AUGUSTO, physician, scientist, consultant; b. Quito, Ecuador, Nov. 7, 1943; came to U.S., 1967; s. Manuel Eduardo and Angela Alicia (Narvaez) P.; m. Lydia Zulema Bohorquez, 1970; children: Patricio, Pablo, Carlos, Katherine. BS, Gonzaga U., 1968; PhD, U. Ill., 1971; D of Medicine & Surgery, Ctrl. U. Ecuador, 1974. Diplomate Am. Bd. Internal Medicine, Am. Bd. Nephrology. Asst. prof. pharmacology Ctrl. U. Sch. Medicine, Quito, Ecuador, 1971-74; staff nephrologist, internist Nat. Naval Med. Ctr., Bethesda, 1979-84; asst. prof. medicine Uniformed Svcs. U. Health Scis., Bethesda, Md., 1980-83; head nephrology divsn. Nat. Naval Med. Ctr., Bethesda, 1983-84; med. dir. El Paso (Tex.) Dialysis Ctr., 1986-89, Nephrology, Internal Medicine & Hypertension Ctr., El Paso, 1987—; asst. prof. medicine Tex. Tech. Sch. Medicine, El Paso, 1989—; med. dir. BMA Dialysis Ctr., El Paso, 1989-95; dir. Total Renal Care, 1995—; staff internist, nephrologist Columbia Med. Ctrs., Sierra Med. Ctr., Southwestern Gen. Hosp., R.E. Thomason Gen. Hosp., Rio Vista Rehab. Ctr., Providence Meml. Hosp., William Beaumont Army Med. Ctr. Author: Farmacologia Hormonal, 1974; contbr. articles to profl. jours. and books. Served with USN, 1979-84. Fellow ACP, Interam. Coll. Physicians and Surgeons; mem. AMA, Nat. Kidney Found., Tex. Med. Assn., Am. Soc. Nephrology, Mayo Clinic Alumni, El Paso County Med. Assn., Am. Heart Assn. (pres. 1996-97, bd. dirs. El Paso divsn. 1994—), S.W. Renal Soc. (pres. 1991-92), S.W. Assn. Hispanic Am. Physicians (pres. 1993, Outstanding Pres. award 1993), Ecuadorean Acad. Medicine. Fellow ACP, Interam. Coll. Physicians and Surgeons; mem. AMA, Nat. Kidney Found., Tex. Med. Assn., El Paso County Med. Assn., Am. Heart Assn. (pres. 1996-97, bd. dirs. El Paso divsn. 1994—), S.W. Renal Soc. (pres. 1991-92), S.W. Assn. Hispanic Am. Physicians (pres. 1993, Outstanding Pres. award 1993), Ecuadorean Acad. Medicine, Mayo Clinic Alumni Assn. Office: NIH Ctr 1701 N Mesa St Ste 101 El Paso TX 79902-3503

PEABODY, WANDA NELL, secondary school educator; b. Newgulf, Tex., Oct. 6, 1952; d. Floyd Edwin and Florence Elizabeth (Lee) Bell; m. Patrick Timothy Peabody Sr., Jan. 6, 1973; 1 child, Patrick Timothy Jr. BS in Edn., S.W. Tex. State U., 1974; MEd in Guidance and Counseling, U. Houston, Victoria, Tex., 1980. Cert. secondary tchr., Tex. Tchr. math. Hurst (Tex.)-Euless Bedford Ind. Sch. Dist., 1974-75; tchr. h.s. math. Boling (Tex.) Ind. Sch. Dist., 1981-91, Van Vleck (Tex.) Ind. Sch. Dist., 1975-79, 93—; student coun., team and cheerleading sponsor Van Vleck Ind. Sch. Dist., 1975-79, math. coord., 1993—; advisor Dist. 14 Student Coun., 1985-91; student coun. sponsor, Univ. Interscholastic League coord. Boling Ind. Sch. Dist., 1981-91. Mem. ASCD, Nat. Coun. Tchrs. of Math., Assn. Tchrs. and Profl. Educators, Tex. Classroom Tchrs. Assn. Home: Rt 1 Box 49A Bay City TX 77414

PEACE, BERNIE KINZEL, art educator, artist; b. Williamsburg, Ky., Oct. 20, 1933; s. Edgar and Ida M. (Miller) P.; m. Sylvia A. Hitchcock, Dec. 19, 1956; children: Anthony P., Tracy A. Peace-Gantzer. AB in Art, Berea Coll., 1954; MFA in Painting, Ind. U., 1957. Prof. art West Liberty (W.Va.) State Coll., 1960-95, prof. emeritus, 1995—; invitee arts and letters series Gov.'s Mansion, 1993. One-man shows include Oglebay Inst., Wheeling, W.Va., 1963, Washington & Jefferson Coll., Washington, Pa., 1968, Huntington (W.Va.) Galleries, 1969, W.Va. U., Morgantown, 1971, Weirton (W.Va.) Community Ctr., 1973, N.E. Mo. State U., Kirksville, 1987, Mus. Fine Arts, Oak Ridge, Tenn., 1988, The Art Store, Charleston, W.Va., 1992; group shows include Ky. State Fair, Louisville, 1960, Upper Ohio Valley Art Show, Wheeling, 1961, Grove City (Pa.) Coll. Invitational, 1962, 63, Bethany (W.Va.) Coll. Art Exhbn., 1963, 68, Steubenville (Ohio) Art Assn. Ann. Exhibit, 1964, 65, 69, 88, 91, Mint Mus. Art., Charlotte, N.C., 1967, 70, 71, Butler Inst. Am. Art, Youngstown, Ohio, 1967, Charleston (W.Va.) Art Gallery, 1970, 71, 72, 74, 77, Westmoreland County Mus. Art, Greensburg, Pa., 1970, 71, 74, Purdue U., 1972, New Orleans Mus. Art, 1973, Richard Hackett Galleries, Parkersville, W.Va., 1974, Pitts. Watercolor Soc., 1974, 75, The Country Studio, Hadley, Pa., 1976, 3-Rivers Arts Festival, Pitts., 1976, Upshur County Ctr. Creative Arts, Buckhannon, W.Va., 1976, Erie Art Ctr., 1977, Wayne County Arts Coun., Ceredo, W.Va., 1978, Delf Norona Mus., Moundsville, W.Va., 1979, Stifel Fine Arts Ctr., Wheeling, W.Va., 1979-80, 83-85, 88-89, 91-93, Gallery G, Pitts., 1979, 42d Ann. Exhbn. Contemporary Am. Paintings, Palm Beach, 1980, Nat. Competitive Exhbn. Painting and Sculpture, 1981, Owensboro (Ky.) Mus. Art, 1982, Art Store Gallery, Charleston, 1984, 90-93, Cultural Ctr., Charleston, 1985, 87, 89, 93, W.Va. State Coll., 1986, 87, Washington & Jefferson Coll., Washington, Pa., 1991, Sunrise Mus. Downtown, Charleston, 1991, USX Bldg. Lobby Tower, Pitts., 1992, 93, State Capitol Bldg., Charleston, 1993, West Liberty State Coll., 1995, others. With U.S. Army, 1957-60. Recipient numerous awards including 1st prize Steubenville Art Assn., 1965, Grumbacher Medal of Merit, 1989, 92, Albert and Jane Wilson Meml. award, 1993, Best of Show award Upper Ohio Valley Art Show, Wheeling, 1967, 82, award State W.Va. Permanent Collection, 1972, Judges' Choice award Bethany Coll. Fall Ann., 1976, Best of Show award, 1991, award of Excellence Allied Artists of W.Va., 1990. Mem. Allied Artists of W.Va. Home: Washington Farms Wheeling WV 26003

PEACH, PAUL E., physician, medical facility administrator; b. Owensboro, Ky., June 2, 1943; s. Elbert B. and Ermal M. (Bennett) P. Student, So. Meth. U., 1961-63; BS, Ind. U., 1965, JD, 1969; student, U. New Orleans, 1977-79; MD, La. State U., 1983. Bar: Ind., 1970; diplomate Am. Bd. Phys. Medicine and Rehab. Atty. pvt. practice Indpls., 1970-72; staff atty La. Dept. Health & Human Svcs., New Orleans, 1972-77; resident La. State U. Charity Hosp., New Orleans, 1983-84, Wadsworth VA Hosp., Cedars-Sinai Hosp., L.A., 1984-86; med. dir. Roosevelt Warm Springs (Ga.) Inst. for Rehab., 1986—; pvt. practice atty., New Orleans, 1972-77; clin. assoc. prof. Ctr. for Rehab. Medicine Emory U., Atlanta, 1987—. Author: (with others) Late Effects of Poliomyelitis, 1991, Effect of Compliance in Treatment Outcomes in Patients with Post-Polio Syndrome, 1991. Fellow Am. Acad. Phys. Medicine and Rehab.; mem. Med. Assn. Ga., Tri-County Med. Assn. Ga. (pres. 1990-91, 93-96), Ga. Soc. Phys. Medicine and Rehab. (pres. 1989-90, 95-96), Am. Acad. Electrodiagnostic Medicine (assoc.), Am. Hosp. Assn. (governing bd. 1988-91, del. rehab. sect. 1990). Home: Roosevelt Inst Box 336 Warm Springs GA 31830 Office: Roosevelt Inst for Rehab Box 1000 Warm Springs GA 31830-0268

PEACOCK, VALERIE LYNN, paralegal; b. Tallahassee, Nov. 6, 1962; d. William Stanley and Valerie Jo (Tate) P. AA with honors, Tallahassee C.C., 1982; BS in Bus. Communication, Fla. State U., 1986. Cert. legal asst., Ga. With Fla. House of Reps., Tallahassee, 1980-84; with office of registrar Fla. State U., Tallahassee, 1984-85; tchr. Leon County Sch. Bd., Tallahassee, 1986-87; legal asst. Dept. of Ins.-Receivership, Tallahassee, 1987-88, B.K. Roberts, Baggett, LaFace & Richard, Tallahassee, 1988; paralegal specialist criminal div. Fla. Atty. Gen., Tallahassee, 1988—; mem. adv. bd. Nat. Ctr. Paralegal Tng., Miami and Ft. Lauderdale, Fla., 1990—; with paralegal studies program Rollins Coll. Ctr. for Lifelong Edn., 1992—. Mem. Jr. League of Tallahassee, 1992—, bd. dirs. 1993—, cmty. pub. rels. chmn., 1993—, chmn. internat. pub. rels. com. 1992-93; vol. missionary local ch. to Port-au-Prince, Haiti, 1985, mem. adminstrv. bd. local ch., Tallahassee, 1988—; atty gen. rep. Ptnrs. in Excellence, Tallahassee, 1990; bd. dirs. Am. Heart Assn., 1992—, v.p., 1996—; chmn. Children's Miracle Network, 1993, mem. cmty. bd. 1994—; Olympic torchbearer, cmty. hero, 1996; pres. Call Care of Fla., 1996. Recipient Pres.'s award Am. Heart Assn., 1996; finalist Vol. of Yr., Tallahassee and Leon County, 1994; named Cmty. Hero and Olympic Torchbearer, 1996 Olympics in Atlanta. Mem. Fla. Supreme Ct. Hist. Soc., Friends of Maclay Gardens, Pi Kappa Phi, Phi Sigma Soc., Phi Theta Kappa. Republican. Office: Atty Gen Criminal Div The Capitol Tallahassee FL 32399-1050

PEADEN, GLENNIS FAYE, minister; b. Brewton, Ala., Oct. 18, 1939; d. Leonard and Myrtie (Blucker) Whitfield; m. Addison Peaden, Apr. 14, 1956; children: Doy, Keenan. A. in Div., Zoe Coll., Jacksonville, Fla., 1995, postgrad., 1995—. Founder Outreach Ministries, Pensacola, Fla., 1970—; founder, dir. day care Pensacola, 1971—; condr. seminars in field. Author: Angels are Real, 1994, Miserably Married and Divorced, 1996, My Favorite Recipes, 1996; album/cassettes Its Me Again Lord, 1980, Lean on You Lord, 1992, His Namae Excellent, 1994. Home: 5828 Twin Oaks Dr Pace FL 32571-8379

PEAK, JAMES MATTHEW, fund raising executive; b. Canton, Ill., Feb. 21, 1936; s. Merle Harry and Hilda (Sepich) P.; m. Julia Lord, Nov. 22, 1962; children: Cynthia, Matthew, Mark, Katherine. BA, U. Tex., El Paso, 1958. Cert. fund raising exec. Agt. trainer Penn Mut. Life Ins., El Paso, 1965-70, gen. agt., Albuquerque 1970-73; gen. agt. Mass. Mut. Life Ins., El Paso, 1973-76; dir. devel. U. Tex., El Paso, 1977-89; chief devel. officer, pres. Providence Meml. Hosp. Found., 1989-91; with dist. relations Council for Advancement and Support of Edn., Tex., 1984-89, devel. rep. SW dist., 1987-89; fund raising cons., S.W. Dist. IV Case, Tex., 1977-89, conf. dir., 1985—. Contbr.: A Handbook of Proven Strategies and Techniques, 1982. Bd. dirs. Am. Cancer Soc., El Paso, 1958-83, El Paso Arts Alliance, 1984-86; mem. El Paso Estate Planning Coun., 1984-96. Served with U.S. Army, 1958-61. Recipient Outstanding Service to Students award U. Tex.-El Paso, 1980, Disting. Service award, 1982. Mem. Assn. Healthcare Philanthropy, Nat. Soc. Fund Raising Execs. (cert.), El Paso Assn. Life Underwriters (v.p. 1973-76), New Eng. Alumni Trust (exec. com. 1987-89). Roman Catholic. Lodges: K.C. (bd. dirs. 1973-75), Lions (v.p. 1984-87, pres. 1987—). Avocations: fishing, sports. Home and Office: 4832 Costa De Oro Rd El Paso TX 79922-1703

PEARCE, BETTY MCMURRAY, manufacturing company executive; b. Hastings, Nebr., Oct. 11, 1926; d. Frank Madry and Scereta (Mudd) McMurray; BS in Aerospace, U. Tex., Austin, 1949; 1 child, Karen A. Harsley. Draftsman, Koch & Fowler, Civil Engrs., Dallas, 1945-47; with Ling Temco Vought-Aircraft Products Group-Aircraft Maintenance and Support Group, Dallas, 1949—, project engr., 1955-77, engrng. project mgr., 1977-83, dir. engrng., 1983-89, engrng. mgr. advanced sys. concepts, 1989-90; program mgr. PAMPA 2000, 1990-92; ret., 1992; dir. LTV Fed. Credit Union, v.p. LTV Mgmt. Club; cons. Active Aux. St. Joseph's Hosp.; pres. St. Andrews Catholic Ch. Coun., Fort Worth, 1977-78; mem. Bishop's Adv. Coun. Fort Worth Diocese, 1980-87, chmn. svc. com., 1980-81, pres., 1981-82, 84-85; mem. Allied Cmtys. of Tarrant, 1982—. Mem. AIAA, Tech. Mktg. Soc. Am. Home: 2829 Princeton St Fort Worth TX 76109-1763

PEARCE, JAMES WALKER, electronics engineer; b. Ft. Ord, Calif., Aug. 23, 1951; s. Robert Edwin and Catherine Porcher (White) P.; m. C. Karen Edwards, Apr. 5, 1980; children: Ryan C., Loren M. BSEE, Cornell U., 1973, MEE, 1974. Registered profl. engr., Tenn. Devel. assoc., fusion energy div. Oak Ridge (Tenn.) Nat. Lab., 1974-80; sr. systems engr. Tech. for Energy Corp., Knoxville, Tenn., 1980-87, prin. Electronics Engring, 1987-90, mgr. electronics engring., 1991-94; sr. product engr. Computational Systems, Inc., Knoxville, 1994—; cons. IT Corp., Knoxville, 1986-87, Perceptics Corp., Knoxville, 1986-87; bd. dirs. Clinch River Aero, Inc., Oak Ridge, 1982-88, pres., 1990—. Personnel mgr. Oak Ridge Civic Music Assn., 1978. Mem. Cornell Soc. Engrs., Aircraft Owners and Pilots Assn., Internat. Arabian Horse Assn. Home: 254 Babbs Rd Lenoir City TN 37771-3616 Office: Computational Systems Inc 835 Innovation Dr Knoxville TN 37932-2563

PEARCE, JENNIFER SUE, real estate appraiser; b. Jacksonville, Fla., Nov. 1, 1954; d. Marvin William and Betty Mae (White) Robinson; m. James Zenous Pearce Jr., Mar. 30, 1974; children: Keith Bryan, Kevin Patrick. Student, Baylor U., 1983, U. Ga., 1985; cert., Jacksonville U., 1986. Cert. residential and comml. real estate appraiser, Fla. Broker, sales Watson Realty Corp., Jacksonville, 1979-82; sr. resdl. appraiser Page Aspinwall Appraiser, Jacksonville, 1982-90; owner Jennifer Pearce Appraiser, Jacksonville, 1991—; instr. real estate appraisal Fla. Community Coll., 1987; commissioned by Ednl. Testing Svc. to establish exam for certification of appraisers in state of Fla. Mem. Appraisal Inst., Am. Acad. State Cert. Appraisers (charter), Daus. of the Nile. Home: 4807 Avon Ln Jacksonville FL 32210-7505 Office: 1938 Blanding Blvd Jacksonville FL 32210-3263

PEARCE, JOHN Y., lawyer; b. New Orleans, Mar. 26, 1948; s. John Young II and Marina (Harris) P.; m. Marjorie Pamela Doyle, May 22, 1971; children: Andrea Elizabeth, Roger Wellington. BA, La. State U., 1973, JD, 1976. Bar: La. 1977, U.S. Dist. Ct. (ea., mid. and we. dists.) La., U.S. Ct. Appeals (5th and 11th cirs.). Assoc. Doyle, Smith & Doyle, New Orleans, 1977-79, ptnr., 1979-80, mng. ptnr., 1980-84; ptnr. Montgomery, Barnett, Brown, Read, Hammond & Mintz, New Orleans, 1984—. Sgt. U.S. Army, 1969-71. Mem. ABA, La. Bar Assn. (chmn. mineral law coun. 1994-95), New Orleans Bar Assn. (exec. com., pres.-elect 1996-97). Republican. Episcopalian. Office: Montgomery Barnett Brown Read Hammond & Mintz 1100 Poydras St New Orleans LA 70163-1100

PEARCE, SARA MARGARET CULBRETH, middle school educator; b. Camilla, Ga., Oct. 20, 1949; d. Max Ronald and Sara Emily (Rivers) Culbreth; children: Ford Pearce, Brad Pearce. BS in Edn., U. Ga., 1971; MEd, Ga. State U., Atlanta, 1974. Tchr. 5th and 6th grades Carver Elementary Sch., Columbus, Ga., 1971-78; tchr. 5th grade Gould Elementary Sch., Savannah, Ga., 1979; tchr. 7th grade Edwards Middle Sch., Conyers, Ga., 1981-91; tchr. Salem High Sch., Conyers, 1991-93, Meml. Mid. Sch., Conyers, 1993—. Recreation, all-star, premier and classic coach Rockdale Youth Soccer Assn., Conyers, 1984—, dir., 1990; youth, H.S. and coll. soccer referee. Named Rockdale County Tchr. of the Yr. 1991, Edwards Middle Sch. Tchr. of the Yr. 1990, Math./Sci. Outstanding Tchr. in Ga., 1990. Mem. NEA, Ga. Assn. Educators, Rockdale Assn. Educators, Nat Coun. Tchrs. Math., Ga. Coun. Tchrs. Math., Assn. for Supervision and Curriculum Devel. Methodist. Home: 548 Sugar Valley Trl SE Conyers GA 30208-3826

PEARCE, STEPHEN LAMAR, management consultant; b. Bryan, Tex., Nov. 25, 1950; s. Stephen D. and Mabel Louise (Rawls) P.; m. Rhonda Dee Greig, Mar. 24, 1982; 1 child, Joshua Davis Gray. BS in Indsl. Tech., Tex. A&M U., 1978, MBA, 1985, PhD in Bus. Adminstrn., 1995. Svc. engr. Dresser Titan, Laredo, Tex., 1981-83; owner Pearce Fabrications, Anderson, Tex., 1983-87; pres. Stephen L. Pearce Assocs., Bryan, 1986—; asst. prof. indsl. distbn., asst. dir. rsch. Tex. A&M U., College Station, 1991-95; vis. asst. prof. Tex. A&M U., College Station, 1986-91. Contbr. articles to profl. jours. With U.S. Army, 1971-72. Mem. Distbn. Rsch. and Edn. Found. (panel 1991-95). Republican. Methodist. Home and Office: Stephen L Pearce Assocs 3709 Valley Oaks Bryan TX 77802-4910

PEARL, ROBERTA LOUISE (ROBERTA GETMAN), lawyer, arbitrator, mediator; b. New Brunswick, N.J., Jan. 8, 1933; d. Murray Filzer and Claire (Golokow) Weinrebe; divorced; children: Daniel, Michael, Poppy, Jason. BA in French Lit., Ind. U., 1970, JD, 1975. Bar: Ind. Arbitrator, mediator Conn. State Bd. Mediation and Arbitration, 1978-86, Austin Dispute Resolution Ctr., 1989-95, Tex. Arbitration/Mediation Svcs., 1993-96; coord., ombudsman alternative dispute resolution program Office Atty. Gen. Tex., Austin, 1995—; arbitration and mediation appts. Fed. Mediation and Conciliation Svc., 1978—, Am. Arbitration Assn., 1978—, Tex. Accts. and Lawyers for the Arts, 1993—, Juvenile Ct., Austin, 1994—. Bd. dirs. Tex. Soc. Sculptors, Austin, pres., 1995-96; mem. faculty Elisabet Ney New Sculpture Conservancy, Austin, 1992—. Home: 1410 Travis Heights Blvd Austin TX 78704-2531 Office: Office Atty Gen Tex PO Box 12548 Austin TX 78711-2548

PEARL, WILLIAM RICHARD EMDEN, pediatric cardiologist; b. N.Y.C., Nov. 1, 1944; s. William Emden and Sara (Gilston) P.; m. Karlyn Katsumoto, July 9, 1978; children: Jeffrey, Kristine. BA, Queens Coll., 1966; MD, SUNY, Bklyn., 1970. Diplomate Am. Bd. Pediatrics, Am. Bd. Pediatric Cardiology. Intern Roosevelt Hosp., N.Y.C., 1970-71; resident N.Y. Hosp.-Cornell Med. Ctr., N.Y.C., 1971-72; fellow Albert Einstein Coll. Medicine, N.Y.C., 1972-74; asst. prof. U. Hawaii, Honolulu, 1974-76; asst. prof. Tex. Tech. Med. Sch., El Paso, 1976-82, assoc. prof., 1982-92; chief pediatric cardiology William Beaumont Army Med. Ctr., El Paso, 1976-94; assoc. prof. med. branch U. Tex. Med. Br., Galveston, 1994—; cons. Miami (Fla.) Children's Hosp., 1988, Driscol Children's Hosp., Corpus Christi, Tex., 1992, Thomason Hosp., El Paso, 1976-92. Contbr. articles to profl. jours. Col. USAR, 1974-92. N.Y. State Bd. Regents scholar, 1962-66, Fed. Health Careers scholar, 1967-70; NIH fellow, 1972-73; recipient Dept. of Army Commendation for outstanding sci. achievement, 1984. Fellow Am. Acad. Pediatrics, Am. Coll. Cardiology; mem. Am. Heart Assn. (coun. on cardiovascular disease in the young 1982). Office: U Tex Med Br Children's Hosp 301 University Blvd Galveston TX 77550-2708

PEARSON, ANTHONY ALAN, minister; b. Tucson, Feb. 21, 1954; s. Arthur and Evelyn Virginia (Horne) P.; m. Marsha Lee Emory, May 3, 1985; children from previous marriage: Jonathan A., David N., Timothy A., Mark A., Monty B. Grad., Bapt. Bible Coll., Springfield, Mo., 1975; ThM, Tabernacle Bible Inst., Dedham, Mass., 1978; BA, Houston Bapt. U., 1988; postgrad., Southwestern Bapt. Theol. Sem., 1991—; DD (hon.), Homestead Coll., 1979; postgrad., S.W. Tex. State U., 1995—. Ordained to ministry Baptist Ch. Pastor, founder Calvary Met. Tabernacle, Norwood, Mass., 1976-79; prin. Calvary Bapt. Sch., Arcola, Tex., 1979-80; pastor Grace Bapt. Ch., Tri-Cities, Tex., 1981-82, Meadowbrook Bapt. Ch., Houston, 1983-93. Author: (booklets) Biblical Spotlight on Tongues Movement, 1975, Short History of Baptists in the North East, 1978, God's Love Letter: The Bible, 1979, The Unforgivable Sin. Life mem. Houston Livestock Show and Rodeo. 1st lt. Tex. SG, 1985-87. Presdl. scholar Southwestern Bapt. Theol. Sem., 1988, 90. Mem. Biblical Archeology Soc., Tex. State Reading Assn., Am. Hist. Soc., Archaeol. Inst. Am., Meadowbrook Karate Club, Alpha Chi, Theta Alpha Kappa.

PEARSON, CHARLES THOMAS, JR., lawyer; b. Fayetteville, Ark., Oct. 14, 1929; s. Charles Thomas and Doris (Pinkerton) P.; m. Wyma Lee Hampton, Sept. 9, 1988; children: Linda Sue, John Paddock. B.S., U. Ark., 1953, J.D., 1954; postgrad., U.S. Naval Postgrad. Sch., 1959; A.M., Boston U., 1963. Bar: Ark. bar 1954. Practice in Fayetteville, 1963—; dir. officer N.W. Comms., Inc., Dixieland Devel., Inc., Jonlin Investments, Inc., World Wide Travel Svc., Inc., Okliania Farms, Inc., N.W. Arl. Land & Devel., Inc., Garden Plaza Inns, Inc. Word Data, Inc., M.P.C. Farms, Inc., Fayetteville Enterprises, Inc., NWA Devel.Co., Delta Comm., Inc.; past. dir., organizer N.W. Nat. Bank. Adviser Explorer Scouts, 1968—; past pres. Washington County Draft Bd.; past pres. bd. Salvation Army. Served to comdr. Judge Adv. Gen. Corps USNR, 1955-63. Mem. ABA, Ark. Bar Assn., Washington County Bar Assn., Judge Advs. Assn., N.W. Ark. Ret. Officers Assn. (past pres.), Methodist Men (past pres), U. Ark. Alumni Assn. (past dir.), Sigma Chi (past pres. N.W. Ark. alumni, past chmn. house corp.), Alpha Kappa Psi, Phi Eta Sigma, Delta Theta Phi. Republican. Methodist. Clubs: Mason (32 deg., K.T., Shriner), Moose, Elk, Lion, Metropolitan. Office: 36 E Center St Fayetteville AR 72701-5301

PEARSON, JIM BERRY, JR., employee resource officer; b. Wichita Falls, Tex., Sept. 25, 1948; s. Jim Berry and June Louise (Young) P.; m. Cynthia Ann Medlin, Nov. 9, 1985. Cert. mediator. Community organizer VISTA, Pitts., 1969-71; youth dir. East Liberty YMCA, Pitts., 1971-72; aide, therapist technician Austin State Sch., Austin, Tex., 1972-80; labor organizer Communications Workers of Am., Austin, Tex., 1980-90; employee resource officer Austin State Hosp., 1990-96; human resource dir. Capital Area State-Operated Cmty. MHMR Svcs., Austin, 1996—; exec. bd. rep. Communications Workers Am./Tex. State Employees Union, Austin, 1987-90; trustee Austin Cen. Labor Coun. AFL-CIO, Austin, 1983-84. Vol. AFL-CIO Polit. Action Com., 1980—; mem. Labor Party Advs., Tex. Populist Alliance; del. founding conv. Labor Party, 1996. Recipient Vols. in Politics award Nat. ALF-CIO, Washington, 1984, Peacemaker award Travis County Dispute Resolution Ctr., 1993. Mem. Comm. Workers Am./Tex. State Employees Union Local 6186 (founding mem.). Home: 2501 Wilson St Austin TX 78704-5436 Office: Austin State Hosp 4110 Guadalupe St Austin TX 78751-4223

PEARSON, MARGARET DONOVAN, former mayor; b. Nashville, Oct. 29, 1921; d. Timothy Graham and Nelle Ligon (Schmidt) Donovan; m. Jimmie Wilson Pearson, Aug. 2, 1946 (dec. Oct. 1978). BS, Vanderbilt U., 1944, MA, 1950; MS, U. Tenn., 1954. Cryptanalysist Army Signal Corps, Washington, 1944-45; phys. edn. tchr. Nashville Bd. Edn., 1945-46; tchr. English, phys. edn. White County Bd. Edn., Sparta, Tenn., 1946-57; spl. edn. supr. Tenn. Dept. Edn., Cookeville, 1957-65; staff devel. dir. Tenn. Dept. Edn., Nashville, 1965-84; ret., 1984; 1st woman alderman City of Sparta, 1987-91, 1st woman mayor, 1991-95. Mem. U.S. Ret. Sr. Vol. Program, 1985—; dist. dir. Tenn. Mcpl. League, 1987-94, 1st woman elected as v.p.; mem. Tenn. Gov.'s Com. Employment of Disabled, 1989—. Recipient Cmty. Leader award Wal-Mart; Am. Speech, Lang. and Hearing Assn. fellow, 1971; Ky. Col.; Tenn. Col. Mem. Sparta C. of C., Rotary (1st woman elected pres.). Methodist. Home: 114 Highland Dr PO Box 22 Sparta TN 38583-0022

PEARSON, PATRICIA KELLEY, marketing representative; b. Carrollton, Ga., Jan. 21, 1953; d. Ben and Edith (Kelley) Rhudy; m. Ray S. Pearson, June 4, 1976; children: Chad, Jonathan, Kelly. BA in Journalism, Ga. State U., 1974; BSN, West Ga. Coll., 1990. RN Fla. Pub. rels. asst. Grady Meml. Hosp., Atlanta, 1974-77; editorial asst. Childers & Sullivan, Huntsville, Ala., 1977-78; sales rep. AAA Employment Agy., Huntsville, 1978-80; editor Wright Pub. Co., Atlanta, 1980-82; elect./electronic drafter PRC Cons., Atlanta, 1980-87; researcher Dept. Nursing at West Ga. Coll., Carrollton, 1989-90; med./surg. nurse Tanner Med. Ctr., Carrollton, Ga., 1989-90, Delray Community Hosp., Delray Beach, Fla., 1990-91; sales rep. Innovative Med. Svcs., 1991-94; with staff devel., employee rels. Beverly Oaks Rehab. and Nursing Ctr., 1994-95; sales rep./pub. rels. rep. Columbia HCA, Melbourne, Fla., 1996—. Vol. Project Response. All-Am. scholar U.S. Achievement Acad., 1990, recipient Nat. Coll. Nursing award, 1989. Mem. NOW, Space Coast Bus. Writer's Guild, Omicron Delta Kappa. Democrat. Home: 139 Jamaica Dr Cocoa Beach FL 32931-2825

PEARSON, R. JOHN C., epidemiologist, educator; b. Birmingham, England, Aug. 17, 1929; came to the U.S., 1968; s. Arthur Samuel and Gwyneth Elsie (Paddock) P.; m. Joyce Underwood, Dec. 15, 1962; children: Daniel C.W., Jeffrey A., Amy N. BA, Cambridge U., 1951, MB, BCHIR, 1954, MA, 1955; MPH, Yale U., 1960. Intern Birmingham, 1955; resident in pediatrics Louisville Children's Hosp., 1958-59, Yale New Haven (Conn.) Hosp., 1961-62; lectr., asst. prof. epidemiology and pub. health Yale U., New Haven, 1960-61, 62-64, assoc. dean, asst. prof. med. sch., 1969-71; sr. rsch. fellow med. care rsch. Manchester (United Kingdom) U., 1964-68; asst. prof. Brown U., Providence, 1968-69; assoc. prof. epidemiology and community medicine Ottawa (Canada) U., 1971-76; prof., chmn. community medicine W.Va. U., Morgantown, 1976—; cons. W.Va. Med. Inst., Charleston, 1992—, Pan Am. Health Orgn., Bogota, Colombia, 1966; mem. adv. com. W.Va. Bur. Pub. Health, Charleston, 1976—; chief gen. practice Royal Ottawa Hosp. for Spl. Rehab., 1973-75; chmn. planning com. 1st Nat. Preventive Medicine Ann. Conf., 1984; pres. Can. Assn. Tchrs. Social and Preventive Medicine, 1975-76, Tristate Occupl. Med. Assn., 1986-87, W.Va. State Health Edn. Coun., 1983-84, Morgantown Vis. Homemaker Svc., 1988-89; bd. dirs. Morgantown Hospice, 1982-88, 89-94; vis. lectr. in pub. health W.Va. Sch. Osteo. Medicine, 1988-94. Contbr. articles to profl. jours. and chpts. to books. Capt. British mil., 1956-58. WHO Exch. of Rsch. Workers fellow, 1965, traveling fellow Coun. of Europe, 1968. Mem. Am. Coll. Preventive Medicine, Assn. Tchrs. Preventive Medicine, Internat. Epidemiology Assn., W.Va. Med. Soc. Episcopalian. Home: 312 Euclid Ave Morgantown WV 26505-6629 Office: U WVa Byrd Health Sciences Ctr Morgantown WV 26506-9145

PEARSON, ROBERT EDWIN, psychiatrist; b. Toledo, Apr. 29, 1923; s. Albin L. and Elizabeth (Christ) Pearson; m. Karen S. Kamerschen, June 18, 1983; m. Katherine L. Gerrie, Oct. 15, 1955 (dec. 1981); children—Robert A., Michael A., Barbara A., Eric J., Brian S., Katherine E. B.S., Wayne U., 1949, M.D., 1952. Diplomate Am. Bd. Psychiatry and Neurology. Intern Highland Park (Mich.) Gen. Hosp., 1952-53; gen. practice medicine Boyne City, Mich., 1953-66; resident in psychiatry Traverse City State Hosp., Mich., 1966-69, dir. adult services, 1969-83; practice psychiatry, Houston, 1983—. Contbr. articles to profl. jours. Served to capt. AUS, 1941-46; ETO. Fellow Am. Soc. Clin. Hypnosis (pres. 1969-70, chmn. Edn. and Research Found. 1972-73), Soc. Clin. and Exptl. Hypnosis, AAAS. Roman Catholic. Home and Office: 10044 Lynbrook Dr Houston TX 77042-1558

PEARSON, SELA, poet, speaker; b. Bklyn., Aug. 10, 1952; d. Thomas Turner and Thelma (Brown) Razor; m. Nassar Anwar Jonathan. BS, St. Joseph's Coll., Bklyn., 1988. LPN. Psychiat., pediat. nurse Syosset (N.Y.) Hosp., 1974-78; sales agent Combined Life Ins. Co. N.Y., Albany, 1978-80; med., surg. nurse Bapt. Med. Ctr., Bklyn., 1980-86; nurse counselor Riker's Island Prison Hosp., Queens, N.Y., 1986-88; clinic nurse St. Christopher Ottilie, Queens, 1988-90; intensive case mgr. AIDS Ctr. Queens County, 1990-92; quality assurance, utilization rev. nurse Vanderbilt U. Med. Ctr., Nashville, Tenn., 1992-94; program dir. Boys and Girls Club, Franklin, Tenn., 1994-95; spkr., writer, nurse Akanke Creations, Brentwood, Tenn., 1996—; cons. Murphy Alternative Ctr., Nashville, 1996, Serendipity House, Nashville, 1996, Family and Ednl. Adv. Assocs., Inc., Nashville, 1996, Growing In Grace Leadership Sch., Nashville, 1996; storyteller, presenter poetry recitals. Author: New York Poetry Foundation Anthology, 1986, Beyond the Stars, 1995 (Editors Choice 1995), Sela's Sounds of Silence, 1995; performer (video) A Soulful Journey, 1995, The Magic of Peace, 1996, Our Voices, 1996; contbr. articles, poetry to jours., mags. Vol. Williamson County Libr., Franklin, 1995—, Boys and Girls Club, Franklin, 1996—; bd. dirs. Nashville Peace Action, 1996—; mem. New Gospel Singers Choir, 1995—. Recipient Vol. Svc. award Berksheire Nursing Ctr., West Babylon, N.Y., 1977. Mem. Brentwood Early Risers Toastmasters (v.p. membership 1996—, recipient various awards), Tenn. Writers Alliance, Harpeth Storytelling Group, Nat. Storytelling Assn., Internat. Soc. Poets (Poets Choice award 1995, Internat. Poet of Merit award 1995), Tenn. Writers Group Franklin, Tenn. Assn. Perpetuation Preservation Storytelling. Office: Akanke Creations 117 Brooklyn Ave North Babylon NY 11704

PEARSON-SHAVER, ANTHONY LLOYD, pediatrician, educator; b. Cleve., July 8, 1952; s. Harrison Peter Shaver and Ida E. (Pearson) Taylor. BA in Music, Wesleyan U., Middletown, Conn., 1974; MD, U. Cin., 1979. Diplomate Am. Bd. Pediatrics. Intern in pediatrics Children's Hosp. Med. Ctr., Akron, Ohio, 1979-80, resident in pediatrics, 1980-82; fellow pediatric critical care Children's Hosp. Pitts. (Pa.), 1984-86; asst. prof. pediatrics Med. Coll. Ga., Augusta, 1986—, med. dir. pediatric transport team, 1990—; nat. faculty pediat. advanced life support course Am. Heart Assn., Atlanta, 1988—. Contbr. chpts. to books, articles to profl. jours. Den leader Boy Scouts Am., Augusta, 1986-89, asst. scout master, 1989-92. With USPHS, 1982-84. Fellow Am. Acad. Pediatrics; mem. AMA, Soc. Critical Care Medicine. Office: Med Coll Ga 1120 15th St # 8415 Augusta GA 30901-3157

PEATTIE, ROBERT ADDISON, engineering educator; b. Greenwich, Conn., Aug. 8, 1956; s. Robert A. and Nancy (Hyatt) P. BS, Trinity Coll., 1979; PhD, Johns Hopkins U., 1988. Teaching asst. Johns Hopkins U., Balt., 1980-83, rsch. asst., 1984-85; asst. prof. Tulane U., New Orleans, 1989—. Contbr. articles to profl. jours. Mary A. Terry fellow Trinity Coll., 1979, Postdoctoral fellow Johns Hopkins U., 1988-89; recipient NSF Rsch. Initiative award, 1990. Mem. Am. Phys. Soc., Am. Soc. Mechanics, Biomed. Engring. Soc. (chair fin. 1993-95), Sigma Xi, Alpha Eta Mu Beta. Office: Tulane U Dept Biomed Engring New Orleans LA 70118

PEAVY, DAN CORNELIUS, orthodontist; b. San Antonio, Jan. 26, 1939; s. Dan C. and Mary (Terrell) P.; m. Harriet Williams, Nov. 9, 1941; children—Daniel, Gardner. BS, So. Meth. U., 1962; DDS, Baylor U., 1962, MSD Orthodontics, 1964. Diplomate Am. Bd. Orthodontics. Pvt. practice orthodontics, San Antonio, 1966—; clin. prof. dept. orthodontics, U. Tex. Dental Sch., San Antonio, 1972—; adv. dir. NCNB Fort Sam Houston Mil. Bank, 1972-92; dir. Nat. Bank Fort Sam Houston Bank. Mem. devel. bd. Inst. Texan Cultures, Health Careers High Sch.; trustee Baylor Coll. Dentistry, 1972-83, San Antonio Med. Found., 1984; mem. city coun. Alamo Heights, 1989—; trustee Tex. Mil. Inst., 1992—. Capt. USAF, 1964-66, Japan, with Res, 1966-68. Fellow Am. Coll. Dentistry, Internat. Coll. Dentistry, Acad. Gen. Dentistry, Dentistry Internat.; mem. Am. Assn. Orthodontists, ADA, Southwestern Soc. Orthodontists (del., dir. 1985), San Antonio Dist. Dental Soc. (pres. 1984), Tex. Assn. Orthodontists (pres. 1984), Baylor Orthodontic Alumni Assn. (pres. 1975), Baylor Alumni Assn., Omicron Kappa Upsilon. Republican. Presbyterian. Clubs: Conopus (pres. 1972), German, San Antonio Country, Tex. Cavaliers (officer 1988, day aide 1989), Order of Alamo (pres. 1974), Argyle, Gireau. Lodge: Rotary. Home: 627 Lamont Ave San Antonio TX 78209-3643 Office: 100 W Olmos Dr San Antonio TX 78212-1954

PECK, CLAUDIA JONES, associate dean; b. Ponca City, Okla., Feb. 1, 1943; d. Claude W. and Josephine Jones; children: Jody Athene, Cameron Guthrie. BS, U. Okla., 1972; MS, U. Mo., 1976; PhD, Iowa State U., 1981. Instr. econs. Iowa State U., Ames, 1980-81; asst. prof. consumer studies Okla. State U., Stillwater, 1981-85, assoc. prof., 1985-88, prof., 1988-89; assoc. dean for rsch. and grad. studies U. Ky., Lexington, 1989—, faculty assoc. Sanders-Brown Ctr. on Aging, 1991. Contbr. articles to profl. jours. Recipient Lela O'Toole Rsch. award Okla. Home Econs. Assn., 1988, Merrick Found. Teaching. award Okla. State U., 1987. Mem. Am. Assn. Family and Consumer Scientists (v.p. 1990-92), Am. Coun. on Consumer Interests (pres. 1994-95, Applied Rsch. award 1985), Missouri Valley Econ. Assn. (v.p. 1994-96), Sigma Xi (pres. 1993-94). Office: U Ky 102 Erikson Hall 0050 Lexington KY 40506-0050

PECK, ROBERT DAVID, educational foundation administrator; b. Devil's Lake, N.D., June 1, 1929; s. Lester David and Bernice Marie (Peterson) P.; m. Lylia June Smith, Sept. 6, 1953; children: David Allan, Kathleen Marie. BA, Whitworth Coll., 1951; MDiv, Berkeley (Calif.) Bapt. Div. Sch., 1958; ThD, Pacific Sch. Religion, 1964; postgrad., U. Calif., Berkeley, 1959-60, 62-63, Wadham Coll., Oxford U., Eng., 1963. Music tchr. pub. schs. Bridgeport, Wash., 1954-55; prof., registrar Linfield Coll., McMinnville, Oreg., 1963-69; asst. dir. Ednl. Coordinating Coun., Salem, Oreg., 1969-75; assoc. prof. Pacific Luth. U., Tacoma, 1976-79, U. Puget Sound, Tacoma, 1977; v.p. John Minter Assocs., Boulder, Colo., 1979-81, Coun. Ind. Colls., Washington, 1981-84; adminstrv. v.p. Alaska Pacific U., Anchorage, 1984-88; pres. Phillips U., Enid, Okla., 1988-94, chancellor, 1994-95; chmn. The Pres. Found. for Support of Higher Edn., Washington, 1995—; pres. Phillips U. Ednl. Enterprises Inc., 1994-95; cons. Higher Edn. Exec. Assocs., Denver, 1984—; owner Tyee Marina, Tacoma, 1975-77; yacht broker Seattle, 1977-79. Author: Future Focusing: An Alternative to Strategic Planning, 1983, also articles. Dem. county chmn., McMinnville, 1968, Dem. candidate for state Ho. of Reps., McMinnville, 1969; pres. McMinnville Kiwanis, 1965-69. Cpl. Signal Corps, U.S. Army, 1952-54. Carnegie Corp. grantee, 1982, 84. Mem. Okla. Ind. Coll. Assn. (sec. 1989—). Mem. Christian Ch. Office: Pres Found for Support Higher Edn Western Office PO Box 529 Phoenix AZ 85001-0529

PEDDICORD, KENNETH LEE, academic administrator; b. Ottawa, Ill., Apr. 5, 1943; s. Kenneth Charles and Elizabeth May (Hughes) P.; m. Patricia Ann Cullen, Aug. 2, 1969; children: Joseph, Clare. BSME, U. Notre Dame, 1965; MSNE, U. Ill., 1967, PhD, 1972. Registered profl. engr., Tex. Rsch. nuclear engr. Swiss Fed. Inst. for Reactor Rsch., Würenlingen, Switzerland, 1972-75; asst. prof. nuclear engring. Oreg. State U., Eugene, 1975-79, assoc. prof. nuclear engring., 1979-82; prof. nuclear engring. Tex. A&M U., College Station, 1983—, head dept. nuclear engring., 1985-88, asst. dir. rsch. Tex. Engring. Experiment Sta., 1988-91, dir. Tex. Experiment Sta., 1991-93, assoc. dean coll. engring., 1990-91, interim dean coll. engring., 1991-93, interim dep. chancellor engring., 1993-94, assoc. vice chancellor for strategic programs, 1994—; vis. scientist Joint Rsch. Centre-Ispra Establishment, EURATOM, Ispra, Italy, 1981-82; cons. EG&G Idaho, Inc., Idaho Falls, Idaho, 1979, Portland (Oreg.) Gen. Electric Co., 1980, Battelle Human Affairs Rsch. Ctr., Bellevue, Va., 1984, Los Alamos (N.Mex.) Nat. Lab., 1984-89, Pa. Power & Light, Allentown, Pa., 1986, Argonne Nat. Lab., Idaho Falls, 1989, Univs. Space Rsch. Assn., Houston, 1989—, Ark. Dept. Higher Edn., Little Rock, 1990; speaker in field; mem. Nat. Rsch. Coun. Com. on Advanced Space Based High Power Techs., 1987-88, NASA OAET Aerospace Rsch. and Tech. subcom., 1987—, SP-100 Materials Sci. Rev. Com., DARPA/NASA/DOE, 1984-86, Nuclear Engring. Edn. for Disadvantaged, 1978—, sec., 1978-80, vice chair, 1985-88, chair, 1988-91; John and Muriel Landis Scholarship Com., 1979—, chair, 1985—; mem. adv. bd. for nuclear sci. and engring., 1984-86; mem. tech. program com. Internat. Conf. on Reliable Fuels for Liquid Metal Reactors, 1985-86; mem. Tex. Transp. Inst. Rsch. Coun., 1987—, Tex. A&M Rsch. Found. Users' Coun., 1989—. Contbr. articles to profl. jours. Recipient Best Paper award AIAA 9th Ann. Tech. Symposium Johnson Space Ctr., 1984. Mem. ASME, NSPE, Am. Nuclear Soc. (cert. governance 1983, 84, 85, Materials Sci. and Tech. Divsn. Chmn's. award 1989, mem. materials sci. and tech. disvsn. exec. com. 1983-86, sec.-treas. 1985-86, vice-chmn./chair-elect 1986-87, chair 1987-88, bd. dirs. 1988-91, mem. edn. divsn. exec. com. 1979-82, sec.-treas. 1982-83, vice-chmn./chair-elect 1983-84, chair 1984-85, mem. student activities com. 1976—, chair 1978-81, Oreg. sect. Edn. com. 1976, 79, 80, Oreg. sect. bd. dirs. 1977), Am. Soc. Engring. Edn., Tex. Soc. Profl. Engrs., Univ. Space Rsch. Assn. (mem. sci. coun. engring.), Pi Tau Sigma, Alpha Nu Sigma. Office: Office of Chancellor John B Connally Bldg 301 Tarrow St Fl 7 College Station TX 77840-1801

PEDEN, ROBERT F., JR., retired lawyer; b. Ft. Worth, July 26, 1911; s. Robert F. and Laura (Phillips) P.; LLB, Cumberland U., 1933; m. Virginia LeTulle, May 25, 1939. Bar: Tex. 1934; practice law, Bay City, 1934-91; ret. 1991; city atty., Bay City, 1935-38, 65-79; county atty. Matagorda County, Tex., 1939-46, 50-54. Bd. dirs. Bay City Library Assn., 1969-88; pres. men. of ch. South Tex. Presbytery, 1959. Mem. ABA, Am. Judicature Soc., State Bar Tex., Matagorda County Bar Assn. (pres. 1961-62, v.p. 1967-69), Lambda Chi Alpha. Presbyterian (clk. session 1969-71, elder 1969—). Rotarian (v.p. 1968-69, pres. 1969-70). Club: Knife and Fork (dir. 1968-69, pres. 1970-71). Home: PO Box 1245 Bay City TX 77404-1245

PEDERSEN, GEORGE J., engineering company executive, computer support company executive; b. 1935. Student, Rutgers U., 1952-53. Contracts mgr. VitroLabs, West Orange, N.J., 1953-68; with Mantech Internat. Corp., Fairfax, Va., 1968—; now chmn. bd., CEO., pres. ManTech Internat. Corp. Office: ManTech Internat Corp 12015 Lee Jackson Hwy Fairfax VA 22033-3300*

PEDERSON, NELS E., molecular virologist, educator; b. Wilmington, Del.. AB, Duke U., 1980; PhD, Pa. State U., 1988. Postdoctoral fellow E.I. DuPont de Nemours & Co., Inc., Wilmington, 1987-90; asst. prof. microbiology Sch. of Medicine East Carolina U., Greenville, 1991—. Office: East Carolina Univ Sch of Medicine Dept Microbiology/Immunol Greenville NC 27858

PEDERSON, TONY WELDON, newspaper editor; b. Waco, Tex., Oct. 27, 1950; s. Lloyd Moody and Ida Frances (Walker) P.; m. Julianne Kennedy, Mar. 21, 1974. B.A., Baylor U., 1973; M.A., Ohio State U., 1976. Sports writer Waco (Tex.) Tribune, Tex., 1970-73; sports writer Houston Chronicle, 1974-75, copy editor, 1976-80, sports editor, 1980-83, mng. editor, 1983—; adj. faculty U. Houston, 1977-79. Mem. Houston Com. Fgn. Rels. Mem. Nat. AP Mng. Editors Assn., Tex. AP Mng. Editors Assn. Methodist. Office: Houston Chronicle Pub Co 801 Texas St Houston TX 77002-2906

PEDRAJA, LUIS GREGORIO, theology educator; b. Cienfuegos, Cuba, May 25, 1963; came to U.S., 1971; s. Luis Ramon and Gladys E. (Chanfrau) P.; m. Amber LaMont, Jan. 6, 1996. BA, Stetson U., 1984; MDiv, So. Bapt. Sem., Louisville, 1987; PhD, U. Va., 1994. Ordained to ministry Baptist Ch., 1984. Pastor Radcliff (Ky.) Bapt. Mission, 1986-88, Lambs Rd. Bapt. Ch., Charlottesville, Va., 1991-93; prof. U. Puget Sound, Tacoma, 1993-94; prof. theology So. Meth. U., Dallas, 1994—; panelist Hispanic Am. Protestant Project, Dallas, 1994—. Pres. U. Va. Habitat for Humanity, 1992-93; mem. disaster action team ARC, Va., Tacoma, Dallas, 1992—, asst. sector coord. for disaster action team, Dallas, 1995-96, 1st officer, 1996—. Recipient Presdl. Preaching award So. Bapt. Sem., 1984, grants in field; named to Outstanding Young Men of Am., 1987. Mem. Am. Acad. Religion (chair Hispanic Am. group 1994—), Ctr. for Process Studies, N.Am. Paul Tillich Soc., Assn. Edn. Teologica Hispana. Democrat. Office: So Meth U Perkins Sch Theology Dallas TX 75275

PEEBLES, E(MORY) B(USH), III, lawyer; b. Hattiesburg, Miss., May 3, 1943; s. E.B. Jr. and Lee (Baldwin) P.; m. Celeste H. Hodges; children: E.B. IV, Catharine Celeste, Thomas Hill. BA, Vanderbilt U., 1965; LLB, U. Ala., 1967. Bar: Ala. 1967, U.S. Dist. Ct. (so. dist.) Ala., U.S. Ct. Appeals (5th and 11th cirs.), U.S. Supreme Ct. Assoc. Armbrecht, Jackson, DeMouy, Mobile, Ala., 1967-72; ptnr. Armbrecht, Jackson, DeMouy, 1972—; dir. Loyal Am. Life Ins. Co., Mobile, 1991-95; bd. dirs. South Ala. area Bank of Ala. Chmn. sports com. Mobile Area C. of C., 1988-90; bd. dirs. Am.'s Jr. Miss Orgn., Mobile, 1983-90; active Mobile area coun. Boy Scouts Am., 1979—; mem. Sr. Bowl Com., Mobile, 1978—; chmn. trustees Maritime Mus. of Mobile. Mem. ABA (chmn. fin. svcs. com., tort and ins. practice sect. 1989-90, comml. fin. svcs. com. bus. law sect. 1984—), Ala. Bar Assn., Maritime Law Assn. U.S., Southeastern Admiralty Law Inst., Internat. Bar Assn., Am. Soc. Internat. Law, Inter-Am. Bar Assn., Ala. Law Inst. (mem. governing coun. 1975—, corp. law com., letters of credit com.), Mobile Touchdown Club (pres. 1987-88). Office: 1200 AmSouth Ctr Mobile AL 36602

PEEBLES, LUCRETIA NEAL DRANE, principal; b. Atlanta, Mar. 16, 1950; d. Dudley Drane and Annie Pearl (Neal) Lewis; divorced; 1 child, Julian Timothy. BA, Pitzer Coll., 1971; MA, Claremont Grad. Sch., 1973, PhD, 1985. Special edn. tchr. Marshall Jr. High Sch., Pomona, Calif., 1971-74; high sch. tchr. Pomona High Sch., 1974-84; adminstr. Lorbeer Jr. High Sch., Diamond Bar, Calif., 1984-91; prin. Chapparal Mid. Sch., Moorpark, Calif., 1991-92, South Valley Jr. High Sch., Gilroy, Calif., 1992—; co-dir. pre-freshman program, Claremont (Calif.) Coll., 1974; dir. pre-freshman program, Claremont Coll., 1975; cons., Claremont, 1983—. Author: Negative Attendance Behavior: The Role of the School, 1985. Active Funds Distbn. Bd.-Food for All, 1987—, Funds Distbn. Task Force-Food for All, 1986; mem. Adolescent Pregnancy Childwatch Task Force. Named Outstanding Young Career Woman Upland Bus. and Profl. Women's Club, 1978-79; Stanford U. Sch. Edn. MESA fellow, 1983, NSF fellow Stanford U., 1981, Calif. Tchrs. Assn. fellow, 1979, Claremont Grad. Sch. fellow, 1977-79, fellow Calif. Edn. Policy Fellowship Program, 1989-90; recipient Woman of Achievement award YWCA of West Edn., 1991. Mem. Assn. Calif. Sch. Adminstrs. (Minigrant award 1988), Assn. for Supervision and Curriculum Devel., Nat. Assn. Secondary Sch. Principals, Pi Lambda Theta. Democrat. Am. Baptist. Home: 970 Sidney Marcus Blvd NE # 1214 Atlanta GA 30324

PEEBLES, RUTH ADDELLE, secondary education educator; b. Livingston, Tex., Dec. 9, 1929; d. Andrew Wiley and Addelle (Green) P. BA, East. Tex. Baptist Coll., 1951; M of Religious Edn., Southwestern Baptist Seminary, Ft. Worth, 1955; MA, Sam Houston State U., 1968. Instr. of religion and Baptist student dir. Ea. N.Mex. U., Portales, 1955-58; Baptist student dir. Madison Coll., Harrisonburg, Va., 1958-60; youth dir. Garden Oaks Baptist Ch., Houston, 1960-62; history tchr. Livingston Ind. Sch. Dist.,

1962-84. Editor: Pictorial History of Polk County, Texas, 1976; author: There Never Were Such Men Before, 1987. Bd. dirs. Polk County Libr. and Mus., Livingston, 1980-83, Polk County Heritage Soc., 1987-89. Recipient Cmty. Svc. award Polk Cunty C. of C., 1980, Hist. Preservation awards Polk County Heritage Soc., 1987, Tex. State Hist. Commn., 1989, SCV Cert. of Appreciation, 1993, Ladies Appreciation medal SCV, 1994. Mem. Daughters of the Republic of Tex., Tex. State Hist. Assn., Tex. State Hist. Found., Hood's Tex. Brigade Assn., Polk County Heritage Soc., Atascosito Hist. Assn., Fort Delaware Soc. Baptist.

PEELER, ALEXANDRA ANN, public relations executive; b. Simpson, Pa., Apr. 11, 1938; d. Alexander Joseph and Ann Billie (Orsefskie) David; m. David Holmes Peeler, Feb. 20, 1968; children: Kirsten and Heather, Paula. BA, Mercyhurst Coll., 1960; postgrad., Marquette U., 1962-64; MFA in Film, Radio, TV, Columbia U., 1969. Bibliographer asst. Libr. Congress, Washington, 1964; mgr. records Opportunities Industrialization Ctr., Erie, Pa., 1965-66; caseworker City of N.Y., 1967-68; asst. dir. pub. affairs Johns Hopkins Med. Instn., Balt., 1971-74; project coord. Neighborhoods Uniting Project, Brentwood, Md., 1975-76; rsch. assoc. Cath. U. Am., Washington, 1976-77; asst. dir. Parish Outreach Nat. Conf. Cath. Charities, Washington, 1977-82; med. writer Franklin Square Hosp., Balt., 1983-85; dir. publs. Cath. Charities U.S.A., Alexandria, Va., 1986-90; dir. comm. Cath. Charities U.S.A., Alexandria, 1990—; freelance writer and producer, Balt., 1972-86. Author: Parish Social Ministry, 1986, (filmstrip) Action Strategies to Prevent Nuclear War, 1982; producer, writer: (filmstrip) Welfare Reform, 1978, Excellence award U.S. Indsl. Film Festival 1978, (film) My Ethnic Neighborhood (with Barbara Mikulski), 1976, Montessori: An Introduction for Parents, 1972. Mem. Internat. Assn. Bus. Communicators (first place Feature Writing 1985), Am. Soc. Assn. Execs., Pub. Rels. Soc. Am., Cath. Press Assn. (awards 1987-92). Democrat. Roman Catholic. Office: Cath Charities USA 1731 King St Alexandria VA 22314-2720

PEELER, BOB, state official; b. Gaffney, S.C., 1952; s. Smith and Sally (Bratton) P.; m. Bett Carter; children: Caroline, Robert, Jr. V.p. Peeler's Milk; former chmn. Cherokee County Sch. Bd., S.C. State Bd. Edn.; now lt. gov. State of S.C.; founding mem. advancement bd. Coll. Commerce, Clemson U. Mem. S.C. Dairy Assn. (past pres.), Cherokee County C. of C. (past pres.), Sertoma Internat. (life), Rotary (Gaffney chpt.), Masons, York Rite. Republican. Methodist. Office: Office Lt Gov PO Box 142 Columbia SC 29202-0142

PEELER, RAY DOSS, JR., lawyer; b. Bonham, Tex., May 4, 1929; s. Ray Doss and Opal (Porter) P.; children: William Bryan, Maribel Porter. BA with high honors, U. Tex., 1948, LLB, 1951. Bar: Tex. 1951. Sole practice, Bonham, 1953—; dist. and county atty., Fannin County, 1960-61; pres. Fannin Bank, Windom, Tex., 1963-70, chmn. bd. dirs., 1970—; chmn. bd. dirs. 1st Nat. Bank, Bonham, 1972-86. Del. Dem. Nat. Conv., 1960; trustee S.B. Allen Meml. Hosp., Bonham, 1962-85; chmn. Bonham United Fund, 1959; pres. Bonham Indsl. Found., 1965-85. Served to capt. USAF, 1951-53. Mem. ABA, State Bar Tex., State Jr. Bar Tex. (v.p. 1959-60), Tex. Horticulture Soc. (pres. 1974-76), Tex. Pecan Growers Assn. (pres. 1974-76), Bonham C. of C. (pres. 1958), Fannin County Hist. Soc. (hon. life, sponsor 1954-60), Phi Beta Kappa, Phi Gamma Delta, Phi Alpha Delta. Mem. Christian Ch. (Disciples of Christ). Clubs: Bonham Golf (bd. dirs. 1958-61), Quail Hollow Country. Lodge: Rotary (pres. Bonham chpt. 1957), Masons. Home: 1912 Nancy Lea Dr Bonham TX 75418-2725 Office: 302 Peeler Bldg Bonham TX 75418

PEET, RICHARD DWAYNE, county judge; b. Binghamton, N.Y., May 5, 1942; s. Clarence and Mary (Moses) P.; m. Carol Maxine Smith, Aug. 24, 1968; children: Tawrin, Tarin, Tracy. BS in Edn., Midwestern State U., 1969. Cert. tchr., Tex. Tchr. Whitney Point (N.Y.) Schs., 1969-71, Pampa (Tex.) H.S., 1971-94, Clarendon Coll., Pampa, 1975-95; mayor City of Pampa, 1989-95; county judge Gray County, Pampa, 1995—. Mem. Tex. Edn. 2000, 1995. Sgt. USAF, 1962-66. Tex. Cmty. Block grantee, 1989-93. Home: 2230 Duncan Pampa TX 79065 Office: 202 N Russel Pampa TX 79065

PEFLEY, CHARLES SAUNDERS, real estate broker; b. Portsmouth, Va., Sept. 4, 1943; s. William R. and Dorothy (Everett) P.; m. Audrey Diane Bennett, Aug. 15, 1977 (div. Sept. 1983). BA in Polit. Sci., Old Dominion U., 1967; JD, U. Balt., 1971; postgrad., Johns Hopkins U., 1972. Lic. real estate broker. V.p. Saxis Island Devel. Corp., Virginia Beach, Va., 1965-72, Pefley, Inc., Virginia Beach, Va., 1972-77; ptnr. Pefley Realty Co., Virginia Beach, 1977—; pres. Pfley Realty Corp., Camden, N.C., 1983—; ptnr. Mickey Properties, Virginia Beach, 1983-87, C.J.S. Enterprises, Virginia Beach, 1986—, Pefzar Realty, Rockville, Md., 1986—, Kelben Properties, Rockville, Md., 1983—; pres. Pefley Realty Corp., Camden, N.C., Bold Realty and Realty Co., Inc., Fair Rental Group, Inc., Centurian Residential Realty Corp., Budget Realty Devel. Corp. Served with U.S. Army, 1968-69. Mem. Tidewater Bd. Realtors. Democrat. Lutheran. Home: 1808 Arctic Ave Virginia Beach VA 23451-3306 Office: Pefley Realty Corp PO Box 291 Camden NC 27921-0291

PEINADO, ARNOLD BENICIO, JR., consulting engineer; b. El Paso, Tex., Oct. 22, 1931; s. Arnold Benicio Sr. and Themis Irene (Molina) P.; m. Rosa de la Torre, July 12, 1954; children: Arnold B. III, Stephen Anthony, Melissa Ann. BS in Engring., Johns Hopkins U., 1952; MS, MIT, 1953. Registered profl. engr., Calif., N.M., Tex. Job supt. Home Constrn. Co., El Paso, 1953-54; staff engr. Simpson & Strata, San Francisco, 1956-59; pres. A. B. Peinado & Sons, Cons. Structural Engrs., El Paso, 1959-71, Peinado, Peinado & Navarro, Cons. Engrs., El Paso, 1971-80; exec. v.p. AVC Devel. Corp., El Paso, 1975-89; pres. AVC Wood Products, Inc., El Paso, 1979-89, Coronado Wood Products Internat., Inc., El Paso, 1988—; exec. v.p. Coronado Engrs. Internat., Inc., El Paso, 1988—; bd. dirs. El Paso br. Fed. Res. Bank of Dallas, 1976-81. Mem. Inter City Group El Paso and Juarez, Mex., 1983—, Tex. bd. advisors Mountain States Tel. & Tel.; vice chmn., bd. dirs. Sierra Med. Ctr. and Hosp., El Paso, 1979-84; state bd. dirs. Cons. Engrs. Coun., Austin, Tex., 1974-76; bd. dirs. Devel. Bd. U. Tex. El Paso, 1984-89; bd. dirs., pres. Pan Am. Contractors Assn., 1971-74. With U.S. Army, 1954-56. People of Vision honoree Tex. Soc. to Prevent Blindness, 1982; named Mem. of Yr. Pan Am. Contractors Assn., 1974. Fellow Tau Beta Pi; mem. ASCE (pres. El Paso chpt. 1971-72), Tex. Soc. Profl. Engrs. (Young Engr. of Yr.1966, Engr. of Yr. 75, pres. El Paso chpt. 1969-70), El Paso Assn. Builders (v.p. 1986-89), Nat. Soc. Profl. Engrs., Granaderos de Galvez (gov. 1986), El Paso Renaissance 400 (bd. dirs.), El Paso C. of C. (bd. dirs., v.p., pres.), Rotary. Home: 5729 Mira Grande Dr El Paso TX 79912-2005 Office: Coronado Engrs Internat Inc 5748 N Mesa St El Paso TX 79912-5427

PEIRCE, ANNE GRISWOLD, dean; b. Plymouth, N.H., May 27, 1951; d. Charles and Nancy (Taylor) Griswold; m. Nathaniel Peirce, Aug. 30, 1975; 1 child, Elizabeth. BSN, U. N.H., 1974; MSN, Boston U., 1977; PhD, U. Md., 1987. Instr. No. Essex C.C., Haverhill, Mass., 1978-79; tchg. asst. U. Md., Balt., 1986, lectr., 1985-87; asst. prof. nursing Seton Hall U., South Orange, N.J., 1987-89; asst. dean undergrad. studies Sch. of Nursing Columbia U., N.Y.C., 1989-92, dir. doctoral studies, 1992-96; dean, prof. of nursing U. Miss. Med. Ctr., Jackson, 1996—; project dir. N.Y. Acad. Medicine, N.Y.C., 1991-92; content rev. exper Decision Support and Outcomes Nurses Care Planning, 1991; content expert Principles and Practice of Nursing Rsch., 1991; gen. steering com. N.J. Dept. Higher Edn., Trenton, 1990. Author: (book) Flow Charts: Clinical Decision Making in Nursing, 1983; contbg. author: Nursing Issues in the 1990s, 1993; contbr. articles to profl. jours. Mem. Jr. League, Balt., 1984-87, Princeton, N.J., 1987-95, N.Y., 1995—. Mem. ANA, AACN, NLN, So. Coun. on Collegiate Edn., Sigma Theta Tau, Alpha Epsilon Delta. Office: The Univ Miss Med Ctr Sch of Nursing 2500 N State St Jackson MS 39216-4500

PEIRIS, ALAN NILRATHAN, medical educator; b. Colombo, Sri Lanka, Sept. 25, 1952; came to U.S., 1983; s. Peter Velin and Edith Doreen Peiris; m. Elizabeth Kay Davidson, Sept. 30, 1983; children: Emma, Alistair. Grad., U. London, MD, 1977, PhD in Nutrition, 1990. Asst. prof. medicine Med. Coll. Wis., Milw., 1986-89; asst. prof. medicine U. Louisville, 1989-91, assoc. prof., 1992-93; prof. medicine East Tenn. State U., Johnson City, 1993—; Author: Photographic Quiz in Medicine, 1984; reviewer for med. jours. including New Eng. Jour. Medicine, Metabolism, Jour. Clin. Endocrinology and Metabolism; contbr. articles to profl. jours. Fellow ACP; mem. Royal Coll. Physicians, Endocrine Soc., Am. Physiol. Soc., Ctrl. Soc. for Clin. Rsch. Office: VAMC-151 Mountain Home Johnson City TN 37608

PEISER, JOHN GEORGE, accountant, consultant; b. Chgo., June 2, 1944; m. Liora Rappaport, June 29, 1969; children: Daniela Jacqui, Gary Dean. BSc, U. Witwatersrand, South Africa, 1965, BSc (hon.), 1969; M in Bus. Leadership, U. South Africa, Pretoria, 1977. CPA. Researcher Nat. Inst. for Pers. Rsch., Johannesburg, South Africa, 1966-69; various mgmt. positions Lindsay Saker, Johannesburg, South Africa, 1970-76, bd. dir. pers., 1976 -78; mgr. human resource planning & devel. Fox & Jacobs, Dallas, 1978-83, regional sales dir., 1984-85; pres. Sidran, Inc., Dallas, 1985-90; CPA, pntr., exec. cons. Peiser & Peiser, CPAs, Dallas, 1990-93; ptnr., exec. cons. Goldin Peiser & Peiser, CPAs, L.L.P., Dallas, 1993—; Bd. dirs. Solomon Schechter Acad. Dallas, chmn., 1984-86. Bd. dirs. Shearith Israel Congregation, Dallas, 1983-86, Zionist Orgn. Am., Dallas; pres. Yavneh Acad. of Dallas, 1993—. Mem. AICPA, Am. Inst. Tng. and Devel., Nat. Assn. Cert. Valuation Analysts, Tex. Soc. CPA, Inst. Personnel Rsch. (branch chair, 1974-75). Office: Goldin Peiser & Peiser CPAs LLP 470 Signature Pl II 14785 Preston Rd Ste 470 Dallas TX 75240-7882

PELAEZ, ROLANDO FEDERICO, economics educator, consultant; b. Washington, May 5, 1940; s. Rolando Juan and Maria Gertrudis (Bringuier) P. BS, La. State U., 1962, MA, 1964; PhD in Econs., U. Houston, 1973; postgrad., Rice U., 1978-79. Teaching fellow U. Houston-Univ. Park, 1970-71, instr., 1971-73; asst. prof. N.Mex. State U., 1973-74, Southeastern La. U., 1976; asst. prof. U. Houston-Downtown, 1977-80, assoc. prof. fin. Coll. Bus., 1987—; assoc. prof. U. St. Thomas, 1980-87; expert witness forensic economist; vis. asst. prof. U. Houston-Univ. Park, 1974-75; spkr., presenter confs. in field. Contbr. articles to profl. jours. OAS doctoral fellow, 1970. Mem. Am. Econ. Assn., Am. Statis. Assn., So. Finance Assn., Southwestern Econ. Assn., Southwestern Finance Assn., Western Econ. Assn., Nat. Assn. Forensic Economists. Home: 8318 Daycoach Ln Houston TX 77064-8202

PELL, JONATHAN LAURENCE, artistic administrator; b. Memphis, Oct. 20, 1949; s. Burton Marshall and Eleanor (Leopold) P. BA, U. So. Calif., 1971. Interior designer Gene Morse Assocs., Wichita, Kans., 1971-77; mgr. Internat. Artists Mgmt., N.Y.C., 1977-79, Robert Lombardo Assocs., N.Y.C., 1979-80; TV producer Sta. WNET, N.Y.C., 1980-83; dir. publicity John Curry Skating Co., N.Y.C., 1983; prodr. Jerome Kern Centennary Gala Town Hall, N.Y.C., 1984; dir. artistic administration The Dallas Opera, 1984—; vocal competition judge Pavarotti Competition, George London Awards, Ctr. for Contemporary Opera, Marguerite McCammon Competition, San Antonio Opera Guild, Richard Tucker award, others; tchr. master classes for young singers Can. Opera Co., S.W. Chpt. NATS. Scenic and Costume designer for plays, musicals and ballets for various cos., 1970-76; host The Dallas Opera Radio Hour, WRR, 1994—. Bd. dirs., chmn. nat. auditions com., mem. award selection com. Richard Tucker Music Found. Mem. Opera Am. Office: Dallas Opera 3102 Oak Lawn Ave Ste 450 Dallas TX 75219-4259

PELLATT, ROSE FELICE, non-profit agency executive; b. Bklyn., May 5, 1943; d. Augustine and Pasqualina (Leuzzi) Frisina; m. Raymond Edward Pellatt, Nov. 30, 1964 (dec. Dec. 1983); children: Mark Edward, Cara Lee. Student, Hunter Coll./CUNY, 1961-62; AAS, Isothermal C.C., Spindale, N.C., 1985; BSIS, U. S.C., Spartanburg, 1986; MPA, U. S.C., Columbia, 1994. Owner, fin. mgr. River Rd. Svc. Sta., Wading River, N.Y., 1975-79; owner, store mgr. Tryon (N.C.) Glass & Mirror, 1980-82; adminstrv. asst. Early Edn. Ctr., Highland, N.Y., 1983-84; scheduler Patterson for Congress Campaign, S.C. 4th Dist., 1986; staff asst. U.S. Ho. of Reps., Spartanburg, 1987-93; acct. The Salvation Army, Spartanburg, 1994—; coord. 4th Dist. Congl. Classroom, 1988-92. Sec. Spartanburg County Dem. Party, 1994-96; vol. Am. Diabetes Assn., Columbia, S.C., 1985-92. Grad. Leadership Spartanburg, 1990; named Mem. of Yr., Spartanburg chpt. Am. Diabetes Assn., 1988. Mem. Am. Soc. Pub. Adminstrs.

PELLER, MARCI TERRY, real estate executive; b. Upland, Pa., Nov. 5, 1949; d. Max Maclyn and Lucille Eugenia (Zucker) P. AA, Harcum Jr. Coll., Bryn Mawr, Pa., 1971; student, Villanova U., 1971-73. With sales dept. William H. Cartwright Real Estate, North Palm Beach, Fla., 1985-91; realtor-assoc. Fin. Realty Group, Lake Park, Fla., 1991—; owner, operator Atlas Bookkeeping Svcs., 1996—. Republican. Jewish. Office: Fin Realty Group 9498 Alternate A1A Lake Park FL 33403-1439

PELLETIER, NANCY ANNE, obstetrical and gynecological nurse, educator; b. St. Louis, June 16, 1951; d. David Cooper Hill and Cenith Lorraine Gore; m. Russell Dean Pelletier, June 16, 1972; children: Kyle, Lindsay, Bradley. Cert. in practical nursing, Alexandria Hosp. Sch. of Practical Nursing, 1971; cert. in health edn., U. Md., 1973; AAS magna cum laude, No. Va. C.C., 1984. LPN, Va.; RN, Va. LPN in pediatrics Alexandria (Va.) Hosp., 1971-72, LPN in medications, 1972-73, LPN in post partum and intensive care nursery, 1977-84, nurse post partum and float pool, 1984-85, childbirth educator, 1978—; sch. nurse, tchr. health edn. Alexandria City Pub. Schs., 1973-76; lead nurse Ob-Gyn Assocs. No. Va., Alexandria, 1984-91; lead ob-gyn nurse Kaiser Permanente of Mid-Atlantic Region, Woodbridge, Va., 1991—; advisor Vocat. Edn. Clubs Am., Washington, 1974. Author: (pamphlet) A Nurse Discusses Your Cesarean Delivery, (teaching tool) Test Your Pregnancy Knowledge. Mem. NAACOG, Am. Soc. for Psychoprophylaxis in Obstetrics (cert. ACCE), Phi Theta Kappa.

PELLI, MOSHE, Judaic studies educator; b. Israel, 1936; came to U.S., 1957; married; 2 children. BS in Journalism/Liberal Studies, NYU, 1960; PhD in Modern Hebrew Lit., Dropsie Coll., 1967. Asst. prof. dept. Oriental lang. and lit. U. Tex., Austin, 1967-71; sr. lectr. dept. Hebrew lit. Ben-Gurion U., Beer Sheva, Israel, 1971-74; assoc. prof. modern Hebrew lang. and lit. Cornell U., Ithaca, N.Y., 1974-78; assoc. prof. Erna Michael Coll. Yeshiva U., N.Y.C., 1978-84; assoc. prof. fgn. langs. U. Cen. Fla., Orlando, 1985-88, prof., 1989—, dir. Judaic studies program, 1985—; vis. prof. dept. religious studies Rice U., Houston, 1970-71; vis. prof. dept. Hebrew lit. Hebrew U., Jerusalem, 1971-72, Tchrs. Coll., Beer Sheva, 1973-74, Melbourne (Australia) U., summers/1977-78; vis. prof. Bklyn. Coll., Lehman Coll., CUNY, 1979-80; exec. dir. Hanoar Haivri, 1962-66, Hebrew Month, 1962-66; vis. scholar Oxford Ctr. for Postgrad. Hebrew Studies, summers/1984, 91, Inst. Jewish Studies, Hebrew U., Jerusalem, summer/1991. Author: (Hebrew texts) Introduction to Modern Hebrew Literature in 18th and 19th Centuries, 1972, (Hebrew) Moses Mendelssohn: Bonds of Tradition, 1972, Struggle for Change, 1988, Getting By in Hebrew, 1984, Age of Haskalah, 1979, also 2 novels, 1961, 65, 8 children's books in Hebrew, 1963-80, and 3 collections of texts, 1971-72; editor Niv Hebrew Lit. Quar., 1957-66; founding editor Lamishpaha, 1964-66, editor, 1983-85; contbr. articles, revs., short stories to profl. publs. Recipient Abraham Friedman Prize for Hebrew Culture in Am. award Hebrew Lang. and Culture Assn. of Am., 1992, Coll. of Arts and Scis. Disting. Rschr. award, 1996, U. Ctrl. Fla. Univ. Disting. Rschr. award, 1996; recipient grants Am. Coun. Learned Studies, 1971, 77, Fla. Endowment Humanities, 1985-86, T.O.P. Jewish Found., 1986-87, Lucius N. Littauer Found., 1990, Fla.-Israel Inst., 1991, Joseph Meyerhoff Fund, 1991; recipient Svc. citation Adult Inst. for Jewish Life, 1987, Meml. Found. for Jewish Culture fellowship, 1996; named scholar-in-residence Temple B'nai Israel, Clearwater, Fla., 1989; Dropsie Coll. fellow, 1962. Mem. Assn. for Jewish Studies, Am. Acad. Religion, Am. Soc. 18th Century Studies, Nat. Assn. Profs. of Hebrew (exec. coun. 1978-84, membership sec. 1982-84), World Union Jewish Studies, Am. Acad. Jewish Rsch. Home: 1140 Washington Ave Winter Park FL 32789-5657 Office: U Cen Fla PO Box 161990 Orlando FL 32816-1990

PELLICONE, WILLIAM, artist, sculptor, writer, architect; b. Phila., Apr. 12, 1915; s. Emilio and Amelia (Practico) P.; m. Marle Guzzette, July 1964 (div. 1992); m. Ilka Bartel, Aug. 5, 1992. Student, Temple U., Pa. Acad. Fine Arts. lectr. art Phila. Parkway Mus., Queens Settlement, N.Y., U. Iowa, Iowa City, Delaware Sch. Sys., Converse Coll., S.C., Ednl. Alliance, N.Y. One-man shows include Allen Stone Gallery, N.Y., Beryl Lush Gallery, Phila., Trylon Gallery, Southampton, N.Y., Capricorn Gallery, Bethesda, Md., Opus 127 Gallery, Soho, N.Y.C., Harpers Coll., Binghamton, N.Y., Phoenix Gallery, N.Y., Creighton Univ., Nebr., Gallery East, East Hampton, N.Y., Frederick Spratt Gallery, San Jose, Calif.; group shows include Allan Stone Gallery, N.Y., Egan Gallery, N.Y., Alan Gallery, N.Y., Betty Parsons Gallery, N.Y., Tanager Gallery, N.Y., Phoenix Gallery, N.Y., M & L Gallery of Fine Art, N.Y., Arsenal Gallery, N.Y., Camino Gallery, N.Y., Trylon Gallery, N.Y., March Gallery, N.Y., Capricorn Gallery, Bethesda, Md., Brata Gallery, N.Y., Art Alliance, Phila., Landmark Gallery, N.Y., Tenth St. Days, N.Y., Profile Gallery, N.Y., Noho Gallery, N.Y., Gallery East, East Hampton, N.Y., Marie Pellicone Gallery, N.Y., Parish Mus., Southampton, N.Y., Elaine Benson Gallery, Bridgehampton, N.Y., Belanthi Gallery, Bklyn.; permanent collections include Met. Mus. Art, N.Y.C., Boston Mus., Smithsonian Inst., Washington, Am. Broadcasting Collection, Iowa Mus., Iowa City, Bayonne (N.Y.) Mus., Martin-Rathburn Gallery, San Antonio. With Merchant Marines, 1943-45, France. Grantee Barnes Found., Temple U., Pa. Acad. Fine Arts, Greek Govt., others. Republican. Home and Office: 101 Myers Creek Rd Dripping Springs TX 78620-3302

PELLOCK, JOHN MICHAEL, child neurologist; b. Passaic, N.J., Dec. 25, 1943; s. John and Laura (Holubko) P.; m. Mary Lee Miller, June 27, 1970; children: Mary Kathryn, John Michael. BA, Johns Hopkins U., 1965; MS, Fairleigh Dickinson U., 1967; MD, St. Louis U., 1971. Diplomate Nat. Bd. Med. Examiners, Am. Bd. Psychiatry and Neurology, Am. Bd. Pediatrics; lic. physician, Mo., N.J., N.Y., Md., Va. Intern, resident in pediatrics Med. Coll. Va., Richmond, 1971-73, asst. prof. neurology, 1978, asst. prof. pediatrics, 1979; fellow Columbia Presbyn. Med. Ctr., N.Y.C., 1973-76; instr. neurology and pediatrics U. Health Scis., Bethesda, Md., 1976-78; assoc. prof. neurology and pediatrics Va. Commonwealth U., Richmond, 1984-88, prof. neurology and pediatrics, 1988—, chmn. epilepsy divsn., 1993—; prof. pharmacy and pharms. Med. Coll. Va./Va. Commonwealth U., Richmond, 1994, chmn. child neurology divsn., 1995; mem. academic staff D.C. Children's Hosp., Nat. Med. Ctr., Washington, 1976-78; mem. staff Med. Coll. Va. Hosp., 1978—, Children's Hosp., Richmond, 1986—, St. Mary's Hosp., Richmond, 1988—, Nat. Naval Med. Ctr., Bethesda, 1976-78; cons., lectr. and presenter in field. Editor: Neurologic Emergencies in Infancy and Childhood, 1984, Pediatric Epilepsy, Diagnosis and Therapy, 1993, Neurologic Emergencies in Infancy and Childhood, 2d edit., 1993, A Textbook of Epilepsy, 5th edit., 1997, Pediatric Epilepsy, 2d edit., 1997; guest editor Seizure Disorders, Pediatric Clinics North America, 1989, Promise and Progress in the Treatment of Epilepsy, Neurology, 34, 1993, Seminars in Child Neurology; editor jours. Practice of Pediatrics, 1980-88, Drug Evaluations, 1991-96; (newsletter) Child Neurology Soc., 1986-88; contbr. numerous articles and abstracts to profl. jours. Eucharistic minister St. Edward's Cath. Ch., Bon Air, Va., 1980—; profl. advisor Va. Capital of March of Dimes, 1980-86; bd. dirs. Cath. Charities of Richmond, 1981-93 (Cert. of Appreciation 1993). Lt. comdr. USNR, 1968-78, hon. discharge. Recipient Cert. of Appreciation, S.C. Epilepsy Assn., 1985; named Best Drs. in Am., Woodward/White Inc., 1993, 94, Am. Men and Women of Sci., 1994; Am. Acad. Pediatrics fellow, 1972; grantee NIH, 1972-74, 78, 84, 87—, Burroughs Wellcome Co., 1980-82, 84-86, 91—, Boots Pharms., Inc., 1984-85, Ciba-Geigy, 1988, 92-93, A.H. Robins, 1984-85, GD Searle Co., 1986, Abbott Labs., 1986-88, 90—, Parke Davis/Warner Lambert, 1988—, Carter-Wallace, 1991-95, DHHS, 1986—, Med. Coll. Va., 1989-93, Janssen Rsch. Found., 1989-97, others. Fellow Am. Acad. Neurology, Am. Acad. Pediatrics; mem. AMA, Am. Epilepsy Soc. (edn. com. 1991-94), Epilepsy Found. Am., Epilepsy Assn. Va. (bd. dirs. 1979—, profl. adv. bd. 1983—, chmn. 1983-88), Va. Neurol. Soc., Med. Soc. Va., Va. Pediat. Soc., Child Neurology Soc. (exec. com. 1988-90, editor newsletter 1986-88, membership com. 1982-86, 88-90), Itnernat. Child Neurology Assn., Itnernat. League Against Epilepsy (commn. 1994), Richmond Pediatric Soc., Richmond Acad. Medicine, USN Neurol. Soc. Office: Med Coll Va/Va Commonwealth PO Box 980211 MCV Station Richmond VA 23298

PELOSOF, HENRI VIDAL, physical medicine and rehabilitation physician, educator; b. Marseille, France, Apr. 9, 1934; came to U.S., 1960; m. Anne Gelfand, Nov. 7, 1969; children: Serena, Lorraine. Faculty of Sci. degree, U. Paris, 1955; Faculty of Medicine degree, U. Rene Descartes, 1960. Diplomate Am. Bd. Phys. Medicine and Rehab.; lic. physician Tex., N.Mex. Rotating intern Miriam Hosp., Providence, 1960-61; resident in phys. medicine and rehab. Inst. Rehab. Medicine NYU Med. Ctr., N.Y.C., 1963-66; chief resident phys. medicine and rehab. Bellevue Hosp., N.Y.C., 1965; med. coord. World Rehab. Fund USAID, 1967-68; dir. rehab. svcs. Miriam Hosp., Providence, 1969-70; asst. prof. dept. phys. medicine and rehab. Baylor Coll. Medicine, Houston, 1970-73; attending physician, chief amputee svc. Tex. Inst. for Rehab. and Rsch., Houston, 1970-73; clin. asst. prof. phys. medicine and rehab. Southwestern Med. Sch., Dallas, 1992—; attending physician, chief phys. medicine and rehab. sect. St. Paul Med. Ctr., Dallas, 1974—; cons. med. staff Presbyn. Hosp.; staff physician VA Hosp., Dallas. Author: (with others) Elective Levels of Amputation of Lower Extremities According to Modern Techniques of Prosthetics, 1968; author: (movies, with others) Comprehensive Rehabilitation of a Quadruple Amputee, 1973, Myoelectric and Me, 1972; contbr. articles to profl. jours. Lt. French Army Med. Corp., 1961-63. Decorated Algerian Campaign medal. Mem. AMA, Am. Acad. Phys. Medicine and Rehab., Am. Assn. Electromyography and Electrodiagnosis, Tex. Med. Assn., Tex. Soc. Phys. Medicine and Rehab. (pres. 1990-91), Dallas County Med. Soc., Dallas Metroplex Phys. Medicine and Rehab. Soc. (pres. 1984). Office: Ste 614 Lockbox 54 8210 Walnut Hill Ln Dallas TX 75231

PELTON, JAMES RODGER, librarian; b. St. Louis, Mar. 21, 1945; s. Norman C. and Leona V. (Schulte) P.; m. Sandra Lee Birdsell, Mar. 29, 1969; 2 daus., Joni Lee, Vicki Sue. B.A., U. Mo., 1967, M.L.S., 1969. Br. librarian Scenic Regional Library, Union, Mo., 1968-71; adminstr. Daniel Boone Regional Library - Columbia Center, Columbia, Mo., 1971-78; cons. La. State Library, Baton Rouge, 1978-80; dir. Shreve Meml. Library, Shreveport, La., 1980—. Mem. ALA, La. Library Assn. Home: 3201 Old Mooringsport Rd Shreveport LA 71107-3926 Office: 424 Texas St Shreveport LA 71101-3522

PEMBERTON, LISA SUZANNE, English language and oral communications educator; b. Benton, Ark., Sept. 2, 1963; d. Johnny Bruce and Linda Joyce (Woolem) P. BS in English, Henderson State U., 1984; MS in English, Ark. State U., 1992. Cert. secondary tchr., Ark. Instr. Hughes (Ark.) H.S., 1984—; part-time instr. East Ark. C.C., Forrest City, 1988—. Author: An Anchor of the Faith: A Study of the Episcopal Catechism, 1992; co-author (curriculum) Integrated Am. History and Lit., 1996. Recipient Profl. Devel. award S.E. Regional Assn. Tchr. Educators, 1984, Tchr. of Yr. award Henderson State U., 1996. Episcopalian. Home: PO Box 1145 710 Main Hughes AR 72348 Office: Hughes Pub Schs PO Box 9 Hughes AR 72348

PEN, RONALD ALLEN, music educator, music critic; b. Chgo., Feb. 22, 1951; s. Rudolph Theodore and Yvonne (Fillis) P.; m. Helen Stanley Behr; 1 child, Robin Stanley. BA, Washington & Lee U., 1973; MA, Tulane U., 1982; PhD, U. Ky., 1987. Chair fine arts dept. Latin Sch. Chgo., Ill., 1973-79, St. Martin's Sch., Metairie, La., 1979-83; prof. music U. Ky., Lexington, 1988—; organist, choirmaster Holy Trinity Ch., Georgetown, Ky., 1984—; music critic Lexington (Ky.) Herald-Leader, 1988—. Author: Introduction to Music, 1992; contbr. articles to profl. jours. Mem. Am. Musicological Soc., Coll. Music Soc., Sonneck Soc. for Am. Music (program chair), Am. Studies Assn., Appalachian Assn. Sacred Harp Singers (dir. 1983—). Episcopalian. Office: Univ Ky 105 Fine Arts Bldg Lexington KY 40506

PENA, MODESTA CELEDONIA, retired principal; b. San Diego, Tex., Mar. 3, 1929; d. Encarnacion E. and Teofila (Garcia) P.; BA, Tex. State Coll. for Women, 1950, MA, 1953, cert. supr., 1979; cert. prin. Tex. A&I U., 1961, cert. supt., 1981. Tchr. English, San Diego (Tex.) High Sch., 1950-76; asst. supt. curriculum and instrn. San Diego Ind. Sch. Dist., 1976-80; gifted edn. resource tchr. William Adams Jr. High Sch., Alice, Tex., 1980-83, asst. prin. for instrn., 1983-88; faculty Bee County Coll., 1975-76. V.p., San Diego PTA, 1963; charter mem. Duval County Hist. Commn., 1975—; reporter Duval Co. Hist. Com., 1988—. Newspaper Fund Inc. fellow, 1964; recipient Adolfo Arguijo Day award, 1990; named Outstanding Sr. of Duval County, Grayfest, 1992; named to San Diego Hall of Honor, 1995. Mem. Tex. State Tchrs. Assn. (rec. sec. 1952-53, 63-64, 1st v.p. 1957-58, 66-67, pres. 1961), Delta Kappa Gamma (rec. sec. chpt. 1972-74, first v.p. 1974-76, pres. 1976-78, achievement award 1985, chpt. parlimentarian, 1984-88, state com. Eula Lee Carter Meml. Fund, state com. constn., area coord. state com. pers., state recording sec., state com. nominations, state achievement award 1996),

Phi Delta Kappa (treas. chpt. 1978-79, rec. sec. chpt. 1983-84). Home: PO Box 353 306 W Gravis Ave San Diego TX 78384-2604

PENA, RAYMUNDO JOSEPH, bishop; b. Corpus Christi, Tex., Feb. 19, 1934; s. Cosme A. and Elisa (Ramon) P. D.D., Assumption Sem., San Antonio, 1957. Ordained priest Roman Catholic Ch., 1957; asst. pastor St. Peter's Ch., Laredo, Tex., 1957-60, St. Joseph's-Our Lady of Fatima, Alamo, Tex., 1960-63, Sacred Heart, Mathis, Tex., 1963-67, Christ the King and Our Lady of Pillar Parishes, Corpus Christi, 1967-69; pastor Our Lady of Guadalupe Parish, Corpus Christi, 1969-76; v.p. Corpus Christi Diocesan Senate of Priests, 1970-76; aux. bishop of San Antonio, 1976-80; bishop El Paso, 1980-95, Brownsville, Tex., 1995—; mem. secretariat to Prep. Synod of Bishops for Am. Mem. Nat. Conf. Cath. Bishops, U.S. Cath. Conf. (chmn. bishops' com. for hispanic affairs 1987-90, bishops' com. for ch. in L.Am. 1994—). Home: Rt 8 Box 629 7600 Old Military Rd Brownsville TX 78522 Office: PO Box 2279 Brownsville TX 78522-2279

PENA, RICHARD, lawyer; b. San Antonio, Feb. 13, 1948; s. Merced and Rebecca (Trejo) P.; m. Carolyn Sarah Malley, May 25, 1979; 1 stepchild, Jason Charles Schubert. BA, U. Tex., 1970, JD, 1976. Bar: Tex. 1976, Colo. 1986. Pvt. practice law, Austin, 1976—; instr. bus. law St. Edwards U., Austin, 1983, Austin Community Coll., 1981-82; broker Tex. Real Estate Commn., 1980—; sports editor, Austin Light newspaper, 1982. Bd. dirs. Ctr. for Battered Women, Austin, 1979-82, Austin Assn. Retarded Citizens, 1980-82; chmn. Austin Travis County Mental Health/Mental Retardation Pub. Responsibility Comm., 1979-84; chmn. pvt. facilities monitoring com. Austin Assn. Retarded Citizens, 1981; bd. dirs. Boys Club of Austin, 1987-88. Named One of Outstanding Young Men Am., Jaycees, 1982. Fellow Tex. Bar Found. (mem. bd. trustees 1994, sec., treas. 1994, vice chair 1995, chair 1996); mem. State Bar of Tex. (bd. dirs. dist. 9 1991—, exec. com., 1992—, chmn. minority representation com. 1991-92, chmn. profl. devel. com. 1991-92, policy manual com. 1993, mem. ABA nominating com. 1990, fed. judiciary appointments com. 1984-86, opportunities for minorities in the profession com. 1990-91, mem. advtg. review com.), Travis County Bar Assn. (trustee lawyer referral svc. 1984-85, bd. dirs. 1986-88, sec. 1988, pres. elect, 89, pres. 1990-91, chmn. jud. screening com. 1987, chmn. 1988-89, ins. com. 1988, 89, chmn. law day banquet com. 1988-89, lawyer referral svc. com. 1983-84, bd. trustees 1984-86, membership com. 1989), Capitol Area Mexican Am. Lawyers (pres. 1985, Outstanding Hispanic Lawyer Austin 1989), Legal Aid Soc. Cen. Tex. (bd. dirs. 1984), Austin Young Lawyers Assn., Tex. Trial Lawyers Assn., Austin C. of C. (leadership Austin 1985-86). Democrat. Home: 107 Top O The Lake Dr Austin TX 78734-5234 Office: Law Office of Richard Pena 901 S Mo Pac Expy Austin TX 78746-5747

PENALOZA, BETTY RAQUEL, international affairs consultant; b. Lima, Peru, Oct. 4, 1947; came to U.S., 1970; d. Hernan and America (Ortiz) P.; m. Ray D. Roy Sr., Mar. 23, 1974 (div. Feb. 1989). BBA, U. St. Thomas, 1992, postgrad., 1993-94. Adminstrv. asst. Petroperu, Lima, 1968-70; adminstrv. asst. Petroperu, Houston, 1970-74, buyer, 1974-88; petroleum attache Consulate of Peru, Houston, 1974-87; buyer Serpimpex, S.A., Houston, 1991-93; owner Am. Victoria Trading Co., Houston, 1994—. Vice-chair Loop Program, End Hunger Network, 1993; vol. Mayor's Office, NAFTA Liaison, 1993. Named First Woman Elected Sec. of the Consular Corps, Consular Corps Houston, 1987. Mem. Consular Corps (hon. life).

PENCE, DANNY B., parasitology educator, researcher; b. Louisville, Jan. 18, 1943; s. Denny W. and Nellie G. (Harrison) P.; m. Cynthia M. Brown, June 26, 1991; 1 child, Kristin. BS, Western Ky. State U., 1965; MS, La. State U. Med. Ctr., New Orleans, 1967, PhD, 1970. Instr. La. State U. Med. Ctr., 1970-72; asst. prof. pathology Tex. Tech. U. Health Sci. Ctr., Lubbock, 1973-75, assoc. prof. pathology, 1976-75, prof. pathology, 1986—; editor Jour. Wildlife Disease, 1986-91. Contbr. articles to profl. jours., chpts. to books. Recipient Disting. Svc. award, Wildlife Disease Assn., 1991. Mem. Wildlife Disease Assn. (coun. officer, 1993-96). Office: Texas Tech U Dept Pathology 3601 4th St Lubbock TX 79430

PENCE, HOBERT LEE, physician; b. Campton, Ky., July 14, 1941; s. Bruce Elmer and Elva (Banks) P.; m. Marsha Lee Sweet, June 29, 1962; children: Robert, Ryan, Stefanie. BS, Ohio State U., Columbus, 1963, MD, 1968. Residency Walter Reed Gen. Hosp., Washington, 1969-71, fellowship in allergy and clin. immunology, 1971-73; allergy and immunology pvt. practice, Louisville, 1975—; asst. clin. prof. medicine U. Louisville, 1976-81; assoc. clin. prof. PediatricsU. Louisville Health Scis. Ctr., 1981-95. Contbr. articles to profl. jours. V.p. Jefferson County Med. Soc., Louisville, 1984-86; pres. Greater Louisville Allergy Soc., 1990-92. Major U.S. Army, 1969-75. Mem. Southeastern Allergy Assn. (1st v.p., pres. elect, pres. 1996). Office: Kentuckiana Allergy 9113 Leesgate Rd Louisville KY 40222-5003

PENDARVIS, DONNA KAYE, elementary secondary school educator, adminstrator; b. New Orleans, June 19, 1959; d. Ray Haddox and Nita Sims; 1 child, Krista. BS, U. So. Miss., 1979; MEd, William Carey Coll., 1982, EdS, 1984; MEd in Guidance and Counseling, Southeastern La. U., 1992. Cert. elem. tchr., Miss., La.; lic. profl. counselor. Tchr. Sumrall (Miss.) Elem. Sch., 1979-88; tchr. kindergarten Washington Parish Sch. Bd., Franklinton, La., 1988-89; elem. tchr. Columbia (Miss.) Acad., 1989-92; counselor and adminstr. St. Tammany Parish, Covington, La., 1992-94; counselor Sixth Ward Jr. H.S., Covington, 1996—; counselor, adminstr. Varnado (La.) H.S., 1994-96; mem. La. Disting. Educator Team. Grantee Miss. Power Found. Mem. NEA, ASCD, Am. Assn. Math. Tchrs., Am. Fedn. Tchrs., Miss. Fedn. Tchrs., La. Edn. Assn., Lamar County Classroom Tchrs. Assn., Washington Parish Reading Assn., Miss. Pvt. Sch. Assn., La. Counselors Assn., La. Vocat. Assn., La. Adminstrn. Sch. Employees Assn., Chi Omega Iota. Home: 276 C Lakeview Dr Slidell LA 70458 Office: Sixth Ward Jr High Sch 72360 Hwy 41 Pearl River LA 70452

PENDER, MICHAEL ROGER, engineering consultant, professional society administrator; b. Bklyn., Feb. 18, 1926; s. Horace Gibson and Lilian Frances (Higgins) P.; m. Francina Joan Krosschell, June 4, 1949; children: Michael Roger, Jr., William J., Robin Jane, Richard A., John A. AB, Dartmouth Coll., 1949, MS in Civil Engring., 1950. Registered profl. engr., Fla., N.Y., N.H.; diplomate Am. Acad. Environ. Engrs. Project engr. Madigan-Hyland, Inc., L.I., 1950-60; dir. state exhibits N.Y. World's Fair, Flushing, 1960-65; commr. pub. works, Town of Hempstead (N.Y.), 1966-77, Nassau County, Mineola, N.Y., 1978-82; supt. pub. works Village of Valley Stream (N.Y.), 1982-85; tech. advisor N.Y. State Assembly, Albany, 1985-86; cons. engr. Boyle Engring. Corp., Sarasota, Fla., 1987—; exec. dir. World's Fair Collectors Soc., 1968—; mem. Sarasota County Pub. Utilities Adv. Bd., 1986-87; vice-chmn. Solid Waste Mgmt Adv. Bd., 1992—, Sarasota County Water & Sewer Adv. Bd., 1995—. Contbr. articles to profl. jours. Treas. Town of Hempstead Local Devel. Corp., 1967-86, Town of Hempstead Ind. Devel. Agy., 1973-86, Nassau County Local Devel. Corp., 1978-83; pres. Univ. Club of L.I., Hempstead, 1985-86. Sgt. U.S. Army, 1945-46. Named Profl. Engring. Mgr. of Yr., N.Y. State Soc. Profl. Engrs., 1979. Fellow ASCE (life), Fellow, Inst. Transp. Engrs. (life); mem. NSPE (life, v.p. 1982-84), Fellow, Fla. Engring. Soc., Am. Pub. Works Assn. (life;pres. 1984-85, chmn. Suncoast br., 1993-94; one of Top Ten Pub. Works Ofcls. in U.S. 1973), Sarasota County C. of C., Dartmouth Club of Sarasota (pres. 1991-93), Sarasota Sister Cities Assn. (treas. 1990—). Republican. Episcopalian. Lodge: Rotary (pres. Sarasota Bay 1992-93). Avocation: photographing railroad depots. Home: 6639 Waterford Ln Sarasota FL 34238-2639 Office: Worlds Fair Collectors Soc PO Box 20806 Sarasota FL 34276-3806

PENDERGRASS, EWELL DEAN, communications executive; b. Houston, Dec. 24, 1945; s. Ewell Burl and Mary LaVerne (Sharp) P.; m. Linda Jo Williams, 1973; children: William Dean, Douglas Aaron, Nagaya Jo. AAS, Westark Community Coll., 1979. Communication technician Murdock Communication, Ft. Smith, Ark., 1966-73; electronics technician City of Ft. Smith, 1973—, now electronics supr.; co-owner LED Communications, 1975—; broadcast engr. Sta. KWHN, 1972-73, Sta. KFSA, 1975-76. Mem. Am. Water Works Assn., Ark. Water Works and Pollution Control Assn. (chmn., Western dist. dir.), Ark. Dept. Pollution and Ecology Wastewater Lic. Bd; mem. Ark. Lic. Com. Democrat. Methodist. Club: Border Amateur Radio (pres. 1974-75). Home: 1106 Country Meadow Ln Cedarville AR 72932-9524 Office: 3900 Kelley Hwy Fort Smith AR 72904

PENDERGRAST, BRYNDA MARIE, elementary school educator; b. Johnson City, Tenn., Sept. 11, 1941; d. Lester E. and June (Wofford) Burnette; m. James Hugh Pendergrast, June 12, 1960; children: James, Stephen. BS, Miss. State Coll. for Women, 1963; MEd, U. So. Miss., 1976; postgrad., Copiah-Lincoln C.C., 1983, 89; gifted cert., Alcorn U., 1991. Tchr. Washington Elem. Sch., Natchez, Miss., 1963-65; tchr. Braden Elem. Sch., Natchez, 1966-68, Adams County Christian Sch., 1969-73, Trinity Episcopal Sch., 1974-78, Morgantown Jr. High Sch., 1978-89, Natchez Mid. Sch., 1989—; mem. sch. improvement, sch. discipline coms.; math club, nat. jr. honor soc. advisor; mem. state com. for computer software evaluation; project SEED evaluator. Interpreter for deaf, svcs. at First Bapt. Ch., Jefferson County Hosp., Youth Ct.; Youth Sunday Sch. divsn. dir. and tchr. First Bapt. Ch.; dir. Ch. Summer Camp, Vacation Bible Sch. dir.; puppet dir. Youth Puppet Team. Named Outstanding Jr. Mem. DAR, 1974. Mem. Nat. Coun. Tchrs. Math., Miss. Coun. Tchrs. Math. (coord. math. contest), Miss. Ednl. Computing Assn. (charter, state awardee for excellence in sci. and math. teaching 1994). Home: 100 Traceside Dr Natchez MS 39120-9277 Office: Natchez Mid Sch 1221 Martin Luther King Natchez MS 39120

PENDERY, EDWARD STUART, deputy county judge; b. Dayton, Ky., June 1, 1931; s. Edward Stuart and Marguerite Garnet (Owens) P.; m. Nancy Jean Burck, Aug. 22, 1958; children: Michael Edward, Darren Frederick, Eric Christopher. Student, U.S. Tech. Sch., 1952. R.R. dep. chief clk. N.Y. Ctrl. R.R., Cin., 1950-51; R.R. comml. agt. C & WC Rlwy., Cin., 1955-58; salesman Pittsburg Paint & Glass, Cin., 1958-63; ops. mgr. Am. Laundry/Econo Sales, Cin., 1963-67; pvt. practice I.P.C.S. Pub., Ft. Thomas, Ky., 1967-68, 74-86; mag. sales and display ads staff Cin. (Ohio) Mag., 1969-74; dep. county judge Campbell County Ky., Newport, Ky., 1986—. Editor, originator: (tabloids) North Ky. Sports Scene, 1976—, Bellevue News, 1980—, Shopping Guides, 1980—. Chmn. site group North Ky. U., Highland Heights, 1968; chmn. study group Ft. Thomas (Ky.) Sch. Sys., 1970; dir. North Ky. U. Norse Club, Highland Heights, 1971-89, Famous Stars H.S. Program, Bellevue, Ky., 1978-94; mem. Bellevue Civic Assn., 1980—, North Ky. Adminstrs. Group, Newport, 1986-94, Libr. Site Com., Cold Spring, Ky., 1993-94, Nat. Alliance Bus., 1993. Staff sgt. USAF, 1951-55. Named Ky. Col., Ky. Gov., 1967; recipient Meritorious Svc. award Cub Scouts, 1968. Mem. Am. Assn. Ret. Persons, Elks, Am. Legion, North Ky. U. Norse Club. Democrat. Home: 38 Homestead Pl Fort Thomas KY 41075-1225

PENDLETON, JANICE BISHOP, company executive; b. Birmingham, Ala., Sept. 7, 1947; d. Lee O'Neal and Ovilee (Bryant) Bishop; m. Hubert Lee Hiott, Jr., Feb. 12, 1969 (div. 1978); children: Stephen Lee, Christopher Allan; m. Romie Robert Pendleton III, June 5, 1981. Student, Jacksonville State U., 1965-68. Pres. Auto Classics, Birmingham, 1982-83; owner Precious Memories, Birmingham, 1982-83; pres. Pendleton Enterprises, Birmingham, 1993—; sec., treas. ISC Tech., Birmingham, 1980—. Author: The Assignment, 1991, William Thomas Zackery Brown, 1992, The Zoo, 1993. Republican. Baptist. Home: 802 Sherman Oaks Dr Birmingham AL 35235

PENDLETON, RICHARD F., logistics systems analyst; b. Phila., Jan. 3, 1940; s. Theodore Francis and Jean Caroline (Moxley) P.; m. Barbara Ann Ezzell, Nov. 9, 1967; children: Sarah Kimberly, Brian Richard. BA, Gettysburg (Pa.) Coll., 1963; MS, Troy (Ala.) State U., 1982. Commd. 2d lt. U.S. Army, 1963, advanced through grades to lt. col., 1982, ret., 1990; dir. intergrated logistics support Nichols Rsch. Corp., Huntsville, Ala., 1990-96, sr. mem. tech. staff, 1996—; sr. logistics systems analyst Logistics, Engring., Environ. Support Svcs., Inc., 1996—. Mem. City Planning Commn., Hartselle, Ala., 1992-96. Mem. Am. Def. Preparedness Assn. (life), Ordnance Corps Assn. (life), Assn. U.S. Army (life), Soc. Logistics Engrs., Air Def. Arty. Assn. (life), U.S. Naval Inst., U.S. Army Command and Gen. Staff Coll. (life). Republican.

PENFIELD, ADDISON PIERCE, broadcaster, marketing specialist; b. Meriden, Conn., Sept. 6, 1918; s. Luther George and Mildred Wetherill (Pierce) P.; m. Virginia Marie Cameron, Sept. 23, 1939; children: Addison P. Jr., Cameron Wallace, Nancy Sue Penfield Wease, Sandra W. Penfield Suggs. AB, Duke U., 1940. Sports commentator WPTF Radio, Raleigh, N.C., 1939-41; Duke sports info. broadcaster Duke U., Durham, N.C., 1941-42; sports and news broadcaster WSB Radio, Atlanta, 1942-44; news, sports, spl. events broadcaster WRNY Radio, Rochester, N.Y., 1946-50; news dir. WIS Radio, columbia, S.C., 1950-52; news and sport broadcaster WBIG Radio, Greensboro, N.C., 1952-62, WSJS Radio and TV, Winston-Salem, N.C., 1963-64, WKXR Radio, Asheboro, N.C., 1965—; play-by-play football announcer Atlantic Refining Co., Phila., 1938-41, 46-50; mgr. Duke Football Network, Durham, 1952-63, 67-69, 74-75; mktg. specialist Regional Consol. Svcs., Asheboro, 1988—. Columnist Asheboro Courier-Tribune, 1969. Chmn. Asheboro Housing Authority, 1983—; bd. dirs. Am. Cancer Soc., Asheboro, 1991-94; bd. dirs., v.p. Asheboro/Randolph C. of C., 1972-74. 1st lt. U.S. Army, 1944-46. Recipient Lee Kirby award D. Mizio's Restaurant, 1953, Svc. to Sports award Asheboro Sports Coun., 1974; named Sportscaster of Yr., N.C. AP, 1953, Sportscaster of Yr., Hot Stove League, 1970. Charter mem. Atlantic Coast Sports Writers (pres. 1956); mem. Carolinas Golf Writers Assn. (life, v.p. 1958), Soc. Profl. Journalists, Nat. Sportscasters and Sports Writers Assn. Republican. Episcopalian. Home: 625 Corwith St Asheboro NC 27203-4274 Office: Regional Consol Svcs 221 S Fayetteville St Asheboro NC 27204-1883

PENG, LIANG-CHUAN, mechanical engineer; b. Taiwan, Feb. 6, 1936; came to U.S., 1965, naturalized, 1973; s. Mu-Sui and Wang-Su (Yang) P.; diploma Taipei Inst. Tech., 1960; M.S., Kans. State U., 1967; m. Wen-Fong Kao, Nov. 18, 1962; children: Tsen-Loong, Tsen-Hsin, Lina, Linda. Project engr. Taiwan Power Co., 1960-65; asst. engr. Carlson & Sweatt, N.Y.C., 1966-67; asst. engr. Pioneer Engrs., Chgo., 1967-68; mech. engr. Bechtel, San Francisco, 1969-71; sr. specialist Nuclear Services Co., San Jose, Calif., 1971-75; sr. engr. Brown & Root, Houston, 1975; stress engr. Foster Wheeler, Houston, 1976; staff engr. AAA Technologists, Houston, 1977; prin. engr. M.W. Kellogg, Houston, 1978-82; pres., owner Peng Engring., Houston, 1982—; instr. U. Houston; condr. piping tech. seminars. Chmn. South Bay Area Formosan Assn., 1974, No. Calif. Formosan Fedn., 1975. Registered profl. engr., Tex., Calif. Developer: (computer progarams) SIMFLEX; condr. seminars in field. Mem. ASME, Nat. Soc. Profl. Engrs. Buddhist. Home: 3010 Manila Ln Houston TX 77043-1312

PENLAND, ARNOLD CLIFFORD, JR., college dean, educator; b. Asheville, N.C., Oct. 8, 1933; s. Arnold Clifford and Pearl (Bailey) P.; m. Jean Wall (div. 1967); 1 child, Marcia Jean; m. Joan Eudy; 1 child, Elizabeth Bailey. BS, Western Carolina U., 1956; MA, Vanderbilt U., 1959; MEd, Duke U., 1966; PhD, Fla. State U., 1983. Tchr. of music Reidsville (N.C.) Pub. Schs., 1956-60; supr. of music Raleigh (N.C.) Pub. Schs., 1960-67; supr. of music and rsch. Smoky Mt. Cultural Arts Devel. Assn., Sylva, N.C., 1967, 1968-69; state supr. of music State Dept. of Edn., Columbia, S.C., 1969-70; assoc. prof. of music U. of Fla., Gainesville, 1970-80, prof. of music, 1980—, assoc. dean and prof. Coll. of Fine Arts, 1981—; prog. dir. Raleigh Cultural Ctr., Inc., 1962-67; music dir. various ch. choirs, N.C. and Fla., 1956-80; ednl. cons. Nat. Grass Roots Opera, Co., Raleigh, 1962-67, bd. dirs. Fla. League of the Arts. Contbr. articles to profl. jours. Mem. Gainesville Cultural Commn., 1975-76, v.p. Alachua County Arts Coun., Inc., 1976-77; bd. dirs. Arts Coun. of Raleigh, Inc., 1963-65. Recipient Disting. Service Citation, Federated Music Clubs of N.C., 1966; grantee Office of Edn., 1967-69. Mem. Nat. Assn. Acad. Affairs Adminstrn. (pres. 1990-92, bd. dirs. 1992-96), Reg. Assn. Acad. Affairs Adminstrn. (pres. 1985-86), Music Educators Nat. Conf., Coll. Music Soc. (life), Lions (v.p. Raleigh chpt. 1963-66), Kiwanis (Kiwanian of Yr. 1989-90, bd. dirs. 1992-96), Order of Omega, Phi Delta Kappa (pres. North Ctrl. Fla. chpt. 1985-86), Sigma Phi Epsilon. Democrat. Presbyterian. Office: U Fla Coll Fine Arts 115800 Gainesville FL 32611-5800

PENLAND, JOHN THOMAS, import and export and development companies executive; b. Guntersville, Ala., Mar. 31, 1930; s. James B. and Kathleen (Bolding) P.; m. Carolyn Joyce White, May 30, 1961; children—Jeffrey K., Mark A., Michael J. B.A., George Washington U., 1957. Vice pres., dir. Rouse, Brewer, Becker & Bryant, Inc., Washington, 1957-63; staff mem. SEC, Washington, 1963-67; pres., dir. INA Trading Corp., Phila., 1968-69; v.p. INA Security Corp., Phila., 1967-69; v.p. Shareholders Mgmt. Co., Los Angeles, 1969, sr. v.p., 1970, exec. v.p., 1970-73, pres., 1973-75, also bd. dirs.; v.p. Shareholders Capital Corp., L.A., 1972-73; v.p., dir. several mut. funds managed by Shareholders Mgmt. Co., 1970-75; pres., chmn., CEO, HMO Internat. and its subs., L.A., 1975; founder, pres., chmn. Pendlar Corp., Atlanta, 1977—; chmn., pres. Bella Vista Developers, Inc., Albuquerque, 1977—; chmn. CompuComp Corp., Atlanta, 1977-81; chmn., pres. Fran Stef Corp., N.Y.C., 1982-89; pres., chmn. Engineered Products Corp., Dandridge, Tenn., 1983-90; founder, chmn., CEO Am. Accessories Inc., Covington, Ga., 1983—; founder, pres., chmn. United Am. Products Corp., Dandridge, 1983-89; founder, chmn. Chamisa Properties, Inc., Albuqueque, 1988-94, Glorieux Ltd., Atlanta, 1988—, Ga. Ptnrs. Ltd., Covington, 1988-94; founder, chmn., dir. Premier Trading Internat., Inc., Atlanta, 1989—; founder, dir. Chamisa Enterprises, Inc., Covington, 1990—; founder, mng. ptnr. Ft. Hill Ptnrs., Knoxville, Tenn., 1990-93; chmn. Einson Freeman & Detroy Corp., Fair Lawn, N.J., 1978-83; founder, dir., pres. West Point Contract Packaging, Inc., Winston-Salem, N.C., 1991—; founder, mng. ptnr. Harbor View, Ltd., Fernandina Beach, Fla., 1992-94; founder, chmn. West Point Tech. Assembly, Inc., Winston-Salem, N.C., 1993—; dir., pres. BKP Industries, Inc., Monroe, Ga., 1995—. Served with AUS, 1948-55. Republican. Episcopalian. Home: PO Box 549 Social Circle GA 30279-0549 Office: 3261 Highway 278 NE Covington GA 30209-3103

PENN, DAWN TAMARA, entrepreneur; b. Knoxville, Tenn., July 22, 1965; d. Morton Hugh and Virginia Audra (Wilson) P. AS, Bauder Fashion Coll., Atlanta, 1984; postgrad., U. Tenn., 1986; grad., Rasnic Sch. Modeling, Knoxville, 1986. Gen. mgr. Merry-Go-Round, Knoxville, 1984-86; mgr., dancer Lady Adonis Inc. Performing Arts Dance Co., Knoxville, 1987-90; owner, pres. Lady Adonis, Inc. Performing Arts Dance Co., Knoxville, 1990—, also chmn.; owner/pres. Penn Mgmt. and Investment Co. Comml. Real Estate, Knoxville, 1989—; deputized bonded rep. Knox County Sheriff's Dept., Knoxville, 1989-90; fgn. dance tours include Aruba, Curacao, Caracas, Barbados, Ont., Que., Montreal, Nfld., Labrador, N.S., New Brunswick; cons. The John Reinhardt Agy., Winston-Salem, N.C., 1987—, Gen. Talent Agy., Monroeville, Pa., 1990—, Xanadu, Inc., Myrtle Beach, S.C., 1991—. Author, editor: Lady Adonis Performing Arts promotional mag., 1988; TV and motion picture credits include: Innocent Blood, 1992, The Phil Donahue Show, N.Y.C., 1989, 91. Coord. bridal fair Big. Bros./Big Sisters Knox County, Knoxville, 1985, 86; judge Southeastern Entertainer of Yr. Pageant, Knoxville, 1992—, Miss Knoxville U.S.A. Pageant, Knoxville, 1990—; active Knoxville Conv. and Visitors Bur., 1993-94. Recipient 1st Pl. award for swimsuit TV comml. and runway modeling Internat. Model's Hall of Fame, 1986, 1st Pl. award for media presentation Modeling Assn. Am. Internat., 1986; nominee The Pres.'s Commn. on White House Fellowships, U.S. Office Pers. Mgmt., 1994-95. Mem. Internat. Platform Assn., Profl. Assn. Diving Instrs. (cert.). Methodist. Home: 5109 Ridgemont Dr Knoxville TN 37918-4539 Office: Lady Adonis Inc/Penn Mgmt Ste 4 7320 Old Clinton Hwy Knoxville TN 37921-1064

PENN, HUGH FRANKLIN, small business owner; b. Morgan County, Ala., Aug. 15, 1917; s. Charles Franklin and Bessie Melinda (Praytor) P.; m. Marynelle Walter, Nov. 12, 1939 (dec. Dec. 1993); children: Hugh Franklin, Charles Phillip, Beverly Ann; m. Martha Ann Jordan Phillips, Feb. 11, 1994. Student, U. Ala., 1936-37. Asst. purchasing agt. for contractors constructing Huntsville Arsenal and Redstone Arsenal, Ala., 1941-43; purchasing agt. U.S. Army Air Force, Courtland Army Air Field, Ala., 1943-46; owner, mgr. Hugh Penn Lumber Co., Hartselle, Ala., 1946-60; owner, mgr. C.F. Penn Hamburgers, Hartselle, 1958-81, chmn. bd., 1981—; postmaster City of Hartselle, 1957-81; office mgr., realtor assoc. Charlie Penn Realty, 1981-85; bd. dirs. Terrell Industries, Inc. Moderator Morgan County Baptist Assn., 1955, 56; chmn. Hartselle Bd. Zoning Adjustment, 1956-76; founder, bd. dirs. Hartselle Downtown Action Com., 1971—; bd. dirs. Morgan County Combined Fed. Campaign, 1971-81, Hartselle Clean City Assn. 1990-93; apptd. to aging adv. coun. North Cen. Ala. Regional Coun. Govt., 1991; bd. dirs., trustee North Cen. Ala. Mental Health Found., 1992. Recipient Hartselle Civitan Unselfish Svc. award, 1995. Mem. Nat. Assn. Post Masters U.S., Hartselle C. of C. (pres. 1976-77); appointed mem. City of Hartselle Industrial Devel. Bd., 1995—. Republican. Baptist. Lodge: Kiwanis (life, Legion of Honor award 1977, Perfect Attendance award 1992). Home: 424 Crescent Dr SW Hartselle AL 35640-3825 Office: PO Box 8 Hartselle AL 35640-0008

PENN, HUGH FRANKLIN, JR., psychology educator; b. Hartselle, Ala., Jan. 28, 1941; s. Hugh Franklin and Marynelle (Walter) P.; m. Susan Irwin Adams, June 5, 1976; children: Charles Bracken, Caryn Elizabeth. BS, Florence State Coll., 1964; MA, Florence State Univ., 1967; grad. ednl. specialist, U. Ala., 1972, PhD, 1982. Psychology tchr. Hartselle (Ala.) H.S., 1964-89, sch. counselor, 1989-91, spl. svcs. counselor, 1991—; psychology instr. Calhoun C.C., Decatur, Ala., 1970—; chmn. bd. North Ctrl. Ala. Mental Health Bd., 1984-87, bd. dirs.; pres. of advisors Ala. Assn. Student Couns., 1970; ea. states head advisor So. Assn. Student Couns., 1973-74; mem. adv. bd. Mental Health Assn. Morgan County, 1996—. Named Outstanding Young Educator of Ala., Ala. Jaycees, 1973. Mem. APA, ACA, Coun. for Exceptional Children, Learning Disabilities Assn., Am. Sch. Counselor Assn., Autism Soc. Am., Orton Dyslexia Soc., Hartselle C. of C. (Thomas Guyton Humanitarian award 1994). Methodist. Home: 412 Aquarius Dr SW Hartselle AL 35640-4000 Office: Hartselle City Schs 130 Petain St SW Hartselle AL 35640-3228

PENN, JOHN G., plastic and reconstructive surgeon; b. Johannesburg, South Africa, May 26, 1942; came to U.S., 1967.; s. Jack and Diana (Malkin) P.; m. Jean Rosalyn Frenkel, Dec. 8, 1965; children: Juliet Susan, Robert Justin. MD, U. Witwaterstrand, Med. Sch., 1965. Diplomate Am. Bd. Plastic Surgery. Intern Johannesburg Gen. Hosp. Group; resident in gen. surgery Peter Bent Brigham Hosp., Boston, 1967-69; fellow in gen. and plastic surgery Brenthurst Clinic, Johannesburg, 1969-70; resident in plastic surgery U. Pitts., 1972-74; pvt. practice Johannesburg, 1974-77, Winter Park, Fla., 1977—; chmn. dept. plastic surgery Winter Park Meml. Hosp., 1982-86, dept. surgery, 1988-90, mem. various coms., mem. staff Fla. Hosp., Orlando; lectr. and presenter in field. Editor Aesthetic Surgery Quar., 1995—. Bd. dirs. Plastic Surgery Ednl. Found., 1993-96; chmn. strategic planning com. Am. Assn. Accreditation of Ambulatory Surg. Facilities Inc., 1995—, co-chmn. symposium com., 1977, bd. dirs., 1995—. Fellow ACS, Royal Coll. Surgeons Edinburgh; mem. Am. Soc. Plastic and Reconstructive Surgeons (spkrs. bur. 1984, plastic surgery product assessment com. 1986-87, chmn. pub. edn. com. 1989-92), Am. Soc. Aesthetic Plastic Surgery (pub. rels. com. 1986, bd. dirs. 1995-96, v.p. 1996-97), Internat. Albert Schweitzer Colloquium, Southeastern Soc. Plastic and Reconstructive Surgeons, Fla. Soc. Plastic and Reconstructive Surgeons, Orange County Med. Soc., Rotary Internat. Office: 1925 Mizell Ave Ste 303 Winter Park FL 32792-4155

PENN, PHILIP JULIAN, lawyer; b. Anchorage, May 11, 1955; s. Percy Junius and Jeanne Naomi (Johnson) P.; m. Rita Elaine Edwards, Feb. 20, 1993. AB, Duke U., 1977; JD, N.C. Ctrl. Law Sch., 1981. Bar: N.C. 1981. Law clerk Henry E. Moss/Paul C. Bland, Durham, N.C., 1981; pvt. practice Durham, 1981, 83-84; ptnr. Sloan, Moss & Penn, Durham, 1982; assoc. atty. Malone, Brown & Matthewson, P.A., Durham, 1982; fed. jud. law clerk U.S. Dist. Ct., Greensboro, N.C., 1982-83; appeals referee N.C. Employment Security Commn., Winston-Salem, N.C., 1984-87; asst. pub. defender 26th Defender Dist., Charlotte, N.C., 1987-92; asst. atty. gen. Virgin Islands Govt., St. Croix, 1992-93; mgr. Knova Bookstore, 1995; pvt. practice Charlotte, 1996; bd. dirs. chmn. legis. and legal issues com. N.C. Gov's. Waste Mgmt. Bd., Raleigh, N.C., 1991-92; adv. bd. mem. Mecklenburg Community Corrections, Charlotte, 1992. Author: Colorblind is a Spiritual State of Mind, 1993. Bd. dirs. Neighborhood Justice Ctr., Winston-Salem, 1987, Recovery Inc., Charlotte, 1994, Portraits of Colors, 1996; alt. del. N.C. Rep. Party, Winston-Salem, 1987; mentor Queens Coll., Charlotte, 1990-92; facilitator New Options for Violent Actions, Mecklenburg County, N.C., 1992. Recipient African-Am. Image award Queens Coll., 1992; named to Outstanding Young Men of Am., 1983, 86. Mem. Tuskegee Airmen, Inc., Kappa Alpha Psi (lt. strategus 1990). Republican. Roman Catholic. Home: Apt 1B 2500 Eastway Dr Charlotte NC 28205-3924

PENN, WILLIAM ROBERT, critical care nurse; b. Grundy, Va., June 30, 1961; s. Thomas J. and Kathleen (Little) P.; m. Mona Lisa Penn, Apr. 21, 1984; children: Andrew Robert, Emily Louise, William Samuel. ADN, Va. Appalachian Tricoll., Abingdon, 1986; BSN, Ea. Ky. U., 1991. RN, Ky.;

cert. emergency nurse, ACLS, trauma nursing care course, BLS instr., PALS. Staff nurse med.-surg. unit Grundy Hosp. Inc., 1986-87; staff nurse telemetry unit Cen. Bapt. Hosp., Lexington, Ky., 1987; staff nurse ICU preceptor Good Samaritan Hosp., Lexington, 1988-90, staff nurse preceptor emergency room, 1990—; part-time LPN instr. Cen. Ky. Vocat. Tech. Inst., 1991-94. Mem. Emergency Nurses Assn. (sec. Bluegrass chpt. 1992-93).

PENNINGER, FRIEDA ELAINE, retired English language educator; b. Marion, N.C., Apr. 11, 1927; d. Fred Hoyle and Lena Frances (Young) P. AB, U. N.C., Greensboro, 1948; MA, Duke U., 1950, PhD, 1961. Copywriter Sta. WSJS, Winston-Salem, N.C., 1948-49; asst. prof. English Flora Macdonald Coll., Red Springs, N.C., 1950-51; tchr. English Barnwell, S.C., 1951-52, Brunswick, Ga., 1952-53; instr. English U. Tenn., Knoxville, 1953-56; instr., asst. prof. Woman's Coll., U. N.C., Greensboro, 1956-58, 60-63; asst. prof., assoc. prof. U. Richmond (Va.), 1963-71; chair., dept. English Westhampton Coll., Richmond, 1971-78; prof. English U. Richmond, 1971-91, Bostwick prof. English, 1987-91; ret., 1991. Author: William Caxton, 1979, Chaucer's "Troilus and Criseyde" and "The Knight's Tale": Fictions Used, 1993, (novel) Look at Them, 1990; compiler, editor: English Drama to 1660, 1976; editor: Festschrift for Prof. Marguerite Roberts, 1976. Fellow Southeastern Inst. of Mediaeval and Renaissance Studies, 1965, 67, 69. Democrat. Presbyterian. Home: 2701 Camden Rd Greensboro NC 27403-1438

PENNINGTON, DONALD HARRIS, physician; b. Clarksville, Ark., Sept. 13, 1945; s. John Powers and Verna Olive (Harris) P.; m. Susan Myree Snyder, Aug. 27, 1966 (div. Aug. 1982); children: Thomas Walter, Aimee Myree, John Herrick. BA, U. of the Ozarks, 1968; MD, U. Ark., 1972; wine diploma, Calif. Dept. Agr., 1973. Intern St. Vincent Infirmary, Little Rock, 1973; physician, founding ptnr. Clarksville Med. Group, P.A., 1972-93; physician Mercy Med. Svcs., Inc., Ft. Smith, Ark., 1993—; cons. family planning svcs. Ark. State Bd. of Health, 1973-93. Founding mem., musician Ft. Douglas (Ark.) Backporch Bluegrass Symphony, 1976-91; acoustic double bassist River Valley Jazz Union, Russellville, Ark., 1991—. Bd. dirs. Johnson County Regional Hosp., Clarksville, 1973-82; asst. ch. organist 1st United Meth. Ch., Clarkville, 1968—, full time organist 1st Presbyn. Ch., 1994—; active ACLU, Planned Parenthood Fedn., The League to Make a Difference, Sierra Club Legal Defense Fund, The Nature Conservancy; mem. Nat. Trust for Hist. Preservation, 1982—. Mem. AMA, Assn. Am. Physicians for Human Rights, Nat. Trust for Historic Preservation, Ark. Med. Soc. (county del. 1972—), Ark. Acad. Family Practice, Sierra Club, Legal Def. Fund, Drug Policy Found., Am. Guild Organists. Democrat. Home: 317 N Johnson St Clarksville AR 72830-2931

PENNINGTON, JAMES RICHARD (RIC PENNINGTON), real estate appraiser; b. Crockett, Tex., June 30, 1951; s. Clifford and Esta Faye (Morrow) P.; children: James Richard III, Daniel Frank. BBA in Fin., U. Tex., 1973. Lic. real estate broker, Tex.; gen. state cert. real estate appraiser, Tex. Rsch. asst. Win Properties, Houston, 1975-76; sales assoc. Jim West & Co., Houston, 1975-76; assoc. appraiser William Behrs, MAI, Houston, 1976-78, Dominy, Ford & Assoc., Houston, 1978-79; sr. appraiser Joseph Blake & Assoc., Houston, 1979-80; owner Pennington & Assoc., Crockett, Tex., 1980—; CEO S.L. Adams Co., Austin, Tex., 1993—, Adams-Reck Environ. Inc., 1993—; v.p. Key Adams, Austin; with property tax divsn. Tex. State Comptr.'s Office, 1996—; instr. real estate appraisal San Jacinto Jr. Coll., Clear Lake City, Tex., 1979-80; expert witness 3d, 12th, 77th and 349th Jud. Dist. Cts. Tex. Adminstrv. bd. chmn. 1st United Meth. Ch., Crockett, 1986; past pres., v.p., dir. Dowdell Pub. Utility Dist., Houston, 1976-79; chmn. bd. equilization, 1976-79; chmn. planning and zoning commn. City of Crockett, 1988-90, mem. bd. adjustments, 1986-88. Mem. Appraisal Inst. (regional profl. standards panel 1989-94), Soc. Real Estate Appraisers (admissions com. Houston chpt. 1988, Sr. Real Property Appraiser award 1982), Austin Bd. Realtors, Nat. Assn. Realtors, Tex. Assn. Realtors, Spring Creek Country Club (dir. 1990-92). Home: 604 N 7th Crockett TX 75835

PENNINGTON, RICHARD J., police chief. Chief of police New Orleans. Office: 715 S Broad Ave New Orleans LA 70151

PENNY, WILLIAM LEWIS, lawyer; b. Memphis, Sept. 4, 1953; s. Charles B. and Dorothy R. (Rivers) P.; m. Linda Brown, Sept. 8, 1979; 1 child, Joseph Martin. BA, U. Tenn., 1975; JD, Nashville Sch. Law, 1981. Bar: Tenn. 1981, U.S. Ct. Appeals (6th cir.) 1981. Program evaluator Office of Comptroller, State of Tenn., Nashville, 1975-80; mgr. compliance and audit Tenn. Dept. Edn., Nashville, 1980-82; chief environ. counsel Tenn. Dept. Health and Environment, Nashville, 1982-84, asst. commr., gen. counsel, 1984-91; gen. counsel Tenn. Dept. Environment and Conservation, Nashville, 1991-92; prin. Law Firm of Manier, Herod, Hollabaugh & Smith, Nashville, 1992—. Bd. dirs. Hosp. Hospitality House, chmn., 1993. Mem. ABA (vice chair dispute resolution com. adminstrv. law sect.), Tenn. Bar Assn. (chmn. environ. law sect. 1991, 92), Nashville Bar Assn. (chair environ. law com.), Assn. Govt. Accts. (editor newsletter, Nashville 1977-79, sec. Nashville chpt. 1979-80, bd. dirs. chpt. 1980-84). Methodist. Home: 6501 Cornwall Dr Nashville TN 37205-3041 Office: Manier Herod Hollabaugh & Smith 2200 One Nashville Pl 150 4th Ave N Nashville TN 37219-2415

PENROSE, CYNTHIA C., health plan administrator, consultant; b. Manila, Nov. 24, 1939; came to U.S., 1940; d. Douglas Lee Lipscomb Cordiner and Jane (Sturgeon) Edises; m. Douglas Francis Penrose, July 11, 1959 (div. 1981); children: Vicki Lynn, Lee Douglas; m. Alan Harrison Magazine, Aug. 30, 1984. BA, U. Calif.-Berkeley, 1963; MBA, U. Santa Clara, 1977. Cert. social svcs. V.p., dir. employment Resource Ctr. for Women, Palo Alto, Calif., 1973-78; bus. planner Raychem Corp., Menlo Park, Calif., 1979; adminstrv. mgr. Electric Power Research Inst., Palo Alto, 1979-83; sr. ptnr. MB Assocs., Washington, 1983-88; dir. ops. Utility Data Inst., Washington, 1984-85; dir. ops. Randmark, Inc., 1986-87; coordinator mkt. devel. for Mid-Atlantic States Kaiser Foundation Health Plan, Washington, 1987-88, asst. to assoc. regional mgr., 1988-94; market planner MetraHealth, Vienna, Va., 1995; exec. staff asst. United HealthCare, Vienna, 1995, dir. strategic planning, splty. cos., 1996—; bd. dirs. and treas. Unique Enterprises, Washington, 1985-87; sec. Wesley Property Mgmt. Co., 1987-89; bd. dirs. Wesley Housing Devel. Corp., 1988-89. Bd. dirs., v.p. LWV, Berkeley and Palo Alto, 1966-73; bd. dirs., sec. Am. Hospice Found., 1995—; chmn. program adv. council Resource Ctr. for Women, Palo Alto, 1980-83; mem. Affirmative Action Adv. Com. Palo Alto, 1975-76. Mem. Peninsula Profl. Women's Network (v.p. 1981-82), U. Calif. Alumni Assn., AAUW (Bicentennial br. sec. 1986-88), Capitol Area Soc. Healthcare Planning and Mktg., LWV. Democrat. Episcopalian. Avocations: swimming; nutrition and health; reading. Home: 1302 Chancel Pl Alexandria VA 22314-4707 Office: United Health Care 8330 Boone Blvd Ste 300 Vienna VA 22182

PENTECOST, WILLIAM RONALD, insurance company executive; b. Ashland City, Tenn., July 7, 1958; s. William Kenneth and Annie Mai (pace) P.; m. Dana Kathyn Griffin, June 9, 1978; 1 child, Lenora Kathryn. Grad., Nashville Sch. of Preaching, 1978; AS, Nashville State Tech. Coll., 1982. Programmer Newspaper Printing, Nashville, 1980-83; programmer, analyst Harvey Freeman, Nashville, 1983-85; program mgr. Permanent Gen. Ins., Nashville, 1985-91; v.p. of MIS/data processing Graward Gen. Ins., Nashville, 1991-95; v.p. co. ops. U.S. Auto Ins., Nashville, 1995—; min. Pleasant View (Tenn.) Ch. of Christ, 1993—; pres. Ind. Cons. Unltd., Inc., 1996. Deacon Chapel Hill Ch. of Christ, White Bluff, 1989-93. Republican. Mem. Ch. of Christ. Home: 327 Sanders Ln Ashland City TN 37015 Office: US Auto Ins Co 209 14th Ave N Nashville TN 37203-3415

PENTON, HAROLD ROY, JR., chemical company executive, researcher; b. New Orleans, Apr. 17, 1947; s. Harold Roy and Heulette Mable (Addison) P.; m. Cherri Edenfield, Dec. 20, 1969; 1 child, Harold Roy III. BS in Chemistry, Fla. State U., 1969; PhD in Chemistry, Ga. Inst. Tech., 1973. Sr. rsch. chemist Am. Enka Co., Asheville, N.C., 1973-74, Akzo B.V., Arnhem, The Netherlands, 1974-75; rsch. group leader Am. Enka Co., 1974-77; rsch. chemist Ethyl Corp., Baton Rouge, 1977-81, sr. rsch. chemist, 1981, R&D mgr., 1981-87, comml. devel. dir., 1987-91, dir. European R&D, 1991-94; tech. dir. Albemarle Corp., Baton Rouge, 1994—; adj. prof. U. N.C., Asheville, 1975-77. Author: Inorganic Polymers, 1987, Handbook of Elastomers, 1989. Recipient Fellowship grant NSF, 1969-73. Mem. Am. Chem. Soc., Indsl. Rsch. Inst., Product Devel. and Mgmt. Assn. Home: 232 Shady Oaks Ct Baton Rouge LA 70810

PEPLOWSKI, CELIA CESLAWA, librarian; b. Montreal, June 4, 1918; came to U.S., 1923; d. Stanley and Wladyslawa (Fabisiak) P. BA and BS with honors, Tex. Woman's U., 1953; MALS, U. Wis., 1955. Substitute libr. Shorewood (Wis.) Pub. Libr., 1955; cataloger, libr. periodical svcs. Arlington (Tex.) State Coll., 1955-56; head libr. English sect. U. of the Sacred Heart, Tokyo, 1956-57; base libr. Sioux City (Iowa) AFB/53rd Fighter Group, USAF, 1957-59; substitute libr. Milw. Sch. Bd., 1959-61; head tech. svcs. Milw. Downer Coll., 1961-63; cataloger, reference libr. Sterling Mcpl. Pub. Libr., Baytown, Tex., 1964-67, acting city libr., 1964-65; asst. extension supr. Mobile (Ala.) Pub. Libr., 1967-68, adminstrv. asst., pers. officer, 1968-69, internat. trade ctr. libr., 1969-70, supr. main libr., 1970-87, substitute libr., 1995—. Mem. AAUW (historian Mobile br.), ALA (subscription books rev. com. 1973-75), Wis. U. Alumni Assn., Tex. Woman's U. Alumni Assn., Pi Lambda Theta, Beta Phi Mu. Home: 217 Berwyn Dr W Apt 209 Mobile AL 36608-2119

PEPPER, MARY JANICE, educational consultant; b. Pearsall, Tex., Oct. 1, 1942; d. Muriel Newton and Jane (Harbour) Moore; m. Clifton Gail Pepper, Feb. 19, 1961; children: John David, James Newton, Jeffery Michael. Student, U. Tex., 1960, 65, 76. Bus. mgr. Natalia (Tex.) Independent Sch. Dist., 1967-71; statistician Tex. Edn. Agy., Austin, 1971-72; mgr. bookkeeping div. Tex. Ednl. Cons. Svc. Inc., Austin, 1972-76, adminstrv. v.p., 1976-82, v.p., COO, 1982-93, pres., 1993—; team tchr. edn. program. U. Tex., Austin, 1985; lectr. Tex. Assn. Secondary Sch. Prins., Austin, 1988. Editor: Sch. Fin. Newsletter, Update for Sch. Adminstrs. Sec. Community Indsl. Found., Natalia, 1969-71, Medina County Water Control and Improvement, Natalia, 1970-71; mem. adv. com. Tex. Edn. Agy. Mem. Tex. Assn. Sch. Bus. Ofcls. (instr. 1987-88, chair coord. task force on sch. acctg. Tex. Edn. Agy. 1991—), Mended Hearts (sec. 1989-90, newsletter editor 1990-91). Baptist. Home: 16048 Hamilton Pool Rd Austin TX 78738-7401 Office: Tex Ednl Consultative Svcs Inc PO Box 18898 Austin TX 78760-8898

PERALTA, ANTONIO MARTINEZ, family physician; b. Legaspi, Luzon, The Philippines, Nov. 20, 1937; came to U.S., 1972; s. Federico Aseneta and Maria Luisa (Martinez) P.; m. Celia Elepano, June 20, 1970; children: Antonio Jr., Alan, Anne Marie, Michael-Andrew. BS, U. of the East, Manila, The Philippines, 1960; MD, Far Eastern U., Manila, The Philippines, 1966. Intern Englewood (N.J.) Hosp. Assn., 1977-78; resident in family practice Yonkers (N.Y.) Gen. Hosp., 1978-80; emergency rm. physician Mattie Wills Hosp., Richland, Va., 1979-82; pvt. practice family medicine Whitewood, Va., 1982-83, Bradshaw, W.Va., 1983-90; assoc. physician Merit Med. Group Managed Care, Richlands, 1990-96; physician Columbia-Clinch Valley Med. Ctr., Richlands, 1996—. Vol. physician Tri-County Med. Clinic, Richlands, 1991—. Capt. M.C. Philippine Army. Fellow Am. Acad. Family Physicians; mem. So. Med. Assn., Tazewell County Med. Soc. (treas. 1995), S.W. Va. Assn. of Philippine Physicians (pres. 1992-94). Republican. Roman Catholic. Home: 737 Sandy Ln Richlands VA 24641 Office: Columbia-Clinch Valley Medical Center Ste 1100 Richlands VA 24641

PERCHIK, BENJAMIN IVAN, operations research analyst; b. Passaic, N.J., May 3, 1941; s. Morris and Frances (Antman) P.; m. Ellen Mae Colwell, Aug. 25, 1963; children: Joel, Dawn. BA, Rutgers U., 1964; m. Mary L. Westcott, Jan. 25, 1994; postgrad. N.Y. Inst. Tech., 1964-65. Quality control E.R. Squibb Corp., New Brunswick, N.J., 1964-67; edn. specialist Signal Sch., Ft. Monmouth, N.J., 1967-74; edn. specialist Armor Sch., Ft. Knox, Ky., 1974-75, ops. rsch. analyst, 1975-78; ops. rsch. analyst HQ TRADOC, Ft. Monroe, Va., 1978-80; ops. rsch. analyst Army Materiel Command, Alexandria, Va., 1980—, exec. officer USAREUR ORSA Cell, 1988-90; chmn. supervisory com. credit union, 1985-88, 91—; cons. Delta Force, Carlisle Barracks, Pa., 1982-84, Internat. Policy Inst., 1983-85, World Future Soc., 1982—; nat. coord. Mensa Investment SIG, 1983—; coord. econ. forecasting group Met. Washington Mensa, 1983—; chmn. security com. Watergate at Landmark, 1985-88. Author: ADP Program and Repair, 1972; writer, editor, pub. internat. newsletter Speculation and Investments, 1983—. Chmn. credit com. Darcom Fed. Credit Union, 1982-85. Mem. Inst. Mgmt. Scis., Internat. Platform Assn., Ops. Rsch. Soc. Am., Old Dominion Boat Club. Office: 5001 Eisenhower Ave Alexandria VA 22333-0001

PEREDNEY, CHRISTINE BOOTH, social worker, educator; b. Athens, Ga., Sept. 12, 1944; d. James Henry and Dorothy Elizabeth (Isbell) Booth; m. Michael Stanley James Peredney, Jan. 24, 1970; 1 child, Christopher Lee. BS, U. Ga., 1966, MS, 1971; cert., Ga. State U., 1979; student, USAF Adminstrv. Sch., 1969; postgrad., LaSalle Extention U., 1971. Cert. elem. tchr., adminstr., gifted edn. tchr., Ga. Psychometrist U. Ga. Guidance Ctr., Athens, 1966-67; tchr. Dekalb Bd. Edn., Decatur, Ga., 1967-68; presch. tchr. Playcare at Tucker, Ga., 1972-74; tchr. Gwinnett Bd. Edn., Lawrenceville, Ga., 1976-86; sr. caseworker Walton County Family and Child Svc., Monroe, Ga., 1987-91, prin. caseworker, 1992-94; PEACH case mgr. DeKalb County Family and Children Svcs., 1994—; agy. rep. Ga. County Welfare Assn., Monroe, 1988-90; mem. tchr. adv. com. Gwinnett Bd. Edn., 1982, 83, 85, sch. coord. tapestry art festival, 1984-86; speaker in field. Choir leader Smoke Rise Baptist Ch., 1990—, pres. Sunday sch., 1992-93, choir sect. leader, 1992-93; mem. honors program com. U. Ga., 1982-83; co-leader Girl Scouts U.S., Scott AFB, Ill., 1969-70. 2d lt. USAF, 1968-70. Mem. Lilburn Women's Club (club woman of yr. 1988, corr. sec. 1989-90, edn. chmn. 1984-86, chmn. conservation 1990-91, co-chmn. home life dept. 1995), Alpha Delta Kappa, Phi Beta Kappa, Phi Kappa Phi. Office: DeKalb County Family & Children's Svcs 178 Sams St Decatur GA 30030-4134

PERETTI, BURTON WILLIAM, history educator; b. San Francisco, Jan. 6, 1961; s. William H. and Giken G. (Koerner) P.; m. Genevieve R. Innes, June 17, 1995. BA, Pomona Coll., 1982; MA, U. Calif., Berkeley, 1985, PhD, 1989. Vis. asst. prof. U. Kans., Lawrence, 1989-92; vis. lectr. U. Calif., Berkeley, 1992-93, Colo. Coll., Colorado Springs, 1993-94, Mid. Tenn. State U., Murfreesboro, 1994-95; asst. prof. Pellissippi State Tech. C.C., Knoxville, 1995—; cons. NEH, 1993, Ednl. Testing Svc., Princeton, N.J., 1992—. Author: The Creation of Jazz, 1992, Jazz as History, 1996, Jazz in American Culture, 1997. Mem. Am. Hist. Assn., Am. Studies Assn. Office: Pellissippi State Tech CC PO Box 22990 Knoxville TN 37933-0990

PEREZ, ALFREDO, business executive; b. 1946. With Torano & Co., Esteli, Nicaragua, 1966-78, Miami, Fla., 1978-83; pres. Ctrl. Am. Tobacco Corp., Miami, Fla., 1979—, ASP Enterprises Inc., Miami, Fla., 1982—. Office: ASP Enterprises Inc 2100 NW 99th Ave Miami FL 33172-2208

PEREZ, GUIDO O., medical educator; b. Santa Clara, Las Villas, Cuba, Dec. 16, 1938; came to U.S., 1961; s. Alex and Maria T. (Martinez) P.; m. Kathleen A. Sullivan, Aug. 12, 1965 (div. 1984); children: Michael, Lawrence, Brian. MD, U. Miami, 1965. Diplomate Am. Bd. Nephrology & Medicine. Instr. Albert Einstein, N.Y.C., 1968-69; asst. prof. U. Conn., Hartford, 1970-72, U. Miami, Fla., 1972—; vis. prof. U. Geneva, 1991—; co-dir. Clin. Rsch. Ctr. U. Miami, 1978-80; chief dialysis unit VA Hosp., Miami, 1972—; dir. renal pathophysiology tchg. U. Miami, 1988—; lectr. in field. Author chpts. in books; contbr. articles to profl. jours. Mem. Kidney Found S. Fla., 1991—. Recipient Arnold Lehman award U. Miami, 1965. Fellow ACP; mem. Am. Soc. Nephrology, Internat. Soc. Nephrology, Latin Am. Soc. Nephrology (sec. 1988-92), So. Soc. Clin. Investigation, Alpha Omega Alpha. Office: VA Hosp 1201 NW 16th St Miami FL 33125-1624

PEREZ, JEFFREY JOSEPH, optometrist; b. Aberdeen, Md., July 26, 1952; s. Jack Joseph and June C. (Champlin) P.; m. Sharon S. Cooper, June 10, 1979; children: Justin Joseph, Ashley Mary Louise. BA, U. Miss., 1974; BS, So. Coll. Optometry, 1977, OD, 1979. Assoc. with Dr. W.H. Starr, Gulfport, Miss., 1979-80; pvt. practice optometry, Gulfport, 1980—. U. Miss. scholar, 1974. Mem. Am. Optometric Assn., Men's Sr. Baseball League, Miss. Optometric Assn. (bd. dir., chmn. pub. rels. com. 1989), South Miss. Optometric Soc., Jaycees, Omega Delta. Roman Catholic. Club: Biloxi Alumni Band. Lodge: Elks. Home: 2473 Greenview Dr Gulfport MS 39507-2213 Office: 12296 Ashley Dr Gulfport MS 39503-2737

PEREZ, JORGE LUIS, manufacturing executive; b. Jaguey Grande, Matanzas, Cuba, Nov. 29, 1945; came to U.S., 1960; s. Adalberto Aquileo and Esther Mireya (Haedo) P.; m. Olga Maria Gonzalez, Mar. 7, 1970; children: Jorge Alejandro, Ricardo Javier. BS in Commerce & Engring. Sci., Drexel U., 1969, MBA, 1981. Jr. indsl. engr. IBM Corp., East Fishkill, N.Y., 1969-70; assoc. indsl. engr. IBM Corp., East Fishkill, 1970-71, sr. assoc. indsl. engr., 1972-75, staff indusl. engr., 1976-77; ops. rsch. analyst IBM Corp., Princeton, N.J., 1977-80; fin. program adminstr. IBM Corp., Franklin Lakes, N.J., 1980-82; mgr. production control IBM Corp., Boca Raton, Fla., 1983-85; project mgr. div. IBM Corp., Boca Raton, 1986-88, program mgr., 1988-92; v.p. Beehive Grill of Coral Springs, Inc., 1994. Author: (manuals) Machine Tooling, Transportation Forecasting, Workload Planning, Measurement, 1972-81. Exec. com. Palm Beach (Fla.) County Rep. Party, 1989; pres., bd. dirs. Palm Beach Farm Workers Coun., 1989; pres. Wee Bee Tots, Inc., Wee Bee Tots of Wellington, Inc., Little Learners Real Estate, Inc. Mem. Am. Prodn. & Inventory Control Soc. (v.p. membership com. 1984-85), Inst. Indsl. Engrs. (sr. mem., pres. 1974-75, excellence award, 1975). Republican. Roman Catholic. Home and Office: 11383 Little Bear Way Boca Raton FL 33428-2632

PEREZ, JOSEPHINE, psychiatrist, educator; b. Tijuana, Mex., Feb. 10, 1941; came to U.S., 1960, naturalized, 1968. BS in Biology, U. Santiago de Compostela, Spain, 1971; MD, 1975. Clerkships in internal medicine, gen. surgery, otorhinolaryngology, dermatology and venereology Gen. Hosp. of Galicia (Spain), 1972-75; resident in gen. psychiatry U. Miami (Fla.), Jackson Meml. Hosp. and VA Hosp., Miami, 1976-78; practice medicine specializing in psychiatry, marital and family therapy, individual psychotherapy, Miami, Fla., 1979—; nuclear medicine technician, EEG technician, supr. Electrographic Labs., Encino, Calif., 1963-71; emergency room physician Miami Dade Hosp., 1975; attending psychiatrist Jackson Meml. Hosp., 1979—, asst. dir. adolescent psychiat. unit, 1979-83; mem. clin. faculty U. Miami Sch. Medicine, 1979—, clin. instr. psychiatry, 1979—. Mem. AMA (Physicians' Recognition award 1980, 83, 86, 89), Am. Assn. for Marital and Family Therapy (cert. clin. mem., treas. 1982-84, pres.-elect 1985-87, pres. 1987-89), Am. Psychiat. Assn., Am. Med. Women's Assn., Assn. Women Psychiatrists, South Fla. Psychiat. Soc. Office: 420 S Dixie Hwy Ste 4A Coral Gables FL 33146-2222

PEREZ, LUIS ALBERTO, lawyer; b. Havana, Cuba, Dec. 22, 1956; came to U.S., 1961; s. Alberto and Estela (Hernandez) P. BBA cum laude, Loyola U., New Orleans, 1978, JD, 1981. Car: La. 1981, U.S. Dist. Ct. (ea. and mid. dists.) La. 1981, U.S. Ct. Appeals (5th and 11th cirs.) 1981, U.S. Dist. Ct. (we. dist.) La. 1983, D.C. 1989, U.S. Dist. Ct. (D.C. cir.) 1989, U.S. Ct. Appeals D.C. 1989, U.S. Supreme Ct. 1989, Tex. 1994. Ptnr. Adams and Reese, New Orleans, 1981—; chmn. internat. practice group Adams & Reese. Dir. Mayor's Hispanic/Latin Am. Adv. Bd. New Orleans, 1989; gov. appointee Pan-Am. Commn. for State of La., 1990-91. Mem. ABA, La. Bar Assn., Fed. Bar Assn., D.C. Bar Assn., State Bar Tex., Hispanic Lawyers Assn. La. (pres. 1988-94), U.S. Hispanic C of C. (pres. 1988-93), Beta Gamma Sigma. Office: Adams and Reese 4500 One Shell Sq New Orleans LA 70139-4501

PEREZ-CRUET, JORGE, psychiatrist, psychopharmacologist, psychophysiologist; b. Santurce, P.R., Oct. 15, 1931; s. Jose Maria Perez-Vicente and Emilia Cruet-Burgos; m. Anyes Heimendinger, Oct. 4, 1958; children: Antonio, Mick, Graciela, Isabelle. BS magna cum laude, U. P.R., 1953, MD, 1957; diploma psychiatry McGill U., Montreal, Que., Can., 1976. Diplomate Am. Bd. Psychiatry and Neurology, Nat. Bd. Med. Examiners, Am. Bd. Geriatric Psychiatry; lic. Can. Coun. Med. Examiners; cert. in quality assurance. Rotating intern Michael Reese Hosp., Chgo., 1957-58; fellow in psychiatry Johns Hopkins U. Med. Sch., 1958-60, instr., then asst. prof. psychiatry, 1962-73; lab. neurophysiologist and psychomatic lab. Walter Reed Army Inst. Rsch., Washington, 1960-62, cons., 1963-65; rsch. assoc. lab. chem. pharmacology NIH, Bethesda, Md., also rsch. assoc. adult psychiatry br. and lab. clin. sci. NIMH, Bethesda, 1969-73; psychiatry resident diploma course in psychiatry McGill U. Sch. Medicine, Montreal Gen. Hosp., 1973-76, Montreal Children's Hosp., 1975; prof. psychiatry U. Mo.-Mo. Inst. Psychiatry, St. Louis, 1976-78; chief psychiatry svc. San Juan (P.R.) VA Hosp., pharmacy and therapeutic com. 1978-92; also prof. psychiatry U. P.R. Med. Sch., 1978-92; prof. psychiatry U. Okla. Health Scis. Ctr., Okla. City VA Med. Ctr., 1992—; spl. adviser on mental health P.R. Senate, P.R. sec. health, 1989; spl. cons. NASA, 1965-69; cons. divsn. narcotic addiction and drug abuse NIDA, 1972-73. Capt. M.C., USAR, 1960-62; sr. surgeon USPHS, 1969-71, med. dir., 1971-73. Recipient Coronas award, 1957, Ruiz-Arnau award, 1957, Diaz-Garcia award, 1957, Geigy award, 1975, 76, AMA Recognition award, 1971, 76, 81, Horner's award, 1975, 76, Pavlovian award, 1978, Recognition cert. Senate of P.R., 1986, cert. of merit Gov. of P.R., 1986. Fellow Interam. Coll. Physicians and Surgeons, Royal Coll. Physicians and Surgeons Can. (sr., cert.); mem. Am. Psychiat. Assn., Am. Physiol. Soc., Pavlovian Soc., Am. Fedn. Clin. Rsch., Am. Assn. Geriatric Psychiatry, Am. Soc. Clin. Pharmacology and Therapeutics, Am. Soc. Pharmacology and Experimental Therapeutics, Soc. Neurosci., Nat. Assn. Healthcare Quality, Internat. Soc. Rsch. Aggression, Okla. Psychiat. Assn., Am. Soc. Clin. Psychopharmacology, Menninger Found., Okla. Assn. Health Care Quality. Roman Catholic. Home: 3304 Rosewood Ln Oklahoma City OK 73120-5604 Office: Oklahoma City VA Med Ctr 921 NE 13th St Oklahoma City OK 73104-5007

PEREZ DE LA MESA, MANUEL JOSE, company executive; b. Habana, Cuba, Mar. 20, 1957; came to the U.S., 1961; s. Manuel Adolfo Oscar and Olga Marta (Cuervo) Perez de la Mesa; m. Ana Lidia Vidal, June 19, 1982; children: Rosario, Manuel, Cristina. BBA in Fin., Fla. Internat. U., 1977; MBA in Controllership, St. John's U., 1980. Fin. analyst Latin Am. Sea-Land Svc., Inc., Ft. Lauderdale, Fla., 1977-79; sr. fin. analyst Sea-Land Svc., Inc., Edison, N.J., 1979-80; regional contr. Latin Am. Sea-Land Svc., Inc., Ft. Lauderdale, 1980-82; ops. auditor IBM, San Jose, Calif., 1982-85; advisory pricing staff IBM, Bethesda, Md., 1985-87; asst. corp. contr. Del Monte Fresh Produce Inc., Coral Gables, Fla., 1987-88; v.p. fin. and ops. Latin Am. Del Monte Fresh Produce Inc., San Jose, Costa Rica, 1988-90; v.p. ops. S.Am. Del Monte Fresh Produce Inc., Santiago, Chile, 1990-91; v.p. planning and devel. Del Monte Fresh Produce Inc., Coral Gables, 1991-94; CFO Gemaire Distbrs. Inc., Deerfield Beach, Fla., 1994; chmn. Agribusiness, Caribbean/Latin Am. Action, Washington, 1991-93; dir., investment banking consulting Latin Fin. Inc., N.Y.C., Miami, Mexico City, 1993—. Mem. Inst. Mgmt. Acctg. Home: 15885 W Prestwick Pl Miami Lakes FL 33014-6523

PÉREZ-GONZALEZ, ESMERALDA, principal, educator; b. Alice, Tex., Sept. 7, 1963; d. Felipe Perez and Cora Cantu Perez Carrillo. BS, Corpus Christi State U., 1987, MS, 1993; AA, Del Mar Coll., 1987. Tchr. Holy Family Sch., Corpus Christi, Tex.; prin. Archbishop Oscar Romero Middle Sch., Corpus Christi, Tex. Title VII Bilingual Edn. Fellowship grantee, Gov. Fellowship award, 1994. Mem. Tex. Assn. Bilingual Edn., PTA, Nat. Cath. Edn. Assoc., Assoc. Supervision, Curriculum Devel., Nat. Assoc. Secondary Sch. Prin., Year Round Edn., Tex. Middle Sch. Assoc., Nat. Middle Sch. Assoc., Nat. Coun. of tchrs. of Math., tex. Coun. of Tchrs. of Math. Home: 7130 Everhart Rd #23 Corpus Christi TX 78413

PERIMAN, PHILLIP, physician, photographer; b. Memphis, Tex., Dec. 5, 1938; m. Judith L. Koob, Apr. 17, 1965; children: Theresa Alice, Benjamin Rufus, Laura Grace. BA, Yale U., 1961; MD, Washington U., St. Louis, 1965. Diplomate Am. Bd. Internal Medicine, Am. Bd. Hematology, Am. Bd. Med. Oncology, Am. Bd. Diagnostic Lab. Immunology; lic. physician, Mo., Tex., N.Mex.; cert. CPR. Rsch. fellow sch. medicine Washington U., 1962, 63, 64; intern in internal medicine Bellevue Hosp./NYU Sch. Medicine, N.Y.C., 1965-66, resident in internal medicine, 1966-67; rsch. lab. cell biology Nat. Cancer Inst./NIH, Bethesda, Md., 1967-69, sr. staff fellow, 1971; rsch. fellow Sir William Dunn Sch. Pathology, Oxford (England) U., 1970; asst. prof. medicine divsn. gen. medicine George Washington U., 1971-73, asst. prof. medicine divsn. hematology and oncology, 1974-76, adj. prof. genetics grad. sch. arts. and scis., 1975-76, assoc. prof. medicine divsn. hematology and oncology, 1976; assoc. prof., assoc. chmn. Regional Acad. Health Ctr. Tex. Tech U. Health Scis. Ctr., Amarillo, 1976-81, chief divsn. hematology/oncology dept. internal medicine, 1976-85, clin. prof. dept. internal medicine, 1982; med. dir. Don and Sybil Harrington Cancer Ctr., Amarillo, 1981-92, pres., 1986-92, dir. electron microscopy lab, physician in hematology and oncology, 1992—; mem. utilization rev. com. George Washington U. Med. Ctr., 1971-72, rsch. com., 1972-76, internship interviewing com., 1972-76, animal rsch. com., 1972-73, search com. for dean for continuing edn., 1974-75, oncology com., 1974-76; chmn. bldg. and site com. Coffee Meml. Blood Ctr. Amarillo, 1980-82, pres., 1981; sr. student advisor

Tex. Tech U. Health Scis. Ctr., 1976—, dean;s subcom. for Amarillo VA Hosp., 1977-81, faculty appointment com., 1977-81, rsch. com. Amarillo VA Hosp., 1977-82, bldg. com., 1979-81, assoc. chmn.'s com., 1976-81, chmn. libr. com., 1978-79, rsch. com., 1983-87, grad. edn. com., 1982-87; chmn. instl rev. com. High Plains Bapt. Hosp. Amarillo, 1979-80, chmn. cancer com., 1979-86; mem. credentials com. Northwest Tex. Hosp., Amarillo, 1980-86, cancer com., 1984; mem. cancer com. St. Anthony's Hosp., Amarillo, 1983-89; chmn. Tex. Regional Oncology Group, 1983-89; chmn. Workgroup State Task Force on Cancer, 1985-86. Contbr. numerous publs. to profl. jours.; photographs exhibited in one man shows Lost Circus Gallery, 1990, Don Harrington Discovery Ctr., 1990, Odessey Gallery, 1991; group shows include Lost Circus Gallery, Amarillo, 1989, O.H.M.S. Cafe and Gallery, Amarillo, 1989, Lubbock Art Assn., 1990, Tex. Photograph Soc., 1990, 92, Amarillo Coll./West Tex. State U., 1991, Odessa Coll., 1993, Nancy Wilson Scanlan Art Gallery, Helm Fine Arts Ctr., St. Stephen's Episc. Sch., Austin, 1996; represented in various pvt. collections; works published in Parallels, 1992, Photo Metro, 1992. With USPHS, 1967-69. Grantee Nat. Cancer Inst., 1972-75, 72-76, 76-78, George Washington U. Med. Ctr., 1974, Tex. Tech U. Health Scis. Ctr., 1979-80, Meadows Found., 1981-82, 87, Ortho Biotech, Inc., 1993; named Man of Yr., Amarillo Globe News, 1980; Paul Harris fellow Amarillo Rotary, 1990. Fellow ACP; mem. AAAS, AMA, Am. Soc. Clin. Oncology, Am. Soc. Hematology, Internat. Assn. for Study Lung Cancer, Internat. Soc. Hematology, Tex. Med. Assn., Potter-Randall County Med. Soc. Home: 1804 N Julian Blvd Amarillo TX 79102-1434 Office: 1500 Wallace Blvd Amarillo TX 79106-1794

PERKEL, ROBERT SIMON, photojournalist, educator; b. Jersey City, Apr. 23, 1925; s. Louis Leo and Flora Sonia (Levin) P.; BS, NYU, 1948; MS, Barry U., 1964; postgrad. Columbia U. Owner, operator Gulfstream Color Labs., Miami Beach, Fla., 1955-61; graphic instr. Dade County Pub. Schs., 1962-66; freelance photojournalist, 1967—; rep. News Events Photo Svc., Ft. Lauderdale, Fla.; instr. photography Broward Community Coll., 1982-92; rep. Patch Communications, Titusville, Fla., 1985-88; pub. Biograph/Communications, North Miami Beach, Fla., 1987-90; contbr. photo stories, and photographs to numerous mags. and indsl. trade publs. including Women's World, Merck, Sharp & Dohme's Frontline Mag., Gt. Am. Combank News, Nat. Utility Contractor, Mainstream, Nat. Jewish Monthly, Delta Digest, Textile Rental, Sprint Communicator, Rag, the All-Music Mag., DAV Mag., Hallandale Digest, Miami Herald, record jacket C.P. Records, Inc.; exhibited at Met. Mus. and Art Center, Coral Gables, Fla., Mus. of Fine Arts, Boston. Former publicity dir. Coun. for Internat. Visitors of Greater Miami; Served with AUS, 1943-46; ETO. Recipient Community Spirit award Zonta Club Greater Miami, 1980. Fellow Nat. Press Photographers Found.; mem. NYU Alumni Fedn. (Leadership award for 1982-83 fund campaign), Barry U. Alumni Assn., Nat. Press Photographers Assn. (life), Nielsen Media Rsch., DAV (nat. citation for disting. service 1969, trustee Jack Schwartz chpt., past comdr. Miami Beach-Surfside chpt.), Steamship Hist. Soc. Am. (S.E. Fla. chpt.), Am. Legion, Alpha Mu Gamma. Clubs: Mus. of Art (Fort Lauderdale). Home: 617 SE 16th St Apt 3 Fort Lauderdale FL 33316-2629

PERKINS, DAVID MARK, railroad executive, forest resource consultant; b. Hannibal, Mo., Dec. 6, 1958; s. John Wesley and Betty Jane (Vaughn) P.; m. Elizabeth Lynn Vincent, Aug. 20, 1983; children: Mary Elizabeth and Anna Lea. BS in Forest Mgmt., Tex. A&M U., 1982; MBA, Stephen F. Austin State U., 1989. Resource mgr. Nat. Forests in Tex., Lufkin, 1983-87; asst. to pres. Angelina & Neches River RR, Lufkin, 1989-90, v.p., asst. gen. mgr., 1990-91, pres., gen. mgr., 1991—. Bd. dirs. Lufkin Nat. Bank, 1993—, Angelina County C. of C., 1992, Pineywoods Found., Lufkin, 1991—, Am. Heart Assn., Lufkin, 1990-93, Tex. Forestry Mus., Lufkin, 1990-93, Meml. Med. Ctr. of East Tex., Lufkin, 1990—, Angelina Beautiful Clean, 1991-93; chmn. Lufkin Coun. Leadership, 1992-93; mem. Econ. Devel. Coun. Mem Am. Short Line R.R. Assn. (bd. dirs. 1992—), Pineywoods Transp. Club (bd. dirs. 1990-91), Kiwanis (bd. dirs. Lufkin chpt. 1991-92), Angelina County A&M Club (chmn. 1992). Republican. Baptist. Office: Angelina & Neches River RR co 2225 Spence PO Box 1328 Lufkin TX 75902-1328

PERKINS, FREDERICK MYERS, retired oil company executive; b. Tallahassee, Fla., Oct. 7, 1928; s. Frederick Myers and Nancy Evelyn (Turner) P.; m. Rosemary Ross, Dec. 21, 1950; children: Lucille Lambert Reed, Nancy Evelyn Cavanagh, Matthew Myers. B.Ch.E., U. Fla., 1951, M.S., 1952. Prodn. research engr. Humble Oil & Refining Co., Houston, 1952-62, prodn. staff coordinator, 1963-65; reservoir engr. Humble Oil & Refining Co., New Orleans, 1965-66; prodn. mgr. Humble Oil & Refining Co., Corpus Chrisiti, Tex., 1966-70; petroleum economist Standard Oil Co. N.J., N.Y.C., 1962-63; dep. mng. dir. Esso Australia Ltd., Sydney, 1970-72; gen. mgr. natural gas Exxon Co. U.S.A., Houston, 1972-76, v.p. prodn., 1976-79, dep. mgr. producing Exxon Corp., 1979-80, v.p. gas, 1980-85, v.p. producing, 1985-86; pres. Exxon Prodn. Research Co., Houston, 1986-93; ret., 1993. Patentee in field. Served with U.S. Army, 1946-47, PTO. Mem. Soc. Petroleum Engrs., Galveston Country Club, Petroleum Club.

PERKINS, JAMES FRANCIS, physicist; b. Hillsdale, Tenn., Jan. 3, 1924; s. Jim D. and Laura Pervis (Good) P.; A.B., Vanderbilt U., 1948, M.A., 1949; Ph.D., 1953; m. Ida Virginia Phillips, Nov. 23, 1949; 1 son, James F. Sr. engr. Convair, Fort Worth, Tex., 1953-54; scientist Lockheed Aircraft, Marietta, Ga., 1954-61; physicist Army Missile Command Redstone Arsenal, Huntsville, Ala., 1961-77; cons. physicist, 1977—. Served with USAAF, 1943-46. AEC fellow, 1951-52. Mem. Am. Phys. Soc., Sigma Xi. Contbr. articles to profl. jours. Home and Office: 102 Mountain Wood Dr SE Huntsville AL 35801-1809

PERKINS, JAMES MORRIS, psychiatrist; b. Monroe, Ga., Feb. 15, 1929; s. James Hugh and Myrtice Louelle (Brown) P.; m. Delaine Durdin, June 21, 1952; 1 child, Penelope Susan Perkins Kurland. BA, Emory U., 1951, MD, 1955. Diplomate Am. Bd. Psychiatry and Neurology. Coord. resident tng. dept. psychiatry Emory Sch. Medicine, Atlanta, 1959-60, exec. asst. dept. psychiatry, 1960-62; dep. chief of psychiatry Emory Clinic Psychiatry Sect., Atlanta, 1962-68; with psychoanalytic tng. Columbia Emory Psychoanalytic Sch., 1964-68; pvt. practice Atlanta, 1968—. Pres. Medlock PTA, Atlanta, 1960-61; cons. in mental health Ga. PTA, 1963-64. Capt. U.S. Army, 1956-58. Fellow Am. Psychiat. Assn., So. Psychiat. Assn., Ga. Psychiat. Assn. (bd. trustees 1967-79, pres. 1975-76); mem. AMA, Med. Assn. Atlanta, Atlanta Yacht Club, Bay Point Yacht Club. Methodist. Office: 3400 Peachtree Rd NE Atlanta GA 30326-1107

PERKINS, LOIS ELAINE, art educator, nurse assistant; b. Asbestos, Que., Can., June 23, 1937; came to U.S., 1940; d. Paul Ernest and Gertrude Anne Bouthillier; m. Harold Lea Perkins, Jan. 19, 1960 (div. Feb. 1962); 1 child, Paul Bouthillier Perkins. BFA, Fla. Atlantic U., 1981. Lic. art therapist, Fla.; cert. nurse asst. Instr., pottery, painting Broward County (Fla.) Sch. System, 1975-89; instr. painting Broward C.C., Coconut Creek, Fla., 1985-89; freelance artist, 1989—; tchr. painting City of Deerfield Beach, Fla., 1994—; judge local and county art shows, Fla.; instr. youth program Fla. Atlantic U. Exhibited in group shows at Boston Globe Show, 1955, Boston Mus. Fine Arts, 1960, Alamance County Festival, N.C., 1960, N.H. League of Arts and Crafts, Concord, 1960-61, D'Onofrio Studio, Serendipity, Miami, Fla., 1964, Beaux Arts, Las Olas Festival, Ft. Lauderdale, Fla., 1963-71, N.Y. Furniture Show, N.Y.C., 1965, Broward C.C., Coconut Creek, Fla., 1980, Broward Art Guild, 1980, 82, Am. Savs. Bank, Pompano Beach, 1984, Curzon Gallery, Boca Raton (Fla.) Hotel, Soc. Four Arts, Palm Beach, Fla., 1988, 91, Judge James R. Knott Ctr. for Hist. Preservation, Delray, Fla., others; represented in permanent collections Pompano Beach City Libr., Hebei Province, China; represented in pvt. collections; newspaper columnist Paint Drops, 1996—. Vol. art therapy Salvation Army, Homestead, Fla.; mem. cmty. appearance com., Pompano Beach, Fla., 1980-81; mem. Hist. Soc., Pompano Beach, 1985-86, Pompano Beach 2000 Plus, 1995. Mem. Fla. Profl. Artists, Inc., Fla. Roster for Fla. Arts in Edn., N.H. League of Arts and Crafts, Sumi-E Soc. Am., Broward Art Guild, Gold Coast Water Color Soc., Norton Artists Guild, Coral Springs Artist Guild, Artist Equity Assn. Methodist. Home: 436 NE 25th Ave Pompano Beach FL 33062-4832

PERKINS, MARIE MCCONNELL, real estate executive; b. Mobile, Ala., June 26, 1938; d. Emanuel and Mary Thelma (Lyons) Andrews; m. Michael Reid Perkins, Jan. 23, 1993; children: Angela Denise McConnell Young, Robin McConnell Wade, Dana McConnell Scott. Grad. high sch., Mobile. Lic. real estate broker. Sales assoc. Roberts Bros. Inc., Mobile, 1974-78, broker assoc., 1978-79; real estate cons. Century 21 Regional Staff South, Mobile, 1979-80; broker, owner ERA Marie McConnell Realty, Inc., Mobile, 1980—, Baldwin County, Ala., 1989—; state dir. Relo-Inter-City Relocation, 1984—. Contbr. articles to mags., newspapers. Bd. dirs. Mobile Cystic Fibrosis Assn., 1987, Penelope House, 1990-94, 92 Cath. Social Svcs.; chmn., organizer Adopt-A-Family program, Mobile, 1984-94; mem. Regional Adv. Coun. for State of Ala., SBA, also chair Women in Bus. for State of Ala. Recipient Career Woman award Gayfers Career Club, Mobile, 1979, Small Bus. of Yr. award C. of C., 1989, Leadership award Scholarship Women's Coun. Realtors, 1993; named Sales Person of Yr., Am. Real Estate Inst., 1978, Broker of Yr., 1980, First Lady of Mobile, 1990. Mem. Nat. Assn. Realtors, Ala. Assn. Realtors (state dir. 1983-85, 88-90), Mobile County Bd. Realtors (bd. dirs., organizer Crime and Missing Children watches, staff instr., Realtor of Yr. 1983), Mobile and Baldwin County Assn. Realtors, Mobile Area C. of C. (exec. com., vice chmn. communication, chmn. Pride Involvement Coun. 1991-92, Small Bus. of Yr. 1989), Women's Coun. Bd. Realtors (Mobile chpt. pres. 1994), Mobile & Baldwin County Home Builder's Assn., Bienville Club. Republican. Baptist. Office: ERA Marie McConnell Realty 824 Western American Dr Mobile AL 36609-4107

PERKINS, MARVIN EARL, psychiatrist, educator; b. Moberly, Mo., June 1, 1920; s. Marvin Earl and Nannie Mae (Walden) P.; A.B., Albion Coll., 1942; M.D., Harvard U., 1946; M.P.H. (USPHS fellow), Johns Hopkins U., 1956; L.H.D., Albion Coll., 1968; grad. U.S. Army Command and Gen. Staff Coll., 1966, U.S. Army War Coll., 1972; m. Mary MacDonald, May 24, 1943 (div.); children: Keith, Sandra, Cynthia, Marvin, Mary, Irene; m. 2d, Sharon Johnstone, May 20, 1978; 1 dau., Sharon. Intern, Henry Ford Hosp., Detroit, 1946-47; post surgeon, hosp. comdg. officer Fort Eustis, Va., 1948; resident physician psychiatry Walter Reed Army Hosp., Washington, 1949-52; chief psychiatry br., psychiatry and neurology cons. div. Office U.S. Army Surgeon Gen., Washington, 1952-53, chief records rev. br., 1953-55; chief psychiat. svcs. div. D.C. Dept. Pub. Health, 1955-58, chief bur. mental health, 1959-60; lectr. Johns Hopkins U., Balt., 1960-65; adj. prof. Columbia U., 1961-67; prof. psychiatry Mt. Sinai Sch. Medicine of CUNY, 1967-72; clin. prof. psychiatry Coll. Physicians and Surgeons, Columbia U., 1972-77; prof. psychiatry N.Y. Coll. Medicine, 1977-78; prof. behavioral medicine and psychiatry U. Va. Sch. Medicine, 1978—; dir. N.Y.C. Community Mental Health Bd., 1960-68, commr. mental health svcs., 1961-68; dir. psychiatry Beth Israel Medical Center, N.Y.C., 1967-72, dir. Morris J. Bernstein Inst., 1968-72; dir. Community Mental Health Svcs. Westchester County, 1972-77; dir. psychiatry Westchester County Med. Center, 1977-78; med. dir. Mental Health Svcs. of Roanoke Valley, 1978-82; med. dir. Roanoke Valley Psychiat. Ctr., 1980-82, pres. med. staff, 1985-86; med. dir., pres. med. staff Catawba Hosp., 1988-91; psychiat., mental hygiene clinic VA Med. Ctr., Salem, Va., 1992-95; cons. psychiatrist Blue Ridge Cmty. Svcs., 1992—; med. dir. partial hospitalization program Alleghany Regional Hosp., Low Moor, Va., 1995—. With AUS, 1943-46; col. M.C. Res. ret. Diplomate in psychiatry Am. Bd. Psychiatry and Neurology; certified mental hosp. adminstr. Am. Psychiat. Assn. Fellow Am. Psychiat. Assn. (life), N.Y. Acad. Medicine (life); mem. AMA, Group Advancement Psychiatry, Roanoke Acad. Medicine, N.Y. Psychiat. Soc., Neuropsychiat. Soc. Va., Med. Soc. Va., State Hist. Soc. Mo. (life), Res. Officers Assn. (life) Mil. Order of World Wars (perpetual). Home: 3728 Forest Rd SW Roanoke VA 24015-4510 also: PO Box 20437 Roanoke VA 24018 Office: 1604 Boulevard Salem VA 24153 also: 865 Roanoke Rd Daleville VA 24083

PERKINS, ROBERT EDGEWORTH, retired automotive executive; b. Melbourne, Fla., Aug. 3, 1921; s. Patrick Edgeworth and Norma (Van Buren) P.; m. Lurlene Varner, July 11, 1941 (dec. Nov. 1981); 1 child, Jo Ann; m. Louise Kilgor Walker, Aug. 20, 1983. With U.S. Naval Shipyard, Charleston, S.C., 1946-50; auto salesman McKesshan Olds, Charleston, 1950-53; factory rep. Chrysler, Dodge Divsn., Lows, S.C., 1953-56; pres. Glover Motors, Ashville, N.C., 1956-73; Pres., founder Perkins Corp., Charleston, S.C., 1975—. Editor (newsletters) Houseboat News, 1971—, Hearing News, 1995—. Pres., founder Remount Rd. Civic, Charleston, 1948, Carolina Hearing Aid Bank, Charleston, 1995—; commdr. U.S. Power Squadron, Ashville, N.C., 1973; With U.S. Army, 1940-46. Mem. Houseboat Assn. Am. (founder, pres. 1971—), Charleston Rod and Reel Club (pres. 1993-96). Republican. Episcopalian. Home: 4940 N Rhett Ave North Charleston SC 29405

PERKINS, ROBERT EUGENE, foundation administrator; b. Pittsfield, Mass., Oct. 20, 1931; s. L. Warren and Gladys (Bell) P.; m. (dec.); children: Stephen, Deborah Smith, Kimberly Robell. BA, Sioux Falls Coll., 1956, LHD (hon.), 1975; MA, Columbia U., 1957; DSc (hon.), Fla. Inst. Tech., 1983; LittD (hon.), U. Sarasota, 1986. Tchr., adminstr. Canton (S.D.) Pub. Schs., 1957-61; dir. admissions Sioux Falls (S.D.) Coll., 1961-65, dean students, 1965-70; pres. Ringling Sch. Art & Design, Sarasota, Fla., 1970-81; exec. dir. Selby Found., Sarasota, Fla., 1981—; Bd. dirs. Manatee C.C., Bootstrap Found., Sarasota Pub. Schs. Found., USF Search Com. for Selby Chair on Econs., Jr. Achievement; instr. New Leaders Coun., Sarasota. Author: The Maestro, 1970, The First 50 Years, Ringling Sch. of Art and Design, 1982, The Selby Impact! Twenty Six Years, 1984. Bd. dirs. Southeastern Coun. Founds., Atlanta, 1982-88; adv. bd. Sarasota Ballet, Sarasota County Arts Coun., Jr. League, Sarasota, Coun. on Children and Youth, Cmty. Found. Sarasota County, Selby Ctr., Human Svcs. Ctr., bd. dirs. Paul Harris fellow; recipient Champion Higher Edn. award Fla. Pvt. Coll. Pres., 1991, A.O. Larsen Disting. Alumni award Sioux Falls Coll., 1988; named Disting. Citizen of Yr., Sarasota, 1988, South Sarasota County, 1990. Mem. Nat. Coun. Founds., Southeastern Coun. Foundations, Fla. Charitable Found. Group, Rotary (pres. 1972, nominating com. mem. R.I. 1978, gov. 1979, Rotarian of the Decade 1980s, Sarasota Rotarian of Yr. 1985), Univ. Club. Presbyterian. Home: 3424 S Lockwood Ridge Rd Sarasota FL 34239-6623 Office: Selby Found 1800 2nd St Ste 905 Sarasota FL 34236-5992

PERKINS, SUE DENE, journalist; b. Wichita Falls, Tex., Jan. 12, 1946; d. Darrye Clayton and Josephine Marie (Hall) P. BA, North Tex. State U., 1968; MA, Stephen F. Austin State U., 1980; postgrad., Angelo State U., 1979. Cert. tchr., Tex. Mag. editor Haire Pubs., N.Y.C., 1968-69; women's editor Arlington (Tex.) Daily News, 1970; police reporter editor Arlington (Tex.) Daily News, 1972; mag. editor Tex. Assn. Bus., Houston, 1972-74; editor in ho. pubs. P.R. Am. Assn. Respiratory Therapy, Dallas, 1974-76; asst. employee pub. rels. Gen. Telephone, San Angelo, 1976-79; dir. student publs. Stephen F. Austin State U., Nacogdoches, Tex., 1980-83, founder Women in Comm. chpt., 1982; instr. journalism Tex. A&M Univ., College Station, 1983-84; owner photo supply Photo-Graphics Co., Lufkin, Tex., 1985-88; adv. student pubs. Diboll (Tex.) Ind. Sch. Dist., 1987-97; editor Escapees, Inc., Livingston, Tex., 1997—; computer cons. Deep East Tex. Coun. Govt., Lufkin, 1990, Region VII Edn. Svc. Ctr., Kilgore, Tex., 1994. Editor: (mags.) Handbags & Accessories, 1968-69, Tex. Industry, 1972-74, (newspaper) Arlington Daily News, 1970-72, (newsletter) Am. Assn. for Respiratory Therapy Bull., 1974-76. Pres. Wheeler Cemetery Assn., Corrigan, Tex., 1992, v.p., 1993; sec. Youth for Christ, Diboll, Tex., 1993-95. Named Outstanding Ex-Student, Electra (Tex.) Alumni Assn., 1981-82. Mem. Journalism Educators Am., Tex. Journalism Edn. Assn., Tex. Classroom Tchrs. Assn., Order Ea. Star. Baptist. Home: RR 1 Box 106 Corrigan TX 75939-9739 Office: Diboll High Sch 1000 Harris St Diboll TX 75941-9762

PERKINSON, DIANA AGNES ZOUZELKA, import company executive; b. Prostejov, Czechoslovakia, June 27, 1943; came to U.S., 1962; d. John Charles and Agnes Diana (Sincl) Zouzelka; m. David Francis Perkinson, Mar. 6, 1965; children: Dana Leissa, David. BA, U. Lausanne (Switzerland), 1960; MA, U. Madrid, 1961; MBA, Case Western Res. U., 1963; cert. internat. mktg. Oxford (Eng.) U., 1962. Assoc. Allen Hartman & Schreiber, Cleve., 1963-64; interpreter Tower Internat. Inc., Cleve., 1964-66; pres. Oriental Rug Importers Ltd., Cleve., 1979—; pres. Oriental Rug Designers, Inc., Cleve., 1980—; pres. Oriental Rug Cons., Inc., Cleve., 1980—; chmn. Foxworthy's Inc., Ft. Myers, Naples, Sanibel, Fla.; bd. dir. Beckwith & Assocs., Inc., Cleve., Secura Inc., Dallas, Dix-Bur Investments, Ltd., Real Estate By Design. Trustee, Cleve. Ballet, 1979, exec. com., 1981; mem. Cleve. Mayor's Adv. Com.; trustee Diabetes Assn. Greater Cleve.; mem., chmn. grantsmanship Jr. League of Cleve., 1982; mem. mem. Cleve. Found.-Women in Philanthropy, 1982; trustee Ft. Myers Symphony, 1990. Mem. Women Bus. Owners Assn., Oriental Rug Retailers Am. (bd. dir. 1983), Cleve. Racquet Club, Recreation League, The League Club (Naples, Fla.), Hillbrook Club, Univ. Club (Ft. Myers, Fla.), Captiva Yacht Club. Republican. Roman Catholic. Home: Ravencrest PO Box 477 Sanibel FL 33957-0477 Office: Foxworthys Inc 2430 Periwinkle Way Sanibel FL 33957-3207 also: 17001 Captiva Rd Captiva Island FL 33924

PERKINSON, DIANA MUNSEY, lawyer; b. Pearisburg, Va., Apr. 13, 1947; d. Garland and Rowena Mae (White) Munsey. AB, Randolph Macon Woman's Coll., Lynchburg, Va., 1969; LLB, U. Va., 1972. Bar: Va. 1973. Ptnr. Perkinson & Perkinson, Roanoke, Va., 1972—. Mem. Va. State Bar, Va. Trial Lawyers Assn., Assn. Trial Lawyers Am., Va. Women's Lawyers Assn. Office: 115 Kirk Ave SW Roanoke VA 24011-1601

PERKOWITZ, ROBERT MICHAEL, management executive, consultant; b. Evanston, Ill., June 21, 1954; m. Lisa Renstrom, May, 1996; children: Thomas, Alex. BS in Social Thought, Lake Forest (Ill.) Coll., 1980; MBA, Lake Forest Grad. Sch. Mgmt., 1981; postgrad., Harvard Bus. Sch., 1988. Pres. Perkowitz Window Fashions, Highland Park, Ill., 1973-76; pres. Tempo Industries, Inc., Vernon Hills, Ill., 1975-88; chmn. Tempo Industries, Inc., Vernon Hills, 1988-92; chmn., pres. Home Fashions, Inc., Westminster, Calif., 1988-93; pres. Joanna Window Decor, Charlotte, N.C., 1993-95, Paradigm Mgmt., Inc., Charlotte, 1995—; chmn. Merchandise Sales, Inc., San Fernando, Calif., 1996—; bd. dirs. Smith & Noble, Corona, Calif., 1996—. Mem. Citizens Adv. Bd. Mecklenburg County, Charlotte, 1996—. Office: Paradigm Mgmt Inc 3817 Bonwood Dr Charlotte NC 28211-1752

PERLMUTTER, BARRY ARTHUR, marketing and sales engineering executive; b. N.Y.C., Oct. 16, 1954; s. Jack and Pearl (Maged) P.; m. Michelle Susan Olshan, July 12, 1984; children: Jason, Bryan. BS in Chemistry, SUNY, Albany, 1975; MS in Environ. Sci. and Tech., Washington U., St. Louis, 1976; MBA in Fin., Mgmt. Info. Sys., U. Ill., Chgo., 1982. Environ. scientist EPA, Chgo., 1978-82; sr. mgr. mktg. Pall Corp., East Hills, N.Y., 1982-88; v.p. mktg., sales and engring. Rosenmund Inc., Charlotte, N.C., 1988—. Contbr. articles to profl. jours. Active United Way, Charlotte, 1990-91. Mem. Am. Mktg. Assn., Internat. Soc. Pharm. Engring. Office: Rosenmund Inc 9110 Forsyth Park Dr Charlotte NC 28273-3881

PERRET, DONNA C., art gallery director; b. Jackson, Miss., June 23, 1949; m. Richard Johnson. BS, Miss. State Coll. for Women, 1972. Asst. dir. mut. funds dept. Howard, Weil, Labouisse & Friedrichs, 1972-75; founder Warehouse Arts Dist., New Orleans, 1984; dir. Galerie Simonne Stern, New Orleans, 1983—, ptnr., 1985—; v.p. policy and planning Arts Coun./Art Table, Inc., N.Y.C., 1996; bd. dirs. Arts Coun. of New Orleans, mem. House Com., Longue Vue Gardens, 1994; guest lectr. in field, including Internat. Coun. of Shopping Ctrs., 1996, Pensacola Mus. of Art, 1995, others. Chmn. Mayor's 1994 Arts Award luncheon, 1994; mem. Women's Profl. Coun. Arts. Coun. of New Orleans, 1992-93; exec. bd. dirs. Contemporary Arts Ctr., 1989-92; exec. bd. dir. Riverfront Civic Assn., 1985-88; founding adv. bd. La. Children's Mus., 1984, others.

PERRET, GERARD ANTHONY, JR., orthodontist; b. New Orleans, Feb. 13, 1959; s. Gerard A. and Marie M. (Gamino) P.; m. Catherine J. McMahon, 1996. BS in Chemistry, U. N.C., 1981; DDS, La. State U., 1986, cert. orthodontics, 1989. Clin. asst. prof. La. State U. Sch. Dentistry, New Orleans, 1986-87; pvt. practice dentistry Lakeside Dental Group, Metairie, La., 1986-87; pvt. practice orthodontics Jacksonville, Fla., 1989-91, Tampa, Fla., 1991—; founder, pres. Orthogap, Inc., Tampa, 1993—. Patentee in field. Active New Tampa Cmty. Coun. Mem. ADA, Am. Assn. Orthodontists, Fla. Assn. Orthodontists, Hillsborough County Dental Soc., Hillsborough County Dental Rsch. Clinic, So. Assn. Orthodontists, Rotary (pres.-elect New Tampa), Omicron Kappa Upsilon. Office: 14201 Bruce B Downs Blvd Ste 2 Tampa FL 33613-3913

PERRIN, ROY ALBERT, JR., real estate developer; b. New Orleans, Feb. 26, 1940; s. Roy Albert and Beverly Addie (Switzer) P.; m. Kathleen Anne Munch; children: Roy Albert III, Robyn Perrin Richmond. BS in Engring., Tulane U., 1961, MS, 1962. Registered profl. engr., La., Miss., Tex. Sales engr. Allan J. Harris Co., Inc., Metairie, La., 1965-70; sales engr. Alexander Industries, Inc., Houston and New Orleans, 1970-72, v.p., 1973-78, pres., chief exec. officer, 1979-85; pres. comml. real estate Stewart Enterprises, Inc., Metairie, 1985-94; pres. Stewart Comml. Real Estate, Inc., Metairie, 1994—. Mem. Gov.'s Task Force, Port of New Orleans, 1982-83; bd. dirs., fin. com. World Trade Ctr., New Orleans, 1985—; mem. exec. com. New Orleans coun. Boy Scouts Am., 1987—. 1st lt. USAF, 1962-65. Hon. harbormaster, Port New Orleans. Mem. ASME, Arnold Air Soc., Navy League, Soc. Naval Architects and Marine Engrs., Bienville Club, Metairie Country Club, Rotary Club Metairie (Paul Harris fellow 1983). Office: Stewart Comml Real Estate Ste 1010 111 Veterans Memorial Blvd Metairie LA 70005-3046

PERRIN, SARAH ANN, lawyer; b. Neoga, Ill., Dec. 13, 1904; d. James Lee and Bertha Frances (Baker) Figenbaum; m. James Frank Perrin, Dec. 24, 1926. LLB, George Washington U., 1941, JD, 1964. Bar: D.C. 1942. Assoc. atty. Mabel Walker Willebrandt, law office, Washington, 1941-42; atty. various fed. housing agys., 1942-69, asst. gen. counsel FHA, Washington, 1959-60, asst. gen. counsel HUD, Washington, 1960-69; sec. Nat. Housing Conf., Washington, 1970-80; rsch. cons. housing and urban devel., Palmyra, Va., 1970-76; acting sec. Nat. Housing Rsch. Coun., Washington, 1973-80; bd. dirs. Nat. Housing Conf., 1972—. Mem. Rep. Presdl. Adv. Commn., 1991-92, Senatorial Com.; trustee Found. for Coop. Housing, 1975-80; mem. Blue Ridge Presbytery Div. Mission, Presbyn. Ch., 1979-80, Friends of Fluvanna County Libr. Mem. ABA, Fed. Bar Assn., Women's Bar Assn. D.C. (pres. 1959-60), Nat. Assn. Women Lawyers, George Washington Law Assn., Charlottesville Area Women's Bar Assn., Fluvanna County Bar Assn., Fluvanna County Hist. Soc. (pres. 1973-75, exec. com. 1985-89), Order Eastern Star, Presbyn. Women (pres. Fork Union chpt. 1972-80, sec. 1980-94), Phi Alpha Delta (internat. pres. 1955-57, internat. adv. bd.). Home: Solitude Plantation Palmyra VA 22963

PERRY, BARBARA ANN, political science educator; b. Louisville, Ky., Jan. 24, 1956; d. Louis Raymond and Lillian Rose (Grenewald) P. BA, U. Louisville, 1978; MA, U. Oxford, England, 1985; PhD, U. Va., 1986. Compliance officer Louisville-Jefferson County Human Rels. Commn., 1978-79; asst. prof. U. Ctrl. Fla., Orlando, 1986-89; asst. prof. Sweet Briar (Va.) Coll., 1989-92, assoc. prof., 1992—; jud. fellow U.S. Supreme Ct., Washington, 1994-95; mem. faculty adv. bd. Thomas Jefferson Ctr., Charlottesville, Va., 1995—. Co-author: Freedom and the Court, 1994, Civil Rights and Liberties Under the Constitution, 1993, Unfounded Fears: Myths and Realities of a Constitutional Convention, 1989; author: A "Representative" Supreme Court?, 1991. Advisor Pub. Leadership Edn. Network, Washington, 1989—. Fellow Va. Found. for Humanities, 1995-96, Sweet Briar Coll., 1995-96; recipient Teaching Excellence award Sears Roebuck Found., 1990-91. Mem. Am. Polit. Sci. Assn., So. Polit. Sci. Assn., Midwest Polit. Sci. Assn. (exec. coun. 1993—). Roman Catholic. Office: Sweet Briar Coll Box 69 Sweet Briar VA 24595

PERRY, BERYL HENRY, JR., government official, accountant; b. Windsor, Va., Apr. 19, 1956; s. Beryl Henry Sr. and Georgia (Nurney) P.; m. Mary Lovette Vinson, Oct. 20, 1979; children: Beryl Henry III, Nicholas Lloyd. BBA, Christopher Newport Coll., 1978. CPA, Va. Acct. ITT Gwaltney, Inc., Smithfield, Va., 1978-79, A. Lee Rawling's CPA's, Smithfield, 1979-82; comptroller V.H. Monette, Inc., Smithfield, 1982-84; treas. County of Isle of Wight, Va., 1984—. Mem. AICPA, Va. Soc. CPAs, Treas. Assn. Va. (officer), Va. Assn. Locally Elected Constl. Officers (officer), Peanut Growers Assn., Va. Farm Bur., Tidewater Treas. Assn. (officer), Jaycees, Ruritan (past pres., dist. gov.), Masons, Kiwanis. Democrat. Baptist. Lodges: Ruritan (past pres., dist. gov.), Masons, Kiwanis. Home: 11021 Foursquare Rd Windsor VA 23487-8002 Office: Office of Treas Courthouse Isle of Wight VA 23397

PERRY, DONNY RAY, electrician; b. Amarillo, Tex., Apr. 29, 1959; s. Ernest Elwood and Donnie Mae Perry; m. Tina Marie Conn, Sept. 9, 1988; children: Contessa, Jason, Stephen, Christopher. Cert. in fiber optics, Tex. State Tech. Inst., 1988; student, Amarillo Coll., 1990—. Electrician Mason & Hanger, Amarillo, 1979—; mem. negotiating com. Mason & Hanger, 1989-90, mem. sick leave and team concept coms., 1991, mem. elec. safety com., 1992, mem. job track analysis and procedure adherence coms., 1993.

Mem. Internat. Brotherhood Elec. Workers, Metal Trades Coun. (negotiating com. 1989-90, exec. bd. 1989-90, co-chair elec. safety com. 1995—, team leader Hazard Identification Team 1995—, legis. and polit. action com. 1996—, apprenticeship com. 1996—), Phi Theta Kappa, Nat. Dean's List.

PERRY, E. ELIZABETH, social worker, real estate manager; b. Balt., Oct. 2, 1954; d. James Glenn and Pearl Elizabeth (Christopher) P.; 1 child, Linden Andrew. AA, C.C. of Balt., 1973; B in Art, Psychology, Social Work, U. Md., Balt., 1975, MSW, 1978. Asst. grant coord. Md. Conf. Social Concern, Balt., 1975; dir. social svcs. West Balt. Cmty. Health Care Corp., 1978-80; tng. counselor NutriSystem Inc. of Md., Balt., 1983-86; counselor/psychotherapist Switlik Elem. Sch., Marathon, Fla., 1988-89; program dir. emergency shelter Children's Home Soc., Miami, 1990-91; health educator, spokesperson Rape Treatment Ctr., Miami, 1991-94; CEO, pres. bd. Child Assault Prevention Project, Miami, 1993—; self-employed in real estate rehab. and mgmt., 1980—; pub. spkr. on women's and children's issues/sexual assault issues, 1990—. Bd. dirs. Partnership Way, 1993-95, ACHIEVE, 1995—; pub. citizen Dem. Nat. Com. Mem. AAUW, NOW (bd. dirs. Dade County 1994-95), Nat. Abortion Rights Action League, Amnesty Internat., People for the Am. Way, Psi Chi, Phi Theta Kappa. Democrat. Home: 5161 Alton Rd Miami Beach FL 33140 Office: Child Assault Prev Project Omni Mall Ste 1195 1601 Biscayne Blvd Miami FL 33132-1224

PERRY, EVELYN REIS, communications company executive; b. N.Y.C., Mar. 9; d. Lou L. and Bertl (Wolf) Reis; m. Charles G. Perry III, Jan. 7, 1968; children: Charles G. IV, David Reis. BA, Univ. Wis., 1963; student Am. Acad. Dramatic Arts, 1958-59, Univ. N.Mex., 1963-64. Lic. real estate broker, N.C. Vol. ETV project Peace Corps, 1963-65; program officer-radio/tv Peace Corps, Washington, 1965-68; dir. Vols. in Svc. to Am. (VISTA), Raleigh, N.C., 1977-80; exec. dir. CETA Program for Displaced Homemakers, Raleigh, 1980-81; cons. exec. dir. to Recycle Raleigh for Food and Fuel, Theater in the Park, 1981-83, Artspace, Inc., Raleigh, 1983-84; pres., chief exec. officer Carolina Sound Comm., MUZAK, Charleston, S.C. and 12 counties in S.C., 1984—; pub. rels. account exec. various cos., Washington, Syracuse, N.Y., 1969-71; cons. pub. rels. and orgn. Olympic Organizing Com., Mexico City, 1968; cons. pub. rels., fundraising, arts mgmt. pub. speaking, Ill., Pa., N.C., 1971-77; orgnl. and pub. speaking cons. Perry & Assocs., Raleigh, 1980—. Mem. adv. bd. Gov.'s Office Citizen Affairs, Raleigh, 1981-85; mem. Involvement Coun. of Wake County, N.C., Raleigh, 1981-84; mem. Adv. Coun. to Vols. in Svc. to Am., Raleigh, 1980-84; mem. Pres.'s adv. bd. Peace Corps, Washington, 1980-82; v.p., bd. dirs. Voluntary Action Ctr., Raleigh, 1980-84, bd. dirs., Charleston, 1988-94; sec. bd. dirs. Temple Kahil Kadosh Beth Elohim, 1987-89, sec. fin., 1989-90, v.p. programming, 1990-93, v.p. adminstrn. 1993-95; bd. dirs. Chopstik Theater, Charleston, 1989-90; del., chmn. S.C. Delegation to White House Conf. Small Bus., 1995. Mem. N.C. Coun. of Women's Orgns. (pres., v.p. 1982-84), Charleston Hotel and Motel Assn., N.C. Assn. Vol. Adminstrs. (bd. dirs. 1980-84), S.C. Restaurant Assn., Nat. Assn. Women Bus. Owners, Internat. Planned Music Assn. (bd. dirs. 1986—, newsletter editor), NAFE, Nat. Fedn. Ind. Businesses (mem. adv. bd. 1987—, chmn. guardian adv. coun. 1994—), Internat. Platform Assn., Theaterworks (bd. dirs. 1994—), Charleston C. of C. Office: Carolina Sound Comm Inc 1941 Savage Rd Ste 200G Charleston SC 29407

PERRY, GLENDA LEE, health science librarian; b. Booneville, Ark., Mar. 21, 1940; d. Earnest Asa and Susan Mae (Aaron) P. BS in Elem. Edn., Ark. Tech. U., 1962; MS in Libr. Sci., La. State U., 1972. Elem. sch. tchr. Ark. Pub. Schs., 1962-64, sch. libr., 1965-74; monograph acquisitions libr. U. Tenn. Health Sci. Ctr. Libr., Memphis, 1979-82, serials libr., 1975-78, 82-87; health scis. libr. Met. Nashville Gen. Hosp., 1987—. Mem. Med. Libr. Assn. (sr. mem. Acad. of Health Information Profls.), Mid Tenn. Health Sci. Librs. Assn. (sec.-treas. 1992-94), Tenn. Health Sci. Librs. Assn. (union list com. 1988-91). Office: Met Nashville Gen Hosp 72 Hermitage Ave Nashville TN 37210-2110

PERRY, HELEN, educator, nurse; b. Birmingham, Ala., Mar. 4, 1927; d. Van Mary Ellenol (Thornton) Curry; m. Charlie Pitts, May, 1960; 1 child, Charlenia; m. George Perry (dec. 1989); children: Hattie Mae (dec.), George Jr., Jose. Student, LaSalle Extension U., Chgo., 1968, Georgetown U., 1979; Doctorate/Mayanuis Mosaic Soc., Duke Univ., San Antonio, 1979. Lic. practical nurse; paramedic. Supply tchr. City Bd. Edn., Birmingham, 1977—; notary pub., Ala., 1975—; nurse home health U. Ala. at Birmingham Hosp., 1988—. Vol. ARC, Birmingham, 1970—; mem. crime watch Am. Police, Washington, 1989; mem. Hall of Fame Pres. Task Force, Washington, 1983-91; nominee Nat. Rep. Com., Washington, 1991, 92; selected VIP Guest delegate Rep. Nat. Conv., Houston, 1992, fin. com. fundraiser Middleton for Congress Campaign '94, Dist. # 59 Bd. Reps.; life mem. Rep. Presdl. Task Force, Washington, 1992; trustee Nat. Crime Watch, 1989, adv. bd. Am. Security Coun., Va., Washington, 1969-91; mem. Nat. Congl. Com. Adv. Bd., Washington; mem. Nat. Law Enforcement Assn., 1989; min. Greater Emmanuel Temple Holiness Ch., Birmingham, 1957—, ordained elder, vice-champion of mother bd.; mem. Jefferson County Rep. Exec. Com.; chair Harriet Tubman Rep. Com.; mem. Image Devel. Adv. Bd.; mem. Coalition for Desert Storm, various others. Recipient cert. of appreciation Pres. Congl. Task Force, 1990, Diamond award U.S.A. Serve Am., 1992, award Ala. Sheriff Assn., 1989, Navy League, 1989-91, Rep. Presdl. award Legion of Merit, 1994, cert. of appreciation Rep. Nat. Commn., 1994, nominated Presdl. Election Registry Rep. Presdl. Task Force, 1992; named Good Samaritan Law Enforcement Officers, Royal Proclamation Royal Highness Kevin, Prince Regent of Hutt River Province, 1994, Royal Ceremonial Jewel. Mem. LaSalle Extension U. Alumni (life mem.), Ala. Nurses Assn., Nat. Assn. Unknown Players. Home: 201 W Ann Dr SW Birmingham AL 35211-4935

PERRY, JAMES FREDERIC, philosophy educator, author; b. Washington, Jan. 21, 1936; s. Albert Walter and Helene Anna Maria (Neumeyer) P.; m. Sandra Jean Huizing, Feb. 18, 1957 (div. May 1972); children: Sandra Elaine, James Frederic Jr., Bartholomew; m. Roberta Schofield, June 6, 1984. Student, Princeton U., 1953-56, Marietta (Ohio) Coll., 1958-60; BA with honors in Philosophy, Ind. U., 1962, PhD in Philosophy of Edn., 1972. NDEA fellow in philosophy U. N.C., 1962-65; instr. N.C. State U., Raleigh, 1965-66; Univ. fellow Ind. U., 1971; adj. lectr. Ind. U., Bloomington, 1972-75; prof. philosophy Hillsborough Community Coll., Tampa, Fla., 1975—. Author: Random, Routine, Reflective, 1989; contbr. articles to profl. jours. Precinct committeeman Dem. Party, Tampa, 1988—. Nat. Def. Edn. Act fellow U. N.C., 1962-65, Univ. fellow Ind. U., 1970-71. Mem. AAUP (pres. Fla. conf. 1986-89, chair com. "A" on acad. freedom 1989—), C.C. Humanities Assn. (so. divsn. exec. bd. 1981-89), Internat. Soc. Philos. Enquiry, Internat. Congress for Critical Thinking and Moral Critiques (founding mem. S.E. coun. 1991), Soc. for Values in Higher Edn., Princeton Alumni Assn. of Fla. Suncoast (sec. 1983-86, pres. 1986-95), Mensa, Authors Guild, Textbook and Acad. Authors Assn. Office: Hillsborough C C PO Box 10561 Tampa FL 33679-0561

PERRY, JEAN PETERS, elementary school principal; b. Wilkes-Barre, Pa.; d. Frederick Simon and Lucy (Khachan) Peters; m. Leonard Thomas Perry, Sept. 2, 1963; children: Laura Victoria Perry, Leonard Thomas Perry. BA in Elem. Edn., Clemson (S.C.) U., 1972, MEd in Reading, 1977, Cert. in Elem. Adminstrn., 1981, postgrad., 1982-96. Sec., Cyrus Eaton chmn. C&O Rwy. Co., Cleve., 1959-62; sec. to chmn./pres. Greater Cleve. Associated Found., Cleve., 1962-67; editor Vocat. Edn. Media Ctr. Clemson U., 1967-69; tchr. D.W. Daniel H.S., Central, S.C., 1972-73, Pickens (S.C.) Elem., 1973-78, Central (S.C.) Elem., 1978-81; asst. prin. McKissick Elem., Easley, S.C., 1981-82; prin. Morrison Elem., Clemson, S.C., 1982-89, Ben Hagood Elem., Pickens, S.C., 1989—. Mem. Nat. Assn. Elem. Sch. Prins., S.C. Assn. Elem. Sch. Prins., Kiwanis Club of Pickens (pres. 1993-94). Democrat. Roman Catholic. Home: 104 Evergreen Dr Clemson SC 29631 Office: Ben Hagood Elem 435 Sparks Ln Pickens SC 29671

PERRY, LEWIS CHARLES, emergency medicine physician, osteopath; b. La Plata, Mo., Apr. 22, 1931; s. Lewis C. and Emily B. Perry; m. M. Sheryl Gupton, Oct. 30, 1953; children: David, Susan, Stephen, John. BS, U. Mo., 1958; postgrad., Louisville Presbyn. Sem., 1958-60; DO, Kirksville Coll. Osteo. Medicine, 1967. Intern Midcities Meml. Hosp., Arlington, Tex.; parish min. Presbyn. Bd. Nat. Missions, Canada, Ky., 1960-62; intern Mid Cities Meml. Hosp., Arlington; pvt. practice, Ingleside, Tex., 1968-72, Tucson, 1972-81; emergency physician Tucson Gen. Hosp., 1981-88, pres. med. staff, 1978-79, clin. instr., 1981-88; emergency physician Meml. Med. Ctr. East Tex., Lufkin, 1988—; clin. instr. Osteo. Coll. Pacific, Pomona, Calif., 1985-88. Pres. Helping Hands, Ingleside, 1969-72; bd. dirs., pres. Salvation Army, Tucson, 1978-81; commr. Cub Scouts Am., Tucson, 1975-76; bd. dirs. Unity of Tucson, Inc., 1986-88; pres. bd. dirs. Unity of Nacogdoches, 1993-94. 1st lt. USAF, 1952-56. Named Physician of Yr., Tucson Gen. Hosp., 1978; recipient God and Country award Boy Scouts of Am., 1960. Mem. Am. Legion, Rotary (recipient God and Country award), Masons, Scottish Rite, Shrine. Home: 1 Columbia Ct Lufkin TX 75901-7212

PERRY, LOIS JOY, non-profit corporation executive; b. Richards Landing, Ont., Can., Aug. 19, 1952; arrived in U.S., 1953; d. Floyd Carleton and Carolyn Lanier (Hassell) Barnes; m. Robert Charles Motton, June 12, 1977 (div. Feb. 1986); children: Robert Jeffrey, Philip Charles; m. Harry Montford Perry, Dec. 31, 1986 (dec. Oct. 1992). B of Religious Edn., Ont. Bible Coll., Toronto, Can., 1974. lic. property and casualty agt., life and health agt.; chartered profl. ins. woman. Office mgr. State Farm Ins., Virginia Beach, Va., 1985-88, owner, agt., 1988-94; co-founder, pres. Visionetics, Inc., Virginia Beach, 1990-95; founder, pres. High Impact Ministries, Inc., Virginia Beach, Tulsa, 1993—; Atlanta, 1993—; bd. dirs. Nineveh Music, Chesapeake, Va., 1993-94. Author: Million $ Planning: One Step at a Time, 1993; singer, songwriter: (album) Fresh New Day, 1994. Co-founder, pres. Christian Songwriters Network, Chesapeake, 1993; mem., organizer Christian Coalition, Virginia Beach, Tulsa and Atlanta, 1993—; dir. Ladies Ensemble, Norfolk, Va., 1993. Recipient Search for Talent Trophy, York Search for Talent, Toronto, 1980, Nat. Sales Achievement award Nat. Assn. Life Underwriters, 1992. Mem. Nat. Assn. Profl. Saleswomen, Virginia Beach Assn. Life Underwriters (sec. 1991-92, v.p. 1992-93, pres. 1993-94), Tulsa So. Tennis Club, Broad Bay Country Club. Republican. Evangelical. Office: High Impact Ministries Inc PO Box 88217 Atlanta GA 30356-8217

PERRY, NELSON ALLEN, radiation physicist, radiological consultant; b. Louisville, Mar. 26, 1937; s. Leslie Irvin and Sue Helen (Harris) P.; m. Sarita Sue Cornn, Apr. 28, 1956; children: Melody S. Bruck, Kimberly D. Horne. AS, Campbellsville (Ky.) Coll., 1954; BS, U. Louisville, 1961; MS, U. Okla., 1966. Cert. hazard control mgr., hazart material mgt.; lic. med. physicist, Tex. Assoc. prof. Ind. Christian U., Indpls., 1974-76; asst. prof. Ind. U., Indpls., 1971-75; instr. Ind. Voc. Tech. Coll., Indpls., 1968-76; health physicist Michael Reese Hosp., Chgo., 1966-68; radiation safety officer St. Francis Hosp., Beech Grove, Ind., 1968-76, Ind. U., Indpls., 1971-74; radiation safety officer U. South Ala., Mobile, 1976—, assoc. prof., 1981—; radiol. cons. Perry Radiol. Cons., Inc., 1974—; radiol. cons., 1974—. Contbr. articles to profl. jours. Named Ky. Col., 1964; USPHS trainee, 1965-66. Mem. Am. Assn. Physicists in Medicine, Health Physics Soc., Ala. Health Physics Soc. (sec. 1977-79, pres. 1980-81). Republican. Baptist. Office: U South Ala 257 CSAB Mobile AL 36688

PERRY, PATRICIA H., English language educator; b. Durham, N.C., Mar. 25, 1946; d. Joseph Junest and Claretta (Higgins) Harris; m. Jerrold V. Harris. BA in English, N.C. Cen. U., 1979, MLS, 1982; PhD in English, SUNY, Stony Brook, 1991. Asst. libr., dir. Learning Resource Ctr. St. Paul's Coll., Lawrenceville, Va., 1981-84, instr., asst. prof. English; asst. prof. English Va. Commonwealth U., Richmond, 1993—; vis. lectr. in English Mt. Holyoke Coll., South Hadley, Mass., 1990-91. Author: The Philosophies and Praxes of Paulo Freire and Peter Elbow. Five Coll. fellow; PEW grantee St. Paul's Coll.; Marilyn & Ira Heehler scholar, Ruth Miller scholar. Mem. MLA, Nat. Coun. Tchrs. English, Beta Phi Mu, Alpha Kappa Mu. Office: Dept of English Virginia Commonwealth Univ Richmond VA 23284-2005

PERRY, ROBERT LEE, non-profit association executive; b. Aurora, Mo., Jan. 4, 1945; s. Bob L. and Lena M. (Smith) P.; m. Nancy B. Whitlow, Aug. 15, 1964 (dec. May 1993); children: Douglas, David; m. Marilyn C. Nelson, Aug. 9, 1993; 1 child, Seth. BS in Edn., S.W. Mo. State U., 1966; MDiv, Midwestern Theol. Sem., 1970, DMin, 1980. Pastor Mt. Zion Bapt. Ch., Sparta, Mo., 1965-67; social worker Mo. Divsn. of Welfare, Springfield, 1966-67; pastor Smith Fork Bapt. Ch., Osborn, Mo., 1968-70, Pisgah Bapt. Ch., Excelsior Springs, Mo., 1970-73; cons. Fgn. Mission Bd., SBC, Oaxaca, Mex., 1974-75; pastor Capital City Bapt. Ch., Mexico City, Mex., 1975-80, First Bapt. Ch., Excelsior Springs, 1980-84; dir. Clay-Platte Bapt. Assn., Kansas City, Mo., 1984-88; exec. dir. Mt. Vernon Bapt. Assn., Annandale, Va., 1988—; bd. dirs. Midwestern Bapt. Sem., Kansas City, Mo., Washington Coll. and Seminary, Falls Church, VBGB Extension Bd., Richmond, Va. Author: Models for Multihousing Ministry, 1989, Pass the Power, Please, 1995; co-author: Values-Based Tactical Planning, 1994, Futuropting: Scenario Planning, 1996. Mem. fin. com. Bapt. World Alliance, McLean, Va., 1990—. Office: Mt Vernon Bapt Assn 7100 Columbia Pike Annandale VA 22003

PERRY, SARAH TERESA ANDERSON (TERI PERRY), nurse manager, critical care nurse; b. Flushing, N.Y., Jan. 14, 1957; d. John Thomas and Dorothy Reu (James) Anderson; m. Dennis Michael Perry Sr., Oct. 17, 1981; children: John Thomas, Clayton Foster. ADN, Augusta (Ga.) Coll. Sch. Nursing, 1979; BSN, Med. U. of S.C., 1985, MSN, 1987. Shift supr. ICU U. Hosp., Augusta, Ga.; staff nurse III Roper Hosp., Charleston, S.C.; nurse mgr. Med. U. of S.C. Med. Ctr., Charleston, mem. biomed. ethics com., 1988-94; nurse mgr. CCU Med. Coll. of Ga., Augusta, 1994-96; nurse mgr. cardiology svc. line Med. Coll. Ga., Augusta, 1996—; mem. biomed. ethics com. Med. Coll. Ga., 1995—; registry coord. Nat. Registry of Myocardial Infarction 2, 1994—. Mem. AACN (pres. Charleston chpt. 1989-90, officer CSRA chpt.), S.C. Nurses Assn., Sigma Theta Tau. Home: 4826 Rocky Shoals Cir Evans GA 30809

PERRY, SHARON LYNN YORK, religious organization administrator, educator; b. Logan, W.Va., Aug. 14, 1952; d. Charles Everett and Annis Rae (Dyer) York; m. Bartholomew Perry, May 24, 1975. Student, Bible Inst., Parkersburg, W.Va., Elkins, W.Va., 1970-80; B. in Cosmetology, Mamie Scott, Parkersburg, 1974. State evangelist, soloist, pianist, pastor's wife Ch. of God, Beckley, W.Va., 1976-78, 81-83; soloist, pianist Ch. of God, White Sulphur Springs, W.Va., 1988-90, dist. ladies ministries pres., 1988-90; state ladies ministries bd. mem. Ch. of God, Beckley, W.Va., 1990-94; ch. music dir., ladies Bible tchr. Mallory (W.Va.) Ch. of God, 1990-94, tchr. Sunday Sch., 1990-93; tchr. Sunday Sch., soloist, pianist, youth worker, counselor program dir. Ch. of God, Monclo-Sharples, W. Va., 1995—; state seminar speaker Ch. of God, Princeton, W.Va., 1991, Petersburg, W.Va., 1991, Ripley, W.Va., 1993, dir. music, Mallory, 1991-93, ladies choir dir., Beckley, 1991-94. Contbg. author: Women of Devotion, 1991. Area fund collector Children's Cancer Soc., Beckley, 1990; dist. l.m. pres. Anti-Abortionist Campaign, White Sulphur Springs, 1988-90, Fight Against Child and Adult Pornography, White Sulphur Springs, 1989; active W.Va. Chs. Flood Relief and Food and Clothing Distbn., 1994-95, disaster relief, 1996—. Office: Drawer E Sharples WV 25183

PERRY, STEPHEN CLAYTON, manufacturing executive; b. Atlanta, Feb. 9, 1942; s. Clayton Henry and Elizabeth Hill (Staples) P.; m. Bonnie Janet Bentley, Nov. 27, 1965; 1 child, Beverly Elizabeth. B in Indsl. Engring., Ga. Inst. Tech., 1964; MBA, Harvard U., 1968; postgrad, George Washington U., 1991—. Indsl. engr. Union Carbide Corp., Columbia, Tenn., 1964; sys. analyst metals and controls divsn. Tex. Instruments, Attleboro, Mass., 1967; with Exxon Corp., 1968-86, gen. mgr. Toledo Scale Corp. subs. Reliance Electric Co., Worthington, Ohio, 1984-89; pres. Toledo Scale Corp. (subs Ciba-Giegy), 1989-90; pres., CEO Easco Hand Tools, Inc., 1990; instr. George Washington U., 1991-94; pres. mfg. divsn. Leucadia, Inc., 1995—. Bd. dirs. Ctr. Sci. and Industry, Columbus, Ohio, 1984-89; mem. Berkeley Heights Twp. (N.J.) Com; 1977-79, dep. mayor, police commr., 1978, mayor, 1979; mem. Clemson U. Pres.'s Adv. Coun., 1990-93. Served to capt., inf., AUS, 1964-66. Ethyl Corp. scholar, 1964; Pillsbury fellow, 1968. Mem. Scale Mfrs. Assn. (pres. 1987-89). Republican. Baptist. Home: 6600 Old Chesterbrook Rd Mc Lean VA 22101-4611

PERRY, STEVEN ELLIOTT, marine corps officer; b. Cranston, R.I., Mar. 15, 1955; s. James Lawrence and Lillian Elaine (Luther) P.; m. Margaret Mery Rudowski, June 18, 1977; children: Benjamin James, Lauren Elaine. BS, Providence Coll., 1977; MBA, Coll. William and Mary, 1989. Commd. 2d lt. USMC, 1977, advanced through grades to maj., 1994; requirements officer MCCDC, Quantico, Va., 1992-95; head support br. Marine Corps Base, Quantico, 1995—; mktg. dir. Homenet Inc., Fredericksburg, Va., 1996. Decorated Army Commendation medal, Navy Commendation medal. Mem. Lions Club (bd. dirs.). Republican. Roman Catholic. Home: 6202 Cranston Ln Fredericksburg VA 22407 Office: USMC 2013 Barnett Ave Quantico VA 22134

PERRY, THOMAS AMHERST, English literature and language educator; b. Beaver City, Nebr., Apr. 26, 1912; s. Thomas Charles and Mable Laura (Avis) P.; m. Lora Margaret Turner, June 20, 1937; children: Laura E. Perry Massie, Robert Thomas, Timothy T., Charles Lee. BA with honors, Park Coll., 1934; MA, U. Iowa, 1936, PhD, 1943; postgrad., Oxford (Eng.) U., 1964. Prin. grade sch., Des Moines, N.Mex., 1934-35; asst. prof. English, Park Coll., Parkville, Mo., 1936-42; instr. U. Iowa, Iowa City, 1943; prof., dept. head Ctrl. Meth. Coll., Fayette, Mo., 1943-63; Fulbright lectr. Am. lang. and lit. U. Bucharest, Romania, 1963-64; Hermann Brown prof. English, Southwestern U., Georgetown, Tex., 1964-65; prof. English, East Tex. State U., Commerce, 1965-80, head dept., 1969-72, prof. emeritus lit. and langs., 1980—; vis. prof. English, U. Mo., Columbia, 1951-52, U. Autonoma Estado Mex., Toluca, 1959, N.E. Mo. State U., Kirksville, summer 1965; mem. com. on doctorate in English, Fedn. North Tex. State Univs., 1972-75; mem. com. on Variorum Glossary, World Shakespeare Congress, Vancouver, B.C., Can., 1970-71; mem. steering com. Romanian Studies Congress, Auckland, New Zealand, summer 1973. Author: A Bibliography of American Literature Translated into Romanian, 1984, From These Roots and Other Poems, 1996; co-author: Romanian Poetry in English Translation: an Annotated Bibliography, 1989, with supplement An Update with Over 60 Newer Poets, 1996; contbr. articles and criticsmm to profl. jours., poems and poem transls. to lit. mags. Past mem. Fayette Libr. Bd.; past mem. local bd. Salvation Army, Commerce; mem. exec. com. Hunt County Rep. Party, Greenville, Tex., 1970-80; past mem. adminstrv. bd. Meth. Ch., Fayette; past mem. adminstrv. bd. 1st Meth. Ch., Commerce. Recipient Disting. Alumnus award Park Coll., 1984; Smith-Mundt grantee, Toluca, 1959, Rsch. Assocs. travel grantee U. Bucharest and U. Cluj, 1968, Am. Coun. Learned Socs. rsch. grantee, Romania, 1978. Mem. MLA (sr. bibliographer 1969—), Comparative Lit. Assn. Am., Shakespeare Assn. Am., Am. Lit. Translators Assn., Internat. Comparative Lit. Assn., Internat. Shakespeare Assn., Am. Romanian Acad. Arts and Scis., Romanian Studies Assn. (exec. bd. 1946-48), Soc. Romanian Studies, Tex. Assn. Coll. Tchrs., Tex. Folklore Soc., Omicron Delta Kappa. Home: 214 Brookhaven Ter Commerce TX 75428 Office: Tex A&M U--Commerce Dept Lit and Langs Commerce TX 75428

PERRYMAN, THOMAS RUBEN, arts administrator, artist; b. Augusta, Ga., May 31, 1952; s. Robert Miller and Mary Wilmoth (Collins) P.; m. Roseann Seymour Rush, Aug. 16, 1986. BA in Arts Adminstrn., East Carolina U., 1975; MBA, Appalachian State U., 1990. Asst. dir. Associated Artists, Winston-Salem, N.C., 1980-85; spl. programs dir. Arts Coun., Inc., Winston-Salem, 1983-84, fund dr. asst., 1984; curator of edn. Hickory (N.C.) Mus. Art, 1985-87; exec. dir. Piedmont Arts Assn., Martinsville, Va., 1987-90; asst. dir., curator of exhbns. Hickory Mus. of Art, 1990—; regional adviser Va. Commn. for Arts, Richmond, 1988-91; bd. dirs. Va. Arts Coalition, Arlington, 1988-90; mem. selection com. Piedmont Craftsmen, Inc., Winston-Salem, 1990; v.p. N.C. Mus. Coun., 1993—. Visual artist, with numerous works in corp. and pvt. collections. Mem. Gov.'s Task Force for Promotion of the Arts, Richmond, Va., 1990—. Mem. Kiwanis, Beta Gamma Sigma. Episcopalian. Home: 634 25th Ave NW Hickory NC 28601-1254 Office: Hickory Mus of Art PO Box 2572 243 3d Ave NE Hickory NC 28601

PERSCHMANN, LUTZ INGO, shoe company executive, real estate consultant; b. Berlin, Prussia, Fed. Republic Germany, June 27, 1940; came to U.S., 1967; s. Walter and Ursula (Zitzow) P.; m. Shaunna M. Rassmussen, July 20, 1977 (div. Nov. 1985); 1 child, Shaunna Marie. AA in Bus. Adminstrn., Daytona Beach Community Coll., 1974; BSBA in Mgmt., U. Cen. Fla., 1976. Acct. Treuhandgesellschaft Deutscher Apotheken, Hannover, Fed. Republic Germany, 1958-61; sr. acct. VIVO-Schaper K.G., Hannover, 1963-67; mgr. front office Marlin Beach Hotel, Ft. Lauderdale, Fla., 1967-68; acct. Peat, Marwick, Mitchel and Co., Ft. Lauderdale, 1968-69; dir. purchasing ACTS Computing Corp., Detroit and Daytona Beach, 1974-75; mgr. bus. ops. COMPU-TIME, Inc., Ft. Lauderdale and Daytona Beach, 1969-74; realtor, assoc. Goldman Gallery of Homes, Daytona Beach, 1976-78; pres., realtor Ingo Internat. Investments, Inc., Daytona Beach, 1978—; v.p. Spiess Shoe Corp., Daytona Beach, 1986—; mng. dir. U.S. Walter and Assocs., Dusseldorf, Germany, 1983-86; v.p. Fla. Shoe Import, Inc., 1990-93. Pres. World Trade Coun. Volusia County, Daytona Beach, Fla., 1983-85; liaison, bd. dirs. Cmty. Housing Resources Bd., Daytona Beach, 1986-90; mem. adv. bd. Leadership Daytona, treas., 1990-93, 95—. With German Navy, 1961-63. Mem. Nat. Assn. Accts. (pres. Daytona Beach chpt. 1973-74), Daytona Beach C. of C. (bd. dirs. 1983-85, transp. com. 1983-90, congl. action com. 1983-94, steering com. internat. trade coun. 1988—), Daytona Beach Bd. Realtors (profl. disputes mediator 1987-92), German-Am. Commerce and Culture Soc., German-Am. Trade Inst. (exec. dir. U.S.), Am. Heart Assn. (bd. dirs. 1993—). Lutheran. Home: 1182 Suwanee Rd Daytona Beach FL 32114-5917 Office: Spiess Shoe Corp 804 Mason Ave Ste C Daytona Beach FL 32117-4719

PERSKY, ALLAN LEE, writer; b. Aberdeen, S.D., May 6, 1943; s. Nathan and Daurice (Ribnick) P. BA, U. Tex., 1971; MA, U. Ariz., 1976, PhD, 1979. Lectr. U. Ariz., Tucson, 1976-81; asst. prof. St. Mary's Univ., San Antonio, 1981-82, So. Univ., New Orleans, 1983-88, McNeese State U., Lake Charles, La., 1988-90, CUNY, Hiroshima, Japan, 1992-93; assoc. editor The Am. Economist, N.Y.C., 1988—. Author: The Mechanical Part of Microeconomics, 1983; contbr. articles to profl. jours. Mem. Am. Econ. Assn., So. Econ. Assn., Western Econ. Assn. Jewish. Home: 4110 West City Ct #52 El Paso TX 79902

PERSON, LAWRENCE, writer, editor; b. Houston, Apr. 14, 1965; s. Murray Wayne and DeLois Anne (Crouch) P. BFA, U. Tex., 1987. Editor Freedom Bulletin, Washington, 1991, Citizens' Agenda, Fairfax, Va., 1992, Nova Express, 1992—. Author (short story) Details, 1991, Huddled Masses, 1992, Salvation, 1992. Program dir. Tex. Rev. Soc., Austin, 1986-87; founder, pres. Students for Kemp U. Tex. chpt., Austin, 1987. Recipient Dishonorable Mention, Bulmer Lyton Contest U. Calif., San Jose, 1986, Felix Morley Meml. prize honorable mention Inst. Humane Studies, 1987. Mem. Sci. Fiction Writers Am., Turkey City Writers Workshop (organizer). Republican. Home and Office: PO Box 27231 Austin TX 78755

PERSON, RUTH JANSSEN, academic administrator; b. Washington, Aug. 27, 1945; d. Theodore Armin and Ruth Katherine (Mahoney) Janssen. BA, Gettysburg (Pa.) Coll., 1967; AMLS, U. Mich., 1969, PhD, 1980; MS in Adminstrn., George Washington U., 1974. Head of reference/asst. prof. Thomas Nelson C.C., Hampton, Va., 1971-74; lectr. U. Mich., Ann Arbor, 1975-79, coord. of continuing edn., 1977-79; asst. prof. Cath. U., Washington, 1979-85, assoc. prof., 1985-86, assoc. dean Sch. of Libr. and Info. Sci., 1983-86; dean Coll. Libr. Sci. Clarion (Pa.) U., 1986-88; assoc. vice chancellor U. Mo., St. Louis, 1988-93; v.p. for acad. affairs, prof. bus. adminstrn. Ashland (Ohio) U., 1993-95; v.p. acad. affairs Angelo State U., San Angelo, Tex., 1995—; reviewer U.S. Dept. Edn., Washington, 1987-89, 92; trustee Pitts. Regional Libr. Ctr., 1986-88; chair publs. com. Assn. of Coll. and Rsch. Librs., Chgo., 1986-90; cons. United Way, Alexandria, Va., 1985; cons.-evaluator North Ctrl. Assn., 1993-95. Co-editor: (book) Academic Libraries: Their Role and Rationale in Higher Education, 1995; editor: (book) The Management Process, 1983; editl. bd. Coll. & Rsch. Librs., 1990—; contr. articles to profl. jours. Mem. Strategic Planning Task Force, Ashland C. of C., 1994; bd. dirs. Alternatives for Living in Violent Environs., Inc., St. Louis, 1992-94; commr. Commn. for Women, Anne Arundel County, Md., 1984-86; mem. Citizens Adv. Bd., Clarion, Pa., 1986-88; mem. Olivette, Mo. Human Rels. Commn., 1992-94, San Angelo Bus. and Profl. Women's Club, 1995—, pres.-elect 1996—; mem. bldg. design oversight com. San Angelo Mus. Fine Arts, 1995—; mem. com. Cactus Jazz Festival, 1995—. Fellow Am. Coun. Edn., 1990, Harvard Inst. Ednl. Mgmt., 1989, Rackham fellow U. Mich., 1976; ACE fellow Ariz. Bd. Regents, 1990-91; recipient Washington Woman award Washington Woman mag., 1986. Mem. ALA (com. on accreditation 1993—), Am. Assn. Univ. Adminstrs. (bd. dirs. 1993—), Coun. for the Preservation of Anthropol. Records (bd. dirs.), Psi Chi, Beta Phi Mu, Pi Lambda Theta, Kappa Delta

Pi, Phi Alpha Theta. Lutheran. Home: 5218 N Bentwood Dr San Angelo TX 76904 Office: Angelo State U Box 11008 ASU Station San Angelo TX 76909

PERSONS, W. RAY, lawyer, educator; b. Talbottan, Ga., July 22, 1953; s. William and Frances (Crowell) P.; m. Wendy-Joy Mottley, Sept. 24, 1977; children: Conrad Ashley, April Maureen. BS cum laude, Armstrong State Coll., 1975; JD, Ohio State U., 1978. Bar: Ga. 1979, U.S. Dist. Ct. (so. dist.) Ga. 1980, U.S. Dist. Ct. (no. dist.) Ga. 1986, U.S. Ct. Appeals (11th cir.) 1986. Assoc. Troutman, Sanders, Lockerman & Ashmore, Atlanta, 1978-79; atty. Nat. Labor Rels. Bd., Atlanta, 1980-82; legis. counsel U.S Ho. Reps., Washington, 1983-86; atty. Mack & Bernstein, Atlanta, 1986-87; ptnr. Arrington & Hollowell, Atlanta, 1987-95, Swift, Currie, McGhee & Hiers, Atlanta, 1995—; adj. prof. litigation Ga. State U., Atlanta, 1989—; spl. asst. atty. gen. State of Ga., Atlanta, 1988—. Master Am. Inns of Ct. (Lamar chpt.); mem. ABA, ATLA, Am. Bd. Trial Advocates, State Bar Ga., Atlanta Bar Assn., Lawyers Club of Atlanta. Republican. Roman Catholic. Office: Swift Currie McGhee & Hiers Ste 300 1355 Peachtree St NE Atlanta GA 30309-3238

PERUGINI, DANIEL FRANCIS, physician, military officer; b. Phila., Oct. 7, 1946; s. Daniel and Grace (De Stefano) P.; m. Coleta C. Van De Laar, May 30, 1970; children: Daniel C., Angela N. BA in Biology, La Salle U., 1968; DO, U. Health Scis., 1973; grad., U.S. Army Command and Gen. Staff Coll., 1981, Indsl. Coll. Armed Forces, 1992. Diplomate Am. Bd. Family Practice, Am. Osteo. Bd. Family Practice. Col. U.S. Army, 1973—; intern Brooke Army Med. Ctr., San Antonio, 1973-74; resident in family practice DeWitt Army Community Hosp., Va., 1974-76; attending physician dept. family practice DeWitt Army Community Hosp., 1976-78, asst. chief and residency dir. dpet. family practice, 1978-80; surgeon 8th inf. divsn. U.S. Army, Bad Kreuznach, Germany, 1981-83; chief dept. family practice Dwight Davie Eisenhower Army Med. Ctr., Augusta, Ga., 1983-87; comdr. U.S. Med. Element, Honduras, Calif., 1987; cons. primary care and family practice Office of Surgeon Gen., 1987-91; comdr., CEO Winn Army Community Hosp., Ft. Stewart, Ga., 1992-95; dep. comdr. clin. svcs., dir. med. edn. Dwight David Eisenhower Army Med. Ctr., Augusta, Ga., 1995—. Fellow Am. Acad. Family Physicians; mem. Uniformed Svcs. Acad. of Family Physicians (bd. dirs. 1978-82), Am. Osteo. Assn., Am. Coll. Osteo. Family Physicians, Assn. Mil. Osteo. Physicians and Surgeons, Assn. Mil. Surgeons of U.S., Am. Coll. Physician Execs. Office: Dwight David Eisenhower Med Ctr Fort Gordon Augusta GA 30905

PERUMPRAL, JOHN VERGHESE, agricultural engineer, administrator, educator; b. Trivandrum, Kerala, India, Jan. 14, 1939; came to U.S., 1963; s. Verghese John and Sarah (Geverghese) P.; m. Shalini Elizabeth Alexander, Dec. 27, 1965; children: Anita Sarah, Sunita Anna. BS in Agrl. Engring., Allahabad (UP India) U., 1962; MS in Agrl. Engring., Purdue U., 1965, PhD, 1969. Postdoctoral rsch. assoc. agrl. engring. dept. Purdue U., West Lafayette, Ind., 1969-70; asst. prof. agrl. engring. dept. Va. Poly. Inst. and State U., Blacksburg, 1970-78, assoc. prof., 1978-83, prof., 1983-86, Wm. S. Cross Jr. prof., head dept. biol. systems engring., 1986—. Contbr. over 30 articles to scholarly and profl. jours. Mem. Am. Soc. Agrl. Engring. (outstanding faculty award student br. 1976, 81, cert. teaching excellence 1979, assoc. editor, transaction of ASAE 1985-86), Fluid Power Soc., Sigma Xi, Alpha Epsilon. Presbyterian. Office: Va Poly Inst and State U Biol Sys Engring Dept Blacksburg VA 24061

PESANTE, ANGEL EDUARDO, insurance executive; b. Santurce, P.R., Apr. 6, 1952; s. Eduardo and Carmen (Martinez) P.; m. Melba Enid Ortiz, Dec. 27, 1975; children: Eduardo Jose, Melissa Querube. BS in sci., U. P.R., 1974; MA in Mgmt./Human Resources, Ctr. Mich. U., 1983. Commd. U.S. Army, 1974-95, advanced through grades to lt. col.; comdr. Co. C, 3d Battalion, 6th Brigade U.S. Army, Ft. Dix, N.J., 1981-83; chief tng. program mgmt. U.S. Army Sch. of Americanos, Ft. Berriez/Ft. Gulick, Panama, 1984-87; chief liaison Honduran Joint Armed Forces Joint Task Force - So. Command, Tegucigalpa, Honduras, 1987-88; spl. asst. to chief of staff Allied Forces So. Europe (NATO), Naples, Italy, 1989-92; chief office def. rep. U.S. Embassy, San Jose, Costa Rica, 1992-94; dir. tng. and doctrine U.S. Army Sch. of Americas, Ft. Benning, Ga., 1995; ins./corr. specialist Am. Family Life Assurance Co., Columbus, Ga., 1995—; translator softball event Atlanta Com. Olympic games, 1996. Recipient Def. Meritorious Svc. medals U.S. Dept. Def., 1989, 92, 94, Minister of Pub. Security award Govt. Costa Rica, 1994, Spl. Honor Contbn. award Govt. Rep. of Honduras, 1986; Proclamation in Hispanic Celebration, Mayor, City of Columbus, Ga., 1996. Mem. Internat. Network (parliamentarian 1995). Roman Catholic. Office: American Family Life Assurance Corp 1932 Wynnton Rd Columbus GA 31999-0001

PESCH, BARBARA HASIER, special education educator; b. Chgo., Aug. 1, 1951; d. John Joseph and Gloria Ann (Neuman) Hasier; m. Aly Abdelnabi, Oct. 12, 1979; children: Gabriel, Joseph, Adam. BS, So. Ill. U., 1974; MEd, Ga. State U., 1981. Cert. spl. edn. tchr., Ga. Clk. Chgo. Pub. Libr., 1968-70; tchr. elem. edn. Chgo. Pub. Schs., 1975-77; tchr. Bartow County Schs., Cartersville, Ga., 1979-81, Fulton County Bd. of Edn., Atlanta, 1981—; supr. student tchr. Ga. State U., Atlanta, 1987. Den mother Boy Scouts Am., Forest Park, Ga., 1983-85, Dallas, Ga., 1989-90. Mem. Am. Fedn. Tchrs., Coun. for Exceptional Children, Internat. Reading Assn., Alpha Delta Kappa. Home: 7597 Harmony Rd Temple GA 30179-9802 Office: Harriet Tubman Elem Sch 2861 Lakeshore Dr Atlanta GA 30337-4419

PESHKIN, SAMUEL DAVID, lawyer; b. Des Moines, Oct. 6, 1925; s. Louis and Mary (Grund) P.; m. Shirley R. Isenberg, Aug. 17, 1947; children—Lawrence Allen, Linda Ann. B.A., State U. Iowa, 1948, J.D., 1951. Bar: Iowa 1951. Ptnr. Bridges & Peshkin, Des Moines, 1953-66, Peshkin & Robinson, Des Moines, 1966-82; Mem. Iowa Bd. Law Examiners, 1970—. Bd. dirs. State U. Iowa Found., 1957—, Old Gold Devel. Fund, 1956—, Sch. Religion U. Iowa, 1966—. Fellow Am. Bar Found., Internat. Soc. Barristers; mem. ABA (chmn. standing com. membership 1959—, ho. of dels. 1968—, bd. govs. 1973—), Iowa Bar Assn. (bd. govs. 1958—, pres. jr. bar sect. 1958-59, award of merit 1974), Inter-Am. Bar Assn., Internat. Bar Assn., Am. Judicature Soc., State U. Iowa Alumni Assn. (dir., pres. 1957). Home: Apt 2064 6735 E Greenway Pkwy Scottsdale AZ 85254

PESOLA, GENE RAYMOND, physician, educator; b. Oct. 21, 1952; s. Raymond Lloyd and Helen Eleanor Pesola; m. Helen Rostata, Jan. 5, 1991; 1 child, Gene Richard. BS in Biology magna cum laude, Mich. Technol. U., Houghton, 1974; MD, Wayne State U., 1979. Diplomate Am. Bd. Internal Medicine, also sub-bds. pulmonary medicine and critical care medicine; cert. BCLS, ACLS, ATLS, PALS. Intern Harlem Hosp., N.Y.C., 1979-80; resident U. Tenn. Affiliated Hosps., Memphis, 1980-82; fellow in pulmonary medicine Mt. Sinai Hosp. and Affiliates, N.Y.C., 1982-84; fellow in critical care medicine Meml. Sloan-Kettering Cancer Ctr., N.Y.C., 1984-85, rsch. fellow, 1985-87; asst. prof. medicine and anesthesia Albert Einstein U., Bronx, N.Y., 1988-89; attending physician Mt. Vernon (N.Y.) Emergency Room, 1989-90; rschr. cell/molecular pharmacology and exptl. therapeutics Med. U. S.C., Charleston, 1991-94; attending physician critical care and emergency medicine N.Y. Cmty. Hosp., Bklyn., 1989—; attending physician dept. emergency medicine St. Vincent's Hosp., N.Y.C., 1994—; asst. prof. emergency medicine N.Y. Med. Coll., 1995—. Contbr. chpts. to books, numerous articles to profl. jours.; reviewer for numerous jours. including CHEST and Intensive Care Medicine. Recipient various awards; grantee Am. Fedn. Clin. Rsch., 1992; Pharm. Mfrs. Found. fellow, 1992-94.

PESUT, TIMOTHY S., investment advisor, professional speaker, consultant; b. Gary, Ind., June 30, 1956; s. Anton and Virginia Udean (Carahoff) P.; m. Michelle Angela Durdov, May 25, 1985; children: Ariel Fay, Caitlin Michelle. AAS in Elec. Engring. Tech., Purdue U., 1978, AAS Supervision, BS Elec. Engring. Tech., 1980. CFP Coll. Fin. Planning; cert. funds specialist, trust and estate planning advisor, investment mgmt. cons.; registered investment advisor. Cardiology clin. rsch. assoc. Cordis Corp., Miami, Fla., 1980-82, neurosurg. specialist, 1982; investment broker A. G. Edwards Sons, Merrillville, Ind., 1982-86, Shearson Lehman, Sarasota, Fla., 1986-88; portfolio mgr. Prudential Securities, Inc., Venice, Fla., 1988-91; registered investment advisor First Southeastern & Co., Sarasota, Fla., 1991—; arbitrator Am. Arbitration Assn., 1992—; founder Inst. of Cert. Estate Planners. Columnist Money Talks, 1988—, Money Mgmt., 1991—. Guardian ad litem 12th Dist. Ct., Sarasota, 1988—; mem. adv. bd. Wilkinson Sch., Sarasota H.S.; bd. dirs. Jr. Achievement of Sarasota County; founding mem. Anthony Robbins Found., 1990. Cpl. USMC, 1974-76. Mem. Profl. Assn. Diving Instrs. (Divemaster), Nat. Speakers Assn., Toastmasters Internat. (gov. divsn. 1, 1994-95, lt. gov. mktg. 1996-97, dist. treas. 1995-96, Area Gov. of Yr. 1994). Republican. Methodist. Office: First Southeastern & Co 1819 Main St Ste 601 Sarasota FL 34236-5984

PET-EDWARDS, JULIA JOHANNA AGRICOLA, systems engineering educator, researcher; b. Leiden, The Netherlands, May 28, 1955; came to U.S., 1956; d. Willem and Helena Maria (Van Zijp) Pet; m. William Benton Edwards, Nov. 27, 1982. BS in Math., Western Mich. U., 1979; MS in Systems Sci., Mich. State U., East Lansing, 1982; PhD in Systems Engring., Case Western Res. U., 1986. Instr. Lansing (Mich.) Community Coll., 1981-83; asst. prof. U. Va., Charlottesville, 1986-93, U. Ctrl. Fla., Orlando, 1993—; cons. Environ. Systems Corp., Charlottesville, 1987-88, Nat. Capitol Systems, Washington, 1989-91; dir. grad. programs sys. engring. dept. U. Va., 1989-93. Author: Risk Assessment and Decision Making Using Test Results, 1989; assoc. contbg. editor: Jour. Internat. Abstracts in Ops. Rsch., 1987—. Recipient Woman of Achievement award Woman's Faculty and Profl. Assn. of U. Va., 1992; Waldo Sangren scholar Western Mich. U., 1978; rsch. grantee Va. Environ. Endowment, 1988-92, TRW, Inc., 1989-93, NASA, 1993-95, Office of Naval Rsch., 1995-96, Olin Chem., 1996—. Mem. IEEE, Inst. Indsl. Engrs. (editor ops. rsch. divsn. newsletter), Am. Soc. for Engring. Edn., Inst. for Ops. Rsch. and Mgmt. Sci., Soc. for Risk Analysis, Sigma Xi, Tau Beta Pi (Eminent Engr.). Home: 4615 Ocean Beach Blvd Cocoa Beach FL 32931-3617 Office: U Ctrl Fla Indsl Engring/Mgmt Systems Orlando FL 32816

PETER, JANET (ERICA CARLE), writer, historian; b. Milw., Mar. 19, 1924; d. Harry John Otto and Beulah Marie (Paulsen) Zurheide; m. Carl Wehr Peter, Aug. 28, 1954; children: Eric John, Carl Wehr, Jr., Heidi Sue Ball. BS Occupl. Therapy, U. Wis., 1946. Home talent dir. Empire Producing Co., Kansas City, 1948-49; recreation dir. Goodwill Industries, Milw., 1949-50; radio, TV writer, prodr. Manson Gold Miller Adv., Mpls., 1952-54; tchr. math., composition Brookfield (Wis.) Acad., 1964-71; edn. columnist Milw. County News, 1973-76; edn. columnist, edn. editor Wis. Report, Brookfield, 1976-83. Vol. Wis. Leg. Rsch. Com., Brookfield, 1973-96. Author: Give Us The Young, 1974, Why Things Are The Way They Are, 1996. Home: 4605 SW Bimini Circle S Palm City FL 34990 Summer Home: # 309 13335 Watertown Plank Rd Elm Grove WI 53122

PETERMAN, GINA DIANE, English language educator; b. Harriman, Tenn., Aug. 30, 1957; d. James Stanley and Ann (Adkins) P. BA in French cum laude, Tenn. Tech. U., 1979, MA in English, 1984; PhD in 20th Century Am. Lit., U. S.C., 1992. Tchr. Gallatin (Tenn.) Pub. Schs., 1980-81; grad. teaching asst. Tenn. Tech. U., Cookeville, 1981-84; instr. English Abilene (Tex.) Christian U., 1984-87; grad. teaching asst. U. S.C., 1987-89; copy editor Bruccoli Clark Layman Pub., 1990; asst. editor Bibliography of Am. Fiction: 1919-1988, 1991; editorial asst. dept. English U. S.C., 1988-91; asst. prof. English Campbell U., Buies Creek, N.C., 1992—; conductor writing workshops. Contbr. articles to profl. jours. Mem. Am. Culture Assn. of the South, Eudora Welty Soc., Philol. Assn. of Carolinas, Soc. for Study of So. Lit., South Atlantic Modern Lang. Assn., Phi Kappa Phi, Omega Rho Alpha. Office: Campbell Univ Dept English Buies Creek NC 27506

PETERS, BOBBY G., mayor; children: Kelly, Jennifer. BS in Criminal Justice, Columbus Coll., M in Edn.; JD, Woodrow Wilson Law Sch. Bar: Ga. Mayor City of Columbus, Ga., 1994—; detective Muscogee County Sheriff's Dept.; instr. criminal justice So. Union State Coll.; past mem. Columbus Coun. Active Calvary Bapt. Ch. Named one of 10 Outstanding Young Men of Am., 1982. Office: Office of Mayor PO Box 1340 Columbus GA 31902

PETERS, DAVID FRANKMAN, lawyer; b. Hagerstown, Md., Aug. 15, 1941; s. Harold E. and Lois (Frankman) P.; m. Jane Catherine Witherspoon, Aug. 21, 1965; children: Catherine, Elizabeth. BA, Washington and Lee U., 1963; LLB, Duke U., 1966. Bar: Va. 1966, U.S. Dist. Ct. (ea. and we. dists.) Va., U.S. Ct. Appeals (2d, 4th, 6th, 7th and D.C. cirs.). Assoc. Hunton & Williams, Richmond, Va., 1966-73, ptnr., 1973—. Pres. Children's Home Soc. Va., Richmond, 1977-78, bd. dirs., 1970-91; trustee Westminster-Canterbury Corp., 1995—; elder, trustee 1st Presbyn. Ch., Richmond. Mem. ABA, Va. Bar Assn. (chmn. adminstrn. law com. 1985-88), Richmond Bar Assn. Lodge: Kiwanis. Home: 3 Windsor Way Richmond VA 23221-3232 Office: Hunton & Williams 951 E Byrd St Richmond VA 23219-4074

PETERS, DIANE PECK, artist; b. Corpus Christi, Tex., May 14, 1940; d. Wilfred John and Mayme Alice (Mitchell) Peck; m. George Peters, Dec. 20, 1958 (dec.); children: George Peters III, Louise Irene, Marie Diane, Wilfred John (dec.). Student, Del Mar Coll., 1958, 81, 82, U. Okla., El Cobano, Mexico, 1972, 73, 75, La. Tech. U., 1973, Master Class Edward Betts, Pensacola, Fla., 1978, 84. Owner Diane Peters Art Studio, Corpus Christi, Tex., 1969-87; artist, designer Olszewski Stained Glass Co., Corpus Christi, 1969-73; owner Diane Peters Art Studio, Lake Corpus Christi, Tex., 1987—. Artist: The New Spirit of Watercolor, 1989; contbr. articles to profl. jours.; exhibited in group shows at World Trade Ctr., Salmagundi Club, Nat. Arts Club, Allied Artist Am., Kotller Gallery, N.Y.C., Raymond Duncan Galleries, Paris, Hacienda El Cobano, U. Okla., Colima, Mexico, Owensboro Mus. Fine Arts, Birmingham Mus. Art, Columbus Mus. Arts and Sci., Marion Koogler McNay Art Inst.; represented in permanent collections at Corpus Christi Mus., Incarnate Word Acad., Sundial II Gallery, Order of Incarnate Word and Blessed Sacrament. Donator paintings Art Community Ctr., Corpus Christi, 1989; alt. mural artist City of Corpus Christi, 1983. Recipient Best of Show awards Art Community Ctr., Corpus Christi, 1989, Brownsville (Tex.) Internat. Art Exhbn., 1991, 93. Mem. LWV, Am. Watercolor Soc. (assoc.), Allied Artist Am. (assoc.), Ky. Watercolor Soc. (John Herweck award 1977, 84), Southwestern Watercolor Soc., Art Assn. Corpus Christi (pres. 1968), Art Guild Corpus Christi (sec., treas. 1969-73), Art Community Ctr., Watercolor Soc. Corpus Christi, Incarnate Word Acad. Alumni (pres. 1963, 64). Roman Catholic. Home and Office: Diane Peters Art Studio HCR2 Box 6546 Sandia TX 78383-9405

PETERS, DOUGLAS ALAN, neurology nurse; b. Portsmouth, Va., Oct. 4, 1968; s. Terrance Gene and Pamela (Haffner) P. BA in Philosophy, Va. Poly. Inst. and State U., 1992; BSN summa cum laude, James Madison U., 1995. RN, Va. Photojournalist CVNI/The Greene County Record, Stanardsville, Va., 1992; nursing asst. Rockingham Meml. Hosp., Harrisonburg, Va., 1993-95; clin. nurse Bapt. Hosp., Pensacola, Fla., 1995-96; neurology nurse Tallahassee Meml. Regional Med. Hosp., 1996—; quality control team advisor/assoc. Bapt. Health Care, Pensacola, 1995—. Vol. hospice unit Rockingham Meml. Hosp., 1994-95, Tallahassee Dem. Com., 1996—. Mem. Nat. League for Nursing, Alpha Chi Sigma, Phi Sigma Pi. Home and Office: 7601 N 9th Ave # 235 Pensacola FL 32514 Office: Escambia County Jail Crisis Intervention Team and Clinic PO Box 17789 Pensacola FL 32522

PETERS, ESTHER CAROLINE, aquatic toxicologist, pathobiologist, consultant; b. Greenville, S.C., May 9, 1952; d. Otto Emanuel and Winifred Ellen (Bahan) P.; m. Harry Brinton McCarty, Jr., May 27, 1984; children: Rachel Elizabeth, William Brinton. BS, Furman U., 1974; MS, U. South Fla., 1978; PhD, U. R.I., 1984. Rsch. asst. Environ. Rsch. Lab., U.S. EPA, Narragansett, R.I., 1980-81; grad. rsch. asst. U. R.I., Kingston, 1981-84; assoc. biologist JRB Assocs., Narragansett, 1984-85; postdoctoral fellow Dept. of Invertebrate Zoology, Nat. Mus. Natural History, Washington, 1985-86, resident rsch. assoc., 1986-89; rsch. fellow Registry Tumors in Lower Animals, Nat. Mus. of Natural History, Washington, 1987-91; sr. scientist Tetra Tech, Inc., Fairfax, Va., 1991—; sci. adv. panel Project Reefkeeper, Am. Littoral Soc., Miami, Fla., 1988—; courtesy asst. prof. Dept. Marine Sci., U. South Fla., St. Petersburg, 1987—; cons. The Nature Conservancy, Arlington, Va., 1991. Author: (with others) Pathobiology of Marine and Estuarine Organisms, 1993, Disease Processes of Marine Bivalve Molluscs, 1988; contbr. articles to profl. jours. Recipient Nat. Rsch. Svc. postdoctoral tng. fellowship NIH, Bethesda, Md., 1987-91. Mem. AAAS, Am. Fisheries Soc., N.Y. Acad. Scis., Soc. for Environ. Toxicology and Chemistry, Soc. Invertebrate Pathology, Sigma Xi. Office: Tetra Tech Inc 10306 Eaton Pl Ste 340 Fairfax VA 22030-2201

PETERS, GERALD ALAN, biology educator; b. Monroe, Mich., Mar. 3, 1943; s. Wilson Eugene Peters and Dorothy June (Hartman) Goetz; m. Bonnie L. Winans, 1965; children: Ann Marie, Kimberly Lorraine. BS in Biology-Chemistry, Ea. Mich. U., 1966; PhD in Botany, U. Mich., 1970. Rsch. technician U. Mich., 1966, univ. fellow, teaching fellow in genetics and biology, 1967-69; postdoctoral fellow Charles F. Kettering Rsch. Lab., 1970-72, staff sci., 1972-76, investigator, 1976-80, asst. mission mgr., sr. investigator, 1980-83; program mgr. biol. nitrogen fixation program USDA/GRGO, 1982, tech. dir., rsch. leader, 1983-84; rsch. leader Battelle-C.F. Kettering Rsch. Lab., 1984-86, rsch. leader, assoc. dir. rsch. program devel., 1986-87; assoc. prof. biology Va. Commonwealth U., Richmond, 1987-90, prof. biology, 1990—, dir. grad. program in biology, 1991-93; guest Acad. Sinica, People's Republic of China, 1979; mem. adv. panel UNOP studies at IRRI, 1983; authority on biology Azolla-Anabaena symbiosis; lectr., presenter, mem. confs., symposia and workshops in field. Mem. editorial bd. Symbiosis, 1985—; cons. editor Plant and Soil, 1988-93; reviewer sci. jours.; contbr. articles to profl. jours. Grantee NSF, 1974-79, 78-81, 82-86, USDA, 1979-83, 83-86, 87-89, USAID, 1984-87, 88-89, 91. Mem. AAAS, Botanical Soc. Am. Home: 2313 Adelphi Rd Richmond VA 23229-3205 Office: Va Commonwealth U Dept Biology 816 Park Ave Richmond VA 23284-9011

PETERS, JOHN, sales executive; b. Oklahoma City, May 13, 1954; s. Joe J. and Nancy Lu (Scouil) R.; m. Beverly Lynn Powley, Aug. 16, 1974 (div. Oct. 1989); children: Stephenie Kate. BS in bus. adminstrn., Okla. State U., 1976. Sales supply div. Bethlehem Steel, Okla. City, 1977-81; div. sales Global Fluids Inc., Lafayette, La., 1981-82; sales cons. Petro-Graphic Analysis, 1983-84, 1984—. Mem. Soc. Petroleum Engrs., Nat. Alliance Bus. Republican. Methodist. Home: 8608 Glenwood Ave Oklahoma City OK 73114-1223

PETERS, KENNETH EARL, educator; b. Detroit, June 24, 1940; s. Earl John and Mildred Eleanor (Rautio) P.; m. Ellen Mearns McAfee, June 19, 1965; children: Kathryn Peters Vizachero, Kenneth McAfee. BA, Albion Coll., 1962; MA in U.S. History, U. Mich., 1963, PhD in Am. Culture, 1972. Tchr. Seaholm H.S., Birmingham, Mich., 1963-66; asst. prof. Roosevelt Sch., Ea. Mich. U., Ypsilanti, 1967-69, Benedict Coll., Columbia, S.C., 1971-73; asst. prof., assoc. prof. Coll. Applied Profl. Scis., U. S.C., Columbia, 1984-95. Writer, editor The Profl., 1984-95; compiler, writer: First-Hand Observations of the Charleston, S.C. Earthquake of 1886 and Other Earthquake Materials, 1986; writer, presenter 90 " Constitutional Minutes" S.C. Ednl. Radio, 1987. Mem., pres. Sch. Improvement Couns., Seven Oaks Elem., Irmo Mid. Sch., Columbia, 1979-85. Named Fraternity Advisor of Yr. U. S.C., Columbia, 1989, 96, Outstanding Freshman Advocate U. S.C., Columbia, 1992. Mem. S.C. Hist. Assn., Thomas Cooper Soc. (membership chmn. 1991-92, 93-94, bd. mem.), Torch CLubs Internat. (program chmn., v.p., pres. Columbia chpt. 1993, 94), Tau Kappa Epsilon, Alpha Phi Omega. Republican. Presbyterian. Home: 921 Sugar Mill Rd Chapin SC 29036-8703 Office: U SC Coll Applied Profl Scis Columbia SC 29208

PETERS, MARY HELEN, real estate agent; b. Cape Girardeau, Mo., July 6, 1934; d. Wilmer Joseph and Ruby Madyliene (Knight) Lichtenegger; m. George Thomas Peters, May 25, 1952 (dec. Oct. 1992); children: Jennifer Susan Peters Dunlap, Gregory Thomas, Douglas Steward. BS in Edn., Ark. State U., 1974, MS in Edn., 1976. Cert. K-12 libr., bus. edn., secondary tchr., Ark. Tchr. bus. Westside H.S., Jonesboro, Ark., 1974-77, libr. media specialist, 1977-89; libr. media specialist Jonesboro H.S., 1989-95; agent Prime Real Estate, Jonesboro, 1989-95; CEO Prime REal Estate L.L.C., Jonesboro, 1996—, Mary Helen Enterprises, L.L.C., Jonesboro, 1996—, Am. Lifestyle Homes, L.L.C., Jonesboro, 1996—; condr. workshops in field, including Ark. Ednl. TV Network, 1988; mem. selection and guidance com. for audio-visual Ark. Dept. Edn., 1986-89. Com. chmn. for election cir. judge Ark. 2d Jud. Dist., 1994. Mem. ASCD, NEA, Internat. Coun. of Shopping Ctrs., Assn. Ednl. Comm. and Tech. (mem. divsn. sch. media specialists), Ark. Edn. Assn., Ark. Libr. Assn., Ark. Assn. Sch. Libr. Media Educators, Ark. Assn. for Instrnl. Media, N.E. Ark. Libr. Assn., Jonesboro Pub. Educators Assn., Ark. State U. Faculty Women's Club (pres. 1973-74), Phi Kappa Phi, Phi Delta Kappa, Kappa Delta Pi, Pi Omega Pi, Delta Kappa Gamma (pres. Pi chpt. 1984-86, exec. com. and exec. bd. Kappa State Ark. 1984-95, 1st v.p., 1989-91, pres. 1991-93, past pres. 1993-95, condr. workshops 1987—, mem. internat. golden gift com. 1994—, Internat. Golden Gift award 1988). Home: 2804 Turtle Creek Dr Jonesboro AR 72401-6943 Office: Prime Real Estate LLC 1923 Stadium Dr Jonesboro AR 72401-4977

PETERS, RANDOLPH WILLIAM, small business owner; b. Walterboro, S.C., Nov. 9, 1954; s. Laurie William and Catherine (Butler) P.; divorced; children: Laura Shea, William Taylor; m. Marilyn B. Rose. Student, Palmer Bus. Coll., Charleston, S.C., 1973-76. Disc jockey, sales mgr. Sta. WALD Radio, Walterboro, 1966-74; sales exec. Sta. WKTM Radio, North Charleston, S.C., 1974-75; outside sales rep. Sears, Walterboro, 1975-76; pres., mgr. Lowcountry Office Supply, Inc., Walterboro, 1976—; pres., gen. mgr. Charleston Copier and Fax Machines, Inc., North Charleston, 1992—; authorized Xerox metro agent Charleston, Dorchester, and Berkley counties of S.C., 1992—. Bd. mem. Colleton County Rice Festival; bd. dirs. Colleton-Walterboro C. of C.; active fundraising March of Dimes, Am. Heart Assn. Recipient Palmetto Boys State award Am. Legion, 1972. Mem. Dogwood Hills Country Club (bd. dirs. 1991-94), Elks (chmn. bd. trustees 1989—, past exalted ruler), Shriners, Masons. Methodist. Home: 8 Duffers Ct Apt B Charleston SC 29414-6844 Office: 5290 Rivers Ave Ste 305 North Charleston SC 29406

PETERS, ROBERT TIMOTHY, circuit judge; b. Memphis, Dec. 28, 1946; s. Rhulin Earl and Bertie Nichols (Moore) P.; m. Ruth Audrey Allen, Dec. 11, 1973; children: Lindsay Elizabeth, Christopher Andrew. AA, St. Petersburg Jr. Coll., 1969; BA, U. Fla., 1971, JD, 1973. Bar: Fla. 1973, U.S. Dist. Ct. (mid. dist.) Fla. 1977, U.S. Ct. Appeals (5th cir.) 1981; cert. real estate lawyer. Ptnr. Goza, Hall & Peters P.A., Clearwater, Fla., 1973-84; sole practice Clearwater, 1984-95; apptd. cir. judge Fla., 1995—; Gov. Fla.'s appointee Condominium Study Commsn., Clearwater, 1990-91. Columnist Clearwater Sun newspaper, 1985—. 1st Lt. U.S. Army, 1966-68, Vietnam. Decorated Silver Star, Purple Heart, Bronze Star with oak leaf cluster. Mem. Fla. Bar (condominium and planned devel. com.), Clearwater Bar Assn. address: PO Box 6316 Clearwater FL 34618-6316

PETERSEN, ERIC CHARLES, archaeologist; b. Omaha, Aug. 3, 1954; s. Ernest Chris and Elisabeth Gyda (Larsen) P. BA, Doane Coll., 1976; MA, U. Nebr., 1984. Ind. archaeologist Omaha, 1984-91; archaeologist Colo. Dept. Transp., Denver, 1991, Dept. Ark. Heritage, Little Rock, 1992-94, Office Cultural Affairs, Santa Fe, 1994—. Champe fellow U. Nebr., 1984. Mem. Soc. Am. Archaeology, Archaeol. Conservancy. Office: Office Cultural Affairs 228 E Palace Ave Santa Fe NM 87501-2013

PETERSEN-FREY, ROLAND, manufacturing executive; b. Hamburg, Fed. Republic Germany, Aug. 17, 1937; came to U.S., 1958; s. Georg and Erna (Coltzau) P.-F.; m. Pamela Susan Mobley, Feb. 2, 1993; children: Martin, Anya, Daniel. BA in Fin., CUNY, 1967, MA in Fin., 1970. Asst. v.p. Mfrs. Hanover, N.Y.C., 1961-70; v.p. gen. mgr. Rusch Inc., N.Y.C., 1970-75; CEO, chmn. bd. dirs. Inmed Corp., Atlanta, 1975-89; chmn. bd. Burrellco, Inc., Atlanta, 1989-90; bd. dirs. Albert Internat., Gainesville, Ga.; chmn. bd. Magnolia Studios, Atlanta, 1991—; mng. ptnr. Bunter Holdings Ltd., Atlanta, chmn. bd. Bd. dirs. Metro. Atlanta chpt. ARC. Served with U.S. Army, 1959-61. Fellow Inst. Dirs. Republican. Club: WCT Peachtree Tennis (Atlanta). Office: Magnolia Studios Inc 120 Interstate N Ste 444 Pky E Atlanta GA 30339

PETERSON, ALLEN JAY, lawyer, educator; b. Los Alamos, N.C., Oct. 26, 1949; s. Lyle Jay and Lois May (Richards) P.; m. Beverly White, May 27, 1989; children: Elizabeth Bishop, Adam Bryant. AA, St. Petersburg Jr. Coll., 1969; BA, Davidson Coll., 1971; postgrad., Harvard U., 1972; JD, U. N.C., 1976. Bar: N.C. 1974, U.S. Dist. Ct. (we. dist.) N.C. 1976. Ptnr. James, McElroy & Diehl, Charlotte, N.C., 1976-84, Howell & Peterson, Burnsville, N.C., 1984-87, Norris & Peterson, Burnsville, N.C., 1987-94; v.p., gen. counsel North State Foods, Inc., 1995—; constnl. law instr. U. N.C., Charlotte, 1977-78. Sunday sch. tchr. Higgins Meml. Meth. Ch., Burnsville,

1991-93, mem. adminstrv. bd., 1990-93. Mem. Am. Assn. Trial Lawyers, N.C. Acad. Trial Lawyers. Home: RR 6 Box 944 Burnsville NC 28714-9632

PETERSON, BONNIE LU, mathematics educator; b. Escanaba, Mich., Jan. 19, 1946; d. Herbert Erick and Ruth Albertha (Erickson) P. AA, Bay de Noc C.C., 1966; BS, No. Mich. U., 1968, MA in Math., 1969; EdD, Tenn. State U., 1989. Tchr. Lapeer (Mich.) High Sch., 1969-70, Nova High Sch., Ft. Lauderdale, Fla., 1970-79, Hendersonville (Tenn.) High Sch., 1979—; adj. faculty Vol. State C.C., Gallatin, Tenn., 1989—; chair Sumner County Schs. Tchrs. Insvc., Gallatin, 1990-92; mem. math. specialist team State of Tenn., 1991-93; spkr. in field. Mem. edn. com. Vision 2000-City of Hendersonville, 1993-94. Tenn. State Bd. grantee, 1989-92; Woodrow Wilson fellow, 1993; State-Level Presdl. awardee, 1994, 95, 96; Tandy Scholars award, 1995. Mem. ASCD, Nat. Coun. Tchrs. Math. (chair workshop support com. 1990), Tenn. Math. Tchrs. Assn., Mid. Tenn. Math. Tchrs. Assn. (pres.), Phi Delta Kappa (past pres.). Home: 1081 Coon Creek Rd Dickson TN 37055-4014

PETERSON, DAVE LEONARD, psychologist; b. Memphis, Nov. 29, 1952; s. Leroy Leonard and Mary Elizabeth (Linker) P.; m. Eleanor M. Hjelvik, Aug. 14, 1980. Student, U. Wis., 1972-74; BA, Sonoma State U., Rohnert Park, Calif., 1976; MA, U.S. Internat. U., San Diego, 1982, PhD, 1990. Psychology intern, 1986; forensic psychologist, forensic psychology coord. Ctrl. State Hosp., Milledgeville, Ga., 1995—; staff sr. psychologist Winnebago (Wis.) Mental Health Inst., 1992-95. Mem. APA, Am. Psychology and Law Soc., Ga. Psychol. Assn., Mid. Ga. Psychol. Assn., Psi Chi. Home: 253 Ivey Dr SW Milledgeville GA 31061 also: Box 2233 Sylacauga AL 35150 Office: Ctrl State Hosp Forensic Svc Divsn Milledgeville GA 31062

PETERSON, DAVID GLENN, retired career officer; b. Seattle, May 4, 1952; s. Wilbur Glenn and Donna Jean (Nielsen) P.; m. Marjorie Ann Erickson, Aug. 6, 1977; 1 stepchild, David Charles Erickson. BA in Social Studies, McKendree Coll., 1978; postgrad., U. Okla., 1981-87. Correctional officer Minn. State Reformatory, St. Cloud, 1973-75; commd. 2d lt. U.S. Army, 1976, advanced through grades to maj., 1987, served in 7th infantry div., 1975-76, adminstrv. officer Armor Sch., 1976-80, served in 1st armored div., 1980-81, 83-84, comdr. 501st adjutant gen. co., 1981-83, deputy adjutant gen. mil. dist. Washington, 1984-87, pers. policy analyst hdqrs. dept. Army, 1987-94; ret., 1994; dir. adminstrn. Nat. Presbyn. Ch., Washington, 1994—. Elder Nat. Presbyn. Ch., Washington, 1990—; bd. dirs. Westhampton Mens Condominuim Assn., 1989-93; trustee N.Y. Ave. Presbyn. Ch., Washington, 1985-87. Mem. Retired Officers Assn., Rails to Trails Conservancy, Nat. Assn. of Ch. Bus. Adminstrn. Republican. Home: 943A S Rolfe St Arlington VA 22204-4542

PETERSON, DAVID JAMES, English language educator, librarian, archivist; b. Jacksonville, Fla., May 7, 1968; s. Rodney W. Peterson and Faith Louis (Kiefer) P. BA, St. Leo (Fla.) Coll., 1990; MA, U. Ga., Athens, 1992. Tech. svcs. St. Leo (Fla.) Coll. Libr., 1986-90, Ireton Libr. Marymount U., Arlington, Va., 1987-88; archivist asst. Hargrett Libr. U. Ga., Athens, 1990-93; instr. English Dept. U. Ga., Athens, 1991%; features editor The Monarch, St. Leo (Fla.) Coll., 1987-90. Author (poems) The Literary Magazine, 1989; contbr. articles to profl. jours. Named Outstanding Humanities scholar Delta Epsilon Sigma, St. Leo Coll., Fla., 1989, 90, Helen S. Lanier scholar U. Ga., 1996. Mem. Modern Lang. Assn., South Atlantic Modern Lang. Assn., Delta Epsilon Sigma, Kappa Gamma Pi, Sigma Tau Delta. Home: 120 Woodland Way Athens GA 30606 Office: University of Georgia Parkway Dr # 252 Athens GA 30606-4950

PETERSON, GARY MICHAEL, neuroscientist, educator; b. San Jose, Calif., Apr. 14, 1951; s. Victor Herbert and Anita Charlotte (Robinson) P.; m. Roberta Margaret Ashcraft, June 10, 1972; children: Juanita Marie Thornton, Sarah Margaret. BA in Psychology magna cum laude, Humboldt State U., 1973; PhD in Neurosci., U. Calif., San Diego, 1979. Postdoctoral fellow dept. anatomy and neurobiology Washington U., St. Louis, 1979-80; postdoctoral fellow Devel. Neurobiology Lab., Salk Inst., San Diego, 1980-83; asst. specialist dept. anatomy U. Calif., Irvine, 1983-85; postgrad. rsch. biologist U. Calif., San Diego, 1985-86; asst. prof. dept. anatomy and cell biology Sch. Medicine East Carolina U., Greenville, N.C., 1986-91; assoc. prof. dept. anatomy and cell biology Sch. Medicine East Carolina U., Greenville, N.C., 1991—, adj. assoc. prof. depts. biology and physiology, 1987—; speaker, rschr. in field; vis. prof. Univ. Health Scis., Antigua, 1995, 96; vis. prof. dept. neurology U. Kuopio, Finland, 1992, Anatomisches Inst., U. Freiburg, Germany, 1990, 91; tchr. for neuroanatomy U. Autónomia de Guadalajara, Mex., 1991; interviewed on WITN TV, Greenville, 1988. Contbr. articles to profl. publs., textbooks; author abstracts in field. Fellow NIH, 1981-83, Alexander von Humboldt Found., 1990; grantee NIH, 1981-83, N.C. United Way, 1987, 88, N.C. Bd. Sci. and Tech., 1987-88, Alzheimer's Disease and Related Disorders Assn., 1987-88, 88-92, So. Regional Ednl. Bd., 1988, Am. Paralysis Assn., 1989, Fogarty/NIH, 1994-96; Vasa Order of Am. scholar, 1969; named Disting. Alumnus, Humboldt State U., 1982. Mem. Soc. for Neurosci., Internat. Brain Rsch. Orgn., Am. Assn. Anatomists, N.C. Soc. for Neurosci., N.C. Assn. for Biomed. Rsch., Cajal Club. Office: East Carolina U Sch Medicine Greenville NC 27858-4354

PETERSON, HOLGER MARTIN, electrical engineer; b. Colman, S.D., Nov. 16, 1912; s. Peter and Karen Marie (Jensen) P.; m. Myrtle Berthine Teigen, Mar. 26, 1939; children: Robert Kent, Janice Marie (Peterson) Priddy. BS in Elec. Engring., S.D. State U., 1933. Chief draftsman bridge dept. S.D. Highway Commn., Pierre, 1935-39; draftsman U.S. Army Corps of Engrs., Tulsa, Okla., 1939-40; tech. instr. Army Air Corps, Rantoul, Ill., 1940-41; supr. Plans & Programming Mgr. USAF Tech. Tng. Command, Biloxi, Miss., 1941-50, Sheppard AFB, Tex., 1950-70; program mgr. Individual Devel. Ctr., Wichita Falls, Tex., 1970-72, cons., 1972-80; owner, mgr. Creative Leaded Glass Co., Wichita Falls, 1981-92; mem. Commn. on Disability, 1990-93. Editor (tech. manuals, extension courses) Aircraft Maintenance, 1941-42, 1968-70. Recipient Exceptional Civilian Svc. award USAF, 1961. Mem. Elks. Democrat. Lutheran. Home and Office: 4810 Marsha Ln Wichita Falls TX 76302-4006

PETERSON, JOHN EDGAR, JR., retired agricultural executive, textile company executive; b. Radford, Va., Mar. 26, 1916; s. John Edgar and Mary Elizabeth (Dolan) P.; BS in Bus. Adminstrn., Va. Polytech. Inst., 1936; m. Mary Jane Crowell, May 8, 1943; children: John Edgar III, Mary Stuart Peterson Henegar, William Early. Jr. auditor Arthur Andersen & Co., N.Y.C. and Atlanta, 1937-39, sr. auditor, 1939-44; sec.-treas. Magnet Cove Barium Corp., Jamestown, Tenn. and Houston, 1944-46; asst. to contr. Burlington Industries, Inc., Greensboro, N.C., 1946-47, sec.-treas., dir. Burlington Mills Internat. Corp., 1947-48, co-divsn. mgr., 1948-49, divsn. contr., 1949-56, area contr., 1956-58, asst. corp. contr., 1958-70, asst. corp. v.p., from 1970, now ret.; chmn. bd. dirs., pres. Lane Processing, Inc., 1985-86, now ret.; chmn. bd. trustees The Lane Processing Trust, 1985-96; dir., sec.-treas. Everetts' Lake Corp., 1958—; examiner, trustee U.S., trustee Bankruptcy Ct., 1982-87; examiner, trustee The Evergreens, Inc., 1982—; former commr. Greensboro Housing Authority. Mem. adv. coun. Paplin Coll. Bus. Va. Polytech. Inst., 1969—. CPA, N.Y., Ga., Tenn., N.C.; cert. internal auditor. Mem. Am. Inst. CPAs, N.C. Soc. CPAs, Inst. Internal Auditors. Presbyterian. Clubs: Starmount Forest Country, Off Island Gun, Three Lakes (dir.), Brush Creek Hunting (dir.), Masons, Tar Heel State Seniors. Home: 1001 Kemp Rd W Greensboro NC 27410-4517

PETERSON, MARK FREDERICK, business administration educator; m. Susan Mende, Aug., 1975. AB in Psychology magna cum laude, Duke U., 1975; AM in Orgnl. Psychology, U. Mich., 1977, PhD in Orgnl. Psychology, 1979. Asst. prof. dept. mgmt. and orgnl. scis. Wayne State U., Detroit, 1979-80; asst. prof. dept. psychology U. Miami, 1980-83, assoc. prof. dept. gen. bus., mgmt. and orgn., 1983-85; assoc. prof. Tex. Tech. U., Lubbock, 1985-90, prof. mgmt. area, 1990—; dir. Program in Internat. Leadership and Mgmt., Inst. Mgmt. and Leadership Rsch., Tex. Tech. U., Lubbock, 1990—, dir. Japanese Studies Program, 1990—; adv. bd. Coll. Bus. Adminstrn., Tex. Tech. U., 1988-90, 93—; lectr. various univs., rsch. ctrs. and confs.; program chair 10th Internat. Assn. Cross Cultural Psychology Congress, Nara, Japan, 1990; ad hoc reviewer Adminstrv. Sci. Quar., Jour. Applied Psychology, Jour. Occupational Psychology, Jour. Mgmt., Acad. Mgmt. Jour. Contbr. numerous chpts. to books, articles, tech. reports to conf. procs. and profl. jours.; mem. editorial bd. Group and Organization Studies, 1985—, Jour. Mgmt., 1989-92. NIMH grad. traineeship, 1979; Fulbright fellow, Japan Program, 1986-87; Vis. scholar Wharton Sch., U. Pa., 1992; recipient Tex. Tech. Coll. Bus. Adminstrn. Ann. Rsch. award, 1990, N.E. Asia Coun. travel award, 1988; grantee U.S. Dept. State, 1981, U. Miami Sch. Bus., 1981, 82, 85, Japanese Ministry Edn., 1981, U.S. Dept. Edn., 1981-82, Keyes Co., Realtors, 1983, Navy Pers. R&D Ctr., 1984, 85, Japan-U.S. Friendship Commn., 1990. Mem. Internat. Assn. Applied Psychology, Internat. Assn. Cross-Cultural Psychology (program chair 1990), Acad. Mgmt. (health care program com. 1980-85, rsch. methods program com. 1988, mgmt. devel. program com. 1989), Acad. Internat. Bus., Soc. Indsl. and Orgnl. Psychology, So. Mgmt. Assn. (internat. bus. program com. 1985), S.W. Acad. Mgmt. (health care program com. 1985). Home: 6606 Norfolk Ave Lubbock TX 79413-5903 Office: Texas Tech Univ PO Box 4320 Lubbock TX 79409-0007

PETERSON, MARK LEE, research chemist; b. Waukesha, Wis., Aug. 28, 1958; s. Thomas Lee and Mary Marie (Cook) P.; m. Eileen Marie Larkin, Sept. 21, 1991. BS, St. Norbert Coll., 1980; PhD, Washington State U., 1987. Sr. rsch. chemist Monsanto Co., St. Louis, 1990-93; process devel. sr. scientist Advanced ChemTech, Louisville, 1993-94, mgr. chem. prodn./rsch. and devel., 1994-95, mgr. comml. ops., corp. v.p., 1996—. Contbr. articles to profl. jours. Postdoctoral fellow U. Minn., 1987-89; recipient Nat. Rsch. Svc. award NIH, 1989. Mem. AAAS, Am. Chem. Soc., Am. Peptide Soc., KC, Phi Lambda Upsilon. Roman Catholic. Home: 3603 Briarglen Ln Louisville KY 40220-5036

PETERSON, NORMA JO, elementary school educator; b. Knoxville, Tenn., Dec. 26, 1938; d. Henry Beecher and Dorotha (Gross) P. BS, U. Tenn., 1960; MA, E. Tenn. State U., 1976. Cert. Career Ladder Level III elem. tchr. Elem. tchr. Knox County-Halls Elem. Sch., Knoxville, 1960-63; adminstrv. asst. Southeastern Region-Ch. of the Brethren, Bridgewater, Va., 1963-64; dir. Children's Work Nat. Office-Ch. of the Brethren, Elgin, Ill., 1964-69; elem. tchr. Prince George's County-Seabrook Elem. Sch., Seabrook, Md., 1969-70, Kingsport (Tenn.) City Schs., Kingsport, 1970—. Recipient Outstanding Educator award, Kingsport City Schs., Tenn., 1986. Mem. NEA, Tenn. Edn. Assn., Kingsport Edn. Assn., Delta Kappa Gamma, Phi Kappa Phi, Pi Lambda Theta. Home: 4100 Prescott Dr Johnson City TN 37601-1048

PETERSON, PETE, congressman. Mem. from Fla. U.S. Ho. of Reps., Washington. Office: US Ho of Reps 306 Cannon House Off Bldg Washington DC 20515

PETERSON, RICHARD LEE, county government official, engineering consultant; b. Kearney, Nebr., Oct. 2, 1945; s. Jack and Beulah (Paul) P.; m. Leslie Pinkham, Apr. 7, 1969 (div. Aug. 1969); 1 child, Keddrin Glenn; m. Emily Braswell, Sept. 5, 1986. BSCE, U. Nebr., 1970; MCE, Tex. A&M U., 1973; student in urban transp., Carnegie-Mellon U., 1978. Registered profl. engr. Tex., Nebr., Calif. Engr. Nebr. Dept. Roads, Lincoln, 1970-72; research asst. Tex. Transp. Inst., College Station, 1973, asst. research engr., 1981-86; chief traffic engr. City of Ft. Worth, 1973-77, transp. planning coordinator, 1977-78, asst. dir. dept. transp., 1978-80; pres., chief exec. officer 5 & 10 Transp. Services, College Station, 1980-87; asst. dir. Dallas County Pub. Works Dept., 1987—; mem. Transp. Research Bd. Co-author: (book) Rail Transportation and Other Modes, 1987. Served with U.S. Army N.G., 1966-72. Hwy. Safety fellow Fed. Hwy. Adminstrn., Tex. A&M U., 1972, Urban Transp. fellow Urban Mass Transp. Adminstrn., Pitts and Europe, 1978. Named Tex. Transp. Engr. of Yr., 1988. Mem. ASCE, NSPE (sec., treas. Lincoln chpt. 1971-72), Am. Soc. Mil. Engrs., Inst. Transp. Engrs. (pres. Tex. sect. 1985-86, sect. rep. 9th dist. 1986-88, tech. coun. 1989-91), Tex. Inst. Transp. Engrs. (v.p. 1984-85, tech. coun. dept. 5 chmn. 1989-92). Home: 6202 Parkdale Dr Dallas TX 75227-3615 Office: Dallas County Pub Works Dept 411 Elm St Dallas TX 75202-3317

PETERSON, ROBERT STEPHEN, administrator cultural organization; b. Erie, Pa., June 10, 1947; s. Oren Bruce and Lorraine Frances (Bessolo) P. BBA, U. Cin., 1970. Mgr. Gant/Shaw, Lexington, Ky., 1970-73, United Reproductions, Ft. Lauderdale, Fla., 1973; asst. to pres. Bond Chem. Co., Ft. Lauderdale, 1973-74; admissions rep., asst. dir. Art Inst. Ft. Lauderdale, 1974-76, v.p., dir. admissions, 1976-88, coll. dir., 1988; sr. v.p. Art Insts. Internat., Pitts., 1988—; bd. trustees, 1989—. Columnist: Good Times Art Lesiure Mag., 1978-82. Mem. Portside Harbordale Civic Assn., Ft. Lauderdale, Fla., 1986-88; nat. judge Miss Nat. Teenager, 1989, 90, 91. Mem. Fla. Art Assn., Fla. Assn. of Coll. Registrars and Admissions Officers (citation 1988), Fla. Pub. Rels. Assn. (sec. 1979-80), Ft. Lauderdale Advt. Fedn., Distributive Edn. Clubs Am. Republican. Roman Catholic. Home: 1628 E Las Olas Blvd Fort Lauderdale FL 33301-2385 Office: 300 6th Ave Ste 800 Pittsburgh PA 15222-2511

PETERSON, SANDRA DEE, elementary school educator; b. Salt Lake City, Sept. 3, 1946; d. Thomas Jr. and Tillie Marie (Uzelac) Jackson; m. Michael George Smith, June 7, 1969 (div. June 7, 1989); children: Meggan, Renae Smith, Brandon Smith; m. Stephen Earl Peterson, Dec. 21, 1993. BS in Elem. Edn., U. Utah, 1969; postgrad., Webster U., 1996—. Tchr. St. Joseph's Cath. Sch., Boise, 1969, Fruitland Elem. Sch., Kennewick, Wash., 1969-70, Franklin Elem. Sch., Boise, 1970-74, Ysleta Ind. Sch. Dist., El Paso, Tex., 1986—; tchr. Youth Opportunities Unltd. Valley View Mid. Sch., El Paso, Tex., 1986-89; chmn. tech. com. Desert View Mid. Sch., El Paso, 1995-96; judge, problem capt. coord., judge trainer, State of Tex. judge, sch. coord. Odyssey of the Mind, El Paso, 1983-96; fellow W. Tex. Writing Project. U. Tex., El Paso, 1991. Contbr. article to profl. jour. Area rep. Mothers' March March of Dimes, Pocatello, Idaho, 1975; mem. long range planning com. Shirley Leavell branch YWCA, El Paso, Tex., 1978; legis. chmn., v.p. E. El Paso Rep. Women, 1977-79; mem. bd. Storybook Pre-Sch. St. Paul's Meth. Ch., El Paso; leader Girl Scouts Am., El Paso, 1981-86; mem. com. troop 279 Boy Scouts Am., 1990-93; dir. Christian edn. St. Christopher's Episcopal Ch., El Paso, 1990-93, mem. vestry, 1993-96; life hon. mem. PTA, El Paso, 1983—. Mem. Tex. Classroom Tchrs. Assn. (faculty rep.). Republican. Episcopalian. Home: 1950 Paseo Arena El Paso TX 79936 Office: Ysleta Sch Dist Desert View Mid Sch 1641 Billie Marie El Paso TX 79936

PETERSON, SCOTT LEE, music retailer; b. Neresheim, Germany, July 18, 1959; came to U.S., 1962; s. Raymond Bertram and Betty Myra (Holburn) P. BS in Econs., George Mason U., 1984. Dir. edn. Jordan Kitt's Music, College Park, Md., 1984-86, asst. mdse. mgr., 1986-87, msde. mgr., 1987-89, dir. mktg., 1989-91, asst. mgr., 1991-92, mgr., 1992-94; pres. ABC Music (ABBA, Inc.), Plymouth, Mass., 1994-95; mortgage banker Douglas-Michaels Co. L.P., Springfield, Va., 1995—. Mem. Dumfries (Va.) Magisterial Civic Assn., 1991—. Mem. Nat. Assn. Young Music Mchts., Nat. Eagle Scout Assn., Masons (master). Home: 8766 Old Colony Way Alexandria VA 22309-1545

PETERSON, STEVEN P., economics educator, consultant; b. Weston, W. Va., Sept. 24, 1954; s. Paul Emerson and Rosemary Catherine (Sullivan) P.; m. Joyce Carol Likes, June 26, 1990. BA, Bowling Green State U., 1976, MA, 1980; PhD, Ind. U., 1989. Assoc. instr. Ind. U., Bloomington, 1983-89; asst. prof. Va. Commonwealth U., Richmond, 1989-95, assoc. prof., 1995—; ind. cons. Crestal Investment Bank, Richmond, 1996—. Contbr. articles to profl. jours. Mem. Am. Econ. Assn., Econ. Sci. Assn. Office: Va Commonwealth U 1015 Floyd Ave Richmond VA 23184-4000

PETERSON, WESTLEY DEZELL, magazine editor; b. St. Louis Park, Minn., Feb. 17, 1960; s. Donald Robert and Lois (Taylor) P.; Laura Lee Nelson, July 10, 1987; children: Robert DeZell, David Taylor. BS, U. Wis., 1984. Editl. asst. Car Collector, Atlanta, 1984, asst. editor, 1985-86, mng. editor/exec. editor, 1987-90, editor, 1990—; profl. appraiser Classic Car Appraisal Svc., Roswell, Ga., 1984—. Judge, mem. adv. com. Burn Found. Concours; judge Meadow Brook Hall Concours; mem. selection com. Meguiar's Award, Milestone Car Soc. Mem. Atlanta Press Club, Packard Club, Class Car Club Am. Office: Car Collector 1241 Canton St Roswell GA 30075-3618

PETERSON, WILLIAM CANOVA, architect; b. Cleve., Nov. 3, 1945; s. William Canova Peterson and Phyllis Imogene (Hill) Smith; m. Anne Lee Deitz, June 3, 1967 (div. Nov. 1981); children—Lisa Ann, Amanda Rebecca; m. Patricia Hill, July 4, 1985. B.Arch., Va. Poly. Inst., 1968; postgrad. Va. Commonwealth U., 1975-77. Registered architect, Va. Specification writer R.P. Fox, Architect, Newark, Del., 1970-72; project mgr. Highfill Assoc., Richmond, Va., 1972-73; project architect Wrigh, Jones & Wilk, 1973-79; prin. Canova Assocs., Archs., Mechanicsville, Va., 1979—. Prin. works include Tuckaway Ctrs., 1984, 1992, Yen Ching West, 1985, HOLLY Office Ctr., 1989, New Hanover Presbyn. Ch., 1989, VA Press Assn. Hdqs., 1991, St. Andrews Presby. Ch., 1993. Mem. exec. com. United Va. Bank-Sr. PGA, Richmond, 1984. Served to 1st lt. U.S. Army, 1968-70, Vietnam. Mem. AIA, Constrn. Specifications Inst. (bd. dirs.), Hanover Rotary (pres. 1983, bd. dirs. 1994, Dist. 7600 Govs. spl. rep. 1993). Republican. Roman Catholic.

PETIT, BRENDA JOYCE, credit bureau sales executive; b. Houston, Dec. 8, 1939; d. Clyde and Bess (Dobbin) McBee; m. Emile Petit, June 20, 1958 (div. 1972); children: Michael, Melinda. Student, Coll. of the Mainland, Texas City, Tex., 1986. Sec. La Marque ISD, La Marque, Tex., 1966-77; employment counselor Snelling & Snelling, Texas City, 1977-78; exec. asst. M. Lackey, Inc., Galveston, Tex., 1978-84; mgr. MPMS Credit Bur., Galveston, 1984-88, TRW, Houston, 1988—; speaker at colls., convs., clubs; bd. dirs. Consumer Credit Counseling Svcs. Galveston County. Lifetime mem. Galveston County Fair and Rodeo Assn., Santa Fe, Tex., 1980—; mem. U. Tex. Med. Br. Women's Aux., Galveston, 1984—; bd. dirs. City of La Marque Tax Reinvestment Zone, 1990—; bd. dirs. Internat. Credit Assn. Mem. NAFE, Internat. Credit Assn. Galveston County (bd. dirs.). Democrat. Baptist. Home: 2702 Lake Rd La Marque TX 77568-6517 Office: TRW 450 Gears Rd Ste 130 Houston TX 77067-4512

PETIT, PARKER HOLMES, health care corporation executive; b. Decatur, Ga., Aug. 4, 1939; s. James Percival and Ethel (Holmes) P.; children: William Wright, Patricia Monique, Meredith Katherine. BS in Mech. Engring., Ga. Inst. Tech., 1962, MS in Engring. Mechanics, 1964; MBA, Ga. State U., 1973. Engr. Gen. Dynamics Corp., Fort Worth, Tex., 1966-67; engring. project mgr. Lockheed-Ga. Co., Marietta, 1967-71; pres., founder, chief exec. officer Healthdyne, Inc., Marietta, 1971—; bd. dirs. Atlantic S.E. Airlines, Atlanta, Healthdyne Technologies, Inc., Atlanta, Healthdyne Info. Enterprises, Inc., Marietta, Ga., Matria Healthcare, Inc., Marietta. Author: Primer on Composite Materials, 1968; patentee in field. Chmn. bd. dirs. Sudden Infant Death Syndrome Alliance, Washington, 1986; active nat. adv. coun. Emory U. Med. Sch., Coun. fellows for the Emory, Ga. Tech. Biomed. Tech. Rsch. Ctr.; bd. dirs. Ga. Rsch. Alliance, 1995. 1st lt. U.S. Army, 1964-67. Recipient Humanitarian award La SocieteFrancaise de Bienfaisance, 1981; mem. Tech. Hall of Fame of Ga.; mem. Ga. Tech. Acad. Disting. Alumni, 1994; Internat. Bus. fellow, 1986. Mem. Health Industry Mfrs. Assn., Cobb County C. of C. (bd. dirs. 1980-82), Pi Kappa Phi. Republican. Methodist. Office: Healthdyne Inc 1850 Parkway Pl Marietta GA 30067-8237

PETRAIT, BROTHER JAMES ANTHONY, secondary education educator, Roman Catholic brother; b. Phila., May 4, 1937; s. John Joseph and Antonina Frances (Cizek) P. BA, U. Detroit, 1969; MEd, U. Ga., 1971; postgrad. in Scis. and Edn., 8 Univs. and Colls. in U.S., 1971—. Joined Oblates of St Francis de Sales, Roman Cath. Ch., 1957. Sci. tchr. Salesian H.S., Detroit, 1961-70, Judge Meml. H.S., Salt Lake City, 1972-76, Benedictine H.S., Detroit, 1976-82; sci. tchr. St. Joseph H.S., Ogden, Utah, 1983-88, Fredriksted, V.I., 1988—; tchr. resource agt. Am. Astron. Soc., 1995—; pres. Mich. Assn. of Biology Tchrs., 1978-82, Utah Biology Tchrs. Assn., 1985-88; bd. dirs. Utah Sci. Tchrs. Assn., 1985-88; presenter at workshops, speaker in Chgo., New Orleans, Las Vegas, Detroit, Phila., Salt Lake City, Layton, Orlando, Purdue U., Anaheim, Australian Nat. Univ., Canberra; participant in 8 NSF-funded programs: U. Ga., Christian Bros. Colls., Vanderbilt U., St. Lawrence U., Ball State U., W. Va. U., No. Ariz. U. Contbr. article to teacher's mags. and ednl. jours. including The Am. Biology Tchr., The Sci. Tchr., The Cath. Digest., Congrl. Record. Anti nuclear weapons activist, founder and leader Nuclear Free Utah, Ogden, 1986-88; led boycott against Morton Salt Co., maker of nuclear weapons.. Recipient Outstanding Biology Tchr. award Nat. Assn. Biology Tchrs., 1975, Nat. Finalist in Presdl. awards for excellence in sci. and math. tchg. Nat. Sci. Tchrs. Assn./NSF/The White House, 1995; fellow Access Excellence fellow Genentech Inc. program for Outstanding Biology Tchrs., 1996. Mem. Nat. Sci. Tchrs. Assn. (cert. in biology and gen. sci., Star award 1976, Ohaus awards, 1980, 84), Am. Astron. Soc., Soc. of Amateur Radio Astronomers. Home and Office: Saint Joseph H S Plot 3 Rte 2 Frederiksted VI 00840

PETRAKIS, NICHOLAS LOUIS, physician, medical researcher, educator; b. San Francisco, Feb. 6, 1922; s. Louis Nicholas and Stamatina (Boosalis) P.; m. Patricia Elizabeth Kelly, June 24, 1947; children: Steven John, Susan Lynn, Sandra Kay. BA, Augustana Coll., 1943; BS in Medicine, U. S.D., 1944; MD, Washington U., St. Louis, 1946. Intern Mpls. Gen. Hosp., 1946-47; physician-researcher U.S. Naval Radiol. Def. Lab., San Francisco, 1947-49; resident physician Mpls. Gen. Hosp., 1949-50; sr. asst. surgeon Nat. Cancer Inst., USPHS, San Francisco, 1950-54; asst. research physician Cancer Research Inst., U. Calif., San Francisco, 1954-56; asst. prof. preventive medicine U. Calif. Sch. Medicine, San Francisco, 1956-60, assoc. prof., 1960-66, prof., 1966-91, chmn. dept. epidemiology and internat. health, 1978-88, prof. emeritus, 1991—; prof. epidemiology U. Calif. Sch. Pub. Health, Berkeley, 1981-91; assoc. dir. G.W. Hooper Edn., U. Calif., San Francisco, 1970-74, acting dir., 1974-77, chmn. dept. epidemiology and internat. health, 1979-89; co-dir. Breast Screening Ctr. of No. Calif., Oakland, 1976-81; cons. Breast Cancer Task Force, Nat. Cancer Inst., Bethesda, Md., 1972-76; chmn. Biometry & Epidemiology Contract Rev. Com., Bethesda, 1977-81; mem. bd. sci. counselors, div. cancer etiology Nat. Cancer Inst., Bethesda, 1982-86; mem. scientific adv. com. Calif. State Tobacco-Related Disease Rsch. Program, 1991-93; cons. U. Crete Sch. Medicine, Heraklion, Greece, 1984; bd. dirs. No. Calif. Cancer Ctr., 1991. Contbr. over 200 research papers on breast cancer, med. oncology and hematology. Eleanor Roosevelt Internat. Cancer fellow Am. Cancer Soc., Comitato Reserche Nucleari, Cassacia, Italy, 1962; U.S. Pub. Health Service Spl. fellow Galton Lab., U. London, 1969-70; recipient Alumni Achievement award Augustana Coll., Sioux Falls, S.D., 1979, Axion award Hellenic-Am. Profl. Soc. of Calif., San Francisco, 1984, Lewis C. Robbins award Soc. for Prospective Medicine, Indpls., 1985. Mem. Am. Soc. Preventive Oncology (founding, pres. 1984-85, Disting. Achievement award 1992), Soc. for Prospective Medicine (founding), Am. Assn. Cancer Rsch., Am. Epidemiol. Soc., Am. Soc. Clin. Investigation, Am. Bd. Preventive Medicine (cert.). Home: 335 Juanita Way San Francisco CA 94127-1657 Office: U Calif Sch Medicine Dept Epidemiology and Biostats 1699 HSW San Francisco CA 94143-0560

PETREE, BETTY CHAPMAN, anesthetist; b. Emmetsburg, Iowa, Sept. 25, 1950; d. David Jr. and Wilma Ruby (Jones) Chapman; m. Howard Gray Petree, Sept. 21, 1974; children: Zachary Gray, Lynsey Taylor. Diploma, Davis Hosp. Sch. Nursing, 1970; cert., N.C. Bapt. Hosp. Sch. Nursing, 1974. RN, N.C. Clin. mgr. pre admit testing N.C. Bapt. Hosp., Winston-Salem, chief nurse anesthetist outpatient surgery, 1990—. Author: Anesthesia for Kidney Transplantation, Thoracic Aortic Trauma. Recipient Excellence in Teaching award, 1984, 86, 100 Great N.C. Nurses award, 1992. Mem. AANA (Clin. Practitioner award 1988), NCANA (program chmn. 1984-85), NCBH Anesthesia Alumni (sec. 1975-76, pres. 1993-95).

PETRI, WILLIAM ARTHUR, JR., medical educator, researcher; b. Washington, Dec. 25, 1955; s. William A. and Ann (Emmons) P.; m. Mary Ann McDonald, May 30, 1982; children: Daniel, David, Sarah, Rachel. PhD in Microbiology, U. Va., 1980, MD, 1982. Diplomate Am. Bd. Internal Medicine, Am. Bd. Infectious Diseases. Asst. prof. infectious diseases U. Va., Charlottesville, 1988-92, assoc. prof., 1992—; mem. tropical medicine and parasitology study sect. NIH, 1993-97. Recipient Young Investigator award Burroughs-Wellcome Fund, 1992-94; Lucille P. Markey scholar, 1985-93; named Outstanding Investigator, So. Am. Fedn. Clin. Rsch., 1995. Mem. Am. Soc. Tropical Medicine and Hygiene (chmn. sci. program 1992—), Am. Type Culture Collection (bd. dirs.). Home: 2584 Holkham Dr Charlottesville VA 22901-9533 Office: U Va Health Scis Ctr Rm 2115 MR4 Bldg Charlottesville VA 22908

PETRIE, GEORGE WHITEFIELD, III, retired mathematics educator; b. Pitts., May 6, 1912; s. George Whitefield Jr. and Mabel Margaret (O'Reiley)

P.; m. Dorothy May Koeppen, May 28, 1944 (dec. 1965); children: George Whitefield IV, Charles Richard; m. Mildred Pearl McClary, Jan. 1, 1967 (dec. 1995). BS in Math., Carnegie Mellon U., 1933, MS in Math., 1936; PhD, Lehigh U., 1949. Assoc. prof. math. S.D. Sch. of Mines, Rapid City, 1936-41; piping engr. Pitts. Piping & Equipment Co., 1941-42; navigation instr. USNR Midshipmen's Sch., N.Y.C., 1943-45; spl. engr. Bethlehem (Pa.) Steel Co., 1945-47; asst. prof. math. and astronomy Lehigh U., Bethlehem, 1947-50; system engr., edn. exec. IBM Corp., 1950-66; prof. math. New Coll., Sarasota, Fla., 1966-68; prof., dept. chmn. U. Wis., Green Bay, 1968-76; ret. U. Wis.; cons. IBM Corp., Armonk, N.Y., 1967-77; tax cons. S.E. Bank Trust Co., Sarasota, Fla., 1977-78; supr. testing hydraulic intensifier Bethlehem Steel Co. Contbr. articles to profl. jours. and publs. Treas. Healthcare Resources, Inc., Sarasota, 1983-92; tax cons. Am. Assn. Ret. Persons, Sarasota, 1989-92; pres. Sarasota Inst. Lifetime Learning, 1984-86, Sarasota Cmty. Concert Assn., 1985-87. Mem. Am. Math. Soc., Math. Assn. Am., Am. Guild Organists, Bird Key Yacht Club. Home: 4573 N Lake Dr Sarasota FL 34232-1938

PETRIE, WILLIAM MARSHALL, psychiatrist; b. Louisville, Oct. 19, 1946; s. Garner McReynolds and Claire (Samuels) P.; m. Patricia L. Roberts, Aug. 3, 1968; children: Christopher W., Ellen M., Shelley M.; m. Lori L. Molchin, Oct. 1, 1994. BA, Vanderbilt U., 1968, MD, 1972. Research psychiatrist NIMH, Rockville, Md., 1975-77; asst. prof. dept. psychiatry Vanderbilt Med. Ctr., Nashville, 1977-81, assoc. prof., 1981-82, assoc. clin. prof., 1982-87, clin. prof., 1992—; pvt. practice psychiatry Psychiat. Cons., P.C., Nashville, 1982—, pres., 1996—; clin. instr. Georgetown U. Med. Ctr., 1975-77; cons. psychopharmacology rsch. br. NIMH, 1977-80; rschr. in geriatric psychopharmacology; med. dir. memory Study Ctr., 1987—; chmn. of psychiatry, Parthenon Pavilion, 1994-96; bd. trustees Centennial Mutual Ctr., 1994—. Mem. editorial bd. Gen. Hosp. Psychiatry, 1995—, Audio Digest Psychiatry, 1996—; author numerous articles and book chpts. on psychopharmacology and geriatric psychiatry. Fellow Am. Psychiat. Assn. (pres. mid. Tenn. dist. br. 1986-87); mem. AMA, Tenn. Med. Assn., Am. Assn. Geriatric Psychiatrists, Am. Coll. Psychiatrists. Democrat. Methodist. Office: Psychiat Cons PC 310 25th Ave N Nashville TN 37203-1515

PETRIKOVICS, ILONA, toxicologist; b. Nyiregyhaza, Hungary, Dec. 12, 1953; came to the U.S., 1990; d. Istvan and Erzsebet (Tomasovszky) P.; m. Zoltan Major (dec. 1989); 1 child, David. Degree in chemistry, Lajos Kossuth U., 1979, PhD summa cum laude, 1982; PhD summa cum laude, U. Med. Sch., Debrecen, Hungary, 1985. Rsch. assoc. Lajos Kossuth U., Debrecen, 1979-81; postdoctoral rsch. assoc. U. Med. Sch., 1982-85; rsch. fellow Rsch. Group on Antibiotics Hungarian Acad. Scis., Debrecen, 1985-88; lab. head BIOGAL Pharm. Works, Debrecen, 1988-90; rsch. assoc. Tex. A&M U., College Station, 1990-91, asst. rsch. scientist, 1991—. Author: Advances in the Biosciences, 1993; contbr. articles to profl. jours. Recipient Gordon Rsch. Conf. award, 1992, Travel award Am. Soc. for Pharmacology and Exptl. Therapeutics, 1993. Mem. Pharmacology Soc. Hungary, Soc. Toxicology. Lutheran. Home: # 133 1700 SW Pkwy College Station TX 77840 Office: Tex A&M U Dept Med Pharm Toxicology College Station TX 77843

PETROSKI, HENRY JOSEPH, engineer educator; b. N.Y.C., Feb. 6, 1942; s. Henry Frank and Victoria Rose (Grygrowych) P.; m. Catherine Ann Groom, July 15, 1966; children: Karen Beth, Stephen James. B Mech. Engring., Manhattan Coll., N.Y.C., 1963; MS, U. Ill., 1964, PhD, 1968; DSc (hon.), Clarkson U., 1990. Registered profl. engr., Tex. Instr. U. Ill., Urbana, 1965-68; asst. prof. U. Tex., Austin, 1968-74; engr. Argonne (Ill.) Nat. Lab., 1975-80; assoc. prof. civil engring. Duke U., Durham, N.C., 1980-87, prof., 1987-93, Aleksandar S. Vesic prof., 1993—, prof. history, 1995—, chmn. dept. civil and environ. engring., 1991—, dir. grad. studies, 1981-86. Author: To Engineer is Human, 1985, Beyond Engineering, 1986, The Pencil, 1990, The Evolution of Useful Things, 1992, Design Paradigms, 1994 (Best Book award in Engring. 1994), Engineers of Dreams, 1995, Invention by Design, 1996; writer, presenter TV documentary To Engineer is Human, 1987; engring. columnist Am. Scientist, 1995—. Named fellow NEH, 1987-88, Nat. Humanities Ctr., 1987-88, Guggenheim fellow, 1990-91; recipient Outstanding Engring. Grad. award Manhattan Coll., 1992, Alumni award for disting. svc. Coll. Engring. U. Ill. at Urbana-Champaign, 1994. Fellow ASCE (Civil Engring. History and Heritage award 1993), ASME (Ralph Coats Roe medal 1991), Soc. History Tech., Sigma Xi. Office: Duke U Sch Engring Durham NC 27708-0287

PETRUZZI, ANTHONY JOSEPH, JR., mortgage company executive; b. Newark, Nov. 12, 1946; s. Anthony and Kathrine (Paglio) P.; m. Kathaleen Jane Zaccardi, June 24, 1974; children: Charles Michael, Anthony James. M., Seton Hall U., 1972. Lic. mortgage broker, real estate assoc. Educator Roosevelt Jr. High, Westfield, N.J., 1968-74; with real estate Gen. Devel. Corp., Florham Park, N.J., 1974-80; v.p. Buick 22, Inc., Scotch Plains, N.J., 1980-83; profl. indsl. mgr. Comml. Credit/Control Data, N.Y.C., 1983-85; pres., chief exec. officer Omega Funding, Inc., Middlesex, N.J., 1985-91, Cambridge Mortgage, Inc., Boca Raton, Fla., 1991—. Mem. Fla. Assn. Mortgage Profls. Republican. Roman Catholic. Office: Cambridge Mortgage Inc 660 Linton Blvd Ste 206-f Delray Beach FL 33444-8148

PETRY, HEYWOOD MEGSON, psychology educator; b. Hartford, Conn., Mar. 7, 1952; s. Henry Anthony and Madeline Heywood (Megson) P.; m. Michele Falzett, Sept. 3, 1983; 2 children. BA, Bates Coll., 1974; MA, Conn. Coll., 1976; PhD, Brown U., 1981. Postdoctoral fellow Vanderbilt U., Nashville, 1980-82, Brown U., Providence, 1982-84; asst. prof. SUNY, Stony Brook, 1984-91; assoc. ophthalmology and visual scis. dept. U. Louisville, 1991—, assoc. prof. psychology dept., 1991—. Reviewer profl. jours.; contbr. articles to profl. jours. including Procs. NAS, Brain Rsch., Nature, Jour. Comparative Neurology, Visual Neurosci., Vision Rsch., Progress in Brain Rsch., Psychophysiology, Am. Jour. Psychology. Grad. fellow Conn. Coll., 1974-76; rsch. grantee NIH, 1982-83, 87-93, Fight-for-Sight, Inc., 1992-93; recipient postdoctoral traineeship NIMH, 1980-82, NIH, 1982-84. Mem. Assn. for Rsch. in Vision in Ophthalmology, Optical Soc. Am., Soc. for Neurosci., Sigma Xi. Office: U Louisville Dept Psychology Louisville KY 40292

PETRY, RUTH VIDRINE, assistant principal; b. Eunice, La., Jan. 20, 1947; d. Adea and Ruth Alice (Fox) Vidrine; m. Carson Clinton Petry, June 19, 1976. BA, La. Coll., 1971; MEd, McNeese State U., 1984. Cert. tchr., La. Tchr. jr. high sch. Jefferson Davis Parish, Jennings, La., 1970-72; tchr. high sch. St. Tammany Parish, Mandeville, La., 1972-73, Jefferson Parish, Gretna, La., 1973-81; tchr. jr. high Acadia Parish, Crowley, La., 1981-90; tchr. lang. arts Crowley Jr. High Sch., 1981-90; master tchr. assessor La. State Dept. Edn., Lafayette, 1990-91; tchr. Crowley Mid. Sch., 1991-94, instrnl. asst., 1994-95; exec. dir. Assoc. Profl. Educators of La., Baton Rouge, 1995-96; acting asst. prin. Rayne (La.) H.S., 1996—; writing assessment coord. Crowley Jr. High Sch., 1984-85, mem. faculty insvc. team, 1986-89, chmn. spelling bee, 1983-90, 92-93, co-chmn. interim self study Crowley Jr. High Sch. So. Assn., 1985-86; mem. state selection com. for La. Tech. of Yr., Students of Yr., 1992-93; mem. Tchr. Evaluation Revision Panels, I, III, IV, 1992-93, Prin.'s Evaluation State Com., 1993; presenter workshops in field. Co-sponsor Nat. Jr. Hon. Soc., 1984-90; mem. La. Gov.-Elect's Edn. Transition Team, 1991-92; mem. La. Goals 2000 steering com. on sch. governance and accountability, 1994-95. Named Crowley Jr. High Tchr. of the Yr., 1985-86. Mem. ASCD, Assn. Profl. Educators La. (pres. Acadia chpt. 1988-92, mem. dist. VII state exec. bd., 1990-91, state pres.-elect 1991-92, state pres. 1992-94), Nat. Assn. Secondary Sch. Prins., La. Assn. Sch. Execs., La. Assn. Prins., La. Assn. for Retarded Citizens, Civitans, Delta Kappa Gamma (chpt. pres. 1988-90, state leadership scholar 1993), Phi Delta Kappa. Republican. Baptist. Home: 206 Bruce St Lafayette LA 70503-6102

PETTIETTE, ALISON YVONNE, lawyer; b. Brockton, Mass., Aug. 16, 1952. Student Sorbonne, Paris, 1971-72; BA, Sophie Newcomb Coll., 1972; MA, Rice U., 1974; JD, Bates Coll., 1978. Bar: Tex. 1979, U.S. Dist. Ct. (so. dist.) Tex. 1980, U.S. Ct. Appeals (5th cir.) 1981. Ptnr. Harvill & Hardy, Houston, 1979-83; pvt. practice, Houston, 1983-84; assoc. O'Quinn & Hagans, Houston, 1984-86, Jones & Granger, Houston, 1986-88; pvt. practice, Houston, 1988—. Editor Houston Law Rev. U. Houston, 1976-78. Exercise instr. YWCA, Houston, 1976-81, U. St. Thomas, Houston. NDEA fellow Rice U., Houston, 1972-74; Woodrow Wilson scholar, Tulane U., New Orleans, 1972. Mem. ABA, Assn. Trial Lawyers Am., Tex. Trial Lawyers Assn., Houston Trial Lawyers Assn., Phi Delta Phi, Phi Beta Kappa. Home: PO Box 980847 Houston TX 77098-0847

PETTIGREW, JOHNNIE DELONIA, educational diagnostician; b. Electra, Tex., July 2, 1948; d. John Drew and Dolly Marie (Watkins) Chester; divorced; 1 child, Jan Elise. B Elem. Edn., U. North Tex., 1970, MEd, 1982; postgrad., Tex. Woman's U., 1993—. Cert. elem., kindergarten, learning disabilities, spl. edn. early childhood, gifted edn. tchr., ednl. diagnostician, adminstr., Tex. 2d grade tchr. Azle (Tex.) Ind. Sch. Dist., 1969-70; 3d grade tchr. Decatur (Tex.) Ind. Sch. Dist., 1970-72; kindergarten, spl. edn. tchr. Boyd (Tex.) Ind. Sch. Dist., 1972-74, kindergarten, gifted edn., spl. edn. tchr., 1981-93; spl. edn. tchr. Springtown (Tex.) Ind. Sch. Dist., 1977-81; gifted edn. tchr. Denton (Tex.) Ind. Sch. Dist., 1993-94, ednl. diagnostician, 1994—; cons. in gifted edn., early childhood and drama to various sch. dists., Tex.; adj. prof. U. North Tex., Denton, 1993. Author: (play) The Monks Tale: Romeo and Juliet, 1990, also ednl. materials. Co-founder children's story hour Decatur Pub. Libr., 1970; dir. Wise County Little Theatre, Decatur; life mem. Boyd Ind. Sch. Dist. PTA, 1989, Tex. PTA. Mem. Am. Assn. for Tchg. and Curriculum, Assn. for Childhood Edn. Internat., Am. Edn. Rsch. Assn., Tex. Assn. for Gifted and Talented, Nat. Assn. for the Edn. of Young Children, So. Early Childhood Assn., Phi Delta Kappa, Phi Kappa Phi. Home: PO Box 91 Decatur TX 76234-0091 Office: Denton Ind Sch Spl Edn Svcs 1117 Riney Rd Denton TX 76208

PETTIJOHN, VIKI ANN, English and Spanish languages educator; b. Ft. Worth, Nov. 1, 1947; d. James Newton Jr. and Annie Marie (Spivey) Spencer; m. Carl H. Pettijohn, Feb. 14, 1969 (div. Dec. 1987). BA in English, Tex. Wesleyan U., 1969; MAT in English, Jacksonville U., 1972; PhD in 20th Century Brit. and Am. Lit., Fla. State U., 1994. Tchr. O.D. Wyatt High Sch., Ft. Worth, 1969-70; tchr. English, Spanish Virginia Beach (Va.) Jr. High Sch., 1972-77, Englewood High Sch., Jacksonville, Fla., 1977-84; teaching asst. Fla. State U., Tallahassee, 1985-89, instr. English, 1989-90; isntr. English and Spanish Southwestern Okla. State U., Weatherford, 1990-94, asst. prof., 1994—, dir. freshman English, 1995—; presenter in field. Contbr. papers to pubs. Okla. Found. Humanities grantee, 1991, Okla. Regents grant, 1992, 93. Mem. South Ctrl. Modern Lang. Assn., Okla. Coun. Tchrs. English, Modern Lang. Assn., AAUW. Independent. Presbyterian. Home: 901 N Indiana St Weatherford OK 73096-3635 Office: Southwestern Okla State U Lang Arts Dept Weatherford OK 73096

PETTIS, JOYCE, English language educator; b. Columbia, N.C., Mar. 14, 1946; d. Howard and Victoria Elizabeth (Hill) Owens; m. Bobby Dennis Pettis (dec. June 1990); 1 child, Daryl Pettis; m. Enoch Charles Temple, Dec. 22, 1993; stepchildren: Chanda Temple, Erica Temple. BA in English, Winston Salem State U., 1968; MA in English, East Carolina U., Greenville, 1974; PhD in English, U. N.C., 1983. Tchr. N.C. pub. schs., 1968-72; asst. prof. East Carolina U., 1974-79; assoc. prof. N.C. State U., Raleigh, 1985-93, 96—; vis. assoc. prof. English U. Ala., Huntsville, 1994-96; dir. honors program U. Ala., 1995-96; editl. bd. N.C. Literary Rev., Greenville, 1992—. Author: Toward Wholeness in Paule Marshall's Fiction, 1995; contbr. articles to profl. jours. Danforth assoc., 1981; recipient Coll. of Arts and Scis. Summer Rsch. award N.C. State U., 1989. Mem. Modern Lang. Assn., Coll. Lang. Assn. (Scholarship award 1995), South Atlantic Modern Lang. Assn., Popular Culture Assn. (area chair for African-Am. Culture, 1986-93). Office: English Dept N C State U Box 8105 Raleigh NC 27695

PETTIT, JOHN DOUGLAS, JR., management educator; b. Alice, Tex., Aug. 19, 1940; s. John Douglas and Vivian Iola (Beaman) P.; m. Suzanne McLeod, Aug. 23, 1964; children: Melanie Ann Wilson, David Bryant. BBA, U. North Tex., 1962, MBA, 1964; PhD, La. State U., 1969. Instr. mgmt. Miss. State U., Starkville, 1964-65; grad. asst. La. State U., Baton Rouge, 1965-67, instr. mgmt., 1967-68; asst. prof. bus. Tex. Tech. U., Lubbock, 1968-69; assoc. prof. mgmt. U. North Tex., Denton, 1969-78, prof. mgmt., 1978-95; chair excellence in free enterprise Austin Peay State Univ., Clarksville, Tenn., 1995—; cons. various orgns., 1969-96; mgr., co-owner Pettit's Cleaners/Hatters, Alice, 1992-96; vis. prof. mgmt. Wichita State U., Kans., 1994-95. Co-author: Business Communication: Theory and Application, 6th edit. 1989, 7th edit. 1993, Report Writing for Business, 8th edit. 1991, 9th edit. 1995, Lesikar's Basic Business Communication, 6th edit. 1993, 7th edit. 1996; editl. bd. Organl. Comm. Abstracts, 1980-85, Jour. Bus. Comm., 1987-90, mng. editor, 1990-94. Mem. choir St. Andrew Pres. Ch., Denton, 1985—, diaconate bd. mem., 1988-91; actor, singer Denton Cmty. Theater Summer Prodn., 1988-95. Recipient Master's Degree award Chgo. Bd. Trade, 1963. Fellow Assn. Bus. Comm. (pres., 1st v.p., exec. dir., 1990-94); mem. Southwestern Fedn. Adminstrv. Disciplines (pres., v.p.), Acad. Mgmt., Denton Country Club (bd. dirs.), Blue Key Nat. Hon. Fraternity, Beta Gamma Sigma (hon.), Phi Kappa Phi (hon.), Delta Sigma Pi. Presbyterian. Home: 9122 David Fort Rd Argyle TX 76226 Office: Austin Peay State Univ Coll Bus Clarksville TN

PETTITT, BARBARA JEAN, pediatric surgeon; b. Niagara Falls, N.Y., Feb. 2, 1952; d. Robert Andrew and Joan Marilyn (Boore) P.; m. Richard Allen Schieber, May 24, 1981; children: Christine Pettitt Schieber, Lucy Pettitt Schieber, Brian Pettitt Schieber. BA in Chemistry magna cum laude, Cen. Coll., Pella, Iowa, 1972; D of Medicine, Northwestern U., Chgo., 1976. Diplomate Am. Bd. Surgery with certificates of spl. competence in pediatric surgery and surg. critical care; lic. pediatric surgeon, Calif., Pa., Ga. Student fellow in rehab. medicine Rehab. Inst. Chgo., spring 1974; intern in straight surgery Los Angeles County-U. So. Calif. Med. Ctr., 1976-77, resident in gen. surgery, 1977-81; resident in pediatric surgery Childrens' Hosp. Pitts., 1982-84; asst. prof. surgery and pediatrics dept. Sch. Medicine Emory U., Atlanta, 1985—; mem. staff Henrietta Egleston Hosp. for Children, Atlanta, 1985-86; mem. staff Grady Meml. Hosp., Atlanta, 1985—, chief pediatric surg. svc., 1990—; chief of surgery Hughes Spalding Children's Hosp., 1993—; instr. ATLS, PALS; active various coms. Henrietta Egleston Hosp. for Children, 1985-86, Grady Meml. Hosp., 1986—, Hughes Spalding Children's Hosp., 1992—; lectr., presenter many profl. and ednl. orgns., 1983—. Contbg. author: (with M. Rowe) Pediatric Surgery, 4th edit., 1986; contbr. articles to profl. publs. Bd. dirs., trustees DeKalb Choral Guild, Atlanta, 1988—; pres. Summit Cmty. Assn., 1992—, Harmony Youth Chorus Parent Orgn., 1995—; chairperson health and safety com. Arbor Montessori Sch. Rsch. grantee Rsch. Corp., summer 1971, NIH, 1983-84; Rollscreen full-tuition scholar, 1969-72, Ruth G. White scholar Calif. State P.E.O., 1974-75; recipient 1st prize Bernard Baruch Essay Contest, Am. Congress Rehab. Medicine, 1975; named Outstanding Young Woman of Yr., State pf Pa., 1984, State of Ga., 1986, Disting. Alumna Ctrl. Coll., 1990. Fellow ACS, Am. Acad. Pediatrics (surg. sect., critical care sect.); mem. AMA, Am. Med. Womens' Assn., Southeastern Surg. Congress, Am. Pediatric Surg. Assn., Assn. Women Surgeons, Am. Soc. Parental and Enteral Nutrition, La.A. County-U. So. Calif. Med. Ctr. Soc. Grad. Surgeons, Phi Delta Epsilon (pres. med. sch. chpt. 1974-75, undergrad. midwest regional coord. 1974-75, nat. exec. com. 1976-80, nat. intern-resident liaison com. 1980-85, nat. constn. and bylaws com. 1986—, Isadore Pilot award Chgo. chpt. 1975, nat. svc. award 1976), Soc. Critical Care Medicine, Ga. Surg. Soc., Assn. Surg. Edn. Democrat. Episcopalian. Office: Emory Univ Sch Medicine Dept of Surgery 69 Butler St SE Atlanta GA 30303-3033

PETTUS, MILDRED LOUISE, retired history educator, writer; b. Lancaster County, S.C., Feb. 1, 1926; d. Calvin Hall and Bessie Kathryn (Rodgers) P. BA in History, Winthrop Coll., 1946; MA in History, U. S.C., 1954. Tchr. Kershaw (S.C.) H.S., 1947-48; cotton gin mgr. Pettus Gin Co., Ft. Mill, S.C., 1949-54; tchr. Spartanburg (S.C.) Jr. Coll., 1955-56, Douglas (Ariz.) H.S., 1956-63, Ajo (Ariz.) H.S., 1964-65, Orlando (Fla.) Jr. Coll., 1965-67; asst. prof. Winthrop Coll., Rock Hill, S.C., 1967-89; ret., 1989. Author: Pictorial History of Lancaster County, South Carolina, 1984, The Springs Story, 1986, The Palmetto State, 1989, The Waxhaws, 1993; author (newspaper column) "Nearly History" in York Sect. of Charlotte Observer, 1985—. Recipient Outstanding Publ. Editor award S.C. Confederation of State and Local History Socs., 1994. Mem. York County Geneal. and Hist. Soc. (bd. dirs., editor The Quarterly 1989—). Democrat. Home: 708 Harrell St Rock Hill SC 29730

PETTY, ALYCE MILLER, elementary school educator; b. Mpls., Dec. 31, 1950; d. James C. Miller and Alice (Owens) Nelson; m. Gilbert Barthel Petty, Feb. 28, 1969; children: Tamara, Regina, Gregory. BS, U. North Ala., 1980, Union U., 1989; MEd, Union U., 1993. Phys. edn. tchr. Denmark (Tenn.) Elem. Sch. Treas. Madison Winter Guard, Jackson, Tenn., 1994-95; mem. Tenn. Profl. Instrnl. Devel. Commn., 1994-95; leader Girl Scouts U.S., Florence, Ala., 1976-80; coach Jackson Recreation Dept., 1984-89, AAU Basketball, Jackson, 1994. Mem. NEA, Jackson-Madison County Edn. Assn. (mem. minority affairs com. 1993-94, welfare com. 1993-94, study com. 1994), Tenn. Edn. Assn. (rep. 1989-94), Delta Sigma Theta. Methodist. Home: 18 Sunnymeade Dr Jackson TN 38305 Office: Denmark Elem Sch 1945 Denmark-Jackson Rd Denmark TN 38391

PETTY, JENNY BETH, librarian, educator; b. Houston, Oct. 11, 1941; d. Robert Lee and Gladys Marie (Morgan) McAllister; m. Clyde Lee Tinsley, Aug. 10, 1962 (div. Sept. 1980); children: Thomas Earl, Tonia Elise, Tana Elaine, Trent Lee; m. William Charles Petty, Mar. 26, 1983. BA in French and English, Ouachita Bapt. Coll., Arkadelphia, Ark., 1962; postgrad., Maryville Coll., St. Louis; MA in LS, U. Mo., Columbia, 1983; PhD in LS, Tex. Woman's U., 1993. Tchr. French and English Stamps (Ark.) H.S., 1962-63; elem. libr. Lonedell (Mo.) R-14 Sch., 1978-80; elem. libr. Rockwood Sch. Dist., St. Louis, 1980-85, h.s. media specialist, 1985-87; periodicals libr., asst. prof. Ouachita Bapt. U., Arkadelphia, Ark., 1988—. Author: More Than Books: A 100 Year History, 1986, Promoting Cultural Awareness, 1993; contbr. articles to profl. jours. Mem. ALA, Am. Assn. Sch. Librs., Assn. Coll./Rsch. Librs., Ark. Libr. Assn. (pres.s 1996, chair coll./univ. divsn. 1994-95), Ark. Traveller Storytelling Assn. (adv. bd. 1996—), Children's Lit. Assn. Presbyterian. Home: 917 N 15th St Arkadelphia AR 71923 Office: Ouachita Bapt U 410 Ouachita St Arkadelphia AR 71998

PETTY, KEVIN JOSEPH, medical scientist, educator; b. El Paso, Tex., Apr. 22, 1956; s. Travis H. and Berenice A. (Wieland) P.; m. Mary C. Luke, Sept. 6, 1986. BA with high honors, U. Tex., 1978; PhD, MD, U. Tex. Southwestern, 1984. Diplomate Am. Bd. Internal Medicine; lic. physician Mass., Tex. Resident in medicine Mass. Gen. Hosp., Boston, 1984-87; rsch. assoc., med. staff fellow clin. endocrinology br. Nat. Inst. Diabetes and Digestive and Kidney Diseases, Bethesda, Md., 1987-91; asst. prof. dept. internal medicine U. Tex. Southwestern Med. Sch., Dallas, 1991—. Recipient Henry Christian award for excellence in rsch., 1991; Pfizer scholar for new faculty, 1992. Mem. AAAS, AMA, ACP, Am. Fedn. for Clin. Rsch. (award to trainees in clin. rsch. 1990), Am. Thyroid Assn., Endocrine Soc., Tex. Med. Assn., Dallas County Med. Soc., Alpha Omega Alpha. Office: U Tex Southwestern Med Ctr Dept Internal Medicine 5323 Harry Hines Blvd Dallas TX 75235-8857

PETTYJOHN, FRANK SCHMERMUND, emergency medicine educator; b. Milford, Del., Sept. 28, 1934; s. James K. and Eloise K. (Kelley) P.; m. Jean A. Rovey, July 1, 1961; children: Elise K. Pettyjohn, Ellen E. Pettyjohn. BCE, U. Del., 1956; MD, Hahnemann U., 1963. Diplomate Am. Bd. Internal Medicine, Cardiovasc. Disease, Am. Bd. Preventive Medicine-Aerospace Medicine. Commd. 2d lt. U.S. Army, 1957; advanced through grades to col. U.S. Army, various, 1977; intern, resident Madigan Gen. Hosp. U.S. Army, Tacoma, 1963-69; chief med. staff aeromed. ctr., Lyster Army Community Hosp. U.S. Army, Ft. Rucker, Ala., 1977-80; dir. applied aeromed. rsch. program U.S. Army, Aerospace Med. Rsch. Lab., Fla., 1980-82; commdg. officer Winn Army Comty. Hosp. U.S. Army, Ft. Stewart, Ga., 1982-85; retired U.S. Army, 1986; clin. prof. medicine U. So. Ala. Coll. Medicine, Mobile, 1986-89, prof. medicine, 1989—, chmn. dept. emergency medicine, 1992—; med. dir. Southflite, Aeromed. Helicopter Svc., U. So. Ala. Med. Ctr., Mobile, 1990—; med. staff emergency medicine U. South Ala. Drs. Hosp., Mobile, Knollwood Park Hosp., Mobile, 1991—; med. staff cardiology and internal medicine, Sacred Heart Hosp., Pensacola, Fla., West Fla. Regional Med. Ctr., Pensacola, 1982—, Gulf Breeze (Fla.) Hosp., 1985—. Contbr. articles to profl. jours. Decorated Bronze Star, Legion of Merit, Air medal with two oak leaf clusters. Fellow ACP, Am. Coll. Cardiology, Am. Coll. Chest Physicians, Am. Coll. Preventive Medicine, Coun. Clin. Cardiology (Am. Heart Assn.), Aerospace Med. Assn. (exec. coun. 1979-82); mem. Am. Coll. Emergency Physicians, Soc. Acad. Emergency Medicine, Assn. Acad. Chmn. Emergency Medicine, Am. Coll. Physician Execs., Internat. Acad. Aviation and Space Medicine. Methodist. Home and Office: 607 Silverthorn Rd Gulf Breeze FL 32561-4625

PETZEL, FLORENCE ELOISE, textiles educator; b. Crosbyton, Tex., Apr. 1, 1911; d. William D. and A. Eloise (Punchard) P. PhB, U. Chgo., 1931, AM, 1934; PhD, U. Minn., 1954. Instr., Judson Coll., 1936-38; asst. prof. textiles Ohio State U., 1938-48; assoc. prof. U. Ala., 1950-54; prof. Oreg. State U., 1954-61, 67-75, 77, prof. emeritus, 1975—, dept. head, 1954-61, 67-75; prof., div. head U. Tex., 1961-63; prof. Tex. Tech U., 1963-67; vis. instr. Tex. State Coll. for Women, 1937; vis. prof. Wash. State U., 1967. Effie I. Raitt fellow, 1949-50. Mem. Met. Opera Guild, High Mus. Art, Sigma Xi, Phi Kappa Phi, Omicron Nu, Iota Sigma Pi, Sigma Delta Epsilon. Author Textiles of Ancient Mesopotamia, Persia and Egypt, 1987; contbr. articles to profl. jours. Home: 150 Downs Blvd Apt D205 Clemson SC 29631-2049

PETZOLD, ANITA MARIE, psychotherapist; b. Princeton, N.J., June 2, 1957; d. Charles Bernard and Kathleen Marie (McDonald) P. AS in Bus., Indian River C.C., Ft. Pierce, Fla., 1986; BS in Liberal Studies, Barry U., 1988; MS in Human Svcs. Adminstrn., Nova U., 1989, postgrad., 1989-91; PhD in Human Svcs. Adminstrn., LaSalle U., 1994. Lic. mental health counselor, Fla.; cert. addictions profl.; internat. cert. alcohol and drug abuse counselor; nat. cert. counselor; cert. employee assistance counselor; nat. cert. clin. mental health counselor; nat. cert. addictions counselor; cert. DUI instr. Admissions coord. The Palm Beach Inst., West Palm Beach, Fla., 1985-86; dir. admissions Heritage Health Corp., Jensen Beach, Fla., 1986-89; drug abuse strategy coord. Martin County Bd. of County Commrs., Stuart, Fla., 1989—; mem. Drug Resource Team for the 12th Congl. Dist., Fla., 1990—, Juvenile Justice Assn. of the 19th Jud. Ct., Fla., 1993—; grant writer in field. Vol. Hist. Soc. Martin County, Stuart, 1986—; mem. United Way Martin County, Stuart, 1993; mem. bd. dirs. Cmty. AIDS Adv. Project, Stuart, 1993; chmn. treatment com. Martin County Task Force on Substance Abused Children, Stuart, 1993—. Recipient Outstanding Cmty. Svc. award United Way Martin County, Stuart, 1993. Mem. NASW, Am. Mental Health Counselors Assn., Nat. Criminal Justice Assn., Nat. Assn. Alcoholism and Drug Abuse Counselors, Nat. Consortium Treatment Alternatives to St. Crime Programs, Am. Coll. Addiction Treatment Adminstrs., Am. Labor-Mgmt. Adminstrs., Fla. Alcohol and Drug Abuse Assn. Republican. Roman Catholic. Office: Martin County Bd County Commrs 400 SE Osceola St Stuart FL 34994-2577

PETZRICK, PAUL ARTHUR, JR., army officer; b. Annapolis, Md., Sept. 25, 1955; s. Paul Arthur and Marie Hattie (Nizer) P.; m. Deborah Ida Sue Chester, June 11, 1977; children: Paul Loren, Samantha Marie. BS in Civil Engring., U.S. Mil. Acad., 1977; MS in Sys. Mgmt., U. So. Calif., 1987; postgrad., LaSalle U., Mandeville, La., 1995-96. Commd. 2d lt. U.S. Army, 1977, advanced through grades to maj., 1994; various assignments Ft. Hood, Tex., Frankfurt, Germany, 1977-88; asst. prof. mil. sci. Duke U. Army ROTC, durham, N.C., 1988-93; engr. systems evaluator U.S. Army Operational Evaluation Command, Alexandria, Va., 1993—; dep. comdr. for support Kuwait Emergency Recovery Office, 1991. Contbr. articles to army publs. Sunday sch. tchr., sec. ch. coun. Christ Luth. Ch., Durham, 1989-93; Sunday sch. tchr. Word of Life Ch., Springfield, Va., 1993-95; asst. Sunday Sch. tchr. Calvary Ch. of the Nazarene, Springfield, 1995—; area coord. Bible study leader Officers Christian Fellowship at Duke U., 1988-93; scoutmaster Boy Scouts Am., 1989-96. Decorated Meritorious Svc. medal (2), Army Commendation medal (3), others. Mem. Assn. Grads. U.S. Mil. Acad., Ret. Officers Assn. Republican. Nazarene. Home: 5713 Heming Ave Springfield VA 22151 Office: US Army Operational Eval Command 5713 Heming Ave Alexandria VA 22303-1458

PEVEN, MICHAEL, art educator, artist; b. Chgo., Apr. 12, 1949. AB in Design, U. Ill., 1971; MFA in Photography, Sch. Art Inst. Chgo., 1977. Prof. dept. art U. Ark., Fayetteville, 1977—, chmn. dept. art, 1992—. One-man shows include Amarillo (Tex.) Mus. Art, 1994, Art Ctr. Ozarks, Springdale, Ark., 1994, Lightfantastic Gallery, East Lansing, Mich., 1990, Robert May Gallery, Lexington, Ky., 1990, Artists Book Works, Chgo., 1988, Shepard Coll. Creative Art Ctr., Shepardstown, W.Va., 1988, Southern Light Gallery, Amarillo, Tex., 1987, Art Acad. Cin., 1986, The

Photographer's Cooperative Gallery, Fayetteville, Ark., 1986, Lamar U., Dishman Gallery, Beaumont, Tex., 1985, Ark. Arts Ctr, Little Rock 1985, Wayne St. U., Art Dept. Detroit 1985, Calif. St. U., Art Dept., Fullerton 1985, Pictures, Tulsa 1985, Cameravision Gallery, Los Angeles 1984, Tarrant County Jr. Coll., Photography Gallery, Hurst, Tex. 1983, Photogenesis Gallery, Albuquerque 1982, Blue Sky Gallery, Portland 1982, Tex. Women's U., Denton 1982, Austin Peay St. U., Clarksville, Tenn. 1981, also numerous other galleries 1977-1981; numerous group exhibits 1977—; represented in numerout pub. collections Amon Carter Mus., Ft. Worth, Art Inst. Chgo, Art Metropple Archive, Toronto, Calif. Mus. Photography, Riverside; author: Snatches (or Man Made Wonders), 1979, Prophesy Panorama, 1982, Some Recent Developments, 1984, Outstanding Young Men of America, 1985, The Marriage of Heaven and Hell, part I, The Bachelor Stripped Bare, 1985, Li'l Joey, Up & Down, Roun' & Roun', 1986, Too Scents Worth, 1988, Global Family, 1990, Cradle of Civilization, 1993. Recipient Fulbright Coll. Master Tchr. award, 1992; Fulbright Coll. Arts and Scis. grantee, 1981, 82, 85, 89, 92, U.A. Teaching Acad. grantee, 1992, 93, Graham Found. grantee, 1969, U. Ark. faculty devel. grantee, 1989; Ark. Arts Coun. fellow, 1986, Mid-Am. Arts Alliance/NEA fellow, 1983, VISIONS fellow, 1982, Ark. Arts Coun. photo fellow, 1990. Mem. Soc. Photographic Edn. Home: 514 Mission Blvd Fayetteville AR 72701-3519 Office: U Ark Dept Art 116 F A Ctr Fayetteville AR 72701

PEYMAN, GHOLAM ALI, ophthalmologist; b. Iran, Nov. 7, 1937; s. Mohammed and Taj (Manteghi) P. BS, MD, U. Freiburg, W. Germany, 1962. Diplomate Am. Bd. Ophthalmology. Asst. prof. ophthalmology A. Lincoln Sch. Medicine, U. Ill., Chgo., 1971-74, assoc. prof., 1974-76, prof., 1976-87; prof. ophthalmology La. State U. Eye Ctr., New Orleans, 1987—. Author: Advances in Uveal Surgery, 1975, Intraocular Tumors, 1977, Principles and Practice of Ophthalmology, 1980, Intravitreal Surgery: Principles and Practice, 1986, 94, Vitreous Substitutes, 1995. Recipient Fisher prize Chgo. Ophthal. Soc., 1973; Nat. Eye Inst./NIH grantee, 1989. Mem. Am. Acad. Ophthalmology, Assn. for Rsch. in Vision and Ophthalmology, New Orleans Acad. Ophthalmology, Retina Soc., Vitreous Soc. Office: LSU Eye Ctr 2020 Gravier St Ste B New Orleans LA 70112-2272

PEYRON, DANIEL LOUIS, tax specialist; b. Palmyra, Va., July 10, 1925; s. Daniel L., Sr. and Mary J. (Dupont) P.; m. Betty A. Nonte, Feb. 18, 1955; children: Dana, Mark, Susan, David, Sandra, Betty Jo. BS in Bus. Adminstrn., U. Ala., 1950; student, Georgetown Univ., 1950-51. Cost acct. USN Bur., Washington, 1950-51; auditor Houdaille Hershey, Detroit, 1951-53; budget mgr. Reynolds Metals Co., Louisville, Ky., 1955-60; pres., CEO Peyron Assocs., Inc., Louisville, 1960—; spkr. in field. Author, editor newsletters, 1975—. With U.S. Army, 1943-45, Italy, France. Decorated Purple Heart, Combat Inf. medal. Office: Peyron Assocs Inc 3212 Preston Hwy Louisville KY 40213-1330

PEYTON, GORDON PICKETT, lawyer; b. Washington, Jan. 22, 1941; s. Gordon Pickett and Mary Campbell (Grasty) P.; m. Marjorie G. Parish, June 9, 1962 (div.); children: Janet Porter, William Parish; m. Jean Nye Groseclose, Oct. 20, 1979. BA cum laude, U. of the South, 1962; JD, Duke U., 1965. Bar: Va. 1965, U.S. Dist. Ct. (ea. dist.) Va. 1966, U.S. Ct. Appeals (4th cir.) 1975, U.S. Ct. Mil. Appeals 1980. Asst. city atty., Alexandria, Va., 1966-69; pvt. practice, Alexandria, 1966-82, 88—; v.p. Peyton, Prendergast and Shapiro, Ltd., Alexandria, 1982-84; pres. Peyton & Shapiro, Ltd., 1985-88. Asst. commr. accounts Alexandria Cir. Ct., 1978—; bd. trustees U. of the South, 1972-76, Ch. Schs. in Diocese of Va., 1974-84; sr. warden Immanuel Ch.-on-the-Hill, 1990-91. 1st. lt. USAF Res. ret. Mem. ABA, 4th Cir. Jud. Conf., Va. Bar Assn., Va. State Bar (chmn. 8th dist. grievance com. 1988-90, vice-chmn. disciplinary bd. 1995—), Va. Trial Lawyers Assn., Alexandria Bar Assn. (pres. 1982-83), Am. Judicature Soc., Va. Conf. Commrs. of Accts., Alexandria C. of C. (v.p., dir. 1974-77). Episcopalian. Office: 908 King St # 201 Alexandria VA 22314-3019

PFANNER, HELMUT FRANZ, German language educator; b. Hohenweiler, Vorarlberg, Austria, Nov. 8, 1933; came to U.S., 1957; s. Georg Franz and Luise (Huber) P.; m. Rosemary Griffin, Mar. 16, 1959 (div. 1964); 1 child, Renate; m. Beverly Louise Radcliffe, Sept. 16, 1966 (div. 1988); children: Heidi, Eric, Marta; m. Nasy Inthisone, Dec. 27, 1995. Grad., Tchr. Tng. Coll., Feldkirch, Austria, 1952; student, Kans. U., 1957-58. Cert. elem. and secondary sch. tchr. Tchr. Volksschule Seewald, Fontanella, Vorarlberg, 1952-53, Volksschule Hohenweiler, 1953-57; English tchr. Hauptschule Belruptstrasse, Bregenz, Austria, 1958-59; German instr. U. Wash., Seattle, 1964-67; asst. prof. U. Va., Charlottesville, 1967-69; assoc. prof. U. N.H., Durham, 1969-79; vis. prof. Purdue U., West Lafayette, Ind., 1979-82; prof. German U. N.H., Durham, 1982-86; prof. German, dept. chmn. U. Nebr., Lincoln, 1986-89; prof. German Vanderbilt U., Nashville, 1989—; dir. Summer Inst. German Lang. and Culture U. Calif., Santa Barbara, 1992—. Author: Hanns Johst, Vom Expr. z. Nationalsozial, 1970, Oskar Maria Graf. eine kritische Bibliogr., 1976, Exile in New York: German and Austrian Writers after 1933, 1983; co-editor: O.M. Graf: Beschreibung eines Volksschriftstellers, 1974, O.M. Graf in seinen Briefen, 1984; editor: Exile across Cultures, 1986, Oskar Maria Graf: Reden und Aufsätze aus dem Exil, 1989, Karl Jakob Hirsch: Quintessenz meines Lebens, 1990, World War II and the Exiles: A Literary Response, 1991. Fulbright scholar Kans. U., 1957-58, German Acad. Exch. scholar, 1963-64; Am. Philos. Soc. grantee, 1969, 73, Alexander von Humboldt fellow, 1972-73, 77-78, Am. Coun. Learned Socs. fellow, 1976-77, NEH fellow, 1996-97. Mem. MLA, PEN German Writers Abroad (Am. sec.-treas. 1979—), Internat. Assn. Germanic Studies, Am. Assn. Tchrs. German, German Studies Assn., Internat. Soc. for Exile Studies. Office: Vanderbilt U Dept Germanic Slavic Langs Box 1567 Sta B Nashville TN 37235

PFANNER, TIMOTHY PAUL, gastroenterologist; b. Springville, N.Y., Sept. 15, 1955; s. George Henry and Carol Joan (Fronheiser) P.; m. Nancy Jo Brinkley; children: Sarah Anne, Joy Esther. BS in Pharmacy, U. Tex., 1980, MD, 1985. Intern Tripler Army Med. Ctr., Honolulu, 1985-86; chief occupational medicine Senela Army Depot, N.Y., 1986-88; residency in internal medicine Tripler Army Med. Ctr., 1988-91; staff internal medicine West Point, N.Y., 1991-93; gastroenterology fellow Brooks Army Med. Ctr., Fort Sam Houston, 1993-95; chief dept. medicine Darnall Amry Cmty. Hosp., Fort Hood, Tex., 1995—. Program chmn. Seneca Falls, N.Y. chpt. Am. Heart Assn., 1986-88; deacon First Bapt. Ch., Seneca Falls, 1986-88; sec. Geneva Camp Gideons Internat., 1986-88. Mem. AMA, Am. Coll. Physicians, Am. Soc. Tropical Medicine & Hygiene, Am. Coll. Gastroenterology, Am. Gastroenterol. Assn., Am. Soc. Gastroentestinal Endoscopists, Christian Med. and Dental Soc., Phi Kappa Phi, Rho Chi, Alpha Omega Alpha. Baptist. Office: Darnall Army Cmty Hosp Bldg 30 000 Dept Medicine Fort Hood TX 78628

PFANSTIEL PARR, DOROTHEA ANN, interior designer; b. San Antonio, Nov. 10, 1931; d. Herbert Andraes and Ethel Missouri (Turner) Pfanstiel; m. Thurmond Charles Parr, Jr., Sept. 15, 1951; children: Thurmond Charles, III, Richard Marshall. AA, Coll. San Antonio, 1951. Asst. dean evening divsn. Alamo C.C., San Antonio, 1951; tchr., cons., dir. Humpty Dumpty Early Childhood Devel. Ctr., San Antonio, 1951-58; exec. sec., cons. Thurmond C. Parr, Jr. & Co., San Antonio, 1960-61; founder, pres. Creative Designs, Ltd., San Antonio, 1962—; liaison, coord. Internat. Students Lang. Sch., Lackland AFB, San Antonio, 1959-65. Adv., cons. Urban Renewal Inner City San Antonio, 1959-61. Named Notable Woman of Tex., Awards and Hons. Soc. Am., 1984-85. Republican. Presbyterian. Office: Creative Designs Ltd PO Box 6822 San Antonio TX 78209

PFEFFERBAUM, BETTY JANE, law educator, psychiatry educator; b. Seattle, Sept. 7, 1946; d. Lois (Yager) P.; m. Richard L. Van Horn, May 29, 1988. BA, Pomona Coll., 1968; MD, U. Calif., San Francisco, 1972; JD, U. Okla., Norman, 1993. Bar: Okla. 1993; diplomate Am. Bd. Psychiatry and Neurology with subspecialty in child psychiatry. Intern pediatrics Martin Luther King Jr. Gen. Hosp., Compton, Calif., 1972-73; resident in psychiatry Neuro Psychiat. Inst., UCLA, 1973-76, fellow in child psychiatry, 1975-77; pvt. practice psychiatry, L.A., 1977-78; prof. U. Tex. Med. Sch., Houston, 1978-89; v.p. for edn. U. Tex. Health Sci. Ctr., Houston, 1987-89; prof., chief child sect. dept. psychiatry U. Okla. Health Scis. Ctr., Oklahoma City, 1989—; adj. prof. Oklahoma City U. Sch. Law, 1994—; mem. Okla. Indigent Def. Sys. Bd., 1992-93, Okla. Bd. Mental Health and Substance Abuse Svcs., 1993-99. Contbr. over 100 articles to med. jours. Grad. Leadership Tex., 1988; participant Leadership Okla., 1995. Fellow Am. Psychiat. Assn., Am. Acad. Child and Adolescent Psychiatry, Group for Advancement Psychiatry; mem. ABA, Am. Coll. Psychiatrists, Order of Coif, Phi Beta Kappa, Pi Mu Epsilon. Jewish. Home: 701 NW 14th St Oklahoma City OK 73103-2211 Office: U Okla Health Scis Ctr 920 SL Young Blvd Oklahoma City OK 73104

PFEIFFER, ANDREW HARDING, publication editor; b. L.A., Feb. 2, 1945; s. Andrew Harding and Claire Annette (Bradgate) P. BA, Wittenberg U., 1965; MA in History, Vanderbilt U., 1967. Indexer TV News Archive Vanderbilt U., Nashville, 1973-87; publ. editor Vanderbilt U., 1987—. Editor: Television News Index & Abstracts, 1987-95. Home: 2119 Bernard Ave Nashville TN 37212 Office: Vanderbilt TV News Archive 110 21st Ave S Ste 704 Nashville TN 37203

PFEIFFER, ECKHARD, computer company executive. BA, Nuremberg Business, 1963; MBA, SMU, 1983. Pres. & CEO Compaq Computer, 1991—. Office: Compaq Computer Corp 20555 State Hwy Houston TX 77070

PFEIFFER, FRED NELSON, lawyer; b. San Antonio, Jan. 21, 1938; s. Jesse Anton Pfeiffer and Irma Jene (Duval) Anhorn; m. Lea Gail Hagemann, Feb. 5, 1966 (dec. Nov. 1990); children: Nelson Layne (dec.), Jason Monroe, Michelle Lea, Kathryn Elizabeth; m. Ann Maria Watson, July 3, 1992. BS in Civil Engring., U. Tex., 1959, JD, 1962. Bar: Tex. 1962, U.S. Ct. Mil. Appelas 1967, U.S. Supreme Ct. 1967; registered profl. engr., Tex. Pvt. practice atty. San Antonio, 1963; asst. gen. counsel San Antonio River Authority, 1963-64, asst. mgr. ops., 1964-68, gen. mgr., 1968—; mem. water resources offs. adv. com. Tex. Water Resources Inst., Tex. A&M, 1972—; mem. Western State Water Coun., 1983—; mem. Tex. Adv. Commn. on Intergovtl. Rels., 1971-88, chmn., 1985-88. With Tex. Air N.G., 1962-65, comdr. USNR Res., 1965-82. Mem. Nat. Water Resources Assn. (bd. dirs. 1987—, pres. 1995-96), Tex. Water Conservation Assn. (bd. dirs. 1968—, pres. 1981-82), Tex. Soc. Profl. Engrs., San Antonio Bar Assn., Greater San Antonio C. of C., Rotary (Paul Harris fellow). Lutheran. Office: San Antonio River Authority 100 E Guenther San Antonio TX 78204-1401

PFISTER, RICHARD CHARLES, physician, radiology educator; b. Ypsilanti, Mich., Nov. 27, 1933; s. Emil Robert and Francis Josephine (LeForge) P.; m. Sally DeAnn Haight, Dec. 31, 1956 (div. 1980); children: Kirk Alan, Gary Raymond, Karen Dawn, James Kevin, William Charles. BS, Ctrl. Mich. U., 1958; MD, Wayne State U., 1962. Assoc. prof. radiology Harvard Med. Sch. and Mass. Gen. Hosp., Boston, 1966-89; med. officer FDA, Washington, 1989-90; prof. radiology U. South Ala., Mobile, 1990-92, La. State U., New Orleans, 1993—. Editor, author: Interventional Radiology, 1982. With U.S. Army Med. Corps, 1953-55. Recipient Investigator award NIH, Washington, 1972. Fellow Am. Coll. Radiology; mem. AMA, Soc. Uroradiology (pres. 1984-85), Radiologic Soc. N.Am., Am. Roentgen Ray Soc., Soc. Cardiovascular Interventional. Office: LSU Med Ctr 1542 Tulane Ave New Orleans LA 70112-2825

PFLIEGER, KENNETH JOHN, architect; b. Washington, Feb. 20, 1952; s. Chester John Pflieger and Madeline (Maben) Wineke; m. Katherine Colleran Greeves, Oct. 1, 1977; children: Kristian, Kevin, Karissa. BA in Pre-Architecture, Clemson U., 1975, MArch, 1977. Registered architect. Intern architect Clark Assocs., Inc., Anderson, S.C., 1977-80; project architect Greene & Assocs., Architects, Inc., Greenville, S.C., 1980-83, exec. v.p., 1983-89, pres., 1989-90; pres. ID/A, Anderson, S.C., 1990—; adj. lectr. Coll. Architecture, Clemson U., 1982. Bd. dirs. Hospice of Anderson, 1991—; bd. mgmt. Anderson Family YMCA, 1995—, v.p. for property mgmt.; active Anderson Mayor's Com. on Employment of People with Disabilities. Mem. AIA (bd. dirs. 1990-93, Design-merit award 1986), Std. Bldg. Code Congress Internat., Interfaith Forum Religion, Art and Arch., Nat. Trust for Hist. Preservation, Anderson Area C. of C., Kiwanis (bd. dirs. 1995—), Tau Sigma Delta. Office: ID/A 2303-C N Main St Anderson SC 29621

PFOUTS, RALPH WILLIAM, economist, consultant; b. Atchison, Kans., Sept. 9, 1920; s. Ralph Ulysses and Alice (Oldham) P.; m. Jane Hoyer, Jan. 31, 1945 (dec. Nov. 1982); children: James William, Susan Jane Pfouts Portman, Thomas Robert (dec.), Elizabeth Ann Pfouts Klenowski; m. Lois Bateson, Dec. 21, 1984 (div.); m. Felicia Sprincenatu, 1993. B.A., U. Kans., 1942, M.A., 1947; Ph.D., U. N.C., 1952. Rsch. asst., instr. econs. U. Kans., Lawrence, 1946-47; instr. U. N.C., Chapel Hill, 1947-50, lectr. econs., 1950-52, assoc. prof. econs., 1952-58, prof. econs., 1958-87, chmn. grad. studies dept. econs. Sch. Bus. Adminstrn., 1957-62, chmn. dept. econs. Sch. Bus. Adminstrn., 1962-68; cons. econs. Chapel Hill, 1987—; vis. prof. U. Leeds, 1983; vis. rsch. scholar Internat. Inst. for Applied Systems Analysis, Laxenberg, Austria, 1983; prof. Cen. European U., Prague, 1991. Author: Elementary Economics-A Mathematical Approach, 1972; editor: So. Econ. Jour, 1955-75; editor, contbr.: Techniques of Urban Economic Analysis, 1960, Essays in Economics and Econometrics, 1960; editorial bd.: Metroeconomica, 1961-80, Atlantic Econ. Jour, 1973—; contbr. articles to profl. jours. Served as deck officer USNR, 1943-46. Social Sci. Research Council fellow U. Cambridge, 1953-54; Ford Found. Faculty Research fellow, 1962-63. Mem. AAAS, Am. Statis. Assn., N.C. Statis. Assn. (past pres.), Am. Econ. Assn., So. Econ. Assn. (past pres.), Atlantic Econ. Soc. (v.p. 1973-76, pres. 1977-78), Population Assn. Am., Econometric Soc., Math. Assn. Am., Phi Beta Kappa, Pi Sigma Alpha, Alpha Kappa Psi, Omicron Delta Epsilon. Home and Office: 127 Summerlin Dr Chapel Hill NC 27514-1925

PHAGAN, PATRICIA ELAINE, museum curator; b. May 24, 1955; d. Leonard T. Jr. and Sarah Frances (Thomas) P. BA in Art, Mercer U., 1977; MA in Art History, U. Cin., 1981; MPhil, CUNY, 1989, postgrad. Curatorial intern Mus. Arts and Scis., Macon, Ga., 1983; rsch. asst. High Mus. of Art, Atlanta, 1985-87; curator of prints and drawings Ga. Mus. of Art, U. Ga., Athens, 1987—; rschr. for Jimmy Ernst's book: A Not-So-Still Life: A Child of Europe's Pre-World War II Art World and His Remarkable Homecoming to America, 1984; mem. visual arts panel Ga. Coun. for the Arts, 1996—. Curated exhbns. include Myth, Culture, Narrative: Current Prints by Six Georgia Artists, Ga. Mus. Art, 1989-90, Alan E. Cober: Suite Georgia, 1991, Charles Meryon and Jean-Francois Millet: Etchings of Urban and Rural 19th Century France, 1992-93, Adriaen van Ostate: Etchings of Peasant Life in Holland's Golden Age, 1994, The American Scene and the South: Paintings and Works on Paper, 1930-1946, 1996; contbr. articles to profl. jours. U. Cin. grad. asst., 1977-78, 78-79; CUNY Grad. Sch. grad. asst., 1982-83; CUNY grad. fellow, 1981, 82, dissertation fellow, 1989, Luce Dissertation fellow in Am. Art, 1989; NEA grantee, 1996. Mem. Coll. Art Assn., Am. Art Mus. Office: Univ of Ga Ga Mus Art Athens GA 30602

PHAN, TÂM THANH, medical educator, psychotherapist, consultant, researcher; b. Hue, Vietnam, June 10, 1949; d. Quê'Dinh and Chánh Thi (Tô) P. BA, Adams State Coll., 1979; MA, Western State Coll., 1980; PhD in Nutrition, Am. Coll. Nutrition, 1983; D of Nutrimedicine, John Kennedy Nutrisci., Gary, Ind., 1986; PhD in Counseling, Columbus Pacific U., 1988; DSc, Lafayette U., 1989. Lic. profl. counselor, marriage and family therapist; cert. nutrimedicine specialist. Counselor Lamar U., Beaumont, Tex., 1980-82; cons. Vietnamese Cmty., Golden Triangle, Tex., 1980—. The Wholistic Clinic, Beaumont, 1980—; mem. adv. bd. Internat. Homeopathic Clearance, Mo., 1993—. Author: How Western Culture..., 1988, Natural Preventive Medicine, The Wholitic Approach, 1992, How to Prevent Mental Illness, 1995, How to Prevent Diabetes, 1996. Fellow Internat. Nutrimedicine Assn., Am. Nutrimedicine Assn.; mem. Interant. Alliance of Nutrimedical Therapists, Internat. Holistic Med. Soc. (bd. dirs. 1996, Cert. of Merit 1996). Office: The Wholistic Clinic 1995 Broadway Beaumont TX 77701

PHARO, WAYNE JOSEPH, cardiologist; b. Lafayette, La., Feb. 14, 1955; married. BS, U. Southwestern La., 1976; MD, La. State U., 1981. Diplomate Am. Bd. Internal Medicine. Intern, resident Charity Hosp., New Orleans, 1981-84; fellow in cardiology Brown U. Med. Sch. and affiliated hosps., Providence, 1984-86; hosp. and emergency rm. physician St. Charles Gen. Hosp., New Orleans, 1982-84; emergency rm. physician Thibodaux (La.) Gen. Hosp., 1984, Vets. Hosp., Providence, 1985-86; active staff Thibodaux Gen. Hosp.; dir. Heart Ctr. of Lafourche, La.; cons. staff Our Lady of Sea Gen. Hosp., Galliano, Lakewood Hosp., Morgan City, South La. Med. Ctr., Houma; clin. investigator PACT Human Rsch. Rev., Biotronic Pacemakers. Contbr. articles to med. jours. Fellow Am. Coll. Angiography, Am. Coll. Cardiology, Soc. for Cardiac Angiography and Interventions; mem. AMA, ACP, Am. Heart Assn. (Am. bd. dirs.), Soc. Nuclear Medicine, Lafourche Am. Heart Assn. (pres. 1989-90), La. Assn. Bus. and Industry, La. chpt. Cardiovasc. and Pulmonary Rehab., La. State Med. Soc., Lafourche Parish Med. Soc., Thibodaux C. of C., South Lafourche C. of C., Krew of Chronus, La. State U. Alumni Assn., La. Sheriff's Assn.

PHELPS, ASHTON, JR., newspaper publisher; b. New Orleans, Nov. 4, 1945; s. Ashton Sr. and Jane Cary (George) P.; m. Mary Ella Sanders, Apr. 10, 1976; children—Cary Clifton, Mary Louise, Sanders. BA, Yale U., 1967; JD, Tulane U., 1970. Trainee Times-Picayune Pub. Corp., New Orleans, 1970-71; asst. to pub. Times-Picayune Pub. Corp., 1971-79, pres., pub., 1979—. Bd. dirs. Bur. Govtl. Rsch., New Orleans, 1973-89, Xavier U. of La., New Orleans, 1974-82, Coun. for Better La., 1982-85, Met. Area Com., New Orleans, Ochsner Found. Hosp., New Orleans, 1982—, Internat. House, New Orleans, 1981-83, Pub. Affairs Rsch., New Orleans, 1982-85, La. Children's Mus., New Orleans, 1983-90, Yale Alumni Assn. of La., 1985, Newspaper Advt. Bur. Future of Advt. Com., 1986-89; chmn. Audit Com. of Associated Press, 1986-90. Mem. So. Newspaper Pubs. Assn. (bd. dirs. 1982-85, found. bd. dirs. 1982-83, pres. 1990-91), La. Press Assn. (bd. dirs. 1984-93, v.p. 1989-90, pres. 1991-92). Office: The Times-Picayune 3800 Howard Ave New Orleans LA 70140-1002

PHELPS, CAROL JO, neuroendocrinologist; b. Sendai, Japan, Apr. 20, 1948; d. Harry J. and Helen I. (Davies) P.; m. James B. Turpen, June 13, 1969 (div. Apr. 1982); children: J. Matthew Turpen, John A. Turpen; m. David L. Hurley, Oct. 12, 1985. BS in Zoology, U. Denver, 1969; PhD in Anatomy, La. State U. Med. Ctr., 1974. Postdoctoral fellow NIH, U. Rochester, N.Y., 1974-76; rsch. assoc. Pa. State U., Univ. Park, 1976-77; instr. Pa. State U., 1977-80, postdoctoral scholar, 1980-82; asst. prof. neurobiology U. Rochester, 1982-90; assoc. prof. anatomy Tulane U. Sch. Medicine, New Orleans, 1990-94; prof., 1994—; nat. scientific adv. coun. Am. Fedn. Aging Rsch., N.Y.C., 1988—; rev. coms. Nat. Inst. on Aging, Bethesda, Md., 1993—; editl. bd. Neuroendocrinology, Paris, 1994—, Endocrinology, 1996—, Jour. of Andrology, 1996—. Com. sec., chair Otetiana Coun. Pack 10 Boy Scouts Am., Honeoye Falls, N.Y., 1987-89. NIH fellow, 1974-76; grantee NIH, 1983—. Mem. Am. Assn. Anatomists, Soc. Exptl. Biology and Medicine, Endocrine Soc., Soc. Neurosci. (chpt. pres. 1995-96). Office: Tulane U Sch Medicine Dept Anatomy 1430 Tulane Ave New Orleans LA 70112-2699

PHELPS, CHRISTOPHER PRINE, neuroscientist; b. Westfield, N.J., July 6, 1943; s. Furman Best and Alta Marie (Prine) P.; m. Elizabeth Jean Lowe, June 30, 1969; children: Jessica Elizabeth, Adam Christopher. AB, Lafayette Coll., Easton, Pa., 1965; PhD, Rutgers U., 1973. Postdoct. UCLA Sch. Med., 1973-76; from asst. prof. anatomy to prof. U. South Fla. Coll. Med., Tampa, 1976-91, prof. anatomy, 1991—, prof. pediatrics, 1994—; ad hoc reviewer NSF, Washington, 1981—; cons. NIH, Bethesda, Md., 1990—. Contbr. articles to profl. jours. including Brain Rsch., Endocrinology and Physiology and Behavior. Active Common Cause, Washington, 1971—; leader Boy Scouts Am., Fla., 1990—. Lt. (j.g.) USPHS, 1967. Busch fellow Rutgers U., 1972-73; postdoctoral grantee: NIH/Nat. Inst. Arthritis, Metabolic and Digestive Diseases, 1975-76, NIH/Nat. Inst. Child Health and Human Devel., 1978-82, Whitehall Found., Inc., 1983-86, NIMH/Alcohol and Drug Abuse, Mental Health Adminstrn., 1990-95. Mem. Endocrine Soc., Soc. for Neurosci. (officer Tampa Bay chpt.), Am. Assn. Anatomists. Office: Univ S Fla Coll Medicine Dept Anatomy MDC Box 6 HSC Tampa FL 33612-4799

PHELPS, GERRY CHARLOTTE, economist, minister; b. Norman, Okla., Oct. 15, 1931; d. George and Charlotte LeNoir (Yowell) P.; 1 child, Scott. BA, U. Tex., 1963, MA, 1984; MDiv, San Francisco Theol. Seminary, 1981. Cert. tchr., Calif. Lectr. in econs. U. Houston, 1966-69; pastor United Meth. Ch., Kelseyville, Calif., 1980-82; sr. pastor Bethany United Methodist Ch., Bakersfield, Calif., 1982-84; exec. dir. Bethany Svc. Ctr., Bakersfield, 1982-84; pres., exec. dir. Concern for the Poor, Inc., San Jose, Calif., 1985-92; pastor United Meth. Ch., Flatonia, Tex., 1993—; exec. dir. Coun. Econ. Strategies, Austin, 1992—, CRISES, Austin, 1994—. Mem. Task Force on the Homeless, San Jose, 1987, Santa Clara County, 1991. Recipient commendation Mayor of Bakersfield, 1984, Santa Clara County Bd. Suprs., 1992. Office: CRISES PO Box 4676 Austin TX 78765-4676

PHIBBS, GARNETT ERSIEL, engineer, educator, minister, religious organization administrator; b. Clinchfield, Va., Oct. 12, 1922; s. Willie McDonald and Alma Irene (Horton) P.; m. Aug. 18, 1945 (div. 1972); children: Gerald Edwin, David Miller, Robert Lee. BA, Bridgewater (Va.) Coll., 1943; MRE, Bethany Theol. Sem., 1945; MDiv, Yale U., 1952, STM, 1954; postgrad., Boston U., Princeton U., St. Louis U. Cert. tchr., Calif.; ordained min. Ch. of the Brethren, 1945. Pastor Ch. of the Brethren, Bassett, Va., 1945-50, Champaign, Ill., 1955-56, Wilmington, Del., 1956-57, Glendale, Calif., 1969-70; pastor Niantic (Conn.) Bapt. Ch., 1950-51, Congl. Ch. (now United Ch. of Christ), Killingworth, Conn., 1951-55; exec. dir. Coun. of Chs., Trenton, N.J., 1957-62, Toledo, 1962-69; exec. dir. Citizens Aiding Pub. Offenders, Toledo, 1974-76; engr. Beverly Hills (Calif.) Hotel, 1981-91; mem., cons., leader Parents Without Ptnrs., 1972-90, ; mem. Habitat for Humanity, 1989-91; cons. North Toledo Community Orgn., 1977; co-founder Rescue Crisis Svc.; founder Interfaith Housing Corp., Toledo. Author: Bethel Memory Makers, 1977; contbr. articles to profl. jours. Mem. Toledo Bd. of Cmty. Rels., 1962-69, Ohio State Civil Rights Commn. of N.W. Ohio, Toledo, 1966-68, U.S. Civil Rights Commn., Toledo, 1965-69, Planned Parenthood Bd., Sister City Com. Toledo, Spain; mem., past pres. Kiwanis Internat., 1945-69; founding bd. dirs. West Hollywood Homeless Orgn. founder Charlotte Interfaith Network for Gay and Lesbian Equality; charter mem. Common Cause, Ams. United for Separation Ch. and State. Recipient Community Svc. award NAACP, 1960, So. Calif. Regional award Parents Without Parents, 1980; named Man of the Yr., ACLU, 1969. Mem. Internat. Union Oper. Engrs., Am. Correctional Assn., Am. Assn. for Pub. Adminstrs., Calif. Assn. Marriage and Family Counselors, Halfway House Assn, Parents and Friends of Gays and Lesbians (bd. sec. Time-Out Youth). Democrat. United Church of Christ. Home: 5945 Reddman Rd Charlotte NC 28212

PHIFER, FORREST KEITH, lawyer; b. Port Arthur, Tex., Jan. 3, 1956; s. Ernest Carl and Ollie (Decker) P.; m. Teresa Darlene Jowell, Febr. 20, 1993. BFA, So. Meth. U., 1978; JD, South Tex. Coll. Law, 1988. Bar: Tex. 1989, U.S. Dist. Ct. (ea., no. and so. dists.) Tex. 1990, U.S. Ct. Appeals (5th cir.) 1990, U.S. Supreme Ct. 1994. Briefing atty. 12th Supreme Jud. Dist. Ct. Appeals, Tyler, Tex., 1989-90; assoc. Norman, Thrall, Angle & Guy, Rusk, Tex., 1990-95; city atty. Rusk, 1996—. Pres., co-founder Tyler United Meth. Dist. Singles Coun., 1989-90; bd. dirs. Cherokee County Child and Family Svcs., 1990-93, Cherokee County Health Adv. Bd., 1991—, Cherokee County Indsl. Commn., 1991—; chmn., pres. Rusk*Make It Happen, 1991-92; active So. Meth. U. TV Guild, Dallas, 1977-78, U.S.A. Film Festival, Dallas, 1978. Mem. ABA, ATLA, Tex. Trial Lawyers Assn., Tex. Criminal Def. Lawyers Assn., U.S. Fifth Cir. Bar Assn., Tex. Bar Assn., Coll. State Bar Tex. (pro bono), Cherokee County Bar Assn. (sec.-treas. 1994-95, pres. 1995-96), Rotary (pres. 1992-93), Phi Delta Phi. Office: Law Office of Forrest K Phifer 509 N Main PO Box 829 Rusk TX 75785

PHILBIN, DONALD R., JR., lawyer; b. Oklahoma City, Jan. 25, 1962; s. Donald R. and Sharon K. (Shipman) P.; m. Mary C. McGee, Oct. 9, 1993. BABA, Trinity U., San Antonio, 1984; JD, Pepperdine U., 1987. Bar: Tex., U.S. Dist. Ct. (no., so., ea. and wo. dists.) Tex., U.S. Ct. Appeals (5th and 10th cirs.), U.S. Supreme Ct. Intern U.S. Senator Don Nickles, Washington, 1983, White House, Washington, 1984; assoc. Oppenheimer, Rosenberg, Kelleher & Wheatley, Inc., San Antonio, 1987-92; ptnr. Wheatley, Campagnolo & Sessions, L.L.P., San Antonio, 1992-94, Campagnolo & Philbin, L.C., San Antonio, 1995—; mem. moot ct. bd. Pepperdine U., 1986-87. Mem. Pepperdine Law Rev., 1985-87. Alumni advisor, ex officio mem. bd. trustees Trinity U., 1993-95. Recipient Am. Jurisprudence awards, 1986-87. Mem. Am. Inns of Ct. Home: 208 Luther Dr San Antonio TX 78209

PHILBRICK, JOHN TRACY, medical educator; b. Richmond, Va., Feb. 15, 1947; s. Robert Lawrence and Jane Tower (Arnold) P.; m. Mary Elizabeth Ropka, Oct. 21, 1978; children: Peter Tracy, Michael Bradford. BA, Harvard Coll., 1969; MD, Harvard Med. Sch., Boston, 1973. Diplomate Am. Bd. Internal Medicine, Am. Bd. Emergency Medicine. Intern SUNY, Buffalo, 1973-74, resident, 1976-78; asst. prof. medicine U. Va., Charlottesville, 1980-89, assoc. prof. medicine, 1989—. Lt. USPHS, 1974-76. Fellow ACP. Office: U Va Sch Medicine PO Box 494 Charlottesville VA 22908-0494

PHILIPP, ANITA MARIE, computer sciences educator; b. Evergreen Park, Ill., Sept. 7, 1948; d. Benedict Anthony and Anne Therese (Bolf) Butkus; m. Leslie Howard Philipp, Sept. 6, 1975; children: Leslie Aaron, Renée Marie. BA in Elem. Edn., St. Norbert Coll., 1969; MEd in Ednl. Media, U. Okla., 1978; student, Okla. City C.C., 1980-93, U. Ctrl. Okla., 1994-95. Cert. tchr., Okla., audio-visual specialist, Okla. Tchr. fifth grade Green Bay (Wis.) Bd. Edn., 1970; social ins. rep. Social Security Adminstrn., Chgo., 1970-73; ops. supr. Social Security Adminstrn., Evanston, Ill., 1973; employee devel. specialist Social Security Adminstrn., Chgo., 1973-76; claims rep. Social Security Adminstrn., Oklahoma City, 1976-77, ops. analyst, 1977-78; adj. instr. computer sci. Okla. City C.C., 1985-96; dir. computer edn. St. James Sch., Oklahoma City, 1987-93; adj. instr. computer sci. U. Ctrl. Okla., Edmond, 1996; prof. computer sci. Okla. City C.C., 1996—; ednl. computer cons., 1989—; faculty advisor St. James Light Newspaper; mem. restaurant evaluation team Dunn-Farley Enterprises, San Marcos, Calif., 1978-85. EEO counselor Social Security Adminstrn., Chgo., 1972-73, coord. info. and referral svcs., 1982-83; leader Campfire Girls, Oklahoma City, 1986-89; mem. St. James Sch. Bd. Edn., Oklahoma City, 1987 (St. James sch. devel. com., 1990—, chairperson, interim devel. dir., 1994-96); eucharistic min. St. James Ch. Named among Top 25 Tchrs., Apple Computer/Homeland Stores, 1990. Roman Catholic. Home: 2209 Laneway Cir Oklahoma City OK 73159-5827 Office: Okla City CC 7777 S May Ave Oklahoma City OK 73159-4419

PHILIPPE, SCOTT LOUIS, optometrist; b. Ft. Thomas, Ky., May 31, 1963; s. Jack Joseph and Betty Jane (Mooar) P.; m. Michelle Annette, June 23, 1990. Student, U. Ky., 1981-84; OD, So. Coll. Optometry, 1988. Optometry extern Carolina Optometry Group, Cary, N.C., 1987, Ft. Lee Army Med. Hosp., Petersburg, Va., 1987; optometrist Dr. Jay Philippe, Parker, Colo., 1988-89, Carolina Optometry Group, Charlotte, N.C., 1989-91; pres. Charlotte Optometry Group, PA, 1991—. Participating doctor Vision USA/Am. Optometric Assn., Charlotte, 1991; mem. Hickory Grove United Meth. Choral, 1990—. Mem. Am. Optometric Assn. (contact lens sect. 1988—), N.C. State Optometric Soc. (exec. coun.), Piedmont Optometric Soc.(pres.), Charlotte Rugby Football Club, Phi Gamma Delta. Republican. Home: 8240 County Downs Ln Charlotte NC 28270-0937 Office: 8701 JW clay Blvd Charlotte NC 28262

PHILIPS, CHRISTINE ANN, healthcare executive; b. Atlanta, June 14, 1938; d. Eric Brook and Ann (Dunbar) B.; m. Charles Flemming Philips, June 7, 1959 (div. 1981); children: Christine Ann Clark, Laura Barton Tripp. AA, St. Petersburg (Fla.) Jr. Coll, 1958. Exec. v.p. Pinellas Assn. for Retarded Children, St. Petersburg, 1963-84; exec. dir. Palm Beach Habilitation Ctr., Lake Worth, Fla., 1984—; cons. in field. Pres. United Way Execs. of Palm Beach County, 1994—. Recipient Disting. Svc. award Fla. Assn. Pvt. Residential Svcs. for Mentally Retarded, 1979, Merit award Fla. Dept. Health and Rehab. Svcs., 1980, Michael Goodman award, 1989. Fellow Am. Assn. on Mental Deficiency (Richard B. Dillard southeastern chpt. 1981); mem. Fla. Assn. Rehab. Facilities (bd. dirs. 1986—, Disting. Svc. award 1993), Civitan, Jr. League, Palm Beach Yacht Club. Republican. Episcopalian. Home: 323 Live Oak Ln Boynton Beach FL 33436-7107 Office: Palm Beach Habilitation Ctr 4522 Congress Ave Lake Worth FL 33461-4709

PHILIPS, JOSEPH BOND, III, medical educator; b. Durham, N.C., Mar. 29, 1949; s. Joseph Bond and Sara (Summerlin) P.; divorced; children: Joseph Bond IV, Ian Mallonee. BS in Chemistry cum laude, Washington and Lee U., 1971; MD, U. N.C., 1975. Diplomate Nat. Bd. Med. Examiners, Am. Bd. Pediatrics, Am. Bd. Neonatal-Perinatal Medicine; lic. physician, Ala., N.C. Intern in pediatrics Mt. Siani Hosp., N.Y.C., 1975-76, resident in pediatrics, 1976-77; resident in pediatrics Duke U., Durham, 1977-78; fellow in neonatal-perinatal medicine U. Fla., Gainesville, 1978-80; asst. prof. pediatrics U. Ala., Birmingham, 1980-85, asst. prof. ob-gyn., 1980-87, asst. prof. physiology and biophysics, 1982—, assoc. prof. pediatrics, 1985—, assoc. prof. ob-gyn., 1987—, mem. staff Univ. Hosp.; mem. staff Children's Hosp. Ala., Birmingham, Cooper Green Hosp., Birmingham; mem. region III perinatal adv. com. State of Ala., 1980-85, 1993-96, region VIII perinatal adv. com., 1990-91; mem. ad hoc com. on obstet. care; mem. neonatal ICUs network steering com., chmn. Tolazoline protocol subcom. Nat. Inst. Child Health and Human Devel., 1986-91; vis. assoc. prof. molecular physiology and biol. physics U. Va., 1992-93; mem. ad hoc rev. team Nat. Heart Lung and Blood Inst.; invited lectr. in field. Editor-in-chief Neonatology Grand Rounds., 1984-87; mem. editorial bd. Continuing Edn. for Family Physician, 1980-87, Neonatology Letter, 1982-83; ad hoc reviewer Jour. Pediatrics, Pediatrics, Pediatrics Rsch., Pediatric Pharmacology, Ala. Jour. Med. Scis., Proceedings Soc. for Exptl. Biology and Medicine, Am. Jour. Med. Scis., Devel. Pharmacology and Therapeutics, Can. Jour. Physiology and Pharmacology Jour. Ob-Gyn., Jour. Thoracic and Cardiovascular Surgery, Jour. Vascular Rsch.; contbr. over 156 articles and abstracts to profl. jours., 9 chpts. to books. Robert E. Lee scholar Washington & Lee U., 1968-71; Nat. Rsch. Svc award, sr. fellow Nat. Heart, Lung and Blood Inst., 1992-93, grantee, 1987-90; grantee Ala. Dept. Pub. Health, 1989-91 (2 grants), Burroughs Wellcome, Inc., 1989-90, 91, 91-92, Sherwood Med., 1985-86, Ross Labs., 1985-87, NICHD, 1986-91, NICDH/Nat. Heart, Lung and Blood Inst., 1988-91, 92-93. Mem. AAAS, Am. Acad. Pediatrics, Am. Heart Assn. (grantee 1984-87), Nat. Perinatal Assn., Soc. for Pediatric Rsch., Soc. Critical Care Medicine (Young Investigator award 1985), European Soc. for Pediatric Rsch., Internat. Soc. for Heart Rsch., So. Soc. for Pediatric Rsch. (coord. chmn. perinatal medicine sessions 1990, coord. chmn. poster symposium 1992), Ala. Acad. Sci., Ala. Perinatal Assn., Ala. Soc. Neonatology, Jefferson County Pediatric Soc., Alpha Epsilon Delta. Democrat. Office: U Ala Birmingham 525 Hillman Bldg Birmingham AL 35233

PHILLIPS, ALFREDO O., bank executive; b. Matamoros, Mex., Sept. 2, 1935; s. Howard and Dolores (Olmedo) P.; m. Maureen Greene, Sept. 6, 1960; children: Alfredo, Ricardo, Adriana. Student, U. Mex., 1955, U. London, 1960. Advisor income tax divsn. Mex. Ministry of Fin., 1960-62, chief fiscal planning dept., 1962-63, dep. head banking dept., 1963-65; loan officer Interam. Devel. Bank, Washington, 1965-66; exec. dir. Internat. Monetary Fund, Washington, 1966-70; dep. dir. Bank of Mex., Mexico City, 1970-82; dir. gen., CEO Nat. Fgn. Trade Bank, Mex., 1982-88; ambassador to Can. Mex. Govt., Ottawa, 1989-91; ambassador to Japan Mex. Govt., Tokyo, 1991-92; dep. sec. for housing Mex. Dept. Social Devel., 1992-94; dir. gen., CEO Infonavit, Mex., 1994; mng. dir. N.Am. Devel. Bank, San Antonio, 1995—. Recipient decorations from Brazil, Peru, Venezuela. Office: NAm Devel Bank 425 Soledad Ste 610 San Antonio TX 78205

PHILLIPS, BERNICE CECILE GOLDEN, retired vocational education educator; b. Galveston, Tex., June 30, 1920; d. Walter Lee and Minnie (Rothsprack) Golden; m. O. Phillips, Mar. 1950 (dec.); children: Dorian Lee, Loren Francis. BBA cum laude, U. Tex., 1945; MEd, U. Houston, 1968. cert. tchr., tchr. coord., vocat. tchr., Tex. Dir. Delphian Soc., Houston, 1955-60; bus. tchr. various private schs., Houston area, 1960-65; vocat. tchr. coord. office edn. program Pasadena (Tex.) Ind. Sch. Dist., 1965-68, Houston Ind. Sch. Dist., John H. Reagan High Sch., 1968-85. Bd. dirs. Regency House Condominium Assn., 1991-93. Recipient numerous awards and recognitions for vocat. bus. work at local and state levels. Mem. AAUW (life, Houston Br. v.p. ednl. found. 1987-90, pres. 1992-94, bd. dirs. 1987-96), NEA, Nat. Bus. Edn. Assn. Am. Vocat. Assn. (life), Tex. State Tchrs. Assn. (life), Tex. Classroom Tchrs. Assn. (life), Tex. Bus. Edn. Assn. (emeritus), Vocat. Office Edn. Tchrs. Assn. Tex. (past bd. dirs.), Greater Houston Bus. Edn. Assn. (reporter), Houston Assn. Ret. Tchrs., Tex. Assn. Ret. Tchrs., Delta Pi Epsilon (emeritus), Beta Gamma Sigma. Home: 2701 Westheimer Rd 8H Houston TX 77098-1235

PHILLIPS, BETTIE MAE, elementary school educator; b. Ft. Worth, May 2, 1941; d. Robert Sr. and Charittie Barnes; m. George Vernon Phillips Sr., Aug. 29, 1960 (div. Aug. 1985); 1 child, George Vernon Jr. BS in Elem. Edn., Bishop Coll., 1967; MEd in Early Childhood Edn., East Tex. State U., 1976. Tchr. Dallas Ind. Sch. Dist., 1968—. Author: The Whole Armor, 1979, Petals, 1988, Lights in the Shadows, 1993; composer children's songs Bettie's Songs, Vol. 1, 1987, God's Cloud and There's Love Everywhere, 1994 (recorded by Hilltop Records, included in album America), You and I Free Your Score (recorded by Hilltop Records, included in album Hilltop Country), 1995. Mem. Classroom Tchrs. Dallas. Baptist. Home: 1312 Mill Stream Dr Dallas TX 75232-4604 Office: Bayles Elem Sch 2444 Telegraph Ave Dallas TX 75228-5819

PHILLIPS, BRUCE HAROLD, lawyer; b. Little Rock, Feb. 5, 1962; s. Philip Kirkland and Jayne (Jack) L.; m. Nancy Lee Williams, Nov. 12, 1994. BA in Bus. Adminstrn., U. Ark., Little Rock, 1988; JD, U. Ark., Fayetteville, 1993. Bar: Ark. 1993, Tenn. 1994, U.S. Dist. Ct. (mid. dist.) Tenn. 1994, U.S. Ct. Appeals (6th cir.) 1995. Golf profl. Internat. Golf, Little Rock, 1982-85, Tee-to-Green Golf, Little Rock, 1985-89; assoc. Jack, Lyon & Jones, P.A., Nashville, 1993—. Mem. Phi Alpha Delta. Office: Jack Lyon & Jones PA 11 Music Cir S Nashville TN 37203-4335

PHILLIPS, DAVID GARDINER, V, fundraising consultant; b. Columbia, S.C., Sept. 2, 1958; s. David Gardiner IV and Ruth Preston (Stone) P.; m. Margaret Mary Cronmiller, July 29, 1989; children: Mary Elizabeth, Isabel Gardiner, David Gardiner. BS in Acctg., U. S.C., 1984. Auditor Owen Steel Co., Columbia, S.C., 1984-85; exec. campaign dir. Cmty. Counselling Svc., N.Y.C., 1986-93; chief devel. officer Spoleto Festival, Charleston, 1994-95; pres., CEO Custom Devel. Solutions, Charleston, 1996—. Mem. Nat. Soc. Fundraising Execs. (low county chpt.), Charleston C. of C., Data Processing Mgmt. Assn., Better Bus. Bur., Rotary (Charleston, Breakfast). Democrat. Presbyterian. Home: 4 Allie Ct Isle Of Palms SC 29451 Office: Custom Devel Solutions 4 Allie Ct Isle Of Palms SC 29451

PHILLIPS, DENISE, critical care nurse; b. Orange, N.J., July 11, 1960; d. James Henry Phillips and Gracie Estelle (Reed) Brown. Diploma in nursing, Riverside Hosp. Sch. Nursing, Newport News, Va., 1985; cert. in paralegal studies, Hampton U., 1990. RN, Va., Fla., Md., N.Y.; cert. BLS instr., ACLS; instr. cert. nurse asst. and LPN programs. Nurse asst. Riverside Hosp., Newport News, 1981-86; Riverside Hosp. Riverside Regional Med. Ctr., Newport News, 1986-91; staff nurse Traveling Nurse Corp., Malden, Mass., 1991-93; dir. staff devel. Va. Health Svcs., Inc., Newport News, 1993-95; asst. dir. nursing svcs. James Pointe Care Ctr., Newport News, Va., 1995—; per diem nurse adminstr. Sentara Hampton (Va.) Gen. Hosp., 1994—; asst. dir. of nursing svcs. James Point Care Ctr., Newport News, Va., 1995—; LPN, cert. nurse asst. instr. Career Devel. Ctr., Newport News, 1989-91; lectr. on decreasing profl. liability for healthcare workers, 1990—. Contbr. article to Health Care Digest, 1995. Vol. Williamsburg (Va.) area Girl Scouts U.S., 1990-92. Mem. ACCN, Nat. League of Nursing. Home: 7402 Vernon Pl Newport News VA 23605 Office: 5015 Huntington Ave Newport News VA 23605

PHILLIPS, DON LEE, nursing administrator; b. Kermit, Tex., Oct. 20, 1947; s. Gilbert M. and Mayrene E. (Eubanks) P.; m. Danna Oelker, Aug. 7, 1971; children: Don L. Jr., Charles. ADN, Grayson County Coll., Denison, Tex., 1985. ACLS, ATLS, CEN. Staff nurse operating rm. North Tex. Med Ctr., McKinney, 1985-86, staff nurse emergency rm., 1986-87, charge nurse emergency rm., 1990-91, house supr., 1991-93, med./surge., pediatric mgr., 1993—; operating rm. supr. HCA Wysung Med. Ctr., McKinney, 1987-88; asst. DON Northeast Med. Ctr., Bonham, Tex., 1988-90; cons. and surveyor for acute care hosps. and home health agencies Tex. Dept. Health, 1995—. Coun. adv. bd. Boy Scouts Am., Paris, 1989—, advancement chmn. exec. bd., 1989—. With USN, 1969-71. Mem. Tex. Nursing Students Assn. (state v.p. 1985), Southwest Football Officials Assn., Lions (v.p. 1975), Elks. Home and Office: Rt 3 Box 87B2 Bonham TX 75418

PHILLIPS, DOROTHY ALEASE, lay church worker, educator, freelance writer; b. Durham, N.C., May 11, 1924; d. Clarence Robert and Addie Lee (Outen) Hicks; m. Chester Raymond Phillips, Oct. 10, 1942; children: Cynthia Kaye, Dean Hayward, Kent Vincent. BS in Edn. and English, Bob Jones U., 1954; M in Edn., East Carolina U., 1970. Cert. secondary tchr., N.C. Former writer, illustrator Sunday sch. lit. Ayden (N.C.) Press.; former nat. youth chmn. women's aux. Free Will Bapts.; dir. pub. rels. and Christian edn. Heritage Bapt. Ch., Johnson City, Tenn., 1980-91; tchr. Four Oaks (N.C.) H.S., 1955-56, Smithfield (N.C.) H.S., 1956-61, Farmville (N.C.) H.S., 1963-65, Rose H.S., Greenville, 1965-76, Univ. H.S., Johnson City, Tenn., 1976-78; participant Blue Ridge Mountain Christian Writers Conf., Black Mountain, N.C.; former thcr. journalism Rose H.S., Greenville, N.C.; mem. choirs, Sunday sch. tchr. various Bapt. chs.; speaker at women's retreats and seminars. Home: 1601 Paty Dr Johnson City TN 37604-7636

PHILLIPS, ELVIN WILLIS, lawyer; b. Tampa, Fla., Feb. 27, 1949; s. Claude Everett and Elizabeth (Willis) P.; m. Sharon Gayle Alexander, June 20, 1970; children: Natasha Hope, Tanya Joy, Trey Alexander. BA, U. Fla., 1971; MA, Western Carolina U., 1974, EdS, 1975; JD, Stetson U., 1980. Bar: Fla. 1980, U.S. Dist. Ct. (mid. dist.) Fla. 1981, U.S. Dist. Ct. (so. dist.) Fla. 1982, U.S. Ct. Appeals (11th cir.) 1988. Tchr. Monroe County Schs., Key West, Fla., 1970-73; asst. prin. Habersham County Schs., Clarksville, Ga., 1973-77; assoc. Dixon, Lawson & Brown, Tampa, Fla., 1980-81, Yado, Keel, Nelson et al, Tampa, Fla., 1981; ptnr. Lawson, McWhirter, Grandoff & Reeves, Tampa, Fla., 1981-88, Williams, Parker, Harrison, Dietz & Getzen, Sarasota, Fla., 1988—. Leadership Devel. Program fellow Southern Regional Coun., Atlanta, 1975. Mem. ABA (forum com. constrn. industry 1989-96), Fla. Bar (chmn. 1991-92, vice chmn. 1990-91, mem. benefits com.), Sarasota County Bar Assn., Phi Kappa Phi, Phi Alpha Delta, Phi Delta Kappa. Democrat. Baptist. Home: 3310 Del Prado Ct Tampa FL 33614-2721 Office: Williams Parker Harrison Dietz & Getzen 200 S Orange Ave Sarasota FL 34236-6802

PHILLIPS, FRED YOUNG, technology management educator, researcher; b. Phila., Mar. 11, 1952; s. Herbert Phillips and Cecelia Brandt; m. Hyonsook Oh, July 1, 1979; children: Anna Grace, Gina Dawn. BA, U. Tex., 1972, PhD, 1978; postgrad., Tokyo Inst. Tech., 1975-76. Lectr. grad. ctr. for mgmt. studies U. Birmingham, Eng., 1971; lectr. Aston U., Birmingham, 1971, St. Edwards U., Austin, Tex., 1974; jr. mathematician Gen. Motors Research Labs., Warren, Mich., 1972; research fellow Toyota Co., Tokyo, 1975-76; research assoc. IC2 Inst., U. Tex., Austin, 1976-77, sr. research fellow, 1984—; dir. research and devel. MRCA Info. Services, Austin, 1978-86, v.p., 1986-89; rsch. program dir. IC2 Inst. U. Tex., Austin, Tex., 1989-95; prof., dept. head dept. mgmt. in sci. and tech. Oreg. Grad. Inst., Portland, 1995—; cons., bd. dirs. Biochron Corp., Bethesda, Md., 1984—; cons. Intelliquest, Inc., Austin, 1988; affiliate staff scientist Battelle Pacific N.W. Labs., 1996—. Mem. editl. bd. Mktg. Sci., 1980—, Technol. Forecasting & Social Change, 1996—; contbr. articles on ops. rsch., mktg. and regional sci. to profl. jours. Mem. Informs, Am. Mktg. Assn. (bd. dirs., v.p. fin. Austin chpt. 1986-88), Info. Industries Assn., Western Regional Sci. Assn., Aikido Assn. Am. (bd. dirs. 1979-81, head instr. Tex. 1984-89), Phi Beta Kappa.

PHILLIPS, GARY LEE, principal; b. Hendersonville, N.C., Apr. 28, 1946; s. Claude E. and Catherine Mamie (Lance) P.; m. Barbara Huddleston, June 5, 1976; 1 child, Bartlett Hamilton. BS in Edn., Maryville Coll., 1968; MEd, Ga. State U., 1976; EdS, West Ga. Coll., 1990. Cert. health phys. edn., driver edn. tchr., adminstrn. supervision. Principal Fayette County High Sch., Fayetteville, Ga.; asst. principal Fayette County High Sch.; athletic dir., head football coach Fulton County Bd. Edn., Atlanta; asst. principal, head football coach Johnson County High Sch., Wrightsville, Ga.; asst. football coach, head track coach Cen. Macon (Ga.) High Sch.; coached 1982 Heisman Trophy winner Herschel Walker, Johnson County High Sch.; speaker in field; presenter seminars. Mem. Vision Statement Com., 1988-89, Media Svcs. Com., 1988, Blue Ribbon Com., 1994, co-chair Schs. Overcrowding Com. Named Coach of Yr., Ga. Athletic Coaches Assn., 7 times, Mid. Ga. Coach of Yr., 1979-80, Class A Coach of Yr., 1978; named one of Young Men of Achievement, 1972; recipient Hon. Chpt. Farmer of Yr. award Future Farmers Am., 1988. Mem. ASCD, Ga. Assn. Ednl. Leaders, Ga. Assn. Secondary Sch. Prins., Phi Delta Kappa (rsch. coord. 1992, pres. region 4AAAA 1994, 95, 96—, Excellence in Adminstrn. award 1991). Office: Fayette County High Sch Fayetteville GA 30214

PHILLIPS, GEORGE LANDON, prosecutor; b. Fulton, Miss., May 24, 1949; s. Gilbert L. and Grace (Staker) P. BS, U. So. Miss., 1971; JD, U. Miss., 1973. Bar: Miss. 1973. Assoc. Johnson, Pittman & Pittman, Hattiesburg, Miss., 1980-94; ptnr. Norris & Phillips, 1975-76; county pros. atty. Forrest County, Miss., 1976-80; U.S. atty. So. Dist. Miss., Jackson, Miss., 1980-94; chmn. investigative agys. subcom. U.S. Atty. Gen.'s Adv. Com., 1983-86, mem. law enforcement coordination subcom. and budget subcom., 1986-88; spl. coun. U.S. Senator T. Cochran, 1995—; chmn. AGAC subcom. law enforcement cooperation and victim/witness assistance, 1989-94; instr. Hattiesburg Police Acad., 1977. Bd. dirs. Forrest County Youth Ct.; pres. South Ctrl. chpt. ARC, 1980-81; bd. dirs. Pine Burr Area coun. Boy Scouts Am.; mem. Atty. Gen.'s Adv. Com., 1981-82, 89-91; bd. dirs. Jackson Zoo, 1989-91. Mem. Miss. Prosecutors Assn. (pres.), Fed. Bar Assn., Miss. Bar Assn. (v.p. southern region), Am. Criminal Justice Assn., Nat. Dist. Attys. Assn., Miss. Trial Lawyers, Miss. Quarter Horse Assn. (pres.), Kiwanis. Baptist. Office: Spl Counsel Office of US Sen T Cochran 188 E Capital Ste 614 Jackson MS 39201-2125

PHILLIPS, JAMES DICKSON, JR., federal judge; b. Scotland County, N.C., Sept. 23, 1922; s. James Dickson and Helen (Shepherd) P.; m. Jean Duff Nunalee, July 16, 1960; children: Evelyn, James Dickson, III, Elizabeth Duff, Ida Wills. BS cum laude, Davidson Coll., 1943; JD, U. N.C., 1948. Bar: N.C. 1948. Asst. dir. Inst. Govt., Chapel Hill, N.C., 1948-49; ptnr. firm Phillips & McCoy, Laurinburg, N.C., 1949-55, Sanford, Phillips, McCoy & Weaver, Fayetteville, N.C., 1955-60; from asst. prof. to prof. law U. N.C., 1960-78, dean Sch. Law, 1964-74; circuit judge U.S. Ct. Appeals (4th cir.), 1978—; Mem. N.C. Wildlife Resources Commn., 1961-63; mem. N.C. Cts. Commn., 1963-75; also vice chmn.; chmn. N.C. Bd. Ethics, 1977-78. Served with parachute inf. U.S. Army, 1943-46. Decorated Bronze Arrowhead, Bronze Star, Purple Heart; recipient John J. Parker Meml. award, Thomas Jefferson award, Disting. Alumnus award U. N.C., 1993. Mem. Am. Law Inst. Democrat. Presbyterian.

PHILLIPS, JANE ELLEN, education educator; b. Phila., Sept. 27, 1943; d. Charles Alvan and Dorothy Lilian (Person) P.; m. Vance P. Packard, Aug. 28, 1965 (div. 1973); m. James G. Harrison, Jr., June 24, 1994. BA, Millersville State Coll., 1965; PhD, U. N.C., 1969. Asst. prof. U. N.C., Chapel Hill, 1969-71; from asst. to assoc. prof. U. Ky., Lexington, 1973-92, prof., 1992—, dir. undergrad. studies dept. classics, 1976-88, acting chair dept. classics, 1982, 89, chair dept. classics, 1989—; vis. asst. prof. Ohio State U., summer 1970; adj. instr. Dickinson Coll., 1971-72, Franklin and Marshall Coll., 1971-72, vis. asst. prof., 1972-73; liaison officer for state Latin tchrs. U. N.C., 1969-71; faculty coun. coll. arts and scis. U. Ky., 1979-82, chair, 1981-82, 85-88, com. on ednl. programs self-study, 1980-81, chair subcom. on instrn., ad hoc com. on priorities and plans, 1982-83, 83-84; core faculty Gov. Acad. for Tchrs. Fgn. Languages/U. Tenn., Knoxville, summer 1989; vis. assoc. prof. U. Toronto, 1990-91; sr. fellow Ctr. for Reformation and Renaissance Studies/Victoria U./U. Toronto, 1987-88; cons. dept. classics U. Tenn., 1985-86; sect. organizer Ky. Fgn. Lang. Conf., 1979, 85-86; faculty adviser Tau chpt. Eta Sigma Phi, 1985-88; panelist fellowship cmpetition NEH, 1992-93. Translator, annotator: Collected Works of Erasmus, vol. 46: Paraphrase on John; editor: Erasmus of Rotterdam Society Yearbook, 1993—; translator: Classical Outlook, 1973-74, 77, 81; co-editor: (poetry) Classical Outlook, 1989—; referee Classical Outlook, Classical Jour.; mem. adv. bd., features editor Classical and Modern Lit.; editl. bd. Collected Works of Erasmus, 1992—. Lay min., mng. com. mem. St. Andrew's Episcopal Ch., Lexington, 1980-95; steering and selection com. mem. Hellenic Awards Program, Lexington, 1991—. Woodrow Wilson fellow, 1965-66, Univ. Svc. fellow, 1965-66, NDEA Title IV fellow 1966-69, NEH fellow, 1975-76; grantee Am. Coun. Learned Soc., 1972-73, U. Ky. Rsch. Found., 1974, NEH, 1977-78, 89, U. Ky, 1979. Mem. Archaeol. Inst. Am. (v.p. Lancaster Soc. 1972-73), Am. Philol. Assn. (com. mem. on status women and minorities 1977-80, com. mem. on smaller classics depts. 1982-84, campus adv. svcs. 1992-94), Am. Classical League (nominating com. mem. 1989), Am. Assn. for Neo-Latin Studies, Classical Assn. the Middle West and South (v.p. Ky. 1974-81, com. mem. for promotion Latin mem. 1979-82, chair 1981-82, exec. com. mem. 1993—, program com. mem. 1992-94), Nat. Com. for Latin and Greek, Internat. Assn. for Neo-Latin Studies, Assn. Ancient Historians, Vergilian Soc. (trustee 1980-82, chair scholarship com. 1982), Classical Assn. Southwestern U.S., N.C. Classical Assn. (sec./treas. 1969-70, editor Susquehanna chpt. newsletter 1972-73), Ky. Classical Assn. (editor newsletter 1976-86, pres. 1977-78, exec. bd. 1978-86), Ky. Coun. Tchrs. Fgn. Langs. (bd. dirs. 1977-78), Women's Classical Caucus (clearing house panel 1976, referee 1977), Erasmus Rotterdam Soc. Democrat. Episcopalian. Office: Univ Kentucky Dept of Classics 1015 Patterson Office Tower Lexington KY 40506-0027

PHILLIPS, JEFFREY EDWARD, writer, editor; b. Hartford, Conn., June 1, 1957; s. Edward Finley and Carolyn (Borstel) P. BA in Journalism, U. Mass., 1979. Commd. 2d lt. U.S. Army, 1979, advanced through grades to maj., 1992; line officer Fed. Republic of Germany, 1979-82, Ky., 1982-83, Tex., 1983-88, Israel, Egypt, 1988-89; media rels. officer Corps and Ft. Hood (Tex.) Pub. Affairs Office, 1989-90; pub. affairs officer 1st Cavalry Div., Ft. Hood, 1990-92; writer, editor, 1992—; pub. Taylor Pub. Co., Dallas. Author: America's First Team in the Gulf, 1992; editor: Warren, 1993. Participant in UN Peace Keepers force and Operation Desert Shield and Desert Storm. Home and Office: 614 S 1st St Apt 320 Austin TX 78704-1127

PHILLIPS, JOHN A(TLAS), III, geneticist, educator; b. Sanford, N.C., Jan. 24, 1944; s. John A. and Rachael (Sloan) P.; m. Gretchen Lynch, Aug. 1, 1965; children: Jennifer Allene, John Atlas IV, Charles Andrew, James William. Student, U. N.C., 1962-65; MD, Wake Forest U., 1969. Diplomate Am. Bd. Pediatrics, Am. Bd. Med. Genetics. Intern Children's Hosp. Med. Ctr., Boston, 1969-70, jr. resident, 1970-71, sr. resident, 1973-74, chief resident, 1974-75; asst. prof. Johns Hopkins U., Balt., 1978-82, assoc. prof., 1982-84; prof. pediatrics Vanderbilt U., Nashville, 1984—, prof. biochemistry, 1986—, David T. Karzon chair genetics, 1992—; bd. sci. counselors Nat. Inst. Child Health, Washington, 1984-88; counsilor Ctr. Study Polymorphisme Humain, Paris, 1988—; mem. adv. com. Ctr. Reproductive Biology, Nashville, 1990—; bd. dirs. March of Dimes Birth Defects Found., Nashville, 1986—; mem. adv. bd. Nat. Neurofibromatosis Found., Tenn., 1990—; mem. Tenn. Genetics Adv. Com., Nashville, 1984—. Contbr. to profl. publs. Lt. comdr. USNR, 1971-73. Recipient Sidney Farber award Children's Hosp., Boston, 1975, E Mead Johnson award Mead Johnson Co., 1984; Pediatric Postdoctoral fellow Johns Hopkins U. Sch. Medicine, 1975-77. Mem. Am. Soc. Clin. Investigation, Soc. Pediatric Rsch., Am. Coll. Med. Genetics (founding, bd. dirs. 1995—), Phi Beta Kappa, Alpha Omega Alpha. Office: Vanderbilt U Dept Genetics DD 2205 Med Ctr N Nashville TN 37232

PHILLIPS, JOHN BOMAR, lawyer; b. Murfreesboro, Tenn., Jan. 28, 1947; s. John Bomar Sr. and Betty Blanche (Primm) P.; m. Ellen Elizabeth Ellis, Aug. 9, 1969; children: John Bomar III, Anna Carroll, Ellis Elizabeth. BS, David Lipscomb Coll., 1969; JD, U. Tenn., 1974. Bar: Tenn. 1974, U.S. Dist. Ct. (ea. dist.) Tenn. 1975, U.S. Tax Ct. 1976, U.S. Ct. Appeals (6th cir.) 1980. Assoc. Stophel, Caldwell & Heggie, Chattanooga, 1974-79; ptnr. Caldwell, Heggie & Helton, Chattanooga, 1979-91, Miller & Martin, Chattanooga, 1991—. Author: Tennessee Employment Law, 1989, 2d edit. 1992, Employment Law Desk Book for Tennessee Employers, 1989; editor: The Tennessee Employment Law Update, 1986—; mem. nat. moot ct. team U. Tenn. Law Rev. Pres. Chattanooga State coll. Found., 1992-94, Boys Club of Chattanooga, 1983-84; sec. Tenn. Aquarium, 1989—; chmn. Chattanooga Conv. and Visitors Bur., 1996—; bd. dirs. Vol. Comty. Sch., Chattanooga, 1980-85, Coun. for Alcohol and Drug Abuse, Chattanooga, 1981-83, Creative Discovery Mus., 1994—; mem. Hamilton County Juvenile Ct. Commn., 1995—. Fellow Tenn. Bar Found.; mem. ABA (labor law sect.), Tenn. Bar Assn. (chair labor law sect. 1992-93, Justice Joseph W. Henry award 1986-87), Chattanooga Bar Assn. (bd. govs. 1978-79), Order of Coif, Fairyland Country Club (Lookout Mountain, Tenn.), Walden Club (bd. govs. 1992-95), Mountain City Club, Kiwanis (pres. Chattanooga 1986-87). Mem. Disciples of Christ. Home: 1107 E Brow Rd Lookout Mountain TN

37350-1015 Office: Miller & Martin 832 Georgia Ave Ste 1000 Chattanooga TN 37402-2291

PHILLIPS, JOHN D., media company executive. CEO Metromedia Internat. Group Inc., Atlanta. Office: Metromedia Internat Group Inc Ste 2210 945 E Paces Ferry Rd Atlanta GA 30326-1125

PHILLIPS, JOHN DAVID, communications executive; b. Charlotte, N.C., Nov. 27, 1942; s. Louis and A. Viola (Pack) P.; m. Cheryl Helen Rudd; children: Hunter, Scott, Andrew, Lauren. Student, U. Va., 1962-63. Pres. RMS Distbg., Frankfurt, West Germany, 1965-66, NGK Spark Plugs, Atlanta, 1967-82; pres., chief exec. officer Advanced Telecommunication, Atlanta, 1982-88, also bd. dirs., 1982-88; owner Specialized Hauling Trucking Co., 1987-89; pres., CEO Resurgens Comm. Group, Inc., Atlanta, 1989-93; pres., CEO, bd. dirs. Actava Group, Inc., Atlanta, 1994-95; pres., CEO Metromedia Group Internat. Inc., 1995—, also bd. dirs. Served to capt. USMC, 1963-64. Republican. Methodist.

PHILLIPS, JOHN WILLIAM, II, law librarian; b. Dallas, Nov. 27, 1956; s. John W. and Jacie (Bower) P.; m. Deborah Hansen, Nov. 4, 1995. BS in paralegal studies, Samford U., 1988; JD, Birmingham U., 1995. Law librarian Rives & Peterson, Birmingham, Ala., 1986—. V.p. Christian Legal Soc., 1993—. Mem. Am. Assn. Law Librarians, Am. Bar Assn. (assoc.). Republican. Office: Rives & Peterson Law Firm 505 20th St N 1700 Financial Ctr Birmingham AL 35203

PHILLIPS, JOSEPH BRANTLEY, JR., lawyer; b. Greenville, S.C., Dec. 5, 1931. B.S. in Bus. Adminstrn., U. S.C., 1954, J.D., 1955. Bar: S.C. 1955. Assoc. Leatherwood, Walker, Todd & Mann, Greenville, 1958-63, ptnr., 1963—. Chmn. bd. deacons Presbyterian Ch., 1970-71, pres. Men of Ch., 1968-69, chmn. Christian Service Ctr., 1972-73; bd. dirs. Greenville Urban Ministry, 1978. Mem. ABA, S.C. Bar Assn., Greenville Bar Assn., Greenville Young Lawyers Club (pres. 1961-62), Lawyers Pilots Bar Assn., Kiwanis (pres. 1973). Clubs: Greenville Country (pres. 1977), Commerce Club. Home: 207 Butler Springs Rd Greenville SC 29615 Office: PO Box 87 Greenville SC 29602-0087

PHILLIPS, JOY EUGENIA, counselor, consultant; b. Colon, Panama, Oct. 25, 1938; d. Ernesto Adolfo and Maria Luisa (Chin) Lee; m. R. Lee Phillips, May 19, 1962; children: Melinda, Lynam, Trevor. BA, U. Md., 1984; MEd, George Mason U., 1987; EdD, Va. Poly. Inst., 1993. Intern Community Mental Health Ctr., Prince William County, Va., 1986; counselor Ctr. for Counseling & Devel., Fairfax, Va., 1987; dir. of guidance Linton Hall Mil. Sch., Bristow, Va., 1987-88; instr. George Mason U., Fairfax, 1987-88; presenter, speaker Benedictine Pastoral Ctr., Bristow, 1987-88; guidance counselor Prince William County Schs., Manassas, Va., 1989-95; adj. faculty mem. in psychology No. Va. Community Coll., 1990—; presenter, speaker Archdiocese of Arlington, Va., 1989—; counselor in pvt. practice Manassas, 1995—; on-site supr. practicum students Va. Tech./Prince William County Schs., Manassas, 1989-95; cons. in field; trainer in-svc. Incoming Counselors, Manassas, 1989-95; univ. supr. practicum grad. studnets Virginia Tech., 1992—. Nominated Agnes Meyer Outstanding Tchr. award, 1992, 93; Blue Cross-Blue Shield Va. grantee, 1991. Mem. ACA, Phi Delta Kappa (exec. bd.). Roman Catholic.

PHILLIPS, L(ARRY) SCOTT, portfolio manager; b. Joplin, Mo., Jan. 30, 1962; s. Gary Lester and Judith Ann (Kelley) P.; m. Gina Lee Ray, Feb. 28, 1987; children: Allie Rae, Colin Scott, Luke Corpier. AS in Computer Sci., Mo. So. State Coll., 1984, BSBA in Econs. and Finance, 1984; MA in Econs., U. Ark., 1986. CFA. Student to student worker Bapt. Student Union, U. Ark., Fayetteville, 1986; trust adminstr. Bank of Bentonville, Ark., 1986-88; portfolio mgr. Arvest Trust Co., N.A., Rogers, Ark., 1988-92, fixed income portfolio mgr., 1992—. Co-designer: (boardgame) The Quest, 1985. Sunday sch. tchr. First Bapt. Ch., Bentonville, 1990—. Mem. Ark. Soc. Fin. Analysts. Republican. Office: Arvest Trust Co NA 201 W Walnut St Ste 7 Rogers AR 72756-6664

PHILLIPS, LINDA DARNELL ELAINE FREDRICKS, psychiatric and geriatrics nurse; b. Calgary, Alta., Can., July 23, 1940; came to U.S., 1964; d. Richard and Adeline Ruth (Kuch) Fredricks; m. Marion Rolley Phillips, June 25, 1960 (div. 1962). Cert. in nursing with honors, Broward C.C., Ft. Lauderdale, Fla., 1983. Exec. sec. Grandeur Motor Cars, Pompano Beach, Fla., 1975-80; charge nurse Las Olas Hosp., Ft. Lauderdale, 1983-85; nurse Med. Pers. Pool, Ft. Lauderdale, 1984-85; pvt. duty nurse, Ft. Lauderdale, 1985—; pres., v.p. L.P.R.N. Inc., 1992-93; cons. nurse Waterford Point Condo, Pompano Beach, Fla., 1980-90. Mem. Fla. Nurses Assn., Internat. Platform Assn. Address: 2910 NE 55th St Fort Lauderdale FL 33308-3452

PHILLIPS, LINDA GRAVES, computer educator, legal secretary; b. Jackson, Miss., Nov. 16, 1948; d. Willie Everett and Margaret Evelyn (Watson) Graves; m. William Russell Bennett, III, Nov. 18, 1967 (div. Aug. 1983); children: William Russell Bennett, IV, Anna Britton Bennett; m. Jeffrey S. Phillips, Oct. 1, 1988. Grad., high sch. Proof clk. First Nat. Bank, Jackson, 1966-67; billing clk. T.G. Blackwell Chevrolet Co., Jackson, 1967-68; tech. asst. Chevron Oil Co., Jackson, 1968-70; exec. sec. to gen. mgr. Gt. Lakes Area Exch., Army and Air Force Exch. Svc., 1973; sales Amway, 1974-77; exec. sec. drilling and engrng. ANR Prodn. Co., Jackson, 1980-84; freelance word processor Jackson, 1984-87; word processor Butler, Snow, O'Mara, Stevens & Cannada, Jackson, 1987-88; ind. computer isntr., Jackson, 1988—; instr. MicroAge Computers, Ridgeland, Miss., 1990-93; owner Inside Track, computer students placement svc., 1995—. Author: WordPerfect 4.2 Training Guide, WordPerfect 5.0 Training Guide, WordPerfect 5.1 Training Guide, WordPerfect 5.1 for DOS Legal Training Guide, DOS Training Guide, WordPerfect 5.1 and 6.0 for DOS, The WordPerfect Primers, WordPerfect 5.1 and 6.0 Advanced Training Guides, WordPerfect Primer for WordPerfect 6.0B for DOS, Advanced WordPerfect Primer for WordPerfect 6.0B for DOS. Office: Customized WordPerfect Tng PO Box 194 Madison MS 39130-0194

PHILLIPS, LINDA LOU, pharmacist; b. Mason City, Iowa, Sept. 3, 1952; d. Reece Webster and Bettye Frances (Martin) Phillips. BS in Polit. Sci., So. Meth. U., 1974; BS in Pharmacy, U. Ark., 1976; MS in Pharmacy, U. Houston, 1980. Registered pharmacist, Tex. Pharmacy intern Palace Drug Store, Forrest City, Ark., 1976-77; pharmacy resident Hermann Hosp., Houston, 1978-79; dir. pharmacy Alvin Cmty. Hosp., (Tex.), 1979-80; relief pharmacist Twelve Oaks Hosp., Houston, 1980; cons. pharmacist Health Facilities, Inc., Houston, 1980-81; pharmacy supr. Meth. Hosp., Houston, 1981—; sec. spl. interest group, IBAX Pharmacy, 1990-93; chmn. HBO and Co., Series 4000, materials mgmt. spl. interest group, 1994—. Mem. Am. Soc. Hosp. Pharmacists, So. Meth. U. Alumni Assn., Ark. Alumni Assn., Rho Chi, Pi Sigma Alpha. Republican. Methodist. Club: Girls' Cotillion (bd. dirs. 1983-85). Home: 7400 Bellerive Dr Apt 403 Houston TX 77036-3045 Office: Meth Hosp Pharmacy 6565 Fannin St Houston TX 77030-2704

PHILLIPS, LYN WALTERS, secondary education educator; b. Laurel, Miss., July 21, 1947; d. Troy Lee and Emily Lucille (Bush) Walters; m. Ronald Denman Phillips, Aug. 24, 1969; children: Kristen Leigh, Breckenridge Denman. AA, Jones Jr. Coll., 1967; BS in Journalism, U. So. Miss., 1970, BS in Secondary Edn., 1987; MS in English, William Carey Coll., 1996. Cert. secondary tchr., Miss. Tchr. Hattiesburg (Miss.) H.S., 1986-96, Oak Grove Mid. Sch., Hattiesburg, 1981-86. Editor: Snail Trails, 1989; pub., adviser newspaper Hi-Flashes, 1986—; cons. Am. Jour., 1990—; contbr. articles to profl. jours. Troop leader Girl Scouts U.S., Hattiesburg, 1978-84; vol. ARC, Salvation Army, Spl. Olympics, Hattiesburg, 1980—; v.p. N.E. Lamar Fire Dept., Hattiesburg, 1989—. Mem. Am. Fedn. Tchrs. (cons.), Lounge Lizzard Soc. (charter, pres. 1993-95), U. So. Miss. Alumni Assn. (bd. dirs. 1989-91), Scholastic Journalism Soc., Soc. Profl. Journalists, Journalism Edn. Assn. Baptist. Home: 106 Tall Pines Dr Hattiesburg MS 39402 Office: Hattiesburg H S 301 Hutchinson Ave Hattiesburg MS 39401

PHILLIPS, MARION GRUMMAN, writer, civic worker; b. N.Y.C., Feb. 11, 1922; d. Leroy Randle and Rose Marion (Werther) Grumman; m. Ellis Laurimore Phillips, Jr., June 13, 1942; children: Valerie Rose (Mrs. Adrian Parsegian), Elise Marion (Mrs. Edward E. Watts III), Ellis Laurimore III, Kathryn Noel (Mrs. Philip Zimmermann), Cynthia Louise. Student, Mt. Holyoke Coll., 1940-42, BA, Adelphi U., 1981. Civic vol. Mary C. Wheeler Sch., 1964-68, Historic Ithaca, Inc., 1972-76, Ellis L. Phillips Found., 1960-91; bd. dirs. New Hist. Geneal. Soc., 1990-93; bd. dirs. North Shore Jr. League, 1960-61, 64-65, 68-69, Family Svc. Assn. Nassau County, 1963-69, Homemaker Svc. Assn. Nassau County, 1959-61. Author: (light verse) A Foot in the Door, 1965, The Whale-Going, Going, Gone, 1977, Doctors Make Me Sick (So I Cured Myself of Arthritis), 1979; editor: (with Valerie Phillips Parsegian) Richard and Rhoda, Letters from the Civil War, 1982, Wooden Shoes the story of my Grandfather's Grandfather (F. M. Sisson), 1990, Irish Eyes, family hist. of McTarsneys and Sissons, 1990; editor Jr. League Shore Lines, 1960-61, The Werthers in America-Four Generations and their Descendants, 1987; A B-Tour of Britain, 1986, (Fletcher M. Sisson) Wooden Shoes, Irish Eyes; contbr. articles on fund raising to mags. Mem. New Eng. Hist. Geneal. Soc. (bd. dirs.), N.Y. Geneal. Biographical Soc., Moorings Club, Creek Club, PEO Sisterhood. Congregationalist. Adresss: 1855 Bay Rd #302 Vero Beach FL 32963-4396

PHILLIPS, PATRICIA ALWOOD RICH, librarian; b. Richmond, Va., July 28, 1942; d. Arthur Melville and Mary Wilson (Bellinger) Rich; m. Stanley Josephus Phillips, July 28, 1963; children: Stanley Josephus Jr., Asha Marie. AB in English, U. N.C., 1965, MSLS, 1967; EdD in Gen. Adminstrv. Leadership, Vanderbilt U., 1995. Cataloger Tenn. Tech. U., Cookeville, 1966-75, head catalog dept., 1976-82, coord. bibliographic control, 1981-83; coord. tech. svc. U. of South, Sewanee, Tenn., 1983-1996; assoc. univ. libr. U. Tex. at El Paso, 1996—. Mem. ALA, AAUP (v.p. pub. instrn. 1978-82, v.p. pvt. instrn. 1984-86), Southeastern Libr. Assn., Tenn. Libr. Assn. Democrat. Episcopalian. Home: Apt 1610 345 Shadow Mountain El Paso TX 79912 Office: U of the South Library UTEP El Paso TX 79968-0582

PHILLIPS, PHILIP EDWARD, lecturer in English; b. Fayetteville, Ark., Feb. 7, 1969; s. Carl M. P. and Peggy Sue Parker; m. Elaine Lenore Anderson, Dec. 18, 1993. BA, Belmont U., Nashville, 1990; Cert. Langue Français Moyen 1, U. Cath. de l'Ouest, Angers, France, 1989; MA, Vanderbilt U., Nashville, 1992, PhD, 1996. Tchg. fellow Vanderbilt U., Nashville, 1991-96, lectr. in English, 1996—. Contbr. reviews to EMLS, Byron Jour., Carmina Philosophiae, poems to Vanderbilt Review. Consortium grant Ctr. Renaissance Studies, Newberry Libr., Chgo., 1996. Mem. MLA, Milton Soc. Am., Internat. Boethius Soc. (rec. sec. 1995—, editor newsletter, 1995), Heights Nat. Alumni Assn. (bd. dirs. 1990—), Poe Found., Poe Studies Assn. Democrat. Episcopalian. Home: PO Box 120243 Nashville TN 37212 Office: Vanderbilt U Dept English Nashville TN 37235

PHILLIPS, RICHARD ENGLAND, foreign language specialist, art history educator; b. L.A., Dec. 13, 1950; s. Francis Emery and Marguerite Bernice (England) P.; m. Alicia Luna Flores, Dec. 2, 1975 (div. Oct. 1993); children: Citlalli Luna, Canek Moisés. BA in Spanish, U. Calif., Irvine, 1973; MA in Spanish, U. Calif., Santa Barbara, 1975; postgrad., U. N.Mex., 1978-84; PhD in Art History, U. Tex., 1993. Cert. tchr. Spanish, ethnic studies c.c., Calif. Svc. rep. Spanish Social Security Adminstrn., L.A., 1977-78; teaching asst. art history U. Tex., Austin, 1985-88, asst. instr. art history, 1989-91; prof. art history Savannah (Ga.) Coll. Art and Design, 1992-93; cert. specialist Spanish lang. Tex. Dept. Human Svcs., Austin, 1993-95; asst. prof. Latin Am. art history Va. Commonwealth U., Richmond, 1995—. Author: Processions through Paradise, 1993. Chmn. ind. scholar abroad award com. U. Tex., Austin, 1990. Dissertation travel fellow Samuel H. Kress Found., 1988. Mem. Assn. for Latin Am. Art, Am. Soc. Hispanic Art Hist. Studies, Coll. Art Assn., Sierra Club. Democrat. Unitarian. Home: Apt 1 2331 W Grace St Richmond VA 23220-1968 Office: Va Commonwealth U PO Box 843046 922 W Franklin St Richmond VA 23284-3046

PHILLIPS, ROBERT BENBOW, financial planner; b. Winston-Salem, N.C., Aug. 20, 1959; s. Clifford Clayton and Roberta George (Stouch) P.; m. Christine Theresa Rudolf, Feb. 12, 1994. BS in Biology, Va. Poly. Inst. and State U., 1981; postgrad., Coll. Fin. Planning, 1992—; postgrad. MBA program, Heriot Watt U., Edinburgh, Scotland, 1996—. Registered investment advisor; registered fin. cons.; cert. investment specialist. Pharm. salesman The Sporicidin Co., Washington, 1982-85; stockbroker Legg-Mason, Radford, Va., 1985-87; brokerage mgr. Golden Rule Ins. Co., Roanoke, Va., 1988-91; fin. planner Fin. Planning Svcs.-Internat., Brazil, 1991-95; wholesaler mut. funds Calvert Group, Bethesda, Md., 1995-96; v.p. Schield Mgmt. Co., Denver, 1996—. Mem., past officer Rep. Com. of Va., 1980—. Mem. Internat. Assn. CFP, Internat. Assn. Fin. Planners, Internat. Assn. Registered Fin. Cons., Nat. Assn. Life Underwriters, Ducks Unlimited (officer New River Valley 1980—), Va. Wine Soc., Delta Kappa Epsilon (past officer). Lutheran. Office: PO Box 312 Haymarket VA 20168

PHILLIPS, ROBERT JAMES, JR., corporate executive; b. Houston, Aug. 4, 1955; s. Robert James and Mary Josephine (Bass) P.; m. Nancy Norris, Apr. 24, 1982; 1 child, Mary Ashton. BBA, So. Meth. U., 1976, JD, 1980. Bar: Tex. 1980. Vp., gen. counsel Aegis Shipping Ltd., London, 1980-81; assoc. Bishop, Larrimore, Lamsens & Brown, 1981-82; pres. Phillips Devel. Corp., Ft. Worth, Tex., 1982—; pvt. practice Ft. Worth, 1982-87, 89—; assoc. Haynes and Boone, Ft. Worth, 1988-89; sr. v.p. Am. Real Estate Group, 1989-93, Am. Savs. Bank, N.A., New West Fed. Savs. and Loan Assn., 1989-93, Am. Savs. Bank, Ft. Worth, 1991-92; chmn., CEO creative risk control Environ. Risk Mgmt. Inc., Ft. Worth, 1992-95; bd. dirs. Tex. Heritage, Inc. Bd. dirs., exec. com. Ft. Worth Ballet Assn., 1984-85, Van Cliburn Found.; v.p. planning, bd. dirs., exec. com. Ft. Worth Symphony Orch., 1984-85; bd. dirs. Mus. Modern Art, 1986—; bd. dirs., exec. com., chmn. investment com. Tex. Boys Choir, 1983-85. Mem. ABA, Tex. Bar Assn., Ft. Worth Bd. Realtors, Crescent Club, Phi Delta Phi, Kappa Sigma, Beta Gamma Sigma. Clubs: River Crest Country, Ft. Worth. Home and Office: PO Box 470099 Fort Worth TX 76147-0099

PHILLIPS, SANDRA ALLEN, primary school educator; b. Newport News, Va., Mar. 10, 1943; d. Cecil Lamar and Mary (Schenk) Allen. BS, Appalachian State U., Boone, N.C., 1965; MEd, U. N.C., Charlotte, 1990. Tchr. Rockwell (N.C.) Elem. Sch., 1964-65, Granite Quarry (N.C.) Elem. Sch., 1965-68, Lillian Black Elem. Sch., Spring Lake, N.C., 1970, Berryhill Elem. Sch., Charlotte, N.C., 1970-71, 77—; tchr. J.C. Roe Sch., Wilmington, N.C., 1974-76, mem. tchr. adv. coun., 1995-96; elected to tchr.'s adv. coun. Charlotte-Mecklenburg Schs., 1995-96, 96-97. Named Tchr. of Yr., Berryhill Elem. Sch., 1989. Mem. Profl. Educators N.C., Classroom Tchrs. Assn. Office: Berryhill Elem Sch 10501 Walkers Ferry Rd Charlotte NC 28208-9721

PHILLIPS, SUSAN DIANE, secondary school educator; b. Shelbyville, Ky., Aug. 28, 1955; d. James William and Catherine Elizabeth (Jones) P. B of Music Edn., Eastern Ky. U., 1977; postgrad., U. Ky., 1987. Tchr. music Breckinridge County Schs., Hardinsburg, Ky., 1978, Perry County Schs., Hazard, Ky., 1980-83, Music on the Move, Louisville, 1985-86, Cooter (Mo.) R-4 Sch., 1987-90, Lewis County High Sch., Vanceburg, Ky., 1990—; staff-cavalcade of bands Ky. Derby Festival, Louisville, 1984-86. Dir. Simpsonville (Ky.) United Meth. Ch. Handbell Choirs, 1985-86. Named Ky. Colonel Gov. Commonwealth of Ky., 1979. Mem. Nat. Band Assn., Am. Choral Dirs. Assn., Ky. Educators Assn., Ky. Music Educators Assn., Music Educators Nat. Conf. Office: Lewis County High Sch Lions Ln Vanceburg KY 41179

PHILLIPS, THOMAS EDWORTH, JR., investment executive, senior consultant; b. Danville, Va., July 7, 1944; s. Thomas Edworth Sr. and Jean (Worley) P.; m. Claudia Mitchell, July 23, 1966; children: Kelly Marie, Melissa Joyce. BS in Econs., Va. Tech., 1966; cert. in investments, N.Y. Inst. Fin., 1969; MS in Bus., Va. Commonwealth U., 1973; postgrad., U. Pa., 1989. Cert. investment mgmt. analyst; registered investment adviser. Edn. coord. Prince William County Schs., Manassas, Va., 1966-67; investment broker Conrad and Co., Richmond, Va., 1967-68; investment exec. Paine Webber, Inc., Richmond, 1968—, divisional v.p., 1980—; registered prin. NYSE, NASD, 1987—; mem. access program nat. com. PaineWebber, N.Y.C., 1989-90, mem. dir.'s coun., 1987-88, mem. managed accounts nat. adv. bd., 1991-93; mem. mut. fund Nat. Adv. Coun., 1996—; bd. dirs. Madison Group, Inc., Richmond, Meadowbrook Assocs., Inc., Richmond; speaker in field. Bd. dirs. Va. Non-Profit Housing Coalition, pres., 1992—; chmn. bd. deacons. Mt. Olivet Ch., Hanover, Va., 1984-85; trustee Hanover Acad., Ashland, Va., 1980-84. Rotary Found. fellow, 1989. Mem. Investment Mgmt. Cons. Assn., Capital Soc., Melody Hills Property Owners Assn. (bd. dirs. 1980—), Va. Tech. Alumni Assn., Rotary, Bull and Bear Club, Omicron Delta Epsilon. Baptist. Home: 15058 Melody Hills Dr Doswell VA 23047-2075 Office: PaineWebber Inc 1021 E Cary St Ste 1800 Richmond VA 23219-4000

PHILLIPS, THOMAS ROYAL, judge; b. Dallas, Oct. 23, 1949; s. George S. and Marguerite (Andrews) P.; m. Lyn Bracewell, June 26, 1982; 1 son, Daniel Austin Phillips; 1 stepson, Thomas R. Kirkham. BA, Baylor U., 1971; JD, Harvard U., 1974. Bar: Tex. 1974; cert. in civil trial law Tex. Bd. Legal Specialization. Briefing atty. Supreme Ct. Tex., Austin, 1974-75; assoc. Baker & Botts, Houston, 1975-81; judge 280th Dist. Ct., Houston, 1981-88; chief justice Supreme Ct. Tex., Austin, 1988—; mem. com. on fed.-state rels. Jud. Conf. U.S., 1990-96; chair Tex. Jud. Dists. Bd., 1988—; mem. State Judges Mass Tort Litig. Com., 1991-96; bd. dirs. Elmo B. Hunter Citizens Ctr. for Jud. Selection, 1992-94, Southwestern Legal Found.; mem. Nat. Conf. Chief Justices, 1989—, 1st v.p., 1995—, pres.-elect, 1996—; adv. dir. Rev. of Litigation, U. Tex. Law Sch., 1990—; chair Nat. Mass Tort Conf. Planning Com., 1993-94. Bd. advisors Ctr. for Pub. Policy Dispute Resolution, U. Tex. Law Sch., 1993—; mem. planning com. South Tex. Coll. of Law Ctr. for Creative Legal Solutions, 1993—. Recipient Outstanding Young Lawyer award Houston Young Lawyers Assn., 1986, award of excellence in govt. Tex. C. of C., 1992; named Appellate Judge of Yr., Tex. Assn. Civil Trial and Appellate Specialists, 1992-93. Mem. ABA, Am. Law Inst., Nat. Ctr. for State Ctrs. (vice chair, bd. dirs. 1996—), State Bar Tex. (chmn. pattern jury charges IV com. 1985-87, vice chmn. adminstrn. justice com. 1986-87, advisor fed. code revision project 1996—), Am. Judicature Soc. (bd. dirs. 1989-95, exec. bd. 1995-96), Conf. Chief Justices (bd. dirs. 1993-95, 1st v.p. 1995-96, pres. elect 1996—), Tex. Philol. Soc., Houston Philol. Soc., Houston Bar Assn., Travis County Bar Assn. Republican. Methodist. Office: Tex Supreme Ct PO Box 12248 Austin TX 78711-2248

PHILLIPS, WILLIAM RAY, JR., retired shipbuilding executive; b. West Point, Va., Feb. 23, 1931; s. William Ray and Marjorie Evelyn (Treat) P.; m. Marian Belle Culbreth, Nov. 7, 1953; children: William Ray III, Dana Louise. Attended, Newport News (Va.) Shipbuilding Apprentice Sch., 1949-54; BS, Va. Poly. Inst., 1960; student advanced mgmt. program, Harvard U., 1975. Foreman machine shops and tool rm. Newport News (Va.) Shipbuilding Co., 1964-66, asst. supt. machine shops div., 1966-67, mgr. nuclear constrn., 1967-72, dir. waterfront ops., 1972-75, v.p. yard ops., 1975-79, v.p. mktg., 1979-83, v.p. engrng., 1983-84, sr. v.p. engrng., 1984-87, exec. v.p., 1987-92, pres., CEO, 1992-94, chmn., CEO, 1994-95; ret., 1995; bd. dirs. Newport News Reactor Svcs., Idaho Falls, Idaho, pres.; bd. dirs. Newport News Indsl. Ohio, North Perry, Ohio, chmn., 1992—. Sgt. U.S. Army, 1955-57. Named Engr. of Yr., Peninsula Engrs. Com., 1986. Mem. Soc. Naval Architects and Marine Engrs. (pres.), Navy League U.S. (life), Naval Submarine League, Am. Soc. Naval Engrs., Propeller Club U.S., Seaford Yacht Club (Yorktown, Va., trustee). Republican. Presbyterian.

PHILLIPS, WINFRED MARSHALL, dean, mechanical engineer; b. Richmond, Va., Oct. 7, 1940; s. Claude Marshall and Gladys Marian (Barden) P.; children—Stephen, Sean. B.S.M.E., Va. Poly. Inst., 1963; M.A.E., U. Va., 1966, D.Sc., 1968. Mech. engr. U.S. Naval Weapons Lab., Dahlgren, Va., 1963; NSF trainee, teaching, research asst. dept. aerospace engrng. U. Va., Charlottesville, 1963-67; research scientist, 1966-67; asst. prof. dept. aerospace engrng. Pa. State U., University Park, 1968-74, from assoc. prof. to prof., 1974-80, assoc. dean research Coll. Engrng., 1979-80; head Sch. Mech. Engrng. Purdue U., West Lafayette, Ind., 1980-88; dean Coll. Engrng. U. Fla., Gainesville, 1988—, dean engrng., assoc. v.p. engr. rsch., 1989—; chmn. bd. dirs. North Fla. Tech. Innovation Corp., 1995—; vis. prof. U. Paris, 1976-77; bd. dirs. Tokheim Corp., Fla., Technology Devel. Bd.; adv. com. Nimbus Corp., 1985-90, Hong Kong U. Sci. and Tech., 1990-93, Fla. Bd. Profl. Regulation, 1992—; co-founder, v.p., CEO Inc., 1990—; mem. acad. adv. coun. Indsl. Rsch. Inst., 1990-93; mem. sci. adv. com. electric Power Rsch. Inst., 1994—; bd. dirs. Southeastern Coalition for Minorities in Engrng. Sect. editor Am. Soc. Artificial Internal Organs Jour.; contbr. more than 140 articles to profl. jours., chpts. to books. Bd. dirs. Ctrl. Pa. Heart Assn., 1974-80, U. Fla. Found., 1989-91, 95—; mem. Ind. Boiler and Pressure Vessel Code Bd., 1981-88. Named Disting. Hoosier Engr., 1987, Sagamore of the Wabash, 1988; recipient Career Rsch. award NIH, 1974-78, Surgery and Bioengrig. Study sect., 1988-91, Fla. High Tech. and Industry Coun., 1990-94, So. Tech. Coun., 1991—. Fellow AAAS, AIAA (assoc.), ASME (sr. v.p. edn. 1986-88, bd. dirs. 1995—), N.Y. Acad. Scis., Am. Astron. Soc., Am. Inst. Med. and Biol. Engrng. (founding fellow, chair coll. fellows 1994-95, pres. 1996-97), Am. Soc. Engrng. Edn. (past chmn. long range planning soc. awards 1990—, vice chmn. engrng. deans coun. 1991-93, chair 1993—, bd. dirs. 1994—, 1st v.p. 1994-95, pres. 1996-97), Royal Soc. Arts; mem. Am. Soc. Artificial Internal Organs (trustee 1982-90, sec.-treas. 1986-87, pres. 1988-89), Nat. Assn. State Univs. and Land-Grant Colls. (com. quality of engrng. edn.), Accreditation Bd. on Engrng. and Tech. (bd. dirs. 1989—, exec. com. 1991—, mem. internat. revs. for univs. in Saudi Arabia, USSR, The Netherlands, Kuwait, pres. 1996-97), Univ. Programs in Computer-Aided Engrng., Design and Mfg. (bd. dirs. 1985-91), Am. Phys. Soc., Biomed. Engrng. Soc., Internat. Soc. Biorheology, Fla. Engrng. Soc., Cosmos Club, Fla. Blue Key, Rotary (pres. Lafayette chpt. 1987-88), Sigma Xi, Phi Kappa Phi, Phi Tau Sigma, Sigma Gamma Tau, Tau Beta Pi (eminent engr.). Home: 4140 NW 44th Ave Gainesville FL 32606-4518 Office: U Fla Coll Engineering 300 Weil Hall Gainesville FL 32611-2083

PHILLIPS, ZOLTON JULIUS, III, minister; b. Fort Monroe, Va., June 25, 1936; s. Zolton Julius II and Ruth (Shores) P.; m. Karen Sue Ellis, Aug. 18, 1962; children: Karen Sue Phillips Ward, Zoltan Julius IV. BA, King Coll., 1959; MDiv, Union Theol. Sem., 1963; D of Ministry, McCormick Theol. Sem., 1977. Ordained to ministry Presbyterian Ch., 1963. Pastor Chinquapin and Salem (N.C.) Presbyn. Ch., 1963-66, Waddell Mem and Mitchells Presbyn. Ch., Rapidan, Va., 1966-69, Village Presbyn. Ch., Richmond, Va., 1969-74, St. Stephen Presbyn. Ch., Orlando, Fla., 1974-76, Glenwood Presbyn. Ch., Greensboro, N.C., 1976-79, Pinewood Presbyn. Ch., Goldsboro, N.C., 1979-82, Lafayette Presbyn. Ch., Tallahassee, Fla., 1982-88, Hunting Ridge Presbyn. Ch., Balt., 1988-90; N.E. regional dir. Outreach Found., Charlotte, N.C., 1990-92; pastor Blackstone (Va.) Presbyn. Ch., 1992—; interim pastor Canal St. Presbyn. Ch., New Orleans, 1990; regional dir. Outreach Found., 1990-92. Author: Shorter History of Mitchells Presbyterian Church, 1967; co-author: Problem Pregnancies and Abortion, 1992. Nat. pres. Presbyn. Pro-Life; aux. chaplain USAF, Richmond, 1969-74, Orlando, 1974-76; police chaplain Tallahassee Police Dept., 1982-88; mem. exec. com. Rep. Ctrl. Com. Leon County, Tallahassee, 1982-88; bd. dirs. united svcs. for older adults City of Greensboro; counselor for youth YMCA, Orlando; pres. PTA; co-organizer, counselor Culpeper County Mental Health Ctr.; mem. Gov.'s Coun. on Edn. in Va.; clergy advisor Planned Parenthood; campus min. Fla. Tech. Inst., Med. Coll. Va. Recipient Cert. of Recognition USAF, 1969, Svc. award Westminster Oaks Retirement Ctr. Synod Fla. Mem. Masons. Office: Blackstone Presbyn Ch 301 Church St Blackstone VA 23824-1601

PHILLIS, MARILYN HUGHEY, artist; b. Kent, Ohio, Feb. 1, 1927; d. Paul Jones and Helen Margaret (Miller) Hughey; m. Richard Waring Phillis, Mar. 19, 1949; children: Diane E., Hugh R., Randall W. Student, Kent State U., 1945; BS, Ohio State U., 1949. Chemist Battelle Meml. Inst., Columbus, Ohio, 1949-53; sec. Lakewood Park Cemetery, Rocky River, Ohio, 1972-75; illustrator periodical Western Res. Hist. Mag., Garrettsville, Ohio, 1974-78; illustrator book AAUW, Piqua, Ohio, 1976; art instr. Edison State C.C., Piqua, 1976; watermedia instr. Springfield (Ohio) Mus. Art, 1976-84; juror art exhbns. state and nat. art group, 1980—; painting instr. state and nat. orgns., 1980—; dir. Nat. Creativity Seminars, Ohio Watercolor Soc., Fairborn, 1993-95, 97; lectr. art healing Wheeling (W.Va.) Jesuit Coll., 1994-96. Author: Watermedia Techniques for Releasing the Creative Spirit, 1992; contbr. articles and illustrations to profl. jours.; one-woman shows include Stifel Fine Art Ctr., Wheeling, W.Va., Springfield (Ohio) Art Mus., Zanesville (Ohio) ARt Ctr., Cleve. Inst. Music, Columbus Mus. Art, Cheekwood Mus. of Art, Bot. Hall, Nashville; exhibited in group shows at No. Ariz. U. Art Mus., Flagstaff, 1993, Taiwan Art Edn. Inst., Taipei, 1994; represented in permanent collections at Springfield Mus. Art, Ohio Watercolor Soc., also corp. collections. Gallery dir. Green St. United Meth. Ch., Piqua, 1972-75; pres. Rocky River (Ohio) H.S. PTA, 1971; chmn. Cmty. Health and Humor

Program, Wheeling, 1992. Recipient First awards Watercolor West, riverside, Calif., 1990, Hudson Soc. award Nat. Collage Soc., 1995, Art Masters award Am. Artist Mag., 1996. Mem. Internat. Soc. Study of Subtle Energies and Energy Medicine (art cons. sci. jour. 1992-96, art and healing workshop 1995), Am. Watercolor Soc. (dir. 1991-93, newsletter editor 1992—, Osborne award 1975), Soc. Layerists in Multi-Media (nat. v.p. 1988-93), Ohio Watercolor Soc. (sec. 1979-82, v.p. 1982-89, pres. 1990-96, Gold medal, Best of Show 1993), Nat. Watercolor Soc., Int. Noetic Sci., West Ohio Watercolor Soc. (pres. 1979-80, 2d award 1982), Allied Artists N.Y., W.Va. Watercolor Soc. (First award 1993), Ky. Watercolor Soc., Ga. Watercolor Soc. Home and Office: Phillis Studio 72 Stamm Cir Wheeling WV 26003-5549

PHILP, JAMES RAMSAY, internal medicine educator; b. Kirkcaldy, Fife, Scotland, Mar. 14, 1936; came to U.S., 1969, naturalized; m. Elizabeth Forbes, Sept. 10, 1960; children: Alison, Ian, Graeme. BSc in Microbiology summa cum laude, U. Edinburgh, Scotland, 1961, MB, ChB, 1961, MD, 1968. Diplomate Am. Bd. Internal Medicine, Am. Bd. Infectious Disease, Am. Bd. Allergy and Immunology. House physician chest unit Cameron Hosp., Fife, 1960; house surgeon, then house physician Edinburgh Royal Infirmary, 1961-62; sr. rsch. fellow in radiobiology dept. Aberdeen U., 1964-66; registrar in medicine, then sr. registrar Aberdeen (Scotland) Royal Infirmary, 1964-68, 69-71; rsch. fellow div. infectious diseases and immunology U. Fla., Gainesville, 1968-69, asst. prof. medicine and microbiology, 1969-70; sr. lectr. bacteriology and infectious diseases, lab. dir. St. Mary's Hosp. Med. Sch. Wright-Fleming Inst., London, 1971-73; assoc. prof. infectious diseases and immunology Wake Forest U. Bowman Gray Sch. Medicine, Winston-Salem, N.C., 1973-77, prof., 1977-82; prof. internal medicine, chmn. dept. U. Ala. Sch. Medicine Coll. Community Health Scis., Tuscaloosa, 1992—; lectr. dept. bacteriology U. Edinburgh, 1962-63; lectr. dept. therapeutics and pharmacology Aberdeen U., 1966-71; mem. staff N.C. Bapt. Hosp., Winston-Salem, 1974-92; founding chmn. Drug Info. Svc. Ctr., 1983-87; pres. Capstone Health Svcs. Found., P.C., Tuscaloosa, 1993—; cons. Shands Teaching Hosp., U. Fla., VA Hosp., 1969-70, Heart, Lung and Blood Inst., NIH, 1980, 81, 84, 86, Emory U. Med. Sch., 1991—, Ohio State Coll. Vet. Medicine, U. Cin. Med. Ctr., Med. Coll. Ohio, Med. Coll. Va., 1991—. Author: (monographs) (with R.B. Stewart and L.E. Cluff) Drug Monitoring: A Requierment for Responsible Drug Use, 1977, (with V.D. Morris) The Management of Sore Throat, 1977; contbr. articles and abstracts to med. jours., chpts. to books. Deacon, elder Presbyn. Ch.; trustee Forsyth Country Day Sch., Crisis Control Pharmacy, Winston-Salem; soccer coach. Rsch. grantee Mary Reynolds Babcock Found., 1988-90, U. Ala. Bur. Health Professions, 1991-92, Heart, Lung and Blood Inst., 1991-96. Fellow ACP, Royal Coll. Physicians (Edinburgh) (bd. advisors to editor Procs.), Infectious Diseases Soc. Am.; mem. Am. Fedn. Clin. Rsch., Am. Soc. Microbiology, Brit. Med. Assn., Brit. Soc. for Study Infection, Brit. Soc. Antimicrobial Chemotherapy, Reticuloendothelial Soc., Royal Med. Soc. (Edinburgh), Scottish Soc. Exptl. Medicine, So. Soc. Clin. Investigation. Home: U Ala Box 870326 Tuscaloosa AL 35487 Office: U Ala Sch Medicine Coll Community Health Scis Box 870326 Tuscaloosa AL 35487-0326

PHINNEY, WILLIAM CHARLES, retired geologist; b. South Portland, Maine, Nov. 16, 1930; s. Clement Woodbridge and Margaret Florence (Foster) P.; m. Colleen Dorothy Murphy, May 31, 1953; children—Glenn, Duane, John, Marla. B.S., MIT, 1953, M.S., 1956, Ph.D., 1959. Faculty geology U. Minn., 1959-70; chief geology br. NASA Lyndon B. Johnson Space Center, Houston, 1970-82; chief planetology br. NASA Lyndon B. Johnson Space Center, 1982-89, ret., 1994; NASA prin. investigator lunar samples. Contbr. articles to profl. jours. Served with C.E. AUS, 1953-55. Recipient NASA Exceptional Sci. Achievement medal, 1972, NASA Cert. of Commendation, 1987; NASA rsch. grantee, 1972-94, NSF rsch. grantee, 1960-70. Mem. Am. Geophys. Union, AAAS, Mineral. Soc. Am., Geol. Soc. Am., Minn. Acad. Sci. (dir.), Sigma Xi. Home: 18063 Judicial Way S Lakeville MN 55044-8839

PHIPPS, CAROLYN SISK, secondary educator; b. Memphis, July 19, 1946; d. William Edward and Gladys (Hines) Sisk; m. Hardie M. Phipps Jr., Jan. 22, 1968. BS, Memphis State U., 1968, MEd, 1970. Cert. tchr. English, guidance, adminstrn. and supr. Tchr. Memphis City Schs., 1968—. Recipient Tchr. of Excellence award Rotary Club, 1996, Tenn. Tchr. of English Tn.. Coun. Tchrs. of English, 1996. Mem. Nat. Coun. of Tchrs. of English (past chair of standing com. on affiliate of tchrs. of English), Shelby-Memphis Coun. Tchrs. of English (past pres.), Delta Kappa Gamma. Methodist. Home: 7091 Crestridge Memphis TN 38119 Office: Wooddale High Sch 5151 Scottsdale Ave Memphis TN 38118-4501

PHIPPS, TONY RANDELL, advertising production consultant, singer, record producer; b. Huntsville, Ala., Apr. 14, 1953; s. Elmer Oakley and Effie Lois (Brewer) P; m. Dr. Linda Roberts Phipps. BS, David Lipscomb Coll., 1974; M of Music Edn., Peabody Grad. Sch. Music, 1976; postgrad. in Communications and Psychology, David Lipscomb Coll. and Peabody Grad. Sch. Music, 1976-78. Performer Opryland U.S.A. Showpark, Nashville, Grand Ole Opry and the Nashville Network, 1975-93; advt. cons. Nashville, 1977—; pre., owner Tony Phipps Prodns., Nashville, 1977—; freelance singer, announcer Nashville, 1977—; owner, operator Tony Phipps Prodns., Nashville, 1980—. Writer, producer radio and TV commls., voice overs, 1980—. Mem. AFTRA. Democrat. Mem. Ch. of Christ. Office: PO Box 40123 Nashville TN 37204-0123 Studio: 821 19th Ave S Nashville TN 37203

PHULL, B. S., scientist. Prin. scientist Laque Ctr. for Corrosion Tech., Wrightsville Beach, N.C. Office: Auditorium Cir Hwy 76 Wrightsville Beach NC

PHUNG, NGUYEN DINH, medical educator; b. Ninh Binh, Vietnam, Sept. 25, 1950; came to U.S., 1975; s. Thu Dinh Nguyen and Minh Tuyet Le; m. Thuy Thanh Tran, Sept. 25, 1974; children: The-Ngoc, Khoi-Nguyen, Thien Huong. MD, Saigon Med. Sch., 1973. Diplomate Am. Bd. Internal Medicine, Am. Bd. Allergy and Immunology. Clin. instr. medicine, staff physician U. Okla. Health Scis. Ctr. & Vets. Hosp., Oklahoma City, 1982-84; clin. asst. prof. medicine U. Tex. Med. Sch., Houston, 1989—. Co-author: Practical Allergy & Immunology, 1983; contbr. articles to profl. jours. Mem. ACP, Am. Acad. Allergy and Immunology. Office: Allergy and Asthma Clinic 2905 Milam St Houston TX 77006-3645

PHUPHANICH, SURASAK, neurologist, oncologist; b. Bangkok, Thailand, Apr. 3, 1952; s. Aree and Suthatip (Tantien) P.; 1 child, Sean C.; m. Cynthia D. Phuphanich, Feb. 14, 1989; 1 child, Melissa. BSc, Ramathibodi Hosp., Bangkok, Thailand, 1973; MD, Mahidol U., Bangkok, 1975. Diplomate Am. Bd. Neurology. Rotating intern, resident internal medicine and psychiatry Ramathibodi Hosp., 1975-77; resident in internal medicine St. Francis Hosp., Evanston, Ill., 1977-78; resident in neurology U. Ill. Hosp./West Side VA Hosp., Chgo., 1978-81, chief resident neurology, 1980-81; asst. neurology U. Ill., 1978-80; clin. instr. neurosurgery U. Calif., 1981-82; asst. rsch. neurologist U. Calif., San Francisco, 1982-83; asst. prof. neurology and neurosurgery U. South Fla. Coll. Medicine, 1984-94, assoc. prof. neurology and neurosurgery, 1995—, dir. divsn. neuro-oncology, 1985—, assoc. prof. neurology and neurosurgery, 1995—; chief neurology svc. H. Lee Moffitt Cancer Ctr. and Rsch. Inst. U. South Fla., Tampa, 1987—, neuro-oncology program leader H. Lee Moffitt Cancer Ctr. and Rsch. Inst., 1992—; cons. neurologist James A. Haley Vets.' Hosp., Tampa, 1984—, U. Community Hosp., Tampa, 1984—; mem. med. staff Tampa Gen. Hosp., 1984—; cons. neuro-oncologist St. Joseph's Hosp., Tampa, 1984—; presenter, lectr. in field; physician advisor peer rev. activities Profl. Found. for Health Care, Tampa, 1990-91, Nat. Med. Audit, Inc., San Francisco, 1992—, Keystone Peer Rev. Orgn., Inc., Harrisburg, Pa., 1992—, Blue Cross/Blue Shield of Fla. Peer Rev. Orgn., Jacksonville, 1992-93. Contbr. articles to profl. jours. Rsch. fellow Assn. Brain Tumor Rsch., 1982-84, Am. Cancer Soc. fellow, 1982-83; recipient Nat. Scholastic Achievement award King of Thailand, 1969; grantee Eleanor Naylor Dana Charitable Trust, 1988, Cell Tech., Inc., 1988-90, Radiation Therapy Oncology Group, 1990-92, Radiation Therapy Oncology Group, 1991—, Nova Pharm. Corp., 1990-92, Brain Tumor Coop. Group, 1992—, ECOG, 1993-94. Fellow Am. Acad. Neurology; mem. Am. Soc. Clin. Oncology, Fla. Med. Assn., Hilleborough County Med. Assn., Am. Soc. Neuroimaging, Soc. for Neuro-Sci., Med. Coun. Thailand. Office: H Lee Moffitt Cancer Ctr 12902 Magnolia Dr Tampa FL 33612-9416

PIANTADOSI, CLAUDE ANTHONY, pulmonologist, educator; b. Hudson County, N.J., Dec. 31, 1949. BA in Chemistry, U. N.C., 1971; MD, Johns Hopkins U., 1975. Diplomate Am. Bd. Internal Medicine. Intern Johns Hopkins Hosp., Balt., 1975-76, asst. resident, 1976-77; clin. fellow divsn. allergy and respiratory diseases Duke U. Med. Ctr., Durham, N.C., 1980-81, rsch. assoc., 1981-87, co-dir. F.G. Hall Hypo-Hyperbaric Ctr., 1988-90, dir., 1988—, prof. medicine, 1994—; cons. in diving medicine, Germany, 1984-85, Diver's Alert Network, 1981—; cons. U.S. EPA, 1987-90. Contbr. articles and revs. to profl. jours. Decorated USN Commendation medal; Henry Strong Denison rsch. scholar Johns Hopkins U. Sch. Medicine, 1974; recipient USN Surgeon Gen.'s award in diving and submarine medicine, 1977. Mem. Johns Hopkins Med. and Surg. Assn., Hyperbaric and Undersea Med. Soc., Am. Soc. Clin. Investigation, Internat. Soc. on Oxygen Transport to Tissue, Am. Thoracic Soc., Am. Heart Assn. Coun. on Cardiopulmonary and Critical Care, Oxygen Soc., Phi Eta Sigma, Phi Beta Kappa. Office: Duke U Med Ctr Dept of Medicine Durham NC 27710

PIAZZA, ELIZABETH ANNE, pharmacist, educator; b. Miami, Fla., Oct. 9, 1952; d. Joseph Edward and Doris (Smale) Youhouse; m. Joseph Carmine Piazza, Sept. 13, 1975; children: Joseph Dominick, Andrew John. AA, Miami-Dade C.C., 1974; BS cum laude, U. Fla., 1977; postgrad., U. Fla. Coll. of Pharmacy, 1996—. Registered pharmacist, Fla., Ala. Pharmacist mgr. Dampier's Pharmacy, Keystone Heights, Fla., 1978-82, Rite Aid Corp., Gainesville, Fla., 1982—; clerkship instr. U. Fla. Coll. of Pharmacy, 1985-96, clin. asst. prof., 1996—. Author: Jake the Snake, 1994; contbr. articles to profl. jours. Spkr., vol. Alachua County School Board, Gainesville, 1987—. Recipient Burrough-Wellcome Company award, 1978. Mem. AAAS (mentor), Fla. Pharmacy Assn., Alachua County Assn. Pharmacists (bd. dirs. 1979), Rho-Chi. Home: 4926 NW 38th St Gainesville FL 32605 Office: Rite Aid Corp 4130 NW 16th Blvd Gainesville FL 32605-3506

PICARD, THOMAS JOSEPH, JR., aerospace company executive; b. Boston, Dec. 7, 1933; s. Thomas Joseph and Bertha Mildred (Brightman) P.; BS in Mech. Engring., U. Mass., 1959; MBA, Rollins Coll., 1985; m. Renee E. Coulmas, Aug. 20, 1977; children by previous marriage: T. Gerald, Pamela P. Mfg. engr. Gen. Electric Co., 1959-60; application and sales engr. Masoneilan Div., McGraw Edison Co., 1960-65; v.p. M.D. Duncan & Assocs., Inc., Orlando, Fla., 1965-74, pres., 1974—. Pres., Brookshire Sch. PTA, Winter Park, Fla., 1969-71, Glenridge Jr. High Sch. PTA, Winter Park, 1972-73; v.p. Winter Park Little League, 1968; mem. Orange County Republican Exec. Com., 1973; mem. 35th Internat. Symposium Com., 1988-89. Served with AUS, 1953-55. Named Exec. of Month, Orlando Area, Sta. WDBO, June 1977; profl. tennis umpire. Mem. Instrument Soc. Am. (sr., mem. exec. bd. 1981-83, 89-91, chmn. 1980, dist. v.p. 1981-83, nominating com., chmn. dist. honors and awards com. 1987-89, mem. nat. edn. com., profl. cert. com., parliamentarian 1984-86, dir. edn. dept. 1985-93, v.p. 1989-91, pres's. adv. com. Aerospace Industries div. 1988-91, fin. com. 1990-94, Disting. Svc. award 1996), U.S. Tennis Assn. Rotary Orange County East (charter mem., bd. dirs. 1970-73, 85, 89-92, pres. 1972-73, Paul Harris fellow 1989, under Rotary dir. 1990-92), Masons. Congregationalist.

PICARD-AMI, LUIS ALBERTO, plastic surgeon; b. Waterbury, Conn., Mar. 1, 1958; s. Luis Alberto and Patricia (Vogan) P.; m. Adelita Alvarado, Feb. 21, 1981; children: Alexandra, Luis Demetrio, Alberto Arturo. MD, U. Panama, Republic of Panama, 1983; MSc, McGill U., 1991. Intern Nicolas Solano Gen. Hosp., La Chorrera, Panama, 1984-85; internship Social Security Met. Hosp., Panama City, Panama, 1983-84; microsurgical rsch. Royal Victoria Hosp., Montreal, 1987-88; residency plastic surgery McGill U., Montreal, Can., 1989-91, general surgery residency, 1985-89; fellowship cleft lip & palate surgery U. Miami, 1991; pvt. practice Miami, 1992—. Contbr. articles to profl. jours. With U.S. Army Res., 1989—. Fellow ACS (assoc.), Royal Coll. Physicians & Surgeons of Can.; mem. AMA (Physicians Recognition award 1991-94), Am. Soc. Plastic and Reconstructive Surgery, Can. Soc. Plastic Surgeons (assoc.), Fla. Soc. Plastic and Reconstructive Surgeons, Latin Am. Soc. Plastic Surgeons (sec.), Greater Miami Soc. Plastic and Reconstructive Surgeons, McGill U. Plastic Surgery Soc., Fla. Med. Assn., Dade County Med. Assn., Panamanian Med. Assn. Roman Catholic. Office: 351 NW 42nd Ave Ste 501 Miami FL 33126-5670

PICKARD, HOWARD BREVARD, law educator, consultant; b. Mangum, Okla., Mar. 6, 1917; s. Charles Brevard and Leila Maude (Davis) P.; m. Georgia Lela Martin, Dec. 24, 1940 (dec. Dec. 1973); children: Virginia Ann Robertson, Karen Sue Oliver; m. Sylvia Claudine Thomas, Dec. 27, 1974. BA, U. Okla., 1938, LLB, 1940; LLM, George Washington U., 1948. Bar: Okla. 1940, U.S. Supreme Ct. 1958. From atty. to supervising atty. Office of Gen. Counsel USDA, Washington, 1940-70, dir. consumer svc. div. Office of Gen. Counsel, 1970-72; prof. Cecil C. Humphrey Sch. of Law Memphis State U., 1972-87, prof. emeritus Cecil C. Humphrey Sch. of Law, 1987—. Author: (chpt.) Agricultural Law, 1981. Lt. USN, 1942-45. Mem. Lions Internat. (pres. Arlington, Va. chpt. 1965-66, dist. gov. 1970-71, pres. Germantown, Tenn. chpt. 1975-76, 87-88, dist./state chmn. com. 1972-95), Order of Coif, Phi Beta Kappa. Democrat. Home: 2075 Thorncroft Dr Memphis TN 38138-4016

PICKENS, JIMMY BURTON, earth and life science educator, military officer; b. Silver City, N.Mex., Oct. 7, 1935; s. Homer Calvin and Edna (Burton) P.; m. Joana Holterman, Oct. 7, 1955; children: Kathleen Jo Pickens Grace, Danette Lynn Pickens Fouch. BS, N.Mex. State U., 1957; MEd, U. Ariz., 1971; cert., Abilene Christian U., 1980; postgrad., LaSalle U., 1992—. Cert. secondary sch. tchr., Tex. Commd. 2nd lt. USAF, 1957, advanced through grades to lt. col., 1972; flight instr. USAF, Harlingen, Tex., 1957-60; instr. USAF Acad., San Antonio, 1960-64; edn. cons. USAF, San Antonio, 1972-75; combat aircrew USAF, Vietnam, 1964-67, advisor, 1971-72; instr. USAF Acad., Colorado Springs, Colo., 1967-70; commdr. USAF, Sacramento, Calif., 1975-78; staff officer USAF, Abilene, Tex., 1978-80, ret., 1980; tchr. earth and life sci. Wylie Jr. H.S., Abilene, 1980—; sci. textbook coord. Wylie Ind. Sch. Dist., Abilene, 1980-91, awards coord., 1982-91, mem. coordinating com. Campaign worker Tex. Rep. Party, Abilene, 1978-91; bd. dirs. Wylie Ind. Sch. Dist. United Way, 1983-87; mem. Big Country Ctr. for Profl. Devel. and Tech., Abilene, 1993—; rep. Tex. Mid. Sch. Acad., Austin, 1993-94. Decorated Bronze Star, Air medal with three oak leaf clusters, Cross of Gallantry with Palm (Vietnam); recipient Teaching Excellence award Tenn. Edn. Agy., Austin, 1984; named Tchr. of Yr. Wylie Mid. Sch. PTO, 1990. Mem. Assn. Tex. Profl. Educators (pres. 1982-83), Sci. Tchrs. Assn. Tex., Air Force Assn., Mil. Order of World Wars, Am. Assn. Educators, Wylie Tex. Conservative Acad. Network (charter), Phi Delta Kappa. Republican. Southern Baptist. Office: Wylie Jr HS 4010 Beltway S Abilene TX 79606-5509

PICKENS, WILLIAM STEWART, cardiologist; b. Bentonville, Ark., Dec. 16, 1940; s. William Craig and Mary Elizabeth (McFarland) P.; BS, U. Ark., Fayetteville, 1962; MD, U. Ark., Little Rock, 1966; children from previous marriage: Holly, Heather, Brian; m. Wanda J. Godwin. Diplomate Am. Bd. Internal Medicine (subspecialty cardiovascular diseases). Rotating intern Tampa (Fla.) Gen. Hosp., 1966-67; resident in radiology U. Fla. Med. Ctr., Gainesville, 1970-72; resident in internal medicine, then fellow in cardiology U. South Fla. Med. Center, Tampa, 1972-75; fellow in cardiovascular radiology U. Fla. Med. Center, 1974; staff physician VA Hosp., Tampa, 1974-75; practice medicine specializing in cardiology, Pensacola, Fla., 1976—; mem. staff Baptist Hosp., Sacred Heart Hosp.; asst. prof. radiology and internal medicine U. Ark., Little Rock, 1975-76 clin. assoc. prof. medicine Tulane U., 1983—; v.p. ECG Systems Inc.; bd. dirs. Mobil Diagnostics, 1985—; trustee Peer Rev. Orgn. State Fla., 1986-91. Benefactor Pickens found. for Edn., 1990. Served as officer M.C., USAF, 1967-72; maj. Res. Rockefeller scholar, 1958-59; U. Ark. Alumni scholar, 1958-60; Edn. Found. scholar, 1958-62; Barton Found. scholar, 1965; C.V. Mosby scholar, 1966. Fellow Am. Coll. Cardiology, Am. Council on Clin. Cardiology; mem. Am. Soc. Nuclear Cardiology (founding), Sigma Xi (assoc.), Alpha Omega Alpha, Phi Eta Sigma, Alpha Epsilon Delta. Republican. Episcopalian. Office: 1717 N E St Ste 331 Pensacola FL 32501-6335

PICKERING, CHARLES DENTON, accountant; b. Alamogordo, N.Mex., Aug. 2, 1950; s. Denton Wiley and Mildred Evelyn (Welch) P.; m. Crenda Jo Pack, Oct. 29, 1983; 1 child, John Denton. BS in Acctg., Miss. State U., 1973. CPA, Ohio, Ill., Tenn. Auditor U.S. Govt., 1970-80; sr. auditor Owens-Corning Fiberglas, Toledo, 1980-84; sec. mgr. internal audit Sundstrand Corp., Rockford, Ill., 1984-89, adminstr. bus. conduct and ethics, 1989-92; inspector Guardsmark, Inc., Memphis, 1992-93; mgr. forensic acctg. Network Security Mgmt. (USA) Inc., Memphis, 1993-94; prin. Charles D. Pickering, CPA, CFE, Forensic Acctg., Memphis, 1995-96; v.p. regulatory affairs LTU Internat. Airways, Miami, 1996—. Mem. AICPAs, Nat. Assn. Cert. Fraud Examiners. Home: 2501 NW 107 Ave Coral Springs FL 33065 Office: 100 N Biscayne Blvd Ste 500 Miami FL 33132-6509

PICKERING, CHARLES W., federal judge; b. 1937. BA, U. Miss., 1959, JD, 1968; Hon. Doctorate, William Carey Coll. Ptnr. Gartin, Hester and Pickering, Laurel, Miss., 1961-71; judge Laurel Mcpl. Ct., 1969; pvt. practice Laurel, 1971-72, 80; ptnr. Pickering and McKenzie, Laurel, 1973-80, Pickering and Williamson, Laurel, 1981-90; judge U.S. Dist. Ct. (so. dist.) Miss., Hattiesburg, 1990—. Contbr. articles to Mississippi Law Journal. Mem. ABA, Miss. Bar Assn., Jones County Bar. Assn., State 4-H Adv. Coun., Assn. Trial Lawyers in Am., Miss. Trial Lawyers Assn., U. Miss. Alumni Assn., Jones County Jr. Coll., Jones County Farm Bur., Kiwanis Club. Office: US Courthouse 701 N Main St Ste 228 Hattiesburg MS 39401-3471

PICKERING, JAMES HENRY, III, academic administrator; b. N.Y.C., July 11, 1937; s. James H. and Anita (Felber) P.; m. Patricia Paterson, Aug. 18, 1962; children: David Scott, Susan Elizabeth. BA, Williams Coll., 1959; MA, Northwestern U., 1960, PhD, 1964. Instr. English Northwestern U., 1963-65; mem. faculty Mich. State U., East Lansing, 1965-81; prof. English Mich. State U., 1972-81, grad. and asso. chmn. dept., 1968-75, dir. Honors Coll., 1975-81; dean Coll. Humanities and Fine Arts U. Houston, 1981-90, sr. v.p., provost, 1990-92, pres., 1992-95. Author: Fiction 100, 1974, 78, 82, 85, 88, 92, 95, The World Turned Upside Down: Prose and Poetry of the American Revolution, 1975, The Spy Unmasked, 1975, The City in American Literature, 1977, Concise Companion to Literature, 1981, Literature, 1982, 86, 90, 94, Mountaineering in Colorado, 1987, Wild Life on the Rockies, 1988, A Mountain Boyhood, 1988, The Spell of the Rockies, 1989, Purpose and Process, 1989, Poetry, 1990, In Beaver World, 1990, Rocky Mountain Wonderland, 1991, A Summer Vacation in the Parks and Mountains of Colorado, 1992, Fiction 50, 1993, Knocking Round the Rockies, 1994, Drama, 1994, Fredrick Chapin's Colorado, 1995. Mem. Coll. English Assn. (pres. 1980-81), Phi Beta Kappa, Phi Kappa Phi, Omicron Delta Kappa. Office: U Houston Dept English Houston TX 77204

PICKERING, TIMOTHY LEE, chemical research center administrator; b. Logansport, Ind., Dec. 11, 1940; s. Joseph Franklin and Helen Mae (Brown) P.; m. Dianna Lee Singleton; children: Christopher, Elizabeth, Shannon. BS, Purdue U., 1963; PhD, Princeton (N.J.) U., 1966. Rsch. chemist Union Carbide Corp., Bound Brook, N.J., 1966-69; sr. rsch. chemist Ciba-Geigy Corp., Ardsley, N.Y., 1969-73; project mgr. Pfizer, Inc., Easton, Pa., 1973-75; rsch. scientist Air Products and Chems., Allentown, Pa., 1975-91; asst. dir. NSF Rsch. Ctr. on Adhesives and Composites, Blacksburg, Va., 1991—. Patentee in field. Mem. AAAS, Am. Chem. Soc. Office: 201A Hancock Hall Blacksburg VA 24061

PICKETT, GEORGE BIBB, JR., retired military officer; b. Montgomery, Ala., Mar. 20, 1918; s. George B. and Marie (Dow) P.; BS, U.S. Mil. Acad., 1941; student Nat. War Coll., 1959-60; m. Beryl Arlene Robinson, Dec. 27, 1941; children: Barbara Pickett Harrell, James, Kathleen, Thomas; m. 2d, Rachel Copeland Peeples, July 1981. Commd. 2d lt. U.S. Army, 1941, advanced through grades to maj. gen., 1966; instr. Inf. Sch., Fort Benning, Ga., 1947-50, instr. Armed Forces Staff Coll., Norfolk, Va., 1956-59; comdg. officer 2d Armored Cav. Regt., 1961-63; chief of staff Combat Devel. Command, 1963-66; comdg. gen. 2d inf. div., Korea, 1966-67; ret., 1973; field rep. Nat. Rifle Assn., 1973-85. Decorated Purple Heart with oak leaf cluster, D.S.M. with two oak leaf clusters, Bronze Star with two oak leaf clusters and V device, Silver Star, Legion of Merit with two oak leaf clusters, Commendation medal with two oak leaf clusters. Mem. SAR (pres. Ala. Soc. 1984), Old South Hist. Assn. Episcopalian. Club: Kiwanis. Author: (with others) Joint and Combined Staff Officers Manual, 1959; contbr. articles on mil. affairs to profl. jours. Home: 3525 Flowers Dr Montgomery AL 36109-4719 Office: PO Box 4 Montgomery AL 36101-0004

PICKETT, STEPHEN ALAN, hospital executive; b. Ft. Payne, Ala., Dec. 22, 1953; s. James Benjamin Pickett and Dorothy Jane (Howell) Pickett Fancher; m. Nell Annette Horsley, Mar. 5, 1977; children: Stefanie Leigh, Allison Marie. BBA, U. Montevallo, 1976; MPH, Tulane U., 1995. CPA, Ala. Sr. acct. Ernst & Whinney, Birmingham, Ala., 1976-78; contr. East End Meml. Hosp., Birmingham, 1978, v.p. fin., 1979-84; v.p. fin. W.Va. U. Hosps., Morgantown, 1985-87, exec. v.p., adminstr., 1987-91; adminstr., COO Tulane U. Hosp. and Clinic, New Orleans, 1991-95, CEO, 1995—; bd. dirs. Met. Hosp. Coun., 1991—, Associated Hosp. Svcs., 1991—. Active sustaining mem. campaign Birmingham coun. Boy Scouts Am., 1978; mem. Jefferson County Republican Exec. Com., Birmingham, 1982, First Baptist Ch. New Orleans (fin. com. 1993—). Fellow Healthcare Fin. Mgmt. Assn.; mem. Am. Inst. C.P.A.s, Ala. Soc. C.P.A.s, U. Montevallo Alumni Assn. (life), Alpha Tau Omega Alumni Assn. Baptist. Lodge: Rotary. Home: 185 Lakewood Estates Dr New Orleans LA 70131-8364 Office: Tulane U Hosp & Clinic 1415 Tulane Ave New Orleans LA 70112-2605

PICKETT, STEPHEN WESLEY, university official; b. Billings, Mont., May 27, 1956; s. Wesley William and Carol Ann (Bollum) P. BA, Houston Bapt. U., 1980; MS, U. North Tex., 1988. Cert. elem. tchr., rehab. counselor, Tex. Hosp. tchr. Houston Ind. Sch. Dist., 1981-85; asst. to assoc. dean of students U. North Tex., Denton, 1988-90, asst. coord. disabled student svcs. Office V.P. student affairs, 1990-91, dir. Office Disability Accommodation, 1991—. Co-author: curriculum guide The Newspaper as a Student Communicator, 1982 (winner Exxon Found.'s Impact Two award for creative teaching). Chair Mayor's Com. on Employment of Persons with Disabilities, Denton, 1990; mem. coun.-at-large Sam Houston Area Coun. Boy Scouts Am., Houston, 1975—; grad. Denton C. of C. Leadership Program, 1992; pub. rels. chair leadership Denton Steering Com., 1993-94. Recipient Cmty. Svc. award U. North Tex., 1992, award for svcs. to persons with disabilities North Tex. Rehab. Assn., 1993, Disting. Alumnus award Houston Bapt. U., 1994, Outstanding Alumnus award Ctr. for Rehab. Studies, U. North Tex., 1995. Mem. Assn. Higher Edn. and Disability, Coun. Exceptional Children, Tex. Assn. Coll. and Univ. Student Pers. Adminstrs. (chair multicultural com. 1994-95). Presbyterian. Office: U North Tex Office Disabili 318A Union Bldg 400 Avenue A Denton TX 76201-5874

PICKLE BEATTIE, KATHERINE HAMNER, real estate agent; b. Henrico County, Va., Sept. 30, 1936; d. Laurance Davis and Susan (Mooers) Hamner; widowed 1969; children: Katherine Carter Beattie, Harry Canfield Beattie IV, Margaret Spotswood Beattie; m. Timothy L. Pickle, III, Dec. 29, 1989. Attended, Va. Commonwealth U. Pres. Varina Wood Products, Inc., Gloucester-Mathews County, 1969-75; real estate agt. Nat. Assn. Bd. Realtors, Gloucester-Mathews County, Richmond, Va., 1975—; pres. Varina Wood Products, Inc., 1969-75. Pres. George F. Baker PTA, 1970; v.p. Varina Women's Club, Henrico, Va., 1969-70; sec. Mathews Women's Club, 1992-94; mem. Rep. Women's Club; mem. Va. Mus. Fine Arts, Naples, Fla. Philharm. Ctr. for Arts com. of a thousand. Mem. DAR, Va. Lioins Club, King's Daus., Raleigh Tavern Soc., Colonial Williamsburg, Va. Mus. Fine Arts. Episcopalian. Home: PO Box 317 Gwynn VA 23066-0317

PIEGORSCH, WALTER WILLIAM, statistics educator, statistician; b. New Rochelle, N.Y., Oct. 29, 1958; s. Walter K. and Emmie (Roland) P.; m. Karen Marie Stange, Apr. 22, 1986. BA magna cum laude, Colgate U., 1979; MS, Cornell U., 1982, PhD, 1984. Math. statistician NIH, Durham, N.C., 1984-93; assoc. prof. statistics U. S.C., Columbia, 1993-96, prof. statistics, 1996—; cons. Nat. Inst. Statis. Sci., Research Triangle Park, N.C., 1993-94, 96. Assoc. editor: Ecological & Environ. Stats., 1994—; mem. editl. bd. Environ. and Molecular Mutagenesis, 1994—, Mutation Rsch., 1994—; contbr. sci. articles to profl. jours. Asst. scoutmaster Boy Scouts Am., Chapel Hill, N.C., 1984-86. Sigma Xi grantee, 1982, 83. Fellow Am. Statis. Assn. (liaison officer sect. on environment 1991-92, chmn. program com. 1993-94, Disting. Achievement medal 1993, assoc. editor jour. Am. Statis. Assn. 1996—); mem. Internat. Environmetric Assn. (assoc. editor jour. Environmetrics 1992—), biometric Soc. (sec. Ea. N.Am. region 1995-96), Internat. Statis. Inst., Environ. Mutagen Soc., Consumers Union. Lutheran.

PIÉLAGO, RAMON, insurance company executive; b. Habana, Cuba, June 30, 1929; came to U.S., 1960; s. Ramon and Virginia (Alvarez) P.; 1 child, Ramón. BBA, Habana U., 1952. Pres. Pielago & Assocs., Miami, Fla., 1972—. Mem. Million Dollar Round Table (life). Home: 2333 Brickell Ave #2006 Miami FL 33129 Office: 717 Ponce De Leon Blvd Ste 226 Coral Gables FL 33134-2048

PIEPHO, (EDWARD) LEE, humanities educator; b. Detroit, Jan. 10, 1942; s. Edward Ernest and Dolores Faye (Dowis) P.; m. Susan Brand, June 13, 1964. AB, Kenyon Coll., 1964; MA, Columbia U., 1966; PhD, U. Va., 1972. Instr. Sweet Briar (Va.) Coll., 1969-72, asst. prof., 1972-78, assoc. prof., 1978-83, prof., 1983-94, Shallenberger Brown prof., 1994—, dept. chmn., 1983-86, coord. European civilization program, 1986-89. Translator, editor: Adulescentia: The Eclogues of Mantuan, 1989; contbr. articles to profl. jours. SIMRS fellow, 1979, Dulin fellow Folger Shakespeare Libr., 1989-90, Mednick fellow, 1996. Mem. Internat. Assn. for Neo-Latin Studies, Modern Lang. Assn. Am., Renaissance Soc. Am. Home: Woodland Rd Sweet Briar VA 24595 Office: Sweet Briar Coll Dept English Sweet Briar VA 24595

PIERCE, CATHERINE MAYNARD, history educator; b. York County, Va., Oct. 11, 1918; d. Edward Walker Jr. and Cassie Cooke (Sheppard) Maynard; m. Frank Marion Pierce Jr., Oct. 4, 1940 (dec. 1974); children: Frank Marion III, Bruce Maynard. BS in Sec. Edn., Longwood Coll., Farmville, Va., 1939; postgrad., Coll. William and Mary, Williamsburg, 1948, 58, 68. Tchr. York County Pub. Schs., Va., 1939-45; instr. Chesapeake (Va.) pub. schs., 1946-49, 57-74; cons. Vol. Svcs., Williamsburg, Va., 1975—. Author audio-visual hist. narratives for use in pub. schs., 1965-86. Organizer The Chapel at Kingsmill on the James, Williamsburg, 1987—, chmn. governing bd., 1987—. Mem. DAR (regent Williamsburg chpt. 1980-83). Baptist. Address: Kingsmill on the James 4 Bray Wood Rd Williamsburg VA 23185-5504

PIERCE, DONALD FAY, lawyer; b. Bexley, Miss., Aug. 28, 1930; s. Percy O. and Lavada S. (Stringfellow) P.; m. Norma Faye Scribner, June 5, 1954; children: Kathryn Pierce Peake, D. F. Jr., John S., Jeff G. BS, U. Ala., 1956, JD, 1958. Bar: Ala. 1958, U.S. Ct. Appeals (5th cir.) 1958, U.S. Dist. Ct. (no., mid. and so. dists.) Ala. 1958, U.S. Ct. Appeals (11th cir.) 1982. Law clk. to presiding judge U.S. Dist. Ct. (so. dist.) Ala., 1958-59; ptnr. Hand, Arendall, Bedsole, Greaves & Johnston, Mobile, Ala., 1964-91, Pierce, Carr, Alford, Ledyard & Latta, P.C., Mobile, 1991—. Trustee, UMS Prep. Sch., 1980-87; mem. Products Liability Adv. Coun., 1990—; bd. overseers The Vanderbilt Cancer Ctr., 1994—. 1st lt. U.S. Army, 1951-53. Mem. Ala. Def. Lawyers Assn. (past pres.), Fedn. Ins. and Corp. Counsel, Am. Acad. Hosp. Attys., Internat. Assn. Def. Counsel, Def. Counsel Trial Acad. (bd. dirs. 1983-84), Def. Research Inst. (pres. 1987, chmn. 1988). Baptist. Contbr. articles to profl. jours. Home: 4452 Winnie Way Mobile AL 36608-2221 Office: Pierce Ledyard et al 1110 Montlimar Dr Ste 900 Mobile AL 36609-1732

PIERCE, EDWARD MARTIN, administrator. BS, U.S. Mil. Acad., 1950. Supr., analyst Dept. Army and Dept. Def., chief of office; small bus. and investment counsellor; tchr. internat. bus. and fin. Contbr. articles to profl. jours. Mem. Strategic Mgmt. Soc., Acad. of Mgmt., Am. Fin. Assn., Fin. Mgmt Assn., So. Fin. Assn., Southwestern Fin. Assn., Ea. Fin. Assn., Doctoral Assn. George Washington U. (past pres.). Home: 3124 Peachtree Cir Davie FL 33328-6705

PIERCE, JERRY EARL, business executive; b. Hinsdale, Ill., Aug. 3, 1941; s. Earl and Adeline A. (Zaranski) P.; m. Carol Louise Martin, Aug. 15, 1964; children: Patricia, Barbara, Linda, Bradley. BS, U. Ill., 1964. With R.R. Donnelley & Sons, Chgo., 1964-70; with Western Pub. Co., Racine, Wis., from 1970, nat. pubs. sales mgr., from 1975; pres. Pierce Sale Co., Inc., Restaurant Equipment World, Inc., Heat Transfer Engring. Inc.; chmn. bd. Tech Industries & Nillwork, Inc., 1989-93; pres. B.J. Installation Co., Inc., 1989-91, ROI World Equipment, 1993—; v.p., sec. Savers Clubs Am., Inc. 1st lt. U.S. Army, 1968-70. Mem. Printing Industry Am., Sales and Mktg. Execs., Fla. Restaurant Assn., Food Svc. Cons. Soc., Food Equipment Distbrs. Assn. (bd. dirs. 1994—). Republican. Episcopalian. Clubs: Interlochen Country (Winter Park, Fla.), Cleve. Advt. Patentee refrigeration-to-water utility cost control system. Home: 2171 Sharon Rd Winter Park FL 32789-1210 Office: 213 N Forsyth Rd Orlando FL 32807-5013

PIERCE, JIM, recording industry producer; b. Pasadena, Calif., Nov. 25, 1932; s. Knute Gunderson Nipedal and Genie (Frick) Pierce; m. Verena Gisela von Guaita, Mar. 12, 1953. Student, Tarleton State Coll., Stephenville, Tex., 1952, Modesto (Calif.) Jr. Coll., 1956. Pianist, band leader Nighthawks, Medford, Oreg., 1953-54; pianist Chester Smith Band, Modesto, 1954-58; producer Poppy Records, Modesto, 1956-58; pianist Capitol, RCA Records, Hollywood, Calif., 1958-65, Nashville Nev. Club, Golden Nuggett, Las Vegas, 1961-68; disc jockey Sta. KVEG-Radio, Las Vegas, 1966-68; pianist Grand Ole Opry, Nashville, 1969-85; pianist, producer Round Robin Records, Hendersonville, Tenn., 1972—; producer Playback Gallery II, Ridgewood Records, Miami, Fla., 1984-90; pres. Strawboss Music (BMI), Hendersonville, 1970—, TNT Talent Agy., Madison, Tenn., 1983-86; v.p. Roy Drusky Enterprises, Madison, 1976-84; band leader Nashville Express, Hendersonville, 1990—. Performed on the piano on 18 number one records; produced over 200 chart records, including 4 numer one records, in Billboard and Cash Box Mags.; coord. all-star country concert for 1994 Winter Olympics, Norway. With USAF, 1951-53. Named Ind. Prodr. of Yr., Internat. Ind. Country Music Awards Show, Nashville, 1991, one of Top 5 Prodrs. and Record Labels in U.S. Cash Box Mag., 1992; nominated for Best Ind. Prodr. Cash Box Mag., 1989, Ind. Prodr. of Yr., 1993. Mem. Am. Fedn. Musicians, Country Music Assn., Reunion Profl. Entertainers, Nashville Assn. Talent Dirs.

PIERCE, LINDA RADCLIFFE, librarian; b. Washington, Mar. 28, 1967; d. James Glenn and Lucille Opal (Bernstein) Radcliffe; m. Howard Wilson Pierce, Jan. 2, 1993; children: Virginia Rose, James David. BS in Edn., Va. Tech., 1990; MLS, Cath. U., 1995. Libr. Am. Geol. Inst., Alexandria, Va., 1990—. Vol. firefighter Fairfax Vol. Fire Dept., 1990-92. Mem. Geosci. Info. Soc. (union list of geol. field trip guide books com. 1990—). Roman Catholic. Office: Am Geol Inst 4220 King St Alexandria VA 22302

PIERCE, MARTHA CHILDRESS, dietitian; b. Kingsport, Tenn., Apr. 5, 1938; d. John Earl Childress and Irene Pecktol; m. Harold W. Pierce, Dec. 12, 1964; 1 child, Chuck. BS, U. Tenn., 1960, MPH, 1982. Registered dietitian; cert. tchr., Tenn. Intern Hines (Ill.) VA Hosp., 1961; field nutritionist Atlanta, Chgo., 1961-63; dietitian Piedmont Hosp., Atlanta, 1963; asst. dean U. Tenn., Knoxville, 1963-64; dietitian Lake Shore Mental Health, Knoxville, 1972-74; instr. Roone State Community Coll., Knoxville, 1988; tchr. KAMA Health Discovery Ctr., Knoxville, 1990; dietitian cons. Shannondale Health Care, Knoxville, 1991-92; customer svc. rep. Dillards Dept. Store, 1993—; sampling specialist Fresh Market, Knoxville, 1989-94; substitute tchr. Knox County Schs., Knoxville, 1984-93. Active Operation Health Check H. Sanders Wellness, Ft. Sanders Hosp., Knoxville, 1985-87, crime prevention Knoxville City Police Dept., mobile meals Knoxville Area Cmty. Action; local judge 4-H CLub Divsn. USDA, Knoxville, 1991, 93. Mem. Am. Home Econs. Assn., Knoxville Dist. Dietetic Assn. (historian 1985-89). Republican. Methodist. Home: 8517 Corteland Dr Knoxville TN 37909-2122

PIERCE, RHONDA YVETTE, criminologist; b. Tampa, Fla., Dec. 4, 1959; d. Howard Jr. and Olivia (Powell) P. AA in Criminal Justice, Hillsboro C.C., Tampa, 1979; BS in Criminology, Fla. State U., Tallahassee, 1981. Cert. mgr. of housing. With Tampa Housing Authority, 1982-96, mgmt. coord., 1988-90, lease enforcement officer, exec. asst., 1991, dir. ops., 1992-94, dir. human resources, 1994-95; exec. dir. Sarasota (Fla.) Housing Authority, 1996—. Area youth dir. 11th Episcopal dist. A.M.E. Ch., Tampa, 1991-95, dir. ops., 1992-94, dir. human rels., 1994-96; local youth dir. Mt. Olive A.M.E. Ch., Tampa, 1989-91; exec. dir. Sarasota Housing Authority, 1996—. Recipient Dedicated Christian Svc. award Mt. Olive A.M.E. Ch., 1983. Mem. Nat. Assn. Housing and Redevel. Ofcls. Methodist. Office: Sarasota Housing Authority 1300 6th St Sarasota FL 34236-4977

PIERCE, RICHARD HARRY, research director for laboratory. Rsch. dir. Mote Marine Lab., Sarasota, Fla. Office: Mote Marine Lab 1600 Ken Thompson Pkwy Sarasota FL 34236-1004

PIERCE, ROLANDA LANETTA, medical/surgical nurse; b. Nashville, Sept. 17, 1963; d. James Vince and Mary Louise (Brown) P. BSN, Tuskegee U., 1985; MS in Nursing, Troy State U., 1990; postgrad., Vanderbilt U., 1993. RN, Ala.; cert. clin. specialist, med.-surg. nurse. Relief supr. Fairview Med. Ctr., Montgomery, 1985, charge nurse; staff nurse Jackson Hosp. & Clinic, Montgomery, 1989-89, nurse clinician, 1989-90; ednl. instr. Jackson Hosp. & Clinic, 1990-93; staff nurse Jackson Hosp. and Clinic, 1993—; rsch. cons., analyst Vanderbilt U. Med. Ctr., Nashville, Tenn. Mem. ANA, Ala. Nurses Assn., Sigma Theta Tau, Chi Eta Phi, Delta Sigma Theta. Home: 60 Plus Park Blvd Nashville TN 37217-1024

PIERCE, VERLON LANE, pharmacist, small business owner; b. Greensburg, Ky., July 13, 1949; s. Ogle Lee and Aleene (Hall) P.; m. Brenda Mildred Russell, May 20, 1973; children: Amanda Lee, Daniel Russell. BS in Math. and Chemistry, Western Ky. U., 1972; BS in Pharmacy, U. Ky., 1975. Relief pharmacist Shugart & Willis Drug Store, Franklin, Ky., 1975-78; staff pharmacist Franklin Simpson Meml. Hosp., Franklin, 1976-79; owner, pres. pharmacist Medicine Shoppe, Bowling Green, Ky., 1978—; pres. Westland Drug Inc., Bowling Green, 1984-89; pres. JP Solutions, Inc., DBA Option Care, 1988—; sec. 21st Investment Group, Bowling Green, 1984—. Recipient Franny award Internat. Franchise Assn., 1980; Hall of Fame bust Medicine Shoppe, St. Louis, 1983. Mem. 4th Dist. Pharmacy Group (pres. 1983-84), Ky. Pharmacy Assn., Masons, Shriners. Democrat. Baptist. Avocations: golf, swimming. Home: 1414 Mount Ayr Cir Bowling Green KY 42103-4709 Office: Medicine Shoppe 818 Us 31W Byp Bowling Green KY 42101-2314

PIERLUISI, PEDRO RAFAEL, attorney general; b. San Juan, P.R., Apr. 26, 1959; s. Jorge A. and Doris (Urrutia) P.; m. Maria E. Rojo, June 20, 1981; children: Anthony, Michael, Jacqueline, Rafael. BA, Tulane U., 1981; JD, George Washington U., 1984. Bar: D.C. 1984, U.S. Dist. Ct. D.C. 1985, U.S. Ct. Appeals (D.C. cir.) 1985, P.R. 1990, U.S. Supreme Ct. 1990. Assoc. Verner, Liipfert, Bernhard, McPherson & Hand, Washington, 1984-85, Cole, Corette & Abrutyn, Washington, 1985-90; ptnr. Pierluisi & Pierluisi, San Juan, 1990-93; atty. gen. Govt. of P.R., 1996—; chmn. exec. bd. Forensic Scis. Inst., 1993—, Criminal Justice Info. System, 1993—; chmn. confiscations bd. Govt. of P.R., 1993—. Mem. ABA (mem. ho. of dels., mem. standing com. on substance abuse), Nat. Assn. Attys. Gen. (chair eastern region), Fed. Bar Assn., George Washington U. Internat. Law Soc. (pres. 1982-83), Rotary, Phi Alpha Delta (hon., Munoz chpt.). Office: Puerto Rico Dept Justice PO Box 192 San Juan PR 00902

PIERONI, ROBERT EDWARD, internist, educator; b. Portland, Maine, June 20, 1937; s. Ansel Kirby and Agnes Mary (Dumais) P.; m. Dorothy Louise McDonnell, Oct. 3, 1970; children: Michelle Kirby, Robert Francis. BS, Boston Coll., 1959; MD, Pa. State U., 1971. Chemist Mass. Dept. Pub. Health, Boston, 1962-71; sr. bacteriologist Mass. Dept. Pub. Health, 1971-74; asst. prof. internal medicine U. Ala., Tuscaloosa, 1974-76, assoc. prof. dept. internal medicine and family practice, 1976-81, prof. internal medicine and family practice, 1981—; cons. VA Hosp., Bryce Hosp. and Partlow State Hosp., Tuscaloosa, 1974—. Contbr. more than 250 textbooks, articles and chpts.; mem. editorial bd. various jours. Col. U.S. Army, 1961—. Decorated Bronze Star, 1991, Commendation for Valor; recipient Golden Stethoscope award, 1982, Faculty Recognition award, 1986, Ala. Golden Eagle Humanitarian award Ala. Sr. Citizens Hall of Fame, 1988. Fellow Am. Bd. Internal Medicine (diplomate), Am. Bd. Family Practice (diplomate), Am. Bd. Allergy and Immunology (diplomate), Am. Bd. Geriatric Medicine (diplomate), Am. Bd. Quality Assurance (diplomate); Mem. AMA, ACP, Am. Coll. Allergy and Immunology, Am. Gerontol. Soc., Am. Acad. Family Physicians, Physicians for Human Rights, Undersea and Hyperbaric Med. Soc., C. of C., VFW, Am. Legion. Democrat. Roman Catholic. Home: 398 Riverdale Tuscaloosa AL 35406-1802 Office: U Ala Dept Internal Medicine PO Box 870326 Tuscaloosa AL 35487-0326

PIERRE, CHARLES BERNARD, mathematician, statistician, educator; b. Houston, Dec. 2, 1946; s. Rufus and Charles (Ellis) P.; m. Patsy Randle, Aug. 28, 1970 (div. 1971); m. Cynthia Gilliam, June 28, 1980 (div. 1994); 1 child, Kimberly Keri. BS, Tex. So. U., 1970, MS in Edn., 1974; PhD in Math. Edn., Am. U., 1992. Cert. tchr., Tex., D.C. Comml. photographer Photographics Labs., Houston, 1968-69; elec. engr., mathematician Sta. KPRC-TV, Houston, 1970-71; instr. math. Houston Ind. Sch. Dist., 1971-72, Meth. Secondary Sch., Kailahun, Sierra Leone, West Africa, 1972-73; math. researcher West African Regional Math Program, Freetown, Sierra Leona, West Africa, 1973-77; instr. math. Houston Ind. Sch. Dist., 1977-80, 81-87, Episcopal Acad., Merion, Pa., 1980-81, D.C. Pub. Schs., Washington, 1987-91; instr. math. Houston C.C., 1985-87; asst. prof. math. and computer sci. San Jose State U., 1992-94; assoc. prof. math. scis. Clark Atlanta U., 1994—; African cons. Peace Corps, Phila., 1977, Sierra Leone, West Africa; lectr. math. Tex. So. U., U. Sierra Leone, U. Liberia, Bunambu Tchrs. Coll., Port Loko Tchrs. Coll., Inst. Edn., West Africa; assessment coord. Calif. State U. Alliance for Minority Participation, San Jose, 1994; advisor design team SKYMATH Project, Boulder, Colo., 1994—; assoc. dir. Park City/IAS Math. Inst. Clark Atlanta U., 1994—; participant Inst. History Math., 1994—; cons. in field. Author: Introduction to Coordinate Analytic Geometry, 1974, Mathematics for Elementary School Teachers, 1976; co-author: The Modern Approach to Trigonometry, 1975, A Resource Book for Teachers, 1975, Picture Book for the West African Regional Math. Program, 1975, textbook 6th grade STEM project U. Mont., 1996. Vol. Peace Corps., Sierra Leone. NSF fellow. Mem. ASCD, NAM, Am. Soc. for Quality Control, Am. Math. Soc., Math. Assn. Am. Democrat. Baptist. Home: 3360 Penny Ln Apt C East Point GA 30344-5557

PIERSON, GIL, broadcast executive; b. Providence, Feb. 7, 1947; s. Lionel Armand and Teresa Lea (Graziosi) P.; m. Suzanne Hyle, Mar. 23, 1968 (div. June 1986); children: Kelly, Marleen; m. Barbara Ann McLoughlin, May 30, 1987 (div. Jan. 1995); 1 child, Sean. Degree in pub. rels., Barry U., 1992-94. Registered lobbyist, Fla.; lic. real estate broker; notary pub. Sr. acct. exec. So. Bell, Ft. Lauderdale, Fla., 1970-96; exec. dir. N.E. Alzheimer's Day Care Ctr., Inc., Deerfield Beach, Fla., 1992-94; sr. account exec. Continental Cablevision/U.S. West; real estate broker HUD, Dept. Vet. Affairs. Cand. State Rep., Deerfield Beach, 1992; mem. coun. exec. dirs. United Way; mem. Broward Alzheimer's Coord. Coun.; mem. planning and zoning bd. City of Deerfield Beach; membership dir. Broward County Fair; bd. dirs. Capital Improvement Bond, City of Deerfield Beach; mem. sch. improvement team Quiet Waters Elem. Recipient Area Agy. on Aging Advocacy award; named one of Outstanding Young Men of Am., 1982. Mem. Deerfield C. of C. (Vol. of Yr. 1992, chmn. bd.), Deerfield Beach Kiwanis (v.p. 1990-93), KC (4th deg.), Jaycees (state sec. 1981-82).

PIETRANTONI, MARCELLO, obstetrician-gynecologist; b. Tumbes, South America, Sept. 10, 1955; came to U.S., 1962; s. Mario and Nellie (Estratti) P.; m. Doreen Marie Balzano; children: Dina Palma, Bianca Graciela, Olivia. Student, U. Windsor, Ontario, Can., 1974-75; BS in Biology, Niagara U., 1978; MD, U. Autonoma de Guadalajara, Jalisco, Mexico, 1982. Lic. physician Ariz., Fla., Ky., N.Y. Resident in ob-gyn. SUNY, Buffalo, 1984-87, chief resident, 1987-88; fellow U. South Fla., 1988-90; asst. prof. maternal-fetal medicine U. Ariz. Med. Ctr., 1990-92, U. Louisville (Ky.) Hosp., 1992—; adv. coun. mem. Project Link Jefferson Alcohol & Drug Abuse Ctr.; reviewer and lectr. in field. Mem. editl. bd. Louisville Medicine, 1995-96; contbr. articles to profl. jours. Grantee Otsuka Am. Pharm., Inc.1996—, U. Ariz., U. Ariz. Health Sci. Ctr., Ortho McNeil Pharm., ADEZA Pharm., Alliant Cmty. Trust Fund; Student MaCain fellow, 1989; recipient Berlex Jr. Faculty award, 1993. Fellow Am. Coll. Obstet.; mem. AMA, Am. Diabetes Assn., Pima County Med. Soc., Tucson Med. Soc., Soc. Perinatologist, Am. Inst. Ultrasound in Medicine, Louisville Ob-Gyn. Soc., Jefferson county Med. Soc., Ky. Med. Soc. Office: Univ Louisville ACB Bldg Ob-Gyn Dept Louisville KY 40292

PIGNATARO, EVELYN DOROTHY, trauma clinician, operating room nurse; b. Morristown, N.J., Jan. 24, 1950; d. Joseph Anthony and Dorothy E. (Crothers) P. BS cum laude, Austin Peay State U., 1977; BSN magna cum laude, Barry U., 1987. Cert. surg. technologist; cert. ACLS, TNCCP, CNOR. Surg. technologist Meml. Regional Hosp., Hollywood, Fla., staff nurse operating rm., charge nurse, asst. nurse mgr. Mem. Assn. Surg. Technologists, Sigma Theta Tau.

PIGOTT, JOHN DOWLING, geologist, geophysicist, geochemist, educator, consultant; b. Gorman, Tex., Feb. 2, 1951; s. Edwin Albert and Emma Jane (Poe) P.; m. Kulwadee Lawwongngam, May 28, 1994. BA in Zoology, U. Tex., 1974, BS in Geology, 1974, MA in Geology, 1977; PhD in Geology, Northwestern U., 1981. Geologist Amoco Internat., Chgo., 1978-80; sr. petroleum geologist Amoco Internat., Houston, 1980-81; asst., then assoc. prof. U. Okla., Norman, 1981—; vis. prof. Mus. Natural History, Paris, 1988, Sun Yat Sen U., Kaohsiung, Taiwan, 1991; rsch. dir. 5 nation Red Sea-Gulf of Aden seismic stratigraphy and basis analysis industry consortium, 1992—; internat. energy cons., 1981—; instr. I.H.R.D.C., Boston, 1987-91, O.G.C.I., Tulsa, 1991—. Mem. editl. bd. Geotectonica et Metallogenin Jour., 1992—. Mem. Am. Assn. Petroleum Geologists, Soc. Exploration Geophysicists, Soc. Petroleum Engrs., Geol. Soc. Am., Indonesian Petroleum Assn., Sigma Xi. Roman Catholic; Buddhist. Office: U Okla Sch Geology & Geophysics 100 E Boyd St Norman OK 73019-1000

PIGOTT, MELISSA ANN, social psychologist; b. Ft. Myers, Fla., Jan. 28, 1958; d. Park Trammell and Leola Ann (Wright) P.; m. David H. Fauss, Jan. 1, 1988. BA in Psychology, Fla. Internat. U., Miami, 1979; MS in Social Psychology, Fla. State U., 1982, PhD in Social Psychology, 1984. Rsch. asst. Fla. Internat. U., 1978-79, Fla. State U., Tallahassee, 1980-84; dir. mktg. rsch. Bapt. Med. Ctr., Jacksonville, Fla., 1984-89; rsch. assoc. Litigation Scis., Inc., Atlanta, 1989-91; sr. litigation psychologist Trial Cons., Inc., Miami, 1991-93; dir. rsch. Magnus Rsch. Cons. Inc., Ft. Lauderdale, 1993—; adj. prof. psychology U. North Fla., Jacksonville, 1985-89, Nova Southeastern U., Ft. Lauderdale, 1995—. Author: Social Psychology: Study Guide, 1990, Social Psychology: Instructors Manual, 1990; contbr. articles to profl. jours. Mem. ACLU, Am. Psychol. Assn., Am. Psychol. Law Soc., Amnesty Internat., Civitan Internat., Southeastern Psychol. Assn., Soc. for Psychol. Study of Social Issues, Soc. Personality and Social Psychology, Greenpeace, Psi Chi. Democrat. Office: Magnus Rsch Cons Inc 1305 NE 23rd Ave Ste 1 Pompano Beach FL 33062-3748

PIKE, BONNIE HAYKIN, playwright, lyricist; b. Omaha, Jan. 1, 1939; d. Harry D. and Pauline C. (Nogg) Haykin; m. Larry S. Pike, June 21, 1959; children: Douglas H., Stacey R., Scott H. BA, SUNY, 1979. Instr. humanities Paideia Sch., Atlanta, 1980-83; playwright, lyricist, 1983—; resident playwright The Theatrical Outfit, Atlanta, 1985-88; artistic resident Emory U., Atlanta, 1990-91; resident artist Capital City Opera, Inc., Atlanta, 1995—. Author: (play) Three Brass Monkeys, 1983 (Nat. Play award 1984); (jazz opera) Sweet Sweet Auburn, 1987; (cabaret) Judgement of Dec. 23, 1992; (opera) Pinnochio, 1995. Recipient grant Bur. Cultural Affairs, Atlanta, 1984. Mem. Atlanta New Play Project (pres. 1986-87), Southeastern Playwrights Project.

PIKE, THOMAS HARRISON, plant chemist; b. West Palm Beach, Fla., Oct. 9, 1950; s. Rufus Draper and Dora Marie (Thomason) P.; m. Julie Lynn Simpson, Aug. 19, 1972; 1 child, Thomas Simpson. BS, Baylor U., 1972. Sci. instr. Valliant (Okla.) Pub. Sch., 1975-76; sch. adminstr. Swink (Okla.) Pub. Sch., 1976-81; plant chemist Western Farmers Electric Coop., Ft. Towson, Okla., 1981—; mem. adv. bd. Kiamichi Vo-Tech Sch., Idabel, Okla., 1985-87. Charter mem. Valliant Youth Assn., 1987-91. Mem. ASME (co-chmn. task force 1988-90), ASTM, Nat. Assn. Corrosion Engrs. Home: RR 1 Box 299 Garvin OK 74736-9755 Office: Western Farmers Electric Coop PO Box 219 Fort Towson OK 74735-0219

PILCHER, BENJAMIN LEE, biology educator; b. Corpus Christi, Tex., Feb. 25, 1938; s. John Fuller Pilcher and Maurine (Rogers) Langham; m. Melissa Jane Payne, June 5, 1965; children: Walter Fuller, Stephen Lee. BS, Tex. Tech Coll., 1961, MS, 1963; PhD, U. N.Mex., 1969. Instr., asst. prof. U. Tex., Arlington, 1963-66; grad. asst. U. N.Mex., Albuquerque, 1966-69; prof. biology McMurry U., Abilene, Tex., 1969—, dir. honors program, 1987—; seasonal park ranger Nat. Park Svc., Bandelier Nat. Monument, N.Mex., 1961, 62, 65, 67, 69. Mem., chmn. Citizen's Energy Coun., Abilene, 1980-84. Mem. Cactus and Succulent Soc., Sigma Xi. Presbyterian. Home: 20 Gardenia Cir Abilene TX 79605-6418 Office: McMurry U Biology Dept Abilene TX 79697

PILCHER, JAMES BROWNIE, lawyer; b. Shreveport, La., May 19, 1929; s. James Reece and Martha Mae (Brown) P.; m. Lorene Pilcher; children: Lydia, Martha, Bradley. BA, La. State U., 1952; JD summa cum laude, John Marshall Law Sch., 1955; postgrad. Emory U., 1957. Bar: Ga. 1955. Legal aide to Speaker of Ho. of Reps., 1961-64; assoc. city atty. City of Atlanta, 1964-69; pvt. practice law, Atlanta, 1969—. Exec. committeeman Dem. Exec. Com. of Fulton County, Ga., 1974-86; bd. dirs. Whitehead Boys Club, 1961-89; trustee Ga. Inst. Continuing Legal Edn, 1988-89. Mem. ABA, State Bar Ga. (chmn. 1988-89, gen. practice and trial sect., chmn. criminal law sect. 1986-87), Ga. Assn. Criminal Def. Lawyers (pres. 1980-82), Ga. Trial Lawyers (mem. exec. com. 1980—), Ga. Claimants Attys. Assn. (pres. 1983-84), Nat. Assn. Criminal Def. Lawyers (bd. dirs. 1980-85), Ga. Inst. Trial Advocacy (bd. dirs. 1986-89), South Fulton Bar Assn. (pres. 1987-88), Assn. Trial Lawyers Am., Kiwanis (Peachtree, Atlanta pres. 1983-84, gov. Ga. dist. 1992-93). Presbyterian. Home: 1195 W Wesley Rd NW Atlanta GA 30327-1407 Office: One Northside 75 Atlanta GA 30318-7715

PILGRIM, CAROL ANN, psychology educator; b. Richmond, Va., May 21, 1956; d. William E. and Eleanor Ann (Fowler) P. BA in Psychology, Va. Poly. Inst. and State U., 1978; MS in Psychology, U. Fla., 1983, PhD in Psychology, 1987. Nat. dir. tng. Mammatech Corp., Gainesville, Fla., 1983-86; lectr. psychology U. N.C., Wilmington, 1986-88, asst. prof., 1988-91, assoc. prof., 1991-96, prof., 1996—; mem. univ. union adv. bd. U. N.C., Wilmington, 1986-91, mem. ROTC adv. bd., 1986-90, co-dir. Seahawk Scholarship Run, 1989, 90, mem. adv. bd. Chancellor's Student Health and Wellness Ctr., 1987-89, chairperson, 1987-88, presenter workshops, mem. univ. meetings; dir. ann. breast exam. evaluations Sch. Medicine U. N.C., Chapel Hill, 1988, 89, 90; rsch. cons. Harvard Cmty. Health Plan, 1990, U. Vt., 1989-92, Sch. Medicine SUNY, Stony Brook, Fox Chase Cancer Ctr. and Sch. Medicine Duke U.; presenter in field. Reviewer Prentice-Hall pub.; ad hoc reviewer mental health retardation panel NIH; guest reviewer Jour. Gen. Internal Medicine, 1994, Am. Jour. Mental Retardation, 1993, 94, Am. Psychologist, 1991; mem. bd. editors: (book series) Behavior Analysis and Society; co-author/presenter (video tape) Clinical Examination of the Breast, 1988; contbr. articles to profl. publs. Mem. adv. com. for breast cancer screening New Hanover County, 1987-91; mem. mammography consortium Nat. Cancer Inst., 1989; active Breast Cancer Task Force, 1988-89, Women's Health Network, 1987-89. Rsch. grantee CDC-U. N.C., Chapel Hill, 1986-87, 87-88, Nat. Cancer Inst.-U. N.C., 1987-91, Sci. and Soc. Project Summer Stipend, 1990, Rockefeller Found., 1991-92, NSF, 1993-96, Nat. Inst. Child Health and Devel., 1996—. Mem. APA, Assn. for Behavior Analysis (mem. adv. bd. Behavior Analyst Jour. 1993—, bd. editors 1992-95, active exptl. analysis of human behavior spl. interest group, co-chairperson 1988-91, bd. editors bull. 1991—, co-editor bull. 1988-91), Soc. for Advancement of Behavior Analysis (bd. dirs. 1995—, exec. coun. lat-large rep. 1995—, assoc. editor Jour. Exptl. Analysis of behavior, mem. bd. editors 1992-95), Soc. for Exptl. Analysis of behavior (bd. dirs. 1994—, adv. bd. Cambridge Ctr. for Behavioral Studies), Southeastern Assn. for Behavior Analysis (pres. 1993-94, bd. dirs. 1991-93, program chairperson ann. meeting 1990), Am. Psychol. Soc., N.C. Assn. for Behavior Analysis, Sigma Xi, Phi Beta Kappa, Phi Kappa Phi. Office: U NC at Wilmington Dept Psychology 601 S College Rd Wilmington NC 28403-3201

PILGRIM, JAMES ROLLINS, retail furniture company executive; b. Atlanta, July 16, 1947; s. George Ezra and Lula May (Rollins) P.; children: Kelley P. Watkins, Amy M. Paul. AS, Gainesville Coll., 1970; BS in Edn., U. Ga., Athens, 1972. Div. mgr. Sears Roebuck & Co., Gainesville, 1965-72; mgr. Power Bldg. Products, Athens, 1972-78; salesman Pilgrim-Estes Furniture Co., Inc., Gainesville, 1978-88, v.p., 1988-90; v.p. Pilgrim Holding Co., Gainesville, 1990—; mgr. Loosier of Gainesville DBA Pilgrim-Estes Furniture Co., 1990-95; pres. 45th Trading Co., Inc., Gainesville, 1996—. Mem. Downtown Mchts. Assn. (pres. 1980-84), Chattahoochee Country Club (mem. com. 1992-94), Elks (exalted ruler Gainesville 1994-95, v.p. Ga. chpt. 1995-96, dist. deputy grand exalted ruler, 1996-97). Republican. Methodist. Home and office: 4038 Oak Harbour Cir Gainesville GA 30506-3060

PILKO, ROBERT MICHAEL, lawyer; b. N.Y.C., May 7, 1952; s. Peter J. and Martha (Tonti) P.; m. Amanda Karroll Stansberry, Apr. 25, 1981; (div. May 1992); children: Angela Dawn, Kristina Ann. BS in Psychology, U. Wis., 1974; MBA in Fin., Tex. So. U., 1978; JD, South Tex. Coll. Law, 1992. Analyst Joseph T. Ryerson & Son, Inc., Chgo., 1974-76; mfg. engr. Nat. Steel Products Co., Houston, 1976-78; tech. sales rep. Schlumberger, Johnston div., Tex., La., Can., 1978-80; ops. mgr. Far East Schlumberger Internat., 1980-84; corp. counsel, divsn. and internat. mgr. Stric-Lan Cos. Corp., Houston, 1984—; mng. mem. Robert M. Pilko & Assocs., P.L.L.C., 1994—. Mediator South Tex. Coll. Law Mediation Clinic, 1992; mediator, mem. Tex. Empowerment Network, Inc.; mem. campus asst. team Spring Branch (Tex.) Ind. Sch. Dist., 1993—. Mem. ABA, Am. Corp. Counsel Assn., State Bar of Tex. (corp. counsel and family law sects.), Houston Bar Assn. (family law and oil, gas and mineral law sects.), Houston Young Lawyers Assn., South Tex. Coll. Law Alumni Assn., Soc. Petroleum Engrs., Fin. Mgmt. Soc., U. Wis. Alumni Club (pres. 1988-90). Republican. Presbyterian. Home: 9803 Oak Point Dr Houston TX 77055-4128

PILLAI, RAVIRAJ SUKUMAR, chemical engineer, researcher; b. Bombay, July 29, 1961; came to U.S., 1986; s. Sukumar and Ratnavalli Pillai; m. Bina Menon, Jan. 4, 1995; 1 child, Amit. BS, U. Mysore, India, 1984; MS, U. Ill., Chgo., 1991, PhD, 1993. Rsch. asst. U. Ill., Chgo., 1989-93; postdoctoral scientist Eli Lilly and Co., Indpls., 1993-94; rsch. chem. engr. SRI Internat., Menlo Park, Calif., 1995; sr. scientist GeneMedicine, Inc., The Woodlands, Tex., 1995—. Sci. reviewer Aerosol Sci. and Tech., 1994, Jour. Pharm. Scis.; contbr. articles to profl. jours. Mem. Am. Assn. for Aerosol Rsch., Am. Assn. Pharm. Scientists, Internat. Soc. for Aerosols in Medicine, Sigma Xi. Hindu. Home: Apt 2203 333 Holly Creek Ct The Woodlands TX 77381

PILLAI, SURESH DIVAKARAN, environmental microbiologist, researcher; b. Trichy, India, Nov. 8, 1962; came to U.S., 1986; s. Divakaran Raman Pillai and Rugminy Koopot. BSc in Botany, Loyola Coll., Madras, India, 1983; postgrad., U. Madras, 1983-85; PhD, U. Ariz., 1989. Grad. tchg. asst. U. Ariz., Tucson, 1985-89, grad. rsch. asst., 1985-89, rsch. assoc., 1989, asst. rsch. scientist, 1989-91; rsch. scientist Naval Med. Rsch. Inst., Bethesda, Md., 1991-92; asst. prof. environ. microbiology Tex. A&M U. Rsch. Ctr., El Paso, 1992—; adj. asst. prof. dept. biol. scis. U. Tex., El Paso, 1993—. Contbr. articles to sci. jours. Kate C. Lewis Acad. scholar U. Ariz., 1986-89, Grad. Tuition scholar, 1988. Mem. AAAS, Soil Sci. Soc. Am., Am. Soc. Microbiology. Home: 1208 Rubye Mae Pl El Paso TX 79912-7485 Office: Tex A&M U Rsch Ctr El Paso TX 79927

PILLANS, CHARLES PALMER, III, lawyer; b. Orlando, Fla., Feb. 22, 1940; s. Charles Palmer Jr. and Helen (Scarborough) P.; m. Judith Hart, July 6, 1963; children: Charles Palmer IV, Helen Hart. BA, U. Fla., 1962, JD, 1966. Bar: Fla. 1967, U.S. Dist. Ct. (mid. dist.) Fla. 1967, U.S. Ct. Appeals (2d cir.) 1968, U.S. Supreme Ct. 1971, U.S. Ct. Appeals (3d cir.) 1976, U.S. Ct. Appeals (5th and 11th cirs.) 1981. Assoc. Bedell, Bedell, Dittmar, Smith & Zehmer, Jacksonville, Fla., 1966-70; asst. state atty. 4th jud. cir. Jacksonville, 1970-72; asst. gen. counsel City of Jacksonville, 1972; ptnr. Bedell, Dittmar, DeVault Pillans & Coxe, P.A., Jacksonville, 1972—; mem. Fla. Bd. Bar Examiners, Tallahassee, 1979-84, chmn., 1983-84; mem. Jud. Nominating Commn., 1988-92, chmn., 1990-91, 1st Dist. Ct. Appeal, Tallahassee, 1988-92, chmn., 1990-91. Master Chester Bedell Inn of Ct.; fellow Am. Coll. Trial Lawyers, ABA; mem. Am. Bar Found., Fla. Bar Assn. (mem. profl. ethics com.). Methodist. Home: Villa 110 6740 Epping Forest Way N Jacksonville FL 32217-2687 Office: Bedell Dittmar DeVault Pillans & Coxe PA Bedell Bldg 101 E Adams St Jacksonville FL 32202-3303

PILLSBURY, EDMUND PENNINGTON, museum director; b. San Francisco, Apr. 28, 1943; s. Edmund Pennington and Priscilla Keator (Giesen) P.; m. Mireille Marie-Christine Bernard, Aug. 30, 1969; children: Christine Bullitt, Edmund Pennington III. BA, Yale U., 1965; MA, U. London, 1967, PhD, 1973; DFA, U. North Tex., 1996. Curator European art Yale U. Art Gallery, New Haven, 1972-76; asst. dir. Yale U. Gallery, New Haven, 1975-76; dir. Yale Ctr. Brit. Art, New Haven, 1976-80; chief exec. officer Paul Mellon Ctr. Studies in Brit. Art, London, 1976-80; dir. Kimbell Art Mus., Ft. Worth, 1980—; founding chmn. Villa I Tatti Coun., Harvard U., 1979-84; adj. prof. Yale U., 1976-80, lectr., 1972-76; internat. adv. bd. State Hermitage Mus., 1995—. Author: Florence and the Arts, 1971, Sixteenth-Century Italian Drawings: Form and Function, 1974, David Hockney: Travels with Pen, Pencil and Ink, 1978, The Graphic Art of Federico Barocci, 1978. Trustee Ft. Worth Country Day Sch., 1982-87, 88-94, St. Paul's Sch., Concord, N.H., 1985—, Burlington Mag. Found., London, 1987—; bd. govs. Yale U. Art Gallery, 1990—; chmn. art adv. panel indemnity program Nat. Endowment Arts, 1984-87; mem. vis. com. Sherman Fairchild Paintings Conservation Ctr., Met. Mus. Art, N.Y.C., 1982—; mem. bd. advisors art dept. U. North Tex., Denton, 1990—; mem. art adv. panel IRS, 1982-84. Decorated chevalier Ordre des Arts et des Lettres, 1985; David E. Finley fellow Nat. Gallery Art, Washington, 1970, Ford Found. fellow Cleve. Mus. Art, 1970-71, Nat. Endowment Arts rsch. fellow, 1974, Morse fellow Yale U., 1975. Mem. Assn. Art Mus. Dirs. (trustee 1989-90), Master Drawings Assn. (bd. dirs. 1987—), Coll. Art Assn., Century Club, Ft. Worth Club, Rivercrest Club, City Club. Episcopalian. Home: 1110 Broad Ave Fort Worth TX 76107-1529 Office: Kimbell Art Mus 3333 Camp Bowie Blvd Fort Worth TX 76107-2744

PIMENTEL, JUAN LUIS, JR., health facility administrator, medical educator; b. Boston, Sept. 2, 1959; s. Juan Luis and Claudina M. (Molestina) P.; m. Ana Maria Gumbs, May 10, 1985; children: Diana, Pamela, Eliana. BS, Holy Spirit High Sch., Guayaquil, Ecuador, 1977; MD, Universidad Catolica, Guayaquil, 1985. Diplomate Am. Bd. Internal Medicine and Nephrology. Rural family practice physician Ministry of Health, Ecuador, 1985-86; physician assoc. Atlanta Diabetes Treatment Ctr., 1987; intern in internal medicine Emory U. Affiliated Hosps., Atlanta, 1987-88, resident in internal medicine, 1988-90; fellow in clin. nephrology, renal divsn. Emory U. Sch. of Medicine, Atlanta, 1990-91; renal rsch. fellow in renal metabolic lab. Atlanta Vets. Affairs Med. Ctr. Atlanta Vets. Affairs Med. Ctr., Atlanta, 1991-93; asst. prof. medicine dept. gerontology/geriatric medicine Emory U. Sch. of Medicine, Atlanta, 1993—; staff physician dept. medicine Atlanta Vets. Affairs Med. Ctr., 1993—; med. dir. nursing home care unit Atlanta Vets. Affairs Med. Ctr., Decatur, Ga., 1993—; presenter in field. Contbr. articles to profl. jours. Recipient Disting. Quality of Work award Ecuadorian Air Force, 1986. Mem. ACP, Renal Physicians Assn., Internat. Soc. Nephrology, Nat. Kidney Found. Roman Catholic. Home: 4140 Spring Mnr Tucker GA 30084-2597 Office: Vets Affairs Med Ctr 1670 Clairmont Rd Decatur GA 30033-4004

PINA, ALBERTO BUFFINGTON, real estate company official; b. Mexico City, Sept. 13, 1957; came to U.S., 1961; s. Alberto Benegas and Olive Diane (Buffington) P.; m. Sandra Ann Lahey, May 17, 1985; children: Alberto Brandon, Jason Bryan, Jonathan Austin. BSIA, S.W. Tex. State U., 1982. Cert. tchr., Tex., lic. real estate salesman, Tex. Derrick hand Sterling Drilling Co., MIdland, Tex., 1979-82; carpenter Match Constrn. Co., San Antonio, 1982-83; sales agt. Guy Chipman Co., San Antonio, 1983-86, corp. listing agt., 1986-93; relocation and constrn. adminstr. Advantage Relocation Concepts and LaDuke/Elrod & Assoc. Inc., San Antonio, 1993-94; sales agt. Advantage Realty, San Antonio, 1994—. Mem. Nat. Assn. Realtors., Tex. Assn. Realtors, San Antonio Bd. Realtors. Republican. Episcopalian. Home: 3155 Eisenhauer Rd San Antonio TX 78209-3542 Office: Advantage Realty 2161 NW Military Hwy San Antonio TX 78212-3359

PINAC, ANDRÉ LOUIS, III, obstetrician, gynecologist; b. New Orleans, Dec. 8, 1955; s. André Louis Jr. and Patricia Elaine (Ledet) P.; m. Deborah Bordelon LaFleur, Nov. 4, 1989; 1 child, Amy Elizabeth; 1 stepchild, Robby Nicholas LaFleur. BS, U. Southwestern La., 1977; MD, La. State U., New Orleans, 1981. Diplomate Am. Bd. Ob-Gyn. Resident ob-gyn La. State U. Affiliated Hosps., New Orleans, Lafayette, Lake Charles and Baton Rouge, 1981-85; practice medicine specializing in ob-gyn Opelousas, La., 1985—; chief of staff Doctor's Hosp. Opelousas, 1993-94; participant Cmty. Health Fair, Opelousas, 1987—; bd. dirs. Drs. Hosp. of Opelousas. Safety officer St. Landry Parish; bd. dirs. Little League, 1992-94. Named Duke at Mardi Gras Festival, Opelousas Garden Club, 1994. Fellow Am. Coll. Ob-Gyn; mem. AMA, So. Med. Assn., La. State Med. Soc., St. Landry Parish Med. Soc., Opelousas Cath. Soccer Assn. (pres. 1991-93), Alpha Phi Alpha (life), Sigma Alpha Epsilon. Roman Catholic. Office: Ste A 839 Creswell Ln Opelousas LA 70570-8936

PINCUS, LAURA RHODA, investor, accountant; b. Bklyn., Jan. 19, 1923; d. Sam and Esther (Boimel) Shore; m. William Pincus, Jan. 31, 1942 (dec. Jan. 1994); children: Irene, Stephan. Student, La Salle Inst., N.Y.C., 1940, C.W. Post, L.I. N.Y., 1960-62. Statis. typist Feinberg & Spaulder, N.Y.C., 1939-40, acct., 1948-58; owner Pincus Plumbing, Northport, N.Y., 1958-80; office mgr. James Robinson, N.Y.C., 1960-61; owner Pincus Plumbing, San Diego, 1980-87, Laura's Ltd., Wellington, Fla., 1987—. Youth program dir. Young Men's Hebrew Assn., Bklyn., 1939-41; founder East Northport Jewish Ctr., L.I., N.Y.; active Tifereth Israel Synagogue of San Diego, 1980-87, Tempe Beth Torah-Wellington, 1987-96; mem. Nat. Coun. Jewish Women, Palm Beach sect., 1991—; founder, treas. B'nai Kodesh, 1996—. Mem. Copperfield Assn., B'nai B'rith (life, bd. dirs., pres. Horizon chpt.), Hadassah (life), Brandeis Club (life, auditor Brandeis Palm Beach East chpt.), Am. Red Mogen David for Israel (life, founder San Diego Tikvah chpt. 1982-87, Wellington chpt. 1990, pres. Tikvah chpt. 1982-87, pres. Wellington chpt. 1990—). Home: 12884 Buckland St West Palm Beach FL 33414-6223

PINDLE, ARTHUR JACKSON, JR., philosopher, researcher; b. Macon, Ga., May 26, 1942; s. Arthur Jackson Sr. and Beatrice Rosetta (Williams) P.; 1 child, Zhinga D. BS in Physics, Morehouse Coll., 1964; MA in Philosophy, Yale U., 1973, MPhil, 1974, PhD in Philosophy, 1978. Physicist IBM, Inc., Poughkeepsie, N.Y., 1964, Naval Ordinance Station, Indian Head, Md., 1966-69, Satellite Experiment Lab, Suitland, Md., 1970-71; philosophy prof. Fayetteville (N.C.) State U., 1976-83; pres. HRG, Inc., New Orleans, 1983—; dir. rsch. NITRT, Inc., New Orleans, 1993—; mem. bd. advs. Inst. Philosoph. Rsch., Boulder, Colo., 1980-83. Contbr. articles to profl. jours. Mem. Dem. Nat. Com., 1993-96. Home: 5000 Good Dr New Orleans LA 70127 Office: NITRT Inc 5000 Good Dr New Orleans LA 70127

PINE, CHARLES, retail executive; b. Tucson, June 3, 1943; s. Gale Oren and Evelyn Jeannette (Burnett) P.; m. Brenda Elaine Porterfield, Jan. 14, 1967; children: Kenneth Charles, Kevin Scott. Student, Old Dominion Coll., Norfolk, Va., 1961-63, U. N.C., 1987. Asst. mgr. Woolworth, Norfolk, 1963-67; mgr. Woolworth, High Point, N.C., 1967-68; asst. mgr. Belk, Orangeburg, S.C., 1968-72; div. mdse. mgr. Belk, Myrtle Beach, S.C., 1978-82; mdse. mgr. Belk of Asheville, N.C., 1982-83, store mgr., 1983-84, v.p., 1984-85, sr. v.p., 1985—; sales rep. Atlantic Boutique Jewelry, Charlotte, N.C., 1972-76; mgr. Collins Dept. Store, Myrtle Beach, 1976-78; bd. dirs. 1st Citizens Bank, Asheville. Bd. dirs. Better Bus. Bur., Asheville, 1984—, Daniel Boone coun. Boy Scouts Am., 1984, Salvation Army, Asheville, 1984—; vol. United Way, Asheville, 1967—, mem. capital funds com., 1988—; trustee Western Carolina U., 1989—; bd. advisors Mars Hill Coll., 1994; chmn. Reynolds Vol. Fire Dept. Republican. Methodist. Mem. Asheville Mchts. Assn. (bd. dirs. 1983—), Asheville C. of C. (bd. dirs. 1987—), Sales/Mktg. Exec. Club (bd. dirs. 1982—), Kiwanis (v.p. 1982—), Mars Hill Coll. (bd. advisors 1994), Reynolds Vol. Fire Dept. (chmn.). Republican. Methodist. Office: Belk of Asheville 5 S Tunnel Rd Asheville NC 28805-2218

PINEIRO, EDUARD EFRALY, anesthetist; b. Camaguey, Cuba, Feb. 9, 1952; came to U.S., 1954; s. Efrain and Aracely (Leon) P. ASN, So. Coll., Collegedale, Tenn., 1975; BS, Sienna Heights Coll., Adrian, Mich., 1979. Cert. RN anesthetist. Staff anesthetist Beyer meml. hosp., Ypsilanti, Mich., 1979-85, Holmes Regional Med. Ctr., Melbourne, Fla., 1986-88; chief anesthetist Humana Hosp., Fla., 1988-89; free-lance anesthetist Indialantic, Fla., 1990-92; chief anesthetist North Fla. Anesthesia Cons., P.A., Jacksonville, Fla., 1992—. Annexation com. Indialantic City Govt. Mem. Am. Assn. Nurse Anesthetist, Fla. Assn. Nurse Anesthetist, Aircraft Owners and Pilots Assn. Republican. Home: 2165 Herschel St Jacksonville FL 32204

PINGREE, DIANNE, sociologist, educator, mediator; b. Dallas; m. Harlan Pingree. AA summa c Home and Office: 1004 Porpoise Austin TX 78734

PINKENBURG, RONALD JOSEPH, ophthalmologist; b. Houston, Nov. 25, 1940; s. William Joseph and Winnie Vale (Downs) P.; BA cum laude, U. St. Thomas, 1963; MD, Baylor U., 1967; m. Patricia Anne Regan, Oct. 21, 1967; children: Lisa, Anne Marie, Steven, Renée. Intern, U. Iowa, 1967-68; resident U. Okla., 1971-74, asst. clin. prof. ophthalmology, 1974-88; assoc. clin prof. opthalmology, U. Tex. Health Sci. Ctr., Tyler, 1988-93; gen. practitioner So. Calif. Permanente Med. Group-Kaiser Found. Hosp., Fontana, 1970-71; pvt. practice medicine specializing in ophthalmology, Tyler, Tex., 1974—; mem. staff Med. Center Hosp., Tyler, Mother Francis Hosp., Tyler. Bd. trustees, Tex. Med. Assn. Ins. Trust, 1988-89, chmn. bd. trustees, 1989—; served with USAF, 1968-70. Fellow ACS, Royal Soc. Medicine, Tex. Soc. Opthalmology and Otolaryngology; mem. AMA, Smith County Med. Soc. (pres. elect 1991-92, pres. 1992-93), Tex. Med. Assn. (chmn. com. assn. ins. programs 1981-88), Tex. Ophthalmology Assn. (pres. elect 1987-88, pres. 1988-89), Am. Acad. Ophthalmology, Am. Intraocular Implant Soc., Retina Found. SW (bd. med. advisors). Roman Catholic. Home: 311 Cumberland Rd Tyler TX 75703-5412 Office: 820 S Baxter Ave Tyler TX 75701-2225

PINKERTON, HELEN JEANETTE, health care executive; b. Chattanooga, Mar. 17, 1956; d. Jesse Robert and Irene Louise (Boyd) Pinkerton. BS, U. Tenn.-Knoxville, 1979, MPH, 1980. Dir. Hypertension/Diabetes Program Alton Park Health Ctr., Chattanooga, 1981—; bd. dirs. Bethlehem Cmty. Ctr., Hospice of Chattanooga; Contbr. to Tenn. Hypertension Control Manual, 1984, 2nd Edit., 1995. Dir. Choirs, fin. officer First Baptist Ch., Hixson; Community Services Club, 1986— (sec.); mem. Chattanooga Jaycees, Chattanooga Hunger Coalition. Doak scholar, 1977. Mem. NAFE, So. Health Assn., Tenn. Pub. Health Assn., Am. Diabetes Assn. (bd. dirs.), Hypertension Coalition (chmn. 1984—), Am. Cancer Soc. (bd. dirs.), Neighbors for Life (chairperson, Am. Cancer Soc.), Alton Park C. of C. (council mem. 1982-86), Alpha Kappa Alpha. Democrat. Avocations: walking, reading, singing, jogging. Home: 5419 Moody Sawyer Rd Hixson TN 37343 Office: Alton Park Health Ctr 100 E 37th St Chattanooga TN 37410-1401

PINKLETON, RANDY FRANKLIN, veterinarian; b. Petersburg, Va., Sept. 21, 1956; s. Willie Franklin and Elizabeth Francis (Williamson) P.; m. Debbie L. Nichols; children: Jacquelyn, Alexandria. BS in Biochemistry, Va. Poly. Inst., 1978; DVM, U. Ga., 1981. Pres. Petersburg Animal Hosp., 1985-91, Vet. Enterprises Inc., Chesterfield, Va., 1991-95; area v.p. The Pet Practice, Chesterfield, 1995-96; group v.p. Vet. Ctrs. of Am., Chesterfield, Va.; pres. Bd. Veterinary Medicine, Va., 1994-96. Mem. So. Vet. Med. Fedn. (bd. dirs. 1990-96), Va. Vet. Med. Assn., Am. Vet. Med. Assn. Office: VEI 7330 Beach Rd Chesterfield VA 23832

PINKSTON, ISABEL HAY, minister, writer, educator, therapist; b. Cambridge, Ohio, Oct. 30, 1922; d. Wilmer Martin and Mary Nola (Clark) Hay; m. Benedict George Dudley, Mar. 12, 1969 (dec. Feb. 1974); m. Robert Sherrill Pinkston, May 1, 1984 (dec. Dec. 1985). BA cum laude, Monmouth (Ill.) Coll., 1944; postgrad. in Christian edn., Wheaton (Ill.) Coll., 1948-49; M of Therapeutic Counseling, Open Internat. U., Sri Lanka, 1994. Ordained to ministry Nat. Assn. Congl. Chs., 1985. Instrumental and vocal music tchr. United Presbyn. Mission Sch., Frenchburg, Ky., 1944-48; dir. Christian edn. United Presbyn. Ch., Zanesville, Ohio, 1949-51; Christian edn. dir. A.R. Presbyn. Ch., Augusta, Ga., 1952-55; mem. staff Koinonia Found., Pikesville, Md., 1956-66; min., pres. bd. dirs. Ch. Religious Rsch., Inc., Grand Island, Fla., 1988-94; pres. Spiritual Devel. Internat., Inc., Eustis, Fla., 1996—; del., participant Internat. Conf. Paranormal Rsch., Ft. Collins, Colo., 1988-89; tchr. psychography course Sancta Sophia Sem., 1991; spkr. Conf. of Internat. Inst. of Integral Human Scis. and Spiritual Scis. Fellowship, 1994, 95, Ann. Conf., World U., 1994. Author: (biography) Seed-Sower for God's Kingdom, 1987, Understanding Homosexuality, 1993; co-editor: Psychography, 1990; editor: (newsletter) Koinonia Epistle, 1957-66, Religious Rsch. Jour., 1988-96, Religious Rsch. Press, 1988-96. Mem. Internat. Coun. Cmty. Chs. (del. 1988—), Assn. for Past-Life Rsch. and Therapy (workshop leader 1989). Home and Office: Spiritual Devel Internat Inc 931 North Shore Dr Eustis FL 32726

PINNADUWAGE, LAL ARIYARITNA, physicist, educator; b. Gonapinuwala, Sri Lanka; came to U.S., 1979; s. Noris Appu and Eminona (Kariyawasam) P.; m. Purnima Damayanthi Senanayake, July 20, 1983; children: Sesha, Nilmini. BS, U. Sri Lanka, Colombo, 1978; MS, U. Pitts., 1980, PhD, 1986. Asst. lectr. U. Sri Lanka, 1978-79; teaching asst. U. Pitts., 1979-80, rsch. asst., 1980-86; postdoctoral fellow U. Tenn., Knoxville, 1986-90, adj. asst. prof., 1991—; rsch. assoc. Oak Ridge (Tenn.) Nat. Lab., 1990—. Contbr. articles to profl. jours. Mem. Am. Phys. Soc. Office: Oak Ridge Nat Lab Bldg 45005 MS 6122 PO Box 2008 Oak Ridge TN 37831-2008

PINNIX, JOHN LAWRENCE, lawyer; b. Reidsville, N.C., Oct. 8, 1947; s. John Lawrence and Esther (Cobb) P.; m. Sally Auman, June 15, 1985; children: Jennifer Elizabeth Haigwood, William C. Haigwood. BA, U. N.C., Greensboro, 1969; JD, Wake Forest U., 1973; MA, U. N.C., Greensboro, 1975. Bar: N.C. 1973, D.C. 1981; U.S. Dist. Ct. (ea. dist.) N.C. 1977, U.S Dist. Ct. (mid. and we. dists.) N.C. 1981; U.S. Ct. Appeals (4th cir.) 1981; U.S. Supreme Ct. 1981. Assoc. Fagg, Fagg & Nooe, Eden, N.C., 1973-74; spl. counsel Adminstrv. Office of the Cts., Morganton, N.C., 1975-76; ptnr. Allen and Pinnix (formerly Barringer, Allen & Pinnix), Raleigh, N.C., 1977—. Contbr. articles to profl. jours. Alt. del. Dem. Nat. Conv., Miami, 1972, rules com., Washington/Atlanta, 1988; bd. dirs. Farmworkers Legal Svcs., Raleigh, 1990-92. Mem. Am. Immigration Lawyers Assn. (founding mem. Carolinas chpt. 1980, treas. 1981-84, 86-87, chpt. co-chmn. 1984-85, 87-88, chmn. nat. chpt. congl. network com. 1990—, nat. bd. govs. 1993—), Am. Immigration Law Found. (trustee 1992—, vice chair 1994—), N.C. Bar Assn. (chmn. immigration and nationality law com. 1989-91), N.C. State Bar (immigration law specialty com. bd. legal specialization 1996—), U. N.C. Greensboro Alumni Assn. (bd. dirs. 1975-76, bd. dirs. Excellence Found.). Baptist. Home: 716 Pebblebrook Dr Raleigh NC 27609-5345

PINO, JOSEPH DAVID, sound designer; b. Fairbanks, Alaska, Feb. 17, 1962; s. John Joseph and Marion Mae (Schauer) P.; m. CathyEllen Slisky, Dec. 10, 1994. BA in Theatre Arts, Ind. U. Pa., 1984; MFA, U. Va., 1988. Tech. dir. Lime Kiln Arts, Lexington, Va., 1987-88; head engr. Blues Alley, Balt., 1988-89; resident sound designer Alley Theatre, Houston, 1989—. Mem. ACLU. Democrat. Lutheran. Home: PO Box 66311 Houston TX 77266-6311 Office: Alley Theatre 615 Texas St Houston TX 77002-2710

PINSON, ARTIE FRANCES, elementary school educator; b. Rusk, Tex., June 20, 1933; d. Tom and Minerva (McDuff) Neeley; m. Robert H. Pinson, Dec. 14, 1963 (div. Nov. 1967); 1 child, Deidre R. BA magna cum laude, Tex. Coll., 1953; postgrad., U. Tex., 1956, North Tex. U., 1958, 63, New Eng. Conservatory, 1955, 57, 59, 62, Tex. So. U., 1971-72; MEd, U. Houston, 1970. Music tchr. Bullock High Sch., LaRue, Tex., 1953-59; music tchr., 9th grade English tchr. Story High Sch., Palestine, Tex., 1959-64; 3d to 6th grade gifted and talented math. tchr. Turner Elem. Sch., Houston, 1964-66; 3d, 5th and 6th grade tchr. Kay Elem. Sch., Houston, 1966-70; 6th grade tchr. Pilgrim Elem. Sch., Houston, 1970-75; 3d to 6th grade math. tchr. Pleasantville Elem. Sch., Houston, 1975-79; kindergarten to 5th grade computer/math. tchr. Betsy Ross Elem. Sch., Houston, 1979—, instrnl. coord., tchr. technologist; instrnl. coord.; lead tchr. math./sci. program Shell/Houston Ind. Sch. Dist., 1986-87, Say "Yes" program, 1988-89; math. tchr. summer potpourri St. Francis Xavier Cath. Ch., 1991; math. tchr. sci. and engrng. awareness and coll. prep. program Tex. So. U., 1993, 94, 95, 96; presenter confs. in field; condr. tchr. tng. workshops. Author computer software in field; contbr. articles to mags. Musician New Hope Bapt. Ch., Houston, 1991—, Sunday sch. tchr.; pianist Buckner Bapt. Haven Nursing Home, Houston, 1990-91; mem. N.E. Concerned Citizens Civic League. Recipient Excellence in Math. Teaching award Exxon Corp., 1990. Mem. Assn. African Am. Math. Educators (Salute to Math. Tchrs. award 1991, treas. 1991-93, sec. 1993—), Nat. Coun. Tchrs. Math., Tex. Coun. Tchrs. Math. (Excellence in Math. Tchg. award 1988), Houston Coun. Tchrs. of Math. (Excellence in Math. Tchg. award 1993), Heoines of Jericho, Palestine Negro Bus. and Profl. Women (charter mem.). Home: 5524 Makeig St Houston TX 77026-4021 Office: Betsy Ross Elem Sch 2819 Bay St Houston TX 77026

PINSON, CHARLES WRIGHT, transplant surgeon; b. Albuquerque, May 29, 1952; s. Ernest Alexander and Jean Elizabeth (Farnsworth) P. Student, Miami U., Oxford, Ohio, 1970-72; BA, U. Colo., Boulder, 1972, MBA, 1976; MD, Vanderbilt U., 1980. Diplomate Am. Bd. Surgery, Nat. Bd. Med. Examiners, Tenn., Mass., Oreg. Resident gen. surgery Oreg. Health Scis. U., Portland, 1980-86; fellow gastrointestinal surgery Lahey Clinic, Burlington, Mass., 1986-87; fellow transplant surgery Harvard U., Boston, 1987-88; dir. liver transplant program Vets. Affairs Western region, Portland, 1989-90, Oreg. Health Scis. U., Portland, 1988-90; interim chmn. dept. surgery Vanderbilt U., Nashville, 1993-95, chief divsn. hepatobiliary surgery and liver transplantation, 1990—, vice chmn. dept. surgery, 1995—; dir. Vanderbilt Transplant Ctr., Nashville, 1993—; mem. adv. bd. Pacific N.W. Transplant Bank, Portland, 1989-90, Tenn. Donor Svcs., Nashville, 1991—. Contbr. articles to profl. jours., chpts. to books. Bd. dirs. ARC, Nashville, 1992-94, Am. Liver Found., 1992—. Postdoctoral fellow Am. Heart Assn., Oreg., 1983-84. Mem. Soc. Univ. Surgeons, Soc. Surg. Oncology, Am. Soc. Transplant Surgeons, So. Surg. Assn., Western Surg. Assn., North Pacific Surg. Assn. (sci. program 1990-92), Sigma Xi, Phi Beta Kappa, Alpha Omega Alpha. Office: Vanderbilt Transplant Ctr 801 Oxford House Nashville TN 37232

PINTOR, ALFONSE MICHAEL, III, community health nurse, educator; b. San Antonio, Nov. 15, 1943; s. Alfonso Jr. and Mable (Herrera) P. ADN, Galveston (Tex.) Coll., 1972; BA, U. St. Thomas, Houston, 1975; MA in Edn., U. Houston, Clear Lake City, 1977; postgrad., U. Tex., 1978. Cert. emergency room nurse, trauma nurse specialist. Instr. nursing Laredo (Tex.) Jr. Coll., Lee Coll., Baytown, Tex.; DON St. Joseph Hosp., Houston; specialist surveyor dept. regulatory svcs. State of Ga., Atlanta; instr. home health survey process Health Care Financing Adminstrn., Balt., 1994; expert panel mem. home health agy. assessment process evaluation project U. Colo., 1994. Mem. Episcopal AIDS Task Force, Atlanta; mem. ARC Disaster Relief. Mem. Assn. Quality Assurance Profls. Home: 35 Wiley Bottom Rd Savannah GA 31411-1363

PIORKOWSKI, JOSEPH D., JR., lawyer, military officer, educator, physician; b. Chester, Pa., Nov. 21, 1956; s. Joseph D. Piorkowski and Elizabeth C. Bell; m. Marjorie Eldridge, Aug. 4, 1984; 1 child, Joseph D. III. BA cum laude, Hofstra U., 1976; DO, Phila. Coll. Osteo. Medicine, 1980; JD magna cum laude, Georgetown U., 1988; MPH, Johns Hopkins U., 1992. Diplomate Am. Bd. Preventive Medicine, Am. Bd. Legal Medicine, Am. Osteo. Bd. Family Practice, Nat. Bd. Examiners for Osteo. Physicians and Surgeons; lic. physician, Md., D.C.; bar: Md., D.C., U.S. Dist. Ct. D.C., U.S. Dist. Ct. Md., U.S. Ct. Appeals (4th and D.C. cirs.); cert. instr. advanced trauma life support; cert. advanced cardiac life support. Commd. ensign USN, 1977, advanced through grades to capt., 1996, flight surgeon fighter squadron 31/carrier air wing THREE, staff physician U.S.S. Kennedy, substance abuse coord., 1982-84; flight surgeon Naval Air Facility, peer review coord. Navy Med. Clinics USN, Washington, 1984-88, head Naval Air Facility Med. Clin., 1986-88; intern in psychiatry Nat. Naval Med. Ctr., Bethesda, Md., 1980-81; law clk. to Hon. Oliver Gasch U.S. Dist. Ct. D.C., 1988-89; assoc. Williams & Connolly, Washington, 1989—; instr. Mil. Tng. Network, Dept. Def., 1986—; adj. prof. law Georgetown U. Law Ctr., Washington, 1992—, clin. asst. prof. dept. surgery Georgetown U. Med. Ctr., 1995—. Contbr. articles to profl. jours. Acad. honors scholar Hofstra U., 1976. Fellow Am. Coll. Preventive Medicine, Am. Coll. Legal Medicine, Aerospace Med. Assn. (assoc.); mem. ABA (litigation sect., health law sect.), Soc. of U.S. Naval Flight Surgeons, Soc. for Epidemiologic Rsch., Assn. of Mil. Surgeons of U.S., Am. Osteo. Assn., Am. Coll. Family Practitioners, Order of Coif, Delta Omega, Psi Chi. Office: Williams & Connolly 725 12th St NW Washington DC 20005-3901

PIOTROWSKI, SANDRA A., elementary education educator; b. Buffalo, May 8, 1949; d. Edward and Loretta (Kasprzyk) Grabowski; m. Daniel J. Piotrowski, June 1, 1970; 1 child, Mark. BS, Rosary Hill Coll., Buffalo, 1971; postgrad., U. North Fla. Cert. tchr., Fla. Elem. tchr. Sacred Heart Sch., Jacksonville, Fla., Spurlin Sch., Jacksonville, St. Paul's Sch., Jacksonville. Mem. ASCD, Fla. Assn. Supervision and Curriculum Devel. Home: 4625 Herta Rd Jacksonville FL 32210-6949

PIPER, J. K. See GILES, KATHARINE EMILY

PIPER, JOHN RICHARD, political science educator; b. Sewickley, Pa., Oct. 2, 1946; s. John Hubert and Carol Elizabeth (Coleman) P.; m. Hoa Thuy Pham, June 6, 1970; 1 child, Carolyn Hoa. BA, Pa. State U., 1968; MA, Cornell U., 1971, PhD, 1972. Prof. polit. sci. Blackburn Coll., Carlinville, Ill., 1972-76; asst. prof. polit. sci. U. Tampa (Fla.), 1976-80, assoc. prof. polit. sci., 1980-83; prof. polit. sci. U. Tampa, Fla., 1983—, chmn. dept. history, polit. sci. and sociology, 1990-96; dir. honors program, 1996—. Author: Ideologies and Institutions: American Conservative and Liberal Governance Prescriptions Since 1933; contbr. articles to profl. jours. Vice-chmn. Tampa Bay World Affairs Coun.; mem. Tampa Bay Com. on Fgn. Rels., 1989—, Common Cause, 1990—, Fla. Consumer Action Network, Tallahassee, 1987—. Recipient Outstanding Educator award Blackburn Coll., 1974, Louise Loy Hunter award U. Tampa, 1981, award for teaching excellence Sears Roebuck Found., 1990; Fulbright-Hays grantee, 1988. Mem. Am. Polit. Sci. Assn., AAUP, Omicron Delta Kappa, Phi Beta Kappa, Pi Kappa Phi. Democrat. Office: Univ of Tampa 401 W Kennedy Blvd Tampa FL 33606-1450

PIPER, MARGARITA SHERERTZ, retired school administrator; b. Petersburg, Va., Dec. 20, 1926; d. Guy Lucas and Olga Doan (Akers) Sherertz; m. Glenn Clair Piper, Feb. 3, 1950; children: Mark Stephen, Susan Leslie Piper Weathersbee. BA in Edn., Mary Washington Coll. of Fredericksburg, 1948; MEd, U. Va., 1973, EdS, 1976. Svc. rep. C&P Telephone, Washington, 1948-55, adminstrv. asst., 1955-56, svc. supr., 1956-62; tchr. Culpeper (Va.) County Pub. Schs., 1970-75, reading lab dir., 1975-80; asst. prin. Rappahannock (Va.) County Pub. Schs., 1980-81, prin., 1981-88, dir. pupil pers., spl. programs, 1988-95; ret., 1995; chair PD 9 regional transition adv. bd. Culpeper, Fauquier, Madison, Orange and Rappahannock Counties, Va., 1991-94; vice chair Family Assessment and Planning Team, Washington, 1992-95. Recipient Va. Gov. Schs. Commendation cert. Commonwealth of Va., 1989-93. Mem. NEA, Va. Edn. Assn., Va. Coun. Adminstrs. Spl. Edn., Va. Assn. Edn. for Gifted, Rappahannock Edn. Assn. Democrat. Episcopalian.

PIPER, THOMAS SAMUEL, minister, consultant; b. Racine, Wis., Feb. 26, 1932; s. Wallace William and Margaret Alice (Lahr) P.; m. Mary Alice Smith, Mar. 12, 1955; children: Daniel Thomas, David Michael, Grace Susan Piper Gonzales. BS, Lawrence U., 1954; ThM, Dallas Theol. Sem., 1969. Ordained to ministry Christian Ch., 1982. Mng. editor Good News Broadcaster mag., Lincoln, Nebr., 1969-82; pastor adminstrn. and edn. Faith Bible Ch., Sterling, Va., 1982-86; pres., cons. Ministries in Sync, Sterling, 1986—; mem. writers conf. faculty Mt. Hermon (Calif.) Christian Conf., 1978-80, Christian Writers Inst., Wheaton, Ill., 1980; mem. pres.'s coun. Loudon County, Good News Jail and Prison Ministry, Arlington, Va., 1984-86; pres. local chpt. Christian Ministries Mgmt. Assn., Washington, 1987, 88; mem. Christian Mgmt. Assn., 1989-90, Nat. Assn. Ch. Bus. Adminstrs., 1986-90. Contbr. numerous articles to profl. jours. With USN, 1956-58. Mem. Voice of Bibl. Reconciliation (bd. dirs. 1991-93), Dallas Theol. Sem. Assn. (pres. local chpt. 1991-93), Internat. Assn. Bus. Communicators (life, pres. local chpt. 1977-79). Republican. Home and Office: Ministries in Sync 1307 E Holly Ave Sterling VA 20164-2614

PIPES, PAUL RAY, county commissioner; b. Truscott, Tex., Oct. 1, 1928; s. David and Maggie (Brown) Pipes; m. Linda Mullins, Dec. 17, 1961; children: Dana, Tricia. BBA, Sam Houston U., 1956, MEd, 1971. Acct. Pan Am. Petroleum Corp., Thibodaux, La., 1956-61; bus. tchr. Brenham (Tex.) H.S., 1962-90; county commr. Washington County, Brenham, 1991—. With U.S. Army, 1951-53, Korea. Decorated Def. Disting. Svc. medal. Republican. Methodist. Home: 2106 Jane Ln Brenham TX 77833 Office: Washington County Horton Loop Brenham TX 77833

PIPKIN, MARVIN GRADY, lawyer; b. San Angelo, Tex., Nov. 15, 1949; s. Raymond Grady and Lillie Marie (Smith) P.; m. Dru Cheatham, July 24, 1971; children: Lacey Elizabeth, Matthew Todd. BBA, U. Tex., 1971, JD, 1974. Bar: Tex. 1974, U.S. Dist. Ct. (we. dist.) Tex. 1979, U.S. Ct. Appeals (5th cir.) 1983. Assoc. Green & Kaufman, San Antonio, 1974-79, ptnr., 1979-82; ptnr. Kendrick & Pipkin, San Antonio, 1982-93, Drought & Pipkin L.L.P., San Antonio, 1993—; mem. coms. on ethics and admissions Tex. Supreme Ct., admissions com.; adv. dir. Trinity Nat. Bank, San Antonio, 1983; bd. dirs. Allied Am. Bank, San Antonio, First Interstate Bank, San Antonio. Bd. dirs. Monte Vista Hist. Assn., San Antonio, 1975-78. Fellow Tex. Bar Found., San Antonio Bar Found.; mem. ABA, Tex. Assn. Def. Counsel, Tex. Bar Assn., San Antonio Bar Assn. Republican. Methodist. Home: 2 Dorchester Pl San Antonio TX 78209-2203 Office: Drought & Pipkin LLP 112 E Pecan St Ste 2600 San Antonio TX 78205-1528

PIPKIN, WADE LEMUAL, JR., reference librarian; b. Seminole, Okla., Apr. 9, 1945; s. Wade Lemual and Jimmie Jeanne (Midkiff) P.; m. Pamela Nan Jackson, July 19, 1975. BA in History, U. Okla., 1967, MA in History, 1970, MLS, 1973. Catalog libr. Ga. So. Coll., Statesboro, 1973-74, ref. libr., 1974-77; acquisitions libr. Kilgore (Tex.) Coll., 1977-81, libr. dir., 1981-93, reference libr., 1993—. Bd. dirs. Kilgore Cmty. Concert Assn., 1989—; chairperson nominating com. East Tex. Profl. Credit Union, Longview, 1991. 1st lt. U.S. Army, 1970-72. Mem. Tex. Libr. Assn. (dist. sec. 1990-91, 94-95), Tex. Jr. Coll. Tchrs. Assn., Lions (past 1st yr. dir., past 2d yr. dir.), East Tex. Health Scis. consortium (sec. 1980-83), Forest Trail Libr. Consortium (sec. 1990-91). Democrat. Mem. Christian Ch. Home: 2603 Spruce St Kilgore TX 75662-4150 Office: Kilgore Coll 1100 Broadway Blvd Kilgore TX 75662-3204

PIPPIN, JAMES ADRIAN, JR., middle school educator; b. Rockingham, N.C., Aug. 6, 1954; s. James A. Sr. and Essie Juanita (Rorie) P. BS, Appalachian State U., 1976; MEd, Columbus Coll., 1982. Tchr. Eddy Jr. High Sch., Columbus, Ga., 1976-89; dir. N.C. Agrl. Extension Svc., Penn 4-H Ctr., Reidsville, 1980-89, Millstone 4-H Camp, Ellerbe, N.C., 1993; tchr. Arnold Middle Sch., Columbus, Ga., 1989—; mem. multicultural curriculum com., sick leave bank com., textbook adoption com. and tech. com. MCSD; tchg. program participant Found. Internat. Edn., Inverness, Scotland, 1986, Dunedin, New Zealand, 1989; curriculum devel. program participant Ga. Dept. Edn., Germany, 1989, 91; adv. com. Deutsche Welle Video, 1992, 95; internat. edn. adv. com. Ga. Dept. Edn., 1993—. Author: The Physiological and Psychological Effects of Space Flight Environments on Blood Glucose and Circadian Rhythms of the Human Body; contb. author: (curricuums) World Studies, Germany and Georgia: The Search for Unity, Education in Thailand, Germany Unity and Disunity: Ubersichten; Overview of the Federal Republic of Germany, Images of Germany: Past and Present, The Olympic Spirit; A Worldwide Connection, Vol. III. Mem. discovery gallery com. Columbus Mus. Arts & Scis., curriculum devel. com. Atlanta Com. for Olympic Games. Named Ga. Tchr. Yr., 1986, Ga. State Semi-Finalist NASA Tchr. Space Program, 1985; recipient Project award TV Worth Teaching, CBS, 1987; Fulbright Study-Tour scholar, Taiwan and Thailand, 1992. Mem. ASCD, NEA (congl. contact team), Columbus Social Sci. Alliance (bd. dirs.), Ga. Assn. Educators, Nat. Coun. Social Scis., Ga. Coun. Social Scis. (bd. dirs.), Musogee Assn. Edn. (v.p., 2d v.p., chmn. policies and grievences com., legis. com., chmn. officer nominating com.), Columbus Hist. Soc., Columbus Hist. Dist. Preservation Soc. (bd. dirs.), Chattahoochee Valley Archaeol. Soc., Phi Alpha Theta, Phi Delta Kappa.

PIPPIN, LINDA SUE, pediatrics nurse, educator; b. Abingdon, Va., Sept. 10, 1954; d. James Robert and Mary (Reedy) P. ADN, Midlands Tech. Coll., 1988. Registered pediatric nurse, S.C.; RNC, ANCC. RNC Lexington Med. Ctr., West Columbia, S.C., 1988—; adj. faculty Midlands Tech. Coll., 1990-95; PALS instr. Lexington Med. Ctr., 1994, mem. various hosp. coms., 1992—. Super sibling tchr. Lexington Med. Ctr., 1994, hosp. adventure instr., 1993—; tchr. Sunday sch. Grace Chapel, West Columbia, 1982—, sponsor Pioneer Club, 1992—; vol. Spl. Olympics, 1995—. Mem. Soc. Pediatric Nurses.

PIRKLE, ESTUS WASHINGTON, minister; b. Vienna, Ga., Mar. 12, 1930; s. Grover Washington and Bessie Nora (Jones) P.; m. Annie Catherine Gregory, Aug. 18, 1955; children: Letha Dianne, Gregory Don. BA cum laude, Mercer U., 1951; BD, MRE, Southwestern Bapt. Sem., 1956, ThM, 1958; DD, Covington Theol. Sem., 1982. Ordained to ministry So. Bapt. Conv., 1949. Pastor Locust Grove Bapt. Ch., New Albany, Miss.; speaker Camp Zion, Myrtle, Miss. Author: Wintertime, 1968, Preachers in Space, 1969, Sermon Outlines Book, 1969, Are Horoscopes All Right?, 1971, I Believe God, 1973, Who Will Build Your House?,1978, The 1611 King James Bible: A Study by Dr. Estus Pirkle, 1994; producer religious films: If Footmen Tire You, What Will Horses Do?, 1973, The Burning Hell, 1975, Believer's Heaven, 1977. Home and Office: PO Box 80 Myrtle MS 38650-0080

PIRRUNG, MICHAEL CRAIG, chemistry educator, consultant; b. Cin., July 31, 1955; s. Joey Matthew and Grace (Fielman) P. BA, U. Tex., 1975; PhD, U. Calif., Berkeley, 1980. NSF postdoctoral fellow Columbia U., N.Y.C., 1980-81; asst. prof. Stanford (Calif.) U., 1981-89; sr. scientist Affymax Rsch. Inst., Palo Alto, Calif., 1989; assoc. prof. Duke U., Durham, N.C., 1989-94, prof., 1994—; dir. Duke U. program in biol. chemistry, 1994—, dir. biotechnology for bus., 1993—; cons. Am. Cyanamid, 1992—, Wyeth-Ayerst, 1995—, Chroma Xome 1995—; sci. advisor Affymax Rsch. Inst., 1991—. Recipient Newcomb Cleveland prize AAAS, 1991, Intellectual Property Owners Disting. Inventor award, 1993, Outstanding Young Tex. Ex., U. Tex. Ex-Students Assn., 1995. Fellow AAAS, John Simon Guggenheim Mem. Found.; mem. Am. Chem. Soc., Am. Soc. Plant Phys. Office: Duke U Dept Chemistry PM Gross Lab PO Box 90346 Durham NC 27708-0346

PISSINOU, NIKI, computer studies educator; b. Bafia, Cameroon; came to U.S., 1978; d. John and Parskevi P.; m. Kia Makki. BS in Indsl. & Systems Engring., Ohio State U.; MS in Computer Sci., U. Calif., Riverside; PhD in Computer Sci., U. So. Calif., 1991. System engr. SOCAMBAM; teaching asst. U. So. Calif., rsch. asst.; sr. rsch. scientist Datatech; asst. prof. The Ctr. Advanced Computer Studies; adj. prof. Nat. Supercomputer Ctr. COmtbr. articles to profl. jours. Office: Ctr Advanced Computer Study 2 Rex St Lafayette LA 70504

PITASI, JUDY, nurse; b. Oneida, Tenn., June 29, 1950; d. Roy Vernon and Hattie (Turner) Cadle; m. Joseph Anthony Pitasi, June 29, 1984; children: Lauren Leigh, Marc Andrew. Diploma, U. Tenn., 1970; grad., USAF Flight Nurse Course, 1979, USAF Nursing Mgmt. Sch., 1982, Aeromedical Ground Coord. Sch., 1983. Charge nurse Shepherd Spinal Ctr., Atlanta; supr. Met. Hosp., Atlanta. Mem. Nat. Rep. Senatorial com.; mem. Nicholas Gibbs Hist. Soc. Maj. USAF, 1974-87. Named Outstanding Jr. Officer Ga., 1984. Mem. Res. Officers Assn. (v.p. 1982, nat. com. 1980-84), Emergency Dept. Nurses Assn., Assn. Mil. Surgeons U.S. Baptist. Republican.

PITMAN, SHARON GAIL, school counselor; b. Dayton, Ohio, June 13, 1946; d. Finley Andrew and Lena Kay (Wells) Jennings; m. Benjamin Pitman III, Jan. 19, 1980; children: Elizabeth Ann (dec.), Emily; stepchildren: Scott, Todd. BS in Edn., Miami U., Oxford, Ohio, 1968, MEd in Edn., 1970; sch. counseling cert. Ga. State U., 1979, MEd in Counseling, 1981; EdS in Guidance and Counseling, Ga. State U., 1989. Tchr. pub. schs., Hamilton, Ohio, 1968-73, Gwinnett County, Ga., 1973-80; sch. counselor Buford Middle Sch., Ga., 1981-89, Duluth (Ga.) Mid. Sch., 1989—; conductor workshops in field. Fellow Am. Assn. Counseling and Devel.; mem. Am. Sch. Counseling Assn. (Nat. Mid. Sch. Counselor of Yr. 1989), Ga. Sch. Counselors Assn. (Mid. Sch. Counselor of Yr. 1988). Office: Duluth Mid Sch Duluth GA 30136

PITT, ROBERT ERVIN, environmental engineer, educator; b. San Francisco, Apr. 25, 1948; s. Wallace and Marjorie (Peterson) P.; m. Kathryn Jay, Mar. 18, 1967; children: Gwendolyn, Brady. BS in Engring. Sci., Humboldt State U., 1970; MSCE, San Jose State U., 1971; PhD in Civil and Environ. Engring., U. Wis., 1987. Registered profl. engr., Wis.; diplomate Am. Acad. Environ. Engrs. Environ. engr. URS Rsch. Co., San Mateo, Calif., 1971-74; sr. engr. Woodward-Clyde Cons., San Francisco, 1974-79; cons. environ. engr. Blue Mounds, Wis., 1979-84; environ. engr. Wis. Dept. Natural Resources, Madison, 1984-87; assoc. prof. depts. civil and environ. engring. and environ. health scis. U. Ala., Birmingham, 1987—; mem. Resource Conservation and Devel. Coun., Jefferson County, Ala., 1992-94; mem. com. on augmenting natural recharge of groundwater with reclaimed wastewater NRC, 1991-94; Ala. state dir. for energy and environment U.S. DOE EPSCOR, 1992-94; guest lectr. U. Gesamthochschule, Essen, Germany, 1994. Author: Small Storm Urban Flow and Particulate Washoff Contributions to Outfall Discharges, 1987, Investigation of Inappropriate Pollutant Entries into Storm Drainage Systems, 1994, Potential Groundwater Contamination from Intentional and Non-Intentional Stormwater Infiltration, 1994, Stormwater Quality Management, 1996, Groundwater Contamination from Stormwater Infiltration, 1996; co-author: Manual for Evaluating Stormwater Runoff Effects in Receiving Waters, 1996; author software in field. Asst. scoutmaster Boy Scouts Am., Birmingham, 1988-94. Recipient 1st Pl. Nat. award U.S. Soil Conservation Svc. Earth Team, 1989, 94, award of recognition USDA, 1990, 1st Pl. Vol. award Take Pride in Am., 1991; Fed. Water Pollution Control Adminstrn. fellow, 1970-71, GE Engring. Edn. fellow, 1984-86. Mem. ASCE, Soc. for Environ. Toxicology and Chemistry, N.Am. Lake Mgmt. Soc. (Profl. Speakers award 1992), Water Environ. Fedn. (1st Pl. Nat. award 1992), Am. Water Resources Assn., Ala. Acad. Sci., Sigma Xi. Office: U Ala Birmingham Dept Civil/Environ Engring 1150 10th Ave S Birmingham AL 35294-4461

PITT, WOODROW WILSON, JR., engineering educator; b. Rocky Mount, N.C., Aug. 14, 1935; s. Woodrow Wilson Pitt and Stella Marie (Whitley) Wiggins; m. Katherine Ann Morton, Jan. 1, 1958; children: Deborah Ann, Abigail Marie, Katherine Elizabeth. BSChemE, U. S.C., 1957; MS, U. Tenn., 1966, PhD, 1969. Registered profl. engr., Tenn., Tex. Devel. engr. Oak Ridge (Tenn.) Nat. Lab., 1960-72, sr. devel. engr., 1972-81, sect. head, 1981-89; vis. prof. Tex. A&M U., College Station, 1989-90, prof. dept. nuclear engring., asst. dept. head, 1991—. Inventor multi-sample rotor assembly for blood function preparation, differential chromatography; contbr. articles to profl. jours. Councilman Oak Ridge City Coun., 1983-89. Lt. (j.g.) USN, 1957-60. Spl. fellow U.S. AEC, 1966-67; recipient IR-100 awards, 1971, 80. Fellow AIChE; mem. ASTM, NSPE, Am. Nuclear Soc., N.Y. Acad. Scis., Water Pollution Control Fedn., Tenn. Soc. Profl. Engrs. (trustee polit. action com. 1988-90), Sigma Xi, Tau Beta Pi. Methodist. Home: 702 Summerglen Dr College Station TX 77840-2333 Office: Tex A&M U Dept Nuclear Engring 129 Zachry College Station TX 77843

PITTAS, PEGGY ALICE, psychology educator; b. Staunton, Va., Oct. 15, 1944; d. Russell Alexander and Anna Francis (Hodge) Sheffer; m. Panayiotis Alecou Pittas, May 23, 1970; 1 child, Alexia. BA in Psychology, Bridgewater Coll., 1966; MA in Psychology, Dalhousie U., N.S., Can., 1969. Counseling psychologist Dalhousie U. Counseling Ctr., Halifax, N.S., 1968-71; asst. prof. psychology Lynchburg (Va.) Coll., 1971-78, assoc. prof. psychology, 1978—; chmn. dept. psychology Lynchburg Coll., 1974-78, 81-82, 84-87; behavioral cons. Blue Ridge Emergency Med. Svc., Lynchburg, 1977-83; cons. Can. Welfare Coun., Ottawa, 1969. Author: Blow Your Little Tin Whistle, A Biography of Richard Clarke Sommerville, 1992; editor St. George Greek Cookbook, 1986; contbr. 10 book vols., 1982. Bd. dirs. Lynchburg League of Women Voters, 1978-79, 94—, Lynchburg Area Mental Health Assn. 1975-81, Community Mental Health Svc. Bd., 1978-81. Recipient grant Mednick Found., 1979; named one of Outstanding Young Women in Am., 1976, 77. Mem. AAUP, Va. Psychol. Assn., Va. Acad. Scis., Gerontol. Soc. Am., Psi Chi, Phi Kappa Phi. Democrat. Greek Orthodox.

PITTMAN, BARBARA SCHOONOVER, counselor; b. Oklahoma City, Dec. 1, 1935; d. Lindley D. and Helen Letisha (Holaday) Schoonover; m. Harrison Victor Pittman, Jr., Feb. 4, 1962; children: Harrison Victor III, Laura Allison. BS, Miss. State Coll. for Women, 1957; MS, Fla. State U., 1962; EdS, Miss. State U., 1987. Lic. profl. counselor. Co-owner Mitre Box Frame Shop, Yazoo City, Miss.; prin. St. Clara Acad./St. Mary's Ch., Yazoo City; instr. health/phys. edn. Gardner-Webb Coll., Boiling Springs, N.C.; owner, therapist New Horizons Counseling Ctr., Yazoo City and Jackson, Miss. Nat. bd. dirs. YWCA USA. Recipient 20 Yrs. Vol. Svc. award ARC. Mem. ASCD, Am. Clin. Mental Health Counselors Assn., Miss. Clin. Mental Health Counselors Assn. (past pres., organizer , 1st chair pvt. practitioner of Miss.), Miss. Assn. Marriage and Family Therapists (bd. dirs., pres.), Internat. Assn. Marriage and Family Therapists.

PITTMAN, BERNICE NUNNALLY, primary care nurse; b. Ogeechee, Ga., July 8, 1940; d. Corrie and Manda Jane (Robinson) Nunnally; m. Jesse James Pittman (div.); children: Roshawn, Duane, Darryl, Roberta, Robert, James (dec.). AA, Armstrong State Coll., Savannah, Ga., 1972. Cert. in new procedures and equipment. Staff and charge nurse Candler Gen. Hosp., Savannah, U.S. Naval Hosp., Beaufort, S.C., Hillhaven Convalescent Ctr., Savannah; staff nurse Candler Gen. Hosp., Savannah; sch. nurse bd. edn. Broad Oaks Psychiat. Hosp., Savannah. With USN, 1958-59. Mem. Ga. Nurses Assn. Home: 1520 Cloverdale Dr Savannah GA 31401-7813

PITTMAN, NATALIE ANNE, paralegal; b. Detroit, Apr. 17, 1952; d. George Jack and Catherine Helen (Platusich) Ochenski; children: Erik Garrett Pittman, Jason Christopher Pittman; m. John Robert Pittman, Dec. 16, 1977; stepchildren: Mark Allen, David Robert. AS with highest honors, Cen. Tex. Coll., 1985. Bd. cert. legal asst. civil trial law, Tex. Owner, mgr. pet store, Killeen, Tex., 1977-85; paralegal Silverblatt Law Office, Killeen, 1985—; corp. sec. Am. Budgerigar Soc., Inc., Killeen, 1986—; also bd. dirs.; spkr. legal asst. program Ctrl. Tex. Coll., Killeen, 1986—, adv. com., 1989—, instr., 1991—; editorial adv. Office Mgmt. and Legal Ethics, 1995; bd. dirs. Heart of Tex. Hospice; show promoter Thunder in the Hills Drum Corps, 1993—; mem. show promoters task force Drum Corps Internat., 1994—. Editorial advisor Know Your Pet-Budgerigars, 1987. Spokesperson Concerned Citizens Quality Edn., Killeen, 1981; pres. Pebble Sch. PTA, Killeen, 1984; active Killeen H.S. Band Boosters, 1987—, pres., 1991-93; Help One Student To Succeed (HOSTS) tutor Killeen Ind. Sch. Dist., 1993-94; umpire state softball tournaments, 1976; active polit. and civic orgns. Mem. State Bar Tex. (legal asst. divsn.), Heart of Tex. Assn. Legal Profls. (pres. 1996—), Nat. Notary Assn., Dallas-Ft. Worth Exhbn. Budgerigar Club (show sec. 1989), Heart 'O Tex. Exhbn. Budgerigar Club (founding). Republican. Roman Catholic. Home and Office: 1704 Kangaroo Ave Killeen TX 76543-3334

PITTMAN, VIRGIL, federal judge; b. Enterprise, Ala., Mar. 28, 1916; s. Walter Oscar and Annie Lee (Logan) P.; m. Floy Lasseter, 1944; children—Karen Pittman Gordy, Walter Lee. B.S., U. Ala., 1939, LL.B., 1940. Bar: Ala. bar 1940. Spl. agt. FBI, 1940-44; practice law Gadsden, Ala., 1946-51; judge Ala. Circuit Ct., Circuit 16, 1951-66; U.S. dist. judge Middle and So. Dist. Ala., 1966-71; chief judge U.S. Dist. Ct. for Ala. So. Dist., 1971-81, sr. judge, 1981—; periodically sits as judge U.S. Ct. Appeals 11th Cir., 1981—; lectr. bus. law, econs. and polit. sci. U. Ala. Center, Gadsden, 1948-66. Author: Circuit Court Proceedings in Acquisition of a Tract of Right of Way, 1959, A Judge Looks at Right of Way Condemnation Proceedings, 1960, Technical Pitfalls in Right of Way Proceedings, 1961. Mem. Ala. Bd. Edn., 1951; trustee Samford U., 1974-90, 92—. Lt. (j.g.) USN, 1944-46. Mem. Ala. State Bar, Etowah County Bar Assn. (pres. 1949), Omicron Delta Kappa. Democrat. Baptist. Office: US Dist Ct PO Box 465 Mobile AL 36601-0465

PITTMAN, WILLIAM CLAUDE, electrical engineer; b. Pontotoc, Miss., Apr. 22, 1921; s. William Claude and Maude Ella (Bennett) P.; m. Eloise Savage, Apr. 20, 1952; children: Patricia A. Pittman Ready, William Claude III, Thomas Allen. BSEE, Miss. State Coll., 1951, MSEE, 1957. From electronic engr. to supr. elec. engring. dept. U.S. Army Labs., Redstone Arsenal, Ala., 1951-59; supr. electronic engr. to aero. engring. supr. NASA/Marshall Space Flight Ctr., 1960; electronic engr. Army Missile Labs., 1962-82; program mgr. Army Labs. and R&D Ctr., Redstone Arsenal, 1982—; organizer numerous sci. and tech. confs. Author patents, reports, papers. Sgt. USMC, 1940-46, PTO. Recipient Medal of Honor, DAR, Meritorious Civilian Svc. award Dept. Army, 1993. Fellow AIAA (assoc.; chmn. Miss.-Ala. chpt. 1981-82, Martin Schilling award 1980); mem. IEEE (sr. life), NSPE, First Marine Div. Assn., DAV, IRE (chmn. Huntsville sect. 1957-58), Madison Hist. Soc., SAR (pres. Tenn. Valley chpt. 1984-85, Ala. Soc. 1990-91, Cert. 1991, Patriot medal), Tau Beta Pi, Phi Kappa Phi, Kappa Mu Epsilon. Home: 704 Desoto Rd SE Huntsville AL 35801-2032 Office: US Army Missile Command Huntsville AL 35809

PITTS, BILL, museum director; b. Castleton, Kans., Jan. 7, 1934. BA, Northwestern State Coll., Alva, Okla., 1957; postgrad., Northwestern State Coll., We. Wash. Coll. Edn., Portland (Oreg.) State Coll. Curator Northwestrn State Coll. Mus., Alva, Okla., 1964-74; dir., curator Santa Fe Trail Ctr., Larned, Kans., 1974-83; dir. State Mus. of Okla. Hist. Soc., Oklahoma City, 1983—; adj. instr. Emporia (Kans.) State U., 1978-83; grant evaluator Inst. Mus. Services, 1980—. Mem. coordinating com. Promotion of Kans. History, 1979-83; mem. council Kans. Com. for Humanities, 1980-83; panel mem. Okla. Arts and Humanities Council, 1966-73; mem. Okla. Hist. Soc. Mem. Am. Assn. Mus. (past Okla. rep.), Am. Assn. State and Local History, Mountain-Plains Mus. Conf., Okla. Mus. Assn. (regional rep. 1984-85, past pres.), Kans. Mus. Assn. (past pres.), Santa Fe Trail Assn. (pres. 1991-95), Westerners Internat., Toastmasters Internat. Home: 2600 NW 16th St Oklahoma City OK 73107 Office: Okla Hist Soc Hist Bldg 2100 N Lincoln Blvd Oklahoma City OK 73105-4915

PITTS, BRYAN, performing company executive. Artistic dir. Ballet Okla., Oklahoma City. Office: Ballet Okla 7421 N Classen Blvd Oklahoma City OK 73116-7129

PITTS, GARY BENJAMIN, lawyer; b. Tupelo, Miss., Aug. 23, 1952; s. Dextar Derward Pitts and Eva Margaret (Holcomb) Bush; m. Nicole Palmer; children: Andrew Ross, Caitlan Taylor. Student, U. Miss., Oxford, 1970-71, Coll. Charleston (S.C.), 1971-73; BA, McGill U., Montreal, Que., Can., 1973-74; JD, Tulane U., New Orleans, 1979. Bar: Tex. 1979, U.S. Ct. Appeals (5th cir.) 1980. Assoc. Julian & Seele, Houston, 1979-84, Ogletree, Pitts & Collard, Houston, 1984-85; ptnr. Pitts & Collard LLP, Houston and Dallas, 1985—. Organizer, legal counsel for Neighborhood Watch Coalition. Capt. USNG, 1975-87. Mem. ATLA, Maritime Law Assn. (proctor in Admiralty 1980—). Office: Pitts & Assocs 8866 Gulf Fwy Ste 117 Houston TX 77017-6528

PITTS, GRIFF D., academic administrator; b. Urbana, Mo., Mar. 8, 1932; s. Griff D. and Fannie (Doran) P.; m. Sharon Dee Christy, Nov. 22, 1967; children: Nancy Rae, Steven G. BA, Pepperdine U., 1953; MA, Ariz. State U., 1959; PhD, Northwestern U., 1970. Dir. counseling and placement W.Va. State Coll., 1966-67; asst. dean to assoc. dean to dean for student affairs Northeastern Ill. U., Chgo., 1967-78, prof. in student counseling, 1967-78; dean for student devel. S. E. Mo. State U., Cape Girardeau, Mo., 1978-83; academic dean Lamson Jr. Coll., Phoenix, Ariz., 1985-89; vice provost, chief acad. officer for coll. sys. Phillips Coll., Gulfport, Miss., 1989-96; dean acad. affairs Masters Inst., San Jose, Calif., 1996—; acting v.p. student affairs Northeastern Ill. U., 1967-68, 74-75; sr. ednl. cons. Advance Schs. Inc., Chgo., 1971-75. Author: Counseling Methods, 1981, Counseling Theories, 1981; contbr. to profl. jours. Academic scholar Pepperdine U., 1950-53; recipient Special Achievement award Pepperdine U., 1953, G. H. Mayr Found. Leadership award Pepperdine U., 1953; Onward House Rsch. fellow, Chgo., 1966, Kellogg fellow Kellogg Found., Mich., 1976-77; named Educator of the Year Ariz. Pvt. Sch. Assn., Ariz., 1986. Mem. Am. Assn. Higher Edn., Am. Counseling Assn., Am. Coll. Personnel Assn., Nat. Career Devel. Assn., Am. Vocat. Assn., Assn. Counseling Edn. and Supervision, Assn. Supervision and Curriculum Devel., Am. Vocat. Assn., Psi Chi, Kappa Delta Pi, Phi Delta Kappa (v.p. 1992, 93). Democrat. Ch. of Christ. Home: PO Box 28713 San Jose CA 95159

PITTS, JACQUELINE IONE, secretary, poet; b. Lansing, Mich., June 17, 1937; d. Clifford Charles and Florence Lavina (Davis) Mallery; m. Levon Pitts, Feb. 19, 1959; children: John, Michael. Grad. high sch., Flushing, Mich., 1955. Sec. GM, Flint, Mich., 1956-86, Ala. River Pulp Co., Perdue Hill, 1990—. Author: Piney Wood Poems, 1992, Aesthetically Yours, Jacqueline, 1994. Pianist, poet Mt. Pleasant Meth. Ch., Evergreen, Ala., 1989—. Home: Box 142 Rt 1 Evergreen AL 36401 Office: Ala River Pulp Co Inc County Rd 39 Claiborne Mill Perdue Hill AL 36470

PIVER, WILLIAM CRAWFORD, civil engineer, consultant; b. Washington, N.C., Apr. 12, 1947; s. William Jr. and Sara Elizabeth (Early) P.; m. Jackie Ann Gerard, Oct. 30, 1970; children: April Denise and Courtney Lorraine. BArch, N.C. State U., 1972, BSCE, 1972. Registered profl. engr., N.C. Engr.-in-tng. Ebasco Services, Inc., Bridge City, La., 1972-73; engr. Peirson & Whitman Internat., Inc., Raleigh, N.C., 1973-76, head sys. planning, 1976-79, exec. v.p., 1979-83; owner William C. Piver & Assoc., Raleigh, 1983—; sec.-treas. bd. dirs. Internat. Commodities, Inc., Raleigh, 1994—. With USMC, 1966-68, Vietnam. Mem. N.C. World Trade Assoc., Capital Area Manufactured Housing Assn., Garner C. of C., Greater Raleigh C. of C. (mem. small bus. owners forum com. 1993-95, new mem. mentor, mem. ins. com. 1993-94). Episcopalian. Home: 2709 Scottsdale Ln Raleigh NC 27613 Office: William C Piver & Assoc 805 Spring Forest Road #950 Raleigh NC 27609

PIZZAMIGLIO, NANCY ALICE, performing company executive; b. Oak Park, Ill., Aug. 22, 1936; d. Howard Joseph and Marian Louise (Henne) Gilman; m. Ernest George Lovas, May 17, 1957 (div. Nov. 1976); children: Lori Dianne, Randall Gilman; m. Albert Theodore Pizzamiglio, Mar. 27, 1978. Student, North Tex. State U., 1955-56. Stewardess North Cen. Airlines, Chgo., 1956-57; receptionist Leo Burnett Advt. Agy., Chgo., 1957-59; office mgr. Judy Stallons Employment Agy., Oak Brook, Ill., 1973-75; mgr. and escort Prestige Vacations, Inc., Oak Brook, Ill., 1975-76; corp. dir. Al Pierson Big Band U.S.A., Inc., Aubrey, Tex., 1976—, Al Pierson, Ltd., Aubrey, Tex., 1978—; corp. pres. Gilman, Inc. Artists Mgmt., Aubrey, Tex., 1982—; owner Dancing Horse Ranch, Aubrey, Tex., 1983—; bus. mgr. Guy Lombardo's Royal Canadians, Aubrey, Tex., 1989—. Editor: (newsletter) Property Owners Assn., 1972-73; contbr. articles to profl. jours. Recipient expert award NRA, 1952. Mem. U.S. Lipizzan Registry (bd. dirs. 1986-89), Dallas Dressage Club (bd. dirs. 1988-94), Am. Horse Shows Assn., Am. Quarter Horse Assn., U.S. Dressage Fedn. (qualified rider 1989, third/all breeds, first level 1989, first/all breeds, fourth level 1991, third Vintage Cup, fourth level 1991, third all-breeds first level 1992, third vintage cup first level 1992). Republican. Episcopalian. Address: Gilman Inc Artist Mgmt 34201 FM 428 East Aubrey TX 76227

PLACE, DALE HUBERT, former state commissioner; b. Parkersburg, W.Va., May 14, 1937; s. Frederick Russell and Evelyn Marie (Fleming) P.; m. Dora Lee Huber, June 4, 1960; children: John David, Steven Christopher. BS, Abilene Christian U., 1964, MEd, 1965; MS, S.W. Tex. State U., 1976. Vocat. rehab. counselor Tex. Edn. Agy., Abilene, 1965-67, vocat. rehab. supr., 1967-69; mental health cons., program specialist Tex. Rehab. Commn., Austin, 1973-85, dep. commr. disability determination div., 1973-85, dep. commr. programs, 1985-87, dep. commr. adminstrv. and support svcs., 1987-92; with D.D. & P. Internat. Mktg., 1992—, Provident Comms., Inc. and DP Ventures, Inc. Author: (with others) Aspects of Disability, 1969. Active Boy Scouts Am., Austin, 1989. With USAF, 1955-59. Recipient Commr.'s Citation SSA, 1984, Regional Commr.'s Citation, 1984, Service Sponsor award League United Latin Am. Citizens, 1986, Citation for Outstanding Services Automated Info. and Telecommunications Council, 1988. Mem. Nat. Rehab. Assn. (life), Nat. Rehab. Counseling Assn. (pres. 1970), Nat. Rehab. Adminstr. Assn., Kiwanis. Republican. Mem. Ch. of Christ. Home and Office: 707 Birch Brook Dr Leander TX 78641

PLANK, (ETHEL) FAYE, editor, photographer, writer; b. St. Francisville, Ill., Oct. 15, 1912; d. Perry Austin and Nellie Sarah (Hardin) Winget; m. Edward Earl Plank, July 10, 1934 (dec. Mar. 1986); children: Earleen F., Eugene Earl, Richard J. Student, Tex. Wesleyan U., West Tex. State U., N.Mex. U., San Antonio Coll., U. So. Miss., Ea. N.Mex. U., U. N.Mex., Drake U., Rutgers U., Dartmouth U., U. Colo., Amarillo Coll., Frank Phillips Coll., Permaian Basin Jr. Coll. Pvt. tchr. art Hereford, Tex., 1960-64; office mgr., bookkeeper West Tex. Devel. Co., Hereford, 1964-70; publicity writer Cowbelles, 1970-74; mng. editor Curry County Times, Clovis, N.Mex., 1974-77; writer advertising and news State Line Tribune, Farwell, Tex., 1977-82; corresp. Lubbock (Tex.) Avalanche Jour., 1977-82, Amarillo (Tex.) Globe News, 1977-86; owner, mgr. Ideas Unltd. (pub. rels. firm), 1977-82; owner, editor, pub. Your Paper, N.Mex., 1977-82; women's editor, photographer Dalhart (Tex.) Daily Texan, 1983—; former writer advt. Spl. Roping and Rodeo, Clovis, Pioneer Days, Clovis, Curry County Fair, Clovis; mem. spl. commr. on publicity and promotion Mesa Redonda Cowboy Camp Mtg., N.Mex., 1980-82, with publicity Federated Rep. Women's Club, Clovis, 1976-82, Clovis Bus. and Profl. Women's Club, 1977-82; with publicity and promotion Miss Rodeo N.Mex. Pageant, 1977-82, Curry County Farm and Livestock Bur., 1977-82; spl. assignments, photographer N.Mex. Stockman, Albuquerque, N.Mex. Farm and Ranch Mag. Publicity chmn., bd. dirs. Keep Dalhart Beautiful; publicity chmn., v.p. Dalhart Ctrl. United Meth. Women; v.p., program chmn., pres. Dalhart Wesleyan Group, Ctrl. United Meth. Ch.; publicity chmn. Dalhart Youth Ctr. Bd.; bd. dirs., task force Dalhart Sr. Citizens; chmn. Dalhart Writer's Group; leader 4-H Club, Hereford, Camp Fire Club, Hereford; active sch. bd. Hereford Ind. Sch. Dist., 1960-62; active Methodist Women's Fellowship, Hereford Red Cross (Gray Lady, chmn.), Hereford Art Guild, Hereford Meth. Ch. Recipient 4-H Leaders award, 1952, Citizen of Yr. award Hereford Lions Club, 1960, appreciation award Am. Nat. Red Cross, 1965, N.Mex. Cowbelle of Yr. award, 1973, Community Leaders and Noteworthy Am. award, 1975-76, award of merit Miss Rodeo N.Mex. Pageant, appreciation award FFA, Pvt. Enterprise award Federated Club Women Am., 1978, Cert. Appreciation, Nat. Heart Edn. Assn., 1979, Golden Quill award N.Mex. Farm and Livestock Bur., 1981, Woman of Achievment award N. Mex. Press Women, 1981, Woman of Achievement award Nat. Fedn. Press Women, 1981, N.Mex. Friend of 4-H award Curry County, 1984, Dallam, Tex., County, 1984, Disting. Proud Ptnr. award Keep Tex. Beautiful, 1988, 89, Cert. merit, O. P. Schnabel Status Citizen, 1992, Outstanding Spl. Promotion award Am. Cancer Soc., ACE award 1990-91, 91-92, Recognition award 1991-92, Pace Setter award 1993, Edn. award 1993, Tex. Sch. Bell award Distinction, Tex. Retired Tchrs. Assn., 1991, Appreciation award Tex. Press Women, 1993, Merit award Kcet Tex. Beautiful Individual Leadership, 1994, Appreciation cert. Tex. Press Women, 1994-95, Merit award HOSTS, 1995; named Citizen of Yr., Dalhart (Tex.) Area C. of C., 1993. Mem. Nat. Fedn. Press Women (bd. dirs., regional chmn.-Tex., N.Mex., Colo., Okla., La.), Panhandle Press Assn., Tex. Press Assn., Soc. Profl. Journalists, N.Mex. Press Women (past pres.), Ea. N.Mex. Press Women (past pres.), N.Mex. Farm and Livestock Bur. (info. dir., former bd. dirs.), Am. Nat. Cowbelles (chmn. beef edn.), N.Mex. Cowbelles (state bd., legis. chmn., publicity, news media, TV dir.), Cattle Capital Cowbelles (local pres.), Bus. and Profl. Women's Club (v.p., pres.), Republican Women's Club (publicity chmn., Curry County Rep. Ctrl. com.), Pilot Club, PTA (pres.). Republican. Methodist.

PLATMAN, ROBERT HENRY, religious educator; b. Rochester, N.Y., Jan. 30, 1925; s. Henry Benjamin and Edna Estella (Ostrander) P. BA, Ohio Wesleyan U., 1945; MDiv, Seabury-We. Theol. Sem., 1950; PhD, NYU, 1974. Ordained priest Episc. Ch., 1950. Curate Trinity Episc. Ch., Highland Park, Ill., 1950-51, St. Michael and All Angels Episc. Ch., Dallas, 1951-53; rector St. Bede's Episc. Ch., Syosset, N.Y., 1953-90; adj. priest St. Boniface Episc. Ch., Sarasota, Fla., 1991—; prof. religious edn. George Mercer Sch. Theology, Garden City, N.Y., 1970-90; chmn. commn. Christian and Jewish rels. Diocese L.I., Garden City, 1970-72, commn. on ch. music, 1977-78. Contbr. articles to profl. jours. Mem. Religious Edn. Assn. U.S. and Can., Soc. for Sci. Study of Religion, Assn. Profs. and Rschrs. in Religious Edn. Home: 2112 41st St W Bradenton FL 34205

PLATSOUCAS, CHRIS DIMITRIOS, immunologist; b. Athens, Greece, Apr. 17, 1951; came to U.S., 1973; s. Dimitrios Evagelos and Maria (Tsonidis) P.; m. Emilia L. Oleszak, Oct. 18, 1985. BS, U. Patras (Greece), 1973; postgrad., Purdue U., 1974; PhD, MIT, 1978. Rsch. fellow/assoc. Meml. Sloan-Kettering Cancer Ctr., N.Y.C., 1978-80, asst. mem., 1980-85, asst. prof., 1981-85, head lab. biol. response modifiers, 1981-85; assoc. prof. dept. immunology M.D. Anderson Cancer Ctr., Houston, 1985-89, prof., dep. chmn., 1989-93, Ashbel Smith professorship, 1991-92, H.L. and O. Stringer professorship in cancer rsch., 1992-93; L.H. Carnell prof. and chmn. dept. microbiology, immunology Temple U. Sch. Medicine, Phila., 1993—; biotech. cons., sci. reviewer study sects. NIH, Bethesda, 1982—. Contbr. numerous articles to profl. jours. Nat. Rsch. Svc. award NIH, 1978-79; NIH grantee, 1982—, Am. Cancer Soc. grantee, 1980-91. Mem. Am. Assn. Immunologists, Am. Soc. Hematology, Am. Assn. Biochem & Molecular Biology, Am. Assn. Pathologists. Greek Orthodox. Office: Temple U Sch Medicine Dept Microbiology and Immunology 3400 N Broad St Philadelphia PA 19140-5196

PLATT, GEOFFREY, JR., cultural administrator; b. N.Y.C., Jan. 13, 1941; s. Geoffrey and Helen (Choate) P.; m. Hope Gifford Forsyth, Sept. 7, 1974; children: Lucy Forsyth, Rufus Choate. BA, Harvard Coll., 1963; MBA, Harvard Bus. Sch., 1973. Field rep. Community Concerts Inc., N.Y.C., 1964-65; mgr. N.J. Symphony Orch., Newark, 1966-69; assoc. dean Aspen (Colo.) Music Festival & Sch., 1969-71; dir. program devel. Colo. Coun. on the Arts, Denver, 1973-75; dir. Arts Coun. New Orleans, New Orleans, 1975-80; exec. dir. Nat. Assembly of State Arts, Washington, 1980-84; chief of staff to U.S. Rep. Michael L. Strang, Washington, 1985-87; dir. govt. affairs Am. Assn. Mus., Washington, 1987-91; exec. dir. Maymont Found., Richmond, Va., 1992—. Bd. dirs. Greater New Orleans Ednl. TV, New Orleans, 1979-80; trustee Washington Revels, Washington, 1990-92. Mem. Met. Club (Washington), Century Assn. (N.Y.C.). Home: 100 Williamson Ct Richmond VA 23229-7763 Office: Maymont Found 1700 Hampton St Richmond VA 23220-6819

PLATT, JEFFREY LOUIS, surgery educator, immunology educator, pediatric nephrologist; b. Mt. Vernon, N.Y., Mar. 21, 1949; s. Charles Alfred and Paula (Rosenblum) P.; m. Agnes M. Schipper. BA in Politics with honors, NYU, 1971; postgrad., Columbia U., 1971-73; MD, U. So. Calif., 1977. Diplomate Am. Bd. Pediatrics, Nat. Bd. Med. Examiners. Intern in pediatrics Children's Hosp. L.A., 1977-78, resident, 1978-79, Della M. Mudd resident, 1979-80; med. fellow in pediatric nephrology U. Minn., Mpls., 1980-85, instr. dept. pediatrics, 1985-86, asst. prof., 1986-88, assoc. prof. pediatrics and cell biology and neuroanatomy, 1988-92; prof. surgery, pediatrics and immunology depts. Duke U., Durham, N.C., 1992—, Dorothy W. and Joseph W. Beard prof. exptl. surgery, 1994—. Mem. editl. bd. Transplantation, Transplant Immunology, Xenotransplantation; contbr. more than 200 articles to med. jours. Recipient Clinician-Scientist award Am. Heart Assn., 1983-88, Established Investigator award, 1988-93. Mem. AAAS, Am. Heart Assn. Coun. of the Kidney in Cardiovascular Disease, Am. Heart Assn. Coun. Basic Sci., Internat. Soc. Nephrology, Am. Assn. Immunologists, Am. Fedn. Clin. Rsch., Am. Soc. Nephrology, Am. Assn. Pathologists, Soc. for Devel. Biology, Clin. Immunology Soc., Soc. Pediatric Rsch., Soc. Glycobiology, Soc. Exptl. Biology and Medicine, Alpha Omega Alpha. Office: Duke U Med Ctr Box 2605 Durham NC 27710

PLAUCHÉ, PRIMA, library director; b. Picayune, Miss., Mar. 14, 1949; d. Charles A. and Jessie D. (Welsh) Thomas; m. Henry Hester Plauché Jr., May 30, 1992; 1 child from previous marriage: Charles Joseph Wusnack. BEd, U. Miss., 1972; MSLS, U. So. Miss., 1981. Libr. Coast Episc. Schs., Bay St. Louis, Miss., 1972-74; dir. Hancock County Libr. System, Bay St. Louis, 1975—; mem. Miss. Statewide Info. Network Task Force, Jackson, 1994—; bd. dirs. Fahey Drug Co., Inc., Bay St. Louis, Libr. Found. Hancock County, Bay St. Louis. Mem. editl. adv. com. Miss. Coast Mag., 1996. Chair goal IV Hancock 2000 Com., 1994-96; mem. exec. com. Hancock County Rep. Ctrl. Com., 1992—. Mem. Miss. Libr. Assn. (legis. chair 1995-96), ALA, Hancock County C. of C. (edn. com. 1985—). Office: Hancock County Libr System 312 Highway 90 Bay Saint Louis MS 39520-3532

PLAVSIC, BRANKO MILENKO, radiology educator; b. Zagreb, Yugoslavia, Croatia, Feb. 14, 1947; came to U.S., 1989; s. Milenko and Nevenka P.; m. Valerie H. Drnovsek, Aug. 26, 1991. MD, U. Zagreb, 1972, MS, 1974, PhD, 1975. Asst. prof. U. Zagreb, 1986, prof. radiology, chief abdominal radiology, 1988; prof. radiology, vice-chmn., dir. abdominal radiol./rsch. Tulane U., New Orleans, 1991—. Co-author: (with A.E. Robinson, R.B. Jeffrey) Gastrointestinal Radiology: A Concise Text, 1992; contbr. articles to profl. jours. Home: 4460 Lennox Blvd New Orleans LA 70131-8348 Office: Tulane U Med Ctr Dept Radiology 1430 Tulane Ave New Orleans LA 70112

PLEACHER, DAVID HENRY, secondary school educator; b. Reading, Pa., Dec. 29, 1946; s. John K. and Isabel Kathleen (Moyer) P.; m. Carol Elizabeth Jackson, June 8, 1968; children: Amy Elizabeth, Michael David, Sarah Catherine. BA in Math., Hartwick Coll., 1968; MS in Edn., James Madison U., 1971. Cert. tchr., Va. Tchr. Arlington (Va.) County Pub. Schs., 1968, Fairfax County Pub. Schs., Herndon, Va., 1968-73; tchr., dept. chair Winchester (Va.) City Schs., 1973—; instr. James Madison U., Harrisonburg, Va., 1982-87; lectr., instr. Lord Fairfax C.C., Middletown, Va., 1986-89; project mem. Computer Software Devel. Project, 1985-90; participant Math. Inst. Woodrow Wilson Found., Princeton, 1986. Co-editor: (computer column) Va. Math. Tchr., 1982-84; author computer programs; contbr. articles to profl. jours. Recipient Presdl. award in excellence in math and sci. teaching NSF, Washington, 1985, Homer "Pete" Ice Svc. award Handley High Athletic Dept., 1991, Tandy Tech. Scholars award Tandy Corp./T.C.U., Washington, 1992. Mem. NEA (life), Va. Edn. Assn., Winchester Edn. Assn., Nat. Coun. Tchrs. Math. (presenter at confs.), Va. Coun. Tchrs. Math. (presenter at confs., William Lowry Outstanding Math Tchr. 1987), Valley Va. Coun. Tchrs. Math., Math. Assn. Am., Coun. Presdl. Awardees in Math. Presbyterian. Home: 304 Caroline Ave Stephens City VA 22655 Office: John Handley High Sch PO Box 910 Winchester VA 22604-0910

PLESS, LAURANCE DAVIDSON, lawyer; b. Jacksonville, Fla., Dec. 22, 1952; s. James William Pless III and Anne (Dodson) Martin; m. Dana Halberg, June 20, 1980; children: Anna Amesbury, William Davidson, Deane Ahlgren. AB with distinction, Duke U., 1975; JD, U. N.C., Chapel Hill, 1980. Assoc. Neely & Player, P.C., Atlanta, 1980-86, ptnr., 1986-92; ptnr. Welch, Spell, Reemsnyder & Pless, P.C., Atlanta, 1992—. Contbr. articles to profl. jours. Vol. Saturday Vol. Lawyer's Found., Atlanta, 1980—. Mem. ABA, Lawyer's Club of Atlanta, Atlanta Bar Assn., Capital City Club. Democrat. Episcopalian. Home: 25 Palisades Rd NE Atlanta GA 30309-1530 Office: Welch Spell Reemsnyder & Pless Ste 2020 400 Colony Sq Atlanta GA 30361-6305

PLICHTA, THOMAS FRANCIS, real estate executive; b. Wyandotte, Mich., Apr. 10, 1952; s. Frank R. and Wanda (Latta) P.; m. Marlene Kovacs, June 14, 1975; children: Brandon Travis, Thomas Francis Jr., Drew Robert. B.A. with honors, Mich. State U., 1974; M.B.A., Wayne State U., 1978. C.P.A., Mich., Tex. Mgr. Deloitte Haskins & Sells, Inc., Detroit, 1974-79; v.p., treas. Condo Marine Properties, Detroit, 1980-81, Paul Bosco & Sons, Dallas, 1982; exec. v.p., COO, CFO Barge Assocs., Inc., Dallas, 1982-85, also dir.; pres. Assoc. Prime Equities, Inc., Dallas, 1984-85; pres. Prime Devel., Inc., Dallas, 1985-86; CFO Metro-Flex Excarating, Inc., Lewisville, Tex., 1987—; vice chmn. dir. Med. Bldg. Corp., Dallas, 1985-86. Recipient Disting. Advisor of Yr. award Jr. Achievement Assn. Southeastern Mich., 1977, Disting. Alumni award Taylor Ctr. High Sch., 1988. Mem. Am. Inst. C.P.A.s, Mich. Assn. C.P.A.s, Tex. Soc. C.P.A.s, Beta Alpha Psi. Roman Catholic. Home: 205 Coyote Ct Lewisville TX 75067 Office: Metroplex Excavating Inc PO Box 1287 Lewisville TX 75067-0607

PLOFCHAN, THOMAS KENNETH, college official; b. Detroit, July 16, 1937; s. Peter Paul Plofchan and Elsie S. (Nogafsky) Bronikowski; m. Paula Grimberg, Aug. 26, 1961; children: Elizabeth, Thomas Kenneth Jr., Margaret, Paul, Peter, Daniel, Jennifer. BA in Music, U. Notre Dame, 1959; MA in Counseling and Guidance, U. Detroit, 1963; postgrad., U. Mich., Dearborn, 1964-65, Columbia U., 1965, Wayne State U., 1966-75. Tchr., choral dir. St. James High Sch., Ferndale, Mich., 1959-63; counsellor Berkley (Mich.) High Sch., 1963-66; asst. dir. admissions Wayne State U., Detroit, 1966-69, internat. student edn. credential analyst grad. div., 1966-69; dir. admissions Marygrove Coll., Detroit, 1969-74, dean continuing edn. and community svcs., 1972-79, dean adminstrv. affairs, dir. planning and budgeting, 1979-82, v.p. for instnl. advancement, 1982-86; v.p. for instnl. advancement U. of Incarnate Word, San Antonio, 1986—; mem. Nat. Com. on Gift Annuities, 1992—. organist St. Piux X Ch., San Antonio, 1986—; mem. Fiesta San Antonio Commn., 1990—. Mem. Nat. Soc. Fund Raising Execs. (cert. fund raising exec. 1992, nat. bd. dirs. 1990-91, nat. assembly 1992—, nat. task force on tax issues 1993-94, chpt. compliance task force 1994—, exec. com. San Antonio chpt. 1988-95, pres. 1990-91, govt. rels. liaison 1992-94, liaison Found. 1992-93), Greater San Antonio C. of C. (chamber diplomat 1989-92, edn. com. 1993—), North San Antonio C. of C., Hispanic C. of C., Alamo Heights C. of C. (bd. dirs. 1991-94), Kiwanis (bd. dirs. N.E. San Antonio 1991—, treas. 1992-93, v.p., pres.-elect 1993-94, pres. 1994-95). Home: 73 Campden Cir San Antonio TX 78218-3007 Office: U of Incarnate Word 4301 Broadway St San Antonio TX 78209-6318

PLONK, WILLIAM MCGUIRE, retired minister; b. Franklin, N.C., Aug. 19, 1925; s. Thomas Motley and Mary Louise (McGuire) P.; m. Nancy Marie Moore, June 29, 1957; children: Mary Evelyn Plonk Lucas, William McGuire Plonk, Jr. BS, Davidson Coll., 1949; BD, Union Theol. Seminary, Richmond, Va., 1954. Ordained to ministry Presbyn. Ch., 1954. Pastor Lawrenceville (Va.) Presbyn. Ch., 1954-56, Rivermont Presbyn. Ch., Chester, Va., 1956-58; youth minister First Presbyn. Ch., Greensboro, N.C., 1958-61; pastor Westminster Presbyn. Ch., Columbia, S.C., 1961-66, Covenant Presbyn. Ch., Spartanburg, S.C., 1966-69, Bow Creek Presbyn. Ch., Virginia Beach, Va., 1969-72; spl. agt. Jefferson Standard Ins. Co., Norfolk, Va., 1972-73; exchange pastor St. Stevens and West Church of Scotland, Broughty Ferry, Scotland, 1972; pastor Makemie/Naomi Makemie Presbyn. Chs., Accomac, Onancock, Va., 1974-90; interim pastor Manokin Presbyn. Ch., Princess Anne, Md., 1991, 92; stated supply Clark Presbyn. Ch., Daugherty, Va., 1993—. Dist. chmn. Boy Scouts Am. 1st lt. U.S. Army, 1944-46. Mem. Rotary (pres. Onancock Club, Paul Harris Fellow 1993), Drummondtown-Lee Ruritan Club (pres.). Home: PO Box 553 23359 Cross St Accomac VA 23301-0553

PLONSEY, ROBERT, electrical and biomedical engineer; b. N.Y.C., July 17, 1924; s. Louis B. and Betty (Vinograd) P.; m. Vivian V. Vucker, Oct. 1, 1948; 1 child, Daniel. BEE, Cooper Union, 1943; MSEE, NYU, 1948; PhD, U. Calif., Berkeley, 1955; postgrad. med. sch., Case Western Res. U., 1969-71; D of Technol. Scis., Slovak Acad. Scis., 1995. Registered profl. engr., Ohio. Asst. prof. elec. engring. U. Calif., Berkeley, 1955-57; asst. prof. elec. engring. Case Inst. Tech., Cleve., 1957-60, assoc. prof., 1960-66, prof., 1966-68, dir. bioengring. group, 1962-68; prof. biomed. engring. Sch. Engring. and Sch. Medicine Case Western Res. U., 1968-83, chmn. dept., 1976-80; vis. prof. biomed. engring. Duke U., Durham, N.C., 1980-81, prof., 1983-96, prof. biomed. engring., Hudson prof. engring., 1990-93, Pfizer-Inc.-Edmond T. Pratt Jr. Univ. prof. biomed. engring., 1993-96; Pfizer-Inc.-Edmond T. Pratt Jr. Univ. prof. emeritus Duke U., Durham, 1996—; mem. biomed. fellowships rev. com. NIH, 1966-70; mem. tng. com. Engrs. in Medicine and Biology, 1972-73, cons., 1974—; cons. NSF, 1973-93; mem. internat. sci. adv. com. Ragnar Granit Inst., Tampere (Finland) U. Tech., 1992—; ad hoc mem. sci. adv. com. Whitaker Found., 1989-91. Author: (with R. Collin) Principles and Applications of Electromagnetic Fields, 1961, Bioelectric Phenomena, 1969, (with J. Liebman and P. Gillette) Pediatric Electrocardiography, 1982, (with T. Pilkington) Engineering Contributions to Biophysical Electrocardiography, 1982, (with J. Liebman and Y. Rudy) Pediatric and Fundamental Electrocardiography, (with R.C. Barr) Bioelectricity: A Quantitative Approach, 1988, (with J. Malmivuo) Bioelectromagnetism, 1995; mem. editorial bd. Trans. IEEE, Biomed. Engring, 1965-70; assoc. editor, 1977-79, editorial bd. TIT Jour. 1971-81, Electrocardiology Jour., 1974—, Medical and Biological Engineering and Computing, 1987—; procs. editor Engring. in Medicine and Biology, 17th Ann., Conf., 1965. Mem. com. on electrocardiography Am. Heart Assn., 1976-82; v.p. Your Schs., Cleveland Heights, Ohio, 1968-69, 73-75; provisional trustee Am. Bd. Clin. Engrs., 1973-74, pres. 1975, trustee, 1976-85. With AUS, 1944-46. Recipient sr. postdoctoral award NIH, 1980-81. Fellow AAAS, IEEE (chmn. Cleve. chpt. group on biomed. electronics 1962-63, chmn. publs. com. group on engring. in medicine and biology 1968-70, v.p. adminstrv. com. 1970-72, pres. 1973-74, chmn. fellows com. Engring. in Medicine and Biology Soc. 1986-87-88, v.p. tech. and conf. activities 1991, William S. Morlock award 1979, Centennial medal 1984, co-program chair ann. conf., Paris 1992, chmn. awards com. 1996); mem. AAUP, NAE (bioengring. peer com. 1988-91, chair 1990-91, nominating com. 1991-92, mem. com. 1992-94, program adv. com. 1996—, NRS postdoctoral rsch. associateships evaluation panel 1987-90), Am. Inst. Med. and Biol. Engring. (founding fellow 1992—), Alliance for Engring. in Medicine and Biology (treas. 1976-78), Biomed. Engring. Soc. (bd. dirs. 1975-78, 79-83, pres. 1981-82, chmn. affiliations com. 1987-89, ALZA Disting. lectr. 1988), Am. Physiol. Soc., Am. Soc. Engring. Edn. (bd. dirs. biomed. engring. divsn. 1978-83, chmn. 1982-83). Office: Duke U Dept Biomed Engring Durham NC 27706

PLOPPER, BRUCE LOREN, journalism educator; b. Syracuse, N.Y., Dec. 1, 1945; s. Loren Brandt and Eleanor Ruth (Hess) P.; m. Deborah Susan Patterson, Nov. 15, 1975; children: John Loren, Kelly Claire. BS in Psychology, Mich. State U., 1967; MA in Social Psychology, So. Ill. U., 1971, PhD in Journalism, 1979. Part time instr. psychology Forest Park C.C., St. Louis, 1971-72; editor Home Savings of Am., L.A., 1974-76; part time instr. journalism So. Ill. U., Carbondale, 1978-79; mng. editor Building News, Inc., L.A., 1979-80; info. svcs. mgr., book divsn. dir. Sci. Rsch. Svcs., Hollywood, Calif., 1980-81; asst. prof. journalism Humboldt State U., Arcata, Calif., 1981-83, Mo. Western State Coll., St. Joseph, 1983-85; asst. prof. journalism U. Ctrl. Ark., Conway, 1985-89, assoc. prof. journalism, 1989-90; assoc. prof. journalism U. Ark., Little Rock, 1990—; lectr. in field. Author: The Problem-Solving Handbook for High School Journalism Advisers, 1992, Mass Communication Law in Arkansas, 1997; contbr. articles to profl. jours. and newspapers. Mem. Journalism Edn. Assn., Ark. Press Women, Investigative Reporters and Editors, Assn. Edn. in Journalism and Mass Comm. (law divsn. liaison to Soc. Profl. Journalists and Reporters com. 1991-92, history divsn., newspaper divsn., scholastic journalism divsn.), Soc. Profl. Journalists (v.p. Ark. profl. chpt. 1988-89, co-chair scholarship com. 1990—, freeedom of info. watchdog com. 1990-92). Home: 5 New Oxford Rd Conway AR 72032-7403 Office: U Ark Little Rock Dept Journalism 2801 S University Ave Little Rock AR 72204-1099

PLOTT, MONTE GLENN, journalist; b. Winston-Salem, N.C., Feb. 19, 1952; s. Bobby Glenford and Elizabeth Rebecca (Manuel) P.; m. Patricia G. Etheridge, July 3, 1982; 1 child, Micah Etheridge. BA in Journalism, U. N.C., 1974. Reporter Winston-Salem Jour., 1974-75; corr. AP, Charlotte, 1975-80; reporter, writer Post-Dispatch, St. Louis, 1980-82; rewrite editor USA Today, Washington, 1982-83; reporter, writer Jour.-Constitution, Atlanta, 1983-88; editor-in-chief Billian Pub., Atlanta, 1988—, editl. dir., 1992—; v.p. Billian/Trans World Pub., 1996—. Author: Flashes of Fire, 1974. Recipient Folio Editl. Excellence award, 1994; Disting. scholar U. N.C. Sch. Journalism, 1972, Scripps-Howard scholar, 1972. Mem. Mag. Assn. Ga. (bd. dirs. 1996). Office: Billian Pub 2100 Powers Ferry Rd NW Atlanta GA 30339-5014

PLOUFFE, LEO, JR., reproductive endocrinologist; b. Montreal, Que., Can., Nov. 26, 1957; s. Leo and Yvette (LaFontaine) P.; m. Evelyn Woodward White, Sept. 22, 1990. Diploma Collegiate Studies, Ahuntsic Coll., Montreal, 1975; MD CM, McGill U., Montreal, 1980. Diplomate gen. ob-gyn. and reproductive endocrinology. Resident in ob-gyn. McGill U., Montreal, 1980-85; fellow in reproductive endocrinology Med. Coll. Ga., Augusta, 1985-87, asst. prof., 1987-92, assoc. prof. endocrinology, 1992—, chief sect. reproductive endocrinology, 1994—. Fellow Am. Coll. Ob-Gyn., AAAS; mem. Am. Soc. for Reproductive Medicine. Office: Med Coll Ga Dept OB-Gyn Augusta GA 30912

PLUFF, STEARNS CHARLES, III, investment banker; b. Biloxi, Miss., Jan. 30, 1953; s. Stearns Charles Jr. and Patricia Elizabeth (Diaz) P.; m. Joan Marie Jay Jones, May 28, 1987; children: Micleah Frances, Ashleigh Nicole. BA, U. Miss., 1975. Supr. Host Internat., New Orleans, 1975-77; contractor Greg Edwards & Co., Falls Church, Va., 1977-80; registered rep. Donald Sheldon & Co., Houston, 1982-85; sr. v.p. GMS Group Inc., Houston, 1985—; dir., sr. v.p. MMP Investments, Inc., Cary, Ill., 1989—; pres. R.P. Telekom U.S.A., Warsaw, 1993—. Vol. Petrosky Elem. Sch., Alief, Tex., 1991—, Girl Scouts U.S., Houston, 1991—. Mem. Chi Psi. Home: GMS Group Inc 15210 La Mancha Houston TX 77083 Office: 5075 Westheimer Rd Ste 1175 Houston TX 77056-5606

PLUMLEY, JOSEPH PINKNEY, JR., public relations educator, consultant; b. Atlanta, Sept. 3, 1944; s. Joseph Pinkney Sr. and Julia (West) P.; m. Patricia Susan Stone, June 10, 1967 (div. Aug. 1983); m. Laurie Ann Gray, June 30, 1984; children: Bradford Christian, Jennifer Elizabeth, Stephanie Anne. BA in Journalism, U. Ga., 1967; student Air. Def. Officer basic course, U.S. Army, 1969, U.S. Army, 1968; student Aviation Sch., U.S. Army, 1969, student Air Def. officer advanced course, 1974; MEd, U. Ga., 1975, EdS, 1976, EdD, 1978; student, U.S. Army Command and Gen. Staff Coll., 1978, U.S. Army Inspector Gen. Sch., 1983. Commd. 2nd lt. U.S. Army, 1968, advanced through grades to lt. col., 1984, student officer basic course, 1968, student aviation course, 1969; served Vietnam, 1970-71; commdg. officer HHB 31st Air Def. Bde U.S. Army, 1972-73; asst. prof. mil. sci. U. Ga., 1974-78; commdg. officer U.S. Army Missile Control Ctr., Wurzburg, Germany, 1978-79; instr. Boston U., 1978-81; exec. officer 37th Air Def. Bn., Schweinfurt, Germany, 1979-81; rsch. dir. U.S. Army Pers. and

Fin. Ctr., Ft. Benjamin Harrison, Ind., 1981-84; asst. prof. Ball State U., Indpls., 1981-84; dep. chief of staff U.S. Army Combined Arms Ctr., Ft. Leavenworth, Kans., 1984-85, insp. gen., 1985-86; ret. U.S. Army, 1988; prof. mil. sci. U. Ala., Tuscaloosa, 1987-88, asst. prof. pub. rels., 1988-94; owner, pres. Plumley & Assocs. Pub. Rels. Cons., Tuscaloosa, 1988—. Author: Writing for Mass Communication, 1994; editor So. Pub. Rels. Jour., 1993-94; contbr. articles to profl. jours. Bd. dirs. YMCA Tuscaloosa, 1989—, Black Warrior coun. Boy Scouts Am., 1986-90. Decorated Bronze Star, Cross of Gallantry, 21 Combat Air medals; recipient Spirit of Freedom award Exch. Club Ala., Montgomery, 1989; named Sr. Practitioner, So. Pub. Rels. Fedn., 1994. Mem. Pub. Rels. Soc. Am., Pub. Rels. Coun. Ala. (pres. 1992, state v.p. 1993, state treas. 1991, bd. dirs. 1991-92), Exch. Club Tuscaloosa (pres. 1989, bd. dirs. 1989-95), Sigma Nu (faculty advisor 1986-94). Republican. Episcopalian. Home: 415 Vantage Pt Tuscaloosa AL 35406-2381 Office: Univ Ala Coll Comm 415 Vantage Pt Tuscaloosa AL 35406-2381

PLUMMER, EDWARD RAY, radio announcer, writer, reporter; b. Flemingsburg, Ky., Sept. 3, 1964; s. Edward Estill and Bernice Mae (Muse) P. BS, Morehead (Ky.) State U., 1987. Lic. radiotelephone operator FCC. Intern, vol. WKMY-FM, Morehead, 1983; desk worker Cooper Hall, Morehead, 1983-86; sr. sports dir., producer, writer, reporter, anchor Newscenter 12, Morehead, 1985-87; census enumerator U.S. Census Bur., Flemingsburg, 1989; cook., gen. maintenance worker Shoney's Restaurant, Morehead, 1990-94; radio announcer, anchor, writer, reporter, music dir. WFLE, Flemingsburg, 1994—; corr. Country Music Examiner mag. Recipient scholarship; nominated Music Dir. of Yr. (country divsn.) Acad. of Ind. Recording Artists, 1996. Mem. Lambda Chi Alpha. Methodist. Home: PO Box 224 Flemingsburg KY 41041 Office: WFLE-AM/FM Fleming County Broadcasting 1 Radio Dr Flemingsburg KY 41041-9400

PLUMMER, MICHAEL KENNETH, financial consultant; b. Jacksonville, Fla., Apr. 24, 1954; s. Kenneth Albert and Edith Lorraine (O'Brien) P.; m. Amy Forté, 1992; 1 child, Brian Michael. BBA in Econs., U. North Fla., 1976; MS in Real Estate, Ga. State U., 1993, postgrad., 1993—. Econ. analyst Barnett Banks of Fla., Jacksonville, 1976-78; exec. v.p. Home Owners Warranty Corp., Jacksonville, 1978-80; market analyst Plantec Corp., Jacksonville, 1980-81; assoc. Laventhol & Horwath, Miami and Denver, 1981-84; sr. mgr., nat. coord. corp. real estate consulting svcs. KPMG Peat Marwick (formerly Peat, Marwick, Main & Co.), Atlanta, 1984-91; sr. mng. dir. IRE Advisors, Atlanta, 1991—. Mem. Gov.'s Econ. ADv. Com., Fla., 1982-84; econ. cons. Atlanta com. for 1996 Olympic Games. Fla. Bankers Assn. scholar; named Eagle Scout Boy Scouts Am., 1972. Mem. Urban Land Inst. Republican. Methodist. Office: IRE Advisors 303 Peachtree St NE Atlanta GA 30308-3201

PLUMMER, PAUL JAMES, telephone company executive; b. Scottsbluff, Nebr., Aug. 3, 1946; s. Virgil Frank and Helen Louise (Hultberg) P.; m. Pamela Lee Purdom, June 26, 1976; 1 child, Brittany Lane. BA, U. Nebr., 1968; postgrad., Platte Coll., 1974-75; MBA, U. Iowa, 1982. With Gen. Tel. Co. of the Midwest, 1968-82, div. traffic supr., Columbus, Nebr., 1969-75, div. traffic mgr., Columbia, Mo., 1975-78, labor relations adminstr., Grinnell, Iowa, 1978-79, labor relations mgr., 1979-82, Compensation and services mgr., 1982; staff specialist customer service GTE Svc. Corp., Stamford, Conn., 1982-83, group specialist customer service, 1983-84, customer services mgr., 1984-87, ops. support planning mgr., 1987-89, mgr. strategic planning telephone ops., Irving, Tex., 1989-95; mgr. bus. devel. GTE Intelligent Network Svcs., Inc., 1995-96; group product devel. mgr. Cityscape, 1996—. Active Boy Scouts Am.; vol. Nat. Marrow Donor Program, Tex. Scholar's Program; pres. Brook Meadows Homeowners Assn.; chmn. citizen's adv. com. Grapevine-Colleyville Ind. Sch. Dist., 1989-93; pres. St. Vincent Episcopal Sch. Parent-Tchr. Club, 1993-95. Mem. Am. Assn. Personnel Adminstrn., Ind. Telephone Pioneer Assn., Personnel Mgmt. Assn. Columbia (exec. bd. dirs., 1st v.p. 1975-78), Brookmeadows Homeowner's Assn. Episcopalian. Clubs: Optimist (past pres. Columbus, Nebr., lt. gov. Nebr. 1973-74), Elks. Home: 2808 Meadowview Dr Colleyville TX 76034-4753 Office: 5525 N MacArthur Blvd Ste 320 Irving TX 75038

PLUMMER, ROBERT EUGENE, educational administrator; b. Ft. Worth, Sept. 7, 1931; s. George G. and Edith (Yates) P.; m. Sandra Sue Cope, Nov. 6, 1959 (div. July 1986); children: David Lee, Steven Paul; m. Mary Beth Maris, Dec. 28, 1987; 1 child, Robert Jones. BBA, U. North Tex., 1958, BS, 1959, MEd, 1963. Tchr. West Covina (Calif.) Unified Sch. Dist., 1963-66, U. North Tex., Denton, 1966-67, Tex. Wesleyan U., Ft. Worth, 1967-68; adminstr., tchr. San Diego Unified Sch. Dist., 1968-70; tchr. Ft. Worth Ind. Sch. Dist., 1970-71, coord. intercultural rels., 1971-74, prin. Oakhurst Elem. Sch., 1974-77, prin. Tanglewood Elem. Sch., 1977-83, coord. elem. magnets/Montessori, 1983-86, prin. South Hi Mount Elem. Sch., 1986-93, prin. Bruce Shulkey Elem. Sch., 1993—. Chmn. bd. dirs. Tarrant County Am. Heart Assn., 1984-85; lifetime mem. PTA; bd. dirs. Am. Heart Assn., Ft. Worth, 1975—, chmn., 1984-85; bd. dirs. Regional XI Blood Bank, Ft. Worth, 1981—, chmn., 1990—; del. to Pisa (Italy) Conf., City of Ft. Worth, 1984. Lt. U.S. Army and USAF, 1951-53, Korea. Recipient svc. plaque March of Dimes, 1975, Key to City, Ft. Worth, 1981, Bd. Mem. of Yr. award Am. Heart Assn., 1977-78, appreciation plaque Carter Blood Bank, appreciation award Optimist Club, 1990, Optimist of Yr. award, 1919, leadership award Ft. Worth Classroom Tchrs., 1990, mayor's cert. of recognition City of Ft. Worth, 1990; Paul Harris fellow Rotary Club Ft. Worth South, 1996. Mem. Colonial Country Club (tennis chair 1973—), Kiwanis (life, pres. Ft. Worth S.W. club 1974-75, lt. gov. internat. 1975-76, Disting. Lt. Gov. award 1976-77, Disting. Svc. award 1976, Appreciation award 1977, others), Phi Delta Kappa (scholar 1982, pres. 1972-73, Svc. Key 1972, Adminstr. of Yr. 1982). Republican. Methodist. Home: 408 Chisolm Trl Hurst TX 76054-3007 Office: Ft Worth Ind Sch Dist 5533 Whitman Ave Fort Worth TX 76133-2619

PLUMSTEAD, WILLIAM CHARLES, quality engineer, consultant; b. Two Rivers, Wis., Nov. 2, 1938; m. Peggy Bass, July 19, 1959 (div. July 1968); children: William Jr., Jennifer; m. Vicki Newton, June 27, 1981. Student, U. Fla., 1956-58, Temple U., 1966-72, Albright Coll., 1973-75; BSBA, Calif. Coast U., 1985, MBA, 1989. Registered profl. engr., Calif. V.p. U.S. Testing Co., Inc., Hoboken, N.J., 1963-76; div. mgr. Daniel Internat., Inc., Greenville, S.C., 1976-83; group mgr. Bechtel Group, Inc., San Francisco, 1983-89; prin. engr. Fluor Daniel, Inc., Greenville, 1989-94; pres. Plumstead Quality and Tech. Svcs., Greenville, S.C., 1994—. Author: (with others) Code/Specification Syndrome, 1976, NDT Laboratories Update, 1991, NDT in Construction, 1991, NDT-A Partner in Excellence, 1994; contbr. articles to profl. jours. Bd. dirs. Piedmont Food Bank, 1994-97. Fellow Am. Soc. Nondestructive Testing (coun. chmn. 1985-88, nat. sec., treas. 1992-93, nat. v.p. 1993-94, pres. 1994-95, chmn. bd. dirs. 1995-96); mem. ASTM (sec. 1989-93, vice chmn. 1994-96, chmn. 1996—), Toastmasters Internat. (pres. local chpt. 1990-91, Competent Toastmaster award 1986, Able Toastmaster award 1993). Home and Office: Plumstead Quality Tech Svcs 806 Botany Rd Greenville SC 29615-1608

PLUNKETT, JACK WILLIAM, writer, publisher; b. Dallas, May 17, 1950; s. Ivan Wayne and Waltina Lee (Roark) P.; m. Lynn Ann Richards (div.); 1 child, Jack W. Plunkett Jr.; m. Mary Lee Hartfelder, Dec. 8, 1972 (div.); children: Altus W., Robert L. Pres. Plunkett Properties Corp., Dallas, 1968-74; ind. mktg. cons. Dallas, 1974-83; mgr. ptnr. Brown-Plunkett, Waxahachie, Tex., 1983—; pub. Plunkett Rsch. Ltd. (formerly Corp. Jobs Outlook), Galveston, Tex., 1986—; editor, publisher Dream Trips! Newsletters, Galveston, 1988—; CEO Cafe Lite Inc., 1990—; spl. cons. Houston Symphony, 1996—. Author: The Almanac of American Employers, 1985, 94, 96, Plunkett's Health Care Industry Almanac, 1995, Plunkett's InfoTech Industry Almanac, 1995, Plunkett's Financial Services Industry Almanac, 1996, Plunkett's Retail Industry Almanac, 1996. Chmn. Mayor's Libr. Fundraising Com., Boerne, Tex., 1988-89; founding pres. Greater Boerne Area Econ. Devel. Corp., 1986-87; dir. Boerne Area Comty. Ctr., 1983-86; area chmn. Lamar Smith for Congress, Boerne, 1986; bd. dirs. Boerne Econ. Devel. Econ. Coun., 1992—, Galveston Hist. Found., 1996—, Sch. of Nursing, U. Tex. med. Br., 1996—, Strand Theater, 1996—; trustee Galveston County United Way, 1996—. Named outstanding chmn. Boy Scouts Am., 1983, Community Vol. of Yr., Boerne Area C. of C., 1989. Mem. Rotary (pres. Boerne chpt. 1988-89), The Centurions. Republican. Office: Plunkett Rsch Ltd PO Drawer 8270 Galveston TX 77553-8270

PLUNKETT, JOSEPH CHARLES, electrical engineering educator; b. Centerville, Tenn., Dec. 3, 1933; s. Harold D. and Lorraine (Lewis) P. B.S., Middle Tenn. State U., 1964; B.S.E.E., U. Tenn., 1966; M.S.E.E., Ga. Inst. Tech., 1973; Ph.D., Tex. A&M U., 1978. Registered profl. engr., Mass. Devel. engr. Martin Marietta Co., Orlando, Fla., 1966-69; research engr. Raytheon Co., Wayland, Mass., 1969-71, IIT Research Inst., Annapolis, Md., 1971-72, Tex. A&M U., College Station, 1974-77; assoc. prof. elec. engring. Calif. State U.-Fresno, 1977-80, prof., 1980-93, chmn. dept., 1980-84, 89-92, prof. emeritus, 1993—; cons. Author numerous articles in field. Served to capt. Ordnance Corps, USAR, 1958-66. Mem. IEEE, Nat. Soc. Profl. Engrs., N.Y. Acad. Scis., Sigma Xi, Eta Kappa Nu. Republican. Mem. Ch. of Christ.

PLYLAR, DEBORAH KOCH, musician, music educator; b. Durham, N.C., Jan. 21, 1960; d. William Julian and Dorothy (Clarke) Kock; m. John Russell Plylar, Jr., July 2, 1983. B in Music, N.C. Sch. Arts, 1982. Co-prin. trumpet Winston-Salem (N.C.) Symphony, 1980-82; prin. trumpet Piedmont Opera Orch., Winston-Salem, 1980-82; trumpeter, exec. dir. S.W. Brass, Phoenix, 1982—; v.p., faculty Plylar Acad. Music, Phoenix, 1982—; co-dir. Ariz. Brass Workshop, Phoenix, 1983-84; instr. Mesa (Ariz.) C.C., 1983-85, Grand Canyon U., 1983-87. Editor: Lip Energizer, 1994, Quick Warmup, 1994, Classic Melodies, 1994, Buzzing for Brass, 1994; arranger 1812 Overture for brass, 1992. Presdl. scholar U. Miami, 1977. Mem. Am. Fedn. Musicians, Internat. Trumpet Guild, S.W. Brass Soc. (v.p. 1991—). Home: 2311 W Windrose Dr Phoenix AZ 85029

PLYLER, CHRIS PARNELL, dean; b. Washington, Mar. 21, 1951; s. Glenn Parnell and Doris Eleanor (Oswald) P.; m. Allison Rose Lord, Aug. 4, 1979; children: Benjamin, Patrick, Christen. BA, Clemson U., 1973; MEd, U. S.C., 1975; PhD, Fla. State U., 1978. Dir. male housing Coll. Charleston, S.C., 1975-76; asst. to pres. Fla. State U., Tallahassee, 1976-77; asst. to assoc. chancellor faculty and pers. rels. State U. System Fla., Tallahassee, 1977-78; assoc. dean acad. affairs U. S.C.-Salkehatchie, Allendale, 1978-82; dir. grad. regional studies U. S.C., Aiken, 1982-84, assoc. chancellor student svcs., 1984-90; dean U. S.C., Beaufort, 1990—; mem. adv. bd. S.C. Nat. Bank, Aiken, 1988-90, Palmetto Fed. Savs. and Loan Assn. Treas. bd. dirs. ARC, Aiken, 1984-90; bd. dirs. Boys and Girls Club, Beaufort, 1990—, Hitchcock Rehab. Ctr., Aiken, 1988-90. Mem. Am. Assn. for Higher Edn., Nat. Assn. for Student Pers. Adminstrn., S.C. Coll. Pers. Assn., So. Assn. for Coll. Student Affairs, Nat. Inst. Conf. for Regional Campus Adminstrn., Sea Island Rotary, Aiken Sunrise Rotary (bd. dirs. 1986-90), Aiken Sertoma Club, Phi Delta Kappa, Omicron Delta Kappa. Home: U SC Beaufort 370 Cottage Farm Dr Beaufort SC 29902-5968 Office: U SC 801 Carteret St Beaufort SC 29902-4601

POBLETE, RITA MARIA BAUTISTA, physician, educator; b. Manila, May 19, 1954; came to U.S., 1980; d. Juan Gonzalez and Rizalina (Bautista) Poblete. BS, U. Philippines, 1974, MD, 1978. Diplomate Am. Bd. Internal Medicine and Infectious Disease. Intern, resident Wayne State U./Detroit Med. Ctr., 1982-85, fellow in infectious disease, 1986-87; fellow in infectious disease Chgo. Med. Sch./VA Hosp., North Chicago, Ill., 1985-86; fellow in spl. immunology U. Miami (Fla.)-Jackson Meml. Hosp., 1987-89; adj. clin. instr. dept. of medicine U. Miami, 1989-90, asst. prof. medicine, 1990-94; infectious disease cons. Cedars Med. Ctr. and Mercy Hosp., Miami, 1994—. Contbr. articles to med. jours. Mem. Am. Soc. for Microbiology, Am. Soc. Internal Medicine, World Found. Successful Women. Office: Cedars Med Ctr 1295 NW 14th St Ste E Miami FL 33125-1600

POCHICK, FRANCIS EDWARD, financial consultant; b. Metuchen, N.J., May 28, 1931; s. Frank Stephen and Bertha Barbara P.; student Rutgers U., 1949-50, 54-55; m. Shirley Ann Elliott, Feb. 16, 1957; children: Bonnie Lynn, Keith Francis. Agt., New Eng. Mut. Life Ins. Co., Newark and New Brunswick, N.J., 1958-61; agt. Lambert M. Huppeler Co., Inc., N.Y.C., 1962-64, cons., 1964, sr. cons. employee benefits, 1968-87, fin. cons. Francis E Pochick Assocs., 1987—. Active adv. bd. Mercer Fund, Cmty. Found. N.J., 1986—, Rec. for the Blind, Princeton, 1989, charitable devel. officer Nat. Found., Inc., 1992, Nat. Coun. on The Aging, Planned Giving Coun. 1994 com. bd. health Princeton Coun. Planned Giving, 1993; v.p. The Benefits Planning Co., Ltd., Charlottesville, Va., 1995. Served with USMC, 1951-54. Mem. Am. Soc. Pension Actuaries, Nat. Assn. Life Underwriters, Internat. Assn. Fin. Planners, Estate Planning Council, Lions, Glenmore Country Club. Home: 1451 Bremerton Ln Keswick VA 22947-9147 Office: PO Box 518 Keswick VA 22947-0518 also: No Jersey Br 30 Two Bridges Rd Fairfield NJ 07004-1530

PODBESEK, KATHERINE J. WOOFTER, critical care nurse, administrator; b. Weston, Lewis County, W. Va., Nov. 27, 1957; d. Lewis Clayton and Norma Jean (Nicholson) Woofter; m. Roy Podbesek, May 26, 1984. Student, Alderson-Broaddus Coll., 1976-77; AAS in Nursing, Salem Coll., 1980. Cert. ACLS. Staff nurse II W. Va. U. Med. Ctr., Morgantown, 1980-82, staff nurse neurosurg. unit, 1982; staff nurse coronary care unit Riverside Regional Med. Ctr., Newport News, Va., 1983-85, renal dialysis staff nurse, 1985-87, cardiac cath. lab. RN, 1987, head nurse renal dialysis unit, 1987-90, renal coord., 1988-90; head nurse REN Corp., USA, Newport News, Va., 1990-92; mid-atlantic regional mgr. REN Corporation, U.S.A., Nashville, 1992-93; nurse post anesthesia care unit Mary Immaculate Hosp., Newport News, Va., 1994-95; dialysis mgr. Sentara Hampton Gen. Hosp., Hampton, Va., 1995—. Mem. Am. Nephrology Nurses Assn. (Tidewater chpt. pres. elect), Nat. Kidney Found., Coun. Nephrology Nurses Technicians (program planning com.1987-90), Va. Renal Adminstrs. Assn. (bd. dirs. 1992-93), Tidewater Area Kidney Patients Assn. (adv. bd. 1988-93). Home: 7390 Battery Dr Gloucester Point VA 23062-2604

PODGOR, ELLEN SUE, lawyer, educator; b. Bklyn., Jan. 30, 1952; d. Benjamin and Yetta (Shilensky) Podgor. BS magna cum laude, Syracuse U., 1973; JD, Ind. U., Indpls., 1976; MBA, U. Chgo., 1987; LLM, Temple U., 1989. Bar: Ind. 1976, N.Y. 1984, Pa. 1987. Dep. prosecutor Lake County Prosecutor's Office, Crown Point, Ind., 1976-78; ptnr. Nicholls & Podgor, Crown Point, 1978-87, instr. Temple U. Sch. Law, 1987-89; assoc. prof. law sch. St. Thomas U., Miami, Fla., 1989-91, Ga. State U., Atlanta, 1991—. Author: White Collar Crime In A Nutshell, (with Israel Borman) White Collar: Law & Practice; assoc. editor Ind. Law Rev., 1975-76; contbr. articles to legal jours.; mem. adv. bd. BNA Criminal Practice Manual. Del. Ind. Dem. State Conv., 1982. Mem. ABA, Ind. Bar Assn., Nat. Assn. Criminal Def. Lawyers. Democrat. Jewish. Office: Ga State U Coll Law PO Box 4037 Atlanta GA 30302-4037

PODGORNY, GEORGE, emergency physician; b. Tehran, Iran, Mar. 17, 1934; s. Emanuel and Helen (Parsian) P.; came to U.S., 1954, naturalized, 1973. B.S., Maryville Coll., 1958; postgrad. Bowman Gray Sch. Medicine, 1958; M.D., Wake Forest U., 1962; m. Ernestine Koury, Oct. 20, 1962; children: Adele, Emanuel II, George, Gregory. Intern in surgery N.C. Bapt. Hosp., Winston-Salem, 1962-63, chief resident in gen. surgery, 1966-67, in cardiothoracic surgery, 1967-69; sr. med. examiner Forsyth County, N.C., 1972—; dir. dept. emergency medicine Forsyth Meml. Hosp., Winston-Salem, 1974-80; sec.-treas. Forsyth Emergency Services, Winston-Salem, 1970-80; clin. prof. emergency medicine East Carolina U. Sch. Medicine, Greenville, 1984—, chmn. residency rev. com. on emergency medicine, 1980-88; mem. Accreditation Coun. for Grad. Med. Edn. Dir. Emergency Med. Svcs. Project Region II of N.C., 1975—; chmn. bd. trustees Emergency Medicine Found.; chmn. residency rev. com. emergency medicine Accreditation Coun. Grad. Med. Edn.; founder Western Piedmont Emergency Med. Svcs. Coun., 1973; mem. N.C. Emergency Med. Svcs. Adv. Coun., 1976-81; assoc. prof. clin. surgery Bowman Gray Sch. Medicine, Wake Forest U., Winston-Salem, 1979—. Bd. dirs. Piedmont Health Systems Agy., 1975-84; trustee Forsyth County Hosp., Authority, 1974-75; bd. dirs. N.C. Health Coordinating Coun., 1975-82, Medic Alert Found. Internat. Fellow Internat. Coll. Surgeons, Internat. Coll. Angiology, Royal Soc. Health (Great Britain), Royal Soc. Medicine, Southeastern Surg. Congress; mem. Am. Coll. Emergency Physicians (charter, pres. 1978-79), AMA, (chmn. coun. of sect. emergency medicine 1978-90, alt. del. for Am. Coll. Emergency Physicians, 1990—), Am. Bd. Emergency Medicine (pres. 1976-81). Contbr. articles to profl. publs. on trauma, snake bite and history of medicine; editorial bd. Annals of Emergency Medicine, Med. Meetings. Home and Office: 2115 Georgia Ave Winston Salem NC 27104-1917

POE-BORDEN, AUDREY, writer, business educator; b. Memphis, May 15, 1926; d. William Arthur and Ethel Lula (Mincey) Poe; m. Arthur Murray Borden, Aug. 5, 1955 (div. Oct. 1975); children: Erica, Ross, Mark, Lindsay, Andrew, Anthony. BS in English and Edn., U. Memphis, 1947; MS in Journalism, Columbia U., 1950; PhD, Columbia Pacific U., 1995. Photojournalist Comml. Appeal-Scripps Howard newspapers, Memphis, 1948-55; writer Gen. Features Corp., N.Y.C., 1950-55; writer, broadcaster Turkish Radio, Ankara, Turkey, 1952-55; spl. edn. tchr. Perry County Schs., Linden, Tenn., 1982-84; spl. edn. tchr. CDC Lewis County Schs., Hohenwald, Tenn., 1985-87, spl. edn. tchr. TAG, 1994—; spl. edn. tchr. Memphis City Schs., 1987-91; cons., writer Inst. for War and Peace Reporting, London, 1991—; bd. dirs. Lewis County Edn. Found., Analytix, Inc., Solytix, Inc., Vesta Svcs., Inc., Software Constrn. Co., Inc. Home: Buffalo River Farm Box 459 Hohenwald TN 38462 Office: Inst War & Peace Reporting, 33 Islington High St, London N19LH, England

POFF, RICHARD HARDING, state supreme court justice; b. Radford, Va., Oct. 19, 1923; s. Beecher David and Irene Louise (Nunley) P.; m. Jo Ann R. Topper, June 24, 1945 (dec. Jan. 1978); children: Rebecca, Thomas, Richard Harding; m. Jean Murphy, Oct. 26, 1980. Student, Roanoke Coll., 1941-43; LL.B., U. Va., 1948, LL.D., 1969. Bar: Va. 1947. Partner law firm Dalton, Poff, Turk & Stone, Radford, 1949-70; mem. 83d-92d congresses, 6th Dist. Va.; justice Supreme Ct. Va., 1972-89, sr. justice, 1989—; Vice chmn. Nat. Commn. on Reform Fed. Crime Laws; chmn. Republican Task Force on Crime; sec. Rep. Conf., House Rep. Leadership. Named Va.'s Outstanding Young Man of Year Jr. C. of C., 1954; recipient Nat. Collegiate Athletic Assn. award, 1966, Roanoke Coll. medal, 1967, Distinguished Virginian award Va. Dist. Exchange Clubs, 1970, Presdl. certificate of appreciation for legislative contbn., 1971, legislative citation Assn. Fed. Investigators, 1969, Thomas Jefferson Pub. Sesquicentennial award U. Va., 1969, Japanese Am. Citizens League award, 1972; named to Hall of Fame, Am. Legion Boys State, 1985. Mem. Bar Assn., VFW, Am. Legion, Pi Kappa Phi, Sigma Nu Phi. Clubs: Mason, Moose, Lion. Office: Va Supreme Ct 100 N 9th St Richmond VA 23219-2335

POGNONEC, YVES MAURICE, steel products executive; b. Rennes, Bretagne, France, Jan. 21, 1948; came to U.S., 1983; s. Jean P. and Simone J. (Boudot) P.; m. Veronique Geffroy, May 14, 1987; children: William, Lucie. M in Engring., Centrale Paris, 1970; MA in Bus., CPA, Paris, 1982. Cons. Office of Graham Parker, Paris, 1972-75; sales mgr. fittings dept. Vallourec S.A., Paris, 1975-79, mgr. engring. dept., 1980-82; v.p. mktg. and sales Vallourec Inc., Houston, 1983-88, exec. v.p., 1989—; advisor French Fgn. Trade Counselors, Houston, 1987—. Lt. French Air Force, 1970-71. Mem. Assn. Ecole Centrale (v.p. U.S. S.W. chpt. 1989—), Nat. Assn. Steel Pipe Distbrs. (bd. dirs. 1990—). Office: Vallourec Inc 1990 Post Oak Blvd Ste 710 Houston TX 77056-3812

POGUE, WILLIAM REID, former astronaut, foundation executive, business and aerospace consultant; b. Okemah, Okla., Jan. 23, 1930; s. Alex W. and Margaret (McDow) P.; m. Jean Ann Pogue; children: William Richard, Layna Sue, Thomas Reid. B.S. in Secondary Edn., Okla. Bapt. U., 1951, D.Sc. (hon.), 1974; M.S. in Math., Okla. State U., 1960. Commd. 2d lt. USAF, 1952, advanced through grades to col., 1973; combat fighter pilot Korea, 1953; gunnery instr. Luke AFB, Ariz., 1954; mem. acrobatic team USAF Thunderbirds, Luke AFB and Nellis AFB, Nev., 1955-57; asst. prof. math. USAF Acad., 1960-63; exchange test pilot Brit. Royal Aircraft Establishment, Ministry Aviation, Farnborough, Eng., 1964-65; instr. USAF Aerospace Research Pilots Sch., Edwards AFB, Calif., 1965-66; astronaut NASA Manned Spacecraft Center, Houston, 1966-75; pilot 3d manned visit to Skylab space sta.; now with Vutara Services of Springdale, Ark. Decorated Air medal with oak leaf cluster, Air Force Commendation medal, D.S.M. USAF; named to Five Civilized Tribes Hall of Fame, Choctaw descent; recipient Distinguished Service medal NASA, Collier trophy Nat. Aero. Assn.; Robert H. Goddard medal Nat. Space Club; Gen. Thomas D. White USAF Space Trophy Nat. Geog. Soc.; Halley Astronautics award, 1975; de la Vaalx medal Fedn. Aeronautique Internat., 1974; V.M. Komarov diploma, 1974. Fellow Acad. Arts and Scis. of Okla. State U., Am. Astron. Soc.; mem. Soc. Exptl. Test Pilots, Explorers Club, Sigma Xi, Pi Mu Epsilon. Baptist (deacon). Home: 4 Cromer Dr Bella Vista AR 72715 Office: Vutara Services PO Box 150 Hindsville AR 72738

POHL, JOHN JOSEPH, JR., retired mechanical engineer; b. Newport News, Dec. 4, 1927; s. John Joseph and Christine (Gentile) P.; m. Irene Lewis, June 30, 1951 (dec.); 1 child, John Joseph. BSME, Va. Poly. Inst & State U., 1951. Staff trainee Newport News Shipbuilding Co., 1951-55, nuclear engr., 1955-59, group leader, 1959-88, program security officer in R & D, 1988-92. Contbr. articles to profl. jours. Ofcl. Spl. Olympics, 1985—; docent Mariner's Mus., 1995—. 1st lt. U.S. Army, 1946-47, 51-53. Named Engr. of the Yr., Peninsula Engrs. Council, 1988. Mem. ASME, Soc. Naval Architects and Marine Engrs., Engrs. Coun. (hon. pres. 1990—), Propeller Club U.S., Am. Legion, KC. Home: 7 Stanton Ct Newport News VA 23606-2925

POINDEXTER, BARBARA GLENNON, secondary school educator; b. Dallas, Oct. 19, 1937; d. Victor and Ruth (Gaskins) Ward; m. Noble Turner Poindexter, Aug. 2, 1994; 1 child, Victoria Angela Glennon Betts. BS, Tex. Woman's U., 1958; postgrad., Kans. State U., 1969-70. Cert. tchr. S.C., Kans., N.Mex., Tex. Drama and English tchr. Linn (Kans.) High Sch., 1968-69; tchr. Mosquero (N.Mex.) High Sch., 1973-74, Sumter (S.C.) Sch. Dist., Maywood Sch., 1974-76, Harleyville (S.C.) High Sch., 1976-78, Hampton (S.C.) High Sch., 1978-79, Centerville Sch., Cottageville, S.C., 1979-80; tchr. English Scurry-Rosser Sch., Scurry, Tex., 1981-82; tchr. French and Spanish Christ the King, Dallas, 1982-83; tchr. French and English, chmn. fgn. lang. dept. Wilmer-Hutchins High Sch., Dallas, 1983—. Mem. Theta Alpha Phi. Democrat. Methodist. Home: 5315 Maple Springs Blvd Dallas TX 75235 Office: Wilmer-Hutchins High Sch 5520 Langdon Rd Dallas TX 75241-7148

POINDEXTER, JOHN BRUCE, entrepreneur; b. Houston, Oct. 7, 1944; s. George Emerson and Rose Ellen (McDowell) P.; B.S.B.A. with honors, U. Ark., 1966; M.B.A., N.Y. U., 1971, Ph.D. in Econs. and Fin., 1976. Assoc., Salomon Bros., N.Y.C., 1971-72; v.p. Lombard, Nelson & McKenna, N.Y.C., 1972-73; v.p., registered prin. Dominick & Dominick, Inc., N.Y.C., 1973-76; sr. v.p. Smith Barney Venture Corp., N.Y.C., 1976-83; gen. partner First Century Partnership, N.Y.C., 1980-83; mng. partner KD/P Equities, ptnr. Kellner, DiLeo & Co., N.Y.C., 1983-85; mng. ptnr., J.B. Poindexter and Co., L.P., 1985-94; chmn. bd. dirs. J.B. Poindexter & Co., Inc., 1994—; chmn. bd. dirs. Truck Accessories Group, Inc., Southwestern Holdings, Inc., adj. assoc. prof. L.I. U. Author various monographs. Trustee Blackhorse Assn. Served to capt. U.S. Army, 1966-70; Vietnam. Decorated Silver Star, Bronze Star (2), Purple Heart (2), Soldier's medal, others. Mem. Beta Gamma Sigma, Alpha Kappa Psi. Club: Metropolitan, N.Y.C., Argyle (San Antonio), Coronado (Houston). Office: 1100 Louisiana St Houston TX 77002

POINDEXTER, KENNETH WAYNE, automobile executive; b. Gladewater, Tex., July 31, 1937; s. Chester Earl and Mildred (Holt) P.; m. Ellen Landers, Jan. 21, 1972; 1 child, Kenna Marie Kempton. Grad. high sch., Stephens, Ark. Editor The Ouachita Citizen, Camden, Ark., 1960-62; advt. mgr. The Camden News, 1962-66; ops. mgr. Cam-Tel Co., Camden, 1967-79; owner Am. Pulpwood Co., Ogemaw, Ark., 1979-90; propertior Poindexter Gen. Mercantile, Ogemaw, 1983-90; pres., dealer prin. Ken Poindexter Autoplex, Inc., Marshall, Tex., 1991—; pres. Ark. Cable TV Assn., 1976. Editor Ouachita County Hist. Quar. (Best in Ark. 1988-90). Elected Justice of the Peace, Ouachita County, 1962-82; chmn. Ouachita County Election Commn., 1984-86, Ouachita County Dem. Ctrl. Com., 1984-86; bd.dirs. Ouachita County Hist. Soc., Camden, 1991; elder Eastern Hills Ch. of Christ, Marshall, Tex. Mem. Stephens C. of C. (pres. 1985-87, Citizen of Yr. 1986), Buena Vista/Ogemaw Water Assn. (charter pres., bd. dirs. 1982-90), Stephens Lions Club (pres. 1982), Nat. Soc. of Sons of Am. Revolution. Mem. Ch. of Christ. Home: 603 Ambassador Blvd Marshall TX 75670-4703 Office: Ken Poindexter Autoplex Inc 1803 E Grand Ave Marshall TX 75670

POINDEXTER, RICHARD GROVER, minister; b. Carthage, N.C., June 9, 1945; s. Romie Dallas and Mollie (Underwood) P.; m. Glenda Joyce Tudor, Feb. 23, 1968; children: Tonya Joyce, Amanda Caroline. BA in Sociology,

N.C. State U., 1967; MDiv., New Orleans Bapt. Theol. Sem., 1973. Ordained to ministry So. Bapt. Conv., 1972. Assoc. pastor, youth dir. Amite Bapt. Ch., Denham Springs, La., 1971-72; Sunday sch. cons. Canal Blvd. Bapt. Ch., New Orleans, 1973; pastor First Bapt. Ch., LaGrange, N.C., 1973-77, Anderson Grove Bapt. Ch., Albemarle, N.C., 1977-86, Rankin Bapt. Ch., Greensboro, N.C., 1986-96, First Bapt. Ch., Haw River, N.C., 1996—; cons. Challenge to Build, Bapt. State Conv. of N.C., Cary, 1977—; mem. Brazil Mission Trip, Piedmont Bapt. Assn., Greensboro, 1989. State chaplain N.C. Army Nat. Guard, Raleigh, 1996; trustee Christian Action League N.C., Raleigh, 1985—. Office: First Bapt Ch 508 E Main St Haw River NC 27258

POINTER, SAM CLYDE, JR., federal judge; b. Birmingham, Ala., Nov. 15, 1934; s. Sam Clyde and Elizabeth Inzer (Brown) P.; m. Paula Purse, Oct. 18, 1958; children: Minge, Sam Clyde III. A.B., Vanderbilt U., 1955; J.D., U. Ala., 1957; LL.M., NYU, 1958. Bar: Ala. 1957. Ptnr. Brown, Pointer & Pointer, 1958-70; judge U.S. Dist. Ct. (no. dist.) Ala., Birmingham, 1970-82, chief judge, 1982—; judge Temp. Emergency Ct. Appeals, 1980-87; mem. Jud. Panel Multi-dist. Litigation, 1980-87; mem. Jud. Conf. U.S., 1987-90; mem. Jud. Coun. 11th Cir., 1987-90, mem. standing com. on rules, 1988-90, chmn. adv. com. on civil rules, 1990-93. Bd. editors: Manual for Complex Litigation, 1979-91. Mem. ABA, Ala. Bar Asn., Birmingham Bar Assn., Am. Law Inst., Am. Judicature Soc., Farrah Order of Jurisprudence, Phi Beta Kappa. Episcopalian. Office: US Dist Ct 882 US Courthouse 1729 5th Ave N Birmingham AL 35203-2000

POKKY, ERIC JON, pharmacist; b. Ft. Worth, Oct. 24, 1957; s. Arne Huntus and Helen Theodora (Tienvieri) P.; m. Catherine Ann Miller, June 13, 1987; 1 child, Allison Christine. Student, U. Tex., Arlington, 1976-80; BS in Pharmacy, U. Houston, 1983; postgrad., Midland (Tex.) Coll., 1984. Cert. anticoagulation therapist; cert. Parkinson's disease therapist. Rec. engr. Hallmark Prodns./Sundown Rec. Studios, Friendswood, Tex., 1980-83; salesman, cons. Future Sys., Midland, 1983-86; pharmacist Town and Country Drug, Odessa, Tex., 1983-92; outpatient pharmacy supr. Med. Ctr. Hosp., Odessa, 1992-95, clin. pharmacy coord., 1995—; pres. ECF Cons. Svcs., 1989—. Fellow Am. Soc. Cons. Pharmacists; mem. Am. Pharm. Assn., Am. Soc. Consulting Pharmacists, Permian Basin Pharm. Assn. (v.p. 1986-88, pres. 1988—), Permian Basin Immunization Coalition, Tex. Children's Health and Safety Initiative, Am. Soc. Hosp. Pharmacists, Am. Soc. Cons. Pharmacists, Tex. Soc. Hosp. Pharmacists, Tex. Pharm. Assn. (del. to house 1994—), West Tex. Pharm. Assn., Kappa Psi (sec. 1982-83). Republican. Lutheran. Home: 4420 Haner Dr Odessa TX 79762-4671 Office: Med Ctr Hosp PO Box 7239 Odessa TX 79760-7239

POKORNY, ALEX DANIEL, psychiatrist; b. Taylor, Tex., Oct. 18, 1918; s. John Robert and Olga Frances (Susen) P.; m. Jeanice Brooke Allen, Mar. 13, 1948; children: Martha, Ross, Ellen, Sally. BA, U. Tex., 1939; MD, U. Tex., Galveston, 1942. Diplomate Am. Bd. Psychiatry and Neurology. Psychiatrist VA Hosp., Houston, 1949-55, chief psychiatry and neurology svc., 1955-73; from instr. to prof. psychiatry Baylor Coll. Medicine, Houston, 1949-89, acting chmn. dept. psychiatry, 1968-72, vice chmn. dept. psychiatry, 1972-89, ret. Editor (with others) 7 books, including Phenomenology and Treatment of Anxiety, 1979, Phenomenology and Treatment of Alcoholism, 1980, Phenomenology and Treatment of Psychosexual Disorders, 1983, Phenomenology and Treatment of Psychiatric Emergencies, 1984; editor numerous publs.; contbr. 100 articles to profl. jours. Capt. U.S. Army, 1943-46. Recipient Amersa award for Excellence in Med. Edu. Assn. Med. Edn. & Rsch. Substance Abuse, 1989, Dublin award Am. Assn. Suicidology, 1992. Fellow AAAS, Am. Psychiat. Assn. (life), Am. Coll. Psychiatrists (life); mem. Soc. Psychophysiological Rsch. Home: 813 Atwell St Bellaire TX 77401-4718

POLAN, NANCY MOORE, artist; b. Newark, Ohio; d. William Tracy and Francis (Flesher) Moore; m. Lincoln Milton Polan, Mar. 28, 1934; children: Charles Edwin, William Joseph Marion. AB, Marshall U., 1936. One-man shows include Charleston Art Gallery, 1961, 67, 73, Greenbrier, 1963, Huntington Mus. Art, 1963, 66, 71, N.Y. World's Fair, 1965, W.Va. U., 1966, Carroll Reese Mus., 1967; exhibited in group shows Am. Watercolor Soc., Allied Artists of Am., Nat. Arts Club, 1968-74, 76-77, 86, 87, 91-95, Pa. Acad. Fine Arts, Opening of Creative Arts Center W.Va. U., 1969, Internat. Platform Assn. Art Exhibit, 1968-69, 72-74, 74, 79, 85-86, 88-90, (Gold medal Best of Show 1991, 2d award painting 1994, 1st award watercolor), Allied Artists W.Va., 1968-69, 86, Joan Miro Graphic Traveling Exhbn., Barcelona, Spain, 1970-71, XXI Exhibit Contemporary Art, La Scala, Florence, Italy, 1971, Rassegna Internazionale d'Arte Grafica, Siena, Italy, 1973, 79, 82, Opening of Parkersburg (W.Va.) Art Center, 1975, Art Club Washington, 1992, Pen & Brush, 1992-93, others. Hon. v.p. Centro Studie Scambi Internazionale, Rome, Italy, 1977. Recipient Acad. of Italy with Gold medal, 1979, 86, Norton Meml. award 3d Nat. Jury Show Am. Art, Chautauqua, N.Y., 1960; Purchase prize, Jurors award, Watercolor award Huntington Galleries, 1960, 61; Nat. Arts Club for watercolor, 1969; Gold medal Masters of Modern Art exhbn., La Scala Gallery, Florence, 1975, gold medal Accademia Italia, 1984, 1986, diploma Internat. Com. for World Culture and Arts, 1987, Philip Isenberg Watercolor award Pen & Brush, 1995, many others. Mem. AAUW, DAR, Nat. Mus. Women Artists (charter), Allied Artists W.Va., Internat. Platform Assn. (3rd award-painting in ann. art exhbn. 1977, Gold medal for Best of Show 1991, 1st award for painting 1994), Huntington Mus. Fine Arts (life), Tri-State Arts Assn. (Equal Merit award 1978), Sunrise Found., Composers, Authors, Artists Am., Inc., Pen and Brush, Inc. (Watercolor exhbn. 1993, Grumbacher golden palette mem., Grumbacher award 1978), W.Va. Watercolor Soc. (charter mem.), Nat. Arts Club, Leonardo da Vinci Acad. (Rome), Accademia Italia, Vero Beach Arts Club, Riomar Bay Yacht Club, Guyan Golf and Country Club, Huntington Cotillion (charter mem.), Mass. Hist. Soc. (hon.), Sigma Kappa. Episcopalian. Address: 2106 Club Dr Vero Beach FL 32963 also: 2 Prospect Dr Huntington WV 25701

POLAND, MICHELLE LIND, medical/surgical and critical care nurse; b. Wheeling, W.Va., Apr. 5, 1956; d. Edwin Ray and Mona Markeeta (Miller) P. Diploma, Belmont Tech. Coll., St. Clairsville, Ohio, 1976, ADN, 1982; BSN, Wheeling Jesuit Coll., 1990, MSN, 1996. Cert. critical care nurse, advanced cardiac life support, pediatric advanced cardiac life support. Staff nurse Peterson Hosp., Wheeling, 1976-81, Wheeling Hosp., 1982—; instr. nursing edn. CPR. Active Big Bros. and Big Sisters Orgn. Recipient Glorium award. Mem. ANA, AACN, W.Va. Nurses Assn., Alpha Sigma Nu, Sigma Theta Tau, Alpha Rho. Methodist. Home: 61 Schuberts Ln Wheeling WV 26003-4621

POLAND, PHYLLIS ELAINE, secondary school educator, consultant; b. Norwood, Mass., May 10, 1941; d. Kenneth Gould Vale and Mildred Eloise (Fisk) Arnold; m. Thomas Charles Poland, June 6, 1968 (div. Nov. 1991); 1 child, Sherilyn Ann Poland Colon. AB in Math., Ea. Nazarene Coll., 1963; BS in Math., Nova U., 1986. Cert. secondary tchr., Fla. H.S. math. tchr. Burrillville, R.I., 1963-64; jr. H.S. math. tchr. Quincy, Mass., 1964-65; math. tchr. Seekonk (Mass.) H.S., 1965-68, Howard Jr. H.S., Orlando, Fla., 1968-74, Lake Highland Prep. Sch., Orlando, Fla., 1977-81, Lake Brantley H.S., Altamonte Springs, Fla., 1981—. Mem. coun. Joy Club Ctrl. Nazarene Ch., 1988—, adult edn. sec., 1990—, mem. choir, 1986—. Grantee NSF, 1969, 70, 71, 72. Mem. NEA. Home: 401 Navarre Way Altamonte Springs FL 32714-2224

POLANSKY, JOEL JUSTIN JONES, public administrator, information specialist; b. Cleve., Jan. 1, 1953; s. Joseph Jr. and Carol Anne (Chilcott) P.; s. Donald Kirby Jones (stepfather). AA/AS in Art Illustration Tech., Brevard Community Coll., Cocoa, Fla., 1974; PE in Plant Engring., St. Augustine Tech., Fla., 1976; BPA, U. Ctrl. Fla., 1994. Prin. Polansky Enterprises, Melbourne, Fla., 1975—; info. specialist U.S. Congressman Jim Bacchus, Fla., 1992—; cons. Johnson Controls-PanAm World Svcs., Storage Tek, TAD Tech. Svcs., DBA Systems and others; author, educator RMJ Planning Group. Rep. State Fla. Democratic Election Com. Brevard County Fla. 1993—. Mem. Am. Soc. Pub. Adminstrs., Pub. Adminstr. Club (treas. 1992-93). Democrat. Home and Office: Polansky Enterprises 592 N Wickham Rd Apt 15 Melbourne FL 32935-8798

POLANSKY-JOSEPH, ISA, information management director, consultant. BA, Hofstra U., Hempstead, N.Y., 1971; MLS, St. John's U., Jamaica, N.Y., 1974. Cert. Media Prodn., N.Y., 1976. Libr./media specialist N.Y. City Bd. Edn., Bklyn., 1971-80; dir. Info. Svcs. Fla. Atlantic U. South Atlantic Regional Resource Ctr., Plantation, Fla., 1980—. Author: The Least Restrictive Environment for Exceptional Students, 1987. Office: Fla Atlantic U S Atlanta Reg Resource Ctr 1236 N University Dr Plantation FL 33322-4724

POLEMITOU, OLGA ANDREA, accountant; b. Nicosia, Cyprus, June 28, 1950; d. Takis and Georgia (Nicolaou) Chrysanthou. BA with honors, U. London, 1971; PhD, Ind. U., Bloomington, 1981. CPA, Ind. Asst. productivity officer Internat. Labor Office/Cyprus Productivity Ctr., Nicosia, 1971-74; cons. Arthur Young & Co., N.Y.C., 1981; mgr. Coopers & Lybrand, Newark, 1981-83; dir. Bell Atlantic, Reston, Va., 1983—; chairperson adv. coun. Extended Day Care Community Edn., West Windsor Plainsboro, 1987-88. Contbr. articles to profl. jours. Bus. cons. project bus. Jr. Achievement, Indpls., 1984-85. Mem. NAFE, AICPAs, Nat. Trust for Hist. Preservation, Ind. CPA Soc., N.J. Soc. CPAs (sec. mems. in industry com.), Princeton Network of Profl. Women. Home: PO Box 2744 Reston VA 22090-0744 Office: Bell Atlantic Video Svcs Co 1880 Campus Commons Dr Reston VA 22091-1512

POLEN-DORN, LINDA FRANCES, communications executive; b. Cleve., Mar. 23, 1945; d. Stanley and Mildred (Kain) Neuger; m. Samuel O. Dorn; children: Lanelle, Brian, Adam, Dawn. BA cum laude, U. Miami, 1967; MBA, Nova Southeastern U., 1993. Reporter Miami (Fla.) News, 1966-67; writer Miamian Mag., 1967-68; dir. pub. rels. Muscular Dystrophy Assn., Miami, 1968-72; cons., adv. and pub. rels. Ft. Lauderdale, 1974-77; pub. rels. writer J. Cory and Assocs., Ft. Lauderdale, Fla., 1978-79; account supr. Maizner & Franklin, Fla., 1979-86; v.p. mktg., communications mgr. Glendale Fed. Bank, Fla., 1986-95; prod. mktg. mgr. Ryder Sys., Inc., Miami, 1995—. Sustaining mem. Mus. Art., Ft. Lauderdale, 1986—, Philharmonic Soc., Ft. Lauderdale, 1987—. Mem. Internat. Assn. Bus. Communicators, Pub. Rels. Soc. Am., Am. Mktg. Assn., Broward C. of C. (vice chmn. govt. affairs 1984-85). Office: Ryder System Inc 3600 NW 82 Ave Miami FL 33166

POLHEMUS, MARY ANN, elementary school principal, educator; b. Adrian, Mich., May 3, 1947; d. Charles Robert and Melva Jane Bartholomew; BS, La. State U., 1969; MEd, U. Houston, 1972; m. John Philip Polhemus, Mar. 25, 1972; 1 child, Sara Jane. Tchr., Houston Ind. Sch. Dist., 1969-75, reading cons., 1975-80, reading and lang. arts cons., 1980-81, secondary reading supr., 1981-84, elem. prin., 1984—. Mem. accreditation team Tex. Sch. Improvement Initiative, 1988-93. Mem. Assn. for Supervision and Curriculum Devel., Internat. Reading Assn., Nat. Council Tchrs. English, Delta Kappa Gamma. Republican. Cons., Spelling for Writing series Charles E. Merrill Pub. Co., 1979-80. Home: 1414 Briar Bayou Dr Houston TX 77077-2004

POLICASTRO, ANTHONY MICHAEL, retired military officer, pediatrician; b. Bklyn., Nov. 27, 1946; s. Anthony Albert and Philomena (Pucci) P.; m. Joan Eleanor Lober, June 20, 1970; children: Lorraine Angela, Barbara Ann, Denise Marie. BS in Biology with honors, Manhattan Coll., 1968; MD summa cum laude, SUNY, Bklyn., 1972. Diplomate Am. Bd. Pediatrics. Resident in pediatrics Tufts New Eng. Med. Ctr., Boston, 1972-75; commd. capt. USAF, 1975, advanced through grades to col.; pediatrician USAF, Dover AFB, Del., 1975-76; pediatrician Malcolm Grow Med. Ctr. USAF, Andrews AFB, Md., 1976-80, asst. chairperson pediatrics, 1980-82, dir. med. edn., 1982-84; chief hosp. services USAF Hosp., Upper Heyford, Eng., 1984-86; hosp. comdr. 363 med. group USAF, Shaw AFB, S.C., 1986-89; hosp. comdr. 1st Med. Group USAF, Langley AFB, Va., 1989-95; sr. v.p. med. affairs Nanticoke Meml. Hosp., Seaford, Del., 1995—; clin. assoc. prof. pediatrics Uniformed Services U. of Health Scis., 1977-93. Contbr. articles to profl. jours. Recipient Make it Click award Nat. Safety Council, 1982. Fellow Am. Acad. Pediatrics (Make it Click award 1982); mem. Assn. Mil. Surgeons U.S., Soc. Devel. and Behavioral Pediatrics. Roman Catholic. Home: Rt 5 Box 23 B Seaford DE 19973

POLICHINO, JOSEPH ANTHONY, JR., wholesale company executive; b. Houston, Oct. 17, 1948; s. Joseph Anthony and Josephine Adeline P.; student Spring Hill Coll., 1966-67; A.A. cum laude, S. Tex. Jr. Coll., 1969; student U. Houston, 1969-71; m. Jean Elliott McDowell, Oct. 7, 1978; children: Joseph Anthony III, Sara Gale. Sales posting clk. Jax Beer Co., Houston, 1971-72, route salesman asst., 1972; sales supr. Nat. Beverage Co., Houston, 1972-74, pres., 1974-76; owner, pres. Coors Northeast Distbg. Co., Houston, 1976-84; founder, v.p. Alessandra Import Co., Houston, 1980-86; exec. v.p. Internat. Brands, 1984-92, founding ptnr., mktg. dir. Hillman Internat. Brands, Ltd., 1992—; cons. to radio medium and small bus. reorgnl. and personal devel. Bd. dirs. Houston Livestock Show and Rodeo, 1978—, Houston Muscular Dystrophy Assn. Exec. Com., 1977-91, Bill Williams Capon Charity Dinner, 1977-95, Strake Jesuit Coll. Prep. Sch., 1986—, Houston Proud, 1989-91; commr. City of West University Place (Tex.), 1981-83, councilman, 1983-85. Mem. Sons of Bosses Internat. (regional v.p. 1974-75), Jesuit Coll. Prep. Alumni Assn. (pres. 1977-79), Houston Citizens C. of C. (dir. 1977—), Nat. Beer Wholesalers Assn., Wholesale Beer Distbrs. Tex., Harris County Wholesale Beer Distbrs. Assn. Roman Catholic. Club: Toastmaster.

POLICINSKI, EUGENE FRANCIS, author, newspaper editor; b. South Bend, Ind., Aug. 31, 1950; s. E.T. and Margaret C. (O'Neill) P.; m. Kathleen Beta O'Donnell Powell, Aug. 19, 1972; children: Ryan, David. Degree in journalism and polit. sci., Ball State U., 1972. Corr. Gannett News Svc., Washington, 1979-82; Washington editor USA Today, Arlington, Va., 1982-83, page one editor, 1983-89, mng. editor sports, 1989-96; host, commentator USA Today Sky Radio, Arlington, 1992-95. Founding editor USA Today Baseball Weekly, 1991. Named one of 100 Most Important People in Sports Sporting News, 1992, 93, 95; inducted into Ball State U. Journalism Hall of Fame, 1989. Mem. Am. Soc. Newspaper Editors (com. chmn. 1989—), Associated Press Sports Editors (com. chmn. 1989-96).

POLICY, JOSEPH J., publisher, television producer; b. Youngstown, Ohio, July 12, 1945; s. Vincent James and Anna Marie P.; m. Carole A., May 10, 1969; children: Amy Annette, Holly Ann. BS, U. Md., 1969. Staff TV dir. WDCA-TV, Washington, 1964-68; mgmt. tng. program Triangle Publs., Phila., 1968-72; promo. dir. WFBG-AM-FM-TV, Altoona, Pa., 1972-74, WQXI-TV, Atlanta, 1974-76, WWL-TV, New Orleans, 1976-78; sta. mgr. WPEC-TV, West Palm Beach, Fla., 1978-81; gen. editor Nat. Enquirer, West Palm Beach, Fla., 1981-89; v.p., dir. corp. mktg. Am. Media, West Palm Beach, Fla., 1989—; cons. Coca-Cola, Atlanta, 1972-76, Kearney, Internat., Atlanta, 1972-76, Amiel Industries, Atlanta, 1972-74. Creator/editor: (mags.) Soap Opera Mag., 1991, Country Weekly Mag., 1994; producer: (TV spl.) Prime Time Country: A Country Weekly Tribute, 1995-96. With U.S. Army, 1969-72, Far East. Recipient 17 Addy awards Fla. Advt. Assn., 1978-81, BPA Nat. award Broadcast Prom. Assn., 1981, J.R. Stram Grant, U. Md. Mem. Nat. Assn. TV Program Execs., Nat. Acad. TV Arts & Scis., Country Music Assn. Republican. Roman Catholic. Office: American Media Inc 600 E Coast Ave Lantana FL 33462-4538

POLIS, SHERI HELENE, marketing and education professional; b. Phila., Sept. 25, 1956; d. Joseph H. and Belle (Oslick) P. BA, Pa. State U., 1978; studied music, Neupauer Conservatory, Phila., 1978-84; MPA, Harvard U., 1985. Nat. sales coord. The Lowry Group, Westlake Village, Calif., 1980-85; dir. mktg. and ops. Travel Trust Internat., Washington, 1985-86; exec. dir. The Learning Annex, Phila., 1987-89; regional edn. dir. Bank Adminstrn. Inst., Voorhees, N.J., 1989-91; regional exec. Robert Morris Assocs., Phila., 1991-96; career cons. Vocalist numerous performances throughout Pa. and N.J; contbr. numerous articles to profl. jours. Bd. dirs. Burlington County chpt. Am. Cancer Soc. Mem. NAFE, Am. Soc. Profl. and Exec. Women, Women in Communications Inc. Home: 2524 Chatsworth Dr Elizabethtown KY 42701

POLITES, MICHAEL EDWARD, aerospace engineer; b. Belleville, Ill., Mar. 19, 1944; s. Matthew Charles and Edith Louise (Schwarz) P. BS in Sys. and Automatic Controls, Washington U., St. Louis, 1967; MSEE, U. Ala., 1971; PhD in Elec. Engring., Vanderbilt U., 1986. Aerospace rsch. engr., guidance, navigation and control sys. NASA/Marshall Space Flt. Ctr. Structures & Dynamics Lab, Huntsville, Ala., 1967-95; supervisory chief, instrumentation and control divsn. Astrionics Lab. NASA/Marshall Space Flight Ctr., Huntsville, Ala., 1995—. 4 patents in field; contbr. numerous articles to profl. jours.; referee various jours. and confs. Recipient 59 NASA awards in the field. Fellow AIAA (assoc., guidance navigation and control tech. com. 1990—, digital avionics tech. com. 1996—); mem. IEEE (sr. Outstanding Engr. Huntsville sect. 1995), ASME, Am. Astronautical Soc. (session co-chmn. 1995 & 97 Guidance and Control Conf.), Mensa, Tau Beta Pi, Eta Kappa Nu, Pi Tau Sigma. Office: NASA Marshall Space Flight Ctr Astronics Lab Huntsville AL 35812

POLITO, SUSAN EVANS, insurance agency official; b. Wyandotte, Mich., Nov. 27, 1957; d. Robert Franklin and Betty Lorraine (Nehlsen) Evans; m. Anthony A. Polito, Apr. 27, 1991; children: Lauren Marie, Daniel Anthony. Student, Pasco-Hernando C.C., New Port Richey, Fla., 1975-76; Assoc. in Automation Mgmt., Ind. Ins. Agts. Am., 1988. Cert. profl. ins. woman NAIW; cert. ins. counselor. Dep. tax collector Pasco County Tax Collector, New Port Richey, 1977-79; agt. Fla. No-Fault Ins., Tampa, 1979-81; personal lines mgr. Courtesy Ins., Inc., Clearwater, Fla., 1981-83; personal risk mgr. Shelton & Connelly Ins., Clearwater, 1983-85; asst. adminstrv. mgr. Shonter & Shonter, Inc., Pinellas Park, Fla., 1985-94; agt. John Russell Ins., Inc., 1994-96; mgr. personal ins. divsn. Fessler Agy., Inc., 1996—; mem. agt.'s adv. bd. Progressive Ins. Co., Tampa, 1990-91. Director's asst. Marty Lyons Found. Fla. chpt., 1989. Kay Cooper Meml. scholar Profl. Ins. Agts. Am., 1988. Mem. Nat. Assn. Ins. Women Internat. (Royal Ins. Automation Essay award 1989), Fla. Assn. Ins. Agts., Ind. Ins. Agts. of Am., Ins. Women Upper Pinellas (officer/dir. Clearwater chpt. 1982-89, Ins. Woman of Yr. award 1983), Ind. Insurers Greater St. Petersburg (exec. bd. dirs. 1987-91, bd. dirs. 1989-92, sec.-treas. 1989-91). Republican. Lutheran.

POLITZ, HENRY ANTHONY, federal judge; b. Napoleonville, La., May 9, 1932; s. Anthony and Virginia (Russo) P.; m. Jane Marie Simoneaux, Apr. 29, 1952; children: Nyle, Bennett, Mark, Angela, Scott, Jane, Michael, Henry, Alisa, John, Nina. BA, La. State U., 1958, JD, 1959. Bar: La. 1959. Assoc., then ptnr. firm Booth, Lockard, Jack, Pleasant & LeSage, Shreveport, 1959-79; judge U.S. Ct. Appeals (5th cir.), Shreveport, 1979—, chief judge, 1992—; vis. prof. La. State U. Law Center; bd. dirs. Am. Prepaid Legal Services Inst., 1975—; mem. La. Judiciary Commn., 1978-79; mem. U.S. Jud. Conf., 1992—, exec. com., 1996—. Mem. editl. bd. La. State U. Law Rev., 1958-59. Mem. Shreveport Airport Authority, 1973-79, chmn., 1977; bd. dirs. Rutherford House, Shreveport, 1975—, pres., 1978; pres. Caddo Parish Bd. Election Suprs., 1975-79; mem. Electoral Coll., 1976. Served with USAF, 1951-55. Named Outstanding Young Lawyer in La., 1971, Outstanding Alumnus La. State U. Law Sch., 1991; inducted in La. State U. Hall of Distinction, 1992. Mem. Am. Bar Assn., Am. Judicature Soc., Internat. Soc. Barristers, La. Bar Assn., La. Trial Lawyers Assn., Shreveport Bar Assn., Justinian Soc., K.C., Omicron Delta Kappa. Democrat. Roman Catholic. Office: US Ct Appeals 300 Fannin St Rm 5226 Shreveport LA 71101-3074

POLITZ, NYLE ANTHONY, lawyer; b. Lake Charles, La., May 7, 1953; s. Henry Anthony and Jane Marie (Simoneaux) P.; m. Catherine Bordelon, May 28, 1977; children: Brandon, Jared, Caroline. Student, La. State U., Shreveport, 1971-72, U. Guadalajara, 1972, La. State U., 1972-74; JD, La. State U., 1977. Bar: La. 1978, U.S. Dist. Ct. (ea., mid. and we. dists.) La. 1978, U.S. Ct. Appeals (5th cir.) 1979. Assoc. Booth, Lockard, Jack, Pleasant & LeSage, Shreveport, La., 1978-79; ptnr. Booth, Lockard, Politz, LeSage & D'Anna, L.L.C., Shreveport, 1979-96; assoc. Patrick W. Pendley P.L.C., Plaquemine, La., 1996—; lectr. La. State Univ., Shreveport. Resolutions com. La. Dem. Party, 1980; bd. dirs. Liberty Bank & Trust, Greenwood, La., 1980-86. Mem. ABA, ATLA, La. State Bar Assn. (ho. of dels. 1986—), La. Trial Lawyers Assn. (bd. govs. 1983-94), Shreveport Bar Assn. (exec. com. 1983-85, 93-94, bd. dirs. pro bono project, chmn. 1993-94), N.W. La. Trial Lawyers Assn. (treas. 1987-90), Henry V. Booth Am. Inn of Ct., KC. Democrat. Roman Catholic. Office: Patrick W Pendley APLC 58005 Meriam St Plaquemine LA 70765

POLIZZI, ALLESSANDRIA ELIZABETH, English language educator; b. Fresno, Calif., Mar. 16, 1971; d. James Patrick Polizzi and Suzanne Elizabeth (Barile) Manning; m. Kevin Michael McClanahan, Oct. 26, 1991. BA, Calif. State U., Fresno, 1993, MA, 1995. Writing tutor Ednl. Opportunity Program, Fresno, 1990-93; tchg. fellow Calif. State U., 1993-95; tchg. fellow dept. English, U. North Tex., Denton, 1995—; instr. Internat. English Inst., Fresno, 1994, Fresno City Coll., 1994-95. Editor: Fine Print, 1993-95, Critical Explorations, 1995. Mem. MLA, South Ctrl. MLA. Democrat..... Office: U North Tex Dept English Denton TX 76203

POLK, MELISSA LEIGH, nurse; b. Honolulu, Aug. 11, 1965; d. Charles Bland and Mary Elizabeth (Maddux) P. Student, So. Union Jr. Coll., 1983-84; AA, Albany Jr. Coll., 1986; student, Darton Coll., 1986-89; BSN, Albany State Coll., 1992. Nurse East Albany (Ga.) Med. Ctr., 1991, Pub. Health Svc., Albany, 1991-93; ob. gyn. nurse Colquett Regional Med. Ctr., Moultrie, Ga., 1996—. With USAF, 1994-96. Mem. ANA, Ga. Nurses Assn., Nat. League Nursing, Sigma Theta Tau Internat.

POLK, RONALD THOMAS, marketing executive; b. Cleve., Sept. 16, 1958; s. Richard T. and JoAnne E. (Uht) P.; m. Elizabeth Sloan Waggener, June 20, 1981; children: Jonathan William, Stephen Thomas. BA in Polit. Sci. and Communications, Denison U., 1980. Media planner Grey Advt., N.Y.C., 1980-81; media analyst Meldrum & Fewsmith Advt., Cleve., 1981-82; media supr. Wendy's Internat., Inc., Dublin, Ohio, 1982-84, mgr. media, 1984-87, dir. media svcs., 1987-89; dir. media Hardee's Food Systems, Inc., Rocky Mount, N.C., 1989-93, dir. media and nat. advt., 1993—; guest lectr. Ohio State U., Columbus, 1983-87, Denison U., Granville, Ohio, 1981-82. Mem. Advt. Fedn. (Columbus). Republican. Roman Catholic. Home: 1236 Green Tee Ln Rocky Mount NC 27804-9633 Office: Hardee's Food Systems Inc 1233 Hardees Blvd Rocky Mount NC 27804-2029

POLLACK, ROBERT HARVEY, psychology educator; b. N.Y.C., June 26, 1927; s. Solomon and Bertha (Levy) P.; m. Martha Dee Katz, Aug. 20, 1948; children: Jonathan Keith, Lance Michael, Scott Evan. BS, CCNY, 1948; MS, Clark U., Worcester, Mass., 1950, PhD, 1953. Lectr. U. Sydney, Australia, 1953-61; spl. rsch. fellow Columbia U., N.Y.C., 1960-61; chief div. congitive devel. Inst. Juvenile Rsch., Chgo., 1960-63, dep. dir. rsch., 1963-69; from clin. asst. prof. to clin. assoc. prof. rsch. U. Ill. Coll. Medicine, Chgo., 1962-67; prof. psychology U. Ga., Athens, 1969-86, chair grad. program. exptl. psychology, 1970-78, chair grad. study com., 1978-86; prof. emeritus, 1986-96; chair grad. program in life-span psychology U. Ga., Athens, 1988-96. Editor: The Experimental Psychology of Alfred Binet, 1969; contbr. over 100 articles and chpts. to profl. publs. Cpl. U.S. Army, 1945-46. Grantee Nat. Inst. Child Health and Human Devel., 1965, 67, 72, 78. Fellow AAAS, Am. Psychol. Assn.; mem. Am. Assn. Sex Edn., Counsellors and Therapists, Gerontol. Soc. Am., Australian Psychol. Soc., Soc. for Researching Child Devel., Soc. for Sci. Study Sex, Sigma Xi. Democrat. Office: U Ga Dept Psychology Athens GA 30602

POLLACK, ROBERT WILLIAM, psychiatrist; b. N.Y.C., May 22, 1947; s. George and Esther P.; m. Pam Gregory, Sept. 15, 1984; 1 child, Jessie. BS in Biology, Yale U., 1969; MD, SUNY Downstate Med. Ctr., Bklyn., 1973. Diplomate Am. Bd. Psychiatry and Neurology. Tng. resident U. Fla., 1973-76, chief resident Dept. of Psychiatry, 1975-76; asst. prof. Dept. of Psychiatry U. Fla., Gainesville, 1976-77; clin. asst. prof. dept. psychiatry Shands Hosp., Gainesville, 1977—; chief dept. psychiatry Fla. Hosp., Orlando, 1983, 84; clin. dir. assessment and evaluation team West Lake Hosp., Longwood, Fla., 1984-87, clin. dir. intensive evaluation unit, 1987-89; med. dir. Fla. Psychiat. Assocs., Winter Park, 1989—, Fla. Psychiat. Mgmt., Winter Park, 1990—, FPM Behavioral Health, 1993—; med. dir. consultation, liaison svc., and spl. med. unit Winter Park Meml. Hosp., 1992. Contbr. 4 articles to profl. jours.; author sci. reports. Chmn. Retinitis Pigmentosa Casino Night, Orlando, 1988-92; vice-chmn. nat. championship com. U.S. Blind Golfers Assn., 1991-92, chair 48th ann. championship com., 1992-93; bd. dirs. Tennis with a Different Swing, Orlando, 1988-92. Mem. Alaqua Country Club (bd. dirs.). Office: FPM Behavioral Health 1276 Minnesota Ave Winter Park FL 32789-4833

POLLARD, ALTON BROOKS, III, religion educator, minister; b. St. Paul, May 5, 1956; s. Alton Brooks Jr. and Lena Laverne (Evans) P.; m. Jessica Juana Bryant, July 14, 1979; children: Alton Brooks IV, Asha Elise. BA, Fisk U., 1978; MDiv, Harvard U., 1981; PhD, Duke U., 1987. Ordained to ministry Am. Bapt. Conv., Progressive Bapt. Conv., 1979. Pastor John Street Bapt. Ch., Worcester, Mass., 1979-82, New Red Mountain Bapt. Ch., Rougemont, N.C., 1984-86; asst. prof. religion St. Olaf Coll., Northfield, Minn., 1987-88; asst. prof. religion Wake Forest U., Winston-Salem, N.C., 1988-92, assoc. prof., 1992—; assoc. min. Emmanuel Bapt. Ch., Winston-Salem, 1988; dir. Kemet Sch. Knowledge, 1990—; vis. asst. prof. U. N.C., Greensboro, 1991; bd. dirs. Crisis Control Ministry, Winston-Salem. Author: Mysticism and Social Change, 1992; assoc. editor Black Sacred Music, 1987—; contbr. articles to religious jours. Mem. adv. bd. Worcester County Sch. Bd., 1980-82; mem. community problem solving com. United Way, Winston-Salem and Forsyth County, 1990—; mem. Community AIDS Awareness Campaign, Winston-Salem, 1991; mem. Leadership Winston-Salem, Class of 1993; bd. dirs. North Carolians Against Racist and Religious Violence, 1993-94. Pew grantee Wake Forest U., 1990. Mem. Soc. for Study Black Religion, Religious Rsch. Assn., Am. Acad. Religion, Assn. for Sociology Religion, Soc. for Sci. Study Religion. Home: 2026 Storm Canyon Rd Winston Salem NC 27106-9772 Office: Wake Forest U PO Box 7212 Winston Salem NC 27109-7212

POLLARD, JOHN OLIVER, lawyer; b. American Falls, Idaho, Dec. 25, 1937; s. Donald Lusher Pollard and Gertrude Marie Schelecter Chaney; m. Patricia Gheen Dyer, June 10, 1961 (div. 1966); 1 child, Ariane Raquel; m. Carol Virginia Foard, Apr. 27, 1968; children: Ashley Carol, Jennifer Leigh. BA, Am. U., 1965; JD, U. N.C., 1973. Bar: N.C. 1973. Indsl. relations mgr. Carolinas Branch, Associated Gen. Contractors, Charlotte, N.C., 1965-68; dir. labor relations and personnel Nello L. Teer Co., Durham, N.C., 1968-71; atty., ptnr. Blakeney & Alexander, Charlotte, N.C., 1973—; bd. dirs. Ingles Markets, Inc., Ashville, N.C., 1987—. Staff mem. N.C. Law Rev., Chapel Hill, N.C., 1973. Bd. mem., past chmn., legal counsel The Relatives, Inc., Charlotte, N.C., 1985—; bd. mem., past pres. Advs. for Children in Ct., Inc., Charlotte, 1985-93; mem. Mecklenburg County Per. Commn., Charlotte, 1984-91. Mem. ABA, N.C. Bar Assn., Quail Hollow Country Club, Charlotte City Club. Republican. Protestant. Home: 4310 Arbor Way Charlotte NC 28211-3814 Office: Blakeney & Alexander 3700 NationsBank Plz Charlotte NC 28280-0001

POLLITT, PHOEBE ANN, school nurse; b. Washington, Mar. 29, 1954; d. Daniel Hubbard and Jean Ann (Rutledge) P.; m. David Randolph Paletta, July 1, 1977 (div. Dec. 1989); children: Douglas, Andrew. BS in Nursing, U. N.C., 1977; MA in Edn., Appalachian State U., 1989; PhD in Curriculum and Instrn., U. N.C., Greensboro, 1994. Pub. health nurse Durham County Health Dept., Durham, N.C., 1977-80; disability devel. specialist Appalachian Devel. Evaluation Ctr., Boone, N.C., 1980-81; home health nurse Watauga County Health Dept., Boone, 1981-82; nursing instr. Caldwell C.C., Lenoir, N.C., 1989-91; adj. prof. nursing Winston-Salem (N.C.) State U., 1990—; sch. nurse, health edn. coord. Watauga County Schs., Boone, 1991—; sec. Watauga County Adolescent Pregnancy Coalition, Boone, 1991—; mem. exec. com. Watauga County Healthy Carolinas 2000, Boone, 1993—; mem. statewide exec. com. Smoke Free 2000, Raleigh, 1994; mem. exec. bd. Watauga County Alcohol and Other Drugs Coun., Boone, 1993. Contbr. articles to profl. jours. Alumni fellow Appalachian State U., 1988, 89; recipient Certs. of Appreciation, Am. Heart Assn., 1992, 93, Hospitality House, 1987, 88, 89, Outstanding Vol. award N.C. Gov. Jim Hunt, 1989, Plaque of Appreciation, OASIS, 1992, Hist. Article award N.C. Hist. Soc., 1994; grantee Arts Coun., 1982, Appalachian State U., 1989, U. N.C., Greensboro, 1991, Healthful Living Sect., Dept. Pub. Instrn., 1992, 93, Janirve Corp., Asheville, N.C., 1992, Project Assist, 1996, N.C. Dept. Pub. Instrn., 1996, Watauga Ednl. Found., 1996. Mem. ANA, N.C. Nurse Assn. (named Great 100 Nurses 1995), Sch. Nurse Assn. N.C. (mem. exec. com., membership chair 1994), Dist. 23 Nurse assn., Sigma Theta Tau. Democrat. Unitarian-Universalist. Home: 554 Dogwood Rd Boone NC 28607 Office: Watauga County Bd Edn Box 1790 Hwy 194 Boone NC 28607

POLLOCK, CANDACE MARIE, reporter; b. Bridgeport, Conn., July 4, 1970; d. Richard Stephen and Sheila Ann (Provost) P. BA in Journalism, Northwestern State U., Natchitoches, La., 1994, BS in Biology, 1994; postgrad., Ohio State U., 1996—. Gen. assignment reporter Alexandria (La.) Daily Town Talk, 1993-95; gen. assignment and bur. reporter The Daily Advertiser, Lafayette, La., 1995-96; agr. reporter Ohio State Comm. and Tech., Columbus, 1996—. Projects coord. Vols. of Am., Alexandria, 1995; vol. asst. zookeeper Alexandria Zoo, 1995; del. conf. Nat. Young Leadership Coun., Washington, 1989. Fellow Coun. for Advancement of Sci. Writing, Madison, Wis., 1994. Mem. Soc. Profl. Journalists, World Wildlife Fund, Phi Kappa Phi. Roman Catholic.

POLLOCK, EKS WYE, III, oil company executive; b. Tulsa, Jan. 29, 1957; s. Eks Wye Jr. and Martha Elizabeth Pollock; m. Dee Lee Anderson, Sept. 3, 1984; children: Eks Wye IV, Angelica. BS in Geol. Engring., U. Okla., 1980. Cons.-geologist various oil cos., Oklahoma City, 1980-91; owner SanDollar Exploration, Oklahoma City, 1987—; pecan farmer Pollock's Pecans, Ada, Okla., 1989—; mgr. Fairfax Ops. Co., Oklahoma City, 1992—; cons. Montgomery Exploration, Oklahoma City, 1992—; cons. Monexco Corp., Dallas, 1988-94. Active Life Loyal Sigs. Mem. Am. Assn. Individual Investors, Am. Assn. Petroleum Geologists, Soc. Petroleum Engrs., Okla. Pecan Growers Assn., Tulsa Geol. Soc., Oklahoma City Geol. Soc. Republican. Office: SanDollar Exploration Co PO Box 539 Oklahoma City OK 73101-0539

POLLOCK, HARLAN, plastic surgeon, educator; b. Columbus, Ohio, Oct. 17, 1937; s. Abe M. and Anne (Mankier) P.; m. Hannah Kay Berger; children: Todd Alan, Tami Ellen Pollock Prengler, Stacy Pollock Olesky. BS, Ohio State U., 1958, MD, 1962. Diplomate Am. Bd. Surgery, Am. Bd. Plastic and Reconstructive Surgery. Intern Parkland Hosp., Dallas, 1962-63, resident in gen. surgery, 1963-67, courtesy staff, 1971—, cons. staff, 1992—; burn fellow surg. rsch. unit U.S. Army Burn Ctr., Brooke Med. Ctr., San Antonio, 1967-68; resident in plastic surgery Walter Reed Gen. Hosp., Washington, 1968-70; pvt. practice, Dallas, 1971—; clin. instr. U. Tex. Southwestern Med. Sch., Dallas, 1971—; mem. staff Presbyn. Hosp. Dallas, 1971—, chmn. plastic surgery sect., 1983-88. Contbr. articles to med. jours. Bd. dirs., past. pres. Jewish Cmty. Ctr. Dallas; bd. dirs. Jewish Family Svcs., Dallas Summer Musicals. Lt. col. MC, U.S. Army, 1967-71, Vietnam. Decorated Bronze Star. Fellow ACS; mem. AMA, Am. Soc. Plastic and Reconstructive Surgeons, Assn. Mil. Plastic Surgeons, Am. Soc. Aesthetic Plastic Surgery, Lipolysis Soc. N.Am., Tex. Soc. Plastic Surgeons (pres.), Tex. Med. Assn., Dallas Soc. Plastic Surgeons (founding, past pres.), Dallas County Med. Soc. Republican. Office: 8305 Walnut Hill Ln Ste 210 Dallas TX 75231-4203

POLLOCK, LINDA ANNE, history educator; b. London, Oct. 4, 1955; d. Raymond Anthony Willimott and Mary Dodds Norquay; m. Iain Forbes Pollock, July 1, 1978 (div. Feb. 1989); m. Dino Cinel, Oct. 28, 1989; 1 child, Sophia. MA, U. St. Andrews, Scotland, 1978, PhD, 1982. Lectr. Churchill Coll., U. Cambridge, Eng., 1987-88; asst. prof. Tulane U., New Orleans, 1988-89, assoc. prof., 1989-93, prof. history, 1993—; mem. adv. bd. The Seventeenth Century jour., Durham, Eng., 1989. Author: Forgotten Children: Parent-child Relations from 1500 to 1900, 1983, paperback edit., 1983, 85, 87, Japanese edit., 1988, Spanish edit., 1990, 94 (nat. book prize 1984), A Lasting Relationship. Parents and Children over Three Centuries, 1987, paperback edit., 1990, With Faith and Psychic: The Life of a Tudor Gentlewoman, Mary Grace Mildmay 1552-1620, 1993, 95; contbr. articles and revs. to profl. publs. Recipient postdoctoral rsch. award Social Sci. Rsch. Coun., 1978-81, 83-86; fellow Churchil Coll., 1983-87, Huntington Libr., 1985, 88, Brit. Acad., 1986-88, Twenty-seven Found. Archive, 1987, Wellcome Found., 1987-88, Folger Shakespeare Libr., 1993; grantee Am. Philos. Soc., 1989, Tulane U., 1991. Mem. Am. Historians Assn., Conf. on Brit. Studies. Democrat. Home: 8011 Hickory New Orleans LA 70118 Office: Tulane U Dept History St Charles Ave New Orleans LA 70118

POLLOCK, MICHAEL ELWOOD, historian, genealogist; b. Washington, July 12, 1951; s. Carlton Elwood and Agnes Magdalen (Gavalchick) P. BA in Govt., Russian Studies, Coll. William and Mary, 1973; MA in Russian Area Studies, Georgetown U., 1978. Clerk/genealogist DAR, Washington, 1974-77; pres. Lineage Search Assocs., Inc., Mechanicsville, Va., 1977—. Asst. editor Lambert Publs., Washington, 1986-88; editor, pub. Frederick Findings, Mechanicsville, 1988—, Pollock Potpourri, Mechanicsville, 1992—, Morgan Migrations, Mechanicsville, 1993—; compiler: Marriage Bonds of Henrico County Virginia, 1984, Morton Family of Southside Virginia, 1984, Marriages of York County Virginia, 1994; contbr. mags. Del. Va. Rep., 1969-80, precinct capt., 1976-80, elections judge, 1981-88. Mem. Assn. Profl. Genealogists (founding), Clan Pollock Assn. (Va. commr. 1995), Va. Genealog. Soc., Alumni Band Orgn. Coll. William and Mary (founding). Baptist. Office: Lineage Search Assocs 7315 Colts Neck Rd Mechanicsville VA 23111-4233

POLLOCK, NEAL JAY, electronics executive; b. Phila., Feb. 4, 1947; s. Sol J. and Shirley (Buchsbaum) P. BA in Physics, U. Pa., 1968; MS in Engring. Sci., Pa. State U., 1972; MBA, Temple U., 1975; postdoctoral, George Washington U., 1978-82. Student trainee Naval Air Devel. Ctr., Warminster, Pa., 1964-68, physicist, 1968-69, electronics engr., 1969-75, plans and programs asst., 1975-76; asst. for interface Naval Air Systems Command, Washington, 1976-78, budget and fin. mgr., 1978-79, asst. program mgr. for acoustic sensors, 1979-84; project engr. Naval Sea Systems Command, Washington, 1984-87; br. head, supr. electronics engring. Space and Naval Warfare Systems Command, Washington, 1987-90, div. head, 1990-93, tech. assessment mgr., program exec. office, space comm. & sensors, 1993—; exec. sec. internat. steering com. Multifunctional Info. Distbn. System, 1994—; EEO counselor Naval Sea Sys. Command, Washington, 1986, sexual harassment avoidance trainer, 1993—, acquisition reform trainer, 1994—; chmn. comms. Quality Mgmt. Bd., 1992-93; bd. dirs. Juliette's Macrobiotic Svcs., Inc., pres., 1996—; mem. specifications and stds. improvement policy bd. SPAWAR. Co-author: Extended Radiometer Analysis-The Point Target; contr.: Organizations in a Changing Society, 1977. United commr. Boy Scouts Am., 1975-76; vol. income tax asst. Ayuda and Spanish Catholico, Washington, 1976-77; active, life mem. Save the Redwoods League, San Francisco, 1987, Nat. Aquarian Soc., Nature Conservancy, Charlottesville, Va., 1988, Archeological Conservancy, Nat. Parks and Conservation Assn., 1990—, Suriname termites and Hawaii dolphins expdns. Earthwatch; active mem., patron sponsor Pearl Buck Found., Prevention of Blindness Soc., Internat. Rescue Com., others; vol. Race for the Cure (for breast cancer), Washington, 1996; officer of elections Arlington County, chief, 1996—; del. Va. State Rep. Conv., 1993; vol. Washington Race for the Cure, 1996—. Recipient Combined Fed. Campaign Eagle award, 1990, 91, 92, 93, 94, 95, 96; USN Student Engring. Devel. scholar, 1964, NSF scholar Stevens Inst. Tech., 1963, Phila. Mayor's scholar. Mem. NRA (life), Nat. Space Soc., Assn. Scientists and Engrs. (life, keyman 1987), U.S. Holocaust Mus. (charter), Alaska Natural History Assn. (life), Pa. State Alumni Assn. (life), Clipper Club (life), Admirals Club (life), Ionosphere Club (life), Worldclub (life), Amb.'s Club (life), Red Carpet Club (life), U.S. Air Club (life), Delta Crown Club (life), Arctic Circle Club, Crossed-the-Line Club, Antarctic Pendulum Club, Antarctic Discoverer's Club, Antarctican Soc., C.G. Jung Inst. Chgo. (life), Northeast H.S. Alumni Assn. (life), Pa. State U. Alumni Assn. (Washington chpt.), U. Pa. Alumni Assn. (life, Washington chpt.), Nat. Birdfeeding Soc., Forum Grad. Assn. (charter, v.p. 1994-95, bd. dirs.), Friends of Garlic, Arlington Cooperative Assn. (life), Thomas Jefferson Pronaos Ancient Mystical Order Rosae Crucis (master 1980-82, Atlantis Lodge sec. 1984-85, treas. 1985-88, chmn. conv. 1980, patron), Mensa (millenium), Masons (32 degree), Antarctican Soc., Planetary Soc., The Arlington Coop. (life mem.), Beta Gamma Sigma. Republican. Jewish. Home: 2500 S Fern St Arlington VA 22202-2538 Office: PEO-SCS-21A 2451 Crystal Dr Arlington VA 22245-5200

POLO, RICHARD JOSEPH, engineering executive; b. Barranquilla, Colombia, Oct. 14, 1936; s. Pedro Pastor and Clotilde (Verano) P.; m. Ana Isabel Cepeda, Feb. 1, 1958; children: Richard J. Jr., James Alan. BCE, NYU, 1957; MS in Structural Engring., Iowa State U., 1963, PhD in Structural and Nuclear Engring., 1971; disting. grad., Command and Gen. Staff Coll., Ft. Leavenworth, Kans., 1970; grad., Inter-Am. Def. Coll., Ft. McNair, Washington, 1977; MBA, Marymount U., 1986. Registered profl. engr., Md., Iowa, Fla., Pa., Conn., N.Y. Commd. 2d lt. U.S. Army, 1957, advanced through grades to col., 1979, various positions, 1957-79; asst. dir. civil works Pacific U.S. Army Office Chief of Engrs., 1979-80; corps engr., engr. brigade comdr. U.S. Army, Ludwigsburg, Fed. Republic Germany, 1980-83; dep. study dir. U.S. Army Office Chief of Staff, Washington, 1984-85; ret. U.S. Army, 1985; v.p. constrn. inspection Kidde Cons. Inc., Balt., 1985, sr. v.p. constrn. inspection, 1986, exec. v.p., 1986-89, corp. sec., 1988-89, also bd. dirs.; v.p. Fla. region CRSS, Miami, 1989-90; CEO, program dir. CRSS/WRJ joint venture, 1989-90; assoc. v.p., dep. divsn. dir. fed. programs Greiner, Inc., Miami, 1991-92; dir. engring. & project ops. CKC (OSC), Miami, 1993-94; dir. L.Am. ops., dir. engring. devel. GeoSyntec Cons., Boca Raton, 1994-96; dir. Miami ops. ICF Kaiser Engrs., Inc., 1996—; pres. Amerint, Miami, 1994—, Am. Enterprises Internat., Inc., Polo Mortgage-Plus, Miami, 1993—; bd. dirs. KCI Holdings, 1988-90. Contbr. articles on mil. and structural engring. to profl. jours. Inventor arcuate space frame. Cmty. comdr. and sr. U.S. rep. Ludwigsburg Mil. Cmty., 1980-83. Decorated Legion of Merit with bronze oak leaf cluster, Bronze Star, others; Brookings Institution Fed. Exec. fellow, 1983-84. Fellow Soc. Am. Mil. Engrs. (bd. dirs. El Paso chpt. 1967-68, pres. Stutttgart chpt. 1980-82); mem. ASCE, NSPE, Md. Soc. Profl. Engrs., Va. Soc. Profl. Engrs. (dir. no. Va. chpt. 1985-89, pres. elect 1988-89), Assn. U.S. Army (pres. Ludwigsburg chpt. 1980-83), Fla. Engring. Soc., Army-Navy Club Coral Gables (dir. 1994—, sec. 1995-96, v.p. 1996—), Greater Miami C. of C. (trustee 1989-92), Country Club Coral Gables, Rotary, Sigma Xi, Phi Kappa Phi, Tau Beta Pi, Chi Epsilon, Psi Upsilon (pres. Delta chpt. 1956-57). Republican. Roman Catholic. Home and Office: Amerint/Am Enterprises Int 430 Sunset Rd Miami FL 33143-6339 Office: ICF Kaiser Engrs Inc 3750 NW 87th Ave Miami FL 33178

POLOZOLA, FRANK JOSEPH, federal judge; b. Baton Rouge, Jan. 15, 1942; s. Steve A. Sr. and Caroline C. (Lucito) P.; m. Linda Kay White, June 9, 1962; children: Gregory Dean, Sheri Elizabeth, Gordon Damian. Student bus. adminstrn., La. State U., 1959-62, JD, 1965. Bar: La. 1965. Law clk. to U.S. Dist. Ct. Judge E. Gordon West, 1965-66; assoc. Seale, Smith & Phelps, Baton Rouge, 1966-68, ptnr., 1968-73; part-time magistrate U.S. Dist. Ct. (mid. dist.) La., Baton Rouge, 1972-73, magistrate, 1973-80, judge, 1980—; adj. prof. Law Ctr., La. State U., 1977—. Bd. dirs. Cath. High Sch. Mem. FBA, La. Bar Assn., Baton Rouge Bar Assn., Fed. Judges Assn., 5th Cir. Dist. Judges Assn., La. State U. L Club, KC, Omicron Delta Kappa. Roman Catholic. Office: US Dist Ct Russell B Long Fed Bldg & US Courthouse 777 Florida St Ste 313 Baton Rouge LA 70801-1717

POLSTER, ELEANOR BERNICE, management educator, university administrator; b. Liberty, N.Y., Apr. 13, 1948; d. Philip and Ann Winitsky; m. Harvey Polster, Jan. 24, 1971. BA, Boston U., 1969; postgrad., U. Miami, 1969-71; MBA, Fla. Internat. U., 1981. Grad. teaching asst. U. Miami, Coral Gables, Fla., 1970-71; sr. benefits analyst Conn. Gen. Life Ins. Co., Miami, Fla., 1971-77; ins. sec. Dr. Selig Snow, South Miami, Fla., 1977, Drs. Silverstein and Halpern, South Miami, 1977-80; grad. asst. Fla. Internat. U. Coll. Bus. Adminstrn., Miami, 1980-81, asst. grad. counselor, 1981, vis. counselor, 1981, counselor, instr. orgn. and mgmt., 1981—, coord. undergrad. counseling, 1990-94; coord. of Weekend BBA Fla. Internat. U., 1994-95; mem. faculty senate Fla. Internat. U. Coll. Bus. Adminstrn., Miami, 1983-87; grad. coord. Fla. Internat. U., 1995—. Mem. Phi Alpha Theta. Jewish. Office: Fla Internat U University Park Campus Miami FL 33199

POLSTER, JOYCE SCHUMANN, nurse educator; b. Vernon, Tex., Dec. 20, 1943; d. John J. and Alice (Schoppa) Schumann; m. Duane L. Polster, Aug. 7, 1965; children: Matthew S., Ryan W., Emmet L. Diploma in Nursing, Wichita Gen. Hosp., Wichita Falls, Tex., 1964; BSN, West Tex. A&M U., 1978, MSN, 1982. Cert. cmty. health nurse, gerontol. nurse, nursing adminstr. Office nurse English & Hunt Clinic, Lubbock, Tex., 1965-66; nurse/educator Lubbock Ind. Sch. Vocat. Nursing, 1967-70; field, clinic nurse Amarillo (Tex.) Bi-City-County Health Dept., 1977-78; charge nurse/nurse mgr. High Plains Bapt. Hosp., Amarillo, 1979-81; nurse/educator Northwest Tex. Hosp. sch. Nursing, Amarillo, 1982-84, West Tex. A&M U., Canyon, 1984-91, Amarillo Coll., 1992—; cons. Otter-Tern, Inc., Amarillo, 1988—. Designer/author: (software) Examplan: Analysis of Nursing Exam, 1987; designer/editor: (software) Examplan: Analysis, 1991, Examplan Version 2.0, 1993, Examplan Version 3.0, 1996; author: (booklets) Examplann - User Documentation, 1993, Examplan - User Guide, 1996. Mem. Bd. Christian Edn., Trinity Luth. Sch., 1995—. Named Vol. of the Yr., ARC, Amarillo chpt., 1987. Mem. Tex. Nurses Assn. (Dist. II bd. dirs., sec./editor 1992-93), Sigma Theta Tau. Lutheran. Home: 2416 Hansford Amarillo TX 79106 Office: Otter-Tern Inc PO Box 2245 Amarillo TX 79105

POLUCCI, ASHLEY V., staff nurse; b. Bennington, Vt., Nov. 28, 1955; s. John Dominic and Bernice Elva (Lavanway) P. ASN, Regents Coll., Albany, N.Y., 1976; BA, North Adams State Coll., 1977; BSN, U. Ctrl. Fla., Daytona, 1996. RN, BLS, ENPC, TNCC, CEN, CCRN, ACLS. Staff nurse ER, ICU, CCU Travcorps, Inc., Malden, Mass., 1979—; staff nurse surg. ICU Albert Einstein Sch. Medicine, N.Y.C., 1989; staff nurse ICU Dartmouth Hitchcock Med. Ctr., Lebanon, N.H., 1991-92; nurse Club Med, Port St. Lucie, Fla., 1991; camp nurse Camp Thoreau in Vt., Thetford Center, 1992-94; staff nurse ER Desert Hosp., Palm Springs, Calif., 1993-94, Grady Meml. Hosp., Atlanta, 1993; staff nurse post-op open heart Ormond Meml. Hosp., Ormond Beach, Fla., 1994; staff nurse ER Halifax Med. Ctr., Daytona Beach, Fla., 1994-96; staff nurse-emergency Middletown (Ohio) Regional Hosp., 1996—; mgr. North Adams Ambulance Svc., North Adams, Mass., 1978-79; participant Project EFECT, 1995-96. Mem. ANA, ONA, ENA, ACCN, Internat. Assn. Turtles.

POMERANTZ, JERALD MICHAEL, lawyer; b. Springfield, Mass., July 9, 1954; s. Lawrence Louis Pomerantz and Dolores (Barez) Chaudoir. BA in Econs. cum laude, Brandeis U., 1976; JD, Vanderbilt U., 1979; student, Am. Inst. Banking, 1983-86. Atty. McAllen, Tex., 1979-80, Weslaco, Tex., 1980-85; gen. counsel, sec. Tex. Valley Bancshares, Inc., Weslaco, 1985-87; atty. for Hidalgo County Rural Fire Prevention Dist., Tex., 1982-88; atty. SBA, Harlingen, Tex., 1987; pvt. practice Weslaco, Tex., 1987-88, 89—, Dallas, 1988-89; assoc. Shank, Irwin, Dallas, 1988; atty. Security Bank Shares, F.M., Dallas, 1988-89; adv. dir. South Tex. Fed. Credit Union; atty. Elsa (Tex.) Housing Authority, 1993—. Mem. Weslaco Charter Review Com., 1981-82, Weslaco 65th Birthday Celebration Com., 1984; polit. adv. com. to elect Ramon Montalvo, Weslaco, 1985, 86, 89, Orlando "Mickey" Pedraza for City Commr. com., Weslaco, 1987; drafted S.B. 139 (amending Tex. bus. and commerce code sect. 9.402(g)) regular session Tex. Legislature, 1989, S.B. 140, 1989, enacted as H.B. 2005 (amending Tex. Credit Code sect. 1.06) regular session Tex. Legislature, 1993. Recipient continuing edn. award Banking Law Inst., 1992. Mem. Tex. Assn. Bank Counsel (bd. dirs. 1993-96, govt. rels. com., long range planning and membership com.), State Bar Tex., Conf. on Consumer Fin. Law, Coll. State Bar Tex. (bd. dirs. 1990-95), Hidalgo County Bar Assn. Home and Office: PO Box 10 Weslaco TX 78599-0010

POMEROY, WYMAN BURDETTE, business owner, consultant; b. Flint, Mich., Feb. 5, 1932; s. Burdette Talmadge and Bernice (Caywood) P.; m. Anna Lee Farley, May 23, 1953; children: Brian Lee, David Michael. Student, Eastern Mich. Coll. Commerc, 1951; student, U. Mich., 1972-73, 75, Mott Community Coll., 1972-75, Oakland Community Coll., 1974. Commanding officer 5th Dist. fire marshal div. Mich. State Police, Paw Paw, 1955-79; fire investigator Fla. State Fire Marshall, Tampa, 1979-80; pres. W.B. Pomeroy & Assocs., Inc., Brandon, Fla., 1980—; pvt. practice comml. property mgmt. Highland Properties of Gulfcoast, Ltd., Hillsborough and Pinellas Counties, Fla.; cons. hazardous materials code fire marshal divsn. Mich. State Police, Paw Paw, 1978, cons. pub. assn. code, 1978. With prodn. and lighting coms. Houghton Lake (Mich.) Playhouse, 1967-71. Staff sgt. USAF, 1951-55, ETO . Recipient Citation, Justice Ct., 1966, Cert. of Appreciation, Flint Fire Dept., 1977, Letter of Appreciation, FBI, 1980. Mem. Am. Soc. Safety Engrs., Internat. Assn. Arson Investigators, Fla. Adv. Commn. on Arson Prevention, Nat. Fire Protection Assn., Arson Coop. of Fla., Lions. Office: WB Pomeroy & Assocs Inc PO Box 2042 Brandon FL 33509-2042

POMMERENKE, ROGER LEE, electronics engineer; b. Kansas City, Mo., Apr. 20, 1946; s. Gustav Adolf and Irene Mildred (Cole) P.; children: Robert, John. BSEE, Lafayette Coll., 1968; MA, Lynchburg Coll., 1987. Registered profl. engr., Va. Internat. field engr. Gen. Electric Overseas Co., Fos-sur-Mer, France, 1972-81; system engr. Gen. Electric, Salem, Va., 1981-92, quality engr., 1992—. Contbr. articles to profl. jours. Vol. Mill Mt. Cmty. Theatre, Roanoke, 1988—. Mem. Roanoke Ski Club (bd. dirs., pres. 1987—, Nastar Gold medal 1994), C. of C. Ambs. (com. chmn.). Home: 5735 Equestrian Dr Roanoke VA 24018-4604 Office: GE Rm 700 1501 Roanoke Blvd Salem VA 24153-6422

POND, JESSE EARL, historical association administrator; b. St. Louis, Jan. 15, 1917; s. Jesse Earl Sr. and Susan Brant (Jackels) P.; m. Edith Anne Mary Lazar, Dec. 5, 1947; children: Susan Mary (dec.), Mark George, Laura Elizabeth, Jesse E. III , Katherine Anne. BS, Menlo Coll., 1953. Photographer for comml. photographer St. Louis, 1933-39, labor foreman for large iron foundry, 1939-46; prodn. mgr. heavy elec. equipment mfr. San Francisco, 1946-49; dep. sheriff County of San Mateo, Redwood City, Calif., 1949-53; v.p. mfg. appliance mfr. Santa Cruz, Calif., 1953-58; facilities adminstr. electronics mfr. Falls Church, Va., 1959-63; prin. mem. Jesse Pond Co., Inc., McLean, Va., 1964—; pres. Pearl Harbor History Assocs., Inc., Sperryville, Va., 1985—; nat. treas. Pearl Harbor Survivors Assn., Inc., McLean, 1974-82. Author: The Square Peg: A Tight Fit in a Tin Can, 1993. Mem. Fairfax County Republican Com., Fairfax, Va., 1962-80; chmn. Rappahannock County Republican Com., Washington, Va., 1982-87. Named Hon. Admiral, State of Tex., 1980, State of Nebr., 1982. Mem. Kiwanis, Lions. Lutheran.

PONDER, BLAIR ARLAN, computer programmer; b. Brownwood, Tex., Dec. 5, 1968; s. Thomas Arlan and Beverly Revé (Lynn) P.; m. Saterra Lei Linn, Feb. 24, 1990; 1 child, Makenzi Elizabethe. Student, Angelo State U., 1987-88, Howard Payne U., 1988-89, Cmty. Coll. of the Air Force, 1992. Mail clerk customer svc. So. Savings & Loan, Brownwood, 1987; cashier, asst. dept. mgr. Wal-Mart, Brownwood, 1988-89; sub. tchr. Early (Tex.) Ind. Sch. Dist., 1989; asst. mgr. J. Riggings, Fort Worth, 1992-93; mgr. J. Riggings, 1993-94; customer rels. Wesco Aircraft, Fort Worth, 1995; computer programmer, trainer Distribution Data Mgmt. Sys., Keller, Tex., 1995—; procedures writer Distribution Data Mgmt. Sys., Keller, 1995-96. Contbr. articles to profl. jours. Com. mem. Boy Scouts Am., Brownwood, 1987-96. With USAF, 1989-92. Recipient Eagle Scout award Boy Scouts Am., Brownwood, 1987. Mem. Boy Scouts Am., Order of the Arrow-Boy Scouts Am. (dist. chief), Phi Mu Alpha Sinfonia, DeMolay. Democrat. Home: 4949 Vega Ct W Fort Worth TX 76133

PONDER, JAMES ALTON, clergyman, evangelist; b. Ft. Worth, Jan. 20, 1933; s. Leo A. and Mae Adele (Blair) P.; BA, Baylor U., 1954; MEd, Southwestern Bapt. Theol. Sem., 1965; DD, Covington Theol. Sem., 1996; m. Joyce Marie Hutchison, Sept. 1, 1953; children: Keli, Ken. Ordained to ministry Baptist Ch., 1953; pastor Calvary Bapt. Ch., Corsicana, Tex., 1953-57, First Bapt. Ch., Highlands, Tex., 1957-62, Ridglea West Bapt. Ch., Ft. Worth, 1963-66, First Bapt. Ch., Carmi, Ill., 1966-67; dir. evangelism Ill. Bapt. State Conv., 1968-70, Fla. Bapt. Conv., 1970-81; pres. Jim Ponder Ministries, Inc., 1981—, Life Internat., Inc., 1993—; dir. Inst. World Evangelism div. Jim Ponder Ministries; preacher Crossroads radio program; fgn. mission bd. evangelist in various countries of Asia, Central Am., Middle East, 1960—; project dir. Korea Major Cities Evangelization Project, 1978-80; evangelist ch. revivals, area crusades and evangelism confs., 1951—; mem. faculty Billy Graham Schs. Evangelism, 1970—; co-founder Ch. Growth Inst. Fla., 1976; co-dir. Ch. Growth Crusades, 1978-79; founder, dir. Inst. World Evangelism (I-Owe), 1987—; pres. Conf. Fla. Baptist Evangelists, 1986-87, Fellowship of Bapt. World Ministries, 1992—; sports announcer Sta. KIYS, Waco, Tex., 1950-54; speaker worldwide missionary radio broadcast Crossroads with Jim Ponder. Mem. Fellowship Christian Athletes, Smithsonian Instn., N. Am. Soc. Church Growth, Acad. Evangelism in Edn., Acad. Evangelism Profs. Republican. Club: Kiwanis. Author: The Devotional Life, 1970; Evangelism Men...Motivating Laymen to Witness, 1975; Evangelism Men...Proclaiming the Doctrines of Salvation, 1976; Evangelism Men...Preaching for Decision, 1979, The Way to Christ, 1994; author, video tchr. Becoming a Witness; contbr. articles to religious publs.; speaker in field. Home: 2000 N Countryside Cir Orlando FL 32804-6914 Office: PO Box 547995 Orlando FL 32854-7995

PONOROFF, LAWRENCE, law educator, legal consultant; b. Chgo., Sept. 10, 1953; s. Charles Melvin and Jean Eileen (Kramer) P.; m. Monica J.

Moses, July 25, 1981; children: Christopher J., Devon E., Laura J., Scott C. AB, Loyola U., Chgo., 1975; JD, Stanford U., 1978. Bar: Colo. 1978, Ohio 1988, U.S. Dist. Ct. Colo., U.S. Dist. Ct. (no. dist.) Ohio, U.S. Ct. Appeals (10th cir.). Assoc. Holme Roberts & Owen, Denver, 1978-84, ptnr., 1984-86; asst. prof. law U. Toledo, 1986-88, assoc. prof. coll. of law, 1988-90, prof. law, assoc. dean academic affairs, 1990-92, prof., 1990-95; prof. Tulane U. Sch. Law, New Orleans, 1995—; vis. prof. Wayne State U. Law Sch., 1993; cons. long range planning subcom. of com. on adminstrn. of bankruptcy system Jud. Conf. of the U.S. Co-author (with S.E. Snyder) Commercial Bankruptcy Litigation, 1989. Mem. ABA, ABI. Home: 6025 Pitt St New Orleans LA 70118 Office: Tulane Law Sch Coll Law 6329 Freret St New Orleans LA 70118

PONSONBY, DAVID PEMBERTON, sports medicine researcher; b. Dalwallinu, Australia, Jan. 31, 1948; came to U.S., 1982; s. Douglas Henry and Olive Lorraine (Patterson) P. BA, U. East Anglia, Norwich, Norfolk, Eng., 1970; MEd, Mercer U., 1973. Cert. tchr., Ga.; nat. lic. U.S. Soccer Coaching Fedn., 1973. Substitute tchr. Avon Schs., Bristol, Eng., 1973, 76-81; rsch. dir. Nautilus Sports/Med. Ins. Australia, Melbourne, 1981-82, Sports Medicine Clins. Am., Dallas, 1982-84; exercise technologist North Tex. Back Inst., Plano, 1984-85; mem. nat. staff Nautilus Sports/Med. Inds., Ft. Worth, 1986-87; personal trainer Key Clinics, Dallas, Irving, Tex., 1987-88; rehab. dir. Valley Ranch Rehab. Ctr., Irving, 1989; rschr. Parker Chiropractic Coll., Irving, 1990-93; cons. Medisport, Frisco, Tex., 1993-95; rsch. cons. Sdi Sys., Inc., Richardson, Tex., 1995—. Author: Soccer Fitness, 1978; contbg. author: The Athlete's Guide to Sports Medicine, 1981, Especially for Women, 1983, Sports Medicine: The Lower Extremity, 1988. Hon. coord. spl. events Am. Indian Heritage Ctr. Tex., Dallas, 1991—. Internat. travel fellow U. East Anglia, 1970. Mem. Greater Dallas Bicylists. Home: 9660 Williford Trl Frisco TX 75034-2576 Office: Sdi Sys Inc 1701 N Greenville Ave #702 Richardson TX 75081

PONTE, CHARLES DENNIS, pharmacist, educator; b. Waterbury, Conn., Jan. 17, 1953; s. Americo Joseph and Irene (Poirier) P. BSc in Pharmacy, U. Conn., 1975; D Pharmacy, U. Utah, 1980. Diplomate Am. Acad. Pain Mgmt.; cert. diabetes edn.; bd. cert. pharmacotherapy specialist. Intern Woodbury (Conn.) Drug Co., 1975; hosp. pharmacy resident Yale-New Haven Hosp., 1975-76, ambulatory staff pharmacist, 1976-78; prof. clin. pharmacy, family medicine Robert C. Byrd Health Scis. Ctr. of W.Va. U., Morgantown, 1980—, also dir. PharmD program; mem. adv. bd. ambulatory care and family practice Annals Pharmacotherapy, Cin., 1985—; mem. adv. panel on family practice U.S. Pharmacopeial Conv., Inc., Rockville, Md., 1990—; mem. vis. faculty Upjohn Co., Kalamazoo, 1986; coord. Sch. Pharmacy, Spencer State Tng. Ctr., 1984-88; participant Practical Aspects of Diabetes Care: Conf. for Pharmacy Educators, 1989; chmn. Van Liere Rsch. Convocation for Med. Students, 1990; mem. splty. coun. on nutritional support pharmacy practice Bd. Pharm. Spltys., 1994—. Contbr. to profl. publs. Grantee Robert Wood Johnson Found., 1981. Fellow Am. Coll. Clin. Pharmacy, Am. Soc. Hosp. Pharmacists (practice interest adv. panel 1990-92); mem. Am. Coll. Clin. Pharmacy, Am. Coll. Clin. Pharmacology, Soc. Tchrs. Family Medicine, Am. Diabetes Assn. (pres. W.Va. affiliate 1985-86), Sigma Xi, Phi Kappa Phi, Phi Lambda Sigma, Rho Chi. Roman Catholic. Office: WVa U Robert C Byrd Health Sci Ctr Sch Pharmacy Morgantown WV 26506

PONTIFLET, ADDIE ROBERSON, nurse, educator; b. Decatur, Ga., Oct. 25, 1943; d. Emory Alexander and Emma Kate (Wilson) Roberson; m. Derrick Mayes, Dec. 12, 1965 (div. Apr. 1966); 1 child, Pamela Denise; m. Theodore Hubert Pontiflet, Nov. 17, 1972. RN diploma, Kings County Hosp. Ctr., Bklyn., 1964, nurse anesthetist diploma, 1973; BS, St. Joseph's Coll., 1975; MSEd, U. So. Maine, 1983. RN, Va.; lic. nurse practitioner, Va. Staff nurse Montifiore Hosp., Bronx, N.Y., 1964-66; head nurse Downstate Med. Ctr., Bklyn., 1967-68; in svc. instr. Kings County Hosp. Ctr., Bklyn., 1968-70; anesthetist Bklyn. Hosp., 1973-74; clin. instr. Ga. Bapt. Med. Ctr., Atlanta, 1976-80; assoc. dir. Mercy Hosp. Sch. of Anesthesia, Portland, Maine, 1980-86; asst. prof. nurse anesthesia Med. Coll. Va., Va. Commonwealth U., Richmond, Va., 1986—. Bd. dirs. YWCA, Portland, 1982-85, Last Stop Gallery, Richmond, 1988-89. Mem. Am. Assn. Nurse Anesthetists (cert.), Va. Assn. Nurse Anesthetists, Phi Delta Kappa. Office: Va Commonwealth U Med Coll PO Box 226 Richmond VA 23202-0226

POOL, MICHAEL LEE, psychiatrist; b. Berwyn, Ill., Feb. 11, 1951; s. Marion Alton and Frances (Jones) P.; m. Dale Paige Allison, June 8, 1974; children: Gregory Arthur, Jeffrey Michael. BA in Psychology with highest honors, U. N.C., 1973, MD, 1977. Diplomate Am. Bd. Psychiatry. Resident in psychiatry N.C. Meml. Hosp., Chapel Hill, 1977-81; chief resident Consult Liaison Svcs., Chapel Hill, 1978; psychiatrist Tenn. Psychiatry and Psychopharmacology Clinic, P.C., Knoxville, 1981—, sec., treas., 1984—; clin. instr. psychiatry U. Tenn., Memphis, 1984—. Contbr. articles to profl. jours. Cons. Samaritan Cons. Ctr., Knoxville, 1983-87; cons. com. Ch. St. United Meth. Ch., Knoxville, 1989-90. Sol W. Ginsburg fellow Group for Advancement of Psychiatry, Cherry Hill, N.J., 1979-80. Mem. AMA, Am. Psychiatric Assn., Knoxville Acad. Medicine, Tenn. Med. Assn., Tenn. Psychiatric Assn., So. Med. Assn. Office: Tenn Psychiatry & Psychopharmacology 9401 Park West Blvd Knoxville TN 37923-4202

POOLE, ANITA JOYCE, marketing and publishing company executive; b. Galveston, Tex., Oct. 27, 1950; d. Donald Wayne and Mary Alice (Anderson) Lawson; m. Richard Barton Poole, July 31, 1971; 1 child, Brian Andrew. AS in Nursing, Cooke County Coll., Gainesville, Tex., 1978. RN, Tex. Staff nurse Westgate Med. Ctr., Denton, Tex., 1978-84; nursing dir. Brookwood Recovery Ctr., Denton, 1984-86; coord. provider rels. Sanus Tex. Health Plan, Inc., Dallas, 1986-88; pres. Lawson and Lee Pub., Denton, 1987—; dir. mktg. WynRose, Inc., Dallas, 1988-89, Innovative Healthcare Systems, Inc., Dallas, 1989-91; dir. account svcs. CORPHEALTH, Inc., Ft. Worth, 1991-93, v.p. provider devel., 1993—; chmn. profl. staff exec. com. Brookwood Recovery Ctr., Denton, 1985-86; cons. managed healthcare firms, Dallas, 1988. Editor: Finger Theatrics: Fine Motor Development for Young Children, 1988. Co-founder pediatric hosp. orientation program Westgate Med. Ctr., 1983-84; chmn. childsafe program Denton Assn. for Edn. Young Children, 1979-80. Nursing scholar Cooke County Coll., 1976-78. Home: 2004 North Lake Trl Denton TX 76201-0604 Office: CORPHEALTH Inc 1300 Summit Ave Ste 600 Fort Worth TX 76102-4420

POOLE, BRYAN CADENHEAD, banker; b. Greenville, Ala., Jan. 9, 1950; d. Henry Grady and Olive Jeanette (Bryan) Cadenhead; divorced; 1 child, Olivia Lawrence. BSBA with high honor, Auburn U., 1972; MBA, U. Ala., Tuscaloosa, 1973; grad. in banking, La. State U., 1980. Asst. cashier Am-South Bank, Birmingham, Ala., 1973-76; credit analyst First Ala. Bank Inc., Montgomery, 1976-77; credit officer First Ala. Bancshares, Montgomery, 1977-91; sr. v.p., regional credit officer 1st Ala. Bank, Montgomery, 1991—, regional loan quality control mgr., 1991—; speaker, condr. tng. sessions. Mem. Robert Morris Assocs. (bd. dirs. Montgomery 1993—), Auburn U. Alumni Assn., Phi Kappa Phi.

POOLE, GALEN VINCENT, surgeon, educator, researcher; b. Pewee Valley, Ky., Apr. 13, 1951; s. Galen Vincent and Audrey (Taylor) P.; m. Carol Ruth Shepherd, Aug. 11, 1974; children: Erin Ruth, Matthew Shepherd. AB, Hanover Coll., 1973; MD, U. Ky., 1978. Diplomate Am. Bd. Surgery; added qualifications in surg. critical care. Intern, resident in surgery Bowman Gray-Wake Forest U., Winston-Salem, N.C., 1978-85; asst. clin. prof. Sch. Medicine U. Ill., Urbana, 1986-89; assoc. prof. Med. Ctr. U. Miss., Jackson, 1989-93, prof. surgery, 1993—. Author: Abdominal Wound Dehiscence, 1987; contbr. more than 70 articles to profl. jours. Chmn. Miss. State Com. on Trauma, Jackson, 1993—; dir. Trauma, Surg., and Critical Care, Jackson, 1989—; mem. adv. coun. Emergency Med. Svcs., Jackson, 1993—. Maj. USAF, 1985-89. Fellow ACS, Southeastern Surg. Congress; mem. Am. Assn. for Surgery of Trauma, Soc. of Univ. Surgeons, Soc. for Surgery of the Alimentary Tract, Soc. for Critical Care Medicine, Alpha Omega Alpha. Home: 145 Summerwood Dr Jackson MS 39208-9075 Office: U Miss Med Ctr Dept Surgery 2500 N State St Jackson MS 39216-4500

POOLE, GEORGE WILLIAM, human resources specialist, consultant; b. Raleigh, N.C., Feb. 16, 1932; s. George Raymond and Mary Lucile (Sullivan) P.; m. Tamara Holliday, Feb. 15, 1958; children: Shawn William, Judith Lucile, Holliday Ann, Patrick Sullivan. BA in Psychology, U. N.C., 1957. Cert. pers. cons. Rep. Sinclair Oil Co., Charlotte, N.C., 1957-58; pers. mgr. Burlington Industries, Inc., Greensboro, N.C., 1958-63; pers. dir. Pine States Creamery, Raleigh, 1963-65, Athey Products Corp., Wake Forest, N.C., 1965-67; pres. Nat. Employment Svc., Raleigh, 1967—. Author: Start-up Power, 1993, What's the Color of Your Underwear?, 1994; contbr. articles to profl. jours. Bd. dirs. Jr. Achievement of East N.C., Raleigh, 1978—, Mayor's Commn. for the Handicapped, 1970-81, Drug Alert, 1974-91; exec. com. ARC, Raleigh, 1968-75, N.C. State Championship Horse, Raleigh, 1984—. With USN, 1951-55. Recipient three 1st place awards Nat. Assn. Pers. Cos., 1969, Bronze award Nat. Jr. Achievement, 1986. Mem. Raleigh C. of C., Lions (life N.C. Lions Assn. for Blind), U. N.C. Chapel Hill Alumni Assn. Republican. Roman Catholic. Office: Nat Employment Svcs PO Box 6505 Raleigh NC 27628-6505

POOLE, JENNIFER CLARK, nurse; b. Tupelo, Miss., Oct. 11, 1958; m. James M. Poole, Aug. 1981. ADN, Miss. U. for Women, Columbus, 1984. Cert. neonatal intensive care nurse; cert. regional trainer neonatal resuscitation; cert. pediatric ALS; cert. instr. CPR. Staff nurse, nursery and neonatal ICU North Miss. Med. Ctr., Tupelo, 1984-86, 87-88, staff and charge nurse surg. ICU, 1986-87, charge nurse neonatal ICU, 1988-91, nurse auditor, 1991-94, MIS analyst/educator, 1996—; instr. continuing edn., 1995. Mem. Assn. Women's Health, Obstetrics & Neonatal Nurses, Nat. Assn. Neonatal Nurses, Miss. Nurses Assn. (pres., 2d v.p. dist. 25, bd. dirs., Pediatric/Neonatal Nurse of Yr. 1990, Critical Care Nurse of Yr. 1991).

POOLE, MAX CALVIN, endocrinology educator; b. Salisbury, N.C., July 18, 1950; s. Louie Calvin and Frances Louise (Agner) P.; m. Susan Marie Pell, June 16, 1979; 1 child, Aaron. BS in Biology, U. N.C., Charlotte, 1972; PhD in Endocrinology, Med. Coll. Ga., 1978. Postgrad. rschr. Med. Coll. Ga., Augusta, 1978-79; rsch. assoc. East Carolina U. Sch. Medicine, Greenville, N.C., 1979-80, asst. prof., 1980-86, assoc. prof., 1986—; asst. dean East Carolina Grad. Sch., Greenville, 1994—; spkr. in field. Contbr. articles to profl. jours. Mem., EMT Ea. Pines Rescue Squad, Pitt County, N.C., 1985—; chair Pitt. County Dem. Party, 1991-95, State of N.C. Internship Coun., Raleigh, 1993—, Simpson Vol. Fire Dept. Dist. Commn., Pitt County, 1992—; vice-chair Cmtys. in Schs., Pitt County, 1993—. Recipient Cmty. Progress Svc. award Concerned Citizens for Justice, Pitt County, 1993. Mem. Endocrine Soc., Sigma Xi, Cmty. Fellowship Club (pres. 1992-93). Baptist. Home: 1324 Boyd-Galloway Rd Grimesland NC 27837 Office: E Carolina U Sch Medicine Dept Anatomy and Cell Biology Greenville NC 27858

POOLE, RICHARD WILLIAM, economics educator; b. Oklahoma City, Dec. 4, 1927; s. William Robert and Lois (Spicer) P.; m. Bertha Lynn Mehr, July 28, 1950; children: Richard William, Laura Lynne, Mark Stephen. B.S., U. Okla., 1951, M.B.A., 1952; postgrad., George Washington U., 1957-58; Ph.D., Okla. State U., 1960. Research analyst Okla. Gas & Electric Co., Oklahoma City, 1952- 54; mgr. sci. and mfg. devel. dept. Oklahoma City C. of C., 1954-57; mgr. Office of J.E. Webb, Washington, 1957-58; instr., asst. prof., assoc. prof., prof. econs. Okla. State U., Stillwater, 1960-65; prof. econs., dean Coll. Bus. Adminstrn. Okla. State U., 1965-72, v.p., prof. econs., 1972-88, Regents Disting. Svc. prof., prof. econs., 1988-93, emeritus v.p., dean, Regents Disting. Svc. prof./prof. econ., 1993—; cons. to adminstr. NASA, Washington, 1961-69; adviser subcom. on govt. rsch. U.S. Senate, 1966-69; lectr. Intermediate Sch. Banking, Ops. Mgmt. Sch., Okla. Bankers Assn., 1968-89; lectr. internat. off-campus programs, Okla. City U., 1994-96. Author: (with others) The Oklahoma Economy, 1963, County Building Block Data for Regional Analysis, 1965. Mem. Gov.' Com. on Devel. Ark.-Verdigris Waterway, 1970-71, Gov.'s Five-Yr. Econ. Devel. Plan, 1993; past v.p., bd. dirs., past chmn. Mid-Continent Rsch. and Devel. Coun. 2d lt., arty. U.S. Army, 1946-48. Recipient Delta Sigma Pi Gold Key award Coll. Bus. Adminstrn., U. Okla., 1951, Merrick Found. Tchg. award on Am. Free Enterprise Sys., 1992, Disting. Alumni award Okla. State U., 1995; inductee Coll. Bus. Adminstrn. Hall of Fame, Okla. State U., 1993, Stillwater Hall of Fame, 1996, Payne County Hist. Soc. and Stillwater C. of C., 1996. Mem. Southwestern Econ. Assn. (past pres.), Am. Assembly Collegiate Schs. Bus. (past bd. dirs.), Nat. Assn. State Univs. and Land Grant Colls. (past chmn. commn. on edn. for bus. professions), Southwestern Bus. Adminstrn. Assn. (past pres.), Okla. C. of C. (past bd. dirs.), Stillwater C. of C. (past bd. dirs. and pres.), Beta Gamma Sigma (past bd. dirs.), Phi Kappa Phi, Phi Eta Sigma, Omicron Delta Kappa. Home: 815 S Shumard Dr Stillwater OK 74074-1136

POOLE, RICHARD WILLIAM, JR., secondary school educator; b. Norman, Okla., Apr. 13, 1951; s. Richard W. and Lynn (Mehr) P.; m. Sonya Lee, Mar. 20, 1982; 1 child, Amanda Lee. BS in Social Studies, Okla. State U., Stillwater, 1976. Tchr., coach West Jr. H.S., Ponca City, Okla., 1976-80; tchr., coach Ponca City Sr. H.S., 1980-92, Am. history tchr., supr. jr. high athletics, 1992—. Served with USNR, 1969-71, Viet Nam. Mem. Lions Club (tail twister 1992, v.p. 1993, pres. After 5 club 1994), Elks. Democrat. Methodist. Home: 1306 El Camino St Ponca City OK 74604-4011

POP, EMIL, research chemist; b. Tirgu Mures, Romania, Aug. 12, 1939; came to U.S., 1983; s. Victor and Rosalia (Graf) P.; m. Elena Petrina Petri, Apr. 28, 1964; 1 child, Andreea Christina. BS, Babes-Bolyai U., Cluj., Romania, 1961; PhD, Inst. Chemistry, Cluj. and Supreme Coun. for Sci. Titles, Dept. of Edn. Bucharest, Romania, 1973. Chemist Chem.-Pharm. Rsch. Inst., Cluj, Romania, 1962-65, rsch. sci., group leader, 1965-78, prin. rsch. sci., group and compartment leader, 1978-83; postdoctoral rsch. assoc. Dept. Medicinal Chemistry, Coll. Pharmacy, U. Fla., Gainesville, 1983-86; rsch. sci. Pharmatec, Inc., Alachua, Fla., 1986-87, group leader, 1987-89, assoc. dir. chem. devel., 1989-92 , dir. chemistry, 1992; dir. chemistry Pharmos Corp., Alachua, 1992-95, sr. dir. chemistry, 1995—. Contbr. articles to profl. jours.; inventor in field. Recipient N. Teclu award Romanian Acad. Sci., 1980. Fellow Am. Inst. Chemists; mem. AAAS, Am. Chem. Soc., Am. Assn. Pharm. Sci., Internat. Union Pure and Applied Chemistry, N.Y. Acad. Scis., Internat. Soc. Quantum Biology and Pharmacology, Assn. de Pharmacie Galenique Industrielle. Greek Catholic. Achievements include design and synthesis of pharmaceutical compounds in particular prodrugs and brain specific chemical drug delivery systems; M.O. calculations. Home: 810 SW 51st Way Gainesville FL 32607-3856

POPE, ANDREW JACKSON, JR. (JACK POPE), retired judge; b. Abilene, Tex., Apr. 18, 1913; s. Andrew Jackson and Ruth Adelia (Taylor) P.; m. Allene Esther Nichols, June 1½, 1938; children: Andrew Jackson III, Walter Allen. BA, Abilene Christian U., 1934, LLD (hon.), 1980; LLB, U. Tex., 1937; LLD (hon.), Pepperdine U., 1981, St. Mary's U., San Antonio, 1982, Okla. Christian U., 1983. Bar: Tex. 1937. Practice law Corpus Christi, 1937-46; judge 94th Dist. Ct., Corpus Christi, 1946-50; justice Ct. Civil Appeals, San Antonio, 1950-65; justice Supreme Ct. of Tex., Austin, 1965-82, chief justice, 1982-85. Author: John Berry & His Children, 1988; chmn. bd. editors Appellate Procedure in Tex., 1974; author numerous articles in law revs. and profl. jours. Pres. Met. YMCA, San Antonio, 1956-57; chmn. Tex. State Law Libr. Bd., 1973-80; trustee Abilene Christian U., 1958—. Seaman USNR, 1944-46. Recipient Silver Beaver award Alamo council Boy Scouts Am., 1961, Distinguished Eagle award, 1983; Rosewood Gavel award, 1962, St. Thomas More award, St. Mary's U., San Antonio, 1982; Outstanding Alumnus award Abilene Christian U., 1965; Greenhill Jud. award Mcpl. Judges Assn., 1980; Houston Bar Found. citation, 1985; San Antonio Bar Found. award, 1985; Disting. Jurist award Jefferson County Bar, 1985; Outstanding Alumnus award U. Tex. Law Alumni Assn., 1988; George Washington Honor medal Freedom Found., 1988; Disting. Lawyer award Travis County, 1992. Fellow Tex. Bar Found. (Law Rev. award 1979, 80, 81); mem. ABA, State Bar Tex. (pres. jud. sect. 1962, Outstanding Fifty Years Lawyer award 1994), Order of Coif, Nueces County (pres. 1946), Travis County Bar Assn., Bexar County Bar Assn., Tex. Philos. Soc., Austin Knife and Fork (pres. 1980), Am. Judicature Soc., Tex. State Hist. Assn., Tex. Supreme Ct. Hist. Soc. (v.p.), Sons of Republic of Tex., Christian Chronicle Coun. (chmn.), Masons, K.P. (grand chancellor 1946), Alpha Chi, Phi Delta Phi, Pi Sigma Alpha. Mem. Ch. of Christ. Home: 2803 Stratford Dr Austin TX 78746-4626

POPE, JESSE CURTIS, theology and religious studies educator; b. Corpus Christi, Tex., Feb. 22, 1955; s. Jesse Rondo and Doris Mae (Whisman) P.; m. Mary Ann Norman, Apr. 17, 1976; children: Jesse Morris, Ashley Elizabeth, Courtney Rebecca, Brianne Leah. AA, Fla. Coll., 1975; BA, Harding U., 1977, MA in Religion, 1978; PhD, Fla. State U., 1990. Min. Ctrl. Ch. of Christ, McAlpin, Fla., 1974-75, Noble Hill Ch. of Christ, Brighton, Mo., 1974, 76, Citizenship Ch. of Christ, McCrory, Ark., 1976-78, Harpersville (Ala.) Ch. of Christ, 1978-81, Moultrie Rd. Ch. of Christ, Thomasville, Ga., 1981-84, Northwood Ch. of Christ, Northport, Ala., 1984-92; min. Carrollwood Ch. of Christ, Tampa, Fla., 1992—, elder, 1994—; prof. Bible Fla. Coll., Temple Terrace, Fla., 1992—; evangelist in field; chmn. profl. devel. com. Fla. Coll., Temple Terrace, 1993—, fin. resources com., 1995—. Contbr. articles to profl. jours. Den leader Boy Scouts Am., Northport, 1986-90, asst. scoutmaster, 1990-92; mem. Nat. Congress Am. Indians, 1993—. Named One of Outstanding Young Men of Am., Jaycees, 1980, 84. Mem. Am. Soc. Ch. History, Bibl. Archael. Soc., Soc. Bibl. Lit., Descendants of Mex. War Vets., Evang. Theol. Soc., Sons of Confederate Vets (chaplain 1990-92), Sons of the Republic of Tex. Republican. Ch. of Christ. Home: 9403 Alanbrooke St Temple Terrace FL 33637-4960 Office: Fla Coll 119 Glen Arven Ave Tampa FL 33617

POPE, MARY ANN IRWIN, artist, designer; b. Louisville, Mar. 8, 1932; d. James Cecil Irwin and Margaret T. Taylor; m. Richard Coraine Pope, Nov. 25, 1954; children: Margaret Neil, Zachary Taylor, Richard Trent. Draftsman U.S. Army, Louisville, 1953-54; fashion artist Byck's, Louisville, 1956-59; freelance fashion artist, Louisville, 1960-66; design asst. Planning, Huntsville, Ala., 1979—; tchr. Huntsville Art League, 1966-78. One woman shows include Birmingham So. U., Ala., 1974, Montevallo Coll., Ala., 1977, 79, U. Ala., Huntsville Gallery, 1979, Kauffman Gallery, Houston, 1986, Isabel Anderson Comer Mus., Sylacauga, Ala., 1989; exhibited numerous group shows Water Tower Galleries, Ky., 1991, Armory Gallery, Montgomery, Ala, 1994, also in Ky., Ala., Ill.; represented in permanent collections Fine Arts Mus. of South, Mobile, Ala., Mint Mus. Art, Charlotte, N.C., Huntsville Mus. Art, Ala., Kennedy-Douglas Ctr. for the Arts, 1994, and numerous other pub. and pvt. collections. Recipient Merit award Art Quest, 1985, Purchase award Aqueous 84 Ky. Watercolor Soc., 1984, Purchase award, 1994, Purchase prize Piedmont Painting Exhibition Mint Mus. Art, Charlotte, 1972, Birmingham Mus. Art Biennial, 1985, Award of Excellence, Merit award Ga. Watercolor Soc., 1993, Purchase award, Aqueous, 1993,1984, Purchase award Watercolor West, 1995, and numerous other awards. Mem. Watercolor USA (corr. sec. nat. hon. soc., Mus. award Springfield Art Mus., Mo., 1982, 84, 89, Purchase prize 1989), Ky. Watercolor Soc. (bd. mem. 1977, Purchase award 1993), Birmingham Art Assn., Ala. Art League, Watercolor Soc. Ala. (adv. bd. 1988-89, asst. treas. 1989-90, pres. 1994-95). Home and Office: 1705 Greenwyche Rd SE Huntsville AL 35801-2113

POPE, RANDALL PATRICK, art director; b. McLean, Va., Apr. 24, 1966; s. Cadesman Jr. and Barbara Evelyn (Wagner) P.; m. Robin Leigh Ruddle, Nov. 19, 1988; children: Ethan Samuel, Abigail Caitlin. BFA, James Madison U., 1988. From asst. art dir. to art dir. Home Buyer Publ., Inc., Herndon, Chantilly, Va., 1988—; art dir. Log Home Living mag., 1989— (Ozzie awards 1989, 94). Office: 4200-T Lafayette Center Dr Chantilly VA 22021

POPE, ROBERT DANIEL, lawyer; b. Screven, Ga., Nov. 29, 1948; s. Robert Verlyn and Mae (McKey) P.; m. Teresa Ann Mullis, Jan. 26, 1981; children: Robert Daniel Jr., Veronica Teres, Jonathan Chase, Byron Christopher, Jessica Victoria. BS in Criminal Justice magna cum laude, Valdosta (Ga.) State Coll., 1975; JD, John Marshall Law Sch., Savannah, Ga., 1980. Bar: Ga. 1981, U.S. Dist. Ct. (no., mid. and so. dist.) Ga. 1983, U.S. Ct. Appeals Ga. 1982. Pvt. practice Cartersville, 1981—; mem. Valdosta Indigent Def. Atty. Panel, 1981-83, Bartow County Indigent Def. Panel, Cartersville, 1987-91, So. Dist. of Ga. Indigent Def. Panel, Brunswick, 1982-84; mem. Cobb County Cir. Defender's Panel for Indigent Criminal Def., Marietta, Ga., 1986—. Recognized as one of most successful criminal def. lawyers Cobb County Cir. Defenders Office, 1994. Mem. Ga. Assn. Criminal Def. Lawyers, Ga. Bar Assn. (criminal law sect.), Am. Criminal Justice Orgn. (Valdosta chpt. pres. 1974-75). Home: 74 Spruce Ln Cartersville GA 30120 Office: 140 W Cherokee Ave Cartersville GA 30120

POPE, ROBERT DEAN, lawyer; b. Memphis, Mar. 10, 1945; s. Ben Duncan and Phyllis (Drenner) P.; m. Elizabeth Dante Cohen, June 26, 1971; 1 child, Justin Nicholas Nathanson. AB, Princeton U., 1967; Diploma in Hist. Studies, Cambridge U., 1971; JD, Yale U., 1972, PhD, 1976. Bar: Va. 1974, D.C. 1980. Assoc. Hunton & Williams, Richmond, Va., 1974-80; ptnr. Hunton & Williams, Richmond, 1980—. Contbg. author: Disclosure Rules of Counsel in State and Local Government Securities Offerings, 2d edit., 1994. Mem. adv. com. Va. Sec. of Health and Human Svcs. on Continuing Care Legislation, 1992—; mem. Anthony Commn. on Pub. Fin.; adv. coun. dept. history Princeton U., 1987-91; mem. Mcpl. Securities Rulemaking Bd., 1996—. Mem. Govt. Fin. Officers Assn. (com. on govtl. debt and fiscal policy), Va. Bar Assn. (chmn. legal problems of elderly 1982-88), Nat. Assn. Bond Lawyers (treas. 1984-85, sec. 1985-86, pres. 1987-88, bd. dirs. 1982-89, Bernard P. Friel medal for contbns. to pub. fin. 1994), Am. Acad. Hosp. Attys., Yale Law Sch. Assn. (exec. com. 1985-88), Bond Club Va. (bd. dirs. 1990—, v.p. 1993-94, pres. 1994-95), NCCJ (Richmond area bd.), Phi Beta Kappa. Republican. Episcopalian. Home: 8707 Ruggles Rd Richmond VA 23229-7918 Office: Hunton & Williams PO Box 1535 951 E Byrd St Richmond VA 23219-4040

POPE, ROBERT GLYNN, telecommunications executive; b. Greenville, Tex., Dec. 5, 1935; s. Edwin R. P.; m. Shirley Hall, Dec. 30, 1958; children: Kenneth, Richard, David. BSME, So. Meth. U., 1958. Registered profl. engr. Chief engr. Southwestern Bell Telephone Co., Houston, 1973-77; v.p. staff Tex. Southwestern Bell Telephone Co., Dallas, 1977-78, v.p. centralized svcs., 1978-80; v.p. residence and pub. svcs. Southwestern Bell Telephone Co., St. Louis, 1980-81, v.p. transition, 1981-83, v.p. strategic planning, 1983; v.p. corp. devel. Southwestern Bell Corp., St. Louis, 1984-86, vice-chmn. corp. devel., 1986-88, vice chmn. corp. devel., chief fin. officer, 1988-90, vice chmn., chief fin. officer, 1990-94, now vice chmn., bd. dirs.; mem. Adv. Bd. Battery Ventures; bd. dirs. Boatmen's Bancshares Corp., Cullen/Frost Bankers, Inc. Trustee Maryville U.; mem. governing bd. Luth. Med. Ctr. With U.S. Army, 1959. Mem. NSPE, Mo. Soc. Profl. Engrs., Media Club St. Louis, Univ. Club, Golf Club Okla., Old Warson Country Club, St. Louis Club. Office: Southwestern Bell Corp PO Box 2933 175 E Houston 6th Fl San Antonio TX 78299-2933*

POPE, STEPHANIE MARIE, classicist, educator; b. Abilene, Tex., Apr. 19, 1953; d. Walter Steele and Ida Nora (Vickery) P. BA, Randolph-Macon Woman's Coll., 1975; MA, U. Cin., 1976. Latin tchr. Norfolk (Va.) Acad., 1977—; sec. North Am. Cambridge Classics Project, Amherst, Mass., 1987-96; cons. for Cambridge Latin course Cambridge Univ. Press, N.Y.C., 1989—; cons. Excel, Inc., Barrington, Ill., 1990—; dir. N.Am. Cambridge Classics Project, Amherst, 1996—. Author (workbook) Worksheets to Accompany C.L.C. Culture, 1994. Sec., v.p., pres. P.E.O., Norfolk, 1977—. Mem. Am. Classical League, Classical Assn. Middle and Western States, Classical Assn. Va. (v.p. 1993-94). Office: Norfolk Acad 1585 Wesleyan Dr Norfolk VA 23502

POPE, WILLIAM L., lawyer, judge; b. Brownsville, Tex., Nov. 5, 1960; s. William E. and Maria Antonieta P. AA, Tex. Southmost Coll., 1980; postgrad., U. Tex., 1980-81, Tex. Christian U., 1982, Tex. Coll. Osteo. Medicine, 1982-83; JD, Baylor U., 1986. Bar: Tex. 1986, U.S. Dist. Ct. (so. dist.) Tex. 1988, U.S. Supreme Ct. 1990. Assoc. Adams & Graham, Harlingen, Tex., 1986-91, ptnr., 1991—; mcpl. ct. judge City of La Feria, Tex., 1987—. Mem. ABA, Tex. State Bar Assn., Cameron County Bar Assn. Mem. Ch. of Christ. Office: Adams & Graham L L P PO Box 1429 Harlingen TX 78551-1429

PORCHER, ARTHUR GIGNILLIAT, III, association administrator; b. Ft. Belvoir, Va., Nov. 3, 1953; s. Arthur Gignilliat, II and Ruth Adele (Webb) P.; m. Jay Lynn Dailey, Sept. 1, 1990; children: Boone Postell, Julia Callaway; m. Rebecca Lynn Burkhardt, July 2, 1977 (div. 1981); 1 child, Arthur Gignilliat IV. BSc in Bus. Adminstrn., U. Cen. Fla., 1977, BA in Psychology, 1991. Br. mgr., loan officer Security Fed. Savings, Vero Beach, Fla., 1977-80; asst. gen. mgr. Deerfield Groves Co., Vero Beach, 1980-82; cons. Third Wave Systems, Inc., Seattle, 1982-86; controller Evergreen Programs, Seattle, 1984-86; acctng. mgr. Wall Systems, Inc., Orlando, Fla., 1986-90; mental health counselor Project III Ctrl. Fla., Orlando, Fla., 1990-

92; adminstr. Orlando Foot and Ankle Clinic, 1992-94; v.p. adminstrn. Goodwill Industries of Ctrl. Fla., Orlando, 1994-96; exec. dir. Youth Options, Orlando, 1996—. Co-Author: Helping Chronically Addicted Adolescents, 1993. Episcopalian. Home: 30 Forest Cir Orlando FL 32803-6246

PORENSKI, HARRY STEPHEN, material engineer; b. Louisville, June 23, 1945; s. Harry Stephen Sr. and Nellie Adelade (Jeffries) P.; m. Geraldine Crawford, Aug. 1967; 1 child, Lisa Marie. BA in Edn., U. Ky., 1968; MS in Physics, U. Louisville, 1977. Sci., math. tchr. Jefferson County Bd. Edn., Louisville, 1969-71; mfg. supr. Brown & Williamson Tobacco Co., Louisville, 1972-74, rsch. physicist, 1974-89; sr. material engr. Brown & Williamson Tobacco Co., Macon, Ga., 1989—. Mem. Am. Physical Soc. Republican. Baptist. Home: 100 Wexford Circle Bonaire GA 31005 Office: Brown & Williamson Tobacco 2600 Weaver Rd PO Box 1056 Macon GA 31298

PORIES, WALTER JULIUS, surgeon, educator; b. Munich, Germany, Jan. 18, 1930; came to U.S., 1940; s. Theodore Francis and Frances (Lowin) P.; m. Muriel Helen Aronson, Aug. 18, 1951; children: Susan E., Mary Jane, Carolyn A., Kathy G.; m. Mary Ann Rose McCarthy, June 4, 1977; children: Mary Lisa, Michael McCarthy. BA, Wesleyan U., Middletown, Conn., 1952; MD with honors, U. Rochester, 1955. Diplomate: Am. Bd. Surgery, Am. Bd. Thoracic Surgery. Intern Strong Meml. Hosp., Rochester, N.Y., 1955-56, resident, 1958-62; chmn. dept. surgery Wright-Patterson AFB, Ohio, 1952-67; asst. prof. surgery and oncology U. Rochester, 1967-69; prof. surgery and assoc. chmn. dept. surgery U. Cleve., 1969-77; prof. surgery and biochemistry East Carolina U., Greenville, N.C., 1977—, chmn. dept. surgery, 1977-96; chief surgery Pitt County Meml. Hosp., 1977-96; prof. surgery U. Health Scis. of Uniformed Svcs., 1982—; founder, assoc. dir. Rochester Cancer Ctr., 1967-69; founder, dir. Cleve. Cancer Ctr., 1972-77, Hospice of Cleve., 1975; founder, chmn. bd. Hospice of Greenville, 1981; med. dir. Home Health Care of Greenville, 1978-83; founder, chmn. bd. Ctr. for Creative Living, 1985-91; pres., chmn. Eastern Carolina Health Orgn. and Echo Mgmt. Orgn., 1994—; vis. scholar NIH, 1996. Author: Clinical Applications of Zinc Metabolism, 1974; editor: Operative Surgery series, vols. 1-4, 1979-83, Office Surgery for Family Physicians, 1985; editor in chief Current Surgery, 1990—; editor Nat. Curriculum for Residency in Surgery, 1988—, mem. residency rev. com., 1992—; contbr. articles to profl. jours. Bd. dirs. Boy Scouts Am., Cleve., 1974-77, Greenville Arts Mus., 1980-82; pres., CEO, chmn. bd. dirs. Ea. Carolina Health Orgn. Maj. USAF, 1955-67; col. USAR, 1979-91, comdr. USAF Hosp., Durham, N.C.; activated Desert Shield, 1990. Decorated Legion of Merit; Thorndyke scholar, 1948-51; recipient McLester award USAF, 1966, Miss. Magnolia Cross, 1989, Presdl. citation for Desert Shield, 1994; named to Hon. Order of Ky. Cols., 1965. Fellow ACS, Am. Coll. Cardiology, Am. Coll. Chest Physicians; mem. Soc. for Vascular Surgery, Soc. Surg. Oncology, Soc. Univ. Surgeons, Am. Surg. Assn., Soc. Environ. Geochemistry (past pres.), Residency Rev. Com. for Surgery, So. Surg. Assn., Soc. for Thoracic Surgery, Ea. Carolina Health Orgn. (pres., chmn. bd. 1994—), Assn. Programs Dirs. in Surgery (pres. 1995-96), N.C. Surg. Assn. (pres. 1995-96), Greenville Country Club, Sigma Xi, Phi Kappa Phi. Republican. Roman Catholic. Home: Deep Sun Farm 7464 NC 43 N Macclesfield NC 27852 Office: East Carolina U Dept Surgery Greenville NC 27858

PORTALES, MARCO ANTONIO, English language educator, executive assistant; b. Edinburg, Tex., Oct. 22, 1948; s. Toribio Narvaez and Maria del Carmen SalvaTierra (Moya) P.; m. Candida Rita Abrams, Feb. 12, 1972; children: Carlos Antonio, Marie Cristina. Student, Pan Am. U., 1966-68; BA in English, U. Tex., 1970; PhD in English, SUNY, Buffalo, 1974. Asst. prof. Englsh U. Calif., Berkeley, 1974-79; dean of Arts and Scis. Tex. Southmost U., Brownsville, 1987-88; assoc. prof. lit. U. Houston, Clear Lake, 1979-89, prof. lit., 1989-91; prof. English Tex. A&M U., College Station, 1991—, dir. undergrad. studies, 1992-93, interim dir. Race and Ethnic Studies Inst., 1993-94, faculty rep. Hispanic Profl. Network, 1991—, prof. English, exec. asst. to pres., 1996—; book reviewer N.Y. Times Book Rev., 1984; vis. scholar NEH, 1992; book cons. Harper Collins, D.C. Heath, U. Tex. Press, 1992; book manuscript reader U. Tenn. Press, 1988, 90; presenter Tex. A&M U., 1992, 93, Am. Lit. Assn. Conf., San Diego, 1990, 92, Am. Studies Assn. Conv., Toronto, 1989, Purdue U., 1989, MLA Afro-Am. Forum, St. Louis, 1985, Westbrook Coll., Portland, Maine, 1985, MLA Conf., San Francisco, 1987, U. Houston, 1983, MLA Conv., L.A., 1982, among others. Author: Youth and Age in American Literature, 1989; contbr. articles to profl. jours. Recipient scholarship U. Tex., 1969-70; fellow SUNY, Buffalo, 1970-74. Mem. Multi-Ethnic Lit. of U.S. (pres. 1992-94, sec. 1988-90, program chair 1985-87, assoc. editor MELUS 1982-88, mem. editorial bd. 1980-82). Roman Catholic. Office: Tex A&M U Dept English College Station TX 77843

PORTEOUS, THOMAS CLARK, retired newspaper editor; b. New Orleans, La., July 10, 1910; s. Alfred Jones and Catherine Dorothy (Plaisance) P.; m. Maragaret Clay Mack, Jan. 9, 1996; children: Cathy Sutton, Thomas Alfred, David Clarke, Donald B., Sarah, John Cross. BA, Rhodes Coll., 1934. Reporter, city editor, polit. columnist Memphis Press-Scimitar, 1934-81; editor Collierville (Tenn.) Herald, 1981-89, assoc. editor, 1989-96; retired, 1996. Author: Southwind Blows, 1948; contbr. articles to profl. jours. Sgt. U.S. Army, 1944-46. Nieman fellow Harvard U., 1946-47. Democrat. Roman Catholic. Home: 508 Dogwood Dr NW Lawrenceville GA 30245-7482

PORTER, ALLEN WAYNE, bail bondsman; b. Pueblo, Colo., June 14, 1936; s. Leo Irwin and Lillian Pearl (Hanson) P.; m. Doris R. Gardner, Nov. 22, 1957 (div. July 1981); 1 child, Irwin Bryant; m. Mabel Leigh Blankenship, Sept. 1, 1981. AS in Security Adminstrn., Tidewater Community Coll., Chesapeake, Va., 1976; BS in Polit. Sci., Christopher Newport Coll., Newport News, Va., 1981. Cert. pvt. security and fire arms instr., Va. Enlisted USN, 1954, advanced through grades to chief petty officer, 1968, ret., 1973; ins. fraud investigator Wackenhut Corp., Norfolk, Va., 1973-76; mgr. investigations for Va. and N.C. Wackenhut Corp., Virginia Beach, Va., 1976-78, dist. mgr. for Va. and N.C., 1978-81; bail bondsman Chesapeake and Portsmouth, Va., 1981—; assoc. prof. criminal justice Thomas Nelson Jr. Coll., Newport News, 1978. Lectr. on security, criminal justice system, bail bonding to various clubs. Mem. Nat. Assn. Chief Police (v.p. 1979-80, named to Am. Police Hall of Fame Legion of Honor 1980), Va. Sheriff's Assn., Chesapeake Bonding Assn. (sec.), Fleet Res. Assn., Masons. Republican. Home and Office: 205 Allen Dr Chesapeake VA 23320-5439

PORTER, BETTY MELISSA GRIFFITH, nursing education administrator; b. Greenup, Ky., Aug. 28, 1940; d. Ruben David and Virgie J. (Rose) Griffith; m. Arvis Porter, Dec. 29, 1962; children--Anthony Wayne (dec.), Roger Dewane. Diploma in nursing Kings' Daus. Hosp. Sch. Nursing, Ashland, Ky., 1961; B.S., Morehead State U., 1971, M.H.Ed., 1973, M.S., 1977, Ed.S., 1977; B.S.N., U. Ky., 1979, M.S.N., 1981, Ed.D., 1984, cert. family nurse practitioner, 1995. Staff nurse Kings' Daus. Hosp., 1961; team leader U. Ky. Med. Ctr., Lexington, 1962; nurse in physician's office, Morehead, Ky., 1964-68; asst. prof. nursing Morehead State U., 1972-79, acting coordinator A.D.N. program, 1979-80, head dept. nursing and allied health sci., 1983-92, 95—, prof. nursing, 1988—; workshop presenter; mem. exec. bd. Area Health Edn. System, 1976-79. Recipient Disting. Faculty award Morehead State U. Sch. Applied Scis. and Tech., 1979. Mem. Ky. Nurses Assn. (pres. dist. #19 1972-75, pres. 1987-89), Am. Nurses Assn., Nat. League Nursing, Ky. League Nursing (chmn. membership 1979-80, Nurse Educator of Yr. 1986), AMA Aux., Ky. Med. Assn. Aux., Ky. Council Higher Edn. (sub-com. on nursing edn. 1979), Sigma Theta Tau (research com. delta Psi chpt. 1982). Republican. Baptist. Avocations: needlepoint, gardening, water sports.

PORTER, CHARLES RALEIGH, JR., lawyer; b. Waco, Tex., Sept. 22, 1922; s. Charles Raleigh and Virginia Louise (Bowen) P.; m. Alice Mungall, Sept. 16, 1946; children—Charles Raleigh III, Melissa Ann, Alice Marguerite, Daniel Bowen. BBA, U. Tex., 1943, JD, 1949. Bar: Tex. 1948, U.S. Dist. Ct. (so. dist.) Tex. 1949, Ct. Appeals (5th cir.) 1955, U.S. Dist. Ct. (we. dist.) Tex. 1972, U.S. Dist. Ct. (no. dist.) Tex. 1977. Asst. Nueces County Attys. Office, Corpus Christi, Tex., 1949-50, Dist. Attys. Office, Corpus Christi, 1950-53; ptnr. Anderson & Porter, Corpus Christi, 1953-63, Sorrell, Anderson & Porter, 1964-68, Porter, Rogers, Dahlman & Gordon, 1969—; dir. Tex. Commerce Bank-Corpus Christi; mem. adv. bd. dirs. Frost Nat. Bank, San Antonio. Bd. dirs. Meth. Home, Waco; mem. exec. bd. Perkins Sch. Theology, So. Meth. U. Lt. (j.g.) USNR, 1944-46, PTO. Fellow ABA, Tex. Bar Found.; mem. Nueces County Bar Assn. (pres. 1959-60), Tex. Assn. Def. Counsel, Internat. Assn. Def. Counsel, U. Tex. Law Sch. Alumni Assn. (bd. dirs.), Masons (32 degree). Republican. Methodist. Home: 33 Blue Heron St Rockport TX 78382 Office: Porter Rogers Dahlman & Gordon 1 Shoreline Pla 800 N Shoreline Blvd Ste 800 Corpus Christi TX 78401-3700

PORTER, DOUGLAS TAYLOR, athletic administrator; b. Fayetteville, Tenn., Aug. 15, 1928; s. Waudell Phillip and Sophia Mae (Taylor) P.; m. Jean Butcher, Apr. 18, 1953; children: Daria C., Blanche E., Douglas V. BS, Xavier U., 1952; MS, Ind. U., 1960. Asst. football coach St. Augustine High Sch., Memphis, 1955, Xavier U., New Orleans, 1956-60; dir. athletics, head football coach Miss. Vocat. Coll., Itta Bena, Miss., 1960-65; assoc. dir. athletics, coach Grambling (La.) State U., 1966-73; head football coach Howard U., Washington, 1974-78; dir. athletics, head football coach Ft. Valley (Ga.) State Coll., 1979—; pres. Nat. Athletic Steering Com., Ft. Valley, 1990—. Lt. U.S. Army, 1951-54. Mem. Am. Alliance of Health, Phys. Edn. and Dance, Nat. Assn. of Collegiate Dirs. of Athletics, Sigma Pi Phi, Alpha Phi Alpha (pres. 1983-87), Phi Delta Kappa. Democrat. Roman Catholic. Home: 107 College Ct Fort Valley GA 31030-3216 Office: Ft Valley State Coll 1005 State College Dr Fort Valley GA 31030-3262

PORTER, EXA LYNN, librarian; b. Stillwater, Okla., Sept. 6, 1945; d. John Albert and Exa Oneil (Dunn) Roth; m. Patrick Earl Porter, Aug. 27, 1966; children: Vanessa Lynn Porter Cannon, Stephen Patrick. BS, Abilene Christian Coll., 1966; MLS, Sam Houston State U., 1982; EdD, U. Houston, 1994. Cert. secondary edn. tchr., learning resources, Tex. Math. tchr. Patrick Henry Jr. High Sch., Houston, 1978-79, Sam Houston High Sch., Houston, 1979-80, Kingwood Middle Sch., Humble, Tex., 1980-82; reference libr. North Harris Coll., Houston, 1982—; chair faculty senate social com. North Harris Coll., 1985-88, mem. steering com. for self-study for accreditation, 1989-90. Bible class tchr. Lake Houston Ch. of Christ, Humble, 1982—. Mem. Tex. Jr. Coll. Tchrs. Assn., Tex. Libr. Assn. (dist. VIII chair, local arrangements chair), ALA. Home: 7327 Misty Morning Humble TX 77346 Office: North Harris Coll 2700 WW Thorne Dr Houston TX 77073

PORTER, HAYDEN SAMUEL, computer science educator; b. Cin., June 2, 1945; s. Hayden Samuel and Thelma (Wulfeck) P.; m. Patricia Maloney, Sept. 28, 1967; children: Hayden, Emily. BS, U. Cin., 1967, PhD, 1973. Postdoctoral fellow U. Fla., Gainesville, 1973-76; sr. mem. tech. staff Computer Sci. Corp., Silver Springs, Md., 1976-79; pres. A2D, Co., Inc., Greenville, S.C., 1981—; Daniel disting. prof. computer sci., chmn. Furman U., Greenville, 1979—. Author: Exploring Macintosh, 1989, Exploring Macintosh Applications, 1989, Exploring Microsoft Works, 1991, Essentials of Lotus 1-2-3 for Macintosh, 1992; contbr. articles to profl. jours. Grantee in field. Mem. Am. Geophys. Union, Am. Phys. Soc., IEEE, Assn. for Computing Machinery (activity monitor 1983—), Sigma Xi.

PORTER, HOWARD LEONARD, III, health policy consultant; b. Denver, July 12, 1945; s. Howard Leonard and Margaret (Johnson) P.; m. Mary Ellen Biciste, June 22, 1968; 1 child, Andrew James. BA, Monmouth (Ill.) Coll., 1967; MS, U. Ill., Champaign, 1968; MBA U. Fla., 1995. Pres. The Porter Co., 1968—; sr. v.p. HCI Preferred Care, Inc., Auberndale, Fla., 1992—; v.p. Roswell E. Johnson Inst. Comm. Rsch., 1992—. Served with Med. Svc. Corps, USAF, 1969-72. Mem. Phi Kappa Phi (hon.). Republican. Presbyterian. Contbr. articles to profl. publs. Home: 2068 Katie Ct Winter Haven FL 33884-3113 Office: PO Box 7533 Winter Haven FL 33883-7533

PORTER, JAMES FRANKLIN, psychologist; b. White Plains, N.Y., Sept. 21, 1951; s. Franklin Wright and Mary Ellen (Herrick) P.; m. Julie Reinberg, Sept. 1, 1991; 1 child, Leah Michelle. BA, Webster Coll., St. Louis, 1974; MS, U. Tex., Dallas, 1980; PhD, U. North Tex., 1992. Lic. psychologist, Tex. Eligibility and social worker Tex. Dept. Human Resources, Dallas, 1974-76, 78-80; caseworker II Heart of Tex. Mental Health/Mental Retardation Ctr., Waco, 1980-84; lic. profl. counselor in pvt. practice Wace and Dallas, 1983-95; psychol. assoc. various orgns., Dallas, 1987-90; psychol. assoc. Timberlawn Mental Health Sys., Dallas, 1990-94, clinic dir. and clin. psychologist, 1994—; psychology clin. and cons. practice Irving, Tex., 1994—. Peer reviewer Jour. Personality and Social Psychology, 1995, Jour. applied Social Psychology, 1995; contbr. articles to profl. jours. Mem. APA, Tex. Psychol. Assn., Am. Soc. Clin. Hypnosis, N.Y. Acad. Scis. Office: Timberlawn Mental Health System 420 Decker Dr #160 Irving TX 75062

PORTER, JAMES KENNETH, retired judge; b. Newport, Tenn., Apr. 6, 1934; s. John Calhoun and Bessie Betis (Crouch) P.; m. Evelyn Janet Rhodes, Sept. 17, 1955; children: Jane Caroline, James Kenneth Jr. BS, U. Tenn., 1955, JD, 1957. Bar: Tenn. 1957, U.S. Dist. Ct. (ea. dist.) Tenn. 1958, U.S. Ct. Appeals (6th cir.) 1971. Ptnr. Porter, Porter & Dunn, Porter & Porter, Newport, 1957-74; state rep. Tenn. Gen. Assembly, Nashville, 1961-65, minority fl. leader, 1963-65; county atty. Cocke County, Tenn., 1961-63, commr. County Election Commn., 1966-72, chmn., 1968-70; mem. Tenn. Senate, Nashville, 1972-74; state cir. judge 4th Jud. Cir., Newport, 1974-93; ret., 1993; state presiding judge 4th Jud. Cir., Newport, 1984-86, 88-90, 1992-93; judgeship nominee U.S. Dist. Ct. (ea. dist.), Tenn., 1986; Tenn. Ct. Appeals nominee, 1990; del. S.E. Law Rev. Conf., Durham, N.C., 1957, Nat. Conf. State Legislator Leaders, Boston, 1963; discussion leader Nat. Jud. Coll., Reno, 1981, faculty adviser, 1982; mem. Gov.'s Correction Overcrowding Commn., Nashville, 1985-86. Contbr. articles to U. Tenn. Law Rev., 1956-57, editor in chief, 1957. Active Farm Bur., 1962-82; mem. adv. coun., trustee Walters State Community Coll., Morristown, Tenn., 1975-86. Mem. ABA (Tenn. jud. del. 1984), Tenn. Jud. Conf. (v.p. 1980-81), Tenn. Trial Judges Assn. (bd. dirs. 1976-86, pres. 1982-85), Tenn. Bar Assn. (spl. trial counsel 1973-76), Cocke County Bar Assn., Smoky Mountain Country Club (bd. dirs. 1964-67, v.p. 1966-67), Order of Coif, Sigma Alpha Epsilon (Highest Effort Law award 1986), Phi Delta Phi. Republican. Baptist. Home: 306 North St Newport TN 37821-2413 Office: 106 S Mims Ave Newport TN 37821-3125

PORTER, JAMES WATSON, ecology and marine science educator; b. Tiffin, Ohio, Oct. 5, 1946; s. Edwards N. and Augusta (Watson) P.; m. Karen Glaus, Jan. 1, 1972; 1 child, Delene W. BS in Biology, Yale Coll., 1969; PhD in Biology, Yale U., 1973. Asst. prof. Sch. Natural Resources U. Mich., Ann Arbor, 1973-77; assoc. prof. dept. zoology U. Ga., Athens, 1977-84, prof., 1984-93, prof. Inst. Ecology, 1993—; Smithsonian predoctoral fellow ,,,sithsonian Tropical Rsch. Isnt., Balboa, Republic of Panama, 1971-72; curator invertebrates U. Ga. Mus. Natural History, Athens, Ga., 1985—; coord. Foun. Fellows Program U. Ga., 1984-87, grad. coord. Inst. Ecology, 1992—, assoc. dir., 1993-96. Editor Ecology, 1975-80; contbr. articles to profl. jours. Grantee NSF, 1978—, EPA, 1985—. Democrat. Episcopalian. Home: 125 Cloverhurst Cir Athens GA 30606 Office: U Ga Inst Ecology Athens GA 30602

PORTER, JOAN MARGARET, elementary education educator; b. Vernon, Tex., Dec. 25, 1937; d. Elton Lonnie and Clara Pearl (Yeager) Smith; m. Claude Walker Porter, Feb. 13, 1960; children: Jolene Porter Mohindroo, Richard Euin, Vonda Sue, Darla Ailese Porter Blomquist. BA, Wayland Bapt. U., 1960; M in Elem. Edn., Ea. N.Mex. U., 1981, bilingual endorsement, 1982. cert. classroom tchr., N.Mex. ESL tchr. Jefferson Elem. Sch., Lovington, N.Mex., 1979-81, tchr. first grade, 1981-82; tchr. bilingual first grade Jefferson Elem. Sch., Lovington, 1982-89; tchr. bilingual first grade Highland Elem. Sch., Plainview, Tex., 1989-91, 1992—, tchr. first grade, 1991-92, tchr. bilingual first grade, 1992-95, tchr. bilingual second grade, 1995-96; vol. tchr. Cert. Adult Literacy, Lovington. Mem. PTA, Assn. Tex. Profl. Educators, Delta Kappa Gamma (profl. affairs com. chmn. 1991), Phi Kappa Phi. Southern Baptist. Home: 101 Juanita St Plainview TX 79072-7625 Office: Highland Elem Sch 1707 W 11th St Plainview TX 79072-6439

PORTER, LEAH LEEARLE, biological researcher; b. Remington, Va., Sept. 19, 1963; d. James Wallace and Earline Yvonne (Moore) P. BS, U. Md., 1985; MS, Cornell U., 1990, PhD, 1993. Biol. technician U.S. Dept. Agr., Beltsville, Md., 1981-85; agrl. cons. Md. Dept. Agr., College Park, 1985; cons., office mgr. Carpigraphics, Inc., Beltsville, 1985-86; grad. rsch. asst. Cornell U., Ithaca, N.Y., 1986-94; cons., mktg. asst. LeEarle Enterprises, Ithaca, 1988-94; mgr. internat. project Glahe Cons. Group, Washington, 1994-95; rsch. mgr. Chem. Mfrs. Assn., Washington, 1995—; cons., mktg. asst. Le Earle Enterprises, Ithaca, 1988-93. Md. State Senate scholar, 1984-85; faculty grad. fellow Cornell U., 1986-87. Fellow N.Y. Acad. Scis.; mem. Am. Phytopathological Soc., Assn. Women in Sci., Black Grad. and Profl. Students, Alpha Chi Sigma, Zeta Phi Beta. Democrat. Baptist. Office: 1300 Wilson Blvd Arlington VA 22209

PORTER, WAYNE RANDOLPH, dermatologist; b. Washington, Jan. 10, 1948; s. James Randolph and Betty Rose (Burgess) P.; BS, MIT, 1970; MD, Duke U., 1973. Intern, U. Miami Affiliated Hosps., 1973-74, resident in internal medicine U. Miami Sch. Medicine (Fla.), 1973-76, resident in dermatology, 1976-78, clin. instr., then asst. prof. dermatology, 1978-85, assoc. prof., 1985—; practice medicine specializing in dermatology, North Miami Beach, 1978—; mem. staff U. Miami-Jackson Meml. Hosp., North Shore Med. Ctr., Parkway Regional Med. Ctr., Aventura Hosp. Diplomate Am. Bd. Internal Medicine, Am. Bd. Dermatology. Mem. med. adv. bd. Dade-Broward chpt. Lupus Found. Am. Fellow Internat. Soc. for Dermatologic Surgery, Am. Acad. Dermatology, Am. Assn. Dermatologic Surgeons; mem. AMA, Dade County Med. Assn., Fla. Med. Assn., Fla. Dermatology Soc., Miami Dermatol. Soc., So. Med. Assn., ACP, Internat. Soc. Pediatric Dermatology, Miami Dermatol. Soc. (pres.). Club: Bath Club (Miami beach). Home: 3550 Rockerman Rd Miami FL 33133 Office: 909 N Miami Beach Blvd Miami FL 33162-3712

PORTER, WILMA JEAN, university director; b. Sylacauga, Ala., May 30, 1931; d. Harrison Samuel and Blanche Leonard Butcher; m. Douglas Taylor Porter, Apr. 18, 1953; children: Daria Cecile, Blanche Evette, Douglas Vincent. BS, Tuskegee U., 1951; MS, Mich. State U., 1966; PhD, Iowa State U., 1980. Asst. dietitian Miss. State Tb Sanatorium, 1951-52; therapeutic dietitian dept. of hosp. City of N.Y., S.I., 1952-53; libr. asst. Mississippi Valley State Coll., Itta Bena, Miss., 1963-65; asst. prof. Grambling (La.) State U., 1966-75, Howard U., Washington, 1976-80; country dir. U.S. Peace Corps, Tonga, 1980-82; asst. dir. internat. programs Ft. Valley (Ga.) Coll., 1983-84, dir. Inst. Advancement, 1984-88; dir. Sch. Home Econs., Tenn. Technol. U., Cookeville, 1989—; project dir. Capitol Hill Health and Homemaker, Washington, 1982-83; interim dir. Inst. Advancement Alcorn State U., Lorman, Miss., 1988-89. Author lab. manual for quantity foods, 1977; editor: (cookbook) Some Christmas Foods and Their Origins from Around the World, 1983. Convenor Nat. Issues Forums, Ga. and Tenn., 1985—; citizen participant Nat. Issues Forums Soviet Dialogue, Newport Beach, Calif., 1988; bd. dirs. Leadership Putnam, Cookeville, 1990-94; chmn. Tenn. Technol. U. campaign United Way, 1989; mem. devel. and planning com. Peach County Ft. Valley, 1985-87; mem. Peach County Heart Fund Dr., 1986-88; participant People to People Citizens Amb. program U.S./China Women's Issues Program, 1995. Title III grantee U.S. Dept. Edn., 1986, 87; Tenn. Dept. Human Svcs. grantee, 1993, 94. Mem. AAUW (program chair 1991-92, pres. Cookeville br. 1993-94), Am. Home Econs. Assn., Am. Dietetic Assn., Nat. Coun. Adminstrs. Home Econs., Tenn. Home Econs. Assn., Tenn. Dietetic Assn. Democrat. Roman Catholic. Home: 512 Fisk Rd Cookeville TN 38501-2925

PORTERFIELD, NOLAN, English language educator, writer; b. Milliken, Colo., Feb. 26, 1936; s. Afton Arthur and Ora Oneda (Beattie) P.; m. Peggy Pearce, Dec. 21, 1956 (div. 1980); 1 child, Kelly Lynn; m. Erika Brady, Sept. 20, 1981. BA, Tex. Tech. U., 1962, MA, 1964; PhD, U. Iowa, 1970. Reporter Gallup (N.Mex.) Daily Ind., 1955; advt. mgr. Lamesa (Tex.) Daily Reporter, 1955-56, pub., 1956-58; instr. English S.E. Mo. State U., Cape Girardeau, 1964-70, asst. prof. English, 1970-74, assoc. prof. English, 1974-78, prof. English, writer-in-residence, 1978-95; cons. Smithsonian Press, Washington, 1981-86. Author: A Way of Knowing, 1971 (Best Novel of Tex. Inst. of Letters 1971), Jimmie Rodgers, 1979 (ASCAP award 1979), Last Cavalier: The Life and Times of John A. Lomax, 1996; editor: Trail to Marked Tree, 1968; contbr. short stories to nat. mags. With U.S. Army, 1958-60. Mem. Am. Folklore Soc., Assn. for Recorded Sound Collections. Home: 564 Boyce Fairview Rd Alvaton KY 42122-9648

PORTIS, CHARLES MCCOLL, reporter, writer; b. El Dorado, Ark., Dec. 28, 1933; s. Samuel Palmer and Alice (Waddell) P. BA, U. Ark., 1958. Reporter The Comml. Appeal, Memphis, 1958, Ark. Gazette, Little Rock, 1959-60, N.Y. Herald Tribune, N.Y.C., 1960-64. Author: Norwood, 1966, True Grit, 1968, The Dog of the South, 1979, Masters of Atlantis, 1985, Gringos, 1991. Sgt. USMC, 1952-55, Korea. Presbyterian. Home: 7417 Kingwood Rd Little Rock AR 72207-1734

PORTIS, EDWARD BRYAN, political science educator; b. Seattle, July 27, 1945; s. Everett E. and Jacquelin G. (Gates) P.; m. Susan Lemmon, Jan. 12, 1974; children: Margaret, Catherine, Elizabeth. BA, Eastern Mont. Coll., 1968; MA, U. S.D., 1969; PhD, Vanderbilt U., 1973. Vis. instr. Fisk U., Nashville, 1971; vis. asst. prof. Vanderbilt U., Nashville, 1972-74; vis. lectr. U. Ga., Athens, 1974-77; asst. prof., then prof. Tex. A&M U., College Station, 1978—; vis. prof. U. Salford, Eng., 1988-89. Author: Max Weber and Political Commitment, 1986, Reconstructing the Classics, 1994; author, editor: Political Theory and Policy Science, 1988; co-editor Jour. Politics, 1993—, book review editor, 1987-93. Office: Tex A&M U Dept Polit Sci College Station TX 77843

PORTMAN, GLENDA CAROLENE, forensic document examiner; b. Ponca City, Okla., Oct. 8, 1946; d. Thomas Harold and Betty Lou (Russell) Godwin; m. David Edwin Portman, Jan. 22, 1967; children: Stephanie Lynn, Stacey Leigh. BA, Okla. State U., 1969. Forensic document examiner Tulsa, 1987—. Editor Jour. Questioned Document Examination, 1995—; contbr. articles to profl. jours. Mem. Ind. Assn. Questioned Document Examiners (cert. document examiner, dir. 1988-90, sec. 1992-97, Pres.'s award 1996), Assn. Cert. Fraud Examiners (cert. fraud examiner, dir. 1996), PEO (officer 1982—). Episcopalian. Office: 10809 S Sandusky Tulsa OK 74137

PORTMAN, GLENN ARTHUR, lawyer; b. Cleve., Dec. 26, 1949; s. Alvin B. and Lenore (Marsh) P.; m. Katherine Seaborn, Aug. 3, 1974 (div. 1984); m. Susan Newell, Jan. 3, 1987. BA in History, Case Western Res. U., 1968; JD, So. Meth. U., 1975. Bar: Tex. 1975, U.S. Dist. Ct. (no. dist.) Tex. 1975, U.S. Dist. Ct. (so. dist.) Tex. 1983, U.S. Dist. Ct. (we. and ea. dists.) Tex. 1988. Assoc. Johnson, Bromberg & Leeds, Dallas, 1975-80, ptnr., 1980-92; ptnr. Arter, Hadden, Johnson & Bromberg, Dallas, 1992-95, Arter & Hadden, Dallas, 1996—; chmn. bd. dirs. Physicians Regional Hosp., 1994-96; mem. exec. bd. So. Meth. U. Sch. Law, 1994—; lectr. bankruptcy topics South Tex. Coll. Law, State Bar Tex. Asst. editor-in-chief Southwestern Law Jour., 1974-75; contbr. articles to profl. jours. Firm rep. United Way Met. Dallas, 1982-92; treas. Lake Highlands Square Homeowners Assn., 1990-93. Mem. ABA, Am. Bankruptcy Inst., State Bar Tex. Assn., Dallas Bar Assn., So. Meth. U. Law Alumni Assn. (council bd. dirs., v.p. 1980-86, chmn. admissions com., chmn. class agt. program 1986-89, chmn. fund raising 1989-91), 500 Club Inc., Assemblage Club. Republican. Methodist. Home: 9503 Winding Ridge Dr Dallas TX 75238-1451 Office: Arter & Hadden 1717 Main St Ste 4100 Dallas TX 75201-7302

PORTMAN, SUSAN NEWELL, lawyer; b. El Dorado, Kans., Sept. 12, 1953; d. Richard and Denise (Beaudequin) Newell; m. Glenn A. Portman, Jan. 2, 1987. BS in Math., U. Okla., 1975; JD summa cum laude, Am. U., 1982. Bar: Tex. 1983, U.S. Dist. Ct. (no. dist.) Tex. 1983. Math. statistician U.S. Dept. Labor Bur. Labor Statistics, Washington, 1975-76; assoc. Johnson, Bromberg & Leeds, Dallas, 1983-87; div. counsel Nat. Gypsum Co., Dallas, 1987-88, corp. counsel, 1988-91, sr. corp. counsel and asst. sec., 1991-93. Treas. Lake Highlands Square Homeowners Assn., Dallas, 1991-93. Named Deans fellow Am. U., recipient Mussey Prize. Mem. So. Meth. U. Sch. Law Corp. Coun., 500 Inc. Club, Pi Mu EPsilon, Alpha Lambda Delta. Democrat. Presbyterian. Home and Office: 9503 Winding Ridge Dr Dallas TX 75238-1451

POSEY, CLYDE LEE, business administration and accounting educator; b. Tucumcari, New Mex., Dec. 27, 1940; s. Rollah P. and Opal (Patterson) P.; m. Dora Diane Vassar; children: Amanda Fox, Julia Forsythe, Rebecca; m. Judith James Jerry, July 31, 1991; stepchildren: David Jerry, Georgia Kenyan. BBA, U. Tex., El Paso, 1963; MBA, U. Tex., 1965; postgrad., U. So. Calif., 1968; PhD, Okla. State U., 1978. CPA, Calif., La., Tex. Lab. aide FBI, Washington, 1959-60; acct. Lipson, Cox & Colton (now Deloitte & Touche), El Paso, Tex., 1962; auditor Main & Co. (now KPMG Peat

Marwick), El Paso, 1963; teaching asst. U. Tex., Austin, 1963-65; tax cons. Peat, Marwick, Mitchell & Co., Dallas, 1965-66; cons. Roberson, Martin, Horg and Ryckman, Fresno, Calif., 1967; CPA pvt. practice Fresno, Ruston, Calif., La, 1966—; asst. prof. Calif. State U., Fresno, 1966-76; assoc. prof. La. Tech. U., Ruston, 1978-84, prof., 1984—; vis. asst. prof. Ctrl. State U., Edmond, Okla., 1971-72, U. Okla., Norman, 1976-78; cons. J. David Spence Accountancy Corp., Fresno, 1974-76; many coms. at La. Tech. U. including acad. senator, new faculty welcoming com., acctg. scholarship chmn.; faculty senate rep.; Faculty Consortium, St. Charles, Ill., 1993; expert witness Superior Ct. Calif. Contbr. numerous articles to profl. jours., bus. mags., newspapers, also book reviews; presentations to profl. meetings. Past bd. dirs. Goodwill, Inc., Ctrl. Calif.; ch. deacon and mem. many coms.; pres., treas., state scripture coord. Gideons Internat. Ruston Camp; rep. United Way La. Tech. U., Ruston. With USCG, 1965. Recipient El Paso CPA's Outstanding Jr. scholarship, Standard Oil scholarship, Price Waterhouse scholarship, Outstanding Educator award Gamma Beta Phi, 1986. Mem. AICPA, Am. Acctg. Assn. (La. membership com. chmn.), Am. Inst. for Decision Scis. (program com. chmn. acctg. track), Tex. Soc. CPAs, Am. Tax Assn. (internat. tax policy subcom.), Beta Gamma Sigma (pres.), Beta Alpha Psi. Baptist. Home: 2700 Foxxwood Dr Ruston LA 71270-2509 Office: La Tech U CAB 129A Ruston LA 71272

POSEY, DANIEL EARL, analytical chemist; b. Corpus Christi, Tex., Apr. 9, 1947; s. Earl Lloyd and Mary Lucille (Williams) P.; m. Mary Jewell King, Dec. 7, 1968; children: Amanda America, Matthew Daniel. BS in Chemistry, U. Houston, 1970. Rsch. technician Getty Oil Co. Exploration & Prodn. Rsch. Labs., Houston, 1968-69; lab. mgr. Inst. for Rsch., Inc., Houston, 1969-79, Am. Convertors, El Paso, Tex., 1979-84; tech. dir. Inst. for Rsch.-Austin, 1984-86; cons. chemist Spectro Chem Inc., Austin, 1986-88; quality engring. supr. Advanced Micro Devices, Austin, 1988—; sect. mgr. Advanced Micro Devices, Austin, Tex., 1994—; mem. Internat. Nonwoven & Disposables Assn., N.Y.C., 1981-83. Contbr. tech. papers to scholarly jours. Recipient Tech. Svc. award Am. Convertors R&D, 1981, Tech. Mgmt. award, 1982; recipient Cert. of Achievement, Am. Men and Women of Sci., 1986. Fellow Am. Inst. Chemists; mem. Am. Chem. Soc., Am. Soc. for Quality Control, Phi Eta Sigma. Republican. Office: Advanced Micro Devices Mail Stop 551 5204 E Ben White Blvd Austin TX 78741

POSEY, SANDRA DENISE, occupational health nurse; b. Baton Rouge, Sept. 24, 1958; d. Johnnie and Louise (Jones) P. BSN, Union Coll., Nebr., 1980; MN, La. State U., New Orleans, 1985. Cert. Adult Nurse Practitioner, Occupational Health Nurse, Hearing Conservationist, Spirometry. Staff charge nurse Our Lady of the Lake Med. Ctr., Baton Rouge, 1980-82, Woman's Hosp., Baton Rouge, 1982-83; sch. nurse East Baton Rouge Parish Sch., Baton Rouge, 1983-85; prof. Southern U., Baton Rouge, 1985-88; med.-surg. mgr. Millinocket Regional Hosp., Millinocket, Maine, 1988-90; adult nurse practitioner Shady Grove Hosp., Rockville, Md., 1990-91; med. svcs. supr. Kaiser Aluminum and Chem. Corp., Gramercy, La., 1991—; prin. advisor Katahdin Area Health Edn. Ctr., Millinocket, Maine, 1989-90; prin. investigator Pvt. Classification Validation Tool, 1984, Diabetic Assessment Tool, 1985, Preceived Stressors Identified by Diabetics, 1985. Author: Patient Handbook of Diabetic Recipes, 1985. Mem. Community Svc. Disaster Relief, Baton Rouge, 1980—, Berean's Sch. Bd. Com., Baton Rouge, 1985-87; cons. Oakwood Coll. Youth Motivational Task Force, huntsville, Ala., 1991-94; lectr. black history Shady Grove Hosp., Rockville, Md., 1991; woman's coord. Berean Ch., Baton Rouge, 1994. Mem. Am. Occupational Health Nurses, La. State Nursing Assn., Am. Red Cross, Sigma Theta Tau, Chi Beta Phi. Mem. Seventh Day Adventist Ch. Office: Kaiser Aluminum & Chem Corp PO Box 3370 Gramercy LA 70052

POSNER, GARY JAY, educational consulting company executive; b. Dec. 31, 1946; married. BA in Bus. Adminstrn., Mich. State U., 1968, MA in Adminstrn., 1971. Dir. employee benefits, dir. employee compensation and benefits, dir. employee rels., chief negotiator Mich. State U., East Lansing, 1968-78; dir. pers. svcs. Cornell U., Ithaca, N.Y., 1978-82; v.p. human resources U. Pa., Phila., 1982-84, v.p. adminstrn., 1984-86; pres. Univ. Search Cons., Phila. and Raleigh, N.C., 1986-88; v.p. Kaludis Cons. Group, Nashville, 1988-93; ptnr., prin. Ednl. Mgmt. Network, Nashville and Nantucket, Mass., 1993—.

POST, ROSE ZIMMERMAN, newspaper columnist; b. Morganton, N.C., Oct. 2, 1926; d. Samuel Sinai and Anna (Pliskin) Zimmerman; m. Edward Martin Post, July 8, 1947; children: David Bruce, Phyllis Post Lebowitz, Samuel Michael, Jonathan Alan, Anna Susan. BA, U. N.C., Greensboro, 1948; postgrad., U. N.C., 1972-74; LittD (hon.), Catawba Coll., 1981. Reporter Salisbury (N.C.) Post, 1951-83, columnist, 1983—; adj. prof. journalism Catawba Coll., Salisbury, 1988-89. Mem. Temple Israel PTA, Salisbury, 1950-80s; bd. dirs. Nat. Coun. Jewish Women; various offices numerous orgns. Recipient Ernie Pyle award Scripps Howard News, 1989, O Henry award N.C. AP News Coun., 1991, 92, 95, N.C. Working Press Excellence in Writing award, 1988, 89, 90, 93; named Citizen of Yr. Salisbury Civitan Club, 1976, Woman of Achievement Salisbury B&PW, 1971, N.C. Journalism Hall of Fame, 1996. Mem. AAUW, NCCJ, Nat. Assn. Newspaper Columnists (1st pl. for gen. columns 1994), N.C. Press Women (sec. 1983, 2d v.p. 1984, 1st v.p. 1985, pres. 1986), N.C. Press Club. Democrat. Jewish. Home: 125 E Corriher Ave Salisbury NC 28144-2427 Office: Salisbury Post 131 W Innes St Salisbury NC 28144-4338

POSTER, DON STEVEN, internist, hematologist, oncologist; b. N.Y.C., Nov. 19, 1950. BA, Pace U., N.Y.C., 1970; DO, U. Osteopathic Health Sci., Des Moines, 1973. Diplomate Am. Bd. Internal Medicine, Am. Bd. Med. Oncology, Am. Bd. Hematology (fellow). Intern USPHS Hosp., S.I., 1973-74; resident in medicine SUNY and Northport VA Hosp., 1975-77; fellow hematology and oncology Roswell Park Meml. Inst., Buffalo, 1977-79; investigator NCI/NIH, Bethesda, Md., 1979-81; med. oncologist North Miami Beach, Fla., 1981—. Editor: Treatment of Nausea and Vomiting, 1981; contbr. articles to profl. jours. Bd. dirs. United Charities, Hollywood, Fla., 1989. With USPHS, 1978-81. Am. Cancer Soc. fellow, 1977-79. Fellow Am. Coll. Clin. Pharmacology, Am. Coll. Medicine.

POSTMA, HERMAN, physicist, consultant; b. Wilmington, N.C., Mar. 29, 1933; s. Gilbert and Sophia Postma; m. Patricia Dunigan, Nov. 25, 1960; children: Peter, Pamela. BS summa cum laude, Duke U., 1955; MS, Harvard U., 1957, PhD, 1959. Registered profl. engr., Calif. Summer staff Oak Ridge Nat. Lab., 1954-57, physicist thermonuclear div., 1959-62, coleader DCX-1 group, 1962-66, asst. dir. thermonuclear div., 1966, asso. dir. div., 1967, dir. div., 1967-73, dir. nat. lab., from 1974; v.p. Martin Marietta, 1984-88, sr. v.p., 1988-91; vis. scientist FOM-Inst. for Plasma Physics, The Netherlands, 1963; cons. Lab. Laser Energetics, U. Rochester; mem. energy rsch. adv. bd. spl. panel Dept. Energy; bd. dirs. Nashville br. Fed. Res. Bank Atlanta, ICS Corp., PAI Corp., ORAS, Inc., M4 Corp. Mem. editorial bd. Nuclear Fusion, 1968-74; contbr. numerous articles to profl. jours. Bd. dirs. The Nucleus; chmn. bd. trustees Hosp. of Meth. Ch.; mem. adv. bd. Coll. Bus. Adminstrn., U. Tenn., 1976-84, Energy Inst., State of N.C.; bd. dirs., exec. com. Tenn. Tech. Found., 1982-88, Venture Capital Fund; vice chmn., commr. Tenn. Higher Edn. Commn., 1984-92; trustee Duke U., 1987—, Pellissippi State Coll., 1991—; chmn. Meth. Hosp. Found., 1990; mem. adv. bd. Inst. Pub. Policy Vanderbilt U., 1986-88, conf. chmn. 1987. Fellow Am. Phys. Soc. (exec. com. div. plasma physics), AAAS, Am. Nuclear Soc. (dir.); mem. C. of C. (v.p. 1981-83, chmn. 1987), Indsl. Rsch. Inst., Gas Rsch. Inst. (adv. bd. 1986-88), Phi Beta Kappa, Beta Gamma Sigma, Sigma Pi Sigma, Omicron Delta Kappa, Sigma Xi, Pi Mu Epsilon, Phi Eta Sigma. Home: 104 Berea Rd Oak Ridge TN 37830-7829

POSTON, BEVERLY PASCHAL, lawyer; b. Birmingham, Ala., Aug. 21, 1955; d. Arthur Buel and Nellie Jo (Weaver) P.; m. Richard F. Poston, Aug., 1992. BA with honor, U. North Ala., 1976; JD, Birmingham Sch. Law, 1982. Bar: Ala. 1982, U.S. Dist. Ct. (no. dist.) Ala. 1982, U.S. Ct. Appeals (11th cir.) 1983. Assoc. St. John & St. John, Cullman, Ala., 1982-84; pvt. practice Cullman, 1984-85, 92—; ptnr. Paschal & Collins, Cullman, 1986-92. Pres. Cullman County Hist. Soc., 1986-87, bd. dirs., 1996—. Named one of Outstanding Young Women Am., 1984; recipient Citiation of Honor, Young Career Women Program, 1989. Mem. ABA, ATLA, Ala. Trial Lawyers Assn., Cullman County Bar Assn., Pilot Club Internat. (Sweetheart award Cullman 1985), Cullman Bus. and Profl. Women's Assn. (young careerist award). Home: 1797 County Road 972 Cullman AL 35057-5861 Office: 905 2nd Ave SW Ste D 905 Cullman AL 35055-4224

POSTON, IONA, nursing educator; b. Charleston, S.C., Sept. 11, 1951; d. Fulton C. and Laura M. (Wolfe) P. BSN, Med. U. of S.C., 1973; MSN, Med. Coll. of Ga., 1979; PhD, U. Fla., 1988. Instr. Clemson (S.C.) U., 1979-81; asst. prof. U. N.C., Greensboro, 1981-85; assoc. in nursing Fla. State U., Tallahassee, 1989; assoc. prof. East Carolina U., Greenville, N.C., 1989—. Contbr. articles to profl. jours. Alden B. Dow Creativity Ctr. fellow, 1993; HBO & Co. nurse scholar, 1995. Mem. So. Nursing Rsch. Soc., NLN, Soc. Pediat. Nurses, AAUP, Sigma Theta Tau.

POSTON, JANICE LYNN, librarian; b. Louisville, Mar. 30, 1965; d. William Kenneth and Loretta Frances (Reece) Ferguson; m. Boyce Day Poston, Jan. 9, 1988. BS in Elem. Edn. with high honors, U. Louisville, 1987; MA in Sch. Media Librarianship, Spalding U., 1992. Part-time libr. page Louisville Free Pub. Libr., 1981-91; elem. sch. tchr. Jefferson County Pub. Schs., Louisville, 1988-91; cataloging svcs. libr. Spalding U. Libr., Louisville, 1991—. Active Christian edn. bd. River City Ch. of God. Mem. Ky. Libr. Assn. Republican. Pentecostal. Office: Spalding U Libr 853 Library Ln Louisville KY 40203

POTKAY, ADAM STANLEY, English language educator; b. Trenton, N.J., Jan. 11, 1961; s. Stanley Eugene and Barbara Marie (Krogulski) P.; m. Monica Brzezinski, May 23, 1991; 1 child, Aaron Joseph. BA, Cornell U., 1982; MA, Johns Hopkins U., 1986; PhD, Rutgers U., 1990. Teaching asst. Johns Hopkins U., 1984-85; lectr. Rutgers U., 1986-88; asst. prof. Coll. William & Mary, 1990-96; Assoc. prof., 1996—. Author: Manners of Reading: Essays in Honor of Thomas R. Edwards, 1992, The Fate of Eloquence in the Age of Hume, 1994, Black Atlantic Writers of the Eighteenth Century, 1995; editor: Eighteenth-Century Life; contbr. articles to profl. publs. Louis Bevier fellow, 1989-90, Rutgers Grad. Sch. Excellence fellow, 1985-89, William and Mary Alumni fellowship award for Excellence in Teaching, 1996. Mem. Am. Soc. 18th-Century Studies, Modern Lang. Assn., David Hume Soc. Office: Coll William & Mary Dept English Williamsburg VA 23187

POTOTSCHNIK, JOHN MICHAEL, artist; b. St. Ives, Cornwall, Eng., Nov. 14, 1945; Came to U.S., 1946; s. Ernest Felix and Patricia Mary (Symons) P.; m. Marcia Janet Forward, Oct. 16, 1971; children: Jonathan Matthew, Andrew Alexander. BFA, Wichita State U., 1968; postgrad., Art Ctr. College, Pasadena, Calif., 1969-71, Lyme Acad. Fine Arts, 1993. Freelance comml. illustrator Dallas, 1972-81. One-man shows include Corsicana (Tex.) Living Arts Ctr., 1989, The Wichita (Kans.) Gallery Fine Art, 1990, invitational, 1991, The Birmingham Trust, Kreymer House, Wylie, Tex., 1991; invitationals: 12th Midwest Gathering Artists, Carthage, Mo., 1989, 13th, 1991, 15th, 1992 (Founder's Choice award), 6th Ann. Best of West, Plano, Tex., 1989, 7th, 1990, 8th, 1991, Tex. Art Gallery, Dallas, 1991, 92, Am. Legacy Gallery, Kansas City, 1992; competition 7th Bosque County (Tex.) Conservatory Fine Arts, 1992 (John Steven Jones fellos, Best of Show, Artist's Choice); pub. collections City of Carrollton, Tex., Collin County (Tex.) Courthouse, Ponca City (Okla.) Art Assn., Wichita Ctr. for Arts, Wichita Sedgwick County Hist. Mus.; pvt. collections Abio & Adleta Realtors, Dallas, Adobe Oil, Midland, Tex., Leggett & Platt, Carthage, Otis Engring., Dallas, Schlumberger, Houston, Tex. Oil and Gas Corp., Dallas; represtnted in permanent collections The Wichita Gallery Fine Art, Am. Legacy Gallery, G. Stanton Gallery, Dallas, Guildhall, Inc. (publ.), Ft. Worth; subject various newspaper revs.; TV interviews Kaleidoscope, Sta. KAKE, Ch. 10, Wichita, 1986, Art About Town, cable, Garland, Tex., 1986, Weekday, Telecable, Plano, Tex., 1987, 1992. Capt. USAF, 1968-72. Recipient George Washington honor medal Freedoms Found. at Valley Forge, Pa., 1984, 86, 92, 95, First Place award Am. Artist Mag., 1990, hon. mention The Artist's Mag., 1992, Top 30 award The Artist's Mag., 1994-95. Mem. Oil Painters Am., Artists and Craftsmen Assn. (editor newsletter 1983-85, 1st v.p. 1985-86, pres. 1986-88), Plano Art Assn. (pres. 1994-95), Copley Soc., Boston, Am. Soc. Classical Realism. Home and Studio: 6944 Taylor Ln Wylie TX 75098-7720

POTTER, ANTHONY NICHOLAS, JR., hospital security executive, consultant; b. N.Y.C., Jan. 6, 1942; s. Anthony Nicholas Sr. and Alta Lorene (Downing) P.; m. Patricia Anne Tlumac, Apr. 4, 1964 (div. Oct. 1981); children: Merika Elizabeth, Victoria Hope Nora; m. Cheryl Kay Dittman, Oct. 15, 1983. AA, Westchester C.C., 1970; BS in Criminal Justice, U. Cin., 1975. Cert. protection profl., security trainer, healthcare protection adminstr. Chief police Tampa Internat. Airport, Fla., 1970-73; prin. cons. Booz, Allen & Hamilton, Cin., 1973-75; chief police City of Danville, Ill., 1976-78; police commr. City of York, Pa., 1978-80; v.p. Omni Internat. Security, Atlanta, 1980-83; exec. dir. Internat. Assn. Shopping Ctr. Security, Atlanta, 1981-90; dir. pub. safety Emory U. Sys. of Healthcare, Atlanta, 1990—; cons. shopping ctr. developers, operators, retailers; faculty mem. Internat. Coun. Shopping Ctr. Mgmt. Insts., 1970-85; expert witness security matters fed. and state cts. Author: Shopping Center Security, 1976, Recommended Security Practices for Shopping Centers, 1987; contbr. articles to profl. jours. Various positions local, coun., regional, nat. Boy Scouts Am., 1950—. Served to sgt. USMC, 1959-65. Recipient Disting. Svc. award Internat. Security Conf. 1970; Merit award Security World Mag., 1972, Lindberg Bell award IAHSS, 1992. Fellow Am. Acad. Forensic Scis.; mem. Met. Atlanta Crime Commn., Internat. Assn. Chiefs Police (pvt. security com. 1978-85), Internat. Assn. Profl. Security Cons. (bd. dirs. 1988-91), Am. Soc. Hosp. Engring. (safety and security mgmt. com. 1993—), Am. Soc. Indsl. Security (chmn. St. Petersburg chapt. 1970-71, chmn. nat. transp. security com. 1971-74, regional v.p. region VI 1975-76, com. standards and codes 1977-80, chmn. legis. com. 1986-87, pvt. security svcs. coun. 1988-90, profl. certification bd. 1991), Internat. Assn. Healthcare Safety and Security (Ga. state chmn. 1991—, tng. and edn. com. 1992—). Republican. Mem. Disciples of Christ Ch. Avocations: model railroading, gun collecting, scuba diving. Home: 2992 Randolph Rd NE Atlanta GA 30345-3600 Office: Emory U Crawford Long Hosp 550 Peachtree St NE Atlanta GA 30308-2225

POTTER, CLEMENT DALE, public defender; b. McMinnville, Tenn., Dec. 22, 1955; s. Johnnie H. and Elnora (Harvey) P.; children: Cory, Sarah, John Warren. BS, Middle Tenn. State U., 1984; JD, U. Tenn., 1987; cert., Tenn. Law Enforcement Acad., 1980. Bar: Tenn. 1987, U.S. Dist. Ct. (ea. dist.) Tenn. 1989. Pvt. practice law McMinnville, 1987-89; city judge City of McMinnville, Tenn., 1988-89; pub. defender 31st Dist. State Tenn., McMinnville, 1989—. Asst. to gen. editor Tools for the Ultimate Trial, 1st edit., 1985. Mem. Warren County Kiwanis Club, McMinnville, 1984-89, pres., 1986-87; mem. Leadership McMinnville, 1989, chmn., 1995-96; TSSAA H.S. Football referee. Staff sgt. USAF, 1974-80. Named McMinnville Warren County C. of C. Vol. of Yr., 1995; recipient D. Porter Henegar & Fred L. Hoover Sr. Bell Ringer award, 1995. Mem. ABA, Cheer Mental Health Assn. (dir. 1988—, pres. 1991—), Harmony House Inc. (dir. 1993-95), Noon Exch. Club McMinnville (dir. 1992—, sec. 1994, pres.-elect 1995, pres. 1996—). Office: Pub Defender 31st Dist PO Box 510 314 W Main St Mc Minnville TN 37110

POTTER, CYNTHIA JEAN, library director; b. Ft. Worth, Apr. 8, 1949; d. Carter Jr. and Suzanne (DeForest) Johnson; m. James Daniel Potter, July 17, 1970 (div. May, 1990); children: Blake Daniel, Blair Carter. BS, Tex. Wesleyan Coll., 1971; MLS, Tex. Woman's U., 1988. Cert. tchr., Tex., Tex. sch. libr. Tchr. elem. sch. Carter Park Elem. Sch., Ft. Worth, 1971-73; ref. libr. Tex. Wesleyan U., Ft. Worth, 1988-89, head of ref. and circulation, 1989-94, dir. W. Libr., 1995—; libr. cons. Pediat. AIDS Project Caht. Charities, United Way, Ft. Worth, 1992, St. Alban's Episcopal Ch., Arlington, Tex., 1994-96; libr. rsch. William James Magnet Sch. Ft. Worth Ind. Sch. Dist., 1991-94. Compiler: (book) Participatory Science Books for Students K-6th, 1988. Sunday sch. tchr. St. Alban's Episcopal Ch., Arlington, Tex., 1996; vol. Rep. Party, N. Tex. area, 1980—. Mem. ALA, Am. Assn. Higher Edn., Assn. Coll. and Rsch. Librs., Tex. Libr. Assn. Republican. Episcopalian. Office: Tex Wesleyan U 1201 Wesleyan St Fort Worth TX 76105

POTTER, ERNEST LUTHER, lawyer; b. Anniston, Ala., Apr. 30, 1940; s. Ernest Luther and Dorothy (Stamps) P.; m. Gwyn Johnston, June 28, 1958; children: Bradley S., Lauren D. A.B., U. Ala., 1961, LL.B., 1963, LL.M., 1979. Bar: Ala. 1963, U.S. Dist. Ct. (no. dist.) Ala. 1964, U.S. Ct. Appeals (5th cir.) 1965, U.S. Supreme Ct. 1972, U.S. Ct. Appeals (11th cir.) 1982. Assoc. Burnham & Klinefelter, Anniston, Ala., 1963-64; assoc. Bell, Richardson, Cleary, McLain & Tucker, Huntsville, Ala., 1964-66, ptnr., 1967-70; ptnr. Butler & Potter, Huntsville, 1971-82; pvt. practice, Huntsville, 1983—; bd. dirs. VME Microsystems Internat. Corp., Inc.; mem. faculty Inst. Bus. Law and Polit. Sci., U. Ala.-Huntsville, 1965-67. Contbg. author: Marital Law, 1976, 2d edit. 1985. V.p. No. Ala. Kidney Found., 1976-77; treas. Madison County Dem. Exec. Com., 1974-78; bd. dirs. United Way Madison County, 1982-87, Girls Inc., Huntsville, 1988—, pres., 1991. Mem. Ala. Law Inst., ABA, Ala. Bar Assn., Madison County Bar Assn., Phi Beta Kappa, Order of Coif. Episcopalian. Home: 1284 Becket Dr SE Huntsville AL 35801-1670 Office: 200 Clinton Ave W Huntsville AL 35801-4918

POTTER, HAROLD CLAUDE, philosopher; b. Waukegan, Ill., Sept. 11, 1941; s. Claude Allen and Stella Eve (Zaborski) P.; m. Barbara Rae Marr, Aug. 18, 1962 (div. Sept. 1991); children: Deborah Renee, Chris Michele. BS, Ill. Inst. Tech., 1963; MS, U. Ill., 1964; PhD, Cornell U., 1970. Mem. tech. staff Bell Labs., Reading, Pa., 1963-77; Pvt. practice Lake County, Ill., 1977-78, Breckingridge County, Ky., 1978—. Author: One Realtist's Guide to Insurance-A Philosophic Commentary, 1991, A Mathematical Depiction of Simple Emotional Character, 1993. Home: US 60 Home Court Box 37 Hardinsburg KY 40143-0037

POTTER, KAREN, library director; b. Harrodsburg, Ky., Sept. 5, 1950; d. Sol J. and Virginia (Baruth) P. BA, Ky. Wesleyan Coll., 1975; MLS, U. Ky., 1980. Head Ky. rm. Owensboro (Ky.) Pub. Libr., 1975-81; libr. dir. Nelson County Pub. Libr., Bardstown, Ky., 1981-85, Altamonte Springs (Fla.) City Libr., 1985-92; dir. libr. svcs. Maitland (Fla.) Pub. Libr., 1992—. Mem. Fla. Pub. Libr. Assn. (chair Friends and Trustees Divsn.), Fla. Libr. Assn., Ctrl. Fla. Libr. Assn., Freedom to Read Found., Beta Phi Mu. Office: Maitland Pub Libr 501 S Maitland Ave Maitland FL 32751-5621

POTTER, ROBERT DANIEL, federal judge; b. Wilmington, N.C., Apr. 4, 1923; s. Elisha Lindsey and Emma Louise (McLean) P.; m. Mary Catherine Neilson, Feb. 13, 1954; children: Robert Daniel, Mary Louise, Catherine Ann. AB in Chemistry, Duke U., 1947, LLB, 1950; LLD (hon.), Sacred Heart Coll., Belmont, N.C., 1982. Bar: N.C. 1951. Pvt. practice law Charlotte, N.C., 1951-81; chief judge U.S. Dist. Ct. (we. dist.) N.C., 1984-91, dist. judge, 1991—, now sr. judge. Commr. Mecklenburg County, Charlotte, 1966-68. Served to 2d lt. U.S. Army, 1944-47, ETO. Mem. N.C. Bar Assn. Republican. Roman Catholic. Club: Charlotte City. Office: US Courthouse 250 Federal Bldg 401 W Trade St Charlotte NC 28202

POTTS, ETHELDA OAKS, library director; b. Booneville, Miss., Dec. 31, 1934; d. Owen Candler and Mary Ernestine (Smiley) Oaks; m. Lester Eugene Potts, Jr., Sept. 6, 1959; 1 child, Daniel Christian. BS, Miss. U. for Women, 1961; postgrad., U. Ala., 1962, 70. Cert. media specialist. Tchr. English Joe Cook Jr. High Sch., Columbus, Miss., 1960-64, Carrollton (Ala.) High Sch., 1964-65, Aliceville (Ala.) High Sch., 1966-70; tchr. English, libr. Pickens Acad., Carrollton, 1970-74; dir. Aliceville Pub. Libr., 1976—. Founder, pres., dir., treas. Aliceville Little Theatre, 1977—; officer New Era Arts Club, Aliceville, 1965—; charter mem. Aliceville Hist. Preservation Soc., 1980—; dir. Aliceville Civic Chorus, 1989; dir., soloist Choir of Aliceville First United Meth. Ch., 1966-85. Recipient Outstanding Citizen of Yr. award Aliceville C. of C., 1982. Mem. ALA, Aliceville Friends of Libr. Office: Aliceville Pub Libr 416 3rd Ave NE Aliceville AL 35442-2207

POTTS, JAMES LAFAYETTE, internist, cardiologist, health facility administrator; b. Cornelius, N.C., May 19, 1935; m. Virginia E., Oct. 29, 1960; children: Rodney L., Regina L., Kimberly L. BS, N.C. Ctrl. U., 1957; MD, Meharry Med. Coll., 1967. From asst. prof. to assoc. prof. SUNY Upstate Med. Ctr., Syracuse, 1972-87; prof. medicine SUNY Health Sci. Ctr., Syracuse, 1987-94; chief cardiology Meharry Med. Coll., Nashville, 1994—; chmn. dept. medicine Meharry Med. Coll., 1995—. Bd. dirs. Urban League Ctrl. N.Y., Syracuse, 1990-94. Served in USCG, 1959. Fellow Am. Coll. Cardiology; mem. Assn. Black Cardiologists, Am. Coll. Physician Execs., Am. Heart Assn. (coun. clin. cardiology). Office: Meharry Med Coll 1005 DB Todd Blvd Nashville TN 37208

POTTS, ROBERT LESLIE, academic administrator; b. Huntsville, Ala., Jan. 30, 1944; s. Frank Vines and Helen Ruth (Butler) P.; m. Irene Elisabeth Johansson, Aug. 22, 1965; children: Julie Anna, Robert Leslie. Student Newbold Coll., Eng., 1963-64; BA, So. Coll., 1966; JD, U. Ala., 1969; LLM, Harvard U., 1971. Law clk. to chief judge U.S. Dist. Ct. (no. dist.) Ala., 1969-70; researcher Herrick, Smith, Donald, Farley & Ketchum, Boston, 1970-71; lectr. Boston U., 1971, U. Ala., 1973-75, 88; ptnr. Potts & Young, Florence, Ala., 1971-84; gen. counsel U. Ala. System, 1984-89, pres. U. North Ala., 1990—; active Nat. Adv. Com. on Instnl. Quality and Integrity, 1994—; bd. dirs. Bank Ind., Florence, 1975-85; adv. com. Rules Civil Procedure, Ala. Supreme Ct., 1973-88; mem. Ala. Bd. Bar Examiners, 1973-79, chmn., 1983-86; trustee Nat. Conf. Bar Examiners, 1986-96, chmn., 1994-95, Ala. State U., 1976-79, Oakwood Coll., 1978-81; pres. Ala. Higher Edn. Loan Corp., 1988-93. Mem. ABA, Ala. Bar Assn. (pres. young lawyers sect. 1979-80). Contbr. numerous articles to profl. jours., edn. and schs. Office: U North Ala University Station Florence AL 35632

POU, LINDA ALICE, interior designer, architectural designer; b. Huntsville, Ala., Oct. 26, 1942; d. Louis and Lillian Maurice (Garvin) Grabensteder; m. Robert LeRoy Pou, Aug. 27, 1965; children: Susan Caroline, Stephanie Lynn. B of Interior Design, Auburn U., 1964; postgrad., Ecoles D'Art Americaines, 1964. Interior designer Martin Interiors, Huntsville, Ala., 1963, Blance Reeves Interiors, Atlanta, 1964-65, Militare, Atlanta, 1965, Loveman's Dept. Store, Huntsville, Ala., 1966, Southeastern Galleries, Charleston, S.C., 1967; draftsman Brown Engring., Huntsville, Ala., 1967-68, Naval Electronics Systems Command, S.C., 1968, Leland Engrs., Charleston, S.C., 1968-69; owner Drafting Svc., Mobile, Ala., 1977-78, The Design Svc., Prattville, Ala., 1980-92; The Design Svc., Savannah, Ga., 1992—. Composer songs including (adult anthems), Sing for Joy, 1983, Sing Hallelujah to the Lord, He's the Rainbow in My Life, 1984, (children's)ùLord of Harvest, 1984, Sing a Song to the Lord of Earth, 1985, (children's musical) Six Myths of Christmas, 1986; compiler and editor book of poetry, Nana's Legacy. Mem. jr. bd. Florence Crittendon Home for Unwed Mothers, Mobile, Ala., 1977-79, Prattville Planning Commn., 1980-92, chmn., 1985-88, vice-chmn., 1988-92; mem. Prattville Hist. Re-devel. Authority, 1988-89; children's choir dir. 1st United MEth. Ch., 1979-83, 87-89, adminstrv. bd., 1987-89, bldg. commn., 1987-89, trustee, 1990-92; mem. Savannah Symphony Women's Guild, 1993—. Mem. ASCAP, Spinners (treas. 1982-83), Prattville C. of C., Garden Club of Savannah (2nd v.p. 1995-97), Alpha Gamma Delta. Home and Office: 202 E 45th St Savannah GA 31405-2216

POUDRIER, JOEL PHILIP, marine corps officer; b. Fitchburg, Mass., May 19, 1967; s. Joseph Roman Lloyd and Judith Rosemary (Spates) P.; m. Celia Porreca, Aug. 16, 1986. Student, Worcester State Coll., 1990-91; BA in Polit. Sci. with honors, Coll. of Holy Cross, 1994. Enlisted man USMC, 1986-90, commd. 1st lt., 1994; intelligence officer Marine Medium Helicopter Squadron 365, Jacksonville, N.C., 1996, 26th Marine Expeditionary unit Air Combat Element, Jacksonville, 1996—. Contbr. poetry to mags. and jours. Home: 25 Longstaff St Jacksonville NC 28540 Office: Marine Medium Helicopter Squadron 365 PSC Box 210226 Jacksonville NC 28545

POULTON, BRUCE ROBERT, former university chancellor; b. Yonkers, N.Y., Mar. 7, 1927; s. Alfred Vincent and Ella Marie (Scanlon) P.; m. Elizabeth Charlotte Jerothe, Aug. 26, 1950; children: Randall Lee, Jeffrey Jon, Cynthia Sue, Peter Gregory. B.S. with honors, Rutgers U., 1950, M.S., 1952, Ph.D., 1956; LL.D., U. N.H. Research instr., then asst. prof. Rutgers U., 1952-56; assoc. prof., then prof., chmn. dept. animal and vet. sci. U. Maine, 1958-66, dir. Bangor Campus, 1967-68, dean, dir. Coll. Life Scis. and Agr., 1968-71, v.p. research and pub. service, 1971-75; chancellor Univ. System N.H., 1975-82, also trustee; chancellor N.C. State U., Raleigh, 1982-89; vis. prof. Mich. State U., 1966-67; mem. regional adv. com. Farm and Home Adminstrn.; mem. exec. com., council on research policy and grad. edn. Nat. Assn. State Univs. and Land Grant Colls.; also mem. senate; mem. Gov.'s Econ. Advisory Council, N.H.; mem. selection com. Kellogg Found.; Lectureship in Agr.; chmn. Rhodes scholarship com. for, N.H.; mem. policy devel. com. New Eng. Innovation Group; adv. com. U.S. Command and Gen. Staff Coll. Author articles in field. Bd. dirs. Research Triangle Inst., Microelectronic Ctr., Triangle Univs. Ctr. Advanced Studies, Aubrey Brooks

Found. Served with AUS, 1944-46. Am. Council Edn. fellow acad. adminstrn., 1966-67. Mem. Am. Inst. Nutrition, Brit. Nutrition Soc., Fedn. Am. Soc. Exptl. Biology, Am. Soc. Exptl. Biology, Am. Soc. Animal Sci., Am. Dairy Sci. Assn. (past pres. Eastern div.), AAAS, Sigma Xi, Alpha Zeta. Office: NC State U Office of Chancellor Raleigh NC 27695

POUNDS, BILLY DEAN, law educator; b. Belmont, Miss., Jan. 23, 1930; s. Seth and Warnie (Wroten) P.; m. Genie Smith, June 22, 1952; children: Nancy Angela Pounds Via, Mary Dean Stone. AA, NE C.C., 1950; BS, Miss. State U., 1952, MS, 1953, EdD, 1968. Tchr. Wheeler (Miss.) High Sch., 1952-53; instr. NE Community Coll., Booneville, Miss., 1953-57; paralegal prof. Miss. U. for Women, Columbus, 1959—, dir. paralegal program, 1983—. Author: A Determination and Appraisal Content of Introduction to Political Science, 1968, History of Republic Party in Mississippi, 1964; co-author: Teaching About Communism, 1977. Pres. Lowndes County (Miss.) Kidney Found., 1970, Lowndes County Cancer Soc., 1972. Capt. USAF, 1957-59. Fellow Miss. State U., 1953; named Faculty Mem. of Yr., Miss. Legis., 1988. Mem. Phi Kappa Phi, Gamma Beta Phi, Kappa Delta Epsilon, Phi Delta Kappa, Phi Alpha Theta, Pi Gamma Mu, Pi Tau Chi. Office: Miss U for Women Columbus MS 39701

POUNDS, GERALD AUTRY, aerospace engineer; b. Boaz, Ala., Mar. 21, 1940; s. C.B. and Pauline (DeBord) P.; m. Linda Lee Lindsey, July 29, 1967; children: Kristina Marie, Alissa Michelle. B in Aerospace Engring., Auburn U., 1963, MS in Aerospace Engring., 1965. With Lockheed Martin Aero. Sys., Marietta, Ga., 1960—, mgr. wind tunnels and aircraft sys. test devel.; lectr. U. Tenn. Space Inst., Tullahoma, 1988-95. Contbr. articles to Jour. Aircraft. Vestry, from jr. warden to sr. warden Christ Episcopal Ch., Kennasaw, Ga., 1974-82; mid. adult retreat coord. Mt. Paran Ch. of God, Atlanta, 1986-91. NSF scholar, 1963-64. Fellow AIAA (assoc.; dep. dir. for test, tech. activities com., 1991—, chmn. Atlanta sect.); mem. Supersonic Tunnel Assn. (co. rep.), Subsonic Aerodynamic Testing Assn. (co. rep.). Home: 315 Walton Green Way Kennesaw GA 30144 Office: Lockheed Martin Aero Sys D/73-66 Z-0605 Marietta GA 30063

POUNDSTONE, ROBERT EMMETT, III, mental health services executive; b. Montgomery, Ala., Mar. 6, 1948; s. Robert Emmett II and Margaret (Farley) P.; m. Linda Scott, Aug. 22, 1970; 1 child, Robert Emmett, IV. BA, Auburn U., 1970; JD, U. Ala., 1973. Bar: Ala., U.S. Dist. Ct. (no., mid. and so. dists.) Ala., U.S. Cir. Ct. (11th and 5th cirs.), U.S. Supreme Ct. Atty. Conservation & Natural Resources, Montgomery, 1973-75; staff atty. Mental Health Dept., Montgomery, 1975-78, asst. chief counsel, 1975-78, 1978-79, chief cousel, 1979-81, dir. legal and adminstrv. svcs., 1981-84, currently facilities dir., 1984—, acting commr., 1985-86, Facilities Dir., 1986S. V.p. Montgomery Riverboat Commn., 1978-80, pres., 1980-82; bd. dirs. Montgomery Jaycees, 1975-80; mem. Farrah Law Soc. U. Ala., Tuscaloosa, 1973. Named Outstanding Young Man, 1976; recipient Jaycees Life Membership award Montgomery Jaycees, 1973-84, Community Svc. award Assn for Retarded Citizens, 1986, Appreciation award Ala. Inst. for the Deaf and Blind, 1986, Alliance for the Mantally Ill, 1990. Mem. ABA, Ala. Bar Assn., Montgomery County Bar Assn., Assn. Mental Health Attys. (chmn. 1984-87, pres. 1984-86). Office: Ala Dept of Mental Health 200 Interstate Park Dr Montgomery AL 36109-5403*

POURCIAU, LESTER JOHN, librarian; b. Baton Rouge, La., Sept. 6, 1936; s. Lester John and Pearlie M. (Hogan) P.; m. Rebecca Anne Thomas, 1975; 1 son, Lester John III. B.A., La. State U., 1962, M.S., 1964; Ph.D. (Higher Edn. Act fellow), Ind. U., 1975. Asst. reference librarian U. S.C., Columbia, 1963-64; reference librarian Florence County Pub. Library, Florence, S.C., 1964-65; reference services coordinator U. Fla., Gainesville, 1966-67; dir. libraries Memphis State U., 1970—, assoc. v.p. for acad. affairs, dir. libraries, 1987—; chmn. coun. of head librarians State Univ. and C.C. System Tenn., 1980, 87; acad. assoc. Atlantic Coun. of U.S., Memphis State U.; fgn. expert, vis. lectr. Beijing U. of Posts & Telecomms., Beijing Normal U., Peking U., Renmen U., Qinghua U., Chingqing Inst. Posts & Telecomms., Guizhou Normal U., Republic of China, 1993; fgn. expert/vis. lectr. Beijing U. Posts and Telecom, 1993, Beijing Normal U., 1993, Peking U., 1993, RenMen U., 1993, Tsinghua U., 1993, Chongqing Inst. Posts and Telecom., 1993, Guizhou Normal U., 1993; fgn. expert, vis. lectr. Nanjing U. Posts and Telecom., Anhui Normal U., Beijing U. Posts and Telecom., 1994, Nanjing U. Posts & Telecomms., consulting prof., 1996—; fgn. expert, vis. lectr. Anhui Normal U., Republic of China, 1994. Contbr. articles to profl. jours. Served with USAF, 1955-59. Recipient Adminstrv. Staff award Memphis State U., 1981, Commendation Boy Scouts Am., 1985, Commendation Tenn. Sec. State, 1989, Honor award Tenn. Libr. Assn., 1990; ; named Outstanding Alumnus, La. State U., 1988; named Libr. of Yr., Memphis Libr. Coun., 1989. Mem. Am. Southeastern, Tenn. Libr. Assn., Am. Soc. for Info. Sci., Nat. Assn. Watch and Clock Collectors (chpt. pres. 1983, sec.-treas. 1988, 89), Antique Automobile Am., Mid-Am. Old Time Automobile Assn., Memphis Old Time Car (sec. 1981, pres. 1982, 89), Delta Phi Alpha, Omicron Delta Kappa (Order of Omega), Phi Kappa Phi. Office: Memphis State U U Libr Memphis TN 38152

POURMOTABBED, GHASSEM, medical educator; b. Kermanshah, Iran; arrived in U.S., 1971; s. Aliakbar and Molouk (Ghovaalla) P. MD, U. Tehran (Iran) Med. Sch., 1970. Diplomate Am. Bd. Endocrinology and Metabolism, Am. Bd. Internal Medicine. Pathology resident U. Miss. Med. Ctr., 1971; intern internal medicine Med. Coll. of Ohio, 1972, resident internal medicine, 1972-74; fellow in endocrinology and metabolism Med. U. S.C., 1974-75, Johns Hopkins U., Balt., 1975-76; rsch. assoc. endocrine sect. Gerontology Rsch. Ctr. NIH, Bethesda, Md., 1977-79; asst. prof. medicine divsn. endocrinology and metabolism U. Tenn. Health Sci. Ctr., Memphis, 1989-93, assoc. prof. medicine divsn. endocrinology and metabolism, 1993—; staff U. Tenn. Bowld Hosp., Memphis, VA Med. Ctr., Memphis, Regional Med. Ctr.; cons. St. Francis Hosp., Bapt. Meml. Hosp., Memphis; grant reviewer for com. on rsch. U. Tenn., Coll. of Medicine, 1992; lectr. in field. Mem. Endocrine Soc., Am. Diabetes Assn. Office: U Tenn at Memphis 951 Court Ave Rm 340M Memphis TN 38103-2813

POWE, RALPH ELWARD, university administrator; b. Tylertown, Miss., July 27, 1944; s. Roy Elward and Virginia Alyne (Bradley) P.; m. Sharon Eve Sandifer, May 20, 1962; children: Deborah Lynn, Ryan Elward, Melanie Colleen. BS in Mech. Engring., Miss. State U., 1967, MS in Mech. Engring., 1968; PhD in Mech. Engring., Mont. State U., 1970. Student trainee NASA, 1962-65; research asst., lab. instr. Miss. State U., 1968, instr. dept. mech. engring., 1968; research asst., teaching asst. Mont. State U., Bozeman, 1968-70, asst. prof. dept. mech. engring., 1970-74; assoc. prof. Miss. State U., 1974-78, prof., 1979-80, assoc. dean engring., dir. engring. and indsl. research sta., 1979-80, assoc. v.p. research, 1980-86, v.p., 1986—; chmn. bd. dirs. Coalition of Experimental Program to Stimulate Competitive Rsch. States, 1994-96; bd. dirs. Gulf Univs. Rsch. Consortium, Tenn.-Tombigbee Project Area Coun.; rep. rsch. coun. Nat. Assn. State Univs. and Land Grant Colls., So. Growth Policies Bd., Miss. Mineral Resources Inst., Sci. and Tech. Coun. States. Disting. Engring. fellow Coll. Engring.; active Miss. Univ. Res. Authority, Coun. on Rsch. Policy, So. Growth Policies Bd.; rep. Miss. Mineral Resources Inst.; gov. rep. Sci. and Tech. Coun. of States; cons. energy conservation programs, coal fired power plants, torsional vibrations, accident analysis; dir. Miss. Energy Rsch. Ctr., 1979-81, Ctr. for Environ. Studies, 1980—; univ. rep. on lignite task force, rep. on bd. dirs. Miss.-Ala. Sea Grant Consortium, chmn. of Council Oak Ridge Associated Univs., rep. to Tenn.-Tombigbee project area coun.; chmn. Miss. Rsch. Consortium; mem. S.E. Univs. Rsch. Assn. Named Outstanding Egr., Engring. Socs. Contbr. articles to profl. jours. Mem. Miss. Econ. Coun., univ. coord. United Way, 1983, 85; tchr. adult Sunday Sch. class 1st Bapt. Ch. Recipient Ralph E. Teeter award Soc. Automotive Engrs., Commdr.'s award Pub. Svc. U.S. Dept. Army, 1995; named Outstanding Engr. in No. Miss. Joint Engr. Soc., Pub. Svc. Commdr.'s award U.S. Army. Fellow ASME; mem. Nat. Assn. State Universities and Land Grant Colls., Starkville Cmty. Theatre Wing. Edn., Wind Energy Soc. Am., Miss. Acad. Scis., Miss. Engring. Soc., Toastmasters, Starkville Quarterback Club, Rotary, Starkville C. of C. (bd. dirs.), Blue Key, Sigma Xi (Miss. State U. research award), Tau Beta Pi, Kappa Mu Epsilon, Pi Tau Sigma, Phi Kappa Phi, Omicron Delta Kappa. Baptist. Lodge: Rotary. Avocations: hunting, fishing, gardening. Home: 110 Pinewood Rd Starkville MS 39759-4128 Office: Miss State U PO Box 6343 Mississippi State MS 39762-6343

POWELL, ANICE CARPENTER, librarian; b. Moorhead, Miss., Dec. 2, 1928; d. Horace Aubrey and Celeste (Brian) Carpenter; student Sunflower Jr. Coll., 1945-47, Miss. State Coll. Women, 1947-48; B.S., Delta State Coll., 1961, M.L.S., 1974; m. Robert Wainwright Powell, July 19, 1948 (dec. 1979); children: Penelope Elizabeth, Deborah Alma. Librarian, Sunflower (Miss.) Pub. Library, 1958-61; tchr. English, Isola (Miss.) High Sch., 1961-62; dir. Sunflower County Library, Indianola, Miss., 1962—; mem. adv. coun. State Instl. Library Services, 1967-71; mem. adv. bd. library services and constrn. act com. Miss. Library Commn., 1978-80, mem. pub. library task force, 1986—; mem. Pub. Library Standards Com., 1988—; mem. state adv. coun. adult edn., 1988-92; mem. steering com. NASA community involvement program Miss. Delta Community Coll., 1990, adult edn. adv. com.; mem. Dist. Workforce Coun., 1994—, Mid Delta Enpowerment Zone Alliance, 1995—; commn. mem. Mid-Delta Empowerment Zone Alliance. Mem. AAUW, NOW, ALA (speaker senate subcom. on illiteracy 1989, honoree ALA 50th Anniversary 1996), Miss. Library Assn. (exec. dir. Nat. Library Week 1975, steering com. 1976, chmn. Right to Read com. 1976, co-chmn., 1987, chmn. legis. com. 1979, chmn. intellectual freedom com. 1975, 80, mem. legis. com. 1973-86, 96, chmn. membership com. 1982, pres. 1984, chmn. nominating com. 1986, chmn. election com. 1989, mem. registration com. 1991—, mem. membership com., mem. nominating com. 1994, mem. publicity com. 1996, mem. fiscal mgmt. com. 1996, mem. awards com. 1996, Peggy May award 1981), Sunflower County Hist. Soc. (pres. 1983-87), Delta Coun. Methodist. Home: PO Box 310 Sunflower MS 38778-0310 Office: Sunflower County Libr 201 Cypress Dr Indianola MS 38751-2415

POWELL, BOONE, JR., hospital administrator; b. Knoxville, Tenn., Feb. 9, 1937; married. BA, Baylor U., 1959; MA, U. Calif., 1960. Adm. intern Marin Gen. Hosp., Greenbrae, Calif., 1959; adm. resident Baptist Meml. Hosp., Memphis, 1960-61; asst. adminstr. Hendrick Med. Ctr., Abilene, Tex., 1961-69, assoc. adminstr., 1969-70, adminstr., 1970-73, pres., 1973-80; pres. Baylor Health Care System, Dallas, 1980—. Contbr. articles to profl. jours. Mem. Am. Coll. Healthcare Execs., Tex. Hosp. Assn. (chair community svc., trustee). Office: Baylor Health Care System 3500 Gaston Ave Dallas TX 75246-2045

POWELL, DAVID THOMAS, JR., retired association administrator; b. Nashville, Dec. 29, 1941; s. David Thomas and Georgia Juanita (Pennington) P.; m. Carolyn DeLorees Sissom, Aug. 25, 1960; children: David Thomas III, Sheryl Renae, Natalie Sue, Joel Brian. Student, St. Leo's Coll., St. Leo, Fla., 1975. Enlisted USAF, 1959, advanced through grades to master sgt., 1976, ret., 1979; meteorologist Sta. KVET-CASE Radio, Austin, Tex., 1979-80; weather technician Nat. Weather Svc., Huron, S.D., 1980-82, Chattanooga, Tenn., 1982—; regional councilman Nat. Weather Svc. Employees Orgn., Tenn., Ga. and Ala., 1982-84; exec. v.p. Nat. Weather Svc. Employees Orgn., 1984-89, nat. pres., 1989-95, chief labor negotiator, 1985-89; interface and coord. with various legislators; participant in drafting legis., coord. legis. betwen Ho. of Reps. and Senate coms. or subcoms.; cons. meteorology and labor/mgmt. matters. Judge Regional Sci. Fair, Chattanooga, 1983, 87. Named Mil. Airlift Command Tech. Advisor of Yr., 1977. Mem. Internat. Platform Assn. Democrat. Baptist. Home: 1007 Green Pond Rd Soddy Daisy TN 37379-3924

POWELL, ERIC KARLTON, lawyer, researcher; b. Parkersburg, W.Va., July 23, 1958; s. James Milton and Sarah Elizabeth (Gates) P. BA in History, W.Va. U., 1980, BSBA, 1981; JD, Western State U., Fullerton, Calif., 1987. Bar: Ga. 1992, W.Va. 1993, U.S. Dist. Ct. (we. dist.) W.Va. 1993. Reference libr. Western State U., 1984; tchr. acctg. Rosary H.S., Fullerton, 1984-85; law clk. Zonni, Ginnochio Taylor, Santa Ana, Calif., 1986-93; temp. law sch. Gibson, Dunn & Crutcher, Irvine, Calif., 1993; pvt. practice, Parkersburg, 1993—. Asst. scoutmaster Boy Scouts Am., Parkersburg, 1981-83. Mem. ABA, ATLA, W.Va. Trial Lawyers Assn., Nat. Eagle Scout Assn., Elks, Delta Theta Phi. Republican. Presbyterian. Home: 2002 20th St Parkersburg WV 26101-4125 Office: 500 Green St Parkersburg WV 26101-5131

POWELL, GARY L., biochemistry educator; b. Fullerton, Calif., Jan. 24, 1941; s. Lee D. and Dorothy D. (Dunphy) P.; m. Constance Marie Andrews, June 26, 1965; children: Gregory Lee, Andrew Scott. BS, UCLA, 1962; PhD, Purdue U., 1967. Asst. prof. Clemson (S.C.) U., 1967-73, assoc. prof., 1973-79, prof., 1979—; NIH trainee Washington U. Sch. Medicine, St. Louis, 1967-69; vis. prof. dept. chemistry U. Oreg., Eugene, 1975-76; guest prof. Max Planck Inst. for Biophys. Chemistry, Goettingen, Germany, 1983-84; coop. exch. scientist NSF, Goettingen, 1983-84; guest scientist Biology dept. Brookhaven Nat. Lab., Upton, N.Y., 1996—. Chmn. rsch. com. Am. Heart Assn. S.C. Affiliate, 1989-92, chmn. peer review group Ga./S.C. Affiliate, 1991; chmn. bicycle paths com. City of Clemson, 1992-94. Fulbright fellow, 1983-84. Methodist. Office: Clemson U Dept Biol Scis PO Box 341903 Clemson SC 29634-1903

POWELL, J(OHN) KEY, estate planner, consultant; b. Dallas, Dec. 14, 1925; s. Floyd Berkeley and Eloise (Saddler) P.; m. Ann Penniman, July 14, 1950; children: Nena Ann, Scott Key, Elliott Edward. U. Ala., Tuscaloosa, 1946-47, U. Ala., Tuscaloosa, 1949-50, So. Meth. U., Dallas, 1947-48, Am. Coll., Bryn Mawr, Pa., 1973. CLU. Agt. Life Ins. Sales, Tuscaloosa, 1950-54; agt., sales mgr. John Hancock, Lubbock, Tex., 1954-57; asst. supt. gen. agys. John Hancock, Boston, 1957-59; gen. agt. S.C. John Hancock, Columbia, 1959-85; cons. Creative Giving Concepts, Columbia, 1989—; vice chmn. First Sun South Corp., Columbia, 1990—. Pres. John Hancock Gen. Accounts Assn., Boston, 1969-70, Columbia Rotary Club, 1985-86; pres. Gen. Agts. and Mgrs. Assn., Columbia, 1974-75, nat. bd. dirs., Washington, 1975-77; chmn. Ctrl. Carolina Cmty. Found., Columbia, 1987-89, Richland Mem. Hosp. Ctr. Cancer Rsch., Columbia, 1988-89; immediate past chmn. Salvation Army; bd. dirs. Midlands Tech. Coll. Found. With USAAC, 1943-45. Mem. Nat. Assn. Life Underwriters, Citizens Advocating Decency and Revival of Ethics (past chmn.), U. S.C. Med. Sch. Ptnrs. Found. Republican. Presbyterian. Home: 212 Holliday Rd Columbia SC 29223-3124 Office: Creative Giving Concepts PO Box 11408 Columbia SC 29211-1408

POWELL, JULIAN ANTHONY, psychologist; b. Alexandria, Va., Dec. 23, 1945; s. Orbun Victor and Hazel Yvonne (Ogle) P.; m. Linda Elaine Woodlief, May 11, 1966 (div. Apr. 1971); 1 child, Maria Elana; m. Lynn Louise Keddie, Oct. 11, 1986. BS in Psychology, Campbell U., Buies Creek, N.C., 1968; MA in Clin. Psychology, East Carolina U., Greenville, N.C., 1975. Lic. psychol. assoc., cert. employee assistance profl. Psychol. asst. Cherry Hosp., Goldsboro, N.C., 1968-69; psychol. program mgr. N.C. Div. Prisons, Greenville, 1970—; adj. faculty Meredith Coll., Raleigh, N.C., 1972, Pitt C.C., Greenville, 1975, East Carolina U., 1975-92; employee assistance program counselor Pitt Meml. Hosp., Greenville, 1988-91; cons. trainer Am. Correctional Assoc., Laurel, Md., 1989—; cons. N.C. Bd. Examiners Practicing Psychologists, Boone, 1993-96; pres. Coastal Employee Assistance Program Corp., Surf City, N.C., 1992—; cons. N.C. Bd. Psychology, 1993—, bd. dirs. Bd. dirs. steering com. Pitt County Borrower Corp., Greenville, 1989-92. Mental Health scholar N.C. Dept. Human Resources, 1969, 70. Mem. Am. Assn. Correctional Psychologists, N.C. Correctional Assn., Pitt County Mental Health Assn., Cape Fear Psychol. Assn. Home: PO Box 3387 Topsail Beach NC 28445 Office: NC Div Prisons PO Box 1058 Burgaw NC 28425-1058

POWELL, LANE HOLLAND, family sociology educator; b. Gadsden, Ala., Aug. 25, 1941; d. James P. and Mary B. (Fernamburg) Holland; m. Robert Z. Powell, Feb. 23, 1963; children: Steve, Sharon, Jim. BA, Sanford U., 1963; MRE, New Orleans Bapt. Sem., 1968; PhD in Family Studies, Tex. Tech. U., 1984. Cert. Family Life Educator, 1990—. News dir. New Orleans Bapt. Sem., 1963-68; pub. rels. cons. Milledgeville, Ga., 1969-74; editor women's mag. Women's Missionary Union, So. Bapt. Conv., Birmingham, Ala., 1977-78; instr. family studies Tex. Tech U., Lubbock, 1979-84; family life educator/counselor Crossroads Samaritan Counseling Ctr., Lubbock, 1982-86; asst./assoc./full prof. human devel. and family studies Samford U., Birmingham, 1986—, chair, dept. family and consumer edn., 1991—; lectr. in field; nat. chmn. tng. and cert. Assn. Couples in Marriage Enrichment, Winston-Salem, N.C., 1987-90. Author: To Listen, To Love, 1984, The Dating Book, 1989, Holding Out for True Love, 1996; author videotape series Generation to Generation, 1991. Mem. Assn. Couples in Marriage Enrichment (bd. dirs. 1988-90), Am. Assn. Pastoral Counselors (profl. affiliate). Mem. Sanford Sociol. Assn. (founder, sponsor 1989), Assn. Couples in Marriage Enrichment (bd. dirs. 1988-90), Am. Assn. Pastoral Counselors, The Growing Pl. Office: Samford U 800 Lakeshore Dr Birmingham AL 35229-0001

POWELL, LEWIS FRANKLIN, III, lawyer; b. Richmond, Va., Sept. 14, 1952; s. Lewis F. Jr. and Josephine (Rucker) P.; m. Lisa T. LaFata; children: Emily, Hannah. BA, Washington & Lee U., 1974; JD, U. Va., 1978. Bar: Va. 1978, U.S. Dist. Ct. (ea. and we. dists.) Va. 1979, U.S. Ct. Appeals (4th cir.) 1979, U.S. Ct. Appeals (2d cir.) 1983, U.S. Ct. Appeals (11th cir.) 1992, U.S. Supreme Ct. 1985. Law clk. to judge U.S. Dist. Ct. (ea. dist.), Richmond, 1978-79; from assoc. to ptnr. Hunton & Williams, Richmond, 1979—; pres. young lawyers conf. Va. State Bar, 1986-87. Bd. dirs. William Byrd Cmty. Ho., Richmond, 1982-87, Boys Club of Richmond, 1984-90, Maymont Found., Richmond, 1987-92, St. Christopher's Sch., Richmond, 1989—. Mem. Richmond Bar Assn. (chmn. improvement justice com. 1982-83), 4th Cir. Jud. Conf., Am. Law Inst. Office: Hunton & Williams Riverfront Plz East Tower 951 E Byrd St Richmond VA 23219-4040

POWELL, LOUISE FOX, real estate developer; b. Hickory, N.C., June 14, 1925; d. Lester Lee and Vesta Boliek Fox; m. Nelson Sherril Powell, May 23, 1953 (dec.); children: Cynthia Louise, Joan Marie, Suzanne Jayne. Grad. in Bus., King's Coll., Charlotte, N.C., 1942. Time study engr. Glenn L. Martin Co., Balt., 1942-44; owner, mgr. Isenhour Fabric Co., Lenoir, N.C., 1949-53; rsch. mgr. Alfred Politz Rsch., Tampa, Fla., 1957-63; cemetary sales mgr. Southea. Advt. and Sales, Hickory and Atlanta, 1954-56; owner, mgr. Louise Powell Realty, Hickory, 1964—; pres., owner Benson-Fox Assocs., Ltd., Hickory, 1986—; owner, mgr. Fairway Shopping Ctrs., Inc., Hickory, 1989—. Leader Girl Scouts U.S., Hickory and Tampa, 1967—; active First United Meth. Ch., Hickory; mem. Hickory Mus. Arts, 1983—, Am. Legion Aux., Hickory, 1973—, Hickory Cmty. Theatre. Home: 1235 10th Street Blvd NW Hickory NC 28601-2367

POWELL, MARY LUCAS, museum director. Dir., curator Mus. of Anthropology, Lexington. Office: Mus Anthropology 211 Lafferty Hall Lexington KY 40506 Office: U Ky 330 W Virginia Ave # A Lexington KY 40504-2641

POWELL, MICHAEL VANCE, lawyer; b. San Diego, Sept. 30, 1946; s. Jesse Vance and Mable Louise (Cagle) P.; m. Sarada Marie Hughes, Dec. 23, 1967; children: Marilyn Jean, Michael Benjamin. AB, Davidson Coll., N.C., 1968; MA, U. Tex., 1972, JD with honors, 1974. Bd. cert. civil appellate law Tex. Bd. Legis. Specialization. Law clk. to judge U.S. Ct. Appeals (9th cir.), 1974-75; assoc. Rain Harrell Emery Young & Doke, Dallas, 1975-80, ptnr., 1980-87; mem. Locke Purnell Rain Harrell, Dallas, 1987—. Elder St. Barnabas Presbyn. Ch., Richardson, Tex. Home: 7312 Tophill Ln Dallas TX 75248-5642 Office: Locke Purnell Rain Harrell 2200 Ross Ave Dallas TX 75201-7903

POWELL, PATRICIA ANN, secondary school educator; b. Covington, Ga., Apr. 6, 1956; d. John Doyle Sr. and Pauline Josephine (Thompson) Dunn; m. Jackie Lee Powell, May 10, 1980; 1 child, Jackie Lee II. BS, Lee Coll., 1978; MEd in Adminstrn. and Supervision, U. Tenn., 1993. Br. loan officer Am. Nat. Bank and Trust, Chattanooga, 1979-81; tchr. math. Hamilton County Schs., Chattanooga, 1983-85; customer svc. rep. First Union Nat. Bank, Atlanta, 1986-88; instr. tech. bus., typing DeKalb County Schs., Decatur, Ga., 1989; grad. asst. U. Tenn., Chattanooga, 1991-93; tchr. math. Hamilton County Sch. Sys., 1993-96; instr. English, bus. math. and bus. skills Urban League Bus. Skills Tng. Ctr., Chattanooga; mem. adj. faculty Chattanooga State Tech. C.C., 1991-92; joint stds. rep. for sch. consolidation, 1995-96. Co-author: Career Orientation-Grade 8, 1985 (monetary award 1984-85); singer African Americans Against Blood Disorders Benefit, Atlanta, 1994. Singer, Mayor's Office Performing Artists Against Drugs, Atlanta, 1990; vol. Chattanooga Comty. Kitchen, 1990—; tutor, coord. math., reading United Way's Adult Reading Program, Chattanooga, 1991—; instr. aerobics Am. Heart Assn., Chattanooga, 1991—; vol. Warner Park Zoo, Chattanooga; treas. Looking to the Word Ministries, Inc., 1985-94; v.p. parents group 1st Cumberland Child Devel. Ctr., 1992-94; sch. rep. Joint Stds. Com. for Consol., 1995-96, Diversity Com. for Consol., 1996-97. Outstanding Classroom Tchr. nominee, 1993-94; recipient Black Grad. fellowship U. Tenn., Chattanooga, 1992, 93; named Woman of Yr. and Mrs. Congeniality, Mrs. Chattanooga-Am. Pageant, 1990; Endowment scholar, 1977-78. Mem. NAFE, AAUW, Hamilton County Edn. Assn. (chmn. minority affairs com. 1995-97), Chattanooga Area Math. Assn. (v.p. mid. schs. 1996-97), Friends of Zoo Preservation Group, Delta Sigma Theta, Kappa Delta Pi (pres., v.p. 1993-95). Home: PO Box 24912 Chattanooga TN 37422-4912

POWELL, REBECCA GAETH, education educator; b. Westlake, Ohio, Oct. 23, 1949; d. John Paul and Ione Roxanne (Poad) Gaeth; m. Jerry Wayne Powell, June 14, 1991; children: Justin Matthew (dec.), Ryan Michael. B Music Edn., Coll. of Wooster (Ohio), 1971; MEd, U. N.C., 1976; D in Edn., U. Ky., 1989. Cert. curriculum and instrn. Elem. tchr. Rittman (Ohio) Elem., 1971-72; presch. tchr. YWCA, Durham, N.C., 1974-76; spl. reading tchr. Claxton Elem. Sch., Asheville, N.C., 1977; instr. and dir. reading, cert. program Mars Hill (N.C.) Coll., 1977-80; health educator Hot Springs (N.C.) Health Program, 1984-85; asst. prof. Ky. State U., Frankfort, 1989-93; assoc. prof. Georgetown (Ky.) Coll., 1993—; Ky. primary sch. rschr. U. Ky. Inst. on Ednl. Reform, Lexington, 1993—; ednl. cons. Jessamine County Schs., Nicholasville, Ky., 1992-93, Dade County Schs., Miami, Fla., 1995; tchr. educator, trainer, participant pilot project Ky. Tchr. Internship Program, Frankfort, 1990—; chmn. Alliance for Multicultural Edn., Ky., 1993-95; coord. Ctrl. Ky. Whole Lang. Network, 1991-93; mem. Ky. Multicultural Edn. Task Force, 1995—. Editor: (monograph series) Alliance for Multicultural Education, 1994-95; contbr. articles to profl. jours. Dissertation Year fellow U. Ky., Lexington, 1988-89. Mem. Nat. Assn. Multicultural Edn., Nat. Coun. Tchrs. English, Nat. Conf. Rsch. in English, Am. Ednl. Studies Assn., Ky. Coun. Tchrs. English, Alliance for Multicultural Edn. Office: Georgetown Coll 400 E College St Georgetown KY 40324-1628

POWELL, ROBERT BURNEY, real estate broker; b. Columbia, S.C., Nov. 12, 1929; s. Robert Burney and Virginia Louise (Vincenzi) P.; m. Clara Melrose Fraser, 1951 (dec.); m. Wilma Joyce Turner Clauder Boothe, Nov. 19, 1976 (div. July 1986); children: Marvin Ray, Gloria Virginia Dani, Don E. Clauder, Arthur Lee Clauder, Candiss Caye Little, Paul Bradley Clauder. Student, U. Ga., 1946-50, So. Meth. U., 1950-51, Tex. Tech U., 1954-57, U. Houston, 1963-64, Houston C.C. Sys., 1985-87. Lic. real estate broker, Tex. Ins. engr. Continental Cos. of N.Y., Atlanta and Dallas, 1946-48; spl. ins. agt. Continental Cos. of N.Y., N.Y.C., 1948-59; state ins. agt. Nat. of Hartford (Conn.) Group, 1959-62; real estate broker, 1962—, The Constitution Agy., Houston, 1980—. Composer piano music; contbr. poems to National Anthology of Poetry, 1946. Mem. com. Nat. Rep. Com., Nat. Dem. Com.; pres. Campbell Woods Civic Club, Houston, 1962-77; mem. com. Clean Houston, City of Houston, 1980—; mem. com. Spring Branch Assn., Neighborhood Civic Assn., Houston, 1986—; mem. Panda Houston Police Dept., 1994—. Recipient honors Ins. Inst. Am., 1948, 50, Hon. Order of Blue Goose, 1950. Mem. Nat. Assn. Realtors, Tex. Assn. Realtors, Houston Assn. Realtors (mem. Make Am. Better Com. 1980-83), Masons. Mem. Unity Ch. of Practical Christianity. Home and Office: 10479 Norton Dr Houston TX 77043-2126

POWELL, ROBERT JACKSON, III, insurance agent; b. Durham, N.C., Dec. 30, 1947; s. Robert Jackson and Catherine (Gant) P.; m. Clarine Gatling Pollock, June 13, 1970; children: Robert Jackson IV, Graham Pollock, John Gatling, Catherine Gant. BA, Davidson Coll., 1969; MBA, U. N.C., 1971. Analyst R.s. Dickson, Powell, Kistler & Crawford, Charlotte, N.C., 1971-73; rsch. dir. The Powell Group, Inc., Charlotte, N.C., 1973-75; sales v.p. Moroil Corp., Charlotte, N.C., 1975-76; agt. The Equitable Soc. N.Y., Greenville, N.C., 1976—; mng. dir. Plan Security Assocs., Greenville, N.C., 1982—; bd. dirs. Moroil Corp., Glen Raven Mills, Inc., Burlington, N.C. Fin. chmn. St. Paul's Episcopal Ch., Greenville, 1992-94; chmn. St. Peter's Cath. Sch., Greenville, 1990—; pres. Greenville Soccer Assn., 1990-93, County Family Violence Commn., Greenville, 1988-91. Capt. U.S Army, 1971-80. Named Friend of Yr. St. Peter's Sch., Greenville, 1992. Mem. NALU, Am. Assn. CLU/ChFC, Million Dollar Round Table, Rotary

(Greenville chpt. pres. 1988-89). Epsicopalian. Home: 511 Bremerton Dr Greenville NC 27858-6502 Office: Plan Security Assocs 3105 C S Evans St Greenville NC 27858

POWELL, STEVEN LOYD, minister; b. Dixon, Ill., Feb. 27, 1954; s. Elmer Loyd and Eleanor Mae (Ritchey) P.; m. Kathryn Ann Benda, Nov. 25, 1975; children: Julie Ann, Phillip Loyd, Stephanie Michelle. Student, Cen. Bible Coll., 1972-75. Ordained to ministry Assemblies of God, 1980. Co-pastor Peace Chapel Assembly of God, Morris, Ill., 1975-77; pastor Mt. Vernon (Ill.) First Assembly of God, 1977-80; sr. pastor First Assembly of God, Hammond, Ind., 1980-89, Bethel Temple Assembly of God, Tampa, Fla., 1989—; youth rep. southeastern sect. Ill. Dist. Assemblies of God, Carlinville, Ill., 1978-80; adviser Joy Fellowship, Northwest Ind. Dist., 1980-82; presbyter Ind. dist. Assemblies of God, Indpls., 1982-89; founder, exec. producer, host "Come Alive" program First Assembly of God, Hammond, Ind., 1983-85. Local adviser Women's Aglow, Morris, Ill., 1975-77, Homewood, Ill., 1982-87; area bd. adviser Women's Aglow Chgo., 1988-89; area exec. chmn. World Wide Pictures, Mt. Vernon, Ill., 1978-79; bd. regents North Cen. Bible Coll., Mpls., 1986-89; nat. bd. govs. Am. Coalition for Traditional Values, 1984-88; bd. dirs. Lake County Econ. Opportunity Coun., Hammond, 1985-88, mayor's rep., 1988-89; founder, exec. dir. soup kitchen Caring Hands, Hammond, 1986-89; task force mem. Project Self-Sufficiency, Hammond, 1987-89; com. mem. Hammond Long-Range Planning Commn., Hammond, 1988-89. Named for Svc. with Distinction, Revivaltime Choir, 1972-74, one of Outstanding Young Men of Am., U.S. Jaycees, 1979; recipient Disting. Svc. Award Hammond Jaycees, 1988, Good Samaritan award 1st Assembly of God Caring Hands, 1989, Key to City of Hammond, Mayor of Hammond, 1989. Office: Bethel Temple Assembly of God 1510 W Hillsborough Ave Tampa FL 33603-1208

POWELL, THOMAS ERVIN, accountant, consultant; b. Trion, Ga., Mar. 19, 1947; s. Ervin and Myrtice (Wike) P.; m. Lana Lois Lang, June 20, 1976; children: Thomas Christopher, Alissa Lynne, Ashley Beth. BS, U. Ctrl. Fla., 1974, MS, 1977; postgrad. studies, U. Fla., 1979. CPA, Fla.; cert. internal auditor. Pub. acct. KPMG Peat Marwick, Orlando, Fla., 1974-75, Arthur Andersen & Co., Orlando, 1975-77; instr. acctg. U. Ctrl. Fla., Orlando, 1977-81; dir. Inst. Internal Auditors, Altamonte Springs, Fla., 1981-95; pres. The Powell Group, Inc., Windermere, Fla., 1996—, 1996—; mem. accreditation com. Am. Assembly Collegiate Schs. Bus., 1992-93. Author: Examination Writer's Guide, 1981, rev. edit., 1995; mem. editl. bd. Issues in Acctg. Edn. Jour., 1995—. Vice chmn. audit bd. City of Orlando, 1990-95; treas. Christian Endowment Found., 1996—; chmn. Practice Advising Coun. With USAF, 1967-71. Mem. AICPA, Am. Acctg. Assn. (profl. exam. com. 1986-89, 93—, audit edn. conf. com. 1990-93, v.p. profl. practices 1994-96, chmn. practice adv. coun. 1996—), Internat. Platform Assn., Inst. Internal Auditors, Fla. Soc. CPAs (edn. com. 1990-93, legis. com. 1991), Nat. Assn. Corp. Dirs., Beta Alpha Psi (adv. coun. 1993—, Alumnus of Yr. U. Ctrl. Fla. 1992), Beta Gamma Sigma. Republican. Baptist. Home: 1938 Maple Leaf Dr Windermere FL 34786 Office: The Powell Group Inc PO Box 766 Gotha FL 34734

POWELL, WANDA GARNER, librarian; b. Dresden, Tenn., Nov. 16, 1940; d. Lewis C. and Mary (Coleman) Garner; m. William C. Powell, Oct. 26, 1963; children: Gena Rae, Elizabeth Lewis. BS, U. Tenn., Martin, 1971; MA, Murray (Ky.) State U., 1976. Sec. Bay Bee Shoe Co., Dresden, 1958-67; clk. U. Tenn., Martin, 1967-71; tchr., libr. Gleason (Tenn.) High Sch., 1971-76; libr. Dresden High Sch., 1976—; career ladder evaluator State of Tenn., Nashville, 1984-85, career ladder III, 1986; pres. Women's Missionary Union, 1986-91. chair bd. dirs. Weakley County Pub. Libr., 1993—. Mem. Weakley County Edn. Assn. (pres. 1981-82), United Teaching Profls., DAR, Phi Delta Kappa, Delta Kappa Gamma (pres. Beta Omega chpt. 1990-92). Democrat. Baptist. Home: RR 1 Box 241 Dresden TN 38225-9735

POWELL, WILLIAM ARNOLD, JR., retired banker; b. Verbena, Ala., July 7, 1929; s. William Arnold and Sarah Frances (Baxter) P.; m. Barbara Ann O'Donnell, June 16, 1956; children: William Arnold III, Barbara Calhoun, Susan Thomas, Patricia Crain. BSBA, U. Ala., 1953; grad., La. State U. Sch. Banking of South, 1966. With Am. South Bank, N.A., Birmingham, Ala., 1953—, asst. v.p., 1966, v.p., 1967, v.p., br. supr., 1968-72, sr. v.p., br. supr., 1972-73, exec. v.p., 1973-79, pres., 1979-83, vice chmn. bd., 1983-93, also bd. dirs.; pres. AmSouth Bancorp., 1979—; bd. dirs. AmSouth Bank Fla., AmSouth Bancorp. Bd. dirs. United Way Found.; trustee Ala. Hist. Soc., Ala. Ind. Colls.; bd. visitors U. Ala.; past pres. United Way, campaign chmn., 1987; mem. pres.'s coun. U. Ala., Birmingham; bd. dirs. Warrior-Tombigbee Devel. Assn., Birmingham Mus. Art, Brookwood Med. Ctr.-AMI, Big Bros./Big Sisters of Greater Birmingham. Lt. AUS, 1954-56. Mem. Birmingham Area C. of C. (bd. dirs.), The Club, Mountain Brook, Birmingham Country Club, Green Valley Country Club (Birmingham). Home: 2114 Hickory Ridge Cir Birmingham AL 35243-2925

POWELL, WILLIAM COUNCIL, SR., service company executive; b. Burlington, N.C., Nov. 5, 1948; s. Thomas Edward Jr. and Annabelle (Council) P.; m. Jacqueline Garrison, July 3, 1976; children: William C. Jr., Ashley C. Student U. S.C., 1968-69; BS Va. Mil. Inst., 1971; MBA, Wake Forest U., 1974; postgrad. Elon Coll., 1974. Lic. real estate broker, N.C. Adminstrv. assoc. Carolina Biol. Supply Co., Inc., Burlington, 1971-91, also bd. dirs.; v.p. Bobbitt Labs., Burlington, 1974-77, pres., 1977-82; owner HEADS, Inc., 1978—, pres., 1984—; owner Ashwil Acres Farm, Mebane, N.C., 1981—; pres. Granite Diagnostics, Inc., Burlington, 1981-84, UST Specialists Inc., 1991—; owner Powell Real Estate, Burlington, 1979—, chmn. bd. dirs.; bd. dirs. Excalibur Lock Co., Inc., Burlington, past chmn.; v.p. Warren Land Co., 1990-94, pres., 1994—; v.p. fin., bd. dirs. Environ. Responsible Bus. Inc., 1992—; mem. Babcock Sch. Alumni Coun. Wake Forest U., 1981-85; bd. dirs. Waubun Labs., Inc., Schriever, La.; mgr. Macon Farm, 1992-95; chmn. bd. Ensci Corp., Inc., 1991-95, CEO, 1994-95; ptnr. Port Assocs., 1987, Port Assocs. II, 1992—; chmn. bd. Netpath Inc., 1995-1996, Pres. Stratonet Inc., 1996—, advisors Elon Coll. (N.C.), 1984-86, bd. visitors, 1987-92; bd. advisors Duke U. Marine Lab., Beaufort, N.C., 1985-92; mem. adv. panel Air Quality Compliance Panel State of N.C. Dept. Environ. Health and Natural Resources, 1994—; guardian mem. Boy Scouts Am., Burlington, 1985; trustee Dr. T.E. Powell Jr. Trust, 1989-95; v.p. fin. Cherokee Coun. Boy Scouts of Am., 1990-92, exec. bd., 1990-94, exec. bd. Old N. State Coun, 1994-95. Capt. USAR, 1971-79. Recipient Bill Fish Cert. State of S.C., 1983, 2 Bill Fish Certs. State of N.C., 1990, Sower's award Duke U., 1985, N.C. Gov.'s Cup for Billfishing, 1991. Mem. NRA, Newcomun Soc. N.Am. (life mem.), Billiard Congress Am., Am. Angus Assn., Billard and Bowling Inst. Assn., N.C. Forestry Assn. (legis. affairs com., 1994—), Ducks Unltd. (area chmn. 1985-87), N.C. Chpt. Safari Club Internat. (state pres. 1985-88, lifetime mem.), Aircraft Owners and Pilots Assn., Cessna Owner Orgn., Atlantic Coast Conservation Assn. (lifetime), Alamance Wildlife Club (bd. dirs. 1992-95), Rolls Royce Owners Club, N.Am. Hunting Club (life), Found. N.Am. Wild Sheep (lifetime), Chaine des Rotisseurs (chevalier 1991), Brotherhood of the Knights of the Vine (master knight 1991), 10 Point Hunt Club, Am. Angus Assn., Nat. Wild Turkey Fedn., Quail Unltd., N.C. Cattlemans Assn., Nat. Cattlemans Assn., Inc., Debordieu Club, Alamance Country Club, Debordieu Beach Club, Litchfield Carriage House Club. Home: 1109 W Front St Burlington NC 27215-3610 Office: HEADS Inc 2608 NC Hwy 100 Elon College NC 27244 also: Stranbet Inc 2260 S Church St Burlington NC 27215

POWELL HILL, ELIZABETH T., singer, small business owner; b. San Antonio, Feb. 5, 1954; d. Elijah and Mattie B. Tyler; m. Frederick Powell, Apr. 16, 1977 (div.); children: Frederick Powell, Michael Powell; m. James LaRue Hill, Mar. 10, 1989; 1 child, Victoria Hill. Degree in Applied Science, St. Philip's Coll., 1987, AA, 1989. Lic. fin. broker, real estate investor. Sec. San Antonio Light Newspaper, 1979-80; bus. owner T. Powell Express Co., San Antonio, 1982—; singer pop rock various locations, 1985—; owner Queen Elizabeth Enterprise Global Wealth Builder, San Antonio, 1996—. Author: (song) Just Seeing You, 1985, (book) The Elizabeth Powell Letters, 1992; designer curio dress, 1989; copyright original works as author, 1992. Founder Perfect Abundant Life Mockulisaphen Ch., San Antonio, 1996. Recipient Trophy award for Best Performer Inner City Prodns., 1986, 1st Runner up trophy for performance Elks Lodge, 1990. Mem. Am. Fedn. Musicians, Internat. Platform Assn. Office: T Powell Express Co PO Box 200643 San Antonio TX 78220-0643

POWER, ELIZABETH HENRY, consultant; b. Hickory, N.C., Sept. 28, 1953; d. William Henry Power and Katheryn Otis (Smith) Nelson. Cert. in creative writing, N.C. Sch. Arts, 1971; BA in Sociology, U. N.C., Greensboro, 1977; MEd in Human Resources Devel., Vanderbilt U., 1997. With adoption and foster home recruitment Davidson County Dept. Human Svcs., Nashville, 1980-81; behavioral cons. Nutri-System Weight Loss Ctr., Nashville, 1982-84; corp. sec., cons. Quantum Leap Cons., Inc., Nashville, 1984-86; pres., owner EPower & Assocs., Brentwood, Tenn., 1980-84, 86—; owner MPD/DD Resource & Edn. Ctr., Nashville, 1991-93; cons. GM/Saturn, 1988-96. Author: If Change Is All There Is, Choice Is All You've Got, 1990, Managing Our Selves: Building a Community of Caring, 1992; co-author, editor: Circle of Love: Child Personal Safety, 1984; contbg. author: Nonprofit Policies and Procedures, 1992, More than Survivors: Conversations with Multiple Personality Clients, 1992, also articles. Vol. West Chester (Pa.) Women's Resource Ctr., 1977; vol. instr. theology Lay Acad. Episc. Diocese Western N.C., Asheville, 1976-77; mem. Burke County Coun. Status Women, Morganton, N.C., 1977-79, sec., 1978; vol. Western N.C. Flood Com., 1977-78; exec. dir. N.C. Rape Crisis Assn., Raleigh, 1979, Foothills Mental Health Ctr., Morganton, 1978-79; mem. task force, writer, convener, facilitator N.C. Gov.'s Conf. Mental Health, 1979; trainer, vol. Rape House Crisis Ctr., Nashville, 1979-81; vol., trainer Rape and Sexual Abuse Ctr., Nashville, 1981-82, bd. dirs., 1981-82; mem. quality circles steering com. Tenn. Dept. Human Svcs., 1980-81; program cons. Women's Resource and Assistance Program, Jackson, Tenn., 1988-92; bd. dirs. Life Challenge Tenn., 1989-91. Recipient numerous awards N.C. Dept. Mental Health/Mental Retardation, 1979, State of N.C., 1979, Central Nashville Optimist Club, 1982, Waco YWCA, Waco, Tex., 1985. Mem. NAFE, Internat. Soc. for Traumatic Stress Studies. Democrat. Home and Office: PO Box 2346 Brentwood TN 37024-2346

POWER, JACQUELINE LOU, accounting educator; b. Little Rock, May 7, 1937; d. Jack Arthur King and Lucie Owen (Brack) Bourdon; m. Billy Joe Power, June 9, 1956 (dec. June 1985); children: Melanie Lou Power Wick, Aaron King Power. BA in Physics, Math., North Tex. State U., 1960; MBA, U. Tex., Tyler, 1986; PhD in Acctg., Tex. A&M U., 1993. Radiol. physicist Phillips Petroleum Co., Idaho Falls, Idaho, 1962-65; instr. math. Muscogee County Schs., Columbus, Ga., 1966-67; instr. phys. sci. Tyler Ind. Schs., 1971-72; instr. physics and math. Tyler Jr. Coll., 1973-74; co-owner A & B Outdoor Sports Ctr., Tyler, 1970-83; lectr. acctg. Tex. A&M U., College Station, 1989-92; instr. acctg. Blinn Coll., College Station, 1992-93; asst. prof. acctg. Tex. A&M Internat. U., Laredo, 1993—. AEC fellow in radiol. physics, 1960-61, Tex. A&M U. Merit fellow, 1987-88. Mem. Am. Acctg. Assn. Republican. Episcopalian. Home: 8107 Estate Dr Laredo TX 78045 Office: Texas A&M International Univ 5201 University Blvd Laredo TX 78041

POWER, SHERRY DECKER, English language educator; b. DeLeon, Tex., July 15, 1946; d. Silas Melton and Mayme Lou (Dickey) Decker; m. Thomas Franklin Power, May 4, 1969; children: Jason Derek, Dana Elizabeth. BA, Tarleton State U., 1991, MA, 1994. Adj. faculty Tarleton State U., Stephenville, Tex., 1993-96; occasional faculty Tex. Christian U., Fort Worth, 1994-96. Pres. Comanche (Tex.) Newcomers Club, 1983-84; county coord. Am. Heart Assn., Comanche, 1983-84, sec., 1984-85. All-Am. scholar U.S. Achievement Acad., 1989. Mem. MLA, Nat. Coun. Tchrs. English, Tex. Coun. Tchrs. English, Conf. on Coll. Composition and Comm., Epsilon Sigma Alpha (pres. 1978-79). Democrat. Baptist. Home: 106 Aztec Circle Comanche TX 76442 Office: Tarleton State Univ Box T-159 Tarleton Sta Stephenville TX 76402

POWERS, CLIFFORD BLAKE, JR., communications researcher, consultant; b. Macon, Ga., July 15, 1960; s. Clifford Blake Sr. and Virginia (Davis) P. BA in Journalism with honors, Columbia Coll., 1983; MS in Communications, U. Tenn., 1989. Photographic intern Playboy, Chgo., 1983; corr.-at-large SpaceWorld Mag., 1983-86; sr. sci. writer Schneider Svcs. Internat., Arnold AFB, Tenn., 1985-87; grad. rsch. asst. U. Tenn., Knoxville, 1988-89; writer II Space & Def. div. Essex Corp., Huntsville, Ala., 1990-96; owner, cons., info. and ednl. products, mktg. Powers Comm., Madison, Ala., 1996—; project mgr. Spacelab J, USML-1, TSS-1 Astro 2, USML-2 missions; instr. sci. Faulkner U., Huntsville, 1990-91. Author: The Soviet Watchers, 1990, (with others) Unlocking The Mysteries of the Universe: A Guide to Astro-1 Observations, 1990, Astro-1 Postmission Summary Report, 1991, Spacelab J: Microgravity and Life Sciences, 1992, The First United States Microgravity Laboratory 1992, The First Mission of the Tethered Satellite System, 1992, USML-1 90-Day Science Report, 1992, Astro-2 Continuing Exploration of the Invisible Universe, 1994, Continuing Exploration of the Invisible Universe: A Guide to Astro-2 Targets, 1995, NASA's Microgravity Science Laboratory: Illuminating the Future, 1996, others; contbr. articles to SpaceWorld Mag., Chgo. Sun-Times and others. Recipient Right Stuff award Space Acad., Huntsville, 1986, NASA Commendation for USML-1, 1992, Group Achievement award NASA (Astro-1 Space Classroom), 1992, Group Achievement Award NASA (Astro-1 Pub. Affairs team), 1992, Disting. Tech. Commn. award 1st Mission of Tethered Satallite System, 1993, Best of Show award Birmingham and Huntsville STC chpt., The First Mission of the Tethered Satellite System, 1993; Group Achievement award, 1993, Excellence in Tech. Communication award (Information Brochures) Huntsville/N. Ala. chpt. SIC, Astro-2 Continuing Exploration of the Invisible Universe, numerous other awards, especially from NASA; Bickle scholar, 1988-89. Mem. Nat. Assn. Sci. Writers (assoc.), N.Y. Acad. Scis., Pub. Rels. Soc. Am., Kappa Tau Alpha. Home and Office: 3003 Flag Cir Apt 2514 Madison AL 35758-1980

POWERS, DONALD TYRONE, artist; b. Madison, Tenn., May 20, 1950; s. Willard and Ruby Lee (Harvey) P.; m. Jeanne Elizabeth Donaldson, Mar. 16, 1977; children: Nathanael Walden, Daniel Everett. Ed., Tenn. Technol. U. Artist, art dir. Tenn. State Mus., 1973-78; represented by Gerold Wunderlich & Co., N.Y.C.; lectr. contemporary realism Columbus Mus. Art, 1985. One-man shows include East Tenn. State U., Fine Arts Gallery, U. of South, First Tenn. Nat. Corp., Hunter Mus. Art, Chattanooga, Harmon Meek Gallery, Morris Fine Arts, Scottsdale, Ariz.; exhibited in group shows at Butler Inst. Am. Art, Albrecht Art Mus., Coll. of William and Mary, Minn. Mus. Art, Sherry French Gallery, N.Y., Southeastern Ctr. for Contemporary Art, Winston-Salem, N.C., Kalamazoo Art Inst., Okla. Art Ctr., Tulsa, Riverside Art Mus., L.A., Babcock Galleries, N.Y., 1993, Kennedy Galleries, N.Y., 1993, Middlebury Coll., Vt., 1993, Alterman and Morris Gallery, Houston, 1993, Cumberland Gallery, Nashville, 1994, Albany Inst. History and Art, 1994, Owensboro (Ky.) Mus. Fine Art, 1994, Westmoreland Mus. Art, Greenburg, Pa., 1994, Md. Inst. Coll. and Art, Balt., 1994, Berzins and Robert Fine Arts, Scottsdale, Ariz., 1994; represented in permanent collections Hunter Mus. Art, Chattanooga, Ga. Mus. Art U. Ga., Athens, Nat. Portrait Gallery, Smithsonian Instn., Washington, Butler Inst. Am. Art, Youngstown, Ohio, Mus. Modern Art, Haifa, Lyndhurst Found., Chattanooga, Am. Acad. and Inst. Arts and Letters, N.Y.C., Carter Presdl. Libr., Atlanta, 1st Tenn. Nat. Corp., Memphis, Remington Rand Corp., Princeton, N.J., Am. Nat. Bank and Trust Co., Chattanooga, Witt, Gaither, Whitaker, Chattanooga, United Dominion, Ltd., Toronto, Tibet House, N.Y.C., Stephens Overseas, Inc., Atlanta, also pvt. collections incl. Southern Assets Mngmnt., Longleaf Partners, Memphis, Emory U, Atlanta; author: The Artist as a Native, 1993. Home: Box 3295 217 Edgewood Dr Thomasville GA 31792-4510

POWERS, ELDON NATHANIEL, computer mapping executive; b. Wichita, Kans., Feb. 14, 1932; s. Ernie Lee and Bessie Othella (Loomis) P.; m. Betty Jean Zeigler, Sept. 4, 1954; children: Rebekah Jean, Robert John, Samuel Tyler. Student, Friends U., 1950-51; BA in Missions, Central Bible Coll., 1954; BA in Modern Lang. Edn., Evangel Coll., 1963; MS in Math., Tulsa U., 1971. Pastor Assembly of God Ch., Hays, Kans., 1955-60; data processing technician Gospel Pub. House, Springfield, Mo., 1960-63; data processing analyst Amoco Prodn. Co., Oklahoma City, 1963-65; research scientist Amoco Prodn. Co., Tulsa, 1965-67, staff research scientist, 1968-81; sr. system analyst Electro Mech. Research, Bloomington, Minn., 1967-68; mgr. info. service Fox Drilling Co., Tulsa, 1981-82; pres. ENP Software, Inc., Sapulpa, Okla., 1982-92; computer mapping specialist PowersTech, Tulsa, 1992—; cons. in field. Contbr. articles to profl. jours.; author various computer programs including automatic contouring and geol. subsurface structural analysis; co-author Jupiter Mapping System. Adv. bd. Cen. Okla. Vocat. Tech. Sch., Sapulpa, 1986-89. Mem. Computer Oriented Geol. Soc., Internat. Assn. Math. Geology. Democrat. Methodist.

POWERS, ESTHER SAFIR, organization design consultant; b. Tel Aviv, Sept. 1, 1948; arrived in Can., 1953, came to U.S., 1977; d. Nisan and Batia (Epstein) Safir; children: Jared Barnet, Eliott Robert. MusB, McGill U., Montreal, Que., Can., 1969; MusM, Ga. State U., 1982, PhD, 1985. Music tchr. North York Bd. Edn., Toronto, Ont., 1969-77; pres. Ested Mgmt., 1975-77, Mescon Group, Atlanta, 1985-95; cons. PeopleTech, 1995—. Contbr. articles to profl. jours., chpt. to book. Pres. bd. dirs. Montessori Sch., Atlanta, 1978; vol. Nat. Coun. Jewish Women, Atlanta, 1990; mem. Ga. Exec. Womens Network; bd. dirs. Coun. Battered Women, 1994—. Mem. Nat. Assn. Sch. Karate, Internat. Soc. for Performance Improvement (pres. Atlanta chpt. 1984-85, conf. mgr. 1983-84, internat. v.p. 1988-90, internat. pres. 1991-92, presdl. citation 1988, presdl. award 1989, leadership award 1990). Office: PeopleTech 1040 Crown Pointe Pky # 570 Atlanta GA 30338-4777

POWERS, EVELYN MAE, education educator; b. Norfolk, Va., Aug. 4, 1946; d. Albert Earl and Dorothy Mae (Weller) P.; m. Curtis Grubb Fitzhugh, June 21, 1969 (div. 1981). BA in Spanish, James Madison U., 1968; MEd in Curriculum & Instrn., Fgn. Langs., U. Va., 1976, PhD in Social Founds. of Edn., 1985. Spanish teacher pub. high schs., Va., 1969-77; grad. instr., instr. U. Va., Charlottesville, 1977-85; adj. and part-time faculty Va. Commonwealth U., Richmond, 1985-88; asst. prof. edn. Lycoming Coll., Williamsport, Pa., 1988-91; asst. prof. social founds. of edn. E. Carolina U., Greenville, N.C., 1991—. Mem. Am. Ednl. Studies Assn., N.C. Founds. of Edn. Profs., So. Atlantic Philosophy of Edn. Soc. (yearbook editor 1994-98, archivist 1993-96), Phi Delta Kappa. Home: 307 Joseph St Greenville NC 27858-9242

POWERS, FRANCIS GARY, JR., municipal official; b. Burbank, Calif., June 5, 1965; s. Francis Gary and Claudia Sue (Edwards) P. Student, Calif. State U., Northridge, 1983-87; BA in Philosophy, Calif. State U., L.A., 1991; MPA, George Mason U., Fairfax, Va., 1994. Adminstrv. asst. Rancho Vista Devel. Co., Palmdale, Calif., 1984-86; pers. adminstr. Pardee Constrn. Co. sub. Weyerhaeuser, L.A., 1988-89; field rep. Alan Parker Constrn., L.A., 1989-90; adminstr. asst. dept. pub. and internat. affairs George Mason U., Fairfax, 1992-94; asst. registrar City of Fairfax, 1994-95; officer of election City of Fairfax, 1994; chmn. 14th Ann. Pub. Administrn. Consortium Conf., Arlington, Va., 1994 (exec. dir. mktg. cons., 1995—); Downtown Fairfax Coalition, 1994. Founder, pres. The Young Californians, L.A., 1986-88; asst. campaign mgr. Va. State Del. Race, Fairfax County, Va., 1993; founder Francis Gary Powers Mus. and Inst. for Study of Civil War, 1996. Mem. Am. Soc. for Pub. Adminstrs., MPA Student Assn. (founder, pres. 1992). Office: PO Box 178 Fairfax VA 22030-0178

POWERS, JACK W., development executive; b. Ft. Wayne, Ind., Oct. 28, 1929; s. Dorsey Byrl and Winnifred Cecelia (Kundred) P.; m. Ruth Margaret Ollhoff, Aug. 23, 1952; children: Tod W., David E., Alicia A., Laura J. B.S., Purdue U., 1952, M.S., 1956, Ph.D., 1957. Regional dir. Research Corp., Atlanta, 1969-75, v.p. resource devel., N.Y.C., 1975-79; v.p. external affairs Rensselaer Poly. Inst., Troy, N.Y., 1979-81; v.p. devel. Davidson Coll., N.C., 1981-85, St. Andrews Presbyterian Coll., Laurinburg, N.C., 1985-88; pvt. cons., 1988—. Mem. Am. Chem. Soc., Nat. Soc. Fund Raising Execs., Council for Advancement and Support of Edn., Sigma Xi. Republican. Presbyterian. Lodge: Masons (grand master Ripon, Wis. 1967-68). Avocations: golf, sailing, fishing. Home and Office: Jack Powers & Assocs 105 N Cherrywood Ln Pisgah Forest NC 28768-9500

POWERS, RUNAS, JR., rheumatologist; b. Jackson's Gap, Ala., Dec. 11, 1938; s. Runas and Geneva (Burton) P.; m. Mary Alice Shelton, Feb. 4, 1969; children: Tiffany, Trina, Runas Coley III. BS, Tenn. State U., 1961; MD, Meharry Med. Coll., Nashville, 1966. From intern to resident in internal medicine Hurley Hosp., Flint, Mich., 1966-67, 69-72; postdoctoral fellow Stanford (Calif.) Med. Ctr., 1972-76; pvt. practice Alexander City, Ala. Contbr. with others articles to Jour. of Rheumatology, Alcohol Myopathy and Myoglobinuric Nephrosis. Lt. comdr. MD, USN, 1967-69. Decorated Purple Heart, Bronze Star; named Man of Yr. Alexander City C. of C., 1991. Fellow Am. Coll. Rheumatology; mem. AMA, N.Y. Acad. Sci, Ala. State Med. Assn., Nat. Med. Assn., Am. Fedn. Clinical Rsch. Office: 3368 Highway 280 Ste 108 Alexander City AL 35010-3375

POWERS, W. ALEX, artist; b. St. Charles, Va., Apr. 25, 1940; s. William Coscar and Elsie Mae (Weston) P.; m. Janet Covington, 1980 (div. 1989). BA, Emory & Henry Coll., 1962. Pub. sch. tchr. Henrico and Chesterfield Counties, Richmond, Va., 1962-66, Melbourne (Fla.) High Sch., 1966-67; sci. computer programmer RCA, Cape Kennedy, Fla., 1967-69; self-employed art tchr. Myrtle Beach, S.C., 1969—; juror Pitts. Watercolor Soc. Nat. Exhbn., 1991, Midwest Watercolor Soc. Nat. Exhbn., 1991, Balt. Watercolor Soc., Mid-Atlanta regional, 1992, Tenn. Watercolor Soc. ann. exhbn., 1992, Southeastern Watercolorist VIII, DeLand Mus. Art, 1993, Oreg. Watercolor Soc., The Dalles, 1993, La. Watercolor Soc. 23rd Ann. Internat. Exhbn., New Orleans, 1994; tchr. 12 to 15 workshops per yr. in U.S., Can. and abroad; represented in galleries in S.C., N.C., Va., Md., Mich., Calif. and Toronto. Author: Painting People in Watercolor, A Design Approach, 1989; exhibited in group shows at So. Watercolor Soc., Ga. Watercolor Soc. Nat., Watercolor U.S.A., Springfield, Mo., S.C. Watercolor Soc., 19th Nat. Watercolor Okla., Watercolor Soc. Ala. 52nd Nat., Miss. Watercolor Soc. Nat., Springs Art Show, Lancaster, S.C., Ky. Watercolor Soc. Nat.; numerous pub., corp. and pvt. collections in U.S. and Can. Recipient Best of Show awards Rocky Mountain Nat. Watermedia Exhbn., Golden, Colo., Okla. Gala Nat. Exhbn., Oklahoma City, Southeastern Watercolorists, Deland, Fla., Aqueous '93 Ky. Watercolor Soc. Nat. Exhbn., High Winds medal Am. Watercolor Soc., 1992. Mem. Nat. Watercolor Soc. Home: 401 72nd Ave N Apt 1 Myrtle Beach SC 29572-3814

POYNER, JAMES MARION, retired lawyer; b. Raleigh, N.C., Sept. 18, 1914; s. James Marion and Mary (Smedes) P.; m. Florence I Chan, Feb. 24, 1945; children: Susan Poyner Moore, Chan Poyner Pike, Margaret Poyner Galbraith, Edythe Poyner Lumdsen, James Marion III. B.S. in Chem. Engring, N.C. State U., 1935, M.S., 1937; J.D., Duke U., 1940. Bar: N.C. 1940. Pvt. practice Raleigh, 1946-51; of counsel ptnr. Poyner, Geraghty, Hartsfield & Townsend, Raleigh, 1951-86; of counsel Poyner & Spruill, Raleigh, 1986-95, ret., 1995; co-founder Cameron-Brown Co. (now 1st Union Mortgage Co.); life dir. 1st Union Corp., 1st Union Nat. Bank; chmn. bd. dirs. Eastern Standard Ins. Co., George Smedes Poyner Founds. Inc. Orch. leader, trombonist, arranger, Jimmy Poyner and His Orch., 1933-38. Mem. N.C. Senate, 1955-59; Past chmn. bd. trustees St. Mary's Coll.; past chmn. bd. World Golf Hall of Fame; past chmn. trustees N.C. Symphony Soc. Served with Chem. Warfare Service, AUS, 1942-46. Decorated Legion of Merit. Mem. ABA, N.C. Bar Assn. (pres. 1967-68, dir. 1963-67), Am. Judicature Soc. (dir. 1973-77), Raleigh C. of C. (past pres.), Phi Kappa Phi. Episcopalian. Home: 710 Smedes Pl Raleigh NC 27605-1141 Office: 3600 Glenwood Ave Raleigh NC 27612-4945

POYNOR, ROBERT ALLEN, JR., guidance counselor; b. Franklin, Tenn., Aug. 2, 1939; s. Robert Allen and Agnes Elizabeth (Gillespie) P.; divorced; 1 child, Melissa Dawn Hay. BA, Belmont Coll., Nashville, 1967; MEd, Middle Tenn. State U., 1972, EdS, 1975; postgrad., Tenn. State U. Cert. elem. tchr., elem. guidance counselor, elem. prin.-advanced, Tenn. Teller, mgmt. trainee Third Nat. Bank, Nashville, 1962-67; employment rep. S.S. Bd. of the S.B.C., Nashville, 1967-68; tchr. Sumner County Bd. Edn., Gallatin, Tenn., 1968-69; asst. sec.-treas., br. mgr. Security Fed. Savs. and Loan Assn., Nashville, 1969-71; tchr. Sumner County Bd. Edn., Gallatin, 1971-79, 83-85, prin., 1979-83, guidance counselor, 1985—; mem. textbook adoption com. Sumner County bd. Edn., 1968-69, gifted com., 1980-82. Charter sec. 100 Oaks Sertoma Club, Nashville, 1970; treas. Am. Savs. and Loan Inst., Nashville, 1970. With U.S. Army, 1957-59, France. Mem. ASCD, Tenn. ASCD, Tenn. Assn. Counselor Devel., Mid. Tenn. Assn. for Counselor Devel., United Teaching Profession, Sumner County Elem. Prins. (past pres. 1982-83), Sumner County Edn. Assn. (past pres. 1978-79), Phi Delta Kappa. Baptist. Home: 288 Indian Lake Rd Hendersonville TN 37075-4344

POYNTER, MELISSA VENABLE, real estate broker; b. Bluefield, W.Va., July 11, 1949; d. Robert Vance and Lois Chapman (Smith) Venable; m. Dan D. Poynter, Jan. 16, 1975; 1 child, Melissa. BS, Pikeville (Ky.) Coll., 1971. Tchr. Floyd County (Ky.) Bd. Edn., Prestonburg, 1971-72; counselor Action Now, Inc., Louisville, 1972-73; exec. sec. Louisville Grocery, 1973-75; chief exec. officer Poynter Enterprises, Lexington, Ky., 1978—; residential broker Rector-Hayden Realtors, Lexington, 1977-87; co-owner, broker Ky. Fine Homes, Lexington, 1987-88; broker Rector Hayden Realtors, Lexington, 1988-91, RE/MAX Creative Realty, Lexington, 1991-94; broker/owner Dan & Melissa Poynter, Realtors, Lexington, 1994—; chmn. bd. Most Valuable Pets, Inc., Lexington, 1993—; relocation dir. Re/Max All Star Realty, 1995—. Contbr. articles to profl. jours. Named 1989 Realtor of Yr., Lexington Bd. Realtors. Mem. Nat. Assn. Realtors (cert. nat. profl. stds. instr. 1987—), Realtors Nat. Mktg. Inst. (cert. resdl. specialist Ky. chpt.), Employee Relocation Coun. (cert. relocation prof. 1994—), Real Estate Buyers Agt. Coun. (accredited buyer rep. 1994—), Ky. Assn. Realtors (chmn. profl. stds. com. 1987-89), Lexington Bd. Realtors (chmn. grievance com. 1985-87, chmn. profl. stds. com. 1987-91, Realtor of Yr. 1989). Republican. Methodist. Office: RE/Max All Star Realty 2204 Silktree Ct Lexington KY 40513-1326

POYNTER, RANDOLPH W., county official; b. May 24, 1954; s. Ken and Marian Poynter; m. Libby Hudgins; children: Randolph Jr., David. BS in Criminal Justice, West Ga. Coll., 1976. Builder, developer residential Conyers, Ga., 1976-83; bank officer DeKalb Fed. Savs., Conyers, 1983-89; chmn., CEO Rockdale County Bd. Commrs., Conyers, 1989—; chmn. Atlanta Regional Commn. Mem. Nat. Assn. Counties (transp. and telecom. steering com.), Assn. County Commrs. (1st v.p.), Bd. Mgrs. Republican. Office: Rockdale County Bd Commrs 922 Court St PO Box 289 Conyers GA 30207

PRADE, JEAN NOËL CRESTA, entrepreneur; b. Boulogne, France, Dec. 26, 1946; came to U.S. in 1981; s. Georges and Jip (Barillier) P.; m. Noelle Prade, Jan. 17, 1971 (div. 1978); 1 child, Arnaud; m. Elizabeth Marie, Aug. 23, 1978; 1 child, Fleur. D.E.S. in Polit. Sci., U. Paris, 1972, D.E.S. in Econs., 1973. Asst. Jones-Lang-Wootton, Paris, London, 1972-74; pres. Maison de Thaïlande, Paris, 1974-76, Interonor, Paris, 1976-81, Epicurean Revue Inc., Sarasota, Fla., 1983—; pub. La Lettre Confidentielle; bd. dirs. Chili's Restaurant, Sun State; pres. Le Haras Inc. Author several gastronomical French books, Windows of the World; contbr. numerous articles on gastronomy and high class travels to mags. V.p. Groupe Union Droit, Paris, 1969-73, Scis. Po Alumni, Paris, 1974; indsl. relations judge, Paris, 1978-81. Recipient of Merite Nat. French govt., 1986, Merite Agricole, 1981. Mem. Ordre Des Tastevins, Chaine Des Rotisseurs, Ordre Des Coteaux De Champagne (chambellan), Fla. Thoroughbred Breeders Assn., Internat. Food, Wine & Travel Writers Assn. (regional dir. 1986—), Thoroughbred Owners and Breeders Assn., Cresta Club (St. Moritz), Regine's (Paris), Rolls Royce Owners Club. Roman Catholic. Home: 4619 Higel Ave Sarasota FL 34242-1205 also: Le Haras 14050 NW # C326 Morriston FL 32668

PRATHER, GARY BENTON, manufacturing company executive; b. Sulphur, Okla., Feb. 6, 1947; s. Samuel Benton and Ruby Marie (Wilks) P.; m. Katheryn Reed, 1966 (div. 1967); 1 child, Kellie Rene'. Student, Murray State U., 1965-67, W.V. Vocat. Tech. Inst., Ardmore, Okla., 1966, 67, U. Wis., 1971. Field engr. bowling products divsn. AMF, Little Rock, 1967-68; mgr. plant engrng. Wonder Snack Foods, Oklahoma City, 1968-69; mgr. field engrng. Visual Graphics Corp., Tamerac, Fla., 1970-75; mgr. sales and svc. World Graphics Corp., Dallas, 1976-77, Graphics Sys., Dallas, 1995—; regional mgr. Harris Corp., Dallas, 1977-94. Author: Elect. Troubleshooting, 1984, A History of the Prather Family, 1989. Mem. Sheriffs Assn. Tex., Tex. Police Officers Assn., Dallas C. of C., Frisco (Tex.) C. of C., Lineages, Masons. Home: 9189 Williams Pl Frisco TX 75034-3611 Office: Prather Enterprises PO Box 1225 Sulphur OK 73086

PRATHER, JOHN GIDEON, lawyer; b. Somerset, Ky., Dec. 12, 1919; s. James Frederick and Josephine Linnwood (Collier) P.; m. Marie Jeanette Moore, Oct. 1945; children: John G., Jerome Moore. B.A., U. Ky., 1940, J.D., 1947. Bar: Ky. 1947, U.S. Dist. Ct. (ea. dist.) Ky. 1950. Pros. atty. Somerset, Ky., 1950-63; commonwealth atty. 28th Jud. Dist., 1963-64; sole practice, Somerset; sr. ptnr. Law Offices of John G. Prather, Somerset; dir. First & Farmers Bank, Somerset. Served to lt. USN, 1942-46; Mem. Pulaski County Bar Assn., Ky. Bar Assn. (ethics com., com. on fees), ABA (probate sect.), Def. Research Inst. Democrat. Mem. Christian Ch. (Disciples of Christ). Clubs: Kiwanis (Somerset), Shriners, Odd Fellows, Masons. Office: PO Box 616 Somerset KY 42502-0616

PRATHER, LENORE LOVING, state supreme court presiding justice; b. West Point, Miss., Sept. 17, 1931; d. Byron Herald and Hattie Hearn (Morris) Loving; m. Robert Brooks Prather, May 30, 1957; children: Pamela, Valerie Jo, Malinda Wayne. B.S., Miss. State Coll. Women, 1953; JD, U. Miss., 1955. Bar: Miss. 1955. Practice with B. H. Loving, West Point, 1955-60, sole practice, 1960-62, 65-71, assoc. practice, 1962-65; mcpl. judge City of West Point, 1965-71; chancery ct. judge 14th dist. State of Miss., Columbus, 1971-82; supreme ct. justice State of Miss., Jackson, 1982-92; presiding justice State of Miss., 1993—; v.p. Conf. Local Bar Assn., 1956-58; sec. Clay County Bar Assn., 1956-71. 1st woman in Miss. to become chancery judge, 1971, and supreme ct. justice, 1982. Mem. ABA, Miss. State Bar Assn., Miss. Conf. Judges, DAR, Rotary, Pilot Club, Jr. Aux. Columbus Club. Episcopalian. Office: Miss Supreme Ct PO Box 117 Jackson MS 39205-0117 also: PO Box 903 Columbus MS 39703-0903

PRATHER, RITA CATHERINE, psychology educator; b. Marietta, Ohio, Nov. 20, 1948; d. Lloyd R. Sr. and Rita C. (Alkazin) Peters; m. Robert E. Prather, Dec. 20, 1969. BA, U. Cen. Fla., 1983; MA, La. State U., 1985, PhD, 1989. Lic. clin. psychologist, Tex. Asst. prof. Tex. A&M U., College Station, 1988-89; psychologist Psychol. Assn. Tex., P.C., Houston, 1989-90; postdoctoral fellow U. Tex. Med. Sch. Houston, 1990-91, asst. prof. psychology, 1991—; speaker on pub. rels. U. Tex.-Houston; judge Houston Sci. and Engrng. Fair, 1993-96. Contbr. over 30 articles to profl. jours. and confs. U. Miss. Med. Ctr. rsch. grantee, 1988. Mem. APA (divsn. clin. and health psychology), Houston Psychol. Assn. (speakers bus. 1990—), Soc. Behavioral Medicine, Assn. Advancement Behavior Therapy. Home: PO Box 920814 Houston TX 77292-0814 Office: U Tex Med Sch Psychiatry Dept 1300 Moursund St Houston TX 77030-3406

PRATT, ALICE REYNOLDS, retired educational administrator; b. Marietta, Ohio, Oct. 5, 1922; d. Thurman J. and Vera L. (Holdren) Reynolds. BA, U. Okla., 1943. Reporter, high sch. tchr., 1944-50; asst. dir. Houston office Inst. Internat. Edn., 1952-58, dir. office, 1958-87, v.p., 1976-87, ret. 1987. Decorated Palmes Academiques (France), 1966; Order of Merit (Fed. Republic Germany), 1972; knight Order of Leopold II (Belgium), 1973; named Woman of Yr., Houston Bus. and Profl. Women, 1958; recipient Matrix award Theta Sigma Phi, 1961; Nat. Carnation award Gamma Phi Beta, 1976. Mem. Houston Com. Fgn. Rels., Japan Am. Soc. (Houston), Houston Philos. Soc., Houston-Taipei Soc. (founding mem., pres. 1989-92), Houston-Galveston/Stavanger Sister City Assn. (founding mem.), Sister Cities Internat. (past nat. bd. dirs.), Nat. Coun. Internat. Visitors (past nat. bd. dirs.), Pan Am. Roundtable (bd. dirs.), Inst. Internat. Edn. (bd. dirs. so. regional office),. Houston Forum (past bd. govs.). Republican. Episcopalian.

PRATT, BILLY KENTON, police officer; b. Tampa, Fla., Nov. 27, 1948; s. Billy Paul and Vera (Parnell) P.; m. Vicki Lynn Throckmorton, Jan. 1, 1977; children: Angela Kristina, Billy Paul II. BS in Bus., Oklahoma City U., 1978; grad., FBI Computer Crime Investigation Sch., IRS Fin. Investigation Sch.; MPA, U. Okla., 1991. Office mgr. Lee Optical Co., Oklahoma City, 1968-72; police officer Police Dept. Oklahoma City, 1972-80, sr. police officer, 1980-82, detective, 1982-86, sgt., 1986-89, lt., 1989, capt., 1989—; microcomputer cons. City of Oklahoma City, 1984—; computer security cons. Control Data Corp., Mpls., 1986; cert. govt. fin. mgr., 1993. Adviser police explorer post Boy Scouts Am., 1978; bd. dirs. Big Bros.-Big Sisters, 1989—. Mem. Internat. Assn. Chiefs of Police, Fraternal Order Police, Internat. City-County Mgrs. Assn., Govt. Fin. Officers Assn. Republican. Mem. Ch. Christ. Office: Oklahoma City Police Dept 701 Colcord Dr Oklahoma City OK 73102-2256

PRATT, CHARLES BENTON, pediatric oncologist; b. Madison, N.C., Aug. 7, 1930; s. Charles Benton and Margaret (Clark) P.; m. Sarah Jane Dillon, Nov. 8, 1958; children: Laura, Margaret, Jane, C. Benton, Stuart. BA, Univ. N.C., 1951; MD, Univ. Md., 1955. Intern Medical Coll. Va. Hosp., Richmond, 1955-56; resident Babies Hosp., N.Y.C., 1958-60, fellow, 1960-61; pvt. practice Richmond, 1961-64; asst. mem. St. Jude Children's Rsch. Hosp., Memphis, 1965-69, assoc. mem., 1969-75, mem., 1975—; prof. pediatrics Univ. Tenn., Memphis, 1985—. Contbr. articles to profl. jours. Vol. Am. Cancer Soc., Memphis, 1975—, Pres. Local Unit, 1986-87, Make-A-Wish-Found., Memphis, 1988—. Capt. U.S. Army, 1956-58. Office: St Jude Childrens Rsch Hosp 332 N Lauderdale Memphis TN 38105

PRATT, DONALD GEORGE, physician; b. Higgins, Tex., Oct. 19, 1946; s. George Horace and Esta Vici (Barker) P. BS in Biomed. Sci., West Tex. State U., 1970; MD, U. Tex., Galveston, 1974. Diplomate Am. Bd. Family Practice, Am. Bd. Radiology (Radiation Oncology). Intern Scott & White Meml. Hosp., Temple, Tex., 1974-75, resident in gen. surgery and pathology, 1975-77, physician, 1979-83; resident in family practice McLennan County Med. Edn. and Rsch. Found., Waco, Tex., 1977-79; physician Family Practice Assocs., El Paso, Tex., 1983; owner, pvt. contractor Minor Emergency Ctrs., Amarillo, Tex., 1983-85; resident in radiation therapy U. Tex., Galveston, 1985-88; ptnr. Cons. in Radiation Oncology, P.A., Amarillo, 1988—, pres., 1994—; dir. dept. radiation oncology Harrington Cancer Ctr., Amarillo, 1994—; pres. Cons. in Radiation Oncology, 1994—; pres. staff Harrington Cancer Ctr., 1995—; prin. investigator Radiation Oncology Group, 1988-95; pres. of staff Harrington Cancer Ctr., 1995—, also bd. dirs. Mem. AMA, Am. Soc. Therapeutic Radiology and Oncology, Am. Acad. Family Physicians, Tex. Med. Assn., Potter/Randall County Med. Soc., Tex. Radiol. Soc. Home: 3623 Tripp Ave Amarillo TX 79121-1809 Office: Cons Radiation Oncology PA 1600 Coulter Dr Ste 402 Amarillo TX 79106-1719

PRATT, DONALD OLIVER, lawyer; b. Belton, Tex., Oct. 31, 1944; s. Oliver and Alice Lorain (Herring) P.; m. Mary Martha Morgan, Sept. 3, 1966; children: David H., William D. AA, Temple (Tex.) Jr. Coll., 1965; BBA, Baylor U., 1968, JD, 1969. Bar: Tex. 1969, U.S. Ct. Mil. Appeals 1969, U.S. Claims Ct. 1972, U.S. Supreme Ct. 1979, U.S. Ct. Appeals (fed. cir.), U.S. Ct. Appeals (5th cir.), U.S. Dist. Ct. (no. dist.) Tex., U.S. Dist. Ct. (we. dist.) Tex. V.p., gen. counsel Broyles & Broyles, Ft. Worth, 1973-75, Cento Industries Inc., Ft. Worth, 1975-78; ptnr. Gandy, Michener, Swindle, Whitaker & Pratt, Ft. Worth, 1978-92, Canterbury, Stuber, Pratt, Elder & Gooch, Dallas, 1992—. Author: Construction Contractors Legal Handbook, 1984, Construction Contracting for Uncle Sam, 1992. Capt. U.S. Army, 1969-73. Fellow Am. Coll. Constrn. Lawyers; mem. ABA (pub. contract sect., com. constrn.), Nat. Panel Constrn. Arbitrators and Mediators, Am. Arbitration Assn., Tex. Bar Assn., Dallas County Bar Assn., Petroleum Club, Woodhaven Club. Republican. Baptist. Office: Canterbury Stuber Pratt Elder & Gooch Ste 1300 5400 Llyndon b Johnson Fwy Dallas TX 75240

PRATT, DOROTHY JANE, environmental executive; b. Detroit, Feb. 17, 1943; d. Lawrence Arthur and Alice Eugenia (Palmer) Pratt; m. John D. Shilling; children: Kaile Lawrene Shilling, Anne Kaitlin Shilling. BS in Zoology, U. Mich., 1964; PhD in Polit. Sci., MIT, 1974. Group leader Environ. Assessment and Strategy The Mitre Corp., McLean, Va., 1975-79; chief, Environ. Ops. and Strategy The World Bank, Washington, 1979-88, chief, Office for Earth Summit Coordination, 1989-92, adv., v.p. Environmentally Sustainable Devel., 1992-93; pres., CEO The Mountain Inst., Franklin, W.Va., 1994—. Recipient Global 500 Environ. award U.N. Environ. Program, 1988. Mem. World Wide Network of Women in Environ. and Devel. (trustee), Millenium Inst. Found. for Internat. Tng., IUCN Internat. Com. on Environmental Edn., IUCN Specialist Group on Sustainable Use of Wild Species. Home: RR 2 Box 661 Purcellville VA 22132-9007 Office: Woodlands Mountain Inst Main And Dogwood St Franklin WV 26807

PRATT, JACK E., SR., hotel executive; b. 1927. Commd. USAF, 1942, advanced through grades, resigned, 1951; ptnr. Wes-Tex Vending Co., 1951—; founder, ptnr. Dairy Queen, Mineral Wells, Tex., 1954-64, Bonanza Steakhouse Restaurants, Tex., 1964-68; chmn., CEO Pratt Hotel Corp., Dallas, 1968—. Office: Pratt Hotel Corp 13455 Noel Rd Ste 2200 Dallas TX 75240

PRATT, JACK E., JR., hotel and casino executive. With Wes-Tex Vending Co., 1951—; also chmn., dir. Pratt Hotel Corp., Dallas. Office: Hollywood Casino Corp 13455 Noel Rd # 48 Dallas TX 75240-6620

PRATT, JOHN EDWARD, law educator; b. Key West, Fla., June 29, 1945; s. Lloyd Edward and Marilyn June (Havercamp) P.; m. Sharon Louise Brown, Aug. 31, 1968; 1 child, Randolph Winfield. BA, So. Meth. U., 1967, JD, 1974. Bar: Tex. 1974, U.S. Dist. Ct. (no. dist.) Tex. 1975. Ptnr. Schuerenberg, Grimes & Pratt, Mesquite, Tex., 1974-77; asst. city atty. City of Dallas, 1978-80; mem. faculty Cedar Valley Coll., Lancaster, Tex., 1981—. Pres. Friends of Mesquite Pub. Libr., Tex., 1975-77; del. Dem. State Conv., Houston, 1988; pres. Ponderosa Estates Homeowners Assn., 1986—. Served to lt. USNR, 1967-71. Mem. State Bar Tex., Acad. Legal Studies in Bus., Tex. Jr. Coll. Tchrs. Assn., Cedar Valley Coll. Faculty Assn. (pres. 1983-85, 93-95), ACLU, Mensa Internat., NAACP. Democrat. Home: 1001 Villa Siete Mesquite TX 75181-1237 Office: Cedar Valley Coll 3030 N Dallas Ave Lancaster TX 75134-3705

PRATT, MARK ERNEST, mechanical engineer; b. Jackhorn, Ky., Nov. 22, 1939; s. James Corbit and Anna Marie (Johnson) P.; m. Yvonne Rose, Sept. 13, 1958; children: Mark Ernest Jr., Mary Yvonne, Bobby Lee, James Paul. Student, I.C.S. Ctr., Scranton, Pa., 1983. Registered profl. engr., Fla. Engr. Mercy Hosp., Miami, Fla., 1965-70; chief engr. Palmetto Gen. Hosp., Hialeah, Fla., 1970-72, Osteo. Gen. Hosp., North Miami Beach, Fla., 1972-77; owner, operator N. Am. Van Lines, Ft. Wayne, Ind., 1977-78; dir. plant ops. Internat. Hosp., Miami, 1978-79, Cypress Hosp., Pompano Beach, Fla., 1979-81, Johnston Meml. Hosp., Abingdon, Va., 1981-87, North Ridge Med. Ctr., Ft. Lauderdale, Fla., 1988-90; adminstrv. dir. plant ops. St. Jude Med. Ctr., Kenner, La., 1990-91; mechanic Bristol (Va.) Compressors, 1991-94; bldg. and grounds supt., dept. corrections, divsn. instl. svcs. Marion (Va.) Correctional Treatment Ctr., 1994—. With U.S. Army, 1955-56. Mem. Am. Soc. Hosp. Engrs., Nat. Fire Protection Assn., Fla. Hosp. Engrs. Assn., Nat. Assn. Power Engrs. (instr. 1980-81, chpt. pres. 1980-81). Baptist. Home: 9613 Pratt Ln Abingdon VA 24210 Office: Marion Correctional Treatment Ctr PO Box 1027 502 E Main St Marion VA 24354

PRATT, MICHAEL FRANCIS, physician and surgeon, otolaryngologist; b. Washington, Dec. 14, 1950; s. James William and Eleanor Mary (LeVangie) P.; 1 child, James Michael. BS, U. Md., 1972; MD, U. Md., Balt., 1980. Diplomate Am. Bd. Otolaryngology. Intern Naval Hosp., San Diego, 1980-81, resident in otolaryngology, 1982-86; instr. George Washington U., Washington, 1974-76; from clin. instr. to asst. prof. Med. U. S.C., 1987-89; asst. prof. Eastern Va. Med. Sch., Norfolk, 1989-94, assoc. prof., 1994—, dir. residency tng., 1989—, vice chair dept. otolaryngology/head and neck surgery, 1994-95. Editorial reviewer The Laryngoscope Jour., 1994—, Head and Neck Jour., 1994—; contbr. articles to profl. jours.; lyricist In Memorium, 1992. Bd. dirs. Va. ProMusica, Norfolk, 1991-93; advisor Golf Com., Norfolk, 1992—; mem. planning com. DePaul Charity Golf Com., Norfolk, 1990—. Decorated Navy Commendation medal with gold star. Fellow ACS, Am. Acad. Facial Plastic and Reconstructive Surgery (Shuster award 1986), Am. Laryngol., Rhinol. and Otol. Soc. (Fowler award 1995), Am. Soc. Head and Neck Surgery, Am. Acad. Otolaryngology/Head and Neck Surgery; mem. Soc. Univ. Otolaryngoly/Head and Neck Surgery, Va. Soc. Otolaryngology (bd. dirs. 1994—). Office: Atlanta Ear Nose and Throat Assn #235 5555 Peachtree Dunwoody Rd Atlanta GA 30342

PRATT, ROBERT THOMAS, JR., journalist, editor; b. New Orleans, Sept. 14, 1959; s. Robert Thomas and Norma Lidia (Alvarez) P. BA in Journalism, Baylor U., 1981. Communications specialist Brookshire Grocery Co. Inc., Tyler, 1984-85; with T.B. Butler Pub. Co., Tyler, Tex., 1981—, East Tex. reporter, 1981-83; city hall reporter Tyler Morning Telegraph, 1984, religion editor, coord. polit. news, 1986—; religion editor, coord. polit. news Tyler Courier-Times, 1986—. Bd. dirs. Meals on Wheels, Tyler, 1987—, Habitat for Humanity Smith County, Tyler, 1991—, Assn. Retarded Citizens, Tyler, 1991—. Recipient Keyman award Tyler Jaycees, 1983, Pathfinder award PATH Orgn., Tyler, 1987, 1st place awards N.E. Tex. Press Assn., 1990; named Outstanding Young Man Am., 1984. Mem. Religion Newswriters Assn., East Tex. Baylor Club (reporter 1986-89). Republican. Presbyterian. Home: 400 Grande Blvd Apt 1802 Tyler TX 75703-4175 Office: TB Butler Pub Co Inc 410 W Erwin St Tyler TX 75702-7133

PRATT, ROBERT WAYNE, computer maintenance executive; b. Lubbock, Tex., Aug. 28, 1967; s. A.C. and Beth (Crawford) P.; m. Isabel Rivero. Grad. high sch., Lubbock. Sales rep. Responsive Svcs. Internat. Corp. (formerly Data Enterprises), Lubbock, 1984-85, v.p. mktg., exec. v.p., 1985-96; owner IRP Internat., 1996—; bd. dirs. Responsive Svcs. Internat. Cor. (formerly Data Enterprises). Campaign worker Lubbock County Rep. Party Exec. Com; western region dir. Tex. Young Rep. Fedn.; on-camera fundraiser PBS. Named Nat. Extemporaneous Speaking Champion, Office Edn. Assn., 1985, Regional Debate Champion, Univ. Interscholastic League, 1983, 84. Mem. West Tex. Data Processing Mgmt. Assn. (pres., chmn. region membership promotion, Eager Beaver award), Young Capitalists of Lubbock (founder), Lubbock County Young Reps. (pres.). Office: IRP 2504 32d St Lubbock TX 79410-3434

PRATT, SHARON L., secondary and elementary education educator; b. Terrell, Tex., Dec. 5, 1946; d. Cecil and Bobbie Lou (Hodge) Brown; m. John E. Pratt, Aug. 31, 1968; 1 child, Randolph W. BS in Edn., U. North Tex., 1969, MS, 1980; ESL cert., East Tex. U., 1987. Cert. elem., English tchr., reading specialist, ESL tchr., Tex. Tchr. Mesquite (Tex.) Ind. Sch. Dist.; elem. tchr. sci. U.S. Govt., Manama, Bahrain; secondary tchr. McDonald Mid. Sch., Mesquite; tchr. ESL and reading improvement North Mesquite High Sch., 1991-92, 96—; adj. faculty devel. reading Cedar Valley C.C., Lancaster, Tex., 1992-95; secondary tchr. Robert T. Hill Mid. Sch. Dallas Ind. Sch. Dist., 1995-96; ESL and reading tchr. North Mesquite H.S., Dallas, 1996—; tchr. ESL and adult edn. classes Dallas Ind. Sch. Dist.; instr. ESL class Eastfield Community Coll., Mesquite. Author: (poem) Sea Shell. Mem. TESOL, Internat. Reading Assn., Tex. State Reading Assn. Home: 1001 Villa Siete Mesquite TX 75181-1237 Office: North Mesquite High Sch 18201 LBJ Fwy Mesquite TX 75150

PRAVEL, BERNARR ROE, lawyer; b. Feb. 10, 1924. BSChemE, Rice U., 1947; JD, George Washington U., 1951. Bar: D.C. 1951, Tex. 1951, U.S. Supreme Ct. 1951. Ptnr. Pravel, Hewitt, Kimball and Krieger, Houston, 1970—. Patent editor George Washington U. Law Rev., 1950. Precinct chmn. Houston Rep. Com., 1972-74. Served to lt. (j.g.) USNR. Fellow Am. Bar Found., Tex. Bar Found.; mem. ABA (chair intellectual property sect. 1991-92), Tex. Bar Assn. (chmn. patent, trademark sect. 1968-69, bd. dirs. 1976-79, Outstanding Contbn. 1982), Nat. Coun. Patent Law (chmn. 1970-71), Am. Intellectual Property Law Assn. (pres. 1983-84), Houston Intellectual Property Law Assn. (pres. 1983-84, Outstanding Svc. award 1986), Order of Coif, Kiwanis, Tau Beta Pi. Home: 10806 Oak Hollow St Houston TX 77024-3017 Office: Pravel Hewitt Kimball and Krieger 1177 West Loop S Fl 10 Houston TX 77027

PRAY, DONALD EUGENE, foundation administrator, lawyer; b. Tulsa, Jan. 16, 1932; s. Clyde Elmer and Ruth Annette (Frank) P.; m. Margaret Morrow, June 12, 1953; children: Melissa, Susan; m. Lana J. Dobson, Nov. 18, 1985. BS in Petroleum Engring., U. Tulsa, 1955; LLB with honors, U. Okla., 1963. Bar: Okla. 1963, U.S. Dist. Ct. (no. dist.) Okla. 1965, U.S. Supreme Ct. 1965. Assoc. firm Fuller, Smith, Mosberg, Davis & Bowen, Tulsa, 1963-65; ptnr. firm Schuman, Deas, Pray & Doyle, Tulsa, 1965-68, Pray, Scott & Livingston, and predecessor firm Pray, Scott, Williamson & Marlar, Tulsa, 1968-79; chmn., mem. exec. com. firm Pray, Walker, Jackman, Williamson & Marlar (merged with firm Walker & Jackman), Tulsa, 1979-95; exec. dir. Donald W. Reynolds Foundation, Tulsa, 1995—. Bd. dirs. Grace & Franklin Bernsen Found., U. Tulsa, St. Johns Med. Ctr., Philbrook Art Mus, Tulsa Ballet Theater., exec. v.p. Served to capt. USAF, 1955-57. Fellow Am. Bar Found.; mem. ABA (econs. com.), Tulsa Estate Planning Forum (pres.), Tulsa Mineral Lawyers Sect. (pres.). Republican. Presbyterian. Clubs: Summit (pres.). Office: Donald W Reynolds Foundation 7130 S Lewis Ste 900 Tulsa OK 74136

PRAYSON, ALEX STEPHEN, drafting and mechanical design educator; b. Tulsa, Okla., June 24, 1939; s. Stephen Alexander and Frances Prayson; children: Stephen, David, Timothy, Anthony. AS, Edison Tech., 1967; DC, Cleveland Coll., 1972; AA, Summit U., 1996. Diplomate Am. Bd. Chiropractic Examiners. Owner Prayson Candies Co., Tulsa, 1963-68; cartographer Howard Needles Tammen and Bergendoff, Kansas City, Mo., 1968-71; supr. M. J. Harden Assocs., Kansas City, 1971-81; asst. prof. Tulsa Jr. Coll., 1981—; advisor Phi Theta Kappa, Tulsa, 1991—. Author: A Love-Hate Anthology, 1993, Cad Systems Operation, 1996; inventor Taffy-Pull. Mem. selection com. Ahepa Civic Youth Svc. Award, Tulsa, 1992—. Named Most Disting. Regional Advisor, Phi Theta Kappa, Tulsa, 1994-95, Robert Giles Disting. Advisor Internat. award Phi Theta Kappa, 1995-96. Mem. Am. Design and Drafting Assn., Okla. Tech. Soc., Tulsa Jr. Coll. Faculty Assn. Home: 2534 E 20th St Tulsa OK 74104-5810

PRECHT, WILLIAM FREDERICK, environmental specialist; b. N.Y.C., Dec. 26, 1956; s. Frederick C. and Ursula I. (Sennholt) P.; m. Joni Ferden, July 27, 1991; children: Lindsey Leona, Chandler Ilsa. BA in Geology, Marine Sci., SUNY, 1978; MS in Earth Sci., Adelphi U., 1981; MA in Marine Geology and Geophysics, U. Miami, 1994; postgrad. in ocean scis., Nova U. Cert. profl. geologist; registered profl. geologist, Pa. Staff geologist Phillips Petroleum Co., Denver, 1981-84; sr. staff geologist Champlin Petroleum Co., Denver, 1984-86; prin. rsch. scientist Reef Resources & Assocs., Billings, Mont., 1986-87; sr. rsch. scientist Reef Resources & Assocs., Miami, Fla., 1987-93; sr. environ. specialist Consulting Engring. & Sci., Miami, 1993-94; environ. dir. Consul-Tech. Engring., Inc., Miami, 1994—; adj. faculty marine scis. Northeastern U., 1987—. Contbr. over 65 articles and abstracts to profl. jours; invited lectr., speaker to over 50 univs. and profl. assns. Pres. Miami Geol. Soc. 1990-91. Recipient fellowship U. Miami, Texaco, 1987-88. Mem. Internat. Soc. for Reef Studies, Soc. for Sedimentary Geology (chmn. carbonate rsch. group 1992-94, Presentation Sci. Excellence award 1985), Am. Assn. Petroleum Geologists (adv. bd. treatise on petroleum geology 1987—, coord. vis. geologists com. 1987—, soc. del. 1990-93), Am. Inst. Profl. Geologists (cert. profl. geologist). Democrat. Home: 7310 Ponciana Ct Miami Lakes FL 33014 Office: Consul-Tech Engring Inc 10570 NW 27th St # 101 Miami FL 33172-2151

PREJEAN, LOUISE MARIE, elementary school educator; b. Alexandria, La., Sept. 22, 1957; d. R.J. and Joan (Montegut) Williams; m. André Henry Prejean, Sept. 4, 1979; 1 child, Neil. BA, U. Southwestern La., 1980, MEd, 1994. Cert. art and elem. tchr., La. Artist, metalsmith Arnaudville, La., 1980—; tchr. Acadiana Arts Coun., Lafayette, La., 1990-94, St. Genevieve Elem. Sch., Lafayette, 1994—; activity coord. Festival Internat., Lafayette, 1990-94; grant artist Acadiana Arts Coun., Lafayette, 1990-94. Den leader, unit commr. Boy Scouts Am., Lafayette, 1986-90, seminar instr., 1990-94; vol. Lafayette Natural History Mus., 1989-93. Mem. La. Educators Assn., Internat. Reading Assn., Soc. N.Am. Goldsmiths, Kappa Delta Pi. Republican. Roman Catholic. Home: RR 2 Box 500 Arnaudville LA 70512-9537

PREMO, MARY KATHARYN (CASSIE), English language and women's studies educator; b. Detroit, Apr. 13, 1967; d. Elmer Robert Premo and Blanche Lillie (Kolar) Hopkins. BA in Comparative Lit., U. Va., 1989; MA in Comparative Lit., U. S.C., 1991; PhD, Emory U., 1996. Adj. instr. English Midlands Tech. Coll., Columbia, S.C., 1991-96, Columbia Coll., 1996—. Contbr. poetry and articles to profl. jours.

PREMPREE, THONGBLIEW, oncology radiologist; b. Thailand, Feb. 1, 1935; s. Korn and Kam (T.) P.; m. Amporn Lohsuwand, Apr. 27, 1963. Pre-Med., Chulalongkorn U., Thailand, 1954; MD, Siriraj U. of Med. Sci., Thailand, 1958; PhD in Radiobiology, John Hopkins U., 1968. Diplomate Am. Bd. Radiology; Fellow in Am. Coll. Radiology. Instr. Dept. Radiology John Hopkins U., Balt., 1968-69; asst. prof. John Hopkins U. Dept. Radiol. Scis., Balt., 1969; staff mem. Dept. of Radiology Ramathibodi Hosp. Mahidol U., Bankok, Thailand, 1969-70; dir. radiobiology Dept. Therapeutic Radiology Tuft New England Med. Ctr., Boston, 1970; asst. prof. sch. of medicine John Hopkins U., Balt., 1971-74; assoc. prof. dept. radiology U. Md. Hosp., Balt., 1974, acting dir., assoc. prof., 1977-79, prof., chief, div. radiation oncology, 1979-83; prof., chmn. dept. radiation oncology U. Hosp., Jacksonville, Fla., 1983—. Contbr. over 100 articles to scientific jours. Recipient PhD Fellowship awards John Hopkins U., 1963-68. Mem. Am. Soc. Therapeutic Radiobiologists, Am. Coll. Radiology, AAAS, AMA,

Radiation Research Soc., Fedn. Am. Scientists, Radiol. Soc. N. Am., The John Hopkins Med. & Surgical Assn. Home: 104 Lamplighter Island Ct Ponte Vedra Beach FL 32082-1940 Office: U Fla 655 W 8th St Jacksonville FL 32209-6511

PRENGAMAN, R. DAVID, company executive. Sr. v.p. R & D, RSR Corp., Dallas. Office: RSR Corp 2777 Stemmons Fwy Ste 1800 Dallas TX 77207

PRESCOTT, WILLIAM BRUCE, minister; b. Denver, Dec. 30, 1951; s. William Rex and Betena Naomi (Fletcher) P.; m. D. Kylene Winters, Nov. 24, 1973; children: William Doyle, Candice Joy. BS in Corrections, U. Albuquerque, 1973; MDiv, Southwestern Bapt. Sem., 1978, PhD, 1986. Ordained minister in Bapt. Ch., 1976. Youth minister Sandia Bapt. Ch., Albuquerque, 1974-75; pastor Clairette (Tex.) Bapt. Ch., 1976-79; instr. philosophy and religion Tarrant County Jr. Coll. NW Campus, Ft. Worth, 1984-86; pastor Easthaven Bapt. Ch., Houston, 1987—; adj. prof. Southwestern Bapt. Theol. Sem., HBU Extension, Houston, 1987-90; police chaplain Houston Police Dept., 1987—; trustee S.E. Area Ministries, Houston, 1988—; mem. exec. bd. Union Bapt. Assn., 1987—, Bapt. Gen. Conv. Tex., 1993—, Tex. Bapts. Committed, 1990—; coord. coun. Coop. Bapt. Fellowship, 1994—, mem. Tex. exec. com., 1996—, Tex. steering com., 1994—; spkr. confs. in field. Book reviewer to Southwestern Jour. Theology; contbr. articles to profl. jours. Served on BGCT Bapt. Distinctives Com., 1994—, BGCT Exec. Bd. Nominatin Com., 1996—, CBF Theol. Edn. Ministry Group, 1994-95, CBF Bapt. Principles Ministry Group, 1995—, CBF Adminstrv. Coun. Structure Com., 1996, CBF Adv. Coun., 1996—, CBF Info. Systems Mgmt. Project Team, 1996—, chmn. CBF Bapt. Distinctives Partnership Team, 1995—; trustee San Andres U., San Andres Island, San Andres Found. Named one of Outstanding Young Men of Am., Jaycees, 1984. Mem. Am. Acad. Religion, Ams. United Separation Ch. & State, So. Bapt. Alliance, Baptists Committed, People for the Am. Way. Democrat. Home: 2203 Bisontine St Friendswood TX 77546-2391 Office: Easthaven Bapt Ch 9321 Edgebrook St Houston TX 77075-1249

PRESLAR, ANDREW BASIL, English language educator; b. Asheville, N.C., May 20, 1959; s. Basil Alexander Preslar and Helen Louise (Turner) Floyd; m. Mary Jane Robin, Mar. 12, 1996. BA in Liberal Arts, U. Tex., 1981; MA in English, Lamar U., 1987. Lectr., tchg. fellow Lamar U., Beaumont, Tex., 1983-87; lectr. Lamar U., Beaumont, 1989-93; instr. Lamar U., Orange, 1993—; head circulation Mary & John Gray Libr., Beaumont, 1987-89; cons. Gulf Coast Regional Maritime Ctr., Orange, 1995. Author: (reference book) Masterplots, 1996, (anthology) Treasury of Best-Loved Poems, 1994; author, contbr. Review of Texas Books, 1988—, assoc. editor., 1989-93. Advisor Phi Theta Kappa-Alpha Nu Gamma chpt., Orange, Tex., 1995—; leadership tng. facilitator Phi Theta Kappa, Orange, 1996. Recipient Writing Achievement award Nat. Coun. Tchrs. English, 1976. mem. ASCD, Order of Demolay (life), Sigma Tau Delta (chpt. pres. 1986-87). Home: 3104 8th St Port Arthur TX 77642 Office: Lamar Univ 410 Front St Orange TX 77630

PRESLAR, LEN BROUGHTON, JR., hospital administrator; b. Concord, N.C., Aug. 13, 1947; s. Len B. and Billie M. (James) P.; m. Joyce W. Whittington, July 11, 1971; children: Bradley E., Whitney A., Andrew C. BA, Wake Forest U., 1971; MBA, U. N.C., Greensboro, 1980. Admissions clk. N.C. Bapt. Hosp., Winston-Salem, 1969-71, systems analyst, 1971-72, budget mgr., 1973, contr., 1973-75, v.p. fin. mgmt., 1975-88, pres., chief exec. officer, 1988—; bd. dirs. Planters Nat. Bank, Winston-Salem, Amos Cottage, Inc. Co-chmn. cabinet United Way, Winston-Salem, 1989—; bd. dirs. N.C. chpt. ARC, 1989—; deacon local Bapt. ch. Fellow Hosp. Fin. Mgmt. Assn. Republican. Baptist. Office: NC Bapt Hosp Medical Center Blvd Winston Salem NC 27157*

PRESLEY, BRIAN, investment company executive; b. Evansville, Ind., Dec. 28, 1941; s. Harry and Ruth P.; B.S. in Bus. Adminstrn., U. Evansville, 1963; M.B.A. Mich. State U., 1964; diploma Wharton Sch., U. Pa., 1995, m. Mary Nell Minyard, Aug. 17, 1972; children—Debra, Cynthia, David, Jeffrey, Clark, Gregory, Steven. Market research analyst Stanley Works, New Britain, Conn., 1964-68; tax shelter coordinator F.I. Dupont, Memphis, 1968-73; v.p. Bullington Schas, Memphis, 1973-75; pres., mng. gen. ptnr. Presley Assocs., Memphis, 1965-93; pres., CFO CSG, Inc., Memphis, 1975—; gen. ptnr. various real estate and oil and gas partnerships, 1974-1986; pres. Cooper St. Group Securities, Inc., 1983-86 ; div. mgr. Advantage Capital Corp. (divsn. SunAmerica, Inc.), 1986-89, reg. v.p., 1989, CEO 1990-94, mng. dir., mkt. strategist, 1995; pres. Presley Adv. Inc., pub. Presley Adv. Letter; instr. fin. div. continuing edn. Memphis U. Bd. dirs. Apt. Council Tenn., 1980-86, sec.-treas., 1982-83; pres. Memphis Apt. Council, 1983; mem., U. Evansville Nat. Alumni Bd., 1988-91. Producer 2 daily radio stock market commentary shows, 1988; fin. commentator Sta. WEVU-TV (ABC), Ft. Myers/Naples, 1988-89. Mem. Internat. Assn. Fin. Planners (mem. broker dealer adv. coun., 1993—), Admirals Club (life), Naples Sailing and Yacht Club, Pi Sigma Epsilon, Beta Gamma Sigma, Tau Kappa Epsilon Alumni Assn. (pres. Memphis area 1979-80). Presbyterian. Host syndicated radio show for sr. citizens, 1979-81. Home: 425 17th Ave S Naples FL 34102 Office: 1600 S Federal Hwy Pompano Beach FL 33062

PRESLEY, DELMA EUGENE, museum director, educator; b. Tallulah Lodge, Ga., May 16, 1939; s. W.F. and Addie (Franklin) P.; m. Beverly Brown Bloodworth, June 17, 1961; children: Jonathan Worth, Susan Franklin, Edwin Brockman. AB, Mercer U., 1961; BD, So. Sem., Louisville, 1964; PhD, Emory U., 1969. Instr. Columbia (S.C.) Coll., 1967-69; asst. prof. Ga. So. U., Statesboro, 1969-72, assoc. prof., 1972-79, prof. English, 1979—, dir. mus., 1982—; mem. folklife adv. bd. Ga. Coun. for Arts, Atlanta, 1986; founder Sci. Edn. Network for S.E., Statesboro, 1988—. Coauthor: Okefinokee Album, 1981; author: The Glass Menagerie: An American Memory, 1990; editor: Dr. Bullie's Notes, 1976. Pres. Bulloch County (Ga.) Hist. Soc., 1980-81; moderator Savannah (Ga.) Presbytery, 1980; cochmn. Edgewood Acres Neighborhood Assn., Statesboro, 1993—. Named Prof. of Yr., Ga. So. U., 1980; recipient Govs. award in humanities State of Ga., 1986; younger humanist fellow NEH, 1974-75. Mem. Am. Assn. Mus., Southeastern Mus. Conf., Ga. Assn. Mus. (adv. bd. 1984—, pres. 1990-91, Mus. Profl. award 1991), Rafthands of Altamaha (founder, pres. 1982-85). Democrat. Home: 106 S Edgewood Dr Statesboro GA 30458-5524 Office: Ga So U Mus Box 8061 Statesboro GA 30460

PRESLEY, PRISCILLA, actress; b. Bklyn., May 24, 1945; m. Elvis Presley, 1967 (div. 1973). Studies with Milton Katselas; student, Steven Peck Theatre Art Sch., Chuck Norris Karate Sch. Prin. Bis and Beau; co-executor Graceland, Memphis. Appearances include (films) The Naked Gun, 1988, The Adventures of Ford Fairlaine, 1990, The Naked Gun 2 1/2, 1991, The Naked Gun 33 1/3, 1994, (TV series) Those Amazing Animals, 1980-81, Dallas, 1983-88, (TV movie) Love Is Forever, 1983; prodr. (TV movie) Elvis and Me, 1988. Office: William Morris 151 S El Camino Dr Beverly Hills CA 90212-2704

PRESMEG, NORMA CHRISTINE, mathematics educator, researcher; b. Germiston, Transvaal, South Africa, Oct. 12, 1942; came to U.S., 1990; d. Christian Brandt and Erika Eunice (De Barzellini) Parnell; m. Christopher Raymond Presmeg, July 8, 1978 (div. June 1989); children: Charmaine, Justine, Neale. BSc, Rhodes U., Grahamstown, South Africa, 1962; BSc with honors, U. Natal, Durban, South Africa, 1963, BEd, 1969, MEd, 1980; PhD, Cambridge U., 1985. Tchr. Natal Edn. Dept., 1965-82; lectr. U. Durban-Westville, 1986-90; asst. prof. dept. curriculum and instrn. Fla. State U., Tallahassee, 1990-94, assoc. prof., 1994—, math. edn. program leader, 1995—; cons. Leon County Schs., Fla., 1990—. Contbg. author: Mathematics Education and Culture, 1986; editor, author: Mathematics Education for Pre-Service and In-Service Teachers, 1991; contbr. articles to profl. jours. Ch. leader Christian Sci. Ch., Margate, South Africa, 1978-82, 1st reader, Durban, 1986-90. Scholarship Univ.'s for the U.K., 1983-85, scholar Human Scis. Rsch. Coun., 1983-85; grantee U. Durban-Westville, 1987-89. Mem. Nat. Coun. Tchrs. of Maths., Math. Assn. Am. Office: Fla State U Curr & Instrn Box 3032 Tennessee St Tallahassee FL 32306

PRESSLEY, LUCIUS C., psychiatrist; b. Chester, S.C., July 19, 1928; s. Lucius Crawford and Mildred Cornell (Cassels) P.; m. Margaret Lindsay Burnside, Oct. 4, 1969; children: Elizabeth, Crawford, John. AB, Duke U., 1949; MD, Med. U. S.C., 1961. Diplomate Am. Bd. Psychiatry & Neurology. Resident U. N.C. Sch. Medicine, Chapel Hill, 1962-65; tchg. psychiatrist Wm. S. Hall Psychiat., Columbia, S.C., 1966—; clin. assoc. prof. Med. U. S.C., Charleston, 1973—, Augusta, 1988—; clin. prof. psychiatry U. S.C. Sch. Medicine, Columbia, 1981—, asst. dean continuing med. edn., 1994; lectr. grad. sch. nursing U. S.C., 1972-73; disting. adj. prof. U. S.C. Coll. Pharmacy, 1978-82; cons. S.C. Dept. Corrections, Columbia, 1985-86, Dorn Veterans Hosp., Columbia, 1986—. Co-editor: Essays in the History of Psychiatry, 1980, A Symposium on Public Research, 1987. Bd. dirs. Health Resources Found., Columbia, 1972-93, 3 Rivers Health Sys. Agy., Columbia, 1981-87. Served in U.S. Army, 1951-53. Fellow Am. Psychiat. Assn.; mem. SAR. Republican. Episcopal. Home: 2815 Canterbury Rd Columbia SC 29204 Office: Wm S Hall Psychiat Inst 1800 Colonial Dr Columbia SC 29201

PRESSON, FRANCIS TENNERY, credit union official; b. Jackson, Tenn., Oct. 31, 1925; s. Norman Z and Mary Isabelle (Tennery) P.; student W. Tenn. Bus. Coll., 1948-49, U. Tenn., 1954; m. Harriet Francis Shires, June 17, 1950; 1 child, Stephen Francis. Car insp. Ill. Central Gulf R.R., Jackson, 1942-86; treas., mgr. ICG Fed. Credit Union, Jackson, 1960—. Mem. Madison County Democratic Exec. com., 1976—; mem. Stadium Com. for City of Jackson, 1970-90; bd. dirs. Credit Bur. Jackson, Tenn., 1991-93). Served with USNR, 1942-45. Mem. Am. Mgmt. Assn., Tenn. Credit Union League (dir. 1973-80, 91—, treas., vice chmn.), VFW (trustee post 1848 1990-92), Brotherhood Ry. Carmen. Baptist. Club: K.P. Home: 407 Lambuth Blvd PO Box 3266 Jackson TN 38303 Office: ICG Fed Credit Union 20 Redbud St PO Box 3334 Jackson TN 38303

PRESSON, GINA, journalist, news and documentary production company executive; b. Nuremberg, Germany, Sept. 1, 1959; parents Am. citizens; d. Gerald Vann Presson and Gail Anne (Carter) Presson Nichols; m. William Michael Hammesfahr, Apr. 25, 1987. BA cum laude, Duke U., 1981. Intern reporter, field producer Sta. WTVD-TV, Durham, N.C., 1979-81; assoc. producer, producer, writer, fill-in reporter Sta. KXAS-TV, Dallas/Ft. Worth, 1981-84; reporter, anchor Sta. KFDX-TV, Wichita Falls, Tex., 1984-85; reporter, producer Sta. WTVR-TV, Richmond, Va., 1985-86; reporter Sta. WWBT-TV, Richmond, 1986-88; owner, reporter, producer Presson Perspectives, Clearwater, Fla., 1988—; prodr. Tampa (Fla.) Com. of 100, 1989, Poynter Inst. for Media Studies, 1990—, Leadership Am. and A Presdl. Classroom for Young Ams., 1993; reporter, prodr. Sta. WEDU-TV, Tampa, 1988—, Sta. WTSP-TV, 1992, Sta. WUSF-Radio, 1993. Prodr. program Everyday Heroes, PBS, 1994. Mem. Pinellas Healthy Start Coalition (appointee); publicist First Presbyn. Ch. Svc. Com., St. Petersburg, Fla., 1990—, Habitat for Humanity, Richmond, 1987-88, Children's Miracle Network, Richmond, 1986-88. Recipient Gold medallion Broadcast Promotion and Mktg. Execs., 1982, 10th Dist. Addy award (5 states), Ft. Worth Ad Club, 1982, 83, Tops award Dallas Ad Club, 1982, Best Spot award Tex. Assn. Broadcasters, 1982, 83, Tops award Dallas Ad Club, 1982, Best Spot award Tex. Assn. Broadcasters, 1983, 4th Pl. award in News Spl., Internat. N.Y. Fest., 1992, 94, Gabriel award, 1993, Fla. AP award, 1993, 3rd Pl. Green Eyeshade award (5 states), 1994. Mem. Soc. Profl. Journalists (dept. regional dir. 1990—, pres. Tampa chpt. 1989-90, fund raiser 1988-89, award 1993, dep. chair nat. profl. devel. com.), Duke U. Alumni Assn., Leadership Am., Alpha Delta Pi. Office: Presson Perspectives 600 Druid Rd E Clearwater FL 34616-3912

PRESTON, CHARLES GEORGE, lawyer; b. Fairbanks, Alaska, Nov. 11, 1940; s. Charles William and Gudveig Nicoline (Hoem) P.; m. Hilde Delphine van Stappen, Mar. 12, 1970; children: Charles William, Stephanie Delphine, Christina Nicoline. BA, U. Wash., 1963, MPA, 1968; JD, Columbia U., 1971. Bar: Wash. 1971, D.C. 1981, U.S. Dist. Ct. D.C. 1981, U.S. Dist. Ct. (we. dist.) Wash. 1971, U.S. Ct. Appeals (9th cir.) 1972, U.S. Ct. Appeals (4th cir.) 1979, U.S. Ct. Appeals (5th cir., D.C. cir.) 1978, U.S. Ct. Appeals (2d cir.) 1980, U.S. Ct. Appeals (11th cir.) 1981, U.S. Supreme Ct. 1977, U.S. Ct. Claims 1982, U.S. Ct. Appeals (fed. cir.) 1982, U.S. Ct. Appeals (1st cir.) 1984, U.S. Ct. Appeals (3d, 6th & 7th cirs.) 1987, Va. 1987, U.S. Dist. Ct. (ea. dist.) Va. 1989, U.S. Dist. Ct. (we. dist.) Wash. 1971, U.S. Dist. Ct. (no. dist.) Calif. 1981, U.S. Bankruptcy Ct. Va. 1990. Assoc. Jones, Grey, Bayley & Olson, Seattle, 1971-72; atty. and asst. counsel for litigation Officer of Solicitor, U.S. Dept. Labor, Seattle, 1972-76, Washington, 1976-81; atty. Air Line Pilots Assn., Washington, 1981-82; mng. ptnr. MacNabb, Preston & Waxman, Washington, 1981-86, Preston & Preston, Great Falls, Va., 1986-95, Charles G. Preston, P.C., 1995—; pres. Preston Group, Inc. 1989—. Lectr. seminars. Mem. ABA, Wash. State Bar, D.C. Bar Assn., Va. Bar Assn., Tng. Law Inst. (pres. 1985—), Gt. Falls Bus. and Profl. Assn. (pres. 1990), The Serbian Crown, Va. (pres. 1989—). Office: Charles G Preston PC 746 Walker Rd Ste 24 Great Falls VA 22066-2636

PRESTON, DEBORAH ELAINE, English language educator; b. Atlanta, June 6, 1965; d. James Edward, III and LeNora Ellen (Lovejoy) P.; m. Lincoln Humphrey Jones, Dec. 11, 1984 (div. July 1988); m. William Michael Raley, Jr., Mar. 16, 1991. BA in Theatre, Fla. State U., 1986, MA in English, 1988; PhD in English, Tulane U., 1988—. Instr. English Dekalb Coll., Lawrenceville, Ga., 1992-95, asst. prof., 1995—. Mem. MLA, Am. Assn. Women in Cmty. Colls., Assn. for Theatre in Higher Edn., South Atlantic Modern Lang. Assn. Office: Dekalb Coll. 5155 Sugarloaf Pkwy Lawrenceville GA 30243

PRESTON, KATHERINE KEENAN, music educator; b. Hamilton, Ohio, Dec. 7, 1950; d. Clem F. Jr. and Mary Elizabeth (Zink) Imfeld; m. Daniel F. Preston, Oct. 8, 1971; 1 child, William Clement Preston. Student, U. Cin., 1969-71; BA in Liberal Arts, The Evergreen State Coll., 1974; MusM, U. Md., 1981; PhD in Musicology, CUNY, 1989. Staff writer, photog. researcher New Grove Dictionary of Am. Music, N.Y.C., 1981-86; freelance music researcher N.Y.C. and Washington, 1982-90; vis. asst. prof. Coll. William and Mary, Williamsburg, Va., 1989-92, asst. prof. music history, 1992-95, assoc. prof. music history, 1995—; cons. to Discovery Prodns., 1991; mem. editl. rev. bd. Symposium, 1989—. Author: Scott Joplin, 1987, Music for Hire: The Work of Journeymen Musicians in Washington, D.C., 1875-1900, 1992, Opera on the Road: Traveling Opera Troupes in the United States, 1825-1860, 1993; editor: Irish American Theater, vol. 10 in Nineteenth-Century American Musical Theater, 1994; text editor: (booklet) Jazz Piano, 1988; reviewer for books and mags.; contbr. articles to profl. jours.; author 23 radio scripts. CUNY fellow, 1981-84, Jr. Rsch. fellow Inst. for Studies in Am. Music, 1981-84, Newberry Libr. fellow, 1985-86, Sinfonia Found. rsch. asst. grantee, 1986-87, Phila. Ctr. for Early Am. Studies Travel and Rsch. grantee, 1986-87, Coll. William and Mary summer faculty grantee, 1992, 93. Fellow Am. Coun. Learned Socs.; mem. The Coll. Music Soc. (mem. editl. bd. 1993), Am. Musicol. Soc. (student rep. 1982-83, sec.-treas. Capital chpt. 1984-88, rep. to nat. coun. 1993—), Sonneck Soc. for Am. Music (program com. 1984, Capital area rep. 1985-89, Irving Lowens award com. 1989-91, mem. handbook com. 1991-93, chair conf. mgmt. com. 1993, chair Lowens award com. 1995—), Alpha Lambda Delta, Pi Kappa Lambda. Office: Dept Music Coll William and Mary Williamsburg VA 23185

PRESTON, RODNEY LEROY, animal science educator; b. Denver, Jan. 11, 1931; s. Leon Leroy and Florence Irene (Roberts) P.; m. Barbara Joan Doile, Mar. 12, 1950; children: Linda M. Preston Vroegindewey, David E., Diane E. Preston Patterson. BS with high distinction, Colo. State U., 1953; MS in Animal Nutrition, Iowa State U., 1955, PhD in Animal Nutrition/ Vet. Physiology, 1957. Asst. prof., assoc. prof., prof. animal sci. U. Mo., Columbia, 1957-69; prof. animal sci. Ohio State U. and Ohio Rsch. Devel. Ctr., Wooster, 1969-75; prof., chmn. dept. animal sci. Wash. State U., Pullman, 1975-82; endowed and hon. Thornton disting. prof. Tex. Tech. U., Lubbock, 1982-96; Paul W. Horn prof. Tex. Tech U., Lubbock, 1994, dir. Burnett Ctr. for Beef Cattle Rsch. and Teaching, 1986-96; ret., 1996; Former mem. com. on animal nutrition NAS-NRC; former mem. design or study teams U.S. AID, Lesotho and Egypt; lectr. various European countries, also South Africa, Zimbabwe, Japan, Mex. and Brazil. Former editor applied sect. Jour. Animal Sci.; contbr. numerous articles and abstracts to sci. jours., chpts. to books. Capt. USAF, 1957-59. Recipient Outstanding Young Faculty Mem. award U. Mo., 1964, rsch. award Tex. Tech U. Coll. Agrl. Scis., 1989, Barnie E. Rushing faculty disting. rsch. award Tex. Tech Dads and Moms Assn., 1990; spl. fellow NIH, The Netherlands, 1964-65. Mem. Am. Soc. Animal Sci. (past pres., Animal Industry award 1996), Am. Inst. Nutrition, Plains Nutrition Coun., Sigma Xi, Alpha Zeta, Gamma Sigma Delta, Phi Kappa Phi. Home and Office: PO Box 3549 Pagosa Springs CO 81147-3549

PRESTON, THOMAS LYTER, public relations executive, crisis management, anti-terrorism consultant; b. Carrollton, Ky., Sept. 25, 1934; s. Thomas Jefferson and Mary Lyter (Robertson) P.; m. Carolyn Louise Points, June 1, 1957; 1 child, Matthew Thomas. AB in Journalism, U. Ky., 1956; postgrad., U. Wash., 1958. Editor The News-Democrat, Carrollton, 1956-57; pub., pres. The Cynthiana (Ky.) Pub. Co., 1959-68; pres. Preston Pub. Rels., Lexington, Ky., 1968-75; pres., chief exec. officer The Preston Group, Inc., Lexington, 1975—; chmn. of bd., 1991—; spl. asst. to the Gov., Commonwealth of Ky., and commr. Ky. Dept. Pub. Info., Frankfort, 1971-74; spl. asst. to U.S. Senate, Washington, 1975; adj. prof. U. Ky., Lexington, 1976-81, Ea. Ky. U., Richmond, 1979; lectr. Fla. State U., Tallahassee, 1989; bd. visitors Dept. Pub. Rels. Fla. State U., 1990—, Sch. Pub. Rels. Ea. Ky. U., 1990—; developer corp. strategies in anti-terrorism and workplace violence; bd. dirs. Woodford Bank & Trust Co., Versailles, Ky.; mem. nat. courts and cmty. com. Nat. Ctr. State Courts; leader seminars in crisis control, reputational mgmt., corporate terrorism and workplace violence response. Contbr. articles to profl. publs. 1st lt. U.S. Army, 1956-59, 61. Mem. Coll. Fellows PRSA (accredited, chmn. East ctrl. dist., 1989-90, pres. thoroughbred chpt. 1987-88), Counselors Acad., Fla. Pub. Rels. Assn., The Lafayette Club (bd. dirs. 1988-94). Home: 4290 Mccowans Ferry Rd Versailles KY 40383-9692 Office: The Preston Group Inc 450 Old East Vine St Lexington KY 40507-1544

PRESTRIDGE, PAMELA ADAIR, lawyer; b. Delhi, La., Dec. 25, 1945; d. Gerald Wallace Prestridge and Peggy Adair (Arender) Martin. BA, La. Poly. U., 1967; M in Edn., La. State u., 1968, JD, 1973. Bar: U.S. Dist. Ct. (mid. dist.) La. 1975, U.S. Dist. Ct. (so. dist.) Tex. 1982, U.S. Ct. Appeals (5th cir.) 1982, U.S. Supreme Ct. 1990. Law clk. to presiding justice La. State Dist. Ct., Baton Rouge, 1973-75; ptnr. Breazeale, Sachse & Wilson, Baton Rouge, 1975-82, Hirsch & Westheimer P.C., Houston, 1982-92; pvt. practive atty. Houston, 1992—. Counselor Big Bros./Big Sisters, Baton Rouge, 1968-70; legal cons., bd. dirs. Lupus Found. Am., Houston, 1984-93; bd. dirs. Quota Club, Baton Rouge, 1979-82, Speech and Hearing Found., Baton Rouge, 1981-82, The Actors Workshop, Houston, 1988-93; active Tex. Accts. and Attys. for the Arts. Recipient Pres.'s award Lupus Found. Am., 1991, cert. of appreciation Assn. Atty. Mediators, 1992. Mem. ABA, La. Bar Assn., Tex. Bar Assn., Houston Bar Assn., Houston Bar Found., Assn. Atty. Mediators (bd. dirs. 1994-96, Citation for Outstanding Mems. 1993), Profl. Atty.-Mediators Coop. (v.p. 1994, bd. dirs. 1994-96, pres. 1995), Phi Alpha Delta. Eckankar. Home: 908 Welch St Houston TX 77006-1312 Office: Phoenix Tower Ste 3300 PO Box 130987 Houston TX 77219-0987

PRETLOW, CAROL JOCELYN, fashion and communications consultant; b. Salisbury, Md., Nov. 9, 1946; d. Kenneth H. and Vivian Virginia (Hughes) P. B.A., Fisk U., 1976; M.A., Norfolk State U., 1982; postgrad. Antioch Law Sch., 1984-85; JD, Am. U., 1991, LLD, 1996. Fashion columnist The Smithfield Times (Va.), 1977-80; talk show hostess Sta. WAVY-TV, 1978-81; fashion editor Tidewater Life Mag., 1979; reporter, asst. news dir. Sta. WNSB News, Norfolk, Va., 1980-81; press sec. Com. to Elect Fred D. Thompson Jr. Treas. Isle of Wight County, 1981; ind. fashion cons., Smithfield, Va., 1982—, publicist, 1987—; fashion reporter Sta. WRAP Radio, Norfolk, 1986-87; fashion coord. Theresa's Boutique, Franklin, Va., 1989—; adj. prof. communication Paul D. Camp Community Coll., Franklin, 1986-87; entertainment fashion editor Citizens Press Am. Newspaper, Portsmouth, Va.; fashion publicist, cons. Carrie's House of Fashion, Smithfield, Va.; legal program advisor Commonwealth Coll., Hampton, 1994—; vis. prof. Elizabeth City State U., 1994; pre-law advisor Nofolk State U. Coord. Sesquitricentennial Celebration, Isle of Wight County, 1984.

PRETO-RODAS, RICHARD A., foreign language educator; b. N.Y.C., May 30, 1936; s. Manuel and Beatrice Alina (Carvalho) Preto-R. B.A., Fairfield U., 1958; M.A. in Philosophy, Boston Coll., 1960; M.A. in Spanish, U. Mich., 1962, Ph.D. in Romance Langs. (fellow Rackham Sch. Grad. Studies 1965), 1966. Instr. U. Mich., 1964-66; asst. prof. U. Fla., 1966-70; assoc. prof. U. Ill., Urbana-Champaign, 1970-74; prof. U. Ill., 1974-81, chmn. Spanish, Italian, 1978-81; dir. lang. U. South Fla., Tampa, 1981-89, prof. lang., 1989—; cons. MLA; Fulbright vis. prof. comparative lit. Université Stendhal, Grenoble, France, 1994-95. Author: Negritude as A Theme in the Poetry of the Portuguese-Speaking World, 1971, Dialogue and Courtly Lore in Renaissance Portugal, 1971; co-author: Cronicas Brasileiras: A Portuguese Reader, 1980, rev. 1994 as Cronicas Brasileiras, Nova Fase, 40 Historinhas of C.D. de Andrade, 1983; co-editor, contbr: Empire in Transition: The Portuguese World in the Time of Camoes, 1985; contbg. editor: Handbook of Latin American Studies, 1983—; contbg. reviewer World Lit. Today, 1986—. NDEA fellow, 1965. Mem. MLA, Am. Council on Teaching Fgn. Langs., Am. Assn. Tchrs. of Spanish and Portuguese, Phi Beta Kappa. Democrat. Home: 4483 Vieux Carre Cir Tampa FL 33613-3057 Office: CPR-107 U South Fla Tampa FL 33620

PREWITT, WILLIAM CHANDLER, financial executive; b. Phila., Aug. 23, 1946; s. Richard Hickman and Jean Mary (Simpkins) P.; m. Karen Ruth Padgett, May 15, 1971. BA in History, Transylvania Coll., 1968; cert., Coll. Fin. Planning, 1985; MS in Fin. Planning, Coll. for Fin. Planning, 1991. Dist. exec. Cen. N.C. Coun., Albemarle, 1971-74, Transatlantic Coun., Heidelburg, Fed. Republic Germany, 1974-78; field dir. Dutchess City Coun., Hyde Park, N.Y., 1978-80; prin. Prewitt Properties, Charleston, S.C., 1980—, William C. Prewitt Cert. Fin. Planner, Charleston, S.C., 1986—; registered rep. First Investors Corp., Charleston, S.C., 1982-83; lectr. Coll. of Charleston, 1987—, Trident Tech. Coll., Charleston, 1987—, Charleston So. Univ. Deacons 1st Presbyn. Ch., Rockingham, N.C., 1972-74; elder 1st Scots Ch., Charleston, 1990-93; treas. South Carolinians to Limit Congl. Terms, 1991—; sec. Hist. Ansonborough Neighborhood Assn., Charleston, 1987-90; bd. dirs. Christian Family Y, 1991—, pres., 1995—. 1st lt. USMCR, 1968-71. Named as One of 200 Best Fin. Advisors, Worth Mag., 1996. Mem. SAR (chpt. treas. 1996—), SCV, S.C. Soc. Cert. Fin. Planners (pres. 1985-87, chmn. bd. dirs. 1988-90), Inst. Cert. Fin. Planners, Internat. Assn. Fin. Planners (registry 1986-92), Nat. Assn. Personal Fin. Advisors (pres. s. region 1994-96, chmn. ethics and standards com. 1996—, nat. bd. dirs. 1996—), Internat. Churchill Soc., Navy League (pres. 1992, chmn. bd. 1993, Charleston coun.). Republican. Home: 33 Hasell St Charleston SC 29401-1604 Office: 15 Broad St Charleston SC 29401-3030

PREYSZ, LOUIS ROBERT FONSS, III, management consultant, educator; b. Quantico, Va., Aug. 1, 1944; s. Louis Robert Fonss, Jr., and Lucille (Parks) P.; m. Patricia Dianne Yelland; children: Louis Robert Fonss IV, Christine Elizabeth, Michael Anthony, Daniel Timothy. BA, U. Wis., Madison, 1968; MBA, U. Utah, Salt Lake City, 1973; postgrad. Stonier Grad. Sch. Banking, Rutgers U., 1983, The Command and Gen. Staff Coll., Ft. Leavenworth, Kans., 1986. Teaching and rsch. asst. U. Utah, 1972-73; mktg. and pers. officer Security 1st Nat. Bank of Sheboyan (Wis.), 1973-76; mktg. dir. 1st Nat. Bank Rock Island (Ill.), 1976-77; asst. v.p., mktg. sales mgr. 1st Nat. Bank Birmingham (Ala.), 1977-78; v.p., mktg. mgr. Sun 1st Nat. Bank Orlando (Fla.), 1978-80; pres. Preysz Assocs. (Fla.), 1980—; asst. prof. mgmt. and banking Flagler Coll., St. Augustine, Fla., 1982—; mem. part-time faculty U. Wis., 1973-76, Fla. Inst. Tech., 1976-77, St. Ambrose Coll., Davenport, Iowa, 1976-77, U. Cen. Fla., 1979-81, Columbia Coll. (Mo.), 1981-82; mem. Tng. and Profl. Devel. Coun., Bank Mktg. Assn., 1976-78, chmn., 1978; mem. mktg. and pub. rels. com. Wis. Bankers Assn., 1975; v.p. Ala. Automated Clearing House Assn., 1978; mem. Wis. Automated Clearing House Assn., 1975-76; speaker to numerous internat., nat. and state assns.; host to daily FM radio program Money Issues. Mem. Rep. Presdl. Task Force, 1982-86, Rep. Nat. Com., 1980-89; bd. dirs. Cath. Charities Bur. Inc., 1988-89, v.p., 1989; bd. dirs. United Way St. Johns County, 1989-95, chmn., 1991-95; bd. dirs. Grace Cmty. Ch., 1996—. Capt. U.S. Army, 1968-72; officer Fla. Army N.G.; charter mem. U.S. Com. for Battle Normandy Mus., 1989; charter mem. Reagan Presdl. Libr. Fellow Soc. Advancement Mgmt. Honor Soc. (internat. v.p., bd. dirs. 1984—, Mgmt. Excellence award 1990); mem. U. Wis. Alumni Assn., U. Utah Alumni Assn., N.G. Officers Assn., Phi Gamma Delta. Clubs: St. Augustine Officers. Lodge: Rotary (Paul Harris fellow). Author: How to Introduce a New Service, 1976; Energy Efficiency Programs and Lending Practices for Florida's Financial Institutions, 1980; Credit Union Marketing, 1981, An Effective Management Structure for Multi-Bank Holding Companies, 1983,

Credit Union Strategic Marketing, 1993; contbg. editor: Target Market, an Instructional Approach to Bank Cross Selling of Services, New Accounts Training Manual, 1977; Tested Techniques in Bank Marketing, 1977; contbg. author: Rapid Debt Reduction Strategies, 1990, The Debt Free Army, 1993; mem. editorial rev. bd. SAM Advanced Mgmt. Jour.; contbr. articles to mags. Republican. Office: PO Box 1027 Saint Augustine FL 32085-1027

PRIAULX, DAVID LLOYD, marketing executive; b. Newton, Iowa, Aug. 11, 1949; s. Dwight Lloyd and Audrey L. (Walker) P.; m. Sherry Lavern Groom, Oct. 10, 1970; children: Christina Kay, Jason Robert. Student, Marshalltown Community Coll., Iowa, 1968-69. Engring. draftsman Maytag Co., Newton, Iowa, 1970-76; parts sales asst. Maytag Co., 1976-81, supr. parts sales and approved svc., 1981-87; sales adminstr Maytag Customer Svc., Cleveland, Tenn., 1987-88; mgr. parts mktg. Maytag Customer Svc., 1988-94, dir. parts mktg., 1994—. Bd. dirs. Bd. of Edn., Newton, 1986-87. With U.S. Army N.G., 1969-75. Mem. Maytag Mgmt. Club (bd. dirs. 1986). Republican. Baptist. Home: 148 Champion Dr NW Cleveland TN 37312-7114 Office: Maytag Customer Svc 240 Edwards St SE Cleveland TN 37311-6035

PRIBOR, HUGO CASIMER, physician; b. Detroit, June 12, 1928; s. Benjamin Harrison and Wanda Frances (Mioskowski) P.; m. Judith Elinor Smith, Dec. 22, 1955: children: Jeffrey D., Elizabeth F., Kathryn A. BS, St. Mary's Coll., 1949; M.S., St. Louis U., 1951, Ph.D., 1954, MD, 1955. Diplomate Am. Bd. Pathology. Intern Providence Hosp., Detroit, 1955-56; resident pathologic anatomy and clin. pathology NIH, Bethesda, Md., 1956-59; field investigator gastric cytology rsch. project Nat. Cancer Inst., Bowman-Gray Sch. Medicine, Winston-Salem, N.C., 1959-60; assoc. pathologist, dir. clin. lab. Bon Secours Hosp., Grosse Pointe, Mich., 1960-63; pathologist, dir. labs. Samaritan Hosp. Assn., East Side Gen. Hosp., Detroit, 1963-64, Anderson Meml. Hosp., Mt. Clemens, Mich., 1963-64; cons. pathologist Middlesex County Med. Examiners Office, New Brunswick, N.J., 1964-73; dir. dept. labs., chief pathologist, sr. attending physician Perth Amboy (N.J.) Gen. Hosp., 1964-73; chmn., chief exec. officer Ctr. Lab. Medicine, Inc., Metuchen, N.J., 1968-77; v.p. med. affairs Damon Corp., Med. Svcs. Group, 1977-78; exec. med. dir. MDS Health Group, Inc., Red Bank, N.J., 1978-80; med. dir. Internat. Clin. Labs., Inc., Nashville, 1981-88; med. dir. SmithKline Beechman Clin. Labs., Nashville, 1990—; physician, pathologist Assoc. Pathologists (P.C.), Nashville, 1981—; rsch. assoc. dept. pathology St. Louis U. Sch. Medicine, 1954-55; instr. pathology Bowman-Gray Sch. Medicine, Winston-Salem, N.C., 1959-60; asst. prof. chemistry U. Detroit, 1961-64; instr. pathology Wayne State U. Sch. Medicine, Detroit, 1961-64; clin. assoc. prof. dept. pathology Med. Sch. Rutgers U., The State U., New Brunswick, N.J., 1966-68; cons. Health Facilities Planning and Constrn. Svc., USPHS, HEW, Rockville, Md., 1970-71; prof. biomed. engring. Coll. Engring., Rutgers, The State U., New Brunswick, N.J., 1971-75, 80-82; chmn. bd. trustees St. Mary's Coll., Winona, Minn., 1972-74, chmn. fin. com., 1971-72; clin. prof. pathology Vanderbilt U. Sch. Medicine, Nashville, 1981—. Author: (with G. Morrell and G. H. Scherr) Drug Monitoring and Pharmacokinetic Data, 1980, The Laboratory Consultant, 1992; contbr. articles to profl. jours. Fellow Am. Soc. Clin. Pathologists (Silver award 1968); mem. AMA , Am. Assn. Exptl. Pathology, Coll. Am. Pathologists (chmn. subcom. 1974-78), Internat. Acad. Pathology, Pan Am. Med. Assn. (life), N.J. State Med. Soc., Acad. Medicine N.J. (chmn. clin. pathology sect. 1965-67), N.J. Soc. Pathologists (exec. com. 1965-67), Sigma Xi. Republican. Roman Catholic. Home: 6666 Brookmont Ter #1111 Nashville TN 37205

PRICE, ALAN THOMAS, business and estate planner; b. Balt., Nov. 11, 1949; s. Alvah Thompson and Doris Elaine (Cole) P.; m. Page Angela Jennings, Sept. 1978 (div. 1980); m. Lauren Ann St. Clare, Aug. 12, 1983 (div. 1992). BS, U. N.C., 1972. CLU; chartered fin. cons.; cert. estate and bus. analyst, fin. planner; registered fin. planner. Mgmt. trainee Sears, Atlanta, 1972-73; ins. agt. Aetna Life & Casualty, Atlanta, 1973-76, Pilot Life/New Eng. Life, Virginia Beach, Va., 1976-81; owner, pres. Page II Prodns., Inc., Norfolk, Va., 1981—; founding prin. 1s Fin. Resources, 1989; veteran judge Miss U.S.A. Pageant System. Fin. columnist News-Herald, 1985-86. Active Mus. Marine Scis., Virginia Beach, 1986—, Hope Found., Windsor, N.C., 1987—, Va. Stage Co., Va. Pops Orch. Named Man of Yr., Pilot Life, Tidewater, Va., 1978, 79, 80. Fellow Life Underwriter Tng. Coun.; mem. Million Dollar Roundtable (life and qualifying), Internat. Assn. Registered Fin. Planners, Am. Coun. Ind. Life Underwriters, Am. Soc. CLU's, Internat. Assn. Fin. Planning (dir. 1987-88), Inst. Cert. Fin. Planners, Nat. Assn. Life Underwriters, Sales and Mktg. Execs., Ct. of the Table, Tidewater Estate Planning Coun., Tidewater Builders Assn., Cen. Bus. Dist. Assn., Hampton Roads C. of C. Methodist. Home: 2645 River Rd Virginia Beach VA 23454-1224 Office: First Fin Resources/Page II Prodns Inc 1 East Chase Ste 1111 Baltimore MD 21202

PRICE, ALEXANDER, retired osteopathic physician; b. Stepanitz, Russia, Mar. 7, 1913; came to U.S., 1921; s. Abraham and Mariam (Cohen) P.; m. Frances Ahrens, 1944 (dec. Sept. 1987); children: John O., Carl A. BA, U. Pa., 1936; DO, Phila. Coll. Osteo. Medicine, 1941; postgrad., Columbia U., 1947-57. Diplomate Am. Osteo. Bd. Internal Medicine, Am. Osteo. Bd. Cardiology. Intern Warren Hosp., Phillipsburg, N.J., 1941-43; postgrad. in cardiology and internal medicine; pvt. practice Camden and Cherry Hill, N.J., 1943-44, 46-80, 82-87, Ft. Lauderdale, Fla., 1980-82; mem. med. staff Met. Hosp., Phila., 1948-63, chief staff, 1961-63; mem. med. staff Cherry Hill (N.J.) Hosp., 1960-87, chmn. dept. medicine, 1960-72, chmn. div. cardiology, 1960-80; ret., 1996; assoc. clin. prof. medicine Phila. Coll. Osteo. Medicine, 1965-80; clin. prof. medicine N.J. Sch. Osteo. Medicine, Rutgers U., Camden, 1970—; physician, cons. in cardiology Primary Health Care Clinic, Broward County, Fla., 1991—. Contbr. numerous articles to osteo. medicine jours. Vol. Medivan (home health care for elderly poor, indigent, disabled), Broward County, Fla., 1988—. With M.C., AUS, 1944-45, MTO. Fellow Am. Coll. Osteo. Internists (pres. 1974-75, Meml. lectr. ea. div. 1970, Meml. lectr. nat. div. 76, Disting. Svc. award 1977), Coll. Physicians Phila.; mem. Am. Osteo. Assn., N.J. Osteo. Assn., Masons. Home: 1071 NW 85th Ave Fort Lauderdale FL 33322-4622

PRICE, B. BYRON, museum director. Dir. Panhandle-Plains Hist. Mus., Canyon, Tex., until 1987; exec. dir. Nat. Cowboy Hall of Fame and Western Heritage Ctr., Oklahoma City, 1987—. Office: Nat Cowboy Hall Fame & Western Heritage Ctr 1700 NE 63rd St Oklahoma City OK 73111-7906

PRICE, CAROLINE LEONA, personnel consulting company executive; b. N.Y.C., Dec. 13, 1947; d. Richard Gustave and Ruth Leonora (Kling) Schlegel; m. Harold Edmond Price, Sept. 27, 1969; children: Jonathan (dec.), Matthew. AA, Concordia Jr. Coll., Bronxville, N.Y., 1967; student, Wagner Coll., Bregenz, Austria, 1967-68; BA, Lehman Coll., CUNY, 1969. Tchr. Dept. Def. Sch. System, Brindisi, Italy, 1970-71; prin. social welfare exec. Putnam County Dept. Social Svcs., Brewster, N.Y., 1971-75; pers. dir. to patent trader, Mt. Kisco, N.Y., 1976-77; tchr. English as fgn. lang. Arbeiterkammer, Feldkirch, Austria, 1978-84; office mgr. Peachtree Temps., Inc., Peachtree City, Ga., 1984-85; office adminstr. Chip & Dale, Peachtree City, 1985-87; rsch. dir. Borman/Gray, Atlanta, 1987-88; owner, prin. Caprice Cons., Peachtree City, 1988-94; assoc. Ward Howell Internat., Atlanta, 1994—; founding chmn. So. Conservation Trust, Inc., 1993-95. Chmn. Peachtree City Planning Commn., 1989-92, McIntosh Recreation Complex Bond Commn., Peachtree City, 1989; mem. Fayette County Solid Waste Com., Fayetteville, Ga., 1989-90, Fayette County Bicentennial Com., 1986; candidate Fayette County Bd. Commrs., 1990; mem. City Coun., Peachtree City, 1992—; founding mem. Peachtree City Compassionate Friends, 1990; bd. dirs. West Fayette YMCA, 1991-95. Mem. Atlanta Researcher's Roundtable (sec. 1989-90, pres. 1996), Am. Bus. Women's Assn. (pres. McIntosh charter chpt. 1989-90, Woman of Yr. award 1990), Regional Leadership Inst. (Atlanta regional commn.). Lutheran. Home: 2403 Ashford Park Peachtree City GA 30269-1448

PRICE, CHARLES GRATTAN, JR., retired insurance agency executive; b. Harrisonburg, Va., May 31, 1919; s. Charles Grattan and Julia Page (Pleasants) P.; m. Kathleen Violette Nutter Price, Mar. 15, 1940 (dec. 1992); children: Julia Kathleen, Melinda Marshall, Charles Grattan III. BS in Mech. Engring., Va. Poly. Inst., Blacksburg, 1940. Mech. engr. Chesapeake Western Ry., Harrisonburg, Va., 1940-41; officer U.S. Army, 1941-45; cons. pvt. practice, Vt., Pa., 1946; with ins. agy. C.G. Price & Sons, Inc., Harrisonburg, Va., 1946-78; ret., 1978; ind. railroad dieselization survey cons., 1946-47. Author: The Crooked and Weedy, 1992, Reminiscences of a Rambling Railroader, 1993, Robert E. Lee's Railroad, 1994. Maj. USAR, 1947-54. Mem. Rlwy. and Locomotive Hist. Soc., Nat. Rlwy. Hist. Soc., Railroadiana Collectors Assn., Elks (lodge 450), Am. Legion (post 27). Presbyterian. Home: 531 Ott St Harrisonburg VA 22801-3218

PRICE, CRAIG GAMMELL, medical liability management consultant, editor, publisher; b. Oakland, Calif., Sept. 6, 1947; s. Leslie Dean and Maurine (Gammell) P.; m. Anna Kwan Tai Lam, July 20, 1970 (div. 1985); children: Meriah, Morgan; m. Mia Rangel, Aug. 4, 1992; 1 child, Sierra Rose. BA, Chaminade Coll., 1974; BS, cert. Physician Asst., Baylor U., 1977; MBA, Houston Bapt. U., 1980. Physician asst. Baylor Coll. Medicine, Houston, 1977-80; v.p. Med. Accountability Group, Houston, 1981-84; pres. Internat. Med. Mktg., Mirandola, Italy, 1984-86, Craig G. Price and Assocs., Austin, San Antonio, 1986—; editor, owner Meriah-Morgan Press, San Antonio, 1990—; cons. United Svcs. Automobile Assoc. Property and CAsualty Co., San Antonio, 1989—, Med. Rsch. Inst., San Antonio, 1991—, Med. Dispute Resolution Svcs., Inc., San Antonio, 1992—, Tex. Workers Compensation Commn., Dallas, 1992—. Author: (textbooks) Strains, Sprain and Automobiles, 1991, Impairment and Disability Ratings, 1992; contbr. articles to profl. jours. Active neighborhood assn. With U.S. Army, 1971-74. Home: 14131 Kings Mdws San Antonio TX 78231-1717 Office: Craig G Price Assocs 8452 Fredericksburg Rd # 144 San Antonio TX 78229-3317

PRICE, DANIEL O'HAVER, retired mathematics educator, statistician; b. Palatka, Fla., Sept. 12, 1918; s. Charles Henry and Lillian (O'Haver) P.; m. Doris Mae Carter, June 21, 1945 (div. Feb. 1985); children: Phil, Karen, Gary; m. Marion Albinson Conner, June 5, 1988. BS, Fla. So. Coll., 1939; MA in Sociology, U. N.C., 1942, PhD in Sociology, 1948. High sch. sci. tchr. Summerlin Inst., Bartow, Fla., 1939-40; from lectr. to prof. U. N.C., Chapel Hill, 1947-66; prof., dept. head U. N.C., Greensboro, 1978-88, prof. emeritus, 1988; prof., dept. head U. Tex., Austin, 1966-78; adj. prof. U. North Fla., Jacksonville, 1990; vol. algebra tutor, Robert E. Lee High Sch., Jacksonville, 1993; dir. Inst. for Rsch. Social Sci., Chapel Hill, 1957-66; cons. NSF, Washington, 1964-76; study sect. mem. NIH, Washington, 1960-72; cons. Bur. the Census, Washington, 1958-68, Inst. Life Ins., N.Y., 1964-68, U.S. Office Econ. Opportunity, 1966-69; vis. lectr. dept. social rels. Harvard U., spring, 1950; vis. prof. computation ctr. MIT, summer, 1957. Author: (with M.J. Hagood) Statistics for Sociologists, 1952, (with M.E. Burgess) An American Dependency Challenge, 1963, (with others) When a City Closes its Schools, (with M. Sikes) Rural-Urban Migration Research in U.S., 1974; editor: The 99th Hour: The Population Crisis in the United States, 1967; contbr. articles to profl. jours. Capt. USNR, ret. Fellow Am. Statis. Assn. (chmn. social stats. sect. 1970, chmn. com. for selection fellows 1975-80, chmn. com. prizes and awards 1981); mem. Population Assn. Am. (sec.-treas., 1st v.p.), So. Demographic Assn. (past. pres.), Pi Gamma Mu, Pi Mu Epsilon. Democrat. Home: 1537 Avondale Ave Jacksonville FL 32205-8507

PRICE, DONALD WAYNE, lawyer; b. Moline, Ill., Sept. 1, 1961; s. Henry Lewis and Barbara Nell (Jones) P.; m. Belinda Louise Burleigh, May 14, 1988; 1 child, Donald Cameron. BA, La. State U., 1986, JD, 1989. Bar: La. 1989, U.S. Dist. Ct. (mid. dist.) La. 1990, U.S. Dist. Ct. (ea. and we. dists.) La. 1991, U.S. Ct. Appeals (5th cir.) 1992. Law clk. La. Supreme Ct., New Orleans, 1989-90; ptnr. Dué, Smith, Caballero, Price & Guidry, Baton Rouge, 1990—. Mem. ABA, Assn. Trial Lawyers Am., La. State Bar Assn., La. Trial Lawyers Assn., Baton Rouge Bar Assn., Order of Coif, Phi Kappa Phi. Democrat. Episcopalian. Office: 8201 Jefferson Hwy Baton Rouge LA 70809-1623

PRICE, DOUGLAS ARMSTRONG, chiropractor; b. Pitts., Feb. 17, 1950; s. Walter Coachman and Janet (Armstrong) P.; m. Ann Georgette Martino, Jan. 31, 1989; 4 children. BA, Brown U., 1972; D Chiropractic, Life Chiropractic Coll., Atlanta, 1983. Diplomate Am. Bd. Chiropractic Examiners; cert. rehab. doctor; life extension physician; independent medical examiner, Fla. Owner, CEO Athletic Attic-Westshore, Tampa, Fla., 1976-80, Applied Biomech. and Musculoskeletal Rehab., Tampa, 1989—, All Am. Chiropractic Clinic; pvt. practice Tampa, 1984-94, Manalapan, Fla., 1994—; dir. Myofascial Therapy Found. Producer therapeutic exercise video for cervical and lumbar rehab.; contbr. articles to profl. jours. Magnetic Resonance Imaging fellow; named to Brown U. Athletic Hall of Fame; Southeastern Masters Champion Shotput, Discus, 1990-91. Fellow Am. Coll. Sports Medicine, Chiropractic Rehab. Assn., Am. Gerontology Assn.; mem. APHA, Am. Chiropractic Assn., Fla. Chiropractic Assn., Hillsborough County Chiropractic Soc. (bd. dirs. 1990-93, pres. 1992-93), Palm Beach Chiropractic Soc. Democrat. Roman Catholic. Home: 731 N Atlantic Dr Lantana FL 33462-1911 Office: 204 S Ocean Blvd Manalapan FL 33462-3312

PRICE, EUGENE, newspaper editor; b. Elizabeth City, N.C., Jan. 5, 1929; s. Charles Edward and Lena Jane (Duncan) P.; m. Gloria Enid MacCormack, Dec. 24, 1950; children: Joyce, Susan, Bonnie, Charles, John. Student, East Carolina U., 1948-49, George Washington U., 1949-50. Reporter The Independent, Elizabeth City, 1946-48, Greenville (N.C.) Daily Reflector, 1948-49; press sec. to U.S. Congressman Herbert Bonner, Washington, 1949-50; city editor Goldsboro (N.C.) News-Argus, 1952-54, mng. editor, 1955-68, editor, mng. editor, 1968-91, editor emeritus, columnist, 1991—; waterfront reporter Norfolk Virginian-Pilot, 1954-55. Past pres. Tuscarora coun. Boy Scouts Am.; chmn. N.C. Wildlife Resources Commn., Raleigh, 1987-89. Sgt. 1st class U.S. Army, 1950-52. Recipient Disting. Svc. award Goldsboro Jaycees, Disting. Citizen and Silver Beaver awards Boy Scouts Am., Goldsboro, Conservation Svc. award Ducks Unltd. Mem. N.C. AP Club (past pres.), N.C. Press Assn. (past pres. dailies div., 30 writing awards), Ea. N.C. Press Assn. (past pres.). Republican. Episcopalian. Home: 130 Quail Dr Dudley NC 28333-9518 Office: Goldsboro News-Argus PO Box 10629 Goldsboro NC 27532-0629

PRICE, GAIL ELIZABETH, corporate communications specialist, author, educator; b. Camden, N.J., Apr. 19, 1945; d. Joseph Washington and Elizabeth (Ahern) P.; m. Robert Alan Price, Apr. 5, 1969 (div. 1974); 1 child, Benjamin Joshua; m. Donald Ferrill Liscomb, Nov. 2, 1985; stepchildren—Dawn, Chance, Samuel, Lindy, Amy, Liberty, Mary. A.B. in Polit. Sci. History, Douglass Coll., 1967; M.A. in Social Scis., Antioch U., 1969; M.A. in Lit. and Writing, Rutgers U., 1979; postgrad. Temple U., 1976-77, Glassboro State U., 1976. Cert. tchr., Calif. tchr. Balt. Pub. Schs., 1967-69; tchr. Unified Sch. Dist., San Francisco, 1969-74; instr. Camden County Coll., N.J., 1976-79; instr. Phila. Coll. Art, 1976-79; instr. Rutgers U., Camden, N.J., 1977-79; regional tng. coord. Legal Svcs. Corp., Phila., 1980-84; dir. pub. rels. Rocco Inc., Harrisonburg, Va., 1984-88; dir. corp. communication WLR Foods, Hinton, Va., 1988—; adj. prof. communication arts James Madison U., 1985-88; pres. The Country Pl., Luray, Va., 1985—; cons., writing instr. various univs., cos. and assns. Author-editor: (monthly column) Clearinghouse Review, 1983-86. Author: The Community as Textbook, 1970, Training Skills Development Manual, 1982; author/editor Dimensions, 1989—, Rocco Messenger, 1984-88; contbr. articles to profl. jours. Women's platform writer for George McGovern's Presdl. Campaign, 1972; organizer, pres. Melville St. Neighbors, Phila., 1982-84; coord. WLR Foods United Way Drive, 1988—, Rocco United Way Drive, Harrisonburg, 1984-88, trustee, exec. com. United Way Harrisonburg-Rockingham, 1988-93; mem. Rockingham Meml. Hosp. Found. Bd., 1987-92; mem. pub. relations council Va. Rural Exposition, 1988—. Recipient Recognition of Service award Legal Services Corp., 1984; inductee Douglass Soc., 1996. Mem. Am. Soc. Tng. and Devel. (v.p. 1983-84; Nat. recognition 1984), Internat. Assn. Bus. Communicators, Pub. Relations Soc. Am. (accredited 1990), Va. Poultry Fedn. (legis. and pub. rels. com. 1990—), Harrisonburg-Rockingham C. of C. (bd. dirs. 1985-93), Luray/Page County C. of C. (pres. 1995, bd. dirs.), Working Women's Forum (Working Woman of Yr. 1994), Pub. Rels. coun. Shenandoah Valley (founder, pres. 1995—). Democrat. Roman Catholic. Home: Price-Liscomb Farm 1 Fort Liscomb Rd Luray VA 22835 Office: WLR Foods Inc PO Box 7000 Broadway VA 22815-7000

PRICE, GAIL ELIZABETH, research firm executive; b. Jacksonville, Fla., 1940; d. Roy Melvin Price and Claire Elizabeth (Baxter) Lee; m. William Pershing Geiger (div. 1982); children: Richard, Stuart, Terri; m. Jerome A. Ross, June 25, 1988. BS, U. Md., 1962. Rsch. asst. CIA, Langley, Va., 1958-62, 70-82, Griffith & Werner, Hollywood, Fla., 1982-84; prin. G.E. Price & Assocs., Ft. Lauderdale, Fla., 1984—. Mem. Exec. Women's Club, Ft. Lauderdale Profl. Women's Club. Republican. Baptist. Office: GE Price & Assocs 4701 N Federal Hwy # 480 B 7 Lighthouse Point FL 33064

PRICE, GEORGE DWIGHT, airline repair specialist; b. Pittsfield, Mass., Mar. 11, 1932; s. George and Delia (Daley) P.; m. June Dobert; children: Dwight, Candace, Sheryl, Linda. AAS, Hudson Valley Tech. Inst., 1957; student, U. Bridgeport, Conn., 1957-67. With Avco-Lycoming Div., 1957-75; product engr. Aviation Power Supply Inc., Burbank, Calif., 1975-78, Nat. Airmotive Corp., Oakland, Calif., 1978-80; overhaul and repair engr. Garrett Turbine Engine Co., Phoenix, 1980, sr. overhaul engr., 1980-81, main coord. programs, 1981-82, sr. repair devel. engr., 1982-83; sr. repair devel. engr. Garrett Airline Svcs. Div., Phoenix, 1983-86, supr. repair devel. engring., 1986-87; mgr. repair devel. Garrett Airline Repair Co., Anniston, Ala., 1987-93; supr. repair devel. engr. Alliedsignal Aerospace Co., Phoenix, 1993-94; cons. GDP Turbine Technologies, 1994—. Contbr. articles to profl. jours. With USAF, 1950-54. Mem. ASME, Am. Soc. of Metals, K.C. (trustee Mesa, Ariz. chpt. 1987—). Republican. Roman Catholic. Home: 1256 River Ridge Rd Norfork AR 72658-9604

PRICE, GREGORY N., economist, educator; b. New Haven, Conn., Mar. 13, 1961; s. Prince A. and Janice (Dixon) P.; m. June 28, 1986; children: Stephen, Julia. BA, Morehouse Coll., 1982; MA, U. Wis., 1984, PhD, 1993. Instr. Glendale (Ariz.) Coll., 1986-87; lectr. Black studies U. Wis., Milw., 1989-91; asst. prof. econs. N.C. A&T State U., Greensboro, 1991—.

PRICE, HOWARD CHARLES, chemist; b. South Gibson, Pa., Feb. 26, 1942; s. Howard Thomas and Rachael Emma (Michael) P.; m. Delores Ann Wilson, July 1, 1967; children: Susanne, Thomas. BS, Dickinson Coll., Carlisle, Pa., 1963; postgrad., Brown U., Providence, 1963-64; PhD, SUNY, Binghamton, 1971. NIH postdoctoral fellow Albert Einstein Coll. Medicine, Bronx, 1970-71; asst. prof. chemistry Marshall U., Huntington, W.Va., 1971-77, assoc. prof., 1978-80; sr. rsch. chemist Adv. Tech. Dept., Zimmer Inc., Warsaw, Ind., 1981-83, rsch. & devel. mgr., 1984-86, rsch. & devel. group mgr., 1987-88; R & D dir. Rsch. Labs., Warsaw, Ind., 1988-90; R & D devel. dir. Advanced Technology Dept., Zimmer Inc., Warsaw, Ind., 1991-92; dir. materials technology divsn. Family Health Internat., Research Triangle Park, N.C., 1992-95; vis. prof. Ohio U., Ironton, 1973-74. Contbr. articles to profl. jours.; author: Pennsylvania Game News, 1982; patentee in field. Band booster Warsaw Community High Sch., 1985-89. 1st lt. U.S. Army, 1964-66. Grantee, Spectroscopy Soc. of Pitts., 1980, Sigma Xi, 1975, NSF and Marshall U., 1973-80. Mem. ASTM, ASM, Am. chem. Soc. (sect. treas. 1975-76), Soc. for Biomaterials, Orthopaedic Rsch. Soc., Soc. Plastics Engrs., N.Y. Acad. Scis., Tissue Engring. Soc., Sigma Xi. Home: 1032 Lakeshore Dr Wendell NC 27591-8640 Office: Four M PO Box 549 Wendell NC 27591

PRICE, JAMES ELDRIDGE, police officer, emergency medical technician; b. Knoxville, Tenn., Oct. 14, 1952; s. J. Eldridge and Doris O. (Lilley) P.; m. Donna J. Jarnagin, July 28, 1984; children: Jessica D., Theron J. BS in Pub. Adminstrn., U. Tenn., 1976. Announcer Sta. WRGS, Rogersville, Tenn., 1967-70, Sta. WKGN, Knoxville, 1970-72, Sta. WROL, Knoxville, 1972-74; security supr. Ft. Sanders Presbyn. Hosp., Knoxville, 1974-76; dep. sheriff Knox County Sheriff's Dept., Knoxville, 1976-78; police officer Morristown (Tenn.) Police Dept., 1978—; cons. Morristown and Hamblen Counties, 1989—; mem. Hosp. Med. Response Emergency Mgmt. Agy., 1987-94; bd. dirs. Morristown-Hamblen Emergency Med. Svcs., 1991-94; adj. prof. criminal justice Walters State C.C., 1995-96. Mem. Morristown Emergency Rescue Squad, 1987-94. Recipient mayor's citation for action above and beyond call of duty City of Morristown, 1989, Gov.'s Highway Safety grant City of Morristown, 1994. Mem. Fraternal Order of Police (sec. local chpt. 1984-87), Police Benevolent Assn., Internat. Wildlife Fedn., Nat. Geog. Soc., Greenpeace, Masons (worshipful master Hamblen lodge 1992), Scottish Rite Club (pres. 1993, 94), Shriners. Democrat. Home: 1125 Heykoop Dr Morristown TN 37814-6121 Office: Morristown Police Dept PO Box 1283 Morristown TN 37816-1283

PRICE, JEANNINE ALLEENICA, clinical psychologist, computer consultant; b. Cleve., Oct. 29, 1949; d. Q. Q. and Lisa Denise (Wilson) Ewing; m. T. R. Price, Sept. 2, 1976. BS, Western Res. U., 1969; MS, Vanderbilt U., 1974; MBA, Stanford U., 1985. Cert. alcoholism counselor, Calif. Health Service coordinator Am. Profile, Nashville, 1970-72; exec. dir. Awareness Concept, San Jose, Calif., 1977-80, counselor, 1989—, exec. dir., 1989-90, v.p. Image Makers (formerly Awareness Concepts), 1994—; mgr. employee assistance program Nat. Semiconductor, Santa Clara, Calif., 1980-81; mgmt. cons. employee assistant programs. Mem. Gov.'s Adv. Council Child Devel. Programs. Mem. Am. Bus. Women's Assn., NAFE, AAUW, Coalition Labor Women, Calif. Assn. Alcohol counselors, Almaca. Author: Smile a Little, Cry a Lot, Gifts of Love, Reflection in the Mirror, The Light at the Top of the Mountain, The Dreamer, The Girl I Never Knew, An Act of Love, Walk Toward the Light.

PRICE, JOANNE, financial executive; b. Louisville, May 23, 1938; m. James E. Price, Feb. 10, 1979; children: Rosemarie, Donna Jean, James, Robert, John, Elke. BS, U. Md., 1988. Asst. controller Wald, Harkrader, and Ross, Washington, 1976-80; controller The Sporting Club, McLean, Va., 1980-88; fin. exec. Artificial Decorations Unltd., Alexandria, Va., 1990—; pres. Hansel and Gretel Nurseries and Child Devel. Ctr., 1988—; v.p. fin. ops. Info. Resources Mgmt. Cons. Corp., 1988—. Active St. Labre Indian Sch. Mem. Nat. Assn. Legal Adminstrs., Am. Inst. Profl. Bookkeepers, Univ. Md. Alumni Assn. (charter), Phi Kappa Phi, Alpha Sigma Lambda, Century Club. Presbyterian. Home: 6856 Heatherway Ct Alexandria VA 22315-3916 Office: Artificial Decorations Unltd 6856 Heatherway Ct Alexandria VA 22315-3916

PRICE, JOE SEALY, law enforcement officer; b. Coleman, Tex., Feb. 27, 1933; s. Joe Collin and Thelma Lou (Boyd) P.; m. Peggy Littlefield LaBuff, June 1954 (div. 1955); 1 child, Roy Earl LaBuff; m. Elizabeth Earldeen Eddins, June 8, 1956; children: Joe Sealy Jr., Michael Raymond, Robert Wayne. Student, Lee Coll., 1982; BS in Law Enforcement Adminstrn., Pacific Western U., 1985; grad., Law Enforcement Mgmt. Inst., 1993. cert. master peace officer Tex. Com. on Law Enforcement Officer Standards Edn. Asst. mgr. Guardian Fin. Corp., Houston, 1954-55; mgr. Installment Credit Corp., Houston, 1955-56; dep. constable Montgomery County Constable Office, Splendora, Tex., 1956-58; dep. sheriff Montgomery County Sheriff's Dept., Conroe, Tex., 1958-59; chief dep. sheriff Kendall County Sheriff's Dept., Boerne, Tex., 1959-60; warrant officer City of Houston Police Dept., 1960-69; dep. sheriff Harris County Sheriff's Dept., Houston, 1969-73; patrolman Galena Park (Tex.) Police Dept., 1973-74, detective sgt. criminal investigation divsn., 1975-85, chief detectives, 1985-89, sgt., shift comdr. patrol divsn., 1989-90, detective sgt. criminal investigation divsn., 1990—, lt. criminal investigation divsn., 1994—, lt. patrol divsn., 1996—. Mem. swine auction com. Houston Livestock Show and Rodeo, 1987; bd. dirs. Trinity Valley Trailriders for Boys Harbor, Houston, 1986-87. Served with USN, 1950-53. Named Detective of the Yr., 100 Club, 1981. Mem. Galena Park Police Assn. (pres. 1975-85), Tex. Mcpl. Police Assn. (v.p. 1981, bd. dirs. 1975-87), Harris County Organized Crime Unit, Metro Crime Coun., Combined Law Enforcement Assn. of Tex. (bd. dirs. 1986—), Masons (32 degree), Shriners, Arabian Knights. Home: 1909 Fm 1942 Rd Crosby TX 77532-6348 Office: Galena Park Police Dept 2000 Clinton Dr PO Box 46 Galena Park TX 77547

PRICE, JOHN RANDALL, theology educator, researcher; b. San Marcos, Tex., Nov. 19, 1951; s. Elmo Churchill and Maurine Grace (Atkings) P.; m. Beverlee Fae Shaw, Aug. 14, 1976; children: Elisabeth, Elisha, Erin, Jonathan, Emilee. BS, S.W. Tex. State U., 1974; ThM, Dallas Theol. Sem., 1981; PhD, U. Tex., 1993. Dir. World of the Bible Tours, San Marcos, Tex., 1982-92; instr. U. Tex., Austin, 1990-92; prof. Ctrl. Tex. Bible Inst., Austin, 1992-93; pres. World of the Bible Ministries, Inc., San Marcos, Tex., 1993—; adj. prof. Liberty U., Lynchburg, Va., 1995—, Tyndale Theol. Sem., Ft. Worth, 1996—; exec. bd. Pre-Trib Rsch. Ctr., Washington, 1994—. Author: Teachers Study Bible, 1992, Ready to Rebuild, 1992, Desecration and Restoration of the Temple, 1993, In Search of Temple Treasures, 1994, Secrets of the Dead Sea Scrolls, 1996; editor: Tyndale House Publ., Wheaton, Ill., 1992-96; mem. adv. bd.: Messianic Times, Toronto, 1993—. Mem. Soc.

Biblical Literature, Evang. Theol. Soc. Office: World of the Bible Ministri 110 Easy St San Marcos TX 78606-7336

PRICE, JUDITH, emergency nurse, administrator; b. N.Y., Feb. 4, 1947; d. Isidore and Evelyn (Simpkins) Price; m. Charles Reed Corn, July 26, 1987. AAS, CUNY, 1966, BA, 1975; BSN, Va. Commonwealth U., 1985; MSN, Barry U., 1993. RN, Fla., Calif., Va., N.Y.; CEN; cert. in nursing adminstrn.; cert. ACLS, PALS, CPR instr., Trauma Nurse Core Curriculum Provider. Staff nurse, relief charge nurse emergency dept. Mt. Sinai Hosp., N.Y.C.; nurse clinician emergency dept. Med. Coll. Va., Richmond; clin. educator emergency dept. Jackson Meml. Hosp., Miami, Fla.; nursing adminstr. Palmetto Gen. Hosp., Miami; dir. emergency svcs. Cedars Med. Ctr., Miami; QI/IC coord. Columbia Cedars, Miami. Mem. Dade County Mrg. Trauma Adv. Com.; mem. adv. bd. North Dade Health Ctr. Mem. ANA, Fla. Nurses Assn., Emergency Nurses Assn. (past pres. Fla. state, past pres. Dade-Broward chpt., treas. Dade-Broward chpt.), Am. Trauma Soc. (past bd. dirs. Fla. divsn., past v.p. Fla. divsn.), Sigma Theta Tau. Home: 3637 NE 168th St Miami FL 33160

PRICE, KENNETH PAUL, clinical psychologist, educator; b. Boston, Oct. 22, 1947; s. Hillel and Miriam (Port) P.; m. Gloria Ray Huberman, June 20, 1971; children: Sarah Lucia, David Alexander. Cert., Hayim Greenberg Inst., Jerusalem, 1966; BJEd, Hebrew Coll., 1969; BA magna cum laude, Brandeis U., 1970; PhD in Clin. Psychology, SUNY, Stony Brook, 1975. Lic. and cert. psychologist, Tex. Practicum in child and adult psychotherapy SUNY Psychol. Svcs., Stony Brook, 1971-72, intern, 1972-73; instr. psychology SUNY, Stony Brook, 1973, rsch. assoc. Rsch. Found., 1974-75; clin. intern VA Hosp., Northport, N.Y., 1973-74, clin. psychologist, 1975; instr. to asst. prof. dept. psychiatry divsn. psychology U. Tex. Southwestern Med. Sch., 1976-80; pvt. practice Dallas, 1980—; part-time lectr. dept. continuing edn. SUNY, Stony Brook, 1975; adj. asst. prof. edn. Grad. Sch. Edn., C.W. Post Coll., L.I. U., 1972-75. Author: (with G. Price) Instructor's Manual and Resource Book, 1974, (with R.J. Gatchel) Clinical Applications of Biofeedback: Appraisal and Status, 1979; editor: (with others) Contemporary Readings in Psychopathology, 1974, 2d edit., 1978; contbr. chpts. to books, articles to profl. jours. Bd. dirs. Zionist Orgn. Am., chmn. program com., 1980—. Nat. Migraine Found. grantee, 1976-77, Roche Psychiat. Svc. Inst. Stress grantee, 1976, U. Tex. Southwestern Med. Sch. instnl. rsch. grantee, 1976, dissertation grantee, SUNY, 1974, NIMH undergrad. rsch. grantee in psychology, 1969-70; Herbert H. Lehman fellow, 1970-74. Mem. APA, Assn. for Advancement of Behavior Therapy, Soc. of Behavioral Medicine, Tex. Psychol. Assn., Dallas Psychol. Assn. Home: 7202 Wester Way Dallas TX 75248-1549 Office: Pain and Stress Ctr 12800 Hillcrest Rd Ste 116 Dallas TX 75230-1514

PRICE, LESTER LEE, naval aviator; b. Eufaula, Ala., Jan. 3, 1955; s. Lester Johnson and Jill (Howell) P.; m. Deborah Demus, Apr. 23, 1994; children: Elisabet, Lacey, Daniel, Kevin, Marissa, Chris, Kathryn. BS, U.S. Naval Acad., 1978; MA, U.S. Naval War Coll., Newport, R.I. Chief engr. USS Fidelity, Panama City, Fla., 1979-81; pers. officer Patrol Squadron 46, Moffett Field, Calif., 1982-85; exec. asst., instr. U.S. Naval Acad., Annapolis, Md., 1985-88; targeting program coord. Chief of Naval Ops., Washington, 1988-90; ops. dept. head Patrol Squadron 26, Brunswick, Maine, 1991-93; instr. Tactical Tng. Group Atlantic, 1993-96; weapons officer USS George Washington (CUN-73), 1996—. Sub-editor (revision): Knight's Modern Seamanship, 1986, Division Officer's Guide, 1987. Recipient Navy Commendation medal, 1988. Mem. Naval Acad. Alumni Assn., Naval Acad. Athletic Assn., Nat. Eagle Scout Assn. (officer rep. 1985-88). Republican. Methodist. Home: 1060 San Marco Rd Virginia Beach VA 23456 Office: Tactical Tng Group Atlantic 2132 Regulus Ave Virginia Beach VA 23461-2199

PRICE, LINDA RICE, community development administrator; b. Norman, Okla., Sept. 17, 1948; d. Elroy Leon and Esther May (Wilson) Rice; m. Michael Allen Price, May 17, 1970; children: Justin R, Mathew Lyon. BA in Am. History, U. Okla., 1970, M. Regional and City Planning, 1975. Dir. U. Okla. Crisis Ctr., Norman, 1969-70; cardio-pulmonary technician Bethany Med. Ctr., Kansas City, Kans., 1970-72; mgr. congressional campaign Barsotti for Congress, Kansas City, 1972; planning intern City of Seminole (Okla.), 1973-74, City of Tecumseh (Okla.), 1974-75; planner I City of Norman, 1975-76, planner II, 1975-80, community devel. coord., 1980-96, asst. dir. planning and cmty. devel. for revitalization, 1996—; adj. prof. U. Okla., Norman, 1986-93; cons. in field, Norman, 1980—. Past pres., mem. LWV Norman, 1979—; chmn. Norman Arts & Humanities Coun., 1983-86; bd. dirs. Women's Resource Ctr., Norman, 1991-92; v.p. Oakhurst Neighborhood Assn., Norman, 1991-94; mem., past pres. bd. Thunderbird Clubhouse, 1992-95. Named to Leadership Norman, Norman C. of C., 1992, for Exemplary Mgmt. Practice, The Urban Inst., 1989, for Outstanding Performance, HUD, 1988; recipient Citation of Merit, Okla. State Hist. Preservation, 1991, Spl. Recognition, Okla. Hist. Soc., 1991. Mem. Am. Inst. Cert. Planners (cert.), Am. Planning Assn. (sec. Okla. chpt. 1980-82), Planning and Women (regional coord. 1987-90), Assn. Cen. Okla. Govt. (areawide planning and tech. adv. com. 1979—), Nat. Community Devel. Assn., (state whip 1988—, chair nat. membership 1994-96), Homeless Here Coalition, Social Svcs. Coordinating Coun. Democrat. Presbyterian. Office: City of Norman PO Box 370 Norman OK 73070-0370

PRICE, MARILYN JEANNE, fundraising and management consultant; b. N.Y.C., Jan. 24, 1948; d. George Franklin and Mary Anastasia (Barnishin) Lawrence; student Temple Bus. Sch., 1964-66; student U. Md., 1973-74; 1 child, Kimberly Jean. Asst. to sr. printing and paper buyer ARC, Washington 1965-67; conf. planner for classified mil. confs. Nat. Security Indsl. Assn., Washington, 1967-69; fund devel. office asst. Nat. Urban Coalition, Washington, 1970; direct mail/membership coordinator Common Cause, Washington, 1970-72; mgr. direct mail fund raising Epilepsy Found. of Am., Washington, 1973-76; exec. v.p. Bruce W. Eberle & Assocs., Vienna, Va., 1977-81; pres. Response Dynamics, Inc., Vienna, Va., 1981-83; v.p. The Best Lists, Inc., Vienna, 1981-83; pres. The Creative Advantage, Inc., Fairfax, Va., 1983—, Creative Mgmt. Services, Inc., Fairfax, 1987—; cons. in field. Asst. to Young Citizens for Johnson, 1964; vol. Hubert Humphrey campaign, 1968, George McGovern campaign, 1972. Recipient Silver Echo award, Direct Mail/Mktg. Assn. Internat. competition for mktg. excellence, 1980. Mem. Nat. Soc. Fund Raisers, Direct Mail Mktg. Assn., Non-Profit Mailers Fedn., Assn. Direct Response Fundraising Council (bd. dirs., treas.), Direct Mktg. Club. Home: 9614 Lindenbrook St Fairfax VA 22031-1121 Office: The Creative Advantage 9401 Lee Hwy Ste 205 Fairfax VA 22031-1803

PRICE, MARTY G., librarian; b. Clarksburg, W.Va., Nov. 23, 1952; s. Robert E. and Mary Jane (Powell) P.; m. Carolyn E. Adams, July 27, 1985; children: Robert W., Allison. BA, Fairmont State U., 1974; MA, U. Chgo., 1976; MLS, U. Mich., 1990. Learning resource ctr. dir. Mary Holmes Coll., West Point, Miss., 1993. Democrat. Office: Mary Holmes Coll PO Box 1257 West Point MS 39773

PRICE, MARY ANN, plant virologist; b. Baton Rouge; d. Thomas Henry and Esther Lee (Robson) P. BS in Microbiology, La. State U., 1978, PhD in Biochemistry, 1991. Rsch. assoc. La. State U., Baton Rouge, 1978-85; postdoctoral rsch. assoc. Wash. State U., Pullman, 1992-93, Citrus Rsch. and Edn. Ctr., Lake Alfred, Fla., 1993—. Contbr. articles to profl. jours. Mem. AAAS, NAFE, Am. Soc. Virology (assoc.), Iota Sigma Pi, Mu Sigma Rho. Home: 2409 8th St Apt 4 Winter Haven FL 33881

PRICE, PAMELA CHAMPION, art educator; b. San Francisco, June 9, 1944; d. John Clyde and Lorraine Clair (Weber) Champion; m. Joel Roderick Price, July 18, 1970. BA in Printmaking, Painting and Drawing, Ga. State U., 1967; MFA in Printmaking, U. Ga., 1970. Teaching asst. Univ. Ga., Athens, 1967-70, instr., 1968-70; adj. instr. Univ. Tex. Permian Basin, Odessa, 1974-75, coord. art, 1975-76, lectr., 1976-77, asst. prof., 1977-83, assoc. prof., 1983-90, prof., 1990—, chmn. art dept., 1992—, Mr. and Mrs. Louis Rochester Prof. of Fine Arts, 1994—; adv. bd. mem. Women's Ctr., Univ. Tex. Permian Basin, 1986-88; editorial adv. bd. mem. Collegiate Press, Alto Loma, Calif., 1990—. One-woman shows include Art Inst. for Permian Basin, Odessa, 1989, San Angelo (Tex.) Mus. Fine Arts, 1988, Univ. Tex. Permian Basin, 1976, 80, 85, Sul Ross State Univ., Alpine, Tex., 1985, Western Tex. Coll., Snyder, 1981, Coll. of S.W., Hobbs, N.Mex., 1980; represented in permanent collections Equitable Corp., Chgo. Art Inst. for Permian Basin, Ark. Art Ctr., Little Rock, Archtl. Arts, Inc., Dallas, Southwestern Bell Tex. Collection, Redstone Arsenal Bank, Ala., Ga. Commn. on Arts. Exhbn. com. mem. Art Inst. for Permian Basin, 1990—; active 20/20 Foresight, Odessa, 1990—. Recipient Minnie Piper Stevens award Minnie Piper Found., 1992; named Amoco Outstanding Tchr., Amoco Found., 1985. Mem. Univ. Art Assn. (faculty advisor 1978—),. Office: U Tex of Permian Basin 4901 E University Blvd Odessa TX 79762-8122

PRICE, ROSALIE PETTUS, artist; b. Birmingham, Ala.; d. Erle and Ellelee (Chapman) Pettus; AB, Birmingham-So. Coll., 1935; MA, U. Ala., Tuscaloosa, 1967; m. William Archer Price, Oct. 3, 1936. Instr. Birmingham (Ala.) Mus. Art, 1967-70, Samford U., 1969-70. Painter in watercolors, casein, oil and acrylic; One-man shows include Samford U., 1964, Birmingham Mus. of Art, 1966, 73, 82-83, Town Hall Gallery, 1968, 75, South Central Bell, 1977, Birmingham Southern Coll., 1992; represented in permanent collections Birmingham Mus. Art, Springfield (Mo.) Art Mus., U. Ala. Moody Gallery of Art, many others. Bd. dirs. Birmingham Mus. of Art, 1950-54, vice chmn., 1950-51; bd. trustees Birmingham Music Club, 1956-66, rec. sec., 1958-62. Recipient purchase award Watercolor USA, 1972; named to Watercolor USA Honor Soc., 1986. Mem. Nat. Watercolor Soc., Nat. Soc. Painters in Casein and Acrylic (W. Alden Brown Meml. award 1970, Joseph A. Cain Meml. award 1983), Birmingham Art Assn. (pres. 1947-49, Best Watercolor award 1950, Little House on Linden purchase award 1968), So. Watercolor Soc., Watercolor Soc. Ala. (sec. 1948-49), La. Watercolor Soc., Pi Beta Phi. Episcopalian. Clubs: Jr. League of Birmingham (chmn. art com. 1947-50), Window Box Garden. Home: 2831 Highland Ave S # 616 Birmingham AL 35205-1843 Office: 2132 20th Ave S Birmingham AL 35223-1002

PRICE, SHERYL O'REAR, pediatrics, women's health and community health nurse; b. Durham, N.C., June 12, 1949; d. Harry B. and Charlotte Emily (Grove) O'Rear; m. Danny G. Price, Mar. 31, 1970; 1 child, Michael B. ADN, Walker Coll.-Walker Tech. Sch., 1985; PharmD program postgrad., Samford U., 1996—. Cert. pediatric nurse, pediatric advanced life support. Media specialist Walker Coll., 1985-87; staff nurse, newborn ICU U. Ala. Hosps., Birmingham, 1987-88; staff nurse, nursery Walker Regional Med. Ctr., Jasper, 1988-90; quality assurance nurse Alacare Home Health, Jasper, 1990-91; spl. care nurse The Children's Hosp. Ala., Birmingham, 1991-96.

PRICE, TOMMYE JO ENSMINGER, community health nurse; b. Shreveport, La., Oct. 10, 1943; d. Joe Pirkle and Edith Pipes (Whitmeyer) Ensminger; m. Murphy Briscoe Price, June 5, 1965; children: John Briscoe, Meredith Jo. BSN, Northwestern State U., 1965. Staff nurse Waterman Meml. Hosp., Eustis, Fla.; office nurse James C. Penrod, MD, Tallahassee, Fla.; staff nurse Highlands (N.C.) Cashiers Hosp.; county coordinating nurse Miss. State Dept. of Health, Raleigh. Mem. ANA, Miss. Nurse's Assn. Home: PO Box 521 Raleigh MS 39153-0521

PRICE, WILLIAM ANTHONY, real estate broker; b. Augusta, Ga., Feb. 25, 1938; s. John Patrick and Lillian (Morgan) P.; m. Barbara Jean Bliss, Aug. 6, 1960; children: Cynthia Dee Price Anfindsen, William Anthony Jr., Christel Lee Price Hammond. BS in Commerce, Spring Hill Coll., 1959. Lic. real estate broker, Ga., S.C. Sales assoc. John B. Murray Co., Augusta, Ga., 1959-69; gen. sales mgr. Bolton & Wakeley Realty Co., Augusta, 1969-71; sales mgr. comml. div. Blanchard & Calhoun Real Estate Co., Augusta, 1971-79, v.p., sales mgr. comml. div., 1979-88; v.p., sales mgr. Blanchard & Calhoun Comml. Corp., Augusta, 1988—. Mem. Augusta Bd. Realtors (pres. 1969, bd. dirs., mem. Masters Club, Realtor of Yr. 1969), Ga. Assn. Bds. Realtors (bd. dirs. 1969, chmn. profl. standards com. 1970-72), Nat. Bd. Realtors, Augusta Country Club, K.C. Republican. Roman Catholic. Home: 2704 Downing St Augusta GA 30909-3735 Office: Blanchard & Calhoun Comml First Union Tower Ste 400 Augusta GA 30901

PRICHARD, ELLA GAYLE WALL, publishing company executive; b. New Orleans, Mar. 17, 1941; d. Samuel Relerford Jr. and Irma Letitia (Roberts) Wall; m. Lev Herrington Prichard III, Dev. 16, 1962; children: Lev H. IV, Margaret Elaine Prichard Fagan. BA, Baylor U., 1963. Reporter The Caller-Times, Corpus Christi, 1962-64; freelance writer Sunday Sch. Bd., So. Bapt. Conv., Nashville, 1977-84; ptnr. The Write Group, Corpus Christi, 1989—; cons., spkr. Texans' War on Drugs, Austin, 1983-85; field reader U.S. Bd. Edn., Washington, 1988-94; cons. Baylor U., Waco, 1991. Editor cookbook: Fiesta, 1973. Founding pres. Coastal Bend Families in Action, Corpus Christi, 1981-83; vice chmn. City of Corpus Christi Landmark Commn., 1977; sec. Nat. Fedn. of Parents for Drug-Free Youth, Washington, 1984-85; bd. regents Baylor U., Waco, 1992—; local pres. Tex. PTA, 1980-81, 83-84. Recipient Cert. of Appreciation for Vol. Svc., State of Tex., 1981, 85, H.H. Reynolds award for disting. svc. to students Baylor U., 1995. Mem. Jr. League of Corpus Christi (rec. sec. 1976-77, Vol. of Yr. 1976, 82), Baylor Alumni Assn. (life, bd. dirs. 1991-94), Corpus Christi Country Club, Corpus Christi Yacht Club, Corpus Christi Town Club. Baptist. Home: 5252 Greenbriar Dr Corpus Christi TX 78413

PRICHARD, JOHN DAVID, minister; b. Burnwell, W.Va., July 19, 1948; s. Joseph and Agnes Arvada (Fisher) P.; m. Drema Kay Clark, Apr. 11, 1970; children: Angela Kay, John David II. AB, Nazarene Bible Coll., 1980; postgrad., U. Bibl. Studies, Bethany, Okla., 1989. Ordained minister Ch. of the Nazarene, 1981. Pastor, zone youth dir. Dille (W.Va.) Ch. of the Nazarene, 1975-77; pastor Craigsville (W.Va.) Ch. of the Nazarene, 1980-82, Walton (W.Va.) Ch. of the Nazarene, 1982-84, Marion (Va.) Ch. of the Nazarene, 1984-88, Beckley (W.Va.) First Ch. of the Nazarene, 1988-95; Charleston (W.Va.) South Hills Ch. of the Nazarene, 1995—; ch. planter Va. Dist., Wytheville, 1985-86; area coord. Va. Nazarene Dist., Marion, 1987-88; dist. adult dir. W.Va. South Dist., 1990—; cafeteria mgr. W.Va. Dist. Campgrounds, 1990—; dist. coll. recruiter Nazarene Bible Coll., Colorado Springs, Colo., 1990—; small ch. growth trainer W.Va. South Dist. Ch. of the Nazarene. Chmn. Libr. Commn., Walton, W.Va., 1983-84; dir. Weekday Religious Edn. Program, Marion, 1985-86; co-chair Greater Beckley Area Crusade, 1993; mem. Beckley Ministerial Assn.; vol. hospice chaplain Raleigh County Hospice Group, 1993-95. With USN, 1966-70, Vietnam. Recipient Gt. Commn. Leadership award W.Va. South Dist., 1990; named Alumnus of Yr., W.Va. South Dist., Nazarene Bible Coll., Colorado Springs, 1990. Mem. Am. Acad. Ministry. Democrat. Office: South Hills Ch of the Nazarene 1565 Smith Rd Charleston WV 25314

PRIDDY, MARGARET MORGAN, critical care nurse; b. Richmond, Va., Apr. 27, 1954; d. James Thomas Jr. and Margaret Fifield (Merriam) P.; m. James Edwards Bush, Dec. 16, 1989; children: Christopher Harrison, Morgan Bush. BSN, Med. Coll. Va., 1981; MS in Nursing, Duke U., 1986. CCRN, cert. ACLS and PALS instr. Edn. staff nurse Highsmith Rainey Hosp., Fayetteville, N.C., 1983-87; instr. Fayetteville Tech. Community Coll., N.C., 1987-88; clin. nurse specialist in surgery Cape Fear Valley Med. Ctr., Fayetteville, N.C., 1988-90, clin. nurse specialist in critical care, 1990-95; case mgr. cardiology Cape Fear Valley Med. Ctr., Fayetteville, 1995—. Named to N.C. Great 100 Nurses The Great 100 of N.C., Inc. 1992. Mem. AACN, Am. Holistic Nursing Assn., Sigma Theta Tau. Home: 234 Murray Hill Rd Fayetteville NC 28303-4910

PRIDE, CHARLEY, singer; b. Sledge, Miss., Mar. 18, 1939; m. Rozene Pride, Dec. 28, 1956; children—Kraig, Dion, Angela. Grad. high sch. Formerly with constrn. cos., refining plants; profl. baseball player with Detroit, Memphis Red Sox, Birmingham Black Barons (all Negro Am. League), Los Angeles Angels (Am. League). Appeared with WSM Grand Ole Opry, Nashville, 1967, Lawrence Welk Show, ABC-TV; appeared on Joey Bishop Show, ABC-TV; appeared with Ralph Emery Show, WSM-TV, Nashville; appeared with Syndicated Bill Anderson, Bobby Lord and Wilburn Brothers, Hee Haw, Tom Jones Show, Flip Wilson Show, Johnny Cash Show, numerous other TV shows; recorded for RCA; albums include: Country Charley Pride, Charley Pride Sings Heart Songs, Charley, Happiness, She's Just Sunday, Happiness of Having You, Charley Pride IN Person, Christmas in My Hometown, Did You Think to Pray, Roll on Mississippi, There's a Little Bit of Hank in Me, You're My Jamaica, Best of Charley Pride, The Best There Is, Greatest Hits, Night Games, Power of Love, Country Feelin, Songs of Love, A Sunshiny Day, Charley Pride Live, 1994; recorded songs Kiss an Angel Good Mornin', Snakes Crawl at Night, Let the Chips Fall, Day You Stopped Loving Me, Does My Ring Hurt Your Finger, Let Me Help You Work It Out, Is Anyone Goin' to San Antone, Afraid of Losing You Again, Let Me Live, One of These Days, Whole Lotta Love; (Named Most Promising Male Artist, Country Song Roundup 1967, Male Vocalist of Year, Country Music Assn. 1971, 72, Entertainer of Yr. in Country Music 1971, winner Grammy awards for best scored rec. 1971, for best country vocal 1972, Trendsetter award Billboard 1970, Top Male Vocalist award Cashbox, Photoplay Gold Medal award 1976). Served with U.S. Army, 1956-58. Address: CECCA Prodn PO Box 670507 Dallas TX 75229-0507

PRIDE, FLEETWOOD MARTIN, III (FLEET PRIDE), education administrator, consultant; b. Dover-Foxcroft, Maine, May 30, 1948; s. Fleetwood Jr. and Marion Josephine (Caster) P.; m. Betty Ruth Wiley, July 24, 1974 (div. Aug. 1982); children: Robert Christopher, Tiffany Inez. AA, Gulf Coast Community Coll., Panama City, Fla., 1973; BA in Religion, Fla. State U., 1978; postgrad., LaSalle U., St. Louis, 1989—. Asst. to dean of students Fla. State U., Tallahassee, 1976-82; faculty chmn. Century Coll., Tallahassee, 1984-86; dir. regulatory affairs United Coll., N.Y.C. and Ft. Lauderdale, Fla., 1986-88; dir. svcs. Pride and Assocs., Tallahassee, 1987-89; dir. edn. Career Insts. of Am., Miami Beach, Fla., 1988-90; acad. coord. Branell Coll., Tallahassee, 1990-93; dir. Branell Inst., Coll. Pk., Atlanta, 1993-94; pres. S.W. Fla. Coll., Ft. Myers, 1994—; pres. Accent Techs. and Sun Micro, Tallahassee, 1983-91, Am. Career Inst., Tallahassee, 1987-92; v.p. Computech and Softech, Tallahassee, 1982-87; dir. svcs. Pride and Assocs., Tallahassee and Miami, 1987—; inst. dir. Edn. Crop. Am., Tallahassee, Atlanta and Nashville, 1990-94. Bd. dirs. Tallahassee Symphony Orch., 1985-93, v.p. fundraising, 1987-88; bd. dirs. ARC Big Bend chpt., Tallahassee, 1987-90; bd. dirs., v.p. Very Spl. Arts of Fla., 1988-90. With USAF, 1967-73, capt. USARNG, 1978-94. Mem. Fla. Assn. Accredited Pvt. Schs., Ga. Pvt. Sch. Assn., Music Educators Nat. Conf., Tyndall Aero Club, Tallahassee Symphony Guild (pres. 1985-86), Leadership Tallahassee Alumni Assn., Internat. Bus. Edn. Assn., Nat. Bus. Educators Assn., MENSA. Republican. Methodist. Home: 2736 Raintree Cir Tallahassee FL 32308-3828 Office: Am Career Inst 1704 Thomasville Rd # 131 Tallahassee FL 32303-5759

PRIDHAM, THOMAS GRENVILLE, retired research microbiologist; b. Chgo., Oct. 10, 1920; s. Grenville and Gladys Etheral (Sloss) P.; m. Phyllis Sue Hokamp, July 1, 1943 (dec.); children: Pamela Sue, Thomas Foster, Grenville Thomas, Rolf Thomas, Montgomery Thomas; m. Edna Lee Boudreaux, Mar. 6, 1995. BS in Chemistry, U. Ill., 1943, PhD in Bacteriology, 1949. Instr. bacteriology U. Ill., Champaign-Urbana, 1947; rsch. microbiologist No. Regional Rsch. Lab., USDA, Peoria, Ill., 1948-51, 53-65, U.S. Indsl. Chems., Balt., 1951-52; supr. tech. ops. Acme Vitamins, Inc., Joliet, Ill., 1952-53; sr. rsch. biologist U.S. Borax Rsch. Corp., Anaheim, Calif., 1965-67; supervisory rsch. microbiologist No. Regional Rsch. Ctr. USDA, Peoria, 1967-81, head agrl. rsch. culture collection No. Regional Rsch. Lab., 1967-81; ret., 1981; cons. Mycogen Corp., San Diego, 1985-87; U.S. sr. scientist Fed. Republic Germany, Darmstadt, 1977. Contbg. author: Actinomycetales: The Boundary Microorganisms, 1974, Bergey's Manual of Determinative Bacteriology, 1974, Synopsis and Classification of Living Organisms, 1982; mem. editorial bd. Jour. Antibiotics, 1969-81; contbr. articles to Jour. Bacteriology, Applied Microbiology, Phytopathology, Actinomycetes, Mycologia, Devel. Indsl. Microbiology, Jour. Antibiotics, Internat. Bull. Bacteriological Nomenclature Taxonomy, Antibiotics Ann., Antimicrobial Agts., Chemotherapy, also others. With USNR, 1943-45, with Rsch. Res., 1945-54, lt. ret. Fulbright scholar, Italy, 1952; grantee Soc. Am. Bacteriologists, 1957. Fellow Am. Acad. Microbiology (ASM state network 1991—); mem. Am. Soc. Microbiology (com. mem., workshop presenter), Soc. Indsl. Microbiology, Mycol. Soc. Am., U.S. Fedn. Culture Collections (v.p. 1981). Episcopalian. Home: 38 Mayo Branch Brandy Keg Prestonsburg KY 41653

PRIEM, RICHARD GREGORY, writer, information systems executive, entertainment company executive; b. Munich, Sept. 18, 1949; came to U.S., 1953; s. Richard Stanley and Elizabeth Teresa (Thompson) P.; m. Janice Lynne Holland, July 27, 1976; children: Michael John, Matthew Warren (dec.), Kathryn Elizabeth. BS in Radio-TV-Film, U. Tex., 1970; grad. with Distinction, U.S. Mil. Police Sch., 1973, 77; MEd in Ednl. Tech., U. Ga., 1979; postgrad., Coll. William and Mary, 1981-82. Cert. fraud examiner. Radio personality, sales exec. KOKE, Inc., Austin, Tex., 1968-73; commd. 2d lt. U.S. Army, 1973, numerous positions including asst. prof. dept. behavioral scis. and leadership U.S. Mil. Acad., staff officer anti terrorism and inspector gen., 1973-94; exec. v.p. It's Your Party, Herndon, Va., 1992—; dep. divsn. mgr. Sci. Applications Internat. Corp., McLean, Va., 1994-95, McLean, 1995—; cons. Dallas Cowboys Football Club, 1981; scouting coord. Army Football, 1983-85. Contbr. articles to profl. jours. Mem. Assn. Cert. Fraud Examiners, Internat. Soc. for Performance Improvement, Am. Soc. Indsl. Security Internat., Phi Kappa Phi, Kappa Delta Pi, Alpha Epsilon Rho. Home: 15386 Twin Creek Ct Centreville VA 22020-3742 Office: Sci Application Internat Corp 1710 Goodridge Dr Mc Lean VA 22102-3701

PRIESMAN, ELINOR LEE SOLL, family dynamics administrator, mediator, educator; b. Mpls., Jan. 19, 1938; d. Arthur and Harriet Lucille (Premack) Soll; m. Ira Morton Priesman, Mar. 30, 1958; children: Phillip Sherman, Artyce-Joy Erin. PhD, Union Inst., 1993. Cert. mediator, Va.; cert. family life educator. Nursery sch. tchr. Jewish Comty. Ctr., Santa Monica, Calif., 1958-59; head tchr. Altrusa Day Nursery, Battle Creek, Mich., 1959-60; prin. Arlington/Fairfax Jewish Ctr., Arlington, Va., 1966-67; tchr. grades 1-10 Congregation Olam Tikvah, Fairfax, Va., 1970-75; dir. Creative Play Nursery Sch., Fairfax, Va., 1970-71; tchr. high sch. Temple Sinai, Washington, Va., 1976-78; prin. Congregation Olam Tikvah, Fairfax, Va., 1975-76; asst. to pres.-emeritus Coun. for Advancement and Support of Edn., McLean, Va., 1987-90; cons. to univ. Union for Experimenting Colls. and Univs., McLean, Va., 1988-90; dir. family dynamics inst. Fairfax; mem. doctoral com. Union Inst., Cin., 1991-92, 93—; faculty mentor Ea. U., Albuquerque, 1993—. Author: The Empowered Parent, 1993, A New Perspective on Parenting, 1994 (Spanish, Korean translations 1996), A New Perspective on Parenting for Attorneys and Mediators, 1995; editor: Empowered Parenting newsletter, 1991-92. Pres. No. Va. Artistic Skating Club, Manassas, 1983-85; chair edn. com. Olam Tikvah Synagogue, Fairfax. Recipient Pres.'s award Olam Tikvah Synagogue, 1976. Mem. N.Am. Soc. Adlerian Psychology, Nat. Coun. on Family Rels., Children's Rights Coun., Acad. Family Mediators, No. Va. Mediation Svc. (mediator), Hadassah (life, Alexandria chpt. pres. 1966-67, Esther award 1965). Jewish. Office: Family Dynamics Inst 9302 Swinburne Ct Fairfax VA 22031-3027

PRIEST, HARTWELL WYSE, artist; b. Brantford, Ont., Can., Jan. 1, 1901; d. John Frank Henry and Rachel Thayer (Gavet) Wyse; m. A.J. Gustin Priest, Aug. 4, 1927; children: Paul Lambert, Marianna Thayer. BA, Smith Coll. Former tchr. graphic art Va. Art Inst., Charlottesville; former lectr. on prints and lithography; juror art exhbn. Unitarian Ch., 1993. One-woman shows include Argent Gallery, N.Y.C., 1955, 58, 60, 73, 77, 81, Va., 1969, 71, Nantucket, Mass., 1956, Ft. Lauderdale, Fla. Art Ctr., 1956; Pen & Brush, N.Y.C., 1973, 91, invitational retrospective exhbn. McGuffey Art Ctr., Charlottesville, Va., 1984, Va., N.Y., 1984, 88; work represented in permanent collections Library of Congress Washington, Norton Gallery, Palm Beach, Fla., Soc. Am. Graphic Artists, Hunterdon County Art Ctr., Longwood Coll., Smith Coll., Va. Mus., Richmond, Carnegie Mellon U. and numerous others; solo exhbn. of prints McGuffey Art Ctr., Charlottesville, Va., 1988, 90, 93, Woodstock Artist Gallery, 1990, Soc. Am. Graphic Artists, 1988-89, 92, Bombay, 1989, U. Va. Hosp., 1989, Bergen Mus. Art and Sci., 1991; represented in group shows McGuffey Gallery, 1988, 94, Gallery Show, Richmond, Va., 1988, Nat. Assn. Women Artists, Florence, Italy, 1972, N.Y.C., 1989, 96, ann. show Ojibway Hotel Club, Pointe au Baril, Georgian Bay, Ont., Can., 1991, Soc. Am. Graphic Srts, N.Y.C., 1989, 92, Woodstock, N.Y. Art Assoc., 1990, McGuffey Art Ctr., Charlottesville, Va., 1990, 94, Pen and Brush ann. Graphic Show, N.Y.C., 1991 (award for etching Spring, Ada Rosario Cecere Meml. award), Bergen Mus., N.J., 1991, Ojibway Club, Ont., Can., 1991; Pen and Brush Christmas exhbn., 1994-95, Showing of a Video, Harrisonburg, Va.; represented in traveling group shows Nat. Assn. Women Artists, Puerto Rico, 1987, India, 1989, N.Y.C., 1994; pvt. collection U. Va. Hosp., Charlottesville, 1989; subject of TV documentary Hartwell Priest: Printmaker, 1995. Recipient awards for lithograph Field Flowers, Longwood Coll., 1965, Nat. Assn. Woman Artists, 1965, lithograph West Wind, A Buell award, 1961, print Streets of Silence, T. Giorgi Meml. award, 1973, lithograph Blue Lichen, Pen & Brush, 1984, award for collage, 1985; 1st award for graphics Blue Ridge Art Show, 1985, Gene A. Walker award for print Glacial Rocks, 1986, award for print Blue Ridge Show, 1987, Philip Isenburg award for graphic PreCambrian Rock Pattern, 1988, Ada R. Cecere Meml. award Pen and Brush, 1991, Art award Piedmont Coun. Arts, 1993. Mem. Nat. Assn. Women Artists (Travelling Printmaking Exhbn. 1987-89), Pen and Brush, Soc. Am. Graphic Artists, Washington Print Club, 2d St. Gallery, Charlottesville, McGuffey Art Ctr. Home: 41 Old Farm Rd Charlottesville VA 22903-4725

PRIEST, MELVILLE STANTON, retired consulting hydraulic engineer; b. Cassville, Mo., Oct. 16, 1912; s. William Tolliver and Mildred Alice (Messer) P.; m. Vivian Willingham, Mar. 22, 1941 (dec.); m. Virginia Young, Dec. 16, 1983. BS, U. Mo., 1935; MS, U. Colo., 1943; PhD, U. Mich., 1954. Registered profl. engr., Ala., La., Miss. Jr. engr. U.S. Engrs. Office, 1937-39; from jr. to asst. engr. Bur. Reclamation, 1939-41; from instr. to assoc. prof. civil engring. Cornell U., 1941-55; prof. hydraulics Auburn (Ala.) U., 1955-58, prof. civil engring., head dept., 1958-65; dir. Water Resources Research Inst., Miss. State U., 1965-77; UN adviser on hydraulics, Egypt, 1956, 57, 60; Mem. Ala. Bd. Registration Profl. Engrs., 1962-65. Contbr. articles to profl. jours. Fellow ASCE (pres. Ala. 1962, exec. com., pipeline div. 1971-74), Am. Water Resources Assn. (dir. 1973-75), Sigma Xi, Tau Beta Pi, Chi Epsilon, Pi Mu Epsilon. Address: PO Box 541 Starkville MS 39760

PRIEST, SHARON DEVLIN, state official; b. Montreal, Quebec, Can.; m. Bill Priest; 1 child, Adam. Tax preparer, instr. H & R Block, Little Rock, 1976-78; account exec. Greater Little Rock C. of C.; owner, founder Devlin Co.; mem. Little Rock Bd. Dirs., 1986—; vice mayor Little Rock, 1989-91, mayor, 1991-93; Sec. of State State of Arkansas, 1994—; bd. dirs. Invesco Inc., New Futures. Bd. dirs., past pres. Metroplan (Environ. Svc. award 1982), YMCA, Southwest Hosp.; mem. Advt. and Promotion commn., Ark. Internat. Visitors Coun., Pulaski Are Transp. Svc. Policy Com., St. Theresa's Parish Coun., Exec. com. for Ark. Mcpl. League, Nat. League of Cities Trans. and Communications Steering Com. and Policy Com., adv. bd. M.M. Cohn., Little Rock City Beautiful Commn., 1980-86; former bd. dirs. Downtown Partnership, Southwest YMCA, 1984, 86, sec.; former mem. Community Housing Resource Bd., 1984-86, Pub. Facilities Bd. Southwest Hosp., 1985-86, Southwest Merchants' Assn., 1985—, 2d v.p., 1985; chmn. Little Rock Arts and Humanities Promotion Commn.; led petition dr. for appropriation for Fourche Creek Plan 7A. Recipient of the Fighting Back Freedom Fighter award, 1995, recipient of Environ. Svc. award from the Little Rock Metroplan Comm. Mem. Leadership Inst. Alumni Assn. (4 Bernard de la Harpe awards). Office: Office of Secretary of State State Capitol Bldg 256 Little Rock AR 72201

PRIESTER, GAYLE BOLLER, engineer, consultant; b. Mpls., July 1, 1912; s. George Charles and Lulu May (Boller) P.; m. Rachel Edith Miller, Sept. 3, 1938; children: Peggy Lu, George William, Phyllis Ann. B in Mech. Engring., U. Minn., 1933; MS, Harvard U., 1934; Mech. Engr., Case Inst. Tech., 1943. Registered profl. engr., Md. Industry rep. Mpls. Gas Light Co., 1934-35; application sales engr. Carrier Corp., N.Y.C., Chgo., Mpls., 1935-41; instr., asst. prof., assoc. prof. Case Inst. Tech., Cleveland, 1941-46; cons. Bur. Ships U.S. Navy, 1942-44; air conditioning engr. Balt. Gas & Electric Co., Balt., 1946-73, chief civil engr., 1973-77; pvt. practice cons. engr. Balt., 1977-89, Advance, N.C., 1989—; dir. Accreditation Bd. for Engring. and Tech., 1976-82. Co-author: (textbook) Refreigeration and Air Conditioning, 1948, rev. 2d edit., 1956; contbr. numerous articles to tech. publs., chpts. to handbooks. Sec. Stoneleigh Comty. Assn., Balt. County, 1947-48, Boy Scout Troop Com., 1952-54; pres. Stoneleigh Elem. Sch. PTA, Balt. County, 1952-53; maj. United Appeal Campaign, Balt., 1953; bd. dirs. Alzheimer's Triad N.C. chpt., 1990-93, treas., 1992-93; elder Clemmons Presby. Ch. Recipient Disting. Svc. award ASHRAE (Balt. chpt.), 1972. Fellow ASHRAE (chpt. pres. 1946, 50, 53, regional chmn. 1965-67, treas. 1970-71, Disting. Svc. award 1968, Disting. 50 Yr. Svc. award 1984); mem. Tau Beta Pi. Republican. Club: Bermuda Run.

PRIESTER, HORACE RICHARD, JR., quality assurance professional; b. Charleston, S.C., Nov. 3, 1936; s. Horace Richard and Pearl (Hinely) P.; widowed; children: Horace Richard III, David Eugene, Cheryl Priester Burns; m. Carole Ledford, Aug. 10, 1985; children: Charles Wayne Blackburn Jr., Carl Ashley Blackburn. BS in Chem. Engring., Clemson U., 1958. Asst. chief chemist Savannah (Ga.) Foods & Industries, Inc., 1968-73, chief chemist, 1973-78, chief chemist refineries, 1978-89, corp. dir. quality assurance, 1990—; bd. dirs., lectr. Sugar Processing Rsch. Inst., New Orleans; referee U.S. Nat. Com. on Sugar Analysis, 1990—; mem. U.S. Nat. Com. on Sugar Analysis, 1982—. Mem. U.S. Cane Sugar Refiners Assn. (tech. com.), Sugar Industry Technologists (lectr.), Inst. Food Technologists, Soc. Soft Drink Technologists, Gideons. Southern Baptist. Office: Savannah Foods & Industries Inc PO Box 710 Savannah GA 31402-0710

PRIESTLEY, G. T. ERIC, manufacturing company executive; b. Belfast, Northern Ireland, May 7, 1942; came to U.S., 1990; s. Thomas John McKee P.; m. Carol Elizabeth Gingles Nelson, June 8, 1966; children: Peter, Gaye, Simon. BS, Queens U., 1963; postgrad. Bus. Sch., Harvard U., 1989. Sales trainee Burroughs Machines Ltd., 1963-64; dealer, sales devel. Regent Oil Co., 1964-66; ops. mgr. RMC (Ulster) Ltd., 1967-70; distbn. mgr. Bass Charrington, Ireland, 1970-71; dir., gen. mgr. Farrans Ltd., 1971-80; dir., CEO Redland plc/British Fuels/Cawoods, 1980-88; dir. Bowater plc, London, 1988-90; pres., CEO Rexam Inc., Charlotte, N.C., 1990-96; exec. v.p., COO Jefferson Smurfit Corp., St. Louis, 1996—. Bd. advisors U. N.C., Charlotte. Mem. Moortown Golf Club, Aloha Golf Club, Royal Ulster Yacht Culb, Quail Hollow Golf and Country Club, Boone Valley Country Club. Home: 9114 Winged Bourne Charlotte NC 28210-5946 Office: Jefferson Smurfit Corp 8182 Maryland Ave Saint Louis MO 63105

PRIEST-MACKIE, NANCY RAY, nutrition consultant; b. Tampa, Fla., Dec. 1, 1934; d. Tommy Rex and Louise Virginia (Pierce) Priest; m. Harry Arendt Mackie, Aug. 6, 1983 (dec. 1991); children from previous marriage: Barbara Ellen, Allison Claire, Samuel Priest, Marjorie Lee. BS in Dietetics, Maryville Coll., 1956; postgrad., Nicholls State U., Thibodaux, La., 1979; MPH, Tulane U., 1981. Lic. dietetian, La.; lic. nutritionist. Clin. dietitian Baton Rouge (La.) Gen. Hosp., 1956-57; research dietitian East La. State Mental Hosp., Jackson, 1957-58; instr. Nicholls State U., Thibodaux, La., 1977-79; clin. dietitian East Jefferson Gen. Hosp., Metairie, La., 1980, Highland Park Hosp., Covington, La., 1981-83; renal cons. Washington Parish Dialysis Ctr., Bogalosa, La., 1985-86, St. Tammany Parish Dialysis Ctr., Covington, La., 1983-89; nutrition cons. Hope St. Nutrition Clinic, Covington, 1983—; renal cons. Home Intensive Care, Hammond, La., 1988-96, Renal Treatment Ctrs., Inc., New Orleans, 1989-91; cons. quality care dialysis Dialysis Ctr., Hammond, La., 1988—, Bogalusa (La.) Cmty. Med. Ctr., 1990-96, St. Helena Parish Dialysis Ctr., 1994—, Renal Mgmt. Assn., New Orleans, 1996—; schizophrenia rschr. Tulane U. Med. Sch., Jackson, La., 1957-58; dir. Hope St. Exptl. Weight Loss Clinic, Covington, 1987, Hadden Hall adv. coun. St. Tammany Coun. on Aging, Inc., 1987—. Author: A First Novel; also other writings. Pres. Golden Meadow Homemakers, La., 1960-61; bd. pres. Council on Aging, Lafourche Parish, La., 1964-66. Mem. Am. Dietetic Assn. (registered), Renal Dietitians Assn., New Orleans Dietetic Assn., Bus. and Profl. Women, Cons. Nutritionists La., La. Cons. Dietitians in Pvt. Practice, A Practice Group of Am. Dietetic Assn. (chmn.). Home and Office: Hope St Nutrition Clinic Ltd 138 N New Hampshire St Covington LA 70433-3236

PRIGMORE, CHARLES SAMUEL, social work educator; b. Lodge, Tenn., Mar. 21, 1919; s. Charles H. and Mary Lou (Raulston) P.; m. Shirley Melaine Buuck, June 7, 1947; 1 child, Philip Brand. A.B., U. Chattanooga, 1939; M.S., U. Wis., 1947, Ph.D., 1961; extension grad., Air War Coll., 1967, Indsl. Coll. Armed Forces, 1972. Social caseworker Children's Svc. Soc., Milw., 1947-48; social worker Wis. Sch. Boys, Waukesha, 1948-51; supr. tng. Wis. Bur. Probation and Parole, Madison, 1951-56; supt. Tenn. Vocat. Tng. Sch. for Boys, Nashville, 1956-59; assoc. prof. La. State U., 1959-64; edni. cons. Coun. Social Work Edn., N.Y., 1962-64; exec. dir. Joint Commn. Correctional Manpower and Tng., Washington, 1964-67; prof. Sch. Social Work, U. Ala., 1967-84, prof. emeritus, 1984—, chmn. com. on Korean relationships; Fulbright lectr., Iran, 1972-73; vis. lectr. U. Sydney, 1976; cons. Iranian Ministry Health and Welfare, 1976-78; frequent lectr., workshop leader. Author: Textbook on Social Problems, 1971, Social Work in Iran Since the White Revolution, 1976, Social Welfare Policy Analysis and Formulation, 1979, 2d edit., 1986; editor 2 books; contbr. articles to profl. jours. Adv. Com. for Former Prisoners of War VA, 1981-83; chmn. Prisoner of War Bd., State of Ala., 1984-89; state comdr. Am. Ex-Prisoners of War, Ala., 1985-86, nat. legis. officer, 1985—, nat. dir., 1989-92, nat. sr. vice comdr., 1993—, nat comdr., 1994-95; gov.'s liaison U.S. Holocaust Meml. Coun., 1983-89; mem. Ala. Bd. Vets. Affairs, 1986-89, Ala. Bicentennial Commn. on Constn., 1987-90; bd. dirs. Community Svcs. Programs of W. Ala., 1985-89, others in past. Served to 2d lt. USAAF, 1940-45, prisoner of war, Germany, 1944-45; lt. col. Res., ret. Decorated Air medal with oak leaf cluster; recipient Conservation award Woodmen of the World, 1971; Fulbright rsch. fellow Norway, 1979-80. Fellow Am. Sociol. Assn., Royal Soc. Health; mem. Acad. Cert. Social Workers, Nat. Coun. Crime and Delinquency, Tuscaloosa Country Club, Capitol Hill Club, Alpha Kappa Delta, Beta Beta Beta. Home: 923 Overlook Rd N Tuscaloosa AL 35406-2122 Office: PO Box 870314 Tuscaloosa AL 35487-0314

PRILLAMAN, BOB MAURICE, paper corporation executive; b. Bassett, Va., Feb. 4, 1933; s. Owen Henry and Betty Mildred (Hickman) P.; m. Lillias Estelle Bidwell; children: Robert Owen, Cathy Mildred, Mary Loucille. BBA, Ga. State U., 1960. Sr. v.p. Caraustar Industries, Austell, Ga., 1969—, Austell Box Bd., 1972—; pres., chmn. Macon (Ga.) Recycling, 1975—, Columbus (Ga.) Recycling, 1975—, Paper Recycling, Doraville, Ga., 1979—; chmn. bd. Sweetwater Paper Bd., Austell, 1988—, Camden (N.J.) Paper Bd., 1988—. Bd. dirs. Marietta (Ga.) Ballet, 1988, Cobb Gen. Hosp., Austell, 1989—, Cobb County Girl's Club, Marietta, 1989—; mem. bd. trustees Kennesaw (Ga.) State Coll., 1989—; chmn. Cobb County Pension Fund; dir. Pnomia Health System, 1994—. Cpl. U.S. Army, 1953-55, ETO. Mem. Am. Paper Inst. (chmn. paper recycling com. 1987—), Cobb County C. of C. (bd. dirs. Marietta chpt. 1982), Rotary (pres. Austell chpt. 1979). Republican. Methodist.

PRIMEAUX, HENRY, III, automotive executive, author, speaker; b. New Orleans, Nov. 16, 1941; s. Henry Jr. and Ethel (Ritter) P.; m. Jane Cathrine Velcich, July 23, 1960; children: Joann Primeaux Longa, Lisa, Henry Joseph. Student, La. State U., New Orleans, 1959-63. Compt. Jimco, New Orleans, 1965-66; owner, mgr. Picone Seafood, New Orleans, 1966-67; v.p. NADW Inc., Metairie, La., 1967-78, Am. Warranty Corp., L.A., 1978-80; pres. F&I Warranty Corp., Arlington, Tex., 1980-87; exec. v.p. F&I Mgmt. Corp., Arlington, 1980-87; pres., chief exec. officer Primco Corp., Arlington, 1987-91; pres. Crown Autoworld Automobile Dealership, Tulsa; cons., corr. Wards Auto Dealer, Deetroit, 1987—, weekly TV program Automotive Satellite TV Network; cons. Nissan Motor Co., L.A., 1988-89, Convergent div. Unisys, Hunt Valley, Md., 1988-90; cons. Mercedes-Benz N.Am.; cons. Automatic Data Processing. Writer Auto Age mag.; author: F&I Handbook. Mem. Rep. Task Force, Rep. Senatorial Inner Circle; bd. dirs. Okla. Spl. Olympics, John Starks Found., Tulsa Ballet, Jr. Achievement, YCMA, Boy Scouts U.S., Children's Med. Ctr.; mem. athletic com. Tulsa Pub. Schs.; mem. nat. adv. bd. GM Sch. to Work Initiative. With USN, 1959-61. Mem. Am. Internat. Automobile Dealers Assn., Assn. of F&I Profls. (bd. dirs. 1990—, pres. 1994), Nat. Auto Dealers Assn. (pres. Tulsa chpt. 1994, Time Quality Dealer of Yr. 1994). Roman Catholic. Home: 10504 S Hudson Pl Tulsa OK 74137-7056 Office: Crown AutoWorld 4444 S Sheridan Rd Tulsa OK 74145-1122

PRINCE, ANNA LOU, composer, music publisher, construction company executive; b. Isabella, Tenn.; d. Ulysses Gordon and Della Carrie (Hawkins) P.; children: Sandra, Teresa, vandi. Diploma Carolina Sch. Broadcasting, 1966; Zion diploma, Israel Bible Sch., Jerusalem, 1970; diploma S.W. Tech. Coll., 1970; student United Christian Assn., 1976; MusD, London Inst. Applied Rsch., 1991; Diplomatic Diploma, Acad. Argentina de Diplomacia, 1993; PhD (hon.) Australian Inst. Co-ordinated Rsch., Victoria, 1993; Diploma of Honors of Internat. Affairs, Institut Des Affaires Internationales, Paris, 1994. Lic. Bible tchr. United Christian Acad. Songwriter Hank Locklin Music Co., Nashville, 1963-70; entertainer 1982 World's Fair, Knoxville, Tenn., 1982; ptnr., owner Prince Wholesale Bait Co., Canton, N.C., 1976-82, Grad Builders, Canton, 1982-86, Prince TV Co., 1986-94; music publisher Broadcast Music, Inc., Nashville, 1982—; mem. production staff, talent coord. (TV series) Down Home, Down Under, 1989-90. Songs recorded on RCA: I Feel a Cry Coming On, 1965 (#1 in Eng.), Best Part of Loving You, (#1 in Eng.), Anna, 1969 (Billboard 1970, recorded in Ireland 1974, hit in Europe and New Zealand); over 20 songs recorded to date; appeared Grand Ole Opry, 1970; host TV talk show, Cable Channel 19, 1989—. Cand. for county commnr. Democratic party Macon County, N.C., 1984; bd. dirs. Macon County Taxpayers Assn., Inc., 1984, v.p., 1984-86; bd. dirs. Head Start, Topton, N.C., 1969-73. Nominated Disting. Women N.C., N.C. Council on Status of Women, 1984, Jefferson award WYFF TV and Am. Inst. for Pub. Service, Outstanding Bus. Woman Small Bus. Adminstrn., 1984. Mem. BMI, Internat. Parliament Safety and Peace (life, dept. fgn. affairs, dep. mem. assembly), Nashville Songwriters Assn. Internat. (moderator, tchr. 1984-86), Country Music Assn., Reunion Profl. Entertainers, Fraternal Order Police, C. of C., Order of Knight of Templars (dame), Lofsensic Order (dame), Maison Internationales des Intellectuals. Democrat. Office: 313 Gallatin Rd S Madison TN 37115-4006

PRINCE, GEORGE EDWARD, pediatrician; b. Erwin, N.C., Nov. 25, 1921; s. Hugh Williamson and Helen Herman (Hood) P.; m. Millie Elizabeth Mann, Nov. 26, 1944; children: Helen Elizabeth, Millie Mann, Susan Hood, Mary Lois. MD, Duke U., 1944. Diplomate Am. Bd. Pediatrics, Am. Bd. Med. Examiners. Intern Boston Children's Hosp. Harvard Svc., Boston, 1944-45; resident pediatrics Children's Hosp., Louisville, 1945-47; instr. pediatrics U. Louisville, 1947; founder Gastonia (N.C.) Children's Clinic, 1947, pediatrician, 1947-86; pub. health physician Gaston County Health Dept., Gastonia, N.C., 1986-95, med. dir., 1995-96; chmn. bd. dirs. Carolina State Bank; bd. dirs. So. Nat. Bank, Gastonia, 1979-95, Hospice, Gastonia, 1987-92; organizer, dir. AIDS Adv. Coun., Gaston County, N.C., 1988-94; coord. N.C. chpt. Pediatric Rsch. in Office Setting, 1986-92. Contbr. articles to profl. jours. Mem. Gaston County Human Rels. Com., Gastonia, 1966; mem. Sch. Health Adv. Coun., Gaston County, 1980-96. Maj. USAF, 1955-57. Recipient Balthis Heart Assn. award Gaston County, 1981, Good Ambassador award Health Dept., 1986. Fellow Am. Acad. Pediatrics (pres. N.C. chpt. 1984-86); mem. AMA, N.C. Pediatric Soc. (hon., pres. 1970), N.C. Med. Soc., Gaston County Med. Soc. (pres. 1966), Rotary (pres. 1984), County Club (bd. dirs. 1975-76). Democrat. Methodist. Home: 2208 Cross Creek Dr Gastonia NC 28056-8808 Office: Gaston County Health Dept 991 Hudson Blvd Gastonia NC 28052-6430

PRINCE, GRACE ROSENE SIMMONS, consulting dietitian; b. Union City, Tenn., Jan. 4, 1935; d. Dewey Benjamin and Jewel LaVerne (Brown) Simmons; m. John Calvin Prince, June 28, 1959 (dec. Apr. 1963); children: Deborah Rosene, Mari Loy. BS in Home Econs., U. Tenn., Martin, 1957; MS in Child Devel. and Family Rels., U. Tenn., Knoxville, 1971; postgrad., Mich. State U., 1975, Ea. Ky. U., 1975. Lic. dietitian/nutritionist. Asst. adminstrv. dietitian Barnes Hosp., St. Louis, 1957-59, intern in dietetics, 1959; asst. adminstrv. dietitian Obion County Gen. Hosp., Union City, Tenn., 1960-61; assoc. prof. Inst. Agriculture, U. Tenn., Knoxville, 1963-73; traveling cons. dietitian Medco Facilities Corp., Evansville, Ind., 1973-74; coord. dietetics Ea. Ky. U., Richmond, 1974-76; chief clin. dietitian Food Svcs. Mgmt. divsn. Marriott Corp., Washington, 1976-78; assoc. prof. food prodn. and nutrition U. Md., Princess Anne, 1977-80; asst. dir. nutrition and dietary St. Mary's Hosp., Huntington, W.Va., 1981-82; dir. dietary dept. Trevecca Health Care, Nashville, 1987-88; ind. cons. nutrition Nashville, 1987-96, dietitian in pvt. practice, 1994-96; pvt. patient cons.; corp. cons. Con Agra Foods, Rebentorra Sysco Foods, hosps. Recipient Nat. Recognition and State award, 1973, State award for radio tape interview Agrl. Extension Edn., 1973. Mem. NAFE, Am. Dietetic Assn. (registered), Sports and Cardiovascular Nutritionists, Am. Diabetes Assn. (Outstanding Contbn. awards 1976-81), Nashville Dietetic Assn. (mem. various coms.), Dietitians in Bus. and Industry, Cons. Nutritionists in Pvt. Practice. Baptist. Office: 108 Mockingbird Rd Nashville TN 37205-1830

PRINCE, JACQUELYNNE BOLANDER, nurse, consultant; b. Norfolk, Va., July 4, 1955; d. Jack C. Bolander and Particia (Loud) Bolander Melvin; m. John Martine Prince, Jr., Oct. 1, 1977; children:Emily Alene, John Ryland, Christopher. B.S., Med. Coll. of Va., 1978; M.S., Tex. Woman's U., 1985. Cert. critical care registered nurse, med.-surg Clin. Nurse Specialist. Staff nurse Med. Coll. of Va., Richmond, 1978-80; asst. nurse coord. Parkland Hosp., Dallas, 1980-82, supr., 1982-83; head nurse N.C. Meml. Hosp., Chapel Hill, 1983-85; coord. critical care edn. Wise Appalachian Regional Hosp., Wise, Va., 1985-86; coord. continuing edn. Norton (Va.) Community Hosp., 1986-91, mem. bd. dentistry State of Va., 1991-92; clin. nurse specialist Fort Sanders Parkwest Hosp., Knoxville, 1992-96, Allergy Asthma & Sinus Ctr., Knoxville, 1996—; cons. in field. Contbr. articles to profl. publs., chpt. in book. Instr. Advanced Cardiac Life Support, Am. Heart Assn., Dallas, Chapel Hill, N.C., 1980—; chmn. health adv. com. Norton City Schs.; chmn. Wise Sch. Dance, 1987-89, bd. dirs., 1987-91; v.p. PTA. Mem. ANA, Assn. Critical Care Nurses (bd. dirs.), N.C. Meml. Collaborator Practice Com., Wise County Med. Soc. Auxilliary (pres. 1988, chmn. health com. 1989-91, v.p. 1991), Parkland Woman's Club (project svc. chmn. 1980-83). Baptist. Avocations: skiing, quilting, reading, running. Home: 809 Bennett Pl Knoxville TN 37909-2348 Office: Allergy Asthma & Sinus Ctr 800 Weisgarber Rd Ste 200 Knoxville TN 37909

PRINCE, LARRY L., automotive parts and supplies company executive; b. 1937. With Genuine Parts Co., Atlanta, 1958—, v.p., then group v.p., 1977-83, exec. v.p., 1983-86, pres., chief oper. officer, 1986-90, chief exec. officer, 1989—, chmn. bd. dirs., 1990—, also bd. dirs. Office: Genuine Parts Co 2999 Circle 75 Pky NW Atlanta GA 30339-3050

PRINGLE, SAMMIE, SR., academic administrator; b. Charleston, S.C., July 1, 1942; s. Jerry and Annie Mae (Capers) P.; m. Alene Doris Barnes, Aug. 17, 1979; children: Sandra, Darren, Sammie Jr., Troy, Bryce, Vanessa. BS in Math., Benedict Coll., 1964; M Computing Sci., Tex. A&M U., 1971; EdD in Ednl. Adminstrn., Clark Atlanta U., 1993. Commd. 2d lt. USAF, 1964, advanced through grades to lt. col., ret., 1986; asst. prof., adminstr. Morris Brown Coll., Atlanta, 1986-91; adminstr. Trenholm State Tech. Coll., Montgomery, Ala., 1991-93; asst. v.p. for acad. affairs, adminstr. Albany (Ga.) State U., 1993—; adj. instr. Elec. Computer Program Inst., Omaha, 1975-78, Troy State U., Montgomery, 1979-81, Ala. State U., Montgomery, 1981-84; faculty intern Army Inst. for Rsch., Atlanta, 1987; pastor Blue Springs Bapt. Ch., Albany. Mem. John David Kelly Consistory, Kiwanis Internat., Zaha Temple, Masons, Omega Psi Phi, Alpha Kappa Mu. Home: 2505 College Park Ln Albany GA 31705 Office: Albany State U 504 College Dr Albany GA 31705-2717

PRIOR, RICHARD EDMON, classics educator; b. Syracuse, N.Y., Aug. 29, 1962; s. Edmon Richard and Stella F. (Beaulieu) P. BA, U. N.C., Greensboro, 1984; MA, U. Md., 1991; PhD, U. Buffalo, 1994. Secondary sch. tchr. Tidewater, Va., 1984-89; teaching asst. U. Md., College Park, 1989-91, U. Buffalo, 1991-94; asst. prof. classics Furman U., Greenville, S.C., 1994—. Author: 501 Latin Verbs, 1995; contbr. articles to Arethusa, Am. Jour. Philology. Mem. Am. Philological Assn., Classical Assn. Atlantic States, Classical Assn. ofr Middle West and So. States, Am. Classical League. Quaker. Office: Furman U Greenville SC 29613

PRIOR, RICHARD MARION, physics educator; b. Dunedin, Fla., July 17, 1942; s. Walter K. and A. Dorothea (Garrison) P.; children: Steven, Sharon. BS, U. Fla., 1964, MS, 1965, PhD, 1968. Rsch. assoc. U. Notre Dame, Ind., 1968-70; prof. U. Ark., Little Rock, 1970-89; prof., chmn. physics dept. West Ga. Coll., Carrollton, 1989-94, North Ga. Coll., Dahlonega, 1994—. Mem. Am. Phys. Soc., Am. Assn. Physics Tchrs. Democrat. Office: North Ga Coll Physics Dept Dahlonega GA 30597

PRIOR, WILLIAM ALLEN, electronics company executive; b. Benton Harbor, Mich., Jan. 14, 1927; s. Allen Ames and Madeline Isabel (Taylor) P.; m. Nancy Norton Sayles, July 7, 1951 (div. Oct. 1971); children: Stephanie Sayles, Alexandra Taylor, Robert Eames, Eleanor Norton; m. Carol Luise Becker-Ehmck, Oct. 30, 1971; children: Michael Becker-Ehmck, Jeffrey Renner. AB in Physics, Harvard Coll., 1950, MBA, 1954. Salesman IBM, Mineola, L.I., N.Y., 1950-52; sales engr. Lincoln Electric Co., Cleve., 1954-57; ptnr. Hammond Kennedy & Co., N.Y.C., 1957-66; v.p. The Singer Co., N.Y.C., 1967-68; pres. Tansitor Electronics, Bennington, Vt., 1969-71, Aerotron Inc., Raleigh, N.C., 1971-82; v.p. J. Lee Peeler & Co., Durham, N.C., 1986-89; pres. Accudyne, Inc., Raleigh, 1990—; dir. Carroll's Foods, Warsaw, N.C.; chmn. Royal Blue Capital, Inc., Raleigh. Cpl. USAAF, 1945-46, Germany. Mem. IEEE, North Ridge Country Club (Raleigh), Raleigh Racquet Club, Harvard Club of N.Y.C., 50 Group. Republican. Home: 329 Meeting House Cir Raleigh NC 27615-3133 Office: Accudyne Inc 5800 Machines Pl Raleigh NC 27616

PRISANT, L(OUIS) MICHAEL, cardiologist; b. Albany, Ga., Dec. 25, 1949; s. Bennie Martin and Mozelle (Cosper) P.; m. Rose Corinth Trincher, June 28, 1975; children: Michelle Elizabeth, Louis Michael. BA, Emory U., 1971; MD, Med. Coll. Ga., 1977. Diplomate Am. Bd. Internal Medicine, Am. Bd. Cardiovascular Diseases, Am. Bd. Geriatric Medicine, Am. Bd. Clin. Pharmacology, Am. Bd. Forensic Medicine, Nat. Bd. Med. Examiners. Intern Med. Coll. Ga., Augusta, 1977-78; resident Med. Coll. Ga., 1978-80; chief med. resident, 1979-80; cardiology fellow Med. Coll. Ga., 1980-82, instr., 1982-83, asst. prof. medicine, 1983-89, assoc. prof. medicine, 1989-94, prof., 1994—, dir. fellowship tng. program, 1996; cons. in field; lectr. in field. Contbr. 90 articles and 89 abstracts to profl. jours., 6 chpts. to books; author of 7 monographs; manuscript reviewer med. jours. FOE grantee, 1989, Rorer, 1989, Am. Cyanamid, 1988, Sandoz, 1989-93, Merck, 1990-92, Squibb, 1991, Lorex, 1991, NIH, 1991, Lederle, 1993, Ciba-Geigy, 1993. Fellow ACP, Am. Coll. Cardiology, Am. Coll. Clin. Pharmacology, Am. Coll. Chest Physicians, Am. Coll. Forensic Examiners; mem. AMA (Physician's Recognition award 1982-95), AAUP, Am. Fedn. Clin. Rsch., Am. Heart Assn., Am. Soc. Echocardiography, Am. Soc. Hypertension, Am. Soc. Internal Medicine, Internat. Soc. for Hypertension in Blacks, Ga. Heart Assn., Assn. for Advancement Med. Instrumentation, Ga. Med. Care Found., Med. Assn. Ga., Richmond County Med. Soc., Ahlquist Soc. (pres.), AMA Physician, Phi Delta Epsilon, Alpha Phi Omega, Tau Epsilon Phi. Jewish. Office: Med Coll Ga Sect Cardiology Rm CK-151 Augusta GA 30912-3150

PRITCHETT, ANNE MCDONALD, medical association administrator; b. Christchurch, New Zealand, Aug. 22, 1967; parents Am. citizens; d. Daniel Welch Jr. and Eunice (Utterbock) McDonald; m. William W. Pritchett IV, July 26, 1992. BA, Va. Poly. Inst. and State U.; MPB in Policy Studies, George Mason U., 1997. Asst. mng. editor Aerospace Med. Assn., Alexandria, Va., 1990; from editorial asst. to dir. editorial svcs. CSR, Inc., Washington, 1990-94, also sr. writer/editor; sr. assoc. Cygnus Corp., Rockville, Md., 1994-96; dir. pub. affairs and govt. rels. Am. Med. Women's Assn., Alexandria, 1996—. Mng. editor newsletter What's Happening in AMWA, 1996. Vol. Nova Mental Health Inst., Fairfax, 1984; vol. various polit. campaigns. Mem. Am. Soc. Assn. Execs., Greater Washington Soc. Assn. Execs., Pub. Rels. Soc. Am., Va. Tech Alumni Assn., Chesapeake Bay Found., Nature Conservancy. Roman Catholic. Home: 1227 Weatherstone Ct Reston VA 20194 Office: Am Med Women's Assn 801 N Fairfax St Ste 400 Alexandria VA 22314

PRITCHETT, LOIS JANE, administrator, counselor, educator; b. Phoenix; d. Harold Bruce Brown and Cora Jane (Burgin) Goodrich; m. David Lowrey Pritchett, Nov. 26, 1976; m. Lloyd Graper, Mar. 29, 1964 (dec. Dec. 1975); 1 child, Samuel Blair. A.B. in Edn., U. Ky., 1963; M.A. in Guidance and Counseling, Georgetown Coll., 1975; Ed.S. in Counseling, U. So. Miss., 1981. Cert. school psychologist, adminstr., supr., counselor, tchr., reading program specialist. Tchr., Monticello Sch. System, N.Y., 1963-65, Fayette County Sch. System, Lexington, Ky., 1965-72, 76-77, 84—; coord. Chpt. 1 Programs, presenter SE Regional Conf., 1987; tchr. Ocean Springs Sch. System, Miss., 1977-78, counselor/sch. psychologist, 1978-84. Den mother Pine Burr council Boy Scouts Am., 1980; Sunday Sch. tchr. 1st Bapt. Ch., Ocean Springs, 1982-84; cons. for teenage workshop Biloxi-Ocean Springs Jr. Aux., 1984. Recipient Outstanding Personnel and Guidance Program award Miss. Personnel and Guidance Assn., 1981, Outstanding Reading Advantage Program award U.S. Dept. Edn., 1992. Mem. IRA (Bluegrass Coun. pres.), Nat. Bd. Cert. Counselors, Am. Assn. for Counseling and Devel., Am. Sch. Counselors Assn., Assn. Supervision Curriculum Devel., Cen. Ky. Ednl. Adminstrs., Ky. Assn. Sch. Adminstrs., Internat. Reading Assn. (Blue Grass council), Fayette County Sch. Adminstrs. Assn., Ky. Assn. Sch. Adminstrs., Ky. Assn. Supervision and Curriculum Devel., Henry Clay Band Boosters (bd. dirs.), Alpha Delta Kappa, Phi Delta Kappa. Democrat. Baptist. Avocations: raising plants, drawing, painting, bridge. Office: Fayette County Pub Schs 701 E Main St Lexington KY 40502-1601

PRIVETT, CARYL PENNEY, lawyer; b. Birmingham, Ala., Jan. 7, 1948; d. William Kinnaird Privett and Katherine Speake (Binford) Ennis. BA, Vanderbilt U., 1970; JD, NYU, 1973. Bar: Ala. 1973, U.S. Dist. Ct. (so. dist.) Ala. 1973, U.S. Dist. Ct. (no. dist.) Ala. 1974, U.S. Ct. Appeals (5th cir.) 1974, U.S. Ct. Appeals (11th cir.) 1981. Assoc. Crawford & Blacksher, Mobile, Ala., 1973-74, Adams, Baker & Clemon, Birmingham, 1974-76; asst. U.S. atty. no. dist. Ala. U.S. Atty.'s Office, U.S. Dept. Justice, Birmingham, 1976-92, first asst. U.S. atty., 1992—. Bd. dirs. Legal Aid Soc., Birmingham, 1986-88, pres., 1988; sec., founder Lawyers for Choice, Ala., 1989-92; bd. dirs. Planned Parenthood Ala., Birmingham, v.p., 1986-91; chair domestic violence com. City of Birmingham, 1989-91; sustaining mem. Jr. League Birmingham; active Downtown Dem. Club, Birmingham. Recipient Cert. in Color Photography U. Ala., Birmingham, 1989, Commr.'s Spl. citation Food and Drug Adminstrn.; named one of Outstanding Young Women Am., 1977, 78. Mem. ABA, Fed. Bar Assn. (pres. Birmingham chpt. 1979), Birmingham Bar Assn., Ala. Bar Assn., Downtown Club. Presbyterian. Home: 30 Norman Dr Birmingham AL 35213-4310 Office: US Attys Office 1800 5th Ave N Ste 200 Birmingham AL 35203-2112

PROCOPIO, JOSEPH GUYDON, lawyer; b. Paterson, N.J., May 1, 1940; s. Joseph A. and V. Genevieve (Kievitt) P.; m. Joanne Julia Roccato, June 30, 1962 (div. Aug. 1980); children: Jennifer Tehani, Joseph Christian; m. Frances Mary Hansen Schmieder, April 16, 1988; stepchildren: Timothy James Schmieder, Julie Ann Schmieder. BS, U.S. Naval Acad., 1962; MS in Ops. Rsch., Naval Postgrad. Sch., 1971; JD, Cath. U. Am., 1979; LLM, George Washington U., 1987. Bar: Va. Commd. ensign USN, 1962, served to comdr., 1978, ret., 1983; gen. counsel, sec. Presearch, Inc., Fairfax, Va., 1983-85; dir. bus. devel., then v.p. corp. communications ERC Internat., Fairfax, Va., 1985-90; pres., CEO Advanced Engring. Group, Inc., Fairfax, 1990-92; chmn., CEO JP Fin. Group Ltd., Fairfax, 1992—; prin. The Poets Group, 1996; bd. dirs. Solomon Group; prin. The Millenium Group, Ltd. (formerly Ashley-Boden-Keenan, Inc.). Decorated Bronze Star, Meritorious Svc. medal, 3 Joint Svc. Commendation award, Nat. Def. medal (Cambodia), Navy Achievement medal, Combat Action ribbon. Mem. Internat. Inst. Strategic Studies, Va. Bar Assn., The Atlantic Coun., World Affairs Coun. Washington, George Washington U. Law Alumni Assn., U.S. Naval Acad. Alumni Assn., U.S. Naval Acad. Class of 1962 Assn. (bd. dirs. 1978-80, 87—, spl. asst. to pres. 1984-87), Nat. Eagle Scout Assn., Capital Soc., The Tower Club. Home: 10637 Canterberry Rd Fairfax VA 22039-1927 Office: JP Fin Group Ltd Fairfax VA 22039

PROCTOR, CHARLES LAFAYETTE, II, mechanical engineer, educator, consultant; b. Crawfordsville, Ind., Nov. 21, 1954; s. Charles Lafayette and Marjorie E. (Purdue) P.; m. Dixie Lee Huffer, May 22, 1976; children: Christina Nicole, Courtney Alexandra, Daniel Charles Doyal. BSME, Purdue U., 1976, MSME, 1979, PhD, 1981. Registered profl. engr., Fla. Asst. prof. mech. engring. U. Fla., Gainesville, 1981-86, assoc. prof., 1986—, dir. Combustion Lab., 1981-89, mem. grad. studies faculty, 1982-87, mem. doctoral rsch. faculty, 1987-94; presenter tech. meetings, mem. Fed. Emergency Mgmt. Agy. Emergency Mgmt. Inst. on Designing Bldg. Fire Safety; mem. hazardous waste incinerator permit writers workshop; pres. Proctor Engring. Rsch. & Cons., Inc., Gainesville, 1984—; pres. ENVIRECO, Inc., Gainesville, 1986-92; owner, mgr. Third Millenium Techs., 1995—. Contbr. articles to profl. jours., also ency. sects. Mem. ASTM (sec. 1984-86, chmn. com. on thermal processes 1986-91), ASME (regional oper. bd. 1986-88, Region XI Gator Sect. chmn. 1996, BPPE bd. 1996, Region XI Ouststanding Faculty Advisor award 1986), AIAA, Am. Soc. Engring. Edn., Soc. Automotive Engrs., Combustion Inst. (oper. bd. eas. sect. 1985-91), Nat. Fire Protection Assn., Air and Waste Mgmt. Assn., Human Factors and Ergonomics Soc., Biomed. Engring. Soc., Pi Tau Sigma. Methodist. Home: 69 Turkey Creek Alachua FL 32615 Office: U Fla Dept Mech Engring Gainesville FL 32611

PROCTOR, CLAUDE OLIVER, Russian language educator; b. Ahoskie, N.C., June 9, 1938; s. Claude Oliver and Helen Louise (Lassiter) P.; m. Doris Merle Stricker, July 7, 1962; children: Christopher Michael, Gabriel Marcus. Student, Davidson Coll., 1956-58, Syracuse U., 1962-63; BGE, U. Nebr., Omaha, 1966; MA, U. Notre Dame, 1974; Tchr.'s cert. with distinction, Southwestern U., 1981; PhD, U. Tex., 1990. Commd. 2d lt. USAF, 1966, advanced through grades to maj., 1977; Russian linguist USAF, Tex., Alaska and Turkey, 1958-67; intelligence officer USAF, West Germany, 1968-70; chief fgn. lang. dept. Air Force Sch. Applied Cryptol. Scis. USAF, Tex., 1971-72; Soviet area specialist Def. Lang. Inst. USAF, Calif., 1974-77; asst. prof. Russian, chmn. strategic langs. USAF Acad. USAF, Colo., 1977-80; ret. USAF, 1980; legal edn. officer Prosecutor Coun., Austin, Tex., 1980-83; dir. S.W. Lang. Svc., Georgetown, Tex., 1983-86; asst. instr. U. Tex., Austin, 1986-88; prof. Russian Ctrl. Tex. Coll., Killeen, 1989—; comml. Russian translator. Author: Soviet Press Translation, 1980, The Analysis of Soviet Press Propaganda: A Case Study of Soviet Polemics in the Sino-Soviet Conflict, 1960-69, 73, Illustrated International Dictionary, 1990, Evaluation of Quality in a Russian-English Machine Translation System, 1990, Multilingual Dictionary of American Sign Language, 1994. Merit badge counselor Lone Star coun. Boy Scouts Am., 1980—; booth chmn. Colorado Springs Intercultural Festival, 1979; mem. Interagy. Task Force for Indochina Refugees, 1975-76; mem. Georgetown City Charter com., 1995; commr. planning and zoning, 1996—. Mem. Am. Coun. for Tchrs. Russian, Tex. Fgn. Lang. Assn., Air Force Assn., Assn. Former Intelligence Officers, Lions, Sertoma, Rotary Internat. (dir. internat. svc. com. 1987-89, mem. world community svc. com. 1988, Paul Harris fellow 1993), Gamma Theta Upsilon, Sigma Phi Epsilon. Lutheran. Home: 1712 Mccoy Pl Georgetown TX 78626-6108 Office: SW Lang Svcs PO Box 1131 Georgetown TX 78627-1131

PROCTOR, DAVID RAY, lawyer; b. Nashville, Apr. 18, 1956; s. Raymond Douglas and Margaret Florence (Coffey) P.; m. Robbin Lynn Fuqua, May 12, 1984 (div.); children: Rachael Lynne, Benjamin David. AA in Polit. Sci., Cumberland Jr. Coll., 1976; BA in Polit. Sci., Vanderbilt U., 1978; JD, Cumberland Sch. Law, 1981; LLM in Taxation, U. Fla., 1983. Bar: Ala. 1981, Tenn. 1983, U.S. Tax Ct. 1983. Law clk. to presiding justice Ala. Supreme Ct., Montgomery, 1981-82; assoc. Thrailkill & Goodman, Nashville, 1983-84; v.p. taxes Alfa Mut. Ins. Co., Montgomery, 1984—. Contbg. editor Cumberland Law Rev., 1980-81; contbr. articles to profl. jours. Tchr. Rsch. Bd., Birmingham, Ala., 1980; active Montgomery Area United Way, 1985—; mem. stewardship com. Montgomery Bapt. Assn.; treas. Taylor Rd. Bapt. Ch., 1994-95, asst. treas., 1996—. Mem. ABA, Nat. Assn. Mut. Ins. Cos. (tax com. 1988—), Ala. Bar Assn., Tenn. Bar Assn., Sunrise Exch. Club Montgomery (treas. 1989-91), Phi Alpha Delta, Pi Sigma Alpha. Baptist. Home: 7016-B Watchman Cir Montgomery AL 36116 Office: Alfa Mut Ins Co 2108 E South Blvd Montgomery AL 36116-2410

PROCTOR, GAIL LOUISE BORROWMAN, home health nurse, educator, women's health nurse; b. Schenectady, N.Y., Oct. 4, 1952; d. Roy Edwin Jr. and Earla Jehnette (Reycroft) Borrowman; m. William Alton Proctor Jr., Nov. 26, 1977; 1 child, Rebecca Louise. Diploma, Ellis Hosp. Sch. Nursing, 1973; BS in Health Scis., SUNY, Saratoga Springs, 1977. RN, Fla., N.Y., S.C., N.C.; cert. childbirth instr., nursing asst. instr. Pvt. practice childbirth educator Rochester, N.Y., 1983-87; staff nurse, educator birthing ctr. Women's Ctr. of Martin County, Stuart, Fla., 1987-88; staff nurse obstets. Martin Meml. Hosp., Stuart, 1988-90; nurse mgr., obstetrics office nurse, 1990-93; pvt. practice specializing in childbirth edn. Stuart, 1990-93; dir. profl. svcs. Home Health Agy., 1993-96; clin. coord., supr. Shands Homecare, Stuart, Fla., 1996—; vocat. instr. Martin County Sch. Bd., 1993-94. Fellow Am. Coll. Childbirth Educators; mem. Am. Soc. Psychoprophylaxis in Obs. Home: 1605 E 14th St Stuart FL 34996-5818 Office: Shands Homecare 900 NE Ocean Blvd Ste 218 Stuart FL 34996-1519

PROCTOR, MARK ALAN, real estate executive, television panelist, commentator; b. Daytona Beach, Fla., June 3, 1948; s. John George and Christine (Crosier) P.; m. Carolyn Louise Morgan, July 24, 1982; 1 child, Morgan Alan. AA, Miami-Dade Community Coll., Miami, Fla., 1968; BA, Fla. Internat. U., 1975; postgrad., Fla. State U., 1978. Pub. relations asst. Woody Kepner & Assoc., Inc., Miami, 1968-70; dir. admission World Jai-Alai, Inc., Miami, 1970-75; sales assoc. R.C. Peacock & Co., Miami, 1975-77; systems cons. Fla. Game & Fish Commn., Tallahassee, Fla., 1977-79; communications dir. Fla. Dental Assn., Tampa, Fla., 1980-81; sales mgr. Gen. Devel. Corp., Tampa, 1981-83; broker-salesman Select Properties & Investment Corp., Tampa, 1983-87; pres. Proctor Properties, Brandon, Fla., 1987—; mem. Hillsborough County Indsl. Devel. Authority, Tampa, 1988—, vice chmn. 1991-92, 93-94; mem. Hillsborough County Housing Resource Bd.,1989—, pres., 1991-92, 92-93; mem. policy bd. Tampa Com. of 100, 1988-89; participant Joint Civil Orientation Conf., U.S. Dept. Def.; gov.'s appointee State of Fla. Growth Mgmt. Com., 1993; bd. dirs. Homes for Hillsborough, Inc.; pres. Dist. Six, Inc., 1994—. Editor, contbr. articles to Wildlife Inventory, 1979; contbr. articles to Fla. Dental Jour., 1980-81, Fla. Conservation News, 1986, Tampa Realtor, 1986; regular guest analyst weekly current events TV show Tampa Bay Week, Sta. WEDU-Channel 3, 1993—, Bayside, Sta. WTOG-Channel 44, 1994—. Pres. Hillsborough Assn. Chambers, Tampa, 1988-89, Arts and Crafts Cmty. Edn. Svcs., Inc. Tampa, 1991-92; pres. Rep. Exec.Com., Tampa, 1984; mem. Pres. Roundtable of Greater Brandon, 1989-90, co-chair Highlighting Hillsborough Paint Your Heart Out, 1992, 93-94, Brandon Balloon Festival and Marathon, 1994, alumni assn. Leadership Hillsborough, 1994-95; ch. moderator United Ch. of Christ, 1994. Recipient Comty. Svc. award 1989, Greater Brandon; named outstanding vol. Bay Area Youth Svcs., Tampa, 1984, Up & Comer of Yr., Price Waterhouse-Tampa Bay Bus. Jour., 1988, to Pres. Coun. U. S. Fla. Coll. Bus. Adminstrn., Tampa, 1989. Mem. Greater Tampa Assn. Realtors (pres. 1990, chmn. exec. bd. 1991, Realtor of Yr. 1985, W.H. Copeland award for outstanding comty. svc. 1991, Civic Achievement award 1991), Fla. Assn. Realtors (state dir. 1987-90, chmn. local govt. subcom. 1990, issues mobilization com. 1991, dist. v.p. 1994, Honor Soc. 1988-90), Nat. Assn. Realtors (congl. coord. 1987-89, polit. affairs com. 1991), Women's Coun. Realtors (affiliate), Real Estate Investment Coun., Greater Brandon C. of C. (pres. 1988,. Republican. Home: 1716 Silverwood Dr Brandon FL 33510-2643 Office: Proctor Properties 409 S Kings Ave Brandon FL 33511-5919

PROCTOR, MARTHA JANE, library manager; b. Panama City, Fla., Oct. 12, 1941; d. Thomas Pierpont and Maude Laveta (McCormick) Morgan; m. Charles Lafayette Proctor, July 9, 1971 (div. Jan. 31, 1977). AA, Gulf Coast C.C., 1961; BA, Fla. State U., 1963, MS in Libr. Sci., 1965; postgrad., U. Windsor, Ontario, Can., 1974-75. Cert. libr., S.C. Tchr. Bay County Schs., Panama City, Fla., 1963-64; reference libr. Atlanta Pub. Libr., 1966; ext. libr. N.W. Regional Pub. Libr., Panama City, 1966-67; reference libr. engring. U. Fla., Gainesville, 1967-70; libr. Fla. R & D ctr. Pratt & Whitney Aircraft, West Palm Beach, Fla., 1970-72; social sci. section head Windsor Pub. Libr., Ontario, Can., 1973-75; pub. libr. cons. Divsn. Libr. Svcs./Fla., Tallahassee, 1978-82; libr. coord. Durham (N.C.) Tech. C.C., 1985-90; regional br. head Charleston (S.C.) County Libr., 1990—; bd. dirs. Ednl. Opportunity Ctr., Charleston. Editor (newsletter) Orange Seed, 1978-82, Special Library Association Florida, 1969-71, (ann. directory) Florida Library Directory, 1978-82. Mem. Planned Parenthood, 1986—, Humane Soc. Am., 1990—; tech. rev. com. Charleston AFB, 1994—. Mem. ALA, S.C. Libr. Assn. (chmn. intellectual freedom com., 1996), Low Country Libr. Assn., Am. Assn. Ret. Persons, Gamma Phi Beta. Home: 5722 St Angela Dr Charleston SC 29418

PROCTOR, RONALD EUGENE, academic administrator, educator, consultant; b. Norfolk, Va., Jan. 7, 1947; s. Oliver Watkins and Christine (Eason) P.; m. Sandra Brown, Aug. 27, 1972; 1 child, Kimberle Nichole. BS in History Edn., Hampton Inst., 1968, MA in Ednl. Adminstrn., 1974; EdD in Social Sci. Edn., Rutgers U., 1976. Lectr. Douglass Coll., New Brunswick, N.J., 1974-76; asst. v.p. acad. affairs Norfolk (Va.) State U., 1976—; auditor Va. Social Sci. Assn., Richmond, 1984-85; v.p. Norfolk State U. Faculty Senate, 1985-86; nat. chmn. Conf. Minority Pub. Adminstrn., Washington, 1993-94. Author econ. impact study Norfolk State U. Rsch. Bull., 1986; co-author article to Va. Social Sci. Jour., 1984; cons. housing history Norfolk: A Historical Account of a Black Community, 1985; researcher agy. report Human Svc. Needs of Portsmouth, Va., 1987. Mem. Virginia Beach (Va.) Community Devel. Corp., 1986; mem. Virginia Beach Tomorrow Task Force, 1986; active Hutton YMCA, 1990, Tidewater Health Care, Virginia Beach, 1993. Capt. U.S. Army, 1969-74. Recipient Rsch. award U.S. Legal Svcs. Corp., Washington, 1982, Inst. Svcs. to Edn., Washington, 1982; named Tchr. of Yr., Norfolk State U., 1984; Pub. Svc. fellow U.S. Dept. Edn., 1991. Mem. ASPA (pres. 1986-87), Kappa Alpha Psi, Hiawatha Social and Beneficial Club, Phi Delta Kappa. Home: 4764 Berrywood Rd Virginia Beach VA 23464-5868 Office: Norfolk State U Office of Acad Affairs 2401 Corprew Ave Norfolk VA 23504-3907

PROCTOR-SAUFLEY, DIANA, medical/surgical nurse, consultant; b. Houston, Nov. 20, 1963; d. Terrell William and JoAnn Fonteno (Farrar) Proctor. AS, San Jacinto Coll., LaPorte, Tex., 1985. Cert. in enterostomal therapy. Floor nurse, team leader St. Lukes Hosp., Houston; charge nurse Rosewood Hosp., Houston; office nurse Med. Clinic of Houston; wound closure specialist Kinetic Concepts, Houston.

PRODAN, JAMES CHRISTIAN, university administrator; b. Colombus, Ohio, Jan. 4, 1947; s. Nicholas Mackley and Muriel Eileen (Bennett) P.; m. Carol Ann Cochran, Mar. 4, 1994; children: Christopher, Tana. BS, Ohio State U., 1969; MMus, Catholic U. Am., 1972; DMA, Ohio State U., 1976. Musician U.S. Army Band, Washington, 1969-72; asst. prof. U. Akron, Ohio, 1975-79; prof. U. N.C., Greensboro, 1979—; assoc. dean sch. music U. N.C., 1989—. Bd. dirs. Vol. Ctr., Greensboro, 1989-95; worship and music com. Christ Luth. Ch., 1988. Mem. Nat. Assn. Schs. Music, Nat. Soc. Fund Raising Execs., Internat. Double Reed Soc. (libr., exec. com.), Am. Fed. Musicians, Nat. Assn. Coll. Wind and Percussion Instrs., Music Educators Nat. Conf., N.C. Music Music Educators Assn., Coll. Music Soc., Music Tchrs. Nat. Assn., Intrnat. Soc. for Music Edn. Republican. Lutheran. Home: 5510 Rutledge Dr Greensboro NC 27455 Office: U NC Greensboro Sch Music Greensboro NC 27412

PROFETA, PATRICIA CATHERINE, librarian; b. Plainfield, N.J., July 31, 1958; d. Henry Stanley and Geraldine Ann (Schilling) Budzinski; m. Geoffrey Victor Profeta, Mar. 30, 1985; children: Katherine Elizabeth, Michael Geoffrey. BA, Douglass Coll., 1979; MLS, Rutgers U., 1981. Reference libr. Rutgers U.-Dana Libr., Newark, 1981-88, N.J. Inst. Tech. Libr., Newark, 1989-92; head libr. svcs. Indian River C.C., Ft. Pierce, Fla., 1992—; co-chairperson Fla. Libr. Paraprofl. Workshop, Ft. Pierce, 1993-95, chairperson, 1995—. Co-contbr. chpt. to: Guidelines for Writing Theses and Dissertations, 1990, 2nd edit., 1992; contbr. articles to profl. publs. Vol. J.A. Thompson Elem. Sch., Vero Beach, Fla., 1994—. Mem. ALA, Fla. Libr. Assn., Fla. Assn. Cmty. Colls. (mem. social com. exec. bd. Indian River C.C. chpt. 1995, sec. 1995-97), Coll. Ctr. for Libr. Automation (mem. resource cooperation sharing com. 1994-97, mem. circulation standing com. 1993-97). Office: Indian River CC Learning Resources Ctr 3209 Virginia Ave Fort Pierce FL 34981-5541

PROFETA, SALVATORE, JR., chemist; b. Phila., May 1, 1951; m. Catherine Mary Cherry, Sept. 20, 1980; children: Luisa, Theresa. BA, Temple U., 1973; PhD, U. Ga., 1978. Postdoctoral fellow chemistry dept. Fla. State U., Tallahassee, 1979-80; postdoctoral fellow pharm. chemistry dept. U. Calif., San Francisco, 1980-81, teaching fellow, 1981-82; instr. chemistry dept. La. State U., Baton Rouge, 1982-84; sr. scientist Allergan Pharms., Inc., Irvine, Calif., 1984-87; project mgr. computational chemistry Glaxo Rsch. Inst., Research Triangle Park, N.C., 1987-90, head chemistry systems, 1990-93; dir. N.C. Supercomputing Ctr. Rsch. Inst. at MCNC, Research Triangle Park, 1993-95; prin. computational chemist Ceregen/Monsanto, St. Louis, 1996—; cons. CADD-CAMM Smith, Kline & French, Phila., 1980-82, Squibb Rsch. Inst., Princeton, N.J., 1982-84; mem. allocation com. N.C. Supercomputing Ctr., 1989-94. Mem. editorial bd. Jour. Molecular Graphics, 1989—; contbg. editor Chem. Design Automation News, 1991—; contbr. articles to Jour. Am. Chem. Soc. NSF fellow, 1976-78; Petroleum Rsch. Found. grantee, 1984-88. Fellow N.Y. Acad. Scis.; mem. Am. Chem. Soc. Office: Ceregen/Monsanto 800 N Lindbergh Blvd U3E Saint Louis MO 63167

PROFICE, ROSENA MAYBERRY, elementary school educator; b. Natchez, Miss., Oct. 8, 1953; d. Alex Jr. and Louise V. (Fuller) Mayberry; m. Willie Lee Profice, Feb. 12, 1977; children: Jamie Martez, Alesha Shermille. BS in History, Jackson State U., 1974, MS in Elem. Edn., 1975, Edn. Splty. in Elem. Edn., 1977. Cert. elem. reading and social studies tchr., Miss. Tchr. reading Ackerman (Miss.) H.S., 1975-76, North Hazlehurst (Miss.) Elem. Sch., 1976-79; tchr. reading and elem. edn. Natchez-Adams Sch. Sys., Natchez, 1979—. Mem. NEA, Miss. Assn. Educators, Concerned Educators of Black Students, Internat. Reading Assn., Nat. Alliance Black Sch. Educators, Natchez Assn. for the Preservation of Afro-Am. Culture (bd. dirs. 1996-97), Linwood Circle Ruritan Club (bd. dirs. 1992-93, sec. 1994-95), Jackson State U. Alumni Assn., 100 Black Women, Zion Hill #1 Bapt. Ch. Democrat. Baptist. Home: 11 Elbow Ln Natchez MS 39120-5346

PROPHETT, ANDREW LEE, political science educator; b. Lynchburg, Va., Mar. 1, 1948; s. Elisha and Evatna (Gilliam) P. BS in History, Hampton U., 1970; MEd in Social Studies, U. Ill., 1972; postgrad., U. Va., 1986-91. Cert. tchr., N.J. and Va. Tchr. U.S. and African history Camden (N.J.) H.S., 1970-85; tchr. social studies Randolph-Henry H.S., Charlotte Court House, Va., 1986—; instr. polit. sci. and African-Am. history Southside Va. C.C., Keysville, 1988—; mem. Campbell County (Va.) Sch. Bd.; trustee, chmn. edn. com. Staunton River Adv. Commn., Randolph, Va., 1994—; summer participant Armonk Inst. Study Tour of Germany, 1995. Mem. Campbell County Dems., Rustburg, Va., 1986—; pres. Campbell County NAACP, Rustburg, 1992—; mem. youth adv. bd. Gethsemane Presbyn. Ch., Drakes Branch, Va., 1994—, deacon, 1995—. Mem. NEA, Va. Edn. Assn., Va. Geog. Soc., Phi Delta Kappa. Democrat. Presbyterian. Home: RR 1 Box 268 Brookneal VA 24528-9631 Office: Randolph-Henry H S PO Box 668 Charlotte Court House VA 23923

PROPST, HAROLD DEAN, retired academic administrator; b. Newton, N.C., Feb. 7, 1934; s. Charles Clayton and Sarah Isabel (Hilderbrand) P. B.A., Wake Forest Coll., 1956; M.A., Peabody Coll., 1959, Ph.D., 1964; LL.D., Mercer U., 1985. Tchr. Vandalia Pub. Schs., Ohio, 1959-60; instr. Wake Forest Coll., Winston-Salem, N.C., 1960-61; asst. prof. English, Radford Coll., Va., 1962-64, assoc. prof., 1964-65, prof., 1965-69, chmn. dept. English, 1965-66, 68-69; dean Armstrong State Coll., Savannah, Ga., 1969-76, v.p. for acad. affairs, 1976-79; vice chancellor for acad. devel. Univ. System Ga., Atlanta, 1979-81, exec. vice chancellor, 1981-85, chancellor, 1985-94. Editor: (novel) John Brent, 1970; contbr. articles to profl. jours., monographs, books. Bd. visitors Radford Coll., 1970-74; former pres. bd. Family Counseling Ctr., Savannah; former pres. bd. Family Counseling Ctr., Savannah; former bd. dirs. Savannah Symphony, Savannah Heart Assn., Alliance Theatre, Atlanta; mem. So. Region Edn. Bd., 1985-94. With USN, 1956-58. Fellow Carnegie Found., 1958, Ford Found., 1960; recipient Disting. Alumnus award Wake Forest U., 1986. Mem. Am. Assn. State Colls and Univs. (com. on accreditation 1982-86), Acad. for Ednl. Devel. (study com. on campus govt. 1976-77). Baptist.

PROSSER, BRUCE REGINAL, JR. (BO PROSSER), minister, consultant; b. Milledgeville, Ga., Sept. 23, 1953; s. Bruce R. Prosser Sr. and Sarah (Dukes) Ellington; m. Gail Ford, June 26, 1976; children: Jamie Lynn, Katie Beth. BBA, Ga. Coll., 1975; MRE, So. Sem., 1979, MDiv, 1980; postgrad., U. Ga., 1988-89, N.C. State U., 1990. Ordained to ministry Hardwick Bapt. Ch., 1978. Assoc. pastor Shepherdville (Ky.) First Bapt. Ch., 1979-82, Cen. Bapt. Ch., Warner Robins, Ga., 1982-84; min. edn., adminstr. First Bapt. Ch., Roswell, Ga., 1984-89; assoc. pastor Forest Hills Bapt. Ch., Raleigh, N.C., 1989-94; min. edn. Providence Baptist Ch., 1995—; mng. ptnr. Creative Consultation Svcs.; chaplain Phi Delta Theta Frat., Ga. Coll., 1974-75, North Roswell PTA, 1985-87; pres. Met. Religious Educators, Atlanta, 1987-88. Author: Promotion Plus!, 1992, (with others) Single Adult Leadership, 1991, Church Administration from A-Z, 1994; contbr. chpts. to books, articles to profl. publs. Assoc. dir. Met. Enlargement Campaign, Atlanta, 1988-89; facilitator N.C. State Leadership Devel. in Creativity, Humor, and Total Quality. Mem. So. Bapt. Religious Edn. Assn. Office: Providence Baptist Ch 4921 Randolph Rd Charlotte NC 28211-4002

PROSSER, JEAN VICTORIA, social worker, therapist; b. Chgo., June 3, 1924; d. Edward and Victoria Isabella (Johnson) P.; m. Aug., 1953 (div.). BA, Roosevelt U., 1948; MSW, U. Ill., 1957. Lic. social worker, therapist, Fla. Caseworker Ill. Dept. of Pub. Aid, Chgo., 1948-54; instr. in med. social work U. Ill. Hosps., Chgo., 1957-60; social worker Firman House Presbytery of Chgo., 1960-65; social worker U. Chgo. Hosps., 1965-69; sch. social worker Sch. Dist. 161, Flossmoor, Ill., 1969-86; part-time social work therapist Ind. Child Abuse Relief Enterprises, Daytona Beach, Fla., 1987-91; pvt. practice Daytona Beach, 1991—; bd. dirs. Daytona Neurol. Assocs. Rehab. Ctr. Active Habitat for Humanity. Mem. NASW (Social Worker of Yr. award 1994), NAACP, , Soc. for Clin. Social Workers, Sigma Gamma Rho. Democrat. Presbyterian. Home: 105A Wood Duck Cir Daytona Beach FL 32119-1345

PROTHRO, JERRY ROBERT, lawyer; b. Midland, Tex., Dec. 22, 1946; s. Jack William Prothro and Nita Marie (Stovall) Milligan; m. Leslie Joan Lepar, Aug. 15, 1970 (div. 1994); children: Laura Kay, Evan Jackson. BA, Southwestern U., 1969; JD, U. Tex. Sch. Law, 1972. Lawyer, capt. U.S. Army, JAGC, 1972-76; assoc. Turpin, Smith & Dyer, Midland, 1976-85; ptnr. Boyd, Sanders, Wade, Cropper & Prothro, Midland, 1985-91; pvt. practice Dallas and Midland, Tex., 1991—; mem. admissions com. M/O div. U.S. Dist. Ct. for Western Dist. Tex., 1987—; speaker in field. Treas., v.p. Southwestern U. Alumni Bd., Georgetown, Tex., 1980-90, pres.-elect, 1991, pres., 1992-94, trustee, 1992-94; adminstrv. bd. First United Meth. Ch., Midland, 1989—; chmn. Permian Basin AIDS Coalition Bd., 1994; active Midland County Hist. Commn., 1980-85. Named Univ. scholar Southwestern U., 1969; recipient Disting. Svc. medal U.S. Army, 1974. Mem. Midland County Young Lawyers (pres. 1979-80), Midland County Bar Assn., 5th Cir. Bar Assn., Pi Kappa Alpha Social Frat., Blue Key Leadership Frat., Pi Gamma Mu Social Sci. Frat. Methodist. Office: PO Box 93 Midland TX 79702-0093 also: 4107 Hawthorne Ste A Dallas TX 75219

PROTO, PAUL WILLIAM, government consulting company executive; b. New Haven, Mar. 1, 1954; s. Cosmo and Nina (Aceto) P.; m. Carol Lynn Culver, May 3, 1986; children: Melissa, Nicole, Cosmo. AS, Dean Jr. Coll., 1974; BA, U. Redlands, 1976; MA, U. Mich., 1981. Sr. advocate Legal Svcs., Inc., Bridgeport, Conn., 1976-81; govt. benefit cons. Disability Svcs., Inc., Southfield, Mich., 1981-86; pres. Govt. Entitlement Svcs., Southfield, 1986-93, Social Security Cons. Svcs., Tampa, Fla., 1992—; v.p. advocacy and edn. Govt. Benefit Specialists, Tampa, 1993—; cons., lectr. Legal Svcs., Inc., Washington, 1977-79. Author: A Stroll Through the Maze: The Social Security Process, 1993, Navigating Rough Waters. . .Understanding the Relationship Between Workers' Compensation and Federal Benefits, 1994; scriptwriter for videotape Social Security Disability and You, 1992. Bd. dirs. Social Security Task Force, Conn., 1978-81; mem. Mayor's Alliance for People with Disabilities, Tampa, 1993—. Named Employer of Yr., Pontiac (Mich.) Jaycees, 1991. Mem. Worker Compensation Claim Profls. (instr. 1993-94), Nat. Orgn. Social Security Claim Reps. Home: 15864 Sanctuary Dr Tampa FL 33647-1075

PROVASEK, EMIL FRANK, JR., small business owner; b. Ft. Worth, Aug. 11, 1957; s. Emil F. and Rema Maxine (Dennis) P. BSEE, U. Tex.-Arlington, 1979. Sr. microwave systems engr. Gen. Dynamics Corp., Ft. Worth, 1979-91; mgr. Causey's Rare Coins, Ft. Worth, 1991—. Mem. IEEE, Am. Numismatic Assn., Tex. Coin Dealer Assn. (bd. dirs.), Eta Kappa Nu. Roman Catholic. Home: PO Box 150411 Fort Worth TX 76108-0411 Office: 1806 Layton Ave Fort Worth TX 76117

PROVINCE, WILLIAM ROBERT, librarian; b. Kansas City, Kans., Nov. 11, 1946; s. Samuel B. and Dorothy E. (Lines) P.; m. Doris F. Woody, Apr. 11, 1970; children: Scott D., Christopher A. BS in Edn. and Social Studies, Ctrl. Mo. State U., 1968, MS in Edn. and Instrnl. Media Tech., 1975; MA in LS, U. Mo., 1983. Life cert. tchr., Mo. Secondary tchr. Chillicothe (Mo.) Pub. Schs., 1968; tchr. social studies and indsl. arts Bogard (Mo.) Pub. Schs., 1973-74; libr. Winfield (Mo.) Pub. Schs., 1975-76; tchr., libr. Bur. Indian Affairs, Wanbiee, S.D., 1977-79; libr. Haskell Indian Jr. Coll., 1979-83, Dept. Army, Ft. Riley, Kans., 1983-85; libr. USAF, Minot AFB, N.D., 1985-87, Chanute AFB, Ill., 1987-91; libr. 81st TRWG (Air Edn. and Tng. Command), Keesler AFB, Miss., 1991—. With USAF, 1968-73. Home: 104 Winchester Dr Ocean Springs MS 39564 Office: McBride Libr Fl 3010 512 Larcher Blvd Keesler AFB MS 39534-2342

PROVINE, LORRAINE, mathematics educator; b. Altus, Okla., Oct. 6, 1944; d. Claud Edward and Emmie Lorraine (Gasper) Allmon; m. Joe A.

Provine, Aug. 14, 1966; children: Sharon Kay, John David. BS, U. Okla., 1966; MS, Okla. State U., 1988. Tchr. math. U.S. Grant High Sch., Oklahoma City Schs., 1966-69; tchr. East Jr. High Sch., Ponca City (Okla.) Schs., 1969-70; tchr. Ponca City High Sch., 1978-79, 81-96; lectr. dept. math. Okla. State U., Stillwater, 1996—. Mem. NEA, Coun. for Exceptional Children, Internat. Soc. Tchrs. in Edn., Math. Assn. Am., Nat. Coun. Tchrs. Math., Sch. Sci. and Math. Assn., Okla. Edn. Assn., Okla. Coun. Tchrs. Math., Assn. Women in Math., Ponca City Assn. Classroom Tchrs. (treas. 1983-86, 91-96), Okla. Assn. Mothers Clubs (life, state bd. dirs. 1977-87, pres. 1984-85), Delta Kappa Gamma (treas. 1996—). Republican. Baptist. Home: 1915 Meadowbrook St Ponca City OK 74604-3012 Office: Okla State U Dept Math MS 408 Stillwater OK 74078-1058

PRUCZ, JACKY CAROL, mechanical and aerospace engineer, educator; b. Bacau, Romania, Dec. 25, 1949; came to the U.S., 1981; s. Carol Haim and Rella (Kaltmann) P.; m. Migri Marlene Caner, Oct. 25, 1972; children: Shirley, Roni. BS, Israel Inst. Tech., 1972, MS, 1979; PhD, Ga. Inst. Tech., 1985. Project engr. Israeli Air Force, Tel Aviv, 1972-75, test engr., 1975-77, sr. rsch. engr., 1977-81; grad. rsch. asst. Ga. Inst. Tech., Atlanta, 1981-85; assoc. prof. mech. and aero. engring. W.Va. U., Morgantown, 1985—, asst. dir. concurrent engring. rsch. ctr., 1988—; dir. structures lab. W.Va. U., 1986-88, chmn. faculty search com., 1986-88; chmn. workshops at nat. confs., 1987—. Contbr. chpt. to book and articles to profl. jours. Captain Israeli Air Force, 1973-81. Mem. AIAA, ASME, Am. Soc. Engring. Edn., Soc. for Advancement Materials and Processing Engring., Am. Soc. Composites, Internat. Orgn. for Standardization, Mech.Vibration and Shock, Computer-Aided Acquisition and Logistics Support Initiative. Home: 109 Greenwood Dr Morgantown WV 26505-2555 Office: WVa U Mech Aero Engring PO Box 6106 Morgantown WV 26506-6106

PRUD'HOMME, ALBERT FREDRIC, securities company executive, financial planner; b. New Rochelle, N.Y., Dec. 19, 1952; s. Albert O. and Rita R. (Moshier) P.; m. LuAnn Winfield, June 29, 1985; children: Cherilyn, Alicia. BA, Mercer U., 1975. Sales rep. Met. Life Ins. Co., N.Y.C., 1975-82; sales agt. Ohio Nat. Life, Cin., 1977-82; pres. Scepter Securities Inc., Charlotte, N.C., 1982-91; with Lyons Fin., The Advisors Group, and Acacia Fin. Group, Charlotte, 1991—; bd. dirs. Lyons Fin. Group Advisors, Inc. Pres. Belmont Abbey Coll. Athletic Found., 1985-87; bd. dirs. Charlotte Youth for Christ. With U.S. Army, 1972-74. Recipient Estate Planning award Winthrop Coll., 1981. Mem. Inst. CFPs (cert.), Internat. Assn. Fin. Planning, Charlotte Soc. Inst. CFPs (pres. 1994—). Democrat. Presbyterian. Home: 3608 Chevington Rd Charlotte NC 28226-4931 Office: 5950 Fairview Rd Charlotte NC 28210-3104

PRUD'HOMME, ECK GABRIEL, JR., physician, consultant; b. Texarkana, Tex., Feb. 8, 1924; s. Eck Gabriel and Mary Anderson (Young) P.; m. Margaret Peavy Murray, Jan. 24, 1948; children: Ann Clark, Kay Eleanor. Student, Tex. A&M Coll., 1941-43, Rice U., 1947; BS in Meterology, U. Chgo., 1949; MD, U. Tex. Med. Br., Galveston, 1952. Cert. Am. Soc. Addiction Medicine. Intern Hermann Hosp., Houston, 1952-53; pvt. practice Winnie, Tex., 1953-57, Ft. Worth, 1957-77; CEO, med. dir. Schick Shadel Hosp., Ft. Worth, 1977-88; pvt. cons. Ft. Worth, 1988—. Contbr. articles to profl. jours. Pres., bd. dirs. Ft. Worth CLU, 1969-75 (Civil Libertarian of Yr. award 1973); founding dir., pres. Ballet Concerto, Ft. Worth, 1968-82, Ft. Worth City Ballet, 1975—; chmn. Tarrant County Task Force on Alcoholism, Ft. Worth, 1980-81; advisor Tex. Com. Alcohol and Drug Abuse, Austin, 1989 (William Heatly award 1990). Fellow Am. Acad. Family Physicians (charter); mem. AMA, Tex. Chem. Dependency Assn. (founding dir., pres. 1979—), Tarrant County Med. Soc., Better Influence Assn. (pres., bd. dirs. 1979), Kiwanis (pres. 1958). Roman Catholic. Home and Office: 6304 Genoa Rd Fort Worth TX 76116-2028

PRUETT, CLAYTON DUNKLIN, biotechnical company executive; b. Montgomery, Ala., June 16, 1935; s. William Rogers and Myra Eleanor (Ganey) P.; m. Barbara Clapp, Feb. 22, 1974; children: Christopher Blair, Tyler Michael. BSCE, Auburn U., 1956. Profl. engr., Ala. Lt. USAF, 1957; staff assoc. Gen. Atomic div. Gen. Dynamics, La Jolla, Calif., 1964-68; exec. v.p. Enviro-Med Inc., La Jolla, 1968-73; chmn. bd. CDP Svcs., Inc., Atlanta, 1973—; pres., CEO Advanced Cancer Techs., Inc., Atlanta, 1988-95. Bd. dirs. Am. Cancer Soc., 1986-90, U. Calif., San Diego Cancer Ctr. Found, 1989—, Nat. Childhood Cancer Found., 1990—. Mem. San Diego Yacht Club. Home: PO Box 2304 Rancho Santa Fe CA 92067-2304 Office: CDP Svcs Inc 1050 Crown Pointe Pky Atlanta GA 30338-7707

PRUETT, LILIAN PIBERNIK-BENYOVSZKY, music educator; b. Zagreb, Croatia, Yugoslavia, Oct. 15, 1930; came to U.S. 1950; naturalized 1955; d. Ivan I. and Mathilde (von Benyovszky) Pibernik; m. James Worrell Pruett, July 20, 1957; children—Mark Worrell, Ellen Sharon. Student Mozarteum, Salzburg, Austria, 1946-50; A.B., Vassar Coll., 1952; M.A., U. N.C., 1957, Ph.D., 1960. Instr. Miss Hall's Sch., Pittsfield, Mass., 1952-54, U. N.C., Chapel Hill, 1960-63; asst. prof. N.C. Central U., Durham, 1965-68, assoc. prof., 1968-73, prof. of mus., 1973—; pianist N.C. Piano Trio, 1967-82. Author and editor: (with others) Directory of Music Research Libraries: Czechoslovakia, Hungary, Poland, Yugoslavia, reciew editor, 1981-92; Gen. editor Earley Keyboard Jour., annual Publication of Southeastern History, and Mid Western Hist. Keyboard Soc., Mem. Am. Musicological Soc. (southeast chpt. pres. 1957-60, sec., treas. 1973-75), Am. Assn. for the Advancement of Slavic Studies, Southeastern Hist. Keyboard Soc. Home: 343 Wesley Dr Chapel Hill NC 27516-1520 Office: NC Cen U Durham NC 27707

PRUITT, ALICE FAY, mathematician, engineer; b. Montgomery, Ala., Dec. 17, 1943; d. Virgil Edwin and Ocie Victoria (Mobley) Maye; m. Mickey Don Pruitt, Nov. 5, 1967; children: Derrell Gene, Christine Marie. BS in Math., U. Ala., Huntsville, 1977; postgrad. in engring., Calif. State U., Northridge, 1978-79. Instr. math. Antelope Valley Coll., Quartz Hill, Calif., 1977-78; space shuttle engr. Rockwell Internat., Palmdale, Calif., 1979-81; programmer, analyst Sci. Support Svcs. Combat Devel. and Experimentation Ctr., Ft. Hunter-Liggett, Calif., 1982-85; sr. engring. specialist Loral Vought Systems Corp., Dallas, 1985-92; mgr. new concept devel. army tactical sys. and tech. Nichols Rsch. Corp., Huntsville, Ala., 1992—. Mem. DeSoto (Tex.) Coun. Cultural Arts, 1987-89. Mem. AAUW (sch. bd. rep. 1982, legal advocacy fund chairperson 1989-91), Toastmasters Internat., Phi Kappa Phi. Republican. Methodist. Office: Nichols Rsch Corp PO Box 40002 4040 S Memorial Pkwy Huntsville AL 35815-1502

PRUITT, DENNIS ALAN, educational administrator, consultant; b. Norfolk, Va., Mar. 28, 1950; s. Harold P. and Leola V. Pruitt; m. Patricia Rasberry, children: Kaitlyn Lee, Christopher Payne, Dennis Alan Jr., Matthew Keith. BA, Armstrong State Coll., Savannah, Ga., 1972; MEd, West Ga. Coll., 1975; EdD, U. S.C., 1995. Dir. Meml. Ctr. Armstrong State Coll., 1972-77; asst. to v.p. academic affairs East Tenn. State U., 1977-78, asst. dir. Univ. Ctr., 1977-79; adminstrv. asst. to v.p. students U. S.C., 1980-81, dir. Univ. Union, 1981-83, acting dean of student affairs, 1983, v.p. student affairs, dean, 1985—; facilitator, presenter leadership retreats various colls. & univs., 1975-95; co-dir. NASPA-NPI, 1989-91; cons. alcohol and drug grant U. Southern Miss., 1987, Nat. Resource Group, Ohio State U., 1992. Bd. dirs. Rape Crisis Network, Columbia, S.C., 1995-96, Crimestoppers, Columbia, 1993-94; chmn. United Way, U. S.C., 1988-89. Recipient Bob E. Leach award NASPA, 1990, Disting. Svc. award, 1986, 87, 88, Disting. Alumni award Armstrong State Coll., 1988. Mem. NASPA, NACA, Am. Mgmt. Assn.. Methodist. Office: U. S.C. 112 Russell House Columbia SC 29208

PRUITT, GARY WAYNE, human resources professional; b. Evergreen Park, Ill., July 27, 1942; s. Harry W. and Mildred E. (Wagner) P.; m. Veronica T. Miller, Nov. 28, 1970; 1 child, Kristine L. BS, Ill. Wesleyan U., 1964; MBA, U. Memphis, 1987. Cert. compensation professional. Mgr. human resources Holiday Inns, Inc., Memphis, 1978-82; dir. compensation Wendy's Internat., Inc., Dublin, Ohio, 1982-84; from mgr. compensation to sr. internat. human resources adv. Federal Express Corp., Memphis, 1984—; pres. GVK Svcs., Inc., Germantown, Tenn., 1995—. Alderman City of Germantown, 1992—, vice mayor, 1996—; vice chmn. Shelby County Rep. Party, Tenn., 1995—; bd. dirs. Germantown Cmty. Theatre, 1993—, Germantown Performing Arts Ctr., 1994—. Sgt. U.S. Army, 1966-68, Germany. Mem. Am. Compensation Assn. (regional v.p. 1986-89). Methodist. Home: 7511 Neshoba Rd Germantown TN 38138

PRUITT, WILLIAM CHARLES, JR., minister, educator; b. Reed, Okla., May 31, 1926; s. William Charles and Helen Irene (Sanders) P.; m. Ellen Ruth Palmer, Aug. 25, 1953; children: Philip, Suzanne, John. BS, Stephen F. Austin State U., 1956, MEd, 1958; BD, MRE, Bapt. Missionary Assn. Theol. Sem., 1959, DRE, 1963; MLS, East Tex. State U., 1963. Ordained to ministry Bapt. Missionary Assn. Am., 1955. Pastor Mt. Pleasant Bapt. Ch., Bedias, Tex., 1955-60, Calvary Bapt. Ch., Commerce, Tex., 1960-63, Glenfawn Bapt. Ch., Laneville, Tex., 1963-66, New Hope Bapt. Ch., Winkler, Tex., 1966-70, Pleasant Ridge Bapt. Ch., Centerville, Tex., 1970-74, Redland Bapt. Ch., Centerville, 1970-79, Concord (Tex.) Bapt. Ch., 1983—; dir. libr. svc., instr. Bapt. Missionary Assn. Theol. Sem., 1958-67, prof. missions and religious edn., 1967-72; instr. psychology Jacksonville Coll., 1971-76; asst. dir. East Tex. Adult Edn. Coop., 1973-93; supr. Adult Learning Ctr. Rusk State Hosp., 1988-96. Tex. wing chaplain CAP, 1971-77; exec. dir. Armed Forces Chaplaincy Com., Bapt. Missionary Assn. Am., Jacksonville, Tex., 1965-95. Mem. Mil. Chaplains Assn. U.S., Lions. Home: Rte 8 Box 327 Jacksonville TX 75766 Office: PO Box 912 Jacksonville TX 75766-0912

PRUS, JOSEPH STANLEY, psychology educator, consultant; b. Glen Cove, N.Y., Mar. 9, 1952; s. Joseph Stanley and Constance Mary (Lamp) P.; m. Audrey Kaye Mink, Apr. 19, 1980; children: Erin Marie, Elizabeth Lauren Scudder. Student, St. John Fisher Coll., Rochester, N.Y., 1970-72; BA, U. Ky., 1974, MA, 1975, PhD, 1979. Lic. sch. psychologist, S.C., Ky.; nat. cert. sch. psychologist. Coord. psychology human devel. program U. Ky., Lexington, 1978-79, assoc. dir. human devel. program, 1979-80; from asst. to assoc. prof. Winthrop U., Rock Hill, S.C., 1980-89, prof., 1989—, dir. Office of Assessment, Sch. Psychology Program, 1988—; cons. Cardinal Hill Hosp., Lexington, 1977-80, U. Ariz., Tucson, 1984-85, Lancaster (S.C.) Mental Retardation Bd., 1987—; numerous presentations in field. Author: Handbook of Certification for School Psychologists, 1989; also numerous articles. Bd. dirs. Wesley Found., 1985-87; chmn. bd. dirs. Rock Hill Girls' Home, 1987-91. Recipient Disting. Prof. award Winthrop U., 1989; numerous grants from state and nat. agys. Mem. APA, NASP (presdl. citation 1993, 96), S.C. Assn. Sch. Psychologists (Outstanding Contbns. to Sch. Psychology award 1991), Phi Beta Kappa, Psi Chi. Home: 2430 Colebrook Dr Rock Hill SC 29732-9411 Office: Winthrop U Dept Psychology Rock Hill SC 29733

PRUSSIN, JEFFREY A., management consultant; b. Bklyn., Aug. 11, 1943; s. Samuel and Shirley (Solomon) P.; m. Judith H. May; children: Aaron Justin, Leya Monique. AB, UCLA, 1965; MA, Johns Hopkins U., 1967. Dir. edn. and tng. Group Health Assn. Am., Washington, 1971-72; mgr. prog. devel. Health System div. Westinghouse, Columbia, Md., 1972-73; prin. Health Care Orgn., Delivery & Fin. System, Kensington, Md., 1973-80; exec. asst. for policy Bur. Health Facilities, HHS, Washington, 1980-81; exec. v.p. Comprehensive Am. Care, Miami, Fla., 1981-84; sr. v.p. Internat. Med. Ctrs., Miami, 1984-86; pres. Health Sys. Devel. Corp., South Miami, Fla., 1986—; cons. in field; lectr. in field; adj. prof. U. Miami, Fla., 1982—; vis. asst. prof. Oreg. State U., Eugene, 1970; adj. asst. prof. Linfield Coll., Oreg., 1969-70, Portland State U., 1969-70. Contbr. numerous articles to profl. jours.; author: Health Maintenance Organization Legislation in 1973-74, 1974, Employee Health Benefits: HMOs and Mandatory Dual Choide, 1976, Results of a State-of-the-Art Review of Health Assurance for the Elderly, 1979, (with Judith M. Prussin), Health Services and the Elderly: A Comprehensive, Annotated Bibliography, 1982, (with Jack C. Wood), Topics in Health Care Financing: Private Third Party Reimbursement, 1975. Mem. Fla. Assn. Health, Maint. Orgns. (pres. 1985-86), Group Health Assn. Am. Office: Health Systems Devel Corp PO Box 432160 Miami FL 33243-2160

PRUZZO, JUDITH JOSEPHINE, office manager; b. Oklahoma City, July 11, 1945; d. Joseph Michael and Mary Amelia (Reinhart) Engel; m. Neil Alan Pruzzo, Aug. 20, 1966 (dec. Sept. 1991); children: Maria Pruzzo Richards, Eric Alan, Brian Samuel, Lisa Michelle. BS in Pharmacy, Southwestern Okla. U., 1968. Registered pharmacist, Mo., Okla., Tex.; cert. by Coun. Homeopathy. Nurse's aide Valley View Hosp., Ada, Okla., 1963-64; pharmacy technician Gibson Pharmacy, Ada, Okla., 1966; pharmacist Trinity Luth. Hosp., Kansas City, Mo., 1968-69, Rsch. Hosp., Kansas City, Mo., 1969-73, East Town Osteo. Hosp., Dallas, 1973; office mgr., profl. homeopath Neil A. Pruzzo, DO, P.A., Richardson, Tex., 1975-91; profl. homeopath, nutritional counselor Pruzzo Clinic, Inc., Richardson, 1992—; lectr., presenter homeopathy and weight loss. Mem. Dallas Symphony Assn., 1992—, Stradivarious patron, 1994—. Women's Bowling Assn. scholar, 1963; named Ada Dist. Dairy Princess, Okla. Dairy Princess Contest, 1965. Mem. Internat. Found. Homeopathy, Nat. Ctr. Homeopathy, Am. Pharm. Assn., Homeopathic Assn., Naturopathic Physicians (assoc.), Southwestern State U. Alumni Assn. (life), Kappa Epsilon (life, v.p. 1967-68). Home: 4303 Shadow Glen Dr Dallas TX 75287-6828 Address: 8345 Walnut Hill Dallas TX 75231

PRYBUTOK, VICTOR RONALD, business educator; b. Phila., Sept. 25, 1952; s. Albert and Dorothy (Welt) P.; m. Gayle Linda Trofe, Apr. 11, 1987; 1 child, Alexis Nicole. BS, Drexel U., Phila., 1974, MS in BioMath and Environ. Health, 1976, 80, PhD Environ. Analysis and Applied Stats., 1984. Tchr. math. Sch. Dist. Phila., 1976-78; lectr. stats. Drexel U. Coll. Bus. and Adminstrn., 1980-84; sr. biostatistician Campbell Soup Co., Camden, N.J., 1984-85; asst. prof. quantitative methods Drexel U. Coll. Bus. and Adminstrn., 1985-91; dir. Drexel U. Ctr. for Quality and Productivity, 1986-91; assoc. prof. mgmt. sci. U. North Tex., Denton, 1991—, dir. Ctr. for Quality and Productivity, 1991—; adj. asst. prof. Drexel. U., 1984-85, Phila. Coll. Textiles and Sci., 1984-85; cons. Pa. Health Care Cost Containment Coun., Harrisburg, 1987, 88; cons. to dept. rsch. nursing Thomas Jefferson U., Phila., 1989-92. Contbr. over 30 articles to profl. jours., over 50 conf. procs., presentations and internal reports. Mentor to gifted child Phila. Sch. System, 1988-89. Fellow HEW, 1978-80. Mem. (sr.) Am. Soc. for Quality Control (cert. quality engr., quality auditor, exec. bd. 1990-91, Irwin S. Hoffer award), Delaware Valley Partnership for Quality and Productivity (founder). Office: U North Tex Dept Bus Computer Syst Denton TX 76203

PRYE, ELLEN ROSS, graphic designer; b. Waynesboro, Va., Mar. 12, 1947; d. John Dewey and Betty Lou (Hardman) Ross; m. Warren Douglas Drumheller, June 7, 1969 (div. 1987); children: Amy Heather Drumheller, Warren Daniel Drumheller; m. John Paul Prye, July 24, 1993. BS, James Madison U., 1990. Cert. tchr. art K-12, Va/. Graphic artist The News-Virginian, Waynesboro, 1990-92, advt. prodn./composing mgr., 1992-94; graphic designer The Humphries Press, Inc., Waynesboro, Va., 1994—. Recipient Distinction award Shenandoah Valley Art Ctr., 1989, 1st pl. award for design of newsletter Printing Industries of Va., 1995, 1st pl. for design of brochure, 1995. Mem. Va. Press Assn. (1st pl. color automotive advt. merit cert. 1991, 1st pl. color health, profl. svcs. advt. merit cert. 1991, 1st pl. color food and drugs, variety advt. merit cert. 1993). Presbyterian. Home: 1830 S Talbott Pl Waynesboro VA 22980-2252 Office: The Humphries Press Inc 1400 Hopeman Pkwy Waynesboro VA 22980

PRYOR, DAVID, U.S. senator. Mem. from Ark. U.S. Senate, Washington. Office: US Senate 267 Russell Senate Off Bldg Washington DC 20510

PRYOR, SHEPHERD GREEN, III, lawyer; b. Fitzgerald, Ga., June 27, 1919; s. Shepherd Green Jr. and Jeffie (Persons) P.; m. Lenora Louise Standifer, May 17, 1941 (dec.); m. Ellen Wilder, July 13, 1984; children from previous marriage: Sandra Pryor Clarkson, Shepherd Green IV, Robert Stephen, Patty Pryor Smith (dec.), Alan Persons, Susan Lenora Pryor. BSAE, Ga. Inst. Tech., 1947; JD, Woodrow Wilson Coll. Law, Atlanta, 1974. Bar: Ga. 1974, U.S. Dist. Ct. (no. dist.) Ga. 1974, U.S. Ct. Appeals (5th cir.) 1974, U.S. Ct. Appeals (11th cir.) 1982, U.S. Supreme Ct. 1977; registered profl. engr. Ga., comml. pilot. engr. Hartford Accident and Indemnity Co., 1947-56, nuclear engr. Lockheed Ga. Co., 1956-64, research and tech. rep., 1964-87, real estate salesman Cole Realty Co. and Valient Properties, 1955-74, Sole practice of law, Atlanta, 1974—. Past pres. Loring Heights Civic Assn.; past mem. Sandy Springs Civic Assn. Devonwood Br.; former trustee Masonic Children's Home of Ga. Served to capt. U.S. Army, 1942-45, USAFR, 1942-55. Mem. Ga. Bar Assn., Ga. Trial Lawyers Assn., Mensa, Intertel, Soc. Automotive Engrs., Assn. Old Crows, The Old Guard of the Gate City Guard (fin. officer, bd. advisors Reinhardt Coll.), Sigma Delta Kappa, Pi Kappa Phi, Kappa Kappa Psi. Republican. Methodist. Lodges: Masons, Shriners Address: 135 Spalding Dr NE Atlanta GA 30328-1912

PRYOR, WILLIAM DANIEL LEE, humanities educator; b. Lakeland, Fla., Oct. 29, 1926; s. Dahl and Lottie Mae (Merchant) P. AB, Fla. So. Coll., 1949; MA, Fla. State U., 1950, PhD, 1959; postgrad. U. N.C., 1952-53. Pvt. art study with Florence Wilde; pvt. voice study with Colin O'More and Anna Kaskas; pvt. piano study with Waldemar Hille and audited piano master classes of Ernst von Dohnányi. Asst. prof. English, dir. drama Bridgewater Coll., 1950-52; vis. instr. English Fla. So. Coll., MacDill Army Air Base, summer 1951; grad. teaching fellow humanities Fla. State U., 1953-55, 57-58; instr. English, U. Houston, University Park, 1955-59, asst. prof., 1959-62, assoc. prof., 1962-71, prof., 1971—; assoc. editor Forum, 1967, editor, 1967-82; vis. instr. English, Tex. So. U., 1961-63; vis. instr. humanities, govt. U. Tex. Dental Br., Houston, 1962-63; lectr. The Women's Inst., Houston, 1967-72; lectr. humanities series Jewish Community Center, 1972-73; originator, moderator weekly television and radio program The Arts in Houston on Stas. KUHT-TV and KUHF-FM, 1956-57, 58-63. Contbg. author: National Poetry Anthology, 1952, Panorama das Literaturas das Americas, vol. 2, 1958-60; contbr. articles to scholarly jours.; dir. Murder in the Cathedral (T.S. Elliot), U. Houston, 1965; performed in opera as Sir Edgar in Der Junge Lord (Henze), Houston Grand Opera Assn., 1967; played the title role in Aella (Chatterton), Am. premiere, U. Houston, 1970. Bd. dirs. Houston Shakespeare Soc., 1964-67; bd. dirs., program annotator Houston Chamber Orch. Soc., 1964-76; narrator Houston Symphony Orch., Houston Summer Symphony Orch., Houston Chamber Orch., U. Houston Symphony Orch., St. Stephen's Music Festival Symphony Orch., New Harmony, Ind.; narrator world premier of The Bells (Jerry McCathern), 1969, U. Houston Symphony Orch., 1969, Am. premier Symphony No. Seven, Antartica (Vaughn-Williams), Houston Symphony Orch., 1967, L'Histoire du Soldat (Stravinski), U. Houston Symphony Orch., 1957, Am. premier Babar the Elephant (Poulenc-Francais), Houston Chamber Orch., 1967, Le Roi David (Honegger), 1979, Voice of God in opera Noye's Fludde (Britten), St. Stephen's Music Festival, 1981; bd. dirs., program annotator Music Guild, Houston, 1960-67, v.p., 1963-67, adv. bd. 1967-70; bd. dirs. Contemporary Music Soc., Houston, 1958-63; mem.-at-large bd. dirs. Houston Grand Opera Guild, 1966-67; mem. repertory com. Houston Grand Opera Assn. 1967-70; bd. dirs. Houston Grand Opera, 1970-75, adv. bd., 1978-79; mem. cultural adv. com. Jewish Community Center, 1960-66; bd. dirs. Houston Friends Pub. Library, 1962-67, 73-75, 1st v.p., 1963-67; adv. mem. cultural affairs com. Houston C. of C., 1972-75; adv. bd. dirs. The Wilhelm Schole, 1980—, Buffalo Bayou Support Com., 1985-87. Recipient Master Teaching award Coll. Humanities and Fine Arts U. Houston, 1980, Favorite Prof. award Bapt. Student Union, U. of Houston, 1991. Mem. MLA, Coll. English Assn., L'Alliance Francaise, English-Speaking Union, Alumni Assn. Fla. So. Coll., Fla. State U., Am. Assn. U. Profs., South Cen. Modern Lang. Assn., Conf. Editors Learned Jours., Coll. Conf. Tchrs. English, Nat. Council Tchrs. of English, Am. Studies Assn., Phi Beta (patron), Phi Mu Alpha Sinfonia, Alpha Psi Omega, Pi Kappa Alpha, Sigma Tau Delta (cited as an Outstanding Prof. of English U. Houston chpt. 1990), Tau Kappa Alpha, Phi Kappa Phi, Caledonian Club (London). Episcopalian. Avocations: tennis, racquetball, swimming, traveling. Home: 2625 Arbuckle St Houston TX 77005-3929 Office: U Houston English Dept University Park 3801 Cullen Blvd Houston TX 77004

PRZYBYZEWSKI, LESLIE CAMILLE, mathematics educator; b. Big Spring, Tex., June 18, 1955; d. Joseph Mac Montgomery and Emily Reese Dann; m. Joseph Stanaslous Przybyzewski, June 20, 1992; children: Jocelyn, Keely, Danny Eagan. AA, Mt. Wachusett C.C., Gardner, Mass., 1980; BS in Math. Edn. magna cum laude, Columbus Coll., 1989; M in Applied Math., Auburn U., 1991, postgrad., 1991-92. Grad. asst. Auburn (Ala.) U., 1991-92; math. instr. Tuskegee (Ala.) U., 1992-96; tutor Sylvan Hearing Ctr., 1996—. Mem. Collegiate Curriculum Reform and Cmty. Action, Greensboro, N.C., 1994-95, 95-96. Recipient scholarship Ga. Bd. Regents, 1975, Columbus Coll., 1987-88, 88-89. Mem. AAUP, MAA, Pi Mu Epsilon, Kappa Delta Pi. Methodist. Home: 465 Lee Rd 227 Smiths AL 36877

PSARIS, AMY CELIA, manufacturing engineer; b. Bklyn., June 18, 1963; d. Arnold S. and Ellen Marion (Wachtel) Levitt. BSME, U. Tex., 1985; MBA, U. Mich., 1991. Registered profl. engr., Mich. Mfg. engr. BOC Power Train GM, Flint and Pontiac, Mich., 1985-91; balance engr. BOC Power Train GM, Flint, 1987-88; sr. mgr. engr. Orbital Engine Co., Tecumseh, Mich., 1991-92; sr. project engr. Johnson & Johnson Corp., Austin, Tex., 1992-93, prodn. team leader, 1993-94; mfg. engr. Ford Motor Co., 1994—. Mem. vis. com. U. Tex. Mech. Engring. Dept., Austin; lit. vol. Williamson County Literacy Coun., 1992-93; mem. Austin Civic Wind Ensemble; tutor Vols. for Adult Literacy, 1987-88; mem. Friends of Alec (U. Tex. Coll. Engring.), Friends of LBJ Libr., Leadership Round Rock. Mem. ASME, Mich. Soc. Profl. Engrs. (bd. dirs. 1987-90, Young Engr. of Yr. 1988, MathCounts chmn. 1988), Soc. Mfg. Engrs., Saginaw Valley Engrs. Coun. (banquet publicity chmn. 1987-88), Tex. Exes Alumni Orgn. Office: Ford Motor Co PO Box 1587 QMP Bldg Maildrop 619 Dearborn MI 48121

PSENCIK, PENNY LYNN, flight nurse; b. Covina, Calif., Nov. 15, 1956; d. Max Cyrus and Alice Elizabeth (Pierce) Birka; m. John Lloyd Psencik, July 2, 1977; 1 child, Ann Elizabeth. ADN, Odessa Coll., 1981; cert. paramedic, Okla. County Community Coll., Oklahoma City, 1990. RN, Tex., Okla.; cert. emergency nurse, cert. flight registered nurse. Charge nurse, staff nurse Rankin (Tex.) Hosp., 1981-82; emergency rm. and pediatrics staff nurse Shannon West Tex. Meml. Hosp., San Angelo, 1979-81, 83-85; emergency rm. staff nurse Midland (Tex.) Meml. Hosp., 1982-83, 85-86; emergency dept. staff nurse City of Faith, Tulsa, 1986-87; emergency rm., ICU charge nurse, patient care coord. Stillwater (Okla.) Med. Ctr., 1987-90; flight nurse Med Flight, Okla. Med. Ctr., Oklahoma City, 1989-91; trauma coord. Life Flight Nurse, Galveston, 1991—. ACLS and Neonatal Advance Life Support instr., coord. Am. Heart Assn., 1987—, bd. dirs., 1989-90. Mem. Am. Trauma Soc., Nat. Flight Nurses Assn., Emergency Nurses Assn. (Trauma Nurse Core Curriculum instr., coord. 1987—, Basic Trauma Life Support instr. 1988—, Pediatric Advance Life Support instr. 1991—, Emergency Nurse Pediatric course instr. 1994). Home: 11343 30th Ave North Texas City TX 77591 Office: U Tex Med Br 301 University Blvd Galveston TX 77550-1073

PTASZKOWSKI, STANLEY EDWARD, JR., civil engineer, structural engineer; b. N.Y.C., June 11, 1943; s. Stanley Edward and Elsie Helena (Heihs) P. AAS, Acad. Aeronautics, Flushing, N.Y., 1967; BS in Civil Engring., U. Mo., 1975. Registered profl. engr., Tex., profl. sanitarian, Tex. Engr. Brown & Root, Inc., Houston, Tex., 1975-79; sr. engr. Marathon Marine Engring. Co., Houston, 1979-84, Gen. Dynamics, Ft. Worth, 1984-91, Bridgefarmer & Assocs., Dallas, 1991-93; prin. Pasko Consultants, Arlington, Tex., 1993—; sr. site constrn. engr. Raytheon Svc. Co., Ft. Worth, 1994—. Mem. AIAA (sr.), Nat. Soc. Profl. Engrs., Tex. Soc. Profl. Engrs., Soc. Profl. Bldg. Designers (cons., sec.). Lutheran. Home: 2002 Park Hill Dr Arlington TX 76012

PUBANTZ, JERRY JAMES, political science educator; b. May 7, 1947; m. Gloria Annunziata; 4 children. BS in Fgn. Svc., Georgetown U., 1969; MA, Duke U., 1972, PhD, 1973. Instr. polit. sci. Duke U., 1971; asst. prof. politics Converse Coll., 1973-76, mem. grad. faculty, 1974-76; prof. polit. sci. Salem Coll., Winston-Salem, N.C., 1976—, chmn. dept. history and polit. sci., 1981-87, 93-96; adj. instr. N.C. Sch. of the Arts, 1983-84, U. Prince Edward Island, Can., 1984, dept. polit. sci. U. N.C., Greensboro, 1981-82, 84, 86, 92-97, dept. polit. sci. Guilford Coll., 1985, 88-89, 96, dept. politics Wake Forest U., 1990, 92-94, 96—; bd. dirs. MidSouth U.S. A/Russia NIS Trade Coun.; mem. nat. adv. bd. Mid. East Policy Coun.; nat. edn. cons. Mid. East Policy Coun., 1986-91; resource person Nat. Fedn. State Humanities Couns., 1984-87; past holder numerous adminstrv. and com. positions. Contbr. to numerous acad. and profl. publs. including Modern Ency. of Russian and Soviet History, Politics and Policy, Pre-law Adviser's Handbook, Observer News Enterprise, others. Grantee Am. Assn. Colls., Ctr. for Theoretical Studies U. Miami, Exxon Ednl. Fun, Shell Corp., S.W. Inst. for Rsch. on Women U. Ariz., Tucson, Ctr. for European Studies U. N.C., Chapel Hill; fellow Islamic and Arabian Devel. Studies Duke U.,

NDEA; scholar Georgetown U., Chrysler Corp. Mem. N.C. Polit. Sci. Assn., So. Assn. for Advancement of Slavic Studies, Am. Polit. Sci. Assn. Internat. Studies Assn., So. Assn. Pre-law Advisors, Sigma Pi, Pi Gamma Mu, Pi Sigma Alpha, Phi Beta Kappa. Office: Salem Coll Dept Polit Sci Winston Salem NC 27108

PUBILLONES, JORGE, transit adminstration administrator; b. Guantanamo, Oriente, Cuba, Apr. 19, 1954; s. Felipe Reinaldo and Maximina (Gonzalez) P.; m. Ingrid Kastorsky, Aug. 6, 1989. BA, Queens Coll. CUNY, 1981; BS in Engring., Fla. Internat. U., 1986, MPA, 1990. Cert. profl. in labor rels. Bus mechanic Met. Dade County Transit Adminstrn.-Metrobus, Miami, 1980-83, transit shop supr., 1983-87; transit prodn. coord. Met. Dade Transit Agy., Miami, 1987-91, tech./spl. projects administr., 1991-95; rail prodn. coord. Metro Dade Transit Agy., Miami, 1995—; employee rep. Govt. Supr. Assn. Fla., Miami, 1986-89. Mem. Rep. Nat. Com., Washington, 1990—; elder Seventh Day Adventist Ch., Pompano Beach, Fla., 1990—. Recipient Appreciation cert. Nat. Found. for Cancer Rsch., 1983, Profl. cert. in HVAC Design, Fla. Internat. U., 1986, Pub. Mgmt. award, 1990, Pub. Pers. Mgmt. and Labor Rels. award Fla. Internat. U., 1981, Recognition cert. Ind. U., 1992. Mem. Am. Soc. for Pub. Adminstrn., DAV. Republican. Seventh Day Adventist. Home: 14461 Lexington Pl Davie FL 33325-6330 Office: Metro Dade Transit Agy 6601 NW 72d Ave Miami FL 33166-3029

PUCHTLER, HOLDE, histochemist, pathologist, educator; b. Kleinlosnitz, Germany, Jan. 1, 1920; came to U.S., 1955; d. Gottfried and Gunda (Thoma) P. Cand. med., U. Würzburg, 1944; Md, U. Köln, 1949; MD, U. Köln, Germany, 1951. Rsch. assoc. U. Köln, 1949-51, resident in pathology, 1951-55; rsch. fellow Damon Runyon Found., Montreal, Que., Can., 1955-58; rsch. assoc. Med. Coll. Ga., Augusta, 1959-60, asst. rsch. prof., 1960-62, assoc. rsch. prof., 1962-68, prof., 1968-90, prof. emerita, 1990—. Assoc. editor Jour. Histotech., 1982-94; mem. editorial bd. Histochemistry, 1977-90. Honored at Symposium on Connective Tissues in Arterial and Pulmonary Diseases, 1980. Fellow Am. Inst. Chemists, Royal Microscopical Soc.; mem. Royal Soc. Chemistry, Am. Chem. Soc., Histochem. Soc. Gesellschaft Histochemie, Anatomische Gesellschaft, Ga. Soc. Histotech. (hon.). Office: Med Coll Ga Dept Pathology Augusta GA 30912

PUCKETT, JAMES MANUEL, JR., genealogist; b. Oakman, Ga., Dec. 8, 1916; s. James Manuel and Alma (Willkie) P.; student West Ga. Coll., Emory U.; m. Robbie Horton, Sept. 13, 1944; 1 son, James William (dec.). Retail mcht., 1937-42; with Treasury Dept., 1944-53; public acct., 1955-60; feature writer Ga. Geneal. Soc. quar., 1965-75; genealogist, lectr., 1965—. Mayor of Oakman, 1940-42. Served with USNR, 1942-44. Fellow Ancient Monument Soc., Heraldry Soc., Am. Coll. Genealogists; mem. SAR, Am. Coll. Heraldy, Am. Hist. Assn., Archaeol. Inst. Am., Sons Confederate Vets., Am. Hist. Assn., Soc. Am. Archivists, Order Stars and Bars (Ga. comdr. 1966-70), Nat. Hist. Soc., So. Hist. Soc., Orgn. Am. Historians, Ctr. for Study of the Presidency, Internat. Platform Assn., Ga. Geneal. Soc., Nat. Geneal. Soc., Nat. Mus. Am. Indian (charter), Civil War Trust (charter). Home: 1563 Runnymeade NE Atlanta GA 30319-2130

PUCKETT, MARY CHRISTINE, logistics management specialist; b. Oklahoma City, Oct. 3, 1955; d. William Lytle and Johnny I. (Jones) Powell; Michael Earl Puckett, Oct. 28, 1972; 1 child, Melissa Cathryn Puckett. BBA in Mgmt., U. Okla., 1993. Sec. U.S. Govt., Fort Meade, Md., 1974; personnel specialist U.S. Govt., Vicenza, Italy, 1975-77; sec. U.S. Govt., Tinker AFB, Okla., 1978-79, supply specialist, 1979-81, inventory mgmt. specialist, 1982-86, program mgr., 1986—. Troop leader Girl Scouts, Moore, Okla., 1979-85; mem. PTA, Moore, Okla., 1979-89; pres. High Sch. PTA, Moore, Okla., 1989-91. Mem. Golden Key Nat. Honor Soc., Tinker Mgmt. Assn., Beta Gamma Sigma, Phi Kappa Phi. Democrat. Roman Catholic. Home: 3013 Broadway Ter Moore OK 73160-7543 Office: US Govt OC-ALC/LCPM Tinker AFB OK 73145

PUCKETT, STANLEY ALLEN, realtor, marketing and management educator, historian; b. Dayton, Ohio, July 21, 1951; s. Russell Elwood and Dorothy Christine (Hoskins) P.; m. Kum Cha Pak, July 28, 1986; children: Thomas Abraham, Jacqueline Sue. BGS, U. Ky., 1974; MSM, Troy State U., Eng., 1983; PhD, Sussex Coll., Eng., 1987. Asst. prof. mktg. Lamar U., Beaumont, Tex., 1987-88; asst. prof. mgmt. Grambling (La.) State U., 1988-93; realtor Tourtelor Bros., Inc., St. Petersburg, Fla., 1994-95, Tourtelot Bros, Inc., St. Petersburg, Fla., 1994-95, Century 21 Am. Dream Realty, Inc., St. Petersburg, Fla., 1995—; edn. cons. Hyndai Mgmt. Devel. Inst., I-chon, Korea, 1986-87; bus. cons. NAF Contracting Office, Ft. Polk, La., 1990; free enterprise fellow Students in Free Enterprise, Inc., Springfield, Mo., 1989-90; admissions liaison USAF Acad., Colorado Springs, Colo., 1989-96; adj. prof. Union Inst. Grad. Sch., Tampa Coll., U. South Fla. Author: Social Marketing, 1988; contbg. author: Great Ideas for Teaching Marketing, 1991; editor chpts.: History of the 8th Air Force, 1986, 87-88, 89-92, History of U.S. Central Command, 1992-94. Lt. col. USAFR, 1975-96, ret. Named to Honorable Order of Ky. Colonels, 1974. Mem. Am. Assn. Individual Investors, Ret. Officers Assn., Air Force Assn., Res. Officers Assn., Nat. Assn. Realtors, Fla. Assn. Realtors, Fla. Suncoast Bd. Realtors. Republican. Christian Ch. (Disciples of Christ). Home: 6420 Pine St NE Saint Petersburg FL 33702-7658 Office: Century 21 Am Dream Realty Inc 6669 54th Ave N Saint Petersburg FL 33709-1502

PUCKETT, THOMAS ROGER, entrepreneur, minister; b. Oklahoma City, Sept. 3, 1948; s. Delmer A. (Ducat) and Greta Sophia (Faucette) Puckett; m. Sallie Diane Hill, Aug. 30, 1968 (div. Aug. 1972); 1 child, Thomas Roger Jr.; m. Mary Ann Smith, July 30, 1976; children: Stephen Bradford, Laurel Christin. BBA in Mgmt., U. Ctrl. Okla., 1970. Ordained min. Northside Bible Ch., Oklahoma City, 1982. Sales and mktg positions Various Truck, Trailers, Commodities, Futures Orgns., Oklahoma City, 1977-85; assoc. pastor Northside Bible Ch., Oklahoma City, 1983-87, pastor, min., 1987—; program dir. S.W. Radio Ch., Oklahoma City, 1986-90; entrepreneur Bun Sav'r Fitness & Health, Oklahoma City, 1992-95, SUMbody Products, Oklahoma City, 1995—. Author, editor: The Comparator Letter, 1992-93; host: (weekly radio broadcast) Northside Bible Ch., Oklahoma City, 1982-89; inventor/patentee in field. Mem. Oklahoma City chpt. for Autistic Citizens. Recipient 1st degree black belt Jack Hwang's Inst. Karate, Oklahoma City, 1966, 6th degree black belt Internat. Martial Arts Fedn., Oklahoma City, 1995. Republican. Home: 2608 Abbey Rd Oklahoma City OK 73120-3403 Office: SUMbody Products PO Box 14844 Oklahoma City OK 73113-0844

PUERLING, JOANNE RENEE, information specialist; b. Lemoore, Calif., June 16, 1965; d. Peter Nicholas and Helene Adele (Baudoin) P. BA, U. N.C., Charlotte, 1987. Clk./typist USAF Utilities, Bolling AFB, D.C., 1983-87; adminstrv. asst. Embassy of Japan, Washington, 1987-88; adminstrv. asst., project asst. ASTD, Alexandria, Va., 1988-93; project mgr., sr. mgr. Am. Prodn. and Inventory Control Soc., Falls Church, Va., 1993-95; info. specialist Hughes Info. Tech. Systems, Reston, Va., 1995—. Tutor ESOL, No. Va. Literacy Coun., Alexandria, 1987-88; vol. comm. Telecomms. Exch. for the Deaf, Alexandria, 1987, Christmas in April, 1988. Mem. Spl. Librs. Assn. Roman Catholic. Home: 207 Skyhill Rd # 6 Alexandria VA 22314-5119

PUFFE, PAUL, minister; b. Crookston, Minn., May 22, 1953; s. Esthel Royal and Elaine Amelia (Radi) P.; m. Eleanor Ann Billmeyer, Dec., 1974; children: P. Alexander, Daniel, Timothy. BS, MIT, 1975; MDiv, Concordia Seminary, St. Louis, 1979; MA, U. Mich., 1984. Ordained to ministry Luth. Ch.-Mo. Synod, 1979. Pastor St. Thomas Luth. Ch., Ann Arbor, Mich., 1979-84; asst. prof. Concordia U. at Austin, Austin, Tex., 1984—; dir. preseminary program Concordia Luth. Coll., Austin, Tex., 1985—, chmn. religion div., 1985-87. Mem. Soc. Bibl. Lit., Am. Schs. of Oriental Rsch. Office: Concordia Luth Coll 3400 N I35 Austin TX 78705

PUGH, JOYE JEFFRIES, educational administrator; b. Ocilla, Ga., Jan. 23, 1957; d. Claude Bert and Stella Elizabeth (Paulk) Jeffries; m. Melville Eugene Pugh, Sept. 21, 1985. AS in Pre-law, S. Ga. Coll., 1978; BS in Edn., Valdosta State Coll., 1980, MEd in Psychology, Guidance and Counseling, 1981; EdD in Adminstrn., Nova U., Ft. Lauderdale, Fla., 1992. Cert. tchr., adminstr., supr., Ga. Personnel adminstr. TRW, Inc., Douglas, Ga., 1981-83; recreation dir. Ocilla (Ga.), Irwin Recreation Dept., 1983-84; exec. dir. Sunny Dale Tng. Ctr., Inc., Ocilla, 1984—; pres. and registered agt. Irwin County Resources, Inc., Ocilla, 1988—, Camelot Ct., Inc., 1994—. Contbr. articles on handicapped achievements to newspapers, mags. (Ga. Spl. Olympics News Media award, 1987, Assn. for Retarded Citizens News Media award, 1988). Adv. bd. Area 12 Spl. Olympics, Douglas, Ga., 1984-88; pres. Irwin County Spl. Olympics, 1984—, mem. adv. task force Spl. Olympics Internat. for 6-7 yr. olds, 1995—, elected to Ga. Spl. Olympics bd. dirs., 1995-98, serve on the comm. and mktg. com. for Ga. Spl. Olympics, 1995-96; exec. dir., fund raising chmn. Irwin Assn. for Retarded Citizens, Ocilla, 1984—; arts and crafts chmn. Ga. Sweet Tater Trot 5k/1 Mile Rd. Races, 1993—; bd. dirs., com. mem., mktg. com. Ga. Spl. Olympics, 1995—; founder, chmn. Joseph Mascolo Celebrity Events, 1985—. Recipient Spirit of Spl. Olympics award Ga. Spl. Olymics, Atlanta, 1986, Cmty. Svc. award Ga. Assn. for Retarded Citizens, Atlanta, 1987, Govs.' Vol. award Ga. Vol. Awards, Atlanta, 1988, Presdl. Sports award AAU, Indpls., 1988, Humanitarian award Sunny Dale Tng. Ctr., Inc., Ocilla, 1988, Golden Poet award New Am. Poetry Anthology, 1988, Outstanding Coach-Athlete Choice award Sunny Dale Spl. Olympics, Ocilla, 1992, Dist. Coach award, 1993, Outstanding Unified Sports Ptnr. of Yr. award, 1995, Coach of Yr. award, 1996; carried Olympic Torch, Ocilla, Ga., 1996; Ga. Spl. Olympics State Gold medalist Golf Unified Team, 1996, State Silver medalist Unified Table Tennis Team, 1996, State Bronze medalist Master's Unified Softball Team, 1995. Mem. DAR, Mut. Unidentified Flying Object Network (Ga. state sect. dir., asst. state dir.), Ga. State Assn. for Retarded Citizens, Ctrs. Dirs. Ga., Ocilla Rotary Club (program dir. 1995—, bd. dirs. 1995—, sec. 1996—), Sunny Dale Unified Track Club (founder 1991—), Sunny Dale Unified Track Club (founder 1991—), Sunny Dale Ensemble (founder), Ocilla/Irwin County C. of C. Baptist. Home: 201 Lakeside Cir Douglas GA 31533-9656 Office: Sunny Dale Tng Ctr Inc Mascolo Dr Box 512 Ocilla GA 31774-9801

PUGH, THOMAS DOERING, architecture educator; b. Jacksonville, Fla., May 27, 1948; s. William Edward Jr. and Lina Lillian (Doering) P.; m. Virginia Margaret McRae, June 14, 1972; children: Rachel McRae, Jordan Faith, Nathan Calder. B in Design, U. Fla., 1971, MA in Architecture, 1974. Asst. prof. architecture U. Ark., Fayetteville, 1976-78; pres. Thomas D. Pugh Constrn. Co., Inc., Fayetteville, Ark., 1978-87; assoc. prof. Fla. A&M U. Sch. Architecture, Tallahassee, 1987—; interim dir. Inst. Bldg. Scis. Fla. Argl. and Mech. U., Tallahassee, 1991-93, dir., 1993—; vis. rsch. fellow Tech. U. Eindhoven, The Netherlands, 1993-94; chmn. radon adv. bd. Fla. State U. Sys., 1988—; mem. Fla. Coordinating Coun. on Radon Protection; juror Progressive Arch.-AIA Nat. Archtl. Rsch. Awards, 1995; mem. rsch. policy bd. AIA/Assn. Collegiate Schs. of Arch., 1996—; mem. edn. com. Odyssey Sci. Ctr., Tallahassee, 1995—. Bd. dir. Tallahassee Habitat for Humanity, 1987-92; crew leader Habitat for Humanity Internat., Americus, Ga., 1988, 90. Recipient Bronze medal Fla. Assn. AIA, Gainesville, 1975; Named Vol. of Yr. Tallahassee Dem. and Vol. Tallahassee, Inc., 1991. Mem. ASCE (sec. spl. task com. radon mitigation 1990-91), Assn. Collegiate Schs. Architecture (coun. on archtl. rsch. 1994). Democrat. Lutheran. Office: Fla A&M Univ Sch Architecture 1936 S Martin Luther King Tallahassee FL 32307-4200

PUJOL, THOMAS JOSEPH, exercise and applied physiology educator; b. Bunkie, La., Mar. 20, 1962; s. Raymond John and Ethylene (Williamson) P.; m. Kelley Jo Kruse, Aug. 7, 1993. BS, Northeast La. U., 1985, MEd, 1987; EdD, U. Ala., 1991. Tchg. and rsch. asst. U. Ala., Tuscaloosa, 1987-91; asst. prof. La. Tech. U., Ruston, 1991—; cons. cardiac rehab. Lincoln Gen. Hosp., Ruston, 1995. Reviewer La. Assn. Health, Phys. Edn., Recreation and Dance Jour., 1994—; contbr. articles to profl. jours. Mem. Am. Coll. Sports Medicine, U. Ala. Alumni Assn. (North La. chpt. pres. 1994-95). Republican. Roman Catholic.

PULIDO, MIGUEL LAZARO, marketing professional; b. Havana, Cuba, Dec. 17, 1934; s. Jose Fabriciano and Maria Dolores (Perez) P.; m. Janie Ham, Nov. 28, 1980; 1 child, Michael James. AE, Sugar Techs., Havana U., 1956; MS, La. State U., 1961, PhD, 1965; completed Exec. Program, U. Va., 1986. Agrl. engr. Agrl. and Indsl. Bank Cuba, Havana, 1956-58, mgr. agrl. and eastern devel. div., 1958-59; agrl. engr. Productora Superfosfatos, Havana, 1959-60; asst. mgr. Tech. Svcs. div. Velsicol Chem. Co., Chgo., 1965-67; v.p. internat. mktg. Buckman Labs., Memphis, 1985—. Editor Jour. Fitopatologia, 1969-74; contbr. articles to profl. jours. Fellow Pan Am. U., 1960-62. Mem. AAAS, Am. Phytopathol. Soc., Weed Sci. Soc., Plant Growth Regulator Soc., Biol. Soc., Internat. Sugarcane Techs. Soc., Tech. Assn. Pulp and Paper Industry. Republican. Office: Buckman Labs Internat Inc 1256 N Mclean Blvd Memphis TN 38108-1241

PULLEN, J(OHN) MARK, computer science and engrineering educator. BSEE, W.Va. U., 1970, MSEE, 1972; DSc in Computer Sci., George Washington U., 1981. Registered profl. engr., W.Va. Assoc. prof. dept. elec. engring. U.S. Mil. Acad., West Point, N.Y., 1983-85; IEEE Congl. fellow U.S. Congl. Staff, Washington, 1985-86; program mgr. Def. Advanced Rsch. Projects Agy., Washington, 1986-88, dep. dir., 1989-91, program dir., 1991-92; assoc. prof. computer sci. (computer networking) George Mason U., Fairfax, Va., 1992—. Contbr. papers to conf. procs., profl. publs. Fellow IEEE (com. mem., vice chmn. Tech. Policy Coun., Harry Diamond award for Distributed Simulation.commd. and ctrl. network 1995); mem. Assn. Computing Machinery, Armed Forces Comms.-Electronics Assn., Eta Kappa Nu, Phi Kappa Phi. Office: George Mason Univ Dept Computer Sci Fairfax VA 22030

PULLEN, RICHARD OWEN, lawyer, communications company executive; b. New Orleans, Nov. 6, 1944; s. Roscoe LeRoy and Gwendolen Sophia Ellen (Williams) P.; m. Frances G. Eisenstein, Jan. 24, 1976 (div. 1986). B.A. in Econs., Whitman Coll., 1967; J.D., Duke U., 1972. Bar: D.C. 1973. Fin. mgmt. trainee Gen. Electric Co., Lynn, Mass., 1967-69; sr. atty. domestic facilities div. Common Carrier Bur., FCC, Washington, 1972-79, atty. advisor Office of Opinions and Rev., 1979-81; chmn. definitions and terminology of joint industry, govt. com. for preparation of U.S. Proposals 1977 Broadcasting Satellite World Adminstrv. Radio Conf.; v.p. Washington office Contemporary Comm. Corp., New Rochelle, N.Y., 1981-91; v.p., gen. counsel Comm. Innovations Corp., New Rochelle, 1991—. With USCGR, 1967-75. Mem. ABA, Fed. Comm. Bar Assn., Fed. Bar Assn., Internat. Platform Assn. Republican. Unitarian.

PULLIAM, STEVE CAMERON, sales executive; b. Martinsville, Va., May 1, 1948; s. Richard Cameron and Pauline Elsie (Haynes) P.; m. Sharon Elizabeth Richards, Nov. 25, 1972; children: Christina Elizabeth, Lindsay Anne. BS in Elec. Engring., Va. Poly. Inst. and State U., Blacksburg, 1971. With tech. mktg. program Gen. Electric, N.C., Mass, 1971-74; sales engr. Gen. Electric, Balt., 1974-77; product specialist Gen. Electric, Waukesha, Wis., 1977-79; mgr. sales support Gen. Electric, Waukesha, 1979-81; area sales mgr. Gen. Electric, Tampa, Fla., 1981-83, dist. sales mgr., 1983-89, zone sales mgr., 1989-92; program mgr., 1992-94; owner Steve Pulliam Enterprises. Bd. dirs. Tampa Unity, Inc., 1982-91. Mem. Elfun Soc., Va. Tech. Alumni Assn., Rotary. Office: 131 Glen Cannon Dr Pisgah Forest NC 28768-9611

PULSIFER, ROY, transportation, financial and business consultant; b. Schenectady, Oct. 20, 1931; s. Joseph R. and Marie (Phillips) P.; B.A., Columbia U., 1953, M. Internat. Affairs, 1958, J.D., 1958; m. Maryann Foreman, Dec. 18, 1963. Bar: N.Y. 1958, U.S. Supreme Ct. Enforcement officer Internat. Air Transport Assn., N.Y.C., 1959-60; atty. adviser FAA, Washington, 1960-63; with CAB, Washington, 1963-82, asst. chief, routes div., office gen. counsel, 1968-70, asst. dir. Bur. Operating Rights, 1970-78, assoc. dir. for licensing programs and policy devel. Bur. Domestic Aviation, 1978-82; transp. and fin. cons. Served with AUS, 1954-56. Recipient Meritorious Service award CAB, 1975. Co-author, project dir. govt. studies; contbr. articles to profl. jours. Home: 210 Lawton St Falls Church VA 22046-4508

PUMARIEGA, JOANNE BUTTACAVOLI, mathematics educator; b. Coral Gables, Fla., May 27, 1952; d. Ciro Charles and Rosaria Frances (Calabrese) Buttacavoli; m. Andres Julio Pumariega, Dec. 26, 1975; children: Christina Marie, Nicole Marie. BA in Math. and Edn. magna cum laude, U. Miami, 1973, MA in Math., 1974; postgrad., U. Houston, 1991-92. Cert. secondary math. tchr., Tex., Fla., Tenn., N.C. Grad. tchg. asst. U. Miami, Coral Gables, 1973-74; substitute tchr. Dade County Pub. Schs., Miami, 1975; math. instr. Miami Dade C.C., 1975-76; math. and G.E.D. instr. Durham (N.C.) Tech. Inst., 1976-77; math. instr. Durham H.S., 1977-78, Durham Acad., 1978-80, Univ. Sch. of Nashville, 1980-83; pvt. practice math. instr. Houston, 1984-86; tutor Clear Lake Tutoring Svc., Houston, 1987-90; pvt. practice, S.A.T, lang. instr. League City, Tex., 1990-92; pvt. practice math. and S.A.T. instr. Johnson City, Tenn., 1996—; instr. lang. Nelson Elem. Sch., Columbia, 1993-96; instr. fgn. langs. and math. Lonnie B. Nelson Elem. Sch., Columbia, S.C. Chair bd. edn. St. Mary Parish, League City, 1988-90, lector, 1992; C.C.E. tchr. St. John Neumann Cath. Ch., Columbia, S.C., 1993-95, lector, 1992—; treas. St. Thomas More Women's Club, Houston, 1985-86; v.p., then pres. housestaff med. wives Duke U., Durham, N.C., 1978-80. Mem. Newcomers of Greater Columbia (chair pub. rels. chpt. 1993, 95), Newcomers of Greater Colo. (com. chair coord. 1994-95), Welcome Neighbors of Bay Area (v.p., program chmn. 1991-92), Tex. Med. Aux., Bay Area Med. Wives, East Tenn. State U. Faculty Women's Club, Phi Kappa Phi, Kappa Delta Pi, Alpha Lamba Delta (Woman of Yr. 1972), U. S.C. Faculty Women's Club (v.p. 1993-94, pres. 1994-95, parliamentarian/advisor 1995-96). Roman Catholic. Home and Office: 2 Roundtree Ct Johnson City TN 37604

PUMPHREY, GERALD ROBERT, lawyer; b. Flushing, N.Y., May 31, 1947; s. Fred Paul and Anne (Afferman) P.; m. Joann DeLillo, Oct. 6, 1968; children: Gerald, Christopher, Elena. BBA, St. John's U., 1969, MBA, 1974; JD, Nova U., 1978. Bar: Fla. 1978. Assoc. Walden & Walden, Dania, Fla., 1978; v.p. legal services Golden Bear, Inc., North Palm Beach, Fla., Jack Nicklaus & Assocs., Air Bear, Inc., also bd. dirs., v.p., sec. Triple P, Inc., 1978-83; sole practice, 1983—. Bd. advisors Benjamin Sch. Found. Athletics Assn., 1980-83; coord. Benjamin Sch. Found., Inc.; mem. golf com. St. Clare's Sch., pres. Home and Sch. Assn., 1983-84; bd. dirs. Deaf Svc. Ctr. Palm Beach County Inc., 1988-89. Mem. ABA, Palm Beach County Bar Assn., North Palm Beach County Bar Assn. (pres. 1991-92), Palm Beach Gardens C. of C. (counsel 1983-87), No. Palm Beaches C. of C. (counsel 1987—), Kiwanis (charter mem., bd. dirs. Palm Beach Gardens 1983-87), Rotary (North Palm Beach 1987—), Phi Alpha Delta. Office: Ste 300 11000 Prosperity Farms Rd Palm Beach Gardens FL 33410

PURCELL, HENRY, III, real estate developer; b. Watertown, N.Y., Dec. 21, 1929; s. John Cecil and Elizabeth (Hathway) P.; m. L. Betty Collier; children: Robert William, Catharine E. H. Purcell Reynolds, Elizabeth J.M. BS in Mil. Engring., U.S. Mil. Acad., 1953; MBA in Econs. and Fin., U. Utah, 1975; postgrad., Princeton, 1960-61. Cert. Middle East specialist, Turkish linguist. Commd. 1st lt. U.S. Army, Augsburg, Republic of Germany, 1953; advanced through grades to lt. col. U.S. Army, 1967; commdr. Co. K. 1st regiment, 5th infantry div. U.S. Army, Augsburg, Fed. Republic of Germany, 1955-56; chief translation, U.S. Mil. Mission to Turkey U.S. Army, Ankara, Turkey, 1957-59; batallion commdr., tng. div. U.S. Army, Ft. Ord, Calif., 1965; sr. regimental adv. 7th ARVN regiment, 5th ARVN div. U.S. Army, South Vietnam, 1966, adv. G3 plans, III Corps ARVN, 1966-67; with Middle East Plans div., U.S. Strike Commd. U.S. Army, Tampa, Fla., 1968-70; asst. chief staff, G5 101st Airborne/Ambl div. U.S. Army, I Corps, South Vietnam, 1970; with G3Plans, Iv Corps ARVN U.S. Army, South Vietnam, 1970, sr. regimental adv. 32d regiment, 1971; with war plans div., deputy chief of staff, ops., The Pentagon U.S. Army, 1971; Middle East Specialist U.S. Readiness command U.S. Army, Tampa, Fla., 1972-74; retired U.S. Army, 1974; Middle East specialist U.S. Attache's Office, Ankara, Istanbul, 1961-63; with Spacos, G3 Plans and nuclear weapons employment div. NATO, Izmir, Turkey, 1963-65; pres. Henry Purcell, Inc., Tampa, 1976—, Warn-a-Prowler Inc., Tampa, 1994—. Pres. Nat. Sojourners, Tampa, 1969, 70, 72, Wilson Jr. High Sch. PTA, Tampa, 1977; commdr. Heroes of '76, Tampa, Fla., 1969, 70. Decorated DFC, Bronze Star for Valor, Cross of Gallantry, Gold Star, Silver Star (Vietnam), 10 Air medals, Army Commendation medal. Mem. Unified Constrn. Trades Bd., Nat. Assn. Realtors, Fla. West Coast Roofing Assn., Nat. Builders Assn., Greater Tampa C. of C. (com. of 100 1980—), Nat. Assn. Ind. Fee Appraisers (dir. Tampa chpt. 1994—). Office: 825 W Platt St Tampa FL 33606-2251

PURCELL, NANCY LOU, alcohol/drug abuse services executive; b. Reading, Pa., Nov. 26, 1934; d. Russel Louis Button ad Helen Geneve (Wichrowski) Shuker; m. John Joseph Crimmins, Dec. 19, 1953; (div. 1982); children: John B. Crimmins, Mark A. Crimmins, Cathy A. Crimmins; m. Grant S. Purcell, May 20, 1989. Sec. US Navy, NH Security Agy., Wash., 1952-55, Harvard U., Cambridge, Mass., 1956-58; personnel mgr. 3B's Corp., Columbia, S.C., 1972-75; mgr., buyer Card N Such, Columbia, S.C.; mgr., trainer Casual Corner, Columbia, 1979-82; dist. mgr. Casual Corner, 1982-85; co-owner, buyer Grant Purcell, Hilton Head, S.C., 1985-89; wardrobe cons., pvt. practice Charleston, S.C., 1981-89; v.p., co-owner Charleston (S.C.) Ctr. for Relapse Prevention, 1992—; dir. mktg. Fenwick Hall Hosp., 1990-91; cons. S. Bell Mktg. SCN Bank, Bankers Trust Bob Capes Realty, Christian Women's Assn, Profl. Women's Club, Columbia, 1981-89. Mem. Nat. Orgn. for Women, Christian Women, Bus. Profl. Women. Democrat. Protestant. Office: Charleston Ctr Relapse Prevention 125G Wappoo Creek Dr Charleston SC 29412-2119

PURCELL, SARAH C. (SALLY), English language educator; b. Ypsilanti, Mich., Oct. 24, 1932; d. Donald and Sarah Emily (Simons) Cameron; m. Jack Allen Purcell, Nov. 11, 1950; children: Jack Allen Jr., Michael David, Stephen Cameron, Scott Winfrey. BA in English, Coastal Carolina Coll., 1985; MA in English, U. S.C., 1989. Grad. asst. dept. English U. S.C., Columbia, 1986-89; part-time instr. English Coastal Carolina Coll., Conway, S.C., 1985-86, adj. prof., 1989—; tutor writing ctr. Coastal Carolina U., 1995-96. Vol. Hospice Horry County, Conway, 1982-85. Mem. MLA, South Atlantic MLA, Nat. Coun. Tchrs. of English. Lutheran. Home: 110 Limestone Ln Conway SC 29526 Office: Coastal Carolina Univ PO Box 1954 Conway SC 29526

PURCELL, WILLIAM PAXSON, III, state legislator; b. Phila., Oct. 25, 1953; s. William Paxson Jr. and Mary (Hamilton) P.; m. Deborah Lee Miller, Aug. 9, 1986; 1 child, Jesse Miller. AB, Hamilton Coll., 1976; JD, Vanderbilt U., 1979. Bar: Tenn. 1979, U.S. Ct. Appeals (6th cir.) 1985, U.S. Supreme Ct. 1986. Staff atty. West Tenn. Legal Svcs., Nashville, 1979-81; asst. pub. defender Metro Pub. Defender, Nashville, Tenn., 1981-84, sr. asst. pub. defender, 1984-85; assoc. Lionel R. Barrett, P.C., Nashville, 1985-86; ptnr. Farmer, Berry & Purcell, Nashville, 1986-90; mem. Tenn. Ho. of Reps., Nashville, 1986-96, also majority leader, 1990-96; chmn. select com. on children and youth Tenn. Ho. of Reps., 1989-96; exec. dir. Vanderbilt Legal Aid Soc., 1978-79; chmn. NCSL Assembly of State Issues, 1995; chmn. policy makers' program adv. bd. Danforth Found. Mem. exec. com. 6th dist. Dems., Nashville, exec. com. 6th dist. Dems., Nashville, 1986-88, mem. Tenn. State Ho. of Reps., Nashville, 1986-96, Majority leader, 1990-96, chmn. human svcs. com. Nat. Conf. State Legislatures, Washington, 1993. Toll fellow Coun. State Govts., 1988; named Legislator of Yr. Tenn. Conservation League, Dist. Attys. Gen. Conf. Mem. ABA, Tenn. Acad. Pediatricians, Tenn. Bar Assn., Nashville Bar Assn., Dem. Legis. Leaders Assn. (chmn. 1994—). Methodist. Home: PO Box 60331 Nashville TN 37206-0331 Office: 18 A Legislative Plz Nashville TN 37243

PURCHASE, HARVEY GRAHAM, veterinary medicine researcher; b. Lvingstone, Zambia, Aug. 8, 1936; came to U.S., 1961; s. Harvey Spurgeon and Vera Margaret (Cooper) P.; m. Nancy Ruth Schneider, July 6, 1963; children: Deborah Ruth, Kenneth Graham. BS, U. Witwatersrand, Republic of South Africa, 1955; B in Vet. Sci., U. Pretoria, Republic of South Africa, 1959; MS, Mich. State U., 1965, PhD, 1970. Gen. practice vet. medicine Republic of South Africa, Eng., 1959-61; research veterinarian Agr. Research Service, U.S. Dept. Agr., East Lansing, Mich., 1961-74; nat. program leader U.S. Dept. Agr., Beltsville, Md., 1974-83, sci. advisor, 1983-88; dir. research Sch. Vet. Medicine Miss. State U., Beltsville, 1988—; assoc. prof. Mich. State U., East Lansing, 1970-74. Editor: Isolation and Identification of Avian Pathogens, 1980; contbr. over 200 articles on vet. sci. to profl. jours., 1961—. Asst. scoutmaster Boy Scouts Am., Md., 1980-85, advisor Explorer Post, 1989-96; active Trinity Presbyn. Ch., Starkville, Miss., 1989—. Recipient Arnold Theiler medal U. Pretoria, 1959, Arthur S. Fleming award Washington Jaycees, 1972, Tom Newman Meml. award Poultry Stock Soc., 1973, William H. Spurgeon award Pushmataha Dist. Boy Scouts Am., 1995, Dean's Pegasus award Coll. Vet. Medicine Miss. State U., 1995. Mem. AVMA, Royal Coll. Vet. Surgeons, Am. Coll. Vet. Microbiologists (sec.

treas. 1989-96, chair bd. govs. 1996), Adv. Bd. Vet. Specialties (sec. 1988-95), Poultry Sci. Assn. (program chmn. 1985, sect. editor jour. 1986-89, CPC Internat. award 1971). Club: Tupelo Squares Sq. Dance (Tupelo, Miss.). Home: 1108 Yorkshire Rd Sherwood Forest Starkville MS 39759 Office: Miss State U Sch Vet Medicine PO Box 9825 Mississippi State MS 39762-9825

PURDOM, R. DON, insurance claims consultant; b. Amarillo, Tex., Dec. 14, 1926; s. Cecil Jack and Ella Emen (Billadeau) P.; m. Billie Frances Roberson, Nov. 18, 1949 (dec. Nov. 1984); children: Robert Don Jr., Lisa Purdom Carlson, Miles Thomas; mem. Joan Blake, Feb. 22, 1986. CPCU. Sr. v.p., dir. Highlands Ins. Co., Houston, 1957-89; ins. claim cons. Conroe, Tex., 1990—; chmn. Tex. Adjusters Licensing Bd., 1973-89. Contbr. articles to profl. jours. Councilman City of Panorama Village, Tex., 1991—. With CIC, 1944-46, PTO. Named Outstanding Man, San Angelo Jaycees, 1955. Mem. Arbitration Forums, Inc. (arbitrator), Masons, Houston Club. Republican. Presbyterian. Home and Office: 21 Winged Foot Dr Conroe TX 77304-1155

PURDON, KEVIN ERIC, food service executive; b. Elkins Park, Pa., May 20, 1955; s. Robert David and Evelyn Hilda (Ganong) P.; m. Peggy Diane Reider, May 8, 1977; children: Kevin, Brooke, Nicolas. BS in Acctg., Oral Roberts U., 1977. CPA; cert. fin. planner. Jr. acct. cost acctg. C-E Natco-Div. Combustion Engring., Tulsa, Okla., 1977-78, cost acct., 1978-79, acct. budgets and forecasts, 1979-80, sr. acct. , budget analyst, 1980-81, fin. analyst, mfg., 1981-83, asst. to sr. v.p. mfg., 1983-85; sr. fin. analyst Cotton Petroleum Corp., Tulsa, 1985-87; v.p. fin. Johnson-Purdon Restaurants, inc., Cedar Rapids, Iowa, 1987-88, Alan Herrman Chevrolet-Geo, Inc., Marlow, Okla., 1989-91; pres. P.C. Restaurants, Inc., Tulsa, 1988-91; dir. internat. planning and control Assocs. Corp. N.Am., Irving, Tex., 1992-94; v.p. operational acctg. Assocs. Ins. Group, Irving, Tex., 1995—; bd. dirs. Agapex Ltd., Denver, J & J Automotive, Inc., Willingboro, N.J. Inventor auto solar battery charger, 1985. Youth coach, YMCA, Bedford, Tex., 1988. Recipient Coach of Yr. award, Mid-Cities Basketball Assn., Bedford, 1989-90. Mem. Nat. Assoc. Accts., U.S. Chess Fedn. Republican. Home: 2500 Fox Glenn Cir Bedford TX 76021-2672

PURDUE, GARY FREDERICK, surgeon, educator; b. Boston, Aug. 19, 1945; s. Frederick Newberry and Isabel Wilde (Wrigley) P.; m. Laurel Patricia Addleman, Apr. 29, 1978; children: Ian, Heather, Keith, Kyle. BS in Ceramic Engring., Alfred (N.Y.) U., 1970; MD, Jefferson Med. Coll., Phila., 1976. Diplomate Am. Bd. Surgery with added qualifications in surg. crit. care. Intern Mercy Hosp., Pitts., 1976-77, gen. surgery resident, 1977-81; fellow U. Tex. Southwestern Med. Ctr., Dallas, 1981-82, asst. prof., 1982-88, assoc. prof., 1988-94, prof., 1994—; co-dir. burn unit Parkland Meml. Hosp., Dallas, 1986—, pres. med. staff, 1992-93, chief trauma svcs., 1994-95. Author: (with others) Child Abuse-A Medical Reference, 1990, Decision Making in Trauma, 1991; mem. editorial bd. Jour. Burn Care & Rehab., 1990—; contbr. articles to profl. jours. With USN, 1966-68. Recipient Disting. Svc. award for community svc. Dallas Hist. Soc., 1986. Fellow ACS; mem. Am. Burn Assn. (fellow 1982-83), Am. Assn. Surgery of Trauma, Internat. Soc. for Burn Injuries, Southwestern Surg. Congress, Soc. Critical Care Medicine. Office: U Tex Southwestern Med Ctr 5323 Harry Hines Blvd Dallas TX 75235-9158

PURI, RAJENDRA KUMAR, business and tax specialist, consultant; b. Hoshiarpur, Punjab, India, Dec. 22, 1932; came to U.S., 1965, naturalized, 1969; s. Harbans Lal and Satya Vati (Jerath) P.; children: Neena, Veena, Ram. BS, Agra U., 1952; diploma in Russian Lang. and Lit., U. Delhi, 1958; BA, U. Wash., 1968, MBA, 1969; MS in Taxation, Golden Gate U., 1982. Customs officer Govt. of India, New Delhi, 1955-60; asst. treas. Merc. Bank Ltd., New Delhi, 1960-65; mem. staff Peat, Marwick, Mitchell & Co., CPAs, Seattle, 1969-70; state exminer State of Wash., 1970-72, asst. supervising state examiner, 1972-74, supervising state examiner, 1974-77; sr. internal auditor Lockheed Corp., Sunnyvale, Calif., 1977-79, sci. programming analyst Lockheed Missle and Space Co., Sunnyvale, 1979-80, data processing specialist, 1980-84, sci. programming specialist, 1984-88; chief acct. Tex. Dept. Health, Austin, 1989-90; dir. internal audit, internal auditor Tex. Workers' Compensation Commn., Austin, 1990-95; bus. and tax cons., 1996—. Del., Wash. State Rep. Conv., 1976, Snohomish County Rep. Conv., 1976; Rep. nominee for state auditor, Washington, 1976; spl. advisor U.S. Congl. Adv. Bd., 1982-83. Mem. AICPA, Inst. Internal Auditors. Home: 2608 Hunlac Cv Round Rock TX 78681-7107

PURIFOY, JUDITH LYNN, telemetry nurse; b. Weirton, W.Va., June 21, 1960; d. Glen L. and Virginia A. (Thomas) Bolen; m. Ottis Purifoy, July 4, 1983. AS, W.Va. No. Community Coll., 1980. RN; cert. BLS, ACLS, coronary care; trauma cert. Med.-surg. nurse North Broward Med. Ctr., Pompano Beach, Fla., 1980-84, pediatric nurse, 1984-89, nurse telemetry/relief charge, 1990—; nurse pediatric intermediate care/telemetry newborn nursery Wuesthoff Hosp., Rockledge, Fla., 1989-90. Home: 1098 NW 4th Ave Boca Raton FL 33432-2553

PURNELL, CHARLES GILES, lawyer; b. Dallas, Aug. 16, 1921; s. Charles Stewart and Ginevra (Locke) P.; m. Jane Carter; children: Mimi, Sarah Elizabeth, Charles H., John W. Student Rice Inst., 1938-39; BA, U. Tex., 1941; student Harvard Bus. Sch., 1942; LLB, Yale U., 1947. Bar: Tex. 1948. Ptnr. Locke, Purnell, Boren, Laney & Neely, Dallas, 1947-89, Locke, Purnell, Rain & Harrell, 1989-90, of counsel, 1990—; exec. asst. to Gov. of Tex., Austin, 1973-75. Bd. dirs. Trinity River Authority of Tex., 1975-81; vice chmn. Tex. Energy Adv. Council, 1974. Served to lt. U.S. Navy, 1942-45; PTO. Mem. ABA, Tex. Bar Assn., Tex. Bar Found. Episcopalian. Clubs: Yale, Dallas Country, Dallas Petroleum, La Jolla (Calif.) Beach and Tennis. Home: # 1 Saint Laurent Place Dallas TX 75225 Office: Locke Purnell Rain Harrell 2200 Ross Ave Ste 2200 Dallas TX 75201-6766

PURSELL, CLEO WILBURN, church official; b. Ft. Worth, Feb. 16, 1918; d. Charles P. and Eltrie Lee (Tice) Dalton; m. Paul Edgar Pursell, Feb. 16, 1939 (dec. 1973). Grad. high sch. Ordained to ministry Nat. Assn. Free Will Bapts., 1939. Asst. pastor various chs., Okla., 1939-57; pres. Okla. State Aux., First Okla. and First Mission Dists.; officer Calif. State Aux., 1960; 2nd v.p., youth chmn. Woman's Nat. Aux. Conv. 1946-48, 52-55, nat. study chmn., 1955-57, exec. sec.-treas., Nashville, 1963-85. Author: Missionary Education of Our Youth, 1955, Woman's Auxiliary Manual, 1965, Triumph Over Suffering, 1982, Death and Dying, 1982, Anne, You're Super, 1990; columnist: Words for Women Contact Mag., 1966-70; editor Co-Laborer, 1963-85, (newsletter) The Minister's Wife, 1965-94; contbr. articles to profl. jours. Prominent in youth work, Okla., 1939-57; tchr. dist. and state Sunday Sch. workshops. Mem. Women's Fellowship Federated Women's Missionary Socs. (treas. Bristow, Okla., 1955). Home: 1148 Vultee Blvd Apt 12 Nashville TN 37217-2108

PURSLEY, CAROL COX, psychologist; b. Chattanooga, Dec. 7, 1951; d. George Edwin and M. Sue (Clarke) Cox; m. James V. Pursley; 1 child, Drew Vinson; stepchildren: Nancy, John. BS, U. Tenn., 1973, MS, 1975; PhD, U. Ky., 1983. Registered rehab. supplier, Ga.; cert. rehab. counselor; lic. psychologist, Ky., Ga.; lic. profl. counselor, Ga.; diplomate Am. Bd. Forensic Examiners. Dir. rehab. Goodwill Industries, Knoxville, Tenn., 1975-77; rsch. and evaluation asst. region IV rehab. continuing edn. U. Tenn., Knoxville, 1977; crisis intervention cons., job placement counselor KACRC, Knoxville, 1977-78; instr., cons. region IV rehab. continuing edn. program U. Tenn., Knoxville, 1978-79; teaching/rsch. asst. U. Ky., Lexington, 1979-80; rehab. specialist Internat. Rehab. Assocs., Louisville, 1980; psychologist and assoc. clin. staff Ea. State Hosp., Lexington, 1981-84; rehab. cons. Southeastern Transitions, Atlanta, 1985-86; pvt. practice rehab. cons. Marietta, Ga., 1986—; rehab. counselor U.S. Dept. of Labor OWCP Program, 1987—; pvt. practice psychotherapy and testing Marietta and Atlanta, 1994—; allied health prof. Ridgeview Inst., 1994-95, clin. psychology staff mem., 1995—; assessments/group therapy, allied health profl. for Rehab. Evaluation and Comprehensive Treatment Program Kennestone Hosp. at Windy Hill, Marietta, 1988-92; clin. assoc. Am. Bd. Med. Psychotherapists, 1986—; strategy meeting cons. Sony Music Entertainment, N.Y.; cons. ADA; expert witness Ga. Composite Bd. Profl. Counselors, Social Workers and Marriage and Family Therapists, 1991—; cons. to Gov.'s Rehab. Adv. Com., 1990. Chairperson-elect Vol. State Rehab. Counseling Assn., Knoxville. 1976; mem. Mayor's Adv. Com. for Handicapped, Knoxville, 1974-76. Facility Improvement grantee s.e. region Rehab. Svcs. Adminstrn., 1975-77, Facility Establishment grantee United Cerebral Palsy, 1977. Mem. APA, Am. Coll. Forensic Examiners, Ga. Psychol. Assn., Ky. Psychol. Assn., Nat. Assn. Rehab. Providers in Pvt. Sector (rsch. and tng. com. 1988-94), Pvt. Rehab. Suppliers of Ga. (chairperson ethics com. 1989-91, named person of distinction state PRSG chpt. newsletter 1990, ethics com. 1986-92), Phi Kappa Phi. Office: 2520 E Piedmont Rd Ste F Marietta GA 30062-1700

PURSLEY-CROTTEAU, MARGARET SUZANNE, psychiatric nurse, substance abuse professional; b. Augusta, Ga., Oct. 18, 1949; d. Norman B. and Florence M. (Morris) Pursley; m. Gary D. Crotteau, Aug. 24, 1985; 1 child, Elizabeth Ann. BSN, Med. Coll. Ga., 1977, MSN, 1981, PhD, 1995. RN, Ga., S.C.; cert. addictions nurse; cert. adult psychiat. clin. nurse specialist. Psychiat. clin. nurse, asst. chief nurse, clin. specialist drug and alcohol Eisenhower Army Med. Ctr., Ft. Gordon, Ga., 1981-86, instr., 1984, 85, 86; dir. adolescent psychiat. substance abuse program Charter Hosp. Augusta, 1986-87; charge nurse chem. dependency unit, adminstrv. supr. Augusta Regional Med. Ctr., 1990-94; asst. prof. comty. health nursing Med. Coll. Ga., 1995—; instr. Augusta Coll., 1983, Med. Coll. Ga., Augusta, 1989-90, U. S.C., Aiken, 1991-94; cons. to chief U.S. Army Nurse Corps, Washington, 1986; cons. chem. dependency nurse liaison program Humana Hosp., Augusta, 1990-92; cons. staff devel. Behavioral Health Ctr., Univ. Hosp., Augusta, 1990-91. Maj. U.S. Army Res. Nurse Corps, 1979-86.

PURVIS, GEORGE FRANK, JR., life insurance company executive; b. Rayville, La., Nov. 22, 1914; s. George Frank and Ann Mamie (Womble) P.; m. Virginia Winston Wendt, May 16, 1942; children: Virginia Reese (Mrs. William H. Freshwater), Winston Wendt, George Frank III. AA, Kemper Mil. Sch., 1932; LLB, La. State U., 1935. Bar: La. bar 1935. Sole practice Rayville, 1935-37; atty. Office Sec. State State of La., Baton Rouge, 1937-41; also dep. ins. commr. State of La., 1945-49; atty. La. Ins. Dept., also spl. asst. to atty. gen., 1937-41; with Pan-Am. Life Ins. Co., New Orleans, 1949—, exec. v.p., 1962-64, pres., chief exec. officer, 1964—, chmn. bd., 1969—, also bd. dirs.; pres., bd. dirs. Compania de Seguros Panamericana, S.Am.; pres. Pan-Am. de Colombia Compania de Seguros de Vida, S.A.; chmn., bd. govs. Internat. Ins. Seminars, Inc., 1984—; mem. Industry Sector Adv. Com. for Trade Policy Matters, 1986; lectr. ins. law Tulane U., New Orleans, 1949-56; bd. dirs. 1st Nat. Bank Commerce in New ORleans, Republic Airlines, Inc., 1st Commerce Corp., So. Airlines-Republic Airlines, Pan Am de Mex. Cos. de Seguros Sobre la Vida, S.A., 1964-88; dir. Northwest Airlines, 1986-87. Compiler, author: Louisiana Insurance Code, 1948; contbr. articles to profl. jours. Chmn. big donors com. New Orleans Christmas Seal Campaign, 1961, gen. campaign chmn., 1962, chmn. profl. group VIII, 1963; vice chmn. New Orleans United Fund campaign, 1965, gen. chmn., 1967; pres. Tb Assn. Greater New Orleans, 1967, La. State U. Found., 1967, YMCA, New Orleans, 1968—, Internat. House, 1977, Met. Area Com., 1979; geog. chmn. U.S. Savs. Bond Campaign, Greater New Orleans, 1971; mem. Bd. City Park Commrs., 1965-79, mem. bd. commrs. Port of New Orleans, 1979—, pres. bd. commrs., 1982; chmn. S.S. Huebner Found. Ins. Edn., 1977—, Bus. Task Force on Edn., Inc., 1980—; mem. adv. bd. Bapt. Hosp., 1985—, Salvation Army, 1986—; bd. dirs. Family Svc. Soc. New Orleans, Council for a Better La., New Orleans Philharm. Symphony Soc., Summer Pop Concerts, Bur. Govt. Rsch. New Orleans; mem. Govs. Cost Control Commn., 1981-89; trustee Greater New Orleans Found., 1987—, chmn. bd. trustees La. Ind. Coll. Fund Inc., 1987-88, mem. 1987—. Served with USNR, 1941-45. Decorated Order of Vasco Nunez de Balboa (Panama); named Alumnus of Yr., La. State U., 1975, role model Young Leadership Coun., 1993; recipient award Inst. for Human Understanding, 1975, Weiss Meml. award, 1976, Vol. Activist award, 1978, award of excellence Greater New Orleans Fedn. Chs., 1983, Disting. Svc. award Navy League, 1983, Humanitarian award Nat. Jewish Hosp./Nat. Asthma Ctr., 1984, internat. ins. award Internat. Ins. Adv. Coun., 1986, 1st ann. award for outstanding efforts in promoting trade with L.Am., Rotary Club, 1987, Hall of Fame award La. State U., 1987, Man of Yr. award Fedn. Ins. and Corp. Counsel, 1988, Integritas Vitae award Loyola U. of South, 1991, Bus. Hall of Fame award Jr. Achievement, 1993, cert. of appreciation La. Air N.G., 1995; selected role model Young Bus. Leadership Coun., 1993. Mem. ABA, La. Bar Assn., La. Law Inst., Am. Judicature Soc., Assn. Life Ins. Counsel, Am. Life Conv. (past chmn. legal sect., exec. com., v.p. La., chmn. 1972), Health Ins. Assn. Am. (dir., chmn. 1970), Ins. Econs. Soc. Am. (chmn. 1980-81), La. Assn. Legal Res. Life Ins. Cos. (pres. 1963-68), New Orleans Assn. Life Underwriters (award for Loyal and Unselfish Service to the Ins. Industry 1987), Internat. Trade Adminstrn. (industry sector and functional adv. coms. for trade policy matters), C. of C. Greater New Orleans Area (dir., pres. 1970), Phi Delta Phi, Omicron Delta Kappa, Delta Kappa Epsilon. Episcopalian. Home: 5501 Dayna Ct New Orleans LA 70124-1042

PURVIS, RONALD SCOTT, financial counselor, real estate executive; b. Cleve., Apr. 17, 1928; s. Samuel Martin Jr. and Dorothea (Scott) P.; m. Lynne Willis, Dec. 20, 1963; children: Ward S., Blair P. Snyder, Heather Leigh Ann. BS, U.S. Naval Acad., 1953; B Individualized Study, George Mason U., 1984. CLU, Chartered Fin. Cons., registered gen. securities prin. Enlisted USN, 1946, advanced through grades to lt. comdr., 1966, hon. discharged, 1972; gen. agt. Can. Life Assurance, Washington, 1972-88; pres. RSVP Realty, McLean, Va., 1985—, Purvis Corp./RIA, Falls Church, Va., 1986—. Del. Rep. Convs., Va., 1975—. Purvis Peak, Antarctic mountain, named in his honor. Mem. D.C. Soc., SAR (asst. registrar 1982-84, chaplain 1989-91, treas. 1991-92, state sec. 1992-94, sr. v.p. 1994-95, state pres. 1995-96, registrar and alt. nat. soc. trustee 1996—), Assn. Naval Aviation, Masons, Shriners. Home: 27310 Baylys Neck Rd Accomac VA 23301-0058 Office: Purvis Corp/RIA 3415 Lakeside View Dr Falls Church VA 22041-2454

PURYEAR, ARLENE SCURRY, elementary school educator; b. Newberry, S.C., July 15, 1960; d. Wilbur Dwight and Callie Rae (Edwards) Scurry; m. Robert Eugene Puryear, May 16, 1981; children: Jennifier Ashleigh, Kaitlyn Nicole. BS in Elem. Edn., Lander U., 1981, MED in Elem. Edn., 1987, postgrad., 1988, 91-92; postgrad., U. S.C., 1988-90, 93, U. Okla., 1990, Clemson U., 1993. Cert. elementary education, middle sch. math and sci. Tchr. Hollywood Elem. Sch./Saluda (S.C.) Dist. 1, 1981-96, chair dept. sci., 1988-96; tchr. Ridge Spring (S.C.) Monetta Elem. Sch., 1996—; owner, voice performer and coach Ashlyn Arts Studio, 1988—;enrichment instr. Lexington 1, 1993; mem. Saluda Dist. 1 sci. dist. Basic Skills Assessment Plan curriculum guide com., Basic Skills Assessment Plan test dist. level math. testing task force, dist. curriculum com., sch. discipline com., Hollywood crisis team, sponsor Young Astonauts Club, 1988—, invention convention; mem. State Scuref Pre-coll. Sci. and Math. Edn. Com.; sci. con. S.C. Edn. Dept., summer 1996; presenter in field. Recording artist contemporary gospel musical group Scurry Sisters. Summer youth and children dir., music instr. vacation bible sch. Red Bank Bapt. Ch., 1988-95; tchr. youth, youth choir dir. 1st Cavalry Balt. Ch., 1989-91; active Saluda County Fine Arts Coun.; area coord. bike-a-thon, St. Jude Rsch. Hosp., 1993; instr. vacation bible sch. Ridge Assn. So. Bapt., 1990, youth instr., 1994, pres. youth com.; sec. Hollywood Parent Support Orgn., PACE, 1993. Recipient STAR award S.C. Palmetto Tchrs.; grantee S.C. Ednl. Incentive Act, 1990-91, Project Wild, 1992-93. Mem. ASCD, Nat. Sci. Tchrs. Assn. (regional bd. dirs. 1993, presenter Calif. coun. 1994, presenter Phila. conf. 1995), S.C. State Sci. Orgn., S.C. Environ. Assn., S.C. Math. Coun., Palmetto State Tchrs. Assn., Women Involved in Rural Electric (v.p.), Walley Bryan Caravan Camping Internat. (past pres. Palmetto State). Home: RR 2 Box 140-b Leesville SC 29070-9407 Office: Ridge Spring Monetta Elem Sch PO Box 386 Ridge Spring SC 29129

PURYEAR, JAMES BURTON, college administrator; b. Jackson, Miss., Sept. 2, 1938; s. Harry Henton and Doris (Smith) P.; m. Joan Copeland, June 13, 1965; children: John James, Jeffrey Burton, Joel Harry. BS, Miss. State U., 1960, MEd, 1961; PhD, Fla. State U., 1969. Lic. profl. counselor, Ga. Assoc. dir. YMCA, Starkville, Miss., 1962-64, dir., 1964-65; dir. fin. aid Fla. State U., Tallahassee, 1967-69; asst. dir. student affairs Med. Coll. of Ga., Augusta, 1969-70, dir. student affairs, 1970-86, v.p. student affairs, 1986—. Adv. bd. mem. Ga. Fed. Bank, Augusta, 1978-85; chmn. bd. First Bapt. Ch., Augusta, 1978-80; pres. Learning Disabilities Assn., Augusta, 1987, PTA, 1994; bd. dirs. Augusta Tng. Shop for Handicapped, 1994—; exec. bd. mem. Boy Scouts Am. Yearbook Dedication MCG Student Yearbook, 1975; scholar Med. Coll. Ga., 1988; recipient Svc. to Mankind award Sertoma, 1988. Mem. Nat. Assn. Student Pers. (S.E. regional bd. 1985), Am. Coll. Pers. Assn., So. Assn. Coll. Student Affairs, Rotary (pres. 1978, Paul Harris fellow 1985). Baptist. Office: Student Affairs Med Coll Ga Augusta GA 30912

PURYEAR, JOAN COPELAND, English language educator; b. Columbus, Miss., May 10, 1944; d. John Thomas and Mamie (Cunningham) Copeland.; m. James Burton Puryear, June 13, 1965; children: John James, Jeffrey Burton, Joel Harry. BA summa cum laude, Miss. State U., Starkville, 1965; MA, Fla. State U., 1969; EdD, U. Ga., 1987. Cert. tchr., Ga. English instr. Fla. State U., Tallahassee, 1965-69, Augusta (Ga.) Coll., 1987-88; head English dept. Augusta Tech. Inst., 1989-93; chairperson gen. edn. and devel. studies, 1993—, mem. dean's coun., mgmt. team and grant proposal team, 1994—; chmn. State Exec. Bd. English, Ga., 1990-92, East Ctrl. Consortium English, Ga., 1990-92; mem. Augusta Tech. Inst. Tech. Com., 1990—; chmn. Capital Funds Raising Family Campaign, Augusta Tech. Inst., vice chmn. Capital Fund Raising Cmty. Campaign; mem. and co-chmn. Continuous Improvement Coun., 1996—, Augusta Tech. Inst.; facilitator Total Quality Mgmt. Tech. Tng.; mem. exec. steering com. Continuous Improvement Coun.; chmn. editing com. Augusta Tech. Inst. Self Study, 1992-93, chmn. long range planning goals and objectives com., 1994. Mem. Cmtys. in Schs., 1996—; trustee Augusta Tech. Inst. Found. Bd., 1996—; co-pres. Davidson Fine Arts Sch. PTA, 1995, co-pres. bd. boosters, 1996; pres. Med. Coll. Spouse's Club, Augusta, 1972; dir. Women's Mission Orgn., First Bapt. Ch., Augusta, 1982, dir. Youth Sunday Sch., 1992—, chmn. 175th Anniversary, 1992, deacon, 1996—, mem. ministerial adv. com. Mem. Modern Lang. Assn., Nat. Coun. Tchrs., Am. Vocat. Assn., Ga. Vocat. Assn., So. Assn. Colls. (accreditation team 1994), Phi Theta Kappa (adv. 1992—). Baptist. Office: Augusta Tech Inst 3116 Deans Bridge Rd Augusta GA 30906-3375

PUSTILNIK, DAVID DANIEL, lawyer; b. N.Y.C., Mar. 10, 1931; s. Philip and Belle (Gerberholtz) P.; m. Helen Jean Todd, Aug. 15, 1959; children: Palma Elyse, Leslie Royce, Bradley Todd. BS, NYU, 1952, JD, 1958, LLM, 1959; postgrad., Air War Coll., 1976. Bar: N.Y. 1959, U.S. Supreme Ct. 1962, Conn. 1964. Legis. tax atty. legis. and regulations div. Office Chief Counsel, IRS, Washington, 1959-63; atty. Travelers Ins. Co., Hartford, Conn., 1963-68; assoc. counsel Travelers Ins. Co., Hartford, 1968-73, counsel, 1973-75, assoc. gen. counsel, 1975-87, dep. gen. counsel, 1987-93; mem. adv. coun. Hartford Inst. on Ins. Taxation, 1978-93, vice chmn., 1991-92, chmn., 1992-93. Grad. editor NYU Tax Law Rev., 1958-59. Trustee Hartford Coll. for Women, 1985-91; life sponsor Am. Tax Policy Inst. Served to col. USAFR. Kenneson fellow NYU, 1958-59. Fellow Am. Coll. Tax Counsel; mem. ABA (chmn. ins. cos. com. 1976-78), Am. Coun. Life Ins. (chmn. co. tax com. 1982-84), Am. Ins. Assn. (chmn. tax com. 1979-81), Assn. Life Ins. Counsel (chmn. tax sect. 1991-93), Twentieth Century Club, Sea Pines Country Club. Democrat. Jewish.

PUTMAN, (JAMES) MICHAEL, lawyer; b. San Antonio, May 12, 1948; s. Harold David and Elizabeth Finley (Henderson) P.; m. Kris J. Bird. B.B.A., S.W. Tex. State U., 1969; J.D., St. Mary's U., 1972. Bar: Tex. 1972, U.S. Dist. Ct. (we. dist.) Tex. 1980, U.S. Ct. Appeals (5th and 11th cirs.) 1981; cert. personal injury trial law specialist Tex. Bd. Legal Specialization. Ptnr. Putman & Putman (inc. 1981), San Antonio, 1972-81, officer, dir., 1981—. Mem. ATLA, State Bar Tex., Nat. Employment Lawyers Assn., Tex. Trial Lawyers Assn. (assoc. dir. 1995, dir. 1996), San Antonio Trial Lawyers Assn. (dir., officer 1975—), Am. Bd. Trial Advocates. Office: Tower Life Bldg Fl 27 San Antonio TX 78205

PUTNAM, JOANNE WHITE, college financial aid administrator, bookkeeper; b. Chattanooga, Nov. 27, 1945; d. Joseph Mitchel and Virginia (Spencer) White; m. Richard Wocester Putnam, Dec. 23, 1967; children: Joseph Worcester, Charles Jason. BS, Emory U., 1967. Sci. programmer Lockheed Ga. Co., Marietta, Ga., 1967-71; bookkeeper Dr. Richard Worcester Putnam, Blairsville, Ga., 1973—; admissions staff Young Harris (Ga.) Coll., 1984-86, dir. fin. aid, 1986—. Contbr. articles to profl. jours. Mem. Union County Hist. Soc., 1980—, Creative Study Club, Atlanta, 1976—; youth advisor Sharp Meml. United Meth. Ch., 1991-93. Mem. Ga. Student Fin. Aid Adminstrs. (program com. 1989-90, nominating com. 1988-89), So. Assn. Student Fin. Aid Adminstrs., Nat. Assn. Student Fin. Aid Adminstrs., Garden Club of Ga. Inc. (chmn. hydroponics 1979-81, chmn. horticulture 1981-83, dir. laurel dist. 1983-85, chmn., advisor laurel dist. 1985—), Nat. Coun. State Garden Club Inc. (master flower show judge 1989—, landscape design critic 1985—, gardening cons. 1985—), Blairsville Garden Club (pres. 1977-79, awards and legislation chmn. 1989-93). Home: PO Box 2059 Blairsville GA 30514 Office: Young Harris Coll PO Box 247 Young Harris GA 30582-0247

PUTNAM, KIMBERLY ANN, freelance writer, editor; b. Findlay, Ohio, May 28, 1959; d. George Glenwood and Dorothy Marie (Smith) Gochenauer; m. Mike D. Putnam, Mar. 9, 1980; 1 child, Jack E. BA in English, U. Findlay, 1982. Asst. editor ASHRAE, Atlanta, 1984-85; editor Profl. Publs., Atlanta, 1985-88; mktg. coord. Assoc. Regional Acctg. Firms, Atlanta, 1988-89; freelance writer and editor, Atlanta, 1989—; mktg. cons. for med. practices, 1991-93; editor Physician's Mktg. and Mgmt., Atlanta, 1990-92, Med. Practice Mgmt. Assn., Atlanta, 1992-93. Ghostwriter: The Economic Case for Growth through Acquisition and Merger, 1992; editor: Georgia-Pacific brochures and newsletters, 1992-93; writer CPA Mkty. Report, CPA Pers. Report, 1994—. Democrat. Presbyterian. Home and Office: 3465 Plantation Rdg Acworth GA 30101-4375

PUTT, B. KEITH, religion educator; b. Corinth, Miss., May 26, 1955; s. Billy C. and Era Mae (Spencer) P.; m. Sherry R. Burns, Aug. 3, 1974; children: Jonathan, Christopher. BA, Blue Mountain Coll., 1977; MDiv, Southwestern Sem., 1980; MA, Rice U., 1990; PhD, 1995. Doctoral adj. Southwestern Sem., Ft. Worth, 1981-83; asst. prof. religion Houston Bapt. U., 1984-90; assoc. prof. Southwestern Bapt. Theol. Sem., Ft. Worth, 1990—; interim pastor Lakeside Bapt. Ch., Houston, 1986-88, First Bapt. Ch. Alief, Houston, 1989-90, Congress Ave. Bapt. Ch., Austin, 1994. Mem. Am. Acad. Religion, Nat. Assn. Bapt. Profs. of Religion, Soc. of Christian Philosophers. Home: 5806 Melstone Dr Arlington TX 76016-2757 Office: Southwestern Sem PO Box 22000 Fort Worth TX 76122

PYDYNKOWSKY, JOAN ANNE, journalist; b. Ft. Riley, Kans., Oct. 2, 1951; d. Fredrick Albert and Mary Elizabeth (O'Connor) Gadwell; m. Michael Stanley Pydyknowsky, Mar. 14, 1981; children: Deborah Findley, Alexandra Pydynkowsky, Royce. BA in Journalism, U. Ctrl. Okla., 1991, MEd in Journalism, 1993. Trust clk. Ill. Nat. Bank, Rockford, 1974-75; engring. aide Barber Colman, Rockford, 1976-77; draftsperson Gen. Web, Rockford, 1979-80, Keeson, Ltd., Rockford, 1981; editor Oklahoma City Marriage Encounter, 1988-89, 94-95; humor columnist UCO Vista, Edmond, Okla., 1990-91; city editor Guthrie (Okla.) Daily Leader, 1991-92; substitute tchr. Edmond (Okla.) Pub. Schs., 1993-94; with N.W. News, Piedmont, Okla., 1994-95, South Oklahoma City Leader, 1995-96; staff writer, columnist, reporter, photographer N.W. News, Piedmont-Surrey Gazette, Okarche Chieftain, Piedmont, 1996—; city editor Okarche Chieftain, Piedmont, 1996—; copywriter, cons., Edmond, 1991—, photographer, 1990—, cartoonist, 1984—, humorist, 1990—; columnist, contbg. writer N.W. News, Piedmont, Okla., 1994-95; reporter and assoc. editor: All About Kids/South Oklahoma City Leader, 1995-96. Asst. leader Boy Scouts Am., Edmond, 1993-95; league coach Young Am. Bowling Alliance, Edmond, 1993—; counselor Oklahoma City YWCA Rape Crisis, 1986-88; mem. Tiaras Jr. Women's Honor Soc., 1990-91; mem. selection com. Okla. Journalism Hall of Fame, 1990. Recipient awards State Fair of Okla., 1983-96, Feature Writing award Okla. chpt. Soc. Profl. Journalists, 1994, six awards, 1995; first place Feature Writing award, State Fair of Okla. Better Newspaper Contest, 1995. Mem. Soc. Profl. Journalists (pres. U. Ctrl. Okla. chpt. 1990, treas. 1989, 91), Kappa Tau Alpha. Roman Catholic. Home: 301 Reynolds Rd Edmond OK 73013-5121

PYLE, GERALD FREDRIC, medical geographer, educator; b. Akron, Ohio, Dec. 22, 1937; s. Russell Roy and Ruth (Martin) P.; m. Carole Wood, Aug. 29, 1959; children: Eric, Frances. BA, Kent State U., 1963; MA, U. Chgo., 1968, PhD, 1970. Cartographer, Rand McNally, Chgo., 1962-64; research geographer Ency. Britannica, Chgo., 1964-65; cartographer U. Chgo., 1965-70; asst. to full prof. U. Akron, Ohio, 1970-80; prof. geography and earth sci. U. N.C., Charlotte, 1980—; prof. health promotion, 1995—; vis. fellow Macquarie U., Sydney, Australia, 1988; research dir. Center for

Urban Studies, Akron, 1973-80; tech. dir. Akron Area Census File, 1974-80; vis. scholar U. S.C., 1977. Author: Heart Disease, Cancer and Stroke in Chicago, 1971, Spatial Dynamics of Crime, 1974, Applied Medical Geography, 1979, Diffusion of Influenza: Patterns and Paradigms, 1986, (with Shannon and Bashshur) The Geography of AIDS, 1990, (with Shannon) Medical Atlas of the Twentieth Century, 1993; sr. editor Med. Geography, Social Sci. and Medicine, 1977-84; book rev. editor Social Sci. and Medicine, 1990—. Recipient Scholars medal First Citizen's Bank, 1992. Grantee Ill. Regional Med., 1969, Law Enforcement Adminstrn. Agy., 1972, 74, NSF, 1979, 82, Nat. Geog. Soc., 1988, NRC, 1995. Fellow Ohio Acad. Sci.; mem. Assn. Am. Geographers (Rsch. Honors S.E. divsn. 1994), Nat. Council Geog. Edn., Phi Kappa Phi. Democrat. Anglican. Current work: Continued research in spatial diffusion of infectious diseases and the location of health care delivery facilities. Subspecialty: Regional epidemiology. Home: 9801 Belt Rd Midland NC 28107-9057 Office: U NC Dept Geography and Earth Sci Charlotte NC 28223

PYLE, THOMAS ALTON, instructional television and motion picture executive; b. Phoenix, Sept. 8, 1933; s. Thomas Virgil and Evelyn B. (Redden) P.; m. Victoria K. Bileck, Apr. 21, 1957; children: Pamela V., Brett T. BA, Ariz. State U., 1956. Freelance unit mgr. theatrical motion picture industry, N.Y.C. and L.A., 1956-60; v.p. sales Depicto Films Corp., N.Y.C., 1960-65; prodr. John Sutherland Prodns., N.Y.C. and L.A., 1965-67; v.p. mktg. Audio Prodns. Ednl. Svcs., N.Y.C., 1967-71; exec. v.p. Data Plex Systems, N.Y.C., 1971-74; divsn. pres., exec. prodr. Sterling Inst. Video Prodns., Washington, 1974-80; pres. Applied Video Concepts, Inc., Washington, 1980-83; pres., CEO Nat. Sci. Ctr. Found., Burke, Va., 1983-85; CEO Network for Instrnl. TV, Inc., Reston, Va., 1987—; active in new bus. and project fundraising; bd. dirs. Nati. ITFS Assoc., Cmty. Ednl. Svcs., Balt., So. Fla. Instrnl. TV, Delaware Valley Ednl. Telecomms. Network, Inc., St. Louis, Instrnl. Opportunities, Inc.; cons. Wireless Cable Industry, 1993—. Writer, dir., producer film on Pres. John F. Kennedy, 1962; producer film biography on Pres. Lyndon B. Johnson, 1964. V.p. Dexter Park Assn., Spring Valley, N.Y., 1968-74, Solaridge Cluster Assn., Reston, Va., 1990. Recipient 27 awards from nat. and internat. film and video festivals, also 2 Commendation awards White House, 2 Acad. award nominations. Mem. AAAS, Internat. Platform Assn., N.Y. Acad. of Scis. Republican. Methodist. Office: Network Instructional TV 11490 Commerce Park Dr Ste 110 Reston VA 20191-1532

PYLES, ADRIENNE MAUGHAN, elementary school educator; b. Birmingham, Ala., Sept. 6, 1967; d. Robert Ferrell and Margie Lynn (Anderson) Maughan. BS, U. Ala., 1993. Cert. tchr. class B. Sales assoc. Parisian, Inc., Hoover, Ala., 1986-89; sec. BMI Refractories, Birmingham, Ala., 1989-92; facilitator's aide Hoover City Schs., 1993-94, 4th grade tchr., 1994—; mem. sci. textbook and curriculum adoption com., Hoover, 1995-96; chairperson Profl. DEvel. Com., Hoover, 1995-96; various presentations. Mem. NEA, Ala. Edn. Assn., Ala. Aerospace Tchrs. Assn., Hoover Edn. Assn. (rep. 1995-96). Home: 2820 Bridlewood Ter Helena AL 35080 Office: South Shades Crest Elem Sch 3770 S Shades Crest Rd Hoover AL 35244-4123

QIAN, ZHAOMING, translator, critic, literature educator; b. Shanghai, China, July 25, 1944; s. Shaozhong Qian and Wenjing Chen; m. May Fang Wang, Jan. 1, 1969; children: Yuyan, Yuli. BA, Beijing Fgn. Studies U., 1967, MA, 1980; PhD, Tulane U., 1991. Editorial asst. Beijing Fgn. Studies U., 1984-86, asst. dir. translation studies, 1985-86, lectr. English, mng. editor, 1982-86; instr. English and Asian lit. Tulane U., New Orleans, 1986-91; asst. prof. English U. New Orleans, 1991-96, assoc. prof. English, 1996—. Author: Orientalism and Modernism: The Legacy of China in Pound and Williams, 1995; editor: Annotated Shakespeare: The Sonnets, 1990; contbr. articles to profl. jours. H. D. Fellow Beinecke Libr. Yale U., 1992-93. Mem. MLA, South Ctrl. MLA, Ezra Pound Soc., William Carlos Williams Soc., Wallace Stevens Soc. Office: U New Orleans Dept English New Orleans LA 70148

QUALEY, THOMAS LEO, JR., human services administrator; b. Kearny, N.J., Dec. 3, 1946; m. Jeanne P., Dec. 26, 1970; children: Kathlyn Jeanne, Theresa Marie. BA, Coll. Santa Fe, 1969; BSN, McNeese State U., 1986, MSN, 1995; MSHHA, U. Ala., Birmingham, 1975. Cert. gerontol. nurse, cert. nursing adminstr., advanced nursing facility adminstr. Health planner New Orleans Area Health Systems Agy.; adminstr. Oak Park Care Ctr., Lake Charles, La., Jefferson Davis Nursing Home, Jennings, La.; health care cons. Contbr. article to profl. jour. With U.S. Army, 1972-75. Fellow Royal Soc. Health; mem. Am. Coll. Health Care Adminstrs., Sigma Theta Tau (charter Kappa Psi chpt., v.p.). Home: 318 E Norwood Dr Jennings LA 70546-6028

QUALLS, CHARLES WAYNE, JR., veterinary pathology educator; b. Oklahoma City, Feb. 8, 1949; s. Charles Wayne and Mary Opal (Howard) Q.; m. Cheryl Lynn Lightfoot, Aug. 9, 1969; children: Kerry Lynn, Julie Elizabeth. BS, Okla. State U., 1971, DVM, 1973; PhD, U. Calif., Davis, 1980. Diplomate Am. Coll. Vet. Pathologists. Postdoctoral fellow U. Calif., Davis, 1973-77; asst. prof. La. State U., Baton Rouge, 1977-82; assoc. prof. Okla. State U., Stillwater, 1982-87, prof. vet. pathology, 1988—, acting head dept. vet. pathology, 1991-92. Mem. editl. bd. Jour. Toxicology and Environ. Health, Vet. Pathology, Bull. Environ. Toxicology; contbr. articles to profl. jours., chpts. to books. Grantee Dept. of Def., U.S. Army Rsch. and Engring. Program, others. Mem Soc. Toxicologic Pathologists, Soc. Environ. Toxicology and Chemistry, Internat. Acad. Pathology, Am. Vet. Med. Assn. (student sponsor 1983—), Phi Kappa Phi, Phi Zeta. Home: 3118 Timberlake Stillwater OK 74075 Office: Okla State U Dept Vet Pathology Stillwater OK 74078

QUALLS, ROBERT GERALD, ecologist; b. Boone, N.C., May 20, 1952; s. Edward Spencer Qualls and Lynn Brown Heffner. MPH, U. N.C., 1981; PhD, U. Ga., 1989. Rsch. assoc. U. N.C., Chapel Hill, 1979-83; asst. rsch. prof. Duke U., Durham, N.C., 1989-96; asst. prof. dept. environ. and rsch. sci. U. Nev., Reno, 1996—. Contbr. articles to profl. jours. NSF rsch. grantee, 1982, EPA acad. rsch. grantee, 1982; NSF Dissertation Improvement awardee, 1985; recipient Internat. Assn. on Water Pollution Founders award for best paper in Water Rsch., 1986. Mem. Soil Sci. Soc. Am., Ecol. Soc. Am. Presbyterian. Home: 5020 Ambrose Dr Reno NV 89509 Office: U Nev MS 199 Dept Environ & Rsch Sci Reno NV 89557

QUALLS, ROBERT L., manufacturing executive, banker, former state official, educator; b. Burnsville, Miss., Nov. 6, 1933; s. Wes E. and Letha (Parker) Q.; m. Carolyn Morgan, Feb. 10, 1979; 1 dau., Stephanie Elizabeth. BS, Miss. State U., 1954, MS, 1958; PhD, La. State U., 1962; LLD, Whitworth Coll., 1974; DBA (hon.), U. of the Ozarks, 1984. Prof., chmn. div. econs. and bus. Belhaven Coll., Jackson, Miss., 1962-66; asst. to pres. Belhaven Coll., 1965-66; asst. prof. finance Miss. State U., State College, 1967-69, adj. prof., 1969-73; sr. v.p., chmn. venture com. Bank of Miss., Tupelo, 1969-73; v.p. Wesleyan Coll., Macon, Ga., 1974; pres. U. of the Ozarks, Clarksville, Ark., 1974-79; mem. cabinet Bill Clinton Gov. of Ark., 1979-80; exec. v.p. Boatmen's Bank of Ark., Little Rock, 1980-85; chmn., CEO, dir. Boatmen's, Harrison, Ark., 1985-86; pres., dir. First Bank Fin. Services, Inc., 1980-85, Advt. Assocs., Inc., 1980-85; pres., chief oper. officer Baldor Electric Co., Ft. Smith, Ark., 1986—, CEO, 1992; mktg. cons. Ill. Central Industries, Chgo., 1964; mem. faculty, thesis examiner Stonier Grad. Sch. Banking, Rutgers U., 1973-86; mem. faculty Miss. Sch. Banking, U. Miss., 1973-78; course coordinator Sch. Banking of the South, La. State U., 1978-88, Banking Sch., Duke U., 1977; lectr. Southwestern Sch. Banking, So. Meth. U., 1983; adj. prof. bus. adminstrn. U. Central Ark., 1985-86. Author: Entrepreneurial Wit and Wisdom, 1986; co-author: Strategic Planning for Colleges and Universities: A Systems Approach to Planning and Resource Allocation, 1979; mem. editorial adv. bd.: Bank Mktg. Mag., 1984-86. Chmn. cmty. svc. and continuing edn. com. Tupelo Cmty. Devel. Found., 1972-73; mem. Miss. 4-H adv. coun., 1969; active Boys Scouts Am.; mem. Lee County Dem. Exec. Com., 1973-74; trustee Wal-Mart Found., 1975-79, Oklahoma City U., 1990-95; trustee, mem. exec. com. U. Ozarks, 1982-88; mem. Pres.'s Roundtable U. Ctrl. Ark., 1982-87; mem. exec. com. Coll. Bus. Adv. Bd., U. Ark., Little Rock, 1980-85; bd. dirs. U. Ark. Med. Sch. Found., 1991—, Ark. Inst., 1991-94, Associated Industries Ark., treas., 1993-94,v.p., 1994-95. Lt. AUS, 1954-56. Found. for Econ. Edn. fellow, 1964; Ford Found. faculty research fellow Vanderbilt U., 1963-64; recipient Pillar of Progress award Johnson County, 1977. Mem. Am. Bankers Assn. (mktg. planning and rsch. com. 1972-73), Ark. Coun. Ind. Colls. and Univs. (chmn. 1978-79), Johnson County C. of C. (pres. 1977), Fort Smith C. of C. (dir. 1995—), Blue Key, Omicron Delta Kappa, Delta Sigma Pi, Sigma Phi Epsilon (citation 1977), Masons (32 deg.), Clarksville Rotary (pres. 1979). Presbyterian. Office: Baldor Electric Co 5711 S 7th St Fort Smith AR 72901-8394

QUANT, HAROLD EDWARD, financial services company executive, rancher; b. Aug. 21, 1948; s. Harold Atwell and Dorothy Ann Quant; m. Michelle Bumpers, June 27, 1982; children: Andrew, Angela, Emily. BSBA, San Jose State U., 1976. Account exec. Dun & Bradstreet, San Jose, Calif., 1970-81; pres. Telecredit Collection Svcs., Inc., L.A., 1981-85; v.p. FCA, Arlington, Tex., 1986-90; pres., CEO Creditwatch, Inc., Arlington, 1990—, chmn. bd. dirs. Sgt. USMC, 1965-70, Vietnam. Decorated Bronze Star, Purple Heart. Mem. City Club. Republican. Mem. United Ch. of God. Office: Creditwatch Inc 1200 E Copeland Rd # 400 Arlington TX 76011-2655

QUARLES, PEGGY DELORES, secondary school educator; b. Dalton, Ga., July 14, 1947; d. Henry Lemuel and Mae Bradford (Hester) Q. BA, Trevecca Nazarene Coll., 1969; MEd, U. Ga., 1981; EdS, West Ga. Coll., 1987. English tchr. Darlington County Schs., Lamar, S.C., 1969-78, Murray County Schs., Chatsworth, Ga., 1978—; mem. Shakespeare Inst., NEH, Washington, 1985, Writing Inst., Boulder, Colo., 1988, Italian Renaissance Inst., Del., Ohio and Florence, Italy, 1990, Women in Renaissance Inst., Richmond, Va., 1992. Vol. ARC, 1987—; mem. Dalton Little Theater, 1980—; bd. dirs. Friends of Libr., 1989-92. Named Tchr. of Yr., Murray County Bd. Edn., 1989. Mem. NEA, Nat. Coun. Tchrs. English, Ga. Coun. Tchrs. English (H.S. English Tchr. of Yr. 1994-95), Carpet Capital Running Club (pres. 1980-82, v.p. 1993-94), Lesche Literary Club.

QUATTLEBAUM, WALTER EMMETT, JR., telephone company executive; b. Midville, Ga., Dec. 22, 1922; s. Walter Emmett and Eva (Bagley) Q.; student Murrey Vocational Sch., Charleston, S.C., 1941, U. Hawaii, 1943; m. Dorothy Evelyn Clewis, Oct. 19, 1946; children: Walter Emmett III, Amalia Ann. Former owner Fla. Telephone Exchange, Sneads, Cottondale, Grand Ridge, Bonifay, Westville, and Seagrove Beach, Quattlebaum Telephone Supply Co., Quattlebaum Investments, also Spanish Trail Motel, Bonifay, Fla.; v.p., dir. Seminole Telephone Co., Donalsonville, Ga.; now investment analyst Quattlebaum Investments and others. Author: Journey of Intrigue and Success. City councilman, Sneads, 1950-52, pres. City Council, 1953. Served with AUS, 1944-46. Mem. Fla. Telephone Assn., Telephone Pioneers Am. Methodist. Office: Quattlebaum Investments PO Box 36 Bonifay FL 32425-0036

QUATTLEBAUM, WILLIAM FRANKLIN, lawyer; b. Bradenton, Fla., Apr. 10, 1953; s. Marion C. and Elizabeth Marie (Stephenson) Q. BS in Advt. and Comm. summa cum laude, U. Fla., 1975, JD, 1978. Bar: Fla., 1979. Atty. Fla. Dept. of Ins., Tallahassee, 1979-80; press sec. Richard Stone U.S. Senate Campaign, Tallahassee, 1980; atty. Fla. Ho. of Reps., Tallahassee, 1980-84; press sec., exec. asst. Fla. Dept. Banking and Fin., Tallahassee, 1984-86; dep. mgr. Bob Graham U.S. Senate Campaign, Tallahassee, 1986; asst. dir. Fla. Health Care for the Uninsured, Tallahassee, 1987; adminstrv. law judge Fla. Div. Adminstrv. Hearings, Tallahassee, 1987—. Mem. Fla. Blue Key Club (pres.), Omicron Delta Kappa, Kappa Tau Alpha. Office: Divsn Adminstrv Hearings 1230 Apalachee Pky Tallahassee FL 32399-6577

QUENCER, ROBERT MOORE, neuroradiologist, researcher; b. Jersey City, Nov. 14, 1937; s. Arthur Bauer and Isabell (Moore) Q.; m. Christine F. Thomas, Sept. 16, 1972; children: Kevin, Keith. BS, Cornell U., 1959, MS, 1963; MD, SUNY, Syracuse, 1967. Diplomate Am. Bd. Radiology, Nat. Bd. Med. Examiners; cert. of added qualifications in neuroradiology. Intern Jackson Meml. Hosp., Miami, Fla., 1967-68; resident in radiology Columbia U., N.Y.C., 1968-71, fellow in neuroradiology, 1971-72; asst. prof. Downstate Med. Ctr., Bklyn., 1972-76; assoc. prof. U. Miami, 1976-79, prof., 1979-92, chmn., prof., 1992—, chief sect. neuroradiology, 1976-86, dir. divsn. magnetic resonance imaging, 1986-92; vis. prof. U. Tenn. Coll. Medicine, Memphis, 1982, Downstate Med. Ctr. Coll. Medicine, Bklyn., 1992, U. Vt. Coll. Medicine, Burlington, 1983, N.Y. Med. Coll., Valhalla, 1984, U. Va. Sch. Medicine, Charlottesville, 1984, U. Ky. Sch. Medicine, Lexington, 1985, Yale U. Sch. Medicine, New Haven, 1986, Columbia U. Sch. Medicine, N.Y.C., 1986, The Mayo Clinic & Found., Rochester, Minn., 1987, Med. Coll. Va., Richmond, 1988, U. Pa. Sch. Medicine, Phila., 1988, Harvard U. Sch. Medicine/Mass. Gen. Hosp., Boston, 1989, U. Conn., Farmington, 1990, Kumamoto, Japan, 1993, U. Man., Can., 1992; Phaler lectr. Phila. Roentgen Soc., 1995; dir. programs in dept. radiology U. Miami Sch. Medicine, 1984, 86, Med. Coll. Wis., Tucson, 1990, 92, Kauai, Hawaii, 1991, Whistler, B.C., 1990; guest lectr. at ASEAN Congress of Radiology, Malaysia, 1992, Royal Australia Radiology Soc., Brisbane, 1993; adv. cons. NIH, 1987, 90; sci. merit reviewer V.A., 1987; presenter, lectr. in field. Author: Neurosonography, 1988; dep. editor Am. Jour. Neuroradiology, 1984—; assoc. editor for neuroimaging Yearbook of Neurology and Neurosurgery, 1991—; book reviewer Am. Jour. Neuroradiology, 1984—, Paraplegia, 1989—, Radiographics, 1991—, Pediatrics, 1993—; mem. editorial bd. Jour. Clin. Neuro-Ophthalmology, 1980—; contbr. articles to profl. jours. Pres. Am. Soc. Neuroadiology, 1994-95; prin. investigator NIH Grant on imaging/pathology of spinal cord injury. Lt. (j.g.) USN, 1959-61. Fellow Am. Coll. Radiology, Am. Soc. Neuroradiology (pres. 1994-95, program com. 1985-89, 92, editl. com. 1984—, publs. com. 1984—); mem. AMA, Radiol. Soc. N.Am. (program subcom. on neuroradiology 1990-94), Southeastern Neuroradiol. Soc. (founder, pres. 1980-81, examiner for bd. certification in radiology and neuroradiology), Dade County Med. Assn., Soc. Chmn. Acad. Radiology Depts., Fla. Radiol. Soc. (magnetic resonance com. 1991-92), Alpha Omega Alpha. Office: U Miami 1150 NW 14th St Miami FL 33136-2137

QUENTEL, ALBERT DREW, lawyer; b. Miami, Fla., Nov. 27, 1934; s. Charles Edward Jr. and Alberta Amelia (Drew) Q.; m. Paula Staelin Hagar, Feb. 9, 1957; children: Albert D. Jr., Stephen C., Marshall Lee, Paul G., Peter E., Michael J. BA, U. Fla., 1956, JD with honors, 1959. Bar: Fla. 1959. Assoc. Mershon, Sawyer, Johnston, Dunwody & Cole, Miami, 1959-64, ptnr., 1965-71; princ. Greenberg, Traurig, Hoffman, Lipoff, Rosen & Quentel, P.A., Miami, 1971—. Editor-in-chief U. Fla. Law Rev., 1959; contbg. author: Florida Real Property Practice, 1965, Real Estate Partnerships Selected Problems and Solutions, 1991, Commercial Real Estate Finance, 1993. Mem. Gov.'s Growth Mgmt. Adv. Com., Tallahassee, 1985-87; bd. dirs. Nat. Parkinson Found., Miami, 1980—, v.p., 1985—. Mem. NRA (life 1989—), Am. Coll. Real Estate Lawyers, Urban Land Inst., Fla. Bar Assn. (chmn. pub. rels. com. 1970-72, chmn. editorial com. jour. 1972-73), Lions (pres. Key Biscayne, Fla. club 1973), Miami Club (pres. 1991-92), Bath Club, Blue Key, Beta Theta Pi (pres. local chpt. 1954-55), Phi Eta Sigma, Phi Kappa Phi. Republican. Congregationalist. Home: 3410 Poinciana Ave Miami FL 33133-6525 Office: Greenberg Traurig Hoffman Lipoff Rosen & Quentel PA 1221 Brickell Ave Miami FL 33131-3200

QUERBES, BETTY-LANE SHIPP, interior designer, real estate agent; b. Mayersville, Miss.; d. Byron Cadmus and MaryLucille (Lane) Shipp; m. Andrew C. Querbes Jr., Dec. 21, 1950; children: Renee Lane, Andrew IV, Maura Colette. Student, Centenary Coll., 1949-51, La. State U., Shreveport, 1972-74. Designer, salesperson Dunn Furniture Co., Inc., Shreveport, La., 1976; interior designer, buyer Dunn Furniture Co., Inc., 1977-82, advertising specialist, 1978-82; columnist, feature writer The Times, Shreveport, 1974-87; co-owner, designer Prothro-Querbes Interior Design, Shreveport, 1982—; real estate salesperson, Andrew Querbes, Jr., Inc., Shreveport, 1975—. Mem. orgnl. com. Live Oak Retirement Ctr., Shreveport; active lay resources task force First Meth. Ch. of Shreveport, 1989—, chair lay resources and leadership devel., 1991-92; sec. La. chpt. Am. Lung Assn., 1987-90, v.p., 1990-93, pres., 1993—; mem. Commn. for Bi-Centennial of Constn. of U.S., 1987-91; chmn. Mayor's Com. to Fight Veneral Disease, Shreveport; pub. rels. specialist Shreveport Mental Health Assn.; v.p. Caddo Bossier Day Care Assn.; treas. Jr. League Shreveport, pres. 1971-72; acquisitions chmn. Spring Street Mus., 1988-90, chmn. bd. dirs., 1990-94. Mem. Am. Soc. Interior Designers (v.p. No. La. assn. 1991-92, pres.-elect 1992—), DAR (pelican chpt.), Nat. Soc. Colonial Dames in Am. (sec. Shreveport com. 1987-90, co-chair Shreveport com. 1994—), Shreveport Med. Soc. (tobacco com.), Demoiselle Club Shreveport (past sec., chmn.), Cotillion Cub Shreveport (gen. chmn. 1977), Chi Omega Alumnae (past pres.). Democrat. Methodist. Home: 321 Corinne Cir Shreveport LA 71106-6003 Office: Prothro Querbes 7035 Sand Beach Blvd Shreveport LA 71105-4929

QUESTER, ALINE OLSON, research director, economist; b. Rockford, Ill., Feb. 9, 1943; d. Rudolph H. and Ethel M. (Hagge) Olson; m. George H. Quester, June 20, 1964; children: Theodore, Amanda. BA, Wellesley Coll., 1965; MA, Tufts U., 1968, PhD, 1976. Instr. in econs. Boston U., 1966-68; asst. prof. econs. SUNY, Cortland, N.Y., 1971-76, assoc. prof. econs., 1976-81; sr. economist Ctr. for Naval Analyses, Alexandria, Va., 1981-86, 87-92, rsch. dept. dir., 1992—; sr. staff economist Coun. Econ. Advisors, Exec. Office of the Pres., Washington, 1986-87. Mem. editl. bd. Social Sci. Quar., 1978—; contbr. articles to profl. jours. Mem. adv. bd. Women's Internat. Security, 1994—. Fellow Woodrow Wilson Found., 1966-68. Mem. Am. Econ. Assn., Mil. Operation Rsch. Soc., Phi Beta Kappa. Home: 5124 37th St N Arlington VA 22207-1862 Office: Ctr for Naval Analyses 4401 Ford Ave Alexandria VA 22302-1432

QUEVEDO, HECTOR ADOLF, operations research analyst, environmental scientist; b. Juarez, Mex., June 25, 1940; came to U.S., 1973; s. Robert and Margaret (Urias) Quevedo Endlich; m. Gloria Guijarro, June 2, 1971; children: Gloria, Hector. BA, U. Tex., El Paso, 1966; MS in Environ. Scis., U. Okla., 1972, PhD in Environ. Scis., 1977. Part-time instr. maths. U. Tex., El Paso, 1977-80; environ. engr. El Paso Natural Gas Co., 1978-79; systems analyst U.S. Army, White Sands Missile Range, N.Mex., 1980-84, Ft. Bliss, Tex., 1985—. Democrat. Home: 11148 Voyager Cove St El Paso TX 79936-3007

QUICK, EDWARD RAYMOND, museum director, educator; b. L.A., Mar. 22, 1943; s. Donald Russell Quick and Gertrude Ruth (Albin) Thornbrough; m. Ruth Ann Lessig; children: Jeannette Lee, Russell Raymond. BA, U. Calif., Santa Barbara, 1970, MA, 1977. Adminstr. supr. Civil Service, Santa Ana, Calif., 1971-75; sr. computer operator Santa Barbara Rsch. Ctr., 1975-77; asst. collections curator Santa Barbara Mus. Art, 1977-78; registrar Montgomery (Ala.) Mus. Fine Arts, 1978-80; asst. dir. Joslyn Art Mus., Omaha, 1980-85; dir. Sheldon Swope Art Mus., Terre Haute, Ind., 1985-95, Berman Mus., Anniston, Ala., 1995—; adv. Ind. Arts Commn., Indpls., 1986-91; mem. Arts in Pub. Places Commn., Terre Haute, Ind., 1986-93; bd. dirs. Arts Illiana, Terre Haute, 1986-91; pres. Friends Vigo County Pub. Libr., 1988-95, treas., 1990-93. Author: Code of Practice for Couriering Museum Objects, 1985, Gilbert Brown Wilson and Herman Melville's "Moby Dick", 1993, The American West in the Berman Collections, 1996; co-author: Registrars in Record, 1987. Bd. dirs. Vol. Action Ctr., Terre Haute, 1987-90, Terre Haute Cmty. Relief Effort for Environ. and Civic Spirit, 1989. With USAF, 1961-65, Air N.G., 1979-96. Mem. Am. Assn. Mus., Assn. Ind. Mus., Am. Assn. State and Local History, Internat. Coun. Mus., Rotary Internat., Alpha Gamma Sigma. Republican. Office: Berman Mus 840 Museum Dr PO Box 2245 Anniston AL 36202-6261

QUICK, JERRY RAY, academic administrator; b. Gosport, Ind., July 3, 1939; s. Waldo C. and M. Marguerite (Goss) Q.; m. Elizabeth Ahlemeyer, June 10, 1962; children: Patrick, Andrew. BS, Ind. State U., 1961; MS, Ind. U., 1965. Tchr., coach MSD Washington Twp., Indpls., 1961-63; assoc. dir. housing Ind. State U., Terre Haute, 1963-75; asst. v.p. Ctrl. Mich. U., Mt. Pleasant, 1975-85; assoc. vice chancellor for bus. Vanderbilt U., Nashville, 1985-89; v.p. fin. and adminstrn. U. Ala., Huntsville, 1989—; mem. task force U.S. Dept. Edn., Washington, 1981-84; mem. accreditation teams So. Assn. Colls. and Schs., 1993—. Contbr. articles to profl. jours. and chpts. to books. Bd. dirs. Better Bus. Bur., Nashville, 1988-89; active Mayor's Commn. on Efficiency, Nashville, 1989. Mem. Nat. Assn. Coll. and Univ. Bus. Officers (editl. bd. 1987-92), So. Assn. Coll. and Univ. Bus. Officers, Nat. Assn. Coll. Aux. Svcs., Ala. Assn. Coll. and Univ. Bus. Officers, Assn. Coll. and Univ. Housing Officers (pres. 1979-80), Huntsville C. of C., Rotary Club of Huntsville. Home: 2513 Garth Rd Huntsville AL 35801 Office: U Ala Huntsville MDH 131 Huntsville AL 35899

QUIDD, DAVID ANDREW, paralegal; b. Chicago Heights, Ill., Sept. 8, 1954; s. John Richard and Mary (Wingate) Q. BA in Polit. Sci., U. New Orleans, 1976; postgrad., La. State U., 1976-79; paralegal cert., U. New Orleans, 1990. Coord. vols. Carter/Mondale Re-election Commn., New Orleans, 1980; paralegal Kitchen & Montagnet, New Orleans, 1981-84, Herman, Herman, Katz & Cotlar, New Orleans, 1985-92; freelance paralegal Metairie, La., 1992—. Pres. Alliance for Good Govt., Jefferson Parish, La., 1982, Young Dems. La., 1975-77; mem. Jefferson Parish Dem. Exec. Com., 1983-87, 89-96, chmn., 1990-93, treas., 1994, vice chmn., 1995; mem. Dem. State Ctrl. Com., 1996—. Mem. Nat. Fedn. Paralegal Assns. (primary rep. 1995—), New Orleans Paralegal Asss. (treas. 1991-94). Roman Catholic. Home: 1141 Papworth Ave Metairie LA 70005-2338

QUIGLEY, JOHN FRANCIS, clergy member, minister; b. Wilmington, Del., Mar. 8, 1951; s. John Francis and Mildred Annette (Norstrom) Q.; m. Kerry Faith Clouse, Aug. 17, 1974; children: John Francis III, Erin Ruth, Brendan Charles. BA in Humanities, Belhaven Coll., 1986; MDiv, Reformed Theol. Seminary, Jackson, Miss., 1989. Ordianed to presbyn. ministry, 1994. Asst. pastor, dir. Christian edn. First Presbyn. Ch., Meridian, Miss., 1993-95; minister Ward Presbyn. Ch., Livonia, Mich., 1995—. With USAF, 1971-75. Republican. Presbyterian. Home: 32043 Maine St Livonia MI 48150 Office: Ward Presbyn Ch 17000 Farmington Rd Livonia MI 48154-2947

QUIGLEY, JOHN JOSEPH, special education educator; b. Auburn, N.Y., May 28, 1946; s. Thomas Edward and Mary Agnes (Brechue) Q.; m. Nancy Louise Crehan, June 7, 1969 (div. 1979); 1 child, Kris Renae. BS, U. Cen. Mich., 1970; MA, U. No. Colo., 1976. Cert. tchr., spl. edn. tchr., Fla. Tchr. of socially maladjusted Dade County Schs., Miami, Fla., 1970-71, tchr. of trainable mentally handicapped, 1971-74, tchr. profoundly mentally handicapped, 1974-75, tchr. multiply handicapped, hearing impaired, 1975-77, tchr. hearing-impaired total communication, 1977—; tchr. Habilitation for the Handicapped, Miami, 1972-81; cons. in trainable mentally handicapped curriculum devel., Duval County, Fla., 1973; master tchr. assoc. Gulfstream Elem. Sch., 1984-87; impact tchr. developer Dade Pub. Edn./Nat. Tchr. Network, 1991-92; adj. prof. U. Miami, 1991-92. Mem. Fla. Educators of Hearing Impaired, United Tchrs. Dade, Deaf Svc. Bur. Home: 10776 N Kendall Dr # 1 Miami FL 33176-1484 Office: Gulfstream Elem Sch 20900 SW 97th Ave Miami FL 33189-2354

QUILLEN, LLOYD DOUGLAS, oil and gas executive; b. Red House, Ky., Sept. 9, 1943; s. Carter Livingston and Irene (Bolson) Q.; m. Leslie J. Johnsen (div. Jan. 1980); children: Tracey, David; m. Debra Gale Wagner, Aug. 7, 1982; children: Justin, Meghan, Bradley. BA, U. Ky., 1965, JD, 1969; student, Emory U., 1966-67. Bar: Ky., 1970, Tex., 1986. Atty. Phillips Petroleum Co., Denver, 1970-76; mgr. real estate and claims Phillips Petroleum Co. Euro. Afr., London, 1976-79; dir. govt. and comml. affairs Phillips Petroleum Co. & Subs., Lagos, Nigeria, 1979-82; mgr. internat. gas devel. Phillips Petroleum Co., Bartlesville, Okla., 1982-84; dir. laws and regulations Phillips 66 Natural Gas Co., Bartlesville, Okla., 1984-88; mgr. bus. devel. and mktg. HUFFCO/VICO Indonesia Co., Jakarta, Indonesia, 1988-93; cons. Govt. of Nigeria, Lagos, 1977-82; gas cons. LNG/Internat. Gas, Houston, 1993—. Charter mem. Statue of Liberty Ellis Island Found., N.Y.C., 1983; pro bono counsel Landmark Preservation Council, Bartlesville, 1986-87, Washington County Sr. Citizens, Inc., Bartlesville, 1987—; cubmaster Boy Scouts Am. Recipient Speak Out award Am. Petroleum Inst., 1972; named to hon. order Ky. Cols., 1969. Mem. Ky. Bar Assn., Tex. Bar Assn., Houston Vols. Lawyers Assn. Republican.

QUILLIAM, JAMES DAVID, air force officer; b. Niagara Falls, N.Y., Aug. 22, 1959; s. Reginald Joseph and Jacqueline Mary (Raleigh) Q.; m. Mary Kathleen Freedman Quilliam, July 15, 1995. BS in Bus. Adminstrn., Norwich U., Northfield, Vt., 1981; MBA, Fla. Inst. Tech., Melbourne, 1987; PhD in Indsl. Orgnl. Psychology, U.S. Internat. U., San Diego, 1995. Aircraft weapons sys. officer RF-4 USAF Tactical Squadron Reconnaissance, Zweibrucken Air Base, Germany, 1982-83; acquisition contracting officer USAF Eastern Space and Missile Ctr., Satellite Beach, Fla., 1984-87; edn. with industry USAF Exec. Internship Lockheed Corp., Sunnyvale, Calif.,

1988-89; acquisition contracting officer USAF Sec. of Air Force Spl. Projects, L.A., 1989-93; asst. prof. USAF ROTC Detachment 055 UCLA, L.A., 1993-95; flight comdr. strategic sys. USAF Quality Inst., Montgomery, Ala., 1995—. Contbr. articles to profl. jours. Maj. USAF, 1981—. Recipient Outstanding Faculty award U. Phoenix, Southern Calif., 1992. Mem. APA, Am. Soc. for Quality Control. Roman Catholic. Office: AFQI/DO 625 Chennault Cir Maxwell AFB AL 36112-6425

QUIN, JOSEPH MARVIN, oil company executive; b. Vicksburg, Miss., Aug. 18, 1947; s. Billy Henry Quin and Cele (Burdette) Peterson; m. Terry Gage, June 12, 1973; children—William C., Elizabeth G. B.B.A., U. Miss., 1969; M.B.A., U. Va., 1972. Dir. planning and devel. Ashland Chem. Co., Dublin, Ohio, 1978-81, adminstrv. v.p., 1981-83; treas. Ashland Oil Inc., 1983-87; adminstrv. v.p. fin., treas. Ashland Chem. Co., Ky., 1987-92, sr. v.p., CFO, 1992—; bd. dirs. Ashland Coal, Inc., AECOM, Inc., Ky. Electric Steel, Inc. Episcopalian. Office: Ashland Inc PO Box 391 Ashland KY 41105-0391

QUINN, CAROLYN ANNE, special education educator; b. Ft. Bragg, N.C., Oct. 13, 1950; d. John Arthur and Daisy (Brake) Cook; m. Daniel Dennis Quinn, Oct. 27, 1973; 1 child, Patrick Quinn. BS in Edn., Ga. So. U., 1972; MEd, Ga. State U., 1978. Tchr. Gracewood State Sch., Augusta, Ga., 1972-74; tchr. Gwinnett County Pub. Schs., Lawrenceville, Ga., 1974-78, instructional lead tchr., 1978—; bd. dirs. Gwinnett County Spl. Olympics, Lawrenceville (Spirit of Spl. Olympics award 1987); advisor Assn. Persons with Severe Handicaps, Atlanta, 1985—; advisor, bd. dirs. Autistic Group Tng. Home. Co-editor: (video tape) Assessing Severe Students, 1987. Active Leadership Gwinnett. Fellow Gwinnett Assn. Retarded Citizens (past pres. div. mental retardation 1983-85, T.W. Briscoe award 1988); mem. Ga. Coun. Exceptional Children (pres. 1987-90). Home: 2880 Brookside Run Snellville GA 30278-5943 Office: Suwanee Ctr 670 Highway 23 NW Suwanee GA 30174-2145

QUINN, CHARLES TREMAN, pediatrician; b. Phoenix, Nov. 26, 1968; s. Gary C. and Laela L. (Bell) Q.; m. Celia Jenkins, Nov. 4, 1995. BS, Tex. Christian U., 1990; MD, U. Tex., Dallas, 1994. Resident in pediatrics U. Tex. Southwestern Med. Ctr., 1994—. Mem. AMA, AAAS, Am. Acad. Pediatrics, Tex. Med. Assn., Dallas County Med. Soc., N.Y. Acad. Scis., Phi Beta Kappa, Alpha Omega Alpha. Home: 14332 Montfort Dr Apt 8407 Dallas TX 75240 Office: Children's Med Ctr 1935 Motor St Dallas TX 75235

QUINN, DAVID W., building company executive; b. 1942. BA, Midwestern U. Ptnr. Arthur Andersen, Dallas, 1967-84; COO Alpert Cos., 1984-87; exec. v.p. Centex Corp., Dallas, 1987—, also bd. dirs. Office: Centex Corp 3333 Lee Pky Dallas TX 75219-5111

QUINN, JANITA SUE, city secretary; b. Breckenridge, Tex., Apr. 14, 1950; d. Doyle Dean and Peggy Joyce (Melton) Allen; m. John Lloyd Rippy, June 27, 1969 (div. Mar. 1976); children: Johna DeAnn, Jason Allen; m. Ervel Royce Quinn, Jan. 31, 1987; stepchildren: Amy Talitha, Jason Ervel. Student, Odessa (Tex.) Jr. Coll., 1968-70, U. Tex. of Permian Basin, Odessa, 1978-79, 85-86. New accts. clk. State Nat. Bank, Odessa, Tex., 1975-76; accts. receivable clk. Woolley Tool Corp., Odessa, Tex., 1976-78; data entry operator M-Bank, Odessa, Tex., 1978-79; asst. county treas. Ector County, Odessa, Tex., 1979-83, county treas., 1983-88; office mgr., co-owner Nat. Filter Svc., Inc., San Antonio, 1988-91; temporary employment Kelly Temporary Svcs., Abilene, Tex., 1991; sec. Pride Refining, Inc., Abilene, Tex., 1991-93; city sec. City of Eastland, Tex., 1993—. Mem., treas., bd. dirs. Family Outreach Svc. Taylor County; vol. tchr. Parenting for Parents and Adolescents; recorder, del. West Tex. Corridor II Com., Eastland and Dallas, 1993; county del. Taylor County dem. Party, Abilene, 1992; state del. Tex. Dem. Party, Dallas, 1991; pres., charter mem. Bluebonnet chpt. City Secs. Region 6 Group, 1994-96. Named Outstanding Mcpl. Clk., Bluebonnet Chpt. Mcpl. Clks./Sec., 1994. Mem. Tex. Mcpl. Clks. Assn., Bluebonnet Chpt. Mcpl. Clks. (founder, pres. 1995—), County Treas. Alumni Assn. (recorder 1991-93), Rotary Internat. Democrat. Ch. of Christ. Office: City of Eastland 416 S Seaman St Eastland TX 76448-2750

QUINN, JOHN COLLINS, publishing executive, newspaper editor; b. Providence, Oct. 24, 1925; s. John A. and Kathryn H. (Collins) Q.; m. Lois R. Richardson, June 20, 1953; children: John Collins, Lo-anne, Richard B., Christopher A. A.B., Providence Coll., 1945; M.S., Columbia U. Sch. Journalism, 1946. Successively copy boy, reporter, asst. city editor, Washington corr., asst. mng. editor, day mng. editor Providence Jour.-Bull., 1943-66; with Gannett Co. Inc., Rochester, N.Y., 1966-90; exec. editor Rochester Democrat & Chronicle, Times-Union, 1966-71; gen. mgr. Gannett News Service, 1967-80, pres., 1980-88, v.p. parent co., 1971-75, sr. v.p. news and info., 1975-80, sr. v.p., chief news exec. parent co., editor USA TODAY, 1983-89; exec. v.p. Gannett Co., Arlington, Va., 1983-90; trustee Gannett Found., Arlington, 1988-91; trustee, dep. chmn. Freedom Forum, Arlington, 1991—. Named to R.I. Hall of Fame, 1975, Editor of Yr. Nat. Press Found., 1986; recipient William Allen White citation, 1987, Women in Communications Headliner award, 1986; Paul Miller/Okla. State U. medallion, 1988. Mem. AP Mng. Editors (past dir., nat. pres. 1973-74), Am. Soc. Newspaper Editors (dir., chmn. editorial bd., chmn. conv. program, nat. pres. 1982-83). Roman Catholic. Home: 365 S Atlantic Ave Cocoa Beach FL 32931-2719 Office: Freedom Forum 1101 Wilson Blvd Arlington VA 22209-2248

QUINN, JOHN MICHAEL, physicist, geophysicist; b. Denver, May 8, 1946; s. Leonard Simon and Winifred Ruth (Doolan) Q.; m. Pamela Dagmar Shield, May 28, 1983. BS in Physics, U. Va., 1968; MS in Physics, U. Colo., 1982. Physicist U.S. Naval Rsch. Lab., Washington, 1967-73; prin. engr. Singer Simulation Products, Silver Spring, Md., 1973-74; rsch. physicist U.S. Naval Rsch. Lab, Washington, 1979-80; geophysicist U.S. Naval Oceanog. Office, Stennis Space Ctr., Miss., 1974-79, 82-85, geophysicist, mathematician, 1985—; investigator Polar Orbiting Geomagnetic Survey Experiment, 1990—; prin. investigator Def. Meteorol. Satellite Program Polar Orbiting Geomagnetic Survey Ext., 1991—; chmn. com. on earth and planetary geomagnetic survey satellites Internat. Assn. Geomagnetism and Aeronomy, 1991—, mem. internat. geomagnetic ref. field com., 1989—. Author: Epoch World Geomagnetic Model, 1985, 90, 95. With U.S. Army, 1968-71. Mem. Am. Geophys. Union, Am. Math. Soc., European Geophys. Soc., Math. Assn. Am. Home: 2732 S Braun Way Lakewood CO 80228-4954 Office: US Geog Survey Magnetics Group Fed Ctr MS 966 Denver CO 80225-0046

QUINN, MICHAEL WILLIAM, public affairs specialist; b. Detroit, Apr. 26, 1949; s. Hubert James and Carolee (Sproull) Q.; m. Deborah Cooper, Feb. 11, 1978; children: Michelle Diane, Brooks William. BA in Journalism, U. S.C., 1975, M in Mass Communications, 1976. Pub. info. officer USAR, Ft. Jackson, S.C., 1977-79, chief command info. div., 1979-85; pub. affairs officer IRS, Columbia, S.C., 1985—; instr. Midlands Tech. Coll., Columbia, 1976-80; adj. prof. U. S.C., 1991—. Maj. USAR, 1968—. Mem. Pub. Rels. Soc. Am. Democrat. Methodist. Office: IRS 1835 Assembly St Columbia SC 29201-2430

QUINN, ROBERT WILLIAM, physician, educator; b. Eureka, Calif., July 22, 1912; s. William James and Norma Irene (McLean) Q.; student Stanford U., 1930-33; M.D., C.M., McGill U., 1938; m. Julia Rebecca Province, Jan. 21, 1942 (dec. Apr. 1994); children—Robert Sean Province, Judith D. Rotating intern Alameda County Hosp., Oakland, Calif., 1938-39; postgrad. tng. internal medicine U. Calif. Hosp., San Francisco, 1939-41, research fellow internal medicine, 1940-41; postgrad. tng. internal medicine Presbyn. Hosp., N.Y.C., 1941-42; research fellow Yale U., 1946- 47, instr. preventive medicine, 1947-49; assoc. prof. preventive medicine and student health U. Wis., 1949-52; prof., head dept. preventive medicine and public health Vanderbilt U., 1952-80, emeritus prof., 1980; dir. venereal disease and tuberculosis control Met. Nashville Health Dept. Bd. dir. Planned Parenthood Assn. Nashville; adv. com. Family Planning Tenn. and Nashville; vol. Vanderbilt U. Vets. Med. Ctr., 1992, Teen Clinic Nashville Planned Parenthood Assn., 1992-93. Served as capt. M.C., USN, 1942-46, USNR 1946-77. Diplomate Am. Bd. Preventive Medicine. Mem. Am. Acad. Preventive Medicine, Infectious Diseases Soc. Am., Middle Tenn. Heart Assn. (pres. 1957), Assn. Am. Med. Colls., Nashville Acad. Medicine, Assn. Tchrs. Preventive Medicine, Am. Public Health Assn., Am. Epidemiol. Soc., Am. Venereal Disease Assn., Physicians for Social Responsibility (pres. Greater Nashville chpt.). Club: Belle Meade Country. Author med. articles. Home: 508 Park Center Dr Nashville TN 37205-3430

QUINN, SONDRA, science center executive. BA, Pa. State U., 1962; MEd, U. Pitts., 1965; postgrad., U. Calif., Berkeley, 1986. Pres. Orlando (Fla.) Sci. Ctr., Inc.; mem. Fla. Sci. Edn. Improvement Adv. Com.; advisor scholastic sci. project Scholastic, Inc.; former chair steering com. Ctrl. Fla. Non-Profit Group for Quality Improvement; mem. rev. panel NSH, NEH, Inst. Mus. Svcs., Dept. Energy, Fla. Divsn. Cultural Affairs Sci. Mus. Programs. Mem. bus. leadership Orlando City of Light Program; active Art Svcs. Coun., Boy Scouts Am., State of Fla. Task Force for Comprehensive Plan to Improve Math., Sci. and Computer Edn. Recipient Cmty. Leader of Yr. award, Woman of Yr. award in Arts and Culture Phi Delta Kappa, 1995. Mem. Fla. Assn. Mus. (past bd. dirs., regional membership coord., head sci. sect., Mus. Svc. Lifetime achievement award 1996), Am. Assn. Mus. (bd. dirs. 1992-95, various coms.), Assn. Sci. and Tech. Ctrs. (bd. dirs., chair exhibit svcs. com., former chair new and developing mus. com., program com., human resources com., former v.p. small mus.). Office: Orlando Sci Ctr Inc 777 E Princeton St Orlando FL 32803

QUINN-MUSGROVE, SANDRA LAVERN, political science educator; b. Grand Rapids, Mich., Oct. 30, 1935; d. Rex Earl and Lavern Emaline (Conner) Nowland; m. James Fenton Arbing, July 16, 1954 (div. 1966); m. C. John Quinn, Nov. 16, 1966 (div. 1986); children: Joan B., John J., Jane M., Julie T., Sandra M.; m. Freddy G. Musgrove, Oct. 24, 1986. BA, U. Las Vegas, 1975, MA, 1976; PhD, Claremont Grad. Sch., 1978. Interior decorator Montgomery Ward, Grand Rapids, 1964-66; mdse. specialist Montgomery Ward, N.Y.C., 1966-72; asst. community affairs dir. Sta. KORK-TV, Las Vegas, 1975-76; exec. officer Norman Kaye R.E. Inc., Las Vegas, 1976-78; dir. edn., writer Polit. Rsch., Dallas, 1978-80; prof., dept. chmn. San Jacinto Coll., Houston, 1980-88, dir., 1985—; prof. Our Lady of Lake U., San Antonio, 1988—; mem. speaker's bur., 1980—; dir. Friendswood Indsl. Devel. Corp., Texas; ptnr. QUIMUS, Tri-County Analysts, Friendswood, 1984—. Co-author: America's Royalty: All the Presidents Children, 2d edit., 1995, How to Pass An Essay Exam, 1983, Texas Government: Its Moral Foundations, 1993, Auctions for Amateurs, 1993; (newspaper columns) On Education, 1984-92, Jus' Thinking 'bout, 1992—, How to Pass Objective Exams, 1991; contbr. articles to profl. jours. Program dir. Am. Bus. Women's Assn., Pearland, Tex., 1982-83; founder Friendswood Literary Forum, 1980; del. Rep. Nat. Conv., 1981; bd. dirs. Ft. Sam Houston Comml. Dist. Commn. Recipient Outstanding Member award Multiple Sclerosis Assn., Las Vegas, 1977. Mem. AAUP (pres.), Southwestern Social Scis. Assn., Women in Polit. Sci., Southwest Humanities Assn., Southwest Polit. Sci. Assn. Roman Catholic. Home: 6209 Warlodge San Antonio TX 78238 Office: Our Lady of the Lake U 24th St San Antonio TX 78285

QUINTANA, ROLANDO, industrial engineer; b. Havana, Cuba, Feb. 13, 1958; came to U.S., 1962; s. Rolando Pascual and Hilda (Davila) Q.; m. Maria del Carmen Ochoa, June 29, 1991. BS, U. Tex., El Paso, 1985, MS in Engring., 1986; PhD in Engring., N.Mex. State U., 1995. Registered profl. engr., Tex.; cert. quality engr. Mech. estimator, safety cons. El Paso, 1980-84; indsl. engr., tech. writer Allen Bradley Co., El Paso, 1986; ops. rsch. analyst U.S. Civil Svc., Ft. Bliss, Tex., 1986-90; instr. computer info. sys. El Paso C.C., 1990—; adj. prof. indsl. engring. U. Tex., El Paso, 1992—; evaluator NSF, Washington, 1993; methods and ergonomics track chmn., speaker Ann. Border Conf. on Mfg. and Environment, El Paso, 1993. Author: Interactive Bus Scheduling System, 1986 (Nick Hoage award 1987), (computer software) Tiempo-A Time Study Management System, 1988, Systematic Performance Rating, 1993. Active Mex.-Am. Legal Def. and Edn. Fund, El Paso, 1993, Flood Damage Prevention Bd. Appeals, El Paso, 1993, Tex. Alliance of Chicanos in Higher Edn., El Paso, 1993. Recipient Nat. Intelligence Cert. Distinction, Def. Intelligence Agy./CIA, 1992. Mem. NSPE, Inst. Indsl. Engrs. (sr., treas., bd. dirs. 1992-93), Am. Soc. Quality Control, Am. Soc. Safety Engrs., Data Processing Mgmt. Assn. (v.p. 1993), Tex. Soc. Profl. Engrs. Democrat. Roman Catholic. Office: El Paso C C 915 Hunter Dr El Paso TX 79915-1914

QUIRANTES, ALBERT M., lawyer; b. Cuba, Jan. 25, 1963; came to U.S., 1966; s. Alberto adn Haydee (Mendez) Q. B in Bus., U. Miami, Fla., 1984; JD, U. Fla., 1987. Bar: Fla. 1988, U.S. Dist. Ct. (so. dist.) Fla. 1990, U.S. Dist. Ct. (mid. dist.) Fla. 1990, U.S. Ct. Appeals (11th cir.) 1990, U.S. Supreme Ct. 1991, U.S. Dist. Ct. Ariz. 1991. Pub. defender Ct. 8th cir., Gainsville, Fla., 1988-89; pvt. practice Miami, Fla., 1989—; sr. ptnr. Ticket Law Ctr., P.A., Miami, Fla., 1990—. Mem. Fla. Traffic Ct. Rules Com., Tallahassee, 1991—. Mem. Fla. Assn. Criminal Def. Attys., Dade Bar (cts. com. 1992—, criminal cts. com. 1992—), Latin C. of C., Jaycees. Home and Office: 1800 NW 7th St Miami FL 33125-3504

QUIRK, KENNETH PAUL, accountant; b. Lake Charles, La., Aug. 29, 1953; s. Charles Patrick and Helen (Lejeune) Q.; m. Teresa Ann Tucker, Mar. 26, 1982 (div. Mar. 1988); 1 child, Heather Marie. BS in Acctg., McNeese State U., 1978; postgrad. MBA on-line, U. Phoenix, 1995—. CPA, La. Staff acct. Quirk, Cargile, Hicks & Reddin, Lake Charles, 1979-80, Browning-Ferris Industries, Lake Charles, 1980-81, La. Savs. Assn., Lake Charles, 1981-90, Calcasieu Marine Nat. Bank, Lake Charles, 1990-96, Hibernia Nat. Bank, Lake Charles, 1996—. Author fin. acctg. software sys. Mem. Young Men's Bus. Club, Lake Charles, 1986-90, Girl Scouts U.S., Lake Charles, 1989-90. Mem. AICPA, Soc. La. CPAs, Assn. for Computing Machinery. Republican. Episcopalian.

QUITERIO, MANUEL LAWRENCE, III, army officer; b. Hartford, Conn., July 11, 1958; s. Manuel Lawrence and Eva (Vincente) Q.; m. Helen Sian Jones, June 5, 1982; children: William Peter, Megan Rose. BA in Internat. Rels., U. Conn., 1980, MA in L.Am. Studies, 1981; postgrad., Command & Gen. Staff Coll., 1990; MS in Strategic Intelligence, Joint Mil. Intelligence Coll., Washington, 1995. Commd. U.S. Army, 1980—, advanced through grades to maj., 1993; tng. officer D-29 Attack Helo Battalion, Ft. Campbell, Ky., 1985-86; attack sect. leader 1-101 Attack Helo Bn., Ft. Campbell, 1986-87, asst. ops. officer, 1987-88; battalion ops. officer 1-126 Attack Helo Bn., Quinset Point, R.I., 1988-89; co. comdr. 1-126 Attack Helo Bn., Quonset Point, R.I., 1989-90; battalion logistics officer S4 1-126 Attack Helo Bn., Qu0nset Point, R.I., 1990-91; tng. officer Combat Aviation Brigade - CATB, Ft. Hood, Tex., 1991-94; aviation liaison officer ARNG Readiness Ctr., Arlington, Va., 1995—. Mem. Assn. U.S. Army, Army Aviation Assn. Am., Army N.G. Assn. (life). Republican. Episcopalian. Home: 4510 Gilbertson Rd Fairfax VA 22032 Office: Army National Guard Readiness Ctr 111 S George Mason Dr Arlington VA 22204

RABIDEAU, PETER WAYNE, university dean, chemistry educator; b. Johnstown, Pa., Mar. 4, 1940; s. Peter Nelson and Monica (Smalley) R.; m. Therese Charlene Newquist, Sept. 1, 1962 (div.); children—Steven, Michael, Christine, Susan; m. Jennifer Lee Mooney, Nov. 15, 1986; children: Mark, Leah. B.S., Loyola U., Chgo., 1964; M.S., Case Inst. Tech., Cleve., 1967; Ph.D., Case Western Res U, Cleve., 1968. Postdoctoral asst. U. Chgo., 1968-69, instr., 1969-70; asst. prof. Ind. U.-Purdue U., Indpls., 1970-73, assoc. prof., 1973-76, prof., 1976-90, chmn. dept. chemistry, 1985-90; dean Coll. Basic Scis. La. State U., Baton Rouge, 1990—; program officer NSF, 1988-89. Contbr. numerous articles to profl. jours. Recipient research award Purdue Sch. Sci. at Indpls., 1982. Mem. AAAS, Am. Chem. Soc. (chmn. Ind. sect. 1974, councilor 1981-90). Home: 15160 Old Oak Ave Baton Rouge LA 70810-5546 Office: La State U Office of the Dean 338 Choppin Baton Rouge LA 70803

RABIN, ALAN ABRAHAM, economics educator; b. N.Y.C., June 16, 1947; s. Sidney and Claire R. B.A., Hamilton Coll., 1969; Ph.D., U. Va., 1977. NSF trainee U. Va., 1970-71, 71-72; intern Coun. Econ. Advisors, 1971; asst. prof. Calif. State U.-Northridge, 1973-74, Georgetown U., Washington, summer 1975; asst. prof. econs. U. Tenn.-Chattanooga, 1977-81, assoc. prof., 1981-86, prof., 1986—. Contbr. articles to profl. jours. NDEA fellow, 1969-70; U. Tenn.-Chattanooga faculty research grantee, 1982. Mem. Am. Econ. Assn., So. Econ. Assn., Atlantic Econ. Soc., We. Econ. Assn., U. Tenn. Chattanooga Council Scholars, Omicron Delta Epsilon. Jewish. Avocations: sports; stamp collecting; bridge. Home: 409 Cameron Cir Apt 806 Chattanooga TN 37402-1513 Office: U Tenn-Chattanooga Dept Economics Chattanooga TN 37403

RABINOWITZ, WILBUR MELVIN, container company executive, consultant; b. Bklyn., Feb. 18, 1918; s. Harry A. and Caroline (Simmons) R.; m. Audrey H. Perlmutter, Apr. 30, 1944; 1 child, Michael B. PhB, Dickinson Coll., 1940; JD, Harvard U., 1943. Gen. mgr. J. Rabinowitz & Sons, Inc., Bklyn., 1945-67; pres. J. Rabinowitz & Sons, Inc., 1967-81, pres. emeritus cons., 1981-95; pres. Met. Glass & Plastic Containers, 1967-81; trustee Mendeleyev U., Moscow, 1991—. Author: Almost Everywhere. Pres. Rabinowitz Found., N.Y.C., 1967—; trustee Dickinson Coll., Carlisle, Pa., 1975—. With AUS, 1943-45, ETO. Mem. Nat. Assn. Container Distbrs. (past pres.), U.S. Power Squadrons (past comdr.), Explorers Club, Marco Polo Club. Home: 2800 S Ocean Blvd Apt Phlm Boca Raton FL 33432

RABON, WILLIAM JAMES, JR., architect; b. Marion, S.C., Feb. 7, 1931; s. William James and Beatrice (Baker) R; m. Martha Ann Hibbitts, Mar. 7, 1987. BS in Arch., Clemson (S.C.) Coll., 1951; BArch, N.C. State Coll., 1955; MArch, MIT, 1956. Registered architect, Calif., Ky., N.C., Ohio, Pa., Ga. Designer archtl. firms in N.Y.C. and Birmingham, Mich., 1958-61; designer, assoc. John Carl Warnecke and Assocs., San Francisco, 1961-63, 64-66, Keyes, Lethbridge and Condon, Washington, 1966-68; prin. archtl. ptnr. A.M. Kinney Assocs. and William J. Rabon, Cin., 1968-85; v.p., dir. archtl. design A.M. Kinney, Inc., Cin., 1977-85; v.p., dir. programming svcs. Design Art Corp., 1977-85; sr. architect. John Portman & Assocs., Atlanta, 1985-88; dir. architectural design Robert and Co., Atlanta, 1988-89; studio dir., design prin. Carlson Assocs., Atlanta, 1990-93; prin. Rosser Internat., 1993—; lectr. U. Calif., Berkeley, 1963-65; asst. prof. archtl. design Cath. U. Am., 1967-68. Prin. works include Kaiser Tech. Ctr., Pleasanton, Calif. (Rsch. Devel. Lab. of Yr. award), 1970, Clermont Nat. Bank, Milford, Ohio, 1971, Pavilion bldg. Children's Hosp. Med. Ctr., Cin. (Cin. AIA design award), 1973, EG&G, Hydrospace, Inc., Rockville, Md. (Potomac Valley AIA design award), 1970, Mead Johnson Park, Evansville, Ind. (Rsch. Devel. Lab. of Yr. merit award), 1973, Hamilton County Vocat. Sch., Cin., 1972, hdqrs. lab. EPA, Cin., 1975, Arapahoe Chem. Co. Rsch. Ctr., Boulder, Colo. (Rsch. Devel. Lab. of Yr. award 1976, Concrete Reinforced Steel Inst. Nat. Design award, Regional AIA Design award), 1976, corp. hdqrs. Ohio River Co., Cin., 1977, Children's Hosp. Therapy Ctr., Cin. (Cin. AIA design award 1978, award of merit Am. Wood Council 1981), VA Hosp. addition, Cin. (Cin. ASHRAE Design award 1980), NALCO Chem. Co. Rsch. Ctr., Naperville, Ill. (Ohio and Cin. AIA design awards 1980, 81), 1980, Proctor & Gamble-Winton Hill Tunnel, Cin. (Ohio AIA design award), 1978, Toyota Regional Ctr., Blue Ash, Ohio (Ohio AIA and Ohio Masonry Council combined design award 1981), planning cons. Nat. Bur. Standards, Republic of China, 1982, East and West fleet hdqrs. and Data Ctr. Librs. of Royal Saudi Arabian Navy, 1985, corp. hdqrs. The Drackett Co., Cin., 1983, corp. hdqrs. Brown & Williamson, Louisville, 1984, Inst. Paper Sci. and Tech., Atlanta, 1989, 93, Animal Sci. Complex, Athens, Ga., 1996. 1st lt. AUS, 1951-53, Korea. Decorated Silver Star, Bronze Star with V device, Bronze Star, Purple Heart with bronze cluster; MIT Grad. Sch. scholar, 1956; Fulbright scholar, Italy, 1957-58. Mem. AIA, Nat. Council Archtl. Registration Bds.

RABOW, STEPHEN DOUGLAS, multimedia consultant, author, publisher; b. Buffalo, Aug. 28, 1953; s. Julian Marshal Rabow and Claire (Cantor) Grinberg; m. Kimberly Anne White, June 7, 1992; 1 child, Aaron Victor. BS, Evergreen State Coll., Olympia, Wash., 1978. Radio personality various radio stas., Seattle, 1978-86; nat. program dir. YESCO/Foreground Music, Seattle, 1981-83; ind. TV producer KCPQ-TV, Seattle, 1984-86; TV personality, producer WWSB-TV, Sarasota, Fla., 1986—; entertainment cons. Sarasota, 1986—, author, pub., 1991—; pres. Rabow Comm. Arts, Sarasota, 1991—. Author/editor (annually) Official Guidebook to Sarasota, 1992—, Suncoast Offshore Grand Prix, 1992—, (semi-annually) Official German Language Guidebook to Florida's West Coast, 1996—. Recipient Fla. Emmy award Nat. Acad. TV Arts and Scis., 1989, Nat. Iris award Nat. Assn. TV Programmers Internat., 1990. Office: Rabow Comm Arts PO Box 15332 Sarasota FL 34277

RABUN, JOSETTE HENSLEY, interior design educator; b. Wichita Falls, Tex.; m. John Stanley Rabun, June 4, 1960; children: John S. Jr., Julie Lynne. BEd, Midwestern State U., Wichita Falls, 1964; BS with honors, U. Tex., 1974; MS, U. Tenn., 1979, PhD, 1984; postdoctoral fellow, U. York, Eng., 1988. Registered interior designer. Grad. teaching asst. interior design and housing U. Tenn., Knoxville, 1978-79, instr. dept. textiles, merchandising and design, 1980-81, asst. prof., 1983-86, assoc. prof. textiles, retailing and interior design, 1988-96, assoc. prof., interior design program coord. interior design program Coll. Architecture & Planning, 1996—; asst. prof. interior design divsn. U. Tex., Austin, 1979-80; asst. prof. USIA faculty exch. program Yarmouk U., Irbid, Jordan, 1985; assoc. prof. dept. interior design Va. Commonwealth U., Richmond, 1987-88; interior designer Weiser/Cawley Interiors, Marietta, Ohio, 1975-76; ptnr. Design Affiliates, Inc., Knoxville, 1984; owner J.S. Rabun & Assocs., Knoxville, 1977-86, 88—; interior design cons. Yarmouk U., Irbid, 1986; interior cons. Loudon Heritage Assn., 1990, Revitalization Project for Downtown Loudon/Madisonville, Tenn., 1990, Comty. Design Ctr., Del Rio, Tenn., 1991, Renovation of Residence, Knoxville, 1993, Comty. Design Ctr., Knoxville, 1990—; co-presenter seminars on hist. preservation, Slovakia, Rumania, and Poland. Author: (with Robert Meden) Historic Preservation and Rehabilitation, 1992; contbr. chpt. (with Betty Treanor) Popular American Housing: A Reference Guide, 1995; contbr. articles to profl. jours., chpts. to books. Bd. visitors Found. Interior Design Edn. Rsch., 1984—. Co-recipient State Historic Preservation award State Daus. of Colonial Wars, 1984; recipient teaching and pub. svc. award U. Tenn., 1982, Faculty Rsch. award Coll. Human Ecology, 1986, 2d pl. award Nat. Trust Student Competition, 1991; grantee U. N.H., Durham, 1984, Historic Preservation for Revitalization of Elizabethton and Erwin, Tenn., 1991, Mabry-Hazen Hist. Found., Knoxville, 1993, U. Tenn., 1994. Mem. Am. Soc. Interior Designers (mem. several state chpts. 1991—, award for hist. preservation 1990, state ednl. award 1994), Interior Design Educators Coun. (fin. chairperson 1990, chairperson South region 1988-90, bd. dirs. 1988-90, mem. tenure and promotion com. 1986-90, continuing edn. unit internat. conf. 1995, 96, Presdl. citations 1991, 94), Nat. Coun. Interior Design Qualification (item writer and team leader theory and history 1993-94, coord. identification and application 1994—), Nat. Trust Hist. Preservation, Nat. Coun. Preservation Edn., Illuminating Engr. Soc., Phi Kappa Phi, Omicron Nu. Office: U Tenn Interior Design Program Coll Architecture & Planning 1700 Volunteer Blvd Knoxville TN 37996-2100

RACE, GEORGE JUSTICE, pathology educator; b. Everman, Tex., Mar. 2, 1926; s. Claude Ernest and Lila Eunice (Bunch) R.; m. Annette Isabelle Rinker, Dec. 21, 1946; children: George William Daryl, Jonathan Clark, Mark Christopher, Jennifer Anne (dec.), Elizabeth Margaret Rinker. M.D., U. Tex., Southwestern Med. Sch., 1947; M.S. in Pub. Health, U. N.C., 1953; Ph.D. in Ultrastructural Anatomy and Microbiology, Baylor U., 1969. Intern Duke Hosp., 1947-48, asst. resident pathology, 1951-53; intern Boston City Hosp., 1948-49; asst. pathologist Peter Bent Brigham Hosp., Boston, 1953-54; pathologist St. Anthony's Hosp., St. Petersburg, Fla., 1954-55; staff pathologist Children's Med. Center, Dallas, 1955-59; dir. labs. Baylor U. Med. Center, Dallas, 1959-86; chief dept. pathology Baylor U. Med. Center, 1959-86, vice chmn. exec. com. med. bd., 1970-72; cons. pathologist VA Hosp., Dallas, 1955-71; adj. prof. anthropology and biology So. Meth. U., Dallas, 1969; instr. pathology Duke, 1951-53, Harvard Med. Sch., 1953-54; asst. prof. pathology U. Tex. Southwestern Med. Sch., 1955-58, clin. assoc. prof., 1958-64, clin. prof., 1964-72, prof., 1973-94, prof. emeritus, 1994—, dir. Cancer Center, 1973-76, assoc. dean for continuing edn., 1973-94, emeritus assoc. dean, 1994—; pathologist-in-chief Baylor U. Med. Ctr., 1959-86, prof. biomed. studies Baylor Grad. sch., 1989-94; chmn. Baylor Rsch. Found., 1986-89; prof. microbiology Baylor Coll. Dentistry, 1962-68, prof. pathology, 1964-68, prof., chmn. dept. pathology 1969-73, dean A. Webb Roberts Continuing Edn., 1973-94; spl. advisor on human and animal diseases to gov. State of Tex., 1979-83. Editor: Laboratory Medicine (4 vols.), 1973, 10th edit., 1983; Contbr. articles to profl. jours., chpts. to textbooks. Pres., Tex. div. Am. Cancer Soc., 1970; chmn. Gov.'s Task Force on Higher Edn., 1981. Served with AUS, 1944-46; flight surgeon USAF, 1948-51, Korea. Decorated Air medal. Fellow Coll. Am. Pathologists, Am. Soc. Clin. Pathologists, AAAS; mem. AMA (chmn. multiple discipline research forum 1969), Am. Assn. Pathologists, Internat. Acad. Pathology, Am. Assn. Med. Colls., Explorer's Club (dir., v.p. 1993—), Sigma Xi. Home: 3429 Beverly Dr Dallas TX 75205-2928

RACE, GEORGE WILLIAM DARYL, psychiatrist; b. Dallas, Oct. 12, 1950; s. George Justice and Annette Isabel (Rinker) R.; m. Carol Diane Webb, Aug. 30, 1979 (div. Apr. 1985); 1 child, Christopher Ryan; m. Elizabeth Randolph Clopton Wallenstein, Oct. 1, 1989; stepchildren: Joshua C. Wallenstein, Eric L. Wallenstein. BA with honors, So. Meth. U., 1972; MD with high honors, U. Tex., Galveston, 1976. Diplomate Am. Bd. Psychiatry and Neurology; lic. physician, Tex. Resident in psychiatry Timberlawn Psychiat. Hosp., 1976-79; pvt. practice psychiatry and geropsychiatry Austin, Tex., 1979—; pres. Geropsych, Inc., Austin, 1989—; adminstrv. med. dir. Spl. Care program St. David's Pavilion, Austin, 1989—; med. dir. Spl. Care program Holy Cross Hosp., Austin, 1986-89; med. dir. Charter Lane Hosp., Austin, 1986-87, med. dir. adult psychiat. unit, 1986-87; med. dir. adult med./geropsychiat. program Shoal Creek Hosp., Austin, 1983-85; mem. behavioral sci. faculty Ctrl. Tex. Med. Found., 1988-90. Mem. adv. coun. Austin Groups for Elderly, 1991—; bd. dirs., past pres. Family Eldercare, 1984-86; mem. bd. Austin area Mental Health Assn., 1992—; mem. adv. com. Friends of St. David's, 1992-94; mem. Prodr.'s Cir. KLRU Pub. TV, 1991—; chmn. So. Meth. U. Alumni, Austin, 1994—. Recipient Recognition of Achievement award Family Eldercare of Austin, 1986. Fellow Am. Psychiat. Assn.; mem. AMA, Am. Coll. Physician Execs., Tex. Med. Assn. (aging and long term com. 1990—, chmn. 1991-92, physician health and rehab. com. 1990-92), Tex. Soc. Psychiat. Physicians (socioecons. com. and constn. and bylaws com. 1990-94), Tex. Geriatrics Soc., Ctrl. Neuropsychiat. Assn., Travis County Med. Soc. (bd. dirs. 1987-89, sec., treas. 1994—), Austin Psychiat. Soc., Westwood Country Club (Austin), Admirals Club (Austin), Austin Assembly, Bachelors Club Austin, Alpha Omega Alpha, So. Meth. Alumni Assn. (chmn. alumni group 1994—, bd. dirs. 1995—). Home: 1407 Wooldridge Dr Austin TX 78703-2529 Office: 720 W 34th St Austin TX 78705-1205

RACHMAN, BRADLEY SCOTT, chiropractic physician; b. Reading, Pa., July 23, 1961; s. Roger Stuart Rachman and Lanie Brenda (Chertok) Stuart; m. Amy Sue Rachman, Oct. 14, 1994; children: Nicole, Carly, Mackie. D of Chiropractic, Palmer U., 1986. Diplomate Nat. Bd. Chiropractic Examiners. Asst. dir. student affairs Palmer U., Davenport, Iowa, 1984-86; dir. Rachman Chiropractic, Ft. Myers, Fla., 1986—; dir. Multi-Disciplinary Symposium, Sanibel, Fla., 1989—; keynote speaker Am. Holistic Nurses Assn., Gainsville, Fla., 1988. Author: American Red Cross-Backtalk, 1987; (textbook) Peripheral Neurology Workbook, 1986. Dir. spinal health program ARC, Ft. Myers, 1987, also bd. dirs. H. Neilsen scholar, 1985. Mem. Fla. Chiropractic Assn. (dir. 1990-92), Tri-County Chiropractic Soc. (pres. 1990-91). Home: 8721 Cajuput Cv Fort Myers FL 33919-1843 Office: Rachman Chiropractic 12734 Kenwood Ln Ste 84 Fort Myers FL 33907-5638

RACINE, BRIAN STANLEY, telecommunications executive; b. Orange, N.J., Apr. 17, 1963; s. Franklin Louis R. and Joan Ann Pfeiffer. BA, Belmont Abbey Coll., 1986. Customer support rep. BTI, Raleigh, 1992-93, major acct. rep., 1993, project leader, 1993-96; project mgr. Fujitsu Network Comms., Raleigh, 1996—. Mem. AAAS, IEEE, Engring. Mgmt. Soc., Comms. Soc., Profl. Comm. Soc. Democrat. Roman Catholic. Home: 3210 J Walnut Creek Pkwy Raleigh NC 27606 Office: Fujitsu Network Comms 4403 Bland Rd Raleigh NC 27609

RACKERS, THOMAS WILLIAM, physicist; b. Ft. Thomas, Ky., Apr. 1, 1955; s. Paul William and Geraldine (Cox) R.; m. Thelma J. Cox, June 18, 1977; 1 child, Teresa Dawn. BA cum laude, Thomas More Coll., Ft. Mitchell, Ky., 1975; MS, Ohio State U., 1977, PhD, 1984. Rsch. assoc. dept. physics Ohio State U., Columbus, 1981-84; rsch. physicist rsch. and technol. dept. Naval Coastal Sys. Ctr., Panama City, Fla., 1984-91; rsch. physicist coastal rsch. and tech. dept. NSWC Coastal Systems Sta., Panama City, 1992—; mem. exec. comms. North Am. Data Gen. Users Group, co-chmn. Cent. Ohio Users of Data Gen. Equipment, Columbus, 1981-84; ind. computer cons. Judge Three Rivers Sci. and Engring. Fair, Panama City, 1985-89; vol., actor Kaleidoscope Theatre, Panama City, 1987—, bd. dirs., 1994—; active mentor program Jr. Mus. Bay County, Fla., 1988-89; guitarist St. John the Evangelist Cath. Ch. Folk Choir, Panama City, 1984—, co-dir., 1990-94, dir., 1995—; sec. Long Glass Youth Bowling League, 1993-94. Mem. Mensa, Bay Line Model R.R. (Panama City condr. 1987-89), St. Andrews Bay NTRAK (chmn. 1989-90), Sigma Pi Sigma. Roman Catholic. Home: 2012 Pattho Ln Lynn Haven FL 32444-5411 Office: NSWC Coastal Systems Sta Code 120B Panama City FL 32407-7001

RACKIN, MARK HENRY, electrical engineer; b. Jersey City, Mar. 4, 1944; s. Harold and Anne (Shafir) R.; m. Irene Gottlieb, Aug. 26, 1967; children: Philip Daniel, Mitchell George. Student, MIT, 1961-63; BSEE, Newark Coll. Engring., 1966; MSEE, Northwestern U., 1968. Registered profl. engr., Fla. Electronics engr. Hewlett-Packard, Berkeley Heights, N.J., 1966; from sr. engr. to group leader Motorola, Inc., Chgo., Plantation, Ill., Fla., 1967-80; sys. mgr. Siemens Telecom., Boca Raton, Fla., 1980-82; chief engr. Solid State Sys., Atlanta, 1982-90; tech. dir. Cortelco,Inc., Atlanta, 1991-93; v.p. engring. Arnica, Inc., Dallas, 1993, Pelican Sys. Group, Inc., Norcross, Ga., 1993—. Inventor in field with patents. Mem. IEEE, Am. Radio Relay League.

RADER, STEVEN PALMER, lawyer; b. Charlotte, N.C., Dec. 30, 1952; s. Alvin Marion Jr. and Shirley Ninabelle (Palmer) R. AB, Duke U., 1975; postgrad., Stetson U., 1975-76; JD, Wake Forest U., 1978. Bar: N.C. 1978, U.S. Dist. Ct. (ea. dist.) N.C. 1979. Assoc. Wilkinson and Vosburgh, Washington, N.C., 1978-81; pvt. practice Washington, 1981-88; spl. asst. to sec. N.C. Dept. Human Resources, Raleigh, 1988-89, asst. dir. office legal affairs, 1989-91, gen. counsel, 1991-93; ptnr. Wilkinson & Rader, P.A., Washington, 1993—; commr. Nat. Conf. on Commrs. of Uniform State Laws, 1985-93; gen. counsel N.C. Rep. Party, 1992—. Mem., sec. City of Washington Human Rels. Coun., 1981-83; chmn. Beaufort County Rep. party, Washington, 1983-87, 1st Congl. Dist. Rep. party, N.C., 1985-92; v.p. East Main St. Area Neighborhood Assn., 1983-85. Mem. N.C. State Bar, 2d Jud. Dist. Bar, Beaufort County Hist. Soc. (v.p. 1981-85, pres. 1985-86). Lutheran. Home: PO Box 1901 Washington NC 27889-1901 Office: Wilkinson & Rader PA PO Box 732 Washington NC 27889-0732

RADER, TODD DAVID, elementary education educator; b. Morganton, N.C., Aug. 6, 1966; s. David Berry and Betsy Elizabeth (Hutchins) R. Degree in elem. edn., Warren Wilson Coll., 1994. Cert. elem. tchr. Instr. Presbyn. Learning Ctr., Morganton, N.C., 1983-94; attendant Warren Wilson Day Care, Savannah, N.C., 1990; tchr., maintenance worker Early Learning Ctr., Savannah, 1991-92; tchr. 3d grade Burke County Pub. Schs., Rutherford College, N.C., 1994—. Democrat. Presbyterian. Home: 716 D W Union St Morganton NC 28655

RADEWAGEN, AMATA COLEMAN, government affairs advisor, advocate; b. Dec. 29, 1947; d. Peter Tali and Nora (Stewart) Coleman; m. Fred Radewagen, Dec. 4, 1971; children: Erika, Mark, Kristen. BS, U. Guam, 1975. Exec. sec. Office of Del.-at-Large for Am. Samoa, Washington, 1971-72; asst. to assoc. dir. OEO, Washington, 1972-73; asst. to undersec. U.S. Dept. Health, Edn. and Welfare, Washington, 1973-75; dep. dir. Washington Pacific Assocs., 1975-82, Pacific Islands Washington Office, 1984—; govt. affairs advisor Am. Samoa Power Auth., Washington, 1995-96; Chief diplomatic corr. Washington Pacific Report, Washington and Pago Pago, Am. Samoa, 1987—. nat. Rep. Committeewoman, Pago Pago, 1986—; mem. founding bd. dirs. Washington Roundtable Asian pacific press, 1987-90; asst. sgt. at arms Rep. Nat. Conv., Houston, 1992; del. Samoan Women's Health Fund, Pago Pago, 1992, 96, spokesperson, 1993—; REp. Congl. nominee Am. Samoa, 1994, 96; mem. Women's Fgn. Policy Group, Ind. Women's Forum. Mem. Internat. Womens Media Found., Am. Samoa Soc. (Washington), Hawaii State Soc., Capitol Hill Club (life). Roman Catholic. Home: PO Box 6171 Pago Pago AS 96799 Office: Am Samoa Power Auth PO Box 26142 Alexandria VA 22313

RADEZ, DAVID CHARLES, financial planning and investment company executive; b. Cobleskill, N.Y. Apr. 23, 1946; s. John Edward and Cora (Drumm) R. B.S., Union Coll., Schenectady, 1968; M.P.A., Cornell U., 1970; cert. real estate studies NYU, 1978. Asst. dir. Kings County Hosp. Ctr., Bklyn., 1970-73; adminstrv. coordinator Meml. Hosp., N.Y.C., 1973-74; dir. clin. ops. Exec. Health Examiners, N.Y.C., 1974-76; real estate salesman Heights-Cranford, Bklyn., 1976-80; real estate broker Whitebread-Nolan, N.Y.C., 1980-81, Montague St. Realty, Bklyn., 1981-82, First Investors Corp., Lexington, Ky., 1984-85, FSC Securities Corp., Lexington, 1985-88, Money Matters, Inc., 1985—, Multi-Fin. Securities, Lexington, 1988-92; real estate cons., Lexington, 1982—. Assoc. agt. Union Coll. Ann. Fund, 1975-92. Mem. Bluegrass Estate Planning Council, Inst. Cert. Fin. Planners. Office: Money Matters Inc 120 Normal Ave PO Box 903 Morehead KY 40351

RADFORD, EDWARD W., small business owner, retired military officer; b. Greenville County, S.C., 1947. BS in Mech. Engring., Ga. Tech. U., MS in Indsl. Mgmt., PhD in Econs. Commd. 2d lt. U.S. Army, 1968, advanced through grades to lt. col., retired; platoon leader MACV, Vietnam, company cmmdr.; owner, mgr. The Radford Co., Radford Storage Systems, Radford Equip. Co, Buford, Ga. Bd. dirs. Gwinnette County Hosp. System, Gwinnette County Housing Authority, Boy Scouts of Am., Ga.; deacon First Bapt. Ch., Buford, Ga.; dep. cmmdr. Ga. State Defense Force, 1996—. Decorated Silver Star, Bronze Star w V, Air Medal, Republic Vietnam Crosss of Gallantry (twice). Mem. The Old Guard of the Gate City Guard. Home: PO Box 1643 Buford GA 30518

RADFORD, GLORIA JANE, retired medical/surgical nurse; b. Kansas City, Mo., Nov. 8, 1927; d. Henry H. and Ruby (Robinson) Calkins; m. William M. Radford, Jan 5, 1952; children: Barbera, Paul, Brenda. Diploma, Kansas City Gen. Hosp., 1948; BS in Profl. Arts, St. Joseph's Coll., 1983; BS in Nursing, Hampton U., 1984. RN, Va. Staff nurse operating room Kansas City (Mo.) Gen. Hosp., 1948-51, Norfolk (Va.) Gen. Hosp., 1953-54; indsl. nurse Physician's Group Practice, North Kansas City, Mo., 1951-53; staff nurse Casualty Hosp., Washington, 1959-60; various mgmt. nursing positions DePaul Hosp., Norfolk, 1961-81; DON Hillhaven Rehab. and Convalescent Ctr., Norfolk, 1981-82; staff nurse Sentara Leigh Hosp., Norfolk, 1983-93. Mem. ANA (cert.), Va. State Nurses Assn. Home: 1549 Sagewood Dr Virginia Beach VA 23455-3529

RADFORD, LINDA ROBERTSON, psychologist; b. Winnipeg, Man., Can., Nov. 6, 1944; came to U.S., 1954; d. William and Edith Aileen (Wheatley) Robertson; 1 child, Drew Richard; m. Richard D. Polley, Sept. 21, 1991. BA, Seattle Pacific U., 1970; MEd, U. Wash., 1972, PhD, 1980. Lic. psychologist, Fla.; cert. clin. hypnotherapist. Dir. support svcs. Highline-West Seattle Mental Health Clinic, 1973-75; rsch. asst. in human affairs Battelle, Seattle, 1976-80, rsch. scientist, 1982-87; sr. cons. Martin Simmonds Assoc., Seattle, 1980-82; pres., owner R.R. Assocs., Seattle and Miami, 1982—; pres. PGI Inc., Miami and London, 1989—; pvt. clin. psychologist Bay Harbor Island, Fla., 1991—, West Palm Beach, Fla., 1991—; chmn., chief exec. officer Swiver Corp., North Miami, Fla., 1994—; chair Swiver Corp., 1994—; vis. sr. assoc. Joint Ctr. for Environ. and Urban Problems, North Miami, Fla., 1986-88; cons. Health Ministry Govt. Thailand, Bangkok, 1989—. Contbr. articles to profl. jours. Community Mental Health Ctr fellow, Seattle, 1972-73. Mem. Am. Psychol. Assn., Am. Soc. Clin. Hypnosis, N.Y. Acad. of Sci. Home: 9264 Bay Dr Surfside FL 33154-3026 Office: 1160 Kane Concourse Ste 401 Bal Harbour FL 33154-2020 also Office: Ste 680 1645 Palm Beach Lakes Blvd West Palm Beach FL 33409

RADHAKRISNAMURTHY, BHANDARU, biochemistry educator; b. Vemulapalli, India, July 1, 1928; came to U.S., 1961; s. Rajeswararao Bhandaru and Sathyavathi Banda; m. Sakuntala Kandukuri Bhandaru, Sept. 5, 1953 (dec. Nov. 2, 1981); children: Rajeswararao, Uma Kalagnanam, Hema, Srinivas; m. Sulochana Yallapragada, Mar. 20, 1983. BS, Nizam Coll., Hyderabad, India, 1951; MS, Osmania U., Hyderabad, India, 1953, PhD, 1958. Chemist Sir Silk Ltd., Sirpur, India, 1953; rsch. scholar Osmania U., Hyderabad, 1953-55, lectr., 1955-61; rsch. assoc. La. State U. Sch. Medicine, New Orleans, 1961-62, instr., 1962-65, asst. prof., 1965-68, assoc. prof., 1968-74, prof., 1974-92; prof. biochemistry Tulane U., New Orleans, 1992—; rsch. grants reviewer La. Heart Assn., New Orleans, 1972-88, NIH, Bethesda, Md., 1989-91, Med. Rsch. Coun., Ottawa, Ont., Can., 1988—, Vets. Affairs, Livermore, Calif., 1987—. Contbr. over 184 articles to profl. jours. Pres. Hindu Temple Soc., New Orleans, 1978-89; trustee Sri Satyanarayana Temple, Kenner, La., 1991—. Fulbright travel grantee, 1961; rsch. grantee La. Heart Assn., 1972, NIH, 1976—, Health Effects Inst., Cambridge, Mass., 1990-92. Mem. AAAS, Soc. for Complex Carbohydrates, Am. Heart Assn., Soc. for Exptl. Biology and Medicine, Am. Chem. Soc., Am. Soc. for Biochemistry and Molecular Biology. Hindu. Office: Tulane Univ Sch Pub Health 1430 Tulane Ave # 29 New Orleans LA 70112-2699

RADLEY, MARY ANN, oil company executive; b. Lethbridge, Alta., Can., Dec. 22, 1945; d. Clarence Lethbridge and Mary Elizabeth (Alfrey) R. BS, U. Lethbridge, 1969; MSE, U. Tex. Arlington, 1976. Hydrologist Freese & Nichols Consulting Engrs., Fort Worth, 1976-80; oil and gas explorer Corpus Christi, Arlington, Tex., 1977-81; pres., treas. Borean Oil Co., Corpus Christi, Arlington, 1981—. Mem. Hickory Creek Hunt (treas. 1990—, Buttons 1988, Colors 1989). Home and Office: 1721 Spring Lake Dr Arlington TX 76012

RADULESCU, DOMNICA VERA MARIA, education educator; b. Bucharest, Romania, June 16, 1961; d. Gheorghe Ioan and Stella (Vinitchi) R.; children: Alexander, Nicholas. Grad., Loyola U., Chgo., 1985; MA, U. Chgo., 1986, PhD, 1992. Lectr. U. Chgo., 1988-92; asst. prof. Washington and Lee U., Lexington, Va., 1992—; dir. University Theatre, U. Chgo., 1990, Washington and Lee U., 1993-95. Actress: The Bridge, Romania, 1980-82; author: André Malraux: The "Farfelu" As Expression of the Feminine and the Erotic, 1994. Grantee NEH; recipient Albatross award Albatross Pub. House, Bucharest, 1983. Mem. MLA, Am. Assn. Tchrs. of French, Malraux Soc. Romanian Orthodox. Home: 9 Jordan St Lexington VA 24450-1976 Office: Washington And Lee U Lexington VA 24450

RADZYKEWYCZ, DAN THEODORE, retired Air Force officer, educator; b. Sadowa, Wysznia, Ukraine, Mar. 7, 1942; came to U.S., 1949; s. Julian and Antonia Anna Radzykewycz; m. Mary Christine Lebedowicz, June 21, 1966; children: Roxanne, Dan Theodore Jr. MA, U. Md., 1966; PhD, Internat. Inst. for Advanced Studies, St. Louis, 1980. Commd. 2d lt. USAF, 1964, advanced through grades to lt. col., 1983, ret., 1991; editor, writer Hdqrs. Pacific Air Forces, Hickam AFB, Hawaii, 1972-75; speech writer to sec. of Air Force Washington, 1975-78; rsch. historian USAF Hist. Rsch. Ctr., Maxwell AFB, Ala., 1978-81; mem. faculty Air Command and Staff Coll., Maxwell AFB, Ala., 1981-83; plans officer U.S. Pacific Command, Camp Smith, Hawaii, 1983-87; mem. mil. then civilian faculty Air War Coll., Maxwell AFB, 1987-95; chief curriculum mgmt. Asia-Pacific Ctr. for Security Studies, Honolulu, 1996—; instr. U. Md., College Park, 1967-69; mem. adj. faculty U. Hawaii System, Honolulu, 1974-75, Auburn U., Montgomery, Ala., 1969-72, 79-81, 91-95, Troy State U., Montgomery, 1972, 78-80, 88-95. Author: Vietnamese Air Force, 1973; editor Corona Harvest series, 1973-75, Project CHECO series, 1973-75; contbr. articles to profl. publs. Decorated Meritorious Svc. medal with three oak leaf clusters. Mem. Pi Sigma Alpha. Office: Asia-Pacific Ctr 2255 Kuhio Ave Ste 1900 Honolulu HI 96815-2600

RAESE, JOHN R., steel company executive; b. 1950. Grad., W. Va. U., 1972. Active in various exec. positions Greer Industries, Morgantown, W. Va., 1972—; pres. Greer Steel Co., Morgantown. Office: Greer Steel Co PO Box 1900 Morgantown WV 26507

RAFAIDUS, DAVID MARTIN, health and human services planner; b. Hamtramack, Mich., Jan. 4, 1956; s. George S. and Emilia Helen (Mazak) R. BS, Cen. Mich. U., 1978; M in Urban Planning, U. Mich., 1980; postgrad. pub. mgmt., Fla. Atlantic U., 1988; site evaluation, planning & devel., Harvard U., 1988. Mem. staff Mich. Mcpl. League, Ann Arbor, 1978-79; teaching fellow dept. urban and regional planning U. Mich., Ann Arbor, 1980; planner dept. cmty. devel. City of Lafayette, La., 1980-82; coord. zoning dept. planning and devel. mgmt. City of Lafayette, 1982-83, devel. mgr. dept. planning and devel. mgmt., 1983-86; county planner Palm Beach County Dept. Planning, Zoning & Bldg., West Palm Beach, Fla., 1986-96; health and human svcs. planner Palm Beach County Cmty. Svcs. Dept., West Palm Beach, Fla., 1996—. Mem. Am. Planning Assn., Palm Beach County Planning Congress, World Future Soc., KC (4th degree), Lambda Chi Alpha. Roman Catholic. Home: 6073 Brandon St Palm Beach Gardens FL 33418-1486 Office: Palm Beach County Cmty Svcs Dept 810 Datura St West Palm Beach FL 33401-5204

RAFEY, LARRY DEAN, microbiologist, clinician; b. St. Louis, Mar. 30, 1948; s. Ernest George and Roslyn (Broida) R. BS, Am. U., 1981; postgrad., Georgetown U., 1981, Howard U., 1992-95. Microbiologist First Medic, McLean, Va., 1973-93; clin. rschr. in gen. and preventive medicine Green Med. Ctr., Vienna, Va., 1995-96; with Gateway Med. Clinic, DeFuniak Springs, Fla., 1996—; ops. dir. CCD Cons.-Forensic Sci. Svcs., Alexandria, Va., 1991-95; mem. infectious diseases del. to China and Vietnam, 1993. Fellow Am. Acad. Physician Assocs.; mem. Am. Soc. Tropical Medicine and Hygiene, Am. Soc. Clin. Pathologists, N.Y. Acad. Scis., Golden Key, Beta Kappa Chi. Home: PO Box 99 Argyledria FL 32422

RAFTERY, WILLIAM A., management consultant; b. N.Y.C., Sept. 11, 1925; s. John J. and Clara A. (Martino) R.; m. Vivian A. Moncton, Aug. 29, 1953; children: Donna Lynn, Linda Leighanne, Vivian. BA in Econs., Tufts U., 1948; MBA, NYU, 1952. V.p. mktg. Signal-Stat Corp., Bklyn., 1948-62; exec. v.p. Surelock Mgmt. Co., Newark, 1956-62; pres. Technorm Corp., Linden, N.J., 1954-62, Motor and Equipment Mgmt. Assn., Englewood Cliffs, N.J., 1962-91, Raftery Cons., Pinehurst, N.C., 1991—; dir. Am. Soc. Assn. Execs., Washington, 1982-86, Maval Mfg. Co., Twinsburg, Ohio, 1991—. 1st lt. USN, 1943-46.

RAGAN, CAROLYN LANCASTER, secondary school educator; b. Hawkinsville, Ga., May 3, 1937; d. Albert Rayford and Belle Iola (Ashley) Lancaster; m. Charles Cecil Becham, Dec. 10, 1955 (dec. 1984); children: Debra B. Johnson, Tammy B. Watson, Timothy M.; m. William Leon Ragan Jr., Nov. 22, 1986. AA with honors, Middle Ga. Coll., 1974, AS with honors, 1975; BS in English Edn. summa cum laude, Columbus Coll., 1979. English tchr. Beechwood Acad., Marshallville, Ga., 1974-77, Baker Acad., Hawkinsville, 1979-84; English/spl. edn. tchr. Hawkinsville High Sch., 1985—; chmn. English dept. Baker Acad., 1979-84; chmn. spl. edn. dept. Hawkinsville H.S., 1987—; sponsor Beta Club, Hawkinsville, 1979-84, Acad. Bowl, 1979-84, Students Against Drunk Driving, 1986—, Future Ga. Educators, 1995—. Campaign mgr. Pulaski County Sheriff, Hawkinsville, 1980, 84, 92, Pulaski County Commr., 1988; mem. com. Am. Heart Assn., Hawkinsville, 1985-88, Am. Cancer Soc., 1990; vol. Habitat for Humanity, Americus, Ga., 1996—. Named Star Tchr., Ga. C. of C., 1982; selected as torch bearer for World Olympics by Coca Cola Corp., Atlanta, 1996. Mem. Nat. Coun. Tchrs. English, Profl. Assn. Ga. Educators, Delta Kappa Gamma., Phi Kappa Phi. Home: 203 Turner St Hawkinsville GA 31036

RAGANS, ROSALIND DOROTHY, textbook author, retired art educator; b. Brooklyn, N.Y., Feb. 28, 1933; d. Sidney Guy Gordon and Beatrice (Zuckerman) Safier; m. John Franklin Ragans, July 31, 1965; 1 child, John Lee. BFA, CUNY-Hunter Coll., 1955; MEd, Ga. So. Coll., 1967; EdD, U. Ga., 1971. Cert. tchr. art, Ga. Tchr. art Union City (N.J.) Bd. Edn., 1956-62; tchr. 1st grade Chatham Bd. Edn., Savannah, Ga., 1962-64; instr. art Ga. So. U., Statesboro, 1964-69, asst. prof., 1969-76, assoc. prof., 1976-89, prof. emeritus, 1989—; keynote speaker art edn. confs., Ind., 1987, 88, Ark., Wis., 1989, Md., 1990, others. Author: (textbooks) ArtTalk, 1988, 2d edit., 1994, Exploring Art, 1990, Understanding Art, 1990. Mem. Nat. Assn. Educators (life), Ga. Assn. Educators (life), Nat. Art Edn. Assn. (Southeastern Art Educator of Yr. 1991, Nat. Art Educator of Yr. 1992), Ga. Art Edn. Assn. (Ga. Art Educator of Yr. 1990), Pilot Club Internat. (Ga. dist., Ga. Profl. Handicapped Woman of Yr. 1988). Jewish. Home: 198 Wendwood Dr Statesboro GA 30458-5467

RAGHU, RENGACHARI, alternative medicine, nutrition, biotechnology and chemistry consultant, agriculture consultant; b. Amur, Tamilnadu, India, Mar. 22, 1943; came to U.S., 1975; s. Rengachari Veeraraghavachari and Sakunthala Krishnaswamy Rengachari; m. Kamala Rengan, Dec. 1, 1972; children: Anand, Adithya. HMB, Hanemann Homeopathic Inst., Bangalore, India, 1963; MS, Annamalai U., Chidambaram, India, 1965; MBA, S.P. Mandalia's Inst., Bombay, 1973; PhD, Bhaba Atomic Rsch. Ctr., Bombay, 1974. Asst. mgr. Amoor (India) Estates, 1962-65; mgr. Sakunthala Chemists, Tiruvarur, India, 1962-65; sr. rsch. fellow TB Ctr, Madras, India, 1965-68; sr. sci. officer Bhaba Atomic Rsch. Ctr., Bombay, 1968-75; dir. rsch. divsn. ob-gyn. Meharry Med. Coll., Nashville, 1975-85; chief clin. chemistry Apollo Hosps., Madras, 1985-89; rsch. cons. Vanderbilt U., Nashville, 1988-89; chmn. clin. biochemistry Nat. Chiropractic Coll., Lombard, Ill., 1989-90; pres. Internat. High Tech. Transfer, Nashville, 1990—. Contbr. over 50 articles to sci. publs.; inventor no-share syringe. Bd. dirs. March of Dimes, Nashville, 1979-83, Juvenile Diabetes Fedn., Nashville, 1983-85, Jr. C. of C., Nashville, 1981-83; mem. bd. trustees Hindu Cultural Ctr., Nashville, 1983-90; mem. commerce adv. com. State of Tenn., Nashville, 1980-84; intern Mr. Bob Clement, U.S. House of Reps., U.S. Congress, Washington, 1994; mem. nat. steering com. Davidson County, Nashville, State of Tenn. Clinton/Gore '96 Campaign. March of Dimes fellow, N.Y., 1975-78; rsch. grantee Nat. Cancer Inst., Washington, 1981-86. Fellow Indian Phytopathology Soc. (life); mem. Am. Clin. Chemists, Soc. Biol. Chemists, Soc. Exptl. Biol. Medicine, Soc. Pharmacology, Soc. Preventive Medicine. Democrat. Home: 822 Kendall Dr Nashville TN 37209-4512 Office: Internat High Tech Transfer 822 Kendall Dr Nashville TN 37209-4512

RAGLAND, INES COLOM, principal; b. Washington, Mar. 12, 1947; d. Jose Luis Sr. and Frances Yerby (Pannill) Colom; m. Benjamin Michael Ragland, Dec. 17, 1977 (div. May 1991); children: Michelle Elizabeth, Rachael Christine. BA in Secondary Edn., Longwood Coll., 1969, MS in Secondary Adminstrn., 1992. Clk. Va. State Water Control Bd., Richmond, 1969; tchr. Spanish Richmond City Pub. Schs., 1969-74; planning supr. Va. State Water Control Bd., 1974-78; asst. prin., tchr., prin. Grove Ave. Bapt. Christian Sch., Richmond, 1978-83; guidance tchr., asst. prin. Victory Christian Acad., Richmond, 1990—; cons. in field. Mission participant, El Salvador, 1992. Mem. ASCD. Office: Victory Christian Acad 8491 Chamberlayne Rd Richmond VA 23227-1550

RAGLAND, WYLHEME HAROLD, minister, health facility administrator; b. Anniston, Ala., Dec. 19, 1946; s. Howard and Viola (Pearson) R.; children from previous marriage: Frederick, Seth. BA, Jacksonville State U., 1973; MDiv., Emory U., 1975; D in Ministry, Vanderbilt U., 1978. Ordained deacon United Meth. Ch., 1974, elder, 1976. Pastor Center Grove United Meth. Ch., Huntsville, Ala., 1975-77, King's Meml. United Meth. Ch., Decatur, Ala., 1977—; dir. pastoral svcs. North Ala. Regional Hosp., Decatur, 1984—, also employee assistance ofcl.; staff devel. tng. coord., 1994; bd. dirs. Bd. of the Ordained Ministry, Birmingham, Ala., Ethnic Minority Ministries, Commn. on Ch. and Safety, Birmingham; del. North Ala. Ann. Conf., Birmingham, 1991. Contbr. articles to various publs. Mem. adv. bd. The Albany Clinic, Decatur, 1989—; mem. N.W. Counseling Ctr., Decatur, 1990—, Cmty. Unity of Decatur, 1989—, Morgan Coutny Hist. Commn., Decatur, 1988—; mem. NAACP, 1993, Ala. Dem. Conf., 1994, Mayor's Task Force, 1994, QUEST Recovery Adv. Com., 1994; vol. Meals on Wheels Christmas in Apr., 1995. Protestant fellow Rockefeller Found., 1973-75. Mem. Ala. Chaplains Assns., Decatur Dist. Mins. Assn., Employee Assistance Soc., Sigma Tau Delta, Pi Gamma Mu, Phi Alpha Theta. Home: 511 Walnut St NE Decatur AL 35601-1941 Office: North Ala Regional Hosp Hwy 31 Decatur AL 35601-4918

RAGSDALE, GEORGE ROBINSON, lawyer; b. Raleigh, N.C., Mar. 26, 1936; s. George Young and Susan (Jolly) R.; m. Adora Prevost, Oct. 20, 1962; children: John Robinson, George Young II, Adora P. AB, U. N.C., 1958, LLB, 1961. Asst. to chief counsel U.S. Senate Subcom. on Constnl. Rights, Washington, 1961-62; law ptnr. Bailey & Ragsdale, Raleigh, 1962-65; legal counsel to Dan K. Moore, Gov. of N.C., Raleigh, 1965-68; judge Superior Ct. of N.C., Raleigh, 1968-70; ptnr. Moore, Ragsdale, Liggett, Ray & Foley, Raleigh, 1970-86, LeBoeuf, Lamb, Leiby & MacRae, Raleigh, 1987-93, Ragsdale, Liggett & Foley, 1994—; lectr. N.C. Assn. Def. Counsel. Trustee U. N.C., Chapel Hill, 1979-87, vice-chmn. bd. trustees, 1983-84, chmn., 1984-85; trustee U. N.C. Endowment, 1980—, chmn., 1984-85; bd. dirs. U. N.C. Instnl. Devel. Found., Inc., 1985—, U. N.C.-Chapel Hill Found.; bd. visitors U. N.C., The Ednl. Found., Inc. Mem. ABA, N.C. Bar Assn., Wake County Bar Assn., Assn. Bar of City of N.Y., Def. Rsch. Inst., Raleigh C. of C., Kiwanis, Sphinx Club of Raleigh, Terpsichorean Club, Raleigh Execs. Club, Carolina Country Club, Laurel Ridge Country Club. Episcopalian. Office: Ragsdale Liggett & Foley 2840 Plaza Pl PO Box 31507 Raleigh NC 27622

RAGSDALE, RICHARD ELLIOT, healthcare management executive; b. St. Louis, Dec. 20, 1943; s. Billie Oscar and Isabelle (Roques) R.; m. Anne Elizabeth Ward, Aug. 20, 1968; children: Richard, Kevin, Bethany. BBA, Ohio U., 1965; M in Internat. Commerce, Thunderbird Grad. Sch. Internat. Mgmt., 1968. Asst. treas. Chase Manhattan Bank, N.Y.C., 1968-73; v.p., treas. Hosp. Affiliates Internat., Nashville, 1973-80; v.p., treas., chief fin. officer INA Health Care Group, Dallas, 1980-81; sr. v.p., chief fin. officer, dir. Republic Health Corp., Dallas, 1981-83, sr. exec. v.p., dir., 1983-85; chmn. Community Health Systems Inc., Brentwood, Tenn., 1985—, Great No. Health Mgmt., Ltd., London, 1986-89; bd. dirs. RehabCare Group, Inc., St. Louis; chmn. ProMed Co., Inc. Ft. Worth, Tex., 1994—. Coach Spring Valley Athletic Assn., Dallas, 1985; trustee Watkins Inst., 1988-94; trustee Benton Hall Sch., 1988—, chair, 1991—; trustee Maryville Coll., 1990—, chair, 1992—. Recipient Thunderbird Disting Alumni award Entrepreneurship, 1990, Jonas Meyer Disting. Alumni award, 1993. Mem. Fedn. Am. Hosps. (legis. commn. 1984-95). Republican. Office: Community Health Systems Inc 155 Franklin Rd Ste 400 Brentwood TN 37027-4646

RAHAL, PARAMVIR SINGH, physician; b. Jalandhar, Punjab, India, Feb. 14, 1964; came to U.S., 1991; s Shangara Singh and Joginder (Kaur) R.; m. Simrita Minhas, Jan. 7, 1990; 1 child, Harman K. Diploma in pre-med., Guru Nanak Dev U., Amritsar, India, 1981; MD, Med. Coll., Amritsar, 1986. Diplomate Am. Bd. Internal Medicine; lic. physician, Calif., Mich., Punjab. House officer dept. medicine and surgery Med. Coll., Amritsar, 1987-88; med. officer Ruby Nelson Hosp., Jalandhar, Punjab, India, 1990-91; intern U. Louisville, Ky., 1991-92; resident in internal medicine U. Louisville, 1992-94; fellow in gastroenterology Providence Hosp. and Med. Ctrs., Southfield, Mich., 1994-96; gastroenterologist Kaiser Permanente, Bakersfield, 1996—; presenter in field. Contbr. articles and abstracts to publs. Mem. AMA, ACP, Am. Coll. Gastroenterology, Am. Gastroent. Assn., Ky. Med. Assn. Home: 901 Mohawk St # 52 Bakersfield CA 93309

RAHALL, NICK JOE, II (NICK RAHALL), congressman; b. Beckley, W.Va., May 20, 1949; s. Joe and Alice Rahall; children: Rebecca Ashley, Nick Joe III, Suzanne Nicole. AB, Duke U., 1971. Staff asst. U.S. Senator Robert C. Byrd, 1971-74; sales rep. Sta. WWNR, Beckley, 1974; pres. Mountaineer Travel Co., Beckley, 1975-77, W.Va. Broadcasting, 1980—; mem. 95th-104th Congresses from 4th (now 3rd) W.Va. dist., Washington, 1977—; mem. transp. and infrastructure com. with subcom. on r.r.'s and surface transp., mem. resources com. with subcom. on energy and mineral resources and nat. parks, forests and lands; bd. dirs. Rahall Comm. Corp. Del. Dem. Nat. Conv., 1972, 74, 78, 80, 84, 88, 92; W.Va. chmn. March of Dimes, 1979. Named Young Man of Year, Beckley Jaycees, 1972; Outstanding Young Man in W.Va., W.Va. Jaycees, 1977; recipient Achievement award Logan Cripple Children Soc., 1978; Citizenship award K.C., 1978, Disting. Svc. award Am. Fedn. Govt. Employees W.Va., 1984, Young Dem. of Yr. Dem. Nat. Conv., 1980, Outfitter of Yr. Profl. Outfitters, 1987, Seneca award Sierra Club 1988, River Conservation award Am. River 1988; named Coal Man of Yr. Coal Industry News, 1979. Mem. NAACP, NRA, Elks, Moose, Masons (33d degree) Shriners. Presbyterian. Office: US Ho of Reps 2269 Rayburn HOB Washington DC 20515-4803

RAHM, NANCY LEE, music education director; b. Huntingdon, Tenn., May 25, 1934; d. W. Deward and Robert Nell (Belew) Tate; m. Otto R. Rahm, Jan. 20, 1957; children: Deward R., Charles A., Robert L. AB, Lambuth Coll., 1956; postgrad., Memphis State U. Cert. music, early childhood, elem., adminstrn. supr. Dir., music edn. Jackson (Tenn.)-Madison County Sch. System, 1967—; tchr. Memphis City Schs., 1956-57, 64-67, Alaska On Base Schs., Anchorage, 1957-58. Mem. NEA, Music Educators Nat. Conf., Am. Orff Schelwerk Assn., Tenn. Edn. Assn., Jackson-Madison County Edn. Assn. (sec.), Am. Choral Dirs. Assn., Alpha Delta Kappa, Phi Delta Kappa. Office: 310 N Parkway Jackson TN 38305-2712

RAHMAN, RAFIQ UR, oncologist, educator; b. Mirali, Pakistan, Mar. 3, 1957; came to U.S., 1985; s. Rakhman and Bibi (Sana) Gul; m. Shamim Ara Bangash; children: Maryam, Hassan, Haider. BS, MB, U. Peshawar, Pakistan, 1980. Bd. cert. internal medicine, med. oncology; lic. physician Pa., Ala., Ky. House officer in internal medicine Khyber Teaching Hosp.-U. Peshawar, Pakistan, 1980-81, house officer in gen. surgery, 1981, jr. registrar med. ICU, 1983-84; jr. registrar internal medicine Khyber Teaching Hosp., 1981-82; sr. registrar internal medicine Khyber Teaching Hosp.-Lady Reading Hosp. & Postgrad. Inst., Peshawar, 1984-85; Audrey Meyer Mars fellow in med. oncology Roswell Park Cancer Inst., Buffalo, 1985-86; resident in internal medicine SUNY-Buffalo Gen. Hosp.-Erie County Med. Ctr.-VA Med. Ctr., 1986-88; chief resident in internal medicine SUNY-Buffalo-Erie County Med. Ctr., 1988; fellow in hematology and med. oncology SUNY-Buffalo-Roswell Park Cancer Inst., 1989-90; hematologist, med. oncologist Daniel Boone Clinic and Harlan A.R.H., 1991-92; clin. asst. prof. medicine U. Ky., 1991—; attending physician, hematology/med. oncologist Hardin Meml. Hosp., Elizabethtown, 1993—, chief medicine, 1996; tchr. med. students Med. Sch., SUNY; participant CALGB protocol studies Roswell Park Cancer Inst., investigator. Editor English sect. Cenna mag. Cenna; contbr. articles to profl. jours. Mem. Pakistan Med. & Dental Coun., Ky. Med. Assn., Harlan County Med. Soc., Hardin-LaRue County Med. Soc. Home: 400 Briarwood Cir Elizabethtown KY 42701-8913 Office: 1107 Woodland Dr Ste 105 Elizabethtown KY 42701-2749

RAIA, CARL BERNARD, commercial real estate executive and developer; b. Houston, Nov. 23, 1931; s. Sam B. and Mary F. (Barzilla) R.; m. Micheline Fauret, June 9, 1956 (dec. Oct. 1990); children: Marylyn, Carlene LoDuca, Carl B. Jr. BS, U. Houston, 1954. Lic. realtor, Tex. Pres. Fonmeadow Devel., Inc., Houston, 1975—; v.p. Vulcan Properties, Inc., Investment Co., 1970; ptnr. M&R, Investment Co., 1970; owner Carl Raia Realty, Houston, 1964—; pres. RaiCom Realty, Inc., Houston, 1995—; pres., chmn. bd. KSBJ Ednl. Found., Humble, Tex., 1988-90. Chmn. Jesus Rally, Houston, 1979-81. With U.S. Army, 1954-57. Mem. Nat. Assn. Realtors, Tex. Assn. Realtors, Houston Assn. Realtors, Nat. Assn. Home Builders, Tex. Assn. Builders, Greater Houston Builders Assn., Full Gospel Businessmen's Internat., Houston Cath. Charismatic Ctr., K.C. Roman Catholic. Office: 7211 Regency Square Blvd Houston TX 77036-3137

RAICHE, BERNARD MARCEL, psychotherapist, heath care consultant; b. Manchester, N.H., Sept. 5, 1944; s. Marcel L. and Therese (Norman) R.; m. Jean Adams, Aug. 25, 1979. BS, Springfield Coll., 1967; EdD, U. Maine, 1977; MSW, U. Wis., 1982; MBA, Marquette U., 1986; JD, Cath. U. Am., 1996. Tchr. Milford (N.H.) Area Jr./Sr. H.S., 1967-68; counselor, tchr. Parkside Jr. High Sch., Manchester, 1968-71; sch. counselor Bow (N.H.) Meml. Sch., 1971-75; tech. coord. U. Maine Tchr. Corps Project, Orono, 1977-79; coord. counseling and pers. svc. Marquette U., Milw., 1981-85, dir. edn. clinic, 1983-87, dir. tchr. edn., 1985-87; exec. dir. Richie McFarland Children's Ctr., Stratham, N.H., 1987-88; dir. child and adolescent psychiat. svcs. Brookside Hosp., Nashua, N.H., 1988-91; assoc. adminstr. Psychiat. Ctr. of Mich. Hosp., New Baltimore, Mich., 1991-92; dir. spl. projects northeast region Nat. Med. Enterprises, 1992-94; health care cons., 1994—; dir. partial hosp. programs Psychiat. Inst. Washington, 1995-96; pvt. practice psychotherapist Washington, 1996—; psychotherapist Lakeside Family Counseling, Mt. Clemens, Mich., 1992, Inner Dynamics, Milw., 1983-87; outpatient therapist Seacoast Mental Health Ctr., Exeter, N.H., 1988-91; counselor Maine Maritime Acad., Cartine, Maine, 1976-77. Contbr. articles to profl. jours. Mem. NASW, ABA, ATLA, Am. Assn. Marriage and Family Therapists, Am. Coll. Healthcare Execs., Am. Health Lawyers Assn. Home: 3440 Hidden Meadow Dr Fairfax VA 22033-1114

RAIDER, LOUIS, physician, radiologist; b. Chattanooga, Sept. 7, 1913; s. Leaha Reevin; m. Emma Silberstein, Oct. 19, 1940; children: Lynne Dianne, David Bernard, Paula Raider Olichney. BS, Bklyn. Coll., 1935; MD, Dalhousie U., 1941. Diplomate, cert. Am. Bd. Radiology. Intern Met. Hosp., N.Y.C., 1940-41, resident in radiology, 1941-42; resident in radiation therapy Bellevue Hosp., N.Y.C., 1942-43; fellow in cancer therapy NIH, N.Y.C., 1943-44; chief of radiology Vets. Hosp., New Orleans, 1947-50; radiologist, chief radiology Providence Hosp., Mobile, Ala., 1950-76; clin. prof. Med. Sch. U. South Ala., Mobile, 1987—. Contbr. articles to profl. jours. Maj. AUS, 1944-47. Fellow Am. Coll. Radiology, Am. Coll. Chest Physicians; mem. Radiol. Soc. N.Am., Am. Roentgen Ray Soc., AMA, Ala. Acad. Radiology (pres. 1970-71, Silver medal 1989), So. Med. Assn. (chmn. sect. radiology 1973-74), Soc. Thoracic Radiology, So. Radiol. Conf., Am. Soc. Emergency Radiology. Democrat. Jewish. Home: 1801 S Indian Creek Dr Mobile AL 36607-2309 Office: Hosp U South Ala 2451 Fillingim St Mobile AL 36617-2238

RAIFORD, ROBERT CHARLES, army officer; b. San Antonio, July 29, 1950; s. Robert Walter and Marjorie Alice (Bantley) R.; m. Robin Lynn Stillings, Nov. 23, 1974 (div. Apr., 1990); children: Erica Lynn, Robert Charles Jr.; m. Cynthia Ann Shuba, Apr. 20, 1991. BSEE, Tex. A&M U., 1972, MSEE, 1975; postgrad., Indsl. Coll. Armed Forces, 1995—. Commd. 2nd lt. U.S. Army, 1972, advanced through grades to col., 1995; co. cmmdr. B Co. 16th Signal Bn., Ft. Hood, Tex., 1977; quality assurance and test engr. USACEEIA-Europe, Worms, Germany, 1978-81; aide to comdg. gen. U.S. Army Info. Systems Command, Ft. Huachuca, Ariz., 1981-84; G-3 ops. officer 11th Signal Brigade, U.S. Army, Ft. Huachuca, 1985; staff officer The Joint Staff U.S Armed Forces, Washington, 1986-89; liason officer Exec. Office Comms. System, Washington, 1989-91; product mgr. All Source Analysis System, McLean, Va., 1991-95. Vol. ticket mgr. Hexagon Inc. (charity), Washington; sec. Springfield Glen (Va.) Homeowner's Assn., 1994. Named Disting. Grad. U.S. Army Signal Sch., Ft. Gordon, Ga., 1972, 78; Nat. Merit scholar, 1968; U.S. Army fellow, 1972. Mem. IEEE, Tau Beta Pi, Eta Kappa Nu. Lutheran. Home: 8000 Middlewood Pl Springfield VA 22153-1928 Office: Indsl Coll Armed Forces Ft Lesley J McNair Nat Def Univ Washington DC 20319-6000

RAIJMAN, ISAAC, gastroenterologist, endoscopist, educator; b. Empalme, Sonora, Mex., July 6, 1959; came to U.S., 1985; s. Jose and Amalia (Langsam) R. MD, Nat. Autonomous U., Mexico City, 1985; postgrad., Nat. U. Houston, U. Wis., 1985. Diplomate Am. Bd. Internal Medicine, Am. Bd. Gastroenterology. Resident in medicine Mt. Sinai Hosp., Milw., 1986-88, chief resident, 1989; clin. fellow in therapeutic endoscopy Wellesley Hosp., Toronto, Ont., Can., 1992-93; rsch. fellow in gastroenterology U. Tex., Houston, 1989-90, clin. fellow, 1990-92, asst. prof. medicine, 1993—, dir. therapeutic endoscopy, 1993—, asst. prof. M.D. Anderson Cancer Ctr., 1993—. Author: Pancreas, 1993, Bockus Textbook of Gastroenterology, 1993; also numerous articles. Mem. Am. Coll. Gastroenterology, Am. Gastroenterology Assn., Internat. Assn. Pancreatology, Am. Soc. Gastrointestinal Endoscopy, Am. Soc. Internal Medicine. Office: 6414 Fannin Ste G125 Houston TX 77030-1501

RAILSBACK, LOREN BRUCE, geologist; b. Richmond, Ind., Nov. 22, 1957; s. John Warren and Patricia Ann (Jackson) R.; m. Celeste Michelle Condit, Feb. 14, 1978. BA in History, U. Iowa, 1980, BS in Geology, 1981, MS in Geology, 1983; PhD in Geology, U. Ill., 1989. Exploration geologist Shell Oil Co., New Orleans, 1983-85; asst. prof. U. Ga., Athens, 1989-94, assoc. prof., 1994—. Contbr. articles to profl. jours. Recipient Rsch. grant NSF, 1992. Fellow Geol. Soc. Am.; mem. Geochem. Soc., Am. Assn. Petroleum Geologists, Internat. Assn. Sedimentologists. Office: Univ Ga Dept Geology Athens GA 30602-2501

RAILTON, WILLIAM SCOTT, lawyer; b. Newark, July 30, 1935; s. William Scott and Carolyn Elizabeth (Guiberson) R.; m. Karen Elizabeth Walsh, Mar. 31, 1979; 1 son, William August; children by previous marriage: William Scott, Anne Greenwood. BSEE, U. Wash., 1962; JD with honors, George Washington U., 1965. Bar: D.C. 1966, Md. 1966, Va. 1993, U.S. Patent Office 1966. Assoc., then ptnr. Kemon, Palmer & Estabrook, Washington, 1966-70; sr. trial atty. Dept. Labor, Washington, 1970-71, asst. counsel for trial litigation, 1971-72; chief counsel U.S. Occupational Safety and Health Rev. Commn., Washington, 1972-77; acting gen. counsel U.S. Occupational Safety and Health Rev. Commn., 1975-77; ptnr. Reed, Smith, Shaw & McClay, Pitts., 1977—; lectr. George Washington U. Law Sch., 1977-79, seminar chmn. Occupational Safety and Health Act, Govt. Inst., 1979—; lectr. Practicing Law Inst., 1976-79. Author: (legal handbooks) The Examination System and the Backlog, 1965, The OSHA General Duty Clause, 1977, The OSHA Health Standards, 1977; OSHA Compliance Handbook, 1992; contbg. author: Occupational Safety and Health Law, 1988, 93. Regional chmn. Montgomery County (Md.) Republican party, 1968-70; pres. Montgomery Sq. Citizens Assn., 1970-71; bd. dirs., pres. Foxvale Farms Homeowners Assn., 1979-82; pres. Orchards on the Potomac Homeowners Assn., 1990-92; dir. Great Falls Hist. Soc., 1991-94; scoutmaster Troop 55 Boy Scouts Am., 1993—. With USMC, 1953-58. Recipient Meritorious Achievement medal Dept. Labor, 1972, Outstanding Service award OSHA Rev. Commn., 1977. Mem. ABA (mgmt. co-chmn. occupational safety and health law com. 1995—), Md. Bar Assn., Va. Bar Assn., Bar Assn. D.C. (vice chmn. young lawyers sect. 1971), Order of Coif, Sigma Phi Epsilon, Phi Delta Phi. Home: 10102 Walker Lake Dr Great Falls VA 22066-3502 also: East Tower 1301 K St NW #1100 Washington DC 20005

RAIMONDO, LOUIS JOHN, psychiatrist; b. N.Y.C., Jan. 9, 1959; s. Louis John and Josephine Anne (Christiano) R. BS, Fordham U., 1981; MD, SUNY at Buffalo, 1985. Diplomate Nat. Bd. Med. Examiners. Resident psychiatry N.Y. Med. Coll. Consortium at Westchester, Valhalla, N.Y., 1985-89; staff psychiatrist Danbury (Conn.) Hosp., 1987-89, Westch County Crisis Intervention Svcs., Valhalla, 1989-90; clin. asst. prof. psychiatry N.Y. Med. Coll., Valhalla, 1990—; med. staff Columbia Med. Ctr., Halifax Med. Ctr., Meml. Hosp., Daytona Beach, Fla., 1989—, Atlantic Shores Hosp., 1990-94; chief of staff Atlantic Shores Hosp., Ormond Beach, Fla., 1993-94; psychiat. med. dir. Columbia Home Health Care, Ormond Beach, Fla., 1994—; med. dir. partial hospitalization programs Quality Life Ctr., Daytona Beach/West Volusia, 1994—; med. dir. Columbia Behavioral Health Unit, 1996—; speaker and cons. in field. Recipient Clin. Excellence in Psychiatry award Sandoz Corp., 1989. Mem. AMA, Am. Psychiat. Assn. (conv. presenter), Fla. Med. Assn., Volusia County Med. Soc., Am. Acad. Forensic Examiners (bd. cert.), Fla. Psychiat. Soc., Phi Beta Kappa. Home: 103 Sand Dunes Dr Ormond Beach FL 32176-2183 Office: East Coast Ctr Psychiatry 595 W Granada Blvd Ste 2E Ormond Beach FL 32174-5190

RAINBOLT, DAVID EUGENE, banker; b. Norman, Okla., Jan. 7, 1956; s. Harry E. and Jeannine (T.) R.; m. Mary Stevenson, Dec. 15, 1979 (div. Aug. 1987); 1 child, Adam D.; m. Kim Phillips, Oct. 6, 1990. BBA, U. Okla., 1978; MBA, Tulane U., 1979. Sr. credit analyst Republic Bank, Dallas, 1980, comml. loan officer, 1980-82; pres. Trencor, Inc., Oklahoma City, 1982-84; chief fin. officer BancFirst, Oklahoma City, 1984—; bd. dirs. BancFirst, Oklahoma City, BancFirst Corp., Trend Venture Corp.; mng. ptnr. Aero-Meridian Ptnrs., Oklahoma City, 1987—; trustee Okla. Tchrs. Retirement System, Oklahoma City, 1988—. Bd. dirs. Okla. Arts Inst., Oklahoma City, 1988—, Jr. Achievement, Oklahoma City, 1988—; bd. dirs., treas. Leadership Okla., Inc., Oklahoma City, 1989—; trustee Okla. Med. Rsch. Found., Oklahoma City, 1988—, Big Bros. Oklahoma City, 1983-89; exec. bd. Last Frontier coun. Boy Scouts Am., 1990—. Mem. Okla. State C. of C. (treas., bd. dirs. 1988—), Okla. Bankers Assn. (bd. dirs. 1987-88, named one of Oklahoma's Future Banking Leaders, 1989, Leadership Oklahoma City (adv. bd. 1988-89), Leadership Okla. (treas., bd. dirs. 1989—), Rotary, Okla. Meml. Union (trustee 1989—). Office: BancFirst 101 N Broadway PO Box 26788 Oklahoma City OK 73126-0788*

RAINBOLT, H.E., bank executive; b. 1929. With Fed. Nat. Bank & Trust, Shawnee, Okla., 1950-89, chmn. bd. dirs., 1967-89; chmn. Bancfirst, Oklahoma City, 1989—; bd. dirs. Trencor Inc., Oklahoma City, Sentinel Petroleum Co. Inc., Oklahoma City. Office: BancFirst 101 N Broadway Ave Oklahoma City OK 73102*

RAINES, EDGAR FRANK, JR., historian; b. Murphysboro, Ill., Aug. 17, 1944; s. Edgar Frank and Mary Bernice (Mohlenbrock) R.; m. Gretchen Rose Beuscher, Aug. 9, 1976 (div. Dec. 1982); 1 child, Edgar Jacob; m. Rebecca Celia Robbins, June 20, 1987. BA, So. Ill. U., 1966, MA, 1968; PhD, U. Wis., 1976. Asst. acad. dean Silver Lake Coll., Manitowoc, Wis., 1976-79; historian Office of Air Force History, Washington, 1979-80, U.S. Army Ctr. of Mil. History, Washington, 1980—; chmn. book selection com. Mil. Classics Seminar, Washington, 1984-86, 89-92. Co-author: The Army and the Joint Chiefs of Staff, 1986. Sec. of the Army fellow Dept. of the Army, 1987. Mem. Am. Hist. Assn., Orgn. Am. Historians, Soc. Mil. History, Soc. History in the Fed. Govt., Ill. State Hist. Soc., Wis. Hist. Soc. Office: US Army Ctr of Mil History 1099 14th St NW Washington DC 20005-3419

RAINES, IRENE FREEZE, real estate broker; b. Gadsden, Tenn., Nov. 13, 1924; d. Fred Dozier and Donnie May (Flippo) Freeze; m. James Athel Raines, 1944; children: Shirley Carol Canady, Carey Athel, David Anthony. Cert., Memphis Sch. Commerce, 1943; student, Jackson State Community Coll., 1978-84. Grad. Realtors Inst., 1986. Insp. Wayne Knitting Mills, Humboldt, Tenn., 1959-69; legal sec. Emison & Emison, P.C., Alamo, Tenn., 1969-79; affiliate broker Hale Herndon Agy., Humboldt, 1979-84; broker Raines Real Estate Agy., Alamo, 1984—. Clk. Chancellor's Office, Alamo, 1979; mem. Crockett County (Tenn.) Dem. Exec. Com., 1976; tchr. Sunday sch., dir. Women's Missionary Union, Bapt. Ch. Mem. Nat. Assn. Realtors, Tenn. Assn. Realtors (edn. com. 1987-88, chaplain), Corckett County C. of C. (charter mem., membership 1991—). Home: RR 2 Box 554 Bells TN 38006-9564 Office: Raines Real Estate Agy 469 S Bells St Alamo TN 38001-1928

RAINES, JEFF, biomedical scientist, medical research director; b. N.Y.C., Sept. 5, 1943; s. Otis J. and Mildred C. (Wetzler) R.; B.S. in Mech. Engring., Clemson U., 1965; M. in Mech. Engring., U. Fla., 1967; MD Harvard U., 1968; Ph.D. in Biomed. Engring. (NIH fellow), M.I.T., 1972; children: Gretchen Christena, Victoria Jean. Mem. staff M.I.T., Cambridge, 1968-70; biophysicist dept. surgery Mass. Gen. Hosp., Boston, 1972-77, dir. Vascular Lab., 1972-77; instr. surgery Harvard Med. Sch., Boston, 1973-77; preceptor Harvard/M.I.T. Sch. Health Scis., 1976-77; research dir., dir. Vascular Lab., Miami (Fla.) Heart Inst., Miami Beach, 1977-88; adj. prof. bioengring. U. Miami, Coral Gables, 1977—; prof. surgery U. Miami (Fla.) Sch. Medicine, 1977—, prin. investigator series NIH programs and pharm. firms, 1977—; Harvard Travelling fellow lectr. in Europe, 1975. Recipient Apollo Achievement award NASA, 1969. Fellow Am. Coll. Cardiology, Am. Coll. of Radiology, Am. Assn. of Physicists in Medicine; mem. Biomed. Engring. Soc., Instrument Soc. Am., Am. Heart Assn., Internat. Cardiovascular Soc., Cardiovascular System Dynamics Soc. (founding mem.; editor 1976—, pres. 1980-82), New Eng. Cardiovascular Soc., AAAS, ASME, Kiwanis, Sigma Xi, Tau Beta Pi. Republican. Presbyterian. Clubs: La Gorce Country, Harvard, M.I.T. Contbr. numerous articles on biomechanics, cardiovascular diagnosis, dynamics and instrumentation to sri. jours.; patentee med. devices; developer math. models of arterial hemodynamics and clin. use of autotransfusion. Home: 770 Claughton Island Dr Miami FL 33131 Office: U Miami Sch Medicine R-669 PO Box 16069 Miami FL 33101-6069

RAINES, STEPHEN SAMUEL, franchising, consulting and development firm executive, lawyer; b. Los Angeles, Aug. 2, 1945; s. Harold Charles and Florence (Pynoos) S.; m. Judith Amanda Masterson, July 18, 1981; children: Jennifer, Jeffrey. BA, UCLA, 1967; JD, Loyola U., Los Angeles, 1971. Bar: Calif. Assoc. Thorpe, Sullivan, Clinnin & Workman, Los Angeles, 1971-75; v.p., gen. counsel United Rent-All, Inc., Los Angeles, 1975-80; pres. UDC Properties, Inc., L.A., 1977-80, Nat. Franchise Assocs., Inc., Atlanta, 1980—; v.p. and bd. dirs. M&R Advt., Inc., Atlanta; franchising cons. U.S. SBA, Atlanta, 1982—, Ga. Bus. Devel. Ctrs., Atlanta, 1982—; instr. Loyola U., L.A., 1971-72, L.A. Community Colls., 1972-75, U.S. Sml. Bus. Devel., Atlanta, 1982—, Ga. State U., Atlanta, 1982—; instr. leadership program Ga. Vietnam Vets., Atlanta, 1982—. Bd. dirs., sec. Vets. Resource Bus. Council, Atlanta, 1986. Served with USAR, 1968-74. Law fellow Loyola Law Sch. of L.A., 1970-71; recipient State of Ga. Bus. Adv. of Yr. award, 1987, Ga. Outstanding Citizen award, 1987. Mem. ABA, Calif. Bar Assn., Internat. Bar Assn., U.S. Supreme Ct. Bar Assn., Atlanta C. of C., Atlanta Venture Capital Forum (charter), Am. Mgmt. Assn., Gwinnett County C. of C. Home: 240 Lake View Ct Lavonia GA 30553-2018 Office: Nat Franchise Assocs Inc 3473 Satellite Blvd Ste 201 Duluth GA 30136-4658

RAINES, THOMAS EDWARD, county official; b. Pensacola, Fla., Oct. 29, 1964; s. Thomas Edward and Mary Delores (Reed) R. AS in Fire Sci. Tech., Pensacola Jr. Coll., 1985; BAS in Resource Mgmt., Troy State U., 1992, MPA in Justice Adminstrn., 1993. Comm. specialist II Escambia Emergency Mgmt., Pensacola, 1984-85; jud. security officer Escambia County Cts., Pensacola, 1985-91; dep. sheriff Escambia County Sheriff's Office, Pensacola, 1991-94; resource officer Escambia County Schs., Pensacola, 1994-95; sr. criminal justice officer Escambia County 1st Jud. Cir., Pensacola, 1995—; adj. instr. Pensacola Jr. Coll., 1986-88; part-time instr. trainer Escambia County Vocation Ctr., Pensacola, 1993—. Coord., com. chair ARC, Pensacola, 1987—; fire fighter/driver instr. Escambia County Vol.. Fire Dept., Pensacola, 1980-90; com. mem., counselor Boy Scouts Am., Pensacola, 1984-93; employee rels. bd. Escambia County, 1989-93; mem. promotions bd. Police Benevolent Assn., Pensacola, 1992. Recipient Life Saving medal Escambia County Sheriff, 1992; named Vol. of the Yr., ARC, 1987. Mem. Am. Soc. Pub. Adminstrn., Conf. of Minority Pub. Adminstrs., Criminal Justice Adminstrs. Conf., Am. Soc. Law Enforcement Trainers, Acad. Polit. Sci., Alpha Sigma Lambda. Democrat. Roman Catholic. Home: 3732 Raines Pensacola FL 32514 Office: First Judicial Circuit 4th Fl 190 Governmental Ctr Pensacola FL 32514

RAINES, TIM D., real estate corporation executive; b. Everett, Wash., May 8, 1950; s. Richard Thomas and Arvilla Mae (Chick) R.; m. Virginia N. McLaurin, July 21, 1977. BA, U. Ala., Tuscaloosa, 1968-72; MA, U. Alabama, Birmingham, 1977; postgrad., U. Calif., 1976-77. Community planner HUD, Birmingham, 1972-77; dir., program planning and eval. HUD, Atlanta, 1977-83, dir. regional ops. div., 1983-87; exec. v.p. chief operating officer Sanbury Corp., Atlanta, 1987-92; prin. Profit, Inc., 1992—. Pres. Stonington Homeowners Assn., Atlanta, 1980-83; patron Atlanta Ballet, 1978—; sponsor Pub. TV (WPBA), Atlanta, 1980—. Recipient Cert. of Recognition William A. Jump Found., 1978. Mem. Am. Soc. Pub. Adminstrs., Am. Mgmt. Assn., Atlanta Zool. Soc. Home: 8315 Ison Rd Atlanta GA 30350-3129

RAINESS, ALAN EDWARD, psychiatrist; b. N.Y.C., Sept. 24, 1935; s. George W. and Ida Rainess; m. Alice Maree Haber, June 5, 1968; children: Alice Jeanne Rainess Kules, James Alan (dec.). AB, Columbia Coll., 1957; MD, U. Paris, 1965. Diplomate Am. Bd. Psychiatry and Neurology. Intern Meadowbrook Hosp., East Meadow, L.I., 1965-66; resident in psychiatry N.Y. VA Hosp., N.Y.C., 1966-67; teaching fellow in psychiatry Harvard Med. Sch., Boston, 1967; chief resident in psychiatry Boston City Hosp., 1967; resident in psychiatry Walter Reed Med. Ctr., Washington, 1970-72; clin. dir. St. Elizabeth's Hosp., Washington, 1973-76; asst. chief psychiatry Andrews AFB Hosp., Camp Springs, Md., 1976-80, chief neurology, 1989-91; resident in neurology Wilford Hall USAF Med. Ctr., San Antonio, 1980-83; chief medicine and neuropsychiatry Air Univ. Hosp., Maxwell AFB, Ala., 1983-89, chief neurology, 1991-94; psychiatrist Manhattan Psychiat. Ctr., N.Y.C., 1994—; asst. clin. prof. psychiatry Georgetown U. Med. Sch., Washington, 1974-79; assoc. prof. neurology and psychiatry Uniformed Svcs. U. Health Scis., Bethesda, Md., 1989-94. Maj. U.S. Army, 1968-73, col. USAF, 1976-94, ret. Fellow Am. Psychiat. Assn.; mem. Am. Soc. Psychoanalytic Physicians (pres. N.Y. chpt. 1996), Am. Acad. Psychoanalysis (psychiat. assoc.), Masons. Home: 345 E 93rd St Apt 22H New York NY 10128-5522 Office: Manhattan Psychiat Ctr New York NY 10035

RAINEY, GORDON FRYER, JR., lawyer; b. Oklahoma City, Apr. 26, 1940; s. Gordon F. and Esther (Bliss) R.; m. Selina Norman, Aug. 3, 1968; children—Kate, Melissa, Gordon III. B.A. in English, U. Va., 1962, LL.B., 1967. Bar: Okla. 1967, Va. 1968. Assoc. Rainey, Flynn, Wallace, Ross & Cooper, Oklahoma City, 1967-68; assoc. Hunton & Williams, Richmond, Va., 1968-75, ptnr., 1975—; bd. dirs. Bon Secours Richmond Health Sys., Inc.; chmn. of exec. com. Hunton & Williams, dir. Crestar Fin. Corp., Crestar Bank, Weidmuller North Am., Inc., Health Corp. of Va., Meml. Regional Med. Ctr., Inc.; bd. mgrs. U. Va. Alumni Assn.; trustee Ch. Schs. Diocese Va.; campaign chmn. United Way of Greater Richmond, 1982, trustee, 1981-84; bd. dirs., past pres. Sheltering Arms Hosp., 1984; trustee Sheltering Arms Found.; chmn. Gov.'s Econ. Devel. Adv. Coun. Dist. 12; mem. Gov.'s Blue Ribbon Strike Force Commn. on Govtl. Reform; past mem. bd. govs. St. Catherine's Sch.; past chmn. bd. dirs. Leadership Met. Richmond; mem. Mayor's Emergency Shelter Task Force, 1981; past pres., bd. dirs. Met. Bus. Found. Served to 1st lt. U.S. Army, 1962-64, Korea. Recipient Communication and Leadership award Toastmasters Internat., 1983. Mem. ABA (sect. on bus. law, banking law com., mem. com. on devel. in investment services), Richmond Metro C. of C. (bd. dirs., past chmn.). Republican. Episcopalian. Clubs: Forum (Richmond, Va.). Office: Hunton & Williams Riverfront Plz East Tower 951 E Byrd St Richmond VA 23219-4040

RAINEY, ROBERT EDWARD, human resources management consultant; b. Erie, Pa., Apr. 6, 1943; s. Thomas James and Ellen Elizabeth (Stockman) R.; B.A. in Psychology, Gannon Coll., Erie, 1969; M.A. in Indsl.-Orgnl. Psychology, U. New Haven, 1976; m. Marie Fava, Sept. 2, 1967; children—R. Gregory, Allison E. Supr. recruiting Welch Foods, Inc., Westfield, N.Y., 1969-72; mgr. mgmt. devel. and recruiting Pepsico Internat., Purchase, N.Y., 1972-76; mgr. mgmt. and orgn. devel. Am. Can Internat. Co., Greenwich, Conn., 1976-78; dir. human resources Mitsubishi Aircraft Internat., Inc., Dallas, 1978-82; v.p. Drake Beam Morin, Inc., Dallas, 1983-85, sr. v.p., San Antonio, 1985-88; pres. Outpath Counseling Svcs. Inc, Ft. Worth, 1988—; mem. adj. faculty U. Tex. at Arlington ; cons. in field. Served with USNR, 1962-65. Mem. Am. Compensation Assn., Nat. Orgn. Devel. Network, Dallas Personnel Assn., Psi Chi. Republican. Roman Catholic. Lodge: Rotary. Home: 5502 Summit Ridge Trl Arlington TX 76017-1234

RAINEY, TERRY LEE, music educator, director; b. Miami, Fla., June 5, 1967; s. Terry Lee Sr. and Olivia Marilyn (Meyers) R.; m. Cindy Renea Bradshaw, Apr. 4, 1992; children: Terry L. III, Randy. BS in Music Edn. magna cum laude, U. Ala., 1990; postgrad., Jacksonville State U., 1991, Ga. So. U., 1994—. Cert. music tchr., Ga., Ala. Music instr. U. Ala., Tuscaloosa, 1989-90; dir. bands, music tchr. Wadley (Ala.) H.S. and Elem. Schs., 1990-91; dir. bands Albany (Ga.) Mid. Sch., 1991-92; music tchr., chorus dir. Sixes Elem. Sch., Canton, Ga., 1992-93; dir. bands, head music dept. McIntosh County Acad., Darien, Ga., 1993—; choir dir. Darien United Meth. Ch., 1994—. Composer vocal music, ch. hymn. Sunday sch. tchr. First United Meth. Ch., Wadley, 1991-92, Canton, 1992-93. U. Ala. scholar, 1987-90. Mem. Ga. Music Educators Assn., Phi Kappa Lambda, Phi Mu Alpha Sinfonia (pres. 1988-90, citation of excellence 1990).

RAINS, CURTIS RAY, educational administrator; b. Princeton, N.C., Jan. 25, 1944; s. William Henry and Betty Thelma (Daughtry) R.; m. Mary Rachel Edwards, July 23, 1995; children: Kim, Kris, Greg. BS, N.C. State U., 1967, MEd, 1971; EdD, Nova U., 1984. Tchr., prin. Johnston County Bd. Edn., Smithfield, N.C., 1967-76; prin. Wayne County Bd. Edn., Goldsboro, N.C., 1976-82; exec. asst. State Dept. Pub. Instns., Raleigh, N.C., 1982-83; spl. asst. Wayne County Bd. Edn., 1983-84; supt. Jones County Bd. Edn., Trenton, N.C., 1985-93; asst. dean U. N.C., Wilmington, 1993-94; cons. State Dept. Pub. Instns., 1994-95; prin. Asheville (N.C.) Pub. Schs., 1996—; chmn. State Testing Commn., Raleigh, 1992-93; coun. mem. Lenoir C.C., Kinston, N.C., 1985-93. Dem. Com., Trenton, 1985-93; chair supt. coun. N.C. Sch. Bd., 1990. Mem. N.C. Assn. Ednl. Personnel (state administr. of yr. 1990, dist. 12 adminstr. of yr. 1989), N.C. Consortium for Advt. of Pub. Edn. (bd. dirs. 1986-93), Masons. Baptist. Home: 103 Rough Pointe Ct Asheville NC 28806 Office: Asheville City Schs 197 S French Broad St Asheville NC 28801

RAINS, GLORIA CANN, environmentalist company executive; b. Atlanta, Feb. 12, 1928; d. Norman Douglas and Jane (McCurdy) Cann; m. John H. Rains Jr., Jan. 15, 1946 (dec. 1983); children: Michael W., Gordon C., Deborah C., John H. III. Freelance writer, cons. Palmetto, 1976—; chmn. ManaSota-88, Inc., Palmetto, 1976—; producer, host ManaSota-88 and the Environ., Brandenton, Fla., 1989-91; pres. ManaSota-88 Inc., Palmetto, 1991—; pres., bd. dirs. Environ. Confedn. S.W. Fla., Ft. Myers, 1976-85; bd. dirs., sec. Fla. div. Izaak Walter League of Am., Palmetto, 1976-80, Manatee chpt., Brandenton, 1976-80. Chmn. natural resources com. Manatee LWV, 1988-89; mem. Gov.'s Phospate Related Radiation Task Force, Fla., 1980-84, Gov.'s Hazardous Waste Policy Adv. Com., Fla., 1983-85, Gov.'s Local Govt. Study Commn., Mantee County, Fla., 1976-77, Mantaee County Pollution Control Bd., 1985-91. Mem. Air & Waste Mgmt. Assn., AAAS, Nat. Coalition Against the Misuse of Pesticides, Save Our Bays (bd. dirs. 1991), Pub. Citizen, Tampa Bay Nat. Estuary Com. Democrat. Home: 5314 Baystate Rd Palmetto FL 34221-8756

RAINS, MARY JO, banker; b. Konawa, Okla., Oct. 27, 1935; d. Albert Wood and Mary Leona (Winfield) Starns; m. Billy Z. Rains, June 17, 1956; 1 child, Nicky Z. Student Okla. Sch. Banking, 1969, Seminole Jr. Coll., 1970-72, E. Central State U., 1978-79, Okla. State U., 1987, Pontotoc County Adult Vocat. Tech. Ctr., 1987; diploma Am. Inst. Banking, 1981, 83. Acctg. divsn. Universal C.I.T., Oklahoma City, 1953-56; cashier Okla. State Bank (name changed to Bancfirst), Konawa, 1957-89, sr. v.p., 1989-95, sr. v.p., br. mgr. 1995—. Sec. 1st Baptist Ch., Konawa, 1969-79, mem. budgeting com., 1982-92, chmn. fin. com., 1994. Mem. Okla. Bankers Assn. (dir. women's div. 1974-76), Konawa C. of C., Am. Legion., Order Eastern Star. Home: RR 2 Box 28 Konawa OK 74849-9704 Office: PO Box 156 Konawa OK 74849-0156

RAINWATER, JOYCE KELLEY, special education educator, consultant; b. Gainesville, Tex., Feb. 1, 1937; d. Emerson H. and Ruth (Sanders) Kelley; children: Kelley Lynn, Kathryn Lee. BSC, Tex. Christian U., 1959, BA in Edn., 1970; spl. edn. cert., E. Tex. U., 1973; postgrad., Tex. Woman's U. Cert. spl. edn. tchr. Bd. dirs. Goodwill Industries, Ft. Worth. Mem. Coun. Exceptional Children, Assn. for Children with Behavior Disorders, Assn. Tex. Profl. Educators (bldg. rep.), Ft. Worth Woman's Club, Tex. Christian U.Century Club, Chi Omega Alumni Assn. Mem. Disciples of Christ Ch. Home: 6600 Foxpointe Rd Fort Worth TX 76132-4453

RAISINGHANI, MAHESH (MIKE) SUKHDEV, software consultant; b. New Delhi, India, Apr. 28, 1967; arrived in U.S., 1989; s. Sukhdev and Vanita R.; m. Prabhreet Raisinghani, June 26, 1993. Student, Redbridge Tech. Coll., London, 1986; B in Commerce, Osmania Univ., Hyderabad, India, 1989; MBA, U. Central Okla., 1990; MS, U. Tex., 1992; MS in Mgmt. Info. Systems, U. Tex., Arlington, 1992, postgrad., 1995—. Mktg. exec. IBM, Fort Worth, Tex., 1991-92; microsystems support specialist U. Tex., Arlington, Tex., 1993—; bus. assoc. Nat. Consulting Network, Dallas, 1993—. Mem. Mktg. Club (pres. 1989-90), Data Processing & Mgmt. Assoc. (v.p. 1990-91), Toastmasters, Rotary Club (pres. 1986-89). Home: 408 S Oak St # 501 Arlington TX 76010 Office: U Tex Box 19437 701 S Nedderman Dr Arlington TX 76019

RAJ, ANIL, shipbuilding executive; b. Kabul, Afghanistan, Sept. 10, 1950; came to U.S., 1972; s. Bhoj and Laj (Adlakha) R.; m. Linda Ann Trimble, Oct. 21, 1978; children: Nicole Ann, Marc Alexander. BS in Marine Engrng., Marine Engrng. Coll., Calcutta, India, 1972; BS in Naval Arch., U. Mich., 1974. Cert. marine engr. Naval architect Brown & Root, Inc., Houston, 1974-77, engrng. mgr., 1982-87; sr. staff naval architect Gulf Fleet Marine Corp., New Orleans, 1977-79, area ops. mgr., 1980-82; dir. engrng., prodn. and procurement Trinity Marine Group & Assoc. Cos., New Orleans, 1987-88; v.p. Trinity Marine Group & Assoc. Cos., Gulfport, Miss., 1988—; sr. v.p. Trinity Marine Group & Assoc. Cos., 1996—; mem. exec. control bd. Gulf Coast Regional Maritime Ctr. U. New Orleans, 1994—. Contbr. articles to profl. publs. Vol. tutor Operation Mainstream Adult Edn. Program, Slidell, La., 1987-89. Nat. Merit scholar Marine Engrng. Coll., 1968-72, Goodrich scholar U. Mich., 1973, 74. Mem. Soc. Naval Architects and Marine Engrs. (chmn. tech. rsch. com., chmn. offshore com. transp. and installation 1984-87, chmn. various coms. Tex. sect. 1976-80, 82-87, chmn. various coms. Gulf sect. 1988-92, exec. com. Tex. and Gulf sects., mem. T&R advanced craft nat. steering com., mem. ship prodn. nat. steering com., mem. nat. exec. coun. 1983, 92, host chmn. nat. ship prodn. com. ann. meeting), Royal Inst. Naval Architects, Am. Soc. Naval Engrs., Ship Builders Cccoun. Am., Am. Def. Preparedness Assn., Off-shore Marine Svc. Assn., U.S. Navy League, Nat. Ship Bldg. Rsch. Program (exec. control bd. 1993—), Tammany Yacht Club. Home: 407 Christian Ln Slidell LA 70458 Office: Trinity Marine Group Inc 13085 Seaway Rd Gulfport MS 39503-4607

RAJAGOPALAN, MELAPPALAYAM SRINIVASAN, microbiologist; b. Nerur, Tamil Nadu, India, Sept. 5, 1952; s. M.R. and Saroja Srinivasan; m. Kala (Krishnamurthy) R., June 8, 1980; children: Sadhana, Vibha. BS in Biology, Mahajana Coll., India, 1972; MS in Microbiology, Christian Med. Coll., India, 1975; PhD of Microbiology, Christian Med. Coll., 1983. Rsch. asst. ICMR Tuberculosis Rsch. Ctr., Madras, India, 1975-78; from rsch. fellow to rsch. assoc. ICMR Ctr. for Virology, Vellore, India, 1978-84; postdoctoral fellow U. Calif., San Francisco, 1984-86; rsch. assoc. dept. microbiology U. Ky., Lexington, 1986-87; from staff scientist to head virology dept. Nat. Inst. Immunology, New Delhi, India, 1987-89; assoc. scientist Lovelace Med. Found., Albuquerque, 1989-92; pres. Ky. Biosafety Cons., Inc., Lexington, 1992—. Contbr. chpt. to book and articles to profl. jours. Mem. Am. Soc. Microbiology, Soc. for Exptl. Biology and Medicine, Indian Immunology Soc. (life), Indian Assn. Med. Microbiologists (life), Ky. Safety & Health Network. Office: Ky Biosafety Cons Inc PO Box 23407 Lexington KY 40523-3407

RAKOW, B.J., management consultant; b. Chgo., Nov. 14, 1938; d. Meyer S. and Lee S. (Siegel) Kaplan; m. Allen Rakow, Jan. 8, 1959; children: Sherry Superfine, Joseph Steven, Scott. MS in Adult Edn./Tng. Mgmt., Fla. Internat. U., Miami, 1974; postgrad., Fla. Atlantic U., Boca Raton, 1980; PhD in Clin. Psychology summa cum laude, U. Ill., 1963. Owner Sherry Jewelry Co., Miami, 1968-72; assoc. dir. Inst. for Women Fla. Internat. U., 1974-75; mgr. tng. and devel. Am. Savs. and Loan Assn., Miami, 1975-76; dir. corp. tng. and exec. devel. Jordan Marsh of Fla., Miami, 1976-80; mgmt. cons. Kane Assocs., Miami and Tampa, Fla., 1980-82; tng. adminstr. State Atty.'s Office, Miami, 1982-83; v.p. mktg. Citibank (Fla.), Miami, 1983-89; mgmt. cons. Fla./Caribbean Region Right Assocs., Miami, 1989-91; dir. Fla. Dislocated Workers Assistance Ctr. Fla. Dept. Labor and Employment Security, 1991-93; dir. profl. svcs. Right Assocs., Miami, 1993—; workshop leader Dade County Sch. Bd., Miami, 1993-94; adj. prof., seminar leader Ctr. for Bus. and Industry, Miami-Dade C.C. Contbr. articles to Miami Herald, 1993. Mem. bus. adv. coun. Barry U. Mem. ASTD, AAUP, Am. Mktg. Assn. Office: Right Assocs 8350 NW 52nd Ter Ste 400 Miami FL 33166-7709

RALEY, WILLIAM L., agricultural executive; b. 1917. With citrus industry, 1958—; bd. dirs. First Commerce Bank, Winter Haven, Fla. Mem. Dundee (Fla.) Citrus Growers Assn. (pres., bd. dirs.).

RALIS, PARASKEVY, art educator, artist; b. N.Y.C., Sept. 16, 1951; d. Harry and Katerina (Koumi) R. AA, Miami-Dade Community Coll., 1970; BFA, Fla. Internat. U., 1973; MS, Nova U., 1977. Tchr. Miami (Fla.) Park Elem. Sch., 1973-80; instr. visual arts, photography Am. Sr. High Sch., 1980-81; tchr. Holmes Elem. Sch., 1981-84, Horace Mann Jr. High Sch., 1983-85; instr. magnet program visual arts, photography R.R. Moton South Ctr. for the Expressive Arts, 1984—, head dept. fine arts spl. area, 1986-89, 93-94, magnet lead tchr., 1992-93; magnet dept. head R.R. Moton South Ctr. for the Expressive Arts, Miami, 1993-94; chairperson grant writing com. R.R. Moton Expressive Arts Ctr., 1990; mem. SBM Sch. Cadre, 1993-94, R.R. Moton's Sch. Based Mgmt. Cadre, 1994-95. Prin. works include Twenty-First M. Allen Hortt Meml. Exhbn., Contemporary Reflections of the 19th Century, 1979, Media Plus, 1980, Inception, 1981, Artspace, 1982, Class Impressions, 1983, Southern Exposure, 1986; exhibited in group shows at Met. Mus. Art and Art Ctr., Coral Gables, Fla., 1986, Broward C.C. Fine Arts Gallery, 1985, Mus. Art, Ft. Lauderdale, 1979, 84, North Miami Mus. and Art Ctr., 1983, Fla. Internat. U., 1980, Nat. Exhibit Am. Art, Chautauqua, N.Y., 1985, Images I Miami Dade C.C., 1988, Omni Internat. Mall Artworks Gallery, 1990, 91, 92, The Ctr. for Visual Comms., 1993, Sheldon Lurie Art Against AIDS Auction IV, Biltmore Hotel, Coral Gables, Fla., 1994, Rex Art Tchrs. Exhibit, 1996, Jacqueline Hinchey Sipes Invitational Art Exhibit, Miami, 1996; inventor first art game in U.S. History, 1978; Photog. of James Brown, 1981. Mem. Dade County Art Tchrs. Assn. (bd. dirs., publicity chmn., Pres.'s award 1984), Fla. Art Educators Assn. (presenter 1994), United Tchrs. of Dade (liaison to Dade Art Educators Assn. 1981-94, 95—, arts advocacy chair for Dade Art Educators 1996—), Fla. Art Edn. Assn. (chair photography com. conv. 1990), Dade Art Educators (pres. 1996—). Greek Orthodox. Home: 798 NE 71st St Miami FL 33138-5718 Office: RR Moton S Ctr for Excellence 18050 Homestead Ave Exp Arts Ctr Miami FL 33157-5529

RALSTON, GILBERT ALEXANDER, writer, educator; b. L.A., Jan. 5, 1912; s. Alexander Gilbert and Jeanette (Johnston) R.; grad. Pasadena Coll., 1929-32; grad. Am. Acad. Dramatic Arts, 1935; B.C.A., Sierra Nev. Coll., 1972; D in Psychology, Fielding Inst., 1983, PhD in Health Sci., 1987, Columbia Pacific U., 1986; m. Mary K. Hart, Dec. 20, 1938; children—Michael, David. Actor, stage mgr. theatre prodns. N.Y.C., 1931-35; writer, dir. radio shows NBC, N.Y.C., 1936-38; prodn. supr. Compton Advt., Inc., N.Y.C., West Coast, 1939-42; organizer, mgr. radio dept. Proctor & Gamble, Cin., 1943-47, exec. producer inc. TV div., 1947-50; free lance producer TV films, 1950-55; exec. producer in charge TV drama CBS, 1955, dir. network programs originating in N.Y.C., 1956; producer High Adventure documentaries with Lowell Thomas, 1957; chmn. sch. communication arts Tahoe (Cal.) Paradise Coll., 1968; dean sch. communicative arts Sierra Nevada Coll., Incline Village, Nev., 1960-73, pres., 1973-83, pres. emeritus, 1983—; pres. Ralston Sch. Communicative Arts, Genoa, Nev., 1971—, Ralston Sch. Massage; v.p. Rule of Three Prodns., Los Angeles, 1973—; lectr. Fordham U., City Coll. City U. N.Y., Loyola U. of Los Angeles, St. Mary's Coll. of Calif. Mem. Authors Guild, ASCAP, Western Writers Am., Writers Guild Am., Am. Massage and Therapy Assn. Author: Ben, 1972; (with Richard Newhafer) The Frightful Sin of Cisco Newman, 1972; Dakota Warpath, 1973; Dakota: Red Revenge, 1973; Dakota Cat Trap, 1974; Dakota Murder's Money, 1974; Dakota: Chain Reaction, The Deadly Art, 1975, The Third Circle, 1976, The Tao of Touch, 1983, Gods Fist, 1989, Hamelin House, 1989, Hunter Fentress, 1990, Fattura Della Morte, 1990, others. Author screenplays: No Strings Attached, 1962; A Gallery of Six, 1963; A Feast of Jackals, 1963; Cockatrice, 1965; Kona Coast, 1967; Night of the Locust, 1969; Ben, 1971, Third Circle, 1975, Sure, 1975. Author screen adaptations: Willard (by Stephen Gilbert), 1970; Bluebonnet (by Boris Sobelman and Jack H. Robinson), 1971; Dakota Red, 1987. Author scripts for TV under sometime pseudonym Gil Alexander: High Adventure, Naked City, Route 66, Follow the Sun, Bus Stop, The Untouchables, Alcoa Theatre, Ben Casey, Richard Boone Show, 12 O'Clock High, The Name of the Game, Daktari, Laredo, Combat, Big Valley, Gunsmoke, Amos Burke, Slattery's People, Alfred Hitchcock, Star Trek, It Takes a Thief, O'Hara, Cannon, numerous others. Address: PO Box 490 Sullivans Island SC 29482-0490

RALSTON, RUTH ANNE, women's health nurse; b. Staunton, Va., May 15, 1958; d. Thomas Edward and Betty Lee (King) Graham; m. Daniel Thomas Ralston, Aug. 15, 1981; children: Anne Katherine, Adam Thomas, Alison Brooke Rebecca. BS in Biology, Longwood Coll., 1981; ADN, Piedmont Va. C.C., 1985. RN, Va. Med./surg. staff nurse Montgomery County Hosp., Blacksburg, Va., 1985-86; staff/charge nurse obstetrics and nursery Martha Johnson Hosp., Charlottesville, Va., 1986-88; office nurse mgr. Bruce D. Campbell MD, med. office, Free Union, Va., 1988-94, William B. Freedman, M.D., Cardiologist, Charlottesville, 1995—; childbirth instr., labor coach Martha Jefferson Hosp., 1991—. Mem. Internat. Childbirth Edn. Assn. (cert. childbirth educator). Democrat. Home: 4235 Viewmont Rd Earlysville VA 22936-9722

RAMAGE, MARTIS DONALD, JR., banker; b. Tupelo, Miss., Oct. 6, 1957; s. Martis Donald and Helen Frances (Estes) R. AA, Itawamba Jr. Coll., Fulton, Miss., 1978; BBA in Banking and Fin., U. Miss., 1980; grad., Mid South Sch. of Banking, 1989. Mgmt. trainee Peoples Bank & Trust Co., Tupelo, 1981-82, asst. cashier, 1983-89, asst. v.p., 1989-90, v.p., 1990-93, 1st v.p., 1993—; sec. Peoples Holding Co., 1993-96, v.p., 1996—. Author: Our Ramage Family, 1986, Mississippi Society SAR 1909-1993; co-editor: The Peoples Bank & Trust Co-In Partnership with the Community, 1989; editor N.E. Miss. Hist. Geneal. Soc. Quar. Sec., treas. United Way of Greater Lee County, Tupelo, 1988-89, Leadership Lee; pres. Itawamba Jr. Coll. Alumni Assn., Fulton, Miss., 1982-83, Friends of Lee County Libr., 1995—, pres. 1995—; bd. dirs. Brice's Battlefield Commn., Inc., 1995—; bd. trustees Miss. Dept. Archives and Hist., 1996—; chmn. Christmas Festival Com., Tupelo, 1990-91; mem. bd. Tupelo Artists Guild. Mem. SAR (trustee 1992-94, pres. Miss. 1991-92, Silver Good Citizenship medal 1990), SCV, Mil. Order of Stars and Bars, Am. Inst. Banking (pres. Tupelo chpt. 1986-87), Ole Miss. Alumni Assn. (bd. dirs. 1991-94), Tupelo Luncheon Civitan Club, Masons, Bank Adm. Inst. (North Miss. chpt. pres. 1994-95, v.p. 1990-94), Sons of the Revolution (v.p. Miss. chpt. 1994—), Miss. Hist. Soc. (bd. dirs. 1995—). Home: 4218 Ridgemont Dr Belden MS 38826-9785 Office: Peoples Bank & Trust Co 209 Troy St Tupelo MS 38801-4827

RAMAPRASAD, SUBBARAYA, medical educator; b. Mysore, India, May 20, 1954; came to the U.S., 1980; s. Puttaniah and Sharadamma Subbaraya; m. Padma, Sept. 28, 1987; 1 child, Sanjay. PhD, Indian Inst. Sci., 1979. Instr. U. Ark. Med. Scis., Little Rock, 1989-91, asst. prof., 1991-94, assoc. prof., 1995—. Contbr. articles to profl. jours. Grantee NIMH, 1994, Ark. Sci. Tech. Authority, 1991. Mem. Internat. Soc. Magnetic Resonance Medicine, N.Y. Acad. Sci., Sigma Xi. Hindu. Home: 5 Sams Cove Little Rock AR 72212 Office: U Ark Med Sci Dept Radiol 4301 W Markham St Little Rock AR 72205

RAMASWAMY, JEGADHABI NACHIAPPAGOUNDAR, environmental engineer, state agency executive; b. Jegadhabi, Madras, India, June 11, 1931; came to U.S., 1967; s. Kaliappa Nachiappa and Kumarayee (Ammal) Goundar; m. Visa Karuppana, Jan. 20, 1956; children: Sampath, Mythili. BE in Civil Engring., U. Madras, India, 1954, MSc in Pub. Health Engring., 1962; PhD in Environ. Engring., W.Va. U., 1970. Registered profl. engr., Fla. Engr. Pub. Health Engring. and Mcpl. Works Dept., Madras, India, 1954-67; rsch. assoc. W.Va. U., Morgantown, 1969-70; chief sanitary engr. Zimmerman, Evans & Leopold, Augusta, Ga., 1970-73; design group mgr. Clyde Williams & Assocs., South Bend, Ind., 1973-78; project mgr. Williams & Works, Grand Rapids, Mich., 1978-80; prof. environ. engring. Anna U., Madras, 1980-84; prof. engr. supr. Dep. Environ. Protection, Tallahassee, Fla., 1984—. Contbr. articles to profl. jours. Grantee Dept. Sci. and Tech., New Delhi, 1982. Mem. Am. Acad. Environ. Engrs. (diplomate). Home: 6719 Pasadena Dr Tallahassee FL 32311-8489 Office: Dept Environ Protection 2600 Blairstone Rd Tallahassee FL 32399-6516

RAMBANA, ANDREA MARIE, nursing educator; b. Kingston, Jamaica, Dec. 29, 1961; d. George Albert and Lilieth Theresa (Watts) Russell; m. Richard Craig Rambana, Dec. 7, 1986; children: Michelle, Andrew. Nursing Diploma, Jackson Meml. Hosp. Sch. of, Nursing, Miami, 1984; BSN, Barry U., 1991. RNC. Med. unit staff nurse Jackson Meml. Hosp., Miami, 1984, staff nurse labor and delivery unit, 1985-88; newborn spl. care unit staff nurse Jackson North Maternity Ctr., Opa-Locak, Fla., 1989-92; nursing clin. educator Jackson North Maternity Ctr., Opa-Locak, 1993—; neonatal resuscitation program instr. Am. Acd. Pediatrics, Miami, 1991—; coord./instr. babysitting course, Jackson North Maternity Ctr., 1993—; CPR instr., 1993; coord. sibling and parent safety courses class, 1996. Participant: (TV series) Healthy Babies, Happy Parents, 1994. Mem. AWHOON, Sigma Theta Tau. Roman Catholic. Office: Jackson North Maternity Ctr 14701 NW 27th Ave Opa Locka FL 33054-3350

RAMBUSS, RICHARD, English language educator; b. Buffalo. BA, Amherst Coll., 1983; MA in English, Johns Hopkins U., 1986, PhD in English, 1990. Asst. prof. English Kenyon Coll., Gambier, Ohio, 1990-92; assoc. prof. Tulane U., New Orleans, 1992—. Author: (book) Spenser's Secret Career, 1993; contbr. essays to profl. jours. Mem. MLA, Renaissance Soc. of Am., Spenser Soc. Office: Tulane U English Dept New Orleans LA 70118

RAMER, HAL REED, academic administrator; b. Kenton, Tenn., June 8, 1923; s. Claude Orion and Dixie Clayton (Carroll) R. BS, George Peabody Coll., 1947; MSW, U. Tenn., 1952; PhD, Ohio State U., 1963. Asst. dean men Ohio State U., Columbus, 1953-58, dir. internat. house, 1958-60, staff asst. to pres., 1960-62; asst. commr. State Dept. Edn., Nashville, 1963-70; founding pres. Vol. State C.C., Gallatin, Tenn., 1970—; bd. dirs. Sumner Regional Health Sys., Inc. Mem. adv. bd. First Union Bank Mid. Tenn., Hendersonville, Tenn., com. March of Dimes, Gallatin; trustee Nashville United Way, 1970s; bd. govs. Aquinas Coll., Nashville, 1967—; bd. dirs. Y.M.C.A.; former chmn. Tenn. Fulbright-Hays Sch. Commn. With USAAF, 1943-45; col. Tenn. Def. Force. Recipient Distinctive Svc. award Devel. Coun. Peabody Coll., Nashville, 1960s, Distinguished Svc. award Tenn. Dept. Edn., 1970, Outstanding Leader award Vanderbilt U. chpt. Phi Delta Kappa, 1987, Gov.'s Svc. award State of Tenn., 1993, Sertoma Club Svc. to Mankind award, 1995-96, Disting. Alumnus award Peabody Coll., 1996; named Rotarian of the Yr., 1979; Paul Harris fellow Rotary Internat., 1981. Mem. Am. Legion, Coun. Pres. C.Cs. (chmn. state Tenn. 1988-89), Tenn. Coll. Assn. (pres. 1985-86), Nat. Alumni Assn. Peabody Coll. (pres. 1970-71, bd. trustees), Tenn. Acad. Sci., Tenn. and Sumner Co. Hist. Socs. (bd. dirs.), English Speaking Union Internat. (Nashville chpt.), So. Assn. Colls. and Schs., Univ. Club Nashville, Gallatin and Hendersonville C. of C., Torch Club Internat., Alpha Tau Omega, Kappa Phi Kappa, Alpha Phi Omega, Phi Delta Kappa. Methodist. Home: 148 Kenner Ave Nashville TN 37205-2219 Office: Vol State CC Office of Pres 1480 Nashville Pike Gallatin TN 37066-3188

RAMEY, ROBERT HOMER, JR., theological seminary educator; b. Danville, Va., Sept. 27, 1929; s. Robert Homer and Helen Lee (Tesh) R.; m. Jane Robbins McGarry, June 28, 1952 (dec. Nov. 1983); children: Robbin Ramey Dorrier, Robert McGarry, Andrea Ramey Mize; m. Gail Pannill Anderson, Oct. 25, 1986. BA, BS, Hampden-Sydney (Va.) Coll., 1951, DD, 1975; BD, Union Theol. Sem. in Va., Richmond, 1954, ThM, 1955, DMin, 1974. Ordained to ministry Presbyn. Ch. U.S.A., 1954. Asst. pastor White Meml. Presbyn. Ch., Raleigh, N.C., 1955-56; pastor St. Andrew Presbyn. Ch., Lynchburg, Va., 1957-63, Knox Presbyn. Ch., Norfolk, Va., 1963-67, Selwyn Ave. Presbyn. Ch., Charlotte, N.C., 1967-74, Meml. Dr. Presbyn. Ch., Stone Mountain, Ga., 1974-79; prof. ministry Columbia Theol. Sem., Decatur, Ga., 1979-95. Author: The Minister's Role in Evangelism, 1985, Discoveries on the Way, 1991, (with others) Living the Christian Life, 1992, Growing Church Leaders, 1995, The Pastor's Start-Up Manual, 1995. Home: 3632 Prestwick Dr Tucker GA 30084-2421

RAMIREZ, ANA MILAGROS, psychologist; b. Santurce, P.R., Oct. 14, 1946; d. Angel Daniel Ramirez-Albite and Elba Hayeé Ramirez; m. Manuel G. Viloria-Hernández, Oct. 19, 1974. BSc in Home Econs., U. P.R., 1963-66, MA in Profl. Counseling and Guidance, 1971; PhD in Psychology, Caribbean Ctr. Advance Studies, 1976. Diplomate and bd. cert. forensic examiner. Profl. counselor P.R. Jr. Coll., Rio Piedras, 1972-74; child psychologist Head Start Program, San Juan, P.R., 1974-76; dir. community mental health ctr. Dept. Health, San Juan, 1976-79; pvt. practice Rio Piedras, 1976-87; prof. psychology Inter Am. U., P.R., 1979-81, 85-87; psychol. resident Edmund S. Bartlett & Assocs., Orlando, Fla., 1987-90; counselor Employee Assistance Program, Orlando, 1987-91; cons. Personal Performance Program, Orlando, 1987-91; supervised pvt. practice Orlando, Fla., 1991-96; psychol. cons. Hispanic Pastors of Presbyn. Ch., nationwide, 1996—; Mem. Gov.'s Com. for Employment of Handicapped, San Juan, 1980-84, Women's Issues Cons. Com., 1985-87, Bd. Ethnic Minorities Affair, Washington, 1981-83. Marriage counselor Cath. Ch., P.R. 1968-74. Recipient Meritorious Svc. awards P.R. Psychol. Assn., 1978, Pres.'s Com. Employment of Handicapped, 1982. Mem. APA, P.R. Psychol. Assn. (v.p. 1977-78, pres. 1978-79, chair various coms. 1980-85, cand. examinig bd. of the state, 1983-85, main speaker P.R. Legislature Bill Practice in Psychology, 1977-82). Democrat.

RAMIREZ, ENRIQUE RENE, social sciences educator; b. Mayaguez, P.R., Feb. 10, 1930; s. Sergio Ramirez and Ofelia Rivera-Zapata; m. Lydia Gonzalez, Sept. 29, 1951; children: Enrique, Hector, Pierangeli, Roxanna. BA, Okla. State U., 1975, MA, 1976, PhD, 1979. Writer, rschr. U.S. Army, Fort Dix, N.J., 1963-66; pers. supr. U.S. Army, Vietnam, 1970-71; writer, rschr. White Sands Proving Grounds, Las Cruces, N.Mex., 1956-58; instr., ROTC Okla. State U., Stillwater, 1968-70, instr., 1976-79; prof., chmn. Tex. Coll., Tyler, 1979-92; dir. history and geography Tyler Jr. Coll., 1992—; Disting. panelist Nat. Grad Fellows program U.S. Dept. Edn., 1986—; coord. internat. studies Southwestern Internat. Consortium, 1984—; chmn. Cmty. Devel. Commn., Tyler, 1989—; lectr. in field. Author: Encounter of Two Worlds: The Mexican Experience, 1991; editor: Newspaper Voz Hispana, Tyler, 1987-89. Chmn. Community Devel. Comm., 1988—; Pres. East Tex. Coun. on World Affairs, Tyler, 1988-89, Hispanic Assn. East Tex., 1989—; commr. Clean Tyler Commn., 1984-85; rep. Conf. on Fgn. Policy/Dept. State, Washington, 1988; bd. dirs. United Way of Greater Tyler; 1986—, Ct. Apptd. Advocates, 1990—, Parents Svc. Ctr., 1990—, Am. Cancer Soc., 1988—, ARC, 1987—, TV Prog. Mundo Hispano, 1990—; precinct chmn. Dem. party. Fulbright-Hays scholar Soviet Studies/U.S. Dept. Edn., 1989, Brazilian Studies, 1991; recipient award United Negro Coll. Fund/MacArthur Found., Spain, 1983, Sears-Roebuck Found. Prof. of Yr. award, Tyler, 1991, Okla. Regents for Higher Edn. Rsch. award, Stillwater, 1979; fellow Students in Free Enterprise, 1988. Mem. Southwestern Social Scis. Assn., Kiwanis. Roman Catholic. Home: 2807 Apache Trl

Tyler TX 75707-9317 Office: Tyler Jr Coll 510-2441 PO Box 9020 Tyler TX 75711-9020

RAMIREZ, MANUEL FERNANDO, surgeon, career officer; b. Mayaguez, P.R., Apr. 22, 1950; s. Ferdinand and Edith (Arroyo) R.; div. Oct. 1986; children: Manuel Jr., Juan, Adriana; m. Diana L. Luttrull, June 20, 1990; 1 child, Anthony. BS, U. P.R., 1972, MD, 1976. Diplomate Am. Bd. Surgery. Commd. 2d lt. U.S. Army, 1976, advanced through grades to col., 1992; intern Tripler Army Med. Ctr., Oahu, Hawaii, 1976-77; resident in gen. surgery Walter Reed Army Med. Ctr., Washington, 1977-81; chief gen. surgery svc. Noble Army Hosp., Ft. McClellen, Ala., 1981-84; vascular fellowship Walter Reed Army Med. Ctr., Washington, 1984-85; asst. chief vascular surgery Brooke Army Med. Ctr., Ft. Sam Houston, Tex., 1985-89; chief vascular surgery Eisenhower Army Med. Ctr., Ft. Gordon, Ga., 1989—, chief gen. surgery, 1993—; also dir. gen. surgery residency program, 1993—; physician advisor U.S. Mil. Med. Group, El Salvador, 1986. Fellow ACS, Interam. Coll. Physicians and Surgeons; mem. AMA, Assn. Program Dirs. in Surgery, Am. Soc. Gen. Surgeons, Soc. Am. Gastrointestinal Endoscopic Surgeons, Internat. Soc. for Endovascular Surgery. Republican. Roman Catholic. Home: 147 Stone Mill Dr Martinez GA 30907-1659 Office: US Army Dept Surgery Eisenhower Army Med Ctr Fort Gordon GA 30905

RAMIREZ, MARIA C(ONCEPCIÓN), educational administrator; d. Ines and Carlota (Cruz) R. BA, Incarnate Word Coll., San Antonio, 1966; MEd, U. Tex., Austin, 1979; postgrad., S.W. Tex. State U., San Marcos, 1980. Cert. elem. tchr., bilingual tchr., supr. Elem. tchr. regular and bilingual Edgewood Ind. Sch. Dist., San Antonio, 1966-69; elem tchr. regular and bilingual Austin (Tex.) Ind. Sch. Dist., 1969-74, bilingual program coord., 1974-89; instrnl. coord. Austin Ind. Sch. Dist., 1989-91, helping tchr., 1991-96, bilingual instrnl. coord., 1996—. Mem. NAFE, ASCD, Tex. Assn. for Bilingual Edn., Austin Area Assn. for Bilingual Edn., Austin Assn. for Pub. Sch. Adminstrs., Tex. Assn. Hispanic Sch. Adminstrs.

RAMIREZ, MICHAEL P., editorial cartoonist; b. Tokyo; s. Ireneo Edward and Fumiko Maria R. Syndicated cartoonist Copley News Svc., 1986—; cartoonist The Comml. Appeal, Memphis, 1990—. Recipient Pulitzer Prize for editorial cartooning, 1994. Office: The Commercial Appeal 495 Union Ave Memphis TN 38103-3242

RAMIREZ, RALPH HENRY, nurse, corporate executive; b. Oakland, Calif., Sept. 25, 1949; s. Hector Ramirez and Genevieve (Figueroa) Ingraham. BS in Nursing, San Jose State U., 1974. RN; cert. critical care nurse. DON nursing Chgo. Ctr. Hosp., 1980-84; adminstr. Med. Profls. Supplemental Staffing, Chgo., 1984-85; pres. Progressive Svcs., Chgo., 1985-92; v.p. Seville Internat. Tours, Inc., 1990—; pres. Progressive Health Svcs. Ctrs., Inc., 1992-94, Merchants Nat. Fin. and Mgmt., Houston, 1994-95; ops. mgr. Ravenswood Home Care, Chgo., 1995—. Contbr. articles to profl. jours. Sponsor nursing symposium, Chgo., 1991—; bd. dirs. AIDS Found. of Chgo., 1991—, chmn. Gala com., 1993, 94; co-chair Bonaventure House Benefit, 1993. Mem. Am. Biog. Inst. (Disting. Leadership award for Outstanding Svc. to Nursing Profession, Golden Acad. award), Chgo. Nurses Assn., Ill. Nurses Assn., Sigma Theta Tau. Democrat. Roman Catholic. Home: 4334 N Hazel St Apt 1708 Chicago IL 60613-1444 Office: Ravenswood Home Care 4600 N Ravenswood Ave Chicago IL 60640-4510

RAMIREZ DE LA PISCINA, JULIAN, diversified financial services company executive; b. Madrid, Apr. 17, 1956; came to U.S., 1984; s. Julian Ramirez de la Piscina and Bienvenida Pena. MBA, U. Complutense, Madrid, 1979. Lic. economist, lawyer. Future mgr. trainer Internat. Computers Ltd., ICL, London, 1980-81; fin. mgr. Moncainsa, Guatemala, 1981; mgr. adminstrn./fin. Mac Lines, Madrid, 1982-83, Warner Home Video, Madrid, 1984; gen. mgr. Constral, Cancun, Mex., 1984-86; CEO Grupo Inmobiliario Turistico, G.I.T., Caribbean area, 1986—; adviser ICL, Madrid, 1981, Fiscal Corp. Svcs., Madrid, 1981-84. Sgt. armed forces, Madrid, 1976-81. Mem. championship Spanish Rugby team, Nat. League, Spain, 1973. Mem. Lawyers Assn. of Spain. Mem. PSP polit. party. Home: 2451 Brickell Ave Apt 11M Miami FL 33129-2420 Office: Radisson Inverrary Resort 3501 Inverrary Blvd Miami FL 33129

RAMOS, MANUEL ANTONIO, JR., pulmonologist; b. Lima, Peru, Dec. 17, 1959; arrived in U.S., 1962; s. Manuel and Rosa (Palao) R. BS with Hons., cum laude, U. Miami, 1980; MD, Tulane U., 1984. Diplomate Am. Bd. Internal Medicine, diplomate Subspecialty of Pulmonary Disease. Intern Tulane Hosps., New Orleans, 1984-85; resident in medicine Jackson Meml. Hosp., Miami, Fla., 1985-87, fellow in pulmonology, 1987-90; pvt. practice in pulmonology Plantation, Fla., 1990—; sec. dept. medicine Plantation Gen. Hosp. Contbr. articles to profl. jours. Active Archbishops of Miami Charity Drive Guild. Fellow Am. Coll. Chest Physicians; mem. AMA (Physicians Recognition award 1990, 95), ACP, Am. Thoracic Soc., Am. Soc. Internal Medicine, Broward County Med. Assn. (Salvation Army Clinic, Ft. Lauderdale 1991—), Plantation C. of C. Office: 7050 NW 4th St Ste 301 Plantation FL 33317-2247

RAMOS, RAUL, surgeon; b. Sabinas, Coahulla, Mex., Oct. 30, 1942; s. Raul and Carmen (Lopez) R.; m. Hilda Mazquiz de Ramos, Mar. 1, 1992; children by previous marriage: Raul, Maria, Ana, Veronica. MD, U. Nuevo Leon, Mex., 1966. Diplomate Am. Bd. Surgery, Am. Bd. Colon and Rectal Surgery. Intern Bapt. Meml. Hosp., San Antonio, 1966-67, mem. active staff, chmn. dept. surgery, 1983-84, 89-90; clin. asst. prof. surgery U. Tex. Health Sci. Ctr., San Antonio, 1973-78, head divns. proctology, 1973—, clin. assoc. prof. surgery, 1978-89, dir. residency program colon and rectal surgery, 1979-82, clin. prof. surgery, 1989—; mem. active staff Santa Rosa Med. Ctr., S.W. Tex. Meth. Hosp., Audie Murphy Meml. VA Hosp., San Antonio Humana Hosp., St. Luth's Luth. Hosp., Bexar County Hosp. Dist.; vis. prof. U. Nuevo Leon, Monterrey , Mex., 1976, 80, Assemblea Nacional de Cirjuanos, Mexico City, 1976, Mil. Med. Sch., Mexico City, 1980, 81, Socieda Mex. Cirjanos Puebla, 1990, Loyola Univ., 1992, U. Guanajuato, mex., 1992, Institutos Technologico Estudios Superiores en Monterrey, 1993; examiner Am. Bd. Surgery, 1990; presenter numerous seminars. Mem. AMA, ACS, Am. Soc. Colon and Rectal Surgeons (mem. coun. 1981-82), Tex. Med. Assn., Tex. Soc. Colon and Rectal Surgeons (pres. 1977, 78), Tex. Soc. Colo-Rectal Surgeons (sec. 1977)Associacion de Cirujanos de Noreste A.C., Sociedad Colombiana de Gastroenterologia, Sociedad Colombiana de Cirujanos de Colon y Recto, Sociedad Chilena de Cirugia, Sociedad Chilena de Proctologia, Sociedad mexicana de Cirjuanos de Colon y Recto, Collegium Internatcionale Chirurgia Digestivae, Internat. Soc. Univ. Colon and Rectal Surgeons, So. Med. Assn. (v.p. sect. colo-rectal surgery 1979, chmn. 1980, sec. 1981, 82, 83), Priestly Surg. Soc., Bexar County Med. Soc. (bd. dirs. 1990-92, chmn. exhibits com.), Gen. Surg. Soc. San Antonio (v.p. 1979, pres. 1980), Sociedad Medica Hispano-Americano de Tejas (sec. 1979, pres. 1986), San Antonio Surg. Soc. (pres. 1986-87), Aust Soc., Mayo Alumni. Office: Colon and Rectal Assocs San Antonio 7950 Floyd Curl Dr Ste 101 San Antonio TX 78229-3916

RAMOS, ROSE MARY, elementary education educator; b. San Antonio, Aug. 8, 1942; d. Henry Barbosa and Bertha Alice (Cuellar) Gonzalez; m. Jesus Ramos Jr., Sept. 11, 1965; children: Rebecca Anne, Veronica Anne. BS in Elem. Edn., Our Lady of Lake U., San Antonio, 1965; MA in Edn., U. Houston, 1992. Cert. elem. educator, kindergarten, reading specialist, bilingual and ESL. Tchr. San Antonio Ind. Sch. Dist., 1965-89, Ft. Bend County (Tex.) Ind. Sch. Dist., 1989—; acad. adv. com. Ft. Bend I.S.D., 1996. Mem. Nat. Space Soc., Tex. State Reading Assn., Tex. Educators of Speakers of Other Langs., Greater Houston Area Reading Assn., San Antonio Conservation Soc., Internat. Reading. Assn. Democrat. Roman Catholic. Home: 3614 Belle Grove Ln Sugar Land TX 77479-2257

RAMOS-CANO, HAZEL BALATERO, social worker, early childhood educator, food service director, executive chef, innkeeper, caterer; b. Davao City, Mindanao, Philippines, Sept. 2, 1936; came to U. S., 1960.; d. Mauricio C. and Felicidad (Balatero) Ramos; m. William Harold Snyder, Feb. 17, 1964 (div. 1981); children: John Byron, Snyder, Jennifer Ruth; m. Nelson Allen Blue, May 30, 1986 (div. 1990); m. A. Richard Cano, June 25, 1994. BA in Social Work, U. Philippines, Quezon City, 1958; MA in Sociology, Pa. State U., 1963, postgrad., 1966-67. Cert. exec. chef, Am. Culinary Fedn. Faculty, tng. staff Peace Corps Philippine Project, University Park, Pa., 1961-63; sociology instr. Albright Coll. Sociology Dept., Reading, Pa., 1963-64; research asst. Meth. Ch. U.S.A., State College, Pa., 1965-66; research asst. dept. child devel. & family relations Pa. State U., University Park, Pa., 1966-67; exec. dir. Presbyn. Urban Coun. Raleigh Halifax Ct. Child Care and Family Svc. Ctr., 1973-79; early childhood educator Learning Together, Inc., Raleigh, 1982-83; loan mortgage specialist Raleigh Savings & Loan, 1983-84; restaurant owner, mgr. Hazel's on Hargett, Raleigh, 1985-86; admissions coord., social worker Brian Corp. Nursing Home, Raleigh, 1986-88, food svc. dir., 1989-90; regional dir. La Petite Acad., Raleigh, 1989-90; asst. food svc. mgr. Granville Towers, Chapel Hill, N.C., 1990-92; mgr. trainee Child Nutrition Svcs. Wake County Pub. Sch. System, Raleigh, N.C., 1993-94; food svc. dir. S.W. Va. 4-H Ednl. Conf. Ctr., Abingdon, 1994-95; caterer, owner The Eclectic Chef's Catering, 1995—; innkeeper, owner Love House Bed and Breakfast, 1996—; cooking instr. Wake Cmty. Tech. Coll., Raleigh, 1986-92; freelance caterer, 1964-95; chair Internat. Cooking Demonstrations Raleigh Internat. Festival, 1990-93. Pres. Wake County Day Care United Coun., 1974-75, N.C. Assn. Edn. Young Children (Raleigh Chpt.), 1975-76; bd. mem. Project Enlightenment Wake County Pub. Schs., 1976-77; various positions Pines of Carolina Girl Scout Council, 1976-85; chmn. Philippine Health and Medical Aid Com., Phil-Am Assn. Raleigh 1985-88 (publicity chmn.); elder Trinity Presbyn. Ch., Raleigh, 1979-81, bd. deacons, 1993-94. Recipient Juliette Low Girl Scout Internat. award, 1953, Rockefeller grant Rockefeller Found., 1958-59, Ramon Magsaysay Presidential award, Philippine Leadership Youth Movement, 1957; Gov.'s Cert. Appreciation State N.C., 1990, Raleigh Mayor's award Quality Childcare Svcs., 1990. Mem. Am. Culinary Fedn., Presby. Women, Raleigh, (historian 1975-76), Penn State Dames (pres. 1968-69). Democrat. Office: Love House Bed & Breakfast 210 E Valley St Abingdon VA 24210

RAMOS-RODRIGUEZ, ISABEL, education educator; b. Rio Piedras, P.R., Sept. 3, 1958; d. Roberto and Rosa Angeles Ramos. BA in Secondary Edn., U. P.R., 1976, MEd in sch. adminstrn., 1982, edn. specialist, 1984, PhD in Adult Edn. and Sch. Adminstrn. and Supn., 1987. Grad. asst. U. South Fla., Tampa, 1984-90; prof. U. P.R., Rio Piedras, 1987—. Contbr. articles to profl. jours. Recipient award Home Econs. Assn. P.R., 1979, MA Coll. of Edn. Grad. Studies awardee. Mem. Phi Kappa Phi, Kappa Delta Pi, Phi Delta Kappa (pub. rels. com. 1988). Office: U PR Rio Piedras Campus Rio Piedras PR 00924

RAMP, WARREN KIBBY, orthopedist, educator; b. N.Y.C., Aug. 19, 1939; m. Anita Decker; 2 children. BS, SUNY, Oneonta, 1963; MS in Zoology, Colo. State U., 1964; PhD, U. Ky., 1967. Asst. prof. dept. oral diagnosis Sch. Dentistry, U. N.C., Chapel Hill, 1970-76, assoc. prof. dept. oral and maxillofacial surgery, 1976-79; asst. prof. dept. pharmacology Sch. of Medicine, U. N.C., Chapel Hill, 1971-76, assoc. prof. dept. pharmacology, 1976-79; assoc. prof. dept. pharmacology and toxicology Sch. Dentistry, U. Louisville, 1979-82, prof. dept. oral biology, 1982-87, prof. dept. oral health, 1987-91; prof. dept. pharmacology and toxicology Sch. Medicine, U. Louisville, 1982-91; sr. scientist dept. of orthopaedic surgery Carolinas Med. Ctr., Charlotte, N.C., 1991—; vis. scientist Dental Rsch. Ctr., Emory U., Atlanta, 1986, adj. scientist, 1987-88; vis. scientist Marine Sci. Rsch. Ctr., U. N.C., Wilmington, 1989-92; adj. prof. dept. biology U. N.C., Charlotte, 1992—, divsn. of health and phys. edn. Va. Poly. Inst. and State U., Blacksburg, 1993—; dir. oral biology grad. program, 1979-84; chmn. dept. oral biology Sch. of Dentistry, U. Louisville, 1983-86; mem. numerous coms. U. N.C., U. Louisville. Asst. editor Bone and Mineral, 1986-92, mem. editl. bd., 1992-94; contbr. numerous articles to profl. jours. Grantee U. N.C., 1970-79, Distilled Spirits Coun. of the U.S., Inc., 1977-78, U. N.C. Rsch. Coun., 1979, U. Louisville Dental Rsch. Com., 1980-81, NSF, 1980-84, U. Louisville Grad. Sch., 1981, Am. Found. for Dental Health, 1983-85, Smokeless Tobacco Rsch. Coun., Inc., 1987-91, Winkler Found./Charlotte Mecklenburg Hosp. Authority, 1993-96; predoctoral fellow NIH, 1964-67, postdoctoral fellow, 1967-70. Mem. AAAS, Am. Physiol. Soc., Am. Soc. for Bone and Mineral Rsch., Internat. Bone and Mineral Rsch. Soc., Orthopaedic Rsch. Soc., Soc. for Exptl. Biology and Medicine, Soc. Biomaterials, Sigma Xi. Home: 5356 Hillingdon Rd Charlotte NC 28226-7360 Office: Baxter Orthopaedic Rsch Lab Carolinas Med Ctr PO Box 32861 Charlotte NC 28232-2861

RAMSAY, JAMES GORDON, anesthesiologist, educator; b. Victoria, B.C., Can., Mar. 28, 1953; came to U.S., 1990; m. Jennifer Brooks; children: Allison, Paul, George. BSc, U. B.C., 1975, MD, 1978. Diplomate Am. Bd. Anesthesiology. Intern Ottawa (Can.) Civic Hosp., 1978-79; resident in anesthesia McGill U., 1979-83; asst. prof., assoc. prof. anesthesiology McGill U., Montreal, Can., 1983-89; assoc. prof. anesthesiology Emory U. Sch. of Medicine, Atlanta, 1990—; chair sci. program Soc. Cardiovascular Anesthesiologists, 1995-96, Soc. Critical Care Anesthesiologists, 1991-92.

RAMSAY, MICHAEL LANDON, middle school educator; b. Dallas, Sept. 14, 1969; s. Tom and Laurie Ramsay. BS in Edn., Baylor U., 1993. Tchr., coach Euless (Tex.) Jr. H.S., 1993—; counselor Kanakuk Kamp, Branson, Mo., 1988-94. Leader FCA, Euless, 1993-95. Home: 6334 N MacArthur Irving TX 76039 Office: Euless Jr H S 306 Airport Fwy Euless TX 76039

RAMSBOTTOM-LUCIER, MARY, physician, medical educator; b. Pretoria, South Africa, June 15, 1960; came to U.S., 1961; d. Charles Antony and Mary Genevieve (Lynch) Ramsbottom; m. Ralph William Lucier Jr., July 5, 1991. BSc in Biochemistry, McGill U., Montreal, Que., Can., 1981, MDCM, 1985; MPH, U. Wash., 1991. Diplomate Am. Bd. Internal Medicine, Nat. Bd. Med. Examiners. Intern, then resident in internal medicine St. Francis Hosp. and Med. Ctr., Hartford, Conn., 1985-88, chief resident/clin. fellow in internal medicine, 1988-89; fellow in acad. primary care Sch. Medicine, resident in preventative medicine Sch. Pub. Health and Community Medicine U. Wash., Seattle, 1989-91, chief resident Sch. Pub. Health and Community Medicine, 1990-91, instr. Sch. Medicine, 1991; clin. scholar divsn. gen. internal medicine and geriatrics U. Ky., Lexington, 1991-92, asst. prof. divsn. gen. internal medicine and geriatrics, 1991—; mem. staff U. Ky. Med. Ctr., 1991, Lexington VA Med. Ctr., 1991; clin. preceptor clerkship students Sch. Medicine U. Ky., 1991—; coord. course on human health, 1993-94, interviewer med. sch. applicants, 1993—, co-chmn. healthy human task force, 1992-94; coord. primary care residents psychosocial and preventative medicine curriculum U. Ky. Med. Ctr., 1991-93, coord. primary care residents rural rotation, 1992-93, asst. dir. gen. internal medicine fellowship, coord. gen. internal medicine fellows seminar, coord. primary care and deriatrics rsch. conf., 1992—, residents psychosocial and preventative medicine curriculum, 1991-93; cons. Ky. Med. Review Orgn., clin. coord. pattern analysis, 1992-94; coord. internal medicine ambulatory course, 1996—; dir. Merek Found. Faculty Devel. Program, 1996—. Reviewer Jour. Gen. Internal Medicine, Archives of Internal Medicine Health Svcs. Rsch.; contbr. articles to med. jours. VA Ambulatory Care fellow, 1994-96, residency tng. grantee, HRSA, 1992-94; Ciba-Geigy summer rsch. scholar McGill U., 1983; grantee Ind./Ky. Med. Rev. Orgn., 1992-93, 93—; recipient Master Tchr. award, 1994. Mem. ACP, Soc. Gen. Internal Medicine (presenter nat. meetings 1989, 90, 92, 93, 94), Am. Coll. Preventive Medicine, Am. Fedn. Clin. Rsch. (chmn. preventive medicine abstract selection com. 1993, moderator preventive medicine abstracts 1994), Assn. Health Svcs. Rsch.; Soc. Gen. Internal Medicine (career choice task force, 1993, managed care task force, 1996, CME coord. for so. region, 1996). Office: U Ky Div Gen Int Med/Geriat K506 Kentucky Clinic Lexington KY 40536

RAMSEY, BILLY MACK, design educator, design consultant, artist; b. Center, Tex., Jan. 31, 1947; s. John D. and Avis M. Ramsey; m. Patricia Delatin, Sept. 23, 1970; children: Matthew Kelly, Alex Taylor. BFA, La. Tech. U., 1969, MFA, 1975. Registered interior designer, Tex. Graphic designer John Guth and Assocs., Architects and Engrs., Shreveport, La., 1968-69, Accent Art Inc., Washington, 1970-72; freelance designer, 1973—; asst. prof. dept. art Memphis State U., 1975-78; from asst. to assoc. prof. dept. home econs. Stephen F. Austin State U., Nacagdoches, Tex., 1978-88; coord. interior design, assoc. prof. dept. environ. design U. So. Miss., Hattiesburg, 1988-89; coord. interior design, assoc. prof. dept. architecture U. Southwestern La., Lafayette, 1989-93; coord. interior design, assoc. prof. Columbus (Ohio) Coll. Art and Design, 1993—; design cons., graphic design Lafayette Parish Sch. Bd., 1992; design cons. graphic design, commd. drawings Am. Gen. Ins. Corp., Tex., 1989-90; design cons. Annex Renovations, Sarah's Sch., Early Learning Ctr., Lafayette, 1990; design cons., archtl. renderings, graphics Vermilionville-Hist. Bayou Attraction, Lafayette, 1990-91; design cons. Stephen F. Austin State U., Nacagdoches, 1989. Exhibited in group show La. Tech. U., 1990; exhibited in one man show S.W. Tex. State U., 1987. Graphics cons. Lafayette Parish Sch. Bd.; vol. March of Dimes; graphics PTA; vol., sponsor St. Jude's Children's Hosp.; mural designer Nacogdoches Meml. Hosp., Our Lady of Wisdom Cath. Ch.; parent liaison, vol. Boy Scouts Am.; design cons. Vermilionville-Hist. Bayou Attraction. With USAF, 1969-73. Recipient Faculty award Design Comm. Assn., 1992. Mem. Interior Design Educators Coun. (1st pl. award 1989), Am. Soc. Interior Designers (Design Educator award 1988), Tex. Assn. Interior Designers, Found. for Interior Design Edn. Rsch. (bd. visitors 1985). Democrat. Methodist. Home: 5000 W Congress St Apt 4D Lafayette LA 70506-6424

RAMSEY, BONNIE JEANNE, mental health facility administrator, psychiatrist; b. Tucson, Dec. 9, 1952; d. William Arnold Jr. and Doris Marie (Gaines) R. BS cum laude, U. S.C., 1971-75, MD, 1981. Diplomate Am. Bd. Psychiatry and Neurology; lic. child and adult psychiatrist S.C., N.C., Ga. Chief resident in psychiatry William S. Hall Psychiat. Inst., Columbia, S.C., 1983, unit dir. adolescent girls, 1986-89; chief child and adolescent inpatient program William S. Hall Psychiat. Inst., Columbia, 1989—, interim dir. child and adolescent div., 1989-92; interim chmn. child and adolescent div. dept. neuropsychiatry U. S.C., Columbia, 1989-92; instr. Sch. of Medicine U. S.C., Columbia, 1986-89, asst. prof. Sch. of Medicine, 1989—. Mem. choir Trinity Meth. Ch., West Columbia, 1981—, vice chmn. bd. trustees, 1989—, trustee, 1990—, mem. at large adminstrn. bd., 1993—; adv. coun. Habitat for Humanity. Named one of Outstanding Young Women of Am., 1985. Mem. AMA (del. residents physician sect. 1983, 84, 86, housing staff sect. 1988—), Am. Psychiat. Assn. (local sec.-treas., pres. 1981—), Am. Acad. Child Psychiatry, S.C. Med. Soc., Columbia Med. Soc., Palmetto Soc. United Way. Methodist. Office: William S Hall Psychiat Inst PO Box 202 Columbia SC 29202-0202

RAMSEY, DAVID JED, medical researcher, computer consultant; b. Manhatten, Kans., May 27, 1950; s. Jed Jr. and Frances Mae (Ewart) R.; m. Janice Ellison, Apr. 15, 1972; children: Bethany Deanne, Emily Michelle. BS, Lamar U., 1972; MS, U. Houston, 1977, PhD, 1982. Instr. lectr. U. Houston Clear Lake, 1983-85, Houston Community Coll., 1985, Brazosport Coll., Lake Jackson, Tex., 1985; programmer, analyst U. Tex. M.D. Anderson Cancer Ctr., Houston, 1985-88; rsch. assoc., database adminstr. U. Tex. Sch. Pub. Health, Houston, 1988—; owner, cons. Bright Idea Computing, Houston, 1991—. Contbr. articles to profl. jours. Precinct judge Harris County Dem. Party, Houston, 1990—; constrn. com. mem. Houston Habitat for Humanity, 1987—. Grad. fellow NSF, 1975-78. Democrat. Office: P O Box 20186 1200 Hermann Pressler Dr Houston TX 77030-3900

RAMSEY, DONNA ELAINE, librarian; b. Charlotte, N.C., Oct. 10, 1941; d. William A. Epps and Mabel P. Tatum; m. Reginald E. Ramsey, Apr. 9, 1979 (dec.); children: Ona, Reginald, Gina Clark. BA, Johnson C. Smith U., 1969; MSLS, Clark Atlanta U., 1971. Reference libr. Barber Scotia Coll., Concord, N.C., 1971-73; head libr. Friendship Jr. Coll., Rock Hill, S.C., 1973-77; asst. serials libr. N.Mex. State U., Las Cruces, 1977-81; info. libr. El Paso Pub. Libr., 1981; supervisory libr. tech. svcs. br. U.S. Army Air Def. Artillery Sch., Ft. Bliss, Tex., 1985-89, libr., 1989-92; libr. U.S. Army Sgts. Maj. Acad. Learning Resource Ctr., Ft. Bliss, 1992—. Contbr. articles to profl. jours. Chair Internat. Trends and Svcs., Links, Inc., El Paso, 1993—; v.p. Blacks in Govt., El Paso, 1992—; life mem. NAACP, El Paso, 1989—; treas. Fed. Women's Program Com., Ft. Bliss, 1990; program chair Black Employment Program Com., Ft. Bliss, 1990-91. Recipient Cert. of Appreciation, IRS, El Paso, 1993, Friends of the Libr., El Paso, 1993; ACRL Mellon fellow Libr. Mgmt., Oberlin Coll., 1975-76. Mem. ALA (steering com., social responsibilities roundtable, task force on women 1977-78, vice-chair staff orgns. roundtable 1991-92, chair staff orgns. roundtable 1992-93, Cert. Achievement Black Caucus 1992), Delta Sigma Theta (life). Episcopalian. Home: PO Box 6769 El Paso TX 79906-0769

RAMSEY, INEZ LINN, librarian, educator; b. Martins Ferry, Ohio, Apr. 25, 1938; d. George and Leona (Smith) Linn; m. Jackson Euguene Ramsey, Apr. 22, 1961; children: John Earl, James Leonard. B.A. in Hist. SUNY-Buffalo, 1971; M.L.S., 1972; Ed.D. in Audiovisual Edn., U. Va., 1980. Librarian Iroquois Central High Sch., Elma, N.Y., 1971-73, Lucy Simms Elem. Sch., Harrisonburg, Va., 1973-75; instr. James Madison U., Harrisonburg, 1975-80, asst. prof., 1980-85; assoc. prof. 1985-91, prof. 1991—; mem. Va. State Library Bd., Richmond, 1975-80; cons. Contr. to Enclopedia, articles to profl. jours.; author (with Jackson E. Ramsey): Budgeting Basics, Library Planning and Budgeting; project dir. Oral (tape) History Black Community in Harrisonburg, 1977-78; storyteller, puppeteer. Rsch. grantee James Madison U., Harrisonburg, 1981, Commonwealth Ctr. State Va., 1989. Mem. ALA, Am. Assn. Sch. Librarians, Assn. Edn. Communications Tech. (exec. bd. DSMS 1989—), Higher Edn. Media Assn. (sec., treas. 1989—), Children's Lit. Assn., Puppeteers Am., Nat. Assn. Preservation and Perpetuation of Storytelling, Va. Ednl. Media Assn. (sec. 1981-83, citation 1983 pres. 1985-86, Educator of Yr. award 1984-85, Meritorious Service award 1987-88), Phi Beta Kappa (pres. Shenandoah chpt. 1980-81), Higher Edn. Media Assn. (sec. treas., 1989—), Beta Phi Mu. Home: 282 Franklin St Harrisonburg VA 22801-4019 Office: James Madison U Dept Secondary Edn Sci Harrisonburg VA 22807

RAMSEY, JETTIE CECIL, county official; b. Daytona Beach, Fla., Aug. 31, 1925; s. Joseph James and Nonnie (Mann) R.; B.B.A., Massey Coll., 1955; postgrad. Fla. Jr. Coll., 1968, 73, Ga. U., 1972, Fla. Technol. U., 1972, U. Colo., 1983; m. Pauline Cordelia Thaden, May 9, 1942 (dec.); children—Wilson Lujack, Joseph Cecil (dec.), Pauline Diana (dec.); m. Mary Lou Gratz Kernie, Oct. 17, 1987. Engr., Duval Engrng. & Constrn. Co., Jacksonville, Fla., 1946-66; with Office of Sheriff, Duval County, Fla., 1966—, warden Duval County Prison, 1969-71, rehab. officer, 1971-73, supt. jails, 1973—. Author: Road Back to the Mainline. Mem. Duval County Exec. Com., 1958—; capt. Jacksonville Police Res., 1968-75; troop scoutmaster Boy Scouts Am., 1962-64. Served with USNR, 1943-46. Mem. So. Genealogists Soc., VFW (vice comdr. 1975), Correctional Officers Assn., Fla. Peace Officers Assn., Fraternal Order Police, Assn. Preservation Tenn. Antiquities, Aasns. Aviation Ordnancemen, Soc. Confederate Vets., Masons (32 deg., worshipful master, Shriners, Order Eastern Star (worthy patron 1960, 81, 90, 92), Navy Alumni Club, Jacksonville Quarterback Club. Democrat. Home: 1039 Hood Ave Jacksonville FL 32254-2303 Office: 451 N Catherine St Jacksonville FL 32202-2501

RAMSEY, KATHLEEN SOMMER, toxicologist; b. Port Washington, Wis., June 2, 1947; d. Harrison Wilson and June Kathleen (Hansen) S.; m. Glenn A. Ramsey, Oct. 4, 1975; 1 child, David A. BA, Ripon Coll., 1969; PhD, U. Iowa, 1973. Diplomate Am. Bd. Toxicology. Rsch. assoc. U. Wis., Milw., 1969; instr. Baylor Coll. Medicine, Houston, 1973-74, USPHS rsch. fellow, 1974-76; rsch. chemist Shell Devel. Co., Houston, 1976-77; toxicologist Shell Oil Co., Houston, 1977-80; dir., cons. toxicologist Toxicon Corp., Magnolia, Tex., 1980—; mem. nat. adv. rsch. resources coun. NIH, Bethesda, Md., 1974-78; bd. dirs. Reid Road Mcpl. Utility Dist., Houston, 1982-95; guest lectr. U. Tex. Sch. Pub. Health, Houston. Contbr. articles to profl. jours. Paramedic Cy-Fair Vol. Fire Dept., Houston, 1983-87; dir. Harvest Bend Home Owners Assn., Houston, 1984-86. U. Iowa grad. fellow, Iowa City, 1969-73; recipient Nat. Rsch. Svc. award NIH, Bethesda, 1975. Mem. Am. Coll. Toxicology, Assn. Water (bd. dirs.), Am. Chem. Soc., Nat. Sci. Tchrs.' Assn. Office: Toxicon Corp 26535 Fm 2978 Rd Magnolia TX 77355-3035

RAMSEY, MICHAEL LEE, financial planner; b. Charleston, W.Va., Sept. 6, 1947; s. Emery Lester and Kathleen (McGraw) R.; m. Katherine Butterfield, July 3, 1985; children: Frank G. Selbe, Hunter Stewart Todd Selbe, Mac Wilson Laing Selbe. BA, W. Va. Univ., 1969. Campaign staff Hoff for Senate, Rutland, Vt., 1970; news editor Raleigh Register, Beckley, V.Va., 1971-76; pub. rels. Ind. Cons., Roanoke, Va., 1976-80; projects mgr. Roanoke C. of C., Roanoke, Va., 1980-84; exec. dir. Roanoke Conv./Visitors Bureau, Roanoke, Va., 1984-87; client svcs. SFCS, Inc., Roanoke, Va., 1989-90; dir. client svcs. Motley & Assocs., Roanoke, Va., 1990-95; financial planner/agt. The Principal Financial Group, Roanoke, Va., 1995—; corp. sec. Roanoke Valley Devel. Co., 1980-88, Va. Mus. of Transp., 1983-85; team leader Va. Govs. Travel Mission, N.Y., 1986-87. Contbg. writer The Roanoke Mag., 1991—, The Assn. Exec., 1995. Bd. dirs. Roanoke Valley Hist. Mus., 1992—; pres. Blue Ridge Parkway Assn., 1985-87, Festival in the

Park, Roanoke, 1984. Episcopalian. Home: 3015 Carolina Ave Roanoke VA 24014 Office: The Principal Fin Group 120 Day Ave SW Roanoke VA 24016

RAMSEY, SALLY ANN SEITZ, retired state official; b. Columbus, Ohio, Feb. 15, 1931; d. Albert Blazier and Mildred (Dodson) Seitz; m. Edward Lewis Ramsey, Apr. 11, 1953 (div. 1962); children: Edward Lewis, Sylvia Ann Mitchell. BA, Ohio State U., 1952, MA, 1955, postgrad., 1963-66; postgrad. St. Mary Coll.-Xavier, Kans., 1962. Rsch. engr., then sr. rsch. engr. N.Am. Aviation, Inc., Columbus, Ohio, and Downey, Calif., 1962-67; legis. intern State of Ohio, 1964-65; rsch. and info. officer Ohio Dept. Urban Affairs, Columbus, 1967-68; adminstrv. specialist Ohio Dept. Devel., Columbus, 1968; assoc. planner, then sr. planner Div. State Planning, Fla. Dept. Adminstrn., Tallahassee, 1968-76; econ. analysis supr., then econ. analyst Fla. Dept. Commerce, 1976-93; ret., 1993; congl. campaign cons., 1966. U.S. Econ. Devel. Adminstrn. fellow, 1978-79. Mem. ASPA, DAR, Fla. Econs. Club, Kappa Kappa Gamma, Pi Sigma Alpha. Episcopalian. Home: 2429 Merrigan Pl Tallahassee FL 32308-2346

RAMSEY, VIRGINIA CAROL MARSHALL, middle school educator; b. Alcoa, Tenn., Aug. 7, 1935; d. Arthur Glenn and Dorothy Alexander (Huff) Marshall; m. David Lawrence Ramsey, July 5, 1957; children—Stephanie Lea, Jennifer Lynne, Thomas Marshall. B.A., Maryville Coll., 1957; Ed.M., W. Ga. Coll., 1981; Ed.S., U. Ga., 1984. Cert. tchr., counselor, art supr., data collector, tchr. art. Instr. art Maryville Coll., Tenn., 1957-58; supr. art Alcoa City Sch. System, Tenn., 1958-59; art instr. Cobb County Pub. Schs., Marietta, Ga., 1972—, Cobb Community Sch., Marietta, 1980-83; bd. dirs. Student Art Symposium, Athens, Ga.; presenter art shows, confs., 1972, 80, 84, 87. Author: Student Teacher Handbook, 1982. Mem. Kennestone Hosp. Guild, Marietta, 1967—; mem. Bells Ferry Homeowners Assn.; mem. Cobb PTA, 1967—, treas., 1974-76, pres., 1970-71, 76-77; mem. Sprayberry High Sch. Booster Club, 1972-86; panelist Gov.'s Conf. on Career Devel., Macon, 1972; leader Girl Scouts U.S.A., 1971-72; v.p. Sprayberry Adv. Council, Marietta, 1981-82, pres., 1982-86; active Robert Woodruff Mus. Art, 1969—, Cobb Arts Coun., 1975—, Marietta/Cobb Fine Arts Orgn., 1970—. Mem. Nat. Art Edn. Assn., Ga. Art Edn. Assn. (mid. sch. chmn. 1984-87, high sch. chmn. 1977-79, Art Tchr. of Yr. State of Ga. 1988-89), Ga. Assn. Educators, Atlanta Area Art Tchrs. Assn., Cobb County Assn Educators, Huguenot Soc. (v.p. Tenn. 1974-75), Delta Kappa Gamma. Republican. Presbyterian. Avocations: photography, hiking, bridge, golf, history, painting. Office: Mabry Sch Cobb County Sch System 2700 Jims Rd Marietta GA 30066-1414

RAMSEY, WILLIAM DALE, JR., petroleum consultant; b. Indpls., Apr. 14, 1936; s. William Dale and Laura Jane (Stout) R.; m. Mary Alice Ihnet, Aug. 9, 1969; children: Robin, Scott, Kimberly, Jennifer. AB in Econs., Bowdoin Coll., 1958. With Shell Oil Co., 1958-95, salesman, Albany, N.Y., 1960, merchandising rep., Milton, N.Y., 1961-63, real estate and mktg. investments rep., Jacksonville, Fla., 1963-65, dist. sales supr., St. Paul, 1965-67, employee relations rep., Chgo., 1967-69, spl. assignment mktg. staff-adminstrn., N.Y.C., recruitment mgr., Chgo., 1970-72, sales mgr., Chgo., 1973-75, sales mgr., Detroit, 1975-79, dist. mgr. N.J. and Pa., Newark, 1979-84, Mid-Atlantic dist. mgr. (Md., D.C., Va.) 1984-87, econ. advisor head office, Houston, 1987-89; mgr. mktg. concepts head office, Houston, 1989-94, mgr. tech. head office, Houston, 1994-95, prin. Ramsey Cons., 1995—; dir. N.Am. Fin. Services, 1971-72; lectr., speaker on energy, radio, TV, appearances, 1972—; guest lectr. on bus. five univs., 1967-72; v.p., dir. Malibu East Corp., 1973-74; prin. Robotics Rsch. Consortium, 1991—; mem. Am. Right of Way Assn., 1963-65. James Bowdoin scholar Bowdoin Coll., 1958. Active Chgo. Urban League, 1971-75; mem. program com., bus. adv. council Nat. Rep. Congl. Com., 1981-87, rep. nat. com., 1994—; mem. Gov.'s Council on Tourism and Commerce, Minn., 1965-67; mem. Founders Soc., Detroit Inst. Arts, 1978-80; bd. dirs. N.J. Symphony Orch. Corp., 1981-85. Capt. U.S. Army, 1958-60. Mem. Internat. Svc. Robot Assn., N.J. Petroleum Council (exec. com. 1979-84 vice chmn. 1982-84), Midwest Coll. Placement Assn., Md. Petroleum Council (exec. com. 1984-87). Presbyterian. Clubs: Ponte Vedra (Fla.); Bowdoin Alumni (Houston); Morris County (N.J.) Golf; Kingwood (Tex.) Country, Houston Soc. Club; Bethesda (Md.) Country. Author: Corp. Recruitment and Employee Relations Organizational Effectiveness Study, 1969; Inventor 6 patents pending. Office: Ramsey Consulting PO Box 311 Kingwood TX 77339

RAMZY, IBRAHIM, pathologist, educator; b. Alexandria, Egypt, Dec. 1, 1936; came to U.S., 1978; m. Faye Ramzy, Aug. 23, 1959; children: Joseph I., Peter I. MB, BChir, Cairo (Egypt) U., 1958, diploma Med. Scis. in Pathology, 1962, MD, 1965. Diplomate Am. Bd. Pathology. Intern Cairo U. Hosp., Cairo, 1959-60, with dept. Pathology, 1960-65; lectr. in Pathology various univs., Can., Egypt, 1965-67; instr. in Pathology U. Toronto (Can.), 1968-69; clin. asst. prof. Pathology U. Western Ont., London, Can., 1970-73; clin. assoc. prof. to clin. prof. Pathology and Ob-gyn. U. Western Ont., London, 1973-78, assoc. prof. Pathology and Ob-gyn., 1977-78; prof. Pathology and Ob-gyn., chief Anatomic Pathology U. Tex. Health Sci. Ct., San Antonio, 1981-86; prof. Pathology and Ob-gyn. Baylor Coll. Medicine, Houston, 1986—; chief Anatomic Pathology, dir. Cytopathology, sr. attending The Meth. Hosp., Houston, 1989—; cons. in gynecol. oncology various hosps., 1976—; pathologist, dir. cytopathology Victoria Hosp., London, 1970-78; vis. prof. dept. ob-gyn. U. Western Ontario, London, dept. pathology U. Cairo, 1980, med. sch. Iowa U., 1993; dir. cytopathology Med. Ctr. and VA Hosps., San Antonio, 1978-86, cytotech. sch. Med. Ctr. Hosp., San Antonio, 1978-86; attending pathologist, dir. cytopathology The Meth. Hosp., Houston, 1986-89; attending pathologist Harris County Hosp. Dist., Houston, 1986—. Author: Testicular Disorders, 1974, Essentials of Gynecologic and Obstetric Pathology, 1983, Clinical Cytopathology and Aspiration Biopsy: Fundamental Principles and Practice, 1990; contbr. chpts. to books, articles to profl. jours. Fellow Coll. Am. Pathologists; mem. AMA, Internat. Acad. of Cytology, Internat. Soc. Gynecol. Pathologists, Internat. Acad. of Pathology, Royal Coll. Physicians and Surgeons of Can., Papanicolaou Soc. of Cytopathology, Am. Soc. Clin. Pathologists, Am. Soc. Cytopathology (v.p. 1992-93, pres.-elect 1993-94, pres. 1994-95), Can. Soc. Cytology (pres. 1974-75), Can. Med. Assn., Tex. Soc. Cytology (pres. 1982, 83), Tex. Soc. Pathologists (pres. 1994-95), Tex. Med. Assn., Harris County Med. Soc., Ont. Med. Assn. Home: 3763 Robinhood St Houston TX 77005-2027 Office: Dept Pathology Baylor Coll Medicine One Baylor Pla Houston TX 77030

RANDALL, BILL VERL, retired oil company executive; b. Nowata, Okla., July 26, 1925; s. Max Willard and Clarice (Lowe) R.; m. Delores DeSirey; children: Donald Ray, Nancy Sue. BSCE with high distinction, Okla. State U., 1949. Registered profl. engr., Okla. Analytical chemist E.I. duPont, Clinton, Iowa, 1949-51; rsch. engr., rsch. assoc. Amoco, Tulsa, 1951-76, rsch. supr., 1976-81; tng. mgr. Amoco, Egypt, 1981-83; spl. rsch. assoc. Amoco, Tulsa, 1983-84; drilling cons. specializing internat. drilling ops. Tulsa, 1985—; spl. drilling assignments in Egypt, including cons. for Gulf of Suez Petroleum Co. Author more than 45 tech. papers in field; holder of 20 patents. Sgt. U.S. Army, 1943-46, ETO. Mem. Soc. Petroleum Engrs., Internat. Assn. Drilling Contractors (various offices including chmn. sub-com. on controlled deviation drilling), Am. Petroleum Inst. Office: Randall Consulting Inc 4526 E 104th St Tulsa OK 74137-6201

RANDALL, CAROLYN MAYO, chemical company executive; b. Atlanta, June 11, 1939; d. Frank and Winifred (Layton) Mayo; m. James Allen Hall, Dec. 28, 1960 (dec. 1973); children: James Allen Hall Jr., Christopher Mayo Hall, Charlotte Ann Hall O'Neal. BA, U. Ga., 1959. Ptnr. Mayo Chem. Co., Marietta, Ga., 1989—. Bd. dirs. Mayo Edn. Found; active Alliance Theater Atlanta, Salvation Army Aux., Voters Guild Met. Atlanta, Friendship Force Atlanta, Kennestone Hosp. Cancer Group, Am. Cancer Soc. Mem. Cobb County Gem & Mineral Soc. (trustee), S.E. Fedn. Mineralogical Soc. (historian), Atlanta Preservation Soc., Nat. Trust Historic Preservation, Ga. Trust Hist. Preservation, Nat. Meml. Day Assn., Better Films Assn. Met. Atlanta (bd. dirs.), Ret. Officers Assn. (ladies aux. bd. dirs.), Ga. Mineral Soc., Native Atlantians Club, 100 Club (pres.), The Frogg Club, Terrell Mill Estates Women's Club (bd. dirs.), Dobbins AFB OFficers Wives Club (bd. dirs.), Alpha Chi Omega, Atlanta Steinway Soc. (bd. dirs.), French-Am. Ch. of C., Raban Gap Nacoochee Guild, Freedoms Found. of Valley Forge, Atlanta Butterfly Club, Make A Wish Found., The Etowah Found., The Civil War Trust. Republican. Episcopal. Home: 3244 Beechwood Dr Marietta GA 30067-5420

RANDALL, DAVID CLARK, medical educator, medical researcher; b. St. Louis, Apr. 23, 1945; s. Walter Clark and Gwendolyn Ruth (Niebel) R.; m. Lea Carol Wylder, Sept. 1, 1985; children: Christopher C., Matthew F., Benjamin W. BA, Taylor U., 1967; PhD, U. Wash., 1971. Asst. prof. divsn. behavioral biology Johns Hopkins U. Sch. Medicine, Balt., 1972-75; asst. prof. dept. physiology U. Ky., Lexington, 1975-78, assoc. prof., 1978-85, prof., 1985—; instr. Asbury Coll., Wilmore, Ky., 1979—; vis. assoc. prof. dept. neurobiology and behavior SUNY, Stony Brook, 1981; dir. grad. studies dept. physiology and biophysics U. Ky., 1981-84, joint prof. grad. ctr. biomed. engring. 1987—, exec. com., 1990-92. Contbr. numerous articles to profl. jours., chpts. to books. Active behavioral medicine br. NIH, Nat. Heart, Lung and Blood Inst., 1982—. Mem. Am. Heart Assn. (various coms., bd. chmn. Ky. affiliate 1994-96), Am. Physiol. Soc., Am. Sci. Affiliation, Nat. Assn. Biomed. Rsch., Applied Rsch. Ethics Nat. Assn., Fedn. Am. Socs. Exptl. Biology, Internat. Autonomic Soc., Internat. Soc. Gravitational Physiology, Christian Med. Dental Soc., Pavlovian Soc. Am. (exec. com. 1983—, pres. 1983), Soc. Neurosci. Office: U Ky Coll Medicine Dept Physiology Lexington KY 40536-0084

RANDAZZO, ANTHONY FRANK, geology educator; b. Staten Island, N.Y., Sept. 20, 1941; s. Anthony and Elizabeth (DeFazio) R.; m. Lynne Schmeiser, Aug. 21, 1965; children: Kirk, Jeff. BS, CCNY, 1963; MS, U. N.C., 1965, PhD, 1968. Asst. prof. U. Fla., Gainesville, 1967-72, assoc. prof., 1972-77, assoc. dean rsch., 1977-82, dir. rsch., 1982-88, prof., 1977—, dept. chmn., 1988-95; co-prin. Geohazards, Inc., Gainesville, 1985—; chmn. State Bd. Profl. Geologists, Tallahassee, 1987-97. Contbr. articles to profl. jours. NSF fellow, 1966; Fulbright scholar, 1995-96. Fellow Geol. Soc. Am.; mem. Soc. Sedimentary Geology, Am. Geophys. Union. Home: 1925 NW 27th St Gainesville FL 32605-3862 Office: U Fla PO Box 117340 Gainesville FL 32611-7340

RANDAZZO, GARY WAYNE, newspaper executive; b. Georgetown, Tex., Sept. 23, 1947; s. Frank Birchmans and Edna Earle (Forbis) R.; m. Joyce Sue McNorton, Oct. 7, 1966; children: Gary Wayne Jr., Vanessa Rene, Michael Jason, Daniel Paul. BBA, U. Tex., 1974; MBA, Tex. A&I U., Corpus Christi, 1976. Instr. Del Mar Coll., Corpus Christi, 1974-76; bus. mgr. Corpus Christi Caller-Times, 1976-81; pres., pub. Huntsville (Tex.) Item, 1981-83; pres. Am. Property Data, Houston, 1984-87; gen. mgr. Health Care News, Houston, 1987-89; v.p. sales Houston Chronicle, Houston, 1995—. Mem. Leadership Houston. Mem. Kiwanis. Home: 9610 Oxted Ln Spring TX 77379-6600 Office: Houston Chronicle 801 Texas St Houston TX 77002-2906

RANDOLPH, JENNINGS, JR. (JAY RANDOLPH), sportscaster; b. Cumberland, Md., Sept. 19, 1934; s. Jennings and Mary Katherine (Babb) R.; m. Sue Henderson, May 28, 1966; children: Jennings, Brian Robert, Rebecca Sue. B.A., Salem (W.Va.) Coll., 1963. Sports and promotion dir. Sta. WHAR, Clarksburg, W.Va., 1958-61; sportscaster Sta. KLIF, Dallas, 1963-66; Sta. KMOX, St. Louis, 1966-68; with Sta. KSDK-TV, St. Louis, 1968—; sports dir. Sta. KSDK-TV, 1968-88, spl. sports corr., 1988—, also on nationally televised broadcasts for various sports events.; TV announcer Fla. Marlins Baseball Club, Ft. Lauderdale, 1993—; TV announcer St. Louis Cardinals, 1970-87, Cin. Reds., 1988; mem. NBC's broadcast staff for 1988 Olympics, Seoul, Korea and 1992 Summer Games, Barcelona, Spain; host nationally syndicated The Golf Show. Trustee Salem Coll., 1976-89. With U.S. Army, 1954-56. Inducted into Boys and Girls Clubs of Am. Hall of Fame, 1990. Mem. Nat. Assn. Sportscasters, Delta Tau Delta. Office: The Fla Marlins 2267 NW 199th St Opa Locka FL 33056-2600

RANDOLPH, LYNWOOD PARKER, federal space agency manager, physicist; b. Richmond, Va., May 21, 1938; s. Samuel Lynwood and Ora Estelle (Harris) R.; m. Aug. 27, 1960; children: Leslie Patrice, Lynwood Parker II, Leonard Patrick, Lemuel Preston. BS, Va. State U., 1959; MS, Howard U., 1964, PhD, 1972; postdoctoral study, U. Md., 1975-77, Harvard U., 1982. Physicist Harry Diamond Labs., Adelphi, Md., 1961-67; research physicist Army Material Command, Harry Diamond Labs., Adelphi, 1967-75; program mgr. NASA, Washington, 1975-82; dep. dir. prodn. NASA, 1982-84, chief productivity, 1984-86, chief mgmt. program, 1986-90; mgr. infotech. standards NASA, Washington, 1990-95; dir. The Quality Inst. Clark Atlanta U., 1995—; mem. Nat. Productivity Rev. Bd. Advisors, 1992—; adj. prof. U. D.C., 1975-85, Howard U., Washington, 1980-82; guest lectr. at various univs., secondary schs. and ch. convs. Contbr. articles to profl. jours. Vestryman St. Timothy Episcopal Ch., Washington, 1991; PTA pres. Edgar Allan Poe Sch., Prince George County, Md., 1970; mem. Harvard Bus. Sch. Alumni, Washington, 1982, NAACP; bd. judges Internat. Who's Who in Quality, 1991—. 1st lt. U.S. Army, 1959-61. Recipient Western Exec. Seminar Ctr. award, Denver, 1988, Nat. Def. Edn. Act Fellowship award, 1961-64, U.S. Senate Commendation for Md. Productivity award, 1992. Fellow AIAA (assoc.); mem. IEEE (sr.), AAAS, Am. Phys. Soc., Am. Platform Assn. (v.p. govt. open sys. solutions), Am. Productivity Mgmt. Assn., Nat. Black MBA Assn., Black Ski Club (bd. dirs., photo editor Washington), Alpha Phi Alpha (Montgomery County chpt., chmn. quality mgmt., 2d v.p., strategic planning commn., edn. founders com., youth activities com. Martin Luther King Jr. breakfast com., Man of Yr. 1992, Award of Merit 1994, Ea. Region Alumni Brother of Yr. 1992, 95, Alumni Brother of Yr. 1995), Sigma Pi Sigma (pres. 1956-59, scholarship 1956). Democrat. Home: 3000 Fairhill Ct Suitland MD 20746-2301 Office: Clark Atlanta U 223 James P Brawley Dr SW Atlanta GA 30314

RANDOLPH, NANCY ADELE, nutritionist, consultant; b. St. Louis, Sept. 7, 1941; d. Robert Andrew and Mary Jane (Hilliker) R.; m. John Reginald Randolph-Swainson, Sept. 16, 1989. BS, U. Ariz., 1963; MEd, Boston U., 1971; postgrad., Harvard U., 1983. Intern instn. adminstrn. Mills Coll., Oakland, Calif., 1963-64; staff dietitian St. Lukes Hosp., St. Louis, 1964-65; clin. dietitian New England Deaconess Hosp., Boston, 1965-66; dietitian mgr. The Seiler Corp., Waltham, Mass., 1966-67; instr., acting dir. Whidden Hosp. Sch. Nursing, Everett, Mass., 1967-72; instr. nutrition Northeastern U. Coll. Nursing, Boston, 1972; renal/rsch. dietitian Lemuel Shattuck Hosp., Jamaica Plain, Mass., 1979-81; New England regional dietitian coord. Beverly Enterprises, Virginia Beach, Va., 1985-88; state nutritionist, surveyor Mass. Dept. Pub. Health/Health Care Quality, Boston, 1988-89; cons. nutritionist Randolph Assocs., West Palm Beach and Sarasota, Fla., 1990—; cons. dietitian Jewish Rehab Ctr., Swampscott, Mass., 1972-79, Lenox Hill Rehab. Ctr., Lynn, Mass., 1972-79, Jesmond Nursing Home, Nahant, Mass., 1972-88, numerous other health care facilities in New England, 1972-88. Mem. Am. Dietetic Assn. (cert.), Fla. Dietetic Assn., Cons. Nutritionists Practice Group, Cons. Dietitians in Health Care.

RANDOLPH, ROBERT MCGEHEE, lawyer; b. San Antonio, June 15, 1936; s. Nowlin and Marjorie (McGehee) R.; m. Jeanette Harrison, Feb. 10, 1962; children: Jeanette, Anne, Nowlin. BA, Tex. Christian U., Ft. Worth, 1957; LLB, U. Tex., 1961. Bar: Tex. 1961, U.S. Dist. Ct. (no. dist.) Tex. 1963, U.S. Supreme Ct. 1972, U.S. Ct. Appeals (5th cir.) 1981. Litigation sect. chief Law, Snakard & Gambill, Ft. Worth, 1963—. 1st lt. U.S. Army. Fulbright scholar, 1957-58. Fellow Tex. Bar Found.; mem. Tex. Assn. Def. Counsel, Ft. Worth-Tarrant County Bar Assn., River Crest Country Club, Ft. Worth Club, Alpha Chi. Office: Law Snakard & Gambill 500 Throckmorton St Ste 3200 Fort Worth TX 76102-3819

RANDZA, JASON MICHAEL, engineer; b. Ellwood City, Pa., June 18, 1963; s. Frank Anthony and Jean Ann (Tracy) R. BS in Aerospace Engring., Pa. State U., 1985. Cert. pvt. pilot. Engr. Atlantic Rsch. Corp., Gainesville, Va., 1985-90; control rm. operator Hadson Power #11, Franklin, Va., 1991; tng. coord. LG&E Westmoreland Southampton, Franklin, Va., 1991-96, plant engr., 1996—. Mem. AIAA, Nat. Assn. Rocketry, Pa. State U. Alumni Assn., Tripoli Rocketry Assn., Cousteau Soc., Am. Kitefliers Assn., Tau Beta Pi, Sigma Gamma Tau. Republican. Roman Catholic. Home: 504 Fairlane Blvd New Galilee PA 16141

RANEY, MIRIAM DAY, actress; b. Florence, S.C., Sept. 30, 1922; d. Lewie Griffith and Iola Lewis (Edwards) Day; m. Robert William Raney, Mar. 31, 1946 (div. Sept. 1976); children: Robert William Jr., Miriam, Kevin Paige, Megan. BSM in Voice, Music Edn., U. N.C., Greensboro, 1939-43; student (summers), Julliard Sch. Music, 1942-43; BA in Music History, U. Ark., Little Rock, 1978-81; Certificate, Adam Roarke Film Actors Lab., Irving, Tex., 1989. Singing chorus N.Y.C. Ctr. Opera Co., 1943-44; understudy, singing chorus Oklahoma, Theater Guild, N.Y.C., 1944-45; ingenue lead Connecticut Yankee, Geosan Subway Cir., N.Y.C., 1945; understudy, singing chorus Up In Central Park, Michael Todd, N.Y.C., 1945-46; beauty cons. Mary Kay Cosmetics, Inc., Dallas, 1993-96. Author: slide sound synchronized show Ark. Women in Music, 1982; composer, lyricist: The Bend and the Willows, 1982, Ballad of Petit Jean, 1983; recent stage appearances include Hedda Gabler (Reponde de Capite repertory), 1990, Time of Your Life (Cmty. Theatre of Little Rock), 1991, Our Town, 1991, Evening with Women II (Regional Theatre of Ctrl. Ark.), 1991; appeared in TV program Unsolved Mysteries, 1988; film Killing Time with Aunt Olene, 1988; also commercials tng. films, 1987-96; print model, Little Rock, Memphis, Ft. Worth, 1988-96. Named Illustrious Alumna, U. N.C. at Greensboro, 1945; recipient Thanks Badge Oachita Coun. Girl Scouts U.S., Little Rock, 1965. Mem. AAUW (Little Rock br. legis. com. 1973-79, program com. 1973-79, state rep. for cultural interests 1976-79, 96), Musical Coterie (Little Rock), Cen. Ark. Guild of Organists (pres. student chpt. 1977-80). Democrat. Home: 25 Valley Forge Dr Little Rock AR 72212-2613

RANGNEKAR, VIVEK MANGESH, molecular biologist, researcher; b. Bombay, Dec. 17, 1955; s. Mangesh Vithal and Sanjivani (Dewoolkar) R.; m. Vidya Vivek Varsha Kulkarni, May 15, 1981; children: Vidyuta, Viraj. MSc, U. Bombay, 1979, PhD, 1983. Postdoctoral fellow U. Chgo., 1983-86; rsch. assoc. Rush Med. Ctr., Chgo., 1986-87; asst. prof. U. Chgo., 1988-91; asst. prof. U. Ky., Lexington, 1992-96, assoc. prof., 1996—. Contbr. articles to profl. jours. including Jour. Biol. Chemistry, Nucleic Acids Rsch., Molecular Cell Biology. Mem. AAAS, Am. Soc. Microbiology. Office: U Ky 800 Rose St Lexington KY 40536-0001

RANIERI, WILLIAM J., medical association administrator. Exec. v.p. So. Med. Assn., Birmingham, Ala. Office: So Med Assn PO Box 190088 Birmingham AL 35219

RANKIN, BETTY HILL, special education educator; b. Greensboro, N.C., Aug. 28, 1945; d. Wilson Conrad and Elizabeth (Roper) Hill; m. James Whiten Rankin Jr., July 23, 1967; 1 child, John Hunter. BA in History, Winthrop U., 1967; postgrad., U. South Fla., 1971-72, U. Va., 1973-96, George Mason U., 1976-88. Tchr. English, history Acad. La Castellana, Caracas, Venezuela, 1967-69; tchr. educable retarded Tampa, Fla., 1970-72; tchr. mentally retarded Loudoun County, Va., 1972—; lectr. Smithsonian Instn., 1990; presenter N.Am. Conf. Rehab. Internat., Atlanta, 1993; mem. Loudoun County Tech. Steering Com., 1992-93; advocate for mainstreaming and integration of students with mental retardation. Profiled in: (video) The Land of Our Children, Rally Behind the Virginians, Am. Resources Coalition, 1992; contbr. articles to mags. Active Contact Endometriosis Assn., Inc., Milw.; treas. N.W. Prince William Citzens Assn., Catharpin, Va., 1986—; pres. Save the Battlefield Coalition, Inc., Catharpin, 1988—. Recipient Peace and Internat. Rels. award Va. Edn. Assn., 1992, Civic commendation Prince William County Planning Commn., 1987; named Tchr. of Yr., IBM, 1988; fellow Internat. Exch. of Experts and Info. in Rehab., U. N.H., 1992; Loudoun Edn. Found. grantee in edn., 1994. Mem. NEA, Assn. Retarded Citizens, Coun. for Exceptional Children (nat. presenter 1989), Tchrs. Internat. Exch. (presenter Japan 1992). Home: PO Box 110 Catharpin VA 20143 Office: Sterling Mid Sch 201 W Holly Ave Sterling VA 20164

RANKIN, DON, art educator; b. Fairfield, Ala., Dec. 9, 1942; s. Joseph P. and Edith Mae (Jones) R.; m. Geneal Muckleroy, Aug. 29, 1964; children: Jennifer Carol, David Rhodes/. MFA, Drawing Board Coll. Comml. and Fine Art, 1966; BA in Fine Art, Samford U., 1969. Staff artist Birmingham News, 1969-74; art dir. Martin White & Mickwee Advt., Birmingham, 1974-77; sr. art dir. Stiener/Bressler Advt., Birmingham, 1977-80; pres. Don Rankin, Inc., graphic design, Birmingham, 1980-92; instr. art Samford U., Birmingham, 1992—. Author: Mastering Glazing Techniques in Watercolor, 1985, Painting from Sketches, Photos and Imagination, 1986, Fifty Questions About Watercolor Glazing Techniques, 1988. With U.S. Army, 1963-65. Mem. So. Watercolor Soc. (pres. 1992-94), Watercolor Soc. Ala. (v.p. 1968). Home: 3412 Wellford Cir Birmingham AL 35226-2616

RANKIN, JACQUELINE ANNETTE, communications expert, educator; b. Omaha, Nebr., May 19, 1925; d. Arthur C. and Virdie (Gillispie) R. BA, Calif. State U., L.A., 1964, MA, 1966; MS in Mgmt., Calif. State U., Fullerton, 1977; EdD, U. LaVerne, Calif., 1981. Tchr. Rowland High Sch., La Habra, Calif., 1964-66, Lowell High Sch., La Habra, Calif., 1966-69, Pomona (Calif.) High Sch., 1969-75; program asst. Pomona Adult Sch., 1975-82; dir. Child Abuse Prevention Program, 1985-86; exec. dir. child abuse prevention Calif. Dept. Pub. Svc., 1985-87; instr. Ind. U., Purdue U. Ind., 1993; assoc. prof. speech Ball State U., Muncie, Ind., 1993-94; instr. No. Va. U., 1994—, trainer Loudoun campus, 1996; faculty evening divsn. Mt. San Antonio C.C., 1966-72; asst. prof. speech Ball State U., Muncie, Ind., 1993; instr. No. Va. U., Alexandria, Annandale, Manassas, Woodbridge, 1995—; assoc. faculty dept. comm. and theatre, Ind. U., Purdue U., Indpls., 1993; trainer internat. convs., sales groups, staffs of hosps., others; spkr., writer, trainer, lectr., cons. in field. Columnist, Jackie's World, Topics Newspapers, Indpls.; author: Body Language: First Impressions, Body Language in Negotiations and Sales; contbr. articles to profl. jours. Mem. Fairfax County Dem. Com.; mem. adv. coun., mem. nat. capital chpt. bd. dirs. ARC. Mem. Pi Lambda Theta, Phi Delta Kappa. Home and Office: 7006 Elkton Dr Springfield VA 22152-3330

RANNEY, MAURICE WILLIAM, chemical company executive; b. Buffalo, Jan. 13, 1934; s. Maurice Lynford and Helen Hart (Birdsall) R.; m. Theresa Ann Berthot, Oct. 24, 1953 (div. 1974); children: William, Linda, Laurel, James; m. Elisa Ramirez Villegas, Dec. 21, 1974; 1 stepchild, Elisa. BS in Chemistry, Niagara U., 1957, MS in Organic Chemistry, 1959; PhD in Phys. Organic Chemistry, Fordham U., 1967. Group leader, tech. mgr. Union Carbide Corp., Tarrytown, N.Y., 1957-75; gen. mgr. Union Carbide Japan KK, 1976-80; exec. v.p. Showa Union Gosei Co., Ltd., 1976-80; rep. dir. Union Carbide Svcs. Eastern Ltd., 1976-80; dir. Nippon Unicar Co., Ltd., 1976-80, Union Showa KK, 1976-80; pres. Union Carbide Formosa Co., Ltd., Hong Kong, Tokyo, 1980-82; bus. dir. Union Carbide Eastern, Inc., Tokyo, 1982-85; pres., rep. dir. Union Carbide Japan KK, 1986-94; pres. Union Indsl. Gas Corp.; rep. dir. Oriental Union Chem. Corp., 1980-82; mng. dir. Nippon Unicar Co., Ltd., 1982-85; v.p. internat. Union Carbide Chems. and Plastics Co., 1986-94; vice chmn., rep. dir. Nippon Unicar, 1986-95; pres. Nihon Parylene, 1992-94, pres. Internat. Partnerships, 1995; dir. Seaforms, 1995, Accur-Search, 1995. Author: Flame Retardant Textiles, 1970, Power Coatings, 1971, Synthetic Lubricants, 1972, New Curing Techniques, 1976, Fuel Additives, 1976, Durable Press Fabrics, 1976, Silicones, Vols. I, II, 1977, Reinforced Plastics and Elastomers, 1978, Offshore Oil Technology, 1979, Oil Shale and Tar Sands, 1980, Primary Electrochemical Cell Technology, 1981; contbr. articles to profl. jours. Union Carbide fellow, Mellon Inst. Indsl. Rsch., 1958-60. Home: # 6 Cotton Hall Ln Hilton Head Island SC 29938

RANNEY, ROBERT JOHN, medical consultant; b. Ft. Dodge, Iowa, Apr. 16, 1943; s. Russell Ballou and Maureen Joan (Bannon) R.; m. Roberta Jean Hoover; 1 stepchild, James Rockford Willis. BS, Mo. Valley Coll., 1971; MPA, U. Mo., 1988. Exec. dir. Ctrl. Ozarks Med. Ctr., Richland, Mo., 1980-85; mgr. practice support initiative Am. Acad. Family Physicians, Kansas City, Mo., 1987-89; sr. cons. Nat. Rural Health Assn., Kansas City, 1986-87; chief exec. officer Midwest Rural Health Assocs., Kansas City, 1985-86; owner, cons. Ranney & Assocs., Fairfield Bay, Ark., 1989—; mem. PSI Network Cons., Am. Acad. Family Physicians, Kansas City, 1993-94; presenter seminars various locations; lectr. AMA. Author: Policy and Procedures Manual for Rural Health Clinics, 1992, The Self Starting Rural Health Clinic, 1993; (manual and seminar) Rural Health Clinics in Detail, 1993. Chmn. Midwest Rural Health Assn., 1981-82; co-chmn. Mo. Coalition Health Care, 1983-84. With U.S. Army, 1965-67. Recipient Recognition award Midwest Rural Health Assn., 1983. Mem. Pi Alpha Alpha.

RANSOHOFF, JOSEPH, neurosurgeon; b. Cin., July 1, 1915; s. J. Louis and Doris (Kauffman) R.; m. Rita Mayer, June 1, 1941 (div. Apr. 1984); children: Joan, Joe; m. Lori Cohen, Apr. 7, 1984; children: Jake, Jade. BS,

Harvard U., 1938; MD, U. Chgo., 1942. Diplomate Am. Bd. Neurosurgery. Intern surgery Cin. Gen. Hosp., 1941-42, asst. resident surgery, 1942-44; neurol. svc. Montefiore Hosp., Bronx, N.Y., 1946-47, neurol. surgery, 1948-49; neurosurgeon Columbia Presbyn. Hosp., N.Y.C., 1949-61; chmn. dept. neurosurgery NYU, N.Y.C., 1962-92; prof. neurosurgery U. South Fla., Tampa, 1992—. Contbr. articles to neurosurg. jours. Capt. U.S. Army, 1944-46, ETO. Home: 915 Mooring Cir Tampa FL 33602 Office: Tampa VA 13000 Bruce Downs Blvd Tampa FL 33612

RANSOM, CLIFTON LOUIS, JR., lawyer, real estate investor; b. Houston, May 25, 1935; s. Clifton Louis and Birdelle (Wykoff) R.; m. Dorothy Ellen Peterson, Dec. 25, 1974. BS in Math., Tex. So. U., 1956; BA in Philosophy, St. Joseph's Coll., Rensselaer, Ind., 1964; MA in Bibl. Theology, St. Louis U., 1970; JD, Tex. So. U., 1974; LLM in Taxation, Washington Law Sch., Salt Lake City, 1991. Bar: Tex. 1974, U.S. Dist. Ct. (so. dist.) Tex. 1976, U.S. Ct. Appeals (5h cir.) 1980, U.S. Supreme Ct. 1980, U.S. Tax Ct. 1991; ordained priest Roman Cath. Ch., 1968. Priest Diocese of Galveston-Houston, 1968-74; atty. Tex. Welfare Dept., Houston, 1975-80, Gulf Coast Legal Found., Houston, 1980—. Bd. dirs. Hope Is Victory AIDS Found., Houston, 1993—. Lt. (j.g.) USN, 1957-60. Democrat. Home: 3919 Point Clear Dr Missouri City TX 77459-3710 Office: Gulf Coast Legal Found 1415 Fannin Ste 200 Houston TX 77002

RANSOM, NANCY ALDERMAN, sociology and women's studies educator, university administrator; b. New Haven, Feb. 25, 1929; d. Samuel Bennett and Florence (Opper) Alderman; m. Harry Howe Ransom, July 6, 1951; children—Jenny Alderman, Katherine Marie, William Henry Howe. B.A., Vassar Coll., 1950; postgrad. Columbia U., 1951, U. Leeds (Eng.), 1977-78; M.A., Vanderbilt U., 1971; EdD, Vanderbilt U., 1988. Lectr. sociology U. Tenn.-Nashville, 1971-76; grant writer Vanderbilt U., Nashville, 1976-77, dir. Women's Ctr., 1978—, instr. sociology, 1972, 74, lectr. sociology and women's studies, 1983, 90—; speaker profl. meetings. Vol. counselor family planning Planned Parenthood Assn. of Nashville, 1973-77, bd. dirs., 1978—, v.p., 1981—, pres., 1987-89; mem. planning com. ACE/ACE nat. identification program Women in Higher Edn., 1984-92. Recipient Woman of Achievement award Middle Tenn. State U., 1996; Columbia U. residential fellow, 1951; Vanderbilt U. fellow, 1971. Mem. AAUW, NOW, Am. Sociol. Assn., Nat. Women's Studies Assn., Southeastern Women's Studies Assn., Nat. Women's Polit. Caucus, LWV, Cable Club, Phi Beta Kappa (v.p. Alpha of Tenn. 1994-95, pres. 95—). Office: Vanderbilt U PO Box 1513 Nashville TN 37235

RANTON, JASON DOUGLAS, news writer; b. Waxahachie, Tex., Jan. 5, 1970; s. James Douglas and JoAnn (Samuels) R. BA, Baylor U., 1993. Communications writer Texas State Tech. Coll., 1993-95; student media adviser Baylor U., Waco, Tex., 1995—. Organist First Bapt. Ch., Waco, 1992—. Mem. Soc. of Profl. Journalists (1st Place News Reporting Award, 1993), Coll. Media Advisers, Soc. of Newspaper Design, Am. Guild Organists (sec. ctrl. Tex. chpt. 1994-96). Republican. Baptist. Home: 2301 Gorman Ave Waco TX 76707 Office: Baylor U PO Box 97353 Waco TX 76798

RAO, LAWRENCE MICHAEL, writer, radio producer; b. Bklyn., Apr. 14, 1948; s. Silvio Robert and Mary Veronica (Kennedy) R.; m. Valerie Ann Means, Feb. 2, 1992. BA, Bklyn. Coll., 1969; Assoc. Media and Comm., New Sch. for Dramatic Arts, 1971; MBA, Bklyn. Coll., 1976. Asst. advt. mgr. Gralla Publs., N.Y.C., 1969-71; advt./mktg. mgr., copywriter Hayden Publs., N.Y.C., 1971-74; dir. advt./mktg., sr. staff writer Edelman Pub. Rels. and Advt. Worldwide, N.Y.C., 1975-78; sr. advt. & pub. rels. specialist, mktg. writer Young and Rubicam Advt., Inc., N.Y.C., 1978-83; v.p. corp. comms. Ford Found., N.Y.C., 1983-86; freelance writer N.Y.C., 1986-88; pres., co-owner Radio Vision Broadcast Prodn. Co., N.Y.C., 1988-90; dir. programming, advt. writer Sta. WVAB-AM Radio, Virginia Beach, Va., 1990-91; pres., owner Enigma Media Cons., 1994-95; ind. vintage radio prodr. for U.S. and Can. stas.; on-air broadcaster, radio prodr. Pacifica Radio Network, NBC. Author, editor: City Gates, 1975; voice actor for ind. films and radio commls., N.Y.C. and Va.; writer for radio stas., Va., N.Y.C. and Can.; contbr. articles, stories to profl. publs. Campaign worker Dem. Party, Bklyn., 1960, 64, 68, 72, 76. Roman Catholic.

RAO, PAPINENI SEETHAPATHI, physiologist, educator, researcher; b. Vetapalam, India, Apr. 19, 1937; came to U.S., 1960; s. Papineni Umamaheswara and Sesharatnam (Nayani) R.; m. Uma Rajeswari Nayani, July 19, 1967; children: Karuna, Rajani, Sobha. B of Vet. Sci., Andhra Vet. Coll., Tirupati, India, 1959; MS, U. Mo., 1961, PhD, 1965. Vet. asst. surg. Dept. Vet. Medicine, India, 1959-60; rsch. asst., rsch. assoc. U. Mo., Columbia, 1962-66; from instr. to assoc. prof. St. Louis U. Sch. Medicine, 1966-79; assoc. prof. dept. ob-gyn. and physiology U. South Fla. Coll. Medicine, Tampa, 1979-85, prof., 1985—. Editor: Septic Shock in Obstetrics and Gynecology, 1977; contbr. chpts. to books. Active Cultural Assn. India, Tampa, 1980—. Kiepe scholar U. Mo., 1961-62. Mem. AAAS, AAUP, Am. Physiol. Soc., Shock Soc., Internat. Endotoxin Soc., Soc. for Study of Reprodn. Hindu. Office: U South Fla Coll Medicine 12901 Bruce B Downs Blvd Tampa FL 33612-4742

RAO, VIJAY MOHAN, biochemist; b. Madhira, India, Oct. 7, 1955; came to U.S., 1981; s. Sambasiva Rao and Vanajakshi (Anne) Lella; m. Usha R. Pendurthi, Aug. 20, 1981; children: Varun Lella, Neil Lella. MPhil, Jawaharlal Nehru U., India, 1979, PhD, 1981. Asst. rsch. biochemist Dept. Medicine U. Calif., San Diego, 1985-91, assoc. rsch. biochemist, 1991-93; assoc. prof. dept. biochemistry U. Tex. Health Ctr., Tyler, 1993-96, prof. dept. biochemistry, 1996—. Editl. bd. mem. Haemostasis, 1991—; reviewer New Eng. Jour. of Medicine, Blood, Jour. of Clin. Investigation, Thrombosis and Haemostasis, Thrombosis Rsch.; contbr. numerous articles to profl. jours. Rsch. grants Nat. Heart, Lung and Blood Inst., 1991—, 1992—, NIH, 1989—; recipient Rsch. Career Devel. award NIH, 1991-96. Mem. AAAS, Am. Soc. Hematology, Coun. on Thrombosis, Internat. Soc. on Thrombosis And Haemostasis. Office: U Tex Health Ctr PO Box 2003 Tyler TX 75710-2003

RAPER, JULIA TAYLOR, pediatric and neonatal nurse; b. Bermuda, B.W.I., Mar. 25, 1963; d. Rodney Blake Taylor Sr. and Barbara Alice Hill; m. Bruce Scott Raper, Dec. 3, 1988. BSN, East Carolina U., 1986; MS in Nursing, Duke U., 1988. Cert. neonatal resuscitation program instr., BCLS instr., PALS instr. Staff nurse neonatal ICU Pitt County Meml. Hosp., Greenville, N.C.; pediatric/neonatal ednl. nurse specialist Children's Hosp. Ea. N.C./U. Med. Ctr. East Carolina, Greenville; mem. adj. faculty East Carolina U. Sch. Nursing. Contbr. articles to profl. jours. Mem. Nat. Assn. Neonatal Nurses, Sigma Theta Tau.

RAPF, JOANNA E., English literature and film educator; b. L.A., July 18, 1941; d. Maurice Harry and Louise (Seidel) R.; 1 child, Alexander Maurice Eaton. AB, Pembroke Coll./Brown U., 1963; MA, Columbia U., 1968; PhD, Brown U., 1973. Asst. in script div. Norwood Film Studios, Washington, 1963-64; film rschr. CBS, Washington, 1964-65; asst. fiction editor Saturday Evening Post, N.Y.C., 1965-66; from asst. prof. to prof. English and film U. Okla., Norman, 1973—, Assocs. Disting. lectr., 1988-89; vis. assoc. prof. film studies Dartmouth Coll., Hanover, N.H., 1994-95; rev. panelist NEH, Washington, 1991—; advisor PBS-Am. Masters, N.Y.C., 1990, 92-93; award judge Cowboy Hall of Fame, Oklahoma City, 1994-96. Author: Buster Keaton: A Bio-bibliography, 1995; author essays and articles. Mem. MLA, Univ. Film and Video Assn., Popular Culture Assn., Soc. for Cinema Studies, Keats-Shelley Assn. Office: U Okla Dept English Norman OK 73019

RAPINI, RONALD PETER, dermatology educator; b. Akron, Ohio, Feb. 15, 1954; s. Vincent Thomas and Joann Irene (Tufexis) R.; m. Mary Jo Beigel, June 16, 1979; children: Brianna Marie, Sarina Elizabeth. BS in Biology, U. Akron, 1975; MD, Ohio State U., 1978. Diplomate Am. Bd. Dermatology (bd. dirs.), Am. Bd. Dermatopathology. Assoc. prof. U. Tex. Med. Sch., Houston, 1983-93; prof. and chair dermatology dept. Tex. Tech. U., Lubbock, 1994—. Author in field. Fellow Am. Acad. Dermatology, Am. Soc. Dermatol. Surgery (bd. dirs.), Soc. Investigative Dermatology; mem. AMA, Am. Soc. Dermatopathology (sec.-treas.), Internat. Soc. Dermatopathology. Office: Texas Tech Univ 3601 4th St Lubbock TX 79430-0001

RAPP, CHRISTIAN FERREE, textile home furnishings company executive; b. Paradise, Pa., July 3, 1933; s. Christian F. and Mildred May (Peters) R.; m. Mary Yvonne Kirchner, June 25, 1953; children: Pamela, Linda, Christian. BS, Drexel U., 1961; postgrad., NYU, 1964-67. Cert. mgmt. acct. Bd. dirs., v.p. fin. Gamon-Calmet Meter Corp., Cin., 1963-73, Mack Shirt Corp., Cin., 1974-77; sr. v.p. fin. and adminstrn. Louisville Bedding Co., 1978—. Treas. polit. campaign for Ky. Senate, 1976. With U.S. Army, 1953-56. Mem. Fin. Execs. Inst. (v.p. 1986—), Nat. Assn. Accts., Phi Kappa Phi. Home: 2316 Mohican Hill Ct Louisville KY 40207-1147 Office: Louisville Bedding Co 10400 Bunsen Way Louisville KY 40299-2510

RAPP, JOANNA A., retired geriatrics nurse, mental health nurse; b. Youngsville, Pa., Nov. 22, 1920; d. Wade Hampton and Edith (Hodges) Brazee; m. Ellsworth G. Rapp, Nov. 6, 1976; children: Sallie Angel, Suzanne Herzing. Diploma, Meadville (Pa.) City Hosp., 1941; BS in Nursing Edn., Western Res. U., 1947. Field team nurse Bur. Occupational Health; staff nurse USPHS Hosp., Anchorage; supr. Hale-Makua, Mauia, Hawaii; instr. John Howard Forensic Psychiat. Hosp., Washington; DON, Twinbrooke So. Nursing Facility, Edinburg, Tex., until 1995; ret., 1995. 1st. Lt. ANC, 1944-46. Named Dist. Nurse of Yr. Home: Rt 11 Box 532W Mission TX 78572

RAPPA, HUGH GREGORY, medical educator; b. N.Y.C., July 8, 1956; s. Charles and Norma (Cotilli) R. D of Medicine and Surgery, U. Padova, Italy, 1991. Instr., mem. student adv. bd. Keiser Coll., Ft. Lauderdale, Fla., 1992-95; asst. prof. anatomy, course coord., physician asst. program Nova Southeastern U., Davie, Fla., 1995—. Vol., interpretor ARC, Vicenza, Italy, 1990-91. Mem. Assn. Edn. in Radiol. Scis. Roman Catholic. Home: 3031 N Ocean Blvd Apt 707 Fort Lauderdale FL 33308-7329

RAPPAPORT, MARTIN PAUL, internist, nephrologist, educator; b. Bronx, N.Y., Apr. 25, 1935; s. Joseph and Anne (Kramer) R.; BS, Tulane U., 1957, MD, 1960; m. Bethany Ann Mitchell; children: Karen, Steven. Intern, Charity Hosp. of La., New Orleans, 1960-61, resident in internal medicine, 1961-64; pvt. practice medicine specializing in internal medicine and nephrology, Seabrook, Tex., 1968-72, Webster, Tex., 1972—; mem. courtesy staff Mainland Ctr. Hosp. (formerly Galveston County Meml. Hosp.), Houston, 1968-96, Bapt. Meml. System, 1969-72, 88—; mem. staff Clear Lake Regional Med. Ctr., 1972—; cons. staff St. Mary's Hosp., 1973-79; cons. nephrology St. John's Hosp., Nassau Bay, Tex.; fellow in nephrology Northwestern U. Med. Sch., Chgo., 1968; clin. asst. prof. in medicine and nephrology U. Tex., Galveston, 1969—; lectr. emergency med. technician course, 1974-76; adviser on respiratory therapy program Alvin (Tex.) Jr. Coll., 1976-82; cons. nephrology USPHS, 1979-80. Served to capt. M.C., U.S. Army, 1961-67. Diplomate Am. Bd. Internal Medicine, Nat. Bd. Med. Examiners. Fellow ACP, Am. Coll. Chest Physicians; mem. Internat., Am. Socs. Nephrology, So. Med. Assn., Tex. Med. Assn., Tex. Soc. Internal Medicine (bd. govs. 1994-96), Am. Soc. Artificial Internal Organs, Tex. Acad. Internal Medicine, Harris County Med. Soc., Am. Geriatrics Soc., Bay Area Heart Assn. (bd. govs. 1969-75), Clear Lake C. of C., Phi Delta Epsilon, Alpha Epsilon Pi, Tulane Alumni Assn. Lodge: Rotary. Home: 1818 Linfield Way Houston TX 77058-2324 Office: PO Box 57609 Webster TX 77598-7609

RAPPORT, JOE ROOKS, rabbi; b. Columbus, Ohio, May 26, 1957; s. James Louis and Karlyn Ann (Israelson) R.; m. Gaylia R. Rooks, Oct. 8, 1980; children: Yael, Lev. BA, Coll. of Wooster, 1979; MA in Hebrew Lit., Hebrew Union Coll., 1982; AM/PhD, Washington U., St. Louis, 1988. Ordained rabbi, 1984; cert. secondary sch. tchr. Interim rabbi B'nai El, St. Louis, 1984-85; assoc. rabbi The Temple, Louisville, 1988—; lectr. in Judaic thought U. Louisville/Bellarmine Coll., 1988—; bd. dirs. Jewish Community Ctr., Louisville, 1988-91; del. Nat. Assn. Jewish Community Rels. Couns., Miami, Fla., 1991; mem. inter-agy. com. on Soviet resettlement Jewish Family and Vocat. Svcs., Louisville, 1990—; ptnr. MAZON: A Jewish Response to Hunger, 1988—. Contbr. articles to profl. publs. Co-chair Louisville Coalition for homeless, 1990—, Many People-One Community (Mayor's Commn. on Prejudice), Louisville, 1990—; chair social action Community Rels. Coun., Louisville, 1991—. Rsch. fellow Washington, 1987, rsch. grantee Lilly Endowment, Louisville Inst., 1996; recipient Julie Linker Young Leadership award Jewish Cmty. Fedn., 1990. Mem. Cen. Conf. Am. Rabbis (mem. task force on cults 1984—), Louisville Bd. Rabbis, Religious Action Ctr. of Reform Judaism, NCCJ (chair edn. com. 1990-91), Phi Beta Kappa. Office: The Temple 5101 Brownsboro Rd Louisville KY 40241-6016

RAREY, KYLE EUGENE, anatomy educator, researcher; b. Elwood, Ind., May 13, 1948; s. Del Eugene and B. (Smith) R.; m. Donna Susan Pugh, Nov. 12, 1976; children: Nathaniel John, Elizabeth Suzanne, Jason Michael, Adam Joseph. BA in Zoology, Ind. U., 1969, PhD in Anatomy, 1977. Sci. tchr. in biology George Washington High Sch., Indpls., 1969-71; assoc. instr. dept. anatomy Sch. Medicine, Ind. U., Indpls., 1972-76; instr. dept. anatomy U. Mich., 1977-79; NIH postdoctoral fellow Kresge Hearing Rsch. Inst., Mich., 1979-81, asst. rsch. sci., 1981-84; assoc. prof. dept. anatomy and cell biology Coll. Medicine, U. Fla., Gainesville, 1987-94, resident rsch. coord. dept. otolaryngology, 1988—; prof. dept. anatomy and cell biology coll. medicine U. Fla., Gainesville, 1994—. Contbr. articles to profl. jours.; co-creator computer instrnl. gross anatomy program. Recipient Fla. Blue Key Disting. Faculty award, 1996, Outstanding tchr. of Yr. award, 1987-88, 89-90, 93-94, 95-96, Basic Sci. Tchg. awards, 1994, 96. Mem. AAAS, Am. Assn. Anatomists, Am. Assn. Clin. Anatomists, Am. Assn. Rsch. in Otolaryngology, Am. Acad. Otolaryngology-Head and Neck Surgery (Nat. Rsch. Svc. award 1979-81, Coll. of Medicine Tchr. of Yr. 1988, 90, 94). Office: U Fla Coll Medicine PO Box 100235 Gainesville FL 32610-0235

RASBURY, JULIAN GEORGE, financial services company executive; b. Houston, July 10, 1957; s. Julian George and Willie Ann (Stringer) R.; m. Kathleen Ellen Price, Nov. 10, 1984; 1 child, Lisa Dawn. BBA in Acctg., U. Tex., 1980. CPA Tex. Bd. Pub. Accountancy, Austin, 1993—; cert. funds specialist Inst. Funds Specialists, La Jolla, Calif., 1994—; gen. securities rep. NASD, Rockville, Md., 1992—, gen. securities prin., 1992—, registered investment advisor, 1993—, fin. & ops. prin., 1994—; bd. dirs. First Fin. Group, Houston. Co-author: Professional Standards in Cafateria Plan Administration, 1993. Mem. Big Bros., Pleasant Hill, Calif., 1987. Mem. AICPA, Tex. Soc. CPAs, Employers Coun. on Flexible Compensation (exec. com. 1992-93), Cafateria Plan Adv. Coun., U. Tex. Alumni Assn. Republican. Baptist. Office: First Fin Group 3801 Kirby Dr Fl 7 Houston TX 77098-4117

RASH, WAYNE, JR., journalist; b. Erie, Pa., Nov. 25, 1948; s. Wayne and Elizabeth Susan (Miller) R.; m. Carolyn Louise Hall, Nov. 25, 1972; children: Julia Leigh, Wayne III, Brittany Lynne. BA, Lynchburg (Va.) Coll., 1980. Dep. commr. revenue City of Lynchburg, 1976-80; prin. Am. Mgmt. Systems, Inc., Arlington, Va., 1984-92; mem. review bd. Infoworld. Author: The Novell Connection, 1989, The Executive Guide to Local Area Networks, 1989, WordPerfect Office 3.0: The Basics, 1991, Politics on the Nets, 1996; columnist Byte Mag., 1988-92, cons. editor, 1992-95; columnist The Star Ledger, Newark, 1996—, OS/2 Mag., Windows NT Mag.; cons. editor Byteweek, 1988-92, Computer Digest, 1986-91; editor Byte Information Exchange, 1984—, The Washington Post Computer Showcase, 1992-93; contbr. The Washington Post, 1994—; editor Tech Report/The Washington Post, 1996—; contbg. editor, columnist Comms. Week; contbg. editor Interactive Age, Plane and Pilot, 1995—, others. Pres. Kings Park West Civic Assn., Fairfax, Va., 1986-88; active Citizens Adv. Coun. on Nat. Space Policy, Studio City, Calif., 1986—, Rep. Cen. Com., Richmond, Va., 1976. Lt. USN, 1980-84. Mem. Nat. Press Club, Lions (program chmn. Brookville-Timberlake chpt., Lynchburg 1976-80), Aircraft Owners and Pilots Assn., Am. Flying Club, Exptl. Aircraft Assn. Episcopalian. Office: 11711 Amkin Dr Clifton VA 20124

RASMUS, JOHN CHARLES, trade association executive, lawyer; b. Rochester, N.Y., Dec. 27, 1941; s. Harold Charles and Myrtle Leota (Dybevik) R.; m. Elaine Green Reeves, Mar. 19, 1982; children: Kristin, Stuart, Karin. A.B., Cornell U., 1963; J.D., U. Va., 1966. Bar: Va. 1970, U.S. Supreme Ct. 1974. Spl. agt. Def. Dept., Washington, 1966-70; v.p., adminstrv. officer, legis. research counsel U.S. League Savs. Instns., Washington, 1970-83; asst. to exec. v.p. Nat. Assn. Fed. Credit Unions, 1983-84; sr. fed. adminstrv. counsel, mgr. agency rels. Am. Bankers Assn., 1985—. Mem. ABA, Fed. Bar Assn. (disting. service award 1980, 82, past chmn. long range planning com., past chmn. council fin. instns. and economy), Univ. Club, Masons. Home: 303 Kentucky Ave Alexandria VA 22305-1739

RASMUSSEN, DUANE ARCHER, retired publishing executive, consultant; b. Austin, MN., Nov. 26, 1928; s. Harry Elwood and Geraldine (Archer) R.; m. Delores Ramona Larson, June 8, 1952 (div. Jan. 1986); children: Sherri L. Miller, Eric Duane, Lisa G. Vial, Leif Harry; m. Edith Roseann Wilkinson, Sept. 24, 1987. BA in Journalism, U. Minn., 1951. Prodn. coord. Herald Pub. Co., Austin, 1937-62; adminstrn. asst. Thomson Newspapers, Austin, 1962-65; pub. Thomson Newspapers, Greenville, OH., 1965-68; pres., CEO Sell Pub. Co., Forest Lake, Minn., 1968-93; retired ECM Pub. Inc., Forest Lake, 1993; curator Minn. Letterpress Mus., 1993-95. Pres. Forest Lake Indsl. Corp., Cmty. Scholarship Found., Forest Lake, 1973-93, Fla. United Way, 1980's, founder. With U.S. Army, 1951-54. Mem. Minn. Newspaper Assn. (pres. 1987, chmn. legislation 1977-87), Soc. Profl. Journalists, Am. Legion, U. Minn. Alumni Assn., Forest Lake Rotary Club, Masons, Austin Fidelity Lodge. Lutheran. Home: 520 Beach Blvd Laguna Vista TX 78578

RASMUSSEN, GERALDINE DOROTHY, composer, artist, musician, author; b. Beaverton, Mich., May 12, 1925; d. Edwin Ludwig and Hazel Helen (Colbeck) R.; m. Vance Hatcher, 1950 (div. 1950); m. Henry L. Oppenborn Jr., June 30, 1953 (div.). B in Music Edn., U. Miami, 1947. Music instr. U. Miami, Coral Gables, Fla., 1948-49; stewardess Nat. Airlines, Miami, 1949-51; substitute tchr. U. Miami Sch. Music, 1948; tchr. Our Lady Queen of Martyrs, Ft. Lauderdale, Fla., 1961-62; pvt. piano instr., 1961-65; music tchr. Broward County Schs., Ft. Lauderdale, 1962-63; tchr. St. Anthony's Sch., Ft. Lauderdale, 1963-64; landlord Ft. Lauderdale, 1964-89; freelance portrait artist Miami, Ft. Lauderdale, 1947—; violist U. Miami Symphony, Coral Gables, 1943-47; mezzo-contralto First Congl. Ch. Choir, Coral Gables, 1944-47, Miami (Fla.) Opera Guild, 1944-47; violinist, violist Ft. Lauderdale (Fla.) Symphony, Hollywood (Fla.) Phil., 1956-64. Author: The Invisible Force, 1981, Toronita: Land of Sunshine and Good Will, 1995; composer: (opera) Julius Caesar, 1983, Christopher Columbus, (for voice, piano and flute obligato) The Bataan Death March, 1989, (for tenor, piano and flute) Columbus Quincentennial; composer songs for voice, piano and flute obligato, La Florida, 1995, La Pieta, 1995; exhibited in group shows at Ft. Lauderdale Libr. and Ft. Lauderdale City Hall; also pvt. collections. Founder, dir. Citizens Against Radioactive Pollution, Ft. Lauderdale, 1976-79; inverviewer USA Poll, Ft. Lauderdale, 1989-90; rec. sec. Morning Musicale Ft. Lauderdale, 1990-91, pres., 1992-94. Mem. Fla. Fedn. Music Clubs (pres. Royal Poinciana dist. 1994-96), Internat. Assn. Hydrogen Energy (hon.), Mortar Bd., Sigma Alpha Iota. Republican. Home: 1609 SE 4th St Fort Lauderdale FL 33301-2347

RASMUSSEN, SHARON LEE, news reporter; b. Seoul, Nov. 5, 1974; d. Anthony Edward and Chong Hui (Lee) R. BA in Communications, U. Ala., 1996. Sales assoc. Svc. Mdse., Huntsville, Ala., 1991-93, Tuscaloosa, Ala., 1993-95; assoc. prodr. Sta. WDBB-Channel 17 News, Tuscaloosa, 1995; morning anchor Sta. WUAL-Ala. Pub. Radio, Tuscaloosa, 1995-96; reporter Sta. WDEF-TV, Chattanooga, 1996—. Named Best Radio News Anchor Ala. Broadcaster Assn., 1995, Best Radio Feature Reporter, 1995; Presdl. scholar U. Ala., 1993; recipient Top Scholar award Kappa Tau Alpha, 1996. Mem. Radio TV News Dirs. Assn., Soc. Profl. Journalists. Home: 3217 Bayless Dr Huntsville AL 35805

RASMUSSEN, WAYNE ROGER, law educator, consultant; b. Sioux Falls, S.D., May 8, 1936; s. Ezra Christian and Loretta Mae Belle (Schlafer) R.; m. Carol Joy Longsdorf Prue, June 4, 1960 (div. May 1973); children: Joy, Corbin; m. Mary Dee Fowlkes, May 20, 1973; children: Thomas, Frances, Heather. BA, ThB, St. Paul Bible Coll., 1963; JD, John Marshall Law Sch., Atlanta, 1989. Bar: Ga. 1989, Calif. 1992; CPCU. Claims adjuster Travelers Ins. Co., St. Paul, 1966-70; claims supr. Travelers Ins. Co., Washington, 1970-72; asst. mgr. claims Travelers Ins. Co., Atlanta, 1972-77; asst. v.p. Continental Ins. Co., N.Y.C., 1977-82; mgr. state claims Continental Ins. Co., Charlotte, N.C., 1982-86; pvt. practice, Atlanta, 1989—; prof. law John Marshall Law Sch., 1989—; ins. cons., Atlanta, 1990—. Aux. police officer N.Y. Police Dept., N.Y.C., 1978-82. With USAF, 1954-58. Named Outstanding Prof. of Yr., John Marshall Law Sch., 1992. Mem. Soc. of CPCU (treas. 1980), Soc. of CLU.

RASMUSSON, RANDALL LEE, biomedical engineer; b. Boston, Aug. 1, 1960; s. Gary Henry and Nancy Elaine (Torkelson) R.; m. Audrey Frances Danovitch, June 2, 1988; 1 child, Abraham Roman. BS, Rice U., 1983, MS, 1986; PhD, Duke U., 1991. Asst. rsch. prof. Duke U., Durham, N.C., 1991—. Contbr. articles to profl. jours., chpts. to books; mem. editl. bd. Circulation Rsch., Dallas, 1996. Biomed. Engrng. Rsch. grantee Whitaker Found., Roslyn, Va., 1994. Mem. IEEE, Biophys. Soc. Lutheran. Office: Duke U Dept Biomed Engring PO Box 90281 Durham NC 27708

RASOR, DORIS LEE, secondary education educator; b. Gonzales, Tex., June 25, 1929; d. Leroy and Ora (Power) DuBose; m. Jimmie E. Rasor, Dec. 27, 1947; children: Jimmy Lewis, Roy Lynn. BS, Abilene (Tex.) Christian U., 1949. Part-time sec. Abilene Christian Coll., 1946-50; sec. Radford Wholesale Grocery, Abilene, 1950-52; tchr. Odessa (Tex.) High Sch., 1967—. Author play: The Lost Pearl, 1946. Recipient Am. Legion award, 1946. Mem. AAUW, Classroom Tchrs. Assn., Tex. Tchrs. Assn., NEA, Tex. Bus. Educators Assn., Alpha Delta Kappa (pres. 1976-78). Ch. of Christ. Home: 3882 Kenwood Dr Odessa TX 79762-7018 Office: Odessa High School 1301 Dotsy Ave Odessa TX 79763-3576

RASTEGAR, NADER E., real estate developer, businessman; b. Tehran, Iran, May 12, 1953; came to U.S., 1982; s. Morteza and Rabe'eh (Baghai-Kermani) R.; m. Soheila Gharai, Apr. 1979; children: Roya Z., Scheherazade B., Maryam A. BSc, U. Wis., 1976; MBA, Iran Ctr. Mgmt. Studies, 1979. Pres. Shahgard Indsl. Co., Tehran, 1977, Renafa, Inc., Atlanta, 1984—. Contbr. articles to various publs. Active various profl., historical, philatelical and environ. socs. and groups. Lt. Iranian Armed Forces, 1977-78. Office: Renafa Inc 1603 Lenox Tower N 3400 Peachtree Rd NE Atlanta GA 30326-1107

RATCLIFF, JOHN GARRETT, lawyer; b. Laurel, Miss., Mar. 12, 1945; s. Kalford Compton and Mary Claire (Terry) R.; m. Margaret Warner White, Aug. 9, 1980 (div. 1987); children: Garrett Bateman, Margaret Lindsley; m. Joy Melane Fair, June 30, 1990; 1 child, Thomas Kalford. BA, Southwestern at Memphis (now Rhodes Coll.), 1966; MA, U. Va., 1970; JD, U. Miss., 1973. Bar: Miss. 1973, U.S. Dist. Ct. (no. and so. dists.) Miss. 1973, U.S. Dist. Ct. (so. dist.) Ala., 1973, U.S. Ct. Appeals (5th cir.) 1973, U.S. Dist. Ct. (ea. dist.) La. 1980, U.S. Dist. Ct. (we. dist.) La. 1983, U.S. Supreme Ct., 1983. Founding ptnr. Andalman, Bergmark & Ratcliff, Hattiesburg, Miss., 1973-75; staff atty. North Miss. Rural Legal Svcs., Oxford, 1977. South Miss. Legal Svcs., Biloxi and Pascagoula, 1977-78; pvt. practice law, New Orleans, 1980-83, Shreveport, La., 1983—; assoc. Walker, Feazel & Tooke, Shreveport, 1983, The Allison Law Firm, Shreveport, 1987-88; atty. Indigent Defender Bd., Shreveport, 1984, 86, 87, Northwest La. Legal Svcs., 1992-95; assoc. Randal L. Loon, 1995—. Mem. La. Bar Assn., Miss. Bar Assn., Shreveport Bar Assn., Nat. Lawyers Guild, Delta Theta Phi, Omicron Delta Kappa, Sigma Alpha Epsilon. Unitarian Universalist. Office: 9435 Mansfield Rd Ste 4B Shreveport LA 71118-2948

RATCLIFFE, DAVID NELSON, surgeon; b. Bluefield, W.Va., Sept. 20, 1960; s. Richard Raymond Ratcliffe and Charlotte Ann (Neal) Perdue. BS in Pre-Medicine, Va. Commonwealth U., Richmond, 1983; MS in Human Genetics, U. N.C., 1987; DO, Southeastern U. Health Scis., North Miami Beach, Fla., 1992. Phys. therapy technician Chippenham Hosp., Richmond, 1978-81, orthopaedic technician, 1981-83; labor and delivery/rsch. asst. Charlotte (N.C.) Meml. Hosp., 1983-85; physician's asst. Irving D. Royce, MD, North Miami Beach, Fla., 1990; intern gen. surgery York (Pa.) Hosp., 1992-93; clin. prof. surgery Nova-Southeastern U. Health Scis., North Miami Beach, Fla., 1993—. Mem. AMA, Pineallas County Osteo. Med. Soc., Residents Coun. Suncoast Hosp., Gen. Surg. Club. Home: 1920 Georgiana St # 4 Largo FL 34944 Office: Suncoast Hosp 2528 Indian Rocks Road Largo FL 34644

RATH, FRANCIS STEVEN, lawyer; b. N.Y.C., Oct. 10, 1955; s. Steven and Elizabeth (Chorin) R.; m. Denise Stephania Thompson, Aug. 2, 1980. BA cum laude, Wesleyan U., Middletown, Conn., 1977; JD cum laude, Georgetown U., 1980. Bar: D.C. 1980, U.S. Dist. Ct. D.C. 1981, U.S. Ct. Appeals (D.C. cir.), 1981, U.S. Supreme Ct. 1987, Va. 1988. Atty., advisor Comptr. of the Currency, Washington, 1980-84; assoc. Verner, Liipfert, Bernhard, McPherson & Hand, Washington, 1984-85; founding mem. Wolf, Arnold & Monroig (merged with Burnham, Connolly, Oesterly & Henry), Washington, 1986-88; pvt. practice Great Falls, Va., 1989—; internat. cons. Fried, Frank, Harris, Shriver and Jacobson, 1991-95; counsel Seward & Kissel, Washington, 1995—. Editor: Law and Policy in Internat. Bus., 1979-80; contbg. author Business Ventures in Eastern Europe and Russia; contbr. articles to profl. jours. Trustee Dunn Loring (Va.) Vol. Fire Dept., 1986. Mem. ABA, D.C. Bar Assn., Va. Bar Assn., Bar of U.S. Supreme Ct., U.S. Combined Tng. Assn. (legal com. 1989-91, safety com. 1990-91, bd. govs. 1995—). Home and Office: 1051 Kelso Rd Great Falls VA 22066-2032

RATHBUN, JAMES RONALD, music educator, conductor; b. Ozark, Mo., Mar. 25, 1934; s. James Wayne and Dorothy Marie (Porter) R.; m. Sharon Kay Short, June 10, 1956; children: Rose Marie, Jeffrey James. BS in Edn., diploma in piano, S.W. Mo. State U., 1956; MME, Ind. U., 1957; DMA, U. Iowa, 1976. Music dir. Lockwood (Mo.) H.S., 1957-59, Sullivan (Mo.) H.S., 1959-63; asst. prof. Abilene (Tex.) Christian Sch., 1963-64, prof., 1972—; asst. prof. Angelo State U., San Angelo, Tex., 1964-66; grad. asst. U. Iowa, Iowa City, 1966-68, 70-72; asst. prof. Concord Coll., Athens, W.Va., 1968-70; dir., founder Abilene Chamber Players, 1984-90; adjudicator, Tex., 1980-95. Performances at Carnegie Hall and Kennedy Ctr., 1986; with Taegu (Korea) Philharm. Orch., 1992, 96, Abilene Philharm. Orch., 1996. Music dir. Abilene Opera Assn., 1984, 88. Grantee Nat. Endowment for the Arts, 1984-86. Mem. Music Tchrs. Nat. assn., Tex. Music Tchrs. Assn., Abilene Music Tchrs. Assn., Mus. Abilene (charter), Abilene Opera Assn. (bd. dirs. 1989-92). Home: 1157 Highland Abilene TX 79605 Office: Abilene Christian Univ PO Box 8274 Abilene TX 79699

RATHBURN, CARLISLE BAXTER, III, college administrator; b. Vero Beach, Fla., Mar. 24, 1957; s. Carlisle Baxter Jr. and Mary Elizabeth (Fuller) r.; m. Tamara Susan Thomas, Mar. 22, 1980; children: Beth, Wesley, Carl, Mary. AA, Gulf Coast Community Coll., Panama City, Fla., 1977; BA, Huntington Coll., 1979; PhD, U. Fla., 1982. Rsch. assoc. inst. higher edn. U. Fla., Gainesville, 1980-82; asst. dir. devel. Valencia Community Coll., Orlando, Fla., 1982-84; dir. instl. advancement Galveston (Tex.) Coll., 1984-85, v.p. planning & devel., 1985-88, v.p. administrn., 1988—, v.p. instrn., 1990-91; pres., 1995—. Bd. dirs. Galveston Hist. Found., 1991—, Cmty. in Schs., 1991—, Gulf Coast PIC, 1987—. Mem. Galveston C. of C. (vice-chmn. 1989-91, bd. dirs. 1988-91. 94—, chair-elect 1997), Rotary (Galveston chpt., bd. dirs.). Methodist. Home: 7742 Chantilly Cir Galveston TX 77551 Office: Galveston Coll 4015 Avenue Q Galveston TX 77550-7496

RATHKE, DALE LAWRENCE, community organizer and financial analyst; b. Rangely, Colo., Mar. 16, 1950; s. Edmann Jacob and Cornelia Ruth (Ratliff) R. BA, Yale U., 1971; MA, Princeton U., 1974, ABD, 1977. Dir. internal ops. Assn. of Cmty. Orgns. for Reform Now (ACORN), New Orleans, 1977—; CFO Citizens' Cons. Inc., New Orleans, 1979—; fin. dir. ACORN Housing Corp., New Orleans, 1984—; pres., sec.-treas. Broad St. Corp., New Orleans, 1986—, Elysian Fields Corp., New Orleans, 1986—, Greenwell Springs Corp., New Orleans, 1989—, ACORN Fund, Inc., New Orleans, 1991—, ACORN Beneficial Assn., Inc., New Orleans, 1991—. Pres., sec.-treas. Assn. for Rights of Citizens, New Orleans, 1980—, ACORN Cultural Trust, Inc., 1988—; active Overture to Cultural Season, 1987—, New Orleans Mus. Art, 1990—. Mem. Yale Club of N.Y.C., Princeton Club of N.Y.C. Office: ACORN 1024 Elysian Fields Ave New Orleans LA 70117-8402

RATHMELL, ARETTA JENNINGS, psychiatrist; b. Plainview, Tex., Mar. 28, 1938; d. Noyce Ted and Ara Mae (Pierce) Jennings; children: Karen, Robert, Gregory. BA, Tex. Tech. U., Lubbock, 1959; MD, Tulane U., New Orleans, 1963. Internal medicine resident Meth. Hosp., Dallas, 1964-66; psychiatric resident Timberlawn Psychiatric Hosp., Dallas, 1966-69, full time med. staff, 1969-76; pvt. practice Forest Hill, Dallas, 1976-78, Charter Hosp., Lake Charles, La., 1978-87, Meth. Hosp., Lubbock, Tex., 1987-88, Charter Hosp., Lake Charles, La., 1989—; mem. res. med. staff, Charter Hosp., Lake Charles, La., 1990, 93, 94, assoc. med. dir., 1994—, bd. dirs. 1994-95; bd. dirs. Friends of Gov.'s Program for Children, Lake Charles, 1985, 86, 93—, La. Health Care Rev., Baton Rouge, La., 1980-95; hon. mem. Vietnam Vets. Assn., Lake Charles, 1989—; cons. Big Bros.-Big Sisters, Lake Charles, 1989—. Lectr., mem., key to city mayor's Commn. on Women, Lake Charles, La., 1980—; hon. mem. Vietnam Vets. Assn., Lake Charles, La., 1989—; cons. Big Bros.-Big Sisters, Lake Charles, 1989—. Recipient Minnie Moffit scholarship Moffitt Found., Dallas, 1967; named asst. parish coroner deputy, asst. parish sheriff's deputy Calcasieu Parish, Lake Charles, La., 1976—. Fellow Am. Psychiat. Assn., La. Psychiat. Assn. (pres. and founder Lake Charles chpt. 1992, 93, 94, v.p., sec., treas.), Am. Coll. Med. Quality (pres. local chpt. 1992, 93, 94, 95), Acad. Psychosomatic Medicine, La. Med. Soc. Republican. Methodist. Home: 681 Lakewood Dr Lake Charles LA 70605-2762 Office: 2001 Southwood Dr # B Lake Charles LA 70605-4139

RATHORE, BAJRANG SINGH, software engineer, consultant; b. Borunda, India, July 5, 1935; came to U.S., 1970; s. Anop Singh and Samdar Kumari (Naruka) R.; m. Suraj Kumari Shekhawat, June 1, 1955; 1 child, Rajeshwari. AS, U. Rajasthan, India, 1955, DVM, 1960; MS, Kans. State U., 1965, PhD, 1968. Vet. asst. surgeon Vet. Hosp. Govt. Rajasthan, Bali, 1960-63; grad. rsch. asst. Kans. State U., 1965-67; pool officer Govt. India, Izatnagar, 1967-69; rsch. assoc. Mich. State U., East Lansing, 1970-71; systems mgr. Tesdata Systems Corp., McLean, Va., 1974-82; sr. software engr. C3, Inc., Herndon, Va., 1982-89, Digital Analysis Corp., Reston, Va., 1989-90; sr. staff cons. The Orkand Corp., Falls Church, Va., 1991-96; applications engr. AT&T, Herndon, Va., 1996—. Contbr. articles to profl. jours. Mem. World Poultry Sci. Assn. (life mem.), Sigma Xi, Gamma Sigma Delta. Home: 3310 Applegrove Ct Herndon VA 20171-3941 Office: AT&T 2355 Dulles Corner Blvd Herndon VA 20171

RATLIFF, CHARLES EDWARD, JR., economics educator; b. Morven, N.C., Oct. 13, 1926; s. Charles Edward and Mary Katherine (Liles) R.; m. Mary Virginia Heilig, Dec. 8, 1945; children: Alice Ann, Katherine Virginia, John Charles. B.S., Davidson Coll., 1947; A.M., Duke U., 1951, Ph.D., 1955; postgrad., U. N.C., Harvard, Columbia. Instr. econs. and bus. Davidson Coll., 1947-48, asst. prof., 1948-49; scholar econs. Duke, 1949-51; mem. faculty Davidson (N.C.) Coll., 1951—, prof., 1960—, chmn. dept. econs., 1966-83, Charles A. Dana prof., 1967-77, William R. Kenan prof., 1977-92, prof. emeritus, 1992—; prof. econs. Forman Christian Coll., Lahore, Pakistan, 1963-66, 69-70; summer vis. prof. U. N.C. at Charlotte, 1958, 60, Appalachian State U., 1962, Punjab U., Pakistan, 1963-64, Kinnaird Coll., Pakistan, 1965, Fin. Svcs. Acad., Pakistan, 1966, NDEA Inst. in Asian History, 1968; lectr. U.S. Cultural Affairs Office, East and West Pakistan, 1969-70. Author: Interstate Apportionment of Business Income for State Income Tax Purposes, 1962, A World Development Fund, 1987, Economics at Davidson: A Sesquicentennial History, 1987; co-author textbooks and monographs; contbg. author: Dictionary of the Social Sciences, Distinguished Teachers on Effective Teaching, 1986, Those Who Teach, 1988, Britain-USA: A Survey in Key Words, 1991; mem. editorial bd. Growth and Change: A Journal of Urban and Regional Policy, 1993—; contbr. articles to profl. jours. Mem. Mayor's Com. on Affordable Housing, Davidson, 1996—, Mayor's Com. Comty. Rels., Davidson, 1973-80, chmn., 1973-78; mem. Mecklenburg County Housing and Devel. Commn., 1975-81; mem. exec. com. Mecklenburg Dem. Com., 1967-69, precinct com., 1967-69, 72-74, 89—, issues com., 1979—, nat. bd. dirs. Rural Advancement Fund Nat. Sharecroppers Fund, Inc., 1978-94, exec. com., 1981-94, treas., 1981-94; mem. Mecklenburg County Comty. and Rural Devel. Exec. Com., 1981—; bd. dirs. Bread for the World, Inc., 1983-84, Pines Retirement Comty., 1990—, Crisis Assistance Ministry, 1992—, Davidson Coll. Devel. Corp., 1992-95, Our Towns Habitat for Humanity, 1996—; bd. advisors Mecklenburg Ministries, 1992—. Ford Found. rsch. grantee, 1960-61, Fulbright-Hays grantee, 1973; rsch. fellow Inter-Univ. Com. Econ. Rsch. on South, 1960-61; recipient Thomas Jefferson award Davidson Coll., 1972, Gold medalist Prof. of Yr. award Coun. Advancement and Support of Edn., 1985, Tchg. Excellence and Campus Leadership award Sear Roebuck Found., 1991, Hunter-Hamilton Love of Tchr. award, 1992. Mem. AAUP, So. Econ. Assn. (exec. com. 1961-63, v.p. 1975-76, N.C. corr. So. Econ. Jour.), Am. Econ. Assn., So. Fin. Assn. (exec. com. 1966-68), Nat. Tax Assn. (chmn. interstate allocation and apportionment of bus. income com. 1972-74), Assn. Asian Studies, Fulbright Alumni Assn., Old Catawba Soc., Phi Beta Kappa, Omicron Delta Kappa (Teaching award 1991). Home: 301 Pinecrest St PO Box 597 Davidson NC 28036-0597

RATLIFF, ERIN SUE, elementary education educator; b. Lincoln, Nebr., Dec. 9, 1960; d. Donald Eugene and Genevieve Nickie (Nixon) Allen; m. Mark Timothy Ratliff, Dec. 17, 1987; children: Kelsey Meagan, Kyle James. BS in Elem. Edn. magna cum laude, Tex. Woman's U., 1984. Cert. tchr., Tex. Tchr. Keene (Tex.) Elem. Sch., 1984-88, Crowley Ind. Sch. Dist., Ft. Worth, 1988-91. Mem. ASCD, Internat. Reading Assn., Assn. Tchrs. and Profl. Educators, Tex. State Tchrs. Assn. Republican. Methodist. Office: Crowley Ind Sch Dist Jackie Carden Elem Sch 3701 Garden Springs Dr Fort Worth TX 76123-2375

RATLIFF, EVA RACHEL, elementary education educator; b. Ada, Mich., Mar. 9, 1944; d. Vernon C. and Edith Rachel (Coffey) Loew; m. Wallace Francis Ratliff, July 27, 1968; children: Ronald, Shelia. BA, Ind. Wesleyan U., 1967; postgrad., East Tenn. State U., 1978, U. Tenn., 1977, 82, 85, 87; MA, Columbia U., 1992. Cert. tchr. music 1-12, classroom 1-9. Tchr. music N. Judson (Ind.)-San Pierre Schs., 1967-68, Mississnewa Community Schs., Gas City, Ind., 1968-69, Mercer County Schs., Harrodsburg, Ky., 1969-73; classroom tchr. Hawkins County Schs., Rogersville, Tenn., 1977-80, Knox County Schs., Knoxville, Tenn., 1980—; Twenty-First Century Classrm. Tchr. of Tenn., 1994—; del. Tenn. Edn. Assn., Nashville, 1989-90. Mem. Knoxville Choral Soc., 1986—. Mem. Knox County Edn. Assn. Home: 8016 Wilnoty Dr Knoxville TN 37931-3453 Office: Sarah Moore Greene Elem Sch 3001 Brooks Rd Knoxville TN 37914-6270

RATLIFF, JANICE KAY, legal administrator; b. Odessa, Tex., Aug. 11, 1949; d. Boyce Emery and Fay LaNell (Russell) Albert; m. Richard Wayne Ratliff, May 4, 1974; children: Ryan, Courtney, Ashlee. BS in Secondary Edn., Tex. Tech U., 1971. Cert. secondary tchr., Tex. Recreation counselor Wichita Falls (Tex.) Parks and Recreation Dept., 1967, Austin (Tex.) Parks and Recreation Dept., 1969; rehab. technician Tex. Rehab. Commn., Austin, 1971-76; co-owner, mgr. Locker Room, sporting goods store, Monahans, Tex., 1984-88; contract worker Calame, Linebarger & Graham, Odessa, Tex., 1983-88; area mgr., paralegal, office mgr. Calame, Linebarger, Graham & Peña, Odessa, Tex., 1988—. Pres. Gifted and Talented Parents Orgn., Monahans, 1986; mem. local parent/tchr. orgn. Tatom Life; v.p. Band Booster Club, 1994-96, pres.-elect, 1996-97; Sunday sch. tchr. Ch. of Christ. Recipient dist. 1st place award for poetry Tex. Fedn. Women's Clubs, 1987. Mem. Tex. Assn. Assessing Officers (v.p. Permian Basin chpt. 1994-96), Rotary Internat. (bd. dirs. 1994-96, program chmn. 1994-95, sec. 1996-97), Wednesday Study Club (pres. 1986-88). Republican. Home: 1309 S Murray St Monahans TX 79756-6305

RATNER, PETER JOHN, computer graphics educator; b. London, June 6, 1949; came to U.S., 1958; s. Bedrich Malek and Vera (Koenig) Ratner; m. Sharon M. Hesch, Jan. 31, 1981; 1 child, Ori Paul. BFA, No. Ill. U., 1978, MFA, 1980. Art tchr. Westmer H.S., Joy, Ill., 1973-77; graphic designer Ryan Ins. Group, Inc., Chgo., 1981-83; art dir. Consolidated Distilled Products, Inc., Chgo., 1983, Steven Buyer & Assoc., Inc., Evanston, Ill., 1983-84, Crest Comm., Inc., Oakbrook, Ill., 1984-89; assoc. prof. James Madison U., Harrisonburg, Va., 1989—; 3D multimedia animation artist Light and Sound Prodns., Penn Laird, Va., 1989—. Author: (booklet) Modeling the Human Form on the Computer, 1995; exhibited in group shows at SIGGRAPH, Orlando, Fla., 1994, 95, MacWorld Expo, Boston, 1994, 95, Electronic Entertainment Expo, Calif., 1995, Digital World, Calif., 1994, Show Biz Expo, Calif., 1994, AEC, Washington, 1994, The Mill River Gallery, Ellicott City, Md., 1994, d'Art Ctr., 1994, Art Assn. of Harrisburg, Pa. Gallery, Harrisburg, 1994, Coastal Ctr. for the ARts, 1994, Peoria (Ill.) Art Guild Gallery, 1994, Gallery 57 Contemporary Arts, 1994, The New England Fine Arts Inst., Boston, 1993, Anchorage (Alaska) Mus. of History and Art, 1993, McPherson (Kans.) Coll. Gallery, 1993, Fla. Mus. of Hispanic and Latin Am. Art, 1993, North Valley Art League Gallery, 1993, Chrysler Mus., 1992, U. N.D. Gallery, 1992, Carrier Found. Aux. Gallery, 1992, Forum Gallery, 1992, Decentralized World-Wide Networker Congress, Osaka, Japan, 1992, Kiehle Gallery, St. Cloud State U., 1992, The Stamping Grounds, Royal Oak, Mich., 1992, many others. Recipient Apple Computers Innovation award Apple Computer, 1992. Mem. AAUP. Home and Office: 6391 W Donnagail Dr Penn Laird VA 22846

RATTLEY, JESSIE MENIFIELD, former mayor, educator; b. Birmingham, Ala., May 4, 1929; d. Alonzo and Altona (Cochran) Menifield; m. Robert L. Rattley; children: Florence, Robin. BS in Bus. Edn.with hons., Hampton U., 1951; postgrad., Hampton Inst., 1962, IBM Data Processing Sch., 1960, LaSalle Extension U., 1955. Tchr. Huntington High Sch., Newport News, Va., 1951-52; owner, operator Peninsula Bus. Coll., Newport News, 1952-85; hosp. adminstr. Newport News Gen. Hosp., from 1986; fellow Inst. Politics John F. Kennedy Sch. Govt. Harvard U., 1990; sr. lectr. polit. sci. Hampton U.; elected mayor of Newport News, 1986-90. Mem. Nat. League Cities, bd. dirs., 1975, 2d v.p., 1977, 1st v.p., 1978, pres., 1979-90, active various coms. and task forces; active on adv. bds. and coms. State Dem. Party; mem. exec. com. Va. Mcpl. League, 1974, 2d v.p., 1976, 1st v.p., 1977, pres., 1979; chair state adv. com. U.S. Civil Rights Commn.; apptd. trustee Va. Vet. Care Facility. Recipient Cert. of Merit Daus. of Isis, 2d annual Martin Luther King, Jr. Meml. award Old Dominion U., Sojourner Truth award Nat. Assn. of Negro Bus. and Profl. Women's Clubs, Cert. of Appreciation NAACP, Hampton Inst. Presdl. award for Outstanding Citizenship.

RATZLAFF, DAVID EDWARD, minister; b. Kansas City, Mo., Mar. 12, 1938; s. John Henry and Amy May (Cathcart) R.; m. Shiela Paige Hickerson, June 9, 1958; children: Perry Dean, Kevin Lee, Kalista Kay. BA in Ministry, Nebr. Christian Coll., 1961; MDiv, Memphis Theol. Sem., 1991; D in Ministry, Lake Charles Bible Coll., 1996. Ordained to ministry Christian Ch., 1962. Min. Christian Ch., Neligh, Nebr., 1959-67; owner, mgr. Kordsman Evangelistic Assn., Hiawatha, Kans., 1967-75; sr. min. Christian Ctr., Hiawatha, Kans., 1970-72; salesman Saladmaster Co., Springfield, Mo., 1975-76; ops. coord. Blackwood Bros. Quartet, Memphis, 1976-79, 85; mgr. sales and svc. Elliot Impression Products, Memphis, 1980-85; min. Bethany Christian Ch., Eads, Tenn., 1986-95; owner Soma Co., 1993—; program chmn. exec. commn. on ministry com. for Christian Chs. (Disciples of Christ), Tenn., 1988—; western area moderator, mem. gen. and exec. bds. Region of Christian Ch. of Tenn., 1991-93; small bus. founder, 1993; mem. pastoral adv. bd. Genesis Cirsis Ctr., Memphis, 1994. Co-author: (songbook) Kordsman Presents, 1966; recorded and produced 6 long play albums, 1966-74. Bd. dirs. Memphis Family Link, 1985-86; mem. United Cerebral Palsy, 1983-86; asst. police chief City of Neligh, 1962-67, coordinator, 1965-67. Mem. Nat. Arts and Recording Artists, Collierville Ministerial Assn., Christian Ch. Ministers Memphis. Republican. Mem. Disciples Christ. Home: 545 Col Arlington Rd S Collierville TN 38017-9999

RAU, LEE ARTHUR, lawyer; b. Mpls., July 22, 1940; s. Arthur W. and Selma A. (Lund) R.; m. Janice R. Childress, June 27, 1964; children—Brendan D., Patrick C., Brian T. BSB, U. Minn., 1962; JD, UCLA, 1965. Bar: Calif. 1966, D.C. 1972, Va. 1986, U.S. Dist. Ct. D.C. 1973, U.S. Dist. Ct. (ea. dist.) Va. 1988, U.S. Ct. Mil. Appeals 1966, U.S. Ct. Appeals (D.C. cir.) 1972, U.S. Ct. Appeals (3d cir.) 1975, U.S. Ct. Appeals (6th cir.) 1980, U.S. Ct. Appeals (4th cir.) 1988, U.S. Supreme Ct. 1971. Trial atty. evaluation sect. antitrust div. U.S. Dept. Justice, Washington, 1965-66, appellate sect., 1970-72; assoc. Reed Smith Shaw & McClay, Washington, 1972-74, ptnr., 1975—; former mem. constl. and adminstrv. law adv. com. Nat. Chamber Litigation Ctr. Inc.; sec., bd. dirs. Old Dominion Land Co., Inc. Contbr. articles to profl. jours. Sec. bd. dris. Reston Found., 1982-93; bd. dirs. Reston Interfaith Inc., 1973-89, pres., 1984-88; bd. dirs. Greater Reston Arts Ctr., 1988-96, pres., 1989-91, sec., 1991-95; mem. Washington Dulles Task Force, 1982-91; mem. exec. com. and ops. com. Fairfax-Falls Ch. United Way, mem. regional coun., 1988-92. Capt. JAGC, U.S. Army, 1966-70. Named Restonian of Yr., 1990; decorated Commendation with oak leaf cluster; recipient Best of Reston award. Mem. ABA (antitrust, adminstrv. law, corp. banking and bus., sci. and tech. sects.), D.C. Bar Assn. (past chmn. energy study group), Calif. Bar Assn., U.S. C. of C. (antitrust policy com.). Democrat. Lutheran. Home: 1930 Upper Lakes Dr Reston VA 22091-3620 Office: Reed Smith Shaw & McClay 8251 Greensboro Dr Ste 1100 Mc Lean VA 22102-3809

RAUF, BARBARA CLAIRE, art educator; b. Covington, Ky., Mar. 13, 1944; d. George Christopher and Amelia Barbara (Rudolf) R. BA in Art Edn. magna cum laude, Thomas Moore Coll., 1969; BFA in Painting summa cum laude, U. Cin., 1974; MFA in Painting, U. Pa., 1977. Tchr. various jr. high schs., 1966-73; grad. teaching asst. U. Pa., Phila., 1976-77; asst. prof. art, dept. chmn. Thomas More Coll., Covington, 1977-83, assoc. prof. art, 1983—; commns. include portraits of Dr. Richard de Graff, pres. Thomas More Coll., 1978, Bishop Francis Howard, Chancellor's Room, 1984, Bishop Ackerman, 1984, Bishop William Hughes, 1985, Bishop Mulloy, 1985, Dr. Robert Giroux, pres., 1985, others; lectr. in field. One woman shows at Fine Arts Gallery, Cin., 1974, Thomas More Coll. Gallery, 1978, Art Wall, Unitarian Ch., Cin., 1990, Carnegie Art Ctr., 1992, YWCA Gallery, 1992, Clermont Art Gallery, 1993, CCA Gallery, Cin., 1994, Carnegie Art Ctr., Covington, 1994, TM Gallery, 1994, Dayton Visual Arts Ctr., 1996, So. Ohio Mus., 1996; group shows include Last Picture Show Gallery, Cin., 1975, Inst. Contemporary Art, Phila., 1975, 76, 77, TM Gallery, 1982, San Giuseppe Gallery, Cin., 1989, Zephyr Gallery, Louisville, 1991. Grantee Ky. Found. for Women, 1990, Thomas More Coll., 1987, 89, Greater Cin. Found., 1983, AIDP, 1978, 79; Thomas More scholar, 1986, U. Pa., 1975.

RAUF, ROBERT CHARLES, systems specialist; b. N.Y.C., June 13, 1944; s. Charles Paul and Charlotte E. (Morten) R.; m. Susan E. Amadeo, June 6, 1964; children: Robert, Cheryl. AAS, Dutchess Community Coll., Poughkeepsie, N.Y., 1967; student, Marist Coll., Poughkeepsie, 1967-69. Program designer IBM, Poughkeepsie, 1964-70, mgr. system performance, 1970-75; mgr. job entry system design IBM, Gaithersburg, Md., 1976-77; mgr. office system and design IBM, Raleigh, N.C., 1978-82, mgr. office systems design, 1983-88; mgr. exec. support systems product IBM, Cary, N.C., 1988-93; mgr. info. systems Ambra Computer Corp., 1993-94; mgr. systems devel. Encompass Corp., Cary, 1994—. Home: 207 Custer Trl Cary NC 27513-4701

RAUH, RICHARD PAUL, architect; b. Covington, Ky., Mar. 27, 1948; s. Robert Paul and Pauline (Farmer) R.; m. Mary Darlene Bailey, Oct. 6, 1975. AB, Columbia U., 1970; BArch, MArch., Harvard U., 1974; DMD, U. Ky., 1980. Registered arch., 30 states; lic. dentist, Ky., Va. Asst. prof. U. Ky. Coll. Arch., Lexington, 1976-80, adj. asst. prof., 1980-81; prin. Carpenter/Rauh, Lexington, 1978-80; prin. Rabun Hatch Portman McWhorter Hatch & Rauh Architects, Atlanta, 1981-85; prin. Richard Rauh & Assocs., Archs., Atlanta, 1984—; cons. Macon (Ga.) Heritage Found., City if Cin., Tampa Preservation Bd., Battle House Found., Mobile, Ala., City of Norwood, Ohio, St. Petersburg (Fla.) Preservation, Inc., City of West Palm Beach, Booker Creek Preservation Inc. Works published in numerous books and mags.; works include: Norfolk Hilton Hotel, Va., 1985, Omni Netherland Plaza Hotel restoration, Cin., 1982-83, Bridgeport Plaza Hilton Hotel, Conn., 1985, Carew Tower Block restoration, Cin., 1983-91, master plan Gaines Ctr. for Humanities U. Ky. Lexington, 1984, La Concha Hotel, Key West, Fla., 1986, Carolina Head Injury Ctr., Durham, N.C., 1987, Albany (Ga.) Holiday Inn Hotel, 1989, Shenandoah Head Injury Ctr., Manassas, Va., 1989, Kenner Toy Products Gen. Offices, Cin., 1990, Cin. Club, 1991, Tower Pl.-Emery Arcade Restoration, Cinn., 1991, Urban Design Masterplan, Mobile, Ala., 1993, O'Neil Cinemas, Duluth, Ga., 1994; author (with David G. Wright) Design Courses at Schools of Architecture in Western Europe: A Documentary Study, 1975. Pres., Hist. South Hill Assn., Lexington, 1978-80; bd. dirs. Margaret Mitchell House, Inc., 1987-92, pres. 1989, Preservation Action, Washington, 1988—, City of Atlanta Neighborhood Planning unit (Buckhead) bd., 1996, Planning adv. bd. 1996. Sheldon fellow, Harvard U., 1974-75, Appleton fellow, 1974-75; recipient LUMEN excellence award Illuminating Engring. Soc. N.Am., 1985; Harvard Book award Harvard Club Cin., 1965; U.S. Dept. Interior grantee Ky. Heritage Commn., 1978, U.S. Dept. of HUD Urban Devel. Action grantee, 1988; recipient honor awards Nat. Trust Historic Preservation U.S., 1985, AIA South Atlantic Regional council, 1984, Ga. Assn. AIA, 1984, 88, 89, 94, Ga. Young Arch. award 1988, Ky. Soc. Archs. AIA, 1986, Nat. award Soc. Am. Reg. Archs., 1986, 89, 90, 94, Build Am. award AGC/Motorola, 1992, Greater Cin. Beautiful award City of Cin., 1984, Ohio Hist. Soc., 1987, Fla. Keys Preservation Bd., 1987, City of Miami Beach, 1990, Nat. Hist. Landmark Designation U.S. Dept. Interior, 1995. Mem. Art Deco Soc. Am., Harvard Club of Ga., Harvard Club of Ky., Filson Club (Ky.), Order Ky. Cols. Democrat. Presbyterian. Home: Box 18560 Atlanta GA 31126 Office: Richard Rauh & Assocs 3400 Peachtree Rd NE Atlanta GA 30326-1107

RAULERSON, PHOEBE HODGES, school superintendent; b. Cin., Mar. 16, 1939; d. LeRoy Allen and Thelma A. (Stewart) Hodges; m. David Earl Raulerson, Dec. 26, 1959; children: Julie, Lynn, David Earl, Jr., Roy Allen. BA in Edn., U. Fla., 1963, MEd, 1964. Tchr. several schs., Okeechobee, Fla., 1964-79; asst. prin. Okeechobee Jr. H.S., 1979-81, prin., 1983-84; asst. prin. South Elem. Sch., Okeechobee, 1981-82; asst. prin. Okeechobee H.S., 1982-83, prin., 1984-96, asst. supt. for curriculum and instrn., 1996—; mem. Dept. Edn. Commr.'s Task Force on H.S. Preparation, 1993-94, chair Task Force Tchr. Preparation & Certification, 1995-96. Mem. Okeechobee Exchange Club. Recipient Outstanding Citizen award Okeechobee Rotary Club, 1986; week named in her honor, Okeechobee County Commrs., 1990. Mem. Am. Bus. Women's Assn., Fla. Assn. Secondary Sch. Prins. (pres. 1993-94, Fla. Prin. of Yr. award 1990), Fla. Assn. Sch. Adminstrs. (bd. dirs. 1992-95), Okeechobee Cattlewomen's Assn. Democrat. Episcopalian. Home: 3898 NW 144th Dr Okeechobee FL 34972-0930 Office: Okeechobee County Sch Dist 700 SW 2nd Ave Okeechobee FL 34974-5117

RAULT, JULES, food technologist, consultant; b. Victoria, Mahe, Seychelles, Nov. 19, 1963; came to U.S., 1984; s. Fabien Jules Rault and Doris Medicie (Dyer) Moore; m. Siara Hosein, Mar. 6, 1987. BS, U. Fla, 1991. H.s. tchr. Ministry of Edn., Seychelles, 1983; lab. technologist Nat. Agro Industries, Sechelles, 1983-84; food chemist ABC Rsch. Corp., Gainesville, Fla., 1991-92, food technologist, 1992-93; food technologist R. L. Schreiber, Inc., Pompano Beach, Fla., 1993-94; food cons. Rault Foods, Coconut Creek, Fla., 1994—; mem. Fla. Restaurant Assn., Ft. Lauderdale, 1994. Mem. Fla. Culinary. Office: Rault Foods 2413 NW 49th Ter Coconut Creek FL 33063-3847

RAUNIKAR, ROBERT AUSTIN, cardiology and pediatrics educator; b. Raleigh, N.C., Aug. 9, 1961; s. Robert and Angelum (Leggett) R.; m. Sara Kent, July 10, 1993. BS in Biology cum laude, Presbyn. Coll., Clinton, S.C., 1983; MD, Med. Coll. Ga., 1987. Diplomate Am. Bd. Pediatrics; lic. physician, Ga., S.C.; cert. instr. pediatric advanced life support. Intern, resident dept. pediatrics Med. Coll. Ga., Augusta, 1987-90, fellow sect. pediatric cardiology Ga. Inst. for Prevention Human Illness and Accidents dept. pediatrics, 1990-93, clin. instr., 1993—; presenter and invited lectr. in field. Contbr. articles to med. and profl. jours. Fellow Am. Acad. Pediatrics; mem. Am. Coll. Cardiology, Am. Heart Assn. Baptist. Office: The Children's Hosp Greenville Meml 490 W Faris Rd Ste 550 Greenville SC 29605-3007

RAUSCH, JEFFREY LYNN, psychiatrist, psychopharmacologist; b. Butler, Pa., Jan. 10, 1953; s. John Kenneth and June Alice (Morrow) R.; m. Catherine Rebecca Montgomery, Aug. 24, 1974; children: Jeffrey David, Caroline Rebecca, Lauren Elizabeth. BS in Biology summa cum laude, Mercer U., Macon, Ga., 1974; MD, Med. Coll. Ga., 1978. Resident in psychiatry U. S.C., 1978-80; clin. psychopharmacology rsch. fellow U. Calif., San Diego, 1980-82; staff psychiatrist San Diego VA Med. Ctr., La Jolla, 1980-91; asst. prof. U. Calif., San Diego, 1982-89; assoc. prof. U. Calif., 1989-91, dir. psychoneuroendocrinology lab., 1990-91; acting assoc. chief psychiatry San Diego VA Med. Ctr., 1989-90; prof., vice chmn. dept. psychiatry Med. Coll. Ga., Augusta, 1991—; dir. lab. clin. neurosci. Augusta VA Med. ctr., 1991—; sci. cons. NIMH Study Sect. Contbr. articles to profl. jours. NIMH First award, 1987. Mem. AAAS, Am. Assn. Chairs Depts. Psychiatry, Nat. Alliance Mentally Ill, N.Y. Acad. Sci., Soc. Biol.

Psychiatry, Psychiat. Rsch. Soc. Presbyterian. Office: Med Coll Ga Dept Psychiatry Health Behavior 1515 Pope Ave Augusta GA 30904-5843

RAUSCHENBERG, BRADFORD LEE, museum research director; b. Atlanta, Sept. 11, 1940. BS in Archaeology and Biology, Ga. State Coll., 1963; MA in History, Wake Forest U., 1995. Archaeologist Ga. Hist. Commn., 1963-64; site supr., asst. Stanley South, State Archaeologist of N.C., 1964-66; antiquarian, asst. Dir. Restoration Old Salem, Inc., Winston-Salem, N.C., 1966-73; asst. to dir. Mus. Early So. Decorative Arts, Winston-Salem, 1973-76, rsch. fellow, 1976-87, dir. rsch., 1987-93; dir. rsch. Mus. Early So. Decorative Arts and Old Salem, Inc., Winston-Salem, 1993—; cons., lectr. in field. Author: British Regional Carving (1600-1640), and Furniture (1600-1800), 1984, Wachovia Historical Society: 1895-1995, 1995. With USCG, 1964-72. Recipient Halifax Resolves award, 1986; grantee NEH, 1972-81, Kaufman Americana Found., 1981-82. Mem. Am. Ceramic Circle (grantee), Orgn. Am. Historians, No. Ceramic Soc., So. Hist. Assn., Friends of Swiss Ceramic Circle, Regioanl Furniture Soc., Furniture History Soc., Soc. Hist. Archaeology, Soc. Post-Medieval Archaeology, Soc. Historians Early Am. Republic. Address: 221 Harmon Ct Winston Salem NC 27106-4613 Office: Mus Early So Decorative Arts PO Box 10310 Winston Salem NC 27108-0310

RAVENEL, SHANNON, book publishing professional; b. Charlotte, N.C., Aug. 13, 1938; d. Elias Prioleau and Harriett Shannon (Steedman) R.; m. Dale Purves, May 25, 1968; children: Sara Blake, Harriett. BA, Hollins Coll., 1960. Mktg. asst., sch. dept. Holt, Rinehart & Winston, Inc., N.Y.C., 1960-61; edit. asst. Houghton Mifflin Co., Boston, 1961-64, editor, 1964-73; editorial cons. pvt. practice, St. Louis, 1973-90; sr. editor, co-founder Algonquin Books of Chapel Hill, 1982-91, editorial dir., 1991—. Series editor: Best American Short Stories, 1978-90; editor: Best American Short Stories of the Eighties, 1990, New Stories From the South, 1986—. Recipient Disting. Achievement award Coun. Lit. Mags. & Presses, N.Y.C., 1990. Mem. PEN Am. Ctr. Democrat. Presbyterian. Office: Algonquin Books of Chapel Hill PO Box 2225 Chapel Hill NC 27515-2225

RAWDON, CHERYL ANN, elementary school educator; b. Dallas, June 13, 1957; d. Billy Wayne and Carol Ann (Murdock) R.; 1 child, Meagan. BS, East Tex. State U., 1979. Cert. kindergarten, elem., jr. high sch. reading and English tchr., Tex. Tchr. reading and spelling Canton (Tex.) Ind. Sch. Dist. Jr. High Sch.; tchr. pre lst grade Midlothian (Tex.) Ind. Sch. Dist., tchr. kindergarten. Mem. First Bapt. Ch., Midlothian, tchr. Sunday sch., mem. choir, mission friends tchr., Awana leader; active numerous cmty. orgns. Recipient Golden Poet award, 1989, 90. Mem. Canton Tchrs. Assn. (pres.), Tex. State Tchrs. Assn., Canton Classroom Tchrs. Assn.

RAWLS, FRANK MACKLIN, lawyer; b. Suffolk, Va., Aug. 24, 1952; s. John Lewis and Mary Helen (Macklin) R.; m. Sally Hallum Blanchard, June 26, 1976; children: Matthew Christopher, John Stephen, Michael Andrew. BA cum laude in History, Hampden Sydney Coll., 1974; JD, U. Va., 1977. Bar: Va. 1977, U.S. Dist. Ct. (ea. dist.) Va. 1977, U.S. Ct. Appeals (4th cir.) 1977. Assoc. Rawls, Habel & Rawls, Suffolk, 1977-78, ptnr., 1978-91; ptnr. Ferguson & Rawls, 1991-96, Ferguson, Rawls, MacDonald, Overton & Grissom, P.C., 1996—; sec., bd. dirs. Suffolk Title Ltd., 1986-95; bd. dirs Old Dominion Investors Trust, Inc. 1994—. Deacon Westminster Reformed Presbyn. Ch., Suffolk, 1979-83, elder, clk. of session, 1984-91, 94—; chmn. bd. dirs. Suffolk Crime Line, 1982-90, Suffolk Cheer Fund, 1982—, Covenant Christian Schs., Suffolk, 1982-84; bd. dirs. Norfolk Christian Schs., 1990—, pres. Parent Tchr. Fellowship, 1995—, vice-chn. steering com. for capital campaign, 1996—; mem. adv. bd. dirs. Salvation Army, Suffolk, 1977-95, chmn., 1989-90; chmn. Suffolk Com. on Affordable Housing, 1989-90; bd. dirs. Suffolk YMCA, 1988-90. Mem. ATLA, Suffolk Bar Assn. (past pres.), Va. State Bar, Va. Bar Assn., Christian Legal Soc., Va. Trial Lawyers Assn., Suffolk Bar Assn., Rotary.

RAWLS, HENRY RALPH, biomedical educator; b. Chattahoochee, Fla., Nov. 19, 1935; s. Ralph Brian and Mildred Elizabeth (Evans) R.; m. Andrea Noel Geoffray, June 11, 1978; 1 child, Randall J. Granier. BS, La. State U., 1957; PhD, Fla. State U., 1964. Chemist Dacron Rsch. Lab. E.I DuPont, Kinston, N.C., 1961; photochemistry dept. supr. Unilever Rsch. Lab., Vlaardingen, The Netherlands, 1965-67; sr. rsch. chemist Gulf South Rsch. Inst., New Orleans, 1967-76; asst. to assoc. prof. La. State U. Med. Ctr., New Orleans, 1976-85; staff R&D sci. Gillette Corp., Boston, 1985-88; prof. Health Sci. Ctr. divsn. biomaterials U. Tex., San Antonio, 1988—; mem. stds. com. ADA, Chgo., 1978—; vis. scientist U. Groningen, The Netherlands, 1980; staff assoc. Forsyth Dental Ctr., Boston, 1985-88. Patentee (with others) interpolymeric resin for treatment of teeth, soft and firm denture liners, flouride interpolymeric resin, radiopaque barium-polymer complexes, x-ray opaque metal-polymer complexes, shape conforming dental wedges; contbr. articles to profl. jours. Lt. USN Res., 1957-60. Recipient Rsch. Career Devel. award Nat. Inst. Dental Rsch., 1977; Fogerty fellow NIH, 1980; rsch. grantee, NIH, FDA, 1973—. Fellow Acad. Dental Materials; mem. Am. Chem. Soc., Internat. Assn. Dental Rsch., European Orgn. Caries Rsch., Omicron Kappa Upsilon (hon.). Office: Univ Tex Health Sci Ctr Divsn Biomaterials 7703 Floyd Curl Dr San Antonio TX 78284-7890

RAWLS, NANCY LEE STIRK, nursing educator; b. Upper Darby, Pa., Mar. 11, 1945; d. Leslie W. and Esther Ruth (Cooper) Stirk; m. William D. Rawls; children: Diane Leslie, William D. Diploma, Lankenau Hosp. Sch. Nursing, Phila., 1966; BSN, Med. U. S.C., 1981; MN, U. S.C., 1990. Unit supr. Meadow Haven Nursing Ctr., Rock Hill, S.C., 1981-82; office nurse Lentz-Ross, MD, P.A., Rock Hill, 1982-87; pediatric clin. instr. York Tech. Coll., Rock Hill, 1987-89; asst. prof. nursing Kennesaw State Coll., Marietta, Ga., 1991-95; clin. examiner for so. performance assessment ctr. N.Y. Regents Coll., Atlanta, 1994-96; nursing instr. Chattahoochee Tech. Inst., Marietta, Ga., 1995—. Mem. Sigma Theta Tau, Phi Kappa Phi.

RAWSON, JIM CHARLES, accountant, executive; b. Houston, Apr. 20, 1947; s. Charles Manly and Georgie (Kearse) R.; m. Linda Eidman, Arp. 12, 1968; children: John Erich, Susan Margaret. BBA, Tex. Christian U., 1969. CPA, Tex. Acctg. clk. Tenneco, Inc., Houston, 1969-71; acctg. clk. Projects Am. Corp., Houston, 1971-74, office mgr., 1974-77, v.p., gen. mgr., 1977-82, pres., 1982—. Recipient Bronze award Am. Land Devel. Assn., 1985, Gold award, 1983, Silver award, 1983. Mem. Am. Inst. CPA's, Tex. Soc. CPA's (Houston chpt.), Am. Resort and Residential Devels. Assn., Sports Car Club of Am. Evangelical. Office: Projects Am Corp 6124 Beverlyhill St Houston TX 77057-6610

RAY, ARLISS DEAN, retired environmental consultant; b. Hot Springs, Ark., Apr. 3, 1929; s. Clyde E. and Gladys Lorraine (Wofford) R.; BEngring., Yale U., 1951; MS, Oreg. State U., 1957; PhD, U. Calif., Berkeley, 1962; m. Ardyth Lee Sharman, Aug. 23, 1952 (dec. Feb. 1992); children: Sandra Lee, Nancy Lynn, Laurie Jean, James Clyde; foster child, Joseph T. Yannetti. Asst. prof. environ. engring. Vanderbilt U., 1961-63; assoc. prof., then prof. U. Mo., Columbia, 1963-71; v.p. Woodward-Envicon, also Woodward Clyde Cons., Clifton, N.J. and Houston, 1972-75; pvt. cons., 1975-77; co-founder, 1978, since exec. officer EMANCO Inc., environ. mgmt. and cons., Houston, 1978-94, ret., 1994; adv. EPA, NSF. Served with USNR, 1951-55. Recipient award merit Mo. Water Pollution Control Assn., 1967. Mem. ASCE, Am. Water Works Assn., Air Pollution Control Assn., Water Pollution Control Fedn., Sigma Xi, Tau Beta Pi, Chi Epsilon, Pi Mu Epsilon. Author papers in field. Home: 500 Pakis Rd 2B Hot Springs National Park AR 71913

RAY, BETTY JEAN G., lawyer; b. New Orleans, June 7, 1943; d. William E. George and Iris U. (Berthold) Grizzell; m. Gerald L. Ray, June 9, 1962; children: Gerald L. Ray, Jr., Brian P. BS Psychology, La. State U., 1976, JD, 1980. Bar: La., 1980; U.S. Dist. Ct. (ea., mid. and we. dists.) La. 1981; U.S. Ct. Appeal (5th cir.) 1981. Jud. law clk. 19th Jud. Dist. Ct., Baton Rouge, 1980-81; atty. Jean G. Ray, Baton Rouge, 1981-83; counsel Gulf Stream, Inc., Baton Rouge, 1982-83; staff atty. La. Dept. Justice, Baton Rouge, 1983-84, asst. atty. gen., 1984-87; staff atty. FDIC, Shreveport, La., 1987-88, mng. atty., 1988-94; spl. dep. receiver Receivership Office, La. Dept. Ins., Baton Rouge, 1994-95; spl. counsel Brook, Pizza & van Loon, L.L.P., Baton Rouge, 1995—. Mem. La. Bar Assn., Baton Rouge Bar Assn., Baton Rouge Assn. Women Attys., Order of Coif, Phi Beta Kappa, Phi Delta Phi (scholar 1980). Episcopalian. Home: 1143 Oakley Dr Baton Rouge LA 70806 Office: Brook Pizza & van Loon Ste 402 9100 Bluebonnet Centre Blvd Baton Rouge LA 70809

RAY, BRADLEY STEPHEN, petroleum geologist; b. Ada, Okla., Feb. 15, 1957; s. Walter Lloyd and Betty Louise (McCurley) R. BS in Geology, Baylor U., 1980; MS in Geology, U. Tex., 1985. Cert. geologist. Asst. geologist Hunt Oil Co., Dallas, 1978, geologist, 1979-81; ind. oil and gas producer Dallas, 1981—; chmn. adv. bd. Geol. Info. Libr. Dallas, 1988—; bd. dirs. Global Mapping Internat. Trustee Dallas Bapt. U., 1988-94, Criswell Coll., 1990-92; chmn. The Habitats Project, 1993—; co-chmn. Peoples and Habitats Project, 1994—; mem. Peoples Info. Network. Mem. Am. Assn. Petroleum Geologists, Ind. Petroleum Assn. Am., Soc. Ind. Profl. Earth Scientists, Dallas Geol. Soc., Tex. Ind. Producers and Royalty Owners, Okla. Ind. Petroleum Assn., Geol. Soc. Am., Computer Oriented Geol. Soc., Nat. Stripper Well Assn., Energy Club, Oklahoma City Geol. Soc., Colbert-Tracht Club. Republican. Baptist. Home: 4925 Greenville #1348 Dallas TX 75206 Office: 1348 One Energy Sq Dallas TX 75206

RAY, BRENDA PATTERSON, medical-surgical nurse; b. Talladega, Ala., June 7, 1950; d. William Arvil Patterson and Frankie (Wilson) Woodruff; m. Michael Lee Ray, Oct. 30, 1973; children: Angela, Brandon. LPN, Bessemer State Coll., 1989. LPN, Ky., Ala. Cardiology nurse Brookwood Hosp., Homewood, Ala., 1989-91; nurse ICU Humana of Lexington, Ky., 1991-95; nurse cardiology Brookwood Hosp., Homewood, Ala., nurse cardiac intervention unit Brookwood Med. Ctr., Homewood, 1995—. Pres. Shelby Acad. PTO, Mantenallo, Ala., 1985-87; First Baptist Ch. of Alabaste, Ala. Selected at Brookwood Med as Top 100 employee for, 1996. Mem. Beta Sigma Phi (chpt. pres. 1980-84, Outstanding Woman of Yr. Epsilon Rho chpt. 1984). Republican. Baptist. Home: 131 Old Spanish Trl Montevallo AL 35115-8765 Office: Broakwood Med Ctr 2010 Medical Center Dr Homewood AL 35115

RAY, CHARLES JACKSON, retired surgeon; b. Greenville, Ala., Dec. 20, 1920; s. Winston J. Ray and Frances G. McMallan; m. Betty Shelton, Mar. 21, 1947; 3 children. MD, Tulane U., 1945. Diplomate Am. Bd. Surgeons, Am. Bd. Colon Rectal Surgeons. Intern Charity Hosp., New Orleans, 1945-46; resident in gen. surgery Tulane U., New Orleans, 1948-49; fellow in gen. surgery Ochsner Clin., New Orleans, 1949-52; pvt. practice Meml. Hosp., Chattanooga; assoc. prof. surgery U. Tenn.; ret., 1995. Fellow ACS; mem. AMA. Address: 324 Marina Blvd Mandeville LA 70471-1532

RAY, CREAD L., JR., retired state supreme court justice; b. Waskom, Tex., Mar. 10, 1931; s. Cread L. and Antonia (Hardesty) R.; m. Janet Watson Keller, Aug. 12, 1977; children: Sue Ann (dec.), Robert E., Glenn L., David B., Marcie Lynn, Anne Marie. B.B.A., Tex. A&M U., 1952; J.D., U. Tex., 1957; L.H.D. (hon.), Wiley Coll., Marshall, Tex., 1980. Bar: Tex. 1957. Practiced in Marshall, 1957-59; judge Harrison County, 1959-61; justice 6th dist. Ct. Civil Appeals, Texarkana, 1970-80, Supreme Ct. Tex., 1980-90; ret. Supreme Ct. Tex., Austin, 1990; prin. C.L Ray, Austin, 1991—. Past pres. Marshall Jaycees, Marshall C. of C.; mem. Tex. Ho. of Reps., 1966-70; active local, regional, nat. Boy Scouts Am.; trustee Wiley Coll. Lt. col. USAF, 1952-54, Korea; ret. Recipient various Boy Scouts awards. Mem. State Bar Tex., N.E. Tex. Bar Assn. (past pres.), VFW, Am. Legion, Rotary, Tex. Aggies. Democrat. Methodist. Home: 604 Beardsley Ln Austin TX 78746 Office: 400 W 15th St Ste 600 Austin TX 78701-1647

RAY, DEE ANN, library director; b. Mar. 28, 1938; d. Herman Lee and Jane (White) R. BA in Modern Langs., U. Tulsa, 1959; MLS, U. Okla., 1960; student, various seminars and workshops. Student asst. U. Tulsa Libr., 1956-59; bookmobile asst. Tulsa City-County Libr., 1959; field cons. Okla. Dept. Librs., 1960-63; dir. demonstration svcs. Mo. State Libr., 1964-66; dir. Western Plains Libr. Sys., Clinton, Okla., 1966—; lectr., planner Mark Twain lectr. series Okla. Com. for Humanities; chmn. program subcom. of steering com. Gov.'s Conf. on Librs., 1978-79; freelance photographer, writer. Contbr. weekly column Between the Bookends to area newspapers, Western Okla.; contbr. articles, book revs. and photographs to various publs.; organizer, scripwriter slide/tape programs on librs. history and cmty. events. Bd. dirs. Okla. Hist. Soc., 1987-96, treas., 1992-96; active Custer County Hist. Soc., friends of Clinton Pub. Libr., Washita County Hist. Soc.; mem. coms., past mem. state archives and records commn. Meth. Ch.; chairperson publicity com. humanities project Okla. Image; vice chairperson Custer County Devel. Coun., 1976-77; bd. dirs., vice chairperson Clinton Regional Hosp., 1991-95; mem. Dewey County Hist. Soc., pres., 1991-94. Recipient Kiwanis Citizen of Yr. award, Clinton, 1983, Am. Legion Community Svc. award, 1982; named one of Outstanding Young Women of Am., 1968; named Clinton's Woman of Yr., 1978, First Lady of Yr., Clinton chpt. Beta Sigma Phi, 1974, Hon. col. Okla. N.G., 1985; named to Dewey County Hall of Fame, 1988; Sasakawa fellow/recipient stipend for airfare to Australia, Internat. Friendship Force, 1985; Paul Harris fellow Clinton chpt. Rotary Internat., 1982. Mem. ALA (mem. governing coun. 1975-78, mem. Caldecott-Newberry com. 1976-77, mem. editl. bd. Small Pub. Librs. pamphlet project 1975-79, mem. status of women com. 1977-78), Okla. Libr. Assn. (pres. 1971-72, treas. 1969-70, program chairperson ann. conf. 1970-71, mem. exec. bd. 1973-74, chairperson publicity 1975-76, chairperson search com. for exec. sec. 1976, mem. archival preservation bd., numerous coms., scholar 1959, Disting. Svc. award 1974), Beta Phi Mu. Democrat. Home: 1400 Redstone Dr Clinton OK 73601-5428 Office: Western Plains Libr Sys PO Box 1027 Clinton OK 73601-1027

RAY, EDDYE ROBERT, occupational safety and health professional; b. Tulsa, Jan. 16, 1941; s. Samuel McKeel and Oteka Nathalee (Ammons) R.; m. Dorothy Christine Rohrer, Aug. 12, 1966; children: Robert Harold, William McKeel. BS in Chemistry, East Cen. State U., Ada, Okla., 1968. Cert. safety profl., hazardous material mgr., safety mgr.; registered environ. mgr. Safety inspector ARCO Chem. Co., Sand Springs, Okla., 1968-86; safety specialist ChemLink Petroleum Inc., Sand Springs, 1986-88; pres. Seagull Enteprise and Assocs., Inc., Tulsa, 1988—; instr. engring. extension Okla. State U., Stillwater, 1988—; fire tng. instr. Tex. A&M U., College Station, 1976—. Asst. scoutmaster Boy Scouts Am., Sand Springs, 1987—. With USAF, 1960-64. Mem. Am. Soc. Safety Engrs., World Safety Orgn., Okla. Safety Coun. (chmn. occupational com. 1987-88), Bowhunting Coun. Okla. (pres. 1983-87). Democrat. Baptist. Office: Seagull Enterprise Assocs 212 N Main St Sand Springs OK 74063-7603

RAY, H. M., lawyer; b. Rienzi, Miss., Aug. 9, 1924; s. Thomas Henry and Isabelle (Dunlap) R.; m. Merle Burt, Nov. 28, 1953 (dec. Dec. 1993); children: Howard Manfred, Mark Andrew. J.D., U. Miss., 1949. Bar: Miss. 1949. U.S. atty. No. Dist. Miss. Oxford, 1961-81; pvt. practice law Corinth, Miss., 1949-61, Jackson, Miss., 1981-85, 90—; asst. atty. gen. State of Miss., Jackson, 1986-90; mem. Atty. Gen.'s Adv. Com. U.S. Attys., 1973-78, chmn., 1976; vis. lectr. UN, Asia and Far East, UN (Inst. for Prevention Crime and Treatment of Offenders), Tokyo, 1977; pros. atty. Alcorn County, Miss., 1956-57, 68-61; mem. Miss. Ho. of RReps., 1948-51; mem. Miss. Gov.'s Com. to Study Laws Regarding Use of Deadly Force on Fleeing Felons, 1982-83, Miss. Gov.'s Constl. Study Commn., 1985-86. Co-author: Miss. Workmens' Compensation Act, 1948. Chmn. Corinth-Alcorn County Airport Bd., 1959-61; trustee Alcorn County Public Library, 1959-62. Served with USAAC, 1943-45, ETO; with USAF, 1951-53. Recipient Corinth's Young Man of Yr. award, 1958. Presbyterian (elder). Clubs: Kiwanis (lt. gov. 1955-56, dist. chmn. 1956-57, pres. Corinth 1943-53). Home: 12 Windy Ridge Cv Jackson MS 39211-2904 Office: PO Box 2449 Jackson MS 39225-2449

RAY, HAL ROBERTS, JR., lawyer; b. Wichita Falls, Tex., Sept. 11, 1960; s. Hal Roberts, Sr. and Mary Johnette (Highsmith) R.; m. Nan Victoria Culpepper, June 13, 1987; children: Hal Roberts III, Victoria Eva. BA, U. Tex., 1981, JD, 1984. Bar: Tex. 1984, U.S. Dist. Ct. (no. dist.) Tex. 1985, U.S. Ct. Appeals (5th cir.) 1986, U.S. Dist. Ct. (ea. dist.) Tex. 1991, U.S. Dist. Ct. (we. dist.) Tex. 1995. Law clk. to chief judge U.S. Dist. Ct. (no. dist.) Tex., Lubbock, 1984-85; assoc. Thompson & Knight, Dallas, 1985-88, Ft. Worth, 1990-94; assoc. Sherrill & Pace, Wichita Falls, 1988-90; asst. atty. gen., chief elder law and ins. practices sect. Office of the Atty. Gen., Austin, 1994, chief elder law & pub. health divsn., 1995, chief natural resources divsn., 1995—. Fellow Tex. Bar Found.; mem. ABA, State Bar Tex., U. Tex. Law Alumni Assn., Phi Beta Kappa. Democrat. Methodist. Office: Office of the Atty Gen PO Box 12548 Austin TX 78711-2548

RAY, JAMES ALLEN, oil company executive, petroleum engineer; b. Charleston, W.Va., Oct. 3, 1955; s. James Stewart and Anna Ruth (Harvey) R.; m. Tammi J. Jeffries, Dec. 18, 1980; children: Whitney Anne, Justin Stewart. BS in Petroleum Engring., W.Va. U., 1978. Staff prodn. engr. Ray Resources Corp., Charleston, W.Va., 1978-81; v.p. Ray Resources Corp., Charleston, 1981-92, pres., 1992—; bd. dirs. Charleston (W.Va.) Area Med. Ctr. Found.; bd. advisors Mary Babb Randolph Cancer Ctr., Morgantown, W.Va., 1990—, U. W.Va. Coll. Mineral and Energy Resources, 1996—. Mem. Salina Lodge A.F. & A.M., Royal Order of Jesters Ct. (Charleston, W.Va.), Beni Kedem Shrine. Home: 835 Lower Donnally Rd Charleston WV 25304-2822

RAY, MARILYN ANNE, nursing educator, nursing researcher; b. Hamilton, Ont., Can., Jan. 24, 1938; d. Arthur William Anthony and Elvera Caroline (Montag) R.; m. James L. Droesbeke, Aug. 18, 1979. Diploma, St. Joseph's Hosp. Sch. Nursing, Hamilton, 1958; BSN, U. Colo., Denver, 1968, MSN, 1969; PhD in Nursing, U. Utah, 1981; MA in Anthropology, McMaster U, 1978. RN, Fla.; cert. advanced nursing adminstr., cert. transcultural nurse CTN. Instr. sch. nursing U. San Francisco, 1970-72; asst. prof. sch. nursing McMaster U., 1973-76; asst. prof. U. Colo., 1984-89; Christine E. Lynn eminent scholar sch. nursing Fla. Atlantic U., Boca Raton, 1989-94, prof. sch. nursing, 1995—; Yingling vis. scholar Va. Commonwealth U., Richmond, 1994-95; vis. assoc. prof. U. Colo., 1989—. Contbr. articles to profl. jours. Col. USAFR, 1967—. Recipient Leininger award, 1989. Mem. ANA, Am. Anthrop. Assn., Transcultural Nursing Soc. (cert.), Aerospace Med. Assn. (mem. rsch. com. space medicine br.), Coll. Nurses Ont., Aerospace Human Factors Assn. (charter), Sigma Theta Tau.

RAY, MARY LOUISE RYAN, lawyer; b. Houston, Dec. 8, 1954; d. Cornelius O'Brien and Mary Anne (Kelley) R.; m. Marshall Ransome Ray, Jan. 30, 1982; children: Siobhan Elisabeth Kelley, Johanna Frances Morris, Jonathan Jordan Willson. BA with honors, U. Tex., 1976; JD, St. Mary's Univ., San Antonio, Tex., 1980. Bar: Tex. 1980, U.S. Dist. Ct. (so. dist.) Tex. 1981, U.S. Ct. Appeals (5th cir) 1993, U.S. Supreme Ct. 1994. Assoc. Kelley & Ryan, Houston, 1980-82, R.W. Armstrong, Brownsville, Tex., 1982-83; ptnr. Armstrong & Ray, Brownsville, Tex., 1983-87, Ransome and Ray, P.C., Brownsville, Tex., 1987—. Bd. dirs. Brownsville Soc. for Crippled Children, 1984-95, pres., 1992-93; bd. dirs. Valley Zool. Soc., 1990—, United Way of Southern Cameron County, 1989-95, pres., 1994; bd. dirs. Crippled Children's Found., Brownsville, 1989—; bd. dirs. Episcopal Day Sch. Found., 1995—, pres., 1995-96. Fellow Tex. Bar Found.; mem. Tex. Bar Assn., Cameron County Bar Assn. (bd. dirs. 1990—, v.p. 1996), Tex. Assn. Bank Counsel. Episcopalian. Office: Ransome & Ray PC 550 E Levee St Brownsville TX 78520-5343

RAY, MICHAEL ROBERT, legal assistant; b. E. Herkimer, N.Y., Dec. 9, 1965; s. William Martin and Doris Helen (Wengert) R. Cert. legal asst., Profl. Career Devel., 1991. Cert. legal asst. Freelance legal asst. Myrtle Beach, S.C., 1990-92; legal asst. Collection Cons. Group, Myrtle Beach, 1990-93; CEO On Time Enterprises Inc., Myrtle Beach, S.C., 1991—. Active Rep. Nat. Com., 1993—. Mem. Nat. Lambda Alliance, Nat. Paralegals/Legal Assts., Columbia Legal Asst.'s Assn., Nat. Platform Assn. Office: On Time Enterprises PO Box 100 Myrtle Beach SC 29578-0100

RAY, MICHELLE MORRIS, secondary education educator, mediator; b. Jacksonville, Fla., June 19, 1949; d. Earl Edgar and Mary Virginia (Bennett) Morris; m. James Edward Ray Jr., Aug. 22, 1970 (div. Sep. 1988); children: Jason Scott, Shannon Melissa. BS, Troy State U., 1970; MS, Nova U., 1984, EdD, 1994. Cert. profl. educator, family mediator, Fla. Educator Richards Jr. High, Columbus, Ga., 1970-72, Jefferson County Bd. of Edn., Birmingham, Ala., 1972-75, Holly Hill (S.C.) Sch. Dist., 1975, Gulf Middle Sch., New Port Richey, Fla., 1978-90, Thomas E. Weightman Middle Sch., Zephyrhills, Fla., 1990-96; mediator Consultation and Mediation Ctr., Tampa, New Port Richey, Fla., 1995—; cons. Right Choices, Tampa, Fla., 1994-95, Parenting Your Teen, Tampa, 1995. Guest spkr. Dade City Rotary, 1993; rep., spkr. USEP-FEA, Wesley Chapel, Fla., 1995; vol. Paint Your Heart Out, Tampa, 1994. Mem. FEA, Internat. Reading Assn., Fla. Reading Assn., Pasco Reading Assn. Methodist.

RAY, MIKE WALLACE, media specialist; b. Sebastopol, Calif., Sept. 15, 1952; s. Homer Wallace and Mae Beth (Cain) R.; m. Sherry Ellen Shoemake, July 17, 1982; 1 child, Ean Davis. BS, Ctrl. State U., 1988. Printer, reporter The Yale (Okla.) News, 1965-70, 73, The Pawnee (Okla.) Chief, 1970-72; reporter Lawton (Okla.) Morning Press, 1974-78, Stillwater (Okla.) News-Press, 1978-79, Odessa (Tex.) Am., 1979-80; editor, reporter Muskogee (Okla.) Daily Phoenix, 1980-85; pub. rels. staff Southwestern Bell Telephone, Oklahoma City, 1985-87; mng. editor Oklahoma City (Okla.) Friday, 1988-89; dir. media divsn. Oklahoma Ho. of Reps., Oklahoma City, 1990—; election stringer, reporter Jodat Microspecialties, Oklahoma City, 1988-89; free-lance news writer Okla. Mcpl. League, Oklahoma City, 1989. Mem. Rotary Club, Muskogee, 1982-85, newsletter editor, 1983-84; state coord. Okla. Citizen Bee, Oklahoma City, 1987; membership directory coord. Pub. Rels. Soc. Am., Oklahoma City, 1992. Recipient Pres.'s award Muskogee Rotary Club, 1983-84, first pl. editorial award Okla. Press Assn./Okla. Natural Gas Co., 1973, first pl. editorial writing award, first pl. column writing award Okla. Press Assn., 1984, 85, Merit award Internat. Assn. Bus. Communicators, 1986, first pl. newsletter 1993, third pl. newsletter 1995, Okla. Chpt. Soc. of Profl. Journalists; Upper Case and Award of Merit, Oklahoma City chpt. Pub. Rels. Soc. Am., 1996, others. Mem. Nat. Conf. State Legislatures. Democrat. Mem. Disciples of Christ Ch. Office: Okla Ho of Reps State Capitol Rm B-24 Oklahoma City OK 73105

RAY, RICKEY JOE, philosophy educator, minister; b. Conway, S.C., Sept. 22, 1956; s. Harold Brooks and Jewel Pauline (Sanders) R.; m. Linnéa Linderholm Olson, Dec. 17, 1995. BA, Charleston (S.C.) So. U., 1978; MDiv, So. Bapt. Theol. Sem., Louisville, 1982; PhD, So. Bapt. Theol. Sem., 1988. Adj. prof. philosophy Jefferson C.C. S.W., Shively, Ky., 1984; chaplain Pine Tree Villa Nursing Home, Louisville, 1987-89; adj. prof. philosophy Ind. U. S.E., New Albany, 1989, Western Ky. U., Bowling Green, 1988-89, Tenn. Wesleyan Coll., Athens, 1989-90, U. Tenn. at Chattanooga, 1990, East Tenn. State U., Johnson City, 1990-92, 95—; pastor Elk Garden-Dennison United Meth. Ch., Rosedale, Va., 1990-94, Weaver Union Ch., Bristol, Tenn., 1994-96; com. on Interfaith Dialogue and Inter-religious Concerns, Holston Conf. of the United Meth. Ch., Abingdon, Va., 1994-95. Contbr. articles to profl. jours. Group facilitator Parents Anonymous, Lebanon, Va., 1991-92. Named Outstanding Young Man in Am., 1983; recipient Cmty. Svc. award for Parents Anonymous, Dept. of Social Svcs., Lebanon, 1992. Mem. AAUP, Am. Philos. Assn., Am. Acad. of Religion, Soc. for Philosophy of Religion, Søren Kierekgaard Soc., Am. Simone Weil Soc. Democrat. Home: PO Box 1086 Abingdon VA 24212 Office: Dept Philosophy East Tenn State U Johnson City TN 37614

RAY, RONALD DUDLEY, lawyer; b. Hazard, Ky., Oct. 30, 1942. BA in Psychology and English, Centre Coll., 1964; JD magna cum laude, U. Louisville, 1971. Assoc. Greenebaum, Doll & McDonald, 1971-75, ptnr., 1975-84, 85-86; ptnr. Ray & Morris, Louisville, 1986-89; mng. ptnr. Ronald Ray Attys., Louisville, 1990—; dep. asst. sec. def. Pentagon, Washington, 1984-85; adj. prof. law U. Louisville Sch. Law, 1972-80; commr. Presdl. Commn. on Assigment of Women in Mil., 1992. Author: Military Necessity & Homosexuality, 1993; sr. legal editor: Personnel Policy Manual, Bank Supervisory Policies, The Bank Employee Handbook, 1985-86; mil. historian. State fin. chmn. Nat. Fin. Com. for George Bush for Pres.; chmn. Vietnam Vets. Leadership Program in Ky., 1982-85, Ky. Vietnam Vets. Meml. Fund, 1985-91; trustee Marine Corps Command and Staff Found., 1985-92; mem. exec. com. State Cen. Com., Ky. Rep. Party, 1986-90; mem. Am. Battle Monuments Commn., 1990-93. With USMC, 1964-69; col. USMCR (ret.). Decorated Silver Star medal with gold star, Bronze Star medal, Purple Heart; recipient Nat. Eagle award. Mem. Naval Inst. (life), Marine Corps Res. Officers' Assn. Home: Halls Hill Farm 3317 Halls Hill Rd Crestwood KY 40014-9523

RAY, RUTH ALICE YANCEY, rancher, real estate developer; b. Birmingham, Ala., July 26, 1931; d. John Grayson and Ruth Ethel (Lutman) Yancey; (div. July 1986); children: Virginia Ruth, John Edward, William Arthur. Student, Fla. State U., 1949-50; BS, Appalachian State U., 1954; postgrad., Stetson U., 1966-67, Appalachian State U., 1962-63, Stetson U.,

1964-67. Tchr. pub. schs. Nenana, Alaska, 1955-56; tchr. 1st Christian Ch., Clermont, Fla., 1965-67, Lake County Sch. Bd., Clermont, 1969-70; rancher Rays' Ranch, Clermont, 1963—; pvt. real estate developer Clermont, 1990—. Chmn. Clermont Planning and Zoning Commn., 1973-81; mem. Heart of Fla Girl Scout Coun., 1988—; life mem. Friends of Cooper Mem. Libr., South Lake Art League. Named Conservation Farmer of Yr., State of Fla., 1982. Mem. Lake County Farm Bur. (bd. dirs. 1977-81), Lake County Cattlemen's Assn. (v.p. 1979-81), Lake County Farmer's Home Adminstrn. (bd. dirs. 1984-88, 1990—, chmn. 1985, 88, 90-91), Nat. Cutting Horse Assn. (life), Am. Quarter Horse Assn., Am. Paint Horse Assn., E.S.A. Internat., Daus. of King, Sigma Kappa. Republican. Episcopalian (sr. warden, eucharistic min.). Home and Office: 12932 County Road 474 Clermont FL 34711-8903

RAY, SHIRLEY DODSON, educational administrator, consultant; b. Smithville, Tex., Sept. 20, 1929; d. Pickett James and Marjorie (Dietz) Dodson; m. John Davis Ray, Aug. 12, 1950; children: Ellen Ray Stauffer, Daniel Dodson, John Andrew. BA, Baylor U., 1950; MA, Tex. A&I U., 1964; postgrad., Corpus Christi State U. Cert. supt., mid. mgmt., elem. secondary edn., bus. Tchr., math. cons., coord. elem. instrn. Corpus Christi Ind. Sch. Dist., 1958-73; gen. cons. Ednl. Svcs. Ctr. Region II, Corpus Christi, 1973-78; curriculum dir. Calallen Ind. Sch. Dist., 1978-87; asst. supt. instructional svcs. Calallen Ind. Sch. Dist., Corpus Christi, Tex., 1987-92; ind. elem. cons. Corpus Christi, 1992—; cons. Corpus Christi, 1992—; adj. prof. Corpus Christi State U., 1983—, Tex. A&M U., Kingsville, 1993—; mem. staff NSF, Tex. A&I U., 1973—. Author numerous booklets and pamphlets, math. workshops; writer with com. for EXCET test for suprs. Mem. ASCD, AAUW, Nat. Coun. Tchrs. Math. (tchr. insvc. com.), Tex. Coun. Tchrs. Math. (past pres.), Tex. Assn. Suprs. Math. (past v.p.), Tex. Assn. Supervision and Curriculum Devel. (bd. dirs.), Assn. Tex. Profl. Educators, Phi Delta Kappa (past pres. Kingsville chpt.), Delta Kappa Gamma.

RAY, TIMOTHY BRITT, social worker, lawyer, administrator; b. New Orleans, June 13, 1939; s. Archibald Cole and Eliza Owen (Britt) R.; m. Constance Helen Abbott, Nov. 27, 1964; children: Michael Gregory Owen, Mary Eliza Rebecca. BA, Davidson Coll., 1961; MA, La. State U., 1963; MSW, W. Va. U., 1968; JD, U. Santa Clara, 1976. Bar: Ohio 1981. Chief psychiatric social worker Alameda County, Oakland, Calif., 1974-77; exec. dir. Toledo Legal Aid Soc., 1977-82, Concept House Inc., Miami, 1982-83; counselor youth Fla. Health and Rehabilitative Svcs., Miami, 1983-84; exec. dir. Dist. Ill. Mental Health Bd., Gainesville, Fla., 1984, Older Americans Coun., Gainesville, 1984-90; elderly housing mgr. Gainesville Housing Authority, 1990-92, med. social work supr. Olsten-Kimberly Quality Care, 1993-94; med. social worker Hospice of Marion County, Gainesville, 1994—; chmn. health care services adv. com. Upjohn Co., Gainesville, 1986. Contbr. articles in profl. jours. Chmn. United Way Exec. Dirs. Coun., Gainesville, 1985; appointee Dist. III Alcohol, Drug Abuse and Mental Health Planning Coun.; chmn. Adult and Elderly Svcs. Com., 1987-88; pres. Interagy. Coun., Gainesville, 1986; pres. bd. Bread of Mighty Food Bank, Inc., 1987-90; elder 1st Presbyn. Ch., Gainesville; bd. dirs. Alzheimers Assn., 1989-90, Cmty. with a Heart, Ocala, Fla., 1995; active Fla. Coun. on Aging, Gainesville Human Rels. Adv. Bd., 1989-91. Bd. govs. fellow, 1967. Mem. ABA, Acad. Cert. Social Workers, Nat. Assn. Social Workers, Gainesville Area C. of C., Phi Alpha Delta. Democrat. Presbyterian. Home: 3321 NW 45th Ave Gainesville FL 32605-1459

RAYAN, GHAZI M., surgeon; b. Haifa, Palestine, Dec. 6, 1949; s. Moh H. and Kay K. (Harti) R.; m. Hoda Khatib, Feb. 15, 1962; children: Nadine, Basil. PNS, Alexandria U., Egypt, 1968, MBBCh, 1973. Dipomate Am. Bd. Orthpaedic Surgery; lic. MD, N.C., Md., Okla. Internship Alexandria U., Egypt, 1974-75; physician ARAMCO, Saudi Arabia, 1975; fellow radiology Johns Hopkins Hosp., Balt., 1975; intern, resident gen. surgery South Balt. Gen. Hosp./U.Md., 1976-77; resident orthopedic surgery Union Meml.-Johns Hopkins Hosp., Balt., 1977-80; fellow in hand/microsurgery Raymond Curtis Hand Ctr., Balt., 1980-81; chief hand surgery dept. U. Okla., Oklahoma City, 1981-87; asst. prof. Health Scis. Ctr., Oklahoma City, 1981-86; assoc. prof. U. Okla., Oklahoma City, 1986-91, clin. prof., 1992—; med. dir. hand rehab. Bapt. Med. Ctr., Oklahoma City, 1987-92, dir. hand surgery fellowship program, 1992—. Mem. editoral adv. bd. Orthopaedics Today, 1982—; editor-in-chief Eastern Mediterranean Hand Bull., 1985—; contbr. chpts. to books, numerous articles to profl. jours. Recipient Am. Physician's Recognition award AMA, 1982-84, 84-87, Best Paper award, 1983, 86, 90, Outstanding Tchrs. award U. Okla. Health Scis. Ctr., 1992-93; Harris fellow, 1986. Fellow Am. Acad. Orthopaedic Surgeons; mem. AMA, Johns Hopkins Med. and Surgery Assn., Oklahoma County Med. Soc., Okla. State Med. Soc., Ctrl. Okla. Orthopaedic Ctrl., Arthritis Found., Am. Soc. Surgery of Hand, Ea. Mediterranean Hand Soc., Am. Assn. for Hand Surgery, Orthopaedic Rsch. Soc., Am. Soc. for Reconstructive Microsurgery, So. Med. Assn., Am. Soc. for Peripheral Nerve Surgery, Am. Med. Writers Assn. Office: Upper Extremity Hand & Microsurgery Ctr 3366 NW Expressway St Ste 700 Oklahoma City OK 73112-4418

RAYBECK, MICHAEL JOSEPH, surgeon; b. Danbury, Conn., Oct. 5, 1945; s. Michael Thomas and Edythe Caroline (Tomaino) R. BS, Mt. St. Mary's Coll., Emmitsburg, Md., 1967; MD, Tulane U., 1971. Diplomate Am. Bd. Surgery, Am. Bd. Quality Assurance Utilization Rev. Physicians. Intern in surgery St. Vincent's Hosp. and Med. Ctr., N.Y.C., 1971-72; resident in gen. and vascular surgery Ochsner Found. Hosp., New Orleans, 1974-78; ptnr. Burshan, Raybeck, MD, P.A., Pompano Beach, Fla., 1978-82, Lauderdale Surg. Group, P.A., Ft. Lauderdale, 1982—; med. adv. com. Dept. Profl. Regulation, State of Fla.; pres. med. staff Holy Cross Hosp., 1995, vice chmn. PHO. Bd. dirs. Am. Heart Assn., Ft. Lauderdale, 1988-91. Fellow ACS, Internat. Coll. Surgeons, Soc. Am. Gastrointestinal Endoscopic Surgeons; mem. Am. Soc. Colon-Rectal Surgeons. Republican. Roman Catholic. Office: Lauderdale Surg Group 4701 N Federal Hwy Fort Lauderdale FL 33308-4608

RAYBURN, WILLIAM FRAZIER, obstetrician, gynecologist, educator; b. Lexington, Ky., Aug. 19, 1950; s. Charles Calvin and Charlotte Elizabeth (Ballard) R.; m. Pamela Rae Gilleland, Nov. 27, 1976; children: Lindsay Ann, Britany Beth, Drake Tanner. BS, Hampden Sydney Coll., 1971; MD, U. Ky., 1975. Diplomate Nat. Bd. Med. Examiners, Am. Bd. Ob.-Gyn. (examiner), Divsn. Maternal-Fetal Medicine. Intern family medicine U. Iowa Hosps. and Clinics, Iowa City, Iowa, 1975-76; resident ob.-gyn. U. Ky. Med. Ctr., Lexington, 1976-79; fellow in maternal-fetal medicine dept. ob.-gyn. Ohio State U. Hosps., Columbus, 1979-81; asst. prof. ob.-gyn. U. Mich. Med. Sch., Ann Arbor, 1981-83, assoc. prof. ob.-gyn., 1983-86; assoc. prof. dept. ob.-gyn. and pharmacology U. Nebr. Coll. of Medicine, Omaha, 1985-88, prof. dept. ob-gyn. and pharmacology, 1988-92; prof. dept. ob-gyn. and pharmacology U. Okla. Coll. Medicine, Oklahoma City, 1992—, John W. Records endowed chair, 1992—; chief of obstetrics U. Okla. Coll. of Medicine, Okla. City, 1992—; dir. maternal fetal medicine dept. ob-gyn U. Mich. Med. Ctr., 1981-85, med. edn.; reviewer for Ob and Gyn., Am. Jour. Ob-Gyn., Jour. Reproductive Medicine, Internat. Jour. Gyn. and Ob., New Eng. Jour. Medicine, Jour. Maternal-Fetal Medicine, Jour. Maternal-Fetal Investigation; U. Nebr. Med. Ctr., 1985-92, U. Okla. Health Sci. Ctr., 1992—, Presbyn. Hosp., Okla. City, 1992—. Author: (books) Obstetrics/Gynecology: Pre Test Self Assessment and Review, 1982; (with others), Every Woman's Pharmacy: A Guide to Safe Drug Use, 1983, Obstetrics for the House Officer, 1984, 2d rev. edition, 1988, Every Woman's Pharmacy, 1984, The Women's Health and Drug Reference, 1993, Oklahoma Notes: Obstetrics and Gynecology, 1994, 2d. rev. edit., 1996, Obstetrics and Gynecology for the House Officer, 1996; editor: (with F.P. Zuspan) Drug Therapy in Obstetrics and Gynecology, 1982, 3d rev. edit., 1992; symposia editor Diagnosis and Management of the Malformed Fetus, Jour. Reprod. Medicine, 1982, Operative Obstetrics, Clinics in Perinatology, 1983, Controversies in Fetal Drug Therapy, Clin. Obstetrics and Gynecology, 1991; contbr. 50 chpts. to books, articles to over 170 profl. jours. including Am. Jour. Obstetric Gynecology, Obstetrics Gynecology, Jour. Reproductive Medicine, Am. Jour. Perinatology and many others; also speaker and lectr. at sci. confs. and seminars and author of audio visual ednl. material for universities and in continuing med. edn.; contbr. over 100 abstracts at sci. meetings; reviewer for Ob. and Gyn., Am. Jour. Ob.-Gyn., Jour. Reproductive Medicine, Internat. Jour. Gyn. and Ob., New Eng. Jour. Medicine, Jour. Maternal-Fetal Medicine, Jour. Maternal-Fetal Investigation. Dir. maternal and infant care programs U. Nebr. Med. Ctr., Omaha, 1986-92; U.S. Pharmacopeia Conv. field reviewer, 1983—. Recipient Residents' prize paper award Ky. Ob.-Gyn. Soc., 1978, 79, Faculty Teaching award for Excellence, 1993, 94.car. Fellow Am. Coll. Obstetricians and Gynecologists (Ephraim McDowell) prize paper award 2d pl. 1978, 1st pl. 1979, Searle-Donald F. Richardson Prize Paper award 1980, Best Doctors in Am., 1996); mem. Soc. Perinatal Obstetricians, Assn. of Profs. in Gyn.-Ob., Soc. for Gynecol. Investigation, Teratology Soc., N.Y. Acad. Sci., Neurobehavioral Teratology Soc., Okla. State Med. Soc. Office: U Okla Health Sci Ctr PO Box 6901 4 SP Rm 710 Oklahoma City OK 73190

RAYMER, WARREN JOSEPH, retired allergist; b. Seguin, Tex., Aug. 23, 1920; s. Milam R. and O'TTilie H. (Fischer) R.; m. Viola M. Glover, July 16, 1945. BA in Zoology, U. Tex., 1942; MD, Baylor Coll. of Medicine, 1947. Diplomate Am. Bd. Allergy and Immunology. Intern Methodist Hosp., Houston, 1947-48, resident, 1948-49; resident in internal medicine So. Pacific Hosp., Houston, 1949-50; fellow in allergy U. Va. Hosp., Charlottesville, 1952-53; pvt. practice Houston, 1950-84; ret., 1984; clin. asst. prof. medicine U. Tex., Houston; mem. staff Hermann Hosp., Houston; hon. mem. Park Plaza Hosp., Houston, Diagnostic Hosp., Houston. Contbr. articles to profl. jours. Capt. USMC, Korean War. Fellow Am. Acad. Allergy, Am. Coll. Allergists (pres. 1981-82), Am. Assn. Cert. Allergists; mem. AMA (life), World Med. Assn., Am. Assn. Physicians and Surgeons, Southwest Allergy Forum, Tex. Med. Assn. (life), Tex. Allergy Immunology Soc. (sec./treas.), Harris County Med. Soc., Greater Houston Allergy Soc., N.Y. Acad. Sci., Masons. Office: Houston Allergy Clinic 1213 Hermann Dr # 444 Park Plz Profl Bldg Houston TX 77004

RAYMOND, GEORGE EDWARD, JR. (CHIP RAYMOND), operations research analyst; b. Monterey, Calif., Dec. 26, 1947; s. George Edward and Madeleine (Gordon) R.; m. Elizabeth B. Dees, Aug. 26, 1968 (div. Dec. 1980); children: Madeleine, Anna Marie, Katie; m. Barbara Ann Sullivan, July 7, 1990. BS, N.C. State U., 1972; MBA, George Mason U./Oxford U., 1995. Served to maj. U.S. Army, Ft. Belvoir, Va., 1972-82; sr. cons. KPMG Peat Marwick, Washington, 1982-85; sr. product mgr. Magnavox, Ft. Wayne, Ind., 1985-87; dir. econ. analysis U.S. Army Info. Sys. Software Ctr., Ft. Belvoir, 1987—. Editor: Resource Management for Software Development, 1990. Recipient meritorious svc. award U.S. Army, 1982. Mem. Am. Soc. Mil. Comptrollers, Order Ky. Cols. Republican. Roman Catholic. Home: 10318 Pond Spice Ter Burke VA 22015-3739 Office: USAISSC Software Ctr 6000 6th St Fort Belvoir VA 22060-5506

RAYMOND, KAY E(NGELMANN), Spanish language educator, consultant; b. Cin., Feb. 1, 1939; d. Gerson Silas and Pauline Coleman (Early) Engelmann; m. O. Ralph Raymond II, Feb. 1, 1964 (div. Sept. 1978); 1 child, Jenifer Kay Raymond-Judy. AB, Radcliffe Coll., 1961; MA, Brown U., 1964; PhD, Ind. U., 1983. Lectr. Boston U., 1965-68; lectr. Assumption Coll., Worcester, Mass., 1965-67; instr. Regis Coll., Weston, Mass., 1967-71; assoc. instr. Ind. U., Bloomington, 1972-83; lectr. Emporia (Kans.) State U., 1983-84; asst. prof. U. Ala. at Huntsville, 1984-89, Sam Houston State U., Huntsville, Tex., 1989-94; assoc. prof. Sam Houston State U., 1994—, coord. fgn. langs., 1995. Advisor Internat. Hispanic Assn., Sam Houston State U., 1989—, Sigma Delta Pi, 1990—; vol. translator City of Huntsville, 1993—. Named Top Prof Bapt. Student Ministry Sam Houston State U., 1996, Outstanding Advisor Internat. Hispanic Assn., 1996. Mem. MLA, Asociación de Literatura Femenina, Phi Sigma Iota (life), Pi Delta Phi (hon.), Sigma Delta Pi (hon.). Democrat. Home: 3644 Youpon St Huntsville TX 77340-8920 Office: Sam Houston State U Fgn Langs Box 2147 Huntsville TX 77341

RAYMOND, LEE R., oil company executive; b. Watertown, S.D., Aug. 13, 1938; m. Charlene Raymond. BSChemE, U. Wis., 1960; PhDChemE, U. Minn., 1963. Various engring. positions Exxon Corp., Tulsa, Houston, N.Y.C. and Caracas, Venezuela, 1963-72; mgr. planning Internat. Co. div. Exxon Corp., N.Y.C., 1972-75; pres. Exxon Nuclear Co. div. Exxon Corp., 1979-81, exec. v.p. Exxon Enterprises Inc. div., 1981-83; sr. v.p., dir. Exxon Corp., N.Y.C., 1984-86, pres., dir., 1987-93, chmn., CEO, 1993—; v.p. Lago Oil, Netherlands Antilles, 1975-76, pres., dir., 1976-79; pres., dir. Esso Inter-Am. Inc., Coral Gables, Fla., 1983-84, sr. v.p., dir., 1984—; bd. dirs. J.P. Morgan & Co., Inc., N.Y.C., Morgan Guaranty Trust Co. of N.Y., N.Y.C.; chmn. Am. Petroleum Inst. Bd. dirs. United Negro Coll. Fund, New Am. Schs. Devel. Corp., 1991—, Project Shelter PRO-AM, 1991—, Dallas Citizens Coun.; trustee Wis. Alumni Rsch. Found., 1987—, Bus. Coun. Internat. Understanding, Inc., 1988—; trustee So. Meth. U.; mem. Tri Lateral Commn., U. Wis. Found., Nat. Rep. Senatorial Com.; mem. emergency com. Am. trade; ptnr. emeritus N.Y.C. Partnership; mem. bd. govs. United Way Am.; active Am. Coun. on Germany, Dallas Com. Fgn. Rels., Dallas Wildcat Com., 1993. Mem. Am. Soc. Engring. (nat. adv. coun.), Am. Soc. Royal Bot. Garden (founder), Bus. coun., Bus. Roundtable (policy taxation task force 1993), Nat. Petroleum Coun., Coun. Fgn. Rels., Singapore-U.S. Bus. Coun.

RAYMOND, STEVEN A., computer equipment company executive. Chmn., CEO Tech Data Corp., Clearwater, Fla. Office: Tech Data Corp 5350 Tech Data Dr Clearwater FL 34620-3122

READ, KENNETH FRANCIS, JR., physics educator, researcher; b. Annapolis, Md., Apr. 24, 1959. BS, Stanford U., 1981; MS, Cornell U., 1984, PhD, 1987. Rsch. assoc. Princeton (N.J.) U., 1987-90, rsch. staff mem., 1990; rsch. staff mem. Oak Ridge (Tenn.) Nat. Lab., 1991—; asst. prof. U. Tenn., Knoxville, 1991—; collaborating scientist Oak Ridge Nat. Lab. and U. Tenn. Knoxville, 1993—. Contbr. numerous articles to Physics Letters B. Recipient Andrew D. White fellowship, NSF Grad. fellowship, Cornell U., 1981; Nat. Merit scholar, 1977. Mem. Am. Phys. Soc., Sigma Xi, Phi Beta Kappa. Office: Oak Ridge Nat Lab Bldg 6003 MS 6372 PO Box 2008 Oak Ridge TN 37831

READ, MICHAEL OSCAR, editor, consultant; b. Amarillo, Tex., July 11, 1942; s. Harold Eugene and Madeline (Welch) R.; m. Jill Kay Vanderby, July 6, 1963 (div. Apr. 1967); 1 child, Rebecca Anne; m. Fawn Dale Barby, Apr. 10, 1977; 1 child, Nathan Michael. AA in Chemistry, Amarillo Coll., 1962; BA in Journalism, Tex. Tech. U., 1965. News editor Olton (Tex.) Enterprise, 1963-64; reporter, photographer Lubbock (Tex.) Avalanche-Jour., 1964-67, copy editor, 1967-70, city editor, 1970-72; copy editor Houston Post, 1972-74, systems editor, 1974-89, dir. news tech., 1989-95; electronic media content coord. Houston Chronicle, 1995—; supervisory com. Shell Employees Fed. Credit Union, Houston; bd. dirs. News Media Credit Union, Houston, Meadows (Tex.) Econ. Devel. Corp.; tchr. Let's Compute!, Stafford, Tex., 1985—; cons. Newspaper Pub. Sys., Stafford, 1989—; mem. joint Newspaper Assn. Am.-Internat. Press. Telecomm. Coun. Com. Wire Svc. Standards; mem. adv. bd. Found. for Am. Comms. FACSNET. Author weekly newspaper column, 1977—. Vol. United Way, Houston, 1973—; bd. dirs. Meadows Community Improvement Assn., 1985-95, Meadows Utility Dist., 1988-93. Eldon Durrett scholar, 1961-65. Mem. Am. MENSA, Am. Philatelic Soc., Am. 1st Day Cov. Soc. (life), U.S. Chess Fedn. (life), Soc. Profl. Journalists (conv. com. 1989-90), Press Club of Houston. Home: 12023 Alston Dr Stafford TX 77477-1505 Office: Houston Chronicle 801 Texas Ave Houston TX 77002

REAGAN, LAWRENCE PAUL, JR., systems engineer; b. Honolulu, Nov. 5, 1957; s. Lawrence Paul Sr. and Laura Louise (Sears) R.; m. Ann Marie Decker, Apr. 15, 1989; children: Lawrence P. III, Andrew Scott, Kelly Rene. BS in Mech. & Aerospace Engring., Ill. Inst. Tech., 1979; MS in Acquisition & Contract Mgmt., West Coast U., Santa Barbara, Calif., 1986. Product engr. R.G. Ray Corp., Schaumburg, Ill., 1978-80; launch integration mgr. USAF Hqrs. Space Divsn., L.A. AFB, 1980-84; chief Titan program mgmt. USAF Aerospace Test Group, Vandenberg AFB, Calif., 1984-89; chief joint communication br. USAF Pentagon, Washington, 1989-91; sr. sys. engr. Dynamics Rsch. Corp., Arlington, Va., 1992-96; dir. Md. ops. Dynamics Rsch. Corp., Lusby, 1996—; CEO Jacob's Well, Inc., Lexington Park, Md., 1993—. Contbr. papers to profl. publs. Named Outstanding Young Engr., Air Force Assn. Mem. AIAA, Soc. Logistics Engring., Air Force Assn. Home: PO Box 22 Lusby MD 20657-0022 Office: Dynamics Rsch Corp 1755 Jeff Davis Hwy Ste 802 Arlington VA 22202-3509

REAGAN, PATRICK DENNIS, history educator; b. St. Paul, Mar. 14, 1953; s. Joseph H. and Elizabeth T. (McGraw) R.; m. Reilly West, Feb. 27, 1988. AB with honors in History magna cum laude, Kenyon Coll., Gambier, Ohio, 1975; MA in History, Ohio State U., 1976, PhD in History, 1982. Vis. instr. dept. history Kenyon Coll., 1980-82; asst. prof. dept. history Tenn. Tech. U., Cookeville, 1982-87, assoc. prof. dept. history, 1987-92, prof. dept. history, 1992—; cons. D.C. Heath, Lexington, Mass., 1988—, Houghton Mifflin, Boston, 1989—. Author: America and the War with Iraq, 1991, Student Guide to Accompany The Great Republic, 1992; co-author: Horace Coon, Money to Burn, 1990; co-editor, contbr. Voluntarism, Planning and the State, 1988, For the General Welfare, 1989; contbr. articles to publs.; webmaster Tenn. Tech. History Web Site. Nat. Merit scholar Kenyon Coll., 1971-75, Henry G. Dalton fellow, 1975-76, Ohio State U. presdl. fellow, 1975-79, Nat. Endowment for Humanities, 1984; Eleanor Roosevelt Inst. grantee, 1979, 80. Mem. AAUP (editor state newsletter 1986-89, v.p., pres. local chpt. 1986-88), ACLU, Am. Hist. Assn., Nat. Coun. for History Edn., Soc. for Mil. History, Orgn. Am. Historians, Econ. History Assn., So. Hist. Assn., Soc. for Historians of Am. Fgn. Rels., Bus. History Conf., Phi Beta Kappa. Office: Tenn Tech U Dept History Box 5064 Cookeville TN 38505

REAGAN, THEODORE JOHN, geologist, exploration consultant, oil and gas mineral investment evaluator; b. Oceanside, Calif., Sept. 16, 1927; s. Walter William and Eugenia (Felix) R.; m. Lorraine Coldewey, Apr. 6, 1936; children: Claire R. Reagan Pelegrin, Ryan, Claudia Rene Bynum. BS in Geology, Tex. A&M U., 1952. Staff geologist Union Sulphur and Oil Inc., Houston, Midland and Corpus Christi, Tex., 1954-57; part owner, v.p. T.L.R. Inc., Corpus Christi, 1957-65; part owner, pres. Petroquest Oil and Gas Inc., Corpus Christi, 1958-87; geol. oil and gas exploration cons. Smithville, Tex., 1987—; exploration dir. Petroquest Oil and Gas Inc., 1965-87. 1st lt. U.S. Artillary, 1952-54. Fellow Am. Assn. Petroleum Geologists, Corpus Christi Geol. Soc., Oil and Gas Industries Libr. (pres. 1983).

REASONER, BARRETT HODGES, lawyer; b. Houston, Apr. 16, 1964; s. Harry Max and Macey (Hodges) R.; m. Susan Hardig; children: Matthew Joseph, Caroline Macey. BA cum laude, Duke U., 1986; Grad. Dipl., London Sch. Econs., 1987; JD with honors, U. Tex., 1990. Bar: Tex. 1990, U.S. Dist. Ct. (so. and no. dists.) Tex. 1993, U.S. Ct. Appeals (5th cir.) 1993. Asst. dist. atty. Harris County Dist. Atty.'s Office, Houston, 1990-92; ptnr. Gibbs & Bruns, L.L.P., Houston, 1992—. Mem. Am. Judicature Soc. (bd. dirs. 1994—), State Bar of Tex., Houston Bar Assn. (legal lines com. 1994—), Houston Young Lawyers Assn. (pub. schs./pub. edn. com. 1994—), Order of Barristers. Episcopalian. Home: 6139 Cedar Creek Dr Houston TX 77057-1801

REASONER, ELIZABETH DIANE, public relations executive; b. Birmingham, Ala., Nov. 1, 1949; d. George Wilburn and Martha Overton (Eason) Fulmer; m. Richard Merle Reasoner, Feb. 10, 1968; children: Richard Michael, Robert Mark. Diploma in ch. music, Fla. Bapt. Theol. Coll., 1972; AS, Southwest Bapt. U., 1978; BA, Ottawa (Kans.) U., 1985; MA, Ottawa U., 1994. Substitute tchr. Liberty County Sch. Dist., Bristol, Fla., 1975-76; with dean's office Southwest Bapt. U., Bolivar, Mo., 1977-78; sec., adminstrv. asst. Midwestern Bapt. Theol. Sem., Kansas City, Mo., 1978-87; pub. rels. specialist Ga. Bapt. Conv., Atlanta, 1987-90, assoc. dir. of pub. rels., 1990—; coord. workshops and musical prodns. Midwestern Bapt. Theol. Sem., Kansas City, 1981-84. Editor: Georgia Baptist Digest, 1990; author, editor publicity material, Ga. Bapt. Conv., 1990—, (newsletter) CenterLines, 1989—. Youth dir. Lake Mystic Bapt. Ch., Bristol, 1974-76; associational music dir. Applachacola Assn., Liberty County, Fla., 1975; music dir. Liberty County Early Learning Ctr., 1974. Recipient Cert. of Merit, The Naval Officers Wives League, Pensacola, 1964, Svc. award Midwestern Singers, Kansas City, Mo., 1987; named one of Outstanding Young Women Am., 1982, Alumnus of Yr., Fla. Bapt. Theol. Coll., 1995. Mem. NAFE, Nat. Orgn. Press Women, Bapt. Pub. Rels. Assn. (v.p. 1994-95), Tau Pi Epsilon (pres. 1972-73). Home: 3750 Colonial Trail SW Lilburn GA 30247-5402 Office: Ga Bapt Conv 2930 Flowers Rd S Atlanta GA 30341-5532

REASONER, HARRY MAX, lawyer; b. San Marcos, Tex., July 15, 1939; s. Harry Edward and Joyce Majorie (Barrett) R.; m. Elizabeth Macey Hodges, Apr. 15, 1963; children: Barrett Hodges, Elizabeth Macey Reasoner Stokes. BA in Philosophy summa cum laude, Rice U., 1960; JD with highest honors, U. Tex., 1962; postgrad., U. London, 1962-63. Bar: Tex., D.C., N.Y. Law clk. U.S. Ct. Appeals (2d cir.), 1963-64; assoc. Vinson & Elkins, Houston, 1964-69, ptnr., 1970—, mng.ptnr., 1992—; vis. prof. U. Tex. Sch. Law, 1971, Rice U., 1976, U. Houston Sch. Law, 1977; chair adv. group U.S. Dist Ct (so. dist.) Tex.; mem. adv. com. Supreme Ct. Tex. Author: (with Charles Alan Wright) Procedure: The Handmaid of Justice, 1965; author: (with others) American Economic Policy in the 1980s, 1994. Life trustee U. Tex. Law Sch. Found.; trustee Southwestern Legal Found., 1990—, Baylor Coll. Medicine, 1992—; chair Tex. Higher Edn. Coordinating Bd., 1991; bd. govs. Rice U., 1994—; exec. bd. dirs. Greater Houston Partnership, 1992—; mem. exec. coun. Ex-Student's Assn. U. Tex., 1992—; gov. Houston Forum, 1992—; bd. dirs. Central Houston, Inc., 1993—. Rotary Found. fellow 1962-63; recipient Disting. Alumnus award for cmty. svc. U. Tex. Law Alumni Assn., 1995. Fellow Am. Coll. Trial Lawyers, Internat. Acad. Trial Lawyers, Internat. Soc. Barristers, ABA Found., Tex. Bar Found.; mem. ABA (chmn. antitrust sect. 1989-90), Houston Bar Assn., Assn. Bar City N.Y., Am. Law Inst., Chancellors, Houston Com. Fgn. Rels., Houston Philos. Soc., Philos. Soc. Tex., Am. Bd. Trial Advocates, Century Assn. N.Y.C., Houston Country Club, Rotary Club, Ramada Tex. Club, Eldorado Country Club (Calif.), Castle Pines Golf Club (Castle Rock, Colo.), Cosmos Club of Washington, Galveston Artillery Club, Phi Beta Kappa, Phi Delta Phi. Democrat. Baptist. Office: Vinson & Elkins 2800 First City Tower 1001 Fannin St Houston TX 77002-6760*

REASOR, RODERICK JACKSON, industrial engineer; b. Hampton, Va., Apr. 8, 1953; s. Emmett Jackson and Cora (Keller) R.; m. Anita Marie Knibb, June 29, 1974; children: Rebecca Eileen, Matthew Ryan, Christopher James, Laura Kathleen. BS, Va. Poly. Inst. & State U., 1976, MS, 1981, PhD in Indsl. Engring. and Ops. Rsch., 1990. Registered profl. engr., Va. Indsl. engr. Tenn. Eastman Co., Kingsport, Tenn., 1977-83; program mgr. Mgmt. Systems Labs., Blacksburg, Va., 1983-86; instr. IEOR Va. Poly. Inst. & State U., Blacksburg, 1986-89, asst. prof. indsl. and systems engring., dir. lab., 1989-95; prin. indsl. engr. Eastman Chem. Co., Kingsport, Tenn., 1995—; mem. FE MPH com. Nat. Coun. Examiners for Engring. and Surveying, 1996; cons. in field. Author: (with others) Occupational Ergonomics, 1995; referee jours.; contbr. articles to proceedings. Deacon, elder 1st Christian Ch., Kingsport, Tenn., 1979-83, vice chmn. bd., 1982, sec. bd., 1981, bible sch. supt., 1982-83, chmn. coms., 1979-83, 97—; vol. econ. discussion series for high sch. srs. Kingsport (Tenn.) C. of C., 1983; judge annual product fair Jr. Achievement Kingsport, 1983; vice chmn. bd. Blacksburg Christian Ch., 1985-88, elder, 1988-95, treas., 1989-90, chmn. bd., 1991-92; bd. dirs. Woodbine Homes Assn., Blacksburg, 1990-91, v.p., 1991-92, pres., 1992-93; bd. dirs. Kingsport Youth Soccer Assn., 1997—. Grantee ITT Teves, 1991-92, NSF, 1991-93, Computer Aided Mfg. Internat., 1991-92, Barden corp., 1989-90, Aluminum Co. Am., 1984-85. Mem. Am. Soc. Engring. Edn. (sec.-treas. 1991-92, editor newsletter 1992-93, program chmn. 1993-94, chmn. indsl. engring. divsn. 1994-95), Inst. Indsl. Engrs. (sr., pres. Tri-Cities Tenn. chpt. 1979-83, Award of Excellence 1983, adv. bd. chmn., dir., program chmn. 1985-89, Pride award 1988, bd. dirs. 1988-89, chpt. devel. chmn. 1990-93, asst. dir. dist. III 1990-92, Excellence award 1990, 91), Coll. Industry Coun. Material Handling Edn. (chmn. acad. programs and activities com. 1994-95, adv. bd. 1994-95), Inst. Ops. Rsch. and Mgmt. Scis. (session chmn. fall ann. meeting 1989), Kiwanis (pub. affairs com. 1982-83), Alpha Pi Mu. Home: 1104 Hillsboro Cir Kingsport TN 37660 Office: Eastman Chem Co PO Box 1973 Kingsport TN 37662

REAVES, FRANKLIN C., secondary school educator; b. Mullins, S.C., Aug. 7, 1942; s. Fred and Vestena (Nance) Reaves; m. Algenia Reaves; children: Kathy J., Jacquelyn C., Frankie D., Anthony, Ron, Randy, Dexter, Brandon. BS, Fayetteville (N.C.) State U., 1968; MS, N.C. A&T State U., 1974, N.C. A&T State U., 1982; PhD, U. Santa Barbara, Calif., 1990. Cert. Am. history tchr., adminstr., career edn., N.C. Lectr. Columbus County Schs., Whiteville, N.C. Pastor St. Mary African Meth. Episcopal Ch., Marion S.C. Mem. NEA, ASCD, N.C. Assn. Educators (pres. Columbus County), N.C. Assn. Edn. (black caucus), Nat. Vocat. Assn., N.C. Vocat. Assn., Internat. Platform Assn., Operation Help the Econ. Linkage of the

Poor (nat. pres.), Marion County Concern Citizens Movement (chmn.). Home: PO Box 534 Mullins SC 29574-0534

REAVLEY, THOMAS MORROW, federal judge; b. Quitman, Tex., June 21, 1921; s. Thomas Mark and Mattie (Morrow) R.; m. Florence Montgomery Wilson, July 24, 1943; children—Thomas Wilson, Marian, Paul Stuart, Margaret. B.A., U. Tex., 1942; J.D., Harvard, 1948; LL.D., Austin Coll., 1974, Southwestern U., 1977, Tex. Wesleyan, 1982; LL.M., U. Va., 1983; LLD, Pepperdine U., 1993. Bar: Tex. 1948. Asst. dist. atty. Dallas, 1948-49; mem. firm Bell & Reavley, Nacogdoches, Tex., 1949-51; county atty. Nacogdoches, 1951; with Collins, Garrison, Renfro & Zeleskey, 1951-52; mem. firm Fisher, Tonahill & Reavley, Jasper, Tex., 1952-55; sec. state Tex., 1955-57; mem. firm Powell, Rauhut, McGinnis & Reavley, Austin, Tex., 1957-64; dist. judge Austin, 1964-68; justice Supreme Ct., Tex., 1968-77; counsel Scott & Douglass, 1977-79; judge U.S. Ct. Appeals (5th cir.), Austin, 1979-90; now sr. judge U.S. Ct. Appeals (5th cir.), Austin, TX, 1990—; lectr. Baylor U. Law Sch., 1976-94; adj. prof. U. Tex. Law Sch., 1958-59, 78-79, 88-95. Chancellor S.W. Tex. conf. United Meth. Ch., 1972-93, chancellor emeritus, 1993—. Lt. USNR, 1943-45. Club: Mason (33 deg.). Home: 24 Woodstone Sq Austin TX 78703-1159 Office: US Ct Appeals 903 San Jacinto Blvd # 434 Austin TX 78701-2450*

REBIK, JAMES MICHAEL, otolaryngologist; b. Marshalltown, Iowa, July 10, 1953; s. Hubert James and Donna Jean (Grandgeorge) R.; m. Sue Ellyn Primmer, Dec. 22, 1979; children: Christopher James, Kristin Leigh, Robert James, Jonathan Michael. BA summa cum laude, U. No. Iowa, 1981; DO, Kirksville Coll. Osteo. Med., 1985. Diplomate in otorhinolaryngology and facial plastic surgery Am. Osteo. Bd. Ophthalmology and Otorhinolaryngology; diplomate Nat. Bd. Med. Examiners for Osteo. Physicians and Surgeons; lic. physician, Mo., Iowa, Minn., Tex. Intern Kirksville (Mo.) Osteo Med. Ctr., 1985-86, resident otorhinolaryngology/oro-facial plastic surgery, 1986-90; otolaryngologist Landstuhl (Germany) Army Regional Med. Ctr., 1990-92; chief otolaryngology-head and neck surgery svc. Reynolds Army Community Hosp., Ft. Sill, Okla., 1992-94; with Primary Med. Clinic, Midland, Tex., 1996—. Maj. M.C. U.S. Army, 1990-94. Recipient 1st degree brown belt Gup U.S. Tang Soo Do Moo Duk Kwan Fedn., 1979. Fellow Soc. Mil. Otolaryngologists; mem. AMA, Am. Osteo. Assn., Am. Coll. Ophthalmology and Otolaryngology-Head and Neck Surgery, Assn. Mil. Surgeons U.S., Am. Acad. Otolaryngic Allergy, Am. Acad. Otolaryngology-Head and Neck Surgery, Christian Soc. Otolaryngology-Head and Neck Surgery, Freeborn County Med Soc., Minn. Med. Assn., Pan-Am. Assn. Otorhinolaryngology-Head and Neck Surgery, Tex. Osteo. Med. Assn., Tex. Med. Found., Mensa. Baptist. Home: 7005 Chadwick Ct Midland TX 79707 Office: Westwood Profl Bldg 4214 Andrews Hwy Ste 100 Midland TX 79703

RECTOR, CLARK ELLSWORTH, advertising executive; b. Pilot Mound, Iowa, Apr. 3, 1934; s. Guy Charles and Hazel Catherine (Forney) R.; m. Suzanne Swayze, Aug. 21, 1956; children: Clark Ellsworth, Jr., Leigh Ann, Curtis Allen. BA, Puget Sound, 1959; postgrad., Pacific Luth., 1961-62. Pres. Clark Rector & Assoc., Inc., Austin, Tex., 1967—; chmn. Rector-Duncan Advt., Inc., Austin, 1970—, The Market Builders, Austin, 1985—; trustee Nat. Sales & Mktg. Coun., Washington, 1980—, Inst. Residential Mktg., Washington, 1980-83, pres., 1983. Contbr. articles to profl. jours. Commr. Austin Housing Authority, 1973-77; dir. N.W. Austin Civic Assn., 1974-76; state committeeman Rep. Party of Tex., 1974-76; adv. coun. Small Bus. Adminstrn., San Antonio, 1972-76. With U.S. Army, 1952-55. Mem. Nat. Assn. Home Builders (Bill Molster award 1984), Sigma Chi. Republican. Methodist. Home: 3809 Woodbrook Cir Austin TX 78759-8226

RECTOR, JOHN MICHAEL, lawyer, association executive; b. Seattle, Aug. 15, 1943; s. Michael Robert and Bernice Jane (Allison) R.; m. Mary Kaaren Sueta Jolly, Feb. 8, 1977 (div. 1995). BA, U. Calif., Berkeley, 1966; JD, U. Calif., Hastings, 1969; PharmD (hon.), Ark. State Bd. Pharmacy, 1991. Bar: Calif. 1970, U.S. Supreme Ct. 1974. Trial atty. civil rights div. Dept. Justice, 1969-71; dep. chief counsel judiciary com. U.S. Senate, 1971-73, counsel to Sen. Birch Bayh, 1971-77, chief counsel, staff dir., 1973-77; confirmed by U.S. Senate as assoc. adminstr. to Law Enforcement Assistance Adminstn. and adminstr. of Office Juvenile Justice Dept. Justice, 1977-79; spl. counsel to U.S. Atty. Gen., 1979-80; dir. govt. affairs Nat. Assn. Retail Druggists, Washington, 1980-85; sr. v.p. govt. affairs, gen. counsel Nat. Assn. Retail Druggists, 1986—; chmn. adv. bd. Nat. Juvenile Law Center, 1973-77; mem. Hew panel Drug Use and Criminal Behavior, 1974-77; mem. cons. panel Nat. Commn. Protection Human Subjects of Biomed. and Behavioral Research, 1975-76; mem. bd. Nat. Inst. Corrections, 1977-79; chmn. U.S. Interdepartmental Council Juvenile Justice, 1977-79; mem. bd. com. civil rights and liberties Am. Democratic Action, 1976-80, Pres.'s Com. Mental Health-Justice Group, 1978; com. youth citizenship ABA, 1978-84; mem. Pharm. Industry Adv. Com.; exec. dir., treas. polit. action com. Nat. Pharmacists Assn., 1981—; exec. dir. Retail Druggist Legal Legis. Def. Fund, 1985—, founder, chmn. Washington Pharmacy Industry Forum; mem. numerous fed. narcotic and crime panels and coms.; owner Second Genesis, an antique and furniture restoration co. Mem. editorial bd. Managed Care Law; contbr. articles to profl. jours. Exec. com. small bus. and fin. couns. Dem. Nat. Com.; dir. Dem. Leadership Coun.'s Network, 1989—, bd. advisers, 1992—, Clinton-Gore Washington Bus. adv. com.; bd. dirs. Small Bus. Legis. Coun., 1987—; bd. dirs. Nat. Bus. Coalition for Fair Competition, 1984—. Perry E. Towne scholar, 1966-67; mem. U.S. Atty. Gen.'s Honors Program, 1968-71; recipient Children's Express Juvenile Justice award, 1981. Mem. Calif. Bar Assn., Nat. Health Lawyers Assn., Am. Soc. Assn. Execs. (govt. affrs sect.), Washington Coun. Lawyers, Assn. of Former Senior Senate Aides, Vinifera Wine Growers Assn. Va. (life), Health R Us, Am. League of Lobbyists, Theta Chi. Democrat. Home: 205 Daingerfield Rd Alexandria VA 22314 Office: Nat Assn Retail Druggists 205 Daingerfield Rd Alexandria VA 22314-2833

REDD, MARY ALLEN, writer educator; b. Provo, Utah, Feb. 28, 1939; d. Mark Knight and Phyllis (Sloan) Allen; m. Robert Redd, Jan. 1, 1991. BA, Brigham Young U., 1962, MA, 1963; PhD, U. Md., 1973. Copy editor Harcourt Brace Pub. Co., N.Y.C., 1965-66; asst. prof. Howard U., Washington, 1973-79; lectr. No. Va. C.C., Alexandria, 1979—, George Mason U., Fairfax, Va., 1982—; tech. writer, editor Advanced Tech., Reston, Va., 1980-82; adj. assoc. prof. U. Md., College Park, 1987—. Author: The World of Holly Prickle, 1993, Animals in American Literature, 1983, The Necessary Blankness: Women in Major American Fiction of the Sixties, 1976. Sponsor Childreach, Warwick, R.I., 1988—. Home: 3151 Lindenwood Ln Fairfax VA 22031-1915

REDDICK, W(ALKER) HOMER, social worker; b. River Junction, Fla., Mar. 26, 1922; s. Walker H. and Lillian (Anderson) R.; B.S., Fla. State U., 1951, M.S.W., 1957; m. Anne Elizabeth Hardwick, Sept. 7, 1947; children—Walker Homer, Andy Hardwick (dec.). Chief juvenile probation officer Muscogee County Juvenile Ct., Columbus, Ga., 1952-53; sr. child welfare worker Floyd County Dept. Pub. Welfare, Rome, Ga., 1955-56; chief social worker Montgomery County Dept. Pub. Health, Montgomery, Ala., 1957-59; dir. social services Ala. Bapt. Children's Home, Troy, 1959-64; casework supr. Youth Devel. Center, Milledgeville, Ga., 1964-71; dir. Family Counseling Center, Macon, Ga., 1972-81; cons. Appleton Ch. Home for Girls Group Homes, Macon, 1974-81; community columnist Macon (Ga.) Telegraph, 1980-81. Pres. Council Service Agys., Macon, 1975. Mem. Ala. State Adv. Com. on Children and Youth, 1961-64. Bd. dirs. Middle Ga. Drug Council. Served with AUS, 1940-43. Licensed marriage and family counselor, Ga. Fellow Royal Soc. Health; mem. Nat. Am. Legion, Assn. Social Workers (charter; bd. mem.-at-large Ga. chpt.), Acad. Cert. Social Workers, Am. Assn. Marriage and Family Therapists, Transactional Analysis Study Group of Macon (dir. 1974), DAV, 121st Inf. Assn. (historian 1981—, pres. 1990), Masons. Episcopalian. Editor: The History of the 121st Infantry Regiment Through 1946, The 121st Infantry Regiment Association Into 1990, 1990; contbr. articles to profl. jours. Address: 2485 Kingsley Dr Macon GA 31204-1718

REDDING, G.A., researcher; b. Ft. Crook, Nebr., Feb. 10, 1946; s. George Andrew and Arian Elizabeth (Salman) R.; m. Katherine Elaine Jones, Aug. 6, 1979 (div. June 1983). BA in Mass Comm. and Journalism, U. Denver, 1969; MS in Radio and TV Prodn., Butler U., 1975; MS in Bus. Adminstrn., Ind. State U., 1976. Commd. U.S. Army, 1969, advanced through grades to lt. col., ret., 1990; asst. bur. chief Mil. Press Bur., Multinat. Force and Observers, Sinai, Egypt, 1982-83; exec. officer U.S. Army Audiovisual Ctr., Washington, 1983-85; chief support divsn. Office of the Sec. of Def., Pentagon, Washington, 1985-87, chief resources divsn., 1987-90; adj. staff rschr. Inst. for Def. Analyses, McLean, Va., 1990—. Mem. DAV, Am. Interactive Media Assn. (charter mem.), Interactive Multimedia Assn., Broadcast Edn. Assn., Armed Forces Broadcasts Assn., Radio-TV News Dirs. Assn., Sigma Delta Chi.

REDDING, JOHN ARTHUR, JR., textile manufacturing executive; b. Winston-Salem, N.C., Jan. 27, 1953; s. John Arthur and Wanda Lou (Pegram) R.; m. Martha Ann Young, May 31, 1975; children: Sarah Ann, Laura Blair. BS in Textile Tech., N.C. State U., 1975. Mgmt. trainee Kendall Co., Pelzer, S.C., 1975-76; planner Kendall Co., Lumberton, N.C., 1976-78; sr. indsl. engr. Kendall Co., Franklin, Ky., 1978-81; indsl. engr. mgr. Kayser Roth Corp.-No Nonsense, Lumberton, 1981-83; div. staff indsl. engr. Kayser Roth Corp.-No Nonsense, Greensboro, N.C., 1983-84; dir. indsl. engring. Kayser Roth Corp.-Socks, Greensboro, N.C., 1984-86; dir. tech. Kayser Roth Corp.-Socks, Greensboro, 1986-88, dir. planning, 1988-90; v.p. mfg. svcs. Chipman-Union, Inc., Union Point, Ga., 1990—. Mem. Jaycees, Bowling Green, Ky., 1980-81. Mem. Inst. Indsl. Engrs. (sr.), Nat. Assn. Hosiery Mfrs., Ga. Textile Mfrs. Assn., Am. Assn. Textile Chemists and Colorists, Oconee County Civitan Club. Republican. Methodist. Home: 1010 Rossiter Ter Watkinsville GA 30677-5123 Office: Chipman Union Inc 500 Sibley Ave Union Point GA 30669-1138

REDDING, MARSHALL SIMMS, ophthalmologist; b. Greensboro, N.C., Oct. 14, 1934; s. Herbert Monroe and Ernestine Ida (Fulgham) R.; m. Bobbie Newman (div.); children: Joan Lucille, Rebecca Marie; m. Alice Meads, Dec. 14, 1985. BA, Duke U., 1958, MD, 1966. Intern Portsmouth (Va.) Naval Hosp., 1966-67; resident U.S. Naval Hosp., Phila., 1967-70, Wills Eye Hosp., Phila., 1969-70; staff ophthalmologist U.S. Navy M.C., Long Beach, Calif., 1970-71, Albemarle Hosp., Elizabeth City, N.C., 1971—, Sentara Norfolk (Va.) Gen. Hosp., Sentara Leigh Meml. Hosp, 1987—; med. examiner FAA, 1976—. Trustee Albemarle Hosp., 1974-85, chmn. bd., 1979-85. Capt. USNR ret. Fellow ACS, Am. Acad. Ophthalmology, Am. Coll. Eye Surgeons; mem. AMA (Physician's Recognition award 1971—), Am. Bd. Eye Surgeons, Am. Intraocular Implant Soc., Am. Soc. Cataract and Refractive Surgery, Am. Soc. Clin. Hypnosis, N.C. Med. Soc. (pres. 1982-83), N.C. Coll. Clin. Hypnosis, N.C. Soc. Ophthalmology (pres. 1981-82), Pasquotank-Camden-Currituck-Dare Med. Soc., So. Med. Assn., Lion's Club, Rotary Club. Office: St Luke's Inst Eye Surgery Halifax Bldg 6161 Kempsville Cir Ste 130 Norfolk VA 23502

REDDY, CHANDRASEKHARA K., agronomy educator; b. Annareddipalem, India, July 1, 1953; came to U.S., 1979; s. Rami K. and Mahalaxmi (Menakuru) R.; m. Indravathi Battula, Dec. 13, 1978; children: Ajay, Ashrit. BSc, Andhra Pradesh Agri. U., India, 1974, MSc in Agronomy, 1977; PhD in Agronomy, U. Fla., 1982. Rsch. fellow ICRISAT, Hyderabad, India, 1977-78; rsch. agronomist U. Fla., Gainesville, 1981-83; asst. prof. agronomy Ala. A&M U., Huntsville, 1983-89, assoc. prof., 1989-94, prof., 1994—; organizer workshops. Author: Alternative Production Strategies for Millet and Cowpea in Rainfed Agriculture in Niger, 1988; (with others) Field Experimentation, 1988; contbr. articles to profl. jours. and reports. Recipient Meritorious Svc. cert. Niger Nat. Agrl. Rsch. Inst., 1990, Meritorious Svc. award Govt. of Niger, 1992, Outstanding Rschr. award Ala. A&M U., 1994. Mem. Am. Soc. Agronomy, Internat. Soil Sci. Soc., Assn. Farming Systems Rsch., West African Farming Systems Network. Office: Ala A&M U Meridian St Huntsville AL 35762

REDDY, GOPAL BAIREDDY, engineering educator; b. Palwai, India, May 11, 1950; came to U.S., 1974; s. B. Soogi and B. Govindamma Reddy; m. Shanti Baireddy, June 27, 1981; children: Kasthuri, Madhuri, Sumana, Bhargava. BE, Osmania U., Hyderabad, India, 1974; MS, Tex. Tech. U., 1976; PhD, N.C. State U., 1986. Lectr. U. N.C., Charlotte, 1976-78, 81-83; pool officer Coun. Sci. and Indsl. Rsch., Hyderabad, 1980-81; asst. prof. Fairleigh Dickinson U., Teaneck, N.J., 1986-90, Trenton (N.J.) State Coll., 1990-91; assoc. prof. U. Houston, 1991—; cons. in field. Contbr. articles to Internat. Jour. Heat and Mass Transfer, Internat. Jour. Energy Rsch., Computers in Edn., Internat. Jour. Ambient Energy. Mem. ASME (dir. coll. rels. 1987-90, Outstanding Contribution award 1989), Am. Soc. Engring. Edn. (Outstanding Campus Rep award 1989), Soc. Mfg. Engring., Tau Beta Pi. Home: 35 Fernglen Dr The Woodlands TX 77380-1557 Office: U Houston College Park Houston TX 77204-4083

REDDY, PAUL W., accountant; b. Dallas, Aug. 15, 1940; s. Paul and Aubyn (Jones) R.; m. Pamela Sue Buffington, Oct. 1966; children: Carole Ann, Bradford Paul. BBA, Baylor U., 1963. CPA. With KPMG Peat Marwick, San Antonio, 1964—, ptnr.-in-chg. tax, 1971-78, mng. ptnr., 1978—. Chmn. bd. NCCJ, 1984; pres., chmn. bd. Jr. Achievement South Tex., 1984, San Antonio Festival, 1982; chmn. adv. coun. St. Mary's U. Sch. Bus., 1988-91; mem. adv. coun. U. Tex. Sch. Bus., San Antonio, 1988-90; mem. M Taxation adv. coun. Baylor U., 1985-93. Sgt. USAFR, 1963-69. Mem. AICPA, Tex. Soc. CPA's, San Antonio Soc. CPA's, Ins. Acctg. & Statis. Assn. Republican. Episcopalian. Home: 15634 Mission Crest San Antonio TX 78232-3452 Office: KPMG Peat Marwick 112 E Pecan St Ste 2400 San Antonio TX 78205-1528

REDDY, THIKKAVARAPU AGAMI, mechanical engineer, educator, researcher; b. Nellore, India, Aug. 26, 1953; came to U.S., 1988; s. T. Dayakar and T. Mahalakshmi Reddy; m. Shobha Kamineni, Aug. 13, 1978; children: Agaja, Satyajit. BSME, Inst. Engrs., India, 1978; PhD, U. Perpignan, France, 1982. Rsch. assoc. field rsch. unit Tata Energy Rsch. Inst., Pondicherry, India, 1977-80; affiliated faculty, rsch. engr. II div. energy tech. Asian Inst. Tech., Bangkok, 1983-85, asst. prof. div. energy tech., 1985-86; vis. scientist applied solar calculations unit Blaustein Inst., Inst. for Desert Rsch., Sede Boqer, Israel, 1987; rsch. staff Ctr. for Energy and Environ. Studies Princeton (N.J.) U., 1988-91, lectr. dept. mech. and aerospace, 1989-91; asst. dir. energy systems lab. Tex. A&M U., College Station, 1991—, vis. faculty dept. mech. engring., 1991—; lectr. in field. Author: Design and Sizing of Active Solar Thermal Systems, 1987, (chpt.) Solar Supplemented Convective Drying Systems, 1986, Solar Thermal Systems, 1994; editor: Solar Thermal Components and Systems Testing, 1986; contbr. articles to profl. jours. Recipient scholarship U. Perpignan, 1975-76. Mem. ASHRAE, ASME, Instn. Engrs. (assoc., chartered engr.), Solar Energy Soc. India, Internat. Solar Energy Soc. Office: Tex A&M Univ Dept Mech Engring College Station TX 77843

REDDY, THIKKAVARAPU RAMACHANDRA, electrical engineer; b. Nellore, India, June 4, 1944; came to the U.S., 1979; s. Thikkavarapu Kota and Saraswathi T. (Sivareddy) R.; m. Padmavathi Reddy Kakuturu Thikkavarapu, Aug. 17, 1973; children: Lavanya T., Samatha T. BSEE, Osmania U., 1968; diploma in computer sci., Coll. Engring., Madras, India, 1978. Cert. profl. engr., chartered engr. Supervising engr. APSE Bd., Hyderabad, India, 1969-79; elec. design engr. Sargent & Lundy, Chgo., 1979-80; engr. Bechtel Corp., San Francisco, 1980-82; supr. Bechtel Corp., Athens, Ala., 1989-92; sr. project engr. EGS, Inc., Huntsville, Ala., 1983-84; sr. start-up engr. Gilbert Commonwealth Co., Reading, Pa., 1984-86; cons. Quantum Resources, Decatur, Ala., 1986-87; prin. engr. Ebasco Svcs. Inc., N.Y.C., 1987-89; pres. LSP Internat. Inc., Huntsville, 1992—; guest lectr. gen. interest and wide range of engring. issues. Author: Qualification of Electrical Distribution Components, 1984, Thermal Aging Techniques of Organic Materials, 1984, and others; contbr. articles to profl. jours.; guest lectr. on wide range of engring. issues. Mem. NSPE (Outstanding Profl. award 1991, Profl. Engr. of Yr. award 1996), IEEE (Meritorious Svc. award 1985), Commonwealth Engrs. Coun., Project Mgmt. Inst., Am. Telugu Assn. (life), Telugu Assn. N.Am. (life), Internat. Platform Assn., C. of C. Home: 1213 Willowbrook Dr SE Apt 7 Huntsville AL 35802-3800

REDDY, YENEMALA JAYSIMHA, mechanical engineer; b. Andhra Pradesh, India, May 17, 1968; came to U.S., 1975; s. Yenemala Ramachandra and Yenemala (Uma) R. B in Mech. Engring., Ga. Inst. Tech., 1991. Cert. engr.-in-tng., Ga. Machinist R-B Pump Inc., Baxley, Ga., 1984-85, draftsman, 1985-88, product devel. engr., 1988—, adminstr. govt. contracts, 1988—, test engr., 1988—, v.p., 1992—. Mem. ASME, NSPE, Lions Club (Rookie of Yr. 1992). Republican. Mem. Christian Ch. Office: R-B Pump Inc PO Box 557 # 1 Dixie Dr Baxley GA 31513

REDER, ELIZABETH ANN, elementary school educator; b. Cin., Jan. 26, 1972; d. Norbert Joseph Jr. and Carole Ann (Block) R. Student, Furman U., 1990-92, U. S.C., Spartanburg, 1992; BS in Elem. Edn. summa cum laude, Auburn U., 1994. Cert. elem. tchr., Ala. 4th grade tchr. St. Joseph Cath. Sch., Tuskegee, Ala., 1994—; Mem. Nat. Coun. Tchrs. Math., Nat. Coun. Social Studies, Phi Kappa Phi. Roman Catholic. Home: 2135 Springwood Dr Auburn AL 36830 Office: St Joseph Cath Sch 2009 Montgomery Rd Tuskegee AL 36088

REDMON, AGILE HUGH, JR., allergist; b. Galveston, Tex., Dec. 17, 1924; s. Agile H. and Natalie Mary (Collins) R.; m. Dora Mary Bastiani, May 18, 1957; children—James Joseph, John Gerard. Student Tex. A&M U., 1942-43, U. Southwestern La., 1943-44; M.D., Baylor U., 1948. Diplomate Am. Bd. Allergy and Immunology. Intern U.S. Naval Hosp., San Diego, 1948-49; resident in allergy, 1955-56; resident in internal medicine Baylor/VA Hosp., Houston, 1950-53; assoc. prof. medicine Baylor U., Houston, 1957—; sr. ptnr. Allergy Asthma Assocs., Houston, 1970—. Served with M.C., USN, 1943-48, 53-57. Fellow Am. Acad. Allergy and Immunology (chmn. council local soc. pres.'s); mem. AMA, Tex. Med. Assn., Harris County Med. Soc. (v.p. 1984), Tex. Allergy Soc. (pres. 1984-88), Houston Allergy Soc. (past pres.). Republican. Roman Catholic. Home: 5223 Contour Pl Houston TX 77096-4117 Office: 7505 Fannin St Ste 515 Houston TX 77054-1913

REDMOND, ROBERT, lawyer, educator; b. Astoria, N.Y., June 18, 1934; s. George and Virginia (Greene) R.; m. Georgine Marie Richardson, May 21, 1966; children—Kelly Anne, Kimberly Marie, Christopher Robert. B.A., Queens Coll., 1955; M.Pub.Adminstrn., CUNY, 1962; J.D., Georgetown U., 1970. Bar: D.C. 1971, Va. 1974, U.S. Supreme Ct. 1974. Commd. 2d lt. U.S. Air Force, 1955, advanced through grades to lt. col., 1972, ret., 1978; served as spl. investigations officer, Korea, Vietnam, W.Germany; adj. prof., acad. dir. mil. dist. Washington resident ctr. Park Coll., Parkville, Mo., 1977—; sole practice, Falls Church, Va., 1980—. Precinct capt. Fairfax County Rep. Party (Va.), 1981-87; pres. PTO, Falls Church, 1984-86; treas. Fedn. Cath. Schs. PTO, 1986-87; bd. dirs. Chaconas Home Owners Assn., 1984—, Social Ctr. Psychiat. Rehab., 1987-93. Mem. Assn. Trial Lawyers Am., Va. Trial Lawyers Assn., Fairfax Bar Assn., Assn. Former Air Force Office of Spl. Investigations Agts. (chpt. pres. 1984-86, nat. membership com. 1986—), Comml. Law League, Delta Theta Phi. Roman Catholic. Lodge: K.C. (4th deg.). Home: 7802 Antiopi St Annandale VA 22003-1405 Office: Ste 900-N 7799 Leesburg Pike Falls Church VA 22043-2413

REDRUELLO, ROSA INCHAUSTEGUI, municipal official; b. Havana, Cuba, Dec. 6, 1951; came to U.S., 1961, naturalized, 1971; d. Julio Lorenzo and Laudelina (Vazquez) Inchaustegui; m. John Robert Redruello, Dec. 14, 1972; 1 child, Michelle. AA, Miami-Dade Community Coll., 1972; BS, Fla. Internat. U., 1974. Cert. systems profl. With Fla. Power & Light Co., Miami, 1975-81, records analyst, 1981-84, sr. records analyst, 1984-87, office mgr. Miami Beach Sanitation Dept., 1987—; exec. Mcpl. Dept., 1986-89; police officer patrol divsn. Miami Police Dept., 1989-91, narcotics divsn., 1991—; mem. spl. task force Drug Enforcement Adminstrn. HDTA Group 1, 1994-96; cons. United Bus. Records, Miami, 1985—. Editor South Fla. Record newsletter, 1983-86; editor, producer Files Mgmt. video tape, 1984-85. Rotary Club scholar, 1970. Mem. Assn. Records Mgrs. and Adminstrs. (chpt. chmn. bd. 1985—, chpt. mem. of yr. 1985), Assn. for Info. and Image Mgmt., Exec. Female, Nuclear Info. and Records Mgmt. Assn. (Appreciation award 1985). Republican. Roman Catholic. Avocations: swimming, jazzercise, reading. Office: Miami Beach Police Dept 1100 Washington Ave Miami FL 33139-4612

REECE, MARILYN KING, college dean; b. Cullman, Ala., July 7, 1949; d. John McCarley and Florence Augusta (Freeman) King; m. John Robert Williamson, Aug. 23, 1970 (div. 1987); children: Joan King, Rachel King; m. David Ronald Reece, Apr. 15, 1995. BA, U. Ala., Tuscaloosa, 1971, MA, 1972. Instr. English, N.E. Ala. C.C., Rainsville, 1973-89, dean extended day, 1989—. Mem. MLA, NEA, Nat. Coun. Tchrs. English, Conf. on Coll. Composition and Comm., Ala. Assn. for Women in Edn. Democrat. Office: NE Ala CC PO Box 159 Rainsville AL 35986-0159

REED, ALFRED DOUGLAS, university director; b. Bristol, Tenn., July 18, 1928; s. Roy Theodore and Elizabeth Brown (Tuft) R.; m. Emily Joyce Freeman, Mar. 18, 1950; children: Roy Frederick, Robert Douglas, David Clark, Timothy Wayne, Joseph William. AB, Erskine Coll., Due West, S.C., 1949. Reporter Citizen-Times, Asheville, N.C., 1949-51, city editor, 1953-60, mng. editor, 1962-63, assoc. editor, 1963-66, capital corr., 1959-66; asst. editor The Presbyn. Jour., Weaverville, N.C., 1951-52; assoc. editor Shelby (N.C.) Daily Star, 1961-62; dir. pub. info. Western Carolina U., Cullowhee, N.C., 1966-96, asst. to the chancellor, 1996—; cons. Devel. Office, East Carolina U., Greenville, 1980; bd. dirs. Wachovia Bank and Trust Co., Sylva, N.C., 1969—. Author: Prologue, 1968, Decade of Development, 1984, Our Second Century, 1992, Fulfillment of Promise, 1994; exec. editor: Western, The Mag. of Western Carolina University, 1991-96. Mem. Asheville City Bd. Edn., 1958-62; vice chmn. bd. dirs. Sta. WCQS FM, Western N.C. Pub. Radio Inc., Asheville, 1978-88; bd. dirs. Cherokee Hist. Assn., 1985—, Western N.C. Assn. Comtys., 1985—, Jackson County Fund of N.C. Comty. Found., 1991-93; mem. Hunter Libr. Adv. Bd., 1991—, Pack Place Adv. Coun., Asheville, 1991—. Recipient Paul A. Reid Disting. Svc. award Western Carolina U., 1980, Disting. Svc. award, 1996. Mem. Coun. for Advancement and Support Edn., Pub. Rels. Assn. Western N.C. (bd. dirs., treas.), Coll. News Assn. Carolinas (bd. dirs. 1968-71, 80-82), N.C. Press Assn. (assoc.), Smoky Mountain Host Assn. (bd. dirs., 1st v.p. 1988-96, pres. 1996—). Democrat. Presbyterian. Home: 310 University Hts Cullowhee NC 28723-9691 Office: Western Carolina U Dir Pub Info 528 Robinson Cullowhee NC 28723

REED, CHARLES, mayor; b. Plano, Tex. Oct. 20, 1944; s. Joseph Oscar and Beulah (Robinson) R; m. Sharon Alice Hair, 1978; children: Michael Ray, Suzanne Denise, Robert Patrick. BA, U. Tex., Arlington, 1971. Mayor Waco, Tex, 1990—. Sgt. USAF, 1965-68. Baptist.

REED, CHARLES BASS, academic administrator; b. Harrisburg, Pa., Sept. 29, 1941; s. Samuel Ross and Elizabeth (Johnson) R.; m. Catherine A. Sayers, Aug. 22, 1964; children: Charles B. Jr., Susan Allison. BS, George Washington U., 1963, MA, 1964, EdD, 1970; postgrad. Summer Inst. for Chief State Sch. Officers., Harvard U. Grad Sch. Edn., 1977; D of Pub. Svc. (hon.), George Washington U., 1987; LLD (hon.), Stetson U., 1987; LittD (hon.), Waynesburg Coll., 1988; LHD (hon.), St. Thomas U., 1988. From asst. prof. to assoc. prof. George Washington U., Washington, 1963-70; asst. dir. Nat. Performance-Based Tchr. Edn. Project, Am. Assn. Colls. for Tchr. Edn., Washington, 1970-71; assoc. for planning and coordination Fla. Dept. Edn., Tallahassee, 1971-75, dir. Office Ednl. Planning, Budgeting, and Evaluation, 1975-79; edn. policy coord. Exec. Office of Gov., Tallahassee, 1979-80, dir. legis. affairs, 1980-81, dep. chief of staff, 1981-84, chief of staff, 1984-85; chancellor State Univ. System Fla., Tallahassee, 1985—; Fulbright 50th Anniversary Disting. fellow Peru, 1996; bd. dirs. Fla. Progress Corp., Capital Health Plan; chmn. bd. dirs. Regional Tech. Strategies, Inc. Mem. Coun. for Advancement and Support of Edn., Coun. on Fgn. Rels., Bus.-Higher Edn. Forum, Coun. of 100. Recipient Disting. Alumni award George Washington U., 1987. Mem. Am. Assn. State Colls. and Univs., Am. Assn. for Higher Edn., Am. Coun. on Edn., Fla. Assn. Colls. and Univs., Edn. Commn. of States (exec. com. 1984-87, exec. com. for campus compact project, Disting. Svc. award 1982), So. Regional Ednl. Bd. (vice-chmn. 1988-90, exec. com.), Assn. Governing Bds. of Univs. and Colls., Nat. Assn. Sys. Heads, Golden Key. Democrat. Roman Catholic. Office: State U System Fla Office of Chancellor 325 W Gaines St Tallahassee FL 32399-6557

REED, CHRISTOPHER ROBERT, civil engineer; b. Charleston, W.Va., Feb. 12, 1948; s. Clarence Milton and Anne (Schaffner) R.; m. Mary Dandridge Kennedy, Mar. 4, 1983. Student W.Va. Inst. Tech., 1966-70, 76-77, Ga. State U., 1973-74. Designer, Sverdrup & Parcel, Charleston, 1970-72; assoc. project engr. Mayes, Sudderth & Etheredge, Atlanta, 1973-76; project mgr. Sverdrup & Parcel, Washington, 1976-79; estimator Deleuw, Cather/Parsons, Washington, 1979-80; project mgr. Parsons Brinckerhoff, McLean,

Va., 1980-85; assoc. Loledemian Assocs., Inc., Rockville, Md., 1985-86; assoc. Post Buckley Schuh and Jernigan Inc., Arlington, Va., 1986-89; assoc., dir. mcpl. engring. Loledemian Assocs., Inc., Rockville, 1989-90; mgr. CRS Donohue and Assocs. Inc., Fairfax, Va., 1990-92; asst. dist. location and design engr. VDOT, Fairfax, 1992-95, dist. location and design engr., 1995-96. Mem. Constrn. Specifications I nst., Inst. Transp. Engrs., Am. Assn. Cost Engrs., Am. Ry. Engring. Assn., Soc. Am. Mil. Engrs., Am. Pub. Transit Assn., ASTM, Capital Yacht Club (sec. 1988-89, vice commodore 1990, commodore 1991), Corinthian Yacht Club (fleet capt. 1992, rear commodore, 1993). Home: 320 Culpeper St Warrenton VA 20186-3001 Office: 1601 Orange Rd Culpeper VA 22701

REED, CORY ARTHUR, Spanish literature educator; b. Gloucester, Mass., June 30, 1962; s. Harold E. and Judith E. (Soule) R. AB, Dartmouth Coll., 1984; MA, Princeton U., 1987, PhD, 1989. Asst. prof. Spanish lit. U. Tex., Austin, 1989-95, assoc. prof. Spanish lit., 1995—; cons. various lang. translators, 1989—. Author: (play) When Death Do Us Part, 1981, (book) The Novelist as Playwright, 1993; contbr. articles to profl. jours. Singer, bd. dirs. Austin Choral Union, 1991—. Rsch. grantee U. Rsch. Inst., 1990. Office: U Tex Dept Spanish Batts Hall 110 Austin TX 78703

REED, CYNTHIA KAY, minister; b. Amarillo, Tex., July 10, 1952; d. Carlos Eugene and Marjorie Marie (Daughetee) R. B of Music Edn., McMurry Coll., Abilene, Tex., 1976; MDiv, Perkins Sch. Theol., Dallas, 1991. Ordained to ministry Meth. Ch., 1989; cert. dir. music. Dir. music and Christian edn. Oakwood United Meth. Ch., Lubbock, Tex., 1978-84; dir. music and Christian edn. 1st United Meth. Ch., Childress, Tex., 1976-78, Littlefield, Tex., 1984-86; intern min. 1st United Meth. Ch., Lubbock, 1989-90, assoc. min., 1990-91; min. Meadow and Ropesville United Meth. Chs., 1991-93, Earth (Tex.) United Meth. Ch., 1993—; extern chaplain Meth. Hosp., Lubbock, 1989—, Walk to Emmaus Renewal Movement, Lubbock, 1990—. Com. mem. Life Gift-Organ Donation, Lubbock, 1991; mem. Arthritis Found., Lubbock, 1991. Georgia Harkness scholar Div. Ordained Ministry, 1989. Mem. Christian Educators & Musicians Fellowship, Am. Guild Organists.

REED, DAVID BENSON, bishop; b. Tulsa, Feb. 16, 1927; s. Paul Spencer and Bonnie Frances (Taylor) R.; m. Susan Henry Riggs, Oct. 30, 1954 (div.); children: Mary, Jennifer, David, Sarah, Catherine; m. Catherine Camp Luckett, Apr. 15, 1984. A.B., Harvard U., 1948; M.Div., Va. Theol. Sem., 1951, D.D., 1964; D.D., U. of South, 1972, Episc. Theol. Sem., Ky., 1985. Ordained priest Episcopal Ch., 1952; missionary priest in Panama and Colombia, 1951-58; with Nat. Ch. Exec. Office, 1958-61; mission priest S.D., 1961-63; bishop of Colombia, 1964-72, Ecuador, 1964-70; bishop coadjutor Diocese of Ky., Louisville, 1972-74; bishop of Ky. Diocese of Ky., 1974-94; asst. bishop of Conn. Episcopal Diocese of Conn., Hartford, 1994-95; 1st pres. Anglican Council Latin Am., 1969-72; chmn. standing commn. on ecumenical relations Episcopal Ch., 1979-82; pres. Ky. Coun. Chs., 1988-91; mem. governing bd. Nat. Coun. of Chs. of Christ in U.S.A., 1982-91, mem. exec. com., 1985-91, sec., 1988-91; Anglican co-chmn. Anglican Orthodox Theol. Cons., 1984-94. Bd. dirs. Alliant Health Systems (formerly Norton Kosair Children's Hosp.), Louisville, 1979-94; trustee U. of the South, 1972—, regent, 1979-82; chmn. Louisville United Against Hunger, 1980-84, 86-87; chmn. Presiding Bishop's Com. on Interfaith Rels., 1991—. Mem. Harvard Club of Western Ky. (pres. 1992-94). Democrat. Home: 5226 Moccasin Trl Louisville KY 40207-1634

REED, DIANE GRAY, business information service company executive; b. Trion, Ga., Sept. 5, 1945; d. Harold and Frances (Parker) Gray; m. Harry Reed, Oct. 2, 1982. Student, Jacksonville U., 1963-64, Augusta Coll., 1972-74; BS, Ga. State U., 1981. Various mgmt. positions Equifax Svcs., Inc., Atlanta, 1964-72, field rep., 1972-74, tech. rep., 1974-79, mgr. systems and programs, 1979-84, dir. tech., 1984-86, asst. v.p., 1986—; v.p. info. tech. sector Equifax Svcs., Inc., 1989—; presdl. adv. council Equifax Svcs., Inc., Atlanta, 1984—; cons. Ga. Computer Programmer Project, Atlanta, 1984-86, spkr. Oglethorpe U. Career Workshop, Atlanta, 1986. Bd. dirs. Atlanta Mental Health Assn., 1985-89; bd dirs., pres. Atlanta Women's Network, 1990; bd. dirs. United Way Bd. Bank, Atlanta, 1984-86; chairperson EquiFax United Way Campaign, 1988-89; vol. Cobb County Spl. Olympics, Marietta, Ga., 1984-87; mem. adv. coun. Coll. Bus. Adminstrn. Ga. State U. mgmt. info. systems industry adv. bd. U. Ga.; mem. Leadership Atlanta Class of '92, Girl Scouts Friendship Circle, Friends of Spelman Coll.; vol. coord. Atlanta Partnership Bus. and Edn.; co-chair salute to women of achievement YWCA, 1992; mem. Leadership Am. Class 1994; tech. steering com. 1996 Olympic Games. Named Woman of Achievement, Atlanta YWCA, 1987; recipient Decca award as one of top 10 bus. women in Atlanta, 1992; named to Leadership Am. Class 1994. Mem. Women in Info. Processing, Inst. Computer Profls. (cert.), Soc. Info. Mgmt., Internat. Women's Alliance, Ga. State Alumni, LWV, Atlanta Yacht Club, Kiwanis Internat. (bd. dirs. Atlanta Buckhead chpt.). Office: Equifax Svcs Inc 1600 Peachtree St NW Atlanta GA 30309-2403

REED, ELIZABETH MAY MILLARD, mathematics and computer science educator, publisher; b. Shippensburg, Pa., July 1, 1919; d. Jacob Franklin and Isabelle Bernadine (Dorn) Millard; m. Jesse Floyd Reed, Aug. 5, 1961; 1 child, David Millard. BA, Shepherd Coll., 1941; MA, Columbia U., 1948; postgrad., W.Va. U., U. Hawaii, Columbia U., NSF Summer Insts., Oakland U., 1974-85. Cert. assoc. in tchr. edn., W.Va. Math. tchr. Hedgesville (W.Va.) High Sch., 1941-47, Martinsburg (W.Va.) High Sch., 1948-51, George Washington High Sch. and Territorial Coll. Guam, Agana, 1952-54, Valley Stream (N.Y.) Meml. Jr. High Sch., 1954-55, Rye (N.Y.) High Sch., 1955-57, Elkins (W.Va.) Jr. High Sch., 1971-87; dir. admissions Davis and Elkins Coll., 1957-67, asst. prof. math., 1968-71, adj. prof., 1987—, lectr. geography, 1971-73; pres. Three Reeds Studios, Elkins, 1989—; Vets. Upward Bound, 1989-94; statis. clk. Lord, Abbett & Co., N.Y.C., 1947-48; customer rep. Kay, Richards & Co., Winchester, Va., 1951-52; mem. adj. grad. faculty W.Va. U., Morgantown, 1984-89; mem. adj. faculty Evans Coll. U. Charleston, W.Va., 1989-90; presenter regional and state computer workshops, W.Va. Author: Computer Literacy at Elkins Junior High School, 1983; project dir. (video) Women: Professionally Speaking, 1988. Dir. pilot project Project Bus., Jr. Achievement, Elkins, 1972-78; organizer Randolph County Math. Field Day, Elkins, 1977; initiator Comprehensive Achievement Monitoring, Elkins, 1980; treas. Humanities Found. W.Va., Charleston, 1983-85, pres., 1985-87; vice-moderator quadrant II Presbytery of W.Va. Recipient Presdl. award for Excellence in Tchg. Math. in W.Va., NSF, 1985. Mem. AAUW (pres. W.Va. divsn. 1977-79, editor 1983—, pres. Elkins br. 1966-68, 88-94), W.Va. Coun. Tchrs. of Math., Nat. Coun. Tchrs. of Math., W.Va. Item Writing Workshop-Math. 9-12 (writer 1985-86). Home and Office: 4 Lincoln Ave Elkins WV 26241-3669

REED, GLEN ALFRED, lawyer; b. Memphis, Sept. 24, 1951; s. Thomas Henry and Evelyn Merle (Roddy) R.; m. Edith Jean Renick, June 17, 1972; children: Adam Christopher, Alec Benjamin. BA, U. Tenn., 1972; JD, Yale U., 1976. Bar: Ga. 1976. Project dir. Tenn. Research Coordinating Unit, Knoxville, 1972-73; assoc. Alston Miller & Gaines, Atlanta, 1976-77; assoc. Bordurant Miller Hishon & Stephenson, Atlanta, 1978-81, ptnr., 1981-85; ptnr., King & Spalding, Atlanta, 1985—. Author: Practical Hospital Law, 1979. legal adv. Ga. Gov.'s Commn. on Healthcare, 1994; Gen. counsel Assn. Retarded Citizens-Atlanta, 1979—, pres., 1992-96; vice-chmn. CARE Atlanta adv. bd., 1992-94, chmn., 1994—; v.p. Ga. Network for People with Developmental Disabilities, 1991-92; bd. dirs. Ctrl. Health Ctr., 1989-95, Vis. Nurse Health System, 1991—, chair, 1995—, Sch. Pub. Health Emory U., Atlanta, 1993—. Mem. ABA, Ga. Bar Assn., Acad. Hosp. Attys. (bd. dirs. 1991—, pres.- elect 1996—), Ga. Acad. Hosp. Attys. (pres. 1991-92), Nat. Health Lawyers Assn., Phi Beta Kappa. Methodist. Office: King & Spalding 191 Peachtree St NE Atlanta GA 30303-1740

REED, GUY DEAN, osteopathic physician; b. Kirksville, Mo., Nov. 4, 1922; s. Arthur Guy and Lena (Murphy) R.; m. Elizabeth Marguerite Matheson, Oct. 20, 1957. Student, Wentworth Mil. Acad., 1939-41, Okla. State U., 1941-42, 45-46, Tulane U., 1942-43; DO, Kansas City Coll. Osteo. Medicine, 1949. Diplomate Am. Bd. Family Practice. Intern Okla. Osteo. Hosp., Tulsa, 1949-50; pvt. practice New Lexington, Okla., 1950-55, Newark, Ohio, 1955-57, Tulsa, 1957—, Owasso, Okla., 1958—; staff Tulsa Regional Med. Ctr., 1958-68, Sheridan Village Med. Clinic, Tulsa; pres. Classic Cars, Inc. Served With M.C. AUS, 1942-45. Decorated Silver Star, Bronze Star with oak leaf cluster, Purple Heart. Mem. Am. Bariatrics Assn., Am. Osteopathic Assn., Am. Coll. Gen. Practitioners in Osteopathy and Surgery, Am. Osteo. Assn., Okla. Osteo. Assn., Tulsa Dist. Osteo. Assn., Tulsa Osteo. Assn., Masons. Home: 6775 S Atlanta Ave Tulsa OK 74136-4302 Office: Sheridan Village Med Clinic 6109 E Admiral Pl Tulsa OK 74115-8623

REED, HELEN I., medical, surgical nurse; b. Radford, Va., Aug. 3, 1967; d. Billy Wayne and Beverly Gayle (Sparks) R. Cert. Practical Nursing, Radford City Sch. Nursing, 1986; BSN, Radford U., 1990, postgrad. RN, Va.; cert. med.-surg. nurse ANCC; cert. ACLS provider, CPR instr. Student nurse intern Radford Cmty. Hosp., 1989-90, staff nurse, 1990—; substitute instr. Radford City Sch. Practical Nursing, med. unit continuing edn. coord., preceptor to new staff. Jr. vol. Radford Cmty. Hosp., 1981-85; Sunday sch. tchr., children's sermon leader Meth. Ch. Nette Whitehead nursing scholar, John Nye scholar, jr. vol. scholar. Mem. ANA, NSNA. Methodist. Office: Carilion Radford Cmty Hosp Med Care Unit 700 Randolph St Radford VA 24141-2430

REED, JESSE FLOYD, artist, art educator; b. Belington, W.Va., July 25, 1920; s. Herman Merideth and Desta (Thomas) R.; m. Elizabeth Mae Millard, Aug. 5, 1961; 1 child, David Millard. Student, Grand Ctrl. Art Sch., N.Y.C., 1942, Art Students League, N.Y.C., 1947; BA, Davis and Elkins Coll., 1952; MA, W.Va. U., 1955. Self-employed artist, 1947—; prof. art Davis and Elkins Coll., Elkins, W.Va., 1949—. Exhibited paintings and etchings in numerous shows. Elder, Presbyn. Ch., Elkins, 1992—. Served with U.S. Army, 1942-45. Recipient Merit award W.Va. Dept. Culture and History, 1976, also purchase awards. Mem. Salmagundi Club, Boston Printmakers, Print Club of Albany (Artist of Yr. 1968), W.Va. Watercolor Soc. Republican. Home: 4 Lincoln Ave Elkins WV 26241-3669

REED, JESSE FRANCIS, entrepreneur, artist, inventor, theologian, business consultant; b. Federalsburg, Md., June 6, 1925; s. Homer F. and Lola Irene (Stevens) R.; BFA, Montclair Coll., 1950; DD, Gnostic Sem., 1968; m. Mary Grace Mayo, July 9, 1944; 1 son, Gary. Owner, Reed's Frozen Foods, Paterson, N.J., 1950-59; pres. A.E. Inc., N.Y.C., 1959-72, Intercontinental Bus. Rsch. & Devel. Inc., San Francisco, 1959-72, chmn. bd., pres. Dallas and Washington, 1972—, Intercontinental Oil & Ore Inc., Carson City, Nev. and Dallas, 1972—; chmn. bd., pres. COSMO U.S.A., Inc., Dallas and Washington, 1974—, Internat. Art Exchange Ltd., Dallas and Los Angeles, 1980—; chmn. bd. Gnosis (Self Discovery and Identification Sys.), 1980—. Chmn. bd. Internat. Arts Soc., Inc., Dallas, 1981—; dir. XTR Corp. Bd. dirs. Am. Art Alliance, Inc., Internat. Fine Art, Inc., Worldwide Art Exchange, Inc., IBR&D, Inc. Gnostic Ch. Served with USN, 1942-46. Recipient various Art Show awards in Tex., Calif., N.J., N.Y., Ga., Fla., Wash., Ill., Hawaii, Minn., Nev., N.Mex., Oreg., Mo., Can., Eng., France, Belgium, Norway, Sweden, Denmark, Switzerland, Australia, N.Z. Mem. Screen Writers Guild, Cattlemen's Assn. Inventor protein converter (controlled environ. food prodn. chain), visual edn. system to translate all ednl. disciplines into their pictorial presentations, modular prefabricate bldg. systems, BIO-HAB (a self energizing life-support system employing; bio chemical, wind, solar, voltaic-cell, energy to powerheat-cool and feed humans and animals), solar energy systems, hydroponic systems, plasma energy systems, electric vehicle systems, subliminal learning systems, precious metal recovery/assaying systems, currency system based upon precious metal art creations, estate protection systems, health systems. Office: PO Box 12488 Dallas TX 75225-0488

REED, JOAN-MARIE, special education educator; b. St. Paul, Sept. 8, 1960; d. William Martin Reed and Diana-Marie (Miller) Reed Moss. BA, U. Minn., 1982, BS, 1983; MEd, Tex. Woman's U., 1986. Cert. tchr., Tex. Tchr. emotionally disturbed Birdville Ind. Sch. Dist., Ft. Worth, 1984-86; tchr. emotionally disturbed Goose Creek Ind. Sch. Dist., Baytown, Tex., 1986-92, ctr. leader, 1992-93, dept. chairperson, 1987-91; tchr. emotionally disturbed Conroe (Tex.) Ind. Sch. Dist., 1993-94, Willis (Tex.) Ind. Sch. Dist., 1994-95, Jefferson County Pub. Schs., 1995—; Co-editor: New Teacher Handbook, 1986-87, Behavior Improvement Program Handbook, 1987-88. Mem. NEA, Coun. for Exceptional Children. Congregationalist. Office: Ctrl Lakewood Adolescent Day Treatment Program 1005 Wadsworth Blvd Lakewood CO 80215-5101

REED, JOHN ALTON, lawyer; b. Washington, June 29, 1931; s. John Alton and Emma Powers (Ball) R.; m. Louisa Wardman, June 6, 1953; children: Donna, Joanne, Deborah. AB, Duke U., 1954, LLB, 1956. Bar: Fla. 1956. Assoc. firm Fowler-White, Tampa, Fla., 1956-57; partner firm Rush, Reed & Marshall, Orlando, Fla., 1957-67; judge Fla. 4th Dist. Ct. Appeal, 1967-73, chief judge, 1971-73; judge U.S. Dist. Ct. for Middle Dist. Fla., Orlando, 1973-84; ptnr., chmn. dept. litigation Lowndes, Drosdick, Doster, Kantor & Reed, Orlando, 1985—; mem. com. on standard civil jury instructions Fla. Supreme Ct. Bd. visitors Duke U. Law Sch., 1983—. Mem. Am., Orange County, Fla. bar assns., Am. Judicature Soc. Republican. Episcopalian. Home: 1020 Mayfield Ave Winter Park FL 32789-2613 Office: PO Box 2809 215 N Eola Dr Orlando FL 32802

REED, LEON SAMUEL, policy analyst; b. Warren, Ohio, July 6, 1949; s. Walter Charles and Lois Avalene (Botroff) R. BA in Econs. and Journalism, Antioch Coll., 1971; m. Margaret Smith, Dec. 27, 1975 (div.); m. Lois S. Lembo; children: Samuel Currier, Stephen Walter, Catherine Lois. Project dir. Coun. on Econ. Priorities, N.Y.C. and Washington, 1970-75; sr. mem. profl. staff Joint Com. on Def. Prodn., U.S. Congress, Washington, 1975-77; mem. profl. staff Com. on Banking, Housing and Urban Affairs, U.S. Senate, Washington, 1977-81; analyst TASC, 1981-82, mgr. contingency planning, 1982-85, mgr. indsl. resources dept., 1985-91, dir. indsl. and mfg. scis. div., 1991—; staff writer, photographer Md. Soccer News; bd. dirs. Council on Econ. Priorities, 1971-73; del. White House Conf. on Youth, 1971. Mem. exec. com., Randolph Civic Assn., 1977-83, pres., 1978-80; v.p. North Bethesda Congress of Citizens Assns., 1983-84, pres., 1984-86, sec., 1986-88; mem. Montgomery County Council of Pres., 1982-88, chmn. 1986-87; soccer coach Montgomery Soccer, Inc., 1986—, bd. dir., 1994—. Mem. Disciples of Christ Ch. Co-author: Guide to Corporations, 1973, Report of the National Critical Technologies Panel, 1991; author: Military Maneuvers, 1975, Resource Management: A Historical Perspective, 1988; contbr. Strategic Survey, 1981-82, The American Defense Mobilization Intrastructure, 1983; author numerous congressional and exec. br. reports, mag. and jour. articles.

REED, LOY WAYNE, minister, ministry director; b. Springfield, Mo., June 19, 1948; s. George Wayne and Stella Gertrude (Miller); m. Glenda Ann Shores, Aug. 24, 1968; children: Danna, Dania, Dawn, Diedra. BA in Philosphy, William Jewell Coll., Liberty, Mo., 1970; MDiv, Midwestern Bapt. Theol. Sem., 1978, D of Ministry, 1984. Campus min. Mo. Western Coll., St. Joseph, 1976-77; campus min., adminstr. U. Mo., 1977-80; pastor Harmony Bapt. Ch., Rogersville, Mo., 1980-85; v.p. Mo. Bapt. Convention, Jefferson City, 1986-87; pastor Calvary Bapt. Ch., Columbia, Mo., 1985-91; dir. student ministries Fla. Bapt. Convention, Jacksonville, Fla., 1991—; cons. Reality Enterprises, Jacksonville, 1995—. Contbr. articles to mags. in field. Named Outstanding Young Man Jaycees, 1976, 79, 80. Mem. Nat. Assn. State Student Dirs. Home: 321 Edinburgh Lane Orange Park FL 32073 Office: Fla Bapt Convention 1230 Hendricks Ave Jacksonville FL 32207-8619

REED, MARK LAFAYETTE, III, English literature educator; b. Asheville, N.C., Sept. 26, 1935; s. Mark Lafayette Jr. and Edith (Murphy) Fisher; m. Martha Balch Sibley, Aug. 30, 1958; children: Victoria Fisher Reed Gless, Christina Pickering Reed Dowdy. BA, Yale Coll., 1957; MA, Harvard U., 1958, PhD, 1962. From asst. prof. to prof. U. N.C., Chapel Hill, 1963-71, Lineberger prof. in the humanities, 1986—. Author: Wordsworth: Chronology of Early Years, 1967, Wordsworth: Chronology of Middle Years, 1975; editor: Wordsworth: Thirteen-Book Prelude, 2 vols., 1991; assoc. editor Cornell Wordsworth Series, 1971—; contbr. articles to profl. jours. Bd. advisors Warren Wilson Coll., Swannanoa, N.C., 1976-86; assoc. trustee Wordsworth Trust, Grasmere, Eng., 1975—. Recipient merit award The Asheville Sch., 1985. Mem. MLA, Keats-Shelley Soc., Wordsworth-Coleridge Assn., Elizabethan Club (New Haven, Conn.), Harvard Club (N.Y.C.), Grolier Club (N.Y.C.), Biltmore Forest Country Club. Office: U NC Dept English Chapel Hill NC 27599-3520

REED, TERRY ALLEN, accountant; b. Ft. Payne, Ala., Oct. 13, 1948; s. Carl and Burma (Benefield) R.; B.S. in Acctg., Jacksonville State U., 1971; m. Sharon Elizabeth Phillips, Sept. 11, 1971; children: Allison Elizabeth, Phillip Allen. Staff acct. Goolsby and Walkley, CPAs, Birmingham, Ala., 1971-72; contr. law firm Bradley, Arant, Rose & White, Birmingham, 1972-82; office mgr. firm Haskell Slaughter & Young, Birmingham, 1982-88; adminstrv. dir. Ala. Symphony Assn., 1989-90; gen. mgr. McCain Engring. Co., Inc., 1990-92; contr. Trimmier Law Firm, LLC, Birmingham, 1993-96; contr. Surface Pro Inc., 1996. Treas. Grace United Methodist Ch., Birmingham, 1981-86. Assn. Legal Adminstrs. (Birmingham chpt.). Home: 5724 Overton Rd Birmingham AL 35210-4109 Office: 2109A Lynngate Drive Rd Birmingham AL 35216

REED, VANESSA REGINA, secondary education educator; b. Grenada, Miss., Oct. 4, 1965; d. Willie Mann and Elma Lee (Finley) R. BS in Social Sci. Edn., Miss. Valley State U., 1987; MA in History, Jackson State U., 1988; postgrad., Miss. State U., Meridian, 1991, 92. Cert. tchr. social sci. History tchr. Jackson (Miss.) State U., 1987-88; social studies tchr. Magnolia Mid. Sch., Meridian, 1988-93; U.S. history tchr. Kate Griffin Jr. H.S., Meridian, 1993—. Sunday sch. tchr., dir. children's ch. Mt. Olive Bapt. Ch.; mem. Heroines of Jericho. Mem. Am. Fedn. Tchrs., Sigma Gamma Rho. Democrat. Office: Kate Griffin Jr HS 2814 Davis St Meridian MS 39301-5655

REED, WALTER GEORGE, JR., osteopath; b. Ardmore, Okla., Sept. 10, 1928; s. Walter George and Lillian Dorene (Gee) R.; m. Elaine Carol Collum; children: Jay Walter, David George, Kimberly Sue. BA, Phillips U., 1955; DO, Kansas City Coll. Osteopathy, 1959. Pvt. practice Oklahoma City, 1960-63, Atoka, Okla., 1963-80; flight surgeon USAF, Omaha, 1980-84, Lubbock, Tex., 1984-86; chief med. officer Army Health Clinic, McAlester, Okla., 1986—. Mayor City of Atoka, 1970s; v.p. Atoka Bd. Edn., 1980s. Lt. col. USAF, 1980-86. Mem. Assn. Mil. Osteo. Physicians and Surgeons, Assn. Mil. Surgeons U.S., Masons (32d degree). Mem. First Christian Ch. Home: Rt 3 Box F Mcalester OK 74501 Office: Army Health Clinic Mcalester OK 74501

REEDER, HARRY PAUL, philosophy educator; b. Michigan City, Ind., Dec. 14, 1946; s. George David and Margene Ruth (Draves) R.; m. Donna Kay Berthelemy (div.); m. Meredith Lynn Marble; stepchildren: Lindsay Elizabeth Summersgill, BLythe Faye Summersgill. BA, U. Ill., 1968; MA, U. Waterloo, 1975, PhD, 1977. Asst. prof. U. Tex., Arlington, 1982-86, assoc. prof., 1986—; lectr. Wilfrid Laurier U., Waterloo, Ont., Can., 1978, Nipissing U. Coll., North Bay, Ont., 1979; vis. asst. prof. U. Guelph (Ont.), 1978-80, U. Alberta, Edmonton, Can., 1981-82. Author: Language and Experience, 1984, The Theory and Practice of Husserl's Phenomenology, 1986, The Work of Felix Kaufmann, 1991; co-author: The Literate Mind, 1987, 3d edit., 1990; mem. editl. bd. Orbis Phaenomenologicus; contbr. articles to profl. jours. Rsch. scholar Fritz Thyssen Stifting, 1975-77. Mem. Am. Philos. Assn., Can. Philos. Assn., North Tex. Philos. Assn. (pres. 1988-89), Soc. for Phenomenology and Existential Philosophy, Husserl Circle. Office: U Tex Dept Philosophy PO Box 19527 Arlington TX 76019

REEDER, WILLIAM GLASE, zoologist, museum administrator; b. Los Angeles, Feb. 4, 1929; s. William Hedges and Gladys Ella (Glase) R.; m. Lynn Roseberry Rohrer, Jan. 27, 1951; children: Elisabeth H., Jeffrey W., Heather L., Kathleen A. B.A., UCLA, 1950; M.A., U. Mich., 1953, Ph.D., 1957. Asst. curator ornithology and mammalogy Los Angeles County Mus., 1949-51; vis. asst. prof. zoology UCLA, 1955-56; curatorial asst. Mus. Zoology, U. Mich., 1956-58; asst. prof. zoology U. Wis., Madison, 1958-62, asso. prof., 1962-66, prof., 1966-78; dir. Zool. Mus., 1967-78; prof. zoology, dir. Tex. Meml. Mus., U. Tex., Austin, 1978—. Mem. Am. Soc. Mammalogy, Tex. Antiquities Com. (chmn. 1984—), Soc. Study Evolution, Soc. Systematic Zoology, Am. Arachnological Soc., Am. Assn. Museums, Soc. Vertebrate Paleontology. Home: 7014 Greenshores Dr Austin TX 78730-4307 Office: Tex Meml Mus 2400 Trinity St Austin TX 78705-5730

REEDY, MITSUNO ISHII, artist, painter; b. Furuichi, Osaka, Japan, Jan. 18, 1941; came to U.S., 1961; d. Mitsuyoshi and Teru (Kakehi) I.; m. William Barret Reedy, Apr. 17, 1970 (dec. Apr. 1984); children: Mitsuno Lee, Michele Ann. Student, Laguna Gloria Art Mus. Sch., Austin, Tex., 1976, Elizabeth Ney Mus. Sch., Austin, Tex., 1977-79, Scottsdale (Ariz.) Art Sch., 1992. Author: The Best of Pastel, 1996, The Best of Oil Painting, 1996; works include oil portraits in the State Capitol Rotunda Okla. City, U. Okla. Sch. of Law Courtroom, Greenwood Cultural Ctr., Tulsa; co-translator: How to Talk so Kids will Listen and Listen so Kids will Talk. Mem. Pastel Soc. Am. Democrat. Methodist. Home and Studio: 1701 Denison Dr Norman OK 73069-7491

REEHER, JAMES IRWIN, minister; b. Sharon, Pa., Dec. 6, 1948; s. James William and Lillian (Irwin) R.; m. Marian Powell, Oct. 25, 1969; children: Elizabeth Margret, James Michael. BA, U. Tampa, 1975; MDiv, Emory U., 1978; DD, Boston U., 1989. Ordained to ministry United Ch. Ch., 1978. Min. Christ United Meth. Ch., Tampa, Fla., 1972-75, Lamar United Meth. Ch., Barnesville, Ga., 1975-78, 1st United Meth. Ch., Seffner, Fla., 1986-90; asst. min. Grace United Meth. Ch., Venice, Fla., 1978-79; founding min. 1st United Meth. Ch., Sarasota, Fla., 1980-86; min. Forest Hills United Meth. Ch., Tampa, 1990—; del. bd. ordained ministry Tampa Dist., 1987—; del. stewardship com. Fla. United Meth. Ch., Tampa, 1988—; bd. dirs. Jim Russo Prison Ministries, Bradenton, Fla., 1990—; chmn. anti-gambling campaign Fla. United Meth. Conf., 1986. Founding chmn. East Hillsborough Orgn., Seffner, 1988; bd. dirs. Life Enrichment Sr. Ctr., Tampa, 1990—. Recipient Outstanding Religious Leader award Sarasota Jaycees, 1985. Mem. Assn. for Clin. Pastoral Edn., Alban Inst., North Tampa Ministerial Assn. Democrat. Home: 3020 Saint Charles Dr Tampa FL 33618-3238 Office: Forest Hills United Meth Ch 904 W Linebaugh Ave Tampa FL 33612-7858

REEMELIN, ANGELA NORVILLE, dietitian consultant; b. Pitts., Apr. 28, 1945; d. Richard Gerow and Kathleen Taylor (Brannen) Norville; m. Philip Barrows Reemelin, Nov. 17, 1973; children: Richard Barrows, Kathleen Easson. BS, U. Tenn., 1967; dietetic intern, Emory U., 1968. Cert. water safety instr. Adminstr. dietitian Servomation of Atlanta, 1968-70; food svc. dir. ARA Food Svcs., Norfolk, Va., 1970-80; cons. Jacksonville, Fla., 1980—; cons. William T. Hall Convalescent Home, Portsmouth, Va., 1975-79. Recipient Outstanding Young Dietitian award Tidewater Dietetic Assn., 1974; Best of Show in sewing FFWC State Arts Festival, 1985, 86, 87. Mem. ARC (30 yr. Vol. award), ADA, Am. Soc. Hosp. Food Svc. Adminstrs., Jr. Womans Club Orange Park (pres. 1986-87, v.p., fundraiser, membership chair, Outstanding Dist. Pres. 1987), U. Tenn. Alumni Assn. (pres. 1982-84, bd. govs. 1984-85), Omicron Nu. Roman Catholic. Home: 601 Lorn Ct Orange Park FL 32073-4228

REEP, ROBERT GREGG, SR., mayor; b. Warren, Ark., June 17, 1954; s. Robert Ellis and Eloise (Galloway) R.; m. Beverly Ann Holloway, Sept. 3, 1982; 1 child, Robert Gregg Jr. BA in Polit. Sci., U. Ark., Monticello, 1976. Dir. community devel. City of Warren, Ark., 1975-86; mayor Ark. Recycling and Mktg. Bd., 1987—; chmn. Ark. Recycling and Mktg. Bd., Little Rock, 1993—. Mem. Warren Lions Club. Democrat. Baptist. Home: 409 N Walnut St Warren AR 71671-2130 Office: City of Warren 104 N Myrtle St Warren AR 71671-2706

REES, FRANK WILLIAM, JR., architect; b. Rochester, N.Y., June 5, 1943; s. Frank William and Elizabeth R. (Miller) R.; m. Joan Mary Keevers, Apr. 1, 1967; children: Michelle, Christopher. BS in Architecture, U. Okla., 1970; postgrad., Harvard U., Boston, 1979, 90; OPM, Harvard U., 1990. Registered architect, 36 states; cert. Nat. Coun. Archtl. Registration Bds. Sales mgr. Sta. KFOM, Oklahoma City, 1967-70; project architect Benham-Blair & Affiliates, Oklahoma City, 1970-75; pres., CEO, founder Rees Assocs., Inc., Oklahoma City, 1975—; pres., chmn. bd. Weatherscan Radio Network, Oklahoma City, 1973-78; chmn. bd. Weatherscan Internat., Oklahoma City, 1972-78; pres. Frontier Communications, Oklahoma City, 1980-84; chmn. architecture bd. U. Okla., Norman, 1988-91. Past pres. Lake Hefner Trails, Oklahoma City, Hosp. Hospitality House, Oklahoma City, Oklahoma City Beautiful; mem. Leadership Oklahoma City. Mem. AIA, Am. Assn. Hosp. Architects, Am. Healthcare Assn., Tex. Hosp. Assn., World Pres. Orgn., Nat. Assn. Sr. Living Industries. Home: 1104 Stone

Gate Dr Irving TX 75063-4676 Office: Ste 200 3102 Oak Lawn Dallas TX 75219-4241

REES, JAMES CONWAY, IV, historic site administrator; b. Richmond, Va., May 5, 1952. BA, Coll. William & Mary, 1974; MPA, George Washington U., 1978. Reporter, photographer Newport News Daily-Press, 1974; coord. radio and television programming The Coll. William & Mary, 1974-78; mng. editor The William & Mary Mag., 1978-82; promotions dir. Va. Shakespeare Festival, 1980; dir. annual giving and pub. info. The Coll. William & Mary, 1978-80, dir. annual support and corp. rels., 1980-81, dir. capital support, 1981-82; asst. dir. devel. Nat. Trust Historic Preservation, 1982-83, assoc. dir. devel., 1983; dir. devel. and comms. Historic Mount Vernon, 1983-85, assoc. dir., 1985-94, resident dir., 1994—; exec. v.p. Mount Vernon Inn, Inc., 1994—; Mem. bd. dirs. Va. Shakespeare Festival, Washington Area Chpt. WIlliam and Mary Alumni Soc. Mem. Nat. Trust for Historic Preservation, Friends of the Nat. Symphony, WETA Pub. Television. Mem. Am. Film Inst., Va. Assn. Mus. (pres. 1991-94). Methodist. Home: 710 A St NE Washington DC 20002 Office: Mount Vernon Ladies Assn Mount Vernon VA 22121

REES, LANE CHARLES, industrial relations consultant; b. Longview, Tex., June 23, 1951; s. Holly Elias and Charlene Elizabeth (Quin) R.; m. Brenda Faye Anderson, July 1, 1978; children: Brian Andrew, Lauren Catherine. BBA in Mgmt. magna cum laude, Tex. A&M U., 1973, MEd in Ednl. Adminstrn., 1978. Pers. rep. Tex. A&M U., College Station, 1973-77; v.p. Brazos Gen. Svcs., Bryan, Tex., 1977-78; successively personnel office supr., wage and salary administrator, employee relations rep., sr. employee relations rep. ARCO, various cities, Tex., 1979-83; from sr. employee rels. rep. to employee rels. dir. ARCO, Anchorage and Kuparuk, Alaska, 1983-87; dir. employee rels. ARCO, Prudhoe Bay, Alaska, 1987-90, dir. human resources dept. engring., 1990-94; sr. human rels. advisor Algeria and engring. exploration Arco Internat. Oil and Gas, Plano, Tex., 1994—; ptnr. Rees and Assocs., Anchorage and Tex., 1978—. Mem. editorial staff Conf. Leadership, 1978. Vice-chmn. Rep. Party of Ala., 1993-94, chair, 1994; mem. ctrl. com. State of Ala., 1990-94; chmn. utility regulatory commn. municipality of Anchorage, 1989-91; mem. com. sec. United Meth. Com. Commn., Nashville, 1988—; evangelism chmn., mem. adv. coun. St. John United Meth. Ch., Anchorage, 1986-91, chmn. adminstrv. bd., 1991-93; trustee Nat. Found. Evangelism, Lake Junaluksa, N.C., 1988-96, exec. com., 1995—; conf. lay leader Ala. Missionary Conf.-Meth. Ch., 1992-94; chmn. evangelism and mem. adminstrv. bd. 1st United Meth. Ch., Allen, Tex., 1995—, lay del. to ann. conf., 1995—. Recipient Denman award Alaska Missionary Conf. of United Meth. Ch., 1989, Legis. citation State of Alaska, 1989. Mem. Acad. Mgmt., Tex. A&M U. Assn. Former Students (nat. councilman 1987-91, bd. dirs. 1996—), Am. Numismatic Assn., Alaska Soc. SAR (pres. 1989-90, trustee Nat. Soc. 1991-94, Silver Good Citizenship award 1989), Phi Eta Sigma, Phi Kappa Phi, Sigma Iota Epsilon (pres. 1972-73), Beta Gamma Sigma. Home: 406 Del Rio Ct Allen TX 75013 Office: Arco Internat 2300 W Plano Pky Plano TX 75075-8427

REESE, ANGELA KATHLEEN, curriculum director; b. Sandersville, Ga., July 19, 1958; d. Billy Charles and Janice Kathleen (Morris) Hodges; m. Kenneth G. Bunch, June 10, 1982 (div. July 1989); children: Kenny, Billy; m. Robert W. Reese, Jan. 9, 1992; 1 child, Kristie. BS in Early Childhood Edn., Ga. Coll., 1980, M in Adminstrn. and Supervision, 1985; specialist in edn., U. Ga., 1988. Cert. ednl. adminstrn. and supervision. Kindergarten tchr. Jones County Sch., Gray, Ga., 1980-81, Fulton County Schs., Atlanta, 1981-82; tchr. grades 4-6, adminstr. Denver Pub. Schs., 1982-84; tchr. grades 3-6, adminstr. Bibb County Schs., Macon, Ga., 1984-89, curriculum dir., 1989—, mid. sch. prin., 1996—; cons. Bibb County Schs., Macon, 1985—, Ga. Coll., Macon, 1990—, Ga. Ednl. Tech. Ctr., Macon, 1990—; presenter in field. Author: Bibb County Pre-K Handbook, 1994, Bibb County Elementary Science Fair Manual, 1995; co-author: Georgia Elementary School Vocabulary, 1988. Collaborative coun. coord. Pre-K Collaborative Coun., Dept. Family and Children's Svc., Macon/Bibb County Health Dept., Child Care Networks, Bibb County Pub. Schs., Macon, 1994-95; mem. Macon Edn. Improvement Team-C. of C., 1995-96; cmty. bd. mem. Wesleyan Coll. Masters Program, Macon, 1995-96. Named Outstanding Educator of Yr., Jaycees, Macon, 1995-96. Mem. ASCD, Ga. ASCD, Ga. Assn. for Curriculum and Instrnl. Supervision, Ga. Coun. Internat. Reading Assn., Profl. Assn. Ga. Educators, Ga. Assn. Ednl. Leaders, Phi Kappa Phi. Home: 1268 Craddock Way Macon GA 31210 Office: Bibb County Schs 484 Mulberry St Macon GA 31201-7906

REESE, CATHERINE CAROLINE, political scientist, educator; b. Nashville, Apr. 10, 1962; d. Charles Henry III and Carolyn Nell (Christnacht) R. BA in Polit. Sci., Rhodes Coll., 1984; MPA, Memphis State U., 1989; D of Pub. Adminstrn., U. Ga., 1995. Counselor eligibility Tenn. Dept. Human Svcs., Memphis, 1984-89; rsch. asst., edn. program specialist Carl Vinson Inst. Govt./U. Ga., Athens, 1989-95; asst. prof. dept. govt. N.Mex. State U., Las Cruces, 1995—. Mem. Am. Soc. Pub. Adminstrn. (pub. budgeting and fin. sect.), Am. Polit. Sci. Assn. Office: NMex State Univ 348 Breland Hall Las Cruces NM 88003

REESE, EDWARD JAMES, JR., computer scientist; b. San Antonio, Aug. 8, 1957; s. Edward James Sr. and Kathy (Veitch) R.; m. Pamelia Kay Oxendine, Sept. 28, 1979; children: Dawn Alicia, Paul Christopher. AAS in Avionics Systems Tech., C.C. of the Air Force, 1985, AAS in Tech. Instrn., 1986, AAS in Electronic Engring. Tech., 1990; BS in Computer Sci. summa cum laude, Park Coll., 1986; MS in Computer Sci., Midwestern State U., 1994. Cert. master instr.; cert. Oracle master Oracle Edn. Svcs., 1993; cert. Oracle Database adminstr. Chauncey Group Internat., 1996. Commd. USAF, 1975, advanced through grades to master sgt.; avionic systems technician 67 Tactical Recon Wing USAF, Bergstrom AFB, Tex., 1976-84, tech. instr. 423 Field Tng. Detachment, 1984-89; info. sys. supt. 82 Field Tng. Group USAF, Sheppard AFB, Tex., 1989-95; ret. USAF, 1995; database adminstr. Oracle Rockwell Automation, 1995—. Cubmaster pack 230 Boy Scouts Am., Wichita Falls, Tex., 1991-93. Mem. Internat. Oracle Users Group Am., Planetary Soc.

REESE, JAMES CARL, JR., drilling engineer; b. Magnolia, Ark., July 25, 1949; s. James Carl and Vivian Marcelle (Thompson) R.; m. Zenaida Salazar, Mar. 16, 1977; 1 child, Michelle Nicole. BS, La. Tech. U., 1971; MS, Va. Tech. U., 1972. Svc. engr. Dowell Schlumberger, Venezuela, 1972-73; supr., engr. Dresser Minerals Internat. Inc., Singapore, 1973-77; drilling engr. Amoco Prodn. Co., Egypt, 1977-78; sr. drilling engr. Amoco Prodn. Co., Philippines, 1978; staff drilling engr. Trinidad Oil Co., 1978-80, Houston, 1980-84; sr. staff drilling engr. Amoco Prodn. Co., Monrovia, Liberia, 1984-86, Houston, Copenhagen, India, Congo, 1987-91; drilling supt. Amoco Prodn. Co., Houston, 1991-92, Amoco Norway, Stavanger, 1992—. Mem. Soc. Petroleum Engrs. Republican. Methodist. Office: Amoco Prodn Co PO Box 3092 Houston TX 77253-3092

REESE, MARC CHARLES, operations administrator; b. Selma, Ala., Feb. 6, 1962; s. Eugene A. and Peggy J. (Stallings) R.; m. Marilyn E. Jenny, Aug. 24, 1985; children: Sarah, Christine, Katherine. BS in Engring. Ops., N.C. State U., 1984. Design engr. Hunter Mktg., Raleigh, N.C., 1985, Brown, Edwards & Miller Engrs., Raleigh, N.C., 1985-86; field engr. Beaman Corp., Greensboro, N.C., 1989-90, engring., quality assurance mgr., 1990-92, ops. mgr., prodn. control, 1992-94; dir. of fin., admin. purchases & materials Morris & Assoc., Raleigh, N.C., 1994—. Capt. U.S. Army, 1986—. Decorated Army Commendation medal. Mem. Soc. Am. Mil. Engrs. Democrat. Presbyterian. Home: 1716 Misty Meadow Ln Garner NC 27529-5046 Office: Morris & Assoc PO Box 1046 Raleigh NC 27602

REESE, PATRICIA ANN, retired editor, columnist; b. Superior, Nebr., Mar. 14, 1954; d. Robert John and Billie Jo (Gooch) R. BS in Wildlife Ecology, Communications, Okla. State U., 1976. Proofreader Ada (Okla.) Evening News, 1976-77, reporter, 1977-81, wire editor, 1981-85, city editor, 1985-92, sects. editor, 1992, ret., 1992. Bd. dirs. Ada Arts and Humanities Coun., 1981-85, 92-95, 96—, historian, 1982-83, sec., 1983-85, 92-95, 96—, newsletter editor, 1996—; charter mem. Seekers dept. Tanti Study Club, Ada, 1982. Recipient Carl Rogan News Excellence award Associated Press/Okla. News Execs., 1986, 90, 91, 92, Best Column award Okla. Natural Gas, 1991. Mem. Am. Mus. Natural History, Archaeology Inst. Am., Okla. Lupus Assn., Ada Cmty. Theatre II, Okla. Press Assn., Internat. Ceramic Inst., Soc. Environ. Journalists. Democrat. Home: RR 4 Box 118 Ada OK 74820-9407

REEVE, SCOTT WAYNE, chemical physics educator; b. Mpls., Sept. 16, 1961; s. Joseph W. Reeve and Dorothy (Erickson) Buckman; m. Debra K. Ingram, July 20, 1992. BA in Chemistry, Augsburg Coll., 1987; PhD, U. Minn., 1992. Rsch. asst. U. Minn., Mpls., 1987-92; postdoctoral rschr. Office Naval Rsch., China Lake, Calif., 1992-94; asst. prof. chem. physics Ark. State U., Jonesboro, 1994—; reviewer Ark. Acad. Sci., Jonesboro, 1994-95, Internat. Conf. for Thin Films and Metall. Coatings, San Diego, 1993-94; speaker in field. Contbr. articles to profl. jours. With U.S. Army, 1979-82. Recipient Contrell Coll. Sci. award Rsch. Corp., 1995-97; rsch. grantee Ark. Space Grant Consortium, 1994-95, U.S. Dept. Energy ERIE Program, 1994-95. Mem. Am. Chem. Soc., Am. Vacuum Soc., Soc. for Applied Spectroscopy, Coun. for Undergrad. Rsch., AAUP, Sigma Xi. Lutheran. Office: Ark State U Dept Chemistry PO Box 419 State University AR 72467

REEVES, ALEXIS SCOTT, journalist; b. Atlanta, Feb. 4, 1949; d. William Alexander and Marian (Willis) Scott; m. Marc Anthony Lewis, Sept. 14, 1968 (div. 1973); m. David Leslie Reeves, Mar. 16, 1974; children: Cinque Scott, David Leslie, Jr. Student Barnard Coll., 1966-68; student Spelman Coll., 1989-90, Regional Leadership Inst., 1992. Reporter, asst. city editor, cable TV editor, mgr. video edit., v.p. community affairs Atlanta Jour. & Constn., Atlanta, 1974-93; dir. Diversity for Cox Enterprises Inc., 1993—; vis. instr. summer program for minority journalists, Berkeley, Calif., 1980, 81, 84, 85, 87 Grady High Sch., Atlanta, 1982-83; journalist-in-residence Clark Coll., Atlanta, 1983. Researcher, writer: The History of Atlanta NAACP, 1983 (NAACP award, 1984). Recipient Disting. Urban Journalism award Nat. Urban Coalition, 1980. Michele Clark fellow Columbia U. Sch. Journalism, 1974. Named one of 100 Top Black Bus. & Profl. Women, 1986; recipient Acad. Achievement award YWCA, 1989. Mem. Nat. Assn. Media Women (Media Woman of Yr. award, 1983, Media Woman of Yr. nat. award 1983, pres. Atlanta chpt. 1985-87), Atlanta Assn. Black Journalists (Commentary Print award 1983), Nat. Assn. Black Journalists, Sigma Delta Chi (bd. dirs. 1980-84, treas. 1985-88). Moderator, First Congl. Ch., 1982-92. Office: Cox Enterprises Inc PO Box 105357 1400 Lake Hearn Dr NE Atlanta GA 30348

REEVES, DIANNE L., artist; b. Milw., Apr. 8, 1948; d. John J. and Bernice M. (Hendricksen) Kleczka; m. Robert A. McCoy, Oct. 15, 1983 (div. June 1988). BFA, U. Wis., Milw., 1968; student, Mus. Fine Arts, Houston, 1974-77, 83, Glassell Sch. Art, Houston, 1980-83. Instr. papermaking Glassell Sch. Art, 1984-85. Exhibited in solo shows at Women and Their Work Gallery, Austin, Tex., 1988, Moreau Galleries/Hamms Gallery, Notre Dame, Ind., 1991, The Martin Mus. of Art, Waco, Tex., 1996; internat. exhibns. include Leopold-Hoesch Mus., Duren, Germany, 1991, 92, 93, galleries in Netherlands and Basel, Switzerland, Copenhagen, 1996, Kunghälvs, Bollebygds, Sweden, 1996; exhibited in numerous group exhbns.; author: (ltd. edit.) From Fiber to Paper, 1991. Bd. dirs., sec. Friends of Dard Hunter, Inc., 1993-94. NEA/Tex. fellow Mid-Am. Arts Alliance/NEA, 1986; recipient awards for art work. Mem. Internat. Assn. Hand Papermakers and Paper Artists (co-chair nominating com. 1993-94), Women and Their Work, Inc., Sierra Club, Tex. Fine Arts Assn., Austin Visual Arts Assn. Home and Studio: 1103 S 3rd St Austin TX 78704

REEVES, GENE, judge; b. Meridian, Miss., Feb. 27, 1930; s. Clarence Eugene and May (Philyaw) R.; m. Brenda Wages, Sept. 26, 1980. JD, John Marshall U., 1964; cert. judge spl. ct. jurisdiction. Bar: Ga. 1964, U.S. Ct. Appeals (11th cir.) 1965, U.S. Supreme Ct. 1969. Ptnr., Craig & Reeves, Lawrenceville, Ga., 1964-71; sole practice, Lawrenceville, 1971-85; prin. Reeves Law Firm, 1985-94; judge City Ct., Lawrenceville, 1969-70, Magistrate Ct. of Gwinnett County, Ga., 1994—. Served to sgt. USAF, 1951-54. Mem. ABA, GTLA, ATLA, Am. Jud. Soc., Gwinnett County Bar Assn. (pres. 1970-72), Criminal Def. Lawyers Assn. Baptist. Home: 221 Pineview Dr Lawrenceville GA 30245-6035 Office: 125 Perry St Lawrenceville GA 30245

REEVES, JAMES FRANKLIN, art broker; b. Hunstville, Ala., July 4, 1946; s. Henry Homer and Marjorie Elinore (Jordan) R.; m. Marion Cecelia Kretzer, Sept. 25, 1978; 1 child, Ceoric Alexander. BA in Art History, U. Ala., 1970; MA in Art History, Vanderbilt U., 1981. Asst. to dir., curator Hunstville (Ala.) Mus. Art, 1973-76; art broker McCormick House, Huntsville, 1976—. Author: Fine Arts, 1993, Kildare, 1994. Sgt. USAF, 1966-70. Home and Office: 2005 Kildare St NW Huntsville AL 35811-1813

REEVES, JOHN MERCER, II, international trade finance professional; b. Sanford, N.C., July 26, 1954; s. Charles Mercer Jr. and Sarah Frances (Crosby) R.; m. Jo Ann Funderburke, Dec. 30, 1978; children: Caroline Elizabeth, Rebekah Ann, John M. III. BCE, N.C. State U., 1977, MCE, 1978; MBA, Duke U., 1983. Engr. Nello L. Teer Co., Durham, N.C., 1973-83; mgmt. cons. Matthews Young & Assocs., Chapel Hill, N.C., 1983-85; pvt. practice option trader Durham, 1985-86; founder Med. Products Search, Inc., Durham, 1986-87; pvt. practice mgmt. cons. Chapel Hill, 1988; pvt. practice real estate developer Durham, 1990-92; merger and acquistion intermediary Allen Comml. Svcs., Raleigh, N.C., 1992-94; founder, pres. First Exim Fin. Ltd., Charlotte, N.C., 1994; bd. dirs. Digital Recorders Inc., Research Triangle Park, N.C., World, Horizon Fin. Svcs., Hastings, England. Mem. com. Durham C. of C. Named Paul Harris fellow Rotary Internat., 1990. Mem. S.W. Durham Rotary Club (bd. dirs. 1983-87). Republican. Presbyterian. Office: 1st Exim Fin Ltd 343 W Main St Durham NC 27701-3215

REEVES, LYNDA P., physical education educator; b. Queens, N.Y., Feb. 16, 1958. BS in Phys. Edn., SUNY, Cortland, 1980; MS in Phys. Edn., James Madison U., 1984; PhD in Phys. Edn., Tex. Women's U., 1991. Cert. phys. edn. tchr., Va., Tex., Tenn. Adapted phys. edn. tchr. Grafton Sch., Berryville, Va., 1980-82; instr., women's athletic coord. Shenandoah Coll., Winchester, Va., 1982-86, women's basketball coach, 1982-83, women's volleyball coach, 1981-86, women's tennis coach, 1984-86; teaching asst. Tex. Women's U., Denton, 1986, adapted aquatics instr., 1987—; tchr. Stonegate Elem. Sch., Bedford, Tex., 1988; adapted phys. edn. specialist Parker County Co-op Spl. Svcs., Weatherford, Tex., 1989-91; physical edn. specialist Aledo (Tex.) Indep. Sch. Dist., 1991-92; asst. prof. motor devel., spl. edn. and early childhood East Tenn. State U., Johnson City, 1992—. Presentor YMCA, Irving, Tex., 1988; mem. Handicapped Awareness Week, Denton, 1987; coord. Jump Rope for Heart, Winchester, 1984-91; aquatic and basketball coach Spl. Olympics, Denton and Winchester, 1986, 87, track and field coach, 1993—. U.S. Achievement Acad. scholar, 1989, 91; recipient Acad. All Am. Collegiate award, 1987. Mem. AAHPERD (presenter conv.), SDAAHPERD (chmn., conv. presenter), Nat. Assn. for the Edn. Young Children, Tenn. Assn. for Health, Phys. Edn., recreation, and Dance (chair, conv. presenter), Coun. for Exceptional Children. Home: 2423 Huffine Cir Johnson City TN 37604-7059 Office: E Tenn State Univ PO Box 70654 Johnson City TN 37614-0654

REEVES, MARK THOMAS, lawyer, architect; b. Miami, Fla., June 8, 1955; s. Joseph James and Anita Laura (Flynn) R. BArch, U. Miami, 1978, MArch, 1980, JD, 1984. Bar: Fla. 1985; registered architect, Fla. Architect Connell Assocs., Inc., Coral Gables, Fla., 1980-84; assoc. Sparber, Shevin, Shapo & Heilbronner, P.A., Miami, Fla., 1984-88, Honigman, Miller, Schwartz and Cohen, West Palm Beach, Fla., 1988-89; ptnr. Steel, Hector & Davis, Miami, 1989—; faculty fellow Henry King Stanford Residential Coll., U. Miami, Coral Gables, 1987-90. Contbr. articles to profl. jours. Vice chmn. Miami Heritage Conservation Bd., 1988; trustee Carrollton Sch. Sacred Heart, Coconut Grove, Fla., 1991—. Recipient Young Architects Recognition award Progressive Architecture Mag., 1987. Mem. AIA (bd. dirs. Miami chpt. 1986-87, v.p. 1987-91, Outstanding Svc. award 1987), U. Miami Alumni Assn. (bd. dirs. 1987-89, v.p. 1994), Am. Arbitration Assn. (panel 1984—), Leadership Miami Alumni Assn. Republican. Roman Catholic. Home: 3020 Seminole St Miami FL 33133-3238 Office: 4000 SE Financial Ctr Miami FL 33131

REEVES, MARY ELIZABETH, education educator, researcher; b. Bossier City, La., Sept. 3, 1964; d. Bert Lee and Doris Elizabeth (Eddy) R.; m. Eric John Fountain, Dec. 19, 1987. BS, La. State U., Shreveport, 1987; MA, La. State U., 1990, PhD, 1993. Cert. secondary math. educator, La. Tchr. Bossier Parish Sch. Bd., Benton, La., 1987-88; asst. prof. N.W. State U., Natchitoches, La., 1992—. Contbr. articles to profl. jours. Mem. AAUW, ASCD, Nat. Coun. Tchrs. Math., Am. Ednl. Rsch. Assn. Office: Northwestern State Univ Divsn Of Education Natchitoches LA 71497

REEVES, MICHEAL AARON, aerospace corporation executive; b. Bryan, Tex., Feb. 7, 1943; s. William Otho Reeves and Pearl Louise Smith Newton; m. Katherine Keys, Nov. 21, 1987; 1 stepchild, Yelon Katherine Clement. BA in Edn., Cen. State U., Edmond, Okla., 1967; MS in Acctg., U. Houston, Clear Lake, 1977. Tech. writer/editor ITT- Fed. Elec. Co., Houston, 1967-71; fin. analyst The Boeing Co., Houston, 1971-77; pres., gen. mgr. Houston Export Crating (HECCO), Houston, 1977-84; v.p. fin. and adminstrn., corp. officer ILC Space Systems, a Div. ILC Dover, Inc., Houston, 1984-93; sr. v.p. aerospace sector, corp. officer Enterprise Adv. Svcs., Inc., Houston, 1993—. Bd. dirs. Houston Port Bur., 1980-84; mem. Houston Livestock Show and Rodeo, 1969—; gen. chair Lunar Rendezvous Festival, Houston, 1992-93. Named Disting. Alumnus, U. Houston at Clear Lake, 1988. Mem. Nat. Contract Mgmt. Assn., Clear Lake Area C. of C. (dir. 1988-90, v.p. 1989-90), U. Houston-Clear Lake Alumni Assn. (pres. 1980-87). Democrat. Baptist. Home: 630 Shorewood Dr Seabrook TX 77586-4610 Office: Enterprise Adv Svcs Inc 6671 Southwest Fwy Ste 550 Houston TX 77074-2218

REEVES, PEGGY LOIS ZEIGLER, accountant; b. Orangeburg, S.C., May 12, 1940; d. Joseph Harold and Lois Vivian (Stroman) Zeigler; m. Donald Preston Reeves, Sept. 9, 1961. Degree in Secretarial Sci., Coker Coll., 1960. Sec. Ladson Beach, CPA, Orangeburg, 1960-61; acctg. clk. Milliken & Co., Laurens, S.C., 1962-67, sec., 1967-73, mgmt. trainee, 1973, plant contr., 1973-74, 76-81; cost acctg. supr. Milliken & Co., Spartanburg, S.C., 1974-76, 81—. Chair bd. dirs. Enoree (S.C.)-Lanford Fire dist., 1982—, treas., 1988—; mem. alumni exec. bd. Coker Coll., 1996—. H.L. Jones scholar Coker Coll., 1959-60. Mem. Inst. Mgmt. Accts. (sec. 1991-94, v.p. membership 1994-95, v.p. adminstrn. and fin. 1995-96, pres.-elect 1996—), Profl. Secs. Internat. (v.p., rec. sec., Sec. of Yr. 1973). Baptist.

REEVES, RAYMOND EDWARD, editor; b. New Orleans, July 7, 1964; s. Dorothy Elizabeth (McClure) R.; m. Linda Carol (Caraway), Nov. 19, 1994. BS in Journalism, U. So. Miss., 1986. Sports writer Columbus (Miss.) Comml. Dispatch, 1987-90; asst. sports editor Natchez (Miss.) Dem., 1990-91; mng. editor alumni pub. U. So. Miss. Alumni Assn., Hattiesburg, 1991—; advisory brd. USM Baptist Student Union, Hattiesburg, 1994—. Recipient 3d Pl. award for Best Sports Feature, Miss. Press Assn., 1989, 1st Pl. award for Best Sports Columnist, Miss. Press Assn., 1990, 2d Pl. award for Best Alumni Mag., Coll. Pub. Rels. Assn. Miss., 1995. Baptist. Office: So Miss Alumni Assn USM Box 5013 Hattiesburg MS 39406

REEVES, TERRY K. PRICE, college administrator; b. Dunn, N.C., July 23, 1968; d. James Leslie and Mary Margaret (Price) Myles. BS, Livingstone Coll., 1990. Lundy endowed chair sec. Campbell U., Buies Creek, N.C., 1990-92; adminstrv. asst. St. Augustine's Coll., Raleigh, N.C., 1992-95; coord. acad. support svcs. St. Augustine's Coll., Raleigh, 1995-96. Contbr. editor St. Augustine's Coll. Personnel Newsletter, 1992-93; prodn. asst. Enterprise Newsletter, Campbell U., 1990-92. Youth leader, supt. Sunday sch. Trinity AME Zion Ch., Dunn, N.C., 1990-96. Recipient Christian Edn. award Trinity AME Zion Ch., 1993. Mem. Episcopal Ch. Women, Alpha Kappa Alpha. Home: 609 E Granville St Dunn NC 28334 Office: St Augustine's Coll 1315 Oakwood Ave Raleigh NC 27610

REEVES, WILLIAM BOYD, lawyer; b. Easley, S.C., Mar. 24, 1932; s. William C. and Elise B. (Brooks) R.; m. Rose Mary Weil, Sept. 7, 1957 (dec. Nov. 1977); 1 dau., Gabrielle; m. Gladys Frances Brown, Nov. 24, 1978; children: Stephanie, William. B.A., Furman U., 1954; LL.B., Tulane U., 1959. Bar: La. 1959, Ala. 1960, U.S. Supreme Ct 1971. Law clk. to U.S. Dist. Judge, So. Dist. Ala., 1959-61; assoc. firm Armbrecht, Jackson & DeMouy, 1961-65; ptnr. Armbrecht, Jackson, DeMouy, Crowe, Holmes & Reeves, Mobile, 1965—. Chancellor St. Lukes Episcopal Ch. and Sch., 1973—. Served to capt. U.S. Army, 1954-56. Fellow Am. Coll. Trial Lawyers, Am. Coll. Legal Medicine, Internat. Soc. Barristers; mem. ABA., Ala. State Bar, La. State Bar, Mobile Bar Assn. (pres. 1981), Internat. Assn. Ins. Counsel, Fedn. Ins. and Corp. Counsel, Maritime Law Assn. U.S. (exec. coun. 1988-90), Ala. Defense Lawyers Assn. (past pres.), Southeastern Admiralty Law Inst. (past pres.), Nat. Bd. Trial Advocates, Am. Bd. Trial Advocates (pres. Ala. chpt. 1986-87), Am. Bd. Profl. Liability Attys., Nat. Health Law Assn., Assn. Profl. Liability Attys., Athelstan Club, Mobile Country Club, Internat. Trade Club, Bienville Club, Propeller Club, Masons. Home: 3755 Rhonda Dr S Mobile AL 36608-1733

REEVY, ANTHONY WILLIAM, university development officer; b. Lubbock, Tex., Aug. 2, 1961; s. William Robert and Carol May (Jones) R.; m. M. Caroline Weaver, June 23, 1990. BS in Chemistry, N.C. State U., 1983, BS in Civil Engring., 1983; MBA in Mktg., U. N.C., 1986; MS in Mass Comms., Miami U., 1988. Asst. promotion and devel. WMUB FM, Oxford, Ohio, 1986-87; devel. asst. WAMU FM, Washington, 1987-89, corp. rels. assoc., 1989-90; devel. dir. WFAE FM, Charlotte, N.C., 1990-94; dir. of libr. devel. N.C. State U., 1994—. Author: non-fiction short stories, poetry. Mem. N.C. Rail Trails (historian, bd. dirs.), Nat. Ry. Hist. Soc. Home: 2222 W Club Blvd Durham NC 27705-3236 Office: The Libraries NC State U Box 7111 Raleigh NC 27695-7111

REGAN, LINDA ANNE, insurance agent; b. Summitt, N.J., Jan. 9, 1957; d. Steven George and Anne M. (Vivian) Fasold; m. Kevin M. Regan, Dec. 7, 1985; children: Anne M., Evan M. Student, Eckerd Coll., 1980. Claims rep. Ohio Casualty Ins. Co., St. Petersburg, Fla., 1973-74; comml. rep. Nat. Ins. Assoc., St. Petersburg, 1974-82, Baynard Bros. Ins., St. Petersburg, 1982-83; comml. underwriter Hull and Co. Inc., Gainesville, Fla., 1983-84; sr. underwriter Harvey, Percy & Jones Inc., Tampa, Fla., 1984-85; office mgr. Aanco Underwriters Inc., St. Petersburg, 1985-86; comml. rep. Wittner, Klutts & Co., St. Petersburg, 1986-88; office mgr. Italiano Ins. Svcs., Englewood, Fla., 1988-90; ins. agt. James T. Blalock Agy., Venice, Fla., 1991-93, Gifford-Heiden Ins. Agy., Venice, 1993—; v.p. Insurors Allied Svc. Corp., Englewood, 1991—; instr. individual devel. program. Editor (newsletter) The Bull., 1989-91. Volunteer Englewood Community Hosp., 1990, Adopt A Hwy. Program, Englewood, 1990, 91, Vineland Elem. Sch., Englewood, 1991. Mem. Fla. West Coast Ins. Women (pres. Pt. Charlotte chpt. 1992-93, pres. 1994-95, treas. 1995-96, Ins. Woman of Yr. 1991), Fla. Assn. Ins. Agts., Profl. Inst. Agts. Assn., Nat. Assn. Ins. Women (Fla. coun. sec. 1988-90), Ins. Women of St. Petersburg (bd. dirs. 1988, v.p. 1989-90), Bus. and Profl. Women's Club (bd. dirs. Englewood chpt. 1989—). Republican. Episcopalian. Home: 7410 Cape Girardeau St Englewood FL 34224-8004

REGAN, SIRI LISA LAMBOURNE, gifted education educator; b. New Orleans, May 2, 1956; d. George William Hugh and Roma Schilling (Philebar) Lambourne; m. Stephen E. Regan, July 21, 1978; 1 child, Addie R.F.R. BA in English Edn., U. New Orleans, 1977, M in Edn. Curriculum and Instrn., 1981, postgrad. Cert. tchr., La. Tchr. Roosevelt Middle Sch., Kenner, La., 1977—; presenter in field; dir., coord. La. Writing Project Jefferson Parish, 1989-90; co-dir. Greater New Orleans Writing Project Inst., 1990, audio-visual coord., 1992—, comuter project coord., 1995—. Contbr. articles to profl. jours. Named La. Middle Sch. Tchr. of Yr. La. State Dept. Edn., 1989, Tchr. of Yr. Southeastern Regional Middle Sch. , 1989; recipient Valley Forge Freedom Found. Educator's medal, 1989-90, Young Careerist award JeffersonBus. and Profl. Women's Club, Key to City of Kenner, 1989. Mem. Nat. Assn. Bilingual Educators (cert.) Nat. Coun. Tchrs. English (cert.), Nat. Middle Sch. Assn., La. Middle Sch. Assn., Coun. Learning Disabilitis, Coun. Exceptional Children, S.E. La. Profl. Assn. Gifted and Talented, Kappa Delta Phi, Phi Delta Kappa, Alpha Theta Epsilon. Meth. Home: 508 Roseland Pky New Orleans LA 70123-3948 Office: Roosevelt Mid Sch 3315 Maine Ave Kenner LA 70065-3806

REGEL, TERRY LYNN, quality systems administrator; b. Marks, Miss., Oct. 19, 1950; s. Carl Fred and Francis Louise (Hayes) R.; m. Patricia Ann Huebschman, Dec. 21, 1973. ASc, N.W. Miss. Jr. Coll., Senatobia, 1971; BA, U. Miss., 1974; MDiv, New Orleans Bapt. Theol. Sem., 1977. Registered quality systems lead auditor Registrar Accreditation Bd., lead assessor Registration Bd. for Assessors. Quality control mgr. Chloride, Inc., Florence, Miss., 1977-86; quality sys. mgr. Alcoa Fujikura, Ltd., Brentwood,

Tenn., 1986—. Co-author: After the Quality Audit: Closing the Loop on the Audit Process, 1996. Sr. mem. Am. Soc. Quality Control (cert. quality auditor, cert. quality engr., sect. chairperson 1985-86), Am. Statis. Assn. Office: Alcoa Fujikara Ltd 105 Westpark Dr Brentwood TN 37027-5010

REGINI, JUDITH L., insurance company professional; b. La Marque, Tex., Nov. 13, 1953; d. Henry Thomas and Nell Beatrice (McNary) Shields; m. Alvine H. Regini, June 29, 1973. ABA, Coll. of the Mainland, Texas City, Tex., 1989; BBA in Mgmt., U. Houston, 1992. Compliance coord. Am. Nat. Ins. Co., Galveston, Tex. Contbr. articles to newsletters, jours. Choir dir. Our Lady of Lourdes Ch., Hitchcock, Tex., 1986—; bd. dirs. Cath. Charities, Galveston County, 1994—, chairperson, 1996—. Fellow Life Office Mgmt. Assn. (assoc. customer svc. designation 1992); Phi Theta Kappa, Alpha Chi. Roman Catholic. Home: PO Box 532 Hitchcock TX 77563-0532 Office: Am Nat Ins Co One Moody Pla # 1436 Galveston TX 77550

REGIS, NINA, librarian, educator; b. Corinth, Miss., Oct. 19, 1928; d. W.C. and Mary Isabelle (Rushing) Hanner; m. George Regis, Sept. 5, 1949 (dec. Jan. 6, 1990); 1 child, Simonne Marie. BA, Bridgewater (Mass.) State U., 1971, MEd, 1975; MALS, U. South Fla., 1981. Cert. libr., tchr. Geneal. libr., asst. rschr. to curator New Bedford (Mass.) Pub. Libr., 1963-71; assoc. libr. New England Hist. Geneal. Soc., Boston, 1972-73; media specialist, libr. Brevard County Schs., Port Malabar Elem. Sch., Palm Bay, Fla., 1978-90; libr., faculty Brevard C.C., Palm Bay, 1990—. Developer and organizer libraries, 1968, 80, 91—. Mem. ALA, Fla. Assn. C.C.s, Libr. Assn. of Brevard County, Internat. Platform Assn., Phi Kappa Phi, Beta Phi Mu. Office: Brevard Community Coll Melbourne Campus Libr 3865 N Wickham Rd Melbourne FL 32935-2310

REGISTER, ANNETTE ROWAN, reading educator; b. Doctors Inlet, Fla., Apr. 5, 1931; d. Ernest Ambors and Frances Perlena (Monroe) R.; Henry Ira Register, Oc. 31, 1954; 1 child, Andrew Henry. RN, Grnville Gen.Hosp.Sch.of Nursi, Greenville, 1948-51; BS, Tex. Woman's U., Denton, 1954; MEd, U. Fla., Gainesville, 1959; SEd, Fla. State U., 1983. Instrn. dir. nursing edn. Alachua Gen. Hosp., Gainesville, Fla., 1955-57; pub. sch. tchr. Okaloosa County, Ft. Walton Beach, Fla., 1966-93; v.p., Internation Training in Communication Ft. Walton Beach, Fla.; active Inst. Sr. Profls. Okaloosa Walton C.C. Pres. United Meth. Women, Ft. Walton Beach, Fla., 1985-87, dist. v.p.; pres. Okaloosa Reading Coun., 1976-80. Mem. Phi Delta Kappa (1st v.p.). Methodist. Office: Okaloosa County Sch Bd 10 Lowery Pl SE Fort Walton Beach FL 32548

REGYNSKI, JANET ELIZABETH, medical/surgical nurse, orthopedic nurse; b. Mitchell, S.D., Aug. 11, 1952; d. John Paul and Marjorie Jane (Oltmans) Falk; children: Joshua, Duane, Debra. Diploma, Meth. Sch. of Nursing, 1975; student, S.D. State U., Brookings, Mid. Tenn. State U., Dakota Wesleyan U. Charge nurse, asst. head nurse St. Joseph Hosp., Mitchell; charge nurse Bedford County Gen. Hosp., Shelbyville, Tenn.; staff nurse Mid. Tenn. Med. Ctr., Murfreesboro. Home: 203 Fox Ln Shelbyville TN 37160-6754

REHBEIN, EDWARD ANDREW, minister, geologist, consultant; b. Portland, Oreg., Aug. 13, 1947; s. Edward Louis and Marjorie Ann (Simshaw) R; m. Phyllis Jean Boyer, June 23, 1973; children: Matthew Louis, Angela Mae. BS in Geology, Calif. Inst. Tech., 1969. Geologist U.S. Forest Svc., Elkins, W.Va., 1972-74, U.S. Geol. Survey, Billings, Mont., 1974-76; coal geologist W.Va. Geologic Survey, Morgantown, 1977; cons. Morgantown, 1978; geologist Allied Corp., Beckley, W.Va., 1979; sr. exploration geologist Kerr-McGee Corp., Beckley, 1980-82, regional mgr. exploration, Reno, Nev., 1983-85; exploration geologist, Oklahoma City, 1985-88; assoc. min. Ch. of Christ, Beckley, W.Va., 1989-90, min., 1990—; pres. M&R Computer Sales and Svc., Inc., Beckley, W.Va., 1989-90. Author: Remembering God's Word, 1991; contbr. articles to profl. jours. and mags. Mem. Am. Assn. Petroleum Geologists. Club: Shotokan Karate Am. Office: N Beckley Ch of Christ PO Box 951 Beckley WV 25802-0951

REHM, BOBBY LEE, marketing executive; b. Kansas City, Mo., Dec. 8, 1953; s. Roy D. and Wylma J. (Anderson) R.; m. Marsha L. Tunnell, May 24, 1980; children: Kathryn, Shannon, Madeline. BS in Journalism, U. N.Tex., 1977. Advt. rep. Lewisville Daily Leader, 1977-78; v.p. Sasco Cosmetics, Inc., 1978-82, G. Brigham Co., 1982-83; sales rep. Paul Revere Life Ins. Co., 1983-85; v.p. mktg. Western Federal Savings & Loan Assn., Dallas, 1985-88, Southwest Corp. Federal Credit Union, Dallas, 1988—. Pres. Coppell (Tex.) Mcpl. Utility Dist., 1983-95; mem. Coppell 2000 Planning Commn., 1988. Methodist. Home: 137 Glenwood Dr Coppell TX 75019-5808

REICH, ALAN ANDERSON, foundation administrator; b. Pearl River, N.Y., Jan. 1, 1930; s. Oswald David and Alma Carolyn (Anderson) R.; m. Gay Ann Forsythe, Dec. 19, 1954; children: James, Jeffrey, Andrew, Elizabeth. B.A., Dartmouth Coll., 1952; diploma in Slavic Studies, Oxford U., 1953; M.A., Russian Inst., Middlebury Coll., 1953; M.B.A., Harvard U., 1959; LLD (hon.), Gallaudet Coll., 1981, Dartmouth Coll., 1992. Exec. Polaroid Corp., Cambridge, Mass., 1960-70; dep. asst. sec. ednl. and cultural affairs Dept. State, Washington, 1970-75; spl. asst. to sec. HEW, 1976-77; dep. asst. sec. commerce, dir. Bur. East-West Trade, Dept. Commerce, 1977-78; pres. U.S. Council for Internat. Yr. of Disabled Persons, Washington, 1978-81, Nat. Orgn. Disability, Washington, 1982—, Bimillennium Found., 1982—, Disability 2000 CEO coun., 1991—. Chmn. Sudbury (Mass.) Community United Fund, 1962, 66; mem. U.S. del. WHO Gen. Assembly, 1970; pres. Nat. Paraplegia Found.; chmn. bd. dirs. Paralysis Cure Research Found., bd. dirs. of the Healing Community, chmn. People-to-people Com. for Handicapped; Impact Found., 1986—; chmn. World Com. on Disability, 1985—. Served to 1st lt. inf. AUS, 1953-57. Named to U.S. Army Inf. OCS Hall of Fame, 1994; recipient Sevier award for svc. to handicapped, 1994. Mem. Paralyzed Vets. Am., Cosmos Club, Achilles Club (London), Beta Theta Pi. Republican. Methodist. Home: 6017 Copely Ln Mc Lean VA 22101-2507 Office: Nat Orgn on Disability 910 16th St NW Ste 600 Washington DC 20006-2903

REICH, DAVID LEE, library director; b. Orlando, Fla., Nov. 25, 1930; s. P.F. and Opal Katherine (Wood) Reichelderfer; m. Kathleen Johanna Weichel, Aug. 2, 1954 (div. Sept. 1964); 1 son, Robert Weichel. Ph.B. magna cum laude, U. Detroit, 1961; A.M. in L.S. (Carnegie Library Sci. Endowment scholar), U. Mich., 1963. Tchr. English Jefferson Davis Jr. Sch., San Antonio, 1961-62; dir. engring. library Radiation Inc., Melbourne, Fla., 1963-64; asst. to dir. libraries Miami-Dade Jr. Coll., Miami, Fla., 1964-65; dir. learning resources Monroe County Community Coll., Monroe, Mich., 1965-68; dep. dir. Dallas Pub. Library, 1968-73; dep. chief librarian The Chgo. Pub. Library, 1973-74, commr., 1975-78; dir. Bd. Library Commrs., Commonwealth of Mass., Boston, 1978-80; exec. sec. New Eng. Library Bd., Augusta, Maine, 1980-82; dir. Lakeland Pub. Library, Lakeland, Fla., 1983—; vice chmn. New Eng. Library Bd., 1979-80; libr. cons. Macomb County C.C., Warren, Mich., 1967; chmn. adv. com. to libr. tech. asst. program El Centro Coll., Dallas, 1969-71; mem. inter-task working group Goals for Dallas, 1968-70, mem. Dallas Area Libr. planning coun., 1970-73; mem. adv. coun. dept. libr. sci. No. Ill. U., 1975-78; v.p., pres.-elect Tampa Bay Libr. Consortium, 1985-86, pres., 1986-87. Co-author: The Public Library in Non-traditional Education, 1974; Contbr. articles to library jours. Bd. dirs. The Villas II Homeowners Assn., 1994-96. Sgt. U.S. Army, 1952-55. Recipient Disting. Alumnus award U. Mich., 1978; William B. Calkins Found. scholar Orlando, 1963. Mem. ALA (coun.-at-large 1968-72, 75-79), S.E. Libr. Assn., Fla. Libr. Assn. (sec.-treas. coll. and spl. librs. divsn. 1965, steering com. mcpl. librs. caucus 1983-84, chmn. 1984-85, exec. bd. 1984-87), Soc. Fla. Archivists (exec. bd. 1994-96, sec. 1966-67), Fla. Pub. Libr. Assn. (pres. 1987-88, exec. bd. 1988-89, 94-95, editor newsletter 1992-93, 96—, chmn. libr. adminstrn. divsn. 1992, friends and trustees divsn. 1993, 95), Alumni Assn. U. Mich. (pres. Libr. Sch. alumni 1973). Home: 3929 Old Road 37 Villa 134 Lakeland FL 33813-1058 Office: Lakeland Pub Libr 100 Lake Morton Dr Lakeland FL 33801-5347

REICH, MICHAEL, electronics engineer; b. N.Y.C., Apr. 6, 1943; s. Sidney and Sylvia (Slackman) R.; m. Roberta Sandra Meritz, Aug. 14, 1966; children: Andrew Paul, Richard Ryan, Evan. BEE, CCNY, 1971; MS in Adminstrn., George Washington U., 1977; postgrad., Fed. Exec. Inst., 1986. Project engr. Naval Electronics Systems Engring. Activity, St. INigoes, Md., 1971-75, tech. svcs. head, 1975-84; exec. dir. Naval Electronic Systems Engring. Ctr., Charleston, S.C., 1984-94; dept. head In-Svc. Engring. Naval Command, Control and Ocean Surveillance Ctr., Charleston, S.C., 1994—. Mem. engring. 200 steering com. The Citadel; mem. com. for tech. devel. Charleston Trident Econ. Devel. Bd., mem bd. of dirs., Trident United Way. Recipient Meritorious Civilian Svc. award USN, 1987, Superior Civilian Svc. award USN, 1992. Mem. IEEE, Fed. Exec. Inst. Alumni Assn., Toastmasters Internat. Home: 2633 Marsh Creek Dr Charleston SC 29414-6578 Office: Nise East 4600 Marriott Dr Charleston SC 29406-6556

REID, AUDLEY GEORGE, religion and philosophy educator; b. Montego Bay, Jamaica, Nov. 9, 1941; came to U.S., 1979; s. Felis Isaiah and Grace (Cramsie) R.; m. Verna Alice Warren, Aug. 27, 1966; children: Gail Patrie, Audley George Jr., Seana Loree. Diploma in theology, U. London, 1966; BA with honors, U. W.I., 1972; M Theol. Studies, Emory U., 1982; PhD, Union Inst., 1995. Min. of religion United Theol. Coll., Jamaica, 1966-77, Jamaica Bapt. Union, Trelawny, 1966-77; area officer Jamaica Adult Literacy Assn., Trelawny, 1972-74; coord. Ministry of Edn., Kingston, Jamaica, 1974-76; resource person Bapt. Conv. of Ont., Toronto, Can., 1977-79; asst. prof. Allen U., Columbia, S.C., 1981-82; life and health ins. agt. Sun Life & Seaboard Life, Toronto, 1984-86; real estate agt. Re/Max Internat., Toronto, 1988-90; prof. Fla. Meml. Coll., Miami, 1990—; adj. prof. Union Inst., Cin., 1994—; sec. bd. govs. United Theol. Coll., Kingston, 1972-77; justice of peace, Trelawny, 1967-77. Contbr. articles to profl. jours. Mem. Land Authority Bd., Manchester, Jamaica, 1972-77; v.p. Vaughan Liaison Com., Toronto, 1977-79; pres. Cmty. Forum, Toronto, 1978-81; mem. Black Archives Found., Miami, 1995—. Emory U. grantee, 1980, 82, Bush grantee, 1995. Mem. U. W.I. Guild of Grads, Black Archives Found. (acad. award 1995), Smithsonian Instn. (nat. mem.), Kiwanis Internat. (hon., founding pres. Upper Trelawny chpt. 1973-74, Outstanding Pres. award 1974). Democrat. Baptist. Home: 3400 Foxcroft Rd # 214 Miramar FL 33025 Office: Fla Meml Coll 15800 NW 42nd Ave Opa Locka FL 33054-6155

REID, CAROLYN KAY, language educator; b. Foster, Ky., May 14, 1963; d. Alvin Richard and Clara Ellen (Taylor) Bishop; m. Brian Lee Reid, July 8, 1983; children: Barton Andrew, Brett Taylor, Brennan Matthew. BA in English, No. Ky. U., 1987, BA in Edn., 1994. Tchr. substitute Pendleton County Bd. Edn., Falmouth, Ky., 1990-92; tchr. Pendleton County Bd. Edn., Falmouth, 1994—. Musician Grassy Creek Christian Ch., Demossville, Ky., 1992—, Sun. sch. tchr., 1996—. Republican. Home: 1008 Sycamore St Falmouth KY 41040 Office: Pendleton County HS Rte 1 Box 224 Falmouth KY 41040

REID, DONALD WAYNE, investment management executive, researcher; b. Cullman, Ala., Sept. 4, 1952; s. Herman L. and Opal Aline (Gerstman) R.; m. Rebecca Gail Cravens, Mar. 16, 1985; children: Lindsey Michelle, Whitney Blair. BS, Auburn U., 1974; MS, U. Ga., 1978; PhD, U. Ky., 1981. Acct. Ernst & Ernst, Chattanooga, 1975-76; rsch. asst. U. Ga., Athens, 1976-78, assoc. prof., 1986-90; rsch. asst. U. Ky., Lexington, 1978-81, asst. prof., 1981-86; assoc. prof. U. South Ala., Mobile, 1990-91; co-dir. rsch. Eden Fin. Corp., Chgo., 1989-91; co-dir. quantitative equity rsch. Weiss, Peck & Greer, Chgo., 1991—. Contbr. articles to profl. jours. Mem. Chgo. Quantitative Alliance. Office: Weiss Peck & Greer 311 S Wacker Dr Chicago IL 60606-6627

REID, DONNA JOYCE, small business owner; b. Springfield, Tenn., June 25, 1954; d. Leonard Earl Reid and Joyce (Robertson) Kirby; m. Kenneth Bruce Sadler, June 26, 1976 (div. Apr. 1980); m. John Christopher Moulton, Oct. 18, 1987 (div. Dec. 1992); m. Peter Leatherland, Apr. 3, 1993. Student, Austin Peay State U., Clarksville, Tenn., 1972-75. Show writer, producer WTVF-TV (CBS affiliate), Nashville, 1977-83, promotion producer, 1983-85, on-air promotion mgr., 1985-86; gen. mgr. Steadi-Film Corp., Nashville, 1986-90; co-owner Options Internat., Nashville, 1990—. Big sister Buddies of Nashville, 1981-87. Named to Honorable Order of Ky. Cols. John Y. Brown, Gov., 1980; recipient Significant Svc. award ARC, 1982, Clara Barton Communications award, 1983. Mem. NAFE, Nat. Assn. TV Arts and Scis., Nat. Film Inst., Nat. Assn. Broadcasters, Internat. Platform Assn. Methodist. Office: Options Internat Inc 913 18th Ave S Nashville TN 37212-2102

REID, GINGER MEREDITH, school counselor, educator; b. Atlanta, Dec. 5, 1969; d. Ronald Davis Balser and Temme Barkin-Leeds; m. Wayne Dale Reid, II, Aug. 12, 1995. BA in Psychology, Emory U., 1993; MEd in Sch. Counseling, Ga. State U., 1995. Cert. sch. counselor, Ga. Summer day camp counselor Frog Hollow Day Camp, Atlanta, 1988-91; tchr., counselor Haverty Hollow Pre-Sch. Enrichment Program, Atlanta, 1991-92, 93-96; rsch. asst. Emory Univ., Atlanta, 1992-93; sch. counselor Dacula (Ga.) Mid. Sch., 1996—. Mem. Ga. Sch. Counselors Assn., Ga. Assn. Play Therapy, Ga. Sch. Age Care Assn., Phi Bet Kappa, Psi Chi. Jewish. Home: 1702 Defoors Mill Ct Atlanta GA 30318 Office: Dacula Mid Sch 6th Grade Counselor Office Dacula GA 30211

REID, HELEN VERONICA, dean; b. Reading, Eng., Sept. 25, 1956; d. Alan A. and Teresa H. (Thatcher) Ware; m. Gary B. Reid, May 29, 1976; children: Robert, Jennifer, Kristen. BA in Biolgoy, U. Tex., Austin, 1976; BSN, U. Tex., Arlington, 1978; MSN, Tex. Women's U., Denton, 1983. CCRN; cert. CPR instr. Asst. nurse coord., staff nurse, float pool nurse Parkland Meml. Hosp., Dallas, 1979-83, float pool nurse, 1987-93; instr. Trinity Valley Community Coll., Kaufman, Tex., 1983-86, freshman team leader, 1986-90; dean health occupations Trinity Valley C.C., Kaufman, Tex., 1990—. Mem. Nursing Network on Violence Against Women, Tex. Assn. Vocat. Nurse Educators, Orgn. for ADN (sec. 1988-92, nom. com. chair 1995-96), Tex. C.C. Tchrs. Assn., Tex. Assn. of Jr. and C.C. Instructional Adminstrs., Sigma Theta Tau. Home: 4332 Crestover Dr Mesquite TX 75150-4452

REID, JOAN LORAINE, primary school educator; b. Bklyn., June 1, 1971; d. Joseph Johnson and Ena May Reid. BS in Edn., Ga. So. U., 1994. Tchr. Chatham County Pub. Schs., Savannah, Ga., 1994; kindergarten tchr. Dade County Pub. Schs., Miami, Fla., 1994—. Mem. ASCD, Internat. Reading Assn., Alpha Kappa Alpha. Home: 1411 SW 88 Way Pembroke Pines FL 33025 Office: Dade County Public Schools 3250 NW 207th St Opa Locka FL 33056-1379

REID, JOSEPH WILLIAM, accountant; b. Gainesville, Ga., Apr. 23, 1955; s. William Lowell and Barbara ann (Trowbridge) R.; m. Elizabeth Chara Sudduth, July 12, 1986; children: Patrick Bennett, Alexandra Mackenzie. BBA in Acctg., U. Ga., 1977. CPA, Ga. Staff acct. KPMG Peat Marwick LLP, Atlanta, 1977-81, mgr., 1981-83, sr. mgr., 1983-88, ptnr., 1988—; S.E. Mergers and Acquisitions Practice. Active Retarded Citizens of Atlanta, bd. dirs., treas., chmn. fin. com., 1990—. Mem. Am. Inst. CPAs, Ga. Soc. CPAs. Home: 575 Leather Hinge Trl Roswell GA 30075-4184 Office: KPMG 303 Peachtree St NE Ste 2000 Atlanta GA 30308-3252

REID, KATHERINE LOUISE, artist, educator, author; b. Port Arthur, Tex., Mar. 25, 1941; d. Clifton Commodore and Helen Ross (Moore) Reid. BA, Baylor U., 1963; postgrad. in design and illustration, Kans. City Art Inst., 1964; MEd, U. Houston, 1973; cert. supervision U. Houston-Clear Lake City, 1980; postgrad. San Jacinto Coll., 1982. Cert. art educator, profl. supr., Tex. Litho reproduction artist Hallmark Cards, Kansas City, Mo., 1963-64; tchr. art high sch. Pasadena Ind. Sch. Dist. (Tex.), 1964-77, supr. art, gifted and talented and photography, 1977-85; supr. art and photography InterAct, 1985-90, instrl. specialist art, 1990—, photography, tutor act art, 1990-93, instrl. specialist in art and special programs, 1993-96, rsch planning , data disaggregation, 1996—, dir. summer, winter program; 4 MAT learning styles trainer DuPont Leadership Devel. Process Trainer, Selective Rsch., Inst., tchr. perceiver specialist, performance quality systems trainer, coop. learning trainer, outcome based edn. trainer, integrated unit devel. and authentic assessment trainer The Greater Gulf Coast Adminstr. Assessment Project, Assessor, 1991; head crafts, asst. dir. winter discovery program-ski camp Cheley Colo. Camps, Denver, Estes Park, 1967-75; mem. awards com. John Austin Cheley Found., 1990-92; staff artist, media workshop, Tex. Edn. Agy., Austin, summer 1961; art enrichment tchr. Port Arthur Ind. Sch. Dist. (Tex.), summer 1961; head crafts Camp Waluta, Silsbee, Tex., summer, 1960; mem. Tex. Edn. Agy., Art Leadership Inst., 1989, 90, Tracking Rsch. Com., 1991, Core Strategic Planning Team, 1992—, Outcome Based Edn. Dist. Planning Com., 1991-92, Quality Systems Improvement Team, 1991-92, Outcome Based Edn. Com. Exit Outcomes, 1991. Author: Through Their Eyes, 1989; inventor, patentee Pet Car Seat, U.S.A. Mem. Friends of Fine Arts-Baylor U., Waco, Tex., 1981—; mem. Scholastic Art awards Regional Bd., Houston, 1978-84, Tex. Edn. Agy. Art Leadership Inst., 1989, 90; bd. dirs. Houston Council Student Art Awards, Inc., 1984—. Named Tchr. of Yr. Pasadena Ind. Sch. Dist., 1975; Outstanding Secondary Educator of Am., 1975; Tex. Art Educator of Yr., 1985. Mem. ASCD, Tex. Assn. Supervision and Curriculum Devel., Tex. Art Edn. Assn. (rep. editor newsletter 1982-85, chmn. supervision div. 1982-83, v.p. membership 1978-80, chmn. pub. info. com., regional chmn. youth art month 1980-82; regional chmn. membership com. 1976-78, pres. elect 1986, sec. 1991-93), Tex. Alliannce for Arts Edn. (bd. vice chmn. 1984-86, treas. 1988-90), Nat. Art Edn. Assn. (conv. com. 1977, 85), Houston Art Edn. Assn. (sec. 1969),Nat. Assn. for Supervision and Curriculum Devel., Delta Kappa Gamma (2d v.p. 1984-86). Baptist. Home: 106 Ravenhead Dr Houston TX 77034-1520

REID, KENDALL MARTIN, librarian; b. Richmond, Va., Jan. 28, 1946; s. Emmet Kendall and Jane Frances (Davenport) R.; m. Sharon Ann Winters, May 7, 1988. BA in English, Randolph-Macon Coll., 1967; MA in English, Wake Forest U., 1977; MLS, U. N.C., 1983. Cert. libr., Va. Tchr. Bedford County (Va.) Pub. Schs., 1967-70, Oak Ridge (N.C.) Acad., 1970-72; head reserved book room Wake Forest U., Winston-Salem, N.C., 1973-87, reference libr., 1984-87; reference libr. Chesapeake (Va.) Pub. Libr., 1987-90, head reference svcs., 1990-95, sr. reference libr., 1995—; instr. Ctr. for R&D in Law-Related Edn. Law Sch. Wake Forest U., 1987; presenter in field. Mem. Am. Conf. for Irish Studies, Va. Libr. Assn. Home: 2502 Chesapeake Ave Hampton VA 23661 Office: Chesapeake Pub Libr System 298 Cedar Rd Chesapeake VA 23320

REID, LYLE, judge; b. Brownsville, Tenn., June 17, 1930; m. Elizabeth W.; children: Betsy, Martha Lyle. BSBA, U. Tenn., JD, 1956. Asst. state atty. gen. State of Tenn., Nashville, 1961-63; county atty. Haywood County, Brownsville, Tenn., 1964-86; atty. Reid & Banks, Brownsville, Tenn., 1963-66; assoc. judge Tenn. Ct. Criminal Appeals, Tenn., 1987-90; chief justice Tenn. Supreme Ct., Nashville, 1990-94; deputy commr. Dept. Commerce & Ins., Tenn. With USAF, Korea. Mem. ABA, Am. Bar Found., Tenn. Bar Assn. Democrat. Methodist. Office: Tenn Supreme Ct 321 Supreme Ct Bldg 401 7th Ave N Nashville TN 37219-1406

REID, RALPH WALDO EMERSON, management consultant; b. Phila., July 5, 1915; s. Ralph Waldo Emerson and Alice Myrtle (Stuart) R.; m. Ruth Bull, Dec. 7, 1946; 1 child, Robert. Student, Temple U., 1932-34. BS, Northwestern U., 1936; MA, U. Hawaii, 1938; PhD, Harvard U., 1948. Cert. mgmt. cons. Asst. to v.p. Northwestern U., Evanston, Ill., 1938-40; chief mcpl. govt. br., spl. asst. govt. sect. Supreme Comdr. Allied Powers, 1946-47; spl. asst. Under Sec. of Army, 1948-49; chief Far Eastern affairs div. Office Occupied Areas, chief econs. div. Office Civil Affairs and Mil. Govt., Dept. of Army, 1950-53; asst. to dir. U.S. Bur. of Budget, Washington, 1953-55, asst. dir., 1955-61; resident mgr. A.T. Kearney Inc., Washington, 1961-72, mng. dir., Tokyo, 1972-81, cons., Alexandria, Va., 1981—; former dir. Nihon Regulator Co., Tokyo, Yuasa-Ionics Ltd., Tokyo, Japan DME, Tokyo. Served to comdr. USNR, 1941-46, PTO. Decorated Commendation Ribbon, USN; Order of Rising Sun 3d class (Japan); recipient Exceptional Civilian Service award U.S. Army, 1954. Mem. Inst. Mgmt. Consultants, Am. Polit. Sci. Assn. Republican. Am. Baptist. Clubs: Cosmos, Capitol Hill (Washington); Union League (Chgo.). Home: 412 Monticello Blvd Alexandria VA 22305-1616 Office: A T Kearney Inc PO Box 1405 Alexandria VA 22313-1405

REID, ROBIN ANNE, English language educator, writer; b. Moscow, Idaho, Nov. 1, 1955; d. Rolland Ramsay and Eileen Margaret (Harris) R. BA, Western Wash. U., 1979, MA in Creative Writing, 1981; MA in English, Middlebury Coll., 1984; PhD, U. Wash., 1992. Asst. prof. dept. lit. and langs. Tex. A&M U., Commerce, 1993—. Bd. dirs. Commerce Humane Assn., 1995. Office: Tex A&M U Dept Lit and Langs Commerce TX 75429

REID, ROSALIND, magazine editor; b. Iowa City, Nov. 16, 1954; d. Isaac Errett and Eleanor Mary Reid; children: Sarah C. Herndon, Kathryn A. Herndon. AB in Journalism, Polit Sci., Syracuse U., 1975; MA in Pub. Policy Scis., Duke U., 1981. Reporter and columnist Lewiston (Maine) Daily Sun, 1975-77; staff writer The News and Observer, Raleigh, N.C., 1979-80, The Cary (N.C.) News, 1981-84; asst. news dir. N.C. State U., Raleigh, 1984-90; assoc. editor Am. Scientist, Research Triangle Park, N.C., 1990-91, mng. editor, 1991-92, editor, 1992—; mem. adv. bd. Dragonfly Mag., 1995—. Recipient Best Local Column award Maine Press Assn., 1977, HEW Pub. Svc. fellowship, Duke U., 1977-78. Mem. Nat. Assn. Sci. Writers, Phi Beta Kappa. Office: Am Scientist 99 Alexander Dr Research Triangle Park NC 27709

REID, WILLIAM HOWARD, psychiatrist; b. Dallas, Apr. 10, 1945; s. Howard Clinton and Lucile (Lattanner) R. BA, U. Minn., 1966, MD, 1970; MPH, U. Calif.-Berkeley, 1975. Diplomate Am. Bd. Psychiatry and Neurology, Am. Bd. Forensic Psychiatry, cert. in adminstrv. psychiatry. Intern, U. Calif.-Davis, 1970-71, resident in psychiatry, 1973-75; with Nebr. Psychiat. Inst., Omaha, 1977-86; med. dir. Colonial Hills/Hosp., San Antonio, 1986-89; med. dir. Tex. Dept. Mental Health and Retardation, Austin, 1989-96; prof. psychiatry U. Tex. Med. Sch., 1989—, Tex. A&M Coll. Med., 1991—. With M.C., AUS, 1971-73. Mem. Am. Psychiat. Assn., AMA, Am. Acad. Psychiatry and the Law (pres. 1988-89). Author: The Psychopath: A Comprehensive Study of Antisocial Disorders and Behaviors, 1978, Psychiatry for the House Officer, 1979, Basic Intensive Psychotherapy, 1980, The Treatment of Antisocial Syndromes, 1981, Treatment of the DSM-III Psychiatric Disorders, 1983, The Treatment of Psychiatric Disorders, 1989, Training Guide for the DSM-III-R, 1989; Editor-in-chief: Psychiatric Update Ser., 1995—; co-editor: Terrorism: Interdisciplinary Perspectives, 1983, Assaults Within Psychiatric Facilities, 1983, Unmasking the Psychopath, 1986, DSM IV Training Guide, 1995, Treatment of Psychiatric Disorders, 3rd edit., 1996; contbr. articles to sci. jours.; composer 25 mus. compositions. Office: PO Box 49817 Austin TX 78765

REID, WILLIAM JAMES, mining machinery executive; b. Cowdenbeath, Scotland, Jan. 18, 1941; came to U.S., 1968; s. William and Sheila (Davidson) R.; m. Thelma Rear, Sept. 27, 1969; children: Judith, Robert. Nat. cert. Mining Engring, Ashington County Tech. Coll., Northumberland, England, 1961. Student apprentice British Coal, England, 1958-63; sales engr. Huwood Ltd., England, 1964-68; mining engr. Huwood-Irwin Co., Irwin, Pa., 1968-71; mgr. mining sales Huwood-Irwin Co., 1971-74, gen. sales mgr., 1974-77, v.p., 1977-79; internat. sales dir. Huwood Ltd., England, 1979-81; exec. v.p. Am. Longwall Mining Corp., Abingdon, Va., 1981-83, pres., 1983-93; pres. Am. Longwall Face Conveyors Inc., Abingdon, Va., 1993-96, Internat. Longwall Cons., Abingdon, Va., 1996—, Internat. Engertainment Assocs., 1996—; apptd. to Nat. Coal Coun. by Sec. Energy, 1994-96; dir. Virginia Coal Coun., 1994-96, 96-99. Trustee Sullins Acad., Bristol, Va., 1984. Recipient Overseas medal British Instn. of Mining Engrs., 1992. Mem. AIME (treas. 1978), North Eng. Inst. Mining and Mech. Engrs. (assoc.), Nat. Mining Assn. (bd. govs. mfrs. divsn. 1991—), Greater Irwin Area C. of C. (bd. dirs. 1977). Presbyterian. Home: Millway Nog 526 Whites Mill Rd Apt 6 Abingdon VA 24210-2956 Office: Internat Longwall Cons Millway Nog 526 Whites Mill Rd Abingdon VA 24210-2956

REID, WILLIAM MICHAEL, mechanical engineer; b. Ames, Iowa, July 12, 1954; s. Richard James and Mary Lou (Moore) R. BS, Mich. State U., 1979. Registered profl. engr., Tex. Project engr. PRINTEK, St. Joseph, Mich., 1983-85; design engr. Tex. Instruments, Dallas, 1979-81, lead engr., 1981-83, project engr., 1985-88, proposal mgr., 1989, program mgr., 1989, 90—; cons., Dallas, 1987—. Mem. Texins. Republican. Roman Catholic. Home: 2412 Sherbrooke Ln McKinney TX 75070 Office: Tex Instruments Inc M/S 860 PO Box 84 Sherman TX 75091

REIF, JOHN HENRY, computer science educator; b. Madison, Wis., Aug. 4, 1951; s. Arnold and Jane (Chess) R.; m. Jane Anderson; children: Katie, Emily. BS in Applied Math. and Computer Sci., Tufts U., 1973; MS in Applied Math., Harvard U., 1975, PhD in Applied Math., 1977. Rsch. asst.

Harvard U., Cambridge, Mass., 1975-77; rsch. assoc. U. Rochester, N.Y., 1977-78, asst. prof. computer sci. dept., 1978-79; asst. prof. computer sci. dept. Harvard U., Cambridge, 1979-83, assoc. prof., 1983-86; prof. computer sci. dept. Duke U., Durham, N.C., 1986—; pres. RSIC, Inc., Durham, 1987—; cons. IBM Watson Rsch. Inst., Yorktown Heights, N.Y., 1983-84, Thinking Machines, Inc., Cambridge, Mass., 1985—, NASA Goddard Space Flight Ctr., Geenbelt, Md., 1985—, Microelectronics Ctr. N.C., Research Triangle, 1986-88. Editor: VLSI Algorithms and Architectures, 1986, Synthesis of Parallel Algorithms, 1993. Fellow IEEE, Assn. for Computing Machinery; mem. Am. Math. Assn., Soc. for Indsl. and Applied Math. Office: Duke U Box 90129 Computer Sci Dept Durham NC 27708-0129

REIFF, DOVIE KATE, urban planner; b. Birmingham, Ala., Nov. 5, 1931; d. Roy Humes and Lou Ada (Erwin) Petty; married, Dec. 25, 1956 (div. Dec. 1977); children: Donna Lynn Reiff Jayanathan, Benjamin Lyle, Johanna Carol Davis. BArch, U. Pa., 1954, M in City Planning, 1969, postgrad. in city and regional planning, 1975. Registered architect, Pa. Architect Oskar Stonorov Architect, Phila., 1954-57; research asst. Inst. Environ. Studies, Phila., 1967-68; sr. planner Montgomery County Planning Commn., Norristown, Pa., 1969-71; urban planner Wallace McHarg Roberts & Todd, Phila., 1971-74; research analyst Del. Valley Regional Planning Commn., Phila., 1974-77; recreation planner U.S. Heritage Conservation and Recreation Service, Phila., 1977-80; community planner U.S. Gen. Services Adminstrn., Phila., 1980-85; vol. urban planner U.S. Peace Corps, Kathmandu, Nepal, 1986-87; program devel. planner Chattanooga Neighborhood Enterprise Inc., 1987-88; environ. planner dept. urban planning City of Birmingham, 1989-92; planning cons., 1992—; mem. exec. com. Phila. chpt. Am. Inst. Planners, 1970-75; bd. dirs. Phila. chpt. AIA, 1978-79, mem. architects in govt. com., Washington, 1984-85. Participant nat. conf. Pres.'s Com. on Employment of Handicapped, Washington, 1974-76; regional del. Gov.'s Coun. on Handicapped, Harrisburg, Pa., 1975, Birmingham Urban Forestry and Tree Commn., 1990-92, Tenn. Urban Forestry Coun., 1993—; vol. Laurel House Women's Shelter, Norristown, Pa., 1985, GSA Adopt-a-Sch. Program, Phila., 1985, Birmingham Ptnrs. in Edn., 1990, VISTA vol. East Tenn. Cmty. Design Ctr., 1994-95; vol. Family Friends, 1996. Brunner grantee AIA, N.Y.C., 1974. Mem. Am. Inst. Cert. Planners, Am. Planning Assn., Nat. Trust for Hist. Preservation. Home: 212 Sunnybrook Trail Signal Mountain TN 37377-1859

REILLY, MICHAEL ATLEE, financial company executive, venture capital investor; b. Ft. Worth, Dec. 10, 1948; s. Thomas William and Alma Margaret (Cox) R.; m. Beverly Ann Yates, Dec. 27, 1974; children—Atlee Michael, Asher Yates, Anson Marcus, Austin Thomas, Axton Carter. B.A., U. Tex., 1971. Ptnr. Michael A. Reilly Co., Dallas, 1971-75, Reilly-Ginsburg, Dallas, 1975-80; pres., CEO Ryan Cos., Arlington, Tex., 1980-90; pres., CEO Reilly Bros., Arlington, 1990—. Chmn. bd. trustees Charitable and Ednl. Found., Arlington, 1976—, Stars for Children Tex., Arlington, 1983—; trustee Ryan/Reilly Sch. Urban Land Studies, U. Tex.-Arlington, 1982—, Childrens Trust Fund State of Tex; vice chmn. Troy Aikman Found. Mem. Urban Land Inst. Office: Reilly Bros Property Co 1000 Ballpark Way Ste 304 Arlington TX 76011-5169

REIMAN, SUE ELLEN, theatre company administrator, actress; b. Oak Park, Ill., Mar. 12, 1955; d. Pat James and Virginia Ann (Dickison) Schmidt. BFA, U. Okla., 1976, MA, 1988. Box office mgr. Dallas Ballet, 1977-78; studio theatre mgr. U. Okla., Norman, 1979-81; co. mgr. Prairie Dance Theatre, Oklahoma City, 1981-83, Street Players Theatre, Norman, 1986-88; mng. dir. Okla. Shakespeare in the Park, Edmond, 1988—; adj. faculty U. Ctrl. Okla., Edmond, 1996—. Mem. Shakespeare Theatre Assn. Am. (Sec. 1991-92). Democrat. Office: Okla Shakespeare in the Park PO Box 1171 Edmond OK 73083

REIMER, KEITH BRIAN, sales executive, marketing professional; b. N. Adams, Mass., Feb. 6, 1957; s. Morton Sterling and Dorothy Ann (Phelps) R.; m. Michele Ann Hawkins, Sept. 10, 1983; children: Justin Keith, Chase William. BS, Bridgewater State Coll., 1979. On-premise mgr. Lone Star Distributors, Dallas, 1985-88; regional mgr. Domecq Importers, Larchmont, N.Y., 1988-89; nat. sales mgr. Varesources, Inc., Garland, Tex., 1989-91; v.p. sales, mktg. Compuquick, Inc., Garland, Tex., 1991—; instr. Garland (Tex.) Small Bus. Assn. Chmn. Tex. Scholars, Garland, 1992—; bd. dirs. BEST steering com. Garland Ind. Sch. Dist., 1992—; coach Pee-Wee football Hillside Acad., Garland, 1995; deacon So. Garland Bapt. Ch., 1995—. Baptist. Home: 3334 Sunrise Dr Garland TX 75043 Office: Compuquick Inc 2302 Guthrie Ste 160 Garland TX 75043

REINBOLD, DARREL WILLIAM, energy engineering specialist; b. Louisville, Nov. 13, 1960; s. Paul William and Betty Lou (Buechler) R.; m. Theresa Marie Morris, June 17, 1989; children: Jessica Marie, Elizabeth Ashley. Cert. heating, air condit., refrig., Pleasure Ridge Pk. Vocat. Sch., Louisville, 1978; AAS, U. Louisville, 1987, BS in Occupational Edn., 1987; cert. universal technician, Esco Inst., 1994. Lic. journeyman HVAC mechanic, Ky. Apprentice pipe fitter A & A Mech., Louisville, 1978-80; heating, ventilation, air conditioning technician Prudential Heating and Air Conditioning, Louisville, 1980-87; heating, ventilation, air conditioning mechanic U. Louisville, 1988-89; svc. sys. specialist Honeywell Inc., Louisville, 1989-93; air conditioning estimator Ware Energy, Louisville, 1993—. Mem. baseball team U. Louisville, 1980-81. Mem. Assn. of Energy Engrs., Honorable Order Ky. Cols. Home: 3219 LaVel Ln Louisville KY 40216-1217 Office: Ware Energy 4005 Produce Rd Louisville KY 40218-3007

REINBOLD, JANICE KAY, school librarian; b. Anderson, Ind., Aug. 19, 1943; d. Norman E. and Ruth (Van Meter) Folsom; m. Paul E. Reinbold, June 11, 1965; 1 child, Sheila Kay (dec.). AB in Elem. Edn., Olivet Nazarene U., 1965; MA in Edn., So. Nazarene U., 1973; MLS, U. Okla., 1981. Elem. tchr. Tippecanoe Ind. Sch. Dist., Lafayette, 1965-67, Hearne (Ind.) Sch. Dist., 1967-70, Western Heights ISD, Oklahoma City, 1972-74; libr. So. Nazarene U., Bethany, Okla., 1976—; adv. bd. Bethany Libr. City Coun., 1992-94. Mem. Cathedral Choir Bethany First Nazarene Ch., 1974—. Mem. Phi Delta Lambda Honor Soc. Office: RT Williams LRC So Nazarene U 4115 N College Bethany OK 73008

REINERT, JAMES A., entomologist, educator; b. Enid, Okla., Jan. 26, 1944; s. Andrew J. and Emma Reinert; m. Anita Irwin; children: Travis J., Gina N., Mindy K., Melanie B., Gregory W., Teresa J. BS, Okla. State U., 1966; MS, Clemson U., 1968, PhD, 1970. Asst. state entomologist U. Md., College Park, 1970; asst. prof. entomology to prof. entomology Ft. Lauderdale Rsch. and Edn. Ctr., U. Fla., 1970-84; resident dir., prof. entomology Rsch. and Ext. Ctr., Tex. A&M U. Sys., Dallas, 1984-94; prof. entomology Tex. A&M Univ. System, Dallas, 1994—. Contbr. over 275 articles to profl. jours. NDEA fellow, 1968; recipient Porter Henegar Meml. award., So. Nurserymen's Assn., 1982. Mem. Inter-Turfgrass Soc., Entomol. Soc. Am., Fla. Entomol. Soc. (v.p. 1983, pres. 1984, Entomologist of Yr. 1985), Fla. State Hort. Soc. (v.p. 1982), S.C. Entomol. Soc., Rsch. Ctr. Adminstrs. Soc. (v.p. 1994, state rep. 1991-92, sec. 1993), Dallas Agr. Club (bd. dirs. 1989, v.p. 1990, pres. 1991). Roman Catholic. Home: 3805 Covinton Ln Plano TX 75023-7731 Office: Tex A&M Univ Rsch and Ext Ctr 17360 Coit Rd Dallas TX 75252-6599

REINHARD, ANDREW, archaeologist; b. Winston-Salem, N.C., June 5, 1972; s. Paul Norris and Janice Cone (McCrum) R. BA in Archaeology and BA in Writing, U. Evansville, Ind., 1994; MA in Archaeology, U. Mo., 1996. Editl. intern Archaeology Mag., N.Y.C., summer 1992; rsch. asst. Mus. of Art and Archaeology, Columbia, Mo., 1994-96; collections mgmt. intern Nelson-Atkins Mus. of Art, Kansas City, Mo., summer 1995; excavator/cataloger Poggio Civitate Excavation, Murlo, Italy, summer 1991; excavator, asst. photographer Isthmia (Greece) Excavation, summer 1996. Author: Athenium Janiform Head-Vases, 1996. Recipient Vigil Honor, Order of the Arrow, 1989. Home: 15099 Stillfield Pl Centreville VA 22020-1145

REINHARD, JOHN FREDERICK, JR., scientist, educator; b. Bronxville, N.Y., Sept. 2, 1951; s. John Frederick and Ingeborg (Mantel) R.; m. Ellen Woodward, Jan. 10, 1976; children: John, Paul, Erich. MS, MIT, 1977, PhD, 1980; postdoctoral fellow in pharmacology, Yale U., 1980-82. Sr. scientist Burroughs Wellcome Co., Research Triangle Park, N.C., 1982—; adj. assoc. prof. U. N.C., Chapel Hill, 1993—; vis. scientist Wellcome Rsch. Labs., Beckenham, Kent, U.K., 1991-92; reviewer Program Project Grant, Dept. Neurology, UMDNJ, Piscataway, 1990; chmn. spl. rev. com. NIH, 1990, chmn. adhoc com., neurology A study sect., 1991, chmn. spl. emphasis panel, neurology B2 study sect., 1993. Contbr. articles to sci. and profl. jours.; patentee in field. NIH postdoctoral fellow, 1978; recipient Nat. Rsch. Svc. award NIMH, 1980. Mem. Am. Soc. Pharmacology and Exptl. Therapeutics, Internat. Soc. Neurochemistry, Soc. Neurosci., European Brain and Behavior (hon.), Brit. Brain Rsch. Soc. (hon.), Sigma Xi, Rho Chi, Phi Sigma. Office: Glaxo Wellcome Co 5 Moore Dr Research Triangle Park NC 27709

REINHARDT, CAROL KENT, library supervisor; b. Denver, Jan. 2, 1945; d. Norman and Helen Luella (Fritz) Howard; m. William Charles Reinhardt, June 23, 1965 (div. Aug. 1992); children: Norman Andrew, Aaron Joel. AA, Gaston Coll., 1975. Tchr. Gaston County Schs., Gastonia, N.C., 1977-79; br. libr. supr. Gaston County Pub. Libr., Dallas, N.C., 1980—; bd. dirs. Gaston Sch. of the Arts; coord. poetry residency project Gaston County Schs., 1996; mem. task force Gaston County Arts-in-Edn., 1996—, coord NEA regional dance on tour, 1996. Bd. dirs. Gaston Dance, Inc., Gastonia, 1992—; project dir. United Arts Coun., Gastonia, 1988—, Gaston County Women's Orgn., 1990—; mem. Gaston County Mus. Art and History, 1986—, Friends of the Gaston County Pub. Libr., 1981—, project coord., 1989—; project coord. Foothills Yarnspinners Story League, 1989—; mem. Gaston County Hist. Soc. Recipient Outstanding Programming award Pub. Libr. Assn., 1992, 93, N.C. Pub. Libr. Dir.'s Assn., 1989, 90, Outstanding Svc. commendation Gaston County Commrs., 1989, 91, 92, 93, 96, Alumnus of Yr. award, 1996, Children and Youth Program Achievement award Nat. Assn. Counties, 1996. Mem. DAR, N.C. Libr. Assn., Pilot Club. Home: 1700 Old Spencer Mountain Rd Dallas NC 28034-9211 Office: Gaston County Pub Libr 105 S Holland St Dallas NC 28034-2013

REINKE, LESTER ALLEN, pharmacologist; b. Davenport, Nebr., Sept. 29, 1946; s. Herman D. and Alma I. (Grosshans) R.; m. Carol S. Paulsen, Sept. 1, 1968; children: Jonathan P., Lisa S. BS, U. Nebr., 1969, MS, 1975, PhD, 1977. Registered pharmacist, Nebr. Postdoctoral fellow U. N.C., Chapel Hill, 1977-80; asst. prof. U. Okla. Health Sci. Ctr., Oklahoma City, 1980-86, assoc. prof., 1986-92, prof. pharmacology, 1992—. Contbr. articles to profl. jours., chpts. to books. Pres. Gatewood Neighborhood Assn., Oklahoma City, 1988-89, Gatewood Area Patrol, Oklahoma City, 1988-89, Redeemer Luth. Ch., Oklahoma City, 1991-93. With U.S. Army, 1969-73. Recipient Provost Rsch. award U. Okla. Health Sci. Ctr., 1984; John E. Fogarty fellow Fogarty Found./NIH, 1989-90; rsch. grantee Nat. Cancer Inst., 1980-86, Nat. Inst. Alcohol Abuse-Alcoholism, 1987—. Mem. Am. Soc. for Pharmacology and Exptl. Therapeutics, Internat. Soc. for Biomed. Rsch. on Alcoholism, Internat. EPR Soc., Oxygen Soc. Lutheran. Home: 1302 NW 21st St Oklahoma City OK 73106-4020 Office: U Okla Dept Pharmacology COP 239 PO Box 26901 Oklahoma City OK 73190

REINTGEN, DOUGLAS SCOTT, surgical oncology educator, researcher; b. Latrobe, Pa., July 22, 1953; s. Robert Joseph and Patricia Lou (Cunningham) R.; m. Margaret Ann Palmer, Sept. 10, 1978 (div. Dec. 1982); m. Ellen Verena Jorgensen, Nov. 19, 1988; children: Christian, Michael. BA, Duke U., 1975, MD, 1979. Intern Duke U Med. Ctr., Durham, N.C., 1979-80, jr. asst. resident in surgery, 1980-81, rsch. fellow in surg. oncology, 1981-83, sr. asst. resident, 1983-86, chief resident in surgery, 1986-87; asst. prof. surgery U. South Fla., Tampa, 1987-91, assoc. prof., 1991-95, prof., 1995—; program leader in cutanous oncology Moffitt Cancer Ctr., Tampa, 1992—. Guest editor Annals Plastic Surgery, 1992, Jour. Surg. Oncology, 1993; editor: Cancer Screening, 1996; editl. bd. Annals Surg. Oncology, 1993. Named One of Best Cancer Specialists in Country, Good Housekeeping mag., One of Best Doctors in Am., Woodward/White, Inc. Mem. ACS, Soc. Surg. Oncology, Soc. Acad. Surgery, Southeastern Surg. Soc., Bassett Surg. Soc. (pres. 1995), Sabiston Surg. Soc. Republican. Roman Catholic. Home: Moffitt Cancer Ctr 16010 Gatwick Ct Tampa FL 33647 Office: Moffitt Cancer Ctr 12902 Magnolia Dr Tampa FL 33612-9416

REIS, MELANIE JACOBS, women's health nurse, educator; b. Merced, Calif., Apr. 17, 1954; d. John William Jr. and Josephine Bernice (Jarecke) Jacobs; children: Jillian, Steve. BSN, Fla. State U., 1976; MN, U. Fla., 1986; postgrad., U. Cen. Fla. Cert. childbirth educator, nurse practitioner in ob-gyn. Clin. instr. labor and delivery U. Cen. Fla., Orlando, 1989, 95, 96, academician instr., 1992; instr. high risk labor and deliver Valencia Community Coll./Orlando Regional Med. Ctr., 1988, 91; labor and delivery staff nurse Orlando Regional Med. Ctr., 1981-89, perinatal clin. nurse specialist (outcomes mgmt.), 1990—; instr. normal and high risk labor and delivery U. Cen. Fla., Orlando; perinatal nurse specialist Healthdyne Perinatal Svcs., Orlando, 1989-90; presenter in field. Mem. AWHONN, Am. Soc. Psychoprophylaxis in Obstetrics, Sigma Theta Tau. Home: 7724 Wicklow Cir Orlando FL 32817-1581 Office: Arnold Palmer Hosp for Children & Women 92 W Miller St Orlando FL 32806-2029

REISIN, EFRAIN, nephrologist, researcher, educator; b. Cordoba, Argentina, Feb. 25, 1943; came to U.S., 1979; s. Maximo and Elisa Reisin; m. Ilana Hershkovitz, Sept. 6, 1971; children: Eyal, Thalia Alexis. MD, Nat. U., Cordoba, 1966. Intern internal medicine Nat. U. Cordoba-Clinicas Hosp., 1966; resident Jimenes Diaz Found., Madrid, 1966-68; resident Chaim Sheba Med. Ctr., Tel Hashomer, Israel, 1968-71, fellow in nephrology, 1971-74, staff physician nephrology, 1974-77; rsch. fellow in hypertension Health Sci. Ctr., Winnipeg, Man., Can., 1977-78; vis. scientist in hypertension Nat. Health Welfare Can., Winnipeg, Man., 1978-79; Ochsner vis. scientist in hypertension Ochsner Found. Hosp., New Orleans, 1979-82; from asst. prof. to assoc. prof. medicine La. State U., New Orleans, 1982-89, prof. medicine, 1989—; dir. dept. nephrology Med. Ctr. Charity Hosp., New Orleans, 1985—; panelist Consensus Conf., NIH, Bethesda, Md., 1991. Author numerous articles and book chpts. on hypertension and nephrology; conducted 1st research study documenting positive effects of weight reduction in treatment of hypertension, 1978 (citation classic Inst. Sci. Info. 1988). 1st lt. Israel Army, 1971-72. Grantee Nat. Health and Welfare Can., 1978-79, Am. Heart Assn., 1980-81, also several pharm. cos., 1984—. Fellow ACP, Am. Coun. High Blood Pressure Rsch., Am. Heart Fund, Am. Coll. Clin. Pharmacology (counselor south ctrl. regional chpt. 1991-92), Am. Fedn. Clin. Rsch., So. Soc. for Clin. Investigation; mem. Internat. Soc. Nephrology, Internat. Soc. Hypertension, Am. Soc. Nephrology, Am. Soc. Hypertension, Coun. Nephrology, Am. Heart Assn., Inter-Am. Soc. Hypertension, Orleans Parish Med. Soc. Office: La State U Sch Medicine 1542 Tulane Ave New Orleans LA 70112-2825

REISMAN, ROSEMARY MOODY CANFIELD, writer, humanities educator; b. Des Moines, Iowa, Nov. 18, 1927; d. V. Alton and Lois Gloria (Slee) Moody; m. Michael Ellison Canfield, Sept. 6, 1952 (div. May 1961); children: Michael, John Charles, Celia Catherine, Christopher James; m. Maurice Reisman, May 10, 1986 (dec. 1990). BA in English, U. Minn., 1949, MA in English, 1952; PhD in English, La. State U., 1971. Reporter Ames Tribune, summer 1944; writer, actor Sta. WOI Pub. Radio, Ames, Iowa, 1944-48; dir., writer children's plays Sta. KASI, Ames, 1949; tchg. asst. U. Minn., 1949-52; writer Sta. WOI-TV, Ames, summer 1952; writer, show host Sta. WDGY, Mpls., 1952-54; instr. La. State U., 1961-69, NDEA fellow, 1969-71; asst. prof. English Troy (Ala.) State U., 1971-80, assoc. prof., 1980-90, chairperson dept. English, 1985-90, prof., 1990-94; mem. honors coun. Troy State U., 1985-94, mem. honors faculty, 1986-94, mem. acad. coun., 1989-92, mem. faculty adv. coun., 1990-92, Rhodes scholar instnl. rep., 1987-91; adj. prof. Charleston So. U., 1996—; coord. sr. honors seminar Coll. of Charleston, 1996—; writer, cons. Baton Rouge State Times—Morning Adv., 1963-70; prodr., writer Perspectives project films Ala. ETV, 1977-80; chairperson conf. sessions South Ctrl. Soc. for 18th-Century Studies, 1988, Southeastern Am. Soc. for 18th Century Studies, 1991, 93; chairperson workshop Ala. Coun. Tchrs. of English, fall 1987; grant writer, project dir. Ala. Humanities Found., 1980, 89, asst. project dir. summer grad. course, 1990, presenter various instns., 1985-94; NEH grant writer, project dir. Ala. Pub. Libr. Sys., 1977-80; past presenter, lectr. Read Ala.! program, most recently NEH conf., 1989, various pub. librs. for Auburn Ctr. for Arts and Humanities, 1989-90; presenter numerous lectures and lectr. series, various instns., 1970—. Author: Perspectives: The Alabama Heritage, 1978; co-author: Contemporary Southern Women Fiction Writers, 1994; chairperson editl. adv. bd. Ala. Lit. Rev., 1986-94; mem. editl. bd. Biog. Guide to Ala. Lit., 1985—; guest editor spl. issue Ala. English 7, spring 1995; contbr. essays, articles and revs. to lit. publs. Baldwin County Humanities scholar Ala. Humanities Found., 1983, 84; finalist Ingalls award for Outstanding Tchg., 1991. Mem. NEA, AAUW (past pres.), AAUP, MLA, South Atlantic MLA, Assn. Depts. of English (mem. exec. com. 1991-94), Assn. Coll. English Tchrs. of Ala. (state pres. 1986-88, mem. steering com.), Ala. Edn. Assn., Fitzgerald Soc., Troy State U. Edn. Assn. (pres. 1990-93), Low Country Assn. (pres. 1996—), Phi Beta Kappa (past pres. S.E. Ala. assn., del. to nat. triennial coun. 1991, alt. 1994), Gamma Beta Phi (nat. pres. 1978-79, cert. of merit 1979). Democrat. Episcopalian. Home and Office: 121 Innisbrook Bend Summerville SC 29483-5084

REISNER, ROBERT F., software executive; b. Cold Spring, N.Y., July 9, 1948; s. Robert R. and Margaret L. (Cayer) R.; m. Elaine M. Kearns, Dec. 25, 1949; children: Joshua, Kristina, Megan. BA in Bus., Marist Coll., 1971; MBA, So. Ill. U., 1977. Computer specialist IBM Corp, Poughkeepsie, N.Y., 1967-71; mktg. IBM Corp, Trenton, N.J., 1971-75; mgr. computer svcs. RCA Corp., Cherry Hill, N.J., 1975-80; dir. fin. analysis RCA Corp., Princeton, N.J., N.Y., 1980-86; cons. fin. analysis GE Corp., Fairfield, Conn., 1986-88, mgr. productivity programs, 1988-90; mgr. fin. corp. staff GE Capital Corp., Stamford, Conn., 1990-92; pres., CEO, general mgr. GE Capital Communication Svcs., Atlanta, 1992-94; sr. v.p. bus. devel. & ventures GE Capital Bus. Svcs., Atlanta, 1994-95; prs., CEO LEX2000 Inc., Atlanta, 1995—. Home: 3262 Belmont Glen Dr Marietta GA 30067-9117 Office: LEX2000 Inc Ste 700-120 2900 Delk Rd Marietta GA 30067

REISTER, DAVID BRYAN, systems analyst; b. L.A., Feb. 22, 1942; s. Bryan and Helen Ross (Jones) R.; m. Willa Katherine Fletcher, Sept. 7, 1963; children: Austen Elisabeth Freeda, Fletcher Bryan. BS in Engring. Physics with highest honors, U. Calif., Berkeley, 1964, MS in Nuclear Engring., 1966, PhD in Engring. Sci., 1969. Asst. prof. SUNY, Buffalo, 1968-74; rschr. Inst. Energy Analysis, Oak Ridge, Tenn., 1974-85; sys. analyst computer sci. and math. divsn. Oak Ridge Nat. Lab., 1985—. Contbr. articles to profl. jours. Mem. IEEE, AAAS, Sigma Xi. Home: 10366 Rather Rd Knoxville TN 37931-2123 Office: Oak Ridge Nat Lab Bldg 6025 MS 6364 Oak Ridge TN 37831-6364

REISZ, SARA NOYES, publisher, lawyer; b. San Jose, Calif., Jan. 26, 1953; d. Trigg and Elizabeth Barnum Noyes; m. John P. Reisz, Mar. 6, 1981; children: Carey, Betsy, Katie. BS, Ctr. Coll., Danville, Ky., 1974; JD, U. Louisville, 1979. Cert. Tourism Mgmt. Profl. Ky. Tourism Coun., We. Ky. U.. Assoc. Greenebaum, Doll & McDonald, Louisville, 1979-82; publisher Editl. Svcs. Co., Louisville, 1990—. Vestry mem. Cavalry Episcopal Ch., Louisville, 1996—. Mem. Ky. Tourism Coun., Louisville and Jefferson Counties Convs., Visitors Bur., Ky. Bar Assn., Louisvlle Bar Assn., Jr. League of Louisville (sustainer adv. bd. 1995—). Democrat. Episcopalian. Office: Editl Svcs Co 812 S 3rd St Louisville KY 40203-2214

REITZ, DOUGLAS JOHN FRANK, airline captain, computer consultant; b. Salisbury, Rhodesia, May 7, 1955; came to U.S., 1980; s. Francis Charles Deneys and Zeta Ann (Runham) R.; m. Judy Ann White, Mar. 31, 1978; 1 child, David Douglas. Dir. ops. Aviex Jet, Inc., Houston, 1980-84; capt. Am. Airlines, Dallas, 1984—; computer cons., 1983—. Flight lt. Rhodesian Air Force, 1973-80. Recipient Sword of Honor, Rhodesian Air Force, 1974. Mem. Allied Pilots Assn. Home: 2134 Sevilla Way Naples FL 34109

REKAU, RICHARD ROBERT, architect; b. Chicago Heights, Ill., June 6, 1936; s. Robert Richard and Charlotte (Ryan) Rekau Altier; m. Carolyn Pritchett, Dec. 20, 1962; 1 son, Ryan Richard. B.Arch., B.S., Ga. Tech Inst., 1965. Registered architect Ga., N.C., Ala., Fla., Md., S.C., Tenn.; cert. Nat. Council Archtl. Registration Bds. Project mgr. John Portman & Assocs., Atlanta, 1970-76; assoc. Herndon & Harris, Atlanta, 1976-77; v.p. Devel. Contractors, Inc., Atlanta, 1979-81; pres. Richard R. Rekau, Architect, P.C., Atlanta, 1977—; pres. Rekau Properties, 1984—. Prin. works include Lanier Plaza, Gainesville, Ga. Corp. Plaza N.W., Atlanta, Pkwy. Village, Macon, Ga., Carrollton (Ga.) Crossroads Shopping Ctr., Tuxedo Park, Atlanta, Griffin (Ga.) Mall. Mem. Ga. Canoeing Assn., Gainesboro 500, Tuxedo Park, Carrollton Crossroads, Festival Ctr. Indigo Run, Hilton Head, S.C., Park Centre Commons, Ocala, Fla., Perimeter Village, Atlanta. Work recipient Better Buckhead award 1987. Mem. AIA, SMPS, Hist. Preservation Found. N.C., Nat. Trust Hist. Preservation, Ga. Tech Alumni Assn. Home: 1771 Beverly Woods Ct Atlanta GA 30341-1418 Office: 1800 Century Pl NE Ste 270 Atlanta GA 30345-4304

REKTORIK-SPRINKLE, PATRICIA JEAN, Latin language educator; b. Robstown, Tex., Feb. 19, 1941; d. Julius and Elizabeth Lollie (Ermis) Rektorik; m. Edgar Eugene Sprinkle, June 22, 1963; children: Julie Anne, Mark. BA in English and Latin, Our Lady of the Lake Coll., San Antonio, 1963, MA, 1967; doctoral student, Tex. A&M U., 1968-74, U. North Tex., 1987—. Cert. secondary tchr., Tex. Latin and English tchr. Ysleta Independent Sch. Dist., El Paso, Tex., 1963-64, El Paso Independent Sch. Dist., 1964-65; instr. Our Lady of the Lake Coll., 1965-66; rhetoric and composition instr. Tex. A&M U., College Station, 1968-69, 72-74, Harford Community Coll., Bel Aire, Md., 1970-71; Latin tchr. Denton (Tex.) Pub. Schs., 1974—; mem. residents adv. com. Tex. Acad. Math. and Sci., Denton, 1987-88; chmn. Latin reading competition Nat. Jr. Classical League, Miami, Ohio, 1988-93; mem. methodology com. Am. Classical League, 1993-95; dir. Tex. State Jr. Classical League Conv., 1996; presenter workshops in field; mem. Tex. State Textbook Adv. Com., 1989-90. Costume designer Denton Cmty. Theater, 1984; choir dir. Immaculate Conception Ch., Denton, 1985-87; chmn. costume competition Tex. State Jr. Classical League, 1987—, exec. bd. sponsor, 1981—. Arthur Patch McKinlay scholar, 1986, 91. Mem. Am. Classical Assn., Classical Assn. of the Mid-West and South, Metroplex Classics Assn. (constl. adv. com. 1988), Classics Assn. Southwestern U.S. (pres. 1987-88), Tex. Classics Assn., Tex. Fgn. Lang. Assn. (chmn. hon. mem. 1988-89, chmn. local arrangements 1977). Roman Catholic. Office: Billy Ryan High Sch 5101 E McKinney St Denton TX 76208-4630

RELLER, L. BARTH, medical microbiologist, physician, educator. Prof. medicine and pathology Med. Ctr. Duke U., Durham, N.C. Recipient Becton Dickinson award in clin. microbiology Am. Soc. Microbiology, 1991. Office: Duke Univ Med Ct Box 3938 Durham NC 27710

REMINE, WILLIAM HERVEY, JR., surgeon; b. Richmond, Va., Oct. 11, 1918; s. William Hervey and Mabel Inez (Walthall) ReM.; m. Doris Irene Grumbacher, June 9, 1943; children: William H., Stephen Gordon, Walter James, Gary Craig. B.S. in Biology, U. Richmond, 1940, D.Sc. (hon.), 1965; M.D., Med. Coll. Va., Richmond, 1943; M.S. in Surgery, U. Minn., Mpls., 1952. Diplomate Am. Bd. Surgery. Intern Doctor's Hosp., Washington, 1944; fellow in surgery Mayo Clinic, Rochester, Minn., 1944-45, 47-52; instr. surgery Mayo Grad. Sch. Medicine, Rochester, Minn., 1954-59, asst. prof. surgery, 1959-65, assoc. prof. surgery, 1965-70, prof. surgery, 1970-83, prof. surgery emeritus, 1983—; surg. cons. to surgeon gen. U.S. Army, 1965-75; surg. lectr., USSR, 1987, 89, Japan, 1988, 90, Egypt, 1990; lectr. Soviet-Am. seminars, USSR, 1987, 89. Sr. author: Cancer of the Stomach, 1964, Manual of Upper Gastro-intestinal Surgery, 1985; editor: Problems in General Surgery, Surgery of the Biliary Tract, 1986; mem. editorial bd. Rev. Surgery, 1965-75, Jour. Lancet, 1968-77; contbr. 200 articles to profl. jours. Served to capt. U.S. Army, 1945-47. Recipient St. Francis surg. award St. Francis Hosp., Pitts., 1976, disting. service award Alumni Council, U. Richmond, 1976. Mem. ACS, AAAS, Am. Assn. History of Medicine, AMA, Am. Med. Writers Assn., Am. Soc. Colon and Rectal Surgeons, Soc. Surgery Alimentary Tract (v.p. 1983-84), Am. Surg. Assn., Assn. Mil. Surgeons U.S., Internat. Soc. Surgery, Digestive Disease Found., Priestley Soc. (pres. 1968-69), Central Assn. Physicians and Dentists (pres. 1972-73), Central Surg. Assn., Soc. Med. Cons. Armed Forces, Mayo Clinic Surg. Soc. (chmn. 1964-66), Soc. Head and Neck Surgeons, Soc. Surg. Oncology, So. Surg. Assn., Western Surg. Assn. (pres. 1979-80), Minn. State Med. Assn., Minn. Surg. Soc. (pres. 1966-67), Zumbro Valley Med. Soc., Sigma Xi; hon. mem. Colombian Coll. Surgeons, St. Paul Surg. Soc., Flint Surg. Soc., Venezuelan Surg. Soc., Colombian Soc. Gastroenterology, Dallas So. Clin. Soc., Ga. Surg. Soc., Soc. Postgrad. Surgeons Los Angeles County, Japanese Surg. Soc., Argentine Surg. Digestive Soc., Bassanese Surg. Assn. (Italy), Tex. Surg. Soc., Omicron Delta Kappa, Alpha Omega Alpha, Beta Beta Beta, Kappa Sigma. Methodist. Home: Sawgrass Players Club 8212 Seven Mile Dr Ponte Vedra Beach FL 32082-3129

REMINGTON, WILL MYRON, engineering executive; b. Montevallo, Mo., July 24, 1940; s. Cecil Spencer and Opal Marie R.; m. Valerie Joyce Buzzelli, Dec. 26, 1962; children: Mark Douglas, Matthew SPencer, Victoria Marie. BS, U.S. Mil. Acad., 1962; MS in Engring., Purdue U., 1968; M Mgmt., Northwestern U., 1990. Registered profl. engr., Pa. Commd. 2d lt. U.S. Army, 1962, advanced through grades to lt. col.; with 237th Engr. Battalion, Heilbronn, Fed. Republic Germany, 1963-66; platoon leader Co. C. 237th Engr. Bn., 1963-64; platoon leader ADM D Co. 237th Engr. Battalion, 1964-65; commdr. D Co. 237th Engr. Battalion, 1965-66; ops. officer 19th Engr. Battalion, Bong Son, Vietnam, 1968-69; ops. officer 2d Engr. Battalion, Camp Castle, Korea, 1972-73, asst. divsn. engr., 1973; comdr. 518th Engr. Co., Ft. Kobbe, Canal Zone, 1974-76; hdqrs. commandant U.S. So. Command, Quarry Heights, Canal Zone, 1976; mgr. Natural Gas Pipeline Co. Am., Lombard, Ill., 1977-92; ret. U.S. Army, 1990; v.p. Stoner Assocs., Inc., Houston, 1992—. Elder Evangelical Free Ch., Naperville, Ill., 1986-92; chmn. Evangelical Covenant Ch., 1982-83. Decorated Bronze Star, Air medal, Meritorious Svc. medal, Joint Svcs. Commendation medal. Mem. West Point Soc. of Greater Houston (bd. dirs.). Office: Stoner Assocs Inc 5177 Richmond Ave Ste 900 Houston TX 77056-6736

REMIREZ, ANTONIO, physician; b. Boonesville, Ark., Dec. 14, 1962; s. Mario Jose and Gemma Maria (Salgueiro) R.; m. Sheri Annette Pope, July 17, 1982; children: Andria Annette, Emily Ada. BS, Baylor U., Waco, Tex., 1985; MD, Baylor U., Houston, 1989. Diplomate Am. Bd. Internal Medicine. Intern, resident St. Luke's Episcopal Hosp., Houston; physician in pvt. practice Beaumont, Tex., 1994—; physician Kelsey Seybold Clinic, Houston, 1992-94. Mem. ACP, Tex. Med. Soc., So. Med. Assn., Jefferson County Med. Assn., Phi Beta Kappa, Alpha Epsilon Delta, Alpha Chi Alpha. Office: 4222 College Beaumont TX 77707

RENARD, MEREDITH ANNE, marketing and advertising professional; b. Newark, Apr. 12, 1952; d. W. Edward and Lois E. (Velthoven) Young; m. Robert W. Renard, Nov. 11, 1995. BA, Caldwell Coll., 1974. Advt., pub. rels. asst. Congoleum Corp., Lawrenceville, N.J., 1974-77; account mgr. Saatchi & Saatchi Compton, N.Y.C., 1977-82; dir. advt., sales promotion Singer Sewing Co., Edison, N.J., 1982-86, dir. product mktg., 1986-88, dir. nat. accounts, 1988-90; sr. mktg. rep. Walt Disney World Co., Lake Buena Vista, Fla., 1990-91; div. mktg. rep. Vista Advt., Walt Disney World Co., Lake Buena Vista, Fla., 1991-92; mgr. advt. Walt Disney World Co., Lake Buena Vista, Fla., 1992-94, mgr. Fla. tourist mktg., 1994—. Contbr. articles to profl. jours. Vol. North Brunswick Dem. Orgn., 1985-87; pub. rels. mgr. Cultural Arts Com., North Brunswick, 1986-87; props chair Adult Drama Group, North Brunswick, 1986-87; mem. mktg. com. Vol. Ctr. Ctrl. Fla., 1993-94. Mem. Fla. Direct Mktg. Assn., Cen. Fla. Direct Mktg. Assn. (bd. dirs. 1990-92). Democrat. Episcopalian. Office: Walt Disney World Co PO Box 10000 Orlando FL 32830-1000

RENAU, LYNNE SCHOLL, publisher, writer; b. Louisville, Oct. 17, 1942; d. Wilbur Schurch and Louise (Gutermuth) Scholl; m. Donald I. Renau, Dec. 21, 1961; children: Christian Elizabeth, A. Michal. BA, U. Louisville, 1963, MSW, 1968. Cert. social worker, Ky. Mus. curator The Filson Club, Louisville, 1979-86; dir. admissions Mt. Holly Nursing Ctr., Louisville, 1986-88; curator, archivist Ky. Derby Mus., Louisville, 1988-93; pub. Herr House Press, Louisville, 1994—. Author: Racing Around Kentucky, 1995, Jockeys, Belles and Bluegrass Kings, 1996, Freebee, The Story of a Good-for-Nothing Horse, 1996. Recipient Isaac Murphy award Churchill Downs, Inc., 1996. Mem. Beargran/St. Matthews Hist. Soc. (life), Ky. Dressage Assn. (sec. 1995-96), The Filson Club (endowment). Christian Scientist. Home and Office: 726 Waterford Rd Louisville KY 40207

RENDA, ROSA A., special education educator; b. Jamaica, N.Y., Nov. 3; d. Liborio and Josephine (Finamore) Lombardo; m. Philip F. Renda, Mar. 30, 1980; children: Felicia-Anne, Philip Jr. BA, Molloy Coll., 1971; MEd, St. John's U., Jamaica, N.Y., 1973; postgrad., L.I. U., 1977. Tchr., asst. prin. St. Rose of Lima, Massapequa, N.Y., 1967-73, Acad. of St. Joseph, Brentwood, N.Y., 1973-79; tchr. Sewanhaka H.S., Floral Park, N.Y., 1979-81, Queen of the Rosary Acad., Amityville, N.Y., 1981-86; tchr. Blessed Trinity, Ocala, Fla., 1987-93, math. coord., 1993-94; S.E.D. tchr. Emerald Ctr., Ocala, Fla., 1994; tchr./children's supr. for the emotionally/mentally disturbed Marion Citrus Mental Health, Ocala, 1994—; tchr. for autistic children Maplewood Sch., Ocala, 1996—. Author: Teaching Metrics, 1975. Vol. Nassau County Rep. Club, Hempstead, N.Y., 1974-76. Mem. ASCD, NEA, Nat. Coun. Tchrs. Math., Nat. Cath. Edn. Assn., Nassau/Suffolk Math. Tchrs., Women of the Moose, Columbiettes, K.C. Aux. Roman Catholic.

RENDE, TONI LYNN, principal, counselor; b. Alamo, Tenn., Dec. 6, 1957; d. Weldon Simmons and Gladyn Brown; m. Salvatore David Rende, Mar. 7, 1981; children: David, Derek. BS magna cum laude, Union U., Jackson, Tenn., 1979; MS, Memphis State U., 12980; MEd, U. Tenn., 1987. Cert. tchr., guidance counselor, Tenn. Ednl. social worker Alamo Dept. Pub. Health, 1979-80; ednl. rsch. specialist Hamilton County Govt., Chattanooga, 1980-82; guidance counselor Lakeview High Sch., Chattanooga, 1982-84; tchr. spl. edn. Chattanooga City Schs., 1985-86; ednl. diagnostician, now adj. prof. U. Tenn., Chattanooga, 1987—; guidance counselor Hickory Valley Christian Sch., Chattanooga, 1990—, prin., 1991-96; cons. Attention Deficit Disorder Support Group, Chattanooga, 1990—; mem. Sta. WRCB Children's Panel, Chattanooga, 1990—; network mem. Mid. Tenn. State U. Dyslexic Chair, Chattanooga, 1990; mem. exec. com. Young Author's Conf. Adv. bd. Children's Ctr., U. Tenn., Chattanooga. Mem. Christian Assn. Psychol. Svcs., Coun. Exceptional Children, Alpha Chi, Pi Gamma Mu, Alpha Delta Kappa. Republican. Methodist. Office: Hickory Valley Christian Sch 6605 Shallowford Rd Chattanooga TN 37421-1707

RENDIN, ROBERT WINTER, environmental health officer; b. Jamaica, N.Y., Oct. 21, 1949; s. Anthony and Gertrude Helen (Winter) R.; m. Janet Elizabeth Meyer, Apr. 8, 1972; children: Cheryl, Valerie, Scott. BS, Rutgers U., 1971; MS in Environ. Health, E. Tenn. State U., 1974; postgrad., U.S. Marine Corps Command & Staff Coll., 1985-86, Tulane U., 1994-95. Commd. lt. (j.g.) USN, 1974, advanced through grades to comdr.; environ. health officer U.S. Naval Hosp., San Diego, 1988; chief preventive medicine U.S. Naval Hosp., Taipei, Taiwan, 1976-78; chief occupational and preventive medicine U.S. Naval Hosp., Great Lakes, Ill., 1978-81; environ. health officer U.S. Navy Atlantic Fleet, Norfolk, Va., 1981-84; chief environ. health svc. Navy Environ. & Preventive Medicine Unit, Virginia Beach, Va., 1984-85; med. planner 1st Marine Force Svc. Support Group, Camp Pendleton, Calif., 1986-87, 4th Marine Div., New Orleans, 1987-90; exec. officer Naval Biodynamics Lab., New Orleans, 1990-92, comdg. officer, 1992-95; dep. dir. preventive medicine and health promotion Navy Environ. Health Ctr., Norfolk, Va., 1995-96, dep. dir. Preventive Medicine and Health Promotion, 1996—. Contbr. articles to profl. jours. Decorated Navy Commendation award (2), Meritorious Svc. medal (2); recipient Combined Svc. Hon. award Republic of China, 1977. Mem. U.S. Naval Inst., Nat. Environ. Health Assn. (registered sanitarian), Uniformed Svcs. Environ. Health Assn., Phi Kappa Phi. Lutheran. Home: 646 Edgewood Arch Chesapeake VA 23320 Office: Navy Environ Health Ctr 2510 Walmer Ave Norfolk VA 23513-2617

RENDON-PELLERANO, MARTA INES, dermatologist; b. Sept. 19, 1957; d. Uriel and Rosa Rendon. BA and Scis., U. P.R., Mayaquez, 1977; postgrad., Autonoma U., Santo Domingo, Dominican Republic, 1977-79; MD, U. P.R., San Juan, 1982. Diplomate Am. Bd. Internal Medicine, Am. Bd. Dermatology; lic. physician, Fla., Tex., Pa., ACLS, Drug Enforcement Adminstrn. Intern and resident in internal medicine Albert Einstein Med. Ctr., Phila., 1982-85; resident in dermatology Parkland Meml. Hosp., Southwestern Med. Sch., Dallas, 1985-88; emergency rm. physician Pottsborough (Tex.) Med. Clinic, 1985-86; coord. dermatology clinic Kayser Permanente Med. Assn. Tex., Dallas, 1986-88; dermatology assoc. Dermatology Ctr., Dallas, 1988-89; staff physician Southwestern Med. Sch., Vets. Hosp., Dallas, 1988-89; clin. asst. prof. dept. deramtology U. Miami (Fla.) Sch. Medicine, 1989—; chief dept. dermatology Cleveland Clinic Fla., Ft. Lauderdale, 1989—; mem. adv. bd. South Fla. Vis. Lectureship Series, 1991-92; mem. rsch. bd. advisors Medecis Corp. Featured on TV shows and in popular mags.; contbr. articles to profl. jours., chpts. to books. Recipient Radio Klaridad award for best sci. work, Miami, 1990. Fellow Am. Acad. Dermatology; mem. ACP (assoc.), AAUW, Womens Med. Assn., Womens Dermatol. Soc., Cuban-Interam. Dermatol. Soc., Women of Spanish Origin, Tex. Med. Assn., Miami Dermatology Soc., Fla. Med. Assn., Broward Dermatology Soc., Broward County Med. Assn., Etta Gamma Delta. Roman Catholic. Office: Cleveland Clinic Fla 3000 W Cypress Creek Rd Fort Lauderdale FL 33309-1710

RENDZIO, ROBERT JOSEPH, safety director, aviation accident investigator; b. Passaic, N.J., Sept. 8, 1953; s. Joseph John and Arlene Mary (Sautner) R. BA in Safety, Embry Riddle Aero U., Daytona, Fla., 1983; MS, U. Denver, 1990. Flight sch. Fort Wolters, Tex., Ft. Rucker, Ala., 1972-73; helicopter pilot B Co., 7th Squadron 1st Calvary, Ft. Knox, Ky., 1973-76; fire prevention mgr. 235th Attack Helicopter Co., Germany, 1976-80; safety mgr. 4th Squadron, 9th Calvary, Fort Hood, Tex., 1980-83; accident investigator U.S. Army Safety Ctr., Fort Rucker, Ala., 1984-90; safety dir. Ctrl. Ops. Military Intelligence, Honduras, 1990-92; safety dir. Ala. Fixed Wing Flight Detachment, Fort Rucker, 1992-93; pres. Safety Rsch. Corp. Am., Daleville, Ala., 1993; safety dir. Ctrl. Am. Military Intelligence Battalion, Honduras, Calif., 1990-92; fire rsch. analyst U.S. Army Safety Ctr., Fort Rucker, Ala., 1985-90. Contbr. articles to profl. jours. Recipient Army Commendation medals, 1979, 92, Meritorious Svc. medal, 1983, 87, 88, 91, Legion of Merit, 1993, U.S. Army Headquarters. Mem. Internat. Soc. Air Safety Investigators, Am. Soc. Safety Engrs., Internat. Aeronautique Assn. Republican. Roman Catholic. Office: Safety Rsch Corp Am Ste C 807 Donnell Blvd Daleville AL 36322

RENEAU, DANIEL D., university administrator. Prof., head dept. biomed. engring. La. Tech. U., Ruston, 1973-80, v.p. acad. affairs, 1980-87, pres., 1987—. Office: La Tech U Tech Station PO Box 3168 Ruston LA 71272*

RENEAU, MARVIN BRYAN, military officer, business educator; b. Wharton, Tex., Jan. 22, 1939; s. Marvin Cecil Reneau and Bessie Marie (Petrash) Ward; m. Doris Faye Martin, Jan. 2, 1957; children: Terran Bryan, Kevin Troy, Shannon Lyn. BS, U. Tampa, Fla., 1971; MS, Am. Tech. U., U. Cen. Tex., 1978; MA, Webster Coll., 1979, PhD, 1996. Commd. 2d lt. U.S. Army, 1964; advanced through grade to col. USAR, 1990; co. comdr., armor U.S. Army, Vietnam, 1968; engring. ops. mgr. U.S. Army, Ft. Sam Houston, Tex.; chief, tng. support div. U.S. Army, 1989; sr. tng. analyst U.S. Army, Ft. Sam Houston, Tex.; cons. U.S. Army C.E., Ft. Worth, 1978—, Army Rsch. Inst., Boise, Idaho, 1987—, Army Tng. Bd., Ft. Monroe, Va., 1987—; asst. prof. bus. Incarnate Word Coll., San Antonio. Author: Beneath the Canopy, 1978, And Where the Rockets Can't Reach, 1993; contbr. articles to profl. jours. Mem. Army Mut. Aid Fund, Arlington, Va., 1968; acad. advisor Incarnate Word Coll., San Antonio, 1981; vol. counselor DAV, San Antonio, 1980; referral agt. United Way, San Antonio, 1988. Comdr. USAR. Decorated Bronze Star, Purple Heart, 3 Meritorious medals, 2 Air medals (1 for valor), 3 Army Commendation medals, Army Achievement medal, Conbar Infantryman badge, Rep. of Vietnam Cross of Gallantry with palm, Legion of Merit, commd. admiral in Tex. Navy; names to Hon. Order Ky. Cols. Mem. Am. Mktg. Assn., ASTD, Assn. U.S. Army, Mil. Order of Purple Heart, NSW Leagues, Fed. Mgrs. Assn., S.W. Mktg. Assn., Res. Officer Assn., Orders and Medals Rsch. of Great Britain, Alpha Kappa Psi (sponsor). Methodist. Home: PO Box 39292 San Antonio TX 78218-1292

RENEE, LISABETH MARY, art educator, artist, galley director; b. Bklyn., July 28, 1952; d. Lino P. and Elizabeth M. (Dines) Rivano; m. John S. Witanowski, May 15, 1982. Student, U. Puget Sound, 1972-74; BA in Art, SUNY, Buffalo, 1977; MFA, L.I. U., 1982; EdD, U. Ctrl. Fla., 1996. Cert. art tchr., Fla. Adj. faculty L.I. U., Greenvale, N.Y., 1980-82, Rollins Coll., Winter Park, Fla., 1982; art tchr. Phyllis Wheatley Elem. Sch., Apopka, Fla., 1983-85, McCoy Elem. Sch., Orlando, Fla., 1985-86, Lake Howell H.S., Winter Park, Fla., 1986-93; adj. faculty U. Ctrl. Fla., 1994-95, vis. instr., 1995-96; gallery dir., prof. West Campus Valencia (Fla.) C.C., 1996—; adj. faculty Valencia C.C., 1995-96; dir. So. Artists Registry, Winter Park, 1984-87; cons. Fla. Dept. Edn., 1989-90, mem. curriculum writing team for arts edn. program; mem. com. Fla. Bd. Edn. Task Force for Subject Area Subtest of Fla. Tech. Cert. Exam.; visual arts dir. Very Spl. Arts Ctr. Fla. Fest, 1996; presenter at profl. confs. Author: The Phenomenological Significance of Aesthetic Communion, 1996; editor: Children and the Arts in Florida, 1990. Visual arts dir. Very Spl. Arts Ctrl. Fla. Festival, 1995; mem. local Sch. Adv. Coun., Winter Park, 1992. Grantee Found. for Advancement of Cmty. Throught Schs., 1991, Divsn. Blind Svcs. Invision, 1995, Tangelo Park Project, 1995; ACE scholar Arts Leadership Inst., 1993-96; recipient Tchr. Merit award Walt Disney World Co., 1990. Mem. NEA, ASCD, Nat. Art Edn. Assn., Fla. Art Edn. Assn. (regional rep. 1989-94), Seminole County Art Edn. Assn., Coll. Art Assn., Caucus on Social Theory and Art Edn., Women's Caucus for Art, Phi Kappa Phi, Kappa Delta Pi. Home: 20 Cobblestone Ct Casselberry FL 32707-5410 Office: Valencia CC West Campus Humanities Dept MC 4-11 Orlando FL 32802

RENEGAR, ROBERT MILTON, golf equipment design consultant and manufacturer; b. Shelbyville, Tenn., Sept. 6, 1948; s. Robert Wayne and Jessica Brown (Compton) R.; m. Theresa Lynn Higgins, Dec. 27, 1969; 1 child, Robert Calloway. BS in Aerospace Tech., Mid. Tenn. State U., 1974, MA in Indsl. Studies, 1980. Prodn. supr. Continental Can Co., Perry, Ga., 1975-77; divsn. engr. Kellwood Co., Perry, Ga., 1977-79; sr. mgr. indsl. engring. Fed. Express Corp., Memphis, 1979-85; pres., CEO Performance Golf Corp., Nashville, 1985-87; dir. R&D Pro-Group, Inc., Chattanooga, 1987-90, Ben Hogan Golf Co., Ft. Worth, 1990-91; cons. golf club design Rader Rsch., Murfreesboro, Tenn., 1991—. Sgt. USAF, 1969-72.

RENICK, FRED TAYLOR, JR., dentist; b. San Antonio, Aug. 21, 1941; s. Fred Taylor and Florence Otillie (Rueger) R. Student, U. Va., 1959-62; BS, East Tenn. State U., 1964; DDS, Med. Coll. Va., 1968. Dentist Martinsville, Va., 1970—; pres., dir. Chatmoss Corp., Martinsville, 1993—; ptnr. Magna Vista Partnership, Ridgeway, Va., 1993—. Capt. U.S. Army Dental Corps, 1968-70. Mem. ADA, Fedn. Dentaire Internat., Va. Dental Assn., Patrick Henry Dental Soc. (sec.-treas. 1972-74, pres. 1974-76). Presbyterian. Home: 224 Rives Rd Martinsville VA 24112 Office: 604 E Church St Martinsville VA 24112

RENICK, TIMOTHY MARK, philosophy and religious studies educator; b. Camden, N.J., Mar. 16, 1959; s. Charles Matthew and Rose Mary (Arnos) R. BA summa cum laude, Dartmouth Coll., 1981; MA, Princeton U., 1984, PhD, 1986. Legis. asst. U.S. Congress, Washington, 1980; lectr. English Darmouth Coll., 1980-81; lectr. Religion Princeton U., 1983-84; prof. philosophy and religion Ga. State U., Atlanta, 1986—; chmn. religion studies U. Ctr. Ga., 1990-92. Contbr. articles to profl. jours. Named Disting. Honors Prof., Ga. State U., 1995; recipient Outstanding tchr. award, Coll. Arts and Scis., Ga. State U., 1990, and Blue Key Nat. Honor Soc., 1995; recipient Assn. of Princeton Grad. Alumni Tchg. award in religion, 1985. Mem. Soc. Christian Ethics, Am. Acad. Religion, 19th Century Studies Assn., Phi Beta Kappa. Office: Ga State U Dept Philosophy Atlanta GA 30303

RENNER, GLENN DELMAR, agricultural products executive; b. Greeneville, Tenn., Nov. 18, 1925; s. Charles Dana and Lula Lucille (Hilton) R.; m. Gladys June Brooks, June 30, 1945; children: Glenna June, Joan Phyllis. BA, Tusculum Coll., 1948; MS, U. Tenn., 1950. Sales trainee Parks Belk Co., Greeneville, 1946-47; tchr., coach Greene County Schs., Greeneville, 1947-48; tchr. City of Greeneville Schs., 1950-54; salesman personal insurance co., Greeneville, 1954-76; real estate owner, pres. Brook Glen Farm Supply, Inc., Greeneville, 1976—. Rep. Tenn. Legis., Greeneville, 1965-66; elected commr. Greene County, 1990, 94. Mem. Soc. Real Estate Appraisers (pres. 1968, award 1963), Greeneville Bd. Realtors (bd. dirs., pres. 1964, 71), Greeneville C. of C. (pres. 1986), Kiwanis (pres. Greeneville chpt. 1989—), Shriners (v.p. 1989, pres. 1991). Republican. Methodist. Home: 104 Reed Ave Greeneville TN 37743-4529 Office: Brook Glen Farm Supply Inc 609 W Irish St Greeneville TN 37743-5203

RENO, DAWN ELAINE, writer, photographer, educator; b. Waltham, Mass., Apr. 15, 1953; d. Donald Earle and Elaine Bess (Gordon) Brander; m. Robert Gene Reno, Feb. 25, 1978; 1 child, Jennifer. AA in Journalism, Bunker Hill C.C., 1976; BA in Creative Writing, Johnson State Coll., 1990; MFA in Fiction, Vt. Coll., 1996. Reporter/ad sales rep. New Eng. Antiques Jour., Ware, Mass., 1987-90; contbg. reporter Black Ethnic Collectibles Mag., Silver Spring, Md., 1989-94; asst., contbg. editor Vt. Woman Mag., Burlington, 1989-90; instr. Ch. Street Ctr., Burlington, 1989-91, C.C. of Vt., Morrisville, 1989-91, The Knowledge Shop, Orlando, Fla., 1991-94, Daytona Beach (Fla.) C.C., 1991—; freelance writer, photographer Reno's Lit. Svc., Deltona, Fla., 1976—; instr. Daytona Beach C.C., 1992-96; lectr. Volusia County Schs., Deltona, 1992—; presenter workshops and seminars. Author: Jenny's First Friend, 1984, Jenny Moves, 1984, Collecting Black Americana, 1986, American Indian Collectibles, 1989, American Country Collectibles, 1990, Advertising Collectibles, 1993, All That Glitters, 1993 (award 1994), Native American Collectibles, 1994, Collecting Romance Novels, 1995, The Silver Dolphin, 1995, Contemporary Native American Artists, 1995, The Encyclopedia of Black Collectibles, 1996. Mem. Arts Coun. of Volusia County. Va. Ctr. for Creative Arts fellow, 1990. Fellow Vt. Studio Colony; mem. Soc. Children's Books Writers and Illustrators, League Vt. Writers. Democrat.

RENSHAW, AMANDA FRANCES, retired physicist, nuclear engineer; b. Wheelwright, Ky., Dec. 10, 1934; d. Taft and Mamie Nell (Russell) Wilson; divorced; children: Linda, Michael, Billy. BS in Physics, Antioch Coll., 1972; MS in Physics, U. Tenn., 1982, MS in Nuclear Engring., 1991. Rsch. asst. U. Mich., Ann Arbor, 1970-71; teaching asst. Antioch Coll., Yellow Springs, Ohio, 1971-72; physicist GE, Schenectady, N.Y., 1972-74, Union Carbide Corp., Oak Ridge, Tenn., 1974-79; rsch. assoc. Oak Ridge Nat. Lab., 1979-91, mgr. strategic planning, 1991-92, liaison for environ. scis., 1993-96; ret., 1996; asst. to counselor for sci. and tech. Am. Embassy, Moscow, 1990; asst. to dir. nat. acid precipitation assessment program Office of Pres. U.S., 1993-94. Contbr. articles to profl. jours. Mem. AAUW, Am. Women in Sci., Am. Nuclear Soc. (Oak Ridge chpt.), Soc. Black Physicists. Home: 1850 Cherokee Bluff Dr Knoxville TN 37920-2215

RENSHAW, DARYL CURTIS, retired army officer, management consultant; b. Ft. Benning, Ga., Sept. 1, 1955; s. John Curtis Renshaw and Estelle Elizabeth (Creel) Drendell; m. Gaynelle Elizabeth Powers, Apr. 15, 1977; children: Emily Sharon, Kathleen Elizabeth. BA, Southeastern Coll., Lakeland, Fla., 1977; MPA, Troy State U., 1992. Child care worker, supr. Polk Regional Detention Ctr., Bartow, Fla., 1974-77; infantryman 82d Airborne Div. U.S. Army, Ft. Bragg, N.C., 1977-78; platoon leader, staff officer, co-cmdr. 9th Infantry Div. U.S. Army, Ft. Lewis, Wash., 1978-83; tactics instr., co. cmdr. Infantry Sch. U.S. Army, Ft. Benning, Ga., 1983-87; war plans officer 7th Corps U.S. Army, Stuttgart, Fed. Republic Germany, 1987-90; liaison officer to USAF 81st Tactical Fighter Wing RAF Bentwaters, U.K., 1990-92; plans and programs officer 3rd Army/U.S. Army Ctrl. Command, Ft. McPherson, Ga., 1992-95; evaluation cons. Am. Found. Abused Children's Therapy, REAP divsn., L.A., 1995-96; corp. trainer and project mgmt. cons. Interaction Bus. Systems (IBS) Conversions, Largo, Fla., 1996—. Chmn. fund raising program Mt. Zion Baptist Ch., Jonesboro, Ga., 1994, mem. leadership and long-range planning com., 1992—. Recipient meritorious svc. medals U.S. Army, 1987, 90, 92, 95, commendation medals, 1983, 93, achievement medal, 1982. Mem. Pi Alpha Alpha. Home: 10100 Sailwinds Blvd #106 Largo FL 33773-1921 Office: IBS Conversions Inc Ste 300 801 West Bay Dr Largo FL 33770

RENSINK, JACQUELINE B., secondary school educator; b. Spruce Pine, N.C., May 17, 1954; d. Joe and Virginia Dare (Grindstaff) Biddix; m. Michael Lynn Rensink, Apr. 2, 1988; 1 child, Sarah Jane Buchanan. MusB, Appalachian State U., 1976, MA, 1983, specialist in mid. grades edn., 1990. Cert. level A music, N.C., level G middle grades edn., N.C. Band dir. Mitchell County Sch. System, Bakersville, N.C., 1977, tchr., 1981—; mem. supt. adv. coun. Mitchell County Sch. System, 1986-88, site-based mgmt. team Harris Mid. Sch., Spruce Pine, 1992-93; student-tchr. supr. Harris Mid. Sch., 1988, 89, 90; coord. World Day Festival Harris Mid. Sch, 1988—. Organist Cen. Bapt. Ch., Spruce Pine, 1990—; bd. dirs. Winterstar-Fairway Assn., Burnsville, N.C., 1992-93. Named Tchr. of Yr., Harris Mid. Sch., 1992, 94. Mem. NEA, Nat. Coun. Social Studies, N.C. Assn. Educators (treas. 1987-88, 91-92, assn. rep. 1992-93), N.C./Nat. Geographic Alliance, N.C. Coun. Social Studies, Delta Kappa Gamma. Republican. Baptist. Home: 290 Winterstar Loop Burnsville NC 28714-9536 Office: Harris Middle Sch 231 Harris St Spruce Pine NC 28777-3119

RENT, CLYDA STOKES, academic administrator; b. Jacksonville, Fla., Mar. 1, 1942; d. Clyde Parker Stokes Sr. and Edna Mae (Edwards) Shuemake; m. George Seymour Rent, Aug. 12, 1966; 1 child, Cason Lynley Rent Helms. BA, Fla. State U., 1964, MA, 1966, PhD, 1968; LHD (hon.), Judson Coll., 1993. Asst. prof. Western Carolina U., Cullowhee, N.C., 1968-70; asst. prof. Queens Coll., Charlotte, N.C., 1972-74, dept. chair, 1974-78, dean Grad. Sch. and New Coll., 1979-84, v.p. for Grad. Sch. and New Coll., 1984-85, v.p. acad. affairs, 1985-87, v.p. community affairs, 1987-89; pres. Miss. U. for Women, Columbus, 1989—; bd. dirs. Trustmark Nat. Bank, Trustmark Corp.; cons. Coll. Bd. N.Y.C., 1983-89; sci. cons. N.C. Alcohol Rsch. Authority, Chapel Hill, 1976-89; bd. mem. So. Growth Policies Bd., 1992-94; mem. adv. bd. Nat. Women's Hall of Fame; rotating chair Miss. Instns. Higher Learning Pres.' Coun., 1990-91; commn. govtl. rels. Am. Coun. Edn., 1990-93; adv. bd. Entergy/Miss., 1994—, Freedom Forum First Amendment Ctr, 1996 ; Rhodes Scholar selection com. Miss. Mem. editl. rev. bd. Planning for Higher Education, 1995; author rsch. articles in acad. jours.; speeches pub. in Vital Speeches; mem. editl. bds. acad. jours. Trustee N.C. Performing Arts Ctr., Charlotte, 1988-89, Charlotte County Day Sch., 1987-89; bd. visitors Johnson C. Smith U., Charlotte, 1985-89; exec. com. bd. dirs. United Way Allocations and Rev., Charlotte, 1982-88; bd. advisors Charlotte Mecklenburg Hosp. Authority, 1985-89; bd. dirs. Jr. Achievement, Charlotte, 1983-89, Miss. Humanities Coun., Miss. Inst. Arts and Letters, Miss. Symphony, Miss. Econ. Coun.; chair Leadership Miss. and Collegiate Miss.; chmn. bd. dirs. Charlotte/Mecklenburg Arts and Sci. Coun., 1987-88; Danforth assoc. Danforth Found., St. Louis, 1976-88, Leadership Am., 1989; golden triangle adv. bd. Bapt. Meml. Hosp.; pres. So. Univs. Conf., 1994-95; mem. commn. govt. rels. Am. Coun. Edn., 1990-93. Recipient Grad. Made Good award Fla. State U., 1990, medal of excellence Miss. U. for Women, 1995; named Prof. of Yr., Queens Coll., 1979, One of 10 Most Admired Women Mgrs. in Am., Working Women mag., 1993, One of 1000 Women of the 90's, Mirabella mag., 1994; Ford Found. grantee, 1981; Paul Harris fellow, 1992. Mem. Am. Assn. State Colls. and Univs. (bd. dirs. 1994-96), Sociol. Soc., So. Assn. Colls. and Schs. (mem. commn. on colls. 1996), N.C. Assn. Colls. and Univs. (exec. com. 1988-89), N.C. Assn. Acad. Officers (sec.-treas. 1987-88), Soc. Internat. Bus. Fellows, Miss. Assn. Colls. (pres. 1992), Newcomen Soc. U.S., Internat. Women's Forum, Univ. Club, Rotary. Office: Miss U Women Pres Office Box W 1600 Columbus MS 39701-9998

RENTERIA, CHERYL CHRISTINA, retired federal agency administrator; b. Corpus Christi, Tex., May 11, 1944; d. C.J. and Nazelle (Smart) Casey; m. Carlos Raymundo Renteria, Oct. 17, 1975; children: Crissa Cybele, Cori Renee. Grad. Inst. U.S. & World Affairs, Am. U., 1965; BA, Tex. Christian U., 1966. Inventory mgmt. specialist Tinker AFB, Oklahoma City, 1966-67; with U.S. Dept. HUD, 1967-94; resident initiatives coord., program mgr. region VI U.S. Dept. HUD, Ft. Worth, 1988-92; mgr. Office of Pub. Housing, 1993-94; ret., 1994; cons., 1995-96; co-chair Pointe Shoe Boutique, 1995-96. Pres. Dallas Office Orgn. Women, 1974-75; treas. Fed. Woman's Program Coun., Dallas, 1977-78; bd. dirs. Ballet Guild, Ft. Worth, 1984—, treas., 1985, v.p., 1986-88, programs chmn., 1990, 91, 92, 93, 94; bd. dirs. lectr. series U. Tex., Arlington, 1987-91, Dance Theatre, Arlington, 1987-91; bd. dirs. Planned Parenthood North Tex., 1986-90, Coun. Advisors, 1990-95; vol. Tex. Christian U. LINKS, Campfire, 30 yr. reunion com.; treas. Arlington Speech/Debate Booster Club, 1994; rec. sec. Ft. Worth Panhellenic Coun., 1994-96; permanent housing subcom. City of Arlinton Priority Home, 1995; co-chmn. Pointe Shoe Boutique, 1995-96; vol. Prevent Blindness. Smith scholar, 1966. Mem. Women in Govt., (pres. 1989-90), Fed. Bus. Assn., Women's Policy Forum, Theater Arlington Guild, Internat. Sister Cities, Opera Guild Ft. Worth, Friends Univ. Tex. Libr., Symphony Soc. Tarrant County (editor newsletter 1984), Jr. Woman's Club Decorteque (v.p. 1977), Woman's Club Ft. Worth, Delta Gamma (pres. house corp. 1985, 86, bd. dirs. 1987—, chair Province leadership seminar 1987, corr. 1984). Home: 1115 Montreau Ct Arlington TX 76012-2737

RENTNER, JAMES DAVID, financial analyst; b. Milw., Mar. 4, 1940; s. Rudolph E. and Lucille L. Rentner; m. Judith Ann Radler, Apr. 11, 1964; children: Tracy Laine, Shannon Kay. BA, Valparaiso U., 1962; MBA, Calif. State U., Fullerton, 1967. Personnel dir. Anaconda Wire and Cable, Orange,

Calif., 1967-69; v.p. Arrow Group Ind., Pompton Plains, N.J., 1969-76; gen. mgr. Fonas, Inc., Latrobe, Pa., 1976-79; prin. Rentner's for Children, Spokane, Wash., 1979-86; account exec. E.F. Hutton, Spokane, 1980-85; v.p. Quantum Planning and Investment, Spokane, 1985; ptnr., v.p. Willoughby Holin and Rentner Inc., Plantation, Fla., 1986—. Active Young Reps., Spokane, 1979-86. Capt. USMC, 1962-65. Fellow Rotary (sustaining, membership com. Spokane chpt. 1980-86, bd. dirs. Coral Springs, Fla. chpt. 1986—, program chmn. 1986-87, Paul Harris award 1988); mem. So. Fla. Fin. Analyst Soc. Baptist. Office: Willoughby Holin Rentner 4440 Pga Blvd Ste 308 Palm Beach Gardens FL 33410-6541

RENTOUMIS, ANN MASTROIANNI, psychotherapist; b. New Haven, Apr. 27, 1928; d. Luigi Mastroianni and Marion Dallas; m. George Rentoumis, June 27, 1959; children: Michael, Mary, Anne. BA in Psychology, Vassar Coll., 1949; postgrad., Boston U., 1949-50; MS in Social Work, Columbia U., 1952. Diplomate Am. Bd. Social Work; lic. cert. social worker; lic. marriage and family therapist. Child and adolescent therapist Bklyn. Psychiat., 1952-55; family therapist Community Svc. Soc., N.Y.C., 1955-58; psychotherapist Bleuler Psychotherapy Ctr., L.I., N.Y., 1958-60, Adolescent Psychiat. Clinic, Tex. Children's Hosp., Houston, 1975-76; pvt. practice, Houston, 1976-77; pvt. practice Lauderdale Psychiat. Group, Ft. Lauderdale, Fla., 1978-90; pvt. practice, Pompano Beach, Fla., 1990-93; psychotherapist New River Group, Ft. Lauderdale, 1993—. Pres. Pine Crest Sch. Mothers Club, 1985-86; v.p. Opera Soc., 987-88; bd. govs., v.p. exec. bd. Fla. Philharm Soc., 1988-90, bd. dirs., 1990—. Named Woman of Yr., Am. Cancer Soc., 1989, Golden Rule award J.C. Penney, 1990. Fellow Am. Orthopsychiat. Assn.; mem. Am. Assn. Marriage and Family Therapists, Am. Group Therapy Assn., Fla. Assn. Psychotherapists, Harbor Beach Surf Club (v.p. 1986-90). Home: 1535 E Lake Dr Fort Lauderdale FL 33316-3205 Office: New River Group 1700 E Las Olas Blvd Fort Lauderdale FL 33301-2408

RENTZ, TAMARA HOLMES, software consultant; b. Austin, Tex., Nov. 23, 1964; d. Thomas Michael and Elizabeth Dianne (Ames) Holmes; m. Christopher Michael Rentz, Sept. 21, 1991. BS in Speech/Orgnl. Comm., U. Tex., 1987. Cert. meeting facilitator; notary public State of Tex. Mgr. PC Sta., Inc., Austin, 1985-86; telecom. advisor Internat. Talent Network, Austin, 1986-87; mktg. rep. Wm. Ross & Co., Austin, 1987; life ins. rep. A.L. Williams, Austin, 1987-88; exec. sec. Adia Temporaries/SEMATECH, Austin, 1988; tng. adminstr. SEMATECH, Austin, 1988-89, data coord. equipment improvement program, 1989-90, user group program mgr., 1992-93; pres. Innovative Bus. Solutions, Austin, 1994—. Mem. Austin Software Coun. Home and Office: 4004 Love Bird Ln Austin TX 78730-3522

REPASKY, MARK EDWARD, oil and gas company executive; b. Mueyguez, P.R., Sept. 7, 1956; s. Robert E. and Pauline M. (Kinney) R.; m. Ivy D. Wilde, June 3, 1978. BS in Petroleum Engring., U. Wyo., 1978. Registered profl. engr., Colo. Engr. No. Natural Gas Co., Tulsa, 1978-80; petroleum engr. Nortex Oil and Gas Co., Denver, 1980-84; sr. petroleum engr. Tex. Oil and Gas Co., Denver, 1984-87; mgr. project Tex. Oil and Gas Co., Dallas, 1987-88; v.p. Panda Resources, Inc., Tulsa, 1988-93; pres. Marker Petroleum, Inc., Tulsa, 1993—. Patentee in field. Richardson Trust scholar, 1974-77. Mem. Soc. Petroleum Engrs., Nat. Soc. Profl. Engrs., Nat. Gas Men's Assn. Home: 8086 S Yale Ave # 195 Tulsa OK 74136-9003 Office: Marker Petroleum Inc 5727 S Lewis Ave Ste 720 Tulsa OK 74105-7148

REPETTO, ALLISON W., agricultural company executive; b. 1926. Owner Orange Blossom Groves, Clearwater, Fla., 1946—. With USN, WWII. Office: Orange Blossom Groves 18200 Us Highway 19 N Clearwater FL 34624-6513

REPPERT, JEFFREY ROY, procurement analyst, systems administrator; b. Pottstown, Pa., June 20, 1957; s. Leroy Samuel and Mary Esther (Becker) R.; m. Silvia Helena Campos, Sept. 4, 1983. BA in Psychology, Seton Hall U.; BS in Bus. Adminstrn., Materials Mgmt., Bloomfield Coll.; MBA, U. Phoenix. Cert. purchasing mgr. Nat. Assn. Purchasing Agts. Contract specialist U.S. Navy Exchange Hdgtrs., Staten Island, 1985-92; procurement analyst U.S. Coast Guard, Washington, 1992—; Computer cons. Blue Mountain Acad., Harrisburg, Pa., 1985. CPO U.S. Navy, 1979-85, Navy Reserve, 1985—. Mem. Nat. Contract Mgmt. Assn. Republican. Seventh Day Adventist. Home: 7839 Enola St Apt 104 Mc Lean VA 22102

RESCH, MARY LOUISE, social services administrator; b. David City, Nebr., Oct. 26, 1956; d. Ernest John and Mary Jean (Roelandts) Cermak; m. Eugene Joseph Resch, Apr. 28, 1979. BS in Psychology, SUNY, Albany, 1984; MS in Counseling and Edn. with high honors, U. Wis., Platteville, 1986. Enlisted U.S. Army, 1974, advance through ranks to sgt., 1982; bomb disposal tech. U.S. Army, Ft. Riley, Kans., 1977-79; bomb disposal instr. U.S. Army, Indian Head, Md., 1979-80; resigned U.S. Army, 1985; instr., intern family advocacy Army Community Svc., U.S. Army, Ft. Belvoir, 1986; sr. counselor, child therapist Community Crisis and Referral Ctr., Inc., Waldorf, Md., 1986-87; adminstr. Walter Reed Army Med. Ctr. USDA Grad. Sch., Washington, 1987-88; contract mgr. USDA Grad. Sch., Ft. Jackson, S.C., 1988-91; pres. Athena Cons., Columbia, S.C., 1991-93; dir. spl. programs Newberry (S.C.) Commn. on Alcohol and Drug Abuse, 1993-95; resource devel. coord. Cities in Schs.-SC, Inc., Columbia, 1995—; human svcs. cons., Washington, 1986-87; adj. instr. Coker Coll., Ft. Jackson, 1989-95. Mem. NAFE, ACA, Nat. Contract Mgmt. Assn. (fellow, former pres., mentor), Mil. Educators and Counselors Assn., Com. Mil. Edn. S.C. Republican. Lutheran. Home: 1016 Harvey Killian Rd Chapin SC 29036-7807 Office: Cities in Schs SC Inc PO Box 773 1200 Catawba St Columbia SC 29202

RESNIK, KIM, communications executive; b. N.Y.C., Aug. 8, 1948; d. David and Elizabeth (Gellhorn) Resnik; m. Eric J. Weeks, Mar. 28, 1968 (div. Sept. 1981); m. Jeffrey M. Gerth, Oct. 27, 1984. BA in English and Am. Lit. cum laude, Brandeis U., 1972; postgrad., Eastern Wash. U., 1979-82, Ga. State U., 1995—. Elem. sch. tchr. Pownal, Vt., 1972-79; pub. rels. dir. Alliance Theater Co., Atlanta, 1982-85, mktg. dir., 1985-88; cons. in mktg. and computer system design, 1988-89; dir. comms. Atlanta History Ctr., 1989—; founder, co-head Heritage Mktg. Group, Atlanta, 1991—. Author poetry pub. in jours. V.p. cultural affairs Buckhead Bus. Assn., Atlanta, 1992—, grad. Leadership Devel. Program, 1994. Mem. Pub. Rels. Soc. Am., Am. Mktg. Assn., Am. Assn. Mus., Southea. Mus. Conf., Atlanta Press Club. Office: Atlanta History Ctr 130 W Paces Ferry Rd NW Atlanta GA 30305-1353

RESO, ANTHONY, geologist, earth resources economist; b. London, Eng., Aug. 10, 1934; s. Harry and Marion (Gerth) R.; came to U.S., 1940, naturalized, 1952. AB, Columbia Coll., N.Y.C., 1954; MA, Columbia U., 1955; postgrad. U. Cin., 1956-57; PhD (fellow) Rice U., 1960; postgrad. Grad. Sch. Bus. U. Houston, 1964-68. Instr. geology Queens Coll., Flushing, N.Y., 1954; geologist Atlantic Richfield Corp., Midland, Tex., 1955-56; asst. prof. geology and curator invertebrate paleontology Pratt Mus., Amherst (Mass.) Coll., 1959-62; staff rsch. geologist Tenneco Oil Co., Houston, 1962-86; geol. mgr. Peak Prodn. Co., Houston, 1986—, v.p., 1988—. Cons. in geol. rsch. Tenn. Gas and Oil Co., 1960-61; lectr. U. Houston, 1962-65; vis. prof. Rice U., 1980; mem. bd. advisers Gulf Univs. Rsch. Corp., Galveston, Tex., 1967-75, chmn., 1968-69; dir. Stewardship Properties, Houston, 1968—. Recipient rsch. grants Am. Assn. Petroleum Geologists, 1958, 59, Geol. Soc. Am., 1958, Eastman Fund, 1962; NSF fellow, 1959. Fellow Geol. Soc. Am. (com. investments 1984-95, chmn. 1985-92, budget com. 1993-95, Disting. Svc. award 1996), AAAS; mem. Am. Assn. Petroleum Geologists (life, com. convs. 1977-83, chmn. 1980-83, gen. chmn. nat. conv. 1979, com. on investments 1982-88, chmn. com. group ins. 1986-88, treas. 1986-88; Disting. svc. award 1985, found. trustee assoc. 1991), Paleontol. Soc., SEPM Soc. for Sedimentary Geology (com. on investments 1990—, chmn. 1992-95), Paleontol. Rsch. Instn., Tex. Acad. Sci., Houston Geol. Soc. (v.p. 1973-75, pres. 1975-76, chmn. constn. revision com. 1981, Disting. svc. award 1985), English-Speaking Union U.S. (dir. Houston chpt. 1978—, v.p. 1982-88, 94—, mem. scholarship com. 1988—, chmn. 1991—), Varsity C Club, Sigma Xi, Sigma Gamma Epsilon, Beta Theta Pi. Episcopalian. Contbr. profl. jours. Home: 1801 Huldy St Houston TX 77019-5767 Office: care Peak Prodn Co PO Box 130785 Houston TX 77219-0785

RESSLER, PARKE E(DWARD), lawyer, accountant; b. Lancaster, Pa., Aug. 21, 1916; s. Parke H. and Sadie (Weiser) R.; B.S., U. Pa., 1947; B.B.A., Baylor U., 1947, LL.B., 1952, J.D., 1969; M.B.A., U. Houston, 1949; m. Margaret B. Tucker, June 3, 1944; children—Nancy Parke, Margaret Anne. Agt. Internal Revenue Service, 1947-50; part time instr. Baylor U., 1950-65; admitted to Tex. bar, 1952, since practiced in Waco; asso. firm Edwin P. Horner. Mem. Am. Inst. C.P.A.'s, Tex. Soc. C.P.A.'s, Am., Tex., McLennan County bar assns., Am. Assn. Atty.-C.P.A.'s, Phi Alpha Delta, Delta Sigma Pi. Mem. Christian Ch. Rotarian. Clubs: Ridgewood Country, Hedonia, Ridgewood Yacht, Baylor Bear. Home: 2209 Arroyo Rd Waco TX 76710-1626 Office: 4800 Lakewood Dr Waco TX 76710-2966

REST, GREGORY JOEL, legislative analyst; b. New Orleans, July 18, 1956; s. Heinrich F. J. and Eleanor Mae (Riske) R.; m. Jane Riley Peterson, Oct. 23, 1982. BA summa cum laude, U. Mich., 1978; postgrad., Stanford U., 1978-79; PhD, Rand Grad. Sch., 1985. Grad. fellow Rand Corp., Santa Monica, Calif., 1980-85; chief legis. analyst Joint Legis. Audit and Rev. Commn./Va. Gen. Assembly, Richmond, 1985—; mem. Va. Prison and Jail Forecast Tech. Rev. Com., Richmond, 1993, 95—; mem. adj. faculty Va. Commonwealth U., 1995—. Co-author: (book) Funding the Standards of Quality, 1988, Proposal for a Revenue Stabilization Fund, 1991, Revenue Forecasting in the Executive Branch, 1991. Bd. trustees First Congl. UCC, Chesterfield, Va., 1992—; co-author Va. Constl. Amendment for Revenue Stabilization Fund, 1992. Recipient Practitioner award Fin. Publs., Inc., 1993. Mem. Nat. Legis. Program Evaluation Soc. (methodology award com. 1992-93). United Ch. of Christ. Home: 3313 Kensington Ave Richmond VA 23221-2303 Office: Joint Legis Audit/Rev Commn Capitol Sq 1100 Gen Assembly Bldg Richmond VA 23219

RESTER, ALFRED CARL, JR., physicist; b. New Orleans, July 11, 1940; s. Alfred Carl and Willietta (Voth) R.; m. Blanche Sue Bing, June 20, 1964 (div. Jan. 20, 1985); children: Andrea Dawn, Karen Alane; m. Sherry Alice Warren, Dec. 12, 1985. BS, Miss. Coll., 1962; MS, U. N.Mex., 1964; PhD, Vanderbilt U., 1969. Postdoctoral fellow U. Delft, Netherlands, 1969-70, scientist first class, 1970-71; guest prof. U. Bonn (Germany) Dept. Physics, 1972-74; asst. prof. Emory U., Dept. Physics, Atlanta, 1975-76; assoc. prof. Tenn. Tech. U., Dept. Physics, Cookeville, Tenn., 1976-77; vis. assoc. prof. U. Fla., Dept. Physics, Gainesville, 1978-81; assoc. rsch. scientist U. Fla. Space Astronomy Lab., Gainesville, 1981-88; dir. U. Fla. Inst. for Astrophysics and Planetary Exploration, Alachua, 1988-93; pres., CEO Constellation Tech. Corp., St. Petersburg, Fla., 1992—; cons. Lockheed Ga., Marietta, 1976, Oak Ridge (Tenn.) Nat. Lab., 1976-77. Editor: High Energy Radiation Background in Space, 1989; contbr. articles to profl. jours. Recipient Antarctica Svc. medal NSF-USN, 1988; grantee various fed. agys. Mem. AAAS, Am. Phys. Soc., Am. Astron. Soc., Sigma Xi Sci. Rsch. Soc. Office: Constellation Tech Corp 9887 4th St N Ste 100 Saint Petersburg FL 33702-2451

RESTINO, MARYANN SUSAN REYNOLDS, pharmacist; b. Ridley Park, Pa., Nov. 24, 1962; d. William Ernest and Rosemary Catherine (Rehill) Reynolds; m. Mark John Restino, Oct. 26, 1991; children: Katelyn Elizabeth, Amanda Catherine. BS in Pharmacy, Phila. Coll. Pharmacy and Sci., 1985; D Pharmacy, U. Tex., 1987. Lic. pharmacist, N.C., Tex., Va. Hosp. pharmacy intern Mercy Cath. Med. Ctr., Darby, Pa., 1982-85; pharmacist Eckerd Drug Co., San Antonio, 1986-87; staff pharmcist Bexar County Hosp. Dist./Med. Ctr. Hosp., San Antonio, 1985-87; resident Med. Coll. Va. Hosps., 1987-88; staff pharmacist Warm Springs Rehab. Hosp., San Antonio, 1990; asst. prof. U. Tex., San Antonio, 1988-90, Phila. Coll. Pharmacy and Sci., 1990-91; pharmacy edn. coord. N.C. Bapt. Hosp., Winston-Salem, 1991-95, asst. dir. pharmacy, 1995—; dir. drug info. ctr. Phila. Coll. Pharmacy and Sci., 1990-91, adj. asst. prof. info. sci., 1991; adj. clin. asst. prof.. Sch. Pharmacy, Campbell U., Buies Creek, N.C., 1992—; clin. asst. prof. Sch. Pharmacy, U. N.C., Chapel Hill, 1992—; adj. prof. physiology and pharmacology Bowman Gray Sch. Medicine, 1996—; presenter in field; bd. dirs. Cmty. Clinic, Inc., San Antonio, 1988-90; mem. pharmacy and therapeutics com. Bexar County Hosp. Dist., 1988-90. Contbr. articles to profl. publs., chpt. to textbook; editor N.J. Hosp. Assn. Newsletter, 1991-93; tech. editor Am. Druggist, 1990—; asst. editor Drugdex Info. System, 1988—; reviewer jours. in field. Gratnee Bowman-Gray Sch. Medicine/N.C. Bapt. Hosp., SunHealth, 1993, 95, Am. Coll. Clin. Pharmacy, 1989—. Mem. Am. Coll. Clin. Pharmacy (membership com. 1990-92, clin. practice affairs com. 1993-95, chmn. clin. practice affairs com. 1994—, Spring Forum com. 1996), N.C.-Triangle Coll. Clin. Pharmacy, Am. Soc. Hosp. Pharmacists (com. on therapeutics task forces 1989-91), N.C. Soc. Hosp. Pharmacists (program com. 1993—, pharmcotherapy SIG adv. group 1993—, Continuing Excellence award 1993, 94, 95, Innovative Practice award 1996), Rho Chi. Republican. Roman Catholic. Home: 6224 Highland Brook Dr Clemmons NC 27012-7411 Office: NC Bapt Hosp Dept Pharmacy Medical Center Blvd Winston Salem NC 27157

RESTIVO, JANET DI MARIA, elementary school educator, education consultant; b. Hempstead, N.Y., Apr. 27, 1948; d. S. Charles and Anne (Sancetta) Di Maria; m. Robert Edward Restivo, Jan. 30, 1971; children: Thomas, Brian, Christopher, Angela, Betsy, David. BS in Elem. Edn., Math., Sci., Adelphi U., 1970, MA in Early Childhood Edn., 1990. Cert. gifted edn. Tchr., grade 1,2 Plainedge Pub. Sch., Seaford, N.Y., 1970-71, 71-72; tchr. reading, reading video-graphics Uniondale (N.Y.) Ind. Sch. Dist., 1972-73; leap gifted magnet grades 1,2,3,5 Carrollton (Tex.)/Farmers Branch Ind. Sch. Dist., 1989, 1993-94, staff devel., 1989-96, tchr. math. title I inclusion, 1994-95, tchr. math. grade 7, 1996—; trainer new tchrs.; chairperson Quality Improvement Coun. Mem. ASCD, Kappan. Home: 3107 Andrew Ln Carrollton TX 75007

RETSKIN, BILL ALLAN, real estate broker; b. Bklyn., Aug. 11, 1942; s. Harold and Mimi (Mitkoff) R.; m. Karin Ann Tipping, June 20, 1970 (div. 1992); 1 child, Jessica Rebbakah; m. Cindy Sue Murray, Nov. 19, 1995. BS in Zoology, U. Miami, 1960-64, BA in Philosophy, 1965; postgrad., George Mason U., 1991-94. Bd. cert. realtor N.C., 1995. CEO Alexandria (Va.) Leather, 1974-83; cons. Keep Track Ltd., Alexandria, 1980-84; instr. computers Computer Learning Ctr., Springfield, Va., 1984-87; computer analyst Ronson Mgmt. Corp., Alexandria, 1989-90; instr. computers Ashton-Tate, L.A., 1988-90; dir. Am. Mail & Graphics, Sheville, N.C., 1992-94; real estate auctioneer, broker Bill Retskin R.E. Auctions, Asheville, N.C., 1995-96; programming instr. U. D.C, 1983-85, N.O.V.A. Adult Edn. Dept., 1983-84; owner, mgr. I Love You Gift Co., 1978-84, Old Dominion Tee Shirt Co., 1976-80. Author, editor: 1939 N.Y. World's Fair Matchcovers, 1989, Matchcover Collector's Priceguide & Resource Book, 1992, The Mathcover Collector's Price Guide, 1994, 2d edit., 1997; editor: The Front Striker Bulletin, 1984—; contbr. articles to profl jours. Mem. Asheville Bus. Achievers Assn., Asheville Bd. of Realtors, N.C. Bd. of Realtors, Auctioneers Assn., N.C. Nat. Auctioneers Assn., Rotary, Am. Matchcover Collecting Club (bd. dirs.). Office: American Matchcover Collecting Club PO Box 18481 Asheville NC 28814

RETTIG, TERRY, veterinarian, wildlife consultant; b. Houston, Jan. 30, 1947; s. William E. and Rose (Munves) R.; m. Helen Rettig, Mar. 12, 1996; children from previous marriage: Michael Thomas, Jennifer Suzanne. B.S. in Zoology, Duke U., 1969, M.A.T. in Sci., 1970; D.V.M., U. Ga., 1975. Resident veterinarian, mgr. animal health The Wildlife Preserve, Largo, Md., 1975-76; wildlife veterinarian Dept. Environ. Conservation State of N.Y., Delmar, 1976-77; owner Atlanta Animal Hosp., 1976—; sec., dir. Atlanta Pet Supply, Inc., 1983-89; cons. Six Flags Over Ga., Yellow River Game Ranch, Stone Mountain Park Animal Forest, Atlanta Zoo. Author: (with Murray Fowler) Zoo and Wild Animal Medicine (Aardvark award 1978), 1978, 2d edit., 1986 (Order of Kukukifuku award 1986); contbr. articles to profl. jours. Del. Dekalb County Republican Conv., 1983; mem. Roswell United Meth. Ch., Boy Scouts Am., 1954—, mem. troop coun., asst. scoutmaster, scout master, Philmont expedition leader, 1988, 89. Spl. scholar Cambridge U. Coll. Vet. Medicine, 1973-74. Mem. AVMA, Ga. Vet. Med. Assn., Greater Atlanta Vet. Med. Assn., Dekalb Vet. Soc., Acad. Vet. Medicine, Am. Assn. Zoo Veterinarians, Am. Assn. Zool. Parks and Aquaria, Nat. Wildlife Health Found., Nat. Wildlife Assn., Atlanta Zool. Soc., Am. Fedn. Aviculturists, Cousteau Soc., Am. Assn. Avian Veterinarians, Am. Animal Hosp. Assn., Internat. Wildlife Assn., Soc. Aquatic Veterinary Medicine, Am. Buffalo Assn. Methodist. Home: 5005 Kimball Bridge Rd Alpharetta GA 30202-5649 Office: Atlanta Animal Hosp 5005 Kimball Bridge Rd Alpharetta GA 30202-5649

RETTON, MICHAEL ANTHONY, municipal official; b. Fairmont, W.Va., Feb. 9, 1962; s. Joseph and Judith Mae (Costello) R.; m. Ronda Jo Parrish; children: Trevor Michael, Lauren Michelle. BSCE, W.Va. U., 1984; postgrad., U. Va., 1986, George Washington U., 1987. Registered profl. engr. Va., W.Va., Md., profl. surveyor, W.Va. Project engr. Dewberry & Davis, Fairfax, Va., 1984-87; project mgr. Stevenson Engring. Inc., Fairfax, 1987-89, Patton, Harris, Rust, Assoc., P.C., Leesburg, Va., 1989-91; dist. engr. W.Va. Bur. Pub. Health, Philippi, 1991-94; city engr., dir. pub. works City of Bridgeport, W.Va., 1994—. Pres. SS Peter & Paul Sch . Found., Monongah, 1995-96. Mem. Am. Water Works Assn., Nat. Coun. Examiners for Engrs. and Surveyors. Home: 1302 Fox Lair Pl Fairmont WV 26554 Office: City of Bridgeport 156 Thompson Dr Bridgeport WV 26330

REUSCHLING, THOMAS LYNN, academic administrator, consultant; b. Conneaut, Ohio, Dec. 28, 1942; s. Fred Leonard and Florice Lucille (Corlew) R.; m. Dorothy Ellen Ford, Sept. 8, 1962; children: Renee, Tracy. BA, Hiram (Ohio) Coll., 1964; MBA, Kent State U., 1966; D. Bus. Adminstrn., U. Colo., 1970. Asst. prof. Kent State U., 1969-73; dir. Sch. Bus. U. No. Iowa, Cedar Falls, 1973-78; dean Sch. Bus. U. Richmond, Va., 1978-88; pres. St. Andrews Presbyn. Coll., Lauringburg, N.C., 1988-94, Fla. So. Coll., Lakeland, 1994—. Pres. Jr. Achievement of Richmond, 1985-86, Carolina Intercollegiate Athletic Conf., 1993-94; bd. dirs. United Way of Richmond, 1987-88; bd. dirs. United Way of Ctrl. Fla., 1995—; deacon, elder River Rd. Presbyn. Ch., Richmond; treas. Ind. Coll. Fund N.C. NDEA fellow U. Colo., 1966-69.

REVEL, RICKY JOE, producer, songwriter; b. Paris, Tenn., Oct. 19, 1956; s. Joe Hulie and Betty (Hanna) R.; m. Jenniffer Diane Scott, Sept. 17, 1983; 1 child, Erica Dianne. Grad. high sch., Paris. Exclusive songwriter King Coal Music, Loretta Lynn Entertainment, Nashville, 1977-79; jingle producer RJR Custom Commls., Henry, Tenn., 1980-82, So. Jingle Network, Paris, 1982-88; with TV prodn. Total Bus. Corp., Paris, 1985-88, pres., owner, 1987-88; film & video producer, dir. Evans & Assocs., Brentwood, Tenn., 1989-90; founder Electronic Media Svcs. Am., Paris, 1991—; entertainer Mail Pouch Express, 1977-81; music tchr. Lonardo Piano Co., Paris, 1983-84; record producer Jen-Ric Studio, Paris, 1984-88, Brentwood, 1989; advt., mktg. cons. So. Advt. and Mktg., Paris, 1984-88; founder Son of the South Pub., 1990—. Albums include Songs of the North & South (East & West), 1989, Making It in America, 1992; composer numerous songs, 1973—. Music dir. Young Life orgn., Paris, 1987. Mem. Am. Fedn. Musicians, Soc. European Stage Authors and Composers. Baptist. Home and Office: RR 3 Box 204C Paris TN 38242-9346

REVELEY, WALTER TAYLOR, III, lawyer; b. Churchville, Va., Jan. 6, 1943; s. Walter Taylor and Marie (Eason) R.; m. Helen Bond, Dec. 18, 1971; children: Walter Taylor, George Everett Bond, Nelson Martin Eason, Helen Lanier. AB, Princeton U., 1965; JD, U. Va., 1968. Bar: Va. 1970, D.C. 1976. Asst. prof. law U. Ala., 1968-69; law clk. to Justice Brennan U.S. Supreme Ct., Washington, 1969-70; fellow Woodrow Wilson Internat. Ctr. for Scholars, 1972-73; internat. affairs fellow Coun. on Fgn. Rels., N.Y.C., 1972-73; assoc. Hunton & Williams, Richmond, Va., 1970-76, ptnr., 1976—, mng. ptnr., 1982-91; lectr. Coll. William and Mary Law Sch., 1978-80. Author: War Powers of the President and Congress: Who Holds the Arrows and Olive Branch, 1981; mem. editorial & mng. bds. Va. Law Rev., 1966-68; contbr. articles to profl. jours. Trustee Princeton U., 1986—, Presbyn. Ch. (U.S.A.) Found., 1991—, Va. Hist. Soc., 1991—, Union Theol. Sem., 1992—, Andrew W. Mellon Found., 1994—, Va. Mus. Fine Arts, 1995—, pres. 1996—; bd. dirs. Fan Dist. Assn., Richmond, Inc., 1976-80, pres., 1979-80; bd. dirs. Richmond Symphony, 1980-92, pres., 1988-90, pres. symphony coun., 1994—; bd. dirs. Presbyn. Outlook Found. and Book Svc., 1985—, pres., 1992—; bd. dirs. Va. Mus. Found., 1990—; elder Grace Covenant Presbyn. Ch. Mem. ABA, Va. Bar Assn., D.C. Bar Assn., Richmond Bar Assn., Am. Soc. Internat. Law, Am. Judicature Soc., Am. Bar Found., Princeton Assn. Va. (bd. dirs. 1981—, pres. 1983-85), Edn. Lawyers (chmn. Va. State Bar sect. 1992-95), Raven Soc., Knickerbocker Club (N.Y.C.), Country Club Va., Downtown Club, Order of Coif, Phi Beta Kappa, Omicron Delta Kappa. Home: 2314 Monument Ave Richmond VA 23220-2604 Office: Hunton & Williams Riverfront Pla East Tower 951 E Byrd St Richmond VA 23219-4040

REVERCOMB, HORACE AUSTIN, III, judge; b. Richmond, Va., Sept. 22, 1948; s. Horace Austin Jr. and Mary Virginia (Kelley) R.; m. Annie S. Anthony, July 10, 1976; children: Brian Austin, Suzanne Melanie. BA, Pembroke State U., 1971; JD, George Mason U., 1977. Bar: Va. 1978. Pvt. practice law King George, Va., 1978-82; ptnr. Revercomb & Revercomb, King George, 1982-90; judge Gen. Dist. Cts. of 15th Jud. Dist. Va., 1990—; spl. justice Cir. Cts. of 15th Jud. Dist., 1987—. Mem. Va. Bar Assn., Fredericksburg Area Bar Assn., Va. Trial Lawyers Assn. Methodist. Home: PO Box 216 King George VA 22485-0216

REVERE, VIRGINIA LEHR, clinical psychologist; b. Long Branch, N.J.; d. Joseph and Essie Lehr; m. Robert B. Revere; children: Elspeth, Andrew, Lisa, Robert Jr. PhB, U. Chgo., 1949, MA, 1959, PhD, 1971. Lic. cons. clin. psychologist, Va. Intern, staff psychologist Ea. Mental Health Reception Ctr., Phila., 1959-61; instr. Trenton (N.J.) State Coll., 1962-63; staff psychologist Trenton State Hosp., 1964-65, Bucks County Psychiat. Ctr., Phila., 1965-67; assoc. prof. Mansfield (Pa.) State U., 1967-77; clin. rsch. psychologist St. Elizabeth Hosp., Washington, 1977-81, tng. psychology coord., 1981-83, staff psychologist, 1985-91; child psychologist Community Mental Health Ctr., Washington, 1983-85; pvt. practice Alexandria, Va., 1980—; cons., lectr. in field. Author: Applied Psychology for Criminal Justice Professionals, 1982; contbr. articles to profl. jours. Recipient Group Merit award St. Elizabeth's Hosp., 1983, Community Svc. award D.C. Psychol. Assn., 1978, Outstanding Educator award, 1972; traineeship NIH, USPHS, Chgo., 1963-65; fellow Family Svcs. Assn., 1958-59. Mem. APA, No. Va. Soc. Clin. Psychologists, Va. Acad. Clin. Psychologists. Home: 9012 Linton Ln Alexandria VA 22308-2733 Office: 5021 Seminary Rd Ste 110 Alexandria VA 22311-1923

REVUELTA, RENÉ SERGIO, marine scientist, educator; b. La Habana, Cuba, Sept. 9, 1956; s. René Juan and Yolanda Paula (López) R.; m. Maria Soledad Tosteson, June 17, 1984 (div. 1993); children: Zinfandel, Luna. BA, U. Miami, 1978; PhD in Marine Scis., U. P.R., 1986. Grad. rsch. assoc. dept. marine scis. U. P.R., Mayaguez, 1978-86; postdoctoral fellow dept. biology and McCollum-Pratt Inst. Johns Hopkins U., Balt., 1986-88; postdoctoral assoc. divsn. marine and atmospheric chemistry U. Miami, Fla., 1988-89; asst. prof. dept. natural scis. Miami-Dade C.C., 1989-92, assoc. prof., 1992—. Editor: Physical Geography, 5th edit., 1993; contbr. articles to profl. jours. Mem. AAAS, Nat. Geog. Soc., Am. Mus. Nat. History (assoc.), Geol. Soc. Am. Home: P O Box 902020 Homestead FL 33090 Office: Miami-Dade CC Dept Natural Scis 500 College Ter Homestead FL 33030-6009

REW, WILLIAM EDMUND, civil engineer; b. Corning, N.Y., Nov. 24, 1923; s. Robert James and Clara (Neal) R.; m. Jean Ella Ohls, Aug. 16, 1947 (dec.); children: Virginia Ann, Robert James, John Edward. BE, Yale U., 1954, M in Engring., 1955. Registered profl. engr., N.Y., Fla., Calif., Ill. Project engr. Texaco & Affiliate, USA and Saudi Arabia, 1955-62; sr. engr. Martin-Marietta Corp., Cape Kennedy, Fla., 1962-63, Chrysler Corp, Cape Kennedy, 1963-65, The Boeing Co., Cape Kennedy, 1965-70; project mgr. Brevard Engring. Co., Cape Canaveral, Fla., 1970-74; city engr. City of Vero Beach (Fla.), 1974-77; resident engr. Post, Buckley, Schuh & Jernigan, Miami, Fla., 1977-85; mgr. Keith & Schnars, P.A., West Palm Beach, Fla., 1985-90; pvt. practice consulting Lake Placid, Fla., 1990—. Active Dem. Party of Brevard County. 1st lt. U.S. Army, 1942-46, ATO. Scholar of 2d rank Yale U., 1953, grad. scholar, 1955. Fellow ASCE (chmn. Fla. ann conv. 1971, Engr. of Yr. 1974); mem. NSPE, Soc. Am. Mil. Engrs. (bd. dirs. 1982-83), Fla. Engring Soc. (chpt. pres. 1976), Yale Club, Browning Assn. Club. Episcopalian. Home: 1425 S Washington Blvd NW Lake Placid FL 33852-4031

REX, DAVID LAWRENCE, project manager; b. Elizabeth, N.J., Oct. 26, 1935; s. Harland Earl and Kathryn Elizabeth (Murphy) R.; m. Ann Ivy

Dipple, Sept. 26, 1964 (div. Dec. 1995); children: Harland Edward, Bradley David. BS in Mech. Engring., U. Wis., Madison, 1958. Registered profl. engr., Tex. Project engr. Bechtel Corp., San Francisco, 1961-67; sr. project engr. Arabian Am. Oil Co., Dhahran, Saudi Arabia, 1967-83; project mgr. Creole Prodn. Svcs. Inc., Houston, 1983-85, Frederic R. Harris, Suez, Egypt, 1986-88; constrn. mgr. Morton Thiokol Inc., Karnack, Tex., 1988; project mgr. Bechtel Corp., Houston, 1988-92, Morrison Knudsen, Cleve., 1992-94; sales engr. McCracken & Assocs., Bristol, Tenn., 1994-95; sales rep. Touch Controls, Inc., Oceanside, Calif., 1996—. Life mem. Rep. Nat. Com. Capt. USAFR, 1958-61. Mem. VFW, U.S. Cycling Fedn., Nat. W Club, Kingsport Bicycle Assn., Res. Officers Assn., Am. Legion, U. Wis. Alumni (life), USCG Alumni Assn., Airport Christian Ch., Disciples of Christ, U. Wis. Alumni Assn. (life), Beta Theta Pi. Home: 777 Lebanon Rd Kingsport TN 37663 Office: 1561 Ft Henry Dr Ste 4 Kingsport TN 37664-2538

REX, LONNIE ROYCE, religious organization administrator; b. Caddo, Okla., May 11, 1928; s. Robert Lavern and Lennie Cordy (Gilcrease) R.; m. Betty Louise Sorrells, Apr. 8, 1949; children: Royce DeWayne, Patricia Louise, Debra Kaye. MusB, Oklahoma City U., 1950; DD (hon.), Am. Bible Inst., 1970. Advt. mgr. Oral Roberts Evang. Assn., Tulsa, 1955-57; bus. mgr. T.L. Osborn Found., Tulsa, 1957-69; gen. mgr. Christian Crusade, Tulsa, 1969-80; sec.-treas. David Livingstone Missionary Found., Tulsa, 1970-80, pres., 1980—; dep. dir. gen. Internat. Biog. Assn.; bd. dirs. Intra-Ch. Pension Fund, Bethany, Okla.; speaker internat. confs. Eng., Hungary, Korea, Singapore, Spain, N.Y.C. Author: Never a Child, 1989. Mem. Internat. PHC Loan Fund; bd. dirs. Armand Hammer United World Coll. of Am. West, 1993—. Recipient Merit award Korea, 1975, Moran medal Republic of Korea, Humanitarian award Senator Hugh Scott, 1983, Svc. to Mankind award Internat. Biog. Congress, Spain, 1987, Internat. Lions Club award; named Outstanding Humanitarian of Yr., Am. Biog. Inst., 1987, Man of Yr., 1990, 1993; knighted in Moscow, 1993. Mem. Knights of Malta (Sword of Svc. 1996), Phi Beta Kappa. Home: 6919 S Columbia Ave Tulsa OK 74136-4328 Office: David Livingstone Missionary Found 6555 S Lewis Ave Tulsa OK 74136-1010

REYES, GUILLERMO ANTONIO, cardiologist; b. Houston, Jan. 26, 1965; s. Luis A. Reyes and Alba Luz (Montes) R. BS in Biochemistry, Tex. A&M U., 1986; MD, Baylor Coll. of Medicine, 1991. Intern, resident in internal medicine Baylor Coll. of Medicine, Houston, 1991-94, fellow in cardiology, 1994—. Elder, deacon 7th Day Adventist Ch., Houston, 1991-94. Recipient Baylor Scholarship award, 1986, 87. Mem. AMA, ACC. Home: 12329 Nesmith Dr Houston TX 77035-5419

REYES, JOSE ANTONIO, SR., minister; b. Canovanas, P.R., May 24, 1940; s. Dionisio Reyes and Antonia (Rodriguez) R.; m. Olfa R. Martinez, May 30, 1964; 1 child, Jose A. BA in Edn., U. P.R., 1962; MA, Sch. Theology, Cleveland, Tenn., 1984; D Ministry, Logos Sch., 1985. Ordained to ministry Ch. of God of Prophecy, 1969. Youth dir. Ch. of God of Prophecy, Rio Piedras, P.R., 1956-58, pastor, 1963-68; mission rep. for Latin Am. Ch. of God of Prophecy, Cleveland, Tenn., 1969-75, internat. radio speaker, 1969—, internat. asst. gen. overseer, 1981—; pres. Hispanic Nat. Religious Broadcasting, Parsippany, 1985-88; v.p. Nat. Orgn. Advancement of Hispanic, 1983-86; com. mem. Hispanic Task Force of Am. Bible Soc., 1985-87; mem. Hispanic Commn., Nat. Assn. Evangelicals, Carol Stream, Ill., 1988—; exec. com. Nat. Religious Broadcasters, 1990-93, bd. dirs., 1990—; founding mem. Alliance Nat. Evang. Ministries, 1993—; pres. ref. com. Latin Am. Christian Comm., 1992—; mem. exec. com. Washington for Jesus, 199—; founding mem. Israel Christian adv. coun., 1996. Author: The Hispanics in USA - A Challenge, An Opportunity for the Church, 1984; author 10 Bible Study Guides on books of the Bible, 1985-90. Recipient Excellence in Hispanic Program Producer award Nat. Religious Broadcasters, 1988, Excellence in Ministry award Internat. Ministry Com., 1990. Mem. Spanish Voice of Salvation Sponsorship Club (pres.). Republican. Home: 3816 Northwood Dr NW Cleveland TN 37312-3805

REYES, MARÍA ELENA, academic program director; b. Eagle Pass, Tex.; d. Jorge Vargas and Maria Claudia (Cardona) R.; div.; children: Paul David, Benjamin, Jenny, Matthew. BA in Sociology and English cum laude, Pan-Am. U., 1973; MA in Secondary Edn., Sul Ross U., 1988; PhD in Curriculum and Instrn., U. Tex., 1991. Part-time Spanish tutor lang. lab. U. Tex., Austin, 1968-70; state caseworker Tex. Welfare Dept., Pharr, 1971-75; tchr. English Eagle Pass H.S., 1978-88; supr. student tchrs. English edn. dept. U. Tex., Austin, 1988-90, rsch.-tchg. asst. to prof. emeritus Don Americo Paredes, 1990-91, cons. Grad. Sch., 1991-92, project dir. Hispanic Mother-Dau. Program, 1992—; vol. United Farm Workers, McAllen, Tex., 1970-73; intern in urban studies, Pan Am. U., 1971-72; rsch. asst. focus group series U. Tex. Sch. Nursing, 1990; developer Lang. Arts IV Course Eagle Pass H.S., 1986, mgr. migrant tutoring program; advisor, bd. dirs. SMART Student Orgn., U. Tex., Austin, cons. Mex. Am. Health Professions Orgn., pres. Chicana/o Grad. Students Assn., minority recruiter, mem. adv. bd. Ctr. for Mex.-Am. Studies; trainer Family Math program; presenter in field. Author: The 1995 Guide to the Top 25 Colleges for Hispanics, 1995; contbr. articles to Hispanic Mag. Mem. KLRU Cmty. Bd., 1995-96, 4-H Aerospace Task Force, Mendez Mid. Sch. PTA; bd. dirs. Found. for Women's Resources Conf., Austin; head Bilingual Students' Support Group Martin Jr. H.S. PTA; vol. tutoring program Bedichek Mid. Sch. Recipient Nat. Hispanic Achievement award, 1995, cert. appreciation Eagle Pass H.S. Student Coun., 1985; rsch. fellow U. Tex. at Austin Ctr. for Mex.-Am. Studies, 1991, Title VII fellow, 1990-91, Univ. Grad. fellow, 1988-91, Urban Studies fellow Pan Am. U., 1973. Mem. ASCD, AAUW (adv. panel, Internat. Fellowship Awards Panel 1995—), Am. Assn. Higher Edn., Exec. Women in Tex. Govt., Expanding Your Horizons (Austin chpt.), Hispanic Assn. Colls. and Univs., U. Tex. Latina Women's Caucus, Tex. Assn. Chicanos in Edn., Kappa Delta Pi (v.p. U. Tex., Austin), Phi Kappa Phi.

REYES, RAUL GREGORIO, surgeon; b. Tegucigalpa, Morazan, Honduras, June 18, 1928; came to U.S., 1939; s. Julio Gregorio and Mercedes Ofelia (Mazzoni) Reyes-Zelaya; m. Blanca Lidia Milla, Apr. 2, 1993; children: Tyra, Kimberly. BS, Georgetown U., 1945; MD, George Washington U., 1950. Diplomate Nat. Bd. Med. Examiners, Am. Bd. Surgery. Intern Charity Hosp., New Orleans, 1950-51; resident Emergency Hosp./George Washington U., Washington, 1951, Charity Hosp., New Orleans, 1952-55; chief thoracic surgery San Felipe Hosp., Tegucigalpa, 1955-56; assoc. to ptnr. Browne-McHardy Clinic, New Orleans, 1955-60, 60-73; med. dir. New Orleans Indsl. Clinic, 1956-58; chief of surgery and orthopedics Lallie Kemp Regional Hosp., Independence, La., 1987-89, med. dirs., 1988-89; owner, pres. Raul G. Reyes, A Med. Corp., New Orleans, 1973—; owner, pres. Internat. Maritime Med. Svcs., New Orleans, 1978—, Catracho Enterprises, New Orleans, 1975—, Phys. Therapy Svcs. of New Orleans, 1975—; faculty La. State Univ. Sch. Medicine, 1953—, others. Inventor in field; contbr. articles to profl. jours. Chmn. Rep. Hispanic Assembly, New Orleans, 1983; pre-cand. Nat. Party, Honduras, 1985; founder Literacy Ctrs. of Honduras, 1991; presdl. candidate Christian Dem. Party of Honduras, 1994. Named to Hon. Consul of Honduras, Hon. Citizen, City of New Orleans. Mem. Am. Coll. Surgeons, AMA, So. Med. Assn., La. State Med. Soc., Orleans Parish Med. Soc., Colegio Medico de Honduras. Roman Catholic. Office: PO Box 15379 New Orleans LA 70175-5379

REYES, RICARDO RAMON, internist, infectious disease physician, immunologist; b. Apr. 27, 1952; m. Isabel Maria Cordoba, Mar. 12, 1977; children: Ricky, Ana Maria. BS, U. Panama; MD, U. Panama Sch. Medicine, 1972. Diplomate Am. Bd. Internal Medicine, Am. Bd. Infectious Diseases. Intern St. Thomas Hosp., Panama, 1976-77, Aquilino Tejeira Hosp., Penonome, Panama, 1977-78; resident in Internal Medicine Gorgas Army Hosp., Ancon, Panama, 1978-81; fellow in infectious disease U. Ky. Med. Ctr., Lexington, 1981-83; mem. staff infectious disease Centro Medico, Paitilla, Panama, 1983—; asst. prof. Clin. Medicine U. Miami (Fla.), 1988-91; attending physician Internal Medicine Spl. Immunology U. Miami Jackson Meml. Hosp., 1988-91, clin. dir. Spl. Immunology Clinic, 1989-91; staff physician Cleveland Clinic Fla., Ft. Lauderdale, 1991—; phys. diagnosis preceptor U. Ky. Med. Ctr., Lexington, 1982-83; cons. Gorgas Army Hosp., Panama, 1983-88, Gorgas Meml. Lab., 1984-88. Fellow ACP; mem. Am. Soc. for Microbiology, Infectious Disease Soc. Am., Internal Medicine Soc. Panama, Infectious Disease Soc. Panama (sec.-treas. 1984-86), Broward County Med. Assn., Fla. Med. Assn. Home: 8601 Dundee Ter Hialeah FL 33016-1402 Office: Cleveland Clinic Fla 3000 W Cypress Creek Rd Fort Lauderdale FL 33309-1710

REYNA, WANDA WONG, early childhood education educator; b. Houston, Nov. 29, 1950; d. Jerry and May (Chan) Wong; m. Carl Glenn Reyna, Aug. 31, 1974; 1 child, Aaron Kyle. AA, San Jacinto Jr. Coll., 1971; BA, U. Houston, 1977, MS, 1985. Cert. home econs., kindergarten, learning disabilities and early childhood edn. and mid-mgmt. tchr., Tex. Tchr. Pasadena (Tex.) Ind. Sch. Dist., 1980—. Mem. Kappa Delta Pi. Office: Sparks Elem Sch 2503 Southmore Ave Pasadena TX 77502-1429

REYNAL, DAVID WEBB, municipal official; b. New Britain, Conn., Dec. 19, 1950; s. Claude Jules and Mildred Gertrude (Hart) R.; m. Deborah L. Roberts, June 19, 1976; children: Joshua Claude, Matthew George. BS in pol. sci., Rensselaer Polytech. Inst., 1973; M in pub. adminstrn., Syracuse U., 1974. Fin. coord. City of Utica, N.Y., 1974-75; sr. adminstrn. analyst City of Newport News, Va., 1975-77; town mgr. Town of Clarksville, Va., 1977-80; program mgr. Va. Dept. Housing & Community Devel., Richmond, 1980; town mgr. Town of Ashland, Va., 1980—. Bd. dirs. Ctrl. Va. Waste Mgmt. Authority, 1990-93, Va. Assembly Future Growth Regional Meeting, Williamsburg, Va., 1993, Ashland-Hanover C. of C., 1989-90; bd. of elders and deacons New Found. Ch. of Christ (chmn. 1990-94), Pamunkey Regional Jail Authority (sec. 1992—). Office: Town of Ashland P O Box 1600 101 Thompson Ashland VA 23005

REYNOLDS, BARBARA C., mental health educator, academic dean; b. Syracuse, N.Y.; d. Robert J. Clark; m. George L. Reynolds, June 9, 1962 (dec.); children: George L. III, Katherine C. BSN, Syracuse U., 1952; MPH, U. Minn., 1968, PhD, 1989. Asst. prof. U. Cin., 1968-75; ind. human resources cons. Cin., 1975-76; asst. prof. sch. pub. health U. Minn., 1976-82; asst. prof. Vanderbilt U., Nashville, 1986-90, N.Y. Med. Ctr. Sch. Nursing, Coll. Mt. St. Joseph; dean sch. nursing Tenn. Tech. U., Cookeville, 1991—. Contbr. articles to profl. jours. Mem. ANA, Tenn. Nurses Assn., Deans and Dirs. Schs. of Nursing in Tenn. (treas.), Leadership Putham Alumni Assn. (pres. 1995-96), Leadership Putnam (bd. dirs. 1996—), Rotary (Cookeville chpt.), Sigma Theta Tau, Phi Kappa Phi. Home: 1078 Independence Ct Cookeville TN 38501-3378

REYNOLDS, BILL See **ARCHER, WILLIAM REYNOLDS, JR.**

REYNOLDS, CYNTHIA MICHELLE, librarian, writer; b. Greensburg, Ky., June 13, 1972; d. Jerald Eugene and Judy Mae (Wright) R. BA in English and Art History, Centre Coll., Danville, Ky., 1994; postgrad., U. Ky., 1996—. Writer, Lexington, Ky., 1994—; libr. clk. Lexington Pub. Libr., 1995—; grad. asst. spl. collections and archives U. Ky., 1996—. Presdl. scholar Centre Coll., 1990-94, Mitchell and Cooper scholar, 1992-94, Brown scholar, 1993-94. Mem. ALA, Writers' Critique Group, Creative Writing Practice Group, Phi Beta Kappa, Phi Sigma Iota.

REYNOLDS, DON WILLIAM, geologist; b. Centerburg, Ohio, Apr. 6, 1926; s. Loren William and Charlotte Lonas (Hunt) R.; m. Betty Jeannette Spears, Sept. 4, 1953; children: Don William, Jr., Richard Allen (dec.), Brenda Gay. BS, Ohio State U., 1952. Registered profl. geologist, Calif. Mgr., Geochem. Engring. Inc., Midland, Tex., 1950-52; geologist Union Oil Co. Calif., Midland, 1953-66, dist. exploration geologist, Anchorage, 1966-68, area geologist, Bakersfield, Calif., 1968-76, dist. devel. geologist, Ventura, Calif., 1976-86; dist. devel. geologist mid-continent dist., Oklahoma City, 1986-89, regional mgr. mid-continent devel., 1989-90, advisor geology, 1990-92; gen. ptnr. Reynolds Farm, 1979—; sec. IFP Inc., Austin, 1989—; chmn. bd. Future Petroleum Corp., 1992—. Pres. Park Stockdale Civic Assn., Bakersfield, 1970, Clearpoint Home Owners Assn., Ventura, 1980-86; chmn. Kern County Freeway Com. Bakersfield, 1970-73. Served wtih USAF, 1944-45. Mem. Am. Assn. Petroleum Geologists, West Tex. Geol. Soc. (sec. 1965-66), Kans.-Okla. Oil and Gas Assn. (nomenclature com. 1987-92), San Joaquin Geol. Soc. (treas. 1974-75), Am. Assn. Petroleum Geologists (sec. Pacific sect. 1975-76). Republican. Methodist.

REYNOLDS, DON WILLIAM, JR., computer software company executive, financial analyst; b. Midland, Tex., Aug. 31, 1960; s. Don William and Betty Jeanette (Spears) R. BS, U. Calif., Berkeley, 1982; MBA, U. Tex., 1991. Fin. analyst Northrop Corp., Hawthorne, Calif., 1982-83; consulting assoc. Kaplan, Smith & Assocs., Glendale, Calif., 1983-87; managing cons. Treasury Svcs. Corp., Santa Monica, Calif., 1987-89; pres. Austin Software Foundry, 1989—; bd. dirs. Intelligent Fin. Perspectives, Austin, Future Petroleum Corp., Dallas; lectr. U. Tex., Austin, 1993—; active Austin Software Coun., 1993—. Author: PowerBuilder Desktop: The Authorized Guide, 1994. Home: 3409 Spotted Horse Trl Austin TX 78739-5729 Office: Austin Software Foundry Ste 190 Bldg 8 500 Capital of Texas Hwy Austin TX 78746

REYNOLDS, GEORGE ANTHONY, JR., engineering executive; b. Columbia, S.C., May 5, 1961; s., George Anthony and Flora Mae (La Coste) R.; m. Katherine Alison Albea, Apr. 14, 1984; children: Amanda Kate, William Anthony. BSME, Clemson U., 1983; postgrad., U. Ala., Huntsville, 1985. Design engr. Motorola, Plantation, Fla., 1983-85; sr. engr. Chrysler, Huntsville, Ala., 1985-88; prin. engr. NCR, Liberty, S.C., 1988-91, project leader, 1991-94; mgr. mech. engring. Sensormatic Electronics, Boca Raton, Fla., 1994-96, dir. product engring., 1996—. Mem. editl. quality audit panel Electronic Packaging & Prodn. Mag., N.Y.C., 1992. Advisor Clemson U. Mech. Engring. Endowment Fund; pres. Seagate Homeowners Assn. Mem. ASME (assoc.), NRA, S.E. Pro/Engr. User Group (pres. 1992-93), Nature Conservancy, Nat. Wildlife Fedn., Ducks Unltd., Fla. Sheriff's Assn. (life), Men of Achievement 1996, Fla. Wildlife Fedn., Tau Beta Pi, Phi Kappa Phi, Alpha Tau Omega (mem. alumni adv. bd. Eta Pi chpt. 1993-94). Republican. Presbyterian. Home: 927 Seagate Dr Delray Beach FL 33483-6617 Office: Sensormatic Electronic Corp 951 Yamato Rd Boca Raton FL 33431-0700

REYNOLDS, H. GERALD, lawyer; b. Alexander City, Ala., July 16, 1940; s. James H. and Melba V. (Scott) R.; m. Mary Alice McGiboney, Sept. 3, 1960; children—Cathy, Gerre, Amy, Richie. B.A., Auburn U., 1962; J.D., Cumberland Sch. Law, 1965. Bar: Ala. 1965, Fla. 1977. Ptnr. King and Reynolds, Alexander City, 1965-66; sole practice, Alexander City, 1966-71; corp. counsel U.S. Pipe and Foundry, Birmingham, Ala., 1971-72; environ. counsel Jim Walter Corp., Tampa, Fla., 1972-87, Walter Industries Inc., 1988— ; judge Ct. Common Pleas, Tallapoosa County, Ala., 1967-68; mem. faculty Alexander City State Jr. Coll., 1966-71; ad hoc instr. Coll. Pub. Health Grad. Sch. U. South Fla., 1988-90. Mem. Ala. Constl. Revision Commn., 1970-75; mem. Ala. Democratic Exec. Com., 1970-72. Mem. Fla. Bar Assn. (chmn. eviron. and land use law sect. 1981-82, vice chmn. continuing legal edn. com. 1980-94). Methodist. Contbr. articles to legal jours.

REYNOLDS, HERBERT HAL, academic administrator; b. Frankston, Tex., Mar. 20, 1930; s. Herbert Joseph and Ava Nell (Taylor) R.; m. Joy Myrla Copeland, June 17, 1950; children: Kevin Hal, Kent Andrew, Rhonda Sheryl. BS, Trinity U., 1952; MS, Baylor U., 1958, PhD, 1961; ScD (hon.), Baylor Coll. Dentistry, Seinan Gakuin U., Japan. Entered USAF, 1948, advanced through grades to col., 1966; service in Japan, Europe; dir. research (Aeromed. Lab.), Alamogordo, N. Mex., 1961-67; comdr. (Air Force Human Resources Lab.), San Antonio, Tex., 1968; ret., 1968; exec. v.p. Baylor U., Waco, Tex., 1969-81, pres., 1981-95, chancellor, 1995—. Contbr. articles to profl. jours. Mem. Sigma Xi, Alpha Chi, Omicron Delta Kappa, Mortar Bd., Kappa Kappa Psi, Beta Theta Pi. Office: Baylor U Office of Chancellor Waco TX 76798

REYNOLDS, JOHN FRANCIS, foreign language educator; b. Boston, Oct. 23, 1942; s. John F. and Margaret E. (Leary) R.; m. Geraldine A. Randall, Aug. 15, 1978. BA, Tufts U., 1964; MA, Tuebingen (Germany) U., 1967; PhD, U. Va., 1970. Tchr. Kant Gymnasium, Berlin, 1964-66; asst. prof. German U. Va., Charlottesville, 1971-77, assoc. prof. German, 1985-87; asst. prof. German Colby Coll., Waterville, Maine, 1978-85, Longwood Coll., Farmville, Va., 1987-89; dir. internat. studies Longwood Coll., Farmville, 1988-91; assoc. prof. Longwood Coll., Farmville, Va., 1989-91, prof., 1991—. Editor: C.F. Gellerts Briefwechsel, vol. 1, 1983, vol. 2, 1987, vol. 3, 1991, vol. 4, 1996; co-author: C.F. Gellerte Gesammelte Schriften, 1980—. Fulbright fellow, Cologne, Germany, 1970-71, fellow Am. Coun. Learned Soc., Harvard U., 1975-76, Alexander von Humboldt Found., Aachen, Germany, 1981-82, 83-84, Internat. Rsch. and Exch., Leipzig, Germany, 1987. Mem. Am. Assn. Tchrs. German (pres. Maine chpt. 1982-84, pres. Va. chpt. 1990-92), Fgn. Langs. in Va., Va. Coun. for Internat. Edn. (pres. 1992-94), Delta Phi Alpha (nat. pres. 1992-93, nat. sec.-treas 1994—), Lessing Soc. Office: Longwood Coll 201 High St Farmville VA 23909-1899

REYNOLDS, JOHN TERRENCE, oil industry executive; b. Madison, Wis., Oct. 2, 1944; s. John Francis and Evelyn Ruth (Straus) R.; m. Diane Marie Princl-Reynolds, Sept. 3, 1966; 1 child, Channing. BSME, U. Wis., 1967, MS in Metallurgical Engring., 1968. Engr. Shell Chem. Co., Denver, 1968-70, Royal Dutch/Shell, The Hague, The Netherlands, 1970-72; sr. engr. Shell Devel. Co., Houston, 1972-75, Shell Oil Co., Houston, 1975-78; staff engr. Shell Oil Co., Deer Park, Tex., 1978-81; engring. mgr. Shell Oil Co., Anacortes, Wash., 1981-87; engring. advisor Shell Oil Co., Houston, 1987—; chmn. inspection codes com., 1989—, inspection subcommittee, 1993—, Am. Petroleum Inst., Washington. Author: Mechanical Integrity of Refinery Equipment, 1993, The New In-Service Piping Inspection Code, 1993. Recipient of numerous certificates of appreciation. Mem. ASME, Am. Soc. for Metals, Nat. Assn. Corrosion Engrs., Am. Petroleum Inst., Nat. Petroleum Refiners Assn. Office: Shell Oil Co 3333 Highway 6 S Houston TX 77082-3101

REYNOLDS, MARJORIE LAVERS, secondary school educator; b. Collingwood, Ont., Can., Jan. 10, 1931; d. Henry James and Laura (Wilson) Lavers; m. John Horace Reynolds, Aug. 17, 1963; children: Steven, Mark. BA, U. Toronto, 1953; MS, U. Minn., 1957; PhD, U. Wis., 1964; AS, State Tech. Inst. Knoxville, 1982. Registered dietitian. Rsch. dietitian Mayo Clinic, Rochester, Minn., 1957-59; rsch. dietitian Cleve. Met. Gen. Hosp., 1959-60; rsch. assoc. U. Tenn., Knoxville, 1963-66; instr. Ft. Sanders Sch. Nursing, Knoxville, 1967-76, State Tech. Inst., Knoxville, 1982-88; substitute secondary sch. tchr. Knox County Schs., Knoxville, 1989-93. Contbr. articles to biochem. and nutrition jours.; newsletter editor Juvenile Diabetes Found., Knoxville, 1985-93. Sec. Midway Rehab. Ctr., Knoxville, 1987—; mem. LWV, Knoxville, 1965—. Mem. Knoxville Dist. Dietetic Assn. (pres. 1971-72, Outstanding Dietitian 1973-1974), Tenn. Dietetic Assn. (pres. 1973-74, Outstanding Dietitian 1973-74), Omicron Nu. Democrat. Presbyterian. Home: 7112 Stockton Dr Knoxville TN 37909-2534

REYNOLDS, MARY ELIZABETH FONTAINE, office administrator; b. New Orleans, Feb. 15, 1931; d. Edgar Benjamin Sr. and Clothilde Marie (Sicard); m. James Louis Reynolds, June 8, 1955; children: Mary Elizabeth, Mary Catherine Anderson, James Louis Jr., Mary Clothilde. BA, Newcomb Coll., 1953. Office adminstr. James L. Reynolds, M.D., New Orleans, 1978—; sec. treas. La. Smoked Products Inc., New Orleans, 1988-94. Chmn. Overture to the Cultural Season, New Orleans, 1972; chmn., founding com. Heart Ambassadors, New Orleans, 1972. Recipient Key to the City New Orleans, 1972. Mem. Orleans Club. Republican. Roman Catholic. Home: 808 Rue Decatur Metairie LA 70005-3462

REYNOLDS, MEGAN BEAHM, primary and elementary education educator; b. Lima, Ohio, Aug. 29, 1955; d. Walter Clarence and Jo Ann (Wood) Beahm; m. Dale Myron Reynolds, Aug. 28, 1976 (div. July 1983); 1 child, Emily Jo Reynolds. BS, Tenn. Wesleyan Coll., 1977; postgrad., U. Tenn., 1986-88. Cert. elem. and early edn. tchr., Tenn. Tchr. adult basic edn. Athens (Tenn.) City Schs., 1977-78; asst. dir. Child Shelter Home, Cleveland, Tenn., 1978; tchr. kindergarten First Bapt. Presch./Kindergarten, Cleveland, 1978-80; teller, bookkeeper C & C Bank Monroe County, Sweetwater, Tenn., 1982-83; substitute elem. tchr. Knox County Schs., Knoxville, Tenn., 1983-85, elem. tchr., 1985-87, tchr. kindergarten, 1987—; career ladder III Knox County Schs., Knoxville, 1993; mem. adv. bd., grade-level chairperson Norwood Elem. Sch., Knox County Schs., 1990-93, mem. adopt a sch. com., 1992-93, S team rep., 1991-92. Editor Norwood Elem. Yearbook, 1989-90. Parent helper Girl Scouts U.S., 1986-90; neighborhood collector Am. Heart Assn., 1987—; v.p. Norwood Elem./Knox County Schs. PTO, 1991-92; Norwood rep. Ft. Kid, 1990-91; youth counselor Middlebrook Pike Meth. Ch., mem. Costa Rica missions team; active participant Vols. of Am. Mem. NEA, Tenn. Edn. Assn., Knox County Edn. Assn., Knox County Assn. Young Children, Children and Adults with Attention Deficit Disorder (presch. Summer intervention program, parent/sch. comms. program 1995—). Methodist. Home: 8525 Savannah Ct Knoxville TN 37923 Office: Norwood Elem Sch 1909 Merchants Dr Knoxville TN 37912-4714

REYNOLDS, NANCY F., public relations counselor, registered nurse; b. Columbia, S.C., July 16, 1946; d. George Harold and Gladys Anita (Howie) Franklin; m. Fred J. Carter, June 15, 1968 (dec. 1969); m. Richard Edward Mancill, III, July 4, 1974 (div. 1981); children: Elizabeth Buxton, Caroline Anita; m. Joseph Craig Reynolds, Dec. 1, 1984. BSN, U. S.C., 1968, MEd, 1972, undergrad. student, 1986-88. RN, S.C. Staff nurse Columbia Hosp., Columbia, S.C., 1968; clin. instr. U. S.C. Coll. of Nursing, Columbia, 1969-73; dir. recruitment and career develop. program U. S.C. Coll. of Nursing, 1972-73; state supr. health occupation S.C. Dept. of Edn., 1974; marriage and family counselor pvt. practice, Murrells Inlet, S.C., 1975-78; pres. and partner Small Oaks, Murrells Inlet, 1978-80; adminstr. Upjohn Health Care Svcs., Columbia, 1980-82; area adminstr. S.C. Cmty. Long Term Care, Columbia, 1982-88; pres., owner Reynolds & Reynolds, Columbia, 1988—. Press Media Women of S.C., chpt. pres. 1990-91; Polit. Action Com. chmn. S.C. Nurses Assn., 1990-94, Legislative Com. chmn., 1982-85; bd. dirs. S.C. Nurses Found., 1990-93, Public Relations Soc. of Am., 1991-94, Killingsworth Home, 1989-92, Shandon United Meth. Ch.; active in numerous other cmty. endeavors. Named to Com. of 100 Cen. Carolina Econ. Devel. Alliance, 1995; recipient Communicator of Achievement award Media Women of S.C., Pres. award S.C. Nurses Assn., 1994, numerous 1st pl. awards in comms. contests; fellow Amy Viglione Cockcroft Leadership Devel. program U. S.C. Coll. Nursing. Mem. ANA, Greater Columbia C. of C., Columbia World Affairs Counc., Public Relations Soc. of Am., Nat. Fedn. of Press Women. Independent. Methodist. Home: 125 S Waccamaw Ave Columbia SC 29205

REYNOLDS, RICHARD CLAY, writer, editor; b. Quanah, Tex., Sept. 28, 1949; s. Jessie Wrex and Pauline (Faught) R.; m. Julia Ann Kavanagh, Jan. 22, 1972; children: Wesley Eliot, Virginia Anne. BA in History, U. Tex., 1971; MA in English, Trinity U., San Antonio, 1974; PhD in Modern Letters, U. Tulsa, 1979. Grad. tchg. fellow U. Tulsa, 1974-77; instr. English Tulsa Jr. Coll., 1977-78, Claremore (Okla.) Coll., 1977-78; assoc. prof. English Lamar U., Beaumont, Tex., 1978-88; prof., novelist in residence U. North Tex., Denton, 1988-92, assoc. dir. Ctr. Texas Studies, 1990-92; freelance writer, editor, cons., 1992—; vis. prof., writer in resident Villanova (Pa.) U., 1994, Tex. Woman's U., 1991; judge Jesse Jones award Tex. Inst. Letters, 1993; fiction judge New Tex. Fiction award, 1991, 92, 93, Rice U. Lit. Festival First Novel award, 1993; mem., cons. Lit. Initiative Task Force, Tex. Commn. Arts, 1992; reader, cons. The Whitston Press, SMU Pres, U. Nev. Press, U. North Tex. Press, Bakersville Pubs., Ltd., ALE Pubs.; editor, cons. Applied Earth Scis., Inc.; lectr. various colls., univs., orgns. and workshops. Actor, dir. prodn. Tulsa Little Theatre, 1976-77, Beaumont Cmty. Players, 1979-88; dir. prodn., producer Beaumont At Mus., 1985; assoc. editor Lamar Jour. Humanities, 1980-88; editor Tex. Writers' Newsletter, 1989-92; editorial cons. Texas Goes to War, 1991; fiction editor New Texas '91 and New Texas '92, Am. Lit. Rev., 1990-92; author: The Vigil, 1986, Agatite, 1986, Stage Left: Development of American Social Drama, 1986, Taking Stock: A Larry McMurty Casebaook, 1989, Franklin's Crossing, 1992, One Hundred Years of Heroes, 1996; contbr. articles to profl. jours. V.p. Denton Area Little League, 1990-93; bd. dirs. Denton Fall Baseball, Inc., 1993. Nat. Endowment for Arts fellow, 1994; recipient awards Tex. Inst. Letters, 1988, Western Writers Am., 1989, Nat. Faculty, 1990, Friends of Libr. award, Key to City of Ft. Worth, 1992, Violet Crown Fiction award, 1992, ALE award, 1993. Pulitzer prize for fiction, 1992. Mem. MLA, PEN Ctrl.-PEN West, Western Writers Am., Tex. Inst. Letters, Author's Guild, South Ctrl. MLA, Western Am. Lits. Assn., Tex. Assn. Creative Writing Tchrs., Associated Writing Programs. Home: 909 Hilton Pl Denton TX 76201-8605

REYNOLDS, RICHARD LOUIS, lawyer; b. Baton Rouge, Sept. 10, 1953; s. Louis Baker and Mildred (Close) R.; m. Wendie Daigle, Nov. 23, 1978; children: Lindsey Michelle, Keith Richard. BS, La. State U., 1975; JD,

Loyola U., New Orleans, 1978. Bar: La. 1978, U.S. Dist. Ct. (ea. dist.) La. 1978, U.S. Ct. Appeals (5th cir.) 1982, U.S. Supreme Ct. 1982. Law clk. 22nd Jud. Dist. Ct., Covington, La., 1978-79; ptnr. Liberto and Reynolds, Covington, 1979-80; contract atty. Mental Health Advocacy Service, Baton Rouge, 1982-83; pvt. practice Covington, 1980-88; dir. Richard Reynolds and Assocs., Covington and Metairie, La., 1988—; asst. dist. atty. Covington, 1984-86, 87-93; instr. Delgado C.C., New Orleans, 1986-87; cons. NBKA, 1988; pres. Strategic Title and Appraisal Svcs., Inc. Columnist: The Northshore Journal. Bd. dirs. Alpha House, Covington, 1986-90, River Forest Acad. Sch.; campaign mgr. for candidate for La. Senate, 1983; mem. exec. com. St. Tammany Parish Dem. Com., 1983; active La. Dem. Ctrl. Com., 1983; Webelos den leader Den 2, Pack 112, Istrouma coun. Boy Scouts Am., 1995-96. Mem. ABA, La. Bar Assn., Covington Bar Assn., Assn. Trial Lawyers Am., La. Trial Lawyers Assn., St. Tammany Bd. Realtors, St. Tammany Home Bldrs. Assn., Rotary (Paul Harris fellow 1987, pres. 1988-89), Optimists. Office: Richard Reynolds & Assocs 610 S Tyler St PO Box 2130 Covington LA 70433

REYNOLDS, SIDNEY RAE, marketing communications executive; b. Alliance, Nebr., June 27, 1956; d. Harold Edward and Dolores Jean (Bestol) James; m. Eddie Ellis Reynolds, May 27, 1975; children: Ashley Dawn, Tyler John. BAgr, Kans. State U., 1977. Asst. editor Harvest Pub. Co., Lansing, Mich., 1977-78, assoc. editor, 1978-80; assoc. editor Harvest Pub. Co., Topeka, 1980-82; editor Specialized Agrl. Publs., Raleigh, N.C., 1982-88, editorial dir., 1984-88; rep. NCH Corp., Raleigh, N.C., 1988-89; pres. Wordcraft, Inc., The Signature Agy., Raleigh, 1987—. Contbr. articles to profl. jours.; developed models for integrated mktg. agys. and pub. rels. measurement, 1987—. Advisor Episcopal Youth Group, Wake Forest, N.C., 1986-89, Raleigh, N.C., 1987—. Named Writer of Yr., Harvest Pub. Co., 1978. Mem. Am. Agrl. Editors Assn., Women in Comms. (bd. dirs. 1978-79), Soc. Profl. Journalists (reorgnl. chairperson 1985-88), Spurs Club (nat. v.p. 1976-78), Agrl. Communicators Club (pres. Manhattan Kans. chpt. 1976), Rotary (treas. Raleigh-Millbrook chpt. 19992-94, v.p. 1994-95, pres. 1995-96, dist. comms. com. chair 1996—), Am. Mktg. Assn., Coun. for Entrepreneurial Devel., Sigma Delta Chi, Gamma Sigma Delta, Alpha Zeta. Home: 437 R Perkerson Rd Spring Hope NC 27882 Office: 183 Wind Chime Ct Ste 100 Raleigh NC 27615

REYNOLDS, WILLIAM BRADFORD, lawyer; b. Bridgeport, Conn., June 21, 1942; s. William Glasgow and Nancy Bradford (DuPont) R.; m. Marguerite Lynn Morgan, June 27, 1964 (div. Feb. 1987); children: William Bradford Jr., Melissa Morgan, Kristina DuPont, Wendy Riker; m. Clare Alice Conroy, Aug. 29, 1987; 1 child, Linda Matisan. BA, Yale U., 1964; LLB, Vanderbilt U., 1967. Bar: N.Y. 1968, D.C. 1973, U.S. Supreme Ct. 1971. Assoc. Sullivan and Cromwell, N.Y.C., 1967-70; asst. to Solicitor Gen. U.S. Dept. Justice, Washington, 1970-73; ptnr. Shaw, Pittman, Potts & Trowbridge, Washington, 1973-81; asst. atty. gen. Civil Rights div. U.S. Dept. Justice, Washington, 1981-88, counselor to Atty. Gen., 1987-88; ptnr. Ross & Hardies, 1989-91, Dickstein, Shapiro & Morin, 1991-94, Collier, Shannon, Rill & Scott, 1994—; chmn. Archtl. Transp. Barriers Compliance Bd., 1982-84. Editor-in-chief Vanderbilt Law Rev., 1966. Disting. scholar Free Congress Found., 1989-93, Disting. fellow Nat. Legal Ctr. for Pub. Interest, Washington, 1989-90. Mem. ABA, Fed. Bar Assn., D.C. Bar Assn., Order of Coif. Republican. Episcopalian.

REYNOLDS, WILLIAM MACKENZIE, JR., lawyer; b. Sumter, S.C., June 9, 1921; s. William MacKenzie and Helen (Janes) R.; m. Nancy Nash, Apr. 14, 1950; children: Helen Janes, William MacKenzie III. BS, The Citadel, 1942; JD, U. S.C., 1975. Bar: S.C. 1975. Commd. 2d lt. USAF, 1942, advanced through grades to col., 1963, ret., 1971; assoc. Nash & Chappell, Sumter, 1975-78; ptnr. Reynolds & Reynolds, Sumter, 1978—; bd. dirs. Nat. Bank S.C., Sumter, Sumter Casket Co.; master in equity County of Sumter, 1984-93. Decorated Legion of Merit, Disting. Flying Cross, Air medal. Mem. Sumter County Bar Assn., U.S. Law Sch. Alumni Assn. (bd. dirs. 1979-89), Order of Daedalians. Episcopalian. Home: 78 Nash St Sumter SC 29150-3219 Office: Reynolds & Reynolds 3 Law Range PO Box 396 Sumter SC 29151-0396

RHEA, MARCIA CHANDLER, accountant; b. Columbia, S.C., Apr. 27, 1956; d. Foster Frazier and Virginia Elizabeth (Goude) Chandler; m. Randall W. Rhea, Aug. 23, 1980. AA, Bauder Coll., Atlanta, 1975; BA magna cum laude, Coll. of Charleston, S.C., 1981; postgrad., CPA studies. Cert. tax practice ptnr., notary pub., S.C., CPA, S.C. Writer, prodr. U.S. Army C.E., Charleston, 1984; mng. ptnr. Care/Share Prodns., Charleston, 1981—; ptnr. Chandler Rhea, CPA, Johns Island, S.C., 1987—; agt. Deering Lit. Agy.; media cons., roving reporter Worldfest-Charleston Internat. Film Festival, 1994. Author: Does It Have to Happen Again?, From Hell's Angel to Heaven's Saint; author (screenplays) The Carolina Storyteller, The Life Shift; contbr. articles to mags. and profl. jours.; prodr. various films. Adult tchr. Ashley Rivers Bapt. Ch.; mem. Tri-County Advocates for Women on Bds. and Commns. for S.C. Recipient Outstanding Acad. Achievement award Coll. of Charleston. Mem. AICPA, Am. Soc. Notaries, S.C. Assn. CPAs, S.C. Motion Picture TV Assn., Script Writers of S.C., Inc., Screenwriters Guild of Charleston (charter), Acctg. Assn., Coll. of Charleston Alumni, Film Soc. Coll. Charleston (bd. dirs.), Phi Kappa Phi, Phi Mu. Republican. Baptist. Office: 3226 Maybank Hwy Ste 1 PO Box 508 Johns Island SC 29455

RHOADES, MARYE FRANCES, paralegal; b. Ft. Defiance, Va., Jan. 29, 1937; d. Silas Caswell Sr. and Mary Ann Frances (James) Rhodes; m. Minter James Rowe, May 1964 (div. 1968); children: Margaret Frances Omar, James Robert; m. Robert Charles Rhoades Jr., July 25, 1980. Student, Coll. W.Va., 1956-58, 68, U. Charleston, 1962-63, 74, 89, Antioch U., 1972-73; grad., Mike Tyree Sch. Real Estate, 1984, Evans Coll. Legal Studies, 1990. Educator Nicholas County Sch. System, Summersville, W.Va., 1958-61; edit. staff, columnist, staff writer, reporter, photographer Beckley Newspapers Corp., 1962-76; Educator Raleigh County Bd. Edn., Beckley, W.Va., 1967-68; exec. editor, columnist Local News Jour., Whitesville, W.Va., 1976-77; libr. bookmobile, asst. ref. libr., outreach coord. Raleigh County Pub. Libr., Beckley, 1977-78; agt. Combined Ins. Co., Chgo., 1978-79; legal sec., paralegal W.Va. Legal Svcs. Inc., Beckley, 1979-82; paralegal Applachian Rsch and Defense Fund Inc., Beckley, 1982-83; exec. dir., owner Rhoades and Rowe, Beckley, 1983-85; paralegal patinet advocate Comty. Health Sys. Inc., Beckley, 1986-96; pvt. practice Beckley, 1996—. Contbr. articles to mags. State bd. dirs., pub. resl. LWV, Beckley; pub. rels., various coms. Raleigh County Dem. Women, Beckley; sec., pub. rels. Orchard Valley Women's Club, Crab Orchard, W.Va.; trustee Fraternal Order Ealges; pub. rels., various coms. Loyal Order Moose, Beckley, Beckley Profl. Bus. Women; com. mem. Nat. Coalition to Save the New River; sales rep. So. U.S. Rep. to U.S. Mil. Acad., West Point, N.Y.; mem. Am. Legion Aux., Mullens, W.Va. Mem. NEA, Classroom Tchrs. Assn., Nat. Paralegal Assn., Nat. Fedn. Paralegals Assn., Nat. Ind. Paralegals Assn., Nat. Com. Save Soc., Sec. Medicare, Nat. Legal Aid and Def. Assn., Nat. Orgn. Social Security Claimants Reps., State Soc. Sec. Task Force, Nat. Vets. Legal Svcs. Project Inc., W.Va. U. Alumni Assn., Community AIDS Edn. Com., W.Va. Edn. Assn. Democrat. Pentacostal Holiness. Home: PO Box 416 Mac Arthur WV 25873-0416 Office: Benefit Advocates PO Box 416 Mac Arthur WV 25873-0416

RHOADES, RICHARD GARDNER, government research executive; b. Northampton, Mass., Aug. 15, 1938; s. Lawrence Duncan and Marion Cushman (Hollister) R.; m. Martha Dale Turner, July 29, 1967; children: Lawren Michelle, Anna Elizabeth, Jennifer Lee. B of Chem. Engring., Rensselaer Poly. Inst., 1960, PhD, 1964; MS in Mgmt., MIT, 1977. Rsch. chem. engr. U.S. Army Missile Command, Redstone Arsenal, Ala., 1965-74, dir. for propulsion, 1974-81, assoc. dir. for tech., 1981-89, assoc. dir. for sys., 1989—; chmn. exec. com. Joint Army Navy Air Force Propulsion Group, Washington, 1978-80; chmn. planning group Army Material Command Vision 2000, Washington, 1990-91. Inventor in field; contbr. articles to tech. jours. Vice chmn. rev. bd. Huntsville Alliance for Sci. Progress, 1990-94; treas. Monte Sano PTA, Huntsville, 1979-82, Monte Sano United Meth. Ch., Huntsville, 1983—. Capt. U.S. Army, 1963-65. Recipient Exec. Rank award Pres. of U.S., 1986, 88, 91, Firepower award Am. Def. Preparedness Assn., 1989, Exceptional Civilian Svc. award Sec. of Army, 1993. Mem. AIChE, Assn. of U.S. Army (bd. dirs. 1991—), Monte Sano Club (treas. 1981-83). Office: Missile Rsch Devel/Engring AMSMI-RD Redstone Arsenal AL 35898

RHOADS, STEPHEN DOUGLAS, architect; b. Phila., Oct. 13, 1957; s. Kenneth Douglas and Phyllis Aileen (Simmet) R.; m. Joan Deborah Lawrence, Oct. 5, 1985; children: Sarah Douglas, Alexander Lawrence. BS in Design, Clemson U., 1979, BArch, 1981. Registered architect. Designer Richardson Corp., Chester Hts., Pa., 1979-80; architect, designer Martin Orgn., Phila., Atlanta, 1982-85; assoc. design prin. Neal, Prince & Ptnrs., Greenville, S.C., 1985-86; project architect CRSS Architects, Greenville, 1986-90; design dir. Jacobs-Sirrine, Greenville, 1990—; prin. Stephen D. Rhoads, Greenville, Anderson, S.C., 1986—; adj. prof. Clemson (S.C.) U., 1994—. Constructor Habitat for Humanity, Clemson, 1994. Mem. AIA (sec.-treas. Greenville chpt. 1995, chair design com. 1993-94, v.p. 1996, dir. S.C. chpt. 1996, Excellence in Architecture award South Atlantic region 1992, Honor award S.C. chpt. 1992, Honor award Greenville sect. 1995, various design awards), Inst. Bus. Designers Carolinas, Air Force Regional Civil Engrs., Cons. Engrs. S.C. Home: 205 W Faris Rd Greenville SC 29605 Office: Jacobs-Sirrine Archtl Group 1041 E Butler Rd Greenville SC 29606-5456

RHODEN, MARY NORRIS, educational center director; b. Greenville, S.C., Jan. 3, 1943; d. Tony and Carrie Thelma (Reuben) Norris; 1 adopted child, Scottie Brooks-Rhoden. BS in Biology, Allen U., Columbia, S.C., 1966; postgrad., Atlanta U., 1967-68. Dir., tchr. MSR Learning Ctr., Riverdale, Ga., 1989—. Author poetry. Vol. Buffalo Soldiers Monument Commn., Ft. Leavenworth, Kans., 1991—; developed letters for nat. campaign to petition Congress, Postmaster Gen. to issue Buffalo Soldiers Stamp. Recipient Cert. Appreciation NAACP, Greenville, S.C., 1979, Wheat St. Bapt. Ch., Atlanta, 1989. Mem. Alpha Kappa Alpha, Alpha Kappa Delta. Democrat. African Meth. Episcopal Ch. Office: MSR Learning Ctr 7037 Shangrila Trl Riverdale GA 30296-2138

RHODEN, WILLIAM GARY, lawyer; b. Aiken, S.C., June 20, 1955; s. Thomas Gary and Catherine (Moseley) R.; m. Paula Jean Henderson, Aug. 8, 1981. BS in Psychology, U. S.C., Aiken, 1977; JD, U. S.C., 1980. Bar: S.C. 1981, U.S. Dist. Ct. S.C. 1982, U.S. Ct. Appeals (4th cir.) 1985. Lab. asst. psychology dept. U. S.C., Aiken, 1975-77; asst. dir. Greer (S.C.) YMCA, 1977-78; law clk. U.S. Atty. Office, Greer, 1977-78; intern U.S. Justice Dept., Columbia, S.C., 1980-81; staff atty. Office of Atty. Gen. State of S.C., Florence, 1981; asst. atty. gen. Office of Atty. Gen. State of S.C., Charleston, S.C., 1981-83; asst. solicitor 7th Jud. Cir., Spartanburg, S.C., 1984-86; pvt. practice Gaffney, S.C., 1986—. Bd. dirs. Cherokee Children's Home, S.C. Peach Festival. Mem. ABA, Cherokee County Bar Assn. (sec.-treas. 1988-96, pres. 1996—), Rotary (Paul Harris fellow), Phi Alpha Delta. Home: 119 College Dr Gaffney SC 29340-3002 Office: 221 E Floyd Baker Blvd PO Box 1937 Gaffney SC 29342

RHODENBAUGH, SUZANNE WADLEY, poet; b. Tampa, Fla., Dec. 9, 1944; d. William Morrill, III and Marguerite Evelyn (Douglas) W.; m. Richard Raymond Jaworski, Mar. 10, 1964 (div. Oct. 1967); 1 child, Suzanne Levy; m. Thomas Richard Rhodenbaugh, Dec. 18, 1976; stepchildren: Justine, Aaron. BA in Eng., U. So. Fla., 1966; MPH in Med. Care Adminstrn., U. Mich., 1974; MFA in Creative Writing, Vermont Coll., 1987. Bibliographer U. So. Fla. Libr., Tampa, 1966-67; field rep. U.S. Office Econ. Opportunity, Atlanta, 1967-69; asst. dir. consumer health Inst. Health and Soc., Washington, 1971-72; spl. asst. to dir. United Mine Workers of Am. Health and Retirement Fund, Johnstown, Pa., 1974-77; cmty. organizer Takoma Park, Md., 1977-84; adj. instr. So. Conn. Colls., Hamden, New Haven, others, 1986-89; tchr. expository writing tutorial-by-mail Johns Hopkins U., Balt., 1989-93; freelance writer, 1980—; vis. writer Quinnipiac Coll., Hamden, Conn., 1989. Author: A Gold Rain at Lonelyfarm, 1990, Gardening Where the Land Remembers War, 1992; contbr. poetry, essays to publs. Activist Westmoreland Area Cmty. Orgn., Takoma Park, 1978-84; organizer Eckert for City Coun. Campaign, Takoma Park, 1981; chmn. cmty. organizing Save Our Cmty. Schs., Takoma Park, 1981-83; chmn. Dalmat for City Coun. Campaign, Takoma Park, 1983. Farrar scholar Bread Loaf Writers' Conf., 1988; Vermont Artists' Studio poetry fellow, 1993. Democrat. Home: 3332 Kensington Ave Richmond VA 23221

RHODES, ANN L., theatrical producer, invester; b. Ft. Worth, Oct. 17, 1941; d. Jon Knox and Carol Jane (Greene) R.; student Tex. Christian U., 1960-63. V.p. Rhodes Enterprises Inc., Ft. Worth, 1963-77; owner-mgr. Lucky R Ranch, Ft. Worth, 1969—, Ann L. Rhodes Investments, Ft. Worth, 1976—; pres., chmn. bd. ALR Enterprises, Inc., Ft. Worth, 1977-93; pres. ALR Prodns., Inc., 1993—. Bd. dirs. Tarrant Coun. Alcoholism, 1973-78, hon. bd. dirs., 1978—; bd. dirs. N.W. Tex. coun. Arthritis Found., 1977-84; adv. bd. Stage West, 1987—, Hip Pocket Theatre, 1994—; bd. dirs. Circle Theater, 1987-94, Arts Coun. of Ft. Worth and Tarrant County, 1991-94; bd. govs. Ft. Worth Theatre, 1989—; mem. pro-arts bd. TCU Coll. Fine Arts & Communications, 1994; exec. com. Tarrant County Rep. Party, 1964-69; bd. dirs. Live Theatre League Tarrant County, 1993—, Casa Mañana Theatre, 1993—, exec. com., 1995—. Recipient various svc. awards, including Patron of Yr. award Live Theatre League Tarrant County, 1992-93. Mem. Jr. League Ft. Worth, Addison and Randolph Clark Soc. Tex. Christian U., Alpha Psi Omega, Kappa Kappa Gamma. Episcopalian. Office: Ste 908 Ridglea Bank Bldg Fort Worth TX 76116

RHODES, CHERYLE KEMBLE, elementary school educator; b. Youngstown, Ohio, Jan. 16, 1951; d. Charles Martin Kemble and Dorothy May (Stewart) Smiley; m. Michael Lester Rhodes, June 29, 1973; children: Gary Michael, Amy Christine, Angela Marie. BS in Elem. Edn. magna cum laude, Lamar U., 1987, postgrad., 1996—. Elem. tchr. Port Arthur (Tex.) Ind. Sch. Dist., 1987-94; math. tchr. Nederland (Tex.) Ind. Sch. Dist., 1994—; cons., tchr. Minority Math. and Sci. Edn. Coop., Austin and Port Arthur, Tex., 1989—; math. cons. Tex. Higher Edn. Coord. Bd., Austin, 1989—, Tex. Mid. Sch. Conf., Beaumont, 1994—. Author: Poetic Anthology; co-author Cultural Contextual Module, 1995; contbr. poetry and essay to religious jours. Recipient Scholorship, Am. Bus. Womens Assn., Beaumont, 1986. Mem. Tex. ASCD, Assn. Tex. Profl. Educators, Tex. Elem. Prins. Supervision Assn. Baptist. Home: 2022 10th St Port Neches TX 77651 Office: Ctrl Mid Sch 220 17th St Nederland TX 77627

RHODES, GENE PAUL, small business owner; b. Houma, La., Feb. 2, 1955; s. Kirby Francis and Jenny (Kraemer) R.; m. Sally Ann Romano, June 7, 1975; children: Chris Michael, Corey Francis, Cade Anthony. AS, Nicholls State U., 1975; cert. in banking, La. State U., 1984, degree in banking, 1987. Sr. computer operator Terrebonne Bank and Trust, Houma, La., 1975-78; mgr. computer ops. First Nat. Bank of Jefferson, Gretna, La., 1979-80, v.p., mgr. info. systems, 1980-86, v.p. info. systems and ops., 1986-87; v.p. info. systems, ops. and admintrn. South Savs. and Loan, Slidell, 1987-90; owner Svc. Master Quality Svcs., Houma, 1990—, Automation Cons. of La., Houma, 1991—; computer cons. Luke Constrn., Houma, La. 1977-78. Pres. Greenacres Subdiv. Civic Assn., Bourg, La., 1986-87. Mem. Am. Mgmt. Assn., Bank Adminstrn. Inst., Data Processing Mgmt. Assn. (bd. dirs. New Orleans chpt. 1983-89, pres. chpt. 1987-88). Republican. Roman Catholic. Club: Terrebonne Sportsmens League. Home: 4015 Kerr Dr Bourg LA 70343-3637 Office: PO Box 766 Houma LA 70361-0766

RHODES, JAMES DEVERS, psychotherapist; b. Midland, Tex., Apr. 28, 1955; s. James Ireland and Loys Ruth (McElrath) R.; m. Moira Sheelagh Josephine Fox Elmore, June 21, 1986. BS, Tex. Christian U., 1978; MEd, U. North Tex., 1991. Lic. profl. counselor, Tex.; lic. chem. dependency counselor, Tex.; nat. cert. addictions counselor II.; nat. cert. clin. hypnotherapist. Substance abuse technician Tarrant Coun. Mental Health-Mental Retardation, Ft. Worth, 1986; substance abuse counselor CPC Millwood Hosp., Arlington, Tex., 1986-89; family therapist Parkside Lodge-Westgate, Denton, Tex., 1989-90; co-dependence therapist, dir. Parkside Outpatient Svcs., Ft. Worth, 1990-91; psychotherapist Behavioral Health Unit La Hacienda Treatment Ctr., Hunt, Tex.; pvt. practice Kerrville, Tex., 1991—; peer evaluator Tex. Bd. Alcoholism and Drug Counselors, Austin, 1988—; allied staff La Hacienda, Charter Hosp., Hill Country Crisis Coun.; practicum supr. Hill Country Coun. on Alcoholism, Hill Country Ind. House, Sid Peterson Regional Hosp.; ct. cons. 216th Dist. Ct., Kerrville, Tex.; clin. supr. Youth Habitat Tex.; adj. psychology faculty San Antonio Coll. Author: Adult Recovery Handbook, 1988. Cmty. liaison Mid-South Redevel. Assn., Ft. Worth, 1979-83; mem. Fairmount Assn., Ft. Worth, 1979-84; bd. dirs. Mid-South Housing Coop. Study, Ft. Worth, 1983, Ctr. Point Alliance for Progress. Mem. ACA, Tex. Assn. Alcoholism and Drug Counselors, Nat. Assn. Alcoholism and Drug Abuse Counselors, Tex. Counseling Assn., Tex. Mental Health Counselors Assn. (treas.), Matt Talbot Retreat Movement (sec. 1989-91), Nat. Assn. Eagle Scouts, Order of Arrow, Rotary, Hill Country Men's Rehab. House (dir.). Episcopalian. Office: The Comfort Zone 180 Guadalupe Plz Kerrville TX 78028

RHODES, KAREN LESUEUR PACKARD, writer; b. Long Beach, Calif., Apr. 12, 1947; d. Arden and Martha Shideler (Reed) Packard; m. M. Keys Rhodes, Feb. 20, 1971; children: Martha, Elizabeth. BA, Fla. State U., 1969, MS cum laude, 1970. Librarian Jacksonville (Fla.) Pub. Libr., 1970-72; staff nurse various hospitals, Jacksonville, Fla., 1979-83; freelance writer Middleburg, Fla., 1990—. Author: Booking Hawaii Five-O: An Episode Guide and Critical History of the 1968-80 Detective Series, 1996; writer and cons. for articles: Classic TV, 1996. Lt. (j.g.) with USCGR, 1976-90. Mem. Libr. of Congress Assoc., Planetary Soc., Phi Beta Kappa.

RHODES, KRIS EVON, academic program director; b. Raymondville, Tex., Apr. 7, 1963; d. Robert Dale Rhodes and Clara Mae (Caldwell) Mazurek; m. Gregg S. Pilgreen, June 21, 1984 (div. Apr. 1987); m. John R. Busley Jr., Oct. 15, 1989. BA in Pub. Adminstrn., Stephen F. Austin State U., 1986, MS in Agr., 1994. Coord. off-campus housing Stephen F. Austin State U., Nacogdoches, Tex., 1984-85, 1991-92, coord. sponsored programs, dir. corp. and found. rels., 1993—; sales rep. East Tex. Garden Ctr., Nacogdoches, Tex., 1987-88; mgr. Cook's Nursery, Nacogdoches, Tex., 1988-91; coord. contracts and grants Tex. State Tech. Coll., Marshall, Tex., 1992-93; presenter workshops. Contbr. articles to profl. jours. Harry S. Cole scholar, 1991-92. Mem. Tex. Assn. Nurserymen, Tex. Com. Natural Resources, Nat. Coun. U. Rsch. Adminstrs. (Quinten S. Mathews award 1991), Rotary Internat. Democrat. Office: Stephen F Austin State U Box 13024 SFA Station Nacogdoches TX 75962

RHODES, LAWRENCE, insurance executive; b. Houston, June 23, 1946; s. Edward H. and Evelyn R. (Jinks) R.; m. Sheila R. Cain, May 30, 1991; children: Gregory, Michael, Ashley, Jennifer, Shelly. BS, U. Houston, 1970. Cert. ins. counselor. Computer run coord. Lockheed Electronics, Houston, 1967-70; asst. mgr. bond dept. Travelers Ins. Co., Houston, 1970-78; v.p. Kelley, Simmons Holland Ins., Houston, 1978-84; sec.-treas. Kelley-Rhodes Ins., Inc., Houston, 1984-94; pres. KRB & Assocs., Houston, 1994—; mem. adv. bd. Associated Gen. Contractors, Houston, 1992-95; instr. Ind. Ins. Agts., Houston, 1989—. Mem. Bd. Constrn. Fin. Mgmt. Assn. (bd. dirs. 1989-95). Republican. Office: KRB Assocs 3500 S Gessner # 202 Houston TX 77063

RHODES, ROBERTA ANN, dietitian; b. Red Bank, N.J., Apr. 11; d. Franklin Galloway and Frances (Kieswetter) DuBuy; m. Albert Lewis Rhodes, Feb. 10, 1978; 1 child, Juliet. BS, Fla. State U., 1977, MS, 1988. Lic. dietitian, Fla., Ga. Clin. dietitian Archbold Hosp., Thomasville, Ga., 1988-90; nutritionist Women, Infant and Children program, Tallahassee, 1990-91; sr. mgmt. clin. and adminstrv. dietitian Sunrise Community, Inc., Tallahassee, 1991-93; clin. svcs. specialist Heritage Health Care Ctr., Tallahassee, 1993-94; clin. dietitian Arbors, Tallahassee, 1994-95; clin. dietitian cons. Southwestern State Hosp., Thomasville, Ga.; clin. dietitian Fla. State Hosp., Chattahoochie, 1995-96, Southwestern State Hosp., Thomasville, Ga., 1996—. Mem. Am. Dietetic Assn., Fla. Dietetic Assn., Sigma Xi, Omicron Nu. Home: 4112 Alpine Way Tallahassee FL 32303-2244

RHODES, STEPHEN MICHAEL, poultry company executive; b. Harrisonburg, Va., Mar. 12, 1949; s. Trovilla Geil and Ogretta (Dove) R.; m. Judy Ann Higgs, June 19, 1971; children: Jeremy, Meridith. AA, Shenandoah Coll., 1969; BA in Biology, Madison Coll., 1971. Mgr. quality control Rocco Farm Foods, Inc., Edinburg, Va., 1971-95, wastewater/environ. mgr., 1996—. V.p., bd. dirs. Plains Youth Baseball League, Va., 1989-91, coach 1984-90; coach pony league, 1991; 1st lt., pres. Broadway Emergency Squad, 1971-77; chmn. coun. on Ministries Sunset Dr. United Meth. Ch., Broadway, 1991, 94—, mem. PPR com., 1994—; coach Timberville Midget League Football, 1985-89; bd. dirs. Community Pk. Bd., Broadway, 1984-86; mem. Rockingham County Recreation Commn., 1990—; pres. Broadway H.S. Athletic Booster Club, 1994-96, v.p., 1996—. Mem. Va. Poultry Industry Lab. (chmn. bd. dirs. 1983, 87), Southeastern Poultry and Egg Fedn. (sci. adv. com. 1983-91). Home: 199 3rd St Broadway VA 22815-9511 Office: Rocco Farm Foods Inc 19992 Senedo Rd Edinburg VA 22824-3172

RHODES-RYAN, GINGER, neonatal nurse practitioner. BS in Nursing, Creighton U., 1978; MSN, Duke U., 1995; neonatal nurse practitioner, Denver Children's Hosp., 1980. RN, N.C., Kans., Colo.; cert. neonatal nurse practitioner. Staff nurse neonatal ICU Denver Children's Hosp., 1978-80; neonatal nurse practitioner Luth. Med. Ctr., Wheat Ridge, Colo., 1980-84; neonatal nurse practitioner St. Mary's Hosp. and Med. Ctr., Grand Junction, Colo., 1984-88; neonatal clin. educator Stormont-Vail Regional Med. Ctr., Topeka, 1988-90; neonatal nurse practitioner Womens Hosp. Greensboro, N.C., 1990-92; neonatal nurse practitioner, dir. Wesley Long Community Hosp., Greensboro, N.C., 1991—. Mem. Nat. Assn. Neonatal Nurses, Assn. of Women's Health, Obstetrics and Neonatal Nurses, Sigma Theta Tau. Home: 2709 Coxindale Dr Raleigh NC 27615-3870

RHYNEDANCE, HAROLD DEXTER, JR., lawyer, consultant; b. New Haven, Conn., Feb. 13, 1922; s. Harold Dexter and Gladys (Evans) R.; 1 son by previous marriage: Harold Dexter III; m. Ruth Cosline Hakanson. BA, Cornell U., 1943, JD, 1949; grad., U.S. Army Command and Gen. Staff Coll., 1961, U.S. Army War Coll., 1970. Bar: N.Y. 1949, D.C. 1956, U.S. Tax Ct. 1950, U.S. Ct. Mil. Appeals 1954, U.S. Supreme Ct. 1954, U.S. Ct. Appeals (D.C. cir.) 1956, (2d cir.) 1963, (3rd cir.) 1965, (4th cir.) 1973, (5th cir.) 1968, (7th cir.) 1973, (9th cir.) 1964, U.S. Temporary Emergency Ct. Appeals 1975, U.S. Dist. Ct. D.C. 1956, U.S. Dist. Ct. (so. and ea. dist.) N.Y. 1963. Pvt. practice Buffalo, Eggertsville, N.Y., 1949-50; examiner/gen. atty. ICC, Washington, 1950-51; atty.-advisor Subversive Activities Control Bd., Washington, 1951-52; trial atty., spl. asst. to atty. gen., asst. U.S. atty. U.S. Dept. Justice, Washington, 1953-62; sr. trial atty., asst. gen. counsel, gen. counsel FTC, Washington, 1962-73; counsel Howrey & Simon, Washington, 1973-76; mng. atty., asst. gen. counsel, corp. counsel Washington Gas Light Co., 1977-87; counsel Conner & Wetterhahn, 1987-90; cons. Fairview, N.C., 1990—; exec. sec. adv. coun. on rules of practice and procedures FTC; mem. Jud. Conf. (D.C. Cir.), 1967—; chmn. legal and regulatory subcom. Solar Energy Com., Am. Gas Assn., Washington, 1978-84; lectr. George Washington U. Law Ctr., 1974; faculty moderator Def. Strategy Seminar Nat. War Coll., 1973; participant spl. programs Indsl. Coll. of Armed Forces, 1962, 69, Armed Forces Staff Coll., 1964. Mem. Leadership Asheville (N.C.) Forum; v.p. bd. dirs. Peninsula Symphony Assn., Palos Verdes Peninsula, Calif., 1989-94; bd. dirs. Help-The-Homeless-Help-Themselves, Inc., Palos Verdes Peninsula, 1991-93. 1st lt. U.S. Army, 1943-46, PTO; col. AUS, 1982—. Mem. ABA, Fed. Bar Assn., D.C. Bar Assn., Bar Assn. of D.C., Washington Met. Area Corp. Counsel Assn. (bd. dirs. 1981-84), Cornell Lawyers Club D.C. (pres. 1959-61), The Selden Soc. (London), Biltmore Forest Country Club (Asheville, N.C.), Montreat (N.C.) Scottish Soc., Res. Officers Assn. (life), Mil. Order Carabao, U.S. Army War Coll. Alumni Assn. (life), Am. Legion, Downtown Club Asheville, Sigma Chi, Phi Delta Phi. Republican. Episcopalian. Home and Office: Eagles View 286 Sugar Hollow Rd Fairview NC 28730-9559

RIBBLE, RONALD GEORGE, psychologist, educator, writer; b. West Reading, Pa., May 7, 1937; s. Jeremiah George and Mildred Sarah (Folk) R.; m. Catalina Valenzuela (Torres), Sept. 30, 1961; children: Christina, Timothy, Kenneth. BSEE cum laude, U. Mo., 1968, MSEE, 1969, MA, 1985, PhD, 1986. Enlisted man USAF, 1956-60, advance through grades to lt. col., 1976; rsch. dir. Coping Resources, Inc., Columbia, Mo., 1986; pres., co-owner Towers and Rushing Ltd., San Antonio, 1986—; referral devel. Laughlin Pavilion Psychiat. Hosp., Kirksville, Mo., 1987; program dir. Psychiat. Insts. of Am., Iowa Falls, Iowa, 1987-88; lead psychotherapist Gasconade County Counseling Ctr., Hermann, Mo., 1988; lectr. U. Tex., San Antonio, 1989—, Trinity U., San Antonio, 1995-96; assessment clinician Afton Oaks Psychiat. Hosp., San Antonio, 1989-91; psychologist Olmos Psychol. Svcs., Inc., San Antonio, 1991-93; vol. assessor Holmgreen Children's Shelter, San Antonio, 1992-93; condr. seminars, revs. for maj. pubs. Author: Apples, Weeds, and Doggie Poo, 1995; contbr. essays to psychol. reference books and poetry to anthologies periodicals, lyrics to popular music; columnist, features editor Feelings, 1993—; public access TV appearances, 1991—. Del. Boone County (Mo.) Dem. Conv., 1984; vol. announcer pub. radio sta., Columbia, 1993; contbg. mem. Dem. Nat. Com., 1983—, Presdl. Congl. Task Force, 1994; vol. counselor Cath. Family and Children's Svc., San Antonio, 1989-91; chpt. advisor Rational Recovery Program for Alcoholics, San Antonio, 1991-92; mem. Pres. Leadership Cir., 1994-95. Recipient Roberts Meml. Prize in Poetry, 1995. Mem. APA, AAUP, NEA, ACLU, Am. Coll. Forensic Examiners, Internat. Soc. for Study of Individual Differences, Internat. Platform Assn. (Poetry award 1995), Bexar County Psychol. Assn., Air Force Assn., Ret. Officers Assn, People for the Am. Way, Poetry Soc. Am., Acad. Am. Poets. Roman Catholic. Home: 14023 N Hills Village Dr San Antonio TX 78249-2531 Office: U Tex Divsn Cultural and Sci San Antonio TX 78249 also: Towers and Rushing Ltd San Antonio TX 78249

RIBEIRO, KAREN LAVETTE, bank administrator; b. Munich, Germany, Jan. 6, 1957; came to U.S., 1966; d. Eldridge Lee and Mary Ann (Feaster) Reese; m. Daniel Rosa, Sr., June 11, 1976 (div. Sept. 1984); children: Daniel Rosa, Jr., Tameka Lea Rosa, India Lacole Rosa. Grad., New Bedford (Mass.) H.S., 1976. Office mgr. YMCA, Winston-Salem, N.C., 1986-92; adminstrv. asst. Wachovia Bank of N.C., Winston-Salem, 1992—. Author: I Will Do A New Thing In You!, 1996. Pres. hospitality com. St. Matthew Ch., 1995-96, missionary com., 1992-95. Apostolic. Home: 4260 Brownsboro Rd E-25 Winston Salem NC 27106

RICAPITO, JOSEPH VIRGIL (GIUSEPPE), Spanish and comparative literature educator; b. Giovinazzo, Bari, Italy, Oct. 30, 1933; came to U.S., 1935; s. Frank and Filomena (Cervone) R.; m. Carolyn Sue Kitchen, Apr. 7, 1958; children: Frank Peyton, Maria Avadna. BA, CUNY, Bklyn., 1955; MA, U. Iowa, 1956; PhD in Romance Langs., U. Calif., L.A., 1966. From instr. to asst. prof. Pomona Coll., Claremont, Calif., 1962-70; from assoc. prof. to prof. Ind. U., Bloomington, Ind., 1970-80; prof. La. State U., Baton Rouge, 1980—, chmn. dept., 1980-85. Author: Bibliografia Razonada y anotada, 1980; editor: La Vida de Laz de Tormes, 1976; translator: Dialogue of Mercury and Charon, 1986, Cervantes's Noveles ejemplares: Between History and Creativity, 1996. Pres. Greater Baton Rouge Am.-Italian Assn., 1984-85. With U.S. Army, 1957-59. Grantee NEH, 1981; named Knight Order of Merit, Republic of Italy, 1988, Knight Order of Queen Isabel, Govt. of Spain, 1990. Mem. MLA, Renaissance Soc. Am., Am. Comparative Lit. Assn., Am. Assn. Tchrs. Spanish and Portuguese, Cervantes Soc. Am. Office: La State U 209 Prescott Hall Baton Rouge LA 70803

RICCITELLI, KEVIN MARK, family practice physician; b. N.Y.C., May 10, 1949; s. James Michael and Frances Ruth (Windish) R.; m. Terri Lee Lashley, Aug. 31, 1973; children: Kris Michael, Heather Dawn, Lindsay Elizabeth. BA, Taylor U., Upland, Ind., 1971; MS, Toledo U., 1976; DO, Ohio U., 1981. Lic. physician Mich., Fla., Okla.; diplomate Nat. Bd. Med. Examiners. Rschr. in biochemistry Med. Coll. of Ohio, Toledo, 1976-77; intern Doctor's Hosp., Massillon, Ohio, 1981-82; physician walk-in ctr. Family Med. Ctrs., Ft. Myers Beach, Fla., 1985-87; pvt. practice Ft. Myers, Fla., 1985-91; resident in radiation oncology Detroit Osteo. Hosp., Highland Park, Mich., 1991-92; site physician Goodyear Corp. Health Dimensions, Lawton, Okla., 1992—. Deacon Western Hills Christian Ch., 1993-94. With U.S. Army, 1971-73; lt. comdr. USPHS, 1982-85. Recipient Commd. Officer award USPHS, Lawton Indian Hosp., 1985, Sandoz Pharm. award, 1979, Purdue-Fredrick Rsch. award Ohio U. Coll. Medicine, 1981. Mem. Am. Osteo. Assn., Okla. Osteo. Assn., Am. Mil. Osteo. Physicians and Surgeons, Am. Coll. Osteo. Family Physicians, Am. Osteo. Coll. Radiology, LaSill Optimist Club. Republican. Home: 4622 NW Meadowbrook Dr Lawton OK 73505-4712 Office: Goodyear Med Ctr One Goodyear Blvd Lawton OK 73505

RICE, ALBERT BROCKHOUSE, college program director; b. Chattanooga, Sept. 9, 1948; s. John L. and Luevinea (Pickett) R.; m. Linda Carol Banks; children: John Raquel Rice, Eric Rice, Albert Brockhouse Rice Jr., Jason O. Banks Rice. AA, Southwestern Christian Coll., Terrell, Tex., 1969; BS, East Tex. State U., 1972; MEd, Ctrl. State U., Edmond, Okla., 1981. Asst. dir. food svc. Langston (Okla.) U., 1982; exec. chef Jeremiah's Restaurant, Shawnee, Okla., 1982-83; adult edn. tchr. Shawnee Pub. Schs., 1983-87; min. Okmulgee (Okla.) Ch. of Christ, 1983-88; adult edn. tchr. Okumlgee Pub. Schs., 1987-88; dir. food svcs. Southwestern Christian Coll., 1991-94, dir. counseling, 1988-94, dir. Upward Bound, 1988—; sch. counselor Boley (Okla.) Pub. Schs., 1979-81; staff asst. Dept. Human Svcs., Boley State Sch. for Boys, 1978-79, program supr., 1976-78, social worker, 1973-76. Recipient Outstanding Black Male award Delta Sigma Theta, 1994. Mem. Tex. Jr. Coll. Tchrs. Assn., Terrell C. of C. (pres.'s club 1989—), Kiwanis (pres. Boley club 1978-79), Kappa Delta Pi, Alpha Phi Alpha. Home: 2300 N Bryan Shawnee OK 74801 Office: Southwestern Christian College 200 Bowser Cir Terrell TX 75160-0001

RICE, ALISON MARIA, editor; b. Mpls., July 5, 1971; d. John Dale and Muriel Irene (Pederson) R. BA in History and English, Coll. of William & Mary, 1993. Editl. intern MSP Comms., Mpls., 1993, Minn. Jour. of Law and Politics, Mpls., 1994; editl. asst. Trout Unltd., Arlington, Va., 1994-95, asst. editor, 1995-96; reporter Fauquier Citizen, Warrenton, Va., 1996—.

RICE, ANTHONY HOPKINS, dean, artist; b. The Philippines, July 21, 1948; s. Lewis Carl and Elizabeth (Hopkins) R.; m. DeeDee Whitlock, June 14, 1986. BFA, Va. Commonwealth U., 1970; MFA, U. N.C., 1972. Catherine Conner prof. painting Wesleyan Coll., Macon, Ga., 1972-85, chmn. dept. visual art, 1981-85; acting dir. Selby Gallery Ringling Sch. Art and Design, Sarasota, Fla., 1985-86, chmn. dept. fine arts, 1985-88, coord. art history program, 1993—, acting dean liberal arts, 1995—; weekly columnist on fine arts Tampa (Fla.) Tribune, 1988-89. Illustrator: (books) Seven Persian Fables, 1983, El Haikai de Flavio Herrera, 1985, A Letter of Columbus, 1990. Cpl. USMCR, 1970-76. Mem. Rotary. Office: Ringling Sch Art and Design 2700 N Tamiami Trl Sarasota FL 34234-5812

RICE, CHARLES EDWARD, bank executive; b. Chattanooga, Tenn., Aug. 4, 1936; s. Charles Edward and Louise (Goodson) R.; m. Dianne Tauscher; children: Danny, Celeste, Michelle. B.B.A., U. Miami, 1958; M.B.A., Rollins Coll., Winter Park, Fla., 1964; grad., Advanced Mgmt. Program, Harvard U., 1975. Vice pres., then pres. Barnett Bank, Winter Park, 1965-71; exec. v.p. Barnett Banks Fla., Inc., Jacksonville, 1971-73, pres., from 1973, chief exec. officer, 1979—, now also chmn., bd. dirs.; bd. dirs. Sprint Corp., CSX Corp. Trustee Univ. of Miami, Rollins Coll. Office: Barnett Banks Inc 50 N Laura St Jacksonville FL 32202-3664*

RICE, DAVID A., metals company executive; b. 1940. PhD in Metallurg. Engrng., Colo. Sch. Mines. With St. Joe Mineral, 1962-69, 80-82, Gulf Resources Chem. Corp., N.Y.C., 1982-84; pres. Savage Zinc Inc., Clarksville, Tenn., 1984—. Office: Savage Zinc Inc 1800 Zinc Plant Rd Clarksville TN 37040

RICE, GEORGE LAWRENCE, III (LARRY RICE), lawyer; b. Jackson, Tenn., Sept. 24, 1951; s. George Lawrence Jr. and Judith W. (Pierce) R.; m. Joy Gaia, Sept. 14, 1974; children: George Lawrence IV, Amy Colleen. Student, Oxford U., 1972-73; BA with honors, Rhodes Coll., 1974; JD, Memphis State U., 1976; Nat. Coll. Advocacy, ATLA, 1978. Bar: Tenn. 1977, U.S. Supreme Ct. 1980. Assoc. Rice, Rice, Smith, Bursi, Veazey, 1976-81, ptnr., 1981—, acting sr. ptnr., 1995. Author: Divorce Practice in Tennessee, 1987, Divorce Lawyer's Handbook, 1989, (video) Divorce: What You Need to Know When it Happens to You, 1990, The Complete Guide to Divorce Practice, 1993, 2d edit., 1997, Visual Persuasion, AIDS and Clients, Prenuptial Agreements, 1996, The Effective Lawyer: Divorce and Personal Injury, 1996; mem. bd. editors Matrimonial Strategist, 1994-96, Hunt, Hide Shoot--a Guide to Paintball, 1996; mem. editl. bd. Active Supreme Ct. Child Support Guidelines Commn., 1989, Family Law Revision Commn., 1990-91. Mem. Timberwolves Paintball Team. Named One of Best Lawyers in Am., 1993, 94. Mem. ABA (conv. lectr. 1993, 94), ATLA, Tenn. Bar Assn. (chmn. family law sect. 1987-88), Memphis Bar Assn. (founding chmn. family law sect.), Tenn. Trial Lawyers Assn. Office: Rice Rice Smith Bursi Veazey & Amundsen 44 N 2nd St Fl 10 Memphis TN 38103-2220

RICE, J. ANDREW, management consultant, tree farmer; b. Cleveland, Tex., July 24, 1953; s. Jakie Andrew and Neva (Richardson) R.; m. Susan Elaine Black, July 29, 1977; children: Faith Ann, Joy Elizabeth, Jakie Weldon, Luke Andrew. BA in Psychology cum laude, Baylor U., 1975; MA in Pub. Mgmt., U. Houston, 1979. Tchr. Tarkington Ind. Sch. Dist., Cleveland, Tex., 1975-76, La Marque (Tex.) Ind. Sch. Dist., 1976-77; jobs coord. Galveston (Tex.) County, 1977-78; adminstrv. asst. City of La Marque, 1978-80; cons. Community Mgmt. Svcs., Houston, 1980-82; owner, cons. Pub. Mgmt., Cleveland, 1982-92; pres. Pub. Mgmt., Inc., Cleve., 1992—. High sch. Sunday sch. tchr. Rural Shade Bapt. Ch.; pres. Tarkington Cmty. Devel. Assn.; mem. Liberty County Hist. Soc.; founding mem. Rice Settlement Cmty. Assn. Mem. World Future Soc., Tex. Farm Bur., Omicron Delta Kappa. Office: Pub Mgmt PO Box 1827 Cleveland TX 77328-1827

RICE, KATHY STRICKLAND, assistant city manager; b. Concord, Ga., Aug. 12, 1947; d. Roger Head and Patricia (Paynter) Strickland; m. C. Matthew Rice, Apr. 12, 1970; children: C. Michael, Adam P., Timothy Burt. BSA, U. Ga., 1970, MPA, 1983. Edn. coord. Action, Inc., Athens, Ga., 1974-78; program dir. Action, Inc., Athens, 1978-80; pers. dir. Clarke County, Athens, 1980-82; planner, researcher E. Cen. Fla., Orlando, Fla., 1982-83; city mgr. Lake Mary, Fla., 1983-86, Gulfport, Fla., 1986-89; dep. asst. city mgr. Clearwater, Fla., 1989-91, deputy city mgr., 1991—; adj. instr. U. South Fla. Grad. Sch. Pub. Adminstrn., 1990—; bd. dirs., sec. to bd. Neighberly Sr. Svcs., 1994—. Pres. Citizens Against Spouse Abuse, St. Petersburg, Fla., 1989; bd. dirs. St. Petersburg Unitarian Universalist Ch., 1986-90; mem. adv. bd. Exec. Fellows Program, Tampa, 1989; mem. Govs.'s Adv. Com. on Unemployment, 1989—; bd. dirs. Palm Shores Retirement Ctrs., 1992-95; mem. adv. task force U. Fla. Pub. Adminstrn. Dept., 1991—; mem. Leadership Pinellas, 1993; treas. Clearwater/St. Petersburg Film Commn., 1993—; bd. dirs. Jazz Holiday Found., 1988-96; mem. mgmt. com. Nat. Estuary Program. Mem. Fla. City and County Mgrs. Assn., Internat. City Mgrs. Assn., Internat. Pers. Mgmt. Assn., Fla. Pub. Pers. Assn., Am. Soc. for Pub. Adminstrn. (pres. Gulf Coast chpt. 1992-93), Fla. Pub. Employee and Labor Rels. Assn., Inst. Govt. Steering Com. Democrat. Home: 720 61st St S Saint Petersburg FL 33707-2429 Office: City of Clearwater 112 S Osceola Ave Clearwater FL 34616-5103

RICE, MARY ESTHER, biologist; b. Washington, Aug. 3, 1926; d. Daniel Gibbons and Florence Catharine (Pyles) R. AB, Drew U., 1947; MA, Oberlin Coll., 1949; PhD, U. Wash., 1966. Instr. biology Drew U., Madison, N.J., 1949-50; rsch. assoc. Columbia U., N.Y.C., 1950-53; rsch. asst. NIH, Bethesda, Md., 1953-61; curator invertebrate zoology and dir. Smithsonian Marine Sta., Smithsonian Instn., Washington, 1966—; mem. adv. panel on systematic biology NSF, Washington, 1977-78; mem. com. on marine invertebrates Nat. Acad. Sci., 1976-81; mem. overseers com. on biology Harvard U., Cambridge, Mass., 1982-88. Assoc. editor Jour. Morphology, Ann Arbor, Mich., 1985-91, Invertebrate Biology, 1995—; editor: (with M. Todorovic) Biology of Sipuncula and Echiura, 1975, 2nd vol., 1976, (with F.S. Chia) Settlement and Metamorphosis of Marine Invertebrate Larvae, 1978, (with F.W. Harrison) Microscopic Anatomy of Invertebrates, Vol. 12, 1993; contbr. articles to profl. jours. Recipient Drew U. Alumni Achievement award in sci., 1980. Fellow AAAS; mem. Am. Soc. Zoologists (pres. 1979), Phi Beta Kappa. Office: Smithsonian Marine Sta 5612 Old Dixie Hwy Fort Pierce FL 34946-7303

RICE, NANCY MARIE, nursing consultant; b. Murphy, N.C., Aug. 3, 1940; d. Berlon and Elizabeth Beryl (Ammons) Lovingood; m. Lewis T. Rice, Jan. 23, 1976; 1 child, Elizabeth Beryl Rembrons Flowers. Diploma, Grady Meml. Hosp., Atlanta, 1961; BA, U. West Fla., Pensacola, 1973; MS, Fla. State U., Tallahassee, 1979. Cert. cmty. health nurse, nursing administr.; diplomate Am. Bd. Quality Assurance and Utilization Review Physicians. Staff nurse Riegel Community Hosp., Trion, Ga., 1961; pub. health nurse Escambia County Health Unit, Pensacola, 1962-63, Santa Rosa County Health Unit, Milton, Fla., 1963-73; pub. health nursing supr. I Leon County Health Unit, Tallahassee, Fla., 1973-77; pub. health nurse Broward County Health Unit, Ft. Lauderdale, Fla., 1977-78; nursing cons. social and econ. svcs. Tallahassee, 1978-79; HMO program specialist social and econ. scvs. program office DHRS Dist. X, Ft. Lauderdale, 1979; pub. health nurse, supr. II Sarasota (Fla.) County Health Unit, 1979-81; health program specialist health program office DHRS Dist X, Ft. Lauderdale, Fla., 1981-83; nursing cons. Dept. Labor, Div. Workers' Compensation, Tallahassee, 1983—. Recipient Cert. of Svc. State of Fla., 10 yr., 20 yr., 25 yrs., 30 yrs., Cert. of Appreciation, 1976, Leon County-Tallahassee Community Action Program. Mem. Am. Nurses Assn., Fla. Nurses Assn., Eta Sigma Gamma. Home: PO Box 13731 Tallahassee FL 32317-3731

RICE, PATRICIA OPPENHEIM LEVIN, special education educator, consultant; b. Detroit, Apr. 5, 1932; d. Royal A. and Elsa (Freeman) Oppenheim; m. Charles L. Levin, Feb. 21, 1956 (div. Dec. 1981); children: Arthur David, Amy Ragen, Fredrick Stuart; m. Howard T. Rice, Dec. 16, 1990 (div. Apr. 1994). AB in History, U. Mich., 1954, PhD, 1981; MEd, Marygrove Coll., 1973. Tchr. reading and learning disabled, cons., Detroit, 1967-76, Marygrove Coll.; coord. spl. edn., Marygrove Coll., 1976-86; adj. prof. Oakland U., 1987-90, U. Miami, 1989-95; edn., curriculum cons. Lady Elizabeth Sch., Jávea (Alicante) Spain, 1988-91; dir. Oppenheim Tchr. Tng. Inst., Detroit; v.p. Mashpelah Cemetary Bd., Ferndale, Mich., 1978—; mem. adv. bd. Eton Acad., Birmingham, Mich., 1991-93; internat. conf. presenter; workshop presenter Dade City Schs., 1992—. Mem. Mich. regional bd. ORT, 1965-68, 86—; mem. youth svcs. adv. com. S.E. Mich. chpt. ARC Bd., 1973-79; mem. Met. Mus., N.Y.C., Seattle Art Mus., Detroit Art Mus., Smithsonian Instn.; v.p. women's aux. Children's Hosp. Mich.; bd. dirs. women's com. United Cmty. Svcs., 1968-73; judge Dade County Schs. for Tchr. Grants, 1996; women's com. Detroit Grand Opera Assn., 1970-75; mem. coms. Detroit Symphony Orch., Detroit Inst. Arts; torch drive area chmn. United Found., 1967-70; bd. dirs. Greater Miami Opera Guild, 1992, Miami City Ballet Dade Guild, 1996—, Opera Ball com., 1992, Lincoln Rd. Walk, chair, 1996, Diabetes Rsch. Inst. & Found. Love & Hope Com., Fla. Concert Assn. Cresendo Soc., 1993—, Villa Maria Angel, 1996—. Mem. NAACP, Navy League (mem. Miami Coun.), Internat. Reading Assn., Nat. Coun. Tchrs. of English, Assn. Supervision and Curriculum Devel., Nat. Assn. Edn. of Young Children, Mich. Assn. Children with Learning Disabilities (edn. v.p., exec. bd. 1976-80), Coun. Exceptional Children, Williams Island Club, Westview Country Club (mem. house com.), Turnberry Isle Clubs (signiture), Phi Delta Kappa, Pi Lambda Theta.

RICE, RICHARD LEE, retired architect; b. Raleigh, N.C., May 4, 1919; s. Robert Edward Lee and Grace Lucille (Betts) R.; m. Cora Belle Stegall, Apr. 12, 1946; children—Richard Lee, Westwood Carter, David Sinclair. BS in Archtl. Engrng., N.C. State U., 1941; grad., U.S. Army Command and Gen. Staff Coll., 1961. Assoc. Cooper-Shumaker, Architects, Raleigh, 1946-47; prin. Richard L. Rice, Architects, Raleigh, 1947-48; assoc. Cooper, Haskins & Rice and predecessor firm, Raleigh, 1948-52, ptnr., 1953-54; ptnr. Haskins & Rice, Architects, Raleigh, 1954-85; prin. Haskins, Rice, Savage & Pearce, Architects, 1985-91, pres., 1985-91; v.p. N.C. Design Found., 1973; pres. N.C. Archtl. Found., 1975; mem. Raleigh Arts Commn., 1978-82, Raleigh Hist. Properties Commn., 1990-92, Raleigh Hist. Dists. Commn., 1991-92. Archtl. works include renovations, Raleigh Meml. Auditorium, 1964, 78, 91 (SE Regional AIA award of merit 1964), Auditorium, 4 high schs. and 13 elem. schs., Raleigh Civic Ctr., stack addition Wilson Libr. U. N.C., Chapel Hill, 1977, Reidsville, N.C. Jr. High Sch.; assoc. architect Raleigh Radisson Hotel, 1980, One Hanover Sq. Office Bldg., 1985, Two Hannover Sq. Office Bldg., 1990, additions and renovations to Raleigh Meml. Auditorium, 1989, 3 indsl. plants, 7 bldgs., Wake Tech. C.C., 50 chs. Pres. Wake County (N.C.) Hist. Soc., 1973-74; mem. N.C. Gov.'s Com. for Facilities for Physically Handicapped, 1970-73; arbitrator Am. Arbitration Assn. With inf. and C.E. U.S. Army, 1941-46, ETO; col. USAR; ret. Decorated Silver Star; Legion of Merit; Bronze Star; Purple Heart. Fellow AIA (pres. N.C. chpt. 1970, Disting. Svc. award N.C. chpt. 1975); mem. Raleigh Council Architects (pres. 1950), Nat. Trust for Hist. Preservation, N.C. State Art Soc., Res. Officers Assn. U.S., Ret. Officers Assn. U.S. (pres. Triangle chpt. 1983), N.C. State U. Gen. Alumni Assn. (pres., chmn. bd. 1960-61, pres. Class 1941, 1986-91), Carolina Country Club, Lions, Torch Club (pres. 1982-83), Phi Eta Sigma, Phi Kappa Phi. Democrat. Baptist.

RICH, ALBERT CLARK, solar energy manufacturing executive; b. Wolfeboro, N.H., Feb. 8, 1950; s. Nelson Barnard and Alberta Louise (Pigon) R.; m. Patricia Ann Murphy, July 16, 1973 (div. Aug. 1975); m. Susan Maura McGee, Jan. 26, 1985; children: Ashley, Katherine, Clark. BA in Polit. Sci. and Research Processes, Principia Coll., 1979; cert., Solar Energy Research Inst., Golden, Colo., 1981. Owner Antique Classic Auto Restoration, Ft. Lauderdale, Fla., 1975-77, AC-Rich & Sun, Herndon, Va., 1979—; founder., pres. Am. Solar Network Ltd., 1989—; pres. Suncorps Inc., Watertown, Mass., 1980-82, Cambridge Alt. Power Co., 1982-83; dist. mgr. Sears/Am. Solar King, Herndon, 1983-85; bd dirs. Monegon Solar, Washington br., 1984; cons. NEEIC, Boston, 1982; chmn. Sec. Energy, Boston, 1983; speaker New Eng. Solar Energy Assn. MIT, Cambridge and Boston, 1983; chmn. solar thermal div. New Eng. Solar Energy Assn., Bay chpt., Boston, 1982-83; contractor White House Pagent of Peace Exhibit. Developer heat cell, heliophase, solar storage tank; inventor, patentee Solar "Skylite" water heater. Organizer Earth Day, Boston, 1982-83, Sec. of Energy, Boston, 1983. Mem. Sacramento Solar Energy Industries Assn. (DOE energy innovation award 1992, DOE energy related inventions program grantee 1994). Home and Office: Am Solar Network Ltd 5840 Gibbons Dr Carmichael CA 95608-6903

RICH, IRENE M., women's health nurse, administrator; b. L.A., Oct. 20, 1950; d. Albert Franklin and Mrs. (Holdeman) Meyers; m. Tommy Lee Rich, Aug. 4, 1973; 1 child, Stacy Leigh. BSN, U. N.C., Greensboro, 1972; MSN, Vanderbilt U., 1984; postgrad., Cath. U. Am. Commd. 2d lt. U.S. Army, 1971, advanced through grades to col.; clin. head nurse labor and delivery U.S. Army Hosp., Ft. Campbell, Ky., 1980-82; chief ambulatory nursing 98th Gen. Hosp., 1984-85, chief maternal and child health nursing, 1986-87, clin. head nurse labor and delivery, 1987-88; head nurse gynecologic oncology Walter Reed Army Med. Ctr., Washington, 1991-92, asst. chief nursing rsch. svc., 1992-94; dir. breast bancer, def. women's health rsch. programs U.S. Army Med. Rsch. and Materiel Command, Ft. Detrick, Md., 1994—, rsch. progrms Osteoporosis, Nuerofibromatosis, %; mem. steering com. Pres.' Nat. Action Plan on Breast Cancer, 1994—, Osteoporosis and Nuerofibromatosis Rsch. Programs. Recipient Nat. Rsch. Svc. award, 1990. Mem. AWHONN (chair), NAACOG (chmn. army sect. 1992—), ANA, Soc. Gynecologic Nurse Oncologists, Sigma Theta Tau. Home: 7936 Carrleigh Pky Springfield VA 22152-1216

RICH, JOHN STANLEY, English language educator; b. Birmingham, Ala., Mar. 5, 1943; s. Stanley Arno and Louise (Truitt) R. BA, U. Ala., 1966; MS, U. Pa., 1968; PhD, U. Ala., 1979. Cert. secondary sch. English. tchr. Instr. English Stillman Coll., Tuscaloosa, Ala., 1968-73; prof. English U. S.C., Aiken, 1979—. Contbr. articles to profl. jours. V.p. Aiken County Hist. Soc., 1983-84. Fulbright scholar, Poland, 1993-94. Mem. Am. Dialect Soc., Am. Name Soc., Nat. Coun. Tchrs. English, South Atlantic Modern Lang. Assn., Southeastern Conf. on Linguistics, Phi Beta Kappa, Phi Delta Kappa. Democrat. Episcopalian. Home: PO Box 2582 Aiken SC 29802-2582 Office: U SC 171 University Pky Aiken SC 29801-6309

RICH, LEE WAYNE, vocational education educator; b. Oceanside, N.Y., July 29, 1951; s. Lee L. Rich and Marjorie (Boyd) Russ; m. Constance Lee Krohne, June 15, 1974; children: Noah, Daniel. BS cum laude, Berry Coll., 1973; MEd, U. Ga., 1979, EdS, 1982. Cert. vocat. educator, Ga., edn. and diversified coop. tng., Ga. Tchr. indsl. arts, soccer coach Jonesboro (Ga.) H.S., 1973-78, coord. diversified coop. tng., 1978-90; vocat. supr. Lovejoy (Ga.) H.S., 1990—; advisor on sys. evaluations of tech prep programs State Dept. Edn., Atlanta, 1996—; chmn. evaluation com. Clayton County Schs., Griffin Tech., Clayton State Coll., Ga., 1991—; adminstr. Atlanta Metro-Tech. Prep. Grant, 1996—. Mem. NEA, Am. Vocat. Assn. (Cert. Excellence 1987), Ga. Vocat. Assn. (Tchr. of Yr. 1987), Ga. Assn. Secondary Prins., Ga. Assn. Ednl. Leaders, Epsilon Pi Tau, Phi Delta Kappa. Home: 7611 Saybrook Trl Jonesboro GA 30236 Office: Lovejoy HS 1587 McDonough Rd Lovejoy GA 30250

RICHARD, RALPH ZACHARY, singer, songwriter, poet; b. Lafayette, La.; s. Eddie Joseph and Marie Pauline (Boudreaux) R. BA, Tulane U., New Orleans, 1972. Singer/songwriter: Bayou des Mysteres, 1976, Mardi Gras, 1977, Migration, 1978, Allons Danser, 1979, Live in Montreal, 1980. Vent D'Ete, 1981, Zack Attach, 1984, Looking Back, 1986, Zack's Bon Ton, 1988, Mardi Gras Mambo, 1989, Women in the Room, 1990, Snake Bite Love, 1992, Cap Enragé, 1996; innovator Cajun and Zydeco musical styles; author: (poetry) Voyage de Nuit, 1988. Cert. Gold Album for Migration, L'industrie Canadienne de l'enregistrement, 1978, Cert. Gold 45 L'Arbre est dans ses feuilles, 1978, Prix de la jeune Chanson Francaise, Ministre de la Culture de France, 1980, Prix Miroir Festival D'été de Québec, 1996; decorated Officier de l'Ordre Des Arts et Lettres de la République Francaise, 1996. Home: PO Box 305 Scott LA 70583-0305

RICHARDS, ASHTON WHITE, dean; b. Boston, Aug. 24, 1960; s. F. Lee and Harriett Stapler (White) R. BA, Syracuse U., 1982; postgrad., Wesleyan U., 1986-89. Dir. alumni affairs, asst. dean of students St. Andrew's Sch., Middletown, Del., 1983-92; asst. dean of students Episc. H.S., Alexandria, Va., 1992-93, dean of students, 1993—. Home: 1200 N Quaker Ln Alexandria VA 22302-3004 Office: Episcopal High Sch 1200 N Quaker Ln Alexandria VA 22302-3004

RICHARDS, BRUCE ALFRED, neurologist; b. North Creek, N.Y., Dec. 12, 1951; s. Alfred Eugene R. and Frances Margaret Peterson-Morey; 1 child, Rachel Margaret. AAS, Adirondack Community Coll., 1972; BA, U. Miss., Oxford, 1978; MD, U. Miss., Jackson, 1982. Intern U. Miss., Jackson, 1982-83; resident in neurology U. Fla., Gainesville, 1986; pvt. practice Gainesville, 1986—; chief neurology Alachua Gen. Hosp., Gainesville, 1986—, chmn. dept. medicine, 1995—. With U.S. Army, 1972-75. Decorated Commendation medal. Mem. AMA, Fla. Med. Assn., Alachua County Med. Soc., Am. Acad. Neurology. Office: 1100 NW 8th Ave Ste A Gainesville FL 32601-4986

RICHARDS, FREDERICK, hematologist/oncologist; b. Aug. 28, 1938; m. Anne Irvine Walters, June 2, 1962; children: Frederick Jr., Laura Anne, Charles Patrick. BS, Davidson Coll., 1960; MD, Med. Coll. S.C., 1964. Diplomate Am. Bd. Internal Medicine, Am. Bd. Hematology, Am. Bd. Med. Oncology. From instr. medicine to assoc. prof. Bowman Gray Sch. Medicine, Winston-Salem, N.C., 1971—. Capt. USAF, 1966-68. Office: Bowman Gray Sch Medicine Medical Ctr Blvd Winston Salem NC 27157

RICHARDS, FREDERICK FRANCIS, JR., manufacturing company executive; b. Payette, Idaho, Jan. 28, 1936; s. Frederick Francis and Dorothy Lucille (Taylor) R.; BS in Indsl. Engrng., So. Meth. U., 1959; MBA, Harvard U., 1961; m. DeAnne Aden, Aug. 10, 1958; children: Frederick Francis III, Craig, Jeffrey. Indsl. engr. Collins Radio Inc., 1955-59; research asst. Harvard U., 1961-62; fin. analyst H.F. Linder & William T. Golden, N.Y.C., 1962-65; pres. Adrich Corp. and subs., Dallas, 1965—; exec. v.p. FSE Corp., Plano, Tex., 1991-92; pres. Resource Locators Inc., Dallas, 1992—; v.p. and prin. Capital Alliance Corp., Dallas, 1985-91; v.p. GTex., Inc., Dallas, 1986-87; pres. Work Lite Dist., Dallas, 1990—, AR Assocs., internat. mgmt. cons., Dallas, 1972—; dir. Dallas Pub. Inc., 1982-84, Aden-Richards Inc., 1979—. Mem. Am. Inst. Indsl. Engrs. (sr.), ASTM, Airplane Owners and Pilot Assn., Am. Soc. Indsl. Security, Internat. Assn. Chiefs Police, Nat. Pilots Assn., Exptl. Aircraft Assn., Tech. Club of Dallas, Harvard Club (N.Y.C.), The Tech. Club of Dallas. Author papers in field; bus. columnist. Home: 3 Cumberland Pl Richardson TX 75080-4926 Office: 1002 N Central Expy Ste 299 Richardson TX 75080-4658

RICHARDS, JERRY CECIL, store owner, writer; b. Dyersburg, Tenn., Jan. 25, 1938; s. Leroy and Dannie Louise (Sutton) R.; m. Ila Ruth Cook, July 20, 1958; children: Tammy Ruth, Jerry Marvin, Timothy Tyrus. Grad. in Bus., Dyersburg State C.C., 1978. Cert real estate broker, Tenn., gen. residential contractor, Tenn.; lic. fed. comm. specialist. Engr. Bellsouth Corp., Memphis, 1956-90; real estate broker Better Homes and Gardens, Jackson, Tenn., 1990-92; shoe store owner Red Wing Shoes, Jackson, Tenn., 1994—. Author: Aisle 12, 1995, Sunset Survivor, 1995, 1 is Missing, 1996; inventor card game. Mem. planning commn. City Bldg. Authority, Dyersburg, 1979; alderman City of Dyersburg, 1979-80. With USAF, 1956-60. Mem. Jaycees (Memphis sec. 1968), Lions (Dyersburg pres. 1979), Comms. Workers of Am. (union rep. and lobbyist 1960-80). Democrat. Southern Baptist. Home: 67 Highland Ridge Cove Jackson TN 38305 Office: Richards Footwear 3740 Us Highway 45 N Jackson TN 38305-7800

RICHARDS, JOHN DALE, sociology and philosophy educator, counselor; b. South Charleston, W.Va., July 31, 1958; s. Guy Edward and Margaret Jane (Gray) R.; m. Susan Lynn McCallister, June 23, 1990. BA, W.Va. State Coll., 1978; MA, Ohio U., 1982, 88. Lic. profl. counselor, W.Va. Bd. Examiners in Counseling; lic. cert. social worker, W.Va. Bd. Social Work Examiners. Family counselor Family Svc. Kanawha Valley, Charleston, W.Va., 1988-93; pvt. practice family counselor South Charleston, 1991-93; asst. prof. W.Va. State Coll., Institute, 1993—; cons. Gov.'s Cabinet on Families and Children, Charleston, 1995, Human Resource Mgmt. Co., Charleston, 1995. Author: Coping with Grief, 1995, (poetry) Uncreated Light, 1995; co-author: The Family Education Experience, 1995. Pres. bd. dirs. Dreikurs Family Edn. Ctr., Charleston, 1995—; mem. adv. bd. Glenwood Family Resource Ctr., Charleston, 1995—. Recipient Dr. W.E.B. Dubois award Alpha Kappa Delta, 1995. Mem. Am. Sociol. Assn., W.Va. Soc. Adlerian Psychology (pres. 1995-96, Dr. Manford A. Sonstegard award 1995), W.Va. Sociol. Assn. (v.p. 1995-96), Masons. Democrat. Home: 1211 Strawberry Rd Saint Albans WV 25177

RICHARDS, LEONARD MARTIN, investment executive, consultant; b. Phila., June 4, 1935; s. Leonard Martin and Marion Clara (Lang) R.; m. Phyllis Janelle Mowrey, Aug. 26, 1961 (div. Aug. 1978); children: Lisa, David Reed. BS, Pa. State U., 1957; MBA, U. Pa., 1963. Asst. to sr. ptnr. Van Cleef, Jordan & Wood, N.Y.C., 1963-68; v.p., portfolio mgr. Bernstein-Macaulay, Inc., N.Y.C., 1968-72; ptnr. G. H. Walker, Laird Co., N.Y.C., 1972-74; v.p., trust officer, mgr. instl. funds group Republic Bank N.A., Dallas, 1974-77; v.p., sr. investment officer, mem. exec. com. Variable Annuity Life Ins. Co., Houston, 1977-88; v.p., sr. investment officer Am. Gen. Series Portfolio Co., 1985-88; bd. dirs., pres. L.M. Richards & Co., Houston, 1982—; bd. dirs. Capital Instl. Svcs., Inc., 1990—, Neurotherapy Mgmt., Inc., 1995—, Trinity Life Ctr., Houston, 1996—. Pres., bd. dirs. Sand Dollar Inc., Houston, 1985-96—; bd. dirs. Houston Chorale, 1988-89. Capt. U.S. Army, 1957-65. Mem. Houston Soc. Fin. Analysts, Assn. Investment Mgmt. and Rsch. Republican. Avocations: skiing, travel, scuba. Home: 9023 Briar Forest Dr Houston TX 77024-7220 Office: LM Richards & Co 4600 Post Oak Place Dr Ste 301 Houston TX 77027-9727

RICHARDS, MARTA ALISON, lawyer; b. Memphis, Mar. 15, 1952; d. Howard Jay and Mary Dean (Nix) Richards; m. Jon Michael Hobson, May 5, 1973 (div. Jan. 1976); m. 2d, Richard Peter Massony, June 16, 1979 (div. Apr. 1988); 1 child, Richard Peter Massony, Jr. Student Vassar Coll., 1969-70; AB cum laude, Princeton U., 1973; JD, George Washington U., 1976. Bar: La. 1976, U.S. Dist. Ct. (ea. dist.) La. 1976, U.S. Ct. of Appeals (5th cir.) 1981, U.S. Supreme Ct. 1988, U.S. Dist. Ct. (mid. dist.) La., 1991. Assoc. Phelps, Dunbar, Marks, Claverie & Sims, New Orleans, 1976-77; assoc. counsel Hibernia Nat. Bank, New Orleans, 1978; assoc. Singer, Hutner, Levine, Seeman & Stuart, New Orleans, 1978-80, Jones, Walker, Waechter, Poitevent, Carrere & Denegre, New Orleans, 1980-84; ptnr. Mmahat, Duffy, & Richards, 1984, Montgomery, Barnett, Brown, Read, Hammond & Mintz, 1984-86, Montgomery, Richards & Ballin, 1986-89, Gelpi, Sullivan, Carroll and Laborde, 1989; gen. counsel Maison Blanche Inc., Baton Rouge, 1990-92; gen. counsel La. State Bond Commn., 1992—; lectr. paralegal inst. U. New Orleans, 1984-89, adj. prof., 1989. Contbr. articles to legal jours. Treas. alumni coun. Princeton U., 1979-81. Mem. ABA, La. State Bar Assn., Fed. Bar Assn., New Orleans Bar Assn., Baton Rouge Bar Assn., Nat. Assn. Bond Lawyers, Princeton Alumni Assn. New Orleans (pres. 1982-86). Episcopalian. Home: 4075 S Ramsey Dr Baton Rouge LA 70808 Office: La State Bond Commn State Capitol Bldg 21st Fl PO Box 44154 Baton Rouge LA 70804

RICHARDS, MELINDA LOU, speech and language pathologist; b. Covington, Tenn., Aug. 11, 1952; d. Clarence M. and Mary Lou (Johnston) R.; m. Douglas C. Wonder, Nov. 27, 1982 (div. 1990). BS in Music Edn. magna cum laude, Tenn. Tech. U., 1974; MMus, U. Tenn., 1979; postgrad., Tenn. State U., 1990-92, U. Tenn., 1993—. Cert. tchr., Tenn. Asst. band dirs., dir. orchs. Greeneville (Tenn.) City Schs., 1974-77; percussionist, asst. timpanist Knoxville (Tenn.) Symphony Orch., 1977-79; commd. 2d lt. USAF, 1979, 1st lt., 1981-83; info. systems mgr. Upper Cumberland Human Resource Agy., Algood, Tenn., 1984-87; speech/lang. pathologist Putnam County Schs., Cookeville, Tenn., 1990—; clin. supr. UT Knoxville, 1996—. With Tenn. Air N.G., 1984—. Decorated USAF Achievement medal, 1986, USAF Commendation medal, 1989, Tenn. Disting. Svc. medal, 1994, Air Reserve Forces Meritorious Svc. medal, 1987, 90, 94. Mem. Am. Speech-Lang. and Hearing Assn., Tenn. Speech-Hearing Assn. (co-chair pub. sch. ad-hoc com., long range planning com., pres.-elect 1996—), Phi Kappa Phi, Kappa Delta Pi, Mu Phi Epsilon, Alpha Psi Omega. Republican. Episcopalian. Home: 1185 E 10th St Cookeville TN 38501-1909

RICHARDS, MICHAEL DULANY, history educator; b. Great Bend, Kans., Nov. 3, 1941; s. Cooper Dulany and R. Jane (Smith) R.; m. Anne Hale Vaughan, Aug. 31, 1961; children: John Michael, David Hale, Arie Christiaan. BA, U. Tulsa, 1962; AM, Duke U., 1964, PhD, 1969. History instr. Sweet Briar (Va.) Coll., 1966-69, asst. prof. history, 1969-74, assoc. prof. history, 1974-82, Samford prof. history, 1982—. Author: Europe, 1900-1980: A Brief History, 1982; editor: Makers of Modern Europe, 1987. Fellow Fulbright Found., The Netherlands, 1965-66, NEH, 1975-76. Office: Sweet Briar Coll Dept History Sweet Briar VA 24595

RICHARDS-KORTUM, REBECCA RAE, biomedical engineering educator; b. Grand Island, Nebr., Apr. 14, 1964; d. Larry Alan and Linda Mae (Hohnstein) Richards; m. Philip Ted Kortum, May 12, 1985; children: Alexander Scott, Maxwell James. BS, U. Nebr., 1985; MS, MIT, 1987, PhD, 1990. Assoc. U. Tex., Austin, 1990—. Named Presdl. Young Investigator NSF, Washington, 1991; NSF presdl. faculty fellow, Washington, 1992; recipient Career Achievement award Assn. Advancement Med. Instrumentation, 1992, Dow Outstanding Young Faculty awd., Am. Soc. for Engineering Education, 1992. Mem. AAAS, Am. Soc. Engring. Edn. (Outstanding Young Faculty award 1992), Optical Soc. Am., Am. Soc. Photobiology. Office: U Tex Dept Elec & Computer Engring Austin TX 78712

RICHARDSON, BARBARA KATHRYN, social worker; b. Magnet Cove, Ark., Nov. 28, 1936; d. Fred Lee and Lillian Catherine (Adkins) R. BA, Mary Hardin-Baylor U., 1961; MSW, Washington U., St. Louis, 1965. Cert. social worker. Sec., Dyke Bros., Little Rock, 1953-55; legal sec. Donalson, Bullard & Kucera, Dallas, 1955-57; pub. welfare worker Henderson County Pub. Welfare, Hendersonville, N.C., 1961-62; child welfare worker Tex. Dept. Pub. Welfare, Belton, 1962-63, adoption worker, Tyler, 1965-66, asst. dir. child welfare, Houston, 1966-69; dir. adoptions Hope Cottage Children's Bur., Dallas, 1970-74; dir. emergency-crisis unit Dallas County Mental Health-Mental Retardation, 1974-76; ednl. contract specialist, continuing edn. bur. Tex. Dept. Human Services, 1977-81, project developer Office Research, Demonstration and Eval., 1981-88, wellness specialist Personnel div., 1988-89; program devel. specialist Family Health Resources and Childrens Protective Svcs., 1989-90; owner Barkrich, Ltd., 1990—. Dem. precinct del., Dallas, 1972. Mem. Nat. Assn. Social Workers (state dir. 1974-75), Acad. Cert. Social Workers, Council on Social Work Edn. (ho. of dels. 1980-82), Gov.'s Club (charter mem. 1992). Home and Office: Barkrich Ltd 506 E 54th St Austin TX 78751-1305

RICHARDSON, BETTY KEHL, nursing educator, administrator, counselor, researcher; b. Jacksonville, Ill., Mar. 24, 1938; d. Alfred Jason and Hilda (Emmons) Kehl; m. Joseph Richardson, June 27, 1959 (div. 1980); children: Mark Joseph, Stephanie Elaine. BA in Nursing, Sangamon State U., 1975, MA in Adminstrn., 1977; MSN, Med. Coll. Ga., 1980; PhD in Nursing, U. Tex., 1985. Cert. advanced nursing adminstrn., clin. specialist child and adolescent psychiat. nursing ANCC; lic. profl. counselor, marriage and family counselor. Instr. nursing Lincoln Land Community Coll., Springfield, Ill., 1978-79; acting dir. nursing MacMurray Coll., Jacksonville, Ill., 1979-81; asst. prof. Sangamon State U., Springfield, 1981-82; adminstr. children and adolescent programs Shoal Creek Hosp., Austin, 1989-90; nursing dir. Austin State Hosp., 1983-89; therapist San Marcos (Tex.) Treatment Ctr., 1989-90; instr. Austin C.C., 1990—; pvt. practice psychotherapy, Austin, 1990—. Advising editor: Parenting in the 90s jour.; contbr. articles to profl. jours. Pres. PTA, 1968. Named Outstanding Nurse, Passavant Hosp., 1958, Nurse of Yr., Tex. Nurses Assn., 1994-95; recipient Plaque for Outstanding Leadership, Austin State Hosp., 1989, plaque for svc. to the poor people of Mexico and C.Am. Internat. Good Neighbor Coun. (Austin chpt.) and U. Area Rotary Club, 1995. Mem. ANA, DAR, Southwest Group Psychotherapy Assn., Tex. Counseling Assn., Rotary (Good Neighbor Coun./Univ. award 1995), Sigma Theta Tau, Phi Kappa Phi. Methodist. Home: 5207 Doe Valley Ln Austin TX 78759-7103 Office: Austin C C 1020 Grove Blvd Austin TX 78759-3300

RICHARDSON, DEBORAH KAYE, clinical nurse specialist, educator; b. Tyler, Tex., Mar. 31, 1953; d. Clarence Bruce and thelma Lee (McCarty) R. BS, Houston Bapt. U., 1975; BSN, Tex. Womans U., Houston, 1983, MSN, 1995. Cert. advanced practice nurse. Hosp. aide M.D. Anderson Cancer Ctr., Houston, 1979-80, med. technologist, 1980-83, clinician, 1983-88, asst. nurse mgr., 1988-91, clin. instr., 1991-95, clinician IV, 1994-96, clin. nurse specialist, 1996—; coord. infusion therapy program Twelve Oak Hosp., Houston, 1990, outreach PICCS program, 1986—. Contbr. articles to profl. jours. Mem. Woodland Heights Assn., Houston, 1991—. Recipient Profl. Growth award Houston Bapt. U., 1974; named Outstanding Nurse Tex. Nurses Assn. Dist. 9; named to Notable Women of Tex. Mem. Oncology Nurses Soc., Nat. Assn. Vascular Access Network, Phi Theta Kappa. Home: 1101 Highland St Houston TX 77009-6516 Office: University Texas MD Anderson Cancer Ctr 1515 Holcombe Houston TX 77030

RICHARDSON, ELEANOR ELIZABETH, marketing professional; b. Durham, N.C., Jan. 16, 1948; d. Thurman Eugene Hogan and Flora Elizabeth (Pope) Teele; m. Fredrick Glenn Richardson, July 16, 1977; children: David, Tammy. BS in Bus., Liberty U., 1990, MBA, 1993. Banking officer State Bank Raleigh, 1977-79, Ft. Knox (Ky.) Nat. Bank, 1980-82, Am. Express, Augsburg and Heidelberg, Fed. Republic Germany, 1982-83; dep. registrar U.S. Army-Europe Vehicle Registry, Heidelberg, 1983-88; mktg. dir. Dept. of Army, Ft. Bragg, N.C., 1989—; tng. dir. Dragon U., Ft. Bragg, 1992-95; tng. dir. for region S.E. Civilian Pers. Ops. Ctr. Asst. Sec. Army for Manpower Rsch. Affairs, Fort Bragg, N.C., 1996—. Mem. Ft. Knox Sch. Bd., 1981-82. Mem. NAFE, Ft. Bragg Officers Club, Fayetteville C. of C., Fayetteville Rotary. Republican. Home: 7701 Pine Ridge Dr Columbus GA 31909 Office: Asst Sec of the Army Soc for RA SECPOC Attn HRD Fort Benning GA 31909

RICHARDSON, ELLIOT LEE, lawyer; b. Boston, July 20, 1920; s. Edward P. and Clara (Shattuck) R.; m. Anne F. Hazard, Aug. 2, 1952; children: Henry, Nancy, Michael. AB cum laude, Harvard U., 1941, LLB cum laude, 1947, LLD (hon.), 1971; other hon. degrees. Bar: Mass. 1949, D.C. 1980. Law clk. Judge Learned Hand, U.S. Ct. Appeals (2d cir.), N.Y., 1947-48, Supreme Ct. Justice Felix Frankfurter, 1948-49; assoc. Ropes, Gray, Best, Coolidge & Rugg, Boston, 1949-53, 55-56; asst. to Mass. Senator Leverett Saltonstall, 1953-54; acting counsel to Mass. Gov. Christian A. Herter, 1956; asst. sec. legis. HEW, 1957-59; U.S. atty. for Mass., 1959-61, spl. asst. to atty. gen. U.S., 1961; ptnr. Ropes & Gray, Boston, 1961-64; lt. gov. Mass., 1965-67, atty. gen. Mass., 1967-69, under sec. state, 1969-70; sec. HEW, 1970-73; sec. def., 1973, atty. gen. U.S., 1973; fellow Woodrow Wilson Internat. Ctr. for Scholars, Washington, 1974-75; ambassador Ct. St. James's, London, 1975-76; sec. commerce, 1976-77; ambassador-at-large, spl. rep. of pres. Law of Sea Conf., Washington, 1977-80; sr. ptnr. Milbank, Tweed, Hadley & McCloy, Washington, 1980-92; personal rep. SG of UN for Nicaraguan Elections, 1989-90; spl. rep. of Pres. of U.S. for multilateral assistance in The Philippines, 1989-94; bd. dirs. Oak Industries, BNFL Inc.; mem. adv. bd. Am. Flywheel Systems; former dir. John Hancock Life Ins. Co. Author: The Creative Balance, 1976; contbr. numerous articles to profl. jours. and others. Former trustee Radcliffe Coll., Mass. Gen. Hosp.; hon. trustee Roger Tory Peterson Inst.; pres. World Affairs Coun., Boston; dir. Mass. Bay United Fund, past chmn. Greater Boston United Fund Campaign; mem. bd. overseers Harvard Coll.; chmn. overseers com. to visit John F. Kennedy Sch. Govt., Harvard U.; mem. overseers com. to visit Harvard U. Law Sch.; bd. dirs. U.S. Coun. Internat. Bus., Urban Inst.; chmn. Coun. on Ocean Law, Hitachi Found., Japan-Am. Soc. Washington; co-chmn. Nat. Coun., UN Assn. U.S.; chmn. overseers com. to visit Harvard Med. Sch. and Sch. Dental Medicine; vice chmn. Citizens Network Fgn. Affairs; mem. Compt. Gen.'s cons. panel; chmn. quality rev. bd. GAO; mem. adv. com. for commemoration World War II, Dept. Def.; bd. dirs. Am. Acad. Diplomacy. Served to 1st lt. inf. U.S. Army, 1942-45. Decorated Bronze Star, Purple Heart with oak leaf cluster, Légion d'Honneur; recipient Jefferson award Am. Inst. Pub. Svc., Thomas Hart Benton award Kansas City Art Inst., Emory R. Buckner medal Fed. Bar Coun., Penn Club award, Albert Lasker Spl. Pub. Svc. award, Neptune award, Meritorious Pub. Svc. award USCG, Harry Truman Good Neighbor award, Spkr. Thomas P. O'Neill Jr. award for pub. svc., Sam Rayburn award, F.D. Roosevelt Freedom medal, and other awards. Fellow AAAS, Am. Bar Found., Mass. Bar Found.; mem. ABA, ASPA, D.C. Bar Assn., Mass. Bar Assn., Harvard U. Alumni Assn. (former elected dir.), Coun. on Fgn. Rels., Am. Law Inst., Am. Soc. Internat. Law, Bretton Woods Com., Am. Acad. Diplomacy, Am. Acad. Social Ins., Internat. Law Assn., Nat. Acad. Pub. Adminstrn., Coun. on Excellence in Govt., DAV, VFW, Am. Legion, Alfalfa Club, F Street Club. Office: Milbank Tweed Hadley McCloy 1825 I St NW Ste 1100 Washington DC 20006-5403

RICHARDSON, EMILIE WHITE, manufacturing company executive, investment company executive, lecturer; b. Chattanooga, July 8; d. Emmett and Mildred Evelyn (Harbin) White; B.A., Wheaton Coll., 1951; 1 dau., Julie Richardson Morphis. With Christy Mfg. Co., Inc., Fayetteville, N.C., 1952—, sec. 1956-66, v.p., 1967-74, exec. v.p., 1975-79, pres., chief exec. officer, 1980—; v.p. E. White Investment Co., 1968-83, pres., 1983—; cons. Aerostatic Industries, 1979—; v.p. Gannon Corp., 1981—; cons. govt. contacts and offshore mfg., 1981—; lectr., speaker in field. Vice pres. public relations Ft. Lauderdale Symphony Soc., 1974-76, v.p. membership, 1976-77, adv. bd., 1978—; active Atlantic Found., Ft. Lauderdale Mus. Art, Beaux Arts, Freedoms Found.; mem. East Broward Women's Republican Club, 1968—, Americanism chmn., 1971-72. Mem. Internat. Platform Assn., Nat. Speakers Assn., Fla. Speakers Assn. Presbyterian. Clubs: Toastmasters, Coral Ridge Yacht Club. Home: 1531 NE 51st St Fort Lauderdale FL 33334-5709 Office: 3311 Fort Bragg Rd Fayetteville NC 28303-4763

RICHARDSON, FRANK H., retired oil industry executive; b. Mar. 15, 1933. BS, South Dakota Sch. Mines, 1955. With Shell Oil Co., Houston, 1955-93, exec. v.p., 1983-88, pres., CEO, 1988-93. Address: 2001 Kirby Dr Ste 504 Houston TX 77019-6033

RICHARDSON, FREDRICK GLENN, consulting company executive; b. Durham, N.C., Mar. 17, 1957; s. Fred G. and Eleanor H. Richardson; m. Carol Thomson, Mar. 10, 1990. BA, N.C. State U., 1981; MBA, Syracuse U., 1989; MA, U.S. Naval War Coll., 1994. Commd. 2d lt. U.S. Army, 1975, advanced through grades to lt. col.; ops. officer 1st pers. command U.S. Army, Schwetzingen, Germany, 1986-87; resource mgmt. officer J.F. Kennedy Spl. Warfare Ctr., Ft. Bragg, N.C., 1989-90; chief officer mgmt. spl. ops. command U.S. Army, Ft. Bragg, 1990-91; chief mgmt. divsn. 22d logistics support command U.S. Army, Dhahran, Saudi Arabia, 1992-93; exec. officer spl. ops. command U.S. Army, Ft. Bragg, 1992-93; chief mil. secretariat J-4, The Joint Staff, Washington, 1994-96; mng. assoc. Coopers & Lybrand Cons., McLean, Va., 1996—. Decorated Legion of Merit, Bronze Star medal. Mem. Am. Soc. Mil. Comptrs., Assn. Govt. Accts., Ret. Officers Assn., Smithsonian Instn. (assoc.), Mensa, N.C. State U. Alumni Assn. (membership dir. 1996—), Clifford Duell Lodge # 756. Office: Coopers & Lybrand LLP 1751 Pinnocle Dr Mc Lean VA 22102

RICHARDSON, GORDON BANNING, insurance company executive, investment consultant; b. N.Y.C., May 19, 1937; s. Ogden Barker and May Thistle (Shirres) R.; m. Judy Carolyn Williams, May 7, 1966; children: Gordon Banning II, Randall S. Student Ashbury Coll., Ottawa, Ont., Can., 1956, Tex. A&M, 1971; BS in Bus. Adminstrn., Boston U., 1962; CLU, Am. Coll., 1974; AEP, NAEDC, 1995. Owner, pres. Ins. Assocs., Caldwell, Tex., 1968—. Recipient Hon. State Farmer award Future Farmers Am., 1975. Mem. Tex. Assn. Life Underwriters (pres. 1989-90), Confederate Air Force (sponsor), Million Dollar Round Table (life), Sigma Alpha Epsilon, Mass Beta Upsilon (life). Baptist. Lodge: Lions (dist. gov. 1981-82).

RICHARDSON, HAROLD EDWARD, literature educator, author; b. Woodstock, Ky., July 13, 1929; m. Antonia Calvert, 1953; children: Shawn Edward, Jill Calvert. BA, Ea. Ky. U., 1952; postgrad. U. Ky., 1949-51; MA, Ea. Ky. U., 1954; AM, U. So. Calif., 1961, PhD, 1963. Tchr. sci., English Bloomfield (Ky.) High Sch., 1952-53; tchr. English Oxnard Union (Calif.) High Sch., 1954-56; creative writing instr. Ventura Jr. Coll., Calif., 1955-56; instr. English, creative writing instr. Fullerton Jr. Coll., Calif., 1956-63; asst. prof. English State U. Calif., Fullerton, 1962; assoc. prof. Ea. Ky. U., Richmond, 1963-65; prof. Ea. Ky. U., 1965-68, U. Louisville, Ky., 1968—; chairperson Ea. Ky. U., 1965-67; vis. prof. English State U. Calif., L.A., Calif., 1967, 71, (summers), U. So. Calif., 1968. Author: William Faulkner: The Journey to Self-Discovery, 1969, (also editor) How to Think and Write, 1971, (with Frederick Shroyer) Muse of Fire: Approaches to Poetry, 1971, Cassius Marcellus Clay: Firebrand of Freedom, 1976, (also editor and commentator) The Best-Loved Short Stories of Jesse Stuart, 1982, Jesse: The Biography of an American Writer-Jesse Hilton Stuart, 1984. Recipient President's Distg. Ach. in Scholarship, Rsch. and Creative Activity award U. Louisville, 1986. Office: U Louisville Dept English 2301 S 3rd St Louisville KY 40292-0001

RICHARDSON, HERBERT HEATH, mechanical engineer, educator, institute director; b. Lynn, Mass., Sept. 24, 1930; s. Walter Blake and Isabel Emily (Heath) R.; m. Barbara Ellsworth, Oct. 6, 1973. SB, SM with honors, MIT, 1955, ScD, 1958. Registered profl. engr., Mass., Tex. Research asst., research engr. Dynamic Analysis and Control Lab. MIT, 1953-57, instr. Dept. Mech. Engring., 1957-58, mem. faculty, 1958-84, prof. mech. engring., 1968-85, head dept., 1974-82, assoc. dean engring., 1982-84; Disting. prof. engring. Tex. A&M U., 1984—; Regents prof. Tex. A&M U. System, College Station, 1993—; dean, vice chancellor engring. Tex. A&M U. Sys., 1984-85; dep. chancellor, dean, dir. Tex. Engring. Expt. Sta. Tex. A&M U., 1985-91; chancellor Tex. A&M U. System, College Station, 1991-93, assoc. vice chancellor engring., 1993—, assoc. dean engring., 1993—; dir. Tex. Trans. Inst., Tex. A&M Univ. Sys., 1993—; with Ballistics Rsch. Lab. Abderdeen Proving Ground, Md., 1958; chief scientist U.S. Dept. Transp., 1970-72; bd. dirs. Foster-Miller Inc., Mass., Ten X Inc., Tex. Utilities Co.; chmn. adv. com. for engring. NSF, 1987-89, adv. com. basic energy scis. U.S. Dept. Energy, 1987-91. Author: Introduction to System Dynamics, 1971; contbr. articles to profl. pubs. Trustee S.W. Rsch. Inst. Officer U.S. Army, 1968. Recipient medal Am. Ordnance Assn., 1953, Gold medal Pi Tau Sigma, 1963, Meritorious Service award and medal Dept. Transp., 1972. Fellow AAAS, ASME (Moody award fluid engring. divsn. 1970, Centennial medallion 1983, Rufus Oldenberger medal 1984, Meritorious Svc. medal 1986, Disting. Svc. award 1986, hon. mem. 1987); mem. NAE (coun. 1986-92, com. on engring. edn.), Am. Soc. Engring. Edn. (Disting. Svc. medal 1993), N.Y. Acad. Sci., Inst. Transp. Engrs., Nat. Rsch. Coun. (gov. bd. 1986-92, chmn. transp. rsch. bd. 1988-89), Sigma Xi, Tau Beta Pi. Office: Tex A&M U Sys CE TTI Bldg MS 3135 College Station TX 77843-3135

RICHARDSON, JASPER EDGAR, nuclear physicist; b. Memphis, Tenn., Nov. 8, 1922; s. Jasper Edgar and Katherine Cecil (Copp) R.; m. Nellie Carolyn Harwell, May 30, 1947; children: Ann Helen, Janet Katherine, Susan Carolyn, Patricia Lynn, Ellen Claire. BS in Physics, Yale U., 1944; MA in Physics, Rice U., 1948, PhD in Physics, 1950. Instr. physics U. Miss., Oxford, 1946-47; asst. prof. Auburn (Ala.) U., 1950-51; A.E.C. fellow Oak Ridge (Tenn.) Inst. Nuclear Studies, 1951-53; physicist U. Tex. M. D. Anderson Hosp., Houston, 1953-55; rsch. physicist Shell Bellaire Rsch. Ctr., Houston, 1955-69; sr. engr. Shell Oil Co., Midland, Tex., 1969-74; staff engr. Shell Oil Co., Houston, 1974-86; ret. Patentee in electronics, oil discovery, measurement; contbr. articles to profl. jours. With USN, 1944-46, Guam. Mem. Am. Phys. Soc., Soc. Petroleum Engrs. Episcopalian.

RICHARDSON, JEAN BROOKS, artist, printmaker; b. Hollis, Okla., Feb. 10, 1940; d. E. Whitson and Mildred E. (Redus) Brooks; m. Ronald A. Richardson, Dec. 29, 1961 (div. 1974); children: Andrea Lynn, Karen Kathleen, Brooks Allen; m. Laurence D. Lucas, Aug. 11, 1977. BFA, Wesleyan Coll., Macon,Ga., 1961. instr. various mus., Oklahoma City, 1971—. Subject of (book) Plains Myths and Other Tales, 1988; subject of articles to profl. jours.; one-woman shows include Enthios Gallery, Santa Fe, 1984, John Szoke Gallery, N.Y.C., 1985, Cogswell Gallery, Vail, Colo., 1986, Robertson Gallery, Beverly Hills, Calif., 1987, Kirkpatrick Ctr. Mus., Oklahoma City, 1988, Four Winds Gallery, Sydney, Australia, 1988, Beth O'Donnell Gallery, Aspen, Colo., 1990, Harrington Galleries, Vancouver, B.C., Can., 1990, Merrill Chase Galleries, Washington, 1991, Lucas Gallery, Telluride, Colo., 1995; represented in permanent collections Am. Embassy, Copenhagen, Minn. Mus. Art, Okla. State Capitol. Mem. Nat. Women in the Arts, Okla. Art Ctr., Individual Artists of Okla. Democrat. Presbyterian. Studio: 1106 NW 50th St Oklahoma City OK 73118-4402

RICHARDSON, JOHN MACLAREN, JR., school superintendent; b. Plainfield, N.J., Nov. 6, 1942; s. John MacLaren and Lucy Lenox (Baker) R.; m. Sharon Rae Kellogg, June 20, 1964; children: Elizabeth R. Updike, John M. III, James Kellogg. AA, George Washington U., 1965, BA, 1969; MA, Grace Theol. Sem., 1993. Bus. mgr. ComMission, Inc., Harrisonburg, Va., 1983-84; cons. in human resources/edn., 1980-88; prin. The Norman A. Whitesel Christian Sch., Mt. Crawford, Va., 1988-90; supt., founding mem. Blue Ridge Christian Sch., Bridgewater, Va., 1990—; bd. dirs. Trinity Christian Sch., Mt. Crawford, Va., 1985-88. Elder Grace Covenant Ch., Harrisonburg, 1988-92. With USN, 1962-66, lt. comdr. USNR, 1966-80. Decorated Nat. Def. medal, USN, 1964, Navy Good Conduct medal, USN, 1966, Armed Forces Reserve medal, USN, 1976. Mem. Internat. Fellowship Christian Sch. Adminstrs., Naval Res. Assn., Res. Officers Assn., Am. Legion, Rotary Internat. Republican. Home: 310 Broad St Bridgewater VA 22812-1718 Office: Blue Ridge Christian Sch PO Box 207 100 Dinkel Ave Bridgewater VA 22812-0207

RICHARDSON, JOSEPH H., company executive; b. 1950. Pvt. practice in law Tallahassee; various mgmt. and exec. positions Fla. Progress Corp. and affiliated cos., 1976—; group v.p., devel. group, pres., CEO Talquin Corp., 1990, sr. v.p. corp. devel., pres., CEO, 1991; sr. v.p. corp. devel. Fla. Progress Corp. Office: Talquin Corp 1 Progress Plz Saint Petersburg FL 33701-4353*

RICHARDSON, K. SCOTT, sales executive; b. Laurens, Iowa, Nov. 3, 1951; s. Kenneth and Lanore R.; m. Theresa Ann Fitzsimmons, Aug. 31, 1974; children: Seth Ian, Aaron Paul, Evan Scott, Claire Elizabeth, Anna Christine. BS in Radiologic Tech., Creighton U., Omaha, 1974; MS, U. Nebr., Omaha, 1976. Spl. procedures tech. Med. Coll. Va., Richmond, 1974-75; chief spl. procedure tech. St. Vincent Hosp., Sioux City, Iowa, 1975; inservice coordinator to radiology mgr. Nebr. Meth. Hosp., Omaha, 1975-78; sales rep. to sr. sales rep. Philips Med. Systems, Inc., Omaha, 1978-81; adminstrv. dir. radiology The Meth. Hosp., Houston, 1981-83; reg. mgr. R.P. Kincheloe Co., Dallas, 1983-84; mgr. sales and svc. R.P. Kincheloe Co., 1984-87, v.p. sales and svc., 1987—. Eucharistic min., svc. min., lector, tchr. continuing Cath. edn., mem. fin. com., mem. bldg. steering com. St. Philips Ch.; T-ball coord. Braeburn Little League, 1989—; coach YMCA Indoor Soccer League, 1987—; mgr. Lewisville Baseball Assn., 1990—, team sponsor, 1990—, bd. dirs., commr., 1992—; active ARC, Glenshire Soccer Club, Braeburn Valley West Swim Team. Mem. Am. Registry Radiologic Technologists, Iowa Soc. Radiologic Technologists, Assn. Univ. Radiology Technologists, Tex. Soc. Radiologic Technologists. Republican. Roman Catholic. Home: 2415 Silverthorne Ct Lewisville TX 75067-3109

RICHARDSON, LAWRENCE, JR., Latin language educator, archeologist; b. Altoona, Pa., Dec. 2, 1920; married. B.A., Yale U., 1942, Ph.D. in Classics, 1952. Instr. classics Yale U., New Haven, 1946-47, instr. to assoc. prof., 1955-66; prof. Duke U., Durham, N.C., 1966-78, James B. Duke prof. Latin, 1978-91, prof. emeritus, 1991—; field archeologist Am. Acad. Rome, 1952-55, Mellon prof., 1980-81; mem. Inst. Advanced Study, 1967-68. Author: Pompeii: An Architectural History, 1988, A New Topographical Dictionary of Ancient Rome, 1992; contbr. articles to profl. jours. Guggenheim fellow, 1958-59; Am. Council Learned Socs. fellow, 1967-68, 72-73; NEH fellow, 1979-80. Mem. German Archeol. Inst. (corr.), Am. Philol. Assn., Archeol. Inst. Am. Office: Duke U West Campus Dept Classical Studies Durham NC 27708

RICHARDSON, LEROY REEVES, medical researcher; b. Miami Beach, Fla., Feb. 2, 1954; s. Van Valentine and Georgianna Duncan (Reeves) R.; m. Rhonda Rose McLawhorn; 1 child, Jason Reeves. BSN, East Carolina U., 1984; MSN, George Mason U., 1994. RN, N.C., Washington. Staff RN, shift supr. Pitt County Med. Ctr., Greenville, N.C., 1984-86, George Washington U. Med. Ctr., Washington, 1986-87; staff RN, shift supr., educator Washington Hosp. Ctr., 1987-94; with neurol. surgery clin. rsch. dept. George Washington U. Med. Faculty Assocs., 1994—. With U.S. Army, 1973-76. Office: George Washington U MFA 2150 Pennsylvania Ave NW Washington DC 20037

RICHARDSON, RICHARD LEWIS, lawyer; b. Balt., Aug. 27, 1952; s. terry Cole and marion cecilia (Kubin) R. AA, U. South Fla., 1973, BA with honors, 1974, MA in Philosophy summa cum laude, 1975; JD, Stetson U., 1979. Bar: Fla. 1979, Fed,. 1980; cert. expert in marital law, Fla., U.S. Dist. Ct. Fla. 1980. Mng. atty. Family Legal Ctrs., Port Richey, Fla., 1980-86; pvt. practice Port Richey, 1986—. Author: Lenin's Materialsm and Empirio-Criticism, 1976. Vol. legal rep. for incompetent juveniles 6th Jud. Cir., Pasco and Pinellas Counties, Fla., 1983—; mem. Pub. Defender's Clinic, St. Petersburg, Fla., 1979. Recipient Award of Participation as Pub. Defender, Pub. Defender's Office, 1979. Mem. ABA (family law sect.), Acad. Am. Trial Lawyers, Fla. Bar Assn. (marital and family law sect.), Themis Acad. Fraternity (v.p. 1971). Home: 10227 Turkey Oak Dr Port Richey FL 34654

RICHARDSON, ROBERT ALVIN, pharmacist; b. Oklahoma City, Apr. 14, 1951; s. Kenneth Alza and Bernice (Bussey) R.; m. Barbara Jean Dial, July 1, 1951 (div. May 1981); children: Kenneth Eugene, Michael Anthony; m. Christi Leigh Miller, Aug. 18, 1956 (div. Jan. 1994); 1 child, Krista Lynn; m. Linda Fay Barrett. BS in Pharmacy, Southwestern Okla. State U., Weatherford, 1975. Registered pharmacist, Tex., N.Mex. Pharmacist Med. Arts Pharmacy, Las Vegas, N.Mex., 1975-76, Graham's Pharmacy, Las Vegas, 1975-76; pharmacist, mgr. Tony's Pharmacy, Las Vegas, 1976-77; hosp. pharmacist Las Vegas Hosp., 1977-78; pharmacist Profl. Pharmacy, Big Spring, Tex., 1978-83; pharmacist, co-owner Munden Pharmacy, Snyder, Tex., 1983-86; pharmacist Eckerd Drug, Sweetwater, Tex., 1985-90; dir. pharmacy Rolling Plains Meml. Hosp., Sweetwater, 1990-94, Trinity Valley Med. Ctr., Palestine, 1994, WalMart Pharmacy, Abilene, 1994—; consulting pharmacist to nursing homes, Big Spring, Tex., 1978-83, Las Vegas, 1977-78. Bd. dirs. Las Vegas/San Miguel C. of C., 1976-77. Mem. Am. Soc. Hosp. Pharmacists. Democrat. Baptist. Lodges: Lions, Rotary (bd. dirs. Las Vegas club 1977-78). Home: PO Box 154 Roscoe TX 79545-0154

RICHARDSON, ROBERT JANECEK, library director; b. Savannah, Ga., July 30, 1945; s. William Blakely and Mildred Ann (Salcedo) R.; m. Janice Amelia Neder, June 10, 1967; children: Robert Jr., Mary Neder Salcedo. AA, Mid. Ga. Coll., 1965; BA, West Ga. Coll., 1967; MSc, Fla. State U., 1971. Tchr. social studies Dublin (Ga.) City Schs., 1967-70; libr., instr. Ga. Coll., Milledgeville, 1971-78; asst. libr. dir. Chattahoochee Valley Regional Libr., Columbus, Ga., 1979-80; libr. dir. Young Harris (Ga.) Coll., 1980—; mem. peer rev. team So. Assn. Colls. and Schs., Atlanta, 1983—; cons. Ga. Mil. Coll. Libr., Milledgeville, 1986, 95. Mem. adminstrv. coun. Sharp Meml. Meth. Ch., Young Harris, 1984-88; trustee Towns County Libr., Hiawassee, Ga., 1980-84, 92—, chmn. 1995—; bd. dirs. Towns-Union Credit Union, Young Harris, 1986—; chair of adhov com. to form Consortia for Private Academic Librs. in Ga., 1995-96; chair of Ga. Private Academic Librs. (GPALS) 1996—; 1996 Ga. Coun. of Media Orgns. (COMO) Svc. award for Continued Involvement and support for joint libr. media confs., 1988-96. Recipient Svc. award Ga. Coun. Media, 1988-96. Mem. Ga. Libr. Assn. (pres. 1989-91, Nix-Jones Svc. award 1993), Ga. Assn. Media Assts. (state advisor 1983-89), Ga. Assn. Instrnl. Tech. (svc. award for continued involvement and support of Joint Annual Libr. Media Conf. 1995). Democrat. Methodist. Office: Young Harris Coll 1 Duckworth Blvd Young Harris GA 30582

RICHARDSON, ROY, management consultant; b. Chgo., Mar. 22, 1931; s. John George and Margaret Beattie (Henderson) R.; BA in Psychology, Macalester Coll., 1952; MA in Labor and Indsl. Relations, U. Ill., 1953; PhD in Indsl. Relations, U. Minn., 1969; m. Mary C. Westphal, May 16, 1970; children: Beth Barnett, Jessica, Adam, Roman, Alexis. With Honeywell, Inc., Mpls., 1956-70, corp. manpower mgr., 1967-70; mgr. manpower devel. and tng. Internat. Harvester, Chgo., 1970-73; dir. personnel U. Minn., 1973-75; v.p. human resources Onan Corp., Mpls., 1975-82; v.p. human resources Graco Corp., Mpls., 1982-84, v.p. human resources and corp. devel., 1985-91; v.p. Human Resources and Quality Mgmt. Systems, 1992-94; pres. Intergrated Mgmt. Systems, 1994—; pres. Pers.l Surveys, Inc., Mpls., 1978-80; dir., chmn. exec. com. Kotz Grad. Sch. Mgmt., St. Paul, 1984-90. V.p. Mpls. Urban League, 1962-64. Recipient Disting. Citizens award City of Mpls., 1964; adj. prof., exec. fellow U. St. Thomas, Mpls. Mem. Soc. for Human Resource Mgmt., U. Minn. Indsl. Rels. Alumni Soc. (dir. 1979-85, pres. 1981), Am. Soc. Quality Ctrl. Republican. Episcopalian. Club: Ford's Colony Country. Author: Fair Pay and Work, 1971.

RICHARDSON, RUTH DELENE, business educator; b. New Orleans, May 27, 1942; s. Daniel Edgar and Allie Myrtle (Skinner) R.; 1 child, John Daniel. B.S., Mars Hill Coll., 1965; M.S., U. Tenn., Knoxville, 1968, Ed.D. (EPDA fellow), 1974. Cert. profl. sec., 1986. Tchr., LaFollette (Tenn) High Sch., 1965-66; instr. Clinch Valley Coll., Wise, Va., 1967-68, U. S.C., Union, 1968-69, Tenn. Wesleyan Coll., Athens, 1969-71, Roane State C.C., Harriman, Tenn., 1971-73; assoc. prof., chmn. dept. bus. edn. and office adminstrn. Ala. State U., Montgomery, 1974-75; assoc. prof. U. South Ala., Mobile, 1975-80; assoc. prof. adminstrv. sys. mgmt. U. North Ala., Florence, 1980-92; prof., 1992—; cons. career edn.; employment tester. Mem. Assn. for Bus. Communication, Nat. Bus. Edn. Assn., Ala. Friends Adoption, Profl. Secs. Internat., Delta Pi Epsilon, Omicron Tau Theta, Phi Delta Kappa, Pi Lambda Theta, Pi Omega Pi. Lutheran. Contbr. articles to profl. jours. Home: 230 Woodcrest Dr Florence AL 35630 Office: U N Ala PO Box 5180 Florence AL 35632

RICHARDSON, SHARON YOUNG, writer, public relations executive; b. Washington, Mar. 13, 1961; d. James Thomas and Evelyn Pollard (Branche) Young; m. Claiborne Turner Richardson II, Nov. 5, 1988; 1 child, Lauren Evelyn. BS in Mass Comm., Va. Commonwealth U., 1983. Reporter Virginian-Pilot, Norfolk, Va., 1983-85; assoc. editor Times News Svc., Springfield, Va., 1985-87; state reporter Times-Dispatch, Richmond, Va., 1987-88; publs. dir. Nat. Assn. Black Journalists, Reston, Va., 1989-90; assoc. editor Assn. Governing Bds. Univ. and Colls., Washington, 1991-93; publs. writer George Mason U., Fairfax, Va., 1993-96; owner Richardson Comm., Woodbridge, Va., 1996—; writing cons. Dynamic Tech. Sys., Alexandria, Va., 1993—. Editor: Economic Prospects for American Higher Education, 1992, Alcohol and Drug Abuse: Policy Guidelines for Boards, 1992. Chairperson publicity com. St. Margaret's Episcopal, Woodbridge, 1994—. Mem. Nat. Assn. Black Journalists, Soc. Profl. Journalists (Sigma Delta Chi Mark of Excellence 1983), Washington Ind. Writers (sec. bd. dirs. 1996—), Washington Assn. Black Journalists. Episcopalian. Home: 11954 Cotton Mill Dr Woodbridge VA 22192-1508

RICHARDSON, STEPHEN GILES, biotechnology company executive; b. Mpls., Sept. 17, 1951; s. Richard Giles and Constance Bernice (Krieg) R.; m. Maureane Hoffman, Mar. 21, 1981. BA cum laude, Wartburg Coll., 1972; MS, U. Iowa, 1974, PhD, 1981; postdoctoral, Duke U., 1982-84. Territory mgr. Wyeth Labs., Phila., 1974-76; research asst. U. Iowa, Iowa City, 1976-82; research assoc. Duke, Durham, N.C., 1982-84; scientist Becton Dickinson Rsch. Ctr., Research Triangle Park, N.C., 1984-86; devel. group leader Dade Internat. (formerly div. Baxter Healthcare), Miami, Fla., 1986; research group leader Organon Teknika Corp., Durham, N.C., 1987-89; R&D sect. head, internat. R&D area mgr., 1989-90; program mgr. divsn. Akzo Nobel, N.V. Organon Teknika Corp., Durham, N.C., 1990-94, assoc. dir., head product devel., 1994—. Contbr. articles to profl. jours.; patentee in field. Co-founder Libertarian Party Minn., Mpls., 1972; exec. sec. Iowa Council to Repeal Conscription, Waterloo, 1971. Mem. Am. Chem. Soc., Am. Assn. Blood Banks, Am. Assn. for Clin. Chemistry, Royal Soc. Chemistry (U.K.), N.Y. Acad. Sci., Electronic Frontier Found., Citizens Internet Empowerment Coalition, Sigma Xi. Home: 5408 Sunny Ridge Dr Durham NC 27705-8552 Office: Organon Teknika Corp Divsn Akzo Nobel NV 100 Akzo Ave Durham NC 27712-9402

RICHARDSON, WANDA LOUISE GIBSON, family practice nurse; b. Dallas; d. Ralph Harrison Gibson and Letha Lee Thompson; children: James L. (dec.), Bruce S., Judith Richardson Holt, Janai Richardson Buentello. Lic. vocat. nurse, Dallas Vocat. Sch., 1960; ADN, Dallas/El Centro Coll., 1981; student, U. Dallas, Irving, 1978. RN, Tex. Staff nurse RHD Hosp., Dallas, 1981; head nurse physicians office, Irving, 1960-80; sr. nurse family practice residency program St. Paul Hosp./U. Tex. Southwestern Med. Sch., Dallas, 1984—. Contbg. columnist Lake Cities Sun News; contbr. poems to anthologies. Vol. tutor Literacy Program, Denton, Tex.; founding mem., mem. choir Cornerstone Bapt. Ch., Plano, 1990; mem. Friends of Libr. of Denton; vol. Big Sisters/Big Bros., Denton. Named one of Notable Women Tex., 1984; recipient Golden Poet award World Poetry, 1991, 92. Mem. Cercle Internat. le Recherches Culturelles et Spirituelles Inc. (charter, officer local chpt.), Nurse Healers Profl. Assn., Dallas Archeol. Soc., Denton J.S. Bach Soc., Dallas Inst. Culture and Humanities, Isthmus Inst. Office: St Paul Hosp 5959 Harry Hines Blvd Dallas TX 75235-6233

RICHARDSON, WILLIAM DONALD, political science educator, consultant; b. Buffalo, N.Y., Mar. 11, 1951; m. Robin Elizabeth Richardson; children: Gregory, Elizabeth. BA, SUNY, Buffalo, 1973, MA, 1975, PhD, 1979. Asst. prof. Ga. State U., Atlanta, 1978-84, assoc. prof. polit. sci., 1984--. Author: Melville's "Benito Cereno", 1987, The American Regime, 1996; contbr. articles to profl. jours. Recipient Dimock award, 1987. Mem. Am. Polit. Sci. Assn., Am. Soc. for Public Adminstrn. (Dimock award), Ga. Assn. of Scholars (v.p. 1990-91, bd. dirs. 1990-94), Southern Polit. Sci. Assn., Northeastern Polit. Sci. Assn. Office: Georgia State Univ Dept Of Political Sci Atlanta GA 30303

RICHARDSON, WILLIAM WIGHTMAN, III, personnel and employee benefits consultant; b. Phila., May 15, 1928; s. William Wightman Jr. and Ruth (Mathers) R.; m. Elizabeth Fritz Rich (div. June 1979); children: William Wightman IV, Brenda Fritz. BA, U. Md., 1954. Commd. 2d lt. USAF, 1951, advanced through grades to capt., 1955; dir. pers. Kinney Nat. Svc. Co., N.Y.C., 1964-67; mgr. human resource sys. Bristol-Myers Co., N.Y.C., 1968-75; dir. employee info. The Coastal Co., Houston, 1976-78; mgr. employee benefits Valero Energy Corp., San Antonio, 1979-90, ret., 1990; cons. on pers. and employee benefits and pers. automation Houston, 1991—; ptnr. Creature Crafts, Bellaire, 1993—. Maj. USAFR ret. Republican. Episcopalian. Home and Office: 4815 Mayfair St Bellaire TX 77401-2313

RICHARDSON, WILLIAM WINFREE, III, lawyer; b. Williamsburg, Va., Aug. 12, 1939; s. William Winfree Jr. and Ellen Blanche (Johnson) R.; m. Constance Diane Niver (div. July 1985); children: Christine Marie, Kenneth Erik. BA, Coll. William and Mary, 1963, Bachelor of Civil Law, 1966, JD, 1967. Bar: Va. 1968. Pvt. practice Providence Forge, Va., 1968—; commr. accounts New Kent Cir. Ct., Providence Forge, 1968—, atty. correctional field unit, 1968—; asst. commr. accounts Charles City Cir. Ct., Providence Forge, 1970—; bd. dirs. C.H. Evelyn Piling Co. Inc., Providence Forge. Advisor Selective Svc. System, New Kent County, Va., 1972. Internat. Order Kings Daus. and Sons scholar, 1957. Mem. ABA, Williamsburg Bar Assn., Va. Trial Lawyers Assn., Am. Judicature Soc., Internat. Platform Assn., Colonial Bar Assn., Phi Alpha Delta, Sigma Pi. Home: Chelsea Plantation West Point VA 23181 Office: PO Box 127 Providence Forge VA 23140

RICHERSON, STEPHEN WAYNE, minister; b. Jackson, Tenn., Sept. 15, 1951; s. Claude Burnette and Mary Cathryn (Greathouse) R.; m. Rebecca Sue Darnell, Sept. 19, 1970; children: Mary Rebecca, Susan Virginia, James Stephen. BSBA, U. Richmond, 1973; MDiv, Southeastern Bapt. Theol. Sem., Wake Forest, N.C., 1979, DMin, 1984. Ordained to ministry Bapt. Ch., 1978. Minister music Hampton (Va.) Roads Bapt. Ch., 1974-76; assoc. minister music and youth Rolesville (N.C.) Bapt. Ch., 1976-78; minister Lea Bethel Bapt. Ch., Prospect Hill, N.C., 1978-80, Menchville Bapt. Ch., Newport News, Va., 1980-87, Westover Bapt. Ch., Richmond, Va., 1987—; br. mgr. Old Point Nat. Bank, Hampton, Va., 1973-76; trustee Va. Bapt. Children's Home, Salem, 1984-85, 878-96, v.p., 1990-91, pres. 1991-96; bd. dirs. Va. Bapt. Gen. Bd., Richmond, 1986-87; faculty Boyce Bible Sch. So. Bapt. Sem., Louisville, 1984-89. Author: Developing a Ministry Dream, 1984. Bd. dirs., swim and dive dir. Shenandoah Comty. Assn., Richmond, 1990-92, pres., 1990-95; soccer coach Reams Rd. Athletic Assn., Richmond, 1988-89; mem. Choral Boosters, PTA, Monacan H.S., Richmond, 1992—; practicum leader Bapt. Theol. Sem., Richmond, 1996-97. Mem. Am. Acad. Ministry, Richmond Bapt. Mins. Conf., Peninsula Bapt. Mins. Conf. (v.p. 1980-87, moderator 1985-86, Pastor of Yr. 1986), Ministerial Support Group Richmond, Chaplain Assn. Chippenham Med. Ctr. Richmond. Office: Westover Bapt Ch PO Box 13048 Richmond VA 23225-0048

RICHERT, HARVEY MILLER, II, ophthalmologist; b. Weatherford, Okla., Aug. 25, 1948; s. Harvey Miller and Catherine Cornelia (Ryan) R.; m. Diana Dee Sisney, Nov. 23, 1966; children: Ronald Lance, Rachelle Lea. BS, Southwestern Okla. State U., 1970; MD, U. Okla., Oklahoma City, 1974. Intern St. Anthony Hosp., Oklahoma City, 1974-75; resident in ophthalmology Tulane U., New Orleans, 1975-78; physician Tucker & Walker Ophthalmology Assocs., Abilene, Tex., 1978-80; ptnr. Tucker, Walker & Richert, Abilene, 1980-86; pvt. practice Abilene, 1986—; med. dir. Lions Eye Bank, Abilene, 1979—; head ophthalmology sect. Humana Hosp., 1984-90, Hendrick Med. Ctr., 1984-92. V.p. Chisholm Trail coun. Boy Scouts Am., 1984-89, 92—, dist. chmn., 1990-92, asst. scoutmaster, 1982-85, scoutmaster, 1985-88. Recipient Scoutmaster of Merit award, Silver Beaver award, Dist. award of Merit, Boy Scouts Am., 1988. Fellow Am. Acad. Ophthalmology, Castroviejo Soc. (assoc.); mem. AMA, Tex. Ophthal. Assn., Tex. Med. Assn., Lions (founders club), Abilene C. of C. Republican. Baptist. Home: 15 Glen Abbey St Abilene TX 79606-5023 Office: 950 N 19th St Ste 200 Abilene TX 79601-2413

RICHESON, HUGH ANTHONY, JR., lawyer; b. Aberdeen, Md., Apr. 22, 1947; s. Hugh Anthony Sr. and Mary Evelyn (Burford) R.; m. Melissa Anne Baum, Apr. 4, 1970; children: Hugh Anthony III, Heidi E., Holly K., Hagin G., Herald Joshua. BBA, U. Richmond, 1969; JD, U. Fla., 1973; student, St. Catherine's Coll., Oxford U., Eng., summer 1973. Bar: Fla. 1974, U.S. Dist. Ct. (mid. dist.) Fla. 1975, U.S. Supreme Ct. 1992. Assoc. Bryant, Dickens, Rumph, Franson & Miller, Jacksonville, Fla., 1974-76, ptnr., 1977; sole practice Orange Park, Fla., 1977-82; ptnr. Smith, Hallowes & Richeson, Orange Park, 1982-83; sole practice Palm Harbor, Fla., 1984—. Pres. Full Gospel Bus. Men's Fellowship Internat., Orange Park, 1983-84, Palm Harbor, 1985-92, field rep., 1987—. Mem. ATLA, Acad. Fla. Trial Lawyers, Clearwater Bar Assn., Fla. Coun. Bar Assn. Pres. (life), Christian Legal Soc., Gideons Internat., Countryside Country Club, Phi Delta Phi. Republican. Methodist.

RICHEY, V. L., steel company executive. Pres. Am. Cast Iron Pipe Co. Address: Am Cast Iron Pipe Co 2930 N 16th St Birmingham AL 35207*

RICHIE, RODNEY CHARLES, critical care and pulmonary medicine physician; b. Big Springs, Tex., Aug. 17, 1946; s. Howard Mouzon and Gloria (Hollingshead) R.; m. Sara Lee Dilley, July 13, 1968; children: Megan Kathryn, Paul Nathan. BA in Chemistry, So. Meth. U., 1968; MD cum laude, Baylor Coll., 1972. Diplomate in Internal Medicine, Pulmonary, Crit. Care and Ins. Medicine. Resident in medicine Baylor Affiliated Hosps., Houston, 1973-75, chief med. resident, 1975, fellow in pulmonary medicine, 1976-77; pvt. practice, pres. Waco (Tex.) Lung Assocs., 1977—; med. dir. Tex. Life Ins., Waco, 1985—. Chmn. med. staff Hillcrest Bapt. Med. Ctr., Waco, 1993; chmn. bd. dirs. GH Pape Found., Waco, 1993. Fellow Am. Coll. Chest Physicians; mem. ACP, AMA, Am. Thoracic Soc., Tex. Club Internists. Episcopalian. Home: 3509 Lake Heights Dr Waco TX 76708-1005 Office: Waco Med Group 2911 Herring Ave Ste 212 Waco TX 76708-3244

RICHKIN, BARRY ELLIOTT, financial services executive; b. N.Y.C., Apr. 14, 1944; s. Harry and Celia (Goldberg) R. BA, Bklyn. Coll., 1964. CLU, cert. in personal fin. planning, NASD. Auditor First Nat. Bank of N.Y., N.Y.C., 1968-70; sr. supr. ABC, N.Y.C., 1970-73; account rep. Met. Life Ins. co., Atlanta, 1973-74; rep. Mixon-Baker Fin. Svcs., Atlanta, 1974-78; owner Barry Richkin Fin. Svcs., Roswell, Ga., 1978—; owner Barry Richkin Philatelics, Roswell, 1991—; cons., owner Benefit Cons. Group, Roswell, 1989—; cons., pres., bd. dirs. Am. Health Network, Roswell, 1982—. Author: Guide to Preferred Provider Organizations, 1986. Mem. Am. Soc. CLU and ChFC, Am. Philatelic Soc., Manuscript Soc., U.S. Postal Hist. Soc., Conn. Hist. Soc. Office: Barry Richkin Fin Svcs PO Box 2071 600 Houze Way Bldg C-6 Roswell GA 30076-1435 also: PO Box 2071 Roswell GA 30076

RICHLEN, SCOTT LANE, federal government program administrator; b. Ames, Iowa, July 23, 1949; s. Ellsworth Mark and Betty Jane (Wegner) R.; m. Deborah Lou Dick, Feb. 6, 1971; children: Mindy Lou, Gwendolyn Anne. BSME, Mont. State U., 1972; M.Engring. in Mech. Engring., U. Idaho, 1982; grad. exec. potential program, Office Pers. Mgmt., 1995. Assoc. engr. Thiokol Chem. Corp., Brigham City, Utah, 1973-75; rsch. engr. EG&G Idaho, Inc., Idaho Falls, 1975-79, sr. program specialist, 1979-84; program mgr. indsl. heat pumps U.S. Dept. Energy, Washington, 1984-87, program mgr. advanced heat exchangers, 1984-94, program mgr. continuous fiber ceramic composites, 1990-95; team leader steel industry R&D U.S. Dept. Energy, 1995—; lectr. profl. extension U. Wis., Madison, 1982-83. Author: (reference text) ASM, Engineered Materials, 1992, Ceramics Information Analysis Center/American Ceramic Society Handbook on Continuous Fiber Reinforced Ceramic Matrix Composites, 1993; editor (conf. procs.) Industrial Heat Exchangers, 1985; inventor, patentee corrosive resistant heat exchanger. Vol. Martha's Table, Washington, 1986—; v.p. Aid Assn for Lutherans, Br. 2792, Annandale, Va., 1988-92. Mem. Precision Aerobatics Model Pilots Assn., No. Va. Control-line Assn. (pres. 1987-89, 91-92), Mont. State Soc. Mont. State U. Alumni Assn. (life). Office: US Dept Energy 1000 Independence Ave SW Washington DC 20585-0001

RICHMAN, MICHAEL B., meteorologist; b. Manhasset, N.Y., May 27, 1954; m. Carol Jean Bistline; 2 children. BA in Geography, SUNY, Plattsburgh, 1976; MS, U. Ill., 1980, PhD in Atmospheric Scis., 1994. Lab. instr. synoptic meteorology SUNY, Plattsburgh, 1975-76; teaching asst. dept. geography U. Ill., Urbana, 1977; grad. rsch. asst. atmospheric scis. sects. Ill. State Water Survey, 1978-79, asst. profl. scientist, 1979-85, assoc. profl. scientist, 1985-86, profl. scientist, 1986-91; rsch. assoc. Cooperative Inst. Mesoscale Meteorol. Studies U. Okla., 1991—, asst. prof., 1994—; chair climate data sets/remotely sensed data 17th Ann. Climate Diagnostics Conf., 1992; organizer, chair joint session on cluster analysis 5th Internat. Meeting Statis. Climatology, 1992; chair sessions on statis. problems in remote sensing of clouds and rainfall and session on theoretical and exptl. stats. 13th Conf. on Probability and Stats. in the Atmospheric Scis., 1996. Assoc. editor: Jour. of Climate, 1989-95; contbr. articles and revs. to profl. jours. Grantee U.S. EPA, 1989-94, NSF, 1991-94, Air Resources Lab., 1993-94, Pitts. Supercomputer Ctr., 1993-94, CRAY Rsch. Inc., 1992-93, Nat. Ctr. for Supercomputing Applications, 1992-93, 90-91, NOAA, 1988-90; Regents scholar, 1972-76. Mem. Am. Meteorol. Soc. (com. on probability and stats. 1983-86, 89-92, 96—, Editors award 1985), Am. Statis. Assn. (engring. and phys. scis. splty. group), Sigma Xi. Office: U Okla Sch Meteorology 100 E Boyd St Norman OK 73019-1000

RICHMOND, ANGIE ANNA ALICE MURRAY, administrative assistant; b. Thibodaux, La., July 6, 1949; d. Edward Justin Paul and Anna Angelina (Himmler) Hebert; m. Daniel William Richmond Jr., July 24, 1993; children: Thomas Joseph Murray, Anthony Michael Murray, Daniel William Richmond III. Speedwriting Cert., Sawyer Secretarial Sch., 1974. Mem. customer svc. staff European Exch. System, Ramstein, Fed. Republic Germany, 1967-68; buyer, expeditor Thurow Electronics, Tampa, Fla., 1968-70; quotation clk. Thomas & Betts Co., Elizabeth, N.J., 1970-75; cost acct., girl Friday Fulton Shirt Co., Elizabeth, 1975-76; office sec. Rapides Parish Police Jury, Alexandria, La., 1977-81, parish sec., 1981—; sec. Rapides Parish Stormwater Mgmt. and Drainage Dist., Alexandria, 1983—. Recipient Journalism award Noncommd. Officers Wives Club, 1967. Mem. Am. Soc. Notaries, Sec.-Treas. Orgn. La. (immediate past pres.), VFW Aux. Democrat. Roman Catholic. Home: PO Box 187 Elmer LA 71424-0187 Office: Rapides Parish Police Jury PO Box 1150 Alexandria LA 71309-1150

RICHMOND, DOUGLAS WERTZ, history educator; b. Walla Walla, Wash., Feb. 21, 1946; s. Henry and Margaret (Wertz) R.; m. Belinda Obdulia Gonzalez, Dec. 29, 1979; 1 child, Soraya. BA, U. Wash., 1968, MA, 1971, PhD, 1976. Asst. prof. U. Tex., Arlington, 1976-82, assoc. prof. history, 1982-92; prof. of history, 1992—. Author: Carlos Pellegrini and the Crisis of the Argentine Elites, 1880-1916, 1989, Venustiano Carranza's Nationalist Struggle, 1893-1920, 1983, others; editor: Essays on the Mexican Revolution, 1979, Essays on the Mexican War, 1986, La Lucha Nacionalista de Venustiano Carranza, 1893-1920, 1986. Mem. S.W. Coun. on Latin Am. Studies. Home: 5608 Atlantis Ter Arlington TX 76016-2137 Office: Univ of Tex Dept History Box 19529 Arlington TX 76019-0529

RICHMOND, PATRICIA NORTHRUP, elementary art educator; b. Rochester, N.y., May 18, 1950; d. Richard and Louise Northrup; m. John Richmond, Mar. 1989. BA, Alma Coll., St. Thomas, Ont., Can., 1968; MEd, Loyola U., Chgo., 1973; postgrad., Coll. William and Mary, 1974, U. Ctrl. Fla., 1990. Cert. tchr. art K-12. Media-action tchr. Henry Lomb Sch., Rochester, N.Y., 1973-75; art tchr. Berkeley Elem. Sch., Williamsburg, Va., 1975-78; dir. children's programs Project on Domestic Violence Salvation Army Emergency Lodge, Chgo., 1978-79; play facilitator Chiswick Family Rescue, London, 1980-81; tchr. Northwestern Meml. Hosp., Chgo., 1982-83; arts adminstr. Focus Inc., Detroit, 1983-86; art tchr. Detroit Pub. Schs., 1986-89, Volusia County Schs., Deland, Fla., 1989—; GED tchr. Met. Correctional Ctr., Chgo., 1978-79; cons., play facilitator Dublin (Ireland) Women's Aid, 1981, Belgium Fedn. Women's Refuges, Leuven, Hasselt, Michelen, 1981; substitute tchr. Chgo. Bd. Edn., 1982-83; workshop tchr., cons. Levine Inst., Detroit; art educator drop out prevention program RESS Discovery Summer Program, Crooms Sch. of Choice, Sanford, Fla., 1992; adj. instr. U. Ctrl. Fla. Daytona Beach campus, Orlando, summers 1994, 95; mem. Ctr. Creative Studies, Detroit, 1987-89. Exhibited in group shows at Pewabic Pottery Student/Faculty Show, summer 1987, Detroit Art Tchrs. Assn. Mich. Gallery, 1988; curator art exhbn. U. Ctrl. Fla. Art for Elem. Edn. Majors Exhbn., 1994. Host family Friendship Force Greater Daytona Beach, Friendship Force New Smyrna Beach, Fla., 1993—, Am. Field Svc., Daytona Beach, 1994-95. Recipient grant Children's Program for Victims of Domestic Violence, McCormick Corp., Chgo., 1978, 79, Arts in Edn. grant Mich. Arts Coun., Detroit, 1984, 85, 86, Golden Apple award Palm Ter. Elem. Sch., Daytona Beach, 1994. Mem. Nat. Art Edn. Assn., Arts for a Complete Edn., Fla. Art Tchrs. Assn., Volusia Art Educator's Assn., Detroit Puppetry Guild (pres. 1987-89), Detroit Art Tchrs. Assn. (bd. mem. 1985-89), Fla. Craftsman Coun., Fla. Art Edn. Assn., Puppeteers of Am. Home: 4043 S Waterbridge Cir Port Orange FL 32119-9616 Office: Palm Ter Elem Sch Art Dept 1825 Dunn Ave Daytona Beach FL 32114-1250

RICHMOND, ROBERT PAUL, chemical engineer, retired; b. Washington, Dec. 25, 1922; s. Paul and Helen Roberta (Moore) R.; m. Marian Alice Kraynak, Sept. 6, 1947; children: Barbara, Nancy. BSChE, MIT, 1943; JD, U. Balt., 1954. Registered profl. engr., La. Chem. engr. Exxon Co., Balt., 1943-58, Baton Rouge, 1958-88; ret., 1988; mfg. mgr. Lube India Ltd., Bombay, 1968-69; supt. lubes process Esso Singapore Ltd., 1973-75. With USN, 1944-46. Mem. SAR (Baton Rouge chpt. pres., La. state treas., Patriot 1995). Democrat. Lutheran. Home: 5242 N Woodmere Fairway Scottsdale AZ 85020-6456

RICHMOND, ROBERT SOUTHWICK, pathologist; b. Honolulu, May 3, 1939; s. Albert Marion and Alice Evelyn (Southwick) R.; m. Marjorie Price Barton, June 24, 1960 (div. Oct. 1976); children: Sarah Price Richmond Beach, Katherine Barton Richmond; m. Ileana Jacoubovitch Grams, Sept. 7, 1980 (div. 1990); 1 child, Miranda Susan Alice; m. Kathleen Hall Mavournin, Nov. 21, 1993. BA, Harvard U., 1959; MD, Washington U., St. Louis, 1964. Diplomate and anat. and clin. pathology, blood banking and transfusion medicine Am. Bd. Pathology. Intern in pathology Johns Hopkins Hosp., Balt., 1964-65, resident in anatomic pathology, 1965, 1968-70; resident in anatomic pathology Cornell Med. Ctr.-N.Y. Hosp., 1968; resident in lab. medicine-clin. pathology Johns Hopkins Hosp., 1970-72; pathologist Nix Hosp., San Antonio, 1972-73, 76-78; med. dir. Red Cross Regional Blood Ctr., Balt., 1973-76; assoc. prof. pathology James H. Quillen Sch. Medicine, East Tenn. State U., Johnson City, 1976—; locum tenens practitioner pathology, 1981—. Served to capt. U.S. Army, 1966-67. Fellow Coll. Am. Pathologists, Am. Soc. Clin. Pathologists; mem. AMA, Am. Soc. for Microbiology. Democrat. Episcopalian. Address: 344 Seven Oaks Dr Knoxville TN 37922-3411

RICHTARIK, MARILYNN JOSEPHINE, English language educator; b. Madison, Wis., Oct. 11, 1965; d. Alfred Andrew and Marilynn Ruth R. AB, Harvard U., 1988; MPhil, Oxford U., 1990, DPhil, 1992. Part-time instr. No. Ariz. U., 1992-93; postdoctoral rsch. fellow U. British Columbia, 1993-95; asst. prof. Ga. State U., 1995—. Author: Acting Between the Lines: The Field Day Theatre Company and Irish Cultural Politics, 1980-84, 1995. Killam fellow Killam Trust, Can., 1993; Rhodes scholar Rhodes Trust, Oxford, 1988, Green Rsch. scholar, Green Coll., Vancouver, Can., 1994. Mem. MLA, Am. Conf. for Irish Studies, Can. Assn. for Irish Studies, Internat. Assn. for the Study of Irish Lit. Democrat. Office: Ga State U Dept English University Plaza Atlanta GA 30303-3083

RICHTER, CAROL DEAN, sales representative; b. Cummings, Ga., May 14, 1940; d. William Ralph and Mildred Mae (Heard) Bottoms; m. Cary James Simmons, July 5, 1959 (div.); children: Joel Perry, Carlton Wesley, Rebecca Lynn; m. Robert Warren Richter Sr., July, 1970 (div.); 1 child, Robert Warren Jr. Student, Unity Sch. of Christianity, Unity Village, Mo., 1974—; AS in Mental Sci., First Ch. of Religious Sci., 1979; degree in Aesthesiology, Derma-Clinic, 1990, The Heal Ctr., Atlanta, 1990. Cert. aesthesiology. Transcriptionist Med. Coll. Hosp., Charleston, S.C., 1960-64, St. Joseph's Infirmary, Atlanta, 1965-70; med. sec. Coal Mountain Clinic, Cummings, 1971-74; transcriptionist Northside Hosp., Atlanta, 1974-89, Gwinnett Med. Ctr., Lawrenceville, Ga., 1989-93; cert. image cons., 1986-90; esthetician Classy You Salon, Duluth, Ga., 1991-92, You-Nique Salon, Buford, Ga., 1990-92; distbr. Amway Distbrs. Assn., Ada, Mich., 1970—; owner, pres. Richter Rallies, Lawrenceville, 1970—. Mem. North Ga. Mountain Planning and Devel. Commn., Gainesville, 1970-74; bd. dirs. Breakthru House, Decatur, Ga., 1975-81. Mem. Internat. Platform Assn.

RICHTER, LAWRENCE MCCORD, municipal government official; b. Thomasville, Ga., Feb. 27, 1954; s. John Agustus Richter and Helen (McCord) Mellon; m. Charlotte Maxwell, Aug. 24, 1979; children: Wanda, David. Student, Seminole C.C., Sanford, Fla., 1972-73. Engring. technician City of Altamonte Springs, Fla., 1975—; mem. Transp. Tech. Commn., Orlando, Fla., 1988—. Mem. Am. Pub. Works Assn., Inst. Transp. Engrs. (Fla. sect.). Democrat. Baptist. Office: City of Altamonte Springs 225 Newburyport Ave Altamonte Springs FL 32701-3642

RICHTER, WILLIAM, JR., technical management consulting executive; b. Bklyn., Aug. 20, 1934; s. William and Emma (Zehender) R.; m. Eleanor E. Wharton, Nov. 1956; children: Mike S., John E., Kathryn L. AAS, N.Y. C.C., 1956; BSEE, NYU, 1957; MBA, U. Ala., 1970. Program mgr., group engr. Walleye, GPS, Mil Systems, Titan, Gemini Martin Marietta, Denver, 1960-67; program mgr. Skylab Martin Marietta, Huntsville, Ala., 1967-75; from dir. mil. space systems, program dir. space station, mgr. system integration .MX to program mgr. Manned Manuvering Unit Martin Marietta, Denver, 1975-89; mgr. program devel., space and launch sys. SCI Sys. Inc., Huntsville, 1989-96; pres. Guest Assocs. Inc., 1996—; assoc. prof. Met. State U., Denver, 1964-67. Mem. sch. bd. Cherry Creek, Colo., 1976. Recipient Collier trophy, 1982, Group Achievement award NASA, 1987, Pub. Svc. Group Achievement medal NASA, 1988. Mem. AIAA (sr.), Am. Soc. Quality Control (pres. 1963-65), Am. Def. Preparedness Assn., Armed Forces Comms. and Electronics Assn. Home: 1715 Drake Ave SE Huntsville AL 35802-1042 Office: PO Box 1000 Mail Stop 206 8600 S Meml Pkwy Huntsville AL 35807

RICHTON, SAMUEL M., physician; b. Pittsfield, Mass., Aug. 17, 1948; m. Marsha Lee Richton, May 25, 1975; children: Jonathan, Joshua, Jeanette, Simcha, Jesse. BS, U. Mass., 1970; MS, Yale U., 1972; MD, Yeshiva U., 1975. Diplomate Am. Bd. Pediatrics, Nat. Bd. Med. Examiners. Resident in pediatrics Rainbow Babies and Childrens Hosp., Cleve., 1975-77; fellow in pediatrics U. Md., Balt., 1977-78, Harvard Med. Sch., Boston, 1978-80; fellow in medicine Children's Hosp., Boston, 1978-80; physician Diabetes Med. Group, L.A., 1980-81; asst. prof. U. Ill. Coll. of Medicine, Chgo., 1981-84, Chgo. Med. Sch., 1984-87; dir. endocrinology Cook County Children's Hosp., Chgo., 1984-87, Miami Children's Hosp., 1987—; med. dir. South Fla. Diabetes Camp, Miami, 1987—. Fellow Am. Acad. Pediatrics; mem. Am. Diabetes Assn., Internat. Diabetes Fedn., Am. Fedn. for Clin. Rsch., Lawson Wilkens Pediat. Endocrine Soc. Office: Miami Childrens Hosp 3100 SW 62nd Ave # 122 Miami FL 33155-3009

RICKARD, RUTH DAVID, retired history and political science educator; b. Fed. Republic Germany, Feb. 20, 1926; came to U.S., 1940; d. Carl and Alice (Koch) David; m. Robert M. Yaffe, Oct. 1949 (dec. 1959); children: David, Steven; m. Norman G. Rickard, June 1968 (dec. 1988); 1 stepson, Douglas. BS cum laude, Northwestern U., 1947, MA, 1948. Law editor Commerce Clearing House, Chgo., 1948; instr. history U. Ill., Chgo., 1949-51; instr. extension program U. Ill., Waukegan, 1960-67; instr. history Waukegan Schs., 1960-69; original faculty, prof. western civilization, polit. sci. Coll. of Lake County, Grayslake, Ill., 1969-92; mem. Inter-Univ. Seminar on Armed Forces and Soc.; mem. Hospitality Info. Svc. for Diplomatic Residents and Families affiliate Meridian Internat. Ctr. Author: History of College of Lake County, 1987 (honored by city of Waukegan 1987), (poem) I Lost My Wings, 1989, Au Revoir from Emeritusdom, 1993, Where are the Safety Zones, 1994; spkr. on various ind. radio and TV programs; contbr. articles to profl. jours. Mem. Econ. Devel. Com., Waukegan, 1992-93. Scholar Freedoms Found. Am. Legion, Valley Forge, Pa., 1967. Mem. AAUW (pres. Waukegan chpt. 1955-57, scholarship named for her 1985), LWV (charter, v.p. Waukegan chpt.), Nat. Press Club D.C. (co-writer/editor NPC History), Phi Beta Kappa.

RICKS, JOHN PAUL, management consultant; b. Greenwood, Miss., Mar. 1, 1955; s. James Vernon and Myrdice Mae (Bailey) R. AA, Miss. Delta Jr. Coll., 1975; BSBA, Delta State U., 1978. Ptnr. Rick's Motor Svc., Greenwood, Miss., 1960-81; v.p. MMR Enterprises, Ltd., Greenwood, 1981-83; pres. Creative Concepts, Greenwood, 1983—; mktg. cons. MMR Enterprises Ltd., Greenwood, 1985-88. Sustaining mem. Rep. Nat. Com., Washington, 1975-83. With Miss. N.G., 1990—. Mem. Am. Mktg. Assn., Beta Alpha Scholars Soc., Phi Theta Kappa, Delta Mu Delta, Phi Kappa Phi. Republican. Baptist. Home and Office: Creative Concepts PO Box 44 Greenwood MS 38935-0044

RICO, DAVID M., physician, researcher; b. Brownwood, Tex., June 6, 1951; s. Ignacio W. and Betty (Luna-Sanchez) R. BS, Okla. City U., 1981; DO, Okla. State U., 1986. Family practice intern La. State U., Shreveport/Monroe, 1986-87; family practice resident U. Ark. for Med. Scis., Little Rock, 1988-90; rsch. assoc. Dept. of Endocrinology VA Hosp., Little Rock, 1987-91; lt., commd. med. officer USPHS, 1987-90; with U. Ark. for Med. Scis., Little Rock, 1987-90; faculty devel., rsch. fellow Health Scis. Ctr. U. Ariz., Tucson, 1992-93; W.K. Kellogg-NACHC fellow in cmty. health W.K. Kellogg Nat. Assn. Cmty. Health Ctrs., 1992-94; chief med. officer USPHS Indian Health Svc., Okmulgee, Okla., 1994—; rsch. cons. U.S. Naval Rsch. Inst., Bethesda, Md., 1989. Contbr. numerous articles to profl. jours. Spokesperson/advocate Am. Indian Inst., Okla. City/Norman, 1989, Wellness & Native Men Conf., Albuquerque, 1993. Nat. Med. Fellowship Found. scholar Okla. State U., 1982-84. Mem. Am. Acad. Family Physicians, So. Med. Assn., Tri Beta. Office: Chief Med Officer USPHSIHS-Tribal Health Sys PO Box 126 Okmulgee OK 74447-0126

RICORDI, CAMILLO, surgeon, transplant and diabetes researcher; b. N.Y.C., Apr. 1, 1957; m. Valerie A. Grace, Aug. 8, 1986; children: M. Caterina, Eliana G., Carlo A. MD, U. Milan (Italy) Sch. Medicine, 1982. Trainee in gen. surgery San Raffaele Inst., Milan, 1982-85; NIH trainee Washington U. Sch. Medicine, St. Louis, 1985-88; attending surgeon San Raffaele Inst., Milan, 1988-89; asst. prof. to assoc. prof. surgery U. Pitts., Pa., 1989-93; prof. surgery, chief divsn. cellular transplantation U. Miami, Fla., 1993—, scientific dir. and chief acad. officer, 1996—; reviewer of applications for grants Can. and Am. Diabetes Assns., Juvenile Diabetes Found., NIH; chmn. First and Third Internat. Congresses of Cell Transplant Soc., Pitts., 1992, Miami, 1996, 5th Internat. Congress on Pancreas and Islet Transplantation, Miami, 1995, others; mem. editl. bd. Transplantation, Transplantation Sci., Cell Transplantation, Transplantation Procs., Jour. Tissue Engring. Editor: Pancreatic Islet Cell Transplantation, 1992, Methods in Cell Transplantation, 1995; contbr. over 200 chpts. to books and articles to jours. including Immunology Today, Jour. Clin. Investigation, New England Jour. Medicine, Hepatology, Diabetes, Transplantation, Endocrinology, Procs. NAS, USA, Am. Jour. Physiology, Surgery, Nature, Lancet, many others. Recipient Juvenile Diabetes Found. Internat. Rsch. Grant award, 1988—, NIH trainee award, 1986-88; grantee NIH, 1993—. Mem. AAAS, Cell Transplant Soc. (founder, pres. 1992-94), Am. Soc. Transplant Surgeons, Internat. Pancreas and Islet Transplant Assn. (cofounder), The Transplantation Soc., Am. Diabetes Assn. (Rsch. award 1996), Am. Fedn. Clin. Rsch., Diabetes Rsch. Internat. Network (founder, chmn. 1994—), Nat. Diabetes Coalition (co-founder 1994—). Home: 72 S Hibiscus Dr Hisbiscus Island Miami Beach FL 33139 Office: U Miami Diabetes Rsch Inst 1450 NW 10th Ave Miami FL 33136-1011

RIDDER, PAUL ANTHONY, newspaper executive; b. Duluth, Minn., Sept. 22, 1940; s. Bernard H. and Jane (Delano) R.; m. Constance Louise Meach, Nov. 6, 1960; children: Katherine Lee Pennoyer, Linda Jane, Susan Delano Cobb, Paul Anthony, Jr. B.A. in Econs., U. Mich., 1962. With Aberdeen (S.D.) Am. News, 1962-63; With Pasadena (Calif.) Star News, 1963-64; with San Jose (Calif.) Mercury News, 1964-86, bus. mgr., 1968-75, gen. mgr., 1975-77, pub., 1977-86, pres., 1979-86; pres. Knight-Ridder Newspaper Div., Miami, Fla., 1986—; pres. Knight-Ridder, Inc., Miami, 1989—, also bd. dirs.; bd. dirs. Seattle Times, Knight-Ridder, Inc., Newspaper First. Bd. dirs. United Way; mem. adv. bd. Ctr. for Econ. Policy Devel. Stanford U., U. Mich.; mem. pres.' adv. bd. U. Mich. Named Calif. Pub. of Yr., 1983, Newspaper Exec. of Yr., Ad Week, 1991. Mem. Fla. C. of C. (bd. dirs., coun. of 100), Cypress Point Club, Indian Creek Club, Pine Valley Golf Club. *

RIDDICK, DOUGLAS SMITH, horticultural industrialist, industrial designer; b. High Point, N.C., Sept. 28, 1942; s. Delmar Smith and Irene Douglas (Sparks) R.; m. Marcia Ann, Feb. 24, 1968; children: Eric Smith, Adrea Anne. Student, Columbus (Ohio) Coll. Art and Design, 1961-65, U. Bridgeport, 1965-66; BFA, U. Del., 1978. Indsl. designer Harper Landell & Assocs., Phila., 1967-70, ILC Industries, Dover, Del., 1970-75, Leeds Travelwear, Clayton, Del., 1975-76, DuPont Co., Glasgow, Del., 1976-79, Consumer Electronics Div. RCA, Indpls., 1979-80; designer Brayton Internat. Coll., High Point, N.C., 1981; owner Riddick Landscape Nursery, Archdale, N.C., 1980—; greenhouses and nursery mgr. Riddick Garden Ctr. and Landscaping, Inc., Archdale, N.C., 1980—. Patentee; designer indsl. instruments in field. Mem. Dover Bicentennial Com., 1975-76, Gov. DuPont's Com. Promotion of Solar Energy and subcom. Consumer Protection, 1978-79. Recipient Best in Packaging award Print Casebooks III, Washington. 1977, Excellence in Advt. award Am. Assn. Nurserymen, 1981. Mem. AAAS, Am. Horticultural Soc., Nat. Space Soc., Planetary Soc. Baptist. Club: Bicycle Club Del. (coordinator 1974-78, pres. 1979). Home and Office: 7125 Turnpike Rd Archdale NC 27263-7726

RIDDLE, CHARLES ADDISON, III, state legislator, lawyer; b. Marksville, La., June 8, 1955; s. Charles Addison Jr. and Alma Rita (Gremillion) R.; m. Margaret Susan Noone, Mar. 24, 1978; children: Charles Addison IV, John H., Michael J. BA, La. State U., 1976, JD, 1980. Bar: La. 1980, U.S. Dist. Ct. (mid. and we. dists.) La. 1983, U.S. Ct. Appeals (5th cir.) 1988, U.S. Supreme Ct. 1991, U.S. Ct. Vets. Appeals 1994. Assoc. Riddle & Bennett, Marksville, 1980; pvt. practice Marksville, 1981—; mem. La. Ho. of Reps., Baton Rouge, 1992—; reelected La. House of Reps., Baton Rouge, 1995-. Elected La. State Dem. Cen. com., Avoyelles Parish, 1983-87, Parish Exec. Demo. Com. 1987-91. Mem. Avoyelles Bar Assn. (pres. 1987-88), Bunkie Rotary (bd. dirs.), Marksville Lions, Marksville C. of C. (pres. 1988-92). Office: 208 E Mark St Marksville LA 71351-2416

RIDDLE, CHARLES DANIEL (DAN RIDDLE), biomedical educator; b. Spartanburg, S.C., Jan. 21, 1945; s. Robert Charles and Nell Grace (Eubanks) R.; 1 child, Ashley Mya. BS in Biology, Clemson U., 1967, MS in Zoology, 1969. Dir. audiovisual lab. Spartanburg Meth. Coll., 1969; tchr. Prevocat. Jr. High Sch., Spartanburg, 1970-71; biomed. instr. Greenville (S.C.) Tech. Coll., 1971—. Mem. Greenville County Coun., 1977-78; pres. Edwards Forest Recreation Assn., Taylors, 1988. 2d lt. U.S. Army, 1969-70. Recipient resolution for svc. Greenville County Coun., 1979. Mem. S.C. Soc. Radiologic Technologists, S.C. Tchrs. Assn., Human Anatomy and Physiology Soc. Baptist. Office: Greenville Tech Coll Pleasantburg Dr Greenville SC 29607-2510 Address: 2005 Gap Creek Rd Greer SC 29651-7878

RIDEOUT, JANET LITSTER, chemist; b. Bennington, Vt., Jan. 6, 1939; d. John Ramage and Elizabeth Dinwiddie (Dewey) Litster; m. Ralph L. Rideout Jr., Mar. 3, 1973. AB, Mt. Holyoke Coll., 1961, MA, 1963; PhD, SUNY, Buffalo, 1968. Rsch. chemist exptl. therapy dept. Burroughs Wellcome Co., 1968-70, sr. rsch. chemist exptl. therapy dept., 1970-79, group leader exptl. therapy dept., 1979-83, group leader organic chemistry dept., 1983-88, asst. div. dir. organic chemistry div., 1988-91; assoc. divsn. dir. organic chemistry divsn. Burroughs Wellcome Co., Triangle Park, N.C., 1991-94; dir. chem. dept. Inspire Pharms., Inc., Durham, N.C., 1995-96, sr. dir. discovery, 1996—; bd. dirs. Burroughs Wellcome Employee Credit Union, 1981-90, pres., 1983-85, treas., 1985-87, sec., 1987-89. Editor: Nucleosides, Nucleotides and Their Biological Applications, 1983; patentee in field. Allied Chem. fellow, 1966-67; Skinner Found. fellow, 1962; Dupont study grantee, 1961; recipient Disting. Chemist award N.C. Inst. Chemists, 1994. Fellow Am. Inst. Chemists (life, bd. dirs. 1994-96); mem. AAAS, Am. Chem. Soc., N.Y. Acad. Scis.

RIDER, JOHN ALLEN, II, business educator, paralegal; b. Gage, Okla., Mar. 11, 1928; s. George Henry Rider and Laurenna Agnes Meek; m. Audrey Claudine Baker, July 16, 1961; children: Micheile Renee Rider Brown, John Allen III. BS, Northwestern Okla. State U., 1952; MA, U. Wyoming, 1956; EdD, U. Nebr., 1966; postgrad., U. Ky. Cert. profl. tchr., Tenn., Iowa. Court reporter, stenographer USN, 1946-48; dep. ct. clk., ct. reporter Ellis County, Okla., 1948-49; tchr. bus. Rozel (Kans.) Rural High Sch., 1952-53, Norwich (Kans.) High Sch., 1953-54, Bluff City (Kans.) High Sch., 1954-56; instr. Black Hills State Coll., Spearfish, S.D., 1956-58; tchr. bus. Balboa (C.Z.) High Sch., 1958-60; instr. Northwestern Coll., Orange City, Iowa, 1958-60, chair divsn. edn., 1962-64; asst. prof. Northwestern State Coll., Alva, Okla., 1962-63; teaching asst. U. Nebr., Lincoln, 1963-64; head bus. edn. program, assoc. prof. U. N.Mex., Albuquerque, 1966-70; prof. West Tex. State U., Canyon, 1970-74; chair prof. occupational edn. divsn. Coffeyville (Kans.) Community Jr., 1974-75; assoc. prof. East Tenn. State U., Johnson City, 1975-94, coord. bus. edn. program, 1985-94; ret., 1994; cons. various bus.; pres. bd. dirs. Enid Literacy Coun., 1996—, also tutor. Active Johnson City Literacy Coun., v.p./tutor trainer, 1978-80; active Enid Literacy Coun., bd. mem. 1996—; relief worker, registrar Mid-Am. yearly meeting Friends Ch., Wichita, 1981; cons. yearly meeting N.C. Soc. Friends, 1987. Recipient Meritorious award West Tex. Bus. Tchr., 1970-74, Outstanding Edn. Grad. award Northwestern Okla. State U. Alumni Assn., 1995; named Tchr. of Yr., Dist. 16 Tex. Bus. Edn. Assn., 1973. Mem. NEA (life), Am. Vocat. Assn. (life), Nat. Bus Edn., Nat. Assn. Tchr. Edn. (life, bus. and office edn.), Tex. State Edn. Assn., Tenn. Bus. Edn. Assn. (treas., pres.-elect, pres., past pres., Educator of Yr. 1986), So. Bus. Edn., Kiwanis (Johnson City exec. bd. 1975-80, 92), Am. Legion (King's Mt. post), SAR (former sec., pres. Panhandle-Plains chpt., Tex. soc.), Holt County (Mo.) Hist. Soc. (charter, life). Republican. Home: 3002 N Grant St Enid OK 73702-1619

RIDER, RICHARD WALTER, career officer; b. Alexandria, Va., Jan. 25, 1945; s. Paul Loren and Ruth Helen (Buchholz) R.; m. Flora Barker, Sept. 14, 1974; 1 child, Richard-Paul Roy. BS, Coll. Environ. Sci. and Forestry, 1966, MS, 1969. Commd. 2d lt. USAF, 1968, advanced through grades to col., 1978; v.p. Paul Rider Warehouse, Ballston, N.Y., 1979-90; warehouse mgr. Lubricant Packaging and Supply, Albany, N.Y., 1990-93; res. disaster preparedness officer USAFR, Glens Falls, N.Y., 1980-85, squadron comdr. 933d Civil Engr. Squadron, Griffiss AFB, N.Y., 1985-93, chief readiness divsn. Directoriate of Civil Engr. HQ Air Force Res., Robins AFB, Ga., 1993—. Councilman Town of Ballston, 1981-93, dep. supervisor, 1988-93; bd. dirs. Christmas in April, Macon, Ga., 1995—. Decorated Bronze Star. Mem. Air Force Assn., Res. Officers Assn., VFW, Nat. Rifle Assn. Republican. Lutheran. Home: 100 Twin Oaks Ct Warner Robins GA 31088-7722

RIDER, ROGER ALAN, lawyer; b. Sweickley, Pa., May 28, 1945; s. Joseph W. and Evelyn M. (Kuntzman) R.; m. Nancy Lucille Huston, May 8, 1982; children: Matthew Huston, Zachary Alan Huston. BS in Psychology, U. Houston, 1971, JD magna cum laude, 1974. Bar: Tex. 1974. Assoc. Butler, Binion, Rice, Cook & Knapp, Houston, 1974-80, ptnr., 1980-82; founding ptnr. Mayor Day & Caldwell, Houston, 1982-90; founder Rider & Assocs., Houston, 1990-96; ptnr. Doyle, Rider, Restrepo, Harvin & Robbins, 1996—; sec., treas., v.p., pres.-elect, pres. Houston Young Lawyers Assn., 1976-81; speaker, instr. U. Houston Law Ctr., 1991, 92; faculty Tex. Legal Svcs. Ctr., 1993. Editor Houston Law Review, 1974. Mem. steering com. numerous judicial election campaigns, Houston, 1991—; mgr., coach youth sports YMCA, Houston, 1987-93; mgr. youth sports United Ch. Athletic League, Houston, 1993—; mgr., coach youth baseball West Univ. Little League, Houston, 1990—. Cpl. USMC, 1966-68, Vietnam. Fellow Houston Bar Found. (life), Tex. Bar Found. (life); mem. ABA (torts and ins. practice sect. 1985-94), Tex. Bar Assn. (Cert. of Merit 1986), Houston Bar Assn. (sec. 1987-89, dir. 1981-85, 90, Pres.'s award 1980, 90, 91), Inns of Ct. (chmn. bd. dirs. 1990-92), Order of Barons (pres. 1974). Home: 2064 Timber Ln Houston TX 77027-4118 Office: Rider and Assocs 600 Travis St Ste 1500 Houston TX 77002-2911

RIDGILL, MARC WAYNE, protective services official; b. Greensboro, N.C., June 26, 1959; s. Wayne Oren and Betty Jean (Welborn) R.; m. STephanie Gail Wainscott, May 26, 1990; 1 child, Seth. BAS in Justice and Policy Studies, Guilford Coll., Greensboro, 1994. Cert. advanced law enforcement, N.C. Justice Acad. Police officer Greensboro Police Dept., 1985—. Inventor (bd. game) Throttle, 1995. Mem. Greensboro Police Club (bd. dirs.). Office: Greensboro Police Dept 300 W Washington St Greensboro NC 27402

RIDGWAY, HELEN JANE, chemist, consultant; b. Ft. Worth, Aug. 10, 1937; d. Ralph Pope and Virginia Leah (Link) R. AS, Arlington (Tex.) State Coll., 1957; BA, North Tex. State Coll., Denton, 1959; MS, Baylor U., Waco, Tex., 1963, PhD, 1968. Rsch. asst. Wadley Rsch. Inst., Dallas, 1960-68; sr. investigator Wadley Insts. Molecular Medicine, Dallas, 1968-86, chmn. chemistry, 1986-92; R & D hemostasis mgr. Helena Labs., Beaumont, Tex., 1993—; cons. Helena Labs., Beaumont, 1986-92. Contbr. articles to sci. jours. AAUW scholar, 1955, 56. Fellow Internat. Soc. Hematology; mem. Am. Chem. Soc., Am. Heart Assn. (coun. on thrombosis).

RIDGWAY WHITE, LURENE JANE, neonatal nurse; b. Lindsay, Okla., Aug. 31, 1958; d. Jack Elijah and Geneva Clydene (Mariott) Matheson; m. Phillip H. Ridgway, May 11, 1996. AAS, Okla. State U., Oklahoma City, 1989; student, Cen. State U., Edmond, Okla., 1977-82. Cert. neonatal rescusication program instr.; cert. breastfeeding educator. Abstractor of land titles Co-Data, Inc., Oklahoma City, 1984-89; charge nurse Deaconess Hosp., Oklahoma City, 1993-94; resource nurse VHA Health Link, Oklahoma City. Mem. Phi Theta Kappa. Home: 11424 Walters Ave Oklahoma City OK 73162-1315 Office: Ste 675 4013 NW Expressway Oklahoma City OK 73116

RIDLEN, LILLIAN MAY HEIGLE, public relations, sales and marketing executive, writer, inventor; b. New Orleans, Nov. 15, 1946; d. Joseph Manuel and Lillian Mae (Theriot) H.; m. Larry Vinson Ridlen, Dec. 28, 1968; children: Larry V. Jr., Kenneth C., Jennifer C. Degree in Nursing, Orleans Parish Sch. Practical Nursing, 1969. Nurse So. Bapt. Hosp., New Orleans, 1970-72; pres. Sunshine & Co., LaPlace, La., 1983-86, The Gift Gallery, LaPlace, 1984-85; v.p. La. Bartending Inst., Kenner, Baton Rouge and New Orleans, 1986-87; dir. La. Bartending Inst., 1987-89; pub. rels. officer, sales and mktg. dir. Universal Fast Foods of LaPlace, Chalmette and Marrero, 1989—; nurse St. Charles Manor Nursing Ctr., 1989—; owner, pres. Ton-Lil Pub. Co., LaPlace, 1990—, Who Dunit and Co./Hair Salon and Gifts, LaPlace, 1996—; rosary and jewelry designer. Author: A Sampling of Southern Cooking, 1985, A Home Study Course in Bartending, 1989; co-author: Songs of the Wind, 1995; composer, lyricist songs; lyricist Tony's Song for artist Wayne Presley; inventor Santa's Snack Pack; author poetry pub. in anthologies, 1996. Organizer Mothers for Safe Edn. St. John the Bapt. Parish, La., 1984. Poetry selected for inclusion in world record effort by Internat. Soc. of Poets, 1994; recipient Poet Editors Choice Outstanding Achievement in Poetry award Nat. Libr. Poetry Editors, 1995; nominated for Poet of Yr. award Internat. Soc. Poets, 1995, 96. Mem. NAFE, Internat. Soc. Poets. Democrat. Roman Catholic.

RIDLEY, BETTY ANN, educator, church worker; b. St. Louis, Oct. 19, 1926; d. Rupert Alexis and Virginia Regina (Weikel) Steber; m. Fred A. Ridley, Jr., Sept. 8, 1948; children: Linda Drue Ridley Archer, Clay Kent. BA, Scripps Coll., Claremont, Calif., 1948. Christian sci. practitioner, Oklahoma City, 1973—; tchr. Christian sci., 1983—; mem. Christian Sci. Bd. Lectureship, 1980-85. Trustee Daystar Found.; mem. The First Ch. of Christ Scientist, Boston, Fifth Ch. of Christ Scientist, Oklahoma City. Mem. Jr. League Am. Home: 7908 Lakehurst Dr Oklahoma City OK 73120-4324 Office: Suite 100-G 3000 United Founders Blvd Oklahoma City OK 73112

RIDLEY, CLARENCE HAVERTY, lawyer; b. Atlanta, June 3, 1942; s. Frank Morris Jr. and Clare (Haverty) R.; m. Eleanor Horsey, Aug. 22, 1969; children: Augusta Morgan, Clare Haverty. BA, Yale U., 1964; MBA, Harvard U., 1966; JD, U. Va., 1971. Bar: Ga. 1971. Assoc. King & Spalding, Atlanta, 1971-77, ptnr., 1977—; bd. dirs. Haverty Furniture Cos., Inc., mem. exec. com., 1992—, vice chmn. bd. dirs., 1996—. Author: Computer Software Agreements, 1987, 2d edit., 1993; exec. editor Va. Law Rev., 1970-71. Chmn. St. Joseph's Hosp. Found., Atlanta, 1986-89; trustee St. Joseph's Health Svcs., 1987—, chmn. fin. com., 1992-96, vice chmn. bd. trustees, 1996—. Roman Catholic. Home: 2982 Habersham Rd NW Atlanta GA 30305-2854 Office: King & Spalding 191 Peachtree St Atlanta GA 30303

RIDLEY, MARION BERTON, otolaryngologist/facial plastic surgeon, medical educator; b. Whitwell, Tenn., Nov. 14, 1956; s. Billy Joe and Bonnie Lynn (Cagle) R. BA magna cum laude, U. Tenn., Chattanooga, 1978; MD, U. Tenn., Memphis, 1982. Diplomate Am. Bd. Otolaryngology, Am. Bd. Facial Plastic and Reconstructive Surgery. Intern and resident U. Tenn. Hosps., Memphis, 1982-84; resident Johns Hopkins Hosp., Balt., 1984-87, instr., 1987-88; fellow U. Mich., Ann Arbor, 1988-89; asst. prof. surgery U. South Fla., Tampa, 1989-96, assoc. prof., 1996—; asst. chief otolaryngology H.L. Moffitt Cancer Ctr. and Rsch. Inst., Tampa. Author: (chpt.) Facial Plastic and Reconstructive Surgery, 1991, Medical Clinics of North America, 1993, Otolaryngology Head and Neck Surgery, 1994, The Larynx, 1995; contbr. articles to profl. jours. Fellow Am. Acad. Otolaryngology/Head and Neck Surgery, Am. Acad. Facial Plastic and Reconstructive Surgery, Am. Coll. Surgeons, Am. Soc. Head and Neck Surgery, Soc. Head and Neck Surgeons, Am. Bronchoesophagologic Assn.; mem. AMA, Johns Hopkins Med. and Surg. Assn., Fla. Soc. Otolaryngology/Head and Neck Surgery (pres. 1996-97). Democrat. Episcopalian. Office: Univ South Florida 12902 Magnolia Dr Ste 3057 Tampa FL 33612-9416

RIDOLPHI, LUCY ELIZABETH, writer, public relations professional; b. Montgomery, Ala., Mar. 11, 1957; d. Julian Maddox and Lucy Elizabeth (Howard) R. BA, Huntingdon Coll., 1979. Editl. asst. Hatton Brown Publs., Montgomery, 1979-81; prodn. asst. Ala. Pub. T.V., Montgomery, 1983; editl. asst. Ala. Travel and Tourism, Montgomery, 1983-84; pub. rels. dir. Ala. C. of C., Montgomery, 1984-85, Huntingdon Coll., Montgomery, 1985-90; editl. asst. B.A.S.S. Inc., Montgomery, 1991-93; staff writer Montgomery Adviser, 1994-95; freelance writer Montgomery, 1995—. Vol. Sundance Film Festival, Salt Lake City, 1992—. Home: 2256 Rosemont Dr Montgomery AL 36111-1009

RIECK, WILLIAM ALBERT, secondary school educator, professor; b. Hackensack, N.J., Jan. 15, 1942; s. William Emanual and Grace Adeline (Bormann) R.; m. Judith Ann Klindt, Apr. 18, 1965; children: Melissa, William Albert Jr. BA, Jersey City State Coll., 1963; MA, Montclair (N.J.) State Coll., 1966; DEd, Loyola U., Chgo., 1976. Asst. prof. Trenton (N.J.) State Coll., 1966-69; area mgr. Dupont Chem., Chgo., 1969-72; chemistry tchr. Lockport (Ill.) High Sch., 1972-74; asst. prin. Oak Forrest (Ill.) High Sch., 1974-75; prin. Evanston (Ill.) Twp. High Sch., 1975-76, Rock Island (Ill.) High Sch., 1975-77, Fallsburg (N.Y.) High Sch., 1977-80, Hicksville (N.Y.) High Sch., 1980-83, Nottingham High Sch., Trenton, 1982-90; head dept. curriculum and instruction U. Southwestern La., Lafayette, 1991—. Contbr. articles to profl. jours. Mem. Hamilton (N.J.) Say No to Drugs Com., 1987—, Hamilton Citizens for Edn., 1989—; advisor DeMolay chpt., Hamilton Sq., N.J., 1987—; trustee First Presbyn. Ch., Levittown, N.Y.,

1981-84. Recipient Disting. Alumnu award Jersey City State Coll., 1983, Citation, N.J. Gen. Assembly, 1983, Cert. of Appreciation, N.Y. Congress Parents and Tchrs., 1982; NSF grantee, 1968, 1994-95. Mem. Nat. Assn. Secondary Sch. Prins. (Svc. award 1989), N.J. Prins. and Suprs. Assn. (exec. coun. 1985—, Svc. award 1989), Assn. for Supervision and Curriculum Devel., Mercer County Prins. and Suprs. Assn. (sec. 1988—), Masons, Shriners (youth com. chmn. 1975-80). Presbyterian. Home: 108 Shadowbrush Bend Lafayette LA 70506-7852 Office: U Southwestern La Maxim Doucet Hall # 410 PO Box 42051 Lafayette LA 70504-2051

RIEDER, ROLAND CONRAD, foundation administrator; b. L.A., July 25, 1931; s. Cecil Clyde and Cecilia Rosemond (LeMon) R. BA, UCLA, 1953, MA, 1955; PhD, Harvard U., 1958. Cert. coll. tchr., Mich. Instr. Mich. State U., East Lansing, 1955-58; jr. govt. aide China Lake (Calif.) Naval Base, 1958-60; archivist Nat. Archives, Washington, 1960-63; prof. history/math. Brandon Hall Found., Dunwoody, Ga., 1963-77, dean of faculty, 1977-84, dir., 1984-96, dir. emeritus, 1996—. Author: Provisional Government of Cuba, 1963; contbr. articles to profl. jours. Mich. State U. Grad. Coun.. fellow, 1956, Harvard Grad. fellow, 1958. Mem. Assn. Am. Archivists (nat. del. 1963—), Am. Ordnance Assn., Southern Assn., Ga. Assn., Phi Beta Kappa. Home: 1701 Brandon Hall Dr Dunwoody GA 30350-3706 Office: Brandon Hall Foundation 128 Northern Ave #14 Decatur GA 30350

RIEGER, SAM LEE, insurance company executive; b. Durango, Colo., May 14, 1946; s. Lee Roy and Ruth (Harris) R.; student U. Tex., 1964-68; m. Pamela J. Robinson, Apr. 7, 1973. Sales agt. Prudential Ins. Co., Dallas, 1970-72; sales supr. Great Am. Res. Inc. Co., San Antonio, 1972-74, dir. manpower devel., 1974-76, agy. mgr., Austin, Tex., 1974-76, S.W. Agy., San Antonio, 1976-82, v.p. sales, Dallas, 1982-85; regional dir., 1985-91, nat. sales cons., 1991—; pres. DalCity Assocs., Inc., 1986—. Served with U.S. Army, 1969. Recipient Nat. Mgmt. award Gen. Agts. and Mgrs. Conf., 1979, 80, 81, 82, 87. C.L.U. Mem. Nat. Assn. Life Underwriters, Dallas Assn. Life Underwriters, Gen. Agts. and Mgrs. Assn. (bd. dirs.). Republican. Methodist. Home: 6139 Copperhill Dr Dallas TX 75248-4978 Office: 13760 Noel Rd Ste 214 Dallas TX 75240-4329

RIENNE, DOZIE IGNATIUS, structural engineer; b. Awka, Nigeria, July 22, 1954; s. James O. and Joy I. Rienne; m. Charlotte Roberts, Feb. 6, 1982; children: Tonnia, Chovia, Brittany. BS in Engring Tech., Constrn. Mgmt, Okla. State U., 1988; postgrad. in Civil Engring., LaSalle U. Project mgr. DF Young Constrn. Co., Dallas, 1981-84; constrn. mgr. VB Cons. Group, Oklahoma City, 1984-88; programs dir. Riennes Corp., Chickasha, Okla., 1989—. Editor: The Role of the Construction Managers, 1992, The Code Plus Built Homes, 1992. Mem. Am. Plywood Assn. (cert., profl. builder and remodeler). Office: Riennes Constrn Co 1524 S 1st St Chickasha OK 73018-5908

RIERSON, ROBERT LEAK, broadcasting executive, television writer; b. Walnut Cove, N.C., Sept. 5, 1927; s. Sanders C. and Anna (Cox) R.; m. Barbara Eugenia McLeod, Sept. 23, 1950 (dec. Feb. 1988); children: Barbara Elaine, Richard Troy. Student, Duke U., 1945-46, Davidson Coll., 1946-47; BS in Speech cum laude, Northwestern U., 1948. Program dir., program ops. mgr. WBT Radio and WBTV, Charlotte, N.C., 1948-66; program mgr. WJBK-TV, Detroit, 1966-69, WTOP-TV, Washington, 1969-71; dir. broadcasting WCBS-TV, N.Y.C., 1971-73; pres. Rierson Broadcast Consultants, N.Y.C., 1973-75; program exec. Grey Advt., N.Y.C., 1975-77; v.p., dir. programming Dancer-Fitzgerald-Sample, N.Y.C., 1977-80; exec. producer Corinthian Prodns., N.Y.C., 1980-82; dir. news programming CNN TV, Atlanta, 1982—. Producer-creator TV show ABCs of Democracy, 1965; producer, writer TV show George Washington's Mt. Vernon, 1970; creator, writer TV series 24 Days of Christmas, 1978. Bd. dirs. Mich. Coun. Chs., Detroit, 1968-69, ARC, Charlotte, 1960-62; 1st v.p. Charlotte Oratorio Singers, 1960-66. Lt. USNR, 1952-54. Recipient Edn. award Charlotte Jr. Woman's Club, 1961, George Washington Honor medal Freedoms Found., 1970; named Young Man of Yr., 1960. Mem. Nat. Assn. Radio-TV Program Execs. (charter mem., bd. dirs. 1964—), Radio-TV News Dirs. Assn., Order of Long Leaf Pine. Republican. Mem. Moravian Episcopal Ch. Home: 3068 Vinings Ridge Dr NW Atlanta GA 30339-3771 Office: Turner Program Svcs 1 Cnn Ctr NW Atlanta GA 30303-2705

RIES, EDWARD RICHARD, petroleum geologist, consultant; b. Freeman, S.D., Sept. 18, 1918; s. August and Mary F. (Graber) R.; student Freeman Jr. Coll., 1937-39; A.B. magna cum laude, U. S.D., 1941; M.S., U. Okla., 1943, Ph.D. (Warden-Humble fellow), 1951; postgrad. Harvard, 1946-47; m. Amelia D. Capshaw, Jan. 24, 1949 (div. Oct. 16, 1956); children: Rosemary Melinda, Victoria Elise; m. Maria Wipfler, June 12, 1964. Asst. geologist Geol. Survey S.D., White River area, 1941; geophys. interpreter Robert Ray Inc., Western Okla., 1942; jr. geologist Carter Oil Co., Mont., Wyo., 1943-44, geologist Mont., Wyo., Colo., 1944-49; sr. geologist Standard Vacuum Oil Co., Assam, Tripura and Bangladesh, India, 1951-53, sr. regional geologist N.V. Standard Vacuum Petroleum, Maatschappij, Indonesia, 1953-59, geol. adviser for Far East and Africa, White Plains, N.Y., 1959-62; geol. adviser Far East, Africa, Oceania, Mobil Petroleum Co., N.Y.C., N.Y., 1962-65; geol. adviser for Europe, Far East, Mobil Oil Corp., N.Y.C., 1965-71, sr. regional explorationist Far East, Australia, New Zealand, Dallas, 1971-73, Asia-Pacific, Dallas, 1973-76, sr. geol. adviser Rsch. Geology, 1976-79, assoc. geol. advisor Geology-Geophysics, Dallas, 1979-82, sr. geol. cons., 1982-83; ind. internat. petroleum geol. cons. Europe, Africa, Sino-Soviet and S.E. Asia, 1986—. Grad. asst., teaching fellow U. Okla., 1941-43, Harvard, 1946-47. Served with AUS, 1944-46. Mem. AAAS, Am. Assn. Petroleum Geologists (assoc. editor 1978-83, 50 Yr. Mem. Svc. award 1993), Geol. Soc. Am., Am. Geol. Inst., Nat. Wildlife Fedn., Nat. Audubon Soc., N.Y. Acad. Sci., Soc. Exploration Geophysicists, Wilderness Soc., Am. Legion, Phi Beta Kappa, Sigma Xi, Phi Sigma, Sigma Gamma Epsilon. Republican. Mennonite. Club: Harvard (Dallas). Author numerous domestic and internat. proprietary and pub. hydrocarbon generation and reserve evaluations, reports and profl. papers. Home and Office: 6009 Royal Crest Dr Dallas TX 75230-3434

RIESSER, GREGOR HANS, arbitrage investment adviser; b. Riga, Latvia, Apr. 13, 1925; came to U.S., 1948; s. Hans Edward and Gilda (Von Scherf) R.; m. Joanna Gray (dec. Aug. 1991); children: Cindy Laughlin, William Riesser; m. Edith Naparst, Dec. 19, 1992; stepchildren: Nicole Naparst, Harold Naparst. MS in Chemistry, U. Geneva, Switzerland, 1949; PhD, U. Calif., Berkeley, 1952. Rsch. chemist Shell Chem. Co., Houston, 1952-70, catalysis bus. ctr., 1970-73; sr. staff chemist Shell Devel. Co., Houston, 1973-84; spkr. on long-term options, scores and primes, arbitrages, dual funds and the stock market; mem. bd. arbitrators NASD. Featured in Forbes, Houston Post, Houston Chronicle. Mem. Am. Assn. Individual Investors, Houston Computer Investment Assn. (dir. 1990—), Guru award). Unitarian. Home and Office: 2309A Nantucket Dr Houston TX 77057-2956

RIETSCHEL, ROBERT LOUIS, dermatologist; b. New Orleans, Oct. 9, 1946; s. Frederick Arnt and Estelle Marie (Fleckinger) R.; m. Connie Joanne Dent, Sept. 3, 1966; children: Eric, Penny. BA, North Tex. State U., 1968; MD, U. Tex., Galveston, 1972. Diplomate Am. Bd. Dermatology. Med. intern Letterman Army Med. Ctr., San Francisco, 1972-73, dermatology researcher, 1973-74; resident in dermatology Brooke Army Med. Ctr., San Antonio, 1974-77, staff dermatologist, 1977-79; assoc. prof. dermatology Emory U. Sch. Medicine, Atlanta, 1981-85, acting chmn. dept. dermatology, 1984-85; assoc. chmn. dept. dermatology Ochsner Clinic, New Orleans, 1985-88; chmn. dept. dermatology, 1988—. Contbr. articles to profl jours. Cubmaster, Boy Scouts Am., Decatur, Ga., 1983-84. Served to maj. U.S. Army, 1971-79. NIOSH grantee, 1981-84. Fellow Am. Acad. Dermatology, Soc. for Investigative Dermatology; mem. AMA, N.Am. Contact Dermatitis Group (sec. 1985-93), Am. Contact Dermatitis Soc. (sec. 1989-93, pres. 1993-95). Republican. Lutheran. Office: Ochsner Clinic 1514 Jefferson Hwy New Orleans LA 70121-2429

RIFE, LISA JUNE DELANEY, physical education educator; b. Richlands, Va., May 28, 1965; d. Everett and Wanda Sue (Clevinger) D. BS, Radford U., 1989. Cert. tchr. health, phys. edn., K-12, driver's edn., Va. Health, phys. edn. Dickenson County Schs., Haysi, Va., 1990-91; health, phys. edn., driver's edn. tchr. Haysi High Sch., Dickenson County Pub. Schs., 1990—; specialty corps band asst. Haysi H.S., 1990-91, basketball cheerleader coach, 1990-92, B-team basketball coach, 1990-92, coord. Jump Rope for Heart, 1990—, volleyball coach varsity and jr. varsity, 1993—. Team leader Dickenson County 4-H club, 1990—. Mem. Va. Phys. Health Edn., Recreation and Dance, AAPHERD. Home: RR 2 Box 525A Grundy VA 24614-9802 Office: Haysi High Sch Main St Haysi VA 24256

RIFFE, STACY CHRISTINE, secondary school educator; b. Beckley, W.Va., Aug. 16, 1970; d. Clinton Gilbert and Frances Loise (Martin) Forren; m. Vincent Rodger Riffe, Apr. 17, 1993. Student, So. W.Va. C.C., Pineville; BA in Edn., Glenville State Coll., 1993; postgrad., CGS, Charleston, W.Va. Cert. tchr., W.Va. Waitress Pineville (W.Va.) Restaurant, 1988; teller Bank of Oceana, W.Va., 1988-90; substitute tchr. Fayette County Bd. Edn., Fayetteville, W.Va., 1993; teller 1st State Bank and Trust, Rainelle, W.Va., 1993; tchr. math. Jackson County Bd. Edn., Ripley, W.Va., 1993—; presenter Ctr. for Profl. Devel., Charleston, 1993—; tech. specialist Jackson County Bd. Edn., Ripley, 1995—; cheerleading coach Ripley H.S., 1996—. Sponsor Young Christians Club, Ripley, 1993—; pianist West Ripley Bapt. Ch., 1993—; pianist, alto Hill Top Quartet, Ripley, 1995—. Mem. NEA, W.Va. Edn. Assn., Jackson County Tchr. Assn. Home: 229 Simmons Dr Ripley WV 25271 Office: Ripley HS # 2 School St Ripley WV 25271

RIFKIN, NED, museum director; b. Florence, Ala., Nov. 10, 1949; s. Arthur Robert and Ina Blanche (Steinberg) R.; m. Diann Carole Kleinman, Mar. 4, 1976; children: Moses Kleinman, Amos Kleinman. BA, Syracuse U., 1972; MA in Art History, U. Mich., 1973, PhD in Art History, 1976. Asst. prof. dept. art U. Tex., Arlington, 1977-80; curator, asst. dir. New Mus. Contemporary Art, N.Y.C., 1980-84; curator contemporary art Corcoran Gallery Art, Washington, 1984-86; chief curator exhbns. Hirshhorn Mus. and Sculpture Garden, Washington, 1986-90, chief curator, 1990-91; dir. High Mus. Art, Atlanta, 1991—.

RIGBY, KENNETH, lawyer; b. Shreveport, La., Oct. 20, 1925; s. Samuel and Mary Elizabeth (Fearnhead) R.; m. Jacqueline Carol Brandon, June 8, 1951; children: Brenda, Wayne, Glen. BS magna cum laude, La. State U., 1950, JD, 1951. Bar: La. 1951, U.S. Ct. Appeals (5th cir.) 1966, U.S. Supreme Ct. 1971, U.S. Tax Ct. 1981, U.S. Ct. Appeals (11th cir.) 1982. Ptnr. Love, Rigby, Dehan & McDaniel, 1951—; adj. prof. of law LSU Law Ctr., 1990—; mem. Marriage-Persons Com. La. Law Inst., 1981—, mem. council, 1988—. Sec. mandatory continuing legal edn. com. La. Supreme Ct., 1987-95. Served with USAAF, 1943-46. Fellow Am. Acad. Matrimonial Lawyers, Am. Coll. Trial Lawyers; mem. ABA, Shreveport Bar Assn. (pres. 1973-74), La. State Bar Assn. (chmn. com. on continuing legal edn. 1974-75, chmn. family law sect. 1981-82, bd. of govs. 1986-88). Methodist. Contbr. articles to profl. jours. Office: Transcontinental Tower 330 Marshall St Ste 1400 Shreveport LA 71101-3015

RIGDON, DAVID TEDRICK, air force officer, geneticist, director; b. Laurel, Miss., Jan. 27, 1948; s. James T. and Marie T. (Taylor) R.; m. Elizabeth Sue Jones, June 1, 1973; children: Angela Denise, Michael David. BS in Biology, U. Ala., 1970; MD cum laude, U. Miss., 1975. Diplomate Am. Bd. Pediats., Am. Bd. Med. Genetics. Commd. USAF, 1975, advanced through grades to col., 1991; intern in pediats. USAF Med. Ctr., Keesler AFB, Miss., 1975-76, resident in pediats., 1976-78; fellow in med. genetics U. Ala., Birmingham, 1978-80; med. geneticist USAF Med. Genetics Ctr., Keesler AFB, 1980-85, dir. Air Force Med. Genetics Ctr., 1985—; cons. Surgeon Gen. USAF, Miss. State Dept. Health; clin. asst. prof. pediats. Uniformed Svcs. Univ. of Health Scis., F. Edward Herbert Sch. Medicine, Bethesda, Md. Contbr. articles to profl. jours. Recipient Physician's Recognition award AMA, 1978, 81, 84, 87, 90, 93, 96. Fellow Am. Acad. Pediats.; mem. Am. Soc. Human Genetics, So. Genetics Group, Alpha Omega Alpha. Republican. Methodist. Office: Air Force Med Genetics Ctr 81 MDOS/SGOT Rm 1A 132 301 Fisher St Keesler AFB MS 39534-2508

RIGDON, EDWARD EUGENE, business educator; b. Homestead AFB, Fla., Aug. 26, 1959; s. Edward E. Rigdon and R. Alyeen (King) Smith; m. Mary A. Hart, Mar. 21, 1992; 1 child, Hannah. BA, U. Ala., 1981, PhD, 1990; postgrad., Cath. U. Leuven, Belgium, 1982-83; MBA, U. Chgo., 1984. Instr. Miss. State U., Starkville, 1988-89; asst. prof. Ga. State U., Atlanta, 1989-96, assoc. prof., 1996—; co-chmn. Symposium on Advanced Casual Modeling, Atlanta, 1992; co-founder SEMNET, Internet discussion list on structural equation modeling. Mem. editorial rev. bd. Structural Equation Modeling; contbr. articles to Jour. Mktg. Rsch., Multivariate Bahavioral Rsch., others. Mem. Am. Mktg. Assn., Phi Beta Kappa, Beta Gamma Sigma. Office: Ga State U Mktg Dept Univ Plz Atlanta GA 30303

RIGG, CAROL MARGARET ELIZABETH RUTH, calligrapher, calligraphic designer, visual arts educator; b. Pitts., Dec. 14, 1928; d. Carl Hazlett and Ruth Standish (Massey) R. BA, Fla. State U., 1951; MA, Presbyn. Sch. Christian Edn., 1955; MFA program, Chgo. Art Inst., 1963. Art. dir. bd. publs. Fla. State U., Tallahassee, 1950-53; art editor motive mag., Nashville, 1954-65; artist-in-residence Fla. Presbyn. Coll., St. Petersburg, 1965-66; prof. visual arts Eckerd Coll., St. Petersburg, 1967-93; prof. emerita Eckerd Coll., 1993—; founder, Possum Press, St. Petersburg, 1969; lectr. Princeton Divinity Sch., 1972. Exhibited works in more than 60 solo art shows; calligraphy featured on two CBS-TV shows, 1969, 71; solo calligraphy exhibit, Cultural Olympics, Seoul, Korea, 1987; author: Calligraphy of the Americas, 1977-95. Pres. Nashville Artists Guild, 1960-62. Fulbright grantee, 1972. Mem. Fla. Gulfcoast Soc. Scribes (founder, pres. 1976-78), Fla. Artist Group, Am. Calligraphic Arts Assn. Quaker. Office: Eckerd Coll PO Box 12560 Saint Petersburg FL 33733-2560

RIGGINS-EZZELL, LOIS, museum administrator; b. Nashville, Nov. 18, 1939; d. Percy Leon and Lula Belle Prather (Traughber) Von Schmittou; 1 son, Nicholas. B.S., Belmont Coll., 1968; postgrad., U. Western Ky., 1969-72, George Washington U., 1978. Cert. tchr., Ky., Tenn. Tchr. Ky. Pub. Schs., Adairville, 1962-71; tour supr. Tenn. State Capitol, Nashville, 1972-74; curator of extension services Tenn. State Mus., Nashville, 1975-77, curator edn., 1977-81, exec. dir., 1981—. Chmn. Nashville Flight of Tenn. Friendship Force, Caracas, Venezuela, 1977, Tenn. Am. Revolution Bicentennial Arts Competition, 1976, Gov.'s Quicentennial Com., 1991-92; bd. dirs. Tenn. State Mus. Found., Inc., 1981—, Zool. Soc. Mid. Tenn., 1986-88, So. Folk Cultural Revival Project, 1986-93, Tenn. Pres. Trust, 1989—, Hist. Coun., Girl Scouts U.S.; mem. commning. com. USS Tenn., 1990; keynote speaker nat. forums Corp. Philanthropy Report, Chgo., Atlanta, 1991. Named Woman for Lears, Lears Mag., 1990, Tenn. Woman of Distinction, 1993. Mem. Southeastern Mus. Conf. (edn. com., rep. to Am. Assn. Mus. council, publs. advt. com. 1983), Inter Mus. Council of Nashville (chmn. edn. 1980-81), Am. Assn. Mus., Am. Assn. State and Local History (edn com. 1988-90), Am. Fedn. Art., Art Dirs. Forum. Office: Tenn State Mus 505 Deaderick St Nashville TN 37219-1402

RIGGS, CARL DANIEL, higher education administrator, biologist; b. Indpls., Dec. 7, 1920; s. Josiah Miller and Margaret Helen (Schleicher) R.; m. Patricia Bynum, June 1, 1952; children: Margaret Clare Riggs Johnson, Carl D., Jeffrey B., Catherine. BS in Zoology, U. Mich., 1944, MS in Zoology, 1946, PhD in Zoology, 1953. Teaching fellow dept. zoology U. Mich., Ann Arbor, 1946-47; instr. to prof. dept. zoology U. Okla., Norman, 1948-65, dean Grad. Coll., 1965-71, v.p. grad. studies, 1966-71, acting provost, 1970-71; v.p. for acad. affairs U. South Fla., Tampa, 1971-80, acting pres., 1977-78, dean Grad. Sch. and coordinator univ. research, 1980-86, interim dean Coll. Pub. Health, 1983-84;dir. Ctr. for Excellence in Math., Sci., Computers and Tech.; pres. Conf. So. Grad. Schs., 1986-87; cons. NSF, NIH, CGS. Mayor pro tem, Norman, 1963-64; bd. dirs. and long range planning com. United Way of Greater Tampa; bd. dirs. Tampa Mus. Art, 1979-84, pres., 1980-81; bd. dirs. Children's Home, Inc., 1974—, pres., 1984-86, also mem. exec. com.; chmn. Scouting for the Handicapped, Gulf Ridge council Boy Scouts Am., 1974-86. Served with USAF. Recipient Conservation Edn. award Sears Roebuck Found., 1966; grantee NSF, 1957-66, NASA, 1966-70, John S. Zink Found., 1976, 70; fellow NDEA, 1966-70. Fellow Okla. Acad. Sci. (pres. 1966-67); mem. AAAS, Am. Inst. Biol. Scis., Am. Fisheries Soc., Am. Soc. Ichthyologist and Herpetologists, Fla. Acad. Sci., Phi Beta Kappa, Sigma Xi, Phi Kappa Phi, Beta Gamma Sigma, Omicron Delta Kappa. Democrat. Presbyterian. Contbr. articles on biology to profl. jours. Office: U South Fla Sca # 464 Tampa FL 33620

RIGGS, DAVID LYNN, company executive; b. Tulsa, Oct. 9, 1943; s. William Lynn and Ruth Elizabeth (Murray) R. AA, Northeastern A&M Coll., Miami, Okla., 1964; BS, Northeastern State U., Tahlequah, Okla., 1966; grad., Borcher Aviation Sch., Tahlequah, Okla., 1966. Cert. in design tech. V.p., gen. mgr. William L. Riggs Co., Inc., Tulsa, 1966—. Trustee Tulsa Bible Sch. Mem. SAR, SCV, Electric Auto Assn. (v.p. 1980—), Indsl. Technology Soc., Am. Design Drafting Assn., Sons Union Vets., Soc. War 1812, Soc. Mil. Order Stars and Bars, Cherokee Nation of Okla., Phi Theta Kappa (Mu chpt.). Office: 600 S 129 E Ave Tulsa OK 74108

RIGGS, DEBORAH KAY, critical care, pediatrics nurse; b. Grafton, W.Va.; m. Thomas R. Riggs, Feb. 12, 1988; children: Kayla Ann, Kimberly Inez. BSN, Alderson-Broaddus Coll., Philippi, W.Va., 1981; MS in Nursing, W.Va. U., 1984. RN, W.Va., Mass., S.C., Tex. Staff nurse med.-surg. unit Louis A. Johnson VA Hosp., 1981-86, staff nurse ICU, infection control nurse, 1986-88; sr. staff nurse cardiovascular ICU, Children's Hosp., Boston, 1988-90; staff nurse emergency and ICU East Cooper Hosp., 1990-92; instr. W.Va. U. Sch. Nursing, Morgantown, 1985-88. Founder, primary nurse clinician Shack Neighborhood Health Clinic, 1985-88; vol. Am. Heart Assn., 1981-88, ARC, 1981-88, People's Hospice, 1985-88; pres. Neighborhood Assn., 1994—; Sunday sch. tchr., 1993-94, 96-97; v.p. affairs March of Dimes. Mem. AACN, AMA, Tex. Med. Assn., Northeast Pediatric Cardiology Nurses Assn., Candelighters, TMA, TMCA, Sigma Theta Tau (program com. Alpha Chi chpt. 1989-90). Home: 5427 Tortuga Trl Austin TX 78731-4540

RIGGS, LAWRENCE WILSON, electronics executive; b. Wilmington, Del, Aug. 25, 1943; s. Wilson Nathaniel and Dorothy Elnora (Robbins) R.; m. Ann Rae Holbert, Aug. 12, 1978; children: Lawrence W. Jr., Natalie Marie Goodwin, Loretta Lynn Bunker. Student, U. Ariz., 1965-67; cert. in engring., Heathkit Continuing Edn., 1977. Asst. mgr. Panafax corp, Hayward, Calif., 1978-80; diagnostic supr.facsimile div. NEC Am., Inc., Santa Clara, Calif., 1980-83, regional svc. mgr. facsimile div., 1983-85; regional svc. mgr. NEC Am., Inc., Atlanta, 1985-87; nat. svc. mgr. facsimile/svc. div. Savin Corp., Atlanta, 1987-90; dir. customer svc. ops. Audiofax Inc., Marietta, Ga., 1990-91, dir. sales/tech. support ops., 1991-94; dir. prodn., procurement, tech. support ops., 1994—; pres., CEO CompuFAX, U.S.A.; v.p. Tele-Enterprises, Atlanta, 1988—. Inventor: Tele-Cube, 1988, Savin Image Roll, 1988. Fellow Assoc. Field Svc. Mgrs. Internat. Home: 225 Farm Ct Roswell GA 30075-4250 Office: Audiofax Inc 2000 Powers Ferry Rd Ste 200 Marietta GA 30067-9480

RIGGS, MARY LOU, investment executive; b. Ashland, Ky., June 16, 1927; d. John Russell and Elizabeth (Prichard) Fields; m. James Webster, June 16, 1951 (dec. 1969); children: Mary Elizabeth Cohen, Martha Ann Lowry, Marjorie Louise Pike. BA, U. Ky., 1949. Pres. Clothier Corp., Huntington, W.Va., 1981, MLR, Inc., Huntington, 1982, Clothier Investment, Huntington, 1985—. trustee Huntington Mus. Art, 1972-90, Marshall Univ. Artists Series, 1975-76, Salem Acad. and Coll., Winston-Salem, 1984-89, also bd. visitors, 1993-96; elder Presbyn. Ch. Mem. Jr. League Huntington (exec. bd.), Jr. League Garden Club (v.p. Huntington chpt.). Presbyterian. Home: 2109 Holswade Dr Huntington WV 25701-5335

RIGGS, PENNY KAYE, cytogeneticist; b. Laredo, Tex., Aug. 24, 1965; d. Michael Gene and Karen Ann (Redic) R. BS in Biology, Purdue U., 1987, MS in Animal Cytogenetics, 1991; PhD in Molecular Genetics, Tex. A&M U., 1996. Rsch. assoc. Purdue U. Cytogenetics Lab., West Lafayette, Ind., 1987-91; Regents' fellow Tex. A&M U., College Station, 1991-92, grad. rsch. asst., 1992—. Author: (with others) Advances in Veterinary Science, 1990, Methods in Molecular Medicine, 1996. Pres. Vet. Med. Student Coun. Recipient Grad. Travel award Purdue U. Dept. Animal Sci., 1990, Grad. Rsch. grant and Travel award Tex. A&M U. Coll. of Vet. Medicine, 1995; Aerospace Postdoctoral fellow U. Houston/Johnson Space Ctr., 1996—. Mem. Am. Genetic Assn., Am. Assn. for Lab. Animal Sci., Tissue Culture Assn., Gamma Sigma Delta. Office: Radiation Biophysics Lab Dept Veterinary Pathobiology SD4 NASA Johnson Space Ctr Houston TX 77058

RIGGS, ROBERT DALE, plant pathology/nematology educator, researcher; b. Pocahontas, Ark., June 15, 1932; s. Rosa MacDowell and Grace (Million) R.; m. Jennie Lee Willis, June 6, 1954; children: Rebecca Dawn, Deborah Lee, Robert Dale Jr., James Michael. BS in Agr., U. Ark., 1954, MS, 1956; PhD, N.C. State U., 1958. Grad. asst. U. Ark., Fayetteville, 1954-55, asst. prof., 1958-62, assoc. prof., 1962-68, prof., 1968-92, univ. prof., 1992—; grad. asst. N.C. State U., Raleigh, 1955-58. Editor 2 books, 1980, 92; contbr. articles to profl. jours.; inventor fungal control of nematodes. Recipient John W. White award Coll. Agr. and Home Econs., 1989, Honor award for Rsch. in Environ. Protection USDA, 1994. Fellow Soc. of Nematologists (v.p. 1991-92, pres.-elect 1992-93, pres. 1993-94, editor-in-chief jour. 1987-90); mem. So. Soybean Disease Workers (Disting. Svc. award 1987), U. Ark. Alumni Assn. (Dist. Faculty Achievement award 1993), Am. Phytopathological Soc. (Outstanding plant pathologist in so. region 1994), Wash. Helm. Soc., Sigma Xi, Gamma Sigma Delta. Democrat. Baptist. Home: 1840 Woolsey Ave Fayetteville AR 72703-2557 Office: U Ark 217 Plant Sci Fayetteville AR 72701

RIGGS, SONYA WOICINSKI, elementary school educator; b. Newhall, Calif., Oct. 9, 1935; d. Jack Lewis Woicinski and Mittie Mozelle (Bennett) Gillett; m. Eugene Garland Riggs, Dec. 21, 1956; children: Georgia Ann, Madeline Sue, Dana Eugene. BS in Elem. Edn., U. Tex., 1970; MEd in Reading Edn., S.W. Tex. State U., 1980. Cert. elem. tchr., Tex.; cert. reading specialist K-12. Sec. state govts., Nebr./Tex., 1955-57; piano instr. Elgin, Tex., 1961-66; tchr. 1st grade Elgin Elem. Sch., Elgin, 1967-69, tchr. Music 3rd/4th grades, 1971-72, tchr. 4th grade, 1972-73; pres. El Tesoro internacionale, 1973-74; sec. region office Planned Parenthood/World Population, Austin, 1975-76; tchr. 8th-12th grades Giddings (Tex.) State Sch., 1976-78; tchr. 4th/5th grades Thorndale (Tex.) Ind. Sch. Dist., 1979-80; tchr. remedial reading Brazosport Ind. Sch. Dist., Freeport, Tex., 1980-81; tchr. 6th grade reading and chpt. I Bastrop (Tex.) Mid. Sch., 1981-94, Bastrop Intermediate, 1994—; developer Enrichment Ctr., Bastrop Intermediate, 1995-96. Contbr. articles to Shih Tzu Reporter, 1993 French Bulldog Ann., French Bullytin, Boston Quar., Golden Retriever World; contbr. poetry to anthologies Garden of Life, 1996, Best Poems of 1996, Of Sunshine and Daydreams, 1996. Mem. Elgin Band Boosters, 1970-83, sec., 1976. Mem. Assn. Tex. Profl. Educators (campus rep. 1996-97), Austin Kennel Club (bd. dirs. 1990-91, 95—, sec. 1996-97), Am. Shih Tzu Club (edn. and rescue com. mem. south ctrl. regional hearing com.), French Bulldog Club Am. (rescue com.), Mission City Ring Stewards Assn., Internat. Soc. Poets, Austin Writers League.

RIGGS, SUZANNE MARIE, critical care nurse; b. Wheeling, W.Va., Feb. 13, 1963; d. William Edward and Mary Ann (Jacob) Simon; m. Donald Gregory Riggs, Nov. 14, 1987; children: Gregory Allen, Kassandra Elizabeth. Diploma, Ohio Valley Gen. Hosp. Sch. of Nursing, 1985; student, Ohio U., St. Clairsville, 1983. Nurse's aide Heartland-Lansing Care Ctr., Bridgeport, Ohio, 1983-84; staff nurse Fairfax Hosp., Falls Church, Va., 1985-87; staff nurse Ohio State U. Hosps., Columbus, 1987-92, renal med. transplant unit, 1987-90; cardiology telemetry unit, 1990-91, centralized scheduling dept., 1991-93; RN Ctrl. outpatient scheduling Ohio Valley Med. Ctr., Wheeling, W.Va., 1993—. Mem. Ohio Nurses Assn.

RIGGSBY, ERNEST DUWARD, science educator, educational development executive; b. Nashville, June 12, 1925; s. James Thomas and Anna Pearl (Turner) R.; m. Dutchie Sellers, Aug. 25, 1964; 1 child, Lyn-Dee. BS, Tenn. Polytech. Inst., 1948; BA, George Peabody Coll. Tchrs., 1952, George Peabody Coll. Tchrs., 1953; MA, George Peabody Coll. Tchrs., 1956, EdS, 1961, EdD, 1964. Vis. grad. prof. U. P.R., Rio Piedras, George Peabody Coll., 1963-64; prof. Auburn (Ala.) U., Troy (Ala.) State U., Columbus (Ga.) Coll.; pres. Ednl. Developers, Inc., Columbus, Ga.; vis. grad. prof. George Peabody Coll., 1963-64; vis. lectr. Fla. Inst. Tech., summers 1967-77. Contbr. articles to profl. jours. Col., USAF, 1944-85. Named to Aerospace Crown Cir., 1984; elected to Aerospace Edn. Hall of Fame, 1982. Fellow AAAS; mem. Nat. Sci. Tchrs. Assn., World Aerospace Edn. Assn. (v.p. for the Ams.). Home: Columbus State U Columbus Coll Columbus GA 31907-5645

RIGHTER, ROBERT WILLMS, history educator; b. Stockton, Calif., July 26, 1933; s. Cornelius E. Righter and Margaret Willms; m. Patricia J. Hansen, 1961 (div. 1983); children: Trisha L., Bonnie Beth; m. Sherry L Smith, June 7, 1986. BA, Willamette U., 1955; MA, San Jose State U., 1963; PhD, U. Calif., Santa Barbara, 1968. Instr. San Jose (Calif.) State U., 1967-69; asst. prof. Calif. State Poly. Inst., Pomona, 1969-73; from asst. to assoc. prof. U. Wyo., Laramie, 1973-88; from assoc. prof. to prof. U. Tex., El Paso, 1988—. Author: Crucible for Conservation, 1982, The Making of a Town, 1985; editor: A Teton Country Anthology, 1990, Wind Energy In America: A History, 1996. Fulbright fellow, 1993; recipient Beveridge award Am. Hist. Assn., 1985. Mem. Am. Wind Energy Assn., Orgn. Am. Historians, Am. Soc. Environ. Historians (awards com. 1992-93), Forest History Assn., Western History Assn. Office: U Tex Dept History El Paso TX 79968-0001

RIGHTS, GRAHAM HENRY, minister; b. Winston-Salem, N.C., Jan. 14, 1935; s. Douglas LeTell and Cecil Leona (Burton) R.; m. Sybil Critz Strupe, Sept. 7, 1963; children: Susan Elizabeth, John Graham. BA, U. N.C., 1956; BD, Yale U., 1959; postgrad., Moravian Theol. Sem., 1959-60, U. Edinburgh, Scotland, 1965-66; DD (hon.), Wofford Coll., 1989. Ordained to ministry Moravian Ch., 1960. Pastor Union Ch., Managua, Nicaragua, 1960-63, Managua Moravian Ch., 1960-65, Mayodan (N.C.) Moravian Ch., 1966-72, Messiah Moravian Ch., Winston-Salem, 1972-81; exec. dir. Bd. World Mission Moravian Ch., Bethlehem, Pa., 1981-83; pres. exec. bd. so. province Moravian Ch., Winston-Salem, 1983-95; pres. exec. bd. world-wide Moravian Ch., 1991-94; pastor First Moravian Ch., Greensboro, N.C., 1995—. Author: On the Roof of the World, 1961. Bd. dirs. Crisis Control Ministry, Forsyth County, 1976—, Ecumenical Inst., 1995—, Salemtowne Retirement Comty., 1996—, Moravian Ch. Found., 1988—, Moravian Music Found., 1996—. Home: 208 S Elam Ave Greensboro NC 27403 Office: 304 S Elam Ave Greensboro NC 27403

RIGSBY, CAROLYN ERWIN, music educator; b. Franklinton, La., Apr. 11, 1936; d. Sheldon Aubrey and Edna Marie (Fussell) Erwin; m. Michael Hall Rigsby, May 30, 1959; 1 child, Laura Elaine Rigsby Boyd. B in Music Edn., Northwestern State U., La., 1958; MEd, Nicholls State U., 1970. Cert. vocal music tchr. k-12. Music tchr. Terrebonne Parish Sch., Houma, La., 1958-81, 81-83; music coord. Terrebonne Parish Sch., Houma, 1983-84; music tchr. Pasadena (Tex.) Ind. Sch. Dist., 1988—. Mem. Tex. Music Educators Assn., Packard Automobile Classics, Lone Star Packard Club, Delta Kappa Gamma (pres. 1988-90). Republican. Methodist. Home: 16014 Mill Point Dr Houston TX 77059-5216

RIGSBY, LEE SCOTT, chemist, consultant; b. Ashland, Ky., Sept. 16, 1947; s. Leo Samuel and Gertrude (Woled) R.; m. Judith Eileen Greene, July 6, 1969; 1 child, Noel Scott Rigsby. BS in Chemistry, Marshall U., 1979; MBA, Xavier U., 1991. Shift supr. Armco Steel Corp., Ashland, 1974-77; lab. mgr. Tri-State Testing Co., Inc., Ashland, 1977-79, v.p., 1979-80; mgr. tech. svcs. Ashland Coal Inc., Huntington, W.Va., 1981-86; dir. tech. divsn. Standard Labs. Inc., Ashland, 1986-92; pres. Vanguard Solutions, Inc., Ashland, 1992—. Contbr. articles to profl. jours. Mem. ASTM (com. chmn. 1994), Am. Soc. for Quality Control (com. chmn. 1994), Am. Chem. Soc., Soc. Mining Engrs. Office: Vanguard Solutions Inc 2104 13th St Ashland KY 41101-3520

RIGSBY, LINDA FLORY, lawyer; b. Topeka, Kans., Dec. 16, 1946; d. Alden E. and Lolita M. Flory; m. Michael L. Rigsby, Aug. 14, 1963; children: Michael L. Jr., Elisabeth A. MusB, Va. Commonwealth U., 1969; JD, U. Richmond, 1981. Bar: Va. 1981, D.C. 1988. Assoc. McGuire, Woods, Battle & Boothe, Richmond, Va., 1981-85; dep. gen. counsel Crestar Fin. Corp., Richmond, 1985—. Recipient Disting. Svc. award U. Richmond, 1987; named Vol. of Yr. U. Richmond, 1986, Woman of Achievement, Met. Richmond Women's Bar, 1995. Mem. Va. Bar Assn. (exec. com. 1993-96), Richmond Bar Assn. (bd. dirs. 1992-95), Va. Bankers Assn. (chair legal affairs 1992-95), U. Richmond Estate Planning Coun. (chmn. 1990-92). Roman Catholic. Home: 10005 Ashbridge Pl Richmond VA 23233-5402 Office: Crestar Fin Corp 919 E Main St Richmond VA 23219-4625

RIKE, LINDA STOKES, real estate broker; b. Washington, Sept. 6, 1949; d. James Edgar Stokes and Corrine (Pollard) Holloway; children: Wyatt, Kelinda. AB, East Carolina U., 1971, MA in Edn., 1973; grad. realtors inst., U. N.C., 1988. Lic. real estate broker, N.C.; cert. residential specialist Realtor's Nat. Mktg. Inst. Rehab. counselor State of Fla., Miami, 1973-75; instr. Miami/Dade Schs., Miami, 1974-75; tchr. Carteret County Bd. Edn., Beaufort, N.C., 1975-76; owner Calico Kitten Childrens Apparel, Morehead City, N.C., 1980-83; real estate broker N.C., 1985—. Bd. dirs. Carteret County Friends of Symphony, 1987-89; mem. N.C. Mus. Art, 1984—, Beaufort Hist. Soc., N.C., 1984—, Friends of N.C. Maritime Mus., 1986—. Mem. Nat. Assn. Realtors, Nat. Assn. Real Estate Appraisers (cert.), Morehead City-Carteret County Bd. Realtors, Carteret County Assn. Real Estate Appraisers, Carteret County C. of C., Beaufort Hist. Soc., Carteret County Friends N.C. Symphony, Friends N.C. Maritime Mus. Methodist. Home: PO Box 1721 Morehead City NC 28557-1721 Office: Linda Rike Real Estate PO Box 2929 Atlantic Beach NC 28512-2929

RIKER, DAVID LEWIS, medical services executive; b. Atlanta, Aug. 12, 1958; s. Elmer Lewis and Belle Holbert (Stamper) R.; m. Loralei Joyce Wisbeski, Aug. 31, 1980 (div. 1991); m. Wendy Marie Wood, Aug. 12, 1992. BS, Fla. So. Coll., 1980. Vol. capt. Fire Dist. No. One of Polk County, Lakeland, Fla., 1981-93; EMT Polk County Emergency Med. Svcs., Bartow, Fla., 1982-93; basic life support instr. Am. Heart Assn., Lakeland, Fla., 1985—; EMT Polk Community Coll., Winter Haven, Fla., 1988-94; first responder, rescue coord. Ridge Vocat. and Tech. Ctr., Winter Haven, 1988-94; founder, pres., chief exec. officer Rescue Assocs., Inc., Lakeland, 1987—; search & resuce instr. Vol. Air Search Inst., Anchorage, 1989-91. Author: (instr. guide) Forty Hour Rescue Manual, 1988, Elevator Rescue Manual, 1990. Conductor Frat. Order Police Assocs. Lodge #46, Lakeland, 1989. Recipient Disting. Svc. citation Atlanta-Fulton County Civil Def., 1977, Award of Merit, 1978, Cert. of Commendation EMT of the Yr., 1988; named Outstanding Vol. Couple ARC, 1980. Mem. Nat. Assn. for Search and Rescue, Internat. Soc. Fire Svc. Instrs., Search and Rescue Soc. of B.C. Home: 1603 Rachael Ln Lakeland FL 33805-7541

RILEY, ALISON DUCRO, middle school educator; b. Port Sulphur, La., May 10, 1968; d. Allen Melvin and Mary Deloris (Bagas) Ducro; m. Irvin Gilbert Riley, Jan. 14, 1994. B Music Therapy, Loyola U., New Orleans, 1994. Mid. grade tchr. St. Jude Sch., Archdiocese of New Orleans, Port Sulphur, 1993—. Sponsor Nat. Jr. Beta Club, St. Jude Sch. Choir, 1995. Mem. Alpha Kappa Alpha. Democrat. Roman Catholic. Home: # 3711 3200 Rue Parc Fontaine New Orleans LA 70131 Office: St Jude Sch PO Box 36 Port Sulphur LA 70083

RILEY, ARCH WILSON, JR., lawyer; b. Wheeling, W.Va., Jan. 15, 1957; s. Arch W. Sr. and Mary List (Paull) R.; m. Sally Ann Goodspeed, Aug. 9, 1980; children: Ann Jerome, Sarah Paull. BA in French and Econs., Tufts U., 1979; JD, W.Va. U., 1982. Bar: W.Va. 1982, U.S. Dist. Ct. (no. and so. dists.) W.Va. 1982. Assoc. Riley & Yahn, Wheeling, 1982, Riley & Broadwater, Wheeling, 1982-83; ptnr. Riley & Riley, L.C., Wheeling, 1983-92, Bailey, Riley, Buch & Harman, L.C., Wheeling, 1993—. Pres. Upper Ohio Valley Crisis Hotline Inc., Wheeling, 1987-88; chmn. Human Rights Commn., Wheeling, 1985; committeeman Ohio County Dem. Execs., Wheeling, 1984-88; bd. dirs., pres. No. Panhandle Behavioral Health Ctr., Wheeling, 1988-89;bd. dirs. Ohio Valley ARC, Wheeling, 1988; del. 1988 Dem. Nat. Conv. Mem. W.Va. State Bar, W.Va. Bar Assn., Ohio County Bar Assn. (sec. 1983-84), Wheeling Country Club, Ft. Henry Club. Presbyterian. Office: Bailey Riley Buch & Harman PO Box 631 Wheeling WV 26003-0081

RILEY, ARTHUR ROY, consulting engineer; b. Wink, Tex., Oct. 10, 1930; s. Lincoln Harold and Wylie Edna (Box) R.; m. Betty Lynn Weddle, Jan. 24, 1953; children: Cynthia Lynn, Nina Marion, Julia Beth, Arthur Roy Jr. BSME, Miss. State U., 1953. Registered profl. engr., La., Tex. Petroleum engr. ea. divsn. Exxon Corp. USA, New Orleans, 1955-62; tech. sales rep. Exxon Chem. Co., Lafayette, La., 1962-70; pres. Arthur Chems., Inc., Lafayette, 1970-75; pres. Arthur Engrs., Inc., Lafayette, 1975-80, Spring, Tex., 1980—; pres. McCain Prodn. Co., Inc., Spring, 1985-92, Gopher Tool Co., Spring and Lafayette, 1980, Chart-X Corp., Spring, 1990—; cons. petroleum engr. various drilling and prodn. cos., La., Tex. and N.Mex., 1975-90; cons. drilling engr. DOE-SPR, New Orleans, 1979-80, DOE-Las Vegas-Geothermal, S.W. La., Houston, 1981, Vertec divsn. Bow Valley Ind., Denver, 1984-85. Del. Tex. Dem. Conv., Houston, 1988. 1st lt. USAF, 1953-55, Korea. Mem. Soc. Petroleum Engrs., Inst. Shaft Drilling Tech. Republican. Baptist. Office: Arthur Engrs Inc 9530 Enstone Cir Spring TX 77379-6605

RILEY, ESTHER POWELL, English language educator, editor; b. Charlottesville, Va., Jan. 11, 1941; d. John Mason and Gladys Lindsay (Farris) Powell; m. William C. Riley, Feb. 9, 1974. BA, Westhampton Coll., Richmond, Va., 1962; MA, U. Va., 1967; PhD, U. Tenn., 1992. Tchr. English, Brookland Jr. H.S., Richmond, 1962-68, William Fleming H.S., Roanoke, Va., 1968-76; tchr. Kempsvilel H.S., Virginia Beach, 1979; mem. adj. faculty U. Richmond, 1976, Tidewater C.C., Virginia Beach, Va., 1977-81, Walters State C.C., Morristown, Tenn., 1986-89; rschr. Bogalusa (La.) Heart Study, 1981-84; asst. prof. Voorhees Coll., Denmark, S.C., 1984-86; instr. dept. English, East Tenn. State U., Johnson City, 1989—. Contbr. articles to profl. jours. and Dictionary Lit. Biography. Bd. dirs., sec. Little Theatre, Greeneville, Tenn., 1991—. Mem. MLA, Am. Soc. for 18th Century Studies, Greeneville Country Club (bd. dirs. 1990—), Phi Kappa Phi, Phi Kappa Epsilon. Home: 281 Grapevine Trail Greeneville TN 37745-0414 Office: East Tenn State U PO Box 70683 Johnson City TN 37604

RILEY, HAROLD JOHN, JR., business executive; b. Syracuse, N.Y., Nov. 13, 1940; s. Harold John and Esther Emma (Denmark) R.; m. Diane Marie Slattery, June 15, 1963; children—Beth Ann, Thomas, Patrick. B.S. in Indsl. Engring., Syracuse U., 1961; postgrad., Harvard Bus. Sch., 1985. Mfg. tng. program Gen. Elec. Co., various locations, 1961-63; various mfg. assignments Crouse-Hinds Co., Syracuse, 1963-74; gen. mgr. Midwest Elec., Chgo., 1974-77; v.p., gen. mgr. Crouse Hinds Distbn. Equipment Div., Earlysville, VA., 1977-79; v.p. Crouse-Hinds Co., Syracuse, 1979-82; exec. v.p. Cooper Industries Inc., Houston, 1982-92, pres., chief oper. officer, 1992-95, pres., CEO, 1995—, also bd. dirs., chmn., 1996; bd. dirs. Wyman-Gordon Co., North Grafton, Mass. Bd. dirs. Jr. Achievement Southeast Tex., Houston Ctrl., Houston Symphony, The Greater Houston Partnership, The Houston Forum, The Mus. Fine Arts, Houston, Jr. Achievement, Inc. Mem. Mfrs. Alliance for Productivity Improvement, The Bus. Roundtable, Houston Club, Lakeside Country Club, Farmington Country Club. Republican. Roman Catholic. Home: 3669 Chevy Chase Dr Houston TX 77019-3009 Office: Cooper Industries Inc PO Box 4446 Houston TX 77210-4446

RILEY, JAMES ALAN, English language educator; b. Pine Bluff, Ark., Mar. 28, 1956; s. James Taylor and Margaret Ann (Langan) R.; m. Tammy Lea Morris, June 26, 1994; children: James Isaac, Christopher Alan, Welch Davis, Chip Davis. BA, U. Ctrl. Ark., 1977; MA, U. Ark., 1981; PhD, Ohio U., 1986. Tchg. assoc. U. Ark., Fayetteville, 1978-81; asst. prof. Ohio U., Athens, 1986-87; assoc. prof. Pikeville (Ky.) Coll., 1987—. Founding editor: (literary mag.) The Pikeville Review, 1987—. Ky. Arts Coun. fellow, 1988, Ohio Arts coun. fellow, 1987; NEA grantee, 1991. Home: 3345 E Shelbiana Rd Pikeville KY 41501 Office: Pikeville Coll Sycamore St Pikeville KY 41501

RILEY, TIMOTHY DENNIS, lawyer; b. Brownsville, Tex., Feb. 15, 1954; s. Hugh Hamilton and Serena L. (Tumlinson) R.; m. Rita Faye Vermoilen, Aug. 24, 1974; children: Sunday S., Easton E., T. Braden. BBA in Mktg., U. Tex., 1974; JD cum laude, U. Houston, 1982. Bar: Tex. 1983; bd. cert. civil trial law and personal injury trial law, Tex. Assoc. litigation sect. Butler & Binion, Houston, 1983-86; ptnr. Floyd, Taylor & Riley, LLP, Houston, 1986-95, Riley & Harris, L.L.P., Houston, 1995—; lectr. South Tex. Coll. Law, Houston, 1986, 87, 88, Pesi Continuing Legal Edn. Program, Houston, 1989, 90. Del. Tex. State Dem. Conv., Houston, 1988, Dist. 15, 1992. Fellow Tex. Bar Found., Houston Bar Found. (life); mem. Houston Bar Assn. (litigatoin sect., chairperson com. for interprofl. rels. physicians 1990), Houston Law Rev. Alumni Assn. (dir., v.p. 1995-96). Democrat. Presbyterian. Home: 3111 Kettering Dr Houston TX 77027-5503 Office: Riley & Harris LLP 1301 Mckinney St Ste 3440 Houston TX 77010-3093

RILEY, WILLIAM J., pediatrician, educator; b. Covington, Ky., Mar. 30, 1947; s. Fleming Charles and Aileen Marcella (Frisch) R.; m. Rebecca Jane Whitfield, Sept. 27, 1967; children: Aaron, Chad. BS, Xavier U., 1967; MD, U. Ky., 1971. Diplomate Am. Bd. Pediatrics and Pediatric Endocrinology. From asst. prof. to prof. U. Fla., Gainesville, 1982-93; prof. U. Tex., Houston, 1993—. Maj. U.S. Army, 1975-78. Fellow Am. Acad. Pediatrics; mem. Lawson Wilkins Pediatric Endocrinology Soc., Am. Diabetes Assn. Office: Health Sci Ctr U Tex 6431 Fannin St Houston TX 77030

RINALDI, RICHARD A., manufacturing company executive; b. Waterbury, Conn., Mar. 16, 1940; s. S. Rinaldi; m. Peggy Rinaldi; children: Matthew, Richard. BSME, Rensselaer Poly. U., M in Mgmt. With Gen. Electric, Okonite Corp.; v.p. sales mktg. Gen. Cable Co.; group v.p. Gulf and Western Mfg. (now Wickes Co.), 1981-86; pres., chief exec. officer Am. Thread Co., Charlotte, N.C., 1986—. Mem. Am. Mgmt. Assn., Soc. Automotive Engrs., Am. Soc. Metals, Nat. Elec. Mfg. Assn., Charlotte Textile Club. Office: Am Thread Co 8757 Red Oak Blvd Charlotte NC 28217-3991

RINDE, JOHN JACQUES, internist; b. Przemysl, Poland, Jan. 3, 1935; came to U.S., 1952; s. Maurice and Stella (Klein) R.; m. Toni Igel, June 21, 1959; children: Debbie Ann, Barbara Gail. BS, MIT, 1957, MS, 1958, MME, 1959; MSEE, Poly. Inst. Bklyn., 1965; MD, U. Ark., 1975. Cert. profl. engr.; diplomate Am. Bd. Internal Medicine. Sr. engr. Sperry Gyroscope Co., Great Neck, N.Y., 1959-67, 70-71; v.p. Olson Assocs. Inc., Huntington, N.Y., 1967-69; sr. engr. Hydrosystems, Inc., Farmingdale, N.Y., 1969-70; physician Clearwater, Fla., 1978—. NSF fellow, 1958. Mem. ACP, Am. Soc. Internal Medicine, Fla. Med. Assn., Pinellas County Med. Soc. (bd. govs. 1989-92). Office: 1305 S Fort Harrison Ave Clearwater FL 34616-3301

RINDERKNECHT, MICHAEL ANTHONY, physician's assistant; b. Chilicothe, Mo., Jan. 11, 1955; s. William Russel and Evangeline (Miller) R.; m. Charlynn Marie Campbell-Wurst, May 21, 1976 (div. May 1986); children: Matthew, Cristen, William; m. Marilee Kay Roost, May 20, 1995. AS in respiratory therapy, Armstrong State Coll., 1991, BS, 1993; MS in Anesthesia, Emory U., 1995. Cert. physician's assistant anesthesia. Respiratory therapist Meml. Med. Ctr., Savannah, Ga., 1989-93; physician's asst. Anesthesiology Cons., Savannah, 1995—. Mem. Am. Assn. Anesthesia Assocs., Sports Car Club Am., Nat. Bd. Respiratory Care. Republican. Baptist. Home: 1111 Cobb Rd Savannah GA 31410 Office: Anesthesiology Cons 415 Eisenhower Dr Ste 6 Savannah GA 31406-2633

RINDERKNECHT, ROBERT EUGENE, internist; b. Dover, Ohio, Apr. 27, 1921; s. Henry Carl and Mary Dorothy (Walter) R.; m. Janice Marie Rausch, Oct. 14, 1966; children: Mary Ellen, William A., Janis E. BS, Case Western Reserve U., 1943, MD, 1945. Diplomate Am. Bd. Internal Medicine. Intern Grasslands Hosp., Valhalla, N.Y., 1945-46; resident U. Hosps. Cleve., 1948-49, VA Hosp., Cleve., 1949-51; internist pvt. practice, Dover, Ohio, 1951-79; ret., 1979; trustee Physicians Ins. Co. Ohio, Columbus, 1978-79. Pres. Tuscarawas County (Ohio) Heart Br., 1962-64, 75-77, East Ctrl. Ohio Heart Assn., Canton, 1967-69. Fellow ACP; mem. Masons, Shriners, Elks. Republican. Presbyterian. Home: 121 Dewitt Circle Daphne AL 36526-7740

RINDSBERG, ANDREW KINNEY, geologist, educator; b. Houston, May 19, 1953; s. Donald N. and Ruth W. (Weber) R. BS in Geology, Stanford U., 1975; MS in Geology, U. Ga., 1983; PhD in Geology, Colo. Sch. Mines, 1986. Instr. Auburn (Ala.) U., 1985-86, asst. prof., 1988; asst. prof. S.E. Mo. State U., Cape Girardeau, 1987-88; geologist Geol. Survey Ala., Tuscaloosa, 1989—. Contbr. articles, reports to profl. jours. and guidebooks. Nat. merit scholar Stanford U., 1971-75; rsch. grantee Sigma Xi, 1978, 82, NSF doctoral enhancement grantee Colo. Sch. Mines, 1982, summer grantee dept. geology, 1985. Mem. Internat. Paleontol. Assn., Paleontol. Soc., Paleontol. Rsch. Instn., Soc. for Sedimentology (formerly Soc. Econ. Paleontologists and Mineralogists), Conchologists Am., Am. Malacol. Union, Nat. Assn. Geology Tchrs., Geol. Soc. Am., Ala. Acad. Sci., Ala. Geol. Soc., Ala. Natural History Soc., Sigma Xi. Episcopalian. Office: PO Box O Tuscaloosa AL 35486

RINEHART, HARRY ELMER, retired sales executive; b. Monessen, Pa., Nov. 9, 1921; s. Harry F. and Stella (Shirey) R.; m. Janet M. Herschell, Mar. 19, 1949 (dec. Feb. 1986); children: Donna C., Ellen L., Scott M. BBA, U. Miami, 1943; MBA, Harvard U., 1948. Salesman Nat. Gypsum Co., Buffalo, 1949-53; asst. dist. mgr. Nat. Gypsum Co., Jacksonville, Fla., 1953-62, dist. sales mgr., 1962-86; exec. dir. Exec. Service Corps N.E. Fla.; chmn. bd. dirs. Hospice of Meth. Hosp., Jacksonville. Elder, clk. of session South Jacksonville Presbyn. Ch., 1987—. Capt. USNR, PTO, Korea. Mem. U. Miami Alumni Assn. (chmn. 1987, Outstanding Svc. award 1986), Rotary (pres. South Jacksonville chpt. 1984), San Jose Country Club, Jacksonville Quarterback Club (dir.), The Champions Club, Am. Legion (post 0088), Sigma Chi (life), Alpha Phi Omega (life). Republican. Presbyterian. Home and Office: 6848 La Loma Dr Jacksonville FL 32217-2612

RINEHART, JAMES FORREST, sales executive; b. Kansas City, Mo., Dec. 1, 1950; s. Kenneth Perry and Eleanor Louise (Lane) R.; m. Betty Keller, Feb. 3, 1973; children: Erica Christine, Andrew James. BA, U. Fla., 1972; M of Social Sci., Syracuse U., 1991, postgrad., 1991—. Roanoke, Va. sales rep. Johnson & Johnson, Skillman, N.J., 1975-76, Fla. account mgr., 1976-77, Charlotte, N.C. dist. sales mgr., 1977, Atlanta dist. sales mgr., 1977-78; So. area sales mgr. Schering Labs., Kenilworth, N.J., 1978-80; dir. nat. advt. sales Whittle Communication, LP, Knoxville, Tenn., 1980-82, v.p. field mktg., 1982-83; nat. sales mgr. Chattem, Inc., Chattanooga, 1983-85, v.p. sales, 1985—. Mem. Coun. on Peace Rsch. in History, 1992—; founding mem. Mediation Svcs. Task Force for Chattanooga, 1991—; active Program on Analysis and Resolution of Conflict, Syracuse U., 1991—. Capt. USAR, 1972-80. Democrat. Presbyterian. Home: 22 Rock Crest Dr Signal Mountain TN 37377-2302 Office: Chattem Inc 1715 W 38th St Chattanooga TN 37409-1248

RING, JAMES EDWARD PATRICK, mortgage banking consulting executive; b. Washington, Feb. 12, 1940; s. Edward Patrick and Eleanor (Sollers) R.; m. Kathleen Murphy, Aug. 10, 1979; children: Christopher James, Daniel Edward Patrick. Student, Holy Cross Coll., Worcester, Md., 1958-59; BSEE, U.S. Naval Acad., 1963; MBA in Fin., Wharton Sch. Bus., U. Pa., 1972. Lic. securities broker, comml. pilot. Fin. analyst Exec. Office of the President, Washington, 1972-74; sr. budget analyst Bd. Govs. Fed. Res. System, Washington, 1974-77; dir. fin. planning Fed. Home Loan Mortgage Ins., Washington, 1977-83; dir. mktg. Ticor Mortgage Ins., Falls Church, Va., 1983-84, G.E. Mortgage Ins., Mc Lean, Va., 1985-86; sr. v.p. First Chesapeake Mortgage, Beltsville, Md., 1986-88; v.p. G.E. Capital Mortgage Corp., McLean, 1988-94; cons. Mortgage Dynamics, McLean, 1994—. Vol. Big. Bros. Am., Washington, 1973-81; pres. U.S. Naval Acad. Class of 1963 Found., 1983-96. Lt. USN, 1963-69. Mem. Wharton Club (Washington), U.S. Naval Acad. Alumni Assn., Army-Navy Country Club. Republican Roman Catholic. Home: 1716 Stonebridge Rd Alexandria VA 22304-1039 Office: 1355 Beverly Rd Ste 300 Mc Lean VA 22101-5723

RINGER, CATHARINA WIN, elementary education educator; b. Syracuse, N.Y., Dec. 4, 1968; d. John Edmund and Catharina Henderika (Schong) Phillips; m. John Frederick Toomey, June 17, 1989 (div.); 1 child, Jonathan Fletcher; m. William Thomas Ringer, Sept. 23, 1995. BA in Elem. Edn. summa cum laude, N.C. Ctrl. U., Durham, 1995. Cert. elem. tchr., N.C. Tchr. asst. Chapel Hill-Carrboro City Schs., N.C., 1992-95; tchr. Durham (N.C.) Pub. Schs., 1996—, mem. math. and sci. leadership team. Clara Thompson scholar N.C. Ctrl. U., 1995. Mem. N.C. Coun. Tchrs. Maths. Home: 180 BPW Club Rd No R-7 Carrboro NC 27510 Office: Hillandale Elem Sch 2730 Hillandale Rd Durham NC 27705-2655

RINK, CHRISTOPHER LEE, information technology consultant, photographer; b. Fullerton, Calif., May 20, 1952; s. Wesley Winfred and Doreen (Warman) R.; m. Donna Marie Wootton, Feb. 25, 1989; children: Christopher Lee, David E., Caroline S. BS in Acctg., No. Ill. U., 1974, MBA, 1976. Teaching asst. No. Ill. U., Dekalb, 1974-76; region acct. Hewlett-Packard Co., Chgo., 1976-77, systems programmer, 1977-80; pres. Amity Systems Assocs., Elmhurst, Ill., 1978-81; programming mgr. Hewlett-Packard Co., Chgo., 1980-81, systems engr., 1981-84; response ctr. engr. Hewlett-Packard Co., Atlanta, 1984-86, info. tech. mgr., 1986-90, info. tech. cons., 1990—; established response ctr. info. tech. dept. Hewlett-Packard, Atlanta, 1986, tech. dir., 1990, established info. tech. resource mgmt. group, established corp.-wide remote ref. sys.,designer corp-wide network printing strategy; project mgr. New Ams. Data Ctr. Author (manual) Stock Market Analysis System, 1976; designer Hewlett-Packard centralized call mgmt. systems, 1990; author computer programs. Coord. Ptnrs. in Edn. Cobb County, Atlanta, 1987-89. Mem. Inforum INner Cir., Interex, Computer Measurement Group. Home: 3409 Bonaire Crossing Marietta GA 30066 Office: Hewlett Packard Co 20 Perimeter Summit Blvd Atlanta GA 30319

RINNE, AUSTIN DEAN, insurance company executive; b. Hermann Henry and Marie (Knudsen) R.; m. Martha Jo Runyan, Dec. 29, 1941; children: Erik Knudsen, Barbara Jane Rivera; student Ind. U., 1938-40, grad. Purdue U., 1947. Spl. agt. Northwestern Mut. Life, Indpls., 1946-56, dist. agt., 1956-58, gen. agt., Dallas, 1958-84, gen. agt. emeritus, 1984—; chmn. bd. dirs. Communication and Mgmt. Assocs., Ann Arbor, Mich. Bd. dirs., v.p. English Speaking Union, Dallas, 1972—; bd. dirs. Dallas Opera, 1984—, Taca Boaro, Dallas Cultural Arts Assn. Served to capt. USAF, 1941-45, ETO. Decorated Purple Heart, Air Medal with Cluster, POW medal, Presdl. Unit citation Happy Warriors WWII pilots, 1995; recipient Trail Boss award S.W. Gen. Agts. and Mgrs. Assn., 1993. Mem. Dallas Estate Planning Coun. (pres. 1965-66), Dallas Assn. Life Underwriters (bd. dirs. 1960-63, Hall of Fame 1989, SW Mgmt. Trial Boss award 1993), Million Dollar Roundtable (life), Dallas Knife and Fork (pres., bd. dirs. 1986—), Mil. Order World Wars, English-Speaking Union (dir., v.p. Dallas chpt. 1972—), Sertoma (pres. Dallas chpt. 1967-68, Sertoman of Yr. 1990), Phi Kappa Psi Alumni Assn. (pres. 1951-52), Ind. U. Alumni Assoc. (pres. Dallas/Ft. Worth 1968-69), Phi Kappa Psi (exec. council 1972-76, endowment bd. 1989—, Dallas sales and mktg. chpt. bd. 1969-72), Park City Club, Dallas Country Club, Northshore Club. Republican. Methodist. Home: 4311 Bordeaux Ave Dallas TX 75205-3719 Office: 3102 Oak Lawn Ave Ste 650 Dallas TX 75219-4271

RINTA, CHRISTINE EVELYN, nurse, air force officer; b. Geneva, Ohio, Oct. 4, 1952; d. Arvi Alexander and Catharina Maria (Steenbergen) R. BSN, Kent State U., 1974; MSN, Case Western Res. U., 1979. CNOR. Staff nurse in oper. rm. Euclid (Ohio) Gen. Hosp., 1974-76, oper. rm. charge nurse, 1977-79; commd. 1st lt. USAF, 1979, advanced through grades to lt. col.; staff nurse oper. rm. Air Force Regional Hosp., Sheppard AFB, Tex., 1979-82; staff nurse oper. rm., asst. oper. rm. supr. Regional Med. Ctr. Clark, Clark Air Base, Philippines, 1982-83; chief, nurse recruiting br. 3513th Air Force Recruiting Squadron, North Syracuse, N.Y., 1983-87; nurse supr. surg. svcs. 432d Med. Group, Misawa Air Base, Japan, 1987-89; course supr./instr. oper. rm. nursing courses 3793d Nursing Tng. Squadron, Keesler Med. Ctr., Keesler AFB, Miss., 1989-92; asst. dir., then dir. oper. rm. and ctrl. sterile supply Keesler Med. Ctr., Keesler AFB, Miss., 1992-93; comdr., enlisted clin. courses flight 383d Tng. Squadron, Sheppard AFB, Tex., 1993-94; comdr., officer clin. courses flight 383rd Tng. Squadron, Sheppard AFB, Tex., 1994-95; comdr. enlisted courses flight 383rd Tng. Squadron, Sheppard AFB, Tex., 1995—. Decorated Air Force Commendation medal, Air Force Achievement medal, Meritorious Svc. medal. Mem. ANA, Ohio Nurses Assn., Assn. Operating Rm. Nurses, Air Force Assn., Sigma Theta Tau. Home: 14 Pilot Point Dr Wichita Falls TX 76306-1000 Office: 383d Tng Squadron 939 Missile Rd Ste 3 Sheppard AFB TX 76311-2262

RIO, FRANCESCO A., tropical medicine and public health specialist; b. Padova, Italy, Apr. 22, 1955; s. Gian Riccardo and Argentina (Barberi) R.; m. Rebecca J. Bailey, June 10, 1995. MD, U. Bologna, Italy, 1986; diploma in Tropical Medicine, Liverpool Sch O Tropical Med., 1988; cert. in Malaria Control, WHO, Switzerland, 1989; MPH, U. Ferrara, Italy, 1990. Health planner and adminstr. CESTAS (NGO), Boké Republic Guinea, 1990-92; cons. (writing guidelines) UNICEF Conakry-Rep. of Guinea, 1992; cons. in epidemiology SANIPLAN mbh (Germany), Mamou-Rep. of Guinea, 1992, 93; chief of project Italian Nat. Cooperation, Cobija, Bolivia, 1992-93; cons. tropical diseases WHO, Geneva, 1993, 94; vis. prof. (malaria) U. Lübeck, Germany, 1993. Fellow Royal Soc. Tropical Medicine (UK), Royal Soc.

Medicine; mem. Am. Soc. Tropical Medicine, Am. Pub. Health Assn., Italian Soc. Tropical Medicine, Italian Soc. Parasitology. Home: 1318 11th Ave S Birmingham AL 35205 Office: WHO, 20 Ave Appia, 1211 Geneva Switzerland

RIOS, EVELYN DEERWESTER, columnist, musician, artist, writer; b. Payne, Ohio, June 25, 1916; d. Jay Russell and Flossie Edith (Fell) Deerwester; m. Edwin Tietjen Rios, Sept. 19, 1942 (dec. Feb. 1987); children: Jane Evelyn, Linda Sue Rios Stahlman. BA with honors, San Jose State U., 1964, MA, 1968. Cert. elem., secondary tchr., Calif. Lectr. in music San Jose State U., 1969-75; bilingual cons., then assoc. editor Ednl. Factors, Inc., San Jose, 1969-76, mgr. field research, 1977-78; writer, editor Calif. MediCorps Program, 1978-85; contbg. editor, illustrator The Community Family Mag., Wimberly, Tex., 1983-85; columnist The Springer, Dripping Springs, Tex., 1985-90; author, illustrator, health instr. textbooks elem. schs., 1980-82. Choir dir. Bethel Luth. Ch., Cupertino, Calif., 1965-66, Bethel Luth. Ch., 1968-83; dir. music St. Aban's Ch., Bogota Colombia; organist Holy Spirit Episcopal Ch., Dripping Springs, Tex., 1987-94; music dir. Cambrian Park (Calif.) Meth. Ch., 1961-64; chmn. Dripping Springs Planning and Zoning Commn., 1991-93. Mem. AAUW, Am. Guild Organists (dean 1963-64), Phi Kappa Phi (pres. San Jose chpt. 1973-74). Episcopalian. Home and Office: 23400 FM 150 Dripping Springs TX 78620

RIOS, JUAN-ERNESTO, elementary education educator; b. Ciudad Acuña, Coahuila, Mexico, Mar. 1, 1951; came to the U.S., 1961; s. Fidel Treviño and Maria (Briones) R.; m. Diana Ochoa (div.); 1 child, Nicholas Fidel; m. Ramona Gamboa; children: Edwardo-Ernesto, Luis-Antonio. BS, Angelo State U., 1974. Cert. bilingual tchr. Mail clk. Angelo State U., San Angelo, Tex., 1970-74; bilingual tchr. Lubbock (Tex.) Ind. Sch. Dist., 1970—, Dallas Ind. Sch. Dist., 1986-87; tutor Lubbock (Tex.) Ind. Sch. Dist., 1974-96. Ch. leader Templo Bapt. Ch., Lubbock, 1980-96. Sgt. Army Nat. Guard, 1977-96. Republican. Home: 1304 47th St Lubbock TX 79412 Office: Lubbock Ind Sch Dist Jackson Elem 201 Vernon Ave Lubbock TX 79415

RIOS, JULIE A., education educator; b. Caracas, Venezuela, Sept. 13, 1945; d. Hector and Olimpia (Leon) Parraga; m. Ramon N. Rios, Apr. 15, 1966; children: Julie, Ramon, Hector, Gustavo. BS, Teresiano Coll., Caracas, 1968. Tchr. asst. Adventure Bay, Coconut Creek, Fla., 1990-92, first asst., 1992-93, head tchr., 1993-96; active workshops: puppet, reading and pre-sch. music, Nova U., Fla., 1996. Author: Just the Way You Are, 1996 (Hon. Mention Writer's Internal Forum award 1996); inventor: Boxy Book, 1995, Theater Book, 1996, Tent House, 1995. Vol. nurse asst. Internat. Red Cross, Caracas, 1967-69. Recipient Amigos de los Ninos award Venezuelan Red Cross, 1968. Mem. Children's Book Writer, Am. Soc. Inventors. Home: 802 Cypress Blvd # 204 Pompano Beach FL 33069

RIPLEY, JOHN WALTER, academic administrator; b. Welch, W.Va., June 29, 1939; m. Molin B. Ripley, May 9, 1964; children: Stephen B., Mary D., Thomas H., John M. BSEE, U.S. Naval Acad., 1962; MS, Am. U., 1976. Commd. 2d lt. USMC, 1962, advanced through grades to col., 1984, ret., 1992; polit./mil. planner Office of Joint Chiefs of Staff, Washington; asst. prof. history Oreg. State U., Corvallis, 1972-75; dir. divsn. English and history U.S. Naval Acad., Annapolis, Md., 1984-87; commanding officer Naval ROTC unit Va. Mil. Inst., Lexington, 1990-92; pres. So. Va. Coll., Buena Vista, 1992-96, chancellor, 1992—; lectr. in field. Decorated Navy Cross, Legion of Merit (2), Silver Star, Bronze Star (2), Purple Heart. Mem. Phi Alpha Theta. Office: Southern Virginia College One College Hill Dr Buena Vista VA 24416

RIPLEY, R(OBERT) KENYON, JR., journalist; b. Virginia Beach, Va., Aug. 3, 1950; s. Robert Kenyon and Martha Phillips (Van Patten) R.; m. Vickie Louise Corbett, Aug. 5, 1972. BA in Journalism, U. N.C., 1972. Editor, The Branch Inter-Varsity Christian Fellowship, Madison, Wis., 1972-75; editor-pub. Spring Hope (N.C.) Enterprise, 1975-90, 92—; editor Nashville (N.C.) Graphic, 1990-92; pub. Triangle East Bus. Jour., Spring Hope, 1991—. Author: Soul Food and Perples, 1971; contbr. articles to His mag. Chmn. bd. dirs. Spring Hope Libr., 1980—; mem. Spring Hope Planning Bd., 1984—; chmn. Spring Hope Revitalization Commn., 1982-96; founding dir. Big Bros./Big Sisters of Nash and Edgecombe Counties, Rocky Mount, N.C., 1984—; bd. dirs. Carolina Gateways Partnership. Named Disting. Vol. of Yr. Nash-Rocky Mount United Way, 1989, Bd. Mem. of Yr., 1991. Mem. N.C. Press Assn. (bd dirs., winner 8 press awards 1975—), Ea. N.C. Press Assn. (bd. dirs., v.p., pres.), N.C. Assn. Cmty. Newspapers (pres. 1981-82), Soc. Profl. Journalists, N.C. Editl. Writers Conf. (chmn., bd. dirs.), Spring Hope Lions (v.p., pres., regional and zone chmn.). Democrat. United Methodist. Home: 111 Circle Dr PO Box 185 Spring Hope NC 27882 Office: Spring Hope Enterprise 113 Ash St PO Box 399 Spring Hope NC 27882

RIPLEY, VICKIE CORBETT, hospital pharmacist; b. Bailey, N.C., June 17, 1950; d. Bobby Jones and Mary Lou (Ayers) Corbett; m. Robert Kenyon Ripley Jr., Aug. 5, 1972. BS in Pharmacy, U. N.C., 1973; paramedic cert., Nash Community Coll., Rocky Mount, N.C., 1987. Registered pharmacist, N.C. Pharmacy intern Madison (Wis.) Gen. Hosp., 1974-75; staff pharmacist Nash Gen. Hosp., Rocky Mount, 1975-76, Southside Pharmacy, Inc., Spring Hope, N.C., 1976-86, Raper Drugs, Inc., Rocky Mount, 1980-86; dir. pharmacy Community Hosp. Rocky Mount, 1986—, sec. pharmacy and therapeutics com., 1986—, chmn. safety com., 1990—; infection control com., 1989, perf. improvement com., 1993, customer svc. coun., customer svc. trainer, 1994, joint commn. on accreditation of healthcar orgn. task force, 1990—; practitioner, instr. U. N.C. Chapel Hill Sch. Pharmacy, 1987—; instr. paramedic pharmacology Nash. Community Coll., 1988—; instr. basic life support Community Hosp. Rocky Mount, 1988—; mem. Area L pharmacy adv. bd. Area Health Edn. Ctrs.. Mem. Gibson Meml. Chancel Chancel Choir, Spring Hope, 1978—, rocky Mount Civic Chorus, 190-82; assoc. dir. music, choir dir., chmn. worship com. Gibson Meml. United Meth. Ch., 1992—; mem. Tree Bd., Town of Spring Hope, 1992-93; mem. Drug Awareness in Spring Hope; vol. paramedic Strong Creek Fire Rescue, Inc., Rocky Mount, 1985-88. Mem. N.C. Pharm. Assn., N.C. Soc. Hosp. Pharmacists, Am. Soc. Hosp. Pharmacists, Am. Pharm. Assn., Area Health Edn. Ctrs. (Area L pharjacy adv. bd.), Kappa Epsilon. Democrat. Methodist. Home: PO Box 185 Spring Hope NC 27882-0185 Office: Community Hosp Rocky Mount 1771 Jeffreys Rd Rocky Mount NC 27804-6341

RIPPE, PETER MARQUART, museum administrator; b. Mpls., Dec. 16, 1937; s. Henry Albert and Zelda (Marquart) R.; m. Maria Boswell Wornom, Aug. 10, 1968. BA, U. Puget Sound, 1960; MA, U. Del., 1962. Dir. Confederate Mus., Richmond, Va., 1962-68; exec. dir. Harris County Heritage Soc., Houston, 1968-79, Roanoke Mus. Fine Arts (Va.), 1979-89, P. Buckley Moss Mus., Waynesboro, Va., 1989—; mem. Roanoke Arts Commn., 1983-90. Fellow Old Deerfield Found., 1958, H.F. duPont Winterthur Mus., 1960-62, chmn. Blue Ridge TV, Roanoke; bd. dirs. Augusta-Staunton-Waynesboro Visitors Bur. Mem. Am. Assn. Mus. (chmn. small mus. com. 1981-83, sr. examiner, 1983—, councillor-at-large 1985-88), Tex. Assn. Mus. (pres. 1975-77, Tex. award 1979), Va. Assn. Mus. (pres. 1983-84), Southeast Mus. Conf. (chmn. awards com. 1986-89), Rotary (Waynesboro chpt.), Waynesboro Club. Democrat. Lutheran. Home: 149 Brook Ct Waynesboro VA 22980-5559 Office: P Buckley Moss Mus 150 B Buckley Moss Dr Waynesboro VA 22980-9406

RIPPEE, YVETTE M., nurse; b. Topeka, Kans., Dec. 2, 1955; d. Claude Elmo and Harriet Annette (Mauldin) R.; m. Michael J. Baker, June 1, 1984; children: James, Joseph. AS, Memphis State U., 1978; student, Rhodes Coll., 1973-75. Cert. high risk perinatal nurse, cert. fetal monitoring. Staff nurse Denver Gen. Hosp., S.W. Tex. Meth. Hosp., San Antonio; asst. nurse mgr. Regional Med. Ctr., Memphis, staff nurse.

RIPPEL, JEFFREY ALAN, library director; b. Moberly, Mo., June 19, 1945; s. Charles Kenneth and Mildred Agnes (Dodge) R.; m. Mary Elizabeth Burton, Oct. 25, 1969; children: Sarah, Andrew. BA, Fla. State U., 1967; MLS, U. Tex., 1973. Cert. county librarian, Tex., profl. librarian, S.C. Br. librarian Waco (Tex.) Pub. Library, 1974-76; dir. Victoria (Tex.) Pub. Library, 1976-78; dep. dir. Greenville (S.C.) County Library, 1978-81; dir. Longview (Tex.) Pub. Library, 1981-88, Lubbock (Tex.) City-County Library, 1988—. Contbr. articles to profl. jours. Bd. dirs. Lubbock Area Coalition for Literacy. Capt. USAF, 1967-72. Mem. ALA, Tex. Library Assn., Lubbock Area Library Assn. (past pres.). Home: 2627 22nd St Lubbock TX 79410-1615 Office: Lubbock City-County Libr 1306 9th St Lubbock TX 79401-2798

RIPPETOE, SANDRA ELAINE, dietitian; b. Louisville, May 11, 1962; d. Edward Earl and Patricia Lynn (Smith) R.; m. Bennett Wade Muncy II, Nov. 28, 1986. BA in Psychology, U. Ky., 1984, BS in Dietetics, 1994; MA, Lexington Theol. Sem., 1989. Registered dietitian, Am. Dietetic Assn.; lic. dietitian, Ky. Assoc. mental health Charter Ridge Hosp., Lexington, Ky., 1984-93; clin. nutritionist Woodford County Health Dept., Versailles, Ky., 1994—. Mem. Am. Dietetic Assn., Am. Diabetes Assn., Ky. Dietitic Assn., Bluegrass Dietetic Assn., Soc. Nutrition Edn., Ky. Nutrition Coun., Ky. Pub. Health Assn., Phi Beta Kappa, Phi Upsilon Omicron. Democrat. Office: Woodford County Health Dept 229 N Main St Versailles KY 40383-1240

RIPPLE, ROCHELLE POYOUROW, educational administrator, educator; b. N.Y.C., Apr. 23, 1936; d. Gerald G. and Hortense (Philips) Bernheimer; m. Julian D. Ripple, Mar. 15, 1985; children: Mitchell, Jill, David. AAS, Fashion Inst. Tech., 1955; Pace U.; BPS, 1974; MEd, Temple U., 1977, EdD, 1990. Cert. tchr. of handicapped, Pa.; cert. prin., sch. supt., Wyo. Fashion designer Skampalon, Inc., N.Y.C., 1955-60; tchr. fashion design Pleasantville (N.Y.) Cottage Sch., 1969-74; spl. edn. tchr. Horsham Clinic, Ambler, Pa., Phila., 1974-78; fed. project dir. Montgomery County Intermediate Unit, Norristown, Pa., 1978-80; exec. dir. Northeast Wyo. Bd. Coop. Ednl. Services, Gillette, Wyo., 1980-86; teaching assoc. Temple U., Phila., 1986-88; dir. vocat.-tech. edn. Ulster County BOCES, New Paltz, 1988-90; prof. ednl. adminstrn. Columbus Coll., 1990. Pres., Yorktown (N.Y.) Community Rels. Coun., 1967-70; mem. adv. bd. Sheridan (Wyo.) Coll. Mem. LWV. Pace U. Trustee scholar, 1973; named Woman of Yr., Beta Sigma Phi, 1982. Mem. ASCD, Council for Exceptional Children, Am. Assn. Sch. Adminstrs., Assn. Retarded Citizens, Assn. Serverely Handicapped, Phi Delta Kappa. Contbr. article to profl. jour. Home: 612 Rudgate Rd Columbus GA 31904-2927 Office: Columbus Coll Dept Edn Columbus GA 31907-5645

RISCUTA, DORUTU HONORIUS, writer; b. Brasov, Romania, Dec. 4, 1960; came to U.S., 1991; s. Sabin ion Riscuta and Olga ioan Apostoaia. MS summa cum laude in Linguistics, U. Bucharest, 1986. Tchr. English and German Pucioasa (Romania) High Sch., 1986-91; assoc. prof. English Acad. Econ. Scis., Bucharest, Romania, 1990-91; writer, 1991—; founder success psychology; tennis profl. Worldgate Athletic Club, Herndon, Va., 1992—. Author: Become Rich and Loved, 1993.

RISDEN, NANCY DIKA, mathematics educator; b. Englewood, N.J., Sept. 14, 1948; d. John and Dorothy Louise (Eisberg) Macris; m. Dennis Richard Risden, Apr. 6, 1974; children: Jeannine, Steven, David. BS, Ursinus Coll., Collegeville, Pa., 1970; MA, Montclair State Coll., Upper Montclair, N.J., 1976. Cert. postgrad. prof. tchr. secondary math., Va., N.J. Tchr. math. West Essex Regional Mid. Sch., North Caldwell, N.J., 1970-71, South Jr. H.S., Bloomfield, N.J., 1971-79; substitute tchr. Oldham County Mid. Sch., Oldham County, Ky., 1981-82; instr. math. Watterson Coll., Louisville, 1984; tchr. math. Duke U. Hosp. Sch., Durham, N.C., 1988-90; substitute tchr. York County Pub. Schs., Yorktown, Va., 1991-93; tchr. math. Tabb Mid. Sch., Yorktown, 1993—. Treas. Mangum Primary Sch. PTA, Durham County, 1988-89; cookie chmn. Girl Scouts U.S., Durham County, 1989; den leader cub scouts Boy Scouts Am., Durham County, 1988-91, com. chairperson pack 104, Yorktown, Va., 1991-95. Mem. NEA, Va. Edn. Assn., York County Edn. Assn., Nat. Coun. Tchrs. Math., Va. Mid. Sch. Assn., Order Ea. Star N.J. (Worth Matron 1975-76, Grand Adah 1976-77). Presbyterian. Home: 113 Daphne Dr Yorktown VA 23692-3220 Office: Tabb Middle School 300 Yorktown Rd Yorktown VA 23693-3504

RISHER, THOMAS DOUGLAS, SR., music educator; b. Meridian, Miss., Aug. 3, 1950; s. Charles Alfred Sr. and Gertrude (Viverette) R.; m. Harriett Ann Myrick, Sept. 23, 1975; children: Kelli Ann, Thomas Douglas Jr. AA, East Miss. Jr. Coll., Scooba, 1969; B Mus. Edn., U. So. Miss., Hattiesburg, 1973; MA in Tchg., U. West Ala., Livingston, 1978. Cert. tchr., Miss. Band dir. Enterprise (Miss.) H.S., 1973-74; dir. bands East Miss. Jr. Coll., Scooba, 1974-78; asst. prof. music U. North Ala., Florence, 1978—. Musician (drummer) Miss. Jr. Miss Pagent Orch., Meridian, 1968—, Miss Miss. Pagent Orch., Vicksburg, Miss., 1968-79, Opryland U.S.A., Nashville, 1980, 81, Sammy Kaye, Ray McKinley, Les Eloart, WarrenCovington, Bob Crosby, Anity Bryant Orchs., 1968—, Roger Williams (orch.), Cmty. Big Band, Florence, 1978—. Mem. AAUP, Am. Fedn. Musicians, Percussive Arts Soc., Not So Modern Drummers, Kappa Kappa Psi. Republican. Presbyterian. Office: U North Ala Box 5040 Irwin St Florence AL 35632-0001

RISLEY, JOHN STETLER, physics scientist, educator; b. Seattle, Mar. 3, 1942; s. Henry Morrow and Helen (Stetler) R.; m. Dellaine Anderson, July 24, 1965; children: Renelle Dee, James Stetler, Steven Robert. BS cum laude, U. Wash., 1965, MS, 1966, PhD, 1973. Rsch. asst. dept. physics U. Wash., Seattle, 1966-73, rsch. assoc., 1973-75; vis. asst. prof. physics U. Nebr., Lincoln, 1976; asst. prof. physics N.C. State U., Raleigh, 1976-79, assoc. prof., 1979-84, prof., 1984—; sec.-treas. IXth Internat. Conf. on Physics of Electronic and Atomic Collisions, Seattle, 1975, mem. program com. Xth Internat. Conf., Paris, 1977, sec., 1977-89; co-chmn. Conf. on Computers in Physics Instruction, Raleigh, N.C., 1988; dir. The Academic Software Libr., 1989—; judge computer software contest Compters in Physics, 1990—. Author: Physics Problems: A Guide to Using the Computer Tutorials in Physics 1 by Control Data, 1987; editor: Physics Academic Software, 1987—, Software for Engineering Students, 1991—; editor: (with E.F. Redish) Computers in Physics Instruction: Abstracts of Contributed Papers, 1988, Computers in Physics Instruction: Software, 1988; editor: (with R. Geballe) Physics of Electronic and Atomic Collisions: Abstrats of Invited Papers, 1976; column editor The Physics Teacher, 1983-88; mem. editl. bd. Am. Jour. Physics, 1984-87, Computers in Physics, 1987-93, Instructional Materials Ctr., 1987-91; contbr. articles to Phys. Rev., Phys. Rev. Letters, Rev. Sci. Instruments, Jour. Physics, Physics Tchr., Computers in Physics. Recipient Disting. Svc. citation Am. Assn. Physics Tchrs., 1992. Fellow AAAS, Am. Phys. Soc. (mem. program com. divsn. electron and atomic physics 1978-79, 84-87, mem. com. internat. sci. affairs 1993-95). Home: 5303 Sendero Dr Raleigh NC 27612-1809 Office: NC State U Dept Physics Raleigh NC 27695-8202

RISTIG, KYLE GREGORY, engineer; b. Ft. Smith, Ark., Dec. 10, 1954; s. William Marcus and Chrys (Olson) R. BS in Engring., Ark. Tech., 1976; MBA, La. Tech., 1984, MA in Counseling, 1987. Field engr. Ark. La. Gas Co., Shreveport, La., 1977-80; engr. transmission Ark. La. Gas Co., 1980-84; engr. gas control ARKLA, Shreveport, 1984-85; engr. planning ARKLA, 1985-87; supr. bus. analysis ARKLA Energy Resources, Shreveport, 1987-90; mgr. employee rels. and tech. tng. ARKLA Pipeline Group, Shreveport, 1990—; instr. La. Tech. U., Barksdale AFB, 1987—. Mem. Civitans, Shreveport, 1988. Mem. ASTD, ASME (chmn. Arkaltex sect. 1989-91), ISPI. Republican. Methodist. Home: 105 Marrero Dr Shreveport LA 71115-2727

RITCHEY, JAMES SALEM, office furniture manufacturing company executive; b. Birmingham, Ala., June 15, 1950; s. Salem E. and Edna (George) R.; m. Rhonda Waddell, Jan. 20, 1989; children: Barry, John. BS in Acctg., U. Ala., 1972, MBA, 1981. CPA, Ala. Staff acct. Ernst & Young, Birmingham, 1971-74; asst. contr. United Chair Co., Inc., Leeds, Ala., 1974-81, contr., 1981-83; v.p. fin. Office Group Am. (United Chair Co., and Anderson Hickey Co.), Leeds, 1983-89, exec. v.p., 1989-91; pres. Office Group Am. (United Chair Co. and Anderson Hickey Co.), Leeds, 1991—; CPA. Named Acctg. Alumni of Yr., U. Ala., Birmingham, 1987. Mem. AICPA, Ala. Soc. CPA's, Nat. Assn. Accts. (past chpt. pres., Branhart-Strawn award 1982), Alpha Beta Psi. Office: Office Group Am 114 Churchill Ave NW Leeds AL 35094-1458

RITCHLIN, MARTHA ANN, occupational therapist; b. Jacksboro, Tex., Oct. 20, 1953; d. Carl Alton and Julia Ann (Jones) Rumage; divorced; children: Carl Allen, Julie Marie. BS, Tex. Women's U., 1976, postgrad., 1986. Occupational therapist Wichita Gen. Hosp., Wichita Falls, Tex., 1977-79; dir. occupational therapy Red River Hosp., Wichita Falls, 1979-83, Bethania Regional Health Care Ctr., Wichita Falls, 1983-87; occupational therapist Girling Home Health, Wichita Falls, 1984-85, Wichita Home Health, Wichita Falls, 1984-86, Outreach Home Health Svcs., Seymour, Tex., 1987—, N. Tex. Easter Seal Rehab. Ctr., Wichita Falls, 1988—; owner, therapist Community Occupational Therapy Svcs., Wichita Falls, 1988—; dir. occupational therapy Wichita Falls (Tex.) State Hosp., 1991—; cons., speaker Muscular Dystrophy Assn., Wichita Falls, 1986, Advantage Sr. Citizens Club, Wichita Falls, 1988, Stroke Club, 1986; cons., activity dir. Clay County Hosp., Henrietta, Tex., 1986-87. Cons., vol. Wichita County Juvenile Detention Svcs., Wichita Falls, 1980; mem. task force State Task Force on Assistive Tech., Tex., 1989—; bus. mem. Ptnrs. in Edn. Named Notable Women of Tex., 1985. Mem. Tex. Occupational Therapy Assn., Am. Occupational Therapy Assn., World Fedn. Occupational Therapy. Baptist. Home: 107 N 12th St Jacksboro TX 76458 Office: Graham Gen Hosp Graham TX 76458

RITTELMEYER, JOHN MOSAL, JR., manufacturer representative, paper company executive, financial consultant, investor; b. Atlanta, Mar. 16, 1935; s. John Mosal and Jane Elizabeth (Torbert) R. Grad. in Indsl. Mgmt., Ga. Inst. Tech., 1958. Sec.-treas. Rittelmeyer and Co., Inc., Atlanta, 1958-87, Crescent Corp., Atlanta, 1972-86, Nassau Corp., Atlanta, 1972-77; mng. ptnr. Ritco Properties, Atlanta, 1966-86, Beta Properties, Atlanta, 1976-86, JGN Properties, Atlanta, 1977-90, RE Properties, Atlanta, 1979-80; mem. Ga. Engring. Soc., Atlanta, 1960-70, Bldg. Owners and Mgrs., Atlanta, 1965-86. Mem., dir. Atlanta Jr. C. of C., Atlanta, 1960-73. Mem. Atlanta Kiwanis, Capital City Club.

RITTER, DENNIS DANIEL, JR., oil industry executive; b. New Orleans, Jan. 19, 1952; s. Dennis D. and Jane (Schayot) R.; m. Carol Ellen Laing, June 7, 1975; children: Marcella Anne, Jared Scott. Student, La. State U., JD, 1977. Bar: La. 1977, Tex. 1992. Land analyst Shell Oil Co., New Orleans, 1977-78, landman, 1978-80, sr. landman offshore divsn. coastal La. ops. desk, 1980-81, dist. landman offshore divsn. coastal La. dist., 1981; asst. land mgr. Nicklos Oil & Gas Co., Houston, 1981-85, land mgr., 1984-91; regional land mgr. Sandefer Oil & Gas Co., Houston, 1984-85, land mgr., 1985-91, land and legal mgr., 1991; land mgr., asst. gen. counsel Preston Oil Co., The Woodlands, 1991—; mem. adv. coun. La. Mineral Law Inst., 1991-94. Mem., usher Woodlands United Meth. Ch.; regional adult vol. leader Sam Houston Area Coun. Boy Scouts Am., asst. scoutmaster Troop 772, 1993—, asst. cubmaster Pack 772, 1988-93. Mem. La. Bar Assn., Tex. State Bar Assn., Am. Assn. Profl. Landmen, Houston Assn. Profl. Landmen (dir. 1991-93), North Houston Assn. Petroleum Landmen, Petroleum Landmen's Assn. New Orleans, Lafayette Assn. Petroleum Landmen. Home: 6 Crescent Falls Ct Spring TX 77381-2688 Office: Preston Exploration LLC PO Box 7520 The Woodlands TX 77387-7520

RITTER, FREDERICK EDMOND, plastic surgeon, educator; b. Cin., Aug. 21, 1959; s. Edmond J. and Alexandra (Engel) R.; m. Christina Weltz, Aug. 2, 1993. BS, U. Cin., 1980; MD, Washington U., St. Louis, 1984. Intern, resident U. Medicine and Dentistry N.J., 1984-90; resident in plastic and reconstructive surgery U. Calif., San Francisco, 1990-92; asst. prof. surgery Duke U., Durham, N.C., 1992—. Contbr. chpts. in books and articles to profl. jours. Republican. Office: Duke Univ Med Ctr Rm 142 Baker House Durham NC 27710

RITTER, GUY FRANKLIN, structural engineer; b. Detroit, Feb. 9, 1933; s. Guy Franklin and Ethel (Reed) R.; m. Peggy Anne Maloy, Sept. 20, 1954; children: Constance Elaine, Margaret Anne, Sallie Reed. BS in Architecture, Ga. Inst. Tech., 1954, B Arch. Engring., 1955; MS in Bldg. Engring., MIT, 1956. Registered profl. engr., Ga., Fla., S.C., N.C., Ala., Tenn. Structural detailer I.E. Morris Assocs., Atlanta, 1955-56; structural engr. Morris, Boehmig & Tindel, Atlanta, 1956-58; dist. structural engr. Portland Cement Assn., Atlanta, 1958-61; sr. structural engr. Lindsey Tucker Ritter, Albany, Ga., 1961-74; v.p. Lindsey & Ritter, Inc., Albany, 1974-79; pres., chief exec. officer Lindsey & Ritter, Albany, 1979—. Mem. Ga. Industrialized Bldgs. adv. com., 1990—; dir. Structural Engrs. Risk Mgmt. Coun., 1989-92. Recipient Value Engr. award GSA, 1974. Mem. ASCE, NSPE, Coalition of Am. Structural Engrs. (nat. vice chmn. 1995-96), Am. Cons. Engrs. Coun., Am. Concrete Inst., Prestressed Concrete Inst., Rotary (local pres. 1983-84). Republican. Presbyterian. Office: Lindsey & Ritter Inc 423 Pine Ave Albany GA 31701-2534

RITTER, WILLIAM STANLEY, physician; b. West Palm Beach, Fla., Dec. 13, 1951; s. William Clarke and LaVerne (Sijkora) R.; m. Sara Ann Deaver, May 20, 1977. BA with distinction, Cornell U., 1973; MD, U. Miami Sch. Medicine, 1977. Diplomate Nat. Bd. Med. Examiners. Intern Mt. Sinai Med. Ctr., Miami Beach, Fla., 1977-78, resident, 1978-79; chief medical resident Mt. Sinai Med. Ctr., Miami Beach, 1979-80; internist Stuart (Fla.) Med. Group, 1980-87, 91—, pres., 1985-87, 91—; internist Treasure Coast Med. Specialists, Stuart, 1987-91, v.p., 1987, sec., 1988-96; pres. Balboa Bldg. Ptnrship, Stuart, 1985-96; chmn. dept. medicine Martin Meml. Hosp., Stuart, 1983, chmn. credentials com., 1987, chmn. pharmacy and therapeutics com., 1993, 95-96. Recipient Julia Fisher Papper award U. Miami Sch. Medicine, 1976. Mem. Am. Soc. Internal Medicine, Am. Coll. Physicians, Phi Beta Kappa, Phi Kappa Phi, Alpha Omega Alpha. Home: 4825 SE Manatee Ter Stuart FL 34997-6997 Office: Stuart Med Group 417 Balboa Ave Stuart FL 34994-2327

RITTSCHOF, DANIEL, biology educator; b. Ariz., Feb. 26, 1946; s. Fred Paul and Beverly Jean (Johnson) R.; m. Josephine Bagenski, May 24, 1980; children: Jeanne, Clare. BS in Zoology, U. Mich., 1968, MS in Zoology, 1970, PhD, 1975. Postdoctoral fellow biochemistry dept. U. Calif., Riverside, 1975-78; rsch. physiologist UCLA Sch. Medicine, 1978-80; marine scientist U. Del., Lewes, 1980-82; from rsch. assoc. to assoc. prof. zoology Duke U., Beufort, N.C., 1982-91, assoc. prof. zoology, 1991—; cons. EI Du Pont Corp., 1994—; antifouling tech. adv. bd. Nova Bioscis. Ltd., 1995—; vis. assoc. prof. Hong Kong U. Sci. and Tech., Kowloon, 1995-96. Ray Lankester fellow Marine Biol. Assn., 1996. Mem. Am. Soc. Zoologists, Assn. Chemoreception Scis., Benthic Ecology Soc., Crustacean Soc., Internat. Soc. Chem. Ecology, European Soc. Comparative Endocrinology, European Marine Biol. Assn. Office: Duke U Marine Lab Beaufort NC 28516

RITZ, JOHN MICHAEL, education educator; b. Latrobe, Pa., Oct. 31, 1948; s. John Edward and Catharine May (Mills) R.; m. Sally Louise Ward, July 18, 1970; 1 child, Molly. BS, Purdue U., 1970; MS, U. Wis., Stout, 1974; EdD, W.Va. U., 1977. Tech. tchr. Nova High Sch., Ft. Lauderdale, Fla., 1970-72; faculty asst. U. Wis.-Stout, Menomonie, 1973-74; tng. assoc. W.Va. U., Morgantown, 1974-77; prof., chmn. Old Dominion U., Norfolk, Va., 1977—; bd. dirs. Tidewater Tech. Assocs., Virginia Beach, Va. Author: Exploring Communication, 1996, Exploring Production Systems, 1990. With U.S. Army, 1971-73, Fed. Republic of Germany. Recipient Tonelson award Old Dominion U., 1982. Mem. Internat. Tech. Edn. Assn. (Disting. Tech. Educator 1986, Meritorious Svc. award 1990), Coun. on Tech. Tchr. Edn. (treas. 1981-85, pres. 1996—, Tech. Tchr. Educator of Yr. 1993), Va. Tech. Edn. Assn. (pres. 1983). Office: Old Dominion U 4600 Hampton Blvd Norfolk VA 23508

RITZ, PAUL STEPHEN, library manager; b. Glencoe, Minn., Apr. 26, 1952; s. Rudolph Albert and Meta Eldoris (Deutschlander) R.; m. Beatrice Ilene Fanelli Boyza (div.). BA, Bowling Green (Ohio) State U., 1974; MS in Libr. Sci., Case Western Res. U., 1980. Notary pub. Asst. mgr. B. Dalton Bookseller #32, Toledo, Ohio, 1975-78; with Western Res. Hist. Soc. Libr., Cleve., 1973, 78, Cleve. Pub. Libr., 1979-80; gen. reference libr. Shaker Heights (Ohio) Pub. Libr., 1979-80; head children's libr. Cuyahoga County Pub. Libr., 1981-85; with Clearwater Pub. Libr. System, 1985—, libr. II br. supr., 1988—; chair ways and means com. Cuyahoga County Pub. Libr.; literacy tutor and spokesperson. Mem. South East Libr. Assn. (awards com.), Ch. and Synagogue Libr. Assn. (local br. v.p.), Fla. Pub. Libr. Assn. (chair of adult svcs. divsn., chair profl. devel. com.), Am. Tolkien Soc. (nat. sec., founder revs. editor), North Greenwood Assn. (sec. publicist), NAACP, YALSA (chair sci.-fiction genre com.), Sci. Fiction Club (past pres, publicist), Computer Club (past pres., publicist)., Avengers, 007, Dark Shawdows, Lincoln Club, Bells Club, Children's Lit. Club. Office: Clearwater Pub Libr System North Greenwood 1250 Palmetto St Clearwater FL 34615-4335

RITZEL, FREDERICK HOWARD, marketing manager; b. Balt., May 27, 1966; s. Frederick Howard Ritzel Jr. and Penny Ellen (Shettle) Crawford; m. Keri Lynne Kenison, Dec. 1, 1990. BBA, Radford U., 1989; MBA, Ga. So. U., 1992. Advt. asst. Envision Advt. Design, Radford, Va., 1989; advt. sales rep. Capital-Gazette Newspapers, Annapolis, Md., 1989-91; mktg. mgr. Commonwealth Coll., Virginia Beach, Va., 1993—. Mem. networking com. C. of C., Hampton Roads, 1994—. Mem. Am. Mktg. Assn., Alpha Beta Gamma. Home: 2924 Sour Gum Ct Virginia Beach VA 23456

RIVAS, ERNESTO, newspaper columnist; b. N.Y.C., Dec. 19, 1924; s. Gabry and Sara (Solis) R.; m. Cocó, Dec. 8, 1969; children from previous marriage: Sara, Patricia, Estrella, Ernesto Jr., Rene, Regina; children: Martín Javier, Gabriela. B of Arts and Sci., Colegio Centroamérica, Granada, Nicaragua. Press div. clk. UN, N.Y.C., 1947-48; reporter La Nueva Prensa, Managua, Nicaragua, 1949-52; dir. Radio Panamericana, Managua, 1952-60; with pub. rels. dept. Nicaragua Mission to UN, N.Y.C., 1960-62; dir. news Radio 590, Managua, 1963-66; columnist La Noticia, Managua, 1967-77; with pub. rels. dept. Emp. Nacional de Luz y Fuerza, Managua, 1978-79; UPI corr., Managua, 1979-80; columnist Diario Las Américas, Miami, Fla., 1981—. Mem. UDN 1981-86, Acción Democrética, Miami, 1986—. Republican. Roman Catholic.

RIVENBARK, REMBERT REGINALD, shipbuilding executive; b. St. Paul, S.C., Sept. 9, 1912; s. Reginald Vernon and Kathleen Francis (Fussell) R.; m. Marie Barbour, July 20, 1932; children: Patricia Pate, Rembert Reginald, Herbert William Barbour. Grad., Goldsboro (N.C.) High Sch. Foreman bottling dept. Coca Cola Bottling Co., New Bern, N.C., 1927-32; with Barbour Boat Works, New Bern, 1932—, successively bookkeeper, office mgr., gen. mgr., v.p., gen. mgr., 1945-57, pres., 1957—, bd. chmn., 1957—; bd. chmn., pres. Marine Trading Corp., New Bern, 1948-89. Mem. N.C. Med. Assn. (hon.), Am. Mgmt. Assn., U.S. C. of C., Am. Boat Builders Assn. (pres. 1960), Am. Ordinance Assn., Crippled Children's Assn. (life), N.C. Wildlife Assn., N.C. Fisheries Assn., N.Y. Athletic Club, East Carolina Yacht Club (charter mem.), New Bern Golf and Country Club, Mason, Shriner, Elks, Rotary. Home: 114 Trent Shores Dr New Bern NC 28562-7749 Office: 522525 Tryon Palace Dr New Bern NC 28560

RIVERA, ANGEL LUIS, chemical engineer; b. Bayamon, P.R., Oct. 7, 1950; s. Luis and Felicita (Lopez) R.; m. Marta V. Rivera, Mar. 21, 1975; children: Luis E., Mayra Lynn, Carlos A. BAChemE, U. P.R., Mayaquez, 1974, MS in Nuclear Engring., 1976; PhD in Environ. Engring., Northwestern U., Evanston, Il., 1981; MBA, U. Tenn., 1986. Devel. engr. Oak Ridge (Tenn.) Nat. Lab., 1980-84, group leader, 1984-86, project mgr., 1986-89, program mgr., 1990—. Contbr. articles to profl. jours. and publs. Mem. Am. Chem. Soc., Am. Inst. Chem. Engrs., Am. Assn. Cost Engrs., Am. Mgmt. Assn., IEEE Computer Soc., Tau Beta Pi. Home: 107 Garnet Ln Oak Ridge TN 37830-5601 Office: Oak Ridge Nat Lab PO Box 2003 Oak Ridge TN 37831-2003

RIVERA, MARLYN FELICIANO, medical facility administrator; b. Hormigueros, P.R., Oct. 25, 1954; came to U.S., 1976; d. Pascual Feliciano Padilla and Guillermina (Rodriguez) Casiano; m. Jorge Luis Rivera Burgos, June 20, 1976; children: George Rivera Jr., Daniel Ivan Rivera. BS, Coll. Agr., Mayaguez, P.R., 1976. Lab. specialist Blue Ridge Hosp., Charlottesbille, Va., 1979-81; office mgr. Jorge L. Rivera MD, 1984—. Author: El Flamboyan newsletter, 1985-87, 93-95. Mem. Club Demas de P.R. (pres. 1985-87, 93—). Republican. Baptist. Office: Jorge L Rivera MD 7390 Barlite Blvd Ste 300 San Antonio TX 78224-1339

RIVERA, OSCAR R., lawyer, corporate executive; b. Havana, Cuba, Dec. 8, 1956; s. Alcibiades R. and Marian (Fernandez) R.; m. Diana J. Bartnett; children: Peter, Taylor. BBA, U. Miami, 1978; JD, Georgetown U., 1981. Bar: Fla. 1981, U.S. Dist. Ct. (so. dist.) Fla. 1982, U.S. Tax Ct. 1982. Assoc. Corrigan, Zelman & Bander P.A., Miami, Fla., 1981-83; ptnr. Siegfried, Rivera, Lerner & De La Torre P.A., Miami, 1984—; adj. prof. law U. Miami, 1987—. Asst. mgr. campaign to elect Michael O'Donovan, Miami, 1976; mem. youth adv. bd., Miami, 1975-78, youth planning council Dade County, Miami, 1975-78. Mem. ABA, Cuban Am. Bar Assn., Internat. Coun. Shopping Ctrs. (v.p. Fla. polit. action com., v.p. Fla. govtl. affairs com., chmn. so. divsn. U.S. divisional govt. affairs), Little Havana Kiwanis, Orange Key, Omicron Delta Kappa, Phi Kappa Phi.

RIVERA-URRUTIA, BEATRIZ DALILA, psychology and rehabilitation counseling educator; b. Bayamón, P.R., Jan. 16, 1951; d. José and Carmen B. (Urrutia) Rivera; m. Julio C. Ribera, July 1, 1978; 1 child, Alejandra B. BA, U. P.R., 1972, MA, 1975; PhD, Temple U., 1982. Staff psychologist Learning Plus, Inc., Phila., 1979-80; cons. Hispanic Mental Health Inst., Phila., 1981-82; staff psychologist J.F. Kennedy Community Mental Health Ctr., Phila., 1982-83; prof. U. P.R., Rio Piedras, 1983—; cons. Jewish Employment & Vocat. Svcs., Phila., 1980; staff psychologist San Juan VA Hosp., Rio Piedras, 1990—. Contbr. articles to profl. jours. Vol. Parroquia San Juan Apóstol y Evangelista, Caguas, P.R., 1988-90, ARC, San Juan, 1990. Faculty U. P.R. instnl. rsch. grantee, 1986-87. Mem. P.R. Psychol. Assn. (bd. editors jour. 1984-89, bd. dirs. 1989-91), P.R. Lic. Bd. Psychologists (pres. ethics com. 1991-92). Home: Roble D 23 Arbolada Caguas PR 00725 Office: PO Box 22724 San Juan PR 00931-2724

RIVERÓN, ENRIQUE PEDRO, artist; b. Cienfuegos, Cuba, Jan. 31, 1902; came to U.S., 1927; s. Enrique and Maria Esperanza (Garcia) R.; m. Adria Delhort, 1928 (div. 1933); m. Noella S. Wible, Dec. 7, 1933 (dec.); 1 child, Patricia Maria Riverón Lee. Diploma, Villate Acad., Havana, Cuba, 1920; postgrad., San Fernando Royal Acad., Madrid, 1924-25, La Colarouse Acad., Paris, 1925-27, La Grand Chaumiere Acad., Paris, 1925-27. Illustrator, cartoonist newspapers and mags. Havana, 1920-58, Madrid, 1925-26, Buenos Aires, 1928, Rio de Janeiro, 1928-29, Santiago, Chile, 1929, Mexico City, 1930; illustrator, cartoonist New Yorker, Vanity Fair, Modern Screen, N.Y.C., 1927, Cine Mundial, Modern Screen, N.Y.C., 1930-45, Walt Disney, L.A., 1938-39, 1958—. One-man shows include Assn. Paris Amerique-Latine, 1926, Delphic Studios, N.Y., 1936, Lyceum Gallery, Havana, 1955, Galeria Sudamericana, N.Y., 1957, Wichita Art Mus., 1958, Gallery Modern Art, Sante Fe, 1961, Birgen Sandzen Meml. Gallery, Lindsborg, Kans., 1964, The Gallery, Ft. Lauderdale, 1965, Ft. Lauderdale Art Mus., 1966, Sala de Exposiciones U. P.R., 1967, Norbert Gallery, Houston, 1973, Bacardi Art Gallery, Ft. Lauderdale, 1974, Barbara Gillman Art Gallery, Miami, 1979, De Armas Gallery, 1980, Lowe Art Museum, 1980, (retrospective) SIBI Art Gallery, Miami, 1984, Bacardi Art Gallery, Miami Youth Mus., 1987; exhibited in group shows at Am. Artist's Congress Gallery, Hollywood, 1938, Galeria Sudamericana, N.Y.C., 1957, Southeast Banking Corp., Miami, 1973, Mus. Modern Art Latin Am., OAS, Washington, 1978, Equitable Gallery, N.Y.C., 1981, Instituto Cultural Domecq, A.C., Mexico City, 1986, Cuban Mus. Art and Culture, 1989, Ctr. Contemporary Art, Miami-Dade Main Libr., 1991, Villa du Parc-Centre D'expositions et D'echanges, Geneva, 1994, numerous others; competitions: San Diego 20th Ann. Soc. Ind. Artists, Grand Ctrl. Galleries, 1936, Denver Art Mus., 1949, Atlanta Art Assn. Galleries, 1960, Ft. Lauderdale Art Mus., 1966, 67, 72, Am. Painting Soc. of Four Arts, Palm Beach, 1971, 72, 75, others. Recipient scholarship, France, Spain, Italy, 1924, award Nat. Salon, Havana, 1935, Purchase prize Wichita Art Assn., 1958, 1st prize Emily Lowe Art Exhbn., 1961, 2d prize Bacardi Gallery, 1969, Hon. mention and Winners' Exhbn. award 12th Ann. Hortt Meml. Exhbn., 1970, Hon. mention 3d Ann. Pan Am. Art Exhbn., 1971, Cintas Found. Lifetime Achievement award, 1988. Mem. Group of Latin Am. Artists (founder).

RIVERO-POTTER, ALICIA, Spanish language educator. BA in Spanish and French, Rutgers U., 1976; MA in Hispanic Studies, Brown U., 1979, PhD in Hispanic Studies, 1983. Lectr. in Spanish Gustavus Adolphus Coll., St. Peter, Minn., 1981-83; asst. prof. Spanish U. N.C., Chapel Hill, 1983-90, assoc. prof. Spanish, 1990—. Author: Huidobro, Borges, Fuentes y Sarduy, 1991; mem. editl. bd., reader Hispanófila, 1991—, Ometeca: Humanities and Science, 1996—; mem. editl. bd. Ediciones Discurso Literio, 1987-90; mem. adv. bd., reader Romance Notes, 1987—; reader Studies in the Romance Languages and Literatures, 1987—, PMLA, 1995, Wayne State U. Press, 1995; reader-advisor South Atlantic Rev., 1988-89; contbr. poetry to anthologies, articles to profl. jours. Arts and Scis. fellow U. N.C., 1993. Mem. MLA, N.E. MLA, South Atlantic MLA, Soc. for Lit. and Sci., Latin Am. Studies Assn., Instituto Internat. Literatura Iberoamericana, Assn. Internat. Hispanistas, Phi Beta Kappa. Office: U N C Dept Romance Langs CB # 3170 238 Dey Hall Chapel Hill NC 27599-3170

RIVERS, JOHN MINOTT, JR., real estate developer; b. Charleston, S.C., May 28, 1945; m. Kathleen Hudson, Nov. 10, 1979. AB in Polit. Sci., U. N.C., Chapel Hill, 1967. Pres. Rivers Enterprises, Inc., Riverwood Devel. Corp., Chattooga Devel. Corp.; mem. adv. com. urban studies Coll. Charleston, 1975, exec. com. Miss. U.S.A./Universe, 1978, sustaining mem. Trident 2000; chmn. CBS TV Network Affiliates, 1982-83, govt. rels. com., 1980-87; organizer Bank of S.C., 1987; bd. dirs. Regional Devel. Alliance, chmn. mktg. com., 1994—. Explorer, mem. adv. bd. Charleston Coun. Boy Scouts Am., 1973-74; mem. com. Roper Hosp. Fund Drive, 1973-74; divsn. pres. United Way, 1974, vice chmn. budget bd., 1974, chmn., 1975, pacesetter divsn., 1976, mem. exec. com., 1975; fund raiser Spoleto U.S.A., 1978; bd. dirs. YMCA Mil. Svcs. Ctr., 1972-78, chmn. publicity com., 1977; treas. Charleston Travel Industry Devel. Coun., 1976, bd. dirs., 1977-78; mem. City Charleston All-Am. com., 1977-78, chmn., 1978; co-chmn. Charleston Area Campaign United Negro Coll. Fun, 1977-78; mem. City Charleston Clean Cmty. Sys. Com., 1977-79, chmn. subcom., 1978-79; mem. Charleston Area Cmty. Rels. com., 1977-78, vice chmn., 1979-82; mem. bd. trustees Ashley Hall, 1983-92, fund raising com. 1983—; mem. adv. bd. The Citizens and So. Nat. Bank S.C., 1974-86; bd. dirs. The Citizens & So. Nat. Bank S.C. Trust, 1981-86; mem. Gibbes Mus. Art, S.C. Hist. Soc., St. Cecilia Soc., St. Philips Episcopal Ch.; pres. adv. coun. Med. U. of S.C., 1994-95; cons. Trident Econ. Devel. Authority, 1994; chancellor's club U. N.C. Chapel Hill, 1987—, nat. devel. coun. 1989—, Wilson libr. fellows mem., 1993—; bd. trustees Choate Sch., 1990-94, exec. com., 1991-92, chmn. of compensation com., 1991-92; commn. mem. S.C. Edns. TV, 1983—, chmn. of new bldg. com., 1989—; exec. com., dir. Cheeha-Combahee Plantation, 1991—; mem. Charleston Mus.; sponsor Charleston Symphony Orch., Nat. Wild Turkey Fedn. Mem. S.C. Broadcasters Assn. (bd. dirs. endl. found. 1982-83), Charleston Indsl. Assn. (sec. 1975-80, bd. dirs. 1975-86, v.p. 1981-86), S.C. State C. of C. (bd. dirs. 1978-81), U. N.C. Alumni Assn. (life, bd. visitors 1989-92), U.S. Naval Supply corps Alumni Assn., Nat. Audubon Soc., Carolina Yacht Club, Yeaman's Hall Club, Wade Hampton Golf Club, High Hampton Golf and Country Club, Chatooga Club, U.S. Croquet Assn. (chmn. internat. rels. com. 1993—), Ducks Unltd., Everglades Club, Piedmont Driving Club. Office: PO Box 21050 Charleston SC 29413-1050

RIVERS, MARIE BIE, broadcasting executive; b. Tampa, Fla., July 12, 1928; d. Norman Albion and Rita Marie (Monrose) Bie; m. Eurith Dickinson Rivers, May 3, 1952; children—Eurith Dickinson, III, Rex B., M. Kells, Lucy L., Georgia. Student, George Washington U., 1946. Engaged in real estate bus., 1944-51, radio broadcasting, 1951—; pres., CEO, part owner Sta. WGUN, Atlanta, 1951—, Stas. KWAM and KJMS, Memphis, Sta. WEAS-AM-FM, Savannah, Ga., Stas. WGOV and WAAC, Valdosta, Ga., Sta. WSWN and Sta. WBGF, Belle Glade, Fla.; owner, chairperson, pres., CEO Sta. WCTH, Islamorada, Fla.; pres., CEO The Gram Corp., real estate com. Creative Christian Concepts Corp., 1985, pres., CEO Ocala, 1986; owner Suncoast Broadcasting Inc. Author: A Woman Alone, 1986; contbr. articles to profl. jours. Mem. Fla. Assn. Broadcasters (bd. dirs.), Ga. Assn. Broadcasters (bd. dirs., William J. Brooks award for exceptional svc. to radio broadcasting 1995), Coral Reef Yacht Club (Coconut Grove, Fla.), Palm Beach Polo and Country Club, Kappa Delta. Roman Catholic. Office: 11924 Forest Hill Blvd Ste 1 West Palm Beach FL 33414-6257

RIVERS, OTIS THOMAS, sales executive; b. Hampton, S.C., Sept. 19, 1961; s. John Calhoun Rivers Jr. and Mary Frances (Lightsey) Owens. BS in Agrl. Econs., Clemson U., 1983. Br. mgr. Simmons Irrigation Co., Hilton Head Island, S.C., 1983-84; state sales rep. Simmons Irrigation Co., Walterboro, S.C., 1984-85; div. mgr. Meadowbrook Enterprises, Savannah, Ga., 1985; sales rep. Brown & Williamson Tobacco Co., Hilton Head Island, 1986; dist. sales mgr. turf div. Rain Bird Sales Inc., Anderson, S.C., 1986-88; mgr. regional sales, turf div. Garden Am. Corp., Anderson, 1988-90; pres. Phillip Rivers Corp., Inc., Anderson, 1988-90, OTR Inc., Anderson, 1990—. Mem. Hilton Head Island Jaycees (Outstanding Mem. award 1985), Chi Psi Alumni Assn. (sec., treas. 1985—), Lodge: Masons. Republican. Lutheran. Lodge: Masons. Office: PO Box 5750 Anderson SC 29623

RIVERS, WILLIAM ELBERT, English language educator; b. Wadesboro, N.C., Apr. 8, 1946; s. Elbert Elmore and Helen Loreen (Sanders) R.; m. Alicia Anne Hickman, June 8, 1968 (div. 1997); children: Anna Lorraine, William Evan, Ashleigh Elaine. BA, Wofford Coll., 1968; MA, U. N.C., 1971, PhD, 1976. From asst. prof. to assoc. prof. English Auburn (Ala.) U., 1975-83; assoc. prof. English U. S.C., Columbia, 1983—, dir. freshman composition, 1987-91, prin. investigator NCR Document Validation Lab., 1987-94. Author/editor: Business Reports: Samples From the Real World; author: Issues and Images, 1993; contbr. articles to profl. jours. Mem. MLA, Nat. Coun. Tchrs. English, Soc. for Tech. Comm., Assn. Tchrs. of Tech. Writing, Kiwanis, Phi Beta Kappa. Methodist. Office: University of South Carolina Dept of English Columbia SC 29208

RIVERS-LUCEY, AMANDA HOPE, elementary school educator; b. Chesterfield, S.C., Dec. 25, 1968; d. Louis Davis Sr. and Nina Gertrude (Morris) Rivers; m. Kevin Patrick Lucey, Oct. 8, 1994. BS, Winthrop U., 1995. Cert. tchr., N.S. Kindergarten, 1st and 2d grade tchr. Best of Am., Inc., Statesville, N.C., 1995—; presenter N.C. Assn. Edn. Young Children, 1996—; area coord. Job Tng. Partnership Assn., Mooresville, N.C., 1994-96. Recipient Cir. of Excellence award Hampton Inn, Memphis, 1993. Mem. ASCD. Home: 175 Sunshine Dr Mooresville NC 28115 Office: Best of America Inc 115 Cooper St Statesville NC 28677

RIVES, THOMAS NELSON, minister; b. Memphis, May 18, 1946; s. Malcomb Eldridge and Dorothy Bell (Nelson) R.; m. Dianne Saleeby, Dec. 17, 1967; children: Thomas N. Jr., Ashley Dianne. BS in Edn., Memphis State U., 1971; postgrad., Southwestern Sem., 1977-79. Ordained to ministry Bapt. Ch., 1975. Min. youth Whitehaven Bapt. Ch., Memphis, 1970-74, 1st Bapt. Ch., Cleve., 1974-77; assoc. pastor 1st Bapt. Ch., Hurst, Tex., 1977-79; min. recreation Red Bank Bapt. Ch., Chattanooga, Tenn., 1979-83; assoc. pastor 1st Bapt. Ch., Tampa, Fla., 1983-86, Bay Area Bapt. Ch., Tampa, 1986-94; pastor Carrollwood Bapt. Ch., Tampa, 1994—. Author: (pamphlet) Bring on the Clowns, 1990; author: The Twelve. Sgt. U.S. Army, 1967-70. Recipient Army Commendation medal U.S. Army, 1969, Gov.'s Religious Commnedation, 1982. Mem. Recreation Assn. Fla Bapt. (pres. 1986-89), Fellowship Christian Magicians, Clowns of Am., World Clown Assn., Tampa Bay Bapt. Assn. (moderator 1994-95). Home: 15009 Sunglow Ct Tampa FL 33624 Office: Carrollwood Baptist Church 5395 Ehrlich Rd Tampa FL 33625-5534

RIVIERE, JIM EDMOND, pharmacologist, educator; b. New Bedford, Mass., Mar. 3, 1953; s. Raymond R. Riviere and Gertrude E. Pelletier-Riviere; m. Nancy Ann Monteiro-Riviere, May 31, 1976; children: Christopher, Brian, Jessica. BS, MS, Boston Coll., 1976; DVM, PhD, Purdue U., 1980. Lic. to practice vet. medicine; diplomate Am. Bd. Forensic Examiners, Am. Bd. Forensic Medicine. From asst. prof. to assoc. prof. N.C. State U., Raleigh, 1981-88, prof., 1988-92, Burroughs-Wellcome disting. prof. pharmacology, 1992—, dir. Cutaneous Pharmacology and Toxicology Ctr., 1989—; cons. for govt. and pharm. cos.; mem. com. on revision U.S. Pharmacopeia, 1995—. Editor 5 books; author over 250 rsch. manuscripts; holder 3 patents in field. Recipient Ebert prize Am. Pharm. Assn., 1991, Outstanding Rsch. award N.C. State U. Alumni Assn., 1993, Disting. Alumni award Purdue U., 1991, numerous rsch. grants. Fellow Am. Acad. Vet. Pharmacology and Therapeutics (editor 1989-92); mem. Am. Assn. Pharm. Scientist, Soc. Toxicology, Am. Vet. Med. Assn., Am. Coll. Forensic Examiners, Am. Med. Writers Assn. Office: NC State U 4700 Hillsborough St Raleigh NC 27606-1428

RIVNER, MICHAEL HARVEY, neurologist; b. Bklyn., Sept. 26, 1950; s. Norman and Carol (Simson) R.; m. Roberta Fran Gottlieb, Aug. 13, 1978; children: Asher, Joshua, Peter, Harold. BA, Duke U., 1972; MD, Emory U., 1978. Diplomate Am. Bd. Psychiatry and Neurology, added qualifications in clin. neurophysiology; diplomate Am. Bd. Electrodiagnostic Medicine. Intern, resident in neurology Med. Coll. Ga., Augusta, 1978-82; from fellow to assoc. prof. neurology Med. Coll. Ga., 1982—; cons. neurology Eisenhower Med. Hosp., Ft. Gordon, Ga., 1982—, VA Med. Ctr., Augusta, 1982—. V.p., campaign chmn. Augusta Jewish Found., 1994, pres., 1995-96; treas. CSRA Swim League, Augusta, 1993—; treas. Augusta Jewish C.C. Fellow Am. Acad. Neurology; mem. Am. Assn. Electrodiagnostic Medicine (equipment com. 1984-87, tng. program com. 1989-92, edn. com. 1992—, chmn. edn. com. 1994—), Southeastern Neuromuscular Group (pres. 1996—). Office: Med Coll Ga EMG Lab Augusta GA 30912

RIZZETTA, CAROLYN TERESA, musical instrument, sound recording entrepreneur; b. Chgo., June 22, 1942; d. Frank Thomas and Teresa Margaret (Sylvester) Peter; m. Samuel Charles Rizzetta, Apr. 23, 1966. Student, Art Inst. Chgo., 1961-63; BA, Rosary Coll., 1964, MLS, 1965. Reference librarian Art Dept. Chgo. Pub. Library, 1965; freelance illustrator Macmillan Pub. Co., N.Y.C., 1966; registrar, cataloger Kalamazoo (Mich.) Pub. Mus., 1967; asst. librarian Def. Nuclear Agy., Washington, 1968-69; serials cataloger Library of Congress, Washington, 1970-73, with intern, 1971-72; head of serials U. Va., Charlottesville, 1974-77; musical instrument maker Valley Head, W.Va., 1978-83; bus. mgr. Rizetta Music, Inwood, W.Va., 1984—. Illustrator Invertabrate Zoology, 1969. Mem. Am. Craft Council, Guild of Am. Luthiers. Home and Office: Rizzetta Music PO Box 510 Inwood WV 25428-0510

ROACH, DAVID GILES, computing and information systems manager; b. Wisner, La., Oct. 26, 1948; s. David and Annie Laura (Hanks) R.; m. Vivian Viola Curry, July 23, 1967. BS in Math., Northeast La. U., 1970; MSc in Math. and Geology, U. Miss., 1975. Grad. teaching asst. computer ctr. Northeast La. U., Monroe, 1970-72; grad. asst. computer ctr. U. Miss., University, 1972, user svcs. mgr., 1973-74, asst. dir. user svcs., 1974-78; assoc. dir. computer ctr. Office Computing & Info. Systems, University, 1978-88, dep. dir. computing and info. sys., 1988—; apptd. mem. Miss. Info. Tech. Svcs. Bd., 1994—; chmn. Miss. Higher Edn. Rsch. Network Policy and Planning Com., 1992-94; chmn. bd. dirs. DEC Computer User Soc. S.E. U.S., 1977-78; voting rep. IBM Share, 1981—, CDC Users Group, 1987-90, Amdahl Users Group, 1986—, Cray Users Group, 1991—. Contbr. article to profl. jour. Planning com. mem. Oxford (Miss.)/Lafayette County Sesquicentennial, 1987; bd. dirs. Oxford/Lafayette County Rep. Party, 1987, Oxford/Lafayette County United Way, 1987-90; sustaining mem. Yocona Area Coun. Boy Scouts Am., 1981—. Mem. Assn. Computing Machinery, Spl. Interest Group on Univ. and Coll. Computing Svcs., Miss. Hist. Soc., Oxford Lions (pres. 1986-87, Lion of Yr. 1986-87, Svc. award 1992-93). Methodist. Home: PO Box 2241 University MS 38677-2241 Office: Computing & Info Systems Rm 305 Powers Hall University MS 38677

ROACH, EDGAR MAYO, JR., lawyer; b. Pinehurst, N.C., June 2, 1948; s. Edgar Mayo Sr. and Rhuamer (Richardson) R.; m. Deborah Day, Oct. 10, 1970; children: Edgar Mayo III, John Clifton. BA, Wake Forest U., 1969; JD with honors, U. N.C., 1974. Bar: N.C. 1974, Va. 1976, U.S. Ct. Appeals (4th cir.) 1976. Law clk. to judge U.S. Ct. Appeals (4th cir.), Abingdon, Va., 1974-75; assoc. Hunton & Williams, Richmond, Va., 1975-80; ptnr. Hunton & Williams, Raleigh, N.C., 1981-94; sr. v.p. Va. Power, Richmond, 1994—. Home: 3142 Monument Ave Richmond VA 23221-1457 Office: Va Power 1 James River Plz Richmond VA 23219-3229

ROACH, JOHN VINSON, II, retail company executive; b. Stamford, Tex., Nov. 22, 1938; s. John V. and Agnes M. (Hanson) R.; m. Barbara Jean Wiggin, Mar. 31, 1960; children: Amy, Lori. BA in Physics and Math., Tex. Christian U., 1961, MBA, 1965. V.p. Radio Shack, 1972-75, Radio Shack Mfg., 1975-78; exec. v.p. Radio Shack, 1978-80; gen. mgr. data processing Tandy Corp., Ft. Worth, 1967-73, pres., 1980—, chief exec. officer, 1981—, chmn., 1982—, also bd. dirs.; bd. dirs. Justin Industries. Bd. dirs. Van Cliburn Found.; chmn. bd. Tex. Christian U. Mem. Ft. Worth Club, City Club, Colonial Country Club. Office: Tandy Corp 1800 1 Tandy Ctr Fort Worth TX 76102

ROACH, JON GILBERT, lawyer; b. Knoxville, June 17, 1944; s. Walter Davis and Lena Rose (Chapman) R.; m. Mintha Marie Evans, Oct. 22, 1977; children: Jon G., II, Evan Graham. B.S., U. Tenn., 1967, J.D., 1969. Bar: Tenn. 1970, D.C. 1981, U.S. Ct. Appeals (6th cir.). Assoc. Stone & Bozeman, Knoxville, 1970-71; pvt. practice, Knoxville, 1971-83; city atty., dir. of law, Knoxville, 1976-83; ptnr. Peck, Shaffer & Williams, Knoxville, 1983-90, Watson, Hollow & Reeves, P.L.C., 1990—; mem. faculty Knoxville Bus. Coll., 1973-74; mem. Tenn. Commn. on Continuing Legal Edn. and Specialization of Tenn. Supreme Ct. Active Big Bros., Big Sisters of Knoxville, Am. Cancer Soc., Jr. Achievement. Mem. ABA, Tenn. Bar Assn. (mem. ho. of dels.), Knoxville Bar Assn., D.C. Bar Assn. Democrat. Baptist. Club: Kiwanis (East Knoxville). Home: 1701 River Shores Dr Knoxville TN 37914-6023 Office: Watson Hollow & Reeves PLC PO Box 131 1700 Plaza First Tenn Knoxville TN 37929-9701

ROADEN, ARLISS LLOYD, retired higher education executive director, former university president; b. Bark Camp, Ky., Sept. 27, 1930; s. Johnie Samuel and Ethel Nora (Killian) R.; m. Mary Etta Mitchell, Sept. 1, 1951; children: Janice Arletta Roaden Skelton, Sharon Kay Roaden Hagen. Grad., Cumberland Coll., 1949; AB, Carson Newman Coll., 1951; MS, U. Tenn., 1958, EdD, 1961; PhD (hon.), Cumberland Coll., 1986; DLitt (hon.), Tusculum Coll., 1992. With Oak Ridge Inst. Nuclear Studies, 1957-59, Auburn U., 1961-62; mem. faculty Ohio State U., 1962-74, prof. edn., 1967-74, acting dean Coll. Edn., 1968-70, vice provost for research, dean Grad. Sch., 1970-74; pres. Tenn. Tech. U., 1974-85, pres. emeritus, 1985—; dir. Tenn. Higher Edn. Commn., Nashville, 1985-95, exec. dir. emeritus, 1995—; summer vis. prof. Marshall U., 1961, U. So. Calif., 1964, Ind. U., 1967; cons. ednl. instns., 1961—; pres. Tenn. Coll. Assn., 1978; chmn. sci. and tech. com. Am. Assn. State Colls. and Univs., 1980; chmn. task force on program and instl. assessment State Higher Edn. Exec. Officers', 1987, pres. 1993-94, chmn. coun. postsecondary accreditation liaison com., 1986-88, exec. com., 1988-95, pres. elect 1992-93; mem. exec. bd. trustees Southern Assn. Colls. and Schs., 1986—, chair communications com., 1990—, mem. task force, 1990—; mem. Southern Regional Edn. Bd., 1985—, chmn. procedures com. for reviewing bylaw changes and revisions, 1988-89; mem. exec. com., state rep., treas., chair Internal Audit Com., 1990-91, Edn. Commn. States, 1987-90; mem. Tenn. Econ. Cabinet Coun., 1988—, chmn.m 1988-91, bd. dirs. 1988—Fgn. Lang. Inst.; treas., chair Internal Audit Com., 1990-91; mem. Performance Standards in Vocat.-Tech. Edn. Working Group, U.S. Dept. Edn., 1990. Co-author: The Research Assistantship: Recommendations for Colleges and Universities, 1975; editor: Problems of School Men in Depressed Urban Areas, 1967; contbr. articles to profl. jours. State chmn. Tenn. Cancer Soc. Crusade, 1986-88, bd. dirs., 1987—; mem. exec. bd., commr. Mid. Tenn. coun. Boy Scouts Am., 1987-88, mem. nat. coun., 1988—, chmn. scouts membership rels. com.; mem. Phi Delta Kappa Found., 1965—, past chmn. bd. govs., mem. futures and diamond jubilee coms., 1989—; chmn. Blue Ribbon Com. To Respond to Edn. Goals, 1990; bd. dirs. Nat. Project 714, 1986—, pres.-elect, 1987-88, chmn., 1988-89; pres. alumni assn. bd. Cumberland Coll., 1987-88, chmn. devel. bd., 1994—; adult Sunday sch. tchr. Woodmont Bapt. Ch., chmn. pers. com. , 1989—. With U.S. Army, 1951-53. Research grantee Phi Delta Kappa Internat., 1968; named Distinguished Alumnus Cumberland Coll., 1970; recipient Distinguished Alumni and Faculty Centennial medallion Coll. Edn., 1970, Distinguished Service award Council Grad. Students, 1974; both Ohio State U.; recipient Silver Beaver award Boy Scouts Am., Rotarian of Yr., 1984; Eagle Scout honoree Middle Tenn. Coun. Boy Scouts Am., 1989, others. Fellow Oxford Soc. Scholars; mem. AAAS, Am. Assn. Higher Edn., Acad. Polit. and Social Scis., Am. Ednl. Rsch. Assn. (chmn. publs. com. 1979-80), Nat. Soc. Study Edn., Nat. Assn. State Colls. and Land Grant Univs.,, Lions (bd. dirs. Nashville 1988-90, pres. 1991-92, zone chmn. 1992-93, vice dist. gov. 1995), Rotary (bd. dirs.), Order of Lion and Eagle, Phi Kappa Phi, Phi Delta Kappa (Disting. Svc. award Ohio State U. chpt. 1974), Kappa Phi Kappa, Kappa Delta Pi. Baptist.

ROAN, FORREST CALVIN, JR., lawyer; b. Waco, Tex., Dec. 18, 1944; s. Forrest Calvin and Lucille Elizabeth (McKinney) R.; m. Vickie Joan Howard, Feb. 15, 1969 (div. Dec. 1983); children: Amy Katherine, Jennifer Louise. BBA, U.Tex., Austin, 1973, JD, 1976. Bar: Tex. 1976, U.S. Dist. Ct. (we. dist.) Tex. 1977, U.S. Ct. Appeals (5th cir.) 1977, U.S. Supreme Ct. 1979, U.S. Ct. Appeals (11th cir.) 1981. Prin. Roan & Assocs., Austin, 1969-71; counsel/com. dir. Tex. Ho. of Reps., 1972-75; assoc. Heath, Davis & McCalla, Austin, 1975-78; prin. Roan & Gullahorn, P.C., Austin, 1978-85, Roan & Autrey (formerly Roan & Simpson), P.C., 1986—; bd. dirs. Lawyers Credit Union, chmn., 1982, 83; bd. dirs. pub. law sect. State Bar Tex., 1980-

84; chmn. Fin. Counseling and Intermediation, Inc.; dir. Am. Bankers Gen. Agy. With Tex. Army N.G., 1966-74. Fellow Tex. Bar Found.; mem. Tex. Assn. Def. Counsel, ABA, Travis County Bar Assn., Knights of the Symphony, Tex. Lyceum Assn. (v.p., bd. dirs. 1983-87), Austin C. of C. Methodist. Clubs: Met., Austin, Headliners. Lodges: Masons, Shriners (Parsons Masonic Master 1976-77). Office: Roan & Autrey 710 First Bank Tower 400 W 15th St Austin TX 78701-1647

ROANE, DAVID JAMES, JR., auditor; b. Petersburg, Va., Nov. 11, 1960; s. David James Roane, Sr. and Anne (Vest) Savage; m. Bonnie L. Dear, Dec. 3, 1983; two children. BS, Va. Commonwealth U., 1984. CPA, Va.; cert. info. systems auditor. Audit intern Continental Fin. Services Co., Richmond, Va., 1983-84, staff auditor, 1984-85; EDP auditor Life Ins. Co. of Va., Richmond, 1985-86; EDP auditor James River Corp., Richmond, Va., 1986-88, sr. EDP auditor, 1990—; technologies group specialist Mgmt. Info. Systems, 1989-90. Treas. Civic Assn., Chester, Va., 1985-91; chmn. fin. com. Matoaca United Meth. Ch., 1990-92, chmn. adminstrv. bd., 1993-95. Methodist. Home: 2665 Mistwood Forest Dr Chester VA 23831-7032

ROATH-ALGERA, KATHLEEN MARIE, massage therapist; b. Binghamton, N.Y., Feb. 7, 1952; d. Stephen James and Virginia Mary (Purdy) Roath; m. Parker Newcomb Wheeler Jr., Sept. 18, 1971 (div. June 1976); 1 child, Colleen Marie Wheeler; m. John M. Algera, Feb. 14, 1981. AS in Phys. Edn., Dean Jr. Coll., Franklin, Mass., 1971; BS in Edn., Boston U., 1977; postgrad., U. Ctrl. Fla., Orlando, 1981-82; grad., Reese Inst. Massage Therapy, Oviedo, Fla., 1988. Lic. massage therapist; master practitioner in myofascial release. Counselor Dept. Def., Orlando, 1979-84; tchr. Divine Mercy Cath. Sch., Merritt Island, Fla., 1984-85; courier Emery Worldwide, Orlando, 1985-89; massage therapist, dir., owner Massage Therapy Clinic of Titusville, Fla., 1989—; instr., supr. clin. internship Reese Inst., 1992-95; assoc. Todd Jaffe, M.D., 1995-96. Mem. Am. Massage Therapy Assn., Fla. State Massage Therapy Assn. (pres. Brevard County 1992—, Therapist of Yr. 1991-92), Nat. Cert. Bd. Therapeutic Massage and Bodywork (recert. chair 1994—). Home: 5528 River Oaks Dr Titusville FL 32780 Office: Massage Therapy Clinic Titusville 3410 S Park Ave Titusville FL 32780-5139

ROBBE, ADRIAN DONALD, military officer; b. Pitts., May 21, 1952; s. Domenic Michael and Matilda (Quintina) R.; m. Donna F. Robbe, June 14, 1974; children: Melissa Ann, Jennifer Lynn, Matthew Benjamin, Sarah Beth.; BS, U.S. Mil. Acad., 1974; MS in Mech. Engring., Calif. State U., Sacramento, 1975; student, Def. Systems Mgmt. Coll., Ft. Belvoir, Va., 1981, Armed Forces Staff Coll., Norfolk (Va.) Naval Base, 1987-88; M in Religious Edn., Tabernacle Bapt. Theol. Sem., Virginia Beach, Va., 1996. Asst. chief Agena Launch Ops. Divsn. 6555th Aerospace Test Group, Patrick AFB, Fla., 1975-78; chief Titan III Launch Vehicle Integration 6555th Aerospace Test Group, Patrick AFB, 1978-79; structural integrity engr. Wright Aero. Labs., Wright-Patterson AFB, Ohio, 1980-81; B-1B Engine Integration mgr. Aero. Systems Divsn., Wright-Patterson AFB, 1981-82, F-15/F-16 F110 Engine Application Mgr., 1982-83, exec. officer alt. fighter engine source selection, 1983-84; chief R & D officer Assignments Br. Air Force Mil. Pers. Ctr., Randolph AFB, Tex., 1984-87; ops. analyst Supreme Allied Command Atlantic (NATO), Norfolk, Va., 1988-92; chief Nuc. Requirements Br. HQ Air Combat Command, Langley AFB, Va., 1992—; air combat comdr. Langley AFB, 1996—. Author: (book) A Defense of the Textus Receptus and the King James Authorized Version, 1996; (booklet) An Exposition of Proverbs 22:6, 1996,A Practical Guide for Planning, Organizing, and Implementing Old Fashioned Day on the Farm Churchwide Family Fellowship, 1996. Editor: The Combat Edge Safety Magazine. Children's dept. Sunday Sch. Tabernacle Bapt. Ch., Virginia Beach, Va. Decorated Air Force Meritorious Svc. medal, Air Force Mil. Pers. Ctr., Randolph AFB, Tex., 1987, Def. Meritorious Svc. Medal Supreme Allied Command Atlantic, Norfolk, Va., 1992. Home: 1021 Goldleaf Ct Virginia Beach VA 23464 Office: Air Combat Command 130 Andrews St Ste 302 Langley AFB VA 23665

ROBBEN, MARY MARGARET, portrait artist; b. Bethesda, Md., Oct. 30, 1948; d. John Otto and Mary Margaret (McConnaughy) R. Student, Ohio U., 1967-71; B.Visual Art, Ga. State U., 1984. Visual merchandising staff Macy's Dept. Store, Union City, Ga., 1985-86; embroidery designer So. Promotions, Peachtree City, Ga., 1987-90; portrait artist Personal Touch Portraits, Peachtree City, Ga., 1991-95, Margy's Portraiture, Peachtree City, 1996—. Mortar Bd. scholar, 1984. Fellow Internat. Biographical Ctr. (life); mem. AAUW, Ga. State U. Alumni Assn., Golden Key, Am. Bus. Women's Assn., Nat. Mus. of Women in the Arts. Home and Office: 207 Battery Way Peachtree City GA 30269-2126

ROBBINS, CHRISTOPHER LINDSAY, federal government official; b. Durham, N.C., Nov. 29, 1941; s. George Lindsay and Blanch Geneva (Atkins) R.; m. Emily Carol Guy Robbins; children: Matthew Christopher, Suzanne Michelle, Christine Carol, Elizabeth Marie. BS in History, U. Tenn., 1966. Inventory mgmt. asst. AMC Supply Mgmt. Intern Sch., Rock Island, Ill., 1966-67; inventory mgmt. specialist Missile Command, Redstone Arsenal, Ala., 1967-70; supply mgmt. asst. Cecil Field NAS, Jacksonville, Fla., 1970-71; inventory mgmt. specialist Gen. Materiel & Parts Ctr., New Cumberland, Pa., 1971-72; staff officer Matcom, Zweibrucken, Germany, 1972-74; officer, specialist Supervisory Supply Mgmt. USAMMAE/MMC, 1974-76; supervisory supply mgmt. officer U.S. Garrison, U.S. Army Garrison, Md., 1976-79; staff mgr., logistical analyst U.S. Army Materiel Command, Alexandria, Va., 1979-83, 91—; supply sys. analyst HQ U.S. Army Europe, Heidelberg, Germany, 1983-91. Home: 6328 Sharps Dr Centreville VA 22020

ROBBINS, EARL L., oil operator; b. Detroit, Mar. 9, 1921; s. Louis and Ida Robbins; m. Dorothy D. Robbins, Nov. 12, 1949 (div. Mar. 1974); children—T. Paul, Louis J., Loralee. BA, Wayne State U., 1949; MBA, U. Chgo., 1951. Owner, Enurtone of Tex., Houston, 1951-55; v.p. Continental Securities Co., Houston, 1955-57; owner, mgr. Robbins & Co., Houston, 1957-59; div. mgr. Great Books, Houston, 1960-96; owner, mgr. Robbins Oil Co., Houston, 1996—; exec. v.p. Solar Contractors, Inc.; CEO Wealth Co. Bus. Cons. Bd. dirs. Cancer League, Houston, 1983-84, Children's Resource and Info. Soc.; chmn. Alley Theater Gala, Houston, 1983; life mem. Houston Livestock Show, 1978-81; chmn. Cheesecake Hall of Fame. Served to maj. USAAF, 1941-46. Decorated Air medal; recipient Disting. Service award Am. Diabetes Assn., Houston, 1982. Mem. Associated Builders and Contractors Greater Houston (membership dir.), Wealth Corp. Sales and Bus. Conss. Office: Robbins Oil Co PO Box 35322 Houston TX 77235-5322

ROBBINS, HONEY-MIAM, financial executive; b. Toronto, Ont., Can., Apr. 10, 1930; came to U.S., 1965; d. Daniel David and Fannie (Schidlowski) Serott; m. Julian Pearson, Mar. 25, 1951 (div. 1973); m. Nat Robbins, Jan. 25, 1976 (dec. Sept. 1988); children: Cheryl Beth Pearson Elbrand, Debra Pearson Abelow, Geoffrey. Student, McGill U., 1948-49, U. Miami, Denver, 1949-50, 68-69; grad., Coll. for Fin. Planning, Denver, 1985. Cert. fin. planner; registered investment advisor, Wash., Fla. Pres. Star Investment Group, Montreal, 1964-65; registered rep., dist. mgr. Investors Diversified Svcs., Miami, Fla., 1974-77; registered rep., fin. planner Nat. Life Vt. and Equity Svcs., Miami, Fla., 1977-79, Mony Life & Mony Securities, Coral Gables, Fla., 1979-83, 1st Fin. Investment Svcs., Coral Gables, Fla., 1983-86; pres. Honath Inc. and Fin. Svcs., Miami, 1981—; cons. World Bus. Brokers, Miami, 1981—, Stetson Co., Miami, 1986—; assoc. broker Evensky, Brown Investments, Inc., Coral Gables, 1986-90, Comprehensive Fin. Svcs., Severna Pk., Md., 1991, IFG Securities Network, Inc., Atlanta, 1996; investment advisor SEC, Washington, 1987. Pres. Temple Beth Am Sisterhood, Miami, 1967; life mem. Sunshine Cancer Group, Miami, 1975. Mem. Internat. Assn. Fin. Planning (bd. dirs. 1976, sec. 1977, Cert Merit 1986), Internat. Bd. Cert. Registered Fin. Planners, Inst. Cert. Fin. Planners (bd. dirs. South Fla. Soc. 1991-92). Republican. Jewish. Office: Honath Fin Svcs 14720 SW 83rd Ave Miami FL 33158-1915

ROBBINS, JANE LEWIS, elementary school educator; b. New Iberia, La., Dec. 14, 1942; d. William Lewis and Maurine (James) R. BS, U. Okla., 1965; ME, So. Methodist U., 1972; postgrad. Tex. Women's U., 1981, 83, 85; edn. adminstrn. cert. East Tex. State U., 1991. Tchr., Lone Grove Ind. Sch. Dist. (Okla.), 1964-65, Concord-Carlisle (Mass.) Regional Sch. Dist., 1966-67, Newton (Mass.) Pub. Schs., 1967-68, Highland Park Ind. Sch. Dist., Dallas, 1968—, Highland Pk. instrnl. specialist, dist. appraiser, coord. dist. gifted and talented, coord. student tchrs., mentor new tchrs., coord. instrnl. leadership program, interim elem. prin., 1990-93; asst. prin. McCulloch Intermediate Sch., Dallas; instr. reading clinic So. Meth. U., 1972-75, Sch. Edn., summer 1978, adj. prof. Div. Ednl. Studies; chmn. English dept. McCulloch Middle Sch.; regional coordinator Tex. Acad. Pentathlon, 1985-89. Mem. ASCD, Tex. Assn. Improvement Reading, Tex. Assn. Gifted and Talented, Assn. Children with Learning Disabilities, Internat. Reading Assn. (North Tex. Coun.), Tex. Elem. Prins. and Suprs. Assn. (Acad. III), Nat. Coun. Tchrs. of English, Tex. Mid. Sch. Assn, Mid. Sch. Consortium, Tex. Assn. Secondary Sch. Prins., Pi Beta Phi, Delta Kappa Gamma. Republican. Episcopalian.

ROBBINS, WILLIAM DAVID, retired police officer; b. Martins Ferry, Ohio, Dec. 22, 1930; s. Harold David and Hazel Clareice (Burnett) R.; m. Marion M. Ruckh, May, 1953; children: Christine Diana Gary, David Rock; m. Evelyn Clair Farley, Nov. 19, 1977; 1 child, Michael Allen. Student, U. Louisville, 1978, U. Ga., 1980. Officer Wheeling (W.Va.) Police Dept., 1957-76, detective, 1976-91, lt., 1991-94. With U.S. Army, 1952-53, Korea. Decorated Bronze Star; recipient numerous citations and commendations for police work. Mem. Fraternal Order of Police, Masons. Democrat. Roman Catholic. Home: 58 Mount Wood Rd Wheeling WV 26003-2631

ROBEAU, SALLY GARWOOD, secondary school educator; b. Corpus Christi, Tex., Nov. 19, 1933; d. Robert B. and Hazel V. (Priour) Garwood; m. Joseph Ruel Robeau, June 5, 1954; children: James, Stephan, David, Catherine, Cheri. BS in Edn., Tex. A&I Univ., Kingsville, 1973, MS in Edn., 1979. Cert. secondary tchr., Tex. Rep. Southwestern Bell Tel. Co., Dallas, Houston, 1954-55; sec. A.G. Edwards & Co., Houston, 1955-56; tchr. Calallen ISD, Corpus Christi, 1973—. Author: Of Pride and Pioneers, 1964. Chmn. Nueces County Hist. Commn., Corpus Christi, 1984-86; pres. bd. dirs. Nuecestown Schoolhouse Hist. Ctr., Corpus Christi, 1986—; life mem. Calallen PTA. Named Tchr. of Yr., Daughters Republic Tex., DAR. Mem. Tex. State Hist. Assn., Nueces County Hist. Soc. Methodist. Home: 14233 Fairway Corpus Christi TX 78410 Office: Calallen ISD 4602 Cornett Corpus Christi TX 78410

ROBEL, RONALD RAY, history educator; b. Oak Park, Ill., Mar. 21, 1934; s. Raymond J. and Mildred A. (Boeche) R. BA, Grinnell Coll., 1956; MA in History, U. Mich., 1957, MA in Far East Lang. and Lit., 1965, PhD in History, 1972. Lectr. U. Md., Far East Div., 1962-64; vis. instr. U. Wis., Madison, 1965-66; instr. history U. Ala., Tuscaloosa, 1966-72, asst. prof. history and Chinese, 1972—, dir. Critical Lang. Ctr., 1985—, dir. Asian studies, 1989—. Mem. Assn. for Asian Studies, Nat. Assn. Self-Instructional Lang. Programs (pres. 1992-94), Ala. Assn. Historians, Ala. Assn. Fgn. Lang. Tchrs., Chinese Lang. Tchrs. Assn. Home: 8 Country Club Cir Tuscaloosa AL 35401-1340 Office: Critical Langs Ctr Box 870246 Tuscaloosa AL 34287-0246

ROBELOT, MILTON PAUL, deacon, architect; b. New Orleans, Oct. 31, 1909; s. Amedeé William and Eva (Trepagnier) R.; m. Mary Lucille Bright, July 20, 1938; 1 child, Katherine Marie Robelot Floyd. BArch, Tulane U., 1932; postgrad., Tex. A&M U., 1939; MS, Miss. State U., 1943. Registered architect, Tenn., Va., Mo.; ordained to ministry Roman Catholic Ch. as deacon, 1974. Deacon St. Dominic Ch., Kingsport, Tenn., 1974—; architect Milton P. Robelot AIA, Kingsport, Tenn., 1948—; chaplain Civitan, Kingsport, 1991—. Mem. AIA (emeritus), Tenn. Soc. Architects (emeritus), KC (chaplain 4th degree), Moose (past dep. supreme gov.), Elks (past exalted ruler). Home: Crown Colony 98 Periwinkle Pl Kingsport TN 37660-7121

ROBERSON, DEBORAH KAY, secondary school educator; b. Crane, Tex., Jan. 15, 1955; d. David B. and Virginia L. (King) Cole; m. Larry M. Roberson; children: Justin, Jenai, Julie. BS in Secondary Edn., Coll. S.W., 1981; MA in Sch. Adminstrn., Sul Ross State U., 1991. Cert. biology and history tchr., mid-mgmt. cert., supt. cert., Tex., biology and history tchr., Okla. Sci. and social studies tchr. Andrews (Tex.) Ind. Sch. Dist., 1987-95; forum tchr.- gifted social studies program, social studies dept. chair Ctrl. Mid. Sch. Broken Arrow (Okla.) Pub. Schs., 1995—; mem. 7th grade history curriculum com. Andrews Ind. Sch. Dist., 1988, mem. outdoor classroom com., 1989-90, chair sci. curriculum com., 1989-90, chair health curriculum com., 1990-91, mem. Tex. pub. schs. open house com., 1989-90, 92-93, mem. dist. textbook com., 1990-91; secondary edn. rep. Ptnrs. in Parliament, Berlin, 1993; site-based com. Broken Arrow Pub. Schs., 1995—, B.A.S.I.S. com., 1995—, nat. history day coord. Ctrl. Middle Sch., 1995, geography bee coord., 1995—, tech. com., 1996—, mem. discipline com., 1996, mem. remediation com., 1996—, Tools for Tomorrow Conf. com., 1996—, others. Livestock leader Andrews County 4-H Program, 1985-89; vol. Am. Heart Assn., Andrews, 1988; vol., team mother Little League, Andrews, 1990; vol., treas. Mustang Booster Club, Andrews, 1993-95. Recipient Appreciation awards Mustang Booster Club, 1993, 94, VFW Ladies Aux. Post 10887 award, Broken Arrow, 1996—. Mem. AAUW, Nat. Assn. Secondary Sch. Prins., Nat. Staff Devel. Coun., Assn. Tex. Profl. Educators (pres. local unit 1992-93, mem. resolutions com. 1994-95, appreciation award 1993, sec. region 1993-94, v.p. region 1994-95), ASCD, Tex. Assn. Supervision and Curriculum Devel., Tex. Network for Continuous Quality Improvement, Nat. Coun. Social Studies, Okla. Assn. Supervision and Curriculum Devel., Okla. Alliance Geographic Edn. Home: 708 N Sweet Gum Ave Broken Arrow OK 74012 Office: Broken Arrow Pub Schs Ctrl Mid Sch 210 N Main St Broken Arrow OK 74012

ROBERSON, MARK ALLEN, physicist, educator; b. Lufkin, Tex., Nov. 12, 1961; s. Roy and Thelma (Weist) R. AAS, Angelina County Jr. Coll., 1982; BSEE, Tex. A&M U., 1984; MS, Stephen F. Austin State U., 1989; PhD, Tex. Tech. U., 1994. From rsch. asst. to instr. Tex. Tech. U., Lubbock, 1990-95; instr. Vernon (Tex.) Regional Jr. Coll., 1995—. Robert A. Welch Found. fellow, 1991-94. Mem. AAAS, Am. Phys. Soc., Materials Rsch. Soc., Sigma Pi Sigma. Office: Vernon Regl Jr Coll Vernon TX 76384-4092

ROBERSON, PAULA KAREN, biostatistician; b. Memphis, Nov. 26, 1952; d. Joseph Paul and Venita Rose (Adams) R.; 1 child, Elizabeth Lourdes. BS, So. Meth. U., 1974; PhD, U. Wash., 1979. Chief biostatis. & data processing group Health Effects Rsch. Lab., U.S. EPA, Cin., 1979-81; asst. mem. biostatis. St. Jude Children's Rsch. Hosp., Memphis, 1982-93, vice chair biostatis. and info. systems, 1986-91; assoc. prof. pediatrics U. Ark. for Med. Sci., Little Rock, 1993—; dir. biostats. Ark. Cancer Rsch. Ctr., 1995—; vis. faculty U. Nebr. Med. Ctr., Omaha, 1992-93; cons. in field; mem. NIH study sect., 1994—. Contbr. numerous articles to profl. jours. Clk. of session Evergreen Presbyn. Ch., Memphis, 1987, 91; session mem. First Presbyn. Ch., Little Rock, 1995—. Mem. AAAS (sect. com., stats. sect. 1995-99), APHA, Am. Statis. Assn. (coun. of chpts., sec.-treas. 1991-96, com. on membership 1992-98, pres. Cen. Ark. chpt. 1995-96), Soc. for Clin. Trials, Am. Soc. Clin. Oncology, So. Soc. Pediat. Rsch., Biometric Soc. (regional adv. bd. 1984-86, 91-93). Office: Ark Cancer Rsch Ctr Div Biostats 4301 W Markham Slot 752 Little Rock AR 72205

ROBERSON, RICHARD W., company executive; b. 1947. BS, U. South Fla., 1970. Audit mgr. Peat, Marwick, Mitchell & Co., Largo, Fla., 1969-77; contr. Eckerd Fleet Inc. Eckerd Corp., 1978—. Office: Eckerd Fleet Inc. 8333 Bryan Dairy Rd Clearwater FL 33518

ROBERSON, RONALD WILLIAM, industrial hygienist; b. Middletown, Ohio, Aug. 21, 1950; s. Wilbur and Arnita Mae (Lovelace) R.; m. Sherrill Ann Erickson, Aug. 18, 1979; children: Jason Scott, Jessica Leigh, Jeremy Todd. BS Chemistry, Miami U., Oxford, Ohio, 1972. Chemist Stauffer Chem. Co., Tarpon Springs, Fla., 1972-83; indsl. hygienist Bendix Corp., Largo, Fla., 1983; corp. indsl. hygienist Sensidyne, Inc., Clearwater, Fla., 1984—. Deacon Northwood Presbyn. Ch., Clearwater, 1991-92, elder, 1996—. Mem. ACS, ASTM, Am. Indsl. Hygiene Assn. (dir. Fla. chpt. 1986-89), Environ. Info. Assn. Home: 1631 Dale Cir S Dunedin FL 34698-4732 Office: Sensidyne Inc 16333 Bay Vista Dr Clearwater FL 34620-3130

ROBERSON, WILLIAM RALPH, dean, artist, educator; b. Ripley, Miss., Feb. 15, 1939. Studnet, Memphis State U., 1957-58; BFA, Memphis Acad. Arts, 1968; postgrad., Ind. U., 1968-69. Prof. Memphis Coll. Art, 1969—, grad. faculty, 1987—, mem. grad. sch. coun., 1987—, assoc. dean, 1992—; co-owner Antique Shop, Memphis; lectr. and presnter workshops in field. Represented in permament collections State of Tenn. Crafts, Nashville, Am. Pub. Powe Assn., Washington, Acalia Mutural Life Ins. Co., Washington, Malone and Hyde, Inc., Memphis, First Tenn. Corp., Memphis, Holiday Inn Corp. Hdqs., Memphis, Nat. Bank Commerce, Memphis, United Va. Bank, Richmond, Jones, Day, Reaves and Pogue, Attys., Inc., Washington, Finnegan, Henderson, Facabow, Garrett and Dunn, Attys., Inc., Washington. Memphis Acad. Arts fellow, 1968. Mem. Tenn. Artist Craftsmen Assn. (v.p. 1973), Tenn. Arts Commn. (adv. panel 1991-92, 93-94), Memphis Coll. Art Alumni Assn. (v.p. 1992-93, 93-94). Office: Memphis Coll Art Overton Park 1930 Poplar Ave Memphis TN 38104-2756

ROBERT, HENRY FLOOD, JR., museum official; b. El Dorado, Ark., Feb. 26, 1943; s. Henry Flood and Margery (Hay) R.; m. Mary Beth Parkey, Apr. 20, 1968; children—Spencer Flood, Erika Ashley. B.F.A., Ariz. State U., 1970, M.F.A., 1973; diploma, Inst. Arts Adminstrn., Harvard U., 1977. Dir. Meml. Union Gallery, Ariz. State U., 1969-70; asst. dir. Univ. Art Mus., 1970-72, Loch Haven Art Center, Orlando, Fla., 1973-74; dir. Montgomery (Ala.) Mus. Fine Arts, 1974-79, Joslyn Art Mus., Omaha, 1979—; guest curator Soleri Exhbn., Whitney Mus. Am. Art, Corcoran Gallery Art, Mus. Contemporary Art; exhbn. dir. Art Inc.: American Paintings from Corp. Collections. Author: Paolo Soleri: Arcology and the Future of Man, 1975, Venetian Drawings from the Collection of Janos Scholz, 1976, Corporate Collections in Montgomery, 1976, American Paintings: 1900-1939, 1976, The George Verdak Collection: Eras of the Dance, 1976, Anne Goldthwaite 1869-1944, 1977, Walter Gaudnek Retrospective, 1978. Mem. Internat. Council Museums, Am. Assn. Museums (visitation com. for accreditation), Assn. Art Mus. Dirs. Episcopalian.

ROBERT, JOSEPH CLARKE, historian, consultant; b. State College, Miss., June 2, 1906; s. Joseph Clarke and Hallie Christian (Cavett) R.; m. Evelyn Mercer Bristow, June 15, 1931 (dec.); children: Frank Chambers, Carol Mercer Robert Armstrong; m. Sara Cross Squires, May 12, 1985 (dec.). AB magna cum laude, Furman U., 1927, LLD, 1959; MA, Duke U., 1929, PhD, 1933; LittD, Washington and Lee U., 1958; LHD, Med. Coll. Va., 1962. Ranger-historian Nat. Park Service, Yorktown, Va., 1934; instr. history Ohio State U., Columbus, Ohio, 1934-38; from asst. prof. to prof. Duke U., 1938-52, assoc. dean Grad. Sch., 1949-52; pres. Coker Coll., Hartsville, S.C., 1952-55, Hampden-Sydney Coll., Va., 1955-60; prof. history U. Richmond, Va., 1961-67, William Binford Vest prof. history, 1967-71, prof. history emeritus, 1972—; cons. Psychol. Cons., Inc., Richmond, 1966, Newport News Shipbldg. & Dry Dock Co. (Va.), 1961-64, others. Author: The Tobacco Kingdom, 1938; The Road From Monticello, 1941; The Story of Tobacco in America, 1949; Ethyl: A History of the Corporation and the People Who Made It, 1983; Gottwald Family History, 1984; contbr. articles to profl. jours. Pres. S.C. Asssn. Colls., 1952-53. Watauga fellow Harvard U., 1929-30, Duke U. fellow, 1930-31, Fund for Advancement of Edn. travel and study grantee, 1960-61, Humanities fellow U. N.C., Duke U., 1966-67. Fellow Am. Coll. Dentists (hon.); mem. So. Hist. Assn. (life), Va. Hist. Soc. (pres. emeritus), Richmond Acad. Medicine (sect. on history of medicine, hon.), Commonwealth Club, Forum Club, Phi Beta Kappa, Omicron Delta Kappa, Sigma Chi. Presbyterian. Home: 103 Tuckahoe Blvd Richmond VA 23226-2224

ROBERT, NICHOLAS JAMES, hematolgist, oncologist; b. Quebec City, Can., Nov. 3, 1948; came to U.S., 1976; s. Francois and Marie F. (Chauveau) R.; m. Katherine F. Box, July 8, 1972; children: Katherine, Michael. BSc, McGill U., 1970, MD, 1974. Diplomate Am. Bd. Internal Medicine, Am. Bd. Anatomic Pathology, Am. Bd. Med. Oncology, Am. Bd. Hematology, Am. Bd. Med. Examiners. Intern, resident in medicine Royal Victoria Hosp., Montreal, 1974-76; resident in anatomic pathology Mass. Gen. Hosp., Boston, 1976-78, chief resident anatomic pathology, 1978-79; fellow in hematology Brigham and Women's Hosp., Boston, 1979-80; fellow in med. oncology Dana Farber Cancer Inst., Boston, 1980-81; clin. fellow in pathology/medicine Harvard Med. Sch., Boston, 1977-81; asst. prof. medicine U. Conn. Health Ctr., 1981-84; asst. prof. medicine, pathology, radiation oncology Tufts U. Sch. Medicine, 1984-91. Reviewer Am. Jour. Hematology, Breast Cancer Rsch. & Treatment, Breast Disease, J.A.M.A., Jour. Clin. Oncology, Jour. Oncology, New England Jour. Medicine; contbr. articles to profl. jours. Grantee Am. Cancer Soc., numerous others. Mem. Am. Cancer Soc. (profl. edn. com. 1982-83, co-chmn. student health care profl. com. 1988-90, editl. bd. 1989-90, bd. dirs. 1989-91), Am. Soc. Clin. Oncology. Office: Fairfax Hematology/Oncology 3289 Woodborn Rd #230 Annandale VA 22003

ROBERTS, BILL GLEN, retired fire chief, investor, consultant; b. Deport, Tex., June 2, 1938; s. Samuel Westbrook and Ann Lee (Rhodes) R.; m. Ramona Ryall, June 1, 1963 (dec. Nov. 1988); 1 child, Renee Ann. Student, So. Meth. U., 1968, North Tex. State U., 1974; grad. paramedic course, U. Tex. Southwestern Med. Sch., 1974; grad. Exec. Program for Fire Service, Tex. A&M U., 1978; AAS, El Centro Jr. Coll., Dallas, 1980; grad. exec. fire officer program, Nat. Fire Acad., 1989. With Dallas Fire Dept., 1958-82, lt., 1964-67, capt., 1967-71, div. fire chief, 1971-79, asst. fire chief, 1979-83; fire chief Austin (Tex.) Fire Dept., 1983-94; tech. bd. dirs. Found. Fire Safety, Washington, 1982-85; adj. faculty Nat. Fire Acad., 1981-86; aft. State Life of Indpls., Dallas, 1962; owner Personnel Testing Lab., Dallas, 1963; real estate salesman Dale Copus Realtor, Dallas, 1963-66; salesman intercommunications equipment Chandler Sound, Dallas, 1966-67; field engr. IBM Corp., Dallas, 1968; cons. U. Tenn., 1974, Ga. Inst. Tech., 1974, Tex. Dept. Health Resources, 1973-78, Rand Corp., Washington, Mission Rsch., Santa Barbara, Calif., Macro. Author: EMS Dallas, 1978; (with others) Anesthesia for Surgery Trauma, 1976, EMS Measures to Improve Care, 1980; contbr. articles to periodicals. Com. chmn. Dallas Jaycees, 1962-65; mem. task force Am. Heart Assn., Austin, 1973-83; bd. dirs. Brackenridge Hosp., 1989, Rehab. Hosp. Austin, 1992-94, Austin Police Pensions Bd., 1989, Capitol Area coun. Boy Scouts Am., 1989-92. Recipient John Stemmons Service award Dallas Fire Dept., 1979; Internat. Assn. Fire Chiefs scholar, 1967. Mem. Internat. Assn. Fire Chiefs, Nat. Fire Protection Assn., Nat. Critical Care Inst., Am. Heart Assn., Am. Trauma Soc. (founder), Am. Assn. Trauma Specialists, Nat. Assn. Emergency Med. Technicians, Tex. Assn. Emergency Med. Technicians, ACS, North Tex. Coun. of Govts. (regional emergency svc. adv. coun. 1973-79), Internat. Rescue and First Aid Assn., Found. Fire Safety (tech. bd. dirs. 1982-85), Tex. Assn. Realtors, Austin World Affairs Coun., People to People Internat., Rotary Internat. Methodist. Home: 3 Highlander Rd Asheville NC 28804-1112

ROBERTS, CANDICE KAY, realty association executive; b. Nashville, Dec. 30, 1956; d. James H. Beazley and Idalia H. Davis Dowlen; m. L. Douglas Roberts, Feb. 26, 1977; 1 child, Bob. BBA, Middle Tenn. State U., Murfreesboro, 1978. Front gate cashier Opryland USA, Nashville, 1974-75; front desk mgr. Holiday Inn, Murfreesboro, 1981-83; admisntrv. asst. Rutherford County C. of C., Murfreesboro, 1983-87; exec. dir. Leadership Rutherford, Murfreesboro, 1985-92; adminstr. asst. in sales prodn. Courier Printing, Smyrna, Tenn., 1992-94; exec. v.p. Rutherford County Assn. Realtors, Murfreesboro, 1994—. Sec. exec. com. United Way of Rutherford County, Murfreesboro, 1991; campaign worker, county elections, Murfreesboro, 1994; troop scouting coord. Boy Scouts Am., 1984-96. Named Vol. of Yr., Rutherford County Heart Unit, 1985. Mem. Am. Soc. Assn. Execs., Am. Heart Assn., Leadership Rutherford Inc., Nat. Assn. Realtors (assn. execs. profl. devel. subcom. 1996—). Methodist. Home: 1003 Houston Dr Murfreesboro TN 37130 Office: Rutherford Co Assn Realtors 225 W College St Murfreesboro TN 37130-3531

ROBERTS, CASSANDRA FENDLEY, investment company executive; b. Port St. Joe, Fla., Sept. 24, 1951; d. Pope and Sophie Virginia (McGee) Fendley; m. Charles Stanton Roberts, Aug. 7, 1971; 1 child, Davis McGee. BSBA, Edison State Coll., 1983. Sales assoc., v.p. Cooper Corp., Atlanta, 1979-85; sales assoc., broker WTM Investments, Atlanta, 1985-92, v.p., 1992—. Mem. Nat. Bd. Realtors, Ga. Bd. Realtors, Atlanta Bd. Realtors. Office: WTM Investments Inc PO Box 13256 Atlanta GA 30324-0256

ROBERTS, CECIL KENNETH, lawyer; b. Tyler, Tex., Mar. 31, 1930; s. Cecil Kelly and Blanche Lulu (Cash) R.; m. Cary N. Thornton, Sept. 1, 1951; children: Kenneth Kelly, Cristina Cary. BBA, U. Tex., Austin, 1950, JD, 1951; LLM, U. Tex., 1953; AMP, Harvard U., 1971. Bar: Tex. 1952.

Atty. Exxon Co., U.S.A., Houston, 1954-64, N.Y.C., 1964-65; chief atty. refining, environment and labor rels. law Houston, 1965-67, adminstrv. mgr. Baytown refinery, 1967-68, mgr. pub affairs dept., 1969-72; exec. asst. to pres. Exxon Corp., N.Y.C., 1972-73, dep. mgr. pub. affairs dept., 1973-74, assoc. gen. counsel, 1974-79; gen. counsel Exxon Co., U.S.A., Houston, 1979-92; v.p., gen. counsel Exxon Corp., Dallas, 1993-95; of counsel Fulbright & Jaworski, Houston, 1995—; bd. dirs. Nat. Ctr. for State Cts., 1986-89; mem. steering com. Com. for Jud. Merit Election. Trustee Southwestern Legal Found., 1993—, U. Tex. Law Found., 1992—; bd. dirs. Landmark Legal Found., Kansas City, Mo., 1980—, vice chmn., 1987-93; mem. bd. visitors U. Tex. Law Sch., Austin; mem. bd. visitors Stanford U. Law Sch., 1980-84, mem. law and econs. adv. com., 1983-87. Recipient Paul C. Reardon award Nat. Ctr. for State Cts., 1990; named Outstanding Alumni, U. Tex. Sch. Law, 1993. Fellow Am. Bar Found.; mem. ABA, Tex. Bar Assn., Houston Bar Assn., Am. Law Inst., Am. Petroleum Inst. (gen. com. on law), Assn. Gen. Counsel, Am. Arbitration Assn. (bd. dirs. 1993—), Petroleum Club (bd. dirs.), River Oaks Country Club, Las Colinas Country Club, Univ. Club (N.Y.C.), Monterey Peninsula Country Club. Office: Fulbright & Jaworski 1301 Mckinney St Ste 5100 Houston TX 77010

ROBERTS, CHARLES AUGUSTUS, JR., journalist; b. Long Beach, Calif., Jan. 19, 1948; s. Charles A. and Margaret A. (Leggett) R.; m. Cheryl A. Romo, Apr. 25, 1981; 1 child, Michael. BA in History and Journalism, Calif. State U., Long Beach, 1970. City editor Lakewood (Calif.) Herald Am., 1973-74; reporter Anaheim (Calif.) Bulletin, 1974-76; reporter county courts Orange County Register, Santa Ana, Calif., 1976-79; reporter state house Orange County Register, Sacramento, 1979-85; corr. United Press Internat., Sacramento, 1985; bur. chief L.A. Daily Jour., Sacramento, 1985-86, Washington, 1986-94; sr. writer L.A., 1994-96, exec. editor, 1996—; pres. Orange County Press Club, Santa Ana, Calif., 1978, Orange County chpt. Soc. Profl. Journalists, Sanat Ana, 1979, Ctrl. Calif. chpt. Soc. Profl. Journalists, Sacramento, 1982; regional dir., nat. bd. Soc. Profl. Journalists, 1982-85. Sgt. U.S. Army, 1970-72. Recipient Silver Medallion State Bar of Calif. Media awards, 1995 Watchdog award Orange County Press Club, Santa Ana, 1981, Best News Story Soc. Profl. Journalists Ctrl. Calif., Sacramento, 1981, 82, Gold Medallion State Bar, 1996, 1996 Greater L.A. Press Club Best Series. Office: Los Angeles Daily Journal 915 E 1st St Los Angeles CA 90012-4050

ROBERTS, DAVID GLEN, marketing director; b. Plainview, Tex., Feb. 8, 1952; s. Doris Glen and Anna Grace (Mathis) R. Student, Tex. A&M U., 1970-71, Dallas Bapt. Coll., 1971-75; BA in Comm., U. Tex. Permian Basin, 1987. Lic. minister Bapt. Ch. Profl. stuntman, actor, 1972-76; mgr. Channel 100, Midland, Tex., 1976-78; owner D.G. Roberts Land Mgmt., Midland, Tex., 1978; regional mktg. dir. Nochar Inc.-Region 11, Midland, Tex., 1990—; cons. EPA, Indpls., 1991—. Appeared in film Drive In, 1976; theatre appearance at Globe Theatre, Odessa, Tex., 1975, Shakespeare in the Park, Dallas, 1976. Chair Midland County Libertarian Party; exec. com. Dist. 31 Tex. Libertarian Party; organizer Sons of Liberty, Midland, 1990—. Mem. Am. Assn. Petroleum-Landmen (registered land profl.), Five Aces, NRA, Tex. State Rifle Assn. Libertarian. Office: Diamond Developers 3105 Barkley Ave Midland TX 79701-6215

ROBERTS, DELMAR LEE, editor; b. Raleigh, N.C., Apr. 9, 1933; s. James Delmer and Nellie Brockelbank (Tyson) R. BS in textile mgmt., N.C. State U., 1956; MA in journalism, U. S.C., 1974. Product develop. engr. U.S. Rubber Co. (Uniroyal), Winnsboro, S.C., 1959-64; process improvement engr. Allied Chemical Co., Irmo, S.C., 1965-67; assoc. editor S.C. History Illustrated Mag., Columbia, 1970; editor-in-chief, editl. v.p. Sandlapper-The Mag. of S.C., Columbia, 1968-74; mng. editor, art dir. Law Practice Mgmt. Mag. at the ABA, Chgo., Ill., 1975—. Editor: The Best of Legal Economics, 1979; freelance editor and/or designer of over 35 books. With U.S. Army, 1956-58. Hon. fellow Coll. of Law Practice Mgmt., Ann Arbor, Mich., 1995. Mem. Soc. Profl. Journalists, Capital City Club (Columbia), Phi Kappa Tau.

ROBERTS, DON E., accountant; b. Bluefield, W.Va., Feb. 16, 1934; s. Frank P. and Lila T. (Thornburg) R.; m. Jacquelyn Joan Ballard, Dec. 30, 1956 (div. 1978); children: Donna, Bruce, Susan; m. Pamala Sue Allen, Nov. 25, 1978; children: Daryl, Dwight. Student, The Citadel, 1952; BSBA, Concord Coll., 1956; postgrad., U. of South Fla., 1977. Sr. acct. Lee W. McLain, CPA, Sarasota, Fla., 1956-62; prin. Don E. Roberts Co., Sarasota, 1962—; leader 17 piece dance band "The Sophisticates". Treas. Sarasota (Fla.) 4H Found., 1966-76, treas. Sarasota Fair Assn., 1967-79. Named Hon. Mem. Sarasota 4H Found., 1978. Mem. Fla. Soc. Enrolled Agts. (pres. Sarasota chpt. 1986-88, Fla. pres. 1990-91), Fla. Accts. Assn. (pres. Sarasota chpt. 1966-69, mem. Fla. exec. bd. 1966-69), Nat. Assn. Enrolled Agts., Nat. Assn. Pub. Accts., Kiwanis Internat. (treas. Sarasota 1957-64, sec. 1966-68, 25 yr. Legion of Honor award 1984, 30 yr., 1989, 35 yr., 1994, life mem. 1988). Republican. Episcopalian. Home: 4873 Old Ranch Rd Sarasota FL 34241-9581 Office: Don E Roberts Co 3212 Southgate Cir Sarasota FL 34239-5514

ROBERTS, EDWIN ALBERT, JR., newspaper editor, journalist; b. Weehawken, N.J., Nov. 14, 1932; s. Edwin Albert and Agnes Rita (Seuferling) R.; m. Barbara Anne Collins, June 14, 1958; children: Elizabeth Adams, Leslie Carol, Amy Barbara, Jacqueline Harding. Student, Coll. William and Mary, 1952-53, NYU, evenings 1955-58; AA in Coll. & Cmty. Svc., St. Petersburg Jr. Coll., 1994. Reporter N.J. Courier, Toms River, 1953-54, Asbury Park (N.J.) Press, 1954-57; reporter Wall Street Jour., N.Y.C., 1957, editorial writer, 1957-63; news editor Nat. Observer, Silver Spring, Md., 1963-68, columnist, 1968-77; editorial writer, columnist Detroit News, 1977-78, editorial page editor, 1978-83; editor editorial page Tampa Tribune, 1983—. Author: Elections, 1964, 1964, Latin America, 1965, The Smut Rakers, 1966, Russia Today, 1967; Editor anthology: America Outdoors, 1965. Recipient Disting. Reporting Bus. award U. Mo., 1969; Pulitzer prize for distinguished commentary, 1974. Mem. Am. Soc. Newspaper Editors, Nat. Conf. Editorial Writers. Office: 202 S Parker St Tampa FL 33606-2308

ROBERTS, ELLIOTT C., SR., public health educator; b. Balt., Jan. 20, 1927; married. BA, Morgan State U.; MA, George Washington U. Bus. mgr. Provident Hosp., Balt., 1953-58, asst. adminstr., 1958-60; chief acct. Crownsville (Md.) Hosp. Ctr., 1960-62, asst. supr., 1962-65; exec. asst. Mercy-Douglass Hosp., Phila., 1965, exec. dir., 1965-69; exec. dir. Harlem Hosp. Ctr., N.Y., 1969-72; commr. hosps. Detroit Gen. Hosp., 1972-77; exec. dir., asst. sec. Charity Hosp. New Orleans, 1977-80; v.p., assoc. project dir. Hyatt Med. Mgmt. Svcs., Chgo., 1980-81; dir., CEO Cook County Hosp., Chgo., 1981-84; prof. dept. health systems mgmt. Tulane U., New Orleans, 1984-94; prof. Coll. St. Francis; CEO Med. Ctr. La., New Orleans; prof. dept. health sys. rsch. and pub. health La. State U., New Orleans, 1994—; active Pro Pac Commn., Washington, 1990—. Mem. Am. Coll. Healthcare Execs. (del.), Assn. Am. Med. Colls. (del., bd. dirs.), Am. Hosp. Assn. (life, trustee 1971-76, Honor award 1993, Life Membership award 1993), Ill. Hosp. Assn. (trustee 1982-84). Office: La State U 1600 Canal St New Orleans LA 70112*

ROBERTS, EMILY BURGIN, writer, editor, communications consultant; b. Little Rock, June 14, 1956; d. Stewart H. and Laura (Glasscock) Burgin; m. John R. Denton II, Jan. 26, 1974 (div. Feb. 22, 1984); children: John Reid III, Stewart Paul; m. Thomas Edward Roberts, Sept. 7, 1996. AA with hons., U. Ark., 1994, BA summa cum laude, 1996. Assoc. dir. comms. Heifer Project Internat., Little Rock, 1981-84; editor Ark. Retail Grocers Assn., Little Rock, 1985-87; writer, editor Burgin Pub. Svcs., N. Little Rock, Ark., 1988—; assoc. editor The U. Ark. Little Rock Forum, Little Rock, 1994-95, mng. editor, 1995-96; editor The Trucker, Belmont Pub., Little Rock, 1996—; intern U. Writing Ctr., 1995; mem. adv. memberships N. Little Rock Sch. Dist. Bd. Edn., 1990-92, mem. adv. bd. Project Promise, 1991-93, Citizens Adv. Com. 1989, Key Communicator, 1988-89; mem. Pulaski Vo-Tech cashier-checker tng. adv. bd., 1986-87. Speechwriter: North Little Rock Millage campaign, 1985-87; editor: Arkansas Banker, 1987, Arkansas Grocer News, 1985-87, Foodline, 1987-90. Past pres. Belwood Elem. PTA, 1988-89; vol. Little Rock Pub. Schs., 1981-84, N. Little Rock Pub. Schs., 1987-92, hunger relief projects Ark. Inter-faith Hunger Task Force, 1985-90. Donaghey scholar U. Ark., 1994-96, Dick Neal Meml. Scholarship, 1994; U. Ark. Bookstore grantee, 1994; recipient Golden Apple award Vols. in Pub. Schs., 1983, nat., regional awards Food Industry Assn. Execs. Assn., G.J. Francis Jr. Meml. awward, 1994. Mem. Soc. Profl. Journalists (Outstanding Graduate 1996), Ark. Press Women (regional awards 1989, 90), Nat. Fedn. Press Women (nat. awards 1989, 90), Ballroom Latin and Swing Dance Assn. (founding dir. 1993), Ark. Assn. Rabbit Breeders (founding dir. 1981), Little Rock Bop Club. Home: 2416 South Dr North Little Rock AR 72118 Office: Burgin Pub Svcs 2416 South Dr North Little Rock AR 72118

ROBERTS, ESTHER LOIS, piano educator, composer, writer; b. Rockwood, Tenn.; d. Reva Gretchen (Crowder) H. BA in Biology, U. Tenn., Knoxville, BA in Botany, BM in Piano Lit./Pedagogy, MM in Piano Lit./Pedagogy. Class piano instr. U. Tenn., Knoxville; piano instr. Cadek Conservatory of Music U. Tenn., Chattanooga; pvt. piano instr. Knoxville. Composer (youth choir cantata) Children of Love, (soprano solo) Corn Husk Moon; author: (children's book series) Sam the Horse, Sam Gets Ready for School, others, 1996. Pres., exec. bd. Shangri-La Therapuetic Acad. of Riding, Knoxville. Mem. Philippine Am. Assn. East Tenn., Music Tchrs. Nat. Assn., Knoxville Music Tchrs. Assn., Knoxville Guild of Piano Tchrs., Am. Musicians Coll., Am. Indian Horse Registry, Great Smoky Mountain Indian Horse Club (pres.), Crossroads Dressage Soc. (v.p., exec. bd.). Home and Office: Starlight Farm PO Box 32663 Knoxville TN 37930

ROBERTS, GARY LYNN, dentist; b. Lubbock, Tex., Aug. 11, 1950; s. Andrew Florence Roberts and Winona Louise (Kelso) Williams; m. Teresa Shelton, Aug. 7, 1971; children: Michael Zachary, Joshua Bradley. BS in Zoology, La. State Univ., 1973; DDS, Baylor Coll. Dentistry, 1977. Instr. Baylor Coll. Dentistry, Dallas, 1977-78; pvt. practice Shreveport, La., 1978—. Fellow Peirre Fanchard Acad., Internat. Coll. Dentistry; mem. ADA, La. Dental Assn. (editor 1988-96, pres.-elect 1996-97). Republican. Episcopalian. Office: 8510 Line Ave Shreveport LA 71106

ROBERTS, GERRY REA, elementary school educator, organist; b. Brady, Tex., Nov. 13, 1940; d. Willie Melvin and Mary Catherine (Brown) Howard; m. Leslie Wayne Templeton, July 28, 1961 (div. Feb. 1977); children: Todd Wayne, Gwen Marie; m. Harold James Roberts Jr., Sept. 24, 1977. Student, Sam Houston State U., 1959-60; MusB, U. Houston, 1962, postgrad., 1964-65; grad., North Tex. State U., 1966, Stephen F. Austin U., 1983; postgrad., East Tex. State U., 1984, Memphis State U., 1984-85, Las Vegas U., 1985. Cert. music tchr., 1-12, Tex., elem. tchr., 1-6, Tex., cert. music tchr., elem.-sec. (K-12), elem. edn. (K-8), Okla.; cert. Orff-Schulwerk levels I, II, III. Music tchr. Deer Park (Tex.) Ind. Sch. Dist., 1962-63, Dallas Ind. Sch. Dist., 1963, Richardson (Tex.) Ind. Sch. Dist., 1964-68; kindergarten tchr. Houston Ind. Sch. Dist., 1971, tchr. 1st grade, 1974-78; tchr. music Klein (Tex.) Ind. Sch. Dist., 1978-90; music tchr. grades 1-6 Choctaw (Okla.)-Nicoma Park Sch. Dist., Okla., 1993—. Pianist, mus. dir. 1960 Playhouse, 1979; pianist prodns. Klein Forest H.S., 1984-86, Klein H.S., 1987-90; singer Houston Symphony Chorale, 1960-62, Richardson Choral Club, 1963-64, Jeffrey Ross Chorale, 1988-89, Tomball (Tex.) Comty. Ch., 1988-90, Oklahoma City Met. Chorus, 1994-96, Okla. Master Chorale, 1996—. Organist St. Paul's Presbyn. Ch., Houston, 1975-77, Lakewood United Meth. Ch., Tex., 1978-80, Windwood Presbyn. Ch., Cypress, Tex., 1981-90; Music dir. 1st United Meth. Ch., Choctaw, 1990-93; handbell dir., organist St. Matthews United Meth. Ch., 1994-96. Recipient Tex. Pianist 2nd Pl. award Tex. Music Tchrs. Assn, 1959; Jesse Jones Foundation scholar, 1959, Houston 1st Pl. award-piano Houston Music Tchrs. Assn., 1959; Sam Houston State U. scholar, 1959, U. Houston scholar, 1960. Mem. NEA, Okla. Educators Assn., Music Educators Nat. Conf., Nat. Music Tchrs. Assn., Am. Guild Organists, Am. Guild of English Handbell Ringers, Inc., The Choristers Guild, Tex. Music Educators Assn., Tex. Tchrs. Assn., Klein Educators Assn., Okla. Music Tchrs. Assn., Okla. Kodály Educators, Kodály Educator Am., Am. choral Dirs.' Assn., Okla. Choral Dirs.' Assn., Okla. Orff-Schulwerk Assn., Am. Orff-Schulwerk Assn. (cert. levels I-III), Gulf Coast Orff-Schulwerk Assn., Sigma Alpha Iota (v.p. Houston alumni chpt. 1971-72, Sword of Honor 1972). Republican. Home and Office: RR 1 Box 799 Harrah OK 73045-7498

ROBERTS, H(UBERT) WILSON, JR., counselor; b. Oxford, Miss., Feb. 20, 1944; s. Hubert Wilson and Sally (Hartwell) R.; m. Donna Ruth Else, Aug. 29, 1965; children: Lesli Deanna, Lindsey Ruth. BBA, Memphis State U., 1971, MS, 1990. Lic. contractor and counselor. Mgr. loan servicing dept. Thomas & Hill, Inc., Memphis, 1967-71; comptroller loan svc. dept. Thomas & Hill, Inc., Charleston, W.Va., 1971-73; mgr. constrn. lending Thomas & Hill, Inc., Memphis, 1973-75; loan broker Mortgage Mktg. Svcs., Memphis, 1975-79; contractor New Colony Homes, Inc., Memphis, 1979—; counselor Memphis Recovery Ctrs., 1991; TV program producer Community Programming Network/Memphis Cablevision, 1989—; dir. Recovery Repertory Theatre, Memphis, 1991. Mem. Kappa Delta Pi (Lambda Gamma chpt.). Republican. Home and Office: 6843 Stone Gap Cv Memphis TN 38141-8564

ROBERTS, JAMES HAROLD, III, lawyer; b. Omaha, Aug. 11, 1949; s. James Harold Jr. and Evelyn Doris (Young) R.; m. Marilyn Novak, June 29, 1974; children: Jessica Noël, Meredith Caitlin. BA, U. Notre Dame, 1971; JD, St. Louis U., 1974. Bar: Iowa 1974, U.S. Ct. Mil. Appeals 1974, U.S. Supreme Ct. 1979, D.C. 1981. Govt. contract atty. U.S. Gen. Acctg. Office, Washington, 1978-83, U.S. Dept. Treasury, Washington, 1983-88; pvt. practice Manatt Phelps & Phillips, Washington, 1988—. Editor St. Louis U. law rev., 1973-74. Served to capt. JAGC, U.S. Army, 1974-78, lt. col. USAR/NG, 1978—. Mem. ABA (pub. contract law sect.), D.C. Bar Assn., Fed. Bar Assn. Roman Catholic. Home: 308 N Monroe St Arlington VA 22201-1736 Office: Manatt Phelps & Phillips 1501 M St NW Ste 700 Washington DC 20005-1700

ROBERTS, JAMES L., JR., state supreme court justice; b. June 8, 1945; m. Rose D. Roberts. BA, Millsaps Coll., 1967; MBA, Miss. State U., 1968; JD, U. Miss., 1971; grad., Nat. Jud. Coll., 1988. Pvt. practice Pontotoc County, Miss., 1971-84; chancellor 1st Chancery Ct. Dist., Miss., 1988-92; assoc. justice MS Supreme Ct, Jackson, MS, 1992—; prosecuting atty. Pontotoc County, 1972-84; speaker in field. Commr. pub. safety State of Miss., 1984-88; mem. Northeast Mental Health-Mental Retardation Commn., 1972-88; chmn. task force hearings Gov.'s Alliance Against Drugs, 1986-87; Sunday sch. leader, ch. officer Pontotoc United Meth. Ch. Recipient Herman C. Galzier award Miss chpt. Am. Soc. Pub. Adminstrn., 1985. Mem. ABA (jud. divsn.), Miss. Bar Assn., 1st Jud. Dist. Bar Assn., Pontotoc County Bar Assn., Miss. Conf. of Judges, Nat. Coun. Juvenile and Family Ct. Judges, Nat. Coll. Probate Judges, Millsaps Coll. Alumni Assn., Miss. State U. Alumni Assn., U. Miss. Alumni Assn., Rotary Club, Omicron Delta Kappa, Delta Theta Phi, Alpha Kappa Psi, Kappa Sigma, Pi Alpha Alpha (hon.). Office: MS State Supreme Ct PO Box 117 Carol Gartin Bldg Jackson MS 39205*

ROBERTS, JANIS ELAINE, small business owner, adjuster, nurse; b. Dallas, Apr. 20, 1956; d. Bill and Betty Lou (Chace) Howard; m. Richard Travis Roberts, Jr., July 2, 1982. BSN, Tex. Woman's U., 1978, MSN, 1984. RN, Tex. Staff, charge and head nurse Irving (Tex.) Community Hosp., 1977-81; grad. nurse, charge nurse Dale County Hosp., Ozark, Ala., 1978; nurse, staff telemetry nurse St. Paul Med. Ctr., Dallas, 1981-83; asst. adminstr. People Care, Dallas, 1983; asst. DON, Westgate Med. Ctr., Denton, Tex., 1983-84; claims analyst Caronia Corp., Dallas, 1985-90; nurse Lewisville (Tex.) Meml. Hosp., 1990-91; propr., claims analyst Profl. Analysis Svcs., Inc., Lewisville, 1990—; instr. ADN and vocat. nurse programs El Centro Coll., Dallas, 1981-83. Mem. Am. Soc. for Healthcare Risk Mgmt., Am. Assn. Legal Nurse Cons. (bd. dirs. Dallas chpt. 1996, pres.-elect Ft. Worth chpt. 1996), North Tex. Soc. for Healthcare Risk Mgmt. (sec. 1993-94, pres. 1994-96), Dallas Claims Assn. Republican. Baptist. Office: Profl Analysis Svcs Inv 1098 Holly Ln Lewisville TX 75067-5710

ROBERTS, JIMMY DAN, educational administrator; b. Orange, Tex., July 8, 1955; s. Upton Knight and Emily (Caillier) R.; m. Wanda L. Williams, Nov. 12, 1982. BA in Curriculum and Instrn., McNeese State U., 1976; postgrad., Lamar U., 1979-80, U. Tex., 1981-83; MEd in Curriculum and Instrn., Tex. A&M U., 1988. Cert. tchr., supr., Tex. Math tchr. Morgan City (La.) Jr. H.S., 1976-77; social studies tchr. Bridge City (Tex.) Ind. Sch. Dist., 1977-81; pre-sch. tchr. Creative World, Austin, 1982-83; mktg. dir., artist Archon-Architectural Illustrations, Austin, 1981-84; social studies tchr. Bremond (Tex.) Ind. Sch. Dist., 1984-88; curriculum coord. Ctrl. Tex. Tech. Prep, Temple, 1992-95, project dir., 1995—; adv. bd. Ctrl. Tex. Quality Work Force, Temple, 1995—, Bell County Coalition for Family Involvement, Belton, 1995—, TQM/Tech Prep, Temple, 1994. Adv. bd. Temple Pub. Works, Temple, 1995—; commr. Temple Planning and Zoning, 1992-95; adv. bd. Temple Bldg. and Stds., 1995—, Bridge City Bd. Adjustments, 1980-81. Mem. ASCD, Am. Vocat. Assn., Nat. Tech. Prep Network, Nat. Assn. of Bus. Office: Temple Coll 2600 S First St Temple TX 76504

ROBERTS, JOHN KENNETH, JR., life insurance company executive; b. Omaha, Mar. 4, 1936; s. John Kenneth and Vera Blanche (Graham) R.; m. Carol Jean Baer, July 1, 1961; children: John Kenneth III, Susan Beth. Student, Cornell Coll., Mount Vernon, Iowa; B.A. in Actuarial Sci., U. Iowa. With Pan-Am. Life Ins. Co., 1959—; pres., chief exec. officer Pan-Am. Life Ins. Co., New Orleans, 1984—; dir. Whitney Nat. Bank of New Orleans, Whitney Holding Corp. Bd. dirs., past chmn. United Way Greater New Orleans Area, also past campaign chmn.; bd. dirs. Children's Hosp., New Orleans, YMCA, New Orleans. Fellow Soc. Actuaries; mem. Am. Acad. Actuaries, Life Office Mgmt. Assn. (bd. dirs., pres. bd. trustees, past chmn.), Health Ins. Assn. Am. (bd. dirs., chmn. pub. rels. policy com. 1993-94), Am. Coun. Life Ins. (bd. dirs. 1992), New Orleans Country Club. Lutheran. Home: 453 Fairfield Ave Gretna LA 70056-7033 Office: Pan-Am Life Ins Co 601 Poydras St New Orleans LA 70130-6029*

ROBERTS, JOSEPHINE ANASTASIA, English literature educator; b. Richmond, Va., Nov. 11, 1948; d. John and Anastasia (Leuty) R.; m. James Frederick Gaines, July 19, 1975; 1 child, John Manley. BA, Coll. William and Mary, 1970; MA, U. Pa., 1971, PhD, 1975. Teaching asst. U. Pa., Phila., 1971-75; asst. prof. La. State U., Baton Rouge, 1975-80, assoc. prof., 1980-86, prof., 1986-91, William A. Read chair, 1991—. Author: Architectonic Knowledge in the New Arcadia, 1978, Richard II: Annotated Bibliography, Vols. I, II, 1988; editor: The Poems of Lady Mary Wroth, 1983, The Countess of Montgomery's Urania, Vol. I, 1995. NEH grantee, 1989-91, Newberry Libr. grantee, 1988, Am. Philos. Soc. grantee, 1988, Henry E. Huntington Libr. grantee, 1980. Mem. Renaissance English Text Soc. (exec. coun. 1986—), MLA, Shakespeare Assn. Am., Renaissance Soc. Am., AAUP, South Cen. MLA, South Cen. Renaissance Assn. Home: 464 Wilton Dr Baton Rouge LA 70815-6567 Office: La State U Dept English Baton Rouge LA 70803

ROBERTS, JUDITH MARIE, librarian, educator; b. Bluefield, W.Va., Aug. 5, 1939; d. Charles Bowen Lowder and Frances Marie (Bourne) Lowder Alberts; m. Craig Currence Jackson, July 1, 1957 (div. 1962); 1 child, Craig, Jr.; m. Milton Rinehart Roberts, Aug. 13, 1966 (div. 1987). BS, Concord State Tchrs. Coll., 1965. Libr., Cape Henlopen Sch. Dist., Lewes, Del., 1965-91; with Lily's Gift Shop, St. Petersburg, Fla., 1991—. Pres. Friends of Lewes Pub. Libr., 1986-90; chmn. exhibits Govs. Conf. Librs. and Info. Svcs., Dover, Del., 1978; mem. Gov.'s State Library Adv. Coun., 1987-91. Mem. ALA, NEA, Del. State Edn. Assn., Sussex Help Orgn. for Resources Exchange (pres. 1984-85), Del. Library Assn. (pres. 1982-83), Del. Learning Resources Assn. (pres. 1976-77). Methodist.

ROBERTS, KAREN BARBARA, art educator; b. Bklyn., May 20, 1953; d. Sol and Adele (Barnett) R.; m. Donald F. Baret, Jr. BA, U. Miami, 1971; MA, Mich. State U., 1972; PhD, SUNY, Binghamton, 1985. Sr. prof. art Broward C.C., Pompano Beach, Fla., 1973—, chmn. dept., 1973-82, dir. Honors Inst. north campus, 1993-95; lectr., cons. Fakes and Forgeries Assn., 1985—; lectr. Ft. Lauderdale (Fla.) Mus. Art, 1989—, Hollywood (Fla.) Art and Culture Ctr., 1989-90, Friends of Mus., Ft. Lauderdale, 1978—, community librs., Broward County, Fla., 1975—, Caucus Women Artists, 1975—. Exhibited in group show Ft. Lauderdale Mus. Art, 1990; presented in permanent collection Ft. Lauderdale Mus. Art. Mem. Broward Theatre Performing Arts, Ft. Lauderdale, 1990—. Recipient Prof. of Yr. Broward C.C., 1991, Endowed chair award, 1992-95. Mem. Coll. Art Assn., Gold Coast Watercolor Soc. (pres. 1994-95), Broward Art Guild, Ft. Lauderdale Mus. Art. Office: Broward Community Coll 1000 Coconut Creek Blvd Pompano Beach FL 33066-1615

ROBERTS, KATHLEEN MARY, school system administrator; b. Syracuse, N.Y., Apr. 15, 1947; d. Casimer and Lorrayne Arletta (Molloy) Piegdon; m. James C. Roberts, June 29, 1968 (div. Sept. 1988). BA, Cen. State U., Edmond, Okla., 1968, MEd, 1971; PhD, U. Okla., 1977. Cert. tchr., prin., supt., Okla.; cert. supt., N.Y. Tchr. Putnam City Schs., Oklahoma City, 1960-72; reading specialist Moore (Okla.) Pub. Schs., 1973-74; reading specialist Crooked Oak Pub. Schs., Oklahoma City, 1974-77, supt., 1990-95; rsch. assoc. Oklahoma City Pub. Schs., 1977-80; supt. Okla. Dept. Corrections, Oklahoma City, 1980-86, Healdton (Okla.) Pub. Schs., 1986-90, Piedmont (Okla.) Pub. Schs., 1995—. Contbr. articles to profl. publs. Bd. dirs. United Meth. Prism Ministry, Oklahoma City, 1986—, Children's Shelter, Ardmore, Okla., 1989-90; mem. State Vocat. Edn. Coun., Oklahoma City, 1980-85. Recipient citation Okla. State Senate, 1986. Mem. ASCD, Internat. Reading Assn., Am. Assn. Sch. Adminstrs., Okla. Assn. Sch. Adminstrs., Phi Delta Kappa, Alpha Chi, Kappa Delta Phi. Democrat. Roman Catholic. Office: Piedmont Schs 713 Piedmont Rd N Piedmont OK 73078

ROBERTS, LYNNE JEANINE, physician; b. St. Louis, Apr. 19, 1952; d. H. Clarke and Dorothy June (Cockrum) R.; m. Richard Allen Beadle Jr., July 18, 1981; children: Richard Andrew, Erica Roberts. BA with distinction, Ind. U., 1974, MD, 1978. Diplomate Am. Bd. Dermatology, Am. Bd. Pediatrics, Am. Bd. Laser Surgery. Intern in pediats. Children's Med. Ctr., Dallas, 1978-79, resident in pediats., 1979-80; resident in dermatology U. Tex. Southwestern Med. Ctr., Dallas, 1980-83, chief resident in dermatology, 1982-83, asst. instr. dermatology and pediatrics, 1983-84, asst. prof., 1984-90, assoc. prof., 1990—; physician Cons. Dermatol. Specialists, Dallas, 1990-93; pres. Lynne J. Roberts, MD, PA, Dallas, 1993—; dir. dermatology Children's Med. Ctr., Dallas, 1986—; dermatology sect. chief Med. City Dallas Hosp., 1994-95, 95—. Contbr. articles to profl. jours., chpts. to books. Recipient Scholastic Achievement Citation Am. Med. Women's Assn., 1978. Fellow Am. Acad. Dermatology, Am. Acad. Pediatrics, Am. Soc. Laser Medicine and Surgery (bd. dirs. 1994—); mem. Soc. Pediatric Dermatology, Am. Soc. Dermatologic Surgery, Tex. Med. Assn., Dallas Zool. Soc., Dallas Arboretum, Kappa Alpha Theta, Alpha Omega Alpha. Office: 7777 Forest Ln Ste B314 Dallas TX 75230-2518

ROBERTS, MARGOT MARKELS, business executive; b. Springfield, Mass., Jan. 20, 1945; d. Reuben and Marion (Markels) R.; children: Lauren B. Phillips, Debrah C. Herman. B.A., Boston U. Interior designer Louis Legum Furniture Co., Norfolk, Va., 1965-70; buyer, mgr. Danker Furniture, Rockville, Md., 1970-72; buyer W & J Sloane, Washington, 1972-74; pres. Bus. & Fin. Cons., Palm Beach, Fla., 1976-80, Margot M. Roberts & Assocs., Inc., Palm Beach, 1976—; dealer 20th century Am. art and wholesale antiques Margot M. Roberts, Inc., Palm Beach, 1989—; v.p., dir. So. Textile Svcs. Inc., Palm Beach. Pres. Brittany Condominium Assn., Palm Beach, 1983-87; v.p. South Palm Beach Civic Assn., 1983-88, South Palm Beach Pres.'s Assn., 1984-88; vice chmn. South Palm Beach Planning Bd., 1983-88, 90-91; elected town commr. Town South Palm Beach, Fla., 1991-92, elected vice mayor, 1992-93, elected mayor, 1993—; apptd. Commn. on Status of Women of Palm Beach County, 1992-95; voting mem. Palm Beach County Mcpl. League, 1992-95; vice chair Commn. Status of Women of Palm Beach County, 1994-95. Mem. Nat. Assn. Women in Bus., Palm Beach C. of C. Republican. Office: Town Hall South Palm Beach 3577 S Ocean Blvd Palm Beach FL 33480-5706

ROBERTS, MARIE DYER, computer systems specialist; b. Statesboro, Ga., Feb. 19, 1943; d. Byron and Martha (Evans) Dyer; BS, U. Ga., 1966; student Am. U., 1972; cert. systems profl., cert. in data processing; m. Hugh V. Roberts, Jr., Oct. 6, 1973. Mathematician, computer specialist U.S. Naval Oceanographic Office, Washington, 1966-73; systems analyst, programmer Sperry Microwave Electronics, Clearwater, Fla., 1973-75; data processing mgr., asst. bus. mgr. Trenam, Simmons, Kemker et al, Tampa, Fla., 1975-77; mathematician, computer specialist U.S. Army C.E., Savannah, Ga., 1977-81, 83-85, Frankfurt, W. Ger., 1981-83; ops. rsch. analyst U.S. Army Contrn. Rsch. Lab., Champaign, Ill., 1985-87; data base adminstr., computer systems programmer, chief info. integration and implementation div. U.S. Army Corps of Engrs., South Pacific div., San Francisco, 1987-93; computer specialist, IDEF repository coord., Functional Process Improvement Expertise, Defense Info. Systems Agy., Arlington, Va., 1993-95; computer specialist Ctr. Integration Def. Info. Systems Agy., MacDill AFB, Fla., 1995—. instr. computer scis. City Coll. of Chgo. in Franfurt, 1982-83. Recipient Sustained Superior Performance award Dept. Army, 1983, Nat. Performance Review Hammer award V.P. Gore, 1996. Mem. Am. Soc. Hist. Preservation, Data Processing Mgmt. Assn., Assn. of Inst. for Cert. Computer Profls., Assn. Women in Computing, Assn. Women in Sci., NAFE, Am. Film Inst., U. Ga. Alumni Assn., Sigma Kappa, Soc. Am. Mil. Engrs. Author: Harris Computer Users Manual, 1983.

ROBERTS, MARY LOU, school psychologist; b. Green Bay, Wis., Sept. 28, 1950; d. Elmer David and Leona Theodora (Puyleart) DeGrand. BA in Elem. Edn. and English, U. Wis., Oshkosh, 1972, student, 1977; MS in Counseling Psychology, U. Cen. Tex., 1989; student, U. Hawaii, 1988. Lic. sch. counselor, Tex.; lic. profl. counselor, Tex.; lic. marriage and family therapist, Tex.; cert. tchr., Tex., Wis., Hawaii. Kindergarten tchr. Howard-Suamico ISD, Green Bay, 1972-78; elem. tchr. St. Anthony's Sch., Kalihi, Hawaii, 1978-80, Ave. E. Copperas Cove (Tex.) ISD, 1983-85; elem. tchr. Killeen (Tex.) ISD, 1985-89, sch. psychologist, 1989—; parent teaching cons. Chpt. I Killeen ISD, 1989—, tchr. inservice training, 1989—, child psychologist, 1989—, cons. family and community counselor, 1989—, community speaker, 1988—. Author: (handbook) Counseling Sessions for Small Groups, 1990; editor, reviewer: Let's Learn More About Responsibility, 1991. Vol. Families In Crisi Inc., Killeen, 1987-89; presenter Family Fair Killeen Ind. Sch. dist., 1989; mentor for two at-risk children in Killeen; sch. bd. mem. St. Joseph Sch., Killeen. Mem. AACD, Am. Bus. Women of Am. (scholarship 1985, ways and means com. chmn. Globe chpt. 1986), Tex. Fedn. Tchrs. U. Cen. Tex. Alumni Assn., Tex. Assn. Counseling Devel., Tex. Sch. Counselor Assn., Mid-Tex. Assn. for Counseling Devel. (sec. 1990-92). Democrat. Roman Catholic.

ROBERTS, NANCY MIZE, retired librarian, composer, pianist; b. Corsicana, Tex., Apr. 19, 1931; d. Edward Harvey and Llora Inez (Huffman) Mize; m. Sam Butler Roberts, Jan. 27, 1928 (dec.); children: Sam Butler Roberts Jr., John Daniel Roberts (dec.). Attended, Corsicana H.S. Cert. county librarian. Inventory clerk Oil City Iron Works, Corsicana, 1949-51; programmer KAND Radio, Corsicana, 1959-60; librarian Corsicana Public Library, 1966-69; owner dress shop Hang-Up, Corsicana, 1969-70; librarian Corsicana Public Library, 1970-73; women's editor Corsicana Daily Sun, 1973-75; librarian Corsicana Public Library, 1975-96. Composer: (church anthems) Clap Your Hands, Two Commandments, God Moves in A Mysterious Way, I Must Tell Jesus. Mem. bd. dirs. Warehouse Living Arts. Recipient Lifetime Achievement award Northeast Tex. Library Assn., 1996. Mem. Women's Clubhouse Orgn. Democrat. Baptist. Home: 1443 W 3d Ave Corsicana TX 75110

ROBERTS, (GRANVILLE) ORAL, clergyman; b. nr. Ada, Okla., Jan. 24, 1918; s. Ellis Melvin and Claudius Priscilla (Irwin) R.; m. Evelyn Lutman, Dec. 25, 1938; children: Rebecca Ann (dec.), Ronald David (dec.), Richard Lee, Roberta Jean. Student, Okla. Bapt. U., 1942-44, Phillips U., 1947; LLD (hon.), Centenary Coll., 1975. Ordained to ministry Pentecostal Holiness Ch., 1936, United Meth. Ch., 1968. Evangelist, 1936-41; pastor Fuquay Springs, N.C., 1941, Shawnee, Okla., 1942-45, Toccoa, Ga., 1946, Enid, Okla., 1947; began worldwide evangelistic ministry thru crusades, radio, TV, printed page, 1947; founder Oral Roberts Evangelistic Assn., Inc., Tulsa, 1948, Univ. Village Retirement Center, 1970, City of Faith Med./Research Ctr., 1981, Healing Outreach Ctr., 1986; founder, pub. Abundant Life mag., Daily Blessing (quar. mag.); founder, chancellor Oral Roberts U., Tulsa, 1963—; founding chmn. Internat. Charismatic Bible Ministries. Author: over 50 books including: If You Need Healing, Do These Things, 1947, God is a Good God, 1960, If I Were You, 1967, Miracle of Seed-Faith, 1970, autobiography The Call, 1971, The Miracle Book, 1972, A Daily Guide to Miracles, 1975, Better Health and Miracle Living, 1976, How to Get Through Your Struggles, 1977, Receiving Your Miracle, 1978, Don't Give Up, 1980, Your Road to Recovery, 1986, Attack Your Lack, 1985, How I Learned Jesus Was Not Poor, 1989, How to Resist the Devil, 1989, Fear Not!, 1989, A Prayer Cover Over Your Life, 1990, Is God Your Source?, 1992, 11 Major Prophecies For You in 1992, 1992, Unleashing the Power of Praying in the Spirit, 1993; also numerous tracts and brochures, Bible commentaries. Recipient Indian of Yr. award Am. Broadcasters Assn., 1963; Okla. Hall of Fame, 1973; Oklahoman of Yr., 1974. Club: Rotary. Office: Oral Roberts U 7777 S Lewis Ave Tulsa OK 74171-0003*

ROBERTS, RAYMOND URL, geologist; b. Camp Kilmer, N.J., Oct. 4, 1949; s. William Martin and Francis (Prozibek) R.; m. Pamela Ruth Mercer, June 15, 1980. BS in Geology, Oreg. State U., 1977. Cert. profl. geologist. With command ctr. Salem Police Dept., Oreg., 1977-78; geologist Core Labs., Oklahoma City, 1978-80, Gulf Oil Co., Oklahoma City, 1980-81; exploration geologist Sabine Corp., Oklahoma City, 1981-85, Terra Resources, Oklahoma City, 1985-89; exploration mgr. Optima Exploration, Inc., Okla. City, 1990-92; cons., 1992-94; hydrologist Superfund Project, Okla. Dept. Environ. Quality, 1994—. Sec. Trinity Luth. Ch., Norman, Okla., 1985-86, v.p. 1986-87, pres. 1987-89; tribal mem. citizens bd. Pottawatomi Indians. Served with U.S. Army, 1967-71, Vietnam. Contbr. over 15 articles and short stories to publs. Mem. Am. Inst. Profl. Geologists. Democrat. Lutheran. Avocation: writing. Home: 9925 Aztec Dr Norman OK 73071-5907

ROBERTS, ROBERT, III, lawyer; b. Shreveport, La., July 22, 1930; s. Robert and Mary Hodges (Marshall) R.; m. Susan F. Forrester, Mar. 16, 1974; children: Robert (dec.), Marshall, Francis T. Kalmbach Jr., Ellen K. Tizian, Lewis K.F. Kalmbach, Samuel A. Kalmbach. BA, La. State U., 1951, JD, 1953. Bar: La. 1953, U.S. Dist. Ct. (we. dist.) La. 1958, U.S. Ct. Appeals (5th cir.) 1966, U.S. Ct. Appeals (8th cir.) 1968, U.S. Supreme Ct. 1975. Assoc., then ptnr. and shareholder Blanchard, Walker, O'Quin & Roberts and predecessor, Shreveport, 1955—. Former pres. Family Coun. and Children's Svcs.; former mem. Peabody study com. Caddo Parish Schs.; former chmn. legal div. United Way. 1st lt JAGC, U.S. Army, 1953-55. Mem. ABA, La. State Bar Assn. (former chmn. mineral law sect., former mem. ho. dels., former mem. bd. govs.), La. State Law Inst. (sr. officer, law reform agy. coun. 1962—, mineral code adv. com., civil code lease adv. com.), Soc. Bartolus, Shreveport Bar Assn. (pres. 1981), Shreveport Club, Pierremont Oaks Tennis Club. Office: Blanchard Walker O'Quin & Roberts PO Box 1126 Shreveport LA 71163-1126

ROBERTS, RONNIE SPENCER, chemical engineering educator, researcher; b. Pascagoula, Miss., June 5, 1943; s. H. Spencer and Lois (Bosarge) R.; m. A. Gayle Trellue, July 8, 1984; 1 child, Ryan Spencer. BS in Chem. Engring., U. Miss., 1966; MS in Chem. Engring., U. Tenn., 1972, PhD in Chem. Engring., 1976. Process engr. Monsanto Co., La., Iowa, 1966-69; prof. chem. engring. Ga. Inst. Tech., Atlanta, 1976—; cons., mem. sci. bd. Stake Tech., Ottawa, Can., 1979-81; cons. Forensic Technologies Inc., Annapolis, Md., 1989—, Milliken Corp., LaGrange, Ga., 1991—. Contbr. articles to profl. jours., chpt. to books. Mem. AIChE (sect. chair 1972-79, sect. vice chair 1972-78, divsn. vice chair 1978-81). Office: Georgia Inst Tech Sch Chemical Engineering Atlanta GA 30332-0100

ROBERTS, ROSE HARRISON, social services administrator, consultant; b. Ripley, Miss., Mar. 30; d. Charles Edgar and Rosa Nell (Smith) Dickerson; m. Bobby R. Harrison, June 9 (div. 1972); children: Pat, Ava Jordan, Kim; m. James L. Roberts, Jr., Sept. 30, 1984. BS, Blue Mountain (Miss.) Coll., 1957; MSW, Tulane U., 1970. Lic. clin. social worker, Miss.; qualfied clin. social worker, diplomate clin. social worker. Social worker Miss. Dept. Pub. Welfare, Ripley, 1963-68; dist. supr. Miss. Dept. Pub. Welfare, Pontotoc, 1970-85; EEO coord. Miss. Dept. Pub. Welfare, Jackson, 1985-86, bur. dir., 1986-88; dir. New Beginnings, Inc., Tupelo, Miss., 1988—; adj. assoc. prof. U. Miss., Oxford, 1974-83; field instr. Miss. So. U., Hattiesburg, 1985-88; cons. nursing homes, Ripley, 1975—; Pontotoc County bd. dirs. Region III Mental Health Com., Tupelo, 1990—. Mem. Blue Print for Hope. Mem. Acad. Cert. Social Workers. Home: PO Box 485 Pontotoc MS 38863-0485

ROBERTS, SANDRA, editor; b. Humboldt, Tenn., July 22, 1951; d. Harold and Margaret (Headrick) R.; m. Parker W. Duncan Jr., Aug. 11, 1990. Student, Tex. Christian U., 1969-70; BS, U. Tenn., 1972; MLS, Peabody Coll. Libr. The Tennessean, Nashville, 1975-82, editorial writer, 1982-87, editorial editor, 1987—. Pres. Women's Polit. Caucus, Nashville, 1982. Recipient John Hancock award John Hancock Co., 1983, Freedom award Tenn. Trial Laywers Assn., 1988. Mem. Am. Soc. Newspaper Editors, Nat. Conf. Editorial Writers, Sigma Delta Chi (Nat. Headliner award 1982). Mem. Christian Ch. Office: The Tennessean 1100 Broadway Nashville TN 37203-3116

ROBERTS, SCOTT BOYD, psychologist; b. Waynesburg, Pa., Sept. 3, 1955; s. Rolland Boyd and Mary Alene (Cowell) R.; m. Margaret Teresa Crouse, July 27, 1985; children: Haddie Lauren, Olivia Mary. BA, Waynesburg Coll., 1982; MA, Ind. U. Pa., 1985. Lic. psychologist. Psychol. assoc. Centerville Clinics, Inc., Frederickton, Pa., 1985-88; psychotherapist Fairmont (W.Va.) Gen. Hosp., 1988-96; program dir. geriatric psychiatry unit, 1996—. Trustee Rogersville (Pa.) United Meth. Ch., 1994—, adminstrv. bd., 1994—; bd. dirs. Greene Assn. Retarded Citizens, Waynesburg, Pa., 1994—. Mem. Pa. Psychol. Assn. Republican. Home: PO Box 394 1st St Rogersville PA 15359 Office: Fairmont Gen Hosp 1325 Locust Ave Fairmont WV 26554

ROBERTS, THOMAS GEORGE, retired physicist; b. Ft. Smith, Ark., Apr. 27, 1929; s. Thomas Lawrence and Emma Lee (Stanley) R.; m. Alice Anne Harbin, Nov. 14, 1958 (dec. 1994); children: Lawrence Dewey, Regina Anne; foster child, Marcia Roberts Dale; m. Betty Howard McElyea, July 28, 1995. AA, Armstrong Coll., 1953; BS, U. Ga., 1956, MS, 1957; PhD, N.C. State U., 1967. Research physicist U.S. Army Missile Command, Huntsville, Ala., 1958-85; cons. industry and govt. agys., 1970—; owner Technoco, Huntsville. Contbr. articles to profl. jours. Patentee in field. Served to sgt. USAF, 1948-52. Fellow Am. Optical Soc.; mem. Am. Phys. Soc., IEEE, Huntsville Optical Soc. Am. (pres. 1980, 92). Episcopalian. Club: Toastmaster Internat. (pres. 1963). Current work: Laser physics, optics, particle beams and instrumentation; diagnostic devices and techniques development. Subspecialties: Laser physics; Plasma physics. Office: Technoco PO Box 4723 Huntsville AL 35815-4723

ROBERTS, THOMASENE BLOUNT, entrepreneur; b. Americus, Ga., Sept. 5, 1943; d. Thomas Watson and Mary Elizabeth (Smith) Blount; m. Henry Lee Roberts, Apr. 24, 1970 (div. 1991); 1 child, Asha Maia. Student, Fisk U., 1960-63; BA, Morris Brown Coll., 1965; MA, Atlanta U., 1970, postgrad., 1979-82; postgrad., Clark Atlanta U. Social worker Gate City Day Nursery Assn., Atlanta, 1965-66; ticket agt. Delta Air Lines, Inc., Atlanta, 1966-68; clk. accounts payable Kraft Foods, Inc., Decatur, Ga., 1968; cons. family svcs. Atlanta Housing Authority, 1970-72, supr. family svcs., 1972-73, mgr. family relocation, 1974-79; grad. rsch. asst. Sch. Edn. Atlanta U., 1979-82; city coun. asst. City of Atlanta, 1984-88, rsch. asst. Dept. Pub. Safety, 1988; dir. govtl. rels. Morris Brown Coll., Atlanta, 1988-93; owner TBR Ent., Atlanta, 1993—; adminstrv. analyst human svcs. City of Atlanta, 1995—; researcher/intern Project Focus Teen Mother Program, Atlanta, 1981-82; moderator Nat. Black Women's Health Project, Atlanta, 1985; workshop leader Assn. Human Resources Mgrs., Atlanta, 1989; pres.'s rep. U. Ctr. Devel. Corp., Inc., 1989-93; cons. entrepreneur devel. workshop Morris Brown Coll. Chairperson Ida Prather YWCA Cmty. Bd., Atlanta, 1985-90; bd. dirs. YWCA Met. Atlanta, 1986-90, Met. Atlanta Coalition 100 Black Women, 1988-90, 92—, sec., mem. bd. dirs., 1994—, Hammonds House Mus., 1995—; active fund dr. com. Jomandi Prodn., 1988-89; v.p. maj. gifts com. Camp Best Friends, City of Atlanta, 1989; mem. Multi-Cultural Leadership Group, Gov.'s Coun. on Developmental Disabilities. Mem. Atlanta-Trinidad/Tobago Exch. (sec., treas. 1983-89, Pt. of Spain cert. 1986), Nat. Polit. Congress Black Women (corr. sec. 1989-90), Nat. Assn. for Equal Opportunity Higher Edn. (coll. liaison 1988-93), Coun. for Advancement-Support of Edn., Info. Forum, Atlanta Urban League, Inc., Nat. Assn. for Equal Opportunity in Higher Edn. (Disting. Alumni award 1991), Nat. Soc. Fund-Raising Execs. (cert. 1992), Nat. Soc. Fund-Raising Execs. Leadership Inst., Friends of Morehouse Sch. Medicine, Delta Sigma Theta (pub. rels. asst. 1986-89). Home: 1817 King Charles Rd SW Atlanta GA 30331-4909 Office: TBR Enterprises Ste A-3165 2740 Greenbriar Pky SW Atlanta GA 30331-2614

ROBERTS, W. MARK, pediatric hematologist/oncologist; b. Kansas City, Mo., July 18, 1958; s. Dewey And Martha Marie (Lambert) Roberts; m. Robyn L. Pilcher, June 20, 1992; children: Kristen Blake, Ian Stuart, Colin Payne. BA in Biology, U. Mo., 1982; MD, U. Mo. Med. Sch., 1982. Diplomate Am. Bd. Pediatrics. Resident in pediatrics Children's Mercy Hosp., Kansas City, Mo., 1982-85; fellow in pediatric hematology/oncology St. Jude Children's Rsch. Hosp., Memphis, 1985-88; asst. prof. dept. pediatrics U. Tenn., Memphis, 1988-94; assoc. prof. divns. of pediatrics Univ. Tex. Anderson Cancer Ctr., 1994—; asst. mem. dept. hematology/oncology St. Jude Children's Rsch. Hosp., 1988-94. Mem. AAAS, Am. Acad. Pediatrics, Am. Cancer Soc., Am. Soc. Mocrobiology, Am. Soc. Hematology, Am. Soc. Clin. Oncology, Am. Fed. Clin. Rsch., Children's Cancer Group. Office: U Tex MD Anderson Cancer Ctr Divsn Ped Box 087 1515 Holcombe Blvd Houston TX 77030

ROBERTS, WILLARD JOHN, secondary school educator; b. Bumcombe County, N.C., Mar. 3, 1933; s. John Woodridge and Gladys Mary (Medford) R. BS, East Carolina U., 1955; MA, Appalachian State U., 1975, EdS, 1976; EdD, Miss. State U., Starkville, 1985. Cert. supr., secondary prin., tchr., Miss., Ala., Tenn. Tchr., coach, athletic dir. Harnett County (N.C.) Bd. Edn., 1955-56, Henderson County (N.C.) Bd. Edn., 1956-58, McDowell County (N.C.) Bd. Edn., 1958-61; tchr. Petersburg (Va.) Bd. Edn., 1961-62, Buncombe County (N.C.) Bd. Edn., 1962-63, 63-67, Fairfax County (Va.) Bd. Edn., 1967-71; security officer Wackenhut security divsn. Singer Furniture, Lenior, N.C., 1973; security officer Blue Ridge Shoe Co., Boone, N.C., 1974-76; day detective Howard Family Room Furniture, Starkville, Miss., 1976-77; spl. police security officer Johnston-Tombigbee Furniture Mfg. Co., Inc., Columbus, Miss., 1977-79; with Oxford Security Svcs. Bryan Foods, West Point, Miss., 1980-82; night security, night desk clk. mgr., night auditor Univ. Motel, Starkville, Miss., 1981—. Mem. Sr. Coalition, United Srs. Assn., Inc., Nat. Com. to Preserve Social Security and Medicare, Am. Immigration Control Found., We The People, Ams. for Immigration Control. Home: PO Box 1464 Starkville MS 39760

ROBERTS, WILLIAM DAN, data processing executive; b. London, Ohio, July 10, 1952; s. Deane Lamar and Dolly Luretta (Slyh) R.; children: Jessica Diane, Stephanie Michelle, William Joseph; m. Kathryn McLaughlin, Nov. 30, 1990. BS in Applied Sci., Miami U., 1974; MBA, Morehead State U., 1980. Computer programmer Ashland (Ky.) Oil Inc., 1974-79; quality assurance analyst NCR, Dayton, Ohio, 1979-80; project leader fin. systems Armco Inc., Middletown, Ohio, 1980-83; mgr. fin. systems Federated Dept. Stores, Cin., 1983-84; mgr. data adminstrn. Boeing Computer Svcs., Kettering, 1985-91; founder Intryss Incorp., Ohio, 1987—; pvt. practive mgmt. cons. W. Dan Roberts Co., Inc., Centreville, Va., 1991—; mem. bd. dirs. Front Royal and Warren County Indsl. Park Corp. Author, copyright (Computer System) Intryss Cash Mgmt. System, 1987, Stock Option Exercise Mgmt. System, 1993, ExerTalk Voice Response System For Executive Stock Options, 1994, ExerStat Broker Communications Software, 1994; pub. newsletter Mgmt. Cons. Critical Path. Explorer scout Boy Scouts Am., Middletown, Ohio, Vienna, 1989, 90; mem. Boeing Exec. Potential Program, 1991; asst. archery divsn. Jr. Olympics, 1994, dir. archery divsn., 1995-96; bd. dirs. Front Royal & Warren County Indsl. Park Corp. Mem. Assn. for Sys. Mgmt., Boeing Mgmt. Assn. (sec. 1989-90), Isaac Walton League Am., Nat. Archery Assn. Am., Va. Archery Assn., Nat. Field Archery Assn., Dayton Amateur Radio Assn., Warren County Amateur Radio Emergency Svc., Gross # 953, Masons. Methodist. Home: 15382 Twin Creek Ct Centreville VA 22020-3742 Office: W. D. Roberts Co Inc PO Box 2168 Centreville VA 22020-8927

ROBERTSON, DALE WAYNE, minister; b. Anderson, S.C., Apr. 6, 1954; s. William Eural and Avis Louise (O'Barr) R.; m. Beth Brown, Nov. 21, 1978; children: Miranda Renee, Christi Alisha. BTh, Brainerd Theol. Seminary, Spartanburg, S.C., 1985; MTh, Immanuel Bapt. Theol. Seminary, Peachtree City, Ga., 1988, MDiv, 1989, DD, 1990. Lic. and ordained to ministry So. Bapt. Conv., 1981. Assoc. evangelist Greater Life Evangelism Assn., Owasso, Okla., 1978-81; minister First Bapt. Ch., Colcord, Okla., 1981-83, Bowman (Ga.) Bapt. Ch., 1983-85, Morningside Bapt. Ch., Valdosta, Ga., 1985—; chmn. evangelism com. Hebron Assn., Elberton, Ga., 1984, Valdosta (Ga.) Assn., 1989; mem. com. on order of bus. Ga. Bapt. Conv., Atlanta, 1989, v.p., 1990, moderator, 1990, vice moderator, 1991, mem. pers. com., 1991, mem. resolutions com., 1991, nominating com., 1995-96, structure study com., 1995-96, time place preaching com., 1995-96, mem. com. on coms., 1991; pres. Ga. Bapt. Preaching conf., 1993-94. Mem. Valdosta Bapt. Assn. (moderator 1992-94), Ga. Alumni Luther Rice Sem. (treas. 1993-94, pres. 1994-95). Home: 1125 N Lakeshore Dr Valdosta GA 31602 Office: Morningside Baptist Church PO Box 2445 Valdosta GA 31604-2445

ROBERTSON, DAVID, pharmacologist, educator; b. Sylvia, Tenn., May 23, 1947; s. David Herlie and Lucille Luther (Bowen) R.; m. Rose Marie Stevens, Oct. 30, 1976; 1 child, Rose. B.A., Vanderbilt U., 1969, M.D., 1973. Diplomate Am. Bd. Internal Medicine, Am. Bd. Clin. Pharmacology. Intern, Johns Hopkins U., Balt., 1973-74, asst. resident, 1974-75, asst. chief service in medicine, 1977-78; fellow in clin. pharmacology Vanderbilt U., Nashville, 1975-77, asst. prof. medicine and pharmacology, 1978-82, assoc. prof., 1982-86, prof., 1986—, prof. neurology, 1991—; dir. clin. research ctr., 1987—; dir. Ctr. for Space Physiology and Medicine, 1989—; dir. Med. Sci. Tng. Program, 1993—; pclin. rsch. specializing in gene therapy and disorders of blood pressure regulation, Nashville, 1978—; mem. staff Vanderbilt Hosp., Burroughs Wellcome scholar in clin. pharmacology, 1985-91. Author: (with B.M. Greene and G.J. Taylor) Problems in Internal Medicine, 1980, (with C.R. Smith) Manual of Clinical Pharmacology, 1981, (with Italo Biaggioni) Disorders of the Autonomic Nervous System, 1995, Primer on the Autonomic Nervous System, 1996; editor-in-chief Drug Therapy, 1991-94; editorial bds. Jour. Autonomic Nervous System, Clin. Pharm. and Therapeutics, Clin. Autonomic Rsch., Am. Jour. Med. Sci., Current Topics in Pharmacology. Recipient Research Career Devel. award NIH, 1981, Grant W. Liddle award for leadership in rsch., 1991; Adolph-Morsbach grantee Bonn, Germany, 1968; Logan Clendening fellow Reykjavik, Iceland, 1969. Fellow Am. Heart Assn. Council Hypertension and Circulation, ACP (teaching and research scholar 1978-81); mem. Am. Autonomic Soc. (pres. 1992-94), Am. Acad. Neurology, Soc. Neurosci., Am. Inst. Aeronautics and Astronautics, U.S. Pharmacopeial Conv., Nat. Bd. Med. Examiners, Aerospace Med. Assn. (space station sci. and applications com.), FDA Consortium Rare Disorders, Rare Disorder Network, Am. Fedn. for Clin. Research, Am. Soc. Clin. Investigation, Assn. Am. Physicians, So. Soc. for Clin. Investigation, Am. Soc. for Clin. Pharmacology and Therapeutics, Phi Beta Kappa, Alpha Omega Alpha (hon., bd. dirs. 1995—). Baptist. Home: 4003 Newman Pl Nashville TN 37204-4308 Office: Vanderbilt U Clin Rsch Ctr 21st Ave S Nashville TN 37232-2195

ROBERTSON, DEREK ALVA, finance director; b. Kingston, Jamaica, May 2, 1964; s. Byron Maurice Willan and Rita Allison (Wyke) R.; m. Shanta Denin Walker, Jan. 14, 1995; 1 child, Ryan Stanberry. BS in Econs., U. W.I., 1985; MBA, CUNY, 1991; postgrad., U. Houston. Adminstrv. ofcr. Ministry of Fgn. Affairs, Kingston, Jamaica, 1985-86; economist Planning Inst. of Jamaica, Kingston, 1986-87; project analyst Nat. Devel. Bank of Jamaica, Kingston, 1987-89; dir. adminstrn. Nat. Hemophilia Found., N.Y.C., 1990-94; fin. dir. Gulf State Hemophilia Treatment Ctr./U. Tex. Health Sci. Ct., Houston, 1994—; chmn. sub-com. on products and therapeutics Maternal and Child Health Bur., Nat. Hemophilia Program of HHS, Bethesda, Md., 1995—. Mem. Am. Soc. Assn. Execs., Black Law Students Assn., Jamaica Coll. Alumni Assn. (sec. 1993-94). Office: Gulf States Hemophilia Ctr U Tex Health Sci Ctr 6410 Fannin Ste 416 Houston TX 77030

ROBERTSON, EARLENE, elementary school educator; b. Marshall, Tex., Oct. 8, 1948; d. John L. Taylor, Sr. and Bobbie Jean Fields-White; divorced; children: Emily, Danielle, Evan. BS, Wiley Coll., 1972; MEd in Guidance, Prairie View A & M Univ., 1977. Cert. elem. tchr. Tex., counselor, Tex. Tchr. DeKalb Ind. Sch. Dist., Tex., 1973-74, Karnack Ind. Sch. Dist., Tex., 1974-80, Marshall Ind. Sch. Dist., Tex., 1980-84, North Forest Ind. Sch. Dist., Houston, 1984-87, Houston Ind. Sch. Dist., Tex., 1987—; grade chmn. Dogan Elem. Sch., Houston, 1991-93, chmn. site based mgmt. com., 1992-93, tchr.-coord. after sch. tutorials, 1994—. V.p. United Meth. Women of Crestmont Park Ch., Tex., 1985-89, pres., 1989-93, lay leader, choir mem., usher, mem. Ruth Cir., 1992-94; dist. coord. Christian Personhood, Houston-South. Mem. Congress of Houston Tchrs. (bldg. rep. 1991—), Nat. Assn. Profl. Women. Democrat. Office: Dogan Elem Sch 4202 Liberty Rd Houston TX 77026-5824

ROBERTSON, HERBERT CHAPMAN, JR., geoscience consulting company executive; b. Dallas, Nov. 18, 1928; s. Herbert Chapman Sr. and Sarah Grace (Foraker) R. BA, So. Meth. U., 1951, MS, 1959. Geologist Research, Inc., Dallas, 1952-54; seismologist Geophys. Surveys, Inc., Dallas, 1957-59; geologist Exploration Surveys, Dallas, 1959-61; research assoc. Teledyne-Geotech, Dallas, 1961-73; sr. geophysicist PEXCON, Dallas, 1973-75; supr. U.S. Geol. Survey, Washington, 1975-81; sr. geophysicist Mobil Exploration Co., Dallas, 1981-82, Sun Exploration Co., Dallas, 1982-84; pres. The Herbert Robertson Co., Inc., Dallas, 1984—; Dept. of Def. tech. cons. to prin. investigator So. Meth. U., Tex., 1984, mgmt. cons. 1989—. Contbr. articles to profl. jours. Served as cpl. U.S. Army, 1954-56. Mem. Soc. Exploration Geophysicists (Silver cert. 1984), Am. Geophys. Union. Republican. Presbyterian. Home and Office: 2116 Housley Dr Dallas TX 75228-2044

ROBERTSON, JACK CLARK, accounting educator; b. Marlin, Tex., Apr. 27, 1943; s. Rupert Cook and Lois Lucille (Rose) R.; m. Caroline Susan Hughes, Oct. 23, 1965; children: Sarah Ellen, Elizabeth Hughes. Student, Rice U., 1961-63; B.B.A. with honors, U. Tex., Austin, 1965, M.in Profl. Acctg., 1967; Ph.D., U. N.C., 1970. C.P.A., Tex. Tax acct. Humble Oil and Refining Co., Houston, 1964-65; auditor Peat, Marwick, Mitchell & Co., Houston, 1965-66; acct. Wade, Barton, Marsh C.P.A.s, Austin, Tex., 1966-67; asst. prof. U. Tex., Austin, 1970-74; assoc. prof. U. Tex., 1974-79, Price Waterhouse auditing prof., 1979-84, C.T. Zlatkovich Centennial prof. acctg., 1984—; acad. assoc. Coopers & Lybrand, N.Y.C., 1975-76; acad. fellow U.S. Securities and Exchange Commn. Office of the Chief Acct., Washington, 1982-83; Erskine fellow U. Canterbury, Christchurch, New Zealand, 1988; lectr. in field. Contbr. articles to profl. jours. Lay reader St. Matthews Episcopal Ch., Austin, 1972-75, mem. vestry, 1973-75, 77-79, 84-86, treas., 1974-75, 77—, chmn. bldg. fund, 1976-87, chmn. everymen. canvass, 1980, sr. warden, 1986; del. Diocese of Tex. Coun., 1993-95. Mem. AICPA, Am. Acctg. Assn. (chmn. auditing sect. 1978-79, chmn. auditing stds. com. 1980-81, chmn. SEC liaison com. 1983-84), Tex. Soc. CPAs (vice chmn., profl. ethics com. 1986-94, 95—, Presdl. citation 1994), Assn. Cert. Fraud Examiners (regent emeritus, cert.), Phi Kappa Phi, Beta Gamma Sigma, Beta Alpha Psi. Office: Univ of Tex CBA 4M 202 Dept Accounting Austin TX 78712

ROBERTSON, JAMES COLE, consultant; b. Washington, June 8, 1929; s. Gordon and Florence Virginia (Cole) R.; m. Pauline Taylor, May 27, 1957; children: Lindsay Gordon, Preston Taylor. AS, Okla. State U., 1950; BS, U. So. Calif., 1954. Inspector Factory Ins. Assn., Charlotte, N.C., 1954-56; sr. instr. U. Md., College Park, 1956-62; asst. state fire marshal State Md., Balt., 1962-64, state fire marshal, 1964-82; cons. Nat. Fire Protection Assn., Quincy, Mass., 1982-85; dir. Dept. Emergency Svcs., Gainesville, Fla., 1985-86; asst. chief Gainesville Fire-Rescue Dept., 1986-88; regional rep. so. and ctrl. states Nat. Fire Protection Assn., Quincy, 1988-93; cons. Mizelle, Hodges & Assocs., Inc., Gainesville, 1993—. Author: Introduction to Fire Prevention, 4th edit., 1995. Mem. Alachua County Hist. Commn., Gainesville, 1987—. Comdr. USCGR, ret. Mem. Fire Marshals Assn. N.Am. (hon. life, pres. 1969-70), Nat. Fire Protection Assn. (life, com. chmn. 1972-82), Sons Confederate Vets. Camp (1st lt. comdr. Fla. divsn.), Gainesville Sunrise Rotary. Republican. Episcopalian. Home: 3235 NW 31st St Gainesville FL 32605-2164 Office: Mizelle Hodges & Assocs Inc PO Box 716 Gainesville FL 32602-0716

ROBERTSON, JOHN MICHAEL, education educator; b. Petersburg, Va., Oct. 11, 1961; s. John Ronald Robertson and Fay Carol (Parrish) Wade; m. Pamela Lynne Mingea R., May 19, 1984; children: Erin Michelle, John David, Caitlyn Anne. Student, Richard Bland Coll., 1980-81; BA, Va. Commonwealth U., 1984; MA, U. Va., 1988, PhD, 1993. Editor, rschr. Ctr. for Nat. Security Law, Charlottesville, Va., 1987-89; prof., cons. Am. Mil. U., Manassas Park, Va., 1995—. Contbr. articles to profl. jours. Mem. U.S.

Strategy Inst., U.S. Naval Inst., Navy League U.S., Phi Kappa Alpha. Home and Office: 12 Barkley Ln Palmyra VA 22963

ROBERTSON, K. JOY, pulmonary/critical care educator; b. San Antonio, May 29, 1936; d. William Homer and Catherine (Wright) R. MD, U. Tex., Dallas, 1962. Staff physician U. Tex. Student Health Ctr., Austin, Tex., 1963-65; med. cons. Tex. Instruments, Dallas, 1965-67; intern. John Peter Smith Hosp., Ft. Worth, 1967-69; resident Parkland Meml. Hosp., Dallas, 1969-70; fellowship Southwestern Med. Sch. U. Tex., Dallas, 1970-72; chief, respiratory therapy VA Hosp., Dallas, 1972-80, asst. chief, pulmonary medicine dept., 1972-80; asst. prof. internal medicine U. Tex. Health Sci. Ctr., Dallas, 1972-81; med. dir., respiratory therapy Assoc. of Arts, El Centro Coll., Dallas, 1974-76; asst. clin. prof. medicine U. Tex. Health Sci. Ctr., Dallas, 1981-84; faculty dir., svc. plan medicine U. Tex. Health Sci. Ctr., 1981-84, assoc. prof. medicine, 1984—, svc. plan faculty dir., Aston Med. Ctr., 1984—; med. dir., R/MICU Parkland Meml. Hosp., 1987-96; med. dir., cardio-pulmonary medicine Zale-Lipshy U. Med. Ctr., 1993-95; adv. coun. NHLBI, 1985-90. Com. mem. Dallas Zoo, 1992—. Mem. Tex. Thoracic Soc. (pres. 1979-80, councillor at large 1975-81, rep. to Am. Assn. Respiratory Bd. Med. Adv. 1976-82), Am. Lung Assn. (pres. Dallas area 1979-81, 1982-83, exec. com. 1979-83, annual awards com. N.Y. 1982-83, adult lung com. N.Y. 1983-84, Edward Livingston Trudeau medal com. N.Y. 1983-84). Office: Univ Tex SW Med Ctr Pulm Crit Care Med 5323 Harry Hines Blvd Dallas TX 75235-9034

ROBERTSON, KAREN LEE, county official, acoustical consultant; b. Whittier, Calif., Mar. 21, 1955; d. Lethal Greenhaw Robertson and Lloydine Ann (Pierce) Robertson-Reese; children: Kimberlee Ann Kubski, Krista Linn Robertson. Student Calif. State U. Acoustical technician Hilliard & Bricken, Santa Ana, Calif., 1977-79, John J. Van Houten, Anaheim, Calif., 1979; prin. Robertson & Assocs., Boulder, Colo., 1980; acoustical technician David Adams & Assocs., Denver, 1980; v.p. engring. John Hilliard & Assocs., Tustin, Calif., 1985—; acoustical specialist County of Orange, Santa Ana, 1980-87; airline access, noise officer John Wayne Airport Adminstrn. of Orange County, 1987-92; chair Noise Abatement Com., 1987-92; chair DFW Noise Forum, 1992—; sr. noise compatibility planner Dallas/Ft. Worth Internat. Airport, 1992-95, mgr. noise compatibility, 1995—. mem. advanced subsonic transport noise reduction steering com. NASA/FAA, 1993—; mem. airports coun. Internat.-N.Am. Environ. Affairs Com. Co-author Land Use/Noise Compatibility Manual, 1984; editor Noise Element of General Plan, 1984. Speaker in field. Mem. acoustical adv. bd. Orange County, 1985-92; mem. Calif. Noise Officers Forum, 1987—. Recipient Achievement award Nat. Assn. Counties, 1986, 90, 91, Orange County Achievement award, 1990, Woman Achievement award, 1991. Mem. Acoustical Soc. Am. (bd. dirs. 1985-86), Transp. Research Bd. (tech. mem. 1985—), Nat. Assn. Noise Control Ofcls., Community/Indsl. Noise Control Assn., Inst. Noise Control Engring. (affiliate), Calif. Assn. Window Mfrs. (STC Task Group 1985). Republican. Office: Dallas/Ft Worth Internat Airport PO Box 619428 Dallas TX 75261-9428

ROBERTSON, MARK WAYNE, investment specialist; b. St. Louis, June 28, 1929; s. Harold LaGrand and Mabel Margaret (Mangels) R.; 1 child, A. Rafael Nuncio. Student, U. Houston, 1949-51. Cost acct. Mo. Pacific Railroad, Houston, 1951-55; contract adminstr. Air Cruisers Co., Belmar, N.J., 1955-57; right of way cons. Tex. Hwy. Dept., Houston, 1957; land mgr. Houston Natural Gas Co., 1957-71; adminstrv. asst. Houston Pile Line Co., 1971-84; real estate broker, investor, 1975—; pvt. practice as investor Kerrville, Tex., 1984—; co-owner several small businesses and distributorships. Profl. artist. Fundraiser John Tower for Senator, Houston, Am. Heart Assn., Houston, 1971-81; officer Mended Hearts Assn., Houston, 1971-81; 2d v.p. Hill County Art Foun., Kerrville, 1989-92, treas., 1990-91, adv. bd. 1996—; sr. mem. Soc. Ambs. St. Joseph Hosp., 1989—; adv. Butt Holdworth Libr., 1991; cultural adviser to mayor. Cpl. U.S. Army, 1951-53. Mem. Internat. Right of Way Assn. (officer 1958-83), Kerrville Art Club (pres. 1990), Art League of Houston, Nat. Soc. Painters in Casein and Acrylic, Allied Artists in Am., River Art Group. Roman Catholic.

ROBERTSON, MICHAEL WAYNE, automation company executive; b. Odessa, Tex., May 26, 1958; s. Gary Lee and Pedie Fern (Wilson) R.; m. Kim Syrice Waldrop, July 8, 1978; children: Syrice Rene, Shanna Mischelle. Grad. H.S., Odessa, 1976. Welder, leadman Challenger Rig, Odessa, 1976-78; pvt. practice contract welder Odessa, 1978-81; field supr. JBI Paint Systems, Ft. Worth, 1981-83; owner M.K. Erectors, Arlington, Tex., 1983-86; assembly supr. Fared Robot Systems, Ft. Worth, 1986-89; ptnr. Metro Automation, Inc., Grand Prairie, Tex., 1989—. Mem. Soc. Mfg. Engrs., Sports Car Club Am. Republican. Office: Metro Automation Inc 1475 Avenue S # 300 Grand Prairie TX 75050-1207

ROBERTSON, RANDALL BALL, marketing professional, sporting events promoter; b. Batesville, Ark., Oct. 25, 1954; s. William Joseph and Carol (Barnett) R.; m. Patricia Alice Schenck, Apr. 1, 1978; children: Alice Hannah, Alexander James, Alistair Graham. BA, Rhodes Coll., 1976. V.p. mktg. Schenck Co., Orlando, Fla., 1980-86; pres. R.B. Robertson & Co., Inc., Winter Park, Fla., 1986—; event mktg. mgr. Golden Bear Internat., North Palm Beach, Fla., 1994—; mktg. cons. Arnold Palmer Enterprises, Orlando, 1989-91, Internat. Mgmt. Group, Cleve., 1989-90. Music editor (LP record) Fannie Bell Chapman Gospel Signer, 1978; sound producer (16 mm film) Four Women Artists, 1978 (1st pl. profiles San Francisco film festival 1978). Founder, chmn. The Film Group, Orlando Mus. Art, 1981-83; mgr. Preventing Alcohol Abuse Task Force, Beer Industry of Fla., 1984; pres. Assoc. Bd. Dirs. Orlando Mus. Art; vol. United Cerebral Palsy, 1984-85, Winter Park Community Playground, 1987; assoc. bd. dirs. Fla. Citrus Sports Assn., 1984-85; mem. City of Winter Park Environ. Rev. Bd., 1989-90, Leadership Orlando, 1985, Ctrl. Fla. Capital Funds Com. Field Rev. Team, 1984, All Saints Episcopal Ch. St. Gregory and Chamber Singer Choirs, 1991. Home: 227 Park Ave Palm Beach FL 33480-3808 Office: Golden Bear Internat Inc 11780 Us Highway 1 North Palm Beach FL 33408

ROBERTSON, SAMUEL LUTHER, JR., special education educator, therapist; b. Houston, Apr. 28, 1940; s. Sam L. and Portia Louise (Burns) R.; children: Samuel Luther IV, Sean Lee (dec.), Ryan William, Susan Elizabeth (dec.), Henry Philmore. BS, McMurry U., 1969; MA, Hardin-Simmons U., 1973; PhD, U. Tex., 1993. Cert. tchr., adminstr., counselor, Tex.; lic. chem. dependency counselor, lic. clin. mental health counselor, alcoholism and drug counselor, Tex. Instr., coach, athletic dir. Tex. and La. schs., 1969-94; social worker, supr. Children's Protective Svcs., Abilene, Tex., 1978-79; instr., adminstr. Harlandale Sch. Dist., San Antonio, 1980-84, 87-90; adminstr. night sch. Harlandale Ind. Sch. Dist., San Antonio, 1988-89; instr. Edgewood Ind. Sch. Dist., San Antonio, 1985-87; developer, instr., integrated unit program San Antonio, 1990—; CEO The Educative Inst., San Antonio, 1992—; CEO Educative Therapeutic Processes, San Antonio, 1972—. Author: (play) The Challenged, 1965: (poem) Trains in the Night, 1969. State co-chmn. Youth for Kennedy-Johnson, Tex., 1960; mem. W. Tex. Dem. Steering Com., Abilene, 1962-63; founding dir. Way Off Broadway Community Theater, Eagle Pass, Tex., 1971-72; founding bd. dirs. Battered Women's Shelter, Abilene, 1978-79; v.p. bd. dirs. Mental Health Assn., San Antonio, 1980-83, bd. dirs Palmer Drug Abuse Program, San Antonio, 1985-87; pres., bd. dir. Alcoholic Rehab. Ctr., 1985-86, 1987-92; mem., vice chmn. Civilian and Mil. Addictive Programs, San Antonio, 1991-92; author, implementer Community Vitalization Program, 1994—. Named Tchr. of Yr. Southside Ind. Sch. Dist., San Antonio, 1970-71, Harlandale Alternative Ctr., San Antonio, 1987-88; Vol. of Yr., Mental Health Assn., San Antonio, 1982, Alcoholic Rehab. Ctr., San Antonio, 1992-93. Mem. ACA, NEA, Am. Mental Health Counseling Assn., Tex. State Tchrs. Assn., Am. Ednl. Rsch. Assn., Am. Assn. Sch. Adminstrs., Tex. Assn. Alcoholism and Drug Abuse Counselors, Nat. Alcoholism and Drug Abuse Counselors, N.Mex. Mental Health Counselors Assn., Phi Kappa Phi, Kappa Delta Pi. Episcopalian. Home: 14015 Big Tree San Antonio TX 78247 Office: Educative Therapeutic Processes 339 E Hildebrand Ave San Antonio TX 78212-2412

ROBERTSON, SYLVIA DOUGLAS, middle school educator; b. Lynchburg, Va., June 25, 1952; d. Alfred Lynch and Rena (Irvin) Douglas; m. Lawrence Edward Robertson, Apr. 26, 1975 (div. May 1985); 1 child, Lawrence Edward Jr. BA, Cedar Crest Coll., 1974; MEd, Lynchburg Coll., 1990. Cert. tchr., Va. Tchr. 7th grade Big Island (Va.) Elem. Sch., 1974-89; tchr., team leader 7th grade Bedford (Va.) Mid. Sch., 1989—, tchr., grade level chairperson 7th grade, 1993-94. Facilitator Police, Pub. Educators and Peer Counselors Utilizing the Leadership of Students at Risk, Bedford, Va., 1991-92; vol. Free Clinic Ctrl. Va., Inc., Lynchburg, Va., 1993. Mem. Nat. Coun. Tchrs. Math., Nat. Sci. Tchrs. Assn., Nat. Energy Edn. Devel. Project, Bedford County Edn. Assn., Va. State Reading Assn., Va. Mid. Sch. Assn., Piedmont Area Reading Coun., Kappa Delta Pi, Phi Delta Kappa, Alpha Delta Kappa (corr. sec. 1993—), Alpha Kappa Alpha. Home: Rte 7 Box 122 Arbor Ct Madison Heights VA 24572 Office: Bedford Mid Sch 503 Longwood Ave Bedford VA 24523-3401

ROBERTSON, TED ZANDERSON, judge; b. San Antonio, Sept. 28, 1921; s. Irion Randolf and Aurelia (Zanderson) R.; m. Margie Gardner. Student, Tex. A&I, 1940-42; LL.B., St. Mary's U., San Antonio, 1949. Bar: Tex. 1949. Chief civil dept. Dist. Atty.'s Office, Dallas County, Tex., 1960-65; judge Probate Ct. 2, Dallas County, 1965-69, Juvenile Ct. 2, Dallas County, 1969-75, 95th Dist. Ct., Dallas County, 1975-76, Ct. Civil Appeals, 5th Supreme Jud. Dist., Dallas, 1976-82, Supreme Ct. Tex., Austin, 1982; of counsel Frank Branson P.C., Dallas, 1989—; guest lectr. So. Meth. U., Dallas, Dallas County Juvenile Bd., Tex. Coll. of the Judiciary, 1970-82. Active Dallas Assn. for Retarded Children; active Dallas County Commn. on Alcoholism, Dallas County Mental Health Assn. Served as yeoman USCG, 1942-46. Recipient Golden Gavel St. Mary's U., San Antonio, 1979; named Outstanding Alumnus St. Mary's U., 1981. Mem. Am. Judicature Soc., Tex. Bar Assn., Dallas Bar Assn., Dallas County Juvenile Bd. Democrat. Methodist. Lodges: Masons; Lions. Home: 6233 Highgate Ln Dallas TX 75214-2157 Office: Frank Branson 4514 Cole Ave Ste 1800 Dallas TX 75205-5412

ROBERTSON, VICKI DAWN, adminstrative secretary, writer; b. Miami, Okla., May 17, 1961; d. Elmer Dewitt and Wanda Jean (Stanley) Wynn; m. Stephen Matthew Robertson, June 9, 1984; 1 child, Christopher Michael. AA, Northeastern Okla. A&M U., 1981; BA, Okla. Bapt. U., 1984. Vol. Bapt. Student Union dir. Mission Svc. Corps. So. Bapts., San Francisco, 1984-86; pharmacy technician St. Francis Hosp., Tulsa, Okla., 1986-88; adminstrv. sec. The Williams Cos., Tulsa, Okla., 1988—. Active Chinese children's ministry Nichols Hills Bapt. Ch., Oklahoma City, 1982; Sunday sch. tchr., summer camp tchr. First Assembly, Miami, Okla., 1994; asst. Acteens leader First Bapt. Ch., Miami, 1983-84; active hosp. and deaf ministry Victory Christian Ctr., Tulsa, 1990-92; notary pub. Tulsa County, 1996; fund raising vol. United Way, Tulsa, 1992-94, Muscular Dystrophy Assn., Tulsa, 1995-96. Mem. Williams Office Network, Nat. African Violet Soc., Ministerial Alliance, Phi Theta Kappa. Home: 4209 E 85th Tulsa OK 74137 Office: The Williams Cos PO Box 2848 Tulsa OK 74101

ROBERTSON, WYNDHAM GAY, university official; b. Salisbury, N.C., Sept. 25, 1937; d. Julian Hart and Blanche Williamson (Spencer) R. AB in Econs., Hollins Coll., Roanoke, Va., 1958. Rsch. asst. Standard Oil Co., N.Y.C., 1958-61; rschr. Fortune Mag., N.Y.C., 1961-67, assoc. editor, 1968-74, bd. of editors, 1974-81, asst. mng. editor, 1981-86; bus. editor Time Mag., N.Y.C., 1982-83; v.p. comm. U. N.C., Chapel Hill, 1986-96; bd. dirs. Wachovia Corp., Media Gen. Inc., Capital Cities/ABC, Inc., Equitable Cos. Inc. Contbr. numerous articles to Fortune Mag. Bd. dirs. Mary Reynolds Babcock Found.; trustee U. N.C. Ctr. for Pub. TV. Recipient Gerald M. Loeb Achievement award, U. of Conn., 1972. Mem. Phi Beta Kappa. Episcopalian.

ROBEY, JOHN DUDLEY, transportation executive; b. Stamping Ground, Ky., Aug. 24, 1930; s. Oliver Holmes and Grace Florence (Wasson) R.; m. Nancy Jane Jenkins, June 12, 1954; children: Deborah Jean Thomas, Dennis Preston, Nancy Johnita, Pamela Grace Holland, Johnnie Sue Beth Burchfield. Cert., Ky. State Police Acad., Frankfort, 1956, FBI Nat. Acad., Washington, 1966; student, Ea. Ky. U., 1967-70. Trooper Ky. State Police, Frankfort, 1956-59, sgt., 1959-67, lt., 1967-70, capt., 1970-73, lt. col., 1973-85; sr. v.p. Keyboard Corp., Elizabethtown, Ky., 1985-90, chmn. of bd., 1990-91, chmn. emeritus, 1991—; Trustee Ky. Retirement Systems, Frankfort, 1975—, chmn. bd. trustees, 1982—; dir. div. Motor Vehicle Enforcement Transp. Cabinet, Frankfort, Ky., 1991-92. Staff sgt. USAF, 1950-53, Korea. Mem. FBI Nat. Acad. Assocs. (pres. 1973), Ky. Motor Transport Assn. (bd. dirs. 1990-94), Ky. State Police Retirees Orgn., Ky. State Police Profl. Asns., Mensa, Masons (32 degree). Democrat. Baptist. Home: 311 Sunset Dr Lawrenceburg KY 40342-1460 Office: Ky Retirement Systems 1260 Louisville Rd Frankfort KY 40601-6157

ROBICHAUD, PHYLLIS IVY ISABEL, artist, educator; b. Jamaica, West Indies, May 16, 1915; came to U.S., 1969, naturalized, 1977; d. Peter C. and Rose Matilda (Rickman) Burnett; grad. Tutorial Coll., 1933, Kingston, Jamaica, Munro Coll., St. Elizabeth, Jamaica, 1946; student Central Tech. Sch., Toronto, Ont., Can., 1960-63, Anderson Coll., Can., 1968-69; m. Roger Robichaud, July 22, 1961; children by previous marriage—George Wilmot Graham, William Henry Heron Graham, Mary Elizabeth Graham Watson, Peter Robert Burnett Graham. Sec. to supr. of Agr., St. Elizabeth, 1940-50; loans officer and cashier Confederation Life Assn., Kingston, 1950-53; tchr. art Jamaica Welfare Ltd., 1963; tchr. art recreation dept. New Port Richey, Fla., 1969-77; tchr. art Pasco Hernando Community Coll., New Port Richey, 1977—; demonstrator various organizations including West Pasco Art Guild, New Port Richey, Ace Artists, New Port Richey; propr., mgr. Band Box Dress Shop, Kingston, Jamaica, 1954-57; numerous one-woman shows of paintings including various banks, libraries, Kingston, 1963-64, 67, Toronto, 1968, New Port Richey, 1969, 70, 73, 76, Tampa, Fla., 1974, 75, 76, Omaha Cattle Company restaurant, Clearwater Fla., 1982, Mus. Pasco Hernando Community Coll., New Port Richey, Fla., 1989, 92, Alric C.T. Pottberg Libr. of the PHCC, 1992; numerous group shows, latest being: Sweden House, Tampa, 1977-78, Chasco Fiesta, New Port Richey, 1977, Magnolia Valley Golf and Country Club, New Port Richey, 1978, West Pasco Art Guild, New Port Richey, 1978, 79, 92, Indian Rocks Beach, 1985, Hernando Community Coll. at the Mus. of the Coll., 1989, other cities in Fla.; executed murals, New Port Richey and Kingston; decorated New Port Richey C. of C., also pvt. collections. Patron, St. Alban's 4H Club, 1942; sec. Sunday sch. Ch. of Eng., Kingston, 1937-39. Recipient award T. Eaton Co. of Can., 1961, cert. of merit, Mayor of New Port Richey, 1976, appreciation award New Port Richey Recreation Dept., 1977; award Fla. Heart Fund. Mem. Nat. League Am. Pen Women (v.p. Tampa br. 1978-80, dir. 1969—), West Pasco Art Guild (Blue ribbons 1978, 79, 2d Pl. Mixed Media award 1991), Fla. Fine Arts Guild. Republican. Roman Catholic. Address: 7032 Lenox Dr New Port Richey FL 34653-1920

ROBIE, DIANE C., nursing consultant, medical investigator; b. Whitensville, Mass., Jan. 17, 1942; d. Walter S. and Virginia C. (Griffith) R.; m. Douglas F. Smith, Sept. 13, 1963; 1 child, Frank Vinson. Diploma, Burbank Hosp. Sch. Nursing, Fitchburg, Mass., 1962; BSN, Nova U., Ft. Lauderdale, Fla., 1977. RN, Mass., Fla.; cert. nat. search cons. Clin. nurse orthopedics unit Medox, Inc., Olsten Med. Svcs., Miami, Fla., 1962-67; mgr. med. advisor and disability mgmt. programs Liberty Mut. Ins. Co., Erie, Pa., 1967-70, Jacksonville, Fla., 1972-75; charge nurse orthopedics Victoria Hosp.; head nurse Cathedral Rehab. Ctr., Jacksonville, Fla.; investigator dept. profl. regulation Fla. Office Investigative Svcs., Miami, 1983-84; implementor intervention project nurses Fla. Bd. Nursing, Jacksonville, 1984-85; owner, mgr. Robie Investigations, Inc., Miami, 1985-88; investigator med. quality assurance Fla. Office Investigative Svcs., Miami, 1988—, constrn. investigator (after Hurricane Andrew), 1992-95; missing persons investigator, Miami, 1977-82; speaker in field; geog. rep., alt. chmn. for Dade County Commn. on Study Future Nursing in Fla. Author: (with J. Roberts) Parenting the Adopted Child, 1981; Searching in Florida, a Resource Guide to Public and Private Records, 1982; contbr. article to nursing jours. Mem. ANA, Fla. Nurses Assn., Nat. Assn. Legal Investigators, Fla. Med. Malpractice Claims Coun., Am. Soc. for Indsl. Security, South Fla. Life and Health Claims Assn., South Fla. Investigators Assn. (v.p. 1988). Home: 20948 SW 103rd Pl Miami FL 33189-3609 Office: Agy for Health Care Admin Divsn Med Quality Assurance 8355 NW 53rd St Miami FL 33166-4666

ROBIN, CLARA NELL (CLAIRE ROBIN), English language educator; b. Harrisonburg, Va., Feb. 19, 1945; d. Robert Franklin and Marguerite Ausherman (Long) Wampler; m. Phil Camden Branner, June 10, 1967 (div. May 1984); m. John Charles Robin, Nov. 22, 1984 (div. Dec. 1990). BA in English, Mary Washington Coll., 1967; MA in English, James Madison U., 1974; postgrad., Jesus Coll., Cambridge, Eng., 1982, Princeton U., 1985-86; Auburn U., 1988, U. No. Tex., 1990-91. Cert. tchr. English, French, master cert., Tex. Tchr. 7th grade John C. Myers Intermediate Sch., Broadway, Va., 1967-68; tchr. 10th grade Waynesville (Mo.) H.S., 1968-70; tchr. 6th, 7th, 8th grades Mary Mount Jr. Sch., Santa Barbara, Calif., 1970-72; tchr. 9th grade Forest Meadow Jr. H.S. Richardson (Tex.) Ind. Sch. Dist., 1972-78, tchr. 10th grade Lake Highlands H.S., 1972-84; tchr. 11th, 12th grades Burleson (Tex.) H.S. Burleson Ind. Sch. Dist., 1986—; instr. composition Hill Coll., 1992-94. Contbg. author: (book revs.) English Journal, 1989-94, (lit. criticism) Eric, 1993. Vol. Dallas Theater Ctr., 1990—; mem. Kimbell Art Mus., Ft. Worth, 1990—, Modern Art Mus., Ft. Worth, 1992—, KERA Pub. TV, Dallas, 1990—. Fellow NEH, 1988, 89, 92, 95, Fulbright-Hays Summer Seminar, 1991; ind. study grantee Coun. Basic Edn., 1990; recipient Honorable Mention Tex. Outstanding Tchg. of the Humanities award, 1995. Mem. ASCD, NEA, Nat. Coun. Tchrs. English, Tex. State Tchrs. Assn., Epsilon Nu of Delta Kappa Gamma (1st v.p. 1988-94, v.p. 1992-94). Home: 4009 W 6th St Fort Worth TX 76107-1619 Office: Burleson High Sch 517 SW Johnson Ave Burleson TX 76028-5312

ROBIN, THEODORE TYDINGS, JR., lawyer, engineer, consultant; b. New Orleans, Aug. 29, 1939; s. Theodore Tydings and Hazel (Corbin) R.; m. Helen Jones, June 8, 1963; children: Corbin, Curry, Ted, Phil. BME, Ga. Inst. Tech., 1961, MS in N.E., 1963, PhD, 1967; LLB, Blackstone Sch. Law, 1979. Bar: Calif 1980, U.S. Patent and Trademark Office 1982; registered profl. engr., Ala., Calif. Rsch. engr. Oak Ridge Nat. Lab., 1967; asst. prof. radiology and physics Emory U., 1968-69; project engr. Atomic Internat. div. N.Am. Rockwell, Canoga Park, Calif., 1970-72; engr. mgmt. engring. div. So. Co. Svcs., Birmingham, Ala., 1972-83, mgr. nuclear support and quality assurance, 1989-90, mgr. quality assurance and resources, 1991-92; mgr. Hatch Design Configuration, 1993-94; program mgr. pooled inventory mgmt. program So. Electric Internat., Birmingham, 1984-88; bd. dirs. polit. action com., 1985-87, patent atty. and cons., 1994—. Mem. ABA, ASME (mem. nuc. quality assurance subcom. on standards coordinating 1991-96), Am. Nuc. Soc. (chmn. Birmingham sect. 1987-88, nuclear power plant standards com. 1989-94). Presbyterian. Lodge: Rotary (pres. Shades Valley club 1987-88, chmn. dist. 6860 internat. youth exchange com. 1989-90, R.I. dist. gov. 6860, 1994-95). Research on power plant performance and reliability and effect of coal quality, space radiation effects on human cells, boiling heat transfer, nuclear reactor safety, multi-utility contracting, reliability economics, benchmarking and total quality management; patent law. Home and Office: 4524 Pine Mountain Rd Birmingham AL 35213-1828

ROBINETTE, ANTHONY EDWARD, military officer; b. Ashland, Ky., Dec. 30, 1964; s. Jack Edward and Janet Nicola (Justice) R.; m. Lisa Dawnette Ison, July 29, 1989. BS, U.S. Mil. Acad., 1987. Commd. 2d lt. U.S. Army, 1987, advanced through grades to capt., 1991; asst. logistics officer 1st bn. 10th cav. U.S. Army, Ft. Knox, Ky., 1988, tank platoon leader 1st bn. 10th cav., 1988-89, mortar platoon leader 1st bn. 10th cav., 1989-90, hdqs. troop exec. officer 5th squadron 15th cav., 1990-91, squadron logistics officer 5th squadron 15th cav., 1991-92, dep. chief protocol hdqs., 1992-94; resigned U.S. Army, 1994; prodn. mgr. AK Steel Corp., Ashland, Ky., 1994—. Named Hon. Order of Ky. Cols., 1987. Southern Baptist. Home: 1400 Montgomery Ave Ashland KY 41101-2635 Office: AK Steel Corp Ashland Works Ashland KY 41101

ROBINETTE, BETSYE HUNTER, school psychologist; b. Nashville, Sept. 30, 1960; d. Gerald Sylvan and Eleanor Louise (Felts) Hunter; m. Michael David Robinette, Aug. 13, 1988; 1 child, David. 030PhD, U. Tenn., 1993; MA cum laude, Wheaton (Ill.) Coll., 1984. Lic. psychol. examiner, cert. sch. psychologist, Tenn. Adolescent counselor Mercy Ctr., Aurora, Ill., 1983-84; mental health technician Glendale Heights (Ill.) Community Hosp., 1984; staff psychologist Cumberland River Comprehensive Care Ctr., Harlan, Ky., 1985-86; psychotherapist Family Svc. Ctr., Asheville, N.C., 1987; psychol. examiner Overlook Mental Health Ctr., Knoxville, Tenn., 1987-88; sch. psychology intern Cherokee Mental Health Ctr., Morristown, Tenn., 1989-90; sch. psychologist Knox County Schs., Knoxville, Tenn., 1990-94, Christian Acad. of Knoxville, 1994—; crisis intervention worker RAFT, Inc. Crisis Intervention, Blacksburg, Va., 1981-82; grad. asst. Wheaton Coll., 1984, U. Tenn., Knoxville, 1988-89; clinic coord. U. Tenn., 1989. Missionary Campus Crusade for Christ, Tokyo, 1982. Mem. Am. Psychol. Assn., Nat. Assn. Sch. Psychologists, Tenn. Assn. Sch. Psychologists, Christian Assn. Psychol. Studies, Phi Kappa Phi, Pi Lambda Theta, Psi Chi (v.p. 1981-82). Presbyterian. Home: 1624 Summerhill Dr Knoxville TN 37922-6257

ROBINETTE, BETTY LOU, occupational health and infection control nurse; b. Richlands, Va., Nov. 24, 1941; d. John H. and Eva M. (Crawford) Brown; m. Daniel G. Robinette, Dec. 1, 1961; children: Daniel G. Jr., Brian L., Lisa D. Diploma, Va. Bapt. Hosp., Lynchburg, 1961; tng. infection control, U. Va., 1977. RN, Va. Nurse Highsmith Meml. Hosp., Fayetteville, N.C., 1962; supr., head nurse Clinch Valley Clinic and Hosp., Richlands, Va., 1962-63; nurse Bristol (Tenn.) Meml. Hosp. 1963-65; sch. nurse Wythe County Sch. Bd., Wytheville, Va., 1966-67; staff nurse, supr., infection control practitioner Wythe County Cmty. Hosp., 1972—, employee health nurse cons. infection control programs, 1976—, team leader continuous quality improvement, 1994. Mem. Assn. Practitioners Infection Control, SW Va. AIDS Coalition.

ROBINS, JAMES DOW, counselor; b. Athens, Ga., Oct. 17, 1952; s. Gerald Burns and Fay Ann (Kennan) R.; m. Sharon Eileen Parker, Apr. 12, 1974 (div. 1976). BA in Psychology, SUNY, Albany, 1981; BA in Comm. cum laude, Tex. A&M U., 1981, MA in Secondary Edn., 1982; ABA, cert. legal asst., Southwestern Paralegal Inst., 1984; MS in Guidance and Counseling, Tex. A&M U., 1993. Bar: Tex., 1985; cert. counselor, psychologist, English and speech tchr., legal asst., Tex. Program dir. University City, Inc., Athens, 1971-73; sta. mgr. Bethany Broadcasting, Houston, 1973-76; program coord. for radio and TV, Tex. A&I U., Kingsville, 1977-82; dir. pub. rels. Kleberg Meml. Hosp., Kingsville, 1983-84; legal asst., cons. Kleberg, Dyer, Redford & Weil, Corpus Christi, Tex., 1984-86; tchr. English lit. Brownsville (Tex.) Ind. Sch. Dist., 1986-90; dir. testing and assessment, dir. suicide intervention Kingsville Ind. Sch. Dist., Kingsville, 1993—; counselor Kingsville Ind. Sch. Dist., 1993—; cons. Conner Mus., Kingsville, 1981-82. Author: The School Counselor: A Profession in Transition, 1993; contbr. articles to various publs. Recipient Disting. Svc. award for Excellence in Broadcasting, Tex. A&M, 1980-81. Mem. ACA (profl.), Tex. Counseling Assn., Mensa, The Blues Found. (internat. voting mem.), State Bar of Tex. (legal asst. div. 1985), Am. Counseling Assn., Tex. Counselors Assn., Tex. Sch. Counselors Assn., Tex. Assn. for Humanistic Edn. and Devel., Tex. Assn. for Multi-Cultural Counseling and Devel., Am. Assn. Assessment in Counseling, World Wildlife Fedn., Gulf Coast Counseling Assn., Gulf Coast Assn. for Counseling and Devel., The Blues Found., Phi Delta Kappa , Alpha Chi. Methodist. Home: 515 University Blvd Kingsville TX 78363-4242

ROBINS, ROBERT SIDWAR, political science educator, administrator; b. Spangler, Pa., Apr. 20, 1938; s. Sydney and Katherine (Sidwar) R.; m. Marjorie McGann, Nov. 25, 1959; children: Anthony P., Nicholas A. BA, U. Pitts., 1959; MA, Duke U., 1961, PhD, 1963. Prof. polit. sci. Tulane U., New Orleans, 1965—, chmn. dept. polit. sci., 1979-90, dep. provost, 1991—; acad. visitor Inst. Commonwealth Studies, U. London, 1969-70, 78-79, mem. 1987-88; sr. assoc. mem. St. Antony's Coll., Oxford, Eng., 1972-73; vis. scholar Hastings Ctr., 1982; vis. scientist Tavistock Clinic, London, 1987-88. Author: Political Institutionalization and the Integration of Elites, 1976 (Carnegie Commn. report) Legislative Attitudes Toward Higher Education in Louisiana, 1968, Psychopathology and Political Leadership, 1977, Disease and Political Leadership, 1990; co-author: When Illness Strikes the Leader; contbr. articles to profl. publs. Vice chmn. Elections Integrity Commn., State of La., 1981-82. Recipient Excellence in Teaching award Tulane U., 1978; Fulbright scholar, 1961-62. Mem. Am. Polit. Sci. Assn., Internat. Soc. Polit. Psychology, New Orleans Fgn. Relations Assn. (bd. dirs.). Home: 727 Pine St New Orleans LA 70118-5118 Office: Tulane U Gibson Hall Office of the Provost New Orleans LA 70118

ROBINS, ROSEMARY GAY, Egyptologist; b. Fleet, England, June 28, 1951; came to U.S., 1988; d. John Maurice and Alison (Gerrish) Robins; m. Charles Cameron Shute, Sept. 6, 1980. BA in Chinese with honors, U.

Durham, England, 1972, BA in Egyptology with honors, 1975; DPhil, U. Oxford, England, 1981; PhD, U. Cambridge, England, 1982. Rsch. fellow in Egyptology Cambridge U., 1979-83; hon. rsch. fellow U. Coll., London, 1984-88; affiliated lectr. U. Cambridge, 1987-88; asst. prof. art history Emory U., Atlanta, 1988-94, assoc. prof. art history, 1994—. Author: Egyptian Painting and Relief, 1986, Women in Ancient Egypt, 1993, Proportion and Style in Ancient Egyptian Art, 1994, (with Charles Shute) Rhind Mathematical Papyrus, 1987; contbr. numerous articles to profl. jours. Mem. Egypt Exploration Soc., Internat. Assn. Egyptologists, Am. Rsch. Ctr. in Egypt, Archaeol. Inst. Am., Coll. Art Assn. Office: Emory U Art History Dept Atlanta GA 30322

ROBINS, WILLIAM LEWIS, medical physicist; b. N.Y.C., July 2, 1953; s. Bertram Julius and Charlotte (Cohen) R.; m. Peggy Benison, Mar. 8, 1981; 1 child, Ilana Brooke. BS, Manhattan Coll., 1984; MS, Rutgers U., 1990. Cert. Am. Bd. Radiology, Therapeutic Radiol. Physics. Med. dosimetrist Mt. Sinai Med. Ctr., N.Y.C., 1982-88; med. physicist, cons. G. Zacharopoulos Inc., N.Y.C., 1988-93; med. physicist Meml. Regional Cancer Ctr., Hollywood, Fla., 1993—. Mem. Am. Assn. Physicists in Medicine, Am. Assn. Med. Dosimetrists, Am. Soc. Therapeutic Radiology and Oncology, Am. Coll. Radiology. Home: 500 Cambridge Dr Weston FL 33326-3561 Office: Meml Regional Cancer Ctr 3501 Johnson St Hollywood FL 33021-5421

ROBINSON, ADAM MAYFIELD, JR., surgeon; b. Louisville, Nov. 9, 1950; s. Adam Mayfield and Addie Hilda (Brown) R.; m. Judith Schevtchuk, Dec. 29, 1973 (div. Aug. 1982); m. Yuko Sakurai, Aug. 30, 1984. AB in Polit. Sci., Ind. U., 1972; MD, Ind. U., Indpls., 1976; MBA, U. South Fla., 1994. Diplomate Am. Bd. Surgery, Am. Bd. Colon and Rectal Surgery. Commd. ensign USN, 1977, advanced through grades to capt., 1990; gen. med. officer USN, Ponce, P.R., 1977-78; gen. surgery resident Bethesda (Md.) Naval Hosp., 1978-82; mem. staff gen. surgeon Yokosuka (Japan) Naval Hosp., 1982-84; ship's surgeon USS Midway, Yokosuka, 1982-84; fellow colon-rectal surgery Carle Clinic U. Ill., Champaign, 1984-85; head divisn. colon-rectal surgery Bethesda Naval Hosp., 1985-90, asst. head gen. surgery, 1987-90; chmn. dept. gen. surgery Portsmouth (Va.) Naval Hosp., 1990—, acting med. dir., 1994-96; force surgeon, comdr. Naval Surface Force, U.S. Atlantic Fleet, Norfolk, Va., 1996—. Contbr. articles to profl. jours. Fellow Am. Coll. Surgeons, Am. Soc. Colon and Rectal Surgeons; mem. AMA, Nat. Med. Assn., Assn. Mil. Surgeons of U.S., Assn. Program Dirs. in Surgery (bd. dirs. 1990), Beta Gamma Sigma. Home: 4760 River Shore Rd Portsmouth VA 23703-1518 Office: Comdr Naval Surface Force US Atlantic Fleet 1430 Mitscher Ave Norfolk VA 23551-2494

ROBINSON, ADELBERT CARL, lawyer, judge; b. Shawnee, Okla., Dec. 13, 1926; s. William H. and Mayme (Forston) R.; m. Paula Kay Settles, Apr. 16, 1988; children from previous marriage: William, James, Schuyler, Donald, David, Nancy, Lauri. Student Okla. Baptist U., 1944-47; JD, Okla. U., 1950. Bar: Okla. 1950. Pvt. practice, Muskogee, Okla., 1956—; with legal dept. Phillips Petroleum Co., 1950-51; adjuster U.S. Fidelity & Guaranty Co., 1951-54, atty., adjuster-in-charge, 1954-56; ptnr. Fite & Robinson, 1956-62, Fite, Robinson & Summers, 1963-70, Robinson & Summers, 1970-72, Robinson, Summers & Locke, 1972-76, Robinson, Locke & Gage, 1976-80, Robinson, Locke, Gage & Fite, 1980-83, Robinson, Locke, Gage, Fite & Williams, Muskogee, 1983-95, Robinson, Gage, Fite & Williams, 1995—; police judge, 1963-64; mcpl. judge, 1964-70; prin. justice Temp. Div. 36 Okla. Ct. Appeals, 1981—; pres., dir. Wall St. Bldg Corp., 1969-78, Three Forks Devel. Corp., 1968-77, Rolo Leasing, Inc., 1971—, Suroya II, Inc., 1977—; sec. Muskogee Tom's Inc., Blue Ridge Corp., Harborcliff Corp.; bd. dirs. First Bancshares of Muskogee, Inc., First of Muskogee Corp., First City Bank, Tulsa; adv. dir. First Nat. Bank & Trust Co. of Muskogee; mng. ptnr. RLG Ritz, 1980—; ptnr. First City Real Estate Partnership, 1985-94. Del. to U.S./China Joint Session on Trade, Investment and Econ. Law, Beijing, 1987; chmn. Muskogee County (Okla.) Law Day, 1963; chmn. Muskogee Area Redevel. Authority, 1963; chmn. Muskogee County chpt. Am. Cancer Soc., 1956; pres. bd. dirs. Muskogee Cmty. Coun.; bd. dirs. United Way of Muskogee, Inc., 1980-88, v.p., 1982, pres. 1983; bd. dirs. Muskogee Cmty. Concert Assn., Muskogee Tourist Info. Bur., 1964-68; bd. dirs., gen. counsel United Cerebral Palsy Eastern Okla., 1964-68; trustee Connors Devel. Found., Connors Coll., 1981—, chmn., 1987-89; active Muskogee Housing Authority, 1992-95. With if. AUS, 1945-46. Mem. ABA, Okla. Bar Assn. (chmn. uniform laws com. 1970-72, chmn. profl. coop. com. 1965-69, past regional chmn. grievance com.), Muskogee County Bar Assn. (pres. 1971, mem. exec. coun. 1971-74), Okla. Assn. Def. Counsel (dir.), Okla. Assn. Mcpl. Judges (dir.), Muskogee C. of C., Delta Theta Phi. Methodist. Club: Rotary (pres. 1971-72). Home: 2408 St Andrews Ct Muskogee OK 74403-1657 Office: 530 Court St # 87 Muskogee OK 74401-6033

ROBINSON, BARBARA OLIVIA, food service specialist; b. Richmond, Va., Jan. 25, 1939; d. Caiaphas Cornelius and Rosa Royal (Meekins) R.; m. Herman Edward Robinson, Oct. 15, 1955 (dec. Nov. 1978); children: Arlene, Edward, Rolanda, Ronald. Student, pubs. schs., Va. With Weiman's Bakery, Richmond, 1957-65; cashier Atlantic Thrift, Phila., 1970-73; PC operator, file clk. Presbyn. Hosp., Phila., 1986-89; food svcs. specialist Richmond Community Action Program, 1990—. Co-author: (poems) New Voices of America Poetry, 1980; author: (poems) Hearts on Fire, 1993; editor Bartram Village Civic Assn., 1971-72. Democrat. Baptist.

ROBINSON, BRUCE BUTLER, physicist; b. Chester, Pa., Oct. 13, 1933; s. George Senior and Dorothy Conerly (Butler) R.; m. Dorothy Ross, June 4, 1960; children: Douglas Ross, Christopher Scott. BS in Physics, Drexel U., 1956; PhD in Physics, Princeton U., 1961; MBA, Rider U., 1977. Rsch. assoc. U. Calif., San Diego, 1961-63; rsch. scientist RCA David Sarnoff Lab., RCA, Princeton, N.J., 1963-73; exec. dir., mem. commerce tech. adv. bd. U.S. Dept. Commerce, Washington, 1973-75; dir. policy integration, dir. coal and synfuels policy U.S. Dept. Energy, Washington, 1975-81; sr. science advisor to v.p. rsch. Exxon Rsch. and Engring. Co., Linden, N.J., 1981-84; dep. dir. Office Naval Rsch., Arlington, 1984-87, dir. rsch., 1987-94, dep. dir. sci. and tech., 1994-96; assoc. tech. dir. for sci. and tech. Office Naval Rsch., 1996—; prin. author nat. energy policy plan U.S. Dept. Energy, 1981; U.S. rep. to internat. energy agy., govt. expert group on tech., Paris, 1979-81; mem. internat. team to rev. R&D programs Dutch Ministry Econs. and Fin., The Hague, The Netherlands, 1979; presenter sci. lectures. Contbr. articles to sci. jours. NSF fellow Princeton U., 1956-58, NSF internat. summer fellow, Varenna, Italy, 1962; recipient Meritorious Presdl. Rank award Pres. of U.S., 1989. Mem. IEEE, Am. Phys. Soc., The Oceanography Soc. (founding).

ROBINSON, CHARLES, JR., healthcare administrator; b. Dublin, Ga., Jan. 8, 1943; s. Charles Sr. and Martha (Gibson) R.; m. Belinda Robinson, Aug. 28, 1971; children: Keino, Kipchoge. BS, Ft. Valley State Coll., 1970; MBA, Brenau U., 1988. Auditor Fed. Res. Bank of Atlanta, 1970-74; asst. adminstr. William May Meml. Med. Ctr., Dublin, Ga., 1974-76; adminstr. Sparta (Ga.) Intermediate Care Ctr., 1976-77, Imperial Health Care Ctr., Atlanta, 1983-84; owner, mgr. Home Health Med., Decatur, Ga., 1984-85; bus. mgr. Hughes Spalding Med. Ctr., Atlanta, 1985-86; exec. dir., adminstr. Sadie G. Mays Meml. Nursing Home, Atlanta, 1977-83, exec. dir., CEO, 1986—; bd. dirs. Ga. Assn. Homes and Svcs. for the Aged, Ga. Nursing Home Assn., Ga. Dept. Med. Assistance (Medicaid) Nursing Home Adv. Bd. With U.S. Army, 1961-64. Fellow Am. Coll. Healthcare Adminstrs. (cert); mem. Am. Healthcare Assn., Am. Assn. of Homes for Aging, Ga. Assn. Homes and Svcs. for Aging, Ga. Nursing Home Assn. Office: Sadie G Mays Meml Nursing 1821 Anderson Ave NW Atlanta GA 30314-1835

ROBINSON, CHARLES EMANUEL, systems engineer, consultant; b. Hayes, Clarendon, Jamaica, Jan. 14, 1946; came to U.S., 1986; s. Charles E. and Ethlyn C. (Singh) R.; m. Joy B. Cassanova, July 31, 1971; children: Sonya, Monique, Nicole, Kimberley. Student, Nat. Tech. Schs., L.A., 1966. Radio technician Chin's Radio & TV, Kingston, Jamaica, 1964-66; solid state technician Wonards Radio Engring., Kingston, 1966-68; instrument technician Ewarton Plant, Aluminum Co. Can., Jamaica, 1968-69; sr. field tech. engr. Ruel Samuels Ltd., Kingston, 1969-77; mng. dir. MSS Ltd., Kingston, 1977-80, Robinson Assocs., Mandeville, Jamaica, 1980-86; design engr. Seaboard Electronics, New Rochelle, N.Y., 1985-95, mgr. tech. svc., 1988-95; sys. engr. MobileComm, Ridgeland, Miss., 1995—. Mem. IEEE, Am. Mgmt. Assn. Home: 424 Red River Trail 1084 Irving TX 75063 Office: MobileComm 6221 N O Connor # 116 Irving TX 75039

ROBINSON, CUMMIE ADAMS, librarian; b. Mansfield, La., Sept. 27, 1945; d. Roosevelt and Annie B. Adams; m. Johnnie Robinson Jr.; children: Jared, Cynara, Cynecia. BS, So. U., Baton Rouge, 1967; MSLS, U. So. Calif., 1972; PhD, Walden U., 1992. Cert. tchr., La. Tchr. Compton (Calif.) Unified Schs., 1970-73; libr. Xavier U., New Orleans, 1973-75, Nicholls H.S., New Orleans, 1989—; tchr. Delgado C.C., 1992; adj. faculty So. U., New Orleans, 1994—. Block coord. Nat. Leukemia Soc., New Orleans, 1992—, March of Dimes, New Orleans, 1992—, Muscular Dystrophy Assn., New Orleans, 1988—. Mem. Nat. Coun. Negro Women, Delta Sigma Theta. United Methodist. Home: 5800 Kensington Blvd New Orleans LA 70127-2809 Office: 3820 Saint Claude Ave New Orleans LA 70117-5736

ROBINSON, DAVID BRADFORD, poet, scientific writer; b. Richmond, Va., Apr. 14, 1937; s. Albert Lewis and Martha Ellen (Lovern) R. BS, U. Miami, 1959, MS, 1961; AA, Miami-Dade Community Coll., 1970; DSc, Northwestern Coll., 1978, PhD, 1979. Author: Characteristics of Cesium, 1978, Collected Poems, 1987. Founder Ronald Reagan Rep. Ctr., Washington; exhibitor Statue of Liberty, Port of N.Y., 1986; mem. Heritage Found., 1989; sustaining sponsor Ronald Reagan Presdl. Found., 1987; charter mem. Ronald Reagan Trust; charter mem. Honor Roll Rep. Presdl. Task Force, 1990, life mem., 1989, Commemorative Honor Roll, 1991; mem. Nat. Rep. Senatorial Com. with Presdl. Commn., 1992; founding sponsor, founding mem. Space Life Sta., 1990. Recipient 2d Pl. Amateur Trophy, Capablanca Chess Club, 1964, Presdl. Sports award bicycling, 1976, Presdl. Achievement award Rep. Nat. Com., 1982, Cert. Good Standing Rep. Presdl. Task Force, 1982-85, Presdl. Merit medal, 1982, Appreciation cert. Sen. Paula Hawkins, 1986, Golden Poet Trophy award World of Poetry, 1987, Silver Anniversary Album, Nat. Geog. Soc., 1987, Pres. Ronald Reagan Appreciation cert., 1988, Pres. Bush Congl. Victory Squadron Recognition cert., 1989, Bush Inaugural/Freedom medal, 1989, World Time-capsule cert., 1990, Am. in Space medal, 1990, Pegasus Time Capsule plaque, 1991, Congl. Merit cert. Nat. Rep. Congl. Com., 1992, Battle of Normandy Found. Appreciation award, 1993, Presdl. Legion of Merit medal, 1993, Congl. Order of Liberty award, 1993, Appreciation cert. Sen. Kay Bailey Hutchinson, 1993, Rep. Presdl. award, 1994, Albert Einstein medal Brit. Bur. Degree Promotion, 1994, Cert. of Appreciation, The Golden Heart Club, Mil. Order of Purple Heart Svc. Found., Congl. Order of Freedom, 1995, numerous other awards Rep. Nat. Com., polit. orgns. Mem. Am. Air Mus. (Brit., founder 1991), Battle of Normandy Meml. Mus. (charter 1988), Sigma Xi, Russian Club, Phi Theta Kappa. Home: 715 NE 92nd St Apt 1A Miami FL 33138

ROBINSON, DAVID MAURICE, professional basketball player; b. Key West, Fla., Aug. 6, 1965. Grad., U.S. Naval Acad., 1987. Commd. ensign USN, 1987; with San Antonio Spurs, 1989—; mem. U.S. Olympic Basketball Team, 1988, 92. Recipient Naismith award, 1987, Wooden award, 1987, IBM award, 1990, 91, 94, Schick Pivotal Player award, 1990, 91; named to Sporting News All-Am. First Team, 1986, 87, Sporting News Coll. Player of Yr., 1987, NBA Rookie of Yr., 1990, All-NBA First Team, 1991, 92, All-Star team, 1990-94; named NBA Defensive Player of Yr., 1992, MVP, 1994-95, season MVP, 1995. Office: care San Antonio Spurs 100 Montanta St San Antonio TX 78203-1031*

ROBINSON, DAVID WAYNE, English language educator, researcher; b. Oakland, Calif., July 3, 1958; s. Russell Hiram Beach and Shirley Faye (Robinson) Boylan; m. Caren Jamie Town, June 14, 1996; 1 child, Rosa Elizabeth Town. BA in English, U. Ala., 1980; MA in English, U. Wash., 1982, PhD, 1985. Temporary instr. U. Wash., Seattle, 1985-86; temporary asst. prof. Stetson U., DeLand, Fla., 1986-87; temporary asst. prof. Ga. So. U., Statesboro, 1988-90, asst. prof., 1990-95; dir. program in comparative lit. Ga. So. U., 1992—, assoc. prof., 1995—; reader German quarterly, 1995. Editor: (book, jour. issue) No Man's Land: East German Drama After the Wall, 1995; translator: (play by Christpher Hein) The Knights of the Round Table, 1995; contbr. articles to profl. jours. Mem. Dem. Com., Bulloch County, Ga., 1988-96, chair, 1996—. Fulbright rsch. fellow, East Berlin, 1988. Mem. Am. Comparative Lit. Assn., MLA, Bertolt Brecht Soc., S. Atlantic Modern Lang. Assn., James Joyce Found., Savannah Ave. Neighborhood Assn. Democrat. Home: 361 Savannah Ave Statesboro GA 30458 Office: GA So U English Dept LB 8023 Statesboro GA 30460-8023

ROBINSON, DOUGLAS GEORGE, lawyer; b. Hamilton, Mont., Feb. 24, 1943; s. Clarence Elijah and Frances Carolina (Alonzo) R.; m. Julia Elizabeth Sullivan, 1995; children by previous marriage: Stephen Douglas, Katherine Marielle. B.A. in Econs, U. Wash., 1965; J.D., George Washington U., 1969. Bar: D.C. Legis. asst. Wash. State Legis. Council, Olympia, 1965-66; assoc. firm Arnold & Porter, Washington, 1969-74; dep. gen. counsel Fed. Energy Adminstrn., Washington, 1974-76; mem. issues staff Carter-Mondale Presdl. Campaign, Atlanta, 1976; mem. Carter-Mondale Transition Group, Washington, 1976-77; spl. asst. to adminstr. for maj. energy projects Fed. Energy Adminstrn., Washington, 1977; asst. adminstr. for regulations and emergency planning Econ. Regulatory Adminstrn., U.S. Dept. Energy, Washington, 1977-78; dep. adminstr. for policy Econ. Regulatory Adminstrn., U.S. Dept. Energy, 1978-80, spl. asst. to sec., dep. sec., 1980-81; ptnr. Skadden, Arps, Slate, Meagher & Flom, Washington, 1981—. Editor-in-chief: George Washington Law Rev, 1968-69. Recipient John B. Larner medal George Washington U. Law Sch., 1969; cert. of superior service Fed. Energy Adminstrn., 1974; Outstanding Service medal Dept. Energy, 1979; Disting. Service medal Sec. of Energy, 1981. Mem. ABA (Nat. Pro Bono Publico award 1994), D.C. Bar Assn., Fed. Energy Bar Assn. Office: Skadden Arps Slate Meagher & Flom 1440 New York Ave NW Washington DC 20005-2111

ROBINSON, E. B., JR., bank executive; b. Centreville, Miss., Sept. 14, 1941; s. Emerson B. and Dolly (McGehee) R.; m. Judy M. Treppendahl, Sept. 7, 1963; children: E.B. III, John Green. BS, Davidson Coll., 1963; MBA, Harvard U., 1967. Mgmt. trainee Deposit Guaranty Nat. Bank, Jackson, Miss., 1967-69, investment officer, 1969-71, asst. v.p., 1971-73, v.p., 1973-75, exec. v.p., 1976-79, pres., chief ops. officer, 1979-84; pres., chief ops. officer Deposit Guaranty Corp., Jackson, 1982-84; chmn. and chief exec. officer Deposit Guaranty Nat. Bank and Deposit Guaranty Corp., Jackson, 1984—; bd. dirs. Fed. Res. Bank of Atlanta. Chmn. fin. com. Millsaps Coll., Jackson; treas. Council for Support of Pub. Higher Edn., Jackson; bd. dirs. Columbia Sem., Atlanta. Served with U.S. Army, 1963-65. J. Spencer Love fellow Harvard U., 1963. Mem. Young Pres.'s Orgn., Assn. of Res. City Bankers (govt. relations com.), Dealer Bank Assn. (Glass-Stegall com.), Jackson C. of C. (pres. 1987), Phi Beta Kappa. Presbyterian. Clubs: Country of Jackson; Harvard (N.Y.C.). Office: Deposit Guaranty Corp PO Box 1200 Jackson MS 39215-1200*

ROBINSON, EDWARD NORWOOD, JR., physician, educator; b. Winston-Salem, N.C., Aug. 20, 1953; s. Edward Norwood and Pauline (Gray) R.; m. Pamela Martin Pittman, Apr. 22, 1978; children: Patrick Edward, Alexander Wood. BA, Duke U., 1975; MD, Bowman Gray Sch., Winston-Salem, 1979. Diplomate Am. Bd. Internal Medicine. Intern East Carolina U. Sch. Medicine, Greenville, N.C., 1979-80, resident, 1980-82; postdoctoral fellow U. Utah Sch. Medicine, Salt Lake City, 1982-85, asst. prof. medicine, 1985-86; asst. prof. medicine U. Louisville, 1986-88; chief infectious diseases Louisville VA Hosp., 1987-88; clin. assoc. prof. medicine U. N.C., Greensboro, 1988-93, clin. prof. medicine, 1994—; epidemiologist Greensboro Women's Hosp., 1990—. Contbr. articles to profl. jours. Fellow ACP, Infectious Diseases Soc. Am.; mem. Am. Soc. Microbiology, Am. Med. Infomatics Assn., Cousteau Soc. (founding mem.), Alpha Omega Alpha. Democrat. Methodist. Office: Moses H Cone Meml Hosp 1200 N Elm St Greensboro NC 27401-1004

ROBINSON, FREDERIC MURRY, agricultural products company executive; b. 1934. With Hanes Corp., Winston-Salem, N.C., 1967-69, Pfizer Genetics, Olivia, Minn., 1969-77, Anderson Clayton Seed Co., Belmont, Iowa, 1977-79, Agrigenetics Corp., Wickliffe, Ohio, 1979-88; pres. Delta and Pine Land Co., Scott, Miss., 1988—. Office: Delta & Pine Land Co 1 Cotton Row Scott MS 38772*

ROBINSON, HAROLD IVENS, lumber company executive; b. Puerto Cabezas, Nicaragua, Dec. 2, 1951; came to U.S., 1951; s. Charles Wesley and Anne (Ivens) R.; m. Dodge Hobson, Feb. 21, 1975. BA, Harvard U., 1973, postgrad., 1990. Overseas purchaser, sales mgr. Robinson Forest Products, New Orleans, 1974-79; v.p. Robinson Lumber Co., New Orleans, 1979—, chief fin. officer, 1986—; pres. Robinson Lumber & Export Co., New Orleans, 1993—; mng. dir. Lisco, Arabi, La., 1983-87; bd. dirs. Premier Bank, New Orleans, World Trade Ctr., New Orleans; mem. OPM Harvard Bus. Sch., 1990. Mem. ACLU, Common Cause, Nat. Hardwood Lumber Assn. (cert. insp.), Internat. Hardwood Products Assn. (bd. dirs., pres. 1994-95). Club: Harvard of La. Office: Robinson Lumber Co 4000 Tchoupitoulas St New Orleans LA 70115-1433

ROBINSON, HERMON CLAYTON (ROB), III, real estate broker; b. Lexington, Ky., Sept. 20, 1944; s. Hermon Clayton Jr. and Barbara Alice (Melvin) R.; m. Virginia Marie Sarno, nov. 29, 1986; 1 child, Hermon Clayton IV. BA in Mgmt., U. Ky.; postgrad., U. North Fla. Cert. property mgr. Inst. Real Estate Mgmt. Sales rep. Burroughs Corp., Jacksonville, Fla., 1967-73; v.p. fin. and adminstrn. Barco Contracting Co., Jacksonville, 1973-78; comml. real estate broker Coldwell Banker, Atlanta, 1978-80; owner Pier Floats, Inc., Daytona Beach, Fla., 1980-83; comml. sales rep. CTD Corp., Daytona Beach, Fla., 1981; ptnr. Mason Ave. Bus. Ctr., Daytona Beach, 1981-82; account exec. Merrill Lynch, Daytona Beach, 1982-83; area mgr. ctrl. Fla. Cardinal Industries, Inc., Sanford, Fla., 1983-88; dir. real estate mgmt. CB Comml. Real Estate Group, Orlando and Jacksonville, Fla., 1988-93; pres. HHH Mgmt., Inc., Orlando, Fla., 1993-94, Robinson Real Estate, Inc., Edgewater, Fla., 1995—. Author: (poem) Then in Field of Gold, 1996, Growing Up in The Path Not Taken, 1996. With U.S. Army, 1964-70. Office: Robinson Real Estate Inc 170 N Copy Dr Edgewater FL 32141

ROBINSON, JAKIE LEE, human services administrator; b. Santee, S.C., Feb. 16, 1951; s. Booker T. and Luciel (Holmon) R.; m. Anita Lynne Williams, Aug. 1, 1992. AS in Electronic Instrumentation Tech., Orangeburg Calhoun Tech. Coll., Orangeburg, S.C., 1982; BS in Elec. Engring. Tech., S.C. State U., 1993, MA in Rehab. Counseling, 1994. Cert. Rehab. Counselor. Sr. devel. technician McDonnell Douglas Astronautics Co., Titusville, Fla., 1982-85; tech. publ. analyst Lockheed Space Ops. Co., Kennedy Space Ctr., Fla., 1985-88; tech. tng. instr. Orangeburg Calhoun Tech. Coll., 1989-90; computer room student asst. S.C. State U. Sch. Engring., Orangeburg, 1991-93; vol. clin. counselor Tri-County Alcohol and Drug Commn., Orangeburg, 1993-94; manpower case mgr. Charleston (S.C.) County Grants Adminstrn., 1994—; mem. adv. com. Project Transition-Edisto Health Dist., Orangeburg, 1993-94. Vice-chair, co-founder Concerned Citizens in Action, Summerville, S.C., 1993. With USAF, 1971-74. Mem. Nat. Rehab. Assn., Charleston Trident Assn. Realtors (lics. 1995), Alpha Phi Alpha (chpt. corres. sec. 1995—), Alpha Kappa Mu, Chi Sigma Iota (life). Home: 8515 Kennestone Ln Charleston SC 29420

ROBINSON, JAMES H., banker. Pres., dir. Sun Bank of South Fla., N.A., Ft. Lauderdale. Office: Sun Bank of South Fla N A 501 E Las Olas Blvd Fort Lauderdale FL 33301-2232*

ROBINSON, JOHNNY AUBREY, controller; b. Wilmington, N.C., June 2, 1959; s. Johnnie Lee Jr. and Loralyn Maxine (Ballard) R.; m. Evelina Debra Jones Walker, Apr. 28, 1984 (div. June 1992). BBA, N.C. Ctrl. U., 1981. Life ins. agt. Durham Life Ins., Wilmington, N.C., 1982-83; storekeeper USN, Long Beach, Calif., 1983-86; staff acct. Wells Fargo Armored Svcs., Atlanta, 1986-88, The Gwinnett Daily News, Duluth, Ga., 1988-91; contr. The State Gazette, Dyersburg, Tenn., 1991—. Pres. N.C. Ctrl. Alumni Assn., Atlanta, 1989-91; treas. Dyer County Coalition of Afro-Am. Men, Dyersburg, 1992-94. With USN, 1983-86. Mem. NAACP, Internat. Newspaper Fin. Execs., Nat. Assn. Minority Media Execs., 100 Black Men of West Tenn. Inc., Omega Psi Phi (treas. 1992-94). Home: 830 Hull St Dyersburg TN 38024-3715 Office: The State Gazette 294 US Highway 51 Byp N Dyersburg TN 38024-3659

ROBINSON, KAREN VAJDA, nutritionist. BS in Home Econs., Montclair State Coll., 1980; MS in Health Scis./Dietetics, James Madison U., 1992. Cert. food svc. sanitation mgr., N.J. Dietitian Roosevelt Hosp., Edison, N.J., 1980-85; asst. mgr. UVA (U. Va.) Dining Svcs., Charlottesville, 1985-86; temp. sales sec., mem. banquet prep. staff Boar's Head Inn, Charlottesville, 1986-88; head diet counselor Diet Ctr., Charlottesville, 1986-90; dir. nutrition program Camp Holiday Trails, Charlottesville, 1988; dietetic intern VA Med. Ctr., Hampton, Va., 1991; pub. health nutritionist Cen. Shenandoah Health Dist., Waynesboro (Va.) Health Dept., 1993—; grad. dietetic intern mentor, 1993—; presenter in field. Contbr. articles to local newspapers. Mem. Charlottesville Health Promotion Coalition, 1993—. Mem. Am. Dietetic Assn. (registered), Am. Assn. Family and Consumer Scis. (cert.), Dietitians in Gen. Clin. Practice, Pediatric Nutrition Practice Group, Pub. Health Nutrition Practice Group, Va. Pub. Health Assn. (sec. 1995, awards chair 1996-97), Blue Ridge Dietetics Assn. (mem. exec. bd. 1993—, editor newsletter 1993-96, nat. nutrition month coord. 1993-95, pres.-elect 1995-96, pres. 1996-97), Blue Ridge Jour. Club. Home: 2229 Commonwealth Dr Apt C Charlottesville VA 22901-1526

ROBINSON, KEITH, sales and marketing executive; b. Scunthorpe, Eng., Jan. 31, 1948; s. Albert Henry and Ruby (Stanton) R.; m. Joan Marie, Dec. 26, 1981; children: Stephen A., David K., Mark P. Grad. Fin. and Acctg., Leicester, Eng., 1972. CPA. Various positions Brit. Gas Corp., London, 1967-75; mgr. computer audit Deloitte & Touche, Montreal, Can., 1975-77, Toronto, 1977-79; mgr. acctg. svc. system No. Telecom Ltd., Toronto, 1979-82, nat. dir. ops. & control, 1982-83; nat. dir. ops. & control No. Telecom Inc., Nashville, 1983-86; dir. customer svc. & engring. No. Telecom Inc., Raleigh, N.C., 1986-89; dir. mktg. No. Telecom Inc., Raleigh, 1989-91, dir. U.S. mktg. rels., 1991-93; v.p. sales and mktg. internat. BCI, Inc., Raleigh, 1993—; cons. Auditor Gen. of Can. Fed, Govt., Ottawa, 1976-78, Guyana Bauxite Co., Georgetown, Guyana, 1977-79. Author: (cassette) Audit Report Writing, 1974. Fin. officer United Way, Jr. Achievement; player Brit. Profl. Soccer Team, 1966-67; bd. dirs. U.S. Devel. Soccer League, F.C. Raleigh United, Summerfield North Swim and Racquet Club, Raleigh, 1992-96. Fellow Chartered Cert. Accts.; mem. United Way Capitol Soc. Home: 8205 Oak Leaf Ct Raleigh NC 27615-5116 Office: BCI Inc 8205 Oak Leaf Ct Raleigh NC 27615

ROBINSON, KENNETH LARRY, insurance company executive; b. Carrollton, Ga., Sept. 20, 1944; s. Tommy Esper and Annie Eunie (Bowie) R.; m. Peggy Marie Tally, Jan. 20, 1967 (div. Feb. 1974); 1 child, Toni Marie; m. Malinda Gayle York, Jan. 11, 1975; 1 child, Tommy Eric. Student, U.S. Armed Forces Inst., Quantico, Va., 1964; cert., Life Ins. Mktg./Research Assn., Atlanta, 1982, Life Underwriters Tng. Council, Montgomery, Ala., 1987. Dist. mgr. United Family Life Ins. Co., Atlanta, 1967-77, Mut. Savs. Life Ins. Co., Decatur, Ala., 1978-88; agy. mgr. Robinson Ins. Agy., Montgomery, Ala., 1989; regional mgr. Nat. Security Ins. Co., Elba, Ala., 1989; master mgr., United Family Life Ins. Co., Atlanta, 1975-77; president's advisory coun., Mut. Savs. Life Ins. Co., Decatur, 1985-87, pres.' club, 1987. Recipient Cert. Achievement Cotton States Ins. Co., 1989. Mem. Nat. Assn. Life Underwriters, Lions. Republican. Baptist. Home: 3781 Audubon Rd Montgomery AL 36111-2660

ROBINSON, LARY ALLEN, cardiothoracic surgeon; b. Iola, Kans., Dec. 5, 1946; s. Leo Davis and Lillian Martha (Heuring) R.; m. Susannah L.; children: Schuyler A., Joshua D. BA in Anthropology, U. Kans., 1968; MD, Washington U., 1972. Diplomate Nat Bd. Med. Examiners, Am. Bd. Thoracic Surgery; diplomate in surgery and surg. critical care Am. Bd. Surgery. Resident in gen. and thoracic surgery Duke U. Med. Ctr., Durham, N.C., 1972-81, cardiothoracic fellowship, 1982-83; cardiac surgery clin. and rsch. fellowship St. Thomas' Hosp., London, 1981-82; assoc. prof. surgery U. Nebr. Med. Ctr., Omaha, 1983-94; assoc. prof. surgery U. South Fla., Tampa, 1994—, dir. divsn. cardiovascular and thoracic surgery, 1995—; adv. panel on surg. drugs and devices U.S. Pharmacopoeial Conv., 1985-90, chmn. adv. panel of surg. drugs and devices, 1990-95, 95—; critical care coun. Am. Coll. of Chest Physicians, 1988—; com. on applicants ACS, 1990—; assoc. examiner Am. Bd. Surgery, 1991-95; steering com. sect. on cardiac surgery Am. Coll. of Chest Physicians, 1993—; spl. rev. com. Nat. Cancer Inst., NIH, 1995. Contbr. chpts. to books and articles to profl. jours. Mem. great Am. Smokeout steering com. Am. Cancer Soc., 1984-86;

spkr. for lectr. Bur. of Am. Cancer Soc., 1987-94, Am. Heart Assn., 1987-94; bd. dirs. Student Exch. Internat., 1989-90; rsch. com. Am. Heart Assn., 1990-94, bd. dirs. Douglas County divsn., 1991-94, comm. com. 1992-94. Maj. USAF, 1974-76. Grantee Am. Heart Assn., 1985-87, NIH, 1987-92, Abbott Labs., 1992-94, VA Rsch. grant, 1985-86. Fellow ACS, Am. Coll. Cardiology, Am. Coll. Chest Physicians; mem. Internat. Soc. for Heart Rsch., Am. Heart Assn., David C. Sabiston Jr. Surg. Soc., Assn. for Acad. Surgery, Southwestern Surg. Congress, Soc. of Thoracic Surgeons, Am. Assn. for Thoracic Surgery, Ea. Coop. Oncology Group. Office: H Lee Moffitt Cancer Ctr Rsch Inst 12902 Magnolia Dr Tampa FL 33612-9416

ROBINSON, MAISAH B., language educator; d. Patrick H., Jr. and Bettie (Lacy) R.; m. Antar Stanford Smith. BA, U. Mich., 1981, MA, 1982; PhD, Ga. State U., 1994. Curriculum coord., lectr. Um al-Qura U., Makkah, Saudi Arabia, 1982-83; instr. Eng., bus. Jackson (Mich.) C.C., Jackson Bus. Inst., 1984-87; instr., coord. spl. projects ELS Lang. Ctrs., Atlanta, 1987—; rsch., editl. asst., instr. U. Mich., Ann Arbor, 1980-82; v.p., writer Zak-Grafix Designs, Inc., Atlanta, 1995—. Author: Composition Teacher's Criteria for Good Writing; editor Braun Brumfield Pub., Ann Arbor. Mem. Nat. Coun. Tchrs. Eng., Tchr. Eng. Spkrs. Other Langs., Mortar Bd. Home: PO Box 381 Austell GA 30001

ROBINSON, MARY LOU, federal judge; b. Dodge City, Kans., Aug. 25, 1926; d. Gerald J. and Frances Strueber; m. A.J. Robinson, Aug. 28, 1949; children: Rebecca Aynn Gruhlkey, Diana Ceil, Matthew Douglas. B.A., U. Tex., 1948, LL.B., 1950. Bar: Tex. 1949. Ptnr. Robinson & Robinson, Amarillo, 1950-55; judge County Ct. at Law, Potter County, Tex., 1955-59, (108th Dist. Ct.), Amarillo, 1961-73; assoc. justice Ct. of Civil Appeals for 7th Supreme Jud. Dist. of Tex., Amarillo, 1973-77; chief justice Ct. of Civil Appeals for 7th Supreme Jud. Dist. of Tex., 1977-79; U.S. dist. judge No. Dist. Tex., Amarillo, 1979—. Named Woman of Year Tex. Fedn. Bus. and Profl. Women, 1973. Mem. Nat. Assn. Women Lawyers, ABA, Tex. Bar Assn., Amarillo Bar Assn., Delta Kappa Gamma. Presbyterian. Office: US Dist Ct Rm 226 205 E 5th Ave # F13248 Amarillo TX 79101-1563

ROBINSON, NAOMI JEAN, educational training systems specialist; b. Storm Lake, Iowa, Oct. 10, 1951; d. Wendell and Norma (Wright) R.; B.A., Buena Vista Coll., 1973; M.A.Ed., George Washington U., 1978. Tchr., elem. schs., Storm Lake, Iowa, 1973-75; edn. specialist intern U.S. Army, Fort Monroe, Va., 1976-78, edn. and test specialist, Fort Eustis, Va., 1978-79, tng. systems analyst, White Sands Missile Range, N.Mex., 1979-82, tng. effectiveness analysis study coord., 1983-85, analyst ops. rsch. and tng. systems, 1985-87, edn. specialist, dir. tng. tech. field Advanced Concepts Team, Ft. Huachuca, Ariz., 1987-88, edn. specialist, dir. tng. lab. Tng. Devel. and Analysis Directorate, N.J. N.G. High Tech. Tng. Ctr., Ft. Dix, N.J., 1988-90; program mgr., COR Tng. Devel. and Analysis Directorate for TRADOC tng. mission support contract, 1990-94, chief special projects team, 1994—, acting div. chief tng. rsch and studies div., 1990-91; chief TRADOC tng. Mission Support Contract Br., 1991-94; chmn. Tng. Devel. Revitalization Joint Task Force Pentagon, Washington, 1994-96; dir. ops. support divsn. and exec. officer tng. devel. analysis activity, Ft. Monroe, Va., 1996—. V.p. Young Reps., 1972-73. Mem. NAFE, Federally Employed Women (1st v.p. chpt. 1982-83, 84-85), Human Factors Soc., Iowa Edn. Assn. Republican. Presbyterian. Club: Bus. and Profl. Women. Author: Guidelines for Development of Skill Qualification Tests, 1977, Standard Operating Procedure for TRADOC Training Mission Support Contract, 1991, 92. Home: 18 Bells Cove Dr Apt E Poquoson VA 23662-1555 Office: Comdr HQ TRADOC Tng Devel & Analysis Directorate Attn care ATTG-CD Fort Monroe VA 23651-5000

ROBINSON, NEIL CIBLEY, JR., lawyer; b. Columbia, S.C., Oct. 25, 1942; s. Neil C. and Ernestine (Carns) R.; m. Judith Ann Hunter, Sept. 4, 1971 (div. Nov. 1979); 1 child, Hunter Leigh; m. Vicki Elizabeth Kornahrens, Mar. 2, 1985; children: Neil C. III, Taylor Elizabeth. BS in Indsl. Mgmt., Clemson U., 1966; JD, U. S.C., 1973. Bar: S.C. 1974, U.S. Ct. Appeals (4th cir.) 1974, U.S. Dist. Ct. S.C. 1976. Asst. to dean U. S.C. Law Sch., Columbia, 1973-74; law clk. to judge Charles E. Jr. Simons Jr. U.S. Dist. Ct. S.C., Aiken, 1974-76; assoc. Grimball & Cabaniss, Charleston, S.C., 1976-78; ptnr. Grimball, Cabaniss, Vaughan & Robinson, Charleston, 1978-84; ptnr., pres. Robinson, Wall & Hastie, P.A., Charleston, 1984-91; ptnr., mem. exec. com. Nexsen, Pruet, Jacobs, Pollard & Robinson, Charleston, 1991—; permanent mem. 4th Cir. Jud. Conf., 1982—; pres. Coastal Properties Inst., Charleston, 1981—. Bd. dirs. Southeastern Wildlife Exposition, Charleston, 1987—, pres. 1994—, Charleston Maritime Festival, 1993—, pres. 1994—, Parklands Found. of Charleston County; pres. S.C. Tourism Coun., Columbia, 1991—. Cpl. USMCR, 1960-66. Recipient Order of Palmetto, Gov. David Beasley, S.C., 1996. Mem. ABA, Urban Land Inst. (recreational devel. coun.), S.C. Bar Assn., Fed. Bar Assn., S.C. Def. Trial Lawyers Assn., Hibernian Soc. (mem. mgmt. com. 1984—), Kiawah Club, Haig Point Club, Country Club of Charleston, Phi Delta Phi. Presbyterian. Home: PO Box 121 Charleston SC 29402-0121 Office: Nexsen Pruet Jacobs Pollard & Robinson 200 Meeting St Ste 301 Charleston SC 29401-3156

ROBINSON, PETER CLARK, general management executive; b. Brighton, Mass., Nov. 16, 1938; s. Richard and Mary Elizabeth (Cooper) R.; m. Sylvia Phyllis Petschek, Aug. 26, 1961 (div. 1973); children: Marc Louis, Nicholas Daniel, Andrea Suzanne; m. Sarah Lingham, Jan. 1, 1984. B.S. in Fgn. Service, Georgetown U., 1961; M.B.A., Babson Inst., 1963; AMP, Harvard U., 1986. Asst. supt. prodn. Mass. Broken Stone Co., Weston, 1961-62; night shift supt. Mass. Broken Stone Co., 1962-65, v.p. ops., 1968, v.p., 1969-75, 85-94, sr. v.p., 1995—, also dir.; gen. supt. Berlin Stone Co., 1965-67, v.p. ops., 1968; v.p. Holden Trap Rock Co., to 1975, also dir., v.p., 1985-94, sr. v.p., 1995—; pres. Blount Materials Inc., Saginaw, Mich., 1975-81; v.p. corp. mktg. Blount, Inc., Montgomery, 1978-79, v.p. corp. planning and mktg., 1979-92, v.p. corp. planning and devel., 1992-94; group exec., pres. Blount Agri/Indsl. Corp., 1984-90; pres. P.C. Robinson & Co., Montgomery, 1994—; mem. The Planning Forum; bd. dirs. Mass. Broken Stone Co. Mem. Nat. Stone Assn. (dir., exec. com., chmn. govt. affairs com., chmn. bd.), Am. Mgmt. Assn., Am. Soc. Agrl. Engrs., Newcomen Soc., Engring. Soc. Detroit, Pres. Assn., SME-AIME. Clubs: Montgomery Country, Capital City (Montgomery), Harvard (Boston). Home: 1822 Galena Ave Montgomery AL 36106-1910 Office: Robinson & Co 1067 Woodley Rd Ste C Montgomery AL 36106-2414

ROBINSON, RAYMOND EDWIN, musician, music educator, writer; b. San Jose, Calif., Dec. 26, 1932; s. Elam Edwin and Zula Mai (Hatley) R.; m. Ruth Aleen Chamberlain, Mar. 12, 1954; children: Cynthia Rae, Greg Edwin, David L., Brent Steven, Jeffrey Vernon. BA, San Jose State U., 1956; MMus, Ind. U., 1958, D in Mus. Edn., 1969; LHD, Westminster Choir Coll., 1987; postdoctoral study, Cambridge U., England, 1987-89, Jagiellonian U., Poland, 1995. Instr. music Ind. U., Bloomington, 1958-59; music critic Portland Reporter, 1962-63, Balt. Evening Sun, 1964-68; founder, tchr. seminar for music adminstrs., 1972—; chmn. divsn. fine arts Cascade Coll., Portland, Oreg., 1959-63; dean Peabody Inst., Balt., 1963-69; pres. Westminster Choir Coll., Princeton, N.J., 1969-87; vis. fellow Wolfson Coll. U. Cambridge, Eng., 1987-89; disting. prof. choral studies, choral condr. Palm Beach Atlantic U., West Palm Beach, Fla., 1989—; pres. Prestige Publs. Inc., 1978—;, 1992-95; music critic Palm Beach (Fla.) Post, 1991—; prof. Sch. Ch. Music Knox Theol. Sem., Ft. Lauderdale, Fla., 1989—; choral condr. Palm Beach C.C., Lake Worth, Fla., 1992-93; condr.-in-residence, dir. music First Presbyn. Ch., West Palm Beach, 1989—; spl. guest choral condr. Palm Beach Opera, 1990—; interim condr. Choral Soc. Palm Beaches, 1992; condr. Ray Robinson Chorale, 1994—. Author: The Choral Experience, 1976, Choral Music, 1978; Krzysztof Penderecki, A Guide to His Works, 1983, A Study of the Penderecki St. Luke Passion, 1983, John Finley Williamson: A Centennial Appreciation, 1987; co-author: German Diction for the Choral Singer, 1992, A Bach Tribute: Bach Essays in Honor of William H. Scheide, 1993; editor The Choral Tradition Series, Hinshaw Music Inc., 1978—, Studies in Penderecki, 1994—. Bd. dirs. Balt. Symphony Orch., 1967-69, Am. Boy Choir Sch., 1970-73, N.Y. Choral Soc., 1972—, Palm Beach Atlantic U. choral series Hinshaw Music Inc., 1990—; bd. dirs. Palm Beach County Coun. Arts, chmn. profl. artists com., mem. task force for master plan, 1990-92; mem. cultural plan com. Palm Beach County Cultural Coun., 1992—; mem. task force for edn. Fla. Philharm. Orch., 1994—. Recipient Disting. Alumni Merit award Ind. U., 1975, Disting. Alumni award Sch. Music, 1973, Disting. Alumni award San Jose State U., 1990. Mem. Coll. Music Soc. (life), Am. Choral Dirs. Assn. (life, chmn. rsch. and publs. com. 1986—), Internat. Heinrich Schütz Soc. (chmn. Am. sect. 1984-87), Univ. Club N.Y., Nassau Club Princeton, Govs. Club West Palm Beach. Presbyterian. Home: 2413 Medina Way West Palm Beach FL 33401-8019

ROBINSON, RICHARD DUANE, oil and gas leasor; b. Oklahoma City, Mar. 20, 1950; s. Farris Michael and Edna Mae (Davenport) R. BS in Edn., U. Okla., 1973, BFA in Art, 1975; MA, master teaching cert., U. Tulsa, 1982. Sextant, custodian McFarlin United Meth. Ch., Norman, Okla., 1973-76; bldg. mgr. U. Okla., Norman, 1976-77; freelance artist Hood-Hope Advt. Agy., Tulsa, 1977-79; mgr. night club and bar 20th Century Electric Club, Tulsa, 1977-80; leasor various petro-chem. cos., Maysville, Okla., 1983—. Mem. Garvin County Dem. Cen. Com., Pauls Valley, Okla., 1994—, sec.-treas., 1995-97; mem. Choctaw Nation Okla., 1950—, Paul Valley Chickasaw Coun., Smithsonian Keepers of the Treas., So. Plains Indian Arts and Crafts Cooperative, Andarko, Okla.; mem. Disciple: Becoming Disciples through Bible Study, Maysville United Meth. Ch. Recipient of merit North Shore Animal League, 1989, cert. of appreciation Dem. Nat. Com. Mem. Smithsonian Assocs., U. Okla. Alumni Assn., U. Tulsa Alumni Assn. Methodist. Home: PO Box 23 Maysville OK 73057-0023

ROBINSON, ROBERT ARTHUR, telecommunications marketing administrator; b. Balt., Jan. 30, 1950; s. Robert Archibald and Dorothy Lee (Armstrong) R.; m. Elizabeth Roxanne Kupihea, Sept. 15, 1983; 1 child, Robert Bronson. Degree in Liberal Arts, Everett (Wash.) Coll., 1974. Ops./mktg. mgr. Mar y Sol Investments, San Anselmo, Calif., 1976-87; sales mgr. Cawc, Inc./Cellisys Inc., Santa Rosa, Calif., 1987-88; dist. sales mgr., br. office mgr. Comtech Mobile Telephone Co., Inc., San Francisco, 1988; gen. mgr. McCaw/Cellular One, Santa Rosa, 1988-90; cons. Cellular Technics, Inc., Dublin, Calif., 1990-91; mktg. mgr. U.S. Cellular, Kailua-Kona, Hawaii, 1991-92; mktg. mgr. ea. N.C. cluster U.S. Cellular, 1992-93; area mgr. ea. N.C./Va. cluster U.S. Cellular, Greenville, N.C., 1993—. With U.S. Army, 1970-72, Vietnam. Office: US Cellular 205 Greenville Blvd SW Greenville NC 27834-7698

ROBINSON, ROBERT EARL, chemical company executive; b. Covington, Ky., Aug. 3, 1927; s. Adolph Earl and Frances Elizabeth (Rouse) R.; m. Myrtle Caroline Tonne, June 10, 1951; children: Linda Ann, Carol Eileen Robinson Cranford, Timothy John. AB, Berea Coll., 1949; MS, Purdue U., 1951, PhD, 1953; postgrad., U. Cin., 1962-64. Project leader U.S. Indsl. Chems., Cin., 1953-64; group leader Stauffer Chem. Co., Weston, Mich., 1964-65; rsch. dir. Cardinal Chem. Co., Columbia, S.C., 1965-66; exec. v.p. Lindau Chems. Inc., Columbia, 1966-86, pres., 1986—; dir. Richland Land Devel. Co., Columbia. Contbr. articles to profl. jours. and encys.; 25 patents in field. Fundraiser Am. Cancer Soc., Columbia, 1991; mem. bd. dirs. S.C. Philharmonic Orch., 1993—. With U.S. Army, 1946-47. Fellow Am. Inst. Chemists; mem. AAAS, Am. Chem. Soc. (chair divsn. small chem. bus. 1993, chair elect 1996), N.Y. Acad. Scis., Baker St. Irregulars, Sherlock Holmes Soc. London, Mensa. Home: 6117 Lakeshore Dr Columbia SC 29206-4331 Office: Lindau Chems Inc 731 Rosewood Dr Columbia SC 29201-4633

ROBINSON, RONALD JAMES, petroleum engineer; b. Pueblo, Colo., Mar. 10, 1946; s. James Claude and Doris Loraine Robinson; B.S. in Math. and Physics, So. Colo. State Coll., 1968; M.S. in Physics, Baylor U., Waco, Tex., 1971; Ph.D. in Petroleum Engring., Tex. A&M U., 1974; m. Bonnie Lynn Martin, Aug. 31, 1968; children: Kevin James, Kyle Bryant, Kurt David. With Getty Oil Co., 1973-78, dist. reservoir engr., Bakersfield, Calif., 1975-78; mgr. thermal recovery Grace Petroleum Corp., Oklahoma City, 1978-79; sr. cons. INTERCOMP Resource Devel. and Engring., Houston, 1979-80; supr. thermal research Getty Oil Co., Houston, 1980-81; spl. projects coordinator Getty Research Ctr., Houston, 1981-84; mgr. reservoir engring. research Texaco, Inc., 1984-89; mgr. internat. applications Texaco, Inc., 1989-92; mgr. internat. applications & tech. transfer Texaco, Inc., 1992-94; gen. mgr. Texaco Exploration and Prodn. Tech. Dept., 1994-95; pres. tech. divsn. Texaco, 1996—; chmn. RBR Investments, 1988—; trustee S.W. Rsch. Inst.; bd. dirs. Petroleum Transfer Coun., 1995-96, Sheltering Arms Sr. Svcs., 1996—, Jr. Achievement, 1996—; industry adv. bd. U. Md. Balt. County, 1996—, dept. petroleum engring. Tex. A&M. NASA fellow, 1968. Mem. Can. Inst. Mining, Indonesian/Am. Bus. Assn. (bd. dirs. 1994—), Soc. Profl. Well Log Analysts, Soc. Petroleum Engrs. (dir.), Scientific Rsch. Soc. N.Am., Greater Houston C. of C. (mem. chmn.'s club 1987—), Sigma Xi. Club: Kiwanis. Author papers in field. Office: PO Box 1404 Houston TX 77251-1404

ROBINSON, STEVEN EARL, structural engineer; b. Phila., Jan. 21, 1955; s. Nelson Arlington and Clara Virginia (Mayo) R.; m. Teresa Dames, July 16, 1979 (div. Dec. 1981); 1 child, Donovan Cornell Brown; m. Patricia Marie Hawkins, Aug. 20, 1988; 1 child, Steven Miles. Archtl. engring., N.C. Agrl. and Tech. State U., Greensboro, 1982. Civil engr. U.S. Army Corps Engrs., Jacksonville, Fla., 1983-90; structural engr. U.S. Army Corps Engrs., Jacksonville, 1991—. Bd. dirs. Luth. Social Svcs., Jacksonville, sec., 1990—; leader Boy Scouts Am., Jacksonville, 1985—. Svc. award, 1993, 94. Recipient Excellence Mentor award YMCA Black Achievers Program, 1992. Mem. Soc. Am. Mil. Engrs. (treas. 1989-92), Jacksonville Alumni Extension of Nat. Soc. Black Engrs. (treas. 1996). Presbyterian. Office: US Army Corps Engrs PO Box 4970 Jacksonville FL 32232-0019

ROBINSON, VICTORIA LEE, critical care, medical/surgical nurse; b. Tyler, Tex., Sept. 21, 1958; d. Louis Henry and Katie Mae (Hawkins) Cooper; m. Burl Robinson Jr., Nov. 28, 1976; children: Taryll, Terrence, Tony. Tyler Jr. Coll., Tyler (Tex.) Jr. Coll., 1982; diploma, Tex. Ea. Sch. Nursing, Tyler, 1983; BSN, Tex. Woman's U., 1990. RN, Tex.; cert. critical care. Staff nurse Med. Ctr. Hosp., Tyler, 1983, asst. nurse mgr., 1985-91, nurse mgr. ICU/Critical Care Unit, 1991—; basic life support instr. Mem. AACCN (cert. ACLS, BLS instr.; sec. Great East Tex. chpt. 1990, 91).

ROBINSON, W. LEE, lawyer; b. Rome, Ga., Sept. 24, 1943; m. Irene Scales, 1966; children: Christine, Jacquelyn. BS, Ga. Tech.; MBA, Mercer Univ., 1985, JD, 1985. With Robinson Hardware Store, Macon, Ga., 1954-86; former mem. Ga. Senate, Atlanta, 1975-83; mayor City of Macon, Macon, 1988-92; pvt. practice law Macon, 1985—. 2d. lt. U.S. Army, col. U.S. Army Res. Decorated 3 Bronze Stars. Mem. Macon C. of C. (former bd. dirs.). Mailing: 3824 Overlook Ave Macon GA 31204-1325 Office: 201 2nd St Ste 580 Macon GA 31201-2738 also: PO Box 4852 Macon GA 31208-4852

ROBINSON, WILKES COLEMAN, federal judge; b. Anniston, Ala., Sept. 30, 1925; s. Walter Wade and Catherine Elizabeth (Coleman) R.; m. Julia Von Poellnitz Rowan, June 24, 1955; children: Randolph C., Peyton H., Thomas Wilkes Coleman. AB, U. Ala., 1948; JD, U. Va., 1951. Bar: Ala. 1951, Va. 1962, Mo. 1966, Kans. 1983. Assoc. Bibb & Hemphill, Anniston, Ala., 1951-54; city recorder City of Anniston, 1953-55; judge Juvenile and Domestic Relations Ct. of Calhoun County, Ala., 1954-56; atty. legal dept. GM&O R.R., Mobile, Ala., 1956-58; commerce counsel, asst. gen. atty. Seaboard Air Line R.R., Richmond, Va., 1958-66; commerce counsel Monsanto Co., St. Louis, 1966-70; gen. counsel, v.p. Marion Labs., Inc., Kansas City, Mo., 1970-79; pres. Gulf and Gt. Plains Legal Found., Kansas City, Mo., 1980-85; atty. Howard, Needles, Tammen & Bergendoff, Kansas City, 1985-86, also bd. dirs.; v.p. S.R. Fin. Group, Inc., Overland Park, Kans., 1986-87; judge U.S. Ct. Fed. Claims, Washington, 1987—. Bd. govs. Kansas City Philharmonic Orch., 1975-77. Served with USNR, 1943-44. Mem. Army Navy Country Club, Skyline Club, Univ. Club, Mason, Scottish Rite, Phi Beta Kappa (past treas. Kansas City, Mo. chpt.), Phi Eta Sigma, Phi Alpha Theta, Kappa Alpha. Episcopalian. Home: 2353 S Queen St Arlington VA 22202-1550 Office: US Ct Fed Claims 717 Madison Pl NW Washington DC 20005-1011

ROBISON, CAROLYN LOVE, librarian; b. Orlinda, Tenn., Aug. 9, 1940; d. Fount Love and Martha Desha (Jones) R. BA, Denison U., 1962; MLS, Emory U., 1965; PhD, Ga. State U., 1982. Tchr. Dag Hammarshjold Jr. High Sch., Wallingford, Conn., 1962-64; asst. librarian, lectr. Architecture Library, Ga. Inst. Tech., Atlanta, 1965-67; head circulation Ga. State U., Atlanta, 1967-71, asst. prof., then assoc. prof., asst. librarian, 1971-75, prof., assoc. librarian, 1975—. Active Friends of Atlanta-Fulton County Pub. Library, 1981—. Recipient Woman of Achievement award YWCA, 1989. Mem. ALA, Southeastern Library Assn., Ga. Library Assn., Am. Assn. Univ. Professors, Delta Kappa Gamma, Phi Kappa Phi, Kappa Delta Pi. Republican. Presbyterian. Home: 1057 Capital Club Cir NE Atlanta GA 30319-2662 Office: Ga State U 100 Decatur St SE Atlanta GA 30303-3202

ROBISON, CLARENCE, JR., surgeon; b. Tecumseh, Okla., Dec. 9, 1924; s. Clarence Sr. and Margaret Irene (Buzzard) R.; m. Patricia Antoinette Hagee, May 27, 1951; children: Timothy D., Paul D., John D., Rebecca A. AS, Stanford U., 1943; MD, U. Okla., 1948. Intern Good Samaritan Hosp., Portland, Oreg., 1948-49; fellow pathology and oncology U. Okla., 1949-51; pathologist USAF Hosp., Cheyenne, Wyo., 1951-53; resident in surgery Okla. U. Health Scis.-Va. Svc., Oklahoma City, 1953-56; mem. faculty surgery dept. Okla. U. Health Scis., Oklahoma City, 1956-57, clin. prof. surgery, 1957—; mem. bd. advisors Mercy Health Ctr., Oklahoma City, 1974-81, sec. of staff, 1974-84, chief surgery, 1992-95; bd. dirs. Okla. Found. for Quality Assurance, Oklahoma City. Mem. Commn. on Mission Indian Nations Presbytery, 1980-91; bd. dirs. Found. Sr. Citizens, 1964—; elder Presbyn. Ch.; presdl. elector Dem. Party, 1960. Capt. USAF, 1951-53. Fellow ACS, Southwestern Surg. Soc., Am. Cancer Soc. (past pres. Okla. divsn., exec. com., bd. dirs., nat. del. dir.); mem. AMA (del. organized med. staff sect. Oklahoma City 1989—, alt. del. AMA from Okla. 1991-93, 96—), SAR, Oklahoma County Med. Soc. (bd. dirs. 1989-93), Okla. State Med. Assn. (alt. trustee Okla. 1989-92, trustee 1993-96), Okla. Surg. Assn. (sec., treas. 1966-68), Oklahoma City Surg. Soc. (pres. 1967-69), Oak Tree Sportsman's Club, Petroleum Club, Men's Dinner Club, Masons (32d degree), Shriners. Office: 4200 W Memorial Rd Ste 805 Oklahoma City OK 73120-8305

ROBISON, KENNETH GERALD, former naval officer, national security consultant, historian; b. Great Falls, Mont., Sept. 30, 1938; s. Perry Russell and Ruth Elsie Helen (Johnson) R.; m. Mary Margaret Michele Crovitz, Mar. 6, 1964; children: Karin Michele, Mark Charles. Student, U. Wash., 1958; BA, U. Mont., 1960, postgrad., 1965; MA, George Mason U., 1994. Commd. ensign USN, 1960, advanced through grades to capt., 1980, intelligence officer, 1960; asst. naval attache U.S. Embassy, Stockholm, 1975-78; asst. chief of staff intelligence U.S. Naval Forces Europe, London, 1980-84; dir. plans, policy and requirements Office Naval Intelligence, Washington, 1984-88; ret., 1988; sr. assoc. Booz, Allen & Hamilton, 1988—. Author: Prisoner of War Debrief--Capt. James Bond Stockdale, 1973; contbr. articles to hist. and genealogical jours. Decorated comdr. Order No. Star (Sweden), Legion of Merit, Meritorious Svc. medal with oak leaf cluster, Navy Commendation medal, Presdl. Unit Commendation medal. Mem. Orgn. Am. Historians, Mont. Hist. Soc., Va. Hist. Soc., Nat. Geneal. Soc., U.S. Naval Inst., Navy League, Am. Legion, VFW, Phi Alpha Theta, Delta Sigma Phi. Republican. Presbyterian. Home: 315 Lamplighter Ln Great Falls MT 59405-4168 Office: Booz Allen & Hamilton Inc 1953 Gallows Rd Vienna VA 22182-3934

ROBISON, RICHARD EUGENE, architect; b. Wichita, Kans., Oct. 30, 1951; s. Robert Dale and Corene (Tiffany) R.; m. Manola Cristina Gomez Pantoja, Dec. 20, 1975; children: Amy Elizabeth, Harriet Paige. Student, Baker U., 1969-71; B Environ. Design, U. Kans., 1974. Lic. profl. architect, Kans.; cert. constrn. specifier. Architect U.S. Peace Corps, Khouribga, Morrocco, 1974-75, OFESUR, Valencia, Venezuela, 1975-78; instr. U. Carabobo, Valencia, 1979-80; architect, ptnr. R.G. Asessores SRL, Valencia, 1978-83; architect Van Doren-Hazard-Stallings, Inc., Topeka, 1983-87, Heery Internat., Inc., Atlanta, 1987-92; architect Lord, Aeck, and Sargent, Inc., Atlanta, 1992-94, prin., 1994—; instr. So. Coll. Tech., 1992. Co-author automated specifications writing system Sweet Spec, 1989, Spec System, 1990. Mem. AIA, Spl. Librs. Assn., Constrn. Specifications Inst. Home: 7484 Waters Edge Dr Stone Mountain GA 30087-6132 Office: Lord Aeck and Sargent Inc 1201 Peachtree St NE 400 Colony Sq NE Ste 300 Atlanta GA 30361-6303

ROBLYER, BOB ALLEN, art director, computer graphics consultant; b. Salinas, Calif., Nov. 7, 1955; s. Paul G. and Edna June (Wage) Short; m. Terry Lee Mullican, Aug. 12, 1977; children: Taylor John, Michelle Elyse. BFA, U. Tex., Arlington, 1983. Art dir. Worrell and Assocs., Ft. Worth, 1983-84, Lino Typographers, Ft. Worth, 1984-91, CITGO Petroleum Corp., Tulsa, 1991—. Designer: birth announcement, 1986; graphics dir. Vision quarterly, 1996. Asst. Webelos pack 143 Boys Scouts Am., Sapulpa, Okla., 1994-95, asst. scoutmaster troop 555, Sapulpa, 1995—. Republican. Mem. Ch. of Christ. Home: 451 W Galaxy Rd Sapulpa OK 74066-6801

ROBOCK, LEONARD IRVING, foreign policy consultant; b. St. Paul, May 30, 1922; s. Samuel and Clara (Abromovich) R. BA in Econs., U. Wis., 1946; cert., Oxford U., Eng., 1947; MA in Internat. Rels., Columbia U., 1952. Instr. English Mod. Inst. Langs., Prague, Czechoslovakia, 1947-48; econ. analyst Econ. Coop. Adminstrn., London, 1948-50; instr. internat. rels. Bklyn. C.C., 1952-54; field rep. Great Lakes Fgn. Policy Assn., Cleve., 1955-57; cultural affairs officer U.S. Info. Agy., Phomn Penh, Cambodia, 1957-59; pub. affairs officer U.S. Info. Agy., Chieng ai, Thailand, 1959-60; info. officer U.S. Info. Agy., Bangkok, Thailand, 1960-67; chief thai desk Voice of Am. U.S. Info. Agy., 1967-68; country affairs officer Thailand and Burma U.S. Info. Agy., Washington, 1968-70, cultural affairs officer Australia, 1970-71, career counselor, 1971-74, econs. officer, 1974-78; pub. affairs officer U.S. Info. Agy., Alexandria, Egypt, 1978-80; mem. fgn. svc. grievnace bd. Dept. of State, 1980-84; cons. in field. Author: Radio Reception and Listening Habits in Northeast Thailand, 1964. Vol. Big Bros., Fairfax County, Va., 1985-89, Youth for Understanding, Washington, 1985-94; chmn. Condominium Recycling Com., McLean, Va.; mem. Dem. Nat. Com., Washington, 1989—. Recipient Disting. Alumni award U. Wis. Washington Area Alumni Assn., 1988. Mem. Am. Fgn. Svc. Assn. Home: 8380 Greensboro Dr Apt 823 Mc Lean VA 22102-3521

ROBSON, GORDON MACDONALD, anesthesiologist; b. Bryn Mawr, Pa., Mar. 21, 1953; s. Robert Dalgleish Robson and Jean (Hickman) Fernow; m. Karin Eloise Stout, Dec. 29, 1973; children: Joshua Daniel, Seth Abraham, Hannah Ruth. MusB magna cum laude, Covenant Coll., 1974; MusM, U. Ariz., 1976; MusD, Fla. State U., 1980; DO, Kirksville Coll. Osteo. Med., 1988. Diplomate Am. Bd. Osteo. Med. Examiners, Am. Osteo. Bd. Anesthesiologists. Violin restorer, musician Atlanta, 1976-78; part time instr. of music Kennesaw Coll., Atlanta, 1978; asst. prof. music N.E. Mo. State U., Kirksville, 1980-84; intern Kirksville (Mo.) Osteo. Med. Ctr., 1988-89; resident in anesthesia Parkview Hosp., Toledo, Ohio, 1989-91; resident Ingham Med. Ctr., Lansing, Mich., 1991-92; staff anesthesiologist Tulsa Regional Med. Ctr., 1992—. Mem., choir dir. Redeemer Presbyn. Ch., Atlanta, 1976-78; Sunday sch. tchr., choir dir. Calvary Ch., Tallahassee, 1978-80; leader, choir dir., treas. Grace Bible Ch., Kirksville, 1980-88; mem., choir dir. Cmty. Christian Reformed Ch., Toledo, 1989-92; mem. Christ Presbyn. Ch., Tulsa, 1992—. Named Elizabeth Black Miller scholar Univ. Ariz., 1974-76, Outstanding Young Men of Am., 1984. Mem. Am. Osteo. Assn., Am. Osteo. Coll. Anesthesiologists, Am. Soc. Anesthesiologists, Soc. Cardiovascular Anesthesiologists, Okla. Osteo. Assn., Pi Kappa Lambda. Republican.

ROBSON, JOHN EDWARD, nursing administrator; b. Grove City, Pa., Aug. 4, 1948; s. Clair Eugene and Grace Louise (Winger) R.; m. Shirley Ann Todd, Feb. 7, 1968; children: Daniale Elaine, Chad Edward. Diploma, Alexian Bros. Hosp., Chgo., 1969; BS, Park Coll., Parkville, Mo., 1982; MPA, Troy (Ala.) State U., 1992. Staff nurse Naval Hosp. Memphis, Millington, Tenn., 1969-73; charge nurse, naval officer Naval Hosp., Yokosuka, Japan, 1973-76; charge nurse, flight nurse Naval Hosp. Whidbey Island, Oak Harbor, Wash., 1976-79; outpatient coord., flight nurse Naval Hosp., Corpus Christi, 1979-82; charge nurse, inpatient coord. Portsmouth (Va.) Naval Hosp., 1982-87; asst. DON Cherry Point Naval Hosp., Havelock, N.C., 1987-91; dir. nursing Guantanamo Bay (Cuba) Naval Hosp., 1991-92, Camp Lejeune Naval Hosp., Jacksonville, N.C., 1992-96; exec. officer Cherry Point (N.C.) Naval Hosp., 1996—; rural nursing instr. Emergency Nurses Assn., Wash. State, 1978-79; advisor, flight nurse USCG Sta., Corpus Christi, 1979-82; clin. coord. Naval Base-haitian Migrant Camp, Guantanamo Bay, 1991-92. Mem. High Sch. Boosters, Havelock, 1987-90; coach Babe Ruth Baseball Program, Havelock, 1987-90. Decorated Navy Commendation medal (2); recipient Sharpshooter award U.S. Navy, 1991. Mem. Emergency Nurses Assn. Methodist. Home: 107 Wadkins Blvd New Bern NC 28560-9488 Office: Naval Hosp Camp Lejeune Jacksonville NC 28540

ROBSON, WILLIAM LANE MCKENZIE, pediatrician, medical educator; b. Calgary, Alta., Can., Sept. 1, 1950; s. Gordon Howison and Mary Margaret Robson; m. Judith Kathleen Robson, Nov. 12, 1979; children: Christine M., Karen E. MD, U. Calgary, 1973. Diplomate Am. Bd. Pediatrics, Am. Bd. Pediatric Nephrology; lic. Med. Coun. Can., 1974, lic. physician N.C., S.C.; FLEX certs., parts 1 and 2, cert. in pediatrics, Can., 1978. Pediatric intern Hosp. for Sick Children, Toronto, 1973-74, sr. pediatric resident, 1975-76, fellow in nephrology, 1976-77; acting dir. pediatric ICU Foothills Hosp., Calgary, 1980-81; Med. Rsch. Coun. fellow in renal physiology U. Toronto, 1977-79; acting dir. pediatric ICU Foothills Hosp., Calgary, 1980-81; assoc. dir. edn. pediatric emergency dept. Alta. Children's Hosp., Calgary, 1981-84; head divsn. pediatric nephrology U. Calgary, 1985-93; dir. pediatric nephrology The Children's Hosp./Greenville (S.C.) Hosp. Sys., 1993—; mem. staff Greenville unit Shriners Hosp., 1994—, Alta. Children's Hosp., 1981-93, Rockyview Hosp., Calgary, 1985-86, Foothills Hosp., Calgary, 1979-85, Holy Cross Hosp., Calgary, 1979-82, Calgary Gen. Hosp., 1979-82. Contbr. chpts. to books, over 40 articles, numerous revs., case reports and photographs to profl. jours. Bd. govs. Strathcona-Tweedsmuir Sch., Calgary, 1987-91, vice chmn., 1989-91, chair long-range planning com., fund raising com., acad. com., architect selection com. Rsch. grantee Greenville Hosp. Sys. Coop. Rsch. and Edn. Program, 1994, 95. Fellow Royal Coll. Physicians (Glasgow), Royal Soc. Health, Am. Acad. Pediat. (cert pediat., cert. pediatric nephrology), Royal Coll. Physicians and Surgeons Can.; mem. Internat. Soc. Nephrology, Internat. Soc. Pediatric Nephrology. Office: The Children's Hosp 890 W Faris Rd Ste 250 Greenville SC 29605-4253

ROCHA, OSBELIA MARIA JUAREZ, librarian; b. Odessa, Tex., Aug. 3, 1950; d. Tomas R. and Maria Socorro (Garcia) Juarez; m. Ricardo Rocha, July 8, 1972; children: Nidia Selina, René Ricardo. AA, Odessa Coll., 1970; BA, Sul Ross State U., 1972; MA, Tex. A & I U., 1977; MLS, Tex. Woman's U., 1991. Cert. tchr., reading specialist, Tex. Math. tchr. Del Rio (Tex.) Jr. High Sch., 1972-78; reading tchr. Del Rio High Sch., 1978-79; math. tchr. Ector High Sch., Odessa, 1979-81, Permian High Sch., Odessa, 1981-88; libr. Blackshear Elem. Magnet Sch., Odessa, 1988-93, Bowie Jr. H.S., Odessa, 1993-95, Ector Jr. H.S., Odessa, 1995—. Reviewer of children's and adolescents' books for MultiCultural Rev.; author articles. Mem. NEA, Internat. Reading Assn., Nat. Coun. Tchrs. Math., Tex. State Tchrs. Assn., Tex. Reading Assn., Tex. Libr. Assn., Tex. Coun. Tchrs. Math., West Tex. Assn. Bilingual Edn., Permian Basin Reading Assn., Beta Phi Mu. Roman Catholic. Home: 1717 W 24th St Odessa TX 79763-2309 Office: Ector Jr HS 900 W Clements Odessa TX 79763

ROCHELLE, WARREN GARY, editor, educator, writer; b. Durham, N.C., Nov. 21, 1954; s. Charles Elmer and Ethel Louise (Glosson) R. BA, U. N.C., 1977; MS in LS, Columbia U., 1978; MFA in Creative Writing, U. N.C., Greensboro, 1991, PhD in English, 1997. Libr. Rocky Mount (N.C.) Acad., 1978-80, Colegio Jorge Washington, Cartagena, Colombia, 1980-82; media specialist Wake County Pub. Schs., Raleigh, N.C., 1982-89; rsch. asst. Rsch. Svcs., U. N.C., Greensboro, 1989-90; program asst. MFA Writing Program, U.N.C., Greensboro, 1990-91; asst. to dir., mng. editor, teaching asst. U. N.C., Greensboro, 1991—. Contbr. short stories to Aboriginal Sci. Fiction, Beyond the Third Planet, Forbidden Lines; contbr. poetry to Coraddi, Crucible, The Charlotte Poetry Rev.; author articles. Recipient Jarrard prize Carolinas Speech Comm. Assn., 1995, 1st prize Nat. Fantasy Fair Fedn. Contest, 1990, 1st prize Irene Leach Short Story Contest, 1989. Mem. MLA, Nat. Coun. Tchrs. English, Rhetoric Soc. Am., Sci. Fiction and Fantasy Writers Am., South Atlantic MLA, Sci. Fiction Rsch. Assn. Democrat. Roman Catholic. Office: U NC Greensboro Dept English 132 McIver Bldg Greensboro NC 27412-5001

ROCHON, JOHN PHILIP, cosmetics company executive; b. Sept. 20, 1951; s. Philip Benjamin and Helena Sylvia (McCullough) R.; m. Donna J. Hewitt, Dec. 15, 1972; children: Heidi C., William J., Lauren. BS, U. Toronto, Ont., 1973, MBA, 1976. Plant mgr. Econs. Lab. Ltd., Toronto, 1976-80; dir. mfg. Mary Kay Cosmetics, Ltd., Toronto, 1980-82; contr. mfg. group Mary Kay Cosmetics, Inc., Dallas, 1982-84, corp. contr., 1984, v.p. fin., chief fin. officer, 1984-85, exec. v.p., chief fin. officer, 1986-87, vice chmn. bd., 1987-93; pres., CEO Mary Kay Cosmetics Corp., Dallas, 1993—; also bd. dirs. Mary Kay Cosmetics, Ltd., Dallas; bd. dirs. Mary Kay Holding Corp., Dallas, Strategic Assessment, Inc.; mem. fin. com. U. Tex., Dallas, 1985—. Mem. Cosmetic, Toiletry and Fragrance Assn., Direct Selling Assn., Verandah Club. Republican. Home: 4315 Firebrick Ln Dallas TX 75287-5138*

ROCKEFELLER, JOHN DAVISON, IV (JAY ROCKEFELLER), senator, former governor; b. N.Y.C., NY, June 18, 1937; s. John Davison III and Blanchette Ferry (Hooker) R.; m. Sharon Percy, Apr. 1, 1967; children: John, Valerie, Charles, Justin. B.A., Harvard U., 1961; student, Japanese lang. Internat. Christian U., Tokyo, 1957-60; postgrad. in Chinese, Yale U. Inst. Far Eastern Langs., 1961-62. Apptd. mem. nat. adv. council Peace Corps, 1961, spl. asst. to dir. corps, 1962, ops. officer in charge work in Philippines, until 1963; desk officer for Indonesian affairs Bur. Far Eastern Affairs, U.S. State Dept., 1963; later asst. to asst. sec. state for Far Eastern affairs; cons. Pres.'s Commn. on Juvenile Delinquency and Youth Crime, 1964; field worker Action for Appalachian Youth program, from 1964; mem. W.Va. Ho. of Dels., 1966-68; sec. of state W.Va., 1968-72; pres. W.Va. Wesleyan Coll., Buckhannon, 1973-75; gov. State of W.Va., 1976-84; U.S. senator from W.Va., 1985—, mem. vets. affairs com., fin. com., commerce, sci. and transp. com., chmn. Sen. steel caucus, Bipartisan Com. on Comprehensive Health Care; chmn. Nat. Commn. on Children, natural resources and environ. com. Nat. Govs. Assn., 1981-84. Contbr. articles to mags. including N.Y. Times Sunday mag. Trustee U. Chgo., 1967—; chmn. White House Conf. Balanced Nat. Growth and Econ. Devel., 1978, Pres.'s Commn. on Coal, 1978-80, White House Adv. Com. on Coal., 1980; active Commerce, Sci., and Transp. Com., Fin. Com.; chmn. Vet. Affairs Com. Office: US Senate 109 Hart Senate Bldg Washington DC 20510*

ROCKWELL, ELIZABETH DENNIS, retirement specialist, financial planner; b. Houston; d. Robert Richard and Nezzell Alderton (Christie) Dennis. Student Rice U., 1939-40, U. Houston, 1938-39, 40-42. Purchasing agt. Standard Oil Co., Houston, 1942-66; v.p. mktg. Heights Savs. Assn., Houston, 1967-82; sr. fin. planner Oppenheimer & Co., Inc., Houston, 1982—; 2d v.p. Desk and Derrick Club Am., 1960-61. Contbr. articles on retirement planning, tax planning and tax options, monthly article 50 Plus sect. for Houston Chronicle newspaper. Bd. dirs. ARC, 1985-91, Houston Heights Assn., 1973-77; named sr. v.p. Oppenheimer, 1986—; mem. Coll. Bus. U. found. bd. Houston, 1990, mem. million dollar roundtable, 1991—, mem. ct. of the table, 1991—, Top of Table, 1996—, mem. sys. planned giving coun., 1992—, mem. coll. bus. adv. bd., 1992—, mem. alumni bd., 1987-95; appointed trustee U. Houston Sys. Found., Inc., 1992. Named Disting. Alumnae Coll. Bus. Alumn. Assn. U. Houston, 1992; named YWCA Outstanding Woman of Yr., 1978. Mem. Am. Savs. and Loan League (state dir. 1973-76, chpt. pres. 1971-72; pres. S.W. regional conf. 1972-73; Leaders award 1972), Savs. Inst. Mktg. Soc. Am. (Key Person award 1974), Inst. Fin. Edn., Fin. Mgrs., Soc. Savs. Instns., U.S. Savs. and Loan League (com. on deposit acquisitions and adminstrn.), Houston Heights Assn. (charter, dir. 1973-77), Friends of Bayou Bend, Harris County Heritage Soc., U. Houston Alumni Orgn. (life), Rice U. Bus. and Profl. Women, River Oaks Bus. Womens Exchange Club, U. Houston Bus. Womens Assn. (pres. 1985), Forum Club, Greater Houston Women's Found. (charter). Office: Oppenheimer & Co Inc 1600 Smith St Ste 3100 Houston TX 77002-7347

ROCKWELL, SHERMAN RALPH, JR., sales executive, packaging consultant; b. Birmingham, Ala., Sept. 16, 1949; s. Sherman Ralph and Martha Ellen (Hopkins) R. BA, Samford U., 1971; postgrad., Memphis State U., 1971-72, Ga. State U., 1975. Gen. mgr. The Peasant Restaurants, Inc., Atlanta, 1985, Proof of the Pudding, Inc., Atlanta, 1985-87; gen. mgr. The Olive Garden Italian Restaurants, Huntsville, Ala., 1987-88, Knoxville, Tenn., 1988; area supr. The Olive Garden Italian Restaurants, Atlanta, 1988-90; mgr. off-premise sales The Olive Garden Italian Restaurants, Orlando, Fla., 1990-96; ind. restaurant cons. Orlando, 1996—; nat. accounts mktg. mgr. Heidi's Fine Desserts, L.A., 1996; nat. accounts mktg. mgr. Heidi's Fine Desserts, 1996. Cons. Gen. Mills Restaurants Recycling Com., Orlando, 1990-91. Mem. Nat. Restaurant Assn. (ednl. found.). Democrat. Presbyterian.

ROCKWELL, SUSAN LYNN, educational association administrator; b. Canton, Ohio, Sept. 1, 1957; d. Wilford Edgar Jr. and Florence E. (Fellers) Metzger. BA in English, U. Ala. at Birmingham, 1990, MA in English, 1993; Cert., Coll. Bus. Mgmt. Inst., Lexington, Ky., 1992; postgrad., Ariz. State U., 1993—. Sec. BDM Corp., Las Vegas, Nev., 1978; sec. U.S. Probation Office, Las Vegas, 1979, Sterne Agee & Leach, Birmingham, 1979-80; sec. to libr. U. Ala. at Birmingham, 1981-83, adminstrv. sec. to budget dir., 1984-88, adminstrv. sec. to treas., 1989-91, adminstrv. assoc. to v.p. fin., 1992-93; dir., mng. editor Nat. Assn. for Ethnic Studies, Tempe, Ariz., 1994—; bd. dirs., sec. U. Ala. at Birmingham faculty and staff devel. fund, 1985-91. Mng. editor: (newsletter) The Ethnic Reporter, 1994—, (jour.) Explorations in Ethnic Studies, 1994—, (jour.) Explorations in Sights and Sounds, 1994—. Vol. A Baby's Place, Birmingham, 1991-93; big sister Big Brothers/Sisters, Birmingham, 1985-86; vol. counselor Rape Response, Birmingham, 1984-88. Recipient 1st prize grad. paper Nat. Assn. for Ethnic Studies, 1994, 2d prize grad. rsch. U. Ala. at Birmingham, 1992. Mem. MLA, Assn. for Study of Am. Indian Lit., Soc. for Study of Am. Autobiography, Sigma Tau Delta (pres. U. Ala. at Birmingham chpt. 1991-93). Democrat. Office: Nat Assn for Ethnic Studies Dept English Arizona State University Tempe AZ 85287

RODBELL, MARTIN, biochemist; b. Balt., Dec. 1, 1925; s. Milton William and Shirley Helen (Abrams) R.; m. Barbara Charlotte Ledermann, Sept. 10, 1950; children: Paul, Suzanne, Andrew, Phillip. BA, Johns Hopkins U., 1949; PhD, U. Wash., 1954; DSc (hon.), U. Montpelier, 1992, U. Wash., 1996, U. Geneva, 1996, Va. Commonwealth U., 1996. Nutrition and endocrinology chemist NIH, Bethesda, Md., 1956—; chief lab. nutrition and endocrinology NIAMD, Bethesda, Md., 1972-84; sci. dir. Nat. Inst. Environ. Health Scis., Rsch. Triangle Park, N.C., 1985-89, chief sect. signal transduction, 1989-94; scientist emeritus Nat. Inst. Environ. Health Scis., Rsch. Triangle Park, 1994—. Recipient Supr. Svc. award HHS, 1974, Gairdner Found. award, 1984, Jacobeus award, 1973, Nobel Prize for Physiology or Medicine, 1994. Mem. NAS (Richard Lounsbery award 1987), Am. Soc. Biol. Chemists., Am. Acad. Arts and Scis. Office: NIH Environmental Health Scis Research Triangle Park NC 27709

RODDA, JOHN LOU, finance company executive, financial consultant; b. Phila., Feb. 27, 1932; s. Kermit K. and Henriette (Cave) R.; m. Jacqueline E. Polonsky; children: Stephen B., Stefani B., Michael J. BS, Pa. State U., 1960; MBA, U. Pa., Phila., 1962. Adminstrv. mgr. Ga. Pacific Corp., Atlanta, 1960-69; v.p., CFO Republic Gypsum Co., Hutchinson, Kans., 1969-92; pres. The ABBA Group, Carrollton, Tex., 1992—. Pres. Am. Kennel Club, Okla., 1972; dist. chmn. Boy Scouts Am., Okla., 1975; wing comdr. Civl Air Patrol, Okla., 1977. Decorated Legion of Honor Chapel of Four Chaplains, 1962. Mem. Corp. Dirs. Soc., Nat. Assn. Corp. Treas. (dir. 1986-92), Nat. Assn. Corp. Sec., Tex. Assn. Bus. Brokers. Office: The ABBA Group 1720 N Josey Ln # 104 Carrollton TX 75006

RODEAN, RICHARD WILLIAM, musician, educator; b. Hibbing, Minn., July 22, 1940; s. William Alexander and Katherine (Robbin) R.; m. Trudy Oman, Aug. 17, 1963; 1 child, Kirsta. MusB, Eastman Sch., 1962, MusM, 1964; PhD in Fine Arts, Tex. Tech., 1980. Music tchr. Brighton Schs., Rochester, N.Y., 1962-65; prof., chmn. fine arts U. Tampa, 1966-81; chmn. performing arts Tex. Woman's U., Denton, 1981—; adjudicator Nat. Assn. Schs. Music, Reston, Md., 1987. Bassoonist Fla. Woodwind Quintet, 1974, Wichita Falls Symphony, 1994—; soloist, Faculty Recitals, 1990—; mus. dir. Denton Cmty. Theatre, 1982— (Josh award 1983). Pres. Denton Arts Coun., 1987-89; bassoonist Fla. Gulf Coast Symphony, Tampa-St. Petersburg, 1966-76. Mem. Tex. Assn. Schs. Music, Rotary, Kappa Kappa Psi (pres. 1978-80). Office: Texas Womans University PO Box 425768 Denton TX 76204

RODEFER, JOANNE MARIE, military officer; b. Abington, Pa., Sept. 9, 1953; d. John Power and Marie Claire (Gorman) Flanigan; m. Karl Douglas Rodefer, June 14, 1980. BA, St. Joseph's Coll., 1975; MS, Air Force Inst. Tech., 1980; MS in Nat. Resource Strategy, Indsl. Coll. of Armed Forces, 1996. Commd. 2d lt. USAF, 1975, advanced through grades to col., 1993, officer in charge F-4E aircraft maintenance unit, 1981; chief mission systems br. Hdqrs. USAFE, Ramstein AB, Germany, 1982-84, chief aircraft avionics br., 1984-85; maintenance supr. 363rd Aircraft Generation Squadron, Shaw AFB, 1986-87, comdr., 1988-90; comdr. Equipment Maintenance Squadron, Shaw AFB, S.C., 1987-88, spl. asst. to dep. comdr. for maintenance, 1988; asst. dep. comdr. for maintenance 363rd Tactical Fighter Wing, Shaw AFB, 1990; maintenance staff officer, dir. maintenance USAF, Washington, 1991-93; comdr. 982d tng. group USAF, Sheppard AFB, Tex., 1993-95; C-141 sys. program dir. Warner Robins Air Logistics Ctr., 1996—. Mem. com. Shaw/Sumter Community Coun., Sumter, 1987-90. Paul Harris fellow Rotary Internat. Mem. Soc. Logistics Engrs. (cert. profl. logistician), Air Force Inst. Tech. Alumni Assn., Air Force Assn., Maintenance Officer Assn. (sec., editor Exceptional Release, program mgmt. profl.). Republican. Roman Catholic. Home: 493 Officers' Cir E Robins AFB GA 31098

RODEHEFFER, JONATHAN PAUL, editor; b. Lima, Ohio, Feb. 25, 1942; s. Paul William and Elnor Beulah (Locher) R.; m. Jane Simerl, Aug. 29, 1964; children: Sarah Jane, Emily Verena. BA, Oberlin Coll., 1964; MA, Johns Hopkins U., 1965. Reporter Balt. Sun., 1967-68, 70-73; tchr. Ruhrtal Gymnasium, Schwerte, Fed. Republic Germany, 1973-75; reporter Orlando (Fla.) Sentinel, 1975-79, asst. metro editor, 1979-81, wire editor, 1981—. With U.S. Army, 1968-69, Vietnam. German Acad. Exch. Svc. fellow, 1965. Mem. Phi Beta Kappa. Republican. Unitarian Universalist. Home: 712 Daniels Ave Orlando FL 32801-4004 Office: Orlando Sentinel 633 N Orange Ave Orlando FL 32801-1300

RODENBECK, SVEN E., environmental engineer, consultant; b. Ft. Eustis, Va., Oct. 2, 1955; s. Eric Otto and Herma (Grawi) R.; m. Pamela Jo Foster, July 27, 1991. AA in Gen. Studies, St. Petersburg Jr. Coll., 1975; BS in Gen. Studies, U. Ctrl. Fla., 1978, BS in Environ. Engring., 1978; MS in Environ. Engring., U. Md., 1983; postgraduate Sch. Pub. Health, Tulane U., 1991-93. Registered profl. engr., Md., Fla. Commd. USPHS, 1979; field engr. Indian Health Svc. USPHS, Billings, Mont., 1979; field engr. Rocky Boy (Mont.) Indian Reservation USPHS, 1979-81; environ. engr. pollution control sect., environ. protection br. Divsn. Safety, NIH, Bethesda, Md., 1981-86, environ. compliance officer environ. protection br., 1986-87; environ. engr. office health assessment Agy. for Toxic Substances and Disease Registry, Atlanta, 1987-89, environ. engr. med. waste group office of assoc. adminstr., 1989-90, environ. engr. cons. divsn. health assessment and cons., 1990-91; environ. engr. cons. Tulane U. Sch. Pub. Health and Tropical Medicine, New Orleans, 1991-93; environ. engr. cons., divsn. health assessment and cons. Agy. for Toxic Substances and Disease Registry, Atlanta, 1993-95, acting sect. chief assessment and cons. divsn. health, 1995-96; environ. engr. cons. divsn. health assessment and cons., 1996—; water quality officer Nat. Scout Jamboree, Ft. A.P. Hill, Va., 1989. Contbr. articles to profl. publs.; author report to congress: The Public Health Implications of Medical Waste, 1990. Recipient numerous USPHS awards, including Commendation medal, 1987, 90, Achievement medal, 1984, 89, citation, 1981, Outstanding Unit citation, 1995, Unit Commendation, 1984, 88, 89, 90, 96, Surgeon Gen.'s Exemplary Service medal, 1996, Field Med. Readiness badge, 1996, Engring. Literary awards, 1995. Mem. ASCE, Soc. for Risk Analysis, Water Environ. Fedn., Nat. Wildlife Fedn., Assn. of Mil. Surgeons of U.S. (life), Nat. Audubon Soc., Ret. Officers Assn., Assn. Commd. Corps USPHS, Consumers Union (life), UCF Alumni Assn., Delta Tau Delta (life). Lutheran. Home: 1229 Hadaway Ct Lawrenceville GA 30243-4668 Office: Agy Toxic Substances Disease Registry Mailstop E-32 1600 Clifton Rd NE Atlanta GA 30333

RODENBERG, HOWARD DAVID, emergency medicine educator; b. Chgo., Oct. 18, 1962; s. Joseph Harris and Harriet Ann (Burgheim) R. BA in Biology with distinction, MD, U. Mo., Kansas City, 1986. Diplomate Am. Bd. Emergency Medicine, Nat. Bd. Med. Examiners; cert. ACLS instr. and affiliate faculty, advanced trauma life support, pediatric advanced life support, basic trauma life support; cert. flight surgeon NASA. Resident in emergency medicine Truman Med. Ctr., Kansas City, 1986-89; assoc. prof., chief sect. prehosp. care U. Fla. Coll. Medicine, Gainesville, 1989-95, dir. med. student edn. div. emergency medicine, 1989-91, clin. resource faculty social-ethical issues med. practice, 1989—; med. dir. air flight program Shands Teaching Hosp.-U. Fla., Gainesville, 1989—; sys. med. dir. Alachua County Dept. Fire and Rescue Svcs., Gainesville; cons. Emergency Health Svc., Med. Rescue Internat., Johannesburg, South Africa, 1995-96; rsch. assoc. NASA Kennedy Space Ctr., Fla., 1989; mem. guest faculty Brit. Assn. for Immediate Care, Cambridge, Eng., 1992, 94, 95; vis. cons. in accident and emergency medicine Addenbrooke's Hosp. and Cambridge U. Sch. Clin. Medicine, 1992, 95; vis. lectr. in disaster mgmt. and prehosp. care Ptnrs. of Ams., Colombia, 1992, lectr. Australia, Eng., Scotland, Italy, South Africa; bd. dirs., mem. planning com. North Ctrl. Fla. Trauma Agy., 1990—, co-chmn. med. adv. panel, 1991—; others. Editor: (with I. Blumen) Air Medical Physician's Handbook, 1993, 94, (with T. Martin) Aeromedical Transportation: A Clinical Guide; mem. editl. bd. Air Medicine jour., 1993—; contbr. articles to med. jours., chpts. to books. Mem. emergency med. svc. programs adv. bd. Santa Fe C.C., 1991—; mem. emergency med. svcs. adv. coun., Alachua County, 1991—; mem. North Ctrl. Fla. adv. bd. ACLS, 1991—. Fellow Am. Coll. Emergency Physicians; mem. Air Med. Physicians Assn. (founding, bd. dirs. 1992—, liaison to Aerospace Med. Assn., 1992—), Fla. Assn. Emergency Med. Svcs. Med. Dirs. (bd. dirs. 1990-91, sec.-treas. 1991-92, v.p. 1993-94, pres. 1994-95, N.E. Fla. regional med. advisor 1991-95), Fla.-Colombian Ptnrs. (bd. trustees 1994—), Omicron Delta Kappa, Pi Kappa Phi. Office: Medical Resource Internat, Johannesburg South Africa

RODENHAUSER, PAUL, psychiatry educator; b. N.Y.C., Apr. 9, 1937; s. Paul Charles and Hazel Lucinda (Palmer) R.; m. Geneva M. Hunsinger, Dec. 26, 1960 (div. 1972); children: Eric Paul, Kirsten, Hans David; m. Skye Kathleen Moody, Apr. 21, 1990. BA, Gettysburg Coll., 1959; MD, Jefferson Med. Coll., Phila., 1963. Diplomate Am. Bd. Psychiatry and Neurology. Intern York (Pa.) Hosp., 1963-64; resident The Sheppard and Enoch Pratt Hosp., Towson, Md., 1966-69; pvt. practice (gen. medicine) York, Pa., 1964-66; pvt. practice (psychiatry) Balt., 1969-71; med. advisor to dir. personnel relations Johns Hopkins Hosp., Balt., 1971-74; staff psychiatrist Brook Lane Psychiat. Ctr., Hagerstown, Md., 1974-78; dir. profl. svcs. Brook Lane Psychiat. Ctr., Hagerstown, 1978-81; residency edn. dir. Wright State U. Sch. Medicine, Dayton, Ohio, 1981-86; chmn. dept. psychiatry Wright State U. Sch. Medicine, Dayton, 1986-90; med. dir. Vista Hill Hosp., Chula Vista, Calif., 1990-91; prof. psychiatry, dir. med. student edn. in psychiatry Tulane U. Sch. Medicine, New Orleans, 1991—, asst. dean admissions and curriculum mgmt., 1993—; adj. prof. health system mgmt. Tulane U. Sch. Pub. Health and Tropical Medicine, New Orleans, 1993—. Mem. editorial bd. Adminstrn. and Policy in Mental Health; reviewer Acad. Psychiatry, Acad. Medicine. Fellow Am. Psychiat. Assn.; mem. Am. Assn. Psychiat. Adminstrs. (pres.-elect), Assn. Dirs. Med. Student Edn. in Psychiatry, Am. Coll. Psychiatrists, Alpha Omega Alpha. Home: 501 Burgundy St New Orleans LA 70112-3403 Office: Tulane U Sch Med 1430 Tulane Ave New Orleans LA 70112-2699

RODGERS, BILLY RUSSELL, chemical engineer, research scientist; b. Fitzgerald, Ga., Sept. 5, 1936; s. Jimmie R. and Ruby Doris (Morris) R.; divorced; children: Cheryl, Donna, Angie, Rusty. AA, U. Fla., 1956, BSChemE with high honors, 1966, MS in Engring., 1967; PhD, U. Tenn., 1980. Project leader Shell Devel. Co., 1968-72; group leader Keene Corp. Fluid Handling, Cookeville, Tenn., 1972-74, Oak Ridge (Tenn.) Nat. Lab., 1974-92; sr. engr. Walk Haydel & Assocs., New Orleans, 1992-94; pres. Rodgers USA Enterprises, Orange Park, Fla., 1992—, Intelligent Cons., Orange Park, 1993—; qualifying agt./mgr. Rodgers Constrn. Co., 1996—. Author 3 books in field; contbr. articles to profl. publs. Fellow AIChE (bd. dirs. 1993-97, chmn. fuels and petrochem. divsn. 1992-95, chmn. program com. fuels and petrochem. divsn. 1990-92). Republican. Office: Rodgers USA Enterprises 794 Foxridge Center Dr Orange Park FL 32065-5776

RODGERS, LYNNE SAUNDERS, women's health nurse; b. Winchester, Va., May 11, 1956; d. Ronald Otho and Anne Coleman (Grille) Saunders; m. Joseph Rodgers, Dec. 21, 1985; children: Joseph Anthony, John Robert, Stephanie Lynne. BSN, George Mason U., 1978. Cert. inpatient obstetric nursing, prenatal childbirth educator, Resolve Through Sharing counselor, perinatal grief counselor. Clin. nurse specialist in labor and delivery Bethesda (Md.) Naval Hosp., 1978-87; labor and delivery staff nurse clinician Fairfax Hosp. Assn., Falls Church, Va., 1987—; clinician, staff nurse in obstetrics Fauquier Hosp., Warrenton, Va., 1990—. Mem. Assn. Women's Health Obstetric and Neonatal Nurses. Office: Fauquier Hosp 500 Hospital Dr Warrenton VA 20186-3027

RODGERS, RICHARD MALCOLM, management accountant; b. Montgomery, Ala., June 23, 1949; s. Charles Malcolm and Betty Jean (Gilbert) R.; m. Linda Joyce Meeks, Dec. 9, 1966 (div. Mar. 1970); 1 child, Angela Christina Rodgers Bolin; m. Sharon Lynn Thomas, May 10, 1992. Student, Emory U., 1967-69; BBA magna cum laude, Ga. State U., 1988. Cert. mgmt. acct. Staff acct. Charter Enterprises, Inc., College Park, Ga., 1971-72; contr. Royal Arts & Crafts, Inc., Atlanta, 1972-73; justice of peace Justice's Ct. Dist. 531, Decatur, Ga., 1973-76; chief cost acct. Gen. Assembly Mission Bd., Presbyn. Ch. U.S., Atlanta, 1974-80; internal audit mgr. Waffle House, Inc., Norcross, Ga., 1980-87; acctg. mgr. W.L. Thompson Cons. Engrs., Inc., Atlanta, 1988-90; contr. Hudson Everett Simonson Mullis & Assocs., Inc., Atlanta, 1990-96; freelance cons. and writer, 1995—. Poet, contbg. editor Archon mag., 1968-70 (Anthology award 1970); composer, lyricist: (musical play) Many a Glorious Morning, 1971; playwright, composer, lyricist: (musical play) Take the Money and Run!, 1979, 91. Exec. com. mem. DeKalb County Rep. Party, Decatur, 1969-76; v.p. Ga. Assn. Justices of the Peace and Constables, Warner Robbins, Ga., 1973-74; treas., founding dir. Ga. Bus. Com. for Arts, Inc., Atlanta, 1981-86; sec. Ga. State Poetry Soc., Inc., Atlanta, 1986 (Judge for Chapbook award 1991, 96). Stipe scholar Emory U., 1968. Mem. AAAS, Inst. Mgmt. Accts., N.Y. Acad. Scis., Idealists Internat. (charter), The Dramatists Guild, Golden Key Nat. Honor Soc. (charter), Beta Gamma Sigma, Phi Kappa Phi. Democrat. Episcopalian. Home and Office: 1111 Clairmont Rd # K-2 Decatur GA 30030

RODGERS, ROBERT AUBREY, physicist; b. Huntsville, Ala., May 10, 1967; s. Aubrey and Peggy Joyce (Hairald) R. BS, U. Ala., Huntsville, 1990, MS, 1992; MSHP, Ga. Inst. Tech., 1993. Grad. student physics rschr. Polarization and Lens Design Lab., U. Ala., Huntsville, 1991-92; grad. student med. physics rschr. Emory U.-Ga. Inst. Tech., Atlanta, 1992-94; staff med. health physicist USAF, Lackland AFB, Tex., 1996—. U. Ala.-Huntsville Honor scholar, 1988-89, scholar, 1986-87. Mem. Am. Assn. Physicists in Medicine, Health Physics Soc. (med. sect.), Soc. Nuclear Medicine. Baptist. Home: 9898 Colonnade Blvd 16202 San Antonio TX 78230

RODMAN, RICHARD EUGENE, associate dean; b. Indpls., Sept. 20, 1950; s. Eugene Francis and Juanita D. (Embry) R.; m. Marilyn McPherson, Aug. 11, 1973; children: Gwynn Ellen, Joseph Richard. AB, Ind. U., 1972; MEd, Murray State U., 1974, S.C.T., 1975; PhD, Ga. State U., 1984. Instr. history, reading Kennesaw Coll., Marietta, Ga., 1974-80; dir. self-help devel. Presbyn. Ch. U.S.A., Lesotho, 1980-84, dir. Maseru guidance project, 1982-84, edn. specialist, 1984-86; edn. cons. internat. gen. assembly Presbyn. Ch. U.S.A., Louisville, Ky., 1987-92, global edn. coord. gen. assembly, 1992-96; assoc. dean Warren Wilson Coll., Asheville, N.C., 1996—; bd. dirs. Near E. Sch. Theol., Beirut, 1992-96; faculty philosophy, comparative religion Marija Theol. Sem., Lesotho, 1984-86. Trustee United Bd. C. Higher Edn. Asia, N.Y.C., 1992-96, Lebanese Am. U., Beirut, 1992-96; bd. dirs. KodaiKanal-Woodstock Inst. Found., India, 1992-96. Maj., 1985-86. Mem. Nat. Assn. Fgn. Student Adv., Appalachian Coll. Assn., Assn. Am. Colls. and Univs., Assn. Internat. Educators. Presbyterian. Office: Warren Wilson Coll PO Box 9000 Asheville NC 28815

RODRIGUEZ, ELENA GARCIA, retired pension fund administrator; b. Havana, Cuba, Mar. 21, 1944; came to U.S., 1959; d. Eliseo and Elena (Suarez) Garcia; divorced; children: Victor, Yvonne, Daniel. B in Profl. Studies, Barry U., 1983; MS in Mgmt., St. Thomas U., 1985; postgrad., U. Phila., 1989, UCLA, 1990. With City of Miami, Fla., 1969-95, pension adminstr., 1978-95, ret., 1995. Author: General and Sanitation Pension Benefit Booklet, 1982, Fire and Police Pension Benefit Booklet, 1982, Retirement Planning Booklet, 1985; author numerous programs dealing with pension and acctg. for pension assets. Mem. Leadership Miami, 1985—.

Mem. NASD (arbitrator), Internat. Found. Employee Benefit Plans, Internat. Pers. Mgmt. Assn., Inst. Fiduciary Edn., Fla. Assn. City Clks., New York Stock Exch. (arbitrator), Am. Stock Exch. (arbitrator), Am. Arbitration Assn., Better Bus. Bur. (arbitrator). Republican. Roman Catholic.

RODRIGUEZ, IVAN, professional baseball player; b. Vaga Baja, P.R., Nov. 30, 1971. With Tex. Rangers, 1988—; mem. Am. League All-Star Team, 1992-96, Am. League Silver Slugger Team The Sporting News, 1994. Recipient Gold Glove award, 1992-95. Office: Tex Rangers 1000 Ballpark Way Arlington TX 76011-5168*

RODRIGUEZ, LORRAINE DITZLER, biologist, consultant; b. Ava, Ill., July 4, 1920; d. Peter Emil and Marie Antoinette (Mileur) D.; m. Juan G. Rodriguez, Apr. 17, 1948; children: Carmen, Teresa, Carla, Rosa, Andrea. BEd, So. Ill. U., 1943; MS, Ohio State U., 1944; PhD, U. Ky., 1973. Asst. nutritionist OARDC, Wooster, Ohio, 1944-49; postdoctoral fellow U. Ky., Lexington, 1973-74, pesticide edn. specialist, 1978-89; pvt. cons. Lexington, 1974-79, 89—. Author ext. publs. in field; co-author rsch. publs. and book chpts. in field. Leader 4-H, Lexington, 1962-68. Named Outstanding 4-H Alumni Woman, Ky., 1969. Mem. Vegetation Mgmt. Assn. Ky. (chmn. adv. bd. 1985-89), Am. Chem. Soc. Democrat. Roman Catholic. Home: 1550 Beacon Hill Rd Lexington KY 40504-2304

RODRIGUEZ, LOUIS JOSEPH, university president, educator; b. Newark, Mar. 13, 1933; m. Ramona Dougherty, May 31, 1969; children: Susan, Michael, Scott. BA, Rutgers U., 1955; MA, La. State U., 1957, PhD, 1963. Dean, Coll. Bus. Adminstrn., Alcee Fortier Disting. prof. Nichols State U., Thibodaux, La., 1958-71; dean Coll. Bus. U. Tex.-San Antonio, 1971-72, v.p. acad. affairs, dean faculty, 1972-73; dean Sch. Profl. Studies U. Houston-Clear Lake City, 1973-75, vice-chancellor, provost, 1975-80; pres. Midwestern State U., Wichita Falls, Tex., 1981—, Hardin Found. prof., 1994—; vice chmn. Coun. Tex. Pub. Univ. Pres. and Chancellors, 1992-93; mem. formula and health professions edn. adv. coms. Tex. Higher Edn. Coordinating Bd. Author 4 books; contbr. over 50 articles to profl. jours. Chmn. bd. Tex. Council on Econ. Edn., Houston, 1981-83; bd. dirs. Joint Council on Econ. Edn., N.Y.C., 1981-83, Goodwill Industries Am., Washington, 1976-82, Robert Priddy Found., 1993-96; pres. Wichita Falls Bd. Commerce and Industry, 1988-89, Clear Lake City Devel. Found., Houston, 1976-77, Goals for Wichita Falls, Inc., 1983; mem. internat. adv. com. Tex. Higher Edn. Coordinating Bd. Recipient Tchr. Edn. Supportive Pres. award Am. Assn. Colls. Tchr. Edn., 1991; named Wichitan of the Yr., 1987; Ford Found. grantee, 1964; Fulbright fellow, 1976. Mem. Am. Assn. State Colls. and Univs. (bd. dirs.), So. Assn. Colls. and Schs. (Commn. on Colls.), Assn. Tex. Colls. and Univs. (pres. 1988-89), Rotary (pres. Downtown Wichita Falls club 1990-91). Mem. Ch. of Christ. Home: 2405 Midwestern Pky Wichita Falls TX 76308-2911 Office: Midwestern State U 3410 Taft Blvd Wichita Falls TX 76308-2095

RODRIGUEZ, SUSAN MILLER, geriatrics nurse; b. New Orleans, Sept. 1, 1950; d. Albert John Miller and Patricia (Shields) Di George; m. Fred H. Rodriguez, Jr., Dec. 22, 1973; children: Alison, Fred III, Kathryn, David. BSN, La. State U. Med. Ctr., 1972. RN, La. Home health nurse Home Health Svcs. of La. Inc., New Orleans, 1972-73; assoc. faculty mem. La. State U. Sch. of Nursing, New Orleans, 1973-75; rsch. nurse Tulane U., New Orleans, 1994; personal health coord. Total Health 65, New Orleans, 1994—. Mem. New Orleans Dist. Nurses Assn. (nominating com.1972-74), Faculty Wives Club of La. State U. Med. Ctr. (pres. 1990-91), La. State U. Sch. Nursing Alumni (treas. 1972-73), Sigma Theta Tau. Republican. Roman Catholic. Home: 5105 Green Acres Ct Metairie LA 70003-1005 Office: Total Health 65 Ochsner Clinic 1514 Jefferson Hwy New Orleans LA 70121

RODRIGUEZ, VICTOR M., obstetrician, gynecologist; b. Ponce, P.R., May 17, 1945; m. Nikki C. Roberts. BS magna cum laude, U. P.R., 1968, MD, 1972, MPH magna cum laude, 1975. Diplomate Am. Bd. Obstetrics and Gynecology, Bd. Med. Examiners. Intern in ob-gyn. U. Dist. Hosp., San Juan, P.R., 1972-73, residence in ob-gyn., 1973-76; chief dept. ob-gyn. USAF Regional Hosp., Montgomery, Ala., 1976-79; obstetrician, gynecologist Maxwell AFB, Montgomery, 1976-79; asst. clin. prof. Coll. Medicine, U. Ark., El Dorado, 1979-90; pvt. practice in ob-gyn. El Dorado, Ark., 1979-90, Hot Springs, Ark., 1990, Troy, Ala., 1991-94; asst. prof. Dept. GYN/OB Emory U., Atlanta, 1994-95. Fellow Am. Coll. Obstetricians and Gynecologists; mem. AMA, APHA, Am. Soc. Colposcopy & Cervical Pathology, Am. Assn. Gynecologic Laparoscopists, P.R. Med. Assn., Ark. Pilots Assn., Soc. Air Force Clin. Surgeons U.S., Assn. Mil. Surgeons U.S., U. P.R. Sch. Medicine Alumni Assn. Home: PO Box 191465 Atlanta GA 31119-1465

RODRIGUEZ ARROYO, JESUS, gynecologic oncologist; b. Arecibo, P.R., Jan. 11, 1948; s. Jesus Rodriguez and Blanca Arroyo; m. Annie Arsuaga, June 3, 1972; children: Ivan, Patricia. BS, U. P.R., San Juan, 1968, MD, 1972, postgrad., 1976. Diplomate Am. Bd. Ob-Gyn. Assoc. dir. gynecologic oncology Oncology Hosp., Rio Piedras, P.R., 1978-83; assoc. prof. ob-gyn, dir. gynecologic oncology U. Hosp. Sch. Medicine, Rio Piedras, 1978-85; gynecologic oncologist Met. Hosp., Rio Piedras, 1979-88; obstetrician, gynecologist Auxilio Mutuo Hosp., P.R., 1981-91, San Pablo Hosp., Bayamon, P.R., 1981-91, Ashford Meml. Community Hosp., 1983-91; cons. gynecologic oncology Tchrs. Hosp., Hato Rey, P.R., 1979-85, Hermanos Melendez Hosp., Bayamon, 1979-91; instr. ob-gyn. U. P.R. Sch. Medicine, 1976-78, asst. prof., 1978-83, assoc. prof., 1984, dir. gynecologic oncology sect., 1978-84. Contbr. articles to med. jours. Mem. Citizen Ambassador Cancer Mgmt. Del. to USSR, 1990. Mem. AAAS, Am. Coll. Surgeons, P.R. Med. Assn. (jud. ethical coun. 1990-91), Internat. Gynecologic Cancer Soc., Soc. Gynecologic Oncologists, Dorado Beach Hotel, Caparra Country Club. Home: 1910 Pasionaria St Urban Santa Maria Rio Piedras PR 00927 Office: Caribbean Oncology & Gyn Assn PO Box 194557 San Juan PR 00919-4557

RODRIGUEZ-DIAZ, JUAN E., lawyer; b. Ponce, P.R., Dec. 27, 1941; s. Juan and Auristela (Diaz-Alvarado) Rodriguez de Jesus; m. Sonia de Hostos-Anca, Aug. 10, 1966; children: Juan Eugenio, Jorge Eduardo, Ingrid Marie Rodriguez. BA, Yale U., 1963; LLB, Harvard U., 1966; LLM in Taxation, NYU, 1969. Bar: N.Y. 1968, P.R. 1970. Assoc. Baker & McKenzie, N.Y.C., 1966-68, McConnell, Valdes, Kelley, Griggs, Sifre & Ruiz-Suria, San Juan, P.R.; undersec. Dept. Treasury P.R., 1971-73; mem. Sweeting, Pons, Gonzalez & Rodriguez, 1973-81; pvt. practice Santurce, P.R., 1981-94, Totti, Rodriguez-Diaz & Fuentes, 1994—; bd. dir. Ochoa Indsl. Sales Corp., Ochoa Telecom, Inc., Industrias Vassallo, Inc. Bd. govs. Acqueduct and Sewer Authority P.R., 1979-84; mem. adv. com. collective bargaining negotiation of P.R. Elec. Power Authority to Gov. P.R., 1977-78; bd. govs. P.R. council Boy Scouts Am., mem. transition com., 1984-85; mem. adminstrv. coun. Ballajá. Mem. ABA, N.Y. State Bar Assn., P.R. Bar Assn., AFDA Club, San Juan Yacht Club. Roman Catholic. Home: 1 Calle Fresno San Patricio Guaynabo PR 00968-4601 Office: Suite 1200 416 Ponce de Leon Avenue Hato Rey San Juan PR 00918

RODRIGUEZ-ORELLANA, MANUEL, law educator; b. Rio Piedras, P.R., Mar. 7, 1948; s. Manuel Rodriguez-Ramos and Elena (Orellana-Ramos) Rodriguez; m. Maria Dolores Pizarro-Figueroa, Jan. 30, 1984; 1 child, Laura Elena Rodriguez-Pizarro. BA, Johns Hopkins U., 1970; MA, Brown U., 1972; JD, Boston Coll., 1975; LLM, Harvard U., 1983. Bar: P.R. 1975, U.S. Dist. Ct. P.R. 1976. Staff atty. P.R. Legal Svcs., Inc., San Juan, P.R., 1975-77, dir. consumer law div., 1977-79; dean students Inter-Am. U. Sch. Law, San Juan, P.R., 1979-80, asst. prof. law, 1980-83; assoc. prof. law Northeastern U. Sch. Law, Boston, 1983-89, prof. law, 1989-93; cons. Office Ind. Counsel-Prosecutor of Commonwealth P.R., San Juan, 1985, Office Minority Leader of P.R. Ind. Party, Senate P.R., San Juan, 1985—; vis. scholar Harvard Law Sch., Cambridge, Mass., 1988; electoral commr. Commonwealth P.R., 1989-95; pvt. practice in civil litigation, 1995—; vis. prof. Eugenio M. de Hostas Sch. Law, Mayaguez, P.R., 1995-96. Author: Después de Todo: Poemas de Noche y Circunstancia, 1982. Candidate for resident commr. from P.R. in U.S. Ho. of Reps., 1996. Mem. ABA, Colegio de Abogados de P.R. (bd. govs. 1977-78).

ROE, ALLIE JONES, technical writer; b. Greenville, S.C., Dec. 3, 1950; d. James Richard and Allie McGreg (Singletary) Jones; m. Eugene Bartlett Roe, Aug. 29, 1970 (div. 1986); 1 child, David Michael. AB in English, Valdosta State Coll., 1972; MA in Journalism, Ohio State U., 1982. Instr. II State of Ga. Health Svcs., Valdosta, 1972-74; prodn. asst. Easton (Md.) Publ. Co., 1974-75; sec. office of radiation safety Emory U., Atlanta, 1977-79; asst. mgr. classified The Booster Newspaper, Columbus, Ohio, 1980-81; editorial aide Battelle Columbus Labs., 1983-84; publs. coord. specialist Battelle Project Mgmt. Div., Columbus, 1984-85, adminstv. coord., 1985-87; free-lance editor Am. Ceramic soc., Westerville, Ohio, 1988; tech. writer, editor Resource Internat., Westerville, 1988-89; tech. writer Cons. & Designers, Winter Park, Fla., 1989-91; advanced tech. writer Westinghouse, Orlando, Fla., 1991—. Vol. Am. Heart Assn., Columbus, 1984-88, Am. Cancer Soc., Columbus, 1986-88. Mem. Women in Comms. Inc. (v.p. projects 1986-87, chair job placement com. 1987-89), Nat. Mus. for Women in the Arts (charter 1988—), Altrusa Internat. (v.p. Orlando chpt. 1994), Jr. League Greater Orlando, Phi Kappa Phi. Methodist. Home: 3732 E Grant St Orlando FL 32812-8417

ROE, MICHAEL HENRY, computer specialist, business manager; b. Clarksville, Tenn., Nov. 15, 1944; s. James Maurice and Virgie (Rye) R.; m. Betty Joyce Daniel, Aug. 26, 1967. BS in Indsl. Mgmt., U. Tenn., 1966, MS in Computer Sci., 1975. Applications programmer, analyst Union Carbide Corp.-Nuclear Div., Oak Ridge, Tenn., 1967-72, systems analyst, 1973-80; part-time instr. U. Tenn., Knoxville, 1976; computing specialist Union Carbide Corp.-Nuclear Div., Oak Ridge, 1981-83; dir. data systems Cumberland Med. Ctr., Crossville, Tenn., 1983-90; cons. Mikro Enterprises, 1990—; cons. Tenn. Technol. U., Cookeville, 1982-83, Martin-Marietta, Oak Ridge, 1983-84; adj. faculty Roane State Community Coll., 1991-92. Mem. Cumberland County Playhouse, Crossville, 1976—; bd. dirs. Med. Ctr. Credit Union, Crossville, 1986-95, pres., 1989-95; adminstrv. bd. First United Meth. Ch., Crossville, 1984-87, chmn. stewardship, 1984-88. Mem. IEEE Computer Soc., Tenn. Mountain Writer's Conf. (bd. dirs.), Nat. Storytelling Assn., Tenn. Assn. for Preservation and Perpetuation of Storytelling, Am. Assn. Computing Machinery, Data Processing Mgmt. Assn., United Fund of Cumberland Co. (bd. dirs.), U. Tenn. Alumni Assn. (chpt. treas. 1990, sec.-treas. 1991-92, pres. 1993-94), Mensa, Rotary (treas. Crossville club 1990, sec. 1991, v.p. 1992, pres. 1993, pres. Rotary Found. Cumberland County 1994, 95). Methodist. Office: Mikro Enterprises PO Box 910 Crossville TN 38557-0910

ROE, RADIE LYNN, secondary school educator; b. Stuart, Fla., Nov. 14, 1962; d. Albert R. III and Martha Katherine (Brooks) Krueger; 1 child, Travis; m. Dan C. Roe, May 24, 1990. AB, Ga. Wesleyan Coll., 1984; postgrad., U. Cen. Fla. Tchr. English Brevard County Sch. System, Melbourne, Fla., 1984-86; bank officer, tng. dir. First Nat. Bank and Trust, Stuart, 1987-90; dir. Christian edn. 1st Presbyn. Ch., Stuart, 1990-91; prof. English, Indian River Community Coll., Ft. Pierce, Fla., 1990-91; employment comm. cons. Curtis and Assocs., Grand Island, Nebr., 1992-93; exec. dir. Community HelpCenter, Grand Island, 1993, Martin County Literacy Coun., Stuart, Fla., 1993-94; mgr. ednl. svcs. The Palm Beach Post subs. Cox Enterprises, Inc., West Palm Beach, Fla., 1994-95; with audiotext advt./programming dept. The Stuart (Fla.) News, 1995—; lang. arts tchr. Southport Middle Sch., Port St. Lucie, Fla., 1996—; presch. tchr. Appletree Acad., Palm City, Fla. 1995—. Active Laubach Literacy in Action. Mem. NAFE, Toastmasters, Habitat for Humanity, Audubon Soc. Republican. Lutheran. Home: 4119 SE Jacaranda St Stuart FL 34997-2220

ROE, RAMONA JERALDEAN, lawyer, state official; b. Gassville, Ark., May 27, 1942; d. Roy A. and Wanda J. (Finley) R. B.A., U. Ark., 1964; J.D., U.Ark.-Little Rock, 1976. Bar: Ark. 1976, U.S. Dist. Ct. (ea. and we. dists.) Ark. 1979. Mng. ptnr. Roe & Hunt, Rogers, Ark., 1977-78; pvt. practice, Rogers, Ark., 1978-81, Little Rock, 1982-84, 90-92; assoc. Richardson & Richardson, Little Rock, 1981-82; dep. exec. dir. Ark. Workers' Compensation Commn., Little Rock, 1984-90; legis. atty. Ark. Code Revision Commn., Little Rock, 1992—. Contbr. articles to profl. jours. Recipient Am. Jurisprudence awards U. Ark. Sch. Law, 1971-72, Corpus Juris Secundum award, 1971, Hornbook award, 1971, Am. Judicature award, 1972. Mem. AAUW (treas. 1980), Bus. and Profl. Women (chpt. treas.-v.p. 1978-80), Delta Theta Phi (clk. of rolls 1973-74, tribune 1974-75), Mensa, Lambda Tau. Methodist. Office: Ark Code Revision Commn 1515 W 7th St Ste 204 Little Rock AR 72201-3936

ROE, WILLARD E., agricultural company executive; b. 1919. With W.G. Roe & Co., Inc., Winter Haven, Fla., 1943—; pres., dir. Wm. G. Roe & Sons, Inc., Winter Haven, 1959—. Office: Wm G Roe & Sons Inc 500 Avenue R SW Winter Haven FL 33880-3871*

ROEBUCK, JUDITH LYNN, secondary school educator; b. Huntington, W.Va., Jan. 1, 1946; d. Russell Vance and Janice Lee (Adams) Dickey; m. William Benjamine Roebuck Jr., Mar. 28, 1970; children: Lisa, Paul. AB, Marshall U., 1968; MA, W.Va. U., 1973; postgrad., Marshall U., W.Va. U., 1973—. Cert. tchr., adminstr., W.Va. Tchr. art, English Vinson High Sch., Huntington, 1967-68; tchr. art Wayne (W.Va.) and Crockett Elem. Sch., 1968-69; tchr. art, speech Ona (W.Va.) Jr. High/Mid. Sch., 1969-91; tchr. speech, debate Huntington High Sch., 1991-92; tchr. art Barboursville (W.Va.) High Sch., 1992-94, Midland H.S., Ona, W.Va., 1994—; chmn. related arts team Ona Mid. Sch., 1988-91, mem. sch. improvement team, 1990-91; mem. adv. bd. Teen Inst., Huntington, 1990—, W.Va. Teen Inst., 1995, leader, 1990—; mem. drama and debate program, Huntington, 1991-92, Invitationalism Coun., Huntington, 1990—, Cabell County Curriculum Coun., Huntington, 1991-92, Cabell County Reading Coun., 1991-92, Cabell County Tchrs. Acad., Tchr. Expectancy Student Achievement, W.Va. Health Schs. Program; mediator, trainer Helping Improve Peace, 1994; mentor, tchr. Impact. Contbr. articles to endl. jours. Counselor, Coll. Scouts Program, 1994—. Mem. NEA, DAR (sec. 1988—), Nat. Art Edn. Assn. (curriculum coun., art chmn. 1993-96, county del. 1994), W.Va. Edn. Assn., Cabell Edn. Assn. (membership chmn. 1989-91), Horizons, Phi Delta Kappa. Home: 30 Chris Ln Rt 2 Milton WV 25541 Office: Cabell Midland High Sch Rt 60 East Ona WV 25545

ROEHM, DAN CHRISTIAN, physician, nutritionist; b. Nashville, Feb. 23, 1925; s. Alfred Isaac and Daisy (Harner) R.; children: Marie Louise, Dan Christian Jr., David Clark, Deedra Carolyn. MD, Western Res. U., 1947; PhD in Adaptive Edn. Therapy, Am. Assn. Adaptive Ednl. Therapy, Ft. Lauderdale, 1987; $D. Intern St. Vincent's Charity Hosp., Cleve., 1947-48; resident Vanderbilt U. Thayer VA Hosp., Nashville, Tenn., 1948-49, 51-53; pvt. practice internal medicine Nashville, 1953-59; pvt. practice medicine Ft. Lauderdale, Fla., 1960—; mem. staff Broward Gen. Hosp., Ft. Lauderdale, chief dept. medicine, 1963-64; asst. inst. Clin. Medicine Vanderbilt Med. Sch., 1951-59. Patentee med. and chem. devices; contbr. numerous articles to med. jours. Served to lt. USNR, 1949-51. Fellow ACP; mem. Am. Coll. Advancement in Medicine (dir. 1986—). Republican.

ROEHR, KATHLEEN MARIE, nursing administrator; b. San Francisco, June 24, 1950; d. Robert E. and Patricia L. (Lawler) Tupa; m. Bernard N. Stolzman, June 8, 1996; 1 child, Michael Scott. BSN, U. San Francisco, 1972; MS, U. S.C., 1986. RN, Calif., S.C., CNAA, CHE. Commd. officer U.S. Army, 1971, advanced through grades to col., 1994; staff nurse surg. ICU U.S. Army MEDDAC, Ft. Polk, 1972-73; staff nurse surg. ICU 2d Gen. Hosp., Landstuhl APO, N.Y., 1973-76, asst. chief, 1976-77, head nurse emergency room, 1977-78; clin. staff nurse emergency room Walter Reed Army Med. Ctr., Washington, 1978-79, head nurse emergency room, 1979-81; head nurse emergency room Irwin Army Community Hosp., Ft. Riley, Kans., 1981-82; chief nurse 16th MASH U.S. Army, Ft. Riley, 1982-84; head nurse emergency room Moncrief Army Community Hosp., Ft. Jackson, S.C., 1986-89; chief, clin. ops. analysis br. Health Facilities, 7th MEDCOM, Heidelberg, Fed. Republic Germany, 1989-90; chief health facilities planning div. 7th MEDCOM, Heidelberg, Germany, 1990-91; chief, nursing adminstrn. 67th EVAC Hosp., Wuerzburg, Germany, 1991-92; chief, dept. of nursing 67th EVAC Hosp., 1993—; dep. comdr. nursing 67th Combat Support Hosp., Wuerzburg, 1993-94; chief dept. nursing Reynold Army Cmty. Hosp., Ft. Sill, Okla., 1994-96; asst. chief dept. nursing Brooke Army Med. Ctr., Ft. Sam Houston, Tex., 1996—; presenter numerous confs. Decorated Legion of Merit, Meritorious Svc. medal with 5 oak leaf clusters. Mem. ANA, Am. Orgn. Nurse Execs., Am. Coll. Healthcare Execs., Nat. League Nursing, Tex. Nurses Assn., Sigma Theta Tau. Home: 13339 Demeter Universal City TX 78148

ROEMER, ELAINE SLOANE, real estate broker; b. N.Y.C., Apr. 23, 1938; d. David and Marion (Frauenthal) Sloane; m. David Frank Roemer, June 21, 1959; children: Michelle Sloane Wolf, Alan Sloane Roemer. BBA, U. Fla., 1959; MEd, U. Miami, 1963. CFP; cert. tchr. Tchr. math. and bus. Dade County Pub. Schs., Miami, 1959-80, Miami Dade Community Coll., 1968-80; tchr. edn. Fla. Internat. U., Miami, 1977-80; real estate broker Miami, 1978—; tchr. math. St. Leo's Coll., Miami, 1991-92; mortgage broker, Miami, 1986—; speaker in field. Contbr. articles to profl. jours. Mem. Kendall-Perrine Assn. Realtors (sec., treas. 1992-93, bd. dirs. 1991-92, grievance com. 1990, arbitration com. 1991, pres.-elect 1994, pres. 1995), Fla. Assn. Realtors (rep. dist. 4 1992-95, honor soc. 1995), Nat. Assn. Realtors, NEA, Fla. Edn. Commn., Classroom Tchrs. Assn., Dade County Edn. Assn., Fla. Coun. Tchrs. Math., Fla. Bus. Edn. Assn., Assn. Classroom Educators, Dade County Assn. Ednl. Adminstrs., ASCD, Alpha Delta Kappa. Home: 7705 SW 138th Ter Miami FL 33158-1120 Office: 9036 SW 152nd St Miami FL 33157-1928

ROESELER, WOLFGANG GUENTHER JOACHIM, city planner; b. Berlin, Mar. 30, 1925; s. Karl Ludwig and Therese (Guenther) Ph.D., Philipps State U. of Hesse, Marburg, W.Ger., 1946-49; LL.B., Blackstone Sch. Law, Chgo., 1958; m. Eva Maria Jante, Mar. 12, 1947; children—Marion, Joanie, Karl. Asso. planner Kansas City (Mo.) Planning Commn., 1950-52; city planning dir. City of Palm Springs, Calif., 1952-54; sr. city planner Kansas City, 1954-56; prin. assoc. Ladislas Segoe & Assos., Cin., 1956-64; dir. urban and regional planning Howard, Needles, Tammen & Bergendoff, cons. Kansas City, N.Y.C., 1964-68; owner W.G. Roeseler, Cons. City Planner and Transp. Specialist, Bryan, Tex., 1969—; head dept. urban and regional planning Tex. A&M U., 1975-81, 85-88, prof., 1975-90, dir. Tex. A&M Ctr. Urban Affairs, 1984-88, exec. officer for edn. College of Architecture, 1987-88, prof. emeritus, 1990—. Fellow Inst. Transport Engrs.; mem. Am. Inst. Cert. Planners (life mem.), Am. Planning Assn., Transport Planners Coun., Urban Land Inst. Author: Successful American Urban Plans, 1982. Contbr. articles to profl. jours. Home: 2508 Broadmoor PO Box 4007 Bryan TX 77805-4007 Office: Tex A&M U PO Box 4007 College Station TX 77844-4007

ROESSLER, P. DEE, lawyer, former judge, educator; b. McKinney, Tex., Nov. 4, 1941; d. W.D. and Eunice Marie (Medcalf) Powell; m. George L. Roessler, Jr., Nov. 16, 1963; (div. Dec. 1977); children: Laura Diane, Trey. Student Austin Coll., 1960-61, 62-64, Wayland Bapt. Coll., 1961-62; BA, U. West Fla., 1968; postgrad. East Tex. State U., 1975, U. Tex.-Dallas, 1977; JD, So. Meth. U., 1982. Bar: Tex. 1982, U.S. Dist. Ct. (ea. dist.) Tex. 1983, U.S. Dist. Ct. (no. dist.) Tex. 1983. Tchr., Van Alstyne Ind. Sch. Dist., Tex., 1968-69; social worker Dept. Social Svcs., Fayetteville, N.C., 1971-73, Dept. Human Svcs., Sherman and McKinney, 1973-79, 81; assoc. atty. Abernathy & Roeder, McKinney, 1982-85, Ronald W. Uselton, Sherman, 1985-86; prof., program coord. for real estate Collin County C.C., McKinney, 1986-87, for criminal justice, 1986-91, for legal asst., 1986—; mcpl. judge City of McKinney Mcpl. Ct., 1986-89; mem. Tex. State Bar Com. on Legal Assts., 1990-94, Tex. State Bar Com. on Child Abuse & Neglect, 1996—. Mem. Collin County Shelter for Battered Women, 1984-86, chmn., 1984-85; v.p. Collin County Child Welfare Bd., 1986, pres. 1987-88, 96—, treas. 1989, mem., 1994—; Rep. jud. candidate Collin County, 1986; chmn. bd. Tri County Consortium Mental Health Mental Retardation, 1984-85; mem. Tex. Area 5 Health System Agy., 1979, Collin County Mental Health Adv. Bd., 1978-79; trustee Willow Park Hosp., HCA, 1987-88; chair Collin County Criminal Justice Sub-com., 1987-88; mem. Collin County Pub. Responsibility Com., 1991—, chair, 1994-95; bd. dirs. Ct. Apptd. Spl. Advocates, 1991-95. Mem. Collin County Bar Assn., Plano Bar Assn. Baptist. Avocations: gardening, reading, writing, traveling. Home: 2118 Chippendale Dr Mc Kinney TX 75070-2850 Office: Collin County Community Coll 2200 W University Dr Mc Kinney TX 75070-2906

ROFF, ALAN LEE, lawyer, consultant; b. Winfield, Kans., July 2, 1936; s. Roy Darlis and Mildred Marie (Goodaile) R.; m. Sonyia Ruth Anderson, Feb. 8, 1954; 1 child, Cynthia Lee Roff Edwards; m. Molly Gek Neo Tan, July 21, 1980. BA with honors and distinction, U. Kans., 1964, JD with distinction, 1966. Bar: Okla. 1967. Staff atty. Phillips Petroleum Co., Bartlesville, Okla., 1966-75, sr. atty., 1976-85, sr. counsel, 1986-94; cons. in Asia, 1995—. Mem. editl. bd. Kans. Law Rev., 1965-66. Precinct com. man Rep. Party, Lawrence, Kans., 1963-64; assoc. justice Kans. U. Chancery Club; mem. Kans. U. Young Reps. Elizabeth Reeder scholar U. Kans., 1965-66, Eldon Wallingford award, 1964-66. Mem. ABA, Okla. Bar Assn., Washington County Bar Assn., Phoenix Club (Bartlesville) (bd. dirs. 1985-86, gen. counsel 1986-91), Order of the Coif, Masons, Phi Alpha Delta, Pi Sigma Alpha. Mem. First Christian Ch.

ROGACHEFSKY, RICHARD ALAN, surgeon, educator; b. Rochester, N.Y., Jan. 1, 1961; s. Harry and Miriam (Sher) R.; m. Tara Suzanne Gotler, Apr. 17, 1994. B in Biology, U. Rochester, 1983; MD, Chgo. Med. Sch., 1987. Resident in orthopedics U. Miami, 1992, asst. prof. dept. orthopedics, 1993—. Contbr. articles to profl. jours. Mem. AMA, Am. Bd. Orthopedic Surgeons, Osteoarthritis Rsch. Soc. Office: U Miami Dept Orthopaedics PO Box 016960 D-27 Miami FL 33101

ROGALLO, FRANCIS MELVIN, mechanical, aeronautical engineer; b. Sanger, Calif., Jan. 27, 1912; s. Mathieu and Marie Rogallo; m. Gertrude Sugden, Sept. 14, 1939; children: Marie, Robert, Carol, Frances. Degree in Mech. and Aero. Engring., Stanford U., 1935. With NACA (name changed to NASA), Hampton, Va., 1936-70, Kitty Hawk Kites, Nags Head, N.C.; lectr. on high lift devices, lateral control, flexible wings and flow systems. Contbr. articles to profl. jours. Active Rogallo Found. Recipient NASA award, 1963, Nat. Air and Space Mus. trophy, Lifetime Achievement award Smithsonian Instn., 1992; named to N.C. Sports Hall of Fame, 1987. Mem. Am. Kite Assn., U.S. Hang Gliding Assn. Episcopalian. Home: 91 Osprey Ln Kitty Hawk NC 27949-3839 Office: Kitty Hawk Kites PO Box 1839 Nags Head NC 27959-1839

ROGERS, ARTHUR HAMILTON, III, lawyer; b. Florence, S.C., Apr. 19, 1945; s. Arthur Hamilton Jr. and Suzanne (Wilson) R.; m. Karen Lyn Hess, June 22, 1968; children: Sarah Elizabeth, Thomas Hess. BA, Rice U., 1967; JD, Harvard U., 1970. Bar: Tex. 1970. Assoc. Fulbright & Jaworski LLP, Houston, 1970-74; participating assoc. Fulbright & Jaworski L.L.P., Houston, 1974-77; ptnr. Fulbright & Jaworski, L.L.P., Houston, 1977—; gen. counsel Lifemark Corp., Houston, 1981-82; sec. Mosher, Inc., Houston, 1984—. Dir. Alley Theatre, Houston, 1990—, Autry House, 1994—; mem. exec. com. Rice U. Fund Coun., Houston, 1993—, vice-chair, 1996—. Mem. ABA, State Bar Tex., Assn. of Rice Alumni (treas. 1995—), Ramada-Tejas Club. Episcopalian. Home: 5309 Bordley Dr Houston TX 77056-2323 Office: Fulbright & Jaworski LLP 1301 Mckinney St Fl 51 Houston TX 77010

ROGERS, BARBARA JEAN (B.J. ROGERS), writer, editor; b. Chgo., Apr. 23, 1949; d. Louis Herman and Bernice (Millunchick) Block; m. Malcolm Leland Rogers Jr., Feb. 17, 1979; children: Anna Elizabeth, Sara Randall. BA cum laude, U. Ill., 1971. Freelance proofreader, copy editor, author Thomas Nelson Pubs., Nashville, 1979-94; v.p. Rogers Graphics, Nashville, 1980-82; proofreader, editor Typecraft Co., Nashville, 1982-88; editor publs. and design Vanderbilt U., 1993—; assoc. critic STAGES, 1991—; gen. mgr. Am. Negro Playwright Theatre, Nashville, 1992—; artistic staff asst. Tenn. Repertory Theatre, Nashville, 1990-93; cast mem., bus. mgr. So. Stage Prodns. and Tenn. Repertory Theatre, 1982, prodn. mgr., 1983, gen. mgr., 1985-86; studio booker, Soundshop, Inc., Nashville, 1977; nat. traffic mgr. Sammy & Co., 1975; post-prodn. coord. Studio Seven, Inc., Chgo., 1973-75; mem. libr. staff Chgo. Hist. Soc., 1968-71. Producer, dir. Nashville Arts Hrk Awards, Greater Nashville Arts Found., 1991, Hungry Ear Prodns., 1989. Founding mem. Tenn. Repertory Theatre Artistic Co., 1987; co-founder, artistic dir. Nashville Early Music Ensemble; founding pres. Nashville Opera Chorus, 1989, soprano, 1989—; house mgr., costume designer Dark Horse Theatre/Nashville Shakespeare Festival, 1990-92; costume designer Belmont U. Opera Workshop, Nashville, 1991—, Actors' Playhouse, Nashville, 1993; box office mgr. Kingston Mines Theatre, Gill Community Arts Ctr., Unity Theatre, Chgo., 1969-75; sec. Bellevue (Tenn.) Civic Coun., 1980-81; edn. ctr. dir. Heartlands Acad. Trust. Mem. AFTRA (bd. dirs. Nashville chpt. 1984-92), Actors' Equity Assn., Regional Orgn. Theatres South, Theatre Communications Group, Am. Internat. Reiki Assn.,

Nashville Entertainment Assn. Office: Vanderbilt U Publs Design 850 Baker Bldg 110 21st Ave S Nashville TN 37203-2416

ROGERS, BENJAMIN KIMBLE, music educator, composer; b. Ruston, La., June 5, 1949; s. James Thomas and Laura Nell (Colvin) R.; m. Virginia Ruth Robertson, Dec. 29, 1973 (div. Dec. 1975). MusB, So. Meth. U., 1971, MusM, 1974. Music instr. Eastfield Coll., Mesquite, Tex., 1971-72, Richland Coll., Richardson, Tex., 1972-75; head of guitar dept. So. Meth. U., Dallas, 1973-75; founder Ponderosa Poets, Ruston, 1986—, Ponderosa Pamphlet, Ruston, 1994; co-founder New Millenium Composers' Forum, Ruston, 1994; music therapist Opportunity House, 1990, Second Beginnings, 1994. Composer 55 songs, 1976—, 27 music opuses, 1969—; author: (books of poetry) Returning from the Pyramid, 1982, Crook in the Seam, 1984, The Zodiac, As a Gift, 1992; contbr. numerous poems to anthologies. Campaigner Dem. Party, Ruston, 1968-92. Unitarian. Home: 7254 Hwy 80 Ruston LA 71270-9233

ROGERS, BETTY GRAVITT, research company executive; b. Valdosta, Ga., June 24, 1945; d. Jim Aldine and Ruby Romell (Mann) Gravitt; m. Ennis Odean Rogers, May 8, 1967; children: Catheryne, Charles, Elizabeth, Susanne. Student, Fla. Community Coll., Jacksonville, 1988. Chief exec. officer Info. Rsch. Ctr., Inc., Jacksonville, 1982-96; co-mgr. Sizes Unltd., The Ltd., Tampa, Fla., 1982-96; visual merchandiser, sales cons. The Entertainer, Jacksonville, Fla., 1996—. Mem. Plan and City Bus. and Profl. Women's Club, Phi Theta Kappa, Beta Phi Gamma. Democrat. Methodist. Home: 3549 Chestnut Hill Ct Jacksonville FL 32223

ROGERS, BRENDA GAYLE, educational administrator, educator, consultant; b. Atlanta, July 27, 1949; d. Claude Thomas and Louise (Williams) Todd; m. Emanuel Julius Jones, Jr., Dec. 17, 1978; children: Lavelle, Brandon, Albre Jede, Briana Adanne. BA, Spelman Coll., 1970; MA, Atlanta U., 1971, EdS, 1972; PhD, Ohio State U., 1975; postgrad. Howard U., 1980, Emory U., 1986. Program devel. specialist HEW, Atlanta, 1972; rsch. assoc. Ohio State U., Columbus, 1973-75; asst. prof. spl. edn. Atlanta U., 1975-78, program adminstr., 1978—, CIT project dir., 1977-91, exec. dir. Impact project, 1992—; tech. cons. Dept. Edn., Washington, 1978-93, 96, cons. head start, 1990-91, cons. Gluction Teasting Svcs., 1996—; due process regional hearing officer Ga. State Dept. Edn., Atlanta, 1978-84, adv. bd., 1980-84; regional cons. Access Project, 1995—; mem. parent adv. coun. APS, 1988—; cons. program devel. Ga. Respite Care, Inc., 1988-89; mem. exec. bd., pres. PTA Stone Mountain Elem. Sch., 1989-92; mem. test verification panel Edn. Testing Svcs., Princeton, N.J., 1995-96. Mem. Ga. Assessment Project com., Atlanta Pub. Schs. Adv. Council, 1986—; bd. dirs. Mountain Pines Civic Assn., 1988—; mem. Grady Meml. Hosp. Community Action Network, Atlanta, 1982-83; exec. bd. PTA Shadow Rock Elem. Sch., 1992-94. Recipient disting. service award Atlanta Bur. Pub. Safety, 1982, disting. svcs. award Mountatin Sch. P.T.A., 1995, award Atlanta Pub. Sch. System, 1980, 82, 83, 89-90; fellow Ohio State U., 1972-74, Howard U., 1980; mem. Assn. for Retarded Citizens, Council for Exceptional Children, NAFE, Phi Delta Kappa, Phi Lambda Theta. Democrat. Roman Catholic. Avocation: gourmet cooking. Office: Clark Atlanta U James P Brawley Atlanta GA 30314-3913

ROGERS, C. B., lawyer; b. Birmingham, Ala., July 10, 1930; s. Claude B. Rogers and Doris (Hinkley) Rogers Lockerman; m. Patricia Maxwell DeVoe, Dec. 22, 1962; children: Bruce Lockerman, Evelyn Best, Brian DeVoe. A.B., Emory U., 1951, LL.B., 1953. Bar: Ga. 1953. Adj. prof. litigation Emory U., 1968-70; assoc., then partner firm Powell, Goldstein, Frazer & Murphy, 1954-76; partner firm Rogers & Hardin, Atlanta, 1976—. Fellow Am. Coll. Trial Lawyers; mem. Am. Law Inst., Capital City Club (Atlanta). Democrat. Episcopalian. Home: 1829 W Wesley Rd NW Atlanta GA 30327-2019 also: Brandon Mill Rd Lakemont GA 30335 Office: Rogers & Hardin 2700 Cain Tower 229 Peachtree St NE Atlanta GA 30303

ROGERS, C. B., JR., information services executive; b. 1930; married. B, Gettysburg Coll.; MBA, George Washington U. Sr. v.p. IBM, 1954-87; pres., COO Equifax Inc., 1987-89, CEO, 1989-92, chmn., 1992—, also bd. dirs. Office: Equifax Inc 1600 Peachtree St NE Atlanta GA 30309-2403*

ROGERS, CHARLES RAY, minister, religious organization administrator; b. Grapevine, Tex., Nov. 26, 1935; s. Arlin Avery and Bessie Lorene (Deaton) R.; m. Oma Fay Hines, Aug. 21, 1954; children: Sheree Gay Rogers Saberjissa, Charles Denne Ray, Robin Celeste Rogers Eddins. MS in Christian Edn., Faith Bible Coll., 1980, DD in Humanities (hon.), 1981; D of Ministry in Humanities (hon.), Sem. of Theol. Missions, Escuintla, Guatemala, 1992. Pastor various Bapt. chs., Athens, Dallas, Ft. Worth, 1960-64, various interdenominational chs., Houston, Longview, 1965-69; pres. Evangelism in Action, Ft. Worth, 1969—; bd. dirs. World Ministry Fellowship, Plano, Tex., dir. world missions, 1970—; leader Over 100 Mission, humanitarian trips Evangelism in Action, Ft. Worth, 1976—. Author: Joy, 1979, Handbook for Victorious Living, 1980, How to Develop Christian Love, 1981; vocalist (rec.) Charlie, 1981. Republican. Home: 6417 Rogers Dr Fort Worth TX 76180-4807 Office: Evangelism in Action PO Box 820724 Fort Worth TX 76182-0724

ROGERS, CHERYL LYNN, music and dance educator; b. Tyler, Tex., Sept. 14, 1949; d. Lewis Barton and Edna Elaine (Hunt) Whisenant; m. Carl Michael Rogers, May 23, 1971; children: Jennifer Leigh, Christopher Lewis. AA, Tyler Jr. Coll., 1969; B. Music Edn., North Tex. State U., 1971; MA, Stephen F. Austin State U., 1972. Math. instr. Kilgore (Tex.) Ind. Sch. Dist., 1972-73, jr. high choral dir., 1973-75; instr. music Tyler Jr. Coll., 1975-88, dir. music and dance, 1988—; dir. Concert Chorus, Chamber Singers, Harmony and Understanding, Tyler, 1980—; adjudicator All-Region, All-Area Vocal Auditions, Tyler, 1975—. Mem. Tyler Friends of the Gifted, 1990—; social com. mem. Hollytree Country Club, Tyler, 1989-90; mem. yearbook com. Women's Symphony League, Tyler, 1991-92; mem. adminstrv. bd. Marvin United Meth. Ch., Tyler, 1984—; yearbook commn. chmn. Kilgore Music Club, 1974-75. Grad. Teaching fellow Stephen F. Austin State U., 1971-72. Mem. Am. Choral Dirs. Assn., Tex. Music Educators Conf., Tex. Assn. Music Schs., Tex. Jr. Coll. Tchr. Assn., Nat. Assn. Tchrs. Singing, Tex. Choral Dirs. Assn., Mortar Bd., Alpha Chi, Pi Kappa Lambda, Phi Theta Kappa, Kappa Delta Pi Edn. Honor Soc. Republican. Office: Tyler Jr Coll PO Box 9020 Tyler TX 75711-9020

ROGERS, DEL MARIE, poet, editor; b. Washington, Apr. 11, 1936; d. Delbert Dodd Bruner and Jewel Marie Thomas; m. John R. Rogers (div.); children: Robert, Ruth, Cassie; m. Terence J. Hunt, (div.). BA in English and Philosophy, Baylor U., 1957; MA in English, Vanderbilt U., 1970. Mktg. tech. writer No. Telecom, Richardson, Tex., 1984-85, sr. tech. writer, 1985-87; sr. editor catalog advt. J.C. Penney, Plano, Tex., 1987-94, sr. copywriter, 1994—. Author: (chapbooks) Breaking Free, 1977, To the Earth, 1982, Origins, 1986, (pamphlet) A Course in Dreams, 1984, (book of poetry) Close to Ground, 1990; poetry editor: Café Solo; editor Firewheel Press; co-editor anthology of poems by contemporary women, 1975; contbr. poems to mags. and anthologies. Recipient NEA prize, 1970; poetry grantee NEA, 1974-75; Danforth fellow Vanderbilt U., teaching fellow Vanderbilt U., 1969-70. Mem. PEN U.S.A.-West, Poetry Soc. Am., Acad. Am. Poets. Democrat. Unitarian.

ROGERS, DENNEY H., building contractor; b. Ephesus, Ga., Mar. 24, 1959; s. Lonnie Lee and Vivian (Denney) R.; m. Karen Ann Pifer, Oct. 19, 1991. BA in Math., West Ga. Coll., 1980. Mgr. Rogers Lumber Co., Ephesus, 1977-85; owner Rogers Poultry Farm, Ephesus, 1976—; pres. L.L. Rogers and Son, Inc., Ephesus, 1985—. Mayor City of Ephesus, 1990—. Mem. Heard County Cattlemen's Assn. (v.p. 1985), Ga. FFA Alumni Assn. (dist. dir. 1996), Nat. Eagle Scout Assn., Heard County Lions (v.p. 1984). Democrat. Baptist. Home: 4137 Veal Rd Ephesus GA 30170 Office: LL Rogers and Son Inc 306 Robinson St Franklin GA 30217

ROGERS, EARL F., SR., automotive supply company executive; b. 1923. Gen. mgr. Rogers Auto Parts, 1940-43, 45-51, sole owner, 1951—. Office: Earl Rogers Co Inc 1002 Oak St Conway AR 72032-4353*

ROGERS, FRANCES EVELYN, author, retired educator and librarian; b. Mobile, Ala., Aug. 30, 1935; d. James Richard Graves and Jessie Reynolds (Butler) Lay; m. Jay Dee Rogers, Mar. 22, 1957; children: Laura, Larry. BA, North Tex. State U., 1957; MSLS, Our Lady of the Lake U., San Antonio, 1975. Cert. tchr., libr., Tex. Tchr. Ector County Ind. Sch. Dist., Odessa, Tex., 1958-59; social dir. svc. club Lackland AFB, San Antonio, 1960-61; tchr. San Antonio Ind. Sch. Dist., 1965-70; tchr., libr. Northside Ind. Sch. Dist., San Antonio, 1970-90, ret. Author: (hist. novels) Midnight Sins, 1989, Texas Kiss, 1989, Wanton Slave, 1990, Surrender to the Night, 1991, A Love So Wild, 1991, Sweet Texas Magic, 1992, Desert Fire, 1992, Desert Heat, 1993, Flame, 1994, Raven, 1995, Angel, 1995, Wicked, 1996; (hist. novels under name Keller Graves) Brazen Embrace, 1987, Rapture's Gamble, 1987, Desire's Fury, 1988, Velvet Vixen, 1988, Lawman's Lady, 1988. Sec., vol. Opera Guild San Antonio, 1980—. Recipient Spirit of Romance award Rom Con, 1996. Home: 2722 Belvoir Dr San Antonio TX 78230-4507

ROGERS, FRANCES NICHOLS, assistant principal; b. Fontana Dam, N.C., July 25, 1944; d. Fred Edward and Violet Bernice (Slagle) Nichols; m. Terry William Rogers, July 3, 1970. BA in English, Berea Coll., 1966; MA in Elem. Edn., U. Ky., 1968; postgrad., U. N.C., 1992. Tchr. intern Breathitt County Schs., Jackson, Ky., 1966-68; tchr. elem. sch. Haywood County Schs., Waynesville, N.C., 1968-72, resource program developer, 1972-75, 77-83, asst. prin., 1983-89, 92—, prin., 1989-92; pres. Haywood County Chpt. N.C. Edn. Assn., 1969-70. Author: Mount Zion United Methodist Church: A History 1850-1982, 1982; author of poems; contbr. articles to profl. jours. Mem. Friends of Libr., Waynesville, 1980—, Haywood Animal Welfare Assn., Waynesville, 1980—, Youth for Christ, Waynesville, 1980—. Named Outstanding Young Educator Waynesville Jaycees, 1968-69, Leader of Am. Elem. Edn., 1971. Mem. Tarheel Assn. Prins. and Adminstrs., Haywood County Prins. Assn., Internat. Reading Assn. (sec. local chpt. 1973-74). Methodist. Home: 120 Arrowood Acres Rd Clyde NC 28721-9751

ROGERS, GARRY LEE, minister, medical technician; b. Asheville, N.C., May 29, 1950; s. Kenneth Ledbetter and Annie Faye (Freeman) R.; m. Judy Gaynelle Plemmons, Octo. 6, 1973; children: Angela Dawn, Andrea Gaynelle, Steffan Garry, Shaana Lynette. EMT-IV Tech., Asheville Buncombe Tech. Coll., 1984; B of Ministry, Internat. Bible Sem., Plymouth, Fla., 1985; student N.T. Study Series, Moody Bible Inst., 1985; M in Bible Theology, Internat. Bible Sem., Plymouth, Fla., 1986, DD (hon.), 1986; cert., Fruitland Bapt. Bible Inst., 1994. Lic. to ministry So. Bapt. Conv., 1969, ordained, 1973. Music dir. New Liberty Bapt. Ch., Asheville, 1967-73, assoc. pastor, 1975-76; pastor Mt. Pleasant Bapt. Ch., Hot Springs, N.C., 1973-74, Jones Valley Bapt. Ch., Leicester, N.C., 1976-90, Emmanuel Bapt. Ch., Clyde, N.C., 1990—; med. technician Tempoe Inc., Asheville, 1983-93; sec. New Found. Bapt. Sunday Sch. Conv., Asheville, 1983-85, moderator, 1984-90; mem. gen. bd. Bapt. State Conv., Cary, N.C., 1984-87; trustee Christian Action League, Raleigh, N.C., 1987—, nominating com., 1994; chaplain West Buncombe Fire Dept., 1985-92, Erwin H.S. Bus. Dirvers Assn., 1986. Author: Prayer and Praying, 1986. Vol. fireman and EMT West Buncombe Fire Dept., Asheville, 1983—; pres. Olivette Cmty. Watch, Asheville, 1990—; mem. com. on coms. Haywood Bapt. Assn., 1994—, mem. orientation com., 1996—. Recipient Bold Mission 100% Increase in Giving award, Bold Mission 100% Increase in Baptisms award N.C. Bapt. Conv., 1977-82, 10 Yr. award West Buncombe Fire Dept., 1993. Mem. N.C. Firemans Assn., Buncombe County Sch. Bus Drivers Assn., N.C. Athletic Officials Assn. Democrat. Home: 520 Olivette Rd Asheville NC 28804-9672 Office: Emmanuel Bapt Ch 26 Weaver Dr Clyde NC 28721-9754

ROGERS, GLENDA MAE, quality assurance manager; b. Gadsden, Ala., Apr. 8, 1948; d. Henry and Clara Mae (Bishop) Parrish; m. Michael W. Rogers, Dec. 19, 1971 (div. May 1978); children: April, Shane. BS in Chemistry, Auburn U., 1970. Food chemist Gold Kist Rsch. Ctr., Lithonia, Ga., 1971-74; quality control supr. Jeno's Inc., Doraville, Ga., 1975-82; quality assurance mgr. So. Tea Co., Marietta, Ga., 1982-90; corp. quality assurance mgr. Tetley, Inc., Marietta, 1990—. Co-author: Jour. Am. Oil Chemists, 1991. Mem. Phi Kappa Phi. Republican. Southern Baptist. Office: Tetley Inc 1267 Cobb Industrial Dr Marietta GA 30066-6616

ROGERS, JAMES BENJAMIN, archivist, clergyman; b. Charleston, S.C., Nov. 4, 1944; s. Paul Henry and Louise (Watkins) R.; foster children, Rith Chhim, Sokhen Serey, Bophea Net, Roth Pin. Coll. of Charleston, 1967; M Ch. Music, Southwestern Sem., Ft. Worth, 1975, MDiv, 1979; MS in Info. Sci., U. North Tex., 1994. Cert. Vietnamese translator Def. Lang. Inst. Archival asst. Southwestern Sem., 1972-75, archivist, rare book libr., 1977-78; music min. 1st Bapt. Ch., Pharr, Tex., 1975-76; tchr. ESL, Oakhurst Sch., Ft. Worth, 1978-79; supr. tech. svcs. Baylor Crouch Music Libr., Waco, Tex., 1990-91; archivist, collections mgr. Baylor Collections Polit. Materials, Waco, 1991—; spkr. on ch. history Bapt. Gen. Conv. Tex., Dallas, 1987-88; tchr. ESL Adult Edn. Ctr., Waco, 1991-94. Editor: Cowboys, Cowtown and Crosses, 1986; contbr. articles to profl. jours. Pianist, tchr. Bible Templo Bautista Emanuel, Ft. Worth, 1977-82; missions educator Gambrell Street Ch., Ft. Worth, 1980-89, Cambodian min., 1984-89; active refugee settlement World Relief, Ft. Worth, 1984-89. With Security Agy., U.S. Army, 1967-71, Vietnam. Named to Hall of Honor, Tex. Bapt. Men, 1986. Mem. Soc. S.W. Archivists, Tex. Bapt. Hist. Collection an Soc. (archivist 1972-75, 77-78), Phi Kappa Phi, Beta Phi Mu. Home: 4409-B Stanley Ave Fort Worth TX 76115 Office: Baylor Collections Polit Materials 1000 University Parks Dr Waco TX 76798

ROGERS, JAMES CURTIS, publisher, psychologist; b. Sandston, Va., May 21, 1930; s. James Allen and Julia Pollard (Curtis) R. BA, U. Calif., Berkeley, 1961; BS, William and Mary Coll.; MA, Columbia Pacific, PhD. Sec., treas., CEO Rojet Theatre Co., Atlanta, 1954; prof. Capitol Radio and Electronics Inst., Washington, 1955; tech. writer Guided Missile Rocket dept. RCA Svc. Co., Alexandria, Va., Cherry Hill, N.J.; sec., treas., CEO Hawkeye Records, Iowa City, Iowa, 1961-63; tchr. Calvert County H.S., Prince Frederick, Md., 1964; child protective officer Social Svc. Bur., Richmond, Va., 1964-68; head master Lyceum Ednl. Com., Gloucester, Va., 1968-70; pub. Lyceum Publs., Richmond, Va., 1968-92; producer, agt. YoungStar Prodns., Richmond, 1989-91; pub., editor FutureWend Publs., Richmond, 1991—; ethics cons. The Matrism Orgn., Richmond, 1988—; publs. officer U.S. Coast GuardAux., Richmond, 1986-87. Author: Foreign Language With a Smile, 1965—, The Kidnapping, 1995; editor It's Your Choice Mag., 1993-95; author plays. Adminstr. Julie and Jim Rogers scholarship fund, Richmond, 1988—; scoutmaster Robert E. Lee Coun., Boy Scouts Am., Richmond, 1948-52, sea scout skipper, 1948-52; dir. Children's Theatre Project, Berkeley, 1959. Mem. Thalian Soc., Am. Inst. Hypnosis, Coll. Med. Hypnotists. Office: FutureWend Publs PO Box 7135 Richmond VA 23221-0135

ROGERS, JAMES EDWARD, paper company executive; b. Richmond, Va., Aug. 13, 1945; s. Olin Adair and Marjorie (Aiken) R.; children: James Edward Jr., Catherine, Margaret. BS in Physics, Va. Mil. Inst., 1967; MS in Nuclear Engring., U. Va., 1969; postgrad., Harvard U., 1987. Licensing engr. Va. Electric and Power Co., Richmond, 1969-71; sales engr., sales mgr., v.p. sales and mktg. James River Paper Co., Richmond, 1971-77, 79-82, sr. v.p., gen. mgr., 1977-82; v.p. corp. devel., 1982-87; sr. v.p., group exec., specialty paper bus. James River Corp., Richmond, 1987-92; pres., CEO Specialty Coatings Intl., Richmond, 1992-93; pres. SCI Investors Inc., Richmond, 1993—; chmn., bd. dirs. Custom Papers Group Inc., Richmond; bd. dirs. Owens and Minor, Inc., Richmond, Wellman, Inc., Shrewsbury, N.J., Caraustar Industries, Inc., Austell, Ga., Marine Devel. Corp., Richmond. Bd. dirs. Richmond Childrens Mus., Maymont Found., Richmond, 1987; mem. men's adv. coun. Va. Home, Richmond, Commonwealth Girl Scouts. Mem. Pub. Affairs Group, Storm Trysail Club. Republican. Clubs: Commonwealth (Richmond); Fishing Bay Yacht (Deltaville, Va.) (commodore 1980); N.Y. Yacht (N.Y.C.). Office: SCI Investors Inc 101 Shockoe Slip Ste O Richmond VA 23219

ROGERS, JAMES EDWIN, geology and hydrology consultant; b. Waco, Tex., Feb. 24, 1929; s. Charles Watson and Jimmie (Harp) R.; m. Margaret Anna Louise Bruchmann, Oct. 10, 1957; 1 child, James Fredrick. Student, Rice U., 1947-49, Baylor U., 1953; BS, U. Tex., 1955, MA, 1961. Geologist U.S. Geol. Survey, St. Paul, 1956-59; geologist U.S. Geol. Survey, Alexandria, La., 1959-63, supervisory hydrologist, 1963-85; ind. cons. Alexandria, 1985—; cons. geol. survey for map State of La., Baton Rouge, 1982-85. Author: Water Resources of Kisatchie Well-Field Area Near Alexandria, Louisiana, 1981, Preconstruction and Simulated Postconstruction Ground-Water Levels at Urban Centers in the Red River Navigation Project Area, Louisiana, 1983, Red River Waterway Project - Summary of Ground-Water Studies by the U.S. Geological Survey, 1962-85, 1988; co-author: Water Resources of Vernon Parish, Louisiana, 1965, Water Resources of Ouachita Parish, Louisana, 1972, Water Resources of the Little River Basin, Louisana, 1973. Scoutmaster Boy Scouts Am., Alexandria, 1971, 72. Sgt. U.S. Army, 1950-52, Japan. Mem. Assn. Ground Water Scientists and Engrs., Geol. Soc. Am., Gem Mineral and Lapidary Soc. Ctrl. La. (pres. 1972, 86-87, 94-96), Baton Rouge Geol. Soc., Phi Beta Kappa. Presbyterian. Home and Office: 4008 Innis Dr Alexandria LA 71303-4738

ROGERS, JAMES GORDON, JR., art educator; b. Dec. 16, 1944. AB in English, U. Mo., 1967, MA in Art History and Archaeology, 1983, PhD, 1989. Teaching asst. dept. art history and archeology U. Mo., Columbia, 1977-83, 89; asst. prof. art history William Woods Coll., Fulton, Mo., 1989-90; prof. art history Savannah (Ga.) Coll. Art & Design, 1990-92; asst. prof. art Florida So. Coll., Lakeland, Fla., 1992—; adj. asst. prof. Sch. Arch. and Comty. Design, U. South Fla., 1995—; cons. The Design Ctr., 1977—; lectr. in field. Contbr. articles to profl. jours. Mem. peer rev. com. Fla. Arts Coun.; past bd. dirs. Mid-Mo. chpt. Am. Heart Assn., Sta KBIA Pub. Radio, Columbia, Mo., Columbia Art League, also co-chmn. finance com.; active Nat. Holocaust Meml. Mus. Mem. AAUP, Am. Soc. Hispanic Art Hist. Studies, Soc. Archtl. Historians, Coll. Art Assn. Office: Fla So Coll Lake Hollingsworth Dr Lakeland FL 33803

ROGERS, JAMES TRACY, JR., bank examiner; b. Hazard, Ky., Oct. 14, 1941; s. James T. Rogers and Emma Elizabeth Callahan; m. Vivian Eversole, June 10, 1962 (div. Aug. 1988); children: Goldea Janine, James Samuel; m. Olga M. Rondem, Feb. 3, 1990. BS in Bus. Edn., Ea. Ky. Univ., 1967. Cert. info. system auditor. Tchr. Harrison County Schs., Cynthiana, Ky., 1967-69; asst. nat. bank examiner Comptroller of Currency, Richmond, Ky., 1969-70; asst. nat. bank examiner Comptroller of Currency, Indpls., 1970-78, nat. bank examiner, 1978-80; nat. bank examiner Comptroller of Currency, Houston, 1980—. Mem. EDP Auditors Assn. (cert. info. sys. auditor). Home: 727 Saddlewood Cir Spring TX 77381-1057 Office: Comptroller of Currency 1000 Louisiana St Ste 930 Houston TX 77002-5008

ROGERS, JAMES VIRGIL, JR., retired radiologist and educator; b. Johnson City, Tenn., Oct. 7, 1922; s. James Virgil and Mary Ruth (Collins) R.; m. Mildred Vandivere, June 9, 1945 (div. 1985); children: Rebecca Jean, James V. III, Janet Marie, Susan Margaret; m. Mary Lujean Craven, Mar. 18, 1989. BS, Emory U., 1943, MD, 1945. Intern Kings County Hosp., N.Y.C., 1945-46; resident in radiology Grady Meml. Hosp., Altanta, 1947-48, Emory U. Hosp., Altanta, 1948-50; instr. Emory U. Sch. Medicine, Atlanta, 1950-51, assoc., 1950-53, asst. prof., 1954-60, assoc. prof., 1960-64, prof., 1965-93; ret.; chief radiology svc. Emory U. Hosp., Atlanta, 1971-80, vice chmn. dept. radiology 1973-78, acting chmn., 1978-80; dep. sect. head Emory Clinic, Atlanta, 1971-78, sect. head, 1978-80, chief radiology svc., 1982-91; cons. radiology 3d Army Hdqrs., Atlanta; examiner Am. Bd. Radiology, 1970-79, site inspector for residency programs, 1972-83. Contbr. articles to profl. jours. Pres. PHRC Ga., Atlanta, 1990. 1st lt. U.S. Army, 1946-47. Fellow Am. Coll. Radiology (councilor); mem. Radiol. Soc. North Am., Am. Roentgen Ray Soc., So. Radiologic Conf. (past pres.), Ga. Radiologic Soc. (past pres.), Atlanta Radiologic Soc. (past. pres.), AMA, So. Med. Assn. (past pres. radiology sect.), Druid Hills Golf Club, Am. Legion. Republican. Methodist. Home: 3810 Shore Blvd Oldsmar FL 34677

ROGERS, JANE HOOKS, insurance agent; b. Princeton, Ky., Feb. 15, 1941; d. Samuel Forest and Margaret (Cook) Hooks; m. Don R. Rogers, June 20, 1959; 1 child, Joel Craig. BS magna cum laude, Murray State U., 1971, MA in Edn., 1972. Office mgr., legal sec. Edward H. Johnstone Law Offices, Princeton, Ky., 1960-67; office mgr. Dist. Office Frank A. Stubblefield U.S. Congress, Murray, Ky., 1967-73; instr. U. Ky., Paducah Community Coll., 1973-75; instr., coord. of coop. & experiential edn. Murray (Ky.) State U., 1975-80; ins. agt. Jane Rogers State Farm Ins., Murray, Ky., 1980—; cons. U. South Fla. Coop. Edn. Ctr. Mem. Murray Civic Music Assn., 1980—, sec., treas. 1990. Mem. AAUW (pres. Murray, Ky. 1987-89), Murray Life Underwriters' Assn. (pres. 1985), Coop. Edn. Assn. of Ky. (oustanding contbn. award 1977, pres. 1979-80), Gideons Internat. Aux. (pres. Murray, Ky 1986). Democrat. Baptist. Home: 1205 Dogwood Dr E Murray KY 42071-3252 Office: Jane Rogers State Farm Ins PO Box 408 305 N 12th St Ste B Murray KY 42071

ROGERS, JOE O'NEAL, international mangement consultant; b. Oklahoma City, Dec. 4, 1948; s. Joe O'Neal Rogers and Bette Ruth (Morris) Weber; m. Joanna Catherine Parish Scott, June 28, 1976; children: Sean, Michael, Andrea, Sam, Ashley, Katherine. BA in Econs. and Philosophy, U. Okla., 1971; MA in Econs., Duke U., 1974, PhD in Econs., 1978. Instr. Duke U., Durham, N.C., 1973; lectr. U. of Western Australia, Perth, 1974-76; asst. prof. Wake Forest U., Winston-Salem, N.C., 1977-78; exec. dir. Task Force on Econ. Policy, Washington, 1979-80; chief economist Sen. W. Armstrong, Washington, 1980-81; exec. dir. House Rep. Conf., Washington, 1981-84; amb., exec. dir. Asian Devel. Bank, Manila, Philippines, 1984-86; pres. Rogers Internat., Vienna, Va., 1986—; ptnr. PHH Fantus Cons., Hunt Valley, Md., 1993-96; chairperson, CEO Asian Core Advisors, 1996—; dir. The China Fund Inc., Hong Kong, 1992—, The Taiwan Fund, Inc., Taipei, 1986—; internat. adv. bd. Selinger, Sch. of Bus., Loyola U., Balt., 1995—; chmn. Asian Bus. Network, WTCI, Balt., 1995—.

ROGERS, JOHN ALVIN, retired technical educator, writer, publisher; b. Dennison, Ohio, Dec. 19, 1946; s. William Arlington and Friedarika Albestina (Schulte) R. B of Gen. Studies, N.Mex. Inst. Mining and Tech., 1974; MS in Resource Geography, Oreg. State U., 1976; postgrad., U. Ariz., 1982. Reporter The Evening Chronicle, 1974; cons. writer Forest Service Research Lab, USDA, Corvallis, Oreg., 1976; rsch. assoc. divsn. econ. and bus. rsch. U. Ariz., Tucson, 1977, rsch. assoc. engring. experiment sta., 1977-78, rsch. assoc. Water Research Ctr., 1979, rsch. assoc. Sch. Renewable Natural Resources, 1980-81, rsch. assoc. libr. dept. acquisitions, 1981-82; intern Pima County Assn. Govts., Tucson, 1979; engring. asst. divsn. environ. health Pima County Health Dept., 1980; tutor writing Pima Community Coll., 1982-83, assoc. faculty dept. writing, teaching asst. dept. reading, 1983-84; tech. writer Hamilton Test Systems, Tucson, 1984; sr. tech. writer E-Systems, Inc., Greenville, Tex., 1985-91; adj. prof. geography Tyler (Tex.) Jr. Coll., 1991; ind. cons. documentation and rsch. svcs. Tyler, 1992-93; edn. materials specialist Avalon Software, Tucson, 1993-94; pres. Sci. Probes Tech. Writing, Publ., and Tng. Svcs., Tucson, 1994—; vol. facilitator pub. participation program Pima County Planning Dept., 1978; mem. So. Ariz. Environ. Coun., 1982-85, editor bull., 1982-84, rep. basin study com. 1983-84, pres., 1982-83, chair program and edn. 1983-84; vol. hydrologist Ariz. Land Dept., Tucson, 1983; reader grants Tandy Corp., Tucson, 1983; cons. environmentalist Tex Com. on Natural Resources, 1989-93. Editor Wordsmith's Forge Quar., 1991-93; contbr. articles and papers to profl. publs. Vol. leader wildlife and ecology project Hunt and Rockwall Counties (Tex.) 4-H, 1985-90. With USN, 1967-71, Vietnam, with Res. Mem. VFW, Noncommd. Officers Assn. (life), Vietnam Vets Am. (life), Audubon Soc. (coord. field trips Tucson chpt. 1994), Nature Conservancy, Mus. Natural History. Home: 4716 W Knollside St Tucson AZ 85741-4630

ROGERS, JON MARTIN, financial consultant, financial company executive; b. Piedmont, S.C., June 4, 1942; s. James Robert and Eunice (Ashley) R.; m. E. Jeanette Owen, June 16, 1962; children: E. Elaine, Jonette Marie, Melissa Anne. BS, Clemson U., 1964, MS, 1966; PhD in Fin. Mgmt., LaSalle U., 1994. CLU, Chartered Fin. Cons. Sales rep. Met. Life, Greenville, S.C., 1969-71; dist. sales mgr. Met. Life, Atlanta, 1972-74; regional sales mgr. Met. Life, Milw., 1975-81, Liberty Corp., Greenville, 1982-88; chmn. bd., chief exec. officer Charter Fin. Group, Greenville, 1989—; ptnr. J&J Enterprises, Piedmont, S.C., 1975—; registered securities rep. Royal Alliance Assocs., Inc., N.Y.C., 1986—; adj. prof. Webster U. Mem. C. of C., Greenville, 1985-86; pres. Rep. Party precinct, Piedmont, 1988; bd. dirs. Optomist Club, Greenville, 1985; deacon, chmn. Washington Ch., Pelzer, S.C., 1985-87, 93-94. Capt. U.S. Army, 1967-69, Vietnam. Decorated Bronze Star. Mem. Nat. Assn. Life Underwriters (v.p. 1972-73, recipient awards), Internat. Assn. Fin. Planners, Nat. Assn. Securities Dealers, Million Dollar Round Table, Gideons Internat. Club (S.C. pres. 1985-87), Child

Evangelism Fellowship (bd. dirs. 1988-89), Rotary Internat. (bd. dirs., pres. 1996-97). Baptist. Home: 21 Fairway Dr Piedmont SC 29673-9167 Office: Charter Fin Group Inc 1 Whitsett St Greenville SC 29601-3136

ROGERS, KENNETH ALLAN, social sciences educator; b. Hyannis, Mass., July 17, 1946; s. Kenneth O. and Marguerite L. (Vincent-Wade); m. Donna Lynn Hodges; children: Christina Marie, Angela Lyn; 1 stepchild, April Lynn McKenney. BS in Meteorology, U. Okla., 1970; MA in Internat. Affairs, Calif. State U., 1976; PhD in Internat. Rels., Am. U., 1982. Commd. 2d lt. USAF, 1970, advanced through grades to lt. col., 1986, Russian lang. specialist, 1967-68; weather forecaster USAF, Heidelberg, Germany, 1970-74; Soviet/East European analyst Pentagon, Washington, 1977-81; Internat. Politico-Mil. Affairs Officer USAF, Washington, 1981-83; dir. comparative and area studies USAF Acad., Colorado Springs, Colo., 1984-89, ret., 1989; prof. Ark. Tech. U., Russellville, 1989—; INF Treaty chief U.S. Inspection team Soviet missile facilities, 1988, 89; faculty senate Ark. Tech. U., 1992-93, chair, 1993-94, mission statement rev. com., 1993-94, gen. edn. core rev. com., 1993-94, assessment com., 1993-94, budget com. 1993-94, edn. reform steering com., 1992-94, mid. level alliance, 1992-94, multi-cultural and internat. affairs com., 1990-93, faculty welfare com., 1990-93, sec., 1992-93, others. Contbr. numerous articles to profl. jours. presenter various civic organizations and local schs. Postdoctoral rsch. fellowship U. Edinburgh, 1983-84. Mem. Internat. Studies Assn. (exec. com. Am.-Soviet rels. sect. 1990-93, co-editor newsletter 1987-91, program organizer ann. conf. 1986, 91). Office: Ark Tech U Dept Social Scis Philosophy Russellville AR 72801-2222

ROGERS, KENNETH R., broadcaster, child care center owner; b. Tennell, Ga., Apr. 15, 1942; s. Harley Levi and Corliss (Kinsey) R.; m. Elizabeth P. McClain, May 4, 1965; children: Eric C., Alison M. BA, Clemson U., 1964; MBA, U. S.C., Spartanburg, 1970. Program dir. WAIM Radio-TV, Anderson, S.C., 1965-68; mgr. Multimedia Broadcasting, Greenville, S.c, 1971-90; dept. head Greenville Tech. U. Greenville, S.C., 1973-77; chmn. S.C. Child Coun., S.C. Child Care Assn., Columbia, S.C., 1982-88. Composer This Masquerade, Give Me the Night. Chmn. Greenville Symphony, 1978-82, United Way, Pickens County, S.C., 1993-95, Republican Party of Pickens County, 1994—. Grammy award Am. Music Assn., N.Y.C., 1977, York award, BMI, N.Y.C., 1978. Home: 201 Lena Dr Easley SC 29640 Office: 100 Cross Hill Rd Greenville SC 29607

ROGERS, LON B(ROWN), retired lawyer; b. Pikeville, Ky., Sept. 5, 1905; s. Fon and Ida (Brown) R.; BS, U. Ky., 1928, LLB, 1932; LHD (hon.), Pikeville Coll., 1979, LHD (hon.) Centre Coll. of Ky., 1992; m. Mary Evelyn Walton, Dec. 17, 1938; children: Marylon Walton, Martha Brown, Fon II. Bar: Ky. 1932. Practiced law in Lexington, 1932-38, Pikeville, 1939-80. Dir. East Ky. Beverage Co., Pikeville, 1940-90, Pikeville Nat. Bank & Trust Co., 1979-95. Elder, 1st Presbyterian Ch, Pikeville, Ky., 1947-75; mem. Pikeville City Council, 1951; mem. local bd. SSS, 1958-69; mem. Breaks Interstate Park Commn., Ky.-Va., 1960-68, chmn., 1960-62, 64-66, vice chmn., 1966-68; chmn. Community Services Commn., Pikeville Model Cities, 1969-71; mem. Ky. Arts Commn., 1965-72, Ky. Travel Council, 1967-70, 73-75; pres. Ky. Mountain Laurel Festival Assn., 1971-72. Chmn. bd. trustees Presbytery Ebenezer, U.S.A., 1950-71; trustee Pikeville Coll., 1951-72, 73-79, trustee emeritus, 1979—; trustee Presbytery of Transylvania, 1971-83; mem. bd. nat. missions United Presbyn. Ch. USA, 1954-66; trustee Appalachian Regional Hosps., Inc., 1963-67, Ky. Ind. Coll. Found., 1973-82; bd. dirs. Meth. Hosp. of Ky., 1966-82; mem., Presbyn. Ch., Lexington, 1982—, trustee, 1989-91; am. mem., trustee 2nd Presbyterian Ch.. Mem. Ky. C. of C. (regional v.p. 1962-64, 69-74), Ky. Hist. Soc., S.A.R., Civil War Round Table, Blue Grass Kiwanis (past lt. gov.), Filson Club, Blue Grass Automobile (pres. 1971-74, dir.), Sigma Alpha Epsilon, Phi Delta Phi. Republican. Home: 505 E Main St Lexington KY 40508-2309 Office: 300 E Main St Ste 403 Lexington KY 40507-1539

ROGERS, LON EDMOND, physician; b. Girard, Tex., Oct. 13, 1934; s. Paul Sone Rogers and Gladys Kidd (Fowler) Bird. BA, U. North Tex., Denton, 1955; MD, U. Tex., Dallas, 1959. Diplomate Am. Bd. Pediatrics, Am. Bd. Dermatology. Intern Robert Green Hosp., San Antonio, Tex., 1959-60; resident in pediatrics Children's Med. Ctr., Dallas, 1960-62; asst. prof. medicine U. Tex. Southwestern Med. Sch., Dallas, 1968-74; resident in dermatology Parkland Meml. Hosp., Dallas, 1974-76; pvt. practice medicine Dallas, 1976—. Contbr. articles to med. jours. Served to capt. USAF, 1962-64. Fellow Am. Acad. Dermatology. Office: 7777 Forest Ln Ste B216 Dallas TX 75230-2509

ROGERS, MARK CHARLES, physician, educator; b. N.Y.C., Oct. 25, 1942; s. Gerald and Inez (Kaufman) R.; m. Elizabeth Ann London, Dec. 30, 1972; children: Bradley, Meredith. BA, Columbia U., 1964; MD, SUNY, Syracuse, 1969; MBA, U. Pa., 1991; PhD (hon.), U. Ljubljana Slovenia, 1995. Diplomate Am. Bd. Anesthesiology (examiner 1982—), Am. Bd. Pediatrics. Intern Mass. Gen. Hosp., Boston, 1969-70, resident, 1973-75; resident Boston Children's Hosp., 1970-71; fellow Duke U. Med. Ctr., Durham, N.C., 1971-73; asst. prof. dept. anesthesiology and critical care medicine Johns Hopkins U., Balt., 1977-79, assoc. prof., 1979-80, prof., chmn. dept., 1980-93, assoc. dean Sch. Medicine, 1990-93, dir. pediatric ICU, 1977-93; CEO Duke Hosp. and Health Network, 1993-96; sr. v.p. Perkin Elmer, Wilton, Conn., 1996—; pres. Critical Care Found., Balt., 1981-96; cons. WHO, Bangkok, 1982-83. Editor in chief: Yearbook of Critical Care, 1983-96, Textbook of Pediatric Intensive Care, 1987, 91, 96, Principles and Practices of Anesthesiology, 1990; editor: Perioperative Management, 1989, dep. editor in chief Critical Care Medicine Jour., 1990-96. Maj. U.S. Army, 1975-77. Recipient Club of Mainz award, Mainz, Fed. Republic of Germany, 1981, award Assn. Univ. Anesthetists, 1980; Fulbright scholar, Ljubljana, Yugoslavia, 1990. Mem. Inst. Medicine. Home: 4406 W Cornwallis Rd Durham NC 27705-8126 Office: Perkin Elmer 50 Danbury Rd Wilton CT 06897

ROGERS, MICHAEL BRUCE, orthodontist; b. Augusta, Ga., Oct. 25, 1945; s. Bruce Latimer and Dorothy (Baird) R.; m. Elizabeth Bennett, Dec. 21, 1968; children: Bruce, Kay, Alison, Lisa. Student, Emory U., 1963-65, DDS, 1969; cert. in Orthodontics, Med. Coll. Ga., 1973. Diplomate Am. Bd. Orthodontists. Pvt. practice orthodontia, Augusta, Ga., 1973—; part-time asst. clin. prof. Sch. Dentistry, Med. Coll. Ga., Augusta, 1973—. Capt. Dental Corps U.S. Army, 1971-73. Fellow Internat. Acad. Dental Studies, Am. Coll. Dentists, Ga. Dental Assn. (hon.), Pierre Fauchard Acad., The Internat. Acad. of Dentists; mem. ADA (del.), Am. Assn. Orthodontists (Ga. del., chmn. mem., ethics and judicial concerns, spkr. of house 1996—, bd. trustees), So. Assn. Orthodontists (spokesperson, sec.-treas. 1993-95, dir. 1995), Eastern Dist. Dental Soc. (pres. 1982-83), Ga. Soc. Orthodontists (v.p. 1983-84, pres. 1984-85), Med. Coll. Ga. Orthodontic Alumni Assn. (pres. 1981-83), Augusta Dental Soc. (pres. 1986-87), Psi Omega (pres. 1967-68), Omicron Kappa Upsilon. Roman Catholic. Avocations: golf, boating. Home: 3214 Candace Dr Augusta GA 30909-3259 Office: 3545 Wheeler Rd Augusta GA 30909-6517

ROGERS, NORMA ELIA MARTÍNEZ, nursing educator; b. San Antonio, Jan. 15, 1944; d. Jesse R. and Estela (Chavez) Martinez; m. William L. Rogers (dec.); children: Sean William, Scott Lewis. BSN, Incarnate Word Coll., San Antonio, 1965; MA in Counseling, St Mary's U., San Antonio, 1968; MS in Nursing, U. Tex., San Antonio, 1978; PhD, U. Tex., Austin, 1995. RN, Tex. Assoc. prof. San Antonio Coll.; dir. psychiat. nursing Laurel Ridge Hosp., San Antonio, Villa Rosa Hosp., San Antonio; mem. faculty U. Tex. Health Sci. Ctr.-San Antonio Sch. Nursing. Maj. Nurse Corps, U.S. Army.

ROGERS, OSCAR ALLAN, JR., college president; b. Natchez, Miss., Sept. 10, 1928; s. Oscar Allan and Maria Pinkie (Jackson) R.; m. Ethel Lee Lewis, Dec. 20, 1950; children—Christopher, Christian, Christoff. A.B., Tougaloo Coll., 1950; S.T.B., Harvard U., 1953, M.A.T., 1954; Ed.D., U. Ark., 1960; postgrad. U. Wash., 1968-69; LHD (hon.), Oklahoma City U., 1992,. Ordained to ministry Congl. Ch., 1953, Baptist Ch., 1955, Methodist Ch., 1962. Asst. pastor St. Mark Congl. Ch., Roxbury, Mass., 1951-54; dean-registrar Natchez Jr. Coll., Miss., 1954-56; pres. Ark. Bapt. Coll., Little Rock, 1956-59; dean students prof. social sci. and edn. Jackson State U., Miss., 1960-68, dean Grad. Sch., 1969-84; pres. Claflin Coll., 1984-94, pres. emeritus, 1994—; postdoctoral fellow U. Wash., Seattle, 1968-69; pastor Asbury-Kingsley Charge, Bolton and Edwards (Miss.) United Meth. Ch., 1962-84, Merton (Miss) Cir. United Meth. Chs., 1994-96. Served with USN, 1946-47. Recipient Order of the Palmetto Gov. Campbell (S.C.), 1994. Mem. Conf. Deans of Black Grad. Schs. (pres. 1975-76, treas. 1979-84), AAUP, NAACP, Phi Delta Kappa, Kappa Delta Pi, Alpha Phi Alpha. Democrat. Author: My Mother Cooked My Way Through Harvard with These Creole Recipes, 1973; Mississippi: The View from Tougaloo, 1979. Home and Office: 5932 Holbrook Dr Jackson MS 39206-2003

ROGERS, RAGAN, fundraiser; b. Tulsa, Okla., Aug. 11, 1948; d. Elmer J. and Wilda P. (Studebaker) Chandley. Cert. fund raising exec. Program dir. Okla. Bapt. U., Shawnee, 1972-76; dir. devel. Planned Parenthood, Houston, 1976-77; v.p. Viletta Corp., Houston, 1978-84; dir. devel. Children's Home San Antonio, 1984-85; v.p. Children's Med. Found., Dallas, 1986-91; pres. Rogers & Assocs., Dallas, 1991—; career mktg. bd. Mademoiselle. Bd. dirs. TACA, Dallas, 1987-95; mem. adv. bd. Assistance League, Dallas, 1987-91; hon. life mem. Women's Aux.-Children's Med., Dallas, 1989. Mem. Nat. Soc. Fundraising Execs. (bd. dirs. Dalls chpt. 1988-94, pres. 1993), Phi Theta Kappa. Office: Rogers & Assocs 2510 Ashbury Ct Grand Prairie TX 75050

ROGERS, RALPH B., industrial business executive; b. Boston, 1909; married. Ed., Northeastern U. With Cummins Diesel Engine Corp., Edwards Co., Hill Diesel Engine Co., Ideal Power Lawnmower Co., Indian Motocycle Co., Rogers Diesel & Aircraft Corp., Rogers Internat. Corp., Armstrong Rubber Export Corp.; with Tex. Industries Inc., Dallas, 1950—, chmn. bd., pres., CEO, 1951-75, chmn. bd., 1975—; dir. numerous subsidiaries. Chmn. bd. dirs. Tex. Industries Found.; chmn. emeritus Pub. Communication Found. North Tex., Pub. Broadcasting Svc., Univ. Med. Ctr., Inc.; past bd. dirs. Nat. Captioning Inst.; trustee Northeastern U.; trustee, chmn. emeritus St. Mark's Sch. of Tex.; former chmn. bd. mgrs. Dallas County Hosp. Dist.; founding chmn., chmn. emeritus Dallas Arboretum and Bot. Soc.; pres. Dallas Found. for Health, Edn. and Rsch.; co-founder Children's TV Workshop; founder, chmn. Zale Lipshy Univ. Hosp. Mem. Masons. Office: Tex Industries Inc 1341 W Mockingbird Ln Ste 700W Dallas TX 75247-6905

ROGERS, RICHARD HILTON, hotel company executive; b. Florence, S.C., May 26, 1935; s. Leslie Lawton and Bessie (Holloway) R.; m. Evelyn Pascuito; children: Richard Shannon, Leslie Anne. Student, U. N.C., 1953-55; BA in Bus. Adminstrn. cum laude, Bryant Coll., 1962; postgrad., Memphis State U., 1964. Innkeeper Helmsley Spear, N.Y.C., 1961-62; v.p. Holiday Inns of Am., Memphis, 1962-73; exec. v.p. First Hospitality Corp., Hackensack, N.J., 1974-77; v.p., chief oper. officer Cindy's Inc., Atlanta, 1978-81; v.p. 1982 World's Fair, Knoxville, Tenn.; pres., chief exec. officer Hospitality Internat., Atlanta, 1982-92; dir. franchise devel. Budgetel Inns, Norcross, Ga., 1992—; developer, operator The Warehouse Rest., Oxford, Miss., 1973-75, Beauregard's Rest., Hattiesburg, Miss., 1975-78, Walter Mitty's Rest., Auburn, Ala., 1980-83. Contbr. to profl. jours. Mem. adv. bd. Bethune-Cookman Coll. With USN, 1954-58, Korea. Mem. Am. Hotel/Motel Assn. (mktg. com. 1986-92, adv. coun. 1987-92, industry adv. bd.), Economy Lodging Coun. Home: 245 Rhine Dr Alpharetta GA 30202-5455 Office: Budgetel Inns 6855 Jimmy Carter Blvd Ste 2150 Norcross GA 30084*

ROGERS, RUTHERFORD DAVID, librarian; b. Jesup, Iowa, June 22, 1915; s. David Earl and Carrie Zoe (Beckel) R.; m. E. Margaret Stoddard, June 4, 1937; 1 child, Jane Shelley. B.A., U. No. Iowa, 1936, Litt.D., 1977; M.A., Columbia, 1937, B.S. (Lydia Roberts fellow), 1938; D.Library Adminstrn. (hon.), U. Dayton, 1971. Asst. N.Y. Pub. Library, 1937-38; reference librarian Columbia Coll. Library, Columbia U., 1938- 41, acting librarian, 1941-42, librarian, 1942-45; research analyst Smith, Barney & Co., N.Y.C., 1946-48; dir. Grosvenor Library, Buffalo, 1948-52, Rochester Pub. Library, 1952-54; chief personnel office N.Y. Library, 1954-55; chief reference dept., 1955-57; chief asst. librarian of Congress, Washington, 1957-62; dep. librarian of Congress, 1962-64; dir. univ. libraries Stanford U., 1964-69; univ. librarian Yale U., 1969-85, univ. librarian emeritus, 1985—; dir. H.W. Wilson Co., 1969—; founder, chmn. bd. dirs. Rsch. Librs. Group, Inc.; mem. Exam. Com. for Pub. Librarians' Certs., N.Y. State, 1951-54; mem. U.S. Adv. Coun. Coll. Libr. Resources; bd. govs. Yale U. Press; bd. dirs., v.p. H.W. Wilson Found., 1995—; chmn. program mgmt. com. Internat. Fedn. Libr. Assns. Author: Columbia Coll. Library Handbook, 1941, (with David C. Weber) University Library Administration, 1971; also articles in profl. jours. Served from pvt. to 1st sgt. Air Transp. Command USAAF, 1942-43; from 2d lt. to capt., planning officer, chief, spl. Planning Div., Office Asst. Chief Staff, Plans, Air Transport Command 1943-46. Decorated officier de L'Ordre de la Couronne Belge; recipient U. No. Iowa Alumni Achievement award, 1958, Disting. Alumni award Columbia U. Sch. Libr. Svc., 1992. Fellow Am. Acad. Arts and Scis.; mem. A.L.A. (chmn. com. Intellectual Freedom 1950-51), (1950-60), (2d v.p. 1965-66), (mem. exec. bd. 1961-66), (trustee endowment fund), Assn. Research Libraries (dir., pres. 1967-68), N.Y. Library Assn., AAUP, Bibliog. Soc. Am., Assn. Coll. and Reference Libraries, Blue Key, Kappa Delta Pi, Sigma Tau Delta, Theta Alpha Phi. Clubs: Grolier; N.Y. Library (N.Y.C.), Columbia U. (N.Y.C.), Yale (N.Y.C.); Cosmos (Washington), Kenwood Country (Washington); Roxburghe (San Francisco); Book of Calif. Home: 1111 S Lakemont Ave Apt 605 Winter Park FL 32792-5474

ROGERS, RYNN MOBLEY, community health nurse; b. Georgetown, S.C., Aug. 2, 1950; d. Ralph Edward and Pearl (Hill) Mobley; m. C. Rogers Jr., July 3, 1971 (div. Mar. 1992); 1 child, Julie Pearl. Student, Georgetown County Sch. Nursing, 1970; AS, SUNY, Albany, 1982; AS in Criminal Justice, Georgetown Tech. Coll., 1992; postgrad., 1994. Cert. community nurse, med. asst. Mem. staff Georgetown Meml. Hosp., 1969-71; office nurse Dr. L. Benton Williams, Georgetown, 1971—; jail nurse Georgetown County Detention Ctr., 1991-92; staff devel. nurse Prince George Village, 1992—. Mem. ANA, Am. Assn. Office Nurses, Nat. Assn. Physicians Nurses, S.C. Nurses Assn., Order Ea. Star. Baptist. Home: 217 Beneventum Rd Georgetown SC 29440-9461 Office: 1743 N Fraser St Georgetown SC 29440 also: Prince George Village 901 Maple St Georgetown SC 29440

ROGERS, SHEILA WOOD, elementary and secondary school educator; b. Louisville, May 10, 1949; d. John Cornelius and Gladys Virginia (Moody) Wood; m. Franklin Don Rogers, Mar. 23, 1969; children: Pamela, Rachel. BA in Math., Christopher Newport Coll., 1974; MEd in Computer Edn., Hampton U., 1986. Tchr. Hampton (Va.) City Schs., 1974-86; instructional specialist York County Pub. Schs., Yorktown, Va., 1986-91; tchr. York County (Va.) Schs., 1991—; math. cons. Nat Diffusion Network, Washington, 1988-90; York County rep. Consortium for Interactive Instrn., Norfolk, Va., 1986-91; facilitator Star Schs. Tech. Edn. Rsch. Ctrs., U. Va., Boston, Charlottesville, 1989—; coord. computer contest U. Wis., Peninsula Coun. of Math. of Va., Hampton, Newport News, 1980-86. Pres. PTA, R. E. Lee Elem. Sch., Hampton, 1987-89, C. A. Lindsay Middle Sch., Hampton, 1989-91; pres. on coun. Hampton Coun. of PTAs, 1990-91, 1st v.p., 1991-93; dir. preschool choirs West Hampton Bapt. Ch., Hampton, 1988—. Mem. NEA, ASCD, Va. Edn. Assn., York County Edn. Assn., Va. Coun. Tchrs. Math., Peninsula Coun. Tchrs. Math., Greater Peninsula Swimming Assn. (rep. 1989-96). Baptist. Home: 109 Prince James Dr Hampton VA 23669-3609 Office: Grafton Mid Sch Grafton Dr Yorktown VA 23693

ROGERS, THOMAS PAUL, retail chain executive; b. Morgantown, W.Va., Dec. 29, 1932; s. Paul Martin and Kathryn (Alger) R.; m. Janet Griffith Rogers, Sept. 14, 1963; children: Paul Griffith, Mary Louise, John Martin. BS in Pharmacy, W.Va. U., 1955. V.p. Rogers Pharmacy, Inc., Morgantown, 1955-73; pres. House of Cards, Inc., Morgantown, 1961-86; chmn., CEO Thoughtfulness, Inc., Granville, W.Va., 1986—. Lt. (j.g.) USNR, 1955-58. Mem. Rotary (pres. Cheat Lake club 1987). Office: Thoughtfulness Inc 319 Main St Granville WV 26534

ROGERS, TIFFANY HEATHER, special education educator; b. Guntersville, Ala., Sept. 14, 1970; d. Larry W.D. Rogers and Kathy Melissa (Belvin) Martin. AS, Snead State U., 1990; postgrad., Auburn U., 1993. Resource behavior disorders tchr. Griffin (Ga.)-Spalding Schs., 1993, self contained behavior disorders tchr., 1993-94; spl. edn. tchr. St. Francis Day Sch., Roswell, Ga., 1994—; pvt. nanny, Auburn, Ala., 1991-93, Marietta, Ga., 1994-95. Vol. GARAL, Atlanta, 1994-95, Atlanta Convention and Visitors Bur., 1994-95; vol. coord. Spl. Olympics, Auburn, 1991-93. Mem. ASCD, Ga. Nat. Edn. Assn., Coun. for Exceptional Children. Home: 406 Alicia St Albertville AL 35950

ROGERS, WILLIAM BROOKINS, financial consultant; b. Atlanta, Mar. 31, 1938; s. William Brookins and Mildred (LaHatte) R.; m. Carolyn Ansley Duren, May 28, 1966; children: W. Brandon, Alicia Deanne. BBA in Acctg., Ga. State U., 1965, MBA in Fin., 1968, PhD student in fin., 1968-70. CPA Ga., cert. mediator, arbitrator; state registered nutral mediator and arbitrator. Sr. acct. A.M. Pullen & Co. CPA's, Atlanta, 1964-69; pres., chmn. Ponderosa Internat., Inc., Atlanta, 1970-76; exec. v.p., chief op. ofcr. GRC/Tidewater Group, Atlanta, 1976-79; pres., CEO Atlanta Bil, Inc., 1979-86, Brookins Mgmt. Co., Inc., Atlanta, 1979—, Hilton Enterprises, Inc., Atlanta, 1981-96; bd. dirs. Ranick Ltd., Athens, Ga., 1981-96; lectr. Am. Mgmt. Assn., Atlanta, 1969-75, Bus. Grad. Sch. U. Ala., Tuscaloosa, 1970, Bus. Sch. Augusta State Coll., 1971, Western and Gwinnette Jud. Cirs.; mem. nat. panel of comml. arbitrators Am. Arbitration Assn.; mem. Inst. of Bus. Appraisers. With U.S. Army, 1959-61. Fellow AICPA; mem. Am. Arbitration Assn. (arbitrator nat. panel), Soc. Profls. in Dispute Resolution (assoc.), Inst. Bus. Appraisers, Beta Gamma Sigma, Omicron Delta Kappa, Beta Alpha Psi. Republican. Episcopalian. Home: 5425 Heathridge Terr Duluth GA 30155-5702 Office: Brooking Mgmt Co Inc PO Box 2198 Duluth GA 30136-8449

ROGERS, WILLIAM FENNA, JR., supermarket executive, management consultant; b. Higgsinville, Mo., Dec. 25, 1912; s. William Fenna and Emily S. (Moose) R.; m. Thelma Ann Hooper, June 15, 1940 (dec. Mar. 1982); m. Ethel Allene Burgess, Aug. 6, 1983; stepchildren: Dorothy H. Nance, Linda H. Connors. BA, Ark. Coll., 1933; postgrad. U. Ark., 1933, Tulane U., 1935, U. Fla., 1938-39. Vocat. adv. Nat. Youth Adminstrn., Little Rock, 1936-38; chief field ops. U.S. Employment Svc., Little Rock, 1938-43, chief supr. tng., Washington, 1946-47; asst. dir. Civilian Pers. Divsn., U.S. Dept. Navy, Washington, 1947-55; mem. productivity team Nat. Mgmt. Coun., Paris, 1952; lectr. U.S. Internat. Fair, Amsterdam, 1963; v.p. indsl. rels. Giant Food, Inc., Washington, 1955-75; mgmt. cons., Falls Church, Va., 1975—; trustee Teamster Warehouse Fund, 1956—, Carpet Layers Funds, 1968—; lectr. Am. U., 1949-69; pres. Chateau Devel. Corp., Fairfax, Va., 1978-83. Mem. selection bd. U.S. Postal Svc., 1969-77; elder New York Ave. Presbyn. Ch., Washington, 1948-72, cons. Lincoln commn., 1984—, chmn., 1989—; elder Falls Church Presbyn. Ch., 1980-83, sunday sch. supt., 1984-88; mem. Falls Church Village Preservation and Improvement Soc., 1967—; chmn. bur. edn. and employment Greater Washington Bd. Trade, 1974-76. Served to lt. comdr. USNR, 1943-64. Mem. ASTD (life), Am. Legion Res. Officers Assn., Naval Res. Assn., Alpha Psi Omega, Kappa Gamma, Pi Kappa Delta, Iota Lambda Sigma. Club: Internat. Town and Country (dir. 1959-61) (Fairfax, Va.). Avocations: golf, fishing. Home: 9229 Arlington Blvd # 258 Fairfax VA 22031-2508

ROGERS, WILLIAM H., JR., banker, securities executive. Exec. v.p. Suntrust Securities, Inc., Atlanta; also sr. v.p. finance Suntrust Banks, Inc., Atlanta. Office: Suntrust Securities Inc 25 Park Pl Atlanta GA 30303-2530 also: Suntrust Banks Inc 25 Park Pl Atlanta GA 30303

ROGERS, WILLIAM RAYMOND, college president emeritus, psychology educator; b. Oswego, N.Y., June 20, 1932; s. William Raymond and A. Elizabeth (Hollis) R.; m. Beverley Claire Partington, Aug. 14, 1954; children: John Partington, Susan Elizabeth Howell, Nancy Claire Glassman. BA magna cum laude, Kalamazoo Coll., 1954; BD, U. Chgo. and Chgo. Theol. Sem., 1958; PhD, U. Chgo., 1965; MA (hon.), Harvard U., 1970. Cons., staff counselor Counseling and Psychotherapy Rsch. Ctr., U. Chgo., 1960-62; teaching fellow, counselor to students Chgo. Theol. Sem., 1961-62; asst. prof. psychology and religion, dir. student counseling Earlham Coll., Richmond, Ind., 1962-68; assoc. prof. psychology and religion, assoc. dean of Coll. Earlham Coll., 1968-70; vis. lectr. pastoral counseling Div. Sch. Harvard U., Cambridge, Mass., 1969-70, prof. religion and psychology Div. and Edn. Schs., 1970-80, faculty chmn. clin. psychology and pub. practice, 1970-72, chmn. counseling and cons. psychology, 1979-80; prof. psychology and religious studies Guilford Coll., Greensboro, N.C., 1980—; pres. Guilford Coll., Greensboro, 1980-96, pres. emeritus, 1996—; bd. dirs. Br. Bank and Trust. Author: The Alienated Student, 1969, Project Listening, 1974, Nourishing the Humanistic in Medicine, 1979; Contbr. articles to profl. jours. Bd. dirs. Greensboro Symphony Soc., Greensboro Day Sch., Moses Cone Hosp., Canterbury Sch., Mary Reynolds Babcock Found., Cemala Found. Danforth Found. fellow, Blatchford Traveling fellow U. Chgo. and Chgo. Theol. Sem., 1958. Mem. Soc. Values in Higher Edn., Friends Assn. Higher Edn., Nat. Assn. Ind. Colls. and Univs., N.C. Assn. Ind. Colls. and Univs., So. Assn. Colls. and Schs., Rotary (club pres.). Mem. Soc. of Friends. Home: 5400 Westfield Dr Greensboro NC 27410-9223

ROGERS, WILMA MESSER, retired elementary school educator; b. Jacksonville, Fla., Oct. 15, 1931; d. William and Ruth Esther (Lockett) Messer; m. Lorain Winston Rogers, Aug. 14, 1954 (dec. 1986); children: Winston Bernard, Marlene Denise, William Earl. BS, Hampton (Va.) U., 1953; postgrad. various colls. including, Univ. Miami, Coral Gables, 1960-62, Barry Univ., 1966; MS, Nova U., Ft. Lauderdale, Fla., 1980. Cert. tchr., Fla. Tchr. J.R.E. Lee Elem. Sch., South Miami, Fla., 1953-59; first grade tchr. Liberty City Elem. Sch., Miami, Fla., 1959-66, 72-88, kindergarten tchr., 1972-88, Headstart program tchr., 1966-72; supervising tchr. Early Childhood Program Miami Dade Community Coll., 1975-77; ret., 1988; group chmn. J.R.E. Lee Elem. Sch., 1957-59, Liberty City Elem., 1962-65, 70-82, other leadership roles; vol. Child Watch, Miami, 1982; mem. edn. component Metro-Miami Action Plan, 1979-81. Assoc. editor The Krinon jour., 1980. Dep. registrar Met. Dade County elections, Miami, 1990; mem. Greater Miami Opera; rec. sec. Miami-Dade Nat. Pan-Hellenic Coun., 1985-87; mem. B.O.L.D., Inc. Recipient numerous citations for excellence in tchg., Svc. award Miami-Dade Nat. Pan-Hellenic Coun., 1988. Mem. NAACP, Nat. Congress Parents and Tchrs. (mem. chmn. Liberty City Elem. PTA 1973-78), Dade County Ret. Tchrs. Assn., Fla. Ret. Educators Assn., Dem. Women's Club Dade County, Dem. Black Caucus Fla., Nat. Coun. Negro Women (pres. 1985-86, Svc. award 1983, 88), Top Ladies of Distinction (Miami chpt. pres. 1995, named Top Lady of Yr. 1993, Svc. award 1995), Nat. Alliance of Black Sch. Educators, Family Christian Assn., Phi Delta Kappa, Zeta Phi Beta. Democrat. Baptist. Home: 2017 NW 55th Ter Miami FL 33142-3092

ROGERS, ZORA ROWENA NEREID ESTHER, pediatrician; b. San Francisco, Jan. 28, 1957; d. Edward de Lancey and Esther Edna (Deering) R.; m. Ralph J. Posch, June 11, 1983; children: Konrad and Leila. AB in Biophysics, U. Calif., Berkeley, 1978; MD, U. Calif., San Diego, 1983. Diplomate Am. Bd. Pediatrics, Pediatric Hematology-Oncology; lic. Nat. Bd. Med. Examiners, 1984, Calif., 1984, Tex., 1987. Resident U. So. Calif., L.A., 1983-86, asst. clin. instr., 1986-87; fellow pediatric hematology-oncology U. Tex. Southwestern Med. Ctr., Dallas, 1987-90, asst. instr., instr., 1990-92, asst. prof. pediatrics, 1992—; lectr. Children's Med. Ctr., Dallas, 1988—; instr. BCLS, 1981-83, ACLS, 1987. Mem. nat. med. adv. bd. Aplastic Anemia Found. Am., 1993—, mem. nat. bd. dirs., 1992-93, 95—; vol. physician Camp Jubilee, 1991-93, med. dir., 1994—, bd. dirs., 1993—. Rsch. fellow U. So. Calif. Med. Ctr., 1986-87, Am. Cancer Soc., 1988-89, 89-90, Damon Runyon-Walter Winchell Cancer Rsch. Fund, 1990-93, 91-93. Mem. Am. Soc. Hematology, Am. Acad. Pediatrics, Am. Soc. Pediatric Hematology/Oncology, Am. soc. Clin. Oncology, Tex. Pediatric Soc., Histiocyte Soc., Pediat. Oncology Group. Office: U Tex Southwestern Med Ctr 5323 Harry Hines Blvd Dallas TX 75235-9063 also: Children's Med Ctr Ctr Cancer & Blood Disorders 1935 Motor St Dallas TX 75235

ROGERSON, CONSTANCE JEAN, guidance counselor; b. Staples, Minn., May 17, 1921; d. John Frank and Nina (Hagen) Grace; m. Richard T. Rogerson, May 28, 1944 (div.); children: Thomas, Richard, John. BA in Chemistry, Linfield Coll., McMinnville, Oreg., 1943; postgrad., Fla. State U., 1960-63, Ga. So. Coll., 1968-69. Instr. Everett (Wash.) Jr. Coll., 1944-47, W.Va. U., Morgantown, 1947-49; elem. tchr. Hermiston (Oreg.) Schs., 1950-58; tchr. math. Duval County Schs., Jacksonville, Fla., 1959-60, counselor, 1961—, ret., 1992; vol. counselor Duval County, 1992—; instr. parenting skills Fla. Jr. Coll., Jacksonville, 1968-82. Grantee Fla. Dept. Edn., 1975-76. Mem. Duval Tchrs. United (exec. bd. 1989-91), Delta Kappa Gamma (pres. 1964-68), Kappa Delta Pi. Republican. Home: 5402 Lori Dr S Jacksonville FL 32207-7034

ROGIC, GEORGE, graphic artist; b. Belgrade, Yugoslavia, May 22, 1965; came to U.S., 1965; s. Milorad Mihilo and Zora Fedora (Markovic) R.; m. Diane Calabrese Rogic, Oct. 8, 1992; 1 child, John Mark. BS in Bus. Adminstrn., U. Mo., St. Louis, 1988. Database mgr. Mallinckrodt Med., St. Louis, 1988-89; prodn. mgr. Admore, Inc., St. Louis, 1989-90; creative svcs. mgr. WHRO, Norfolk, Va., 1990—; owner Rogicdesign, Norfolk, 1990—. Art dir. Veer mag., 1992—, Ghent mag., 1992, WHRO mag., 1990 (PIVA award 1993). Mem. Nat. Assn. Desktop Pubs. Office: WHRO 5200 Hampton Blvd Norfolk VA 23508-1507

ROGOSKI, PATRICIA DIANA, financial executive; b. Chgo., Dec. 29, 1939; d. Raymond Michael and Bernice Rose (Konkol) R. BS in Acctg. and Econs., Marquette U., 1961, postgrad., 1965-66; postgrad., NYU, 1966-68, St. John's U., N.Y.C., 1975-76; cert. mgmt. acct., 1979. Sr. fin. analyst Blackhawk Mfg. Co., Milw., 1961-66; mgr., sr. analyst Shell Oil Co., N.Y.C., 1966-71; mgr. data processing Bradford Nat./Penn Bradford, Pitts., 1971-75; asst. mgr. fin. controls ITT, N.Y.C., 1975-79; v.p., comptr. ITT Consumer Fin. Corp., Mpls., 1979-80; sr. v.p. fin. ITT Fin. Corp., St. Louis, 1980-84; v.p., exec. asst., group exec. ITT Coins, Secaucus, N.J., 1984-85; pres. Patron S., Ltd., Wilmington, Del., 1986—; CFO, sr. v.p. Guardsmark, Inc., Memphis, 1989-94; sr. v.p. Peoplemark, Inc., Memphis, 1989-94. Bd. dirs. St. Louis Repertory Theater, 1983-84. Named to Acad. Women Achievers, YWCA, N.Y.C., 1980. Mem. Fin. Execs. Inst., Inst. Mgmt. Acctg., Econ. Club. Office: Patron S Ltd NE Hercules Plz 1313 N Market St Ste 3410 Wilmington DE 19801-1151

ROHACK, JOHN JAMES, cardiologist; b. Rochester, N.Y., Aug. 22, 1954; s. John Joseph and Margaret Elizabeth (McLaughlin) R.; m. Charlotte McCown, Dec. 7, 1980; 1 child, Elisha Monique Feigle. BS, U. Tex., El Paso, 1976; MD, U. Tex., Galveston, 1980. Diplomate Am. Bd. Internal Medicine. Intern internal medicine U. Tex. Med. Br. Hosps., Galveston, 1980-81, resident internal medicine, 1981-83, chief resident internal medicine, 1983-84, fellow cardiology, 1984-86; instr. medicine U. Tex. Med. Br., Galveston, 1983-86; asst. prof. medicine Tex. A&M Coll. Medicine, College Station, 1986-95, assoc. prof., 1995—, sect. chief cardiology, 1989—; assoc. med. dir. Scott and White Health Plan, 1995—; bd. dirs. Health for All Clinic, v.p., 1994-96; mem. Accreditation Coun. on Continuing Med. Edn., 1995—; med. dir. Fitlife Ctr. Tex. A&M U., College Station, 1990—. Bd. dirs. Am. Heart Assn., Brazos Valley College Station, 1987—, Tex. affiliate Austin, 1991—, 1st v.p., 1994-95, pres.-elect, 1995-96, pres., 1996-97. Fellow ACP, Am. Coll. Cardiology (bd. dirs. Tex. chpt. 1992—); mem. AMA (alt del. ho. of dels. 1984-93, del. 1993—, coun. on med. edn. 1995-98), Tex. Med. Assn. (exec. coun. med. student sect. 1981-82, ho. of dels. 1982—, trustee 1994—), U. Tex. Med. Br. Alumni Assn. (trustee 1989—, pres. 1996-97), Brazos Robertson County Med. Soc. (exec. com. 1989—, pres. 1995-96). Office: Scott and White Clinic 1600 University Dr E College Station TX 77840-2642

ROHE, CHARLES H., sports association administrator; b. Chgo., Aug. 9, 1931; s. Walter H. and Naomi S. (Throckmorton) R.; m. Jeanne Floroth Halford (div. Oct. 1970); children: Kevin D., Connie Bishop; m. Dana Dunbar Turner, July 1, 1986; 1 child, Mason Turner. BS, U. So. Miss., Hattiesburg, 1953, MA, 1954. Football, basketball, track coach Hattiesburg H.S., 1954-56; football and track coach U. So. Miss., 1956-58, Furman U., Greenville, S.C., 1958-62, U. Tenn., Knoxville, 1962-71; athletic dir. Va. Tech., Blacksburg, 1971-73; v.p. and adminstr. Pace Mgmt. Corp., Houston, 1973-82; exec. dir. Fla. Citrus Bowl, Orlando, 1982—; mem. bd. dirs., v.p. Cen. Fla. Zoo, 1991—, Orlando Opera Co., 1990—; mem. adminstrn. bd., chmn. sports and recreation com. St. Luke's Methodist Ch. mem. U.S. Olympic Com., Knoxville, Tenn., 1968-76. Named Jaycee of the Yr. S.C. Jaycees, 1961, Nat. Track Coach of the Yr. U.S. Track & Field Fedn., 1967. Mem. Am. Football Coaches Assn. Home: 5379 Isleworth CC Dr Windermere FL 34786 Office: Florida Citrus Sports 1 Citrus Bowl Pl Orlando FL 32805-2459

ROHN, REUBEN DAVID, pediatric educator and administrator; b. Israel, Apr. 12, 1945; came to U.S., 1954; s. Aryeh and Rachel (Brenner) R.; m. Judith Semel, Sept. 6, 1971; 1 child, Karen. BA cum laude, Bklyn. Coll., 1967; MD, N.Y. Med. Coll., 1971. Diplomate Am. Bd. Pediat., Am. Bd. Pediatric Endocrinology, Am. Bd. Pediatrics-Adolescent Medicine. Intern in pediatrics Montefiore Hosp., Bronx, N.Y., 1971-72, resident in pediatrics, 1972-74; fellow in adolescent medicine U. Md. Hosp., Balt., 1974-76; preceptor in pediatrics Johns Hopkins U. Sch. Health Svcs., Balt., 1975-76; asst. prof. dept. pediatrics Ea. Va. Med. Sch., Norfolk, 1976-82; coord. pediatric clerkship Ea. Va. Med. Sch., Children's Hosp. of King's Daughters, Norfolk, 1977-90; prof. dept. pediatrics Ea. Va. Med. Sch., Norfolk, 1989—; adj. prof. chemistry Old Dominion U., Norfolk, 1984—; dir. adolescent medicine/endocrinology Children's Hosp. of King's Daughters, Norfolk, 1976—; mem. curriculum com. Ea. Va. Med. Sch., 1977-79, clerkship coords. com. 1977-90, genetics com., 1978-80, evaluation com. 1979-91, chmn. selectives com., 1981-82, ad hoc com. on consultation, 1982-83, student progress com., 1983-85, student health com., 1985-87, LCME com. on curriculum, 1990-92; mem. child abuse com. Children's Hosp. of King 's Daus., 1976-80, chmn. adolescent adv. com., 1976-80, patient care com. 1980-94, nutrition com. 1980-94, utilization rev. com., 1980-82, med. records com., 1987-89, gen. med./surg. task force com., 1987-88; bd. dirs. Pediatric Faculty Assocs., 1994—; spkr. in field. Reviewer Jour. Adolescent Health Care, 1986—, mem. editorial bd., 1989-92; contbr. articles to profl. jours. Mem. Norfolk Sch. Health Coun., 1977—, mem. ad hoc com. infant screening program for hypothroidism Commonwealth of Va., 1977-79, cons., 1979—; mem. cmty. adv. bd. Norfolk Adolescent Pregnancy Prevention Svc. Project, 1981-83; bd. dirs. Elizabeth River chpt. Am. Diabetes Assn., 1982-85, South Hampton Roads chpt. 1985-93; mem. adv. com. Norfolk-Virginia Beach Jr. League, 1987-88; judge ann. Health Edn. Fair, Norfolk Pub. schs., 1980-94. Recipient grant Bressler Rsch. Fund, 1975-76, Biomed. Rsch. Devel. grant Ea. Va. Med. Sch., 1978, 78-79, 79-80. 81-82, 83-84, Children's Health Found. grant, 1988-89. Fellow Am. Acad. Pediatrics (youth and adolescence com. Va. chpt. 1978—); mem. Soc. Adolescent Medicine (abstract reviewer 1984-91), Lawson Wilkins Pediatric Endocrine Soc., Sigma Xi. Home: 4653 Larkwood Dr Virginia Beach VA 23464-5815 Office: Childrens Hosp Kings Daus 601 Childrens Ln Norfolk VA 23507-1910

ROHR, DWIGHT MASON, news director, radio marketing consultant; b. Covington, Va., July 18, 1952; s. Edward Mason and Betty (Eppling) R.; m. Betty Erwin, Aug. 1, 1977; children: Christopher Mason, Joseph Michael. Student, Dabney S. Lancaster C.C., Clifton Forge, Va., 1985—. Cert. radio operator; cert. radio mktg. cons. Audio engr. WJBR, Wilmington, Del., 1971-72; announcer WASA/WHDG, Havre de Grace, Md., 1972-73; news dir. mktg. WKEY Inc., Covington, 1974—. Active Stonewall Jackson Area coun. Boy Scouts Am., 1990—; dir. cmty. rels. ARC, Covington, 1975—; mem. adv. bd. Salvation Army, Covington, 1995—; elder First Christian Ch. Recipient Scouter of Yr. awrd VFW Post 1033, 1994, Dist. award of merit Boy Scouts Am., 1995; named to Outstanding Young Men of Am., 1980. Mem. Soc. Profl. Journalists, Radio TV News Dirs. Assn., Masons, Scottish Rite. Republican. Home: 347 E Gray St Covington VA 24426

ROHRBOUGH, ELSA CLAIRE HARTMAN, artist; b. Shreveport, La., Sept. 26, 1915; d. Adolph Emil and Camille Claire (Francis) Hartman; m. Leonard M. Rohrbough, June 19, 1937 (dec. Jan. 1977); children: Stephen, Frank, Leonard. Juried exhbns. (painting) Massur Mus. Art, Monroe, La., Mobile (Ala.) Art Gallery, Gulf Coast Juried Exhibit, Mobile, Juried Arts Nat., Tyler, Tex., Greater New Orleans Nat., La. Watercolor Soc. Nat., Ky. Watermedia Nat., So. Watercolor Ann., La. Women Artist, many others. One-woman shows include Le Petit Theatre du Vieux Carre, New Orleans World Trade Ctr.'s Internat. House, Singing River Art Assn., Pascagoula, Miss., La. Font Inn, Pascagoula, Mandeville (La.) City Hall, St. Tammany Art Assn., Covington, La., others; exhibited in groups shows at 1st Guaranty Bank, Hammond, La., St. Tammany Art Assn., Ft. Isabel Gallery, Covington, S.E. La. State U. Mem. Nat. League Am. Pen Women (v.p. S.E. La. br. 1986-87, pres. 1987-92, 94-98), St. Tammany Art Assn. (bd. dirs. 1985-86, 87, instr. 1977-78, classes chmn. 1986-88). Republican. Roman Catholic. Home: 2525 Lakeshore Dr Mandeville LA 70448-5627

ROHRICH, RODNEY JAMES, plastic surgeon, educator; b. Eureka, S.D., Aug. 5, 1953; s. Claude and Katie (Schumacher) R.; m. Diane Louise Gibby, July 3, 1990. BA summa cum laude, N.D. State U., 1975; MD with honors, Baylor Coll., 1979. Diplomate Am. Bd. Plastic Surgery, Nat. Bd. Med. Examiners. Instr. surgery Harvard Med. Sch. Mass. Gen. Hosp., Boston, 1985-86; asst. prof. U. Tex. Southwestern Med. Ctr., Dallas, 1986-89, assoc. prof., 1989—; chief plastic surgery Parkland/Zale Univ. Med. Ctr., Dallas, 1989-91; prof., chmn. dir. plastic surgery U. Tex. Southwestern Med. Ctr., Dallas, 1991—; pres., faculty senate U. Tex., crystal charity ball disting. chair in plastic surgery. Editl. bd. Selected Readings in Plastic Surgery, The Cleft Palate and Craniofacial Jour., Plastic and Reconstructive Surgery Jour.; contbr. articles to med. jours. Bd. dirs. Save-the-Children Found., Dallas, March of Dimes, Dallas; class mem. Leadership Dallas, 1989-90; mem. Adopt-A-Sch., Dallas Summer Mus. Guild, Dallas Mus. Art, Dallas Symphony Assn., Tex. Health Found., Youth Leadership Dallas. Grantee Urban Rsch. Fund, 1982, United Kingdom Ltd. Ednl. Rsch. Fund, 1983, Oxford Cleft Palate Found., 1983, Am. Assn. Plastic Surgeons, 1985, Plastic Surgery Ednl. Found., 1985, 89, 90, U. Tex. Health Sci. Ctr. Dept. Surgery, 1986, Howmedica, 1989, ConvaTec-Squibb, 1989, 91, ConvaTec, 1991. Mem. AAAS, AMA (Thomas Cronin award 1988, 90, Clifford C. Snyder award 1990), Am. Assn. Hand Surgery, Am. Burn Assn., Am. Cleft Palate Assn., Am. Coll. Surgeons, Am. Soc. Law and Medicine, Am. Soc. Maxillofacial Surgeons, Am. Soc. for Surgery the Hand, Am. Soc. Plastic and Reconstructive Surgeons, Am. Trauma Soc., British Med. Assn., Nat. Vascular Malformations Found. Inc. (med. and sci. adv. bd.) Tex. Med. Assn., Tex. Soc. Plastic Surgeons, Mass. Gen. Hosp. Hand Club, Dallas County Med. Soc., Assn. Acad. Chmn. Plastic Surgery, Dallas Soc. Plastic Surgeons, Harvard Med. Sch. Alumni Assn., Inst. for Study of Profl. Risk, Plastic Surgery Rsch. Coun., Reed O. Dingman Soc. Plastic Surgeons, So. Med. Assn. Republican. Roman Catholic. Office: U Tex Southwestern Med Ctr Divsn of Plastic Surgery 5323 Harry Hines Blvd Dallas TX 75235-7200

ROISLER, GLENN HARVEY, quality assurance professional; b. Milw., Apr. 6, 1952; s. George Harvey and Mayme Elvin (Salo) R.; m. Jacqueline Bout, July 27, 1971; 1 child, Renee Jenette. Student electronics tech., DeVry Inst. Tech., Chgo., 1976; student computer engring. tech., Capitol Radio Engring. Inst., Washington, 1980; BA in Econs., N.C. State U., 1992. Instr. scuba Pirate's Cove, Inc., Milw., 1969-70; sr. electronics technician Bendix Field Engring. Corp., Columbia, Md., 1977-79; field engr. Technicare, Inc., Solon, Ohio, 1979; supr. electronics Troxler Labs., Inc., Research Triangle Park, N.C., 1979-81; mgr. prodn. Matrix Corp., Raleigh, N.C., 1981; vendor surveillance specialist Carolina Power and Light Co., Raleigh, N.C., 1981-84, sr. quality assurance specialist, 1984-91, sr. systems analyst, 1991—. Contbr. articles to profl. publs. Served with USN, 1971-77. Mem. Am. Soc. Quality Control (crt. quality engr., reliability engr.), Gamma Beta Phi, Sigma Pi Sigma, Omicron Delta Epsilon. Methodist. Office: Carolina Power & Light Co PO Box 1551 Raleigh NC 27602-1551

ROLAND, BILLY RAY, electronics company executive; b. Grandview, Tex., June 12, 1926; s. Marvin Wesley and Minnie Mae (Martin) R.; m. Ruth Ranell Sheets, Mar. 9, 1950 (div. 1982); children: Carl Ray and Darla Kay (twins); m. Linda Sue Leslie, Feb. 21, 1986 (div. Nov. 1991); m. Martha Kay Redford, May 17, 1993. B.S., Tex. Christian U., 1954. C.P.A., Tex. Ticket and baggage agt. Southwestern Greyhound Co., Ft. Worth, 1943-44, 46-51; supr. acctg. dept. Tandy Leather Co., 1954-60; controller, asst. sec., treas. Tandy Corp., 1960-75, Tandy crafts, Inc., 1975-78; v.p. Tandy Corp., 1978-85, ret. V.p., treas. David L. Tandy Found., 1966—; mng. trustee James L. and Eunice West Charitable Trust, 1980-91; treas. Benjamin F. Johnston Found., 1984—. Served with inf. U.S. Army, 1944-46. Mem. Am. Inst. C.P.A.s, Tex. Soc. C.P.A.s, Ft. Worth Soc. C.P.A.s, Ft. Worth C. of C. Democrat. Methodist. Clubs: Colonial Country, Petroleum, Lake Country Golf and Country. Home: 8937 Random Rd Fort Worth TX 76179-2739

ROLAND, CATHERINE DIXON, entrepreneur; b. Andalusia, Ala., Mar. 9, 1936; d. Charles and Thelma (Chapman) Dixon; m. Henry F. Roland, Dec. 16, 1966 (div. Nov., 1976); 1 child, Charles H.; stepchild, Vickie Roland Little. Student, Huntingdon Coll., 1954-56; BS, Auburn U., 1956-59; MA in History, U. Ala., Tuscaloosa, 1965-66. Sec. Dixon Lumber Co., Inc., Andalusia, 1969-74, v.p., 1974-78; land and timber owner, mgr. Catherine D. Roland & Co., Andalusia, 1978—; owner Sta. WCTA, andalusia, 1947-75, bd. dirs., 1972-75; owner, bd. dirs. D & G Property Ltd., Perth, Australia, 1967—, Covington County Bank, 1979—, So. Nat. Corp., 1985—. Chmn. Thelma Dixon Found., Andalusia, 1981—; mem. Rep. Senatorial Inner Cir., Washington, 1980—, 2d Congl. Com., Montgomery, Ala., 1980—, Andalusia Pub. Libr. Friends, Inc., 1981—; mem. adv. coun. Mises Inst. Auburn (Ala.) U., Auburn and Washington, 1983-85, Coll. Bus. Auburn U., 1987—; mem. Com. of 100, Huntingdon Coll., 1978, trustee, 1978—, vice chmn. bd. trustees 1985-93; bd. dirs. Women Health, Birmingham, Ala., 1978-82, Health Svcs. Found., 1982—, Andalusia Hosp., 1980-82. Named countess Huntingdon Coll., Montgomery, 1978, named to Hall of Honor, 1980; recipient commendation for Outstanding Svc. and Leadership, 1980, Loyalty award, 1988. Mem. DAR, Nat. Soc. Colonial Dames XVII Century, Ams. of Royal Descent, Dames of Magna Charter, Forest Farmers Assn., Ala. Wildlife Fedn., Andalusia Area C. of C., Auburn Alumni Assn., Huntingdon Coll. Alumni Assn. (chmn. Andalusia area chpt. 1983—), Am. Legion, Study Club. Methodist.

ROLAND, MELISSA MONTGOMERY, accountant; b. Houston, Mar. 6, 1961; d. John Edgar and Mariann (Guggino) Montgomery; m. Larry Dean Roland, Sept. 20, 1984. BBA, Tex. A&M U., 1983. CPA, Tex., cert. fraud examiner, Tex. Audit sr. Arthur Andersen & Co., Houston, 1983-87; cons. mgr.-performance improvement group Ernst & Young, San Antonio, 1988-91; COO Roy Smith Shoes, Inc. d/b/a Accenté, Houston, 1991—. Bd. dirs., treas. Grandparents Outreach, San Antonio, 1989—. Mem. AICPA, Tex. Accts. and Lawyers for the Arts (adv. bd.), Tex. Soc. CPAs, Young Reps., Jr. League Houston, S.W. Found. Forum. Presbyterian. Home: 5523 Boyce Springs Dr Houston TX 77066-2401 Office: 3120 Rogerdale Rd Ste 190 Houston TX 77042-4125

ROLAND, PETER SARGENT, otolaryngologist; b. Washington, Apr. 3, 1947; s. Joseph Morgan and Mary Hellen (Banker) R.; m. Miriam Woodhall, Apr. 1, 1977 (div. July 1986); m. Melinda Clair Gill, Feb. 22, 1989; children: Evelyn, Jason, Britney, Kenzey. BA, Rockford Coll., 1969; MD, U. Tex., 1976. Resident in otolaryngology Pa. State U./M.S. Hershey Med. Ctr., Hershey, 1976-80; asst. prof. otolaryngology Uniformed Svcs. U. Health Scis., Washington, 1980-84; fellow in otology, neurotology & skull base surgery EAR Found., Nashville, 1984-85; prof. otolaryngology U. Tex. Southwestern Med. Ctr., Dallas, 1985—; chief otolaryngology Parkland Meml. Hosp., Dallas, 1990—. Served to lt. comdr. USNR, 1980-84. Fellow Am. Otol. Soc., Am. Neurotol. Soc., Am. Acad. Otolaryngology; mem. Alpha Omega Alpha. Home: 2117 Clearspring Dr S Irving TX 75063-3393 Office: U Tex Southwestern Med Ctr 5323 Harry Hines Blvd Dallas TX 75235-7200

ROLAND, RAYMOND WILLIAM, lawyer; b. Ocala, Fla., Jan. 3, 1947; s. Raymond W. and Hazel (Dunn) R.; m. Jane Allen, Dec. 28, 1968; children: John Allen, Jason William. BA, Fla. State U., 1969, JD, 1972. Bar: Fla. 1972, U.S. Dist. Ct. (no. dist.) Fla. 1973, U.S. Dist. Ct. (mid. dist.) Fla. 1985, U.S. Ct. Appeals (5th cir.) 1974, U.S. Ct. Appeals (11th cir.) 1983, U.S. Supreme Ct. 1985; cert. civil trial lawyer; cert. cir. ct. mediator. Assoc. Keen, O'Kelley & Spitz, Tallahassee, 1972-74, ptnr., 1974-77; ptnr., v.p. McConnaughhay, Roland, Maida & Cherr, P.A., Tallahassee, 1978—; mem. exec. bd. NW Fla. chpt. March of Dimes. Bd. dirs. So. Scholarship Found., Tallahassee, 1985-89, v.p. 1989. Mem. Internat. Assn. Def. Coun., Assn. Internat. Droit Assurance, Internat. Soc. Ins. Law (U.S. chpt.), Def. Rsch. Inst., Fla. Bar (mem. Judicial Adminstrn., Selection and Tenure com.), Fla. Def. Lawyers Assn., Tallahassee Bar Assn. (treas. 1979), Kiwanis (life, lt. gov. 1984-85), Capital City Kiwanis Club (Kiwanian of Yr. 1978, pres. 1979), Fla. Kiwanis Found. (life fellow). Republican. Baptist. Home: 1179 Ox Bottom Rd Tallahassee FL 32312-3519

ROLFE, PAULA GRACE, educational administrator; b. Perth Amboy, N.J., Mar. 12, 1942; d. Fredrick Carl and Mae (Sapun) Lamp; m. George William Rolfe, Jr., July 4, 1965; 1 child, George William III. BA, Montclair (N.J.) State Coll., 1964; MS, Ill. State U., 1969; EdD, Auburn U., 1982. Tchr. Edison (N.J.) Twp. Pub. Schs., 1964-67, Pekin (Ill.) Pub. Schs., 1967-68, 1969-70; tchr. Guardian Angel Orphanage, Peoria, 1967-71; substitute tchr. Montgomery (Ala.) Pub. Schs., 1974-77; grad. teaching asst. Auburn (Ala.) U., 1979-80; owner, dir. Sylvan Learning Ctr., Shreveport, La., 1983—. Mem. Mayor's Commn. for Women of Bossier City (La.) Inc., 1987—, 1st v.p., 1990—, pres., 1991-92. Mem. Am. Bus. Women's Assn. (Woman of the Yr. 1988, Srebo chpt. sec. 1990—, pres. 1991-92), Am. Home Econs. Assn., Am. Assn. for Adult and Continuing Edn., Quota Club, Montclair State Coll. Alumni Assn., Ill. State U. Alumni Assn., Auburn U. Alumni Assn. Methodist.

ROLFE, ROBERT MARTIN, lawyer; b. Richmond, Va., May 16, 1951; s. Norman and Bertha (Cohen) R.; m. Catherine Dennis Stone, July 14, 1973; children: P. Alexander, Asher B., Joel A., Zachary A. BA, U. Va., 1973, JD, 1976. Bar: Va. 1976, N.Y. 1985, U.S. Dist. Ct. (ea. and we. dists.) Va. 1976, U.S. Supreme Ct. 1979, U.S. Ct. Appeals (4th cir.) 1976, U.S. Ct. Appeals (2d cir.) 1979, U.S. Dist. Ct. (ea. dist.) Mich. 1985, U.S. Ct. Appeals (D.C. cir.) 1985, U.S. Dist. Ct. (so. dist. and ea. dist.) N.Y. 1985; U.S. Ct. Appeals (7th cir.) 1995. Assoc. Hunton & Williams, Richmond, 1976-83, ptnr., 1983—. Contbr. articles to profl. jours. Bd. dirs. Jewish Family Svcs., Richmond, pres., 1993-95; bd. mgrs., 2d v.p. Congregation Beth Ahabah, 1995—. Mem. ABA (litigation sect., natural resources, energy and environ. law sect.), Va. Bar Assn., Va. State Bar, Richmond Bar Assn., Am. Arbitration Assn. (comml. arbitrators panel), Order of Coif (Alumni award for acad. excellence U. Va. 1976). Home: 18 Greenway Ln Richmond VA 23226-1630 Office: Hunton & Williams Riverfront Plz East Tower 951 E Byrd St Richmond VA 23219-4074 also: 200 Park Ave New York NY 10166-0005

ROLINE, ERIC ALFRED, manufacturing company executive; b. Biggar, Sask., Can., Mar. 5, 1955; came to U.S., 1967; s. Alfred Christain and Antionette (Flavel) R.; m. Virginia Anne McCamey, Aug. 3, 1991; 1 child, Wesley Daniel Idell. BS in Applied Organizational Mgmt., Tusculum (Tenn.) Coll., 1989; AAS in electronics engring. tech., DeVry Inst. Tech., Phoenix, 1975; student, Regis Coll., Colorado Springs, Colo., 1985-86. Electronic technician Nat. Semi-Condr. Inc., Santa Clara, Calif., 1976-77; mem. spl. task force Intel Inc., Santa Clara, 1977; project engr. Cermetek Microelectronics Inc., Sunnyvale, Calif., 1977-80; founding mem. Horizon Cons. Inc., Colorado Springs, 1980-83; dir. tech. svcs. SuperFlow Inc., Colorado Springs, 1983-86; tech. svcs. mgr. Detroit Gasket div. Indian Head Industries Inc., Newport, Tenn., 1986—. Mem. ASTM, SAE, Soc. Mfg. Engrs., Orchid Soc. East Tenn. (trustee 1991-92).

ROLLASON, WENDELL NORTON, social services administrator; b. Winsted, Conn., Aug. 21, 1916; s. George Herbert Sanderson and Helen Hotchkiss (Norton) R.; m. Mary Jane Kemp, 1946 (div. 1971); children: Wendell, Frank, Raleigh; m. Barbara Louise Schott, Oct. 29, 1978. Grad. high sch., Winsted. Supr. Dade County Port Authority, Miami, Fla., 1946-51; exec. dir. Inter Am. Affairs Com., Miami, Fla., 1952-64; exec. dir. Redlands Christian Migrant Assn., Immokalee, Fla., 1966-90, exec. v.p., 1990—; chmn. Gov.'s Adv. Coun. on Farmworker Affairs, 1979, 86, 90; mem. Nat. Commn. on Migrant Edn. appt. by U.S. Senate, 1989-92. Vice chmn. Fla. Interagy. Coordinating Coun. for Infants and Toddlers, 1989-93; chmn. dist. adv. coun. Fla. Dept. Health Related Svcs., 1989-91. Petty officer 1st class USN, 1941-45. Recipient various awards, 1952-93; named One of Fla.'s Greatest Humanitarian Assets, Gov. of Fla., 1985; ann. health award created in his name, 1988; scholarship fund created in his name Migrant Parent Orgn., 1992. Mem. Fla. Assn. Community Health Ctrs. Democrat. Episcopalian. Home: 14940 Old Olga Rd Fort Myers FL 33905-4734

ROLLER HALL, GAYLE ALINE, gifted and talented educator; b. L.A., Dec. 3, 1959; d. Willard E. and Ruby A. (Meek) Roller; m. Samuel Hall, May 20, 1995. BA in Elem. Edn., Hendrix Coll., 1982; M in Elem. Edn., Ark. Tech. U., 1985, MS in Edn. Gifted and Talented, 1992. Cert. elem. edn., gifted K-12. Substitute tchr. Ft. Smith (Ark.) Pub. Schs., 1982-84; grad. asst. Ark. Tech. U., Russelville, 1984-85; gifted and talented tchr. Russellville (Ark.) Schs., 1985-86; gifted tchr., coord. Hartford (Ark.) Sch., 1986—; vis. lectr. Ark. Tech. U., Russellville, 1987-89. Mem. Circle K Svc. Orgn., Conway, Ark., 1978-82, Big Sister Youth Svcs., Conway, 1978-81; asst. leader 4-H Hartford, 1988-93, main leader, 1993-94. Mem. Ark. Edn. Assn. (pub. rels. com. 1990-93), Hartford Edn. Assn. (pres. 1992-94). Baptist. Home: Rt 1 Box 3190 Howe OK 74940 Office: Hartford Sch PO Box 489 Hartford AR 72938-0489

ROLLINS, ALBERT WILLIAMSON, civil engineer, consultant; b. Dallas, July 31, 1930; s. Andrew Peach and Mary (Williamson) R.; B.S. in Civil Engring., Tex. A. and M. U., 1951, M.S. in Civil Engring., 1956; m. Martha Ann James, Dec. 28, 1954; children—Elizabeth Ann, Mark Martin. Engring. asst. Tex. Hwy. Dept., Dallas, 1953-55; dir. pub. works City of Arlington (Tex.), 1956-63, city mgr., 1963-67; partner Schrickel, Rollins & Assos., land planners-engrs., Arlington, 1967—. Mem. Gov.'s Energy Adv. Council; chmn. Tex. Mass Transp. Commn.; bd. dirs. Tex. Turnpike Authority. Served as 1st lt. AUS, 1951-53. Registered profl. engr., Tex., La., Okla. Mem. Internat. City Mgmt. Assn., Nat. Soc. Profl. Engrs., ASCE, Am. Water Works Assn., Water Pollution Control Fedn., Sigma Xi, Phi Eta Sigma, Tau Beta Pi, Phi Kappa Phi, Chi Epsilon. Contbr. articles to profl. jours. Home: 3004 Yellowstone Dr Arlington TX 76013-1166 Office: Suite 200 1161 Corporate Dr W Ste 200 Arlington TX 76006-6819

ROLLINS, GARY WAYNE, service company executive; b. Chattanooga, Aug. 30, 1944; s. Orville Wayne and Grace (Crum) R.; m. Ruth Magness; children: Glen William, Ruth Ellen, Nancy Louise, Orville Wayne. BSBA, U. Tenn., 1967. Sales mgmt. Orkin Exterminating Co., Atlanta, 1967-72, v.p. ops., 1975-78, pres., 1978—; v.p., gen. mgr. Dwoskin, Atlanta, 1972-75; with Rollins, Inc., Atlanta, 1959—, v.p., 1972-84, pres., COO, 1984—, also bd. dirs.; pres. Rollins Supply, Inc., Atlanta; v.p. LOR, Inc., Atlanta, 1978—; bd. dirs. Rollins Leasing Co., Wilmington, Del., Rollins Energy Services, Atlanta, RPC Energy Svcs., Inc. Mem. Atlanta Symphony, 1970—, Atlanta Humane Soc., 1970—, Atlanta High Mus. Art, 1970—, Ga. Structural Pest Control Commn., 1967; founding dir. Tuxedo Park Civic Assn., Atlanta, 1984—. Recipient de Tocqueville Soc. award United Way, 1987. Mem. PADI Open Water Diving, Piedmont Driving Club. Methodist. Club: Cherokee (Atlanta). Office: Rollins Inc 2170 Piedmont Rd NE Atlanta GA 30324-4135*

ROLLINS, GREY JAMES, computer operator, author; b. Rutherfordton, N.C., Sept. 10, 1957; s. William Hugh and Eleanor Louise (Geer) R.; m. Cynthia Ann Nelson, May 28, 1994. BA in Geology and Psychology, U. N.C., 1979. In mainframe ops. U. S.C., Columbia, 1984—. Author: (fiction) To Victor Go the Spoils-Analog, 1990, Invitation to Ecstacy-Analog, 1992, Darwin's Children-Analog, 1993. Mem. Sci. Fiction Writers Am.

ROLOF, MARCIA CHRISTINE, sales executive; b. Green Bay, Wis., Sept. 1, 1950; adopted d. William August Rolof and Marcella S. (Rantanen) R.; m. Gerald W. Mattson, July 5, 1969 (div. 1974); 1 child, Shannon M. Mattson; m. Louis Glenn Mitchell, Nov. 12, 1994. Mgr., sales rep. Cameo Photography, 1980-82; tchr., physically challenged resource coord. U. Wis., 1982-85; dist. mgr. Women's Specialty Retail Group, U.S. Shoe, 1985-90; regional sales dir. Decor/Claire Corp., 1990-93; corp. adminstr. FLC, Inc., Houston, 1993-94; dist. mgr. United Retail Group, Inc., Houston, 1994-96; tutor, reading and lang. Pasadena Ind. Sch. Dist., Houston. Author: Tie the Moon to Your Car (My Cancer, My Way), 1994; author short stories; spokesperson childrens radio program. Network vol. U. Tex. M.D. Anderson Cancer Ctr., Houston, 1993—; vol. counselor R to R Cancer Soc., Houston, 1994. Mem. Houston C. of C., Pasadena C. of C.

ROMAGUERA, JORGE ENRIQUE, internist, educator; b. Cali, Colombia, Dec. 21, 1956. Student, U. P.R., 1974-76, BS magna cum laude, 1978, MD, 1982; student, MIT, 1976. Diplomate Am. Bd. Internal Medicine, Am. Bd. Med. Oncology, Nat. Bd. Med. Examiners; lic. physician, Tex. Intern Univ. Hosp., San Juan, P.R., 1982-85; fellow Univ. Hosp., San Juan, 1985-87; fellow U. Tex., Houston, 1987-88, faculty assoc., 1988-92, asst. internist, asst. prof., 1992—; instr. U. Tex. Med. Sch., 1988-90. Contbr. chpt. in book and articles to profl. jours. Maj. USAR, 1988-94; P.R. Army N.G., 1986-88. Grantee Bristol-Myers Squibb US Pharm. Fellow ACP; mem. AAAS, Am. Soc. Hematology, Am. Soc. Clin. Oncology, Tex. Med. Found., P.R. Soc. Hematology, Phi Kappa Phi. Home: 3010 Stanton St Houston TX 77025-2631 Office: MD Anderson Cancer Ctr 1515 Holcombe Blvd # 68 Houston TX 77030-4009

ROMAGUERA, MARIANO ANTONIO, consulting engineer; b. Mayaguez, P.R., May 4, 1928; s. Jose Mariano and Aminta (Martinez) R.; BS, MIT, 1950; MS, U. P.R., 1975; m. Virginia Casablanca, July 3, 1952; children: Jose Mariano, Jorge Enrique, Alberto, Ana Maria. Asst. engr. Arturo Romaguera, Cons. Engr., Colombia, 1950-51; asst. engr. Ingenio Providencia, Palmira, Colombia, 1951; shift engr. Central Igualdad and Western Sugar Refinery, Mayaguez, 1954; erection engr., asst. project mgr., Pradera Valle, Colombia, 1954-55, plant supt., chief engr., 1955-57; project engr. Ingenior Providencia, Palmira, Colombia, 1957, chief engr. ops. and maintenance, 1958-64; exec. v.p. Romaguera & Vendrell Devel. Corp., Mayaguez, P.R., 1964-68; pres. RomaVel, Inc., Mayaguez, 1965-68, Yagueka Equipment, Inc., 1968-78, Mariano A. Romaguera and Assocs., Engrs., Appraisers and Cons., Mayaguez, 1974—; sr. ptnr. Camino, Romaguera & Assocs., 1976—; sr. ptnr. M/E Appraisers, 1976—; cons. engr. Sugar Corp. P.R., Commonwealth of P.R., Biomass Steam Generation Rsch.; bd. regents Cath. U. P.R. Pres., Yagueka dist. P.R. coun. Boy Scouts Am., 1965-69, mem. exec. bd. P.R. coun.; chmn. ARC, 1966; bd. dirs. Mayaguez YMCA; mem. MIT Ednl. Coun.; mem. bd. regents Catholic U. of P.R. With Army, 1952-54, Korea. Recipient Silver Beaver award P.R. coun.l Boy Scouts Am., 1969. Mem. NSPE, ASME (pres. S.W. P.R. group), Am. Soc. Appraisers, Instituto de Evaluadores de P.R., Colegio Ingenieros y Agrimensores de P.R. (past pres. Mayaguez dist.), Instituto de Ingenieros Mecanicos de P.R., P.R. Soc. Profl. Engrs., Assn. Engrng. Socs., Am. Right of Way Assn., Internat. Soc. Sugar Cane Technologists, P.R. Assn. Real Estate Bds., Mayaguez Bd. Realtors, M.I.T. Alumni Assn., Nu Sigma Beta, Alpha Phi Omega. Roman Catholic. Lodge: Rotary. Home: 16 Calle Peral N Mayaguez PR 00680-4855 Office: PO Box 1340 Mayaguez PR 00681-1340

ROMAIN, BELLA MARY, graphic designer; b. Oakland, Calif., June 16, 1949; d. John Thomas Kondrup and Anna (Rabinowitz) Friedman; m. Stewart Jay Romain, Mar. 19, 1972. Student, SUNY, Stony Brook, 1967-68, Sch. Visual Arts, 1973-75; BFA magna cum laude, West Ga. Coll., 1989. Asst. to editor Dell Pub. Co., N.Y.C., 1968-72; reporter, proofreader Local News, Long Island, N.Y., 1973-76; graphic designer, editor Yellow Book Corp., N.Y.C., 1976-78; freelance graphic designer, editor N.Y.C., 1978-82; owner, graphic designer, editor designplus, Carrollton, Ga., 1982—; publs. cons. West Ga. Coll., Carrollton, 1985—. Paintings exhibited in numerous juried shows, including Alexandria Mus. Art, 1992. Speaker to civic groups, Carrollton, 1993; vol. Amateur Radio Emergency Svcs., Carrollton, 1985—; vol. designer Carroll County Humane Soc., Carrollton, 1993—. Recipient Fine Arts Achievement award Binney & Smith, 1989. Mem. Nat. Mus. Women in Arts, Lions Internat., Am. Bus. Women's Assn., Toastmasters (chair membership local chpt. 1993), Carroll County C. of C., Phi Kappa Phi. Home and Office: 285 Timber Ridge Trl Carrollton GA 30117-8884

ROMANO, ESTEBAN OSCAR, urologist; b. Cordoba, Argentina, Dec. 14, 1949; came to U.S., 1975; s. Fernando Oscar and Lyla Esther (Merino) R.; m. Maria Cristina Grunewald, Dec. 22, 1972; children: Lucia, Esteban, Cristina, Sebastian. MD, U. Nat. Cordoba, 1972; MBA, U. South Fla., 1993. Diplomate Am. Bd. Urology, Am. Bd. Quality Assurance and Utilization Rev. Intern Wilson Meml. Hosp., Johnson City, N.Y., 1977-78, resident in surgery, 1978-79; resident in urology La. State U., New Orleans, 1979-82; pvt. practice, Slidell, La., 1982—; pres. med. staff Slidell Meml. Hosp., 1987-88, dir. quality and utilization, 1990-94, med. dir., 1995, med. adminstrv. officer, 1996—. Active Indian Guides, YMCA, Slidell, 1994. Recipient Physician Recognition award AMA, 1994. Fellow ACS, Internat. Coll. Surgeons, Am. Coll. of Healthcare Execs. Office: Urology Ctr 1051 Gause Blvd Ste 440 Slidell LA 70458

ROMANO, GENO VINCENT, emergency medicine physician; b. Milw., Mar. 4, 1955; s. James Vincent and June Alice (Ranta) R.; m. Mary C. Plawin Gordon, Dec. 24, 1977 (div. July 1989); children: Maria, Charla, Vincent. BS, Concord Coll., 1981; MD, Marshall U., 1985. Bd. cert. Am. Bd. Family Practice. Asst. prof. Coll. Medicine U. Fla., Gainesville, 1988-93; emergency dept. physician Alachua Gen. Hosp., Gainesville, 1994—. Fellow Am. Acad. Family Physicians; mem. AMA, Am. Med. Soc. for Sports Medicine (charter), Am. Coll. Sports Medicine. Home: PO Box 23707 Gainesville FL 32602-3707

ROMAN-RODRIGUEZ, JESSE, medical center administrator, internist; b. Mayaguez, P.R., July 6, 1959; m. Iris M., 1982; children: Veronica, Victoria. BS magna cum laude, U. P.R., 1979, MD, 1983. Diplomate Nat. Bd. Med. Examiners, Am. Bd. Internal Medicine. Intern and resident in internal medicine VA Hosp., San Juan, P.R.; postdoctoral rsch. fellow in cell and molecular biology Washington U., St. Louis, 1987-91, pulmonary medicine fellow, 1986-89; asst. chief pulmonary sect. Atlanta VA Med. Ctr., Decatur, 1991-94, chief, 1994—, med. dir. respiratory therapy, pulmonary div., 1991—; asst. prof. medicine Emory U., Atlanta, 1991—; staff physician Dept. Internal Medicine, Washington U. Sch. Medicine, St. Louis, 1989-91, Barnes Hosp., St. Louis, 1989-91, VA Med. Ctr., St. Louis, 1989-91, dept. medicine, Emory U. Sch. Medicine, 1991—, VA Med. Ctr., Atlanta, 1991—, Grady Meml. Hosp., Atlanta, 1991—; instr. medicine Washington U., 1989-91; lectr. in field; referee for grant evaluation Ga. Am. Lung Assn. Rsch. Awards, clin. investigator devel. award rev. com. NIH, NHLBI. Contbr. articles to profl. jours.; editorial cons. Devel. Biology, Am. rev. of Respiratory Cell and Molecular Biology, Am. Jour. Physiology, Lung Exptl. Rsch., Jour. Cellular Physiology. Am. Lung Assn. rsch. fellow, 1988, Nat. Rsch. Svc. Award fellow, 1988; Am. Heart Assn. grantee, 1992; recipient Am. Lung Assn. Rsch. award, 1992, Dept. Vets. Affairs Rsch. Adv. Group award, 1991, Biomed. Rsch. Support award Washington U., 1990, Minority Med. Faculty Devel. award Robert Wood Johnson Found., 1990; NIH grantee, 1988-89, 93—. Fellow Am. Coll. Chest Physicians, Am. Fedn. Clin. Rsch. (So. sect. Young Faculty award 1991); mem. Am. Soc. Cell Biology (Minority travel award 1989), Am. Thoracic Soc., Soc. Exptl. Biology and Medicine, Am. Lung Assn. (Ga. chpt.), Assn. for Respiratory Health in Minorities (sec.), Am. Heart Assn. (cardiopulmonary coun.), Soc. Clin. Investigation (So. sect.). Home: 2438 Kings Arms Dr NE Atlanta GA 30345-2116 Office: Vets Affairs Med Ctr Dept Medicine (111) Rm 1209 1670 Clairmont Rd Decatur GA 30033-4004

ROMEO, ANTHONY C., air transportation services executive; b. 1953; married. With Overseas Nat. Airways, Detroit, 1971-76, Fleming Internat., Miami, Fla., 1976-82; pres., dir. Miami Aircraft Support, Inc., 1981—; prin. Charter Am., Inc., Miami, 1986—, Support Equipment Leasing, Inc., Miami, 1988—. Office: Miami Aircraft Support Inc 9100 S Dadeland Blvd, Ste 104 Miami FL 33156*

ROMEO, TONY, microbiology educator; b. Batesville, Ark., Dec. 20, 1956; s. Edward Peter and Norma Lee (Johnson) R.; m. Lori Ann Dinello, July 16, 1983. BS in Microbiology, U. Fla., 1979, MS, 1981, PhD, 1986. Postdoctorate Mich. State U., East Lansing, 1986-89; assoc. prof. U. North Tex. Health Sci. Ctr., Ft. Worth, 1989—; cons. Zeneca Seeds, Slater, Iowa, 1992-93; peer rev. cons. NIH/ADAMHA, 1993—; external reviewer Manitoba Health Rsch. Coun., 1993—. Author 23 manuscripts in books and jours. Recipient NSF Divsn. Molecular Biosciences rsch. grant, 1993-97, NIH biomed. rsch. support grant, 1989-93. Mem. AAAS, Am. Soc. for Biochemistry and Molecular Biology, Am. Soc. for Microbiology, Am. Men and Women of Sci. Office: U North Tex Health Sci Ctr 3500 Camp Bowie Blvd Fort Worth TX 76107-2644

ROMERE, MARY ELAINE, public health services manager; b. Erie, Pa., Dec. 31, 1954; d. Charles E. and Elaine (Trabinger) Schwarz; m. Joseph S. Romere III; children: Brie, Wynn. BSN, U. Pitts., 1976; MHA, Ohio State U., 1981. DON, perinatology and gynecology Sinai Hosp. of Detroit, 1983-84; dir. obstetric svcs. Hermann Hosp., Houston, 1985-86; nursing supr. Women's Hosp. of Tex., Houston, 1987-89; mgr. maternal-child health svcs. Meml. S.W. Hosp., Houston, 1989-90; search assoc. Guidry East Barnes and Bono, Inc., Humble, Tex., 1990-92; dir. pediatrics Kingwood (Tex.) Plaza Hosp., 1992-93; health svcs. area mgr. Harris County Health Dept., Houston, 1995—. Mem. Houston Orgn. Nurse Execs., Am. Coll. Healthcare Execs. Home: 1908 Riverlawn Dr Kingwood TX 77339

ROMERO, EMILIO FELIPE, psychiatry educator, psychotherapist, hospital administrator; b. Havana, Cuba, Nov. 12, 1946; came to U.S., 1960; s. Emilio Jose and Isela Maria (Correoso) R. BA cum laude, U. Miami, Coral Gables, Fla., 1966; MD, U. Zaragoza (Spain), 1972. Diplomate Am. Bd. Psychiatry and Neurology (examiner 1987—). Resident in psychiatry U. Tex. Health Sci. Ctr., San Antonio, 1976; assoc. dir. Therapeutic Community for Schizophrenics Audie L. Murphy VA Hosp., San Antonio, 1976-78, staff psychiatrist outpatient psychiatry svcs., 1978-81, dir. outpatient psychiatry svcs., 1981-89, acting chief psychiatry svc., 1989-90, chief psychiatry svc., 1990—; asst. prof. psychiatry U. Tex. Health Sci. Ctr., San Antonio, 1976-87, assoc. prof. psychiatry, 1987-93, prof., 1993—; psychoanalytical cons. Med. Ctr. Hosp., San Antonio, 1981-87; lectr. on dream interpretation, U.S., Can., Europe, S.Am., 1977—; judge Internat. Film Festival on Culture and Psychiatry, 1976, 78; cons. to Donald Sutherland on film Lost Angels, 1988. Co-author: Psiquiatria Clinica Para Estudiantes de Medicina, 1993, Psiquiatria Para No Psiquiatras, 1995; contbr. articles to nat. and internat. profl. jours. Active local TV and radio stas., San Antonio Express News & Light, San Antonio and Diario del las Americas, Miami, Fla., 1973—; mem. art com. San Antonio Mus. Assn., 1988—, mayor's Com. to Receive the King of Spain, San Antonio, 1987; mem. Mex. Rels. Com. to Receive His Holiness Pope John Paul II, San Antonio, 1987. Knighted Sovereign Order of Malta, Rome, 1987; recipient Silver plaque U. Salamanca (Spain), 1982; recognized with proclamation of day in his honor, Dade County, Fla., 1992; named to Austrian Order of Mil. Medicine and Pharmacy, 1994. Fellow Am. Psychiat. Assn., Am. Assn. Social Psychiatry, Am. Coll. Psychiatrists; mem. Tex. Soc. Psychiat. Physicians (chmn. internat. grads. 1985—), Assn. Mil. Surgeons U.S. (internat. com. 1986—, chair 1996), Bexar County Psychiat. Soc. (pres. 1987-88, Leadership award 1988), Sociedad Española de Psiquiatria (Mem. of Honor 1988, Disting. Guest and Citizen City of Salamanca Spain 1990), Austrian Order Mil. Medicine and Pharmacy. Roman Catholic. Home: 141 Twinleaf Ln San Antonio TX 78213-2516 Office: Audie Murphy VA Hosp 7400 Merton Minter St San Antonio TX 78284-5700

ROMERO, JORGE ANTONIO, neurologist, educator; b. Bayamon, P.R., Apr. 15, 1948; s. Calixto Antonio Romero-Barcelo and Antonia (de Juan) R.; m. Helen Mella, June 20, 1970 (div. 1983); children: Sofia, Jorge, Alfredo, Isabel; m. Cheryl Raps, Aug. 1994; 1 child, Jessica. SB, MIT, 1968; MD, Harvard U., 1972. Diplomate Am. Bd. Psychiatry and Neurology. Intern U. Chgo. Hosp. and Clinics, 1972-73; resident Mass. Gen. Hosp., Boston, 1975-78; rsch. fellow in pharmacology NIMH, Bethesda, Md., 1973-75; asst. prof. neurology Harvard Med. Sch., Boston, 1979-92; mem. staff VA Med. Ctr., Brockton, Mass., 1979-92; assoc. physician Brigham and Women's Hosp., Boston, 1980-92; chmn. dept. neurology Ochsner Clin. Baton Rouge, 1993—; cons. Mass. Mental Health Ctr., Boston, 1987-92. With USPHS, 1973-75. Recipient Career Devel. award VA, 1979. Mem. Am. Acad. Neurology. Office: Ochsner Clin Baton Rouge 16777 Medical Center Dr Baton Rouge LA 70816-3228

ROMERO-BARCELÓ, CARLOS ANTONIO, governor of Puerto Rico; b. San Juan, P.R., Sept. 4, 1932; s. Antonio S. Romero and Josefina Barceló; m. Kathleen Donnelly, Jan. 2, 1966; children: Juan Carlos, Melinda Kathleen; children by previous marriage: Carlos, Andrés. BA, Yale U., 1953; LLB, U. P.R., 1956; LLD (hon.), U. Bridgeport, 1977. Bar: P.R. 1956. Mem. Herrero-Frank & Romero-Barceló, 1956-58; ptnr. Rivera-Zayas, Rivera-Cestero & Rúa, San Juan, 1958-63, Segurola, Romero & Toledo, 1963-68; pres. Citizens for State 51, 1965-67; mayor, San Juan, 1969-77; gov. P.R., 1977-85, 92—; pres. New Progressive Party, 1974-85, 89-91; resident commr., 1991—. Recipient Hoey award for Interracial Justice, Cath. Interracial Council of N.Y., 1977, Spl. Gold Medal award Spanish Inst., N.Y., 1979, U.S. Atty.-Gen.'s medal, 1981. Mem. Nat. Govs. Assn., So. Govs. Assn. (chmn. 1980-81), Conf., Nat. League Cities (pres. 1975), U.S. Conf. Mayors (bd. dir.). Roman Catholic. Author: Statehood is for the Poor; contbr. articles to profl. jours. Office: 2243 Rayburn Washington DC 20515*

ROMINE, THOMAS BEESON, JR., consulting engineering executive; b. Billings, Mont., Nov. 16, 1925; s. Thomas Beeson and Elizabeth Marjorie (Tschudy) R.; m. Rosemary Pearl Melancon, Aug. 14, 1948; children—Thomas Beeson III, Richard Alexander, Robert Harold. Student, Rice Inst., 1943-44; B.S. in Mech. Engring, U. Tex., Austin, 1948. Registered profl. engr., Tex., Okla., La., Ga. Jr. engr. Gen. Engring. Co., Ft. Worth, 1948-50; design engr. Wyatt C. Hedrick (architect/engr.), Ft. Worth, 1950-54; chief mech. engr. Wyatt C. Hedrick (architect/engr.), 1954-56; chmn., chief mech. engr. Thomas B. Romine, Jr. (now Romine Romine & Burgess, Inc. cons. engrs.), Ft. Worth, 1956—; mem. heating, ventilating, and air conditioning controls com. NRC, 1986-88. Author numerous computer programs in energy analysis and heating and air conditioning field; contbr. articles to profl. jours. Mem. Plan Commn., City of Ft. Worth, 1958-62; mem. Supervisory Bd. Plumbers, City Ft. Worth, 1963-71, chmn., 1970-71; chmn. Plumbing Code Rev. Com., 1968-69; mem. Mech. Bd., City Ft. Worth, 1974-82, chmn., 1976-82; chmn. plumbing code bd. North Central Tex. Council Govts., Ft. Worth, 1971-75; Bd. mgrs. Tex. Christian U.-South Side YMCA, 1969-74; trustee Ft. Worth Symphony Orch., 1968—, Orch. Hall, 1975—. Served with USNR, 1943-45. Disting. fellow ASHRAE (pres. Ft. Worth chpt. 1958, nat. committeeman 1974—); fellow Am. Cons. Engrs. Coun., Automated Procedures for Engring. Cons. (trustee 1970-71, 75, 1st v.p. 1972-73, internat. pres. 1974); mem. NSPE, Tex. Soc. Profl. Engrs. (bd. dirs. 1956, treas. 1967), Cons. Engrs. Coun. Tex. (pres. North Tex. chpt., also v.p. state orgn. 1965, dir. state orgn. 1967), Starfish Class Assn. (nat. pres. 1970-73, nat. champion 1976), Delta Tau Delta (v.p. West div. 1980-90), Pi Tau Sigma. Episcopalian (vestryman). Clubs: Colonial Country, Rotary. Home: 3232 Preston Hollow Rd Fort Worth TX 76109-2051 Office: Romine Romine & Burgess 300 Greenleaf St Fort Worth TX 76107-2316

ROMO, JOSE LEÓN, library educator; b. Roswell, N.Mex., July 16, 1930; s. Jose L. and Barbara (Romero) R. BA in Theology and Spanish, Coll. of Santa Fe, 1974; postgrad., Colegio Sant' Anselmo, Rome, 1975-76; MA in LS, U. Denver, 1980. Monk Order of St. Benedict, Pecos, N.Mex., 1970-75, 76-78, Rome, 1975-76; reference, libr. instrn. libr. Coll. St. Benedict, St. Joseph, Minn., 1980-84, St. John's U., Collegeville, Minn., 1980-84; reference libr., instr. Laredo (Tex.) Jr. Coll.-Laredo State U., 1984-87; libr. dir. St. Vincent de Paul Sem., Boynton Beach, Fla., 1988—. Latin Am. Affairs scholar, U. N.Mex., 1948-50; U. Denver. Libr. Sci. fellow, 1979-80. Mem. ALA, Am. Coll. and Rsch. Librarians, Am. Theol. Libr. Assn. Office: St Vincent de Paul Sem Libr 10701 S Military Trl Boynton Beach FL 33436-4811

ROMPF, PAUL DOUGLAS, hotel and restaurant administration educator. BA, Mich. State U., 1966, MBA, 1968; PhD, U. S.C., 1992. Instr.-coord. Mid-Fla. Tech. Inst., Orlando, 1972-75; asst. prof. hotel and restaurant adminstrn. U. So. Miss., Hattiesburg, 1975-78, 83-85; faculty and rsch. assoc. U. S.C., Columbia, 1985-94; vis. prof. U. S.C., 1996, Ga. So. U., 1996—; cons. PR Enterprises, 1994-95; dir. Office of Market Rsch., S.C. PRT, 1995; pres. PR Devels., Inc., Arlington, Tex., 1980-86; asst. mgr. Contemporary Hotel, Lake Buena Vista, Fla., 1971-72; asst. mgr. Kellogg Ctr. Mich. State U., East Lansing, 1966-68. Contbr. articles to profl. jours. Sgt. U.S. Army, 1969-70. Grantee S.C. Dept. Parks, Recreation and Tourism, 1993, World Bank, 1987-88, Miss. Vocat. Rehab for Blind, 1985, Miss. Employment Security Commn., 1984. Mem. Greater Columbia Hospitality Sales Assn. (exec. dir. 1989—), S.C. Festival Assn. (ex officio bd. dirs. 1991—, mem. cert. festival planner standing com. 1993), Coun. on Hotel, Restaurant and Instnl. Edn. (dir. 1975, sec. 1978), Greater Columbia Conv. and Visitors Bur. (pub. rels. com.), Am. Mktg. Assn., Assn. Consumer Rschrs., Nat. Restaurant Assn., Southeastern Coun. on Hotel, Restaurant and Instnl. Edn. Home: 900 Country Club Dr # 9 Statesboro GA 30458 Office: Ga Southern Univ PO Box 8034 Statesboro GA 30460

RONAN, WILLIAM JOHN, management consultant; b. Buffalo, Nov. 8, 1912; s. William and Charlotte (Ramp) R.; m. Elena Vinadé, May 29, 1939; children: Monica, Diana Quasha. A.B., Syracuse U., 1934; Ph.D., N.Y. U., 1940, LL.D., 1969; certificate, Geneva Sch. Internat. Studies, 1933. Mus. asst. Buffalo Mus. Sci., 1928-30; with Niagara-Hudson Power Co., 1931; transfer dept. N.Y.C.R.R., 1932; Penfield fellow internat. law, diplomacy and belles lettres, 1935, Univ. fellow, 1936; editor Fed. Bank Service, Prentice-Hall, Inc., 1937; instr. govt. N.Y. U., 1938, exec. sec. grad. div. for tng. in pub. services, 1938, asst. dir., 1940, asst. prof. govt., dir. grad. div. for tng. pub. service, 1940, assoc. prof. govt., 1946-47, prof., 1947, dean, grad. sch. pub. adminstrn. and social service, 1953-58; Cons. N.Y.C. Civil Service Commn., 1938; prin. rev. officer, negotiations officer U.S. Civil Service Commn., 1942; prin. div. asst. U.S. Dept. State, 1943; cons. Dept. State, 1948, Dept. Def., 1954; dir. studies N.Y. State Coordination Commn., 1951-58; project mgr. N.Y. U.-U. Ankara project, 1954-59; cons. ICA, 1955, N.Y. State Welfare Conf.; adminstrv. co-dir. Albany Grad. Program in Pub. Adminstrn.; 1st dep. city adminstr. N.Y.C., 1956-57; exec. dir. N.Y. State Temporary Commn. Constl. Conv., 1956-58; sec. to Gov. N.Y., 1959-66; chmn. interdept. com. traffic safety, commr. Port Authority N.Y. and N.J., 1967-90, vice chmn., 1972-74, chmn., 1974-77; with UTDC Corp., West Palm Beach, Fla.; trustee Crosslands Savs. Bank; chmn. bd. L.I. R.R., 1966-74; chmn. Tri-State Transp. Com., N.Y., N.J., Conn., 1961-67; chmn. interstate com. New Haven R.R., 1960-63; chmn. N.Y. Com. on L.I. R.R., 1964-65; mem. N.Y. State Commn. Interstate Coop., 1961, N.Y. State Com. Fgn. Ofcl. Visitors, 1961, N.Y. State Coordination Commn., 1960; mem. N.Y. Civil Svc. Commn., Temporary State Commn. on Constl. Conv., 1966-67; chmn. N.Y. State Met. Commuter Transp. Authority, 1965-68, Met. Transp. Authority, 1968-74, Tri-Borough Bridge and Tunnel Authority, 1968-74, N.Y.C. Transit Authority, 1968-74, Manhattan and Bronx Surface Transit Operating Authority, 1968-74; chmn. bd., pres. 3d Century Corp., 1974-94; mem. Commn. Critical Choices for Am., 1973—, acting chmn., 1975—; mem. urban transp. adv. com. U.S. Dept. Transp.; sr. adviser Rockefeller family, 1974-80; pres. Nelson Rockefeller Collection, Inc., 1977-80; trustee Power Authority of State of N.Y., 1974-77; cons. to trustees Penn Ctrl. Transp. Co.; vice chmn. bd. CCX, Inc.; sec.-treas. Sarabam Corp. N.V.; chmn., dir. UTDC (U.S.A.) Inc., 1987-88; chmn. UTDC Corp., 1989-94, Transit Svcs. Corp., 1989-94; cons. Herzog Transit Svcs., 1995—, Dime Savs. Bank, Metal Powder Products Inc., Prometech, Inc., Internat. Mining and Metals Inc., Quadrant Mgmt. Inc., 1990—, Ohio Highspeed Rail Authority, 1991-93; chmn. N.Y. and N.J. Inland Rail Rate Com.; dir. Nat. Mgmt. Coun., 1951. Author: Money Power of States in International Law, 1940, The Board of Regents and the Commissioner, 1948, Our War Economy, 1943, (with others), articles in profl. jours.; adviser: Jour. Inst. Socio-Econ. Studies. Mem. U.S. FOA, Am. Public Health Assn.; staff relations officer N.Y.C. Bd. Edn.; Mem. Nat. Conf. Social Work, Nat. Conf. on Met. Areas, Citizens Com. on Corrections, Council on Social Work Edn.; bd. dirs. World Trade Club; adv. bd. World Trade Inst.; mem. 42d St. Redevel. Corp., chmn., 1980-94; mem. Assn. for a Better N.Y.; bd. advisers Inst. for Socioecon. Studies, 1977—; dir. Nat. Health Council, 1980-86; dep. dir. policy Nelson Rockefeller campaign for Republican presdl. nomination, 1964; mem. N.Y. State Gov.'s Com. on Shoreham Nuclear Plant, 1983-85, Nassau County Indsl. Devel. Authority, 1982-90, U.S. Dept. Transp. Com. on Washington and Capital Dist. Airports, 1985-86; bd. dirs. Ctr. Study Presidency, 1986-90, Alcoholism Council of N.Y., 1986—; trustee N.Y. Coll. Osteopathic Medicine, 1986-91. Served as lt. USNR, 1943-46. Mem. NEA, Am. Polit. Sci. Assn., Am. Acad. Pub. Adminstrn., Am. Soc. Pub. Adminstrn., Civil Svc. Assembly of U.S. and Can., Internat. Assn. Met. Rsch. and Devel., Nat. Mcpl. League, Mcpl. Pers. Soc., Citizens Union of N.Y., Nat. Civil Svc. League, Am. Acad. Polit. and Social Sci., L.I. Assn. Commerce and Industry (dir.), Internat. Inst. Adminstrv. Scis., Am. Fgn. Law Assn., Internat. Union Pub. Transport (mgmt. com., v.p.), Am. Pub. Transit Assn. (chmn. 1974-76), Nat. Def. Transp. Assn. (v.p. for Mass transit), Met. Opera Club, Maidstone Club, Devon Yacht Club, Knickerbocker Club, Hemisphere Club, Harvard Club, Creek Club, Wings Club, Traffic Club, Univ. Club, Am. Club Riviera, Beach Club (Palm Beach), Everglades Club. Home: 525 S Flagler Dr West Palm Beach FL 33401-5922 Home: Villa La Pointe Du Cap, Ave de La Corniche, 06230 Saint Jean Cap Ferrat France

RONDEAU, CLEMENT ROBERT, gas industry executive, petroleum geologist; b. Ironwood, Mich., July 6, 1928. BS, Tulane U., 1955. Geol. supr. Texaco, Inc., New Orleans, 1955-63; area mgr. Pubco Petroleum Corp., New Orleans, 1963-69; cons. petroleum geologist Harahan, La., 1969—; owner Natural Gas Exploration Co., Harahan, 1977—. Mem. AAAS, Am. Assn. Petroleum Geologists, Soc. Exploration Geophysicists, New Orleans Geol. Soc., Explorers Club, Internat. Platform Assn., Internat. Oil Scouts Assn., Phi Beta Kappa, Sigma Gamma Epsilon. Democrat. Roman Catholic. Home: 632 Stratford Dr New Orleans LA 70123-3849 Office: Natural Gas Exploration Co 6430 Jefferson Hwy New Orleans LA 70123-5036

RONE, JAMES KELLETT, endocrinologist, career officer; b. Columbia, S.C., Oct. 6, 1961; s. William Eugene and Margaret Louise (Banks) R.; m. Donna Lee Walgamotte, Feb. 14, 1990 (div. Apr. 1994); stepchildren: Shannon Nicole Vaughn, Stephen Daniel Vaughn. BS, U. S.C., 1983, MD, 1987. Bd. cert. internal medicine, 1990, endocrinology, 1993. Commd. lt. USAF, 1983, advanced through grades to maj., 1993; resident in internal medicine Keesler USAF Med. Ctr., Biloxi, Miss., 1987-90, staff endocrinologist, 1992-94; chief of endocrinology USAF Med. Ctr., Biloxi, Miss., 1994—; fellow in endocrinology and metabolism Wilford Hall USAF Med. Ctr., San Antonio, Tex., 1990-92; instr. in medicine Uniformed Svcs. U. Health Scis., San Antonio, 1990-92; clin. asst. prof. medicine U. S. Ala., Mobile, 1992—; quality assurance coord. dept. medicine Keesler USAF Med. Ctr., Biloxi, 1993-96, asst. med. flight comdr., 1996—. Author: (with others) Manual of Medical Care, 1994, (with others) Endocrine & Metabolic Testing Manual, 1994; contbr. articles to profl. jours.; question writer/reviewer Am. Bd. Internal Medicine. Fellow ACP; mem. Soc. Uniformed Endocrinologists, Endocrine Soc., NRA, Am. Thyroid Assn., Am. Diabetes Assn. Episcopalian. Home: 2660 Beach Blvd Apt 21E Biloxi MS 39531-4512 Office: 81st Medical Group/SGHM 301 Fisher St # 401 Keesler AFB MS 39534-2508

RONEY, PAUL H(ITCH), federal judge; b. Olney, Ill., Sept. 5, 1921; m. Sarah E. Eustis; children: Susan M., Paul Hitch Jr., Timothy Eustis. Student, St. Petersburg Jr. Coll., 1938-40; B.S. in Econs, U. Pa., 1942; LL.B., Harvard U., 1948; LL.D., Stetson U., 1977; LL.M., U. Va., 1984. Bar: N.Y. 1949, Fla. 1950. Assoc. Root, Ballantine, Harlan, Bushby & Palmer, N.Y.C., 1948-50; ptnr. Mann, Harrison, Roney, Mann & Masterson (and predecessors), St. Petersburg, Fla., 1950-57; pvt. practice law, 1957-63; ptnr. Roney & Beach, St. Petersburg, 1963-69, Roney, Ulmer, Woodworth & Jacobs, St. Petersburg, 1969-70; judge U.S. Ct. Appeals (5th cir.), St. Petersburg, 1970-81; judge U.S. Ct. Appeals (11th cir.), St. Petersburg, 1981-86, chief judge, 1986-89, sr. cir. judge, 1989—; mem. adv. com. on adminstrv. law judges U.S. CSC, 1976-77; pres. judge U.S. Fgn. Intelligence Surveillance Ct. of Rev., 1994—. With U.S. Army, 1942-46. Fellow Am. Bar Found.; mem. ABA (chmn. legal adv. com. Fair Trial-Free Press 1973-76, mem. task force on cts. and public 1973-76, jud. adminstrn. div., chmn. appellate judges conf. 1978-79, mem. Gavel Awards com. 1980-83), Am. Judicature Soc. (dir. 1972-76), Am. Law Inst., Fla. Bar, St. Petersburg Bar Assn. (pres. 1964-65), Nat. Jud. Coll. (faculty 1974, 75), Jud. Conf. U.S. (subcom. on jud. improvements 1978-84, exec com. 1986-89, com. to review circuit coun. conduct and disability orders 1991-93). Home: Bayfront Tower 1 Beach Dr SE Saint Petersburg FL 33701-3924 Office: US Ct Appeals 11th Circuit 601 Federal Bldg 144 1st Ave S Saint Petersburg FL 33701-4311

RONIS, MARTIN JORN JANIS, pediatrics researcher and educator; b. Huddersfield, Yorkshire, Eng., Apr. 8, 1961; came to U.S., 1985; s. Fritz and Helga (Nicks) R.; m. Lisa Ricketson, May 16, 1992. BA in Natural Scis., Cambridge U., Eng., 1982; PhD in Biochemistry and Physiology, Reading (Eng.) U., 1985. Teaching asst., instr. biochemistry Reading U., 1982-85; postdoctoral rsch. assoc. toxicology program N.C. State U., Raleigh, 1985-87; vis. rsch. assoc. dept. physiol. chemistry Karolinska Inst., Stockholm, 1987-89; instr. dept. pediatrics U. Ark. Med. Scis., Little Rock, 1989-90, asst. prof., 1990-96, tenured assoc. prof. Ark. Children's Hosp. Rsch. Inst., 1996—; ad hoc reviewer sea grant instl. program Hancock Inst. Marine Studies, U. So. Calif., 1990, La. Bd. Regents, LEQSF Grant Program, 1992. Ad hoc reviewer Alcohol: Clin. and Exptl. Rsch., Gastroenterology, others; contbr. articles to profl. jours. Grantee Nat. Inst. Alcohol Abuse and Alcoholism, 1990—, Nat. Inst. Drug Abuse, 1992-95, Nat. Inst. Environ. Health Sci., 1994—, EPA, 1995-96, USDA, 1995—. Mem. Internat. Soc. Study of Xenobiotics, Soc. Toxicology, N.Y. Acad. Sci., Sigma Xi. Democrat. Home: 7214 Apache Rd Little Rock AR 72205-5002 Office: U Ark Med Scis Dept Pediatrics Slot 512B Little Rock AR 72205

RONN, EHUD ISRAEL, finance educator; b. Tel Aviv, Dec. 1, 1950; came to U.S., 1978; s. Menachem F. and Bilha (Kesten) R.; m. Aimee Beth Gerbarg, Dec. 22, 1979; children: David Aaron, Rebecca Anne. BS in Econs. and Mgmt., Technion U., Haifa, Israel, 1976, MS in Econs., 1978; PhD in Fin., Stanford U., 1983. Asst. prof. fin. U. Calif., Berkeley, 1982-88; from vis. asst. prof. to vis. assoc. prof. U. Chgo., 1987-88; assoc. prof. U. Tex., Austin, 1988-96, prof., 1996—; cons. fin. various orgns., Berkeley, Chgo. and Austin, 1982—. Contbr. articles on fin. and econs. to profl.

jours., 1977—. Funding grantee Q Group, Inst. Quantitative Rsch. in Fin., 1985, 88, Inst. Chartered Fin. Analysts, 1988, Prochnow Edni. Found., 1989; award recipient Am. Assn. Ind. Investors and Western Fin. Assn., Colorado Springs, 1986. Republican. Jewish. Office: U Tex Austin Dept Fin Coll & Grad Sch Bus Austin TX 78712-1179

RONZIO, ROBERT ANTHONY, biochemist, educator; b. Colo., Jan. 24, 1938. BA, Reed Coll., Portland, Oreg., 1960; PhD, U. Calif., Berkeley, 1966; D of Naturopathic Medicine (hon.), Bastyr U., 1990. Diplomate in Nutrition Counseling Am. Bd. Nutritional Medicine; cert. nutrition specialist. Assoc. prof. Mich. State U., East Lansing, 1969-77; visual artist Seattle, 1977-80; resource faculty prof. The Evergreen State Coll., Olympia, Wash., 1980-86; prof. med. sci. Bastyr U., Seattle, 1986-91, chair basic med. scis., 1989-91; mem. Disting. Nutrition Faculty Bastyr U., Seattle, Wash., 1986; dir. ednl. svcs. Gt. Smokies Diagnostic Lab., Asheville, N.C., 1993-94; lab. dir. Biotics Rsch. Corp., Stafford, Tex., 1994—. Author: Facts on File, 1990-96, Metabolic Mastery, 1991, Encyclopedia of Nutrition and Good Health, 1997. Coord. Community Sci. Program, Tacoma, 1982-85; educator Push/Excel, Tacoma, 1982-88. Am. Cancer Soc. postdoctoral fellow, U. Wash., 1967-69. Fellow Am. Inst. Chemists; mem. Am. Chem. Soc., Am. Bd. Nutritional Medicine, Am. Coll. Nutrition, Am. Assn. for Environ. Medicine, Am. Oil Chemists Soc., The Oxygen Soc., Inst. Food Technologists, Phi Beta Kappa, Sigma Xi. Office: Biotics Rsch Corp PO Box 36888 Houston TX 77236-6888

ROOKEY, THOMAS JEROME, dean; b. Oswego, N.Y., Oct. 18, 1944; s. Ernest J. and Irene A. (Matthews) R.; m. Rosann Spohn, Mar. 30, 1967; children: Austin, Kristin, Dionna. Student, Siena U., Italy, 1964; BA, SUNY, 1966; MA, Bucknell U., 1968; PhD, Lehigh U., 1972. Rsch. assoc. Pa. Dept. Edn., Harrisburg, 1966-72; rsch. analyst Reach for Better Schs., Phila., 1971-72; assoc. prof. East Stroudsburg (Pa.) U., 1972-76; exec. dir. Ednl. Improvement Ctr., Princeton, N.J., 1976-83; dean Clarion U., Oil City, Pa., 1983-89; acad. dean Medaille Coll., Buffalo, 1989—. Contbr. articles to profl. jours. Mem. Coun., Town of Hightstown, N.J., 1982-83; v.p. Oil City C. of C., 1984-89; mem. exec. bd. United Way, Venango, Pa., 1984-89; mem. County Planning Commn., Venango, 1985-89. With USAF, 1968-69. Named Citizen of Yr. Oil City, 1988; recipient Svc. awrd Venango Video, Oil City, 1989, Excellence award Nat. Assn. State Edn. Dept. Info. Officers, 1981. Mem. Am. Assn. Cmty. and Jr. Coll., Nat. Assn. Campus Adminstrs., Rotary (Pres. 1987), Phi Delta Kappa (Kappan of Yr. 1976). Office: Dublin Campus 101 Kellam Rd Dublin GA 31021-3457

ROOMBERG, SUSAN KELLY, city administrator; b. Corpus Christi, Tex., May 22, 1961; d. Oscar Olie and Barbara Ann (Hodson) Sjerven. BA in English, Psychology, Austin Coll., 1983; M in Pub. Affairs, U. Tex., 1986. Adminstrv. intern Austin (Tex.) Fire Dept., 1983-84; intern to congressman Washington, summer 1984; adminstrv. intern Asst. City Mgrs. Office, Austin, 1984-85, adminstrv. asst., 1985-86; adminstrv. asst. Transp. and Pub. Services Dept., Austin, 1986-87, coordinator adminstrv. services, 1987-89; budget analyst Fin. Svcs. Dept., Austin, 1989-90; budget and mgmt. analyst Office Mgmt. and Budget, City of Alexandria, Va., 1990-94; prin. SKR Assocs., Midland, Tex., 1995—. Trustee merit scholar Austin Coll., 1979-83, Clarence E. Ridley scholar, 1985-86. Mem. LWV (bd. dirs. 1995—), Austin Soc. Pub. Arminstrn., Tex. City Mgmt. Assn. (edn. com. 1986-89, conf. com. 1989-90), Internat. City/County Mgmt. Assn., Lyndon Baines Johnson Sch. Alumni Assn. (sec. nat. bd. dirs. 1987-88, pres. 1989-90, bd. dirs., pres. Austin chpt. 1989-90, bd. dirs. Washington chpt. 1991. 93-94), Alpha Phi Omega, Delta Phi Nu. Presbyterian. Office: SKR Associates PO Box 80565 Midland TX 79708

ROONEY, MICHAEL JAMES, lawyer, educator; b. Bloomington, Ill., Dec. 18, 1947; s. James Patrick and Nellie Mae (Schaefer) R.; children: Dawn Suzanne, Donald Edward, Joseph Michael; m. Deborah Daily, Nov. 27, 1992. BEd, Ill. State U., 1971; JD, U. Ill., 1976. Bar: Ill. 1976, U.S. Ct. Appeals (7th cir.) 1978. Atty. Atty's. Title Guaranty Fund, Inc., Champaign, Ill., 1976-81, v.p., corp. counsel, 1981-83, exec. v.p., 1983-88, pres., 1988-91; bus. devel. dir. Penta Corp., Champaign, 1991-92; v.p., Dallas area mgr. Chgo. Title Ins. co., 1993—; bd. dirs. Ill. Inst. Continuing Legal Edn., Springfield, 1984-93, chmn., 1991-92; vis. asst. prof. Coll. Commerce, U. Ill., Champaign, 1982-87. Author: Searching Illinois Real Estate Titles, 1978, Attorney's Guide to Title Insurance, 1980, rev. edit., 1984; also articles. Pres. Mahomet (Ill.)-Seymour Boosters, 1983-84. Fellow Am. Bar Found. (life), Ill. Bar Found. (charter); mem. ABA (chmn. real property com. gen. practice sect. 1983-87, budget officer 1990-91, coun. mem. 1991-93, mem. commn. on non-lawyer practice 1991-95, real property probate and trust law), Ill. Bar Assn. (sec. real estate sect. coun. 1984-85, vice chmn. 1985-86, chmn. 1986-87, ins. program com. 1988-93, sec. 1989-90, vice chmn. 1990-91, chmn. 1991-92, protect pub. from unauthorized practice of law 1988-93), Internat. Right of Way Assn. (instr. 1983—), Champaign County Bar Assn., Chgo. Bar Assn., Am. Coll. Real Estate Lawyers, Greater Dallas Assn. Realtors, 1993—, curriculum coord. Leadership 1996—, grad. leadership 1995). Home: 818 Pelican Ln Coppell TX 75019-5929

ROOS, SYBIL FRIEDENTHAL, retired elementary school educator; b. L.A., Jan. 29, 1924; d. Charles G. and Besse (Weixel) Friedenthal; m. Henry Kahn Roos, May 8, 1949 (dec. Dec. 1989); children: Catherine Alane Cook, Elizabeth Anne Garlinger, Virginia Ann Bertrand. BA in Music, Centenary Coll., 1948; MEd, Northwestern State U., 1973. Cert. elem. edn. tchr., spl. edn. tchr. Tchr. Caddo Parish Schs., Shreveport, 1968-75, Spring Branch Ind. Schs., Houston, 1975-85; vol. Houston Grand Opera/Guild, 1979—, Houston Mus. of Fine Arts/Guild, 1990—. Author tchrs. guides. Pres. Nat. Coun. Jewish Women, Shreveport, 1958, Houston Grand Opera Guild, 1989-91; bd. dirs. Mus. Fine Arts; area coord. Spl. Olympics, Shreveport, 1974-75; mem. Houston Symphony League, Houston Ballet Guild. With USN, 1944-46. Mem. AAUW (pres. Spring Valley Houston chpt. 1985-87), Houston Grand Opera Guild, Houston Symphony League, Houston Ballet Guild, Mus. of Fine Arts Guild (bd. dirs.), Am. Needlepoint Guild, Delta Kappa Gamma (bd. dirs., treas. 1987-89), Phi Mu. Republican. Home: 10220 Memorial Dr Apt 78 Houston TX 77024-3227

ROOT, HARLAN DAVID, surgery educator; b. Rider Mill, N.Y., Feb. 16, 1926; s. Franklin Fowler and Alice Laurena (Snook) R.; m. Catherine Bradford Friedrich, June 26, 1953; children: David, Susan, Julie, William. AB, Cornell U., Ithaca, N.Y., 1950; MD, Cornell U., N.Y.C., 1953; PhD, U. Minn., 1961. Diplomate Am. Bd. Surgery. Surgery intern U. Minn. Hosps., 1953-54, surgery resident, 1954-60, cardio-thoracic resident, 1962-63; asst. prof. surgery U. Minn., Mpls., 1961-66; assoc. prof. U. Tex. Health Sci Ctr., San Antonio, 1966-68, prof., 1968—; cons. surgeon State Chest Hosp., San Antonio, 1966—, VA Hosp., San Antonio, 1973—. Contbr. numerous articles to med. jours., chpts. to books. Pres. PTA, Mpls., 1960-61. Petty officer 2d class USN, 1945-46. Fellowship Am. Cancer Soc., 1957-58. Fellow ACS (pres. Tex. chpt. 1984-85, bd. govs. 1988-94); mem. Am. Assn. for Surgery of Trauma (pres. 1988-89). Episcopalian. Office: U Tex Health Sci Ctr 7703 Floyd Curl Dr San Antonio TX 78284-6200

ROOT, JAMES BENJAMIN, landscape architect; b. Detroit, Jan. 26, 1934; s. William Jehial and Helen Elizabeth (English) R. BBA, Memphis State U., 1960; B in Landscape Architecture, U. Ga., 1966. Registered landscape architect; lic. real estate agt., Va. Asst. prof. W.Va. U., Morgantown, 1973-75, 93; pvt. practice Charlottesville, Va., 1976-85, 91—; site planner LBA, PH&R, Charles P. Johnson & Assocs., Fairfax, Va., 1986-90; pvt. practice as golf course architect, Charlottesville, 1976—; instr. Parkersburg C.C., 1975, Piedmont Va. C.C., 1981. Author: Fundamentals of Landscaping and Site Planning, 1985; contbr. articles to profl. jours. Mem. Planning Commn., Marietta, Ohio, 1972. Mem. Nat. Golf Found., Elks, Va. Writers Club. Office: PO Box 7017 Charlottesville VA 22906-7017

ROOT, M. BELINDA, chemist; b. Port Arthur, Tex., May 2, 1957; d. Robert A. and Charlene (Whitehead) Lee; m. Miles J. Root, Nov. 8, 1980; children: Jason Matthew, Ashley Erin. BS in Biology, Lamar U., 1979; MBA, U. Houston, 1994. Asst. chemist Merichem Co., Houston, 1979-81, project chemist, 1982-84, instrument chemist, 1984-85, quality assurance coord., 1986-89, product lab. supr., 1989-91; quality control supr. mfg. Welchem Inc. subs. Amoco, 1991—; mgr. Quality Control Petrolite Corp., 1993; mgr. quality control/quality assurance Akzo-Nobel Chems., Pasadena, Tex., 1994—. Editor (newsletter) Merichemer, 1989-91. Mem. MADD, 1989—, PTA, 1988—. Recipient Gulf Shore Regional award Cat Fanciers Assn., 1981, Disting. Merit award, 1990. Mem. NAFE, Am. Soc. Quality Control (cert. quality auditor, quality engr.), Am. Chem. Soc., United Silver Fancier (sec. 1980-82), Lamar U. Alumni Assn., Beta Beta Beta (sec. 1978-79), Beta Gamma Sigma. Office: Akzo-Nobel Chem Inc 13000 Bay Park Dr Pasadena TX 77507

ROOT, RAYMOND FRANCIS, food broker account executive; b. South Glens Falls, N.Y., Oct. 9, 1948; s. Raymond Lawrence and Frances (Seaver) R.; children: Judson Victor, Anna Mayhew. BS magna cum laude, Troy State U., 1977; MBA, Auburn U., 1986. Enlisted U.S. Army, 1967, advanced through grades to capt., 1975, pilot, 1968-77; vol. released; salesman Allen W. Smith Co., Inc., Montgomery, Ala., 1977-83; account exec., gen. mgr. Graham, Bowen & Graham, Montgomery, 1983-87; account exec. Graham/Schulwolf & Assocs., Inc., Montgomery, 1987-89; acct. exec. Budd Mayer Co. of Ala., Montgomery, 1989—. Contbr. photographs and articles to Ala. Exchangite mag., 1986-92. Serving as col. Ala. N.G. Decorated Bronze Star, Purple Heart, Air medal. Mem. Montgomery Food Brokers Assn. (mem. spkrs. bur. 1980—, sec.-treas. 1986-90, 92—), Sales and Mktg. Execs. (bd. dirs., v.p.), DAV, Vietnam Helicopter Pilots Assn., Exch. Club Montgomery (dist. officer 1987-90, dist. pres. 1989-90, Exchangite of Yr., 1989, Outstanding Dist. Dir. 1987). Roman Catholic. Home: 1767 Laurelwood Ln Montgomery AL 36117-4743 Office: Budd Mayer Co of Ala Bldg H 2358 Fairlane Dr Ste 76 Montgomery AL 36116-1609

ROPER, BERYL CAIN, writer, publisher, retired library director; b. Long Beach, Calif., Mar. 1, 1931; d. Albert Verne and Ollie Fern (Collins) Cain; m. Max H. Young, Aug. 22, 1947 (div. 1958); children: Howard, Wade, Debra, Kevin, John R., Christopher; m. George Albert Roper, Mar. 24, 1962 (dec. July 1978); children: Ellen, Georgianne; m. Jack T. Hughes, Sept. 21, 1993. BA, West Tex. State U., 1986; MA, Tex. Womans U., 1989. Libr. clk. Cornette Libr., West Tex. State U., Canyon, 1981-87; dir. Clarendon (Tex.) Coll. Libr., 1988-96; lectr. in history and archaeology; co-owner Aquamarine Publs. Editor, pub.: In the Light of Past Experience, 1989, Transactions of the Southwest Federation of Archaeological Societies, 1993, Greenbelt Site, 1996; author, pub.: Trementina, 1990, Trementina Revisited, 1994; author articles on women and history. Mem. Clarendon Archaeol. Soc. (charter, v.p. 1990-91), Tex. Libr. Assn., Tex. Jr. Coll. Tchrs. Assn., Tex. Intertribal Indian Orgn. (charter), Pi Gamma Mu, Beta Phi Mu, Alpha Chi, Phi Alpha Theta. Republican. Mem. LDS Ch. Office: Aquamarine Publs 1903 3d Ave Canyon TX 79015

ROPER, D'ARCY WENTWORTH, III, association executive; b. Petersburg, Va., Nov. 15, 1944; s. D'Arcy Wentworth II and Sarah Fleming (Heath) R.; m. Patricia Ann Purviance, July 25, 1971 (div. Nov. 1979); children: D'Arcy Wentworth IV, Sara Rebecca; m. Mary Elizabeth Janson, June 5, 1982; stepchildren: Kristina Ann Voerman, Lara Louise Voerman. BS in Bus. Mgmt., Lehigh U., 1968; MS in Sys. Mgmt., U. So. Calif., 1978; diloma in national resource mgmt., Nat. Def. U., Washington, 1989. Commd. ensign USN, 1969, advanced through grades to capt., 1990; supply officer USS Capodanno, Mayport, Fla., 1973-75, USS Coral Sea, Norfolk, Va., 1986-88; officer-in-charge Navy Fin. Office, New London, Conn., 1975-78; logistics officer Mid. East Force, Manamah, Bahrain, 1978-79; asst. supply officer Marine Corps Air Sta., Cherry Point, N.C., 1979-83; logistics plans officer U.S. Naval Supply Sys. Command, Washington, 1983-86; dir. inspections Office Insp. Gen., Dept. Def., Washington, 1989-92; prof. logistics Nat. Def. U., 1992-94; ret., 1994; mgr. tech. svcs. Nat. Inst. Govt. Purchasing, Reston, Va., 1994—; bd. dirs. Cmty. Svc. Credit Union, Groton, Conn., 1975-78. Editor Tech. Bull., 1995—. Vestryman St. David's Episcopal Ch., Ledyard, Conn., 1977-78; vestryman, treas. St. Christopher's Ch., Havelock, N.C., 1979-83; chmn. all night grad. party Robinson H.S., Burke, Va., 1989, 90. Decorated Legion of Merit. Mem. Beta Theta Pi (bd. dirs. Beta Chi House Assn. 1995—). Republican. Home: 5903 Oak Ridge Ct Burke VA 22015 Office: Nat Inst Govt Purchasing 11800 Sunrise Valley Dr Reston VA 22091

ROPER, DONNA KAYE, historian; b. Piedmont, S.C., Dec. 9, 1954; d. Donald Lionel and Evelyn Frances (Cowart) R. BA, U. S.C., 1976, MA, 1989. Registrar, curator Pendleton (S.C.) Dist. Commn., 1978-84, asst. dir., 1985—; sec., v.p., pres. Confederation of S.C. Local Hist. Soc.; bd. dirs. Anderson (S.C.) County Hist. Soc., Palmetto Trust for Hist. Preservation, S.C. Hall of Fame, 1994-95, Pendleton Found. for Black History and Culture, 1996—; project dir. S.C. Humanities Coun. and S.C. Dept. Archives and History grants. Contbr. articles to profl. jours. Officer on exec. bd. Clemson Little Theater, Pendleton, S.C., 1993—. Mem. Greenville County Hist. Soc. Home: 16 King St Piedmont SC 29673-1329 Office: Pendleton Dist Commn 125 E Queen St Pendleton SC 29670 also: PO Box 565 Pendleton SC 29670

ROPER, EDDIE JOE, energy company executive; b. Wichita Falls, Sept. 11, 1950; s. Johnnie Fletcher and Lera Fay (Horn) R.; m. Patsy Ann Wester, Dec. 3, 1977; children: Amber Michelle, Aaron Joseph. BS, Tex. Tech. U., 1973. Driller Tom Brown, Inc., Midland, Tex., 1974-76, tool pusher, 1976-78, drilling supt., 1978-81; pres. Roper Energy Co., Midland, Tex., 1981—; bd. dirs. Internat. Assn. Drilling Contractors, Washington. Mem. chorale Midland-Odessa Sumphony &Chorale, Midland, 1991, 92, 93. Republican. Baptist. Office: Roper Energy Co PO Box 8005 Midland TX 79708-8005

ROPER, HARTWELL H., tobacco company executive. CFO, v.p. Universal Leaf Tobacco Corp. Office: Universal Leaf Tobacco Co Hamilton St at Broad PO Box 25099 Richmond VA 23260-5099*

ROPER, JOHN LONSDALE, III, shipyard executive; b. Norfolk, Va., Jan. 19, 1927; s. John Lonsdale II and Sarah (Dryfoos) R.; m. Jane Preston Harman, Sept. 29, 1951; children: Susan Roper, John Lonsdale IV, Sarah Preston Roper Massey, Jane Harman Roper Van Sciver, Katherine Hayward Roper Stout. BSME, U. Va., Charlottesville, 1949; BS in Naval Architecture and Marine Engring., MIT, 1951. CEO, pres. Norfolk Shipbuilding & Drydock Corp., 1985-91, pres., CEO, 1991—, also bd. dirs.; dir. John L. Roper Corp., Cruise Internat., Inc., The Flagship Group Ltd.; pres., dir. Lonsdale Bldg. Corp. Marepcon Corp.-Internat. With USCG, 1945-46. Mem. Shipbuilders Coun. Am. (bd. dirs.). Episcopalian.

RORIE, CHARLES DAVID, SR., college official; b. Dallas, Jan. 10, 1936; s. Oscar Lee and Sibyl Matilda (Carver) R.; m. Julia Hanora Davenport, Aug. 5, 1961; children: Julie Anne, Peter Patrick, Charles David Jr. AA, Tyler Jr. Coll., 1955; BA, Sam Houston State U., 1961; MS, East Tex. State U., 1964; PhD, U. Tex., 1973; grad. in Ednl. Mgmt., Harvard U., 1985. Counselor, instr. Southwest Tex. Jr. Coll., 1968-71; dean instruction W.Va. Northern Community Coll., 1973-75; asst. dean Cuyahoga (Ohio) Community Coll., 1975-82; dean of coll. Dyersburg State Community Coll., 1982-86; v.p. instrn. and ednl. svcs. Elgin (Ill.) Community Coll., 1986-93; exec. dean, CEO El Paso (Tex.) C.C., 1993—. Designing and implementing video/computer programs in the classroom. Dyersburg (Tenn.) Spl. Olympics, 1983-86. Served with U.S. Army, 1961-62, with Royal Can. Navy, 1965-68. Mem. Am. Assn. Higher Edn., Am. Vocat. Assn., Coun. Occupational Edn., Bentley Drivers Club. Democrat. Episcopalian. Home: 6725 Ridge Top Dr El Paso TX 79904-3914 Office: El Paso CC PO Box 20500 El Paso TX 79998-0500

RORIE, NANCY KATHERYN, elementary and secondary school educator; b. Union County, N.C., May 31, 1940; d. Carl Van and Mary Mildred (Pressley) R. BA, Woman's Coll. U. N.C., 1962; MEd, U. N.C., 1967; EdD, Duke U., 1977. Cert. curriculum and instrnl. specialist, social studies tchr. for middle and secondary levels, English tchr., N.C. Social studies and English tchr. Guilford County Schs., Greensboro, N.C., 1962-67; social studies instr. Lees-McRae Coll., Banner Elk, N.C., 1967-76; social studies tchr. Monroe (N.C.) City Schs., 1977-93; curriculum instrnl. specialist, social studies tchr. Union County Schs., Monroe, N.C., 1993—. Named Woman of Yr., Am. Biog. Inst., 1995, Internat. Woman of Yr, Internat. Biog. Ctr., Cambridge, Eng., 1995-96; recipient: The Twentieth Century Award for Achievement, Internat. Biog. Ctr., Cambridge, Eng. Mem. Prof. Educators N.C., Phi Alpha Theta, Kappa Delta Pi. Democrat. Baptist. Home: 2401 Old Pageland Rd Monroe NC 28112-8163

RORISON, MARGARET LIPPITT, reading consultant; b. Wilmington, N.C., Feb. 6, 1925; d. Harmon Chadbourn and Margaret Devereux (Lippitt) R. AB, Hollins Coll., 1946; MA, Columbia U., 1956; Diplôme de langue, L'Alliance Française, Paris, 1966; postgrad. U. S.C., 1967-70, 81—. Market and editorial researcher Time, Inc., N.Y.C., 1949-55; classroom and corrective reading tchr. N.Y.C. public schs., 1956-65; TV instr. ETV-WNDT, Channel 13, N.Y.C., 1962-63; grad. asst., TV instr. U. S.C., Columbia, 1967-70; instrnl. specialist in reading S.C. Office Instrnl. TV and Radio, S.C. Dept. Edn., Columbia, 1971-81; reading cons. S.C. Office Instructional Tech., 1982—. Active Common Cause. Mem. Internat. Reading Assn., Am. Ednl. Rsch. Assn., Assn. Supervision and Curriculum Devel., Nat. Soc. Study of Edn., Phi Delta Kappa . Episcopalian. Author instrnl. TV series: Getting the Word (So. Ednl. Communications Assn. award 1972, Ohio State award 1973, S.C. Scholastic Broadcasters award 1973), Getting the Message, 1981. Home: 460 S 23rd St Wilmington NC 28403-0200

ROSA, IDAVONNE TAYLOR, community health nurse; b. Ft. Worth, Aug. 10, 1921; d. William Oscar and Minnie Belle (White) Taylor; m. John Moore Rosa (dec.); children: Walter E. Rose, Jimie Lee Rose. Diploma in nursing, U. Cen. Ark., 1974; postgrad., Ark. State U. RN, Ark.; lic. social worker, Ark.; cert. disaster nurse ARC. Vol. Peace Corps, Afghanistan, 1968-72; dir. nursing Pioneer Nursing Home, Melbourne, Ark., 1974-79; dir. ind. living svcs. East Ark. Agy. on Aging, Jonesboro, 1980—; chmn. nursing adv. coun. Delta Tech. Inst., 1994-95. Mem. stering com., Ark. rep. Nat. Silver Haired Congress, 1994-95; del. White House Conf. on Aging, Washington, 1995; tng. coord. disaster com. Craighead County chpt. ARC, 1995—; pres. Mid-Am. Congress on Aging, 1988-89, chmn. presdl. adv. bd., 1990-95. Mem. S.W. Soc. on Aging, Ark. Nursing Home Nurses Assn., Ark. Gerontol Soc. (bd. dirs. 1993-95)). Home: PO Box 141 Jonesboro AR 72403-0141

ROSAMOND, SANDRA PAULINE (SANDI ROSAMOND), secondary education educator; b. Oklahoma City, July 22, 1947; d. Benjamin Franklin and Opal Pauline (Wilson) Creason; 1 child, Francis Wesley Cooke; m. Freedus Edward Rosamond, Mar. 17, 1984. BS in Edn., Cen. Okla. U. (name changed to U. Ctrl. Okla.), 1969; MS in Family Rels. and Child Devel., Okla. State U., 1977, postgrad., 1991-95. Cert. educator, vocat. educator, Okla. Tchr. Oklahoma City Pub. Schs., 1969-70, Ctr. Sch. Dist., Kansas City, Mo., 1970-72; adminstrv. asst. Grad. Sem., Phillips U., Enid, Okla., 1974-75; tchr. pre-sch. Meml. Dr. United Meth. Ch., Tulsa, 1975-77; officer probation Juvenile Bur. Okla. Dist. Ct., Tulsa, 1977-81, fiscal officer, 1981-82; tchr. Liberty Mounds Schs., Mounds, Okla., 1982-83; tchr. L.E. Rader Juvenile Ctr., Sand Springs, Okla., 1983-86, chairperson tchrs., 1983-86, tchr. intensive treatment, 1986-89; trainer/cons., program devel. specialist U. Okla. Nat. Resource Ctr. for Youth Svcs., Tulsa, 1989-92; assoc. mgmt. svcs. Indian Meridian Vocat. Tech. Ctr., Stillwater, Okla., 1992-93; owner, CEO Monarch Environ. Techs., Sand Springs, Okla., 1993-95; staff mgr. Dollar Rent a Car Systems Inc., Tulsa, 1995—; owner Sandi's Crochet Originals; grant reader Okla. State Bd. Edn., Oklahoma City, 1985; presenter workshops and seminars at nat. confs.; instr. Zenger-Miller Tng., Pacific Inst. Tng. Author: Detained and Attended: Detention and Attendant Care Staff Training, 1991; contbr. articles to profl. jours. Chairperson, with curriculum devel. sexuality com. Okla. United Meths., Oklahoma City, 1974-77, bd. dirs. placement and adoption bd., 1975-78; mem. rewrite com. Okla. State Dept. Vocat./Tech. Edn. in Home and Community Services, 1988; nat. trainer Advanced Course for Residential Child Care Workers, 1989-92; trainer Conflict Resolution, 1989-92. Mem. ASCD, ASTD (chpt. sec. 1989, 95), Okla. Vocat. Assn., Am. Vocat. Assn., Children's Instns. and Agys. Inc. (exec. bd. dirs.), Omicron Nu, Phi Kappa Phi. Democrat. Office: 5330 E 31st St Tulsa OK 74135

ROSANDICH, THOMAS JAMES, academic administrator; b. LaCrosse, Wis., May 28, 1954; s. Thomas Peter and Sally (Gentile) R.; m. Mary Ellen, June 21, 1981; children: Jayme, Jillian. Student, U. S. Ala., Mobile, 1977-82; B.Mgmt., Columbia Pacific U., San Rafael, Calif., 1988; M.Sport Sci., U.S. Sports Acad., Daphne, Ala., 1989, postgrad., 1989—. Purchasing coord. U.S. Sports Acad., Mobile, 1982-84; equip. specialist Am. Inst. Sport Design, Mobile, 1984-85; dir. mktg. Sports Internat., Mobile, 1985-86; advisor Minister of Sport, State of Bahrain, Manama, 1987; v.p. devel. U.S. Sports Acad., Riyadh, Saudi Arabia, 1986-88; gen. mgr. Saudi Am. Co. for Sports Tng., Riyadh, 1988-94; dean adminstrn. and fin. U.S. Sports Acad., Daphne, Ala., 1994—; bd. dirs. USSA Internat., Riyadh, Saudi Am. Co. for Sports Tng., Riyadh; cons. in field. Contbr. articles to profl. jours. With U.S. Army, 1972-76. Mem. Am. Legion. Office: 1 Academy Dr Daphne AL 36526-7055

ROSARIO-GUARDIOLA, REINALDO, dermatologist; b. Santurce, P.R., Sept. 17, 1948; s. Tomas and Aurea (Guardiola) Rosario; m. Fe Milagros Rivera, Aug. 19, 1972; children: Amarillis, Reinaldo, Gadiel. BS, U. P.R., 1968, MD, 1972. Rsch. fellow photobiology Harvard Med. Sch., Boston, 1976-77; asst. prof. U. P.R. Sch. of Medicine, Rio Piedras, 1979—; chief, dermatology sect. San Juan VA Hosp., Rio Piedras, 1979—. Bd. dirs. Wesleyan Acad. Guaynabo, P.R., 1990—. Grantee Dermatology Found., 1978. Fellow Am. Acad. Dermatology; mem. P.R. Dermatol. Soc. (pres. scientific com. 1978-79), Harvard-MGH House Officers Club, Alpha Omega Alpha. Office: El Monte Mall Ste 33A San Juan PR 00918

ROSATO, MICHAEL JAMES, dean, education educator; b. Newark, Ohio, Apr. 2, 1960; s. Alfred Angelo and Annetta Belle (Jackson) R.; m. Kimberly Ann Standridge, Nov. 23, 1985; children: Natalie Ann, Nicole Elizabeth, Dominic Hayes, Naomi Katharine. BA, Carson-Newman Coll., 1983; MEd, Tex. Wesleyan U., 1985; EdD, Ind. U., 1993. Pub. sch. tchr. Arlington (Tex.) Ind. Sch. Dist., 1985-87; asst. to dir. of tchr. edn. program Ind. U., Bloomington, 1987-88, assessment asst., 1991; residence coord. Butler U., Indpls., 1988-91; asst. prof. adult edn. Dallas Bapt. U., 1992-95, chair dept. applied studies, 1993-95, assoc. dean applied studies, 1994-95, dir. higher edn. program, dean of edn., assoc. prof. edn., 1995—; sec. univ. faculty coun. Dallas Bapt. U., 1994-95. Mem. Fellowship Las Colinas, Irving, Tex. Named one of Outstanding Young Men of Am. Office: Dallas Bapt U 3000 Mountain Creek Pkwy Dallas TX 75211-9299

ROSCHE, LORETTA G., medical, surgical nurse; b. New Philadelphia, Ohio, Sept. 16, 1934; d. Seldon E. and Margaret (Murphy) Donohue; m. Thomas R. Rosche, Sept. 6, 1954; children: Melanie Rosche Smith, Cynthia Rosche Geeker, Lori Rosche Davis, Julia Rosche Sivyer. Diploma, Lafayette Sch. Nursing, 1984; cert., Jewish Hosp., 1985; student, Am. Healthcare Inst. RN, Va. Office mgr., nurse, surg. asst. to pvt. physician Williamsburg, Va., 1979—; advanced tng. in laparoscopic surgery Abbott Northwestern Hosp., Mpls., 1990; surg. nurse vol. surg. team Esperanza, Amazon region of Brazil, 1988, 91; lectr. various groups including Med. Soc., Rotary, Hand Soc. Named Speaker of Yr. Psi Beta, 1990. Mem. Assn. Hand Care Profls. (co-founder, treas.), Am. Assn. Med. Assts. (cert.), Soc. Laparoendoscopic Surgeons. Home: 128 Country Club Dr Williamsburg VA 23188-1516

ROSE, CHARLES DAVID, consulting company executive; b. Corpus Christi, Dec. 28, 1939; s. Robert Chester and Gladys (Blackmon) R.; m. Mary Ann McKinney, Apr. 23, 1965; children: David, Elizabeth, Katherine. BS in Physics magna cum laude, La. Tech. U., 1964; postgrad., Iowa State U. From engr. to dist. level supr. staff ops. South Ctrl. Bell Telephone Co., 1964-70; mgr. sales and engring. Hycaloader Co., 1970-74; owner Charles Rose Cons., Monroe, La., 1974—. Contbr. numerous articles to profl. jours. Mem. ASTM (various coms.), Am. Statis. Assn., Am. Soc. for Quality Control. Home: 6606 Mapleshade Ln # 11F Dallas TX 75252 Office: Charles Rose Cons PO Box 797425 Dallas TX 75379-7425

ROSE, CHARLES GRANDISON, III (CHARLIE ROSE), congressman; b. Fayetteville, N.C., Aug. 10, 1939; s. Charles Grandison Jr. and Anna Frances (Duckworth) R.; m. Stacye Hefner; children: Charles Grandison IV, Sara Louise, Kelly Josephine. AB, Davidson Coll., 1961; LLB, U. N.C., 1964. Bar: N.C. 1964. Chief prosecutor Dist. Ct., 12th Jud. Dist., 1967-70; mem. 93nd-104th Congresses from 7th N.C. dist., Washington, 1972—; mem. agrl. com., subcom. Specialty Crops and Natural Resources, Gen. Farm Commodities 93nd-104th Congresses from 7th N.C. dist.; co-founder Congl. Rural Caucus; founder Congl. Clearing House on the Future. Pres.

N.C. Young Democrats, 1968. Presbyterian. Office: US Ho of Reps 242 Cannon Bldg Washington DC 20515-0003*

ROSE, CHESTER ARTHUR, accountant, financial planner; b. Roaring Springs, Pa., Sept. 21, 1941; s. Joseph Blair and Elva Blanche (Barnes) R.; m. Marla K. Brattin, Mar. 19, 1967; children: Scott Bains, Brooks Emerson. AA in Acctg., Hershey (Pa.) Jr. Coll., 1961; BS in Acctg., Elizabethtown Coll., 1963; MBA in Acctg., Mich. State U., 1967. Cert. fin. planner, CPA. Commd. lt. USAF, 1964, advanced through grades to maj., 1975, retired, 1984; staff acct. Hahn, Small & Batto, San Antonio, 1984-90, ptnr., 1991-96; tax mgr. Gibbons, Vogel & Co., San Antonio, 1996—; Bd. dirs. Lackland Fed. Credit Union, San Antonio, Hosp. Welcome Lodge of San Antonio. lectr. Care for Elderly, San Antonio, 1990—. Mem. AICPA, Inst. Cert. Fin. Planners. Office: Gibbons Vogel & Co 8620 N New Braunfels Ste 200 San Antonio TX 78217

ROSE, DENNIS NORMAN, manufacturing company executive; b. Medicine Hat, Alberta, Can., Jan. 5, 1948; came to U.S., 1987, naturalized, 1995; s. Norman Cecil Joseph and Anna (Jorgensen) R.; children: Darren Craig, David Christopher. BS, U. Calgary, Alberta, Can., 1971; MBA, York U., Toronto, Ontario, Can., 1977. Registered profl. engr., Ky., Ind., Fla., Ont., Can. Mgr. Mfg. and Engring. Canadian GE, Barrie, Ontario, Can., 1971-79; v.p. Algonquin Industries, Huntsville, Ontario, Can., 1979-85; gen. mgr. Mallory Controls, Woodstock, Ontario, Can., 1985-87; v.p. ops. Mallory Controls, Indpls., 1987-89; exec. v.p. Sargent & Greenleaf, Inc., Nicholsville, Ky., 1989-93; v.p., gen. mgr. New Eng. Machinery, Inc., Bradenton, Fla., 1993-94; mfg. cons., owner, pres. Turnaround, Bradenton, Fla.; owner, pres. Quality Screening and Window Repair, Inc., Sarasota, Fla. Mem. Nat. Soc. Profl. Engrs., Aircraft Owners & Pilots Assn., Am. Soc. for Quality Control, Assn. for Mfg. Excellence. Home: Unit 111 4001 Gulf Dr N Holmes Beach FL 34217

ROSE, DONALD L., physician, educator; b. St. Charles, Mo., July 20, 1911; s. William Albert and Estelle Mattie (Sherry) R.; m. Martha Jane Koontz, Mar. 6, 1937; children: Nancy Kathryn Rose Harling, William Donald. BA, U. Colo., 1933, MA, MD, 1936. Diplomate Am. Bd. Phys. Medicine and Rehab. Intern Miami Valley Hosp., Dayton, Ohio, 1936-37, resident, 1937-38; rsch. assoc. Kettering Inst. Med. Rsch., Dayton, 1938-41; asst. prof. sch. medicine Univ. Kans., Kansas City, 1947-49, assoc. prof., 1949-51, prof., 1951-74, prof. emeritus, 1974—; cons. Phys. Med. Surgeon Gen.'s Office, Washington, 1957-65, nat. cons. USAF, 1959-61; bd. govs. Am. Bd. Phys. Medicine and Rehab., Rochester, Minn., 1957-67. Contbr. chpt. An Atlas of Amputations, 1947, Postgraduate Medicine and Surgery, 1951, Therapeutic Heat, 1958. Med. advisor NFIP Wyandotte County, Kansas City, 1947-60, Johnson County chpt., 1950-60, MDA Kansas City, 1965-74. Fellow Baruch Found., Boston, 1946-47. Mem. AMA, Am. Acad. Phys. Medicine and Rehab. (pres. 1953-54, Disting. Clin. award 1983), Am. Congress Rehab. Medicine (pres. 1957-58), Kans. Med. Soc., Wyandotte County Med. Soc. Republican. Methodist. Home: 16 Eaton Cir Bella Vista AR 72715-5513

ROSE, EDWARD W. (RUSTY ROSE), professional sports team executive. Gen. partner Texas Rangers, Arlington, TX. Office: care Texas Rangers 1000 Ballpark Way Arlington TX 76011-5168*

ROSE, JAMES TURNER, aerospace consultant; b. Louisburg, N.C., Sept. 21, 1935; s. Frank Rogers and Mary Burt (Turner) R.; m. Daniele Raymond, Sept. 15, 1984; children by previous marriage—James Turner, Katharine S. B.S. with high honors, N.C. State U., 1957. Aero. research engr. NASA, Langley Field, Va., 1957-59; project engr. NASA (Mercury and Gemini), Langley Field, Va. and Houston, 1959-64; program systems mgr. McDonnell Douglas Astronautics Co (MDAC), St. Louis, 1964-69; mgr. shuttle ops. and implementation (MDAC) McDonnell Douglas Astronautics Co., St. Louis, 1969-72; mgr. shuttle support (MDAC) St. Louis, 1972-74; dir. space shuttle engring. NASA, Washington, 1974-76; mgr. space processing programs McDonnell Douglas Astronautics Co., St. Louis, 1976-83; dir. electrophoresis ops. in space McDonnell Douglas Astronautics Co (MDAC), St. Louis, 1983-86; asst. adminstr. comml. programs NASA, Washington, 1987-91; aerospace cons., 1992—. Recipient Lindberg award for mgmt. leadership AIAA, 1983, Presdl. Meritorious Rank award, 1989, NASA Exceptional Svc. medal, 1990, Laurels award Aviation Week, 1990, Aerospace Contribution to Soc. award AIAA, 1993. Mem. Phi Kappa Phi. Episcopalian.

ROSE, JONATHAN CHAPMAN, lawyer; b. Cleve., June 8, 1941; s. Horace Chapman and Katherine Virginia (Cast) R.; m. Susan Anne Porter, Jan. 26, 1980; 1 son, Benjamin Chapman. A.B., Yale U., 1963; LL.B. cum laude, Harvard U., 1967. Bar: Mass. 1968, D.C. 1972, U.S. Supreme Ct. 1976, Circuit Ct. Appeals 1977, Ohio 1978. Law clk. Justice R. Ammi Cutter, Mass. Supreme Jud. Ct., 1967-68; spl. asst. to U.S. pres., 1971-73; gen. counsel Council on Internat. Econ. Policy, 1973-74; assoc. dept. atty. gen. U.S. Dept. Justice, 1974-75; dept. asst. atty. gen. U.S. Dept. Justice (Antitrust Div.), 1975-77; asst. atty. gen. Office of Legal Policy, 1981-84; ptnr. firm Jones, Day, Reavis & Pogue, Washington, 1977-81, 84—. Prin. Ctr. for Excellence in Govt.; pres. Yale Daily News Found. 1st lt. U.S. Army, 1969-71. Mem. ABA, D.C. Bar Assn., Mass. Bar Assn., Ohio Bar Assn., Fed. Bar Assn., Am. Law Inst. Republican. Episcopalian. Clubs: Met, Chevy Chase, Union, Yale, Harvard. Office: Jones Day Reavis & Pogue 1450 G St NW Ste 600 Washington DC 20005-2001

ROSE, JUDY HARDIN, mental health nurse; b. Shelbyville, Ky., Sept. 14, 1956; d. T.J. and Martha Bell (Ricketts) Hardin; m. Jake E. Rose Jr., Feb. 14, 1980; 1 child, Natalie Adele. Student, Western Ky. U., Bowling Green, 1974-75; AS, Ky. State U., Frankfort, 1979; BSN, U. Louisville, 1995. Cert. CPR, HIV counselor, jr. Red Cross instr., ARC. Tchr. expectant mother classes Family Med. Ctar., Campbellsburg, Ky.; acting shift supr. Kings Daus. Hosp., Shelbyville; charge nurse Cen. State Hosp., Louisville; med. dir. Rice-Audubon Vocat. Edn., Louisville; charge nurse Johnson-Breckinridge Treatment Ctr. Advisor Youth of Newburg; youth sponsor, youth dir. cross tng. Henry Christian Ch. Home: 4009 Evergreen Rd Crestwood KY 40014-9230

ROSE, MELISSA EVA ANDERSON, small business owner; b. Grayson, Ky., Sept. 24, 1959; d. Thomas Erwin and Betty Jane (Mauk) Hall; m. William David Rose, June 19, 1992. Student, Araphoe Bus. Coll., Denver, 1976-78; BA, Morehead State U., 1979-84. Sales clk. Cases Hardware and Antiques, Olive Hill, Ky., 1970-72; waitress Los Gringitos, Morehead, Ky., 1975; tele-mktg. operator Citi-Corp Fin. Svcs., Denver, 1977-78; model, spokeswoman Ford Agy. NY, N.Y.C., 1979-81; counselor Christian Social Svcs., 1979-81; activities coord. Dept. Corrections, Denver, 1979; pres. ops. Dimensions Unltd. Inc., Denver, 1981—; owner, pres. Dimensions Unltd. Inc., Huntington, W.Va., 1985-96, Unlimited Expressions, Morehead, Ky., 1996—; cons. Home Interior Designs, Inc., Denver, 1985-86; sec. Denver County Real Estate Commn., 1987-88; bd. dirs. Found. for Human Concerns, Morehead, Ky., 1987—, Excalibur Fin. Svc., Olive Hill, Ky., Melissa E. Rose Inc.; cons. Ky. C. of C., Glasgow, 1988—; founder, pres. Unified Fortress Group, Inc., 1989, Gold Link Publs., 1991-92; contr. Alpha Mktg. Corp., 1992-95; owner Mystic Limousine, 1992—. Author: Business Ethics 2nd Moral Values, 1987, Life After Death 2 Cultural Explorations, 1987, Business Marketing-Sales for the 90s, 1992, Secrets Through the Eyes of Stone, 1996 (autobiography). Spokesperson Nat. Rep. Group, Morehead, 1981; chairperson Tiffany's Gold Charity Soc., Denver 1986; sec. Bus. Devel. Soc., Las Vegas, 1987; charter sponsor NATO Culture Exch. in W.Va., NY, 1989. Named Dutchess Hutt River Province, Australia, 1996. Mem. NAFE, Dunn V. Bradstree, Inc., Nat. Assn. Mchts., Encore Gold Purchasing Club, League Human Rights, Nat. Assn. Euroecan Bus. Cmtys., Met. Mus. Art, Smithsonian Instn., Citizens for a Better Govt. (chair), Olive Hill C. of C. Office: Dimensions Unltd Inc 3845 Bluestone Bratton Bridge Rd Morehead KY 40351-9788 also: Golden Link Publs PO Box 869 Olive Hill KY 41164-0869

ROSE, NEAL NICHOLAS, maintenance and construction company executive; b. Altoona, Pa., Feb. 4, 1950; s. William Cornelius and Lucy (Compagnia) R.; m. Janet Marie McPhail, Aug. 11, 1973; children: Kristina Michelle, William Nicholas, Cathryn Suzanne. BS, Edison State Coll., Trenton, N.J., 1984. Cert. safety profl., hazard control mgr.; registered profl. engr., environ. assessor. Safety sypr. Brown and Root, Inc., Houston, 1973-77; sr. safety supr. Koppers Co., Inc., Woodward, Ala., 1977-79; safety dir. B.E. & K, Inc., Wilmington, N.C., 1979-81; safety supt. H.B. Zachry/DuPont, Victoria, Tex., 1981-85; corp. safety specialist The Mundy Co., Pasadena, Tex., 1985-86; mgr. safety and health Milpark Drilling Fluids, Houston, 1986-88; pres. Hazard Control Assocs., Pasadena, 1988-89; dir. Tex. Indsl. Painting Co., Houston, 1989-91; v.p. Viceroy, Inc., Pasadena, 1991—; environ. cons. Hazard Control Assocs., Pasadena, 1984-91; exam proctor Cert. Safety Profl., Houston, 1985-94. Author, instr. Hazardous Waste Worker Training, 1986. Del. Rep. Party, Pasadena, 1988. With USN, 1968-72, Vietnam, 1969-70. Mem. Am. Indsl. Hygiene Assn. (full mem.), Am. Soc. Safety Engrs. (pres. gulf coast chpt. 1990-91), Soc. Human Resource Mgmt. (profl. mem.), Houston Human Resource Mgrs. Assn.

ROSE, NORMAN, lawyer; b. N.Y.C., July 7, 1923; s. Edward J. and Frances (Ludwig) R.; div.; children: Ellen, Michael. B.B.A., CCNY, 1947; J.D., N.Y. Law Sch. 1953. Bar: Fla. 1979, N.Y. 1954, U.S. Dist. Ct. (ea. dist.) N.Y. 1956, U.S. Dist. Ct. (so. dist.) N.Y. 1960, U.S. Dist. Ct. (so. dist.) Fla. 1981, U.S. Ct. Appeals (2d cir.) 1967, U.S. Tax Ct. 1956, U.S. Supreme Ct. 1961. Pvt. practice, N.Y.C., 1954-69, Garden City, N.Y., 1969-79, Ft. Lauderdale, Fla., 1979-91; ptnr. Dean, Falanga & Rose, Carle Pl., N.Y., 1979-81; referee Small Claims Ct., N.Y.C., 1959-69; arbitrator Accident Claims Tribunal, Am. Arbitration Assn., 1960-65; C.P.A., N.Y.C., 1951-57; lectr. in field. Author law note Liability of Golfer to Person Struck by Ball, 1959 (Hon. mention 1960). Pres. Nassau S. Shore Little League, Lawrence, N.Y., 1966-68; treas. 5 Towns Democratic Club, Woodmere, N.Y., 1966-67; chmn. United Fund, Village of Lawrence, 1967. Served to cpt. USAF, 1943-45, ETO. Decorated Disting. Flying Cross (ETO), Air medal, Silver star, Purple Heart, Presdl. Unit citation. Mem. Assn. Trial Lawyers Am. (sustaining), Acad. Fla. Trial Lawyers (sustaining), Broward County Trial Lawyers Assn. (sustaining), N.Y. State Assn. Plantiffs Trial Lawyers, N.Y. State Bar Assn., Fla. Bar, Nassau County Bar Assn. (chmn. med.-legal com. 1975-77), Lawyer/Pilots Bar Assn. Democrat. Jewish. Club: Lawrence Country (bd. govs. 1966-68); Palm Aire Country club, Oaks Golf & Racquet Club, Old Westbury Country (bd. govs. 1975), Lodges: Masons, Shriners. Home: 3200 Port Royale Dr N Fort Lauderdale FL 33308-7809 Office: 1290 E Oakland Park Blvd Fort Lauderdale FL 33334-4443

ROSE, SHARON MARIE, critical care nurse; b. Big Spring, Tex., Feb. 16, 1958; d. William Coleman Smith and Grace Marie (Arnett) Karns; m. Christopher Robin Rose, Jan. 21, 984; 1 child, Crystal Alyss. AAS, Odessa Coll., 1981; BS in Occupational Edn., Wayland Bapt., 1987. Cert. nephrology nurse. Critical care RN Univ. Med. Ctr., Lubbock, Tex., 1981-88; med-surg. instr. Lubbock (Tex.) Gen. Hosp., 1988-89; dialysis RN St. Mary of the Plains Hosp., 1989-91; asst. CCU mgr. St. Mary of the Plains Hosp., Lubbock, 1990-91; health occupations instr. Lubbock Ind. Sch. Dist., 1991-94; in-svc. coord. Dialysis Ctr. Lubbock, Tex., 1994—; tchr. summer session Asst. for Med. Terminology course, 1993; mem. Health Occupations Adv. Com., Lubbock, 1988. Mem. Nat. Kidney Found. Mem. Tex. Health Occupations Assn. (v.p. 1993-94), Health Occupation Students Am. (advisor 1991-94), Tex. Tech. Med. Alliance, Nat. Kidney Found. (coun. nephrology nurses and technicians). Baptist. Home: 4708 31st St Lubbock TX 79410 Office: Dialysis Ctr Lubbock 4110 22nd Pl Lubbock TX 79410

ROSE, STEVEN RAPHAEL, social worker, educator; b. Montreal, Que., Can., Dec. 8, 1952; came to the U.S., 1955; BA, Bklyn. Coll., 1973; MSW, Washington U., St. Louis, 1975; PhD, U. Wis., 1981. Psychiat. social worker Community Counseling Ctr., Quincy, Ill., 1975-77; teaching asst., field instr. U. Wis., Madison, 1977-81; asst. prof. U. Vt., Burlington, 1981-85; lectr. Hebrew U., Jerusalem, 1985-89; assoc. prof. La. State U., Baton Rouge, 1989-96, prof., 1996—; cons. in field. Co-author Task Groups in the Social Services; contbr. articles to profl. jours. and chpts. to books. HHS fellow, 1979-80. Mem. NASW (bd. dirs. Vt. chpt. 1984-85). Office: La State U Sch Social Work Huey P Long Field House Baton Rouge LA 70803

ROSE, SUSAN A. SCHULTZ, retired theological librarian; b. Mountain Lake, Minn., Dec. 22, 1911; d. David. D. and Anna (Eitzen) Schultz; m. Delbert R. Rose, Dec. 27, 1986. BA, John Fletcher Coll., 1940; BSLS, U. Ill., 1946, MLS, 1949; LittD (hon.), Houghton Coll., 1974. Dean women John Fletcher-Kletzing Coll., University Park, Iowa, 1940-45; asst. libr. Bethany (Okla.) Coll., 1946-47; dir. libr. svcs. Asbury Theol. Sem., Wilmore, Ky., 1949-78, ret., 1978; cons. grad. schs. theology librs. The Philippines, 1978-80, 85-86, Nairobi, Kenya, 1983-84, Zagreb, Yugoslavia, 1984, Taiwan, Korea, Japan, 1987, Allahabad, India, 1989, Kericho, Kenya, 1989, Manila, 1990; cons. grad. schs. theology librs. Wesly Bible Seminary, Jackson, Miss., 1987-93, Kaohsiung, Taiwan, 1992, Owerri, Nigeria, 1993; mem. exec. com. 1st Alliance Ch., Lexington, Ky., 1958-61, 66-73; del. to nat. coun. Christian and Missionary Alliance, Columbus, Ohio, 1964, to Nat. Congress on Edn., St. Paul, 1970. Contbr. articles to profl. jours. Sunday sch. tchr. 1st Alliance Ch., Lexington, 1951-70; mem. libr. bd. Withers-Jessamine County Libr., Nicholasville, Ky., 1966-77. Recipient Outstanding Spl. Libr. of Yr. award Ky. Trustees Assn., 1967, Disting. Svc. award Asbury Theol. Sem., 1974, Emily Russell award Assn. Christian Librs. , 1974, Disting. Alumnus award Vennard Coll. (successor to John Fletcher-Kletzing Coll.), 1982. Mem. Am. Theol. Libr. Assn. (ret., exec. sec. 1967-71, dir. 1974-77), Wesley Theol. Soc. (ret.), Christian Holiness Assn., Ky. Libr. Assn. (bd. dirs. 1960—, sect. chair 1966-67). Mem. Christian and Missionary Alliance. Home: Shell Point Village 3905 Lucina Fort Myers FL 33908-1671

ROSE, SUSAN ROGERS, endocrinologist, researcher; b. Salem, Mass., July 14, 1947; d. William Minor Lile and Eloise Everett (Ranney) Rogers; m. Douglas F. Rose, June 13, 1970; 1 child, Matthew F. AB in Psychology, Oberlin Coll., 1969; MEd in Edn., Edinboro Coll., 1971, U. Dayton, 1972; MD, Case Western Res. U., 1980. Diplomate Nat. Bd. Med. Examiners; lic. psychologist, Ohio; lic. sch. psychologist, Ohio. Grant reviewer NIMH, Bethesda, Md., 1969-70; sch. psychologist Southwestern Ohio Region, 1971-73, Parma (Ohio) Pub. Schs., 1973-74, Cleve. Pub. Schs., 1974-76; intern in pediatrics Cleve. Clinic Found., 1980-81, resident in pediatrics, 1981-83; fellow in endocrinology Nat. Inst. Child Health, 1983-86; rsch. asst. prof. pediatrics U. N.Mex. Sch. Medicine, Albuquerque, 1989-92; assoc. prof. pediat. U. Tenn. Sch. Medicine, Memphis, 1992—; adj. scientist devel. endocrinology br. Nat. Inst. Child Health and Human Devel., NIH, Bethesda, 1986—, cons., 1989—; rsch. assoc., prof. pediats., vol. staff U. N.Mex. Sch. Medicine, Albuquerque, 1992—. Author book chpts.; editor Highlights jour., 1993—; contbr. over 70 articles to profl. jours. Sci. fair judge, Albuquerque, 1989-92, Memphis, 1993—. Mem. AMA, Am. Assn. Pediats., Am. Med. Women's Assn., Western Pediat. Rsch. Soc., Lawson Wilkins Pediat. Endocrine Soc., Endocrine Soc., so. Pediat. Rsch. Soc., Growth Hormone Soc. Office: Univ Tenn 848 Adams Ave Memphis TN 38103-2816

ROSEBERRY, ELIZABETH ANN, neonatologist; b. Athens, Ohio, Jan. 26, 1947; d. Horace Hewell and Margaret Elizabeth (Ross) Roseberry; m. Massimo Costa, June 15, 1974 (div. Sept. 9, 1982); m. Matthew Martin Hine, June 14, 1986 (div. Oct. 15, 1989). BS in Biology cum laude, Wake Forest U., 1968; MS in Zoology, Oreg. State U., 1970; postgrad., U. Ariz., 1974-76; MD, U. Tex., Houston, 1985. Diplomate Am. Bd. Pediatrics; lic. physician Tex., Va., W.Va. Lab. technician III Litton-Bionetics, Inc., Bethesda, Md., 1971-74; lab. technician II depts. pharmacology and anesthesiology U. Ariz. Med. Ctr., Tucson, 1974-75, rsch. asst. dept. anesthesiology, 1975-76; rsch. asst. II, dept. lab. medicine, Biol. Scis. Group U. Conn., Farmington and Storrs, 1977-78; technician I Forest Sci. Lab. Tex. A&M U., College Station, 1979-80; rsch. assoc. dept. survery Divsn. Immunology and Organ Transplantation, U. Tex., Houston, 1980-81; resident in pediatrics U. Tex. Med. Br., Galveston, 1985-88, fellow in neonatology, 1988-90; affiliate neonatologist Fairfax Neonatal Assocs., P.C., Falls Church, Va., 1990-92; assoc. neonatologist Pediatrix Med. Group, Charleston, W.Va., 1992—; staff neonatologist Fairfax Hosp., Falls Church, 1990-92, Potomac Hosp., Woodbridge, Va., 1990-92, Women and Children's Hosp., Charleston Area Med. Ctrs., 1992—; Mary Washington Hosp., Fredericksburg, 1993—, Alexandria (Va.) Hosp., 1993—, Virginia Beach (Va.) Gen. Hosp., 1994—; clin. asst. prof. pediatrics W.Va. U. Sch. Medicine, 1993-94. Contbr. articles to profl. jours. Recipient Minnie L. Maffett award, 1989-90. Fellow Am. Acad. Pediatrics; mem. AMA (Physician Recognition award 1988-91, 92—), Tex. Med. Soc., Med. Soc. Va., Prince William County Med. Soc., W.Va. State Med. Assn., Kanawha Med. Soc. Home: 10547 River Run Ct Manassas VA 20112-3007 Office: Pediatrix Med Group 1101 Sam Perry Blvd Ste 310 Fredericksburg VA 22401

ROSEBERRY, RICHARD LEE, secondary education educator, retired coast guard; b. Davenport, Iowa, Aug. 17, 1953; s. Richard Robert and Billie Dawn (Lebkisher) R.; m. Susan June Bublin, June 23, 1989; children: Virginia Leigh Hess-Roseberry, Dawn Marie. BS in History/Govt., U.S. Coast Guard Acad., 1975; MS in Mgmt. Engring., Rensselaer Poly. Inst., 1981. Commd. ens. USCG, 1975, advanced through grades to lt. comdr., 1986-95; ret.; deck officer USCG, Honolulu, 1975-77, Pearl Harbor, 1977-78; coast guard liasion officer Fleet Tng. Group, Pearl Harbor, 1978-80; asst. indsl. mgr. Support Ctr. Govs. Island, N.Y.C., 1981-84, indsl. mgr., 1988-92; chief search and rescue br. Greater Antilles sect. USCG, PR, 1992-95; afloat ops. officer USCG Seattle, 1984-85; resident Inspector Office, Seattle, 1985-88; tchr. physics and chemistry Bishop Verot H.S., Ft. Myers, Fla., 1996—; flotilla staff officer USCG Aux., Seattle, 1987-88, N.Y.C., 1988-92, P.R., 1992-95, Ft. Myers, 1995—. Del. to 1995 Presidency III Conv.; 1st v.p. Cape Coral New Resident Club; newsletter editor Cape Coral Rep. Club; safety officer Cape Coral Power Squadron; mem. Lee County Rep. Exec. Com.; sec. S.W. Fla. Kansas City Chiefs Fan Club. Mem. Inst. Indsl. Engrs., U.S. Naval Inst., U.S. Sailing Assn., Gov.'s Island Boat Club (commodore 1988-90), N.Y. Yacht Club, The Ret. Officers Assn. Republican. Home: 5313 Bay Shore Ave Cape Coral FL 33904

ROSEFIELD, HERBERT AARON, JR., state agency administrator; b. Sumter, S.C., Dec. 5, 1943; s. Herbert Aaron and Virginia (Moise) R.; m. Linda Halpern, Aug. 1967 (div. 1980); children: Scott Michael, Mark Brian; m. Donna Brod Andrews, Oct. 29, 1988; 1 stepchild, Bess Maureen. AB in Psychology, U. N.C., Chapel Hill, 1966; MA in Psychology, U. S.C., Columbia, 1968; EdD, N.C. State U., 1981. Lic. psychologist, N.C. Staff psychologist S.C. Vocat. Rehab., Florence, 1971-73; staff psychologist N.C. Divsn. Prisons, Huntersville, 1973-74, dir. psychol. svcs., 1974-78; correctional adminstr. N.C. Divsn. Prisons, Winston-Salem, 1978-83; command mgr. N.C. Divsn. Prisons, Raleigh, 1983-87, supt., 1987-94, dir. health care, asst. dir., 1994—; instr. Campbell U., Buies Creek, N.C., 1989-90, Fayetteville (N.C.) State U., 1991-94. Sec., bd. dirs. Brotherhood, Temple Beth Or, Raleigh, 1986-88; chmn. bd. dirs. United Way of Hoke County, 1993-94; active Health Care Task Force, 1994—; mem. Nature Conservancy, Environ. Def. Fund. Lt. U.S. Army, 1968-71, Vietnam. Mem. Am. Correctional Assn. (chmn. substance abuse com. 1990-92, mem. program coun. 1986-88, chmn. state pres.' com. 1984-86, mem. health care task force, 1994—), N.C. Correctional Assn. (pres. 1984-85), Am. Correctional Health Svcs. Assn. (chmn. program coun. 1990-92, spl. interest housing and programming for geriatric inmates, editor Corhealth, 1993—), N.C. Law Enforcement Assn., Audubon Soc., Phi Kappa Phi. Jewish. Office: NC Divsn Prisons Health Svcs 831 W Morgan St Raleigh NC 27603-1658

ROSELLI, RICHARD JOSEPH, lawyer; b. Chgo., Mar. 2, 1954; s. H. Joseph and Dolores Roselli; m. Lisa McNelis; children: Nicholas Joseph, Christiana Elise, Alexandra Grace, Michaela Luciana. BA, Tulane U., 1976, JD, 1980. Bar: Fla. 1981, U.S. Dist. Ct. (so. dist.) Fla. 1981, U.S. Ct. Appeals (5th and 11th cirs.); bd. cert. civil trial lawyer. Assoc. Krupnick & Campbell, Ft. Lauderdale, Fla., 1981-84; ptnr. Krupnick, Campbell, Malone Roselli, Ft. Lauderdale, 1984-91, Krupnick Campbell Malone Roselli Buser Slama & Hancock P.A., Ft. Lauderdale, 1991—. Trustee Fla. Democrat. Party. Mem. ATLA, Am. Bd. Trial Advocates, Am. Soc. Law and Medicine, So. Trial Lawyers Assn., Acad. Fla. Trial Lawyers (bd. dirs. 1987—, exec. com. 1990—, sec. 1993, treas. 1994, pres. 1996—, chmn. Fla. lawyers action group-PAC 1996, Golden Eagle award, 1989, Silver Eagle award, 1990), Trial Lawyers for Pub. Justice, Lawyer Pilots Bar Assn., St. Jude Catholic Ch. (mem. edn. and adv. coun.). Office: 700 SE 3rd Ave Fort Lauderdale FL 33316-1154

ROSEMAN, JOSEPH JACOB, flutist; b. Rio Pedras, P.R., July 14, 1964; s. Joseph and Elizabeth (Ubiñas) R. MusB cum laude, U. of Arts, Phila., 1986; MusM summa cum laude, Eastman Sch. Music, Rochester, N.Y., 1990; postgrad., Fla. State U., 1992—; pvt. study with profl. flutists, tchrs., 1982—; DMus, Fla. State U., 1996. Piccolo soloist Phila. Chamber Orch., 1983-85, Allentown (Pa.) Symphony Orch., 1985-88; co-prin. flutist Eastman Wind Ensemble, Rochester, 1988-90; prin. flutist Musica Nova Contemporary Ensemble, Rochester, 1988-89; soloist Pottstown (Pa.) Symphony Orch., 1988-92; prin. flutist/soloist Gibbs Chamber Orch., Rochester, 1989-90; flute instr. community edn. divsn. Eastman Sch. Music, 1989-90; flute instr. Cmty. Music Sch., Allentown, 1990-92; pvt. instr. flute, 1984—; piccolo substitute Pa. Ballet Orch., Phila., 1985-86; flute/piccolo substitute Lehigh Valley Chamber Orch., 1983-92, Phila. Opera Co., 1988-92, Rochester Philharm., 1989-91; flute substitute Concerto Soloists Phila., 1988-92; mem. Roseman/Clearfield Duo, Phila., 1986—; participant woodwind quintet programs Young Audiences of Rochester, 1988-89; band cons. Thomasville (Ga.) H.S., 1993—; band adjudicator Pa. Honors Band, Bethlehem, 1990. Rec. artist (with Eastman Wind Ensemble) CBS/Sony Masterworks, 1990; recital performer Carnegie Hall, N.Y.C., 1985; performer mus. events including Nat. Orchestral Inst., Blossom Music Festival, Aspen Music Festival, New-Coll. Music Festival, Colo. Philharm. Festival, Edinburgh Music Festival, Heidelberg Music Festival; soloist Atlanta Symphony Orch. Recipient Donald Vorhees Music award Allentown Symphony Assn., 1983; Fla. State U. fellow, 1992-93, 93-94, 94-95; Pro-Mozart Soc. of Atlanta scholar, Salzburg, Austria, 1994. Mem. Nat. Flute Assn., Pi Kappa Lambda. Democrat. Roman Catholic. Home: 5001 Lake Front Dr Apt B8 Tallahassee FL 32303-7171

ROSEN, ANA BEATRIZ, electronics executive; b. Guayaquil, Ecuador, May 16, 1950; came to U.S., 1962; d. Luis A. and Luz Aurora (Rodriguez) Moreira; m. Manuel Jose Farina, Dec. 15, 1979 (dec. Apr. 1990); children: Kevin, Mark; m. Michael G. Rosen, June 6, 1992. AA, Latin-Am. Inst., 1971. Adminstr. asst. M&T Chem. Inc., N.Y.C., 1971-75; mgr. sales Singer Products Co., N.Y.C., 1975-78; v.p. Argil Internat. Ltd., N.Y.C., 1978-83; pres. KMA Enterprises Inc., Bklyn., 1983-94, KMA Industries Inc., Palm Beach Gardens, Fla., 1994—; mem. U.S Trade Adv. Bd. Mem. ARC. Mem. NAFE, World Trade Coun. (Palm Beach County), Gold Coast Bus. and Profl. Women of the Palm Beaches. Roman Catholic.

ROSEN, BARRY HOWARD, museum director, history educator; b. Phila., June 26, 1942; s. Robert R. and Sylvia (Chanin) R.; m. Ann Adair Gould, Feb. 14, 1970; 1 son, David Joshua. B.S., Temple U., 1963, M.A., 1966; Ph.D., U. S.C., 1974. Asst. to provost U. S.C., Columbia, 1973-74, asst. to pres., 1974-77, dir. mus., univ. archivist, dir. mus. mgmt. programs, 1975-82; exec. dir. Kansas City Mus., Mo., 1982-86; pres. N.J. Hist. Soc., Newark, 1986-88; pres., CEO Milw. Pub. Mus., 1988—; field reader Inst. Mus. Svcs., Washington, 1981-84. Bd. dirs., pres. Westown Assn., 1988—. Mem. Am. Assn. State and Local History, Am. Assn Mus. (accrediting com. 1982—), Assn. Sci. Mus. Dirs. (chmn. future planning com. 1990—), Natural History Museums 2000 (steering com., 1989—, Southeastern Wis. Amniotrophic Lateral Sclerosis Soc. (bd. dirs. 1990—). Home: 809 Heron Rd Fort Lauderdale FL 33326-3348 Office: Milw Pub Mus 800 W Wells St Milwaukee WI 53233-1404

ROSEN, BENJAMIN MAURICE, venture capitalist, computer company executive; b. New Orleans, Mar. 11, 1933; s. Isidore J. and Anna Vera (Leibof) R.; m. Alexandra Ebere, Sept. 29, 1967; children—Jeffrey Mark, Eric Andrew. B.S., Calif. Inst. Tech., 1954; M.S., Stanford U., 1955; M.B.A., Columbia U., 1961. Engr. Raytheon Corp., Oxnard, Calif., 1955-56; engr. Sperry Corp., Great Neck, N.Y., 1957-59; v.p. Quantum Sci. Corp., N.Y.C., 1961-65; ptnr. Coleman & Co., N.Y.C., 1965-75; v.p. Morgan Stanley & Co. Inc., N.Y.C., 1975-80; pres. Rosen Research Inc., N.Y.C., 1980-83; ptnr. Sevin Rosen Mgmt. Co., N.Y.C., 1981—, chmn. bd., 1982—; also chmn. Compaq Computer Corp, Houston, TX; former founder dir. Lotus Devel. Corp.; mem. bd. overseers and mgrs. Meml. Sloan Kettering Cancer Ctr., N.Y.C.; mem. bd. overseers Columbia U. Grad. Sch. Bus., N.Y.C. Trustee Calif. Inst. Tech., Pasadena. Office: Sevin Rosen Mgmt Co 200 Park Ave New York NY 10166-0005 also: Compaq Computer Corp PO Box 692000 B Houston TX 77269-2000*

ROSEN, ELLEN FREDA, psychologist, educator; b. Chgo., Jan. 28, 1941; d. Samuel Aaron and Clara Laura (Pauker) R. BA, Carleton Coll., 1962; MA, U. Ill., 1965, PhD, 1968. Instr. psychology U. Ill., Urbana, 1966-67; prof. Coll. William and Mary, Williamsburg, Va., 1967—; cons. Ctr. for Teaching Excellence Hampton (Va.) U., 1988-94. Author: Ednl. Computer Software, (with E. Rae Harcum) The Gatekeepers of Psychology, 1993;

contbr. articles to profl. jours. Mem. Soc. for Computers in Psychology (bd. dirs.), Psychonomic Soc., Va. Psychol. Assn., Ea. Psychol. Assn., C.G. Jung Soc. of Tidewater (treas.), Am. Psychol. Soc., Assn. for Anorexia and Bulimia of Va. Office: Coll of William and Mary Dept of Psychology Williamsburg VA 23187

ROSEN, HOWARD ROBERT, lawyer; b. Montreal, Que., Can., Apr. 15, 1960; came to U.S. 1967; s. Kelvin and Binnie Lynn (Michaels) R. ; m. Adrienne Joy Unger, Apr. 11, 1987. BA, Emory U., 1982; JD, U. Miami, 1985. Bar: Fla. 1985. Asst. state atty. Dade County State Atty. Office, Miami, Fla., 1985—. Mem. ABA. Home: 17931 NW 9th Ct Pembroke Pines FL 33029 Office: Dade County State Atty 1350 NW 12th Ave Miami FL 33136-2102

ROSEN, PHILIP TERRY, history educator; b. Syracuse, N.Y., Mar. 22, 1946; s. Theodore and Martha (Mason) R.; m. Jackie McGillivray, May 2, 1970; 1 child, Philip Terry Mason. Student, U. Philippines, 1966-67; BA, Sterling Coll., 1968; postgrad., Universidad Indsl. de Santander, Colombia, 1970; MA, Emporia State U., 1970; PhD, Wayne State U., 1975. Instr. Am. History Wayne State U., Detroit, 1970-73; fellow Smithsonian Inst., Washington, 1974-75; asst. dir. council continuing edn. Marygrove Coll., Detroit, 1977-78, dean div. continuing edn., 1978-80; dean Erie (Pa.) Met. Coll., 1980-84; dir. continuing edn., assoc. prof. history U. Alaska, Anchorage, 1984—. Author: The Treaty Navy, 1919-1937, 1979, Peace and War: U.S. Naval Policies, 1776-1979, 1979, The Modern Stentors: Radio Broadcasters and the Federal Government, 1920-34, 1980; co-author: Hoover and the Historians, 1989; editor International Broadcasting Systems, 1988. Gannon U. Liberty Fund fellow, 1977. Mem. Am. Hist. Assn., So. Hist. Assn., Orgn. Am. Historians, Council Advancement Exptl. Learning. Home: 1615 E Fairview Ave #202A Montgomery AL 36106

ROSEN, STEPHEN LESLIE, lawyer; b. St. Paul, Minn., Nov. 20, 1948. BA, Hamline U., 1970; JD, So. Tex. U., 1974. Bar: Fla. 1974, U.S. Dist. Ct. Fla. 1975, U.S. Supreme Ct. 1980. Atty. Marlow, Mitzel, Ortmayer, Tampa, Fla., 1974-76, Wagner, Cunningham, Tampa, 1976-79, Morris and Rosen, Tampa, 1980-92, Rosen and Osborne, PA, Tampa, 1992—. Author: Worker's Compensation, Florida Bar, 1975, Longshore and Harborworkers Law, Florida Bar, 1978. Mem. Fla. Bar Assn. (chmn. worker's compensation bd. cert. com. 1988-90, chmn. statewide judicial nominating com., 1990-93, chmn. worker's compensation sect. 1992, Bud Adams award 1991). Office: Rosen and Osborne PA 4016 Henderson Blvd Tampa FL 33629-4940

ROSENAU, PAULINE VAILLANCOURT (PAULINE MARIE VAILLANCOURT-ROSENAU), public health educator; b. San Diego, June 14, 1943; d. Earl William and Marguerite (Rosenberger) Hansen; m. Jean Guy Vaillancourt (div.); 1 child, Veronique; m. James Rosenau, June 14, 1987 (div. June 1993). BA, U. Calif., Berkeley, 1965, MA, 1966, PhD, 1972; MPH, UCLA, 1992. Asst. prof. McGill U., 1969-73; assoc. prof. polit. sci. U. du Que., Montreal, Can., 1973-79, prof., 1980-93; assoc. prof. mgmt. & policy scis. U. Tex. Sch. Pub. Health, Houston, 1993—; dir. advance studies program dept. polit sci. U. Que., Montreal, 1977-79; vis. prof. U. de Haute-Normandie, Rouen, France, 1984-85, U. Calif., Irvine, 1988. Author: When Marxists Do Research, 1986, Post-Modernism and the Social Sciences, 1992, Health Care Reform in the 1990s, 1994, (with others) Sondage Politique et Politiques des Sondages au Quebec, 1979; editor: Quebec and the Parti Quebecois, 1979; contbr. articles to profl. jours. Mem. APHA, Can. Polit. Sci. Assn. (bd. dirs. 1975-77, program chair ann. meeting 1981), Soc. Quebecoise de Sci. Politique (bd. dirs. 1977-79). Office: Univ Tex Sch Public Health 1200 Herman Pressler PO Box 20186 Houston TX 77225

ROSENBAUM, DONALD HERMAN, JR., orthopaedic surgeon; b. Gary, Ind., Dec. 30, 1951; s. Donald Herman and Jane Rae (Bond) R.; m. Lola Sicard; 1 child, Christine. BA in Zoology and Pre-Med. Scis., DePauw U., 1974; MHA, Washington U., 1977; DO, Phila. Coll. Osteo. Medicine, 1986. lic., Fla., Pa. Commd. ensign USN, 1979; advanced through grades to comdr. USN, 1993, 1979, 1993; chief ops. mgmt. svc., asst. mil. constrn. liaison officer Naval Regional Med. Ctr., Orlando, Fla., 1977-80; outpatient dept. adminstr., fleet liaison officer Naval Regional Med. Ctr., Naples, Italy, 1980-82; surg. intern, lt. comdr. Naval Hosp., Oakland, Calif., 1986-87; flight surgeon VMFA-451 MAG 31 Marine Corps Air Station, Beaufort, S.C., 1987-90; resident in orthopedics Nat. Naval Med. Ctr., Bethesda, Md., 1990-94; chief dept. orthopedic surgery Jacksonville (Fla.) Naval Hosp., 1994—. Contbr. articles to profl. jours. Named Second Marine Airwing Flight Surgeon of Yr., 1990; recipient Navy Commendation medal, 1982, Humanitarian medal, 1980, Medal of Merit by Italian Govt., 1983, Meritorious Unit Commendation Ribbon 5 stars, 1988, 89, 90, Nat. Def. medal, 1990, Navy Commendation medal, 1990. Mem. AMA, Am. Assn. Orthopaedic Surgeons, Am. Coll. Health Care Execs., Assn. Mil. Surgeons of U.S., Am. Osteo. Assn., Assn. Mil. Osteopathic Physicians and Surgeons, Soc. of U.S. Naval Flight Surgeons. Home: 1847 Commodore Point Orange Park FL 32073 Office: Jacksonville Naval Hosp Dept Orthopedic Surgery 2013 Child St Jacksonville FL 32214-5013

ROSENBERG, GEORGE A., public relations company executive; b. N.Y., Dec. 13, 1945. BA in Pub. Rels., The Am. U., 1967; student, Pace Coll. With Burson-Marsteller, 1969-85; pres., COO Cohn & Wolfe, 1986-92, pres., CEO, 1992-93; mng. dir. Ward Howell Internat., N.Y., 1993—. Office: Cohn & Wolfe 225 Peachtree St NE Atlanta GA 30303-1701*

ROSENBERG, LESLIE KAREN, media director; b. Camden, N.J., Mar. 3, 1949; d. Lorimer and Doris Selma (Kohn) R. BS in Radio, TV, Film, U. Tex., 1971. Continuity dir. WEAT-TV/AM/FM, West Palm Beach, Fla., 1971-74; media buyer Wm. F. Haselmire Advt., West Palm Beach, 1974-75, media dir., 1982-85; program and pub. svc. dir. WTBS-TV, Atlanta, 1975-78; nat. traffic coord. WXIA-TV, Atlanta, 1978-80; sr. sales asst. CBS Radio Spot Sales, Atlanta, 1980-82; acct. exec. WRMF-FM, West Palm Beach, 1985; media dir., acct. exec. Merlin Masters & Nomes Advt., West Palm Beach, 1985-88; pres., media dir. Media Magic Plus, Inc., West Palm Beach, 1988—; advt. coord. Hearx, Inc., West Palm Beach, 1996—; comm. adv. bd. Palm Beach Jr. Coll., Lake Worth, 1972-74; advtsg. coord. HEARX Ltd., 1996—; mem. Internat. Cultural Exchange Program. Talent, author various radio commercials (Addy award 1973, 74), talent various TV commercials (Addy award 1974). Bd. dirs. Lake Worth (Fla.) Playhouse, 1989-92, program co-chmn., 1989-91; producer Lake Worth Playhouse Internat. Cultural Exch. for 1994 trip to Eng., mem. com. for 97 trip to Eng., 1994-97. Mem. Advt. Club of the Palm Beaches (bd. dirs. 1983-85), NAFE, Nat. Acad. Arts & Sciences, Fireside Theatre, U.S. Racquetball Assn. (dir. tournament control 1976-80). Office: Media Magic Plus Inc PO Box 19962 West Palm Beach FL 33416-9962

ROSENBERG, ROBERT MARK, trade association executive; b. N.Y.C., Dec. 8, 1950; s. Walter J. and Anita (Marcus) R.; m. Karen Rosenberg (div.). BSBA, U. Fla., 1973; MS, Fla. State U., 1977; MA, U. Chgo., 1980. Chief Bur. Horse Racing, State of Fla., Miami, dep. dir., then dir. divsn. pari-mutuel wagering, 1980-87; mgr., then dir. govt. affairs Nat. Pest Control Assn., Dunn Loring, Va., 1989—. Office: Nat Pest Control Assn 8100 Oak St Dunn Loring VA 22027

ROSENBERRY, WILLIAM KENNETH, lawyer, educator; b. St. Louis, Aug. 14, 1946; s. William Hugh and Shirley Anne (Love) R.; m. Linda Lou Lang, Aug. 24, 1968 (div. 1985); children: Ashlie Anne, Allison Renee; m. Donna L. Pruitt; stepchildren: Corey David Pruitt, Lindsey Lee Pruitt. BBA, U. Tex., Arlington, 1967; JD, Baylor U., 1970. Bar: Tex. 1970, Colo. 1991, U.S. Dist. Ct. (no. dist.) Tex. 1971; bd. cert. specialist in comml. real estae law, residential real estae law, Tex. Assoc. Hinds & Chambers, Arlington, 1970-71; ptnr. Duke, Rosenberry, Duke & Jelinek, Arlington, 1971-76; pvt. practice, Arlington, 1976—; mem. faculty U. Tex., 1991—; bd. dirs. Equitable Bank, NA, Arlington, Equitable Bankshares, Dallas; gen. mgr. Triple R. Properties. Assoc. editor Baylor Law Rev., 1969. Pres. Pantego Christian Acad. Boosters, Arlington, 1990-92; mem. Arlington City Zoning Bd., 1989-92. Recipient oustanding part-time faculty teaching award dept. real estate and fin. U. Tex., 1992; named to Outstanding Young Men in Am., 1980. Mem. Arlington Bar Assn. (bd. dirs. 1987), Arlington Sportsmans Club, Baylor Bear Club, Arlington Republican Club. Mem. Pantego Bible Ch. Office: 3010 W Park Row Dr Arlington TX 76013-2048

ROSENBLUM, JOHN WILLIAM, dean; b. Houston, Jan. 1, 1944; s. H. William and Susan (Ullmann) R.; m. Carolyn Edith Jones, Sept. 12, 1964; children: J. Christopher, Kathryn, Nicholas. A.B., Brown U., 1965; M.B.A., Harvard U., 1967, D.B.A., 1972. Instr. Harvard U. Bus. Sch., Boston, 1969-72, asst. prof., 1972-75, assoc. prof., 1975-79; prof. Darden Grad. Sch. Bus. Adminstrn., U. Va., Charlottesville, 1979-80, assoc. dean, 1980-82, dean, 1982-93; Tayloe Murphy prof., 1993—; dean Jepson Sch. Leadership Studies, U. Richmond, Va., 1996—; bd. dirs. Chesapeake Corp., Cadmus Comms., Inc., T. Rowe Price Assocs., Comdial Corp., Cone Mills Corp., The Providence Jour. Co. Co-author: Strategy and Organization, 1973, (2d edit.), 1977, Cases in Political Economy-Japan, 1980. Mem. Phi Beta Kappa, Omicron Delta Kappa. Home: RR 3 Box 530 Crozet VA 22932-9319 Office: Univ Richmond Jepson Sch Richmond VA 23173

ROSENBLUM, JOSEPH, English language educator; b. Waterbury, Conn., Dec. 19, 1947; s. Morris and Mary (Twersky) R.; m. Suzanne Helena McCloud, July 4, 1975; 1 child, Ida Elizabeth. BA, U. Conn., 1969; PhD, Duke U., 1975; MLS, U. N.C., 1976. Sr. libr. U. Miss., Oxford, 1976-79; reference libr. Guilford Coll., Greensboro, N.C., 1980-83; lectr. U. N.C., Greensboro, 1980—. Author: Thomas Holcroft, 1995, Shakespeare: An Annotated Bibliography, 1992, (play) Error in Judgement, 1993; editor: The Plays of Thomas Holcroft, 1980, Lives of Mississippi Authors, 1981, American Book Collectors and Bibliographers, 1994, A Bibliographical History of the Book, 1995. Recipient Best Article award Southeastern Libr., 1982, English Detective Fiction 2d prize Oxford Univ. Press, 1990. Mem. Trollope Soc., Charles Lamb Soc., Phi Beta Kappa. Democrat. Home: 215 Woodlawn Ave Greensboro NC 27401-1747 Office: Univ NC at Greensboro Greensboro NC 27412

ROSENBLUM, MARTIN JEROME, ophthalmologist; b. N.Y.C., Apr. 7, 1948; s. Philip and Rita (Steppel) R.; m. Zina Zarin, May 31, 1975; children: Steven David, Richard James. BS, Bklyn. Coll., 1968; MD, U. Ariz., 1973. Diplomate Am. Bd. Ophthalmology, Nat. Bd. Med. Examiners. Intern Cornell U., N.Y.C., 1974-75; resident N.Y. Med. Coll., 1975-78, instr., 1978-79; resident Columbia U., 1977; practice medicine specializing in eye surgery, St. Petersburg, Fla., 1979—; chief ophthalmology, chief surgery Edward White Hosp.; asst. clin. prof. ophthalmology, U. So. Fla.; attending surgeon Columbia St. Petersburg Med. Ctr., St. Anthony's Bayfront Med. Ctr., Palms of Pasadena Amer Soc. for Cataract and Refractive Surgery. Fellow ACS, Am. Acad. Ophthalmology; mem. AMA, Am. Soc. Ophthalmic Plastic and Reconstructive Surgery, Fla. Med. Assn., Fla. Soc. Ophthalmology, Pinellas County Med. Soc. Republican. Jewish. Club: Seminole Lake Country. Avocation: tennis, golf, travel. Home: 9035 Baywood Park Dr Largo FL 33777-4630 Office: 2200 16th St N Saint Petersburg FL 33704-3106

ROSENBLUM, SOL A., medical educator; b. Nashville, May 8, 1926; s. Ernest Noah and Selma (Zhislin) R.; m. Susan Jane Adler, Dec. 5, 1955; children: Jami Lynn Rosenblum Rubens, Jill Allen Rosenblum Garcia, JoAnne. BS, U. Tenn., 1949, MD, 1951; postgrad., Vanderbilt U., 1956—. Intern Michael Reese Hosp., Chgo., 1951-52, fellow cardiology and hematology, 1952-54, med. resident, 1954-56; Asst. clin. prof. medicine Vanderbilt U. Sch. Medicine, Nashville. Fellow Am. Coll. Chest Physicians; mem. Am. Coll. Physicians. Home and Office: 6603 Fox Hollow Rd Nashville TN 37205-3956

ROSENE, LINDA ROBERTS, organizational consultant, researcher; b. Miami, Fla., Nov. 1, 1938; d. Wilbur David and Dorothy Claire (Baker) Roberts; m. Ralph W. Rosene, Aug. 3, 1957; children: Leigh, Russ, Tim. MA, Fielding Inst., 1981, PhD in Clin. Psychology, 1983. Lic. clin. psychologist; lic. Am. marriage and family therapist. Counselor Rapid City (S.D.) Regional Hosp., 1978-81, Luth. Social Svcs., Rapid City, 1978-82; exec. v.p. Target Systems Inc., Dallas and Irving, Tex., 1983-85, cons., 1985—; cons. S.W. Home Furnishing Assn., Dallas, 1984, Northwestern Bell, Omaha, 1985; presenter, developer seminars gest-Accor Retail Assn. of Can., So. Home Furnishings Convs., 1989, Am. Assn. Med. Assts., many others. Pub. Convenience Store News, Nat. Petroleum News, Nat. Home Furnishing Assn.-West news mag., Profl. Furniture Merchants mag.; mem. nat. adv. group Nat. Assn. Convenience Stores; presenter Internat. Sleep Products Assocs., 1990, Profit Mgmt. Systems, 1990, S.E. Buying Assocs., 1990, Nat. Assn. Casual Furn. Retailers, Petroleum Mktg. Edn. Found., 1991, Nat. Petroleum Mktg. & Edn. Found., 1991, Nat. Adv. Group, 1993, Tex. Mini Storage Retailers Assn., 1992, Workforce 2000, 1992, Nat. Adv. Group, 1993, ann. conf. Gen. Elec. Retail Systems, 1993, 94, Va. Petroleum Jobbers Assn., 1993, Ft. Worth, Tex. Pers. Assn., 1994, N.Y. chpt. Young Pres. Orgn., 1994—, Next Generation, Waco, Tex., 1994, Internat. Conf. Shopping Ctrs., 1994, Bank North Tex., 1994, Ky. Grocers Assn., Can. Retailers Cantrex, 1995, 96, Spring Air Dealers Assn., 1995, Mortgage Loan Industry, Weiner & Assocs. Nat. Seminars, 1995—, Nat. Inst. Occupational Health, Safety & Health, 1995, Am. Psychiatric Assn., 1996, World Bus. Acad., 1996, CEO-Network, 1996, Tex. Lic. Marriage & Family Therapist Annual Conv., 1996, Centrex Nat. Conv., Internat. Conf. of Shopping Ctrs., 1996, U.S. Profl. Tennis Assn., 1996, V. Vision Internat., 1996, Presbyn. Hosp., Dallas, 1996, many others; developer copyrighted hiring system, 1985, rev., 1989, copyrighted recruitment tng. system for retail mgmt., 1988, rev., 1989; developer copyrighted coll. recruitment sys. "Place", 1996; speaker in field. Author: Civil War in American Workplace, 1995; pub. Mini Storage Messenger Mag., Recovery, Bed Times; contbr. articles to newspapers and mags. Bd. dirs. Assn. Children with Learning Disabilities, S.D., 1983-84, West River (S.D.) Alcoholism Svcs., 1983-84, Health Adv. Com. of Head Start, S.D., 1980-84, St. Martins Acad., S.D., 1971-75; mem. Rapid City Mayor's Commn. on Racial Conciliation, 1971-73, Nat. Trust for Hist. Preservation; charter mem. Nat. Mus. Women in the Arts; presenter parenting seminar Westminster Presbyn. Ch., Dallas. Named to Nat. Register of Cert. Group Psychotherapists; rsch. grantee Nat. Luth. Ch., 1981. Mem. APA, Am. Group Psychotherapist Assn., Am. Group Psychotherapy Assn. (clin.), Dallas Group Psychotherapist Assn., N.C. Psychol. Assn., Assn. Marriage and Family Therapists, Rotary Internat., S.W. Home Furnishing Assn. Internat. Avocations: aviation, bicycling, racquetball, music, birdwatching. Home: 7005 Deloache Ave Dallas TX 75225-2422

ROSENE, RALPH WALFRED, consulting company executive; b. Davenport, Iowa, Mar. 21, 1938; s. Raymond Walfred and Lavern (Marre) R.; m. Linda Roberts, Aug. 3, 1957; children: Leigh, Russell, Tim. Grad. high sch. Sales Mpls. Star/Tribune, 1958-66, sales mgr., 1966-68; advt. dir. Rapid City (S.D.) Jour., 1968-72, ops. mgr., 1972-74, gen. mgr., 1974-76; chief exec. officer First Am. Systems, Rapid City, 1976-82; sr. ptnr. Target Systems, Inc., Dallas, 1982-85, pres., 1985—; CEO, 1990—; speaker and seminar leader in field. Contbr. to numerous nat. industry publs. Chmn. bd. Community Action Agy., Rapid City, 1970-71. Mem. Rapid City S.D. C. of C. (chmn. bd. 1980), Toastmasters (pres. Dallas chpt. 1986), CEO Network (mem. local bd.). Office: Target Systems Inc 5605 N Macarthur Blvd Ste 280 Irving TX 75038-2630

ROSENFELD, STEVEN IRA, ophthalmologist; b. N.Y.C., Nov. 18, 1954; s. Frederick and Pearl (Stern) R.; m. Lisa Allyson Klar, June 24, 1978; children: Michael, Julie. BA, Johns Hopkins U., 1976; MD, Yale U., 1980. Diplomate Am. Bd. Ophthalmology, Nat. Bd. Med. Examiners. Intern Yale-New Haven Hosp., 1980-81; resident Barnes Hosp., St. Louis, 1981-84; fellow Bascom Palmer Eye Inst., Miami, Fla., 1984-85; ptnr. in pvt. practice Delray Eye Assocs., Delray Beach, Fla., 1985—; clin. instr. Bascom Palmer Eye Inst., 1985-90, asst. clin. prof., 1990—; assoc. examiner Am. Bd. Ophthalmology, Phila., 1993—. Author: Lens and Cataract: The Eye in Systemic Disease; contbr. articles to profl. jours. Recipient Harry Rosenbaum Rsch. award Washington U. Sch. Medicine, 1984; named one of Best Doctors in Am., 1996; Heed Ophthalmic Found. fellow, 1984. Fellow ACS, Am. Acad. Ophthalmology, Soc. Heed Fellows; mem. Castroviejo Corneal Soc., Eye Bank Assn. Am., Fla. Med. Assn., Fla. Soc. Ophthalmology, Assn. for Rsch. in Vision and Ophthalmology, Ocular Microbiology and Immunology Group, Phi Beta Kappa, Alpha Omega Alpha. Office: Delray Eye Assocs 16201 Military Trl Delray Beach FL 33484-6503

ROSENOW, DORIS JANE, critical care nurse, nursing consultant; b. Sharon, Pa., Sept. 13, 1935; d. John J. and Mary F. (Koss) Skertic; m. Galen J. Rosenow, Dec. 14, 1957; children: Mary K. Gage, Gail E. Logan. Diploma in Nursing, St. Anthony de Padua Hosp., Chgo., 1955; BSN and BA in Psychology, Incarnate Word Coll., San Antonio, 1980; MSN, U. Tex. Health Sci. Ctr., San Antonio, 1984; PhD, U. Tex., 1990. RN, Tex.; cert. critical care RN. Critical care nurse Good Shephard Hosp., Longview, Tex., 1977, Brooke Army Med. Ctr., San Antonio, 1978-85; instr. Health Scis. Ctr. Tex. Tech. U., Odessa, 1985-88; asst. prof. Incarnate Word Coll., San Antonio, 1990-91, U. Tex., Galveston, 1991-92; assoc. prof. Tex. A&M, Corpus Christi, 1992—; researcher in field. Contbr. articles to profl. jours. Served to 1st lt. USAF, 1957-60. Mem. ANA, Tex. Nurses Assn., Scientific Rsch. Soc., Sigma Theta Tau (Nat. Honor Soc. 1984), Phi Kappa Phi (Nat. Honor Soc. 1990), Sigma Xi. Home: 15615 Boulder Creek St San Antonio TX 78247-2936

ROSENSTOCK, JOEL, physician; b. N.Y.C., Aug. 28, 1948; s. Frank and Shirley (Kimmelman) R.; m. Marna Jay Berusch, Sept. 15, 1971 (div. Sept. 1978); m. Madelene Blake Caldwell, Jan. 1, 1986; children: Scott Adam, Todd Stuart. BA, Cornell U., 1970; MD, U. Brussels, 1976; MPH, Uniformed Svcs. Univ. Health Scis., 1985. Intern U. Louisville, 1976-77, resident, 1977-78; resident Christ Hosp., Cin., 1979-80; fellow in infectious diseases Nat. Naval Med. Ctr., 1981-83; attending physician Christ Hosp., Cin., 1979-81; commd. ensign USN, 1981, advanced through grades to comdr., 1986, resigned, 1989; assoc. prof. medicine Uniformed Svcs. Univ. Health Sci., Bethesda, Md., 1983-85; officer in charge Naval Sch. Health Scis., Panama, 1986-89; staff physician Piedmont Hosp., Atlanta, 1989—; clin. attending physician NIH, Bethesda, 1983-86. Mem. ACP, Am. Soc. Microbiology, Am. Soc. Tropical Medicine, Assn. Mil. Surgeons U.S., Infectious Disease Soc. Am., Infectous Disease Consortium Ga. (prin. investigator), AIDS Rsch. Consortium Atlanta (prin. investigator). Office: 35 Collier Rd NW Ste 245 Atlanta GA 30309-1603

ROSENTHAL, LEE H., federal judge; b. Nov. 30, 1952; m. Gary L. Rosenthal; children: Rebecca, Hannah, Jessica, Rachel. BA in Philosophy with honors, U. Chgo., 1974, JD with honors, 1977. Bar: Tex. 1979. Law clk. to Hon. John R. Brown U.S. Ct. Appeals (5th cir.), 1977-78; assoc. Baker & Botts, 1978-86, ptnr., 1986-92; judge U.S. Dist. Ct. (so. dist.) Tex., 1992—. Editor topics and comments Law Rev. U. Chgo., 1977-78. Active vis. com. Law Sch. U. Chgo., 1983-86, 94—; mem. devel. coun. Tex. Children's Hosp., 1988-92; pres. Epilepsy Assn. Houston/Gulf Coast, 1989-91; trustee Briarwood Sch. Endowment Found., 1991-92; bd. dirs. Epilepsy Found. Am., 1993—. Fellow Tex. Bar Found.; mem. ABA, Am. Law Inst., Texas Bar Assn., Houston Bar Assn. Office: US Dist Ct US Courthouse Rm 8631 515 Rusk St Houston TX 77002

ROSENTHAL, PAUL EDMOND, lawyer; b. Miami, May 1, 1951; s. David and Helen (Kaplan) R. BA, U. Fla., 1973, JD, 1976. Bar: Fla. 1977, U.S. Dist. Ct. (mid. dist.) Fla. 1977. Asst. city atty. City of Orlando (Fla.), 1977-79, asst. to mayor and council, 1979-80; assoc. Van den Berg, Gay & Burke, Orlando, 1980-81; ptnr. Van den Berg, Gay, Burke, Wilson & Arkin, Orlando, 1982-85, Foley & Lardner, Orlando, 1985—; mem., chmn. 9th Jud. Cir. Nominating Commn., Orlando, 1984-88; atty. City of Ocoee, Fla., 1988—. Mem. ABA, Orange County Bar Assn., Delta Upsilon (sec. alumni club). Democrat. Jewish. Office: Foley & Lardner 111 N Orange Ave Ste 1800 Orlando FL 32801-2387*

ROSENTHAL, RICHARD, law librarian; b. N.Y.C., Jan. 15, 1948; s. Albert Richard and Patricia (O'Neil) R.; m. Iona Elizabeth Parks, Sept. 3, 1977; children: Carolyn, Alan. AA, Nassau Community Coll., 1968; BA, SUNY, Brockport, 1970; MLS, L.I. U., 1972. Sr. librarian Assoc. Library Svc., N.Y.C., 1973-77; libr. assoc. Law Libr. Tulane U., New Orleans, 1977-8l; libr. Milling, Benson, Woodward, New Orleans, 198l-86, Adams & Reese, New Orleans, 1986-91, Scott & Hulse, 1991—. Mem. Am. Assn. Law Librs., Border Libr. Assn., Tex. Libr. Assn., Lions, El Paso Downtown Lion's Club. Roman Catholic. Home: 6841 Orizaba Ave El Paso TX 79912-2305 Office: Tex Commerce Bank Bldg Flr 11 El Paso TX 79901

ROSENTHAL, RICHARD RAPHAEL, allergist, researcher; b. N.Y.C., Apr. 5, 1939; s. Louis and Augusta (Dubovah) R.; m. Eileen Pressman, Jan. 1, 1968. B.A., Rutgers U., 1961, M.S., 1962; M.D., SUNY-Bklyn., 1966. Diplomate Am. Bd. Allergy and Immunology. Intern Kings County Hosp., Bklyn., 1966-67, resident in internal medicine, 1967-68; resident in internal medicine L.I. Jewish Med. Ctr., New Hyde Park, N.Y., 1970-71; fellow in medicine Johns Hopkins U. Sch. Medicine, Balt., 1971-73, asst. in medicine, 1973-74, instr. medicine, 1974-75, asst. prof. medicine clin. immunology div., 1975—; practice medicine specializing in allergy and clin. immunology, Fairfax, Va., 1973—; chief allergy sect. Fairfax (Va.) Hosp., 1973—; cons. Nat. Inst. Allergy and Infectious Diseases, NIH. Served with USPHS, 1968-70. NIH grantee, 1973—. Fellow Am. Acad. Allergy, ACP; mem. AMA (continuing edn. award 1969, 72), Am. Thoracic Soc., Am. Soc. Internal Medicine, Va. Acad. Medicine, Johns Hopkins Med. Soc., Lung Assn. No. Va., Greater Washington Allergy Soc. (sec-treas. 1978), Md. Allergy Soc., Md. Thoracic Soc., Va. Thoracic Soc., Am. Lung Assn., Fairfax County Med. Soc. Club: West River (Md.) Sailing. Mem. editorial bd. Jour. Allergy and Clin. Immunology; contbr. numerous articles to med. jours.; patentee nebulization dosimeter. Home: PO Box 769 Great Falls VA 22066-0769*

ROSENTHAL, SUSAN BARBARA, retired librarian; b. Elberon Park, N.J., Apr. 7, 1946; d. Joseph and Anna (Warar) Rosenthal. B.A., Montclair State Coll., 1967; M.Ed. in L.S., U. Miami, 1973. Cert. media specialist, tchr., Fla., N.J. Tchr., Manasquan Bd. Edn. (N.J.), 1967-71; tech. services librarian Oakland Park Library (Fla.), 1978-92, asst. dir., 1992-93, acting dir., 1993, ret. Author: (mag.) Galumph, 1965-67; contbr. A Micro Handbook for Small Libraries and Media Centers, 1983, 2nd edit., 1986, 3d edit., 1991. Mem. Humane Soc., Broward County, Fla., 1981, WPBT-TV PBS sta., 1975—; charter mem. Mus. of Discovery and Sci., 1989—, U.S. Holocaust Meml. Mus., 1994-96. Recipient St. Cloud Teaching award Société d'Enseignement, St. Cloud, France, 1966, 2 awards Libr. Pub. Rels. Coun., winner, 1983, honorable mention, 1985, cert. appreciation U.S. Holocaust Meml. Mus., 1996. Mem. ALA, Fla. Library Assn. (continuing edn. com. 1980), Fla. Pub. Library Assn., Broward County Library Assn. (treas. 1981-83), Apple Libr. Users Group, Apple Computer Enjoyment Soc. (chpt. sec. 1984-87, corp. sec. 1985-89), Consumers Union, Wilderness Soc., World Wildlife Fund, Environ. Def. Fund, People for Ethical Treatment Animals, Nature Conservancy, Mensa, Procrastinators Club Am., Pi Delta Phi. Office: Bibliothéque Lamienne 1522 NE 34th Ct Oakland Park FL 33334-5381

ROSETT, JACQUELINE BERLIN, financial executive; b. N.Y.C., Aug. 28, 1945; s. Marshall Hamilton and Lenore (Berlin) Rosett. BS in Physics, Columbia U., 1967. With George B. Buck Inc., N.Y.C., 1967-68; pres. Jacqueline Rosett Assocs., N.Y.C., 1968—; cons. in internat. investments. Photographer: The African Ark, 1974. Vol. counselor N.Y.C. Opera Guild, 1982—; chmn. Symphony Design Showcase Shop; 2d v.p. Interacial Interfaith Coun.; mem. Diamond Club San Diego Zool. Soc., 1975—. Mem. Am. Soc. Profl. and Exec. Women, Nat. Assn. Female Execs., Bronx Zoological Soc. Democrat. Jewish. Club: Camerata (events chmn.).

ROSIERE, RANDY EUGENE, range scientist, educator; b. Joplin, Mo., Feb. 13, 1949; s. William E. and Elizabeth A. (Shapland) R. AA, Northeastern Okla. A&M Coll., 1969; BS, Okla. State U., 1971; MS, N.Mex. State U., 1974, PhD, 1978. Cert. profl. animal scientist, Am. Registry Profl. Animal Scientists. Various positions USDA, 1969, 70; lab. technician Okla. State U., Stillwater, 1970, 71; rsch.-teaching asst. N.Mex. State U., Las Cruces, 1972, 73, 75-78; rsch. assoc. Oreg. State U., Burns, 1974; asst. prof. U. Calif., Berkeley, 1978-85; from asst. to assoc. prof. Tarleton State U., Stephenville, Tex., 1985—. Contbr. articles to profl. jours. With inf. divsn. U.S. Army, 1971-77. Mem. Soc. Range Mgmt., Am. Soc. Animal Sci., Nat. Cattlemen's Assn., Tex. S.W. Cattle Raisers Assn., Am. Sheep Industry Assn., Tex. Sheep and Goat Raisers, Am. Registry Profl. Animal Scientists. Republican. Methodist. Office: Tarleton State Univ Agriculture & Natural Resou Mail Drop # 50 Stephenville TX 76402

ROSIN, LINDSAY ZWEIG, clinical psychologist; b. San Antonio, Oct. 28, 1954; s. Morris and Ethel (Rosenberg) R.; m. Susana Aceituno, Sept. 3,

1981; children: Lauren, Melanie. BA, U. Tex., 1975; MA, Xavier U., 1979; PhD, Fla. Inst. Tech., 1985. Lic. psychologist, Tex. Psychology assoc. Dayton (Ohio) Mental Health Ctr., 1980-81, Cin. Neurological Assocs., Cin., 1981-82; intern VA Med. Ctr., Houston, 1982-83; coord. outpatient services Houston Child Guidance Ctr., Houston, 1983-84; fellow Med. Ctr. del Oro Hosp., Houston, 1984-85; staff psychologist Mid-City Mental Health Mental Retardation, Houston, 1985-89; clin. asst. prof. psychology Baylor Coll. Medicine, Houston, 1985—; pvt. practice Houston, 1986—; psychologist St. Joseph Hosp., Houston, 1987—; psychologist cons. Mid-City Mental Health Mental Retardation, Houston, 1989—, Tex. Children's Hosp., 1993—. Contbr. articles to profl. jours. Recipient Outstanding Contbn. to Psychology award, Ohio Assn. Psychologists, 1982. Mem. Am. Psychol. Assn., Tex. Psychol. Assn., Houston Psychol. Assn., Internat. Neuropsychological Soc., Gerontological Soc. Am. Home: PO Box 20671 Houston TX 77225-0671 Office: 3730 Kirby Dr Ste 825 Houston TX 77098-3927

ROSIN, MORRIS, real estate, land development company executive; b. San Antonio, Feb. 21, 1924; s. Berco and Leia (Dupchansky) R.; student Tex. A&M U., 1942, St. Mary's U., 1941, 45-47; m. Ethel Rosenberg; children—Susan, Charles, Lindsay. Sec.-treas. Bimbi Mfg. Co., 1949-67; pres. Bimbi Shoe Co. div. Athlone Industries, San Antonio, 1970-72; v.p. Athlone Industries, Parsippany, N.J., 1967-72; pres. Ardo Pro, San Antonio, 1966-74, Yoakum Bend Corp., San Antonio, 1968—, Broadway Devel. Corp., 1984-90; sec.-treas. R & R Corp., San Antonio, 1970-72. Served with USAAF, 1942-45. Clubs: Masons (32 deg.), Shriners. Home: 101 Westcott #103 Houston TX 77007

ROSINEK, JEFFREY, judge; b. N.Y.C., Sept. 13, 1941; s. Isidore and Etta (Kramer) R.; m. Sandra Gwen Rosen, Aug. 7, 1977; 1 child, Ian David. B.A. in History, U. Miami, 1963, postgrad. in Polit. Sci., J.D., 1974. Bar: Fla., 1974. Tchr., Coral Gables (Fla.) High Sch., 1963-78; sole practice, Miami, Fla., 1974-76; assoc. Tendrich and Todd, Miami, 1976-77; ptnr. Todd, Rosinek & Blake, Miami, 1977-84, Rosinek and Blake, 1984-86; judge Dade County Court, Miami, 1986-89, 11th Jud. Cir., Fla., 1990—; instr. Boston U., 1975; mem. faculty Fla. Coll. Advanced Judicial Studies, 1992—. Chmn. Miami Environ. Research Adv. Com., 1969-73; mem. Miami Beach Transportation commn., Nat. Bicentenial Competition on the constitution & Bill of Rights com., Dade County Youth Adv. Bd., 1973-75; bd. dirs. U. Miami Law Sch., treas. alumni, jud. dir.; past pres. Dade County Young Democrats; mem. Congl. Civilian Rev. Bd., 1975-90, chmn., 1976-78; bd. dirs., treas. Fla. Congl. Com., Legal Services Greater Miami; Fla. chmn. Project Concern Internat.; v.p. Beth David Congregation, 1976-85; bd. trustees Haven Ctr.; bd. dirs., treas., organizer South Miami-Kendall pro bono project Legal Service of Greater Miami, 1983-86; bd. dirs. Fla. Law Related Edn., 1988—, Adv. Program, 1988—; active Dade Coalition for the Homeless, 1992—, Dade County Homeless Trust. 1993—, chmn. criminal justice com.; chmn. Beck Mus. of Judaica, 1989—; 1st v.p. Coral Gables H.S. Parent-Tchrs.-Students Assn., 1995-96, pres., 1996—. Recipient award Jewish Theol. Sem., 1978. Mem. ABA, Dade County Bar Assn., South Miami-Kendall Bar Assn. (past pres.), Coral Gables Bar Assn., Fla. Bar Assn. (jud. nominating procedures com.), Miami Beach Bar Assn. (bd. dirs.), Wig and Robe (chancellor 1973-74), Bar and Gavel Soc., Am. Judges Assn. (bd. govs. 1990-93, sec. 1993-94, 2d v.p. 1993-94, 1st v.p., 1994-95, pres.-elect 1995-96, pres. 1996—), Nat. Court Reporters Assn. (strategic alliance com. 1993). Clubs: Biscayne Bay Kiwanis (disting. past pres., lt. gov. Fla. Dist., Maj. Emphasis chmn., pres. 1994—), Key Internat. (counselor Fla. dist., past pres. 1980-81, pres. 1994-95, Key of Honor 1979, Key Club honoree 1984), Greater Miami C. of C. (Carrefour Housing Corp., v.p. permanent housing for the homeless). Home: 535 Bird Rd Miami FL 33146-1307 Office: 1351 NW 12th St Miami FL 33125-1644

ROSINSKI, JAN, mathematics educator; b. Gorzow, Poland, May 18, 1950; came to U.S., 1983; s. Franciszek and Zofia (Mierzejewska) R.; m. Wanda Maria Kasprzak, 1977; 1 child, Marek. MA in Math., Wroclaw (Poland) U., 1974, PhD in Math., 1975. Asst. prof. math. dept. Wroclaw U., 1976-85; assoc. prof. math. dept. U. Tenn., Knoxville, 1985-91, prof., 1991—; vis. asst. prof. math. dept. La. State U., Baton Rouge, 1983, Case Westen Res. U., Cleve., 1983-84; vis. scientist Cornell U., Ithaca, N.Y., 1990, Ctr. Stochastic Processes U. N.C., Chapel Hill, 1984-85, 91; reviewer NSF, 1986—. Contbr. articles on probability and stochastic processes to profl. jours. Rsch. grantee, Air Force Office of Scientific Rsch., 1986-92, NSF, 1994—. Mem. Am. Math. Soc., Inst. Math. Stats., Bernoulli Soc. Office: U Tenn Dept Math Knoxville TN 37996

ROSKY, THEODORE SAMUEL, insurance company executive; b. Chgo., Apr. 14, 1937; s. Theodore and Lora Marie (O'Connell) R.; m. Jacqueline Reed, Apr. 19, 1958; 1 child, Laura Marie. B.A., State U. Iowa, 1959. Various actuarial positions Conn. Gen. Life Ins. Co., Hartford, 1959-66; assoc. actuary Conn. Gen. Life Ins. Co., 1967-70, controller, 1970-73, 2d v.p., actuary, 1973, v.p., 1973-78; exec. v.p. Capital Holding Corp., 1978-84, exec. v.p., CFO, 1984-91, exec. v.p., 1991-92; bd. dirs. Legend Funds, 1993—, SBM Mut. Funds, 1995—, SBM Certificate Co., 1996—; instr. State U. Iowa, 1958-59, U. Hartford, 1964-66, U. Conn., 1967-68. Bd. dirs. Hartford Coll. for Women, 1974-78, Macauley Theater, 1983-85, Louisville Fund for the Arts, 1980—, Louisville Luth. Home, 1983—, Louisville Orch., 1982-88, 89-95, Ky. Opera, 1992—, Lincoln Found., 1992—, Actors Theatre of Louisville, 1995—, New Performing Arts, Oak and Acorn, 1995—; mem. bd. pensions Evangel. Luth. Ch. Am., 1974-82, 84-87, 89-95. Recipient award Soc. Actuaries, 1958. Fellow Soc. Actuaries; mem. Am. Acad. Actuaries, Southeastern Actuaries Club. Republican. Lutheran. Club: Pendennis. Home: 2304 Speed Ave Louisville KY 40205-1642

ROSLOW, SYDNEY, marketing educator; b. N.Y.C., July 29, 1910; s. Joseph and Anna (Lipman) R.; B.S., N.Y. U., 1931, M.A., 1932, Ph.D., 1935; m. Irma Sternberg, Oct. 21, 1932; children: Richard Jay, Susan Jane, Peter Dirk. Rsch. asst. in market. indsl., pers. rsch. Psychol. Corp., 1931-41; sch. psychologist, mem. bd. edn., Hastings on Hudson, N.Y., 1937-48; pub. opinion rsch. program surveys div. Dept. Agr., 1939-43; founder Pulse, Inc., market and audience rsch. in radio, television, advt. industries, N.Y.C., 1941-78; adj. assoc. prof. Baruch Coll. CUNY, 1967-75; assoc. prof. dept. mktg. Fla. Internat. U., 1976-83, prof. mktg., assoc. dean Coll. Bus. Adminstrn., 1983-90, prof. emeritus, 1990—, acting assoc. dean, 1996—. Contbr. articles to profl. jours. Fellow Am. Psychol. Assn.; mem. Am. Mktg. Assn. (pres. Miami chpt. 1980-82), Market Rsch. Coun. (inducted into Hall of Fame 1992), Radio-TV Rsch. Coun. (past pres.) Radio and TV Execs. Soc., Phi Beta Kappa. Home: 1035 NE 202nd Ter Miami FL 33179-2548 Office: Fla Internat U North Miami Campus North Miami FL 33181

ROSNER, ANTHONY LEOPOLD, chemist, biochemist; b. Greensboro, N.C., Nov. 13, 1943; s. Albert Aaron and Elsie Augustine (Lincoln) R.; m. Ruth Francis Marks, June 19, 1966; 1 child, Rachael. BS, Haverford Coll., 1966; PhD, Harvard U., 1972. Staff fellow NIH-NINDS, Bethesda, Md., 1972-74; gen. dir. Receptor Lab. Beth Israel Hosp., Boston, 1976-83, tech. dir. Chem. Lab., 1981-83; tech. dir. New Eng. Pathology Svcs., Wilmington, Mass., 1983-86, cons., 1986—; dept. adminstr. Brandeis U., Waltham, Mass., 1986-91; rsch. ops. mgr. in newborn medicine Children's Hosp., 1991-92; dir. rsch. Found. for Chiropractic Edn. and Rsch., Arlington, Va., 1992—; cons. Ctr. for Alternative Medicine Beth Israel Hosp., Boston, 1996—; vis. fellow Lab. Molecular Biology, CNRS, Gif-sur-Yvette, France, 1973. Assoc. editor Jour. Manipulative and Physiol. Therapeutics, mem. editl. bd., 1993—; assoc. editor Jour. Neuromusculoskeletal System, sect. editor, 1993—; mem. adv. bd. Alternative Therapies in Health and Medicine; contbr. articles to profl. jours. Harvard U. fellow, 1966. Mem. AAAS, Am. Chem. Soc. (auditor N.E. chpt. 1990—), N.Y. Acad. Scis., Clin. Ligand Assay Soc., Soc. Rsch. Adminstrs. Democrat. Jewish. Home: 1443 Beacon St Apt 201 Brookline MA 02146-4709 Office: Found for Chiropractic Edn & Rsch 1701 Clarendon Blvd Arlington VA 22209-2700

ROSS, ANN DUNBAR, secondary school educator; b. Longview, Tex., Jan. 21, 1945; d. Louie and Myra Lee (Fanning) Dunbar; m. John Reuben Ross, Sept. 9, 1967; children: Jennifer Ann, John Byron. BA in Math., U. Tex., 1968; M in Liberal Arts, So. Meth. U., 1974; Endorsement in Gifted Edn., U. North Tex., 1992. Tchr. math. Dallas, 1968-72, Duncanville (Tex.) High Sch., 1979-89; tchr. math., dept. chairperson Duncanville Ninth Grade Sch., 1989—; vertical team mem. Math. Dept. Duncanville High Sch., 1993—; site based mgmt. mem. Duncanville Ninth Grade Sch., 1993; presenter in field at math. conf. Mem. ASCD, Nat. Coun. Tchrs. Math., Tex. Coun. Tchrs. Math., Tex. Fedn. Tchrs.

ROSS, BRENDA MARIE, elementary school educator; b. New Orleans, May 5, 1944; d. Leslie Carl and Dorothy Marie (McElroy) R. BS, La. State U., 1968, cert. in gifted teaching, 1985. With Orleans Parish Schs., New Orleans, 1968-70, 1970—. Mem. Internat. Reading Assn., Nat. Acad. Games, Assn. for Gifted and Talented Students, New Orleans Acad. Games League, Greater New Orleans Tchrs. of Math., La. Assn. Tchrs. of Math., Delta Kappa Gamma (Pi chpt.). Republican. Episcopalian. Office: Claiborne Sch 4617 Mirabeau Ave New Orleans LA 70126-3540

ROSS, COLIN ANDREW, psychiatrist; b. Sarnia, Ont., Can., July 14, 1950; s. William King and Evelyn Margaret (Bruneau) R.; children: Simeon Leavis, Dana Ceridwen; m. Nancy Eleanor Keys, Feb. 8, 1986; children: Andrew William, Keir Alexander, Micaela Marie. MD, U. Alta., 1981. Resident in psychiatry U. Man., Winnipeg, 1981-85, from asst. prof. to assoc. prof. psychiatry, 1985-91; dir. dissociative disorders unit Charter Behavioral Health System of Dallas, Plano, Tex., 1991—; assoc. clin. prof. psychiatry Southwestern Med. Ctr., Dallas, 1993—. Author: Multiple Personality Disorder, 1989, The Osiris Complex, 1994, Satanic Ritual Abuse, 1995, Pseudoscience in Biological Psychiatry, 1995. Fellow Royal Coll. Physicians and Surgeons of Can., Internat. Soc. for Study of Dissociation (pres. 1993, Pres.'s award 1990, Morton Prince award 1989); mem. Am. Coll. Psychiatrists (Laughlin fellow 1985), Am. Psychiat. Assn., Can. Psychiat. Assn. Office: 1701 Gateway Blvd Ste 349 Richardson TX 75080-3546

ROSS, DANIEL W., English language educator; b. Atlanta, May 29, 1952; s. Robert C. and Evangeline (Durham) R.; m. Cynthia Patricia Yates, June 5, 1976; children: Benjamin Y., Melanie M. AB in Journalism, U. Ga., 1974, MA in English, 1977; PhD in English, Purdue U., 1984. Asst. dir. continuing edn. Brewton-Parker Coll., Mt. Vernon, Ga., 1975-78; tchg. asst. Purdue U., West Lafayette, Ind., 1978-85; asst. prof. English Allentown Coll., Center Valley, Pa., 1985-89; assoc. prof. English Columbus (Ga.) Coll., 1990-95, acting chair dept. English, 1995—. Author: The Critical Response to William Styron, 1995; contbr. articles to profl. jours. Mem. MLA. Baptist. Office: Columbus Coll Dept Lang & Lit Columbus GA 31907

ROSS, DONALD EDWARD, university administrator; b. Mineola, N.Y., June 29, 1939; s. Alexander Walker and Florence M. (Carville) R.; m. Helen Landgren, June 23, 1966; children: Ellen Ross Sarafian, Kevin McAndrew. BFA, N.Y. Inst. Tech., 1962, LLD (hon.), 1978; MS, Hofstra U., 1970. Dean of students N.Y. Inst. Tech., Old Westbury, 1962-68; pres. Wilmington (Del.) Coll., 1968-77; pres., CEO Lynn U. (formerly Coll. of Boca Raton), Fla., 1971—; chmn. adv. com. U.S. Army Command and Gen. Staff Coll. Bd. dirs. Fla. Endowment Fund, 1989—; trustee Boca Raton Community Hosp., 1990—; mem. governing bd. Philharmonic Orch. Fla., 1990—; mem. U.S. Mil. Screening Com. Named Industrialist of Yr., Greater Boca Raton C. of C., 1992, Man of the Yr., City of Hope; recipient Boy Scouts Am. Leadership Svc. award, Boca Raton award, 1991. Mem. Assn. Univ. Pres., Econ. Coun. of Palm Beach County, Royal Palm Yacht and Country, Loggerhead Club, Adirondack League Club, Old Forge Club, City (Boca Raton). Home: 212 Coconut Palm Rd Boca Raton FL 33432 Office: Lynn Univ 3601 N Military Trl Boca Raton FL 33431-5507*

ROSS, DOUGLAS, lawyer, legal academic administrator; b. L.A., July 12, 1948; s. Mathew and Brenda Butler (Boynton) R.; m. Lynne Rose Maidman, June 14, 1970. AB cum laude, Tufts U., 1970; JD with honors, George Washington U., 1973. Bar: Ohio 1973, D.C. 1980, U.S. Supreme Ct. 1976. Asst. atty. gen., antitrust sect. Office of Ohio Atty. Gen., Columbus, 1973-74; spl. asst. U.S. atty. Ea. Dist. Va., Alexandria, 1977; trial atty. antitrust divsn. U.S. Dept. Justice, Washington, 1975-82; atty. advisor Office of Legis. Affairs, 1984-86, Office of Legal Policy, 1987-89, Office Policy Devel., 1989-92; Supreme Ct. counsel Nat. Assn. Attys. Gen., 1982-91; ran advocacy project for states to enhance their effectiveness before Supreme Ct., 1982-91, operated clearinghouse on state constl. law, 1987-91; civil divsn. Appellate Staff, 1992-94, Office of Consumer Litigation, 1994—. Recipient Meritorious award Dept. Justice, 1979, Spl. Achievement award, 1984. Mem. Supreme Ct. Hist. Soc., D.C. Bar Assn., Supreme Ct. Opinion Network (bd. dirs. 1989-91), Arlington County Sports Commn. (chair subcom. on swimming pools 1995—). Jewish. Home: 3153 19th St N Arlington VA 22201-5103 Office: US Dept Justice PO Box 386 Washington DC 20044-0386

ROSS, FRED MICHAEL, organic chemist; b. N.Y.C., Aug. 26, 1921; s. Albert N. and Shirley (Honig) R.; m. Nee Kilar, May 9, 1954; children: Robin, Bonnie, Richard. BS, Mich. Tech. U., 1943. Sr. gas analyst Pure Oil Co., Chgo., 1943-44; chief chem. engr. Multiplate Glass Corp., Jamaica, N.Y., 1945-51; founder, CEO Diamond Dust Co., Inc., Mineola, N.Y., 1952-80; chmn. bd. dirs. Portfolio Mgmt., Inc., Rochester, N.Y., 1976-80; founder, pres. Gemery Corp., Mineola, 1974-80; CEO, chmn. Robonard, Inc., Boca Raton, Fla., 1980—. Contbr. over 40 articles to profl. publs. Campaign chmn. for R. Shaw for Ariz. Ho. of Reps, 1994. Officer USN, 1944-45. Recipient Silver medal for Outstanding Alumnus Mich. Tech. U., 1978. Fellow Am. Inst. Chemists. Office: Robonard Inc 10325 Crosswind Rd Boca Raton FL 33498-4757

ROSS, GLORIA JEAN, artist; b. Terrell, Tex., June 24, 1943; d. John Frederick and Shirley Joe (West) Williams; m. Winston Byrd Ross, Aug. 24, 1963; 1 child, John Winston. BS, Tex. Woman's U., 1965; MS, U. North Tex., 1981, MFA, 1983. Cert. tchr. Art tchr. West Springfield High Sch., Fairfax, Va., 1967-70, Tucker (Ga.) High Sch., 1970-72, The Westminster Sch., Atlanta, 1972-73; art/adult edn. tchr. San Jose (Calif.) Sch. System, 1973-74, Virginia Beach (Va.) Schs., 1975; adult edn. dir. Denton (Tex.) Pub. Schs., 1983-85; prgram dir. Children's Arts and Ideas Found., Dallas, 1985-88; continuing edn. coord. Tex. Woman's U., Denton, 1988-90; freelance artist Plano, Tex., 1990—. One person shows include U. North Tex. Art Gallery, Denton, 1983, Irving Cultural Ctr., Tex., 1986, Trammel Crow Ctr. Gallery, Dallas, 1988, Tex. Woman's U., Denton, Tex., 1990, Eleven East Ashland, Phoenix, 1991, Wichita Falls (Tex.) Art Assn. Gallery, 1992, Del Rio (Tex.) Arts Ctr., 1992; exhibited in group shows Irving (Tex.) Arts Ctr., 1985, Cedar Valley C.C., Cedar Hill, Tex., 1990, Paige-Hansen Art Gallery, Dallas, 1994, Arlington (Tex.) Mus. Art, 1995, Plano (Tex.) Cultural Arts Ctr., 1995, 96, Eastfield C.C., Mesquite, Tex., 1995; represented in collections Hyatt Hotel, Cancun, Mex., Renaissance Hotel, Washington, Harris Hosp., Ft. Worth, Bus. Interiors, Irving, EMSI, Dallas, Oracle Corp., Houston, Pitts Energy, Houston, The Mus. of Photography, Riverside, Calif., Pizza Inn Japan, Texins Credit Union, Richardson, Tex., Capstead Mortgage, Ft. Worth, Northern Telecom, Newark, N.J., Equitable Ins., Dallas, Ga. Street Hotel, Indpls., Fed. Depository Regional Office, Dallas, Harris Hosp., Ft. Worth, Butler and Binion, Dallas, MEPC, Dallas, Trinity Med. Ctr., Ft. Worth Gehad Investments, Dallas, Nat. Athletic Assn., Dallas, NCNB, Dallas, others. Founder, bd. mem. Dallas (Tex.) Women's Caucus for Art, 1983-90, first pres., 1983. Recipient Fellowship award Mid-Am. Arts Alliance, Kansas, Mich., 1993. Mem. So. Graphics Assn. Democrat.

ROSS, HOWARD PHILIP, lawyer; b. Chgo., May 10, 1939; s. Bernard and Estelle (Maremont) R.; m. Loretta Teresa Benquil, 1962 (div.); children: Glen Joseph, Cynthia Ann; m. Jennifer Kay Shirley, 1984. BS, U. Ill., 1961; JD, Stetson Coll. Law, 1964. Bar: Fla. 1964, U.S. Ct. Appeals (5th cir.) 1965, U.S. Ct. Appeals (11th cir.) 1981, U.S. Supreme Ct. 1969; cert. civil trial lawyer; cert. bus. litigator. Assoc. Parker & Battaglia and predecessor firm, St. Petersburg, Fla., 1964-67; ptnr. Battaglia, Ross, Hastings, Dicus & Andrews and predecessor firms, St. Petersburg, 1967-87; ptnr. Battaglia, Ross, Dicus & Wein, P.A., 1987-92, pres., CEO, 1992—; lectr. Stetson Coll. Law, St. Petersburg, 1971-72, adj. prof., 1987. Author: Florida Corporations, 1979; co-author: Managing Discovery in Commercial and Business Litigation, 1993; contbr. articles to profl. jours. Hon. chairperson St. Petersburg br. 1995 Awards Banquet NAACP, 1995. Recipient Woman's Svc. League Best Groomed award, 1979, Fla. Bar merit citation, 1974. Mem ABA, Fla. Bar Assn. (chmn. civil trial certification com. 1993-94), St. Petersburg Bar Assn., St. Petersburg Area C. of C. (bd. govs. 1990-95, v.p. pub. affairs 1992-93, v.p. membership 1993-94, exec. com. 1992-95, counsel 1994-95, dean entrepreneurial acad., Mem. of Yr. 1993-94), Citizen Rev. Com. City of St. Petersburg (chmn. subcom., 1992-94, co-chair 1994—). Republican. Jewish. Office: Battaglia Ross Dicus & Wein PO Box 41100 980 Tyrone Blvd N Saint Petersburg FL 33710-6333 also: 100 N Tampa St Ste 3100 Tampa FL 33602-5835

ROSS, JAMES PATRICK, army officer; b. Eatontown, N.J., May 9, 1968; s. James French and Louise Theresa (Fandozzi) R.; m. Leslie Ann Zier, June 2, 1990; children: Ryan James, Matthew Steven. BS in Econs., U.S. Mil. Acad., 1990. Commd. 2d lt. U.S. Army, 1990, advanced through grades to capt., 1994; battery exec. officer, bn. adj., then brigade adj. U.S. Army Field Arty. Tng. Ctr., Ft. Sill, Okla., 1992-95; battery commd. A-1-78 F.A., Ft. Sill, 1995—. Mem. U.S. Army F.A. Assn. (sec. Ft. Sill chpt. 19994-95), Assn. U.S. Army. Home: 32 Elmont Rd Trenton NJ 08610

ROSS, JAMES ULRIC, lawyer, accountant, educator; b. Del Rio, Tex., Sept. 14, 1941; s. Stephen Mabrey and Beatrice Jessie (Hyslop) R.; m. Janet S. Calabro, Dec. 28, 1986; children: James Ulric Jr., Ashley Meredith. BA, U. Tex., 1963, JD, 1965. Bar: Tex. 1965, U.S. Tax Ct. 1969; CPA, Tex. Estate tax examiner IRS, Houston, 1965-66; tax acct. Holmes, Raquet, Harris & Shaw, San Antonio, 1966-67; pvt. practice law and acctg., Del Rio and San Antonio, 1968—; instr. St. Mary's U., San Antonio, 1973-75; assoc. prof. U. Tex., San Antonio, 1975—. Active Am. Cancer Soc., Residential Mgmt., Inc., Am. Heart Assn. Mem. ABA, Tex. Bar Assn., Tex. Soc. CPAs, San Antonio Bar Assn., San Antonio Estate Planners Coun. Contbr. articles on U.S. and Internat. Estate Planning and Taxation to legal and profl. jours. Home: 3047 Orchard Hl San Antonio TX 78230-3078 Office: 760 Tex Commerce Bank Bldg 7550 IH 10 W San Antonio TX 78229

ROSS, JIM BUCK, state commissioner; b. Pelahatchie, Miss., Aug. 14, 1917; s. E. N. and Emma (Jones) R.; m. Margaret Spann, 1941; children: James Hal, Gwendolyn Barnham. BS, Miss. State U., 1939; LLB, Jackson Sch. Law, 1941. Dealer farm equipment, cattleman, cotton grower Rankin County, Miss., 1945-57; mayor Town of Pelahatchie, 1960-63; mem. Miss. State Senate, 1964-68; commr. Miss. State Dept. Agr. and Commerce, Jackson, 1968—. Served to 1st lt. U.S.Army, 1944-46, PTO. Recipient Natural Resources Conservation award; named Woodman of Yr., Man of Yr. Miss. Seedman's Assn., award Merit Miss. Assn. Conservation Dist. Inc., 1983, award Merit Miss. Hist. Soc., 1984, Disting. Svc. award Catfish Farmers Am., 1986. Mem. VFW, Cystic Fibrosis Assn. (past pres.), Miss. Horse Coun., Miss. Econ. Coun., Miss. State U. Alumni Assn., Miss. Cattlemen's Assn., Am. Legion, Masons (32d degree). Methodist. Home: PO Box 129 Pelahatchie MS 39145-0129 Office: MS Agr & Commerce Dept PO Box 1609 Jackson MS 39215-1609*

ROSS, KATHLEEN, secondary school educator, author, consultant; b. New Orleans, July 5, 1948; d. William H. and Marilyn (Shoop) R.; m. Thomas Warren, Nov. 10, 1979. BS, U. New Orleans, 1971; MST, Loyola U., New Orleans, 1973. Cert. math. tchr., prin., adminstr., supr., supr. student tchrs. Pres., cons. author Math. Assoc. Inc., Harvey, La.; former math. cons. Jefferson Parish Pub. System, Harvey; instr. La. systemic initiative project program Loyola U.; cons., author Addison Wesley Pub. Mem. ASCD, Nat. Coun. Tchrs. Math., Nat. Coun. Suprs. Math., La. Tchrs. Math., Greater New Orleans Tchrs. Math., Textbook Authors Assn., La. Assn. Sch. Execs., Tex. Tchrs. Math., Oreg. Tchrs. Math., La. Coun. Suprs. Math., Phi Delta Kappa. Home: 3900 S Inwood Ave New Orleans LA 70131-8456

ROSS, KENNETH S., business executive; b. 1934. Prin. W.E. Ross & Sons, Inc., Ocilla, Ga., 1966-88; pres. Ocilla Gin Co., 1988—. Office: Ocilla Gin Inc Southside Indsl Park Ocilla GA 31774

ROSS, KNOX WINTON, JR., accountant; b. Jackson, Miss., Oct. 20, 1966; s. Knox W., Sr. and Jean H. Ross; m. Jamie L. Eichelberger, June 9, 1990. B in Profl. Accountancy with honors, Miss. State U., 1988; MBA, U. Ala., 1990. CPA, Miss. Staff cons. Small Bus. Devel. Ctr. U. Ala., Tuscaloosa, 1988-90; sr. acct. Ernst and Young, Jackson, Miss., 1990-93; acct. Breazeale, Saunders & O'Neil, Ltd., Jackson, Miss., 1993-94; sr. acct. Tony G. Chance, CPA, Forest, Miss., 1994—. Mem. Town of Pelahatchie Planning Commn., Pelahatchie Vol. Fire Dept. Mem. AICPA, Miss. Soc. CPAs, Inst. Mgmt. Accts. (bd. dirs.), Forest Rotary club, Morton Lions Club, Phi Gamma Delta, Phi Kappa Phi, Omicron Delta Kappa, Beta Alpha Psi, Beta Gamma Sigma. Republican. Southern Baptist. Home: PO Box 369 Pelahatchie MS 39145-0369

ROSS, LESA MOORE, quality assurance professional; b. New Orleans, Jan. 25, 1959; d. William Frank and Carolyn West Moore; m. Mark Neal Ross, Nov. 30, 1985; children: Sarah Ann, Jacquelyne Caroline. BS in Engring., U. N.C., Charlotte, 1981; MBA in Quality and Reliability Mgmt., U. North Tex., 1991. Seismic qualification engr. Duke Power Co., Charlotte, N.C., 1981-82; quality assurance engr. Tex. Instruments Inc., Lewisville, Tex., 1982-91; compliance mgr. Am. Med. Electronics, Inc., 1992-93; owner Ross Quality Cons., 1993-95; customer quality assurance sect. mgr. Hitachi Semiconductor (Am.) Inc., 1995-96; v.p. quality Ross Networking Cons. Inc., 1996—. Recipient Nat. Sci. Found. Rsch. Grant, U. N.C., Charlotte, 1980. Mem. Am. Soc. Quality Control (cert. quality engr., quality auditor, reliability engr., cert. quality technician, sec. Dallas sect. 1994-95, chair-elect Dallas sect. 1995-96, chair 1996-97), Zeta Tau Alpha (pres. 1984-85). Home: 4925 Wolf Creek Trl Flower Mound TX 75028-1955

ROSS, NORMAN ALEXANDER, retired banker; b. Miami, Fla., Jan. 30, 1922; s. Norman DeMille and Beatrice (Dowsett) R.; children: Isabel, Diana. A.B., Stanford U., 1946; postgrad., Trinity Coll., Oxford U., Eng., 1953; D.H.L., Lincoln Coll., Ill., 1959, Fisk U., 1978, Roosevelt U., 1979; Litt.D., Lake Forest Coll., 1967. Airport mgr. Pan Am. Airways, 1943; asst. to producer Metro-Goldwyn-Mayer, 1943-44; ptnr. Norman Ross & Co., 1947-50; owner Norman Ross Record Club, 1951-52; v.p. pub. affairs First Nat. Bank Chgo., 1968-79, sr. v.p. communications dept., 1979-81, sr. v.p. community affairs, 1981-86; pres. Ross-McElroy Prodns., Inc., 1962-68; sr. affairs commentator Sta. WLS-TV, Chgo., 1989—; radio-TV commentator NBC, ABC, Chgo., 1953-64, ABC, Stas. WGN and WBKB, Chgo., 1964-68; former columnist Chgo. Daily News. Served with inf. AUS, World War II. Decorated cavaliere Dell Ordine Repubblica Italiana, Knight 1st Class Republic of Austria, 1989; U.S. Army Outstanding Civilian Service medal; officier and cross of chevalier Legion of Honor France; recipient Peabody award for TV program Off the Cuff 1964. Mem. Phi Gamma Delta. Clubs: Chgo., Racquet, Oxford, Econ. (Chgo.), Wayfarers, Casino. Home: 1200 N Lake Shore Dr Apt 801 Chicago IL 60610-2347 Office: Pilot Knob Bed & Breakfast Inn PO Box 1280 Pilot Mountain NC 27041-1280

ROSS, PATTI JAYNE, obstetrics and gynecology educator; b. Nov. 17, 1946; d. James J. and Mary N. Ross; B.S., DePauw U., 1968; M.D., Tulane, U., 1972; m. Allan Robert Katz, May 23, 1976. Asst. prof. U. Tex. Med. Sch., Houston, 1976-82, assoc. prof., 1982—, dir. adolescent ob-gyn., 1976—, also dir. phys. diagnosis, dir. devel. dept. ob-gyn.; speaker in field. Bd. dirs. Am. Diabetes Assn., 1982—; mem. Rape Coun. Diplomate Am. Bd. Ob-Gyn, Children's Miracle Network Hermann's Children's Hosp; Olympic torch relay carrier, 1996; founder Women's Med. Rsch. Fund, U. Tex. Med. Sch., Houston. Mem. Tex. Med. Assn., Harris County Med. Soc., Houston Ob-Gyn. Soc., Assn. Profs. Ob-Gyn., Soc. Adolescent Medicine, AAAS, Am. Women's Med. Assn., Orgn. Women in Sci., Sigma Xi. Roman Catholic. Clubs: River Oak Breakfast, Profl. Women Execs. Contbr. articles to profl. jours. Office: 6431 Fannin St Houston TX 77030-1501

ROSS, PHILIP ROWLAND, library director; b. Indiana, Pa., Apr. 7, 1940; s. David Biddle and Miriam Elizabeth (Hill) R.; m. Elaine Lucille George, July 17, 1965; children: Mary Elizabeth, David Bruce. BA, Pa. State U., 1962; MSLS, U. Md., 1969. Postal fin. officer USAF, Tachikawa AFB Tokyo, 1963-65; chief data control and quality control Hdqrs. Air Force Systems Command, Andrews AFB, Md., 1965-68; asst. libr. acquisitions West Liberty (W.Va.) State Coll., 1969-86; dist. mgr. Wheeling (W.Va.) office First Investors Corp., 1986-89; divs. mgr. State of Ark. First Investors Corp., Little Rock, 1989-92; dir. Lonoke (Ark.) Prairie County Regional Libr. System, 1992—; founder, treas.-mgr. West Liberty (W.Va.) State Coll. Fed. Credit Union, 1977-82, chmn. bd., 1984-85; mem. Ark. On Line Network Adv. Com., Little Rock, 1993-96, Libr. Devel. Dist. State Coun., Little Rock, 1993—, vice chmn., 1996. Maj. USAF, 1962-68; maj. Res., 1968-84, ret. Maj. USAF, 1962-68; maj. Res., 1968-84, ret. Decorated various USAF medals and decorations. Mem. Assn. Ark. Pub. Librs. (treas.-sec. 1993, 94, v.p. pres.-elect 1995, prse. 1996), Ark. Libr. Assn. (com. mem. 1994-95, conv. com. 1996), Lonoke, Ark. C. of C., Am. Legion, Lions. Republican. Methodist. Home: 691 Wayne Elmore Rd Lonoke AR 72086-9126 Office: Lonoke/Prairie County Regional Libr System 303 Court St Lonoke AR 72086-2858

ROSS, PHILIPPE EDWARD, biology educator, environmental toxicology researcher; b. Bangor, Maine, Oct. 22, 1949; s. Edward Ernest and Josephine Louise (Brown) R.; m. Linda Carole Yas, June 16, 1972; 1 child, Kie Myfanwy Ross Zuraw. BSc in Biology and Psychology, McGill U., Montreal, Quebec, Canada, 1972, MSc in Biology, 1975; PhD in Biology, U. Waterloo, Ontario, Canada, 1980. Aquatic ecologist BEAK Consultants, Ltd., Mississauga, ON, Canada, 1979-80; asst. prof. U. Montreal, 1980-85; assoc. prof. scientist Ill. Natural History Survey, Champaign, 1985-91; prof. and head biology The Citadel, Charleston, S.C., 1991—; sr. scientific adv. USEPA, Great Lakes Nat. Program, Chgo., 1988-92; mem. technical adv. com. NOAA/Coastal Oceans Program, Silver Spring, Md., 1992—; nat. scientific coord. Nat. Indicator Study, Baton Rouge, La., 1993-94. Recipient Univ. Rsch. fellow Natural Sci. & Eng. Rsch. Coun., Ottawa, Canada, 1980-85. Mem. Am. Soc. Limnology & Oceanography, Internat. Assn. for Great Lakes Rsch. Aquatic Ecosystem Health Mgr. Soc. (sec.), Soc. Environ. Toxicology & Chemistry (pres. Carolina chpt. 1995), Societas Internationalis Limnology, Univ. Club of Chgo. Home: 115 Register Rd. Charleston SC 29409 Office: Dept Biology The Citadel 171 Moultrie St Charleston SC 29409

ROSS, ROBERT CLARK, public relations executive; b. Cleve., May 19, 1945; s. Logan and Laura Myrle (Clark) R.; m. Karen Roberta Frey, Aug. 17, 1968; children: Christopher, Mark. BA in Journalism, Ohio State U., 1968. Pres. Bob Ross Pub. Rels. Svcs., Miami, Fla., 1977-80; ptnr. Schulte Ross & Aguilar, South Miami, Fla., 1980-83, Starr/Ross Corp. Comm., Coral Gables, Fla., 1983-85; pres. Bob Ross and Assocs. Inc., Miami, 1986—. Exec. bd. mem. Fla. Cystic Fibrosis, 1982-89; bd. mem., sec. Am. Lung Assn. Dade Monroe, 1983-91; bd. mem. Am. Lung Assn. Fla., 1988-91. 1st lt. U.S. Army, 1968-70. Named Outstanding Bd. Mem., Am. Lung Assn. Dade-Monroe, 1989. Mem. Pub. Rels. Soc. Am. (accredited, pres. Miami chpt. 1980, nat. nominating com. 1990, membership chair Counselors Acad. 1992-93, mem. exec. com. Counselors Acad. 1994-96, dist. chair 1993). Office: Bob Ross & Assocs 6701 SW 94th St Miami FL 33156-1734

ROSS, SADYE LEE TATMAN, home health geriatrics nurse; b. Albuquerque, Dec. 5, 1937; d. Charles Robert Tatman and Cecilia Marie Zimmer; m. E. Ray Ross, Nov. 16, 1974. Diploma, Henry Ford Hosp., 1959. RN, Miss., Calif.; cert. gerontol. nurse. Head nurse Orange Meml. Hosp., Orlando, Fla., 1963-64; assoc. dir. Coll. of Calif. Med. Affiliates, San Francisco, 1964-65; ICU staff nurse So. Pacific Hosp., San Francisco, 1965-66; office mgr. Mortimer Weiss, M.D., San Francisco, 1966-70; staff nurse Kwajalein (Marshall Island) Missile Range Hosp., 1970-72, nursing supr., 1974-76; nursing svc. supr. St. Francis Hosp., San Francisco, 1972-74; staff nurse Lawrence County Nursing Ctr., Monticello, Miss., 1989-93, South Miss. Home Health, Prentiss, Miss., 1993—. Mem. Nat. Gerontol. Nurses Assn., Sorosis Club (pres. 1992-94). Home: RR 2 Box 372 Silver Creek MS 39663-9504 Office: South Miss Home Health PO Box 663 Prentiss MS 39474-0663

ROSSELLÓ, PEDRO, governor; b. San Juan, P.R., Apr. 5, 1944; m. Maga Nevares, Aug. 9, 1969; children: Juan Oscar, Luis, Ricardo. BS, U. Notre Dame, 1966; MD, Yale U., 1970; MPH, U. P.R., 1981; LLD (hon.), U. Notre Dame, 1995, U. Mass., 1995. Intern straight surgery Beth Israel Hosp., Boston, 1970-71, resident gen. surgery, 1971-74; resident cardiac and burns Mass. Gen. Hosp., Boston, 1972; resident trauma San Francisco Gen. Hosp., 1973; sr. resident pediat. surgery Children's Hosp., Boston, 1974-75, chief resident, pediat. surgery-urology, 1975-76; instr. surgery Harvard Med. Sch., 1975-76; pvt. practice San Juan, 1976-92; asst. prof. surgery U. P.R., 1978-82, assoc. prof. surgery, 1982-92; dir. Dept. Health City of San Juan, 1985-87; chief surgery San Jorge Hosp., San Juan, 1989-92, med. dir., 1990; gov. Puerto Rico, 1996—; lead gov. So. Regional Project Infant Mortality, 1993-95; chair So. States Energy Bd.; mem. intergovtl. policy adv. com. U.S. Trade Rep.; v.p. Coun. State Govts. Contbr. articles to profl. jours. Mem. P.R. Olympic Com., 1982-84, 87-88; v.p. New Progressive Party, 1988-91, pres., 1991—; mem. steering com. Edn. Commn. States; bd. visitors Georgetown U. Law Ctr., Washington. Capt. USNG, 1970-76. Mem. Nat. Govs. Assn. (host. 1996 ann. meeting), So. Govs. Assn. (vice chair), Dem. Govs. Assn. (vice chmn.), P.R. Tennis Assn. (pres. 1982-84), Caribbean Tennis Assn. (pres. 1983-84), Alpha Omega Alpha.

ROSSER, DAVID PENDLETON, chemical engineer; b. Bethesda, Md., Sept. 27, 1945; s. John Hodge and Jewel Maxine (Hutchins) R.; m. Patricia Leigh Crabill, Aug. 5, 1967; children: Christopher, Andrew, Amy, Leanna. BSChemE, U. Md., 1967. Devel. engr. Celanese Corp., Cumberland, Md., 1967-71; devel. engr. Celanese Corp., Shelby, N.C., 1971-73, project engr., 1973-75, product engr., 1975-77, engring. group leader, 1977-78, new product engr., 1978-81; process engr. Celanese Corp., Summit, N.J., 1981-82, tech. svc. engr., 1982-84, prodn. supr., 1984-86; sr. mfg. engr. Hoechst Celanese Corp., Charlotte, N.C., 1986-92, staff engr., 1992—. Editor Charlotte Baha'i Nightingale newsletter, 1994—. Del. Nat. Baha'i Conv., 1981, 82, 89; pres. Assn. Religious Orgns., Plainfield, N.J., 1986; chmn. Spiritual Assembly Baha'is, North Plainfield, N.J., 1984-86, Charlotte, N.C., 1988-89, treas., 1989—; bd. dirs. Hoechst Celanese-Winterfield Elem. Sch. Partnership, 1995—. Mem. AIChE (treas. ctrl. Carolinas sect. 1992—), Soc. Plastics Engrs. (sr.), Soc. Mfg. Engrs. (sr., cert. mgr. technologist, cert. mfg. engr.), N.C. Nature Conservancy, Charlotte Area Clergy Assn. Home: 6743 Rosemary Ln Charlotte NC 28210-7016 Office: Hoechst-Celanese Corp 13800 S Lakes Dr Charlotte NC 28273-6738

ROSSER, JOHN BARKLEY, JR., economics educator; b. Ithaca, N.Y., Apr. 12, 1948; s. John Barkley and Annetta Louise (Hamilton) R.; m. Sue A. Vilhauer, Aug. 31, 1968 (div. 1979); children: Meagan Rebecca, Caitlin Elizabeth; m. Marina R. Vcherashnaya, May 24, 1987; 1 child, Alexandra Ashley. BA, U. Wis., 1969, MA, 1972, PhD, 1976. Project specialist Inst. Environ. Studies, Madison, Wis., 1972-75; planning analyst Dept. Natural Resources, Madison, 1975-76; prof. econs. James Madison U., Harrisonburg, Va., 1976—, Kirby L. Kramer Jr. chair of bus. adminstrn., 1996—. Author: From Catastrophe to Chaos: A General Theory of Economic Discontinuities, 1991, (with M.V. Rosser) Comparative Economics in a Transforming World Economy, 1996; contbr. articles to profl. jours. Mem. Am. Econs. Assn., So. Econs. Assn., Va. Social Sci. Assn. Unitarian. Home: 236 Franklin St Harrisonburg VA 22801-4019 Office: James Madison Univ Dept Economics Harrisonburg VA 22807

ROSSER, RHONDA LANAE, psychotherapist; b. Champaign, Ill., Aug. 29, 1953; d. Neill Albert and Grace Lee (Byers) R.; (div. June 1, 1993); children: Anthony Neill Williams, Joseph Neill Jackson Hogan. BS in Psychology, Guilford Coll., 1975; MEd in Edn., U. N.C., Greensboro, 1979, PhD in Counseling, 1991. Joined 3rd Order of Secular Franciscans/Order of St. Francis. Instr. U. N.C., Greensboro, 1985-88; dir. Montagnard Program Luth. Family Svcs., Greensboro, 1985-88; psychotherapist pvt. practice, Greensboro, 1989—. Contbr. articles to profl. jours. Recipient Presdl. citation U.S. Govt., 1987. Mem. Am. Counseling Assn. (Outstanding Rsch. award 1991), Chi Sigma Iota. Democrat. Roman Catholic (3d order of Secular Franciscans/Order of St. Francis). Home and Office: 2318 W Cornwallis Dr Greensboro NC 27408-6802

ROSSETT, BEN WYOMING, television producer, editor; b. N.Y.C., Aug. 19, 1960; s. Yale and Ruth (Schwartz) R. BA in TV and Mass Media, SUNY, Buffalo, 1980, BA in Speech Comm., 1980; MA in Radio, TV and Film, U. Tex., 1982. News dir., disc jockey Sta. WRUB-AM Radio, Buffalo, 1977-80; comml. prodn. asst. Sta. WKBW-TV, Buffalo, 1980; assoc. news prodr. Sta. KXAN-TV, Austin, 1982; editor, prodn. asst. Videolife Prodns., N.Y.C., 1982-83; TV prodn. specialist Danville (Va.) C.C., 1983-87, Austin (Tex.) C.C., 1987-93; media svcs. coord. St. Philip's Coll., San Antonio, Tex., 1993-96; instr. of radio, TV and film San Antonio Coll., 1994—; editor, producer Kaleidoscope TV Network, 1996—; vice-chmn. Univ. and Fine Arts Cable Channel Adv. Com., San Antonio, 1996. Producer/dir. (video programs) St. Philip's Coll: A Point of Pride in the Community, 1996, The St. Philip's College Learning Resource Center, 1995, (TV series) Kaleidoscope Kitchen, The Way I See It, 1996; actor: Harlequin Dinner Theatre, 1993—, Alamo St. Restaurant and Theater, 1993—. Recipient award for Best Pub. Rels./Mktg. Program, C.C. Assn. for Ednl. Technology, 1995; named Best Support Actor, U.S. Army Forces Command Festival of the Performing Arts, 1995, Best Leading Actor U.S. Army Forces Command Festival of the Performing Arts, 1994. Home: 313 Aransas Ave San Antonio TX 78210 Office: Kaleidoscope TV 1777 NE Loop 410 Ste 300 San Antonio TX 78217

ROSSI, ROBERT JOHN, retired group newspaper executive, consultant; b. Pitts., Jan. 5, 1928; s. John Baptist and Carmella Marie (Pastore) R.; BA, Denison U., 1950; postgrad. 1963; m. Mary Kathryn Rust, June 30, 1951; children: Shannon Elizabeth, Claudia Irene. Advt. dir., bus. mgr. Willoughby (Ohio) News-Herald, 1953-60; advt. dir. Elgin (Ill.) Courier-News, 1960-64; editor and pub. New Albany (Ind.) Tribune and Sunday Ledger, 1964-71; mgmt. cons. Thomson Newspapers, Inc., Chgo., 1971, gen. mgr. So. div., Tampa, Fla., 1972-73; v.p., chief newspaper ops. officer Park Communications Inc., Ithaca, N.Y., 1974-79, 85-95, also dir.; editor, gen. mgr. Courier News, Blytheville, Ark., 1983-85, also Osceola Times, Ark.; bd. dirs. Ky. Opera Assn., Ky.-Ind. Comprehensive Health Planning Coun. With U.S. Army, 1946. Mem. Am. Newspaper Pubs. Assn., So. Newspaper Pubs. Assn., Internat. Execs. Svc. Corps., Filson Club. Republican. Presbyterian. Home and Office: 104 Lendl Ct Cary NC 27511-6694

ROSSI, WILLIAM MATTHEW, lawyer; b. Coldwater, Ohio, June 11, 1954; s. Hugh Dominic and Patricia Jean (Putts) R.; m. Constance Sue Streacker, July 21, 1973; children: Bryan Thomas, Lauren Michelle, Alexandria Marie. BA cum laude, Miami U., Oxford, Ohio, 1977; JD magna cum laude, U. Dayton, 1981. Bar: Ohio 1981, U.S. Dist. Ct. (so. dist.) Ohio 1982, U.S. Supreme Ct. 1986, U.S. Ct. Appeals (6th cir.) 1987, Fla. 1991, U.S. Dist. Ct. (so. and mid. dists.) Fla. 1992, U.S. Ct. Appeals (11th cir.) 1992. Assoc. Milliken & Fitton, Hamilton, Ohio, 1981-83; dep. law dir., chief city negotiator City of Middletown, Ohio, 1984-89; pvt. practice, 1989-92; assoc. Jackson, Lewis, Schnitzler and Krupman, Orlando, Fla., 1992-93; asst. county atty. Sarasota County, Fla., 1993—; bd. dirs. Columbia Inst. Bus., Middletown, 1977-78; lectr. Sawyer Coll., Dayton, 1982-83; small claims referee, 1984-92. Asst. coach Knothole Baseball, Middletown, 1981; bd. dirs. Butler County Mental Health Ctr., Hamilton, 1983-85, Summer Youth Theatre, Middletown, 1985-86; mem. bd. rev. Troop 20 Boy Scouts Am., 1986-87; mem. adv. bd. St. Joseph's Coll. Recipient Am. Jurisprudence award Lawyers Coop. Pub. Co., 1979, 81, Internat. Youth Achievement award Internat. Biog. Ctr. and Am. Biog. Inst., 1982. Mem. ABA, Fla. Bar Assn., Nat. Pub. Employer Labor Rels. Assn., Phi Beta Kappa, Phi Delta Phi (bd. dirs., historian 1979-80). Republican. Roman Catholic. Home: 6215 Aventura Dr Sarasota FL 34241

ROSSIE, CARLOS ENRIQUE, computer school administrator, consultant; b. Havana, Cuba, Oct. 7, 1948; s. Dionisio M. and Edelmira (Blanco) R.; came to U.S., 1966; m. Claudia V. Velilla, Mar. 24, 1972; children—Cynthia Patricia, Claudette Marie, Carlos Fernando. Assoc. in Sci., Miami Dade Jr. Coll., 1970; postgrad., Fla. Internat. U., 1978—; B in Computers, Internat. Coll. of Cayman Islands, 1988; MBA, Internat. Coll., 1990; EdD, Nova Southeastern U., 1994. Dir., owner Programar Computer Sch., Colombia, 1972-78; computer system and procedures analyst, dir. programmers and analysts tng. Burger King Corp., Miami, Fla., 1978-79; asst. v.p. computer dept. Flagler Fed. Savs. and Loans, Miami, 1979-81; dir., owner Fla. Programming Computer Sch., Miami, 1981—; pres. READ (Rossie Ednl. Advisors), Miami, 1994—; computer cons. for Cuban-Am. Orgn. program, Dade County (Fla.), 1981—; computer presentations Dade County High Schs. Author: Cobol Computer Language, 1974 (Best Cobol Book award Columbia, S.Am.), How to Design and Implement a Recruitment Program for International Students, 1994; 3 other computer books and intro. to data processing computer book. Cons. econ. com. Colombian Conservative Party. Roman Catholic. Office: 10415 SW 145th Ave Miami FL 33186-2918

ROSSITER, ALEXANDER, JR., news service executive, editor; b. Elmira, N.Y., Mar. 2, 1936; s. Alexander H. and Eleanor (Howell) R.; m. Sylvia Lee Vanlandingham, June 11, 1960; children: Alexander H. III, Jill Jarrell. BA, Rutgers U., 1958; postgrad., Emory U., 1959. With UPI, 1959-92; newsman Atlanta, 1959-61, Richmond, Va., 1961-63; bur. mgr. Cape Canaveral, Fla., 1963-73; sci. editor Washington, 1973-87, exec. editor, 1987-88, exec. editor, sr. v.p., 1988-91, editor, exec. v.p., 1991-92; asst. v.p., dir. news svc. Duke U., Durham, N.C., 1992—; mem. nat. adv. bd. Knight Ctr. for Specialized Journalism, Colleg Pk., Md., 1988-92. Recipient Grady-Stack medal Am. Chem. Soc., 1987, other journalism awards. Mem. Nat. Assn. Sci. Writers, Edn. Writers Assn. Office: Duke U 615 Chapel Dr Durham NC 27706-2500

ROSSMAN, ROBERT HARRIS, management consultant; b. Phila., Jan. 27, 1932; s. Benjamin Bernard and Vivian (Silnutzer) R.; m. Wanda Ward, Aug. 9, 1980; 1 child, Victoria Anne; children from previous marriage: Rodger Samuel, Robbi Jennifer, Ronni Esther. BS, U.S. Merchant Marine Acad., 1953; MSME with honors, U.S. Naval Postgrad. Sch., 1963; cert. advanced naval architecture, MIT, 1973. Cert. mgr. human resources; cert. value specialist. Commd. ensign USN, 1953, advanced through grades to comdr., 1967, shipboard engr., 1953-55, maintenance and repair officer Reserve Fleet, 1955-57; served as ship supt. Norfolk Naval Shipyard, Portsmouth, Va., 1957-60; maintenance and logistics planning officer Amphibious Squadron Twelve, Little Creek, Va., 1963-65; planning and estimating supt. U.S. Naval Ship Repair Facility, Yokosuka, Japan, 1965-67; design and planning advisor USN, Saigon, Republic Viet Nam, 1967-68; chief prodn. engring. Def. Contract Adminstrn. Svcs., Alexandria, Va., 1968-70; dir. cost reduction Naval Ship Systems Command, Washington, 1970-73; dep. program mgr. new ship class Naval Ship Engring. Ctr., Hyattsville, Md., 1973; ret. USN, 1973; ptnr. Kempter-Rossman Internat., Washington, 1974-91; owner Rossman Assocs. Internat., 1991—; cons. in cost and time reduction, mgmt. improvement, productivity and competition enhancement. Author: (textbook) Function Based Analysis, 1983, Total Cycle Time Reduction, 1992; editor mag. Performance, 1970-73; contbr. articles to profl. jours. Pres. PTA, Fairfax County, Va., 1969-70, Community Civic Assn., Fairfax County, 1970-71; chmn. Boy Scouts Am. and Weblos troops, 1969-71, del. at large 1st Congl. Dist. Rep. Com., N.C., 1989-90; chmn. Chowan County (N.C.) Rep. Com., 1990-92. Decorated USN Commendation medals, Honor medal-1st Class (Republic of Vietnam Armed Forces), Combat Action medal. Fellow Soc. Am. Value Engrs. (v.p. 1970-73, Disting. svc. award 1976); mem. U.S. Merchant Marine Acad. Alumni Assn., Am. Legion, Sigma Xi. Jewish. Home: 110 Old Hertford Rd Edenton NC 27932-9608 Office: Rossman Assocs Internat Speight House 110 Old Hertford Rd Edenton NC 27932-9608

ROSSO DE IRIZARRY, CARMEN (TUTTY ROSSO DE IRIZARRY), finance executive; b. Ponce, P.R., Feb. 9, 1947; d. Jorge Ignacio and Carmen Teresa (Descartes) Rosso Castain; m. Alfredo R. Irizarry Sile, Aug. 29, 1967. BBA, U. P.R., Rio Piedras. Vice pres. Alcay Inc., San Juan, P.R., 1972—, also bd. dirs.; v.p. J.I.C. Corp., M.I.C. Corp.; bd. dirs., now pres. bd. Construcciones Urbanas Inc., Internat. Fin. Corp. Troop leader Girl Scouts U.S.A., 1977-80; bd. dirs. PTA, San Juan, 1978-81, 86-88; activities coord. Colegio Puertorriqueño Niñas, San Juan, 1987-88; judge Miss P.R. Pageant, San Juan 1987-88, 93, 94, 95, Miss World P.R. Pageant, San Juan, 1987-88, Miss World of P.R., 1990; pres. fundacion dept. Oncologia Pediatrica Hosp. Universitario Dr. Antonio Ortiz, 1990, 95-96; organizer Best of Saks Fifth Avenue Benefit, 1991, 92, 93, 94, 95, pres. 1992, 94, 96; com. mem. Make a Wish Found. Coleccion Alta Moda, 1994; mem. com. Museo Ponce Gala, 1994; mem. com. Museo Ponce Coala, 1994; luminaria J.C. Penney, 1994; destellos de la Moda, 1994, 95-96; pres. Best of Saks 5th Avenue Benefit, 1990-96. Named to Ten Best Dressed List, San Juan Star, 1986-87, Hall of Fame of Ten Best Dressed, 1989; recipient luminaria J.C. Penney, 1994. Fellow Assn. Porcelanas; mem. Club de Leones (Garden Hills, P.R., Lady of Yr. award 1978), Caparra Country Club (pres. 1985-86), Club Civicos Damas (judge hat how 1989, in charge spl. events 1992), Mu Alpha Phi. Republican. Roman Catholic. Office: Internat Fin Corp PO Box 8486 Santurce San Juan PR 00910-0486

ROSSOWSKA, MAGDALENA JOANNA, physiology educator, research scientist; b. Warsaw, Poland, Feb. 24, 1938; came to U.S. 1981; d. Czestaw Taracha and Anna Szulakowska-Taracha; m. Wojciech Joseph Rossowski, July 8, 1965; 1 child, Thomas Maciej. MS in Biology, U. Warsaw, 1961; postgrad., Polish Acad. of Sci., Warsaw, 1962-66; PhD in Biochemistry, Inst. of Biochemistry and, Biophysics, Warsaw, 1966. Postdoctoral fellow, instr. Med. Rsch. Ctr., Polish Acad. Sci., Warsaw, 1966-70, asst. prof. dept. neurochemistry, 1970-81; rsch. assoc. dept. biochemistry La. State U., New Orleans, 1982-83, rsch. assoc. Eye Ctr., 1984-89, rsch. assoc. dept. physiology, 1989-91, instr. dept. physiology, 1991-92, asst. prof., 1992—. Contbr. articles to profl. jours. Mem. Solidarity, Polish Acad. Sci., 1980-81, Polish-Am. Assn. of La., New Orleans, 1985—. Office: La State U Med Ctr 23 Theresa Ave New Orleans LA 70119

ROSSOWSKI, WOJCIECH JOZEF, medical educator, research scientist; b. Krakow, Poland, Oct. 9, 1932; came to U.S., 1981; s. Stefan Rafal Rossowski and Maria Kazimiera Kruczek-Rossowski; m. Magdalena-Joanna Taracha, July 8, 1965; 1 child, Tomasz-Maciej. MD, Med. Acad., Poznan, Poland, 1957, PhD, 1961, DSc, 1968. Med. diplomate, Poland. Resident U. Hosp. for Sick Children, Poznan, 1957-61; instr. dept. histology and embryology Med. Acad., Poznan, 1957-61; asst. prof. Inst. Exptl. Pathology Polish Acad. Scis., Warsaw, Poland, 1961-66; assoc. prof. Inst. Nuclear Rsch., Warsaw, 1966-81; cancer rsch. scientist Roswell Park Meml. Inst., Buffalo, 1981-82; rsch. assoc. La. State U. Med. Ctr., New Orleans, 1982-84; rsch. assoc. prof. Tulane U. Sch. Medicine, New Orleans, 1984-95, rsch. prof., 1995—; advisor grad. student thesis Inst. Nuclear Rsch., Warsaw, 1974-81; assoc. mem. European Late Effect Project Group, Bordeaux, France, 1975-81; vis. prof. German Cancer Rsch. Ctr., Heidelberg, Germany, 1976, 77. Contbr. more than 85 rsch. articles and reports to profl. jours. Rep. Solidarity, Inst. Nuclear Rsch., Warsaw, 1980-81. Grantee Fedn. of the European Biochem. Socs., Polish Biochem. Soc., 1965; rsch. grantee German Acad. Exch. program, 1975, Cancer Assn. Greater New Orleans, 1982, Am. Heart Assn., 1983; instnl. grantee Tulane U. Med. Sch., 1986. Mem. AAAS, Polish-Am. Assn. La. Roman Catholic. Office: Tulane U Sch Medicine 1430 Tulane Ave New Orleans LA 70112-2699

ROTE, CAREY CLEMENTS, art educator; b. Worland, Wyo., Dec. 2, 1957; d. Albert Eugene Clements and Ellen (Maverick) Dickson; m. John Christopher Rote, Dec. 27, 1982; children: Sunshine Marie, Christopher Maverick, Brooke Fontaine. BA, Tex. Christian U., 1977; MA, Tulane U., 1980; PhD, U. Tex., Austin, 1987. Lectr. Trinity U., San Antonio, 1983-84, San Antonio Coll., 1985-86, San Antonio Art Inst., 1984-86; researcher Archive for Rsch. in Archetypal Symbolism, N.Y.C., 1986, 92; asst. prof. Corpus Christi State U. (now Tex. A&M U.-Corpus Christi), 1987-92, assoc. prof., 1992—; dir. Weil Gallery, 1988—; presented numerous papers on art; lectr. Art Mus. South Tex., 1989-90. Researcher: Treasures of St. Mark's, 1984, McNay Art Inst., 1980; art critic Corpus Christi Caller-Times, 1989-91; author: (exhbn. catalogues) Benito Huerta, 1989, Jan Tips/Reginald Rowe, 1989, Karin Broker, 1988, Malinda Beeman, 1990, El Corazon del Pueblo, 1991, Of Gods and Kings, 1992, Conflicting Rituals: Sharon Kopriva, 1992, Talleres en Fronteras, 1993, Shared Passions, 1996. Vol. Jr. League, San Antonio, 1980-88, Jr. League, Corpus Christi, 1988-91; bd. dirs. Corpus Christi Ballet, 1990-91, Creative Arts Ctr., 1990-91, Corpus Christi Arts Coun., 1991-94; bd. dirs. Art Mus. South Tex., 1993—. U. Tex. fellow, 1984, Baumberger Endowment fellow, 1981-83, Matilda Geddings Gray Found. fellow, 1979, Corpus Christi State U. fellow, summer 1991; Tulane U. scholar, 1978-80; Corpus Christi State U. faculty rsch. grantee, 1991, Tex. A&M U.-Corpus Christi faculty rsch. grantee, 1995; recipient Josephine Harrold Barnes Achievement award, 1975-77, Internat. Partnership Among Museums award Am. Assn. Museums, 1992. Mem. Coll. Art Assn. Democrat. Episcopalian. Office: Tex A&M U-Corpus Christi 6300 Ocean Dr Corpus Christi TX 78412-5503

ROTENBERG, DON HARRIS, chemist; b. Portland, Oreg., Mar. 31, 1934; s. Morris Hyman and Helen (Harris) R.; m. Barbara Ress, June 29, 1958; children: Laura, Debra. BA, U. Oreg., 1955; AM, Harvard U., 1956; PhD, Cornell U., 1960. Rsch. chemist Enjay Chem. Lab. Exxon Rsch. & Engring. Co., Linden, N.J., 1960-67, sr. rsch. chemist Enjay Polymer Lab., 1967-71; mgr. polymer sci. and engring. Am. Optical Corp., Southbridge, Mass., 1971-75, dir. materials and process lab., 1975-80, v.p. R&D, 1980-85; v.p., gen. mgr. precision products bus. Am. Optical Corp., Southridge, Mass., 1985-88; tech. dir. Coburn Optical Industries, Tulsa, 1988-92; cons. Plastics Tech. Assocs., Tulsa, 1992—; v.p. rsch. and devel. Neolens, Inc., Miami, Fla., 1994-96; mgr. process engring. Sola Optical, Miami, Fla., 1996—. Contbr. articles to Advances in Chem. Series, Jour. Macromolecular Sci.-Chem. Todd Rsch. fellow Cornell U., Ithaca, N.Y., 1956-59. Mem. Am. Chem. Soc. (plastics, polymer and rubber divns., contbr. to jour.), Soc. Plastics Engrs., Radtech Internat., Phi Beta Kappa, Sigma Xi. Home: 4507 E 108th St Tulsa OK 74137-6850 Office: Sola Optical 18963 NE 4th Ct Miami FL 33179

ROTENIZER, R. EUGENE, financial planner, consultant and advisor; b. Hillsville, Va., Oct. 31, 1937; s. William Ray and Ava Marie (Robinson) R.; children: David E., Jeffrey W., Brent N. BS in Bus., Nat. Coll., 1956. CFP, CLU, RFC, registered investment advisor, registered prin. Fin. advisor and planner, money mgr., owner Countrywide Fin. Group, Mt. Airy, N.C., 1973—; pvt. practice fin. cons.; cons., bus. advisor Mount Airy, 1981—; fed. arbitrator Nat. Assn. Securities Dealers. Author: Financial Independence Can Be Yours! How to - For All Ages, 1994; contbr. articles to profl. jours. With U.S. Army, 1957-62. Mem. Nat. Assn. CLUs and ChFCs, Nat. Assn. Realtors, Internat. Assn. Registered Fin. Consultants, Internat. Assn. CFPs. Republican. Baptist. Office: 1253 W Lebanon St Mount Airy NC 27030-2227

ROTH, ALEDA VENDER, business educator; b. Cleve., Oct. 8, 1945; d. Joseph Patrick and Beatrice Vender; m. G. Douglas Roth, Sept. 26, 1970; children: G. Brian, Lauren Carter. BS in Psychology with honors, Ohio State U., 1968; MSPH in Biostats., U. N.C., 1970; PhD in Ops. Mgmt., Ohio State U., 1986. Chief statistician Ark. Children's Colony Ark. State Dept. Human Svcs., 1968-69; rsch. assoc., epidemiologist Epidemiologic Field Sta. Greater Kansas City Mental Health Found., 1970-72, statis. cons. Epidemiologic Field Sta., 1972-74; nat. dir. stats. dept. ANA, 1972-79; grad. teaching and rsch. assoc. faculty mgmt. sci. Ohio State U., 1979-83, grad. teaching and rsch. assoc. acctg. dept., 1983, instr. computer and info. sys. Coll. Engring., 1983-84, instr. faculty mgmt. sci. Coll. Adminstrv. Sci., 1984-85; asst. prof. Sch. Mgmt. Boston U., 1985-89; prin. investigator retail banking futures project, 1986-94, prin. co-investigator rsch. DTT-UNC global mfg. strategy and tech. vision project, 1989—, rsch. assoc. ctr. health rsch. and edn., 1989-93; assoc. prof. dept. health adminstrn. Duke U. Med. Ctr., Durham, 1989-91; assoc. prof. bus. Duke U., Durham, N.C., 1989-93, U. N.C., Chapel Hill, 1993—; adj. faculty mem. Sch. Pub. Health, U. N.C., Chapel Hill, 1972-74; mem. Coop. Health Stats. Sys. Adv. Com., Nat. Ctr. for Health Stats., DHHS, 1974-76; membership svcs. com. Nat. Decision Scis. Inst., 1989-90; adj. rsch. faculty Boston U. Mfg. Roundtable, 1985-90; rsch. adv. com. U. N.C.-Ctr. for Mfg. Excellence, 1989-94; exec. com. U.N.C. Cato Ctr. Applied Bus. Rsch., 1994—; chair, panelist numerous confs. and seminars; presenter and cons. in field. Author: (with M. van der Velde) The Future of Retail Banking Delivery Systems, 1988, Retail Banking Strategies, Opportunities for the 1990s, 1990, World Class Banking: Benchmarking the Market Leaders, 1992 (With C. Giffi and G. Seal) Competing in World Class Manufacturing: America's 21st Century Challenge, 1990; editor: Facts About Nursing, 1972-73 edit., 1974, 1974-75 edit., 1976, 1980-81 edit., 1981, (with J. Jaeger and A. Kaluzny) The Management of Continuous Improvement: Cases in Health Administration, 1993; sr. assoc. editor Manufacturing and Svc. Operations Management, 1996—; assoc. editor Decision Sciences, 1993—, Jour. Ops. Mgmt., 1993—, assoc. editor, Prodn. and Ops. Mgmt. Jour., 1996—, mem. editl. adv. bd. 1991-93; mem. editl. bd., 1996—, mem. editl. rev. bd., 1992-96, assoc. editor OM Review, 1992-94, Benchmarking for Quality and Tech. mgmt., 1993—; mem. editl. bd. Internat. Jour. Prodn. Ops. Mgmt., 1995—; ad hoc referee Mgmt. Sci., Jour. Ops. Mgmt., Decision Scis., Prodn. and Ops. Mgmt. Jour., IEEE Transactions; contbr. articles to profl. jours., chpts. to books. Recipient Book award of excellence Soc. for Tech. Comm., 1992, Kenan Inst. Faculty rsch. award, 1994, Outstanding paper award for excellence Literati Club, London, 1995, Kenan-Flagler Bus. Sch. Disting. Rsch. award 1996, Best Paper award Acad. of Mgmt., 1996, Interdisciplinary Paper award Decision Scis. Inst., 1996; Anna Dice scholar Ohio State U., 1985, O'Herron faculty scholar, 1996; mem. grantee U.S. Quality Coun. II of the Conf. Bd., 1991—, Quality mgmt. Ctr., 1992—; NIMH fellow, 1969-70, U. N.C. Cato Ctr. fellow, 1995, Kenan Inst. fellow, 1995-96. Mem. Prodn. and Ops. Mgmt. Soc. (session chair ann. mtg. 1991, 92, track chair 1994, bd. dirs. 1995—),

Ops. Mgmt. Assn. (sec. 1988-91, bd. dirs. 1988-95, planning com. ann. conf. 1990-91, session chair ann. mtg. 1991), Decision Scis. Inst. (bd. dirs. 1996—), Phi Kappa Phi, Delta Omega. Office: U NC Kenan-Flagler Bus Sch Chapel Hill NC 27599-3490

ROTH, BRIAN ANDREW, project engineer; b. Hartford, Conn., Mar. 31, 1960; s. Charles Vincent and Gail Audrey (Bockus) R.; m. Jacqueline Jordan, Aug. 16, 1986. BSME, U. Tex., 1988. Design engr. Barnes Drill Co., Rockford, Ill., 1988-89, Camco Products and Svcs., Inc., Houston, 1989-94, Baker Oil Tools, Houston, 1994—. Patentee hydraulically actuated well shifting tool, flapper mount for well safety valve, fluid circulation apparatus. Vol. Houston Habit for Humanity, 1989-91. Mem. ASME. Home: Apt 1711 444 E Medical Center Blvd Webster TX 77598-4345 Office: Baker Oil Tools 6023 Navigation Blvd Houston TX 77011-1131

ROTH, DOVER, psychiatrist; b. Bklyn., May 17, 1928; s. Joseph and Millie Roth; m. Charlene Kay Gray, July 25, 1973; children: David, Joel, Steven, Ann. AB in Biol. Scis., U. Tex., El Paso, 1947; MD, Harvard U., Boston, 1951. Diplomate Am. Bd. Psychiatry and Neurology. Resident in psychiatry Boston Psychopathic Hosp., 1952-53; rsch. fellow Harvard U., 1953; chief resident VA Rsch. Hosp., Chgo., 1955-56; pvt. practice, Highland Park, Ill., 1956-92, Lake Forest, Ill., 1956-92; psychiatrist Mental Health Authority Harris County, Houston, 1992-95; med. dir. Benesys, Houston, 1993-94; staff & cons. psychiatrist Univ. Houston Student Health Svc., 1995—; mem. Lake County Bd. Health, 1978-81, pres., 1980; med. dir. Forest Hosp., Des Plaines, Ill.,1957-58, dir. adult unit, 1970-91; chief dept. psychiatry and mental health North Suburban Clinic, Skokie, Ill., 1978-89; cons. Pain Treatment Ctr., Lake Forest Hosp., 1988-92; med. dir. chem. dependency unit Martha Washington Hosp., Chgo., 1989-90; physician adv. Intracorp, Dallas, 1989-92; appeals reviewer Health Direct, Park Ridge, Ill., 1989—; presenter in field; numerous others. With M.C., USN, 1953-55. Fellow Am. Psychiat. Assn. (life), Ill. Psychiat. Assn., Chgo. Soc. Adolescent Psychiatry (founding). Office: U Houston Student Health Ctr 2800 Calhoun Houston TX 77204-3251

ROTH, JAMES JOSEPH, telecommunications engineer; b. Latrobe, Pa.; s. Joseph James and Clara Ruth (Short) R.; m. Patricia Ann Patillo Denton, May 1969 (div. Sept. 1972); m. Lydia Ann Robinson, July 6, 1975. BBA magna cum laude, St. Leo Coll., 1976; MS in Mgmt. Info. Sys., Kennedy Western U., 1993. Served to sr. master sgt. USAF, 1963-83; ret., 1983; sr. staff mem. Contel Info. Sys., Littleton, Colo., 1983-84; assoc. prin. engr. Harris Corp., Melbourne, Fla., 1984-86; sr. sys. designer Grumman Data Sys., Woodbury, N.Y., 1986-87; sr. sys. engr. Grumman Space Sta., Reston, Va., 1987-90; cons. CDI Corp., Arlington, Va., 1990-91; network architect, computer analyst The Computer Mcht., Norwood, Mass., 1992-93; integration cons. THO Exports, Needham, Mass., 1994; vendor mgr. AT&T Bell Labs., Middletown, N.J., 1994-96; cons. Rivert Group, Northbrook, Ill., 1996—, Strong Runds, Milw., 1996—; mem. security and privacy working group Grumman Space Sta, 1987-90, chair sys. engring. group, 1989-90. Author: Tactical Air Command Aircrew Reporting System, 1979; co-author: Tactical Air Command Flying Training Management System, 1976, U.S. Air Force Operations Resource Management System, 1987. Mem. IEEE, Assn. Computing Machinery, VFW, DAV.

ROTH, LANE, communications educator; b. N.Y.C., Apr. 10, 1943. BA, NYU, 1964; MA, Fla. State U., 1974, PhD Mass Communication, 1976. Camera operator Sta. WFSU-TV, Tallahassee, 1973-74; broadcast engr., producer, writer, performer Sta. WFSU-FM, Tallahassee, 1974-76; co-host Sta. WNIN-TV, Evansville, Ind., 1976-77; asst. prof. radio-TV-film U. Evansville, 1976-78; asst. prof. comm. Lamar U., Beaumont, Tex., 1978-82, assoc. prof., 1982—; Bd. dirs. Mental Health Assn. of Jefferson County, 1993—; writer, performer fund-raising promos, Sta. KVLU-FM, Beaumont, 1995—. Author: Film Semiotics, Metz, and Leone's Trilogy, 1983; contbr. articles to profl. mags., jours.; contbr. to acad. books. mem. bd. of dirs. Mental Health Assoc. of Jefferson Co., 1993—. Mem. Internat. Assn. for the Fantastic in the Arts, World Comm. Assn., Märklin Club. Roman Catholic. Office: Lamar U Dept Communications Beaumont TX 77710

ROTH, MARJORY JOAN JARBOE, special education educator; b. Ranger, Tex., May 24, 1934; d. James Aloysius and Dorothy Knight (Taggart) Jarboe; m. Thomas Mosser Roth, Jr., Dec. 22, 1959; children: Thomas Mosser III, James Jarboe. BA in English, Rice U., 1957; MEd in Ednl. Adminstrn., U. N.C., Greensboro, 1981. Cert. tchr.-specific learning disabilities, middle grades lang. arts and social studies, intermediate grades, adminstr.-prin., N.C. Tchr. 4th grade Houston Ind. Sch. Dist., 1957-60; specific lang. disabilities instr. Forsyth Tech. C.C., Winston-Salem, N.C., 1976-77; specific learning disabilities tchr. Forsyth Country Day Sch., Winston-Salem, 1977-80; tchr. 5th grade Winston-Salem/Forsyth County Schs., 1982-83, specific learning disabilities tchr. Mt. Tabor High Sch., 1983-86; part time instr. English and Learning Disabilities Forsyth Tech. C.C., 1986-90; founding pres., prin. Greenhills Sch., Winston-Salem, 1990—. Co-author, co-editor booklets. Sunday Sch. dir., tchr. Galloway Meml. Episcopal Ch., 1960-70, pres., treas., sec. Churchwomen, 1963-74; treas. Elkin Jr. Woman's Club, 1962; chmn. Elkin Heart Fund Drive, 1968; bd. dirs. Hugh Chatham Hosp. Auxillary, 1968, Friends of the Elkin Pub. Libr., 1968-74, chmn., 1970-72, chmn., exhibits chmn. summer reading program; pres. South Surry Heart Assn., 1969; mem. Churchwomen of St. Paul's Episcopal Ch., Winston-Salem, 1982—, Fiddle and Bow Folk Music Soc., Winston-Salem, 1992—. Forsyth fellow NEH, 1985; grantee in field. Mem. ASCD, Children with Attention Deficit Disorder (profl. adv. bd. N.C. Triad chpt. 1990—), Learning Disability Assn. N.C. (sec., bd. dirs. 1981-86), Orton Dyslexia Soc. (sec., bd. dirs. Carolinas br. 1981-85, founding pres. N.C. br. 1987-91, bd. dirs. 1987-96, nat. nominating com. 1992-94). Republican. Home: 940 Fox Hall Dr Winston Salem NC 27106-4431 Office: Greenhills Sch 1360 Lyndale Dr Winston Salem NC 27106-9739

ROTH, OLIVER RALPH, radiologist; b. Cumberland, Md., Nov. 30, 1921; s. DeCoursey Andrew and Mabel (Lathrum) R.; BS, Frostburg (Md.) State Coll., 1942, DSc (hon.), 1980; MD, U. Md., 1950; m. Virginia McBride, June 2, 1943; 1 child, Tiija. Diplomate Am. Bd. Radiology. Resident, Johns Hopkins Hosp., Balt., 1954-57; cancer research fellow Middlesex Hosp., London, 1957-58; founder dept. radiation oncology Presbyn. Hosp., Charlotte, N.C., 1958-62; attending radiologist King's Daus. Hosp., Ashland, Ky., 1962-80; radiologist Our Lady of Bellefonte Hosp., 1981-86; mem. faculty Sch. of Allied Health Shawnee State U., Portsmouth, Ohio, 1986-90; prof. radiology Sch. Medicine Marshall U., Huntington, W.Va., 1990—; mem. adv. com. Ky. Cancer Commn., 1978; bd. dirs. Boyd County chpt. Am. Cancer Soc., 1978. With USN, 1942-45. Commanded to Buckingham Palace, June 17, 1958; recipient Disting. Alumni award Frostburg State U., 1979. Mem. AMA, Am. Coll. Radiology, Radiol. Soc. N.Am., Am. Radium Soc., Royal Faculty Radiology, Brit. Inst. Radiology. Democrat. Lutheran. Club: Shriners (Cumberland, Md.). Book reviewer Radiology, 1954-55. Home: 2912 Cogan St Ashland KY 41102-5230

ROTH, ROBERT, advertising executive; b. 1941. Grad., U. Miami, Fla., 1962. With Suntan West Hotel, Inc., N.Y.C., 1962-65; officer Admktg. Inc., L.A., 1965—; pres., dir., CEO R.M.R. Advt. Corp., Miami, 1976—; officer I.G.T. Svcs., Inc., Miami, 1987—. Office: R M R Advt Corp 1111 Lincoln Rd Miami FL 33139-2452

ROTH, ROBERT ALLEN, systems consultant; b. Chgo., Oct. 26, 1947; s. Ralph Robert and Lucile Emily (Hence) R.; m. Betty Rae Wooten, July 23, 1968 (div. June 1975); children: Robert Allen III, Anna Katherine; m. Carolyn McConnell, Aug. 23, 1980. AA, St. Johns River Jr. Coll., Palatka, Fla., 1967; B Gen. Studies, Rollins Coll., 1969; MBA, U. North Fla., 1974. Cert. sys. profl., computing profl. Various positions, 1968-80; systems mgr. Charter Oil Co.-Alaska Oil Co., Jacksonville, Fla., 1980-81; project leader, lead analyst Halliburton Svcs., Duncan, Okla., 1982; mgr. data adminstrn. and software quality assurance Comm. Satellite Corp., Washington, 1982-83; div. mgr. Automated Scis. Group, Inc., Fairfax, Va., 1983-86; div. dir. Inf. Sys. and Networks (ISN) Corp., Sarasota, Fla., 1986-87; pres., owner, operator ROMAC Enterprises, Sarasota, 1987-92; hdqs. div. mgr. COMPEX Corp., Sarasota, 1987, v.p., gen. mgr. S.E. region, 1991-92; pres., dir. R&D Advanced Tech. Group, Sarasota, Fla., 1992-96; prin. cons. Data Dimensions, Jacksonville, Fla., 1996—. Mem. Rotary (v.p. Sarasota 1991-92, pres. 1992-93, Paul Harris fellow 1992). Home and Office: Data Dimensions 3692 East Wexford Hollow Rd Jacksonville FL 32224-6678

ROTH, ROBERT WILLIAM, computer field engineer; b. Covington, Ky., Sept. 17, 1953; s. Robert John and Barbara (Model) R.; m. Julie Lavonne Zimmerman, Jan. 29, 1982. BA, Morehead State U., 1978; MBA, U. Ky., 1979. Airport mgr. Am. Airlines, Dallas, 1979-85; sales mgr.-airlines Motorola Inc., Dallas, 1985-87; maj. accounts exec. Metromedia Inc., Dallas, 1987-89; field svc. tech. Am. Airlines, Dallas, 1989-90; telecom. network analyst Tulsa, 1990-91; sr. comm. engr. Am. Airlines, Tulsa, 1991-94; computer field engr. Am. Airlines, Cin., 1994—. With U.S. Army, 1972-74, Vietnam. Decorated Silver Star, Bronze Star; named to Hon. Order Ky. Cols., 1975; recipient 1st Pl. award for Best Mktg. campaign KIPA, 1977. Mem. Am. Legion, VFW. Republican. Office: PO Box 619616 MD 3494 Dallas TX 75261-9614

ROTH, STEPHEN L., cardiologist; b. N.Y.C., Feb. 20, 1949; s. Joel and Pauline (Wolf) R.; m. Susan E. Katz, Dec. 24, 1974 (div. Nov. 1994); children: Mark, Jason. BA, NYU, 1970; MD, U. Pa., 1974, PhD, 1976. Intern Bellevue-NYU Med. Ctr., 1976-77, resident in internal medicine, 1977-79, fellow in cardiology, 1979-81; pres. Cardiology Cons. of Hollywood, Fla., 1981—; sr. attending physician Hollywood (Fla.) Meml. Hosp., Hollywood Med. Ctr.; lectr. in field. Recipient AMA Physician Recognition award, 1983, 86, 89, 92, 95. Fellow Am. Heart Assn., Am. Coll. Cardiology, Phi Beta Kappa. Office: Cardiology Cons Hollywood 4700F Sheridan St Hollywood FL 33021

ROTH, WILLIAM STANLEY, hospital foundation executive; b. N.Y.C., Jan. 12, 1929; s. Sam Irving and Louise Caroline (Martin) R.; m. Hazel Adcock, May 6, 1963; children: R. Charles, W. Stanley. AA, Asheville-Biltmore Jr. Coll., 1948; BS, U. N.C., 1950. Dep. regional exec. Nat. council Boy Scouts Am., 1953-65; exec. v.p. Am. Humanics Found., 1965-67; dir. devel. Bethany Med. Ctr., Kansas City, Kans., 1967-74; exec. v.p. Geisinger Med. Ctr. Found., Danville, Pa., 1974-78; found. pres. Baptist Med. Ctrs., Birmingham, Ala., 1978—; sec. Western Med. Systems, Cherokee Cmty. Homes, Cullman Sr. Housing, Dekalb Sr. Housing, Limestone Sr. Housing, Oxford Sr. Housing. Mem.-at-large Nat. council Boy Scouts Am., 1972-86; chmn. NAHD Ednl. Fund, 1980-82; ruling elder John Knox Kirk, Kansas City, Mo., Grove Presbyn. Ch., Danville, Pa. Recipient Silver award United Methodist Ch., 1970, Mid-West Health Congress, 1971; Seymour award for outstanding hosp. devel. officer 1983. Fellow Assn. for Healthcare Philanthropy (life, nat. pres. 1975-76); mem. Nat. Soc. Fund Raising Execs. (pres. Ala. chpt. 1980-82, nat. dir. 1980-84, mem. ethics bd. 1993—, advanced cert. fund raising exec., Outstanding Fund Raising Exec., Ala. chpt. 1983), Mid-Am. Hosp. Devel. Assn. (pres. 1973-74), Mid-West Health Congress (devel. chmn. 1972-74), Am. Soc. for Healthcare Mktg. and Pub. Rels., Ala. Soc. for Sleep Disorders, Ala. Heart Inst., Ala. Assn. Healthcare Philanthropy (pres. 1991-93, chmn. bd. 1993-94), Ala. Planned Giving Coun. (bd. dirs. 1991—, pres. 1994-95), Alpha Phi Omega (nat. pres. 1958-62, dir. 1950—, Nat. Disting. Service award 1962), Delta Upsilon (pres. N.C. Alumni 1963-65). Clubs: Rotary (pres. club 1976-77), Relay House, Summit, Green Valley (bd. govs.), Elks, Order Holy Grail, Order Golden Fleece, Order of The Arrow (Nat. Disting. Service award 1958). Editor Torch and Trefoil, 1960-61. Home: 341 Laredo Dr Birmingham AL 35226-2325 Office: 3500 Blue Lake Dr Ste 101 Birmingham AL 35243-1908

ROTHACKER, KENNETH CHARLES, linguist; b. Bklyn., Dec. 28, 1945; s. Charles Augustus and Florence Elsie (Ahern) R.; children: Ariane-Thérèse, Jordan Albert. Student, Providence Coll., 1963-64; BA in French, St. John's U., 1967; MA in Linguistics, Hunter Coll., N.Y.C., 1976; ABD in Linguistics, CUNY, 1979. Tchr. French, comm. arts St. Brendan's High Sch., Bklyn., 1967-71; tchr. French and Spanish Msgr. McClancy High Sch., Jackson Heights, N.Y., 1972; instructional aide in Spanish New High Sch., Bklyn., 1973; asst. prof. English and ESL SUNY Ednl. Opportunities Ctr., Farmingdale, 1974-84; tchr. English Berlitz Sch. Langs., Atlanta, 1988-90; substitute tchr. French, Spanish, English Pace Acad., Atlanta, 1985; adj. instr. ESL Ga. State U., Atlanta, 1986-87; asst. prof. English Andrew Coll., Cuthbert, Ga., 1987; instr. French composition and Spanish West Ga. Coll., Carrollton, 1989-90; method dir. Berlitz Lang. Sch., Atlanta, 1990—; instr. ESL East-West Found., Atlanta, summer 1987, 89; free-lance translator, Spain, 1984; escort interpreter in French, summer 1967; translator/interpreter U.S. Census Bur., Atlanta, 1985-87. Contbr. articles to profl. jours. NSF grantee, summer 1971. Mem. TESOL, Am. Name Soc., Am. Translators Assn., N.Am. Catalan Soc., Assn. for Computational Linguistics, Atlanta Assn. of Interpreters and Translators. Roman Catholic. Office: Berlitz Language Ctr 3400 Peachtree Rd NE Atlanta GA 30326-1107

ROTHENBERG, MACE LAWRENCE, physician, medical educator; b. N.Y.C., Nov. 9, 1956; s. William Harry and Corinne (Kaufman) R.; m. Joyce Elaine Fryburg, June 12, 1988; children: Stephanie, Bryce. BA, U. Pa., 1978; MD, NYU, 1982. Diplomate Am. Bd. Internal Medicine, Am. Bd. Internal Medicine (Oncology). Intern then resident Vanderbilt U., Nashville, 1985; fellow in med. oncology Nat. Cancer Inst., Bethesda, Md., 1985-88, sr. staff mem., 1988-91, spl. asst. to dir. div. of cancer treatment, 1988-91; asst. prof. medicine U. Tex. Health Sci. Ctr., San Antonio, 1991-95, assoc. prof., 1995—; exec. officer S.W. Oncology Group, San Antonio, 1991—; chmn. devel. therapeutics com., co-chmn. gynecologic cancer com. S.W. Oncology Group, 1991—. Editor: Gynecologic Oncology - Controversies and Developments, 1994; assoc. editor (jour.) Investigational New Drugs, 1991—; contbr. articles to profl. jours. Grantee Nat. Cancer Inst., 1993. Fellow Am. Coll. Physicians; mem. Am. Soc. Clin. Oncology, Am. Assn. Cancer Rsch. Democrat. Jewish. Home: 13255 Hunters Lark St San Antonio TX 78230-2017 Office: Univ Tex Health Sci Ctr 7703 Floyd Curl Dr San Antonio TX 78284-7884

ROTHERY, CHET, business executive; b. Washington, Feb. 5, 1955; s. Chester Grogan Sr. and Mary (Tomlinson) R. BA in Mgmt., Nat. Louis U., McLean, Va., 1990. Sys. analyst Technology Applications Inc., Alexandria, Va., 1983-86; user svcs. con. Fin. Techs., Chantilly, Va., 1986-88, mgmt. analyst, 1988-89, sr. account rep., 1989-90, product support mgr., 1990-91, bus. devel. specialist, 1991-92; bus. sys. analyst Cable/Wireless, Inc., Vienna, Va., 1993-95, enterprise project mgr., 1995-96, sr. mgr. bus. improvement, 1996—. Sec. Concord Mews Civic Assn., Arlington, Va., 1988-90, pres., 1990-91. Mem. Soc. for Tech. Comm. (Excellence award 1990, Merit award 1994). Home: 4013 19th St S Arlington VA 22204-5115 Office: Cable/Wireless Inc 8219 Leesburg Pike Vienna VA 22182

ROTHMAN, DAVID BILL, lawyer; b. N.Y.C., Apr. 25, 1952; s. Julius and Lillian (Halpern) R.; m. Jeanne Marie Hickey, July 7, 1974; children: Jessica Suzanne, Gregory Kozak. BA, U. Fla., 1974, JD, 1977. Bar: Fla. 1977, U.S. Dist. Ct. (so. dist.) Fla. 1980, U.S. Ct. Appeals (5th cir.) 1980, U.S. Supreme Ct. 1981, U.S. Ct. Appeals (11th cir.) 1982, U.S. Dist. Ct. (ea. dist.) Ky. 1985, U.S. Dist. Ct. (mid. dist.) Fla. 1986; bd. cert. criminal trial law Fla. Bd. Asst. state atty. Dade County State Atty.'s Office, Miami, Fla., 1977-80; ptnr. Thornton Rothman, P.A., Miami, 1980—; adj. prof. U. Miami Sch. Law, 1995—; com. mem. Fla. Rules Criminal Procedures, 1990-93, metro Dade Ind. Rev. Panel, 1989—, co-chmn., 1990-91, chmn., 1991-92, 95—; panel mem. fee arbitration 11th Cir. Ct., 1994-96, co-chair, 1995-96. Mem. ABA, Fla. Bar Assn., Dade County Bar Assn. (criminal ct. com. 1984—, chmn. 1987-90, bd. dirs. 1990-93, treas. 1993-94, sec. 1994-95, v.p. 1995-96, pres.-elect 1996—), Nat. Assn. Criminal Def. Lawyers, Fla. Assn. Criminal Def. Lawyers (bd. dirs. statewide, Miami chpt. 1991—, pres. Miami chpt. 1993-94, sec. 1996—). Democrat. Jewish. Home: 9951 SW 127th Ter Miami FL 33176-4833 Office: Thornton & Rothman PA 200 S Biscayne Blvd Ste 3420 Miami FL 33131-2310

ROTHMAN, RICHARD LEE, JR., health facility administrator; b. Canton, Ohio, Mar. 19, 1963; s. Richard Lee Sr. and Grace Neal (Parrish) R. BSA, U. Tenn., 1989; MBA, Clemson U., 1993. Mgr. ops., traffic Milliken & Co., Spartanburg, S.C., 1989-93; mgr. sales, mktg. Milliken & Co., LaGrange, Kansas City, Ga., Mo., 1993-95; dir. ops. Alliance for Quality Care, Knoxville, Tenn., 1995—; adv. bd. mem. Nelco Engring., Greenville, S.C., 1993—. Developed software Cornerstone Logic, 1994. With U.S. Army, 1984-86. Mem. Delta Nu Alpha (v.p. 1988-89). Republican. Presbyterian. Home: 8919 Fox Lake Dr Knoxville TN 37923 Office: Alliance for Quality Care 111 Center Park Dr Ste 100 Knoxville TN 37922-2103

ROTHOLZ, MAX B., agricultural products executive; b. 1920. Pres., dir. Rice Belt Warehouse, Inc., El Campo, Tex., 1962—. Office: Rice Belt Warehouse Inc Highway 59 El Campo TX 77437*

ROUB, BRYAN R(OGER), financial executive; b. Berea, Ohio, May 1, 1941; s. Bernard Augustus and Pearl Irene (Koeblitz) R.; m. Judith Elaine Penman, June 19, 1965; children: Paul, Bradley, Michael. Student, Ohio Wesleyan U., 1959-62; BS, Ohio State U., 1966; MBA, U. Pa., 1978. Mem. audit staff Ernst & Ernst, Cleve., 1966-70; asst. contr. Midland-Ross, Cleve., 1970-73, contr., 1973-81, v.p., 1977-81, sr. v.p., 1981-82, exec. v.p. fin., 1982-84; sr. v.p. fin. Harris Corp., Melbourne, Fla., 1984-93, sr. v.p., CFO, 1993—; mem. fin. coun. II Machinery and Allied Products Inst., Washington, 1978-84, coun. I, 1984—, vice chmn., 1994-95, chmn., 1996—; mem. conf. bd. coun. of CFO's, 1993-96. Mem. adv. coun. Coll. Adminstrv. Scis., Ohio State U., 1978-81; mem. citizen's adv. coun. Westlake (Ohio) Schs., 1981-83; trustee Alcoholism Svcs. Cleve., 1982-84; mem. devel. bd. St. John's Hosp., 1983-84; pres. Westridge Homeowners' Assn., 1977; dir., treas. Tortoise Island Homeowners' Assn., 1988-90; bd. dirs. Easter Seal Soc. of Brevard County, 1993—. Mem. AICPA, Ohio Soc. CPAs, Fin. Execs. Inst. (treas. N.E. Ohio chpt. 1976-78, bd. dirs. 1980-81, 83-84, v.p. 1981-82, pres. 1982-83, bd. dirs. Orlando chpt. 1984—, v.p. 1985-86, pres. 1986-87, nat. bd. dirs. 1987-90, area v.p. 1990-91, chmn. budget and fin. com. 1988-89), Fin. Execs. Rsch. Found. (trustee 1994—, chmn. planning com. 1995—), Westwood Country Club, Eau Gallie Yacht Club (bd. govs., treas. 1990-92). Home: 556 Lanternback Island Dr Satellite Beach FL 32937-4712 Office: Harris Corp 1025 W Nasa Blvd Melbourne FL 32919-0001

ROUGH, HERBERT LOUIS, insurance company executive; b. N.Y.C., Jan. 19, 1935; s. Albert and Jean (Bendeth) R.; m. Fern Sadkin Schultz; children: Lee Michael, Lisa Joi. BS, NYU, 1956. CLU, ChFC. From agt. to dist. mgr. Equitable Life Assurance Soc., N.Y.C., 1961-69; brokerage mgr. Bernard Bergen Cos., Inc., N.Y.C., 1969-73; pres., gen. agt. Rough Agy. Inc., Great Neck, N.Y., 1973—, Comprehensive Planning--Goodman, Ltd., Hicksville, N.Y., 1988—, Rough Agy. Inc. of Fla., Ft. Lauderdale, 1991—; pres., mem. field adv. coun. Am. Gen. Life Ins. Co. of N.Y., Syracuse, 1978-83, Madison Life Ins. Co., N.Y.C., 1974-77; guest spkr. in field; instr. continuing edn. Broward c.C., Fla. Treasurer Gray Wig Repertory Theatre, Hofstra U., Uniondale, N.Y., 1981-84; pres. Heart Assn. of Great Neck, 1977. Capt. USAF, 1956-59. Mem. Life Underwriters Assn., Gold Coast Assn. of Health Underwriters (pres. 1996-97), Nat. Assn. Ind. Life Brokerage Agys., CLU Assn., Knickerbocker Yacht Club, Kiwanis (pres. Great Neck chpt. 1977—). Democrat. Jewish. Office: Comprehensive Planning Group LLC 99 N Broadway Hicksville NY 11801-2905

ROUHANI, BEHNAZ, mathematics educator; b. Dubai, United Arab Emirates, Feb. 4, 1958; came to U.S., 1984; parents Manuchihr and Shams Alzoha Rouhani. Student, St. Albans (Eng.) Coll., 1978; BS with honors, Hatfield (Eng.) Poly., 1982; MA, W.Va. U., 1987, U. Ga., 1994. Asst. sci. officer Nat. Inst. Agrl. Engring., Silsoe, Eng., 1980-81; mktg. info. analyst Kodak Near East, Dubai, 1983-84; teaching asst. W.Va. U., Morgantown, 1985-88; bus. mgr. Modern Optical House, Dubai, 1988-90; instr. Athens (Ga.) Area Tech. Inst., 1990—. United Arab Emirates' Govt. scholar, 1978-82. Mem. Am. Math. Soc. for 2-Yr. Colls.

ROUHANI, SHAHROKH, civil engineering/environmental educator,; b. Tehran, Iran, Mar. 28, 1956; came to U.S., 1974; s. Aboutorab and Parirokh (Garakani) R.; m. Firouzeh Yekta, Aug. 18, 1983; children: Nina, Shiva. BSCE, U. Calif., Berkeley, 1978, BA in Econs., 1978; SM in Engring., Harvard U., 1980, PhD in Environ. Scis., 1983. Registered profl. engr., Ga. Asst. prof. Ga. Inst. Tech., Atlanta, 1983-90, assoc. prof. civil engring., 1990—; sr. cons. Dames & Moore, Atlanta, 1990-95; pres. New Fields, Inc., Atlanta, 1995—; NSF vis. scientist Ctr. Geostats., Nat. Higher Sch. Mines Paris, 1987-88; expert mem. ASTM, EPA, U.S. Geol. Survey, Dept. Def. Geostats. Standardization Com., 1991-96. Co-author: Ground Water, 1991; contbr. articles to profl. publs., chpts. to books., also numerous reports, papers in field. Mem. ASCE (award 1991, chmn. nat. ground water hydrology 1991, chmn. task com. on geostatis. techniques in geohydrology 1987-89, sec. water resources com. Ga. sect. 1988, spl. session organizer 1989, 90, contact mem. task com. 1988-90, symposium organizer 1991), Am. Geophys. Union (assoc. editor Water Resources Rsch. 1989-94), Internat. Water Resources Assn., Am. Water Resources Assn., N.Am. Coun. on Geostats., Internat. Geostatis. Assn., Phi Beta Kappa, Tau Beta Pi, Chi Epsilon, Sigma Chi. Office: Newfields Inc 1201 W Peachtree St Ste 3050 Atlanta GA 30309

ROUNDS, PHILARD LEAON, SR., fundraiser; b. Des Moines, Jan. 9, 1928; s. Clarence Leaon and Alice Rudella (Eitel) R.; m. Shirley Anne Rounds, 1946; children: Rose Ann Rounds Farabough, Philard L. BA, Fla. So. Coll., Lakeland; diploma in Bible, Open Bible Coll., Des Moines. Missionary to Japan, 1950-67; Oral Roberts U., Tulsa, 1967-87, David Livingston Missionary Assn., 1988-89, First United Meth. Ch., 1989—; regional rep. Oral Roberts U., Tulsa, 1967-87; sr. v.p. planned giving David Livingstone Assn., Tulsa, 1987-88; min. planned giving First United Meth. Ch., tulsa, 1989—. Author: Planned Giving Manual, 1989. Fundraising exec. Nat. Soc. Fundraising, Tulsa, 1988—; active alumnus Nat. Planned Giving Inst., Memphis, 1988. With U.S. Army, 1946-49. Mem. Nat. Inst. Planned Giving, Nat. Soc. Fundraising Execs. (pres. ea. Okla. chpt. 1994), Fla. Acad. Scis., Pi Gamma Mu. Republican. Methodist. Home: 6443 S Sandusky Ave Tulsa OK 74136-1626 Office: First United Methodist Ch 1115 S Boulder Ave Tulsa OK 74119-2418

ROUNTREE, HELEN CLARK, anthropology educator; b. Camp LeJeune, N.C., Oct. 8, 1944; d. Henning Ainsworth Jr. and Mildred Ellen (Clark) R. AB summa cum laude, Coll. of William and Mary, 1966; MA in Anthropology, U. Utah, 1968; PhD in Anthropology, U. Wis., Milw., 1973. Instr. in sociology Old Dominion U., Norfolk, Va., 1968-73, asst. prof. anthropology, 1973-80, assoc. prof. anthropology, 1980-91, prof. anthropology, 1991—; cons. Jamestown Settlement Mus., Williamsburg, Va., 1986—, Va. Coun. on Indians, Richmond, Va., 1993—, Md. Commn. on Indian Affairs, Annapolis, Md., 1995—. Author: The Powhatan Indians of Virginia: Their Traditional Culture, 1989, Pocahontas' People: The Powhatan Indians of Virginia Through Four Centuries, 1990, Young Pocahontas in the Indian World, 1995; editor, contbr.: Powhatan Foreign Relations, 1500-1722, 1993. Pub. spkr. to various orgns., Va. and Md., 1989—. Recipient Outstanding Faculty award State Coun. on Higher Edn. Va., 1995. Fellow Soc. for Applied Anthropology; mem. Am. Anthropol. Assn. (life), Am. Soc. for Ethnohistory (pres. 1993-94), Royal Anthropol. Inst. Gt. Britain and Ireland (overseas mem.). Democrat. Episcopalian. Office: Old Dominion U Dept Sociology Norfolk VA 23529

ROUNTREE, VIRGINIA WARD, English language educator; b. Abbeville, Ala., June 21, 1942; d. George Earl and Sue Virginia (Hartley) Ward; m. Thomas Jefferson Rountree, Aug. 12, 1967 (dec. May 1992); 1 child, Carla Daphne. BS in English and Edn., Troy State U., 1963; postgrad., Auburn U., 1964; MA in English, U. Ala., 1968; postgrad., U. South Ala., 1986-88. Tchr. English Lanier H.S., Montgomery, Ala., 1963-65, Tuscaloosa (Ala.) Jr. H.S., 1969-70, Tuscaloosa Acad., 1970-71, Julius T. Wright Sch., Mobile, Ala., 1975-77; adj. lectr. Spring Hill Coll., Mobile, 1992—, U. South Ala., Mobile, 1993—; sr. counselor U. Ala., 1966-67; supervising tchr. Tuscaloosa Pub. Schs., 1969-70, mem. rsch. com., 1969-70. Mem. U. South Ala. Women's Club (sec. 1971-72), Alpha Delta Kappa, Kappa Delta Pi. Episcopalian. Home: 8035 Hilltop Rd Mobile AL 36619-5353 Office: Spring Hill Coll 400 Dauphin St Mobile AL 36602-2402

ROURKE, ARLENE CAROL, publisher; b. N.Y.C.. Pres. Rourke Publs., Vero Beach, Fla., 1984—. Author, pub. books for children on Native Am. people, western history, religion, the environment, animal care and personal relationships, science biographies. Active Ctr. for the Arts, 1985—, Riverside Theatre, Vero Beach, 1985—; mem. ethics com. Turnabout Modeling Sch. and Agy., 1986.

ROUSAKIS, JOHN PAUL, former mayor; b. Savannah, Ga., Jan. 14, 1929; s. Paul V. and Antigone (Alexopoulos) R.; m. Elizabeth Lattimore, Oct. 24, 1987; children: Rhonda, Paul, Thea, Tina. B.B.A., U. Ga., 1952. Commr. Chatham County, Ga., 1965-69; vice chmn. Chatham County, 1969-70; mayor of Savannah, 1970-92; ins. broker Savannah, 1956—. Past pres. Nat. League Cities. With AUS, 1953-56. Named Outstanding Young Man of Savannah, Outstanding Young Man of Ga., 1962, Archon Greek Orthodox Ch., 1988, Outstanding City Ofcl., State of Ga.; recipient Tree of Life award Jewish Nat. Fund, 1983, Pres.'s award Nat. League of Cities, 1991. Mem. Ga. Mcpl. Assn. (past pres.), Am. Legion, Ahepa, Masons, (Shriner, Knight Comdr. 32d deg.). Office: 24 E Liberty St Savannah GA 31401

ROUSCH, BERNARD LAWRENCE, psychiatrist; b. Bklyn., Oct. 23, 1936; s. David and Martha (Felner) R.; m. Tamara Beryl Grodman, Jan. 31, 1959; children: Daniel, Rebekah, Eason, Andrew, Chava, Shana, Sarah. AB in Econs., Syracuse U., 1958; MD, NYU, 1962. Diplomate Am. Bd. of Psychiatry and Neurology. Resident in psychiatry S.W. Med. Sch., Dallas, 1968; dir. Lithium Treatment Ctr. Mid-Cities Psychiatric Ctr., Bedford, Tex., 1968—; vice chief psychiat. dept. Harris Meth.-Hurst-Euless-Bedford Hosp., Bedford, 1988-91; chief psychiat. dept. HCA Richland Hosp., Tex., 1989; clin. dir. adolescent unit Residential Treatment Ctr., Bedford, 1991, chief of med. staff, 1992; clin. asst. prof. Tex. Coll. Osteo. Med., Ft. Worth, 1992; disability examiner S.W. Med. Examiners, Dallas, 1994—. Sr. surgeon USPHS 1962-68, Ft. Worth. Mem. AMA, Am. Psychiat. Assn., Tex. Med. Assn., Tarrant County Med. Soc. Office: Mid-Cities Psychiat Ctr 111-B Bedford Road Bedford TX 76022

ROUSE, EDNA FRANCES, special education educator; b. Welch, W.Va., May 11, 1946; d. Delphin Barr and Shirlie Juanita (Powers) Mabry; m. Malcolm Everett Rouse, Feb. 27, 1965; children: Gwendolan Michelle Rouse Pierce, Mark Everett (dec.). AS with honors, Miss. Gulf Coast Jr. Coll., Wiggins, 1982; BS with honors, U. So. Miss., 1986, MS, 1991, cert. adminstrn., 1996. Tchr. George County Sch. Sys., Lucedale, Miss., 1986—. Mem. NEA, ASCD, Miss. Assn. Educators, Ea. Star. Baptist. Home: 1126 New Hope Church Rd Lucedale MS 39452 Office: Agricola Elem Sch 6165 Highway 613 Lucedale MS 39452-9701

ROUSE, JOHN WILSON, JR., research institute administrator; b. Kansas City, Mo., Dec. 7, 1937; s. John Wilson and Gail Agnes (Palmer) R.; m. Susan Jane Davis, May 3, 1981; 1 son, Jeffrey Scott. A.S., Kansas City Jr. Coll., 1957; B.S., Purdue U., 1959; M.S., U. Kans., 1965, Ph.D., 1968. Registered profl. engr., Mo., Tex. Engr. Bendix Corp., Kansas City, Mo., 1959-64; rsch. coord. Ctr. for Rsch., U. Kans., Lawrence, 1964-68; prof. elec. engring., dir. remote sensing ctr. Tex. A&M U., College Station, 1968-78; Logan prof. engr., chmn. elec. engring. U. Mo., Columbia, 1978-81; dean engring. U. Tex., Arlington, 1981-87; pres. So. Rsch. Inst., Birmingham, Ala., 1987—; mgr. microwave program NASA Hdqrs., Washington, 1975-77; bd. dirs. Protective Life Corp., Ala. Power Co.; chmn. bd. So. Rsch. Techs. Inc. Contbr. articles to profl. jours. Recipient Outstanding Tchr. award Tex. A&M U., 1971; Outstanding Prof. award U. Mo., 1980; Engr. of Yr. Tex. Soc. Profl. Engrs., 1983. Mem. IEEE, Nat. Soc. Profl. Engrs., Am. Soc. Engring. Edn., Internat. Bus. Fellows, Internat. Union Radio Sci., Sigma Xi, Eta Kappa Nu, Tau Beta Pi. Home: 2004 Bridgelake Dr Birmingham AL 35244-1421 Office: Southern Research Institute PO Box 55305 2000 9th Ave S Birmingham AL 35205-2708

ROUSE, LEGRAND ARIAIL, II, retired lawyer, educator; b. Spartanburg, S.C., June 11, 1933; s. LeGrand and Hilda Virginia (Ariail) R.; m. Patricia Adelle White, Aug. 23, 1958; children: LeGrand A. III, Laurie Adelle Rouse-Hazel, Daniel Morris. AB in History and Polit. Sci., Wofford Coll., 1954; LLB, U. S.C.; 1959, JD, 1970; MA in Govt., Am. U., 1969. Bar: S.C. 1959, U.S. Dist. Ct. S.C. 1959, U.S. Ct. Appeals (4th cir.) 1964, U.S. Supreme Ct. 1963. Sole practice, Spartanburg S.C., 1959-63, 68-69; assoc. counsel, jud. improvements subcom. U.S. Senate Judiciary Com., Washington, 1963; profl. staff mem. U.S. Senate P.O. and Civil Service Com., Washington, 1964-68; instructional specialist Office of Instructional TV, S.C. Dept. Edn., Columbia, 1970-73; social studies cons. curriculum devel. S.C. Dept. Edn., 1973-79; spl. asst. legal and legis. affairs to State Supt. Edn., Columbia, 1979-91; spl. asst. to sr. exec. asst. Policy, Rsch., and Leadership, Columbia, 1991; cons. S.C. Council for Social Studies, Columbia, 1973-78; dir. S.C. Council Econ. Edn., Columbia. Author: Government-Politics-Citizenship, tchr. lesson guide, 1971-72; creator, on-camera instr. Government-Politics-Citizenship TV series, 1970-72; project dir. econs. edn. kit for tchrs. grades 1-12: People, Production, Profits, 1977. Mem. S.C. Ho. of Reps., Columbia, 1961-64; alt. del. Nat. Democratic Conv., 1964. Served to 1st lt. USAR, 1955-57. Recipient Schoolmens' medal Freedoms Found. at Valley Forge, 1974. Mem. S.C. Bar Assn., S.C. State Employees' Assn. (pres. 1980-82), Masons, Nat. Sojourners (pres. chpt. 184). Methodist. Home: 1021 Milton Ln Columbia SC 29209-2321

ROUSE, ROSCOE, JR., librarian, educator; b. Valdosta, Ga., Nov. 26, 1919; s. Roscoe and Minnie Estelle (Corbett) R.; m. Charlie Lou Miller, June 23, 1945; children: Charles Richard, Robin Lou. BA, U. Okla., 1948, MA, 1952; MALS, U. Mich., 1958, PhD, 1962; student (Grolier Soc. scholar), Rutgers U., 1956. Bookkeeper C & S Nat. Bank, Valdosta, Ga., 1937-41; draftsman R.K. Rouse Co. (heating engrs.), Greenville, S.C., 1941-42; student asst. U. Okla. and Rice U., 1947-48; asst. librarian Northeastern State Coll., Tahlequah, Okla., 1948-49; acting librarian, instr. library sci. Northeastern State Coll., 1949-51; circulation librarian Baylor U., 1952-53, acting univ. librarian, 1953-54, univ. librarian, prof., 1954-63, chmn. dept. library sci., 1956-63; dir. libraries State U. N.Y. at Stony Brook, L.I., 1963-67; dean libr. svcs., prof. Okla. State U., Stillwater, 1967-87, univ. libr. historian, 1987-92; chmn. dept. libr. edn. Okla. State U., 1967-74; Vis. prof. U. Okla. Sch. Library Sci., summer 1962, N. Tex. State U., summer 1965; acad. library cons.; mem. AIA-Am. Library Assn. Library Bldg. Awards Jury, 1976; bd. dirs. Fellowship Christian Libr. and Info. Specialists. Author: A History of the Baylor University Library, 1845-1919, 1962; editor: Okla. Librarian, 1951-52; co-author: Organization Charts of Selected Libraries, 1973; A History of the Okla. State U. Library, 1992; contbr. articles, book revs., chpts. to publs. in field. Bd. dirs. Okla. Dept. Librs., 1989-92, chmn., 1990-92. 1st lt. USAAF, 1942-45. Decorated Air medal with 4 oak leaf clusters; recipient citation Okla. State Senate, 1987, Rotary Outstanding Achievement award, 1996; named in 150 Prominent Individuals in Baylor's History. Mem. ALA (life, mem. coun. 1971-72, 76-80, 83-84, 84-88, chmn. libr. orgn. and mgmt. sect. 1973-75, planning and budget assembly 1978-79, coun. com. on coms. 1979-80, bldgs. and equipment sect. exec. bd. 1979-80, chmn. bldgs. for coll. and univ. librs. com. 1983-85, chmn. nominating com. libr. history roundtable 1993-94), Okla. Libr. Assn. (life, pres. 1971-72, ALA coun. rep. 1976-80, 83-84, OLA Disting. Svc. award 1979, Spl. Merit award 1987), S.W. Libr. Assn. (chmn. coll. and univ. div. 1958-60, chmn. scholarship com. 1968-70), Internat. Fedn. Libr. Assns. (standing com. on libr. bldgs. and equipment 1976-88), Assn. Coll. and Rsch. Librs. (chmn. univ. librs. sect. 1969-70, mem. exec. bd. and rep. to ALA Coun., 1971-72), U. Mich. Sch. Libr. Sci. Alumni Soc. (pres. 1979-80, Alumni Recognition award 1988), mem. Alumni Found. Com., 1992—, Payne County Ret. Educators Assn. (v.p., pres. elect 1991-92, pres. 1992-93), Okla. Hist. Soc. (com. on Okla. Higher Edn. mus. 1985—), Beta Phi Mu. Baptist (chmn. bd. deacons 1973). Clubs: Archons of Colophon, Stillwater Rotary (dir. 1978-82, pres. 1980-81).

ROUSEFF, RUSSELL LEE, food chemistry educator, researcher; b. Chgo., Nov. 20, 1944; s. Walter and Evelyn Alice Rouseff; m. June Mary-Faye Duren, Aug. 19, 1967; children: Rebecca, Christopher. BS in Chemistry, Wheaton Coll., 1966; MS in Analytic Chemistry, Southern Ill. U., 1968; PhD in Analytic Chemistry, U. Ga., 1972. Chemist Sherwin-Williams Chem. Co. Rsch. Ctr., summers 1964-66; prof. chemistry Polk C.C., Winter Haven, Fla., 1971-74; chemist III sci. rsch. dept. Fla. Dept. Citrus, 1974-77, rsch. scientist I, 1977-81, rsch. scientist II, 1981-85, rsch. scientist III, 1985-87; rsch. prof. food sci. and human nutrition dept. Citrus Rsch. and Edn. Ctr., U. Fla., Lake Alfred, 1987—; Mem. editorial adv. bd. Jour. Agrl. and Food Chemistry, 1982-86, 93—. Co-author: Citrus Fruits and Their Products, 1986; editor: Bitterness in Foods and Beverages, Developments in Food Science Series, 1990; contbr. articles to profl. publs., chpts. to books. Soccer referee U.S. Soccer Fedn., 1990-95. USDA grantee, 1989-92, 92-95. Fellow Am. Chem. Soc. (chmn. local sect., sec./treas. 1974-77, state analytical topic group chmn. 1974-77, nat. mem. chmn. agrl. and food divsn. 1979-83, chmn., program chmn., sec./treas. flavor subdivsn. 1981-86, councilor 1990-93); mem. Inst. Food Technologists (citrus products divsn. sec./treas. 1987-89, sensory divsn., state chmn., program chair 1989-90, exec. com. 1986-88, councilor 1991-95). Office: U Fla Citrus Rsch & Edn Ctr 700 Experiment Station Rd Lake Alfred FL 33850-2243

ROUSSEAU, T(HURL) MARSHALL, museum director; b. Granite City, Ill., Apr. 16, 1933; s. Joseph Carl and Alberta Pearl (Kirkpatrick) R.; m. Jayne Kay Ball, July 6, 1963 (div. Dec. 1, 1977). AB, Valparaiso U., 1955. Copywriter Stix, Baer & Fuller, St. Louis, Mo., 1957-60; advt. dir. Stix, Baer & Fuller, St. Louis, 1968-72; asst. advt. mgr. Neiman Marcus Co., Dallas, 1960-63; sr. copywriter Gardner Advt. Co., St. Louis, 1964-68; sr. v.p. mktg. Robinson's of Fla., St. Petersburg, 1973-86; pres. The Fla. Orchestra, Tampa, 1986-88; v.p. Bay Plaza Cos., St. Petersburg, 1988-90; exec. dir. Salvador Dali Mus., St. Petersburg, 1991—; adj. prof. mus. studies, U. S. Fla., St. Petersburg, 1996. Bd. dirs. Asolo Ctr. for Performing Arts, Sarasota, 1977-87, Salvador Dali Mus., St. Petersburg, 1974—; chmn. bd. govs. Fla. Orch., Tampa, 1983-85; mem. Fla. Arts Coun., Tallahassee, 1984-86. Named Arts Patron of Yr., Pinellas County Arts Coun., Clearwater, Fla., 1981; recipient Silver Medal award St. Petersburg Advt. Club, 1985, Golden Baton award St. Petersburg Symphony Guild, 1987, Disting. Alumnus award, Valparaiso (Ind.) U., 1995. Mem. Mo. Athletic Club. St. Petersburg Yacht Club. Republican. Presbyterian. Home: 639 Cordova Blvd NE Saint Petersburg FL 33704 Office: Salvador Dali Mus 1000 3d St S Saint Petersburg FL 33701

ROUSSEAU, WYATT EASTERLING, pulmonologist, internist; b. Baton Rouge, Mar. 6, 1943; s. Thomas Harrison and Irene Frances (Easterling) R.; m. Eugenia Morris, May 9, 1970 (div. Oct. 1985); children: Jennifer, William Harrison; m. Carolyn Ann Crawford, Apr. 25, 1987. BA, Vanderbilt U., 1965, MD, 1969. Pvt. practice Dallas, 1976—. With USPHS, 1971-73. Fellow ACP, Am. Coll. Chest Physicians, Am. Lung Assn. of Tex. (pres. 1983-84), Am. Lung Assn. (nat. coun. 1995), U. Tex. Southwestern Med. Sch. Alumni (bd. dirs. 1993—). Republican. Episcopalian. Home: 10305 Crittendon Dr Dallas TX 75229 Office: 5439 Glen Lakes Dr Dallas TX 75231

ROUTH, JOHN WILLIAM, lawyer; b. Knoxville, Tenn., Dec. 3, 1957; s. John C. and Mary (Parker) R.; m. Martha Carol Carter, Aug. 6, 1983; children: John Carter, Carol Ann. BA, U. Tenn., 1979, JD, 1983. Bar: Tenn. 1983, U.S. Dist. Ct. (ea. dist.) Tenn. 1983. Assoc. Francis W. Headman, Knoxville, 1983-87, Wm. R. Banks and Assocs., Knoxville, 1987—; judicial commr. Knox County Gen. Sessions Ct., Knoxville, 1992-94. Bd. dirs. Cerebral Palsy Ctr. for Handicapped Adults, Knoxville, 1985-88; chmn. adminstv. bd. Emerald Ave. United Meth. Ch., Knoxville, 1988-90. Mem. Tenn. Bar Assn., Knoxville Bar Assn., Tenn. Assn. Criminal Def. Lawyers, City Salesman Club (v.p. 1988, sec. 1987). Methodist. Office: William R Banks & Assocs 203 W Clinch Ave Knoxville TN 37902-1602

ROUTHENSTEIN, LAWRENCE RICHARD GREEN, software engineer; b. Haverford, Pa., Mar. 5, 1964; s. Warren and Marilyn (Block) R.; m. Lisa Wendy Green, Aug. 25, 1985. BS in Computer Sci., Drexel U., 1987; MS in Computer Sci., Johns Hopkins U., 1992. Sr. computer systems engr. Applied Physics Lab Johns Hopkins U., Laurel, Md., 1987-95; sr. software engr. ISR Global Telecom, Orlando, Fla., 1995—. Developer prototype tactical comms. system analyzer which was adopted as standard equipment by Navy for Aegis cruisers. Recipient scholarship Quest Systems, Phila., 1987, Nat. Merit scholar; nominated for Aegis Excellence award USN. Mem. Assn. Computing Machinery, Pi Mu Epsilon, Phi Eta Sigma. Office: 2600 Lake Lucien Dr Ste 350 Maitland FL 32751-7273

ROUTMAN, DANIEL GLENN, marketing professional, lawyer; b. Birmingham, Ala., July 26, 1961; s. Stanley and Joyce R.; m. Elizabeth Horchow, Mar. 9, 1991; 1 child, Regen. BBA, U. Tex., 1983, JD, 1985. Bar: Tex. 1986. Assoc. Liddell, Sapp, Zivley & LaBoon, Austin, 1986-88, Baker & Botts, Dallas, 1989-91; assoc. gen. counsel Perot '92 Campaign/United We Stand Am., Dallas, 1992-94; prin. Wilson Comms., Dallas, 1994-95; dir. comms. C/Net: The Computer Network, San Francisco, 1996; dir. mktg. AudioNet, Dallas, 1996—. Mem. adv. bd. The Family Gateway, Dallas, 1996—; chmn. jr. assocs. Dallas Mus. Art, 1991-92, Friends of the Ctr. for Human Nutrition U. Tex. Southwestern Med. Sch., 1992-96. Home: 5845 Lupton Dr Dallas TX 75225 Office: AudioNet 2929 Elm St Dallas TX 75226

ROVIS, CHRISTOPHER PATRICK, clinical social worker; b. N.Y.C., Dec. 2, 1950; s. Del Patrick and Patricia Joan (Martin) R.; m. Lorraine Theresa LaPanna, July 26, 1985; children: Lauren Christine, Vincent Christopher. BS, George Mason U., 1973; MSW, Va. Commonwealth U., 1975; cert., Cath. U., 1985; PsyD, Newport U., 1988; cert. in family therapy, Family Therapy Inst., 1984. Lic. clin. social worker, Va., Md. D.C.; diplomate Am. Bd. Examiners in Clin. Social Work. Sr. staff psychotherapist N.W. Ctr. for Community Mental Health, Reston, Va., 1976-84; pvt. practice Tysons Corner Psychotherapy Assocs., Vienna, Va., 1982-91, Ctr. Psychotherapy at Tyson's Corner, Vienna, Va., 1991—. Mem. NASW, Acad. Cert. Social Workers, Greater Washington Soc. for Clin. Social Work. Roman Catholic. Home: 3189 Mary Etta Ln Herndon VA 22071-1620 Office: Ctr Psychotherapy at Tysons Corner 8308 Old Courthouse Rd # B Vienna VA 22182-3809

ROWE, BOBBY LOUISE, art educator; b. Montgomery, Ala., Feb. 15, 1930; d. Herbert and Louise (Barbaree) R. AB, Montevallo U., 1950; MA, Columbia U., 1959; PhD, Fla. State U., 1974. Cert. tchr. K-12 and jr. coll., Fla. Supr. student tchrs. U. Fla. Coll. Edn., Gainesville; assoc. prof. art edn. Mid. Tenn. State U., Murfreesboro; art edn. dir. Cleve. State U.; art curriculum specialist Palm Beach County Sch. Bd., West Palm Beach, Fla.; invited fiber artist, computer imagist, digital photographer; invited lectr. and conf. leader. Mem. Nat. Art Edn. Assn., Am. Edn. Rsch. Assn., Alpha Delta Kappa.

ROWE, BONNIE GORDON, music company executive; b. Buford, Ga., May 3, 1922; s. Bonnie Gordon and Alma (Poole) R.; m. Mary Wilburta Shidler; 1 child, Sharon Lynn; m. Gloria Lucille Fairfax, Feb. 17, 1962 (div.); 1 child, Susan Rebecca. Student Ga. Evening Coll., 1939-41, U. Wichita, 1948-49, Ga. State Coll., 1949-52. Traffic mgr. Bonanza Air Lines, Las Vegas, 1946-48; music tchr. 1948-52; owner Rowe Accordion Distbg. Co., Rowe Accordion Center, Atlanta, 1952-56, Atlanta Music Pub. Co., 1956—, B. Rowe Music Co., Atlanta, 1957—; pres.-treas. B.C.R. Corp. Composer: Accordionique, 1953, Vivolet, 1956, More and More and More, 1964, Dedication, 1964, All I Really See is You, 1965, I Love Only You, 1965, Festival March, 1965, Predudio Reminisci, 1969. Bd. dirs. Sandtown Found., Atlanta. Lt. col. USAAF, World War II, ETO. Decorated Air medals with three oak leaf clusters. Mem. Southeastern Accordion Assn. (past pres.), Nat. Assn. Music Mchts., Atlanta Fedn. Musicians (life mem.), Travelers Protective Assn., Atlanta C. of C., Res. Officers Assn., Ret. Officers Assn., Air Force Assn., Internat. Platform Assn., Am. Legion, Sandtown Civitan Club (past pres., lt. gov., past pres. Met. Atlanta Council), Elks (exalted ruler 1987, 88, 89, past pres. past exalted rulers assn., trustee Union City, state organist Ga. Elks Assn.), Dobbins AFB Officers Club, Gamma Delta Phi. Home: 5085 Erin Rd SW Atlanta GA 30331-7810 Office: 6102 Mableton Pky Mableton GA 30059-4302

ROWE, HENRY THEODORE, JR. (TED ROWE), industrial video producer, director; b. Englewood, N.J., Oct. 8, 1932; s. Henry Theodore and Florence Jane (Bivins) R.; m. Judith Lyttelton Waddell, June 8, 1957 (div. Apr. 1982); children: Henry Theodore III, Lyttelton Waddell, Eliza Ritnour, Virginia Bivins; m. Phyllis Arlene Prevosto, Dec. 26, 1983. Student, Cornell U., 1951-53; BS, St. Lawrence U., 1956; postgrad., Columbia U., 1956-57. Pub. affairs fellow Brookings Instn., Washington, 1961; with IBM Corp., 1957-88; sr. requirements adminstr. IBM Corp., White Plains, N.Y., 1970-76; sr. bus. programs adminstr. IBM Corp., White Plains, also Irving, Tex., 1976-86; cons. mktg. support rep. IBM Corp., Roanoke, Tex., 1986-88; owner Ted Rowe Assocs., Dallas, El Jebel, Colo., 1989—; v.p., bd. dirs. West End Post, Dallas. Co-writer, editor weekly food column Food for Thought. 1st lt. U.S. Army, 1956-57. Mem. Am. Film Inst., Am. Fedn. Musicians, Aspen C. of C. Assn. Republican. Office: Ted Rowe Assocs PO Box 28327 El Jebel CO 81628

ROWE, KATHERINE ELAINE, school counselor, therapist; b. Ada, Okla., Feb. 6, 1951; d. Allen E. and Fannie Mae (Mitchell) Biggs; m. Reginald Dean Rowe, June 3, 1972; children: Regina Kay, Krista Elaine. AS, Murray State Coll., Tishomingo, Okla., 1971; BS, Okla. State U., 1973, MS, 1983, PhD, 1991. Cert. tchr., Okla.; cert. profl. in family and consumer scis. Tchr. Byng Pub. Schs., Ada, 1973-75, 86-93, Maud (Okla.) Pub. Schs., 1976-78, Stratford (Okla.) Pub. Schs., 1982-83; pre-sch. tchr. United Meth. Ch., Ada, 1985-86; asst. prof. Chadron (Nebr.) State Coll., 1993-94; therapist Profl. Counseling Group, Ada, 1996—; counselor Stratford Pub. Schs., 1995—; mem. adv. bd., assessment dept. Mid-Am. Vo-Tech, Wayne, Okla., 1995—. Bd. dirs. March of Dimes, Ada; vol. in polit. campaigns. Nebr. State Dept. Edn. grantee, 1994; At-Risk Counseling grantee Okla. State Dept. Edn., 1996. Mem. Nat. Coun. Family Rels., Am. Assn. Family and Consumer Svcs., Am. Vocat. Assn., Okla. Vocat. Assn., Phi Delta Kappa. Democrat. Methodist.

ROWE, WILLIAM JEFFREY, electrical engineer; b. Columbus, Ga., Mar. 2, 1954; s. William Edmonds and Lillie (Moseley) R.; m. Barbara Herzberg, May 26, 1984; children: Britton Haley, Christine Catherine, William Jeffrey Jr., James Clifford. BA in Econs., Stanford U., 1976; MS in Physics, Ga. State U., 1984; MSEE, U. Fla., 1992. Staff economist U.S. Civil Aeronautics Bd., Washington, 1977-78; econ. rsch. analyst Delta Air Lines, Atlanta, 1978-81; sr. ops. rsch. analyst Lockheed Aeronautical Sys. Co., Marietta, Ga., 1981-83; sr. rsch. engr. Lockheed Aero. Systems Co., Marietta, Ga., 1983-88; sr. engr. Sverdrup Tech. Inc., Eglin AFB, Fla., 1988-90, assoc. prin. engr., 1990-93; project mgr. Sverdrup Tech. Inc./NASA Ames Rsch. Ctr., Moffett Field, Calif., 1993-96; team leader F-22 ground test svcs. Lockheed Martin Aeronautical Sys. Co., Marietta, 1996—; cons. in field. Contbr. articles to profl. jours.; inventor/patentee in field. Mem. IEEE, AIAA (selected sensor systems tech. com. 1991). Roman Catholic. Home: 3706 Thunder Way Marietta GA 30066 Office: Lockheed Martin Aeronautical Sys Co Dept 73-40 Zone 0990 Marietta GA 30063

ROWELL, JOHN THOMAS, psychologist, consultant; b. Lloyd, Fla., Mar. 21, 1920; s. Irvin Caleb and Esther Estelle (Rowden) R.; m. Mabel Zelma Hartwell Mason, Aug. 15, 1942; children: James Roger, Douglas Hugh, Martin Allen. BA, U. Mich., 1949; MA, Fla. State U., 1950, PhD, 1958. RN, Mass. Chief psychologist Milledgeville (Ga.) State Hosp., 1951-57; human factors scientist RAND Corp., Santa Monica, Calif., 1957, System Devel. Corp., Santa Monica, 1957-58; branch head System Devel. Corp., Ft. Lee, Va., 1958-61; group leader System Devel. Corp., Santa Monica, 1961-63; br. mgr. System Devel. Corp., Falls Church, Va., 1963-69; pres. N.C. Leadership Inst., Greensboro, N.C., 1969-72; v.p. Essex Corp., Alexandria, Va., 1972; pres. John Rowell Assocs., Greensboro, 1972-87, New Bern, N.C., 1987-93; cons. indsl. orgns. in southeastern U.S. Co-author: National Document Handling Systems for Science and Technology, 1976; contbr. articles to profl. jours. Bd. dirs. Goodwill Industries, Greensboro, 1973-87, Greensboro Mental Health Assn., Greensboro, 1976-81, Epilepsy Assn. N.C., Greensboro, 1977-81. With U.S. Army, 1943-46. Recipient commendation White House, 1975. Mem. Am. Psychol. Assn., N.C. Psychol. Assn., S.E. Psychol. Assn., Guilford County Psychol. Assn. (pres. 1974, Citation 1975), Rotary (chmn. com.). Republican.

ROWLAND, ARTHUR RAY, librarian; b. Hampton, Ga., Jan. 6, 1930; s. Arthur and Jennie (Goodman) R.; m. Jane Thomas, July 1, 1955; children: Dell Ruth, Anna Jane. A.B., Mercer U., Macon, Ga., 1951; M. Librarianship, Emory U., 1952. Circulation asst. Ga. State Coll. Library, 1952, circulation librarian, 1952-53; librarian Armstrong Coll., Savannah, Ga., 1954-56; head circulation dept. Auburn U. Library, 1956-58; librarian, asso. prof. library sci. Jacksonville U., 1958-61; librarian, asso. prof. library sci. Augusta Coll., 1961-76, prof., libr., 1976-91, libr. emeritus, 1991—; lectr. libr. edn. U. Ga., 1962-66; trustee Augusta-Richmond County Pub. Libr., 1980-93, pres. bd. trustees, 1983-85, v.p. bd., 1988-91; trustee Augusta Regional Libr., chmn., 1984-85; trustee East Cen. Ga. Regional Libr., 1987-93, chmn., 1988-91; chmn. Gov.'s Conf. on Ga. Librs. and Info. Svcs., 1977; del. White House Conf. on Librs. and Info. Sci., 1979; cons. on libr. mgmt. to Govt. of Indonesia, 1986. Author: Bibliography of the Writings of Georgia History, 1966, A Guide to the Study of Augusta and Richmond County, Georgia, 1967, (with Helen Callahan) Yesterday's Augusta, 1976, (with James E. Dorsey) A Bibliography of the Writings on Georgia History 1900-1970, rev. edit., 1978, (with Marguerite F. Fogleman) Reese Library Genealogical Resources, 1988, supplement, 1990, Goodman Cousins, 1988, Rowland Cousins, 1990, New Guide to the Study of Augusta, 1990, Index to City Directory of Augusta, Georgia, 1841-1879, 1991, More Goodman Cousins, 1993, My Fair Grandmother, 1994, Distant Cousins, The Huguenots Connecting Rowland, Bulloch, de Bourdeaux, DeVeaux and Roosevelt Families of S.C., N.C. and Ga., 1995, The Bessent Family of Georgia, 1995, Reeves Family of Georgia, 1996, Descendants of Wiley Reeves, 1996, Rowland-Huckaby Connections, 1996; editor: Reference Services, 1964, Historical Markers of Richmond County, Georgia, rev. edit., 1971, The Catalog and Cataloging, 1969, The Librarian and Reference Service, 1977, Reminiscences of Augusta Marines, 1985; supervising editor (with Heard Robertson) Jour. Archibald Campbell, 1981; contbr. to profl. jours. V.p. Ga. Libr. Assn. Trustees and Friends, 1989-91. With USN, 1948-49. Recipient Nix-Jones award for disting. service Ga. Library Assn., 1981,,Town and Gown award Augusta Coll. Alumni Assn., 1985. Mem. ALA, Am. Assn. State and Local History, Bibliog. Soc. Am., Southeastern Libr. Assn. (hon. life, exec. bd. 1971-72), Ga. Libr. Assn. (hon. life, 2d v.p. 1965-67, 71-73, 1st v.p., pres.-elect 1973-75, pres. 1975-77, chmn. budget com. 1977-79, adv. to pres. 1979-83, 85-92), Ctrl. Savannah River Area Libr. Assn. (past pres., editor union list of serials 1967), Duval County Libr. Assn. (past v.p.), Nat. Geneal. Soc., Ga. Geneal. Soc., N.C. Geneal. Soc., Va. Geneal. Soc., Augusta Geneal. Soc., Richmond County Hist. Soc. (curator 1964-91, pres. 1967-69, founder, editor Richmond County History), Ga. Hist. Soc. (curator emeritus), Ga. Bapt. Hist. Soc., Nat., Young Men's Libr. Assn. (v.p. 1988-91), Ga. Trusts for Hist. Preservation, Hist. Augusta (trustee emeritus), Soc. Ga. Archivists, Kappa Phi Kappa. Baptist. Address: One Seventh St Ste 1503 Augusta GA 30901

ROWLAND, DAVID JACK, academic administrator; b. Columbus, Ohio, June 17, 1921; s. David Henry and Ethel (Ryan) R.; m. Mary Ellen Stinson, Apr. 8, 1944; children: David Allen, Ryan Stinson, Sue Ellen Rowland Summers. BS, Ohio U., 1949; MA, U. Ala., 1951; LittD (hon.), Athens State Coll., 1967; LLD (hon.), Jacksonville State U., 1969. Pres. Walker Coll., Jasper, Ala., 1956-88, chancellor, 1988-95; interim pres. U. Ala./Walker Coll., 1995-96; bd. dirs. First Nat. Bank, Jasper, first Comml. Bancshares, Birmingham, Ala.; chmn. Ala. ACT Bd., Tuscaloosa, 1968—; real estate developer. Chmn. Jasper Indsl. Bd., 1987—; commr. Ala. Mining commn., Jasper, 1976—; mem. Ala. Employer Guard Res. commn., Birmingham, 1988—; trustee Walker Coll.; chmn. adv. bd. Jasper Salvation Army. Col. U.S. Army, 1942-46, ATO. Decorated Legion of Merit; recipient Silver Beaver award Boy Scouts Am., 1972. Mem. Res. Officers Assn. (pres. Jasper chpt.), Summit Club, Met. Dinner Club, Rotary (pres. Jasper 1967-68, Paul Harris fellow), Masons. Home: 1005 Valley Rd Jasper AL 35501-4964 Office: Walker Coll Office of President UAB/Walker College Jasper AL 35501

ROWLAND, PATRICIA ANN, special education educator; b. N.Y.C., Nov. 27, 1956; d. Francis James and Frances Patricia McCarty; m. Robert Michael Rowland, Sept. 2, 1978; 1 child, Kelly Margaret. BA in Edn., Fla. Atlantic U., 1978, MEd, 1987. Tchr., autistic students Palm Beach County Sch. System, West Palm Beach, Fla., 1978-82, tchr., adult mentally handicapped, 1983-85; instr., literacy Palm Beach County Schs./Boca Raton (Fla.) Hosp., 1986-90; instr., literacy/GED Fla. Atlantic U., Boca Raton, 1990—; instr., adult mentally handicapped sr. citizens Palm Beach Habilitation Ctr., Lake Worth, Fla., 1990-93; PALS lab. instr. Pvt. Industry Coun., Delray Beach, 1992—; dir. family literacy program Lincoln Elem. Sch., Riviera Beach, Fla., 1993—. Bd. dirs. Trinity Lutheran Sch., Delray Beach. Grantee Fla. Atlantic U., 1983; recipient pres.'s award Palm Beach County Literacy Coalition, 1995. Fellow Broward/Palm Beach Autistic Soc. (sec. 1981-82); mem. Coun. Exceptional Edn. of Mentally Retarded, Lit. Coalition (chairperson S. Network Palm Beach County 1994—), Adult and Cmty. Educators Fla., Fla. Atlantic U. Alumni Assn. Home: 629 West Dr Delray Beach FL 33445-8715

ROWLETT, BOBBY N., executive of fitness equipment company; b. 1952. Grad., Ark. State U., 1974. Acct. Touche Ross, Memphis, Tenn., 1974-80; treas. Jacuzzi, Inc., Little Rock, Ark., 1980-87; pres. Troxel Co., Inc., Moscow, Tenn., 1987—. Office: Troxel Co Inc Hwy 57 W Moscow TN 38057

ROWLEY, CHARLES KERSHAW, economics educator; b. Southampton, Eng., June 21, 1939; came to U.S., 1984; s. Frank and Ellen (Beal) R.; m. Betty Silverwood, June 19, 1961 (div. 1971); m. Marjorie Isobel Spillets, July 17, 1972; children: Amanda, Sarah. Lectr. U. Nottingham, Eng., 1962-65; lectr., then sr. lectr. U. Kent, Canterbury, Eng., 1965-70; reader U. York, Eng., 1970-72; prof. econs. U. Newcastle, Eng., 1972-83, George Mason U., Fairfax, Va., 1984—, gen. dir. John Locke Inst., 1989—, sr. rsch. assoc. Ctr. for Study of Pub. Choice, 1987-92; cons. Office Fair Trading, London, 1980-83; rsch. assoc. Wolfson Coll., Oxford, 1984—. Author numerous books in econ.and law; editor: Pub. Choice, 1990—; contbr. articles to profl. jours. Grantee Bank of Eng., 1965, Social Sci. Rsch. Coun., London, 1970-72, Dept. Environ., London, 1974-80, Bradley Found., 1988—, Liberty Fund, 1990, 93, John M. Olin Found., 1986. Mem. Mont Pelerin Soc., Am. Econ. Assn., Royal Econ. Soc., Pub. Choice Soc., European Pub. Choice Soc. (pres. 1980-82) Home: 5188 Dungannon Rd Fairfax VA 22030-5414 Office: George Mason U Ctr Study Pub Choice 4400 University Dr Fairfax VA 22030-4443 also: The Locke Inst 4094 University Dr Fairfax VA 22030

ROWSEY, NORA KATHLEEN, management consultant; b. Ypsilanti, Mich., July 1, 1954; d. Eldron Carpenter and Vivian Irene (Fouty) R. LPN, Oakland Community Coll., Royal Oak, Mich., 1980; ASN, U. State N.Y., Albany, 1986; BS in Applied Organizational Mgmt. cum laude, Tusculum Coll., 1989. RN, lic. practical nurse. Staff nurse orthopedics, med. surg. Pontiac (Mich.) Osteo. Hosp., alternate charge nurse ICU, 1987-91; DON nursing Superior Home Health Care, Inc., Maryville, Tenn.; home care cons. Alpha Med., Chattanooga, 1991-94; exec. dir. of profl. svcs. Putnam Home Health Care, Inc., Palatka, Fla., 1994—, Superior Home Care, Jacksonville, Fla., 1994—. Home: 390 A1A Beach Blvd Apt 59 Saint Augustine FL 32084-5992

ROY, ELSIJANE TRIMBLE, federal judge; b. Lonoke, Ark., Apr. 2, 1916; d. Thomas Clark and Elsie Jane (Walls) Trimble; m. James M. Roy, Nov. 23, 1943; 1 son, James Morrison. JD, U. Ark., Fayetteville, 1939; LLD (hon.), U. Ark., Little Rock, 1978. Bar: Ark. 1939. Atty. Rose, Loughborough, Dobyns & House, Little Rock, 1940-41, Ark. Revenue Dept., Little Rock, 1941-42; mem. firm Reid, Evrard & Roy, Blytheville, Ark., 1945-54, Roy & Roy, Blytheville, 1954-63; law clk. Ark. Supreme Ct., Little Rock, 1963-65; assoc. justice Ark. Supreme Ct., 1975-77; U.S. dist. judge then sr. judge Ea. and We. Dists. Ark., Little Rock, 1977—; judge Pulaski County (Ark.) Cir. Ct., Little Rock, 1966; asst. atty. gen. Ark., Little Rock, 1967; sr. law clk. U.S. Dist. Ct., Little Rock and Ft. Smith, 1967-75; Mem. med. adv. com. U. Ark. Med. Center, 1952-54; Committeewoman Democratic Party 16th Jud. Dist., 1940-42; vice chmn. Ark. Dem. State Com., 1946-48; mem. chmn. com. Ark. Constnl. Commn., 1967-68. Recipient disting. alumnae citation U. Ark., 1978, Gayle Pettus Pontz award, 1986, Brooks Hays Meml. Christian Citizenship award, 1994; named Ark. woman of yr., Bus. and Profl. Women's Club, 1969, 76, outstanding appellate judge, Ark. Trial Lawyers Assn., 1976-77, Delta Theta Phi mem. of yr. 1989; named among top 100 women in Ark. bus., 1995; Paul Harris fellow Rotary Club Little Rock, 1992. Recipient disting. alumnae citation U. Ark., 1978, Gayle Pettus Pontz award, 1986, Brooks Hays Meml. Christian Citizenship award, 1994; named Ark. Woman of Yr., Bus. and Profl. Women's Club, 1969, 76, Outstanding Appellate Judge, Ark. Trial Lawyers Assn., 1976-77, Mem. of Yr., Delta Theta Phi, 1989; named among top 100 women in Ark. bus., 1995, Ark. Bus. Top 100 Women in Ark., 1995; Paul Harris fellow Rotary Little Rock, 1992. Office: US Dist Ct 600 W Capitol Ave Rm 423 Little Rock AR 72201-3326

ROY, RICHARD JAMES, lawyer, engineer, consultant; b. New Orleans, Jan. 30, 1944; s. Alphonse Kennision Roy and Elizabeth Louise (Roscoe) McIntosh; m. Elise Schroder, Dec. 26, 1976 (div. Aug. 1979); m. Marci Horne, June 6, 1986; 1 child, Michael. BSME, Tulane U., 1966, JD, 1981. Bar: La. 1981, Tex. 1982. Project mgr. Mech. Constrn., New Orleans, 1965-68; pres. R. J. Roy Constrn., New Orleans, 1968-70; project mgr. Crown Bldrs., Baton Rouge, 1970-71, Belemy Bros., Atlanta, 1971-72; v.p. Construcciones Werl, San Juan, P.R., 1972-78; sr. contract adminstr. Ebasco Services, New Orleans, 1978-81; atty. Raymond Internat., Houston, 1981-85; pres. Gleason Peacock & Roy, Houston, 1985-92, Roy & Assocs., Galveston, Tex., 1992—. Mem. ABA, La. Bar Assn., Tex. Bar Assn., Houston Bar Assn. (ADR com. 1983—, mediator 1986—), Am. Arbitration Assn., ASME, Nat. Soc. Profl. Engrs., Tex. Soc. Profl. Engrs., Nat. Acad. Forensic Engrs. Republican. Office: Roy & Assocs 6025 Heards Ln Ste 4W Galveston TX 77551-5036

ROYAK, ELIZABETH, credit union executive. Chmn. bd., dir. Pinellas County Tchrs. Credit Union, Largo, Fla. Office: Pinellas County Teachers Cr Un 10125 Ulmerton Rd Largo FL 33771-3532*

ROYALL, RICHARD ROYSTER, classical music festival administrator; b. Richmond, Va., May 22, 1941; s. Richard Royster Royall and Blanche May (Allbritton) Gore. BA, Princeton U., 1963; BL, U. Tex., 1967. Rep. Shaw Concerts, N.Y.C., 1968-70; dir. info. James Dick, Concert Pianist, Austin, Tex., 1970-71; treas. James Dick Found., Round Top, Tex., 1971—; mng. dir. Festival-Inst., Round Top, 1971—; mem. exec. com. James Dick Found., Round Top, 1976—. Contbg. writer: New Handbook of Texas, 6 vols., 1996. Mem. Sesqui-Centennial com. State of Tex. for Round Top, 1986. Rotary Internat. student fellow, Heidelberg, Germany, 1963-64. Office: Festival Inst at Round Top PO Box 89 Round Top TX 78954

ROYCE, E. SCOTT, legal researcher, writer; b. Phila., Oct. 26, 1951; s. Robert R. and Henrietta D. (Follmer) R.; m. Julie Ann Floyd, June 9, 1984. BA, U. Va., 1973. Editor, researcher Kephart Comm., Alexandria, Va., 1973-76; legal researcher Nat. Right to Work Legal Def. Found., Springfield, Va., 1973—; mem. com. scholars Agorist Inst., Beverly Hills, Calif., 1986—. Editor So. Libertarian Rev., 1974-78, Freedom in History, 1984-86; contbg. editor New Libertarian, 1976—, Agorist Quar., 1995—; contbr. articles to numerous mags., newsletters and newspapers. Exec. dir. Va. Coll. Rep. Fedn., 1970, Coll. Youth for Garland, 1970, No. Virginians Against Involuntary Servitude, 1979-81; mem. nat. exec. com. Libertarian Party, 1972-74; rsch. dir., speechwriter Beale for Del., 1975, 77; mem. nat. adv. bd. Libertarian-Rep. Alliance, 1975-78; rsch. dir. Callahan for Congress, 1976; mem. nat. adv. bd. Ripon Soc., 1979-80; mem. bd. Washington Peace Ctr., 1979-80; coord. Arlington (Va.) Clark for Pres. Com., 1980; del. 10th Congl. Dist. Dem. Party Conv., 1984. Named hon. Ky. Col., Gov. Louis Nunn, 1971. Mem. ACLU, Orgn. Am. Historians, Peace History Soc. Home: PO Box 10607 Arlington VA 22210-1607

ROYER, DAVID LEE, investment banker; b. Clarksburg, W.Va., Mar. 12, 1952; s. Chris W. and Virginia M. Royer; m. Patricia A. Martin, Aug. 30, 1973 (div. Jan. 1991); 1 child, Amy. BSBA, Salem Coll., 1973; MBA, W.Va. U., 1979. Asst. to v.p. mktg. Mylan Labs., Pitts., 1974-78; internat. sales mgr. Neville Chem. Co., Pitts., 1978-82; pres. Seneca Leasing Co., Pitts., 1982-83; regional lease mgr. Prime Computer Inc., Pitts., 1982-84; regional dir. Heather Fin. Corp., Pitts., 1985-86; nat. dir. sales and mktg. Joy Fin. Co., Pitts., 1986-88; nat. account rep. Transam. Comml. Fin. Corp., Pitts., 1988-90; bus. devel. mgr. Integra Fin. Corp./Integra Bus. Credit Corp., Pitts., 1990-91; v.p. investment analyst NationsBank/NationsBanc Leasing Corp., Tucker, Ga., 1991—; presenter workshops in field. EMT, Doddridge County Ambulance Svc., 1972-73, Harrison County Emergency Squad, 1971-73; lt. Salem (W.Va.) Vol. Fire Dept., 1968-73; bus. advisor Jr. Achievement, Western Pa., 1984; fin. advisor, fin. adv. bd. Ch. of God, World Hdqrs., 1979—. Mem. Ga. Canoe Assn., Atlanta Divers, Atlanta Ski Club, Atlanta Oceans Club (project leader Adopt-a-Stream program 1993—), Atlanta Reef Dwellers. Home: 775 Jackson Bank Pl NW Lilburn GA 30247-6085 Office: NationsBank 2300 Northlake Center Dr Tucker GA 30084-4007

ROYSTON, LLOYD LEONARD, educational marketing consultant; children: Sharon, William, Jayston. AB, Talladega Coll., 1958; MEd, Tuskegee Inst., 1971; EdD, U. Ala., 1980. Cert. tchr., counselor. Tchr. Ala. State Bd. Edn., Dadeville, 1959-63; social caseworker N.Y.C. Social Services, 1963-65; continuing edn. Tuskegee Inst., Ala., 1965-77, dir. human resources, 1980; faculty devel. coordinator U. Ala., University, 1977-80; dean continuing edn. Pensacola Jr. Coll., Fla., 1982-86; sr. assoc. Ednl. Transactions Assocs., 1986—; spl. cons. Ala. A&M U., 1988, assoc. dean Sch. Grad. Studies, 1988-89; head staff and program devel., Tuskegee U., 1990-93; asst. to dir. mktg. rels. Auburn U. Coop. Ext. Svc., 1993—; cons. AID, 1976-78, Multi-Racial Corp., New Orleans, 1970-72. Author: Methods of Teaching Adults, 1968, Planning Practices At Predominantly Black Institutions, 1980. Bd. dirs. PUSH, Pensacola, 1983, Wedgewood Homeowners Assn., Pensacola, 1982, Fla. Inst. Govt., U. West Fla., 1982-86, Pvt. Industry Council, Pensacola, 1984-86; mem. Ganett Found. Scholarship Com., 1984. Recipient Service award Dept. Social Service N.Y.C., 1964, Outstanding service award Ala. Migrant Council, 1974, Youth Services award Tuskegee Inst., 1977, Service award Equal Opportunity Commn., Pensacola, 1985. Mem. Am. Council on Edn., Am. Assn. Adult and Continuing Edn., Talladega Alumni Assn. (v.p. 1984-86), Kappa Delta Pi. Baptist. Avocations: fishing, camping, swimming, specialty cooking.

ROYTMAN, GRIGORY, education educator; b. Odessa, USSR, June 25, 1937; came to U.S., 1979.; s. Lev Moiseevich and Mila Grigorevna (Kachurovskaya) R.; m. Lidiya Petrovna Krylov, Mar. 30, 1970 (div. Apr. 1973). Diploma, Pedagogical Inst., Odessa, 1967; MA in Curriculum and Teaching, Columbia U., 1983, EdM in Curriculum and Teaching, 1983, EdD in Curriculum and Teaching, 1985. Bilingual tchr. Odessa Secondary Sch., 1968-70; English translator tech. info. Tech. News Info., Moscow, 1970-75, 77-78; English tchr. Moscow Secondary Sch., 1975-77; freelance editor tech. translations of Russian jours. Allerton Press Inc., N.Y.C., 1979-80; field cons. Office Ednl. Evaluation N.Y.C. Bd. Edn., 1982; cons. Jewish Ednl. Svc. N.Am., Inc., 1985; Russian lang. instr. Def. Lang. Inst., Monterey, Calif., 1986-90; lectr. Russian Dept. fgn. langs. and lits. Appalachian State U., Boone, N.C., 1990-92, asst. prof. Russian, 1990—; lectr. on acculturation and identity of Russian immigrants, 1985-86; presenter papers in field. Contbr. articles to profl. publs.; translator various short stories, articles. Bilingual edn. grantee Title VII, 1980-83. Mem. MLA, So. Atlantic MLA, Am. Assn. Tchrs. Slavic and East European Langs. Home: 132 Stoney Brook Ct Boone NC 28607 Office: Appalachian State U Dept Fgn Langs and Lits Boone NC 28608

ROZELL, MARK JAMES, political scientist, educator; b. Paterson, N.J., Oct. 26, 1959; s. Robert Morris and Josephine (Imperato) R.; m. Lynda Marie Gucker, June 11, 1983. BA, Eisenhower Coll., 1982; MA, U. Va., 1983, PhD, 1987. Assoc. prof. polit. sci. Mary Washington Coll., Fredericksburg, Va., 1986-95; rsch. assoc. prof. White Burkett Miller Ctr., U. Va., Charlottesville, 1996; assoc. prof. polit. sci. Am. U., Washington, 1996—; media analyst numerous broadcast stas., newspapers, mags., Washington, Va., 1988—; sokr. civic, bus. and govt. groups, Va., Washington, 1988—; lectr. grad. program in congl. studies Cath. U., 1996—. Author: The Press and the Carter Presidency, 1989, The Press and the Ford Presidency, 1992, Executive Privilege, 1994, In Contempt of Congress, 1996, The Press and the Bush Presidency, 1996; (with Clyde Wilcox) Second Coming: The New Christian Right in Virginia Politics, 1996. Fellow Dirksen Ctr., 1995-96, Earhart Found., 1995, NEH, 1992. Mem. Acad. Polit. Sci., Ctr. for Study of Presidency, Am. Polit. Sci. Assn. (rsch. grantee 1994), So. Polit. Sci. Assn., We. Polit. Sci. Assn. Home: 8426 Bowling Green Ct Vienna VA 22180 Office: Amer U Sch Pub Affairs Tenly Campus Washington DC 20016-8083

RUA, MILTON FRANCISCO, retired lawyer; b. San German, P.R., Dec. 8, 1919; s. Urbano F. and Josefa A. (Gonzalez-Ferrer) R.; BA cum laude, U. P.R., 1941, LLB, 1943; m. Barbara Ann Becher (dec. Nov. 1989); children by previous marriage: Milton J., Jaime L. Admitted to P.R. bar, 1943; legal counsel Dept. Finance of P.R., 1943-46; sr. partner Rivera-Zayas, Rivera-Cestero & Rua, San Juan, P.R., 1950-73; founder Milton F. Rua Law Offices, San Juan, P.R., 1973-86; founder, counsellor Banco Mercantil de P.R., Rio Piedras, 1966—, chmn. bd. dirs., 1975—; founder Asso. Ins. Agencies, Inc., San Juan, 1972, Fajardo Fed. Savs. & Loan Assn., 1972—. Mem. bar exam. com. Supreme Ct. P.R., 1955-56; spl. counsel com. natural resources and beautification P.R. Ho. of Reps., 1967-68; mem. citizens com. nuc. plants Environ. Quality Bd. of P.R., 1972; chmn. Electoral Reform Commn., 1973-74; mem. organizing com. First Latin Am. Biennal Graphic Arts, P.R., 1970; bd. dirs. Casa el Libro, chmn., 1960-70; bd. dirs. Inst. of Culture of P.R., 1968-79, Students Art League of San Juan, Mus. P.R., P.R. Found. for Humanities, 1981-84; trustee Advance Ctr. for Studies P.R. and Caribbean, 1986—. Mem. Found. Bar Assn. P.R. (hon. pres. 1976-78), Bar Assn. P.R., Am., Inter-Am. bar assns., Iberoamerican Inst. Aero. Law. Clubs: Bankers, Union League (N.Y.C.), Elks. Address: Cond Din # 10 Candina 10 San Juan PR 00907-1705

RUBBA, ROSE ANN, electronics technician; b. Atlantic City, N.J., May 3, 1965; d. Joseph Paul Rubba Sr. and Rose Francis Butterhof. AS, Atlantic C.C., 1986; Electronics diploma, RETS, Metairie, La., 1987. Asst. PC Ctr. Alton Ochsner Med. Found., New Orleans, 1986-87, electronics technician, 1989—; customer svc. engr. Xerox, Mt. Laurel, N.J., 1987-88; shop technician Adrian Lewis, Inc., Hammonton, N.J., 1988-89. Recipient Peter Francis Edgar award Policeman Daughter scholarship, Atlantic City, 1983, 84, Tchr. Svc. award Kiawanis, Hammonton, N.J., 1983. Mem. Am. Legion (ladies aux.). Home: 2824 Kingman St Apt C Metairie LA 70006-6651 Office: Alton Ochsner Med Found 1516 Jefferson Hwy New Orleans LA 70121-2429

RUBENS, LINDA MARCIA, home health services administrator; d. Harry and Ruth Slutzah; m. Robert A. Rubens; children: Scott, Mark. AS, Fla. Jr. Coll., Jacksonville. Lic. nursing home adminstr. RN U. Hosp. of Jacksonville, 1976-82; dir. nursing Mandarin Manor Nursing Home and Retirement Village, 1982-85, asst. adminstr., 1985-87; dir. nursing P.H.E.O. Med. Ctr., 1987-88; dir. clin. and profl. svcs. Kimberly Quality Care, 1988-90, br. mgr., 1990-93; adminstr. Health Care Mgmt. Cons., Jacksonville, 1993—; exec. dir. Mount Carmel Gardens Retirement Cmty., 1995—; part-time Dept. Labor, Office of Worker's Compensation, 1992—. Past mem. Gerontol. Search Team for Cathedral Found.; past treas. Mayor's Orgn. for Vol. Effort, past bd. dirs.; vice chairperson State-Wide Human Rights Adv. Com., chairperson consumer rels. subcom., 1990—; apptd. to Dist. IV Ombudsman Com., 1982-90, Dist. IV Human Rights Adv. Com., 1989-90; bd. dirs. Mt. Carmel Retirement Cmty., State Mental Health Planning Coun.; chairperson Statewide Human Rights Advocacy Com., State of Fla. Mem. Rehab. Nurses Assn., Dirs. of Nursing Assn. (sec. long term care). Home: 13116 Mandarin Rd Jacksonville FL 32223-1748

RUBENS, PHILIP, communications educator, technical writer; b. Washington, Jan. 13, 1943; s. Maurice and Anna Mae (Kindilien) R.; m. Brenda Knowles, May 4, 1969; children: Theresa Marie Norman, Alesia Lauree Chavez. BA, U. Tex., Arlington, 1970; MA, U. Tex., 1972; PhD, No. Ill. U., 1976. Instr. Braniff Airways, Santiago, Chile, 1966-67; teaching asst. U. Tex. at Arlington, 1970-71, No. Ill. U., DeKalb, 1972-74; asst. prof. William Rainey Harper Coll., Chgo., 1975-76; assoc. prof. Mich. Tech. U., Houghton, 1976-80; prof. visual & tech. comm. Rensselaer Poly. Inst., Troy, N.Y., 1980—; tech. writer Washington Gas Light Co.; dir. comm. Braniff Airways, LTV Aerospace, Gas Dynamics Lab., City of Arlington; sr. rsch. assoc. TechWriting Affiliates, Inc.; cons. in field including Software Group, 1984, N.Y. Edn. Assn., 1981-84, IBM Corp., 1984, 85, 87, TechWriting Affiliates Inc., 1985, 86, 88—, Short Bros., Inc., Belfast, Ireland, 1985, Info. Assocs., 1985, DuPont Corp., 1985, Bell Labs., 1985, U. Leeds, 1986, High Tech., Inc., Tokyo, 1987. Editor: (book) Science and Technical Writing: A Manual of Style, 1993; mem. editorial bd. Mohawk Monitor, 1980—, Roxbury Press, 1986, Iowa Jour. Bus. and Tech. Comm., 1987—, Computers and Composition, 1987—, MIT Press, 1988—. Mem. Smithsonian Inst., Washington, 1976—; faculty advisor Keweenaw Chpt. Soc. for Tech. Comm., 1976-80; mem. Sierra Club, 1980—; dept. rep. Hudson-Mohawk Consortium, 1980-81; sustaining mem. No. Ill. U. Exec. Alumni Assn., 1980—; chair, membership com. Mohawk Chpt. Soc. for Tech. Comm., 1980-81, vice chair, 1981-82; exec. alumni U. Tex. at Arlington, 1981—; mem. Saratoga Sailing Club, 1981—, Saratoga Performing Arts Ctr., 1981—; mem. Westport (Conn.) Hist. Soc., 1985—. Recipient Chgo. Poetry Soc. Award for Outstanding Religious Poetry, Award for Outstanding Children's Poetry, Award for Most Outstanding Poem for Yr., 1975, Writer's Key for Outstanding Writing Ability, Sigma Tau Delta, 1976, Chpt. Achievement award Soc. for Tech. Comm., 1979, Outstanding Article award, 1982, Tchr. of Excellence award N.Y. State English Coun., 1984, Award of Merit for Softbridge Online Tutorial, 1986; MIT Sloan Sch. Mgmt. Rsch. fellow, 1990, Soc. for Tech. Comm. fellow, 1992. Mem. AAAS (edn. com. 1982—, MLA, Am. Bus. Comm. Assn. (chair undergrad. studies com. 1977), Coun. for Programs in Tech. and Sci. Comm. (charter mem., judge CPTSC Logo Competition 1982), IEEE Profl. Comm. Soc. (edn. com. 1986, co-program chair of 1989 conf.), Midwest MLA, Nat. Coun. Tchrs. English (mem. tech. writing com. 1976—), Popular Culture Assn., Sci. Fiction Rsch. Assn., Sci. Writing Educators Group, Soc. for Tech. Comm. (judge internat. audio-visual competition 1985— and others. Home: 303 Bebington Dr Cary NC 27513-1750 Office: Rensselaer Poly Inst Sage Labs Troy NY 12180

RUBENSTEIN, BERNARD, orchestra conductor; b. Springfield, Mo., Oct. 30, 1937; s. Milton and Evelyn Marion (Friedman) R.; m. Ann Warren Little, Aug. 28, 1961; children: Tanya, Stefan Alexei. B.Mus. with distinction, Eastman Sch. Music, U. Rochester, 1958; M.Mus., Yale U., 1961. Assoc. prof. conducting, dir. orch. orgns. Northwestern U., Evanston, Ill., 1968-80. Asst. condr. R.I. Philharm. Orch., 1961-62; condr. music dir. Santa Fe Symphony Orch., 1962-64; condr. Greenwood Chamber Orch., Cummington, Mass., 1968-79; asst. condr. Stuttgart Opera, 1966-68; condr., music dir. Music for Youth, Milw., 1970-80; assoc. condr. Cin. Symphony Orch., 1980-86; music dir. Tulsa Philharm., 1984-96, condr., 1996; guest condr. numerous orchs. including Milw. Symphony Orch., St. Paul Chamber Orch., Guadalajara Symphony Orch., Berlin Radio Orch., Frankfurt Radio Orch., Grant Park Orch., Chgo., die reihe, Vienna, Austrian Radio Orch., Eastman Philharm., Halle Symphony Orch., E. Ger., Warsaw Philharm., St. Louis Little Symphony, W. German Radio Orch., Palazzo Pitti Orch. Florence, Italy, Frankfurt Opera, Tonkuenstler Orch., Vienna, S.W. German Radio Orch., Baden-Baden, Jerusalem Symphony, Anchorage, Hamilton, Ont., Hartford Conn., L.A. Chamber Orch., Austin (Tex.) Symphony, Am. Composers Orch. N.Y.C. Winner internat. conducting competition Serate Musicale Fiorentine, 1965; Fulbright scholar, 1964-66; recipient Charles Ditson award Yale U., 1961, Martha Baird Rockefeller award, 1966-68. Mem. Am. Symphony Orch. League. Office: 1070 Governor Dempsey Dr Santa Fe NM 87501-1078

RUBIN, BERNARD ROSS, osteopathic medicine educator; b. Springfield, Ill., May 10, 1950. BS, U. Ill., Urbana, 1972; DO, Coll. Osteo. Medicine, Chgo., 1976. Diplomate Nat. Bd. Examiners for Osteo. Physicians and Surgeons, Am. Bd. Internal Medicine. Intern Chgo. Osteo. Hosp., Chgo., 1976-77; resident in Internal Medicine Albert Einstein Med. Ctr., Phila., 1977-80, fellow in Rheumatology, 1980-81; fellow in Rheumatology Thomas Jefferson U. Sch. Medicine, Phila., 1981-82; instr. Medicine, fellow in Clin. Immunology Hahnemann U. Sch. Medicine, Phila., 1982-83; asst. prof. Medicine Tex. Coll. Osteo. Medicine, Ft. Worth, 1983-87, chief divsn. Rheumatology, 1985—, assoc. prof. Medicine, 1987-92, prof. Medicine, 1992—. Contbr. chpts. to books, articles to profl. jours. Active Ft. Worth Symphony Soc., Presbyn. Night Shelter Homeless Clinic; v.p., bd. dirs. N.W. chpt. Arthritis Found., 1985-87; bd. dirs. Ft. Worth Opera, 1989—, Ft. Worth Mus. Sci. & History, 1993—, Stage West, 1991—, Casa Manana, 1993—, Easter Seal Soc. Tarrant County, 1990-93, 1st v.p., 1991-92; assoc. med. dir. Arthritis Care Ctr., Ft. Worth. 1991—; sect. chair United Way Tarrant County, 1992, 93. Fellow ACP, Am. Coll. Rheumatology; mem. Osteo. Assn., Am. Coll. Osteo. Internists (pres. Rheumatology sect. 1992-95), Am. Fedn. Clin. Rsch., Dallas-Ft. Worth Rheumatology Club, Tex. Rheumatism Assn. (bd. govs. 1988—, sec.-treas. 1990-91, v.p. 1991-92, pres. 1992-93), Clin. Immunology Soc., Am. Soc. for Bone and Mineral Rsch. Office: U North Tex Health Sci Ctr 3500 Camp Bowie Blvd Fort Worth TX 76107-2644

RUBIN, BURTON JAY, lawyer, editor; b. Bklyn., Jan. 23, 1946; s. Samuel and Sidell (Greenfield) R.; m. Janice Ann Edelstein, Feb. 17, 1974; 1 child, Jennifer Sidell. AB in Biology, Guilford Coll., Greensboro, N.C., 1966; JD, U. N.C., 1969. Bar: Va. 1971; U.S. Ct. Customs and Patent Appeals 1975. Legal editor Labor Rels. Reporter, Bur. Nat. Affairs, Inc., Washington, 1970; asst. editor U.S. Law Week, 1970-74, asst. mng. editor Patent, Trademark and Copyright Jour., 1974-75, mng. editor U.S. Patents Quar., 1975-85; atty. Am. Soc. Travel Agts., 1985-87, gen. counsel, 1987—, pvt. practice, 1990—; cons. Roundhouse Sq. Psychiat. Ctr., Alexandria, Va. Mem. Fairfax County Water Authority, Va.; mem. Fairfax County Police-Citizens Adv. Coun., 1982-83, alt. mem., 1984-85; mem. West Springfield Police-Citizens Adv. Com., 1979-85, chmn., 1981; bd. dirs. Bur. Nat. Affairs, 1984-85; mem. Fairfax County Rep. Com., 1982-85; chmn. adv. com. Assn. Law & Policy, 1996—. Mem. ABA, Am. Soc. Assn. Execs. (legal counsel 1996—). Contbr. articles to profl. jours. Office: Am Soc Travel Agts 1101 King St Alexandria VA 22314-2944

RUBIN, DAVID LEE, French literature educator, critic, editor, publisher; b. Indpls., Sept. 30, 1939; s. Ira Bertram and Jeanne Iva (Gamso) R.; m. Carolyn Dettman, June 12, 1965; 1 child, Timothy Craig. BA, U. Tenn., 1962; cert., U. Paris, 1963; MA, U. Ill., 1964, PhD, 1967. Instr. French U. Ill., Urbana, 1966-67; asst. prof. U. Chgo., 1967-69; asst. prof. U. Va., Charlottesville, 1969-74, assoc. prof., 1974-82, prof. French, 1982—; seminar dir. Folger Inst., 1989; founder Rookwood Press, 1992—; cons. Can. Coun., Etudes littéraires françaises, NEH, numerous univ. presses; lectr., spkr. in field. Author: Higher Hidden Order, 1972, The Knot of Artifice, 1981, A Past with Silence, 1991; editor: The Selected Poetry and Prose of John T. Napier, 1972, La poésie française du premier 17e siècle, 1986, Sun King, 1991; co-editor: La Cohérence Intérieure, 1977, Convergences, 1989, The Ladder of High Designs, 1991, The Fulbright Difference, 1993; founding editor Continuum, 1989-93, EMF; Studies in Early Modern France, 1994, EMF Monographs, 1994; mem. editl. bd. Purdue Monographs, 1975—, Oeuvres et Critiques, 1976—, French Rev., 1986-94; Am. corr. Cahiers Maynard, 1973—, Cahiers Tristan L'Hermite, 1989; contbr. articles to profl. jours., chpts. to books. U.S. State Dept. Fulbright fellow, 1962-63, Woodrow Wilson Found. fellow, 1963-64, Guggenheim Found. fellow, 1980-81. Mem. MLA, ACLU, Farmington Club, Boar's Head Club, Phi Beta Kappa. Home: 520 Rookwood Pl Charlottesville VA 22903-4734 Office: U Va French Dept 302 Cabell Hall Charlottesville VA 22903

RUBIN, JOYCE LINDA, education educator; b. Bklyn., Jan. 25, 1944; d. Nathan and Beatrice (Harris) Rachlin; m. Jerome L. Rubin, June 7, 1964; children: Steven, Shari, Jeffrey. BA in Early Childhood Edn., Bkyn. Coll., 1965, MS in Early Childhood Edn., 1968; D Edn. in Early and Mid. Childhood, Nova U., 1991. Cert. in clin. supervision. Prekindergarten tchr. Project Head Start, Bklyn., 1965; kindergarten tchr. N.Y.C. Bd. Edn., Bklyn., 1965-67; adj. instr. early childhood dept. SUNY, Farmingdale, 1974-77; dir. Giant Step Nursery Sch., 1971-85; instr. dept. early childhood edn. and elem. edn. Fla. Atlantic U., Miami, 1987-88; clin. supr. Tchr. Edn. Ctr., 1991; ednl. cons. Tchr. Edn. Inst., 1988—; adj. instr. Coll. Edn. Fla. Internat. U., 1986-95; asst. prof. early childhood edn. Fla. Atlantic U., 1995-96, Barry U., 1996—; discussion leader Continuing Edn. Program Baldwin Pub. Schs., PACE, 1977-78; developer, instr. various insvc. courses Early Childhood Edn. Coun. Nassau County, N.Y., 1972-85; developer, presenter workshops Miami-Dade C.C., 1991, 92; ofcl. validator Nat. Assn. Edn. Young Children accreditation system, Washington, 1988—; bd. mem. Nassau County Early Childhood Edn. Coun., 1980-85, Day Care Coun. Nassau County, 1981-85; validator Nat. Acad. Early Childhood Programs, 1987—. Creator videotape Television and the Young Child, Selkirk Cable Systems and B'nai Brith Women, 1987. Mem. Nat. Assn. Edn. Young Children, Assn. Childhood Edn. Internat., Fla. Assn. Children Under Six. Home: 10689 NW 17th Ct Coral Springs FL 33071-4280

RUBIN, LARRY JEROME, literature educator; b. Bayonne, N.J., Feb. 14, 1930; s. Abraham Joseph and Lillian (Strongin) R. BA, Emory U., 1951, MA, 1952, PhD, 1956. Instr. English Ga. Inst. Tech., Atlanta, 1955-58, asst. prof., 1958-65, assoc. prof., 1965-73, prof., 1973—. Author: The World's Old Way, 1962 (award Ga. Writers Assn. 1963), Lanced in Light, 1967 (award Dixie Coun. 1967), All My Mirrors Lie, 1975 (award Dixie Coun. 1975); contbr. articles on various authors to profl. jours. Recipient Smith-Mundt lectureship U.S. State Dept., 1961-62; Fulbright lectureship, 1966-67, 69-70, 71-72. Mem. Poetry Soc. Am. (Reynolds lyric award 1961, ann. award 1973), South Atlantic MLA, Coll. English Assn., Nat. Coun. Tchrs. English. Democrat. Jewish. Home: PO Box 15014 Atlanta GA 30333-0014 Office: Ga Inst Tech 225 North Ave NW Atlanta GA 30332-0165

RUBIN, MARK STEPHEN, ophthalmic surgeon; b. Syracuse, N.Y., Dec. 22, 1946; s. Max Leon and Ruth (Dworski) R.; m. Patrizia Silvestri, May 1, 1994; 1 child, Jonathan C. BA, SUNY, Buffalo, 1968; MD summa cum laude, U. Bologna, Italy, 1974. Diplomate Am. Bd. Ophthalmology. Intern Deaconess Hosp., Buffalo, 1976; resident in ophthalmology Wettlauffer Eye Clinic, Buffalo, 1979; chief ophthalmology Augsburg (Fed. Republic Germany) Army Hosp., 1979-80; pvt. practice Modena, Italy, 1980-88; head dept. ophthalmology Fla. Health Care Plan, Daytona Beach, 1988-90; pvt. practice Daytona Beach, Fla., 1990—; cons. USAF, Aviano Air Base, Italy, 1982-88; cons. surgeon Hesperia Hosp., Modena, 1980-88. Author: (with others) Extracapsular Cataract Surgery, 1988; translator: Lasers and Microsurgery, 1986, Ophthalmic Lasers, 1986. Pres., bd. dirs. Ctr. for Visually Impaired, Daytona Beach; cons. Volusia County Health Dept. Fellow Am. Coll. Internat. Physicians, Am. Coll. Surgeons; mem. Italian Order Physicians and Surgeons, Internat. Assn. Ocular Surgeons, Am. Acad. Ophthalmology, Am. Soc. Cataract and Refractive Surgery, Fla. Med. Soc., European Soc. Refractive Surgery, Italian Ophthalmologic Soc., Italian Soc. Profl. Ophthalmologists, Volusia County Med. Soc., Cen. Fla. Soc. Ophthalmology, Volusia County Reef Rsch. Dive Team. Jewish. Home: 891 N Beach St Ormond Beach FL 32174-4002 Office: 570 Memorial Cir Ormond Beach FL 32174-5070 also: 402 N Halifax Ave Daytona Beach FL 32118-4016

RUBIN, MENACHEM M., rabbi, author; b. Romania, June 22, 1922; came to U.S., 1948; s. Jacob Israel and Malka Nechama (Dackner) R.; 3 children. Ordained rabbi, Romania, 1944. Rabbi Yeshurin Congregation, Miami Beach, Fla.; dean Yeshiva, Torah Vyirah U.T.A., Bklyn., 1950-70. Author: Questoin of Jewish Law, Final Solution: History and Research of Holocoust, 1995; contbr. articles to profl. jours. Active various polit. campaigns, Bklyn., 1950—. Recipient Citation, Bklyn. Borough Pres., 1960, various religious/Jewish orgns. in U.S. and Israel, 1970-80. Mem. United Rabbinical Orgn. of Flatbush-Bklyn. (pres.). Home: 1454 Ocean Pkwy Brooklyn NY 11230 Office: Yeshurin Congregation Adas Israel Inst 4200 Sheridan Ave Miami Beach FL 33140-3116

RUBIN, PAUL HAROLD, economist; b. Boston, Aug. 9, 1942; s. Joseph and Freda (Goldhagen) R.; m. Marcia Ann Claybon, June 15, 1964 (dec. Feb. 1973); children: Joseph Saul, Rachel Beth; m. Mariam Hope Moss, July 26, 1985. BA, U. Cin., 1963; PhD in Econs., Purdue U., 1970. Prof. econs. U. Ga., Athens, 1968-82; sr. staff economist Pres. Coun. Economic Advisers, Washington, 1981-82; prof. econs. Baruch Coll. and the Grad. Ctr., N.Y.C., 1982-83; head, consumer protection Bur. Econs., FTC, Washington, 1983-85; chief economist Consumer Product Safety Commn., 1985-87; v.p. Glassman-Oliver Economic Cons., Inc., Washington, 1987-91; prof. econs. Emory U., Atlanta, 1991—; adj. prof. George Washington U. Law Ctr., Washington, 1985-89. Author: Congressmen, Constituents and Contributors, 1982, Business Firms and the Common Law, 1983, Managing Business Transactions, 1990, Tort Reform by Contract, 1993; editor-in-chief Managerial and Decision Economics; contbr. articles to profl. jours. Mem. Am. Econ. Assn., So. Econ. Assn. (v.p. 1994-96), Am. Law and Econs. Assn., Pub. Choice Soc. Republican. Office: Emory U Dept Econs Atlanta GA 30322

RUBIO, PEDRO A., cardiovascular surgeon; b. Mexico City, Dec. 17, 1944; came to U.S., 1970; s. Isaac and Esther; m. Debra Rubio; children: Sandra, Edward, MD, U. Nacional Autónoma de Méx., 1968; MS in Surg. Tech., Pacific Western U., 1981, PhD in Biomed. Tech., 1982. Diplomate Am. Bd. Surgery, Am. Bd. Abdominal Surgery, Am. Bd. Laser Surgery, Am. Bd. Quality Assurance and Utilization Rev. Physicians, Am. Acad. Pain Mgmt., Am. Bd. Forensic Medicine, Am. Bd. Forensic Examiners, Diplomate Mexican bd. Angiology and Vascular Surgery, Infectious Diseases and Gen. Surgery; profl. cert. law enforcement sci., Nat. Com. Profl. Law Enforcement Standards, 1972. Prof. neurology Escuela Normal de Especialización, Secretaria de Educación Publica, Mexico City, 1968-69; asst. instr. dept. surgery Baylor Coll. Medicine, Houston, 1971-76; clin. instr. dept. surgery U. Tex. Med. Sch. Houston, 1978-91; clin. assoc. prof. surgery dept. surgery U. Tex. Med. Sch., Houston, 1991—, profl vascular surgery, Nat U. Mexico Med. Sch., clin. supr. psychiatry residency tng. program Tex. Research Inst. Mental Scis., Houston, 1979-85; surgeon, dir. Cardiovascular Surg. Ctr., Houston, 1976-85, Houston Cardiovascular Inst., 1985-89, Laser Gallbladder Surgery Ctr. of Houston, 1990-94; course dir. Laser Tng. Inst., 1991—, Houston Laser Inst., 1989-91; chmn. surgery dept. Med. Ctr. Hosp., Houston, 1978-94, chmn. emeritus dept. surgery Med. Ctr. Hosp., Houston, 1994—; nat. med. dir., pres., CEO, chmn., Nat. Assn., Preferred Providers, Houston, 1995—, pres. CEO, chmn., bd. Nat. Assn., Preferred Providers, Houston, 1996—; research projects with FDA, NCI, HEW, VA ; pres. exec. com. Houston Chamber Singers, 1982-83. Decorated Palms Honor Cross (hon.), Mex. Army; recipient Recognition diploma bachelor's class Universidad Nacional Autonoma de Mex., 1961, Facultad de Medicina, 1966; named Outstanding Surg. Intern, Baylor Coll. Medicine, 1970-71.Doctor of Humane Letters Loudou Inst. Applied Rsch., Fellow Academia de Ciencias Medicas del Instituto Mexicana de Cultura, Academia Mexicana de Cirugia, ACS (Best Paper award South Tex. chpt. 1976), Am. Coll. Angiology, Am. Coll. Chest Physicians, Assn. Surgeons India (hon.), Soc. Surgeons Nepal (hon.), Internat. Coll. Surgeons (hon.), Knight Grand Cross, The Sovereign and Military Order of Saint John of Jerusalem, Houston Acad. Medicine. Internat. Coll. Angiology, Internat. Coll. Surgeons (N.Am. fedn. sec. 1991-92, pres. U.S. sect. 1988-89, pres. Tex. div. 1983-85, world pres.-elect 1993-94, world pres. 1995, historian 1985-94, chmn. membership com. U.S. sect. 1984-86, 3d pl. sci. motion picture 1980), Israel Med. Assn. USA, Royal Soc. Medicine, Am. Heart Assn. (stroke council), Am. Geriatrics Soc., AMA (Recognition award 1972-95), Am. Trauma Soc., Denton A. Cooley Cardiovascular Soc., Harris County (Tex.) Med. Soc., Houston Surg. Soc. (1st pl. essay 1973, 75), Internat. Assn. Study Lung Cancer, Internat. Cardiovascular Soc., Internat. Soc. Laser Medicine and Surgery, Sociedad Mexicana de Angiologia (1st pl. nat. essay contest 1974), Soc. Internat. Chirurgie, Soc. Am. Gastrontestinal Endoscopic Surgeons, Soc. Laparoendoscopic Surgeons, Soc. for Minimally Invasive Surgery, Southwestern Surg. Congress, Tex. Med. Assn., World Med. Assn., Internat. Coll. Surgeons (world pres.), Phi Beta Delta. Lodge: Rosicrucian. Author: Atlas of Angioaccess Surgery, 1983; Atlas of Stapling Techniques, 1986; contbr. 260 sci. articles to publs.; patentee med. instrumentation. Office: 20682 SweetGlen Dr Porter TX 77365-6385

RUBY, RALPH, JR., vocational business educator; b. Newburgh, N.Y., Apr. 11, 1944; m. Dorothy Nelle Privette; children: Laconya Dannet, Ralph III, Vanessa Rae. AAS, Orange County C.C., 1968; BS, U. Tenn., Knoxville, 1969, MS in Bus. Edn., 1972; EdD, U. Mo., Columbia, 1975. Cert. tchr., adminstr., N.Y. Tchr. keyboarding, bus. law Valley Cen. High Sch., Montgomery, N.Y., 1969-76, chair bus. dept., 1974-75; asst. prof. vocat. bus. edn. U. Ark., Fayetteville, 1976-79; from asst. prof. to prof. bus. edn., coord. vocat. bus. edn. Ark. State U., State University, 1979—; mem. edn. adv. com. 26th Congl. Dist., N.Y.; vis. prof. McGill U., Montreal, Que., Can., 1977; acctg. author Gregg divsn. McGraw-Hill Book Co., 1978—; presenter workshops, tngs. programs. Author: Rough Draft Typing Practice, 1980, Target Type!: Improving Speed and Accuracy, 1987, Word Processing and Editing Techniques, 1988, Real Life Keyboarding Applications: (Word Processor, Data Base, Spreadsheet), 1990, Top Row Target Type, 1991, Starship Speller, 1991, Number Pad Tutor, 1991, Lotus in Your Classroom, 1991, WordPerfect in Your Classroom, 1992, Microsoft Works in Your Classroom, 1993, The Big Board Stock Market (simulation), 1993, PageMaker in Your Classroom, 1993, MS-DOS Made Easy, 1993, WordPerfect for Desktop Publications, 1993, Microsoft Windows in Your Classroom, 1994, Mystery at Laser Age Hardware, 1994, The Class Works, 1994, WordPerfect in Your Classroom Using the MacIntosh, 1994, PageMaker in Your Classroom for Windows, 1996, WordPerfect for Desktop Publishing, 1996, Quattao Pao in Your Classroom, 1996, Espionage at International Electronics, 1996, Microsoft Works for Windows in Your Classroom, 1996, Ami Pro For Windows in Your Classroom, 1996; editor Jour. Edn. for Bus, 1980—, also others. Mem. Am. Vocat. Assn. (life), Nat. Bus. Edn. Assn., So. Bus. Edn. Assn., Nat. Assn. Tchr. Edn. for Bus. and Office Edn. (life), Delta Pi Epsilon, Kappa Delta Pi, Phi Delta Kappa (life). Office: Ark State Univ Coll Business State University AR 72467

RUCKDESCHEL, JOHN CHARLES, oncologist, researcher; b. Newport, R.I., Jan. 5, 1946; s. John Adam and Rita Frances (Riley) R.; m. Maureen Cassidy, June 26, 1986; children: Daniel, Emily. BSc, Rensselaer Poly. Inst., 1967; MD, Albany Med. Coll., 1971. Intern Johns Hopkins U., Balt., 1971-72; fellow Nat. Cancer Inst., Balt., 1972-75; resident Beth Israel Hosp., Boston, 1975-76; asst. prof. medicine Albany (N.Y.) Med. Coll., 1976-79, assoc. prof. medicine, 1979-85, prof. medicine, 1985-91, head div. med. oncology, 1987-91, dir. joint ctr. for cancer and blood disorders, 1989-91; dir., chief exec. officer H. Lee Moffitt Cancer Ctr. and Rsch. Inst., Tampa, 1991—; prof. Univ. South Fla. Coll. Medicine, 1991—. Co-editor: (textbook) Thoracic Oncology, 1989, 95; contbr. articles to med. jours. Recipient Physicians Recognition award AMA, 1994. Fellow Am. Coll. Physicians, Am. Coll. Chest Physicians; mem. Am. Assn. for Cancer Rsch., Am. Soc. Clin. Oncology, Am. coll. Physician Execs., Internat. Assn. for the Study of Lung Cancer, Alpha Omega Alpha. Home: 2506 Mistic Point Way Tampa FL 33611-5061 Office: H Lee Moffitt Cancer Ctr 12902 Magnolia Dr Tampa FL 33612-9416

RUCKELSHAUS, WILLIAM DOYLE, waste disposal services company executive; b. Indpls., July 24, 1932; s. John K. and Marion (Doyle) R.; m. Jill Elizabeth Strickland, May 11, 1962; children: Catherine Kiley, Mary Hughes, Jennifer Lea, William Justice, Robin Elizabeth. B.A. cum laude, Princeton U., 1957; LL.B., Harvard U., 1960. Bar: Ind. 1960. Atty. Ruckelshaus, Bobbitt & O'Connor, Indpls., 1960-68; dep. atty.-gen. Ind., 1960-65, chief counsel office atty.-gen. Ind., 1963-65; minority atty. Ind. Senate, 1965-67; mem. Ind. Ho. of Reps., 1967-69, majority leader, 1967-69; asst. atty.-gen. charge civil div. Dept. Justice, 1969-70; adminstr. EPA, Washington, 1970-73; acting dir. FBI, 1973; dep. atty. gen. U.S., 1973; mem. firm Ruckelshaus, Beveridge, Fairbanks & Diamond, Washington, 1974-76; sr. v.p. law and corp. affairs Weyerhaeuser Co., Tacoma, 1975-85; adminstr. EPA, Washington, 1983-85; pres. William D. Ruckelshaus Assocs., 1985-88; mem. firm Perkins Coie, Seattle, 1985-88; chmn. bd., CEO Browning-Ferris Industries, Inc., Houston, 1988—; bd. dirs. Cummins Engine Co., Monsanto Co., Nordstrom, Inc., Weyerhaeuser Co., Inc. Rep. nominee for U.S. Senate, Ind., 1968. With AUS, 1953-55. Mem. Fed. Bar Assn., Ind. Bar Assn., D.C. Bar Assn., Indpls. Bar Assn. Office: Madrone Investment Group LLC Ste 3700 1000 2d Ave Seattle WA 98104

RUCKER, KENNETH LAMAR, public administrator, educator; b. Atlanta, July 16, 1961; s. Jack Lamar and Priscilla Anne (Anderson) R.; m. Kerri Lynn Hairston; 1 child, Kenneth Lamar II. BSBA, Brenau U., 1991; MPA in Pub. Mgmt., Ga. State U., 1993; postgrad., U. Ga., 1993—. Cert. peace officer, supr., Ga. Law enforcement officer Met. Atlanta Rapid Transit Authority, 1984-93; sch. resource officer Fulton County Bd. Edn., Atlanta, 1993-95; field facilitator Cmtys. in Schs. of Ga., Inc., Atlanta, 1995—, field facilitator Cross Roads program, 1995—; bd. dirs. Benefactors of Edn., Inc., Atlanta; cons. pub. security Fulton County Bd. Edn., Atlanta, 1993-95. Sunday sch. tchr. Simpson St. Ch. of Christ, Atlanta, 1991—; youth motivator Atlanta Pub. Schs., 1988—; bd. dirs. Benefactors Edn., Inc., 1996—. Commd. officer Supply Corps, USNR, 1995—. Doctoral fellow U. Ga. Mem. Am. Soc. Pub. Adminstrn., Nat. Orgn. Black Law Enforcement Execs., Conf. on Minority Transp. Ofcls., Nat. Forum Black Pub. Adminstrs., Internat. Platform Assn., Benefactors of Edn., Inc. (bd. dirs. 1996—), Brenau U. Alumni Club, Ga. State U. Alumni Club, U.S. Naval Inst., Naval Res. Assn., Res. Officer's Assn., Pi Alpha Alpha, Pi Sigma Alpha, Omicron Delta Kappa (cir. pres. 1992-93). Home: 1823 Tiger Flowers Dr NW Atlanta GA 30314-1833 Office: Cmtys in Schs of Ga Inc 1252 W Peachtree St NE Ste 43D Atlanta GA 30309

RUDD, WILLIE, association administrator. Prse. United Furniture Workers Ins. Fund, Nashville. Office: United Furniture Workers Ins Fund PO Box 100037 1910 Airlane Rd Nashville TN 37224

RUDDER, BOBBY JOEL, technology educator; b. Knoxville, Tenn., Apr. 1, 1939; s. Mark Nathaniel and Ruth Cecelia (Harvey) R.; m. Freda Mae Gilbert, July 3, 1965; 1 child, Catherine Michelle. B. Tech. in Inds. Engring. Tcrh., Appalachian State U., 1993, MA in Edn., 1994, Edn. Specialist, 1995; postgrad., E. Tenn. State U., 1996—. Sole propr. Universal Electronics Sales and Svc., Atlanta and Knoxville, 1974-78; tech. support specialist Hitachi Sales Corp. Am., Atlanta, 1978-81; field svc. mgr. ea. zone Mitsubishi Elec. Sales Am., Atlanta, 1981-84; nat. svc. mgr. NEC Technologies, Inc., Wood Dale, Ill., 1984-88; gen. mgr. svc. and engring. AIWI Am. Inc., Moonachie, N.J., 1988; nat. svc. mgr. JVC Svc. and Engring. Corp. Am., Fairfield, N.J., 1989-92; instr. in residence dept. tech. Coll. Fine and Applied Arts Appalachian State U., Boone, N.C., 1993—; developer electronics program Passaic County (N.J.) Vocat. H.S. Past participant nat. skill olympics competition Vocat. Indsl. Clubs Am. With USN, 1961-74. With. Mem. AAUP, Electronics Industries Assn., Consumer Electronics Manufacturers Assn. (past mem. product svc. exec. com., svc. edn. cons. 1992—). Home: 1816 Fieldcrest Circle Johnson City TN 37604 Office: Warf-Pickel Hall East Tenn State Univ Johnson City TN 37608

RUDERT, CYNTHIA SUE, gastroenterologist; b. Cin., Mar. 17, 1955; d. John Wayne and Hilda Wanda (Loftus) R.; children: Ronald Lamar Hilley II, Henry Byron Hilley. BS with honors, U. Ky., 1975; MD, U. Louisville, 1979. Diplomate Am. Bd. Internal Medicine, Am. Bd. Gastroenterology. Intern internal medicine Emory U., Atlanta, 1979-80, resident, 1980-82, fellow gastroenterology, 1982-84, asst. prof. medicine, Emory U., Atlanta, 1984-91; guest speaker Alcoholism Conf., Kanasawa, Japan, 1987; nat. and internat. speaker in gastroenterology; author: Medicine for the Practicing Physician, 3rd rev. edition, 1991, (chpts.) Acute Pancreatitis, Chronic Pancreatitis, Ischaemic Hepatitis, Rudert, C.S. Alcohol Related Symptons. Recipient Newburg award U. Louisville, 1979. Fellow ACP; mem. AMA, Am. Med. Women's Assn., Am. Assn. for Study Liver Disease, Am. Gastroent. Assn., Am. Assn. for Study Liver Diseases, So. Med. Assn., Am. Liver Found., Am. Acad. Scis., Ga. Gastroent. Soc., Med. Assn. Ga., Med. Assn. Atlanta, Atlanta Women's Med. Alliance (founder). Office: 2500 Hospital Blvd Ste 210 Roswell GA 30076-4918

RUDIS, VICTOR AUGUSTINE, research forester, ecologist; b. Boston, Aug. 27, 1950; s. Hans and Stella (Okuniewska) R.; m. Mary R. DeRonde, Aug. 14, 1976; children: Jeffrey, Jonathan. BS in Biology, Boston Coll., 1972; MS in Ecology, Rutgers U., 1975; MS in Forestry, U. Wis., 1978. Instr. Rutgers Prep. Sch., Somerset, N.J., 1972-73; tchg. asst. Rutgers U., New Brunswick, N.J., 1973-74, rsch. asst., 1974; grad. rsch. asst. dept. forestry U. Wis., Madison, 1976-78; planning asst. Wis. Dept. Natural Resources, Madison, 1979; rsch. forester forest inventory and analysis USDA Forest Svc., New Orleans, 1980-83; rsch. forester So. Rsch. Sta. Forest Inventory & Analysis USDA Forest Svc., Starkville, Miss., 1983—. Contbr. articles to profl. publs. V.p. Miss. State U. World Neighbors Assn., Mississippi State, 1990. Mem. Miss. Native Plant Soc. (bd. dirs. 1995-96, pres. 1992-94, editor 1990-91, sec.-treas. 1988-89), Soc. Am. Foresters, Ecol. Soc. Am., U.S. Internat. Assn. Landscape Ecologists, Starkville Swim Assn. (sec. 1996). Office: USDA Forest Svc So Rsch Sta Forest Inventory & Analysis 201 Lincoln Green PO Box 928 Starkville MS 39760-0928

RUDLIN, DAVID ALAN, lawyer; b. Richmond, Va., Nov. 4, 1947; s. Herbert and Dorothy Jean (Durham) R.; m. Judith Bond Faulkner, Oct. 4, 1975; 1 child, Sara Elizabeth. BA with high distinction, U. Va., 1969, JD with honors, 1973. Bar: Va. 1973, U.S. Dist. Ct. (ea. dist.) Va. 1975, U.S. Ct. Appeals (4th cir.) 1975, U.S. Ct. Appeals (10th cir.) 1980, U.S. Ct. Appeals (2d cir.) 1983, U.S. Supreme Ct. 1979. Assoc. gen. counsel U.S. Commn. on Orgn. of Govt. for Conduct of Fgn. Policy, Washington, 1973-75; assoc. Hunton & Williams, Richmond, 1975-82, ptnr., 1982—; adj. faculty William and Mary Coll., Marshall-Wythe Sch. Law, Williamsburg, Va., 1982—, U. Richmond, 1993—; faculty mem. Boulder and S.E. Regional programs Nat. Inst. Trial Advocacy; vis. lectr. U. Va. Sch. Law, Charlottesville, 1980—; mem. Va. Mediation Panel, Am. Arbitration Assn., 1996—; mem. dispute resolution svcs. adv. coun. Supreme Ct. Va. Bd. dirs., ex officio mem. Cystic Fibrosis Found., Richmond; alumni Metro Leadership Richmond, 1988-89; mem. bd. editorial advisors The Environmental Counselor, Chesterland, Ohio, 1989—, The Toxics Law Reporter, Washington, 1988—; bd. dirs., apt. special adv., adv. com. Richmond Juvenile and Domestic Rels. Ct., 1990-94. Author: (book chpts.) Toxic Torts: Litigation Of Hazardous Substances Cases, 1983, 2nd edit., 1992, Federal Litigation Guide, 1989, Corporate Counselor's Guide To Environmental Law, 1989, Sanctions: Rule 11 and Other Powers, 1992; contbr. articles to profl. jours. and mags, chpts. to books. Mem. ABA (chmn. litigation sect. environ. litigation com. 1985-88, co-chmn. litigation sect. liaison with jud. com. 1988-91, vice-chmn. toxic and hazardous substances and environ. law com. tort and ins. practice sect., 1988-91, co-liaison to standing com. on environ. law from environ. litigation com. litigation section, 1988-92, dir. divsn. IV litigation sect. 1991-95, litigation sect. co-chair programs subcom. first amendment & media litigation com. 1993—, mem. litigation sect. task force on specialization 1994—, mem. litigation sect. task force on justice sys. 1994—, litigation sect. liaison to ABA jud. adminstrn. divsn. task force on reduction of litigation cost and delay 1995—, chair litigation sect. 1997 ann. meeting Washington 1995—), Va. Bar Assn. (chair joint com. on alternative dispute resolution with Va. State Bar 1991—), Va. Trial Lawyers Assn., Richmond Bar Assn. (chmn. membership com. 1988-91, mem. judiciary com. 1991-94, mem. continuing legal edn. com. 1994—), Va. Assn. Def. Attys., Ctr. Pub. Resources (products liability com. 1988—, judge Ann. Awards in Alternative Dispute Resolution 1990—). Office: Hunton & Williams Riverfront Pla E Tower 951 E Byrd St Richmond VA 23219-4074

RUDLOFF, WILLIAM JOSEPH, lawyer; b. Bonne Terre, Mo., Feb. 19, 1941; s. Leslie W. and Alta M. (Hogenmiller) R.; m. Rita Howton, Aug. 5, 1965; children: Daniel, Andrea, Leslie, Susan. AB, Western Ky. U., 1961; JD, Vanderbilt U., 1965. Bar: Ky. 1965, Tenn. 1965, U.S. Supreme Ct. 1975; Diplomate Am. Bd. Profl. Liability Attys.; cert. civil trial specialist Nat. Bd. Trial Advocacy. U.S. magistrate Western Dist. Ky., 1971-75. NDEA fellow U. Nebr. 1961-62, U. Ky. fellow. Fellow Ky. Bar Found. (charter life); mem. Am. Bd. Trial Advocates, Am. Counsel Assn., Def. Rsch. Inst., Ky. Def. Counsel, Trial Attys. Am., Am. Coll. Legal Medicine, Internat. Assn. Def. Counsel. Home: 126 Broadway PO Box 146 Smiths Grove KY 42171-0146 Office: 553 E Main St Bowling Green KY 42101-2256

RUDOLPH, ANDREW HENRY, dermatologist, educator; b. Detroit, Jan. 30, 1943; s. John J. and Mary M. (Mizesko) R.; children: Kristen Ann, Kevin Andrew. MD cum laude, U. Mich., 1966. Diplomate Am. Bd. Dermatology. Intern, Univ. Hosp., U. Mich. Med. Center, Ann Arbor, 1966-67, resident dept. dermatology, 1967-70; practice medicine specializing in dermatology, 1972—; asst. prof. dermatology Baylor Coll. Medicine, Houston, 1972-75, assoc. prof., 1975-83, clin. prof., 1983—; chief dermatology svc. VA Hosp., Houston, 1977-82; mem. staff Meth. Hosp., Tex. Children's Hosp., St. Luke's Episcopal Hosp. Served as surgeon USPHS, 1970-72. Regent's scholar U. Mich., 1966. Fellow Am. Acad. Dermatology; mem. Am. Dermatol. Assn., AMA, So. Med. Assn., Tex. Med. Assn., Harris County Med. Soc., Houston Dermatol. Soc. (past pres.), Tex. Dermatol. Soc., Assn. Mil. Dermatologists, Internat. Soc. Tropical Dermatology, Royal Soc. Health, Royal Soc. Medicine, Dermatology Found., Skin Cancer Found., Am. Venereal Disease Assn. (past pres.), Assn. Mil. Surgeons U.S., Am. Soc. for Dermatol. Surgery, Soc. for Investigative Dermatology, S. Central Dermatologic Congress, Mich. Alumni Assn. (life), Alpha Omega Alpha, Phi Kappa Phi, Phi Rho Sigma, Theta Xi. Mem. editorial bd. Jour. of Sexually Transmitted Diseases, 1977-85. Contbr. to med. jours., periodicals and textbooks. Office: 6560 Fannin St Ste 724 Houston TX 77030-2725

RUDOLPH, DEBORAH ANN, materials management executive; b. San Antonio, Dec. 18, 1958; d. James Richard and Lola Mae (Muenchow) R. BS, Tex. A&M U., 1981. Operating rm. technician Sch. Vet. Medicine Tex. A&M U., College Station, 1978-81; cardio-pulmonary technician St. Joseph Hosp., Bryan, Tex., 1981-84; with Argon Med., Athens, Tex., 1985-89, vendor devel. analyst, 1986, master scheduling supr., 1987-88, inventory control supr., 1988-89; buyer/planner Alcon Labs., Inc., Ft. Worth, 1990-91, ops. scheduling supr., 1991, cen. planning master planner, 1992-93; ophthalmic/vision care divsn. planning mgr., 1994—; owner Angel Haven Cattle Co., 1994—. Mem. Nat. Audubon Soc., Nat. Wildlife Fend. Mem. Am. Prodn. and Inventory Control Soc., NAFE. Office: Alcon Labs Inc 6201 South Fwy Fort Worth TX 76134-2001

RUEGER, BRIAN LEE, marine corps officer; b. Dayton, Ohio, July 3, 1970; s. Ronald Lynn and Virginia Alice (Woodman) R. BS in Bus. Mgmt., Elon Coll., 1992. Comm. 2d lt. U.S. Marine Corps, 1993, capt., 1995; co. comdr. U.S. Marine Corps, Camp Lejeune, N.C., 1995—; Adj. lect. Business Mgmt., Park Coll. Decorated Navy Achievement medal. Mem. Omicron Delta Kappa, Omicron Delta Epsilon, Kappa Alpha Order (treas. 1989—). Democrat. Baptist. Home: 2657 Coquina Dr Johns Island SC 29455 Office: Company I 3d Bn 2d Marines PCS Box 20096 Camp Lejeune NC 28542-0096

RUEHLMANN, WILLIAM JOHN, communications educator; b. Cin., Apr. 27, 1946; s. William Edward and Margaret Thelma (Smith) R.; m. Lynn Elise Klausli, Sept. 6, 1969; children: Benjamin Derek, Martha Jill. BA, Am. U., 1968; MA, U. Ariz., 1970; PhD, U. Cin., 1974. English tchr. Elder High Sch., Cin., 1970-71; reporter Ky. Post, Covington, 1974-75; asst. prof. journalism Suffolk U., Boston, 1975-77; feature writer Va. Pilot and Ledger-Star, Norfolk, 1977-93; assoc. prof. communications Va. Wesleyan Coll., Norfolk, Virginia Beach, 1993—; mem. adv. bd. Crippen & Landru, 1994—, Blackware Rev., Virginia Beach, 1995—. Author: Saint With a Gun, 1974, Stalking the Feature Story, 1977; editl. cons. Internat. Polygonics, N.Y.C., 1988-92. Elder 1st Presbyn. Ch., Norfolk, 1982—; bd. dirs. Family Svcs. Tidewater, Norfolk, 1984-92. Staff sgt. U.S. ANG, 1970-74. Recipient Media award Independence Ctr., 1988, 94, Journalism award Va. Press Assn., 1986, 87, 88, 89. Mem. AAUP, Nat. Book Critics Circle, Coll. Media Advisors, Omicron Delta Kappa, Sigma Tau Delta. Office: Va Wesleyan Coll 1584 Wesleyan Dr Norfolk VA 23502

RUFFER, DAVID GRAY, museum director, former college president; b. Archbold, Ohio, Aug. 25, 1937; s. Lawrence A. and Florence A. (Newcomer) R.; m. Marilyn Elaine Taylor, Aug. 23, 1958; children: Rochelle Lynne, Robyn Lynne, David Geoffrey. B.S., Defiance Coll., 1959; M.A., Bowling Green State U., 1960; Ph.D., U. Okla., 1964. Spl. instr. U. Okla., 1963-64; asst. prof. biology Defiance Coll., 1964-68, asso. prof., 1968-73, faculty dean, 1969-73; provost Elmira (N.Y.) Coll., 1973-78; pres. Albright Coll., Reading, Pa., 1978-91, U. Tampa, Fla., 1991-94; exec. dir. Dayton (Ohio) Soc. Natural History, 1995—. Author: Exploring and Understanding Mammals, 1971; contbr. articles to profl. jours. NSF grantee, 1965, 67; Ohio Biol. Survey grantee, 1968-69. Fellow AAAS; mem. Am. Assn. Higher Edn., Animal Behavior Soc., Am. Soc. Mammalogists, Sigma Xi. Methodist. Club: Rotary. Home: 3700 Wales Dr Dayton OH 45405 Office: Dayton Mus Natural History 2600 Deweese Pkwy Dayton OH 45414-5400

RUFFIN, PAUL DEAN, English language educator; b. Millport, Ala., May 14, 1941; s. David Clarence and Zealon (Robinson) R.; m. Sharon Marie Krebs, June 21, 1973; children: Genevieve, Matthew. BS, Miss. State U., 1964, MA, 1967; PhD, Univ. So. Miss., 1974. Instr. Eng. Univ. So. Miss., Hattiesburg, 1971-72, Miss. State Univ., Starkville, 1972-74; prof. Eng. Sam Houston State Univ., Huntsville, Tex., 1975—; dir. Tex. Rev. Press, Huntsville, 1992—. Author: Circling, 1996, Our Women, 1985, The Man Who Would Be God, 1993; editor: That's What I Like About the South, 1993; editor Tex. Rev., 1976—. With U.S. Army, USNG, 1959-65. Mem. Tex. Inst. Letters, Conf. Coll. Tchrs. Eng., South Ctrl. Modern Lang. Assn. Home: 2014 Ave N 1/2 Huntsville TX 77340

RUFFNER, CHARLES LOUIS, lawyer; b. Cin., Nov. 7, 1936; s. Joseph H. and Edith (Solomon) R.; m. Mary Ann Kaufman, Jan. 30, 1966 (div. 1993); children: Robin Sue, David Robert; m. Nanette Diemer, Feb. 26, 1995. BSBA in Acctg., U. Fla., 1958; JD cum laude, U. Miami, 1964. Bar: Fla. 1964, U.S. Dist. Ct. (so. and mid. dists.) Fla. 1964, U.S. Ct. Appeals (5th cir.) 1964, U.S. Ct. Appeals (11th cir.) 1984, U.S. Claims Ct. 1966, U.S. Tax Ct. 1966, U.S. Supreme Ct. 1968. Cert. in taxation. Trial atty. tax div. Dept. Justice, Washington, 1964-67; pres. Forrest, Ruffner, Traum & Hagen, P.A., Miami, Fla., 1967-78; pres. Ruffner, Hagen & Rifkin, P.A., Miami, 1978-81; tax ptnr. Myers, Kenin, Levinson, Ruffner, Frank & Richards, Miami, 1982-84; pres. Charles L. Ruffner, P.A., 1984—; lectr. Fla. Internat. U., Miami. Author: A Practical Approach to Professional Corporations and Associations, 4 edits., 1970, (column) Tax Talk, Miami Law Rev.; editor: Miami Law Rev., 1963-64; contbr. numerous articles on taxation to law jours. Mem. ABA, Fed. Bar Assn., Fla. Bar (exec. council tax sect. 1967-92, 95—, amicus curiae in test case of validity profl. corps.), Dade County Bar Assn., South Fla. Tax Litigation Assn. (chmn. 1986—), Phi Alpha Delta, Phi Kappa Phi. Office: Courvoisier Centre II 601 Brickell Key Dr Ste 507 Miami FL 33131-2650

RUGABER, WALTER FEUCHT, JR., newspaper executive; b. Macon, Ga., Nov. 29, 1938; s. Walter Feucht and Edith Almeda (Maynard) R.; m. Sally Sanford, Oct. 6, 1962; children—Leslie, Christopher, Mark. B.S., Northwestern U., 1960. Corr., editor N.Y. Times, 1965-78; v.p., exec. editor Greensboro Daily News & Record, N.C., 1978-82; pres., pub. The Roanoke Times, Va., 1982—; pres. Landmark Pub. Group; mem. Pulitzer Prize Bd. Bd. dirs. United Way of Roanoke Valley, 1982-88, Roanoke Symphony Soc., 1985—, pres., 1986-88; trustee Hollins Coll. Mem. Am. Newspaper Pubs. Assn., Am. Soc. Newspaper Editors, So. Newspaper Pubs. Assn. Office: Times World Corp PO Box 2491 201-209 W Campbell Ave Roanoke VA 24010

RUGALA, KAREN FRANCIS (KAREN FRANCIS), television producer, painter; b. Memphis, Apr. 27, 1950; d. Ben Porter Francis and Marguerite K. Higginbotham; children: Sarah Helfinstein, Ben Helfinstein. BA in Communication Arts, Rhodes Coll., 1971; MA, U. Mo., 1973. Cert. tchr., Tenn. Secondary sch. tchr. Memphis City Schs., 1971-72; speech tchr. U. Ga., Athens, 1973-75; dir. computer systems installations Planning Rsch. Corp., McLean, Va., 1976-78; dir. account mgmt. TDX Systems, Cable & Wireless, Vienna, Va., 1978-80; cons. telecommunications MCI, Washington, 1985-87; producer Fairfax Cable Access, Merrifield, Va., 1991—; owner Art Promotions, McLean, 1989—. Exhibited paintings in numerous group and one-woman shows including Clark & Co. Gallery, Washington, 1994, McLean Project for Arts, 1992, Hospice of No. Va. Auction Gala, 1992, Capitol Hill Art League, Washington, 1995, Mus. Contemporary Art, Washington, 1996, many others; paintings represented in numerous pvt. collections. Active Family AIDS Housing Found., 1992, Hospice No. Va., 1991, 92, Friends of Vietnam Vets. Meml., 1992; founding bd. mem. Jobs for Homeless People, 1988-90. Office: Art Promotions PO Box 3104 Mc Lean VA 22103-3104

RUGG, PETER, oil company executive; b. Glen Cove, N.Y., Apr. 12, 1947; s. Daniel M. and Carol (Van Zandt) R.; m. Meredith Catlin Phelps, Sept. 12, 1969 children: Charlton Alexander, Courtney Caroline. B.A. Columbia U., 1969, BS in Engring, 1970. Asst. treas. Morgan Guaranty Trust Co., N.Y.C., 1972-74, asst. v.p., 1974-76, v.p., London, 1975-79, v.p., head banking, Hong Kong, 1979-82, v.p. mergers and acquisitions, N.Y.C., 1982-85, v.p. capital markets, 1985-87, v.p. corporate fin., 1987-92; v.p. JP Morgan Securities, 1992-93; sr. v.p., CFO Triton Energy, Dallas, 1993—; adj. prof. fin. Fordham U. Grad. Sch. Bus. Adminstrn., 1987-90. Clubs: New York Yacht (N.Y.C.); Fishers Island (N.Y.); Fishers Island Yacht (past commodore); Northwood Club (Dallas), Royal Hong Kong Yacht Club. Avocations: sailing, skiing, arts, reading. Home: 4 Glenheather Ct Dallas TX 75225 Office: Triton Energy 6688 N Central Expy Dallas TX 75206

RUGGIERI, ELAINE, public relations administrator; b. Kennett Square, Pa., Nov. 20, 1933; d. Arcangelo and Angelina (Leo) R.; m. William S. Satterthwaite Jr., Aug. 13, 1959 (div. 1982); children: Amy Nelson Satterthwaite, Jane Clifford Satterthwaite. AB, Bucknell U., 1955; postgrad., U. Va., 1973-75, 1973-75, NYU, 1983-88. Dir. pub. rels. Darden Grad. Sch. Bus. Adminstrn. U. Va., Charlottesville, 1979—, instr., 1982-85, 88, instr. written communications dept. tng. and devel., 1988—; various writing, editorial and pub. rels. positions, 1955—. Editor mag. Darden Mag., 1979-86, 89—, jour. Fin. Analysts Rsch. Assn., 1981-82; TV show host FOCUS, 1982-86. Recipient George Washington medal Freedoms Found. Valley Forge, 1958, 1st pl. graphics communications award Printing Industries Va., 1984, APEX award of excellence Comm. Concepts Inc., 1993, 94; named one of 100 Top Pub. Rels. Profls., Sch. Mass. Comm., Va. Commonwealth U., 1993. Mem. Pub. Rels. Soc. Am. (accredited), Richmond Pub. Rels. Assn. (dir. chpt. 1996). Office: U Va Darden Grad Sch Bus Adminstrn PO Box 6550 Charlottesville VA 22906-6550

RUGGIERO, LAURENCE JOSEPH, museum director; b. Paterson, N.J., Mar. 25, 1948; s. Salvatore Joseph and Grace Marie (Williams) R.; m. Virginia Frances Fornaci, Mar. 7, 1970; 1 child, John Laurence. BA, U. Pa., 1969, MA, 1979, PhD, 1975; MBA, Boston U., 1978. Asst. prof. history of architecture U. Ill., Chgo., 1973-77; fin. analyst Met. Mus. Art, N.Y.C., 1979-80, asst. to pres., 1980-81; exec. dir. Oakland (Calif.) Mus. Assocs., 1981-85; dir. John and Mable Ringling Mus., Sarasota, Fla., 1985-92; assoc. dir. Charles Hosmer Morse Mus. Am. Art, Winter Park, Fla., 1992—, dir., 1995—; adj. prof. Ringling Sch. Art and Design, Sarasota, 1986-92. Kress Found. fellow, 1971-73. Mem. Fla. Art Mus. Dirs. Assn. (treas. 1987-92), Coll. Art Assn. Am., Am. Assn. Mus., Il Cenacolo (San Francisco). Office: 445 Park Ave N Winter Park FL 32789-3212

RUHM, CHRISTOPHER JOHN, economics educator; b. San Francisco, Apr. 26, 1955; s. John Felix and Maria Bertha (Kirs) R.; m. Maryanna Robin Williams, May 6, 1989; children: William Christopher, Peter Thomas. BA, U. Calif., Davis, 1978; MA, U. Calif., Berkeley, 1981, PhD, 1984. Teaching and rsch. assoc. U. Calif., Berkeley, 1980-84; asst. prof. Boston U., 1984-91; assoc. prof. U. N.C., Greensboro, 1991-94, prof., 1994—. Contbr. articles to profl. jours. Rsch. fellow Brandies U., Waltham, Mass., 1988-90. Mem. Am. Econ. Assn., Internat. Health Econs. Assn., Soc. Labor Economists. Office: U NC Dept Econs Greensboro NC 27412-5001

RUHRUP, CLIFTON BROWN, sales executive; b. Jacksonville, Fla., Nov. 9, 1916; s. Ernest Alfred and Elizabeth L. (Garrett) R. Student, U. Okla., 1934-35, Oklahoma City U., 1946-48; cert. sales mgmt., U. Okla., 1962. From intern trainee to asst. sales mgr. Dolese Bros. Co., Oklahoma City, 1950-54, gen. sales mgr. aggregate div., 1955-61, gen. sales mgr. aggregate and prestress div., 1966—, asst. sec., 1971—. Chmn. bd. dirs. Cen. YMCA, Oklahoma City, 1973-78, named Outstanding Vol. of Yr., 1978, fellow mem., 1978—; bd. dirs. Better Bus. Bur., 1992—; mem. assoc. bd. Associated Bd. Contractors Okla. S/Sgt. USAAF, 1943-46, PTO. Mem. Oklahoma City C. of C., Toastmasters (pres. 1968), Rotary (editor newspaper 1972-76, contbg. editor 1988—, Paul Harris fellow), Phi Eta Sigma. Republican. Mem. First Christian Ch. Office: Dolese Bros Co 20 NW 13th St Oklahoma City OK 73103-4806

RUKEYSER, WILLIAM SIMON, journalist, business executive; b. N.Y.C., June 8, 1939; s. Merryle Stanley and Berenice (Simon) R.; m. Elisabeth Mary Garnett, Nov. 21, 1963; children: Lisa Rukeyser Burn, James William. A.B., Princeton U., 1961; student, Christ's Coll., Cambridge (Eng.) U., 1962-63. Copyreader Wall St. Jour., 1961-62; staff reporter Wall St. Jour., Europe, 1963-67; assoc. editor Fortune mag., 1967-71, mem. bd. editors, 1971-72; mng. editor Money mag., N.Y.C., 1972-80, Fortune mag., 1980-86; dir. internat. bus. devel. Time Inc., 1986-88; editor in chief, exec. v.p. Whittle Communications, Knoxville, Tenn., 1988-91; chmn., chief exec. officer Whittle Books, Knoxville, 1991-94; pres. William Rukeyser, Inc., Knoxville, 1994—; contbg. editor CNN, 1995—; commentator Good Morning America, ABC-TV, 1978-85, CBS Radio Stas. News Svc., 1979-86; bd. dirs. Computational Systems, Inc., Tri-Media Comm., Inc. Mem. jud. com. Union County (N.J.) Med. Soc., 1977-80; co-chair capital campaign Nat. Mental Health Assn., 1984-85; dir., mem. exec. com. Knoxville Mus. Art, Knoxville Symphony Orch.; mem. liaison com. U. Tenn. Med. Ctr.; mem. adv. coun. U. Tenn. Coll. Bus. Adminstrn.; dir. Bijou Theatre Ctr., Knoxville. Home: 1509 Rudder Ln Knoxville TN 37919-8437

RULAND, MIDLRED ARDELIA, retail executive, retail buyer; b. Draketown, Ga., Aug. 11, 1918; m. Harry Morse Ruland, Aug. 19, 1947; children: Hal Morse, Judy Lee Ruland Rigas. BS, West Ga. Coll., 1966. Elem. tchr. New London, Conn., 1947-48, Atlanta, 1948-51, Rome, Ga., 1951-81; mgr. McBrayer Bros. Furniture Co., Rome, 1981—. Rosenwald Found. scholar, 1941-42. Mem. NEA, Nat. Fedn. Ind. Bus. (corr. sec. 1975—), Ga. Edn. Assn. (del. 1964-74), Ga. Home Furnishings Assn., Twickham Garden Club, Rome Pride Assn., Rome C. of C., Alfa Delta Kappa. Republican. Baptist.

RULIFSON, ROGER ALLEN, fisheries and marine science researcher, educator; b. Manchester, Iowa, Nov. 13, 1951; s. Ralph Eugene and Leona Emma (Spiller) R.; m. Gayle Lee Gwennap, June 20, 1981; children: Heather Lynn, Eric Charles. BS in Biology and French, U. Dubuque, 1973; MS in Marine Sci. and Engring., N.C. State U., 1975, PhD in Marine Sci. and Engring., 1980. Biol. tech. II N.C. Coop. Fishery Rsch. Unit, Raleigh, 1975; leader, fish distbn. and vulnerability assessment task Tex. Instruments, Inc., Buchanan, N.Y., 1975-77; rsch. asst. N.C. State U., Raleigh, 1977-80, postdoctoral rsch. assoc., 1980-81; asst. prof. Unity (Maine) Coll., 1981-83; asst. scientist Inst. Coastal and Marine Resources, East Carolina U., Greenville, N.C., 1983-87, assoc. scientist, 1987-93, sr. scientist, 1993—; asst. prof. biology East Carolina U., Greenville, 1983-87, assoc. prof., 1987-93, prof., 1993—; dir. East Carolina U. Field Sta. for Coastal Studies at Mattamuskeet; presenter in field. Referee New Zealand Jour. Marine and Freshwater Rsch., Contbns. Marine Sci., Jour. Exptl. Marine Biology and Ecology, N.Am. Jour. Fisheries Mgmt., Transactions of Am. Fisheries Soc., Proceedings of Southeastern Assn. Fish and Wildlife Agys., U.S. Fish and Wildlife Svc.; rsch. grant reviewer; contbr. over 40 articles to profl. jours. Recipient Conservation Achievement award Gov. State of N.C., 1991; named Water Conservationist of Yr., 1991. Mem. Am. Fisheries Soc. (fisheries scientist, assoc. editor 1991-93), Am. Inst. Fisheries Rsch. Biologists, Estuarine Rsch. Fedn., Sigma Xi. Methodist. Office: East Carolina Univ Inst Coastal/Marine Resourc Greenville NC 27858-4353

RUMAN, MARGARET ANN (PEGGY RUMAN), dental hygienist; b. Athens, Ohio, Aug. 24, 1946; d. Louis Francis and Marjorie Dorothea (Morris) R. BFA, Ohio U., 1968; AS, Camden County Coll., 1974; postgrad., Temple U., 1980—, N.J. Sch. Medicine & Dentistry, 1974-95. Registered dental hygienist, N.J., Fla. Social worker Divsn. Family & Youth Svcs., Red Bank, N.J., 1968-71; dental asst. Dr. Sam. D. Zimmerman, Shrewsbury, N.J., 1971-72; dental hygienist Dr. Sam. D. Zimmerman, Red Bank, 1974-95; health officer Office of Sam D. Zimmerman, Red Bank, 1994-95; instr. Jersey Shore Med., 1988; mem. Dental Hygienist Northeast Region Bd., 1974—. Host dinner musicale Ohio U. sta. WOUB-FM, Athens, 1966-67. Mem. Am. Dental Hygienist Assn., South Seas Plantation Fla., Red Bank (N.J.) Art Alliance, Ctrl. N.J. Dental Hygienist Assn. (presenter, fundraiser 1988-89, pres. 1988-90), Fla. Dental Hygienist Assn., Gulf Coast Dental Hygienist Assn. Republican. Roman Catholic. Home: 7121 Mill Run Cir Naples FL 33942

RUMBAUT, RUBÉN DARIO, psychiatrist, educator; b. Cienfuegos, Las Villas, Cuba, July 10, 1922; came to U.S., 1960; s. Bienvenido and Zoila Rosa (Lopez) R.; m. Carmen Riera, Dec. 8, 1947; children: Ruben G., Luis E., Carlos R., Miryam, Carmen M., Michelle. MD, Havana U., 1946; BA in Journalism, Sch. Journalism, Havana, 1957; grad., Menninger Sch. Psychiatry, 1969. Fellow Am. Bd. Psychiatry and Neurology. Surg. intern Hosp. Emergencias, Havana, 1947, resident in anesthesiology, 1948-49, staff anesthesiologist, 1950-51; staff anesthesiologist Hosp. Curie, Havana, 1951-57, resident psychiatrist, 1957-58; pvt. practice psychiatry Havana, 1957-60; ward supr. Nat. Mental Hosp., Havana, 1959-60; chief VA Mental Hygiene Clinic VA Hosp., Albuquerque, 1961-66; psychiatrist VA Hosp., Topeka, 1966-70; asst. chief psychiatry VA Hosp., Houston, 1971-84; cons.-at-large psychiatry, Houston, 1989—; prof. psychiatry Baylor Coll. Medicine, Houston, 1972-89, prof. emeritus, 1989—. Contbr. articles to profl. jours., chpts. to books; writer, pub. 2 books. Nat. v.p. Cath. Action Youth, Havana, 1943-45; founder Movimiento Humanista Cubano, 1950-53, Cuban Med. Assn. in Exile, 1960. Fellow Am. Psychiat. Assn. (life, v.p. com. Hispanic psychiatrists 1976-78, chmn. com. on internat. med. grads. Tex. bd. 1985-90), Am. Coll. Psychiatrists (emeritus). Roman Catholic. Office: PO Box 231 Sugar Land TX 77487-0231

RUMBERGER, REGINA, retired English language educator; b. Pitts., Aug. 6, 1921; d. Edward T. and Margaret (Berry) Flynn; m. Wilson A. Rumberger, July 31, 1943 (div. 1974); children: Edward, Wilson J., Susan A., Gerard, Paul, Nancy, Joe. BEd, Duquesne U., 1942; MEd, U. Pitts., 1950; grad., State Office Div. Blind Svcs., Ft. Myers, Fla., 1984. Professed Lay Carmelite, 1990. Primary tchr. Allegheny County Pub. Sch., Pa., 1942-43, Sharpsburg (Pa.) Schs., 1943-50; instr. English, Edison C.C., Ft. Myers, 1964-78; ret., 1978; media cons., Lee County and Ft. Myers, 1956; cons., evaluator State of Fla. and Lee County, 1987-88; cons., evaluator Lee County Dept. Transp., Ft. Myers, 1988-90. Chmn. water and safety ARC, Ft. Myers, 1960-65, first aid adminstr., 1965-68; pres. Lee County Med. Aux., 1965-66; consumer rep. Lee County Dept. Transp.; bd. dirs. Met. Planning Orgn., Ft. Myers, 1990—; v.p. S.W. Fla. Curia, 1988—; asst. tour guide to Fr. Stanislaw Pierog, tour dir. Andrew's Pilgrimages, Stockbridge, Mass., 1990—; cons. on accessibility for handicapped Mayor's Alliance, mem. Coun. Disabled, 1991-92; cons., citizen adv. Divsn. Blind Svcs., State of Fla., 1990-91; vol. Lee Mem. Hosp., 1992, Caloosa Retirement Ctr., 1988-96; mem. coun. Lee County Bd. Parks and Recreation, 1994—; mem. citizen's adv. com. Metro. Planning Orgn., 1996—; amb. of Mass. Trans., State of Fla.; spokesperson for disabled Lee County CAC. Recipient award Boy Scouts Am., Ft. Myers, 1967, State of Fla., 1984, Ft. Myers Care Ctr./Lee Convalescence, 1990, Vol. of Yr., State of Fla., 1994, award Caloosa Retirement Ctr., 1996. Mem. AAUW (pub. rels. com. Ft. Myers 1987-90). Roman Catholic. Home: 2140 Cottage St Apt 109 Fort Myers FL 33901-3666

RUMBOUGH, STANLEY MADDOX, JR., industrialist; b. N.Y.C., Apr. 25, 1920; s. Stanley Maddox and Elizabeth (Colgate) R.; m. Nedenia Hutton, Mar. 23, 1946 (div. 1966); children: Stanley H., David P. (dec.), Nedenia Colgate; m. Margaretha Wagstrom, Dec. 21, 1967 (div. 1990); m. Janna Herlow, Mar. 8, 1990. A.B., Yale U., 1942; postgrad. in bus. adminstrn., NYU, 1947-51. Vice pres., dir. Willis Air Service, Teterboro, N.J., 1946-47; v.p., dir. White Metal Mfg. Co., Hoboken, N.J., 1945-61; pres. White Metal Mfg. Co., 1960-61; pres., dir. Metal Container Corp., 1950-59, Am. Totalisator, Balt., 1956-58; chmn. bd. Extrusion Devel. Corp., 1959-61; co-founder, chmn. bd. Elec. Engring. Ltd., 1960-69; chmn. bd. Wallace Clark & Co., 1962-69; co-founder, dir. Trinidad Flour Mills, 1961-72, Jamaica Flour Mills, 1963-66; dir. Telemedia Inc., 1980-89; dir. Dart Industries, 1961-80, ABT Family of Funds, 1983-95; bd. dirs. Internat. Flavors and Fragrances, CUC Internat., Inc.; spl. asst. to sec. Dept. Commerce, 1953; spl. asst. White House charge exec. br. liaison, 1953-55. Chmn. U.S. Com. for UN, 1957-58; co-founder Citizens for Eisenhower, 1951; vice chmn. Citizens for Eisenhower-Nixon Com., 1952; trustee Young Pres. Found., 1957-70, pres., 1962-65; bd. dirs. N.Y. World's Fair Corp., 1961-70, Nat. Conf. on Citizenship, 1973—, Population Resource Ctr., 1978-92, Planned Parenthood of Palm Beach Area, 1979-95, Planned Parenthood Fedn. Am., 1981-84, Kravis Ctr. Performing Arts, Palm Beach Civic Assn.; trustee Libr. for Presdl. Papers, 1966-70, Internat. House, 1959—, Fgn. Policy Assn., 1961-70, Am. Health Found., 1972-76. Capt. USMCR, 1942-46. Decorated Air medal (8), D.F.C. (2). Mem. Chief Execs. Orgn., World Pres.'s Orgn., Def. Orientation Conf. Assn., Racquet and Tennis Club, Internat. Lawn Tennis Club, Maidstone Club, Seminole Club, Bath and Tennis Club, Everglades Club, Nat. Golf Links Am. Club, Zeta Psi. Republican. Home: 655 Island Dr Palm Beach FL 33480-6121 Office: 280 Sunset Ave Palm Beach FL 33480-3815

RUMELY, ROBERT S., mathematician; b. Pullman, Wash., June 23, 1952; s. John Hamilton and Constance Mary (Dudley) R.; m. Cherilyn Marie Caldwell, July 4, 1987; children: Joseph David, Timothy Charles, Jennifer Marie. BA, Grinnell Coll., 1974; PhD, Princeton U., 1978. Instr. Mass. Inst. Tech., Cambridge, 1978-80; postdoctoral vis. fellow Harvard U., Cambridge, 1980-81; asst. prof. U. Ga., Athens, 1981-85; assoc. prof. U. Ga., 1985-90, prof., 1990—; grad. program com. U. Ga., 1986-91, grad. coord. math., 1992-95. Author: Capacity Theory on Algebraic Curves, 1989. Den leader pack 149 Boy Scouts Am., Athens, 1994. Sloan Found. fellow, N.Y.C., 1983-87; NSF grantee, 1979-80, 82-83, 84-85, 88-89, 91-93, others. Mem. Am. Math. Soc. Office: U Ga Math Dept Athens GA 30602

RUMMEL, HAROLD EDWIN, real estate development executive; b. Youngstown, Ohio, Oct. 4, 1940; s. Harold Edward and Florence Louise (Hill) R.; children: Timothy B., Jonathan S., Briana. BS, U. Fla., 1963. Writer, editor various newspapers, Fla., 1958-70; polit. campaign mgr. various state campaigns, Tallahassee, Fla., 1971-79; sr. v.p. Fla. Fed. Sav. Bank, St. Petersburg, 1979-86; pres., chief exec. officer Rummel Cos., St. Petersburg, Fla., Mobile, Ala., 1986—. Active in civic and polit. orgns. Democrat. Home: 1682 Oceanview Dr Tierra Verde FL 33715-2500 Office: Rummel Cos 5401 Central Ave Saint Petersburg FL 33710-8049

RUMP, RONNIE BETH, oil and gas company executive; b. Fremont, Nebr., Mar. 6, 1947; d. Richard Bryant and Margaret Louise (Neff) R. BA in English, Midland Luth. Coll., 1969; JD, Creighton U., 1978; MA in Profl. Devel., Amber U., 1993. Bar: Nebr. Copywriter J. Lipsey and Assocs., Omaha, Nebr., 1968-70; dir. pub. rels. Coll. of St. Mary, Omaha, 1970-73, dean continuing studies, 1973-75; landman Arco Oil and Gas Co., Midland, Tex., 1978-80; dir. recruiting, tng. and devel. Arco Oil and Gas Co., Dallas, 1980-91, sr. tng. specialist mgmt. tng., 1991-93, dir. outplacement svcs., 1993-95; prin. Human Syss. Tech. Consulting Firm, Carrollton, Tex., 1996—; bd. trustees Midland Luth. Coll., Fremont, 1994—. Con. YWCA Women's Resource Ctr., Dallas, 1994. Named Outstanding Young Alumni award Midland Luth. Coll., Fremont, 1983. Mem. ASTD, Internat. Assn. Career Mgmt. Profls., Nebr. Bar Assn., Gray Panthers. Home: 2907 Panorama Carrollton TX 75007

RUMPEL, PETER LOYD, architect, educator, artist; b. Hamilton, Ont., Can., Mar. 25, 1939; s. George Hilburn and Reine (Loyd) R.; children: Hillary, Reine. B.Arch., U. Fla., 1961. Registered architect. Architect Clements, Rumpel, Assocs., Jacksonville, Fla., 1976-84; architect Clements, Rumpel, Goodwin, d'Avi, Jacksonville, 1984—; CRG Archs./Planners, Inc., 1992; assoc. prof. U. Fla., Gainesville, 1984-92; adj. prof. U. Fla., 1982-84; disting. lectr. 1984-92. Prin. works include Fla. Jr. Coll. Jacksonville-N. Campus (honor award Fla. Assn. AIA 1979, merit award Jacksonville chpt. AIA 1972), River Garden Hebrew Home for Aged (Modern Nursing Home of Month award 1971, hon. mention Fla. Assn. AIA 1971, merit award Jacksonville chpt. AIA 1972), Fla. Christian Home Apts. (award merit Fla. Assn. AIA 1973, merit award Jacksonville chpt. AIA 1974, 4th ann. award Outstanding Concrete Structure in Fla. 1974), St. Mary's Episcopal Ch. Renovation (honor award Jacksonville chpt. AIA 1974, award merit Fla. Assn. AIA 1974), Rumpel Residence (first award Jacksonville chpt. Am. Plywood Assn. 1974, honor award Jacksonville chpt. AIA 1974, award merit AIA Homes for Better Living Program 1975), Higginson Residence (merit award Jacksonville chpt. AIA 1974), Sawgrass Harbor Condominiums (award merit Jacksonville chpt. AIA 1975), Sawgrass Golf Club (citation Jacksonville chpt. AIA 1975), Jacksonville Jewish Ctr. (honor award Fla. Assn. AIA 1976, citation Jacksonville chpt. AIA 1977), U. N. Fla. Lab.-Office Bldg. (merit award Jacksonville chpt. AIA 1977), Fla. Jr. Coll., S. Campus, Phase II (honor award Jacksonville chpt. AIA 1977), Drew Bldg. Renovation (merit award Jacksonville chpt. AIA 1978), Mayport Jr. High Sch. (merit award Jacksonville chpt. AIA 1978, award merit Fla. Assn. AIA 1978, First Ann. Gov.'s Design award 1981), T.R.E.E.O. U. Fla. (honor award Jacksonville chpt. AIA 1979, honor award Fla. Assn. AIA 1979), Officer's Conf. Ctr., Camp Keystone (merit award Jacksonville chpt. AIA 1980), St. James Community Life Ctr. (honor award Jacksonville chpt. AIA 1981), U. N. Fla., student activity ctr. (honor award Jacksonville chpt. AIA 1982, award excellence Fla. Assn. AIA 1982), Unenlisted Personnel Housing (award merit ASID 1983), Hurley Manor Elderly Housing (award excellence Jacksonville chpt. AIA 1984), Arlington By the River (honor award Jacksonville chpt. AIA 1984, award excellence Jacksonville chpt. AIA 1984), 120-Bed Nursing Home Care Unit (honor award Jacksonville chpt. AIA 1984, award excellence Concrete Inst. Fla. 1984), Fla. A&M U. Sch. Architecture Bldg. (honor award Jacksonville chpt. AIA 1985), Drew Bldg. (design recognition award Jacksonville area C. of C. 1984, preservation award City of Jacksonville and Jacksonville Hist. Landmarks Com. 1985), Cypress Village Apts. (award for excellence Jacksonville chpt. AIA 1991), Drew Bldg. Renovation (Merit award Jacksonville chpt. AIA. 1989), BEQ & EM Dining Facility (Significant Concrete Structure Fla. First Coast chpt. ACI 1994), Additions and remodeling Pine Forest Elem. Sch. (award for excellence Jacksonville chpt. AIA 1995). Pres. Jacksonville Community Design Ctr.; mem. Jacksonville Hist. Landmarks Com., 1981-84. Served with USMC. Recipient first award nat. competition to design new sch. architecture at Fla. A&M U., 1980. Fellow AIA (honor award Fla. chpt. 1981, John Dyal award Jacksonville chpt. 1985). Democrat. Episcopalian. Home: 133 Marine St Saint Augustine FL 32084-5003 Office: CRG Architects Planners Inc 2111 Corporate Square Blvd Jacksonville FL 32216-1919

RUMPHO-KENNEDY, MARY ELLEN, plant biochemistry educator; b. Faribault, Minn., Aug. 12, 1956; d. Morris Palmer and Blanche Winifred (Miller) Rumpho; m. Robert Alan Kennedy, June 9, 1984; children: Bryce Robert, Curran Patrick; stepchildren: Caleb John, Alex E. BA in Biology, Winona State U., 1978; PhD in Horticulture, Wash. State U., 1982. Rsch. asst. Fed. Water Quality Lab. USDA Forest Svc., Winton, Minn., summer 1978; teaching asst. U. Iowa, Wash. State U., 1978, 79; rsch. asst. Wash. State U., 1979-82; postdoctoral rsch. assoc. Washington State U., 1982-84, asst. prof. courtesy, 1984-85; sr. rsch. assoc. Ohio State U., 1985-87, rsch. scientist, 1987-89; asst. prof. U. Md., 1990-92; assoc. prof. Tex. A&M, 1992—, mem. faculty plant physiology/plant biotechnology, 1993—; vis. rsch. assoc. I.N.R.A. Lab. de Physiologie Vegetale, Bordeaux, France, 1982; vis. adj. lectr. Ohio State U., 1989; faculty rsch. assoc. U. Md., 1989; invited participant profl. seminars, 1979—; lectr. in field. Contbr. articles to profl. jours.; invited to participate in seminars, 1979-96; lectr. in field; reviewer agys. and jours. Sci. Fair judge, 1993-94; presentations at elem., jr. and sr. high schs., 1991. Recipient Sarah Bradley Tyson Found. fellowship, 1981-82, Am. Chem. Soc., NIH, NSF, USDA, Ohio State U., Wash. State U., Tex. A&M honors program grantee. Mem. AAAS, Am. Soc. Plant Physiologists, Phycological Soc., Assn. Women in Sci., Sigma Xi (Student Rsch. award 1990), Gamma Sigma Delta (historian Tex. A&M U. chpt. 1995-96, sec. 1996—). Office: Tex A&M U 522 HFSB Dept Horticultural Scis College Station TX 77843-2133

RUNDELL, ORVIS HERMAN, JR., psychologist; b. Oklahoma City, June 16, 1940; s. Orvis Herman and Virginia Reid (George) R.; BS, U. Okla., 1962, MS, 1972, PhD, 1976; m. Jane Shannon Brians, June 25, 1966; children: Leslie Jane, Anne Reid. Lab. mgr. Okla. Center Alcohol and Drug-Related Studies, Oklahoma City, 1969-76, staff scientist, 1974—; asst. prof. psychiatry and behavioral scis. U. Okla. Health Sci. Center, 1976—; dir. clin. physiology and sleep disorders ctr. Columbia Presbyterian Hosp., Oklahoma City, 1982—; clin. dir. Diagnostic Sleep Ctr. of Dallas, 1989-93; ptnr. Sleep Medicine Assocs., 1994—; cons. in field; mem. instl. rev. bd. U. Okla. Health Sci. Ctr., 1989—. Bd. dirs. Hist. Preservation, Inc., Oklahoma City, 1978-90. Served with USAR, 1963-69. Grantee Nat. Inst. Drug Abuse, Nat. Inst. Alcohol Abuse and Alcoholism, Kerr Found. Fellow Am. Sleep Disorders Assn.; mem. Am. Psychol. Assn., N.Y. Acad. Scis., Psi Chi, Phi Gamma Delta. Author articles, papers in field, chpts. in books; asst. editor Alcohol Tech. Reports, 1976—; cons. editor Psychophysiology, 1974—. Home: 431 NW 20th St Oklahoma City OK 73103-1918 Office: 700 NE 13th St Oklahoma City OK 73104

RUNDHAUG, JOYCE ELIZABETH, biochemist, former nurse; b. Seattle, Sept. 8, 1952; d. Robert Norman and Elsie Elizabeth (Ohm) Ball; m. William George Rundhaug, July 16, 1977. BSN, U. Md., Balt., 1974; PhD, U. Hawaii, 1989. Teaching asst. S.W. Tex. State U., San Marcos, 1978-80; teaching asst. U. Hawaii, Honolulu, 1980-81, rsch. asst., 1982-89; staff fellow Nat. Inst. Environ. Health Sci., Research Triangle Park, N.C., 1989-92; project investigator M.D. Anderson Cancer Ctr. Sci. Park, U. Tex., Smithville, 1992—. Contbr. articles to jours. Cancer Rsch., Carcinogenesis, Jour. Cellular Physiology, Milecular Carcinogenesis. Capt. U.S. Army, 1970-77. Walter Reed Army Inst. Nursing scholar, 1970-74, Achievement Rewards for Coll. Scientists scholar, 1987. Mem. AAAS, Am. Assn. Cancer Rsch., N.Y. Acad. Scis., Phi Kappa Phi. Office: MD Anderson Cancer Ctr Sci Park-Rsch Divsn PO Box 389 Smithville TX 78957

RUNDUS, RAYMOND JOE, English language educator; b. Blue Rapids, Kans., Sept. 25, 1934; s. Paul and Esther Frances (Traxler) R.; m. Constance Jane Orr, Aug. 4, 1955 (div. Jan. 1959); m. Brigitte Obermeyer, June 4, 1959; children: Richard Hans, Ronald Paul, Victoria Rae. BA in English, Coll. of Emporia, Kans., 1955; MA in English, Wayne State U., 1957; PhD in English, U. Nebr., 1969. Cert. permanent 2-yr. coll. tchr., Mich. Grad. asst. Wayne State U., Detroit, 1955-57; tchr. English and French, Caney (Kans.) High Sch., 1960-61, Neodesha (Kans.) High Sch., 1962-64, Hutchinson (Kans.) High Sch., 1964-65; instr., asst. prof. English, Coll. of Emporia, Kans., 1965-70; prof. English, Pembroke (N.C.) State U., 1970—, chmn. dept., 1970-79; vis. prof. Wicbita (Kans.) State U., summers, 1969-70; cons. Johnson County C.C., Shawnee Mission, Kans., 1969, Dillon (S.C.) City Schs., 1972, East Bladen High Sch., Elizabethtown, N.C., 1973; mem. accreditation team N.C. Dept. Pub. Instrn., Raleigh, 1975-77; adj. faculty mem. PhD program Union Inst., 1993—. Editorial asst. Asian Forum, 1974-76; contbr. articles to profl. jours. Chmn. credentials com. Rep. Com. Robeson County, Lumberton, N..C., 1984-85; master of ceremonies, judge pub. speaking contest Robeson County, 4-H, 1984—; planner, master of ceremonies Sonnet Performance, Friends of Libr., Pembroke, 1991-92, pres., 1992-93. With Signal Corps, U.S. Army, 1957-60. Grantee NDEA, 1962, 65, Inst. for Undergrad. Curriculum Reform, U. N.C., 1972, Danforth

Found., 1973, N.C. Humanities Coun., 1974, 75, 76, 92. Mem. AAUP, Nat. Coun. Tchrs. English, South Atlantic MLA, Philol. Assn. Carolinas, Ambs. Club Givens Performing Art Ctr., Native Am. Resource Ctr. (patron). Home: 5512 Tournament Ln Hope Mills NC 28348-9776 Office: U NC at Pembroke 1 University Dr Pembroke NC 28372

RUNNION, CINDIE J., elementary school educator; b. Knoxville, Tenn., Mar. 8, 1958; d. James B. and Josephine Marie (Sykes) Runnion. BS, East Tenn. State U., 1979, MEd, 1989; postgrad., U. Madrid. Sec. Runnion Ent., Newport, Tenn.; tchr. 3rd grade Cocke County Bd. Edn., Newport, 1980—. First Bapt. Ch. meml. scholar. Mem. NEA, ASCD, Tenn. Edn. Assn., Cocke County Edn. Assn. (faculty rep., v.p. 1991-92). Home: 146 New Cave Church Rd Newport TN 37821-7404

RUNYON, MICHAEL, holding company executive. With One Up Enterprises, Inc., Falls Ch., Va., 1977—; pres. U.S. Marine Corp., Falls Ch. Office: One Up Enterprises Inc 7777 Leesburg Pike Ste 406N Falls Church VA 22043-2403*

RUNYON, THEODORE HUBERT, JR., religion educator, minister; b. Tomahawk, Wis., Mar. 20, 1930; s. Theodore H. Sr. and Carol Louise (Jett) R.; m. Cynthia Margaret Guild, June 25, 1955; children: Margaret, David, Stephen. BA, Lawrence U., 1952; BD, Drew U., 1955; ThD, U. Goettingen, Germany, 1958. Ordained to ministry United Meth. Ch. as deacon, 1953, as elder, 1955. Min. to youth Hanson Pl. Cen. United Meth. Ch., Bklyn., 1952-54; pastor Christ United Meth. Ch., Phila., 1954-55; prof. systematic theology Candler Sch. Theology Emory U., Atlanta, 1958—; dir. United Meth. and ecumenical studies, 1980—; co-chmn. Oxford (Eng.) Inst. of Meth. Theol. Studies, 1976-80; mem. exec. com. World Meth. Coun., 1976-81; pres. Emory U. Senate, 1983-84; mem. gen. conf. commn. on Our Theol. Task, 1984-88. Editor: Hope for the Church, 1979, Sanctification and Liberation, 1981, Wesleyan Theology Today, 1985, Theology, Politics and Peace, 1989. Trustee CRISIS INC, Atlanta, 1968-72, Atlanta Assn. for Internat. Edn., 1979-82; mem. exec. com. Japanese Students Assn., Atlanta, 1986—; ministerial mem. Fla. Conf. United Meth. Ch. Recipient Disting. Alumnus award Lawrence U., 1986; named One of Outstanding Educators Am., 1975; Fulbright grantee, 1955-57, 64-65, Danforth Found. grantee, 1971-72, Assn. Theol. Schs. grantee, 1987-88. Mem. AAUP, Am. Acad. Religion, Bonhoeffer Soc., N.Am. Paul Tillich Soc. (pres. 1989-90), Soc. for Values in Higher Edn. Democrat. Home: 780 Houston Mill Rd NE Atlanta GA 30329-4210 Office: Emory U Candler Sch Theology Atlanta GA 30322

RUPERT, DANIEL LEO, elementary education administrator; b. Waynoka, Okla., Nov. 12, 1953; s. Robert Anthony and Georgia Yvonne (Lewis) R.; m. Emily Carol Lummus, June 12, 1977; 1 child, Joshua Daniel. AA, Miss. County C.C., 1979; BA in Social Psychology, Park Coll., 1981; MDiv, New Orleans Bapt. Theol. Sem., 1985; EdS, Miss. State U., Starkville, 1991. Chaplain East Miss. State Hosp., Meridian, 1985-87; dir. of rsch. Am. Family Assn., Tupelo, Miss., 1988-89; cons. Rupert & Assocs., Tupelo, 1989-93; guidance counselor Okolona (Miss.) Elem. Sch., 1993-94, guidance counselor, asst. prin., chpt. 1 coord., 1994-96, prin., 1996—; computer cons. Lee County Schs., Tupelo, 1990. Author: Selected Poems by Author, 1990; co-author: (state core objectives) Health Education Core Objectives for the State of Mississippi, 1991. Prt-time pastor Koinonia Bapt. Mission, Mooreville, Miss., 1992—; mem. Christian Bus. Men's Com., Tupelo, 1989-94. With USAF, 1976-82; capt. USAFR, 1983-91, ret., 1995. Mem. ASCD, Am. Assn. Christian Counselors, United Am. Karate Assn., Christian Martial Arts Instrs. Assn. (bd. dirs.), Miss. Counseling Assn., Tupelo Martial Arts Acad., Luncheon Civitan Club, Chi Sigma Iota. Republican. Southern Baptist. Home: 1931 E Main St PO Box 495 Tupelo MS 38802 Office: Okolona Elem Sch 411 W Main St Okolona MS 38860-1307

RUPP, KELLY S., English language educator; b. Kansas City, Mo., June 25, 1962; d. Jerry Daniel Rogers and Susan (Ehrnman) Todd; m. Gabriel V. Rupp, May 1, 1984; children: Zacharia, Alexandra. BA in English, Pittsburg State U., 1984, MA, 1987. Cert. c.c. tchr., Ariz. English instr., journalism advisor Navajo C.C., Tsaile, Ariz., 1986-91, Redlands C.C., El Reno, Okla., 1991—. Editor: Cow Creek Rev., 1984. Mem. Freedom of Info. Okla., Nat. Coun. Tchrs. English, Okla. Collegiate Press Assn., Okla. Arts Inst. Alumni, Pittsburg State U. Alumni Assn. Democrat. Presbyterian. Home: 406 Cherokee El Reno OK 73036 Office: Redlands C C 1300 S Country Club El Reno OK 73036

RUPPE, ARTHUR MAXWELL, lawyer; b. Boone, N.C., Dec. 15, 1928; s. Arthur Monroe and Floye (Robinson) R.; m. Ruth Marie Ledford; children: Ruth Carol, Sharon Marie, Arthur Maxwell Jr., Susan Lunette. AA, Gardner Webb Coll., 1947; AB, U. N.C., 1950, JD, 1952. Bar: N.C. 1952, U.S. Dist. Ct. (ea. dist.) N.C. 1955, U.S. Ct. Mil. Appeals 1968. Asst. staff, judge advocate U.S. Army, Ft. Bragg, N.C., 1952-55; sole practice Fayetteville, N.C., 1955—. Served to 1st lt. U.S. Army, 1952-55. Mem. ABA, N.C. Bar Assn. (patron), 12 Jud. Dist. Bar Assn., Cumberland County Bar Assn. (pres. 1982-83), K.P. Democrat. Baptist. Home: 336 Summertime Rd Fayetteville NC 28303-4658 Office: 115 S Cool Spring St Fayetteville NC 28301-5723

RUPPERT, SUSAN DONNA, critical care nursing educator, family adult nurse practitioner; b. LaSalle, Ill., Aug. 17, 1953; d. Joseph J. and Phyllis A. (Koontz) Stachowicz; m. Robert M. Ruppert; children: Sarah E., Michael R. AAS in Nursing, Ill. Valley C.C., Oglesby, 1974, AS in Sci., 1975; BSN, No. Ill. U., 1976; MSN, U. Tex. Health Sci. Ctr., San Antonio, 1979; PhD in Nursing, Tex. Woman's U., 1992; FNP, U. Tex. Medical Branch, 1995. CCRN; NP-C, CS. Evening supr. Met. Gen. Hosp., San Antonio, 1978-79; instr. U. Iowa Coll. Nursing, Iowa City, 1979-81; program coord. continuing edn. Meth. Hosp., Houston, 1981-89; assoc. prof. U. Tex. Health Sci. Ctr., Houston, 1989—. Editor: Critical Care Nursing: Clinical Management Through the Nursing Process, 2d edit.; contbr. articles to profl. jours. and books. Recipient Outstanding Young Alumni award No. Ill. U., 1992, Outstanding Houston Nurse award Tex. Nurses Assn., 1995. Mem. AACN (past bd. dirs., Excellence in Critical Care Edn. award 1995), ANA, Am. Acad. Nurse Practitioners, Tex. Nurses Assn. (Nursing Celebration '95 honoree 1995), Soc. Critical Care Medicine, Greater Houston Soc. Critical Care Medicine, Houston Area Nurse Practitioners, Am. Bus. Women's Assn., Sigma Theta Tau (Regional Dissertation award 1992). Home: 4602 Springfield Lakes St Sugar Land TX 77479-2051 Office: U Tex Houston Hlth Sci Ctr 1100 Holcombe Blvd Rm 6.250 Houston TX 77030-3911

RUPPRECHT, NANCY ELLEN, historian, educator; b. Coeur d'Alene, Idaho, Sept. 23, 1948; d. George John and Nancy Berneeda (Baird) R. BA with honors, U. Mo., 1967, MA, 1969; PhD, U. Mich., 1982. Acad. dir. pilot program U. Mich., Ann Arbor, 1971-73, lectr. in women studies, 1973-75; vis. lectr. history U. Mo., St. Louis, 1976-77; vis. instr. of history Wash. U., St. Louis, 1977-79, Grinnell (Iowa) Coll., 1979-81; asst. prof. Oakland U., Rochester, Mich., 1981-83; asst. prof. of history Mid. Tenn. State U., Murfreesboro, 1985-91, assoc. prof., 1991—; dir. women's studies program Middle Tenn. State U., 1988—, publicity dir. women's history month, 1989-92, mem. faculty senate, 1992-95. Contbr. articles to profl. jours. Recipient Cantrel award MTSO, 1995-96. Mem. AAUP (chpt. v.p. 1988-89, pres. 1989-93), AAUW, NOW, Am. Hist. Assn., S.E. Women's Studies Assn., So. Hist. Assn. (chair nominating com. European divsn. 1996—), So. Humanities Assn., Holocaust Studies Assn., Mid. Tenn. Women's Studies Assn., German Studies Assn., Women in Higher Edn. in Tenn., Concerned Faculty and Adminstrv. Women (chpt. v.p. 1993-95, chpt. pres. 1995-96), Assn. of Faculty and Adminstrv. Women (chpt. pres. 1995—). Home: 1106 Jones Blvd Murfreesboro TN 37129-2310 Office: Middle Tenn State U 275 Peck Hall Murfreesboro TN 37132-0001

RUSH, AUGUSTUS JOHN, psychiatrist, educator; b. Glen Ridge, N.J., Dec. 15, 1942; s. Augustus John Jr. and Helen Rush; m. Susan Rush, Dec. 5, 1970 (div. Mar. 1977); 1 child, Matthew; m. Dee Miller, May 31, 1986; 1 child, Augustus John III. AB in Biochemistry cum laude, Princeton U., 1964; MD, Columbia U., 1968. Intern Northwestern U., Chgo., 1968-69; resident U. Pa., Phila., 1972-75; asst. prof. U. Okla. Health Scis. Ctr., Oklahoma City, 1975-78; assoc. prof. U. Tex. Southwestern Med. Ctr., Dallas, 1978-83, Betty Jo Hay prof., 1983-88, Betty Jo Hay Disting. Chair in Mental Health, 1988—; dir. Mental Health Clin. Rsch. Ctr., Dallas, 1987—. uthor: Beating Depression, 1983; co-author: Cognitive Therapy of Depression, 1979, Cognitive Therapy of Depressed Adolescents, 1994; editor: Short-Term Psychotherapies for Depression, 1982; co-editor: Depression: Basic Mechanisms Diagnosis and Treament, 1986—; assoc. editor Biol. Psychiatry, 1994—. Trustee Greenhill Sch., Dallas, 1988-92. Fellow Am. Psychiat. Assn., Am. Coll. Psychiatrists, Am. Coll. Neuropsychopharmacology; mem. Soc. for Psychotherapy Rsch. (pres. 1984-85), Soc. for Biol. Psychiatry (sec.-treas. 1990-94, v.p. 1994, pres. 1996-97), Dallas County Med. Soc. Office: U Tex Southwestern Med Ctr Dept Psychiatry 5959 Harry Hines Blvd Ste 600 Dallas TX 75235-6233

RUSHER, DERWOOD H., II, lawyer; b. Roanoke, Va., Dec. 23, 1954; s. Derwood H. and Edith (McFadden) R.; m. Ashley Simmons, Aug. 15, 1987; 1 child, Paige C. BS, Va. Poly. Inst. and State U., 1977; JD, U. Richmond, 1980. Bar: Va. 1980, N.C. 1987, Ga. 1993, U.S. Dist. Ct. (mid. dist.) N.C. 1987, U.S. Dist Ct. (we. dist.) Va. 1987, U.S. Dist. Ct. (ea. dist.) Va. 1988, U.S. Ct. Appeals (4th cir.) 1980, U.S. Ct. Appeals (7th cir.) 1981, U.S. Ct. Appeals (3d, 5th, 6th, 8th, 9th, 10th, 11th, D.C., Fed. cirs.) 1987, U.S. Supreme Ct. 1987, U.S. Dist. Ct. Ariz. 1990, U.S. Dist. Ct. (no. dist.) Ga. 1993. Assoc. Street, Street, Street, Scott & Bowman, Grundy, Va., 1980-81; atty. Standard Oil Co., Chgo., 1981-84, Lexington, Ky., 1984-86; assoc. Womble, Carlyle, Sandridge & Rice, Winston-Salem, N.C., 1986-92; sr. atty. Rollins, Inc., Atlanta, 1992-95; of counsel King & Spalding, Atlanta, 1996—. Mem. ABA, Phi Kappa Phi, Phi Delta Phi, Beta Gamma Sigma, Sigma Chi. Methodist. Home: 1320 Northcliff Trace Roswell GA 30076-3274 Office: King & Spalding Law Dept 191 Peachtree St Atlanta GA 30303-1763

RUSHING, DOROTHY MARIE, retired historian, educator; b. Bonham, Tex., Aug. 28, 1925; d. Van Bain and Ada Belle (Price) Hawkins; m. J. E. Rushing, Aug. 6, 1960 (dec. 1985); children: Charles Maret, Bill Maret, Bob Maret, Charles Rushing, Martha Rushing Sosebee. BA, Tex. Woman's U., 1972; MA, East Tex. State U., 1974; PhD, U. North Tex., 1981. Cert. history, lang. arts. secondary tchr., Tex. Tchr. pub. schs., 1972-86; instr. East Tex. State U., Commerce, 1972-74, 80-81; teaching fellow U. North Tex., Denton, 1975-76; prof. Richland Coll., Dallas, 1975-95, Collin County Community Coll., McKinney, Tex., 1975-95; historian-archivist J.C. Penney, Inc., Dallas, 1988-95; lectr., Dallas, 1972—; vis. prof. Johns Hopkins U., 1985, U. Va., 1989; statis. analyst Dallas County C.C., 1982; lay rep. N.E. Tex. Libr. System, 1984-89. Editor, author: Texas: The Lone Star State, 1984; contbg. author: Beyond Sundown, 1975, Handbook of Texas, 1996. Decorated Honorary Cross of Lorraine (France); named Outstanding Instr., Richland Coll., 1987; postdoctoral fellow NEH, 1985, 89; grantee Dallas County C.C. Dist., 1984. Mem. Phi Kappa Phi, Sigma Tau Delta, Phi Alpha Theta. Home: 1214 Patricia Ln Garland TX 75042-8041

RUSK, JOHANNA NEPPI-MARIE, secondary education educator; b. Elizabethtown, Ky., Jan. 30, 1970; d. Cecil Gordon and Clara Mae (Thomas) Druen; m. Ryan Edward Rusk, June 5, 1993; 1 child, Jacob Ryan. Student, Harlaxton Coll., England, 1990; BA, U. Evansville, 1992. Cert. tchr., Ind., Ky. Tchr., speech coach Evansville (Ind.) Sch. Corp., 1992-93; tchr. Madison County Schs., Richmond, Ky., 1993-94, Hardin County Schools, Elizabethtown, 1994—; rep. Hardin County Edn. Assn., Elizabethtown, 1994-96, Ky. Edn. Assn., 1994-96; pub. rels. liaison North Hardin H.S., Radcliff, Ky., 1995—; com. mem. Ky. Edn. Assn., 1996—. Mem. Nat. Coun. of Tchrs. of English, Ky. Coun. of Tchrs. of English/Language Arts.

RUSKIN, LES D., chiropractor; b. Detroit, Feb. 26, 1960; s. George J. and Marilyn D. (Moore) R.; m. Anna, Aug. 28, 1987. BS, U. State of N.Y. Regents Coll. Degree, Albany; degree, Sch. Chiropractic, 1986; D of Chiropractic, Life Coll., Marietta, Ga., 1986. Assoc. dr., clinic dir. tng. program Hofmann Chiropractic Ctr., Allen Pk., Mich., 1987-88; clinic dir., assoc. dr. Hamtramck (Mich.) Chiropractic Ctr., 1988-89; clinic dir. Boot Ranch Chiropractic Ctr., Palm Harbor, Fla., 1990—. Mem. Greater Clearwater C. of C., Greater Palm Harbor Area C. of C. Named Outstanding Young Men of Am. Mem. Am. Chiropractic Assn., Internat. Chiropractors Assn., Fla. Chiropractic Assn., Fla. Chiropractic Soc., Mich. Chiropractic Coun., Am. Running and Fitness Assn., Acad. Indsl. Health Cons., Mich. State U. Alumni Assn. (life), Sch. Chiropractic Alumni Assn. (life coll.), Am. Coll. Sports Medicine, Am. Acad. Pain Mgmt., Better Bus. Bur. West Fla. Office: Boot Ranch Chiropractic 336 E Lake Rd Palm Harbor FL 34685-2427

RUSLING, BARBARA N(EUBERT), real estate executive, state legislator; b. St. Louis, Nov. 27, 1945; d. Ralph L. and Rosemary (Stroot) Neubert; m. Randolph H. Wieser, Apr. 23, 1966 (div. Nov. 1983); children: Keith, Steve, Eric; m. Robert Best Rusling, Aug. 2, 1985. BA, Vanderbilt U., 1966; postgrad., Baylor U., 1975. Lic. real estate broker. Appraisal intern Smith Real Estate, Waco, Tex., 1975; resident real estate broker Sanger Suburban Realty, Waco, 1975-81, sales mgr., 1981-83; pres., gen. mgr. Coldwell Banker Hallmark Realty, Waco, 1983—; mem. from dist. 57 Tex. State Ho. Reps., 1995—. Chmn. bd. dirs. YWCA, Waco, 1976-79; dir. Leadership Waco Program, 1986-87; various positions Hist. Waco Found.; bd. dirs. Waco Civic Theatre, Family Counseling Ctr., 1991—, United Way, 1992—, Family Abuse Ctr., 1993—, Waco Better Bus. Bur., 1994—. Mem. Tex. Assn. Realtors (edn. com., strategic planning com. 1983-95, realtor lawyer com. 1985-93), Realtors Nat. Mktg. Inst. (cert.), Waco Bd. Realtors (past bd. dirs., salesman of yr. 1979), Waco C. of C. (bd. dirs. 1990-93), Waco Sailing Club, Kappa Delta. Home: 1635 Meandering Way China Spring TX 76633-2905 Office: Coldwell Banker Hallmark Realty 7101 Bosque Blvd Waco TX 76710-4018

RUSSAC, RANDALL JOSEPH, psychology educator; b. Perth, Australia, Jan. 8, 1947; came to U.S., 1948; s. Joe Russac and Billie Patricia (Hunt) Flynn; m. Julie Ann Bush, Nov. 22, 1971 (div. Sept. 1980); children: Megan, Beth, Adam, Emily; m. Janet Lynn Harris, Aug. 22, 1985. BA in Psychology, U. Wash., 1972; PhD in Psychology, Ariz. State U., 1977. Cert. sch. psychologist, Fla. Assoc. prof. psychology U. North Fla., Jacksonville, 1977—, chmn. dept., 1986-87, dir. Lab. for Rsch. in Neurocognitive Devel., 1985—; ptnr. Weaver and Russac, Cons.; co-owner Tots to Teens Book Orders, Inc., Jacksonville, 1988—. Author Memory Assessment Battery test, 1988. Bd. dirs. Mandarin Libr. Assn., Jacksonville, 1989-90; mem. Jacksonville Community Coun., Inc., 1988—, Greater Jacksonville Families in Action, 1988—. With U.S. Army, 1967-70, Vietnam. Decorated Purple Heart. Mem. Am. Psychol. Soc., SE Psychol. Assn., Cognitive Neurosci. Group Jacksonville (founder, pres. 1987-90). Home: 2057 River Oaks Dr Jacksonville FL 32259-8330 Office: U North Fla 4567 Saint Johns Bluff Rd S Jacksonville FL 32224-2646

RUSSE, CONRAD THOMAS CAMPBELL, accountant; b. Bethesda, Md., July 15, 1954; s. Frederick William Jr. and Constance Oakman (Fagan) R.; m. Deborah Joyce Thompson, June 14, 1980; children: Thomas Campbell, Catherine Alexandra, Caroline Saunders. BS, Duke U., 1977; MBA, Ga. State U., 1982. CPA, Ga., Tenn., N.C. Estimator Advance Builders, Inc., Smyrna, Ga., 1978; contractor B&B Drywalls, Marietta, 1979-81; acct. Evans, Snyder & Co., Atlanta, 1981-82; tax acct. Peat Marwick Mitchell & Co., Charlotte, N.C., 1982-85, Ernst & Whinney & Co., Chattanooga, 1985-86; tax mgr. Costello, Strain & Co, CPAs, Chattanooga, 1986-89; prin. Thomas C. Russe, CPAs, Chattanooga, 1989—; bd. dirs., treas. Visually Impaired Tng. and Learning Ctr., Chattanooga, 1988-93, Chattanooga Tax Practitioners, 1987—, pres., 1991. Membership chmn. Cherokee Area coun. Boy Scouts Am., Chattanooga, 1987, 88; bd. dirs. Allegro Dance Theater, 1990-92. English Speaking Union scholar, 1972-73. Mem. AICPA, SAR, N.C. Assn. CPAs, Ga. Soc. CPAs (mem. taxation com. 1993—), Tenn. Soc. CPAs (taxation com. 1990, 92, tax liaison com. 1992—), Chattanooga Estate Planning Coun., Chattanooga Area C. of C. (seminars chmn. small bus. coun. 1987, 88, steering com. small bus. coun. 1986—), CPA Club (bd. dirs. 1991-92), CPA-Atty. Forum (pres. 1992-94), Chattanooga Golf and Country Club. Episcopalian. Home: 1108 Signal Rd Signal Mountain TN 37377-3122 Office: 407 Chestnut St Ste A 117 Chattanooga TN 37402-4905

RUSSELL, ANDREW MILO, music educator; b. Fredericksburg, Tex., July 16, 1948; s. Daniel Louden and Evelyn Sarah (Allen) R.; m. Sharon Anne Shelburne, June 2, 1968 (div. June 1994); children: Emily Christine, Andrea Layne, Dana Leslie. MusB, U. Houston, 1974; performance cert., Ind. U., 1974; MusM, Ind. U., Bloomington, 1975. Asst. prof. Baylor U., Waco, Tex., 1975-79; assoc. prof. U. Tex., Arlington, 1979—; cons. Tex. Commn. on Arts, Austin, 1985—. Performer numerous concerts, recitals nationwide, 1968—. E-5 with U.S. Army, 1971-74. Mem. Internat. Trombone Assn. (Emory B. Remington award), Am. Fedn. Musicians, Tex. Music Educators Assn., Chgo. Chamber Brass. Democrat. Baptist. Home: 1213 Scott Dr Hurst TX 76053-4223 Office: U Tex PO Box 19105 Arlington TX 76019

RUSSELL, ANGELA PARISH HALL, health care company executive, educator; b. Kingston, Jamaica, Mar. 5, 1953; d. Vernon and Cecelia (Thompson) Parish; m. Sidonia Russell, Aug. 31, 1984; 1 child, Keisha Hall. Cert., N.Y. Inst. Dietitics, 1971; BSN, Herbert H. Lehman Coll., 1976; MA, Columbia U., 1979; PhD, U. Miami (Fla.), 1992. Cert. advanced nurse practitioner, Fla., N.Y.; cert. occupl. health nurse; cert. employee assistance profl.; cert. health edn. specialist; cert. adult nurse practitioner. Dietitian, supr. Cliffside Nursing Home, N.Y., 1971-73; surg. staff nurse Albert Einstein Med. Ctr., N.Y., 1976-79; coronary care nurse S. Miami (Fla.) Hosp., 1979-80; part time coronary ICU Larkin Hosp., 1981-83; occupational health nurse, mgr. So. Bell, Miami, Fla., 1980-91; asst. mgr. Health Svcs. Edn./Promotion-Life Reach, Bell South Corp., Miami, 1991—; pres., CEO APR Health Svcs. Inc., 1993—; nurse practitioner Mt. Sinai Hosp., 1993-95; mem. adj. faculty Fla. Internat. U., 1996; coord. health edn. South Fla., Nashville area, 1990-93; part-time supr. geriatric care East Haven Health Related Facility, N.Y., 1978-79; guest lectr. U. Miami, 1987. Author: Pre-Postnatal Program and EAP External Model for Small Business-Marketing Program, 1995, 96. Vol. prison release program Woman's Detention Ctr. Charles J. Turcotte scholar, 1987; recipient rsch. in excellence award for dissertation, 1992. Mem. Coun. on Nursing and Anthropology, Am. Occupl. Health Nurses Assn. (editl. rev. panel 1987-89, assoc. editor Jour. Health Promotion 1992-94), Fla. State Nursing Assn. Occupl. Health Nurses, Miami Assn. Occupl. Health Nurses, Jamaican Nurses Assn., Phi Lamba Pi, Sigma Theta Tau. Office: APR Health Svcs Inc 9754 W Datura St Miami FL 33157-5431

RUSSELL, ARMISTEAD (TED) GOODE, enviromental engineering educator, consultant; b. Pullman, Wash., Jan. 16, 1957; s. Thomas Solon and Cynthia Ann (Williams) R.; m. Jerri Aleen Fischer, Aug. 14, 1982; children: Samantha M., C. Kurtis. BSin Mech. Engring., Wash. State U., 1979; MS in Mech. Engring., Calif. Inst. Tech., 1980, PhD in Mech. Engring., 1995. Rsch. scientist Calif. Inst. Tech., Pasadena, 1985; asst. prof. mech. engring. Carnegie Mellon U., Pitts., 1985-90, assoc. prof. mech. engring., 1990-94, prof. mech. engring., 1994-96; Ga. Power prof. environ. engring. Ga. Inst. Tech., Atlanta, 1996—; program review coms. EPA, 1987—, Fed. Adv. Com. Act subcom. ozone, particulate matter and regional haze, 1995—; coms. ozone formation and control, risk assessment to toxic air pollutants NRC, 1989-94; subcom. on oxygenated fuels White House Office Sci. Telanology and Policy, 1995-96; vis. prof. Ecole Poly. Fed. de'Lausanne, Switzerland, 1993-95. Recipient Ralph Teetor award SAE, 1988. Mem. ASME, Am. Assn. Aerosol Rsch. (co-chair conf. 1995), Air and Water Mgmt. Assn. Office: Ga Inst Tech 200 Bobby Dodd Way Atlanta GA 30332

RUSSELL, BRENDA FLANNIGAN, critical care, medical/surgical nurse; b. Columbia, S.C., Sept. 1, 1944; d. Mark and Mamie (Miles) Flannigan; children: Craig Stone, Carol Taylor; m. Allan W. Russell, Mar. 31, 1990. AS, Albany (Ga.) Jr. Coll., 1985. RN, Ga.; cert. post anesthesia nurse. Staff nurse post anesthetic unit Atlanta Outpatient Peachtree Dunwoody Ctr., 1991—. Mem. Am. Soc. Post Anesthesia Nurses, Ga. Assn. Post Anesthesia Nurses (pres., v.p., chmn. state seminar com., organizer S.W. and S.E. dists., pres., v.p., nominating chmn.), Ga. Nurses Assn. Home: 5303 Pounds Dr N Stone Mountain GA 30087-3523

RUSSELL, BYRON EDWARD, physical therapy educator; b. Louisiana, Mo., Apr. 27, 1949; s. John Franklin and Nellie Mae (Bryant) R.; m. Anna Jean Talkington, Mar. 25, 1972 (div. Dec. 19, 1979); children: Brad Michael, Audrey Lynn; m. Roberta Louise Snover, May 22, 1982. BS in Microbiology, Colo. State U., 1975; BS in Phys. Therapy, Tex. Tech. Health Sci. Ctr., 1988; MHS in Phys. Therapy, U. Indpls., 1994. Staff therapist Lubbock (Tex.) Gen. Hosp., 1988-89, S.W. Gen. Hosp., San Antonio, 1989-90; dir. phys. therapy Brady/Green Health Ctr., San Antonio, 1990-92; asst. prof. phys. therapy U. Tex. Health Sci. Ctr., San Antonio, 1992-95, Hardin-Simmons U., Abilene, Tex., 1995—; item writer Profl. Exam Svc., N.Y.C., 1996—; editor PT Series, Del-Mar Pubs., 1993-94. Editl. bd. Indsl. Rehab. Jour., 1996. Capt. USAR, 1989—. Mem. Am. Phys. Therapy Assn., Tex. Phys. Therapy Assn. (vice chair ctrl. dist.), Am. Coll. Sports Medicine, Sigma Xi. Baptist. Office: Hardin-Simmons University Box 16065 Abilene TX 79698-6065

RUSSELL, CLIFFORD SPRINGER, economics and public policy educator; b. Holyoke, Mass., Feb. 11, 1938; s. Kenneth Clifford and Helen Alwilda (Springer) R.; m. Louise Pancoast Bennett, Feb. 3, 1965 (div. June 1985); m. Susan Vanston Reid, Sept. 7, 1985; stepchildren: Timothy Taylor Greene, Elizabeth Claussen Greene. BA, Dartmouth Coll., 1960; PhD, Harvard U., 1968. Sr. rsch. assoc. Resources for the Future, Washington, 1968-70, fellow, 1970-73, sr. fellow, 1973-85, div. dir., 1981-85; prof. econs. and pub. policy Vanderbilt U., Nashville, 1986—, dir. Vanderbilt Inst. for Pub. Policy Studies, 1986—. Author: Drought and Water Supply: Implications of the Massachusetts Experience for Municipal Planning, 1970, Residuals Management in Industry: A Case Study of Petroleum Refining, 1973, Steel Production: Processes, Products and Residuals, 1976, Environment Quality Management: An Application to the Lower Delaware Valley, 1976, Freshwater Recreational Fishing: The National Benefits of Water Pollution Control, 1982, Enforcing Pollution Control Laws, 1986; contbr. articles to profl. jours. Trustee, treas. Environ. Def. Fund, N.Y.C., and Washington, 1973-85; mem. Tenn. Gov.'s Energy Adv. Bd., Nashville, 1989-94; trustee Tenn. Environ. Coun., Nashville, 1989-96; pres. 1992-95. Lt. USN, 1960-63. Mem. Assn. Environ. and Resource Econs. (bd. dirs. 1983-85, chmn. workshop com., pres. 1993-94). Home: 1222 Clifftee Dr Brentwood TN 37027-4105 Office: Vanderbilt Inst Pub Policy Studies 1207 18th Ave S Nashville TN 37212-2807

RUSSELL, DAN M., JR., federal judge; b. Magee, Miss., Mar. 15, 1913; s. Dan M. and Beulah (Watkins) R.; m. Dorothy Tudury, Dec. 27, 1942; children—Ronald Truett, Dorothy Dale, Richard Brian. B.A., U. Miss., 1935, LL.B., 1937. Bar: Miss. bar 1937. Practice in Gulfport and Bay St. Louis, Miss.; U.S. judge So. Dist. Miss., 1965—; now sr. judge; Dir. So. Savs. & Loan Assn., Gulfport, Miss. Chmn. Hancock (Miss.) Civic Action Assn., 1964—; Democratic presdl. elector, 1964; chmn. Hancock County Election Commn., 1959-64. Served to lt. comdr. USNR, 1941-45. Mem. Miss. Bar Assn., Hancock County Bar Assn. (v.p. 1964-65), Hancock County C. of C. (pres. 1946), Tau Kappa Alpha, Scribblers. Club: Rotarian (pres. Bay St. Louis, Miss. 1946). Office: US Dist Ct PO Box 1930 Gulfport MS 39502-1930*

RUSSELL, DANIEL N., physicist; b. Munich, 1953; parents Am. citizens; s. Nelson H. and Fifi Eugenia Russell. BA in Zoology, U. S.Fla., 1980, BS in Physics, 1980, MS in Solid State Physics, 1985. Biophysics rsch. asst. U. South Fla., Tampa, 1976-79; pvt. tutor Tampa, 1980-84; adj. prof. math, physics, astronomy Hillsborough C.C., Tampa, 1987-88; with nuclear radiol. control office Norfolk Naval Shipyard, Dept. of Navy, Va., 1989-90; elec. engr. U.S. Dept. Commerce Patent Office, Washington, 1990-92; founder, physics and patent cons., owner Aquellacraft, Tampa, 1985—; lab. instr. U. South Fla., 1982-83; tchr. math. Hillsborough County Coun. Gifted and Talented Students, 1984. Contbr. articles to Internat. Jour. Biometeorology, Bioelectricity, Bioelectrochemistry and Bioenergetics, others; patentee on non-linear tunnel hull boat, 1995. Republican. Home: 151 Barbados Ave Tampa FL 33606-3558 Office: 4601 W Kennedy Blvd Ste 214 Tampa FL 33609

RUSSELL, DAVID EMERSON, consulting mechanical engineer; b. Jacksonville, Fla., Dec. 20, 1922; s. David Herbert and Wilhelmina (Ash) R.; B.Mech. Engring., U. Fla., 1948; postgrad. Oxford (Eng.) U. Mech. engr. United Fruit Co., N.Y.C., 1948-50, U.S. Army C.E., Jacksonville, 1950-54, Aramco, Saudi Arabia, 1954-55; v.p. Beiswenger Hoch and Assocs., Inc., Jacksonville, 1955-57; owner, operator David E. Russell and Assocs., cons. engrs., Jacksonville, 1957—. Chmn. Jacksonville Water Quality Control Bd., 1969-73; bd. dirs. Jacksonville Hist. Soc., 1981-82; mem. Jacksonville

Bicentennial Commn., 1973-79. Served to 2d lt. AUS, 1943-46. Recipient Outstanding Service award City of Jacksonville, 1974. Registered profl. engr., Fla., Ga. Mem. ASME (chmn. N.E. Fla. 1967-68), Nat. Soc. Profl. Engrs., ASHRAE, Fla. Engring. Soc. Episcopalian. Club: University (Jacksonville). Contbr. articles to profl. jours.; holder of 5 U.S. patents. Avocations: world travel, boating, classical music. Home: 4720 Timuquana Rd Jacksonville FL 32210-8231 Office: 110 Riverside Ave Jacksonville FL 32202-4906

RUSSELL, DAVID L., federal judge; b. Sapulpa, Okla., July 7, 1942; s. Lynn and Florence E. (Brown) R.; m. Dana J. Wilson, Apr. 16, 1971; 1 child, Sarah Elizabeth. BS, Okla. Bapt. U., 1963; J.D., Okla. U., 1965. Bar: Okla. 1965. Asst. atty. gen. State of Okla., Oklahoma City, 1968-69, legal adviser to gov., 1969-70; legal adviser Senator Dewey Bartlett, Washington, 1973-75; U.S. atty. for Western dist. Okla. Dept. Justice, 1975-77, 81-82; ptnr. Benefield & Russell, Oklahoma City, 1977-81; chief judge U.S. Dist. Ct. (we. dist.) Okla., Oklahoma City, 1982—. Lt. comdr. JAGC, USN, 1965-68. Selected Outstanding Fed. Ct. Trial judge Okla. Trial Lawyers Assn., 1988. Mem. Okla. Bar Assn., Fed. Bar Assn. (pres. Oklahoma City chpt. 1981). Republican. Methodist. Office: US Dist Ct 3309 US Courthouse 200 NW 4th St Oklahoma City OK 73102-3003

RUSSELL, DONALD STUART, federal judge; b. Lafayette Springs, Miss., Feb. 22, 1906; s. Jesse and Lula (Russell) R.; m. Virginia Utsey, June 15, 1929; children: Donald, Mildred, Scott, John. AB, U. S.C., 1925, LLB, 1928; postgrad., U. Mich., 1929; LLD (hon.), Wofford Coll., Lander Coll., The Citadel, U.S.C., Emory U., Clemson U., C.W. Post Coll. Bar: S.C. 1928. Pvt. practice law Spartanburg, 1930-42, 1938-42, 47-51, 57-63; with Nicholls, Wyche & Byrnes, Nicholls, Wyche & Russell, and Nicholls & Russell, 1930-42; mem. Price Adjustment Bd., War Dept., Washington, 1942; asst. to dir. econ. stabilization, 1942, asst. to dir. war mobilization, 1943; dep. dir. Office War Mobilization Reconversion, 1945; asst. sec. state, 1945-47; pres. U. S.C., 1951-57; gov. S.C., 1963-65, mem. U.S. Senate from S.C., 1965-66, U.S. Dist. Ct. judge, 1967-71; judge U.S. Ct. Appeals, Spartanburg, S.C., 1971—. Mem. Wriston Com. on Reorgn. Fgn. Service, 1954; trustee emeritus Emory U., Atlanta, Converse Coll., Spartanburg, S.C., Benedict Coll., Columbia, S.C. Served as maj. AUS, 1944, SHAEF, France. Mem. ABA, Am. Law Inst., S.C. Bar Assn., Spartanburg County Bar Assn., Phi Beta Kappa. Methodist. Office: US Ct Appeals 4th Ct PO Box 1985 Spartanburg SC 29304-1985

RUSSELL, ELBERT WINSLOW, neuropsychologist; b. Las Vegas, N.Mex., June 4, 1929; s. Josiah Cox and Ruth Annice (Winslow) R.; children from previous marriage: Gwendolyn Marie Harvey, Franklin Winslow, Kirsten Nash, Jonathan Nash; m. Sally Lynn Kolitz, Apr. 2, 1989. BA, Earlham Coll., Richmond, Ind., 1951; MA, U. Ill., 1953; MS, Pa. State U., 1958; PhD, U. Kans., 1968. Clin. psychologist Warnersville (Pa.) State Hosp., 1959-61; clin. neuropsychologist VA Med. Ctr., Cin., 1968-71; dir. neuropsychology lab. VA Med. Ctr., Miami, Fla., 1971-89, rsch. psychologist, 1989—; adj. prof. Nova U., Ft. Lauderdale, 1980-87, U. Miami Med. Sch., 1980-94, U. Miami, 1979—. Author: (with C. Neuringer and G. Goldstein) Assessment of Brain Damage, 1970; (with R.I. Starkey) Halstead Russell Neuropsychology Evaluation System (manual and computer program), 1993; contbr. articles to profl. jours. Fellow APA, Am. Psychol. Soc., Nat. Acad. Neuropsychology; mem. Sigma Xi. Democrat. Soc. of Friends. Home: 6091 SW 79th St Miami FL 33143-5030 Office: 6262 Sunset Dr Ste 228 Miami FL 33143-4843

RUSSELL, FRED MCFERRIN, journalist, author, lawyer; b. Nashville, Aug. 27, 1906; s. John E. and Mabel Lee (McFerrin) R.; m. Katherine Wyche Early, Nov. 2, 1933; children: Katherine (Mrs. Earl Beasley), Ellen (Mrs. Robert Sadler), Lee (Mrs. John Brown, Carolyn Russell. Student, Vanderbilt U., 1923-27. Bar: Tenn. 1928. Atty. Real Estate Title Co., 1928; reporter Nashville Banner, 1929, sports editor, 1930-69, sports dir., 1969-87, v.p., 1955—; chmn. honors ct. Nat. Football Found. and Hall of Fame, 1967-92; So. chmn. Heisman Trophy Com., 1946-92. Author: 50 Years of Vanderbilt Football, 1938, I'll Go Quietly, 1944, I'll Try Anything Twice, 1945, Funny Thing About Sport, 1948, Bury Me in an Old Press Box, 1957, Big Bowl Football, 1963; contbr. to mags. including Saturday Evening Post, 1939-63. A founder Harpeth Hall Sch., 1951, trustee, 1951-55; nat. pres. Vanderbilt Alumni Assn., 1960-61; dir. Children's Regional Med. Center, 1970-72. Recipient Nat. Headliners award, 1936; Grantland Rice award for sports writing, 1955; Jake Wade award, 1966; Coll. Football Centennial award, 1969; writing award Golf Writers Assn. Am., 1972; award for disting. journalism U.S. Olympic Com., 1976; Disting. Am. award Nat. Football Found. and Hall of Fame, 1980; Amos Alonzo Stagg award Am. Football Coaches Assn., 1981; award Nat. Turf Writers Assn., 1983; ed Smith award AP Sports Editors, 1984; named to Tenn. Sports Hall of rame, 1974, Nat. Sportscasters and Sportswriters Hall of Fame, 1988. Mem. Football Writers Assn. Am. (pres. 1960-61), Sigma Delta Chi, Kappa Sigma (nat. man of yr. 1983), Omicron Delta Kappa. Methodist. Clubs: Belle Meade Country, Univ. Lodges: Masons (33 degree), Shriners. Office: Nashville Banner 1100 Broad St Nashville TN 37203

RUSSELL, GEORGE HAW, video production company executive; b. Neosho, Mo., May 22, 1945; s. Kenneth L. and Marjorie (Haw) R.; m. Suzanne Bennett, June 1, 1967; children: Margaret Anne, Marjorie Jane, Karen Lee, George Andrew. BA, La. State U., 1967. Exec. v.p. Ednl. Filmstrips, Huntsville, Tex., 1974-90; chief exec. officer Ednl. Video Network, Huntsville, 1990—; ptnr. The Sam Houston Group Ltd. Liability Partnership, Huntsville, 1991—. Producer ednl. videos Nombres et Couleurs, 1988 (Silver Apple award 1988), Napoleon, 1989 (Silver Apple award 1989), Bullfight, 1990, The French Revolution, 1990; exec. producer Spain's Historic Cities, 1992, Munich's Oktoberfest, 1992, The New Nutriton Pyramid, 1992, The Visual Language of Design, 1992, Florence, 1993, Joan of Arc, 1993, New Food Guide Pyramid, 1993, Cleaning and Maintaining Your VCR, 1993, Arts and Crafts of Mexico, 1993, Understanding Geysers and Hot Springs, 1993, Thoreau at Walden Pond, 1993, French Markets, 1993, Great Zimbabwe, 1993. Bd. govs. Tex. Com. on Natural Resources, Dallas, 1979—; bd. dirs. Gibbs-Powell House Mus., Huntsville, 1984—, Natural Area Preservation Assn., Dallas, 1986—; chmn. forest practices Lone Star Sierra Club, Austin, Tex., 1984—; chmn. Fed. Forest Reform, Washington, D.C., 1991—. Ist lt. U.S. Army, 1971-74. Recipient spl. achievement award Sierra Club, San Francisco 1985, chpt. conservation award 1987, environ. heroes for centennial 1991; named Citizen of Month, Huntsville Item 1988. Democrat. Methodist. Home: 1409 19th St Huntsville TX 77340-5056 Office: Ednl Video Network 1401 19th St Huntsville TX 77340-5057

RUSSELL, GERALD EDWARD, social worker, retired army officer; b. Monticello, Miss., Apr. 7, 1933; s. Jessie Edward and Lavert Virdew (Franklin) R.; m. Nina Merle Holmes, Dec. 17, 1955; children: Tina, Aprile, Glen, Eric. MSW, Tulane U., 1962. Cert. social worker, La.; diplomate Am. Bd. Examiners and NASW in Clin. Social Work. With Dept. Pub. Welfare, Jackson, Miss., 1958-64, supr. child welfare, 1962-64; commd. 1st lt. U.S. Army, 1964, advanced to grade of lt. col., 1979; ret., 1982; chief social work U.S. Army Hosp., Ft. Jackson, S.C., 1964-66; mem. child fellowship program Walter Reed Hosp., Washington, 1966-68; asst. chief social work Brooke Gen. Hosp., Ft. Sam Houston, Tex., 1968-72; chief social work U.S. Army Hosp., Ft. Polk, La., 1972-82, supr. child protection, 1982—. Mem. NASW (cert.), Acad. Cert. Social Workers, La. Assn. Substance Abuse, La. Conf. Social Welfare, La. Soc. Clin. Social Workers. Home: 136 Russell Cir Leesville LA 71446-9011

RUSSELL, GRADY, accountant, educator; b. Pulaski, Tenn., Mar. 17, 1951; s. Alton Levoid and Theresa (Whitlock) R.; m. Melanie Smith, Apr. 13, 1974; children: Mark, Sarah. AA, State Tech. Inst., Memphis, 1973; BA, U. Memphis, 1978; MS in Human Resource Devel., U. Tenn., Knoxville, 1995. Asst. contr., office mgr. Ideal Chem. & Supply Co., Memphis, 1973-77; mktg. coord. Plough Inc., Memphis, 1977-79; office mgr., asst. acctg. mgr. Velsicol Chem. Corp., Memphis, 1979-80; sr. budget analyst City of Memphis Govt., 1980-82; acct., internal auditor U. Tenn., Memphis, 1982-85; dir. restricted funds acctg. State Tech. Inst., Memphis, 1985—; adj. instr. acctg. State Tech. Inst., Memphis, 1992-95. Mem. Memphis Coll. Student Svcs. Assn., West Tenn. Vocat. Assn., Phi Kappa Phi. Baptist. Home: 2914 Suesand Dr Memphis TN 38128 Office: State Tech Inst at Memphis 5983 Macon Cv Memphis TN 38134-7642

RUSSELL, I. JON, medical educator; b. Hammond, Ind., May 3, 1943; s. Stanley Irwin and Lettie Esther (Benson) R.; m. Barbara Ann Runnels, June 7, 1964; children: Steven Jon, Timothy Lee, Deborah Ann. BA in Chemistry, Union Coll., 1965; MS, PhD in Biochemistry, U. Nebr., 1969; MD, Loma Linda U., 1973. Intern in internal medicine Loma Linda U.; resident in internal medicine Mayo Clinic, Rochester, Minn., 1975, fellow in rheumatology, 1978; asst. prof. medicine U. Tex. Health Sci. Ctr., San Antonio, 1978-87, assoc. prof. medicine, 1987—; dir. Univ. Clin. Rsch. Ctr.; past coord. San Antonio Rheumatology Forum; past local adv. bd. chmn. San Antonio Area Chpt. Lupus Found., Inc.; chmn. Am. Coll. Rheumatology non-anticular study group. Contbr. over 50 articles to profl. jours.; editor Jour. Musculoske Path. Mem. Internat. Myopain Soc. (founding pres.). Office: U Tex Health Sci Ctr 7703 Floyd Curl Dr San Antonio TX 78284-6200

RUSSELL, INEZ SNYDER, non-profit organization executive; b. Highland Falls, N.Y., June 29, 1951; d. Charles and Catherine (Collins) Snyder; m. William Edward Russell, Mar. 31, 1984; children: Kenneth Shawn, Charles Daniel. Student, McLennan Community Coll., 1971-72, Baylor U., 1972, 79. Pvt. practice cons. Dallas, Austin, Waco and San Antonio, Tex., 1969-79; instr. Datapoint Corp., Waco, 1979-82; founder, pres. The Last Word, Waco, 1982-89; founder, exec. Friends for Life, Waco, 1989—; counselor U.S. Small Bus. Administrn. Small Bus. Devel. Ctr.; bd. dirs. The Internat. Women's Resource Ctr. Author: (manual) Control User Guide, 1980, Production Inventory Control User Guide, 1980, Integrated Electronic Office System Reference Manual, 1981, Work Order System, 1981; contbr. articles to profl. jours. Tchr. First Bapt. Ch., Hewitt, Tex., 1980—; mem. occupational adv. com. McLennan Community Coll., 1984—; chairperson Wheels For Life program St. Jude Children's Hosp., Waco, 1987. Mem. NAFE, Cen. Tex. Women's Network, Better Bus. Bur., Nat. Coun. on Aging, Nat. Soc. Fund Raising Execs., Greater Waco C. of C. Office: PO Box 23491 Waco TX 76702-3491

RUSSELL, JERRY LEWIS, public relations counselor, political consultant; b. Little Rock, July 21, 1933; s. Jerry Lewis and Frances (Lieb) R.; m. Alice Anne Cason, Feb. 14, 1969; children—Leigh Anne, Andrew J. III, Christopher R.; children by previous marriage—Jerry Lewis III, Susan Frances. B.A. in Journalism, U. Ark., 1958; postgrad. in history U. Central Ark., 1978-82. Pub. relations dir. Little Rock C. of C., 1958; editor, pub. The Visitor, Little Rock, 1959-60; sec.-mgr. Ark. Press Assn., Little Rock, 1960-61; account exec. Brandon Agy., Little Rock, 1961-65; founder, pres. Guide Advt. (now part of River City Enterprises), also River City Pubs., Little Rock 1965-70, 72—; pres. River City Enterprises, 1974—; dir. pub. relations services S.M. Brooks Agy., Little Rock, 1970-72; founder, pres. Campaign Cons., 1974—; pub., editor Grass Roots Campaigning newsletter, 1979—. With AUS, 1953-56. Mem. Ark. Advt. Fedn. (pres. 1967-68), Pub. Relations Soc. Am. (pres. Ark. chpt. 1974), Am. Assn. Polit. Cons., Orgn. Am. Historians, Co. Mil. Historians, Western Hist. Assn., Custer Battlefield Hist. and Mus. Assn. (bd. dirs. 1988-90), Custer Battlefield Preservation Com. (bd. dirs. 1989-94), Ft. Laramie Hist. Assn., Council on Am.'s Mil. Past (state dir. 1979—), So. Hist. Soc., Little Big Horn Assos., Ark. Hist. Soc., Civil War Round Table Ark. (charter pres. 1964-65), Civil War Round Table Assos. (founder 1968, nat. chmn.), Order Indian Wars (founder 1979, nat. chmn.), Circus Fans Assn. Am. (pres. Little Rock chpt. 1981-83), Westerners Internat. (charter pres. Little Rock Corral 1974—), Confederate Hist. Inst. (founder 1979, nat. chmn.), Soc. Civil War Historians (founder 1984, exec. dir.), Ft. Phil Kearny Bozeman Trail Assn. (bd. dirs. 1985-95), Friends of Ft. Davis. Home: 9 Lefever Ln Little Rock AR 72227-3303

RUSSELL, JOHN FRANCIS, retired librarian; b. Mt. Carmel, Ind., Apr. 30, 1929; s. David Freeman and Bertha (Major) R.; B.A., DePauw U., 1951; postgrad. Ind. U., 1951-52; M.A., Johns Hopkins U., 1954; student Cath. U. Am., summer 1955; M.S., Grad. Sch. Library Sci. Drexel U., 1977; m. Edith Raymond Hyde, June 27, 1953; 1 dau., Anne Marie. Tchr. English, Park Sch. Balt., 1954-75, chmn. dept., 1957-75; tchr. speech, dir. Ira Aldridge Players Morgan State Coll., fall 1965-66; tchr. drama Loyola Coll., 1964, 66. Pres. Tchrs.' Assn. Ind. Sch. Balt. Area, 1960-62, advisory bd., 1966-67, chmn. com. on English, 1966-68; exec. com. Assn. Ind. Md. Sch., 1967-68. Dir., costumer Johns Hopkins U. Playshop, 1963-64; lectr. Lecture Group, Woman's Club Roland Park, others, 1964—. Bd. dirs. Balt. area council World Federalists U.S.A., 1961-67, vice chmn., 1964-67, nat. exec. council, 1963-65; bd. dirs. Center Stage, 1964-77; dir. Blvd. Players, pres., 1960-67; dir. Pasadena Little Theatre, v.p., 1979-83, pres., 1983-85, 2d v.p., 1990—; dir. Center Stage Players, New Image Theatre, Theatre Network of Houston, U.S.A. Theatre, Actors Conservatory Tex., v.p., 1990-91; bd. dirs. Unicorn Sch. Acting, 1996—; adv. com. Am. H.S. Theatre Festival, 1995; mem. adminstrv. bd. St. Mark's United Meth. Ch., 1957-67, Towson United Meth. Ch., 1967-77, First United Meth. Ch., 1980-89; sec. Festival Angels, 1982—(outstanding svc. award 1991); community vol. svcs. com., ARC, 1985-90; comprehensive volunteerism adv. com., Sheltering Arms, 1986-89. Recipient Nat. Citation of Merit Am. Shakespeare Festival, 1961; Critics Choice award Houston Post, 1984; certs. of appreciation Sheltering Arms, 1986-89, cer. of recognition, 1988. Mem. Am. Assn. Cmty. Theatre, Harris County Heritage Soc., Am. Film Inst., Nat. Film Soc., Am. Theatre Assn. (v.p. Mid-Atlantic dist. 1967-68, pres. 1968-69, nat. dir. 1970-73, Mid-Atlantic chpt. award for achievement and contbn. to theatre 1973), Secondary Sch. Theatre Assn. (v.p. devel. 1974-75), Tex. Non-Profit Theatre, Nat. (bd. dirs. 1969), Md. (pres. 1969-70) Coun. Tchrs. English, Capital Area Media Educators Orgn. (exec. com. 1970-73, screening chmn. 1971-73), ALA, Tex. Libr. Assn. (audiovisual chmn. conv. planning com. 1981), Council Info. and Referral Svcs. (newsletter editor 1984-86), Tex. Alliance Info. and Referral Svcs. (conv. speaker 1981, 83, 84, 85), Alliance of Info. and Referral Svcs. (conv. speaker 1985), Houston Public Library Staff Assn. (pres. 1981-82), Literacy Vols. Am. (sec. Houston 1984-87, adv. bd. 1989-91, 95-96, bd. dirs. 1992-95, chmn. program com. 1991-93), Reading, Edn. and Devel. Coun. (recruitment chmn., exec. com. 1984-86), Cultural Arts Coun. of Houston/ Harris County, Park Pl. Civic Club (exemplary svc. award 1991), Phi Beta Kappa, Phi Eta Sigma, Beta Phi Mu. Editor: The Secondary School Theatre, 1972-74. Home: 7817 Grove Ridge Dr Houston TX 77061-1405

RUSSELL, JOYCE WEBER, principal; b. Detroit, Feb. 21, 1948; d. Ronald Robert and Eleanor Treva (Burns) Weber; m. James Edward Russell, Mar. 25, 1970; 1 child, Jennifer Eileen. AA, Palm Beach C.C., Lake Worth, Fla., 1968; BA, Fla. Atlantic U., 1970, MA, 1975. Cert. tchr., prin. Tchr. Palm Beach County Sch. Bd., West Palm Beach, Fla., 1970-79, staff devel. specialist, 1979-84; asst. prin. Allamanda Elem., 1984-88; prin. Addison Mizner Elem., Boca Raton, Fla., 1988-90, South Olive Elem., West Palm Beach, 1990-95; adminstr. Safe Schs. AFTER Sch. Programs, Sch. Police, 1995—. Chair Vision 2000 Good Shepherd Meth. Ch., West Palm Beach, 1990-95; mem. Leadership Palm Beach County, 1990-96. Mem. NAESP, ASCD, Fla. Assn. Sch. Administrs., Palm Beach County Adminstr. Assn., Phi Delta Kappa. Office: Sch Bd Palm County Dept Sch Police # 121B 3330 Forest Hill Blvd West Palm Beach FL 33406-5869

RUSSELL, MARGARET JONES (PEG RUSSELL), secondary school educator; b. Durham, N.C., Apr. 25, 1938; d. Roderic O. and Margaret (Moore) Jones; m. Michael Morgan Russell; children: Lauren Skinner, Carol Martin, Seth Russell, Jay Russell. BA, Muskingum Coll., 1961. Ordained deacon Presbyn. Ch., 1970. Tchr. Sarasota (Fla.) County Sch. Bd., 1962-97, Sarasota H.S., 1982-96; sponsor literary mag. Quest, 1988—. Editor: (newsletter) The Mainsail, 1992-95; contbr. poems to profl. pubs. ARC vol. Sarasota Meml. Hosp., 1966-83, aux. vol., 1994—; reader Fla. Studio Theatre, Sarasota, 1980—. Sarasota Herald Tribune scholar, 1993; Fla. Writing Project fellow, 1990. Mem. Nat. Coun. Tchrs. English, Fla. Coun. Tchrs. English, Fla. Freelance Writers, Light Verse Workshop (co-chair 1995), Sarasota Fiction Writers, Meadows Country Club, Alpha Gamma Delta. Republican. Presbyterian. Home: 1150 Willis Ave Sarasota FL 34232-2148

RUSSELL, PATRICIA COOPER, foundation administrator; b. Houston, Feb. 5, 1944; d. Austin Eli and Sarah Lorraine (Rountree) Dawkins; children from previous marriage: Catherine Sloane, Sarah Riley, Patricia Daily; m. Robert B. Russell, Jr., Aug. 3, 1996. BA, Columbia Coll., 1965; grad. Williamsburg Devel. Inst., 1990. Appointments sec. to Congressman Tom Gettys, Washington, 1965; tchr. Lugoff (S.C.) Elem. Sch., 1967-68, Camden (S.C.) Elem. Sch., 1969-70; ombudsman State of S.C., 1970-73; asst. dir. Carolina Cup and Colonial Cup Internat. Steeplechase, Camden, 1973-87; adminstr. Camden Feed Co., 1973-87; office mgr. Camden Tng. Ctr., thoroughbreds, 1973-87; asst. sec. Mulberry Resources, Inc., 1980-82; sec.-treas. Equistar Products Co., 1980-87; mktg. dir. Holiday Inn of Lugoff-Camden, Holiday Inn of Sumter, S.C., 1987-88; dir. Devel. Bapt. Med. Ctr. Found., 1988-89; exec. v.p. S.C. State Mus. Found., Columbia, 1989—. Bd. dirs. Kershaw County Fine Arts Ctr., Columbia Devel. Corp.; sustaining mem. Camden Jr. Welfare League; mem. Inaugural Class, Leadership Kershaw County, 1986-87, participant Statewide Program, 1987-88; adv. com. Charleston Steeplechase; mem. Santee-Lynches Coun. Govts., 1987-88; bd. dirs. Kershaw County unit Am. Cancer Soc., 1980-90; chmn. bd. dirs. Kershaw unit Am. Heart Assn., 1984-86; bd. dirs. Palmetto Balloon Classic, 1983-86; mem. Bd. Appeals, City of Camden, 1985-87; vice chmn. Kershaw County Tourism Adv. Com., 1987-88; adminstrv. bd. Lyttleton St. United Meth. Ch., Camden, 1986-88; chmn. leadership com. Kershaw County, 1988-89; mem. Columbia Action Coun., 1988-90, Columbia Forum, 1988—; adv. com. S.C. Joint Legis. Com. on Cultural Affairs, 1989-96; active Assembly on the Future of S.C., 1989; trustee S.C. bd. Leukemia Soc. of Am., 1987-91; mem. strategic planning com. City of Columbia, 1995-96. Mem. Nat. Soc. Fundraising Execs. (mem. regional bd. 1993-96; Am. Assn. Mus., Media Club of Columbia, Greater Kershaw County C. of C. (v.p. pub. affairs 1983-86, William F. Nettles award 1988), Thoroughbred Assn. S.C. (sec.-treas. 1986-88), Leadership S.C. Alumni (bd. dirs. 1988-93, pres. 1992-93), S.C. Exec. Inst., Future Group of Richland County (cultural resources chair 1994), Newcomen Soc. of the U.S., Co-Chmn., S.C. Bd. Dirs., Greater Columbia C. of C., Capital City Club, Sprindale Hall Club, Univ. Assocs. Club, Rotary (mem. bd. dirs. Columbia, 1993-96, Paul Harris fellow). Methodist. Home: 115 Shallow Brook Dr Columbia SC 29223 Office: SC State Mus Found PO Box 100107 Columbia SC 29202-3107

RUSSELL, PEGGY TAYLOR, soprano, educator; b. Newton, N.C., Apr. 5, 1927; d. William G. and Sue B. (Cordell) Taylor; Mus.B. in Voice, Salem Coll., 1948; Mus.M., Columbia U., 1950; postgrad. U. N.C., Greensboro, 1977; student Am. Inst. Mus. Studies, Austria, 1972, 78; student of Clifford Bair, Nell Starr, Salem Coll., Winston-Salem, N.C., Edgar Schofield, Chloe Owen, N.Y.C.; student opera-dramatics Boris Goldovsky, Southwestern Opera Inst., Ande Andersen, Max Lehner, Graz, Austria; m. John B. Russell, Feb. 23, 1952; children: John Spotswood, Susan Bryce. Mem. faculty dept. voice Guilford Coll., Greensboro, 1952-53, Greensboro Coll., 1971-72; pvt. tchr. voice, Greensboro, 1963—; co-founder, v.p. sales, mktg. Russell Textiles, Inc., 1988; vis. instr. in voice U. N.C., Chapel Hill, 1973-77; founding artistic dir., gen. mgr. Young Artists Opera Theatre, Greensboro, 1983; staged and produced 18 operatic prodns., 1983-91; guest lectr. opera workshop U. N.C., Greensboro, 1990-91; lectr. opera Friends of Weymouth, So. Pines, N.C., 1994; lectr. on music history and opera, High Point, N.C., Center for Creative Leadership, Greensboro, 1979-80, First Presbyn. Ch., 1982; debut in light opera as Gretchen in The Red Mill, Winston-Salem Opera Assn., 1947; debuts include: Rosalinda in Die Fledermaus, Piedmont Festival Opera Assn., 1949, Lola in Cavalleria Rusticana, Greensboro Opera Assn., 1951, Violetta in La Traviata, Greensboro Opera Assn., 1953, Fiordiligi in Cosi fan tutte, Piedmont Opera Co., 1956; appeared as Marguerite in Faust, Brevard Music Center Resident Opera Co., 1967, First Lady in The Magic Flute, Am. Inst. Mus. Studies, Graz, Austria, 1972; mem. Greensboro Oratorio Soc., 1955-59, soprano soloist in The Messiah, 1952, 58, The Creation, 1955, Solomon, 1958; soprano soloist Presbyterian Ch. of the Covenant, Greensboro, 1958-71; guest appearances Sta. WFMY-TV, Greensboro, 1958-62; soprano soloist with Greensboro Symphony Orch., 1964, 80, Eastern Music Festival Orch. 1965, Greensboro Civic Orch., 1980; soloist in numerous recitals including: Wesleyan Coll., 1964, Roanoke Symphony Guild, 1967, Am. Inst. Mus. Studies, Austria, 1972, 78, U. N.C., Chapel Hill, 1974, 75, 76, 77, N.C. Mus. of Art, 1978; recital, masterclass Mars Hill Coll., 1981. Bd. dirs. Music Theater Assocs., Greensboro Friends of Music, N.C. Lyric Opera; judge Charlotte Opera Guild Auditions, 1994. Mem. Friendship Force of Guilford County, Holland, 1985, No. Germany, 1987. scholarship grantee N.C. Arts Council and Nat. Endowment for the Arts, 1991. Mem. Nat. Opera Assn. (chmn. regional opera cos. com. 1985-91, judge vocal competition auditions 1991, 92, 94, chmn. trustees Cofield Endowment 1991), Central Opera Service, Nat. Assn. Tchrs. of Singing (state gov. 1976-82, coordinator Regional Artist Contest 1982-84), N.C. Fedn. Music Clubs (dir. 1956-58), Music Educators Nat. Conf., Greensboro Music Tchrs. Assn. (pres. 1966-67), Symphony Guild (dir. 1977-78), Broadway Theater League (chmn. 1961-63), Atlanta Opera Guild, Civic Music Assn. (chmn. 1963-64), English Speaking Union (bd. dirs. Greensboro chpt., chmn. Shakespeare competition 1995), N.C. Symphony Soc., Piedmont Triad Coun. Internat. Vis. (Appreciation award Nat. Coun. Internat. Visitors 1994), Greensboro Preservation Soc., Guilford County Planning/Devel. Office (Forecast 2015 Com.). Presbyterian. Clubs: Sherwood Swim and Racquet, The Greensboro City. Home: 3012 W Cornwallis Dr Greensboro NC 27408-6730

RUSSELL, PHILLIP RAY, retail executive; b. Malvern, Ark., Jan. 10, 1953; s. Billy Lee and Lucille Virginia (Bowen) R.; m. DeLois Ann Tindell, Jan. 20, 1978; children: Julie Ann, Laura Beth, Sarah Renee. BBA, U. Ark., 1975. Clk. Kroger Co., Malvern, 1971-76; mgmt. trainee Kroger Co., Little Rock, 1976-77; co-mgr. Kroger Co., Pine Bluff, Ark., 1977-78, Monroe, La., 1978-80; store mgr. Kroger Co., Hamburg, Ark., 1980-81, Brinkley, Ark., 1981-82, Jonesboro, Ark., 1982-90; store mgr. Dixie Co., Jonesboro, 1990—; cons. mem. Kroger Store Mgr. Adv. Bd., Memphis, 1985-86, 88-89. Pres. Valley View PTA, Jonesboro, 1986-87; coach Valley View Blazers T-Ball, Jonesboro, 1987; team capt. March of Dimes, Jonesboro, 1986-87; loaned exec., sect. leader, speaker's bur., team capt. Jonesboro United Way, 1982—; mem. adv. bd. Ark. Food Bank, 1987—; v.p. adv. bd. N.E. Ark. Food Bank, 1989-90, 94—, pres., 1990-91, 93-94. Recipient Vol. Gold award Jonesboro United Way, 1984, B.H. Kroger award Kroger Co., 1985, Pres. award Valley View PTA, 1988; Gibson-Duncan scholar, 1971-75. Mem. Jonesboro C. of C., Ark. State U. Indian Club (chief 1984-86), Elks (investigation chmn. 1985-86), Kiwanis, Alpha Kappa Psi (life, treas. 1974-75, Outstanding Pledge 1973), Pi Sigma Epsilon. Republican. Baptist. Home: 1807 Chalet Dr Jonesboro AR 72404-7727 Office: Dixie Co 3402 Stadium Blvd Jonesboro AR 72401-6231

RUSSELL, RALPH TIMOTHY, insurance company executive, mayor; b. Foley, Ala., May 26, 1948; s. Ralph Joseph and Dorothy Eleanor (Peterson) R.; m. Sandra Earle Schultz, May 30, 1970; children: Karen, Kevin, Kenton. BS in Acctg., U. Ala., 1970; MBA, U. South Ala., 1975. Chartered property casualty underwriter. Exec. v.p. Baldwin Mutual Ins. Co., Foley, Ala., 1972—; mayor City of Foley, 1996—; bd. dirs. Baldwin Mutual Ins. Co., 1976—, Riviera Utilities, Foley, 1976—, Gulf Coast Title Ins. Co., Foley, 1978—, Colonial Bank, Foley, 1991—. Pres. South Baldwin United Way, 1981-82; nat. v.p. U. Ala. Alumni Assn., Tuscaloosa, 1978-79; chmn. Foley Pub. Libr., 1975-84, St. Margaret's Ch. Bd., Foley, 1989-90, Baldwin County Econ. Devel. Alliance; treas. South Baldwin Hosp.; mayor Foley, 1996—. Paul Harris fellow, 1986. Mem. Nat. Assn. Mut. Ins. Cos. (chmn. bd. dirs. 1986-94), Ala. Ins. Planning Com. (bd. dirs.), Ins. Edn. Found. (bd. dirs. 1991-94), Soc. CPCU (pres. 1982), South Baldwin C. of C. (past pres.). Roman Catholic. Home: 117 W Rosetta Ave Foley AL 36535-2223 Office: Baldwin Mutual Ins Co 315 E Laurel Ave Foley AL 36535-2617

RUSSELL, ROBERT LEONARD, professional association executive; b. Mt. Vernon, Ill., July 18, 1916; s. Charles Arthur and Edna Mabel (Yearwood) R.; m. Jeanne Lucille Tackenberg, May 21, 1942 (dec. Feb. 1990). Student, St. Petersburg C.C., 1971-72; BS, U. Mid. Fla., 1973, MS, 1974. Reporter Peoria (Ill.) Jour., 1939-42, 46-47, Chgo. Daily News, 1947-57; asst. exec. dir. Profl. Golfers Assn., Dunedin, Fla., 1957-65; exec. dir. United Vol. Services, San Mateo, Calif., 1965-66; reporter St. Petersburg (Fla.) Evening Ind., 1967-70; pres. Aldrich & Assocs., 1967-70; exec. v.p. Fla. Health Care Assn. (formerly Fla. Nursing Home Assn.), Orlando, 1970-77; exec. v.p. Mortgage Bankers Assn. Fla., Orlando, 1977-90, Mortgage Bankers Assn. Cen. Fla., Orlando, 1978-94, Mortgage Bankers Ednl. Found. Fla., Orlando, 1986-90; adminstr. Fla. Health Care Self Insurers Fund, 1972-78; sec.-treas. Mortgage Bankers Fla. Polit. Action Com., 1977-85, treas., 1987-90; pres. Profl. Assn. Svcs., Inc., 1977-81, 90-94, chmn. bd., 1981-90; CEO B. & B. Trust, Ltd., 1994—. Editor: Profl. Golfer mag., 1957-65, Nat. Golfer mag., 1965-66, Communicator, 1977-80, Bull., 1980-81, The Messenger, 1981-90, the newsletter, 1980-94; exec. editor Rx Sports and Travel mag., 1966-67. Elder Park Lake Presbyn. Ch., Orlando, 1979-83, St. Paul's

Presbyn. Ch., Orlando, 1983-87, Presbyn. Ch. of Lakes, 1987-93; mem. coord. coun. Presbytery of Cen. Fla., 1989-90; active Holy Family Cath. Ch., Orlando, 1993—; fin. sec. Holy Family Dr. Phillips Coun., KC, 1994—. With USAAF, 1942-46. Mem. Am. Soc. Assn. Execs. (cert.), Fla. Soc. Assn. Execs., Cen. Fla. Soc. Assn. Exec., Am. Coll. Health Care Adminstrs. (fellow emeritus), Fla. Sheriffs Assn. (hon.), Mortgage Bankers Assn. Fla. (hon. life), Mortgage Bankers Assn. Ctrl. Fla. (hon. life), U.S. Basketball Writers Assn. (life, pres. 1956-57), Football Writers Assn. Am. (bd. dirs. 1955-57), Nat. Rifle Assn. (life), Am. Legion (life), Knights of Columbus. Republican. Home: 7316 Lismore Ct Orlando FL 32835-6150 Office: PO Box 916 Windermere FL 34786-0916

RUSSELL, ROBERT PRITCHARD, ophthalmologist; b. Columbia, S.C., Apr. 30, 1945; s. Austin Henderson and Ruby Mae (Pritchard) R.; m. Olivia Louise Walker, Jan. 22, 1972; children: Robert Pritchard Jr., Denise Olivia. BA with distinction, U. Miss., 1967; MD, U. Miss., Jackson, 1971. Intern Miss. Bapt. Hosp., Jackson, 1971-72; resident U. Med. Ctr., Jackson, 1974-77; pvt. practice ophthalmologist Jackson, 1977—; mem. surg. staff St. Dominic Health Svcs., Jackson, 1977—; cons. Miss. Bapt. Med. Ctr., Jackson, 1977—, River Oaks Hosp., Flowood, Miss., 1981—; attending teaching staff mem. U. Med. Ctr., Jackson, 1977—. Lt. USNR, 1972-74. Mem. Am. Assn. Ophthalmology, Am. Soc. Contemporary Ophthalmology, Internat. Glaucoma Congress, Am. Intraocular Implant Soc., Contact Lens Assn. Ophthalmologists, Am. Acad. Ophthalmology, Phi Kappa Phi, Alpha Epsilon Delta, Phi Eta Sigma, Phi Chi, Sigma Chi. Republican. Home: 139 Royal Lytham Jackson MS 39211-2516 Office: Watkins Med Bldg 1421 N State St Ste 501 Jackson MS 39202-1658

RUSSELL, SCOTT DANIEL, botany educator, electron microscopist; b. Milw., Dec. 8, 1952; s. Erwin D. Russell and Ann McMullen O'Rourke; m. Susan Elaine Nelson, Dec. 17, 1983 (div. 1992); 1 child, Eric Scott; m. Vivian M. Connelly, July 17, 1993. BS in Botany, U. Wis., 1975; MSc in Biology, No. Ariz. U., 1977; PhD in Botany, U. Alta., 1981. Asst. prof. U. Okla., Norman, 1981-87, dir. electron microscope lab., 1984—, assoc. prof. botany, 1987-92, prof. botany, 1992—. Editor: International Review of Cytology, 1992; mem. editorial adv. bd. Phytomorphology, 1990—, Plant Systematics and Evolution, 1991—, Zygote, 1992—; contbr. articles to profl. jours. Grantee, Dept. Edn., Dept. Energy, State of Okla., USDA, NSF, 1982—; recipient Jeanette Siron Pelton award, Bot. Soc. Am., 1987. Mem. Bot. Soc. Am. (mem. election com. 1995—), Microscopy Soc. Am. (LAS rep., Diatome award 1992), Okla. Acad. Sci. (exec. bd., chmn. sect.), Microbeam Analysis Soc., Okla. Soc. Microscopy (pres. 1987-88, sec.-treas. 1990-94), Internat. Soc. Plant Morphologists (editl. adv. bd. 1990—), Internat. Assn. for Sexual Plant Reprodn. Rsch. (webmaster 1996—), WWW-Virtual Libr. Botany (webmaster 1996—), WWW-Virtual Libr. Microscopy (webmaster 1996—). Home: 1629 Wilderness Dr Norman OK 73071-6113 Office: U Okla Dept Botany & Microbiology 770 Van Vleet Oval Norman OK 73069-8816

RUSSELL, SUSAN WEBB, elementary and middle school education educator; b. Richmond, Va., Feb. 18, 1948; d. William Camper and Isabel McLeod (Smith) Webb; m. Russell Christian Proctor, III, Dec. 30, 1972 (div. 1981); 1 child, Alexander Christian Proctor; m. Walter William Russell, III, July 16, 1988; stepchildren: Walter William IV, Brian Earl. AB in English, Fine Arts, and Edn., Randolph-Macon Woman's Coll., 1970. Cert. tchr., Va. Customer svc. rep. Xerox Corp., Richmond, 1970-72; tchr. English grades 7, 8, 9 Am. Internat. Sch., Lagos, Nigeria, West Africa, 1973-75; group travel counselor Dynasty World Travel, Richmond, 1980-81; sec. to dir. athletics and receptionist The Collegiate Schs., Richmond, 1982-84, tchr. English and reading grades 6, 7, 9, 1984-88, tchr. word processing grade 5, 1984-86; tchr. social studies Norfolk (Va.) Acad., 1988-91, tchr. English and reading, 1991—; forensics coach Norfolk Acaad., 1991—. Editor Bulldog News, 1988-90; advisor Bullpup News, 1990-95. Methodist. Office: Norfolk Acad 1585 Wesleyan Dr Norfolk VA 23502-5512

RUSSELL, TIMOTHY JEROME, career officer; b. Compton, Calif., Aug. 29, 1960; s. Larry Arthur R. and Patricia Helena (Collins) Heath; m. Anita Louise Isaeff, Oct. 5, 1985; children: Brenda Nicole, Geoffrey Brandon. AA, Diablo Valley Coll., 1981; BS, Calif. State U., 1983; MA, Iowa State U., 1995. Commd. 2nd lt. U.S. Army, 1985, advanced through grades to maj., 1996; exec. officer B troop 1st squadron 12th cavalry U.S. Army, Ft. Knox, Ky., 1987-88; asst. opers. officer 2nd brigade 1st armored divsn. U.S. Army, Erlangen, Germany, 1989-91, comdr. D co. 4th bn. 70th armor 1st armored divsn., 1991-92; asst. prof. milit. sci. U.S. Army Cadet Command, Ames, Iowa, 1992-95; aide-de-camp U.S. Army Cadet Command, Ft. Monroe, Va., 1995—; Reviewer Armor Mag., 1993. Bd. dirs. United Way Vol. Ctr., Ames, Iowa, 1994. Decorated Bronze Star. Mem. Assn. U.S. Army, Armor Assn. (Order of St. George 1992).

RUSSINOFF, DAVID MICHAEL, computer scientist; b. Richmond, Va., Nov. 16, 1948; s. Albert and Betty Helen (Scherr) R.; m. Lin Anne Shockey, June 10, 1989; children: Joshua Reuven, Solomon. BS, MIT, 1971; MS, NYU, 1977, PhD, 1978; MA, U. Tex., 1983. Instr. Sch. Engring. and Sci. Cooper Union, N.Y.C., 1976; instr. dept. math. NYU, 1975-78, U. Tex., Austin, 1978-81; sr. mem. tech. staff Microelectronics and Computer Tech. Corp., Austin, 1983-91; adj. assoc. prof. dept. computer sci. U. Tex., 1981-94; sr. computing rsch. scientist Computational Logic, Inc., Austin, 1992-94; cons. Sematech, Inc., Austin, 1994, AMD, Austin, 1995—. Author: (chpts.) Specification and Validation Methods, Object-Oriented Databases and Applications; contbr. articles to profl. jours. Mem. Sigma Xi, Phi Kappa Phi. Democrat. Jewish. Home: 1106 W Ninth St Austin TX 78703

RUSSO, LOUIS S., dean, neurology educator; b. Westerly, R.I., Aug. 13, 1944; s. Louis and Rose Anne (Boumenot) R.; m. Sheila Louise Daly, July 27, 1968; children: Lydia Simms, Louis James. Student, Johns Hopkins U., 1962-65; MD, NYU, 1965-69. Diplomate Am. Bd. Med. Examiners, Am. Bd. Psychiatry & Neurology. Intern Mayo Clinic, Rochester, Minn., 1969-70; resident in neurology Mt. Sinai Hosp., N.Y.C., 1970-73; clin. asst. prof. neurology U. Fla. Coll. Medicine, Gainesville, 1974-77; asst. prof. neurology U. Fla. Coll. Medicine, 1977-82, assoc. prof. neurology, 1982-88, prof. neurology, 1988—, interim assoc. dean Jacksonville programs, 1992-94; sr. assoc. dean Jacksonville programs, 1994—; assoc. chmn. dept. neurology, 1982-94, asst. dean Jacksonville programs, 1983-86, interim asst. v.p., 1992-94, asst. v.p., 1994—; pvt. practice neurology, Jacksonville, 1973-77; cons. Fla. Vocat. Rehab. Svcs., 1973—; chief neurology svcs. Univ. Med. Ctr., 1977-94, dir. clin. neruophysiology lab., 1977-94, dir. muscular dystrophy clinic NE Fla. chpt., 1978-94, assoc. med. dir., 1980-83, interim exec. v.p. for med. affairs, 1992-94, exec. v.p. med. affairs, 1994—; mem. numerous coms. U. Fla., U. Med. Ctr.; trustee Jacksonville Faculty Clinic, 1987—, mem. fin. com., 1989-92, chmn. bd., 1992—; mem. joint conf. com. Meml. Hosp., Jacksonville Meml. Hosp., 1976-77; bd. dirs. Mental Health Resource Ctr., Jacksonville, 1989-91; mem. adv. com. Attending Staff Found., 1990-92; lectr. in field. Bd. dirs. Jacksonville Urban League, 1995—, North Fla. chpt. Nat. Multiple Sclerosis Soc., 1977-87, chmn. med. adv. com. 1977-83; Mayor's Ad Hoc Com. on Biotech., 1986; planning com. Leadership Jacksonville Poverty Day, 1987; adv. com. Childrens Hosp., 1992—. Recipient Tchr. award Duval County Family Practice Soc., 1976, Beals award for rsch., 1984; grantee Wallace Labs., 1990-91, Synergen/Syntex, 1993, Nat. Muscular Dystrophy, 1993-94. Fellow Am. Acad. Neurology, Am. Heart Assn. (stroke coun.); mem. Am. Neurol. Assn., Fla. Neurol. Assn., Fla. Med. Assn., Duval County Med. Soc. (bd. dirs. 1984-86, Beals award com. 1985-87) Jacksonville Faculty Practice Assn. (acad. fund bd. govs. 1977-87, bd. dirs., exec. com., fin. com. 1988—, vice-chmn. bd. dirs. 1991-92, chmn. 1992—. Office: U Fla Health Sci Ctr 653 W 8th St Jacksonville FL 32209-6511

RUST, ROBERT FRANCIS, publishing executive; b. Herrick, S.D., Oct. 26, 1927; s. Charles William and Agatha Susan R.; m. Wilma Lorraine LeBeau, Oct. 18, 1948; children: Randal, Roberta, Ann, Mary. Student, U. Houston, 1950-53. Time keeper Vessels Co., Houston, 1950-53; v.p. Gulf Pub. Co., Houston, 1953—. With USAF, 1948-49. Mem. Houston Club. Office: Gulf Pub Co PO Box 2608 Houston TX 77252-2608

RUSTIN, DOWSE BRADWELL, III, credit union executive; b. Charleston, S.C., Sept. 14, 1950; s. Dowse Bradwell, Jr. and Mary Bill (Griffin) R.; m. Ruth Ann Johnson, June 26,1976; children: Dowse Bradwell IV, Sarah Caroline. BS, Coll. of Charleston, 1975; postgrad., U. N.C., 1982. Internal auditor Wachovia Bank & Trust Co. N.A., Winston-Salem, N.C., 1975; retail loan officer, banking officer Wachovia Bank & Trust Co. N.A., Eden, N.C., 1978-81; city office mgr., asst. v.p. Wachovia Bank & Trust Co. N.A., Graham, N.C., 1981-85; pres. Charleston Area Fed. Credit Union, S.C., 1985—; bd. dirs. S.C. Credit Union League, Columbia, 1992-94, treas. bd. dirs., 1994, 2d vice chmn., 1995; mem. supervisory com. Carolina Corp. Credit Union, Columbia, 1991-92; treas. Charleston Area Chpt. Credit Unions, 1990-93, pres., 1994; faculty mem. S.C. Credit Union Lending Sch., Columbia, 1989—; regional spkr. on banking, econs. and disaster recovery planning. Mem. exec. bd. Coll. of Charleston Alumni Assn., 1992; mem. allocations bd. Trident United Way, Charleston, 1991-92. Served with USNR, 1968-74. Mem. S.C. Credit Union Mgmt. Assn., Charleston Trident C. of C. (speakers bur. 1987—), Masons (master mason), Charleston Rod and Reel Club (pres. 1991-92). Republican. Methodist. Office: Charleston Area Fed Credit Union 1845 Sam Rittenberg Blvd Charleston SC 29407-4870

RUSTIN, RUDOLPH BYRD, III, physician; b. Charleston, S.C., May 14, 1957; s. Rudolph Byrd and Mary Pringle (Herrin) R.; m. Sandra Lee Talbott, Nov. 28, 1985; children: Jonathan, Jeffrey. BS in Chemistry cum laude, Hampden Sydney Coll., 1979; MD, Med. U. S.C., 1983. Diplomate Am. Bd. Surgery, Am. Bd. Colon and Rectal Surgery; lic. physician, S.C. Intern Cleve. Clinic Found., 1983-84, resident, 1984-88, chief resident gen. surgery, 1987-88, fellow, 1988-89; private practice colon rectal surgery Charleston, 1989—; clin. assoc. surgery Med. U. S.C., Charleston, 1989—; active staff Roper Hosp., Charleston, St. Francis Xavier Hosp., Trident Med. Ctr.; courtesy staff Baker Hosp., N. Charleston, AMI East Cooper Community Hosp., Mt. Pleasant, S.C.; clin. assoc. Charleston Meml. Hosp.; presenter in field. Fellow ACS, Am. Soc. Colon Rectal Surgeons, Southeastern Surgical Congress; mem. Med. Soc. S.C., S.C. State Med. Assn., S.C. Med. Assn. (del.), So. Med. Assn., Charleston County Med. Soc., Phi Beta Kappa. Office: 125 Doughty St Ste 770 Charleston SC 29403

RUTAN, THOMAS CARL, nurse; b. El Paso, Tex., May 18, 1954; s. Robert Judson and Louisa Almeria Elizabeth (Niccolls) R.; m. Randi Lee Watson, Sept. 17, 1980; children: Thomas Caleb, Susannah Christine, Rebecca Abigail. BSN, U. Tex., 1977, MSN, 1987. RN. Staff nurse U. Burn Ctr., U. Tex. Med. Br. Hosp., Galveston, 1977, U.S. Army Inst. Surg. Rsch., Ft. Sam Houston, Tex., 1978-81; flight nurse U.S. Army Inst. Surg. Rsch., 1979-81; staff nurse Burn Intensive Care Unit, U. Tex. Med. Br. Hosp., Galveston, 1981-83; clin. rsch. nurse Shriners Burns Inst., Galveston, 1983-94, project leader clin. info. systems, 1988-91; asst. dir. med. staff and rsch. adminstrn. Shriners Burn Inst., Galveston, 1991-94; nurse clinician III Blocker Burn Ctr., U. Tex. Med. Br., Galveston, 1994; clin. nurse specialist, dialysis, gen. surg.-Burns U. Hosp. UMDNJ, Newark, 1994—. Capt. U.S. Army, 1978-81. Mem. AAAS, ANA, N.Am. Burn Soc., Tex. Nurses Assn., Am. Burn Assn., N.Y. Acad. Sci., Planetary Soc., Consumers Union, Nature Conservancy. Methodist. Office: UMDNJ 150 Bergen St Newark NJ 07103-2406

RUTFORD, ROBERT HOXIE, geoscience educator; b. Duluth, Minn., Jan. 26, 1933; s. Skuli and Ruth (Hoxie) R.; m. Marjorie Ann, June 19, 1954; children: Gregory, Kristian, Barbara. BA, U. Minn., 1954, MA, 1963, PhD, 1969; DSc (hon.), St Petersburg State Tech U., Russia, 1994. Football and track coach Hamline U., 1958-62; rsch. fellow U. Minn., 1963-66; asst. prof. geology U. S.D., 1967-70, assoc. prof., 1970-72, chmn. dept. geology, 1968-72, chmn. dept. physics, 1971-72; dir. Ross Ice Shelf Project U. Nebr., Lincoln, 1972-75; dir. divsn. Polar Programs NSF, Washington, 1975-77; vice chancellor for research and grad. studies, prof. geology U. Nebr., 1977-82, interim chancellor, 1980-81; pres. U. Tex., Dallas, 1982-94, Excellence in Edn. Found. prof. of geoscis., 1984—; U.S. del. to Scientific Com. on Antarctic Rsch., 1986—, v.p., 1996—; chmn. NRC Polar Rsch. Bd., 1991-95. Mem. editl. bd. Issues in Sci. and Tech., 1991-94. Trustee Baylor Coll. Dentistry, 1989-96. 1st lt. U.S. Army, 1954-56. Recipient Antarctic Svc. medal, 1964, Disting. Svc. award NSF, 1977, Ernie Gunderson award for svc. to amateur athletics S.D. AAU, 1972, Outstanding Achievement award U. Minn., 1993, Lifetime Achievement award, 1995. Fellow Geol. Soc. Am.; mem. Antarctican Soc. (pres. 1988-90), Arctic Inst. N.Am., Explorers Club, Am. Polar Soc., Philos. Soc. Tex., St. Petersburg Acad. Engring. (Russia), Cosmos Club, Sigma Xi. Lutheran. Home: 1882 Quail Ln Richardson TX 75080-3456 Office: Univ Tex Dallas Geosciences Program Richardson TX 75083-0688

RUTH, BETTY MUSE, school system administrator; b. Florence, Ala., Oct. 24, 1943; d. Paul and Mary Lucille (Gresham) Muse; m. Thomas Gary Ruth, Dec. 17, 1965 (div. Sept. 1979); 1 child, Thomas Paul; m. Charles Larry Oliver, Jr., Mar. 10, 1990. BSBA, Athens State Coll., 1982; MBA, U. N.Ala., 1986. Sec., bookkeeper Anderson News Co., Florence, 1963-65; acct. receivable bookkeeper McConnell AFB, Wichita, Kans., 1967-68; legal sec. Reynolds Law Firm, Selmer, Tenn., 1973-74; subs. tchr. Athens (Ala.) City Schs., 1974-78, dir. RSVP, 1978—; del. White House Conf. on Aging, 1995; mem. Nat. Coun. on Aging, 1985—. Active United Way, Athens, 1990-94; sec. Gov.'s Commn. Nat. and Comty. Svc., Ala, 1994; vice chair Tenn. Valley Exhibit Commn., Ala., 1984—; past pres. Athens-Limestone County Beautification Bd., 1991-94; People-to-People internat. del. to People's Republic of China, 1994. Named outstanding project dir. Action, Atlanta, 1985, outstanding woman of Ala., 1989. Mem. NEA, Ala. Edn. Assn., Nat. Assn. RSVP Dirs. (v.p., treas., del. 1985—, svc. award 1993), Region IV Assn. RSVP dirs. (pres., v.p., treas. 1979—, svc. award 1989), Ala. Assn. RSVP Dirs. (v.p., sec., treas. 1978—, Citizens award 1991), Athens State Coll. Alumni Assn. (bd. dirs. 1993—). Mem. Ch. of Christ. Home: 15705 Kings Dr Athens AL 35611 Office: Athens State Coll PO Box 852 Athens AL 35612-0852

RUTH, BRYCE CLINTON, JR., lawyer; b. Greenwood, Miss., Dec. 19, 1948; s. Bryce Clinton and Kathryn (Arant) R.; m. Martha M. Ruth; children: Lauren Elizabeth, Bryce Clinton III. BS, Delta State U., 1970; JD, Memphis State U., 1979. Bar: Tenn., 1979, U.S. Dist. Ct. (mid. dist.) Tenn. 1979, U.S. Ct. Mil. Appeals 1991, U.S. Ct. Appeals (6th cir.), 1994. Criminal investigation spl. agt. IRS, Memphis and Nashville, 1971-82; asst. dist. atty. Dist. Atty. Office, Gallatin, Tenn., 1982-89; asst. pub. defender Pub. Defender's Office, Gallatin, 1989-90; pvt. practice White House, Tenn., 1989—; judge City of Cross Plains, Tenn., 1992—; juvenile ct. referee judge Robertson County, Tenn., 1995—; mem. dist. investigating com. dist. VI Tenn. Bd. Law Examiners, 1989—; mem. child enforcement steering com. Asst. Dist. Atty. Office, 1983-84, chmn. legis. subcom., 1985; lectr. in field. Chmn. fin. com. White House First United Meth. Ch., 1983-88, trustee, 1988-90, chmn., 1990; trustee Vol. State Coll. Found., 1993—; bd. dirs. Crime Stoppers of Sumner County, 1989-94; bd. dirs. White House Youth Soccer, 1992-93, coach, 1987-91; bd. dirs. Sumner County CASA, 1992-93; coach Jr. Pro Football, 1980-85; video cameraman for football team White House H.S., 1991—; mem. Leadership Sumner, 1989; bd. dirs. White House Men's Club, 1981-83, 85-88, v.p., 1984, 88, pres., 1985. Maj. USAR, JAGC, 1983—. Recipient Disting. Expert award for pistol marksmanship U.S. Treasury, Disting. Svc. award City of White House. Mem. NRA, Tenn Bar Assn. (del. 1993—), Sumner County Bar Assn. (chmn. domestic rels. com. 1984-85), White House Area C. of C. (bd. dirs. 1990-95, pres. 1993-94). Office: 3210 Hwy 31W PO Box 68 White House TN 37188

RUTHERFOORD, REBECCA HUDSON, computer science educator; b. Elkhart, Ind., Feb. 24, 1948; d. Charles Melvin Hudson and Eunice Klaire (Lund) Edmonds; m. James Kincanon Rutherfoord, Aug. 31, 1968; children: James Kincanon Jr., Charles Penn. BS, Ind. State U., 1971, MS, 1972, EdD, 1975; MS in Computer Sci., So. Poly State U., Marietta, Ga., 1995. Cert. data processor. Staff asst. Ind. State U., Terre Haute, 1969-71; vocal music tchr. S.W. Parke Schs., Rockville, Ind., 1971-73; fellowship asst. Ind. State U., Terre Haute, 1974-75; vocal music tchr. Slidell (La.) High Sch., 1977-78; programmer, analyst La. State U., Baton Rouge, 1978-79, dir. computer rehab. program, 1979-80; programmer, analyst Hanes Corp., Atlanta, 1980-81; asst. prof. Devry Inst., Atlanta, 1981-83; acting dept. chair So. Poly. State U., Marietta, Ga., 1989-92, prof. computer sci., 1983—, computer sci. grad. program coord., 1996—; cons. The Assocs. Group, Inc., Roswell, Ga., 1986-88, Crawford Communications, Atlanta, 1987; adj. prof. Cobb County Bd. Edn., Marietta, Ga., 1985-87, Joseph T. Walker Sch., Marietta, 1985-86; vis. prof. Leicester (U.K.) Polytechnic, 1990. Choir dir. St. Peter and Paul Episcopal Ch., Marietta, 1981-85, choir mem., 1992—; Christian edn. dir. St. Francis Episcopal Ch., Denham Springs, La., 1978-80; choir mem. St. David's Episcopal Ch., Roswell, 1985-92; bd. dirs., mem. Cherokee Comty. Habitat for Humanity, 1994—. Mem. Data Processing Mgmt. Assn., Assn. Computing Machinery, Sigma Alpha Iota. Republican. Office: So Poly State Univ 1100 S Marietta Pky Marietta GA 30060-2855

RUTHERFORD, JOHN SHERMAN, III (JOHNNY RUTHERFORD), professional race car driver; b. Coffeyville, Kans., Mar. 12, 1938; s. John Sherman and Mary Henrietta (Brooks) R.; m. Betty Rose Hoyer, July 7, 1963; children: John Sherman, Angela Ann. Student, Tex. Christian U., 1956. Profl. race car driver, 1959-94, ret., 1994, driver super-modified race cars, sprint cars, stock cars, midgets, sports cars, Indy cars, Trans-Am cars and formula 5000; mem. Indy Car Racing Inc.; appointed spl. events coord. Indy Racing League, 1995—; pace car driver for Championship Auto Racing Teams, 1992-95; lectr. in field. Host: TV show The Racers; race commentator TV show, NBC, ESPN, CBS, ABC; appeared in numerous TV commercials; art work included in traveling exhbn. Art and Athletes; TV and radio pub. services messages for Nat. Safety Council, Calif. Hwy. Patrol, U.S. Marines, Muscular Dystrophy Assn., Cystic Fibrosis Assn., Boy Scouts, Camp Fire, Shriner's Hosp., Tex. Soc. to Prevent Blindness, Air N.G. Hon. state chmn. Am. Cancer Soc., Tex., Tarrant County Soc. to Prevent Blindness, Emergency Medicine Found., Ft. Worth Kidney Assn., Ft. Worth Burn Ctr.; Ind. chmn. Am. Heart Assn. Named Ft. Worth Newsmaker of Yr., 1974, Driver of Yr. Sport Mag., 1976, Driver of Yr. Auto Race Writers and Broadcasters Am., 1974, 80, Olsonite Driver of Yr., 1980, Corvette Challenge's Sportsman of Yr., 1988, Motorsports amb., 1993; recipient Jim Clark award, 1969, Extra Mile award, 1973, Mim Malloy award, 1974, Eddie Sachs award, 1975, Louie Meyer award, 1992; chosen for Internat. Race of Champions, 1974, 76, 77, 78, 79, 84, chosen Fast Masters, 1993; elected to Tex. Sports Hall of Fame, 1981, Indy 500 Hall of Fame, 1987, Boys Clubs Am.'s Celebrity Hall of Fame, 1987, Tex. Auto Racing Hall of Fame, 1988, Nat. Sprint Car Hall of Fame, 1995, Internat. Motorsports Hall of Fame, 1996, Motorsports Hall of Fame, 1996. Mem. Fedn. Internat. Automobile, Internat. Motors Sports Assn., Exptl. Aircraft Assn., Warbirds of Am., Confederate Air Force, Internat. Aerobatic Club, League Auto Racing (sec., bd. dirs.), Championship Drivers Assn. (bd. dirs.), Nat. Rifle Assn., Air Force Assn., Air Power Coun., Blue Angels Assn., Ft. Worth Boat Club, Shady Oaks Country Club, Lions.

RUTHERFORD, MARY LOUISE MANLOVE, artist; b. Nashville, May 2, 1929; d. William Robert and Mayme (Escue) Manlove; m. Samuel Kenneth Rutherford, Dec. 20, 1952; children: Samuel Kenneth Jr., Kate, Susan. BA, Vanderbilt U., 1951, MA, 1972. lectr. art history. Exhibited oil paintings on canvas in local and regional shows and galleries. Mem. Visual Arts Alliance of Nashville. Home and Studio: 225 Robin Hill Rd Nashville TN 37205-3523

RUTHERFORD, SAMUEL KENNETH, JR., marketing executive; b. Nashville, Dec. 21, 1953; s. Samuel Kenneth and Mary Louise (Manlove) R.; m. Clela Susan Massey, Aug. 18, 1979; children: Samuel Kenneth, William Massey, Madelyn Cathleen. BA, U. Tenn., Knoxville, 1978; MA, Vanderbilt U., 1981. Tech. svc. mgr. Tentex Products, Inc., Nashville, 1982-84, mktg. mgr., 1984-89; proprietor Sam Rutherford Mktg. Svcs., Nashville, 1989—. Mem. ACLU, Amnesty Internat.

RUTHERFORD, VICKY LYNN, special education educator; b. Florence, S.C., Sept. 12, 1947. BS, Hampton U., 1969, MA, 1971; PhD, Mich. State U., 1991. Cert. tchr. French, spl. edn., reading specialist, Va., tchr. spl. edn., S.C. Social worker day care Hampton (Va.) Dept. Social Svc., 1970-72; reading therapist, asst. dir., dir. Bayberry Reading Clinic, Hampton, 1973-77; tchr. reading, English, counselor York County Schs., Yorktown, Va., 1977-85; staff advisor, asst. to course coord. Mich. State U., East Lansing, 1985-90; tchr. autistic Florence (S.C.) Dist. 1 Sch. Sys., 1992-96, tchr. emotionally impaired, 1996—. Instrnl. designer: Addiction Severity Index #1, 1987, #2, 1988, Managing a Diverse Workforce, 1990; designer, trainer: Project Teach, 1991; designer, developer: (video) Camp Takona Summer Experience, 1992. Bass guitarist, Sun. sch. sec., youth worker, Sun. sch. supt. Progressive Ch. of Jesus, Florence, 1992—. Fellow Mich. Dept. Edn., 1987-89. Mem. Internat. Reading Assn. Office: Briggs Elem Sch 1012 Congaree Dr Florence SC 29501-5791

RUTHERGLEN, GEORGE A., law educator; b. Portland, Oreg., Sept. 12, 1949; s. John Alfred and Helen Kathleen (Bero) R.; m. Jessica Rosalind Feldman, Apr. 25, 1975; children: Susannah Kathleen, Michael Francis. AB, U. Calif., 1971, JD, 1974. Bar: Va. 1979, U.S. Dist. Ct. (we. dist.) Va. 1980, U.S. Ct. Appeals (4th cir.) 1980, U.S. Supreme Ct. 1988. Law clk. to judge J. Clifford San Diego, 1974-75; law clk. to justices William O. Douglas, John Paul Stevens Washington, 1975-76; prof. law U. Va., Charlottesville, 1976—; supervising atty. Post-Conviction Assistance Project, 1980—; cons. standing com. on fed. jud. improvements ABA, Ci.go., 1988-89. Author: Major Issues in the 1983 Federal Law of Employment Discrimination, 1988. Mem., chair adv. com. 4th Cir. Rules, Richmond, Va., 1988—. Mem. Order of Coif, Phi Beta Kappa. Democrat. Home: 1698 Rugby Ave Charlottesville VA 22903-5141 Office: U Va Sch Law 580 Massie Rd Charlottesville VA 22903-1738*

RUTLEDGE, MARY ELIZABETH, English language educator; b. Dallas, Nov. 15, 1952; d. Jack Sylvester and Anna Pauline (Fronhoff) R. BA, U. Tex., Arlington, 1974; PhD, U. North Tex., 1996. Cert. secondary English, German, and history tchr. Tchr. English and German Grand Prairie (Tex.) Ind. Sch. Dist., 1974-76, Dallas Ind. Sch. Dist., 1976-93; teaching asst. German U. Tex., Arlington, 1975; organizer Am. Fedn. Tchrs., Dallas, 1983-84; teaching fellow English U. North Tex., Denton, 1994-96; chair excellence in teaching award com. Dallas Ind. Sch. Dist., 1986-89. Author, prodr. (radio program) Adventures with the Anteaters. Ray Stoker Dissertation scholar, 1996. Mem. MLA, AAUW, Nat. Coun. Tchrs. English, South Ctrl. MLA, Golden Key, Alpha Chi, Delta Phi alpha, Phi Kappa Phi. Home: 9601 Forest Ln #914 Dallas TX 75243

RUTLEDGE, ROGER KEITH, lawyer; b. Knoxville, Tenn., Dec. 27, 1946; s. Joseph P. and Jean Mae (Karnes) R.; m. Lily Mee Kin Hee, June 6, 1970; children: Amelia Leilani, Sarah Elizabeth. BA in History with honors, U. N.C., 1968; JD cum laude, Am. U., 1977. Bar: Tenn. 1977, U.S. Dist. Ct. (we. dist.) Tenn. 1978, U.S. Supreme Ct. 1982. Served in U.S. Peace Corps, Nepal, 1968-70; fgn. service officer U.S. Dept. State, Washington and Italy, 1971-76; ptnr. Rutledge & Rutledge, Memphis, 1977—. Editor fiction Carolina Quar., 1967-68; assoc. editor Am. U. Law Rev., 1976-77. Mem. campaign com. Albert Gore Jr. U.S. Senate, Shelby County, 1984, for pres. campaign, 1988; bd. chmn. United Meth. Neighborhood Ctrs., Inc., 1992. Mem. ABA, Tenn. Bar Assn., Memphis Bar Assn. (editor Bar Forum 1986, asst. editor 1987). Democrat. Methodist. Office: Rutledge & Rutledge 1053 W Rex Rd Memphis TN 38119-3819

RUTYNA, RICHARD ALBERT, history educator; b. San Diego, Apr. 10, 1937; s. Micszlav and Mary Elizabeth (Sawyer) R. BA in History, Coll. of William and Mary, Norfolk, Va., 1959; MA in History, Coll. of William and Mary, Williamsburg, Va., 1961; postgrad., U. Va., 1963-66. Tchr. history Granby H.S., Norfolk, 1960-61; instr. history Old Dominion U., Norfolk, 1961-63, asst. prof., 1966-78, assoc. prof., 1978-92, assoc. prof. emeritus, 1992—. Author: Heritage and Horizons: Old Dominion University, 1987; editor: (anthologies) Virginia in The American Revolution I, 1977, Virginia in The American Revolution II, 1983, Conceived in Conscience, 1983; contbr. articles to profl. publs. Sec. 2nd Congl. Dist. Dem. Com., Va., 1968-72, chmn., 1972-75; mem. Dem. State Cen. Com., 1968-75; mem. steering com. Dem. Party, 1972-75. Sgt. USMCR, 1954-62. Mem. Inst. Early Am. History and Culture (assoc.), Phi Alpha Theta. Roman Catholic. Home: 1228 Lowery Ct Norfolk VA 23502-2209

RYAN, CYNTHIA ANN, English language educator; b. Clinton, Ill., Oct. 16, 1963; d. Gerald Francis and Mary Ann (Grady) R.; m. Bruce Thomas McComiskey, May 28, 1994. BS in English, Ill. State U., 1987, MS in English, 1989. Undergraduate tchg. asst. Ill. State U., Normal, 1986-87; grad. instr. Ill. State U., 1987-89; lectr. U. Md. European Divsn., Neuulm, Germany, 1989-90; academic asst. U. Md. European Divsn., Heidelberg, Germany, 1990-92; grad. instr. Purdue U., W. Lafayette, Ind., 1992-94; lectr. East Carolina U., Greenville, N.C., 1995—; mem. exec. com. East Carolina

U. Women's Studies, Greenville, 1995—. Contbr. articles to profl. jours. Mem. Nat. Coun. of Tchrs. of English, Nat. Women's Studies Assn. (spec. caucus on women's ctrs. 1996), Am. Humor Studies Assn., SE Women's Studies Assn., Assn. for Business Comm., Conference on Coll. Comp. & Comm., Modern Language Assn., Phi Kappa Phi. Office: East Carolina U English Dept GCB 2201 Greenville NC 27858

RYAN, DANIEL LUCIOLE, company executive; b. Charles City, Iowa, June 7, 1941; m. Connie Peck, Aug. 19, 1961; children: Timothy Lee, Taressa Linn. BA, State Coll. Iowa, Cedar Falls, 1963; MA, U. No. Iowa, Cedar Falls, 1968; PhD, Pacific Western U., L.A., 1984. Lic. engring. technician, Nebr. Asst. dir. TI Technical Inst., Omaha, 1967-76; asst. dir. NEDS No. Ednl. Devel. Sys., Omaha, 1971-75; coordinating prof. Clemson (S.C.) U., 1976-92; pres. DLR Assocs., Sunset, S.C., 1992—; vis. prof. U. Idaho, Moscow, 1976, Gannon U., Erie, Pa., 1980. Author: Computer-Aided Kinetics for Machine Design, 1981, Computer Programming for Graphical Displays, 1983, Computer Graphics Problems Manual, 1983, Computer-Aided Architectural Graphics, 1983, Mini/Micro Computer Graphics, 1984, Principles of Automated Drafting, 1984, Graphic Communication A CAD Approach, 1986, Graphic Communication, 1987, Graphical Displays for Engineering Documentation, 1987, Nhkkehepkap B Canp (Russian), 1989, Computer-Aided Design, 1989, Tech Sketching and Computer Ill, 1990, CAD/CAE Descriptive Geometry, 1992, Computer-Aided Graphics Design, 1994, Robotic Simulation, 1994; contbr. articles to profl. jours. Home and Office: DLR Assocs Box 11 Sunset SC 29685

RYAN, DAVID ALAN, computer specialist; b. Cin., Nov. 13, 1961; s. James Patrick and Virginia Ann (Stewart) R. BS, Wright State U., 1983; MS, Tex. A&M U., 1988. Statistician U.S. Bur. of Census, Washington, 1988-92, computer specialist, 1992—. Vol. math. modeling Soil Conservation Svc., Washington, 1991—; date modeling vol. Washington Opera, 1992—; data entry/programming vol. Opera Am., Washington, 1990-91; hist. rschr. Gasby's Tavern Mus., Alexandria, Va., 1991—; mem. Bravo! for the Washington Opera, 1991-95. Recipient Vol. Svc. award Soil Conservation Svc., 1992, 93. Mem. Am. Statis. Assn., Capitol PC Users Group, Ballston-Va. Square Civic Assn. (exec. com. 1995—, sec. 1996—). Office: US Bur of Census Econ Planning Coord Divsn Ctr for Econ Studies Washington DC 20233-6101

RYAN, DONNA HARRINGTON, health science association administrator; b. Lafayette, La., Dec. 26, 1945; d. Clifford Litherland and Norma B. (Moorison) Harrington; m. Joseph T. Ryan, Aug. 24, 1968; children: Isaac, Coogan, Sarah. MD, La. State U., 1970; BS cum laude, U. Southwestern La., 1985. Cert. oncology and geriatric medicine Am. Bd. Internal Medicine. Rotating intern La. State U. Divsn. Charity Hosp., New Orleans, resident internal medicine; dir. internal medicine wards Charity Hosp., New Orleans, 1979-84; program dir. Internal Medicine Residency Program, New Orleans, 1980-82; vice-chancellor clin. affairs La. State U. Med. Ctr., New Orleans, 1984-90, acting chancellor, 1985; assoc. exec. dir. Pennington Biomed. Rsch. Ctr., Baton Rouge, 1990—; bd. dirs. CSLA, Baton Rouge. Editor: Mycotoxins, Cancer & Health, 1991, The Science of Food Regulation, 1992, Vitamins and Cancer Prevention, 1993. Bd. dirs. Leukemia Soc. Am., New Orleans, 1983-86, Vols. of Am., New Orleans, 1984-91; mem. Am. Cancer Soc. Edn., New Orleans, 1990—, La. Health Care Authority Gov.'s Transition Team, Baton Rouge, 1991. Recipient Joel Fletcher Acad. scholarship, New Orleans, 1963-66, Optimist Leukemia Professorship, 1981-84, Topper award Outstanding Young Profl. in New Orleans, 1985. Mem. APHA, ACP, Am. Assn. for Cancer Rsch., Am. Soc. Clin. Oncology, Am. Soc. Hematology, Alpha Omega Alpha, Phi Kappa Phi. Office: Pennington Biomed Rsch Ctr 6400 Perkins Rd Baton Rouge LA 70808-4124

RYAN, EILEEN PATRICIA, psychiatrist, educator; b. N.Y.C., July 8, 1957; d. William Matthew and Eileen V. (Clarke) R.; m. Thomas William McNamara, Sept. 28, 1985; children: Liam T., Ellen R. BA, NYU, 1979; DO, Chgo. Coll. Osteo. Medicine, 1984. Cert. gen. psychiatry, child and adolescent psychiatry. Supervising editor McGraw Hill Book Co., N.Y.C., 1979-80; intern Bapt. Med. Ctr., Bklyn., 1984-85; resident, then fellow U. Pitts., 1985-89; asst. prof. psychiatry Western Psychiat. Inst. and Clinic, U. Pitts., 1989-92; med. dir. diagnostic and evaluation ctr. Western Psychiat. Inst., Clinic U. of Pitts., 1989-92; attending psychiatrist DeJarnette Ctr., Staunton, Va., 1992—; asst. prof. psychiatry U. Va., 1992—. Grantee, U. Pitts., 1988. Mem. Am. Pyschiat. Assn., Am. Acad. of Child and Adolescent Psychiatry. Office: DeJarnette Ctr PO Box 2309 Staunton VA 24401-2309

RYAN, ELLEN MARIE, elementary education and gifted education educator; b. Flushing, N.Y.; d. Francis and June Marie Ryan. BA in Elem. Edn., Queens Coll., 1971; MA in Edn., Adelphi U., 1974; MEd in Adminstrn., Stetson U., 1982; postgrad., Fla. Tech., 1988—. Cert. tchr. N.Y.C.; profl. cert. N.Y., Pa., Fla.; cert. tchr., elem. edn. adminstr., early childhood, gifted tchr.; cert. sch. site trainer in tech. Miami Mus. Sci. Tchr. grade 3 Park View Elem Kings Park (N.Y.) Sch. Dist., 1971-75; tchr. grade 6 So. Lehig Sch. Dist., Center Valley, Pa., 1975-77; resource tchr. grades K-6 North Penn Sch. Dist., Lansdale, Pa., 1977-79; tchr. grade 1 Holland Elem., Brevard County Schs., Satellite Beach, Fla., 1979-81; tchr. gifted student program Surfside Elem., Satellite Beach; tchr. grades K-6 Brevard County Schs., 1981—; grant writer, reviewer Grantsmanship Cadre, Brevard Schs., Fla., 1992—; cons. multimedia presentation NSF, State Systemic Initiative, Surfside Elem., Fla. Tech., Melbourne, 1994; cons., trainer, spkr. Surfside Elem., Satellite Beach, 1994, 95; presenter in field. Dir., prodr., photographer various prodns., 1992. Treas. Melbourne (Fla.) Panhellenic, 1987, yearbook chairperson, 1988, installation banquet chair, 1989; publicity chair Holy Name of Jesus Fall Festival, Indialantic, Fla., 1991. Fla. Instrnl. Tech. grantee Fla. Tech., 1991-93, Creative Tchg. grantee Brevard Schs. Found., Fla. Found., Melbourne, 1993, Tchrs. and Tech.-NSF grantee, 1993-95, Multimedia Life Sci. mini grantee Fla. Assn. for Gifted, 1994, Tech. Apprentice Program grantee Bell South Found., 1994—. Mem. Fla. Assn. Computer Educators (integrating tech. into the curriculum 1994—), Fla. Edn. Tech. Conf. (workshop presenter 1994), Delta Kappa Gamma (Beta Sigma chpt. yearbook chairperson, membership chair 1994—), Phi Delta Kappa (Creative Tchg. grants Cape Kennedy chpt. 1993). Office: Brevard County Schs Surfside Elem 475 Cassia Blvd Melbourne FL 32937-3114

RYAN, FRANK J., construction executive. Pres., COO Air Products and Chems., Inc.; bd. dirs. Southdown, Inc., Houston, 1993—, chmn. bd. dirs., 1995—, mem. compensation and benefits com., nominating com. Office: Southdown Inc Citicorp Ctr Ste 2400 1200 Smith St Houston TX 77002-4486

RYAN, J. BRUCE, health care management consulting executive; b. Southbridge, Mass., Mar. 28, 1944; s. Charles J. and Doris (Olney) R.; m. Sarah E. Pattison, Aug. 16, 1993. BSBA in Fin., U. Mass., 1972, MSBA, 1974; MA in Econs., U. Wash., 1976. Regional v.p. Amherst Assocs. Inc., Atlanta, 1976-85; exec. v.p. Jennings Ryan & Kolb, Inc., Atlanta, 1985—; mem. managed care adv. bd. St. Anthony Pub. Mem. editl. rev. bd. Healthcare Fin. Mgmt.; contbr. articles to profl. jours. With U.S. Army, 1968-70. Mem. Healthcare Fin. Mgmt. Assn. (Helen M. Yerger/L. Van Seawell best article award 1990), Soc. for Healthcare Planning & Mktg., Fin. Mgmt. Assn., Am. Assn. Physician-Hosp. Orgns. Home: 1060 Kentucky Ave NE Atlanta GA 30306-3534 Office: Jennings Ryan & Kolb Inc # 500 17 Executive Park Dr NE Atlanta GA 30329-2222

RYAN, JAMES, insurance company executive; b. Pittsburgh, Pa., Jan. 21, 1937; s. Martin Charles and Lucy Elizabeth (Misklow) r.; m. Marlene Sullivan Ryan, Jan. 27, 1973. BA, U. Pitts., U. Louisville. Cert. ins. wholesaler. Chmn. Market Finders Ins. Corp., Louisville, 1972—; com. chmn. Am. Assn. Mng. Gen. Agts., 1988-89; pres. Ky. Lloyd's Agts. Assn., 1985—; bd. dirs. Nat. Assn. Profl. Surplus Lines Office, Inc., 1983-86; pres. Ky. Surplus Lines Assn., Louisville, 1988-89; mem. adv. coun. Essex Ins. Co., 1991-93. Pub. in Best Rev., 1995. Mem. Ky. Thoroughbred Owners & Breeders, Inc., Hon. Order of Blue Goose Internat., Kosair Shrine Temple, Hon. Order of Ky. Col. Named Adv. Coun. Colony Ins. Co., Glen Allen, Va., 1991-93, Hamilton Ins. Co., 1993, Cardinal Ins. Co., 1991-93. Mem. Profl. Ins. Agts., Ind. Ins. Agts. Assn., Am. Assn. Mng. Gen. Agts. (cert., chmn. adv. com. 1991-92, bd. dirs. 1994-96, v.p. zone 3 1995-96, pres.-elect 1996-97, pres. 1997—), Nat. Assn. Profl. Surplus Lines Offices (chmn. legis. com. 1988-89, Published Best Rev. 1995), Am. Assn. of Gen. Agts. Republican. Roman Catholic.

RYAN, JAMES CHRIS, electrical engineer; b. Tulsa, Aug. 28, 1959; s. James L. and Mary E. (Hill) R. BSEE cum laude, Tulsa U., 1986. Engr. Data Gen. Corp., Westboro, Mass., 1986-87; engr. Wiltel, Tulsa, 1987-90, sr. engr., 1990-92, mgr. engring., 1992-94; dir. engring., 1994—. Staff sgt. USAF, 1979-83. Mem. IEEE. Office: Wiltel MS 25-5 PO Box 21348 Tulsa OK 74121

RYAN, JAMES GILBERT, historian, educator, writer; b. Wilmington, Del., Jan. 31, 1947; s. James A. and Audrey May (Davis) Urian; m. Anita Louise Noble, Jan. 20, 1973 (div. Sept. 1978). BA, U. Del., 1970, MA, 1973; MA, U. Notre Dame, 1975, PhD, 1981. Vis. instr. dept. history Purdue U., 1976, 77, 78; lectr. dept. history Pa. State U., Delaware County campus, 1978-79; instr. dept. history U. Notre Dame, summers 1979-80; adj. asst. prof. dept. history Ind. U. at South Bend, 1980-81; adj. asst. prof. dept. polit. sci. Temple U., 1982-84, 85-87; adj. asst. prof. dept. history and politics Drexel U., Phila., 1982-85, 85-87, vis. asst. prof. dept. history and politics, 1985; vis. asst. prof. dept. polit. sci. Muhlenberg Coll., Allentown, Pa., 1987-90; asst. prof. history dept. gen. acad. Tex. A&M U., Galveston, 1990-96; assoc. prof. Tex. A & M U., Galveston, 1996—; vis. researcher Russian Ctr. for Preservation and Study of Documents of Recent History, Moscow, 1993; presenter in field. Author: Earl Browder, 1997; contbr. chpt. to book and articles to profl. jours. Grantee Muhlenberg Coll., 1988, 90, Tex. A&M U., 1990, 91, 92, 93, 95. Mem. AAUP, NEA, Am. Hist. Assn., Orgn. Am. Historians, Historians of Am. Communism (ctrl. com. mem. 1995—), Southwestern Hist. Assn., Tex. Faculty Assn. Democrat. Home: 7302 Heards Ln Apt 313 Galveston TX 77551-1152 Office: Tex A & M Univ Dept Gen Acad PO Box 1675 Galveston TX 77553-1675

RYAN, JAMES HERBERT, security and retail services company executive; b. Petersburg, Va., Feb. 1, 1931; s. Richard Hillsdon and Mary Orgain (Mann) R.; BS, U.S. Mil. Acad., 1955; MA, U. Pa., 1962; MS, George Washington U., 1972; grad. Program for Mgmt. Devel. Harvard U., 1972; PhD, Walden U., 1984; m. Patricia Louise Abbott, June 7, 1955; 1 child, Pamela Louise. Commd. 2nd lt. U.S. Army, 1955, advanced through grades to lt. col., 1968, ret., 1972; gen. mgr. U.S. ops. Ryan Enterprises, Washington, 1970-73; pres. Ford Enterprises, Ltd., Mt. Rainier, Md., 1973-87; pres. James H. Ryan Assocs., Inc., Petersburg, Va., 1987—. Advisor to Sec. of Army, 1975, chief of naval material, 1980-82; mem. Pres.'s Pvt. Sector Survey on Cost Control (Grace Commn.), 1982; bd. govs. USO, 1977-86; pres. Hist. Petersburg Found., 1991-93; vestryman St. Paul's Episcopal Ch., 1994-96. Decorated Legion of Merit, Soldiers medal, Bronze Star, Air medal, Vietnamese Gallantry Cross. Mem. Am. Mgmt. Assn., Nat. Retail Federation, Am. Soc. Indsl. Security, Internat. Assn. Profl. Security Cons. (pres. 1993-95), Ret. Officers Assn., West Point Soc. Ctrl. Va., Rotary Club of Petersburg (pres. 1993-94). Episcopalian. Home: 1666 Westover Ave Petersburg VA 23805-2820 Office: James H Ryan Assocs Inc 520 Grove Ave PO Box 2126 Petersburg VA 23804

RYAN, JAMES WALTER, physician, medical researcher; b. Amarillo, Tex., June 8, 1935; s. Lee W. and Emma E. (Haddox) R.; children: James P.A., Alexandra L.E., Amy J.S. A.B. in Polit. Sci., Dartmouth Coll., 1957; M.D., Cornell U., 1961; D.Phil., Oxford U. (Eng.), 1967. Diplomate: Nat. Bd. Med. Examiners. Intern, Montreal (Que.) Gen. Hosp., McGill U., Can., 1961-62; asst. resident in medicine Montreal (Que.) Gen. Hosp., McGill U., 1962-63; USPHS research asso. NIMH, NIH, 1963-65; guest investigator Rockefeller U., N.Y.C., 1967-68; asst. prof. biochemistry Rockefeller U., 1968; asso. prof. medicine U. Miami (Fla.) Sch. Medicine, 1968-79, prof. medicine, 1979-95; prof. anesthesiology, pharmacology and toxicology Med. Coll. Ga., Augusta, 1995—; sr. scientist Papanicolaou Cancer Rsch. Inst., Miami, 1972-77; hon. med. officer to Regius prof. medicine Oxford U., 1965-67; vis. prof. Clin. Rsch. Inst. Montreal, 1974; mem. vis. faculty thoracic disease divsn., dept. internal medicine Mayo Clinic, 1974; cons. Chugai Pharm. Co., Ltd., Tokyo, Apotex, Inc., Toronto. Contbr. numerous articles on biochem. research and pathology to sci. jours.; patentee in field. Rockefeller Found. travel awardee, 1962; William Waldorf Astor travelling fellow, 1966; USPHS spl. fellow, 1967-68; Pfizer travelling fellow, 1972; recipient Louis and Artur Luciano award for research of circulatory diseases McGill U., 1984-85. Fellow Am. Inst. Chemists; mem. Am. Chem. Soc., Biochem. Soc., Am. Soc. Biol. Chemists, Am. Heart Assn. (mem. council cardiopulmonary diseases 1972—, Council for High Blood Pressure Research 1976—), Microcirculatory Soc., So. Soc. Clin. Investigation, AAAS, N.Y. Acad. Scis., Sigma Xi. Baptist. Club: United Oxford and Cambridge U. (London). Home: 3047 Lake Forest Dr Augusta GA 30909-3027 Office: Med Coll Ga Vascular Biology Ctr Augusta GA 30912

RYAN, JOHN FERGUS, novelist, probation officer, educator; b. Kansas City, Mo., June 6, 1931; s. John Fergus and Fay Sanford (Stukey) R.; m. Carla J. Smith, Aug. 8, 1952; children: John B., Carla E., Andrew D. BS, Memphis State Coll., 1957. Probation officer Tenn. Dept. Correction, Memphis, 1962-94; tchr. English Memphis Coll. Art, 1994—. Author: (novels) The Redneck Bride, 1982, The Little Brothers of St. Mortimer, 1991 (among Notable Novels of the Yr., N.Y. Times 1992). Bd. dirs. ACLU, Nashville, 1995. Sgt. U.S. Army, 1952-54, Korea. Mem. The Authors Guild. Democrat. Unitarian. Home: 1937 Lyndale Ave Memphis TN 38107

RYAN, JOHN M., lawyer; b. Glen Ridge, N.J., May 18, 1936. AB, Dartmouth Coll., 1958; LLB, U. Va., 1963. Bar: Va. 1964. Lectr. at law Marshall-Wythe Sch. Law Coll. William and Mary, 1976-86; ptnr. Vandeventer, Black, Meredith & Martin, Norfolk, Va.; gen. counsel Va. Internat. Terminals, Inc. Trustee John Marshall Found.; bd. dirs. Va. Symphony. Fellow Va. Law Found.; mem. ABA (labor rels., litigation sect.), Va. Bar Assn. (pres. 1988), Maritime Law Assn. of U.S., Norfolk-Portsmouth Bar Assn., Va. State Bar, Nat. Conf. Bar Pres., So. Conf. Bar Pres. Office: Vandeventer Black Meredith & Martin 500 World Trade Ctr Norfolk VA 23510-1617

RYAN, JOHN MICHAEL, municipal employee; b. Dallas, Nov. 30, 1953; s. Tom and Lyla Marie (Smith) R.; m. Pamela Sue White, Jan. 1, 1977; children: Jillian Dawn, Jennifer Leigh, Julianne Michelle. BS, U. Tex., 1977. From dispatcher to purchasing mgr. City of Plano, Tex., 1977—; bd. dirs. North Ctrl. Tex. Regional Cert. Agy., Arlington, 1991—; instr. Lyndon B. Johnson Sch. Pub. Affairs, Austin, Tex., 1992—. Sm. bus. adv. bd. Plano C. of C., 1993—. Named civilian of yr. Plano Police Dept., 1980. Mem. Nat. Inst. Govt. Purchasing, Nat. Purchasing Inst. (dir.-elect 1994—), Tex. Purchasing Mgmt. Assn. (pres. 1994—), Collin County Govt. Purchasers Forum (founders chair 1991—). Office: City of Plano 1520 Avenue K Plano TX 75086

RYAN, LOIS AGNES, secondary mathematics educator; b. Lynn, Mass., Dec. 12, 1942; d. Joseph and Gertrude Mary (Mozar) Zarohian; m. Charles T. Ryan, Jr., June 22, 1969; children: Wayne, Douglas, Ryan. BS in Edn., Salem State., 1964, MS in Edn., 1967. Cert. math. educator, counselor; cert. in computer math. for high sch. math. Math. tchr. Kennedy Jr. High, Peabody, Mass., 1965-69; lab aide math. Frank Day Jr. High, Newton, Mass., 1969-71; nursery sch. tutor Belmont (Mass.) Nursery Sch., 1972-78; spl. needs tutor, edn. cons. Lexington (Mass.) Pub. Schs., Belmont, 1978-86; psychiat. tutor, edn. cons. McLean's Hosp., Belmont, 1984-88; tchr. math. No. Highlands Regional High Sch., Allendale, N.J., 1988-90; edn. cons. Ridgewood, N.J., 1988-90; tchr. math. Bloomfield (N.J.) Pub. Schs., 1990-91, Oakbrook Mid. Sch., Summerville, S.C., 1991-94; Natchitoches Ctrl. H.S., La., 1994-95; math. tchr. Wimfield H.S., La., 1995-96; dept. chair math Hicks (La.) H.S., 1996—; cons. in field; vis. team mem. Mid. States Evaluation, 1989. Host parent Acad. Adventures in Am., Inc., Ridgewood, 1989; vol. Pop Warner Football Assn., Lexington, 1980-88, Cub Scouts and Boy Scouts, Lexington, 1980-90, Ridgewood High Sch. Instrn. Com., 1989-90. Recipient Grant NSF, 1967, 68, Dodge Found. Grant, 1990-91. Mem. NEA, Nat. Coun. Tchrs. Math., Assn. Math. Tchrs. N.J., Bergin County and Essex County Tchrs. Assn., Bloomfield Tchrs. Assn., Eagle Mother's Boy Scouts. Home: 183 Saint Charles Natchitoches LA 71457

RYAN, SUSAN MAGNESS, librarian, educator; b. Takoma Park, Md., May 27, 1958; d. Donald Eaton and Shirley Anne (Lusby) Magness; m. Edward Timothy Ryan, Sept. 1, 1984; 1 child, Shannon Kelsey. BS, Fla. State U., 1981, MS, 1982; MLS, UCLA, 1989. Intelligence officer CIA, Washington, 1983-84; libr., assoc. prof. Stetson U., DeLand, Fla., 1989—. Author: Downloading Democracy: Government Information in an Electronic Age, 1996, Government CD-ROMs: A Practical Guide to Searching Electronic Databases, 1994; series and cons. editor Librs. Unltd., 1994-96; mem. editl. bd. Jour. Govt. Info., 1993-96, column editor, 1994-96; contbr. numerous articles to acad. jours. Bd. dirs. coun. advisors for Sch. Libr. and Info. Studies, Fla. State U., Tallahassee, 1995—. Mem. ALA (mem. govt. docs. round table 1989—, Catharine J. Reynolds award for rsch., govt. docs. round table 1996), Fla. Libr. Assn. (chairperson govt. docs. caucus 1992-93), Ctrl. Fla. Libr. Consortium (chairperson govt. docs. interest group 1991-92). Office: duPont-Ball Libr Stetson Univ Campus Box 8418 Deland FL 32720

RYAN, TERESA WEAVER, obstetrical nurse; b. Dallas, July 18, 1956; d. J.E. and Mary (Davis) Weaver; m. Patrick Hallaron Ryan, Apr. 7, 1991. BS, Troy State U., 1983; BSN, Tex. Christian U., 1987; MSN, U. South Ala., 1994; postgrad., La. State U. RN, Fla.; cert. maternal-newborn nurse ANCC. Intelligence analyst USN, Dallas, 1983-87; enlisted USAF, 1987, advanced through grades to capt. (obstetrical nurse), 1987—; childbirth educator USAF, 1988—. Mem. NOW, Assn. Women's Health, Obstetrical and Neonatal Nurses, Nat. Humane Soc. Educators, People for the Ethical Treatment of Animals, Sigma Theta Tau (sec. 1987—, rsch. grant 1987), Phi Kappa Phi. Roman Catholic. Home: 35 Imperial Woods Dr Harahan LA 70123

RYAN, THOMAS WILLIAM, lawyer; b. Tulsa, Feb. 16, 1953; s. Dean Lawrence and Helen Ladeen (Steinkierchner) R.; m. Mary Ellen Poxon, Jan. 30, 1973; children: Matthew Alan, Jennifer Erin. BA, U. Houston, 1975, JD, 1978. Bar: Tex. 1978. Ptnr. Hart, Ryan & Pfeffer, Houston, 1978-80; contracts adminstr. Texaco Inc., Houston, 1980-85; sr. atty. Total Minatome Corp., Houston, 1985—. Coach youth sports YMCA, Houston, 1990. Mem. KC (adv. 1985-87), State Bar Tex. Office: Total Minatome Corp 909 Fannin St Ste 2200 Houston TX 77010-1007

RYAN, WILLIAM JOSEPH, multimedia and distance education designer; b. Amsterdam, N.Y., Aug. 12, 1958; s. William John and Joann Gail (Birmingham) R. BS, SUNY, Brockport, 1979; MS, Ithaca Coll., 1987; postgrad. Prodn. coord., disc jockey WWBK, Brockport, N.Y., 1979; video prodn. asst. Nat. Tech. Inst for Deaf at Rochester Inst. of Tech., Rochester, N.Y., 1979-80; media specialist Coll. of St. Rose, Albany, 1980-85; video developer Sci. Rsch. Assocs., Chgo., 1987-89; sr. tng. comms. specialist Westinghouse Savannah River Co., Aiken, S.C., 1989—; cons. Infocomm, Internat. Comms. Industries Assn., Internat. TV Assn. Transition Team, 1991-94; mem. nat. stds. com. for. curriculum devel. for multimedia developers and producers/dirs. Contbr. articles to profl. jours.; presenter at tng. and ednl. workshops. Recipient Total Quality Achievement award Environ. Safety, Health and Quality Assurance divsn. Westinghouse Savannah River Co., 1991; grantee Am. Speech-Hearing Assn. and Dept. Edn., 1986. Mem. Internat. TV Assn. (chair electronic com. commn. 1995-96, bd. dirs. Augusta chpt. 1990—, chmn. tech. support svcs. 1989-95, judge and panel host ann. video festival interactive category, 1991—, Nat. Svc. award 1993, 95), Assn. for Applied Interactive Multimedia (bd. dirs. 1993-95), Soc. Motion Picture and TV Engrs., JY-15 Sailing Assn. (editor newsletter), U.S. Sailing Assn., Phi Kappa Phi. Home: 4334 Ridge Cliff Dr Augusta GA 30909-9618 Office: Westinghouse Savannah River Co Video Svcs Bldg 777-10A Aiken SC 29803

RYAN, WILLIAM JOSEPH, communications company executive; b. Nyack, N.Y., Apr. 14, 1932; s. William Joseph and Elizabeth (Langley) R.; m. Jane Householder, June 27, 1970; children: Ashley Allison, William Joseph, III. BA, U. Notre Dame, 1954. TV producer Jules Power Prodn., Chgo., 1954-56; pres., gen. mgr. Radio Naples, Naples, Fla., 1956-70; gen. mgr. Radio Naples (Fla.) div. Palmer Broadcasting, 1970-73; v.p., cable-radio Palmer Broadcasting, Fla. and Calif., 1973-80; v.p. cable Palmer Communications, Naples, 1980-82; pres. Palmer Communications, Inc., Des Moines, 1982-84, pres., chief exec. officer, 1984-95; pres. CEO Palmer Wireless Inc., 1995—; bd. dirs. Norwest Bank, Des Moines, C&S Bank, Ft. Myers, Fla., Naples Cmty. Hosp. State committeeman Rep. Com., Collier County, Fla., 1970-72; pres. Navy League, Naples, local chpt. Am. Cancer Soc.; chmn. Collier County Econ. Devel. Coun.; bd. dirs. Philharm. Ctr. Arts, Naples Philharm. Recipient Walter Kaitz award Nat. Cable TV Assn. Mem. Cable Advt. Bur. (founding chmn., bd. dirs.), Econ. Develop. Coun. (chmn.), So. Cable Assn. (pres.), Fla. Cable Assn. (pres.), Fla. Assn. Broadcasters (pres.), Cable TV Pioneers, Broadcast Pioneers, Cable TV Adminstrn. and Mktg. Soc. (Grand Tammy award 1981), Cellular Telephone Industry Assn. (bd. dirs.), Naples C. of C. (pres.), Royal Poinciana Club. Office: Palmer Wireless Inc 12800 University Dr Ste 500 Fort Myers FL 33907-5337

RYBERG, THOMAS CARL, quality assurance professional; b. Chgo., Sept. 25, 1937; s. William Oscar and Mary Irene (Elliott) R.; m. Beve K. Craig; children: Timothy, Christopher John, Stephen; stepchildren: Stacey, David. BSME, Marquette U., 1959. Standards engr. Cutler Hammer, Lincoln, Ill., 1959-64; standards engr. Cutler Hammer, Bowling Green, Ky., 1964-66, mfg. supr., 1966-67; plant indsl. engr. Cutler Hammer, Athens, Ala., 1967-74, quality assurance mgr., 1968-74, material mgr., 1974-76, plant mgr., 1976-79; ops. mgr. Wolverine Tube, Decatur, Ala., 1979; plant mgr. D.A.B. Industries, Athens, 1979-86; dir. ops. D.A.B. Industries, Troy, Mich., 1983-86; sr. quality engr. Critikon (subs. J&J Co.), Huntsville, Ala., 1986-91, resident mgr. quality, 1991-94; mgr. quality assurance OMC, Calhoun, Ga., 1994—. Pres. Community Rels. Assn., Decatur, 1982; chmn. United Way, Limestone County, Ala., 1981. Recipient Legis. Proclamation award Ho. of Reps., 1978. Mem. Am. Soc. Quality Control (sr. mem., cert. quality engr., cert. quality auditor, chmn. 1991-92, author, editor newsletter 1991-92, Profl. of Yr. award 1991), Inst. Indsl. Engrs. (sr. mem.), Athens C. of C. (pres. 1983). Home: 136 Southmont Dr NE Calhoun GA 30701-9537

RYDER, FRANK GLESSNER, German literature educator, researcher; b. Mpls., Dec. 23, 1916; s. William and Agnes Crocker (Glessner) R.; m. Shirley Ruth Sickels, Aug. 21, 1948; children: Elizabeth R. Napier, Barbara R. Studholme, Mary R. Cullin. BA summa cum laude, U. Minn., 1937, MA, 1938; PhD, U. Mich., 1950. From instr. to prof. German Dartmouth Coll., Hanover, N.H., 1945-63; chmn., prof. German Ind. U., Bloomington, 1963-71; Kenan prof. German lit. U. Va., Charlottesville, 1971-81, Kenan prof. German lit. emeritus, 1981—; vis. prof. Stanford NDEA, Bad Boll, Germany, 1965, U. Wis., Madison, 1967-68, U. Hamburg, Germany, 1970, Monash U., Melbourne, Australia, 1972, Ripon (Wis.) Coll., 1974, U. Oreg., 1974. Editor: George Ticknor's Werter, 1952; translator: The Song of the Nibelungs, 1962; editor, co-editor (including transl.) Goethe, Verse Plays and Epic, Goethe Early Verse, Drama and Prose Plays, 1983, Gottfried Keller, 1982, Literary Fairy Tales, 1983, Romantic Novellas, 1985, German Romantic Stories, 1988, Goethe's Egmont, Iphigenie, Tasso, 1992. Lt. (j.g.) USNR, 1943-46, PTO. Recipient Goethe Gold medal Goethe Inst., Munich, 1970, Outstanding German Educator award Am. Assn. Tchrs. of German, 1995; Fulbright sr. scholar, 1972; Am. Coun. Learned Socs. faculty study fellow, 1951, Ford Found. fellow, 1955-56; selected German Fgn. Office Guest Program, Bonn, 1961. Home: PO Box 29 Batesville VA 22924-0029

RYDER, GENE ED, retired United States Air Force training administrator; b. Canyon, Tex., Sept. 19, 1932; s. Johnny Allen and Rilda (New) R.; m. Mary Louise Wilson, Feb. 16, 1958; children: Carlyn, Katherine, Anita, Valerie. BA in Govt. cum laude, St. Mary's U., 1965; MEd, Our Lady of the Lake U., 1968; PhD in Adminstrn., The Union Inst., 1979. Instr. USAF, Scott, Keesler & Lackland AFB, 1958-65; tng. specialist USAF, Lackland AFB, Tex., 1965-69, tng. evaluator, 1969-72, curriculum coord., 1972-75, supr. curriculum devel., 1975-78, supr. tng. evaluation, 1978-83, tng. advisor, 1983-92; chief tng. policy USAF, Randolph AFB, Tex., 1992-95; ret., 1995; chmn. affiliated schs. adv. panel C.C. of Air Force, Maxwell AFB, Ala., 1984-88; co-chmn. USAF Tng. and Instrnl. Sys. Career Program, Randolph AFB, 1992-95; apptd. to Tex. State Bd. Profl. Counselors, 1995—. Author: Basics of Sunday School Leadership: A Guide for Lay Leaders, 1982. Dir. edn. Calvary Hills Bapt. Ch., San Antonio, 1981-94; coord. state scripture Gideons Internat., Nashville, 1991-94; elected mem. Tex. State Rep. Exec. Com., 1994—. With USAF, 1953-56. Mem. Phi Delta Kappa. Home: 1502 Copperfield Rd San Antonio TX 78251-3324

RYDSTROM, CARLTON LIONEL, chemist, paint and coating consultant; b. Indpls., Dec. 4, 1928; s. Carlton Lionel and Sara Ann (McNeese) R.; m. Kathleen O'Leary, Oct. 21, 1954 (dec.); children: Carlton L. III, Michael, Mary (dec.), Leslie, Patricia, Timothy, Molly; m. Mary L. Murphy, June 13, 1992. BS in Polymer Chemistry, N.D. State U., 1951; MS in Phys. Chemistry, U. Puerto Rico, Rio, Piedras, 1953. Chemist Am. Marietta Co., Kankakee, Ill., 1951-52; chemist, plant mgr. Chinamel Paints, Hato Rey, Puerto Rico, 1952-53; tech. mgr. Midwest Synthetics (Valspar), Rockford, Ill., 1953-55; mng. ptnr. Norcote Co., St. Petersburg, Fla., 1955-71; pres. C.M. Industries, Inc., St. Petersburg, 1971-74, Tuf-top/Norcote Coatings, Inc., St. Petersburg, 1974-80; owner Rydstrom Lab., Inc., St. Petersburg, 1980—; bd. dirs. Stacote Finishes, Ltd., W.I.; cons. Sch. Bds. State of Fla., 1981—, paint and adhesive industries. Pres. parish coun. St. Jude Cath. Cathedral Parish, 1977-78, 78-79, St. Vincent de Paul Pinellas Dist., St. Petersburg, 1988-91; nat. secretariat Cursillo Movement, Roman Cath. Ch., Dallas, 1985-88; dir. Cursillo Movement, Diocese of St. Petersburg, 1995—; dir. St. Vincent de Paul Food Ctr., St. Petersburg, 1988—; chmn. Waterfront Planning Com., St. Petersburg, 1959; mem. bd. dirs. St. Petersburg Cath. H.S., 1977-80. Fellow N.Y. Acad. Sci.; mem. Nat. Assn. Corrosion Engrs., Soc. Coatings Tech. (chmn./pres. 1958-59, Disting. Svc. award 1975), Fla. Paint and Coating Assn. (treas., dir. 1959-75), St. Vincent dePaul Soc. (Top Hat award 1991), Jr. C. of C. (DSA 1960). Republican. Roman Catholic. Home and Office: 6300 25th Ave N Saint Petersburg FL 33710-4128

RYEN, DAG, journalist; b. Ringsaker, Norway, May 13, 1945; came to U.S., 1949; s. Kob and Geggy (Selen) R.; m. Grethe Fribu, Jan. 4, 1970 (div.); m. Lajla Auguste Breien Peersen, Mar. 3, 1978; children: Olve, Trond, Anja, Hild, Tind Shepper. AB, Princeton U., 1967; student, George Washington U., 1967-68; MA, U. Ky., 1992. Assoc. editor Norwegian News Svc., Oslo, 1971-75; dir. pub. rels. Rogaland Theater, Stavanger, Norway, 1975-77; adminstrv. asst. to Mayor, Lexington, Ky., 1977-78; pres. The Helicon Co., Lexington, 1979-87; exec. editor The Coun. of State Govts., Lexington, 1987-95, dir. Ctr. for Internat. Affairs, 1995—; theater critic Lexington Herald-Leader, Lexington, 1986—. Author: This Trembling Land, 1980, Traces: The Story of Lexington's Past, 1987; editor: (mag.) State Government News, 1987-95, Jour. of State Govt., 1987-95. Mem. Ky. Heritage Coun., 1995—; pres. Land and Nature Trust, Lexington, 1981-83, chmn. bd. dirs., 1985-87. McConnell Found. fellow, 1966. Mem. Nat. Press Club, Soc. Profl. Journalists. Home: 4100 Parkers Mill Rd Lexington KY 40513-9733 Office: The Coun of State Govts 3560 Iron Works Rd Lexington KY 40511-8410

RYLES, TIM, state commissioner. Commr. ins., comptr. gen. Ga. Dept. Ins., Atlanta. Mem. Nat. Assn. Consumer Agy. Adminstrs. (former pres.). Office: Ga Dept Ins 716 W Tower 2 Martin Luther King Jr Dr SW Atlanta GA 30334-9008*

RYNEAR, NINA COX, retired registered nurse, author, artist; b. Cochranville, Pa., July 11, 1916; d. Fredrick Allen and Nina Natalie (Drane) Cox; m. Charles Spencer Rynear, Aug. 22, 1934 (dec. May 1941); children: Charles Joseph, Stanley Spencer. RN, Coatesville Hosp. Sch. Nursing, 1945; BS in Nursing Edn., U. Pa., 1954. Interviewer Nat. Opinion Rsch. Ctr., U. Denver, Colo., 1942-47; sch. nurse West Goshen Elem. Sch., West Chester, Pa., 1946-47; pub. health nurse Pa. Dept. Health Bur. Pub. Health Nursing, Harrisburg, 1947-51; staff nurse V.A. Hosp., Coatesville, Pa., 1951-54; staff nurse, asst. head nurse V.A. Hosp., Menlo Park, Calif., 1954-56; asst. chief nursing svc. Palo Alto and Menlo Park VA Hosps., Palo Alto, Menlo Park, Calif., 1956-76; self employed Reno, Nev., 1976—. Author: (poems, musical compositions) Old Glory and the U.S.A., 1989, Mister Snowman, 1988, Dawn Shadow of Lenape, 1988; (poem and song compilation) This Side of Forever, 1990; (musical compositions) Blessed Are Those Who Listen, What Can I Leave, The Hobo's Promise; (childrens' stories) Wilyum of Orange 1st, Lady Harley and Pepper, 1995; contbr. sonnets to Newsletter of N.Am. Acad. Esoteric Studies; paintings represented in numerous pvt. collections. Pres. Chester County Pub. Health Nurses Assn., 1950. Staff nurse Cadet Corps, 1944-45. Mem. VFW Aux. (patriotic instr. 1989-90, chmn. safety div. Silver State #3396 chpt. 1990-91), New Century Rebekah Lodge #244. Methodist. Home and Office: 3476 Harbor Beach Dr Lake Wales FL 33853-8082

RYSKAMP, KENNETH LEE, federal judge; b. 1932; m. Karyl Sonja Ryskamp; 1 child, Cara Leigh. AB, Calvin Coll., 1955; JD, U. Miami, 1956. Bar: Fla. 1956, Mich. 1957, U.S. Supreme Ct. 1970. Law clk. to presiding judge Fla. Ct. Appeals 3d Dist., 1957-59; pvt. practice law Miami, Fla., 1959-61; ptnr. Goodwin, Ryskamp, Welcher & Carrier, Miami, 1961-84; mng. ptnr. Squire, Sanders & Dempsey, Miami, 1984-86; judge U.S. Dist. Ct. (so. dist.) Fla., Miami, 1986—. Office: US Dist Ct 701 Clematis St Fl 4 West Palm Beach FL 33401-5101

RYSTROM, KENNETH FRED, JR., communications educator; b. Bayard, Nebr., Mar. 4, 1932; s. Kenneth Fred and Zella Rae (Borland) R.; m. Sally Ann Hall, June 13, 1954 (div. Nov. 1977); children: Anne, Margaret, Victoria; m. Billie Hodge Campbell, June 9, 1978 (div. 1981). BA in Journalism, U. Nebr., 1954; MA in Polit. Sci., U. Calif., Berkeley, 1955; MA in Journalism, U. So. Calif., 1982, PhD in Polit. Sci., 1984. Reporter The Columbian, Vancouver, Wash., 1957-60; editorial writer Register &Tribune, Des Moines, 1960-65; editorial page editor The Columbian, 1965-72, mng. editor, 1972-77; prof. U. Redlands (Calif.), 1978-84, Va. Polytech Inst. & State U., Blacksburg, 1984—; vis. prof. Wash. State U., Pullman, 1977-78; pres. Nat. Conf. Editorial Writers, 1974. Author: (textbook) The Why, When, How of the Editorial Page, 1983, 2d edit., 1994; co-author: (textbook) Interpreting Public Issues, 1991. 1st lt. U.S. Army, 1955-57, Korea, capt. U.S. Army res., 1962-63. Recipient W. Grad award, 1992, 93, 94. Mem. Soc. Profl. Journalists, Kiwanis, Phi Beta Kappa. Home: 1012 Chateau Ct Blacksburg VA 24060-3676 Office: Va Polytech Inst & State U Communications Studies Blacksburg VA 24061-0311

SAADEH, CONSTANTINE KHALIL, internist, health facility administrator, educator; b. Beirut, Sept. 6, 1957; came to U.S., 1982; s. Khalil Constantine and Angel Janet (Iskendarian) S.; m. Vivian Camille Novni, June 28, 1988 (div. Apr. 1993); 1 child, Charles; m. M. Celeste Gaylor, 1996; 2 children: Charles, McKenzie. BS in Biology-Chemistry, Am. U. Beirut, 1978, MD, 1982. Diplomate Nat. Bd. Med. Examiners, Am. Bd. Internal Medicine, Am. Bd. Allergy and Immunology, Am. Bd. Internal Medicine, Am. Bd. Rheumatology, Am. Bd. Geriatrics, Am. Acad. Pain Mgmt. Intern dept. of medicine U. Miami, Jackson Meml. Hosp., Fla., 1982-83, resident dept. of medicine, 1983-85; fellow in clin. immunology Baylor Coll. of Medicine, Houston, 1985-87; fellow in rheumatology U. Colo. Health Sci. Ctr., Denver, 1987-88, instr. dept. internal medicine, 1988-89; acting chief med. svc. VA Med. Ctr., Amarillo, Tex., 1989, med. svc. staff physician, 1989—; asst. prof. dept. internal medicine Tex. Tech U. Health Scis. Ctr., Amarillo, 1989-91, assoc. prof. internal medicine and pediatrics, dir., 1991—, regional chair internal medicine, dir. residency program, 1992—, assoc. prof. dept. microbiology and immunology, 1992—; mem. grad. med. edn. com. Tex. Tech. U. Health Sci. Ctr.; mem. pharmacy and therapeutics com. N.W. Tex. Hosp.; mem. pharmacy and therapeutics com., R&D com. VA Med. Ctr., faculty appointments com., MPIP com. Tex. Tech. U., program dir., chmn. residency evaluation com., 1992—; lectr. in field. Contbr. articles to profl. jours. Fellow ACP, Am. Acad. Allergy and Immunology, Am. Coll. Rheumatology; mem. AMA, So. Med. Assn. (chmn. rheumatology sect. 1996-97). Home: 7100 Canterbury Amarillo TX 79109 Office: Tex Tech U Health Scis Ctr 1400 Wallace Blvd Amarillo TX 79106-1708

SAADIAN, JAVID, accountant, consultant; b. Tehran, Iran, Dec. 25, 1953; came to U.S., 1971; s. Avshalom and Akhtar (Barookhian) S.; m. Janet Elissa Salins, Dec. 30, 1978; children: Jason, Sarah, Susan. Student, Montgomery Coll., spring 1972; BS in Acctg., U. Md., 1976. CPA, Md., Va. Acct. Lewis Kest and Co., Washington, 1977-78; auditor, sr. acct. Aronson, Greene, Fisher & Co., Bethesda, Md., 1978-80; auditor Price Waterhouse, Washington, 1980-81, contr., 1981-83; dir. fin. Mt. Vernon Ladies Assn. of the Union and subs., 1983-94, dep. dir. for fin. and adminstrn., 1994—; cons. various orgns. Washington met. area, 1979—; mem. U.S. Taxation, Acctg. and Bus. Del. to China and Hong Kong, 1989. Fin. advisor Ft. Hunt Coop. Presch., Alexandria, 1986-89; treas. Collingwood on Potomac Homeowners Assn., Alexandria, 1987-89; mem. budget and fin. com. Mt. Vernon Coun. of Citizens Assns., 1988, treas., 1988-89; treas., mem. fin. com., bd. dirs. Adat Reyim Congregation, 1991, fin. v.p., 1996—. Recipient cert. of merit SBA, Washington, 1976. Mem. AICPA, Va. Soc. CPA's, Am. Soc. Assn. Execs., Fairfax C of C., Mt. Vernon-Lee C. of C. (1982-91), Beta Alpha Psi (chmn. tutoring com. 1976). Jewish. Home: 8636 Oak Chase Cir Fairfax VA 22039-3328 Office: Mt Vernon Ladies Assn Union George Washington Meml Pky Mount Vernon VA 22121

SAARI, JOY ANN, family nurse practitioner, geriatrics medical and surgical nurse; b. Chippewa Falls, Wis., July 14, 1953; d. Harry R. and Hilda R. (Christianson) Harwood; m. Allan A. Saari, Dec. 31, 1973 (dec.); children: Christopher, Erik. BSN summa cum laude, U. Wis., Eau Claire, 1978; postgrad., Blue Ridge Community Coll., Verona, Va., 1987; MSN, FNP, George Mason U., 1995; MSN. RN, Mich., Wis., Va.; FNP, Va.; cert. BLS instr., ACLS. Staff nurse Portage View Hosp., Hancock, Mich., 1979-80; evening supr., asst. dir. nursing Chippewa Manor, Chippewa Falls, 1980-86; staff nurse Bridgewater (Va.) Home, Inc., 1986-90; p.m. charge nurse Medicalodge Leavenworth, Kans., 1990-91; outdoor edn. nurse Montgomery County (Md.) Schs., 1991-93; FNP Leesburg/Sterling Family Practice, 1995—. Capt. USAR Nurse Corps. Mem. Am. Acad. Nurse Practitioners, Nat. League of Nursing, No. Va. Nurse Practitioner Assn., Res. Officer Assn., Am. Legion Aux., Phi Kappa Phi.

SAATKAMP, HERMAN JOSEPH, philosophy educator; b. Knoxville, Tenn., Sept. 29, 1942; s. Herman Joseph and Geneva L. (Mays) S.; m. Dorothy Tyre; children: Barbara, Joseph. BA, Carson-Newman Coll., 1964; MDiv, So. Theol. Sem., 1967; MA, Vanderbilt U., 1970, PhD, 1972. Teaching asst. Vanderbilt U., Nashville, 1968-70; asst. prof. U. Tampa, Fla., 1970-73, assoc. prof., 1973-78, prof. philosophy, 1978-80, Dana prof. philosophy, 1981-85; head dept. philosophy and humanities Tex. A&M U., College Station, 1985-94, 96—, prof., 1985—; adj. lectr. U. So. Fla., 1971, 72; chair dept. philosophy U. Tampa, 1975-83, chair humanities div., 1983-85; chair univ. chamber music series Tex. A&M U., 1985-88, mem. adv. bd. Koriyama, Japan campus, 1989-93, adv. panel on undergrad. edn., 1990, multiple mission task force, chair cmty. scholars subcom., 1990-91, mem. exec. coun. coll. liberal arts, mem., chmn. various coms.; mem. internal bd. advisors Inst. Pacific Asia, 1987-91. Co-author: Frontiers in American Philosophy, vol. 1, 1992, vol. 2, 1996, George Santayana: A Bibliographical Checklist, 1880-1980, 1982; gen. editor: The Works of George Santayana, vol. 1, 1986, vol. 2, 1987, vol. 3, 1989, vol. 4, 1994, The Vanderbilt Library of American Philosophy; contbr. numerous articles and revs. to profl. publs. Fin. com. Brazos Valley Symphony Bd., 1991-92, chair long range planning com., 1991-92, exec. dir. search com., 1991-92, pres., 1988-89, 1st v.p., 1987-88, chair fin. com., 1986-88, devel. com., 1986-88, membership com., 1986-88; bd. dirs. Tex. Com. Humanities, 1992-97, vice-chair, 1995-96, chair, 1996-97. Grantee NEH, 1977—, Inst. History Am. Philosophy, 1976, Gen. Electric, 1976; NDEA fellow, 1968-70. Fellow Sophia; mem. MLA, Am. Philos. Assn. (program adv. com. 1990-92), Arts Coun. Brazos Valley, Assn. Documentary Editing (pres. 1996-97, mem. com. 1995, councilor-at-large 1991-94, chair tech. com. 1989, 90, edn. com. 1986), Assn. Literary & Linguistic Computing, U. Va. Bibl. Soc., Bryan Coll. Sta. Sister Sister City Assn., Inst. Scholarly Editing (nat. adv. bd.), Inst. for Humanities at Salado, Interdisciplinary Group for Hist. Literary Study, Opera and Performing Arts Soc., Santayana Soc. (exec. com.), Soc. Advancement of Am. Philosophy (chair Hermes prize com., mem. Schneider award com., China conf. com., com. fin., exec. com. 1988-90), Soc. Computers and Humanities, Soc. Textual Scholarship, Word Processors Topical Study Group (chair Tex. A&M 1985-87), Tex A&M U. Faculty Club (mem. adv. bd. 1989—, v.p. 1990-91, pres. 1991-92), Phi Beta Delta (mem. activation com. Alpha Eta chpt. 1987), Phi Kappa Phi. Office: Texas A&M Univ Santayana Edition Dept Philosophy College Station TX 77843-4237

SABATINI, SANDRA, physician; b. N.Y.C., Dec. 1, 1940. BS in Chemistry, Millsaps Coll., 1962; MS in Pharmacology, Marquette U., 1966; PhD in Pharmacology, U. Miss., 1968; MD in Internal Medicine, Tex. Med. Sch., 1974. Lic. physician, Ill., Tex. Intern in medicine U. Ill. Hosp., Chgo., 1974-75; asst. prof. U. Tex. Med. Sch., San Antonio, 1968-70; assoc. dir. U. Ill. Hosp., Chgo., 1977-78; asst. prof. U. Ill. Coll. of Medicine, Chgo., 1977-83, assoc. prof. medicine and physiology, 1983-84; attending physician in nephrology VA, Chgo., 1977-84; med. dir. Dialysis Unit U. Ill., Chgo., 1978-84; prof. internal medicine and physiology Tex. Tech. U. Health Sci. Ctr., Lubbock, 1985—, chmn. dept. physiology, 1993—; attending physician in nephrology U. Med. Ctr., Lubbock, 1985—; lab. instr. Millsaps Coll., Jackson, Miss., 1961-62; instr. in pharmacology, Bapt. Hosp. Sch. Nursing, Jackson, 1966-68; merit rev. mem. NSF, 1987, 91, 92; rev. mem. several orgns. including Chgo. Heart Assn., 1984, NIH, 1982, 86, 89-93, Nat. Kidney Found., 1987, 89—, Am. Heart Assn., 1981-84, others. Editorial referee Am. Jour. Kidney Disease, Am. Jour. Physiology, Am. Jour. Nephrology, Annals of Internal Medicine, others; editorial bd. Am. Jour. Nephrology, 1989-93, Seminars in Nephrology, 1984—; ; author numerous publs. and abstracts in field; contbr. articles to profl. jours. Recipient predoctoral fellowship grant, Marquette U., 1963-66, pub. health predoctoral fellow U. Miss. Med. Sch., 1967-69, gen. medicine sci. rsch. grant U. Tex. Med. Sch., 1968-70, post-grad. fellowship award Karolinska Inst., Swedish Med. Coun., 1971, 73, NIH grants, 1979-82, 1984—, Chgo. Heart Assn. grant-in-aid, 1979-85, Nat. Eye Inst. grant, 1979-80, Banes Charitable Trust award U. Ill.,1984-85, U.S. Olympic Com. Rsch. Found. Clin. Study, 1986-87, numerous others awards in field. Fellow Am. Coll. Physicians; mem. AAAS, AAUP, AOA (hon.), Am. Fedn. Clin. Rsch., Am. Heart Assn., Am. Physiol. Soc., Am. Soc. Nephrology, Am. Soc. Pharmacology and Exptl. Therapeutics, Am. Soc. Renal Biochemistry and Metabolism (pres. elect 1994), Cen. Soc. Clin. Rsch., Ill. Kidney Found., Internat. Soc. Nephrology, Italian-Am. Nephrologists, Inc., Nat. Kidney Found. (numerous offices including chmn. several coms.), Nat. Kidney Found. of West Tex. (bd. dirs. 1993—, Outstanding Vol. 1995). Office: Tex Tech U Health Sci Ctr 3601 4th St Lubbock TX 79430-0001

SABAT-RIVERS, GEORGINA, Latin American literature educator; b. Santiago, Oriente, Cuba; came to U.S., 1962; d. José and Balbina (Mercadé) Sabat; m. Armando A. Guernica (div.); children: Armando A., Antonio J., Rodolfo M., Georgina M.; m. Elias L. Rivers, Sept. 19, 1969. MA in Romance Langs., Johns Hopkins U., 1967, PhD in Romance Langs., 1969. Instr. U. Oriente, Santiago de Cuba, 1956-61; asst. prof. Georgetown Visitation Coll., Washington, 1962-63; asst. prof. Western Md. Coll., Westminster, 1963-69, assoc. prof., 1969-73, prof., 1973-78, chair dept., 1974-78; assoc. prof. SUNY, Stony Brook, 1978-86, prof., 1986—, chair dept., 1981-84; vis. prof. U. Calif., Irvine, 1989, U. Iowa, Iowa City, 1994, UNAM, Mexico City. Author: El Sueño de Sor Juana Inés de la Cruz tradiciones literarias y originalidad, 1976, Sor Juana Inés de la Cruz Inundación castálida, 1982, Literatura Femenina conventual: Sor Marcela de San Félix Hija de Lope, 1992, others; mem. editl. bd. Colonial L.Am. Rev., 1990—, Caliope; contbr. articles to profl. jours. Fellow NEH, 1984-85, Fulbright, 1987; Soviet Union Internat. Rsch. and Exch. Bd. grantee, 1986, Summer seminar grantee NEH, 1995. Fellow Am. Philos. Soc.; mem. MLA (del. 1988-93), AAUW, Assn. Internat. Hispanistas, Assn. Internat. Siglo de Oro, Assn. Internat. Cervantes, Inst. Internat. Revista Iberoamericana Lit. (editl. bd. 1987-90).

SABLIK, MARTIN JOHN, research physicist; b. Bklyn., Oct. 21, 1939; s. Martin C. and Elsie M. (Fuzia) S.; m. Beverly Ann Shively, Nov. 26, 1965; children: Jeanne, Karen, Marjorie, Larry. BA in Physics, Cornell U., 1960; MS in Physics, U. Ky., 1965; PhD, Fordham U., 1972. Jr. engr. The Martin Co., Orlando, Fla., 1962-63; half-time instr. U. Ky., Lexington, 1963-65; rsch. assoc. Fairleigh Dickinson U., Teaneck, N.J., 1965-67, instr. physics, 1967-1972, asst. prof., 1972-76, assoc. prof., 1976-80; sr. rsch. scientist Southwest Rsch. Inst., San Antonio, 1980-87, staff scientist, 1987—; local chmn. Intermag. Conf., San Antonio, 1995. Mem. editorial bd. Nondestructive Testing and Evaluation, 1989—; mem. adv. bd. Conf. on Properties and Applications of Magnetic Materials, 1990—, Workshop on Advances in Measurement Techniques and Instrumentation for Magnetic Properties Determination, 1994—, Magnetic Materials, Measurements and Modeling Symposium, 1996; contbr. articles to profl. jours.; referee, patentee in field. Recipient Imagineer award Mind Sci. Found., 1989. Mem. IEEE, Am. Phys. Soc., Am. Geophys. Union, Am. Soc. Nondestructive Testing (chmn. So. Tex. sect. 1983-84), Am. Assn. Physics Tchrs. Roman Catholic. Office: SW Rsch Inst PO Box 28510 San Antonio TX 78228-0510

SACASAS, RENE, lawyer; b. N.Y.C., July 10, 1947; s. Anselmo and Orlanda (Soto) S.; m. Cathy Lee Van Natta, Jan. 24, 1970. BA, Am. U., 1969; JD, Emory U., 1975. Bar: Fla. 1976, U.S. Dist. Ct. (so. dist.) Fla. 1976, U.S. Ct. Appeals (5th cir.) 1976, U.S. Supreme Ct. 1980, U.S. Ct. Appeals (11th cir.) 1983. Law clk. McLarty and Aiken, Atlanta, 1974-76; assoc. Welbaum, Zook, Jones, Williams, Miami, Fla., 1976-79; ptnr. Darrach, Merkin and Sacasas, Miami, 1979-83, Merkin & Sacasas, Miami, 1984-86; of counsel Welbaum, Zook & Jones, Miami, 1986-95; Welbaum, Guernsey, Hingston, Greenleaf & Gregory, Miami, 1996—; asst. prof. bus. law U. Miami, 1985-91, assoc. prof., 1991—, chmn. bus. law dept., 1992—; head master Hecht Residential Coll., 1995—. Mem. ABA, Fla. Bar Assn. (vice chmn. grievance com. 1981-84), Dade County Bar Assn., Latin Am. C. of C., U.S. Jaycees, Cuban Am. Bar Assn., Iron Arrow, Leadership Fla., Phi Sigma Kappa (ET chpt. pres. 1968), Omicron Delta Kappa, Phi Kappa Phi. Contbr. articles profl. jours. Home: 3790 Kent Ct Miami FL 33133-6137 Office: Welbaum Zook & Jones 901 Ponce De Leon Blvd Coral Gables FL 33134-3073

SACHAU, WILLIAM HENRY, auditor, consultant; b. Ridgewood, N.Y., Feb. 6, 1924; s. Hans Richard Koenig and Christiana H. (Betke) S.; BS in Bus. Adminstrn., Duquesne U.. 1950; MBA, U. Denver, 1953; student, Indsl. Coll. Armed Forces, 1962; m. Dorothy Jean Fjone, Nov. 1, 1952; children: Christy Jean. Susan Melinda, William Eric. X-ray technician Presbyn. Hosps. Med. Center. N.Y.C. and Pitts., 1946-50; staff mem. Ralph B. Mayo & Co., C.P.A.s, Denver. 1951-54; auditor Ford Motor Co.. Dearborn, Mich.. 1954-59; auditor Collins Radio Co., Dallas, 1959-60, supr. ops. control, 1960-62, mgr. auditing and procedures. 1962-71, mgr. acctg. and consolidations, 1971-74; mgr. auditing Cities Service Co., Tulsa, 1974-82; audit chmn. Syncrude Ltd., 1980-83; corp. mgr. internal audit Occidental Petroleum, 1983-85, mgr. audit coordination, ops. and systems analyst 1985-87; audit cons., 1987—; instr. So. Methodist U.; lectr., mem. adv. bd. North Tex. U. Mem. Dallas United Fund, 1968-72; active Boy Scouts Am.; judge, timer Pard Swim Team, Richardson, Tex., 1966-73. Bd. dirs. Richardson Credit Union, 1971-76, Karios Counseling Ctr., Tulsa. Served with 13th Armored Divsn., AUS, 1943-45, ETO; 1951-52, 3rd Divsn. Korea; capt. Res. ret. Decorated Bronze Star, Commendation medal, Purple Heart; named Outstanding Mem., Inst. Internal Auditors of Dallas, 1964-65; cert. internal auditor. Mem. AICPAs (com. on internal acctg. control), Inst. Internal Auditors (internat. dir. 1966-67, regional dir. 1967-70, research com. mem. 1970-80, 82-87, internat. sec. 1980-81), Am. Acctg. Assn., Nat. Assn. Accts., Am. Assn. Cost Engrs., Combat Infantrymen's Assn., Chpt. Chaplin, Mil. Order of the Purple Heart. Republican. Lutheran (coun. 1955-68, 75-79, pastoral call com. 1992-93). Contbr. articles to profl. jours. Home and Office: 4123 E 85th St Tulsa OK 74137-1736

SACHSMAN, DAVID BERNARD, communications educator; b. N.Y.C., Aug. 16, 1945; s. Edgar and Susan (Sassower) S.; m. Judith Mittleman, Mar. 15, 1967; children: Jonathan William, Susanne Elizabeth. BA in English, U. Pa., 1967; AM in Comm., Stanford U., 1968, PhD in Comm., 1973. Asst. prof., lectr. Calif. State U., Hayward, 1969-71; asst. prof. Rutgers U., New Brunswick, N.J., 1971-76; spl. corr., copy editor The Home News, New Brunswick, N.J., 1974-77; assoc. prof. Rutgers U., New Brunswick, N.J., 1976-88; sr. Fulbright-Hays scholar U. Nigeria, Nsukka, 1978-79; chairperson dept. journalism Rutgers U., New Brunswick, 1983-88; adj. assoc. prof. U. Medicine and Dentistry of N.J., Piscataway, 1987-89; dean, prof. Calif. State U., Fullerton, 1988-91; west chair of excellence in comm., pub. affairs U. Tenn., Chattanooga, 1991—; mem. editorial bd. Mass. Comm. Rev., San Jose, Calif., 1976—; prin. investigator for externally funded rsch., New Brunswick, N.J., Fullerton, Calif., 1977-91; cons. in field. Co-editor: Media Casebook, 1972, 77, Environmental Reporter's Handbook, 1988; co-author: Media: An Introductory Analysis of American Mass Communications, 1972, 76, 82, The Press and the Suburbs: The Daily Newspapers of New Jersey, 1985, Environmental Risk and the Press, 1987; assoc. editor Advances in Telematics, 1983-86, Mass Comm. Rev., 1984-87; contbr. numerous articles to profl. jours. Trustee The Daily Pennsylvania, Inc., Phila., 1985-88; bd. dirs. Girl Scout Coun. of Orange County, 1989-91, Moccasin Bend Girl Scout Coun., Chattanooga, Tenn., 1991—; bd. dirs., v.p. Girls Inc. of Chattanooga, 1991-94. Recipient award for Rsch. and Journalism, N.J. Chpt. Soc. for Profl. Journalists, 1984, 86, 88, 89; grantee Hazardous Substance Mgmt. Rsch. Ctr., 1985-89, 1985-90, Calif. Dept. Transp., 1990. Mem. Assn. for Edn. in Journalism and Mass Comm., Internat. Comm. Assn., Soc. of Environ. Journalists, Speech Comm. Assn., Investigative Reporters and Editors, Radio-TV News Dirs. Assn., N.J. Profl. Chpt. Soc. Profl. Journalists (pres. 1981-83, bd. dirs. 1984-88), Internat. Comm. Assn., Alpha Phi Gamma. Home: 1002 Centennial Dr Chattanooga TN 37405-4256 Office: U Tenn at Chattanooga 210 Frist Hall Chattanooga TN 37403

SACKS, CHARLES BERNARD, physician, educator; b. Cleve., May 14, 1939; s. Jerry and Frances (Shifrin) S.; m. Lora Jane Glickman, May 2, 1993; children: Eliza, Aaron. BA, Ohio State U., 1961, MD, 1965. Staff psychiatrist Washington Vets. Hosp., 1971-76; asst. clin. prof. Georgetown U., Washington, 1971—; staff psychiatrist Reston Clinic, Fairfax City, Md., 1976-77, Drug Treatment Adminstrn., Washington, 1971-72, Washington Free Clinic, 1971-73, Arlington & Fairfax City Hosp., 1977-88, Group Health Assocs., Washington, 1984-86; psychiatrist pvt. practice, McLean, Va., 1977—, Greenbelt, Md., 1977—; dir. Chevy Chase Psychiat. Clinic, Washington, 1987-89. Maj. U.S. Army, 1969-71. Decorated Bronze medal with Oak Leaf Cluster. Mem. Am. Psychiat. Assn., Md. Med. Assn., Washington Psychiat. Assn., Fairfax and Arlington City Med. Assn., Prince Georges City Assn. Office: 1307 Vincent Pl Mc Lean VA 22101-3615

SADA, FEDERICO G., glass manufacturing executive. Chmn. bd. dirs., CEO Anchor Glass Container Corp., 1993—. Office: Anchor Glass Container Corp 4343 Anchor Plaza Pky Tampa FL 33634-7537*

SADANA, AJIT, chemical engineering educator; b. Rawalpindi, India, Feb. 14, 1947; came to U.S., 1980; s. Jai Chand and Jinder S.; m. Lopa M. Tandon, Jan. 16, 1973; children: Neeti, Richa. MChemE, U. Delaware, 1972, PhDChemE, 1975. Project engr. Enviroengineering, Inc., Somerville, N.J., 1974-75; sr. sci. officer Nat. Chem. Lab., Poona, India, 1975-80; assoc. prof. of chem. engring. U. Miss., University, 1981-90, prof. chem. engring., 1990—; engr. duPont, Inc., Newark, Del., 1989; sr. fellow Naval Rsch. Lab., Washington, 1990, disting. fellow, 1991; cons. NIH, Bethesda, Md., 1993, Oak Ridge (Tenn.) Nat. Lab., 1994, 95, 96. Author: Biocatalysis: Fundamentals of Enzyme Deactivation Kinetics, 1991. Office: U Miss Dept Chem Engring 134 Anderson Hall University MS 38677-9740

SADLER, CHARLES BENJAMIN, JR., pharmacist, real estate associate, marketing professional; b. Petersburg, Va., Feb. 2, 1939; s. Charlie Benjamin and Ellen Elizabeth (Rathine) S.; m. Nancy Marie Newton, June, 1960 (div. Mar. 1979); children: Charles Benjamin III, Tracy Lynn; m. Linda Lee Puryear, Apr. 14, 1979. BS in pharmacy, Med. Coll. of Va., 1960; postgrad., Richard Bland Coll., 1971-72, 76, Va.Commonwealth U., 1972-73; cert. in real estate, Moseley-Flint Coll., Richmond, Va., 1977. Registered pharmacist, Va.; lic. real estate. Pharmacist, instr. John Randolph Hosp., Hopewell, Va., 1960-61; pharmacist Peoples Drugs, Richmond, Va., 1961-63, O.P. Hare Drugs, Petersburg, Va., 1963-65; mgr., pharmacist Super X Drugs, Covington, Danville, Clipton Forge, Va., 1965-68; pharmacist Gray Drug Fair, Hopewell, Col. Hts., Richmond, Va., 1968-88; mgr. pharmacy Standard Drug Store, Petersburg, 1988-91, Phar-Mor Drugs, Colonial Heights, Va., 1991-92, Farmco Drug, 1992-95, Revco D.S., Petersburg, Va., 1996—; pres. CBS Assocs. Internat. Active mem. Smithsonian Inst., Washington, 1965—, Met. Guild Pharmacists, Citizens Choice, Washington, 1984—. Mem. Am. Pharm. Assn., Va. Pharm. Assn. (4th dist.), Va. Commonwealth U. Alumni Assn., Cousteau Soc., Petersburg Jaycees, Kappa Psi. Republican. Baptist. Home: 4104 Birchleaf Ct Chester VA 23831-4618

SADLER, DOLORES ANN (DEE SADLER), retired clinical social worker, psychotherapist; b. N.Y.C., Feb. 18, 1943; d. Gerard R. and Helen C. (Moran) Endres; m. Charles L. Sadler, May 1962 (div. 1975); children: Lynn, Robert, Kristine; m. John K. Hobbins, Aug., 1976 (div. 1978). AAS, County Coll. of Morris, Randolph, N.J., 1981; BA, Rutgers U., 1983, MSW, 1984. Lic. clin. social worker, N.J. Adminstrv. asst. Morristown (N.J.) Rehab. Ctr., 1972-82; social worker Lyons (N.J.) VA Med. Ctr., 1982-84, Americare Rehab., Englewood, Fla., 1984-85; psychotherapist, clin. social worker Med. Ctr. Hosp. psychiat. ctr., Punta Gorda, Fla., 1985-93; pvt.

practice psychotherapy Punta Gorda, 1993-95; supr. grad. students U. South Fla., 1987-93, Barry U., 1987-90, Nova U., 1991-93. Bd. dirs. Heart and Lung Assn. of Charlotte County, 1985-86, Women's Support Ctr., 1994—; bd. trustees Mt. Olive Assn. Tenants, 1983-84; developer Swim, Inc. (for handicapped), 1975-79; organizer Orgn. Handicapped Students, 1979-81; vol. Morris County Hotline, 1982-83; advocate Arts & Culture Assn., Charlotte County, Fla. Mem. NASW, ACLU, NOW, Acad. Cert. Social Workers (cert.), Amnesty Internat., Alumni Assn. Rutgers U. Democrat.

SADLER, LUTHER FULLER, JR., lawyer; b. Jacksonville, Fla., Apr. 10, 1942; s. Luther Fuller and Jane Grey (Lloyd) S.; children: Catherine Winchester, Anna Stephenson Lloyd. BA, Yale U., 1964, LLB, 1967. Bar: Fla. 1967. Ptnr. Mahoney, Hadlow, Chambers & Adams, Jacksonville, 1967-81, Commander, Legler, Werber, Dawes, Sadler & Howell, Jacksonville, 1982-91, Foley & Lardner, Jacksonville, 1991—; gen. counsel Jacksonville C. of C., 1987. Trustee Jacksonville Art Mus., 1984-94, Episcopal Child Care and Devel. Ctrs., Inc., 1990-94. Lt. USNR, 1967-73. Mem. ABA, Fla. Bar Assn. (chmn. corp. banking and bus. law sect. 1979-80), Timuquana Country Club. Episcopalian. Office: Foley & Lardner PO Box 240 200 N Laura St Jacksonville FL 32202-3528

SADLER, WILLIAM JACQUES, social worker; b. Tomah, Wis., Apr. 21, 1959; s. John Weldon and Maureen (Sullivan) S.; m. Danna Bustamante, June 22, 1990; 1 child, Jordan Wyatt. BSW, U. Tex., El Paso, 1986, post-grad., 1986-87; MA in Counseling, Webster U., 1989, cert., 1990; MSW, U. Tex., 1994. Children's protective svcs. specialist Tex. Dept. Human Svcs., El Paso, 1989, social worker children's protective svcs., 1989—; psychotherapist Jewish Family Svcs., 1992-93, Family Sci. of El Paso, 1993-94, Alliance Hosp. of Santa Teresa, N.Mex., 1994. Vol. Tex. Dept. Human Svcs., 1989. Mem. NASW, Tex. Soc. Clin. Social Work, Am. Assn. Marriage and Family Therapists (El Paso chpt.). Democrat. Roman Catholic.

SADOSKI, MARK CHRISTIAN, education educator; b. Bristol, Conn., June 2, 1945; s. Waldmyr John Sadoski and Ruth Elaine (Gustafson) Kantorski; m. Carol Ann Bove, June 28, 1969; 1 child, Thomas Christian. BS, So. Conn. State U., 1968, MS, 1973; PhD, U. Conn., 1981. Cert. reading, English, social studies tchr. Tchr., reading cons. Milford (Conn.) Pub. Schs., 1968-81; assoc. faculty So. Conn. State U., New Haven, 1978-81; prof. edn. Tex. A&M Univ., College Station, 1981—. Mem. editl. bd. Reading Reasearch Quarterly, 1989—, Jour. Reading Behavior, 1990-95, Reading Psychology, 1990—, Jour. Literacy Rsch., 1995—; contbr. over 50 articles to profl. jours. Accident prevention counselor S.W. region FAA, 1989-91. Recipient Disting. Alumnus award So. Conn. State U., 1994. Mem. Internat. Reading Assn. (outstanding dissertation award com. 1983-85, finalist Outstanding Dissertation award 1982), Nat. Reading Conf., Am. Ednl. Rsch. Assn. (outstanding book award com. 1994—), Soc. for Sci. Study of Reading (chair pubs. com. 1996—). Office: Tex A&M Univ Dept EDCI College Station TX 77843

SADOWSKI, CAROL JOHNSON, artist; b. Chgo., Mar. 20, 1929; d. Carl Valdamar Johnson and Elizabeth Hilma (Booth) Johnson-Chellberg; m. Edmund Sadowski, July 9, 1949; children: Lynn Carol Mahoney, Christie Sadowski Cortez. AAS, Wright-Ill. Coll., 1949. Tchr. art Malverne (N.Y.) H.S., 1968-69; artist Valley Stream, N.Y., 1968-76, Hollywood, Fla., 1976—; guest speaker Mus. Art Ft. Lauderdale, Fla., 1991, others; TV appearances on WCGB, Gainesville, WSVN, Miami, Storer and Hollywood Cable. One-woman shows include Mus. Fla. History, 1984-85, 87, Hist. Mus. South Fla., Miami, 1986, Thomas Ctr. Arts, Gainesville, Gla., 1985, 87, Hist. Mus. South Fla., Miami, 1986, Thomas Ctr. Arts, Gainesville, Gla., 1985, 87, Elliott Mus., Stuart, Fla., 1987, Hemingway Mus. & Home, Key West, Fla., 1986, Mus. Fla. History, Tallahassee, 1985, 87, Alliance Francaise de Miami, 1995; commd. painting St. Agustin Antigua Found., St. Augustine, Fla., 1985, Atlantic Bank, Ft. Lauderdale, Fla., Bonnet House Fla. Trust, Ft. Lauderdale, Tropical Art Gallery, Naples, Fla., 1981-83, Tequesta (Fla.) Art Gallery, 1985-89, Gingerbread Square Gallery, Key West, 1990—, Wally Findlay Galleries, Inc., Palm Beach, Key West Graphics, Tamarac. Recipient Hemingway medal Ernest Hemingway Mus., Cuba, 1990, appreciation award City of Hollywood. Mem. Internat. Platform Assn., Broward Art Guild, Fla. Hist. Assn., Ernest Hemingway Soc., Chopin Found., Am. Inst. for Polish Culture, Alliance Francaise de Miami, Internat. Platform Assn., Women in the Arts Nat. Mus. (charter mem.). Home and Studio: 1480 Sheridan St Apt B-17 Hollywood FL 33020-2295

SADRI, MOHMOUD, sociology educator; b. Tehran, Iran, Nov. 17, 1953; came to U.S., 1978; s. Fatollah and Vajiheh (Molai) S. BA, U. Tehran, 1974, MA, 1976; MA, New Sch. Social Rsch., N.Y.C., 1980, PhD, 1988. Asst. prof. Northwestern U., Evanston, Ill., 1988-92, Tex. Women's U., Denton, 1992—. Co-author: Symbolic Interaction, 1993, Durkheim on Division of Labor, 1993; assoc. editor International Journal of Politics, Culture and Society, 1988—; contbr. articles to profl. jours. Vol. Denton Housing Authority, 1992-93, Big Bros. and Sisters. Mem. Am. Sociol. Assn., Internat. Sociol. Assn., Mid-East Studies Assn., Sierra Club. Home: # D 1929 Colorado Blvd Denton TX 76205 Office: Tex Womens U PO Box 23928 Denton TX 76204-1928

SADUN, ALBERTO CARLO, astrophysicist, physics educator; b. Atlanta, Apr. 28, 1955; s. Elvio Herbert and Lina (Ottolenghi) S.; m. Erica Liebman. BS in Physics, Mass. Inst. Tech., 1977; PhD in Physics, MIT, 1984. Asst. prof. Agnes Scott Coll., Decatur, Ga., 1984-90, assoc. prof., 1990—, dir. Bradley Obs., 1984—; adj. prof. Ga. State U., Atlanta, 1986—; rsch. affiliate NASA/Caltech Jet Propulsion Lab., Pasadena, Calif., 1988-90, summer faculty fellow, 1987, 88. Contbr. articles to Nature, Astrophys. Jour., Astron. Jour., Publ. Aston. Soc. of the Pacific, Astrophys. Letters and Communications. Mem. Am. Jewish Com., Atlanta, 1984—. Fellow Royal Astron. Soc.; mem. Internat. Astron. Union, Am. Astron. Soc., N.Y. Acad. Scis. Home: 4739 Springfield Dr Dunwoody GA 30338 Office: Agnes Scott Coll 141 E College Ave Decatur GA 30030-3770

SADUN, LORENZO ADLAI, mathematician; b. Silver Spring, Md., Nov. 3, 1960; s. Elvio Herbert and Lina Amelia (Ottolenghi) S.; m. Anita Elizabeth Glazer, Sept. 4, 1988; children: Rina Ellen, Allan Elvio. BS, MIT, 1981; MA, U. Calif., 1982, PhD, 1987. Rsch. instr. Calif. Tech. Math. Dept., Pasadena, 1987-89; Courant instr. Courant Inst. Math. Scis., N.Y.C., 1989-91; asst. prof. U. Tex., Austin, 1991—. Contbr. articles to profl. publs. Home: 1706 W 30th St Austin TX 78703-1824 Office: U Tex Math Dept Austin TX 78712

SAEGER, DIXIE FORESTER, dietitian; b. Cullowhee, N.C., Oct. 16, 1940; d. James Fred and Thelma (Phillips) Forester; m. Henry E. Saeger, Aug. 6, 1962; 1 child, Jeffrey Alan. BS in Home Econs., Tenn. Tech. U., 1962; MS in Nutrition, U. Tenn., 1978. Registered dietitian. Clin. instr. dietetics U. Tenn., Knoxville, 1980-81; instr. U. Tenn., Chattanooga, 1976-88; clin. dietitian North Park Hosp., Chattanooga, 1979-87; dir. dietetic svcs. Parkwood Health Care Ctr., Chattanooga, 1987-89; clin. dietitian Meml. Hosp., Chattanooga, 1989—. Mem. Am. Dietetic Assn. (practice groups dietitians in nutrition support, dietitians in clin. nutrition mgmt.), Tenn. Dietetic Assn. (chmn. quality assurance 1987-88, chmn. coun. practice divsn. mgmt. 1989-91), Chattanooga Dist. Dietetic Assn. (sec. 1980-82, chmn. ednl. program devel. 1981-82, pres. 1983-84, coun. on practice 1984-89, adminstr. coord. lic. com. 1986, chmn. long range planning com. 1987-88, chmn. coun. practice 1988-89, nominating com. 1992-93, chmn. long range planning 1993-94). Home: 2807 Saint Johns Ln Chattanooga TN 37421-5049

SAFCSAK, KAREN, medical/surgical nurse; b. Pitts., Aug. 18, 1956; d. Joseph and Mary B. (Reis) S. Diploma, OVGH Sch. Nursing, 1977; BSN summa cum laude, Ohio U., 1980. Instr. critical care Ohio Valley Med. Ctr., Wheeling, W.Va., 1982-84; head nurse progressive care Ohio Valley Med. Ctr., Wheeling, 1984-86; critical care clin. rsch. nurse St. Thomas Hosp., Nashville, 1986-88; clin. nurse specialist, researcher Vanderbilt U. Hosp., Nashville, 1988-95; project mgr. critical care rsch. Orlando (Fla.) Regional Med. Ctr., 1995—; lectr. critical care topics, critical care nurse; instr. basic cardiac life support. Contbr. articles to profl. jours.; rev. Clin. Intensive Care jour.. mem. Soc. Critical Care Medicine, Am. Assn. Critical Care Nurses, Phi Kappa Phi. Office: Orlando Regional Med Ctr 1414 Kuhl Ave Orlando FL 32806-2008

SAFF, EDWARD BARRY, mathematics educator; b. N.Y.C., Jan. 2, 1944; s. Irving H. and Rose (Koslow) S.; m. Loretta Singer, July 3, 1966; children: Lisa Jill, Tracy Karen, Alison Michelle. BS with highest honors, Ga. Inst. Tech., 1964; PhD, U. Md., 1968. Asst. prof. U. Md., 1968; post-doctoral researcher Imperial Coll., London, 1968-69; asst. prof. math. U. South Fla., 1969-71, assoc. prof., 1971-76, prof., 1976-86, disting. rsch. prof., 1986—, dir. Ctr. for Math. Svcs., 1978-83, dir. Inst. for Constructive Math., 1985—; sr. vis. fellow Oxford U., 1978. Author: (with A.D. Snider) Fundamentals of Complex Analysis, 1976, (with A.W. Goodman) Calculus, Concepts and Calculations, 1981, (with A. Edrei and R.S. Varga) Zeros of Sections of Power Series; editor (with R.S. Varga) Pade and Rational Approximation: Theory and Applications, 1977, (with R.K. Nagle) Fundamentals of Differential Equations, (with R.K. Nagle) Fundamentals of Differential Equations and Boundary Value Problems, 1993, (with D.S. Lubinsky) Strong Asymptotics for Extremal Polynomials Associated with Weights on R., 1988; editor-in-chief Constructive Approximation Jour., 1983—; editor Jour. Approximation Theory, 1990—, Cambridge Univ. Press, 1995—. Fulbright fellow, 1968-69, Guggenheim fellow, 1978; NSF grantee, 1970-72, 80—; Hon. prof. Zhejiang Normal U. Mem. Am. Math. Soc., Math. Assn. Am., Sigma Xi. Home: 11738 Lipsey Rd Tampa FL 33618-3620 Office: U South Fla Dept Math Tampa FL 33620

SAFFORD, ROBERT EUGENE, cardiologist, health facility administrator, educator; b. Memphis, Sept. 13, 1945; s. Eugene Edis and Louise Margaret (Morse) S.; m. Debra Eleanor Schade, May 30, 1982; children: Brooke Elizabeth, David John. BS in Chem. Engring. magna cum laude, Lafayette Coll., 1967; MS, PhD in Chem. and Biomed. Engring., U. Wis., 1970, 73; MD, Mayo Med. Sch., 1977. Diplomate Am. Bd. Internal Medicine, Subspecialty Bd. in Cardiovascular Disease, Nat. Bd. Med. Examiners; lic. MD, Mass.; lic. Fla. Bd. Med. Examiners, Minn. Bd. Med. Examiners, Fla. Office Radiatin Control. Intern in internal medicine, resident internal medicine Mass. Gen. Hosp., Harvard U. Med. Sch., Boston, 1977-78, 78-80, fellow in cardiology, 1980-82; asst. prof. medicine Mayo Med. Sch. and Univ. Minn., Rochester, 1982-91; cons. in cardiovascular diseases and internal medicine Mayo Clinic, Rochester, 1982-86; cons. in cardiovascular diseases and internal medicine Mayo Clinic, Jacksonville, Fla., 1986-96, chmn. sect. cardiovascular diseases, 1985-96; co-dir. echocardiography lab. and nuclear cardiology lab. Mayo Clinic and St. Lukes Hosp., Jacksonville, Fla., 1990-92, 96—; assoc. prof. medicine Mayo Med. Sch., Jacksonville, Fla., 1992—; chmn. instl. clin. practice com. Mayo Clinic, 1987-88, vice-chmn. bd. govs. Mayo Clinic, Jacksonville, 1988—; exec. med. staff com. St. Lukes Hosp., 1987-88. Mem. editorial bd. Cardiac Clinics of the Mayo Clinic Proceedings, 1984-86, Video J. Echo, 1993; contbr. numerous articles, papers, abstracts to profl. publs. Grantee Sterling-Winthrop Rsch. Inst., 1990, NIH, 1990, Nat. Heart, Lung and Blood Inst., 1991, Genentech Pharms., Inc., 1992, Marion Merrell Dow, Inc., 1992, Mayo Found., 1992, Boots Pharms., 1993, DuPont Merck, 1993. Mem. AMA, Fla. Med. Assn., Duval County Med. Soc., Am. Soc. Echocardiography, Am. Coll. Cardiology, Cardiovascular Soc., Paul Dudley White Soc., Am. Heart Assn. Office: Mayo Clinic 4500 San Pablo Rd S Jacksonville FL 32224-1865

SAFKO, JOHN LOREN, physics and astronomy educator; b. San Diego, Oct. 29, 1938; s. Loren Edmund Caraveau and Lillian Mae (Spitzer) Safko; m. Peggy Jean Ferrell, Aug. 21, 1964; children: Tanya Dawn, John L. Jr. BS, Case Inst. Tech., 1960; PhD, U. N.C., 1965. From asst. prof. to prof. dept. physics and astronomy U. S.C., Columbia, 1964—, prof. dept. physics and astronomy, 1979—, sec. to faculty, 1989-96. Author various astronomy and physics study guides. Fellow AAAS; mem. Am. Assn. Physics Tchrs., Am. Phys. Soc., Am. Astron. Soc., S.C. Acad. Sci. (treas. 1973—), Gen. Relativity and Gravitation Soc. Internat., Sigma Xi. Republican. Methodist. Office: U SC Dept Physics and Astronomy Columbia SC 29208

SAGAN, STANLEY DANIEL, career officer, retired; b. Niagara Falls, N.Y., Jan. 6, 1916; s. Stanley and Kathryn Sagan; m. Eleanor Stella Krzesimowski, Apr. 19, 1941; children: Lawrence S., Deborah E. BA, U. Dayton, 1944. Lic. aircraft pilot. Designer aircraft U.S. War Dept., Dayton, Ohio, 1942-45; instr. U. Dayton, 1946-47, U. Detroit, 1947-48; commd. 1st lt. USAF, Dayton, 1950; advanced through grades to lt. col. USAF, 1971; rsch. and devel. officer USAF, Dayton, 1948-51; spl. staff officer USAF, 1951-55; tech. cons. USAF, San Antonio, 1961-71; ret. USAF, 1971; tchr., bus. mgr. Antonian H.S., San Antonio, 1971-74; aircraft designer Saga Corp., San Antonio, 1974-77; staff com. vocat. edn., Target 90 of San Antonio, 1982-88. Author: Dithyramb, 1996; author of poems; inventor in field. Vol. Rep. party, San Antonio, 1987-88. Recipient cert. of merit San Antonio Archdiocese, 1987, cert. of svc. U.S. Dept. Air Force, 1971. Mem. Soc. of Automotive Engrs., San Antonio Ret. Officers Assn. (v.p., legis. liaison officer 1980-91, bd. dirs. 1996—, Pres.'s award 1986), Mil. Order of World Wars (comdr. 1983-84, nat. officer, chmn. law and order com. 1992-94), Tex. Tchrs. State Assn., Am. Legion (cert. appreciation 1987, adjutant 1977). Roman Catholic.

SAGAWA, SHIRLEY SACHI, lawyer; b. Rochester, N.Y., Aug. 25, 1961; d. Hidetaka H. and Patricia (Ford) S.; m. Gregory A. Baer; children: Jackson Ford Baer, Matthew Sagawa Baer. AB, Smith Coll., 1983; MSc, London Sch. Econs., 1984; JD, Harvard U., 1987. Bar: Md. 1988. Chief counsel youth policy, labor and human resources com. U.S. Senate, Washington, 1987-91; sr. counsel and dir. family and youth policy Nat. Women's Law Ctr., Washington, 1991-93; spl. asst. to Pres. Clinton for domestic policy, 1993; exec. dir., mng. dir., exec. v.p. Corp. for Nat. and Comty. Svc., Washington, 1993—. Mem. exec. bd. Orgn. for Pan-Asian Am. Women, Washington, 1987-89; mem. Women of Color Leadership Coun., 1991-92; vice chair, bd. dirs. Nat. Community Svc. Commn., 1991-93. Recipient Philip V. McGance award Coun. for Advancement of Citizenship, 1991, cert. of recognition Nat. Coun. Jewish Women, 1989, Alexandrine medal Coll. St. Catherine, St. Paul, 1995; Harry S. Truman scholar, 1981; Smith Coll. Alumnae Assn. fellow, 1983, AAUW fellow, 1986. Mem. Md. Bar Assn. Democrat. Episcopalian. Office: Corp for Nat and Community Svc 1201 New York Ave NW Washington DC 20005-3917

SAGE, ANDREW PATRICK, JR., systems information and software engineering educator; b. Charleston, S.C., Aug. 27, 1933; s. Andrew Patrick and Pearl Louise (Britt) S.; m. LaVerne Galhouse, Mar. 3, 1962; children: Theresa Annette, Karen Margaret, Philip Andrew. BS in Elec. Engring, The Citadel, 1955; SM, MIT, 1956; PhD, Purdue U., 1960; DEng (hon.), U. Waterloo, Can., 1987. Registered profl. engr., Tex. Instr. elec. engring. Purdue U., 1956-60; assoc. prof. U. Ariz., 1960-63; mem. tech. staff Aerospace Corp., Los Angeles, 1963-64; prof. elec. engring. and nuclear engring. scis. U. Fla., 1964-67; prof., dir. Info. and Control Scis. Center, So. Methodist U., Dallas, 1967-74; head elec. engring. dept. So. Meth. U., 1973-74; Quarles prof. engring. sci. and systems U. Va., Charlottesville, 1974-84; chmn. dept. chem. engring. U. Va., 1974-75, chmn. dept. engring. sci. and systems, 1977-84, assoc. dean, 1974-80; First Am. Bank prof. info. tech. George Mason U., Fairfax, Va., 1984—, assoc. v.p. for acad. affairs, 1984-85; dean Sch. Info. Tech. and Engring. George Mason U., 1985-96, founding dean emeritus, 1996—; cons. Martin Marietta, Collins Radio, Atlantic Richfield, Tex. Instruments, LTV Aerospace, Battelle Meml. Inst., TRW Sys., NSF, Inst. Def. Analyses, Planning Rsch. Corp., MITRE, Engring. Rsch. Assocs., Software Productivity Consortium; gen. chmn. Internat. Conf. on Sys., Man and Cybernetics, 1974, 87; mem. spl. program panel on sys. sci. NATO, 1981-82; trustee, cons. Ctr. Naval Analysis, 1990-94. Author: Optimum Systems Control, 1968, 2d edit., 1977, Estimation Theory with Applications to Communications and Control, 1971, System Identification, 1971, An Introduction to Probability and Stochastic Processes, 1973, Methodology for Large Scale Systems, 1977, Systems Engineering: Methodology and Applications, 1977, Linear Systems Control, 1978, Economic Systems Analysis, 1983, System Design for Human Interaction, 1987, Information Processing in Systems and Organizations, 1990, Introduction to Computer Systems Analysis, Design, and Applications, 1989, Software Systems Engineering, 1990, Decision Support Systems Engineering, 1991, Systems Engineering, 1992, Systems Management for Information Technology and Software Engineering, 1995; assoc. editor IEEE Transactions on Systems Sci. and Cybernetics, 1968-72; editor: IEEE Transactions on Systems, Man and Cybernetics, 1972—; assoc. editor: Automatica, 1968-81; editor, 1981-96; mem. editl. bd. Systems Engring, 1968-72, IEEE Spectrum, 1972-73, Computers and Elec. Engring., 1972-94, Jour. Interdisciplinary Modeling and Simulation, 1976-80, Internat. Jour. Intelligent Sys., 1986—, Orgn. Sci.-94, 1990; editor Elsevier North Holland textbook series in sys. sci. and engring., 1970-88, John Wiley textbook series on sys. engring., 1989—; co-editor-in-chief Jour. Large Scale Sys.: Theory and Applications, 1978-88, Info. and Decision Technologies, 1988-94, Info. and Sys. Engring., 1995—; contbr. articles on computer sci. and sys. engring. to profl. jours. Recipient Norbert Wiener award, 1980, Joseph G. Wohl career award, 1991, Superior Pub. Svc. award Sec. of the Navy, 1994; Case Centennial scholar, 1980, Award Washington Soc. of Engrs., 1996. Fellow IEEE (M. Barry Carlton award 1970, Centennial medal 1984, Outstanding Contbn. award 1986, Donald G. Fink prize 1994), AAAS (chmn. sect. M 1990), IEEE Sys. Soc.; mem. Man and Cybernetics Soc. (pres. 1984-85, Inst. Mgmt. Scis., Internat. Fedn. Automatic Control (Outstanding Svc. award), Am. Soc. Engring. Edn. (Frederick Emmonds Terman award 1970, Centennial cert. for exceptional contbn. 1993), Washington Soc. Engrs. (award 1996), Inst. for Mgmt. Sci. and Ops. Rsch., Sigma Xi, Eta Kappa Nu, Tau Beta Pi. Home: 8011 Woodland Hills Ln Fairfax VA 22039-2433 Office: George Mason U Sch Info Tech Fairfax VA 22030-4444

SAGE, LOIS ELLIOTT, educational diagnostician; b. Houston, Sept. 21, 1943; d. Charles Herbert and Roberta (Jackson) Elliott; m. Charles A. Sage, June 24, 1967 (div. Oct., 1973); 1 child, Scott Elliott. BS in Elem. Edn., U. Tex., 1965; MEd, U. Houston, 1985. Spanish tchr. Lovett and Bonham Elem. Schs., Houston, 1965-68; 4th grade tchr. Kolter Elem. Sch., Houston, 1968-70; 4th grade tchr. Roberts Elem. Sch., Houston, 1972-74, 3rd grade tchr., 1974-75, 5th grade tchr., 1975-78; 3rd grade tchr. Askew Elem. Sch., Houston, 1978-86; bilingual ednl. diagnostician Fort Bend Ind. Sch. Dist., Houston, 1986—. Recipient Mary Kenner award, Alpha Xi Delta scholarship, Austin, Tex., 1965. Mem. Tex. Ednl. Diagnosticians' Assn., Kappa Delta Pi. Republican. Baptist. Home: 12335 Brandywyne Dr Houston TX 77077-4813

SAGER, DENNIS WAYNE, internist, engineer; b. Richmond, Va., May 25, 1946; s. Martin and Sara (Miller) S.; m. Jeanne Barbara Kaswell, Sept. 2, 1968; children: Lauren, Deborah, Michael, Jill. BS in Aeronautics and Astronautics, MIT, 1968, MS, 1973; MD, Ea. Va. Med. Sch., 1978. Diplomate Am. Bd. Internal Medicine. Trajecory analyst NASA mission control ctr. TRW Systems, Houston, 1968-69; tech. staff design portions FAA en rte air traffic control MITRE Corp., Atlantic City, McLean, Va., 1969-75; intern Wright State U., Dayton, Ohio, 1978-79, resident in internal medicine, 1979-81; pvt. practice Reston, Va., 1981—; chmn. dept. medicine Reston Hosp. Ctr., 1993-94, sec.-treas. med. staff, 1993—; sr. aviation med. examiner FAA, 1982—; advisor Fairfax County Police Officers Retirement Bd., 1983—. Mem. Am. Soc. Internal Medicine, Med. Soc. Va., Fairfax County Med. Soc. Jewish. Office: 1800 Town Center Dr Ste 118 Reston VA 20190-3200

SAHA, PABITRA KUMAR, civil and structural engineering educator, consultant; b. Calcutta, India, Apr. 20, 1949; came to U.S., 1977; s. Mahitosh and Annapurna (Saha) S.; m. Sikha Mondal, June 6, 1976; children: Krishanu, Jishnu. BCE, U. Calcutta, 1971; MS in Civil Engring., U. Ill., 1979, PhD in Civil Engring., 1982. Registered profl. engr., Ala. Engring. trainee Raymach Engring., Calcutta, 1971-72; trainee Howrah (India) Improvement Trust, 1972; civil engr. Bilaney and Co., Calcutta, 1972-74; sr. design asst. Met. Transport Project, Calcutta, 1974; asst. structural engr. Engrs. India Ltd., New Delhi, 1974-77; rsch. asst. U. Ill., Urbana, 1978-81; asst. prof. A&M U., Huntsville, 1982-88, assoc. prof. structural engring., 1988-93, acting chmn. civil engring. dept., 1991-92, prof. civil engring., 1993—; prin. investigator for composite structure rsch. project Nat. Aero Space Plane, Wright-Patterson AFB, 1990-93; prin. investigator for composite structure rsch. project Wright-Patterson AFB, 1993—; co-prin. investigator for non-linear optics and optical materials Minority Rsch. Ctr. NSF Project, Huntsville, 1988-93; cons. M. Shaw Internat., Inc., Huntsville; pres., owner M. Shaw Enterprise, Calcutta, India, 1989—; co-prin. investigator for subsidence monitoring project U.S. Bur. Mines, 1993-96; prin. investigator for computational fluid dynamics rsch. for SBIR project, NASP, Wright-Patterson AFB, 1994-95. Vice pres. Huntsville India Assn., 1988-89, pres., 1989-90. Govt. of India scholar, 1977; recipient Outstanding Tchr. Svcs. award Ala. A&M U., 1987. Mem. ASCE. Home: 1210 Aldridge Dr SE Huntsville AL 35803-2402 Office: Ala A&M U PO Box 367 Normal AL 35762-3670

SAHAI, HARDEO, medical statistics educator; b. Bahraich, India, Jan. 10, 1942; m. Lillian Sahai, Dec. 28, 1973; 3 children. BS in Math., Stats. and Physics, Lucknow U., India, 1962; MS in Math., Banaras U., Varanasi, India, 1964; MS in Math. Stats., U. Chgo., 1968; PhD in Stats., U. Ky., 1971. Lectr. in math. and stats. Banaras U., Varanasi, India, 1964-65; asst. stats. officer Durgapur Steel Plant, Durgapur West Bengal, India, 1965; statistician Rsch. and Planning div. Blue Cross Assn., Chgo., 1966; statis. programmer Cleft Palate Ctr., U. Ill., 1967, Chgo. Health Rsch. Found., 1968; mgmt. scientist Mgmt. Systems Devel. Dept. Burroughs Corp., Detroit, 1971-72; from asst. prof. to prof. dept. math. U. P.R., Mayaguez, 1972-82; vis. research prof. Dept. Stats. and Applied Math. Fed. U. of Ceara, Brazil, 1978-79; sr. research statistician Travenol Labs., Inc., Round Lake, Ill., 1982-83; chief statistician U.S. Army Hqrs., Ft. Sheridan, Ill., 1983-84; sr. math. statistician U.S. Bur. of Census Dept. of Commerce, Washington, 1984-85; sr. ops. rsch. analyst Def. Logistics Agy. Dept. Def., Chgo., 1985-86; prof. Dept. Biostats. and Epidemiology U. P.R. Med. Scis., San Juan, 1986—; cons. P.R. Univ Cons., P.R. Driving Safety Evaluation Project, Water Resources Rsch. Inst., Travenol Labs., Campo Rico, P.R., U.S. Bur. Census, Washington, Lawrence Livermore Nat. Lab., Calif., others; vis. prof. U. Granada, Spain, U. Veracruzana, Mex., U. Nacional de Colombia; vis. prof. U. Nacional de Trujillo, Peru, 1993-94, hon. prof. dept. stats., 1994—; adj. prof. dept. math. U. P.R. Natural Scis. Faculty, 1995—. Author: Statistics and Probability: Learning Module, 1984; author: (with Jose Berrios) A Dictionary of Statistical Scientific and Technical Terms: English-Spanish and Spanish-English, 1981, (with Wilfredo Martinez) Statistical Tables and Formulas for the Biological Social and Physical Sciences, 1996, (with Anwer Khurshid) Statistics in Epidemiology: Methods, Techniques and Applications, 1996, (with Satish C. Misra and Michael Graham) Quotations on Probability and Statistics with Illustrations, 1996; mem. editl. bd. Sociedad Colombiana de Matematicas, P.R. Health Scis. Jour.; contbr. editor Current Index to Stats.; reviewer Collegiate Microcomputer, Comm. in Statistics, Indian Jour. Stats., Jour. Royal Statis. Soc. (series D, The Statistician), New Zealand Statistician, Biometrics, Can. Jour. Stats., Technometrics, Problems, Resources and Issues in Math. Undergrad. Studies; contbr. more than 100 articles and papers to profl. and sci. jours., numerous articles to tech. mags. Active Dept. Consumer Affairs Svcs. Commonwealth of P.R., San Juan, Dept. Anti-Addiction Svcs., Commonwealth of P.R., San Juan., Inst. of AIDS, Municipality of San Juan, VA Med. Ctr. of San Juan, Caribbean Primate Rsch. Ctr., Ctr. Addiction Studies Caribbean Ctrl. U. Recipient Dept. Army Cert. Achievement award, 1984, U. Ky. Outstanding Alumnus award, 1993, medal of honor U. Granada, 1994, plaque of honor U. Nacional de Trujillo, 1994; fellow Coun. Sci. and Indsl. Rsch., 1964-65, U. Chgo., 1965-68, Harvard U., 1979, Fulbright Found., 1982; U.P. Bd. Merit scholar, 1957-59, Govt. India Merit scholar, 1959-64; grantee NSF, 1974-77, NIMH, 1987-90, 91—, NIDA, 1991—. Fellow AAAS, Inst. Statisticians (charter statistician), Inst. Math. and Its Applications (charter mathematician), N.Y. Acad. Scis., Royal Statis. Soc.; mem. Internat. Statis. Inst., Internat. Assn. Teaching Stats., Soc. Epidemiol. Rsch., Inst. Math. Stats., Bernouilli Soc. for Math. Stats. and Probability, Internat. Biometric Soc., Am. Soc. for Quality Control, Am. Stats. Assn., Japan Statis. Soc., Can. Statis. Soc., Inter-Am. Statis. Inst., Internat. Assn. Statis. Computing, Sch. Sci. and Math. Assn., Sigma Xi. Home: Street Dr Gaudier Texidor K-5-B Terrace Mayaguez PR 00680-9998 Office: U PR Grad Sch Pub Health Med Scis Campus Dept Biostats & Epid PO Box 365067 San Juan PR 00936-5067

SAHN, STEVEN ALAN, internist, educator; b. Bklyn., Jan. 25, 1943; s. Irwin H. and Mildred P. Sahn; m. Eleanor Elizabeth Sahn, Nov. 4, 1974; children: Karen, Stacey, James, Michael, Rachel. BA, Duke U., 1964; MD, U. Louisville, 1968. Diplomate Am. Bd. Internal Medicine, Am. Bd. Pulmonary Medicine, Am. Bd. Critical Care Medicine. Intern in internal medicine U. Iowa Hosp., Iowa City, 1968-69, resident in internal medicine, 1969-71; fellow in pulmonary disease U. Colo. Health Sci. Ctr., Denver, 1971-73, instr. medicine, 1973-74, asst. prof. medicine, 1974-78, assoc. prof. medicine, 1978-83; prof. medicine, dir. divsn. pulmonary and critical care Med. Univ. S.C., Charleston, 1983—; vis. prof. U. Calif., San Francisco, 1980, Kans. U. Med. Ctr., Kansas City, 1981, U. Louisville Sch. Medicine,

1982, Wright State U. Med. Sch., Wright-Patterson AFB Hosp., Dayton, Ohio, 1982, Oreg. Health Scis. U., 1982, Vanderbilt U., Nashville, 1984, U. S.C. Sch. Medicine, 1985, U. Ariz. Health Sci. Ctr., Tucson, 1985, 92, 93, Yale U., New Haven, Conn., 1986, Hershey (Pa.) Med. Ctr., 1986, SUNY, Stonybrook, 1987, Dartmouth-Hitchcock Med. Ctr., Hanover, N.H., 1988, Maine Med. Ctr. U. Vt., Portland, Maine, 1988, Fitzsimmons Army Med. Ctr., Denver, 1989, Seton Hall U. Grad. Med. Edn., 1989, Newark, 1989, Loyola U. Med. Ctr., Chgo., 1989, Andrews AFB, Washington, 1990, Keesler AFB, Biloxi, Miss., 1990, U. Rochester, N.Y., U. Ala., Birmingham, 1990, N.Y. Med. Coll., 1990, Temple U. Sch. Medicine, Phila., 1990, U. Milan, Italy, 1990, Georgetown U. Med. Ctr., Washington, 1991, Albert Einstein Sch. Medicine, 1991, Johns Hopkins U. Sch. Medicine, Balt., 1991, Ind. U. Med. Ctr., 1994, Ohio State U. Sch. Medicine, 1994, others; cons. Fitzsimons Army Med. Ctr., 1980-83, 88-90, DHEC of S.C., 1982—, USAF, 1989—, FDA Office of Orphan Product Devel., 1993—; presenter numerous seminars; keynote speaker numerous meetings. Euthor: (with J.E. Heffner) Pulmonary Pearls, 1988, vol. II, 1994, Critical Care Pearls, 1989; editor: (with L.B. Reller and R.W. Schrier) Clinical Internal Medicine, 1979, Pulmonary Emergencies, 1982, Diseases of the Pleura: Seminars in Respiratory Medicine, 1987, Infections of the Pleural Space: Seminars in Respiratory Infections, Vol. III, 1988, (with J.E. Heffner) Internal Medicine Pearls, 1993, (with J.E. Heffner) Cardiology Pearls, 1993, Tuberculosis Pearls, 1996; mem. editorial bd. Chest, 1987—, Pulmonary and Critical Care Update, 1988—; dept. editor Pulmonary and Critical Care Pearls Chest, 1992—, Pulmonary Pearls Jour. Respiratory Disease, 1990—, Critical Care Pearls Jour. Critical Illness, 1990—; cons. to editorial bd. Am. Jour. Diseases of Children, Am. Jour. Medicine, Am. Review Respiratory Diseases, Annals of Internal Medicine, Chest, Critical Care Medicine, Jour. Am. Acad. Dermatoloty, Jour. Am. Med. Assn., European Respiratory Jour., Jour. Applied Physiology, Jour. Intensive Care Medicine, Jour. Laboratory and Clin. Medicine, Jour. Respiratory Diseases, Lung, Mayo Clinic Proceedings, Med. Toxicology, N.Y. State Jour. Medicine, Tubercle and Lung Diseases, Western Jour. Medicine; contbr. articles, reviews and abstracts to profl. jours., chpts. to books. Recipient Young Investigator Pulmonary Rsch. award NHLBI, 1975-77, grantee 1975-77; named one of Outstanding Med. Specialists in the U.S. Town and Country Mag., 1990, one of 400 Best Doctors in Am., Good Housekeeping Mag., 1991; grantee Milheim, 1977-78, Beecham, 1977-78, 82-83, Warner-Chilcott, 1978-79, Squibb, 1978, 79-80, Lilly, 1979-80, 81-82, Boehringer-Ingelheim, 1980, 89-90, Med. Coll. S.C., 1985-86, ALASC, 1985-86, 86-87, 87-88, 88-89, Lederle, 1988-92, Hoescht-Roussel, 1988-90, Support Systems Internat., 1990-92, 92-93, Cutter Biological, Miles, Inc., Glaxo, 1991-92, Schering-Plough, 1992-93, Tap Pharmaceuticals, 1993. Fellow Am. Coll. Chest Physicians (annual meeting com. 1986, gov. S.C. 1988-91, 91-94, organizing com. nat. pulmonary bd. review course 1990, 92, 94, membership com. 1992-93, annual internat. sci. program com. 1993-95, reviewer MKSAP 1994), Am. Coll. Physicians, Am. Coll. Critical Care Medicine; mem. Am. Fedn. Clin. Rsch. (so. sect.), Am. Thoracic Soc. (respiratory care com. 1978-80, rsch. coord. com. 1985-87, annual meeting com. 1985-89, chmn. sci. assembly on clin. problems 1986-87, coun. chpt. reps. 1987-90), Am. Lung Assn. (adv. bd. S.C. coastal br. 1985-87, 89-91, 92-94, med. review com. 1985-89), We. Soc. Clin. Investigation, S.C. Thoracic Soc. (sci. planning com. 1985-86), Charleston County Med. Soc. Home: 10 Cochran Ct Charleston SC 29407-7505 Office: Med U SC Divsn Pulmonary & Critical Care Medicine 171 Ashley Ave Charleston SC 29425-0001

SAHR, MORRIS GALLUP, financial planner; b. Schenectady, Nov. 28, 1928; s. Nathan and Esther (Gallup) S.; m. Sarah Diane Eisenberg, Dec. 23, 1956; children: Evelyn, David, Janet. AB, U. Oreg., 1951, MA, 1953; PhD, Calif. Open U., Oakland, 1978. CFP. Pres. Deposit Mgmt. Svc., Inc., Palmyra, Va., 1978—. Co-author: Your Book of Financial Planning, 1983, Encyclopedia of Financial Planning, 1984, The Financial Planner, 1986, Financial Planning Can Make You Rich, 1987. Chmn. Fairfax County Planning Commn., 1964-68; del. White House Conf. on Aging, 1980, U.S. Congl. Adv. Bd., 1984-87; bd. dirs. Fairfax Indsl. Devel. Authority, 1985-96; adjudicator Am. Arbitration Assn. Recipient award Danforth Found.; named 1 of Top 200 Planners in U.S., Money Mag.; hon. fellow Kennedy Libr., 1985; Paul Harris fellow, 1989. Mem. Internat. Assn. Fin. Planning (founder, 1st pres. Metro Washington chpt.), Inst. Cert. Fin. Planners (nat. govt. affairs com.), Am. Assn. Practicing Fin. Planners (past pres.), Rotary (pres. Fairfax 1984-85), Sr. Leadership Coun. Charlottesville. Home and Office: DMS Inc 61 Wildwood Dr Palmyra VA 22963

SAID, RUSHDI, geologist; b. Cairo, May 12, 1920; came to U.S., 1981; naturalized, 1985; children: Kareem, Sawsan. PhD, Harvard U., 1950; Dr.rer.nat. h.c., Tech. U., Berlin, 1986. Prof. geology Cairo U., 1951-68; head Geol. Survey & Mining Orgn., Egypt, 1968-78; geologist, cons. Washington, 1978—. Author: The Geology of Egypt, 1962, The River Nile, Geology, Hydrology and Utilization, 1993. Mem. Parliament of Egypt, 1964-76; mem. exec. com. Interparliamentary Union, Geneva, Switzerland, 1972-76. Recipient Nachtigal medal Geog. Soc. Berlin, 1986; decorated Sci. and Arts Medal (1st order) Egyptian Govt., 1962. Hon. fellow Geol. Soc. Am., Geol. Soc. Africa; fellow Third World Acad. Sci.; mem. Institut d'Egypte, Egyptian Acad. Sci. Home: 3801 Millcreek Dr Annandale VA 22003-2330

SAIKEVYCH, IRENE A., pathologist; b. Perth Amboy, N.J., Oct. 16, 1950; d. Victor C. and Maria (Shomber) S.; divorced; 1 child, Natalie S. White. BA in Chemistry, U. Ill., 1972; MD, Northwestern, 1976. Diplomate Am. Bd. Med. Genetics; cert. pathologist. Resident Northwestern U., Honolulu, 1976-81; fellow in cytogenetics U. Hawaii, Honolulu, 1982-84, dir. cytogenetics rsch. lab., 1985-92, asst. prof. to assoc. prof. Dept. Pathology, 1982-92; med. dir. clin. cytogenetics Dept. Pathology St. Francis Hosp., Honolulu, 1988-92; staff pathologist Presbyn. Hosp., Charlotte, N.C., 1993—, dir. genetic svcs., 1993—. Contbr. numerous articles to profl. jours. Fellow Am. Coll. Med. Genetics (founder); mem. AAAS, AMA, Coll. Am. Pathologists (cytogenetics resource com. 1987—), Am. Soc. Human Genetics, Am. Soc. Hematology. Office: Presbyn Path Grp Presbyn Hosp Path Lab Med 200 Hawthorne Ln Charlotte NC 28204-2515

SAIKOWSKI, RONALD ALEXANDER, consulting engineer; b. Wichita Falls, Tex., May 15, 1950; s. Alexander Edward and Marie (Balazs) S.; m. Martha Elizabeth Dixon, July 21, 1973; children: Natalie, Emery, Denise. BCE, Tex. Tech. U., 1973. Registered profl. engr., Tex., Okla., Tenn., N.Mex., Colo., Mo. Design engr. Lockwood-Greene Engring., Atlanta, 1973-75; environ. engr. Champion Internat., Atlanta, 1975-77; project mgr. Greiner Engring., Houston, 1977-82; mgr. engring. Montgomery Engring., Houston, 1982-83; owner, pres., bd. dirs. Sitech Engring. Corp., Woodlands, Tex., 1983—; mem. adv. bd. Lower Lake Creek Reservoir Com., Conroe, Tex., 1985-89; pres., bd. dirs. Montgomery County Flood Control Corp., Conroe, 1987-89; pres. Comml. Real Estate Assn., Montgomery County, 1989. Editor newsletter. Precinct chmn. Montgomery County Reps., 1982-96, chmn. candidates com., 1985—, mem. exec. com., 1982-96, del. Nat. Rep. Conv., 1992; mem. adv. com. Congressman Joe Barton, Concoe, 1984-92, chmn. steering com. Richard Smith for State Senate; v.p., bd. dirs. Montgomery County Mcpl. Utility Dist. 46, 1987-89; election judge Montgomery County, 1983-96; mem. steering com. CROP Walk; chmn. mktg. bd. Jr. Achievement, Montgomery County; adv. bd. Child Advocacy Support Assn.; bd. dirs. McCullough H.S., 1993-95, band booster, 1995—; mem. civil engring. adv. coun., Tex. Tech. U., 1996—. Mem. Am. Waterworks Assn., Water Pollution Control Fedn., South Montgomery County C. of C. (chmn. numerous coms., Small Bus. Man of Yr. 1992), Conroe C. of C., Comml. Real Estate Assn., Tex. Tech. Civil Engrs. (adv. coun. 1996—), Montgomery County (bd. dirs. 1987-90, pres. 1989), Edn. for Tomorrow Alliance, Women Helping Women, Tex. Tech. Civil Engring. Acad., Toastmasters, Kiwanis (bd. dirs. Montgomery County 1986-87), Tau Beta Pi, Chi Epsilon. Methodist. Home: 59 Wood Scent Ct The Woodlands TX 77380-2896 Office: Sitech Engring Corp 2202 Timberloch Pl Ste 100 The Woodlands TX 77380-1106

SAINE, BETTY BOSTON, elementary school educator; b. Newton, N.C., Dec. 1, 1932; d. Glenn and Carrie Queen Boston; m. Thomas Paul Saine, Aug. 3, 1968; 1 child, Carrie Ann. BA, Lenoir Rhyne Coll., 1956. Tchr. grade 4 High Point (N.C.) City Schs., 1956-59, Charlotte City Schs./ Charlotte-Mecklenburg Schs., 1959-66; art tchr. grades 1-8 Newton-Conover City Schs., 1966-67; tchr. grade 4 Charlotte-Mecklenburg Schs., 1967-68; tchr. grade 6 Lincolnton (N.C.) City Schs., 1968-70; tchr. grades 5 and 6 Lincolnton City Schs./Lincoln County Schs., 1972-90; ret. Historian, publicity chair beautification com. Sunflower Garden Club, Lincolnton, 1976-87. Mem. Alpha Delta Kappa (various offices and coms.). Methodist. Home: 2492 Pickwick Pl Lincolnton NC 28092-7748

ST. GERMAIN, FERNAND JOSEPH, congressman; b. Blackstone, Mass.; s. Andrew Joseph and Pearl (Talaby) St Germain; m. Rachel O'Neill, Aug. 20, 1953; children: Laurene, Lisette. Ph.B. in Social Sci, Providence Coll., 1948, LL.D., 1965; LL.B., Boston U., 1955; J.S.D. (hon.), Suffolk U., 1976; D.C.L. (hon.), Our Lady of Providence Sem., 1968; D.B.A. (hon.), Bryant Coll., 1981; D.Public Service (hon.), Roger Williams Coll., 1981; LL.B., Brown U., 1985. Bar: R.I. 1956, Fed. 1957, U.S. Supreme Ct. 1983. Mem. R.I. Ho. of Reps., 1952-60; mem. 87th to 100th Congresses from 1st R.I. Dist., 1961-1989, chmn. house com. on banking fin. and urban affairs, 1980-88. Served with AUS, 1949-52. Recipient Silver Shingle award for disting. public service Boston U. Sch. Law Alumni Assn., 1981, Alumni award disting. pub. service Boston U. Sch. Law, 1982. Mem. ABA, R.I., Bar Assn. Fed. Bar Assn., alumni assns. Our Lady of Providence Sem., Providence Coll., Boston U. Law Sch., Am. Legion. Office: 7601 Lewinsville Rd Ste 205 Mc Lean VA 22102

ST. JOHN, BILL DEAN, diversified equipment and services company executive; b. Wewoka, Okla., 1931. BBA, So. Meth. U., 1952. Asst. treas. Seaboard Oil Co., 1954-58; auditor Alford Merony & Co., 1958-60; v.p. fin. Can. Refractories Ltd., 1968; with Dresser Industries Inc., Dallas, 1960—; treas. Ideco div. Dresser Industries, Dallas, 1961-63; fin. contr. Dresser Industries Inc., Dallas, 1970-73, staff v.p. fin. svcs., 1975-76, v.p. acctg., 1976-80; exec. v.p. adminstrn. Dresser Industries, Inc., Dallas, 1980-92, vice chmn., 1992—, CFO, 1993—; Allendale Ins. So. adv. bd., 1995—. With U.S. Army, 1952-54. Mem. AICPA, Mfrs.' Alliance for Productivity and Innovation (fin. coun.), The Conf. Bd. (chief adminstrv. officers coun.), Allendale Ins. So. Adv. Bd. Office: Dresser Industries Inc PO Box 718 2001 Ross Ave Dallas TX 75221-0718

ST. JOHN, HENRY SEWELL, JR., utility company executive; b. Birmingham, Ala., Aug. 18, 1938; s. H. Sewell and Carrie M. (Bond) St. J.; student David Lipscomb Coll., 1956-58, U. Tenn., 1958-59, U. Ala., 1962-64; m. J. Ann Morris, Mar. 7, 1959; children: Sherri Ann, Brian Lee, Teresa Lynn, Cynthia Faye. Engring. aide Ala. Power Co., Enterprise, 1960-62, Birmingham, 1962-66; asst. chief engr. Riviera Utilities, Foley, 1966-71, sec.-treas., gen. mgr., 1971—. Deacon, Foley Ch. of Christ, 1975-82, elder, 1983—; active Am. Cancer Soc., chmn. bd. Baldwin County unit, 1977; bd. dirs. AGAPE of Mobile, 1977-80; treas. Christian Care Ctr., Inc., 1981—; bd. dirs. South Baldwin Civic Chorus, pres., 1979-82 . Mem. IEEE., South Ala. Power Distbrs. Assn. (chmn. 1973-74), Ala. Consumer-Owned Power Distbrs. Assn. (chmn. 1974-75, 82-83, vice-chmn. 1981, sec.-treas. 1980), S.E. Electric Reliability Coun. (assoc.), Mcpl. Electric Utility Assn. Ala. (exec. com., dir. 1971—), Ala. Mcpl. Electric Authority (bd. dir. 1981—, vice chmn. 1981-82, chmn. 1983—), Electric Cities Ala. (bd. dirs., exec. com. 1989—), United Mcpl. Distbrs. Group (bd. dirs. 1972—), Am. Pub. Power Assn. (cable communications com.), Pub. Gas. Assn. Ala. (bd. dirs. 1987-88), South Baldwin C. of C. (pres. 1974, dir. 1972-75, 81-90, 92-95). Clubs: Foley Quarterback (sec.-treas. 1984-85); Gulf Shores Golf (dir. 1974-75), Classic Chevy, Internat. (life mem.), Azalea City Classic Chevy (bd. dirs., exec. com. 1989—, v.p. 1991-92, 96—), Chevrolet Nomad Assn. (bd. dirs. 1992—, v.p. 1993—). Rotarian. Home: PO Box 1817 Foley AL 36536-1817 Office: PO Box PO Box 550 Foley AL 36536-0550

ST. WECKER, PETER GRANT REEVES, pharmaceutical clinical research executive; b. N.Y.C., July 30, 1964; s. Myron Sydney and Wendy Joan St. Wecker. BA in Chemistry, Earlham Coll., 1986; PhD in Physiology, U. N.C., 1994. Pharmacol. rschr. Duke U., Durham, N.C., 1987; acad. programs coord. N.C. Supercomputer Ctr., Research Triangle Park, N.C., 1994; project mgr. assoc. Quintiles, Inc., Research Triangle Park, 1994—. Contbr. articles to profl. jours. Vol. Mus. of Life and Sci., Durham, N.C., 1994—; senator Grad. and Profl. Students, Chapel Hill, 1989-93. Mem. AAAS, Soc. for Neurosci., Drug Info. Assn., Project Mgmt. Inst., Sigma Xi. Office: Quintiles Inc 1007 Slater Rd Durham NC 27703

SAIZAN, PAULA THERESA, oil company executive; b. New Orleans, Sept. 12, 1947; d. Paul Morine and Hattie Mae (Hayes) Saizan; m. George H. Smith, May 26, 1973 (div. July 1976). BS in Acctg. summa cum laude, Xavier U., 1969. CPA, Tex.; notary pub. Systems engr. IBM, New Orleans, 1969-71; acct., then sr. acct. Shell Oil Co., Houston, Tex., 1971-76, sr. fin. analyst, 1976-77, fin. rep., 1977-79, corp. auditor, 1979-81, treasury rep., 1981-82, sr. treasury rep., 1982-86; asst. treas. Shell Credit Inc., Shell Leasing Co., Shell Fin. Co. 1986-88, sr. pub. affairs rep., 1988-89, sr. staff pub. affairs rep., 1990-91, program mgr., 1991-96, sr. program mgr., 1996—. Bd. dirs. Houston Downtown Mgmt. Dist., Greater Houston Conv. and Visitors Bur. (treas.), St. Joseph Hosp. Found., United Negro Coll. Fund, Associated Cath. Charities, Houston, Galveston; mem. adv. coun. U.S. SBA region VI, Houston; acctg. dept. adv. bd. Tex. So. U.; del. White House Conf. on small bus., 1995. Mem. AICPA, NAACP, Tex. Soc. CPAs, Leadership Houston, Greater Inwood Partnership, LWV of Houston, Xavier U. Alumni Assn., Nat. Assn. Black Accts., Nat. Coun. Negro Women, Inc., Nat. Political Congress Black Women, Alpha Kappa Alpha, Phi Gamma Nu, Kappa Gamma Pi. Roman Catholic. Home: 5426 Long Creek Ln Houston TX 77088-4407 Office: Shell Oil Co PO Box 2463 Houston TX 77252-2463

SAJO, ERNO, nuclear engineer, educator, physicist, consultant; b. Budapest, Hungary, Hungary; s. Erno L. F. and Eva (Kemenes) S.; m. Agatha Nicolette Schiller. BS, MS, Tech. U. Budapest, 1983; PhD, U. Lowell, Mass., 1989. Design engr. Eroterv, Budapest, 1983-85; rsch. asst. U. Lowell, 1985-89; assoc. prof. La. State U., Baton Rouge, 1990—. Co-author: English-Hungarian Dictionary of Science and Technology, 1991; contbr. articles to profl. jours. Mem. Am. Nuclear Soc. (faculty advisor student chpt. 1990—), Am. Health Physics Soc. (sec. La. chpt.), Sigma Xi, Alpha Nu Sigma. Office: La State U Nuclear Sci Ctr Baton Rouge LA 70803

SAKAI, PETER A., lawyer; b. McAllen, Tex., Oct. 21, 1954; s. Pete Y. and Rose Marie (Kawahata) S.; m. Raquel M. Dias, Mar. 10, 1982; children: George Y., Elizabeth K. BA, U. Tex., Austin, 1976, JD, 1979. Bar: Tex. 1979. Asst. dist. atty. County of Bexar, San Antonio, 1980-82; pvt. practice San Antonio, 1983-94; assoc. judge Bexar County Dist. Ct., San Antonio, 1994—; hearings arbitrator City of San Antonio, 1983-93; judge Mcpl. Ct., City of Elmendorf, Tex., 1985; juvenile assoc. judge 289th Dist. Ct., San Antonio, 1989-94; city atty. City of Leon Valley, Tex., 1986-90. Contbr. to profl. publs. Bd. dirs. Bexar County Juvenile Vols. in Probation, San Antonio, 1983-93; Japan Am. Soc. San Antonio, 1987-89, Cmty. Cultural Arts Orgn., San Antonio, 1987-92, Bexar County Local Devel. Corp., San Antonio, 1989-94. Mem. ABA, State Bar Tex., San Antonio Bar Assn. Office: Bexar County Courthouse 100 Dolorosa Rm 205 San Antonio TX 78205

SAKAKIBARA, YOSHITAKA, business educator; b. Okazaki, Aichi, Japan, July 9, 1952; s. Kishio and Katsuko S.; m. Hiroko Yamamoto, Dec. 21, 1987; children: Shimon, Naomi. BA, Kyoto U. Fgn. Studies, 1976; MS, U. So. Calif., L.A., 1978, PhD, 1984. TESOL, ACTFL cert. tester. Lectr. U. So. Calif., L.A., 1982-84; asst. prof. U. S.C., Columbia, 1985-91; assoc. prof., 1991—; adj. prof. internat. bus. U. S.C., Columbia, 1986—; prin. Japanese Supplementary Sch., Columbia, 1985—. Contbr. articles to profl. jours. Mem. Acad. Internat. Bus., Assn. Asian Studies, Assn. Tchrs. of Japanese, Comparative and Internat. Edn. Soc. Office: U SC Dept Germanic Langs Columbia SC 29208

SAKS, JUDITH-ANN, artist; b. Anniston, Ala., Dec. 20, 1943; d. Julien David and Lucy-Jane (Watson) S.; student Tex. Acad. Art, 1957-58, Mus. Fine Arts, Houston, 1962, Rice U., 1962; BFA, Tulane U., 1966; postgrad. U. Houston, 1967; m. Haskell Irvin Rosenthal, Dec. 22, 1974; 1 child, Brian Julien. One-man shows include: Alley Gallery, Houston, 1969, 2131 Gallery, Houston, 1969; group shows include: Birmingham (Ala.) Mus., 1967, Meinhard Galleries, Houston, 1977; Galerie Barbizon, Houston, 1980, Park Crest Gallery, Austin, 1981; represented in permanent collections including: L.B. Johnson Manned Space Mus., Clear Lake City, Tex., Harris County Heritage Mus., Windsor Castle, London, Smithsonian Instn., Washington: commns. include: Pin Oak Charity Horse Show Assn., Roberts S.S. Agy., New Orleans, Cruiser Houston Meml. Rm., U. Houston; curator student art collection U. Houston, 1968-72; artist Am. Revolution Bicentennial project Port of Houston Authority, 1975-76. Recipient art awards including: 1st prize for water color Art League Houston, 1969, 1st prize for graphics, 1969, 1st prize for sculpture, 1968, 1st place award for original print, DAR, Am. Heritage Com., 1987. Mem. Art League Houston, Houston Mus. Fine Arts, DAR (curator 1983-85, 93-95, contbr. Tex. sesquicentennial drawing for DAR mag.), Daus. Republic Tex. Home: 2215 Briar Br Houston TX 77042-2959

SALADINO, ANTHONY JOSEPH, aerospace engineer; b. Bridgeport, Conn., Mar. 4, 1959; s. Joseph and Jeannette Anne (Martin) S. BSME, U. Bridgeport, 1981; MS in AE, U. Conn., 1982; PhD in AE, U. Tenn., 1989. Machinist apprentice Assocs. Inc., Milford, Conn., 1976-81; rsch. asst. U. Tenn. Space Inst., Tullahoma, 1983-87; sr. aerospace engr. REMTECH, Inc., Huntsville, Ala., 1987-91; rsch. engr. SECA, Inc., Huntsville, 1992-94; mem. tech. staff and mgr. Dynacs Engring. Co., Renton, Wash., 1995—; presenter confs. Contbr. articles to profl. jours. Mem. AIAA, ASME, N.Y. Acad. Scis., Sigma Xi. Office: Dynacs Engring Co Inc 258 SW 43rd St Bldg 3 Renton WA 98055-4936

SALADINO, TONY JOSEPH, artist; b. New Orleans, June 5, 1943; s. John Vincent and Lena (Randazzo) S.; m. Judy Lynn Lattis, Aug. 28, 1943; children: Dan, Ben, Amy, Ann. BS in mktg., U. New Orleans, 1964. instr. Modern Art Mus. Ft. Worth, 1992, Tarrant County Jr. Coll., 1992, Imagination Celebration Kennedy Ctr. Arts, 1991, Oxbow Summer Sch. Art Saugatuck, Mich., 1991. Represented in permanent collections Wichita Falls (Tex.) Mus. and Art Ctr., Nat. Mus. Fine Arts, Hanoi, N. Vietnam, Parkersburg Art Ctr., W.Va., The Art Complex Mus., Duxbury, Mass., Mus. of Art and Archaeology, U. Mo., Hunterdon Art Ctr., N.J., Mus. Internat. Art, Bahia, Brazil, U. Wis., Kenosha, Nassau County Community Coll., Garden City, N.Y., McNeese State U., Lake Charles, La., U. Dallas, City of Milford, Conn. Home: 660 W Oak Dr Hurst TX 76053-5526 Office: Saladino Studio 756 Norwood Dr Hurst TX 76053-5769

SALAH, SAGID, retired nuclear engineer; b. Seoul, Sept. 2, 1932; came to U.S., 1954; s. Galim and Faiza (Sultan) Salahutdin; m. Ravile Almakay, Apr. 2, 1966; children: Shamil, Kamil, Safiye. BChemE, U. Fla., 1958, MS in Nuclear Engring., 1960, PhD in Nuclear Engring., 1964. Nuclear engr. AEC, Bethesda, Md., 1964-66; sr. design engr. Westinghouse Astronuclear Lab., Large, Pa., 1966-70; sr. sys. engr. Westinghouse Nuclear Energy Sys., Pitts., 1970-73; mem. sys. safety engring. staff U.S. Nuclear Regulatory Commn., Bethesda, 1973-93; ret., 1993; nuclear engring. cons. Oak Ridge (Tenn.) Inst. Nuclear Studies, 1963, 64; instr. U. Md., College Park, 1973-76. Contbr. articles to Nuclear Sci. and Engring. Youth coach Nat. Capital Soccer League, Vienna, Va., 1975-85. Mem. Am. Nuclear Soc. (emeritus, reviewer trans. papers 1972), Sigma Tau. Moslem. Home: 9302 Kilport Ct Vienna VA 22182

SALAM, HALIDE, artist, art educator; b. Calcutta, India, Sept. 25, 1951; came into U.S., 1971; d. Badi Us and Fatema Reza Salam; m. Timothy Edward Archer, May 31, 1980. BA in Psychology, Chittagong (Bangladesh) Girls Coll., 1965; MA in Painting, N.Mex. Highland U., 1973; PhD in Fine Arts, Tex. Tech. U., 1977. Prof. art Radford (Va.) U., 1977—; lectr. in field. One-woman shows include Danville (Va.) Mus., 1986, Bangladesh Art Acad., 1988, Greensboro (N.C.) Artist's League, 1989, Ircica Yildiz Sarayi, Turkey, 1992, 100 Yil Sanat Galerisi, Turkey, 1992, Izmir Resim Ve Heykel Muzesi, Turkey, 1992, Devlet Guzel Sanatlar Galerisi, Turkey, 1993, Flossie Martin Gallery, Radford, Va., 1993, Art Inst. and Gallery, Salisbury, Md., 1995-96; exhibited in group shows at Radford Coll., 1978, Radford U. Kent Gallery, 1977-87, James Madison U., Harrisonburg, Va., 1979, Roanoke Mus., 1981, 82, Danville Mus. Art, 1982, numerous other nat. and internat. group shows; numerous pub. and pvt. collections; subject numerous revs. Mem. Architecture and Design Assn. (bd. dirs. 1990—). Home: 2430 Ridge Rd Blacksburg VA 24060 Office: Radford Univ Dept Art Radford VA 24142

SALANT, NATHAN NATHANIEL, athletic conference executive; b. Bronx, N.Y., June 25, 1955; s. Benjamin B. and Marilyn (Balterman) S. BA cum laude, SUNY, Albany, 1976; JD, Boston U., 1979. Bar: N.J. 1981. Asst. athletic dir. SUNY, Albany, 1979-80, St. Francis Coll., Bklyn., 1981-85; spl. asst. athletic dir. Adelphi U., Garden City, N.Y., 1985-88; commr. Mid. Atlantic States Collegiate Athletic Conf., Chester, Pa., 1988-92; adj. prof. English Widener U., Chester, 1988-92; commr. Gulf South Conf., Birmingham, Ala., 1992—; mem. men's com. on coms. NCAA, 1993—, mem. D-II men's basketball south crtl. regional adv. com., 1995—. Author: This Date in New York Yankees History, 1979, 81, 83, Superstars, Stars and Just Plain Heroes, 1982. Head coach Rockland (N.Y.) OTB Pirates Am. Legion Baseball Team, 1974-76, 77—. Named Coach of Yr., Rockland County Big League, 1979-81, 83, 85-86, 87, 89, N.Y. State Am. Legion, 1987, 89-94. Mem. ABA. Home: 174 Woodmere Creek Ln Birmingham AL 35226-3561 Office: Gulf South Conf 4 Office Park Cir Ste 218 Birmingham AL 35223-2538

SALAS, NESTOR AUGUSTO, real estate executive; b. Havana, Cuba, Aug. 22, 1947; s. Carlos Manuel and Lourdes Perez Lavin; 1 child, Nicholas Alexander. AA, Miami Dade C.C., 1969; BS, N.Y. Sch. Interior Design, 1971. V.p. Salas Furniture, Newark, N.J., 1970-78; pres. NASA Trading, Miami, 1979—, Mortgage Ctr., Miami, 1986-90; realtor Coldwell Banker-Kassner, Miami, 1979—; mortgage broker The Salas Interest, Miami, 1990—. Bd. dirs. Rare Fruit Coun., Miami, 1984. Mem. Fla. Assn. Mortgage Brokers (Miami chpt. chmn. pub. rels. 1988-90), Bd. of Realtors. Office: NASA Enterprises PO Box 430913 Miami FL 33243-0913

SALATICH, JOHN SMYTH, cardiologist; b. New Orleans, Nov. 28, 1926; s. Peter B. and Gladys (Malter) S.; BS cum laude, Loyola U., New Orleans, 1946; MD, La. State U., 1950; m. Patricia L. Mattison, Sept. 26, 1959; children: John Smyth, Elizabeth, Allison, Stephanie. Intern Charity Hosp., New Orleans, 1950-51, resident, 1951-54; practice medicine, specializing in cardiology and internal medicine, New Orleans, 1954-92, Gen. Internal Med. Clinic Tulane Med. Sch., 1992—; dir. EKG dept. Southeastern La. Hosp., Mandeville, La.; prof. clin. medicine La. State U., 1994; mem. staff Touro Infirmary, St. Charles Gen. Hosp.; chmn. dept. medicine Hotel Dieu, 1974-86 pres., New Orleans Emergency Room Corp., Physician Supplemental Services; adv. bd. Bank La., 1960-89; mem. Pres.'s Coun. Loyola U., 1990-92. Bd. dirs. La. Regional Med. Program, 1972. Served to capt. M.C., AUS, 1954-56; Korea. Decorated Medallion of Greek Army. Diplomate Am. Bd. Internal Medicine. Fellow Am. Coll. Chest Physicians, ACP; mem. Am. Heart Assn., La. Heart Assn., New Orleans Acad. Internal Medicine, La. Soc. Internal Medicine, AMA, La. Med. Soc., Orleans Parish Med. Soc., Theta Beta, Alpha Sigma Nu, Delta Epsilon Sigma. Club: New Orleans Country. Contbr. articles to profl. and bus. jours. Home: 433 Country Club Dr New Orleans LA 70124-1038 Office: Nola 70112 144 Elk Pl Ste 1100 New Orleans LA 70112-2636

SALAY, CINDY ROLSTON, technical specialist, nurse; b. Roanoke, Va., July 18, 1955; d. Gilbert Wilson and Elinor Patterson (Sandridge) Rolston; m. John Matthew, July 7, 1988; 1 child, David. AAS, Va. Western Community Coll., 1976; AS, J. Sargeant Reynolds Community Coll., 1982; BS, Va. Commonwealth U., 1984. RN. Operating room RN Henrico Doctors Hosp., Richmond, Va., 1979-80; nursing supr. Johnston Willis Hosp., Richmond, 1980-87; systems analyst, coord. Health Corp Va., Richmond, 1983-87, sr. project leader, 1987-88; sr. systems analyst Hosp. Corp. Am., Nashville, 1987; sr. systems cons. IBAX Healthcare Systems, Reston, Va., 1988-94; sys. analyst MCV Hosps. Info. Sys., Richmond, Va., 1994-95; specialist HBO & Co., Atlanta, Ga., 1995—. Presbyterian. Home: 13800 Sunrise Bluff Rd Midlothian VA 23112-2512 Office: HBO & Company 301 Perimeter Center N Atlanta GA 30346

SALAZAR, RAMIRO S., library administrator; b. Del Rio, Tex., Mar. 3, 1954; s. Jesus and Juanita (Suarez) S.; m. Cynthia Castillo, Dec. 19, 1976 (div. 1990); children: Ramiro Orlando, Selinda Yvette. BA, Tex. A&I U., 1978; MLS, Tex. Woman's U., 1979. Asst. libr. dir. Val Verde County Libr., Del Rio, 1975-76; libr. Robert J. Kleberg Libr., Kingsville, Tex., 1977-78; libr. dir. Eagle Pass (Tex.) Pub. Libr., 1980-84; dir. Main Libr. San Antonio

Pub. Libr., 1984-90; dir. librs. El Paso Pub. Libr., 1991-93, Dallas Pub. Libr., 1993—; chmn. Tex. State Libr. Planning Task Force, 1991-92; active Tex. Women's U. Sch. Libr. and Info. Studies Adv. Bd., 1993—, Alliance for Higher Edn. Libr. Dirs. Coun., 1993—; trustee AMIGOS Bibliographic Coun.; bd. advs. U. N. Tex. Sch. Lib. and Info. Scis., 1993, Booker T. Washington H.S. of Performing and Visual Arts, 1995-96. Chair customer svc. steering com. City of Dallas, 1993—; chair coupon book/resident privilege card task force City of Dallas, 1995-96; active home instrn. program for presch. children Nat. Coun. Jewish Women, 1996—. Recipient H.W. Wilson Staff Devel. award jury, 1995-96. Mem. ALA, Libr. Adminstrn. and Mgmt. Assn. (bldg. and equipment sect., arch. for pub. libr. com. 1993-95, cultural diversity com. 1995—, pres.'s programs com. 1996—), Tex. Mcpl. League (resolutions com. 1995—), Tex. Mcpl. Libr. Dirs. Assn., Pub. Libr. Adminstrs. North Tex., Reforma (exec. bd. dirs.), Tex. Libr. Assn. (chmn. pubs. com. 1992-93, legis. com. 1993-95, ad hoc com. value of pub. librs. 1995—, awards com. 1995—), Jaycees. Democrat. Roman Catholic. Home: PO Box 15031 Dallas TX 75201-0031 Office: Dallas Pub Libr 1515 Young St Dallas TX 75201-5499

SALDANA, ALFONSO MANUEL, lawyer; b. Lima, Peru, Sept. 4, 1960; came to U.S. 1969.; s. Mario J. and Nelly (Davalos) S. BA, U. Miami, 1983; JD, Thomas M. Cooley Law Sch., 1986. Bar: Fla. 1987, U.S. Dist. Ct. (so. dist.) Fla. 1987, U.S. Dist. Ct. (mid. dist.) Fla. 1993, U.S. Ct. Appeals (11th cir.) 1988, U.S. Ct. Appeals (D.C. cir.) 1989, U.S. Supreme Ct. 1996. Student intern Office State Atty., Miami, Fla., 1985; grad. intern Office State Atty., 1986; asst. atty. gen. Office Atty. Gen. Fla., West Palm Beach, 1987-89, Hollywood, Fla., 1989-93; pvt. practice Miami, Fla., 1993—. Campaign asst. Reagan/Bush Presdl. Campaign, 1984. Roman Catholic. Office: PO Box 432832 Miami FL 33243-2832

SALE, THOMAS WIRT, JR., surgeon, educator; b. Hampton, Va., Feb. 26, 1926; s. Thomas Wirt Sr. and Mildred O. (Fields) S.; m. Mary Elizabeth Woodward, Dec. 17, 1949; children: Thomas W. III, Carter Woodward, John Cabell, Sidney Overton Sale Bland. Student, U. Va.; MD, Med. Coll. Va. Diplomate Am. Bd. Surgery. Intern Worcester (Mass.) City Hosp., 1952-54; resident in surgery Boston City Hosp., 1954-57; pvt. practice gen. surgery Hampton, Va., 1957-94; pres. Va. Peninsula Acad. Medicine, Newport News, Va., 1961; asst. prof. clin. surgery Ea. Va. Med. Sch., Norfolk, Va., 1989—; pres. Hampton (Va.) Med. Soc., 1966; pres. med. staff Mary Immaculate Hosp., Newport News, 1962; cons. in surgery VA Hosp., Hampton, 1967-95; bd. visitors Ea. Va. Med. Sch., Norfolk, 1984-91; pres. U.S. sect. Internat. Coll. Surgeons, Chgo., 1993. Contbr. articles to profl. jours. Pres. Va. Peninsula unit Am. Cancer Soc., 1966, Am. Heart Assn., 1970-71; bd. trustees Jamestown-Yorktown Found., Williamsburg, Va., 1981-89; Va. state pres. Nat. Soc. SAR, Louisville, 1992. Staff sgt. U.S. Army, 1944-46, ETO. Decorated Combat Infantrymans badge, Bronze Star medal, 1945; recipient Physician's Recognition award AMA, Chgo., 1969-96, Merit award of honor Internat. Coll. Surgeons, Chgo., 1993. Fellow ACS; mem. NRA (life), Southeastern Surg. Congress, Am. Legion, The Jamestowne Soc., Internat. Brotherhood Magicians (pres. Norfolk ring 1964-66), Gem and Mineral Soc. Va. Peninsula. Episcopalian. Home: 4304 Chesapeake Ave Hampton VA 23669-4638

SALEM, JOSEPH JOHN, jeweler, real estate developer; b. Corpus Christi, Tex., Dec. 29, 1920; s. Sam and Victoria (Moses) S.; m. 1952; children: Chris, Joey, Sam II. LLD (hon.), U. Tex., San Antonio, 1970. Congressman State of Tex., Austin, 1968-76; jeweler Corpus Christi; apptd. Pres.'s Kennedy and Johnson Nat. Coms. on Employment of the Handicapped and Employment of Older Worker, local chmn. state of Tex. com.; past mem. mayor's com. on mental retardation Corpus Christi Police Officers Assn. Mem. Tex. and Nueces County Heart Assn., USO Exec. Com., YMCA; mem. nat. adv. com. Brand Names Found.; mem. Nueces County Dem. Orgn.; sustaining mem. Nat. Dem. Com.; past pres. West Side Pony League; past chmn. rehab. sub com. of long range planning com. UCS; past mem. mayor's com. mental retardation Task Force Com.; past pres. Better Bus. Bur. Capt. USAF, 1941-46. Recipient UMC award Outstanding Man of Yr., Internat. Pres. award Optimists, Local Benny award Corpus Christi's Favorite Businessman, Outstanding Retailer of Yr. award Jewelers Category Brand Names Found., Cert. of Hon. Corpus Christi Classroom Tchrs. Assn., County Auditors Tex. award for Outstanding Svc., South Tex. Legislator of Yr. award Ams. in Action, Meritorious Svc. award Tex. Good Rds. and Transp. Assn., Appreciation award Tex. State Dept. of Am. Legion, Scout-A-Rama cert. Appreciation for Outstanding Work with Boy Scouts, Outstanding Svc. award Corpus Christi Police Officers and Firefighters, cert. Appreciation Boys Clubs Am., cert. Appreciation Navy Wive's Clubs Am., cert. Appreciation Lions Clubs, Kiwanis Clubs, and Civitan Clubs, award for Humanitarian Svcs. to Working People Tex. OCAW; commd. Hon. Tex. Col., Adm. in Tex. Navy; Salem auditorium named in his honor Boys and Girls Club; Salem Ball Pk. named in his honor City of Corpus Christi; Salem St. named in honor; named to Vet. Hall of Fame, 1993. Mem. Corpus Christi C. of C. (mem. mil. affairs, inter-city rels. com., aviation com., Optimists (past pres.), KC. Democrat. Roman Catholic. Office: 4350 S Alameda St Corpus Christi TX 78412-2412

SALEMI, DOMINICK JOHN, lawyer, publisher, writer; b. Bklyn., Mar. 14, 1956; s. Dominick Francis and Joan Ann (Cavallaro) S. BA, U. Notre Dame, 1978; JD, Wake Forest U., 1983. Bar: D.C. 1984. Atty. U.S. Dept. Commerce, Washington, 1984—. Publisher, editor, writer (mag. and recorded works) Brutarian, 1991—. Roman Catholic. Home: 8433 Richmond Ave Alexandria VA 22309 Office: Dept Commerc Commr Patents & Trademarks Washington DC 20231

SALERNO, PHILIP ADAMS, information systems specialist; b. Harrisburg, Pa., Oct. 25, 1953; s. Lewis Gabriel S. and Barbara Ellen (Garlinger) Hardisty. AS, Baylor U., 1975; BS in Med. Tech., Our Lady of the Lake U., 1979. Cert. med. technologist, lab. technologist. Lab. technician U.S. Army, Stuttgart, West Germany, 1971-74; instr., Acad. Health Scis. U.S. Army, Ft. Sam Houston, 1976-80; asst. instr. Baylor U., 1976-78; staff med. technologist M.D. Anderson Hosp., Houston, 1980; lab. supv. Twelve Oaks Hosp., Houston, 1980-83; clin. lab. instr., Acad. Health Scis. U.S. Army, Ft. Sam Houston, 1982-90; dir. current product engring. Community Health Computing, Houston, 1983-94; owner Salerno Systems Group, Houston, 1985-95; sr. project mgr. Systems Xcellence, Dallas, 1995-96; mgr. engring. svcs. Health Cor, Dallas, 1996—. Co-author: Basic Med. Parasitology, 1977. Del. Rep. State Conv., 1986, 88, 90; precinct chmn. Rep. Party of Harris County, Houston, 1988-92; vol. fireman Kentland, Md., 1969-73; bd. dirs. Belmont Park Townhomes, 1993-95. Named Soldier of the Year, U.S. Army Baden Wurtemburg Support Dist., Federal Republic of Germany, 1974. Mem. Soc. Armed Forces Med. Lab. Scientists; assoc. mem. Am. Soc. Clin. Pathologists. Lutheran. Home: 625 Anglewood Dr Richardson TX 75081 Office: Health Cor Ste M-2000 8150 N Central Expwy Dallas TX 75206

SALES, JAMES BOHUS, lawyer; b. Weimar, Tex., Aug. 24, 1934; s. Henry B. and Agnes Mary (Pesek) S.; m. Beuna M. Vornsand, June 3, 1956; children: Mark Keith, Debra Lynn, Travis James. BS, U. Tex., 1956, LLB with honors, 1960. Bar: Tex. 1960. Practiced in Houston, 1960—; sr. ptnr. firm, head litigation dept., mem. exec. com. Fulbright & Jaworski, 1960—; pres. State Bar of Tex., 1988-89. Author: Products Liability in Texas, 1985; co-author: Texas Torts and Remedies, 5 vols., 1986; assoc. editor Tex. Law Rev., 1960; editl. bd. Def. Law Jour.; contbr. articles to profl. jours. Trustee South Tex. Coll. Law, 1982-88, 90—, A.A. White Dispute Resolution Ctr., 1991-94; bd. dirs. Tex. Resource Ctr., 1990-95, Tex. Bar Hist. Found., 1990-96. 1st lt. USMCR, 1956-58. Named among Best Lawyers in Am., 1989-96. Fellow Internat. Acad. Trial Lawyers, Am. Coll. Trial Lawyers (state chmn. 1993-96), Am. Bd. Trial Advocates, Am. Bar Found. (sustaining life, state chmn. 1993—), Tex. Bar Found. (trustee 1991-95, vice-chmn. 1992-93, chmn. 1993-94, chair adv. bd. for planned giving 1994-97, sustaining life mem.), Houston Bar Found. (sustaining life, chmn. bd. 1982-83); mem. ABA (ho. of dels. 1984—, mem. Commn. on IOLTA 1995—), Internat. Assn. Def. Counsel, Nat. Conf. Bar Pres. (coun. 1989-92), So. Conf. Bar Pres., Def. Rsch. Inst., So. Tex. Coll. Trial Advocacy (dir. 1983-87), Fed. Bar Assn., State Bar Tex. (pres. 1988-89, bd. dirs. 1983-87, chmn. bd. 1985-86), Tex. Assn. Def. Counsel (v.p. 1977-79, 83-84), Houston Bar Assn. (officer, bd. dirs. 1970-79, pres.-elect 1979-80, pres. 1980-81), Gulf Coast Legal Found. (bd. dirs. 1982-85), Bar Assn. 5th Fed. Cir., The Forum, Westlake Club (bd. govs. 1980-85), Inns of Ct. (bd. dirs. 1981-84), Ramada-Tejas, Order of Coif. Roman Catholic. Home: 10803 Oak Creek St Houston TX 77024-3016 Office: Fulbright & Jaworski 1301 Mckinney St Houston TX 77010

SALES, JAMES WILLIAM, chemical engineer; b. Mobile, Ala., May 1, 1958; s. John Wesley and Willean (Bondurant) S.; m. Cynthia Lynn Griffis, Feb. 23, 1980; children: James William Jr., Christopher Brandon, Kimberly Nicole, Rebecca Lynn. AS, Patrick Henry Jr. Coll., 1977; BSChemE, U. Ala., 1979. Registered profl. engr., Tenn. Design engr. Eastman Chem. Co., Kingsport, Tenn., 1979-85; project engr. Ectona polyethylene terethalate project Eastman Chem. Co., London, 1985-88; engring. mgr. filtrate purge project Eastman Chem. Co., Columbia, S.C., 1989-90; engring. mgr. Ectona polyethylene terethalate project Eastman Chem. Co., London, 1990-93; engring. mgr. Mex. polyethylene terethalate project Eastman Chem. Co., Mexico City, 1993-94; bus. devel. mgr. fine chems. bus. orgn. Eastman Chem. Co., Kingsport, 1994—. Chmn. deacons First Bapt. Ch., Kingsport, 1995—, Sunday sch. dir., 1994-95; pres. Tellico Hills Home Owners Assn., Kingsport, 1988-89. Mem. AIChE, Kiwanis (sec. 1981-86), Phi Kappa Sigma (treas. 1978-79), Tau Beta Pi, Alpha Chi Omega. Office: Eastman Chem Co 1999 E Stone Dr Kingsport TN 37660-4630

SALGUEIRO, ALEX, restaurant executive; b. Havana, Cuba, Mar. 20, 1954; came to U.S., 1960; s. Francisco Raul and Hortencia (Gonzalez) S.; m. Fonda Gay Maulden, Mar. 22, 1986. AA, Miami Dade C.C., 1975; BA, Fla. Internat. U., 1978. With Burger King Corp., Miami, Fla., 1971-82; project mgr., area mgr. Burger King Corp., Atlanta, 1982-86; v.p., ptnr. Savannah (Ga.) Restaurants Corp., 1986-91; pres., chief exec. officer Savannah Restaurants Corp., 1991—. Republican. Roman Catholic. Clubs: Marshwood, Plantation (Savannah). Lodge: Rotary. Office: 9A Mall Ter Savannah GA 31406-3602

SALINAS, ALBERT, golf course architecture company executive. V.p. Leo Trevino/William Graves Inc., Dallas. Office: Leo Trevino/William Graves 16800 Dallas Pky Ste 180 Dallas TX 75248-1931

SALINAS, BARUJ, artist, architect; b. Havana, Cuba, July 6, 1935; came to U.S., 1959; s. Moises and Regina (Algazi) S.; 1 child, Shari Regina. BArch, Kent State U., 1958. Chief draftsman Calif. Exploration Co., Coral Gables, Fla., 1961-64; draftsman Stresscon, Miami, Fla., 1964-66; chief draftsman Pillsbury Co., Miami, Fla., 1966-70; artist Miami and Barcelona, Spain, 1970—; instr. Winchester Sch. Art, Barcelona, 1992, 93, N.Y. Sch. Visual Arts, Barcelona, 1993. Vol. Amnesty Internat., Paris, 1989-90; art coord. Internat. Com. for Human Rights, Miami, 1993-94, 95-96. Recipient fellowship Cintas Found., 1969, 70, 1st prize Ft. Lauderdale Mus. Art, 1969, 1st prize Cultura P.R., 1983. Democrat. Jewish. Home: 2740 SW 92nd Ave Miami FL 33165-3119

SALINAS, CARLOS FRANCISCO, dentist, educator; b. Iquique, Chile, Apr. 9, 1941; came to U.S., 1972; s. Carlos F. and Victoria (Cerda) S.; m. Maria Asunción Córdova, 1963; children: Carlos Miguel, Claudio Andres, Maria Asunción. BS, U. Chile, Santiago, 1958; DDS, U. Chile, 1963; DMD, Med. U. S.C., 1985. Cert. Fla., 1982, Tenn., 1982, S.C., 1985. Dentist Nat. Health Svc., Viña del Mar, Chile, 1963-65; pvt. practice Viña del Mar, 1963-72; fellow in medicine/genetics Johns Hopkins U., Balt., 1972-74; faculty mem. Med. Univ. S.C., Charleston, 1974-88, assoc. prof., 1988-94, prof., 1994—, dir. divsn. craniofacial genetics, 1981—; dir. craniofacial anomalies and cleft lip palate ctr. Med. U. S.C., Charleston, 1995—; faculty mem. U. Chile, Valparaiso, 1965-74; dentist Dental Ctrl. Clinic for Chilean Navy, Valparaiso, 1964-66; vis. scientist U. Montreal, 1974; internat. cons. Inter-american Coll. Physicians and Surgeons, Ptnrs. of Ams., WHO/Pan Am. Health Orgn. Editor: Genetica Craniofacial, 1979, Craniofacial Anomalies: New Perspectives, 1982, (with R.J. Jorgenson) Dentistry in the Interdisciplinary Treatment of Genetic Diseases, 1980, (with K.S. Brown) Craniofacial Mesenchyme In Morphogensis and Malformations, 1984, (with J.M. Opitz) Recent Advances in Ectodermal Dysplasias, 1988; contbr. articles to profl. jours. Bd. dirs. Ptnrs. Am. (award 1992), East Cooper Cmty. Outreach, S.C. World Trade Ctr., Charleston; chmn. bd. S.C. Hispanic Coalition, 1994—; founder Circulo Hispanoamericano de Charleston, pres. 1978-96; hon. consul of Chile, 1978—. Fogarty Internat. Rsch. fellow; grantee NIH, 1972-74, HEW, 1979-80, 80-81, 81-82, 82-83, 83-84, Dept. Health and Human Svcs., 1983-84, 84-85, March of Dimes Birth Defects Found., 1984-85, S.C. State Health and Human Svcs. Fin. Commn., 1989—. Mem. AAAS, Soc. Craniofacial Genetics (pres. 1985, 92, chmn. membership com. 1993-94), Iberoam. Soc. Human Genetics of N.Am. (v.p. 1992-94, pres. 1994—), Am. Assn. Dental Schs., Am. Soc. Human Genetics, Am. Cleft Palate and Craniofacial Anomalies Assn., Internat. Assn. for Dental Rsch., Am. Assn. for Dental Rsch., Interam. Coll. Physicians and Surgeons (bd. dirs. chpt. faculty and rschrs. 1994—), Incontinentia Pigmenti Found. (sci. adv. coun. 1995—), Med. Assn. P.R. (hon.), Peruvian Soc. Human Genetics (hon.), Med. Soc. Western Dist. P.R. (hon.). Home: 948 Equestrian Dr Mount Pleasant SC 29464-3608 Office: Med Univ SC 171 Ashley Ave Charleston SC 29425-2601

SALINGER, MARION CASTING, international studies educator, poet, consultant; b. Buffalo, May 22, 1917; d. George Alfred and Mary Helen (Knopf) C.; m. Herman Salinger, Nov. 29, 1941; children: Jill Hudson Salinger Winter, Wendy Lang, Jennifer Wilson Salinger Duffy. Student, U. Buffalo, 1936, U. Wis., 1938-40. Journalist Kenmore (N.Y.) Ind. Record, 1934; syndicated journalist Madison, Wis., 1937-39; pvt. sec. library Duke U., Durham, N.C., 1956-60, adminstrv. mgr. Ctr. for internat. Studies, 1966-85, adminstrv. coordinator Can. Studies Ctr., 1979-89; cons. on Canada Forest History Soc., Inc., 1989-92; cons. Human Resources Devel. Internat., 1992—. Poems published in mags. Kaleidoscope, N.Mex. Quar., Fantasy, Little Treasury of World Poetry, Dimension, Archive, Chronicle of Higher Edn.; editor, co-editor numerous articles and monographs; contbr. articles to profl. jours. Recipient Silver medal Women of Achievement, Durham, 1984, Exemplary Mentor award Duke U. Adminstrv. Women's Network, 1992. Mem. Assn. Can. Studies in U.S. (Donner award 1985), Soc. Internat. Devel. (pres. local chpt. 1985-92, Disting. Svc. award 1994), So Atlantic States Assn. for Asian-African Studies (exec. dir. 1980-82), Nat. Coun. Social Studies, P.E.O. Sisterhood (state pres. 1960), Internat. Visitors Coun. (bd. dirs. 1988-93). Democrat. Episcopalian. Office: 3444 Rugby Rd Durham NC 27707-5449

SALINO, JEFFREY ALAN, leasing executive; b. Reading, Pa., Aug. 6, 1960; s. Joseph Frank and Lorraine Helen (Rathgeber) S.; m. Teresa Kathleen Nowak, Oct. 20, 1984; children: Sarah Eileen, Gregory Joseph. Student, U. Vienna, 1980-81; BA in Polit. Sci. and Germanic Lang., George Washington U., 1983. Cert. comml. investment mem. Devel. asst. Stout & Teague Cos., Washington, 1983-85; dir. renewal leasing Greenhoot, Inc., Washington, 1985-87; v.p., regional leasing mgr. Heitman Properties, Arlington, Va., 1987-95, 1995—. Mem. Washington Area Comml. Brokers Coun. Inc. (comml. leasing com. 1983—), Cert. Comml. Investment Mems. (v.p. Md./D.C. chpt. 1995), Washington Assn. Realtors, Soc. for Preservation and Encouragement of Barbershop Quartet Singing in Am. (chpt. sec. 1985-86), Internat. Brotherhood Musicians. Republican. Home: 7867 Vervain Ct Springfield VA 22152-3108 Office: Heitman Properties 1330 Connecticut Ave NW Washington DC 20036

SALISBURY, ALAN BLANCHARD, information systems executive; b. Newark, Jan. 21, 1937; s. Lloyd Wade and Elizabeth Barry (Blanchard) S.; m. Florence Dorothy Conrad, May 21, 1971; children: Katherine Anne, Barbara Lynn. BS with distinction, U.S. Mil. Acad., 1958; MSEE, Stanford U., 1964, PhD, 1973; postgrad., Indsl. Coll. of Armed Forces, Washington, 1978. Commd. 2d lt. Signal Corps U.S. Army, 1958, advanced through grades to Maj. Gen., ret., 1987; asst. prof. U.S. Mil. Acad., West Point, N.Y., 1964-67; chief of data communications 1st Signal Brigade, Republic of Vietnam, 1968-69; tech. adv. Directorate of Mgmt. Info., Washington, 1970-71; dir. U.S. Army Ctr. for Tactical Computer Sci., Ft. Monmouth, N.J., 1975-77; project mgr. Operations Tactical Data Systems, Ft. Monmouth, N.J., 1978-82; program mgr. Joint Tactical Fusion Program, Washington, 1982-84; comdr. U.S. Army Info. Systems Engring., Ft. Belvoir, Va., 1984-87; pres. Contel Technology Ctr., Fairfax, Va., 1987-91; exec. v.p. Microelectronics & Computer Tech. Corp., Austin, Tex., 1991-93; pres. Learning Tree Internat. USA, Inc., Reston, Va., 1993—; bd. dirs. Sybase, Emeryville, Calif., Challenger Ctr. for Space Sci. Edn., Alexandria, Va., TelePad Corp., Herndon, Va.; trustee Mitretek Systems, Inc., McLean, Va.; bd. visitors Software Engring. Inst. Carnegie Mellon U., Coll. of Engring. U. Md.; bd. trustees Mitretek Systems, McLean, Va. Author: Microprogrammable Computer Architectures 1976, numerous articles in profl. jours.; founding editor Journal of Systems & Software, 1979-85. Decorated Bronze Star (2), 1969, D.S.M., 1987. Mem. Inst. for Elec. & Electronic Engrs. (sr.), Assn. for Computing Machinery, Armed Forces Communications & Electronics Assn. (chpt. pres. 1981-82), Phi Kappa Phi, Soc. of the Sigma Xi. Office: Learning Tree Internat 1805 Library St Reston VA 22090-5621

SALISBURY, MARGARET MARY, retired elementary school educator; b. LaGrange, Tex., Oct. 23, 1932; d. Charles Frederick and Hedwig Mary (Fajkus) Meyer; m. Harrison Bryan Salisbury, Jan. 8, 1955; children: Elaine, Kathleen, David, Stephen, Mark, Margaret II. BA, Our Lady of the Lake, San Antonio, 1954; MA, U. Tex., San Antonio, 1975. Lic. elem., secondary edn., English and sch. adminstrn. High sch. tchr. St. Joseph's Sch. for Girls, El Paso, Tex., 1954-55; tchr. 1st grade St. Patricks Cathedral Sch., El Paso, 1955; tchr. 2d grade S.W. Ind. Sch. Dist., San Antonio, 1971-74, tchr. 6th grade, 1974-75, supr. testing, reading, 1975-81, 82-86, jr. high sch. prin., 1981-82, dir. alternative sch., 1986-87, tchr. 3d grade, 1987-96; ret., 1996; pres. Cooperating Tchr./Student Tchr. U. at Tex., San Antonio, 1986-87. Mem. AAUW (chairperson pub. policy com. 1995—), Internat. Reading Assn., Tex. State Reading Assn., Alamo Reading Coun., Reading Improvement, Pres. Club, San Antonio Ret. Tchrs. Assn. Republican. Roman Catholic. Home: 126 Meadow Trail Dr San Antonio TX 78227-1639

SALLEE, BILL, business consultant; b. Muskogee, Okla., June 28, 1929; s. William Everette and Ethyle Phoebe (Youngblood) S.; m. Judith Feger Lindley, July 2, 1950; children: Charles Michael, Rebecca Jane, Paul Lindley. Student, Phillips U., 1946-47, Southeastern State U., 1947-48, Nat. Exec. Inst., 1957, So. Meth. U., 1985. Exec. Boy Scouts Am., 1957-75; spl. events producer Traders Village, Grand Prairie, Tex., 1976-89; bus. mgr. Mauldin Bus. Group, Cedar Hill, Tex., 1989—; owner Channel One Comm., Grand Prairie, 1986-88; pres. Mortgage Connections, Inc., Grand Prairie, 1992—; writer, columnist various newspapers and mags., 1989—; regional and nat. coms. Boy Scouts Am., 1957-75; seminar presentor for CPA groups, 1987-89. Author: Camp Adminstration and Management, 1968; photojournalist various positions, 1972—. Pres. Wranglers Rodeo Club, Grand Prairie, 1987-89; campaign mgr., publicist local elections, 1980—; pres. Grand Prairie Response Against Narcotics and Drugs, 1989—. With USN, 1948-51. Recipient Vol. awards City of Grand Prairie, 1988, 89. Mem. Nat. Assn. of Sportswriters and Sportscasters, Rotary (Very Involved Rotarian, 1988). Republican. Methodist. Home: 1701 British Blvd Grand Prairie TX 75050-7036

SALLIN, MICHAEL, agricultural company executive; b. 1951. MBA, HEC Bus. Sch., Paris, 1973, PhD in Internat. Fin., 1975. Student mission HEC Bus. Sch., South Africa, 1975-78; with Daval Steel Product, Inc., N.Y.C., 1978-80; pres., dir. I. M. G. Enterprise, Inc., Groveland, Fla., 1979—. Office: I M G Enterprise Inc 7836 Cherry Lake Rd Groveland FL 34736-9007

SALLIS, JAMES, writer; b. Helena, Ark., Dec. 21, 1944; s. Chappelle Horace and Mildred Clodine (Liming) S. Student, Tulane U., 1961-63, U. Tex., 1985-87. tchr. intensive writing workshops Clarion (Pa.) Coll., U. Wash., Tulane U., Loyola U.; guest lectr. modern poetry, European lit., art; writer short stories, essays, poetry and trans. Editor New Worlds 1966-68; editor: (anthologies) The War Book, 1972, The Shores Beneath, 1973; features writer, reviewer, columnist Tex. Jazz, 1980-83, lead book reviewer Dallas Morning News, 1981-83; book reviewer Washington Post Book World, L.A. Times, 1993—; author: A Few Last Words, 1972, The Guitar Players, 1982, 94, Jazz Guitars, 1984, The Long-Legged Fly, 1992, Saint Glinglin (translator), 1993, Difficult Lives, 1993, Moth, 1993, Black Hornet, 1994, Limits of the Sensible World, 1994, Renderings, 1995, The Guitar in Jazz, 1996, Ash of Stars: On the Writings of Samuel R. Delany, 1996.

SALLIS, JOHN CLEVELAND, philosophy educator; b. Poplar Grove, Ark., June 8, 1938; s. Chappelle Horace Jr. and Mildred (Liming) S.; m. Lois P., Dec. 27, 1959; children: Lauren Michel Lewis, Kathryn Ann Sallis. BA, U. Ark., 1959; MA, Tulane U., 1962, PhD, 1964. Instr. U. of the South, Sewanee, Tenn., 1964-66; assoc. prof. Duquesne U., Pitts., 1966-70, prof., 1970-83; Arthur J. Schmidt prof. Loyola U., Chgo., 1983-90; W. Alton Jones prof. Vanderbilt U., Nashville, 1990-96; prof. philosophy Pa. State U., 1996—. Author: Phenomenology and the Return to Beginnings, 1973, Being and Logos: The Way of Platonic Dialogue, 1975, The Gathering of Reason, 1980, (German translation 1983), Delimitations: Phenomenology and the End of Metaphysics, 1986 (French translation 1990), Spacings-of Reason and Imagination, 1987, Echoes: After Heidegger, 1990, Crossings: Nietzsche and the Space of Tragedy, 1991, Double Truth, 1994, Stone, 1994; editor: Heidegger and the Path of Thinking, 1970, Radical Phenomenology: Essays in Honor of Martin Heidegger, 1978, Studies in Phenomenology and the Human Sciences, 1981, Merleau-Ponty: Perception, Structure, Language, 1981, Philosophy and Archaic Experience: Essays in Honor of Edward G. Ballard, 1982, Husserl and Contemporary Thought, 1983, Deconstruction and Philosophy: The Texts of Jacques Derrida, 1988, Reading Heidegger: Commemorations, 1993, (with K. Maly) Heraclitean Fragments, 1980, (with H. Silverman and T. Seebohm) Continental Philosophy in America, 1983, (with J. Taminaux and G. Moneta) The Collegium Phaenomenologicum: The First Ten Years, 1988. Recipient Danforth Grad. fellowship, 1959-64, Alexander von Humboldt-Stiftung Dozentenstipendium, 1974-75, Fritz Thyssen-Stiftung Rsch. grantee, 1979, Faculty Rsch. grant Duquesne U., 1981, Pres.' award for Excellence in Scholarship, 1981, Am. Coun. of Learned Socs. fellowship, 1982-83, Alexander von Humboldt-Stiftung grant, 1989, 92-93, NEH grant, 1989. Home: 811 Evansdale Dr Nashville TN 37220-1511 Office: Vanderbilt U Philosophy Dept Nashville TN 37240

SALLOME, SAM, electrical engineer, writer; b. Rochester, N.Y.; s. Charles Russel and Jenny Louise (Caccamise) S. AAS, Rochester Inst. Tech., 1975; BSEE, 1975. Registered profl. engr., Minn.; cert. tchr., Calif. Elec. engr. Eighth Army Faculty Engrs., Korea, 1976-78, U.S. Command, Hawaii, 1978-80, Planning Dept., Design Divsn., Pearl Harbor, Hawaii, 1980-81, Command Fleet Activities, Okinawa, Japan, 1981-82; chief engr. Combined Field Army, Uijongbu, Korea, 1982-84; elec. engr. Hdqrs. V Corps, Frankfurt, Germany, 1984-85, Def. Supply Ctr., Richmond, Va., 1985-87; chief engr. 1st Signal Bd., Army, Seoul, Korea, 1987-91; elec. engr. Def. Supply Ctr., Richmond, 1991—. Author: The Lot, 1996. Home: 10752 W Providence Rd Richmond VA 23236

SALMAGGI, GUIDO GODFREY, former diplomat, opera impresario; b. Bklyn., July 22, 1916; s. Alfredo and Elvira (Canzano) S.; m. Nancy Stair, Feb. 11, 1944 (div. Oct. 1974); child: Linda; m. Maria Gargenti. Grad. h.s., Bklyn.; student, Bklyn. Conservatory of Music, Sch. of Drama & Arts, L.A. Artistic dir. N.Y. Opera Festival, Inc., Washington, 1956-64; artistic advisor Honolulu Symphony Opera, 1960-62; genl. dir. Bklyn. Opera Co., 1960-70; dir. of auditoriums City and County of Honolulu, 1969-71; with pub. rels. Hyatt Regency Waikiki Hotel, Honolulu, 1976-88; vice consul of Italy State of Hawaii, San Francisco, 1967-88. Opera debut in Verdi's La Traviata, N.Y. Hippodrome Theatre, 1938; sang national anthem for all U.S. Presidents from Franklin D. Roosevelt to George Bush; columnist Kahala Press Newspaper, 1972-78. Pres. Sons of Italy, Honolulu, 1969-71; dean Consular Corps. of Hawaii, 1973-75. Sgt. U.S. Army Spec. Svcs., PTO, 1941-45. Recipient Medal of Mil. Merit, U.S. Army, Honolulu, 1945; knighted Commendatore, Sons of Italy, 1988. Roman Catholic.

SALMON, EDWARD LLOYD, JR., bishop; b. Jan. 30, 1934; s. Edward Lloyd Sr. and Helen Bernice (Burley) S.; m. Louise Hack, 1972; children: Catherine, Edward III. BA, U. of the South, 1956; BD, Va. Theol. Seminary, 1960. Ordained to deaconate Episc. Ch., 1960, to priesthood, 1961. Vicar St. Andrew's Ch., Rogers, Ark.; rector St. Andrew's Ch., Rogers, 1963-68; vicar St. James Ch., Eureka Springs, Ark., St. Thomas Ch., Springdale, Grace Ch., Siloam Springs; assoc. St. Paul's Ch., Fayetteville, 1968, rector, 1968-78; rector Ch. St. Michael and St. George, St. Louis, 1978-90; elected bishop Diocese S.C., 1990—; chmn. bd. dirs. Speak, Inc., The Anglican Digest; trustee Univ. of South, Nashotah House Seminary, Voorhees Coll., Denmark, S.C.;pres. Kanuga Confs., Inc.; chmn. Anglican Inst. Office: PO Box 20127 Charleston SC 29413-0127

SALMON, EMILY JONES, historian, editor; b. Richmond, Va., Dec. 12, 1947; m. John S. Salmon, May 27, 1978. BS in Psychology, Va. Commonwealth U., 1970; MA in History, N.C. State U., 1973. Archivist N.C. State Dept. Archives and History, Raleigh, 1971-73; archivist Va. State Libr., Richmond, 1973-78, asst. editor publs. br., 1978-82; assoc. editor, historian, copy editor, computer systems mgr. Publs./Cultural Affairs divsn. The Libr. of Va., Richmond, 1982—; speaker in field. Compiler: Treasurer's Office Inventory, 1977, (with John S. Salmon) Office of The Second Auditor Inventory, 1981; editor: A Hornbook of Virginia History, 3d edit., 1983; co-editor: (with Edward D.C. Campbell Jr.) The Hornbook of Virginia History, 4th edit., 1994; co-author: (with John S. Salmon) Franklin County Virginia, 1786-1986: A Bicentennial History, 1993; reviewer books and exhibits; contbr. numerous articles to profl. jours. Recipient award of Excellence, Printing Industry of the Carolinas, 1994, cert. of commendation Am. Assn. State and Local History, 1994, 95, GODORT award for Notable State Docs., ALA, 1995. Mem. Va. Hist. Soc., Nat. Trust for Hist. Preservation, So. Hist. Assn., Chesterfield Hist. Soc. Baptist. Home: 5102 King William Rd Richmond VA 23225-3024 Office: The Libr of Va 11th St At Capitol Sq Richmond VA 23219

SALOMONE, WILLIAM GERALD, lawyer; b. Flushing, N.Y., Apr. 14, 1948; s. Harry and Mary (Tartaro) S.; m. Mary Jo Piano, July 22, 1978; children: Jennifer Ann, Julie Marie, Joseph William. BCE, Manhattan Coll., 1970; MSCE, UCLA, 1971; PhD in Civil Engring., Purdue U., 1978; JD, U. Fla., 1985. Bar: Fla., U.S. Dist. Ct. (mid. dist.) Fla.; registered profl. engr., N.Y., N.J., Ill., Fla., Md., Ga., Ala. Rsch. fellow UCLA, 1970-71; project engr. Dames & Moore, Cranford, N.J., 1971-75; rsch. asst. Purdue U., West Lafayette, Ind., 1975-78; project mgr. Woodward-Clyde Cons., Chgo., 1978-80; prin. geotech. engr. Fluor Power Svcs., Chgo., 1980-81; v.p., dir. geotech. engring. Bromwell Engring., Inc., Lakeland, Fla., 1981-82; atty. at law Sarasota, Fla., 1986—; Author: Solomon on Mediation: A Practice and Procedure Handbook, Earth And Its People, How Can We Progress, The Presidential Pager; cons. William G. Salomone, Lakeland, 1982-86; pvt. practice cons., Sarasota, 1986—; adj. prof. bus. law U. Fla., 1985-86; adj. prof. U. South Fla., 1985, 90-96, pvt. mediator, Sarasota, 1987—, pvt. arbitrator, Sarasota, 1989—; mediator Fla. Cir. Ct., 1991—, mediator U.S. dist. ct., middle dist., 1996— ; spl. master code enforcement Sarasota County, Fla., 1991, 92; judge Lakeland Regional High Sch. Sci. Fair, 1983, NFL Sunshine Debate Tournament Nat. Forensic League, Sarasota, 1991; chmn. citizens adv. com. Sarasota-Manatee Met. Planning Orgn., 1991-92; vice chmn. citizens adv. com. Sarasota Bay Nat. Estuary Program, 1992-93; invitee Am. environ. law del. to Peoples Republic of China, Japan, Eng., Fed. Republic of Germany and Poland, 1988, 91 for citizens ambassador program People to People Internat. NDEA Title IV fellow UCLA, 1970-71, ; recipient Letters of Commendation, Mayor of Lakeland, Sheriff of Bartow, Fla., Dept. Army C.E. Mem. ASCE (Young Civil Engr. of Yr. 1982, letter of commendation, bd. county commrs.), ASTM, Am. Trial Lawyers Assn., Am. Arbitration Assn. Inc. (panel arbitrators and mediators), Internat. Soc. Soil Mechanics and Found. Engring., NSPE (coll. scholarship com. 1983), Fla. Engring. Soc. (Young Engr. of Yr. 1983, Journalism award 1992), Chi Epsilon, Tau Beta Pi. Office: PO Box 15 Sarasota FL 34230-0015

SALOOM, KALISTE JOSEPH, JR., lawyer, retired judge; b. Lafayette, La., May 15, 1918; s. Kaliste and Asma Ann (Boustany) S.; m. Yvonne Adelle Nassar, Oct. 19, 1958; children: Kaliste III, Douglas James, Leanne Isabelle, Gregory John. BA with high distinction, U. Southwestern La., 1939; JD, Tulane U., 1942. Bar: La. 1942. Atty. City of Lafayette (La.), 1948-52; judge City and Juvenile Ct., Lafayette, 1952-93, ret., 1993; judge pro tempore La. Ct. Appeal 3d Cir., 1992; of counsel Saloom & Saloom, Lafayette, La., 1993—; tech. adviser Jud. Adminstrn. of Traffic Cts.; mem. jud. coun. La. Supreme Ct., 1960-64; bd. dirs. Nat. Ctr. for State Cts., Williamsburg, Va., 1978-84, adv. coun., 1984—, mem. assocs. com., 1986— (Disting. Svc. award Trial Judge on State Level 1988); mem. Nat. Hwy. Traffic Safety Adminstrn. Adv. Com., U.S. Dept. Transp., 1977-80, Nat. Com. on Uniform Traffic Laws, 1986; expert panel Drunk Driving Protection Act U.S. Congress, 1989-91. With U.S. Army, 1942-45. mem. editorial bd. Tulane Law Rev., 1941; contbr. articles to profl. jours. Recipient Civic Cup, City of Lafayette, 1965, Pub. Svc. award U.S. Dept. Transp., 1980, Disting. Jurist award Miss. State U. Pre-Law Soc., 1987, Disting. Svc. award Nat. Ctr. for State Cts., 1988, Disting. La. Jurist award La. State Bar Found., 1992. Mem. ABA (Benjamin Flaschner award 1981, vice chair JAD com. on traffic ct. program 1989-95), Am. Judges Assn. (William H. Burnett award 1982), Nat. Coun. Juvenile Ct. Judges, La. City Judges Assn. (past pres.), La. Juvenile Ct. Judges Assn. (past pres.), Am. Judicature Soc. (panel drafting La. children's code 1989-91), Order of Coif, Equestrian Order of Holy Sepulchre (knight), Oakbourne Country Club, KC. Democrat. Roman Catholic. Home: 502 Marguerite Blvd Lafayette LA 70503-3138 Office: 211 W Main St Lafayette LA 70501-6843

SALTER, DAVID WYATT, secondary school educator; b. Augusta, Ga., Aug. 10, 1950; s. Wyatt Jackson and Annie Lee (Coleman) S.; m. Dorothy Mikell Fishburne, Aug. 11, 1973; 1 child, Caroline Elizabeth. BS, U. S.C., 1973, MEd, 1977, postgrad., 1982-92; postgrad., Clemson U., 1985. Cert. tchr., S.C. Tchr. biology Aiken (S.C.) High Sch., 1973—, chair dept. biology, 1985—; curriculum assoc. for h.s. sci., Sch. Dist. of Aiken County, 1994—, adult edn. tchr., 1976-85; bd. dirs. S.C. Jr. Acad. Sci., 1984—; mem. adult edn. curriculum com. S.D. Dept. Edn., 1984; mem. state textbook com., 1989, 92. Organist Warrenville (S.C.) United Meth. Ch., 1963-91, 93—; speaker Prayer Breakfast for High Sch. Srs. St. John's United Meth. Ch., Aiken, 1984; mem. ednl. adv. com. Aiken County Human Rels. Commn., 1993-95. Recipient Svc. award to S.C. Jr. Acad. Sci., 1994; named Outstanding Tchr. in Math. and Sci., Sm. Nuclear Soc. Savannah River Sect., 1991-92, Midlands Sci. Tchr. of Yr., U. S.C. chpt. Sigma Xi, 1994, S.C. Acad. Sci. award Excellence in Sci. or Math. Teaching, 1995. Mem. NEA, Nat. Biology Tchrs. Assn., S.C. Edn. Assn., Aiken County Edn. Assn., S.C. Acad. Sci., S.C. Assn. Biology Tchrs. (2d v.p. 1993-94, 1st v.p. 1994-95, pres. 1996), S.C. Suprs. Assn., S.C. Sci. Coun., Nat. Sci. Tchrs. Assn., Am. Guild Organists (sub-dean Augusta chpt. 1993-94, dean Augusta chpt. 1994-96). Methodist. Home: PO Box 904 52 Sunnyside Ln Aiken SC 29803-9420 Office: Aiken High Sch 211 Rutland Dr Aiken SC 29801-4007

SALTER, LANORA JEANETTE, corporate financial officer; b. Omaha, Nebr., June 7, 1964; d. Phillip Ray Sr. and Charlene (Sanford) Hinton; m. Howard Douglas Salter, Mar. 26, 1964; children: Ryan Douglas, Erin Jeanette, Evan Tainter. AS, Chattochee Valley C.C., 1988; diploma, Am. Inst. Banking, 1988; BS, Spring Hill Coll., 1995. Office mgr. Zales, Mobile, Ala., 1983-85; customer svc. rep. Columbus (Ga.) Bank & Trust, 1985-88; adminstrv. asst. First Atlanta Bank, Augusta, Ga., 1988-90; customer svc. specialist Am. South Bank, Mobile, 1990-92; v.p. finance adminstrn. Performance Rehab. Assocs., Inc., Fairhope, Ala., 1992—; treas. bd. dirs. AIB, 1989-90. tutor Am. Literacy Coun., 1994. Republican. Episcopalian. Office: Performance Rehab Assoc Inc PO Box 1100 Point Clear AL 36564

SALTER, LEO GUILFORD, mental health services professional; b. Atlanta, Nov. 12, 1937; s. Robert Franklin and Era Mae (Mask) S.; m. Evelyn Sue Clements. BA, Ga. State U., 1962; MEd, U. Ga., 1966; PhD, U. So. Miss., 1972. Lic. clin. psychologist, Fla.. Exec. dir. Human Resources Ctr., Daytona Beach, Fla., 1975-80; asst. dir. ACT Corp., Daytona Beach, 1980-85, dir. psychology svcs., 1986-91; pres. Behavioral Health Svcs., Daytona Beach, 1988—; adj. prof. Stetson U., Deland, Fla., 1980-91; clin. cons. West Volusia Meml. Hosp., Deland, 1988—; bd. dirs. ARCC Corp., Daytona Beach. Author: Labor Research Project, 1968. Del. Fla. State Dem. Conv., Hollywood, 1984; mem. Dem. Exec. Com., Volusia County, 1991. With USN, 1958-62. Recipient Excellence in Crime and Drug Intervention award ARP, Daytona Beach, 1987, Spl. Commendation award Nat. Coun. Cmty. Mental Health, Washington, 1980, Outstanding Svc. award Dist. Mental Health Bd., Volusia County, 1978, Outstanding Vol. Svc. award State of Fla., 1978, Spl. Commendation award Fla. Coun. for Cmty. Mental Health, 1993, Clinician of Yr. award ACT Corp., 1995. Mem. APA, Fla. Psychol. Assn. Home: 1980 Reynolds Rd De Leon Springs FL 32130-3262 Office: ACT Corp 1220 Willis Ave Daytona Beach FL 32114-2810

SALTERS, RICHARD STEWART, engineering company executive; b. St. Johns, Mich., Apr. 4, 1951; s. Stewart Arthur and Mary Ann (Eiseler) S.; m. Patricia Lynn Shumsky, Oct. 23, 1971 (div. Mar. 1982); children: Tiffani, Destiny. BS in Engring., Purdue U., 1974. Field engr. Henkels & McCoy, Inc., Blue Bell, Pa., 1972-77; area mgr. engring. dept. Harris McBurney Co., Inc., Jackson, Mich., 1977-81; project engr. Lambic Telcom, Inc., Ridgewood, N.J., 1981-82; pres. S & H Assocs., Inc., Lafayette, La., 1982—. Mem. Engring. Soc. of Detroit, City Club of Lafayette. Roman Catholic. Office: S & H Assocs Inc PO Box 52721 Lafayette LA 70505-2721

SALTHOUSE, THOMAS NEWTON, cell biologist, biomaterial researcher; b. Fleetwood, U.K., Mar. 8, 1916; came to U.S., 1960; s. William and Edith Alice (Croft) S.; m. Mary Reynolds, Apr. 30, 1942; children: Andrew John, Robert William. Diplomate Royal Microscopical Soc. Sr. technologist U. Coll. E. Africa, Uganda, 1947-56; rsch. assoc. Atomic Energy Can., 1957-60; asst. pathologist E.I. DuPont, 1960-62; sr. scientist E.R. Squibb & Sons, 1962-68; sect. mgr. Ethicon Rsch. Found., 1968-81; vis. prof. bioengineering Clemson U., 1982-88. Author: (with others) Enzyme Histochemistry in Fundamentals of Biocompatibility, 1981, Biocompatibility of Sutures in Biocompatibility in Clinical Practice, 1982, Implant Shape and Surface in Biomaterials in Reconstructive Surgery, 1983; co-editor Soft Tissue Histology in Handbook of Biomaterials, 1986, 2d edit., 1996; editl. bd. Jour. Biomed. Material Rsch., 1978-84; contbr. articles to profl. jours. Recipient Phillip B. Hoffman award, 1974. Fellow N.Y. Acad. Scis., Inst. Biomed. Sci. London, Royal Photographic Soc. London; mem. Soc. for Biomaterials (sec., treas. 1976-78, pres. 1980-81, Clemson award 1978), Inst. Biomed. Scis., Dist. Sci. Ethicon Divsn. of Johnson Johnson (ret.). Home: 2825 Carter Rd Unit 18 Sumter SC 29150-1713

SALTIEL, JACK, chemistry educator; b. Salonica, Greece; s. Albert and Flora (Altcheh) S.; m. Terri Rose Saltiel, Sept. 14, 1965. BA, Rice U., Houston, 1960; PhD, Calif. Inst. Tech., 1964. NSF postdoctoral fellow U. Calif., Berkeley, 1964; prof. chemistry Fla. State U., Tallahassee, 1965—, assoc. chair Grad. Studies, 1993-95; lectr. Robert A. Welch Found., Tex., 1990. Contbr. articles to profl. jours. NSF grantee, 1965—; Alfred P. Sloan Found. fellow, 1971-73. Mem. Am. Chem. Soc., Inter-Am. Photochem. Soc., European Photochem. Assn., Am. Soc. for Photobiology, Sigma Xi, Phi Lambda Upsilon. Office: Fla State U Dept Chemistry Tallahassee FL 32306-3006

SALTMARSH, SARA ELIZABETH, lawyer; b. Jacksonville, Fla., Nov. 15, 1956; d. Ernest Olmstead and Anne (Frankenberg) S. Student, Randolph-Macon Woman's Coll., 1974-76; BA in English with honors magna cum laude, Fla. State U., 1978; postgrad., Iowa State U., 1980-81; JD, U. Tex., 1986. Bar: Tex. 1987; cert. family law. Assoc. Ausley & Slaikeu, P.C., Austin, Tex., 1987-90, Law Offices of Edwin J. Terry, Jr., Austin, 1990-92; pvt. practice law Austin, 1992—; mem. security com. Travis County Commr.'s Ct., 1991-93. Editor: Reference Guide to Travis County Practice, 1991, 92, 93, 95, 96. Givens Disting. scholar, 1974, Lyndon Baines Johnson Meml. scholar, 1976; recipient Am. Jur. award Wills and Estates, 1986, Marital Relations and Divorce, 1986. Mem. ABA, ATLA, Am. Inns of Ct. (barrister), Coll. State Bar Tex., Pro Bono Coll. State Bar Tex., Tex. Acad. Family Law Specialists, Tex. Exes, Travis County Bar Assn. (sec.-treas. family law sect. 1989-90, v.p. 1990-91, pres. 1991-92, bd. dirs. 1991-92, chair mentor program com. 1993-94, 96—), Williamson County Bar Assn., Austin Young Lawyers Assn. (chmn. It's the Law com. 1990-91), Travis County Women Lawyers Assn., Austin Mus. Art, Fla. State U. Alumni Assn. (life), Sierra Club, Phi Beta Kappa, Lambda Iota Tau. Democrat. Office: 805 W 10th St Ste 200 Austin TX 78701-2038

SALTONSTALL, NATHANIEL, educational consultant; b. Dedham, Mass., June 27, 1928; s. Philip Leveritt and Kathryn Elizabeth (Lapham) S.; m. Elizabeth C. Sibley, July 29, 1950; children: Karen Hasler, Timothy S., Susan S. Duncan, Nathaniel. BA, Yale U., 1950; MALS, Wesleyan U., Middletown, Conn., 1956. Tchr. Mooreland H.S., New Britain, Conn., 1952-54; tchr., adminstr. Kingswood Sch., West Hartford, Conn., 1955-62; headmaster Lancaster (Pa.) CDS, 1963-65, Chestnut Hill Acad., Phila., 1966-73, Asheville (N.C.) CDS, 1974-79; cons. Ind. Ednl. Svcs., Inc., Princeton, N.J., 1979-92; mem. bd. Pa. Sch. for Deaf, Phila., 1965-70, Madera Sch., McLean, Va., 1970-74, Ind. Ednl. Svcs., Princeton, 1965-75. Trustee Fla. Conservation Assn., Sarasota, 1985—, Island Inst., Rockland, Maine, 1990—, Pelican Man Bird Sanctuary, Sarasota, 1991-93; trustee, pres. Jameson Point Assn., Rockland, 1988-91. Republican. Episcopalian. Home: 891 Freeling Dr Sarasota FL 34242

SALTS, NANCY LEE, critical care, emergency nurse; b. Deer Run, W.Va., Nov. 19, 1945; d. Ralph A. and Neva A. (Mitchell) Rexrode; m. R.J. Salts, Apr. 20, 1973; children: Jason L., Angela S. AS, Fla. Keys Community Coll., Key West, 1980. RN, Iowa, Nebr., La.; cert. in advanced cardiac life support. ICU and med.-surg. nurse Community Meml. Hosp., Missouri Valley, Iowa; telemetry nurse Bergen Mercy Hosp., Omaha; emergency room and telemetry nurse Immanuel Med. Ctr., Omaha; emergency room pool nurse Pendleton Meml. Meth. Hosp., New Orleans, asst. head nurse emergency dept., 1993—. Vol. co-facilitator for systematic tng. for effective parenting; facilitator Navy Alcohol and Drug Safety Action Program.

SALTZ, IVAN K(ENNETH), data processing executive; b. Ithaca, N.Y., Apr. 12, 1949; s. Fred and Gertrude (Miller) S.; 1 child, Jason Vincent. BSEE, Rensselaer Poly. Inst., Troy, N.Y., 1971. Engr. ADT Security Sys., N.Y.C., 1972-74; software program mgr. Coulter Electronics, Hialeah, Fla., 1974-80; mgr. East sys. engring. Tex. Instruments, Dallas, 1980-85; pres. I-Square Corp., Cooper City, Fla., 1985-95, InfoSci. Inc., Plantation, Fla., 1996—; bd. dirs. Purtech Co., Plantation, Fla. Patentee in field. Mem. IEEE, ACM, Ind. Computer Cons. Assn. Office: InfoSci Inc PO Box 292457 Davie FL 33329-2457

SALTZ, RENATO, plastic surgeon; b. Uruguaiana, Brazil, Aug. 29, 1956; came to U.S., 1982; s. Jayme and Berta Saltz; m. Marcia Bartczak, Mar. 6, 1982; children: Bianca, Felipe. MD, U. Fed. Rio, Grande do Sul, Porto Alegre, 1980; postgrad., U. Ala., 1987-89, Med. Coll. Ga., 1990-92. Diplomate Am. Bd. Surgery, Am. Bd. Plastic Surgery. Mem. med. staff U. Fed. Rio, 1975-80; intern in gen. surgery Jackson Meml. Hosp., Miami, Fla., 1982-83, resident in gen. surgery, 1983-86, chief resident in gen. surgery, 1986-87; resident in plastic surgery U. Ala., Birmingham, Ala., 1987-88; chief resident in plastic surgery U. Ala., Birmingham, 1989, fellow in hand, aesthetic and microsurgery, 1989-90; plastic surgeon Med. Coll. Ga., Augusta, 1990-94, asst. prof. sect. plastic surgery dept. surgery, 1990—; assoc. prof. plastic reconstruct surgery U. Utah, 1994—; dir. microsurgery and rsch. lab. sect. plastic surgery Med. Coll. Ga., Augusta, 1990—; lectr., presenter in field; vis. prof. divsn. plastic surgery W.Va. U., Morgantown, 1989, vis. prof. divsn. plastic surgery, U. Ala., Birmingham, 1991; vis. prof. divsn. plastic surgery Fundação Faculdade Fed. Ciêcias Médicas de Porto Alegre, Brazil, 1993. Contbr. articles to profl. publs., chpts. to books; author videotapes. Recipient 3d prize in resident competition Southeastern Soc. Plastic and Reconstructive Surgeons, 1988, 2d prize in resident competition Southeastern Soc. Plastic and Reconstructive Surgeons, 1989. Fellow ACS, Internat. Coll. Surgeons; mem. AMA, Am. Burn Assn., Am. Soc. Reconstructive Microsurgery, Plastic Surgery Rsch. Coun., Am. Soc. Plastic and Reconstructive Surgery, Inc., Jackson Med. Soc., Brazilian Plastic Surgery Soc., Southeastern Surg. Congress, Richmond County Med. Soc., Rocky Mountain Assn. Plastic and Reconstructive Surgeons. Office: Plastic Surgery 3C-127 50 N Medical Dr Salt Lake City UT 84132-0001

SALTZMAN, EDWARD JACOB, retired pediatrician; b. Phila., Dec. 9, 1926; s. Maurice and Sophia Saltzman; m. Joan Gloria; children: Edward Jr., Joel, Robert. MD, Jefferson Med. Coll., 1949. Diplomate Am. Bd. Pediatrics. Pediatrician Pediatric Assocs., Hollywood, Fla., 1955-90; clin. prof. U. Miami Sch. Medicine, 1962—. Editor: Management of Pediatric Practice, 1989. Capt. USMC, 1953-55. Mem. Am. Acad. Pediats. (chair sect. on adminstrn. and practice mgmt.). Home: 12827 Cinnamon Way Palm City FL 34990

SALTZMAN, IRENE CAMERON, perfume manufacturing executive, art gallery owner; b. Cocoa, Fla., Mar. 23, 1927; d. Argyle Bruce and Marie T. (Neel) Cameron; m. Herman Saltzman, Mar. 23, 1946 (dec. May 1986); children: Martin Howard (dec.), Arlene Norma Hanly. Owner Irene Perfume and Cosmetics Lab., Jacksonville, Fla., 1972—, Irene Gallery of Art, Jacksonville, 1973—. Mem. Cummer Gallery of Art, Jacksonville, 1972—, Jacksonville Gallery of Art, 1972—; mem. Jacksonville and Beaches Conv. and Vis. Bur. Mem. Aircraft Owners and Pilots Assn., USAF Assn., Jacksonville C. of C. (mem. downtown coun.), U.S. C. of C., Ret. Judge Advocates Assn. of USAF (hon.), First Coast Women in Internat. Trade, Cosmetic, Toiletry and Fragrance Assn., Jacksonville Navy Flying Club, Ponte Vedra Club. Democrat. Episcopalian. Home: 2701 Ocean Dr S Jacksonville FL 32250-5946

SALTZMAN, MARVIN, art educator; b. Chgo., June 16, 1931; s. John and Annie (Elizer) S.; m. Jacquelyn L. Friedman, June 20, 1954; children: Paul A., Leslie Saltzman Kriezman. BFA, U. So. Calif., 1958, MFA, 1959. Asst. prof. Ea. Oreg. Coll., La Grande, Oreg., 1962-66, U. So. Calif., L.A., 1966; assoc. prof. U. N.C., Chapel Hill, 1967-71, prof., 1971—; studio chmn. U. N.C., Chapel Hill, 1967-75, chair divsn. of fine arts, 1976-79. Exhibited in group shows at N.C. Mus. of Art, Portland Mus. of Art, L.A. County Mus. of Art, Ackland Mus. of Art, Nat. Acad. of Sci., Coll. Libr. of Congress, N.C. Mus. of Art, others; represented by Novus Inc., Atlanta, Raleigh Contemporary Gallery. Sgt. U.S. Army, 1951-53. Home: 717 Emory Dr Chapel Hill NC 27514

SALVATORI, VINCENT LOUIS, corporate executive; b. Phila., Apr. 22, 1932; s. Louis and Lydia (Tofani) S.; m. Carol Hope Rissmiller, 1989; children: Leslie Ann, Robert Louis, Sandra Ann, Stephanie Marie. Diploma, Temple U., 1954; BSEE, Pa. State U., 1958. Dept. head Radiation Systems, Inc., McLean, Va., 1966-68; founder, v.p. Quest Rsch. Corp., McLean, Va., 1968-80; exec. v.p. QuesTech, Inc., McLean, Va., 1980-88; pres., CEO, QuesTech, Inc., Falls Church, Va., 1988-91, chmn., CEO, 1991—, also bd. dirs.; bd. dirs. QuesTech Svc. Co., QuesTech Pkg., Inc.; chmn. Dynamic Engring., Inc. Author: Investigations into Microwave Multipath Interferometer, 1959,Investigation of Luxembourg Effect Utilizing Cubic Function Solid State Devices, 1960, Factors Influencing Communications with Satellites, 1959. Pres. PTA, Springhill Sch., Fairfax County, Va., 1973. Sgt. USAF, 1948-52. Mem. IEEE, AAAS, Assn. for Corp. Growth (D.C. chpt.), Am. Def. Preparedness Assn., Armed Forces Comm. and Electronics Assn., Am. Mgmt. Assn., Security Affairs Support Assn., Annapolis Yacht Club. Office: QuesTech Inc 7600W Leesburg Pike Falls Church VA 22043-2004

SALYER, JERRY L(EE), judge; b. Binger, Okla., Sept. 20, 1936; s. Ervin D. and Ruth (McCollum) S.; m. Lucy W. Salyer, 1959 (div. 1985); children: Cynthia J., Derek S., Leigh Michelle; m. Sondra J. Goode, 1989 (div. 1992). AA, Cameron Coll., Lawton, Okla., 1956; BA, U. Okla., 1959, JD, 1961; grad., Hastings Coll., 1974. Bar: Okla. 1961, U.S. Ct. Mil. Appeals 1962, U.S. Dist. Ct. (we. dist.) Okla. 1967, U.S. Ct. Appeals (10th cir.) 1971. Assoc. Mosteller, Fellers, Andrews, Snider & Baggett, Oklahoma City, 1961; atty. Judge Advocate Gen. Corps U.S. Army, Columbia, S.C., 1961-65; legal asst. Okla. Supreme Ct., Oklahoma City, 1965-67; ptnr. Batchelor, Salyer & Johnson, Oklahoma City, 1967-79; pvt. practice Oklahoma City, 1979-88; judge State of Okla. Workers' Compensation Ct., Oklahoma City, 1988—, presiding judge, 1993—; atty. Okla. City Urban Renewal Auth., 1967-79, auth. counsel, 1979-88; auth. counsel Oklahoma City Redevel. Auth., 1985-88. Editor: Oklahoma Law Rev., 1961. Pres. We. Okla. chpt. Muscular Dystrophy Assn., Oklahoma City, 1975, v.p., 1974. Col. USAR, 1959—. Recipient diploma in humanities and judging, Am. Acad. Judicial Edn., 1994. Mem. ABA, Okla. Bar Assn., Okla. County Bar Assn., Order of Coif, Phi Delta Phi. Home: 2208 NW 46th St Oklahoma City OK 73112-8845 Office: State Okla Worker's Compensation Ct 1915 N Stiles Ave Oklahoma City OK 73105-4914

SALYER, KENNETH E., surgeon; b. Kansas City, Kans., Aug. 18, 1936; s. Everett A. and Laurene S.; m. Luci Lara-Salyer; children: Kenneth E. Jr., Leigh Green-Salyer. BS, U. Mo., 1958; MD, U. Kans., 1962. Intern Parkland Meml. Hosp., Dallas, 1962-63; resident in gen. surgery Parkland Meml. Hosp., 1963-67; fellow in surgery U. Tex. SW Sch. Med., Dallas, 1965-67; founder, dir. residency tng. program U. Tex. SW Sch. Med., 1969-78; prof. surgery, chair plastic surgery S, 1969-78; resident in plastic surgery U. Kans. Sch. Med., Kansas City, 1967-69; founder, dir. Internat. Craniofacial Inst., Dallas, 1986—; editl. bd. mem. Annals of Plastic Surgery, 1977-79, Jour. of Speech and Hearing Disorders (editl. cons.) 1982, Tex. Medicine (editl. cons.) 1981-85, Jour. of Craniofacial Surgery, 1990—, Italian Jour. Craniomaxillofacial Surgery, 1990—, Argentinian Jour. Plastic Surgery (internat. consultative coun. 1995—). Author: Techniques in Aesthetic Craniofacial Surgery, 1989, Cleft Lip and Palate Treatment Center: A Booklet for Parents, 1994, (with J. Bardach) Surgical Techniques in Cleft Lip and Palate, 1987, 2d edit. 1991, (with others) The Atlas of Craniomaxillofacial Surgery, 1982; editor: Symposium on Plastic Surgery in the Orbital Region, 1976; author various book chpts. Recipient Nat. Inst. Health award public health svc., sr. clin. traineeship Cancer Control Program 1967-69, Plastic Surgery Resident Program Participation award 2nd place 1967-69, scholar. competition (hon. mention) Edn. Found. Am. Soc. Plastic and Reconstructive Surgeons, 1972, Rsch. Grant award Ednl. Found. Am. Soc. Plastic and Reconstructive Surgeons 1975-76, Hektoen Gold medal for original investigation "Spectrum of Rsch. and Clin. Mgmt. of Craniofacial Anomalies" exhibit at AMA, San Francisco 1977, selected hon. mem. Japanese Soc. Craniofacial Surgery 1993, selected chmn. med. adv. bd. Children's Craniofacial Assn. 1993; grantee Internat. NIH Microvascular Surg. Rsch. 1969, Vets. Admin. Hosp. Maxillofacial Rsch. 1972-78, Sid Richardson Found. med. rsch. 1975-76, Gen. Electric Found. for Craniofacial Deformities 1985-87; recipient various awards for videos. Mem. AMA (mem. various coms.), Am. Acad. Pediat. (exec. com. section on plastic surgery, founding mem., sec.-treas. 1987-90, chmn. 1991—), Am. Assn. of Pediat. Plastic Surgery (founding mem., chmn. 1991—), Am. Assn. Plastic Surgery (mem. various coms.), Am. Burn Assn., Am. Cleft Palate Assn. (mem. various coms.), Am. Coll. Surgeons, Am. Soc. for Aesthetic Plastic Surgery, Am. Soc. Maxiofacial Surgery (mem. various coms.), Am. Soc. Plastic and Reconstructive Surgery (mem. various coms.), Am. Soc. for Reconstructive Microsurgery, Argentine Soc. of Plastic Surgery, Children's Craniofacial Assn. (chmn. med. adv. bd.), Chirugio Soc., Craniofacial Biology Group, Dallas County Med. Soc., Dallas Soc. Plastic Surgery, Euro. Assn. for Craniomaxillofacial Surgery, Internat. Coll. Surgeons, Internat. Confederation for Plastic Reconstructive Surgery (founding mem.), Internat. Craniofacial Club, Internat. Craniofacial Travel Club, Internat. Soc. Clin. Plastic Surgery, Internat. Soc. Cranofacial Surgery (hon. mem.), Lipoplasty Soc. of N.A., Inc., McKorkle Soc., Pan-Pacific Surg. Assn., Physicians Art Assn., Plastic Surgery Rsch. Coun., Soc. for Biomaterials, Soc. Craniofacial Genetics, Soc. Head and Neck Surgery, So. Med. Assn., Southwestern Med. Found., Tex. Soc. Plastic Surgery (mem. various coms., pres.-elect 1982-83, pres. 1983-84), Tex. State Med. Assn., Wound Healing Soc. Office: Internat Cranio Inst 7777 Forest Ln C717 Dallas TX 75230

SALYZYN, MARK GREGORY, software and hardware design engineer; b. Urbana, Ill., Jan. 24, 1961; s. Vladmir and Violet Marie (Zadvorney) S.; m. Leslie Estelle Jackson, Aug. 19, 1981 (div. Apr., 1996); children: Nicholas Ross, Trevor Alexander, Athena Leah, Anna Edith; m. Lyna B. Gagnon, June 25, 1996; children: Paul Thomas Jakobsen, Cristel Leya Jakobsen. B Sc. in Engring., U. Alberta, Edmonton, Alberta, Can., 1982. Registered profl. engr., Alberta, Can. Software engr. Genstar Cement, Edmonton, Alberta, Can., 1981; chief design engr. Advanced Digital Engring., Edmonton, Alberta, Can., 1983-95; sr. software engr. Distributed Processing Tech., Maitland, Fla., 1995—; pres. and engr. Drivers R Us, Maitland, Fla., 1990—. Cub leader Boy Scouts Am., Edmonton, Alberta, Can., 1993, 94; dir. pub. svc. NARC No. Alberta Amateur Radio, Edmonton, 1994, 95; dir. USRGRP Edmonton, UNIX User Group, Edmonton, 1995. Mem. Assn. Profl. Engrs., Geologists, Geophysicists of Alberta (cert. profl. engr.). Republican. Roman Catholic. Office: Distributed Processing Tech 140 Candace Dr Maitland FL 32751

SALZER, LOUIS WILLIAM, chemist; b. Cleve., Sept. 3, 1918; s. Louis and Anna (Froelich) S.; m. Shirley R. Robinson, July 2, 1956. BS in Edn., Kent State U., 1940, postgrad., 1941. Chemist/mass spectrometist Standard Oil Co. Ohio, Cleve., 1944-54; tng. engr. mass spectrometry Consol. Electrodynamics, Pasadena, 1954-58; prof. chemistry Fenn Coll., Cleve., 1956-59; devel. scientist B.F. Goodrich Co., Avon Lake, Ohio, 1959-75; on line analytical process instrumentation specialist B.F. Goodrich Co., U.S., Can., France, Italy, Wales, Japan, 1963-72, Venezuela, 1982; cons on line analytical instrumentation/mass spectrometry Dunedin, Fla., 1975—; tng. engr. mass spectrometer atomic energy establishment, India, 1958. Mem. ACS, Instrument Soc. Am. Republican. Lutheran.

SALZMAN, GARY SCOTT, lawyer; b. Portchester, N.Y., May 26, 1963; s. David Stuart and Francine (Selenow) S.; m. Suzanne Sansone, Apr. 2, 1990. BBA, U. Miami, 1985, JD, 1988. Bar: Fla. 1988, U.S. Dist. Ct. (so. dist.) 1989, Colo. 1991, U.S. Dist. Ct. (mid. dist.) Fla. 1992, U.S. Ct. Appeals (11th cir.) 1992, U.S. Supreme Ct. 1992; cert. arbitrator. With Robinson & Greenberg, PA, Coral Gables, Fla., 1988-89, Buchbinder & Elegant, PA, Miami, Fla., 1989, Mishan, Sloto, Hoffman and Greenberg, PA, Miami, 1989-91, Dempsey & Assocs., Winter Park, Fla., 1991-92; pvt. practice law Orlando and Winter Park, Fla., 1992-95; ptnr. Marlowe, Appleton, Weatherford & Salzman, Winter Park, 1996—. Mem. ABA, Fla. Bar (com. rels. with Inst. CPAs 1992-93, bus. litigation com. 1995—), Bus. Exec. Network, Orange County Bar Assn. Office: 1031 W Morse Blvd Ste 105 Winter Park FL 32789-3738

SAMA, MEG E., telecommunications executive; b. Red Bank, N.J., Sept. 20, 1958; d. James A. and Catherine (Carway) Ferrano; m. Anthony L. Sama, Sept. 17, 1983; children: Alison, Patrick, Anthony, Nicholas. Student, Madison Computer Sch., 1977. Data processing clk. Herman's Sporting Goods, Carteret, N.J., 1979-81, revenue coord., 1980—; v.p. fin. Target Mgmt., Port Saint Lucie, Fla., 1987—. Roman Catholic.

SAMADZADEH, FARIDEH ANSARI, computer science educator; b. Tehran, Iran, Jan. 22, 1957; m. Mansur Samadzadeh, May 24, 1979; children: Shahrzad, Nozlee, Shereen. BA in Pub. Rels., Coll. Mass. Comm., Tehran, 1979; MS, U. S.W. La., 1982, MS in Computer Sci., 1987; PhD in Computer Sci., Okla. State U., 1992. Instr. Shokouh's English Inst., Tehran, 1974-79; lectr. computer sci. dept. Okla. State U., Stillwater, 1988-90, instr., 1990-92, asst. rsch. computer scientist, 1992-93, instr., 1993-94; prof. computer sci. Okla. Sch. Sci. and Math., Okla. City, 1994—. Mem. editorial adv. bd. The Computer NewsBoard; tech. reviewer for jours.; panel reviewer and mail reviewer NSF; contbr. numerous articles to profl. confs. NSF grantee, 1992-94, Okla. State U. grantee, 1991-92. Grantee NSF 1994—, Okla. State Regents for Higher Edn., 1992-94, U.S. Dept. Edn., 1992, Okla. State U., 1991-92. Mem. ACM (SIGAPP (Cert. Appreciation 1992), SIGSOFT, SIGCHI, SIGOPS, SIGMETRICS, SIGACT, SIGPLAN, SIGART, IEEE Computer Soc., Sigma Xi, Phi Kappa Phi. Office: Okla Sch Sci & Math 1141 N Lincoln Blvd Oklahoma City OK 73104

SAMBALUK, NICHOLAS WAYNE, auditor; b. Winnipeg, Can., Nov. 5, 1955; s. Nicoli and Mary (Homeniuk) S.; m. Rosalyn Eisterhold, Apr. 5, 1981; children: Nicholas Michael, Eric Preston. BS, Ariz. State U., 1977. CPA, Va.; cert. mgmt. acct.; cert. internal auditor. Auditor Office of Inspector Gen. for Health and Human Services, Jefferson City, Mo., 1978-82, Def. Contract Audit Agy., Ft. Worth, 1982-87; auditing instr. Def. Contract Audit Inst., Memphis, 1987-90; audit supr. Def. Contract Audit Agy., Dallas, 1990-91; program mgr. Hdqrs. Def. Contract Audit Agy., Ft. Belvoir, Va., 1991-96; br. mgr. Def. Contract Audit Agy., Arlington, Tex., 1996—. Mem. AICPA, Nat. Assn. Accts. Democrat. Home: 622 High View Dr Weatherford TX 76086 Office: Def Contract Audit Agy PO Box 968 Arlington TX 76004

SAMFORD, KAREN ELAINE, small business owner, consultant; b. Houston, Aug. 14, 1941; d. George C. and Agnes M. (Phillips) Sanford; m. Jeff E. Samford, Aug. 18, 1938; children: Jeffrey Barton, Keri Lynn. BA in English, History, Tex. Christian U., 1964. Cert. secondary tchr., Tex. Tchr. secondary schs., Tex., La., Mo., 1964-74; saleswoman, 1974-83, corp. trainer, , 1983-86; owner Karen E. Samford Tng. Cons., Plano, 1986—. Republican. Home and Office: 3409 Haversham Dr Plano TX 75023-6109

SAMIIAN, BARAZANDEH, business owner, educator; b. Tehran, May 13, 1939; came to U.S., 1958. B.A., Woodbury U., Los Angeles, 1961; B.A., Immaculate Heart Coll., Los Angeles, 1979; M.A., Webster U., Geneva, 1981; EdD U. North Fla., 1994. 1 child, Mina P. Cullimore. Cons., Design & Architecture, Tehran, 1965-72; bus. cons. multinat. corps., Calif., 1970-77; co-owner Samiian and Solomon Assocs., Geneva, 1978-86; owner, B. Samiian Assocs., Jacksonville, Fla., 1987—; adj. prof. Webster U., Geneva, 1981—, U. North Fla., 1990-95; cons. and lectr. human resources and leadership devel.; regional acad. dir. North Fla. Campuses Webster U., 1995—. Mem. editl. bd. and pubs. com. Multicultural Edn., 1994—. Named Woman of Yr., 1983; recipient Gov's. citation State of Md., 1983. Mem. Nat. Assn. for Multicultural edn. (nat. bd. dirs. 1993—), Internat. Alliance Exec. Women (bd. dirs. 1988-92), Internat. Assn. of Human Resources Info. Mgmt. (bd. dirs. North Fla. 1995—), Phi Delta Phi, Phi Delta Kappa. Office: Webster Univ Jacksonville Met Campus 9423 Ponder Rd Jacksonville FL 32257-4903

SAMMARCO, PAUL, marine science educator. Prof. La. U. Marine Consortium. Address: 8124 Hwy 56 Chauvin LA 70344

SAMPLES, MARTINA, nursing home administrator; b. Phila., Nov. 20, 1942; d. Martin Rulon and Mallette Mary (Holden) Sembach; m. Billy Irwin Samples, May 13, 1987; children: Lauren, Lynne, Michael, Andrew, Toni, Christopher, Roberta, John. AA, Daytona Beach Community Coll., 1978. LPN; lic. nursing home adminstr., Tex. Adminstr. Purple Hills Manor/Gray Enterprises, Bandera, Tex., 1985-86, Comanche View-Nat. Heritage, Ft. Stockton, Tex., 1986-87, Louis Pasteur Care Ctr./Camlu Care Ctrs., San Antonio, 1987-88, Castle Hills Manor/Campbell-White Assocs., San Antonio, 1988-89, Briarcliff Health Care Ctr., Greenville, Tex., 1989-91; mgr. physician orders dept. Cullum Industries Page Drug Nursing Home Svcs., 1992-96; prin. Samples & Assocs., San Antonio, 1992—; adminstr. Our Lady of the Lake Retirement Ctr., McCullough Hail Nursing Ctr., San Antonio, 1996—; sr. long term care cons. Medicare/Medicaid reimbursement, tchr. seminars to long-term care adminstrs.; adj. faculty St. Phillips Coll., San Antonio, 1992—. Mem. NAFE, Tex. Health Care Assn., Tex. Assn. for Homes Svcs. for Aging, Am. Legion, Order Eastern Star, VFW, Nat. Assn. of Miniature Enthusiasts. Republican. Methodist. Home: 860 Dougherty St Prescott AZ 86301

SAMUEL, JAMES RAY, minister, dean; b. Florence, S.C., Apr. 2, 1952; s. Joseph and Jannie (Allen) S.; m. Dellyne Cypress, Aug. 17, 1974; 1 child, Brian James. BA in English, Livingstone Coll., 1975; MDiv, Duke U., 1982; Clin. Pastoral Edn., N.C. Sch. Pastoral Care, 1982; D Ministry, Drew U., 1990. Ordained to ministry A.M.E. Zion Ch., 1979. Sr. pastor Third Creek A.M.E. Zion Ch., Cleveland, N.C., 1980-82, Marable Meml. A.M.E. Zion Ch., Kannapolis, N.C., 1982-84, Soldiers Meml. A.M.E. Zion Ch., Salisbury, N.C., 1984-89, Little Rock A.M.E. Zion Ch., Charlotte, N.C., 1989—; dean Hood Theol. Sem., Salisbury, 1990—, prof. homeletics, prof. contemporary theology; trustee A.M.E. Zion Camp Dorothy Walls, Blue Mountain, N.C., 1982-91; del. 42d Gen. Conf. A.M.E. Zion Ch., St. Louis, 1984, 43d Gen. Conf. A.M.E. Zion Ch., Charlotte, 1988, World Meth. Conf., Singapore, 1991; mem. connectional budget bd. A.M.E. Zion Ch., 1988—. mem. Charlotte Community Rels. Coun., 1989—, Charlotte Minority Affairs Commn., 1989—, Charlotte Area Clergy Assn., 1989—. Recipient Keeper of Dream award Charlotte Community Rels. Coun., 1991. Mem. Assn. Theol. Schs., Assn. Theol. Deans, Masons. Home: 7208 Chadwyck Farms Dr Charlotte NC 28226-2621 Office: AME Zion Ch 401 N Mcdowell St Charlotte NC 28204-2030

SAMUELS, ALAN DANIEL, internist, gastroenterologist; b. Cleve., Mar. 13, 1942; s. John A. and Miriam (Wolf) S.; m. Sharon Winter, June 28, 1964; children: Lauren Ruth, Jill Alison. BA, U. Mich., 1962; MD, Western Res. U., 1966. Intern Mt. Sinai Hosp., Cleve., 1966-67, resident, 1967-68; resident in medicine Duke U. Med. Ctr., 1970-71; pvt. practice, Memphis, 1973—. Maj. M.C., U.S. Army, 1968-70, Vietnam. Fellow U. Chgo., 1971-73. Fellow ACP, Am. Coll. Gastroentrology. Office: Gastroenterology Clinic 1068 Cresthaven Rd Ste 300 Memphis TN 38119-0846

SAMUELS, BERNARD, obstetrician, gynecologist; b. New Orleans, Mar. 6, 1932; s. Robert Nathan and Helen (Cotlar) S.; m. Jeannine Claire Phillips, July 31, 1955; children: Elizabeth, Richard, Keith. BS in Psychology and Chemistry, Tulane U., 1953; MD, La. State U., 1957. Diplomate Am. Bd. Ob-Gyn. Intern Touro Infirmary., 1957-58, resident in ob-gyn., 1958-61; obstetrician, gynecologist The Women's Ctr. for Ob-Gyn., Metairie, La., 1961—; clin. asst. prof. ob-gyn. La. State U. Sch. Medicine/Charity Hosp., New Orleans, 1987—. Contbr. articles to profl. jours. Pres. La. State U. Med. Sch. Alumni Assn., New Orleans, 1991-92, Summer Sch. Alumni Bd., New Orleans, 1986. Named Alumnus of Yr., La. State U. Med. Sch., 1986. Fellow Am. Coll. Ob-Gyn.; mem. AMA, Am. Soc. Fertility and Sterility, Am. Assn. Gynecologic Laparoscopists, Am. Inst. Ultrasound in Medicine, Am. Soc. Abdominal Surgeons, So. Med. Soc., La. State Med. Soc., New Orleans Ob-Gyn. Soc., Jefferson Parish Med. Soc., Gynecologic Laser Soc., Phi Delta Epsilon (pres. 1966). Office: The Womens Ctr of Ob-Gyn 4720 S I 10 Service Rd W Metairie LA 70001-7403

SAMUELS, MICHAEL EDWIN, health administration educator, consultant; b. Logansport, Ind., Sept. 14, 1940; s. Fred and Dorothy Alice (Chappel) S.; m. Sandra Louise Pinkston, June 2, 1963; children: Michael Edwin II, Brian Patrick. BA, Guilford Coll., 1964; MA, George Washington U., 1972; DPH, U. N.C., 1975; LLD (hon.), Kirksville Coll. Osteo. Medicine, 1985. Acting, dir., then dep. dir. primary health care program USPHS, Rockville, Md., 1978-81, dir. migrant health program, 1981-83, dep. dir. Nat. Health Svc. Corps, 1983-84, dept. dir. div. fed. occupational health, 1985-86; prin. asst. to U.S. surgeon gen. USPHS, Washington, 1986-88; asst. to dir. Fogarty Internat. Ctr., NIH, Bethesda, Md., 1984; rsch. fellow Inst. Medicine, NAS, Washington, 1984-85; legis. health aide to Congress Richard Gephardt, U.S. Ho. of Reps., Washington, 1985; prof., chmn. dept. health adminstrn. U. S.C., Columbia, 1988—; cons. on child health AID, Washington, 1987, cons. on HIV and AIDS, 1991; cons. U.S.-Egypt coop. health program USPHS, Cairo, 1992-93; cons. U.S.-Mex. Border Health Assn., El Paso, Tex., 1993; mem. rural health adv. com. Sheps Rsch. Ctr., U. N.C., Chapel Hill, 1989—; mem. Nat. Migrant Health Fellowship Com., 1989—. Co-author: Recruitment and Retention of Physicians for Rural Areas, 1993; mem. editl. bd. Jour. Rural Health, 1990-93; contbr. articles to profl. jours. Mem. AIDS task force S.C. Med. Assn., Columbia, 1990—; chmn. S.C. Gov.'s Task Force on Rural Primary Care, Columbia, 1990-91; bd. dirs. Hampton Devel. Corp., Estele, S.C., 1990—; mem. migrant health coun. S.C. Dept. Health and Environ. Control, Columbia, 1990—. With USN, 1960-62. Recipient surgeon gen.'s medal for outstanding achievement USPHS, 1988, surgeon gen.'s medal of appreciation, 1988; Disting. Alumni award Guilford Coll., 1988, William Miller award for excellence in med. edn. Assn. Colls. Osteo. Medicine, 1989. Mem. Nat. Rural Health Assn. (sec. 1995-97, award 1980, 82, 84), Kirksville Osteo. Alumni Assn. (hon.), Sigma Xi (bd. dirs. 1990-92). Democrat. Episcopalian.

SAMUELS, ROSEMARIE, small business owner, consultant; b. Shreveport, La.. BS, A & M Coll., 1976; MEd, So. U., 1987. Rsch. assoc. animal sci. dept. So. U., Baton Rouge, La., 1980-84; juvenile counselor Comprehensive Health & Social Svc. Ctr., Baton Rouge, La., 1984-87; ednl. programs devel. cons. Baton Rouge, 1987; admissions records mgr., admissions counselor La. State U., Baton Rouge, 1988-93; mental health counselor Appleton/Vilas Psychotherapy and Counseling, Baton Rouge, La., 1994-95; owner, author greeting cards, posters Pardon Me Greetings, Baton Rouge, La., 1995—; cons. La. Dept. Edn., Baton Rouge, 1987, So. U. Sys. Found., 1994; presenter, spkr. in field. Assoc. dir. 100 Black Men of Metro Baton Rouge, 1996—; co-founder, bd. dirs. African-Am. in La. Higher Edn., Baton Rouge, 1990-95, sec., treas.; mem. La. task force on African Trade, Fin. and Devel., Baton Rouge, 1987, teen task force La. Dept. Edn., 1992. Mem. Am. Christian Counselors Assn., YWCA, La. Assn. Spiritual, Ethical and Religious Values in Counseling, La. Counseling Assn., So. U. Alumni Fedn. Office: Pardon Me Greetings PO Box 66886 Baton Rouge LA 70806

SANBERG, PAUL RONALD, medical educator; b. Coral Gables, Fla., Jan. 4, 1955; s. Bernard and Molly (Spector) S. BS with honors, York U., 1976; MS, U. B.C., 1979; PhD, Australian Nat. U., 1981. Postdoctoral fellow Johns Hopkins Med. Sch., Balt., 1981-83; asst. prof. Ohio U., Athens, 1983-86; assoc. prof. U. Cin., 1986-89; prof. Brown U., Providence, 1990-92, U. South Fla., Tampa, 1992—. Grantee NIMH, NIH, Hereditory Disease Found., Huntington's Disease Found.; recipient award Am. Coll. Neuropsychopharmacology, Tourette Syndrome Assn., Sir J.G. Crawford medal, Ore Forro prize CINP. Mem. APA, Soc. for Neurosci., Psychonomic Soc., Internat. Brain Rsch. Orgn., Interant. Behavioral Neurosci. Soc. (pres. 1994), Am. Soc. for Neural Transplant (prs. 1995), Cell Transplant Soc. (pres. 1996). Home: 11751 Pilot Country Dr Spring Hill FL 34610-7912 Office: U South Fla Coll Medicine Dept Surgery MDC 16 12901 Bruce B Downs Blvd Tampa FL 33612

SANBORN, ALLEN FRANCIS, biologist, educator; b. Aurora, Ill., Apr. 22, 1961; s. Maurice Russell and Mary Ann Josephine (Cyrwus) S.; m. Polly Kristine Phillips, July 26, 1992. BS in Gen. Biology, U. Ill., 1983, MS in Biology, 1984, PhD in Physiology, 1990. Grad. teaching asst. sch. life scis. U. Ill., Urbana-Champaign, 1984-89; asst. prof. biology Barry U., 1990-96; assoc. prof., 1996—. Reviewer: Jour. Thermal Biology, Comparative Biochemistry and Physiology; contbr. articles to profl. jours. Nat. Inst. Health Systems and Integrative Biology fellow, 1987-90. Mem. AAAS, Am. Soc. Zoologists, Entomol. Soc. Am., Fla. Entomol. Soc., Microscopy Soc. Am., Southwestern Assn. Naturalists, Sigma Xi. Office: Barry Univ Sch Natural & Health Scis 11300 NE 2d Ave Miami FL 33161-6628

SANBORN, LISA DIANE, elementary education educator; b. Dallas, July 31, 1972; d. James Niles and Sheree Darlene (Sewell) Stacy; m. Craig Burton Sanborn, July 23, 1994. BS, Southwestern Assemblies of God U., Waxahachie, Tex., 1994. Cert. provisional elem. self-contained and provisional elem. English tchr., Tex. Tchr. Joe Lawrence Elem. Sch., Mesquite (Tex.) Ind. Sch. Dist., 1994—, staff devel. specialist, 1995—. Mem. Assn. Tex. Profl. Educators, Mesquite Edn. Assn.

SÁNCHEZ, ELAINE RUBY, academic librarian; b. Austin, Tex., Sept. 8, 1953; d. Hulon C. and Ruby A. Huie; m. Adolfo Sánchez, Aug. 26, 1972; children: Cristal, Laura, Sara. BA in German (hon.), U. Tex., 1975, MLS, 1976. Libr., clerical asst. U. Tex./Dept. Spanish and Portuguese Libr., Austin, 1975; grad. asst., clerical asst. U. Tex./Grad. Scho. of Libr. Scis., 1975-76; receptionist, libr. asst. I U. Tex./Pub. Affairs Libr., 1976-77, serials libr. asst. II, 1977-78, cataloging libr. asst. II, 1978-79; Latin Am. cataloger U. Tex./Gen. Librs., 1984-86; monographs cataloger S.W. Tex. State U. Libr., San Marcos, 1986-87; head cataloging libr. S.W. Tex. State U. Libr., 1987—; spec. interest group chair DRA User's Group, Cataloging/Authorities, (nationwide), 1990-91. Author: (with others) Introducing and Managing Academic Library Automation Projects, 1996; author revs. Sponsor Save the Children, Colombia, Nepal, 1984—; brownie troopleader Girl Scouts Am., Austin, 1985; religious edn. tchr. asst. St. Catherine of Sienna, Austin, 1991, eucharist hourly coord., 1995—. Mem. Tex. Libr. Assn. (sec., treas. coll. and univ. librs. divsn., mem. com., adminstrn. interest group, catalogers and classifiers interest group). Democrat. Roman Catholic. Home: 4704 Trail Crest Crc Austin TX 78735 Office: Alkek Libr SW Tex U 601 University Dr San Marcos TX 78666-4604

SANCHEZ, ISAAC CORNELIUS, chemical engineer, educator; b. San Antonio, Aug. 11, 1941; s. Isaac Jr. and Marce (Aguilar) S.; m. Karen Patricia Horton, Aug. 7, 1976; children: Matthew, Timothy. BS with honors, St. Mary's U., 1963; PhD, U. Del., 1969. Postdoctoral Nat. Bureau Standards, Gaithersburg, Md., 1969-71; assoc. scientist Xerox Corp., Webster, N.Y., 1971-72; asst. prof. U. Mass., Amherst, 1972-77; rsch. chemist Nat. Bureau Standards, Gaithersburg, 1977-86; fellow Alcoa, Pitts., 1986-88; prof. U. Tex., Austin, 1988—; H.A. disting vis. prof. U. Akron (Ohio), 1995. Mem. editorial bd. Jour. Polymer Sci., 1986-92, Polymer, 1987—; contbr. over 90 articles to profl. jours. Bd. dirs. Tex. Alliance for Minorities in Engring., Austin, Tex., 1989-91. Lt. USN, 1963-67. Recipient Cullen Trust Endowed professorship in engring U. Tex., 1992, Bronze medal U.S. Dept. Commerce, 1980, Silver medal, 1983, E.U. Condon award Nat. Bur. Standards, 1983. Fellow Am. Phys. Soc.; mem. AAAS, Am. Chem. Soc., AICE, Materials Rsch. Soc., Soc. Plastics Engrs. (Internat. Rsch. award 1996). Office: Univ Tex Chem Engring Dept Austin TX 78712

SANCHEZ, JAVIER ALBERTO, industrial engineer; b. San Cristobal, Tachira, Venezuela, Apr. 13, 1960; came to U.S., 1977; s. Leonidas and Ana Mireya (Albornoz) S. AA, Butler County C.C., El Dorado, Kans., 1979; BS in Indls. Engring., Wichita State U., 1982, MS in Engring. Mgmt., 1985. Indsl. cons. Ferronikel, C.A., Caracas, Venezuela, 1977-83; project mgr. Trabajos Viales, C.A., Caracas, Venezuela, 1980; applications engr. Major, Inc., Wichita, Kans., 1983; mfg. engr. L.S. Industries, Inc., Wichita, 1983-86; plant mgr. World Wide Mfg., Inc., Miami, Fla., 1986-88; prodn. mgr. Capitol Hardware Mfg. Co., Chgo., 1988-91; product mgr. Ready Metal Mfg.Co., Chgo., 1991-92; engring. tech. resources and materials mgr. Taurus Internat. Mfg. Inc., Miami, 1992-95; materials mgr. Marino Tech., Inc., Miami, 1996; project engr. South Fla. Mfg. Tech. Ctr., Pompano Beach, Fla., 1996—; sr. cons. Ferronikel, C.A., Caracas, 1983—, mgr. internat. ops., 1986—; mem. adv. bd. Plastidrica, C.A., Caracas, 1988—. Recipient scholarship award Venezuelan Govt., 1977, Mariscal Ayacucho award, 1980. Mem. Am. Soc. for Metals, Soc. Mfg. Engrs., Inst. Indsl. Engrs. (sr.), Soc. Safety Engrs., Nat. Safety Coun., Am. Prodn. and Inventory Control Soc., Soc. Plastic Engrs., Am. Inst. Plant Engrs., Nat. Fire Protection Assn., Nat. Assn. Purchasing Mgmt. Roman Catholic. Home: 8357 W Flagler St Ste 308 Miami FL 33144-2072 Office: So Fla Mfg Tech Ctr 1000 W McNab Rd Pompano Beach FL 33069

SANCHEZ, JUAN ANTONIO, cardiovascular surgeon, educator; b. Havana, Cuba, May 8, 1959; came to U.S., 1968; s. Juan A. and Maria D. (Nunez) S.; m. Lise Lucas, Sept. 15, 1984; children: Emily Marie, Eric Michael, Daniel Alexander. BS cum laude, U. Miami, 1980; MD, U. Fla., 1984. Diplomate Nat. Bd. Med. Examiners, Am. Bd. Surgery, Am. Bd. Thoracic Surgery. Intern in surgery Georgetown U. Med. Ctr., Washington, 1984-85, from resident to chief resident in gen. surgery, 1985-89; rsch. fellow in cardiovascular surgery Coll. Physicians and Surgeons Columbia U., N.Y.C., 1989-90; postdoctoral rsch. scientist Coll. Physicians and Surgeons Columbia U., 1989-91; clin. fellow in cardiopulmonary transplantation Yale-New Haven (Conn.) Med. Ctr., 1991, from resident to chief resident in cardiothoracic surgery, 1991-92; instr. in surgery Yale Sch. Medicine, New Haven, 1992-93; asst. prof. divsn. cardiothoracic surgery U. Miami (Fla.) Sch. Medicine, 1993-95; chief sect. thoracic transplantation U. Ky., Lexington, 1995—, 1996—. Contbr. over 70 articles to profl. jours. Lt. comdr. USNR, 1989—. Recipient Ferriaolo-Glenn award, 1993, William Warren and Marie C. Wolff scholarship, 1982-84. Fellow Am. Coll. Angiology, Am. Coll. Cardiology, Royal Soc. Medicine, InterAm. Coll. Physicians and Surgeons; mem. ACS, AMA, Am. Coll. Chest Physicians, Am. HEart Assn. (cardiovascular surgery coun.), Acad. Surg. Rsch., Assn. Acad. Surgeons, Assn. Mil. Surgeons U.S., Internat. Soc. Heart Transplantation, Robert b. Wallace Surg. Soc., Delta Theta Mu, Phi Kappa Phi.

SANCHEZ, MARIA FELISA, foreign language professional; b. Gijón, Asturias, Spain, May 22, 1962; Came to U.S., 1987; d. Jose R. and Maria F. (Viguera) S.; m. C. Lloyd Halliburton, Jan. 6, 1993; children: Carlos David, Lawden Nerea. Lic. in English Philology, U. Oviedo, Spain, 1987; PhD in Hispanic Linguistics, U. Mass., 1992. Teaching asst. Ctrl. Coll., Pella, Iowa, 1987-88, U. Mass., Amherst, 1988-92; asst. prof. La. Tech. U., Ruston, La., 1992—; instr. Spanish La. Sch. for Math., Sci. and the Arts, Natchitoches, 1994—; sponsor editor Edwin Mellen Press, Lewiston, N.Y., 1994—; faculty mem. Edwin Mellon U., Lewiston, 1994—. Mem. MLA, Am. Assn. Tchrs. Spanish and Portuguese, South Ctrl. MLA, Linguistic Soc. Am., Linguistic Assn. the S.W., Philogical Assn. La. Roman Catholic. Home: 873 Parkway Dr Natchitoches LA 71457-5554

SÁNCHEZ, PABLO J., pediatrician, educator; b. Cuba, Nov. 11, 1954; s. Guillermo and Carolina (Parlade) S. BS in Biology, Seton Hall U., 1977; MD, U. Pitts., 1981. Diplomate Am. Bd. Pediats., Am. Bd. Perinatal-Neonatal Medicine, Am. Bd. Pediat. Infectious Diseases. Intern and resident in pediatrics Children's Hosp. Pitts., 1981-84; fellow in neonatology Babies Hosp. Columbia-Presbyn. Med. Ctr., N.Y.C., 1984-86; fellow in pediatric infectious disease U. Tex. Southwestern Med. Ctr., Dallas, 1986-88, asst. prof. pediats., 1988-95; assoc. prof. pediats., 1996—; mem. infection control com. Parkland Meml. Hosp., Dallas, 1988—; lectr. Columbia-Presbyn. Med. Ctr., N.Y.C., 1986, Pub. Health Dept., Dallas, 1987-93, Humana Hosp. and Med. Ctr. Dallas, 1991, Symposium on Congenital and Perinatal Infection, Chgo., 1991, Am. Acad. Pediatrics, New Orleans, 1991, Changing Role of Mycoplasma in Respiratory Diseas and Aids, Scottsdale, Ariz., 1991, Ctr. for Disease Control, Atlanta, 1991, Cirena Found., Cali, Colombia, 1993. Author: (chpts. in books) Current Therapy in Pediatric Infectious Disease, 1988, Principles and Practice of Pediatrics, 1993, Advances in Pediatric Infectious Diseases, 1992, Current Pediatric Therapy, 1993, Infectious Diseases of the Fetus and Newborn Infant, 1993; author articles and revs. Grantee U. Tex. Southwestern Med. Ctr., 1988-89, Am. Lung Assn., 1990-91, SmithKline Beecham Pharms., 1990, Ctrs. for Disease Control, 1990-91, 93-94, Pediatric AIDS Found., 1990-91, Burroughs Wellcome Co., 1993-94, NIAID/NIH, 1993—. Mem. Am. Acad. Pediatrics, Infectious Diseases Soc. Am., Pediatric Infection Soc., Nat. Perinatal Assn., Tex. Perinatal Soc., Tex. Med. Soc. Roman Catholic. Office: U Tex Southwestern Med Ctr 5323 Harry Hines Blvd Dallas TX 75235-7200

SANCHEZ, VANESSA DIANE, special education educator; b. Cleve., Dec. 20, 1964; d. Jimmy and Violena (Johns) Melton; m. Mark Steven Sanchez, June 11, 1993. BS, Nova S.E. Univ., Ft. Lauderdale, Fla., 1995. Hearing impaired interpreter Dade County Schs., Miami, Fla., 1991-92, Leon County Schs., Tallahassee, Fla., 1992-95; spl. edn. tchr. Pinellas County Schs., Largo, Fla., 1995—. Hearing impaired interpreter World Wide Ch. of God, Miami, 1992; sec. Cap Frid, Tallahassee, 1993. Paul Douglas scholar Fla. Dept. Edn., 1993. Mem. Fla. Registry Interpreters for Deaf. Office: Lynch Elem Sch 1901 71st Ave N Saint Petersburg FL 33702

SANDEFER, G(EORGE) LARRY, lawyer; b. Washington, Mar. 2, 1950; s. George Hall and Mary Gray (Babers) S. BS, Auburn U., 1972; JD, U. Fla., 1978. Bar: Fla. 1978, U.S. Dist. Ct. (mid. dist.) Fla. 1978, U.S. Ct. Appeals (5th and 11th cirs.) 1981, U.S. Supreme Ct. 1982. Asst. atty. State of Fla., Clearwater, 1977-86; sole practice Clearwater, 1986-88; assoc. Kimpton, Burke and White, P.A., 1988-90; sole practice Largo, Fla., 1990—. Mem. Indian Rocks Civic Assn.; city commr. Indian Rocks Beach. 1st lt. USAF, 1973-75. Mem. ATLA, Pinellas County Trial Lawyers Assn., Fla. Assn. Criminal Def. Attys., Colo. Bar Assn., Kiwanis.

SANDELL, GEORGE NORMAN, banking executive; b. Camden, N.J., May 28, 1944; s. Norman and Betty Willetta (MacCartney) S. BS, U.S. Mil. Acad., 1966; MA in Fin., U. Fla., 1972. Commd. 2d lt. U.S. Army, 1966, advanced through grades to capt., 1968; resigned, 1970; mortgage officer Gt. Am. Mgmt. Co., Atlanta, 1973-74; asst. v.p. Adair Mortgage Co., Atlanta, 1974-77; 1st v.p. Trust Co. Bank, Atlanta, 1977—. Decorated Bronze Star with oak leaf cluster, Purple Heart. Mem. Atlanta Vietnam Vets. Bus. Assn., Atlanta Gator Club. Home: 1915 Annwicks Dr Marietta GA 30062-5409

SANDER, GARY EDWARD, medical educator; b. New Orleans, Feb. 14, 1947; s. Edward William and Vera Cornibe S.; m. Patricia Elaine Pruett, July 14, 1973; children: Edward, Andrew, Philip. BS in Chemistry summa cum laude, Loyola U., New Orleans, 1968; PhD in Biochemistry, Tulane U., 1971, MD, 1973. Diplomate Am. Bd. Internal Medicine, Am. Bd. Cardiovascular Disease. Intern in internal medicine Walter Reed Army Med. Ctr., Washington, 1974-75, resident, 1975-77, chief med. resident, 1977, attending physician, 1977-80; assoc. prof. medicine Tulane U., New Orleans, 1980-85, prof. medicine, 1985-92; prof. medicine La. State U., New Orleans, 1992—; rsch. internist Walter Reed Army Inst. of Rsch., 1977-80, chief dept. clin. physiology, divsn. of medicine, 1979-80; asst. prof. medicine Uniformed Svcs. U. of the Health Scis., 1978-80; staff physician Mobile Health Care Montgomery County, Md., 1979-80; vis. physician Charity Hosp., New Orleans, 1980—; chief admitting officer VA Med. Ctr., New Orleans, 1980-82, physician-in-charge hypertension screening and treatment program, 1982-92; mem. pharmacy and therapeutics com. Tulane Med. Ctr., 1987-90, utilization rev. com., 1990-92; mem. med. records com. U. Hosp., 1993-94, credentials com., 1994; mem. faculty Pennington Biomed. Rsch. Inst., La. State U., 1992—; mem. instl. rev. bd. La. State U. Med. Ctr., 1992—, dir. cardiovascular fellowship tng. program, 1994—. Assoc. editor: Cardiomyopathy, 1988; guest editor Am. Jour. Cardiology, 1989; contbr. articles to profl. jours. Maj. U.S. Army MC, 1974-80. Grad. Tng. fellow NDEA, 1968-70. Fellow Am. Coll. Physicians, Am. Heart Assn. (cardiopulmonary coun. 1980—, circulation coun. 1983—), Am. Coll. Cardiology (editor newsletter La. chpt.), Am. Coll. Angiology, Am. Coll. Chest Physicians; mem. Am. Fedn. Clin. Rsch., Am. Soc. Pharmacology and Exptl. Therapeutics, Am. Soc. Hypertension, So. Soc. Clin. Investigation, New Orleans Acad. Internal Medicine, Musser-Burch Soc., Alpha Sigma Nu, Alpha Omega

Alpha. Home: 1237 Beverly Garden Dr Metairie LA 70002-1903 Office: La State U Dept of Medicine 1542 Tulane Ave New Orleans LA 70112-2822

SANDERS, BARBARA BOYLES, health services director; b. Charleston, Miss., May 4, 1950; d. Marion Enoch and Bettye Sue (Wright) Boyles; m. James Norton Sanders, June 15, 1974 (div. July 1977). BA in History, Miss. Coll., 1970; MA in History, Delta State U., 1975; postgrad., U. So. Miss., 1974-77. History tchr. McCluer H.S., Jackson, Miss., 1972-74, Laurel (Miss.) Pub. Schs., 1974-77; dir. field svcs. Am. Heart Assn., Little Rock, 1977-81; v.p. Boyles Enterprises, Inc., Jackson, 1981-84; exec. dir. Nat. Multiple Sclerosis Soc., Jackson, 1984-93; nat. exec.-dir. Nat. Assn. EMTS, Clinton, Miss., 1994—; cons. in adminstrn. and devel., Jackson, 1993—; mem. editl. adv. bd. Ed League Cons., Naples, 1996—; adv. bd. Preserve Sight, Jackson, 1993—; adv. bd. ALS Assn., Jackson, 1994—. Sunday sch. tchr. New Covenant Ch., Ridgeland, Miss., 1994—. Mem. Am. Soc. Assn. Execs. Republican. Home: 17 Club Oaks Cir Pearl MS 39208 Office: Nat Assn EMTs 102 W Leake St Clinton MS 39056-4252

SANDERS, BARBARA HEEB, writer, consultant; b. Harrisburg, Ark., May 15, 1938; d. Raymond and Irene (Rice) Heeb; m. Carmack Wilson Sanders, July 6, 1956; children: Gregory Wilson, Stephanie. BS in Edn., Ark. State U., 1963; postgrad., Ark. Coll., 1972-73, 74, East Tex. State U., 1979. Cert. secondary edn. Asst. Poinsett County Tax Assessor's Office, Harrisburg, 1956; sec., clk. Jackson Life Ins. Co., Memphis, 1956-57; owner Heeb, Heeb and Sanders Farms, Harrisburg, 1962-74; cashier Ark. Power and Light Co., Harrisburg, 1963; tchr. Harrisburg Pub. Schs., 1963-66; owner, dir. Ozark Attractions, Inc., Mountain View, Ark., 1976-69; owner Sanders Ranch, Timbo, Ark., 1976-87; dir. tchr. workshops East Tex. State U., Mountain View, 1973-84; freelance writer, cons. Harrisburg, 1987—; owner, bd. dirs. Battle Music Inc., Timbo; advisor, cons. Gov. Bill Clinton, Little Rock, 1981—; cons. Chaplin-Martinov Prodns., Woodland Hills, Calif., 1982—; music dir. Crowley's Ridge Folk Festival, 1972-73; performer numerous festivals and schs.; Poinsett County Motion Picture and Film Commn., 1992—. Feature writer The Modern News, 1990—; editor poetry; performer record albums, 1973, 78; contbr. articles to profl. jours. Member Gov.'s Task Force on Edn., Little Rock, 1973-74, Ark. State Libr. Bd., Little Rock, 1988—, Friends of the Libr. of Craighead County, 1989—; del. Dem. Party State Conv., Little Rock and Hot Springs, Ark., 1978-82; mem. adv. com. H.P. Maddox Sr. Ednl. Found./Ark. Community Found., Inc., 1989—; county coord. U.S. Senator Dale Bumpers, Washington, 1973-74, Gov. Bill Clinton, Little Rock, 1981—; bd. dirs. Folk Music Hall of Fame, Mountain View, 1973; justice of the peace County of Poinsett, 1989-91; mem. Poinsett County Ednl. Planning Com., Harrisburg, 1975, Poinsett County Fair Bd. Assn., 1972-74, N.E. Ark. Forum on Early Childhood Edn., Little Rock, 1974, Poinsett County Farm Bur., 1963—, rice promotion com., 1969; active vol. fund drive Heart Fund, Harrisburg, 1964, Am. Cancer Soc., Harrisburg, 1971, 72, Cystic Fibrosis Rsch. Found., 1970, 71, local chair, 1972; mem. state adv. com. Keep Ark. Beautiful Commn., 1989—; Ark. planner Statue of Liberty Centennial, N.Y.C., 1986; mem. Poinsett County Dem. Women's Club, corr. sec., 1979-81, mem. ways and means com., 1982, mem. state planning com. for nat. meeting, 1986; active local campaign orgns. Mem. Vocat. Bus. Edn. (chmn. adv. coun. 1984—), White House Conf. on Libr. and Info. Svcs. (task force), Rackensack Folklore Soc., Lower Miss. Delta Devel. Commn. (adv. mem.), Harrisburg Garden Club, Delta Kappa Gamma. Mem. Ch. of Christ. Home: 409 E Griffin St Harrisburg AR 72432-2805

SANDERS, CHARLES ADDISON, physician; b. Dallas, Feb. 10, 1932; s. Harold Barefoot and May Elizabeth (Forrester) S.; m. Elizabeth Ann Chipman, Mar. 6, 1956; children: Elizabeth, Charles Addison, Carlyn, Christopher. MD, U. Tex., 1955. Intern, asst. resident Boston City Hosp., 1955-57, chief resident, 1957-58; clin. and rsch. fellow in medicine Mass. Gen. Hosp., Boston, 1958-60; chief cardiac catheterization lab. Mass. Gen. Hosp., 1962-72, gen. dir., 1972-81, physician, 1973-81, program dir. myocardial infarction rsch. unit, 1967-72; exec. v.p. E.R. Squibb and Sons, 1981-84; exec. v.p. Squibb Corp., 1984-88, vice chmn., 1988-89; chief exec. officer Glaxo Inc., Research Triangle Park, N.C., 1989-94, chmn., 1992-95; assoc. prof. medicine Harvard U. Med. Sch., 1969-80, prof., 1980-83; candidate U.S. Senate, 1996; bd. dirs. Mt. Sinai Med. Ctr., N.Y.C.; chmn. Commonwealth Fund N.Y.C.; mem. Inst. Medicine. Mem. editorial bd. New Eng. Jour. Medicine, 1969-72. Chmn. Project Hope; bd. dirs. U. N.C., Chapel Hill; bd. trustees U.N.C., Chapel Hill; mem. Pres. Coun. Advisors on Sci. and Tech. Capt. USAF, 1960-62. Mem. ACP, Am. Heart Assn., Mass. Med. Soc. Office: 100 Europa Dr Ste 170 Chapel Hill NC 27514

SANDERS, DEION LUWYNN, baseball and football player; b. Ft. Myers, Fla., Aug. 9, 1967. Student, Fla. State U. Baseball player N.Y. Yankees, 1988-90, Atlanta Braves, 1991-94, Cin. Reds, 1994; football player Atlanta Falcons, 1989-94, San Francisco 49ers, 1994, Dallas Cowboys, 1995—. Named to Sporting News Coll. All-Am. football team, 1986-88, Sporting News NFL All-Pro Football Team, 1991, 92, 94, Pro Bowl team, 1991-94; recipient Jim Thorpe award, 1988. Address: San Francisco Giants Candlestick Park San Francisco CA 94124*

SANDERS, GEORGIA ELIZABETH, secondary school educator; b. Holmwood, La., July 14, 1933; d. Frederick Rudolph and Susie W. (Hackett) S. Student, La. Coll., 1951-53, La. State U., 1959-60; BS, then MS in Microbiology, U. Southwestern La., 1970; MS in Math., U. So. Miss., 1983. Instr. dept. biology U. New Orleans, 1976-79, instr. dept. math., 1983-86; tchr. East Baton Rouge Parish Schs., 1988-89; tchr. math. St. Tammany Parish, La., 1990—. Mem. NEA, Am. Math. Soc., Math. Assn. Am., Nat. Coun. Tchrs. Math. Home: PO Box 968 Slidell LA 70459-0968

SANDERS, GILBERT OTIS, health and addiction psychologist, consultant, educator, motivational speaker; b. Oklahoma City, Aug. 7, 1945; s. Richard Allen and Evelyn Wilmoth (Barker) S.; m. Lidia Julia Grados-Ventura; 1 child, Lisa Dawn Sanders-Coker. AS, Murray State Coll, 1965; BA, Okla. State U., 1967, U. State of N.Y.; MS, Troy State U., 1970; EdD, U. Tulsa, 1974; postdoctoral studies St. Louis U., Am. Tech. U.; grad. U.S. Army Command and Gen. Staff Coll., Ft. Leavenworth, Kas., 1979. Diplomate Am. Bd. Med. Pschotherapist, Am. Bd. Forensic Examiners. Dir. edn. Am. Humane Edn. Soc., Boston, 1975; chmn. dept. computer sci., dir. Individual Learning and Counseling Ctr., asst. prof. pschology and law enforcement Calumet Coll., Whiting, Ind., 1975-78; rsch. psychologist U.S. Army Rsch. Inst., Ft. Hood, Tex., 1978-79; pvt. practice counseling, Killen, Tex., 1978-79; psychologist U.S. Army Tng. and Doctrine Command Sys. Analysis Activity, White Sands Missile Range, N.Mex., 1979-80; project dir. psychologist Applied Sci. Assocs., Ft. Sill, Okla., 1980-81; pvt. practice counseling, Lake St. Louis, 1981-83; assoc. prof. Pittsburg State U., Kans., 1983-85; pres. Applied Behavioral Rsch. Assocs. (formerly Southwestern Behavioral Rsch.), Oklahoma City, 1985-94; pvt. practice counseling Christian Family Counseling Ctr., Lawton, Okla., 1986-87; psychologist, systems analyst U.S Army Field Artillery Sch.-Directorate of Combat Devels., Ft. Sill, Okla., 1987; psychologist U.S. Army Operational Test and Evaluation Agy., Washington, 1988-89; psychologist, drug abuse program dir. Fed. Bur. of Prisons-Fed. Correctional Inst. El Reno, Okla., 1989-91; psychologist, clin. dir. drug abuse program U.S. Penitentiary, Leavenworth, Kans., 1991-95; pvt. practice psychologist MacArthur Med. and Psychotherapy, Inc. and Acad. Christian Counseling Okla., Oklahoma City, 1992—; adj. prof. bus. and psychology Columbia Coll.-Buder Campus, St. Louis, 1982-84; adj. prof. U.S. Army Command Staff and Gen. Coll., 1983-89, Columbia Pacific U., 1984—, Greenwich U., 1990—, U. Alaska S.E., 1995—. Editor: Evaluation for a Manual Backup System for TACFIRE (ARI), 1978, Training/Humane Factors Implications--Copperhead Operational Test II Livefire Phase, 1979, TRADOC Training Effectiveness Analysis Handbook, 1980, Cost and Training Effectiveness Analysis/TEA 8-80/Patroit Air Defense Missile System, 1980, Cost and Training Analysis/Infantry Fighting Vehicle (Bradley), 1980, Human Factors Implications for the Howitzer Improvement Program, 1989, The Drug Education Handbook, 1995, Therapist Handbook for Drug Treatment, 1996; author research reports. Recipient Kavanough Found. Community Builder award, 1967; named Hon. Col. Okla. Gov. Staff, 1972, Hon. Amb., 1974. Fellow Am. Assn. Psychologists Treating Addictions (diplomate), Am. Forensic Counselors Assn.; mem. APA, ACA, Am. Assn. Marriage and Family Therapists, Am. Mental Health Counselors Assn., Res. Officers Assn., Commd. Officers Assn., U.S. Pub. Health Svc., Pi Kappa Phi, Alpha Phi Omega. Home: 5404 NW 65th St Oklahoma City OK 73132-7747 Office: Mac Arthur Med Inst 7317 N Mac Arthur Blvd Oklahoma City OK 73132

SANDERS, GLEN ARTHUR, television producer; b. Las Vegas, Apr. 5, 1970; s. Arthur Frederick and Donna Marie (Milloy) S. Student, L.I. U., 1988-90; BFA, NYU, 1992. With studio ops. dept. Trinity Broadcast Network, Pembroke Park, Fla., 1985-87; studio cameraman News 12 L.I., Woodbury, N.Y., 1988-92; dir. creative svcs. Sta. KJCT TV-8, Grand Junction, Colo., 1993-94; instr. Art Inst. Fort Lauderdale, Fla., 1995—; producer, video cameraman SANDS Entertainment, Inc., Fort Lauderdale, 1994—. Active Young Profls. for Covenant House, Fort Lauderdale, 1994; mem. steering com. Com. of 100, Fort Lauderdale, 1995; active Fort Lauderdale Film Festival, 1994. Mem. Internat. TV Assn. (pres.-elect Miami chpt., bd. dirs. 1994—), Assn. Ind. Video and Filmmakers, Fla. Motion Picture & TV Assn., NYU Alumni Assn.

SANDERS, HAROLD BAREFOOT, JR., federal judge; b. Dallas, Tex., Feb. 5, 1925; s. Harold Barefoot and May Elizabeth (Forrester) S.; m. Jan Scurlock, June 6, 1952; children—Janet Lea, Martha Kay, Mary Frances, Harold Barefoot III. BA, U. Tex., 1949, LLB, 1950. Bar: Tex. bar 1950. U.S. atty. No. Dist. Tex., 1961-65; asst. dep. atty. gen. U.S., 1965-66; asst. atty. gen., 1966-67; legis. counsel to President U.S., 1967-69; partner firm Clark, West, Keller, Sanders & Butler, Dallas, 1969-79; U.S. dist. judge for No. Dist. Tex., Dallas, 1979—, chief judge, 1989-95. Mem. Tex. Ho. of Reps., 1952-58; Dem. nominee U.S. Senate, 1972. Lt. (j.g.) USNR, World War II. Mem. ABA (chmn. nat. conf. fed. trial judges 1988-89), Fed. Bar Assn. (Disting. Svc. award Dallas 1964), Dallas Bar Assn., State Bar Tex. (jud. conf. U.S. 1989-92, jud. panel on multidistrict litigation 1992—), Blue Key, Phi Delta Phi, Phi Delta Theta. Methodist. Office: US Courthouse 1100 Commerce St Fl 15 Dallas TX 75242-1027

SANDERS, HENRY WALKER, foundation executive; b. Charlotte, N.C., May 13, 1965; s. Ernest Gordon and Grace Wooten (Walker) S.; m. Dabney Lorimer Halyburton, Sept. 23, 1989. BA in Economics/Polit. Sci., U. of the South, Sewanee, Tenn., 1987. Cert. Fin. Planner. Fin. planner assoc. The Teague Group, Charlotte, N.C., 1988-93; dir. of develop. and regional svcs. Found. for the Carolinas, Charlotte, 1993-96; pres. J. Marion Sims Found., 1996—. Mem. Sewanee Club (pres. 1992-96), Charlotte Latin Alumni Bd. (pres. 1993-94). Home: 2240 Sharon Rd Charlotte NC 28207

SANDERS, JAMES NORMAN, marriage, family, individual and group counselor; b. Benington, Okla., Nov. 13, 1930; s. James C. Sanders and Bella (Hodges) Welch; m. Patricia J. Dews, May 27, 1955; children: James Norman Jr., Timothy W. DD, Clarksville Sch. Theology, 1979, ThD, 1980; PhD, ZOE Internat. Coll., Jacksonville, Fla., 1989; Cert. Addiction Profl., Am. Coll. Addictionology and, Maladaptive Behavior, Miami, 1995. Cert. Christian counselor; diplomate Am. Bd. Christian Psychology. Enlisted man USAF, 1948, advanced through grades to master sgt., 1963, manpower systems engr., 1948-68; ret., 1968; asst. adminstrs. Johns Hopkiins Hosp., Balt., 1968-73; cons., 1973-78; exec. v.p. Fla. Beacon Coll., Largo, 1979-82; dir. Christian Counseling Svcs., Vero Beach, Fla., 1983—; cons. health div. Westinghouse Co., Pitts., 1970-72. Co-author: Supervisory Development for Hospital Employees, 1972. Bd. dirs. ZOE Internat. Coll., 1986. Recipient cert. of appreciation State of Md., 1952. Office: The Charles Parker Found for HHS Rsch & Devel 2213 Highland Ave Melbourne FL 32935-6621

SANDERS, JOHN BURTON, pianist; b. Tulsa, June 1, 1932; s. Julian Burton and Pearl (Kinsey) S.; m. Rosemary Roark, June 16, 1954 (div. 1970); children: Charles Alec, Donna Carolyn. BMus, Tulsa U., 1954; BA, U. Tex., 1961, MLS, 1964. Registered piano technician. Pianist First Unitarian Ch. of Austin, 1963—; piano technician Austin, 1957—. With USAF, 1954-57, lt. col. USAF Res., 1957-82. mem. Res. Officers Assn., Ret. Officers Assn., Piano Technicians Guild, Inc. (pres. Austin chpt. 1967-75), Mosquito Assn., Wednesday Morning Music Club. Democrat. Unitarian. Home: 4209 Burnet Rd #201 Austin TX 78756 Office: First Unitarian Ch Austin 4700 Grover Ave Austin TX 78756

SANDERS, JULIA JEAN, primary school educator; b. Hawkinsville, Ga., Sept. 25, 1958; d. Julian and Jeanette (Curry) S. BS in Early Childhood Edn., Valdosta (Ga.) State Coll., 1980; MRE, So. Bapt. Theol. Sem., 1982; M in Early Childhood Edn., Ga. Southwestern Coll., 1986, EdS, 1988. Cert. early childhood edn. tchr., Ga. Tchr. kindergarten Pulaski County Bd. of Edn., Hawkinsville, 1982—; tchr. Support Specialist Endorsement, 1991. Named one of Outstanding Young Women of Am., 1982, Young Careerist for 1991 for Pulaski County and Ga. Southwest Dist., Pulaski County Tchr. of Yr., 1989; recipient Nat. Educator award Milken Family Found., 1991. Mem. Profl. Assn. Ga. Educators, Nat. Assn. Edn. Young Children. Baptist. Home: 224 Mashburn St Hawkinsville GA 31036-1604

SANDERS, KATHEY GOLIGHTLY, child welfare organization executive; b. Dumas, Tex., Aug. 31, 1960; d. Don Ray and Glennetta (Tinnin) G.; m. Mark Evan Sanders, Apr. 20, 1991; 1 child, Kaitlin Glenn Sanders. BA, Okla. Bapt. U., 1982; MDiv., So. Bapt. Theol. Sem., 1985. Artistic adminstr. Ky. Opera, Louisville, 1985-88; dir. student svcs. ACDI Adult Edn., Louisville, 1988-90; dir. coalitions Libr. Found., Louisville, 1990-91; assoc. dir. deve. Ky. Bapt. Homes for Children, Louisville, 1991—. Mem. Nat. Soc. Fund Raising Execs., Nat. Coun. Planned Giving, Nat. Child Care Devel. Assn., Fund Raising Execs. Metro Louisville. Democrat. Baptist. Office: Bapt Homes for Children 10801 Shelbyville Rd Louisville KY 40243-1243

SANDERS, LEON LLOYD, nursing administrator, retired naval officer; b. El Paso, Tex., Jan. 7, 1951; s. Jay Leon and Mona Elma (McClelland) S.; m. Gail Ann Zuidema, May 3, 1970 (div. Dec. 1974); 1 child, Shawn Stephen; m. Emily Irene Lord, Apr. 7, 1978; children: Abygayl, Elisabeth, Jonathon, Anna, Naomi. Diploma, St. John's Sch. Nursing, 1984; BSN, Old Dominion U., 1991; MS, U. Fla., 1993—. RN, La., Fla.; cert. BLS instr., ACLS instr., PALS instr., Am. Heart Assn.; cert. Emergency Nurse, RN Intravenous. Staff nurse orthopedic and neurologic units Meml. Hosp., Lake Charles, La., 1984, staff nurse neonatal ICU, 1984-85; commd. ENS USN, 1985, advanced through grades to lt., 1989; staff nurse orthopedic, neonatal ICU, emergency rm. USN, Portsmouth, Va., 1985-89; nurse mgr. edn. and tng. USN, Jacksonville, Fla., 1991-93, nurse mgr. ICU, 1993-94, nurse mgr. internal medicine, 1994-95, home health nursing, 1995—; speaker in field. Editor, founder newsletter The Cracker Barrel, 1987-89; author computer programs in field. Vol. instr. prehosp. advanced trauma life support U. Hosp., Jacksonville, 1992—, nurse rsch., nursing case mgmt., BLS instr. Pub. Health Office, 1991-92. Mem. Intravenous Nurses' Soc., Golden Key Honor Soc., Sigma Theta Tau, Alpha Chi. Home: 14139 Inlet Dr Jacksonville FL 32225-2000

SANDERS, MARC ANDREW, computer technical consultant; b. Chgo., Apr. 21, 1947; s. Edward and Elizabeth Sanders. BA, Roosevelt U., 1973; MAS, Fla. Atlantic U., 1987. Computer programmer Market Facts, Inc., Chgo., 1973-76, N.E. Ill. Planning Commn., Chgo., 1977; salesman Radio Shack, Tamarac, Fla., 1982-83; sr. analyst/tech. cons. Birch/Scarborough Rsch., Coral Springs, Fla., 1984-91; programmer/analyst Datateam, Inc., Margate, Fla., 1992-93, SIRS, Inc., Boca Raton, Fla., 1994—. Mem. ACM, IEEE Computer Soc., Phi Kappa Phi, Beta Gamma Sigma, Upsilon Pi Epsilon. Democrat. Jewish. Office: SIRS PO Box 9742 Coral Springs FL 33075-9742

SANDERS, MARION YVONNE, geriatrics nurse; b. St. Petersburg, Fla., Dec. 4, 1936; d. Ira Laurey and Maude Mae Cherry Sanders; children: Dwayne Irwin Parker, Princess Charrie Ferrette, Henry, Pelote. BS, Fla. A&M U., 1959; MS, Nova U., Ft. Lauderdale, Fla., 1992. RN, Fla. Staff nurse Lantana (Fla.) TB Hosp., 1960-61, Mercy Hosp., St. Petersburg, 1961; gen. duty nurse VA, Tuskegee, Ala., 1961-62; staff nurse John Andrews Hosp., Tuskegee, 1962-63; gen. duty staff nurse Brewster Meth. Hosp., Jacksonville, Fla., 1963-65, Duval Med. Ctr., Jacksonville, 1965-66; pvt. duty nurse Dist. 2 Registry, Jacksonville, 1966-70; supr. Eartha White Nursing Home, Jacksonville, 1970; staff nurse Bapt. Hosp., Jacksonville, 1971-73, City-County Methadone Clinic, Jacksonville, 1976-78; pvt. duty nurse Home Nursing, Jacksonville, 1982-86; pvt. duty geriatric nursing and gerontology specialist Home Nursing, 1995—. Active St. Stephen African Meth. Episcopal Ch., Jacksonville; advocate for poor, homeless and prisoners; vol. shelter mgr. ARC, Miami, Fla., 1992-94; vol. cmty. activist, Miami, 1994; vol. Jacksonville Cmty. Rels. Bd., 1996. Recipient Cert. of Recognition, Rep. Party, Fla. and Wash., 1990, Rep. Congl. Orgn., 1988, 90, 91. Mem. ANA (mem. polit. action coms.), Fla. Nurses Assn. Republican. Methodist. Home: 4832 N Main St Apt 14 Jacksonville FL 32206

SANDERS, ROBERT MARK, political science educator; b. Bklyn., Feb. 9, 1953. AA in Journalism, Miami-Dade C.C., 1973; BA in Sociology/Anthropology, Fla. Internat. U., 1975, MS in Mgmt., 1975, PhD in Pub. Adminstrn., 1991. Asst. to coord. of doctoral program Fla. Internat. U., Miami, 1984-88, fellowship instr. of pub. adminstrn., 1984-88, instr., 1990-92; asst. prof. polit. sci. Coll. of N.J., Ewing, N.J., 1988-90, U. West Ga., Carrollton, 1992—; with Dade County Comty. Drug Edn. program, 1985-87, City of Davie Govt., 1985-87. Contbr. articles to profl. jours. Active Atlanta Greens, East Bay Animal Referral, Animal Rights Found. Fla., Citizens for a Pure Environ., N.J., Greenpeace, People for Ethical Treatment of Animals, Last Chance for Animals, Pet Rescue Ctr., Performing Arts for Community and Edn., others. Recipient Bayshore Svc. Club scholarships, 1973-76, Miami Men's Fashion Guild scholarship, 1973, Miami-Dade Bd. Trustees grants, 1972-73. Mem. Am. Soc. Pub. Adminstrn., Internat. Inst. Adminstrv. Scis., Internat. Assn. Conflict Mgmt., Ga. Soc. Pub. Adminstrn., South Fla. Soc. Pub. Adminstrn., N.J. Soc. Pub. Adminstrn., Ctr. for Environ. Edn., Am. Fedn. State, County and Mcpl. Employees, Civil Svc. Assn. Office: Univ of West Ga Dept Polit Sci Carrollton GA 30118

SANDERS, RUSSELL EDWARD, protective services official; b. Louisville, Oct. 6, 1949; s. Robert George Sr. and Jean Francis (Stevens) S.; m. Mary Ann Miller, Feb. 12, 1972; children: Scott, Jason. BA in Psychology, U. Louisville, 1976, MEd in Pers. Svcs., 1980, MS in Community Devel., 1987. Firefighter Louisville Fire Dept., 1967-74, sgt., 1974-77, capt., 1977-81, dist. chief, 1986-95; regional mgr. Nat. Fire Protection Assn., Louisville, 1995—; adj. instr. Nat. Fire Acad., Emmitsburg, Md., 1985-86; instr. Western Oreg. State Coll., Monmouth, 1984; cons. numerous locations; tchr. Jefferson County Pub./Cath. Sch. Systems, Louisville, 1976-80; bd. dirs. Gov's. Commn. on Pers. Standards, Frankfort, Ky. Contbr. numerous articles to profl. publs. Tennis coach St. Barnabas Cath. Sch., Louisville, 1985-86; baseball coach Hikes Point Optimist, Louisville, 1988; bd. dirs. Ky. Cmty. Vol. Fire Prevention Program, Louisville, 1986—, Stage One Childrens Theater. Sgt. U.S. Army, 1969-71. Recipient People to watch award Louisville mag., 1988, Dean's Citation/Outstanding Svc. award U. Louisville, 1988; Fed. Emergency Mgr. Agy. fellow Harvard U., 1987. Mem. Nat. Inst. Bldg. Scis. (bd. dirs.), Metro Fire Chiefs Assn. (sec. 1988-89, chmn. 1990-91), Soc. Exec. Fire Officers, Internat. Soc. Fire Svc. Instrs., U. Louisville Alumni Assn. (pres.-elect, sec. Outstanding Alumni award 1987), Commanding Officers Club. Democrat. Roman Catholic. Office: Nat Fire Protection Assn 3257 Beals Branch Dr Louisville KY 40206-3060

SANDERS, SHARON RAYE (SHARRI SANDERS), telecommunications executive, educator; b. Dayton, Ohio, Aug. 25, 1942; d. Robert J. Rapa and Mildred B. Wallace; m. Robert Meredith Sanders, Dec. 28, 1961; children: Robert E., Kenneth B. (dec.). Tchr. cert., U. Tex., 1989, 90. Various positions Rockwell Internat, Bastian-Blessing, others, Mich. and Ill., 1960-79; adminstrv. asst. Tex. Tech. Sch. Medicine, Lubbock, 1980, Thermex Energy Corp., Dallas, 1980-81; exec. asst. Bonser-Philhower Sales, Richardson, Tex., 1982; owner, operator SRS Bus. Svc. Secretarial/Printing, Kaufman, Tex., 1982-89; tchr. Kaufman H.S., 1989-92; prin. ptnr. MetCom of East Tex., Chandler, Tex., 1993—. Author: What's Cooking?, 1988; contbr. poetry to anthologies; contbg. writer Kaufman Herald, 1988-89, The Secretary mag., 1991. Pres. PTA, Allegan, Mich., 1973, sec., 1974; sec. ladies aux. Forest Grove Property Owners Assn., 1993-94; bd. dirs. Forest Grove Property Owners Assn., 1994-96. Recipient Engraved Appreciation award Student Body/Graphic Arts, Kaufman H.S., 1992, 20th Century award for Achievement in Edn., 1994. Mem. NAFE, Nat. League Am. Pen Women (2d place writing contest award 1988), Tex. Printing Instrs. Assn. (sec. 1992), Kaufman C. of C. (bd. dirs. 1983-86), Chandler Lioness Club (co-first v.p., 1995-96). Office: MetCom of East Tex PO Box 1590 Chandler TX 75758-1590

SANDERS, TENCE LEE WALKER, elementary education educator; b. Ridgeville, S.C., June 15, 1937; d. Joseph Thomas and Rosalee (Simmons) Walker; divorced; children: Carsandra, Torin Travis. BS, Allen U., 1960; postgrad. S.C. State Coll., 1960-61, CCNY, 1969-70; MA, Antioch Coll., 1974. Lic. tchr., N.Y., N.J. Tchr. Mary Ford Sch., Charleston, S.C., 1960-61, St. Thomas Apostle Sch., N.Y.C., 1966-72, New Rochelle Sch. System, N.Y., 1972-94, ret., 1994; reading coordinator YWCA, N.Y.C., 1966; tchr. Project Head Start, N.Y.C., 1967, 69. Chairperson awards com. Allen U., 1985-88; Active St. Peters A.M.E. Ch., 1989. Recipient cert. of merit Delta Sigma Theta, 1955, S.C. Hwy. Dept., 1956, William Alanson White Inst. Psychology, Psychiatry and Psychoanalysis, 1971. Outstanding Svc. in Field of Edn. award, Allen U., 1989. Mem. Am. Fedn. Tchrs., N.Y. State United Tchrs., New Rochelle Fedn. United Sch. Employees, Gen. Alumni Assn. Allen U. (pres. Met. N.Y.C. chpt. 1983-93, Oustanding Svc. Beyond Call Duty met. alumni chpt. 1989, Outstanding Leadership and Dedicated Svc. award 1992, Outstanding Leadership, Unwavering Loyalty and Selfless Devotion award 1996), Alpha Kappa Alpha. Democrat. Methodist. Avocation: traveling, theater, dancing, photography. Home: PO Box 5196 Charleston SC 29405

SANDERS, TIMOTHY LEE, therapist, writer; b. Nagoya, Japan, Dec. 1, 1957; s. William Mills and Edith Dorothy (Englert) S.; m. Kati Bowen, Oct. 14, 1988. BS in Psychology, U. Miss., 1981; MS in Counseling Psychology, U. So. Miss., 1985. Lic. profl. counselor, Ala. Bd. Examiners in Counseling, 1993. Outpatient therapist North Ark. Human Svcs. System, Inc., Heber Springs, 1985-87, Marshall-Jackson Mental Health Ctr., Scottsboro, Ala., 1987—; pvt. practice, 1993—; lectr. in field to include Gulf Coast Conf. on Alcohol and Drug Abuse, Orange Beach, Ala., 1993, Ala. Coun. Communty Mental Health Bds., Birmingham, Ala., 1993,Hospice of N.E. Ala., Scottsboro, 1993, Ala. Assn. Addicitons Counselors, Gulf Shores, 1993, Nat. Symposium for Nat. Child Advocacy Ctr., 1993, U. Nebr. grad. Sch., 1993. Author: Male Survivors: 12-Step Recovery Program for Survivors of Childhood Sexual Abuse, 1991, After The War is Over: Long-Term Recovery Strategies for Adult Male Survivors of Childhood Sexual Abuse, 1993; contbr. articles to profl. jours. Vol. Ark. Alliance for Mentally Ill; regional coord. Nat. Sibling and Adult Children Network; mem. Scottsboro-Jackson County Rotary Club; vol. cons. Hospice of N.E. Ala. Mem. ACA, Ala. Counselor's Assn., Sexual Abuse Treatment Info. Network of North Ala. Home: 1149 Pleasant Grove Rd Woodville AL 35776-7260 Office: The Counseling Ctr 233 S Market St Scottsboro AL 35768-1806

SANDERS, WAYNE R., manufacturing executive; b. Chgo., July 6, 1947; s. Ralph G. and Bernice F. (Swanson) S.; m. Kathleen E. Lessard, Aug. 22, 1970; children: Tracy, Amy, Megan. BCE, Ill. Inst. Tech., 1969; MBA, Marquette U., 1972. Fin. analyst Ford Motor Co., Dearborn, Mich., 1972-75; sr. fin. analyst Kimberly-Clark Corp., Neenah, Wis., 1975, dir. bus. planning internat., 1976-80, dir. bus. planning U.S. consumer bus., 1980-81; v.p. strategic planning Kimberly-Clark of Can., Toronto, Ont., 1981-82, pres., 1982-85; sr. v.p. Kimberly-Clark Corp., Dallas, 1986; pres. infant care sector Kimberly-Clark Corp., Neenah, Wis., from 1987; former pres. personal care div. Kimberly-Clark Corp., pres., chief oper. officer world consumer, nonwovens and svc. and indsl. ops., 1990—; pres., CEO Kimberly-Clark Corp., Dallas, 1990-91, chmn., CEO, 1992—, chmn. bd., CEO, 1992—. Elected mem. Neenah Sch. Bd., 1980-81; nat. trustee Boys and Girls Clubs Am., 1994; trustee Marquette U., Milw. Roman Catholic.

SANDERS, WILLIAM EUGENE, marketing executive; b. Asheboro, N.C., Nov. 16, 1933; s. Arthur Ira and Picola (Loftin) S.; m. Velna Elizabeth Sumner, June 8, 1957; children: William Eugene Jr., George Herbert Sumner. AB in Polit. Sci., U. N.C., 1956, postgrad. in Law, 1956-57. Marketing rep. Encyclopaedia Britannica, Greensboro, N.C., 1957-60, Am. Pubs., Chgo., 1960-66; pres. S&W Distbrs., Inc., Greensboro, 1966—. Little league coach Civitans, Greensboro, 1967-68. With U.S. Army Res., 1957-63. Named Hon. Amb. Dept. of Labor, Ky., 1976, Ky. Col., 1976, Hon. Mem. La. Lt. Gov. Staff, 1984; recipient Cert. Appreciation Jefferson Davis Parish Libr., Jennings, La., 1986, Top Sales award Am. Media. Corp., 1996, Marshall Cavendish Top Prodn. award, 1990-91, Mktg. award Am. Media, 1995. Mem. State Libr. Assns. Va., W.Va., La., Gen. Alumni Assn. (co-chairman

Greensboro chpt. 1979-80), Chi Phi. Democrat. Presbyterian. Office: S&W Distbrs Inc 1600H E Wendover Ave Greensboro NC 27405-6837

SANDERSON, DAVID ODELL, insurance broker; b. Tulia, Tex., Sept. 20, 1956; s. Ray Sanderson and Nancy (Allison) Godwin; m. Kathy Ann Gossett, June 30, 1984. BBA, Tex. Tech U., 1980. Chartered fin. cons., CLU. Gen. agt. Southwestern Life Ins. Co., Dallas, 1980—; owner David Sanderson CLU, Chartered Fin. Cons., Abernathy, Tex., 1985—; life mgr. Quisenberry Ins., Lubbock, Tex., 1989-90; ind. ins. broker Abernathy, 1990—; gen. agt. Ohio Nat. Cos., Cin., 1993—; registered rep. The O.N. Equity Sales Co., Cin., 1993—. Tchr. Bible class Sunset Ch. of Christ, Lubbock, 1986—. Named one of Outstanding Young Men of Am., 1985. Mem. Nat. Assn. Life Underwriters (Nat. Quality award 1985-86), Tex. Assn. Life Underwriters (polit. action com., state bd. dirs., v.p. 1991—), Lubbock Area Assn. Life Underwriters (bd. dirs. 1987-89, chmn. polit. action com. 1987-90, chmn. meetings logistics 1990-92, chmn. state legislation com. 1992—), Am. Soc. CLU and ChFC, Lubbock Area Soc. CLU and ChFC (bd. dirs. 1991-93), Lions. Home and Office: 602 10th St Abernathy TX 79311-3004

SANDERSON, MARY LOUISE, medical association administrator; b. Fairmont, W. Va., Oct. 29, 1942; d. Lawrence Oliver and Frances Evelyn (Shuttleworth) Shingleton; m. William W. Olmstead III, Dec. 1966 (div. June 1974); children: William W. IV, Happy; m. Lester F. Davis, III, Oct. 1979 (div. Dec. 1986); m. David S. Sanderson, Sept. 1992. Student, Vassar Coll., 1960-62, Carnegie Mellon, 1962-63. Real estate broker, N.C. Exec. sec. Creative Dining, Raleigh, N.C., 1980-83, Sea Pines Plantation Co., Hilton Head, S.C., 1973-79; adminstr. Am. Bd. Neurological Surgery, Houston, 1983—. Vol. Interact, Raleigh, 1984-86, M.D. Anderson Cancer Ctr./Camp Star Trails, 1994—; docent Mordicai House Hist. Preservation, Raleigh, 1981-83; mem. Reach to Recovery, 1995—. Recipient Vol. award N.C. State Gov., 1986. Mem. Am. Soc. Assn. Execs. Democrat. Episcopalian. Office: Am Bd Neurol Surgery 6550 Fannin St Ste 2139 Houston TX 77030-2722

SANDIDGE, JUNE CAROL, physical education educator; b. Lynchburg, Va., Mar. 16, 1936; d. Fred Brown and Sarah Elizabeth (Cocks) S. BS, Longwood Coll., Farmville, Va., 1959; MEd, U. Va., 1967; cert. advanced grad. studies, Va. Tech. Inst., 1981. Tchr. Roanoke (Va.) City Schs., 1959-65; prof. phys. edn. and recreation Ferrum (Va.) Coll., 1965—; asst. dir. YWCA Camp-on-Craig, Roanoke, 1965-83, dir., 1984-85; interim dir. Henry Forks Svc. Ctr., United Meth. Ch., Rocky Mount, Va., 1986-87, chair bd., 1989-91, cons. ARC, Roanoke, 1986-90, chair S.W. Va. territory, 1988-91, chair Va./D.C. field svc., 1992-95. Chair S.W. Va. Territory, 1988-91, chair Va./D.C. field svc., 1992-95. Recipient Disting. Service Alumni award Longwood Coll., 1984, Honor award for vol. svc. ARC, 1982. Mem. AAUW, AAHPERD, Va. Assn. Health, Phys. Edn., Recreation and Dance (rep. aquatic coun. so. dist. 1991-93), Coun. Nat. Coop. Aquatics, Phi Delta Kappa (pres. 1990-91). Baptist. Home and Office: Ferrum Coll Ferrum VA 24088

SANDLER, NAT HAROLD, psychiatrist; b. Memphis, Feb. 27, 1937; s. Max M. and Ann (Allen) S.; m. Judith Ann Henriott, May 9, 1964; 1 child, Mark. BS, U. Memphis, 1961; MD, U. Tenn., 1963; MPH, U. N.C., 1971. Diplomate Am. Bd. Psychiatry. Intern Norton Infirmary, Louisville, Ky., 1963-64; resident Wayne County Hosp., Eloise, Mich., 1964-67; dir. Bluegrass East Camp Care, Lexington, Ky., 1971-75; pvt. practice Lexington, 1975—; pres. Bluegrass Psychiatric Svc., Lexington, 1988—; chief psychiatry Good Samaritan Hosp., Lexington, 1989-90. Chair NCCJ, Lexington, 1988. Lt. comdr. USNR, 1967-69. Fellow U. N.C., Chapel Hill, 1969-71. Fellow Am. Psychiatric Assn.; mem. AMA, Ky. Psychiatric Assn. (pres. 1990-91). Democrat. Jewish. Office: 1401 Harrodsburg Rd Ste C425 Lexington KY 40504-3772

SANDLIN, ANN MARIE, real estate broker; b. Ft. Worth, Sept. 17, 1940; d. Joseph Gustave Rountree and Jessie Margaret (Piatt) Ford; m. James Gordon Anderson, Apr. 28, 1961 (div. May 1981); children: James Gordon Jr., Edward Joseph; m. George Wilson Sandlin, Nov. 11, 1984. Mail clk. State Comptroller's Dept., Austin, Tex., 1960-62; Realtor, relocation dir., office mgr. Sandlin & Co. Real Estate, Austin, 1976—. Mem. Women's Coun. Realtors (past pres.), Tex. Assn. Realtors (bd. dirs. 1988—, chmn. pub. rels. 1991), Austin Bd. Realtors (bd. dirs. 1990—, pres. 1996), Daus. Republic of Tex. Office: Sandlin & Co PO Box 202738 Austin TX 78720-2738

SANDLIN, BEVERLY RUTH, education educator; b. Eunice, N.Mex., Nov. 15, 1949; d. Robert P. and Minnie Lee (Wilson) Harvey; m. Donald Sandlin, Apr. 12, 1971; 1 child, Pamela Ann. BS in Edn., Ea. N.Mex. U., Portales, 1971; MS, Northwestern La. State U., 1981, Northwestern La. State U., 1982; Ednl. Specialist, Fla. State U., 1991. Cert. tchr., Fla. Tchr. Tucumcari (N.Mex.) Pub. Schs., 1971; dir. Zweibruecken (Fed. Republic of Germany) Pre-Sch., 1973-78; tchr. Vernon Parish Sch. Dist., Leesville, La., 1978-79, Rapides Parish Sch. Dist., Alexandria, La., 1979-81, England AFB (La.) Elem. Sch., 1981-82, Sch. of Hope-ARC, Ft. Walton Beach, Fla., 1982-84, Okaloosa County Sch. Dist., Ft. Walton Beach, 1984-92; instr., coord. child devel. ctr. Okaloosa-Walton C.C., Niceville, Fla., 1992—. Mem. Nat. Assn. Edn. Young Children, So. Early Childhood Assn., Fla. Assn. C.C.'s., Am. Assn. Women C.C.'s, Garnet Key Soc., Phi Delta Kappa, Delta Kappa Gamma, Phi Kappa Phi. Home: 362 Evergreen Ave Niceville FL 32578-1134

SANDLIN, DEBBIE CROWE, critical care nurse; b. Columbia, Tenn., Oct. 1, 1953; d. William Taylor and Jean (Burns) Crowe; divorced; 1 child, Ashley Taylor. AS cum laude, Columbia State Coll., 1973; student, U. Tenn., Nashville, 1974-76. RN, Tenn.; cert. ACLS, BCLS, U.T. critical care curriculum. Charge nurse surg. unit Maury Regional Med. Ctr., Columbia, 1973-74; charge nurse surg. ICU HCA Pk. View Med. Ctr., Nashville, 1974-76; staff nurse post anesthesia care unit HCA Westside Hosp., Nashville, 1976-79; head nurse Parkside Surgery Ctr., Nashville, 1979-85; head nurse Columbia So. Hills Med. Ctr., Nashville, 1985—, post anesthesia care unit nurse, 1985—. Maury Regional Med. Ctr. Auxillary scholar, 1971. Mem. Mid. Tenn. Soc. Post Anesthesia Nurses (founder, pres. 1986, bd. dirs. 1986-88, Outstanding Svc. award 1986-87, pub. newsletter, editor 1986-87, various coms.), Tenn. Soc. Post Anesthesia Nurses (v.p. 1986-87, pres. 1987-88, bd. dirs. 1986-93, state seminar com. chairperson 1993-94, congl. rep. Point Sys. Winner 1987, 88, chair edn. com. 1994-95, chair TSPAN mid-yr. seminar 1996, various coms.), Am. Soc. Post Anesthesia Nurses (Tenn. dir. 1990-93, membership com. 1993-95, ethics com. 1993-94, new products com., exec. com. 1992-93, chair bylaws com. 1992-93, nat. conf. com. 1991-92, amb. to Nat. Assn. Orthopaedic Nurses 1994, Pres. Appreciation award 1992, 93, 94, Amb. award 1995, product evaluation com. 1995-96, liasion to emergency nurses assn. nat. conf. 1995). Home: 508 Michele Dr Antioch TN 37013-4109

SANDMAN, DAVID EDWARD, JR., rehabilitation nurse; b. Cin., Mar. 14, 1959; s. David Edward and Jean Marie (Thiemann) S. Diploma in nursing, Christ Hosp., Cin., 1984; BS in Communication Sci. and Disorders, U. Cin., 1981. RN, Ohio. Rehab. nurse Jewish Hosp., Cin., 1984-86, U. Hosp., Cin., 1986-87; pvt. duty home rehab. nurse RN Registry, Cin., 1987-91; rehab. nurse No. Ky. Rehab. Hosp., Edgewood, 1991—; contract co-statis. analyst rehab. medicine dept. Good Samaritan Hosp., Cin., 1986; presenter in field. Contbr. articles to profl. jours.

SANDMEL, BEN, journalist, musician; b. Nashville, June 8, 1952; s. Samuel and Frances (Fox) S. BA in Folklore, Ind. U., 1976. Fieldwork researcher La. Folklife Program, 1984—; drummer Hackberry Ramblers; presenter, writer La. Folklife Festival; programming cons. New Orleans Jazz and Heritage Festival, Folk Masters Concert Series, Wolf Trap, Vienna, Va. Author record liner notes for more than 75 albums, music criticism for Atlantic Monthly, Rolling Stone; prodr.: (albums) Drinkin' and Stinkin' (Boogie Bill Webb), Cincinnati Stomp (Big Joe Duskin), Cajun Boogie (Hackberry Ramblers); contbr. travel articles to Esquire. Mem. NARAS, Am. Folklore Soc., Press Club of New Orleans (Critical Rev. of Yr. award 1984, 91). Home: 221 Metairie Ct Metairie LA 70001

SANDOVAL, ARTURO ALONZO, art educator, artist; b. Espanola/Cordova, N.Mex., Feb. 1, 1942; s. Lorenzo Sandoval and Cecilia Eulalia (Archuleta) Harrison; (div. Sept. 1982); 1 child, Avalon Valentine Galaglorial. Student, U. Portland, 1959; BA, Calif. State Coll., L.A., 1964, MA, 1969; MFA, Cranbrook Acad. Art, Bloomfield Hills, Mich., 1971. Designer, illustrator Western Lighting Corp., L.A., 1964-66; advt. designer, adult edn. instr. spl. svcs. USN, Yokosuka, Japan, 1966; interior designasst. Walter B. Broderick & Assocs., La Mesa, Calif., 1967; asst. prof. art dept. U. Ky., Lexington, 1974-76, assoc. prof., 1976-86, full prof., 1986—, dir. art dept. Barnhart Gallery, 1976—, curator, 1979—; teaching asst. Calif. State Coll., L.A., 1969, Cranbrook Acad. Art, Bloomfield Hills, 1970; fiber art demonstrator Mus. Art, Grand Rapids, Mich., 1970; batik and tie-dye demonstrator Gwynn's Fabric Shop, Birmingham, Mich., 1970; instr. Calif. State Coll., L.A., 1970, So. Ill. U., Carbondale, 1971, Edwardsville, 1971, 72; presenter various lectures and workshops throughout the U.S., 1973—; juror Mo.Women Festival Arts, St. Louis, So. Ill. U., East St. Louis, 1974, Paramount Arts Assn., Ashland, Ky., 1975, Ind. Weavers Guild, Indpls., 1979, Fed. Corrections Inst., Lexington, 1979, Hawaii Craftsman Hui and Art Dept. U. Hawaii, Manoa, Honolulu, 1982, art dept. Va. Intermont Coll., Bristol, 1982, Arrowmont Sch. Arts and Crafts, Gatlinburg, Tenn., 1984, Ctr. Contemporary Art, U. Ky., Lexington, 1984, Guild Greater Cin.,Carnegie Art Ctr., Covington, Ky., 1989, S.C. Arts Commn., Charleston, 1990, Adams Art Gallery, Dunkirk, N.Y., 1994; visual arts cons. Ky. Arts Commn., Frankfort, 1977; curator Visual Arts Ctr. Alaska, Anchorage, 1982, Ky. Art and Crafts Found., Inc., Louisville, 1985; mem. artist adv. panel Ky. Art and Crafts Found., Louisville, 1986, 87, 92, 93, 94; visual arts cons. Arts Midwest, 1987; artistic advisor Ky. Guild Mktg. Bd., Lexington, 1988, 91, 92, 93; bd. mem. Ky. Guild Mktg. Bd., 1992, Am. Craft Coun., N.Y.C.; vis. artist/critic Allen R. Hite Inst., U. Louisville, 1992; vis. artist Coll. Human Environ. Scis., U. Ky., Lexington, 1993; vis. artist/ lectr. fiber dept. Cranbrook Acad. Art, Bloomfield Hills, Mich., 1994. Exhibited in group shows at Yeiser Art Ctr., Paducah/Paramount Arts Ctr., Ashland/S.E. Cmty. Coll., Cumberland, 1994, Textile Arts Centre, Chgo., 1994, Winnipeg (Man., Can.) Art Gallery, 1994, Riffe Gallery, Ohio Arts Coun., Columbus, 1994, Royal Hiberian Acad., Gallagher Gallery, Dublin, Ireland, Cooper Gallery, Barnsley, South Yorks, Gt. Britain, Shipley Art Gallery,Gateshead, Gt. Britain, 1994, Grand Rapids (Mich.) Art Mus., 1994, Whatcom Mus. History and Art, Bellingham, Wash., The Rockwell Mus., Corning, N.Y., Mus. Art, Washington State U., Pullman,The Hyde Collection, Glen Falls, N.Y., 1994, U. Art Galleries, U. S.D., Vermillion, 1994, Barnhart Gallery, U. Ky., Lexington, 1994, Sawtooth Ctr. Visual Art, 1994, Santa Fe Gallery, Santa Fe Cmty. Coll., Gainesville, Fla., 1994, Liberty Gallery, Louisville, 1994, Asahi Shimbun Gallery, Tokyo, Takashimaya Gallery, Osaka, 1994, Minn. Mus. Art, Landmark Ctr., St. Paul, 1994, S.C. State Mus., Columbia, 1994, Galbreath Gallery, Lexington, 1994, others; represented in permanent collections at Wabash Coll., Crawfordsville, Ind., Greenville County Mus. Art, Greenville, S.C., Mus. Modern Art, N.Y.C., St. Mary's Coll., Notre Dame, Ind., Coll. St. Rose, Albany, N.Y., Bowling Green (Ohio) StateU., U. Notre Dame, Transylvania U., Lexington, U. Ky. Mus. Art, Lexington, Mid-Am. Rare Coin Auction Galleris, Lexington, Henry Luce Found., N.Y.C., Lexington Ctrl. Libr., others. Recipient Alexandra Korsakoff Galston Meml. prize St. Louis Artist's Guild, 1971, Mus. Merit award Mus. Arts and Scis., Evansville, 1972, Creative Rsch. Grant So. Ill. U.-Edwardsville Rsch. Found., 1972, Craftsman fellowship Nat. Endowment for Arts, Washington, 1973, Friend of Mus. award Mus. Arts and Scis., Evansville, 1973, Clay Eugene Jordan ann. bequest prize for crafts St. Louis Artist's Guild, 1973, Teaching Improvement grant U. Ky. Rsch. Found., 1974, Travel grant U. Ky. Rsch. Found., 1977, Judges Choice award Berea (Ky.) Coll., 1978, Handweaver's Guild Am. award, 1978, Fiber award LeMoyne Art Found., Tallahassee, 1981, Elise Strout Merit award Mus. Arts and Scis., Evansville, 1981, Handweavers Guild Am. award, 1983, Martha Ryan Merit award Mus. Arts and Scis., Evansville, 1984, Best of Show award Gayle Willson Galleries, Southampton, 1984, Juror's merit award Brenau Coll., Gainesville, Ga., 1985, Installation Grant Ind. Arts Commn., Ft. Wayne, 1985, All Smith fellowship Ky. Arts Coun., Frankfort, 1987, Merit award Renwick Gallery, Tuscaloosa, Ala., 1988, Merit award Mus. Arts and Scis., Evansville, 1989, Design Grant, Arts and Cultural Coun. for O.A. Singletary Ctr. for Arts, Lexington, 1990, Visual Arts fellowship Nat. Endowment for Arts, Washington, 1992, Hon. award Ky. Crafts Mktg. Bd., Frankfort, 1994. Mem. Lexington Fiber Guild Inc., Louisville Visual Arts Assn., Ky. Art and Craft Found., Inc., Ky. Guild Artists and Craftsmen, Am. Craft Coun. Home: PO Box 25153 Lexington KY 40525-5153 Office: U Ky Dept Art 207 Fine Arts Bldg Lexington KY 40506

SANDS, DON WILLIAM, agricultural products company executive retired; b. Durant, Okla., Aug. 30, 1926; s. William Henry and Mary (Crutchfield) S.; m. Joan Cantrell, Mar. 28, 1947; children: Susan Sands Hendrix, Stan W., Steve J. B.S., Southeastern Okla. State U., 1949. Office mgr. Durant Cotton Oil & Peanut Corp., Okla., 1947-53; asst. mgr. Greenwood Products Co., Graceville, Fla., 1953-57; with Cotton Producers Assn. (changed name to Gold Kist Inc., 1970); exec. v.p., mem. exec. com. Gold Kist Inc., Atlanta, 1978-84, pres., chief oper. officer, mem. exec. com., 1984-88, pres., chief exec. officer, chmn. exec. com., 1989-91; chmn. Golden Poultry Co., Inc. subs. Gold Kist Inc., Atlanta, 1987-92; bd. dirs. Nat. Data Corp., Atlanta, Ga. World Congress Ctr., Atlanta, Bus. Coun. Ga., So. Ctr. for Internat. Studies; chmn. bd. Golden Poultry Co., Inc., Atlanta; mem. Atlanta Dist. Export Coun.; audit com. Nat. Data Corp., Atlanta, 1980. Mem. adv. bd. Inst. Internat. Edn., Atlanta, 1980, Japen-U.S. S.E. Assn., 1975; bd. dirs. Ga. Bd. Industry and Trade, 1979, Bus. Coun. Ga., So. Ctr. for Internat. Studies, Atlanta; chmn. bd. trustee, mem. fin. com. Ga. Coun. on Econ. Edn.; active Pleasant Hill Presbyn. Ch., Duluth, Ga.; past chmn. Ga. World Congress Ctr. With USN, 1944-46. Named to Nat. Peanut Coun. Hall of Fame, 1992. Mem. Nat. Coun. Farmer Coops., Ga. C. of C. (bd. dirs.), Japan-Am. Soc. Ga. (chmn. bd. dirs.), S.E. U.S./Japan Assn. (Ga. adv. bd., chmn.), Atlanta Athletic Club (gen. chmn. 1990 U.S. Womens Open, pres.), St. Ives Country Club (pres. 1990-95). Republican. Presbyterian (elder). Office: Gold Kist Inc 244 Perimeter Center Pky NE Atlanta GA 30346-2302

SANDS, ROBERTA ALYSE, real estate investor; b. N.Y.C., Oct. 7, 1937; d. Harry and Irene (Mytelka) S. BEd, U. Miami, 1960; postgrad., U. Oslo, 1960. Cert. secondary educator biology, Mass. Phys. edn. instr. Key Biscayne and Ludlam Elem. Sch., Miami, 1961-63; sci. tchr. Plantation (Fla.) Mid. Sch., 1969-71, Rickards Middle Sch., Ft. Lauderdale, Fla., 1972-76; founder U. Miami Diabetes Rsch. Inst., 1989. Author: Biology on the Secondary Level, 1970. Vol. Douglas Garden Retirement Home, Miami, 1988-92, Mus. of Art, Ft. Lauderdale, 1988-92, Imperial Point Hosp., Ft. Lauderdale, 1981-83. Mem. AAUW (rec. sec. 1988-92, cultural chair 1993-94, legis. chair Ft. Lauderdale br. 1994-95, women's issue chair Ft. Lauderdale 1994—, edn. chair Pompano Beach br. 1994-96, Recognition of Significant Svc. award 1983). Home: Apt 8S 4250 Galt Ocean Dr Fort Lauderdale FL 33308-6138

SANDS, WILLIE LOUIS, federal judge; b. 1949. BA, Mercer U., 1971, JD, 1974. Chief legal asst. to dist. atty. Macon Jud. Cir., 1974, asst. dist. atty., 1975-78; asst. U.S. atty. U.S. Dist. Ct. (mid. dist.) Ga., 1978-87; with Mathis, Sands, Jordan & Adams, Macon, 1987-91; judge superior ct. Macon Jud. Cir., 1991-93; dist. judge U.S. Dist. Ct. (mid. dist.) Ga., Albany, 1994—; ptnr. Investors Ltd., 1984-91; mem. task force substance abuse Ga. Supreme Ct., 1991—, mem. com. gender equality, 1993—; bd. dirs. Bank Corp. Ga./1st South Bank, N.A. Organist/min. music, officer Steward Chapel AME Ch., 1976—; active Cmty. Found. Ga., Inc.; mem. 30th anniversary planning com. Mercer U., mem. bd. visitors Walter F. George sch. law, 1994—; v.p. Ga. Commn. Family Violence, 1992—; bd. dirs. Macon Symphony, 1992—. 2d lt. Signal Corps, U.S. Army, 1971, res. Acad. scholar Mercer U.; grad. Leadership Macon, 1985, Leadership Ga., 1986. Mem. ABA, Am. Judicature Soc., State Bar Ga. (mem. bench and bar com. 1991—), Macon Bar Assn. (pres. 1991-92), Coun. Superior Ct. Judges (mem. bench and bar com. 1991—), Walter F. George Sch. Law Alumni Assn. (bd. dirs.), Scabbard and Blade Mil. Honor Soc., Alpha Phi Alpha, Sigma Pi Phi, Homosophian Club. Office: US Dist Ct PO Box 1705 Albany GA 31702-1705

SANDSTROM, DIRK WILLIAM, air force officer, hospital administrator; b. Ogden, Utah, Oct. 27, 1963; s. William Arthur and Jeanene Melva (Curtis) S.; m. Lisa Marie Nelson, Dec. 29, 1992; children: Elisabeth, Annette, Matthew Daren. BS cum laude, U. Utah, 1990, MPH, 1994. Rsch. asst. U. Iowa, Iowa City, 1990-92; freelance writer Blackwell Cons., Inc., Salt Lake City, 1993-94; commd. 1st lt. USAF, 1994; asst. adminstr. 7th Med. Group, Dyess AFB, Tex., 1995-96, chief info. officer, 1996—, mem. adv. coun. health care consumer adv. coun., 1995-96; lectr. U. Utah, Salt Lake City, 1993-94, Salt Lake C.C., Salt Lake City, 1993-94; mem. adv. bd. Salt Lake City-County Health Dept., 1993-94. Author: How To Own a Home Business, 1994; editor Utah Pub. Health Assn. Newsletter, 1993-94. Master Boy Scouts Am., Salt Lake City, 1993-94; loaned exec. United Way Abilene, Tex., 1996; dir. combined fed. campaign Dyess AFB, 1996. Mem. Am. Coll. Healthcare Execs., Air Force Assn., Co. Grade Officers Assn., Golden Key, Phi Beta Kappa, Phi Kappa Phi, Beta Sigma. Republican. Mem. LDS Ch. Home: 108 Virginia St Dyess AFB TX 79607-1032 Office: 7th Med Group/7 MDSS/SGSI 697 Hospital Rd Dyess AFB TX 79607-1367

SANDSTRUM, STEVE D., industry manager; b. Ulysses, Kans., Dec. 8, 1953; s. Don Eugene and Alleene (Lawrence) S.; m. Nancy Heinzer, Aug. 28, 1976; 1 child, Andrew. BS in Zoology, Okla. State U., 1976, MS in Engring., 1980. Registered engr. in training. Devel. engr. Phillips Driscopipe, Richardson, Tex., 1984-85, sr. tech. engr., 1985-86, quality assurance specialist, 1986-88; sr. polymer engr. Solvay Polymers, Houston, Tex., 1988; tech. svc. mgr. Poly Pipe Industry, Gainesville, Tex., 1988; group leader Solvay Polymers, Houston, 1988-91, mktg. mgr. profl. engr., 1991-92; industry mgr., 1992—; exec. bd. Plastics Pipe Inst., Wayne, N.J., 1989-91, adv. bd., 1991-94, hydrostatic bd., 1991—; tchr. Okla. State U., Stillwater, 1979-80; pres. Plastics Pipe Inst., Washington, 1995—. Author: (chpt.) Pipeline Rehabilitation, 1987, Above Ground Applications, 1989; editor: Handbook of Polyethylene Pipe, 1991. Pres. Sea Lion Swim Team, Kingwood, Tex., 1995. Recipient rsch. award Gen. Motors, 1981. Mem. NSPE, ASTM (Cert. of Appreciation 1993), Soc. Plastic Engrs., Am. Water Works Assn., Plastics Pipe and Fittings Assn. (pres. 1996), Am. Pub. Works Assn., Tex. Soc. Profl. Engrs., Alpha Phi Mu. Republican. Presbyterian. Office: Solvay Polymers 3333 Richmond Ave Houston TX 77098-3007

SANDUSKY, CAMILLE MARTIN, special education diagnostician; b. Brownwood, Tex., Nov. 12, 1934; d. Dean Donald Martin and Dora (Ely) Allen; m. Judge Edward Sandusky, Jan. 30, 1954; children: Koby Austin, Sam Ely, Ross Edward. BS, Our Lady of the Lake Coll., 1968, MA, 1973. Registered profl. ednl. diagnostician, Tex. Clk. Tex. Transp. Inst., College Sta., 1958-60; tchr. D'Hanis (Tex.) Ind. Sch. Dist., 1968-69, Medina Valley Ind. Sch. Dist., LaCoste, Tex., 1969-70; homebound tchr. Edgewood Ind. Sch. Dist., San Antonio, 1970-72; ednl. diagnostician South San Antonio Ind. Sch. Dist., 1972-76, Devine (Tex.) Ind. Sch. Dist., 1980-81, Hondo (Tex.) Ind. Sch. Dist., 1981-95, Windham (Tex.) Sch. Sys., 1995-96. Mem. S.W. Tex. Property Rights Assn., 1988—; bd. dirs. Medina County Family Life Ctr., 1984-85, 91-96. mem. Coun. Exceptional Children, Tex. Ednl. Diagnostician's Assn., Alamo Area Ednl. Diagnostician's Assn., Delta Kappa Gamma (treas. 1992—). Mem. Ch. of Christ. Home: 3120 C R 4516 Hondo TX 78861-1006

SANFORD, CATHY ELAIN, medical/surgical nurse administrator; b. Dahlonega, Ga., Mar. 8, 1955; d. William Leonard and Bessie Ellene (Chambers) Crow; m. Arthur Sanford, Oct. 8, 1976. Diploma, Brenau Coll. Sch. Nursing, 1976; BSN, North Ga. Coll., 1989; MSA, Ctrl. Mich. U., 1993. Supr. med. surg. Lumpkin County Hosp., Dahlonega, Ga., 1976-77; supr. spl. care Lumpkin County Hosp., Dahlonega, 1977-79, emergency rm. supr., 1979-81, asst. dir. nursing, infection control, insvc. edn., 1981-90; dir. nursing St. Joseph's Hosp., Dahlonega, 1991-96; staff asst. to pres. Chestatee Regional Hosp., Dahlonega, 1996—. Mem. ANA (cert. nursing adminstr., med./surg. nurse), AONE, Employee Health Assn., Assn. Practitioners in Infection Control, Am. Heart Assn. (pres.), Ga. Orgn. Nurse Execs., Ga. Nurses Assn., Eastern Star. Home: RR 8 Box 340 Dahlonega GA 30533-9765

SANFORD, JAMES KENNETH, public relations executive; b. Clyde, N.C., Jan. 23, 1932; s. James Edward S. and Bernice (Crawford) Peebles; m. Alice Pearl Reavis, Sept. 22, 1957; children: Timothy, Scott, Jeannette. AA, Mars Hill (N.C.) Coll., 1952; AB, U. N.C., 1954, MA, 1958. Pub. rels. officer Asheville (N.C.) United Appeal, 1954; reporter, copy editor Winston-Salem (N.C.) Jour., 1957-59, asst. state editor, 1959-61, news editor, 1961-63, editorial writer, 1963-64; dir. pub. info. and publs. U. N.C., Charlotte, 1964-94; pub. rels. cons. Charlotte, N.C., 1994—; cons. Commn. on Future of Mars Hill Coll., 1990-91, City of Charlotte, 1991. Author: Charlotte and UNC Charlotte: Growing Up Together, 1996; co-author: Fifty Favored Years, 1972; contbr. numerous articles to mag. and newspapers. Active attractions com. Charlotte Conv. and Visitors Bur., 1994—, Internat. House Bd., 1995, adv. com. Sta. WTVI Pub. TV, Charlotte, 1986-94; chmn. bd. deacons local ch., 1994-95. With U.S. Army, 1954-56. Elected to N.C. Pub. Rels. Hall of Fame, 1995; recipient Alumnus by Choice award U. N.C. at Charlotte, 1996. Fellow Pub. Rels. Soc. Am. (chmn. S.E. dist. 1991); mem. Coll. News Assn. Carolinas (Lewis Gaston award 1982), Charlotte Pub. Rels. Soc. (pres. 1974, Infinity award 1986), Coun. for Advancement and Support Edn. (asst. dist. chmn. 1975-76), Phi Kappa Phi. Baptist. Home and Office: 1216 Braeburn Rd Charlotte NC 28211-4769

SANFORD, MARSHALL (MARK SANFORD), congressman; b. Ft. Lauderdale, Fla., May 28, 1960; m. Jenny Sullivan; 3 children. BA, Furman U., 1983; MBA, U. Va., 1988. With Goldman Sachs, 1988, CRC Realty, 1988-89; prin. Southeastern Ptnrs., 1989—, Norton & Sanford, 1993—; mem. 104th Congress from 1st Dist. S.C., 1995—. Republican. Office: US Ho of Reps Washington DC 20515

SANFORD, TERRY, lawyer, educator, former United States Senator, former governor, former university president; b. Laurinburg, N.C., Aug. 20, 1917; s. Cecil and Elizabeth (Martin) S.; m. Margaret Rose Knight, July 4, 1942; children: Elizabeth Knight, Terry. AB, U. N.C., 1939, JD, 1946; 30 hon. degrees from colls. and univs. Bar: N.C. 1946, D.C. 1979. Asst. dir. Inst. Govt., U. N.C., 1940-41, 46-48; spl. agt. FBI, 1941-42; pvt. practice Fayetteville, 1948-60; ptnr. Sanford, Adams, McCullough & Beard, Raleigh, N.C. and Washington, 1965-86; gov. State of N.C., 1961-65; pres. Duke U., Durham, N.C., 1969-85, prof. pub. policy, 1992—; mem. U.S. Senate 99th-102d Congresses from N.C., Washington, 1986-93; ptnr. The Sanford Law Firm, PLLC, Raleigh, 1993—; prof. of practice, public policy Duke U., 1992—; pub. gov. Am. Stock Exchange, 1977-83; dir. Study of Am. States, Duke U., 1965-68; mem. Carnegie Commn. Ednl. TV, 1964-67; pres. Urban Am., Inc., 1968-69; chmn. ITT Internat. Fellowship Com., 1974-86, Am. Coun. Young Polit. Leaders, 1976-86; pres. U.S. Del. Inter-Parliamentary Union, 1988-90. Author: But What About the People?, 1966, Storm Over the States, 1967, A Danger of Democracy, 1981, Outlive Your Enemies, 1996. Sec.-treas. N. C. Port Authority, 1950-53; mem. N.C. Senate, 1953-54; pres. N.C. Young Dem. Clubs, 1949-50; del. Nat. Dem. Conv., 1956, 60, 64, 68, 72, 84, 88, 92; chmn. Nat. Dem. Charter Commn., 1972-74; mem. governing bd. Nat. Com. for Citizens in Edn., Am. Art Alliance; trustee Am. Council Learned Socs., 1970-73, Nat. Humanities Center, 1978-86, Meth. Coll., 1958-94, Howard U., 1968-86; chmn. N.C. Mus. Art, 1993—; bd. dirs. Children's TV Workshop, 1967-71, Council on Founds., 1971-76, N.C. Outward Bound, 1981-88; chmn. bd. trustees U. N.C., 1961-65; chmn. So. Regional Edn. Bd., 1961-63, Sta. ACSN (The Learning Channel), 1980-86, Assn. Am. Univs., 1980-81, Nat. Civic League, 1985-86. Served to 1st lt. AUS, 1942-46. Mem. ABA, Am. Acad. Polit. and Social Sci., Coun. Fgn. Rels., Am. Judicature Soc., Nat. Acad. Pub. Adminstrn., AAAS, Phi Beta Kappa. Methodist. Office: Sanford Law Firm 234 Fayetteville St Raleigh NC 27601-1867

SANGANI, BHARAT HIMATLAL, cardiologist; b. Bombay, India, Oct. 20, 1957; came to U.S., 1983; s. Himatlal and Champaben (Gaglani) S.; m. Smita Vakharia, June 1, 1984; children: Nili, Niki. MBBS, Bombay U., 1982. Diplomate Am. Bd. Internal Medicine, Am. Bd. Cardiology. Intern King Edward Meml. Hosp., Bombay, 1981-82; resident in internal medicine Mt. Carmel Med. Ctr., Columbus, Ohio, 1983-86, fellow in cardiology, 1986-88; pres. Coast Cardiology Ctr., Gulfport, Miss., 1988—. Fellow Am. Coll. Cardiology, Am. Coll. Chest Physicians; mem. AMA, Coll. Physicians and Surgeons (India), Royal Soc. Health (England), Am. Heart Assn., Am. Assn. Nuclear Cardiology, Am. Coll. Angiology, Ohio State Med. Assn., Miss. Med. Assn. Office: Coast Cardiology Ctr 1104 Broad Ave Gulfport MS 39501-2414

SANGER, HERBERT SHELTON, JR., lawyer, former government official; b. Oak Hill, W.Va., Aug. 6, 1936; s. Herbert Shelton and Ethel Dean (Layne) S.; m. Rita Adele Baumgartner, Aug. 20, 1958; children: Charles, Carole, Warren, George. A.B. in English and Polit. Sci, Concord Coll., Athens, W.Va., 1958; LL.B., W.Va. U., Morgantown, 1961. Bar: W.Va. 1961, U.S. Supreme Ct. 1976, U.S. Ct. Appeals 5th and 6th cirs. 1973, 10th cir. 1978, 11th cir. 1981, 4th cir. 1982, U.S. Dist. Ct. (ea. dist.) Tenn. 1987, Tenn. 1988. Lifetime del. 6th Cir. Jud. Conf.; staff atty. Office of Gen. Counsel, TVA, Knoxville, 1961-69, asst. gen. counsel power, 1969-72; assoc. gen. counsel litigation and power Office of Gen. Counsel, TVA, 1972-73, dep. gen. counsel, 1973-75, gen. counsel, 1975-86; ptnr. Wagner, Myers & Sanger, P.C., Knoxville, 1986—; asst. prof. law U. Tenn.; Arthur B. Hodges prof. law W.Va. U.; chmn. bd. dirs. TVA Retirement System, 1975-86, Paribas Concorde Trust, Ltd., Regal Cinemas, Inc. Bd. dirs. East Tenn. Found., Knoxville Symphony Soc. Recipient Lawyers Coop award, 1961, Lawyers Title Ins. Co. award, 1961. Mem. ABA, Fed. Bar Assn., W.Va. Bar Assn., Tenn. Bar Assn., Am. Corp. Counsel Assn. (bd. dirs. 1982-87), Internat. Nuclear Law Assn., Knoxville Symphony Soc. (bd. dirs.). Baptist. Home: 5100 Malibu Dr Knoxville TN 37918-4513 Office: Wagner Myers & Sanger PC PO Box 1308 1801 Plaza Tower Knoxville TN 37901-1308

SANGER, STEPHEN THOMAS, secondary school educator; b. Norwalk, Ohio, Nov. 28, 1946; s. Thomas Andrew and Verna Mae (Ruffing) S.; m. Jeannette Eileen Bishop, Dec. 27, 1969; children: Neil Thomas, Aaron Joseph, Katherine Joyce. BA in French, Ohio State U., 1969; MBA, U. Auburn, 1980. Cert. tchr., Fla. Commd. 2d lt. USAF, 1969, advanced through grades to lt. col.; asst. ops. officer Deatchment 5 Aerospace and Rescue and Recovery, Great Falls, Mont., 1974-75; chief air field mgmt. 341 Combat Support Group, Great Falls, 1975-77; sect. comrd., dep. win chief Squadron Officers Sch., Montgomery, Ala., 1977-81; ops. officer Detachment 4, 37 Aerospace Rescue & Recovery Squadron, Jacksonville, Ark., 1981-83; comdr. Detachment 4, 37 Aerospace Rescue & Recovery Squadron, Little Rock/Jacksonville, 1983-85; ops. officer 55 Aerospace Rescue & Recovery Squadron, Ft. Walton Beach, Fla., 1987-89; chief of current ops. 39 Spl. Ops. Wing, Ft. Walton Beach, 1987-89; chief dir. of command and control Hdqrs. Air Rescue Svc., Sacramento, Calif., 1989-93; ret. USAF, 1993; asst. aerospace sci. tchr. West Orange H.S., Winter Garden, Fla., 1994—; adv. bd. McClellan AFB Officers Club, Sacramento, 1991-93; air traffic control bd. Little Rock AFB, Jacksonville, 1980-85, Malmstrom AFB, Great Falls, 1975-77. Editor: Air Navigation, 1981. Decorated DFC, Air medal. Mem. Ret. Officers Assn., Air Force Assn., Order of Daedalians, inst. of Mgmt. Accts., Classroom Tchrs. Assn., U. Ctrl. Fla. Acctg. Soc. Republican. Roman Catholic.

SAN MIGUEL, MANUEL, painter, historian, composer, poet; b. Guayama, P.R., Sept. 29, 1930; s. Manuel and Luisa (Griffo) San M.; m. Sandra Bonilla, July 12, 1969; children: Manuel, Ana. Educated, U. P.R., 1947-51, U. Pa., 1966-68, Arts Students League, N.Y.C., 1968-69. Historian, San Juan Nat. Historic Site, Nat. Park Svc., 1953-63; exec. sec. Acad. Arts and Scis., San Juan, 1963-64; founder of mus. and study collection El Morro Castle San Juan Nat. Hist. Site (U.S. Recipient Commendable Svc. award, 1964, citation for commendable svc. in field of hist. rsch. and interpretation, 1964); painter, writer, musician, 1964—; cons. in field. Exhibited in U. P.R., 1958, 62, Ateneo de P.R., 1962, Pan-Am. Union, Washington, 1963, Bienal Mexico, 1972, Bienal Rio de Janeiro, 1976, Orange County Schs. Mus. Art, Orlando, Fla., 1992, Mus. Modern Art, Paris, 1994, and numerous other nat. and internat. exhbns.; contbr. monographs on historical work in San Juan Nat. Historic Site to U.S. Nat. Archives, Washington; contbr. poetry to anthologies including Anthology of Latin American Poets, vol. III, 1987; rec. artist popular music of P.R. Capt. U.S. Army, 1951-53, Korea. Decorated Bronze Star with valor clasp and oakleaf cluster, Purple Heart, Combat Infantryman Badge, others; recipient citation Nat. Park Svc., 1964, Lifetime Achievement award in cultural arts Govt. of Puerto Rico and Spanish Heritage Found., 1996; named One of Ten Outstanding Hispanic Men, Orlando, Fla., 1991. Mem. VFW (life), Disables Am. Vets. (life), Am. Legion, Acad. Arts and Scis., Ateneo de P.R. (bd. govs. 1959-60), Am. Biog. Inst. (bd. advisors, life mem. bd. govs.), Am. Philatelic Soc. (postal commemorative soc.), Inst. Puerto Rican Culture (cons.), Puerto Rican Philatelic Assn., Internat. Platform Assn., Lions (Lion of Yr. 1962-63). Achievements include documentary research in the restoration of Castillo San Marcos, St. Augustine, Fla., Castillo San Felipe de Barajas, Colombia, South Am., and restoration of San Juan fortifications and city walls. Home: 1214 Howell Creek Dr Winter Springs FL 32708-4516

SAN MIGUEL, SANDRA BONILLA, social worker; b. Santurce, P.R., May 23, 1944; d. Isidoro and Flora (Carrero) Bonilla; m. Manuel San Miguel, July 12, 1969. BA, St. Joseph's Coll., 1966; MS in Social Work, Columbia U., 1970. Case worker Dept. Labor, Migration Div., N.Y.C., 1966-68; clin. social worker N.Y.C. Housing Authority, N.Y.C., 1968-69, Children's Aid Soc., N.Y.C., 1969-71; sr. social worker Traveler's Aid Soc., San Juan, P.R., 1971-74; coord., supr. Dept. Addiction Control Svcs., San Juan, P.R., 1974-77; substance abuse div. dir. Seminole County Mental Health Ctr., Altamonte Springs, Fla., 1978-81; cons. pvt. practice Hispanic Cons. Svcs., Winter Springs, Fla., 1982—; adj. prof. Seminole Community Coll., Lake Mary, Fla., 1986-90; sch. social worker I Seminole County Pub. Schs., Sanford, Fla., 1986-91, lead sch. social worker, 1991—; mem. pres.'s minority adv. coun. U. Ctrl. Fla., 1982—, vice chair, 1982-86, chair, 1986-90; mem. bd. regents EEO adv. com. State Univ. System Fla., 1985-89; bd. dirs. Seminole Cmty. Mental Health Ctr., 1986-94, 95—, v.p., 1988-90, pres., 1990-91; adv. bd. Nat. Devereux Found. Ctrl. Fla., 1993—, women's adv. bd. South Seminole Hosp., Fla., 1994—; v.p.; mem. Fla. Consortium on Tchr. Edn. for Am. Minorities, 1990—; mem. local com. Hispanic Info. and Telecomms. Network, 1990; mem. Seminole County (Fla.) Juvenile Justice Coun., 1993—; mem. statewide student svcs. adv. com. Dept. Edn., Fla., 1993-96; student svcs. adv. group, 1996—; apptd. mem. to NASW Nat. Sch. Social Work Credential Com., Washington, 1996—. Recipient UCF Pres.'s Outstanding Svc. award, Orlando, Fla., 1991, Ponce De Leon Hispanic Comm. Svc. award, Orlando, 1992, Svc. Recognition plaque Seminole Comm. Mental Health ctr., 1991, Leadership plaque Fla. Assn. of Sch. Social Workers, 1994, Outstanding Contbn. to Student Svcs. cert. Fla. Dept. Edn., 1995. Mem. NASW, Fla. Assn. Sch. Social Workers (co-founder minority caucus 1988, columnist quar. newsletter Minority Corner 1988-92, bd. dirs. 1989—, sec. 1990-92, v.p. 1992-93, pres. 1993-94), Sch. Social Work Assn. of Am., Fla. Assn. Student Svcs. Adminstrs., Collegiate Social Workers P.R., Columbia U. Alumni Assn., St. Joseph's Coll. Alumni Assn. Home: 1214 Howell Creek Dr Winter Springs FL 32708-4516 Office: Seminole County Pub Schs 1401 S Magnolia Ave Sanford FL 32771-3400

SANNER, GEORGE ELWOOD, electrical engineer; b. Rockwood, Pa., Aug. 30, 1929; s. Dennis Charles and Alverda (Growall) S.; m. Marjorie Mary Hohman, July 1, 1951; children: George Bradley, Marjorie Rosalie, Cathy Ann. BS, U. Pitts., 1951; postgrad., Johns Hopkins U., 1957-59. Registered profl. engr., Md.; cert. cost acctg. mgmt. Supervisory engr. Westinghouse Electric Corp., Balt., 1952-58, chief scientist, cons. def. and space ctr., 1964-72; chief engr., program mgr. radio div. Bendix Corp., Balt., 1958-64; engring. mgr. jet propulsion labs. Bendix Corp., Pasadena, Calif., 1980-81; pres., gen. mgr. Santron Corp., Balt., 1972-79; v.p. engring. M-Tron Industries div. Curtiss Wright Corp., Yankton, S.D., 1979-80; sr. engring. specialist engring. ctr. Litton Data Systems, New Orleans, 1981-83; cons. engring. mgmt. AIL div. Eaton Corp., Deer Park, N.Y., 1983-87; sr. prin. engr. Am. Electronics Labs, Inc., Lansdale, Pa., 1987-92; cons. Atlanta, 1992—; rep. People to People Tour, various countries, 1978. Patentee in field. Vestryman Immanuel Ch., Sparks-Glencoe, Md., 1969-70; trustee St. Paul's Sch. for Boys, Balt., 1965-67; mem. bishop's secretariat Diocese of L.I., Garden City, N.Y., 1985-87; mem. exec. com. Scriptural Coalition, Diocese of Phila., 1990-92; mem. Rep. Nat. Com., Rep. Presdl. Trust, Nat. Rep. Senatorial Com. A.K. Mellon Found. scholar, 1947-50, Carnegie Inst. Tech. scholar, 1947-51. Mem. IEEE, KC, Quarter Century Wireless Assn., Knights of Columbus. Roman Catholic. Address: 1135 Creekside Way Roswell GA 30076-4368

SAN PEDRO, GERARDO SANTOS, pulmonary and critical care physician, researcher; b. Manila, Philippines, Nov. 13, 1959; came to U.S., 1974; s. Crispin and Nonie (Santos) S.; m. Margaret Rose Woolford, June 16, 1980; children: Jason Timothy, Amy Marie, Austin Brooks, Bethany Rose, Nathan Crispin. BS in Biology, U. Ark., Little Rock, 1980, MD, 1984. Lic. physician Ark., La. Intern U. Ark., Little Rock, 1984-85, resident in internal medicine, 1986-87, fellow in pulmonary and critical medicine, 1987-90; attending physician gen. internal medicine, pulmonary and critical care medicne Univ. Hosp., John J. McClellan Vets. Hosp., U. Ark. Med. Sci, Little Rock, 1990-95; attending physician gen. internal medicine, pulmonary and critical care medicine Univ. Hosp., Overton Brooks VA Hosp., La. State U. Med. Ctr., Shreveport, La., 1995—; cons. tuberculosis program Ark. Dept. Health, Pulaski County, 1987-95, La. Dept. Health, Caddo Parish, 1995—; instr. dept. internal medicine U. Ark. for Med. Scis., 1990, asst. prof. medicine pulmonary and critical care divsn. dept. internal medicine, 1990-95, adj. asst. prof. dept. physiology and biophysics, 1992-95, lectr. Coll. Pharmacy, Coll. Nursing, Coll. Health Related Professions, 1990-95, course dir. phys. exam. sophomore med. students Coll. Medicine, 1993-95, mem. numerous clin. and edn. coms.; med. dir. Pulmonary Functions lab. John L. McClellan Vets. Hosp., Little Rock, 1990-95; assoc. prof. clin. medicine sect. pulmonary and critical care medicine dept. internal medicine La. State U., Shreveport, 1995—, mem. curriculum com., 1995—, edn. com., 1995—, ethics com., 1995—; mem. Am. Thoracic Soc. Assembly on Microbiology, Tuberculosis and Pulmonary Infections Program com., 1996—; manuscript reviewer Clin. Infectious Disease, Respiratory Care; rschr., presenter in field. Contbr. chpts. to books, numerous abstracts and articles to profl. jours. Mem. staff Westside Free Med. Clin. Cath. Social Svcs., Diocese of Little Rock, 1986-95, adult sponsor Cath. Youth Orgn. St. Theresa's Parish, 1987-93; mem. com. Troop 731 County Pines Acad. Windy Pines Assn. Ouachita Girl Scout Coun. Girl Scouts Am., 1992-93; asst. scoutmaster Troop 2 Country Pines Acad. Quapaw Area Coun. Boy Scouts Am., 1992-93. Major Ark. Army N.G., 1990-95, active svc. Saudi Arabia, 1990-91. Decorated Army Commendation medal, 1991, Kuwait Liberation medal, 1991; named Diocesan Vol. of Distinction, Cath. Diocese of Little Rock, 1995. Mem. Am. Thoracic Soc., Ark. Thoracic Soc., Soc. Critical Care Medicine, Alpha Epsilon Delta. Roman Catholic. Office: La State U Med Ctr Sect Pulmonary and Crit Car 1501 King's Hwy Shreveport LA 71130

SANSBURY, BARBARA ANN PETTIGREW, nursing administrator; b. Florence County, Aug. 6, 1951; d. Simon and Mary Magaline (Quillen) Pettigrew; 1 child, Terrence Urice. LPN, Southside Area Vocat. Ctr., 1970; AD, Florence (S.C.) Darlington Tech. Sch., 1978; BSN, Med. U. of S.C., 1987, MSN, 1991. RN, S.C. Staff and charge nurse McLeod Regional Med. Ctr., 1970-91; staff nurse Faith Health Care Facility, Florence, 1983-84; sch. nurse Timmonsville (S.C.) High Sch., 1983-84; clin. instr. Florence Darlington Tech., 1989-90; sr. staff nurse Med. U. S.C., 1991-92; nurse mgr. VA Med. Ctr., Augusta, Ga., 1992-96, nursing care mgr., 1997—. Mem. USAR, ANA (cert. psychiat. nurse), Ga. Nurses Assn. (chair psychiat. and mental health coun.), Chi Eta Phi, Sigma Theta Tau Internat. Home: 3211 Wrightsboro Rd Apt S-2 Augusta GA 30909

SANSING, GORDON H., minister; b. New Orleans, Nov. 16, 1942; s. L. Gordon and Polly (Murphy) S.; m. Elese Williams, Aug. 24, 1963; children: Mark G., Brian W. BA, Miss. Coll., 1964; MTh, New Orleans Bapt. Theol. Sem., 1967, DMin, 1974. Minister of music and youth Washington (Miss.) Bapt. Ch., 1961-62, Firt Bapt. Ch., Florence, Miss., 1962-64; pastor Knoxo Bapt. Ch., Tylertown, Miss., 1964-67; asst. pastor Calvary Bapt. Ch., Jackson, Miss., 1967-69; asst. pastor First Bapt. Ch., Marks, Miss., 1969-76, Pontotoc, Miss., 1976-83, Vicksburg, Miss., 1983—; trustee Blue Mountain Coll., Miss., 1973-82, Miss. Coll., Clinton, 1983-89, 93-96; bd. dirs. Midd West Industries, Vicksburg, Good Shepherd Ctr., Vicksburg. Pres. Vicksburg Civitan Club, 1988-89; dist. chaplain Magnolia Dist. Civitan Club, Miss., 1987-88, lt. gov., 1991-92. Named to Outstanding Young Men of Am., 1972, 74. Office: First Bapt Ch 1607 Cherry St Vicksburg MS 39180-3561

SANSONE, SUSAN MARY, health facility administrator; b. Cin., Aug. 15, 1957; d. Paul Lucian and Florence Margaret (Kaiser) Back; m. Joseph A. Sansone, May 23, 1981; 1 child, Joseph Anthony. Diploma, Deaconess Hosp. Sch. Nursing, 1978; BS magna cum laude in Nursing Mgmt., Coll. Mt. St. Joseph, 1991. Cert. ACLS, BLS, PALS; cert. post anesthesia nurse. Nursing asst. Deaconess Hosp., Cin., 1976-78, staff nurse med./surg., 1978-79, staff nurse ICU/critical care unit, 1979-82, staff nurse recovery rm., 1982-86, post anesthesia care unit asst. mgr., 1986-87, post anesthesia care unit mgr., 1987-93; mgr. post anesthesia care, same day surgery, pre-admissions testing St. Elizabeth Med. Ctr., Edgewood and Covington, Ky., 1993—; mem. rsch. adv. bd. Hill-Rom, Batesville, Ind., 1991—. Mem. Am. Soc. Post Anesthesia Nurses, Ohio Post Anesthesia Nurses Assn., Cin. Post Anesthesia Nurses Assn., Kappa Gamma Pi Honor Soc. Home: 3390 Cherryridge Dr North Bend OH 45052-9522 Office: 1 Medical Village Dr Edgewood KY 41017-3403

SANTA-COLOMA, BERNARDO, secondary school educator, counselor; b. N.Y.C., May 31, 1934; s. Bernardo Santa-Coloma Sr. and Belma Remotti; m. Sofia A. Santa-Coloma, Dec. 22, 1981; children: Ananda, Anita. BA in Humanistic Psychology, U. Calif., Santa Cruz, 1973; MA in Integral Counseling Psychology, Calif. Inst. Integral Studies, San Francisco, 1976; MEd in Secondary Edn., U. Nev., Las Vegas, 1979; 3 level cert., Feuerstein's Instrumental, Enrichment Program; postgrad., U. Sarasota. Cert. secondary edn. tchr. ESl, history, English, Tex.; cert. guidance counselor Tex. Edn. Assn., lic. marriage and family therapist, Tex.; nat. cert. counselor. Mem. tchr. corps., vol. VISTA, Las Vegas, Nev., 1976-79; family counselor, English tutor Diocese of Matamoros and Valle Hermoso Tamps, Mexico, Cath. Family Svcs. and Vol. Ednl. and Social Svcs., Amarillo, Tex., 1980-82; grad. asst. Pan Am. U., Brownsville, Tex.; at-risk program, low-level reading instr. Brownsville Ind. Sch. Dist., 1984-94; basic skills instr. James Pace High Sch., Brownsville; counselor and psychotherapist Family Effectiveness and Devel. Program, Kids in Crisis Teenage Crisis Hotline, La Casa Esperanza Home for Boys; basic adult reading instr. Southmost Coll., ESL Alternative Ctr.; tchr., pvt. practice counselor, Brownsville Ind. Sch. Dist. Alternative Ctr., 1994—. Contbr. articles to profl. jours. in U.S. and Mex. including Integracion Integral, Journey in Matamoros. Vol. VISTA, 1976-79, VISTA Tchr. Corps, Las Vegas, Peace Corps, Thailand, 1979, Vol. Edn./Soc. Svc., Tex., Mex., 1980-82. With USN, 1952-56, medic neuropsychiatric wards San Diego and Guam. Recipient scholarship U. Calif.-Santa Cruz, 1971-73, U. Nev. tchr. corps, 1977-79; named grad. asst. Calif. Inst. Integral Studies, 1974-76. Home: PO Box 3941 Brownsville TX 78523-3941 also: Country Club 2009 Madero Dr Brownsville TX 78521-1734

SANTANGELO, DANIEL L., association administrator. Exec. dir. Fla. Dept. Citrus, Lakeland. Office: Fla Dept Citrus PO Box 148 Lakeland FL 33802

SANTANNA, RICARDO PEREIRA, trade company executive; b. Rio de Janeiro, Nov. 2, 1962; came to U.S., 1986; s. Lauro Andrade and Aurelina Pereira (Noronha) S.; m. Margaret Julie Stephens, June 14, 1987; 1 child, Alexandra. BBA, U. Estacio de SA, Rio de Janeiro, 1986. Adminstrv. surp. CBTU, Rio de Janeiro, 1980-86; mgr. Via Brazil, N.Y.C., 1986-87, U.S. group consolidator, office mgr., 1987-90; pres. Harpal Internat. Co., Coral Springs, Fla., 1990—; cons. Grupo San Fernando, Lima, Peru, 1992—. Office: Harpal Internat Co Ste 7B 2301 W Sample Rd Bldg 1 Pompano Beach FL 33073-3081

SANTI, ELLYN E., mathematics educator. BS, No. Ariz. U., 1971, MA, 1974; postgrad., George Mason U., 1980-82. Cert. tchr., Va. Tchr. math. Flagstaff (Ariz.) Pub. Schs., 1972-76, head math. dept., 1974-76; asst. prof. math. No. Va. C.C., Annandale, Va., 1976—; participant Writing Across the Curriculum Workshops, Annandale, 1992-93. Recipient recognition for outstanding contbns. to edn. No. Va. C.C. Alumni Fedn., 1993. Mem. Am. Math. Assn. Two-Yr. Colls., Va. Math. Assn. Two-Yr. Colls. (regional v.p. 1989-91, coord. spring conf. 1992), Phi Kappa Phi. Office: No Va C C 8333 Little River Tpke Annandale VA 22003-3743

SANTIAGO, RAYMOND, library administrator, educator; b. N.Y.C., July 13, 1949; s. Raymond and Livia Santiago; m. Crystal C. Capelis, May 15, 1979; 1 child, Jason Esrael. BFA, Rochester (N.Y.) Inst. Tech., 1974; MLS, SUNY, Buffalo, 1975. Co-chair, head non-print svcs. World U., San Juan, P.R., 1978-84; libr. Tampa-Hillsborough Pub. Libr. Sys., Fla., 1984-88, section mgr., 1988-90; supr. libr. svcs. Miami-Dade Pub. Libr. Sys., Fla., 1990-91, asst. dir., 1991—; adj. faculty U. South Fla., 1994—. Mem. ALA, Pub. Libr. Assn., Fla. Libr. Assn. Home: 1300 El Rado St Coral Gables FL 33134 Office: Miami-Dade Pub Libr Sys 101 W Flagler St Miami FL 33130-1504

SANTILLI, RUGGERO M., physicist; b. Capracotta, Is, Italy, Sept. 8, 1935; came to U.S., 1967; s. Ermanno and Ida (Conti) S.; m. Carla Gandiglio, June 15, 1965; children: Luisa, Ermanno. PhD in Theoretical Physics, U. Turin (Italy), 1966. With Ctr. Theoretical Physics U. Miami, 1966-67; with dept. physics Boston U., 1967-76; with Ctr. Theoretical Physics MIT, Cambridge, 1976-78; with dept. math., Lyman lab. Physics Harvard U., Cambridge, 1978-83; pres., prof. theoretical physics Inst. Basic Rsch., Cambridge, 1983-91, Fla., 1991—; prof. physics (hon.) Acad. Scis., Kiev, Ukraine; vis. scientist Joint Inst. Nuclear Rsch., Dubna, Russia; organizer 5 Internat. Workshops on Lie-admissible Formulations Harvard U.; co-organizer 5 Internat. Workshops on Hadronic Mechanics, U.S., Italy, Greece, First Internat. Conf. on Nonpotential Interactions and their Lie-Admissible Treatment U. Orléans, France and other internat. confs. Founder, editor-in-chief: Hadronic Jour., Hadronic Jour. Suplement, Algebras, Goups an d Geometries; referee, contbr. over 150 artiles to physics and math. jours., also 12 monographs in theoretical physics. Recipient: Gold Medals for Scientific Merits Molise Province, Italy, City of Orléans, France; nominated among most illustrious applied mathematicians of all times Estonian Acad. Scis. Office: Inst Basic Rsch PO Box 1577 Palm Harbor FL 34682-1577

SANTORE, CARRIE-BETH, computer management professional; b. Torrington, Conn., July 28, 1953; d. Michael and Dolores Leonard S. BA History and Am. Studies cum laude, Conn. Coll., 1975; MA History, U. Conn., 1977; MBA Mktg., Va. Polytechnic Inst., 1988. Analyst CIA, Washington, 1980-90; prin. tng. specialist Quality Sys., Inc., Fairfax, Va., 1990-93, dep. dir. ops. programs, 1993-95; mgr. Proposal Ctr. Quality Systems, Inc., Fairfax, Va., 1995-96; tech. publs. mgr. Sci. & Tech. Analysis Corp., Fairfax, Va., 1996—; Lotus cert. cons., 1994. Bd. dirs., sec. Seminary Walk Condo Assn., Alexandria, Va., 1987-88, editor newsletter, 1986-87; vol. Alexandria Waterfront ARC, 1989-90; mem. com. to devel. internat. studies program Conn. Coll., New London, 1988-89. Mem. SALT, Balt. Washington Info. Systems, AAUW, Women's Nat. Book Assn., Assn. Proposal Mgmt. Profls., Phi Alpha Theta. Office: Sci & Tech Analysis Corp Ste 300 11250 Waples Mill Rd Fairfax VA 22030

SANTORO, ANTHONY RICHARD, academic administrator; b. Feb. 2, 1939; m. Carol Lynne; 1 child, Melissa. AB, Coll. of the Holy Cross, 1960; MA, U. Calif., 1962; PhD, Rutgers U., 1978. Instr. history Monmouth Coll., West Long Branch, N.J., 1963-67; v.p. for adminstrn., chair depts history and philosophy, registrar Briarcliff Coll., Briarcliff Manor, N.Y., 1967-77; v.p. Devel. and Coll. Rels. Ladycliff Coll., Highland Falls, N.Y., 1977-88; pres. St. Joseph's Coll., Standish, Maine, 1979-87; pres. Christopher Newport U., Newport News, Va., 1987-96, pres. emeritus, disting. prof. history, 1996—. Author: Theophanes Chronograhia: A Chronicle of 8th Century Byzantium, 1982; co-author: An Eyewitness to History: The Short History of Nikephoros the Patriarch of Constantinople, 1991. Office: Christopher Newport U Smith Hall 164 Newport News VA 23606-2998

SANTOS, BARBARA LYNN, nurse; b. Great Lakes, Ill.; d. Stanley and Alice (Strzyzewinski) Abstetar; children: Denise, Kimberly. BS in Nursing magna cum laude, Salve Regina Coll., 1984; postgrad., U. Tampa. Staff nurse Newport (R.I.) Hosp.; staff nurse The Miriam, Providence; charge nurse, asst. nurse mgr. Bayfront Med. Ctr., St. Peterburg, Fla.; radiology nurse. Mem. Am. Urol. Assn. Allied.

SANTOS, LISA DIANE, plastic surgeon; b. Lubbock, Tex., Aug. 8, 1959; d. Ray E. and Jo (Edwards) S. MD, Tex. Tech. U. Sch. Medicine, 1984. Intern U. Ky., 1984-85, resident surgery, 1985-87, resident plastic surgery, 1987-89; fellow cosmetic surgery NYU, 1989; pvt. practice plastic surgery pvt. practice, Houston, 1990—; clin. instr. divsn. plastic surgery Baylor Coll. Medicine, Houston, 1991—. Bd. dirs. Hope Ctr., Houston, 1992; active Jr. League, Houston, 1984, River Oaks Bus. Women's Exch. Club, 1992. Named Notable Women Tex., 1984; recipient Janet M. Glasgow Achievement citation, 1984. Fellow ACS; mem. AMA, Am. Soc. Plastic and Reconstructive Surgeons, Tex. Med. Assn., Houston Soc. Plastic Surgeons, Harris County Med. Soc. Office: 6624 Fannin St Ste 1420 Houston TX 77030-2326

SANTOS, LISA WELLS, critical care nurse; b. Richardson, Tex., Oct. 25, 1963; d. Malcolm R.N. and Maitland Anne (MacIntyre) Wells; m. Ignacio Santos, Jr., Dec. 17, 1988. Cert. med. asst., x-ray-lab. technician, Tex. Coll. Osteopathy, 1983; ASN, El Centro Coll., 1988; postgrad., U. North Tex.; BS in Bus. Mgmt., Le Tourneau U., 1993; postgrad., U. Phoenix, 1995—. RN, Tex.; cert. in CPR; cert. case mgr., cert. profl. in health care quality; advanced competency certification in continuity of care; assoc. cert. mgr.; cert. disability analyst, fellow. Med. technologist Family Med. Ctr., Dallas, 1984-85, Beltline Med. Clinic, Dallas, 1985-86; nurse, lab. technician Primacare, Dallas, Plano, Richardson, Tex., 1986-88; charge nurse telemetry unit NME Hosp.-RHD Meml. Hosp., Denton, Tex., 1988-89; nurse ICU Denton (Tex.) Regional Med. Ctr.; nurse Angel Touch, Dallas, 1989; nurse cons. Travelers Ins., Richardson, Tex., 1990-91; med. rev. specialist Nat. Group Life, Las Colinas, Tex., 1991-94; mgr. coordinated care Nat. Group Life, 1994-95; pres. San Cal Health Care Options, Lewisville, Tex., 1994-95; clin. dir. PRN Associated Care/ Am. Care Source, Dallas, 1995—. Contbr. articles to profl. jour. Mem. AACN, NAFE, Nat. Assn. Health Care Quality, Nat. Assn. Quality Assurance Profls., Assn. Nurses in AIDS Care, Case Mgmt. Soc. Am., Am. Assn. Law Ethics and Medicine, Am. Assn. Continuity of Care, Alpha Epsilon Delta, Alpha Beta Kappa, Gamma Beta Phi.

SANTOS, MARIA J., evaluator; b. Barcelona, Spain, Mar. 18, 1963; came to U.S., 1976; d. Evencio and Fermina (Diez) S.; m. Glenn J. McLoughlin, Aug. 18, 1990; children: Caroline Ann McLoughlin, Joseph Evan McLoughlin. BS in Bus. Adminstrn., Villanova (Pa.) U., 1986; MBA, George Washington U., 1991. Evaluator U.S. Gen. Acctg. Office, Washington, 1986—. Editor: Global Network Newsletter, 1989-92 (spl. commendation, 1990). Mem. ASPA, No. Va. Investment Club. Office: US General Acctg Office 441 G St NW Rm 4A48 Washington DC 20548-0001

SANUSI, IRWAN DANIEL, pathology educator; b. Blitar, Java, Indonesia, Feb. 9, 1931; came to U.S., 1970; s. Wie Bo and Tiauw Nio (Oei) Sie; m. Marina Theresia Juniati, Sept. 18, 1960; children: Hani David, August, Monica F. MD, Airlangga U. Sch. Medicine, Surabaya, Indonesia, 1960. Diplomate Am. Bd. Pathology, 1973; med. lic. La., 1972, Tex., 1979. Resident pathology and forensic pathology Airlangga U. Sch. Medicine, 1960-62; resident pathology Med. Coll. Va., Richmond, 1962-63; resident forensic pathology Med. Coll. Va. & Chief Med.'s Examiners Office, Richmond, 1963-64; instr. Airlangga U. Sch. Medicine, 1964-70; resident pathology La. State U. Sch. Medicine, Shreveport, 1970-72; surgical and anatomic pathology La State U. Med. Ctr. and VA Hosp., Shreveport, 1970—; instr. dept. pathology La. State U. Sch. Medicine, 1971-72, asst. prof., 1972-76, assoc. prof., 1976-89, prof., 1989—; chief autopsy svcs. dept. pathology, chief forensic pathology and dermatopathology sect., vis. staff/attending pathologist La. State U. Med. Ctr., 1972—, served on numerous coms., 1975—; cons. and staff pathologist VA Hosp., Shreveport, 1978—; cons. pathologist E.A. Conway Meml. Hosp., Monroe, La., 1979—; med. staff pathologist Physicians and Surgeons Hosp., Shreveport, 1985—. Co-author: An Atlas of Skin Biopsy, Diagnosis by Light and Immuno Microscopy of Vesico-bullous, Connective Tissue Disorders and Vasculitis of the Skin, 1983; contbr. chpts. to books and manuals, more than 24 articles to profl. jours. and 52 abstracts. Mem. AMA, Am. Soc. Clin. Pathologists, Am. Acad. Forensic Scis., Nat. Assn. Med. Examiners, Internat. Acad. Pathologists, Internat. Soc. Dermatopathology, So. Med. Assn., Shreveport Med. Soc. Democrat. Roman Catholic. Office: La State U Sch Medicine 1501 Kings Hwy Shreveport LA 71103-4228

SAPERY, DAVID L., systems analyst; b. N.Y.C., Sept. 6, 1967; s. Stanley L. and Marijane Sapery; m. Fern S. Abrams, Sept. 5, 1993. BA, U. Pa., 1990. Cert. sys. engr. Microsoft Corp. Programmer/analyst Omnicomputer Inc., N.Y.C., 1987-89; staff cons. Price Waterhouse, Columbia, Md., 1990-91; sr. systems architect DataFocus Inc., Fairfax, Va., 1991—. Mem. IEEE, U.S. Fencing Assn. (life, bd. dirs. 1995—, info. sys. coord. 1995—). Office: DataFocus Inc 12450 Fair Lakes Cir Fairfax VA 22033

SAPOUGH, ROY SUMNER, JR., educational administrator; b. Rock Hill, S.C., Nov. 13, 1951; s. Roy Sumner and Janie Lee (Price) S.; m. Bonne Barmore, June 17, 1978; children: William Sumner, Blaksley Rhett. BS in Edn., Ga. So. U., 1976, MEd, 1986, EdS, 1988. Cert. tchr., adminstr., Ga. Tchr. Wayne County Jr. High Sch., Jesup, Ga., 1976-77, Claxton (Ga.) High Sch., 1977-79, Taliaferro County Sch., Crawfordville, Ga., 1980-81, Thomson (Ga.) High Sch., 1981-85; purchasing agt. Hatteras Yacht, High Point, N.C., 1979-80; prin. Glascock County Schs., Gibson, Ga., 1985-87, Norris Mid. Sch., Thomson, 1987-93, Thomson Mid. Sch., 1993—. Mem. ASCD, Nat. Assn. Secondary Sch. Prins., Ga. Assn. Mid. Sch. Prins., Ga. Assn. Ednl. Leaders, Belle Meade Country Club, Kiwanis, Phi Delta Kappa. Republican. Methodist. Home: 1835 Folly Lake Dr Thomson GA 30824-9472 Office: Thomson Mid Sch PO Box 1140 Main St Thomson GA 30824

SAPP, A. EUGENE, JR., electronics executive; b. Winston-Salem, N.C., 1933; married. BEE, Ga. Inst. Tech., 1959. With Tex. Instruments Inc., 1959-62, SCI Systems Inc., Hunstville, Ala., 1962—; v.p. SCI Systems Inc., 1973-80, exec. v.p., 1980—, now pres., chief oper. officer. Office: SCI Systems Inc PO Box 1000 Huntsville AL 35807-4001*

SAPP, NEIL CARLETON, air transportation executive, consultant; b. Miami, Fla., Nov. 22, 1939; s. Alfred Eli and Vera May (Crowson) S.; m. Peggy Joe Brotherton, June 10, 1962; children: Erin Lynn, Kerrie Ellen. BS, U.S. Naval Acad., 1962; postgrad., U. Miami, Coral Gables, Fla. Commd. ensign U.S. Navy, 1962, advanced through grades to lt.; fighter pilot U.S. Navy, Virginia Beach, Va., 1962-67; resigned U.S. Navy, 1967; capt. Nat. Airlines, Miami, Fla., 1967-80, Pan Am. World Airways, Inc., Miami, 1980-91, Delta Air Lines, Inc., N.Y.C., 1991—; mng. ptnr. Sapp & Slaton Fin. Concepts Group, Coral Gables, Fla., 1981-85; chmn., CEO, pres. U.S. Indsl. Dynamics Corp., Miami, 1988-95; pres., COO Iowa Acquisition Group, Inc., 1990-91; v.p. mktg. and corp. devel. The Systema Group, Inc., Miami, 1993-95; pres. Air Transport Equity Corp., 1996—; past chmn. internat. ops., vice chmn. master exec. coun. Nat. Airlines Pilots Assn., Miami; past chmn. spl. corp. ops., profl. stds., flight stds. and tng. Pan Am. N.Y.; bd. dirs. World Export/Import Marts, Ltd., Waterloo, Iowa, 1989-95; bd. advisors The Cesne Inst., Waterloo, 1988—; trustee Pan Am Pilots Retirement Found., Inc., 1996—. Officer affiliate admissions com. U.S. Naval Acad., 1967-95; bd. dirs. St. Thomas Sch., Miami, 1976-77; co-pres. Coral Gables Sr. H.S. PTA, 1983-84; vol. Informed Families of Dade County, Miami, 1984—; vestry St. Thomas Ch., Miami, 1976-79. Mem. Internat. Platform Assn., Delta Airline Pilots Assn. (chmn. profl. stds., flight stds. and tng. 1991-93), Assn. Naval Aviation, Tailhook Assn., U.S. Naval Acad. Alumni Assn., Am. Legion, Naval Inst., Navy League of the U.S., Camarilla Club, Beach Colony Club, Miami Club, Army-Navy Club Washington, Riviera Country Club. Episcopalian. Home: 7201 SW 47th Ct Miami FL 33143-6109

SAPP, WILLIAM DAVID, minister; b. Savannah, Ga., Jan. 29, 1948; s. William McKinley and Ellen Louise (Lewis) S.; m. Linda Powers, Jan. 31, 1970; children: Benjamin D., Matthew P. AB, Mercer U., Macon, Ga., 1968; MDiv, So. Bapt. Theol. Sem., Louisville, 1972, PhD, 1975. Ordained to ministry, Bapt. Ch. Instr. So. Bapt. Theol. Sem., Louisville, 1974-75, assoc. dir. student devel. svcs., 1975-76; dir. orgn. Christian Life Commn. of So. Bapt. Conv., Nashville, 1976-81; pastor First Bapt. Ch., Chamblee, Ga., 1981-91, Derbyshire Bapt. Ch., Richmond, Va., 1991—; pres. Va. Bapt. Pastor's Conf., 1994-95; 1st v.p. Ga. Bapt. Conv., 1984-85; chmn. denominational rels. com. Bapt. Gen. assn. Va., 1993-96; vis. prof. So. Bapt. Theol. Sem., Louisville, 1984; adj. prof. Bapt. Theol. Sem., Richmond, 1996. Contbr. articles to profl. jours., chpts. to books. Mem. AIDS Task Force, DeKalb County, Ga., Atlanta, 1988-90; instnl. rev. bd. Northside Hosp., Atlanta, 1987-91. Mem. West Richmond Rotary Club. Home: 10800 Weather Vane Rd Richmond VA 23233 Office: Derbyshire Baptist Church 8800 Derbyshire Rd Richmond VA 23229

SAPP, WILLIAM ROTHWELL, artist, educator; b. Cape Girardeau, Mo., July 4, 1943; s. William Rothwell and Mary Anna (Heeb) S.; m. Virginia Frances Gohn, 1966 (div. Apr. 1982); m. Julie Anne Vesper, July 3, 1991; 1 child, Adam Nathaniel. BS, U. Mo., 1965, MA, 1967; MFA, Washington U., St. Louis, 1978. Asst. instr. U. Mo., Columbia, 1965-67; asst. prof. Adams State Coll., Alamosa, Colo., 1967-73; assoc. prof. U. Ark., Little Rock, 1978-89; assoc. prof. art U. Ga., Athens, 1989—. Sculptor Perros Vigilantes, 1996. With U.S. Army, 1969-71. Visual Artist grantee Ark. Arts Coun., 1985, Mid-Am. Arts Alliance/NEA, 1986, So. Arts Fedn., 1993, Internat. Arts Programming Network, 1995. Mem. Phi Beta Delta. Office: U Ga Lamar Dodd Sch Art Jackson St Athens GA 30602

SARABIA, FERMIN, psychiatrist; b. Santiago, Oriente, Cuba, Aug. 9, 1931; came to U.S., 1961; s. Enrique and Dulce Maria (Ramos) S.; m. Perla Lucia Perez de Castro, Apr. 19, 1961; children: Anthony F., Perla M., Lillian M., Patricia M. BS, Instituto de Santiago de Cuba, Oriente, 1950; MD, U. Havana, Cuba, 1959. Diplomate Am. Bd. Psychiatry and Neurology. Resident physician Gen. calixto Garcia U. Hosp., Havana, Cuba, 1960-61; rotating intern Orange Meml. Hosp., Orlando, Fla., 1962-63; resident in psychiatry Ctrl. State Griffin Meml. Hosp., Norman, Okla., 1963-66; staff psychiatrist San Antonio State Hosp., 1966-67, clin. dir., 1967-69; part-time psychiatrist Community Guidance Ctr., San Antonio, 1969-70; pvt. practice San Antonio, 1969-93; field rep. Joint Commn. on Accreditation of Healthcare Orgns., San Antonio, 1993—; clin. assoc. prof. psychiatry U. Tex., San Antonio Health Sci. Ctr., 1977-95, clin. prof. psychiatry, 1995—; mem. Tex. Coun. on Disabilities, 1989-90, task force on crimes against disabled, 1990; bd. dirs. Tex. State Bd. of Mental Health/Mental Retardation, 1989—, chmn. audit com., 1989-91, vice chmn., 1991—, mem. pers. com., 1989—; active staff Santa Rosa Med. Ctr., San Antonio, 1968—, Bapt. Meml. Hosp., San Antonio, 1977—; courtesy staff St. Luke's Luth. Hosp., S.W. Tex. Meth. Hosp., Humana Hosp. of San Antonio, others. Contbr. articles to profl. jours. Cons./vol. Halfway House of San Antonio, Inc., 1969—, bd. dirs., 1969—, pres. 1973; mem.-at-large Bexar County Hosp. Dist. Exec. Com., 1982-83; mem. Horizon House adv. Bd., 1980-81, Camino Real Health Systems Agy. Mental Health Task Force, 1977; mem. human rights com. Goodwill Industries, 1970; psychiat. cons. Parallel Sch. for Disturbed Children, 1971-72; bd. dirs. Vis. Nurses Assn., 1973-77; bd. dirs. Club Sembradores de Amistad, 1973-75, 76-77, pres. 1978-79. Recipient Humanitarian award U.S. Cath. Conf., Migration and Refugee Svcs., 1982, Americanism award Nat. Soc. Daus. of Am. Revolution, 1983, Physicians Recognition award AMA, 1973, 76, 79, 82, 85, 88, 91. Fellow Am. Psychiatric Assn.; mem. AMA, Tex. Med. Assn. (mental health/mental retardation com. 1979-83, alcohol and drug abuse com. 1983-86), Bexar County Med. Soc. (bd. censors 1989-91, chmn. bd. censors 1991, bd. dirs. 1991—), Tex. Psychiat. Soc., Sociedad Medica Hispano Americana, Bexar County Psychiat. Soc. (sec.-treas. 1979-81, pres. 1982-83), Am. Soc. Adolescent Psychiatry, San Antonio Soc. Adolescent Psychiatry (pres. 1988-89). Office: 343 W Houston St Ste 903 San Antonio TX 78205-2109

SARACELLI, KRISTINE DORTHIE, systems engineer, consultant; b. N.Y.C., May 24, 1954; d. George R. and Dorothy L. (Weidmann) Stegmann; m. Paul R. Saracelli, June 5, 1982. BS, Ramapo (N.J.) Coll., 1982. Computer ops. staff Marlyn Steel Co., Tampa, Fla., 1977-78; computer ops. supr. IBM, Sterling Forest, N.Y., 1979-83; info. ctr. support staff IBM, Franklin Lakes, N.J., 1983-84; data processing mgr. IBM, Sterling Forest, 1984-86; competitive analysis staff IBM, Montvale, N.J., 1987-88; decision support ctr. facilitator IBM, Southbury, Conn., 1988-89; decision support tech. mgr. IBM, Southbury, 1989-90, methodology devel. staff, 1990-93; cons. IBM Consulting Group, Raleigh, N.C., 1993-94; sr. bus. area mgr. ISSC/IBM, Raleigh, N.C., 1995—; instr. skill dynamics, Thornwood, N.Y., 1992-93; IBM project rep. G.U.I.D.E. Internat., 1993-94 (invited speaker Lisbon, Portugal, 1993). Contbr. articles to profl. jours. Mem. IEEE, Assn. for Computing Machinery, N.C. Quality Assurance Discussion Group (invited speaker Raleigh 1993). Democrat. Methodist. Home: 14200 Wyndfield Cir Raleigh NC 27615-1317 Office: IBM Integrated Sys Solutions Corp 1001 Winstead Dr Cary NC 27513

SARAF, SHEVACH, company executive. Pres. Solitron Devices, West Palm Beach, Fla. Office: Solitron Devices 3301 Electronics Way West Palm Beach FL 33407-4620

SARASOHN, EVELYN LOIS LIPMAN, principal; b. Charleston, S.C., Sept. 17, 1937; d. Hyman Isaac and Gittel (Ingberman) Lipman; m. Nachum Hershel Sarasohn, Aug. 14, 1960; children: Michele Beth, Hyman Isaac, Jeffrey Steven, Jonah Mendel, Jenny Tzipporah. BS in English, Coll. of Charleston, 1959; MEd in Supervision and Adminstrn., The Citadel, 1974. Elem. tchr. Addlestone Hebrew Acad., Charleston, 1959-64, 1964-68, middle sch. math. and sci. tchr., 1968-80, asst. prin. early childhood, 1968-80, computer coord., 1980-81, asst. prin., 1981-90; prin. Addlestone Hebrew Acad., 1990—; test supr. Ednl. Testing Svc., Princeton, N.J., 1971—. Author: Aleph-Bet Readiness, 1980, also video tape. Co-leader parenting group B'rith Shalom Beth Israel Synagogue, 1986-94. Mem. ASCD, Nat. Conf. Yeshiva Prins., S.C. Assn. Children Under Six, Nat. Coun. Tchrs. Math., Internat. Reading Assn., S.C. Assn. Ind. Schs., Jewish. Home: 131 Chadwick Dr Charleston SC 29407-7472 Office: Addlestone Hebrew Acad 1639 Wallenberg Blvd Charleston SC 29407-3507

SARBO, LINDA DIANE, English language educator; b. New Castle, Pa., Apr. 19, 1942; d. Walter Scott and Mary Elizabeth (Shannon) McKee; m. Gerald Victor Sarbo, Dec. 23, 1963 (div. Feb. 1990); 1 child, Shannon Marin. BA in English, Pa. State U., 1963; MA in Composition, U. South Fla., 1992, PhD in Composition and Rhetoric, 1996. Tchr. Mahoning County Schs., Youngstown, Ohio, 1964-67; program dir. Mahoning County Ct., Youngstown, 1967-71; dep. probation officer Marin County Probation Dept., San Rafael, Calif., 1971-76; supr. Dept. Health and Rehab. Svcs., Tampa, Fla., 1976-79; v.p. Am. Transworld Corp., Tampa, 1979-89; tchg. asst. U. South Fla., Tampa, 1992-96, asst. coord. rsch. Coll. Arts and Scis., 1994-95; editl. cons., Tampa, 1992—. Co-editor: White Mule, 1993—; contbr. articles, poetry to various profl. jours. and lit. mags.; author: (instr.'s guide) Becoming an Academic Writer, 1994. Recipient Suncoast Writers Conf. Poetry award, 1993, Am. Acad. Poets award, 1991, 92; Alice Hearne scholar, 1996. Mem. MLA, Nat. Coun. Tchrs. English, Fla. Coun. Tchrs. English, Conf. on Coll. Composition and Comm., Phi Kappa Phi.

SARDANOPOLI, BRUNO SARDI, retired television station sales official; b. Bronx, N.Y., Apr. 30, 1936; s. Anthony and Filomena (Oliveti) S. Student, NYU, 1954-55, U. Hartford, 1958-59. Cust. svc. mgr. Capital Records, N.Y.C., 1959-62; nat. promotions mgr. Colpix Records, N.Y.C., 1962-66; regional sales mgr. Fermodyl Syntex Corp., L.A., 1970-76; gen. sales mgr. Sta. WUAB-TV, Cleve., 1976-81, Sta. WFLD-TV, Chgo., 1981-82; lectr. in field. Pres. honor guard Colonial Color Guard, 1956-58. Mem. Humane Soc., Greenpeace, Audubon Soc. Home: 13785 Exotica Ln West Palm Beach FL 33414-8134

SARGENT, CHARLES LEE, manufacturing company executive; b. Flint, Mich., Mar. 22, 1937; s. Frank T. and Evelyn M. (Martinson) S.; m. Nancy Cook, June 9, 1962; children: Wendy L., Joy A., Candace L. B ME, GM Inst., 1960; MBA, Harvard U., 1962. Reliability engr. AC Spark Plug div. GM, Flint, 1962-63; with Thetford Corp., Ann Arbor, Mich., 1962-95, pres., chmn. bd. dirs., 1974-95; pres., chmn. bd. dirs. Thermassan Corp., 1969-72; chmn. GMI Engrng. and Mgmt. Inst., Flint, Mich., 1995—; pres., owner Quality Best Lifts, Inc., Fort Myers, Fla., 1996—; bd. dirs. First of Am. Bank, Fla.; trustee Lincoln Cons. Schs., 1973-77; GMI Engrng. and Mgmt. Inst., Flint, 1989, chmn. 1995—. Patentee in field. Elder Presbyn. Ch. Recipient Entrepreneurial Achievement award GMI, 1989; named Entrepreneur of the Yr., Harvard Bus. Sch. Club of Detroit, 1981. mem. Barton Hills Country Club (bd. dirs. 1985-87, pres. 1987), Harvard Bus. Sch. Club of Detroit (bd. dirs. 1983-93). Home: 3774 Cracker Way Bonita Springs FL 33923

SARGENT, JAMES O'CONNOR, freelance writer; b. N.Y.C., June 15, 1918; s. Joseph Hughes and Maryann Josephine (O'Connor) S.; m. Mildred Elizabeth Clark, apr. 19, 1949. Student, British Intelligence Sch., Calcutta, India, summer 1944, Fordham U., 1949-51. Ghostwriter, freelance writer, 1949—; founder Washington Writers Group, Washington, 1960—. Editor, rschr., writer (Bell Aircraft Co. in-house publ.) History of the Helicopter, 1952; author: (novellas) You Don't Bury on Christmas, 1960, Interregnum in a Commune, 1968, The Button Man, 1969, Moon in Pisces, 1970, Death in Saigon, 1971, Last Minuet in Washington, 1973, (MWA Anthology) Killers of the Dream, 1974; (screenplay) Queen Victoria and Lady Flora, 1993; (play) Loss of Innocence, 1994; published over 1500 works. Liaison with Peiping Aviators Assn., 1995-96. Maj. USAF, 1942-47. Decorated Bronze Star, Chinese medal of freedom. Mem. 14th USAF Assn., 528th Fighter Squadron Assn. (officer). Home: 1019 Stillbrook Rd Pensacola FL 32514-1629

SARGENT, JOANNE ELAINE, lawyer; b. Miami, Fla., Aug. 6, 1947. BE cum laude, Fla. State U., 1969; ME summa cum laude, Fla. Atlantic U., 1973; JD, Vt. Law Sch., 1985. Bar: Fla. 1986, Vt. 1986, U.S. Ct. Appeals (D.C. cir.) 1989, U.S. Dist. Ct. (D.C.) 1988, U.S. Dist. Ct. (so. dist. trial bar) Fla. 1988, U.S. Dist. Ct. (so. dist.) Fla. 1986, U.S. Dist. Ct. (mid. dist.) Fla. 1989, U.S. Ct. Appeals (11th cir.) 1988, U.S. Ct. Internat. Trade 1986, U.S. Claims Ct. 1988. Law clerk atty. gen.'s office State Dept. Edn., Montpelier, Vt., 1983, 84; law clerk DuFresne and Bradley, P.A., Coconut Grove, Fla., 1985-86; assoc. Sandler, Travis & Rosenberg, P.A., Miami, 1986-88; pvt. practice Coral Gables, 1989-90; career atty. Fla. Ct. Appeal (3d dist.), Miami, 1990—; family alcoholism counselor Detoxification Ctr. Hillcrest Hosp., Pittsfield, Mass., 1974-75; sch. adminstr. Drury Mid. Sch., North Adams, Mass., 1975-76; dir. student svcs. Mt. Greylock Regional High Sch., Williamstown, Mass., 1976-81, tchr. math., sci., 1969-76; presenter ednl. conf. for hearing officers Supreme Ct. of Va., 1985, 86; cons. U. Mass. Bus. adv. counsel Fellowship House, Miami, 1994. Mem. Fla. Bar Assn., Dade County Bar Assn., Coral Gables Bar Assn. (officer, dir. 1994). Office: US Ct Appeal 3d Dist 2001 SW 117th Ave Miami FL 33175-1716

SARKAR, CHITTO PRIYO, family medicine physician, researcher; b. Calcutta, India, June 1, 1951; came to U.S., 1979; s. Bimala Kanta and Labonyamoyee (Mitra) S.; m. Patricia A. Matthews, May 27, 1987; 1 child, Daniel Lee. BSc, Calcutta U., 1969, MSc, 1971, PhD, 1978; DO, Kirksville (Mo.) Coll., 1987. Rsch. assoc. Tulane Med. Ctr., Dept. Biochemistry, New Orleans, 1979-80, Kirksville Coll. Oste. Medicine, 1980-82; rsch. sci. staff Columbia, Mo., 1982-83; intern Botsford Gen. Hosp., Farmington Hills, Mich., 1987-88; resident gen. family practice Oakland Gen. Hosp., Madison Heights, Mich., 1988-89; physician Okeechobee (Fla.) Community Health Ctr., 1989-91; pvt. practice Port St. Lucie, Fla., 1992—; physician Infectious Disease Ctr., Ft. Pierce, Fla., 1992; staff physician Lawnwood Regional Med. Ctr., Ft. Pierce, Fla., Med. Ctr. of Port St. Lucie, Fla.; instr. S.E. Coll. Osteo. Medicine, North Miami Beach, Fla., 1989—. Contbr. articles to profl. jours. Mem. AMA, Am. Osteopathic Med. Assn., Am. Acad. Family Physicians. Democrat. Hindu. Home: 5806 Balsam Dr Fort Pierce FL 34982-3761 Office: St Lucie Family Doctor 7830 S Federal Hwy Port Saint Lucie FL 34952-1422

SARKAR, MOHAMADI ALIBHAI, pharmacy educator, researcher; b. Bombay, India, June 10, 1960; came to U.S., 1985; s. Alibhai Mohammedali and Amena Alibhai S.; m. Preeti Surendra Verma, Apr. 4, 1991. BS in Pharmacy, Bombay U., 1981, MS in Pharm. Tech., 1985; PhD in Pharm. Scis., Va. Commonwealth U., 1990. Registered Pharmacist. Staff Glaxo (India) Ltd., 1980; pharm. supr. Sandoz (India) Ltd., 1981-82; lectr. in pharmaceutics U. Bombay Coll. of Pharmacy, 1982-85; rsch. asst. biopharm. analysis lab. Med. Coll. Va., 1985-86, grad. teaching asst. dept. pharmacy and pharm., 1986-89; assoc. prof. dept. pharm. scis. W.Va. U., Morgantown, 1990—; cons. Mylan Pharms., Morgantown, 1991—, Kabi Pharmacia, Piscataway, N.J., Pharmacia, Inc., Columbus, Ohio. Author: (with others) Immunoassay, 1993; manuscript reviewer; contbr. articles to profl. jours. KV Pharm. Co. grantee 1985-86, Warner-Lambert Ltd. grantee 1989, 90, W.Va. U. Senate Rsch. grantee 1990-91, Am. Cancer Soc. Instnl. Rsch. grantee 1992-93, NIH grantee, 1993, 94, U.S. Dept. Edn. grantee, 1993; recipient First award NIH/NCI, 1994—. Mem. Am. Assn. Pharm. Scientists (chair Symposium in Drug Metabolism SW reg. meeting, 1994), Internat. Soc. Study of Xenobiotics, Soc. of Toxicology. Office: WVa U Rm 2025 Health Scis N Morgantown WV 26506

SARNA, JAN CHRISTOPHER, history educator; b. Little Rock, Ark., June 6, 1954; s. Clement Luke and Frances Josephine (Wallace) S. BA, Hendrix Coll., 1976; MA, Tulane U., 1978. Pvt. tutor of history New Orleans, 1979-85; mgr., co-owner Wholesale Merchandising, New Orleans, 1981-82; faculty, lectr. MARA C.C., Kuantan, Malaysia, 1985-93; faculty dept. of history U. Ark., Little Rock, 1994-95; faculty dept. of liberal arts Henderson State U., Arkadelphia, 1995—; faculty divsn. gen. edn. Cossatot Tech. Coll., DeQueen, Ark., 1996—; adj., cons. Jefferson Parish Schs., Metairie, La., 1983-85; cons. MARA C.C., 1986-92, spl. liaison, 1987, 90, organizer pub. seminar of U.S. edn. and life, 1991. Contbr. articles to profl. jours. Mem. Orgn. of Am. Historians, So. Hist. Assn., Am. Hist. Assn., Civil War Round Table Assocs., Civil War Round Table of Ark. (pres. 1975, v.p. 1995), Internat. Orgn. of Historians of Asia. Roman Catholic. Office: Cassatot Tech Coll PO Box 960 Hwy 70 W De Queen AR 71832

SARNOFF, MARC DAVID, lawyer; b. Bklyn., Dec. 28, 1959; s. Joel Sarnoff and Alaine (Katz) Stagnitta. BA, U. Tampa, 1981; JD, Loyola U., New Orleans, 1984. Bar: La. 1985, Fla. 1986, U.S. Dist. Ct. (so. dist.) Fla. 1986, D.C. 1987. Assoc. Herman, Herman, Katz & Coller, New Orleans, 1984-85; asst. prosecutor Orleans Parish Dist. Atty. Office, New Orleans, 1985-86; assoc. Christenberry & D'Antoni, New Orleans, 1986-87, Law Offices of Howard D. Dillman, Miami, Fla., 1987-91; ptnr. Goldman, Moore and Sarnoff, Miami, 1991-92, Sarnoff & Bayer, Miami, 1992—. Capt. U. Tampa Swimming Team, 1978. Mem. Million Dollar Advs. Forum, Phi Delta Theta (v.p. 1980, 81). Home: 3197 Virginia St Miami FL 33133 Office: Sarnoff & Bayer 3197 Virginia St Miami FL 33133-4545

SARTAIN, JAMES EDWARD, lawyer; b. Ft. Worth, Feb. 9, 1941; s. James F. and May Belle (Boaz) S.; m. Barbara Hardy, Aug. 17, 1962; 1 child, Bethany Sartain Hughes. BA, Tex. A&M U., 1963; LLB, Baylor U., 1966. Bar: Tex. 1966, U.S. Ct. Mil. Appeals, 1971, U.S. Dist. Ct. (no. dist.) Tex. 1974. Staff atty. Dept. Justice, Washington, 1970-72; staff atty. to U.S. Sen. William L. Scott Fairfax, Va., 1972; pvt. practice Ft. Worth, 1973—; sec. Penrose Lumber Co., Abilene, Tex., 1987—, Esprit Comm. Corp., Austin, Tex.; bd. dirs. Emerald Restoration, Inc., Abilene, Tex.; sec. Esprit Comm. Corp., Austin, Tex. Bd. dirs. Ft. Worth Boys Club, 1980-89, Oakwood Cemetery, Ft. Worth, 1979-84. Capt. arty. U.S. Army, Vietnam. Mem. ABA, Abilene Bar Assn., Baylor Law Alumni Assn., Ft. Worth-Tarrant County Bar Assn., Coll. State Bar Tex., Masons, Petroleum Club, Phi Delta Phi. Republican. Presbyterian. Office: 6112 McCart Ave Ste 201 Fort Worth TX 76133

SARUSKI, MICHAEL, interior designer; b. New Orleans, Dec. 26, 1963; s. Bernardo and Rebeca (Mechaber) S.; m. Ana Morel, May 27, 1990; 1 child, Joel Alexander. AA, U. Fla., 1984; BArch, U. Miami, 1987. Lic. interior designer, Fla. Draftsman William Dorsky & Assocs., Miami, 1985; design coord. Triangle Contractors, Miami, 1986, Benson, Bishop, Booth, ASID, Coral Gables, Fla., 1986-87, R. Mickley Interior Design, Miami, 1987; designer L.E. Seitz Assocs., Coral Gables, 1987-88, Lynn Wilson Assocs., Coral Gables, 1988-91, CLDA, Inc., Coconut Grove, Fla., 1991-92; pres., designer Saruski Design Studio, Miami Beach, Fla., 1993—; cons. for comml. interior design firms. Mem. ASID (bd. dirs. 1994-96), Nat. Trust for Hist. Preservation. Office: Saruski Design Studio 420 Lincoln Rd Ste 241 Miami Beach FL 33139-3009

SARVIS, EDWARD EARL, police official; b. Durham, N.C., Jan. 24, 1946; s. Newman Earl and Effie Irene (Baker) S.; m. Donna Lee Morgan, Dec. 17, 1966; children: Edward Earl Jr., Amy Lora, Holly Anne. AAS in Police Sci., Durham Tech. Coll., 1976; B of Adminstrv. Sci., Guilford Coll., 1978. Ins. agt. Met. Life Ins. Co., Durham, N.C., 1968-71; patrol comdr. dist. 1, Durham (N.C.) Police Dept., 1971—, pub. info. officer, 1989—. Pres. bd. elders Grove Park Chapel, Durham, 1978-95; v.p. Mountain Top Youth Camp, Pinacle, N.C., 1978—. With U.S. Army, 1965-68, Vietnam. Recipient Cert., So. Police Inst., 1976, Advanced cert. State of N.C., 1976. Mem. Fraternal Order of Police, VFW. Republican. Office: Durham Police Dept 505 W Chapel Hill St Durham NC 27701-3101

SARVIS, ELAINE MAGANN, assistant principal; b. Conway, S.C., May 11, 1947; d. John Thomas and Gloria (Winkler) Duckett; m. John Wesley Magann, Aug. 2, 1969 (dec. Nov. 1975); children: Christiane, James Wesley; m. Francis Mack Sarvis, Dec. 18, 1982. BA in Elem. Edn., U. S.C., 1969, MEd in Early Childhood, 1976, postgrad., 1990. Cert. elem. adminstrn. tchr., S.C. Tchr. Southside Elem. Sch., Augusta, Ga., 1969-70, Homewood Elem. Sch., Conway, 1970-71, Timmerman Sch., Columbia, S.C., 1972-73, South Conway Elem. Sch., Conway, 1973-74, 1975-76, instructional specialist, 1976-80, tchr., 1980-90; tchr. Horry County Gifted and Talented Program, Conway, 1990-91; mem. com. Horry County Tchr. Incentive Program, Conway, 1989-91; bd. dirs. Horry County Sick Leave Bank Program. Mem. First Bapt. Ch., Conway, 1958—, North Myrtle Beach High Parent Tchr. Orgn., 1990; neighborhood chmn. Am. Heart Assn., Conway, 1978. Named Tchr. of Yr. County of Horry, 1990. Mem. NEA, S.C. Edn. Assn., Horry County Edn. Assn., Horry County Math. Advancement Coun., S.C. Coun. for the Social Studies, Internat. Reading Assn., S.C. Assn. for Children's Sci., Palmetto State Tchrs. Orgn., Alpha Delta Kappa. Republican. Baptist. Home: PO Box 3769 411-34th Ave N North Myrtle Beach SC 29582 Office: South Conway Elem Sch 3001-4th Ave Conway SC 29526

SASEEN, SHARON LOUISE, artist, painter, educator; b. Savannah, Ga., Jan. 23, 1949; d. Edward James and Lois (Howard) Saseen; m. Joseph A. Dillon (div. 1978; 1 child, Edward Saseen Dillon. BFA, U. Ga., 1970, MAE, 1972; MFA in Illustration, Syracuse U., 1988; postgrad., Savannah Coll. Art & Design, 1982-84. Art tchr. James Island Middle Sch., Charleston, S.C., 1973, Savannah/Chatham County Bd. Edn., 1973-79, 1978-79; lower sch. art tchr. Savannah Country Day Sch., 1979-84; artist-in-residence Savannah Art Assn., 1976—; ptnr. Signature Gallery in City Market, Savannah, 1992—; ptnr. Gallery 209, Savannah, 1978—. One woman shows include Savannah Coll. Art and Design, Exhibit A Gallery, 1983, Historic Savannah Found., An Exhbn. Daufuskie S.C. Impressions, 1986, Atlanta Fin. Ctr., 1990, Internat. Oasis Gallery, 1991; exhibited in group shows Hilton Head Island/Pink Island Gallery, 1986, Lord and Taylor of Fifth Ave., 1987; illustrator Where Did My Feather Pillow Come From?, 1982; cover designer Southern Bell Telephone Book, 1991, 92. Recipient Savannah Art Assn. Mem. Show award, 1976; first prize in show award Savannah Arts Festival, 1978, Friedman's award, 1979. Mem. Nat. League Am. Pen Women, Inc.

SASEK, GLORIA BURNS, English language and literature educator; b. Springfield, Mass., Jan. 20, 1926; d. Frederick Charles and Minnie Delia (White) Burns; BA, Mary Washington Coll. of U. Va., 1947; EdM, Springfield Coll., 1955; postgrad. Sorbonne, summer 1953; MA, Radcliffe Coll., 1954; postgrad. Universita per Stranieri, Perugia, Italy, summer 1955; m. Lawrence Anton Sasek, Sept. 5, 1960. Tchr., head dept. jr. and sr. h.s. English, Somers, Conn., 1947-51, 52-59; tchr. English, Winchester (Mass.) pub. schs., 1959-60; faculty La. State U., Baton Rouge, 1961—, asst. prof. English, 1971—, chmn. freshman English, 1969-70; mem. South Ctrl. Conf. on Christianity and Literature. Recipient George H. Deer Disting. Tchr. award La. State U., 1977, Gumbo Favorite Prof., 1978, Disting. Undergrad. Teaching award Amoco Found., 1994. Mem. MLA, AAUP (chpt. v.p. 1981-84), South Ctrl. Modern Lang. Assn., South Ctrl. Renaissance Soc., South Ctrl. Conf. on Christianity and Lit., South Ctrl. Soc. for 18th Century Studies. Address: 1458 Kenilworth Pky Baton Rouge LA 70808-5737

SASS, ANNE MICHELE, pediatric nurse practitioner, clinical nurse specialist; b. N.Y.C., Apr. 17, 1965; d. William Kenneth and Panthie (Hopper) S. BSN, SUNY, Buffalo, 1989; MSN, Emory U., 1995. RN, Tex., Ga. Staff nurse orthopedics Buffalo Gen. Hosp., 1989; charge nurse gen. surgery Millard Fillmore Hosp., Buffalo, 1990; staff nurse newborn nursery, postpartum unit USAF Wilford Hall Med. Ctr., Lackland AFB, Tex., 1990-94; childbirth educator Wilford Hall, 1993-94. 1st lt. USAF, 1990-94. Mem. Nat. Assn. Pediat. Nurse Assocs. & Practitioners, Am. Heart Assn., Internat. Nursing Honor Soc., Sigma Theta Tau (Alpha Epsilon chpt.). Baptist.

SASS, ARTHUR HAROLD, educational executive; b. N.Y.C., Nov. 22, 1928; s. Maxwell Sigmund and Alice May (McGillick) S.; m. Eleanore G. Schmidt, Dec. 31, 1949; children: Nancy, Arlene, Susan, Eric. BS, Oswego (N.Y.) State Coll., 1949; EdM, Rutgers U., 1959, postgrad., 1960-68. Cert. chief sch. adminstr. Tchr. Millsboro (Del.) Pub. Sch. System, 1949-51, Eatontown (N.J.) Pub. Sch. System, 1955-66; coord. coop. indsl. edn. Monmouth Regional High Sch., Tinton Falls, N.J., 1966-68; prin. Mt. Holly (N.J.) Pub. Sch. System, 1968-71; supt. schs. Lumberton Twp. (N.J.) Pub.

Sch. System, 1971-72, Lacey Twp. (N.J.) Pub. Sch. System, 1972-74; analyst mil. pers. Naval Sea Systems Command, Washington, 1975-79; head employee devel. Naval Rsch. Lab., Washington, 1979-83, 85-90; acad. dir. Naval Res. Engring. Duty Officer Sch., Leesburg, Va., 1983-85; pres. DEVPRO, Inc., Warrenton, Va., 1985—; prin. founder Dept. Def. Sci. and Engring. Apprentice Program; established nation's first fed. svc. high sch. coop. indsl. edn. program, 1967. Author: Guide to the Naval Ammunition Depot, 1967; editor: (brochure) Commodore John Barry-Father of the U.S. Navy, 1976. Chmn. Shade Tree Commn., Little Silver, N.J., 1968-75, Rapidan/Rappahannock (Va.) Cmty. Mental Health Ctrs., 1980-81; deacon Warrenton Ch. of Christ, 1985—, elder, 1995; mem. Va. Gov.'s Adv. Bd. for Emergency Med. Svcs., 1994—. With USN, 1952-55; capt. USNR, 1983-88. Recipient Tng. Officers' Conf. Disting. Svc. award, 1988, Outstanding Contbn. to Engring. Edn. and Rsch award George Washington U., 1991. Mem. Am. Soc. Tng. and Devel., Res. Officers Assn. (v.p. Va. chpt. 1982-83), Naval Res. Assn. (Plimsoll Mark award 1975), Am. Soc. Naval Engrs., Navy League, Wash. Acad. Scis., Tng. Dirs. Forum. Republican. Home and Office: 5268 Ambler Dr Warrenton VA 20187-9201

SASS, JAMES ALLEN, navy officer; b. Tampa, Fla., May 31, 1955; s. James Lois Sass and Betty Jean (Denham) Alguire; m. Rose Marie Hammel; 1 child, Jamie Michelle; m. Amanda Sue Hodge, Dec. 2, 1979; children: Kimberly, Michael, Christopher. BS, So. Ill. U., 1982; MA, Webster U., St. Louis, 1993. Commd. USN, 176—, advanced through grades; ocular technician USN Hosp., 1976-82; combat info. officer USS Roanoke, Alameda, Calif., 1983-85; navigator USS Buchanan, San Diego, 1985-87; ops. officer USS Blakely, Charleston, S.C., 1987-89, USS Wainwright, Charleston, 1989-91; instr. U.S. Naval Acad., Annapolis, Md., 1991-93; navigator USS Wasp, Norfolk, Va., 1993-94; requirements officer Staff Chief Naval Ops., Washington, 1995-96; exec. officer USS taylor, Mayport, Fla., 1996—; cons. in field. Asst. cub scouts Boy Scouts Am., 1995-96. Decorated Navy Commendation medals (2). Lutheran. Office: USS Taylor FFG-50 FPO AA 34093-1504

SASS, RONALD LEWIS, biology and chemistry educator; b. Davenport, Iowa, May 26, 1932; s. Erwin Leese and Flora Alice (Puck) S.; m. Joyce R. Moorhead, 1951 (div. 1968); children: Dennise, Andria; m. Margaret Lee Macy, Apr. 4, 1969; children: Hartley, Dennis. BA, Augustana Coll., Rock Island, Ill., 1954; PhD, U. So. Calif., L.A., 1957. Chemist U.S. Army, Rock Island (Ill.) Arsenal, 1951-54; asst. prof. Rice U., Houston, 1958-62, assoc. prof., 1962-66, prof., 1966—, chmn. biology, 1981-87; co-dir. Rice Ctr. for Edn., Houston, 1988—; chair Rice Earth Sys. Inst., Houston, 1990—, Ecology and Evolutionary Biology, 1995—; cons. EPA, Washington, 1990—, Coll. Bd., N.Y.C., 1988—. Contbr. articles on chemistry, biology and biochemistry to profl. jours. NSF predoctoral fellow U. So. Calif., 1954-57, fellow AEC, 1957-58, Guggenheim fellow, 1965, sr. rsch. fellow NRC, 1988. Mem. Internat. Geospher-Biosphere Program (com. chair 1990—). Home: 2406 Wordsworth St Houston TX 77030-1834 Office: Rice U Ecology & Evolutionary Biology Houston TX 77251

SASSAMAN, ANNE PHILLIPS, science administrator; b. La Grange, Ga., Jan. 7, 1944; d. Joe and Bessie (Lewis) Phillips; m. John Robert Ball, Aug. 13, 1966 (div.); children: Kristen Anne, John Robert; m. Jan Frederick Sassaman, Oct. 1, 1983. BS with honors, Auburn U., 1965; PhD, Duke U., 1970. Rsch. assoc. depts. surgery, medicine, biochemistry Duke U., Durham, N.C., 1970-74; rsch. chemist FDA, Bethesda, Md., 1974-76; scientist-adminstr. Nat. Heart, Lung & Blood Inst., Bethesda, 1976-79, chief blood diseases br., 1979-86; dir. div. extramural rsch. and tng. Nat. Inst. Environ. Health Scis., NIH, Research Triangle Park, N.C., 1986—. Contbr. rsch. articles on biochemistry of thrombosis and thrombolysis to sci. jours. Mem. exec. com. coun. on thrombosis Am. Heart Assn., Dallas, 1979-86; mem. exec. bd. Am. Field Svc., Chapel Hill, N.C., 1989-92; vol. Am. Heart Assn., March of Dimes. Mem. AAAS, Am. Soc. Hematology, Internat. Soc. Thrombosis and Haemostatis, N.C. Soc. Toxicology, Assn. for Women in Sci., Sigma Xi. Democrat. Methodist. Home: 534 Caswell Rd Chapel Hill NC 27514-2704 Office: Nat Inst Environ Health Scis PO Box 12233 Durham NC 27709-2233

SASSCER, DONALD STUART, mechanical engineer, nuclear engineer; b. Washington, June 30, 1929; s. Joh M. and Helen M. (Albright) S.; m. Ruth Ester Burgos, June 14, 1958; children: Timothy, James, Julie, David. BSME, U. Utah, 1953; MS in Nuclear Engring., Iowa State U., 1958, PhD, 1964. Prof. Iowa State U., Ames, 1958-64; researcher nuclear rsch. lab. U. P.R., Mayaguez, 1964-74, researcher energy lab., 1974-88, prof. dept. nuclear energy, 1964-74, prof. dept. mech. engring., 1974-88; prof. Triton Coll., Chgo., 1988-90; asst. dir. office of rsch. and spl. projects Northwestern U., Evanston, Ill., 1991-93; cons. Office of Rsch. and Sponsored programs S.W. Tex. State U., Marcos, Tex., 1993-95; ret., 1995; scientist Argonne Nat. Lab., Chgo., 1988-93; cons. Common Wealth Oil Refinery, Ponce, P.R., 1968. Author: (with others) Blomass Energy Development, 1986, Alternative Energy Sources II, 1983, Alternative Energy Sources III, 1983, Tritium, 1973; contbr. articles to profl. jours. 1st. lt. USAF, 1953-55. Spl. fellow U.S. AEC, 1960-61, 61-62; grantee U.S. Dept. Energy, 1971, 72, 73, 74, 76, 77, 80-89, rsch. grantee NASA, 1974-75. Mem. ASME, Am. Soc. for Engring. Edn. Home: 2646 Chestnut Bend San Antonio TX 78232-4659

SASSEEN, GEORGE THIERY, retired aerospace engineering executive; b. New Rochelle, N.Y., July 21, 1928; s. George Thiery and Rosemary (Head) S.; m. Gertrude Bradford, Nov. 11, 1951 (div. Sept. 1980); children: Sharon Sasseen Hudek (dec.), George (dec.), John; m. Margret E. Katorsky, Apr. 1, 1982. BME, Yale U., 1949. Registered profl. engr., Tex. Br. chief-elect spacecraft ops. Kennedy Space Ctr. NASA, Fla., 1961, chief engring. div., 1967-75; Apollo ops. mgr. Kennedy Space Ctr. NASA, 1962-64, chief ground system div., 1964-66; dir. engring. shuttle ops. Kennedy Space Ctr. NASA, Fla., 1975-84; asst. mgr. space sta. Johnson Space Ctr. NASA, Houston, Fla., 1984-86; engring. dir. shuttle ops. return to flight Kennedy Space Ctr. NASA, Fla., 1986-94; ret., 1994. 1st lt. USAF, 1951-53. Named Engr. of Yr. Space Congress, 1971; recipient NASA awards for exceptional svc., outstanding leadership (2), disting. svc., Presdl. Meritorious Exec. award. Mem. Morys Assn. (New Haven), Patrick Officers Club, Cocoa Beach (Fla.) Pow Squadron (comdr. 1975), Moose, Tau Beta Pi. Democrat. Presbyterian. Home: 215 Mizzen Ct Merritt Island FL 32953-3059

SASSER, ELLIS A., gifted and talented education educator; b. Norfolk, Va., June 14, 1946; d. Haywood Ellis and Jessie (Johnson) S.; m. R. Wayne Kitsteiner, June 11, 1983. BA, Emory and Henry Coll., 1968; MA, Va. Commonwealth U., 1976; cert. creative problem solving, Ctr. for Creative Learning, Honeoye, N.Y., 1990, cert. advanced creative problem solving, 1990. Primary tchr. Henrico County Pub. Schs., Richmond, Va., 1968-76; tchr. gifted Henrico County Pub. Schs., Richmond, 1976—; tchr. humanities Three Chopt Gifted Ctr. Henrico County Pub. Schs.; gifted adv. bd. Henrico County Programs for the Gifted, Richmond, 1990—. Recipient R.E.B. award for teaching excellence Greater Richmond Community Found., 1989. Mem. AAUW, NEA, Va. Edn. Assn., Henrico Edn. Assn., Coun. for Exceptional Children, Va. Assn. for Gifted Edn., Va. Hist. Soc., Richmond Area Friends of the Gifted, Richmond Symphony Chorus, 1973-94, West of the Blvd. Civic Assn., Delta Kappa Gamma Soc. Internat. (pres. Gamma Chi chpt. 1994-96). Home: 3223 Floyd Ave Richmond VA 23221-2903 Office: Henrico County Pub Schs Three Chopt Elem Sch 1600 Skipwith Rd Richmond VA 23229-5205

SASSER, JONATHAN DREW, lawyer; b. Monroe, N.C., Mar. 1, 1956; s. Herman Wallace and Faith Belzora (Harrington) S.; m. Debra A. Smith, Feb. 22, 1994. BA with honors, U. N.C., 1978, JD with honors, 1981. Bar: N.C. 1981, N.Y. 1983, U.S. Dist. Ct. (so. and ea. dists.) N.Y. 1983, U.S. Dist. Ct. (no. dist.) Tex. 1983, U.S. Dist. Ct. (ea. dist.) N.C. 1986, U.S. Ct. Appeals (4th cir.) 1987, U.S. Dist. Ct. (mid. dist.) N.C. 1987, U.S. Supreme Ct. 1988. Law clk. to assoc. justice N.C. Supreme Ct., Raleigh, N.C., 1981-82; assoc. Paul, Weiss, Rifkind, Wharton & Garrison, N.Y.C., 1982-86, Moore & Van Allen and predecessor firm Powe, Porter & Alphin P.A., Durham, N.C., 1986-89; ptnr. Moore & Van Allen, Raleigh, 1990—. Editor: Cellar Door, 1977-78. Dem. precinct chmn., Chapel Hill, N.C., 1976-82. John Motley Morehead Found. fellow, Chapel Hill, 1978; John Motley Morehead Found. scholar, Chapel Hill, 1974. Mem. ABA, N.C. State Bar Assn., N.C. Bar Assn., N.Y. State Bar Assn. Baptist. Home: 311 Calvin Rd Raleigh NC 27605-1707 Office: Moore & Van Allen One Hannover Sq Ste 1700 Raleigh NC 27601

SASSER, PATRICIA JANE, sales executive; b. San Antonio, Aug. 11, 1942; d. Andrew Burgess and Dorothy Mae (Ackermann) Eastwood; m. Thomas Michael Myers, Aug. 23, 1964 (div. 1977); children: Gregory Stephen Myers, Amanda Beth Myers, Rodney Travis Myers. BS in Home Econs. Edn., So. Coll. 7th Day Adventist, 1965; MEd in Instrnl. Tech., McNeese State U., 1996. Cert. tchr., Miss., Tenn., Tex. 1st grade tchr. Chattanooga Pub. Sch. System, 1965-66; tchr. Beaumont (Miss.) High Sch., 1966-67; Bass meml. acad. tchr. Gulf Coast Conf. 7th-Day Adventist, Lumberton, Miss., 1966-67; 1st grade tchr. Northside Ind. Sch. Dist., San Antonio, 1967-68; substitute tchr. Cleburne (Tex.) City Schs., 1977-79; tchr. grades. 1-4 Lake Charles (La.) 7th Day Adventist Elem. Sch., 1979-80; with outside sales dept. Copy Systems, Beaumont, Tex., 1980-83; with outside sales dept. Stargraphics, Inc., Beaumont, 1983-87, with outside sales dept., br. mgr., 1987—. Bd. dirs. Christmas in April, Lake Charles, 1993—. Mem. La. Computer Educators, S.W. Louisiana C. of C., C. of C., Kiwanis (com. chmn. Sulphur chpt. 1989—, v.p., 199294, pres., 1994-95, named Kiwanian of Yr. 1993). Home: 3236 W Queen Circle Sulphur LA 70663 Office: Stargraphics Inc 128 State St Lake Charles LA 70605

SASSER, WARREN T., sporting services company executive. With Paragon Golf Constrn.; v.p. Jack Nicklaus Golf Svcs.

SASSER, WILLIAM DAVID, advertising company executive; b. Stillwater, Okla., Nov. 30, 1962; s. William Dow and Virginia Gayle (Roberts) S.; m. Lisa Jan Doyle Graham, Dec. 18, 1993; children: Kristofer Trey, Adam Graham, Karlie Graham. BS in Mktg. and Mgmt., Okla. State U., 1985. V.p. Heartlands Devel. Co., Inc., Perkins, Okla., 1980—, Sasser Co., Perkins, 1984—; pres. Advt. Concepts, Inc., Perkins, 1986—; bd. dirs. Okla. Farmhouse Frat Corp., Stillwater, 1985-92; select cons. Farmhouse Frat. Internat., 1989-91. Co-author: Perkins-Queen City of the Cimarron, 1989. Mem. Centennial 1889 Land Run Com., Okla., 1987; pres. S.W. Housing Preservation Found., Inc., 1989-91, Perkins-Tryin Edn. Found., 1996; area rep. Youth for Understanding Internat., North Cen. Okla., 1987—; vol. alumni coord., Ark., La., Okla., Tex., N.Mex., 1988; bd. dirs. Perkins Hist. Soc., Inc., 1986—, First Christian Ch., Perkins, 1989-96, Perkins Cemetery Assn., 1987—; bd. dirs. Friends of Okla. State U. Libr., 1990-91, Friends of Higher Edn. in Okla., 1990-92, Stillwater Area United Way, 1991—; bd. dirs. Friends of the Thomas-Wilhite Meml. Libr., 1996—, pres., 1996; bd. dirs. Perkins-Tryon Edn. Found., 1995—, pres., 1996; chmn. Perkins Centennial Com., 1987-89; founder Old Ch. Ctr. for Arts. Named Ambassador of Goodwill, Gov. Okla., 1981, one of Outstanding Young Men Am., 1985, 88. Mem. Okla. State U. Alumni Assn. (life, bd. dirs. Payne County Club), Payne County Hist. Soc. (life, Preservation award 1991), Payne County Cattlemen's Assn., Perkins C. of C. (sec. 1987, v.p. 1988-90, pres. 1991), Lions (bd. dirs. Perkins chpt. 1987-92, v.p. 1989-91, pres. 1992-93). Democrat. Office: Advt Concepts Inc 222 N Main St Box 667 Perkins OK 74059

SASSER, WILLIAM JACK, retired federal agency administrator, consultant; b. Arcadia, Okla., Aug. 12, 1934; children: Sam, Steve, Susan, Sandra. BS in Sociology and Psychology, Okla. Bapt. U., 1956; postgrad., S.W. Bapt. Sem., 1957-60, George Washington U., 1966. Lic. comml. pilot with instrument rating. Air traffic control specialist S.W. region FAA Air Route Traffic Control Ctr., Ft. Worth, 1963-65, pers. officer, 1970-71; tech. intern FAA, Washington, 1965-66; employee devel. officer S.W. region FAA, Houston and Ft. Worth, 1966-70; chief tng. br. pers. div. Gt. Lakes region FAA, Des Plaines, Ill., 1971-73; with exec. devel. program Gt. Lakes and ctrl. regions FAA, Des Plaines, Kansas City, Mo., 1973-75; asst. chief airports div. ctrl. region FAA, Kansas City, 1975-76, mgr., 1977-87; mgr. airports div. S.W. region FAA, Ft. Worth, 1987-89, dep. regional adminstr. S.W. region, 1989-95; ret. S.W. region, 1995; pvt. cons. Decatur, 1995—. Home: PO Box 162595 Fort Worth TX 76161

SASTRI, VINOD RAM, polymer chemist, educator; b. Lucknow, India, June 20, 1957; Came to U.S., 1978; s. Darbha Narayan and Prema Lata (Rajan) S. BSc, Madras U., India, 1976; MSc in Chemistry, Indian Inst. Tech., 1978; PhD in Organic Chemistry, Rutgers U., 1984. Postdoctoral fellow Poly. U., Bklyn., 1984-87; sr. rsch. chemist BASF, Clifton, N.J., 1987-88; rsch. chemist Allied Signal, Petersburg, Va., 1989-96; product technologist GE Plastics, Mt. Vernon, Ind., 1996—; adj. prof. Va. Commonwealth U., Richmond, 1992-96. Mem. Am. Chem. Soc., Am. Inst. Chemists, Soc. Plastics Engrs. Democrat. Office: GE Co 1 Lexan Ln Mount Vernon IN 47620-9367

SATRE, PHILIP GLEN, casino entertainment executive, lawyer; b. Palo Alto, Calif., Apr. 30, 1949; s. Selmer Kenneth and Georgia June (Sterling) S.; m. Jennifer Patricia Arnold, June 30, 1973; children: Malena Anne, Allison Neal, Jessica Lilly, Peter Sterling. BA, Stanford U., 1971; JD, U. Calif.-Davis, 1975; postgrad sr. exec. program MIT, 1982. Bar: Nev. 1975, Calif. 1976. Assoc. Vargas & Bartlett, Reno, 1975-79; v.p., gen. counsel, sec. Harrah's, Reno, 1980-83, sr. v.p., 1983-84, pres. Harrah's East, Atlantic City, 1984; pres., CEO Harrah's Hotels and Casinos, Reno, 1984-91; dir., sr. v.p. Gaming Group The Promus Cos., Inc., Memphis, 1988-91, dir., pres., COO, 1991-94, dir., pres., CEO, 1994-95; pres, CEO Harrahs Entertainment, Inc., 1995—; dir., treas. Nat. Judicial Coll., Reno. Active The Stanford Athletic Bd., 1996—. Mem. ABA, Nev. Bar Assn., Calif. Bar Assn., Order of Coif, Phi Kappa Phi, Stanford Alumni Assn. (pres. Reno chpt. 1976-77), Young Pres. Orgn., The Bus. Roundtable.

SATTERFIELD, BENTON SAPP, obstetrician, gynecologist; b. Raleigh, N.C., Nov. 5, 1936; s. George Howard and Alleece Voss (Sapp) S.; m. Emma Garnett Hix, Oct. 5, 1963; children: Benton Sapp, Robert N., E. Carson, William H., T. Bart. BS, N.C. State U., 1958; MD, Duke U., 1962. Rotating intern Med. Coll. Va., 1962, resident in ob-gyn., 1963-65; pvt. practice Raleigh, N.C. Chmn. ARC, Wake County, N.C., 1971-74. Capt. M.C., USAF, 1966-68. Mem. ACS, ACOG, Am. Fertility Soc., N.C. Med. Soc., Wake County Med. Soc. Methodist. Home: 3509 Alleghany Dr Raleigh NC 27609-6307 Office: 2801 Blue Ridge Rd Raleigh NC 27607-6474

SATTERFIELD, MARK EDWARD, consultant, columnist; b. Boston, Mar. 14, 1955; s. Charles Nelson and Anne (Pettingell) S. BA in English, Washington U., St. Louis, 1977; MA in Career Devel., Vt. Coll., 1991. Prin. Wottowa & Assocs., St. Louis, 1977-82; mgr. recruiting restaurant group Pepsi Co., Wichita, Kans., 1982-83; dir. human resources Kraft Inc., Chgo., 1983-87, cons., 1987—; dir. career svcs. Sch. Bus., Emory U., Atlanta, 1987-91; founder, CEO Satterfield Seminars, 1991—; cons. Kraft/Gen. Foods, 1989—, GE, 1987—, Info. Resources, Inc., Chgo., 1989—, Coca-Cola, 1990—. Columnist Atlanta Jour. Constitution, 1990—; author: Business and Career Etiquette, Where the Jobs Are, The Hottest Careers for the 90s, How to Negotiate the Salary or Raise You Deserve; contbr. articles on career change to profl. jours. Recipient Best Article award Dow Jones Nat. Bus. Employment Weekly. Mem. Employment Mgrs. Assn., Am. Mgmt. Assn., Am. Soc. for Tng. and Devel., Coll. Placement Assn. Home: 720 Rio Grande Dr Alpharetta GA 30202-5458

SATULOFF, BARTH, accounting executive, dispute resolution professional; b. Buffalo, Dec. 13, 1945; s. Bernard and Annette (Lurie) S.; m. Gail Lois Seid Jaffe, Aug. 23, 1992. BBA in Acctg., U. Miami, 1967, MBA, 1969. CPA, Fla., N.Y., Ill., La.; registered securities arbitrator, NYSE, AMEX, NASD; cert. state ct. arbitrator, Fla.; spl. master Fla. Pvt. Property & Land Use Cases. Staff acct. Price Waterhouse, Miami, Fla., 1969-71; tax specialist Laventhol & Horwath, Miami, 1973-74; mng. dir. Barth Satuloff, CPA, Miami, 1974—; pres., bd. dirs. Satuloff Bros., Inc., Buffalo, 1974-94, Miami, 1994—; sec., treas. Chartered Investment Rsch. Corp., Miami, 1980-89, also bd. dirs. Mem. endowment fund com. U. Miami, 1979; mem. Estate Planning Coun. Greater Miami, 1974; bd. dirs. Fellowship House Found., Miami, 1980; mem. FICPA Polit. Action Com., 1983, Ctr. for Fine Arts, Hist. Mus. South Fla., The Lowe Art Mus. U. Miami, Nat. Trust Historic Preservation. With Fla. N.G., 1970-76. Mem. AICPA (mem. small bus. taxation com. of tax divsn. 1993-96), ABA (sect. dispute resolution bylaws and directory com., sect. bus. law, forum on enterntainment and sports industries, taxation and bus. law), Fla. Inst. CPAs Ednl. Found., Fla. Inst. CPAs, N.Y. State Soc. CPAs, Ill. Soc. CPAs, Soc. La. CPAs, Miami Country Day Sch. ALumni Assn. (bd. dirs., sec. 1987-93, treas. 1994—), Am. Arbitration Assn. (nat. panel arbitrators and mediators), Audubon Soc., Zool. Soc. Fla., Ducks Unltd. (chmn. Miami chpt. 1991-92, 94-95), Trout Unltd., Nature Conservancy. Home: 9614 SW 134th Ct Miami FL 33186-2253 Office: 9495 Sunset Dr Ste B-275 Miami FL 33173-3253

SATZ, PHYLLIS ROBYNE SDOIA, pianist, composer, conductor, educator; b. N.Y.C., Feb. 23, 1935; d. Candido and Helen (Borsody) Sdoia; m. Barry Satz, Feb. 16, 1957; children: Stephen Mark, Rana Bambi, Michael Eric, Martin Craig. AA summa cum laude, Miami Dade Community Coll., 1981; BA summa cum laude, Fla. Internat. U., 1983; postgrad., U. Miami, Fla., 1983-85. Classical concert pianist, 1952—; dir. Sdoia Satz Music Inst., Miami, Fla., 1983—; music dir. St. Paul's Meth. Ch., Miami, 1985-90, Shores Sch., Miami, 1986-89; instr. music Miami Dade C.C., 1987-90, presents seminars, master classes to music tchrs., orgns. Solo debut Carnegie Hall, N.Y.C., 1952; featured soloist, numerous orchestras, U.S., Can., Mex., Bermuda; author: The Acquired Art of Teaching Music: A Basic Text, 1990; composer: The Life and Times of Mischka The Mouse, 1982, Regrets, 1980, Shma Yisroel, 1981, Silly Songs and Gobbles and Giggles, 1990, Modal Suite for Piano, 1983, Toccata, 1984, Short Suite for a Long Piano, 1985, Keys to Arban, 1987, Rhapsodie Hongroise, 1981, Bluesprechtsong, 1984, Ultimate Question, 1985. Lt., Aux. Police Svcs., N.Y.C., 1965-78. Winner Naumberg Competition, N.Y.C., 1951, Young Am. Artist, 1952, Mus. Artists in the Schs., 1952, Levintritt Piano Competition, 1953. Mem. NAFE, ASCAP, Music Educators Nat. Conf., Music Tchrs. Nat. Assn., Nat. Guild Piano Tchrs., Am. Coll. Musicians, Bandmasters Assn., Trumpet Guild, Organist Guild, Hillel, Phi Theta Kappa. Democrat. Jewish.

SAUDER, MICHAEL HOCKENSMITH, travel agency executive; b. Emporia, Kans., July 14, 1948; s. Earl W. and Stelouise (Hockensmith) S.; m. Margaret Elder, May 22, 1971; children: Aaron, Kyle, Paul. BSBA, U. Kans., 1972. Agt. Internat. Tours, Leavenworth, Kans., 1971; mgr. Internat. Tours, Leavenworth, 1971-72, regional mgr., 1972-73; pres., chief exec. officer Rennert World Travel, Inc., San Antonio, 1973—; mem. pres. adv bd. Braniff Airlines, 1988; bd. advisors Alamo Rent-a-Car, Ft. Lauderdale, Fla., 1987-92; nat. steering com. rep. officers Am. Express Travel Realted Svcs.; mem. adv. coun. U. Tex. at San Antonio Sch. Bus., 1993. Trustee Univ. United Meth. Ch., San Antonio, 1984-87, 88-92; mem. coun. City of Shavano Park (Tex.), 1978-82; fire chief Shavano Park Vol. Dept., 1983-84; chmn. Shavano Park Bd. Adjustments, 1982-88; bd. dirs. N.E. YMCA, San Antonio, 1988-92; bd. dirs., mem. exec. com. Nat. Youth Sports Coaches Assn., 1989—. Recipient Travel Agt. of Yr. award Continental Airlines, 1975, Top Sales Agt. award Mexicana Airlines, 1981; named one of Am. Airlines Top 100 Travel Agts., 1984—, Entrepreneur of Yr. Ernst & Young, 1989. Mem. Am. Soc. Travel Agts. (vice chmn. nat. hotel com. 1979-83), Inst. Cert. Travel Agts. (life, councilor 1977—), Young Pres. Orgn., U. Tex. San Antonio Roadrunners Club (chair membership dr. 1991-92), Rotary, Optimists (v.p. San Antonio chpt. 1976-77). Republican. Methodist. Office: Rennert World Travel 8103 Broadway St San Antonio TX 78209-1917

SAUDER, RANDY JAMES, state legislator, lawyer; b. Dubois, Pa., June 6, 1954; s. Harvey Louis and Dorothy Lee S.; children: Michael Louis, Angela Lynn. BA in Theology, Andrews U., 1979; JD, Detroit Coll. of Law, 1987. Bar: Ga. 1989, U.S. Dist. Ct. Ga. 1989, U.S. Ct. Appeals, 1989. Dean of staff New Friends Youth Camp, Ontario, Canada, 1977; minister Seventh Day Adventist Ch., Canada, 1979-87; law clk. Vandeveer, Garzia, Tomkin, Detroit, 1985-86; assoc. Cochran, Camp & Snipes, Smyrna, Ga., 1987-94; pres. Am. Investment Corp., Atlanta, 1987—; mem. Ga. Ho. of Reps., Smyrna, 1995—; pres. Atlanta Spinal Therapeutic Systems, Smyrna, Ga., 1993. Editor Marietta (Ga.) Rotary Metroliner, 1990-92. Vice chmn. Cascade Adventist Elem. Sch. Bd., Atlanta, 1987-91; vol. Am. Cancer Soc., Cobb County, Ga., 1990, 91; trustee, vice chmn. Smyrna Hosp. Found., 1992, chmn., 1993. Mem. ABA, Ga. Bar Assn. (real estate, corp. banking sects.), Cobb County Bar Assn., Cobb C. of C., Smyrna C. of C., Marietta Metro Rotary Club (sec. 1992-93, Disting. Svc. award 1990-91). Office: 248 Roswell St Marietta GA 30060

SAUERZOPF, MICHAEL ALFRED, software development consultant; b. Allentown, Pa., Oct. 2, 1959; s. Alfred Ignatz and Angela (Sgro) S. BS in Bus., Indiana U. of Pa., 1981. From assoc. sys. rep. to cons. Shaw Sys. Assoc., Inc., Houston, 1982—. Mem. United We Stand. Mem. NRA. Republican. Roman Catholic. Home: 7120 Fondren Rd Houston TX 77036

SAUL, RICHARD STEVEN, communication disorders educator, audiologist; b. Liberty, N.Y., Sept. 28, 1951; s. Jack Aaron and Estelle (Russo) S.; m. Barbara Jean Finegold, July 12, 1980; children: Jessica Rae, Benjamin Jacob. BA, Fla. Atlantic U., 1973; MA, U. Fla., 1976; PhD, SUNY, Buffalo, 1983. Chief audiologist Bethesda Meml. Hosp., Boynton Beach, Fla., 1985-86; asst. prof. So. Ill. U., Carbondale, 1982-85; audiology coord. Vet. Affairs Med. Ctr., Miami, 1986-90; assoc. prof. East Tenn. State U., Johnson City, 1990-93; faculty in audiology Fla. Atlantic U., Boca Raton, 1993—; various state and nat. profl. coms. Ctr. for Geriatrics and Gerontology, 1991—; presenter in field. Contbr. numerous articles to profl. jours. Pres. Sephardi Fedn. Palm Beach County, 1995. Mem. Acoustical Soc. Am., Am. Speech Lang. Hearing Asns., Am. Auditory Soc., Am. Acad. Audiology, Acad. of Rehab. Audiology, Fla. Speech Lang. Hearing Assn. (continuing edn. com. 1994—), Am. Anthropol. Assn. Jewish. Office: Fla Atlantic Univ 500 NW 20th St Boca Raton FL 33431-6415

SAULMON, SHARON ANN, librarian; b. Blackwell, Okla., June 13, 1947; d. Ellis Gordon and Willa Mae Overman; 1 child, John Henry. AA, No. Okla. Coll., 1967; BA, Ctrl. State U., 1969, MBA, 1987; MLS, U. Okla., 1974; postgrad., Okla. State U., 1982. Children's libr. Met. Libr. Sys., Oklahoma City, 1969-74, coord. pub. svcs., 1974-77, asst. chief ext. svcs., 1977-80; reference/special projects libr. Rose State Coll., Midwest City, Okla., 1980-91, head libr., 1991—; adj. faculty Rose State Coll., 1983—; program chair Global Okla. Multi-Cultural Festival, 1993; mem. nat. adv. panel for assessment of sch. and pupb. librs. in support of nat. edn. goals, 1995—; spkr. various civic and profl. orgns. Contbr. articles to profl. jours. Bd. dirs. Areawide Aging Agy., 1974-77; chair Met. Libr. Commn., 1990—, disbursing agt., chair fin. com., 1986-88, long-range planning com., 1985-87; chair bd. dirs. Met. Librs. Network Ctrl. Okla., 1989-90, chair alternative funding com., 1990—, newsletter editor, 1987-89, chair electronic media com., 1987-89. Recipient Outstanding Contbn. award Met. Libr. Sys., Friends of the Libr., 1990, Disting. Svc. award Okla. Libr. Assn., 1995. Mem. AAUW, Am. Libr. Trustee Assn. (pres. 1994-95, 1st v.p., pres. elect 1993-94, newsletter editor 1989-93, chair publs. com. 1987-92, regional v.p. 1985-88, chair speakers bur. com. 1991-92), Assn. Coll. and Rsch. Librs. (Cmty. and Jr. Coll. sect.), Pub. Libr. Assn., Am. Mktg. Assn., Okla. Libr. Assn. (conf. preview editor 1990-91, chair trustees divsn. 1989-90, mem. coms., disting. svc. award 1995). Democrat. Methodist. Office: Rose State Coll Libr 6420 SE 15th St Midwest City OK 73110-2704

SAULS, DON, religious organization administrator, clergyman; b. Eureka, N.C.; m. Marie Brown; children: Donna, Dale. B in Sacred Lit., Holmes Sch. of the Bible, Greenville, S.C., 1967; MA in Adult Edn., N.C. State U., 1984; postgrad., N.C. Wesleyan Coll. Ordained to ministry Pentecostal Free Will Bapt. Ch., 1966. Pastor Pentecostal Free Will Bapt. Ch., Benson, N.C., 1967-74, gen. dir. Christian Edn. dept., 1971-84, gen. supt., 1984—; tchr. Heritage Bible Coll., Dunn, N.C., 1971—, also trustee; chmn. bd. dirs., sec., mem. bd. adminstrn. Pentecostal Fellowship N.Am., 1988-91, Pentecostal and Charismatic Chs. of N.Am.; lectr. U.S. and abroad. Columnist Messienger, 1984—, now editor-in-chief; contbr. articles to jours. in field. Chmn. bd. dirs. Cape Fear Christian Acad.; pres. Harnett County Helpnet. Mem. Kiwanis (former pres. Dunn club, bd. dirs., dir. children's programs dist. 11). Office: Pentecostal Free Will Bapt Ch PO Box 1568 Dunn NC 28335-1568

SAULS, RICHARD LYNN, journalism educator; b. Shellman, Ga., Jan. 11, 1933; s. Edgar Earl Sauls and Mary Alena (Craig) Sauls Christian; m. Helen Esther Braat, June 4, 1952; 1 child, Raymond Kenneth. BA in Religion, So. Coll. 7th Day Adventists, 1956; MA in English, Vanderbilt U., 1962; PhD in English, U. Iowa, 1972. Tchr., prin. Sand Mountain Jr. Acad., L.I., Ala., 1953-55, Pewee Valley (Ky.) Jr. Acad., 1955-58, Nashville Union Jr. Acad., 1958-61; from supervising isntr. English to assoc. prof. English So. Coll. 7th Day Adventists, Collegedale, Tenn., 1961-69, prof. journalism and Enlish, dept. chair, 1989—; from assoc. prof. to prof. English, academic dean

Atlantic Union Coll., South Lancaster, Mass., 1969-86; prof. journalism and English Andrews U., Berrien Springs, Mich., 1986-89; reporter Naples (Fla.) Daily News, summer 1987, staff writer, summer 1988. Author: Language Matters, 1978; contbg. editor East Hamilton County Jour., 1989-93; contbr. articles to profl. jours. Press sec. Lancaster (Mass.) Conservation Commn., 1977-80; bd. dirs. Thayer Conservatory Cmty. Orch., Lancaster, 1980-85. B'nai B'rith scholar, 1950. Mem. So. Soc. Adventist Communicators (v.p. 1991-92), Soc. Profl. Journalists, Assn. for Edn. in Jounralism and Mass Comms., Assoc. Ch. Press. Office: So Coll 7th Day Adventist PO Box 370 Collegedale TN 37315-0370

SAUM, ELIZABETH PAPE, community volunteer; b. Evanston, Ill., Aug. 7, 1930; d. Karl James and Catherine (Schwall) Pape; m. William Joseph Saum, Dec. 31, 1960; children: JeanMarie, Katherine Anne, Mary Elizabeth. BA in English cum laude, Fontbonne Coll., 1952; MA in English, Northwestern U., 1958. Cert. tchr., Ill. Tchr. Our Lady of Perpetual Help, Glenview, Ill., 1952-55, Wilmette (Ill.) Jr. High Sch., 1955-61; dir. religion edn. St. Paul's Ch., Valparaiso, Ind., 1972-76; activities dir. Heritage Manor Nursing Home, Plano, Tex., 1982-84; exec. dir. Jessamine County Assn. Exceptional Citizens, Nicholasville, Ky., 1985-89; ret., 1989. Pres. bd. dirs. Women's Neighborly Orgn., Lexington, 1977-81; mem. Bluegrass Long-Term Care Ombudsman, Lexington, 1984-89, pres., 1986-88; bd. dirs. Women's History Coalition Ky., Midway, 1985-90; bd. dirs. Sr. Citizens East, Louisville, 1991-93, treas., 1992-93; creator, pres. Ky. Women's Heritage Mus., Lexington, 1986-90; adminstrn. coord. Transfiguration Ch., Goshen, Ky., 1991-93. Mem. AAUW (bd. dirs. Ky. br. 1977-81, 85—, named gift honoree 1988, v.p. Ednl. Found. 1988-94, 95-96, co-pres. Ky. chpt. 1994-96, named gift honoree Lexington br. 1987, pres. 1984-86, 88-90, Louisville br. editor newsletter 1990-93, treas. 1991-93, v.p. Ednl. Found. 1991-93), Lexington Newcomers (editor newsletter 1976-78), Trigg County Quilter's Guild (pres. 1995—). Democrat. Roman Catholic. Home: PO Box 1510 Cadiz KY 42211-1510

SAUMELL-MUÑOZ, RAFAEL E., secondary education educator; b. Havana, Cuba, June 20, 1951; came to U.S., 1988; s. Rafael Saumell-Pérez and Pura C. Muñoz-Infante; m. Maria M. Baston-Chils, July 20, 1974; children: Abdel, Michael. Licenciatura Linguistica, U. Havana, 1978; PhD in Spanish, Washington U., St. Louis, 1994. T.v., radio producer Inst. Cubano Radio/TV, Havana, 1975-81; tchg. asst. Washington U., St. Louis, 1988-91; lectr. U. Mo., St. Louis, 1989-90, Webster U., St. Louis, 1991; asst. prof. Sam Houston State U., Huntsville, Tex., 1992—; adv. to pres. Inst. Cubano Radio/TV, 1977-81. Contbr. articles to profl. jours. Mem. Modern Language Assn., Union Escritores y Artistas. Roman Catholic. Office: Sam Houston State U PO Box 2147 SHSU Huntsville TX 77341

SAUNDERLIN, GEORGE RAYMOND, nurse; b. Bridgeton, N.J., Aug. 14, 1950; s. Lester Patrick and Betty Marie (Weldon) S.; m. Mary Meredith Joyce, May 10, 1975; 1 child, George Stephen. BA, Lynchburg Coll., 1972; diploma in Nursing, U. Pa., 1975; BSN, Incarnate Word Coll., 1985. RN, Va.; cert. gastroenterology RN. Staff nurse surg. intensive care unit Pa. Hosp., Phila., 1975-76; staff nurse neuroscience unit Med. Coll. Va. Hosps., Richmond, 1976; staff nurse multisvcs. unit USAF Hosp. Mountain Home, Mountain Home AFB, Idaho, 1977-78; staff nurse obstet. and multisvcs. unit USAF Hosp. Misawa, Japan, 1978-81; staff nurse, asst. charge nurse, divsn. internal medicine USAF Med. Ctr., Lackland AFB, Tex., 1981-85; asst. charge nurse obstet. svc. USAF Hosp. Wurtsmith, Wurtsmith AFB, Mich., 1985-88; staff nurse emergency svcs. Med. Coll. Va. Hosps., Richmond, 1988-89, staff nurse endoscopy ste., 1989—; mem. editorial bd. Gastroenterology Nursing, Pensacola, Fla., 1993—. Capt. USAF Nurse Corps Res. Mem. U.S. Naval Inst., Soc. Gastroenterology Nurses and Assocs. Office: Med Coll Va 12th and Broad St Richmond VA 23298

SAUNDERS, ALEXANDER HALL, real estate executive; b. Tallahassee, Oct. 5, 1941; s. Irvin Jasper and Perry Francis (Watson) S.; m. Pamela Wightman, July 24, 1970; 1 child, Anne Marguerite. AA, Norman Coll., 1961; BA, Mercer U., 1966. Planning adminstr. Ga. Dept. Corrections, Atlanta, 1969-70; mgmt. analyst Ga. Dept. Transp., Atlanta, 1970-71, tng. adminstr., 1971-72, asst. to research and devel., 1972-73, adminstr., asst. to dir., 1974-82; pres. ERA Towne Square Realty, Inc., Stone Mountain, Ga., 1982—. Named one of Top Real Estate Execs. in Am., ERA, 1987. Mem. Nat. Assn. Realtors, Ga. Assn. Realtors, DeKalb Bd. Realtors, ERA North Ga. Brokers Coun. (trustee 1983-86, pres. 1988-89, v.p., dir. fin. 1989-), Metro Listing Svc., U.S. C. of C., DeKalb C. of C., Better Bus. Bur., Alpha Tau Omega, Delta Theta Phi.

SAUNDERS, BARRY WAYNE, state official; b. Roxboro, N.C., June 9, 1944; s. Charlie Clifton and Mary Louise (Mooney) S.; m. Brenda Kaye Bell, Oct. 18, 1987; children: Dara Louise Saunders Lockamy, Erin Elissa (dec.). BA, Campbell u., 1971; MEd, U. N.C., 1974; EdD, N.C. State U., 1990. Tchr. Granville County Sch. System, Oxford, N.C., 1966-69; mental health counselor Vocat. Rehab., Henderson, N.C., 1971-75; staff devel. specialist John Umstead Hosp., Butner, N.C., 1975-82; trainer, asst. mgr., mgr. tng. N.C. Dept. Transp., Raleigh, 1982—; mgr. tng. (on loan from N.C. Dept. Transp.) Gov.'s Office of Quality Improvement, 1995-96; pres. Omicron Cons., Cary, N.C., 1982—. Contbr. articles to profl. jours., poems to N.C. Poetry Soc., 1981. Sec. Dem. Party, Person County, N.C., 1980-84. Mem. Nat. Mgmt. Assn. (bd. dirs. state govt. chpt. 1992-95), Triangle Quality Coun. (bd. dirs. 1995—). Methodist. Home: 312 Montibello Dr Cary NC 27513-2479

SAUNDERS, DORIS EVANS, editor, educator, business executive; b. Chgo., Aug. 8, 1921; d. Alvesta Stewart and Thelma (Rice) Evans; m. Vincent E. Saunders Jr., Oct. 28, 1950 (div. 1963); children: Ann Camille, Vincent E. III. B.A., Roosevelt U., 1951; M.S., M.A., Boston U., 1977; postgrad., Vanderbilt U., 1984. Sr. library asst. Chgo. Pub. Library, 1942-46, prin. reference librarian, 1946-49; librarian Johnson Pub. Co., 1949-66, dir. book divsn., 1961-66, 73-77; prof., coord. print journalism Jackson (Miss.) State U., 1977-96, acting chair dept. mass communication, 1990-96, chair, 1991-96; Disting. minority lectr. U. Miss., Oxford, 1986-96; ret., 1996; pres. Ancestor Hunting, Inc., Chgo., 1982—; dir. community rels. Chgo. State Coll., 1968-70; acting dir. instnl. devel. and community rels Chgo. State Coll., 1969-70; columnist Chgo. Daily Defender, 1966-70, Chgo. Courier, 1970-73; staff assoc. Office of Chancellor, U. Ill. at Chgo. Circle, 1970-73. Host: radio program The Think Tank, 1971-72; writer, producer: (TV) Our People, 1968-70; producer, host: Faculty Review Forum, Sta. WJSU, 1987-93; author: Black Society, 1976; assoc. editor: Negro Digest mag, 1962-66; editor: The Day They Marched, 1963, The Kennedy Years and the Negro, 1964, DuBois: A Pictorial Biography, 1979, Wouldn't Take Nothin' for My Journey (L. Berry), 1981; compiler, editor: The Negro Handbook, 1966, The Ebony Handbook, 1974; pub. Kith and Kin; contbr. to profl. jours., mags. Bd. dirs. Arts Alliance, Jackson-Hinds County, Miss., 1993; mem. com. on racial recognition Diocese of Miss. Mem. NAACP. Democrat. Episcopalian. Address: PO Box 2413 Chicago IL 60690-2413 also: PO Box 10054 Jackson MS 39286

SAUNDERS, DOROTHY ANN, insurance company executive, sales management; b. Roxbury, N.C., Nov. 29, 1932; d. James William and Anna Bell (Wesley) Rice; m. Bernard L. Lewis, June 10, 1950 (dec. Jan. 1957); m. J.R. Saunders, Nov. 26, 1976 (dec. May 1981). Student, Md. U., 1950-53. Bookeeper, office mgr. TTN Cosmetics, Bethesda, Md., 1958; owner, mgr. Donnel's Hall of Gifts, Washington, 1959-63, Gifts, Inc., Washington, 1959-63; with U.S. Govt. Health, Edn., Welfare, Bethesda, 1965-73; owner, mgmt. in sales Dorothy Saunders Ins. Agy., Forest, Va., 1973—; vis. spkr. Bus. & Profl. Woman's Assn., Brookneal, Va., 1986-87; mem. bd. rsch. advisor ABI. Mem. Nat. Trust for Historic Preservation. Fellow Am. Biog. Inst.; mem. Internat. Platform Assn., Am. Lyceum Assn. Democrat. Baptist. Home and Office: RR 1 Box 166D Huddleston VA 24104-9765

SAUNDERS, JIMMY DALE, aerospace engineer, physicist, naval officer; b. Bronte, Tex., Dec. 16, 1948; s. James Howard and Wanda Lee (Lackey) S.; m. Judy Karon Falconer, Aug. 2, 1969; children: Jennifer Rebecca, Rachel Lee, Jason Allan. BS in Physics, U. Miss., 1976; MS in Physics, Naval Postgrad. Sch., Monterey, Calif., 1986. Enlisted USN, 1970, advanced through grades to comdr., 1991; ret., 1993; intelligence officer Comdr. Submarines Mediteranean, Naples, Italy, 1979-82; weapons officer USS George Bancroft, 1982-84; asst. for strategic weapons systems Strategic Systems Programs, Washington, 1987-88, asst. head missile ops., 1988, asst. head missile engring., 1988-90, asst. for advanced systems, 1990-91, head missile engring., 1991-93; asst. dir. Applied Rsch. Labs. U. Tex., Austin, 1994—; staff assoc. Chief Naval Ops. for Spl. Studies, 1989-90, Def. Sci. Bd., 1990; tech. advisor Strategic Arms Reductions Treaty, Geneva, 1990-91. Contbr. article to Phys. Rev. Mem. County Sch. Adv. Coun., Goose Creek, S.C., 1982-84; commr. Springfield (Va.) Youth Football Program, 1990-93; bd. dirs. Springfield Youth Club, 1990-93. Mem. AAAS, Am. Phys. Soc., Am. Soc. Naval Engrs., Sigma Xi. Methodist. Home: 9651 W Hwy 29 Georgetown TX 78628 Office: U Tex Applied Rsch Labs PO Box 8029 Austin TX 78713

SAUNDERS, PATRICIA GENE, textbook editor; b. Tulsa, Okla., Nov. 29, 1946; d. Eugene Merritt and Patricia May (Hough) Knight; m. Joseph Eugene Saunders, June 24, 1989. BA, Baylor U., 1969. Nat. advt. sec. KTVT-TV, Ft. Worth, 1969-71; tchr. Arlington (Tex.) Ind. Sch. Dist., 1971-77, Garland (Tex.) Ind. Sch. Dist., 1977-79; spl. projects assoc. Electronic Data Systems, Dallas, 1979-81; adminstrv. asst. Diversifield Innovators, Dallas, 1981-82; system ops. mgr. Span Instruments, Plano, Tex., 1982-86; data processing mgr. Claire Mfg., Addison, Ill., 1986-87, Everpure, Inc., Westmont, Ill., 1987-88; software cons. Software Alternatives, Inc., Downers Grove, Ill., 1988-89; data processing asst., cons. J&J Maintenance, Inc., Austin, Tex., 1989-90; pres., computer cons. Cardinal Software Solutions, Inc., Austin, 1990-93; editor Holt, Rinehart & Winston, Inc., Austin, 1993—. Contbr. articles to Tex. Hwy. Patrol Assn. Mag., Hill Country Sun, South Austin News, Police Vet. Mem. Smithsonian Instn., N.Y. Met. Mus. Fine Art, Soc. of Children's Book Writers and Illustrators, Austin Writers' League, Baylor Alumni Assn., Nat. Wildflower Ctr. Republican. Baptist. Home: 410 Teal Ln Kyle TX 78640-8888 Office: Holt Rinehart & Winston 1120 Capital Of Tex Hwy S Austin TX 78746

SAUNDERS, PHYLLIS S., business and financial broker, consultant; b. N.Y.C., May 2, 1942; d. Jack and Bella (Bader) Bloom; widowed; children: Todd B., Dean B. Founder, pres. P.S. Export Co., Inc., buying service, money management, consulting, in all types of business and finance for Cen. and S.Am., Bahamas, Caribbean, and third world countries, 1971—; pres. Burnett Enterprises Ltd. Mem. Am. Bus. Women's Assn., Nat. Assn. Women Bus. Owners, Am. Liver Found., Am. Jewish Com., Nat. Home Asthmatic Children, Hope Ctr. Mentally Retarded Children, U. Miami Booster Club, U. Miami Ctr. for Liver Diseases, U. Miami AIDS Research Ctr., Fla., Miami Childrens Hosp., Jewish Home for the Aged, Ctr. Fine Arts, Concert Assn. Fla., Fla. Grand Opera, Miami Ballet, Greater Miami Opera Guild, Fla. Philharm., Lowe Art Gallery, New World Symphony, PBS, Muscular Dystrophy, Multiple Sclerosis, Cerebal Palsy, Am. Cancer Soc., Am. Heart Assn. Republican. Avocations: golf, tennis, aerobics, fishing, boating. Home: 2 Grove Isle Dr Apt 205 Coconut Grove FL 33133-4102

SAUNDERS, RICHARD AMES, ophthalmologist, educator; b. N.Y.C., Nov. 9, 1946; s. Dero Ames and Beatrice (Nair) S.; m. Anne Elizabeth Leslie, Oct. 20, 1973; children: Jean, Carter. AB, Dartmouth Coll., 1969; MD, Columbia U., 1973. Intern, St. Luke's Hosp. Ctr., N.Y.C., 1973-74; resident in ophthalmology Presbyn. Hosp., N.Y.C., 1974-77; fellow Ind. U. Sch. Medicine, Indpls., 1977-78; asst. prof. ophthalmology Med. U. S.C., Charleston, 1978-81, assoc. prof., 1981-90, prof. 1990—. Mem. AMA, Am. Acad. Ophthalmology, Am. Assn. Pediatric Ophthalmology and Strabismus. Avocations: athletics, fishing. Home: PO Box 1431 Folly Beach SC 29439-1431 Office: Med U SC Storm Eye Inst Dept Ophthalmology 171 Ashley Ave Charleston SC 29425-2236

SAUNDERS, SUSAN PRESLEY, real estate executive; b. South Bend, Ind., Feb. 27, 1956; d. William Presley Jr. and Anne Summers (Winburn) S. Student, Converse Coll., 1974-77, Sandhills Community Coll., Southern Pines, N.C., 1978-86. Lic. real estate broker, N.C.; ins. lic., N.C.; notary pub.; accredited Relo coord. With Gouger, O'Neal & Saunders, Southern Pines, 1973-74, 75, Ceralon Mfg., Aberdeen, N.C., 1976; bank teller The Carolina Bank, Aberdeen, 1977-78; from clk. to v.p. fin. G.O.S., Inc., Southern Pines, 1978—. Mem. NAFE, Am. Soc. Profl. and Exec. Women, Am. Inst. Profl. Bookkeepers, Sandhills Area C. of C. (membership com. So. Pines chpt. 1989-94), Moore County Leadership Inst. Democrat. Presbyterian. Home: 130 Pebble Bch Southern Pines NC 28387-2345 Office: GOS Inc 177 W Pennsylvania Ave Southern Pines NC 28387-5428

SAUNDERS, TED ELLIOTT, accountant; b. Nashville, Feb. 19, 1952; s. Owen Felts and Dora Dean (Dorris) S.; m. Susan Sherrill, July 14, 1984; children: Scott Thomas, Shelley Eileen. BS, Mid. Tenn. State, 1973. Asst. mgr. Bill Crooks Foodtown, Nashville, 1974-75; bookkeeper Odom Sausage Co., Inc., Madison, Tenn., 1975-84; partnership acct. Transatlantic Exploration Ltd., Nashville, 1984-86; chief acct. B.A. Pargh Co., Inc., Nashville, 1986-89; comptroller Built More Homes, Inc., Lavergne, Tenn., 1989-92; bus. mgr. St. Edward Ch. and Sch., Nashville, 1992—. Bd. dirs. Tenn. Pride Employees Credit Union, 1977-83; pres. Danbury Condominium Assn., Nashville, 1986-88. Mem. Nat. Assn. Accts. Democrat. Baptist. Office: St Edward Ch and Sch 190 Thompson Ln Nashville TN 37211-2451

SAUNDERS, TRACIE LEE, day care provider; b. Glens Falls, N.Y., Feb. 22, 1960; d. Terry Wayne and Marilyn Teresa (Spano) O'Neil; m. Scott David Saunders, Dec. 12, 1984; children: Christopher Brtholomew, Benjamin Scott, Alexandra Elizabeth. Student, Defense Lang. Inst., 1978-79, 82. SSG, asst. platoon sgt., unit supr. U.S. Army, 1978-86; real estate Pan Am. Svcs., Carmel, Calif., 1987; self employed child care provider, presch. educator Springfield, Va., 1990-96; membership coord. Country Club of Fairfax, Va., 1996—; Author: (children's Story) The Brothers, The Sister and the Witch, 1995, also poetry. Author poetry and children's story The Brothers, The Sister and the Witch, 1995. Environ. activist Newington Forest Cmty. Assn., Springfield, 1996. Lutheran. Home: 8044 Steeple Chase Ct Springfield VA 22153

SAUNDERS, WILLIAM ARTHUR, management consultant; b. Ottawa, Ont., Can., Oct. 13, 1930. BS with honors, McGill U., 1954; MBA in Econs. and Fin., U. Western Ont., 1956, M of Commerce in Econs. and Mktg., 1960. Econ. analyst Imperial Oil Ltd., Toronto, Ont., 1956-63; supr. distbrn. Polysar Ltd., Sarnia, Ont., 1963-69; venture mgr. Polysar Plastics, Inc., Westport, Conn., 1969-77; adv. strategy devel. Gulf Oil Chems. Co., Houston, 1977-82; mgmt. cons. Houston, 1982—; pres. William A. Saunders Co., 1987—. Mem. Soc. Plastics Engrs., Assn. Corp. Growth. Methodist. Home and Office: 7518 Burgoyne Rd Apt 343 Houston TX 77063-3142

SAUR, JOSEPH MICHAEL, software engineer; b. Bklyn., Apr. 3, 1948; s. Joseph Charles and Margaret Mary (McCarthy) Saur; m. Jane Margaret Lent, Mar. 14, 1970; children: Maryellen, Meaghan, Joseph, David, Michael, Gregory, Dawn, Christopher, John, Geoffrey, Caroline, Renée. BS in Biology, St. John's U., 1969; grad. with distinction, Naval War Coll., 1986; BS in Computer Sci., Old Dominion U., 1989, MS in Computer Sci., 1991. First lt. USS Excel, Long Beach, Calif., 1970-71; gunnery officer USS Durham, San Diego, 1972-73; NGFS instr. Navphibscol, Coronado, San Diego, 1974-75; weapons officer USS Patterson, Mayfort, Fla., 1977-78; ops. officer USS Sylvania, Norfolk, Va., 1980-81; officer in charge naval sci. dept. Mass. Maritime Acad., Buzzards Bay, 1982-83; surface ops. officer Fleet Electronic Warfare Support Group, Norfolk, 1984-87; readiness and tng. analysis officer Comnavsurflant, Norfolk, 1988-90; software engr. PRC Inc., Virginia Beach, Va., 1990-95, AMS Inc., Norfolk, Va., 1995—. Contbr. articles to profl. jours. Lt. commdr. USN, 1970-90. Decorated Navy Commendation medal USN, 1984. Mem. Assn. Computing Machinery, Spl. Interst Group on Simulation (assoc. editor newsletter), Mil. Ops. Rsch. Soc., U.S. Naval Inst. Office: AMS Inc 999 Waterside Dr Ste 700 Norfolk VA 23510

SAUR, RONALD GARLIN, personal and organizational development specialist; b. Des Moines, Oct. 5, 1950; s. John Junior and Irene Ellen (Robinson) S.; m. Cheryl Lynn Smith, Dec. 28, 1971; 1 child, Joel Garlin. BA in Math., Graceland Coll., 1972, BA in Math. Edn., 1972; MS in Math., U. Iowa, 1978. Dept. head, high sch. math. Coon Rapids Community Schs., Coon Rapids, Iowa, 1972-73; eighth grade math. instr. Davenport Community Schs., Davenport, Iowa, 1973-75; high sch. math. instr. Davenport Community Schs., Davenport, 1975-81; computer sci. and math. instr. Marycrest Coll., Davenport, Iowa, 1978-83; ops. research analyst U.S. Army Chem. & Materiel Command, Rock Island, Ill., 1981-83; systems programmer, analyst Sun Exploration & Prodn. Co., Dallas, 1983-85; customer edn. instr. Prime Computer, Inc., Dallas, 1985-87, supr. customer edn., 1987-88, mgr. customer edn., 1988-91; instr., cons. Solutec, Inc., Carrollton, 1991-92; co-owner Triad Resource Assocs., Carrollton, Tex., 1989-92; instr. North Lake Coll., Irving, Tex., 1991-92, Networth, Inc., Irving, Tex., 1992—; instr., course developer Interleaf, Irving, Tex., 1993, Eicon Tech., Dallas, 1994. Author/editor computer courses. Pastor, RLDS Ch., Davenport, Iowa, 1979-80, assoc. pastor, Richardson, Tex., 1988-89, adminstrv. dir. 1990-91; block capt. Highlands Homeowner Assn., Carrollton, 1986. Mem. ASTD, IEEE Computer Soc., Assn. Computing Machinery, Nat. Diabetes Assn. (Tex. affiliate), U. Iowa Alumni Assn. Reorganized Ch. of Jesus Christ of Latter Day Saints. Home and Office: 3705 Bishop Hill Dr Carrollton TX 75007-2002

SAUTER, MARSHA JEANNE, elementary school educator; b. Ft. Wayne, Ind., Apr. 13, 1951; d. Donald Paul and Juanita Mae (Foltz) Harsch; m. Michael Charles Sauter, Dec. 11, 1971; 1 child, Paul Michael. Student, Ball State U., 1969-71; BS in Edn. summa cum laude, U. Cin., 1974. Cert. tchr., Ohio, Okla. 6th grade tchr. Norwood (Ohio) Schs., 1974-75, 1st grade tchr., 1975-77; kindergarten tchr. Mason (Ohio) Schs., 1979-81; 1st grade tchr. Oak Park Elem. Sch. Bartlesville (Okla.) Schs., 1988—, primary curriculum coord., 1992-95, 96—, mem. edn. com., 1991—, mem. English/math. textbook selection com., 1992, 93. Jr. H.S. youth advisor Good Shepherd Presbyn. Ch. Bartlesville, 1982-85, Sr. H.S. youth advisor, 1991-92, elder on session, 1985-88, 96—; mem. sunshine squad-crisis line Women Children in Crisis, Bartlesville, 1993—; sec. Bartlesville Cmty. Singers. Grantee Bartlesville Sch. Found., 1992, 94, 95. Mem. NEA, Nat. Coun. Tchrs. Math., Tchrs. Assn. of Whole Lang., Nat. Reading Assn., Okla. Reading Assn., Soc. for Prevention of Cruelty to Animals, Okla. Edn. Assn., Toastmasters (Competent Toastmaster award 1993, sec.-treas. 1994-95, v.p. membership 1995-96), Elks. Home: 365 Turkey Creek Rd Bartlesville OK 74006-8116 Office: Bartlesville Pub Schs Oak Park Elem 200 Forest Park Rd Bartlesville OK 74003-1503

SAVAGE, DIXIE LEE KINNEY, nursing administrator; b. Muscogee County, Ga., Aug. 9, 1949; d. Thomas T. and E. Ruth (Bailey) Kinney; m. Charlie Ray Savage, July 31, 1971; children: Melissa L. Savage Hand, Stephanie Rhea. ADN, DeKalb Coll., 1982; BSN, Med. Coll. Ga., 1990. RN, Ga.; cert. instr. ACLS, Am. Heart Assn. Staff nurse cardiothoracic surgery Emory U. Hosp., Atlanta, 1982-84; from staff nurse ICU, CCU to nursing supr. Humana Hosp. Gwinnett, Snellville, Ga., 1984-94; dir. ambulatory svcs. Columbia Eastside Med. Ctr., Snellville, Ga., 1994—; dir. perioperative svcs. Columbia Eastside Med. Ctr., 1995—. Recipient Nursing Excellence award Humana Hosp. Gwinnett. Mem. AACN (CCRN, mem. adv. com.), Phi Theta Kappa.

SAVAGE, JAMES FRANCIS, editor; b. Boston, July 23, 1939; s. James and Hanora (Enright) S.; m. Sharon Kaye Base, May 29, 1965; 1 son, Sean. A.A., Boston U., 1959, B.S., 1961. Reporter Quincy (Mass.) Patriot Ledger, 1961-63; reporter Miami (Fla.) Herald, 1963-67, investigative reporter, 1967-78, investigations editor, 1978-84, assoc. editor investigations, 1984—; investigative reporter Boston Herald Traveler, 1967. Served with AUS, 1962. Recipient Nat. Headliners award, 1969, Fla. Press Assn. award, 1972, George Polk Meml. award for investigative reporting, 1973, 80, Pub. Service award Nat. A.P. Mng. Editors, 1974, 80, award Fla. Soc. Newspaper Editors, 1974, 75, Nat. Disting. Service award Sigma Delta Chi, 1979, 87, Pulitzer Prize Staff award for Nat. Reporting, 1987, Outstanding Investigative Reporting award Investigative Reporters and Editors, 1988, Disting. Alumni award Boston U. Coll. Communications, 1990, Pulitzer Prize Staff Pub. Svc. award, 1993; Profl. Journalism fellow Stanford, 1974-75. Home: 1004 Orange Is Fort Lauderdale FL 33315-1651 Office: 1 Herald Plz Miami FL 33132-1609

SAVAGE, JAY MATHERS, biology educator; b. Santa Monica, Calif., Aug. 26, 1931; s. Jesse Mathers and Mary Louise (Bird) S.; m. Ruth Louise Byrnes, June 28, 1952 (div. Feb. 1978); children: Nancy Diane, Charles Richard; m. Rebbeca E. Papendick, June 30, 1981. AB, Stanford U., 1950, MA, 1954, PhD, 1955. Asst. prof. biology Pomona Coll., Claremont, Calif., 1954-56; instr. biology U. So. Calif., L.A., 1956-57, asst. prof. biology, 1957-59, assoc. prof. biology, 1959-64, prof. biology, 1982—; chair biology U. Miami, Coral Gables, Fla., 1982-86; assoc. dir. Allan Hancock Found., U. So. Calif., L.A., 1964-82; rsch. dir. Evolution and Ecological Biology Sect., L.A., 1977-82; chmn. NAS com. biol. humid tropics, Washington, 1980-82; commr. Internat. Commn. Zoology, London, 1982. Author: Evolution, 3d edit., 1977, Ecological Aspects of Development in the Humid Tropics, 1982, Introduction to the Herpetofauna of Costa Rica, 1986. Guggenheim Found. fellow, 1963-64, The Explorers Club fellow, 1978; recipient Individual Achievements award Skull and Dagger, U. So. Calif., 1978. Mem. Am. Soc. Ichth and Herbs (pres. 1982), Orgn. Tropical Studies (bd. dirs. 1963—, pres. 1973-80), So. Calif. Acad. Scis. (pres. 1966-68), Soc. Sys. Biol. (pres. 1995-96), Univ. Nat. Oceanaographic Lab Sys. (vice chair 1971-73). Office: Univ of Miami PO Box 249118 Coral Gables FL 33124-9118

SAVAGE, KAY WEBB, lawyer, health center administrator, accountant; b. Piedmont, Ala., Mar. 30, 1942; d. Robert Benjamin and Ellon Marie (Posey) Webb; m. Perry Lauren Savage, Nov. 18, 1961; children: Perry Lauren Jr., Shannon Hunter. BS in Secondary Edn., Jacksonville State Coll., Ala., 1963, AB, 1964; BS, Birmingham-So. Coll., 1987; JD, U. Ala., 1989. Bar: Ala. 1989; CPA, Ala.; cert. secondary tchr., Ala. Tchr. English, Hokes Bluff High Sch., Gadsden, Ala., 1963-64; tchr. sci. and math. McArthur Sch., Birmingham, Ala., 1964-68; tchr. sci. Mountain Brook Jr. High Sch., Birmingham, 1968-69; acct. Robert Resha, CPA, Birmingham, 1984-86; pvt. practice acctg. Birmingham, 1986—, pvt. practice law, 1989—; adminstr. Ala. Orthopaedic and Spine Ctr., Birmingham, 1987—; pres. Aleco, Inc., Birmingham, 1990—, Savage Enterprises, Birmingham, 1985—; bd. dirs. Assoc. Agys. Am., Coastal Bend Oil & Gas Co., Piedmont Ednl. Trust. Pres., sec. Snowcrest Condominium Assn., Snowshoe, W.Va., 1984-88; mem. exec. bd. Rep. Congl. Leadership Coun., Washington, 1988—; mem. Senatorial Trust, Washington, 1989, Presdl. Roundtable, Washington, 1989—, Piedmont Schs. Found., Birmingham Olympic Com., 1990—, Birmingham So. Coll. Arts Coun., 1992—, also gala advisor; v.p. United Cerebral Palsy, mem. multiple sclerosis class, 1995; sponsor U.S. Olympic Team; bd. dis. Piedmont Schs. Found., mem. scholarship com.; del. 1st Moscow Conf. on Law and Econ. Coop.; mem. exec. com. Com. for Fair Cts., 1994—; legis. chmn. Jefferson County Med. Alliance, 1994—, Ala. Med. Alliance, 1995; bd. dirs. End Meml. Found., 1994—. Fulbright fellow, 1964; recipient (5) Am. Jurisprudence awards. Mem. AAUW, Ala. Bar Assn., Ala. Soc. CPAs, Birmingham Bar Assn., Med. Group Mgmt. Assn., Bones Orthopedic Mng. Group, Attys. at Law and CPA U.S.A., Am. Soc. Law and Medicine, Pilot Lawyers Assn., Assn. Agys. Am. (bd. advisors), Coastal Ben Oil and Gas (bd. dirs.), Exec. Women Internat., C. of C. (bd. dirs. 1994—), Ninety Nines, Rotary Club Internat. (dir.), Sigma Delta Kappa (svc. award 1989), Sigma Kappa Delta, Sigma Tau Delta, Pi Gamma Mu. Home: 3815 River View Cir Birmingham AL 35243-4801 Office: 52 Med Park East Dr Ste 115 Birmingham AL 35243

SAVAGE, RICHARD MARK, systems analyst; b. Rockville Centre, N.Y., Feb. 8, 1950; s. Jack Earl and Margaret Ruth (Davis) S.; m. Jean Ann Hively, Sept. 19, 1970; children: Michael A., David A. Cert. in mid-mgmt. with honors, Wilbur Wright Jr. Coll., Chgo., 1974; AA in Sci., Community Coll. of USAF, 1979; assoc. tech. degree, GTE Corp., 1987, Assoc. Mgmt., 1991; BSBA, LeTourneau U., 1996. Enlisted USAF, 1969, advanced through grades to staff sgt., 1973; airman, student security service USAF, Tex., 1969-70; radio communications analyst USAF, Crete, Greece, 1970-72, Shepherd, Eng., 1972-77; instr. USAF, San Angelo, Tex., 1977-79; resigned USAF, 1979; personnel and sales recruiter Interglobal Tech. Services, Austin, Tex., 1979-80; switching services maint. analyst GTE of the Southwest, Baytown, Tex., 1981-83; switching services budget analyst GTE of the Southwest, San Angelo, 1983-85, switching services systems analyst, 1985-87, adminstrn. results supr., 1987-89; sr. adminstr. GTE Telephone Ops., 1989-90; staff adminstr., 1990-94; industry sales, systems mgr. GTE Supply, Irving, Tex., 1994—; cons. to local bus., San Angelo, Dallas Metroplex, 1985—; pres., owner Savage Innovations, San Angelo, Dallas, 1986—. Commr., cubmaster Boy Scouts Am., San Angelo, 1986-87; pres. McGill PTA, San Angelo, 1987-89; mem. adult coun. Sierra Vista Meth. Ch., San

Angelo, 1987-88. Named one of Outstanding Young Men Am., 1985. Office: GTE Supply MC HQA04U03 PO Box 169001 Irving TX 75016-9001

SAVAGE, ROBERT L., political science educator; b. Fort Worth, Feb. 26, 1939; s. Henry Carroll and Helen Marie (Donahue) Goldman; m. Patricia Ann Shipp, Mar. 8, 1959 (div. 1963); 1 child, Georgia Faye; m. Naomi Lee Stedman, Nov. 8, 1963 (div. June 1976); 1 child, Naomi Lynne; m. Barbara Grace Brown, Jan. 4, 1980. AS in Math., Tarleton State Coll., 1961, BA in Govt., 1963; MA in Polit. Sci., U. Houston, 1966; PhD in Polit. Sci., U. Mo., 1971. Asst. prof. Auburn U., Montgomery, Ala., 1971-74; U. Ark., Fayetteville, 1974-77, assoc. prof., 1977-82, prof., 1982—, interim chair, 1988-89, chair, 1989—; mem. adv. bd. dirs. Ark. Household Research Panel, Coll. Bus. Adminstrn. U. Ark., Fayetteville, 1980-87; mem. exec. council Nat. Network State Polls, Tuscaloosa, Ala., 1984-87. Author: (with others) Candidates and Their Images, 1976; editor: (with others) The Orwellian Moment: Hindsight and Foresight in the Post-1984 World, 1989, Politics in Familiar Contexts; Projecting Politics Through Popular Media, 1990; author, co-author monographs and contbr. articles to profl. jours. Staff cons. Ala. Energy Mgmt. Office, Montgomery, 1974; chmn. Community Devel. Com., Fayetteville, 1977-78; regional Humanist Ark. Endowment Humanities, 1978-85. Served with USAF, 1956-59. Grantee U.S. Dept. Housing & Urban Devel. 1975, First Ark. Bank Co. 1979, Ark. Endowment Humanities, 1980, J. William Fulbright Coll Arts & Sci. U. Ark. 1981, Nat. Sci. Found., 1991. Mem. Internat. Communication Assn. (v.p. 1988-90, vice chmn. polit. comm. div. 1986-88, chmn. polit. comm. div. 1988-90), Am. Polit. Sci. Assn., Midwest Polit. Sci. Assn. (mem. editorial bd. Am. Jour. Polit. Sci. 1983-85), Southern Polit. Sci. Assn., Southwestern Polit. Sci. Assn. (exec. council 1981-83, v.p., program chmn. 1987-88, pres. 1990-91), Southwestern Social Sci. Assn. (v.p. 1995-96, pres.- elect 1996—), Polit. Film Soc., Ark. Polit. Sci. Assn. (pres. 1978-79, mem. editorial bd. Midsouth Jour. Polit. Sci. 1990-93) Speech Communication Assn., Southern Speech Communication Assn., Ga. Polit. Sci. Assn., Conf. Fed. Studies, Policy Studies Orgn., Assn. Politics and Life Scis., Pi Sigma Alpha, Phi Kappa Phi. Democrat. Avocations: record collecting, reading. Office: U Ark Dept Polit Sci Old Main 428 Fayetteville AR 72701

SAVAGE, THOMAS YATES, lawyer; b. Fredericksburg, Va., Apr. 13, 1956; s. Joseph L. and Marie (Radolinski) S.; m. Julia Savino, Sept. 1, 1984. BS in Mass Communications, Va. Commonwealth U., 1978; JD, Washington and Lee U., 1982. Bar: Va. 1982. Sole practice Fredericksburg, 1982—. Dist. chmn. Fauquier County Dem. Com., Va., 1985, 90, 95, 96; bd. dirs. Vol. Emergency Families for Children, 1989-93; mem. Friends of Rappahannock, Fredericksburg; chief bd. Goldrein Vol. Fire Dept., Inc., 1989-92. Named one of Outstanding Young Men of Am., 1984, Outstanding Young Virginian, Va. Jaycees, 1993. Mem. ABA, Fredericksburg Area Bar Assn. Roman Catholic. Office: 707 Princess Anne St Fredericksburg VA 22401-5923

SAVEDGE, ANNE CREERY, artist, photographer; b. Richmond, Va., Jan. 29, 1947; d. Leslie Roy Jr. and Dorothy (Rakes) C.; m. Edwin Clement Savedge Jr., Aug. 11, 1967; 1 child, Ross Alan. BS, James Madison U., 1969; M in Art Edn., Va. Commonwealth U., 1977. Art instr. Colonial Heights (Va.) High Sch., 1969-78; instr. Va. Mus. Robinson House, Richmond, 1983-86; vis. artist Office of Youth and Community Svcs., Dinwiddie, Va., 1986-87; artist-in-residence Richmond Children's Mus., 1987-88; instr. Shenandoah Photographic Workshops, 1988; adj. faculty U. Richmond, 1978—; artist-in-residence Va. Mus. of Fine Arts, Richmond, 1984-86, Richmond Children's Mus., 1987—; curator Bedford Gallery Photoshow Longwood Coll., Farmville, Va., 1985, Light Images Gallery Photoshow James Madison U., Harrisonburg, Va., 1985, 1708 East Main Gallery Photoshow, Richmond, 1987, 90; artist Fay Gold Gallery, Atlanta, 1985-87, Nat. Copier Art Show; artist-in-edn. gifted program, Dinwiddie, Va., 1988; instr. Chesterfield Tech. Ctr., 1989—. Solo shows include Marsh Gallery, U. Richmond, 1986, 1708 Gallery, 1994, Baton Rouge, 1991; exhibited in group shows Pleiades Gallery, N.Y.C., 1989, Martin Gallery, Washington, 1989, Midwest Invitational, 1993-94, Mars Gallery, Ariz., 1994, Bloom Gallery, Milan, Italy, 1995; represented in permanent collections Polaroid Internat. Collection, Federal Res. Bank. Adv. coun. Richmond Arts Coun.; evaluation com. Partners-in-Arts; master tchr. Va. State T&I Skills USA Nat. Conf.; chmn. 1708 Gallery Exhbns., 1995-96. Mem. Richmond Artists Assn. (pres. 1978-80, cert. distinction 1980), Soc. for Photographic Edn., Va. Soc. for Photographic Arts (steering com. 1976—, fundraising chmn. 1978—, mem. chmn. 1980-86). Methodist. Home and Office: 5318 Verlinda Dr Richmond VA 23237-3307

SAVEROT, P.M., business executive. Dir. R&D E.R. Johnson Assoc., Inc., Fairfax, Va. Office: ER Johnson Assoc Inc 9302 Lee Hwy Ste 700 Fairfax VA 22031

SAVILLE, MICHAEL J., air force officer; b. Cumberland, Md., Aug. 22, 1957; s. Robert W. and Carole Jean (Minke) S.; m. Janet Bennett, Mar. 24, 1986; 1 child, Jason. BS, W.Va. U., 1979; MPA, Golden Gate U., 1988. Commd. 2d lt. USAF, 1979, advanced through grades to lt. col.; supr. munitions maintenance 49th fighter interceptor sqadron USAF, Griffiss AFB, N.Y., 1979-81; officer munitions staff 425th munitions support squadron USAF, Langley AFB, Va., 1981-83, chief munition maintenance 48th fighter interceptor squadron, 1983-84; chief munitions readiness br. hdqs. U.S. Cen. Air Forces USAF, Shaw AFB, S.C., 1984-86; chief weapons safety 8th tactical fighter wing USAF, Kunsan Air Base, South Korea, 1986-87; logistics resource programmer Dir. Programs & Evaluation USAF, Washington, 1987-92; chief prodn. sect. depot maintenanc divsn. USAF, Wright-Patterson AFB, Ohio, 1993-94, exec. officer Dir. of Logistics, 1994-95; comdr. 19th maintenance squadron USAF, Robins AFB, Ga., 1995—. Decorated Meritorious Svc. medal (2), Air Force Commendation medal (5). Mem. Air Force Assn., Maintenance Officer Assn., Soc. Profl. Journalists, Am. Legion. Republican. United Methodist. Home: 220 Falcon Crest Warner Robins GA 31088 Office: 19th Maintenance Squadron 555 Blunk Rd Robins AFB GA 31098

SAVILLE, R. ALLEN, management consultant; b. El Paso, Tex., May 24, 1945. BA in Polit. Sci., U. Richmond, 1967; JD, U. Va., 1973; M in Urban and Regional Planning, Va. Poly. Inst. and State U., 1976, D in Planning and Mgmt. Sys., 1981. Sr. planner Hayes, Seay, Mattern & Mattern, Roanoke, Va., 1976-79; dir. consulting svcs. The Profl. Group, Richmond, Va., 1979-83; pres. Mgmt. Planning Sys., Inc., Richmond, 1983-84; mgr. consulting svcs. Gary, Stosch, Walls & Co. (merged with Deloitte & Touche), Richmond, 1984-86; nat. dir. consulting skills edn., nat. dir. mgmt. edn. and orgnl. devel. Ernst & Young, Reston, Va., 1986-92; prin. Saville Consulting Svc., Reston, Va., 1992-96, Pritchett & Assocs., Dallas, 1996—. Office: Pritchett & Assocs. 13155 Noel Rd Ste 1600 Dallas TX 75240

SAVING, THOMAS ROBERT, economics educator, consultant; b. Chgo., Dec. 27, 1933; s. Harold John and Frances Josephine (Fillipino) S.; m. Barbara Jean Sorby, Aug. 22, 1959; children: Jason Lee, Nicole Aline. B.A. in Econs., Mich. State U., 1957; M.A. in Econs., U. Chgo., 1958, Ph.D. in Econs., 1960. Asst. prof. U. Wash., Seattle, 1960-61; asst. prof. Mich. State U., East Lansing, 1961-63, assoc. prof., 1965-66, prof., 1966-68; head dept. econs. Tex. A&M U., College Station, 1985-91, dir. Pvt. Enterprise Rsch. Ctr., 1991—, prof. econs., 1968-89, disting. prof. econs., 1989—; pres. RRC, Inc., College Station, 1979-89, chmn. bd., 1989—. Author: Money, Wealth, Economic Theory, 1966. Mem. Am. Econ. Assn., So. Econ. Assn. (pres. 1981-82), Western Econs. Assn. (pres. 1971-72), Econometric Soc., Mont Pelerin Soc. Home: 1402 Post Oak Cir College Station TX 77840-2322 Office: Tex A&M U Pvt Enterprise Rsch Ctr College Station TX 77843-4231

SAVOY, CHYRL LENORE, artist, educator; b. New Orleans, May 23, 1944; d. Frank Peter and Bobby Adrienne (Rawls) S.; 1 child, Bobby Frances. BA, La. State U., 1966; MFA, Wayne State U., 1970. Art tchr. St. Martin's Sch., Detroit, 1969; grad. asst. Wayne State U., Detroit, 1970; asst. prof. fine arts La. State U., Shreveport, 1973-77; asst. prof. sculpture & drawing U. SW La., Lafayette, 1978—; drawing com. U. SW La., 1985, advisor for art and architecture student assn., 1985, acad. student advisor dept. visual arts, 1986, libr. rep., 1986, sculpture com., 1986-87, drawing com., 1986-87, studio position search com., 1988-89, co-chair sculpture position search com., 1988-89, dir. sch. art and architecture search com., 1989-90, coord. sculpture, 1989—, dir., coord. models program, 1989, curriculum com. visual arts dept., 1991, faculty senator 1992-96, ways & means. com. One-person exhbns. at Univ. Art Gallery, Wayne State U., 1970, New Orleans Mus. Art, 1972, Univ. Art Ctr., U. S.W. La., 1983, Maison du Que., Lafayette, 1983, Galeria de Acad. de Artes Plasticas, Monterrey, Mex., 1987, Artists Alliance, Lafayette, 1992, Clark Hall Gallery, Southeastern La. U., Hammond, 1995, Escuela de Humanidades, U. Ams., Puebla, Mex., 1996; exhibited in group shows at 28th Ann. Nat. Drawing and Small Sculpture Show, Corpus Christi, 1994, 15th Ann. Art Exhbn., Columbia, Mo., 1994, Alexaxandria Mus. Art, 1993, Premier Nat. Ann. Exhbn. World Trade Ctr., New Orleans, 1991, La. Arts and Scis. Ctr., New Orleans Contemporary Art Ctr. Mem. art com. R.S. Barnwell Garden and Art Ctr., 1975-76, chair art com., 1976-77. Mem. Artists Alliance, Phi Beta. Home: PO Box 573 Youngsville LA 70592-0573 Office: Visual Arts Dept U SW La PO Box 43850 Lafayette LA 70504-3850

SAWCHUK, WILLIAM SAMUEL, dermatologist; b. Detroit, Dec. 14, 1952; s. William Alexander and Jeanette Mae (Daggan) S.; m. Maureen Patricia O'Connor, May 28, 1988; children: Andrea Elizabeth, Katherine Melissa. BS in Pharmacy, U. Mich., 1976, MD, 1981. Diplomate Am. Bd. Dermatology. Resident in medicine Mass. Gen. Hosp., Boston, 1981-82; dermatology resident Duke U. Med. Ctr., Durham, N.C., 1982-85; med. staff fellow Nat. Cancer Inst., Bethesda, Md., 1985-88; pvt. practice Falls Church, Va., 1988—; cons. Dermatology br. Nat. Cancer Inst., Bethesda, Md., 1988—, Nat. Naval Med. Ctr., Bethesda, 1990—, Water Reed Army Med. Ctr., Washington, 1991—. Contbr. articles to profl. jours. Recipient Stelwagon award ACP, 1986; Bill Reed fellow, 1986. Fellow Am. Acad. Dermatology; mem. AMA, Va. Med. Soc., Washington Dermatology Soc., Fairfax County Med. Soc., Soc. for Investigative Dermatology. Office: 6319 Castle Pl # 2C Falls Church VA 22044-1907

SAWYER, ANITA DAWN, special education educator; b. Harrison, Ark., July 8, 1963; d. Donnie Frank and Myrtle Darline (Curbow) Coxsey; m. Timothy Clarence Sawyer, Mar. 26, 1988; children: Benjamin Aram, Lukas Ryan, Lauren Nicole. AS, North Ark. Cmty. Tech. Coll., Harrison, 1984; BS in Edn., U. Ctrl. Ark., 1986. Cert. spl. edn.-mildy handicapped grades K-12. Jr. and sr. H.S. spl. educator Omaha (Ark.) Pub. Schs., 1986-91; extended yr. svcs. coord. Boone County Spl. Svcs., Harrison, summer 1987; tchr.-leader summer youth program Job Tng. Partnership Act, Harrison, summer 1991; jr. and sr. H.S. spl. educator Alpena (Ark.) Pub. Schs., 1991; indirect svcs. coord. Omaha (Ark.) H.S., 1986-91, Alpena (Ark.) H.S., 1991—, dist. spl. olympics coord., Omaha Pub. Schs., 1987-91, Alpena Pub. Schs., 1991—; adv. bd. mem. Omaha H.S. Future Bus. Leaders Am., 1990-91; coord. transitional svcs. Omaha, 1986-91, Alpena, 1991—; pres. pers. policies committee, Alpena, 1995-96. Vol. internat. cert. Omaha (Ark.) and Ark. Spl. Olympics, 1986-91; fundraising and cmty. contact rep. United Way-Omaha (Ark.) H.S., 1989; spl. olympics coach in bowling, basketball, floor hockey and athletics Alpena (Ark.) and Ark. Spl. Olympics, 1991—. Mem. NEA, Ark. Edn. Assn. (bldg. rep., gen. assembly 1986-90), Omaha Edn. Assn. (v.p. 1986-87, pres. 1987-90, rep.), Coun. Exceptional Children, Omaha Booster Club (v.p. 1988-89), Omaha PTO, Alpena PTO. Baptist. Home: RR 4 Box 391C Harrison AR 72601-9155 Office: Alpena Pub Schs PO Box 270 300 S Denver Alpena AR 72611

SAWYER, DAVID NEAL, petroleum industry executive; b. Paducah, Ky., Sept. 27, 1940; s. David A. and Lois (Neal) S.; children: Laura Kathleen, Allen Neal. BS, La. State U., 1964; PhD, U. Wis., 1969. Registered profl. engr., Tex. Process engr. Shell Chem. Co., Norco, La., 1964-65; instr. chem. engring. U. Wis., Madison, 1969-70; sr. rsch. engr. Atlantic Richfield Co., Plano, Tex., 1970-73; staff reservoir engr. Arco Oil and Gas Co., Dallas, 1973-84; pres. Plantation Petroleum Co., Houston, 1984—; dir. Miss. CO2 Enhanced Oil Recovery Lab., 1990—; cons. in field; presenter, Beijing; presenter seminar internat. mktg. petroleum products, Lagos, Nigeria, 1986, 91; presenter seminar enhanced oil recovery, Lagos, 1991. Author of seminars. Panel mem. Leadership Devel. Seminar, 1986. Recipient Warrior Basin study, U.S. Dept. Energy, 1990-92; NSF fellow, 1965-69. Mem. Geosci. Inst. Oil and Gas Rsch. (state rep., bd. dirs. 1989-92), Am. Soc. Engring. Edn. (presenter 1989), Soc. Petroleum Engrs. (bd. dirs.), AAAS, Tau Beta Pi, Sigma Xi. Office: Plantation Petroleum Inc 3401 Louisiana St Ste 100 Houston TX 77002

SAWYER, MARY CATHERINE, hospital administrator; b. Borger, Tex., Dec. 8, 1931; d. Andrew Rodgers and Mary Elizabeth (Slater) Hill; m. Edmond Eugene Sawyer, Aug. 26, 1963; children: Slater Shane, Anthony Barrett, Maronda Rae. BBA, Tex. Tech U., 1956; cert. in med. records, U. Tex. Med. Br., Galveston, 1957. Registered med. adminstr.; cert. coding specialist. Med. record adminstr. Taylor Hosp., Inc., Lubbock, Tex., 1957-63; pvt. practice cons. Paris, Tex., 1963-79; med. record adminstr., coding specialist St. Joseph's Hosp., Paris, 1979—. Mem. DAR (corr. sec. 1989-91, treas. 1991-93, 1st vice regent 1994-96, def. chmn. 1990-96), Gordon Country Club, Phi Gamma Nu. Methodist. Home: PO Box 128 Deport TX 75435-0128 Office: St Joseph's Hosp PO Box 9070 Paris TX 75461-9070

SAWYER, RAYMOND LEE, JR., motel chain executive; b. New Orleans, Oct. 7, 1935; s. Raymond Lee Sawyer and Eloise Falvy (Searcy) Easley; m. Dolores Jean Young, June 11, 1960; children: Lisa Kay, Linda Faye. BA, Northwestern State U., 1959. Art dir., advt. mgr. Natural Food and Farming Mag., Atlanta, Tex., 1959-66, editor, 1963-66; asst. editor, editor Tourist Court Jour./Southwest Water Works Jour., Temple, Tex., 1966-73; editor Tourist Court Jour./Southwest Water Works Jour., Temple, 1973-75; founding ptnr., sr. v.p. Budget Host Inns, Ft. Worth, 1975-83, pres., chief exec. officer, 1983—. Named Man of Yr. Motel Brokers Assn. Am., 1974; recipient Bob Gresham Meml. award Nat. Innkeeping Assn., 1975. Mem. Am. Automobile Assn. (mem. lodging adv. panel 1990—). Methodist.

SAWYER-MORSE, MARY KAYE, nutritionist, educator; b. Ft. Stockton, Tex.. BA in psychology, Southwest Tex. State U., 1978; MS in nutrition, Incarnate Word Coll., 1987. Lic. dietitian. Nutrition svcs. con. Christian Sr. Svcs., 1985-87; nutrition svcs. cons. The Alternative Adult Day Care Ctr., 1989-90; pvt. con. dietitian, 1990—; exec. dir. Christian Sr. Svcs., 1987-90; community dietitian Health Enhancement Ctr. Humana Hosp. Met., 1990-91; dietetic program dir., asst. prof. U. of the Incarnate Word, San Antonio, Tex., 1991—; Presenter Diabetic Homebound Svcs. Nat. Conf. of Meals-On-Wheels Am., 1989. Innovative Nutrition Svc. Model Southwest Tex. Gerontological Soc. Annual Meeting, 1988. Contbr. articles to profl. jours. Recipient Disting. Rsch. award, 1977, 78, Acad. Excellence award, 1978, YWCA Women's Leadership award, 1988, Creative Tchg./Rsch. award, 1994, Carnation Corp. scholar, 1995. Mem. Am. Dietetic Assn. (sec. 1990-92, nominating com. 1993-94, dietetic educator's practice group), Tex. Dietetic Assn. (pub. rels. officer 1995-96), San Antonio Dist. Dietetic Assn. Office: U of the Incarnate Word 4301 Broadway St San Antonio TX 78209-6318

SAXON, JOHN DAVID, lawyer, policy analyst, educator; b. Anniston, Ala., July 21, 1950; s. J.Z. and Sarah Elizabeth (Steadham) S.; m. Elizabeth Lord, Mar. 10, 1973. BA with honors, U. Ala., 1972, JD, 1977; grad. Exec. Program Stanford U., 1986; MA, U. N.C., 1973. Bar: Ala. 1977, U.S. Dist. Ct. (no. dist.) Ala. 1977, U.S. Supreme Ct. 1983, U.S. Dist. Ct. (mid. dist.) Ala. 1989, U.S. Dist. Ct. (so. dist.) Ala. 1990, U.S. Ct. Appeals (11th cir.) 1990, U.S. Ct. Appeals (5th cir.) 1992. Adminstrv. asst. to acting chief exec. officer U. Ala.-University, 1976-77; assoc. Sirote, Permutt, Friend, Friedman, Held & Apolinsky, P.A., Birmingham, Ala., 1977-78; spl. asst. to Vice Pres. U.S., Washington, 1978-79; counsel subcom. on jurisprudence and govt. rels. Com. on Judiciary, U.S. Senate, Washington, 1979-80, counsel Select Com. on Ethics, 1980-83; dir. corp. issues RCA, Washington, 1983-86; Washington rep., Gen. Electric Co., 1986-87; assoc. counsel U.S. Senate Select com. on secret mil. assistance to Iran and the Nicaraguan Opposition, 1987-88; spl. counsel U.S. Senate Armed Svcs. com., 1988; counsel, Johnston, Barton, Proctor, Swedlaw & Naff, Birmingham, 1988-90; atty. Gathings & Davis, Birmingham, 1990-92; ptnr. Cooper, Mitch, Crawford, Kuykendall & Whatley, 1992-95; pres. and prin. John D. Saxon, P.C., 1995—; adj. instr. polit. communication U. Md., 1982-83; instr. speech communication U. Ala.-University, 1973; instr. speech communication and mgmt. Brewer Jr. Coll., Tuscaloosa, 1975-77; adj. instr. civil litigation Samford U., Birmingham, 1977-78; adj. prof. Washington Coll. Law The Am. U., 1988; vis. scholar The Hastings Ctr., 1983; mem. Am. Observer Delegation, Kettering Found., U.S.-China Task Force, 1986; bd. dirs. White House Fellows Found., 1981-84 , pres., 1983-84; mem. bd. advisers Center for Publ. Law and Service, U. Ala. Sch. Law, 1976-83; bd. trustees Farrah Law Soc., 1988-94, vice-chmn., 1990-92, chmn., 1992-94; bd. dirs. exec. com. mem. U. Ala. Law Found., vice chmn., 1996—; mem. Pres.'s Commn. White House Fellowships, 1983-84, 93—; mem. Washington Local Devel. Corp, 1986-88; chmn. Ala. Clinton for Pres. Campaign, 1992, 96; mem. platform com. Dem. Nat. Conv., 1992, del., 1996; treas. Ala. Dem. Party, 1995—; mem. policy adv. com. The Coalition for Excellence in Edn., chmn., 1991-92; dir. The A+ Rsch. Found.; mem. bd. advisors N.E. Ala. Devel. Forum, 1992—, Nat. Governing Bd. Common Cause, 1992-95, Leadership Birmingham Class of 1993-94; mem. pres. adv. coun. Birmingham So. Coll., 1993—; mem. adminstrv. bd. First United Meth. Ch., 1994—; co-pres. Birmingham Boys Choir Found., 1994-96; asst. scoutmaster Troop 57 Boy Scouts of Am.; pres. Southside Baseball, 1995—; adv. com. The Blackburn Inst., U. Ala.; bd. dir. Miles Coll. Ctr. for Cmty. Econ. Devel., 1995—. Served to 2d lt. U.S. Army, 1974, capt. Res. White House Fellow, 1978-79; named Disting. Mil. Grad., U. Ala., 1972. Mem. ABA (spl. com. litigation sect.), Ala. Bar Assn., Birmingham Bar Assn. (chmn. profl. ethics com. 1991-92, mem. grievance com. 1992—, co-chmn. 1995—), Ala. Trial Lawyers Assn. (bd. govs. 1990-94, exec. com. 1994—), White House Fellows Assn. (pres. 1983-84), Kiwanis Club (Birmingham), Scabbard and Blade, The Order of Barristers, Bench and Bar (Outstanding Sr. award 1977), Downtown Dem. Club (pres. 1992-93), Omicron Delta Kappa, Omicron Delta Epsilon, Phi Alpha Theta, Pi Sigma Alpha. Methodist. Contbr. articles to newspapers and legal publs., chpts. to books.

SAY, BURHAN, physician; b. Istanbul, Turkey, Feb. 26, 1923; came to U.S. 1951; s. Ethem Serif and Ayse Say; m. Elizabeth E. Jackson, Nov. 5, 1955; children: Ahmet Serif, Daniel Demir. MD, U. Istanbul, 1946. Diplomate Am. Bd. Pediatrics, Am. Bd. Med. Genetics. Asst. prof. pediatrics Hacettepe U., Ankara, Turkey, 1960-64, prof. pediatrics, 1964-73; clin. prof. of pediatrics U. of Okla./Tulsa Med. Coll., 1975—; dir. H.A. Chapman Inst., Tulsa, 1982—; v.p. Children's Med. Ctr., Tulsa, 1988—. Contbr. articles to profl. jours. Pres. Am. Cancer Soc., Tulsa, 1980-90, Great Plains Genetics Soc., Tulsa, 1993. Lt. Turkish Army, 1946-48, Turkey. Fulbright scholar, Boston, 1966-68. Home: 6216 E 99th St Tulsa OK 74137-5503 Office: Childrens Med Ctr 5300 E Skelly Dr Tulsa OK 74135-6566

SAYEED, KHALID BIN, political scientist, educator; b. Bellary, India, Nov. 20, 1926; came to U.S., 1952; s. Abdul Rahman and Sayeeda Sayeed; m. Janet Noel Callender, 1954; children: Adil, Miriam. BA, Madras U., 1948, MA, 1948; BSc in Econs., London Sch. Econs., 1951; PhD, McGill U., 1956. Asst. prof. U. New Brunswick, Can., 1959-61; from asst. prof. to prof. Queen's U., Kingston, Ont., Can., 1961-92; prof. emeritus Queen's U., Kingston, 1992—; vis. prof. Duke U., Durham, N.C., 1965, McGill U., Montreal, Que., Can., 1967-69; cons. UN, 1970-71. Author: Pakistan the Formative Phase, 1961, Political System of Pakistan, 1967, Politics in Pakistan: Nature and Direction of Change, 1980, Western Dominance and Political Islam, 1995. Grantee Fulbright, 1953-54, Ford Found., 1957-59, Nuffield, 1961, Cand. Coun., 1967-69, 70-71, 82, 84. Home: 2840 N Ocean Blvd #802 Fort Lauderdale FL 33308

SAYEGH, GLENDA FAYE, elementary school educator; b. Seneca, S.C., Aug. 1, 1953; d. Ernest Daniel and Edith Pauline (Holden) Alexander; m. Mona Nasser, July 20, 1985. AA, Anderson Coll., 1973; BA, So. Wesleyan U., 1975; MEd, Clemson U., 1980, EdS, 1984. Presch., kindergarten educator Tamassee (S.C.) DAR, 1975-76; third grade educator Hart County Pub. Schs., Hartwell, Ga., 1976-77; substitute tchr. Oconee County Pub. Schs., Walhalla, S.C., 1977-78; fourth grade educator Homeland Park Elem. Schs., Anderson, S.C., 1978-80; fifth grade educator Calhoun St. Elem., Anderson, 1980-81, first grade educator, 1989-94, fifth grade educator, 1989—; contracted with Exclamations Model and Talent Agy., Lilburn, Ga., 1994—; lobbyist S.C. State Dept. for S.C. Edn. Improvement Act, Columbia, 1984; mem. Sch. Improvement Coun., Anderson, 1988-90, Anderson Dist. 5 Sci. Curriculum Com., Anderson, 1980, 94. Contbr. articles to profl. jours. Local del. for Republican Party, 1987. Mem. NEA, ASCD, S.C. Edn. Assn., Clemson Alumni Soc., S.C. PTO, Women's Missionary Union, Campus Crusade for Christ. Democrat. Baptist. Home: 217 Westwind Rd Anderson SC 29625-2255 Office: Calhoun Elem Sch 1520 E Calhoun St Anderson SC 29622-0439

SAYER, COLETTA KEENAN, gifted education educator; b. Cleve., July 4, 1950; d. Nicholas Charles and Coletta (Kuonen) Yawarsky; m. Mark Andrew Sayer, June 3, 1977; 1 child, Mark Martin. BA, St. Mary of the Wood Coll., 1972. Classroom tchr. Cath. Diocese of Cleve., 1972-76; learning disabilities specialist Brunswick (Ohio) Bd. Edn., 1976-77; classroom tchr. of gifted Houston Bd. Edn., 1988-91; tchr. ESL Benbrook Elem. Sch. Houston Ind. Sch. Dist., 1991-96. Houston Bus. Com. for Excellence in Edn. grantee, 1989. Mem. ASCD, Houston Classroom Tchrs. Assn. (pres. 1996-97). Roman Catholic. Office: Benbrook Elem Sch 4026 Bolin Rd Houston TX 77092-4711

SAYERS, CHERA LEE, economics educator; b. Lansing, Mich., Apr. 14, 1959; d. Vernon L. and Shirley Ann (Armour) S.; m. S. Nuri Erbas, May 19, 1990; 1 child, Serra April. BA, Mich. State U., 1981; MS, U. Wis., 1984, PhD, 1986. Vis. asst. prof. U. N.C., Chapel Hill, 1987-88, Haverford (Pa.) Coll., 1986-87; asst. prof. U. Houston, 1988-94; rsch. economist, div. econ. analysis Commodity Futures Trading Comm., Washington, 1990-93; adj. prof. econs. Marymount U., Arlington, Va., 1995—; econ. cons. for litigation, 1995—; pub. speaker various univs. and profl. orgns., 1986—; article referee various jours. in economic field. Contbr. articles to profl. jours. Recipient Bd. of Trustees scholarship Mich. State U. 1981, Harry Bullis scholarship U. Wis. 1985. Mem. Am. Econ. Assn., Am. Fin. Assn., Econometric Soc., Com. on Status of Women in the Econs. Profession, Soc. on Non-Linear Dynamics and Econometrics (organizing com.), Fedn. Orgns. for Profl. Women, U. Wis. Alumni Assn., Mich. State U. Alumni Assn., Phi Kappa Phi. Office: Sch Bus Adminstrn Marymount Univ Arlington VA 22207

SAYERS, KATHLEEN MARIE, associate dean; b. Kansas City, Kans., Jan. 5, 1946; d. Harry Patrick and Georgetta (Viets) s.; m. Julian Olivares, June 6, 1975; children: Christopher, Anthony. BA, U. Kans., 1967, MA, 1969; MA, U. Houston, 1983; PhD, U. Tex., 1981. Lectr. Brandeis U., Waltham, Mass., 1975-76; asst. dir. continuing studies lang. programs Rice U., Houston, 1983-86, dir. continuing studies lang. programs, 1986-92, assoc. dean Sch. Continuing Studies, 1991—; cons. Houston Ind. Sch. Dist., 1982. Mem. MLA, Tchrs. of English to Speakers of Other Langs. Internat., Tex. Tchrs. of English to Speakers of Other Langs. IV (pres. 1986, 1st v.p. 1987, 2d v.p. 1988), So. Ctrl. MLA. Office: Rice U Sch Continuing Studies 6100 Main St Houston TX 77005-1892

SAYERS, LAURA KRISTINE, physical education and special education educator; b. Shreveport, La., Mar. 11, 1971; d. Joe Douglas and Martha Jean (Morton) S. BA, La. Coll., 1983; MA, U. New Orleans, 1994. Cert. health and phys. edn. tchr., spl. edn. tchr., La. Adapted motor devel. tchr. Rapides Parish Sch. Bd., Alexandria, La., 1994—; pvt. adapted motor devel. tchr., Pineville, La., 1989-93, New Orleans, 1993-94; presenter in field. Mem. AAHPERD, La. Alliance Health, Phys. Edn., Recreation and Dance, N.Am. Fedn. Adapted Phys. Activity (contbr. to newsletter), Lions, Kappa Delta Pi, Omicron Delta Kappa, Alpha Mu. Baptist. Home: 4325 Clubhouse Dr #B-6 Alexandria LA 71306

SAYERS, MARTHA MCCRAY, retired secondary school educator; b. Monroe, N.C., Dec. 17, 1937; d. Hurley Franklin and Mary Frances (Snyder) McCray; m. Gerald Sidney Sellers, Aug. 1961 (div. Mar. 1974); m. Thomas Garrett Sayers, July 25, 1974; 1 child, Steve Sellers. BA, Furman U., 1960; MEd, U. S.C., 1974. Dir. student activities S.C. Baptist Hosp., Columbia, 1960-62; reading supervisor Lexington County Sch. Dist., Batesburg, S.C., 1968-74; tchr. Batesburg-Leesville Schs., Batesburg, 1974-75, Lexington (S.C.) Schs., 1975-77, Winston-Salem (N.C.) Forsyth County Schs., 1978-85, Cabarrus County Schs., Concord, N.C., 1985-88. Co-author: Graphic Learning, 1981. Vol. entertainer nursing homes, Wolcott-Hall Adams House, Torrington, Conn., 1988-94. Baptist. Home: PO Box 11042 Winston Salem NC 27116

SAYERS, MICHAEL EUGENE, rheumatologist; b. Wichita, Kans., Sept. 20, 1955; s. Lawrence F. and Lois Luella (Glass) S.; m. Sylvia Lynn Liston, Dec. 17, 1978; children: Tara Lynn, Kimberly Jean. BS in Biology, Pitts. State U., 1977; DO, Univ. Health Scis., 1982. Diplomate in internal medicine and rheumatology Am. Bd. Internal Medicine. Rsch. asst. Pitts. State U., 1977-78; intern Sandusky (Ohio) Meml. Hosp., 1982-83; commd. ensign USN, 1983, advanced through grades to comdr., 1993; gen. med. officer Branch Clinic-Key West, Fla., 1983-85, Branch Clinic-Mare Island, Vallejo, Calif., 1985-86; chief resident in internal medicine Naval Med. Ctr., Oakland, Calif., 1986-89; fellow in rheumatology Cleve. Clinic Found., 1989-91; staff rheumatologist dept. internal medicine Naval Med. Ctr., Portsmouth, Va., 1991—. Contbr. articles and presentations to profl. jours.; co-author: Psoriasis, 1994. Recipient Aadel Askari Meml. award, 1990. Fellow ACP, Am. Coll. Rheumatology; mem. Christian Med. Soc. Republican. Home: 10340 Marble Creek Cir Colorado Springs CO 80908 Office: Arthritis Assocs Colorado Springs 625 N Cascade Ave Ste 210 Colorado Springs CO 80903-3271

SAYERS, TRACY LAMAR, holding company executive; b. Atlanta, Oct. 26, 1963; s. Joe Howell and Judy L. (Ward) S.; m. Mary Elizabeth Lockhart, July 25, 1987. BBA, North Ga. Coll., 1985; MBA, Mercer U., 1991. Assoc. dir. devel. North Ga. Coll., Dahlonega, 1988-92; dir. devel. Columbus (Ga.) Regional Health Care System, 1992-96; adj. prof. Columbus (Ga.) Coll., 1992—; chief operating officer The Pezoid Co., Columbus, Ga., 1996—. Author: Coca-Cola: Internationally Speaking, 1992. Campaign coord. Senator Sam Nunn's re-election campaign, Dahlonega, 1989-90; troop leader Boy Scouts Am., Columbus, 1992—; bd. dirs. Girls Club of West Ga., 1993—, Ronald McDonald House of West Ga., 1992—, Am. Heart Assn.; mem. North Ga. Olympic Adv. Panel, 1992—. Recipient Golden Steeple Alumni award North Ga. Coll., 1992; named Exec. of Yr., Columbus Ga., 1994. Mem. Ga. Assn. Devel. Profls. (pres. 1993—), Columbus C. of C. (mem. Leadership Columbus 1993—), Civitan Internat. (treas. 1988-90), Rotary (fellowship com. 1992—). Office: The Pezoid Co PO Box 4252 Columbus GA 31904

SAYFIE, EUGENE JOE, cardiologist, internist, educator; b. Charleston, W.Va., Sept. 13, 1934; s. Snow and Selma (Zakaib) S.; BS magna cum laude, W.Va. U., 1956; MD, Washington U., St. Louis, 1960; m. Suzanne Morin, Feb. 22, 1969; children: Stephanie, Nicole, Lisa, Amy Jo. Practice medicine specializing in internal medicine and cardiology, Miami, Fla.; mem. staff Miami Heart Inst., chief med. staff, 1978-80, chief of medicine, 1981-88, chmn. cardiovasc. dept., 1988—; cons. staff physician Jackson Meml. Hosp., Miami; staff physician Aventura Hosp.; clin. assoc. prof. Sch. Medicine, U. Miami. Bd. dirs. Miami Heart Inst., Heart Assn. Greater Miami; trustee Antiochian Orthodox Christian Archdiocese N.Am., Ransom-Everglades Sch., 1977—. Recipient Silver Meritorious award Miami Heart Inst., 1977. Fellow ACP, Am. Coll. Cardiology, Am. Coll. Angiology, Am. Coll. Chest Physicians; mem. AMA, Am., Fla., Greater Miami (pres. 1981-82, dir.) heart assns., Fla., Dade County Med. Assns., LaGorce Country Club, Bath Club, Alpha Omega Alpha, Phi Beta Kappa. Mem. Eastern Orthodox Ch. Office: 4701 N Meridian Ave Ste 7460 Miami Beach FL 33140-2910 also: 2999 NE 191st St Ste 300 Concord Ctr II Miami FL 33180

SAYKA, ANTHONY, process engineer; b. Merced, Calif., May 1, 1957; s. Harry Michael and Monica (Smith) S. AS, Pikes Peak Community Coll., 1982; BS in Chemistry, U. Colo., 1985; BS in Physics, U. Tex., San Antonio, 1993. Air conditioning and heating contractor Callaway heating & Cooling Co., Panama City, Fla., 1977-80; process engr. NCR Corp., Colorado Springs, 1984-88; rsch. scientist Microtech Rsch. Co., Colorado Springs, 1986-87; sr. process engr. Micron Tech., Boise, Idaho, 1988-89; sr. process engr./patent specialist VLSI Tech., Inc., San Antonio, 1989-95; process engr. Advanced Micro Devices, Austin, Tex., 1995—; broker assoc. Preferral, Inc., Colorado Springs, 1986-87. Patentee in field. Election asst. El Paso County Rep. Party, Colorado Springs, 1984. Mem. Am. Chem. Soc. Roman Catholic.

SAYLOR, MICHAEL J., golf course architecture design company executive. Pres. Bessent, Hammack, Ruckman, Inc., Jacksonville, Fla. Office: Bessent Hammack Ruckman Inc 1900 Corporate Square Blvd Jacksonville FL 32216-1941

SCAFETTA, JOSEPH, JR., lawyer; b. Chester, Pa., May 10, 1947; s. Giuseppe and Mary (Koslosky) S.; m. Teresa M. Talierco, July 4, 1986. BS in Aero. Engring., Pa. State U., 1969; JD, U. Pitts., 1972; M in Patent Law, Georgetown U., 1973; MBA, George Washington U., 1983. Bar: Pa. 1972, U.S. Patent and Trademark Office 1973, D.C. 1978, Va. 1979, U.S. Supreme Ct. 1980, U.S. Ct. Appeals (fed. cir.) 1982. Legal rschr. Arent, Fox, Kintner, Plotkin et al, Washington, 1973; law clk. to presiding judge U.S. Dist. Ct. S.C., Columbia, 1973-74; assoc. Colton & Stone, Arlington, Va., 1975-77, Craig & Antonelli, Washington, 1977-78, Wigman & Cohen, Arlington, 1978-83, Wenderoth, Lind & Ponack, Washington, 1983-86, Cushman, Darby & Cushman, Washington, 1986-87; counsel Russell, Georges & Breneman, Arlington, 1987-91, Young & Thompson, Arlington, 1991-96; pvt. practice Arlington, 1996—; patent counsel QuesTech, Inc., Falls Church, Va., 1983—, Dynamic Engring., Inc. Newport News, Va., 1989—; voting mem. Nat. Commn. for Social Justice, 1995—. Author: Book Review Copyright Handbook, 1979, The Constitutionality/Unconstitutionality of the Patent Infringement Statute, 1979, (with others) Patents on Microorganisms, 1980; editor: An Intellectual Property Law Primer, 1975; contbr. articles to profl. jours. Mem. Consumer Affairs Commn., Alexandria, Va., 1985-87; charter mem. Christopher Columbus Quincentenary Jubilee Com., 1990-93; chair Va. chpt. Commn. for Social Justice, 1987-93; mem. Fairfax County Dem. Com., Falls Church, 1987-89; parliamentarian City Dem. Com., Alexandria, 1985-87. Recipient Robert C. Watson award Am. Patent Law Assn., 1975. Mem. ABA, Am. Arbitration Assn. (mem. comml. panel), Va. Bar Assn., Am. Intellectual Property Law Assn. (mem. awards com. 1983—), D.C. Bar Assn., Patent and Trademark Office Soc., Avanti Italiani (pres. Alexandria chpt. 1981-83), Sons of Italy, Grand Lodge Va. (state pres. 1993-95).

SCALES, DIANN ROYLETTE, librarian; b. Birmingham, Ala., Aug. 15, 1945; d. Alphonso Monroe and Ella (Allen) Scales. BA in Am. History, Miles Coll., Birmingham, Ala., 1966; MA in European History, Atlanta U., 1969, MSLS, 1973. Substitute tchr. C.W. Hayes High Sch., Birmingham, 1967-68; reserve librarian Atlanta U., 1969-73, ref. librarian, 1973-81; ref. librarian Miles Coll., Birmingham, 1981-82, U. Montevallo, Ala., 1984—. Mem. Coalition of 100 Black Women, Birmingham, 1990—. Mem. ALA, Nat. Librs. Assn. (exec. bd. mem.-at-lg. 1989-92), Ala. Libr. Assn. (reference and adult svcs. round table mem.-at-lg. 1990-91), Assn. Social and Behavioral Scientists, So. Hist. Assn., Delta Sigma Theta Sorority, Inc. (corr. sec. 1987-89). Democrat. Baptist. Home: 616 6th St N Birmingham AL 35203-1403 Office: U Montevallo Station 6101 Carmichael Libr Montevallo AL 35115

SCALES, DONALD KARL, dentist, army officer; b. Jacksonville, Fla., Apr. 7, 1960; s. Kenneth Ira and Marjorie Kathleen (Lahr) S. BS in Biology, The Citadel, 1982; DDS, Ind. U., 1989; postgrad., U. North Fla., 1982-85. Mem. affiliate faculty Ind. U. Dental Sch., Indpls., 1988-89; commd. 1st lt. U.S. Army, 1989, advanced through grades to maj., 1995; resident advanced edn. program in gen. dentistry MEDDAC student detachment U.S. Army, Ft. Carson, Colo., 1989-90; gen. dentistry officer 92d med. detachment, infection control officer U.S. Army, Hanau, Germany, 1990-94; chief oral surgery Hanau Dental Clinic, 1990-91; dental surgeon 4th Brigade, 3d Inf. Divsn., Aschaffenburg, Germany, 1991-92; clinic chief Aschaffenburg Dental Clinic, 1992; preventive dentistry officer/pub. health dentist 92d Med. Detachment, Hanau, Germany, 1992-93; clinic chief U.S. Army Dental Clinic, Buedingen, Germany, 1993-94; dep. comdr. 92d Med. Detachment, 1994; dentist 86th Combat Support Hosp., Ft. Campbell, Ky., 1995; sr. med. officer Zone IV, UN Mission in Haiti (U.S. Army Operation Uphold Democracy), 1995-96; dental surgeon 1st Brigade, 101st Airborne Divsn. (AASLT), 1995-96; dental surgeon 5th Spl. Forces Group (Airborne), 1996—; dental cons. Westside Dental Care Ctr., Jacksonville, 1982—; lectr. and presenter in field; mem. exec. coun., mem. quality assurance com. 92nd Med. Detachment, 1991-92, Frankfurt (Germany) Dental Activity, 1993-94, Heidelburg (Germany) Dental Activity, 1994; rep. 7th Med. Command and U.S. European Command Dept. of Def. African Hosp. Project, 1993, Med. Civic Action Program, Kenya, 1996. Com. chmn. Panther edn. assistance program Hanau Am. H.S., 1990-94; CPR instr. Am. Heart Assn., Hanau, 1990-94; instr. dental asst. program ARC, Hanau, 1990-94. Mem. ADA, Acad. Gen. Dentistry, Assn. Mil. Surgeons U.S., Assn. U.S. Army, The Citadel Alumni Assn. (life), Ind. U. Alumni Assn. (life), N.E. Fla. Citadel Club. Office: 5th Spl Forces Group (Airborne) Attn Group Surgeons Office Fort Campbell KY 42223

SCALES, JOHN RICHARD, systems engineer; b. Montgomery, Ala., Nov. 29, 1947; s. Thomas Richard and Anne Ruth (Sheehan) S.; m. Carolyn Ann Gray Revezzo, Aug. 15, 1970 (div. Jan., 1973); m. Camille Gaylord, June 14, 1980; children: Richard, Mary, Stephen. BS in Physics, U. Ala., 1970, MA in Edn., 1977, MS in Ops. Rsch., 1988, PhD in Systems Engring., 1992. Inf. officer U.S. Army, 1970-75; tchr. Lithonia (Ga.) H.S., 1977-81; systems engr. Sci. Application Internat. Corp., Huntsville, Ala., 1981-92; mil. fellow Ctr. for Strategic and Internat. Studies, Washington, 1992-93; sr. systems engr. SAIC, Huntsville, 1993—; comdr. 20th Spl. Forces Group, Huntsville, 1994—; adj. prof. systems engring. U. Ala., Huntsville, 1994—. Author: Options for U.S. Military Support to the UN, 1993; contbr. articles to profl. jours. Coach Recreation League Basketball, Huntsville, 1992-93; treas. Monte Sano Civic Assn., Huntsville, 1994—. Capt.U.S. Army, 1970-75, Vietnam. Mem. Ops. Rsch. Soc. Am., Assn. U.S. Army, Am. Def. Preparedness Assn., Air Force Assn., U.S. Naval Inst. Home: 5130 Panorama Dr SE Huntsville AL 35801-1223 Office: 6725 Odyssey Dr NW Huntsville AL 35806-3301

SCALF, JAMES FRANKLIN, III, architect; b. Nashville, July 10, 1950; s. James Franklin Jr. and Nettie Mai (Caldwell) S.; m. Romayne Linda Rhoads, Aug. 11, 1973; children: Dominetta, Danelese. BArch cum laude, U. Tenn., 1974; postgrad., NYU, 1977, Nashville State Tech. Inst., 1978, 79. Registered architect, Tenn., Miss., Tex., Ark., Va., Fla., Ky., N.C.; cert. single family fee compliance inspector. Instr. art history and aesthetics art dept. Watkins Inst., 1976-80, dir. art dept., 1979-80; prin. James F. Scalf & Assocs., Nashville; chmn. tech. documents com. Nashville dept. Constrn. Specification Inst., 1980, bd. dirs., 1979-81; panelist housing session, human rights forum U. Tenn. Ctr. for Govt. Tng. and Office Handicapped Persons, Dept. Pers., Met. Govt., Nashville, 1981; cons. to pvt., state and fed. clients regarding settlement problems, structural damage involving claims, termite damage and re-roofing; responsible for design and constrn. documents for numerous projects. Contbr. articles to archtl. publs. Recipient Lyzon Art Gallery award Tenn. Art League, 1977. Mem. Nat. Coun. Archtl. Registration Bds., Soc. Archtl. Historians, Archtl. Acoustics Soc., Carolinas Coun. Housing, Redevel. and Codes Ofcls., Fla. Assn. Housing and Redevel. Ofcls., Ky. Housing Assn., Tenn. Assn. Housing and Redevel. Authorities, Nat. Assn. Housing and Redevel. Ofcls. (Southeastern Regional Coun.), Masons (select master 1981, super excellent master 1981, knight templar 1981, life mem. Order of the Bath 1993, past illustrious master Lebanon Coun. Cryptic Mason, numerous other offices). Office: James F Scalf & Assocs 2605 12th Ave S Nashville TN 37204-2597

SCALF, JEAN A. KEELE, medical/surgical, geriatrics and home health nurse; b. Tullahoma, Tenn., Jan. 2, 1955; d. Sam Allen and Helen Virginia (Winkler) Keele; children: William Adam Keele, Mark Allen Scalf. AS, Motlow State Community Coll., Tullahoma, 1984, Cleve. State Community Coll., 1980. Staff and charge nurse Coffee Med. Ctr., Manchester, Tenn.; staff nurse Elk Valley Home Health, Tullahoma; charge and staff nurse Bedford County Nursing Home, Shelbyville, Tenn.; asst. dir. nursing Geriatrics Nursing Ctr., Heber Springs, Ark.; owner, operator Jean's Feline and Basset Hound Emporium, Tullahoma, Tenn. Home: 441 Smith Ln Tullahoma TN 37388

SCALISE, CELESTE, lawyer; b. San Antonio, May 15, 1959; d. Robert and Edna (King) Scalise; m. James S. Boyd Jr., Oct. 6, 1984 (div. Dec. 1988); m. Marshall Bruce Lloyd, May 13, 1989 (div. July 1995). BA, U. Tex., San Antonio, 1979; JD, Tex. Tech U., 1983. Bar: Tex. 1984, U.S. Ct. Appeals (5th cir.) 1984, U.S. Dist. Ct. (so. dist.) Tex. 1985, U.S. Dist. Ct. (no. dist.) Tex. 1990, U.S. Dist. Ct. (we. dist.) Tex. 1991, U.S. Dist Ct. (ea. dist.) Tex. 1992. Field ops. asst. Bur. of Census U.S. Dept. of Commerce, San Antonio, 1980; title examiner, law clk. Lubbock (Tex.) Abstract & Title Co., 1982-83; assoc. Bonilla & Berlanga, Corpus Christi, Tex., 1983-89; sr. assoc. Heard, Goggan, Blair & Williams, San Antonio, 1989-90; assoc. Denton & McKamie, San Antonio, 1990, Joe Weiss and Assocs., San Antonio, 1990; field litigation office Cigna litigation atty. Law Offices of Sean P. Martinez, San Antonio, 1990—; pres. Fountain Rorm, Inc.; mem. adv. group Camino Real Health Systems Agy., Inc., San Antonio, 1978-80. Mem. substance abuse adv. com. Planned Parenthood Bd., Corpus Christi, 1983-85; vice chair Nueces County Mental Health/Mental Retardation Substance Abuse Com., San Antonio, 1987-89; mem. vestry Trinity Episcopal Ch. Mem. Tex. Bar Assn. (govt. lawyers sect., ins. def.), San Antonio Bar Assn., U. Tex. at San Antonio Alumni Assn., Delta Theta Phi. Episcopalian. Home: 2130 W Gramercy Pl San Antonio TX 78201-4822 Office: Law Offices Sean P Martinez 300 Convent St San Antonio TX 78205-3701

SCALISE, GARY DENIS, quality systems engineer; b. Warren, Pa., June 25, 1953; s. Joseph A. Jr. and Anna M. Scalise; m. Robin L. Clark, Feb. 18, 1978 (div. Oct. 1995); 1 child, Danielle L. Student, Drexel U., 1973; BS in Comms., Temple U., 1976; MS in Indsl. Tech., Western Carolina U., 1988. Quality control foreman, engr. GTE/Sylvana Plastics, Warren, 1978-84; quality assurance mgr. GTE/Asheville (N.C.) Plastics, 1984-88, Day Internat., Asheville, N.C., 1990-92; quality engr R&D Ctr. Eaton Corp., Detroit, 1988-90; owner, prin. Scalise Profl. Quality Sys., Asheville, 1992—; mem. adv. bd. Sch. Applied Scis. West Carolina U., 1992—. Author: SPC and Quality Improvement, 1991, also conf. procs. in field. Lead organist Basilica of St. Lawrence, Asheville, 1992—. Mem. Am. Soc. Quality Control (sr. mem.; cert. quality engr.). Roman Catholic. Home: 12 Elmwood Ln Asheville NC 28803

SCAMEHORN, JOHN FREDERICK, chemical engineer; b. York, Nebr., Oct. 26, 1953; s. Denver Alonzo and Mary Esther (Weber) S. BSChE, U. Nebr., 1973, MS, 1974; PhD, U. Tex., 1980. Registered profl. engr. Okla., Tex. Rsch. engr. Conoco, Ponca City, Okla., 1974-77; rsch. asst. U. Tex., Austin, 1977-80; rsch. engr. Shell Devel. Co., Houston, 1980-81; prof. U. Okla., Norman, Okla., 1981-92, Asahi glass chair, 1992—; v.p. Surfactant Assoc. Inc., Norman, 1987—; adv. bd. mem. EPA Hazardous Substance Rsch., Manhattan, Kans., 1989-90; organizer 65th Annual Colloid and Surface Sci. Symposium, Norman, 1991; assoc. editr. Jour Am. Oil Chemists Soc., 1986—; host radio show KGOU, Norman, 1984. Editor: Phenomena in Mixed Surfactant Systems, 1986, Surfactant Based Separation Processes, 1989, Solubilization in Surfactant Aggregates, 1995; contbr. articles to profl. jours. Bd. dirs. Opera Guild U. Okla., 1985-86. Recipient Cert. Appreciation ISEC Am. Chem. Soc., 1992. Mem. Am. Oil Chemists Soc. (mem. at large bd. 1990—), Am. Chemical Soc. (chair. elect. spearations subdivision 1994), Am. Inst. Chemical Engrs. Republican. Office: U Okla 100 E Boyd St Norman OK 73019-1000

SCANCARELLI, JANINE LAURA, linguistics educator, researcher; b. N.Y.C., Sept. 4, 1959; d. Eugene and Adrienne (Hofmann) S.; m. Douglas Duncan, Aug. 15, 1982 (div. Mar. 1985); m. Christopher McMahon, Sept. 28, 1991. BA in Linguistics summa cum laude, Yale U., 1980; Ma in Linguistics, UCLA, 1982, PhD in Linguistics, 1987; postgrad. in law, Stanford U., 1995—. Teaching asst. cons. dept. linguistics UCLA, 1984; instr. dept. English U. Ky., 1986-87, asst. prof. dept. English, 1987-89; asst. prof. dept. English Coll. of William & Mary, Williamsburg, Va., 1989-93, assoc. prof. dept. English, 1993—; presenter in field; cons. Cherokee linguistics Okla. Native Am. Langs. Devel. Inst., Choctaw, 1993. Mem. editorial bd. Lang. and Comm., 1990—; book reviewer; contbr. articles to profl. jours. Recipient Phillips Fund grant Am. Philos. Soc., 1984, Inst. Am. Cultures grant UCLA Am. Indian Studies Ctr., 1984, Summer Faculty Rsch. fellowship U. Ky., summer, 1978, 87, grant NEH, 1989, Jacobs Rsch. Funds grant Whatcom Mus. Soc., 1989-90, Summer Faculty Rsch. grant Coll. William and Mary, 1990, 91, 94, Rsch. grant Coll. William and Mary, 1990, 91, 93. Mem. Linguistic Soc. Am., Soc. for Study of Indigenous Langs. of Ams. Office: Coll William and Mary Dept English Williamsburg VA 23187

SCAPERLANDA, MARÍA DE LOURDES RUIZ, writer, journalist; b. Pinar del Río, Cuba, Aug. 13, 1960; came to U.S., 1962; d. Ignacio Manuel Ruiz and María de Jesus Páez Clausell; m. Michael Anthony Scaperlanda, Dec. 27, 1981; children: Christopher, Anamaría, Rebekah, Michelle. BA in Journalism, U. Tex., 1981; postgrad., St. Mary's U., 1982, U. Okla., 1996—. News asst. The Daily Texan, Austin, 1979-80; pub. info. specialist Austin Parks and Rec., 1980-81; freelance writer Norman, Okla., 1981—; media coord. Cath. Diocese of Austin, 1983-84; mng. editor The Forum Mag., Austin, 1983-86; state corr. Tex. Cath. Press, Austin, 1990-94. Contbr. articlest to Austin Mag., The Family, Columbia, New Covenant Mag., The Lutheran, Catholic Parent Mag., National Catholic Register, Catholic Twin Circle, St. Anthony Messenger, Our Sunday Visitor. Mem. Cath. Press Assn. (Best Personality Profile 2nd Place 1994, Best News Report on Internat. Event 3rd Place 1996, Best Reporting on Local or State Matter 3rd Place, 1996, Best Campaign in the Public Interest 2nd Place, 1996, 3rd Place, 1996, Best Feature 2nd Place 1996), Austin Writers' League. Roman Catholic. Office: 3816 Waverly Ct Norman OK 73072

SCAPERLANDA, MICHAEL ANTHONY, law educator; b. Austin, Tex., Apr. 29, 1960; s. Anthony Edward and Carolyn Ann (Beeler) S.; m. Maria Ruiz, Dec. 27, 1981; children: Christopher, Anamaria, Rebekah, Michelle. BA in Econs., U. Tex., 1981, JD, 1984. Bar: Tex. 1984, D.C. 1985, U.S. Dist. Ct. D.C. 1986, U.S. Dist. Ct. (we. dist.) Tex. 1987. Law clk. to chief justice Tex. Supreme Ct., Austin, 1984-85; assoc. Hogan & Hartson, Washington, 1985-86, Hughes & Luce, Austin, 1986-89; assoc. prof. law Coll. of Law U. Okla., Norman, 1989-95, prof. Coll. of Law, 1995—; vis. assoc. prof. Sch. Law, U. Tex., Austin, summers 1991, 92, 93, 95; couns. Southwestern Bell Telephone Co., Oklahoma City, 1993, 94; roundtable participant Cath. Legal Immigrant Network, Inc., Washington, 1993; chair adv. bd. Immigration Svcs. of Diocese of Austin, 1993-96; pro bono atty. Cath. Charities Immigration Office, Oklahoma City, 1993—. Contbr. articles to legal publs. Mem. Am. Immigration Lawyers Assn. (chair law tchrs. com. 1993-95), K.C., Order of Coif. Office: U Okla Coll of Law 300 W Timberdell Rd Norman OK 73072-6415

SCARBORO, ALLEN, sociologist, educator; b. Pinehurst, N.C., Dec. 31, 1947; s. Charles Arthur and Frances (Allen) S.; m. Cheryl Ann Bostic, Aug. 22, 1969; children: Cristofer Allen, Sean Paul. AB, Kenyon Coll., 1970; MA, Hartford Sem. Found., Conn., 1973; PhD, Emory U., 1976. Instr. social scis. Atlanta Jr. Coll., 1974-75; asst. prof. sociology U. Wis., Platteville, 1976, mem. grad. faculty, 1977-82; asst. prof. sociology and anthropology Millsaps Coll., Jackson, Miss., 1982-85, assoc. prof., 1985-92, prof., 1992-94, chmn. div. social and behavioral scis., 1987-90, chmn. dept. sociology and anthropology, 1987-94; prof. sociology Augusta (Ga.) Coll., 1994—, chmn. dept. sociology, 1994—, bd. regents disting. prof. of tchg. and learning, 1996—; tchr. Colegio Americano de Quito, Ecuador, 1978-79, vis. instr. Pontifical Univ. Catolica del Ecuador, 1978-79; leader numerous workshops, confs., and seminars, including Alverno Coll., 1988-90, Emory U., 1990-91, Princeton U., 1988, Vanderbilt U., 1984, U. Wis., 1979, U. N.C., 1977; presenter numerous symposiums. Contbr. articles to profl. jours. including Sociol. Spectrum, 1991, Assessing Undergrads. in Sociology, 1990, Teaching Sociology, 1989, Women's Studies Ency., many others; co-author: Living Witchcraft: A Contemporary American Coven, 1994. Mem. Ala.-Miss. Sociol. Assn. (pres. 1991-92), Am. Sociol. Assn., Ga. Sociol. Assn., So. Sociol. Soc. Office: Augusta Coll Dept Sociology Augusta GA 30904

SCARBOROUGH, FRANCES SONGER, marketing executive, consultant, public speaker; b. Atlanta, Feb. 13, 1957; d. Francis Harold and Lois Irene (Stringer) S.; m. Rutledge Lee Scarborough. BA in Exptl. Psychology magna cum laude with honors, Ga. State U., 1982. Mgr., stores asst. Pepperidge Farm, Atlanta, 1976-82; mgr. S&A Corp., Atlanta, 1982-83; food and beverage asst. mgr., dir. meetings and banquets, sales dir., dir. mktg. Guest Quarters, Atlanta/Charlotte, 1983-87; hypnotherapist Hypnosis Motivation Inst., Atlanta, 1984-86; handwriting analyst, Atlanta, 1985-86; mktg. and image cons., public speaker Total Mind Cons., Charlotte, N.C., 1987-89; v.p. P.K.G.'s-Charlotte, N.C., 1988-94; exporter WestWorld Internat., LLC, Charlotte, 1994-96; pres. Visian Alliance Network, Inc., Charlotte, 1996—. Mem. NAFE, Blue Key, Psi Chi, Phi Kappa Phi. Avocations: writing, racquetball, gardening. Home: 6120 Old Providence Ln Charlotte NC 28226-6802 Office: Ste N-213 2300 Sardis Rd N Charlotte NC 28227-7712

SCARBOROUGH, JOE, congressman; b. Atlanta, Apr. 9, 1963; m. Melanie Scarborough; Children: Joey, Andrew. BA, U. Ala., 1985; JD, U. Fla., 1990. Atty., 1990—; mem. 104th Congress from 1st Fla. dist., Washington, 1995—, polit. dir. freshman class, 1995—; mem. govt. reform and oversight com., nat. security com.,, co-chmn. New Federalists 195th Congress; bd. dirs. Emerald Coast Pediat. Primary Care, Inc. Tchr. Sunday sch. 1st Bapt. Ch. Mem. Young Lawyer's Assn., Fellowship Christian Athletes, Navy League (bd. dirs.). Republican. Office: US Ho of Reps 1523 Longworth Washington DC 20515

SCARBROUGH, CLEVE KNOX, JR., museum director; b. Florence, Ala., July 17, 1939; s. Cleve Knox and Emma Lee (Matheny) S. B.S., U. No. Ala., 1962; M.A., U. Iowa, 1967. Asst. prof. art history U. Tenn., 1967-69; dir. Mint Mus. Art, Charlotte, N.C., 1969-76, Hunter Mus. Art, Chattanooga, 1976—; pres. N.C. Mus. Coun., 1976; bd. mem. adv. com. Tenn. Arts Commn., 1976-77, chmn. visual arts com., 1978—; mem. art selection com. TVA, 1983—, Provident Life Ins. Co., 1983—; cons. Mus. Assessment Program, 1984-94; grant evaluator Inst. Mus. Svcs., 1985-86; mem. art adv. com. First Tenn. Corp., 1991; lectr. Tenn. Gov.'s Conf. on the Arts, 1991. Compiler, editor: North Carolinians Collect, 1970, Pre Columbian Art of the Americas, 1971, Graphics by Four Modern Swiss Sculptors, 1972, British Paintings from the North Carolina Museum, 1973, Montain Landscapes by Swiss Artists, 1976. Mem. Chattanooga Landmark Com.; mem. City Planning Bd.; Bd. dirs. Chattanooga Conv. and Visitors Bur., 1977-79; advisor Chattanooga Cen. City Council, 1981-85, Tenn. State Mus., 1981, mem. Am. Federation of Arts Adv. Bd., 1987—. Served with USN, 1962-64. Mem. Am. Assn. Museums (accreditation vis. com. 1985-94), Southeastern Mus. Conf. (coun. 1976-80, 86-88, chmn. publs. com. 1979, rep. to Am. Assn. Mus.; bd. dirs. 1986-88), Rotary. Office: Hunter Mus Art 10 Bluff View St Chattanooga TN 37403-1111

SCARBROUGH, GLENDA JUDITH, elementary education educator; b. Hill County, Tex., July 17, 1940; d. Roland Leon and Bessie Bell (Ferguson) Blocker; m. Johnny Ray Scarbrough, Feb. 20, 1959; 1 child, Deborah Lynn Randolph. BS, Coll. of Southwest, Hobbs, N.Mex., 1969; MEd, Sul Ross State U., Alpine, Tex., 1985. Elem. tchr. Andrews (Tex.) Ind. Sch. Dist., 1969-86, reading specialist, 1986—; mem. Tex. Gov.'s Tchrs.' Profl. Practices Commn., 1991-93; mem. Tex. State Textbook Selection Com., 1993. Mem. Assn. Tex. Profl. Educators (campus rep., chpt. pres. 1982-84, regional v.p. 1983-84, pres. 1984-86, state bd. dirs. 1986-90, regional com. for dyslexia guidelines 1987), Delta Kappa Gamma. Home: 306 SW 12th St Andrews TX 79714-6705 Office: 405 NW 3rd St Andrews TX 79714-5014

SCARBROUGH-LUTHER, PATSY WURTH, geographic information systems specialist; b. Paducah, Ky., Dec. 5, 1947; d. James Edward and Olean Barbara (Sietz) Wurth; m. Jerry Leon Scarbrough, Aug. 7, 1965 (div. 1985); children: Tracy Ann, Ashli Michele, Scott Jeremy; m. Robert W. Luther, Feb. 25, 1995. BS magna cum laude, Murray (Ky.) State U., 1988, MS, 1991. Cert. emergency med. technician. Instr. Ky. Cabinet for Human Resources, Frankfort, 1983-93, Vocat. Edn. Region I, Paducah, Ky., 1983-91, Murray State U., 1983-91, Calloway County Red Cross, Murray, 1985-89; exec. dir. Marshall County Red Cross, Benton, Ky., 1985-88; first aid attendant Ohio River Steel, Calvert City, Ky., 1985-86; profl. intern Johnson Controls, Cadiz, Ky., 1986; grad. asst. Murray State U., 1988-91; fellow U.S. Dept. Energy/Oak Ridge (Tenn.) Nat. Lab., 1989-90; postgrad. rsch. fellow U.S. Army Corps Engrs. Constrn. Engring. Rsch. Lab., Champaign, Ill., 1991-92, acting team leader spatial techs. support team, 1992-93; GIS facility mgr. environ. scis. divsn. Oak Ridge (Tenn.) Nat. Lab., 1993-95; mgr. GIS svcs. Solutions to Environ. Problems, Inc., Oak Ridge, 1995-96, AEgis Svcs. Corp., Clinton, Tenn., 1996—; adj. prof. Roane State C.C., Hariman, Tenn., 1996—. Troop leader Kentuckiana Girl Scouts, Benton, 1973-84, fund drive chmn., 1973-84. Mem. LWV, Am. Soc. Safety Engrs., Ky. EMT Instrs. Assn. (instr.), Western Ky. EMT Assn., Am. Soc. Photogrametry and Remote Sensing (Western Great Lake region sec., treas. 1992), Nat. Safety Coun. (cmty. health and emergency svcs. com.), Assn. Women in Sci., Tenn. Geog. Info. Coun., S.E. Regional ARC/INFO Users Group (chair 1995),

Nat. Assn. Environ. Profls., Oak Ridge Area ARC/INFO Users Group (chairperson 1996), Epsilon Pi Tau, Alpha Chi. Democrat. Roman Catholic. Home: 330 Melton Hill Dr Clinton TN 37716 Office: Aegis Svcs Corp PO Box 160 Clinton TN 37717

SCARLETT, ELIZABETH ANN, foreign language educator; b. Bklyn., Apr. 11, 1961; d. Thomas Peter and Mary Elizabeth (Hogan) S.; m. David Edward Wagner, Apr. 23, 1995. BA in Comparative Lit. cum laude, Washington U., 1983; MA in Romance Langs. and Lits., Harvard U., 1986, PhD in Romance Langs. and Lits., 1991. Arts editor Washington U. campus newspaper Student Life, St. Louis, 1979-80; Spanish drill instr. Washington U., St. Louis, 1982-83; English lang. asst. Lycée Polyvalent Paul-Sabatier, Carcassonne, France, 1983-84; Spanish tchg. fellow Harvard U., Cambridge, Mass., 1985-88, 89-91; rschr., writer Harvard Student Agys., Cambridge, 1986, travel guide editor, 1987; vis. asst. prof. dept. English lang. U. Seville, Spain, 1988-89; asst. prof. Spanish dept. Spanish, Italian and Portuguese U. Va., Charlottesville, 1991—. Author: Under Construction: The Body in Spanish Novels, 1994 (Choice award 1995); editor: Let's Go: Spain, Portugal & Morocco, 1988, Let's Go: Mexico, 1988; contbr. chpt. to book. Fulbright French Tchg. Assistantship, Fulbright-Hays Program and French Govt., Carcassonne, France, 1983-84; grantee Harvard U., 1984-91, 85; Sesquicentennial fellow U. Va., 1995. Mem. MLA, Am. Assn. Tchrs. Spanish and Portuguese, Assn. Internat. de Hispanistas, New Novel Assn. Office: Univ Va Dept Spanish Italian & Port 115 Wilson Hall Charlottesville VA 22903

SCARMINACH, CHARLES ANTHONY, lawyer; b. Syracuse, N.Y., Feb. 19, 1944; s. John Louis and Lucy (Egnoto) S.; children: John, Catherine, Karen, Charles, Robert. MA, U. Buffalo, 1965; JD, Syracuse U., 1968. Bar: N.Y. 1968, S.C. 1974. Gen. counsel Sea Pines Co., Hilton Head Island, S.C., 1973-78; sole practice, Hilton Head Island, 1978-83; ptnr. Novit & Scarminach, P.A., Hilton Head Island, 1983-93; bd. dirs. Nations Bank, Hilton Head Island. Chmn. bd. Sea Pines Montessori Sch., Hilton Head Island, 1979-83; bd. dirs. Hilton Head Preparatory Sch., 1984-93, chmn. bd. trustees 1986-93. Maj. U.S. Army, 1968-73. Mem. ABA, S.C. Bar Assn., N.Y. State Bar Assn., Hilton Head Island C. of C. (bd. dirs. 1996—). Democrat. Roman Catholic. Club: Sea Pines. Home: 11 Governors Rd Hilton Head Island SC 29928-4153 Office: Novit & Scarminach PA PO Box 14 Hilton Head Island SC 29938-0014

SCARPACE, PHILIP JAMES, geriatric researcher, administrator, educator; b. Buffalo, Jan. 4, 1948; s. Frank B. and Lauri L. Scarpace; m. Nihal Tumer, May 29, 1989. BS in Physics, Calif. State U., San Jose, 1970; PhD in Biophysics, U. Rochester, 1974. Fellow dept. radiation biology and biophysics U. Rochester, N.Y., 1970-74; NIH rsch. fellow dept. radiation biology and biophysics U. Rochester Med. Ctr., 1974-75; asst. prof. physiology San Diego State U., 1975-76; fellow divsn. endocrinology dept. medicine U. Calif. Sch. Medicine, San Diego, 1975-76; instr. math. Moorpark (Calif.) Coll., 1977-81; asst. prof. math. Calif. State U., Northridge, 1979-81; asst. rsch. prof. dept. medicine U. Calif. Sch. Medicine, L.A., 1977-87; chief molecular biophysics lab. Geriatric Rsch., Edn. and Clin. Ctr. VA Med. Ctr., Sepulveda, Calif., 1977-87; assoc. dir. Ctr. Rsch. on Oral Health and Aging U. Fla., Gainesville, 1988-93, assoc. prof. pharmacology and therapeutics, 1987-94, prof. pharmacology and therapeutics, 1994—; rsch. dir. Geriatric Rsch., Edn. and Clin. Ctr. VA Med. Ctr., Gainesville, 1987—; GRECC rev. panelist, 1991; ad hoc study sect. NIH Study Sect.; Biochem. Endocrinology, 1990; ad hoc reviewer VA Merit Rev. Bd., 1984-90, VA Med./Dental Fellowship, 1990; reviewer rsch. and devel. com. VA Med. Ctr., Sepulveda and Gainesville; symposium chmn. Internat. Congress Gerontology, 1989, Infections, Immunology and Aging, 1989, Current Issues in Geriatric Dentistry, 1990. Assoc. editor: Growth, Devel. and Aging, 1988—, Jour. Gerontology, 1996—; mem. editorial rev. bd. Jour. Gerontology: Biol. Scis., 1992-95; referee (jours.) Endocrinology, Molecular Pharmacology, Am. Jour. Physiology, others; contbr. rsch. articles to med. jours. NIH tng. grantee U. Rochester 1970-74; rsch. grantee VA Merit Rev., 1978-80, 80-83, 83-87, 87-90, 90-94, Am. Lung Assn., 1980-81, U. Fla., 1988-89, 90-91, 92-93, NIH 1988-93, 93-98, Am. Heart Assn., 1992-94. Mem. AAAS, Am. Soc. Pharmacology and Exptl. Therapeutics, Gerontol. Soc. Am. (program chair ann. meeting 1993, symposium chmn. 1990, 91, 93), Tau Delta Phi. Office: VA Med Ctr 1601 SW Archer Rd Gainesville FL 32608-1135

SCAVO, CARMINE PETER FRANCIS, political science educator; b. Bklyn., July 7, 1949; s. Carmelo and Florence Jean (Iovine) S.; m. Kimber Lee Smith, June 13, 1992; children: Nicholas James, Marisa Ann. BA in Am. Govt., U. Va., 1971; postgrad., Coll. William and Mary, 1975-77; PhD in Polit. Sci., U. Mich., 1986. Grant adminstr. Urban Crime Prevention Project, Cin., 1981-83; market rschr. Quantime Corp., Cin., 1983-84; vis. lectr. U. N.C., Greensboro, 1984-85; vis. asst. prof. polit. sci. East Carolina U., Greenville, N.C., 1985-87, asst. prof., 1987-95, assoc. prof., 1995—. Co-author: (monographs) American Voting Behavior, 1984, 85, 92; contbr. articles to profl. jours. Chmn. Cypress group Sierra Club, Greenville, 1988-91. With USCG, 1971-75. Mem. N.C. Polit. Sci. Assn. (v.p. 1996-97). Democrat. Home: 103 Lakeleaf Ct Raleigh NC 27606 Office: East Carolina U Dept Polit Sci Greenville NC 27858-4353

SCERPELLA, ERNESTO GUILLERMO, physician researcher; b. Lima, Peru, Dec. 11, 1960; came to U.S., 1988; s. Juan Severino and Maria Doris (Porth) S.; m. Patricia Del Carmen Campos, Oct. 29, 1988; 1 child, Ernesto Alessandro. MD, Cayetano Heredia U., 1986. Resident internal medicine U. Miami, 1988-91, fellow spl. immunology, 1994-95, asst. prof. medicine, 1995—; fellow infectious disease U. Tex., Houston, 1991-94; mem. infection control com. Pub. Health Trust-Jackson Meml. Hosp., Miami, 1995—; instr. in histology Cayetano Heredia U., Lima, 1980-81. Author numerous scientific articles on areas related to infectious diseases and AIDS; sci. reviewer for several med. jours. Zeneca travel grant Nat. Found. for Infectious Diseases, 1993. Mem. ACP, AMA, Infectious Diseases Soc. of Am. (HIV/AIDS tng. program 1994), Panamerican Assn. of Infectious Diseases. Office: U Miami Sch Medicine 901 NW 17th St Ste D Miami FL 33136-1135

SCHAADT, ROBERT LEE, JR., library director, archivist; b. Bowling Green, Ohio, Mar. 1, 1953; s. Robert Lee and Donna Joan (McCleary) S.; m. Melissa M. Carman, June 25, 1977 (div. Aug. 1986); children: Robert Lee III, Elizabeth Frances; m. Dana Gwen Abshier, May 25, 1990. Student, Ohio U., 1971; BA in History, Oakland U., Rochester, Mich., 1974; MA in History/Archivist, U. Calif., Riverside, 1978. Records, warehouse mgr. Dynatec Corp., Santa Ana, Calif., 1975-76; asst. archivist A.K. Smiley Pub. Libr., Redlands, Calif., 1977-78; state field archivist local records Tex. State Libr., Houston, 1978-83; dir., archivist Sam Houston Regional Libr. & Rsch. Ctr., Liberty, Tex., 1983—; archival/mus. cons. Heritage House Mus., Orange, Tex., 1990—; archival cons. Newton County Hist. Ctr., Newton, Tex., 1989—, Jasper County Archives, Jasper, Tex., 1991-92; hist. cons. Liberty (Tex.) Ct. Hist. Commn., 1983—; mem. Sam Houston Bicentennial Commn. Tex. State Libr., Austin, 1993. Author: History of Hardin County, 1992; editor: Mudbaths to Millionaires: Sour Lake Texas, 1994. Early voting judge Liberty County, Tex., 1990—; chair hist. commn. Trinity Valley Exposition, Liberty, 1987-91; mem. Liberty County Hist. Com., 1983—, Hardin County Hist. Com., Kountze, Tex., 1990—; mem. Tex. ann. conf. Meth. Ch. Commn. on Archives and History, 1996—. Recipient Disting. Svc. award Tex. Hist. Commn., Austin, 1986, Cert. of Appreciation S.F. Austin Bicentennial Commn., 1994, Disting. Svc. award DAR, 1995. Mem. Soc. S.W. Archivists (sec. 1988-92, chair profl. devel. 1981-83, chair fin. com. 1994-95, treas. 1995—), Atascosito Hist. Soc. (sec.-treas. 1983—), Tex. Gulf Coast Hist. Soc., Acad. Cert. Archivists (cert. archivist), Soc. Am. Archivists (com. on cert. 1986-87), S.E. Tex. Mus. Assn. (pres. 1995, bd. dirs. 1996). Democrat. Methodist. Office: Sam Houston Regional Libr & Rsch Ctr Box 310 FM 1011 Liberty TX 77575-0310

SCHABEL, DONALD JACOB, library director; b. Chgo., May 20, 1937; s. Frank Rudolph and Marie Josephine (Waszak) S.; m. Patricia Ann Mackey, June 18, 1960; children: Michael, Mary, Christine. BS in Edn., No. Ill. U., 1959; postgrad., U. Chgo., 1960; MALS, Rosary Coll., River Forest, Ill., 1967. Libr. Chgo. Pub. Libr., 1967-70, asst. chief music dept., 1970-71, chief dept. history, 1971-74, dir. cultural ctr., 1974-77, asst. dir. tech. svcs., 1977-79, dir. tech. svcs., 1979-83; asst. dir. Lexington (Ky.) Pub. Libr., 1983—; cons. So. Pines (N.C.) Pub. Libr., 1987. Contbr. articles to profl. jours. Libr. Aviation Mus. of Ky., 1995—. Mem. Blue Grass Orchid Soc., Phi Mu Alpha. Office: Lexington Public Library 140 E Main St Lexington KY 40507-1318

SCHACHTEL, BARBARA HARRIET LEVIN, epidemiologist, educator; b. Rochester, N.Y., May 27, 1921; d. Lester and Ethel (Neiman) Levin; m. Hyman Judah Schachtel, Oct. 15, 1941; children: Bernard, Ann.Mollie. Student Wellesley Coll., 1939-41; BS, U. Houston, 1951, MA in Psychology, 1967; PhD, U. Tex.-Houston, 1979. Psychol. examiner Meyer Ctr. for Devel. Pediatrics, Tex. Children's Hosp., Houston, 1967-81; instr. dept. pediatrics Baylor Coll. Medicine, Houston, 1967-81, asst. prof. dept. medicine, 1982—; asst. dir. biometry and epidemiology Sid W. Richardson Inst. for Preventive Medicine, Meth. Hosp., Houston, 1981-88, dir. quality assurance, 1988-93; retired 1993; mem. instl. rev. bd. for human rsch. Baylor Coll. Medicine, Houston, 1981-87; mem. devel. bd. U. Tex. Health Sci. Ctr., Houston, 1987—; mem. dean's adv. bd. Sch. Architecture U. Houston, 1987; bd. dirs. Tex. Medical Ctr, 1990-93. Contbr. articles to profl. jours. Vice pres., bd. dirs. Houston-Harris County Mental Health Assn., 1966-67; vice-chmn. bd. mgrs. Harris County Hosp. Dist., Houston, 1974-90, chmn. 1990-92, bd. dirs., 1970-93; trustee Inst. Religion in Tex. Med. Ctr., 1990— bd. mem. Planned Parenthood of Houston, Inc., 1994—, Houston Ind. Sch. Dist. Found., 1993—; sec. Bo Harris County Hosp. Dist. Found. Bd., 1993—. Named Great Texan of Yr., Nat. Found. for Ilietis and Colitis, Houston, 1982, Outstanding Citizen, Houston-Harris County Mental Health Assn., 1985; recipient Good Heart award B'nai Brith Women, 1984, Women of Prominence award Am. Jewish Com., 1991, Mayor's award for outstanding vol. svc., 1994. Mem. APA, APHA, Wellesley Club of Houston (pres. 1968-70). Avocations: golf, tennis, books. Home: 2527 Glen Haven Blvd Houston TX 77030-3511

SCHADER, BILLY WAYNE, oil company executive; b. Fayetteville, Ark., June 23, 1947; s. Earvel and Madge Frey (Watson) S.; m. Janis Lynn Conrad, Aug. 12, 1967; children: Brandon Wayne, Derek Evan. Student, U. Ark., 1965-67, 69-72. Registered profl. engr., Ark. Engrng. asst. Southwestern Energy, Fayetteville, Ark., 1969-72, staff asst., 1972-76, prodn. engr., 1976-81, engrng. mgr., 1981-84; mgr. engrng./prodn. Southwestern Energy, Oklahoma City, 1984—. Leader Boy Scouts Am., Oklahoma City, 1983-84; coach Little League Baseball, Oklahoma City, 1984-87. With USN, 1967-69. Mem. Soc. Petroleum Engrs., Soc. Profl. Enrs. Republican. Baptist. Home: 2805 Lost Rock Trl Edmond OK 73003-4556 Office: Southwestern Energy Prodn Co 5600 N May Ave Oklahoma City OK 73112-4275

SCHAEFER, GEORGE PETER, utility company executive; b. N.Y.C., Nov. 7, 1950; m. Lois Nancy Bedner, July 6, 1974; children: Lauren Jessica, Alexis Carmella. BA, Am. U., 1972; M in Pub. Adminstrn., Syracuse U., 1974. Budget analyst HEW, Washington, 1974-76; policy analyst U.S. Dept. Energy, Washington, 1976-78; assoc. Booz, Allen & Hamilton, Bethesda, Md., 1978-80; dir. energy program The Orkand Corp., Silver Spring, Md., 1980-81; dir. energy fin. Ultrasystems, Irvine, Calif., 1981-82; sr. v.p., mgr. energy project financing Gen. Electric Credit Corp., Stamford, Conn., 1982-88; sr. v.p. European ops. GE Capital Corp., London, 1988-91; sr. v.p. gas industry financing GE Capital Corp., 1991; sr. v.p. internat. bus. devel. GE Capital Corp., Stamford, Conn., 1992-93; v.p. internat. devel. Energy Power Group, Little Rock, 1993-95; mng. dir. fin. Houston Industries Energy, 1995—. Author: (with others) Biomass as Non Fossil Fuel Source, 1978, Energy Project Financing, 1986; also articles. Centennial scholar Case Western Res. U., Cleveland, 1978; named One of Outstanding Young Men of Am., U.S. Jaycees, 1982. Mem. Renewable Energy Inst., Internat. Assn. Energy Economists, Am. Soc. for Pub. Adminstrn. (co-founder sect. on budgeting and fin. 1975; co-founder, bd. govs. Jour. Pub. Budgeting and Fin. 1980). Home: 3 Buckingham Ct Houston TX 77024

SCHAEFER, RICHARD J., communications educator; b. Jamaica, N.Y., Sept. 29, 1951; s. John J. and Eleanor A. (Greene) S.; m. Jo Ann Jecklin, Aug. 23, 1975; 1 child, Adrian Jecklin. BA in English, U. Notre Dame, 1973; MS in Comm., U. Utah, 1987, PhD of Comm., 1992. Editor, prodr. KUTV, Salt Lake City, 1979-83; writer WICAT Sys., Orem, Utah, 1983-84; rsch. asst. KUED-TV, Salt Lake City, 1984-87; tchr. fellow Dept. Comm. U. Utah, Salt Lake City, 1987-90; asst. prof. Dept. Journalism Tex. A&M U., College Station, 1991—. Contbr. articles to profl. jours. Mem. Assn. Edn. in Journalism and Mass Communication, Speech Communication Assn., Internat. Communication Assn., Computer Profls. for Spcial Responsibility. Home: 3902 4th St Bryan TX 77801 Office: Dept Journalism Tex A&M Univ College Station TX 77843-4111

SCHAEFFER, BARBARA HAMILTON, retired rental leasing company executive; b. Newton, Mass., Apr. 26, 1926; d. Peter Davidson Gunn and Harriet Bennett (Thompson) Hamilton; m. John Schaeffer, Sept. 7, 1946; children—Laurie, John, Peter. Student, Skidmore Coll., 1943-46; AB in English, Bucknell U., 1948; postgrad. Montclair State U., 1950-51, Bank St. Coll. Edn., 1959-61, Yeshiva U., 1961-62; student Daytona Beach Coll., 1984. Cert. primary, secondary tchr., N.J. Dir. Pompton Plains Sch., N.J., 1959-62; adviser Episcopal Sch., Towaco, N.J., 1968-70; v.p. Deltona-DeLand Trolley, Orange City, Fla., 1980-81; pres. Monroe Heavy Equipment Rentals, Inc., Orange City, 1981—, also Magic Carpet Travel, 1985-88 cons., founder, pres. TLC Travel Club, Orange City, 1981-88; lectr. on children's art, 1959-70. Contbr. articles to profl. publs. Mem. LWV, AAUW, Internat. Platform Assn., Small Bus. Devel. Regional Ctr. (Stetson U. chpt.), Nat. Trust Historic Preservation. Episcopalian. Avocations: restoring old homes, oil painting, piano, writing. Home: 400 Foothill Farms Rd Orange City FL 32763-5502 Address: PO Box 688 Debary FL 32713-0688

SCHAEFFER, PETER (VIKTOR), urban and regional planning educator; b. Zurich, Switzerland, Aug. 26, 1949; s. Victor and Catharina M. (Sciuchetti) S.; m. Patricia Marie Dresler, June 1, 1976; 1 child, Joseph Victor. Licencitate in Econ., U. Zurich, 1975; MA in Econs., U. So. Calif., 1979, PhD in Econs., 1981. Asst. prof. urban and regional planning U. Ill., Urbana, 1981-88; assoc. prof. U. Colo., Denver, 1987-93, dir. urban and regional planning, 1988-93; prof., dir. divsn. resource mgmt. W.Va. U., Morgantown, 1993—. Mem. editl. bd. Jour. Planning Edn. & Rsch., 1989—, Internat. Regional Sci. Rev., Jour. Planning Lit., 1996—; contbr. articles to profl. jours. Plan commr. City of Urbana, 1984-87; bd. dirs. Internat. Ctr. for Tourism Planning and Design, Denver, 1993-96, Lightstone Found., Moyers, W.Va., 1995—. Mem. AAUP, Am. Econ. Assn., Regional Sci. Assn. (treas. 1987—), Am. Agrl. Econ. Assn., Assn. Collegiate Schs. of Planning. Home: 1006 Deerwood Dr Morgantown WV 26505 Office: W Va U Divsn Resource Mgmt Morgantown WV 26506-6108

SCHAEFGEN, PHILIP P., business owner, consultant, accountant; b. Memphis, Feb. 1, 1958; s. Harold W. Sr. and Gertrude Goelz S. BA, Memphis State U., 1980, postgrad., 1987; cert. in computers, State Tech. U., 1981. CPA, Tenn. Acct. Lewis Jones, CPAs, Memphis, 1976-77, Kenneth Miller, CPAs, Memphis, 1977-78; owner DBA, Memphis, 1978-79; mng. ptnr. P.S. Enterprises, Memphis, 1978-79; mgr. The Escapade, Memphis, 1978-79; with Fed. Express Corp., Memphis, 1980-95, sr. acct., 1983-85, sr. investment and security analyst, 1986-95; mng. ptnr. Schaefgen & Assocs., CPAs, Memphis, 1980—; gen. ptnr. Schaefgen Investments, Memphis, 1989—; owner Soft Source Sys., 1989—; contr. Tiger Internat. Ins. Ltd., 1993-94, v.p., 1993-95, sr. v.p., 1995—; pres. Perfect Green Landscaping, Inc., 1993-95; pres., CEO P. Schaefgen & Assocs., PC, 1995—; bd. dirs. Tiger Internat. Ins. Ltd. subs. of Fed. Express Corp. West Tenn. Venture Capital Corp., 1993, Perfect Green Landscaping, Inc., Memphis, 1985, P. Schaefgen and Assocs., P.C., 1995; bd. dirs. adv. com. Shelby State C.C., Memphis. Contbr. articles to corp. newspaper. Active Suicide Prevention Ctr., Memphis 1976, Nat. Rep. Com.; pres. East Memphis Soccer Assn., 1995—; chmn. Tenn. Employers for Traffic Safety. Mem. AICPA, Soc. CPAs (tax divsn.), Nat. Soc. Tax Profls., Tenn. Assn. Pub. Accts., Tenn. Soc. CPAs, Jaycees (v.p. Memphis chpt. 1989—, bd. dirs. 1988, v.p. of month 1989, dir. of quarter 1988), KC (treas. Memphis chpt. 1984-92), Porsche Club Am. Republican. Roman Catholic. Home: 1183 Huntsman Ln Memphis TN 38120-3303

SCHAFER, EDWARD ALBERT, JR., data processing executive; b. Johnstown, Pa., Sept. 10, 1939; s. Edward A. and Dorothy (Cook) S.; m. Christine A. Ferruzzi, Aug. 27, 1976; children: David E., Kimberly L., Jaime L. BSEE, U. Pitts., 1963. Sales engr. Westinghouse Electric Corp., Pitts., 1963-69; nat. sales mgr. Time Share Peripherals Corp., Bethel, Conn., 1969-75; dist. sales mgr. Versatec, Inc., Boston, 1975-80, Gerber Systems Tech., Boston, 1980-82; regional dir. Intergraph Corp., Reston, Va., 1982-88; v.p., gen. mgr. N.Am. ops. Structural Dynamics Rsch. Corp., Cin., 1988-92; pres., CEO Schafer Holdings, Inc., Palm Harbor, Fla., 1992-94; acct. exec. Sherpa Corp., Palm Harbor, 1994-96; data mgmt. cons. Computervision Corp., Palm Harbor, 1996—. Office: Computervision Corp 4403 Sawgrass Dr Palm Harbor FL 34685-1097

SCHALL, STEWART ALLAN, pediatric cardiologist; b. Bklyn., Aug. 13, 1938; s. Jack and Ruth Schall; m. Beatrice Oritsky, Aug. 4, 1971; 1 child, Rachel. BA, Rutgers U., 1960; MD, U. Pa., 1964. Diplomate Am. Bd. Pediatrics, subspecialty pediatric cardiology. Intern straight pediatrics Bronx Mcpl. Hosp. Ctr., Albert Einstein Sch. Medicine, 1964-65, jr. and sr. resident, 1965-67; fellow Cardiovascular Rsch. Inst. U. Calif. Sch. Medicine, San Francisco, 1969-71; vis. pediatric cardiologist San Francisco Children's Hosp., 1971-72; cons. pediatrician Watts Hosp., Durham, N.C., 1973-76; cons. pediatric cardiologist Wake Meml. Hosp., Raleigh, N.C., 1973-85; attending pediatric cardiologist N.C. Meml. Hosp., 1972—; attending pediatrician,pediatric cardiologist Moses H. Cone Meml. Hosp., Greensboro, N.C., 1985—; attending pediatric cardiologist Women's Hosp., Greensboro, 1990—; cons. pediatric cardiologist Wesley Long Community Hosp., Greensboro, 1991—; asst. prof. pediatrics U. N.C., 1972-78, assoc. prof., 1978—; mem. pediatric teaching svc. Moses H. Cone Meml. Hosp., Greensboro, 1985—. Contbr. articles to profl. jours. Fellow Am. Acad. Pediatrics, Am. Coll. Cardiology; mem. Southeastern Pediatric Cardiology Assn., N.C. Pediatric Soc., N.C. Heart Assn. (bd. dirs. Greensboro divsn.), N.C. Med. Soc., Guilford County Med. Soc. Office: Moses Cone Meml Hosp Pediatric Tchg Svc 1200 N Elm St Greensboro NC 27401-1004

SCHALLY, ANDREW VICTOR, endocrinologist, researcher; b. Poland, Nov. 30, 1926; came to U.S., 1957; s. Casimir Peter and Maria (Lacka) S.; m. Ana Maria Comaru, Aug., 1976. B.Sc., McGill U., Can., 1955, Ph.D. in Biochemistry, 1957; 16 hon. doctorates. Research asst. biochemistry Nat. Inst. Med. Research, London, 1949-52; dept. psychiatry McGill U., Montreal, Que., 1952-57; research assoc., asst. prof. physiology and biochemistry Coll. Medicine, Baylor U., Houston, 1957-62; assoc. prof. Tulane U. Sch. Medicine, New Orleans, 1962-67, prof., 1967—; chief Endocrine Polypeptide and Cancer Inst. VA Med. Ctr., New Orleans; sr. med. investigator VA, 1973—. Author several books; contbr. articles to profl. jours. Recipient Van Meter prize Am. Thyroid Assn., 1969; Ayerst-Squibb award Endocrine Soc., 1970; William S. Middletown award VA, 1970; Ch. Mickle award U. Toronto, 1974; Gairdner Internat. award, 1974; Borden award Assn. Am. Med. Colls. and Borden Co. Found., 1975; Lasker Basic Research award, 1975; co-recipient Nobel prize for medicine, 1977; USPHS sr. research fellow, 1961-62. Mem. NAS, AAAS, Endocrine Soc., Am. Physiol. Soc., Soc. Biol. Chemists, Soc. Exptl. Biol. Medicine, Internat. Soc. Rsch. Biology Reprodn., Soc. Internat. Brain Rsch. Orgn., Mex. Acad. Medicine, Am. Soc. Animal Sci., Nat. Acad. Medicine Brazil, Acad. Medicine Venezuela, Acad. Medicine Poland, Acad. Sci. Hungary, Acad. Sci. Russia, Acad. Medicine Poland. Home: 5025 Kawanee Ave Metairie LA 70006-2547 Office: VA Hosp 1601 Perdido St New Orleans LA 70112-1207

SCHANZER, MARK JOSEPH, petroleum company executive; b. Ithaca, N.Y., Dec. 26, 1957; s. Joseph and Patricia (Bogart) S.; m. Celine Catherine Likoudis, June 20, 1980; children: James Joseph, Sarah Soh-Jung, Rebecca Byul. BS in Acctg., Canisius Coll., 1980; MBA, Averett Coll., 1992. CPA; cert. mgmt. acct. From acct. to supr. Mobil Oil Corp., Dallas, 1981-86; from fin. acct. to scheduling supr. Mobil Oil Corp., Fairfax, Va., 1986-90; trade/credit control mgr. Mobil Supply & Trading, Fairfax, 1990-92, project mgr., 1992, bus. integration team leader, 1993-96, global procurement mgr. utilities, transp. and logistics, 1996; with Mobil Oil Torrance Refinery, Torrance, Calif., 1996—. Mem. Families Adopting Children Everywhere, Fairfax, 1991, Ch. Parish, Cypress, Calif., 1996. Mem. Nat. Assn. Accts., Inst. Cert. Mgmt. Accts., Beta Gamma Sigma. Office: Mobil Oil Torrance Refinery 3700 W 190th St Torrance CA 90504

SCHAPPEL, ARTHUR WALTER, neuropsychiatrist; b. Indpls., Mar. 11, 1917; s. Wilkes Walter and Amelia (Fenstermacher) S.; m. Priscilla K. Smith, June 26, 1943; children: Priscilla Anne Russel, Nan Margaret Barry. AB in Chemistry, Ind. U., 1938; MD, Ind. U., Indpls., 1941. Diplomate Am. Bd. Psychiatry; lic. physician, Ind. Intern City Hosp., Cleve., 1941-42; resident neuropsychiatry Bellevue Hosp., N.Y.C., 1946-48; asst. prof. clin. neurology NYU Sch. Medicine, N.Y.C., 1953-60; pvt. practice neuropsychiatry Forest Hills, N.Y., 1946-88; pres. med. bd. Beckman Downtown Hosp., N.Y.C. Fleet surgeon Port Washington (N.Y.) Yacht Club. Mem. Acad. Neurology, Am. Psychiat. Assn. (pres. Queens County chpt.), Eastern Assn. EEG, N.Y. Acad. Scis. Home: 8407 Atascocita Lake Way Humble TX 77346

SCHAR, DWIGHT C., construction company executive; b. 1942. With Ryan Homes, Washington, 1986-77, NVLand, 1977—, NVR L P, 1980-86; bd. dirs. NVCompanies Inc. Office: NVR L P 7601 Lewinsville Rd Ste 300 Mc Lean VA 22102-2815

SCHARLATT, HAROLD, management company executive; b. N.Y.C., Dec. 9, 1947; s. Bertram and Miriam Louise (Stone) S.; BEd, SUNY, 1969, MA in Liberal Studies, 1973; advanced cert. adminstrn. and supervision, Oxford U., 1975; m. Mary Moore, June 10, 1978. Tchr., in-service instr. N.Y., 1970-77; mgmt. devel. specialist Union Carbide Corp., N.Y.C., 1977, mgmt. devel. cons., 1978-80; regional dir. Vector Mgmt. Systems, Inc., Lexington, Ky., 1980-83; pres. Tng. and Devel. Assocs., Inc., Lexington, 1983—. Mem. Am. Soc. Tng. and Devel., Soc. Human Resource Mgmt., Human Resource Planning Soc., Assn. For Psychol. Type, Human Resource Planning Soc., Assn. for Continuing Edn., Assn. For Quality and Participation. Office: 3608 Bircham Way Lexington KY 40515-1207

SCHARLAU, CHARLES EDWARD, III, natural gas company executive; b. Chgo., Apr. 24, 1927; s. Charles Edward II and Esther (Powell) S.; m. Clydene Yvonne Sloop, Aug. 13, 1960; children: Caryn, Robin, Greg, Charles, Marti. LLB, U. Ark., 1951. Bar: Ark. 1951, U.S. Dist. Ct. (western dist.) Ark. 1951, U.S. Supreme Ct. 1958. Atty. Ark. Western Gas Co., Fayetteville, 1951-61, v.p., 1961-68, pres., 1968-78; pres., chmn. S.W. Energy Co., Fayetteville, 1978—; bd. dirs. C.H. Heist Co., Clearwater, Fla., McIlroy Bank and Trust Co., Fayetteville. Chmn. U. Ark. Devel. Coun., 1989—. With USMC, 1945-46. Mem. ABA, Ark. Bar Assn., So. Gas Assn., Nat. Assn. Mfrs. (bd. dirs. 1986-89), Am. Gas Assn. (bd. dirs. 1987-90), U. Ark. Alumni Assn. (pres. 1972-73), Ark. C. of C. (pres. 1977-79), Beta Gamma Sigma. Methodist. Home: 1506 Sunset Pl Fayetteville AR 72701-1627 Office: Southwestern Energy Co 1083 Sain St Fayetteville AR 72703-6206

SCHARP, ROBERT CHARLES, mining engineer, energy company executive; b. Nebraska City, Nebr., Jan. 21, 1947; s. Hoyt Merwin and Betty Jane (James) S.; m. Cheryl P. Naas, Aug. 8, 1969; children: Paula Jean, Jacob Robert. Engr. of mines degree, Colo. Sch. Mines; Advanced Mgmt. Program, Harvard U., 1987. Mining engr. Phelps Dodge Corp., Morenci, Ariz., 1974-75; chief engr. Kerr-McGee Coal, Gillette, Wyo., 1975-80; mgr. Jacobs Ranch Mine Jacobs Ranch Mine, Gillette, Wyo., 1980-88; gen. mgr. Galatia Mine, 1988-90; v.p. ops. Kerr-McGee Coal, Oklahoma Ciy, 1990-91; pres. Kerr McGee Coal Corp., Oklahoma Ciy, 1991-95; sr. v.p. Kerr McGee Coal Corp., 1995—; pres. SRVP Kerr McGee Corp.; mem. Nat. Coal Coun. Served with U.S. Army C.E., 1970-73, Germany; col. Wyo. N.G., ret. 1993. Mem. Nat. Coal Assn. (bd. dirs.), Am. Mining Congress (bd. dirs.), Soc. Mining Engrs., Ill. Coal Assn., Ill. Mining Inst., Rocky Mountain Coal Mining Inst. (bd. dirs. spl. care), Mid-Continent Oil and Gas Assn. (exec. com.). Address: 5205 Summit Dr Edmond OK 73034-7966

SCHATZ, DESMOND ARTHUR, pediatrician, endocrinologist; b. Johannesburg, South Africa, Jan. 27, 1956; came to U.S.; m. Nadine Segall, Oct. 7, 1980; children: Richard Allan, Megan Renee. MB BCh, U. Witwatersrand Med. Sch., Johannesburg, South Africa, 1979. Diplomate Am. Bd. Pediatrics, Am. Bd. Pediatric Endocrinology; Diploma in Child Health; lic. MD, Fla. Externship dept. pediatrics U. Calif., San Francisco, 1978; intern in internal medicine and surgery Johannesburg (South Africa) Hosp., 1980; med. officer dept. pediatrics 1 Military Hosp., Pretoria, South Africa, 1981-82; pediatric resident U. Fla., Gainesville, 1983-86, pediatric endocrinology fellow, 1986-89, instr. pediatric endocrinology and pathology, 1988-89, asst. prof. pediatric endocrinology, 1989-94, assoc. prof., 1994—; ad-hoc reviewer in field for various profl. jours. Co-editor: Turner Syndrome, 1989, Advances in Experimental Medicine and Biology: Prediabetes, 1989, Immunotherapy of Type I Diabetes, 1989, Proceedings of the 13th International Diabetes Foundation Congress, 1989, Immunology of Endocrine Disease, 1990, Topics in Pediatrics, 1990, Seminars in Immunopathology: Immune Endocrinology, 1992; contbr. to numerous symposia and book chpts.; contbr. numerous articles to profl. jours. Recipient Spl. Recognition award U. Fla., 1984, Awards for Sci. Excellence, U. Fla., 1985-88, scholarship Diabetes, Melbourne, Australia, 1988, Kokomoor award, Outstanding Pediatric fellow U. Fla., 1988; named one of Best Doctors in Am., 1993; grantee in field. Fellow Am. Acad. Pediatrics; mem. Am. Diabetes Assn., Am. Bd. Pediatrics, Internat. Diabetes Fedn., Soc. Soc. for Pediatric Rsch., Fla. Med. Assn., Fla. Pediatric Soc., Alachue County Med. Soc., Lawson Wilkens Pediatric Endocrine Soc., The Endocrine Soc., Soc. Pediatric Rsch. Home: 3639 NW 33d Ter Gainesville FL 32605-2184 Office: U Fla Dept Pediats PO Box 100296 JHMHC Gainesville FL 32610

SCHATZKI, THEODORE RICHARD, philosopher; b. Boston, Jan. 10, 1956; s. Stefan Conrad and Virginia Helen (Todd) S. BA in Applied Math., Harvard U., 1977; BPhil, Oxford U., 1979; MA, U. Calif., Berkeley, 1982, PhD, 1986; postgrad., Freie U., Berlin, 1982-83. Teaching assoc. and asst. dept. philosophy U. Calif., Berkeley, 1980-86; asst. prof. dept. philosophy U. Ky., Lexington, 1986-91, assoc. prof. dept. philosophy, 1991—; co-dir. com. on social theory U. Ky., 1989—, assoc. chmn. dept. philosophy, 1992-93. Author: Social Practices, 1996; contbr. articles to profl. jours. Recipient Disting. Teaching Asst. award U. Calif. Acad. Senate, 1984, Fulbright Rsch. award, Norway, 1993; Humboldt Rsch. fellow Germany, 1993-94, External Rsch. fellow Oreg. Ctr. for the Humanities, 1993-94, Summer Faculty Rsch. fellow U. Ky., 1987, 89, Rotary Internat. fellow, 1982-83, Ralph C. Church fellow U. Calif., 1979-80; Multidisciplinary Feasibility Assessment Program grantee U. Ky., 1989-90, Ky. Humanities Coun. grantee, 1989, Am. Coun. Learned Socs. Travel grantee, 1987. Office: Univ Ky Dept Philosophy Lexington KY 40506-0027

SCHAUDIES, JESSE P., JR., lawyer; b. Knoxville, Tenn., Aug. 27, 1954; s. Jesse P. and Adele (Thompson) S.; m. Elizabeth D. Schaudies, Sept. 15, 1979; children—Jesse P. III, Frederick T., Deneen Adele. B.A. magna cum laude, Duke U., 1976; J.D., Georgetown U., 1979. Ptnr. Troutman Sanders, Atlanta, 1979-94; exec. v.p. Randstad Staffing Svcs., 1994—. Mng. editor Am. Criminal Law Rev., 1978-79. Mem. ABA, Ga. State Bar Assn. (labor sect., litigation sect.), Author's Court Ga. (charter), law revs.; contbr. articles to profl. jours. Republican. Presbyterian. Office: Randstad Staffing Svcs 2015 South Park Pl Atlanta GA 30339

SCHAUER, CATHARINE GUBERMAN, public affairs specialist; b. Woodbury, N.J., Sept. 24, 1945; d. Jack and Anna Ruth (Felipe) Guberman; m. Irwin Jay Schauer, July 4, 1968; children: Cheryl Anne, Marc Cawin. AB, Miami-Dade Jr. Coll., 1965; BEd, U. Miami, 1967; postgrad. Mercer U., 1968, MPA, Troy State U., 1995. Writer, Miami (Fla.) News, 1962-63; tchr. Dade County Schs., Miami, Fla., 1967-68; coord. pub. info. Macon Jr. Coll. (Ga.), 1968-69; writer Atlanta Jour., 1969-72; editor Ridgerunner newspaper, Woodbridge, Va., 1973-75; pub. info. specialist Dept. Interior, Washington, 1980-82; writer Dept. Army, Ft. Belvoir, Va., 1982-84, chief prodn., design and editl., publs. div., 1984-85; head writer-editor SE region U.S. Naval Audit Svc., Virginia Beach, Va., 1986; pub. affairs specialist, tech. rep. for vis. ctr. ops., NASA Langley, 1986-90, project mgr., chmn. 75th anniversary yr., 1991-92; NASA Langley Rsch. Ctr., Hampton, Va., 1987-89, acting head Office Pub. Svcs., 1989, pub. affairs officer for space NASA Langley, 1993—; columnist, writer Potomac News, Woodbridge, 1972-85. Contbr. articles to profl. jours. Historian, publicity chmn. PTO, Woodbridge, 1974; publicity chmn. Boy Scouts Am., Woodbridge, 1974-83, Girl Scouts U.S., Woodbridge, 1974-79; bd. dirs. Congregation Ner Tamid, Woodbridge, 1984-85. Recipient Outstanding Tng. Devel. Support award U.S. Army, 1983; 1st place news writing award and 1st place for advt. design Fla. Jr. Coll. Press Assn., 1964, 1st place feature writing award, 1964, 1st place news writing award Sigma Delta Chi, 1965, 70th anniversary team NASA, 1988, Long Duration Exposure Facility Team award NASA. Mem. Va. Press Women (1st Pl. Govt. Mags. 1991, 3d Pl. Govt. Brochures 1991, 1st Pl. Govt. Brochures 1993, 1st Pl. Govt. Media Campaign 1993, 1st Pl. Govt. Cmty. Svc. Internal Comm. Campaign 1996), Women in Comms., Nat. Fedn. Press Women (life, 1st Pl. Govt. Mag. 1991, 1st Pl. Govt. Media Campaign 1993, 1st Pl. Govt. Internal Comm. Campaign 1996), Internat. Assn. Bus. Communicators (1st Place Mktg. Campaign award 1996). Democrat. Home: 120 Tide's Run Yorktown VA 23692-4333 Office: NASA Langley Rsch Ctr Mail Code 154 Hampton VA 23681-0001

SCHAUER, IRWIN JAY, quality and productivity officer; b. Mar. 8, 1945; m. Catharine Schauer, 1968; children: Cheryl Anne, Marc Cawin. BA in Psychology, U. Miami, 1968; M in Pub. Adminstrn., Troy State U., 1995. Pers. mgmt. specialist Office of Pers. Mgmt., Atlanta and Washington; chief, employee rels. U.S. Secret Svc., Washington; chief, classification and staffing Dept. of Transp., Washington; chief pers. mgmt. sect. NASA Hdqrs., 1982-85, employee rels. officer, 1985; head, placement and position mgmt. br., personnel dir., chief pers. divsn. NASA-Langley Rsch. Ctr., Hampton, Va., 1985-90, quality and productivity officer, 1990—; mem. Hampton Roads Focus on Quality Group; mem. exec. com. Va. Peninsula Total Quality Inst.; Baldrige examiner, Pres.'s Quality Award examiner, 1995, 96. Contbr. articles to profl. jours. Recipient Hon. Badge U.S. Secret Svc. Mem. Internat. Soc. of Pers. Mgmt., Quality and Productivity Mgmt. Assn. Home: 120 Tide's Run Yorktown VA 23692-4333 Office: NASA Langley Rsch Ctr Mail Stop 363 Hampton VA 23681-0001

SCHAVER, MARK J., journalist; b. Glendale, Calif., July 23, 1961; s. Lou Shaver and Marney Catherine (Gorske) Sims; m. Fran Ellers, Sept. 3, 1994; 1 child, Zoe Ellers. BA in Econs. and Pol. Sci., Boston U., 1982; MA in Journalism, U. N.C., 1992. Reporter Wilmington (N.C.) Morning Star, 1989-90, The Courier Jour., Louisville, 1990—. Mem. Soc. Profl. Journalists, Investigative Reporters Editors.

SCHECHTER, ARTHUR LOUIS, lawyer; b. Rosenberg, Tex., Dec. 6, 1939; s. Morris and Helen (Brilling) S.; m. Joyce Proler, Aug. 26, 1965; children: Leslie Schechter Karpas, Jennifer Schechter Rosen. BA, U. Tex., 1962, JD, 1964; postgrad. U. Houston, 1964-65. Bar: Tex. 1964, U.S. Dist. Ct. (ea. and so. dists.) Tex. 1966, U.S. Ct. Appeals (5th cir.), U.S. Supreme Ct. 1976, cert. Tex. Bd. Legal Specialization to Personal Injury Trial Law, 1964-94. Pres. Arthur L. Schechter & Assocs., 1992-94, Schechter & Marshall, L.L.P., 1994—; spkr. Marine Law Seminar, 1983; spkr. in field. Contbr. to Law Rev., 1984. Bd. dirs. Theatre Under the Stars, Houston, 1972-78, Congregation Beth Israel, Houston, 1972-84, pres., 1982-84; pres. Am. Jewish Com., Houston, 1982-84, chmn. fgn. rels. com., chmn. United Jewish Campaign exec. com., chmn. 1993-94; pres. Jewish Fedn. Ctr. Houston, 1994-96; mem. fin. coun. Nat. Dem. Orgn., 1979; mng. trustee, mem. fin. com. Dem. Nat. Com., 1992—, fin. chmn. Tex. Clinton/Gore '96; vice chair Clinton/Gore Jewish Leadership Coun., 1996; v.p., exec. com. Nat. Jewish Dem. Coun., 1992—; mem. Leadership Cir., Dem. Senatorial Campaign Com.; mem. Deans Council, U. Tex. Law Sch. Found., Austin, 1981-84, U.S. Holocaust Coun., 1994—; pres. Beth Israel Congregation, 1988-90; bd. trustees Schlenker Sch. Coun. Recipient Svc. award Congregation Beth Israel, 1976, Pres. award NAACP, 1992, Love award Child Advocate Houston, Benefactor award Jewish Chautaqua Soc., 1995, Nat. Am. Jewish Com. Human Rels. award, 1996. Mem. ATLA, Tex. Trial Lawyers Assn. (chmn. admiralty sect., presenter 1985-87), Jewish Fedn. Houston (bd. mem., v.p., pres. 1994—), Houston Trial Lawyers Assn., Houston Bar Assn. Democrat. Jewish. Home: 19A Westlane Houston TX 77019

SCHECHTERMAN, LAWRENCE, securities arbitration executive; b. Elizabeth, N.J., June 23, 1943; s. Josef and Sylvia (Berger) S.; m. Suzanne Lois Hilzenradt, May 31, 1981; children: Jill Laura, Danielle Sara, Danielle Beth, Nicole Corrin, Gregory Jared. BA, U. Miami, Fla., 1966; JD, Suffolk U., 1969; LLM, NYU, 1973. Tax assoc. Coopers & Lybrand, N.Y.C., 1969-70; assoc. Bendit, Weinstock & Sharbaugh, Newark, 1970-72; pvt. practice, East Brunswick, N.J., 1972-81; gen. counsel Equinox Solar, Inc., Miami, Fla., 1981-83; mem. Lawrence Schechterman, P.A., Boca Raton, Fla., 1983-93; pres. Securities Arbitration Recovery, Inc., Boca Raton, 1993—; pres. B'nai Torah Congregation of Boca Raton Inc., 1987-89, trustee, 1989-91, mem. Author: (poetry) New Dimensions: An Anthology of American Poetry, 1967; contbr. articles to legal jours. Councilman, Twp. of East Brunswick, 1976-80. Office: 3003-C8 Yamato Rd Ste 1082 Boca Raton FL 33434

SCHECTER, ERLINE DIAN, educational administrator; b. El Paso, Tex., Apr. 7, 1956; d. Irving and Jean (Lapowski) S. BA in Elem. Edn., U. Ariz., Tucson, 1978; MEd, Lesley Coll., 1988; cert., Sul Ross State U., 1990. Cert. mid-mgmt., Tex. Tchr. Dept. Def. Dependent Schs., Iwakuni, Japan, 1980-83; elem. tchr. El Paso Ind. Sch. Dist., 1978-80, 83-85, tchr. computers, 1985-92, staff devel., 1992-96; asst. dir. tech. tng. programs, staff devel., 1996—; cons. Region XIX Edn. Svc. Ctr., El Paso, 1985-88, Norton Bros. Computer Ctr., El Paso, 1984-86, Ector County Ind. Sch. Dist., 1989-90. Mem. AAUW, ASCD, Tex. Computer Edn. Assn. (treas.1990-94, Area II dir. 1986-90, electronic editor 1994-95, scholarship chairperson 1996-97), Internat. Soc. for Tech. in Edn., Nat. Coun. Jewish Women, Alpha Epsilon Phi, Phi Delta Kappa. Office: Staff Devel 6500 Boeing Dr # K El Paso TX 79925-1073

SCHEEL, WILLIAM PRESTON, association executive, priest; b. Chgo., Sept. 19, 1936; s. Harvey Andrew and Mildred Jeanette (Preston) S.; m. Rose-Marie Anne Hamilton-Birch, Apr. 23, 1960 (div. Dec. 1986); children: Sarah Alexandra Scheel-Cook, William Christopher; m. Vivian Carol Rowe, June 24, 1989. BA, U. of South, 1959; MDiv, Seabury-Western Theol. Sem., Evanston, Ill., 1962; EdD, U. Mass., 1971. Ordained priest Episcopal Ch., 1962. Vicar Episcopal chs., Red Lake Indian Reservation, Minn., 1962-64; asst. rector St. David's Episcopal Ch., Minnetonka, Minn., 1964-66; chaplain, tchr. Shattuck-St. Mary's Sch., Faribault, Minn., 1966-69; headmaster Christchurch (Va.) Sch., 1971-74, St. Mary's Hall, Burlington, N.J., 1974-80, Berry Acad., Rome, Ga., 1980-83, St. Cyprian's Episcopal Sch., Lufkin, Tex., 1984-86; exec. dir. Southwestern Assn. Episcopal Schs., Dallas, 1986—; cons. various pub. and pvt. schs., 1970—; adj. prof. Berry Coll., Rome, 1980-83; mem. nat. adv. bd. Nat. Coalition for Equality in Learning, Amherst, Mass., 1991-96; chmn. Tex. Pvt. Sch. Accreditation Commn., San Antonio, 1995-97. Editor ShArES newsletter; contbr. book revs. and articles to various publs. Mem. Libr. Co. Burlington, 1975-80; chmn. Hist. Dist. Rev. Bd., Burlington, 1976-80; pres. Friends of Libr., Lufkin, 1984-86. Ford Found. fellow U. Mass., 1969-71. Mem. Tex. Assn. non-Pub. Schs. (bd. dirs. 1985—). Home: 14609 Cambridge Ct Addison TX 75244 Office: Southwestern Assn Epis Schs 5952 Royal Ln Ste 204 Dallas TX 75230

SCHEER, FRANK REEDER, corporate freight traffic administrator, library curator, information specialist; b. Alexandria, Va., Dec. 31, 1950; s. Lloyd Francis and Kathryn Cornelia (Werth) S.; m. Arja Sinikka Seppala, Dec. 31, 1985; children: Frank J.K., Harri L.H. BA, U. Va., 1972; MBA, U. Tenn., 1974, D of Bus. Adminstrn., 1982. Operator Rich. Fred. & Potomac R.R., Alexandria, 1969-70; relief agt.-operator Chesapeake & Ohio Railway, Gordonsville, Va., 1971-73; asst. to trainmaster Norfolk & Western Railway, Decatur, Ill., 1974-76; grad. teaching asst. U. Tenn., Knoxville, 1976-78; mgr. rail ops. analysis U.S. Railway Assn., Washington, 1978-82; staff transp. specialist Va. Power, Richmond, 1982-90; materials distbn. system specialist U.S. Postal Svc., Washington, 1990—; curator Railway Mail Svc. Libr., Alexandria, 1980—. Mem. Am. Soc. Transp. and Logistics (cert.), Assn. for Transp. Law, Logistics, and Policy, Mobile Post Office Soc. (patron), Am. Philatelic Rsch. Libr., Am. Philatelic Soc., T.P.O. & Seapost Soc. Home: 12 E Rosemont Ave Alexandria VA 22301-2325 Office: US Postal Svc 475 L'Enfant Plz SW Rm 1141 Washington DC 20260-6225

SCHEFFLER, STEVE JOHN, communications executive; b. Lincoln, Nebr., Nov. 4, 1967; s. John Richard and Marilyn Ruth (Olsen) S.; m. Catherine Alice Adelman, July 20, 1991; children: Ryan Olsen, Rachel Jean. BJ, U. Tex., 1986-90. Public relations coord. U. Tex. Ex-Students' Assn., Austin, Tex., 1990; staff writer Am. Productivity & Quality Ctr., Houston, 1990-92; comm. specialist/editor Am. Productivity & Quality Ctr., 1992-93, comm. mgr., 1993-95; publ. mgr. North Harris Montgomery C.C. Dist., Houston, 1995—. Recipient Best New Magazine/Journal award for publication excellence, 1993. Mem. Public Relations Soc. of Am. Home: 8 Thrush Grove Pl The Woodlands TX 77381 Office: North Harris Montgomery CC Dist 250 N Sam Houston Pkwy E Houston TX 77060

SCHEIDE, FRANK MILO, communications educator; b. Red Wing, Minn., Apr. 1, 1949; s. Milo Wayne and Genevieve Ione (Richardson) S.; m. Melissa Jo Gard, Oct. 21, 1978 (div. June 1984); m. Elizabeth Susan Dewar, July 29, 1993. BS in History and Polit. Sci. magna cum laude, U. Wis., River Falls, 1971; MA in Cinema Studies, NYU, 1972; PhD in Comm., U. Wis., Madison, 1990. Lectr. comm. U. Wis., River Falls, 1973, instr., 1975-76; asst. film archivist Wis. Ctr. for Theater Rsch., Madison, 1973; teaching asst. U. Wis., Madison, 1973-75; filmmaker in residence Horace Mann Jr. H.S., Sheboygan, Wis., 1976; asst. prof. Ball State U., Muncie, Ind., 1976-77; ind. video prodr., media cons. Fayetteville, Ark., 1983-84; instr. U. Ark., Fayetteville, 1984-91, asst. prof., 1991-95, assoc. prof., 1996—; guest. spkr. Brit. Film Inst., London, 1997; mem. Buster Keaton Celebration Com., Iola, Kans., 1995—; founder, coorganizer U. Ark. Native Am. Symposium, 1995—; cons. Our Charlie Day event St. Peter's Ch., London, 1993; lectr. profl. and ednl. instns., including S.W. Theater Conf., Little Rock, 1979, Nat. Fedn. Local Cable Programmers, 1985, Jefferson County (Ark.) Hist. Mus. Guild, 1987, Hist. Confedn. Ky., 1990; guest lectr. Anthropology Colloquium, 1988; guest speaker Anthropology Club, U. Ark., 1986; film lectr. Fulbright Sch. Pub. Affairs, summer 1986, coord. video project, summers 1987-89; presenter in field. Author: Introductory Film Criticism: A Historical Perspective, 1994; prodr., narrator, dir. many documentaries, tng. and orientation films, other video prodns.; host interview series with Norman DeMarco, Fayetteville Open Channel TV, 1987; writer, prodr. study guide and series of TV programs for telecom. course on comedy of Chaplin and Keaton, U. Ark., 1982; contbr. articles and revs. to profl. jours. and various publs. Hon. mem. Vauxhall Heritage Ctr., St. Peter's Ch., 1993, United Keetoowah Bank of Cherokee Indians, 1992, Jefferson County Hist. Soc., 1987; bd. dirs. Ozark Stage Works, 1993, Native Ams. for Clean Environ., 1989-90; bd. dirs. Fayetteville Open Channel, 1984-87, pres., 1985-86; vol. asst. Film Study Ctr., Mus. Modern Art, N.Y.C., 1972; citizen commentor for study U.S. Dept. Interior, Fayetteville, 1986; cons. Fayetteville Cmty. Devel. Com., 1978. Ford Found. fellow, 1973-74; named one of Outstanding Young Men of Am., 1982; rsch. grantee Ark. Office on Alcohol and Drug Abuse Prevention, 1984, Ark. Endowment for Humanities, 1984, Ark. Arts Coun., 1985, Ctr. for Ark. Regional Studies, 1992; recipient Bread Loaf Writing award Atlantic Monthly, 1969, Certs. of Appreciation, Fayetteville Open Channel, 1986-87, United Keetoowah Band of Cherokee Indians, 1992, 93. Democrat. Methodist. Office: U Ark Dept Comm Kh # 417 Fayetteville AR 72701

SCHEIE, PAUL OLAF, physics educator; b. Marietta, Minn., June 24, 1933; s. Olaf Johan and Selma Pricilla (Varhus) S.; m. Mary Anna Harrison, May 18, 1963; children—Eric, Maren. BA, St. Olaf Coll., Northfield, Minn., 1955; MS, U. N.Mex., 1957; PhD, Pa. State U., 1965. Asst. prof. physics Oklahoma City U., 1958-63; asst. prof. biophysics Pa. State U., State Coll., 1965-73; prof. physics Tex. Luth. Univ., Seguin, 1973—, interim acad. dean, 1976. Contbr. articles to profl. publs. Recipient Faculty Alumni award, Tex. Luth. Coll., 1985. Mem. Biophys. Soc., AAAS, Am. Assn. Physics Tchrs., Am. Phys. Soc., Royal Micros. Soc., Sigma Xi. Lutheran. Lodge: Lions. Avocations: woodworking, gardening. Home: 207 Leonard Seguin TX 78155-5110 Office: Tex Luth Coll Dept Physics 1000 W Court St Seguin TX 78155-5978

SCHEITLIN, CONSTANCE JOY, real estate broker; b. Louisville, Nov. 21, 1949; d. Albert and Esther Joy (Sulzer) Kraus; m. Charles James Scheitlin, Sept. 11, 1982; 1 child, Brittany. Student, U. Louisville, 1974-75, Spencerian Bus. Coll., Louisville, 1968. Lic. salesperson in real estate, Ky.; lic. real estate broker, Fla. Customer svc. rep. Chevron Oil Co., Louisville, 1968-77; acctg. asst. E. Bruce Neikirk, Atty., Louisville, 1978; retail mgr. Stannye's Boutique, Louisville, 1978-85; real estate sales person Louisville, 1970-85; real estate salesperson Venice, 1987-92; legal asst. Andrew Britton, Atty., 1986-92; real estate broker, mgr. Michael Saunders & Co., Venice, 1992-93, Coldwell Banker Agts. Realty, Venice, 1993-95; mgr. Coldwell Banker Residential Real Estate, Venice, 1995-96, regional mgr., property mgmt., 1996—; treas. Stannye's Boutique, Louisville, 1983-85. Chmn. Metro United Way, Louisville, 1975-77; team capt. Greater Louisville Fund for the Arts, 1980-85; mem. South Venice Civic Assn., 1985—; chmn. So. Venice Road and Bridge Trustees, 1989-96. Mem. Venice Area Bd. Realtors (dir. 1992-95), Women's Coun. of Realtors (treas. 1988-89, pres. 1989-90), Sarasota Bd. Realtors, Nat. Assn. Real Property Mgrs. Mem. Ch. of Christ. Office: Coldwell Banker 3322 Bee Ridge Rd Sarasota FL 34239-7213

SCHELL, GEORGE POWELL, information systems educator; b. Jacksonville, Fla., May 18, 1950; s. Wilkie Jay and Norma Jean (Fiske) S.; m. Tracy Friedman, Aug. 13, 1983; children: Robert Wilkie, Amy Abigail. BSBA, U. Fla., 1972, MA in Mgmt. Sci., 1976; PhD in Mgmt. Info. Systems, Purdue U., 1983. Programming instr. Purdential Ins. Co., Jacksonville, 1972; asst. computer lab. dir. Bur. ofEcons. and Bus. Rsch., U. Fla., Gainesville, 1972-76; mgr. math rsch. Wilson Foods Corp., Oklahoma City, 1976-80; prof. U. Tulsa, 1983-89, U. N.C., Wilmington, 1989—; cons. Am. Meat Inst., Pritsker and Assoc., others. Author: Casebook for Management Information systems, 3d-6th edits.; contbr. articles to Info. and Mgmt., Interfaces, Internat. Jour. Policy and Info., others. Vol. Habitat for Humanity,Wilmington, 1992—; coach Odyssey of the Mind, Johnson Elem. Sch., Wilmington, 1993, 94. Mem. Inst. of Mgmt. Sci., Decision Scis. Inst., Assn. for Computing Machinery. Office: U NC Wilmington Cameron Sch Bus Adminstrn Wilmington NC 28403

SCHELL, JOAN BRUNING, information specialist, business science librarian; b. N.Y.C., June 9, 1932; d. Walter Henry and Gertrude Emily (Goossen) Bruning; m. Harold Benton Schell, Aug. 27, 1955 (div. 1978); children: Jeffrey Mark, Sue Lynne. AB, Wittenberg U., 1954; postgrad., Syracuse U., 1963, U. Md., 1965-66; MLS, U. Pitts., 1968. Actuarial, claims asst. Nationwide Ins., Columbus, Ohio, 1954-57; tech. report typist Cornell U., Ithaca, N.Y., 1957; bus. libr. asst. U. Pitts., 1969; bus. reference libr. Dallas Pub. Libr., 1971-73, Pub. Libr. Cin. and Hamilton County, Cin., 1973-79; book selection coord. Pub. Libr. Cin. & Hamilton County, Cin., 1979-83, asst. to main libr., 1983-85; literacy tutor Cin. LEARN, 1985-89; recorder feminist lit. Womyn's Braille Press, Mpls., 1985-89; wellness program asst. Times Pub. Co., St. Petersburg, Fla., 1989-96, Taoist Tai Chi Soc., 1995—; dir. Wittenberg U., Springfield, Ohio, 1988—; bd. dirs. Crazy Ladies Ctr. Inc., Cin., 1989-93; coord. Fla. west coast Old Lesbians Organizing for Change, 1993-95; sec., trustee Clio Found., Inc., 1995—; docent Fla. Internat. Mus., 1994—. Compiler: (reference source) Greater Cincinnati Business Index, 1975-79; editor: New Reference Materials, 1983, 84. Mem. Tampa Bay YWCA Women's Guild, St. Petersburg, 1991-95; vol. NOW Elect Women Campaign, St. Petersburg, 1990-92, Senator Helen G. Davis Reelection, St. Petersburg, 1992. Mem. ALA, Spl. Librs. Assn. (treas., archivist 1974-83), Am. Assn. Individual Investors, Laubach Literary Action, Taoist Tai Chi Soc., Beta Phi Mu Libr. Sci. Hon., Phi Delta Gamma Grad. Women Hon. Address: PO Box 7472 Saint Petersburg FL 33734-7472

SCHELLHAAS, LINDA JEAN, toxicologist, consultant; b. South Haven, Mich., Apr. 27, 1956; d. Richard Louis and Virgene Frieda (Lietzke) Plankenhorn; m. Robert Wesley Schellhaas, May 27, 1990. BA in Biology, Albion Coll., 1978. Pathology rsch. asst. Internat. R&D Corp., Mattawan, Mich., 1978-80; toxicology rsch. coord. Borriston Labs., Inc., Temple Hills, Md., 1980-84; quality assurance coord. Tegeris Labs., Inc., Temple Hills, Md., 1984-85; good lab. practice compliance specialist, staff scientist Dynamac Corp., Rockville, Md., 1985-90; dir. quality assurance Pathology Assocs., Inc., Frederick, Md., 1992-94; pres., regulatory compliance specialist Quality Reviews, Inc., Falling Waters, W.Va., 1990—; instr. regulatory compliance tng. seminars, 1990—. Contbr. articles to profl. jours. Mem. Soc. Quality Assurance, Albion Coll. Fellows, Pi Beta Phi, Phi Beta Kappa. Office: Quality Reviews Inc 1204 Berkeley Dr Falling Waters WV 25419-0755

SCHELLHAAS, ROBERT WESLEY, songwriter, musician; b. Pitts., Feb. 27, 1952; s. Albert Wesley and Florence Elizabeth (Smiley) S.; children: Matthew L., Abigail K., David A.; m. Linda Jean Plankenhorn, May 27, 1990. BA, Thiel Coll., 1974; MDiv, Gordon-Conwell Theol. Sem., 1977; PhD, Calif. Grad. Sch. Theology, Glendale, 1986. Ordained minister Congl. Ch., 1978. Pastor Congl. chs., Everett, Peabody, Mass., 1976-80; chaplain U.S. Army, 1980-88; owner/founder Schellware, Everett, Mass., 1977-89; v.p., founder Quality RVWS, Inc., Falling Waters, 1989—; also bd. dirs. Quality Reviews, Inc., Falling Waters; staff scientist Dynamac Corp., 1989-90; dir. Creative Alternatives Recording, Pub., 1992—; career cons. Author: Toyosaurus Wrex, 1986, Intimacy: Theological and Behavioral Implications, 1986, Personality Preference Inventory (P.P.I.), 1988, Led Zeppelin: My Night as the Right Fifth Member, 1996; ad editor/author: AIDS Ministry in Perspective, 1988, Army monthly newsletters, 1980-85, various pub. articles; composer more than 200 songs; musician with 4 recordings. V.p. Ft. Stewart (Ga.) Sch. Bd., 1980-82; profl. counselor AIDS Ministry; Cub Scout leader Boy Scouts Am., 1981-85; missions dir. Children's Sand and Surf Missions, 1976-79; founder Bette Smiley Endowed Scholar Fund, Laroche Coll., Pitts., 1995. Maj. USAR, 1988—. Recipient Mayor's award in Photography, Everett, 1976. Mem. DAV, SAR, Internat. Found. Gender Edn., Assn. Clin. Pastoral Counseling, Am. Philatelic Soc. Office: Quality Reviews Inc 1204 Berkeley Dr Falling Waters WV 25419-9657

SCHELSKE, CLAIRE L., limnologist, educator; b. Fayetteville, Ark., Apr. 1, 1932; s. Theodore J. and Ida S. S.; m. Betty Breukelman, June 2, 1957; children—Cynthia, John, Steven. A.B., Kans. State Tchrs. Coll., Emporia, 1955, M.S., 1956; Ph.D., U. Mich., 1961. Tchg. and rsch. asst. dept. biology Kans. State Tchrs. Coll., 1952-55, vis. instr., summer 1960; teaching fellow dept. zoology U. Mich., 1955-57; asst. prof. radiol. health dept. environ. health U. Mich. (Sch. Public Health); asst. research limnologist Gt. Lakes Research Div., Inst. Sci. and Tech., 1967-68, assoc. rsch. limnologist, 1969-71, rsch. limnologist, 1971-87; asst. dir. Gt. Lakes Research Div., Inst. Sci. and Tech. (Gt. Lakes Research Div.), 1970-72, acting dir., 1973-76, assoc. prof. limnology, dept. atmospheric and oceanic sci., 1976-87; assoc. prof. natural resources Sch. Natural Resources, 1976-86, prof., 1986-87; Carl S. Swisher prof. water resources U. Fla., Gainesville, 1987—; research fellow Inst. Fisheries Research, Mich. Dept. Conservation, 1957-60; research assoc. U. Ga. Marine Inst., 1960-62; fishery biologist, supervisory fishery biologist, chief Estuarine Ecology Program, Bur. Comml. Fisheries, Radiobiol. Lab., Beaufort, N.C., 1962-66; adj. asst. prof. dept. zoology N.C. State U., Raleigh, 1964-66; tech. asst. Office Sci. and Tech., Exec. Office of Pres., Washington, 1966-67; cons. Ill. Atty. Gen., 1977-79. Author: (with J.C. Roth) Limnological Survey of Lakes Michigan, Superior, Huron and Erie, 1973. Recipient Disting. Alumnus award Emporia State U. (formerly Kans. State Tchrs. Coll.), 1989. Fellow AAAS, Am. Inst. Fishery Rsch. Biologists (regional and dist. dir. South-Cen. Gt. Lakes chpt. 1977-80); mem. Am. Soc. Limnology and Oceanography (sec. 1976-85, v.p. 1987-88, pres. 1988-90), Ecol. Soc. Am. (assoc. editor 1972-75), Internat. Assn. Gt. Lakes Rsch. (editl. bd. 1970-73, chmn. 20th Conf. 1977, assoc. editor 1984-93), Soc. Internat. Limnology. Home: 2738 SW 9th Dr Gainesville FL 32601-9003 Office: U Fla Dept Fisheries and Aquatic Scis 7922 NW 71st St Gainesville FL 32653-3071

SCHENK, JOSEPH BERNARD, museum director; b. Glendale, Ariz., Mar. 28, 1953; m. Jacqueline Van Lienop; children: Brian, Stuart. BA in Mus. Staff Preparation, Huntingdon Coll., 1974; MA in Art Edn., Ball State U., 1979; postgrad., U. Calif., Berkeley, 1986. Exhibits asst. Hunter Mus. of Art, Chattanooga, 1974-75; asst. dir. Alford House/Anderson Fine Arts Ctr., Anderson, Ind., 1976, exec. dir., 1976-79; exec. dir. Okefenokee Heritage Ctr., Waycross, Ga., 1979-83; dir. So. Forest World, Waycross, 1979-83, Chattahoochee Valley Art Mus., LaGrange, Ga., 1983-88, Mobile (Ala.) Mus. of Art, 1988—; bd. dirs. U.S. Sports Acad. Art Mus.; v.p. Ala. Mus. Assn., 1994-96, pres., 1996—; adv. panelist Visual Arts Fellowships, Ala. State Coun. on the Arts, 1994-95, Profl. Touring Panel Ga. Coun. for Arts, 1983-84, PRACSO Panel Ga. Coun. for Arts, 1984-86, Arch. & Environ. Arts Ind. Arts Commn., 1978-79, Mus. Ind. Arts Commn., 1977-79; Ind. rep. Small Mus. Com. Midwest Mus. Conf., 1978-79. Pub. numerous art catalogs; editor newsletter Ga. Assembly of Community Arts Agys., 1987-88. Art juror at numerous pub. and pvt. art shows; bd. dirs. Ga. Alliance for Arts Edn., 1982-84, Assn. Ind. Mus., 1979, Mobile Arts Coun., 1989-90, Ga. Assembly Community Arts Agys., 1986-88; commr. Madison County Hist. Home, Anderson, 1977-79; mem. dedication com., cons. Krannert Fine Arts Ctr., Anderson Coll., 1979; mem. com. forest festival tourism and conventions Waycross/Ware County C. of C., 1979-83; bd. dirs. Southeastern Ga. Travel and Tourism Assn., 1981-83, sec., 1981-82, pres., 1982-83.

Grantee Nat. Endowment for Arts, Ala. State Coun. on Arts, Mobile Arts Coun., Ga. Endowment for Humanities, Ga. Coun. Arts, Ala. Arts Found., Inst. Mus. Svcs., Ga. Gov.'s Intern Program, others; recipient Spark Plug of Yr. award Waycross Jaycees, 1981; Mus. Mgmt. Inst. scholar, 1986. Mem. Am. Assn. Mus., Southeastern Mus. Conf., Ala. Mus. Assn. (v.p. 1994—), Rotary, Mobile United. Home: 6401 Sugar Creek Dr S Mobile AL 36695 Office: Mobile Museum of Art PO Box 8426 4850 Museum Dr Mobile AL 36689

SCHEPER, GEORGE H., nursing administrator; b. King City, Calif., June 20, 1937; d. George H. Sr. and Sally T. (Rassmussen) S.; m. Caroline H. Scheper, May 30, 1980. ADN, North Idaho Coll., 1978. Entered USAF, 1955, advanced through grades to master sgt., 1971, ret., 1975; charge nurse Coeur d'Alene (Idaho) Convalescent Ctr., 1978-79, Queen Anne Villa Care Ctr., Seattle, Wash., 1979-84; dir. nurses Queen Anne Villa Care Ctr., Seattle, 1984-86; hospice nurse, home health nurse Hospice of the Ozarks, Mountain Home, Ark., 1986-88; DON Fulton County Nursing Ctr., Salem, Ark., 1989-91, Retama Manor North, Corpus Christi, Tex., 1991-92; dir. rehab. program Heartland of Corpus Christi, Tex., 1992-93; dir. skilled unit Rehab. Hosp. South Tex., Corpus Christi, 1993-95; mgr. rehab. program Theratx Alameda Oaks Nursing Ctr., Corpus Christi, 1995-96; nursing supr. Harbor View Care Ctr, Corpus Christi, 1996; quality assurance coord. Ideal Healthcare Svcs., Corpus Christi, 1996—. Mem. Air Force Sgts. Assn., Order of Alhambra, Lions. Home: 4630 Coody Ln Corpus Christi TX 78413-2122

SCHERCH, RICHARD OTTO, minister, consultant; b. Balt., Nov. 21, 1926; s. Richard Leopold and Anna Elizabeth (Finger) S.; m. Janice Marie Halbgewachs, June 24, 1951; children: Richard Paul, Leslie Carol, Lisa Beth, Jeremy Thomas. BA, Gettysburg Coll., 1948; BD, Luth. Sch. Theology, Phila., 1951; PhD, Johns Hopkins U., 1959; D Ministry, Lancaster Theol. Sem., 1975; cert. in dispute resolution recognition, Capital U., 1993. Ordained to ministry Luth. Ch., 1951. Mission developer Wichita, Kans., 1951-53; pastor Trinity Luth. Ch., Manhattan beach, Calif., 1953-57; asst. pastor 1st Luth. Ch., Balt., 1957-59; pastor St. Mark's Luth. Ch., Birdsboro, Pa., 1961-65, Zion Luth. Ch., Lebanon, Pa., 1965-71, Shiloh Luth. Ch., York, Pa., 1972-75, Christ Luth. Ch., Paramus, N.J., 1976-81; sr. pastor Emmanuel Luth. Ch., Venice, Fla., 1981-93; owner Bldg. Bridges Consultation Svcs., Sarasota, Fla., 1993—; mission developer Kansas City, Mo., 1959-61; lectr. Chautauqua (N.Y.) Inst., 1963, 64, 65; instr. Johns Hopkins U., Balt., 1957-58, U. Balt., 1958-59; dir. Consult, Inc., Lebanon, Pa.; adj. faculty mem. Luther Coll., Teaneck, N.J., 1977-78, Bergen C.C., Paramus, 1979; chmn. profl. support com. Fla. Synod Luth. Ch. Am., Tampa, Fla., 1982-87, ptnr. in evangelism, Chgo., 1985-91; cons. Fla.-Bahamas Synod, 1993—. Comdr. USNR, 1956-77. Mem. Internat. Transactional Analysis Assn., Venice C. of C., Rotary. Republican.

SCHERF, JOHN GEORGE, IV, lawyer; b. Tuscaloosa, Ala., Oct. 12, 1962; s. John G. III and Roberta Cannon (Timmons) S.; m. Lorie Lankford, Feb. 12, 1994; 1 child, Austin Tyler. AA, Okaloosa Walton Jr. Coll., Niceville, Fla., 1983; BA in Psychology, U. West Fla., 1987; JD, Samford U., 1991. Bar: Ala. 1992, U.S. Dist. Ct. (no. dist.) Ala., 1994. Clk., assoc. Taylor & Robinson, Birmingham, Ala., 1992-93; assoc. Frank S. Buck, P.C., Birmingham, Ala., 1993-95; pvt. practice Birmingham, Ala., 1995—. Mem. Assn. Trial Lawyers Am., Ala. Bar Assn., Ala. Trial Lawyers Assn., Birmingham Bar Assn. Democrat. Methodist. Home: 611 Springs Ave Birmingham AL 35242 Office: Scherf Griffin & Davis LLC 2122 1st Ave N Birmingham AL 35203-4202

SCHERF, ROSALYN FELLER, nurse, writer; b. Phila., Dec. 2, 1946; d. Peter Lawrence and Lillian Ruth (Crandell) Feller; m. Brian Cameron Scherf, Sept. 11, 1982. RN, Thomas Jefferson Med. Coll., Pa., 1968. Lic. Fla., Washington, Pa. Staff nurse, asst. head nurse, head nurse St. Christopher's Hosp. for Children, Phila., 1968-71; charge nurse Variety Children's Hosp., Miami, Fla., 1971-72; staff nurse, relief charge nurse Rochester (N.Y.) Gen. Hosp., 1972-74; staff nurse, relief charge nurse, clin. nurse III Jackson Meml. Hosp., Miami, Fla., 1974-90, rsch. nurse NBSC Ctr., 1980-84; staff nurse, part-time neonatal rsch. nurse Jackson Meml. Hosps., Children's Orthopaedic Hosp., Seattle, 1984-85; part-time neonatal rsch. U. Wash., Seattle, 1985; high frequency ventilation study, 1986; asst. head nurse North Shore Med. Ctr., 1987-88; staff nurse, clinic nurse for neonatal devel. flu, 1987-92, educator, parent/infant case mgr., 1992-95; BLS instr., parent and staff educatgor North Shore Med. Ctr., 1995—; nurse developmental FIU program North Shore Med Ctr., Miami, Fla., 1991-93, nurse educator, 1993-95; per diem home infusion nurse Quantum/Health Resources, 1995—; speaker Tiny Baby Conf., Orlando, Fla., 1985, Nursing Symposium, 1985, Dynamics of Optimal Critical Care Nursing Conf., 1986; lectr. U. Hosp., 1986; coord. First Luth. Ch. Cmty. Health Fair, 1992; co-leader CFIDS Support Group, Broward County, Fla., 1988-94. Author, co-author: (2 book chpts.) BPD-Strategies for Total Patient Care, 1990; author: (poem) Kevin, 1990, (book) Anthony, 1993; co-author multiple rsch. papers from Jackson Meml. Hosp.; author/co-author numerous articles in field. Mem. fund raising com. Broward Wildlife Care Ctr., Broward, Ft. Lauderdale, Fla., 1989. Recipient Bausch and Lomb Sci. award Dobbins H.S., Phila., 1964; named valedictorian Murrell Dobbins Tech. H.S., Phila., 1964. Mem. Fla. Trails Assn., Broward Wildlife Care Ctr., Sierra Club, Friends of Everglades, New Horizons. Democrat. Lutheran. Home: 1060 Tyler St Hollywood FL 33019-1304 Office: North Shore Med Ctr 1100 NW 95th St Fl 3 Miami FL 33150-2038

SCHESSLER, THOMAS GERARD, JR., neonatal intensive care nurse; b. Naples, Fla., Apr. 15, 1960; s. Thomas Gerard Sr. and Edith Ann (Gibbs) S.; m. Gail Marie Schessler, Aug. 13, 1984; children: Trey, Trevor, Tyler. ADN, Polk Community Coll., 1982. RN, Fla.; cert. NALS instr., prepared childbirth instr., breast feeding instr., Registered Nurse Cert., high risk neonatal. House nursing asst. Lakeland (Fla.) Regional Med. Ctr., staff nurse ortho./neuro surg. unit, staff nurse neonatal ICU; charge nurse level III nurse Neonatal Intensive Care Unit Columbia Brandon Regional Med. Ctr.; adj. faculty Polk C.C. Founder, pres. St. Anthony's Cath. Home and Sch. Assn. With USN, 1978-80. Mem. Nat. Assn. Neonatal Nurses, Mid-Fla. Assn. Neonatal Nurses (co-founder, pres.-elect 1988-90, pres. 1990-92). Home: 5605 La Serena Ave Lakeland FL 33809-4261

SCHEUERLE, ANGELA ELIZABETH, pediatrician; b. Syracuse, N.Y., Aug. 13, 1962; d. William Howard and Jane Frances (Walker) S. BS in Biology magna cum laude, U. of the South, 1984; MD, U. South Fla., 1988. Resident in pediatrics Children's Hosp. Med. Ctr., Cin., 1988-91; fellow Inst. for Molecular and Human Genetics Baylor Coll. Medicine, Houston, 1991-95; asst. prof. pediatrics, divsn. med. genetics U. Tex. Med. Sch., Houston, 1995—. Vol. Tampa (Fla.) Big Bros./Big Sisters, 1978-82. Mem. AMA, Am. Soc. Human Genetics, Am. Pediatric Assn., Phi Beta Kappa, Sigma Xi, Alpha Epsilon Delta. Democrat. Office: UTHSC-Houston Dept Pediats Divsn Med Genetics 6431 Fannin MSB 3.144 Houston TX 77030

SCHEWEL, ROSEL HOFFBERGER, education educator; b. Balt., Mar. 1, 1928; d. Samuel Herman and Gertrude (Miller) Hoffberger; m. Elliot Sidney Schewel, June 12, 1949; children: Stephen, Michael, Susan. AB, Hood Coll., 1949; MEd, Lynchburg Coll., 1974; EdS, 1982. Reading resource tchr. Lynchburg Pub. Schs., Va., 1967-75; adj. prof. edn. Lynchburg Coll., 1973-79; cons., seminar leader Woman's Resource Ctr., Lynchburg, 1980-92; assoc. prof. edn. Lynchburg Coll., 1980-92. Trustee, vice chair bd. trustees Lynchburg Coll., Va., 1992—; bd. dirs. Va. Found. for Humanities and Pub. Policy, 1985-90, New Vistas Sch., Lynchburg Human Rights Commn., 1992—, Lynchburg Youth Svcs., 1993—; bd. dirs. Venture Enterprising Women, Planned Parenthood of the Blue Ridge; trustee Va. Mus. of Fine Arts, 1985-90; apptd. Commn. on Edn. for All Virginians, 1990; bd. dirs. Action Alliance for Virginia's Children and Youth, 1995—; bd. trustees Amazement Sq. Children's Mus., 1996—. Recipient Disting. Svc. award NCCJ, 1973, Outstanding Woman in Edn. award YWCA, 1988, Disting. Alumni award Lynchburg Coll., 1993. Democrat. Jewish. Address: 4316 Gorman Dr Lynchburg VA 24503-1948

SCHICHLER, ROBERT LAWRENCE, English language educator; b. Rochester, N.Y., May 16, 1951; s. Alfred James and Elizabeth Johanna (Flugel) S. BA in English, SUNY, Geneseo, 1974, MA in English, 1978; PhD of English, Binghamton U., 1987. Writer, asst. administr. Artists-in-Residence Program, Rochester, N.Y., 1978-79; substitute tchr. City Sch. Dist., Rochester, 1980-82; instr. English Talmudical Inst. Upstate N.Y., Rochester, 1981-82, Binghamton (N.Y.) U., 1983-84; rsch. asst. Medieval and Renaissance Texts and Studies, Binghamton, 1985-86; adj. asst. prof. Rochester Inst. Tech., 1987-89; assoc. prof. English Ark. State U., State University, 1989—; adj. asst. prof. Monroe C.C., Rochester, 1987-89. Author: King of the Once Wild Frontier: Reflections of a Canal Walker, 1993; editor: Lady in Waiting: Poems in English and Spanish, 1994, Abstracts of Papers in Anglo-Saxon Studies, 1988—, Ctr. for Medieval and Early Renaissance Studies, Binghamton, 1986-94, Spillway Publs., Rochester, 1992—; asst. editor: Old English Newsletter, 1986-87, Mediaevalia, Binghamton, 1988-89; contbr. articles to profl. jours. Active Pres's. Nat. Steering Com., 1995—. Mem. Internat. Soc. Anglo-Saxonists, Internat. Ctr. Medieval Art, Medieval Acad. Am., Modern Lang. Assn. Am., South Cen. Modern Lang. Assn., Ark. Philol. Assn. Home: 726 Southwest Dr Apt K-2 Jonesboro AR 72401-7074 Office: Dept English and Philosophy Ark State U State University AR 72467-1890

SCHIEFFELIN, GEORGE RICHARD, educational consultant; b. N.Y.C., July 3, 1930; s. George McKay and Louise (Winterbotham) S. B.A., Hobart Coll., 1953. Ednl. cons. Denver, 1956-62, New Haven, 1962-89, Tampa, Fla., 1989—; dir. Charles Scribner's Sons, N.Y.C., Scribner Book Stores, N.Y.C., Pubs. Realty Co., N.Y.C., 1962-83, Macro Communications, N.Y.C., 1975-83; asst. to lt. gov. of Colo., 1958-59. Trustee Hobart and William Smith Colls., 1969-78, Rocky Mountain Coll., 1989-93, adv. com. Rocky Mountain Coll., 1993—. With AUS, 1953-55. Mem. Morristown Field Club, Univ. Club (Denver), Princeton Club (N.Y.C.), Williams Club.

SCHIEKEN, RICHARD MERRILL, physician; b. Phila., May 6, 1939; s. Benjamin B. and Edythe (Lesser) S.; m. Barbara Lynn Newman, Aug. 23, 1964; children: Julia, William, Shira. AB, LaSalle U., 1961; MD, U. Pa., 1965. Diplomate Am. Bd. Pediatricts. Intern, then resident in pediatrics Children's Hosp. of Pa., Phila., 1965-68, fellow in pediatric cardiology, 1968-70; asst. instr. pediatrics U. Pa., Phila., 1966-67; clin. asst. prof. Sch. Medicine Georgetown U., Washington, 1971-73; with U. Iowa, Iowa City, 1973-82, prof. pediatrics Sch. Medicine, 1980-82, prof. preventive medicine Sch. Medicine, 1981-82; prof., chmn. pediatric cardiology dept. Med. Coll. of Va., Richmond, 1982—; mem. exec. com. Nat. Cholesterol Edn. Program, Bethesda, 1986-96. Contbr. articles to profl. jours. Chmn. epidemiology disease control study sect. NIH, Bethesda, Md. Maj. U.S. Army, 1970-73. Fellow Am. Coll. Cardiology (chmn. preventive cardiovascular disease com. 1984-86), Am. Acad. Pediatrics, Am. Heart Assn. (epidemiology coun.); mem. Nat. Acad. Sci. (diet and health coms. 1986-88). Jewish. Home: 422 September Dr Richmond VA 23229-7318

SCHIFFERS, PEGGY ESPY, management consultant; b. Harrisburg, Pa., Jan. 13, 1943; d. George Jr. and Mary Louise (D'Oliér) Shuman; m. Richard C. Espy, June 13, 1964 (div. Sept. 1974); 1 child, Leigh; m. Edmond A. Schiffers, Jan. 6, 1990; children: Angie, Amy, Pete, Ann, Steve. BA, Wilson Coll., 1964; MEd, Shippensburg State Coll., 1966. Tchr. Carlisle (Pa.) Pub. Schs., 1964-66, Fairfax County Schs., Springfield, Va., 1967-68, Birchwood Sch., Arlington, Va., 1971-74; passport examiner U.S. Dept. of State, Washington, 1974-75; personnel specialist FTC, Washington, 1975-79; prin., cons. Towers Perrin, Washington, 1980-90; v.p. Gannotta, Bray & Assocs., Washington, 1990-91; pres. Schiffers Assocs., Jacksonville, Fla., 1991—. Bd. dirs. PACE Ctr. for Girls, Jacksonville, 1995—; pres. bd. dirs. Fairlington Glen, Arlington, 1979-80. Mem. Soc. Human Resource Mgmt. (cert., nat. com. mem. 1991—), Inst. Mgmt. Cons. (cert.), Am. Compensation Assn., Am. Soc. Assn. Execs. Home and Office: Schiffers Assocs 4401 San Jose Ln Jacksonville FL 32207

SCHIFLETT, MARY FLETCHER CAVENDER, health facility executive, researcher, educator; b. El Paso, Tex., Sept. 23, 1925; d. John F. and Mary M. (Humphries) Cavender; 1 son, Joseph Raymond. BA in Econs. with honors, So. Meth. U., 1946, BS in Journalism with honors, 1947; MA in English, U. Houston, 1971. Writer, historian Office Price Adminstrn., Dallas, 1946-47; asst. editor C. of C. Publs., Dallas, 1947-48; bus. writer Houston Oil, 1948-49; market analyst Cravens-Dargan, Ins., Houston, 1949-52; bus. writer Bus. Week and McGraw-Hill Pub. Co., Houston, 1952-56; freelance writer in bus. econs., banking and ins., 1956-68; spl. projects coord. Ctr. for Human Resources, Houston, 1969-73; dir. publs. Energy Inst., U. Houston, 1974-78; sr. rsch. assoc. Inst. Labor and Indsl. Rels., 1973-80, mem. adj. faculty Coll. Architecture, 1976-85, dir. Ctr. for Health Mgmt., Coll. Bus. Adminstrn., 1980-83; assoc. dir. rsch. and planning Tex. Med. Ctr., Inc., Houston, 1984; dir. spl. projects and pub. affairs Tex. Med. Ctr., 1985-92, asst. v.p., 1993-95, assoc. v.p., 1995—. Bd. dirs. Third Ward Redevelopment Coun., 1993—, Houston Acad. Motion Pictures, 1986-90, Houston World Trade Assn., 1988-91, Friends Hermann Pk., 1995—, mem. exec. com., 1996—. Pres., Houston Ct. Humanities, 1978-80; project dir. Houston Meets Its Authors I-IV, 1980-84; pub. program dir. Houston: Internat. City, 1980-83. Named One of Houston's Women of Yr. YMCA, 1988. Mem. Internat. Coun. Indsl. Editors, World Future Soc., Tex. Folklore Soc., Friends of Libr., Houston C. of C. (future studies com. 1975-84, small bus. coun. 1981-83), Nat. Assn. Bus. Economists, AIA (profl. affiliate), Mortar Bd., Theta Sigma Phi, Alpha Theta Phi, Delta Delta Delta. Methodist. Club: Downtown (pres. 1987-89), River Oaks Rotary (bd. dirs. 1996—, Paul Harris fellow 1996). Lodge: Rotary. Author: (with others) Dynamics of Growth, 1977, Applied Systems and Cybernetics, 1981, The Ethnic Groups of Houston, 1984, Names and Nicknames of Places and Things, 1986. Office: Tex Med Ctr 406 Jesse H Jones Libr Bldg Houston TX 77030

SCHILLER, LAWRENCE RUDOLPH, academic administrator; b. Phila., Mar. 25, 1951; s. Albert Harris and Laura (Weiser) S.; m. Ann Lynn Kleiman, Jan. 11, 1975; children: Rachel, David. BS with highest distinction, Pa. State U., 1968; MD cum laude, Thomas Jefferson U., 1972. Diplomate Nat. Bd. Med. Examiners, Am. Bd. Internal Medicine, Am. Bd. Gastroenterology. Intern dept. internal medicine Temple U. Hosp., 1972-73, resident in internal medicine, 1973-75, chief resident internal medicine, 1975-76; rsch. fellow in gastroenterology U. Tex. Health Sci. Ctr. at Dallas, 1978-80, asst. prof. dept. internal medicine, 1980-85, clin. asst. prof. dept. internal medicine, 1985-92, clin. assoc. prof. dept. internal medicine, 1992—; dir. gastrointestinal physiology lab. Baylor U. Med. Ctr., Dallas, 1985-96, assoc. dir. gastrointestinal rsch. dept. internal medicine, 1985-96; investigator Ctr. for Ulcer Rsch. and Edn., L.A., 1982—; clin. instr. in medicine Temple U. Health Scis. Ctr., Sch. Medicine, Phila., 1975-76; clin. asst. dept. internal medicine The Germantown Dispensary and Hosp., Phila., 1975-76. Author: (with others) Medical Emergency Manual: Differential Diagnosis and Treatment, 1976, Motor Function of the Stomach, 1983, Medical Therapy of Peptic Ulcer Disease, 1981, Textbook of Medicine, 1985, Cecil Textbook of Medicine, 1989, Gastrointestinal Disease: Pathophysiology, Diagnosis, Management, 1994, Principles and Practice of Endocrinology and Metabolism, 1990, Diarrheal Diseases, 1991, others; contbr. articles to profl. jours. Maj. U.S. Army, 1976-78. Recipient Henry Keller Mohler Meml. prize for therapeutics, 1972. Fellow ACP, Am. Coll. Gastroenterology; mem. Jefferson Med. Coll. Alumni Assn. (life), Am. Fedn. for Clin. Rsch., Am. Gastroenterol. Assn., Hobart Amory Hare Honor Med. Soc. (treas. 1971-72), Phi Eta Sigma, Phi Delta Epsilon, Alpha Omega Alpha. Home: 7701 Mullrany Dr Dallas TX 75248-1716 Office: Gastroenterol Divsn Baylor Univ Med Ctr 3500 Gaston Ave Dallas TX 75246-2045

SCHILLING, WILLIAM RICHARD, aerospace engineer, research and development company executive; b. Manheim, Pa., Jan. 12, 1933; s. William Thomas and Ora Lee (Worley) S.; m. Patricia Elise Brigman, June 8, 1957; 1 child, Duane Thomas. BCE, Va. Poly. Inst., 1956; MS in Structural Engring., Pa. State U., 1959; MS in Aero. Engring., U. So. Calif., 1961, Engrs. Degree in Aerospace Engring., 1966. Aerodynamist Douglas Aircraft Co., Santa Monica, Calif., 1956-64; study chmn. Research Analysis Corp., McLean, Va., 1964-72; div. mgr. Sci. Applications, Inc., McLean, 1972-78; pres., chief exec. officer McLean Rsch. Ctr., Inc., 1978-89; exec. v.p. Wackenhut Applied Techs. Ctr., Fairfax, Va., 1989-91; dir. bus. devel., dir. sys. rsch. divsn., bd. dirs. Internat. Devel. and Resources, Inc., Falls Church, Va., 1991—; pres. Systems Rsch. Corp., Falls Church, 1991—; pres., bd. dirs. LaMancha Co., Santa Fe, 1985-89. Contbr. numerous articles to profl. jours. Chmn. com. Boy Scouts Am., McLean, 1968-78; vol. Am. Heart Assn., McLean, 1984-89; bd. dirs., chief exec. officer Internat. Housing Devel., McLean, 1986—. Mem. Assn. U.S. Army, Am. Def. Preparedness, Va. C. of C. Baptist. Home: 6523 Old Dominion Dr Mc Lean VA 22101-4613 Office: Internat Devel & Resources Mosby Bldg Ste 515 10560 Main St Ste 515 Fairfax VA 22030-4900

SCHIMBERG, HENRY AARON, soft drink company executive; b. Chgo., Mar. 3, 1933; s. Arnold and Judith (Aaron) S.; m. Linda Waxberg, June 21, 1975; children: Aaron David, Alexis Leigh. BA, Beloit Coll., 1954. Exec. v.p. Nehi Royal Crown Corp., Chgo., 1970-76; pres. Royal Crown Bottling Co., Los Angeles, 1976-79; pres. bottling ops. Royal Crown Cola Co., Rolling Meadows, Ill., 1979-82; pres., CEO, bd. dirs. Coca-Cola Bottling Midwest, Mpls., 1982-91, Cen. States Coca-Cola Bottling Co., Springfield, Ill., 1985-91, Coca-Cola Bottling Co. of St. Louis, 1986-91, Cin. Coca-Cola Bottling Co., 1986-91, Mid-States Coca-Cola Bottling Co., Paducah, Ky., 1986-91; pres., COO, bd. dirs. Johnston Coca-Cola Bottling Group, Chattanooga, Tenn., 1986-91, Coca-Cola Enterprises Inc., Atlanta, 1991—, Pacific Coca-Cola Bottling Co., Bellevue, Wash., 1992—, Austin Coca-Cola Bottling Co., Dallas; bd. dirs. Johnston So. Co., Chattanooga. Cpl. U.S. Army, 1954-56. Mem. Minn. Soft Drink Assn. (bd. dirs. 1983—), Wis. Soft Drink Assn., Ill. Soft Drink Assn. (pres. 1974-76), Nat. Soft Drink Assn. (exec. bd. 1986—, chmn. 1994—), Coca-Cola Bottlers Assn. (bd. govs. 1986—). Jewish. Office: Coca-Cola Enterprises Inc 2500 Windy Ridge Pkwy Atlanta GA 30339

SCHINDLER, CHARLES ALVIN, microbiologist, educator; b. Boston, Dec. 27, 1924; s. Edward Esau and Esther Marian (Weisman) S.; m. Barbara Jean Francois, Jan. 14, 1955; children: Marian Giffin, Susan, Neal. BS in Biology, Rensselaer Poly. Inst., 1950; MS, U. Tex., 1956, PhD, 1961. Commd. officer USAF, 1951, advanced through grades to maj., 1965; asst. dir. for biology and medicine at atomic weapons tests Armed Forces Spl. Weapons Project, Camp Mercury, Nev., 1953; rsch. scientist USAF, 1954-68; tchr. Norman (Okla.) Pub. Schs., 1968-86; asst. prof. U. Okla., Flagler Coll., 1968-86; cons., sci. supr. Oklahoma City (Okla.) Sch. Dist., 1989-93; cons. Mead Johnson Rsch. Ctr., Evansville, Ind., 1962-72. Contbr. articles to profl. jours. Coun. mem. Norman (Okla.) City Coun., 1967-81, 83-85. Fellow Charles E. Lewis Fellowship Com., Austin, Tex., 1958; rsch. grantee NSF, Norman, 1972. Mem. Soc. Gen. Microbiology, Sigma Xi. Home: 2000 Morgan Dr Norman OK 73069

SCHINE, JEROME ADRIAN, retired accountant; b. Albany, Ga., Nov. 7, 1926; s. Nathan Benjamin and Celia (Hurwitz) S.; m. Marjorie Elizabeth Clark, July 11, 1955; 1 child, Michael Howard. Diploma, North Ga. Jr. Coll., Dahlonega, 1945; BSBA, U. Fla., 1949. CPA, Fla. Staff acct. M.A. Montenegro & Co., Tampa, Fla., 1949-52, ptnr., 1952-70; ptnr. Arthur Young, Tampa, 1970-87; cons., Tampa, 1987—; mem. Fla. Bd. Accountancy, 1982-89, chmn., 1984; pres. Nat. Assn. State Bds. Accountancy, 1989-90. Pres. Tampa Mus. of Art, 1985; v.p. Children's Ctr. Cancer and Dread Disease, Tampa, 1986-87; treas. Hillsborough County Charter Commn., Tampa, 1980; mem. Hillsborough County Local Govt. Commn., 1965. Cpl. U.S. Army Air Corps, 1945-47. Recipient Disting. Alumnus award Fisher Sch. Acctg., U. Fla., 1990. Mem. AICPA (mem. coun. 1973-80), Fla. Inst. CPAs (pres. 1973-74), Temple Terrace Golf and Country Club (pres. 1973). Republican. Jewish. Home: 444 Biltmore Ave Tampa FL 33617-7208

SCHLACHTER, DEBORAH BRISTOW, special education educator, consultant; b. Ajo, Ariz., Dec. 21, 1957; d. John Edward Jr. and Anne Elizabeth (Butler) Bristow; m. James Martin Schlachter Jr., July 25, 1981; children: James Martin, Katie Elizabeth, Joshua Timothy, Jacob Leslie, Jean Nicole. BE, Stephen F. Austin, 1981; MEd, U. N. Tex., 1991. Cert. tchr., Tex. Pvt. practice spl. needs tutor Dallas/Ft. Worth, 1981-91; pvt. practice family in home child care Lancaster, Tex., 1982-89; instr., coord. Cedar Valley Coll., Lancaster, 1989—; tchr. DeSoto (Tex.) Ind. Sch. Dist., 1990-91; kindergarten tchr. Dallas Ind. Sch. Dist., 1991-92, ESL tchr. 1st grade, 1992-93; 4-6th grade Montessori tchr. Dallas Pub. Sch., 1993-95; co-leader strategic planning Lancaster Ind. Sch. Dist., 1992-93. Co-editor: Resource Handbook for Educators on American Indians, 1993-94. Vol. tutor Women's Halfway House, Nacogdoches, Tex., 1980-81; trainer in spl. needs children PTA, Dallas-Ft. Worth, 1990—, active Dallas-Lancaster, 1984—; voting mem. Dallas Native Am. Parent Adv. Com., 1992-94; vol. Harry Stone Montesorri Acad. PTA, v.p., 1995-96, 96-97. Mem. ASCD, AAUW, Nat. Assn. Edn. Young Children, Nat. Indian Edn. Assn., Nat. Mus. Am. Indian, Am. Montessori Soc., So. Assn. Children Under Six, Dallas Assn. Edn. Young Children, Native Am. Rights Funds, Am. Indian Resource and Edn. Coalition. Episcopalian. Home: 532 Laurel St Lancaster TX 75134-3220

SCHLACKS, STEPHEN MARK, lawyer, educator; b. Pittsburg, Kans., Oct. 13, 1955. BA, Austin Coll., Sherman, Tex., 1978; MBA, U. Dallas, 1982; JD, Baylor U., 1986. Bar: Tex. 1987, U.S. Dist. Ct. (so. dist.) Tex. 1987, (no., ea. and we. dists.) Tex. 1988, U.S. Ct. Appeals (5th cir.) 1987, (8th cir.) 1989, U.S. Supreme Ct. 1990. In mgmt. Johnson & Johnson Products, Inc., Sherman, 1978-84; assoc. atty. Wetzel & Assocs., The Woodlands, Tex., 1986-92; ptnr. Hope, Causey & Schlacks, P.C., Conroe, Tex., 1992-96, Schlacks & Denman, The Woodlands, Tex., 1996—; adj. faculty North Harris County C.C., Houston, 1990-91. Leon Jaworski scholar, 1984, Harcourt Brace Jovanovich scholar, 1986. Mem. Fed. Bar Assn., Montgomery County Bar Assn., Tex. Assn. Def. Counsel, Sigma Iota Epsilon, Pi Gamma Mu. Republican. Presbyterian. Home: 5 Cat Feet Ct The Woodlands TX 77381-3043 Office: Schlacks & Denman Attys Ste 110 2202 Timberloch Pl The Woodlands TX 77380

SCHLEGEL, ROB ALLEN, utilities executive; b. El Paso, Tex., Aug. 30, 1949; m. Martha Dee Coker, July 27, 1974; children: Scott and Steven (twins), Michael. BS in Acctg., Abilene Christian U., 1974; MBA in Fin., U. North Tex., 1980. Sec., treas. Affiliated Mgrs. Inc., Amarillo, Tex., 1974-76; v.p., gen. mgr. Aspen Enterprises, Amarillo, Tex., 1976-77; regulatory acct. Tex. Power & Light Co., Dallas, 1977-79, adminstrv. asst. to treas., 1979-80, supr. fin. reports, 1980-82; asst. dist. mgr. Tex. Power & Light Co., Tyler, 1982-85; exec. asst. to v.p. ops. Tex. Electric Svc., Ft. Worth, 1985-86, customer ops. mgr., 1986; dist. mgr. T.U. Electric, Mesquite, 1986—; chmn. bd. Mesquite Econ. Devel. Found., 1996. Bd. dirs. Am. Heart Assn., Mesquite, 1990, Mesquite Symphony Assn., 1990, Mesquite Social Svcs., 1996—; youth soccer coach Mesquite Soccer Assn., 1986-90. Served with USN, Vietnam. Named one of Outstanding Young Men of Am., U.S. Jaycees, 1980, 84, Mesquite Citizen of Yr., 1991. Mem. Assn. MBA Execs., Mesquite C. of C. (bd. dirs., chmn. bd. 1990, Chmn.'s award for exceptional svc. 1987), Rotary (pres. Mesquite chpt. 1992-93). Republican. Home: 1316 Gonzales Dr Mesquite TX 75150-4290 Office: TU Electric 124 W Davis St Mesquite TX 75149-4625

SCHLEGELMILCH, REUBEN ORVILLE, electrical engineer, consultant; b. Green Bay, Wis., Mar. 8, 1916; s. Raymond Adolf and Emma J. (Schley) S.; m. Margaret Elizabeth Roberts, Aug. 22, 1943; children: Janet R., Raymond J., Joan C., Margaret Ann. BS in Elec. and Agrl. Engring., U. Wis., 1938; MS in Elec. and Agrl. Engring., Rutgers U., 1940; postgrad. in elec. engring., Cornell U., 1940-41, Poly. Inst. Bklyn., 1947-51, U. Ill., 1941-42; SM in Indsl. Mgmt., MIT, 1955; postgrad. in elec. engring., Syracuse U., 1956-59, Fed. Exec. Inst., 1982. Registered profl. engr., N.J. Dir. research and devel. Rome Air (Elec.) Devel. Ctr., N.Y., 1955-59; tech. dir. def./space, Westinghouse Elec., Corp. Hdqrs., Washington, 1959-63; mgr. adv. tech. and missiles Fed Systems IBM, Owego, N.Y., 1963-68; gen. mgr., pres. Schilling Industries, Galesville, Wis., 1968-71; mgr. systems design U.S. Army Adv. Systems Concepts Agy., Alexandria, Va., 1971-74; mgr. gun fire control systems, Naval Sea Systems Command, Washington, 1974-80; tech. dir. office research and devel. U.S. Coast Guard Hdqrs., Washington 1980-86; cons. in field, 1986—; govt. cons. electronics, Dept. Def. Research and Devel. Bd., 1949-54; indsl. cons. missile/space, Aerospace Industries Assn., 1959-63; chmn. profl. sci. com. Rome Air Devel. Ctr., 1956-59; mem. nat. com. Engring. Mgmt. Inst. Elec. Engring., N.Y.C., 1956-59. Patentee target position indicator; author tech. reports and articles. Vol. Annandale Christian Community for Action (Va.), 1973—; mem. Winterset Civic Assn., Annandale, 1971—. Alfred P. Sloan fellow MIT, 1954-55. Mem. IEEE (sr. life, sec., vice chmn., chmn. 1956-59, Recognition award 1959), Am. Def. Preparedness Assn. (chmn. So. Tier Empire Post 1967-68, recognition award 1968), NSPE, N.Y. Acad. Scis., Soc. Sloan Fellows MIT. Lodges: Masons, Rotary, Shriners. Home: 8415 Frost Way Annandale VA 22003-2222

SCHLEIFER, NANCY FAYE, lawyer, writer; b. Bellmore, N.Y., Jan. 14, 1950; d. Jerome and Freda (Marks) Beigel; m. Martin David Schleifer, May 9, 1969; 1 chil, Sunny Schleifer Drucker. BA, Fla. Internat. U., 1974; MA, U. Miami, 1976, JD, 1980. Bar: Fla. 1980. Atty. Sparber, Shevin, Sharp & Heilbronner, Miami, 1983-88; pvt. practice law Miami, 1988-89; staff atty. Guardian Ad Litem, Miami, 1988-89; adminstrv. atty. HRS, Dist. XI, Miami, 1990; staff atty. commn. for children Fla. Bar, Miami, 1990-91; dir. The Children's Law Project Nova U. Sch. Law, Ft. Lauderdale, Fla., 1991-93; sole practitioner Miami, 1993—. Author: Litigation Forms and Checklists, 1991; contbr. chpt. to book, articles to profl. jours. Co-dir., organizer Miami Children's Hosp. Cancer Camp, 1991—. Recipient Guardian Ad Litem award. Mem. Fla. Assn. Women's Lawyers (chmn. com. abused and neglected children 1989-90), Fla. Bar (juvenile rules com. 1993—), Dade County Bar (chmn. juvenile ct. com. 1988-89), Interagy. Task Force for Sexually Abused Children. Office: 1395 Coral Way Fl 2 Miami FL 33145-2946

SCHLESINGER, HARVEY ERWIN, judge; b. N.Y.C., June 4, 1940. BA, The Citadel, 1962; JD, U. Richmond, 1965. Bar: Va. 1965, Fla. 1965, U.S. Supreme Ct. 1968. Corp. counsel Seaboard Coast Line R.R. Co., Jacksonville, Fla., 1968-70; chief asst. U.S. atty. Middle Dist. Fla., Jacksonville, 1970-75, U.S. magistrate judge, 1975-91, U.S. Dist. judge, 1991—; adj. prof. U. N. Fla., 1984-91; mem. adv. com. on Fed. Rules of Criminal Procedure to U.S. Supreme Ct., 1986-93; chmn. U.S. Dist. Ct. Forms Task Force, Washington, 1983—. Served to capt. JAGC U.S. Army, 1965-68. Bd. dirs. Pine Castle Ctr. for Mentally Retarded, Jacksonville, 1970-87 , pres., 1972-74. chmn. bd. dirs., 1973-74, 76, trustee Pine Castle Found., 1972-76; trustee Congregation Ahavath Chesed, Jacksonville, 1970—, v.p., 1975-80, pres., 1980-82; v.p. S.E. council Union Am. Hebrew Congregations, 1984-88; asst. commissioner for exploring N. Fla. council Boy Scouts Am., 1983-86, exec. com., 1986—; mem. Boy Scouts Am. Nat. Jewish com. on Scouting, Irving, Tex., 1986-93, recipient Silver Beaver award Boy Scouts Am., 1986; trustee River Garden Home for Aged, 1982—, sec., 1985; co-chmn. bd. govs. Jacksonville chpt. NCCJ, 1983—, presiding co-chmn. 1984-89, nat. bd. trustees, N.Y.C., 1986-93. Recipient George Washington Medal Honor, Freedoms Found, Valley Forge, Pa, 1987, Silver Medallion Humanitarian award Nat. COnf. Christians and Jews, 1992. Mem. ABA (fed. rules of evidence and criminal procedure com. 1979—, Flascher award 1989), Va. Bar Assn., Fla. Bar Assn., Fed. Judges Assn., Nat. Council U.S. Magistrates (pres. 1987, v.p. 1985, pres. elect 1986, sec. 1983, treas. 1984), Jacksonville Bar Assn., Fed. Bar Assn. (pres. Jacksonville chpt. 1974, 75, 81-82), Am. Judicature Soc., Chester Bedell Am. Inns of Ct. (pres. 1992—. Lodge: Rotary (Paul Harris fellow, pres. S. Jacksonville club), Mason (past master, past venerable master, knights commander of Ct. Honour, Scottish rite bodies), Shriner. Office: 311 W Monroe St PO Box 1740 Jacksonville FL 32201

SCHLESINGER, WILLIAM H., biochemist, educator; b. Cleve., Apr. 30, 1950; s. William Lee and Cornelia (Harrison) S.; m. Lisa Dellwo, Oct. 29, 1988. AB, Dartmouth Coll., 1972; PhD, Cornell U., 1976. Asst. prof. U. Calif., Santa Barbara, 1976-80; from. asst. prof. to assoc. prof. Duke U., Durham, N.C., 1980-88, prof., 1988-93, James B. Duke prof., 1993—. Author: Forest Ecosystems, 1985, Biogeochemistry, 1991. Fellow Am. Acad. Arts & Scis. Office: Duke U Phytotron Durham NC 27708

SCHLEUPNER, CHARLES JOHN, internist, educator, health facility administrator; b. Balt., Feb. 12, 1945; s. George Michael Sr. and Blanche Arlington (Moran) S.; m. Lynn Foley, June 17, 1967; children: Mark, David, Ann. BS, Loyola Coll., Balt., 1967; MS, U. Pitts., 1968; MD cum laude, U. Md., 1972. Diplomate in internal medicine and infectious diseases Am. Bd. Internal Medicine; diplomate in med. microbiology Am. Bd. Pathology. Intern in internal medicine U. Utah Med. Ctr., 1972-73, resident in internal medicine, 1973-75, fellow in infectious diseases, 1975-77; chief infectious disease sect. VA Med. Ctr., Salem, Va., 1981-91, chief med. svc., 1992—; assoc. prof. medicine U. Va., Charlottesville, 1981-91, prof. medicine, 1992—; chief med. svcs. VA Med. Ctr., Reno, 1991-92; prof., vice chmn. dept. medicine U. Nev., Reno, 1991-92; co-dir. program in internal medicine U. Va., Salem, 1992—. Contbr. chpts. to books, articles to profl. jours. Fellow ACP, Infectious Diseases Soc. Am. Office: Vets Affairs Med Ctr 1970 Roanoke Blvd Salem VA 24153-6415

SCHLOEMER, NANCY FORD, retired health facility administrator; b. Framingham, Mass., Dec. 8, 1933; d. Reginald and Dorothea (Ryan) Ford; m. James Schloemer, Jan. 22, 1956; children: James (dec.), Susan, Carla. RN, White Plains (N.Y.) Hosp., 1954; BSN, SUNY, Albany, 1981; MS, Long Island U., 1985. Cert. clin. nurse specialist, psychiatric mental health, advanced nursing adminstr. Asst. dir. nursing Fair Oaks Hosp., Summit, N.J., 1978-82; clin. nurse specialist Falkirk Hosp., Central Valley, N.Y., 1982-86; dir. nursing Stony Lodge Hosp., Ossining, N.Y., 1986-89; asst. adminstr. Cape Fear Valley Med. Ctr., Fayetteville, N.C., 1989-92. Mem. Va. Nurses Assn., Sigma Theta Tau. Home: 15465 Pine Green Ln Montpelier VA 23192-9577

SCHLUETER, DAVID ARNOLD, law educator; b. Sioux City, Iowa, Apr. 29, 1946; s. Arnold E. and Helen A. (Dettmann) S.; m. Linda L. Boston, Apr. 22, 1972; children: Jennifer, Jonathan. BA, Tex. A&M U., 1969; JD, Baylor U., 1971, LLM, U. Va., 1981. Bar: Tex. 1971, D.C. 1973, U.S. Ct. Mil. Appeals 1972, U.S. Supreme Ct. 1976. Legal counsel U.S. Supreme Ct., Washington, 1981-83; assoc. dean St. Mary's U., San Antonio, 1984-89, prof. law, 1986—; reporter Fed. Adv. Com. on Criminal Rules, 1988—; chmn. JAG adv. coun., 1974-75. Author: Military Criminal Justice: Practice and Procedure, 1982, 4th edit., 1996; (with others) Military Rules of Evidence Manual, 1981, 3d edit., 1991, Texas Rules of Evidence Manual, 1983, 4th edit., 1995, Texas Evidentiary Foundations, 1992, Military Evidentiary Foundations, 1994; contbr. articles to legal publs. Maj. JAGC, U.S. Army, 1972-81. Fellow Am. Law Inst., Tex. Bar Found. (life), Am. Bar Found. (life); mem. ABA (vice chmn. criminal justice sect. coun. 1991-94, vice chmn. com. on criminal justice and mil. 1983-84, chmn. standing com. on mil. law 1991-92, chmn. editl. adv. bd., Criminal Justice Mag., 1989-91), Tex. Bar Assn. Republican. Lutheran. Office: St Marys U Sch Law 1 Camino Santa Maria St San Antonio TX 78228-8603

SCHLUETER, LINDA LEE, law educator; b. L.A., May 12, 1947; d. Dick G. Dulgarian and Lucille J. Boston; m. David A. Schlueter, Apr. 22, 1972; children: Jennifer, Jonathan. BA, U. So. Calif., 1969; JD, Baylor U., 1971. Bar: D.C. 1973, U.S. Supreme Ct. 1976, Ct. Mil. Appeals, 1990. Govt. rels. specialist hdqrs. U.S. Postal Svc., Washington, 1973-75; staff atty. Rsch. Group, Inc., Charlottesville, Va., 1979-81; pvt. practice Washington, 1981-83; asst. prof. law Sch. Law St. Mary's U., San Antonio, 1983-87, assoc. prof., 1987-90, prof., 1990-94; presenter law Tex. Women Scholars Program, Austin, 1986, 87; bd. dirs Inst. for Comparative and Internat. Legal Rsch. Author: Punitive Damages, 1981-89, 3rd edit., 1995, ann. suppls., Legal Research Guide: Patterns and Practice, 1986, 3rd edit., 1996; editor Cmty. Property Jour. , 1986-88, Cmty. Property Alert, 1989-90; assoc. editor Modern Legal Sys. Cyclopedia, 20 vols., 1990, ann. suppls. Mem. ABA, Bexar County Women's Bar Assn., San Antonio Conservation Soc., Order of Barristers, Phi Alpha Delta. Republican. Lutheran.

SCHLUMBERGER, ROBERT ERNEST, accountant; b. Pitts., Sept. 25, 1951; s. Ernest August Jr. and Barbara Ann (Rodler) S.; m. Mary Cecelia Leahy, Dec. 7, 1974; children: Jennifer Marie, Saralynne Cecelia. BS, Pa. State U., 1974. Mgr. Bradford House Restaurant, Punxsutawney, Pa., 1974-76, Latrobe, Pa., 1976-77, Butler, Pa., 1977-78; owner, acct. Schlumberger Bus. Svcs., Butler, Pa., 1978-88; pres., acct. Schlumberger Acctg. Svcs., Inc., Crystal River, Fla., 1988—; registered rep. H.D. Vest Investment Securities, Inc., Las Colinas, Tex., 1986—. Mem. Nat. Assn. Pub. Accts. Republican. Lutheran. Home: 720 N Dove Pt Crystal River FL 34429-5339 Office: Schlumberger Acctg Svcs Inc 6220 W Corporate Oaks Dr Crystal River FL 34429-8723

SCHLUNK, JURGEN ECKART, German language educator; b. Marburg, Hesse, Ger., May 26, 1944; s. Hans-Joachim and Hildegard (Elsasser) S.; m. Sharon Marie Hemelt, Oct. 18, 1979; 1 child, Andrea Dora. MA, U. N.H., 1968; PhD, Philipps Universitat, Marburg, Ger., 1970. Dramaturg Mcpl. Theatre, Marburg, 1970-71; resident dir. jr. yr. abroad Davidson Coll., Marburg, 1972-73; vis. asst. prof. Franklin & Marshall Coll., Lancaster, Pa., 1973-74; asst. prof. W.Va. U., Morgantown, 1974-80; dramaturg and actor Theater Tri-Buhne, Stuttgart, Ger., 1976-77, 80-81; assoc. prof. W.Va. U., Morgantown, 1981—; vis. prof. Padagogische Hochschule, Heidelberg, Ger., 1985-86; dir. Fgn. Lang. Residence Hall Program, W.Va. U., 1984-88, steering com. mem. Humanites Ctr., W.Va. Humanities Coun., Charleston, 1988—, bd. dirs., 1994—; exec. com. mem. So. Humanities Media Fund Bd. Editor: Martin Walser: International Perspectives, 1987; contbr. articles to profl. jours. Davidson Coll. Richardson scholar, 1966-67; Salzburg Seminar for Am. Studies fellow, 1981; NEH summer seminars, 1982, 85, 89; recipient Outstanding Tchr. award, Coll. Arts and Scis., W.Va. U., 1991. Mem. MLA, South Atlantic MLA, Am. Assn. Tchrs. German (chpt. sec.-treas. 1978-80, 95—, pres. 1983-85), W.Va. Fgn. Lang. Tchrs. Assn., Delta Phi Alpha. Office: W Va Univ Dept Fgn Lang Morgantown WV 26506

SCHMALBECK, RICHARD LOUIS, university dean, lawyer; b. Chgo., Dec. 31, 1947; s. George Louis and Betty Jeanne (Strecker) S.; m. Linda Michaels; children: Suzanne, Sabine. AB in Econs. with honors, U. Chgo., 1970, JD, 1975. Bar: Ohio 1975, D.C. 1977. Asst. to dir. and economist Ill. Housing Devel. Authority, Chgo., 1971-73; assoc. Vorys, Sater, Seymour & Pease, Columbus, Ohio, 1975-76; spl. asst. to assoc. dir. for econs. and govt. Office of Mgmt. and Budget, Washington, 1976-77; assoc. Caplin & Drysdale, Washington, 1977-80; assoc. prof. law Duke U., Durham, N.C., 1980-84, prof. law, 1984-90, 93—, vice chmn. acad. coun., 1984-85; dean U. Ill. Coll. Law, Champaign, 1990-93. Assoc. editor U. Chgo. Law Rev., 1974-75; contbr. articles to profl. jours. Mem. ABA (articles editor jour. 1977-80), Am. Law Inst., Phi Beta Kappa. Office: Duke University Sch of Law PO Box 90360 Durham NC 27708-0360

SCHMALTZ, LAWRENCE GERARD, engineer, consultant; b. Belle Fourches, S.D., Feb. 11, 1957; s. Tony J. and Evalyn Marie (Kouf) S. BSCE, S.D. Sch. of Mines & Tech., 1979; postgrad., U. Phoenix. Registered profl. engr., S.D., Colo., Fla. Engr. Skidmore, Owings & Merrill, Denver, 1979-82; project mgr. U.S. Dept. of Def., Rapid City, S.D., 1982-84; regional mgr. Waste Environ. Tech., Denver, 1986-87; project engr. Canonie Environ. Svcs., Denver, 1988; regional mgr. Burdco Environ., Inc., Longwood, Fla., 1988; v.p. Atcon, Inc., 1989-91; pres. CE Systems, Inc., 1989—, A2L Techs., Inc., 1992—; adj. faculty U. North Fla., 1989—; gen. ptnr. LJS Properties, Rapid City, 1984—; real estate broker Larry G. Schmaltz, Aurora, Colo., 1985-88; pres., cons. Dynamics Cons. & Mgmt., Aurora, 1986-88; instr., trainer in field. Bd. dirs. Cherry Creek Spl. Edn. Adv. Bd., Englewood, Colo., 1985. Mem. NSPE, Profl. Engrs. in Constrn., Fla. Engring. Soc., Fla. Environ. Auditors Assn., Nat. Registry of Environ. Profls. (adv. bd.), Nat. Platform Assn., Nat. Groundwater Assn. Home: 13014 N Dale Mabry Hwy # 334 Tampa FL 33618-2808

SCHMALZ, ROBERT FREDERICK, II, music educator; b. Pitts., Oct. 20, 1941. BSc in Music Edn., Duquesne U., 1963; MA in Music History/Lit., U. Pitts., 1966, PhD in Musicology, 1971. Tchr. instrumental and gen. music Pitts. Pub. Sch., 1964-65; liberal arts acad. advisor U. Pitts., 1965-68, grad. asst., 1966-69, asst. dir. Coll. Arts and Scis. Advising Ctr., 1969-71; asst. prof. music U. Southwestern La., Lafayette, 1972-79, assoc. prof., 1979-86, prof., coord. grad. music programs, 1986—, Ruth Stodghill Girard Endowed prof. music, 1991—; with Pitts. Civic Light Opera Orch., Pitts. Pops Orch., Nixon and Penn Theatre Orch., Pitts., Vermillon Chamber Orch., Lafayette, La., Acadiana Symphony Orch., La. Philharmonic, Pitts., Baton Rouge, Wheeling, McKeesport, Altoona and Johnstown Symphony orchs.; artist; clinician H.N. White Co., 1976-85. Mem. nat. editorial bd. Symposium, Jour. Coll. Music Soc., 1980-86; assoc. editor Explorations in Renaissance Culture, 1984—; performer as orchestral musician with groups backing notable entertainers including Frank Sinatra, Jack Jones, Pearl Bailey, Englebert Humperdinck, Tom Jones, Liberace, Shirley Jones, others; recording artist including 2 LP's, a jazz album and numerous TV and radio commercials/demos; appearances as trombone soloist; contbr. articles to profl. jours. Chmn. bd. dirs. Lafayette Community Concert Band, Inc., 1982-86. Named U. Southwestern La. Disting. Prof., 1979, Ruth Stodghill Girard Endowed Prof. Musics, 1989-93, 93-96; Duquesne U. scholar, 1959-63; U. Pitts. fellow, 1964-66; grantee U. Southwestern La./La. Arts Coun., 1980-81, La. divsn. Arts/Acadiana Arts Coun., 1984, La. Divsn. Arts, 1984, U. Southwestern La., 1981-83, 84, 85, 88, 89, 90, NEH Summer Inst., 1981, 92. Mem. Am. Musicol. Soc. (pres. So. chpt. 1983-86), Coll. Music Soc. (pres. So. region 1983-85), South Ctrl. Renaissance Conf. (pres. 1984-85), Am. Fedn. Musicians, Internat. Trombone Assn., Nat. Assn. Coll. Wind and Percussion Instrs., Renaissance Soc. Am., The Sonneck Soc., Phi Kappa Phi, Pi Kappa Lambda, Phi Mu Alpha Sinfonia. Lutheran. Home: 405 Brentwood Blvd Lafayette LA 70503-4015

SCHMEIDLER, NEAL FRANCIS, engineering executive; b. Hays, Kans., Feb. 29, 1948; s. Cyril John and Mildred Mary (Karlin) S.; m. Lorrinda Mary Brungardt, Jan. 31, 1950; children: Lori Ann, LaNette Renee, Lance Edward, LeAnna Karleen. BS in Math., Fort Hays State U., 1970; MS in Indsl. Engring., Kans. State U., 1973. Master engr. Trans World Airlines, Inc., Kansas City, Mo., 1973-78; chief indsl. engr. U.S. Dept. of the Army, Fort Carson, Colo., 1978-80; staff indsl. engr. U.S. Dept. of Agriculture, Washington, 1980-83; tech. dir. Tech. Applications, Inc., Alexandria, Va., 1983-86; v.p. engring. and tech. svcs. div. Standard Tech., Inc., Bethesda, Md., 1986-88; dir. indsl. engring. and ops rsch. svcs. Operational Technologies Svcs., Inc., Vienna, Va., 1989-91; founder, pres. OMNI Engring. and Tech., Inc., McLean, Va., 1989—; dir. No. Va. Tech. Coun., 1993-95. Guest (radio talk show) Basically Business, 1991; contbr. articles to profl. jours. Mem. info. tech./telecommunications infrastructure com. Commonwealth of Va. Gov.'s Regional Econ. Devel. Adv. Couns., 1994. Named Sr. Engr. of Yr., D.C. Coun. of Engring. and Archtl. Socs., 1991; recipient Spl. Act or Svc. award U.S. Dept. of Army, 1980. Mem. ABA (small bus. com. 1991-92), Inst. Indsl. Engrs. (sr., nat. capital chpt. bd. dirs. 1986-93, Award of Excellence 1982), Air Traffic Control Assn., Am. Soc. for Quality Control, No. Va. Tech. Coun., Human Factors and Ergonomics Soc., Washington Acad. Scis. (bd. mgrs. 1993-96), Kappa Mu Epsilon, Sigma Pi Sigma. Office: OMNI Engring & Tech Inc 7921 Jones Branch Dr # 530 Mc Lean VA 22102-3306

SCHMELZER, CLAIRE DOBSON, nutrition and management educator. BS in Foods and Nutrition, U. Ill., 1969; MS in Pub. Health, U. S.C., 1983; PhD in Hotel and Restaurant Mgmt., Va. Poly. Inst. & State U., 1992. Licensed dietician, Ky. Dietitian Vets. Hosp., Mpls., 1970-71; assoc. dir., clin. dietitian Meth. Hosp., Mpls., 1971-77; dietary cons. Johnson City/Columbia, Tenn./S.C., 1977-79; clin. dietitian Providence Hosp., Columbia, 1978-81; nutrition edn. and tng. coord. State Office of Sch. Food Svc., Columbia, 1981-82; asst. dir. dietary, chief dietitian Providence Hosp., Columbia, 1982-83; temporary asst. prof. dept. nutrition and food sci. U. Ky., Lexington, 1983-85, asst. prof. dept. nutrition and food sci., 1985-90, assoc. prof. dept. nutrition and food sci., 1991-92, program dir. Hospitality Mgmt. Program, 1992—; mem. various univ. coms.; presenter in field. Editorial bd. Jour. Nutrition in Recipe and Menu Devel.; reviewer Internat. Jour. Hospitality Mgmt., Jour. Hospitality and Tourism Rsch.; contbr. articles to profl. jours. Grantee Marjorie S. Stewart Rsch. grant, 1986, U. Ky. Faculty Rsch. grant, 1987, U. Ky. Rsch. Com., 1989, U. Ky. Ctr. for Small Bus. Devel., 1989, Coll. Human Environ. Scis., U. Ky., 1989. Mem. Coun. for Hotel, Restaurant & Instn. Edn., S.E. Coun. for Hotel, Restaurant & Instn. Edn. (bd. dirs. 1987-89, 92-93, sec. 1993-94, pres.-elect, pres. 1995-96), Phi Upsilon Omicron. Office: Univ Ky 120 Erikson Hall Lexington KY 40506-0500

SCHMID, HENRY FREDERICK, construction executive; b. Ft. Meyers, Fla., Dec. 9, 1966; s. Heinrich Otto E. and Elke Marie (Krabbe) S. AA, U. Fla., 1988; BS, Fla. Internat. U., 1991. Quality control mgr. Hewett-Kier Constr., Inc., Homestead, Fla., 1991-95, supt. constrn., 1992-95; constrn. project mgr. I. Giller, Inc., Miami, Fla., 1995—; chmn. Assoc. Genl. Contrs., Miami, 1990-92. Vol. disaster relief FEMA, Florida City and Homestead, Fla., 1992-93; environ. vol. Save the Glades, 1993-94. Mem. Sigma Lambda Chi. Home: 9100 SW 122d Pl #402 Miami FL 33186 Office: I Giller Inc Ste 401 975 Arthur Godfrey Rd Miami Beach FL 33140

SCHMIDEL, JUDITH S., artist, writer, counselor; b. Brunswick, Ga., Feb. 5, 1940; d. William Oscar Smith and Ruth (Goolsby) Royals. Grad. h.s., Atlanta, 1957; student, Augusta State U. Real estate broker Schmidel Realty & Appraisal, 1984-86; real estate appraiser, 1986-90. Designer children's books. Home: 1964 Battle Row Augusta GA 30904

SCHMIDLY, DAVID J., academic administrator, dean; b. Levelland, Tex., Dec. 20, 1943; m. Janet Elaine Knox, June 2, 1966; children: Katherine Elaine, Brian James. BS in Biology, Tex. Tech U., 1966, MS in Zoology, 1968; PhD in Zoology, U. Ill., 1971. From asst. prof. to prof. dept. wildlife fisheries scis. Tex. A&M U., College Station, 1971-82, prof., 1982-96, head dept. wildlife, 1986-92; CEO, campus dean Tex. A&M U., Galveston, 1992-96; chief curator Tex. Coop. Wildlife Coll., College Station, 1983-86; v.p. Tex. Inst. Oceanography, 1992-96; v.p. for rsch. and grad studies, dean grad. sch. Tex. Tech U., Lubbock, 1996—; cons. Nat. Park Svc., Wildlife Assocs., Walton and Assocs., Continental Shelf Assn., LGL; press adv. com. Tex. A&M U., 1983—; charter mem. Tex. A&M U. Faculty Senate, 1983-85; chmn. Scholarship Com., 1978-82; lectr. various workshops and seminars. Author: The Mammals of Trans-Pecos Texas including Big Bend National Park and Guadalupe Mountains National Park, 1977, Texas Mammals East of the Balcones Fault Zone, 1983, The Bats of Texas, 1991, The Mammals of Texas, 1994; contbr. articles to profl. jours. Trustee Tex. Nature Conservancy, 1991—. Recipient Dist. Prof. award Assn. Grad. Wildlife and Fisheries Scis., 1985, Donald W. Tinkle Rsch. Excellence award Southwestern Assn. Naturalists, 1988, Diploma Recognition La Universidad Autonoma de Guadalajara, 1989, La Universidad Autonoma de Tamaulipas, 1990. Fellow Tex. Soc. Sci. (bd. dirs. 1979-81); mem. AAAS, Am. Soc. Mammalogists (life, editor Jour. Mammalogy 1975-78), Am. Inst. Biol. Scis. (bd. dirs. 1993—, coun. affiliate socs. 1989—), Am. Naturalist, Soc. Marine Mammalogy (charter mem.), Soc. Systematic Zoology, The Wildlife Soc. Soc. Conservation Biology, Nat. Geog. Sci. Soc., S.W. Assn. Naturalists (life mem., bd. govs. 1980-86, 91—, pres. 1981, trustee 1986—), Tex. Mammal Soc. (pres. 1985-86), Assn. Systematic Collections (bd. dirs.), Chihuahuan Desert Rsch. Inst. (v.p. bd. scientists 1982—, bd. dirs. 1991), Mexican Soc. Mammalogists, Sigma Xi (v.p. 1986-87, pres. 1987-88), Disting. Scientist award 1991), Beta Beta Beta. Phi Sigma, Phi Kapa Phi. Home: 4404 15th St Lubbock TX 79416 Office: Tex Tech U Holden Hall Box 41033 Lubbock TX 79409-1033

SCHMIDT, ARTHUR LOUIS, retired state senator, businessman; b. Cold Spring, Ky., May 1, 1927; s. Joseph E. and Elizabeth (Bertsch) S.; m. Marian Seibert, Apr. 28, 1951; children: Karen, Marianne. Mgr. mktg. Cin. Bell, 1946-83; dir. Provident Bank of Ky., 1964-93. Mem. City Council, Cold Spring, Ky., 1962-63; mem. Ky. Ho. of Reps., 1963-83; mem. Ky. Senate, 1983-92.

SCHMIDT, BENNO CHARLES, JR., lawyer, educator; b. Washington, Mar. 20, 1942; s. Benno Charles and Martha (Chastain) S.; children by previous marriage—Elizabeth, Benno III; m. Helen Cutting Whitney, 1980; 1 child, Christina. BA, Yale U., 1963, JD, 1966; LLD (hon.), Princeton U., 1986; LittD (hon.), Johns Hopkins U., 1987; LLD (hon.), Harvard U., 1987. Bar: D.C. 1968. Law clk. Chief Justice Earl Warren, U.S. Supreme Ct, Washington, 1966-67; spl. asst., asst. atty. gen. Office Legal Counsel U.S. Dept. Justice, Washington, 1967-69; Harlan Fiske Stone prof. constl. law Columbia U., N.Y.C., 1969-86, dean Law Sch., 1984-86; pres., prof. law Yale U., New Haven, 1986-92; pres., CEO The Edison Project, Knoxville, Tenn., 1992—. Author: Freedom of the Press versus Public Access, 1976; (with A.M. Bickel) The Judiciary and Responsible Government 1910-1921, 1984. Dir. Nat. Humanities Ctr., Chapel Hill, N.C., 1985—. Office: The Edison Project 1240 Old Weisgarber Knoxville TN 37909-2639

SCHMIDT, DALE RUSSELL, lawyer; b. Berea, Ohio, Aug. 8, 1948; s. Russell A. and Dorothy D. Schmidt; m. Donna L. Van Stone, May 30, 1970; children: Ian Fletcher, Inge Brooke. BA, Yale U., 1970; JD, Am. U., 1976. Bar: Va. 1978, D.C. 1980, U.S. Dist. Ct. (ea. dist.) Va. 1996, U.S Tax Ct., U.S. Ct. Appeals (4th cir.) 1978, U.S. Ct. Appeals (D.C. cir.) 1980. Systems dir. Hon. Robert W. Kasten, Jr., Washington, 1977-78; counsel Nat. Elec. Mfrs. Assn., Washington, 1978—; pvt. practice Alexandria, Va., 1987—. Served with U.S. Army, 1970-71. Mem. ABA (chmn. internat. and comparative law com. Adminstrv. Law sect. 1987-90, vice chmn. mem. com. Adminstrv. Law Sect. 1987-90), Greater Washington Soc. Assn. Execs. (chmn. law and legis. com. 1982-84, co-chmn. legis. and media guide com. 1988-90), Am. Soc. Assn. Execs. (Legal sect.), Alexandria Bar Assn. Office: PO Box 26153 Alexandria VA 22313 also: NEMA 1300 N 17th St # 1847 Arlington VA 22209

SCHMIDT, FREDERICK LEE, artist, educator; b. Hays, Kans., Dec. 11, 1937; s. Jacob Robert and Lulu Gertrude (Haas) S.; m. Nancy Siegrist Eiss, July 19, 1959 (div. July 1972); children: Jeffrey Eugene, Pamela Lynn Klustner; m. Linda Sue Bullock, Nov. 18, 1990; 1 stepchild, Heather Hutchison. BA in Art Edn., U. No. Colo., 1962; MA in Painting and Drawing, U. Iowa, 1967, MFA in Painting and Drawing, 1968. Art tchr. Salina (Kans.) H.S., 1962-65, Coll. H.S., U. Iowa, Iowa City, 1967-68; asst. prof. Northwestern Coll., Orange City, Iowa, 1968-70, Western Carolina U., Cullowhee, N.C., 1970-72, Va. Poly. Inst. and State U., Blacksburg, 1972-76; instr. Ark. State U., State University, 1976-77; traveling artist Ark. Arts Ctr., Office State Svcs., various cities, 1977-78; instr. U. Ark., Pine Bluff, 1978-81; art and English tchr. Pulaski County (Ark.) Sch. Dists., 1982-86; tchr. art Little Rock Pub. Schs., 1986—; artist in residence Ark. Arts Coun., 1980-81. One-man shows include Heights Gallery, 1984, Ark. Territorial Restoration, Little Rock, 1986, Northwestern Coll., Orange City, 1987; exhibited in group shows at Ark. Art on Exhibit, Arkadelphia, 1980, 81, 82, Ark. Arts, Crafts and Design Fair, Little Rock, 1977, 80, 81, S.E. Arts Ctr., Pine Bluff, Ark., 1981, Mid-Am. Arts Alliance, Kansas City, Mo., 1979, and others; represented in permanent collections Ark. Coll., Batesville, Ind. Gas Co., Indpls., People's Bank, Tupelo, Miss., Ark. Arts Ctr., Little Rock, Systematics Inc., Little Rock, Gov.'s Office State Capitol, Ark., J.B. Hunt Trucking, Ark., Kimberly-Clark, Ark., St. Vincent Infirmary, Little Rock, 1st Bank of Jacksonville, Ark., Bank of Loanoke, Ark., U. Ark. Med. Campus Eye Clinic, Little Rock, Ark. Best, U. Ark. Med. Sch., numerous others. Campaign worker Ark. Rep. Com., Little Rock, 1985—; runner Ark. Pikes Soc., Little Rock, 1990—. Sgt. USMC, 1954-62. Recipient grand purchase award S.E. Ark. Arts Ctr., 1979, hon. mention purchase award, 1980, 81; award Ark. Art on Exhibit, 1981, best of show award, 1982; best of show award Ark. Arts, Crafts and Design Fair, 1981; also others; grantee Ark. Office Arts and Humanities, 1980, Ark. Arts Ctr., 1990—, rsch. grantee Northwestern Coll., Helen Wurlizer Found.; arts scholar U. Iowa. Mem. Fellowship Bible Ch.

SCHMIDT, GENE, air transportation executive; b. 1928. Formerly with Northwest Airlines; cons. Northwest Aerospace Tng. Corp., Naples, Fla. With U.S. Armed Forces, Korea. Office: Naples City Airport Authority 160 Aviation Dr N Naples FL 34104-3568

SCHMIDT, GLENN FREDERIC, electronics engineer; b. Elmhurst, Ill., Feb. 8, 1966; s. Frederic Lawrence and Darlene Patricia (Thornton) S. BS in Bio-Engring., Tex. A&M U., 1988, MS in Bio-Engring., 1990. Rsch. asst. Tex. A&M U., College Station, 1988-90; hardware engr. Darwel Techs., Garland, Tex., 1990-94, Power Distbn. Inc., Plano, Tex., 1994—. Mem. IEEE, NSPE, Tex. Soc. Profl. Engrs. (engr. in tng.). Republican. Lutheran. Home: 1518 Grinstad Dr Garland TX 75040-9100 Office: Power Distbn Inc 1001 W Park Blvd Apt 152 Plano TX 75075-2661

SCHMIDT, JUNE LAUREL, minister; b. Benton Harbor, Mich., June 5, 1941; d. Laurie Hudspeth-Minton and Julia Montgomery (Rowland) Minton; m. Ronald Edward Rogers, May 28, 1967 (dec.); children: Ronald Edward, Rhonda June; m. Donald Fredrick Schmidt, Dec. 18, 1980; stepchildren: Donald, Karen, Darryl, Lori, Mark. Diplomas in ministry, Gospel Crusade Inst. Ministry, Brandenton, Fla., 1980, 81. Ordained to ministry, Gospel Crusade Ministerial Fellowship, Bradenton, Fla., 1980. Assoc. pastorial trainee Soul's Harbour Ch., Tulsa, Okla., 1980; internat. dir. City of Light Sch. of Ministry, Houston, 1980-82; dir. missions World Bible Way Fellowship, Dallas, 1983-85; pres., CEO His Word to the Nations, Inc., Dallas, Perry, Kans., Sacramento, and Orlando, Fla., and Sewanee, Ga., 1983—; regional dir., Caribbean region and Venezuela Gospel Crusade Ministerial Fellowship, Brandenton, Fla., 1986-96; bd. dirs. Gospel Crusade Ministerial Fellowship, Bradenton, Fla., 1986-96, His Word to the Nations, Inc., Dallas, Perry, Sacramento, Orlando, and Sewanee, 1983—, The Encouragers, Nashville, 1986-91; cons. various internat. ministries, 1980—, Eagles Internat., New Brunswick, Can., 1993-95; supr. Herbalife Internat., 1994—. Editor: The Gospel Crusader, The Shepherd's Reporter, The Harvest Communiqué; contbr. numerous articles to religious publs. Capt., counselor Little League Baseball, Mililani Town, Hawaii, 1970; mem. Internat. Women in Leadership; bd. dirs. various internat. ministries. Mem. Gospel Crusade Ministerial Fellowship, World Bible Way Fellowship. Republican. Non-denominational Pentecostal. Home and Office: 3475 Maple Terrace Dr Suwanee GA 30174

SCHMIDT, LAWRENCE KENNEDY, philosophy educator; b. Rochester, N.Y., Oct. 2, 1949; s. Paul Frederick Schmidt and Rebecca Jane Gilford; m. Monika Reuss, Sept. 2, 1984; 1 child, Kassandra Gaya Reuss-Schmidt. BA, Reed Coll., 1972; MA, U. N.Mex., 1978; PhD, U. Duisburg (Germany), 1983. Instr. Philosophy U. Duisburg, Duisburg, 1979-83, U. N.Mex., Albuquerque, 1984; asst. prof. Philosophy Hendrix Coll., Conway, Ark., 1984-89, chair dept. Philosophy, 1987-92, assoc. prof. Philosophy, 1989—; bd. dirs. Marshall T. Steel Ctr. for the Study of Religion and Philosophy; mem. summer seminar for coll. tchrs. NEH; bd. dirs. Bernd Magnus. Author: (book) The Epistemology of H-G Gadamer, 1985, 2d edit., 1987; editor: (book) The Specter of Relativism, 1995; translator: (book) Hans-Georg Gadamer on Education, Poetry, and History, 1992; contbr. articles to profl. jours. Fulbright scholar, Duisburg, 1977-79; faculty rsch. grantee Hendrix Coll., 1985, 88, 91, 93, 96. Mem. AAUP (pres. Hendrix chpt. 1987-91, 95—), Ark. Philos. Assn., Am. Philos. Assn., Phi Beta Kappa. Office: Hendrix Coll Conway AR 72032

SCHMIDT, PAUL JOSEPH, physician, educator; b. N.Y.C., Oct. 22, 1925; s. Joseph and Anna (Schwanzl) S.; BS Fordham U., 1948; MS, St. Louis U., 1952; MD, NYU, 1953; m. Louise Kern Fredericks, June 18, 1953; children: Damien, Matthew, Thomas, Maria. Intern, St. Elizabeth's Hosp., Boston, 1953-54; staff assoc. Nat. Microbiol. Inst., Bethesda, Md., 1954-55; chief blood bank dept. NIH, Bethesda, Md., 1955-74, asst. chief clin. pathology dept., 1963-65; sr. asst. surgeon, USPHS, 1954, advanced through grades to med. dir., 1964-74; assoc. clin. prof. pathology, then clin. prof. Georgetown U., Washington, 1965-75; dir. S.W. Fla. Blood Bank, Inc., Tampa, 1975-90, pres. 1987-90; head transfusion medicine, Transfusion Medicine Acad. Ctr., 1991—; prof. pathology U. So. Fla., Tampa, 1975—; cons. com. on Blood, AMA, 1964-69; tech. adv. Blood Transfusion Rsch. div. US Army, 1966-74; res. adv. com. Blood Program, ARC, 1967-73; com. Human Rsch., ARC, 1968-74; council on Immunohematology, Am. Soc. Clin. Pathologists, 1968-74; com. Anticoagulant Solutions, NRC-Nat. Acad. Sci., 1968-70; com. Plasmapheresis, NRC-Nat. Acad. Sci., 1969-70; com. Blood Bank Programs, N.Y.C., 1969-70; com. Component Therapy, NRC-Nat. Acad. Sci., 1969; com. standards, Am. Assn. Blood Banks, 1970-85 (chmn. 1981-85); Task Force on Blood Banking, dept. HEW, 1972-73; adv. com. Blood Diseases and Resources, Nat. Heart Lung Blood Inst., 1975-79; cons. to surgeon gen. U.S. Navy, 1976; dir. clin. svcs. ARC Blood Svcs., San Juan, P.R., 1993-95; clin. prof. pathology U. P.R., 1993—, Koppisch lectr., 1994; Molthan Meml. lectr. Pa. Assn. Blood Banks, 1995. Mem. svc. and rehab. com. Fla. div. Am. Cancer Soc., 1976-84; bd. dirs. ARC, Tampa 1978-83 (v.p. 1980); com. Transfusion Transmitted Viruses, Coll. Am. Pathologists 1981-91; com. Transfusion Medicine, Coll. Am. Pathologists, 1981-92; bd. dirs. Am. Blood Commn., 1985-87. Served with U.S. Army, 1944-46. Recipient Jour. Club Rsch. award, NYU, 1952, Silver medal Spanish Red Cross, 1960; Emily Cooley award Am. Assn. Blood Banks, 1974, John Elliott award, 1993. Diplomate Am. Bd. Pathology, Nat. Bd. Med. Examiners. Fellow Coll. Am. Pathologists (emeritus); mem. Am. Assn. Blood Banks (pres. 1987-88), Internat. Assn. History Medicine, Internat. Soc. Blood Transfusion, Fla. Assn. Blood Banks (pres. 1980-81), Cosmos, Rotary. Roman Catholic. Contbr. articles to profl. jours., editorial bd. Transfusion, 1968—, Annals Clinical Lab. Sci., 1971-74, Blood, 1976-77; editor: Progress in Transfusion and Transplantation, 1972; described etiology of renal failure after hemolytic blood transfusion reactions, 1967, Rh null disease, 1967. Office: PO Box 2125 Tampa FL 33601-2125

SCHMIDT, PAUL WICKHAM, lawyer; b. Milw., June 25, 1948; s. Edmund Julian and Barbara (Wickham) S.; m. Cathryn Ann Piehl, June 27, 1970; children: Thomas Wickham, William Piehl, Anna Patchin. BA cum laude, Lawrence U., 1970; JD cum laude, U. Wis., 1973. Bar: Wis. 1973, U.S. Dist. Ct. (we. dist.) Wis. 1973, U.S. Supreme Ct. 1982, D.C. 1988. Atty. advisor Bd. Immigration Appeals, Washington, 1973-76; gen. atty. office of gen. counsel Immigration and Naturalization Service, Washington, 1976-78, acting gen. counsel, 1979-81, 86-87, dep. gen. counsel, 1978-87; assoc. Jones, Day, Reavis & Pogue, Washington, 1987-89, ptnr., 1990-92; mng. ptnr. Fragomen, Del Ray & Bernsen, P.C., Washington, 1993-95; chmn. Bd. of Immigration Appeals, Falls Church, Va., 1995—. Mem. ABA, D.C. Bar Assn., Wis. Bar Assn., Fed. Bar Assn. (immigration sect.). Home: 711 S View Ter Alexandria VA 22314-4923 Office: Bd Immigration Appeals Skyline Tower 5107 Leesburg Pike Ste 2400 Falls Church VA 22041

SCHMIDT, PHILIP S., mechanical engineering educator. Prof. dept. mech. engring. U. Tex., Austin, Douglass prof. Recipient Ralph Coats Roe award ASEE, 1992; named Carnegie Found. Tex. Prof. of Yr., 1994. Office: Univ Tex Dept Mech Engring Austin TX 78712

SCHMIDT, RENÉ R., music educator, organist, choirmaster; b. Glencoe, Minn., Sept. 17, 1952; s. Victor John and Ruth M. (Goodeman) S. BA in Music, Luther Coll., 1974; Master of Music Organ and Harpsichord, So. Meth. U., 1978; PhD in Musicology, U. North Tex., 1992. Music instr. Dallas Ind. Sch. Dist., 1978-81, 85—; adj. music faculty So. Meth. U., 1980, U. North Tex., 1995; mus. instr. St. Philip's Cath. Sch., 1991-92, Skidmore Coll. U. without Walls, fall 1992, 93; dir. children's chorus Lyric Opera Dallas, summer 1990; dir. Dallas Boys Choir, 1989-91, accompanist, asst. dir., 1986-89; organist Christ Episcopal Ch., Dallas, 1976—, choirmaster, 1976—; lectr. summer sch. English Organ Music Cleve. Lodge, Dorking, Eng., 1979; presenter papers in field. Mem. Am. Guild Organists (Dallas chpt., dir. edn. com. 1990-93, exec com. 1987-93, steering com. nat. conv. Dallas 1993-94, dir. recital series com. 1994—), Am. Musicological Soc., Tex. Mus. Educators Assn. Home: 4311 Bowser Ave Apt 204 Dallas TX 75219-2884

SCHMIDT, RICHARD ALAN, management company executive; b. Chgo., Aug. 5, 1943; s. Herman and Lillian (Hirsch) S.; married; children: Mollee A., Michael A. BS, Bradley U., 1966. Purchasing agt. U.S. Ry. Equipment Co., Chgo., 1969-71; product mgr. Lift Parts Mfg. Co., Chgo., 1971-73; gen. mgr. Systems Products Co., Chgo., 1973-74, Highlift Equipment Co., Columbus, Ohio, 1974-81; dir. to pres. Schmidt Mgmt. Inc., Columbus, 1979-88; owner Aero Devel., Inc., Columbus, 1988-90; chmn., CEO Stellar Asset Mgmt., Inc., Naples, Fla., 1990—; pres. Sandcastle Boats, Inc.; pvt. pilot, rated instr. Multi Engine Land & Sea; scuba diver, master diver rating. Columnist material mgmt., 1979; editor, pub. The Risk Report, 1991—; bus. editor WNPL-TV News. Dep. sheriff Perry County, Ohio. Mem. Internat. Materials Mgmt. Soc. (cert. in materials mgmt. and handling, pres. Columbus chpt. 1977, internat. pres. 1977-78), Naples C. of C. (pres. club 1991—), Mensa. Office: Stellar Asset Mgmt Inc 8889 Pelican Bay Blvd Naples FL 33963

SCHMIDT, THOMAS, small business owner, writer; b. Goose Leg, Wis., May 10, 1963; s. Frederick and Ethel (Ramone) S.; m. Mary Francis Glennon, Apr. 21, 1991 (div. July 1995); children: Tracy, Ahmed; m. April Mae Showers, July 6, 1995; 1 child, Kenneth. BA, U. Fla., 1985. Copywriter/janitor The Nibblick Group, Tampa, Fla., 1986-87; copywriter Bourne, Berns & Berle, Pompano Beach, Fla., 1987-88, Manlove & O'Hara, Palm Beach, Fla., 1988-89, Tishman, Freegood & Waring, Miami, Fla., 1989-94; proprietor fruit stand; shrimp boat capt. Author: Floyd!: The Life and Times of Howard McNear, 1995; contbr. articles to profl. jours. Recipient Addy awards Advt. Fedn. Am., 1989-94. Mem. Knights of San Juan (treas. 1993—, Sterling Svc. Cross 1989), Jr. Go-Getters (Man of the Yr. 1990). Libertarian. Lutheran. Home and Office: 2206 S Cypress Bend Dr #404 Pompano Beach FL 33069

SCHMIDT, WALTER, geologist; b. June 28, 1950; s. Waldemar E. and Elizabeth M. (Stover) S.; m. Cheryl Schmidt; children: David, Amber. AS in Ocenaographic Tech., Fla. Inst. Tech., 1970; BA in Geology, U. South Fla., 1972; MS in Geology, Fla. State U., 1977, PhD in Geology, 1983. Rsch. asst. Fla. State U. Sedimentation Lab., 1973-74; asst. geologist N.W. Fla. Water Mgmt. Dist., 1974-75; geologist II N.W. Fla. Dist. Geologist, Fla. Bur. Geology, 1975-79; geologist III Head of geologic framework subsect. Fla. Bur. of Geology, Dept. of Natural Resources, 1979-81, adminstr. geol. investigations sect., 1981-85; state geologist, chief dept. environ. protection Fla. Geol. Survey, Dept. Natural Resources, 1985—; adj. prof. geology dept. Fla. State U., 1985—; adv. bd. Fla. Sinkhole Rsch. Inst., 1985-90; chmn. Big Cypress Swamp Adv. com., 1985—; mem. Gov.'s Outer Continental Shelf Adv. Com., 1985—; legis. appointee Fla. Bd. Profl. Geologists. Contbr. numerous articles to profl. jours. Fellow Geol. Soc. Am. (agy. rep., southeastern sect. com. geology and pub. policy 1989-92, nat. geology and pub. policy com. 1992-93); mem. Assn. of Am. State Geologists (state rep., pres. 1995-96), Soc. for Sedimentary Geology, Southeastern Geol. Soc. (v.p. 1983, pres. 1984, nominating com. 1990), Am. Inst. Profl. Geologists (cert., many coms.), Fla. Acad. Scis. (chmn. geology and hydrology sect.), N.C. Bd. Licensing of Geologists (lic.), S.C. State Bd. Registration for Geologists (lic.), Sigma Xi. Home: 6663 Chevy Way Tallahassee FL 32311-5412 Office: Fla Geol Survey 903 W Tennessee St Tallahassee FL 32304-7716

SCHMITT, FREDERICK ADRIAN, gerontologist, neuropsychologist; b. Cin., July 22, 1953; s. Werner and L. Gerlinde (Adrian) S.; m. Melinda Greenlese, Oct. 16, 1984. B.S., Rensselaer Poly., 1975; Ph.D., U. Akron, 1982. Lic. psychologist, N.C., Ky. Postdoctoral fellow Duke Aging Ctr., Durham, N.C., 1981-83, fellow in geriatrics, 1983-84; vis. asst. prof. psychology, U. N.C., Chapel Hill, 1984-85; rsch. assoc. Duke Med. Ctr., Durham, 1984-85; dir. neuropsychology svc. U. Ky., Lexington, 1985—, assoc. prof. neurology, 1990—, adj. prof. psychiatry, adj. prof. dept. psychology; assoc. Sanders-Brown Ctr. on Aging; cons. NIMH Office AIDS Programs, Am. Found. for AIDS Rsch.; co-dir. Memory Disroders Clinic. Contbr. chpts. to books, articles to profl. jours. Mem. AAAS, APA, Am. Acad. Neurology, Nat. Acad. Neuropsychology, N.Y. Acad. Sci, Gerontol. Soc. Am., Internat. Neuropsychol. Soc., Soc. for Research Child Devel., Soc. for Neurosci. Mem. of Baha'i Faith. Office: U Ky Dept Neurology Chambers Bldg Annex 4 Rm 228E Lexington KY 40536

SCHMITT, JAMES KENNETH, internist, health facility administrator, educator; b. Oakland, Calif., May 26, 1944; s. Malcolm John and Edni Irene (Watchers) S.; m. Norma DeAnn McKenzie, Aug. 17, 1973; children: James Eril, Brian Lawrence. BA, U. Calif., Berkeley, 1966; MD, U. Calif., San Francisco, 1971. Diplomate Am. Bd. Internal Medicine, subspecialty endocrinology and metabolism, subspecialty geriatrics. Intern internal medicine Highland Gen. Hosp. Alameda County Hosps., Oakland, Calif., 1971-72, resident internal medicine, 1972-74; fellow endocrinology metabolic rsch. unit U. Calif., San Francisco, 1976-78; instr. internal medicine U. Nebr., Omaha, 1975-77; instr. internal medicine, asst. rsch. physician U. Calif., San Francisco, 1978-80, asst. clin. prof. medicine, 1988, attending physician Comprehensive Clinic, 1978; attending physician general internal medicine Highland Gen. Hosp. and Naval Regional Med. Ctr., Oakland, Calif., 1981; physician Hunter McGuire VA Hosp., Richmond, Va., 1983-92; assoc. prof. medicine Med. Coll. Va., Richmond, 1992—; chief gen. internal medicine Hunter Holmes McGuire VA Med. Ctr., 1993—; attending physician Triage area McGuire VA Med. Ctr., Richmond, 1983—, Hunter Homes McGuire VA Med. Ctr., Richmond, 1983—, endocrinology svc.. 1983—, emergency rm., 1983-90, primary care clinic, 1983—, extended care clinic, 1983—, gen. internal medicine ward, 1983—; chief endocrinology Portsmouth (Va.) Naval Hosp., 1990-91, attending physician gen. med. wards, 1991; attending physician geriatrics svcs. VA Med. Ctr., Richmond, 1983-91. Editor, author: Medical Consequences of Spinal Cord Injury, 1987; contbr. articles to profl. jours., chpts. to books. With USAF, 1974-76, comdr. M.C., USNR, 1979-83, capt. M.C., 1993—. Fellow ACP; mem. Am. Fedn. Clin. Rsch., Am. Soc. Hypertension, The Endocrine Soc., Am. Diabetes Assn., Phi Beta Kappa. Home: 1900 Castlebridge Rd Midlothian VA 23113-4003 Office: Hunter Holmes McGuire VA Med Ctr 1201 Broad Rock Blvd Richmond VA 23249-0001

SCHMITZ, DOLORES JEAN, primary education educator; b. River Falls, Wis., Dec. 27, 1931; d. Otto and Helen Olive (Webster) Kreuziger; m. Karl Matthias Schmitz Jr., Aug. 18, 1956; children: Victoria Jane, Karl III. BS, U. Wis., River Falls, 1953; MS, Nat. Coll. Edn., 1982; postgrad., U. Minn., Mankato, 1969, U. Melbourne, Australia, 1989, U. Wis., Milw., 1989, Carroll Coll., 1990, Cardinal Stritch, 1990. Cert. tchr., Wis. Tchr. Manitowoc (Wis.) Pub. Schs., 1953-56, West Allis (Wis.) Pub. Schs., 1956-59, Lowell Sch., Milw., 1960-63, Victory Sch., Milw., 1964; tchr. Palmer Sch., Milw., 1966-84, 86-94, unit leader, 1984-86; ret., 1994; co-organizer Headstart Tchg. Staff Assn., Milw., 1968; insvc. organizer Headstart and Early Childhood, Milw., 1969-92; pilot tchr. for Whole Lang., Hi-Scope and Math. Their Way, 1988-93; bd. dirs. Cuurriculum Devel. Ctr. of Milw. Edn. Ctr., 1993-94. Author: (curriculum) Writing to Read, 1987, Cooperation and Young Children (ERIC award 1982), Kindergarten Curriculum, 1953. Former supporter Milw. Art Mus., Milw. Pub. Mus., Milw. County Zoo, Whitefish Bay Pub. Libr., Earthwatch Riveredge Nature Ctr.; vol. fgn. visitor program Milw. Internat. Inst., 1966-94, holiday folk fair, 1976-94, Earthwatch, 1989; lobbyist Milw. Pub. Sch. Bd. and State of Wis., 1986-93; coord. comty. vols., 1990-94. Grantee Greater Milw. Ednl. Trust, 1989. Mem. NEA (life), ASCD, Milw. Kindergarten Assn. (rec. sec. 1986-93), Nat. Assn. for Edn. of Young Children, Tchrs. Applying Whole Lang., Wis. Early Childhood Assn., Milw. Tchrs. Ednl. Assn. (co-chmn. com. early childhood 1984-86), Assn. for Childhood Edn. Internat. (charter pres. Manitowoc chpt. 1955-56), Milw. Educating Computer Assn., Alpha Psi Omega. Roman Catholic. Home: 312 8th Ave Apt 1 Tierra Verde FL 33715-1800

SCHMITZ, MICHAEL LELAND, pediatric anesthesiologist, pediatrician, educator; b. Pana, Ill., June 13, 1960; s. Leland Henry and Doris Marie (Weitekamp) S.; m. Susan Beth Shapiro, July 22, 1990; children: Andrea Lauren, Drew Michael. BS in Chemistry-Biochemistry cum laude, U. Ill., 1982; MD, U. Calif., San Francisco, 1986. Diplomate Am. Bd. Anesthesiology, Am. Bd. Pediat. Resident in pediatrics Harbor-UCLA Med. Ctr., 1986-89; resident in anesthesiology U. Pa. Med. Ctr., Phila., 1989-91; fellow in pediatric anesthesia and pediatric cardiac anesthesia and critical care Children's Hosp. Phila., 1991-92; pediatric anesthesiologist pediat. pain mgmt. svc. Ark. Children's Hosp., Little Rock, 1992—; asst. prof. anesthesiology and pediatrics U. Ark. for Med. Scis., Little Rock, 1992—, dir. anesthesiology residency program, 1995—; lectr., spkr. in field. Contbr. articles and abstracts to med. jours., chpt. to book. Grantee Abbott Labs., 1992. Mem. AAAS, Am. Acad. Pediatrics, Am. Soc. Anesthesiologists, Ark. Soc. Anesthesiologists, Am. Soc. Regional Anesthesia, Internat. Anesthesia Rsch. Soc., Soc. Cardiovasc. Anesthesiologists, Soc. Critical Care Medicine, Soc. Pediatric Anesthesia, Phi Beta Kappa. Office: Ark Children's Hosp Div Pediatric Anesthesia 800 Marshall St Sturgis 319 Little Rock AR 72202-3591

SCHMOKE, L(EROY) JOSEPH, III, corporate finance executive, consultant; b. Detroit, July 15, 1944; s. LeRoy Joseph and Leona Rita (Barkhaus) S.; m. Diana Lynn Dragon, July 12, 1969. BS in Fin., U. Detroit, 1966; postgrad., Wayne State U., 1971-73. Account exec. First Am. Corp., Southfield, Mich., 1967-69; mgr. corp. svcs. Merrill Lynch Pierce Fenner & Smith, Southfield, 1969-74; founder, pres. Versatile Van Works of Detroit, Inc., Livonia, Mich., 1974-77, Am. Radio Distbrs., Dearborn Heights, Mich., 1976-80; founder, pres., dir. University Consultants, Inc., Boca Raton, Fla., 1980—; pres. Fla. Restaurant Investment Corp., Boca Raton, 1983-91, also bd. dirs.; founder, chmn., CEO Healthcare Infonet, Inc., Boca Raton, Fla., 1990—; pres. Mariner Capital, 1984; founder, chmn., treas. Schmoke & McBath Enterprises, Garden City, Mich., 1973-76; exec. v.p. Servico Bus. Sys., Ft. Lauderdale, Fla., 1983; founder Database Ptnrs., L.C. Boca Raton; founder, pres. UCI Physicians & Co., Inc., Boca Raton. Author: Vital Business Secrets for New and Growing Companies, Dow Jones-Irwin, 1989. With USMCR, 1965-71. Mem. Assn. Corp. Growth (internat. v.p.), Seagate Club (Delray Beach, Fla.). Republican. Home: 76 Lariat Cir Boca Raton FL 33487 Office: University Consultants Inc 7601 N Federal Hwy Ste A-220 Boca Raton FL 33487-1657

SCHNARS, JEFFREY, engineering company executive. V.p. Schnars Engring. Corp., Boca Raton, Fla. Office: Schnars Engring Corp # 108 951 Broken Sound Pkwy NW Boca Raton FL 33487-3531

SCHNECK, PAUL BENNETT, computer scientist; b. N.Y.C., Aug. 15, 1945; s. Irving and Doris (Grossman) S.; m. Marjorie Ann Axelrod, Feb. 5, 1967; children: Phyllis Adele, Melanie Jane. BS, Columbia U., 1965, MS, 1966; PhD, NYU Courant Inst. Math. Scis., 1979. Computer scientist Inst. for Space Studies, N.Y.C., 1970-76; program mgr. Goddard Space Flight Ctr., Greenbelt, Md., 1976-79; asst. to dir. Goddard Space Flight Ctr., Greenbelt, 1979-80, chief info. extraction div., 1980-81, asst. dir., 1981-83; head info. sci. div. Office of Naval Rsch., Arlington, Va., 1983-85; dir. Supercomputing Rsch. Ctr., Bowie, Md., 1985-93; chief scientist Inst. Defense Analyses, 1993; fellow Mitre Corp., McLean, Va., 1993-96, dir. info. sys. and fellow, 1994-96; dir. info. sys. and fellow Mitretak Systems, Inc., McLean, Va., 1996—; vice chmn. bd. Nat. Info. Tech. Ctr., 1993, chmn. bd., CEO, 1994, exec. com., 1994—; mem. adv. bd. Inst. Computational Sci. and Informatics, George Mason U., 1995—; mem. adv. bd. computer scis. U. Md., College Park, 1989-96; tchr. Columbia U., Johns Hopkins U., U. Md. Author: Supercomputer Architecture, 1987; contbr. articles to Ency. of Computer Sci. and Tech., Ann. Rev. of Computer Sci., Ency. Phys. Sci. and Tech. Yearbook. Fellow IEEE, Assn. for Computing Machinery; mem. Brit. Computer Soc., Engring. Coun. (chartered engr., Eng.). Office: Mitretek Systems Inc 7525 Colshire Dr Mc Lean VA 22102-7500

SCHNECKENBURGER, KAREN LYNNE, finance executive; b. Peoria, Ill., Sept. 12, 1949; d. Walter Carl and Judith Jane (Grimshaw) S. BS in Acctg., Bradley U., 1971. CPA, Ill. Auditor Ernst & Young, Chgo., 1971-76; controller C.A. Roberts Co., Franklin Park, Ill., 1976-78; mgr. fin. and investments Gould Inc., Rolling Meadows, Ill., 1978-86; treas. Fairchild Industries, Inc., Chantilly, Va., 1986—, The Fairchild Corp., Chantilly, 1991—; v.p., 1992—. Advisor Jr. Achievement, Chgo., 1979-85. Mem. AICPA, Fin. Execs. Inst., Ill. CPA Soc., Chgo. Fin. Exch. Home: 2249 Cedar Cove Ct Reston VA 20191-4100 Office: The Fairchild Corp PO Box 10803 Chantilly VA 20153-0803

SCHNEIDER, ARTHUR, computer graphics specialist; b. Chgo., June 17, 1947; s. George Joseph and Doris Hilda (Hirsberg) S.; m. Marita Rose Scherer (div. 1976); 1 child, Heather Patricia; m. Jayne Bangs, 1986. BA in Radio and TV, Ind. U., Bloomington, 1972. Corp. CAD system specialist Entre Computer Ctr.; computer graphic specialist, system builder ZML/McCann Erickson Worldwide; chief executive officer Applied Computer Graphics, Inc., Louisville; nat. sales leader Entre Computer Ctr.; instr. Bullitt Co. Vocat. Sch.; founder Electronic Imaging Soc. Inc. Mem. World Future Soc., Nat. Trust for Historic Preservation. Office: Applied Computer Graphics Inc 2553 Kings Hwy Louisville KY 40205-2646

SCHNEIDER, CHERYL, human resources professional; b. Mt. Kisco, N.Y., Sept. 10, 1955; d. Walter Michael Schneider and Geraldine (O'Connor) Sadler. BA in Communications and English Edn., U. South Fla., 1978; MS in Human Rels. and Bus., Amber U., 1993; postgrad., U. Dallas, 1993—. Tchr. Readak Ednl. Svcs., New Orleans, 1978-80, Jeannette (La.) Sr. High Sch., 1980-82, Live Oak High Sch., Watson, La., 1982-83; broadcaster Sta. KANE, New Iberia, La., 1980-82, Sta. WFMF-FM, Baton Rouge, 1984; store exec. Mervyn's, Dallas, 1985-89; corp. recruiter Murata Bus. Systems, Dallas, 1989-92; human resources generalist GAF Corp., Dallas, 1992-93; dir. human resources Great Western Press, 1993-94; regional mgr. human resources Popeye's Chicken, Irving, Tex., 1994-96; dir. human resources 1st Data Corp., Pensacola, Fla., 1996—; advisor Mervyn's Employee Assn., 1988-89; traffic reporter WBAP Radio Sta., Dallas, 1996—. Mem. NAFE, Nat. Human Resource Mgmt. Assn., Dallas Pers. Assn., Dallas Human Resources Mgmt. Home: Apt 373 1625 Bulevar Mayor # H-6 Pensacola Beach FL 32561 Office: Popeyes Chicken Ste 500 1231 Greenway Tower Irving TX 75038

SCHNEIDER, CLARA GARBUS, dietitian, consultant; b. Paterson, N.J., Sept. 2, 1955; d. Edward George and Constance (Murray) Garbus; m. Philip John Schneider, July 22, 1978; children: Amy L., Stephen P. BS, U. Del., 1977; MS, U. Md., 1979; postgrad., Marymount U., 1995—. Registered dietitian. Nutritionist Woman, Infant & Children Feeding Program, Leesburg, Va., 1980-81, Barney Sr. Svcs., Washington, 1982-83; cons. dietitian Sharon Nursing Home, Washington, 1984-85, NAS, Washington, 1985; cons. Nat. Assn. WIC Dirs., Balt., 1990; cons. dietitian J.B. Johnson Nursing Ctr., Washington, 1990-93, Am. Inst. for Cancer Rsch., Washington, 1987—, Higher Horizons Head Start, Fairfax, Va., 1985-93, Arlington (Va.) Cmty. Action Program, 1985—; employment exch. coord. for dietitians D.C. Dietetic Assn., 1985—; cons. dietitian Hospice Vis. Nurses Assn. No. Va., 1993—. Author: Diabetic's Brand Named Food Exchange Handbook, 1991; contbr. articles to profl. jours. Active Girl Scouts U.S., Arlington, 1989-95, Boy Scouts Am., 1992—. Mem. AAUW, Am. Dietetic Assn., Cons. Nutritionists of Chesapeake Bay Area, Arlington Nutrition Coun., Assn. of Part-Time Profls. Home and Office: 263 N Bryan St Arlington VA 22201-1418

SCHNEIDER, DENNIS RAY, microbiology educator; b. Sinton, Tex., June 10, 1952; m. Cynthia Diane Schatte, Aug. 21, 1976; 2 children. BA with honors, U. Tex., 1974, PhD, 1978. Post-doctoral fellow Behringwerke AG, Marburg/Lahn, West Germany, 1978-79, U. Mo. Med. Sch., Columbia, 1980-81; rsch. microbiologist New Eng. Nuclear, N. Billerica, Mass., 1981-82; R&D dir. Austin (Tex.) Biol. Lab., 1982-88; adj. assoc. prof. U. Tex., Austin, 1986—; R&D devel. dir. Micro-Bac Internat., Austin, 1988-94; v.p. Micro-Bac Internat., Round Rock, Tex., 1994—. Author: Bioremediation: A Desktop Manual for the Environmental Professional; author chpt. Microorganism Adaptation to Host Defense. Grantee NASA, 1988, 92, 93. Mem. AAAS, Am. Soc. for Microbiology, Mensa, Profl. Assn. Dive Instrs. Office: Micro-Bac Internat 3200 N I H 35 Round Rock TX 78681-2410

SCHNEIDER, FRANK DAVID, family physician; b. Brookline, Mass., Aug. 12, 1961; s. Morris I. and Shirley R. (Freedman) S.; m. Peggy S. Lorton, Aug. 14, 1993; children: Michael, Brian, Daniel, Allison. BA, Boston U., 1983, MD, 1987; MS in Pub. Health, U. Mo., 1992. Diplomate Am. Bd. Family Practice, Nat. Bd. Med. Examiners; lic. physician N.C., Tex. Intern Duke U., Fayetteville, N.C., 1987-88, resident in family practice, 1988-90; acad. fellow, clin. instr. dept. family and cmty. medicine U. Mo., Columbia, 1990-92; asst. prof./dir. predoctoral med. edn. dept. family practice U. Tex. Health Sci. Ctr., San Antonio, 1992—; mem. staff Univ. Hosp., San Antonio, 1992, U. Mo. Hosp. and Clinics, Columbia, 1990; lectr. in field. Editor: FellowNet, 1992-93; contbr. article on family violence to profl. jours. Active San Antonio Health Care Partnership; resident dir., found. trustee N.C. Acad. Family Physicians, 1989-90, resident dir. elect, 1988-89; vol. Columbia Medigroup, 1990-92. Am. Acad. Family Physicians Found. grantee, 1994, HHS grantee, 1995, South Tex. Health Resources Ctr., 1995, U. Tex. Health Sci. Ctr., 1993; Burroughs Wellcome Resident scholar Am. Acad. Family Physicians Cong. Del. and Nat. Conv., 1988; recipient Fayetteville Area Health Edn. Ctr. Resident Libr. award, 1988, Tex. Acad. Family Practice Rsch. award, 1996. Mem. AMA, Am. Acad. Family Physicians, Soc. Tchrs. Family Medicine (program com. Violence Edn. Conf. 1995, chmn. group on violence edn. 1996-98, chmn. group on fellowship tng. 1991-93), N.Am. Primary Care Rsch. Group (reviewer abstracts ann. meeting 1992-93, 95-96, Resident/Fellow award 20th ann. meeting 1992), Tex. Acad. Family Physicians (bd. dirs. Alamo chpt. 1996). Office: U Tex Health Sci Ctr Dept Family Practice 7703 Floyd Curl Dr San Antonio TX 78284-6200

SCHNEIDER, GEORGE WILLIAM, retired aircraft design engineer; b. Riley, Kans., Aug. 17, 1923; s. George William and Helen Juanita (Carey) S.; m. Marguerite Ann Bare, May 7, 1945 (div. Oct. 1977); children: Peggy Diane Schneider Tsolakopolous, Donald Lynn; m. L. Elaine Phillips, Oct. 22, 1977. Student, Wichita State U., 1952-58; BSME in Design, Kans. State U., 1962. Designer Ling Temco Vought, Dallas, 1962-65; lead designer 727 Boeing Airplane Co., Renton, Wash., 1965-66; lead designer 747 Boeing Airplane Co., Everett, Wash., 1966-72; designer 707, 727, 737, AWACS Boeing Airplane Co., Renton, 1972-75; designer DeHavilland Dash 7 Boeing Airplane Co., Toronto, Ont., Can., 1975-77; design engr. Boeing Airplane Co., Morgantown, W.Va., 1977-79; lead designer 757 Boeing Airplane Co., Renton, 1980-81; sr. design engr. Boeing Airplane Co., Oak Ridge, Tenn., 1981-83; ret., 1983; vice chmn. Nat. Agenda Bd., 1995-96. Author books, articles, reports in field. Chmn. com. Explorer scouts Boy Scouts Am., Seattle, 1966-68. Mem. ASME (regional chmn. history and heritage 1991, regional nat. agenda bd. 1992-94, sec. nat. agenda bd. 1994-95, editor Dixie News regional news bull., chmn. govtl. rels. Greenville sect. 1990—, chmn. Greenville sect. 1989-93, chmn. awards and hons.), S.C. Coun. of Engring. Soc. (sec., treas. 1992-93, v.p. 1993-94, pres. 1994-95). Home: 211 Roper Mount Rd Ext Greenville SC 29615-4826

SCHNEIDER, JAYNE B., school librarian; b. Cin., Nov. 9, 1950; d. Neil Kendrick and Edith (Dilworth) Bangs; m. James R. Bronn, June 9, 1973 (div. 1979); m. Arthur Schneider, July 11, 1986; 1 stepdaughter, Heather. BS in Elem. Edn., Ea. Ky. U., 1973; MA in Libr. Sci., Spaulding U., 1978. Tchr., 1st & 2d grades Fort Thomas (Ky.) Pub. Schs./Ruth Moyer Elem., 1973; libr. Lassiter Middle Sch., Ky., 1973—; presenter Nat. Middle Sch. Assn., St. Louis, 1988, Denver, 1989, Assn. of Ind. Media Educators, 1992. Mem. Ky. Hist. Soc., Friends of the Libr.; co-capt. Block Watch. Named Superstar Ky. Ednl. TV; Owen Badgett grantee Louisville Community Grant, 1988. Mem. NEA, ALA, AASL, PTSA (life), Nat. Mid. Sch. Assn., Jefferson County Sch. Media Assn. (treas. 1982-83, sec. 1991-92, newsletter editor 1992-93, pres.-elect 1993-94, pres. 1994-95, nomination chairperson 1996—), Ky. Sch. Media Assn. (bd. dirs. 1994-95). Presbyterian. Home: 2553 Kings Hwy Louisville KY 40205-2646 Office: Lassiter Mid Sch 8200 Candleworth Dr Louisville KY 40214-5552

SCHNEIDER, LAZ LEVKOFF, lawyer; b. Columbia, S.C., Mar. 15, 1939; s. Philip L. and Dorothy Harriet (Levkoff) S.; m. Ellen Linda Shiffrin, Dec. 12, 1968; 1 child, David Allen. BA, Yale U., 1961, LLB, 1964; LLM, NYU, 1965. Bar: D.C. 1965, N.Y. 1965, Fla. 1970. Assoc. Fulton, Walter & Duncombe, N.Y.C., 1965-67, Rosenman, Colin Kaye Petschek Freund & Emil, N.Y.C., 1967-69; assoc. Kronish, Lieb, Weiner, Shainswit & Hellman, N.Y.C., 1969-70; ptnr. Ruden Barnett McClosky & Schuster, Ft. Lauderdale, Fla., 1970-80; pvt. practice, Ft. Lauderdale, 1980-86; ptnr. Sherr, Tiballi, Fayne & Schneider, Ft. Lauderdale, 1987-91, Berger & Davis, P.A., Ft. Lauderdale, 1991—; bd. dirs. Am. Surety and Casualty Holding Co. Mem. Goodwin Biotech., Inc., exec. com. Fla. regional bd. Anti Defamation League, 1972—. Mem. Fla. Bar Assn., Broward County Bar Assn. (chmn. sect. corp. bus. and banking law 1978-80). Jewish. Club: Yale (pres. 1977-79). Grad. editor Tax Law Rev., 1964-65. Office: 100 NE 3rd Ave Fort Lauderdale FL 33301-1176

SCHNEIDER, NANCY REYNOLDS, pathologist; b. Schenectady, N.Y., July 27, 1942; d. Charles Philip Jr. and Ruth Louise (Taylor) Reynolds; m. John Stanley Schneider, July 13, 1968. BA, Ohio Wesleyan U., 1963; MA, U. Mich., 1964; MD, Cornell U., 1981, PhD, 1981. Diplomate Am. Bd. Pathology, Am. Bd. Med. Genetics; lic. Tex. Bd. Med. Examiners. Resident in pathology U. Tex. Southwestern Med. Ctr., Dallas, 1982-85; asst. instr. pathology U. Tex. Southwestern Med. Ctr., 1986, instr. pathology, 1986-87, asst. dir. hemotherapy dept., 1986-87, asst. prof. pathology, 1987-92, dir. cytogenetics lab., 1987—, assoc. prof. pathology, 1992—; attending staff physician Parkland Meml. Hosp., Dallas, 1986—. Contbr. articles to profl. jours. and chpt. to book. Mem. AMA, AAAS, Am. Soc. Clin. Pathologists, Am. Soc. Human Genetics, Tex. Genetics Soc., Coll. Am. Pathologists, Phi Beta Kappa. Office: Univ Tex Southwestern Med Ctr Dept Pathology 5323 Harry Hines Blvd Dallas TX 75235-9072

SCHNEIDER, PETER RAYMOND, political scientist; b. Muskogee, Okla., Aug. 8, 1939; s. Leo Frederick and Tillie Oleta (Cannon) S.; m. Anne Larason, Jan. 22, 1964 (div. 1983); children: Christopher, Geoffrey; m. Adrienne Armstrong, Dec. 19, 1986; 1 child, Robbie. BS, Okla. State U., 1966, MS, 1968; PhD, Ind. U., 1974. News editor No. Va. Sun, Arlington, 1961-62; news writer AP, Balt., 1962, Balt. News-Am., 1962-65; asst. prof. U. Oreg., Eugene, 1974-76; pres. Inst. of Policy Analysis, Eugene, 1976-83; v.p. Am. Justice Inst., Sacramento, 1983; dir. Ctr. for Assessment of The Juvenile Justice Ctr., Sacramento, 1983; v.p. Nat. Partnership, Washington, 1985; sr. rsch. scientist Pacific Inst. for Rsch. and Evaluation, Bethesda, Md., 1984-92, dir. justice div., 1986-89; pres. Inst. of Policy Analysis, Vienna, Va., 1992-95; CEO IPA Internat., Inc., Vienna, 1995—. Contbr. numerous articles to profl. jours., chpts. to books. Recipient Julia Lathrop award Am. Criminal Justice Assn., 1985. Mem. Am. Polit. Sci. Assn., Am. Restitution Assn., Pi Sigma Alpha, Sigma Delta Chi, Phi Kappa Phi, Omicron Delta Kappa, Phi Kappa Theta. Home: 9025 Streamview Ln Vienna VA 22182-1726 Office: IPA Internat Inc 8133 Leesburg Pike Ste 260 Vienna VA 22182-2706

SCHNEIDER, RICHARD HAROLD, university dean, educator; b. N.Y.C., Feb. 14, 1947; s. Sam and Shirley (Steier) S.; children: Samantha Raye, Joanna Elizabeth. AB, U. Fla., 1968, MA, 1973, PhD, 1981; acting dean than assoc. dean, 1990—. Researcher, writer CBS TV News, N.Y.C., 1970-71; teaching and research asst. U. Fla., Gainesville, 1971-73; spl. asst. CBS News Radio, Miami Beach, Fla., 1972; asst. to dir. Urban and Regional Devel. Ctr., Gainesville, 1973-75; instr. Santa Fe Community Coll., Gainesville, 1974-75; research assoc. U. Fla., Gainesville, 1975-78; asst. dir. Fla. Architecture and Bdlg. Ctr., Gainesville, 1979-81; asst. dean Coll. Architecture U. Fla., Gainesville, 1981—, assoc. prof., 1984—, assoc. dean, 1987-90, 91—; acting dean, 1990-91; vis. scholar U. Manchester Inst. Sci. and Tech., 1995-96, U. Ariz., 1996; rsch. cons. Inst. Man. and Sci. Rensselaerville, N.Y., 1973; cons. St. Johns River Water Mgmt. Dist., Palatka, Fla., 1979-80, City of High Springs, Fla., 1978-80, City of Gainesville, 1980-81, Miss. State U., 1989. Contbr. articles to profl. jours. Mem. Neighborhood Design Com., 1987-88; organizer Army Res. Med. Screening Program for Indigent, Gainesville, 1972-74; chmn. ACLU, Alachua County, Fla., 1974-75; mem., chmn. Gainesville Mcpl. Svcs. Com. Research grantee City of Gainesville, 1980, Nat. Inst. Dispute Resolution, 1986, Fla. Dept. Environ. Regulation, 1986. Mem. Nat. Inst. Bldg. Scis., Am. Planning Assn., Am. Inst. Cert. Planners, Landscape Architecture Accreditation Bd. (evaluator 1983—), Archtl. Rsch. Ctr. Consortium (sec. 1986—, v.p. 1992-95, pres. 1995—). Democrat. Jewish. Office: U Fla Coll Architecture 431 Arch Bldg Gainesville FL 32611

SCHNEIDER, ROBERT JAMES, languages educator; b. Saginaw, Mich., Feb. 28, 1939; s. Otto and Jane Elizabeth (Putnam) S. BA in Classics, U. of the South, 1961; M in Medieval Studies, U. Notre Dame, 1963, D in Medieval Latin Lit., 1965. Asst. prof. classics U. So. Calif., L.A., 1965-68; prof. classical langs. Berea (Ky.) Coll., 1968—. Bd. dirs., pres. Richmond (Ky.) Choral Soc., 1986—. Recipinet Seabury Tchg. award Berea Coll., 1989, Acorn Tchrs. award Ky. Advocates for Higher Edn., 1993. Mem. Medieval Acad. Am., Am. Philol. Assn., Ky. Classical Assn., Vergilian Soc., Phi Beta Kappa, Phi Kappa Phi. Home: 325 Dale Rd Paint Lick KY 40461-9723 Office: Berea Coll Cpo # 1860 Berea KY 40404

SCHNEIDER, SANFORD, physician, educator; b. Tappan, N.Y., Feb. 4, 1937; s. Jacob and Ann Georgia (Ritz) S.; m. Joan Helene Schwitz, 1959; children: Lisa, Paul, Marc. B.A., U. Rochester, 1959; M.D., NYU, 1963. Diplomate Am. Bd. Psychiatry and Neurology, Am. Bd. Pediatrics. Intern Duke U., Durham, N.C.; resident in pediatrics and neurology Columbia-Presbyn. Med. Ctr., N.Y.C.; dir. child neurology Loma Linda U., Calif., 1971-93, prof. pediatrics and neurology, 1979-93; prof. neurology, chief child neurology Presbyn. Health Found., Okla. U. Health Sci. Ctr., 1993—; chmn. pediatrics Riverside Gen. Hosp., Calif., 1982-91. Served to capt. USAF, 1966-68. Fellow Am. Acad. Neurology, Am. Acad. Pediatrics.

SCHNEIDER, STEVEN L., company executive. Pres., CEO Trion, Inc., Sanford, N.C. Office: 101 McNeill Rd Sanford NC 27331-0760

SCHNEIDER, WILLIAM JAMES, plastic and reconstructive surgeon; b. Miami, Fla., Dec. 19, 1943; s. James William and Reva (Gross) S.; m. Rebecca Jo Phillips, June 10, 1967; children: James Carter, Jason Christopher, Brian Phillips. BS, Stetson U., 1966; MD, Vanderbilt U., 1970. Cert. Am. Bd. Plastic Surgery. Intern surgery U. Fla., Gainesville, 1970-71, resident surgery, 1971-72, 1970-72; resident surgery Emory U., Atlanta, 1972-75, rsident plastic surgery, 1975-77; pvt. practice Aesthetic Plastic Surgery Assocs., Knoxville, Tenn., 1977—; chief dept. surgery East Tenn. Children's Hosp., Knoxville, 1982, Ft. Sanders Regional Med. Ctr., Knoxville, 1986. Author chpts. in several books; contbr. articles to profl. jours. Pres. Westborough Neighborhood Assn., Knoxville, 1986; coach, commr. West Knoxville Youth Baseball, 1978-85. Fellow Am. Coll. Surgeons; mem. Southeastern Soc. Plastic & Reconstructive Surgeons, Tenn. Soc. Plastic & Reconstructive Surgeons (pres. 1988-90), Am. Soc. Plastic & Reconstructive Surgeons, Am. Soc. for Aesthetic Plastic Surgery, Knoxville Surg. Soc. (pres. 1985), Knoxville Acad. Medicine. Methodist. Home: 8101 Osler Ln Knoxville TN 37909-2130 Office: Aesthetic Plastic Surgery 801 Weisgarber Rd NW Knoxville TN 37909-2780

SCHOBEL, GERHARDT BEAVEN, law enforcement officer; b. St. Petersburg, Fla., Nov. 7, 1955; s. William Allen Schobel and Jacquelyn Lee (Beaven) Allison; m. Terry L. Leak, June 26, 1976. AS in Police Adminstrn., St. Petersburg Jr. Coll., 1975; BA in Criminal Justice, U. South Fla., 1977, MPA, 1994. Div. asst. mgr. Sears Roebuck & Co., St. Petersburg, 1974-80; detective sgt. Pinellas County Sheriff's Office, Largo, Fla., 1980—; pres. Creative Insights Corp. Recipient Appreciation award Am. Soc. Indsl. Security, 1985, three Excellent Svc. awards, one Disting. Svc. award, U.S. Postal Inspection Svc., 1988, U.S. Customs Svc., 1989. Mem. ASPA (exec. bd. dirs. Suncoast chpt.), ASTD, Police Benevolent Assn., Pi Alpha Alpha (past pres. U. South Fla. chpt.). Republican. Office: Pinellas County Sheriff's Office 10750 Ulmerton Rd Largo FL 33778-1703

SCHOELL, WILLIAM FREDERICK, III, marketing educator; b. New Orleans, Dec. 3, 1941; s. William Frederick Jr. and Edith (Maumus) S.; m. Rosalie Bowers, June 7, 1963; children: Shannon Kristine, Bryan Patrick. BS, U. New Orleans, 1963; MBA, U. Ark., 1965, PhD, 1969. Econs. instr. U. Ark., Fayetteville, 1964-66; instr. mgmt. and mktg. U. New Orleans, 1966-68, asst. prof. mktg., 1968-69; assoc. prof. U. Southern Miss., Hattiesburg, 1970-75; prof. U. So. Miss., Hattiesburg, 1975—. Author: (with others) Marketing Essentials, 1993, Introduction to Business, 1993, Contemporary Marketing, 1995, Intro to Canadian Business, 1990. Mem. Am. Mktg. Assn., Midwest Mktg. Assn., Southwest Mktg. Assn., Southern Mktg. Assn., Beta Gamma Sigma. Home: 308 4th Ave Hattiesburg MS 39401-4276 Office: U So Miss PO Box 8122 Hattiesburg MS 39406-8122

SCHOEMANN, RUDOLPH ROBERT, lawyer; b. Chgo., Nov. 2, 1930; s. Rudolph and Anna Elise (Claus) S.; m. Florence Margaret Olivier, May 17, 1952 (div.); children—Peggy Ann Schoemann Salathe, Rudolph Robert III, Richard Randolph (dec.), Rodney Ryan; m. Marie Louise Gandolfo Webb, Dec. 2, 1983. Student, Wabash Coll., Crawfordsville, Ind., 1946-47; B.C.S., Loyola U. of South, New Orleans, 1959, J.D., 1952; B.A., Tulane U., 1966, LL.M. in Admiralty Law, 1981, LL.M. in Internat. Law, 1989; postgrad. U. New Orleans, 1981-82. Bar: La. 1952, U.S. Supreme Ct. 1959, U.S. Ct. Appeals (5th cir.) 1952, U.S. Ct. Appeals (11th cir.) 1981, U.S. Ct. Appeals (D.C. cir.) 1982, U.S. Dist. Ct. Md. 1957, U.S. Dist. Ct. (ea. dist.) La. 1952, U.S. Dist. Ct. (we. dist.) La. 1960, U.S. Dist. Ct. (mid. dist.) La. 1952, U.S. Ct. Mil. Appeals, 1953, U.S. Ct. Customs and Patent Appeals 1953, U.S. Ct. Claims 1953. Assoc. James J. Morrison, New Orleans, 1952-54; ptnr. Smith & Schoemann, New Orleans, 1955-60, Schoemann & Gomes, 1961-63, Schoemann, Gomes, Ducote & Collins, 1963-67, Schoemann, Gomes & Ducote, 1968-74, Rudolph R. Schoemann, 1974-77, Schoemann & Golden, 1978-79, Schoemann, Swaim, Morrison & Cockfield, 1979-80, Schoemann & Assocs., 1980—(all New Orleans). Served with La. N.G., 1949-52, to 1st lt. JAGC, U.S. Army, 1952-53; capt. Res. ret. Mem. ABA, La. Bar Assn., New Orleans Bar Assn., La. Def. Assn., New Orleans Def. Assn., Def. Research Inst., Soc. Naval Architects and Marine Engrs., Fed. Bar Assn. Democrat. Lutheran. Address: 3670 Gentilly Blvd New Orleans LA 70122-4910

SCHOENBUCHER, BRUCE, health physicist; b. Dec. 15, 1943; s. Albert King and Alice Elizabeth (Thomson) S.; m. Patty Jo Parry, Feb. 3, 1965 (div. Feb. 1980); children: Teresa Marie, Bonnie Lynn Schoenbucher Mendoza; m. Nancy Lippincott, Jan. 3, 1987; 1 child, Carly Cramer Cutler. BS in Radiation Protection Engring., Tex. A&M U., 1977, MS in Nuclear Engring., 1982. Lic. med. physicist, Tex.; cert. healthcare safety profl. Health physicist nuclear sci. ctr. Tex. A&M U., College Station, 1971-75, health physicist Coll. Vet. Medicine, 1977-79; mgr. radiation safety programs U. Tex. Med. Br., Galveston, 1980-88, asst. dir. environ. health and safety, 1984-88, radiation safety officer, dir. environ. health and safety, 1988—; radiation safety officer Burn Inst Shriners Hosp. for Crippled Children, Galveston, 1991—; presenter in field. Contbr. articles to profl. pubis. With USN, 1962-71. Mem. APHA, Health Physics Soc. (med. sect. exec. bd. 1993-96, mem. pub. info. com. 1981-84, chmn. 1982-84), South Tex. Chpt. Health Physics Soc. (chmn. ad hoc com. on licensure of med. physicists, chmn. fin. com. 1986-88, treas. 1980-85, pres-elect 1985-86, pres. 1986-87), Am. Assn. Physicists in Medicine, Am. Biol. Safety Assn., Am. Soc. Safety Engrs., Laser Inst. Am., Nat. Fire Protection Assn., Tex. Safety Assn., Galveston C. of C., U.S. Coast Guard Auxilliary, Phi Kappa Phi, Sigma Nu Epsilon, Tau Beta Pi. Office: U Tex Med Br 301 Univ Blvd Galveston TX 77555-0633

SCHOFIELD, BARBARA CURTRIGHT, school administrator; b. Paris, Mo., Dec. 24, 1942; d. W.L. and Karoline (Klein) Curtright; m. Alan Otis Schofield, Apr. 28, 1967 (div. 1986); children: Dianna Kay, Nichol LaVaughn, Theresa Alana. BS, U. Mo., Columbia, 1964; MEd, U. Mo., St. Louis, 1978; Cert. Ednl. Specialist, Southeast La. U., 1986. Cert. ednl. adminstr., La. Tchr. phys. edn. Neal Jr. High Sch., North Chicago, Ill., 1964-66, Deerfield (Ill.) High Sch., 1966-67, Holy Child H.S., Waukegan, Ill., 1970-72; dean of girls Antioch (Ill.) High Sch., 1972-74; dean of students, extra-curricular activities Washington (Mo.) High Sch., 1974-78; phys. edn. tchr. Clearwood Jr. High Sch., Slidell, La., 1978-83; asst. prin. Boyet Jr. High Sch., Slidell, 1983—. Elder 1st Presbyn. Ch., Slidell, 1985-90, 93—, clk. of session, 1993-95, 97—. Mem. ASCD, NEA, La. Assn. Educators (mem. congrl. contact team dist. 1), St. Tammany Assn. Educators (legis. chmn. 1980-81, pres. 1981-83), St. Tammany Adminstrs. Assn. (sec. 1991-92), Alpha Delta Kappa (pres. 1990-92), Delta Kappa Gamma. Office: Boyet Jr High Sch 59295 Rebel Dr Slidell LA 70461-3713

SCHOFIELD, CALVIN ONDERDONK, JR., bishop; b. Delhi, N.Y., Jan. 6, 1933; s. Calvin O. and Mabel (Lenton) S.; m. Elaine Marie Fullerton, Aug. 3, 1963; children: Susan Elaine, Robert Lenton. B.A., Hobart Coll., 1959, S.T.D. (Hon.), 1980; M.Div., Berkeley Div. Sch., 1959, D.D. (hon.), 1979; D.D. (hon.), U. of the South, 1981. Ordained priest Episcopal Ch., 1962; curate St. Peter's Episcopal Ch., St. Petersburg, Fla., 1962-64; vicar St. Andrew's Episcopal Ch., Miami, Fla., 1964-70; rector St. Andrew's Episcopal Ch., 1970-78; bishop coadjutor Diocese S.E. Fla., Miami, 1978-79, bishop, 1980—; exec. bd. Presiding Bishops Fund for World Relief; exec. coun. Episcopal Ch., 1991—. Regent U. of the South, Sewanee, Tenn., 1988—. Capt. chaplain corps USNR, 1960-85; ret., 1985. Mem. Naval Res. Assn., Naval Inst. Republican. Office: 525 NE 15th St Miami FL 33132-1411

SCHOFIELD, JAMES ROY, medical consultant, educator; b. July 12, 1923; s. Arthur Monroe and Grace Pearl (West) S. BS, Baylor U., 1945, MD, 1947; LLD (hon.), Queens U., Kingston, Ont., Can., 1988. Instr. to prof. Baylor U. Coll. Medicine, Houston, 1947-71; asst. dean to acad. dean Baylor U. Coll. Medicine, 1953-71; sec., liaison com. on med. edn. Assn. Am. Med. Colls. and AMA, Washington, 1972-87; ind. cons. on med. edn. Washington, 1987—; mem. transitional coun. United Arab Emirates U., 1986-89; external auditor Sultan Qaboos Coll. Medicine, Muscat, Oman, 1987—; vis. disting. prof. history of medicine, univ. cons. on premed. edn. Baylor U., 1992—; faculty Baylor in the British Isles, 1994—; cons. in field. Author: New and Expanded Medical Schools: Midcentury to the 1980's, 1985; contbr. articles to profl. jours. Bd. dirs. Am-Polish Found., 1995. Capt. M.C., U.S. Army, 1954-57. Recipient disting. Achievement award Baylor U., 1992, Disting. Alumnus award Baylor Coll. Medicine, 1996. Mem. Sigma Xi, Alpha Omega Alpha. Republican. Baptist. Address: 700 Greenwood Ct Georgetown TX 78628-8371

SCHOFIELD, JOHN MARCUS, retired lawyer, writer; b. Peoria, Ill., May 5, 1913; s. Adlai Bassett and Ethel Leigh (Whiting) S.; m. Melba Opal White, June 21, 1939 (div.); children: Beverly, Robert, William, John, Jean; m. Doris Abigail Boatwright, Aug. 21, 1965; children: J. Marcus, James, Candace, Carmen; m. Elizabeth Jane Crocker, Sept. 3, 1977. BS in Banking, U. Ill., 1938; postgrad., Ark. Law Sch., 1942-43. Bar: S.C. 1943, U.S. Dist. Ct. S.C. 1944, U.S. Ct. Appeals, U.S. Supreme Ct. 1950. Ins. adjuster Jack C. Neer Co., Portland, Oreg., 1939-41, Gay and Taylor, Greenville, S.C., 1942-43; pvt. practice law Walhalla, S.C., 1943-65; editor, pub. DuQuoin (Ill.) Panorama, 1965-72; asst. Sunday editor Sarasota (Fla.) Herald Tribune, 1972-82; freelance writer Sarasota, 1982—; mediator Sarasota County Ctr., 1984—. Author: Justice Leads the Way, 1984, On a Lonely Island, 1992, The Lady is Coming to Dinner, 1992. Spkr., Rep. Nat. Com., 1936; sec. S.C. Rep. Com., 1956, spkr., 1964-65; alt. del. Rep. Nat. Conv., San Francisco, 1956; dir. Sarasota/Manatee Univ. of Ill. Alumni Club. Mem. Assn. Ret. Attys. (past officer). Home: 3976 Linwood St Sarasota FL 34232-3728

SCHOFIELD, ROBERTA, artist, consultant, educator; b. Ronceverte, W.Va., July 9, 1945; d. Thomas Robert Schofield Morrison and Ruth Thrasher; m. James Frederic Perry, June 6, 1984. Student, Berea Coll., 1963-64, U. Cin., 1965-69; BA, U. South Fla., 1973, MFA, 1979. Adj. faculty U. South Fla., Tampa, 1979-81; faculty South Fla. Jr. Coll., Avon Park, 1979-82, U. Wis., Eau Claire, 1983-84; interim dir. Fla. Ctr. Contemporary Art, Tampa, 1986-87, ind. curator, 1987—; adj. faculty Saint Petersburg (Fla.) Jr. Coll., 1988; ind. curator Tampa City Coun., 1988-90, 91-94; ind. artist Tampa, 1979—. Exhibits include (solo and two person): Waterworks Visual Art Ctr., Salisbury, N.C., Broward C.C., Pembroke Pines, Fla., Visual Arts Ctr. Northwest Fla., Panama City, St. Petersburg Ctr. for the Arts, Fla., Tampa Bay Performing Arts Ctr., Tampa, Fla., Cudahy's Gallery, Richmond, Va., Clayton Galleries, Tampa, Jacksonville Coalition for the Arts, Art in Pub. Places Gallery, Tampa, Centre Club, Tampa, Stein Gallery, Tampa, Capitol Gallery, Tallahassee, St. Andrew's, Tampa, Hillsborough Community Coll., Tampa, TECO Pla. Gallery, Tampa, Polk Community Coll., Winter Haven, Fla., Tampa Gen., Berry Coll., Rome, Ga., Tampa City Hall, Capricorn Galleries, Bethesda, Md., Latin Quarter Gallery, Tampa, Brandon (Fla.) Cultural Ctr., Jones Intercable, Tampa, The Casements, Ormond Beach, Fla., Jamestown Community Coll., Olean, N.Y., Gallery E, Evergreen, Colo., West Liberty (W.Va.) Coll., Campbellsville (Ky.) Coll., New Coll., Sarasota, Fla., U. Cen. Fla., U. South Fla., Fla. Sch. for the Arts; group exhibits include: Port Royal Plantation, Hilton Head Island, S.C., Dunedin (Fla.) Fine Art Ctr., Raleigh Gallery, Boca Raton, Fla., Ruth Eckerd Hall Performing Arts Ctr., Clearwater, Fla., Sarasota (Fla.), Visual Arts Ctr., Tampa (Fla.) Mus. Art, Polk Mus. Art, Lakeland, Fla., Polk Cmty. Coll., Winter Haven, LeMoyne Art Found., Tallahassee, Gulf Coast Cmty. Coll., Panama City, Fla., Lakeland Ctr. Arts, Octagon Arts Ctr., Clearwater, Fla., Raleigh Gallery, Dania, Fla., Linda Hayman Gallery, Boca Raton, Fla., U. South Fla. Mus., Tampa, Stein Gallery, Tampa, Crescent Gallery, Huntington, N.Y., Miami U., Oxford, Ohio, The Arts Ctr., St. Petersburg (1st. Place 1979, 83), Ridge Art Assn., Winter Haven (Merit award 1979, Best of Show 1986, Equal Merit award 1989), Joan Hodgell Gallery, Sarasota (2nd Prize 1988), Orlando (Fla.) Mus. Art, North Miami (Fla.) Mus. and Art Ctr., Gallery Contemporanea, Jacksonville, Fla., The Soc. of Four Arts (Mary Hulitar award 1982), Palm Beach, Fla., Brea (Calif.) Gallery, Milw. Art Mus., Hanson Galleries, New Orleans, and various others: pub. and corp. collections include: City of St. Petersburg, Polk Mus. Art, Lakeland, Deland (Fla.) Mus. Art, Sterling Winthrop Rsch., Collegeville, Pa., Anchor Glass Container Corp., Tampa, Strathmore Hall Found., Rockville, Md., U. Wis., Eau Claire, Jamestown Community Coll., Valencia Community Coll., Orlando, Barnett Banks, St. Petersburg, Tampa and Jacksonville, Fed. Res. Banks, Miami, Richmond, Va., First Fla. Banks, Clearwater, Lakeland, Orlando, Holland & Knight, Tampa, Gen. Telephone Co., Tampa; executed mural for Guardian ad Litem, Tampa. Bd. dirs. Women's Caucus for Art Fla./West Coast chpt., Saint Petersburg, 1986-90; mem./exhibit coord. Las Damas De Arte, Tampa, 1987-89, v.p. 1996—; chmn. com. Festival Charities, Inc., Tampa, 1991; mem. Coll. Art Assn.; chair Artists Adv. Com. Hillsborough County, 1995—, mem. (ex-officio) Arts Coun. of Hillsborough County, 1995—; founder Ye Loyal Krewe of Grace O'Malley, Tampa, 1992. Grantee Fla. Individual Artist fellowship, 1987, Finalist NLAPW Mature Women's scholarship, 1988, Hillsborough County Arts Coun., 1990; recipient Equal Merit award Lee Scarfone Gallery U. Tampa, 1980, 2d prize Thomas Ctr. Gallery, 1980, 1st prize Equ Claire Arts Coun., 1984, Cert. Excellence Internat. Art Competition, L.A., 1984, Arts Recognition award Tampa/Hillsborough County Arts Coun., 1987; named Disting. Alumna USF Coll. of Fine Arts, 1990. Mem. AAUP (bd. dirs. Fla. conf. 1986-87), Coll. Art Assn., Women's Caucus for Art (elected mem.), Fla. Artists Group, Nat. Assn. Women Artists (elected mem.). Home: PO Box 10561 Tampa FL 33679-0561

SCHON, ALAN WALLACE, lawyer, actor; b. Mpls., Nov. 27, 1946; s. Hubert Adelbert and Jennie (Jamieson) S.; m. Linda Kay Long, June 14, 1969; 1 child, Cynthia Anne. BA, U. Minn., 1969; JD, William and Mary Coll., 1973; grad. Command & Gen. Staff Coll., U.S. Army, 1984. Bar: Minn. 1973, U.S. Dist. Ct. Minn., Alaska 1986, U.S. Dist. Ct. Alaska, U.S. Ct. Appeals (9th cir.) 1988, Va. 1995. Prin. Schon Law Office, Fairbanks, Alaska, 1986-94; owner, pub. Nordland Pub. Co., Hampton, Va., 1991-94; dep. city atty. mcpl. bonds, environ. law, pub.-pvt. econ. devel. funding environ. law City of Hampton, Va., 1994—; nationwide environ. group mgr. Delphi Info. Network, Gen. Videotex Corp., Cambridge, Mass., 1991-94. Author, pub. EnvironLaw, 1991-94; editor William and Mary Law Rev., 1970-73; performer Va. Opera, Norfolk, 1995, 96; film actor Day of the Jackal and Quest: Flight 427 (The Learning Channel). Dir. Alaska State Fair, Fairbanks, 1987-91, Fairbanks Light Opera Theater, Fairbanks, 1991-94; dir., sec. Riding for Am., Inc., 1993—; dir. Interior Alaska Econ. Devel. Ctr., 1993-94. Maj. U.S. Army, 1974-86. Mem. Fairbanks C. of C. (chmn. environ. concerns com. 1992-94). Home: 13 Keeton Ct Hampton VA 23666-2271 Office: Office of City Atty 22 Lincoln St Hampton VA 23669-3522

SCHON, SANDRA DIANE, elementary school educator; b. Oak Park, Ill., May 17, 1961; d. Edwin and Dolores (Donald) Czubakowski; m. Donald Eugene Schon, June 25, 1994. BS in English, Reading, North Tex. State U., 1983. Cert. tchr. English, reading, Tex. Supr. acad. support svcs. So. Ill. U., Carbondale, 1984-87; acct.'s asst. Tex. Woman's U., Denton, 1987-90, memtor trainer, 1995—; tchr. Little Elm (Tex.) Ind. Sch. Dist., 1991—, site-base team mem., 1994—, curriculum devel. mem., 1996—. Named to Outstanding Young Women in Am., 1988; McMath Music scholar, 1979. Mem. ASCD.

SCHÖNHOFF, KATHLEEN MARIE, nursing educator; b. Janesville, Wis., Feb. 23, 1923; d. Patrick Joseph and Mary Anne (Regan) O'Hara; m. Robert lee Schönhoff Sr., Dec. 24, 1971; children: Joseph John, Brian Robert. BS in Nursing, Incarnate Word Coll., 1970, MS in Nursing, 1987; MS in Edn., S.W. Tex. State U., 1974. Prof. nursing San Antonio Coll., 1974—, coord. pediatric nursing, 1990-92, prof. nursing emeritus, 1992; nurse examiner Tex. Dept. Health, San Antonio, 1994—; nurse resource person for film on nursing dept. theatre/comms. dept. San Antonio Coll., 1988; conductor breast self-exam. clinic Holy Cross Family Health Pavilion, San Antonio, 1988; nurse examiner dept. of health Tex. Nurses Found. Mem. Altar Soc. of Our Lady of Grace Parish, San Antonio; mem. profl. adv. com. Vis. Nurses Assn. Mem. AAUP (treas. 1989), ANA (charter mem. Coun. Maternal-Child Nursing 1987—), Nat. League Nursing, Nat. Assn. Hispanic Nurses, Tex. Faculty Assn., San Antonio Symphony Assn., Benefactor's Club (Incarnate Word Coll.), Sigma Theta Tau, Sigma Lambda Chi. Republican. Roman Catholic. Home: 501 Hillside Dr Olmos Park Estates San Antonio TX 78212

SCHOOLEY, CHARLES EARL, electrical engineer, consultant; b. Archie, Mo., Sept. 18, 1905; s. Charles Elias and Virginia Maria (Bone) S.; m. Dorothy S. Alexander, Apr. 29, 1934 (dec. 1965); 1 dau., Dorothy Virginia; m. Dolores Harter, Apr. 1966 (dec. 1993). B.S. in Elec. Engring, U. Mo., 1928. Registered profl. engr., Ga. With Ozark Utilities Co., Bolivar Telephone Co., Mo. Pacific R.R.; transmission engr. Long Lines dept. Am. Tel. & Tel. Co., St. Louis, Kansas City, N.Y.C., 1927-44; co-axial carrier engr., elec. coordination engr. Am. Tel. & Tel. Co., N.Y.C., 1944-48; div. engr. Am. Tel. & Tel. Co., Washington, 1948-49; facility engr., engr. transmission, comml. devel. engr. Am. Tel. & Tel. Co., 1949-51, toll dialing engr., plant extension engr., system planning engr., operating and engring. dep., 1951-53, asst. chief engr., dir. customer products planning, 1956-57; chief engr. So. Bell Tel. & Tel. Co., Atlanta, 1953-55; v.p. operations, dir. Ind. Bell Telephone Co., Indpls., 1957-59; dir. operations, mem. bd. long lines dept. Am. Tel. & Tel. Co., N.Y., 1959-66; dir., v.p. Transpacific Communications Co., Transocean Cable Ship Co., Eastern Tel. & Tel. Co., 1960-66, 9 other Am. Tel. & Tel. subs; v.p., treas., dir. Eds, Inc., Sharon, Conn., 1970-85. Vice pres. Berkshire Hills (Conn.) Music and Dance Assn., 1970-78; v.p., treas. Wingspread Found., 1977—; trustee Brevard (N.C.) Music Ctr., 1994—. Recipient Disting. Service to Engring. medal U. Mo., 1960. Fellow IEEE; mem. Ga. Engring. Soc., Met. Club (N.Y.C.), Hendersonville (N.C.) Country Club, QEBH U. Mo., Delta Upsilon (bd. dirs. 1962-70), Eta Kappa Nu. Address: PO Box 746 Hendersonville NC 28793-0746 also: PO Box 633 Winter Haven FL 33882-0633 also: 210 Crooked Creek Rd Hendersonville NC 28739-6822

SCHOOLEY, KENNETH RALPH, manufacturing company executive; b. Anamosa, Iowa, Jan. 22, 1943; s. Ralph Kenneth and Kathleen Ann (Eilers) S.; m. Sharon Faye Foster, July 11, 1986; children by previous marriage: Blaine Evan, Lynette Kay. Student, Kirkwood Community Coll., Cedar Rapids, Iowa, 1971-75. Asst. warehouse mgr. Trico Auto Parts, Bakersfield, Calif., 1964-65; mail carrier U.S. Post Office, Bakersfield, 1965, Marion,

Iowa, 1965-66; asst. traffic mgr. Cargill Corn Starch & Syrup, Cedar Rapids, 1966-68; traffic mgr. LeFebure Corp., Cedar Rapids, 1968-71; traffic mgr. to mgr. traffic and warehouse Amana Refrigerator, 1971-80; traffic mgr. Service Merchandise Co., Nashville, 1980-84; corp. traffic mgr. U.S.A. Inter City Products, La Vergne, Tenn., 1984-95; logistics mgr. Am. Water Heater Group, Johnson City, Tenn., 1995—. Mem. Iowa Indsl. Traffic League (sec.-treas. 1973-74). Republican. Lutheran. Club: Nashville Traffic. Home: 1412 Colowy Park Dr # 13 Johnson City TN 37604 Office: Am Water Heater Group 101 S Broadway St Johnson City TN 37601-4958

SCHOOLS, CHARLES HUGHLETTE, banker, lawyer; b. Lansing, Mich., May 24, 1929; s. Robert Thomas and Lillian Pearl (Lawson) S.; B.S., Am. U., 1952, M.A., 1958; J.D., Washington Coll. of Law, 1963; LL.D., Bethune-Cookman U., 1973; m. Rosemarie Sanchez, Nov. 22, 1952; children—Charles, Michael. Dir. phys. plant Am. U., 1952-66; owner, 1957—, Gen. Security Co., Washington, 1969—; chmn., pres. Consol. Ventures Ltd.; pres., chmn. bd. McLean Bank (Va.), 1974—, Instl. Environ. Mgmt. Services; chmn. bd. Harper & Co.; chmn., pres. Community Assos. of Va., Associated Real Estate Mgmt. Services; dir. Computer Data Systems Inc., DAC Devel. Ltd., Am. Indsl. Devel. Corp., Intercoastal of Iran; mem. Met. Bd. Trades. Pres., McLean Boys' Club; bd. dirs. D.C. Spl. Olympics, Nat. Kidney Found.; trustee Bethune Cookman Coll., Western Md. Coll., Randolph Macon Acad. Served with USAAF, 1946-47, USAF, 1947-48. Mem. Va. C. of C., Profl. Businessman's Orgn., Alpha Tau Omega. Democrat. Clubs: Georgetown of Washington, Touchdown of Washington, Univ. of Washington, Washington Golf and Country, Pisces (Washington); Halifax (Daytona Beach, Fla.); Masons. Home: 1320 Darnall Dr Mc Lean VA 22101-3006 Office: 1313 Dolley Madison Blvd Mc Lean VA 22101-3926

SCHOONOVER, HUGH JAMES, roofing company executive; b. Buffalo, N.Y., Nov. 3, 1942; s. Lyle L. and Helen Gladys (Mitchell) S.; m. Magdalen Ann Nowikowski, Apr. 11, 1969 (div. Aug. 1980); m. Edith Ann Forner, Jan. 11, 1986. Student, Cuyahoga Community Coll., Cleve., 1964-66, Wright State U., Dayton, Ohio, 1965-66; grad., Real Estate Inst. Lic. real estate broker, mortgage broker; cert. buyer agt. Asst. mgr. Midland Guardian Acceptance Co., Cin., 1964-69; mgr. Am. Loan and Savs., Hamilton, Ohio, 1969-73; salesman Midwest Cemetery Cons., Dayton, 1973-78; pres. Hoover Construction, Dayton, 1978-82; chmn. B&H Industries of S.W. Fla. (DBA Shutterworld, Rolsafe), Ft. Myers, Fla., 1982-92; pres. A Buyer's Agency Realty, Inc., Fla., 1992-96, Abar Martgage Co., Cape Coral, Fla., 1992-96, A Better Applied Roof, Fla., 1996—; chmn. adv. bd. S.W. Fla. div. BBB, Ft. Myers, 1984-89, dir. Miami, 1984-89. With USMC, 1960-64. Mem. Marine Corps League, Sons Am. Revolution (v.p. 1988-89), Am. Legion, Shriners, Moose, Elks. Republican.

SCHOONOVER, JACK RONALD, judge; b. Winona, Minn., July 23, 1934; s. Richard M. and Elizabeth A. (Hargeisheimer) S.; student Winona State Coll., 1956-58; LLB, U. Fla., 1962; m. Ann Marie Kroez, June 18, 1965; children: Jack Ronald, Wayne J. Bar: Fla. 1962. Atty. Wotitzky, Wotitzky & Schoonover, 1962-69, Schoonover, Olmsted & Schwarz, 1969-75; spl. asst. state's atty., State of Fla., 1969-72; city atty. City of Punta Gorda, Fla., city judge, 1973-74; judge 20th Jud. Cir. Ct., Ft. Myers, Fla., 1975-81, 2d Dist. Ct. Appeal, 1981—, chief judge, 1990-92; atty. Charlotte County Sch. Bd., 1969-75, Charlotte County Zoning Bd., Charlotte County Devel. Authority; mem. unauthorized practice law com. 12th Jud. Cir., mem. grievance com. 20th Jud. Cir.; adj. prof. Edison C.C. Tchr. Charlotte County Adult Edn. Assn. Served with USAF, 1952-56. Mem. Am. Legion. Home: 1224 Stratton Ct W Lakeland FL 33813-2348 Office: PO Box 327 Lakeland FL 33802-0327

SCHOPPER, SUE FRANKS, maternal, women's health and medical/surgical nurse; b. Stigler, Okla., Mar. 25, 1938; d. Everett and Ruby (McCaslin) F.; m. Jared B. Schopper, Jan. 27, 1978; children: Robert, Jenny, Melody. Assoc. Diploma Nursing, Bacone Coll., Muskogee, Okla., 1973; BSN, Northeastern State U., Tahlequah, Okla., 1991. RN, Okla. Supr. VA Med. Ctr., Muskogee, 1973-78; charge nurse obstetrics-labor-delivery room, newborn nursery Hastings Hosp., Tahlequah, 1979; charge nurse surg. floor Tahlequah City Hosp., 1983-90; pediatric nurse Pediatric Clinic, Tahlequah, 1990—; RN cons. Green Acres Retirement Ctr., Tahlequah, 1989—. Home: 402 Wheeler St Tahlequah OK 74464-6301 Office: Pediatric Clinic 1607 S Muskogee Ave Tahlequah OK 74464-5430

SCHOPPMEYER, MARTIN WILLIAM, education educator; b. Weehawken, N.J., Sept. 15, 1929; s. William G. and Madeleine M. (Haas) S.; m. Marilyn M. Myers, Aug. 9, 1958; children: Susan Ann, Martin William. B.S., Fordham U., 1950; Ed.M., U. Fla., 1955, Ed.D., 1962. Tchr. Fla. pub. schs., 1955-59; instr., then asst. prof. U. Fla., 1960-63; assoc. prof., then prof. edn. Fla. Atlantic U., Boca Raton, 1963-68; dir. continuing edn. Fla. Atlantic U., 1965-67; mem. faculty U. Ark., Fayetteville, 1968—; prof. edn. U. Ark., 1971-93; univ. prof. U. Ark., Fayetteville, 1993—; program coord. for ednl. adminstrn. U. Ark., 1983-90; mem. Nat. Adv. Coun. Edn. Professions Devel., 1973-76; exec. sec. Ark. Sch. Study Coun., 1976—; evaluator instructional tng. program Nat. Tng. Fund, 1978; bd. dirs. Women's Ednl. and Devel. Inst., 1977-80, Nat. Sch. Devel. Coun., sec., 1989-90, v.p. 1990, pres., 1990-92; mem. oversight com. South Conway (Ark.) County Sch. Dist.; mem. state commn. to study effect of Amendment 59 to Ark. Constn. Author books, monographs, articles in field. Mem. president's coun. Subiaco Acad., 1984-90; chmn. Subiaco Sch. Bd., 1990-93, mem., 1993—. With U.S. Army, 1951-53, Korea. Recipient numerous fed. grants. Mem. NEA, Ark. Edn. Assn. (past chpt. pres.), Ark. Assn. Ednl. Adminstrs., KC, Rotary, Kappa Delta Pi, Phi Delta Kappa, Delta Tau Kappa. Roman Catholic. Home: 2950 Sheryl Ave Fayetteville AR 72703-3542 Office: U Ark 231 Grad Edn Bldg Fayetteville AR 72701

SCHOR, OLGA SEEMANN, mental health counselor, real estate broker; b. Havana, Cuba, Mar. 2, 1951; came to U.S., 1961; d. Olga del Carmen (Hernandez) S.; m. David Michael Schor, Apr. 22, 1979; 1 child, Andrew. A.A., Miami Dade Community Coll., 1971; B.A., U. Fla.-Gainesville, 1973; M.Edn., U. Miami, Fla., 1976; Psy.D., Nova U., 1981; cert. Bert Rodgers Sch. Real Estate, Miami, 1981, Gold Coast Sch. Real Estate, 1988; lic. real estate broker. Teaching asst. U. Fla., Gainesville, 1972-73; counselor U. Miami, Fla., 1974-79; assoc. psychotherapist Linda H. Jamrozy & Assocs., Miami, 1976-78, Interactive Systems, Miami, 1978-79; psychometrist Jackson Meml. Hosp., Miami, 1978-79; assoc. psychotherapist Behavioral Medicine Inst., Miami, 1979-85, Tony Ciminero & Assocs., Miami, 1985-86; lectr. U. Miami, 1976-78, Jackson Meml. Hosp. Sch. Nursing, Miami, 1976; real estate broker The Keyes Co. Realtor, Coral Gables, 1981-88, Keyes Asset Mgmt., Miami, 1988—; sec./treas. bd. dirs. BODS Inc., Miami. Chmn. creative writing Jr. Orange Bowl competition. Recipient Assoc. of Quarter award Keyes Co. Realtors, 1986. Mem. Am. Psychol. and Guidance Assn., Keyes Comml. Roundtable, Keyes Inner Circle, Coral Gables Bd. Realtors, Gulliver Acad.'s Parents Bd., Dade County Mental Health Assn., Million Dollar Sales Club. Club: South Fla. Sailing Assn. (Miami). Avocations: sailing; diving; reading; running; theater; acting; tennis. Office: Keyes Asset Mgmt Inc 1 SE 3rd Ave Fl 11 Miami FL 33131-1700

SCHORB, E(DWIN) M(ARSH), poet; b. Plainfield, N.J., Sept. 12, 1935; s. Edwin Marsh and Mary Ann (McGrath) S.; m. Margaret Patricia Hill; children: Selah Brett, Leslie Helene. Acting and drama student, Neighborhood Playhouse, N.Y.C., 1957-58, Erwin Piscator's Dramatic Workshop, N.Y.C., 1958-59; student, Henry George Sch. Polit. Economy, 1966-68. Author: Poor Boy and Other Poems, 1975, 50 Poems, 1987; contbr. poems to lit. publs., including Am. Scholar, Sewanee Rev., So. Rev., Yale Rev., Carolina Quar., Stand, Frank. N.C. Arts Coun. fellow in lit., 1995-96; grantee Am. Acad. Arts and Letters, Dramatists Guild, Authors League Fund. Home and Office: PO Box 1461 Mooresville NC 28115

SCHORMAN, TEDD J., film producer; b. Lawrence, Mass., Sept. 25, 1947; s. Edward Joseph and Abby Irene (Curry) S.; m. Ellie M. Perron, Jan. 20, 1973; children: Kyle J., Kara M. Grad. high sch., North Andover, Mass. Sr. v.p. Holiday Inn, Memphis, 1975-86; group v.p. Howard Johnson Co., Boston, 1982-86; pres., CEO Sable Enterprises, Inc., Memphis, 1986—. Exec. prodr.: (African wildlife film) Swift and Silent, 1992 (ACE Award 1992), Silent Hunter, 1991 (Discovery Award 1993). Wildlife film donations to various charitable and sch. sys.; bd. dirs. Hotel Motel Assn., Memphis, 1982-85. Office: Sable Enterprises Inc 779 Walnut Knoll Ln Cordova TN 38018-6302

SCHOTT, CLIFFORD JOSEPH, lawyer; b. Newark, N.J., July 28, 1926; s. Clifford J. and Sally V. (Donnelly) S.; m. Nancybelle MacDonnell, July 22, 1951; children: Christylee, Clifford, Sally, Steven, Craig. Student, Upsala U., 1949-51; grad., U. Miami, 1952, JD, 1954. Bar: Fla. 1955, U.S. Dist. Ct. (so. dist.) Fla. 1956, U.S. Ct. Appeals (5th cir.) 1959, U.S. Ct. Appeals (11th cir.) 1981, U.S. Tax. Ct. 1973, Fla. RR and Pub. Utilities Commn. 1963, U.S. Supreme Ct. 1968. Assoc. Holladay & Swann, Miami, Fla., 1955-56; ptnr. Hastings, Thomas & Sheppard, Miami, 1956-57; asst. gen. counsel Dade County Port Auth., Miami, 1957-60; atty., negotiator Eastern Airlines, Inc., Miami, 1960-63; assoc. Carver, Langston & Massey, Lakeland, Fla., 1963-66; ptnr. Wendel & Schott, Lakeland, 1966-68; pvt. practice Lakeland, 1968-83; sr. ptnr. Schott & Dale, P.A., Lakeland, 1983-89; pvt. practice Lakeland, Fla., 1989—; mcpl. judge City of Lakeland, 1967-68; asst. county solicitor County of Polk, Bartow, Fla., 1967-69. Pres., Polk County Assn. Retarded Children, Lakeland, 1966-67, com. chmn., 1967; counsel Ch. of the Resurrection, Lakeland; bd. dirs. St. Joseph's Sch., Lakeland, 1973. With USAAF, 1944-46, ETO. Mem. ABA, Fla. Bar Assn., Lakeland Bar Assn., Assn. Trial Lawyers of Am., Polk County Trial Lawyers Assn. (adv. com. 1983—), Fla. Def. Lawyers Assn. (bd. dirs. 1985—), Internat. Assn. Def. Attys., 10th Judicial Cir. Bar, Lakeland C. of C. (aviation adv. com.), Am. Legion (judge adv. 1978), Rotary (pres. 1969-70), KC (dep. grand knight 1973), Phi Alpha Delta. Republican. Roman Catholic. Home: 2605 Derbyshire Ave Lakeland FL 33803-4100 Office: 908 S Florida Ave Lakeland FL 33803-1177

SCHOTT, LINDA KAY, historian, educator; b. Hondo, Tex., June 7, 1957; d. Rudolph Robert and Elsie Emma (Boehle) S.; m. Horace Jeffrey Hodges, Dec. 22, 1979 (div. Aug. 1985); m. Ralph Joseph Noonan III, May 16, 1987; 1 child, Decker Joseph Schott-Noonan. BA, Baylor U., 1979; MA, Stanford U., 1982, PhD, 1986. Seminar instr. Stanford U., 1984-85; asst. prof. history S.W. Tex. State U., San Marcos, 1985-86, Tex. Luth. Coll., Seguin, 1986-89; asst. prof. history U. Tex., San Antonio, 1989-95, assoc. prof., 1995—, dir. Ctr. for Study of Women and Gender, 1994—; mem. governing bd. Conf. of Women Historians in Tex., 1992-95. Author: Reconstructing Women's Thoughts, 1997, also articles. Mem. Am. Hist. Assn., Orgn. Am. Historians, Berkshire Conf. Women Historians, So. Assn. Women Historians. Democrat. Office: U Tex at San Antonio 6900 N Loop 1604 W San Antonio TX 78249

SCHOTZ, SYLVAN ART, physician; b. Phila., Oct. 15, 1926; s. Max and Erna (Gabel) S. BS, City Coll. N.Y., 1948; MD, SUNY, 1952. Diplomate Am. Bd. Internal Medicine. Asst. clinical prof. medicine U. Miami Sch. Medicine, Miami, 1960—; attending physician Miami Heart Inst., Miami Beach, Fla., 1960—, Mt. Sinai Hosp., Miami Beach, Fla., 1960—. With U.S. Navy, 1945-46. Fellow Am. Coll. Physicians, Am. Coll. Chest Physicians; mem. AMA (Physician's Recognition award 1980), Phi Beta Kappa. Jewish. Office: Sylvan Schotz MD PA 4302 Alton Rd Ste 1010 Miami Beach FL 33140-2878

SCHRADER, WILLIAM CHRISTIAN, III, history educator; b. Louisville, Aug. 6, 1940; s. William Christian Jr. and Willie Thomas (Calvert) S.; m. Juanita Carol Houdeschell, June 6, 1972 (div. 1989); children: Elizabeth, Michael, John. AB, Bellarmine Coll., 1962; postgrad., Friedrich-Alexander U, Erlangen, Germany, 1962-63; MA, Cath. U., Washington, 1966, PhD, 1972. Asst. prof. history Tenn. Tech. U., Cookeville, 1966-72, assoc. prof., 1972-78, prof., 1978—, pres. faculty senate, 1992-94. Contbr. articles and revs. to profl. jours. Cons. Tenn. Com. for Humanities, 1974-75; mem. Cookeville Arts Coun., 1975-80. Fulbright fellow, Erlangen, 1962-63, Woodrow Wilson fellow Cath. U., 1963-64, NEH fellow U. N.C., Chapel Hill, 1978-79; named Outstanding Faculty Tenn. Tech. U., 1970-71, 92-93. Mem. AAUP (pres. Tenn. conf. 1986-88), Southeastern Am. Soc. for 18th Century Studies (archivist-historian 1987—), Cookeville Toastmasters (pres. 1985-86), KC (chancellor 1978-81). Roman Catholic. Home: 110 Westgate Cir # C Cookeville TN 38506-5433 Office: Tenn Tech U Box 5064 Cookeville TN 38505

SCHRAMEK, LYNN BETH GOTTLIEB, communications executive; b. Cin., Mar. 19, 1956; d. Lloyd George Gottlieb and LaVerne (Wolf) Shone; m. Bradley Walter Schramek, July 22, 1989. BA in Journalism, Ohio State U., 1978. Supr. Ohio State U. Music Rm., Columbus, 1976-78; customer svc. rep. Warner Qube, Columbus, 1978; sales rep. Stewart Sandwiches & Coffee Inc., Columbus, 1979; corp. pub. rels. coord. Copco Papers, Inc., Columbus, 1979-83; assoc. dir. communications Ohio Sch. Bds. Assn., Westerville, 1983-84; communications coord. J.C. Penney Casualty Ins. Co., Westerville, 1985-89; dir. pub. rels. Fekete & Co., Columbus, Ohio, 1989; pub. info. officer Ohio Dept. Edn., Columbus, 1990-91; dir. employee comm./publs. Corrections Corp. Am., Nashville, 1992-96; pres. LBS Comm., Pittsford, N.Y., 1996—. Pub. rels. vol. Youth for Understanding Internat. Exch., Columbus, 1990-91; mem. Williamson County Arts Coun. Mem. Internat. Assn. Bus. Communicators (community rels. dir. 1988-89, pres. 1984-85, Disting. Communicator of Yr. Columbus chpt. 1989), Pub. Rels. Soc. Am. (publicity chair 1992). Jewish. Office: LBS Comm 26 Lake Lacoma Dr Pittsford NY 14534

SCHREADLEY, RICHARD LEE, writer, retired newspaper editor; b. Harrisburg, Pa., Jan. 3, 1931; s. Harry Leroy and Flora Rebecca (McQuilken) S.; m. Doris Arlene Sheaffer, Dec. 18, 1952; 1 child, Rhys Leroy. B.A., Dickinson Coll., 1952; M.A., Tufts U., 1968, M.A.L.D., 1969, Ph.D., 1972. Reporter The News and Courier, Charleston, S.C., 1975; asso. editor The Evening Post, Charleston, 1975-76; editorial page editor The Evening Post, 1976-77, editor, 1977-81; exec. editor The Evening Post and The News and Courier, 1981-88; assoc. editor and sr. writer mil. and polit. affairs The News and Courier, 1989. Author: From the Rivers to the Sea, The United States Navy in Vietnam, 1992, Virtue and Valor, The Washington Light Infantry in Peace and in War, 1996. Chmn. Fgn. Affairs Forum of Charleston, 1987-88, mem. steering com., 1989. Served to comdr. USN, 1949-52, 56-73. Mem. Navy League, Ret. Officer Assn., Washington Light Infantry, Army-Navy Club of Washington, Country Club of Charleston. Home: 812 Clearview Dr Charleston SC 29412-4511

SCHREIBER, ALAN HICKMAN, lawyer; b. Muncie, Ind., Apr. 4, 1944; s. Ephriam and Clarrisa (Hickman) S.; m. Phyllis Jean Chamberlain, Dec. 22, 1972; children—Jennifer Aline, Brett Justin. Student DePauw U., 1962-64; B.S. in Bus., Ind. U., 1966, J.D., 1969. Bar: Fla. 1971, U.S. Dist. Ct. (so. dist.) Fla. Asst., State Atty.'s Office, Ft. Lauderdale, Fla., 1971-76; pub. defender 17th Jud. Circuit, Ft. Lauderdale, 1976—; cons. Fla. Bar News on Criminal Law, 1982; lobbyist for indigent funding, Fla., 1980—; apptd. to Supreme Ct. Com. on Racial and Ethic Bias; co-chair Chiles-MacKay task force on criminal justice. Contbr. articles to profl. jours. Mem. Dem. Exec. Com., Ft. Lauderdale, 1980; mem. Plantation Dem. Club, 1983; campaign chmn. Goldstein for Atty. Gen. Fla., 1982. Named Young Dem. of Yr., Broward County Young Dems., 1980; Man of Yr., Jewish War Vets., 1982; recipient B'nai B'rith Pub. Servant award, 1990. Mem. Fla. Bar Assn., Broward County Bar Assn., ABA, Nat. Legal Aid Defenders Assn., Phi Alpha Delta. Home: 885 Orchid Dr Fort Lauderdale FL 33317-1221 Office: 201 SE 6th St Fort Lauderdale FL 33301-3303

SCHRIEFFER, JOHN ROBERT, physics educator, science administrator; b. Oak Park, Ill., May 31, 1931; s. John Henry and Louise (Anderson) S.; m. Anne Grete Thomsen, Dec. 30, 1960; children: Anne Bolette, Paul Karsten, Anne Regina. BS, MIT, 1953; MS, U. Ill., 1954, PhD, 1957, ScD, 1974; ScD (hon.), Tech. U., Munich, Germany, 1968, U. Geneva, 1968, U. Pa., 1973, U. Cin., 1977, U. Tel Aviv, 1987, U. Ala., 1990. NSF postdoctoral fellow U. Birmingham, Eng., also; Niels Bohr Inst., Copenhagen, 1957-58; asst. prof. U. Chgo., 1958-59; asst. prof., then assoc. prof. U. Ill., 1959-62; prof. U. Pa., Phila., 1962-79; Mary Amanda Wood prof. physics U. Pa., 1964-79; Andrew D. White prof. at large Cornell U., 1969-75; prof. U. Calif., Santa Barbara, 1980-91, Chancellor's prof., 1984-91, dir. Inst. for Theoretical Physics, 1984-89; Univ. prof. Fla. State U., Tallahassee, 1992—, Univ. Eminent Scholar prof., 1995—, chief scientist Nat. High Magnetic Field Lab., 1992—. Author: Theory of Superconductivity, 1964. Guggenheim fellow Copenhagen, 1967; Los Alamos Nat. Lab. fellow; Recipient Comstock prize Nat. Acad. Sci.; Nobel Prize for Physics, 1972; John Ericsson medal Am. Soc. Swedish Engrs., 1976; Alumni Achievement award U. Ill., 1979; recipient Nat. Medal of Sci., 1984; Exxon faculty fellow, 1979-89. Fellow Am. Phys. Soc. (v.p. 1994, pres.-elect 1995, pres. 1996, Oliver E. Buckley solid state physics prize 1986); mem. NAS (coun. 1990—), Am. Acad. Arts and Scis., Coun. Nat. Acad. Sci., Royal Danish Acad. Scis. and Letters, Acad. Sci. USSR. Office: Fla State UNHMFL 1800 E Paul Dirac Dr Tallahassee FL 32306-4005

SCHRODER, JACK SPALDING, JR., lawyer; b. Atlanta, July 10, 1948; s. Jack Spalding Sr. and Van (Spalding) S.; m. Karen Keyworth, Sept. 1, 1973; children: Jack Spalding III, James Edward. BA, Emory U., 1970; JD, U. Ga., 1973. Bar: Ga. 1973, U.S. Dist. Ct. (no. dist.) Ga. 1973, U.S. Ct. Appeals (5th cir.) 1973, U.S. Ct. Appeals (11th cir.) 1982. Assoc. Alston & Bird, Atlanta, 1973-78, ptnr., 1978—. Co-editor, contbr. author: Georgia Hospital Law Manual, 1979, 84, 92, Credentialing: Strategies for a Changing Environment/BNa's Health Law and Business Series, 1996. Participant Leadership Ga., Atlanta, 1986, United Way (chmn. legal div.), Atlanta, 1980. Mem. ABA (vice chmn. medicine and law com. 1989-90), Am. Acad. Healthcare Attys. (bd. dirs. 1994—, chmn. med. staff and physician rels. com. 1991-94), Ga. Acad. Hosp. Attys. (pres. 1981-82), State Bar Ga. (bd. govs. 1987-89), Atlanta Coun. Younger Lawyers (pres. 1977-78), Atlanta Bar Assn. (pres. 1982-83), Atlanta Bar Found. (pres. 1991-95). Office: Alston & Bird 1 Atlantic Ctr 1201 W Peachtree St NW Atlanta GA 30309-3400

SCHRODER, JOHN L., JR., retired mining engineer; b. Martinsburg, W.Va.. BS in Mining Engring., W.Va. Sch. Mines, MS, 1941. Registered profl. engr., W.Va., Ky. Jr. engr. H.C. Frick Coke Co. U.S. Steel, Uniontown, Pa., 1941-44; prodn., safety engr. Gay Coal and Coke Gay Mining Cos., 1946-49.; asst. engr. mine planning U.S. Steel, Gary, W.Va., 1949-51, asst. chief engr., 1951-1953; chief engr. U.S. Steel, Lynch, Gary, Ky., 1953-1958; gen. supt. U.S. Steel, Lynch, 1958-70; gen. mgr. coal ops. U.S. Steel, Pitts., 1970-79, v.p. coal ops. resource devel., 1979-81, pres. subsidiary U.S. Steel Mining Co., Inc., 1981-83, ret., 1983; spl. asst. to the pres. Am. Mining Congress, 1983-84; dean Coll. Mineral and Engry Resources W.Va. U., 1984-91, ret., 1991; chmn. Mine Insps. Exam. Bd.; mem Govs. Moore's Energy Task Force. Lt. j.g. USN, 1944-46. Recipient Howard N. Evanson award Soc. Mining, Metallurgy and Exploration, 1991. Mem. AIME (Erskine Ramsay medal 1992), Nat. Mine Rescue Assn., W.Va. Coal Mining Inst., Old Timers Club, King Coal Club. Office: 228 Maple Ave Morgantown WV 26505-6666

SCHROEDER, HARRY WILLIAM, JR., physician, scientist; b. Mpls., Minn., Oct. 1, 1952; s. Harry Williams Sr. and Maria de los Angeles (Melendez) S.; m. Dixie Lee Douglas, Nov. 24, 1979; children: Harry William III, Elena, Jeannette. BS, Tex. A&M U., 1974; PhD, Baylor Coll. Medicine, 1979, MD, 1981. Vis. fellow Yale U., New Haven, 1980; intern, then resident in internal medicine U. Ky., Lexington, 1981-84; sr. fellow med. genetics U. Wash., Seattle, 1984-88; rsch. assoc. Howard Hughes Med. Inst., Seattle, 1986-88; asst. prof. medicine and microbiology U. Ala., Birmingham, 1988-93, assoc. prof. medicine & microbiology, 1993—. RJR Nabisco scholar in immunology, 1989. Fellow Am. Coll. Med. Genetics (founder 1993), Molecular Medicine Soc.; mem. AAAS, Am. Soc. Human Genetics, Am. Fedn. Clin. Rsch., Am. Assn. Immunologists, Clin. Immunology Soc., Soc. for Molecular Recognition, So. Soc. for Clin. Rsch., Am. Coll. Rheumatologists. Office: U Ala TI 378 UAB Station Birmingham AL 35294

SCHROEDER, JAMES WHITE, lawyer; b. Elmhurst, Ill., Apr. 19, 1936; s. Paul W. and Thelma C. (White) S.; m. Patricia N. Scott, Aug. 18, 1962; children: Scott W., Jamie C. BA, Princeton U., 1958; JD, Harvard U., 1964. Bar: Colo. 1964, U.S. Dist. Ct. Colo. 1964, U.S. Ct. Appeals (10th cir.) 1965, U.S. Supreme Ct. 1972, U.S. Dist. Ct. D.C. 1973, U.S. Ct. Appeals (D.C. cir.) 1974, U.S. Ct. Appeals (8th cir.) 1977, U.S. Ct. Appeals (3d cir.) 1981, U.S. Claims Ct. 1983, U.S. Ct. Appeals (fed. cir.) 1983. Ptnr., Moseley, Wells & Schroeder, Denver, 1965-72, Kaplan, Russin & Vecchi, Washington, 1973-92; counsel Whitman & Ransom, Washington, 1992-93; dep. under sec. USDA, 1993—; arbitrator Am. Arbitration Assn. Active Ams. for Democratic Action, Smithsonian Instn., Denver Symphony Orch., Denver Art Mus. Lt., USNR, 1958-64. Am. Field Service scholar, 1953; NROTC scholar, 1954. Mem. ABA, Fed. Bar Assn., Denver Bar Assn., Colo. Bar Assn., D.C. Bar Assn., Cap and Gown Club, Lincoln's Inn Club, City Club Denver (pres. 1972), Princeton Club Washington (pres. 1982-84). Democrat. Home: 4102 Lester Ct Alexandria VA 22311-1121

SCHROEDER, LEILA OBIER, retired law educator; b. Plaquemine, La., July 11, 1925; d. William Prentiss and Daisy Lavinia (Mays) Obier; divorced; 1 child, James Michael Cutshaw; m. Martin Charles Schroeder Jr., Sept. 19, 1969. BA, Newcomb Coll., 1946; MSW, La. State U., 1953, JD, 1965. Bar: La. 1965. Exec. dir. Evangeline Area Guidance Ctr. La. Dept. Hosps., Lafayette, 1955-57; dir. social services dept. East La. State Hosp. La. Dept. Hosps., Jackson, 1957-60; cons. psychiat. social work La. Dept. Hosps., Baton Rouge, 1960-61; research assoc. La. State U., Baton Rouge, 1965-68, asst. prof., 1968-73, assoc. prof., 1973-80, prof., 1980-96; ret., 1996. Author: The Legal Environment of Social Work, 1982, The Legal Environment of Social Work, 1995; contbr. articles to profl. jours. Fellow Am. Orthopsychiat. Assn.; mem. ABA, Nat. Assn. Social Workers, Acad. Cert. Social Workers, La. State Bar Assn., Baton Rouge Bar Assn. Home: 4336 Oxford Ave Baton Rouge LA 70808-4651

SCHROEDER, WALTER ALLEN, lawyer, banker; b. San Francisco, July 29, 1954; s. Carl Walter and Mary (Lee) S.; m. Andrea Maggie Paull, June 3, 1994. BS in Bus. Adminstrn., Georgetown U., 1976; JD, U. Houston, 1979. Bar: Tex. 1979, D.C. 1984, U.S. Dist. Ct. (no. dist.) Tex., 1979, U.S. Dist. Ct. (so. dist.) Tex. 1980, U.S. Dist. Ct. (we. dist.) Tex. 1982, U.S. Ct. Appeals (5th cir.) 1980, U.S. Ct. Appeals (11th cir.) 1981, U.S. Ct. Appeals (D.C. cir.) 1987, U.S. Supreme Ct. 1984. Asst. treas. G.U. Fed. Credit Union, Washington, 1976-77; asst. to pres. U.S.E. Credit Union, Houston, 1977-79; analyst Banc Systems, Inc., Houston, 1979; briefing atty. Tex. Ct. Civil Appeals, Ft. Worth, 1979-80; asst. counsel Am. Ins. Assn., Houston, 1980-81; atty. Rolston & Hausler, Houston, 1981-85, Chamberlain, Hrdlicka, White, Johnson & Williams, 1985-86, Hollrah, Lange & Thoma, 1986-87, Eikenburg & Stiles, 1987-89; v.p., sr. atty. First City Tex.-Houston, N.A., 1989-91; ptnr. Schroeder, Walthall, Sheehan & Slaydon, LLP, Houston, 1991—; apptd. assoc. judge Municipal Ct., City of Houston, Tex., 1995; dir. Fayetteville Bank, 1988-90, Fayetteville Bancshares Inc., 1988-90; dir., v.p. Victorian Owners Assn., Inc, 1989—; v.p. Park Regency Coun. Co-owners, pres. 1985-86, dir. 1985-86, 87-90. Trustee Found. Amateur Radio, Inc. Washington, 1972-76, chmn. audit com., 1975-76; treas. Houston Echo Soc., 1979; apptd. Ethics Commn. City of Houston, 1991-95, chmn., 1992-95. Mem. ABA, D.C. Bar Assn., Houston Bar Assn., State Bar Tex., Tex. Assn. Bank Counsel (co-chmn. corp. counsel sect. 1989-90) Republican. Lutheran. Contbr. articles to profl. jours. Office: 1100 Louisiana St Ste 4850 Houston TX 77002-5222

SCHROER, JANE HASTINGS, nurse practitioner; b. Pender, Nebr., Aug. 24, 1947; d. John Dean and Florence (Meier) Hastings; m. Ronald L. Schroer, May 13, 1967; 1 child, Patricia Schroer Kennedy. LPN, Antonian Sch. Prac. Nursing, Carroll, Iowa, 1966; Diploma, St. Joseph Sch. Nursing, Sioux City, Iowa, 1980; B.Applied Sci., Teikyo Westmar U., LeMars, Iowa, 1985; Women's Health Care Nurse Practitioner, S.W. Med. Ctr./U. Tex., Dallas, 1990. Cert. nurse practitioner Tex., Iowa, Ariz., Nebr., Fla.; RN. Nurse cardiac catheterization lab. Marian Health Ctr., Sioux City, 1980-85; ob-gyn. nurse practitioner Drs. Goodman and Partridge, Chandler, Ariz., 1991-93; nurse practitioner STD Clinic, Austin, Tex., 1994-95; women's health nurse practitioner Round Rock (Tex.) Rural Health Clinic, 1995—. Mem. ACOG (edn. affiliate), Austin Area Nurse Practitioner Assn., Tex. Nurse Practitioner Assn., Tex. Nurses Assn. Republican. Roman Catholic. Home: 2008 Rosemary Ln Round Rock TX 78664 Office: Round Rock Health Clinic 2000 N Mays Ste 109 Round Rock TX 78664

SCHROPP, MARY LOU, public relations executive; b. Havre-de-Grace, Md., Aug. 13, 1947; d. Howard James and Maude Elizabeth (Parker) S.; 1 child, Matthew Austin. Student, George Washington U., 1965-68. Vice pres. Snyder Assoc., Inc., Washington, 1969-76; pres. Health Communications, Inc., Washington, 1976-80; creative services project mgr. U.S. Catholic Conf., Washington, 1980-81; pres., owner MLS Creative Services, Falls

Church, Va., 1981-93; dir. corp. comm. PHP Healthcare Corp., Reston, Va., 1993—. Editor: Electronic Media, Popular Culture and Family Values, 1985; Rehabilitation Facilities Sourcebook, 1984, 85; periodicals, textbooks. Exec. producer videotapes, 1982. Coord. World Communications Day, Washington, 1982-85 ; cons. Cath. Communication Campaign, Washington, 1982-84; fund raising cons. Nat. 4-H Coun., Chevy Chase, Md., 1985-86; v.p. devel. Aviation Rsch. and Edn. Found., Herndon, Va., 1985-91, Campaign for Human Devel., 1992. Mem. Pub. Relations Soc. Am., Washington Independent Writers, Religious Pub. Rels. Coun. (v.p. local chpt. 1981-82, DeRose-Hinkhouse Communications award 1981, 82, 80), Nat. Soc. Fund Raising Execs. Democrat. Office: PHP Healthcare Corp 11440 Commerce Park Dr Reston VA 22091-1544

SCHUBERT, PATRICIA ANN, middle school educator; b. Jacksonville, Fla., Aug. 31, 1949; d. Kermit Lee and Montie Lou (Fletcher) Prime; m. Norman David Schubert, Aug. 23, 1969; children: Travis Lee, Jonathan David. AA in Edn., Santa Fe C.C., Gainesville, Fla., 1990; BA in Edn., U. Fla., 1993, MEd, 1995. Cert. tchr. elem. edn., mid. grades, sci., gifted, Fla. Prep aid Oldtown (Fla.) Elem. Sch., 1980-82; substitute tchr. Gilchrist County Sch. Bd., Trenton, Fla., 1988-90, Alachua County Sch. Bd., Gainesville, 1994-95; sci. tchr. Howard Bishop Mid. Sch., Gainesville, 1995-96, Ft. White (Fla.) Pub. Sch., 1996—. Cub scout leader Boy Scouts Am., North Fla. coun., 1980—; 4-H leader horse project; pianist rock Sink Bapt. Ch., Oldtown, 1978—; leader Girls in Action, So. Bapt. Conv./Woman's Missionary Union, 1988-94; sch. vol. Trenton (Fla.) Elem. Sch., 1987-90, Oldtown elem. Sch., 1978-80. Recipient Dist. Award of Merit, Manatee dist. Boy Scouts Am., 1992. Mem. Golden Key, Kappa Delta Pi, Phi Kappa Phi. Home: 618 S Main St Trenton FL 32693

SCHUCH, CHARLES MICHAEL, medical educator, researcher; b. Raleigh, N.C., Mar. 4, 1955; s. Charles Peter Schuch and Cecile Hope Pate; m. Barbara L. Wall, Jan. 22, 1983; children: Brandon Michael, Zachary Michael. BA, U. N.C., 1977; Cert. in Prosthetics Orthotics, UCLA, 1978. Am. Bd. Cert. in Orthotics and Prosthetics. Prosthetic technician trainee J.E. Hanger, N.E., Raleigh, N.C., 1974; prosthetic orthotic technician N.C. Meml. Hosp., U. N.C., Chapel Hill, 1974-77; resident in prosthetics UCLA, 1978; staff prosthetist orthotist J.E. Hanger, S.E., New Orleans, 1978-80; mgr. patient svcs. Capital Prosthetics and Orthotics, Raleigh, 1981-84; asst. clin. prof. orthopaedics and rehab., assoc. dir. divsn. prosthetics, orthotics and rehab. engring. svcs. U. Va. Med. Ctr., Charlottesville, 1984-88; mgr., clin. prosthetist orthotist J.E. Hanger, S.E., Greenville (S.C.) Orthopedic Appliance Co., Friddle's Orthotic and Prosthetic Labs. Spartanburg, 1988-92; asst. clin. prof., dir. dept. prosthetics and orthotics Duke U. Med. Ctr., Durham, N.C., 1992—; speaker conf. Prosthetic Orthotic Rsch. for 21st Century, Bethesda, Md., 1992; speaker in field. Mem. editl. bd. Jour. Prosthetics and Orthotics, 1990-92, editor, chmn., 1992-96; editor, contbr. Acad. Am. Ency.; contbr. articles to profl. jours. Fellow Internat. Soc. Prosthetics and Orthotics (hon. treas. 1993-94, chmn. bd. dirs. 1991-92, sec. bd. dirs. 1988-91, bd. dirs. 1988-94, chmn. organizing com. 1993, sci. sessions organizing com. 1992, spkr. 1990, 91, cons. above knee tchg. objectives com. 1987); mem. Am. Acad. Orthotists and Prosthetists (bd. dirs. 1990, 92-96, pres. 1995, moderator ann. meeting and sci. symposium 1988, 91, 92, editor jour. procs. ann. symposium 1993), N.C. Soc. Prosthetists and Orthotists (bd. dirs. 1984, 93—). Home: 7005 Tanbark Way Raleigh NC 27615-5360 Office: Duke U Med Ctr Dept Prosthetics Orthotics MO4 Davison Bldg Box 3885 Durham NC 27710

SCHUCK, MARJORIE MASSEY, publisher, editor, authors' consultant; b. Winchester, Va., Oct. 9, 1921; d. Carl Frederick and Margaret Harriet (Parmele) Massey; student U. Minn., 1941-43, New Sch., N.Y.C., 1948, N.Y. U., 1952, 54-55; m. Ernest George Metcalfe, Dec. 2, 1943 (div. Oct. 1949); m. 2d, Franz Schuck, Nov. 11, 1953 (dec. Jan. 1958). Mem. editorial bd. St. Petersburg Poetry Assn., 1967-68; co-editor, pub. poetry Venture Mag., St. Petersburg, Fla., 1968-69, editor, pub., 1969-79; co-editor, pub. Poetry Venture Quar. Essays, Vol. I, 1968-69, Vol. 2, 1970-71; pub., editor poetry anthologies, 1972—; founder, owner, pres. Valkyrie Press, Inc. (name changed to Valkyrie Pub. House 1980), 1972—; cons. designs and formats, trade publs. and ann. reports, lit. books and pamphlets, 1973—; founder Valkyrie Press Roundtable Workshop and Forum for Writers, 1975-79; established Valkyrie Press Reference Libr., 1976-80; pub., editor The Valkyrie Internat. Newsletter, 1986—; exec. dir. Inter-Cultural Forum Villanor Ctr., Tampa, Fla., 1987-94; dir. edn. The Villanor Mus. Fine and Decorative Arts, Tampa, 1994, St. Petersburg, 1994—; pres. Found. for Human Potentials, Inc., Tampa, 1988-94; representative distbr. Marg Art Publs. of India (Bombay), 1992—; mem. pres. coun. U. South Fla., 1993-95; lectr. in field. Judge poetry and speech contests Gulf Beach Women's Club, 1970, Fine Arts Festival dist. 14. Am. Fedn. Women's Clubs, 1970, South and West, Inc., 1972, The Sunstone Rev., 1973, Internat. Toastmistress Clubs, 1974, 78, Beaux Arts Poetry Festival, 1983, 89, 92-96; judge poetry contest Fla. State conf. Nat. League Am. Pen Women, 1989, Tampa Bay Poetry Coun., 1994-96; judge Fla. Gov.'s Screenwriters Competition, 1984—; judge poetry contest Tampa Bay Poetry Coun., 1996. Corr.-rec. sec. Women's Aux. Hosp. for Spl. Surgery, N.Y.C., 1947-59; active St. Petersburg Mus. Fine Arts (charter), St. Petersburg Sister City Com., St. Petersburg Arts Ctr. Assn.; mem. Orange Belt express com. 1988 Centennial Celebration for St. Petersburg; mem. Com. of 100 of Pinellas County, Inc., exec. bd., 1975-77, membership chmn., 1975-77; pub. rels. chmn. Soc. for prevention Cruelty to Animals, 1968-71, bd. dirs., 1968-71, 75-77; founder, mem. Pinellas County Arts Coun., 1976-79, chmn., 1977-78; mem. grant rev. panel for lit. Fine Arts Coun. of Fla., 1979; mem., bd, dirs. Tampa Bay Poetry Found., Inc., 1995—. Named One of 76 Fla. Patriots, Fla. Bicentennial Commn., 1976; a recipient 1st ann. People of Dedication award Salvation Army, Tampa, 1984; named to Poetica Hall of Fame, Tampa Bay Poetry Coun., 1994. Mem. Am. Assn. Museums, Acad. Am. Poets, Fla. Suncoast Writers' Confs. (founder, co-dir., lectr. 1973-83, adv. bd. 1984—), Friends of Libr. of St. Petersburg, Suncoast Mgmt. Inst. (exec. bd.; chmn. Women in Mgmt. 1977-78), Pi Beta Phi. Republican. Episcopalian. Author: Speeches and Writings for Cause of Freedom, 1973. Contbr. poetry to profl. jours. Home and Office: 8245 26th Ave N Saint Petersburg FL 33710-2857

SCHUDER, RAYMOND FRANCIS, lawyer; b. Wickford, R.I., Dec. 27, 1926; s. Rollie Milton and Selma (Ball) S.; AB, Emory U., 1949, JD, 1951; m. Betty Jo Williams, Mar. 14, 1948; children: Gregg Williams, Glen Arva. Bar: Ga. 1951. With Trust Co., Ga., Atlanta, 1951-54; assoc. firm Wheeler, Robinson & Thurmond, Gainesville, Ga., 1954-59; pvt. practice law, Gainesville, 1959-70, 76—; ptnr. Schuder & Brown, Gainesville, 1971-76; Mcpl. ct. judge, Gainesville, 1956-60, 73-75, Magistrate ct. judge, 1985—; bd. dirs. Lanier Securities, Inc. Supr. Upper Chattahoochee Soil and Water Conservation Dist., 1971-74; chief exec. officer, bd. dirs. Charles Thompson Estes Found., Inc., Gainesville. Cpl. USMCR, 1944-50; 1st lt. USAR, ret. Mem. State Bar Ga. (gov. 1966-70), Gainesville-Northeastern (pres. 1969-70) Bar Assn., Am. Legion, V.F.W., Elks. Methodist. Home: 2224 Riverside Dr Gainesville GA 30501-1232 Office: 500 Spring St E Gainesville GA 30501-3792

SCHUELKE, CONSTANCE PATRICIA, mortgage company executive; b. Cedar Rapids, Iowa, Feb. 9, 1953; d. Enno August and Ruth Otilia (Firnhaber) S.; m. Kevin Dennis Curran, May 21, 1983 (div. Dec. 1986); 1 child, Emma Kate Schuelke-Curran. BA, U. Nebr., 1973. Asst. mgr. Jaeger Internat., Atlanta, 1973-75; pres., owner Domani of Florence (Italy), Inc., 1975-82; assoc. broker Downtown Properties, Inc., Atlanta, 1982-85; v.p. Dunwoody Mortgage, Inc., Atlanta, 1985-90; owner, exec. v.p. FSM, Inc. dba First So. Mortgage, Atlanta, 1990-91; v.p. Dunwoody Mortgage, Inc., Atlanta, 1991-95, Regency Mortgage, Atlanta, 1995-96; Vanguard Mortgage Corp., Atlanta, 1996—. Neighborhood adv. Inman Park Civic Assn., Atlanta, 1973—, Castelberry Hill Neighborhood, Atlanta, 1988—; fund raiser Design Industry Found. for AIDS, Atlanta, 1989. Mem. Mortgage Bankers Ga., Ga. Assn. Mortgage Brokers (individual sr.), Midtown Bus. Assn., Atlanta Bd. Realtors, Ravinia Club, Pi Beta Phi, Phi Upsilon Omicron (Hon.), Nat. Honor Soc. Democrat. Home: 35 Ivy Gates Atlanta GA 30342 Office: Vanguard Mortgage Corp Ste 125 4840 Roswell Rd Bldg B Atlanta GA 30342

SCHUETTE, JAMES, biologist; b. West Point, N.Y., Mar. 25, 1962; s. Rober C. and Shirlee J. (Campshure) S.; m. Ayisha Nabin, June 26, 1989 (div. 29, Apr. 1994); children: Charles Anik Nabin, Michaela Fathielah Schuette. BS in Wildlife Mgmt., U. Minn., 1983; MS in Wildlife Ecology, Okla. State U., 1991. Field biologist Minn. Dept. Natural Resources, Thief River Falls, 1983; biol. technician Bur. Land Mgmt., Butte, Mont., 1983; fgn. fisheries observer Nat. Marine Fisheries Svc., Corvallis, Oreg., 1984; field biologist Nat. Park Svc., Cape Hatteras, N.C., 1984; biol. technician U.S. Fish and Wildlife Svc., Bowling Green, Ky., 1984; eagle nest observer U.S. Forest Svc., Carefree, Ariz., 1984; vol. Peace Corps, Ouagadougau, Burkina Faso, Africa, 1985-87; rsch. biologist Assn. Devel. l'Elevage de la Faune Africaine, Nazinga, Burkina Faso, 1987-89; biol. adminstr. Fla. Game and Fresh Water Fish Commn., West Palm Beach, 1991—; co-chair evaluation com. Geographic Info. Sys., Fla. Game and Fish Commn., West Palm Beach, 1991—; Fla. Game and Fish del. Sci. Subcom. Fed. Task Force on Everglades Restoration, West Palm Beach, 1993-95; mem. Sci. Adv. Group for Everglades, West Palm Beach, 1992-95. Coach Little League Baseball, Palm Springs, Fla., 1993-95. Home: 3644 Walden Ln West Palm Beach FL 33406-5633 Office: Fla Game and Fresh Water Fish Commn 551 N Military Trl West Palm Beach FL 33415-1311

SCHUETTE, OSWALD FRANCIS, physics educator; b. Washington, Aug. 20, 1921; s. Oswald Frances and Mary (Moran) S.; m. Kathryn E. Cronin, June 7, 1947; children: Patrick Thomas, Mary Kathryn, Elizabeth Anne. B.S., Georgetown U., 1943; Ph.D., Yale U., 1949. Assoc. prof. physics Coll. William and Mary, 1948-53; Fulbright research prof. physics Max Planck Inst. for Chemistry, 1953-54; sci. liaison officer U.S. Naval Forces, Germany, 1954-58; mem. staff Nat. Acad. Scis., Washington, 1958- 60; dep. spl. asst. for space Office Sec. Def., Washington, 1961-63; prof. physics dept. U. S.C., 1963-92, dit. prof. emeritus, 1992—; vis. prof. Inst. Exptl. Physics, U. Vienna, 1980. Lt. USNR, 1944-46. Fellow AAAS; mem. Am. Phys. Soc., Am. Assn. Physics Tchrs., S.C. Acad. Sci., Sigma Xi. Home: 4979 Quail Ln Columbia SC 29206-4624

SCHUH, MERLYN DUANE, chemist, educator; b. Avon, S.D., Feb. 21, 1945; s. Edward Arthur (dec.) and Amelia (Rueb) S.; m. Judy Anne Swigart, June 1, 1969. BA, U. S.D., 1967; PhD, Ind. U., 1971. Asst. prof. Middlebury (Vt.) Coll., 1971-75; prof. chemistry Davidson (N.C.) Coll., 1975—, James G. Martin prof. chemistry, 1992; adj. prof. chemistry Syracuse (N.Y.) U., 1982-83; vis. prof. chemistry U. N.C.-Chapel Hill, 1996-97. Contbr. articles on gas and solution phase photophysics, laser spectroscopy and protein dynamics to tech. jours. Chmn., bd. dirs. Metrolina Assn. for Blind, Charlotte, N.C., 1980-81. Recipient profl. devel. award NSF, 1981; Dreyfus Found. scholar, 1992-94. Mem. Davidson Lions (all offices). Democrat. Presbyterian. Home: PO Box 704 Davidson NC 28036-0704 Office: Davidson Coll PO Box 1749 Davidson NC 28036-1749

SCHUH, SANDRA ANDERSON, ethics educator; b. Hartford, Conn., Aug. 22, 1947; d. Axel Magna and Dorothy Catherine (Spring) Anderson: m. Edward Walter Schuh, Apr. 10, 1978; Children: Matthew, Bradley. AM, U. Miami, Coral Gables, 1982, PhD, 1986. Philosophy instr. U. Miami, 1986-88, Fla. Atlantic U., Boca Raton, 1988-90; asst. prof. philosophy U. Tampa, Fla., 1990—; ethics cons. U.S. Govt. Dept. of Energy, Washington, 1987, Med. Ethics, Miami; mem. ethic com. Miami Gen. Hosp. Investigator Dept. of Human Resources, 1988; evaluator Fla. Endowment for Humanities, 1990, panelist, Tampa, 1990. Dana Grantee U. Tampa, 1991. Mem. AAAS (pres. 1993), Fla. Philosophic Assn., Am. Philosophic Assn., Am. Soc. for Engring. Edn., N.Y. Acad. Sci., Soc. Women in Sci. Office: U of Tampa Kennedy Blvd Tampa FL 33606-1411

SCHUK, LINDA LEE, legal assistant, business educator; b. Scott Field, Ill., July 19, 1946; d. Frank A. Schuk and Jessie (Bumpass) Stearns; divorced; 1 child, Earl Wade. BBA, U. Tex., El Paso, 1968. Lic. life and health ins. agt., Tex. Acct., traffic mgr. Farah Mfg. Co., El Paso, 1970-71; adminstrv. asst. Horizon Corp., El Paso, 1971-76; adminstrv. asst. in charge office ops. Foster-Scwartz Devel. Corp., El Paso, 1976-78; legal sec. Howell and Fields, El Paso, 1978-80; supr. Southland Corp., San Antonio, Waco, El Paso, 1980-83; sales mgr. Southland Corp., San Antonio, 1983-84, dist. mgr., 1984-87; dist. supr. E-Z Mart Convenience Stores, San Antonio, 1987-89; legal asst. Brock & Brock, San Antonio, 1989—; instr. San Antonio C.C., 1989—. Mem. NAFE. Democrat. Baptist. Home: 11903 Parliment Apt 323 San Antonio TX 78216 Office: Brock & Brock 803 E Mistletoe Ave San Antonio TX 78212-3524

SCHULER, BURTON SILVERMAN, podiatrist; b. N.Y.C., Aug. 4, 1950; s. Irving and Sylvia (Silverman) S.; m. Caroline Davis, Oct. 1989. D Podiatric Medicine, N.Y. Coll. Podiatric Medicine, 1975. Diplomate Nat. Bd. Podiatry Examiners. Pvt. practice Alamogordo, N.Mex., 1975-84, Panama City, Fla., 1984—; dir. Podiatric Pain Mgmt. Ctr.; expert in podiatric malpractice cases. Author: Podiatric Malpractice, 1981, The Agony of De-Feet, A Podiatrist Guide to Foot Care, 1982; contbr. to Collier's Ency., also numerous articles to profl. publs. Active March of Dimes, 1971—; mem. exec. com. Dems. Bay County, Fla.; chmn. 1st congl. dist. com. Fla. Dem. Com. Fellow Acad. Ambulatory Foot Surgery, Am. Acad. Pain Mgmt. (diplomate), Am. Podiatric Circulatory Soc. Office: The Schuler Profl Bldg 2401 W 15th St Panama City FL 32401-1567

SCHULER, THEODORE ANTHONY, civil engineer, city official; b. Louisville, July 1, 1934; s. Henry R. and Virginia (Meisner) S.; m. Jane A. Bandy, July 29, 1979; children: Marc, Elizabeth, Eric, Ellen. BCE, U. Louisville, 1957, M.Engring., 1973. Registered profl. engr., Tenn., Ky.; registered land surveyor. Design, constrn. engr. Brighton Engring. Co., Frankfort, Ky., 1960-65; design engr. Hensley-Schmidt Inc., Chattanooga, 1965-68, assoc. mem., 1969-73, sr. assoc. mem., 1973-75, prin., asst. v.p., head Knoxville office, 1975-81; chief planning engr. engring. dept. City of Knoxville, 1981-96, ret., 1996. Served to lt. (j.g.) USNR, 1957-60. Fellow ASCE. Home: 5907 Adelia Dr Knoxville TN 37920-5801

SCHULL, WILLIAM J., geneticist, educator; b. Louisiana, Mo., Mar. 17, 1922; married, 1946. BS, Marquette U., 1946; PhD in Genetics, Ohio State U., 1949. Head dept. genetics Atomic Bomb Casualty Comsn., Japan, 1949-51; jr. geneticist Inst. Human Biology, U. Mich., 1951-53, asst. geneticist, 1953-56, from asst. prof. to prof. human genetics, med. sch., 1956-72, prof. anthropology, 1969-72; prof. human genetics U. Tex. Grad. Sch. Biomedical Sci., Houston, 1972—; vis. fellow Australian Nat. U., 1969; cons. Atomic Bomb Casualty Comsn., 1954, 56, NIH, 1956—, chmn. genetics study sect., 1969-72; dir. Child Health Survey, Japan, 1959-60; vis. prof. U. Chgo., 1963, U. Chile, 1975; German Rsch. Assn. guest prof. U. Heidelberg, 1970; mem. com. atomic casualties Nat. Rsch. Coun., 1951, subcom. biology Com. Dentistry, 1951-55, com. on collaborative project Nat. Inst. Neurol. Disease and Stroke, 1957—, panel in genetic effects of radiation, WHO, 1958—, panel experts human heredity, 1961—, nat. adv. com. radiation USPHS, 1960-64, bd. sci. counselors Nat. Inst. Dentistry Rsch., 1966-69; dir. Radiation Effects Rsch. Found. and head dept. epidemiology and Japan, 1978-80; adv. Nat. Heart and Lung Inst.; mem. subcom. biology and medicine AEC, human biology coun. Soc. Study Human Biology. Recipient Centennial award Ohio State U., 1970. Mem. AAAS, U.S.Mex. Border Health Assn., Japanese Soc. Human Genetics (hon.), Peruvian Soc. Human Genetics (hon.), Genetic Soc. Chile (hon.), Sigma Xi. Office: U Tex Health Sci Ctr Human Genetics PO Box 20334 Houston TX 77225

SCHULMAN, JOSEPH DANIEL, physician, medical geneticist, executive, reproductive biologist, educator; b. Bklyn., Dec. 20, 1941; s. Max and Miriam (Grossman) S.; m. Dixie A. King; children: Erica N., Julie K. B.A., Bklyn. Coll., 1961; M.D., Harvard U., 1966. Diplomate Am. Bd. Pediatrics, Am. Bd. Ob-Gyn, Am. Bd. Med. Genetics. Intern, resident in pediatrics Mass. Gen. Hosp., Boston, 1966-68; clin. assoc. Nat. Inst. Arthritis and Metabolic Diseases, 1968-70; resident in obstetrics and gynecology and fellow in pediatrics N.Y. Hosp.-Cornell Med. Center, 1970-73; Gilbert and Nat. Found. fellow Cambridge (Eng.) U., 1973-74; head sect. human biochem. genetics Nat. Inst. Child Health and Human Devel., NIH, Bethesda, Md., 1974-83; dir. med. genetics program NIH, Bethesda, Md., 1979-1983; prof. ob/gyn, pediatrics, and genetics George Washington U., 1983-84; dir., CEO Genetics & IVF Inst., Fairfax, Va., 1984—; chmn. Genetics & IVF, Inc., Bethesda, Md., 1988—; prof. human genetics, pediatrics, obstetrics and gynecology Med. Coll. Va., 1984—; with dept. ob-gyn Fairfax Hosp., 1984—; advisor to numerous govt. and private agys. Author 3 books; contbr. numerous articles to med. jours.; editorial bd. Molecular Human Reproduction, 1995—. Served with USPHS, 1968-70, 74-83. Fellow Am. Coll. Obstetricians and Gynecologists; mem. Soc. Pediatric Research, Soc. Gynecologic Investigation, Am. Soc. Clin. Investigation, Am. Soc. Human Genetics, Am. Fertility Soc., Phi Beta Kappa, Sigma Xi. Clubs: Harvard, Cosmos. Office: 3020 Javier Rd Fairfax VA 22031-4627

SCHULTE, FRANCIS B., archbishop; b. Philadelphia, PA, Dec. 23, 1926. Grad., St. Charles Borromeo Sem. Ordained priest Roman Catholic Ch., 1952. Apptd. titular bishop of Afufenia and aux. bishop of Phila., 1981-85; bishop Wheeling-Charleston, W.Va., 1985-89; archbishop New Orleans, 1989—. Office: 7887 Walmsley Ave New Orleans LA 70125-3431

SCHULTE, JAMES MICHAEL, gas industry executive; b. Amarillo, Tex., May 30, 1955; s. Marvin Francis and Helen Gertrude (Actfeld) S.; m. Janet Louise Oppe, June 26, 1982; children: Christopher, Nicholas, Katherine. BBA, West Tex. State U., 1980. Programmer, analyst Mason & Hanger Silas Mason Co., Amarillo, 1980-85; sr. analyst, programmer Diamond Shamrock Corp., Amarillo, 1985-92; supr. gas measurement and systems Maxus Exploration Co., Amarillo, 1992—; computer adv. com. Amarillo Coll., 1992-95. With U.S. Army, 1973-76. Mem. Data Processing Mgmt. Assn. (sec. 1986-87, v.p. 1988, pres. 1989, Best Mem. award 1989), Panhandle Natural Gas Soc. (sec.-treas. 1991-92, v.p. 1992-93, pres. 1993-95). Roman Catholic. Office: Midgard Energy Co Subs of Maxus Energy Co 112 W 8th Ave Amarillo TX 79101-2300

SCHULTZ, CARMEN HELEN, copywriter, translator; b. Caracas, Venezuela, Jan. 22, 1962; came to U.S., 1975; d. Arthur Henry and Alicia M. (Mercedes) S. BA in Fgn. Langs. cum laude, So. Meth. U., 1984; postgrad. studies, Monterey Inst. Internat. Study, 1985-86, U. Tex., Dallas, 1987-94; Bus. Cert., U. Tex., 1995, U. Tex., Austin, 1995. Tech. translator Mobil Oil Exploration & Producing Svcs., Dallas, 1984-85; freelance translator/interpreter Dallas, 1985-87; abstractor/rsch. asst. Rand Corp., Santa Monica, Calif., 1987; Hispanic comm. coord. Mary Kay Cosmetics, Inc., Dallas, 1987-93; bilingual copywriter Rapp Collins Worldwide, Irving, Tex., 1993-94; translator/copy editor Ornelas & Assocs., Dallas, 1994-95; translator, writer Assocs. Corp. of N.Am., Irving, 1995—. Editor/translator: Belleza Total, 1992 (Internat. Mercury award); founder, editor (newsletter) Entérate, 1988 (Hispanic 100 1990, 91); contbg. writer Applause, 1992 (Award of Merit IPBC). So. Meth. U. scholar, 1980-84. Mem. Am. Translators Assn., Am. Lit. Translators Assn., Metroplex Interpreters and Translators Assn., Dallas Hispanic C. of C., Pi Delta Phi, Sigma Delta Pi. Roman Catholic. Home: 7008 Town Bluff Dr Dallas TX 75248-5524 Office: Assocs Corp of North America 250 Carpenter Freeway Irving TX 75062

SCHULTZ, DAVID ANDREW, political science educator; b. Binghamton, N.Y., Jan. 28, 1958; s. Fred L. and Margaret (Schuh) S.; m. Helene Levy, Sept. 10, 1982. BA, Harpur Coll., Binghamton, 1980; MA, Rutgers U., 1982, SUNY, Binghamton, 1986; PhD, U. Minn., 1989. Dir. code enforcement City of Binghamton, 1982-84; planner Opportunities for Broome, Binghamton, 1985-86; asst. prof. Polit. Sci. Gustavus Adolphus Coll., St. Peter, Minn., 1989-91, Trinity U., San Antonio, 1991-94; adj. prof. polit. sci. U. Minn., St. Paul, 1994-95; asst. prof. dept. polit. sci. U. Wis., River Falls; bd. dirs. Hampden Park Foods. Author: Property, Power and American Democracy, 1992, An Introduction to American Government through Microcase, 1992, A Short History of the U.S. Civil Service, 1991; editor: Law and Politics: Unanswered Questions, 1994, The Juris Prudential Vision of Justice Antonin Scalia, 1996. Mem. ACLU (bd. dirs. San Antonio chpt. 1992-93, case com. Minn. chpt. 1988-91, bd. dirs., treas. Minn. chpt.), common Cause (bd. dirs., state pres.).

SCHULTZ, EVERETT HOYLE, JR., radiologist, educator; b. Winston-Salem, N.C., Sept. 13, 1927; s. Everett Hoyle and Etta A. (Transou) S.; m. Nancy M. Jansson, Apr. 15, 1955; children: Susan, Frank, Janet, Sally, s. Pre-med. student, U. N.C., 1945-48; MD, Wake Forest U., 1952; ed. course in radioisotopes, Inst. Nuclear Studies, Oak Ridge, Tenn., 1957. Diplomate Am. Bd. Radiology; lic. physician, N.C., Mass., Fla., Ga. Intern U. Okla. Hosps., 1952-53, resident in radiology, 1954-55; resident in radiology U. N.C., 1955-57, assoc. prof. radiology Sch. Medicine, 1961-67; pvt. practice Cambridge, Mass., 1957-58; asst. in radiology MIT, Cambridge, 1957-58; asst. prof. Coll. Medicine U. Fla., 1958-61; staff radiologist St. Anthony's Hosp., St. Petersburg, Fla., 1967-84, VA Hosp., 1986-87; asst. prof. Coll. Medicine U. South Fla., 1986-87; assoc. prof. Med. Coll. of Ga., 1987—; program chmn. So. Radiol. Conf., 1963, 78, pres., 1964; presenter profl. assns., 1956—. Editorial cons. Yearbook of Cancer, 1964-83; contbr. articles to profl. jours. Fellow Am. Coll. Radiology; mem. N.C. Radiol. Soc. (pres. 1965), Mensa. Home: 608 Aumond Rd Augusta GA 30909-3308 Office: Med Coll Ga Dept Radiology Augusta GA 30912-3910

SCHULTZ, MARILYN ANN, medical/surgical nurse; b. El Paso, Tex., Oct. 22, 1954; d. Roy Henry and Mary Elizabeth (Moseley) S. BA in Edn., Trinity U., San Antonio, 1976, BA in Music, 1976; MA in Music, Trinity U., 1979; ADN, San Antonio Coll., 1985; BSN, U. Tex., San Antonio, 1989, MSN, 1995. RN, Tex.; cert. piano tchr., Tex. Nurse Santa Rosa Med. Ctr., San Antonio, S.W. Tex. Meth. Hosp., Santa Rose Med. Ctr., San Antonio; nurse surgery and orthopedics units N.E. Bapt. Hosp., San Antonio, nurse med. unit, 1992-95; clin. nurse specialist orthopedics dept. Audie L. Murphy Meml. VA Hosp., San Antonio, 1995—. Mem. ANA, San Antonio Music Tchrs. Assn., Assn. for Childhood Edn. Internat., Kappa Delta Pi, Mu Phi Epsilon. Home: 7710 Hartman St San Antonio TX 78209-3141

SCHULTZ, ROBERT BROWN, physician; b. Palo Alto, Calif., Sept. 27, 1921; s. Edwin W. and Anna Francel (Roberts) S.; m. Corinne Marvin, Aug. 7, 1951; children: David Linton, Carolyn Jane. AB, Whitman Coll., 1946; MA, Stanford U., 1948; MD, Yale U., 1952. Diplomate Am. Bd. Pathology. Intern, asst. resident Grace-New Haven Hosp., 1952-54; resident Grace New Haven (Conn.) Hosp., 1955-56; asst. prof. U. Minn., Mpls., 1956-58; from asst. prof. to assoc. prof. U. Md. Sch. Medicine, Balt., 1958-67, prof., acting head dept. pathology, 1967-70; pathologist Lee Meml. Hosp., Ft. Myers, Fla., 1970-74; med. dir. lab. Ft. Myers Community Hosp., 1974-84; med. dir. Edison Regional Blood Ctr., Ft. Myers, 1974—. With USNR, 1942-45. Am. Can. Soc. fellow Childrens Med. Ctr., Boston, 1954-55. Fellow Am. Assn. Blood Banks, Am. Soc. Clin. Pathologists, Fla. Assn. Blood Banks (pres. 1987), Internat. Acad. Pathologists, Coll. Am. Pathologists; mem. Sigma Xi. Republican. Home: 5521 Maeva Ct Fort Myers FL 33919-2612 Office: Edison Regional Blood Ctr 3714 Evans Ave Fort Myers FL 33901-9303

SCHULTZE, LISA JANE, editor; b. Camden, N.J., Aug. 25, 1971; d. William E. and Pamela T. (Grimac) S. AA, St. Petersburg Jr. Coll., Clearwater, Fla., 1993; BA, U. South Fla., 1996. Contbg. editor Tampa Bay Mag., Clearwater, 1993-96; in acctg. dept. Sterile Recoveries, Inc., Clearwater, 1996—; freelance writer, Clearwater, 1993—; staff writer Countryside Cougar, Tarpon Springs, Fla., 1996—. Home: 2761 Haverhill Ct Clearwater FL 34621 Office: Sterile Recoveries Inc 28100 US Hwy 19 N Ste 201 Clearwater FL 34621

SCHULTZE, MARIBETH JANE, psychologist; b. Dayton, Ohio, May 28, 1947; d. Richard Charles and Eileen Rita (Keane) S. BS cum laude, Wright State U., 1969; MA, Clark U., 1973, PhD, 1981. Lic. clin. psychologist, Tex. Resident in clin. psychology Wilford Hall USAF Med. Ctr., San Antonio, 1983; clin. psychologist Sheppard Regional USAF Hosp., Wichita Falls, Tex, , 1983-86; chief psychol. svcs. USAF Hosp., Blytheville, Ark., 1986-87; clin. psychologist Dallas VA Med. Ctr., 1987—; cons. family practice clinic, oral surgery Sheppard Regional Hosp., 1984-86. Contbr. articles to profl. jours. Mem. APA (divsn. clin. neuropsychology 1983—), Internat. Neuropsychol. Soc., Nat. Acad. Neuropsychology, Tex. Psychol. Assn. (Continuing Edn. Achievement award 1984, 85, 86, 87). Office: Dallas VA Med Ctr 4500 S Lancaster Rd Dallas TX 75216-7167

SCHULZ, BRADLEY NICHOLAS, lawyer; b. Staten Island, N.Y., July 1, 1959; s. George Robert Jr. and Mary Jane (Fazakerley) S. BA, Wake Forest U., 1981; JD, N.Y. Law Sch., 1984. Bar: N.Y. 1985, N.C. 1985, N.J. 1985, U.S. Dist. Ct. (ea. dist.) N.C. 1985, U.S. Dist. Ct. (so. dist.) N.Y. 1985. Assoc. Mast, Tew, Armstrong & Morris, P.A., Smithfield, N.C., 1984-85; ptnr. Mast, Morris, Schulz & Mast, P.A., Smithfield, 1986—. Chmn. Young Republicans, Johnston County, Smithfield, 1988. Hankins scholar Wake

Forest U., 1977-81, N.Y. Law Sch. scholar, 1981-84. Mem. ABA, N.C. Bar Assn., N.Y. Bar Assn., N.J. Bar Assn., N.C. Acad. Trial Lawyers, Johnston County Bar Assn., Theta Chi Fraternity. Republican. Episcopalian. Home: 102 Pheasant Run Clayton NC 27520-8301 Office: Mast Morris Schulz & Mast PA PO Box 119 Smithfield NC 27577-0119

SCHULZ, MICHAEL ANTHONY, JR., construction company executive, real estate developer; b. New Orleans, Dec. 17, 1934; s. Michael Anthony and Hilda (Monnin) S.; m. Ann Miller Hawkins; 1 child, Terri Lynn Guidry. BS, La. State U., 1959. Registered profl. engr., La., Miss. Plant mgr. Tidewood Corp., Baton Rouge, 1957-58; engr. La. Concrete Products, Baton Rouge, 1959-61; dept. head Wilson P. Abraham, Baton Rouge, 1961-64; mgr. Odis F. Haymon, Baton Rouge, 1964-67; sec., treas. The Bedford Corp., Baton Rouge, 1967-85; pres. Mike Schulz Constrn., Inc., Baton Rouge, 1985-92; coord. facility mgmt. La. Health Care Authority, Baton Rouge, 1992—. Maj. gen. USAR, 1957-93. Fellow Am. Soc. Civil Engrs.; mem. La. Engring. Soc., Soc. Am. Mil. Engrs., Res. Officers Assn., Sr. Army Res. Comdrs. Assn., Am. Arbitration Assn. (panel of arbitrators). Democrat. Episcopalian. Home: 441 Highland Oaks Dr Baton Rouge LA 70810-5344

SCHULZ, WALTER KURT, accountant, consultant; b. Hamburg, Germany, Apr. 9, 1940; came to U.S., 1970; s. Richard and Karla (Halm) S.; m. Beth Ann Edwards, June 21, 1972; children: Alec, Elli, Peter, Andrew, Heidi. MBA, U. Münster, Germany, 1969; MBA in Acctg., Ohio State U., 1972. Auditor Dr. Kaase, CPA, Bad Oeynhausen, Germany, 1966-71; systems analyst United Airlines, Chgo., 1973-77; v.p. fin. Eickhoff-Nat. Corp., Pitts., 1977-79; div. controller Mobay Corp., Pitts., 1979-86; pres. Infotek/PC Acctg., Charlotte, N.C., 1986—; cons. Westinghouse Corp., Mercy Hosp., Pitts, Charlotte Hornets. Lt. German Air Force, 1960-63. Mem. Am. Mgmt. Assn., Assn. MBA Execs. Republican. Home: 301 Sardis Rd N Charlotte NC 28270-2245

SCHULZ-BEHREND, GEORGE, German language educator; b. Greifswald, Germany, Feb. 12, 1913; came to U.S., 1928; m. Mary Louise Barker Modave (dec.); children: Anita Schoeffler, Paul Hubert; m. Betty Stahl, Aug. 28, 1959. BA in English, U. Colo., 1935, MA in German, 1936; PhD in German, U. Iowa, 1944. Instr. Elkader (Iowa) Jr. Coll., 1938-44; English instr. U. Iowa, Iowa City, 1944-46; instr. German U. Tex., Austin, 1946-65, prof. German, 1965-94, prof. emeritus, 1994—; guest prof. Berlin Free U., 1963, Marburg U., 1966. Editor: Complete Works of Martin Opitz (1597-1639), vol. 1, 1968, vol 2, 1970, vol. 3, 1978-79, vol. 4, 1989-90; translator: Simplicius Simplicissimus, a Novel of the Thirty Years by Grimmelshausen, 1965, 2d rev. edit., 1993. Recipient Honor award Opitz und seine Welt Festschrift, 1990, Gratitude award West German Govt., 1957, Order of Merit, 1988; Fulbright scholar, 1952-53. Mem. MLA, Am. Assn. Tchrs. German. Home: 1100 Gaston Ave Austin TX 78703-2508 Office: U Tex Dept Germanic Langs Austin TX 78712-2508

SCHULZE, ARTHUR EDWARD, biomedical engineer, researcher; b. Richmond, Tex., Nov. 22, 1938; s. Arthur Dorwin and Ida (Bockhorn) S.; m. Sharon Kay Havemann, Sept. 2, 1962; children: Keith E., Mark A. BSEE, U. Tex., 1962, MSEE, 1963; MS Biomed. Sci., U. Tex., Houston, 1968. Registered profl. engr., Tex. Sr. aerosystems engr. Gen. Dynamics, Ft. Worth, 1963-67; rsch. assoc. U. Tex. Grad. Sch. Biomed. Scis., Houston, 1967-68; mgr., biomed. engr. SCI Systems, Inc., Houston, 1968-74; v.p. Telecare, Inc., Houston, 1974-79; gen. mgr. Tex. Sci. Corp., Houston, 1979-81; dir. R & D Narco Bio-Systems, Houston, 1981-84; pres. Narco Bio-Systems, 1984-86; v.p. Lovelace Sci. Resources, Inc., Houston, 1986-92; pres. Healthcare Tech. Group, 1993—. Contbr. articles to sci. publs. Mem. IEEE, Aerospace Med. Assn., Assn. Advancement Med. Instrumentation, AAAS, Biomed. Technology Club. Home: 8807 Mobud Dr Houston TX 77036-5321 Office: Healthcare Tech Group 6901 Corporate Dr Ste 111 Houston TX 77036-5119

SCHULZE, ERIC WILLIAM, lawyer, legal publications editor, publisher; b. Libertyville, Ill., July 8, 1952; s. Robert Carl and Barbara (Mayo) S. BA, U. Tex., 1973, JD, 1977. Bar: Tex. 1977, U.S. Dist. Ct. (we. dist.) Tex. 1987, U.S. Ct. Appeals (5th cir.) 1987, U.S. Dist. Ct. (ea. and so. dists.) Tex. 1988, U.S. Dist. Ct. (no. dist.) Tex. 1989, U.S. Supreme Ct. 1989; bd. cert. civil appellate law Tex. Bd. Legal Specialization, 1990—. Rsch. asst. U. Tex., Austin, 1978; legis. aide Tex. Ho. of Reps., Austin, 1979-81; editor Tex. Sch. Law News, Austin, 1982-85; assoc. Hairston, Walsh & Anderson, Austin, 1986-87; ptnr. Walsh, Anderson, Underwood, Schulze & Aldridge, Austin, 1988—, mng. ptnr., 1993—; editor Tex. Sch. Adminstrs. Legal Digest, Austin, 1986-92, co-pub., 1991—, mng. editor, 1992—. Editor: (legal reference books) Texas Education Code Annotated, 1982-85; editl. adv. com. West's Edn. Law Reporter, 1996—. Del. Tex. State Democratic Conv., 1982, Travis County Dem. Conv., 1982, 84, 86. Recipient Merit award for pubs. Internat. Assn. Bus. Communicators-Austin br., 1983, Merit award for authorship Coll. of State Bar Tex., 1992. Mem. Fed. Bar Assn., Am. Bar Assn., Tex. Bar Assn., Travis County Bar Assn., Bar Assn. of 5th Cir., Defense Rsch. Inst., Nat. Council Sch. Attys., Tex. Council Sch. Attys., Nat. Orgn. Legal Problems in Edn., Toastmasters (pres. Capital City chpt. 1995). Home: 3416 Mt Bonnell Cir Austin TX 78731 Office: Walsh Anderson Underwood Schulze & Aldridge PO Box 2156 Austin TX 78768-2156

SCHUMACHER, CARL JOSEPH, JR., lawyer, educator; b. New Orleans, Sept. 17, 1926; s. Carl J. and Katherine (Bagnetto) S.; m. Leila Flournoy, Sept. 7, 1952; children: Carl David, Steven Stone, Katherine Holliday (dec.), Robert Priestley, Gerald Flourney. B.A., Tulane U., 1947, LL.B., 1950, M.C.L., 1959. Bar: La. 1950. Mem. firm Schumacher Law Corp., New Orleans; lectr. La. State U. Law Sch.; chmn. adv. com. New Orleans Juvenile Ct., 1954-57. Served to ensign USNR, World War II. Fellow Am. Coll. Trial Lawyers; mem. La. Bar Assn., Maritime Law Assn. U.S., U.S. Naval Inst., Bartolus Soc., Kappa Delta Phi, Phi Delta Phi, Kappa Sigma. Roman Catholic. Home: 4616 Perrier St New Orleans LA 70115-3920 Office: 1106 Arabella St New Orleans LA 70115-3102

SCHUMACHER, CYNTHIA JO, secondary education educator, retired; b. Sebring, Fla., Sept. 24, 1928; d. Floyd Melvin and Espage Love (Rogers) S. BA, Fla. State U., 1950, MA, 1951; MS, Nova U., 1978; postgrad., Fla. State U., 1968-69. English tchr. Grady County Sch. System, Cairo, Ga., 1951-53; elem. tchr. Brevard County Sch. System, Melbourne, Fla., 1953-55; elem. tchr., curriculum generalist, secondary tchr. Lake County Schs., Tavares, Fla. area, 1955-85; retired, 1985; mem. Edn. Standards Commn., Fla., 1980-85, Quality Instrn. Incentives Coun., Fla., 1983-84. Author: (poetry) Seeds from Wild Grasses, 1988, Creekstone Crossings, 1993; (poetry and stories) Butterfly Excursions, 1996. Pres. League of Women Voters of Lake County, 1989-91; mem. Lake Conservation Coun., The Nature Conservancy, Habitat for Humanity of Lake County. named Fla. Tchr. of Yr., Fla. Fedn. Women's Clubs, 1966, Lake County Tchr. of Yr., Lake County Sch. Systems, 1985, East Cen. Fla. Tchr. of Yr., finalist State of Fla., 1986; recipient Good Egg award Leesburg Area C. of C., 1991. Mem. Lake County Edn. Assn. (pres. 1971-72, cons. 1985—). Democrat. Roman Catholic. Office: Lake County Edn Assn PO Box 490816 Leesburg FL 34749-0816

SCHUMACHER, THERESA ROSE, singer, musician; b. Muskegon, Mich.; d. Boles and Marguerite (Lassard) Pietkiewicz; m. Glenn O. Schumacher, 1968 (div. 1988); children: Pamela Harrington Boller, Daniel Mark Harrington. BS in Sociology, Fairmont State Coll., 1975. Active W.Va. U. Symphony Choir, 1988—, 93 Fairmont State Coll. Choir; musician with spl. knowledge of music from 1735-1850, Nat. Park Svcs., 1989—. Mem. AAUW, W.Va. Poetry Soc., Morgantown, W.Va. Poetry Soc. Home: PO Box 162 Mannington WV 26582-0162

SCHUMACKER, RANDALL ERNEST, educational psychology educator; b. Oakes, N.D., May 26, 1951; s. Ernest and Helen (Jackson) S.; m. Joanne Cummins, July 24, 1952; children: Rachel Ann, Jamie Maureen. AA, William Rainey Harper Jr. Coll, 1970; BS, Western Ill. U., 1972; MS, So. Ill. U., 1978, PhD, 1984. Rsch. asst. So. Ill. U., Carbondale, 1980-84, assoc. dir. computing, 1984-87; asst. prof. U. North Tex., Denton, 1988-90, assoc. prof., 1991—, rsch. assoc. prof. Unit Health Svcs. Dept. Family Medicine, 1995—; vis. prof. So. Ill. U., 1980-84; vis. scholar U. Chgo., 1996; cons. Tex. Acad. Math. & Sci., Denton, 1993, Carrollton-Farmers Br. (Tex.), 1991-94, Profl. Devel., 1989-92; presenter in field. Contbr. articles to profl. jours. Mem. Am. Psychol. Assn., Am. Ednl. Rsch. Assn., Southwest Ednl. Rsch. Assn., Am. Statis. Assn., Midwestern Ednl. Rsch. Assn., Nat. Coun. Measurement Edn., Phi Delta Kappa. Republican. Lutheran. Office: U North Tex Coll Edn Denton TX 76203

SCHUMAKER, KAREN ANN, education and literacy educator; b. Columbus, Ohio, Sept. 18, 1949; d. Charles Herbert and Mary Agnes Hosey; m. Donn M. Schumaker, Aug. 18, 1972; children: Kurt Andrew, Emily Marie. BS in Elem. Edn., Ohio State U., 1972, MA in Early and Middle Childhood Edn., 1974; postgrad., St. Mary's Coll., Winnona, Minn., 1983-84; PhD in Curriculum and Instrn., U. Tex., 1991. Cert. tchr. Tex., Ohio, Minn.; cert. supervision, mgmt., English, psychology, reding specialist, ESL, child devel., spl. edn. Tchr., sci. coord. Southwestern City Schs., Columbus, 1972-78; career cons. Wyoming City Schs., Cin., 1972-78; title I reading, math instr. Rosemount (Minn.) Ind. Sch. Dist., 1979-81; ESL tchr. Burnsville (Minn.) Cmty. Edn., 1979-85; chpt. one progrm coord. Round Rock (Tex.) Ind. Sch. Dist., 1985-87; prof. S.W. Tex. State U., San Marcos, 1991-93, U. Tex., Austin, 1993-94; instr., rschr. Austin C.C., 1994—; prof. St. Edward's U., Austin, 1994—; exec. bd. mem. Tex. Tchr. Educators, 1993-95; mem. conf. planning com. Coll. Acad. Support Programs, Tex., 1996—. Author (taxonomy) A Study of Teacher Responses to Pupil Connected Reading, 1991; editor Tex. Tchr. Educator's Forum, 1993-95; contbr. articles to profl. jours. Exec. bd. mem., legis. rep. PTSA, Bloomington, Minn., 1989-91; task force participant Bloomington Ind. Sch. Dist. Youth Svc. Task Force, 1989-91, Alternative Sch. Task Force, Bloomington, 1989-91; mem. Austin Jr. Forum, 1992-93; pres. Balcones Country Club Swim Team, Austin, 1992-95. Mem. ASCD, Internat. Reading Assn., Tex. State Reading Assn. (chair facilitators local arrangements com. 1996), Tex. Profs. of Reading (sec./treas. 1994-96), Gifted and Talented Spl. Interest Coun., Phi Kappa Phi, Kappa Delta Pi, Pi Lambda Theta, Kappa Kappa Gamma. Home: 10713 Keystone Bend Austin TX 78750 Office: St Edwards Univ Box 808 3001 S Congress Ave Austin TX 78704-8412

SCHUMAN, BERNARD THOMAS, political science educator; b. Hornell, N.Y., Mar. 24, 1953; s. Bernard K. and Dale (Hood) S.; m. Linda Susan Gognat, Aug. 15, 1986. BS, U. Tulsa, 1975; MPA, U. Tenn., 1991, postgrad., 1993—. Advt. mgr. Bristow (Okla.) News-Record, 1976-78; mgr. pub. rels. Loffland Bros. Co., Tulsa, 1978-87; survey intern-cons. Mcpl. Tech. Adv. Svc., Knoxville, Tenn., 1991; rsch. cons. Social Sci. Rsch. Inst., Knoxville, 1992; budget analyst Tenn. Dept. Fin. and Adminstrn., Nashville, 1992-93; survey rschr. dept. transp. U. Tenn., Knoxville, 1990, tchg. assoc. dept. polit. sci., 1993—. Author: Municipal Water/Wastewater Survey Results, 1991. participant confs. in field. Mem. ASPA, Am. Polit. Sci. Assn., So. Polit. Sci. Assn., Pi Sigma Alpha. Unitarian. Office: U Tenn 1001 McClung Tower Knoxville TN 37909

SCHUMAN, STANLEY H., epidemiologist, educator; b. St. Louis, Dec. 29, 1925; married, 1952; 8 children. MD, Washington U., St. Louis, 1948; MPH, U. Mich., 1960, DPH, 1962; LLD (hon.), Clemson U., 1996. Diplomate Am. Bd. Pediatrics. Intern Jewish Hosp., St. Louis, 1948-49; resident Children's Hosp., St. Louis, 1950-51, Grady Hosp., 1953; clin. instr. pediatrics, sch. medicine Wash. U., 1954-59; from asst. prof. to prof. epidemiology, sch. pub. health U. Mich., Ann Arbor, 1962-73; prof. epidemiology in family practice, coll. medicine Med. U. S.C., Charleston, 1974—, prof. pediatrics, 1976—; med. dir. Agromedicine Program, Clemson Med. U., S.C., 1984—; project dir. S.C. Pesticide Study Ctr., EPA, 1981-84. Author: Epidemiology, 1986, Environmental Epidemiology, 1996. Mem. Am. Epidemiol. Soc., Soc. Epidemiol. Rsch., Coun. Agrl. Sci. Tech., Sigma Xi. Home: 1019 Scotland Dr Mount Pleasant SC 29464-3612 Office: Med U SC Agromedicine Program 171 Ashley Ave Charleston SC 29425-0001

SCHUSSLER, IRWIN, psychiatrist, educator; b. Bklyn., Nov. 14, 1943; s. Jack and Fannie Yetta (Blank) S.; m. Myra Yvette Paget, June 26, 1966; children: Jeffrey Mitchell, Doreen Robyn, Kimberly Beth, Howard, Brian. BS, Bklyn. Coll., 1964; DO, Chgo. Coll. Osteopathic Medicine, 1968. Diplomate Am. Bd. Psychiatry and Neurology, Am. Bd. Gen. Psychiatry and Child Psychiatry, Am. Osteopathic Bd. Neurology and Psychiatry, Am. Bd. Sexology. Intern Interboro Gen. Hosp., Bklyn., 1968-69; resident in gen. psychiatry U. Fla. Coll. Medicine, Gainesville, 1972-74, asst. prof. psychiatry and pediatrics, 1976-77, dir. in-patient psychotherapy, 1976-77, fellow in child and adolescent psychiatry, 1974-76; fellow in human sexual medicine U. Pa., Phila., 1975; practice medicine specializing in psychiatry Ft. Worth, 1977-79; clin. assoc. prof., vice chmn. dept. psychiatry North Tex. State U. Health Scis. Ctr., Tex. Coll. Osteo. Medicine, Ft. Worth, 1979—; bd. dirs. Osteo. Med. Ctr. Tex., med. dir. psychiatry dept.; bd. dirs. Health Care Tex., Mental Health Assn. Contbr. articles to profl. jours. Bd. dirs. Mental Health Assn. Fellow Am. Coll. Neuropsychiatry, Am. Coll. Sexology; mem. Am. Psychiat. Assn., Am. Acad. Child Psychiatrists, Am. Acad. Clin. Psychiatrists, Am. Assn. Sex Educators, Counselors and Therapists, Tex. Soc. Psychiat. Physicians (pres. Tarrant County chpt.), Am. Osteo. Assn., Tex. Osteo. Med. Assn., Fla. Osteo. Med. Assn., Masters and Johnson Found. Jewish. Home: 3712 Myrtle Springs Rd Fort Worth TX 76116-9213 Office: Psychiat Cons Ft Worth 3704 Mattison Ave Fort Worth TX 76107-2619

SCHUTH, MARY MCDOUGLE, interior designer, educator; b. Kansas City, Mo., Jan. 19, 1942; d. William Darnall and Marie DeArmond (Meiser) McDougle; m. Howard Wayne Schuth, Sept. 4, 1965; 1 child, Andrew Wayne. BS in Interior Design, Communications, Northwestern U., 1964; Cert. Basic Mgmt., U. Mo., 1966. Lic. interior designer, La. Interior designer Cottington's Interiors, Glen Ellyn, Ill., 1964-65, Robnett-Putman Interiors, Columbia, Mo., 1966-67, Nu-Idea Furniture Co., New Orleans, 1973, Maison Blanche, New Orleans, 1974-75, Mary M. Schuth Interior Design, Metairie, La., 1977—; instr. interior design U. New Orleans div. Continuing Edn., 1973—; judge model homes U.S. Homes, Mandeville, La., 1978, 80; bd. dirs. Interior Design Adv. Com. Delgado Coll., New Orleans, 1981—; mem. Alpha Chi Omega Frat. housing rev. com., 1991-96; guest lectr. Delta Queen Steamboat Co., 1995-96; spkr. in field. Co-author: cookbook From the Privateers' Galley, 1980; design work featured in profl. jours.; contbr. to Metairie Mag., 1993-94. Recipient 3rd place Batik Design Juried Art Show Columbia (Mo.) Art League, 1969. Mem. AIA (profl. affiliate), Am. Soc. Interior Designers (profl.), La. Landmarks, Alpha Chi Omega, Alumnae Club (New Orleans).

SCHUTTE, OFELIA M., philosophy educator; b. Havana, Cuba, Oct. 12, 1945; came to U.S., 1960; d. José Antonio and Ofelia (Fraga) S. BA, Barry Coll., 1966; MA, U. Miami, 1969, Miami U., Oxford, Ohio, 1970; PhD, Yale U., 1978. Asst. prof. humanities U. Fla., Gainesville, 1978-79, Lilly found. postdoctoral teaching fellow, 1979-80, asst. prof. philosophy, 1979-84, assoc. prof., 1984-94, prof., 1994—. Author: Beyond Nihilism: Nietzsche Without Masks, 1984, Cultural Identity and Social Liberation in Latin American Thought, 1993; mem. editorial bd. Hypatia: A Jour. of Feminist Philosophy, Tampa, Fla., 1990—. Fulbright rsch. fellow Coun. for Internat. Exch. of Scholars, Mexico City, 1985, Bunting Inst. fellow Radcliffe Rsch. Ctr., Cambridge, Mass., 1993. Mem. Am. Philos. Assn., Soc. for Women in Philosophy, Soc. for Phenomenology and Existential Philosophy, Latin Am. Studies Assn., Soc. for Iberian and Latin Am. Thought (pres. 1989-91, exec. officer 1991-94), N.Am. Nietzsche Soc. Office: Univ Fla Dept Philosophy Gainesville FL 32611

SCHWAB, CAROL ANN, law educator; b. Washington, Mo., Mar. 2, 1953; d. Calvin George and Edith Emma (Starke) Schermann; m. Steven Joseph Schwab, May 31, 1975. BA, Southeast Mo. State U., 1975; JD, U. Mo., 1978; LLM, Washington U., St. Louis, 1985. Bar: Mo. 1979, N.C. 1986. Law clk. to presiding justice U.S. Dist. Ct. (we. dist.), Kansas City, Mo., 1979-82; assoc. Bryan, Cave, McPheeters & McRoberts, St. Louis, 1982-84, Smith, Anderson, Blount, Dorsett, Mitchell & Jernigan, Raleigh, N.C., 1985-87; assoc. prof., resource mgmt. specialist N.C. Coop. Extension Svc., N.C. State U., Raleigh, 1988—; instr. legal writing St. Louis U. Sch. Law, 1984. Contbr. articles to profl. jours. Bd. dirs., co-chair fin. com. N.C. chpt. Nat. Com. for Prevention of Child Abuse, 1988-90, pres.-elect, 1990; mem. bd. assocs. N.C. Child Advocacy Inst., 1990-93; mem. Children's Summit Steering Com., 1993. Recipient John S. Divilbiss award U. Mo., 1977. Mem. N.C. Bar Assn. (editor The Will and Way quar. publ. 1990-91, sec. estate planning and fiduciary law sect. 1991-92, coun. mem. 1996—, mem. comm. adv. com. 1991—, mem. tech. adv. com. 1995—, mem. elder law com. 1996—), Mo. Bar Assn. Republican. Roman Catholic. Office: NC State U Campus Box 7605 Raleigh NC 27695

SCHWAB, THERESE MATHES, nursing educator; b. Detroit, Sept. 18, 1935; d. Charles Joseph and Wilhelmina (Kengel) Mathes; m. Francis Schwab, Aug. 29, 1964; children: Mary, Karen, Jodie, Charles. BS in Nursing, Barry U., 1957; MPH in Nursing, U. Minn., 1965; MS in Edn., No. State U., 1975; PhD, Walden U., 1981. Pub. health nurse Washtenaw County Health Dept., Ann Arbor, Mich., 1959-62; nursing coord. Regional Med. Program, Omaha, 1968-73; assoc. prof. U. Wyo., Laramie, 1975-86, U. Tex. Health Sci. Ctr., San Antonio, 1986-95, Tex. A&M U., Laredo, 1995-96, U. Tex., Brownsville, 1996—. Contbr. articles to profl. jours. Recipient Ellogen Meritorious Teaching award, 1986. Mem. APHA, Tex. Nurses Assn., Sigma Theta Tau., Sigma Xi. Home: 3500 Carmen Ave Unit 1205 Rancho Viejo TX 78575

SCHWABE, GEORGE BLAINE, III, lawyer; b. Tulsa, Oct. 10, 1947; s. George Blaine Jr. and Marguerite Irene (Williams) S.; m. Jann Lee Schoonover, July 28, 1972; 1 child, George Blaine IV. BBA, U. Okla., 1970, JD, 1974. Bar: U.S. Ct. Appeals (10th cir.) 1974, Okla. 1974, U.S. Dist. Ct. (we. dist.) Okla. 1974, U.S. Dist. Ct. (no. dist.) Okla. 1985, U.S. Supreme Ct. 1991. From assoc. to ptnr. Crowe & Dunlevy, Oklahoma City, 1974-82; ptnr., dir. Mock, Schwabe, Waldo, Elder, Reeves & Bryant, Oklahoma City, 1982-96, Gable, Gotwals, Moch, Schwabe, Oklahoma City, 1996—; adj. prof. law Oklahome City U.; lectr. numerous CLE programs, Okla. Capt. USAR. Fellow Am. Coll. Bankruptcy; mem. ABA (bus. bankruptcy com. sect. bus. law), Okla. Bar Assn. (pres. 1987-88, bd. dirs. 1985—), Oak Tree Country Club, Okla. City Golf & Country Club, Rotary. Republican. Mem. Christian Ch. (Disciples of Christ). Office: Gable Gotwals Mock Schwabe 1 Leadership Sq Fl 15 Oklahoma City OK 73102

SCHWALKE, MICHAEL ALLEN, general surgeon, surgical oncologist; b. Bethesda, Md., May 3, 1954; s. Joseph Clarence and Carolyn Emmett (Melton) S.; married; 1 child, Michael Allen II. BS cum laude, U. South Fla., 1977; MS, Va. Tech., 1981; MD, Med. Coll. Va., 1985. Cert. in laparoscopic surgery; diplomate Nat. Bd. Med. Examiners; lic. physician; cert. Am. Bd. Surgery. Resident in surgery Brown U., Providence, 1985-89, Med. Coll. Va., 1989-91; asst. prof. surgery/surg. oncology La. State U. Sch. Medicine, Shreveport, 1991-95; gen. surgeon, surg. oncologist in pvt. practice Shreveport, La., 1995—. Contbr. chpts. to books, articles to profl. jours. Stiles grantee, 1992-93, NSABP grantee, 1993-95, NIH grantee, 1995-97. Fellow ACS, Southeastern Surg. Congress (affiliate); mem. AMA, Surg. Assn. La., Shreveport Med. Soc., Humera Surg. Soc., Soc. for Study of Breast Disease. Office: Physicians Plz Ste 3 2514 Bert Kouns Ind Loop Shreveport LA 71118

SCHWANZ, DEBORAH ANN, psychiatric nurse; b. South Bend, Ind., Jan. 1, 1952; d. Ned Christian and Rita Jane (Witucki) S. Diploma in nursing, Meml. Hosp. Sch. Nursing, South Bend, 1973; BS in Health Arts, Coll. of St. Francis, Joliet, Ill., 1991. RN, Fla.; cert. psychiat. and mental health nurse ANCC. House float nurse Meml. Hosp., 1973; psychiat. team leader St. Anthony's Hosp., St. Petersburg, Fla., 1974-81, asst. head nurse, 1981-84, clin. mgr. psychiatry, instr. aggression control techniques, 1984-89; weekend nursing supr. Boley, Inc., St. Petersburg, 1989-92; nurse therapist various nursing homes, St. Petersburg, 1992-93, Physicians' Cmty. Hosp., St. Petersburg, 1993-94; contract psychiat. nurse St. Anthony's Home Health Care, St. Petersburg, 1986-94; psychiat. home health nurse Shands Home Care, Largo, Fla., 1995—; presenter on psychiat. nursing at seminars and workshops, St. Petersburg and Clearwater, Fla., 1984-88. Mem. St. Petersburg Dem. Club. Mem. NOW (past sec. Pinellas chpt.), Mental Health Assn., Meml. Hosp. Sch. Nursing Alumni Assn. Office: 7249 Bryan Dairy Rd Largo FL 33777-1540

SCHWARTZ, BERNARD, law educator; b. N.Y.C., Aug. 25, 1923; s. Isidore and Ethel (Levenson) S.; m. Aileen Haas, Apr. 18, 1950; 1 child, Brian Michael. BSS, CCNY, 1944; LLB, NYU, 1944; LLM, Harvard U., 1945; PhD, Cambridge (Eng.) U., 1947, LLD, 1956; Doctorat d'Universite, U. Paris, 1963. Bar: N.Y. 1945. Mem. law faculty NYU, 1947-92, Edwin D. Webb prof. law, 1963-92; Chapman Disting. prof. law U. of Tulsa, 1992—; cons. Hoover Commn., 1955; chief counsel, staff dir. spl. subcom. legislative oversight U.S. Ho. Reps., 1957-58; Tagore Law lectr., Calcutta, India, 1984; corr. mem. Nat. Acad. Law and Social Scis., Argentina, 1986—. Author: French Administrative Law and the Common Law World, 1954, The Supreme Court, 1957, The Professor and the Commissions, 1959, Introduction to American Administrative Law, 1962, The Reins of Power, 1963, Commentary on the Constitution of the U.S., 5 vols., 1963-68, The Roots of Freedom, 1967, Legal Control of Government, 1972, Constitutional Law: A Textbook, 1972, 2d edit., 1979, The Law in America, 1974, Administrative Law, 1976, 3d edit., 1991, The Great Rights of Mankind, 1977, expanded edit., 1992, Administrative Law: A Casebook, 1977, 4th edit., 1994, Super Chief: Earl Warren and His Supreme Court, 1983, Inside the Warren Court, 1983, The Unpublished Opinions of the Warren Court, 1985, Some Makers of American Law, 1985, Swann's Way: The School Busing Case and the Supreme Court, 1986, Behind Bakke: The Supreme Court and Affirmative Action, 1988, The Unpublished Opinions of the Burger Court, 1988, The Ascent of Pragmatism: The Burger Court in Action, 1990, The New Right and the Constitution, 1990, Constitutional Issues: Freedom of the Press, 1992, Main Currents in American Legal Thought, 1993, A History of the Supreme Court, 1993, The Unpublished Opinions of the Rehnquist Court, 1996, Decision: How The Supreme Court Decides Cases, 1996. Ann. Survey Am. Law dedicated in his name, 1988. Mem. ABA. Office: U Tulsa Coll Of Law Tulsa OK 74104

SCHWARTZ, BONNIE JO, electrical engineer; b. Albuquerque, Dec. 13, 1957; d. Jimmy and Phyllis Ann (Payne) Schaefer; m. John Anton Schwartz, May 19, 1984; children: James Edward, John Austin. BS in Internat. Rels., USAF Acad., 1980; MA in Polit. Sci., Wichita State U., 1987, BSEE, 1989. Cert. engr.-in-tng., Okla. Commd. 2d lt. USAF, 1980, advanced through grades to capt.; crew comdr. Titan II ICBM USAF, McConnell AFB, Wichita, Kans., 1980-84, wing exec. officer, 1984-87; resigned USAF, 1987; statis. process control cons. Boeing Co., Wichita, 1987-90; sr. project mgr. John Zink Co., Tulsa, 1990-91, internat. R&D facility engr., 1991-93, internat. R&D facility mgr., 1993-94, dir. combustion tech., 1994-95; mgr. Pipeline Control Ctr. Koch Industries, Wichita, Kans., 1995—. Trustee Undercroft Montessori Sch., Tulsa, 1991-93; swimming coach Oologah (Okla.) Goldfin Swim Team, 1992—. Mem. Instrument Soc. Am., Mensa Soc., Golden Key Nat. Honor Soc., Tau Beta Pi, Eta Kappa Nu, Pi Mu Epsilon, Pi Sigma Alpha. Republican. Home: 2604 E Central Ave Wichita KS 67002

SCHWARTZ, CHARLES, JR., federal judge; b. New Orleans, Aug. 20, 1922; s. Charles and Sophie (Hess) S.; m. Patricia May, Aug. 31, 1950; children—Priscilla May, John Putney. BA, Tulane U., 1943, JD, 1947. Bar: La. 1947. Ptnr. Guste, Barnett & Little, 1947-70; practiced in New Orleans, until 1976; ptnr. firm Little, Schwartz & Dussom, 1970-76; dist. counsel Gulf Coast dist. U.S. Maritime Adminstrn., 1953-62; judge U.S. Dist. Ct. (ea. dist.) La., New Orleans, 1976—; mem. Fgn. Itelligence Surveillance Ct., 1992—; prof. Tulane U. Law Sch.; lectr. continuing law insts.; mem. Jud. Conf. Com. U.S. on implementation of jury system, 1981-85; mem. permanent adv. bd. Tulane Admiralty Law Inst., 1984—. Bd. editors Tulane Law Rev. Pres. New Orleans unit Am. Cancer Soc., 1956-57; v.p., chmn. budget com. United Fund Greater New Orleans Area, 1959-61, trustee, 1953-65; bd. dirs. Cancer Assn. Greater New Orleans, 1958—, pres., 1958-59, 72-73; bd. dirs. United Cancer Council, 1963-85, pres., 1971-73; mem. com. on grants to agencies Community Chest, 1965-87; men's adv. com. League Women Voters, 1966-68; chmn. com. admissions of program devel. and coordination com. United Way Greater New Orleans, 1974-77; mem. comml. panel Am. Arbitration Assn., 1974-76; bd. dirs. Willow Wood Home, 1979-85, 1989-92; bd. mgrs. Touro Infirmary, 1992—; trustee Metairie Park Country Day Sch., 1977-83; mem. La. Republican Central Com., 1961-76; mem. Orleans Parish Rep. Exec. Com., 1960-75, chmn., 1964-75; mem. Jefferson Parish Rep. Exec. Com., 1975-76; del. Rep. Nat. Conv., 1960, 64, 68; mem. nat. budget and consultation com. United Community Funds and Coun. of Am., 1961; bd. dirs. Community Svcs. Coun., 1971-73. Served to 2d lt. AUS, 1943-46; maj. U.S. Army Res.; ret. Mem.

La. Bar Assn. New Orleans Bar Assn. (legis. com. 1970-75), Fed. Bar Assn., Fgn. Rels. Assn. New Orleans (bd. dirs. 1957-61), 5th Cir. Dist. Judges Assn. (pres. 1984-85), Lakewood Country Club (bd. dirs. 1967-68, pres. 1975-77). Office: US Dist Ct C-317 US Courthouse 500 Camp St New Orleans LA 70130-3313

SCHWARTZ, GERALD, public relations and fundraising agency executive; b. N.Y.C., June 22, 1927; s. George and Martha F. S.; m. Felice P. Schwartz, June 25, 1950: children: Gary R., Gregg R., Wendy L. Student N.C. State U., 1944-45; AB, U. Miami, Fla., 1949, BS, 1950, postgrad., 1966-67. Staff writer Miami Herald, 1941-44; publicity dir. U.S. Army in Europe, 1946-48; editor Miami Beach Sun, 1950-51; fund raising and pub. rels. counselor, Miami, 1952-58; press sec. to Gov. Nebr., 1959-60; exec. v.p. Bar-Ilan U., Ramat Gan, Israel, Israel, 1960-61; prin. Gerald Schwartz Agy., Miami, Fla., 1962—. Dep. chmn. Dem. Midwest Conf., 1958-60; pres. Am. Zionist Fedn. So. Fla., 1970-73, 86-92; nat. v.p. Am. Zionist Fedn., 85-89, 91-93; pres. Pres.'s council Zionist Orgn. Am., 1983-85; bd. dirs. Temple Emanu-El of Greater Miami, Papanicolaou Cancer Research Inst., Miami, 1962-80; vice chmn. Urban League of Greater Miami, 1983-87; vice chmn. City of Miami Beach Planning Bd., 1953-55; bd. dirs. Greater Miami Symphony, 1982-87, Miami Beach Taxpayers Assn.; pres. Civic League Miami Beach, 1985-87; nat. chmn. Friends of Pioneer Women/Na'amat, 1984—; pres. Greater Miami chpt. Assn. Welfare of Soldiers in Israel, 1983-86; chmn. City of Miami Beach Hurricane Def. Com., 1978-86, 90—; trustee South Shore Hosp. and Med. Ctr., Miami, 1987—; exec. vice chmn. South Shore Med. Ctr. Found., 1989—; bd. govs. Barry U., 1985-86; chmn. Econ. Devel. Coun. City of Miami Beach, 1985-91; bd. dirs. Crimestoppers of Dade County, 1991-94, bd. dir.,Jewish Nat. Fund of Am., 1995—. Served with U.S. Army, 1944-46. salem Peace award State of Israel Bonds, 1978., Recipient Jerusalem 3000 award State 0f I Mem. Pub. Rels. Soc. Am. (accredited; treas. So. Fla. chpt. 1962-64), Am. Pub. Rels. Assn. (pres. chpt. 1960-61), Am. Assn. Polit. Cons, Nat. Assn. Fund Raising Execs. (pres. chpt. 1977-78, 1995—), Miami Beach Taxpayers Assn. (bd. dirs. 1994—), Miami Internat. Press Club (bd. dirs. 1991—), Miami Beach C. of C. (v.p. 1978-80, 81-84, 86-87, 96—, pres.-elect 1988-90, trustee 1990—), Lead and Ink, Tiger Bay Club (pres. 1986-88), B'nai B'rith (pres. lodge 1964-66), Theta Omicron Pi, Omicron Delta Kappa, Alpha Delta Sigma (pres. chpt. 1965-67), Zeta Beta Tau. Office: Gerald Schwartz Agy 600 Alton Rd Miami FL 33139-5502

SCHWARTZ, JOYCE GENSBERG, pathologist; b. San Antonio, July 24, 1950; d. Frank and Sara Gensberg; B.A., U. Tex.-Austin, 1971, M.A., 1972; M.D., U. Tex.-San Antonio, 1980; m. Alan R. Schwartz, July 17, 1977. Speech pathologist Northeast Ind. Sch. Dist., San Antonio, 1971-73; vet. asst., 1973-74; resident in pathology U. Tex. Health Sci. Ctr. at San Antonio, 1980-84, mem. faculty pathology 1984-96; med. dir. Corning Clin. Labs., 1996—. Pres. P.I. Nixon Hist. Libr., 1991-92. Recipient Presdl. Teaching award, 1991, Piper Prof. award, 1992; named San Antonio Women's Hall of Fame, 1995. Mem. AMA, Coll. Am. Pathologists (regional commr.), Tex. Soc. Pathologists (sec. 1994-96), Bexar County Med. Assn., Women's Faculty Assn. (pres. 1988-89), San Antonio Soc. Pathologists (pres. 1988-89), Phi Kappa Phi, Alpha Omega Alpha. Jewish. Office: Corning Clin Labs 4771 Regent Blvd Irving TX 75063

SCHWARTZ, LEONARD JAY, lawyer; b. San Antonio, Sept. 23, 1943; s. Oscar S. and Ethel (Eastman) S.; m. Sandra E. Eichelbaum, July 4, 1965; 1 child, Michele Fay. BBA, U. Tex., 1965, JD, 1968. Bar: Tex. 1968, Ohio 1971, U.S. Supreme Ct. 1971, U.S. Dist. Ct. (no., ea., wes. and so. dists.) Tex., U.S. Dist. Cts. (no. and so. dists.) Ohio, U.S. Dist. Ct. Nebr., U.S. Ct. Appeals (5th, 6th, 7th and 11th cirs.). Assoc. Roberts & Holland, N.Y.C., 1968-70; ptnr. Rigely, Schwartz & Fagan, San Antonio, 1970-71; staff counsel ACLU of Ohio, Columbus, 1971-74; ptnr. Schwartz & Fishman, Columbus, Ohio, 1974-79; elections counsel to sec. of state State of Ohio, Columbus, 1979-80; ptnr. Waterman & Schwartz and successor firms, Austin, Tex., 1981-85, Schwartz & Eichelbaum, P.C., Austin, 1985—; gen. counsel Dallas Ind. Sch. Dist. and various other sch. dists.; adj. prof. law U. Tex. Sch. Law, Austin; labor and employment law cons. Tex. Assn. Sch. Adminstrs; condr. workshops in field. Contbr. articles to profl. jours. Mem. chancellor's coun. U. Tex. Sys.; mem. U. Tex. Pres.'s Assocs., Littlefield Soc., Sch. of Law Keeton Fellows. Recipient Outstanding Teaching Quiz Master award U. Tex. Sch. Law, 1968. Mem. ABA, Tex. Bar Assn., Bar Assn. 5th Cir., Fed. Bar Assn., Phi Delta Phi. Democrat. Jewish. Office: Schwartz & Eichelbaum PC One Commodore Plz 800 Brazos Ste 870 Austin TX 78701

SCHWARTZ, MARY REBECCA, pathologist; b. Bremen, Germany, Oct. 7, 1953; parents Am. citizens; d. M.E. and Molly (Rosoff) Schwartz; m. David Allen Cech, Apr. 12, 1981; children: Jacqueline Michelle, Daniel Michael. BA with honors, Stanford (Calif.) U., 1974; MD, Washington U., 1978. Diplomate in ant. and clin. pathology with subsplty. in cytopathology Am. Bd. Pathology. Intern, resident Baylor Coll. Medicine, 1978-82; asst. prof. Baylor Coll. Medicine, Houston, 1978-92, assoc. prof. pathology and dermatology, 1992—; clin. assoc. prof. So. Ill. U., Springfield, Ill., 1989-90; attending pathologist St. John's Hosp., Springfield, 1989-90, The Meth. Hosp., Houston, 1978—; residency program dir. Baylor Coll. Medicine, 1990—. Contbr. articles to profl. jours., chpts. to books. Recipient Merck award Washington U. Sch. Medicine, 1978. Fellow Coll. Am. Pathologists, Am. Soc. Clin. Pathologists; mem. U.S. and Can. Acad. Pathology, Papanicolaou Soc. Cytology, Am. Soc. Cytopathology (chmn. edn. devel. com. 1992-95, chmn. lab. accreditation com. 1995—), Phi Beta Kappa, Alpha Omega Alpha. Office: The Methodist Hospital 6565 Fannin MS 205 Houston TX 77030

SCHWARTZ, MIRIAM CATHERINE, biology educator; b. Tarlac, Luzon, Philippines, Mar. 9, 1964; came to U.S., 1980; d. Conrado Palarca and Elena Obcena (Domingo) Estanislao; m. Jason Jay Schwartz, July 20, 1987. BS in Biology, Calif. State U., L.A., 1985; PhD, Purdue U., 1992. Rsch. asst., rsch. assoc. dept. biol. sci. Purdue U., West Lafayette, Ind., 1988-93, teaching asst., instr., 1988-93; postdoctoral fellow sch. med. Emory U., Atlanta, 1993-94; biology lectr. Spelman Coll., Atlanta, 1994—. Contbr. articles to profl. jours. Aux. vol. Emory Univ. Hosp., Atlanta, 1993—. Mem. Phi Kappa Phi, Golden Key Nat. Honor Soc. Office: Spelman Coll Atlanta GA 30314

SCHWARTZ, SERGIU, concert artist; b. Bucharest, Romania, Dec. 16, 1957; came to U.S., 1981; s. Saul and Clara (Schor) S. Student, Rubin Acad. Music, 1972, MA, 1977; dipl. profl. studies, Hochschule für Musik, 1978; dipl. premier prix artist, Guildhall Sch. London, 1981; dipl. profl. studies, Juilliard Sch., 1985. Concert violinist Joanne Rile Artists Mgmt., Phila., 1983—; artist faculty The Harid Conservatory, Boca Raton, Fla., 1991—; prof. violin Wells Cathedral Sch., Bath, Eng., 1979-81, Pimlico Sch. Music, London, 1979-81, E. Kaufman Cultural Ctr., N.Y.C., 1985-86; vis. artist Fla. Internat. U., Miami, 1995-96. Soloist with Fla. Philharm., 1996, Atlas Camerata of Israel, N.Y.C., 1996, Jerusalem Symphony Orch., 1995, Slovak Philharm., N.Y.C., 1994, Dresden Philharm., Switzerland, 1993, London Soloists Chamber Orch., 1993, 92, Dresden Staatskapelle, Germany, 1992, European Cmty. Chamber Orch., 1992, Am. Youth Symphony, 1992, Mecklenburg Symphony, 1991, Orch. of St. Luke's, N.Y.C., 1991, Bern Symphony, Switzerland, 1990, Polish Nat. Radio and TV Orch., Cracow, 1990, London Symphony Orch., 1989, Grant Park Festival Orch., Chgo., 1988; in recital at Newport Music Festival, R.I., 1996, UCLA Ctr. for Performing Arts, 1995, Interlochen (Mich.) Arts Festival, 1993, Tisch Ctr. for Arts at 92 St. Y, N.Y.C., 1993, Weill Recital Hall at Carnegie Hall, N.Y.C., 1993, 91, L'Ermitage, L.A., 1992, Kuhmo (Finland) Music Festival, 1991, Wigmore Hall, London, 1990, 80, Meany Theatre, Seattle, 1990, Pasadena Auditorium, L.A., 1988, Merkin Hall, N.Y.C., 1986, 85, Kennedy Ctr., Washington, 1985, 83, Music at La Gesse Festival, Toulouse, France, 1983, Acad. of Santa Cecilia, Rome, 1983, Carnegie Recital Hall, N.Y.C., 1982, Mus. Fine Arts, Montreal, Can., 1981; recordings Vox Unique, Arcobaleno, Discover/Koch Internat. Recipient Solo Recitalist award Nat. Endowment for Arts, 1985, Artists Internat. Competition, 1982, Vina del Mar Internat. Violin Competition, 1981, Emily Anderson Internat. Violin Competition, 1979, Tibor Varga Internat. Violin Competition, 1978, award Am.-Israel Cultural Found., 1975. Home: 210 W 70th St #1108 New York NY 10023 Office: The Harid Conservatory 2285 Potomac Rd Boca Raton FL 33431-5518

SCHWARTZ, STEPHEN BLAIR, retired information industry executive; b. Chgo., Oct. 19, 1934; s. Herbert S. and Gertrude (Weinstein) S.; m. Nancy Jean Astrof, Dec. 18, 1955; children: Debra Lee Schwartz Zaret, Susan Beth Schwartz Derene. B.S. in Indsl. Engring., Northwestern U., 1957. With IBM Corp., 1957-92; various mgmt. positions, dir. product programs Harrison, N.Y., to 1977, v.p. Systems Communications div., 1977-81; v.p. Armonk, N.Y., 1982-90; v.p. Am. Far East Corp. subs. IBM Corp. Tokyo, 1982-84; pres., CEO Satellite Bus. Systems, McLean, Va., 1984; v.p., asst. group exec. Telecommunications, 1985-86, v.p., pres. Systems Products Div., 1986-88, v.p., gen. mgr. Application Bus. Systems, 1988-90; sr. v.p. market driven quality Stamford, Conn., 1990-92; bd. dirs. Niagara Mohawk Power Corp., MFRI, Inc. Mem. PGA Nat. Golf Club (Palm Beach Gardens, Fla.). Republican. Jewish.

SCHWARTZBERG, ROGER KERRY, osteopath, internist; b. Bklyn., Mar. 30, 1948; s. Erwin and Edna (Kuchlik) S.; m. Linda Lurie, July 1, 1972 (div. Nov. 1974); m. Vicki Ann Davis, Nov. 28, 1976; children: Jeremy Dylan, Joshua Ryan. BA in Psychology, Syracuse U., 1970; DO, Mich. State U., 1973. Diplomate Am. Acad. Osteopathic Internists. Intern, sr. asst. surgeon USPHS Hosp., S.I., N.Y., 1973-74; med. resident Southeastern Med. Ctr., North Miami Beach, Fla., 1974-77, chief resident, 1975-77; pvt. practice Seminole, Fla., 1977—; active staff Univ. Gen. Hosp., Seminole 1978—, chmn. dept. internal medicine, 1981-82, governing bd. 1981-86, 88—, vice chmn. 1986, 88—, Pinellas Community Hosp., Pinellas Park, Fla., 1980—, chief of staff, 1985-86, Seminole Hosp. and Women's Ctr., Seminole, 1989—; adj. clin. faculty U. New Eng. Coll. Osteo. Medicine, Biddeford, Maine, 1985—; clin. asst. prof. internal medicine, 1987—, Nova Southeastern Univ. Coll. of Osteopathic Medicine, 1987—; clin. asst. prof. internal medicine Kirksville (Mo.) Coll. Osteo. Medicine, 1989—; mem. active staff Suncoast Osteo. Hosp., Largo, Fla., 1982—, Largo Med. Ctr. Hosp., 1990—, St. Petersburg Gen. Hosp., 1991—; clin. assoc. prof. coll. osteo. medicine U. Health Scis., 1992—. Named Educator of Yr. Met. Gen. Hosp., Pinellas Park, Fla., 1985. Fellow Am. Acad. Osteo. Internists (certification bd. 1990); mem. Am. Osteo. Assn., Am. Assn. Physician Specialties, Am. Coll. Osteo. Internists, Fla. Osteo. Med. Assn. (trustee 1985-89), Pinellas County Osteo. Med. Soc. (trustee 1985-89, gov. 1989-90, v.p. 1991—). Jewish. Office: Oakhurst Med Clinic 13020 Park Blvd Seminole FL 33776-3639

SCHWARZ, FERDINAND (FRED SCHWARZ), ophthalmologist, ophthalmic plastic surgeon; b. Trenton, N.J., Dec. 13, 1939; s. Ferdinand and Laura Francis Schwarz; m. Carol Ann Snyder, Feb. 26, 1966; children: Lesley Ann, Jeffrey Ryan, Jason Bradley, Allyson Larner. BSEE, Lafayette Coll., 1961; MD, N.J. Coll. Medicine and Dentistry, 1970; MBA, Winthrop Coll., 1991. Diplomate Nat. Bd. Med. Examiners. Project engr. Astro div. RCA, Princeton, N.J., 1961-66; intern Robert Packer Hosp., Sayre, Pa., 1970-71; resident Guthrie Clinic Ophthalmology/Robert Packer Hosp., Sayre, Pa., 1971-74; Heed fellowship in ophthalmic plastic and reconstructive surgery U. Pa. Med. Sch./Temple Med. Sch./Hahnemann Med. Sch., Phila., 1974-75; pvt. practice Columbia, S.C., 1975—; vice chief med. staff Providence Hosp., Columbia, 1984, chief med. staff, 1985; cons. Dorn VA Hosp., Columbia, 1975—, Moncrief Hosp., Columbia, 1975-89. Contbr. numerous articles to sci. engring. and med. publs., 1962—. Heed (Found.) Ophthalmic fellow, Chgo., 1975. Mem. AMA, S.C. Med. Soc., S.C. Ophthalmology Soc., Cen. S.C. Ophthalmology Soc. (pres. 1983), Soc. Heed Fellows, Palmetto Club, Spring Valley Country Club. Roman Catholic. Home: PO Box 23038 Columbia SC 29224-3038 Office: Drs Schwarz and Milne PA 1655 Brabham Ave Ste 100 Columbia SC 29204-2039

SCHWARZ, PAUL WINSTON, judge, lawyer, business company executive; b. Sacramento, Sept. 24, 1948; s. Egon Ferdinand and Louise (Fulcher) S.; m. Virginia Adams, July 12, 1987; children: Austin Winston, Julie Adams. BA in Philosophy, Calif. State U., San Jose, 1971; JD, Santa Clara U., 1974. Bar: Pa. 1975, U.S. Supreme Ct. 1978, D.C. Ct. Appeals 1987, Va. 1992. Commd. 2d. lt. U.S. Army, 1971, advanced through grades to lt. col., 1992; corp. counsel Oracle Corp., Bethesda, Md., 1992-93; sec., v.p. and corp. counsel Oracle Complex Systems Corp., Arlington, Va., 1992-93; counsel McAleese & Associates, P.C., Washington, DC, 1993-94; apptd. U.S. adminstrv. law judge, 1994. Author: A Roadmap into the World of Federal Contracts, 1989. Decorated Legion of Merit, U.S. Army Gen. Staff Badge award. Mem. ABA (chmn. com. on pub. contract law gen. practice sect. 1991, vice-chmn. judiciary com. 1995), Army and Navy Country Club, Army and Navy Club Washington D.C., Nat. Soc. SAR. Episcopalian. Home: 5336 Sugar Hill Dr Houston TX 77056-2028

SCHWEI, MICHAEL A., assistant principal; b. Milw., July 10, 1956; s. Allen Jacob and Darlene Ann Schwei. BS in Edn., U. Wis., Milw., 1978; MEd, Stephen F. Austin State U., 1995. Cert. tchr., Tex.; cert. in mid-mgmt. With Marino Constrn. Co., Milw., 1978-80; tchr. English Houston Ind. Sch. Dist., 1980-81; tchr. math, computer literacy, journalism Humble (Tex.) Ind. Sch. Dist., 1981-96; mid. sch. asst. prin. Pflugerville (Tex.) Ind. Sch. Dist., 1996—. Named T.P. and Jenny Lou White Outstanding Adminstrn. Edn. Student, Stephen F. Austin State U. Alumni Assn., 1995-96. Mem. ASCD, Assn. of Tex. Profl. Educators, Phi Delta Kappa. Home: 3101 Wells Branch Pkwy #222 Austin TX 78728 Office: Westview Middle School 1805 Scofield Ln Austin TX 78727

SCHWEIBINZ, CARL JOSEPH, learning resources manager; b. Pitts., Oct. 31, 1950; s. Wilbert Roy and Dorothy Joan S.; m. Raquel Otero, Dec. 26, 1970; children: Elizabeth, Raquel. AS, DeKalb C.C., 1979; BS, U. Md., 1990. Enlisted U.S. Army, advanced through grades to staff sgt.; storage equipment specialist U.S. Army, Frankfurt, Germany, 1968-69; photo lab. tech. U.S. Army, Ft. Bragg, N.C., 1970-72, Nurnburg, Germany, 1972-73; photo lab. supr. U.S. Army, Ansbauch, Germany, 1973-75, Ft. Ord, Calif., 1975-76; photographer supr. U.S. Army, Seoul, 1976-77; tng. material writer U.S. Army, Ft. Gordon, Ga., 1977-80; ops. supr., instr. U.S. Army, Lowry AFB, Colo., 1980-84; audiovisual supr. U.S. Army, Augsburg, Germany, 1984-87; sr. aduiovisual tech. U. South Fla., Tampa, 1988-90; ret. U.S. Army, 1987; campus audiovisual tech. to learning resources mgr. Hillsborough C.C., Tampa, 1995—. Mem. Internat. TV Assn. (v.p. 1995-96). Office: Hillsborough Comm Coll PO Box 5096 Tampa FL 33675

SCHWEITZER, GEORGE KEENE, chemistry educator; b. Poplar Bluff, Mo., Dec. 5, 1924; s. Francis John and Ruth Elizabeth (Keene) S.; m. Verna Lee Pratt, June 4, 1948; children: Ruth Anne, Deborah Keene, Eric George. BA, Central Coll., 1945, ScD in Philosophy, 1964; MS, U. Ill., 1946, PhD in Chemistry, 1948; MA, Columbia U., 1959; PhD in History, NYU, 1964. Asst. Central Coll., 1943-45; fellow U. Ill., 1946-48; asst. prof. chemistry U. Tenn., 1948-52, assoc. prof., 1952-58, prof., 1960-69, Alumni Distinguished prof., 1970—; cons. to Monsanto Co., Proctor & Gamble, Internat. Tech., Am. Cyanamid Co., AEC, U.S. Army, Massengill; lectr. colls. and univs. Adv. bd. Va. Intermont Coll. Author: Radioactive Tracer Techniques, 1950, The Doctorate, 1966, Genealogical Source Handbook, 1979, Civil War Genealogy, 1980, Tennessee Genealogical Research, 1981, Kentucky Genealogical Research, 1981, Revolutionary War Genealogy, 1982, Virginia Genealogical Research, 1982, War of 1812 Genealogy, 1983, North Carolina Genealogical Research, 1983, South Carolina Genealogical Research, 1984, Pennsylvania Genealogical Research, 1985, Georgia Genealogical Research, 1987, New York Genealogical Research, 1988, Massachusetts Genealogical Research, 1989, Maryland Genealogical Research, 1991, German Genealogical Research, 1992, Ohio Genealogical Research, 1994, Indiana Genealogical Research, 1996; also 155 articles. Faculty fellow Columbia U., 1958-60. Mem. Am. Chem. Soc., Am. Philos. Assn., History Sci. Soc., Soc. Genealogists, Phi Beta Kappa, Sigma Xi. Home: 407 Ascot Ct Knoxville TN 37923-5807

SCHWEITZER, THEODORE GOTTLIEB, III, United Nations administrator; b. Hannibal, Mo., Aug. 28, 1942; s. Theodore Gottlieb Jr. and Dorothy Lois (Burnett) S. Cert. in French Lang., U. Paris, 1968; BA, U. Iowa, 1970, MA, 1974. Cert. Thai Lang. Am. Univ. Alumnae Assn., Bangkok, 1976, profl. tchr., Iowa. Tchr., librarian Lewis County Schs., Ewing, Mo., 1971-73; head librarian Internat. Sch., Bangkok, 1974-76; info. officer U.S. Army, Udorn, Thailand, 1974-76; dir. media services Am. Sch., Teheran, 1976-77; dir. media svcs. Am. Sch., Isfahan, Iran, 1977-78; refugee officer UN HCR, Geneva and Bangkok, 1979—; founder S.E. Asia Rescue Found., Ft. Walton Beach, Fla., 1981—, Hanoi Fgn. Langs. U., 1992-94. Author: Ted Schweitzer Story, 1985, (with Malcolm McConnell) Inside Hanoi's Secret Archives-Solving the MIA Mystery, 1995. Spl. rep. to Vietnam, Office of the Sec. of Def., Washington, 1992-94. With USAF, 1959-62. Recipient Award of merit SOS Boat people Com., San Diego, 1982, replica of Nobel Peace Prize, UN High Commr. for Refugees, 1981. Mem. Mensa. Republican. Baptist. Home: 762 Sailfish Dr Fort Walton Beach FL 32548-6041 Office: UN High Commr for Refuges, Palais Des Nations, Geneva Switzerland

SCHWENDINGER, CHARLES JOSEPH, public administration educator, researcher; b. Dubuque, Iowa, July 2, 1931; s. Leo James and Loretta Lucille (Meyers) S.; m. Marion Jean Blain, June 11, 1957 (div. 1981); 1 child, Julieanne Schwendinger Wattles; m. Chieko Ikeda, Oct. 13, 1982. BA in History, Va. Mil. Inst., 1957; MPA, U. Okla., 1980, D Pub. Adminstrn., 1991. Commd. 2d lt. U.S. Army, 1957, advanced through grades to lt. col., 1971, served in various locations including Vietnam, 1957-78, ret., 1978; asst. prof. pub. adminstrn. Troy (Ala.) State U., 1986-88, asst. prof., 1989, 91—; lectr. in field. Contbr. to profl. publs. Sgt. U.S. Army, 1949-53. Decorated Bronze Star medal with 2 oak leaf clusters, Air medal. Fellow Pi Alpha Alpha (chpt. pres. 1980-86, 89-90), Pi Sigma Alpha; mem. DAV, VFW, NRA, Am. Soc. Pub. Adminstrn. (coun. mem. Okla. chpt. 1989-90), Internat. City Mgmt. Assn., Am. Legion, Ret. Officers Assn. Roman Catholic. Home: PO Box 6378 Tampa FL 33608-0378 Office: Troy State U Fla Region PO Box 6472 Macdill AFB FL 33608

SCHWERIN, ALAN KENNETH, philosophy educator; b. Johannesburg, South Africa, Mar. 16, 1953; came to U.S., 1985; s. Kenneth Charles and Loretta May (Colyn) S.; m. Helen Griffiths, Jan. 29, 1977; children: Brett, Mia. BComm, U. Witwatersrand, Johannesburg, 1974; BA with honors, Rhodes U., Grahamstown, South Africa, 1977, MA, 1979; PhD, Rice U., 1988. Sr. lectr., philosophy dept. head U. Transkei, South Africa, 1980-85; asst. prof. philosophy McNeese State U., La., 1988-95, Monmouth U., Long Branch, N.J., 1996—. Author: The reluctant Revolutionary, 1989; editor: The Expanding Universe, 1993; contbr. articles to profl. jours. Recipient South Africa Nat. Photographic prizes, 1979; Rice U. fellow, 1986-88; Shearman Rsch. grantee; Human Scis. Rsch. Coun. scholar, 1977, 78. Mem. Am. Philos. Assn., Leibniz Soc., Hume Soc., Acad. Model Aeronautics, So. Soc. for Philosophers and Psychologists. Home: 439 Washington St Lake Charles LA 70605

SCHWETMAN, JOHN WILLIAM, English language professional educator; b. Boston, Jan. 27, 1942; s. Herbert DeWitt and Mary Jean (Knight) S.; m. Jenny Lynn Noe, Apr. 15, 1962; children: Sondra Paige, Melinda Sue. BA in English, Baylor U., 1963, MA in English, 1965; PhD in English, U. Kans., Lawrence, 1974. Asst. instr. Baylor U., Waco, Tex., 1963-65; instr. Cen. Mo. State Coll., Warrensburg, 1965-68; asst. instr. English Kans. U., 1969-72; asst. prof. and prof. Sam Houston State U., Huntsville, Tex., 1972—. Author: Advanced Composition, 1976; contbr. articles to profl. jours. Mem. MLA, Huntsville (Tex.) Audubon Soc. (pres. 1978-79), Medieval Acad. Am., Internat. Soc. of Anglo-Saxonists, S. E. Medieval Assn. (bd. dirs. 1987-90, pres. 1995-97). Democrat. Home: 2404 Avenue S Huntsville TX 77340-5519 Office: Sam Houston State U Huntsville TX 77341

SCHWITTERS, ROY FREDERICK, physicist, educator; b. Seattle, Wash., June 20, 1944; s. Walter Frederick and Margaret Lois (Boyer) S.; m. Karen Elizabeth Chrystal, June 18, 1965; children: Marc Frederick, Anne Elizabeth, Adam Thomas. S.B., MIT, 1966, Ph.D., 1971. Research asso. Stanford U. Linear Accelerator Center, 1971-74, asst. prof., then asso. prof., 1974-79; prof. physics Harvard U., 1979-90; scientist Fermi Nat. Accelerator Lab., Batavia, Ill., 1980-88; dir. superconducting supercollider Fermi Nat. Accelerator Lab., 1989-93; prof. physics U. Tex., Austin, 1994—. Author papers on high energy physics; asso. editor: Ann. Rev. Nuclear and Particle Sci; div. asso. editor: Phys. Rev. Letters. Recipient Alan T. Waterman award NSF, 1980. W.K.H. Panofsky Prize, Am Physical Soc., 1996. Fellow AAAS, Am. Phys. Soc. (W. K. H. Panofsky Prize, 1996), Am. Acad. Arts and Scis. Home: 1718 Cromwell Hill Austin TX 78703 Office: U Tex Dept Physics Austin TX 78712-1081

SCIOLARO, CHARLES MICHAEL, cardiac surgeon; b. Kansas City, Kans., July 5, 1958; s. Gerald Michael and Charleen Gwen (Walter) S.; m. Vicki Lynn Mizell, Sept. 29, 1984; children: Rachel Diane, Lynsey Michelle, Ryan Michael, Jonathan Charles. BA in Biology and Chemistry magna cum laude, Mid Am. Nazarene Coll., 1980; MD magna cum laude, U. Kans., Kansas City, 1984. Diplomate Am. Bds. Gen. Surgery, Thoracic and Cardiac; lic. Ariz., Calif., La., Fla., Kans.; cert. advanced cardiac life support, advanced cardiac life support instr., advanced trauma life support, Calif. x-ray supr. and operator, transesophageal echocardiography. Intern gen. surgery Tucson hosps. surg. program U. Ariz., 1984-85, resident gen. surgery, 1985-86, 87-89, chief resident gen. surgery, 1989-90; biochemistry rsch. fellow U. Kans., Kansas City, 1978-79; instr. surgery Loma Linda U. Med. Ctr., Tucson, 1991-92; staff physician St. Francis Cabrini Hosp., Alexandria, La., 1993-96, Rapides Regional Med. Ctr., Alexandria, 1993-96; instr. surgery Loma Linda (Calif.) U. Med. Ctr., 1991-93; physician divsn. cardiac, thoracic and vascular surgery MacArthur Surg. Clinic, Alexandria, 1993-96, Kunla Multispecialty Clinic, Kansas City, 1996—; staff physician Providence Med. Ctr., Kansas City, 1996—; emergency rm. physician, cons. Nat. Emergency Corp., Tucson, 1986—; part-time emergency care attendent Veteran's Med. Ctr., Tucson, 1985-89, Cigna Urgent Care, 1985-89; with div. cardiac, thoracic and vascular surgery MacArthur Surg. Clin., Alexandria, 1993-96. Author: (manuscripts) Aortic Coarctation in Infants, 1991; researcher, lectr. and presenter in field. Mem. ACS, Am. Coll. Cardiologists, Am. Coll. Chest Physicians, La. Med. Soc., Rapides Med. Soc., Southeastern Surg. Congress, Soc. Thoracic Surgery, Internat. Soc. Intraoperative Cardiovascular Ultrasound, Internat. Coll. Surgons, Internat. Platform Assn., Phi Delta Lambda. Republican. Home: 12839 Century St Shawnee Mission KS 66213 Office: Kanza Ste 300 21 N 12th St Kansas City KS 66102

SCIULLA, MICHAEL GARRI, foundation administrator; b. Bklyn., Dec. 31, 1950; s. Frank and Dolores (Delind) S.; m. Carol Goff, Sept. 4, 1988; 1 child, Logan Michael. BA, Eisenhower Coll., 1973; postgrad., Carleton U., 1973-75. Registered lobbyist U.S. Congress. Reporter Geneva (N.Y.) Times, 1975; legis. asst. U.S. Ho. Reps., Washington, 1975-76, 77-78; reporter V.I. Post, St. Thomas, 1979; v.p., dir. BOAT/U.S., Alexandria, Va., 1980—; bd. dirs. Recreational Boaters Calif., Sacramento. Contbr. articles to profl. jours. Mem. Am. League Anglers and Boaters (bd. dirs., former pres.), Boating Writers Internat., Sport Fishing and Boating Partnership Coun. Office: BOAT/US 880 S Pickett St Alexandria VA 22304

SCIVALLY, BART MURNANE, accountant, auditor; b. Oklahoma City, Mar. 13, 1944; s. Louis Frensley and Mary Helen (Boadway) S.; divorced; children: Amy D., Robyn M., Louis Francis. BS in Bus. Adminstrn., U. Ark., 1969. CPA, Ark. Auditor Div. of Legis. Audit, Little Rock, 1968-73, audit supr., 1974—. Mem. Am. Inst. CPA's, Assn. Govt. Accts. (cert. Govt. Fin. Mgr. 1995). Roman Catholic. Office: Div of Legis Audit 172 State Capitol Little Rock AR 72201-1033

SCOFIELD, LOUIS M., JR., lawyer; b. Brownsville, Tex., Jan. 14, 1952; s. Louis M. and Betsy Lee (Aiken) S.; children: Christopher, Nicholas. BS in Geology with highest honors, U. Mich., 1974; JD with honors, U. Tex., 1977. Bar: Tex. 1977, U.S. Dist. Ct. (ea. and so. dists.) Tex., U.S. Ct. Appeals (5th cir.) 1981, U.S. Supreme Ct. 1984. spkr. Jefferson County Ins. Adjusters, S.E. Tex. Ind. Ins. Agts., Gulf Ins. Co., Dallas, Employers Casualty Co., Beaumont, Tex. Employment Commn., Jefferson County Young Lawyers Assn., Jefferson County Bar Assn., South Tex. Coll. of Law, John Gray Inst., Lamar U., 1991, Tex. Assn. Def. Counsel, 1991; cert. arbitrator Nat. Panel of Consumer Arbitrators; arbitrator BBB; presenter Forest Park H.S., Martin Elem. Sch., St. Anne's Sch. Contbr. articles to profl. jours.; columnist Jefferson County Bar Jour. Patron Beaumont Heritage Soc., John J. French Mus.; bd. dirs. Beaumont Heritage Soc., 1983-84, mem. endowment fund com., 1988; chmn. lawyers divsn. United Appeals Campaign, 1984; grand patron Jr. League of Beaumont, 1989, 90. Fellow Tex. Bar Found., State Bar of Tex. (mentors com. 1995); mem. ABA, Tex. Assn. Def. Counsel (dir. at large 1986-87, v.p. 1987-89, adminstrv. v.p. 1989-90, program chmn. San Diego 1989), Assn. Def. Trial Attys., Def. Rsch. Inst., Am. Judicature Soc., Jefferson County Bar Assn. (disaster relief project 1979, outstanding young lawyer's com. 1980), Beaumont Country Club, Tower

Club of Beaumont, Phi Beta Kappa. Democrat. Episcopalian. Home: 4790 Littlefield St Beaumont TX 77706 Office: Mehaffy & Weber PO Box 16 Beaumont TX 77704

SCOGIN, TROY POPE, publishing company executive, accounts executive; b. Manchester, Ala., Oct. 31, 1932; s. James David and Thelma Katie (Helton) S.; m. Katie Elizabeth Bates, May 26, 1956; children: Norma Kay, Joyce Marie. BA, Howard Coll., 1955; MDiv, So. Baptist Theol. Seminary, Louisville, 1959; MA, Samford U., 1972. Ordained to ministry Baptist Ch., 1956. Pastor West Port (Ky.) Baptist Ch., 1956-58, Providence Baptist Ch., Bellevue, Ohio, 1958-61; chaplain/capt. USAF, Lincoln, Nebr., 1961-64; pastor Sycamore (Ala.) Baptist Ch., 1964-65; sales rep. Houghton Mifflin Co., Boston, 1965-74, regional mgr., 1974-89, spl. asst. to exec. v.p. coll. div., 1989-90, v.p., 1984—, nat. accounts exec., 1990-92; interim pastor Ross Ave. Bapt. Ch. Intercity Mission, Dallas, 1993—; adv. bd. dirs. Ross Ave. Ctr.; faculty Eastfield Coll., 1992—. Chmn. bd. deacons Ross Avenue Bapt. Ch., Dallas, 1991; mem. adv. bd. Ross Avenue Ctr. Mem. Am. Mgmt. Assn., Am. Soc. Tng. Devel., Nat. Coun. Tchrs. English, Tex. Jr. Coll. Tchrs. Assn., Phi Kappa Phi, Omicron Delta Kappa (nat. leadership fraternity pres. 1954), Alpha Phi Omega (nat. svc. fraternity pres. 1952). Democrat. Home: 15742 Havenrock Cir Dallas TX 75248-4219

SCOLLARD, DAVID MICHAEL, pathologist; b. Dickinson, N.D., July 26, 1947; s. Denzil and Audrey Scollard; m. Fredrikke Skinsnes, June 24, 1971; children: Winston, Darikka. BA, St. Olaf Coll., 1969; BS in Medicine, U. N.D., 1971; MD, PhD, U. Chgo., 1975. Cert. Am. Bd. Pathology. Intern U. Hawaii, Honolulu, 1975-76; lectr. in pathology U. Hong Kong, 1976-81; asst. prof. pathology U. Ill., Chgo., 1981-84; assoc. prof. pathology U. Hawaii, Honolulu, 1984-92; chief rsch. pathology GWL Hansen's Disease Ctr., Baton Rouge, 1993—; assoc. prof. pathology LSU Sch. of Medicine, New Orleans, 1993—; vis. asst. prof. U. Chgo., Ill., 1980; field dir. Chiang Mai/Ill. Leprosy Rsch. Project, U. Ill. and Chiang Mai (Thailand) Univ., 1981-84. Contbr. articles to profl. jours. Named Fulbright scholar Prince Leopold Inst. for Tropical Medicine, Antwerp, Belgium, 1990. Mem. Internat. Acad. Pathology, Am. Assn. Microbiology, Am. Assn. Immunology, Internat. Leprosy Assn., Am. Soc. Investigative Pathology. Office: GWL Nat Hansens Disease Ctr at La State U PO Box 25072 Baton Rouge LA 70894-5072

SCOTT, ANN MARTIN, English language educator; b. Knoxville, Tenn., Mar. 24, 1943; s. William Martin and Clara Oleeta (Sallee) Breeding; divorced. B.A., Peabody Coll., 1964; M.A., Fla. State U., 1969, M.L.S., 1972, Ph.D., 1975. Cert. tchr., Tenn., Fla., La. Tchr., Kissimmee Jr. High Sch., Fla., 1967-68; instr. S. Fla. Jr. Coll., Avon Park, 1969-70; chmn. English dept. Lake Placid Jr. High Sch., Fla., 1970-71; asst. prof. Ind. State U., Evansville, 1975-76; assoc. prof. English U. Southwestern La., Lafayette, 1976—, dir. tech. comm. program; cons. Fla. State Dept. Edn., Tallahassee, 1974-75; writer Am. Coll. Testing Program, 1976-86. Editor: Collaborative Technical Writing: Theory and Practice, 1989, Cajun Vernacular English, 1992; contbr. articles to profl. jours. Active Computer Profls. Social Responsibility, Habitat Humanities, Greenpeace, Nature Conservancy, Save the Children. Recipient Experienced Tchr. award HEW, 1968. Mem. Assn. Tchrs. Tech. Writing (mem. coun. programs tech. and sci. comm.), Linguistic Soc. Am., La. Assn. Coll. Composition, La. Coun. Tchrs. English, Assn. Tchrs. Tech. Writing. Avocations: photography, flute, stained glass, stone masonry, camping. Home: PO Box 186 Cecilia LA 70521-0186 Office: U Southwestern La Dept English Griffin Hall Lafayette LA 70504

SCOTT, CAROL LEE, child care educator; b. Monte Vista, Colo., Jan. 10, 1944; d. Robert A. and Thelma G. (Allen) Jay; m. Bates E. Shaw, June 4, 1966 (dec. Feb. 1976); children: Crystal A., Sharon L.; m. James W. Scott, July 23, 1977. BA in Home Econs., Friends U., 1965; MS, Okla. State U., 1973. Cert. in family and consumer scis., child and parenting specialist; lic. profl. counselor. Receptionist Cen. Assembly of God Ch., Wichita, Kans., summer 1965; office worker Henry's Inc., Wichita, 1965-66; tchr. home econs. Wichita High Sch. South, 1966, Cir. High Sch., Towanda, Kans., 1966-68, Fairfax (Okla.) High Sch., 1968-74; tchr. vocat. home econs. Derby (Kans.) High Sch., 1974-75; child devel. specialist Bi-State Mental Health Found., Ponca City, Okla., 1975-87; instr. child care Pioneer Tech. Ctr., Ponca City, 1987—, dir., 1987-89, 93—; cons. Phil Fitzgerald Assocs. Archs., Ponca City, 1980, Head Start Okla., 1981-86; trainer, paraprofl. Child Care Careers, 1980—; validator Nat. Assn. Edn. Young Children 1992—. Contbg. author Child Abuse Prevention Mini Curriculum. Mem. sch. bd. Ponca City Schs., 1982-85, title IV-A parent com., 1985-89; area chmn. Heart Fund, 1985; chmn. edn. com. Dist. XVII Child Abuse Prevention Task Force, Okla., 1985—, treas., 1989—; mem. cultural affairs com. Ponca City Adv. Bd., 1986-89; co-chair Week of the Young Child Com. for Kay County, 1991—. Mem. NEA, Am. Vocat. Assn., Am. Assn. Family and Consumer Scis., Okla. Vocat. Assn., Okla. Assn. Vocat. Home Econs. Tchrs., Okla. Edn. Assn., Okla. Assn. for Edn. Young Children, Okla. Early Childhood Assn., So. Early Childhood Assn., No. Okla. Early Childhood Assn. (chmn. 1992-93, past chmn. 1993-94, exec. coun. at-large 1994-97), Nat. Assn. Vocat. Home Econs. Tchrs., Nat. Assn. for Edn. Young Children (validator for early childhood programs seeking accreditation by divsn. Nat. Acad. Early Childhood Programs 1992—), Friends of Day Care. Republican. Methodist. Home: 414 Virginia Ave Ponca City OK 74601-3436

SCOTT, DAVID G., geneticist; b. Norman, Okla., July 1, 1951; s. Gene J. and Shirley Colleen (Whittle) S.; m. Jutta K. Witte, Sept. 27, 1975. BS, U. Okla., 1979, MS, 1982; PhD, Ind. U., 1987. Rsch. assoc. Mont. State U., Bozeman, 1987-88; from asst. prof. to assoc. prof. S.C. State U., Orangeburg, 1988—. Served in U.S. Army, 1972-75, Germany. NSF grantee, 1989, Pub. Insts. Health grantee, 1990. Mem. Genetics Soc. Am., Animal Behavior Soc., Behavior Genetics Soc. Office: SC State U Biology Dept 300 College Ave Orangeburg SC 29117

SCOTT, DOROTHY MARIE, retired education educator, civic worker; b. Mineral Wells, Tex., Jan. 31, 1921; d. Theophilus J. and Vesta Rebecca (Howson) S. BA, Tex. Woman's U., 1942, MA, 1946; EdD, U. North Tex., 1965. Cert. tchr., supr., adminstr., Tex. High sch. tchr Brownsville (Tex.) High Sch., 1942-45, Corsicana (Tex.) Ind. Sch. Dist., 1945-46; high sch. tchr Tyler (Tex.) Ind. Sch. Dist., 1946-63, dir. secondary instrn., 1963-79; instr. Sch. Edn. and Psychology, U. Tex., Tyler, 1979-83; ret., 1983; instr. jr. colls., Brownsville, 1942-45, Tyler, 1946-48; bd. dirs. Smith County Tchrs. Credit Union, Tyler, 1953-63; mem. exec. bd. East Tex. Study Coun., Commerce, 1966-68; bd. dirs. East Tex. Rsch. and Devel. Ctr., Nacogdoches, 1989—. Contbr. articles to ednl. publs. Vol. Mental Health Assn. Tyler, 1983-85; chmn. bd. dirs. Neighborhood Crime Watch, Tyler, 1988-90; bd. dirs. East Tex. Coun. on World Affairs, 1988-92; mem. selection com. C. of C. Leadership Tyler, 1985; cmty. coord. Gt. Decisions 1989, Tyler. Named Educator of Month, Tex. Sch. Bus. mag., 1967, Woman of Yr., Tyler City Women's Commn., 1989, Woman of Yr. East Tex. Coun. on World Affairs, 1989. Mem. ASCD, Tex. Assn. (pres. 1969), AAUW (pres. Tyler br. 1985-86, bd. dirs. 1987—, Dorothy Scott scholarship named in her honor 1985), Tex. Assn. Univ. Women (bd. dirs. 1984-86), M M Investment Club (pres. 1988-90), Zonta (pres. Tyler 1976-78, Woman of Yr. 1985, 89), Phi Delta Kappa (pres. Rose City chpt. 1979-81), Delta Kappa Gamma (pres. Theta Nu chpt. 1957-58), Smith County Ret. Sch. Pers. (chair scholarship com. 1995-96). Democrat. Baptist. Home: 442 Towne Oaks Tyler TX 75701-9533

SCOTT, EUGENE BENSON, II, general practice and family medicine physician; b. Memphis, Jan. 3, 1950; s. Eugene Benson and Dorothy Elizabeth (King) S.; m. Marilyn Bedgood, June 11, 1971; children: Luke B., Ashley Elizabeth. BS with honors, Northeast La. U., 1972; MD, La. State U., New Orleans, 1975. Diplomate Am. Bd. Quality Assurance and Utilization Review Physicians. Resident in family practice La. State U. Med. Ctr., Shreveport, 1976; gen. practice and family medicine physician Green Clinic-Contempo Office, West Monroe, La., 1977—. Contbr. articles to profl. jours. Recipient grant La. Acad. Sci., 1972, La. Heart Assn., 1972-73, Am. Heart Assn., 1973-74; investigator Eli Lilly and Co., 1989-90. Fellow Am. Acad. Family Physicians; mem. La. State Med. Soc. (5th Dist. Bd. Councillors 1992-97; Bd. Govs. 1992-97, Bd. Dirs. Edn. and Rsch. Found.), Ouachita Parish Med. Soc. (sec.-treas. 1987-88, 91-92), La. Acad. Family Physicians. Home: 745 Forty Oaks Farm Rd West Monroe LA 71291

SCOTT, GARY LEROY, photographic manufacturing executive, photographer; b. Portland, Oreg., May 14, 1954; s. Glenn Howard and Esther Ruth (Robinson) S. Grad., USN Sch. Photography, Pensacola, Fla., 1974; BS, U. Oreg., 1979, MS, 1982. Freelance photographer and filmmaker Scott Cinema and Visual, Inc., various locations, 1969—; computer traffic operator Burlington No. R.R., Portland, 1979-81; instr. U. Oreg., Eugene, 1981-82; S.E. dist. sales mgr. E. Leitz, Inc., 1984-87; mgr. profl. products Fla. div. Fuji Photo Film USA, Inc., Lake Mary, Fla., 1987—; freelance media cons., advt. copywriter, TV and film script writer, 1984—; lectr. in field. Served with USN, 1972-76. U. Oreg. Sch. Journalism research grantee, 1981. Mem. Am. Soc. Mag. Photographers, Profl. Photographers of Am. Republican. Home and Office: PO Box 952619 Lake Mary FL 32795-2619

SCOTT, GEORGE COLE, III, stockbroker, investment advisor; b. N.Y.C., July 9, 1937; s. George Cole Scott II and Anne Blair Clark Martindell; m. Leslie Jane Daniels, Apr. 12, 1969; children: Jane Leslie, Anne Blair, John Cole. BA, U. Wash., 1969. Advt. reporter Am. Weekly, London, 1966-68; stockbroker Anderson & Strudwick, Richmond, Va., 1969-73, Scott & Stringfellow, Richmond, 1973-78, Piper, Jaffray & Hopwood, Seattle, 1978-82, Wheat, First Securities, Inc., Richmond, 1982-87; rep. Anderson & Strudwick, Richmond, 1988—; pres. Closed-End Fund Advisors, Santa Barbara, Calif., 1996— ; dir. Bergstrom Capital Corp., Seattle, 1976—. Co-author: Investing in Closed-End Funds: Finding Value and Building Wealth, 1991; pub., editor; The Scott Letter: Closed-End Fund Report, 1988-96; contbr. to Closed-End Country Fund Report, Barron's and other publs. Founder Seattle-Christchurch, New Zealand Sister City Com. Served with USCG, 1960-64. Contbr. articles to profl. jours. Recipient Disting. Citizen award State of Wash., 1981. Mem. Richmond Soc. Fin. Analysts (assoc.), Democrat. Episcopalian. Clubs: Soc. Cin.; Wash. Athletic (Seattle); Country Club Va. Avocations: freelance writing, travel. Home: 8659 Rio Grande Rd Richmond VA 23229-7822 Office: Anderson & Strudwick 1108 E Main St Richmond VA 23219-3539

SCOTT, GEORGE GALLMANN, accountant; b. Hattiesburg, Miss., July 8, 1928; s. John Havers and Rebecca Evelyn (Gallmann) S.; BS, Millsaps Coll., 1949; m. Patsy T. Womack, June 27, 1953; 1 child, George Gallmann. Accredited tax advisor, 1992. Clk., Spanish Trail Transport, Mobile, Ala., 1949-50, asst. auditor, 1953-55; bookkeeper Met. Engraving & Electrotype Co., Richmond, Va., 1952-53; chief clk. Central Truck Lines of Tampa, Fla., Mobile, 1955-56; gen. auditor M.R.&R. Trucking Co., Crestview, Fla., 1956-66, sec.-treas., 1967-77; pub. acct. enrolled to represent taxpayers before IRS, 1979—. Mem. data processing adv. com. Okaloosa-Walton Jr. Coll., Niceville, Fla., 1965-66, 72-73; mem. Okaloosa County Gen. Advisory Com. for Devel. Vocat. Edn., 1973, 79; bd. dirs. Okaloosa Community Concert Assn., 1982-87; chmn. Crestview Downtown Devel. Bd., 1988-89. With U.S. Army, 1950-52. Accredited in acctg. and taxation Nat. Accreditation Coun. for Accountancy. Mem. Am. Trucking Assn. (nat. acctg. and fin. coun. 1956-77), Southeastern Acctg. and Fin. Coun. (bd. dir. 1974-77), Crestview Downtown Mchts. Assn. (bd. dir. 1980-84, treas. 1980-84), Greater Crestview C. of C. (chmn. bus. ethics com. 1973-74, bd. dir. 1981-83, treas. 1982-83), Fla. Accts. Assn. (bd. govs. 1979-80, pres. N.W. Fla. chpt. 1979-80), Kiwanis, Pi Kappa Alpha. Methodist (choir dir. 1966-83, chmn. ofcl. bd. 1971-73, chmn. fin. com. 1974-75, 79-81, audit com. 1977-86, mem. com. on lay personnel 1979-87, chmn. 1983-87, 89-90, mem. com. on pastor-parish rels. 1980-86, coun. ministries 1985, trustee 1985-87, treas. 1990-95). Home: 244 Seminole Trl Crestview FL 32536-2326

SCOTT, IRENE FEAGIN, federal judge; b. Union Springs, Ala., Oct. 6, 1912; d. Arthur H. and Irene (Peach) Feagin; m. Thomas Jefferson Scott, Dec. 27, 1939 (dec.); children: Thomas Jefferson, Irene Scott Carroll. A.B., U. Ala., 1932, LL.B., 1936, LL.D., 1978; LL.M., Catholic U. Am., 1939. Bar: Ala. 1936. Law libr. U. Ala. Law Sch., 1932-34; atty. Office Chief Counsel IRS, 1937-50, mem. excess profits tax coun., 1950-52, spl. asst. to head appeals div., 1952-59, staff asst. to chief counsel, 1959-60; judge U.S. Tax Ct., 1960-82, sr. judge serving on recall, 1982—. Contbr. articles to Women Lawyers Jour. Bd. dirs. Mt. Olivet Found., Arlington. Mem. ABA (taxation sect.), Ala. Bar Assn., Fed. Bar Assn., D.C. Bar Assn. (hon.), Nat. Assn. Women Lawyers, Nat. Assn. Women Judges, Kappa Delta, Kappa Beta Pi. Office: US Tax Ct 400 2nd St NW Washington DC 20217-0001

SCOTT, JAMES MERLIN, insurance company executive; b. Calera, Okla., June 25, 1934; s. H.M. and Myrtle B. S.; m. Peggy Jo Scott, Sept. 24, 1955; children: Michael, Terri, Cynda, John. BS in Phys. Edn., West Tex. State U., 1955, MEd in Govt., 1958. Salesperson Vickers Pet. Co., Wichita, Kans., 1955-56; basketball, baseball coach Clovis (N.Mex.) Sr. High, 1956-57; asst. dean of men West Tex. State U., Canyon, 1957-58, freshman basketball coach, 1958-61; agt. Mass. Mut., Amarillo, Tex., 1958-64; dist. mgr. Jefferson Standard Life, Amarillo, 1964; agy. v.p. Nat. Old Line, Little Rock, 1964-82; sr. v.p., chief agy. officer Providential Life Ins. Co., Little Rock, 1983—. Mem. Ark. Assn. Health Underwriters (bd. dirs., past pres. 1989-90), Ark. Assn. Life Underwriters (pres. bd. dirs. 1993-94). Republican. Baptist. Office: Providential Life Ins Co 2120 Riverfront Dr Little Rock AR 72202-1747

SCOTT, JOAN, nurse educator, training program administrator; b. Milledgeville, Ga., Feb. 8, 1948; d. Eugene Scott Sr. and Carrie (Ingram) Charles; 1 child, Karla Letrice. BSN, Fla. A&M U., 1970; MSN, Med. Coll. Ga., 1979. Grad. nurse Tallahassee (Fla.) A&M Hosp., 1970-71; charge nurse intensive care unit Baldwin County Hosp., Milledgeville, 1971-72; charge nurse male med. unit Cen. State Hosp., Milledgeville, 1972-77, tng. specialist prin., 1977-80; clin. nurse emergency rm. Med. Ctr. of Cen. Ga., Macon, 1983-86; staff devel. and tng. coord. III Cen. State Hosp., Milledgeville, 1980-90; clin. instr. nursing Macon Coll., 1991—; adj. nursing instr. Ga. Coll., Milledgeville, 1977-80; chairperson admission com. nursing dept. Ga. Coll., Milledgeville, 1978-79, mem. nursing com., 1982-88. Mem. exec. bd. West End Elem. PTA, Milledgeville, 1977-84; leader Girls Scouts U.S., Milledgeville, 1978-90; youth choir leader Wesley Chapel AME Ch., Milledgeville, 1978-86; mem. nursing adv. com. Baldwin Vocat. Tech. Sch., Milledgeville, 1982-83, CETA Program of Practical Nursing Program Adv. Com., Milledgeville, 1982-83; mem. profl. ednl. program Baldwin County chpt. Am. Cancer Soc., 1983-84; chairperson sch. program subcom. Baldwin County chpt. Am. Heart Assn., 1984-85. Me.m Ga. Nurses Assn. (various coms. 14th dist. 1974-88, program rev. subcom. 1986-88), Am. Legion Aux., Delta Sigma Theta Alumnae. Democrat. Office: Cen State Hosp Staff Devel & Tng Dept Milledgeville GA 31062

SCOTT, JOHN FREDRIK, art history educator, consultant; b. Summit, N.J., May 14, 1936; s. Herbert E. and Carmen E. (Anderson) S.; m. Lynn G. Thomson, July 25, 1964; children: Erik A., Elizabeth Cameron. AB, Princeton U., 1958; MAT, Johns Hopkins U., 1962; PhD, Columbia U., 1971. Instr. Bennett Coll., Millbrook, N.Y., 1962-63; rsch. assoc. Met. Mus. Art, N.Y.C., 1968-71; asst. prof. art history Cornell U., Ithaca, N.Y., 1971-77, Rice U., Houston, 1977-81; assoc. prof. art history U. Fla., Gainesville, 1981—. Author catalogs, articles and monograph. Ford Found. fellow, 1966-68, NEH fellow, 1974-75, Joint U.S.-Spanish Commn. fellow, Madrid, 1988, Fulbright fellow, Bogota, 1996. Mem. Gainesville Soc./Archaeol. Inst. Am. (sec. 1991—, pres. 1985-87), Assn. Latin Am. Art History (pres. 1987-88), Coll. Art Assn. Methodist. Home: 3112 NW 57th Ter Gainesville FL 32606-6939 Office: U Fla Art Dept Gainesville FL 32611

SCOTT, JOHN ROLAND, lawyer, oil company executive; b. Wichita Falls, Tex., May 13, 1937; s. John and Margaret S.; m. Joan Carol Redding, Sept. 5, 1959; 1 child, John Howard. LLB, Baylor Sch. Law, Waco, Tex., 1962. Bar: Tex. 1962, Alaska 1970, U.S. Dist. Ct. (we. dist.) Tex. 1965, U.S. Dist. Ct. Alaska 1975. Assoc. litigation sect Lynch & Chappell, Midland, Tex., 1962-65; regional atty. Atlantic Richfield Co., Midland, 1965-79; sr. atty., Anchorage, 1969-77, sr. atty., Dallas, 1977-80; v.p., assoc. gen. counsel Mitchell Energy & Devel. Corp., Houston, 1980-82; asst. gen. counsel Hunt Oil Co., Dallas, 1982-84, v.p., chief counsel, 1984-91; v.p. gen. counsel, 1991—; bar examiner in Alaska, 1974-77. Mem. State Bar Tex. (lectr.), Dallas Bar Assn., ABA, Phi Alpha Delta. Republican. Clubs: Petroleum (Dallas). Office: Hunt Oil Co 1445 Ross Ave Dallas TX 75202-2812

SCOTT, JOHN TARRELL, art educator, sculptor; b. New Orleans, June 30, 1940; m. Anna Rita Smith, Jan. 22, 1966; children: Maria, Tyra, Lauren, Alanda, Ayo. BA, Xavier U. La., 1962; MFA, Mich. State U., 1965, HHD (hon.), 1995; HHD (hon.), Madonna Coll., 1988. Prof. fine arts Xavier Univ. La., New Orleans, 1965—. Exhibited at Gallerie Simonne Stern, New Orleans, 1983—, McIntosh Gallery, Atlanta, 1993—, Horwich Gallery, Santa Fe, 1995—; prin. works include Composition for a City Dance in 3 Movements, 1996, Stony Brook Dance, 1989, Five Rings for Philly Joe, 1993-94; executed mural with 3 dimensional elements River Spirit, 1996; designer Jazz and Heritage Festival, New Orleans, 1993, New Orleans Internat. Airport, 1990; panelist Audubon Inst., New Orleans, 1993, Tulane Sch. Architecture, New Orleans, 1990. Recipient Delgado Soc. award New Orleans Mus. Art, 1996, Links award The Links Inc., 1995. Office: 13020 Carrere Ct Ste B New Orleans LA 70129

SCOTT, KATHY LYNN, peri-operative nurse; b. Waukegan, Ill., Apr. 22, 1962; d. Howard E. and Roberta L. (Richman) S.; m. Robert K. Copeland, July 23, 1988 (div. 1990). ASN, Coll. of Lake County, Grayslake, Ill., 1984, AS in Mid. Mgmt., 1985; student, No. Ill. U., 1980-82. RN, Fla. Staff nurse oncology unit Humana Hosp. of Lucerne, Orlando, Fla., Winter Park (Fla.) Meml. Hosp.; staff devel. coord. Manor Care, Orlando; asst. dir. of nursing Regents Park Nursing Home, Winter Park; oper. rm. staff nurse Fla. Hosp., Orlando. Mem. Assn. Oper. Rm. Nurses, Phi Theta Kappa. Home: 2424 Tree Ridge Ln Orlando FL 32817-2725

SCOTT, KENNETH PLEASANT, JR., life insurance agent; b. Chatham, Va., July 16, 1946; s. Kenneth Pleasant Sr. and Hazel Garnett (Hodnett) S.; m. Jacquelyn Carol Doane; children: Kenneth Pleasant III, Hunter Carrington, Brantley Blair, George Holland. BA in History, Elon Coll., 1969. Foreman Reynolds Tobacco Co., 1969; sales rep. Ennis Bus. Forms, 1969-72; sales cons. Audio Fidelity Corp., 1972-75; dir. new products Hoffman Info. Systems, 1975-76; mgr. Richmond office, Sherwood Comml. Brokers, 1976-77; v.p., prin. Southern Bus. Brokers of Va., 1977-80; pres. K.P. Scott & Co., Inc., 1976-92; v.p., treas., chief fin. officer STW Ltd., DBA Comml. Cafe, 1979-90; pres., chief fin. officer 6th St. Co., DBA Comml. Cafe, 1985-91; agt. N.Y. Life Fin. Svcs., 1992—; pres. 6th St. Marketplace Assn., 1986-87, A Pleasant Group Inc., 1990-92; bd. dirs. Retail Mchts. Assn. Greater Richmond, 1986-92. Organizer, pres. World Invitational Rib Championship, 1986-92; trustee Hargrave Mil. Acad., 1986-92, vice chmn. bd. trustees, 1989-91, sec., 1988; pres. HMA Alumni Assn., 1986-87, bd. dirs., 1984-88; organizing mem. Cultural-Loop Trolley Com., 1986; pres. Tourism Task Force, 1988-89; mem. com. CIAA Tournament, 1987; originator, co-chmn. Richmond Biggest Heart award; treas. St. Stephens Kindergarten, 1985-86, bd. dirs., 1983-86; treas., bd. dirs. Richmond Strikers Soccer Club, 1990—; asst. chmn. Recreational League., 1990-91; v.p. bd., chmn. Boys Travel Program, 1993—. Recipient Disting. Alumnus Achievement award Hargrave Mil. Acad., 1989, Walter R. Davis Trustee of Yr. award, 1990. Episcopalian. Club: Commonwealth (Richmond, Va.). Lodge: Masons. Office: PO Box 8596 Richmond VA 23226-0596

SCOTT, KENNETH R., transportation executive; b. Iowa City. BCE, U. Iowa, 1960; MCE, U. Mo., Rolla, 1966. Commd. U.S. Army, 1961, advanced through grades, 1970; airport project engr. Norfolk (Va.) Airport Authority, 1970-72, asst. airport mgr., 1971-72, exec. dir., 1972—; adj. prof. Embry-Riddle Aero. U. at Norfolk Naval Air Sta. and Langley AFB. Bd. dirs. Norfolk Cmty. Promotion Corp., Va. Aviation and Space Edn. Forum. Mem. Am. Assn. Airport Execs., Va. Airport Operators Coun. Office: Norfolk Airport Authority Norfolk Intl Airport Norfolk VA 23518-5897

SCOTT, KERRIGAN DAVIS, private investor, philanthropist; b. Magdalene, Fla., Sept. 26, 1941; s. Thurman Thomas and Jacqueline (Glenister) S.; children: Katherine, Stephanie, Jennifer. N.D. U. Va., 1964. Pvt. investor, Hilton Head Island, S.C., 1965—. Aide-de-camp to gov. of Tenn. with rank of col. Recipient Presdl. Legion Merit, Shield of Valor medal, White House Letter Commendation. Author: Aristocracy and Royalty of the World, 1983, Hereditary Baron in the Nobility of France. Mem. bd. regents Liberty U., Lynchburg, Va.; bd. dirs. Aid to Hospitalized Vets.; assoc. Library of Congress; pres. The Cittanova Found. Recognized as His Royal Highness, Prince of Cittanova by Govts. of Albania and San Marino (Italy). Episcopalian. Club: Shipyard Plantation Racquet. Home: Hilton Head Plantation 10 Windflower Ct Hilton Head Island SC 29926-1704

SCOTT, LEE ALLEN, SR., securities company executive; b. Daniels, W.Va., Oct. 28, 1940; s. Minor Lee and Margaret Allen (Kay) S.;m. Myrah Lou Erickson, July 15, 1962; children: Elizabeth Ashley, Stephanie Erickson, Lee Allen Jr. BSBA, W.Va. U., 1962; MBA, U. Ky., 1967; CLU; cert. fin. planner, cert. investment mgmt. analyst; chartered fin. cons. Mgmt. trainee Gen. Tel. & Electronics Co., 1965-66; regional group mgr. Prudential Ins. Co., 1967-76; pres. Scott & Assocs., Inc., employee benefit cons., Parkersburg, W.Va., from 1976; pres., chmn. bd., chief exec. officer Union Trust Nat. Bank, 1980-82; sr. v.p. investments Prudential Securities, Inc., Durham, N.C., 1983—. Bd. dirs. Parkersburg YMCA; chmn. W.Va. Found. Ind. Colls., chmn.; pres. Mid Ohio Valley United Fund, Wood County Devel. Authority; bd. dirs. Parkersburg United Fund; trustee Bethay Coll. With USAR, 1963-65. Decorated Army Commendation medal. Mem. Am. Soc. CLU's, Am. Mgmt. Assn., Health Ins. Assn. Am. (chmn. health care com. W.Va.), Inst. Cert. Fin. Planners, Nat. Assn. Life Underwriters, Estate Planning Coun., Registry Fin. Planners (cert. investment mgmt. analyst), Parkersburg Country Club, Elks, Parkersburg Rotary. Methodist. Home: 132 Donegal Dr Chapel Hill NC 27514 Office: Prudential Securities Inc PO Box 52395 3518 Westgate Dr Durham NC 27707

SCOTT, LEE HANSEN, retired holding company executive; b. Atlanta, Sept. 25, 1926; s. Elbert Lee and Auguste Lillian (Hansen) S.; m. Margaret Lee Smith, July 20, 1951; children: Bradley Hansen, Randall Lee. B.E.E., U. Fla., 1949. With Fla. Power Corp., St. Petersburg, 1949-94; dir. constrn., maintenance and operating Fla. Power Corp., 1968-71, v.p. customer ops., 1971-77, sr. v.p. ops., 1977-83, pres., 1983-88, chmn. bd., 1988-90, also bd. dirs.; also bd. dirs. Fla. Progress Corp.; retired, 1994; bd. dirs. Sun Banks; cons. in field. Pres. St. Petersburg chpt. ARC, 1977, Pinellas Com. of 100, 1980, Community Services Council, 1970, St. Petersburg Progress, 1983, Bus. and Industry Employment Devel. Council, 1983; chmn. bd. United Way. Served with USAF, 1944-46. Named Mr. Sun of St. Petersburg, 1990. Mem. Fla. Engring. Soc., IEEE, Elec. Council Fla. (pres. 1979), St. Petersburg C. of C. (v.p. 1980), Fla. C. of C. (pres. 1987-88), Pinellas Suncoast C. of C. (past chmn., chmn. bd. trustees). Presbyterian. Home: 601 Apalachee Dr NE Saint Petersburg FL 33702-2766

SCOTT, LORETTA CLAIRE, elementary education educator; b. Pitts., Jan. 11, 1949; d. Joe and Sarah Margaret (Parise) Ferraro; m. James L. Scott II, May 22, 1971; children: James, Sarah. BS in Edn., Pitts. State U., 1970; MEd, U. Mo., 1989. Cert. tchr., Mo., Va. Tchr. Sunnyview Attendance Ctr., Chetopa, Kans., 1971, Weir (Kans.) Elem. Attendance Ctr., 1971-72, Bullfrogs and Little Fishes, Lebanon, Mo., 1982-83, Columbia (Mo.) Catholic Sch., 1984-91; tchr. Chpt. I math. lab. Alexandria (Va.) City Pub. Schs., 1991-94; tchr. intermediate math. lab. Cora Kelly Magnet Sch., Alexandria, Va., 1994—. Trainer math. insvc. State of Mo., Jefferson City, 1987-89. Recipient Edn. of Achievement award Mo. Coun. Pvt. Edn., 1990. Mem. ASCD, NEA, Va. Edn. Assn., Nat. Coun. Tchrs. Math., Va. Coun. Tchrs. Math. Roman Catholic.

SCOTT, LOUYSE HULSEY, school social worker; b. Toccoa, Ga., Feb. 20, 1952; d. William Floyd Hulsey Sr. and Doris Elaine (Smith) Carter; m. Roy Leon Scott, Jan. 11, 1975. AA, Emmanuel Coll., Franklin Spring, Ga., 1974; BSW, North Ga. Coll., Dahlonega, 1979; MSW, U. Ga., 1983. Lic. master social worker; cert. sch. social worker, pupil pers. dir. Social worker Alpine Psychoeducational Ctr., Gainesville, Ga., 1978-84; sch. social worker Stephens County Schs., Toccoa, Ga., 1984-96. Author: (poetry) Poetry for Everyday People, 1994. Mem. Stephens County Child Abuse Protocol Com., 1992—, Stephens County Domestic Violence Task Force, 1995—, Interagy. Staffing Com., 1994—; chairperson, past treas. Action Cmty. Team for A Drug Free Stephens County, 1990—; vol. Hand-in-Hand Hospice, Toccoa, 1995, Hospice of the Upstate, Anderson, S.C., 1989-90, Stephens County Red Ribbon Campaign, Toccoa. Mem. NASW (Sch. Social Work Specialist credentials), Sch. Social Workers Assn. Ga., Inc. (past membership chair, 9th Dist. Sch. Social Worker of Yr. 1992), Ga. Assn. Educators (sec. local chpt.

1994-96). Baptist. Home: PO Box 202 Carnesville GA 30521-0202 Office: Stephens County Pub Schs Rt 1 Box 75 Toccoa GA 30577

SCOTT, MARK ALDEN, hospital network executive; b. Chattanooga, Dec. 4, 1959; s. Dewey Alden and Rowena (Lowery) S.; m. Donna Ruth Kibble, Sept. 11, 1982; 1 child, Matthew. Student, Tenn. Tech. U., Cookeville, 1978-80, Chattanooga State U., 1981, 93—. Cert. network engr. Programmer Jerry Bell Constrn., Chattanooga, 1986-88; PC specialist Siskin Steel & Supply, Chattanooga, 1988-89; support and network mgr. Tiger Data Systems, Chattanooga, 1989-90, programmer, 1990; system cons. Data Concepts, Chattanooga, 1990—; microcomputer specialist Meml. Hosp., Chattanooga, 1991-93, network mgr., 1993-96, mgr. network svcs., 1996—; programmer Candlelighters, Chattanooga. Mem. Netware Users Internat., Chattanooga Area Netware Users Group (pres.). Republican. Baptist. Home: 8411 Forrest Breeze Dr Chattanooga TN 37416-3223 Office: Meml Hosp 2525 Desales Ave Chattanooga TN 37404-1161

SCOTT, MARTHA SUE, food company executive; b. San Antonio, Aug. 10, 1961; d. Charles and Susie (Lara) S. Student, U. Tex., San Antonio, 1979-82. Crew mem. McDonald's, San Antonio, 1979-80, asst. mgr., 1980-84, store mgr., 1984-88, area supr., 1988—. Recipient Archie award McDonald's, 1981; named Outstanding Store Mgr., 1987, 88, 89. Mem. NAFE. Democrat. Roman Catholic. Home: 802 Inspiration Dr San Antonio TX 78228-1015 Office: McDonald's 6967 San Pedro Ave San Antonio TX 78216-6206

SCOTT, MARY SHY, music consultant; b. Atlanta, July 19, 1929; d. Robert and Flora Shy; m. Alfred Scott, Feb. 11, 1951; children: Alfredene Cheely, Arthur Robert, Alfred Jr. AB, Spelman Coll., Atlanta, 1950; MA, N.Y.U., 1969; HHD (hon.), Miles Coll., 1992. Life Cert. Edn. State Ga. Elem. music specialist Atlanta Pub. Sch., Atlanta, 1950-87; music cons. Atlanta, 1987—. Contbr. articles to profl. jours. Bd. mem. SCLC Nat., 1986, United Negro Coll. Fund, 1990—; Mem. Steward Allen Temple AME Ch., Atlanta, 1989; 3rd v.p. Ednl. Advancement Found., Chgo. Recipient Plaque Meritorious Svc. award -Eta Omega Chpt. Omega Psi Phi Fraternity, 1987, Plaque Peachtree Suburban Chpt. for leadership and dedicated svc., 1988, Paque for Outstanding Contbn. in the Advancement of the Arts Top Ladies of Distinction, Inc., 1988; presented keys to 13 U.S. cities; recipient of 43 Proclamations and Commendations from city and state govts. across the U.S., OUIDAH '92 award, Pres. N.D. Soola, Benin Rep., West Africa, 1993. Mem. Internat. Platform Assn. (pub. speaker), Kappa Alpha Sorority (1st nat. v.p. 1986-90, internat. pres. 1990-94). Home and Office: 2781 Baker Ridge Dr NW Atlanta GA 30318-7258

SCOTT, MIKE, pharmacist, consultant; b. Lockhart, Tex., Apr. 24, 1947; s. Leonard Walter and Bonnie (Hinkle) S.; m. Carolyn Ann Hemme, Aug. 16, 1968 (div. Mar. 1984); children: Michael David, James Daniel; m. Sherry E. Leighton, Jan. 14, 1989; children: Monica Mueller, Amy Mueller, Julie Mueller, Sarah Mueller, Chris Leighton. BS in Pharmacy, U. Tex., 1970. Cert. pharmacist, Tex. Pharmacist Mercer's Pharmacy, Lockhart, 1970-72, Gibson Pharmacy, Lockhart, 1972-73; pharmacist, owner Scott's Pharmacy, Lockhart, 1973—; cons. pharmacist City of Lockhart Hosp., 1971-80, Cartwheel Lodge Nursing Home, Lockhart, 1973-88, Cartwheel Lodge Nursing Home, Luling, Tex., 1980-88, Cartwheel Lodge Nursing Home, Gonzales, Tex., 1983-88, Golden Age Home, Lockhart, 1988-96. Coun. mem. Lockhart City Coun., 1978-87, mayor pro-tem, 1981-87; pres. region 10 Tex. Mcpl. League, Ctrl. Tex., 1985-86; chmn. planning and zoning commn. City of Lockhart, 1987—. 1st lt. U.S. Army, 1970-76. Mem. Tex. Pharm. Assn. (bd. dirs. 1993—, chmn. sect. pharmacy mgmt. 1992-93, treas.-elect 1996-99). Office: Scott's Pharmacy & Florist 1005 W San Antonio St Lockhart TX 78644-2421

SCOTT, NATHAN ALEXANDER, JR., minister, literary critic, religion educator; b. Cleve., Apr. 24, 1925; s. Nathan Alexander and Maggie (Martin) S.; m. Charlotte Hanley, Dec. 21, 1946; children: Nathan Alexander III, Leslie K. AB, U. Mich., 1944; BD, Union Theol. Sem., 1946; PhD, Columbia U., 1949; LittD, Ripon Coll., 1965, St. Mary's Coll., Notre Dame, Ind., 1969, Denison U., 1976, Brown U., 1981, Northwestern U., 1982, Elizabethtown Coll., 1989; LHD, Wittenberg U., 1965; DD, Phila. Div. Sch., 1967; STD, Gen. Theol. Sem., 1968; LHD, U. D.C., 1976; DD, The Protestant Episcopal Theological Seminary in Va., 1985; HumD, U. Mich., 1988; LHD, Wesleyan U., 1989, Bates Coll., 1990; STD, Univ of the South, 1992; DD, Kenyon Coll., 1993, Wabash Coll., 1996; Ordained priest Episcopal Ch., 1960; canon theologian Cathedral St. James, Chgo., 1967-76. dean of chapel, Va. Union U., 1946-47; instr. humanities, Howard U., 1948-51, asst. prof., 1951-53, assoc. prof., 1953-55; asst. prof. theology and literature, U. Chgo., 1955-58, assoc. prof., 1958-64, prof., 1964-72, Shailer Mathews prof. of theology and lit., 1972-76, prof. English, 1967-76; Commonwealth prof. religious studies, U. Va., 1976-81, William R. Kenan prof. religious studies, 1981-90, prof. English, 1976-90, prof. emeritus, 1990—. Author: Rehearsals of Discomposure: Alienation and Reconciliation in Modern Literature, 1952, The Tragic Vision and the Christian Faith, 1957, Modern Literature and the Religious Frontier, 1958, Albert Camus, 1962, Reinhold Niebuhr, 1963, The New Orpheus: Essays toward a Christian Poetic, 1964, The Climate of Faith in Modern Literature, 1965, The Broken Center: Studies in the Theological Horizon of Modern Literature, 1966, Ernest Hemingway, 1966, The Modern Vision of Death, 1967, Adversity and Grace: Studies in Recent American Literature, 1968, Negative Capability: Studies in the New Literature and the Religious Situation, 1969, The Unquiet Vision: Mirrors of Man in Existentialism, 1969, The Wild Prayer of Longing: Poetry and the Sacred, 1971, Nathanael West, 1971, Three American Moralists: Mailer, Bellow, Trilling, 1973, The Poetry of Civic Virtue: Eliot, Malraux, Auden, 1976, Mirrors of Man in Existentialism, 1978, The Poetics of Belief: Studies in Coleridge, Arnold, Pater, Santayana, Stevens and Heidegger, 1985, Visions of Presence in Modern American Poetry, 1993; co-editor Jour. Religion, 1963-77, (with Ronald Sharp) Reading George Steiner, 1994; adv. editor Religion and Lit., Literature and Theology, Callaloo. Fellow Am. Acad. of Arts and Scis.; mem. Soc. Arts, Religion and Contemporary Culture, Soc. for Values in Higher Edn. (Kent fellow), MLA., Am. Acad. Religion (pres. 1986), Century Assn. (N.Y.C.), Quadrangle Club, Arts Club (Chgo.), Greencroft Club (Charlottesville, Va.). Office: U Va Dept Religious Studies Charlottesville VA 22903

SCOTT, OWEN MYERS, JR., nuclear engineer; b. Birmingham, Ala., Oct. 15, 1952; s. Owen Myers and Sarah (Watson) S.; m. Eleanor Eason, July 15, 1978; 1 child, Owen Myers III. BCE, Auburn U., 1977; MBA, U. Ala., Birmingham, 1981; MS Nuclear Engring., Ga. Inst. Tech., 1986. Registered profl. engr., Ala., Fla., Ga., Miss. Physics lab. instr. Auburn (Ala.) U., 1977; civil/structural design engr. So. Co. Svcs., Inc., Birmingham, 1977-84, nuclear analysis engr., 1984-90; sr. nuclear engr. So. Nuclear Co., Birmingham, 1991—; pres. So. Investors, Birmingham, 1994—. Co-author (computer program) radiol. shielding analysis, 1986. Instr., advisor Jr. Achievement/Project Bus., Birmingham, 1982. Recipient Tech. award Electric Power Rsch. Inst., 1995. Mem. Am. Nuclear Soc., ASCE, Nat. Mgmt. Assn., Omicron Delta Epsilon. Presbyterian. Home: 3876 Timberline Way Birmingham AL 35243-2452 Office: So Nuclear Co 40 Inverness Center Pkwy PO Box 1295 Birmingham AL 35201

SCOTT, PATRICK GREIG, language educator, librarian; b. Grimsby, Lincs., U.K., Feb. 20, 1945; came to U.S., 1976; s. James and Jessie (Atkinson) S.; m. Mary Jane Wittstock, Sept. 1, 1973; children: Nancy, Thomas. BA, Merton Coll., Oxford, Eng., 1966, MA, 1970; MA, Leicester (Eng.) U., 1969; PhD, Edinburgh (Scotland) U., 1976. Tutor in English Gindiri Tchr. Tng. Coll., Plateau, Nigeria, 1962-63; tutorial asst. Leicester U., 1968-70; lectr. English Edinburgh U., 1970-76; vis. lectr. Coll. William and Mary, Williamsburg, Va., 1974, 76; vis. assoc. prof. U. S.C., Columbia, 1976-77, assoc. prof. English, 1977-80, prof. English, 1980—; spl. collections coord. Thomas Cooper Libr., Columbia, 1995-96; assoc. univ. libr., 1996—; dir. seminars for sch. tchrs. NEH, 1986, 88, co-dir. Scottish conf., 1990; dir. Robert Burns Project grant S.C. Humanities Coun., 1995; postmaster in modern history Merton Coll., Oxford, 1962. Author: Tennyson's Enoch Arden, 1970, The Early Editions of A.H. Clough, 1977; editor: Victorian Poetry 1830-1870, 1971, Culture and Education in Victorian England, 1990, S.C. Working Papers in Scottish Bibliography, 1993—; editl. bd. Tennyson Soc., 1973-76, Victorians Inst. Jour., 1988—, Stirling-South Carolina Hogg Edit., 1992—. NEH Summer Rsch. fellow, 1991. Mem. Victorians Inst. (sec. 1994-96, pres. 1996—). Home: 1703 Belmont Dr Columbia SC 29206 Office: Univ of South Carolina Dept English Columbia SC 29208

SCOTT, RICHARD KEVIN, army officer; b. N.Y.C., Apr. 6, 1971; s. Richard Nathaniel and Edith Magdaline (Taylor) S. BSBA, BS in Am. Politics, Bucknell U., 1993. Commd. 2d lt. U.S. Army, 1993, advanced through grades to 1st lt.; exec. officer 194th Mil. Police Co., Ft. Campbell, Ky., 1994-95; advanced party comdr. 194th Mil. Police Co., Panama, 1994-95; exec. officer Hdqs. Law Enforcement Command, Ft. Campbell, 1995-96; plans officer Hdqs. and Hdqs. Co. 101st Corps Support Group, Ft. Campbell, 1996—. Active Combined Fed. Campaign, 1993-96. Mem. Assn. U.S.Army, Ft. Campbell Officer's Club, Kappa Alpha Psi. Episcopalian. Home: 1991 Timberline Way Clarksville TN 37042

SCOTT, RICHARD L., health and medical products company executive; b. Kansas City, Mo., 1953. BSBA, U. Mo.; JD, So. Meth. U. Bar: Tex. Pvt. practice, until 1987; chmn., CEO, Columbia/HCA Healthcare Corp., Nashville, 1987—; bd. dirs. Banc One Corp. Recipient silver award as CEO of Yr. Fin. World mag.; named One of Top 25 Performers, U.S. News & World Report, 1995. Mem. Healthcare Leadership Coun., Bus. Roundtable, Bus. Coun. Office: Columbia/HCA Healthcare Corp 1 Park Plz St Nashville TN 40202-1366*

SCOTT, RILLA REBECCA, special education educator; b. Joplin, Mo., Nov. 10, 1947; d. Oliver Quentin and Mary Madeline (Shepherd) S. AA, Crowder Coll., 1967; BS, Mo. So. State Coll., 1969; MS, Pittsburg (Kans.) State U., 1973. Elem. sch. tchr. Westview Sch. C-6, Neosho, Mo., 1969-71; tchr. spl. edn. Lenapah (Okla.) Pub. Schs., 1972-78, Picher (Okla.)-Cardin Schs., 1978—, No. Ottawa County Coop., 1978—; coach Okla. Spl. Olympics, 1973—; bd. dirs. Pathfinders' Spl. Edn. Coop., Bartlesville, Okla., 1977. Vol. Newton County Libr., Neosho. Mem. NEA, Okla. Edn. Assn., Coun. Exceptional Children, Picher-Cardin Classroom Tchrs. Assn. (pres. 1986-87), Friends of Libr., Newton County Hist. Soc., Joplin Geneal. Soc. Mem. Ch. of Christ. Home: 11610 Goldfinch Road Neosho MO 64850 Office: Picher Cardin schs West A St Picher OK 74360

SCOTT, ROBERT EDWIN, law educator; b. Nagpur, India, Feb. 25, 1944; came to U.S., 1955; s. Roland Waldeck and Carol (Culver) S.; m. Elizabeth (Loch) Shumaker, Aug. 14, 1965; children: Christina Elaine, Robert Adam. BA, Oberlin (Ohio) Coll., 1965; JD, Coll. of William and Mary, 1968; LLM, U. Mich., 1969, SJD, 1973. Bar: Va. 1968. From asst. to assoc. prof. Law Sch. Coll. of William and Mary, Williamsburg, Va., 1969-74; prof. law Sch. of Law U. Va., Charlottesville, 1974-82, Lewis F. Powell, Jr. prof. Sch. of Law, 1982—, dean and Arnold H. Leon prof., 1991—. Author: Commercial Transactions, 1982, 91, Sales Law and the Contracting Process, 1982, 91, Contract Law and Theory, 1988, 93. Fellow Am. Bar Found.; mem. Va. Bar Assn. Democrat. Methodist. Home: 1109 Hilltop Rd Charlottesville VA 22903-1220 Office: U Va Sch of Law Charlottesville VA 22903

SCOTT, RONALD WILLIAM, educator, physical therapist, lawyer, writer; b. Pitts., Dec. 19, 1951; s. Richard Jack and Leone Florence (Gore) S.; m. Maria Josefa Barba-Garces, Aug. 5, 1973; children: Ronald William Jr., Paul Steven. BS in Phys. Therapy summa cum laude, U. Pitts., 1977; JD magna cum laude, U. San Diego, 1983; MBA, Boston U., 1986; LLM, Judge Adv. Gen. Sch., Charlottesville, Va., 1988; postgrad., Samuel Merritt Coll., Oakland, Calif. Bar: Calif. 1983, Tex. 1994; cert. orthopaedic phys. therapist. Commd. 1st lt. U.S. Army, 1978, advanced through grades to maj.; atty.-advisor U.S. Army, Frankfurt, Germany, 1983-87; malpractice claims atty. U.S. Army, Ft. Meade, Md., 1988-89; chief phys. therapist U.S. Army, Ft. Polk, La., 1989-92; phys. therapist, clin. instr. Brooke Army Med. Ctr., San Antonio, 1992-94; assoc. prof. dept. phys. therapy Sch. of Allied Health Scis., U. Tex. Health Sci. Ctr., San Antonio, 1994—; presenter numerous profl. seminars on health law, ethics, and quality and risk mgmt.; guest lectr. phys. therapy program Allegheny U., Phila., 1991—, Temple U., Tex. Woman's U., U.S. Army-Baylor U. Author: Healthcare Malpractice, 1990, Legal Aspects of Documenting Patient Care, 1994, Promoting Legal Awareness, 1996; editor: Law Rev., U. San Diego, 1982-83; also articles; mem. editl. adv. bd. PT: The Mag. of Phys. Therapy, 1991—. Merit badge counselor Boy Scouts Am. Mem. ABA, Am. Phys. Therapy Assn. (chair, jud. com., McMillan scholar 1976), Nat. Health Lawyers Assn., Tex. Phys. Therapy Assn., Soc. for Human Resource Mgmt. (presenter Geriatric Rehab. Conf. Cambridge U. 1995, Trinity Coll., Dublin 1996). Democrat. Methodist. Home: 5815 Spring Crown San Antonio TX 78247-5409 Office: U Tex Health Sci Ctr 7703 Floyd Curl Dr San Antonio TX 78284-6200

SCOTT, SIDNEY BUFORD, financial services company executive; b. Richmond, Va., Mar. 3, 1933; s. Buford and Mary (Nixon) S.; m. Susan Elder Bailey, Sept. 19, 1959; children: Sidney Buford Jr., Elizabeth Scott Cech, George Reily Bailey. Student, Yale U., 1951-53; BA, U. Va., 1955; LLD (hon.), St. Paul's Coll., 1982. Chmn. Scott & Stringfellow Inc., Richmond, 1974—, Scott & Stringfellow Fin. Svcs., Richmond; bd. dirs. Ethyl Corp., Gt. Ea. Energy and Devel. Corp.; mem. regional firms adv. com. N.Y. Stock Exch., 1982-85; chmn. bd. trustees Securities Industry Found. for Econ. Edn., 1976-86; trustee Va. Retirement Sys., 1984-94. Bd. dirs. Atlantic Rural Expn., Hollywood Cemetery, Police Benevolent Assn., Richmond Renaissance, Va.; trustee, chmn. Elk Hill Farm, Inc.; bd. visitors U. Va., 1987-94; former vice rector, bd. visitors Va. Commonwealth U.; past chmn. United Way Greater Richmond; vestryman, past sr. warden St. Paul's Episcopal Ch.; bd. dirs., past pres. Sheltering Arms Hosp; past bd. dirs., v.p. Big Bros. Am.; past bd. dirs., chmn. Big Bros. Richmond, Met. Found., also others. Sgt. U.S. Army, 1956-58. Recipient Outstanding Young Man of Yr. award Richmond Jr. C. of C., 1964, outstanding svc. award Va. Coun. on Econ. Edn., 1976, 80, Brotherhood award NCCJ, 1981, George P. Baker medal Joint Coun. on Econ. Edn., 1986, Bd. Mem. of Yr. award Va. Assn. Children's Homes, 1987. Mem. Securities Industry Assn. (governing coun. 1976-78), Raven Soc., Beta Gamma Sigma. Democrat. Home: 7612 Hill Dr Richmond VA 23225-1021 Office: PO Box 1575 Richmond VA 23213-1575

SCOTT, STANLEY VANAKEN, administrator, educator, consultant; b. Lakeworth, Fla., Apr. 20, 1943; s. Claude Huffman and Julia Mae (Pitcock) S.; m. Tatiana E. Scott; children: Shellie Ann, Tobie Lou, Kristopher Kent, Jennifer Ann. BBA, U. Alaska, 1981; MA, Ohio State U., 1985, PhD, 1986. Mapper U.S. Geol. Survey, Denver, 1966-70; contract mgr. Plains Builders, Abilene, Tex., 1970-73; owner, mgr. Allens Park (Colo.) Stables, 1973-77; photomapper Boulder County, Boulder, Colo., 1975-77; mgr. Ambuco Alaska, Anchorage, 1977-79; asst. to dean Coll. Bus. U. Alaska, Anchorage, 1979-81, assoc. prof. mktg., 1990-93; grad. asst. Ohio State U., Columbus, 1982-85; asst. prof. mktg. Boise (Idaho) State U., 1985-90, mem. faculty senate Coll. Bus., 1987-88, 88-89; dean Sch. Bus., Profl. Mktg. Ala. A&M U., Normal, 1993—; mem. exec. bd. Ala. State Small Bus. Consortium, deans' coun., adv. coun. Ala. A&M U.; assoc. Alaska Ctr. Internat. Bus., 1992-93; cons. NPT com. SBDC, 1992, Idaho State Lottery, 1990, Idaho NPT EMD, 1989, Kellog Idaho Gondola, 1988; mem. Idaho Gov.'s Market Plan, 1987. Author Idaho Innovations, 1987-88, Jour. Internat. CNSR Behavior, 1989, Jour. Marketing for Higher Education, 1989, Great Ideas in Teaching Marketing, 1990. Rsch. grantee U.S. West Commn., 1989, Idaho Nat. Engring. Lab, 1988. Fellow Acad. Mktg. Sci.; mem. Am. Mktg. Assn., Ak. Youth Parents Fedn. (bd. dirs.), Internat. Acad. Mktg. and Mgmt., Acad. Bus. Adminstrn., U. Alaska Anchorage Mktg. Mgmt. Club (adv. 1990-93), Beta Gamma Sigma, Pi Sigma Epsilon (advisor 1985-90, Favorite Mktg. Tchr. award 1986, 87, 88). Office: Ala A&M U Office of Dean Sch Bus PO Box 429 # A M U Normal AL 35762-0429

SCOTT, SUZANNE, writer, artist; b. Athens, Ga., Mar. 1, 1940; d. Jane Scott (Terrell) Overby; divorced; children: Elizabeth Atwell, William F. Atwell Jr., Stephanie Atwell Zehr, David Allan Atwell; life ptnr. Lynne Mary Constantine. BA in English, Eastern Mennonite Coll., 1979; MA in English Lit., James Madison U., 1986. Continuity writer WSVA TV-AM-FM, Harrisonburg, Va., 1966-68, 71-72, WBTX-FM, Broadway, Va., 1972; instr. English as 2d lang. Eastern Mennonite Coll., Harrisonburg, 1977-78, instr. English, 1979; teaching asst. English James Madison U., Harrisonburg, 1979-81; writer Psychiatric Insts. Am., Washington, 1981-84; founding ptnr. Community Scribes, Arlington, Va., 1984—; founding ptnr., mng. editor Womens Monthly, 1992—; co-founder, ptnr. Women's Monthly, Arlington, 1992—; artist Arts & Space, Inc., Arlington, 1995—. Co-author: Migraine: The Complete Guide, 1994; contbr. articles to profl. jours. Mem. Nat. Gay & Lesbian Journalist Assn., Washington, 1995—; artist Arts and Space, Inc., 1995—. Meth. Ch. Coll. scholar, 1958; Teaching fellow James Madison U., 1979, 80. Mem. NAFE, Nat. Gay & Lesbian Journalists Assn., Arlington C. of C., Arlington Arts Ctr. Democrat. Methodist. Office: Community Scribes 1001 N Highland St Arlington VA 22201-2142

SCOTT, VERNELL IZORA, lawyer; b. Beaufort, S.C., Oct. 10, 1948; d. Hugh M. and Hattie Mae (Mimms) Washington; m. Edward A. Scott (div. 1988); children: Derek L., Michael Q. AA, Fugazzi Bus. Coll., 1975; BA, Chgo. State U., 1983; JD, Chgo.-Kent Coll. Law, 1988. Bar: Ill. 1989, U.S. Dist. Ct. (7th dist.) Ill. 1989, S.C. 1990, U.S. Dist. Ct. S.C. 1990, U.S. Ct. Mil. Appeals 1992. Assoc. Stanley Hill & Assocs., Chgo., 1989; pvt. practice Beaufort, S.C., 1990—; legal recruiting coord. Burke, Wilson & McIlvaine, Chgo., 1988-89. Bd. dirs. United Communities for Child Devel., Beaufort, 1990, 1st vice chair Beaufort County Dem. Party, 1990-92. Mem. ABA, Am. Trial Lawyers Assn., S.C. Bar Assn., S.C. Trial Lawyers Assn. Office: 907 Bay St PO Box 2357 Beaufort SC 29901

SCOTT, VICKI SUE, school system administrator; b. Pine Bluff, Ark., Feb. 16, 1946; d. John Wesley and Ruby Gray (Whitehead) and Hannah (Lewis) S. BA, Hendrix Coll., 1968; MS in Edn., U. Cen. Ark., 1978, postgrad., 1979-84; postgrad., U. Ark., 1983-85, Ark. State U., 1993-94. Cert. adminstrn., secondary sch. prin., middle sch., secondary health and phys. edn. Tchr., coach Brinkley (Ark.) Pub. Schs., 1968-76, Lonoke (Ark.) Jr. and Sr. High Schs., 1976-77; tchr., coach S.E. Jr. High Sch., Pine Bluff, 1978-92, asst. prin., 1992—, dir. summer sch., 1991, 92; AIDS educator Arkansas River Edn. Svc. Coop., Pine Bluff, 1989-92. Active Leadership Pine Bluff, 1993-94. Scholar Assn. Women Ednl. Suprs., 1985; named Outstanding Young Women of Am., 1974. Mem. ASCD, DAR, Ark. Assn. Ednl. Admisntrs., Nat. Assn. Secondary Prins., Order Ea. Star, Delta Kappa Gamma (scholar 1984), Phi Delta Kappa. Baptist. Home: 3215 S Cherry St Pine Bluff AR 71603-5983 Office: SE Mid Sch 20001 S Ohio St Pine Bluff AR 71601-6901

SCOTT, VIRGINIA R., glass researcher, writer; b. Rogersville, Ala., June 17, 1916; d. William Brown and Emma (Harrison) Reeder; m. Owen Scott, June 25, 1941; children: Anne, Karen, Owen III. BS, Ala. Coll. Women, 1938. Home econs. tchr. Cullman County Sch. Sys., West Point, Ala., 1938-40, Florence (Ala.) City Schs., 1940-46; columnist Rainbow Review Mag., Costa Mesa, Calif., 1973-89, Depression Glass Daze, Otisville, Mich., 1973-90; editor newsletter The Candlewick Collector, 1976—. Author: The Collector's Guide to Imperial Candlewick, 1980. Mem. Ohio Candlewick Club, Michiana Candlewick Assn., Nat. Imperial Glass Collectors Soc. Methodist. Home: 275 Milledge Ter Athens GA 30606

SCOTT, WILLIAM FLOYD, accountant; b. Woodland, Miss., Feb. 26, 1936; s. Robert Fulton and Sarah Etta (Watson) S.; m. Carolyn Marie Pierce, Dec. 12, 1958; children: David, Ricky, Stephen, Julie. BS in Bus. Adminstrn., Delta State U., Cleveland, Miss., 1957. Staff acct. Reynolds Elec. & Engring., Las Vegas, Nev., 1957-62, sr. auditor, 1962-65, dir. internal auditing, 1965-70; sr. staff acct. Davis & Mosher, CPAs, Pasadena, Tex., 1970-72; owner Scott & Co., CPAs, Pasadena, 1972—. Chmn. fin. com. Meml. Bapt. Ch., Pasadena, 1974-80, treas., 1974—. Mem. AICPA, Tex. Soc. CPAs, Pasadena Noon Optimist Club (treas. 1973-75). Office: Scott & Co CPAs 4620 Fairmont Pky Ste 200 Pasadena TX 77504-3328

SCOTT-WABBINGTON, VERA V., elementary school educator; b. Holland, Tex., Jan. 17, 1929; d. John Leslie Scott and Willie Mattie (Dickson) Stafford. BA, Huston-Tillotson Coll., 1950; MA, Roosevelt U., 1965. Cert. elem. tchr., Tex. Tchr. Ft. Hood/Killeen (Tex.) Ind. Sch. Dist., 1951-58, Gary (Ind.) Sch. Dist., 1958-83; tchr. Ft. Worth Pub. Schs., 1983—, key tchr. minority math. and sci. edn. coop., 1989-92; mem. mentorship program Ft. Worth Ind. Sch. Dist.; mem. Nat. Rev. Panel to Review Nat. Coun. of Social Studies Curriculum Stds., 1993; adj. prof. Tex. Weslyan U., Ft. Worth. Active in several polit., civic and social orgns. Recipient Outstanding Achievement in Edn. award Baker Chapel African Meth. Episc. Ch., 1991, NAACP Edn. award, 1992. Mem. Nat. Alliance Black Sch. Educators (tchr. 1991), Am. Fedn. Tchrs., Tex. Fedn. Tchrs., Tex. Alliance Black Educators. Home: 7212 Misty Meadow Dr S Fort Worth TX 76133-7117

SCOTT-WILSON, SUSAN RICE, principal; b. Brownsville, Tenn., Aug. 11, 1942; d. Moreau Estes and E. Estelle (Walker) Rice; m. Charles E. Scott, Feb. 28, 1969 (div. July 1985); children: Tamera W., David W.; m. Lloyd Curlin Wilson, Apr. 7, 1994. BS, U. Tenn., Martin, 1964; EdM, Memphis State U., 1979, EdD, 1989. Cert. master tchr., Tenn. Elem. tchr. Lauderdale County Bd. Edn., Ripley, Tenn., 1964-65; exchange tchr. USIA, Washington, Netherlands, 1986-87; chmn. English dept. Am. Sch. of The Hague, Netherlands, 1987-88; secondary tchr. Haywood County Bd. Edn., Brownsville, Tenn., 1974-86, tchr. vocat. English, 1989-90, dir. adult basic edn., 1990-96; vice prin. Haywood H.S., Brownsville, Tenn., 1995—; mem. curriculum task force Tenn. Dept. Edn., Nashville, 1985-86, mem. collaborative task force, 1989-92. Local elector Tenn. Pres.'s Trust, Knoxville, 1989—; mem. Sister Cities Commn., Brownsville, 1990; com. mem. Ptnrs. in Edn., Brownsville, 1992-93; mem. West Star Leadership, 1993, Tenn. Reorgnl. Improvement Mgmt. Sys., 1994-95; mem. steering com. Fayette County-Haywood County Cmty. Enterprise, Brownsville, 1994—; bd. dirs. YMCA, Brownsville, 1996—. Named Outstanding Tchr. by students U. Chgo., 1989. Mem. NEA, Nat. Coun. Tchrs. English (regional composition judge 1984-86), Am. Assn. Adult and Continuing Edn., Tenn. Edn. Assn., Tenn. Assn. Adult and Continuing Edn., Tenn. Tchrs. Study Coun. (state steering com. 1984-86), Sigma Tau Delta, Phi Delta Kappa. Methodist. Home: 321 N Washington St Brownsville TN 38012-2063 Office: Haywood HS 1175 E College St Brownsville TN 38012-2208

SCOULAR, MARION ETHEL, embroidery educator; b. Haifa, Palestine, Nov. 9, 1935; arrived in U.S., 1963; d. William and Marjorie Faith (Taylor) Reid; m. Nicholas John Scoular, Aug. 16, 1958 (div. Aug. 1967); children: Barrie Gordon, Wendy Ann. Student, Royal Sch. of Needlework, London, 1952-55; cert., Cambridge Inst., 1956; student, St. Osyth's Coll., Clacton, Eng. Home econs. tchr. English H.S., 1956-60; owner, operator Robin Hood Wool Shop, Clemson, S.C., 1964-77; tchr. Callaway Needlecraft Sch., 1970-75, Valentine Assembly for Embroiderers, 1974-76; instr. Birmingham So. Coll., 1981, 82, U. Wis.; tchr. Margaret Boyles Heirloom Sch., Atlanta, 1988, Martha Pullen's Ch., Huntsville, 1988; cons. Am. Sch. of Needlework Pub. Co.; evaluator Counted Thread Socs. Ethnic Study Program; coord. Pinehurst Inst. of Advanced Needle Art, N.C. One woman shows include Greenville County Libr., S.C., Anderson Arts Coun., S.C.; author: Why Call it Blackwork?, 1993, Hardanger, 1994; contbr. articles to profl. jours. Recipient Silver medal City and Guilds of London Inst., 1953, 1st prize award Worshipful Co. of Needlemakers, 1953. Mem. Embroiderers' Guild of Am. (hon., mem. Mid-Atlantic regional sem., 1992, N.Y. regional sem. 1989, sem. tchr. 1969, 74-77, 80-82, 85, 89, 94-96, mid-Atlantic regional touring tchr., many others), Southeastern Yarncrafters Guild (hon.), Am. Needlepoint Guild, Nat. Coun. of Am. Embroiderers. Home and Office: 2840 Skye Ter Duluth GA 30136-6262

SCRAGG, GEORGE HENRY, JR., marketing executive; b. Westchester, N.Y., Sept. 13, 1934; s. George Henry and Blanche (Hudson) S.; m. Marion Nisbett Eells, Sept. 24, 1960; children: Caroline, Marion, Laura. AB, Princeton U., 1956. With sales dept. Harris Intertype Corp., 1962-71; v.p., gen. mgr. Harris Intertype Can., Toronto, 1971-73; v.p. sales Harris Corp., Cleve., 1973-76; v.p. mktg. Mitsubishi Aircraft Internat. Inc., Dallas, 1976-82, Mann Roland U.S.A., Middlesex, N.J., 1983-84; v.p. corp. mktg. Aviall, Dallas, 1984-85, v.p., gen. mgr. aircraft services div., 1985-88, v.p. bus. aviation, 1988-92, sr. v.p. mktg., 1992-94. Pub. Q.B. Beam, Cleve., 1968-86. Served as 1st lt. USAF, 1956-59. mem. Nat. Bus. Aircraft Assn. (chmn. adv. coun.), North Dallas C. of C. (chmn. aviation com. 1986-92) Brook Hollow Golf Club (bd. dirs.), TBARM Club, Garden of the Gods Club. Republican. Episcopalian. Home: 5909 Luther Ln Apt 2004 Dallas TX 75225 Office: 7515 Lemmon Ave Dallas TX 75209-3017

SCRANTOM, JOHN GARDNER, retired company executive; b. Rochester, N.Y., Nov. 10, 1928; s. Issac Elbert and Mattie-Mae (Archur) S.; m. Phyllis Frances Bucci, Jan. 20, 1951 (div. Aug. 1959); children: Sherry, John

Klumpp; m. Caroline Marie Frenz, Jan. 30, 1960; children: William E., John G. Jr., Robert R., Roxanne M. BSBA, U. Rochester, 1953. Acctg. trainee Ford Motor Co., Detroit, 1953-54; treas. Hayden Coy, Rochester, 1954-57; gen. mgr. City Delivery and Storage Corp., Rochester, 1957-60; v.p., gen. mgr. Jacobs Transfer Co., Washington, 1960-63; gen. mgr. Kott Storage & Van, Berwin, Ill., 1963-65; sr. buyer Tex. Instruments Inc., Dallas, 1965-80. Editor Jour. Am. Soc. for Philatelic Pages and Panels, 1983 (Cardinal Spellman award 1986). With USAF, 1946-49. Recipient Most Popular Exhibit award Tex. Stamp Dealer's Assn., 1988. Mem. Am. Soc. for Philatelic Pages and Panels (founder, pres. 1983-89, emeritus 1990—). Republican. Episcopalian. Home: 1138 Princeton Dr Richardson TX 75081-3615

SCRENOCK, GREGORY HOWARD, mortgage company executive; b. Passaic, N.J., Apr. 5, 1961; s. Howard Francis and Doris Louise (Hintenberger) S.; m. Joanne C. McNamara, Sept. 10, 1988; children: Madelyn, Victoria Grace. BA, Rutgers U., Newark, 1983; comparative law cert., U. Rome, 1985; JD, Temple U., 1986. Pre-trial investigator supr. Phila. Com. Pleas & Mcpl. Ct., 1984-86; assoc. Picinich & Selser, P.C., Hackensack, N.J., 1986-87; nat. rep., legal advisor Am. Fedn. Govt. Employees, New Brunswick, N.J., 1987-89; law clk. to Hon. Peter J. O'Brien Stroudsburg, Pa., 1989-91; exec. v.p. Preferred Fin. Corp., Stroudsburg, Pa., 1991-92; pres. Bankers First Mortgage Inc., Tannersville, Pa., 1992-96, Mortgage Lending Svcs. Inc., Tarpon Springs, Fla., 1996—, Owners Equity Mortgage Corp., Tarpon Springs, 1996—; bd. dirs. Achieva Profess Corp., Fla., Conquest & Fin., Fla., Mortgage Lending Svcs. Corp. Rutgers scholar, 1983. Mem. Nat. Assn. Mortgage Brokers, Fla. Assn. Mortgage Brokers, Palm Harbor C. of C., Tarpon Springs C. of C., Rotary Club (Fla.), BPO Elks, Tarpon Springs Yacht Club, Pi Sigma Alpha. Roman Catholic. Home: 1005 Lake Avoca Pl Tarpon Springs FL 34689 Office: Owners Equity Mortgage Corp 101 E Tarpon Ave Tarpon Springs FL 34689

SCREWS, DAVID LAWRENCE See ALLISON, DAVID LAWRENCE

SCRIVNER, BARBARA E., piano educator; b. Medford, Oreg., May 25, 1931; student (piano student of Lawrence Morton), Bob Jones U., 1962-66; corr. student Inst. Children's Lit., Redding Ridge, Conn., 1974-76; children: R. Dick, Lawrence C., Barbara Ann, Betty Jo. Part time sec., Oreg., 1948-50, 60-62, S.C. 74-76, 80-86, Census Bur., S.C., 1980-82; piano tchr., Greenville, S.C., 1963—; instr. more than 90 student/tchr. recitals; freelance pianist, local chs. and restaurants. Active Rep. Nat. Com., Nat. Rep. Senatorial Com., Nat. Rep. Congl. Com., S.C. Rep. Party; vol. Rep. Party, 1992—; coord. hdqs. Greenville County Rep. Party, Greenville, 1993-94; precinct Rep. pres. Greenville # 25, 1993-94. Contbr. column A Life Within, also by-line columns-opinion to Times Examiner, Greenville, 1995—; contbr. articles, letters to newspapers and columns.

SCROGGIN, DAVID FRED, onwer appraisal company; b. Morrilton, Ark., Nov. 26, 1943; s. Eddie S. and geneva H (Corkill) S.; m. Audrey Elaine Fahst, June 3, 1980 (div. Oct. 1986). AS, Delmar U., Corpus Christi, Tex., 1968; student, San Antonio Coll., 1968-69. Cert. personal property appraiser. Mgr. Southwestern Bell Telephone, Tex., 1966-72; exec. v.p. Amigoland, Inc., brownsville, Tex., 1972-73; v.p. Seahorse Transport, Inc., brownsville, 1973-78; pres. Results Internat., L.A., 1978-81; regional mgr. Raypak Inc., Moorpark, Calif., 1981-83; gen. mgr. Rainbow Plastics, El Monte, Calif., 1983-87; pres. Motorsports Mktg. Corp., Atlanta, 1987—. Mem. Internat. Good Neighbor Conf., 1971-75; chmn. ARC, Tex., 1975; bd. dirs. Brownsville C. of C., 1971-73. With USMC, 1960-65. Baptist. Office: Motorsports Marketing Corp PO Box 2545 19 Andrews St Newnan GA 30264

SCRUGGS, CHARLES EUGENE, university administrator; b. Cullman, Ala., Nov. 16, 1937; s. Forrest Perier and Ora Mae (Smith) S.; m. LaDonna Kathryn Loescher, June 13, 1959; children: Melana Teresa, Sabrina Kay. BA, Transylvania U., 1959; MA, U. Ky., 1962, PhD, 1968. Instr. U. Ky., Lexington, 1962; asst. prof. Appalachian State U., Boone, N.C., 1962-65; assoc. prof. Ea. Ky. U., Richmond, 1967-72; prof. U. South Fla., Tampa, 1972-93, dir. internat. programs, 1988—; vis. prof. U. Paris, 1984; chmn. divsn. lang. U. South Fla., Tampa, 1979-80; translator, cons. Cano, Capsas and Assoc., Tampa, 1981-84. Author: Charles Dassoucy: Adventures in the Age of Louis XIV, 1984, Study Abroad in the Eighties, 1986, France: Tradition and Transition, 1989. Sec. Jr. C. of C., Boone, N.C., 1964-65. Haggin fellow U. Ky., 1960, NDEA fellow U. Ky., 1965-67. Mem. Assn. Internat. Educators, Am. Assn. Tchrs. French, Tampa Bay Area Com. on Fgn. Rels., Sister Cities Internat., Alliance Française. Democrat. Presbyterian. Office: CPR 107 4202 E Fowler Ave Tampa FL 33620-9900

SCRUGGS, CHARLES G., editor; b. McGregor, Tex., Nov. 4, 1923; s. John Fleming and Adeline (Hering) S.; m. Miriam June Wigley, July 5, 1947; children—John Mark, Miriam Jan. B.S., Tex. A&M U., 1947. Assoc. editor Progressive Farmer, Dallas, 1947-61, editor, 1962—, v.p., 1964—, exec. editor, 1972, editorial dir., 1973—, editor-in-chief, 1982-87; editorial chmn. So. Progress Pubs., 1987-89; pres. Torado Land and Cattle Co., pres. Tex. Comml. Agr. Council 1953-54; chmn. bd. Sunlean Foods, Inc., 1989—. Author: The Peaceful Atom and the Deadly Fly, 1975, American Agricultural Capitalism. Founding gen. chmn. Chancellors' Century Coun., Tex. A&M U. System, 1987-90; Mem. Gov.'s Com. for Agr., 1950, Tex. Animal Health Council, 1955-61; chmn. So. Brucellosis Com., 1956; pres. Tex. Rural Safety Com., 1957-59; chmn. Nat. Brucellosis Com., 1958-59, 71-72; del. World Food Congress, 1963; pub. mem. U.S. del. 17th Biennial Conf. of FAO, UN, Rome, 1973; chmn. Joint Senate-House Interim Com. Natural Fibers, Tex. Legislature, 1971; mem. coordinating bd. Tex. Coll. and Univ. System, 1965-69; bd. regents Tex. Tech U., 1971-78; founding pres. S.W. Animal Health Research Found. 1961-63, trustee, 1961—. Served to lt. col. U.S. Army; Res., ret. Recipient Christian Svc. Mass Media award, 1995, Abilene Christian U., Southwestern Cattle Raisers award, 1962, Am. Seed Trade Assn. award, 1963, award of honor Am. Agrl. Editors Assn., 1964, Reuben Brigham award Am. Assn. Agrl. Coll. Editors, 1965, Disting. Svc. award Tex. Farm Bur., 1966, Journalistic Achievement award Nat. Plant Food Assn., 1967, Nat. award for agrl. excellence Nat. Agri-Mktg. Assn., 1983, Agrl. Vision award Nat. Forum for Agr., 1994; named Disting. Alumnus Tex. A&M U., 1982. Mem. Am. Agrl. Editors Assn. (pres. 1963), Am. Soc. Mag. Editors, Tex. Assn. Future Farmers Am. (pres. 1940-41), Dallas Agrl. Club (pres. 1951), Nat. Livestock Confedn. Mexico (hon.), The Austin Club, Headliners Club, Alpha Zeta, Sigma Delta Chi.

SCRUGGS, SANDRA LYNN, secondary school educator, writer; b. Springfield, Mass., Nov. 23, 1961; d. Charles Hubert Scruggs and Julia Jo (Talbot) McCool. BS in Sports Medicine, Brigham Young U., 1987; MA in Edn., N.Mex. State U., 1992. Lic. EMT. Tchr., athletic trainer Jefferson H.S., El Paso, Tex., 1987-88; Spanish tchr., athletic trainer Manzano H.S., Albuquerque, 1992-93; physical edn. tchr., athletic trainer Canutillo Schs., Tex., 1993—. Author: (children's book) The Adventures of Willy B., 1996. Missionary LDS, Santiago, Chile, 1988-90; vol. firefighter Mesilla Fire Dept., N.Mex., 1994-96. Mem. Nat. Athletic Trainers' Assn. (cert.).

SCRUPE, MARA A. (MARY SCRUPE), visual artist, sculptor; b. Mpls., Feb. 19, 1955; d. Carolyn A. (Hanson) Sankey; m. Daniel J. Holm, July 19, 1986. BA, Macalester Coll., 1977; MFA, Bard Coll., 1995. Founder, dir. WAVE Gallery, St. Paul, 1984; instr. The Hand Workshop, Richmond, Va., 1988-90; exec. dir. Greater Reston (Va.) Arts Ctr., 1990-91, Second St. Gallery, Charlottesville, Va., 1991-92; visual artist, curator, educator, 1992—; artist-in-residence Mpls. Pub. Schs., 1982-84, Minn. State Arts Bd., 1983-87, 89, Sculpture Space, Utica, N.Y., 1986, Del. Ctr. for Contemporary Arts, Wilmington, 1994; guest lectr. Coll. of Associated Arts, St. Paul, 1983, Macalester Coll., St. Paul, 1983, Colgate U., Hamilton, N.Y., 1986, Munson-Williams-Proctor Art Inst. Sch., Utica, 1986, Vanderbilt U., Nashville, 1988, U. Tenn., Knoxville, 1989, Appalachian State U., Boone, N.C., 1990, Radford (Va.) U., 1991, Sawhill Gallery, James Madison U., Harrisonburg, Va., 1992, Fayerweather Gallery, U. Va., Charlottesville, 1992, others; vis. artist The Miami U., Oxford, Ohio, 1993, Western Mich. U., Kalamazoo, 1993, Walters State C. C., Morristown Tenn., 1993, adj. prof. sculpture, Va. Commonwealth U., Richmond, 1996-97; adj. prof. sculpture Longwood Coll, Farmville, Va., 1995. One-woman shows include Arts Ctr. Minn., Mpls., 1982, Coll. Associated Arts, St. Paul, 1983, WAVE Gallery, St. Paul, 1984, PLUG-IN, Inc., Winnipeg, Can., 1985, Adirondack State Park, Old Forge, N.Y., 1988, Foundry Gallery, Washington, 1990, U. Calif., Riverside, 1991, Peninsula Fine Arts Ctr., Newport News, Va., 1993, Del. Ctr. Contemporary Arts, Wilmington, 1994, Virginia Beach (Va.) Ctr. Arts, 1997, solo exhibition ARC Gallery, Chgo., 1996, Solo Exhibition, VA Commonwealth U., Richmond, 1996, Anderson Gallery; groups shows include W.A.R.M. Gallery, Mpls., 1982, Fed. Res. Bank Exhbn. Program, Mpls., 1985, C.G. Rein Gallery, Mpls., 1985, Martin Gallery, Washington, 1986, Anderson & Anderson Gallery, Mpls., 1986, Macalester Coll. Alumni Invitational, St. Paul, 1987, Second St. Gallery, Charlottesville, Va., 1988, Sarratt Gallery, Vanderbilt U., Nashville, 1988, Chrysler Museum, Norfolk, 1988, Washington Sq. Exhbn. Program, Washington, 1988, 90, Peninsula Fine Arts Ctr., Newport News, Va., 1990, Nat. Ornamental Metals Mus., Memphis, 1991, Sawhill Gallery, James Madison U., Harrisonburg, Va., 1992, U., Tenn., Knoxville, 1992-94, Fayerweather Gallery, U. Va., Charlottesville, 1992, Walters State C. C., Morristown, 1993, Western Mich. State U., Kalamazoo, 1993, Thomas J. Walsh Art Gallery, Fairfield Conn., 1993, Laguna Gloria Art Mus., 1993, Frederic Layton Art Gallery, Milw., 1993, The Ellipse Art Ctr., Arlington Va., 1994, Miami-Dade C.C., Fla., 1994, N.Y. (N.Y.C.) Open Ctr., 1994, Austin Mus. Arts Laguna Gloria Austin, Tex., Artspace New Haven, Conn., Three Rivers Arts Festival, Three Rivers Art Festival of the Carnegie Mus., of Arts, Pittsburg, Pa., McNeese State U. Lake Charles, La., Nexus Found. for Today's Art, Phila., 1994, Pyramid Atlantic Art Ctr., Washington, 1995, Peconic Gallery of Suffolk C.C., Albany, N.Y., 1995, Sage Jr. Coll., Rathbone Gallery, Albany, 1995, Boston Ctr. for the Arts, 1995, Md. Art Place, Balt., 1995, Matrix Workshop of Women Artists, Sacramento, Calif., 1995, Pleiades Gallery, N.Y.C., 1995, Contemporary Artist Ctr., Boston, 1995, Vividian Gallery, N.Y.C., 1995, Soho 20 Gallery, N.Y.C., 1995, Allentown Art Mus., Allentown, Pa., 1996, Muscarelle Mus. Art Coll. of William and Mary, Williamsburg, Va., 1996, 1996, Internat. Sculpture Ctr., Washington, 1996; Public Arts Commn., The Dream Garden, Wilmington Del., Commn by the City of Del., The Del. Ctr. of Horticulture and The Delaware Ctr., for Cont. Arts, 1995; represented in permanent collections including Western Mich. U., Va. Commonwealth U., Med. Coll. Va., Fairfield U., Conn., Blue Cross ad Blue Shield Corp of Del., Commn., John Michael KohlerArt Ctr., Shebl. Mem. fundraising com. AIDS Support Group Charlottesville, 1992—; active Nat. Mus. Women in the Arts, Washington. Recipient Artist-in-Residence award Villa Montalvo Ctr. for Arts, 1987, Artist-in-Residence award Tyrone Guthrie Ctr.-Ireland, 1991, Nat. Site-Specific Sculpture Competitition award U. Calif.-Riverside, 1991, Mildred Victor prize Nat. Sculpture Soc. Centennial Exhbn., 1993, Nat. Outdoor Sculpture Competition award Miami U., 1993, Installation Exhbn. award Sch. 33 Art Ctr., 1994, John J. Humphrey Best of Show award, Three Rivers Arts Fest. of Carnegie Mus. Art, Pitts.; workshop grantee Film in the Cities Performance Program, 1984; grantee COMPAS Comm. Arts Fund, St. Paul, 1984, Minn. State Arts B., 1985, 86, The Ruth Chenven Found., Inc., 1986, Artists Space, N.Y.C., 1988, 89; Artist-In-Residence grantee Mid-Atlantic Arts Found, 1989, Visual Arts Residency grantee Mid Atlantic Arts Found., 1994; fellow Djerassi Found., 1990, 91, ACTS Inst., 1991; Artist-In-Residence fellow MacDowell Colony, 1993. Mem. Internat. Sculpture Ctr., Washington Sculptors Group, Washington Project for Arts, Second St. Gallery, 1708 E. Main Artists Collectivie, Tri-State Sculptors Guild, Coll. Art Assn., Southeastern Coll. Art Assn. Home: 3601 Connecticut Ave NW Apt 517 Washington DC 20008-2449

SCRUPSKI, SCOTT EDWARD, environmental engineer; b. Teaneck, N.J., Feb. 1, 1956; s. Edward Stanley and Florence Sylvia Scrupski; m. Cheryl Lynn Gerlach, June 6, 1981; 1 child, Anna Nicole; 1 stepchild, Elizabeth Virginia Pierce. BS in Environ. Sci., Fla. Inst. Tech., 1980. Cert. asbestos inspector and mgmt. planner. Health inspector Brevard County Health Dept., Melbourne, Fla., 1981-82; constrn. supt. Maronda Homes, Inc., Palm Bay, Fla., 1982; waste water treatment plant operator trainee City of Melbourne, 1982-83; hazardous waste coord. govt. systems sector Harris Corp., Palm Bay, Fla., 1983-85; sr. engr. environ. McDonnell Douglas Aerospace East, Titusville, Fla., 1985-95; sr. environ. engr. McDonnell Douglas Space and Defense Sys., KSC, Fla., 1995—; adj. prof. Brevard C.C., 1993-96. Mem. Profl. Assn. Diving Instrs., Internat. Assn. Environ. Mgrs. Democrat. Jewish. Home: 1334 Glendale Ave NW Palm Bay FL 32907-8066 Office: McDonnell Douglas Space and Defense Sys PO Box 21233, Dept F676 Kennedy Space Center FL 32815

SCUDDER, ROBERT, minister, youth home administrator; b. Monroe, LA., May 1, 1926; s. Lee and Aldyth (Flenniken) S.; m. Mary Nichols, Oct. 28, 1967; children: Lee, Doug, Vicki, Dana. BA in Human Behavior, Newport U., Newport Beach, Calif., 1983. Ordained to ministry So. Bapt. Conv., 1979. Min., tchr. Books 'n Tapes, Shreveport, La., 1974—; counselor Shreveport Counsel Ctr., 1975-80; asst. pastor Woodlawn Bapt. Ch., Shreveport, 1976; exec. dir., adminstr. Joy Home for Boys, Greenwood, La., 1979—; bd. dirs. Johnny Robinson Youth Shelter, Monroe, 1980—; mem. licensing bd. Dept. Health and Hosps. for Group Homes and Adoptions, State of La., 1986-88, 89—. Author: Genesis, 1976, Cults Exposed, 1981, Customs and Prayer, 1983; also child care pamphlet. Served with USN, 1941-43, PTO. Mem. Am. Assn. on Mental Deficiency (religious v.p. 1984-86, Kiwanis (pres. 1971-72, Child Care award 1984). Home: PO Box 550 Greenwood LA 71033-0550 Office: Joy Home for Boys PO Box 550 Greenwood LA 71033-0550

SCURO, JOSEPH E., JR., lawyer; b. Jersey City, Mar. 28, 1948; s. Joseph E. and Phyllis (Amato) S.; m. Virginia Ruth Shaw. BA with honors, Manhattan Coll., 1970; JD, Ohio State U., 1972. Bar: Tex., Ohio, U.S. Dist. Cts., U.S. Ct. Appeals (5th and 10th cir.), U.S. Tax Ct., U.S. Mil. Appeals, U.S. Supreme Ct. Asst. atty. gen. Ohio, 1973-81; chief legal counsel Ohio State Hwy. Patrol, 1975-81; practice law, 1973—; of counsel Nicholas & Barrera, San Antonio and Dallas, 1982-90; counsel to San Antonio, Dallas and Grapevine Police Officers Assns, Combined Law Enforcement Assn. Tex., Alamo Heights Police Officers Assn., Tex. Mcpl. League; former legal adviser, spl. counsel to cities of San Marcos, New Braunfels, Balcones Heights, La Vernia, Poteet, Laredo, Odessa, Dilley, Hondo, Highland Park, Kyle, Universal City, Del Rio, Greenville, Galveston, Arlington, Austin and others; former spl. counsel on tng. San Antonio Police Dept.; former counsel to Bexar County Constable's Assn.; condr. seminars. Contbr. articles on police and law enforcement to profl. jours. Bd. dirs. Nat. Hispanic Arts Endowment. Served to capt. USAF, 1970-75. Fellow Southwestern Legal Found. (sec. 1986-91); mem. ABA, Tex. Bar Assn., Ohio Bar Assn., San Antonio Bar Assn., Columbus (Ohio) Bar Assn., Am. Trial Lawyers Assn., Police Exec. Research Forum, Internat. Assn. Chiefs of Police (legal officer sect.), Ams. for Effective Law Enforcement (bd. advs.), Southwestern Law Enforcement Inst. (bd. advs.), Internat. Soc. Law Enforcement and Criminal Justice Instrs., Fed. Criminal Investigators Assn. (hon.), Ohio Assn. Polygraph Examiners (hon.). Republican. Presbyterian. Office: Main Place Station PO Box 50966 Dallas TX 75250-0966

SCUTT, CHERYL LYNN, communications executive; b. Columbus, Ind., Dec. 7, 1948; d. Russell O. and Hazel Jeannette (Gordon) S. BA in Journalism, Ind. U., 1971. Freelance writer various nat. orgns. various orgns., Bloomington, Ind., 1971—; feature writer, columnist The Herald-Telephone, Bloomington, Ind., 1971-80, asst. lifestyles editor, 1980-83; comm. assoc. United Way of Mid. Tenn., Nashville, 1983-85, asst. comm. dir., 1985-88, v.p. comm., 1988-94; pres. Scutt Comm. Svcs., Antioch, Tenn., 1994—; instr. Ind. U. H.S. Journalism Inst., Bloomington, 1981, 82; presenter in field United Way Am., 1988-93. mem. Nat. Profl. Adv. Mktg. Com./United Way of Am., 1990-92; comm. coun. mem. Nashville Area C. of C., 1993-94; pub. rels. and devel. comm. cons. Adolescent Pregnancy and Prevention Coun., Nashville, 1992-93; pub. rels. com. ARC, Nashville, 1994—; pub. rels. com. League for Hearing Impaired, 1995-96. Recipient Gold award United Way Am., 1984, Silver award, 1984, 85, 87, Spl. Recognition award, 1985, Second Century Initiative award, 1988, 90, 90, 91, 1st Pl. award UPI, 1975, 1st Pl. award Women's Press Club Ind., 1976, 77, 78, 79, 83, Edn. award Am. Lupus Soc., 1981, Diamond award Nashville Advt. Fedn., 1984, 86, 87, 88, 89, Merit award, 1984, 87, 88, 1st Pl. award 7th Dist. Advt. Fedn., 1984, Merit award Nashville chpt. Pub. Rels. Soc. Am., 1988, numerous others. Mem. ASCAP, Soc. Profl. Journalists, N.Am. Assn. Ventriloquists.

SEAB, CHARLES GREGORY, astrophysicist; b. Ft. Benning, Ga., May 26, 1950; s. James A. and Ruby (Jones) S.; m. Peggy R. McConnell, May 9, 1979; 1 child, Jenna R. McConnell-Seab. BS in Physics, La. State U., 1971, MS in Physics, 1974; PhD in Astrophysics, U. Colo., 1982. Engring. analyst, programmer Mid. South Svcs., New Orleans, 1974-77; NRC rsch. assoc. NASA Ames Rsch. Ctr., Mountain View, Calif., 1983-85; rsch. scientist U. Calif., Berkeley, 1985, Va. Inst. Theoretical Astronomy, Charlottesville, 1985-87; vis. asst. prof. U. New Orleans, 1987-89, asst. prof., 1989-91, assoc. prof. astrophysics, 1991-96; prof., 1996—; bd. dirs. Freeport McMoran Obs., New Orleans, 1991—. Author: Astronomy, 1994; contbr. articles to profl. jours., chpts. to books. Capt. USAR, 1971-80. Nat. Merit scholar, 1967-71. Mem. Am. Astron. Soc., Pontchartrain Astronomy Soc., Phi Kappa Phi. Office: U New Orleans Physics Dept Lakefront New Orleans LA 70148

SEABOLT, JAMES DAVIDSON, statistical writer; b. Greensboro, N.C., Oct. 27, 1956; s. Jasper Gibbs Jr. and Helen Sarah (Beogetter) S.; m. Mary Lauren White, Sept. 15, 1984. BA, N.C. State U., 1977, M of Econs., 1979, PhD, 1990. Staff economist N.C. Pub. Staff, Raleigh, 1980-81; statis. writer SAS Inst., Inc., Cary, N.C., 1990—. Contbr. articles to profl. jours. Capt. U.S. Army, 1982-86. Mem. Am. Econ. Assn., Atlantic Econ. Assn., Aikido Assn. Am. Republican. Methodist.

SEABOLT, PATRICIA ANN, peri-operative nurse; b. Richwood, W.Va., Mar. 11, 1955; d. Jack E. and Mildred Ruth (Cowger) S. BSN, Alderson-Broaddus Coll., 1977; MEd, W.Va. U., 1979; M in Nursing Adminstrn., U. S.C., 1987. Staff nurse med. unit W.Va. U. Hosp., Morgantown, 1977-78, staff nurse surgery, 1983-84, asst. nurse mgr., 1984-85; staff nurse ICU/CCU St. Francis Hosp., Charleston, W.Va., 1979-80, asst. dir., dir. staff devel., 1980-83; staff nurse surgery Richland Meml. Hosp., Columbia, S.C., 1985-87; grad. rsch. asst. U. S.C., Columbia, 1986-87; nurse mgr. surgery Charleston Area Med. Ctr., 1987-88; dir. nursing and surg. svcs. Spartanburg (S.C.) Regional Med. Ctr., 1988-90; dir. surg. svcs. St. Joseph Hosp., Lexington, Ky., 1990-93; operational dir. oper. rm. svcs. U. Ky. Med. Ctr., Lexington, 1993—. Mem. Ky. Soc. Post-Anesthesia Nurses, Assn. Oper. Rm. Nurses, Sigma Theta Tau. Republican. Baptist. Office: U Ky Chandler Med Ctr Oper Rm Svcs 800 Rose St Lexington KY 40514

SEAHOLM, MEGAN, history educator, historian; b. New Orleans, Sept. 26, 1949; d. Leonard Howard and Ruth Margaret (Thomas) S.; m. Gregory John Cantrell, June 28, 1980; 1 child, Ellen Seaholm Cantrell. BA, Austin Coll., 1971; MA, Yale U., 1973; PhD, Rice U., 1988. Dir. clinic svcs. Planned Parenthood, Austin, 1978-80; rsch. assoc. The Handbook of Tex., Galveston and Austin, 1986-89; rsch. assoc. Centennial History Project U. Tex. Med. Br., Galveston, 1986-89; lectr. U. Tex., Austin, 1990-96; summer faculty Coll. Bd./Advanced Placement Inst., Houston, Dallas, San Antonio, 1991-93. Author book revs. including Jour. So. History, Southwestern Quar., Social Sci. Quar., Med. Humanities Rev., Annals of Sci. Mem. citizen's adv. bd. to Austin Ind. Sch. Dist. Bd. Trustees, 1994-95; mem. Commn. on Status of Women, 1975-76; co-founder Austin Ctr. for Battered Women, 1986-77. Recipient Presdl. Recognition award Rice U., 1982-84, Capt. Septimus Longscope award for best paper in history Rice U., 1987-88, Best Paper in U.S. history award 1983 Southwestern Hist. Assn., 1983. Mem. AAUP, Am. Hist. Assn., So. Hist. Assn., So. Assn. Women's Historians, Nat. Women's Studies Assn., Nat. Women's Health Network, Nat. Abolition Rights Action League, Tex. Abolition Rights Action League, Amnesty Internat. Democrat. Unitarian. Home: 5409 Salem Hill Dr Austin TX 78745 Office: Univ Tex Garrison Hall Austin TX 78712

SEALE, JAMES LAWRENCE, JR., agricultural economics educator, international trade researcher; b. Memphis, Mar. 12, 1949; s. James Lawrence and Mary Helen (Keefe) S.; m. Colleen Welberry, Sept. 18, 1951. BA, U. Miss., 1972; postgrad., U. Chgo., 1978-79; PhD, Mich. State U., 1985. Agrl. vol. Peace Corps, Tondo, Zaire, 1973-75; agrl. advisor Harvard Inst. for Internat. Devel., Abyei, Sudan, 1978; specialist Mich. State U., Fayoum, Arab Republic of Egypt, 1980-83; asst. prof. agrl. econs. U. Fla., Gainesville, 1985-90, assoc. prof. agrl. econs., 1990-95, prof. agrl. econs., 1995—; vis. prof. U. Leicester (Eng.), 1992, 94, hon. vis. fellow dept. econs., 1995. Author: (with H. Theil and C.F. Chung) International Evidence on Consumption Patterns, 1989; contbr. articles to profl. jours. NIMH scholar U. Chgo., 1978-79; traveling scholar U. Mich., 1979; rsch. fellow Cairo U., 1980-83; McKethan-Matherly rsch. fellow, 1986-88, McKethan-Matherly sr. rsch. fellow, 1991-94. Mem. Am. Econs. Assn., Am. Agrl. Econs. Assn., Internat. Assn. Agrl. Economists, Econometrics Soc., Caribbean Agro-Econ. Soc., Internat. Agrl. Trade Rsch. Consortium, Gamma Sigma Delta. Episcopalian. Home: 1621 NW 65th St Gainesville FL 32605-4127 Office: U Fla Dept Food and Resource 1095 McCarty PO Box 110240 Gainesville FL 32611-0240

SEALE, JAMES MILLARD, religious organization administrator, clergyman; b. Middlesboro, Ky., Oct. 4, 1930; s. Albert Tyler and Edith Josephine (Buchanan) S.; m. Mary Dudley Harrod; children: William Alan, Ann Lynn Seale Hazelrigg. BA, Transylvania U., 1952; BD, Lexington Theol. Sem., 1955, MDiv, 1963, D Ministry, 1981. Ordained to ministry Christian Ch. (Disciples of Christ), 1951. Student pastor various Christian Chs., Ky., 1949-54; pastor 1st Christian Ch., Pikeville, Ky., 1954-58, Erlanger (Ky.) Christian Ch., 1958-61; sr. minister 1st Christian Ch., Mt. Sterling, Ky., 1961-70, Paris, Ky., 1978-82; stewardship sec. Gen. Office Christian Ch., Indpls., 1970-74; adminstr. Christian Ch. Home of Louisville, 1974-77; dir. devel. Christian Ch. Homes Ky., Louisville, 1978; pres. Disciples of Christ Hist. Soc., Nashville, 1983-95. Author: A Century of Faith and Caring, 1983, Forward From The Past, 1991; editor jour. Discipliana, 1983-92. Pres. Kiwanis Club, Pikeville, 1957, Mt. Sterling, 1963, lt. gov., Ctrl. Ky., 1965.

SEALS, GERALD, city manager; b. Columbia, S.C., Sept. 22, 1953; m. Kanet K. Seals. Student, U. S.C., U. Denver, So. Ill. U. City mgr. Glendale Heights, Ohio, Springfield, Ill., Corvallis, Oreg.; adminstr. Greenville County, S.C.; owner, cons. Strategic Alliances Mgmt. Group, Greenville. Author: Taming City Hall, 1995. Bd. dirs. Urban League. Mem. Rotary Internat. Home: 301 Sugar Creek Ln Greer SC 29650 Office: Greenville County Govt Ste 100 301 University Ridge Greenville SC 29601

SEALS, RYAN BROWN, electronics engineer; b. Coleman, Tex., July 23, 1920; s. William Harrison and Ocia Mae (Brown) S.; m. Mary Jo Taylor, Aug. 31, 1941 (div. Feb. 1942); m. Doris Jo Brown, Mar. 29, 1942 (div. Nov. 1961); 1 child, Sandra Jean Seals Harmes; m. Jeanette Ceil Meadows, July 28, 1967. BA, North Tex. Agrl. Coll./Tex. A&M, 1941; BS in Physics and Math., Daniel Baker Coll., 1952; postgrad. So. Meth. U., Tex. Christian U., U. So. Miss., 1953-78. Cert. flight instr. Asst. chief engr. KNET Radio, 1941-42; asst. head electronics tng. Kelly Field, San Antonio, 1942-44; chief engr. KSTA Radio, Coleman, 1947-52; design engr. through project dir. Collins Radio Co., Dallas, 1952-71; cons. electronics, Dallas, Austin (Tex.), Los Angeles, 1972; systems engr., program mgr. Litton Data Systems div., Pascagoula, Miss., 1972-81, sr. staff engr., 1981-87, cons., 1987-92, chief engr. svc. industries, 1992—; instr. Jackson County Jr. Coll., Gautier, Miss., 1972-80. Adviser, Elec. Ectronics Sch., Jackson County Jr. Coll., 1972-86; chief check pilot CAP Squadron Group 3 Miss., 1973-79. Served with USN, 1944-46. Mem. IEEE (sr.), Aircraft Owners and Pilots Assn., Exptl. Aircraft Assn. (chpt. founder, pres. 1980-83, 91, tech. counselor, flight advisor), Internat. Aerobatics Club (chpt. founder, pres. 1979-85, profl. air show pilot, bd. dirs.). Presbyterian. Home and Office: Air Park Estates 6320 Lockheed St Plano TX 75093-6511

SEAMANS, ANDREW CHARLES, editorial and public relations consultant, columnist, author; b. Hillside, N.J., Sept. 10, 1937; s. Thomas Randall and Marie Josephine (Mazur) S.; m. Marion Gloria Lufbery, Aug. 25, 1956 (div. June 1986); children: Andrew Charles, Darryl Wayne, Marion Gloria Seamans Raynor, Dawn Louise Seamans Wheeler. AS cum laude, No. Va. Community Coll., Annandale, 1989. Lic. real estate salesman, Va. Editorial writer U.S. Press Assn., McLean, Va., 1968-70; pub. rels. asst. Nat. Right to Work Com., Washington, 1970; assoc. editor Human Events, Washington, 1970-81; mng. editor Heritage Features Syndicate, Washington, 1981-91; syndicated columnist The Answer Man Creators Syndicate, L.A., 1985—; chief copy editor The Hill Newspaper, Washington, 1996—; bd. dirs., pub. rels. cons. Marine Learning Inst., St. Louis, 1980—. Author: Who, What, When, Where, Why In the World of American History, 1991, Who, What, When, Where, Why In the World of World History, 1991, Who, What, When, Where, Why In the World of Nature, 1992; co-author: Whose FBI?, 1974. Bd. dirs. McLean Little League Baseball, Inc., 1975-83, pres., 1982-83; pres. Rahway (N.J.) Young Rep. Club, 1964-66; chmn. platform com. Union County Young Reps., N.J. Young Reps., various other Rep. orgns. Recipient cert. of appreciation McLean Little League Baseball, 1978, named to Hall of Fame, 1985. Mem. Pub. Rels. Soc. Am., Soc. Profl. Journalists (bd. dirs. D.C. chpt. 1986-87, membership dir. 1986-87, 89-90, dir. pub. info. 1988), No. Va. Assn. Historians, Va. Hist. Soc., Internat. Platform Assn., Nat. Press Club. Episcopalian. Home and Office: Horizon House #603 1300 S Army-Navy Dr Arlington VA 22202

SEANOR, TIMOTHY CRAIG, children's program administrator; b. Dallas, July 26, 1956; s. Edward Raymond and Mary Katherin (Meacham) S.; m. Tammy S. Blaylock, June 26, 1982; children: Zachariah, Sarah. BA, Union U., 1978; MA of Religion Edn., Southwestern Bapt. Theol. Sem., 1980. Min. of edn. Chamberlain Ave. Bapt. Ch., Chattanooga, 1980-81; assoc. editor Probe mag. Brotherhood Commn., Memphis, 1982-83, editor Pioneer mag., 1984-87; dir. Royal Amb. Edn. Dept., Chattanooga, 1987-92; dir. children/Royal Amb., 1992—. Author: Pioneer Adventure Series (Albert McClellen award 1986), Lad Mag., Royal Amb. Leaders Mag., Pioneer Probe Mag., Royal Amb. Campcraft Series; editor mags. Mem. Bapt. Pub. Rels. Assn., So. Bapt. Religious Assn., Ednl. Press Assn. Home: 410 Kingridge Dr Collierville TN 38017-1716 Office: Brotherhood Commn 1548 Poplar Ave Memphis TN 38104-2432

SEAR, MOREY LEONARD, federal judge, educator; b. New Orleans, Feb. 26, 1929; s. William and Yetty (Streiffer) S.; m. Lee Edrehi, May 26, 1951; children: William Sear II, Jane Lee. J.D., Tulane U., 1950. Bar: La. 1950. Asst. dist. atty. Parish Orleans, 1952-55; individual practice law Stahl & Sear, New Orleans, 1955-71; spl. counsel New Orleans Aviation Bd., 1956-60; magistrate U.S. Dist. Ct. (ea. dist.) La., 1971-76, judge, 1976—, chief judge, 1992—; judge Temp. Emergency Ct. of Appeals, 1982-87; adj. prof. Tulane U. Coll. Law; former chmn. com. on adminstrn. of bankruptcy sys., former chmn. adv. com. on bankruptcy rules, former mem. com. on adminstrn. of fed. magistrate sys. Jud. Conf. U.S.; former mem. Jud. Conf. of U.S. and Its Exec. Com.; mem. cir. coun. 5th Cir. of U.S.; founding dir. River Oaks Pvt. Psychiat. Hosp., 1968. Pres. Congregation Temple Sinai, 1977-79; bd. govs. Tulane Med. Ctr., 1977—; former chmn. Tulane Med. Ctr. Hosp. and Clinic, 1980-85. Mem. ABA, La. Bar Assn., New Orleans Bar Assn., Order of Barristers, Order of the Coif (hon.). Office: US Dist Ct C-256 US Courthouse 500 Camp St New Orleans LA 70130-3313

SEARCY, CHRIS JACKSON, obstetrician, gynecologist; b. Enterprise, Ala., Jan. 14, 1953; s. Alfred Houston and Kathryn (Jackson) S.; m. Manera Anne Saloom, Aug. 17, 1974; children: Mary Kathryn, Chris Jackson, Houston Farris. BS, Birmingham-So. Coll., 1975; MD, U. Ala., 1979. Diplomate Am. Bd. Obstetrics and Gynecology. Resident in ob-gyn. U. Ala. Med. Ctr., Birmingham, 1983; pvt. practice specializing in ob-gyn. Columbus, Miss., 1983-86, Riverside Clinic, Jacksonville, Fla., 1986-91; pvt. practice specializing in ob.-gyn. Azalea City Physicians for Women, Mobile, Ala., 1992-93; chief svc. Ob-Gyn. Prime Health, 1993—; clin. asst. prof. ob/gyn U. South Ala., 1994—. Fellow Am. Coll. Ob-Gyn.; mem. AMA, Am. Fertility Soc., Med. Assn. State of Ala., Med. Soc. Mobile County, Mobile Young Physicians Assn., South Ctrl. Ob-Gyn. Soc., Charles E. Flowers Soc. Republican. Episcopalian. Home and Office: 1400 University Blvd S Ste E Mobile AL 36609-7874

SEARCY, LAURA FISCHER, pediatric nurse practitioner; b. Woodhaven, N.Y., Sept. 1, 1954; d. Gustave George and Margaret Joan (Ward) Fischer; m. Alvis I. Searcy, July 9, 1977; children: Brian Devin, Kevin Alan, Kristen Lauren. BS in Nursing, U. Fla., 1976; M in Nursing with honors, Emory U., 1991. cert. pediatric nurse practitioner. Participant grad. nurse internship program Variety Children's Hosp., Miami, 1976-77; staff nurse pediatric intensive care Shands Teaching Hosp., Gainesville, Fla., 1977-78; from Level I to Level II staff nurse various intensive care units Egleston Hosp. Emory U., 1978-81; rsch. nurse dermatology divsn. dept. medicine Emory U., 1981-82; childbith educator Better Birth Found., 1984-86; level III nurse Crawford Long Hosp., Atlanta, 1986-91; pediatric nurse practitioner Emory U. Sch. Medicine, Atlanta, 1991-93, Cobb Pediatrics, Austell, Ga., 1991—; cons. Dowell Elem. Sch. PTA, Sch. Wide Bicycle Safety Edn. Program Rocky Mount Elem. Sch., 1990. Coun. mem. legis. advocacy Nursing, Child Health Edn., Spl. Edn. Issues, 1990—; selected Leadership Cobb Class of 1995-96; vocalist, soloist St. Anne's Ch., 1985-93; classroom and clinic vol., founder, co-chair spl. edn. com. Rocky Mountain Elem. Sch. PTA, 1991, 91-92, 93-94, coord. parent reading tutors program, 1993-94; facilitator Parent to Parent Program, 1992—; mem. Ga. Supporters of the Gifted, 1990—, hospitality chair, 1991-92, legis. chair, 1994-95; dir. music St. Olivers Ch., 1982-84; mem. Cobb County Sch. Bd., 1996. Named Mabel Hamrick scholar, 1990. Mem. Ga. Nurses Assn. (mem. Spkrs.' Bur., state-wide lobbying coord., prescriptive authority coalition, mem. sch. health com. 1991—), Nat. Assn. Pediatric Nurse Assocs. and Practitioners (pres.-elect Ga. chpt. 1991-92, pres. 1992-93, legis. chair 1993—, nat. legis. com. 1993—, grantee Nurse in Washington Internship 1993), Southeastern Regional Nursing Rsch. Soc., Cobb Area Pediatrics Soc., Sigma Theta Tau (scholar 1990), Zeta Tau Alpha. Home: 3666 Heatherwood Dr Marietta GA 30066-4679 Office: Cobb Pediatrics 3911 Mulkey Way Austell GA 30001-1102

SEARCY, MARY LOUISE, private duty nursing assistant; b. Memphis, Tenn., June 15, 1940; d. James and Margaret Louise (Patton) Deese; m. Louis Edward Lemenze, Apr. 7, 1956 (div. Feb. 1960); children: Connie Sue Lemenze Warren, Louis Edward Lemenze, Jr.; m. William Howard S., Oct. 17, 1961 (dec. Dec. 1986). Grad., Dyersburg H.S., 1956. Cert. Nursing Asst. Cashier various grocery & retail stores, Memphis, 1968-1981; sales auditor diamond and gift store, Memphis, 1982-90; pvt. duty nursing asst. various agencies, Memphis, 1989—. Author: Goodbye My Love, 1993. Volunteer: Am. Red Cross, U.S. Navy Hosp., Millington, Tenn., 1991-92, Women's Shelter, Memphis, 1992; nursing advisor, Methodist church, Dyersburg, Tenn., 1990-93, church sec., Dyersburg, 1987-1993. Cert. of Recognition for Leadership, Meth. Ch., Dyersburg, 1984. Republican. Methodist. Home: 6407 Ricks Pl Arlington TN 38002

SEARLES, DAVID SEWALL, JR., real estate executive; b. Detroit, Aug. 5, 1946; s. David Sewall and Beverly P. (Jones) S.; m. Susan Mondoro, Mar. 21, 1968; children: David S. III, Kenneth Devereux, Philip Edward. BA, U. South Fla., 1968; MBA, Harvard U., 1970. Research asst. Harvard Bus. Sch., Boston, 1970-71; v.p. fin. United Resources, Inc., Miami, Fla., 1973-75; pres. Canterbury Realty Co., Atlanta, 1975—, Chase Properties Assocs., LLC, Atlanta, 1977—; CEO, CRT Trust Advisors, Inc., 1990—; v.p. Royal Chase, Inc., Atlanta, 1983—; ltd. ptnr. Tempo Chase Assocs., L.P., Atlanta, 1983—; gen. ptnr. Willeo 120 Investment, LLC, Atlanta, 1984—, Royal Chase Investment Co., Atlanta, 1985—; gen. ptnr., CEO River Oak Holdings, Inc., Atlanta, 1986—; CEO CRT Asset Mgmt., Inc. and Flagship Net Solutions, LLC, Atlanta, 1990—, 1996—. Lector Holy Innocents Episcopal Ch. Mem. SAR, Internat. Order St. Luke the Physician, Appalachian Trail Conf. (life), Horseshoe Bend Country Club. Home: 5030 Nesbit Ferry Ln Atlanta GA 30350-1116 Office: CRT Trust Advisors Inc 400 Embassy Row NE Ste 500 Atlanta GA 30328-1667

SEARLES, JOHN RUMNEY, JR., retired city planner and developer; b. Detroit, Oct. 14, 1912; s. John Rumney Searles and Elisabeth Quincy Sewall; m. Leota Johnson, July 3, 1943; children: Elisabeth, John Rumney III, James Catlin. AB, Princeton U., 1934; MA, Wayne State U., 1940. Rsch. asst. Detroit Bur. Govt. Rsch., 1937-40; asst. to dir. urban redevel. HHFA, Washington, 1946-51; exec. dir. D.C. Redevel. Land Agy., Washington, 1951-62; exec. v.p. Met. Devel. Assn., Syracuse, N.Y., 1962-77; dir. devel. Sutton Real Estate Co., Syracuse, 1977-79; cons. Jacksonville Beach (Fla.) Redevel. Agy., 1980-84; exec. dir. St. Johns Co. Redevel. Agy., St. Augustine, Fla., 1991. Chmn. Vicars Landing Life Care Facility, Ponte Vedra Beach, Fla., 1981-85; mem. Onandaga County (N.Y.) Planning Bd., mem., 1962-79, chmn., 1978-79; mem. site com. St. John's County Libr., St. Augustine, Fla., 1986-92; mem. St. John's County Redevel. Com., 1986-88; mem. infrastructure study com. Jacksonville Cmty. Coun., 1987, mem. garbage study com., 1989; mem. steering com. Fla. Sesquicentennial, 1994. With U.S. Army, 1941-46, PTO. Recipient Rockefeller Pub. Svc. award Princeton U., 1956, Disting. Svc. award City of Washington, 1962. Mem. Nat. Assn. Housing and Redevel. Ofcls. (pres. 1958, Disting. Svc. award 1962), Sawgrass Property Owners Assn. (pres. 1987), Princeton Class of 1934 (Outstanding Achievement award 1971), Ponte Vedra Inn and Club. Home: 44 N Tifton Way Ponte Vedra Beach FL 32082-3319

SEARLES, PAUL DAVID, historian; b. Bangor, Maine, Jan. 1, 1933; s. Paul Joseph and Frances (Colby) S.; m. Mary Sinclair LAwson, June 23, 1956; children: Rachel, Richard, John. BA, Yale U., 1955, MAT, 1970; PhD, U. Ky., 1993; LLD (hon.), U. New Haven, 1976. Mktg. exec. Procter & Gamble, Cin., 1958-62; mktg. cons. Glendinning Cos., Westport, Conn., 1962-69; tchr. high sch. Westport Sch. Bd., 1969-71; peace corps country dir. U.S. Govt., Manila, Philippines, 1971-74; peace corps regional dir. U.S. Govt., Washington, 1974-76; dept. chmn. Nat Endowment for the Arts, Washington, 1976-80; bus. exec. various cos., 1980-90; historian pvt. practice, Owensboro, Ky., 1990—. Author: A College For Appalachia: Alice Lloyd on Caney Creek, 1995, The Peace Corps Experience: Challenge and Change, 1969-76. V.p. Owensboro Symphony Orch., 1990—; trustee 1st Presbyn. Ch., Owensboro, 1994—. 1st lt. USMC, 1955-58. Recipient Golden Harvest award Philippine Govt., 1974. Home and Office: 1907 Littlewood Dr Owensboro KY 42301-4690

SEARS, EDWARD L., English language educator; b. Pratt, Kans., Jan. 27, 1954; s. Melvin Leroy and Deloris Fay (Owens) S. BA in English, West Tex. State U., 1990; MA in English, Tex. Tech. U., 1993. Firefighter Dodge City (Kans.) Fire Dept., 1981-83, Amarillo (Tex.) Fire Dept., 1983-86; tutor Writing Ctr. West Tex. State U., Canyon, 1987-90; tutor Writing Ctr. Tex. Tech. U., Lubbock, 1990-92, tchg. asst., 1990-92; asst. prof. of English South Plains Coll., Levelland, Tex., 1992—; coord. computer-assisted writing South Plains Coll., Levelland, 1995—, mem. technology task force, 1994-95. Ssgt. USAF, 1977-81. Democrat. Office: South Plains Coll 1401 College Ave Levelland TX 79336

SEARS, GORDON MORTIMER, public relations consultant; b. Bristol, Tenn., June 25, 1923; s. Harold Mortimer and Kythe Carlisle (McClellan) S.; m. Mabel Cecilia Waddell, Aug. 28, 1948; children: Kythe Lee, Patricia Gordon, Elizabeth Baker. BA in Journalism, Emory U., 1943. With United Press, 1947-51; account exec. Carl Byoir & Assocs., N.Y.C., 1952-60; pub. rels. dir. Kern County Land Co., San Francisco, 1960-64; v.p. Pacific T.J. Ross and Assocs., San Francisco, 1964-68; exec. v.p. T.J. Ross and Assocs., N.Y.C., 1969-71, pres., 1971-78, chmn., CEO, 1978-86; chmn. Douglas G. Hearle & Assoc., N.Y.C., 1987-89; cons. Columbia, S.C., 1991—; bd. dirs. Roper Ctr. for Pub. Opinion Rsch., Storrs, Conn. Capt. USMC, 1942-52. Mem. Soc. Profl. Journalists, Pub. Rels. Soc. Am., Sertoma Internat., Media Club (Columbia), Kappa Alpha, Omicron Delta Kappa. Republican. Anglican. Home: 317 Park Shore Dr E Columbia SC 29223-6020

SEARS, LESLIE RAY, III, electrical engineer; b. Shirley, Mass., July 26, 1952; s. Leslie Ray Jr. and Claire Lavina (Sanders) S.; m. Vickie Jean Ray, Nov. 20, 1976; children: Valorie Michelle, Rachel Elisabeth, Katie Lynn. BSEE, Carnegie Mellon U., 1974; MBA, U. Utah, 1978. Registered profl. engr., Okla. Prin. engr. II Halliburton Energy Svcs., Duncan, Okla., 1982—. Patentee in field. Capt. U.S. Army, 1974-82. Mem. IEEE, Okla. Home-Based Bus. Assn. (dir., exec. bd. 1986-90). Republican. Presbyterian. Home: 2027 Stoneridge Ln Duncan OK 73533 Office: 2600 S 2d St Duncan OK 73536

SEARS, RALPH WESTGATE, mayor; b. Grand Island, Nebr., Oct. 8, 1922; s. Mark P. and Alma Elizabeth (Westgate) S.; m. Marcia Janis Mockett, June 19, 1948; children: Steven Ralph, Sara Joan Sears Belcher, Randall Jane Sears Rosenberg. BS, U. Nebr., 1948; postgrad., U. So. Calif., 1949-51. Mem. staff Sta. KOLN-Radio, Lincoln, Nebr., 1947-48, Sta. KUSC-Radio, L.A., 1949-51, Sta. KUOA-Radio, Tuscaloosa, Ala., 1951-52; dir. pub. rels. U. Montevallo, Ala., 1956-74; owner Sears Properties, Montevallo, 1980-96; asst. prof. Ala. Coll., Montevallo, 1948-56; pres., owner Sta. WBYE-Radio, Calera, Ala., 1959-84; pres., pub. Shelby County Reporter, Columbiana, Ala., 1967-84. Mem. Montevallo City Coun., 1956-72; mayor City of Montevallo, 1972—; chmn. bd. dirs. Shelby Youth Attention Home; mem. adv. com. Salvation Army, Shelby County. 1st sgt. U.S. Army, 1942-45. Mem. Montevallo C. of C. (past pres., Outstanding Civic Leader award 1982). *Died Feb. 14, 1996.*

SEARS, ROBERT STEPHEN, finance educator; b. Odessa, Tex., May 27, 1950; s. William Bethel and Leola Vernon (Little) S.; Reva Dana Flournoy, Aug. 17, 1973; children: Matthew Stephen, Elizabeth Rea. AAS, Odessa Jr. Coll., 1970; BA summa cum laude, Tex. Tech. U., 1973, MS, 1976; PhD, U. N.C., 1980. Supr. Bethel Enterprises, Odessa, Tex., 1973-74; tchg. asst. Tex. Tech. U., Lubbock, 1974-76, Lubbock Bankers Assn. prof., dir. Inst. Banking and Fin. Studies, 1988—; tchg. asst. U. N.C., Chapel Hill, 1976-79; asst. prof. U. Ill., Champaign, 1979-85, assoc. prof., 1985-88; rsch. prof. Bur. Econ. and Bus., Champaign, 1984; cons. Cameron Brown Mortgage Co., Raleigh, N.C., 1978-80, Howard Savings Bank, Livingston, N.J., 1980; asset mgr., trustee, pvt. investors, 1984—. Author: Investment Management, 1993, (chpt), Modern Real Estate, 1980, 84; assoc. editor Rev. of Bus. Studies, 1989-95, Jour. of Fin. Rsch., 1990-96, Internat. Jour. of Bus., 1995—; contbr. articles to profl. jours. Chmn. fin. com. Temple Bapt. Ch., Champaign, Ill., 1982, bd. deacons, 1982-88, chmn. deacons, lay leader, 1983; Sunday sch. tchr. Carrboro (N.C.) Bapt. Ch., 1977-79; bd. deacons Ind. Ave. Bapt. Ch., Lubbock, 1989—, Sunday sch. tchr., 1991-92, master design com., 1993—; trustee All Saints Episcopal Sch., 1995—. Rsch. grantee Cameron Brown Mortgage Co., Raleigh, N.C., 1978-80, U. Ill, Champaign, 1980-84, 86-87, Investors in Bus. Edn., Champaign, 1980-81, 84. Mem. Am. Fin. Assn., Southwestern Fin. Assn. (pres. 1989-90, v.p., program chmn. 1988-89, sec., treas. 1986-88, bd. dirs. 1984-86, mem. program com. 1985-86, 89—), Fin. Mgmt. Assn. (mem. program com. 1986, 89-94), So. Fin. Assn. (mem. program com. 1986), Western Fin. Assn. (mem. program com. 1986), Ea. Fin. Assn., Lake Ridge Country Club. Republican. Baptist. Office: Tex Tech U COBA PO Box 4320 Lubbock TX 79409-4320

SEARS, WILLIAM JOHN, physiologist; b. Oskaloosa, Iowa, Apr. 13, 1931; m. Orpha Mae Fisk, Sept. 9, 1953; children: Michael, Cheryl, John, Patricia. BS in Zoology, Iowa State U., 1957; MS in Physiology, U. So. Calif., 1966, PhD in Physiology, 1968. Commd. 2d lt. USAF, 1957, advanced through grades to col., 1981; physiol. tng. officer USAF, March AFB, Calif., 1958-61; chief physiol. tng. USAF, Carswell AFB, Tex., 1961-64; grad. instr. U. So. Calif., L.A., 1964-68; chief test facilities br. USAF Sch. Aerospace Medicine, Brooks AFB, Tex., 1968-73, chief crew protection br., 1975-81; exch. officer in physiology Royal Airforce Inst. Aviation Medicine, Farnsborough, U.K., 1973-75; dir. bioenviron. engring. S.W. Rsch. Inst., San Antonio, 1981-82; sr. scientist Tech. Inc., San Antonio, 1982-83; pres. Aerospace Assocs., Inc., San Antonio, 1983—; cons., lectr., presenter in field; mil. cons. in aerospace physiology USAF Surgeon Gen.; sci. advisor in aerospace physiology resident postdoctoral program AFSC Nat. Coun. Contbr. articles, guest referee to profl. publs.; patentee in field. Decorated Legion of Merit. Fellow Aerospace Med. Assn. (Fred A. Hitchcock award for excellence in aerospace physiology); mem. Aerospace Physiologists Soc. of Aerospace Med. Assn., Sci. Rsch. Soc. N.Am., Human Factors Soc., Air Force Assn. (1st Place Sci. award), Ret. Officers Assn., Sigma Xi. Home: 309 Driftwind Dr San Antonio TX 78239-2410

SEAY, BILLY MACK, psychology educator; b. Bismarck, Ark., Nov. 4, 1938; s. Franklin Whitfield and Annie Mildred (Money) S.; m. Nedra Ann Dees, Mar. 7, 1959; children: Delecia Susanne Seay Carey, Franklin Whitfield. BA, So. Ark. U., 1960; MS, U. Wis., 1962, PhD, 1964. From instr. to assoc. prof. psychology La. State U., Baton Rouge, 1964-75, prof., 1975—, dir. honors divsn., 1981-92, dean honors coll., 1992—. Author: Development of Behavior, 1978; contbr. articles to profl. jours. Fellow Woodrow Wilson Found., 1960. Mem. Nat. Collegiate Honors Coun., So. Regional Honors Coun., La. Collegiate Honors Coun. Baptist. Home: 756 Castle Kirk Dr Baton Rouge LA 70808 Office: La State U 201 Honors Ctr Baton Rouge LA 70803

SEAY, CHARLES FRANK, III, educator, systems analyst; b. Austin, Tex., Oct. 19, 1948; s. Charles Frank Jr. and Emily Ann (Moore) S.; m. Joan Stewart, Oct. 13, 1978; children: Charles IV, Michael James, Christine Caldwell. BA, Princeton U., 1971; ThM, Dallas Theol. Sem., 1975; MA, U. Texas at Dallas, 1991, postgrad., 1991—. Tchr. Believers Chapel, Dallas, 1977-84; pastor Grace Cmty. Ch., Lancaster, Tex., 1984-89; sys. analyst, product mgr. Seay Systems, Dallas, 1989—; bd. dirs. Gleaners Internat., Dallas. Presbyterian. Home: 746 Mill Creek Rd Lancaster TX 75146

SEBASTIAN, MICHAEL JAMES, retired manufacturing company executive; b. Chgo., July 8, 1930; s. Michael and Larraine (DeAmicis) S.; m. Sally Ervin, Nov. 29, 1953; children: Michael, Mark, Lisa. B.S. in M.E., Santa Clara U., 1952; A.M.P., Harvard U., 1972. Div. mgr. FMC Corp, Indpls., 1953-77; pres. Rotek, Aurora, Ohio, 1977-78; v.p. Gardner-Denver, Dallas, 1978-79; group pres. Cooper Industries, Dallas, 1979-81; v.p. Cooper Industries, Houston, 1981-82, exec. v.p., 1982—; bd. dirs. Cooper Cameron Corp., Quanex Corp., Gardner Denver Machinery, Inc. Past dir. Weatherford Internat.; mem. adv. bd. U. Houston Ctr. Pub. Policy. Mem. Lakeside Country Club (Houston). Republican. Roman Catholic. Home: 11511 Shadow Way Houston TX 77024-5216 Office: Cooper Industries Inc Ste 5800 600 Travis Houston TX 77210-4446

SEBREN, LUCILLE GRIGGS, retired private school educator; b. Chesterfield, S.C., May 21, 1922; d. Manley Oscar and Clara Blanche (Rivers) Griggs; m. Herbert Lee Sebren, Dec. 19, 1943; children: Herbert Lee Jr., George Hall, Samuel Robert Franklin. BA, Flora Macdonald Coll., Red Springs, N.C., 1942; MEd, Coll. of William and Mary, 1966. Cert. tchr., Va., N.C., S.C. Tchr. Cheraw (S.C.) Elem. Sch., 1942-44; tchr. kindergarten Larchmont Meth. Ch., Norfolk, Va., 1951-53; tchr. Norfolk Acad., 1953-89, supr., cons., adminstr. primary dept., 1970-89, master tchr., cons. elem. grades, 1970-89, asst. to dir. of admissions, 1987—. Contbr. articles to profl. jours. Mem. Va. Symphony and Symphony Aux., Norfolk, 1946—, Norfolk Soc. Arts, 1970—, Chrysler Mus., Norfolk, 1965—, Va. Opera Assn., Norfolk, 1974—; pres. Philanthropic Ednl. Orgn., 1993—. Recipient Disting. Svc. award Norfolk Acad., 1991. Mem. AAUW (sec. exec. bd. 1974-76), Joie de Vivre (treas. 1994—), Old Dominion U. Faculty Wives Club (pres. 1958-60), Town-N-Gown (bd. dirs. 1992—, chaplain 1993—, v.p. 1995-96, pres.-elect 1996-97), Nat. Cathedral Assn., Alpha Delta Kappa Internat. (pres., past state, provincial, nat. pres. 1995—, pres. Va. 1978-80, S.E. region 1981-83, internat. grand chaplain 1983-85, internat. grand pres.-elect 1985-87, internat. grand pres. 1987-89, internat. exec. bd. 1985-91, pres.-elect internat. past state pres. 1993-95, pres. 1995—), Kappa Delta Pi. Republican. Baptist. Office: Norfolk Acad 1585 Wesleyan Dr Norfolk VA 23502-5512

SEBRING, MARJORIE MARIE ALLISON, former home furnishings company executive; Burnsville, N.C., Oct. 8, 1926; d. James William and Mary Will (Ramsey) Allison Shockey; student Mars Hill Coll., 1943, Home Decorators Sch. Design, N.Y.C., 1948, Wayne State U., 1953; cert. home furnishings rep. U. Va., 1982; 1 child, Patricia Louise Banner Krohn. Dir. decorating div. Robinson Furniture, Detroit, 1949-57; head buyer Tyner Hi-Way House, Ypsilanti, Mich., 1957-63; head buyer Town and Country, Dearborn, Mich., 1963-66; instr. Nat. Carpet Inst., 1963-71; owner Adams House, Inc., Plymouth, Mich., 1966-72; exec. v.p. mktg. and sales, regional sales and mktg. mgr. Triangle Industries, L.A., 1972-89; co-owner Markham-Sebring, Inc., St. Petersburg, Fla., 1983-89; dir. contract div. Kane Furniture, 1984-85; co-owner Accessories, Etc., 1985-89; chmn. bd. Heritage Lakes, U.S. Home. Vol. coord. Pasco County Clerk Ct., Suncoast Theatre; mem adv. bd. Webster Coll; charter mem. Presdl. Task Force; pres. Presbyn. Ch. Seven Springs; bd. dirs. Fla. Health and Human Svc.; chmn. bd. dirs. Two Westminster Condominium Assn., Inc. Recipient nat. sales awards, recognition for work with youth and aged; named to Fla. Finest list by Fla. Gov., 1994. Mem. Internat. Home Furnishings Assn., Fla. Home Furnishings Rep. Assn. (officer), Am. Security Coun. (coun.), Williamsburg Found., USCG Aux., Nat. Audubon Soc., Internat. Platform Assn. Republican. Contbr. creative display to Better Homes and Gardens, 1957-64. Home: 4902 Cathedral Ct New Port Richey FL 34655-1486

SECREST, JAMES SEATON, SR., lawyer; b. Middletown, Ky., Dec. 9, 1930; s. Elmer S. and Linney (Witherbee) S.; m. Mary Sue Corum, Sept. 2, 1950; children: James Seaton, Lynne Suzanne. J.D., U. Louisville, 1954. Bar: Ky. 1954. Ptnr. Goad & Secrest, Scottsville, Ky., 1955-62; sole practice, 1962-77; ptnr. Secrest & Secrest, Scottsville, 1977—. City judge pro tem Scottsville, 1955-58; judge Allen County, 1958-61; city atty. Scottsville, 1962-66; atty. Allen County, 1966-89, dep. judge/exec., 1990—; bd. dirs. Barren River Area Devel. Dist., 1970—, mem. regional bd. ethics; bd. dirs. Transfinancial Bank of Scottsville. Mem. Scottsville C. of C. (pres. 1962), Ky. County Attorneys Assn. (pres. 1973), Ky. Assn. Counties (bd. dirs. 1985-86), ABA, Ky. Bar Assn. Republican. Methodist. Club: Rotary (pres. 1960). Home: 10055 New Glasgow Rd Scottsville KY 42164-9534 Office: Secrest & Secrest PO Box 35 210 W Main St Scottsville KY 42164-0035

SECULAR, SIDNEY, federal agency administrator, procurement analyst; b. N.Y.C., Dec. 20, 1940; s. Benjamin and Mollie (Stern) S.; m. Mildred Lucille Vance, Nov. 1, 1969. BA, SUNY, Stony Brook, 1962. Cert. high sch. tchr. Contract asst. U.S. Army, Bklyn., 1962-66; contract specialist USN, Washington, 1966-67, FDA, Washington, 1967-68; contracting officer Dept. Justice, Washington, 1968-81; procurement ctr. rep., counselor to small bus. SBA, Washington, 1986—; mem. consumer bd. Giant Food Corp., WSSC Water Utility; freelance resume writer Silver Spring, Md., 1985-86, 89—; weather forecaster Washington Weatherline, Bethesda, Md., 1982-91, Comprehensive Weather Svcs., 1982-85, Bell Atlantic Telephone Co., 1991—. Activist Citizens to Preserve Old Silver Spring, 1981—, East Silver Spring Citizens Assn., 1981—; vice chmn. Md. Libertarian Party, 1977-78. With U.S. Army, 1963-69. Recipient performance and suggestion awards U.S. DEA and SBA. Mem. Am. Soc. Pub. Adminstrn., Nat. Contract Mgmt. Assn., Am. Meteorol. Soc., Am. Numis. Assn., Area Small and Disadvantaged Bus. Coun., Ctr. Hiking Club (trails dir. 1975), Masons. Home: 740 Silver Spring Ave Silver Spring MD 20910-4661 Office: US SBA Code SBA Arlington VA 22245-5200

SEDLAK, JEFFREY MICHAEL, electrical engineer, career officer; b. Meadville, Pa., Sept. 2, 1958; s. Michael Raymond and Norma Jean (Monnin) S.; m. Cheryl Ann Lind, May 21, 1983; 1 child, Heather Nicole. BS in Elec. Engring., Grove City (Pa.) Coll., 1980; MS in Elec. Engring., Air Force Inst. Tech., 1987. Commd. 2d lt. USAF, 1976, advanced through grades to maj., 1991; fgn. telecom. system analyst Fgn. Tech. Divsn./TQCS, Wright-Patterson AFB, Ohio, 1980-84; computer resources staff engr. Hdqs. Air Force Logistic Command/MMEC, Wright-Patterson AFB, 1984-85; tactical weapon systems analyst Hdqs. USAF/SAGF, Pentagon, Va., 1987-91; chief missile analysis 83d Fighter Weapon Squadron/ADM, Tyndall AFB, Fla., 1991-93; dir. analysis 83d Fighter Weapon Squadron/AD, Tyndall AFB, 1993-94; dep. divsn. chief Def. Info. Sys. Agy./JIEO/JEKN/The Pentagon, Washington, 1994-95, divsn. chief, 1995-96, comdr., global command and control sys. Europe, 1996—; cons. EON Enterprises, Dayton, Ohio, 1987-91. Author: Aircraft to Perform Combat Air Support, 1988, Lasers for Airbase Defense, 1990. Teamworker Polk Christian Educators, Slippery Rock, Pa., 1980; active Officer's Christian Fellowship, Wright-Patterson AFB, 1980-85; counselor Boy Scouts Am., Ft. Lee, Va., 1988; divsn. keyworker Air Force Assistance Fund, Pentagon, 1989; activities dir. Hispanic Heritage Com., Pentagon, 1990; judge Panama City (Fla.) Sci. Fair, 1993. Decorated Air Force Achievement medal, Nat. Def. Svc. medal, Air Force Commendation medal. Mem. Tyndall Officer's Club, Tyndall Yacht Club, Delta Iota Kappa. Office: Def Info Sys Agy JIEO/JEKB The Pentagon Rm BG645 Washington DC 20330

SEDWITZ, JOSEPH LEE, surgeon, gynecologist; b. Youngstown, Ohio, Nov. 15, 1923; s. Samuel Harold and Alice (Brunswick) S.; m. Barbara Beresfort Britton, Sept. 27, 1957; children: Keith Britton, Alicia Leigh. MD, U. Va., 1951. Diplomate Am. Bd. Surgery. Intern George Washington U. Hosp., 1951-55; resident N.J. Naval Hosp., San Diego, 1956-58; pvt. practice surgery Wake Med. Ctr., Raleigh, N.C., 1961—; clin. prof. surgery East Carolina U. Sch. Medicine, Greenville, N.C., 1987—, N.C. U. Sch. Medicine, Chapel Hill, 1996—. Co-author: Surgical History, 1994. Served as comdr. USN, 1956-61. Fellow ACS. Office: Wendell Zebulon Surg Clin 321 Hospital Rd Zebulon NC 27597-2551

SEE, FRENCH AUGUSTUS, farmer, banker; b. Adrian, W. Va., Jan. 15, 1908; s. Clarence Lee and Myrtle (Alverda) S.; m. Hazel Tilder, Dec. 25, 1940; children: Thomas French, Edward James. Student bus., W. Va. Wesleyan Coll., 1930-34; student banking, Buckhannon & Clarksburg Coll., 1934-36; student, Reppert Sch. Auctioneering, Decatur, Ind., 1939. Farming Family Farm, French Creek, W. Va., 1918-30; banker Bank of Adrian (became Adrian Buckhannon Bank), Adrian, Buckhannon, W. Va., 1927-49; builder, organizer, mgr. Buckhannon Livestock Auction Mkt., 1936-46;

banker Union Trust Co., Balt., 1945-47; mgr. Farmer's Livestock Auction Mkt., Winchester, Va., 1947-52; owner, organizer, pres. Va. Livestock Auction Mkt., Winchester, 1956-65; owner, organizer Culpepper (Va.) Livestock Auction Mkt., 1960-75, Marshall (Va.) Livestock Auctin Mkt., 1960-65; stockholder, pres. Balt. Livestock Auction Mkt., 1956-95; bd. dirs. Adrian-Buckhannon (W.Va.) Bank, First Cmty. Banks; livestock cons., Va., W.Va., Md., 1964—. Mem. adv. com. Shenandoah U., Winchester, 1986—; elder, clk. of session French Creek Presbyn. Ch., 1932-46; deacon 1st Presbyn. Ch., Winchester, 1970-85. With U.S. Army, 1942. 4-H scholar (state champion corn grower), 1924. Mem. Emeritus Club W. Va. Wesleyan Coll., Masons, Blue Lodge, Shriners, Am. Legion. Republican.

SEEGERS, GERALD E., recreation facility executive; b. 1933. Grad., Valparaiso U., 1954. From acct. to audit supr. Arthur Andersen & Co., 1956-74; fin. officer Sullair Corp., 1974-77, Dedelow Inc., 1977-78, Tyler Refrigeration, 1978-80, Waste Mgmt., Inc., 1980-92; vice chmn. bd. Discovery Zone, Inc., Fort Lauderdale, Fla., 1992—. Office: Discovery Zone Inc 110 E Broward Blvd Fl 23 Fort Lauderdale FL 33301-3503

SEELEY, DAVID WILLIAM, minister; b. Des Moines, May 21, 1944; s. William Amos S. and Margaret Rose (Owens) Young; m. Janet Kay Hill, Mar. 14, 1964; children: John David, Karen Anne. BA cum laude, Lincoln Christian Coll., 1972; MA, Lincoln Christian Seminary, 1973; postgrad., U. South Fla., 1973-74, Fla. Atlanta U., 1975; BS, Am. Inst. Holistic Theology, 1994, MS, 1995, PhD, 1996. Ordained 1976; cert. pastorial counseling, Liberty Baptist Coll., Lynchberg, Va.; cert. natural health care practitioner Sarasota (Fla.) Sch. Natural Healing Arts, 1992; cert. cranio sacral therapy Upledger Inst., Palm Beach Gardens, Fla., 1992; cert. fin. independence cons., Ill. Asst. mgr. Regal Svc. Station, San Jose, Calif., 1965-66; dep. sheriff Santa Clara County Sheriff's Dept., San Jose, 1966-69; minister Allerton (Ill.) Christian Ch., 1969-70, Arm Prairie (Ill.) Christian Ch., 1970-72, Edgewood (Ill.) Christian Ch., 1972-73; guidance counselor Alva (Fla.) Middle Sch., 1973-76; pres. Good News of Christ, Inc., Englewood, Fla., 1978—; minister Northside Christian Ch. of Christ, Englewood, 1976—; cons. Custom Ch. Book Svc., Orlando, Fla., 1993-94. Contbr. articles to religious publs.; author/pub. newsletters. Mem. Englewood Boosters Club, 1985—. Mem. Englewood Ministerial Assn. (sec. 1978-80), Suncoast Christian Ministers Assn. (pres. 1977-79), Lincoln Christian Coll. Alumni Assn., Southwest Fla. Christian Men's Fellowship, Club Nautico. Republican. Office: Northside Christian Ch of Christ 685 N Indiana Ave Englewood FL 34223-2705

SEELIGSON, MOLLY FULTON, educational consultant; b. Dallas, Sept. 4, 1942; d. Bernard L. and Helen (Smith) Fulton; m. John M. Seeligson, Nov. 26, 1965; 1 child, Michael Bernard. BS, So. Meth. U., 1964. Cert. tchr., Tex. Pvt. tutor Dallas, 1957-71; co-founder, bd. dirs., administr. Clear Spring Sch., Eureka Springs, Ark., 1974-93, exec. dir., 1993-95; bd. dirs. Eureka Springs Child Devel. Ctr., 1975-78, Legacy, Inc., Dallas, First Eureka Springs Bank; founding bd. The Wellness Ctr., 1994; designer La Poynor Ednl. Project, La Rue, Tex.; cons. in field. Author, pub. Sidereal Almanac, 1987—. V.p. Hist. Dist. Mchts. Assn., Eureka Springs, 1972-73. Office: Clear Spring Sch PO Box 142 Eureka Springs AR 72632-0142

SEELIN, JUDITH LEE, rehabilitation specialist; b. Bklyn., Feb. 22, 1941; d. Sidney and Helene Agnes (Minkowitz) S.; m. Mel Schwartz, Sept. 30, 1965 (div. 1983); children: Jeffrey, Robin; m. Arnold Seelin, Oct. 16, 1983. AAS, SUNY, Farmingdale, 1972; BSN, SUNY, Stony Brook, 1973. CRRN, CIRS, CCM. Staff nurse surg. unit L.I. Jewish Med. Ctr., New Hyde Park, N.Y., 1962-67; DON Home Health Aids, Inc., Hempstead, N.Y., 1973-78, Able Home Health Care, Wantagh, N.Y., 1978-84; nursing adminstr. Aides at Home, Inc., Hicksville, N.Y., 1984-86; asst. ADON Savana Cay Manor, Port Saint Lucie, Fla., 1986; Fla. state supr. CCM, Hollywood, Fla., 1987-93; med. team leader Resource Opportunities, Fort Lauderdale, Fla., 1993-95; ind. med. case mgr., 1993-95; W.C. resource nurse Humana Health Care Plan, Mirama, Fla., 1995—; spkr. Am. Inst. Med. Law; adv. bd. mem. Whithal, Boca Raton. Mem. AARN, CMSA. Home: 14090 Fair Isle Dr Delray Beach FL 33446-3395

SEFCIK, JAMES FRANCIS, museum director; b. Troy, N.Y., Jan. 1, 1943; s. Zigmond Adam and Sophie Claire (Konieczny) S.; children: James F. Jr., Jonathan A.; m. Beverly Ann Hansen, May 29, 1982. BS, St. Joseph's Coll., Phila., 1964; MA, Temple U., 1967; postgrad., U. Notre Dame, 1965-69. Asst. prof. history Gannon Coll., Erie, Pa., 1969-74; sr. curator history N.Y. State Mus., Albany, 1974-78, dir. mus. ops., 1978-81; dir. pub. rels. and devel. Chrysler Mus., Norfolk, Va., 1981-84; asst. dir. State Hist. Soc. Wis., Madison, 1984-88; dir. La. State Mus., New Orleans, 1988—; adj. prof. Russell Sage Coll., Troy, 1978-81; vis. prof. Pa. State U., Behrend, spring 1972, Landis Valley Farm Mus., Lancaster, Pa., summer 1975; cons. N.Y. state Am. Revolution Bicenntennial, Albany, 1975-76; Gov.'s designee N.W. Ordinance Bicentennial, 1986-87; chair cultural projects La. Commn. on French Revolution, New Orleans, 1988. Contbr. articles to profl. jours. Wis. rep. Nat. Com. Bicentennial Celebration, 1986-87; appointee French Quarter Festival Com., Mayor City of New Orleans, 1988-94; spl. host Rep. Nat. Conv., New Orleans, 1988. U. Notre Dame fellow, 1968; Gannon Coll. rsch. grantee. Mem. Am. Assn. Mus., Am. Assn. State and Local History (audit com. 1994), La. Assn. Mus. (coun. 1989-94). Office: Louisiana State Museum PO Box 2448 New Orleans LA 70176-2448

SEFCIK, JOHN DELBERT, financial services executive; b. Temple, Tex., Jan. 21, 1921; s. John J. and Annie (Chaloupka) S.; m. Norma Marie Kuzel, May 22, 1942 (div. Sept. 1985); children: John D. Jr., Camille Freitas; m. Christine Gajdica Goodlett, Dec. 13, 1987. Student, Temple Jr. Coll., 1938-39; acctg. grad., Four C. Bus. Coll., 1948-50; A in Mgmt., Brewster Coll., 1956-59; student, So. Meth. U., 1958-70; grad., Civil Def. Staff Coll., Assn. Logistics Ex Sch., Command & Gen. Staff Coll., Indsl. Coll. Armed Forces, Arty. and Civil Affairs Mil. Govt. Sch. Cert. Army logistician. Placement mgr., tax auditor Tex. Employment Commn., 1945-51; with Phoenix Life Ins. Co., 1951-53; mktg. and dist. mgr. Armour Pharm. Co., Inc., 1953-86; regional mgr. ins. and investments, real estate broker Primerica Fin. Svcs., 1987-96. Bd. dirs., gen. chmn. 1st Dallas Mil. Ball, 1965, past pres., 1992-93, mem. to date. Master sgt. U.S. Army, 1940-45; col. USAR, 1948-78. Decorated Legion of Merit, Bronze Star. Mem. 102d Inf. Divsn. Assn. (life, pres., v.p., bd. dirs. , reunion gen. chmn. 1983-89), Res. Officers Assn. (life, nat. chmn. civil preparedness com. 1989-94, numerous other coms., Brigade of Vols., Wall of Gold, Waco chpt. pres. 1951-53, Dallas chpt. pres. 1963-65, Army Tex. dept. v.p. 1963-67, 90th divsn. arty. chpt. pres. 1965-66, pres. 1967-68, Tex. dept. nat. councilman 1968-69, Tex. ROA Conv. Gen. chmn. 1981), Mil. Order World Wars (life), Am. Legion (life), Ret. Officers Assn. (life), 2d INF Indian Head Divsn. Assn., KC (4th degree, Sir Knight Abram J. Ryan Assembly Coun. No 799).

SEGAL, EDWIN S., anthropology educator; b. Troy, N.Y., Nov. 15, 1940; s. Joseph and Bessie (Katz) S.; m. Marcia Deanne Texler, Dec. 23, 1962; children: Shoshanna Abra, Marta Stephanie. BA in Social Sci., Harpur Coll., 1962; MA in Anthropology, Ind. U., 1965, PhD in Anthropology, 1970. Rsch. asst. human rels. area files Ind. U., 1964, rsch. asst. to prof. Peter B. Hammond, 1964, teaching asst., 1964-65, teaching assoc., 1965-66; instr. in anthropology U. Louisville, 1966-70, asst. prof. anthropology, 1970-74, assoc. prof., 1974-81, prof., 1981—; prof. sociology U. Malawi, 1983-85; active numerous coms. U. Louisville; ednl. cons. Urban Edn. Ctr., Louisville, 1971-74; chairperson dept. anthropology U. Louisville, 1971-74, 78-81; adj. curator for anthropology Louisville Mus. History and Sci., 1978-90; bd. dirs. Ind. Consortium for Internat. Programs, U. Louisville rep., 1980-81, 86—, exec. com. 1987—, editor ICIP Bulletin, 1987—; vis. scholar Inst. Social and Econ. Rsch., Rhodes U., Grahamstown, S. Africa, 1992, dept. sociology U. Nairobi, Kenya, 1993. Book reviewer The African Book Publ. Record, Oxford, Eng., 1985—; manuscript reviewer Holt, Rinehart and Winston, 1987—; article referee Jour. Urban Affairs, 1987—; contbr. articles to profl. jours. Systems cons. Jewish Community Fedn., 1987-89; data systems cons. Louisville Youth Orch., 1987-93. Recipinet Fulbright Sr. Lectureship award, 1983-85; grantee U. Louisville, 1988, Ctr. for Sci. Devel., Pretoria, S. Africa, 1992, U. S. Dept. Edn., 1993. Office: U Louisville Dept Anthropology Louisville KY 40292

SEGALL, JAMES ARNOLD, lawyer; b. Columbus, Ohio, Aug. 19, 1956; s. Arthur and Greta Helene (Cohen) S.; m. Janice Faye Wiesen, Mar. 14, 1981; children: Gayle Helene, Aryn Michelle, Craig Lawrence. BA, Coll. of William and Mary, 1978; JD, Washington and Lee U., 1981. Bar: Va. 1981, U.S. Dist. Ct. (ea. dist.) Va. 1981. Assoc. Phelps & King P.C., Newport News, Va., 1981-84, Buxton & Lasris P.C., Yorktown, Va., 1984-85; sole practice Newport News, 1985-89; pres. James A. Segall & Assocs., 1990-91, James A. Segall & Assocs., P.C., 1991-92, Segall & Moody, Newport News, 1992—; lectr. Hampton Roads Regional Acad. Criminal Justice, 1986-89. Bd. dirs. ct.-apptd. Spl. Adv. Program, Newport News, 1986-87, Hamton-Newport News Cmty. Svcs. Bd., 1993—, treas., 1995-96, vice-chair, 1996—; participant coop. office edn. program Newport News Pub. Schs., 1987-90; lectr. vol. programs 7th Dist. Ct. Svc. Unit, 1986-89; active City Newport News Cable TV Adv. Commn., 1990-93, Newport News Dem. City Com., 1990-91; bd. dirs. Rodef Sholom Temple, 1992-94, United Jewish Commun. the Va. Peninsula, Inc., 1990—, chmn. spl. activities and fundraising com., 1990-91, chmn. bylaws com., 1992-93, 95—, campaign coun., 1995—, cmty. rels. coun., 1995—. Mem. ATLA, Newport News Bar Assn., Va. Trial Lawyers Assn., Va. Coll. Criminal Def., Kiwanis, B'nai B'rith (pres. 1989-91), Ruritan (sec. 1985-87), Moose. Home: 306 Dogwood Dr Newport News VA 23606-3728 Office: Segall & Moody 525 Oyster Point Rd Newport News VA 23602-6919

SEGARS, JOHN KELVIN, minister; b. Carnesville, Ga., Aug. 20, 1935; s. Erastus Earl and Octie Irene (Payne) S.; m. Reba Nell Williamson, Nov. 6, 1954; children: Karen Failyer, Jackie Wheat. BTh, Internat. Sem., 1984, ThM, 1984, ThD, 1988, DD, 1985. Ordained to ministry So. Bapt. Conv., 1967. Pastor East Side Bapt. Ch., Winder, Ga., 1967-71, Beacon Height Bapt. Ch., Madison, Ga., 1971-79, Bethlehem (Ga.) First Bapt., 1980-85, Edwards Chapel Bapt., Athens, Ga., 1985—; team leader mission trip to Indian reservation, Fla., 1984; Liberia, 1988, Republic of Panama, 1991, 93, 95; mem. exec. com. Ga. Bapt. Conv., 1972-77, tchr. edn. ext. classes, 1991-92; with tour of Israel, other countries, 1974; pres. Mins.' Conf., 1988; elected preacher various ann. associational meetings. Author: Pneumatologh, 1989. Chaplain Barrow County Jail, 1968-71; bd. dirs. Assn. Youth Camp, 1972-75; chmn. Area Aging Program, Athens, 1983-84, Sr. Citizen Adv. Com., Madison, 1975-78, Winder, 1983. Named Citizen of Month Hi-Y Club, Morgan County, 1979. Mem. Morgan County Bapt. Assn. (moderator 1974-76), Applachee Bapt. Assn. (fin. com. chmn. 1984-85, moderator 1983-85), Sarepta Bapt. Assn. (moderator 1989, personnel com. chmn. 1991), Masons (chaplain 1976-79). Office: Edwards Chapel Bapt Ch 105 Timothy Pl Athens GA 30606-4427

SEHRING, ADOLF, artist, sculptor; b. Urupinsk, Russia, June 8, 1930; came to the U.S., 1949; s. George Henry M. and Clair (Burstin) S.; married, 1992; children: Oliver, Nina, Marc. Student, Acad. Fine Arts, Germany, 1946-49. Pres. A. Sehring Studio Inc., Orange, Va., 1970—, Am. Artist Portfolio Inc., Orange, 1987—; lectr. in field, 1970—. Commd. by the Vatican to paint the ofcl. portrait of Pope John Paul II; works collected in Chrysler Mus., Am. Embassy, Stockholm, Bayly Mus., Victoria and Albert Mus.; represented in 30 galleries. Served with U.S. Army, 1951-53, Korea. Decorated 14 combat medals; recipient Stalin medal for art, 1937, Rias award, 1946; commd. to sculpt Pocahontas bronze, Town of Gloucester, Va., bronze in collection of Pres. Bush. Home: Tetley Plantation Tetley Dr Somerset VA 22972 Office: A Sehring Studio Tetley Plantation Somerset VA 22972

SEIB, BILLIE MCGHEE RUSHING, nursing administrator, consultant; b. Brookport, Ill., Mar. 4; d. Frank and Ila (Paris) McGhee; m. Alfred Rushing, Jan. 2, 1958 (dec.); children: Lisa, Libbi; m. Bob Seib, Mar. 21, 1986. Diploma, DePaul Sch. Nursing, St. Louis, 1947; postgrad. in oper. rm. nursing, Washington U., St. Louis, 1950. Dir. operating room Jennie Stuart Med. Ctr., Hopkinsville, Ky.; clin. mgr. operating room Meml. Med. Ctr., Savannah, Ga.; mgr. operating room Meth. Med. Ctr., Oak Ridge, Tenn.; coord. operating room Parkwest Hosp., Knoxville, Tenn.; mem. oper. rm. pool Ft. Sanders Park West Hosp., Knoxville, 1992-93; geriatric supr. BHCC, Oak Ridge, Tenn., 1993-96; geriatric supervisor Windwood Health Care, Clinton, Tenn., 1996—; cons. Washington, Fla., Ky., Nev. Mem. Assn. Oper. Rm. Nurses (cert., bd. dirs., past pres. East Tenn. chpt.). Home: 133 Lakeview Hills Ln Clinton TN 37716-5957

SEIBEL, HUGO RUDOLF, anatomist, university dean; b. Radautz, Rumania, Nov. 9, 1937; came to U.S. 1952; s. Hugo Josef and Berta (Gertel) S.; m. Edith Edeltrud Kramer, June 14, 1964. BS, Bklyn. Coll., 1960; PhD, U. Rochester, 1967. Coll. sci. asst. Bklyn. Coll., 1960-62; asst. prof. anatomy Med. Coll. Va., Richmond, 1967-70, assoc. prof. anatomy, 1970-75, prof. anatomy, 1975—, curriculum coord., 1976-87, asst. dean medicine, 1984-87, assoc. dean medicine, 1987—. Author: Barron's How to Prepare for the MCAT's, 1976, Essentials of Histology, 1972; contbr. over 130 articles to profl. jours. Recipient Disting. Univ. Tchg. award Va. Commonwealth U., 1988. Mem. AAUP, Am. Assn. Anatomists, Soc. Exptl. Biology and Medicine, Va. Acad. Sci. (co-chair and chair), Sigma Xi (pres.). Office: Med Coll Va Box 565 1101 E Marshall St Richmond VA 23298-5008

SEIBERT, BARBARA ANN WELCH, school librarian; b. Hagerstown, Md., Mar. 31, 1949; d. William Ridings and Betty Louise (Timmons) Welch Clipp; m. Paul Alan Seibert, Aug. 22, 1970; children: Paul Matthew, Gretchen Elizabeth. AA, Hagerstown Jr. Coll., 1969; BS, Shepherd Coll., Shepherdstown, W.Va., 1971; MEd, Tex. A&M U., 1972. Cert. preK-12 libr., 7-12 bus. edn. tchr., Va. Instr. Lynchburg (Va.) Coll., 1980-83, Ctrl. Va C.C., Lynchburg, 1983-85; libr. James River Day Sch., Lynchburg, 1985—. Mem. Lynchburg Pub. Libr. Bd., 1989-92. Mem. ALA, Va. Libr. Assn., Piedmont Area Reading Coun., Va. Reading Assn. (young readers com. 1993—). Home: 3720 Otter Pl Lynchburg VA 24503-3206 Office: James River Day Sch 5039 Boonsboro Rd Lynchburg VA 24503-1801

SEIDMAN, STEPHEN BENJAMIN, computer science educator; b. N.Y.C., Apr. 13, 1944; s. Sylvan and Anne (Levine) S.; m. Barbara Heidemarie Koppe, Aug. 24, 1969; children: Miriam, Naomi. BS, CCNY, 1964; AM, U. Mich., 1965, PhD, 1969. Asst. prof. math. NYU, 1969-72; asst. prof. math. George Mason U., Fairfax, Va., 1972-76, assoc. prof. math., 1976-84, prof. computer sci., 1984-90; prof., dept. head computer sci., engring. Auburn (Ala.) U., 1990-96; prof., chair dept. computer sci. Colo. State U., Ft. Collins, 1996—. Author: Assembly Language programming in Compass, 1987. Mem. IEEE Computer Soc., Assn. for Computing Machinery.

SEIFER, RONALD LESLIE, psychologist; b. Liberty, N.Y., Oct. 23, 1942; s. Leon and Pearl (Treibitz) S.; m. Gail Sandra Eagerman, May 29, 1967; children—David Marc, Robert Eric. BA, Queens Coll., 1964; MA, Northeastern U., 1967; PhD, U. Maine, 1971. Lic. psychologist, Fla., N.Y. Intern psychologist Albert Einstein Coll. Medicine, Bronx, N.Y., 1968-69; psychologist St. Vincent's Hosp., Harrison, N.Y., 1969-71; supervising psychologist Saratoga County Mental Health Ctr., Saratoga Springs, N.Y., 1971-76; psychologist Brevard County Mental Health Ctr., Melbourne, Fla., 1976-79; pvt. practice clin. psychology, Melbourne, 1978—; assoc. med. staff Holmes Regional Med. Ctr., Melbourne, 1979—; coord. TOP Soccer, Fla. Youth Soccer Assn., 1990—. Research fellow Northeastern U., 1964-66. Mem. Am. Psychol. Assn., Am. Soc. Clin. Hypnosis, Fla. Soc. Clin. Hypnosis (treas. 1985-88), N.Am. Soc. Psychology of Sport and Phys. Activity, Biofeedback Soc. Am., Brevard County Psychol. Assn. (pres. 1979-80). Avocations: gardening, fishing. Office: Melbourne Psychiatry 109 Silver Palm Ave Melbourne FL 32901-3125

SEIFERT, ALVIN RONALD, psychologist; b. Wheatland, Iowa, Oct. 22, 1941; s. Alvin A. and Gladys M. (Brinkman) S.; m. Julie Ann Hodgskin, Mar. 29, 1988; 1 child, Matthew Charles. BA, Iowa Wesleyan Coll., 1967; postgrad., Drake U., 1968-70; PhD, U. Tenn., 1975. Diplomate Am. Acad. Pain Mgmt.; cert. biofeedback profl. Asst. prof. Coll. Medicine U. South Fla., Tampa, 1974-88; psychologist VA Med. Ctr., Tampa, 1974-88; pvt. practice Tampa, 1981-88; psychologist Behavioral Inst. Atlanta, 1988—; cons. VA Rsch., Topeka, 1977, East Tenn. State U. Med. Sch., 1981, So. Saw Co., Atlanta, 1989-92. Editor: International Perspectives on Self-Regulation and Health, 1991, Clinical Applied Psychophysiology, 1994. With USN, 1960-64. Grantee Knoxville Children's Found., 1970-74; fellow Japan Soc. for Promotion of Sci., 1991. Mem. APA, AAAS, Assn. for Applied Psychophysiology and Biofeedback (Presdl. award 1992), Am. Psychol. Soc., Soc. for Behavioral Medicine, Soc. for Pscyhophysiol. Rsch. Office: Behavioral Inst Atlanta 5555 Peachtree Dunwoody Rd NE Atlanta GA 30342-1710

SEIFERT, PATRICIA CLARK, cardiac surgery nurse; b. Springfield, Mass., Apr. 4, 1945; d. Thomas W. and Kathleen E. (O'Malley) Clark; m. Gary F. Seifert, Sept. 10, 1966; children: Kristina S. Glenn, Philip A. BA in History, Trinity Coll., 1967; ADN, No. Va. Community Coll., 1976; MS in Nursing, Cath. U. Am., 1988. RN, Va., D.C.; cert. oper. rm. nurse, first asst. nurse. Head nurse cardiac surgery The Fairfax Hosp., Falls Church, Va., 1976-88; adminstrv. dir. The Wash. Hosp. Ctr., Washington, 1988-89; oper. rm. coord., cardiac surgery Arlington (Va.) Hosp., 1989—, Alexandria (Va.) Hosp., 1995—; lectr./cons. in field. Author: (books) Clinical Assessment Tools for Use with Nursing Diagnosis, 1989, Cardiac Surgery, 1994; contbr. chpts. to Alexander's Care of the Patient in Surgery, 10th rev. edit., 1995, Cardiovascular Nursing, 7th rev. edit., 1990, Perioperative Care Planning, 2d rev. edit., 1995, The RN First Assistant: An Expanded Perioperative Role, 2d rev. edit., 1992, Core Curriculum for the RN First Assistant, 2d rev. edit., 1994; contbr. articles to profl. jours. Mem. N.Am. Nurses Nursing Diagnosis Assn., Am. Heart Assn. Coun. on Cardiovasc. Nursing, Assn. Oper. Rm. Nurses (cert. perioperative nurse, RN 1st asst., nat. bd. dirs. 1994-98, pres. No. Va. chpt. 1994-95, numerous scholar awards, Nat. Pres.'s award 1992, nat. nominating com. 1991-93), Va. Nurse's Assn. (dist. 8 bd. dirs. 1987-91, Nurse of Yr. 1984), Sigma Theta (pres. Pes Eta Alpha chpt. 1990-92). Home: 6502 Overbrook St Falls Church VA 22043-1942 Office: 1701 N George Mason Dr Arlington VA 22205-3671

SEIGLER, RUTH QUEEN, college nursing administrator, educator, consultant, nurse; b. Conway, S.C., July 31, 1942; d. Charles Isaac and Berneta Mae (Weaks) Queen; m. Rallie Marshall Seigler, Sept. 1, 1963; children: Rallie Marshall Jr., Scot Monroe. ADN, Lander Coll., 1962; BSN, U. S.C., 1964, MSN, 1980. Pub. health nurse Richland County Health Dept., Columbia, S.C., 1964-66; dir. nurses Columbia Area Mental Health Ctr., 1966-69; program nurse specialist Midlands Health Dist., 1969-72; discharge planner Richland Meml. Hosp., 1972-73, clin. dir., 1973-75; exec. dir. S.C. State Bd. Nursing, 1976-83; v.p. nursing dept. Self Meml. Hosp., Greenwood, S.C., 1983-86; exec. dir. S.C. Commn. on Aging, Columbia, 1986-95; asst. dean Coll. Nursing U. S.C., Columbia, 1995-96, assoc. clin. prof., 1996—; bd. dirs. Queen Gas Co., Barnwell, S.C.; nurse cons. Creative Nursing Mgmt., Mpls., 1984—. Advisor: The Role of County Mental Health Nurse, 1971. Recipient Disting. Alumni award Lander Coll., 1978, career Woman recognition award Columbia YWCA, 1980, William S. Hall award S.C. Assn. Residential Care Homes, 1988, U. S.C. Coll. Nursing Disting. Alumni award, 1993, award for excellence S.C. League for Nursing, 1995, Svc. Recognition award S.C. AARP, 1995; named one of Ten Women of Achievement, S.C. March of Dimes, 1987. Mem. ANA, APHA, S.C. Nurses Assn. (sec. 1965-68, bd. dirs. 1986-88, Excellence award 1984, Recognition award 1984), S.C. Hosp. Assn., S.C. Gerontol. Soc., S.C. Nurses Found., S.C. Healthy People 2000 (vice chair), Partnership for Older South Carolinians (founder, chair bd. dirs.), Columbia Luncheon Club, S.C. Fedn. Older Ams., Evening Mission Action Group, Bd. Nursing Home Examiners, Pilot Club, Inc. (pres. 1988-89), Rotary Internat., Sigma Theta Tau. Presbyterian. Home: 2220 Bermuda Hills Rd Columbia SC 29223-6710 Office: U SC Coll Nursing Dept Adminstrv and Clin Nursing Columbia SC 29208

SELBER, ARLENE BORK, environmentalist; b. Jacksonville, Fla., June 24, 1942; d. Morris and Ethyl (Sigal) Bork; m. H. Joel Selber, Nov. 22, 1964 (div. 1982); children: Blair C., Robin A. BS, Tufts U., 1964; MBA, Jacksonville U., 1983. Internat. mktg. dir. Clow Corp., Jacksonville, 1984-85; dir. mktg. Haztech Inc., Atlanta, 1985-87; asst. v.p. Nuclear Assurance Corp., Atlanta, 1987-88; dir. bus. devel. Ecotek, Inc., Atlanta, 1988-90; v.p. bus. devel. Parsons Engring. Sci., Inc., Charlotte, N.C., 1990-95, Newport News (Va.) Nuclear, 1996—. Advisor, Adv. Com. for Internat. Trade, Sen. Paula Hawkins, Washington, 1984; mem. trade adv. coun. U.S. Dept. Commerce Environ. Techs. Mem. ASME (mixed waste com., vice chmn.), Am. Nuclear Soc., Hazardous Materials Control Resources Inst. (bd. dirs.), Women's Execs., Internat. Soc. for Decontamination and Decommissioning Profls., Laubach Tutor, Charlotte C. of C. (Far East task force 1983-84), High Mus., Jacksonville Track Club (bd. dirs. 1977-83), Women's Execs. Golf League.

SELBY, JOHN HORACE, surgeon; b. Springfield, Mass., Nov. 11, 1919; s. Howard Williams and Ethel (Wagg) S.; AB, Dartmouth Coll., 1941; MD, Boston U., 1944; postgrad. U. Pa., 1948; children by previous marriage: John H., Susan, Sherrill, Lucinda; m. 2d, Carolyn Symes, Feb. 14, 1970. Intern Mary Hitchcock Meml. Hosp., Hanover, N.H., 1944-45; resident New Eng. Deaconess Hosp., 1945-46, Portsmouth Naval Hosp., 1946-48, Mass. Meml. Hosp., 1949-50, Boston City Hosp., 1950-51 (all Boston), practice medicine, specializing in thoracic surgery, Lubbock, Tex., 1952—; chief thoracic surgery Meth. Hosp., Lubbock, 1964-73, 77-79, chief surgery, 1954-56, 64-65; chief of staff St. Mary's Hosp., Lubbock, 1973, chief surgery, 1970; chief surgery Univ. Hosp., 1973; active staff Meth. Hosp., St. Mary's, Health Scis. Center; dir. med. staff affairs Highland Hosp., 1986-92; hon. staff West Tex. Hosp.; cons. staff South Park Hosp., Meml., Seminole, Mercy, Slaton, Cook Meml., Levelland Hosps.; regional med. dir. Tex. Med. Found. Peer Rev. Orgn., 1986-94; med. dir. HMI, Inc, 1986-93; mem. med. care adv. com. Tex. Dept. Human Svcs., 1990-94, chmn. physician payment adv. com., 1991-94; chmn. bd. South Plains Health Systems, 1975-81; mem. Statewide Health Coordinating Coun., 1977-85, exec. com., 1979; clin. prof. surgery Tex. Tech. Med. Sch., 1975—; mem. adv. com. Lubbock County Hosp. Dist. Bd., 1979; trustee, med. dir. All Am. Security Life Ins. Co., 1954-55. Bd. dirs. Tex. Tb Assn., pres., 1967-68; bd. dirs. Lubbock Community Planning Council, 1954-56; chmn. adv. bd. Salvation Army, 1956-57; bd. dirs. Inst. for Internat. Rsch. and Devel.; bd. dirs. Lubbock Area Found., 1983—, treas., 1985. Diplomate Am. Bd. Thoracic Surgery, Am. Bd. Surgery. Fellow A.C.S., Am. Coll. Chest Physicians, Internat. Coll. Surgeons, Internat. Acad. Medicine, Southwestern Surg. Coll.; mem. So. Thoracic Surgery Assn., S.W. Surg. Conf., Am. Thoracic Soc., Tex. Trudeau Soc. (pres. 1959-60), Lubbock-Crosby-Garza County Med. Soc. (pres. 1984), Panhandle S-Plains Med. Soc., Tex. Med. Assn. (ho. of dels. 1979—, com. on health planning 1979-83, coun. on socioecons. 1983-90, chmn. 1985-90), AMA, Am. Cancer Soc. (dir. Tex. div. 1961-63), South Plains Heart Assn. (pres. 1957), Lubbock County Tb Assn. (pres. 1959-60, pres. South Plains Kidney Found. 1989—), Sigma Chi (Order Constantine 1994—). Club: Rotary Internat. (pres. Lubbock 1980-81, dist. gov.'s rep. 1981-82, gov. nominee 1982-83, gov. 1983-84, instr. nat. assembly 1985). Home: Park Tower 1617 27th St Lubbock TX 79405-1451 Office: 1500 Broadway Ste 1207 Lubbock TX 79401-3107

SELCH, ANDREA HELEN, English and American literature educator, writer; b. N.Y.C., May 9, 1964; d. Frederick Richard and Patricia Ann (Bakwin) S. AB, Duke U., Durham, N.C., 1986; MFA, U. N.C., Greensboro, 1990. Editor and columnist The N.C. Ind., Durham, 1986-89; tchr. continuing edn. Duke U., Durham, 1990-92, instr. English dept., 1992—. Contbr. poetry to numerous jours.

SELECMAN, CHARLES EDWARD, business executive; b. Dallas, Sept. 17, 1928; s. Frank A. and Eloise (Olive) S.; m. Nan Harton Nash, May 11, 1951 (div. 1975); children: Mary Lucinda, Nan Elizabeth, Amy Eloise; m. Judith Wallace Pollard, Feb. 6, 1976 (div. 1984); m. Barbara Ann Calvert, Apr. 18, 1985. B.A., So. Meth. U., 1951. Bus. mgmt. clk. Buick Motor div. Gen. Motor Corp., Dallas, 1951-52; pers. dept. Chance Vought Aircraft, Inc., Dallas, 1952-56; div. pers. mgr. U.S. Industries, Inc., Longview, Tex., 1956-64; div. v.p. mktg. U.S. Industries, Inc., 1964-66; div. exec. v.p. Axelson div. U.S. Industries, Inc., 1966-67, div. pres., 1967; corp. v.p. U.S. Industries, Inc., N.Y.C., 1967-68, corp. exec. v.p., dir., 1968-70, pres., 1970-73; vice chmn., CEO U.S. Industries, Inc., 1973-74, also dir.; pres., CEO E.T. Barwick Industries, Inc., 1975-78; ptnr. Marshalese Texas Partners, Dallas, 1978-83; chmn., pres., CEO Input/Output Inc., Houston, 1984-93, chmn., 1993—; dir. Triton Oil & Gas Corp., 1975-93. Mem. Soc. Exploration Geophysicists, Sigma Alpha Epsilon. Office: Input/Output Inc 12300 Parc Crest Dr Stafford TX 77477-2419

SELF, DONALD RAYMOND, marketing educator; b. Mercedes, Tex., Aug. 10, 1944; s. Raymond Ralph and Laura Neil (Drennan) S.; m. Mary Anne Shull, June 2, 1966 (div. Sept. 1987); children: Michelle Self Taylor; m. Robin Sunshine McCullin, Jan. 2, 1988. BA, U. Tex., 1965; MBA, Tex.

A&I U., 1970; DBA, La. Tech. U., 1977. Instr. Southwestern Tex. State U., San Marcos, 1970-72; from asst. to assoc. prof. Ga. Coll., Milledgeville, 1975-79; assoc. prof. Ga. So. Univ., Statesboro, 1979-85; prof. Auburn U., Montgomery, Ala., 1985—. Dir. Coun. on Substance Abuse, Ala., 1993—. Mem. Atlantic Mktg. Assn. (pres. 1989), Mid-South Mktg. Assn. (program chair 1995-96), Mu Kappa Tau, Pi Sigma Epsilon. Office: Auburn U 7700 University Dr Montgomery AL 36117

SELF, MARK EDWARD, communications consultant; b. Tyler, Tex., Dec. 6, 1955; s. Edward and Ruby (Rogers) S.; m. Dianne Logan; children: Patricia Bartlett, Marcile Christine. Student, Tenn. Tech. Sch., 1973-76. Gen. mgr. Gulf Telephone Inc., Beaumont, Tex., 1980-82; gen. sales mgr. CSC Telephone Inc., Tyler, Tex., 1982-83; v.p. sales Teleci Inc., Irving, Tex., 1983-85; cons. Self & Assocs., Grapevine, Tex., 1985—; pres. S&A Equipment Co., Grapevine, 1990—. Fundraiser Freedom Ride Found., Dallas, 1987. Named Outstanding Young Men of Am., 1985. Mem. Am. Hotel and Motel Assn., Nat. Office Machine Dealer Assn., Nat. Fedn. Ind. Bus., Dallas C. of C., Masons. Home: 3442 Spring Willow Dr Grapevine TX 76051-6516 Office: Self & Assocs 1006 Heather Dr Euless TX 76040-4424

SELIG, CAMDEN WOOD, associate athletic director; b. Chapel Hill, N.C., Mar. 29, 1961; s. Julian Wood and Elizabeth Camden Selig; m. Marie Ellen Miller. BA in Psychology, Washington and Lee U., 1983; MS in Sports Adminstrn., Ohio U., 1985; postgrad., U. Va. Adminstrv. asst. to athletic dir. Ohio U., Athens, 1984-85; asst. mktg. dir., dir. ticket ops. Va. Commonwealth U., Richmond, 1985-87; asst. to athletic dir. Va. Commonwealth U., Charlottesville, 1987-88; dir. sports promotions U. Va., Charlottesville, 1988-90, asst. athletic dir. mktg., promotions and corp. rels., 1990—. Vol. fundraiser Habitat for Humanity, 1992—. Home: 114 Harvest Dr Charlottesville VA 22903-4845 Office: U Va Athletics PO Box 3785 University Hall Charlottesville VA 22903

SELIG, OURY LEVY, financial consultant; b. Galveston, Tex., Sept. 24, 1924; s. Andrew Lionel and Freda (Schreiber) S.; m. Miriam Claire Pozmantier, Aug. 22, 1948; children: Michael, Debra, Madeline, James. BBA, U. Tex., 1949, postgrad., 1950; postgrad., U. Houston, 1953-56. Asst. bus. adminstr. of hosp. U. Tex. Med. Br., Galveston, 1952-54; acct. Port of Galveston, 1954-57, asst. auditor, 1957-64, asst. to gen. mgr., 1964-69, dir. fin. and adminstrn., 1966-74, dep. exec. dir., 1974-88. Author: (with E. Kalketenidou) Public Port Financing in the United States, 1994. Life mem. Bay Area coun. Boy Scouts Am., Galveston, 1963—; bd. dirs. Galveston County Jewish Welfare Assn., 1982-84; trustee Galveston Wharves. Sgt. USAF, 1943-46. Recipient Nehemiah Gitelson award, Alpha Epsilon Pi, 1948, Silver Beaver award Boy Scouts Am., 1968, Shofar award, Boy Scouts Am., 1968, Disting. Service award, Galveston Jaycees, 1968. Mem. Am. Assn. Port Auths. (chmn. fin. com. 1972-76, chmn. risk mgmt. com. 1981-85, vice chmn. task force on tax reform 1985-86, Important Svc. award 1987), Tex. Water Conservation Assn. (pres. 1979-80), Galveston Hist. Found., Friars Club. Democrat. Home and Office: 11 Colony Park Cir Galveston TX 77551-1737

SELIG, WILLIAM GEORGE, university official; b. Prince Rupert, B.C., Can., Sept. 25, 1938; s. George Oliver Selig and Minerva Junuetta (Brand) Goodale; m. Judith Margaret Sprague, June 20, 1964; children: Cheryl, Cynthia. BA, Cen. Washington State Coll., 1961, MA, 1968; CAGS, U. Mass., 1972, EdD, 1973. Tchr. Sharon (Mass.) High Sch., 1963-64, Hydaburg (Alaska) Grade Sch., 1964-65, W. Puyallup (Wash.) Jr. High Sch., 1966-69; dir. spl. edn. Northampton (Mass.) Schs., 1969-73, 1974-76; asst. prof. Westfield (Mass.) State Coll., 1973; dir. pupil svcs. Longmeadow (Mass.) Pub. Schs., 1976-80; prof. Regent U., Virginia Beach, Va., 1980-83, dean, prof., 1984-89, provost, 1989—; bd. dirs. Set Net, Virginia Beach; pres. Motivational Teaching Systems, Inc.; spl. edn. adv. bd. dirs. Virginia Beach Pub. Schs.; bd. trustees Klingberg Family Ctrs., New Britain, Conn., 1991—. Author: Training for Triumph, 1984, Loving Our Differences, 1989, Handbook of Individualized Strategies for Classroom Discipline, 1995. Episcopalian. Office: Regent University 1000 Regent University Dr Virginia Beach VA 23464-9803

SELIGSON, DAVID, orthopedic surgeon, educator; b. N.Y.C., Aug. 9, 1942. AB in Chemistry magna cum laude, Harvard U., 1964; MD, Duke U. Med. Sch., 1968. Diplomate Am. Bd. Orthopedics; lic. physican Mass., Vt., Ky., Ind. Intern and jr. surg. resident Harvard Surg. Svc./Boston City Hosp., 1968-70; resident Harvard U., 1973-76; pvt. practice orthopedics; asst. prof. orthopedic surgery U. Vt., Burlington, 1976-82, assoc. prof. orthopedic surgery, 1982-83; prof. dept. orthopedics U. Louisville, 1983—, vice chmn. orthopedics dept., 1992—; vis. prof. Mid-Ctrl. Orthopedic Soc., 1984, Monmouth Med. Ctr., N.J., 1987, Northwestern U., Evanston, Ill., 1993, Jamaica Hosp., L.I., 1993; speaker Ctrl. We. Orthopedic Assn., Brazil, 1993; lectr. in field. Edtl. bd. Jour. Orthopaedic Trauma, 1988—, Jour. Trauma, 1987—, Clin. Orthopaedics and Related Rsch., 1993—, Techniques in Orthopedics, 1986—, assoc. editor trauma, 1992; author: Concepts in External Fixation, 1982, Concepts in Intramedullary Nailing, 1985; contbr. numerous articles to profl. jours., chpts. in books. Lt. comdr. USNR, 1970-72. Grantee Eli Lilly Co., 1983, U. Louisville, 1984, OEC, 1984-85, OREF, 1984-85, USN, 1988—, others; recipient Edwin G. Bovill Rsch. award Orthopedic Trauma Assn., 1989, Sci. Exhibit Achievement award 84th Ann. Sci. Assembly, So. Med. Assn., 1990, Naval Achievement medal Trauma Mgmt. in Vietnam. Fellow ACS, Am. Acad. Orthopedic Surgeons; mem. Am. Assn. for Surgery of Trauma, Kuntscher Kreis Soc. (bd. dirs. 1994), Am. Assn. for Hand Surgery (grantee 1988-89), Orthopedic Trauma Assn. (chmn. bylaws com. 1990), Musculoskeletal Trauma Assn. (founding mem., pres. 1990-91), Health Vols. Overseas. Home: 1213 Old Cannons Ln Louisville KY 40207-4307 Office: U Louisville Dept Orthopedic Surgery Louisville KY 40292

SELKE, CHARLES RICHARD, lawyer, mediator, real estate professional; b. Houston, Dec. 10, 1947; s. Oscar Otto Jr. and Edith Hicks (Hardey) S.; children: Erin Hardey, Lindsay Broussard. BA, U. Tex., 1970, JD, 1972. Bar: Tex., 1972. Pvt. practive Houston, 1974-80; ptnr. Beich & Selke, Houston, 1980-81; sr. v.p., ptnr. The Murphree Co., Houston, 1982-86; sr. v.p. Lowe Enterprises, Inc., Houston, 1987-88, Trione & Gordon, Inc., Houston, 1986-90; exec. v.p. Interstate Realty Corp., Houston, 1990-92; trust mktg. officer No. Trust Bank of Tex., Houston, 1992-93; pres. C. Richard Selke, P.C., Houston, 1992—. Bd. dirs., The McClelland Found., Austin, Tex., 1980—; mem. Chapelwood United Meth. Ch. Mem. State Bar Tex., Houston Bar Assn., Breakfast Club Houston (pres. 1989), Briar Club (bd. dirs.). Office: C Richard Selke PC 3200 Southwest Fwy 33rd Fl Houston TX 77027-7526

SELKE, OSCAR O., JR., physiatrist, educator; b. Houston, Mar. 13, 1917; s. Oscar Otto and Orile Mollie (Medlenka) S.; m. Edith Hicks Hardey, July 10, 1943; children: Charles Richard, Carolyn Selke Brophy, Barbara Selke-Kern, Bruce Hardey. BA, U. Tex., 1938; MD, U. Tex., Galveston, 1941; postgrad., U. Pa., 1945-46. Diplomate Am. Bd. Phys. Medicine and Rehab. Intern, resident Hermann Hosp., Houston, chief phys. medicine and rehab., 1946-76, chief emeritus, 1977—, med. dir. sch. phys. therapy, 1947-65; mem. clin. faculty phys. medicine and rehab. Baylor U. Coll. of Medicine, 1950—, emeritus, 1985—; chief phys. medicine and rehab. Methodist Hosp., 1952-60, St. Luke's Hosp., 1953-63, Tex. Children's Hosp., 1953-63, Ctr. Pavilion Hosp., 1966-77, Park Plaza Hosp., 1975—; mem. clin. faculty phys. medicine and rehab. U. Tex. Post-grad. Sch. of Medicine, 1952-63, U. Tex. Med. Sch., Houston, 1972—; area cons. VA in Phys. Medicine and Rehab., 1950-66; med. adv. bd. United Cerebral Palsy of Tex., 1959-73, bd. dirs., 1967-70, Gulf Coast, 1971-74; bd. dirs. Harris County Cerebral Palsy Treatment Ctr., 1947-50, 68-71, pres., 1952, med. adv. bd., 1947-70; bd. dirs. Muscular Dystrophy Assn. Gulf Coast, pres., 1953; med. adv. bd. Muscular Dystropy Assn. Am., 1972-76; bd. dirs. Child Guidance Ctr. of Houston, 1949-55, Soc. Crippled Children and Adults, Houston, 1958-62; med. adv. bd. Harris County Muscular Dystrophy Assn., 1950-76, Harris County Multiple Sclerosis Soc., 1958-60, Am. Rehab. Found., 1961-66; mem. bd. Am. Registry of Phys. Therapists, 1957-71. Mem. editorial bd. Archives of Phys. Medicine and Rehab., 1957-72. Capt. USAF, 1942-45. Mem. AMA (residency rev. com. phys. medicine and rehab. 1970-75, past chmn. phys. medicine and rehab sect., Cert. of Appreciation 1975), Am. Assn. Electromyography and Electrodiagnosis, Am. Acad. Phys. Medicine and Rehab., Am. Congress Rehab. Medicine, Tex. Phys. Medicine and Rehab. Soc. (past pres.), Tex. State Med. Assn., Harris County Med. Assn., Houston Phys. Medicine and Rehab. Soc. (past pres.). Presbyterian. Home: 3646 Olympia Dr Houston TX 77019-3028

SELKE-KERN, BARBARA ELLEN, university official, writer; b. Houston, Dec. 14, 1950; d. Oscar Otto Jr. and Edith Hicks (Hardey) Selke; m. Homer Dale Kern, May 31, 1985. BS, U. Colo., 1973; MA, U. Tex., 1981, PhD, 1986. Cert. elem. and secondary tchr., Tex. Co-owner Colo. Sound, Denver, 1972-76; tchr. Jefferson County Schs., Lakewood, Colo., 1974-76; dir. Harvest Time Day Care Ctr., Austin, 1976-77; mgr. TourService, Inc., Austin, 1977-82; curriculum specialist U. Tex., Austin, 1982-87, ednl. resources coord., 1987-88, ednl. resources dir., 1988-92; coord. adult vocat. programs Austin (Tex.) C.C., 1992-94, coord. grant devel., 1994-95, exec. asst. to the pres., 1995—. Author (books): Retail Travel Marketing, 1983, Communication Skills, 1984, Orientation to Cosmetology Instructor Training, 1984, Resumes and Interviews, 1984, Competency in Teaching, 1985, Guidelines for the Texas Cosmetology Commission Instructor Licensing Examination, 1985, Effective Communication, 1986, Effective Teaching, 1986, Balancing the Curriculum for Marketing Education, 1987, Bulletin Board Designs for Marketing Education, 1987, Marketing Education I, 1988, Flashcards for Marketing Education, 1988, Glossary for Marketing Education, 1988, Validated Task Lists for Apparel And Accessories Marketing, 1991; co-author: Higher Level Thinking in Marketing Education, 1990; author (computer software): Emergency Aid, 1986, 2nd edit., 1989, Measuring Employee Productivity, 1986, Retail Pricing in Action, 1987, Marketing Fibers and Fabrics, 1989, Physical Distribution, 1991; editor: Training Plans for Marketing Education, 1987, Correspondence, 1988, Instructional Planning, 1988; contbr. articles to profl. jours. Recipient scholarship Am. Bus. Women's Ass., 1985. Mem. Nat. Coun. Resource Devel., Am. Assn. C.C., Tex. Jr. Coll. Tchrs. Assn., Phi Delta Kappa, Kappa Delta Phi, Phi Kappa Phi. Home: 6518B Hart Ln Austin TX 78731-3139 Office: Austin CC 5930 Middle Fiskville Rd Austin TX 78752-4342

SELL, JOAN ISOBEL, mobile home company owner; b. Johnson City, Tenn., May 5, 1936; d. Earl Walter and Jeanne Mason (Lyle) S.; m. Dale L. Moss, Jan. 15, 1956 (div. Nov. 1977); children: Carol Anne, John D. BS, East Tenn. State U., Johnson City, 1961. Cert. tchr., Tenn., Ga. Tchr. Asbury Sch., Johnson City, 1961-62, Richard Arnold High Sch., Savannah, Ga., 1964-66, Windsor Forest High Sch., Savannah, 1966-67, Boones Creek High Sch., Jonesborough, Tenn., 1967-77; co-owner Moss-Sell Mobile Homes, Johnson City, 1978-88; co-owner Biddix Budget Homes, Inc. (formerly Budget Mobile Homes), Johnson City, 1978-87, v.p., sec., 1987—; pres., treas. Budget Homes, Inc. (formerly Biddix Budget Homes), Johnson City, 1988-92; owner McKinley Park, Johnson City, 1970—; sec. Piedmont Fin. Svcs. Inc., 1995—. Mem. Tenn. Manufactured Housing Assn. (state bd. dirs. 1993-95), N.E. Tenn. Manufactured Housing Assn. (pres.), DAR, UDC, Order Ea. Star. Mem. Brethren Ch. Home: 3 Caitlin Ct Johnson City TN 37604-1147 Office: McKinley Park PO Box 5189 Johnson City TN 37603-5189

SELL, STEWART, pathologist, immunologist, educator; b. Pitts., Jan. 20, 1935; s. Oliver Martin and Mary Myra (Stewart) S.; m. Patricia Damon King, June 20, 1958 (div. 1985); children: Sherri Lynn Phillips, Stacy L. Klinke, Sean Stewart, Stephaine King Kinzel; m. Ilze Mara Klavins, Feb. 16, 1991; 1 child, Philip Janus. BS, Coll. of William and Mary, 1956; MD, U. Pitts., 1960. Diplomate Am. Bd. Pathology, Am. Bd. Med. Lab. Immunologists. Intern, asst. resident in pathology Mass. Gen. Hosp., Boston, 1960-62; rsch. assoc. germfree animal rsch. lab. NIAID, NIH, Bethesda, Md., 1962-64; spl. fellow dept. exptl. pathology U. Birmingham (Eng.) Med. Sch., 1964-65; instr., asst. prof., then assoc. prof. pathology U. Pitts. Sch. Medicine, 1965-69; assoc. prof., then prof. pathology U. Calif., San Diego, 1970-82; prof. U. Tex. Med. Sch., Houston, 1982—, chmn. dept. pathology, 1982-87; adj. prof. lab. medicine U. Tex.-M.D. Anderson Cancer Ctr., Houston, 1983; mem. pathology B study sect. NIH, 1972-77; mem. immunology adv. com. Am. Cancer Soc., 1983-88; mem. bd. sci. counsel divsn. cancer biol. diagnosis Nat. Cancer Inst., 1982-86. Author: Immunology, Immunopathology & Immunity, 1972, 5th rev. edit., 1996, BasicImmunology, 1987; editor: Seriological Cancer Markers, 1992, Monoclonal Antibodies in Cancer, 1985, 6 other oncology books. NIH grantee, 1964—. Mem. Am. Assn. Immunologists, Am. Soc. Exptl. Pathology, Am. Assn. Cancer Rsch., Internat. Soc. Oncodevel. Biology and Medicine (bd. dirs. 1972-85), Internat. Acad. Tumor Market Oncology (bd. dirs. 1984—), Am. Soc. Microbiology. Office: U Tex Health Sci Ctr Box 20708 6431 Fannin Houston TX 77225

SELLARS, NIGEL ANTHONY, historian, writer; b. Birmingham, England, Oct. 2, 1954; came to U.S., 1963; s. Robert William and Florence (Thompson) S.; m. Victoria Susan Brown, Dec. 17, 1981 (div. Jan. 1989); m. Nancy Lee Phillips Sellars, Jan. 1, 1990. BA in Psychology, U. Okla., Norman, 1977, BA in Journalism, 1980, MA in Journalism, 1985, PhD in History, 1994. Reporter Moore Monitor, Sooner Pub. Co., Moore, Okla., 1981-84, Daily Okla., Okla. Pub. Co., Oklahoma City, 1984-88; editor Yukon Review Newspaper, Yukon, Okla., 1988; adjunct prof. Dept. Journalism, U. Okla., Norman, Okla., 1990—; grad. teaching asst. Dept. History, U. Okla., Norman, Okla., 1988-94; instr. dept. history U. Okla., 1994—. Author twelve short stories, 1982-94; music album Dougherty's Fancy, 1989; contbr. articles to profl. jours. Recipient Donnell M. Owings award, Dept. History, U. Okla., Norman, 1990, Marshall Gregory award, Okla. Edn. Assn., Oklahoma City, 1986, 88, Carl Rogan award, Okla. AP, Oklahoma City, 1987. Mem. Orgn. Am. Historians, Western History Assn., Okla. Hist. Soc., Am. Hist. Assn., Small Press Writers and Artists Orgn. Office: University of Oklahoma Dept History Norman OK 73019

SELLERS, BEVERLY BURCH, university administrator; b. Geneva, Ala., July 23, 1962; d. Robert and Eris Lucille (Reeves) B.; m. James T. Sellers, Sept. 22, 1984. AA, Enterprise (Ala.) Jr. Coll., 1982; BA, Troy State U., 1984; MA, La. State U., 1989. Nat. cert. counselor. Career counselor Southeastern La. U. Comprehensive Counseling Ctr., Hammond, 1989-94; asst. dir. career devel. svcs. Southeastern La. U., 1994—; conduct career decision making, resume writing, job search and interviewing, and Myers-Briggs Type Indicator workshops and presentations for campus and cmty. orgns. Office: Southeastern La U PO Box 492 Hammond LA 70404-0492

SELLERS, CLEVELAND LOUIS, JR., history educator; b. Denmark, S.C., Nov. 8, 1944; s. Cleveland and Pauline (Taggart) S.; m. Gwendolyn Elfreda Williamson, Dec., 1973; children: Nosizwe Abidemi, Cleveland Lumumba, Bakari. Diploma, Shaw U.; EdM, Harvard U.; EdD, U. N.C., Greensboro. Pers. interviewer City of Greensboro, N.C., manpower planner, manpower planning supr.; instr. U. N.C., Greensboro, 1983-84; supr. residential svcs. Greensboro Housing Auth., N.C.; instr. sociology Denmark (S.C.) Tech. Coll.; assoc. prof. African-Am. Studies U. S.C., Columbia, asst. prof. dept. history. Author: (autobiography) The River of No Return, 1973; cons. (books) In Struggle, 1980, The Orangeburg Massacre, (film) Freedom on My Mind, 1994 (Oscar nominee 1995). Bd. dirs. S.C. State Bd. Edn., Columbia, 1991—; bd. dirs., trustee Voorhees Coll., Denmark, S.C., 1993—; chmn. bd. dirs. Denmark Recreation Ctr., Inc.; field dir. Jackson for Pres., Va., N.C., S.C., W.Va., 1983. Named to S.C. Hall of Fame United Black Fund, Inc., Columbia, 1995. Fellow N.C. Inst. Politics; mem. Am. Hist. Assn., Nat. Assn. State Bds. Edn., So. Conf. Afro-Am. Studies, S.C. Assn. Sch. Adminstrs., Omega Phi Psi (vice basilus 1992-95, Omega Citizen of Yr. 6th dist., Charlotte 1983, Omega Man of Yr. Tau Omega chpt., Greensboro 1988). Episcopalian. Office: U SC Dept History Gambrell Hall Rm 143 Columbia SC 29208

SELLERS, FRED EVANS, accounting educator; b. Lexington, Mo., Feb. 28, 1941; s. James MacBrayer and Rebekah Hall (Evans) S.; m. Katherine Ann Griggs, May 3, 1969; children: Mark Griggs, Rebekah Field. BA in History, Yale U., 1965; MBA, U. Kans., 1976, PhD in Bus., 1984. CPA, Tex. Reporter Kansas City (Mo.) Star, 1965-66, copy editor, 1966-70; copy editor Washington Star, 1970-72, asst. nat. editor, 1972-73; asst. prof. U. Tulsa, 1979-87; assoc. prof. Southwestern U., Georgetown, Tex., 1987—, chair dept. econs. and bus., 1994—; sec., treas. planning com. U. Tulsa Conf. Accts., 1980-87. Contbr. articles to profl. jours. Trustee Wentworth Mil. Acad., Lexington, Mo., 1986—, pres., 1990-92; trustee Williamson County (Tex.) Literacy Coun., 1989-91; treas., bd. dirs. St. John's Presch., Tulsa, 1984-87; conv. del. Episc. Diocese Okla., 1984, 85; audit com. St. John's Episc. Ch., Tulsa, 1983-87; bishop's com. Grace Episc. Ch., 1989, jr. warden, 1989, bishop's warden, 1990; alt. Tex. State Rep. Conv., 1988; treas. Georgetown Area United Way, 1993—. Mem. Inst. Mgmt. Accts. (dir. manuscripts Austin chpt. 1988—), Am. Acctg. Assn. (membership com. 1980-81), AICPA, Tex. Soc. CPAs (ednl. instns. com. Austin chpt.), Rotary. Home: 1610 E 15th St Georgetown TX 78626-7206 Office: Southwestern U Dept Econs and Bus Adminstrn Georgetown TX 78627-0770

SELLERS, GEORGEANNA, English language educator; b. Lexington, N.C., Dec. 23, 1955; d. James Howard Sr. and Ora Caroline (Leonard) S. AA, Davidson County Community Coll., Lexington, 1976; BA in English with honors, U. N.C., Greensboro, 1981, MA, 1984. V.p. Piedmont Freight System, Lexington, N.C., 1979-85; instr. English High Point (N.C.) Univ., 1984—; writing tutor Davidson County Community Coll., 1980-82; vol. tutor-tchr. Lexington City Schs., 1987. Vol. librarian 2d United Ch. Christ, Lexington, 1980—, chair library com., mem. Christian edn. com.; mem. People for the Ethical Treatment Animals. Mem. Nat. Coun. Tchrs. English (mem. Coll. Composition and Communication), Nat. League Families POW's MIA's (campaign promoter, organizer 1986-88), VFW Aux., Amnesty Internat., Phi Theta Kappa. Home: 1752 Burkhart Rd Lexington NC 27292-0700 Office: High Point Univ Dept English Montlieu Ave High Point NC 27262-4029

SELLERS, JOANNE GRANT, community relations executive; b. Miami, Fla., June 19, 1948; d. Joe M. and Phyllis (Ellis) Grant; m. Jack Sellers, Apr. 15, 1978. BS, U. North Ala., 1970. Mgr. cmty. rels. OXY USA, Inc., Tulsa. Pres., bd. dirs. Project Get Together, Tulsa, 1986—; bd. dirs. Energy One Credit Union, 1988—, sec.; bd. dirs. Citizens Crime Commn. Mem. U.S. C. of C. (pub. affairs com. 1988—). Republican. Methodist. Office: OXY USA Inc 110 W 7th St Tulsa OK 74119-1044

SELLERS, MACKLYN RHETT, JR., architect; b. Cheraw, S.C., July 9, 1962; s. Macklyn Rhett and Jackie Rae (Dickens) S.; 1 child, Macklyn Rhett III. BS in Design, Clemson U., 1984, MArch, 1987. Registered architect, S.C.; cert. Nat. Coun. Archtl. Registration Bds. Intern architect Overstreet Archtl. Assn., Anderson, S.C., 1984-85, Freeman-White Architects, Charlotte, N.C., 1985, 86; health care specialist The Edge Group, P.A., West Palm Beach, Fla., 1987; health care specialist Louis P. Batson III Architects, Greenville, S.C., 1987-89, architect, health care specialist, 1989-92; health facilities planner Freeman White Architects, Inc., Charlotte, 1992—, assoc., 1993—; teaching asst. Coll. Architecture, Clemson (S.C.) U., 1986-87, health care components grad. teaching asst., 1987. Editor Pike to Pike, 1982-83. Mem. memls. bldg. com. Christ Ch. Episcopal, Greenville, 1991-92. Mem. AIA, Pi Kappa Alpha (newsletter editor 1982-83, 1st pl. award 1982-83). Episcopalian. Home: 1427 Flintwood Dr Rock Hill SC 29732-1467 Office: Freeman White Architects Inc 8001 Arrowridge Blvd Charlotte NC 28273-5604

SELLERS, TERRY, JR., wood science and technology scientist, educator; b. Quinton, Ala., Sept. 26, 1938; s. Terry and Lillian Nora (Gilchrist) S.; m. Esther Joan Estill, June 5, 1960; children: Kathryn Jill, Lee Anna. BS in Forestry, Auburn U., 1960, MS in Wood Technology, 1961; D of Agr., U. Tokyo, 1993. Dir. quality control Koppers Co., Inc., Morrisville, N.C., 1962-65; mgr. mktg. Reichhold Chems., Tuscaloosa, Ala., 1965-80; prof. wood sci. and tech. Miss. Forest Products Lab. Miss. State U., Starkville, 1980—; assessment referee for domestic and fgn. academia, industry and govt., 1980—; stds. standing com. Dept. Commerce, Washington, 1993-96; adv. coun. Auburn U. Sch. Forestry; lectr., rschr., presenter and cons. in field. Author: Plywood & Adhesive Technology, 1985; (ency.) Composite Materials, 1991; contbr. USDA Forest Svc. Bull., 1989; bimonthly contbg. writer Panel World mag.; contbr. numerous reports and articles to profl. jours.; patentee in field. Recipient numerous grants U.S. industry and govt., 1980—, Cert. Appreciation, Dept. Commerce, 1993. Mem. Adhesion Soc., Am. Chem. Soc., Forest Products Soc. (pres. 1983-84, Meml. award 1979), Japan Wood Rsch. Soc., Soc. Wood Sci. and Tech., Plywood Pioneers Assn., Jaycees, Lions, Alpha Zeta, Gamma Sigma Delta, Phi Eta Sigma, Xi Sigma Pi. Methodist. Home: 1634 Turkey Creek Rd Starkville MS 39759-9225 Office: Miss Forest Products Lab 100 Blackjack Rd Starkville MS 39759-9219

SELLIN, JOSEPH HENRY, gastroenterologist; b. N.Y.C., Mar. 25, 1948; s. Stephen and Regina Sellin; m. Rena Sellin; children: Angela, Jonathan. BA magna cum laude, Amherst Coll., 1969; MD, Albert Einstein Coll. Medicine, 1973. Diplomate Am. Bd. Internal Medicine, sub-bd. in Gastroenterology. Med. intern Montefiore Hosp., Bronx, N.Y., 1973-74, resident in medicine, 1974-76; rsch. fellow in medicine Albert Einstein Coll. Medicine, Bronx, 1976-77; fellow in medicine U. Chgo., 1977-79, rsch. assoc., instr., 1979-80; asst. prof. medicine U. Tex. Med. Sch., Houston, 1980-87, asst. prof. medicine and physiology, 1986-87, assoc. prof. medicine and physiology, 1987-94, prof. medicine and integrative biology, 1994—, dir. div. gastroenterology, 1990—; mem. staff Hermann Hosp., chief gastroenterology, 1990—, chmn. gastrintestinal endoscopy com., 1992—; mem. staff Lyndon Baines Johnson Hosp., St. Joseph's Hosp., Methodist Hosp. Contbr. numerous articles to profl. jours. John Woodruff Simpson fellow, 1969; AGA Marion rsch. scholar, 1984-87; NIH grantee, 1982-85,86-89, 86-90, 89—; recipient several awards. Fellow Am. Coll. Gastroenterology Investigation; mem. Am. Gastroent. Assn., Am. Physiol. Soc., Am. Soc. for Clin. Investigation, Crohn's and Colitis Found. Am. (regional med. advisor 1991-94), Gastrointestinal Rsch. Group, Harris County Med. Soc., Houston Gastroent. Soc., Houston Gulf Coast Ileitis and Colitis Found. (co-chair med. adv. com. 1990-92), Soc. for Exptl. Biology and Medicine, Tex. Med. Assn., Tex. Soc. for Gastroenterology and Endoscopy, Phi Beta Kappa. Office: U Tex Med Sch 6431 Fannin St 4234 MSB Houston TX 77030-1501

SELMAN, JOE B., insurance company executive; b. Oklahoma City, Jan. 31, 1946; s. Paul J. and Letita G. (Whisler) S.; m. Eleanor J. Selman, Aug. 26, 1983; children: Karen L. Hartigan, Linda D. Coker, James J. Student, U. Okla., 1964-66, Elon Coll., 1968, Am. Coll., 1984, 88. Asst. athletic trainer U.S. Naval Acad., Annapolis, Md., 1966-68; assoc. distbr. Zimmer-Baxter, Roanoke, Va., 1968-73; distbr. Zimmer-Selman, Roanoke, 1973-75; pres. Joe B. Selman, Inc., Roanoke, 1975-76; agt. Equitable Life, 1977-95; dist. mgr. Equitable Life, Charlottesville, Va., 1978-81; pres. Benefits Mgmt., Charlottesville, 1981-94; CEO Duke Benefit Svcs., Inc., Charlottesville, 1995—; Am. Sports Underwriters cons. for catastrophic med. ins. plan for student athletes to Nat. Coll. Athletic Assn., Kansas City, Kans., 1983-84. Pres. Charlottesville dist. Va. Student Aid Found., 1991. With USN, 1966-68. Mem. Million Dollar Round Table (life). Episcopalian. Office: Duke Benefit Svcs Inc 2975 Ivy Rd Charlottesville VA 22903

SELMAN, MINNIE CORENE PHELPS, elementary school educator; b. Freedom, Okla., Mar. 25, 1947; d. Maxwell Jack and Mary Elizabeth (Mountain) Phelps; m. Thomas O. Selman, Aug. 8, 1966; children: T. Justin, Jeffrey L. BS in Elem. Edn., Northwestern Okla. State U., 1969; diploma in aerospace sci. and tech. edn., Okla. City U./Internat. Space Academy, 1996. Cert. elem. tchr., early childhood edn. tchr., elem. sci. tchr., Okla.; cert. early experiences insci., Okla. Tchr. Woodward (Okla.) Pub. Sch., 1969-72; pre-sch. tchr. Free Spirit Pre-sch., Woodward, 1974-75; tchr. Montessori Discovery World Pre-sch., Woodward, 1975-78; tchr. kindergarten Woodward Pub. Sch., Woodward, 1978—; host Leaderhip Okla. in the Classroom, 1991; tng. tchr. Okla. State U., Stillwater, 1987, 90. Benefit vol. Western Plains Shelter Orgn., Woodward, 1990, 91; life mem. Plains Indians and Pioneers Hist. Found., Woodward. Woodward Pub. Schs. Ednl. Found. grantee, 1990, 91, 92, NASA/NSTA grantee, 1995. Mem. NEA, Okla. Edn. Assn., Woodward Edn. Assn. (pub. rels. com. 1990—), Nat. Sci. Tchr. Assn. (cert. in elem. sci.), Okla. Sci. Tchrs. Assn. Democrat. Home: 318 Spruce Park Dr Woodward OK 73801-5945

SELMI, WILLIAM, JR., lawyer; b. Phila., June 18, 1937; s. William and Eleanor (Mishler) S.; m. Joan H. Silver, Dec. 4, 1966 (div. 1976); children: William III, Richard Kern; m. Patricia Ann Cantrell, Dec. 29, 1989 (div. 1995). AB, U. Miami, Coral Gables, Fla., 1969, JD, 1972. Bar: Fla. 1972, U.S. Dist. Ct. (so. dist.) Fla. 1973, U.S. Supreme Ct., 1976. Ptnr. Peer & Selmi, Jensen Beach, Fla., 1972-79; pvt. practice law Okeechobee, Fla., 1979—. Pres. Kiwanis Club, Jensen Beach, 1978; bd. dirs. Jensen Beach C. of C., 1977-78, Martin County Dem. Com., Stuart, Fla., 1977, Okeechobee br. ARC, 1990-95, Okeechobee United Way, 1993—. Home: 136 SW 85th

Ave Okeechobee FL 34974-1554 Office: 306 NW 5th St Okeechobee FL 34972-2565

SELTZER, BENJAMIN, neurologist, educator; b. Phila., Aug. 5, 1945; s. Albert P. and Sylvia (Superstein) S.; m. Natalie C. Ross, Oct. 13, 1974; children: Daniel, Jennifer, Peter, Nathan. AB, U. Pa., 1965; MD, Jefferson Med. Coll., 1969. Fellow in neurology Harvard Med. Sch., Boston, 1970-73, lectr. on neurology, 1978-88; staff neurologist Boston City Hosp., 1973-75, Beth Israel Hosp., 1975-88; chief dementia study unit VA Hosp., Bedford, Mass., 1978-88; from asst. to assoc. prof. neurology and psychiatry Boston U. Sch. Medicine, 1978-88; prof. neurology, psychiatry and anatomy, dir. divsn. behavioral neurosci. Tulane U. Sch. Medicine, New Orleans, 1988—; adj. prof. psychology U. New Orleans, 1990—. Contbr. numerous articles to med. and sci. jours. Fellow Am. Acad. Neurology, Royal Soc. Medicine (London); mem. Soc. for Neurosci., Gerontol. Soc. Am. Home: 923 Webster St New Orleans LA 70118-5910 Office: Tulane U Sch Medicine 1430 Tulane Ave New Orleans LA 70112-2699

SELZER, MICHAEL DAVID, sales executive; b. Alvin, Tex., Feb. 15, 1947; s. Ardine and Kathryn Eileen (Rashaw) S.; m. Lynne Pittman, Feb. 19, 1970; children: Marie, Beth, Jennifer. BA, So. Meth. U., 1969; MA, Pepperdine U., 1976. Commd. USMC, 1969, advanced through grades to lt. col., 1986; assignments with 2d Marine Div., 4th Marine Div., 1st Marine Aircraft Wing, Marine Corps Bases, Camp Lejeune, Camp Butler, Def. Logistics Agy.; ret. USMC, 1989; pres., dir. govt. sales worldwide Nautilus, Indpendence, Va., 1989—; founder, gen. mgr. Corp. Freight Cons., 1990. Mem. adminstrv. coun. United Meth. Ch., 1988-89. Mem. Marine Corps Assn., Naval Inst., Am. Prodn. and Inventory Control Soc., Nat. Strength and Conditioning Assn., Mil. Fitness Roundtable (pres. coun. on phys. fitness and sports). Republican. Methodist. Home: 2306 Piedmont Ridge Ct Marietta GA 30062-2513 Office: Nautilus 709 Powerhouse Rd Independence VA 24348

SEME, PHILLIPINE JANE N., education educator, consultant; b. Durban, Natal, S. Africa, May 15, 1957; d. Livingstone Mlungisi and Rebecca Khethiwe (Manzini) S.; m. J.M. Kargbo, Feb. 24, 1996; 1 child, Siphokazi Joice. MS, Okla. State U., 1987; MEd, Harvard U., 1990, EdD, 1993. Tchr. Inanda Sem., Durban, Natal, S. Africa, 1983, Edendale Tech. Coll., Pietermaritzburg, Natal, S. Africa, 1983-85; rsch. asst. Okla. State U., Stillwater, 1986-87; tchg. fellow Grad. Sch. Edn. Harvard U., Cambridge, Mass., 1991-92, rsch. asst. Grad. Sch. Edn., 1993; asst. prof. Old Dominion U., Norfolk, Va., 1993—; tchr. rsch. cons. Breadloaf Sch. English, Middlebury, Vt., 1995—; overseas rep. S. African Tchrr. of English to Spkrs. of Other Langs., Empangemi, 1995—; proposal reviewer Nat. Reading Conf., Chgo., 1996. Book reviewer profl. jours. Grad. scholarship award U.N., N.Y.C., 1987-91, Luth. World Ministries, 1985-87. Mem. Am. Ednl. assn., Nat. Coun. Tchrs. English, Nat. REading Conf., Internat. Reading Assn., Tchrs. of English to Spkrs. of Other Langs., Assn. Supervision and Curriculum. Home: 901E Armfield Cir #104 Norfolk VA 23505 Office: Old Dominiom U ECI Darden Coll Edn Norfolk VA 23529

SEMELKA, RICHARD CHARLES, medical educator; b. Nov. 25, 1959; m. Colleen Black; children: Charles, Claire. Faculty of Sci., U. Manitoba, Can., 1979; Faculty of Medicine, U. Manitoba, 1983. Diplomate Am. Bd. Radiology. Fellow Royal Coll. Physicians and Surgeons of Can. in diagnostic radiology. Intern U. Manitoba, 1983-84, resident in radiology, 1984-88; attending radiologist Med. Ctr., U. Calif. at San Francisco, 1989-90; asst. prof. dept. radiology U. Manitoba, Winnipeg, 1990-92; magnetic resonance imaging rsch. coord. St. Boniface Rsch. Found., Winnipeg, 1990-92; assoc. prof. dept. radiology U. N.C., Chapel Hill, 1992—; dir. magnetic resonance imagin U. N.C., 1992—. Author: (with J.P. Shoenut) MRI of the Abdomen with CT Correlation, 1993; editl. bd. Topics in Magnetic Resonance Imaging, 1993; reviewer Radiology, 1991; contbr. articles to profl. jours.; lectr. in field. Recipient body computed tomography fellowship St. Boniface Gen. Hosp., Winnipeg, 1988, clin. rsch. fellowship in magnetic resonance imaging Med. Ctr., U. Calif. at San Francisco, 1988-90, Manitoba Health Rsch. Coun. indsl. rsch. grant, 1990, Manitoba Health Rsch. Coun. Univ.-Industry collaborative grant, 1992-93, St. Boniface Rsch. Found. grants, 1992-93, 92-94. Mem. Radiol Soc. N.Am., Soc. Magnetic Resonance in Medicine, Am. Roentgen Ray Soc., , Soc. Magnetic Resonance Imaging. Office: Radiology Dept Univ North Carolina Campus Box 7510 Chapel Hill NC 27599

SEMMENS, JAMES PIKE, obstetrician, gynecologist, educator, sexual physiologist; b. Milw., Aug. 16, 1919; s. Thomas Perry and Corinne Middleton (Pike) S.; m. Eve Curtis, Oct. 1, 1982; children by previous marriage: James Alan, Michael Paul, Christine Anne, Gregory George, John Patrick; m. Eve Curtis, Oct. 1, 1982. BS, Marquette U., 1941, MD, 1943. Diplomate Am. Bd. Ob-Gyn., Am. Bd. Sexology; cert. sex therapist. Intern Milw. Hosp., 1943-44; asst. resident in pediatric surgery and pediatrics Milw. Children's Hosp., 1944-45; commd. lt. (j.g.) U.S. Navy, 1943, advanced through grades to capt., 1962; sr. med. officer USS Halsey Powell, 1945-46, Naval Mag., Port Chicago, Calif., 1953-54, rsch. dept. ob-gyn., Portsmouth, Va., 1954-57; vis. clin. instr. ob-gyn. Med. U. S.C., Charleston, Herbert Burwig lectr., 1968; chief of dependents, chief ob-gyn. dept. U.S. Naval Hosp., Charleston, 1957-61, Pensacola, Fla., 1961-63; chief ob-gyn. dept. U.S. Naval Hosp., Oakland, Calif., 1963-69, exec. officer, chief ob-gyn., Long Beach, Calif., 1969-71; assoc. prof. ob-gyn. U. So. Calif. Sch. Medicine, Los Angeles, 1970-71; assoc. clin. prof. ob-gyn. U. Calif. Coll. Medicine-Irvine, 1970-71; ret., 1971; assoc. prof. ob-gyn. Med. U. S.C., 1971-79, prof. ob-gyn., 1979-83, prof. emeritus, 1983—; cons. in field. Author: Teen Age Pregnancy, 1968, Mid Life Sexuality, 1989, Adolescent Experience, 1970; contbr. numerous articles to med. publs.; producer med. films. Fellow ACS, Am. Coll. Obstetricians and Gynecologists (chmn. armed forces dist. 1968-71; chmn. audio-visual edn. com. 1971-73; mem. edn. in family life com. 1973-76), Am. Acad. Family Physicians (charter); mem. AMA, Am. Fertility Soc., S.C. Med. Soc., Charleston County Med. Soc., Alameda County Gynecol. Soc., San Francisco Gynecol. Soc. (courtesy mem.), S.C. Obstet. and Gynecol. Soc., Wis. Med. Soc., Assn. Mil. Surgeons U.S., Pacific Coast Fertility Soc., Internat. Assn. Psychosomatic Ob-Gyn., Am. Assn. Sex Educators, Counselors and Therapists (chmn. S.C. sect. 1978-81, 83—, chmn. southeastern dist., dir. 1981-83), Assn. Sex Therapists and Counselors (pres. 1976-86), Phi Sigma, Kappa Alpha. Home and Office: 2415 Haulover Johns Island SC 29455-6082

SEMORE, MARY MARGIE, abstractor; b. Cowlington, Okla., Feb. 11, 1920; d. William Leonard and Bessie Mae (Bellah) Barnett; m. Jack Sanford Semore, Mar. 3, 1940 (dec. Jan. 1985). Grad. high sch., Wagoner, Okla., 1938. Legal sec. W.O. Rittenhouse, Wagoner, Okla., 1938-40; abstractor Wagoner County Abstract Co., 1941—. Mem. Am. Legion Women's Aux., Wagoner Hist. Soc. Mem. Okla. Land Title Assn., Am. Land Title Assn., Wagoner C. of C., DAR, Daus. Am. Colonists. Democrat. Methodist. Home: 902 S White Ave Wagoner OK 74467-7239 Office: Wagoner County Abstract Co 219 E Cherokee PO Box 188 Wagoner OK 74477

SEMPLE, THOMAS CARL, physical-organic chemist; b. Attleboro, Mass., July 16, 1959; s. Alan R. and Janice L. (Jordan) S.; m. Antonette Marie Gambini, Nov. 17, 1990; children: Alana G., Alexandra C. ScB, MIT, 1981; PhD, Brown U., 1986. Rsch. fellow Yale U., New Haven, 1986-88; process rsch. chemist Shell Chem. Co., Houston, 1988—. Contbr. articles to profl. jours. Mem. AAAS, Am. Chem. Soc., NYAS, Sigma Xi. Home: 401 Falling Leaf Dr Friendswood TX 77546-4521 Office: Shell Chem Co WTC 3333 Highway 6 S Houston TX 77082-3101

SENGUPTA, GUNJA, historian, educator; b. Calcutta, India, Apr. 2, 1962; came to U.S., 1985; d. Dibyendranath and Rukmabai (Duttagupta) S. BA, U. Bombay, India, 1984; PhD, Tulane U., 1991. Asst. prof. dept. history East Tex. State U., Commerce, 1990—; lectr. in field; condr. seminars/workshops in field. Author: For God and Mammon: Evangelicals & Entrepreneurs, Masters & Slaves in Territorial Kansas, 1854-1860, 1996; contbr. articles to profl. jours. Contbg. mem. Dem. Nat. Com. East TEx. State U. Rsch. grantee, 1990-91; Tulane U. Grad. Sch. fellow, 1985-87, teaching assistantship, 1987-90; Tata scholar The J.N. Tata Endowment, Bombay, 1985, Kulkarni scholar, Coelho scholar, Anant Sakharam Bakre Meml. prize, all U. Bombay, Wordsworth scholar and prize, 1983, Daxina fellow, Watumull Found. scholar, Elphinstone Coll. Centennial scholar, Elphinstone Coll. Open Merit scholar, 1981-84. Mem. Am. Hist. Assn., Orgn. Am. Historians, So. Hist. Assn., Assn. of Third World Studies, Phi Alpha Theta. Office: East Texas State Univ Dept History East Texas Sta Commerce TX 75429

SENNETT, HENRY HERBERT, JR., theatre arts educator and consultant; b. Atlanta, Feb. 28, 1945; s. Henry Herbert and Betty Ruth (Wilson) S.; m. Beverly Ann Rodgers, Dec. 9, 1967; children: Cristie Aline, Herbert Alan. BS in Edn., Ark. State U., Jonesboro, 1968; MA, Memphis State U., 1971; MDiv, So. Bapt. Sem., Louisville, 1978; DMin, Midwestern Bapt. Sem., Kansas City, Mo., 1988; MFA, Fla. Atlantic U., 1989. Cert. tchr. Tchr. speech and English Covington (Tenn.) High Sch., 1971-72; freelance designer Lighting by Herb, Memphis, 1972-73; tchr. speech and English Augusta (Ark.) High Sch., 1973-76; instr. drama Jefferson Community Coll., Louisville, 1977-78; pastor Dublin (Ohio) Bapt. Ch., 1979-83, Trinity Bapt. Ch., Searcy, Ark., 1983-85; asst. prof. theatre arts, dept. chair Palm Beach Atlantic Coll., West Palm Beach, Fla., 1985-96; pres. S&R Prodns., Inc., 1995—; assoc. prof. comm. arts, dept. chair La. Coll., Pineville, 1996—; stress mgmt. cons. Palm Beach County Bd. Edn., West Palm Beach, 1988—; freelance cons. theatrical lighting and design, West Palm Beach, 1986—; cons. drama edn. Fla. Dept. Edn., 1991-94; vis. prof. Midwestern Bapt. Sem., Kansas City, Mo., 1988; pres. S & R Prodns., Inc., 1995-96; pres., coord., assoc. prof. Commn. Arts, La. Coll. Author: Theatre in the Church, 1992, Religion and Dramatics: Essays on the Relationship Between Christianity and Theatrical Arts, 1994, author: (play) Stars, 1989. 1st lt. U.S. Army, 1968-70, Vietnam; chaplain USAR, 1984—. Mem. Nat. Assn. Schs. Theatre, Fla. Theatre Edn., Fla. Theatre Conf., South Western Theatre Conf., Assn. Theatre Higher Edn., Blue Key Nat. Honor Soc., Theatre Comm. Group, Pi Kappa Phi (pres. 1965-66). Republican. Baptist. Office: Louisiana College Box 554 Pineville LA 71359-0554

SENSABAUGH, MARY ELIZABETH, financial consultant; b. Eastland, Tex., Aug. 15, 1939; d. Johnnie and L.G. (Tucker) Roberts; m. Dwight Lee Sensabaugh, Dec. 22, 1956; children: Robert Lee, Mark Jay. Student, Odessa Jr. Coll., 1959-63, U. North Tex., 1963-67. Sr. acct. Braniff Internat. Airlines, Dallas, 1967-68; acct. Computer Bus. Services, Dallas, 1968-72; sec.-treas. Robert D. Carpenter, Inc., Dallas, 1972-76; controller Broadway Warehouses, Dallas, 1976-78; asst. controller S.W. Offset, Dallas, 1978-79; sec.-treas., cons. Carpenter, Carruth & Hover, Inc., Dallas, 1979-92; sec.-treas. Roberts, Taylor and Sensabaugh, Inc., Hurst, Tex., 1992—. Mem. Nat. Assn. Women in Constrn. (bd. dirs. Dallas chpt. 1983-84), Internat. Platform Assn., Beta Sigma (pres. Irving, Tex. chpt. 1973-74), NAFE. Home: 702 Hughes Dr Irving TX 75062-5601 Office: 204 W Bedford Euless Rd Ste E Hurst TX 76053-4042

SENSE, KARL AUGUST, physicist, educator; b. Kiel, Schleswig-Holstein, Germany, Mar. 6, 1917; came to U.S., 1929; s. Carl Richard and Charlotte Irma (Neuenfeldt) S.; m. Rita Evelyn Sharp, June 5, 1948 (div. Jan. 1971); children: Karl D., Nancy C., Kurt A., Janet E., Eric M. BA, SUNY, Albany, 1939; MS, U. Minn., 1951. Asst. div. cons. Battelle Meml. Inst., Columbus, Ohio, 1951-58; sr. physicist Atomics Internat. (Rockwell), Canoga Park, Calif., 1958-61; rsch. scientist Astropower subs. Douglas Aircraft, Newport Beach, Calif., 1961-64; project mgr., staff engr. TRW Systems Group, Redondo Beach, Calif., 1964-69; pvt. practice cons. Garden Grove, Calif., 1969-80; engring. specialist satellite systems div. Rockwell Internat., Seal Beach, Calif., 1981-84, ret., 1984; lectr. in physics Calif. State U., Long Beach, 1986. Author: Theory on Determination of Molecular Complexes of Vapors of Binary Systems, 1957, Power Failure Analysis of Satellites in GPS Orbit, 1981; mgr., author: Nuclear-Magnetohydrodynamic Power Systems, 1967; patentee thermionic emitter. Comdr. Am. Legion Post # 286, Garden Grove, 1977; pres. Worthington (Ohio) Luth. Ch., 1957; co-chmn., bd. dirs. Luth. High Sch. Assn. of Orange County, Calif., 1968. 2d lt. USAAF, 1943-45. Fellow AIAA (assoc., Membership award 1991); mem. Am. Phys. Soc. (sr.). Home: 37 Marion Hts Galax VA 24333-4500

SENTELL, JACKIE ROBERTA RATLIFF, secretary; b. Grundy, Va., Feb. 28, 1940; d. Clyde and Maye Marinda (Mitchell) Ratliff; m. Philip Ramon Sentell, June 25, 1961 (dec. Nov. 1982); children: Normandee, Katrinka; adopted Ramon; and 10 foster children. Student, Cin. U., 1958-61, Cin. Bible Coll., 1957-61. Pvt. tchr. music Va., Ga. and Ariz., 1957-92; florist FTD, 1972-84; with Primerica Fin. S.V.P. (formerly A.L. Williams), Ariz. and Va., 1982-94; admission rep. Va. Coll., Roanoke, Va., 1992-94; sr. v.p. PriMerica Fin. Svc., 1994—. Exec. sec. ARC, Grundy, 1990-92; sec., pres. Gilbert (Ariz.) C. of C., 1972-78; chmn. Gilbert Parade, 1972-78; tchr. bible sch., supt. Youth and Women's Group, 1952-90; bd. dirs. Gilbert Fine Arts, 1972-74, Gilbert IDA, 1974-82, Beauty Pageants, 1970's; play dir. Gilbert Fine Art, 1974-84; pres. PTA, 1961-90; dir., music dir., organist Mountain Players, 1961-94. 2d lt. Civil Air Patrol. Named Citizen of the Yr., Town of Gilbert, 1978, Mother of the Yr., Gilbert Christian Ch., 1980, Woman of the Yr., Cen. Ch., 1986; recipient Leadership award CAP, 1990-91. Mem. Kiwanis (pres. 1990-91). Republican. Home: 2002 Langdon Rd SW Apt 24 Roanoke VA 24015-3458

SENTER, LYONEL THOMAS, JR., federal judge; b. Fulton, Miss., July 30, 1933; s. L. T. and Eva Lee (Jetton) S.; married. B.S., U. So. Miss., 1956; LL.B., U. Miss., 1959. Bar: Miss. 1959. County pros. atty., 1960-64, U.S. commr., 1966-68; judge Miss. Circuit Ct., Circuit 1, 1968-80, U.S. Dist. Ct. (no. dist.) Miss., 1980—. Mem. Miss. State Bar. Democrat. Office: US Dist Ct PO Box 925 Aberdeen MS 39730-0925

SENTI, FREDERIC RAYMOND, food safety consultant; b. Cawker City, Kans., Apr. 29, 1913; s. Peter and Jennie (Huiting) S.; m. Alice Geneva Buikstra, Sept. 21, 1939; children: Neal Clinton, Nancy Kay, Patricia Alice. BSCE, Kans. State U., 1935, MS in Chemistry, 1936; PhD in Chemistry, Johns Hopkins U., 1939; DS (hon.), Kans. State U., 1963. Asst., assoc. physicist, physicist, prin. physicist USDA, Ea. Regional Rsch. Lab., Phila., 1941-48; chemist, head analytical physical chemistry & physics div. USDA, No. Regional Rsch. Lab., Peoria, Ill, 1948-54; chief, cereals lab. USDA, No. Regional Rsch. Lab., Peoria, 1954-59, dir., 1959-64; deputy adminstr., nutrition, consumer and indsl. use rsch. USDA, Agrl. Rsch. Svc., Washington, 1964-72, asst. adminstr, nat. program staff, 1972-74; rsch. assoc. FASEB, Life Scis. Rsch. Office., 1974-77, assoc. dir., 1978-83, sr. scientific cons., 1983-86; pvt. practice cons. food safety, 1987—; bd. trustees Am. Type Culture Collection, 1962-72, chmn., 1968-69; chief staff officer com on processed foods for developing countries and domestic food distbn. programs USDA, 1964-74; mem. patent policy com. Fed. Coun. Sci. and Tech., 1964-74; mem. liaison panel food protection com., Nat. Rsch. Coun., 1971-74; cons. AID, Govt. of India, 1966, 68, UN FAO, Rome, 1977; program chmn. World Soy Protein Food Conf., Munich, 1973. Contbr. articles to profl. jours. Mem. sch. bd. Wilder-Waite Community Sch., Peoria County, Ill., 1952-57, pres. sch. bd., 1955-57; mem. sch. bd. Dunlap (Ill.) High Sch., 1958-64, pres. sch. bd., 1961-64; mem. Rotary, Peoria, 1950-64. Fellow AAAS; mem. Am. Soybean Assn. (hon., life), Am. Chem. Soc. (chmn. carbohydrate chemistry div. 1963-64, exec. bd. 1961-66), Am. Assn. Cereal Chemists, Am. Crystallographic Assn., Inst. Food Technologists, Agrl. Rsch. Inst., NAS, Cosmos Club. Home and Office: 3134 N Piedmont St Arlington VA 22207-5330

SENYARD, CORLEY PRICE, JR., engineering executive, consultant; b. Baton Rouge, Feb. 6, 1956; s. Corley P. Sr. and Suzanne (Jackson) S.; m. Kathleen Finley, June 11, 1977; children: Brandy Adelle, Kristen Sheena. BS in Computer Sci., La. State U., 1977; postgrad., Fla. Inst. Tech., 1979-80. Sr. engr. Boeing Aerospace, Wichita, Kans., 1977-79, Harris Corp., Melbourne, Fla., 1979-81; staff prodn. engr. Amoco Prodn. Co., Lafayette, La., 1981-84; sr. staff engr. Quad-S Cons., Inc., League City, Tex., 1984-87, assoc. engr., 1987-89; v.p., engr. Quad-S Consultants, Inc., League City, Tex., 1987-94; nat. mfg. cons. CSC, Chgo., 1994—; bd. dirs. Quad-S Cons., Inc., League City; co-owner CBT, Ltd., Baton Rouge, 1986-93; dir. ops. Computer Scis. Corp., Hanover, Md., 1994; speaker profl. confs. Contbr. articles to profl. jours.; patentee in field. Mem. IEEE, Computer Soc. of IEEE, ACM-Siggraph, Assn. for Computing Machinery. Republican. Office: Computer Scis Corp 1302 Coleman Boylan Dr League City TX 77573-5228

SEPPER, DENNIS LEE, philosophy educator; b. Medina, Ohio, Jan. 26, 1951; s. Joseph Julius and Margaret Martha (Micsko) S.; m. Kathleen Anne Wellman, Aug. 23, 1975; children: Elizabeth Wellman Sepper, Matthew Wellman Sepper. BA, Harvard Coll., 1973; MA, U. Chgo., 1974, PhD, 1981. Lectr. Coll. Notre Dame, Belmont, Calif., 1980-82, Stanford (Calif.) U., 1981-82; asst. prof. U. Dallas, Irving, Tex., 1982-88; assoc. prof. U. Dallas, Irving, 1989—, prof., 1995—; rsch. fellow U. Wis., Madison, 1988-89. Cons. editor Am. Cath. Philos. Quar., Irving, 1990—; author: Goethe Contra Newton, 1988, Newton's Optical Writings, 1994, Descartes's Imagination, 1996; contbr. articles to profl. jours. Study grantee DAAD, Munich, 1977-79, rsch. grantee NEH, 1989-90; fellow Inst. for Rsch. in Humanities, U. Wis., 1988-89. Mem. Am. Philos. Assn., History of Sci. Soc., Metaphys. Soc. Am., Philosophy Sci. Assn., North Tex. Philos. Assn. Roman Catholic. Office: Univ Dallas Philosophy Dept 1845 E Northgate Dr Irving TX 75062-4736

SEPTER, GLENN A., army officer; b. Henderson, Ky., Sept. 25, 1950; s. Robert Baire and Davinna Lavell (Reynolds) S.; m. Debra Sue King, Oct. 20, 1973; children: Leigh Ann, Amanda Michelle, Krista Lynn. BA in Bus. Adminstrn., Columbia Coll., St. Louis, 1987. Commd. 2d lt. U.S. Army, 1973, advanced through grades to lt. col., 1993; supply, logistics, ops. and mgmt. officer various locations, 1981-92; ops. officer U.S. Army Res. Pers. Ctr., St. Louis, 1992-93, br. chief, 1993; dep. chief of staff Hdqrs. 100th Divsn., Louisville, 1993—. Mem. Res. Officers Assn., Louisville Armed Forces Com., Assn. of the Century. Baptist. Home: 2405 Tregaron Ave Louisville KY 40299

SEPULVADO, JOSEPH MICHAEL, computer information scientist; b. Cheyenne, Wyo., Aug. 16, 1952; s. Joseph Martin and Ann Mildred (Shipp) S.; m. Cynthia Marie Howell, July 31, 1982 (div. Aug. 1987); m. Shirley Rae Benham; children: Julie Ann, Angela Dyan. BS, U. Okla., 1972. Cert. data processor, data educator, computer programmer. Sr. systems analyst Pub. Svc. Co. of Okla., Tulsa, 1978-80; application supr. Cotton Petroleum Corp., Tulsa, 1980-81; cons. Forte Info. Svcs., Tulsa, 1981-82; instr. Tulsa Jr. Coll., 1982-84; sr. systems analyst Citgo Petroleum Corp., Tulsa, 1984; cons. Computer Horizons, inc., Jacksonville, Fla., 1984-85, Computer Assistance, Inc., Dallas, 1985-87, IMI Systems, Inc., Dallas, 1987—. With USAF, 1981. Roman Catholic. Home: 1701 Windmire Dr Mesquite TX 75181-1555 Office: IMI Systems Inc 14180 Dallas Pky Ste 450 Dallas TX 75240-4370

SERAFIN, DONALD, plastic surgeon; b. N.Y.C., Jan. 18, 1938; s. Stephen Michael and Julia (Sopko) S.; A.B., Duke U., 1960, M.D., 1964; m. Patricia Serafin; children: Allison Elizabeth, Christina Julia, Donald Stephen, Lara Leigh. Surg. intern Grady Meml. Hosp., Atlanta, 1964-65; resident in surgery Emory U. Hosp., Atlanta, 1965-69; asst. resident in plastic and reconstructive surgery Duke U. Med. Center, Durham, N.C., 1971-73, chief resident, 1973-74; Christine Kleinert fellow in hand surgery U. Louisville Hosp., 1972-73; practice medicine specializing in plastic surgery, Durham; mem. staff Durham County Gen. Hosp.; asst. prof. plastic, reconstructive and maxillofacial surgery Duke U., 1974-77, assoc. prof., 1977-81, prof., 1981-95, chmn. Plastic Surgery Rsch. Council, 1983. Assoc. editor Jour. Reconstructive Microsurgery. Contbr. articles to profl. jours. Served to maj. M.C., USAF, 1969-71, col. M.C., USAR. Diplomate Am. Bd. Surgery, Am. Bd. Plastic Surgery. Recipient Air Force commedation medal, 1971, U.S. Army commendation medal, 1990. Fellow ACS; mem. Internat. Soc. Reconstructive Microsurgery, Am. Soc. Plastic and Reconstructive Surgeons, Am. Assn. Plastic Surgeons, Am. Burn Assn., AMA, Plastic Surgery Research Council, N.C. Soc. Plastic, Maxillofacial and Reconstructive Surgeons, Southeastern Soc. Plastic and Reconstructive Surgeons, Southeastern Med. Dental Soc., Sigma Xi. Office: Duke U Med Ctr PO Box 3708 Durham NC 27710

SERAFINI, ALDO N., radiology educator, medical educator; b. May 2, 1940; naturalized citizen, U.S.; MBChB, U. Witwatersrand, Johannesburg, South Africa, 1966. Diplomate Am. Bd. Nuclear Medicine, diplomate Am. Bd. Internal Medicine; cert. Fla. State Bd. Med. Examiners. Intern Jackson Meml. Hosp., 1967-68, resident in internal medicine, 1968-70, resident in nuclear medicine, 1970-72; instr. dept. radiology U. Miami (Fla.) Sch. Medicine, 1972-73, asst. prof. radiology dept., 1974-78, assoc. prof. radiology, 1978-83, prof. radiology, 1983—, assoc. prof. medicine, 1982-84, prof. medicine dept. medicine, 1984—; attending staff Mount Sinai Med. Ctr., Miami Beach, Fla., 1972-77, U. Miami (Fla.) Hosp. and Clinic, 1977—, U. Miami (Fla.)/Jackson Meml. Med. Ctr., 1977—, Cedars Med. Ctr., Miami, 1985—. Contbr. chpts. to books and articles to profl. jours. Nominated as best doctor in U.S.A., 1993. Office: U Miami Hosp and Clinic Sylvester Comp Cancer Ctr 1611 NW 12th Ave Miami FL 33136-1005

SERIO, FRANCIS G., periodontist educator, researcher; b. N.Y.C., Apr. 19, 1954; s. Joseph and Jane Elaine (Lada) S.; m. Cheryl Lynn Hench, Aug. 29, 1987; children: Andrew Joseph, Grace Marie. BA, Johns Hopkins U., 1976; DMD, U. Pa., 1980; MS, U. Md., 1991. Diplomate Am. Bd. Periodontology. Instr. U. Md. Dental Sch., Balt., 1981-83, 84-86, asst. prof., 1983-84, 86-91, assoc. prof., 1991-93; assoc. prof., chmn. U. Miss. Sch. Dentistry, Jackson, 1993—; cons. Dept. Vets. Affairs, Balt. & Perry Point, Md., 1986-93, Jackson, Miss., 1993—. Author: International Dental Volunteer Organizations: A Guide to Service and a Directory of Programs, 1993; contbr. chpts. to Clark's Clinical Dentistry, 1989,91. Dir. Dominican Dental Mission Project, San Jose de Olca, Dominican Republic, 1982—. Named to Archbishop Molloy High Sch. Hall of Fame, Jamaica, N.Y., 1988; recipient Frank Sinnreich award U. Md., 1992, Pres.'s Vol. Action award Pres. George Bush, Washington, 1991. Mem. ADA (chmn. internat. com. 1990), Am. Acad. Periodontology, Am. Assn. Dental Schs., Health Vols. Overseas (chmn. dentistry overseas divsn. 1990—), Acad. of Dentistry Internat., Nat. Acad. of Practice, Omicron Kappa Upsilon. Roman Catholic. Office: U Miss Sch Dentistry 2500 N State St Jackson MS 39216-4500

SEROKA, JAMES HENRY, social sciences educator, university administrator; b. Detroit, Mar. 5, 1950; s. Henry S. and Mary (Wyoral) S.; m. Carolyn Marie White, June 27, 1970; children: Mihail, Maritsa. BA, U. Mich., 1970; MA, Mich. State U., 1972, PhD, 1976. Labor mkt. analyst U.S. Dept. of Labor, Washington, 1970-71; asst. prof. U. N.C., Greensboro, 1976-77, Appalachian State U., Boone, N.C., 1977-79, So. Ill. U., Carbondale, 1979-81; assoc. prof. So. Ill. U., 1981-87, prof., dir., 1987-88; prof., head div. humanities and social scis. Pa. State U., Erie, 1988-90; prof. U. North Fla., Jacksonville, 1990—; also dir. Ctr. for Pub. Leadership, Jacksonville; dir. Master of Pub. Affairs Program Soc. Ill. U., 1987-88, Rural and Small Town Adminstrn. Project, 1980-85; asst. dir. Appalachian Regional Bur. Govts., Boone, N.C., 1977-79; manpower planning analyst U.S. Dept. Lab., Washington, 1970-71; exchange prof. Fakultet Politickih Nauka, Univerzitet u Beogradu, Yugoslavia, 1986; sr. researcher Coun. for the Internat. Exchange Scholars Yugoslavia, 1980; mem. state adv. com. Gov.'s Rural Affairs Coun. for State of Ill., 1988. Co-author: Political Organizations in Social Yugoslavia, 1986 (Choice award 1987); editor Rural Public Adminstration, 1986; co-editor: Developed Socialism, 1982, Comparative Political Systems, 1990, Yugoslavia: The Failure of Democratic Transformation, 1992; contbr. numerous articles to profl. jours. Recipient Akademischer Austausch Dienst Lang. scholar Fed. Republic of Germany, 1988 and numerous other grants, traveling fellows. Mem. Am. Soc. Pub. Adminstrn. (so Ill. chpt. 1982-83), Nat. Civic League, Am. Polit. Sci. Assn., Internat. Polit. Sci. Assn., Midwest Polit. Sci. Assn., So. Polit. Sci. Assn., Southwestern Polit. Sci. Assn., Western Polit. Sci. Assn., Policy Studies Orgn., Acad. Polit. Sci., Rural Sociol. Assn., Internat. Studies Assn., Am. Assn. Advancement of Slavic Studies, Western Social Sci. Assn., Cmty. Devel. Soc. Office: U North Fla Ctr Local Govt Adminstn 4567 Saint Johns Bluff Rd S Jacksonville FL 32224-2646

SEROW, ROBERT CHARLES, education educator, writer, consultant; b. N.Y.C., Oct. 8, 1947; s. William J. and Dorothea G. Serow; m. Kathleen O'Brien, May 10, 1951; children: Megan, Brian. BA, Fordham U., 1969; MA, Cornell U., 1976, PhD, 1976. Tchr. parochial schs. N.Y.C., 1969-72; rsch. asst. Cornell U., Ithaca, N.Y., 1972-76; cons. Montgomery County Schs., Rockville, Md., 1976-77; mem. faculty N.C. State U., Raleigh, 1977—; vis. faculty U. Mass., Amherst, 1983-84; cons. N.C. Bd. Edn., Raleigh, 1980-81; mem. rsch. adv. bd. Wake County Schs., Raleigh, 1992—; mem. sch. bd. Cardinal Gibbons H.S., Raleigh, 1988-90. Author: Schooling for Social Diversity, 1983, Social Foundations of Education, 1994; contbr. articles to profl. jours. Mem. N.C. Commn. on Nat. and Cmty. Svcs., Raleigh, 1993-97; mem. tech. rev. group Student Literacy Corps, Washington, 1991-94.

Grantee N.C. State U., 1978-79, 84-85, U. N.C., 1991-92, Project Succeed, 1993-97. Mem. Am. Ednl. Rsch. Assn., Am. Assn. for Higher Edn., Nat. Soc. for Exptl. Edn., Am. Evaluation Assn. Office: NC State U PO Box 7801 Raleigh NC 27695

SERRIE, HENDRICK, anthropology and international business educator; b. Jersey City, July 2, 1937; s. Hendrick and Elois (Edge) S.; m. Gretchen Tipler Ihde, Sept. 3, 1959; children: Karim Jonathan, Keir Ethan. BA with honors, U. Wis., 1960; MA, Cornell U., 1964; PhD with distinction, Northwestern U., 1976. Dir. Solar Energy Field Project, Oaxaca, Mex., 1961-62; instr. U. Aleppo, Syria, 1963-64; asst. prof. Beloit (Wis.) Coll., 1964-69, Calif. State U., Northridge, 1969-70, Purdue U., West Lafayette, Ind., 1970-72, New Coll./U. South Fla., Sarasota, 1972-77; tchr. Pine View Sch., Sarasota, 1978; prof. anthropology, internat. bus. Eckerd Coll., St. Petersburg, Fla., 1978—; dir. internat. bus. overseas programs Eckerd Coll., 1981—; sr. rsch. assoc., Human Resources Inst., St. Petersburg, 1988—. Author, editor: Family, Kinship, and Ethnic Identity Among the Overseas Chinese, 1985, Anthropology and International Business, 1986, What Can Multinationals Do for Peasants, 1994; writer, dir. films: Technological Innovation, 1962, Something New Under the Sun, 1963; contbr. articles to Wall Street Jour. and Wall Street Jour. Europe. Tchr. Sunday sch., North United Methodist Ch., Sarasota, 1977—. Exxon scholar, So. Ctr. for Internat. Issues, Atlanta, 1980-81; Presdl. fellow Am. Grad. Sch. Internat. Mgmt., 1991; recipient Leavy award, Freedoms Found., Valley Forge, Pa., 1989. Fellow Am. Anthropol. Assn., Soc. Applied Anthropology; mem. So. Ctr. Internat. Issues, Acad. Internat. Bus., Tampa Bay Internat. Trade Coun., Internat. Soc. Intercultural Edn., Tng. and Rsch. Democrat. Home: 636 Mecca Dr Sarasota FL 34234-2713 Office: Eckerd Coll Dept Internat Bus Saint Petersburg FL 33733

SERTICH, ANTHONY PATRICK, JR., otorhinolaryngologist, facial/plastic surgeon; b. San Antonio, Tex., Aug. 9, 1956; s. Anthony Patrick Sertich and Jeanette Frances Murphy; m. Pamela Gordon, Oct. 3, 1986; children: Anthony Patrick III, John Carl. BS summa cum laude, St. Mary's U., San Antonio, 1977; MD, Southwestern Med. Sch., 1981. Resident in gen. surgery U. South Fla., 1981-83, resident in otolaryngology, head and neck surgery, 1983-86; CEO South Tex. Otorhinolaryngology Assocs., San Antonio, 1986—, Aesthetic Facial Plastic Surgeons of South Tex. Bd. dirs. Am. Cancer Soc. Mem. Tex. Medical Assn. (del. 1988—), Bexar County Medical Soc. Am. (bd. dirs.), Rotary Club. Republican. Roman Catholic. Office: 7711 Louis Pasteur Dr Ste 706 San Antonio TX 78229-3422

SERVER, RONALD DOUGLAS, criminologist, political scientist, lawyer, educator; b. Fort Worth, Oct. 19, 1950; s. Frederick Douglas and Mabel Marie (Brown) S. BA, Prairie View A&M U., 1974; MPA, Tex. Christian U., 1976; JD, South Tex. Coll. of Law, 1984. Bar: Tex. 1985. Adminstrv. intern Tarrant County Hosp. Dist., Fort Worth, 1975-76; asst. city mgr. City of Weatherford, Tex., 1976-77; asst. prof. Prairie View (Tex.) A&M U., 1977-88, coord. criminal justice program, 1989—, interim head social and polit. sci. dept., 1994—; assoc. Glenn Taylor & Assocs., Hempstead, Tex., 1992—. Author: Houston Defender, 1993. Vol. adv. coun. Atty. Gen. Office-CS, Houston, 1992—; parliamentarian Faculty Senate-Prairie View A&M U., 1991—. Named Advisor of the Yr., Prairie View A&M U., 1992. Mem. Tex. Bar Assn., Nat. Acad. Advisement Assn., Southwestern Pre Law Advisors Assn. (v.p. 1996—)., So. Assn. Pre Law Advisors, Nat. Assn. Blacks in Criminal Justice. Democrat. Office: Prairie View A&M U PO Box 748 Prairie View TX 77446-0748

SESSIONS, GEORGE PURD, physician; b. Dawson, Ga., July 9, 1931; s. George Purdee and Jessie Louise (Ferguson) S.; m. Martha Ann Hernandez, June 30, 1960; children: William Dean, Neal Bradley, Annette Elaine. BS, U. Ga., 1952; MD, Med. Coll. of Ga., 1955. Diplomate Am. Bd. Anesthesiology. Intern Macon (Ga.) Hosp., 1955-56; sr. asst. surgeon USPHS, New London, Conn., 1956-58; resident Charity Hosp., New Orleans, 1958-60; instr. in anesthesia Emory U., Atlanta, 1960-61; chief dept. anesthesiology DeKalb Gen. Hosp., Decatur, Ga., 1961-81, Scottish Rite Hosp., Decatur, 1965-74, Decatur Hosp., 1972-82; pres. DeKalb Anesthesia Assocs., P.A., 1970-95. With USPHS, 1956-58. Mem. AMA, Med. Assn. of Ga., So. Med. Assn., Am. Soc. Anesthesiology, Ga. Soc. Anesthesiology (pres. 1972-73). Home: 1658 Mason Mill Rd NE Atlanta GA 30329-4133 Office: DeKalb Anesthesia Assocs PA 2675 N Decatur Rd Ste 309 Decatur GA 30033-6132

SESSIONS, JEFFERSON BEAUREGARD, III, state attorney general; b. Selma, Ala., Dec. 24, 1946; s. Jefferson Beauregard and Abbie (Powe) S.; m. Mary Montgomery Blackshear, Aug. 9, 1969; children: Mary Abigail, Ruth Blackshear, Samuel Turner. B.A., Huntingdon Coll., Montgomery, Ala., 1969; J.D., U. Ala., 1973. Bar: Ala. 1973. Assoc. Guin, Bouldin & Porch, Russellville, Ala., 1973-75; asst. U.S. atty. U.S. Dept. Justice, Mobile, Ala., 1975-77, U.S. atty., 1981-93; assoc., ptnr. Stockman & Bedsole Attys., Mobile, Ala., 1977-81; ptnr. Stockman, Bedsole & Sessions, Mobile, 1993-94; atty. gen. State of Ala., 1996—; mem. U.S. atty's. com. on legis. and rules, 1983-85; mem. U.S. atty. gen's. adv. com., 1987-89, vice chmn. 1989; chmn. controlled substances subcom. U.S. atty. gen's. adv. com., 1992-93. Presdl. elector State of Ala., 1972; mem. bd. trustees, exec. com. Mobile Bay Area Partnership for Youth, 1981—; chmn. adminstrv. bd. Ashland Pl. United Meth. Ch., Mobile, 1982; mem. bd. dirs. Mobile Child Advocacy Ctr., 1988—; chmn. com. on govt., judiciary and law enforcement Coalition for a Drug Free Mobile, 1990-93; 1st v.p. Mobile Lions Club, 1993-94. Capt. USAR, 1975-85. Recipient U.S. Atty. Gen's. award for significant achievements in the war against drug trafficking U.S. Atty. Gen. William P. Barr, 1992. Mem. ABA, Ala. Bar Assn., Mobile Bar Assn., Omicron Delta Kappa. Home: 16 S Lafayette St Mobile AL 36604-1714 Office: Office of Atty General 11 S Union St Montgomery AL 36104-3760

SESSIONS, ROGER CARL, emergency physician; b. Stamps, Ark., Oct. 4, 1944; s. Darrell Inman and Linda Evelyn (Rogers) S.; m. Sherri Lorene Steward, June 12, 1971 (div. Oct. 1981); 1 child, David Steward. BSE, So. Ark. U., 1966; MS, Henderson State U., 1971; DO, Tex. Coll. Osteo. Medicine, 1981. Diplomate Am. Bd. Emergency Medicine. Asst. coach Tex. H.S., Texarkana, 1966-67; track coach Atlanta H.S., Tex., 1967-72; football coach, athletic dir. N.W. H.S., Justin, Tex., 1972-77; intern Dallas-Ft. Worth Med. Ctr., Grand Prairie, Tex., 1981-82, practice emergency medicine, 1987-96; pvt. practice emergency medicine, 1982—; with EmCare, Dallas, 1989-96; dir. emergency dept. New Boston Gen. Hosp., Tex., 1984-87, Mesquite (Tex.) Physician's Hosp., 1987-88, North Tex. Med. Ctr., 1991-93; with Baylor Med. Ctr., Grapevine, Tex., 1996—; rsch. dir. Ferris, Inc., Burr Ridge, Ill. Fellow Am. Coll. Emergency Physicians; mem. AMA, Am. Coll. Sports Medicine, Tex. Coll. Emergency Physicians. Avocation: running.

SETHI, KAPIL DEV, physician; b. Sultanpur, Punjab, India, June 19, 1953; arrived in U.S., 1983; s. Sada Nand and Sumitra (Kataria) S.; m. Ranjit K. Makhni, Feb. 26, 1978; children: Aditi, Gaurav, Ajay. MBBS, CMC, Ludhiana, 1976; MD, PGI, Chandigarh, 1979, DM, 1981; postgrad., Inst. MEd. Edn. and Rsch., 1976-79. Diplomate Am. Bd. Psychiatry and Neurology; bd. cert. in internal medicine India. Rotating intern Christian Med. Coll. and Brown Meml. Hosp., Ludhiana, India, 1975-76; resident teaching, fellow in neurology Inst. of Med. Edn. and Rsch., Chandigarh, India, 1979-81; rsch. fellow, neurology Charing Cross Group of Hosps. Med. Sch., London, 1982-82; registrar neurology Welsh Nat. Sch. Medicine, Morristown Hosp., 1982-83; resident in neurology Med. Coll. Ga., Augusta, 1983-85; asst. prof. neurology Med. Coll. of Ga., Augusta, 1985-91, assoc. prof. neurology, 1991—, dir. movement disorders clinic, 1985—, co-dir. Chemodenervation Clinic, 1990—; staff physician VA Hosp., 1985—; quality assurance com. Med. Coll. Ga. Hosp., phase III curriculum com., 1989-93, libr. com., 1986—; chmn. session on disease of the extrapyramidal motor system World Congress of Neurology, New Delhi, India, 1989; vis. prof. Cleve. Clinic, 1991, U. Ill., Sch. Medicine, Peoria, 1990; lectr. in field. Editl. reviewer Neurology, 1977—, Am. Jour. Dermatology, 1987, Movement Disorders, 1990—, Southern Med. Jour., 1991—, Jour. of Neuropsychiatry and Clin. Neurosci., 1990—, Jour. of Family Practice, 1992—; author: Geriatrics, 1988, Tremor-Current Diagnosis in Neurology, 1993, Paroxysmal Dyskinesias; contbr. chpts. to books and numerous articles to profl. jours. Recipient numerous rsch. grants. Mem. AMA, Royal Coll. of Physicians, Am. Acad. Neurology (co-chmn. session on anterior horn cell 1989), Movement Disorder Soc. (co-chmn. hyperkinetic movement disorders 1993), Am. Assn. of Physicians from India, Assn. of Indian Neurologists in Am. (bd. dirs.). Home: 3709 Merion Dr Augusta GA 30907-9034

SEVERE, JOHN THOMAS, lawyer; b. Perry, Okla., Nov. 17, 1951; s. Claude Otto and Irma Bonita (Nida) S.; m. Karen Suzanne McCracken, Dec. 29, 1973; children: Melissa Marie, John Thomas III. BS, Okla. State U., 1974; JD, Okla. City U., 1978. Bar: Okla. 1978, U.S. Dist. Ct. (no. dist.) Okla. 1978, U.S. Dist. Ct. (we. dist.) Okla. 1982, U.S. Ct. Appeals (10th cir.) 1979, U.S. Supreme Ct. 1982. Asst. city atty. City of Stillwater, Okla., 1978-79, acting city atty., 1979-80; atty. pvt. practice, Stillwater, 1979—, Perry, 1987-92; asst. dist. atty. Payne & Logan Counties, Stillwater, 1981-85. Bd. dirs., v.p., allocations com. chair Stillwater United Way, 1981-83; mem. amb. com. Stillwater C. of C., 1981—; mem. Friends of Scouting, Boy Scouts Am., 1990-95; vol. coach Pks. and Recreation Youth Baseball, Youth Football, 1987-93, YMCA Youth Flag Football, YMCA Youth Wrestling, 1992-93; coach Stillwater Royals Baseball, 1994, Stillwater Cowboys Baseball, 1995, Stillwater Sox Baseball Assn.; founding mem. Stillwater Wrestling Club, 1990, pres., 1990-91, 91-92; bd. dirs. Stillwater LIFE Ctr., 1989-92. Fellow Okla. Bar Found.; mem. ABA, ATLA, Okla. Bar Assn., Okla. Trial Lawyers Assn., Payne County Bar Assn (law day chair 1979, 89, v.p. 1985), Noble County Bar Assn., Pawnee County Bar Assn., Lions Internat., Phi Delta Phi. Democrat. Mem. Christian Ch. (Disciples of Christ). Office: 2317 W 7th Pl Stillwater OK 74074-1902

SEVIER, ELISABETH, French language educator, writer; b. Larissa, Greece, Dec. 15, 1930; came to U.S., 1955; d. Marcel U. and Therese (Tchichekian) Kapelian; m. Robert Wesley Sevier, July 25, 1958; children: Adele, Renee, Lisa. BS in Edn., N.Mex. State U., 1971. Cert. tchr., Okla. Commd. 2d lt. French Army, 1945, advanced through grades to capt., 1953; nurse French Army, France and Indo-China, 1945-53, Hotel Dieu Hosp., El Paso, Tex., 1955-58, Sacred Heart Hosp., Red Bud, Ill., 1959-68; tchr. French Radford Sch. for Girls, El Paso, 1971-75, Edmond (Okla.) Meml. H.S., 1980—. Author: Lisette, 1995. Decorated Croix de Guerre with bronze star, Paris, 1948, Cross of Lorraine, Paris, 1948, Colonial medal, Indo-China, 1953. Mem. NEA, Am. Assn. Tchrs. of French, Okla. Assn. Tchrs. of French (pres. 1983), Phi Kappa Phi, Kappa Kappa Iota. Office: Edmond Meml HS 1000 Fifteenth St Edmond OK 73013

SEVIN, DIETER HERMANN, language and literature professional, educator; b. Mühlanger, Germany, Nov. 5, 1938; came to U.S. 1958; s. Wolf-Dieterich and Erna (Brockmann) S.; m. Ingrid Antje Dirks, June 15, 1963; children: Sonja, Karen. BA, San Jose State U., 1963; MA, U. Wash., 1964, PhD, 1967. Asst. prof. Pacific Lutheran U., Tacoma, Wash., 1967-68; asst. prof. Vanderbilt U., Nashville, 1968-73, assoc. prof., 1973-82, prof., 1982—. Author: Zur Diskussion: A Modern Approach to German Conversation, 3d edit., 1987, Christa Wolf (interpretation), 3d edit., 1995, Wie Geht's? An Introductory German Course, 5th edit., 1995; editor: Die Resonanz des Exils, 1992, Teststrategien in DDR-Prosawerken zwischen Bau und Durchbruch der Berliner Mauer, 1994; contbr. numerous articles on German lit. and culture to profl. jours. Fellow Am. Philos. Soc. (grant 1991), Am. Council of Learned Socs. (grant 1981-82), German Academic Exchange Svc. (grant 1980). Office: Vanderbilt U Dept Germanic And Slav Nashville TN 37235

SEWARD, TROILEN GAINEY, psychologist; b. Petersburg, Va., Nov. 26, 1941; d. Troy L. and Mary (Nester) Gainey; m. William E. Seward III, June 29, 1963; children: Susan Blair, William E. IV. BA, Coll. William and Mary, 1963, MEd, 1980, EdS, 1980; MEd, Va. Commonwealth U., 1977. Elem. tchr. Petersburg, 1963-67; secondary tchr. Surry (Va.) Acad., 1967-76, guidance counselor, 1976-77; headmistress Tidewater Acad., Wakefield, Va., 1977-79; psychologist Peninsula Child Devel. Clinic, Newport News, Va., 1980-82; sch. psychologist Dinwiddie (Va.) Pub. Sch., 1982-89, dir. pupil pers. svcs., spl. edn., 1990-93, dir. student svcs., 1993-95, supt., 1996—; mem. human rights com. Southside Tng. Ctr., Petersburg, 1986—. Trustee Ritchie Meml. ch., Claremont, Va., 1971—; mem. Town Coun., Claremont, 1984-90, mem. fin. com., 1984-90. Mem. Nat. Assn. Sch. Psychologists (del. 1992-94), Va. Assn. Sch. Psychologists (chair cert. and licensure com. 1985-87, legis. chair 1987—, pres. 1989-91), Delta Kappa Gamma, Phi Kappa Phi. Episcopalian. Home: PO Box 266 Claremont VA 23899-0266

SEWPERSHAD, LIONEL, principal; b. Bath, Berbice, Guyana, Sept. 2, 1940; came to U.S., 1964; s. Baldeo and Ramouti (Balkaran) Prasad; m. Leticia Rafaela Detres, Aug. 10, 1967 (div. 1981); children: Leticia Chandini, Ileana Natasha; m. Marta Cecilia Orta Sewpershad, Dec. 31, 1985. BA summa cum laude, Inter Am. U., 1967; MA, Brandeis U., 1981; postgrad., SUNY, Binghamton, 1967-68, U. Miami, 1987—. Elem. sch. tchr. St. Thomas Luth. Sch., Berbice, Guyana, 1958-60; civil svc. clk. II Ministry of Home Affairs, Georgetown, Guyana, 1960-64; lectr. Inter Am. U., San German, P.R., 1968-70; sociologist Planning Secretariat Ministry of Econ. Devel., Georgetown, 1972-74; social worker Dept. Welfare, Christiansted, St. Croix, V.I., 1974-76; tchr. Arthur Richards Jr. High Sch., Frederiksted, St. Croix, 1977-86; asst. prin. Evelyn M. Williams Sch., Mt. Pleasant, St. Croix, 1986-91, Charles H. Emanuel Sch., Kingshill, St. Croix, V.I., 1991-94; instr. U. V.I., Kingshill, 1983—; prin. Pearl B. Larsen Sch., Christiansted, V.I., 1994-95, Juanita F. Gardine Sch., Christiansted, 1995—; dir. adult basic edn. Dept. Edn., Christiansted, St. Croix, V.I., 1991-94. Pres. Mon Bijou Tenant Assn., St. Croix, 1980-83; bd. dirs. Community Action Agy. St. Croix, 1980-83. Mem. ASCD, Caribbean Studies Assn., Frederiksted Lions (pres. 1986-88) St. Croix Ednl. Adminstrs. Assn. (v.p. 1989-91), Caribbean Light Lodge 101, Phi Delta Kappa (pres. chpt. 1496). Home: PO Box 2814 Frederiksted VI 00841-2814 Office: Juanita F. Gardine Sch Christiansted VI 00820

SEXAUER, BRADLEY LESTER, healthcare administrator; b. Evansville, Ind., Aug. 13, 1951; s. Adolph L. and Edna L. (Ernst) S. BA, DePauw U., 1973; MHA, Tulane U., 1976; MBA, U. S.D., Vermillion, 1980. Adminstrv. asst. Tulane Med. Ctr. Hosp., New Orleans, 1976-77; assoc. dir. S.D. Health Systems Agy., Vermillion, 1977-81; mgr. regional planning Humana Inc., Orange Park, Fla., 1981-84; field v.p. Nat. Med. Enterprises, Atlanta, 1984-87; corp. v.p. planning Ingalls Health System, Harvey, Ill., 1987-92; v.p. planning and mktg. Danville (Va.) Regional Med. Ctr., 1992—. Fellow Am. Coll. Healthcare Execs., Soc. for Healthcare Planning and Mktg., Va. Inst. Polit. Leadership U. Va. Home: 228 Oak Creek Dr Danville VA 24541-6269 Office: Danville Regional Med Ctr 142 S Main St Danville VA 24541-2922

SEXSON, STEPHEN BRUCE, educational writer, educator; b. Silver City, N.Mex., May 29, 1948; s. Ralph Dale and Wanda Claudean (McMahan) S.; m. Barbara Jane Davis, May 24, 1968; children: David Paul, Linda Carol. BA in Rhetoric and Pub. Address, Pepperdine U., 1969, MA in Pub. Comm., 1975; EdD in Higher Edn., Okla. State U., 1990. Asst. to supt. Morongo Unified Sch. Dist., 29 Palms, Calif., 1973-77; corp. trainer Merrill Lynch Realty, Dallas, 1979-81; sch. psychologist Texhoma (Tex.) Sch. Dist., 1982-83; assoc. prof., dir. Christian Student Ctr. Okla. Panhandle State U., Goodwell, 1982-84; rsch. resident Okla. State U., Stillwater, 1984-87; mem. spl. programs staff L.A. Unified Sch. Dist., 1987-93; dir. Edwest Edn. Rsch., Burbank, Calif., 1991—; guest lectr. edn. Okla. State U., Stillwater, 1993-94, U. Tulsa, 1993-94; conv. spkr. Merrill Lynch Realty-Relo, Atlanta, 1979. Author: The Magic Classroom, 1995, The Values Rich Teacher, 1996; contbr. articles to profl. jours. Mem. ASCD, Am. Assn. Sch. Adminstrs., Nat. Assn. of Sch. Psychologists, Lions Club, Phi Delta Kappa. Home: 266 Backs Ln #B Placentia CA 92870

SEXTON, BRENDA ATWELL, nursing educator; b. Abingdon, Va., Oct. 20, 1962; d. Carl Edward Jr. and Barbara Jean (Testerman) Atwell; 1 child, Joshua Casey. ADN, Wytheville (Va.) C.C., 1984; BSN cum laude, East Tenn. State U., 1985; postgrad., U. Tenn., 1985—. RN, Va.; Registered Nurse Cert., ANCC, Va.; cert. cmty. 1st aid instr., Va.; cert. ACLS, Va., BLS instr., ARC, Va.; cert. instr. Breast Self-Exam, Testicular Self-Exam and smoking cessation classes, ARC, Va. Staff, charge nurse Bristol (Tenn.) Meml. Hosp., 1985-87; staff nurse Meml. Mission Hosp., Asheville, N.C., 1987-88; staff, relief charge nurse oncology Humana Hosp. Bayside, Virginia Beach, Va., 1988-89; staff nurse orthopedic unit Chesapeake (Va.) Gen. Hosp., 1989-92, clin. nurse educator, 1992—; clin. instr. Tidewater C.C., Portsmouth, Va., 1991. Mem. Am. Soc. Health Edn. and Tng. (Va. chpt.), Educators Awareness Group Hampton Rds., Sigma Theta Tau (Epsilon chpt.). Baptist. Home: 1332 Fallmouth Ct Virginia Beach VA 23464-6320 Office: Chesapeake Gen Hosp 736 Battlefield Blvd N Chesapeake VA 23320-4941

SEXTON, JEAN ELIZABETH, librarian; b. Boone, N.C., June 24, 1959; d. Warren G. and Carol Jean (Smith) S. AA, Chowan Coll., Murfreesboro, N.C., 1979; AB, U. N.C., 1981, MS in Libr. Sci., 1983. Cataloging libr. Pembroke (N.C.) State U., 1983-89, coord. tech. svcs., 1989-92, asst. dir., coord. tech. svcs., 1992—; cons. Whitaker Libr. Chowan Coll., 1989—. Editor Libr. Lines, 1992; contbr. articles to profl. jours. Order of Silver Feather. Mem. N.C. Libr. Assn., Southeastern Libr. Assn., Dickens Fellowship, N.C. Zool. Soc., N.C. Aquariums. Democrat. Baptist. Home: 118 Charles St Apt 3 Lumberton NC 28358 Office: U NC Pembroke Livermore Libr Pembroke NC 28372

SEYDEL, SCOTT O'SULLIVAN, chemical company executive; b. Atlanta, Mar. 29, 1940; s. John Rutherford and Jane (Reynolds) S.; m. Ruth Clark, Apr. 20, 1985; children: John Rutherford II, Rosina Marie, Lael Elizabeth, Scott O'Sullivan, Howard Clark. Student Ga. Inst. Tech., 1959-62, U. Ga. Sch. Journalism, 1962-63; student bus. adminstrn. N. Tex. State U., 1963. With Tex. Textile Mills, Inc., McKinney, 1963-64; personnel dir. 1965 Corp., AZS Corp., Atlanta, 1965, pub. relations dir., 1966, asst. v.p., 1967, asst. exec. v.p., 1968, corp. dir., 1968-71, v.p. diversification, dir. internat. activities, 1969-70; pres. Seydel Cos., Atlanta, 1970—; v.p., dir. SICHEM, Ghent, Belgium, 1975-78, SICO South Africa, Durben, South Africa, 1975—, Siven, S.A., Caracas, Venezuela, 1978-84; v.p. European Homes, Ltd., 1987-91; bd. dirs. Gorden Bailey & Assocs., Seydel Peruana, S.A., Complete Health, Evo Rsch. Inc., Petrock, Inc. Contbr. articles to profl. jours.; patentee in field. Bd. dirs. Coll. Internat. Bus., Ga. State U., Brandalan, Inc., Global Green, Inc.; chmn. Met. Atlanta YMCA (chmn.), 1991—; bd. dirs., chmn. legis. com. Ga. High Tech Alliance, chmn., 1994—; v.p., bd. dirs. African Bus. Devel. Coun.; mem. exec. com. Inst. for Internat. Edn.; dir. Atlanta Triad Edn. Consortium; chmn. bd. advs. Ga. World Congress Inst., 1981-83; trustee Atlanta Internat. Sch. Named Internat. Businessman of Yr. Gov. of Ga., 1988. Fellow Am. Assn. Textile Chemists and Colorists; mem. Internat. Council for Textile Technologists (dir. 1957—, sec. 1971-88), So. Textile Assn., Atlanta Assn. Internat. Edn. (dir.), U.S. C. of C. (exec. res. com., export coun., exec. com. 1989—), Atlanta Benedicts (v.p. 1972, dir. 1971-73), Atlanta Carribean Trade Orgn. (bd. dirs.), Atlanta C. of C. (vice chmn. 1995—), Chi Phi. Clubs: Piedmont Driving (Atlanta), World Trade Club (bd. dirs. 1992). Lodge: Rotary. Home: 1021 West Peachtree Battle Ct NW Atlanta GA 30327 Office: Seydel Cos 4200 Northside Pky NW Atlanta GA 30327-3054

SEYFERT, JEFF LYNN, business educator; b. Seminole, Okla., Feb. 1, 1965; s. Carl J. and Mary W. (Snell) S.; m. Erica R. Nottnagel, Dec. 28, 1991. AA, Seminole Jr. Coll., Seminole, Okla., 1985; BS, Southern Nazarene Univ., 1987; MBA, The Univ. Tulsa, 1989. Residence dir. The Univ. Tulsa, Tulsa, Okla., 1987-90; asst. prof. Southern Nazarene Univ., Bethany, Okla., 1990—; SBI dir. Southern Nazarene Univ., 1991—. Mem. Am. Mktg. Assn. Republican. Home: 806 Ranchoak Dr Yukon OK 73099 Office: Southern Nazarene Univ 6729 NW 39th Expressway Bethany OK 73008

SEYKORA, MARGARET S., psychotherapist; b. N.Y.C., June 18, 1947; d. Stanley Sneider and Janet Pick (Sneider) Smith; m. Sern A. Seykora, Jan. 19, 1968 (div. 1984); m. H. Lester Mower, Jr., Nov. 19, 1993. BS in Journalism, U. Fla., 1970; MA in Edn. and Human Devel. Counseling, Rollins Coll., 1991. Lic. mental health counselor, Fla.; lic. mortgage broker, Fla., lic. real estate broker, Fla. Advt. profl. Gainesville (Fla.) Sun, 1968-75, TV mag. editor, 1968-75, Sunday/lesiure/book editor, 1970; stoneware potter, owner Old Town (Fla.) Pottery, 1975-82; real estate salesperson Jack McCormick Realty, Chiefland, Fla., 1982-85, Coldwell Banker, Orlando, Fla., 1985-90; real estate broker The Hood Group, Inc., Orlando, 1990-92; psychotherapist, facilitator, pres. Personal Dynamics Inst., Altamonte Springs, Fla., 1989—; career instr. The Knowledge Shop, Winter Park, Fla., 1992—; outpatient clin. svcs. supr. Lakeside Alternatives, Winter Park, Fla., 1992—; adj. instr. Seminole C.C., Sanford, Fla., 1992—, Valencia C.C., Winter Park, 1992—. Author/facilitator workshops in field. Mem. Nat. Bd. Counselors, Am. Counseling Assn., Assn. for Specialists in Group Work, Nat. Bd. Realtors. Mem. Ch. of Religious Sci. Office: Personal Dynamics Inst 421 Montgomery Rd Ste 105 Altamonte Springs FL 32714-3140

SEYKOWSKI, ROSEMARY TERESA, operations research, management scientist; b. Pitts., Jan. 29, 1964; d. John Vincent and Rosemarie Magdeline (Mooney) Battles; m. Craig Michael Seykowski, Oct. 12, 1991. Student, Pa. State U., 1981-82; BA in Math., W. Va. U., 1985; MS in Ops. Rsch./Mgmt. Sci., George Mason U., Fairfax, Va., 1994. Instr. W.Va. U., Morgantown, 1982-85; ops. rsch. analyst Sys. Planning and Analysis Inc., Falls Church, Va., 1985-88; sr. sys. analyst Def. Group, Inc., Arlington, Va., 1988-91; asst. prof. CIS dept. No. Va. C.C., Loudoin, Va., 1994-96; sr. ops. rsch. analyst The Mitre Corp., McLean, Va., 1991—. Swimming coach Spl. Olympics, Annandale, Va., 1995; mem. festival com. ARC, Alexandria, Va., 1991-93; catechist vol. St. Bernadette's Ch., Springfield, Va., 1987—. Mem. Inst. for Ops. Rsch. and Mgmt. Sci., Washington Ops. Rsch./Mgmt. Sci. Coun., Mil. Ops. Rsch. Soc., Pi Mu Epsilon. Roman Catholic. Office: Mitre Corporation 1820 Dolley Madison Blvd Mc Lean VA 22102

SEYMOUR, BARBARA LAVERNE, lawyer; b. Columbia, S.C., July 9, 1953; d. Leroy Semon and Barbara Lucile (Youngblood) Seymour. BS, S.C. State Coll., 1975; JD, Georgetown U., 1979; MBA, Harvard U., 1985. Bar: S.C. 1979, Tex. 1984, U.S. Dist. Ct. (ea. dist.) Tex. 1983, U.S. Dist. Ct. (so. dist.) Tex. 1985, U.S. Tax Ct. 1986, U.S. Claims Ct. 1991. Tax atty. Texaco Inc., White Plains, N.Y., 1979-80, Houston, 1980—; mem. IRS Commr.'s Adv. Group; mem. Simplified Tax and Wage Reporting Sys. Working Group; loaned exec. for task force to audit Tex. Employment Commn. by Gov. of Tex., 1987-88. Troop leader Girl Scouts U.S., White Plains, 1979-80, asst. troop leader, Houston, 1981-82; bd. dirs. Sickle Cell Disease Rsch. Found. Tex., Houston, 1986-92, treas., 1986-88, pres., 1988-90, chair 25th anniversary gala, 1996; vol. allocation panel United Way of the Tex. Gulf Coast; mem. Black Exec. Exch. program Nat. Urban League 1980—; mem. bus. adv. coun. S.C. State Coll. Sch. Bus., 1990-93; bd. dirs., exec. com. Houston Area Urban League, 1995—; mem. bus. adv. coun. S.C. State Coll. Sch. Bus., 1990-93. Named One of 50 Outstanding Young Leaders of the Future, Ebony Mag., 1983; recipient Disting. Bus. Alumnus award S.C. State Coll., 1991, Eagle award Nat. Eagle Leadership Inst., 1995; selected for Leadership Houston, Leadership Am., 1990; finalist Five Outstanding Young Houstonians award Jaycees, 1988, one of 10 Foremost Fashionables in Houston, Alpha Kappa Alpha, 1994. Mem. ABA (environ. tax com.), Houston Black Women Lawyers Assn. (sec. 1981-82, treas. 1982-83), Houston Bus. Forum (bd. dirs. 1983, 87-90, treas. 1988-89, sec. 1989-90), Nat. Bar Assn. (com. chmn. 1982-83), S.C. Bar Assn., Tex. Bar Assn., Harvard U. Bus. Sch. Black Alumni Assn. (historian 1985-86), Black Law Alumni Coun. of Georgetown U. Law Ctr., W.J. Durham Soc., The Links, Inc. (v.p. Houston chpt. 1996—, chair 1995 Cotillion), Alpha Kappa Alpha. Democrat. Roman Catholic. Office: Texaco Inc 1111 Bagby St Houston TX 77002-2551

SEYMOUR, NATASHA DENISE, secondary education educator; b. Memphis, Oct. 2, 1972; d. James Edward Sr. and Shirley Faye (Harrison) S. BS, Vanderbilt U., 1994. Tchr. Germantown H.S. Shelby County Schs., Memphis, 1994—. Mem. NEA, ASCD, Nat. Coun. Tchrs. Math. Democrat. Baptist. Office: Shelby County Schs Germantown H S 7543 Poplar Pike Germantown TN

SGANGA, JOHN B., furniture holding company executive; b. Bronx, N.Y., Nov. 21, 1931; s. Charles and Marie (Crusco) S.; B.S. in Acctg. cum laude, Bklyn. Coll., 1961; postgrad. Bernard Baruch Coll.; m. Evelyn Joan Battilana, Jan. 19, 1957; children: Mark, John B. Jr., Matthew. Systems analyst DIVCO, Wayne, N.Y., 1965-67; mgr. mgmt. cons. services Coopers & Lybrand, C.P.A.s, N.Y.C., 1967-74; sr. v.p. fin. and adminstrn. Aurora Products Co. subs. RJR Nabisco, West Hempstead, N.Y., 1974-79; controller Gt. Lakes Carbon Corp., N.Y.C., 1979-80, v.p., 1980-81, sr. v.p. fin., CFO, 1981-86; v.p. Cunard Line, Ltd., N.Y.C., 1988; exec. v.p., CFO Consolidated Furniture Corp. (formerly Mohasco Corp.), Wilmington, Del., 1989—, also bd. dirs. Served with USNR, 1950-54. Mem. Inst. Cert. Mgmt. Cons. (a founder), Inst. Mgmt. Accts., Fin. Execs. Inst. (past chmn. com. M.I.S.). Clubs: Treas.'s, Brookside Racquet and Swim. Contbr. articles to jours. in field; editl. adv. to Financial Management mag. Home: 255 Davidson Ave Ramsey NJ 07446-1003 Office: Consolidated Furniture Corp One Commerce Ctr 1201 N Orange St Ste 790 Wilmington DE 19801-1119

SGRO, BEVERLY HUSTON, state official, educator; b. Ft. Worth, Jan. 12, 1941; d. James Carl and Dorothy Louise (Foster) Huston; m. Joseph Anthony Sgro, Feb. 1, 1964; children: Anthony, Jennifer. BS, Tex. Woman's U., 1963; MS, Va. Poly. Inst. and State U., 1974, PhD, 1990. Cert. tennis teaching profl. Instr. of deaf Midland (Tex.) Ind. Sch. System, 1963-64; speech pathologist Arlington (Tex.) Pub. Sch. System, 1964; rsch. asst. Tex. Christian U., 1964-65; tennis profl. Blacksburg (Va.) Country Club, 1977-81; from coord. for Greek affairs to exec. asst. to v.p. student affairs Va. Poly. Inst. and State U., Blacksburg, 1981-89, dean of students, 1989-93; sec. of edn. Commonwealth of Va., Richmond, 1994—; adj. faculty Coll. Edn., Va. Poly. Inst. and State U.; lectr., presented papers at numerous symposia and convs., 1983—. Trustee Foxcroft Sch., Middleburg, Va., 1989—, pres. bd. trustees, 1993—. Mem. AACD, Nat. Assn. Student Pers. Adminstrs., Am. Coll. Pers. Assn. (sec., com. mem. 1986-88), Omicron Delta Kappa, Phi Kappa Phi, Phi Upsilon Omicron, Pi Lambda Theta, Sigma Alpha Eta, Zeta Phi Eta. Home: 1324 Maple Ave Richmond VA 23216 Office: Educ Office 9th St Office Bldg 5th Fl Richmond VA 23219

SHABAAZ, AHIA, family nurse practitioner; b. Newark, Apr. 13, 1950; d. William F. and Marguerite L. (Brown) Woodson; m. Warren N. Moore, Mar. 25, 1986; children: Mason H. Smith, Theresa L. Smith. BS in Psychology, SUNY, Albany, 1983; BSN, Tenn. State U., Nashville, 1985; MPH, U. Tenn., 1991; MSN, Vanderbilt U., 1995. RN, Tenn.; cert. advanced practice nurse, Tex. Cmty. health nurse Bapt. Hosp. Home Care, Nashville, 1989-91; healthcare cons. Africare, Washington, 1990-91; commd. lt. comdr. USPHS, 1992-94; med. coord. Sierra Leone Red Cross Soc., 1992; dep. dir. Jackson-Hinds Birth Ctr., Jackson, Miss., 1992-93; program dir. Health Care for the Homeless, Bethesda, Md., 1993-94; managed care health cons. Nashville, 1994-96; family nurse practitioner Deep East Tex. Regional Health Ctr., Newton, 1996—; part-time grad. tchg. assoc. U. Tenn., Knoxville; part-time staff nurse labor and delivery unit U. Tenn. Med. Ctr., Knoxville. 1st lt. U.S. Army, 1986-89, capt. USAR, 1989-92. Mem. ANA, Am. Heart Assn., Am. Acad. Nurse Practitioners, Tenn. Nurses' Assn., APHA, Am. Coll. Healthcare Execs, Sigma Theta Tau. Home: 125 Avondale Access Rd Hendersonville TN 37075-5842

SHABAZZ, AIYSHA MUSLIMAH, social work administrator; b. Columbia, S.C., Aug. 9, 1942; d. Jerry James Gadson and Edna Louise (Bellinger) Gadson Smalls; m. Abdullah Muslim Shabazz, July 28; children: Ain, Wali. BA, Fed. City Coll., Washington, 1973; MSW with honors, U. S.C., 1994, postgrad., 1994-95. Cert. child protective svcs. investigator, S.C., adoption investigator, S.C.; lic. social worker and ACBSW; cert. AIDS instr. ARC; lic. notary pub., S.C. Social work asst. Family Service Ctr., Washington, 1966-68; admission counselor Washington Tech. Inst., Washington, 1968-70; program dir. Park Motor Community Ctr., Washington, 1970-75; adminstrv. asst. Neighborhood Planning Council, Washington, 1974-75; substitue tchr. D.C. Pub. Sch. System, Washington, 1974-75; substitute tchr. Dist. I Pub. Schs., Columbia, 1977; home sch. program dir. Community Care, Inc., Columbia, 1977-81; monitor summer program U. S.C., Columbia, 1982; program dir. Dept. Social Services, Columbia, 1984—, case auditor, 1987-88, social worker supr., 1988—, project adminstr. for a alcohol and drug abuse program, 1994—; writer Acad. of Bacholu-Social Workers Exam, 1991; cons. substance abuse resch. program evaln., 1994—. substance abspeaker in field. Bd. dirs. Frederick Douglas Inst., Washington, 1968-69; pres. Park Motor Resident Coun., Washington, 1972-75; expert witness Family Ct.; bd. dirs. Coun. on Child Abuse and Neglect; adv. com., v.p. Benedict Coll. Sch. Social Work, S.C. Protection and Advocacy Handicapped Children; vol. AIDS instr. ARC, 1994; chairperson coordinating com. Voice of the Customer, 1995—. Mem. NASW (bd. dirs. 1993-95), S.C. Child Abuse and Neglect Task Force, AIDS Task Force (chmn. 1987-89). Democrat. Office: Dept Social Services 3220 Two Notch Rd Columbia SC 29204-2826

SHACHNOW, DOUGLAS ALLEN, travel industry educator, writer; b. New Rochelle, N.Y., Sept. 11, 1950; s. Leonard Howard and Peggy (Feldman) S. BS in Fgn. Langs., Georgetown U., 1972. Apartment leasing mngr. Columbus Assoc., N.Y.C., 1970-77; founder, pres. Octagon Cinema Equipment Mfg. Corp., N.Y.C., 1978-82; founding ptnr. Schoen-Douglas Inc., N.Y.C., 1982-85; v.p. adminstrn. Heritage Park Corp., Holmdel, N.J., 1985-86; v.p. mgr. apt. loan orgn. Columbia Equities, Ltd., Scarsdale & Tarrytown, N.Y., 1986-89, Eagle Multi-Linding Corp., Westbury, N.Y., 1989-91; founder, pres. Travcomp Software Co. Inc., Rye, N.Y., 1992—; founder, owner Pacific Hemispheres Cruises and Tours, Palm Beach, Fla., 1994—; ind. cons. travel agency start-ups, Palm Beach, 1995—. Author: (instnl. manual) The B.O.K. Book, 1988, (textbooks) Sea Travel: The Book, 1995, Understanding Tours and Packages, 1996; sys. designer cons. software Cruise Counselor II; contbr. articles to mags. in field. Lectr., instr., docent in origami Morikami-Japanese Mus. and Gardens, Del Rey Beach, Fla., 1994—; founding dir. Friends of Origami Ctr. of Am., N.Y.C., 1982-89. Recipient citation as contbr. to edn. improvement Outside Sales Support Network, 1995. Mem. Cruise Lines Internat. Assn. (assoc.), Inst. Cert. Travel Agts., Nat. Assn. Cruise Only Agys., Pacific Area Travel Assn. (assoc.). Home: 13C Stratford Dr E Boynton Beach FL 33436

SHACKELFORD, ALPHONSO LEON, pharmacist, medical writer; b. Grapevine, Tex., June 4, 1920; s. Alphonso Lee and Ida May (Marriott) S.; m. Frances Chapman, June 30, 1945; children: Alan Eugene, Anne Marr, Sally Sue. BS, Coll. of Ozarks, 1949, DPharm, 1981. Registered pharmacist, Tex. Asst. chief pharmacy service Meth. Hosp., Dallas, 1949-51; pharmacist Myers and Rosser Prescription Pharmacy, Dallas, 1951-52; owner, operator Shackelford Prescription Pharmacy, Dallas, 1952-58; staff pharmacist Nix Meml. Hosp., San Antonio, 1958-60; pharmacy mgr. Sommers Drug Store, San Antonio, 1960-73; owner, cons. Alchem Assocs., San Antonio, 1973-83; staff pharmacist S.W. Gen. Hosp., San Antonio, 1983-87. Columnist Flying Rev., 1985—, news editor, 1986—; mem. edit. bd. Med. Communications. Vol. story teller Inst. Texan Culture, 1986. Served as sgt. USAAF, 1942-45. Mem. Am. Med. Writers Assn. (pres. S.W. chpt. 1979-82), U.S. Pilots Assn., Tex. Pilots Assn. Republican. Episcopalian. Home and Office: PO Box 28072 San Antonio TX 78228-0072

SHACKLEFORD, WILLIAM ALTON, SR., minister; b. Red Springs, N.C., Aug. 5, 1947; s. Purcell and Pearl (Walton) S.; m. Rebecca Belsches, Dec. 2, 1972; children: Kristal Lynn, William Alton Jr. Student, Hampton U., 1965-67, U. Richmond, 1969, 70; DD (hon.), Va. Sem. and Coll., 1990. Ordained to ministry Unity Bapt. Mins.' Conf., 1977. Pastor Cedar Grove Bapt. Ch., Charles City, Va., 1979-82, St. Paul High Street Bapt. Ch., Martinsville, Va., 1986—; past pres. Bapt. Sunday sch. and Bapt. Tng. Union Congress of Va., Sunday sch. Union of Hampton and Adjoining Cities, Unity Bapt. Min.'s Conf., Newport News, Va.; corr. sec. Va. Bapt. State Conv., 1986-96; sr. technician tech. svc. Badishe Corp., Williamsburg, Va., 1967-81, asst. supr. corp. office svcs., 1981-86. Contbr. articles to Martinsville Bull. Apptd. supt. Schs. Adv. Coun.; mem. Child Abuse and Neglect Multidiscipline Team; mem. exec. bd. Martinsville Voter's League, 1987—; mem. overall econ. devel. com., ad hoc drug and alcohol abuse com., past mem. adminstrv. bd. Martinsville Dept. Social Svcs.; mem. adv. coun. Good News Jail and Prison Ministries; past chmn. bd. dirs., mem. adv. com., mem. editl. bd. Patrick Henry Drug and Alcohol Coun.; vice chmn. Martinsville City Sch. Bd., 1991—; past chmn. bd. trustees Va. Sem. and Coll., Lynchburg, Va., 1992-96; v.p. Va. One Ch. One Child, 1992—; mem. edn. com. Va. Mcpl. League, 1993-95. Named Outstanding Min. Nat. Hairston Clan, 1988; recipient Dedicated Svc. award Va.'s One Ch. One Child Program, 1989, numerous others. Mem. NAACP, Smith River Bapt. Assn. (vice moderator), Martinsville and Henry County Ministerial Alliance (various positions). Home: 405 3rd St Martinsville VA 24112-3416 Office: St Paul High Street Bapt Ch PO Box 1003 401 Fayette St Martinsville VA 24114

SHADARAM, MEHDI, electrical engineering educator; b. Tehran, Iran, Apr. 19, 1954; came to U.S., 1976; s. Ali and Masoumeh (Bayram) S.; m. Luz Elena Inungaray, Mar. 24, 1990; 1 child, Jacob Benjamin. BSEE, U. Sci. and Tech., Tehran, 1976; MSEE, U. Okla., 1981, PhD in Elec. Engring., 1984. Registered profl. engr., Tex. Lab. asst. U. Okla. Elec. Engring. Dept., Norman, 1979-81, lab. instr., 1982-84; project engr. Ra Nav Lab., Oklahoma City, 1981-82; asst. prof. U. Tex. Elec. Engring. Dept., El Paso, 1984-90, assoc. prof., 1990—. Contbr. articles to profl. jours. Recipient Faculty Fellowship award Assoc. Western U., 1990, 1991, Advising the Best Thesis award U. Tex. El Paso, 1990, ASEE Faculty fellowship award, 1995, 96. Mem. IEEE (sr. mem., chmn. 1988-90, treas. 1987), Optical Soc. Am., Soc. Photo Optical and Instrumentation Engrs., Eta Kappa Nu. Home: 6518 Jim De Groat Dr El Paso TX 79912 Office: U Tex at El Paso Elec Engring Dept El Paso TX 79968

SHADDEN, MARIE CHRISTINE, criminal justice research professional; b. Oakland, Calif., Jan. 24, 1952; d. James and Barbara Matheney; m. David Shadden, May 10, 1975; 1 child, Michelle. BA in Criminology, U. Calif., Berkeley, 1974; MPA, Golden Gate U., 1989. Cert. instr. and police adminstr. Commd. 2d lt. USAF, 1974; advanced through grades to lt. col., 1991; pub. rels. officer 49th Security Police Squad, Holloman AFB, N.Mex., 1974-77; night ops. Security Police Squad, Spangdahlem AB, Fed. Republic of Germany, 1978-81; exec. asst., instr., commdr., historian Security Police Acad.-Lackland AFB, San Antonio, 1981-84; dir. police tng. Tactical Air Command, Langley AFB, Va., 1984-88; commdr., police chief, dir. security 832 air divsn., edn. officer, asst. prof., AFROTC Ariz. State U., Tempe, 1988-92; ret. USAF, 1992; exec. dir. MADD, Tenn., 1992-94; exec. asst. Tenn. Higher Edn. Commn., 1994, 1994—; assoc. Comty. Rsch. Assocs., Nashville, 1995—; chair DUI rate reduction com. Nashville Prevention Partnership, Nashville, 1993. Author: History of the USAF Security Police, 1947-1980, 1982; contbr. articles and revs. to profl. publs. Cons. pub. rels. Phoenix Friends of the Libr., Ironwood Branch, Ariz., 1991-93; mus. assoc. SP Mus. Found., San Antonio, 1982-84; active Tenn. Hist. Soc., 1994. Recipient Presdl. Vol. cert., 1988. Mem. Mid. Tenn. Ret. Officers Assn. (bd. dirs.), Brentwood Women's Club (chair pub. affairs 1993-94), Tenn. Fed. Women's Clubs (legis. chair). Office: # 100 311 Plus Park Blvd Ste 100 Nashville TN 37217-1025

SHADE, CYNTHIA SPECIA, gifted and talented education educator; b. San Antonio, Apr. 15, 1949; d. Adolph John and Agnes Theodora (Constantine) Specia; m. Vernon Ronnie Shade, Feb. 2, 1969; children: Charles Ronnie, Alethea Estelle. AA, San Antonio Coll., 1969; BA, St. Mary's U., 1970; MA, S.W. Tex. State U., 1974; EdD, Tex. A&M U., 1993. Cert. tchr., supt., mid-mgmt., master tchr., Tex. Tchr. Edgewood Ind. Sch. Dist., San Antonio, 1971-73, coord., 1991—; tchr. North East Ind. Sch. Dist., San Antonio, 1973-91; faculty advisor Princeton Ednl. Testing Svc., 1993—; adj. prof. U. Tex. Extension, Austin, 1994; judge Nat. Endowment for Humanities Young Scholars, 1992. Contbr. articles to profl. jours. Dir. liturgical drama St. Mark's Cath. Ch., San Antonio, 1981-88. Recipient Exemplary Tchg. award Delores Kohl Found., 1990, Outstanding Tchg. of the Humanities Tex. Com. for the Humanities, 1990, Spl. Recognition Publs. San Antonio Conservation Soc., 1989, Excellence Architecture award for Cmty. Excellence, 1989. Mem. AAUW, San Antonio Speech Arts Assn. (pres. 1976-77, poet laureate 1988-91), Nat. Assn. for Gifted Children, Tex. Assn. for Gifted and Talented, Alpha Psi Omega, Kappa Delta Pi (Mu Chi chpt.). Home: 630 Many Oaks San Antonio TX 78232-2727 Office: Edgewood Ind Sch Dist 1930 Herbert Ln San Antonio TX 78227

SHADISH, WILLIAM RAYMOND, psychologist, educator; b. Bklyn., Mar. 11, 1949; s. William R. Shadish Sr. and Maryjane A. (McDerrmott) Cartmell; m. Betty Duke, Aug. 16, 1981. BA in Sociology, Santa Clara U., 1972; postgrad., Calif. State U., Hayward, 1973; MS in Clin. Psychology, Purdue U., 1975, PhD in Clin. Psychology, 1978. Lic. psychologist, Tenn. Staff asst. joint com. on master plan for higher edn. Calif. State Legislature, 1972; core staff therapist Psychol. Svcs. Ctr., Purdue U., 1975-77; intern Memphis Clin. Psychology Internship Consortium, 1977-78; postdoctoral rsch. fellow Ctr. Health Svcs. and Policy Rsch. Northwestern U., Evanston, Ill., 1978-81, instr. dept. psychology, 1979-81; vis. rsch. assoc. Vanderbilt Inst. Pub. Policy Studies, Vanderbilt U., Nashville, 1985-90; dir. rsch. design and stats. program dept. psychology U. Memphis, 1987—, dir. Ctr. for Applied Psychol. Rsch. dept. psychology, 1990—, from asst. prof. to prof. psychology, 1986-90; mem. faculty senate U. Memphis, 1985-87, mem. univ. instnl. rev. bd., 1989-92, active various coms.; presenter many profl. confs. and symposia, instns. including Midwestern Psychol. Assn., Evaluation Rsch. Soc., Soc. Exptl. Social Psychology, Tenn. Assn. Mental Health Ctrs., U. S.D., U. Toledo, U. Wyo., U. Ill., U. Miss., U. Freiburg, Germany, U. Ariz., DePaul U., Dalhousie U., Halifax, N.S.; grant/contract reviewer NIH, NIMH, NSF, others; cons. in field. Co-author: Evaluation Studies Rev. Ann., Vol. 12, 1987, Psychology of Science: Contributions to Metascience, 1989, Foundations of Program Evaluation: Theories of Practice, 1991, The Social Psychology of Science, 1994; author or co-author over 25 book chpts.; editor New Directions for Program Evaluation, 1992-95; sr. guest editor Jour. social Issues, 1989; mem. editl. bd. Am. Jour. Cmty. Psychology, 1987—, Behavior Therapy, 1987-88, Evaluation Studies Rev. Ann., 1986, Jour. Applied Behavioral Sci., 1981—, New Directions for Program Evaluation, 1989-92, Psychological Methods, 1995—, Psychological Methods, 1995—; editl. cons. Am. Psychologist, Am. Jour. Cmty. Psychology, Jour. Abnormal Psychology, Jour. Applied Behavioral Sci., Jour. Gerontology, Jour. Personality, Psychol. Bull., Schizophrenia Bull., others; contbr. more than 50 articles to profl. jours. Pres. adv. bd. Project R.A.P. (Responsible Adolescent Parenting), Memphis, 1990-92, bd. dirs., 1988—; mem. task force on pub. and pvt. sector responsibilities for mental health and substance abuse svcs. Tenn. Dept. Mental Health and Mental Retardation, 1984-85; mem. care home resource com. Mental Health Soc. Memphis and Shelby County, 1984-88, mem. policy task force. 1988. With USAR, 1970-73; with USNG, 1973-76. Rsch. grantee NIMH, 1986-88, Russell Sage Found., 1989-90, State of Ill., 1978-82, NIH, 1988-92, 91-96, 92-96, 93—. Fellow APA (program chairperson divsn. 24 ann. conv. 1989, divsn. 5 ann. conv. 1994), Am. Psychol. Soc. (charter); mem. Am. Evaluation Assn. (charter, bd. dirs. 1991-93, quantitative interest group program chairperson ann. conv. 1991, chairperson task force on devel. of guiding principles for evaluators 1992-94, directory devel. com. 1987, ethics com. 1994-96, pres. elect 1996), Am. Statis. Assn., Am. Assn. Applied and Preventive Psychology, Soc. for Social Studies of Sci. Office: U Memphis Dept Psychology Memphis TN 38152

SHADOAN, WILLIAM LEWIS, judge; b. Galesburg, Ill., July 12, 1931; s. William Parker and Hortense (Lewis) S.; m. Katherine E. Thomson, 1961; children—Ann-Wayne Harlan, Kate, Tom. B.S., U. Ky., 1955; J.D., U. Louisville, 1961. Bar: Ky. 1961, U.S. Dist. Ct. (we. dist.) Ky. 1961. City atty., Wickliffe, Ky., 1963-76; county atty. Ballard County, Ky., 1985—; chief regional judge 1st cir. Wickliffe, Ky., 1983—. Chmn., Ballard County Democratic Party, 1963; trustee Methodist Ch., Wickliffe, 1961-84; adviser Selective Service, Paducah, Ky., 1968; chmn. Wickliffe C. of C., 1967-71; mem. exec. com. Ky. Hist. Soc., Frankfort; vice chmn. Ky. Cert. of Need and Licensure Bd., 1973-84. Named assoc. justice Ky. Supreme Ct., 1984. Served to capt. U.S. Army, 1955-59. Mem. Ky. Health Systems Assn. (vice chmn. 1976-82), ABA, Ky. Bar, Assn. Trial Lawyers Am., Ky. County Ofcls. Bd. (chmn. 1976-80), Miss. River Commn. (chmn. 1976-83), Ky. County Attys. Assn. (pres. 1966-77), First Dist. Bar Assn. (pres.). Lodges: Mason (Wickliffe, 32 degree); Shriners (Madisonville, Ky.); Order of Eastern Star, Elks. Home: RR 2 Wickliffe KY 42087-9804 Office: Ballard Courthouse 4th St Wickliffe KY 42087

SHAFER, JOHN MILTON, hydrologist, consultant, software developer; b. Findlay, Ohio, Mar. 18, 1951; s. Paul Eugene and Mary Ethel (Schwyn) S.; m. Elise Ann Dunne, Apr. 11, 1980; children: Paul Emery, Jessica Elise, Elise Ann. BS in Earth Sci., Pa. State U., 1973; MS in Resource Devel., Mich. State U., 1975; PhD in Civil Engring., Colo. State U., 1979. Cert. hydrologist #218. Asst. rsch. prof. Colo. State U., Fort Collins, 1979-80; rsch. engr. Battelle Meml. Inst., Richland, Wash., 1980-83, sr. rsch. engr., 1983-84; hydrologist Ill. State Water Survey, Champaign, 1984-85, asst. head ground water sect., 1985-90, prin. hydrologist, 1988-91, head hydrology div., 1990-92; assoc. dir., rsch. prof. Earth Scis. and Resources Inst., U. S.C., Columbia, 1992-95, dir., 1995—; cons. pvt. cos., 1984—; owner GWPATH, Columbia, S.C., 1992; v.p. Environ. and Archtl. Signage, Findlay, Ohio; prin. hydrologist, co-owner Applied Hydrogeologic Rsch., Inc., Seattle, 1995—. Developer software, 1987; contbr. articles to profl. jours. Recipient John C. Frye Meml. award in geology, 1991, Ill. Groundwater Sci. Achievement award, 1993. Mem. Intergovt. Coord. Com. Groundwater, Am. Geophys. Union, Am. Inst. Hydrology (pres. Ill. sect. 1985-92), Nat. Ground Water Assn., Ill. Groundwater Assn., Sigma Xi. Republican. Presbyterian. Home: 321 Lake Front Dr Columbia SC 29212-2426 Office: Earth Scis Resouces Inst U SC 901 Sumter St Columbia SC 29201-3961

SHAFER, ROBERTA W. CROW, human resources executive, career marketing consultant, venture capital consultant; b. Long View, Tex., Oct. 31, 1950; d. George Clifford and Marie (Mitchell) C.; m. Gary Stuart Shafer, July 23, 1988. Student U. Ala., 1968-70; A.F.A. in Fine Arts-Drama, Music, Am. Musical & Dramatic Acad., N.Y.C., 1972. Cert. personnel cons., Nat. Assn. Personnel Cons. Exec. trainee/retail merchandising and mgmt. Bergdorf-Goodman, N.Y.C.; account exec., cons. Lawrence Agy., N.Y.C., 1974-77; dist. sales mgr. Career House, Bensalem, Pa. and N.Y.C., 1977-82; dir. research and recruiting Retail Recruiters, Internat., N.Y.C., 1982-83; dir. exec. search/retail and mfg. Lloyd Cons., Inc., N.Y.C. and Chgo., 1983-85; dir. human resources R.P. McCoy Apparel, Ltd. dba Labels for Less, N.Y.C., 1985-87 ; pvt. practice venture capital and human resources consulting, N.Y.C., 1985-89; ind. cons. Donaldson, Lufkin & Jenrette, N.Y.C., 1985; guest lectr. Lab. Inst. Tech., St. John's U., Dowling Coll., N.Y.C., 1985-95; v.p. Ann H. Tanners Co., N.Y.C., 1988-90; pres. Crow-Shafer Assocs., N.Y.C., 1990—, Careercrafters, N.Y.C., 1991-95, Career Crafters Ala., Huntsville, 1995—. Mem. NAFE, Nat. Assn. Personnel Cons., New Bus. Network (charter mem, bd. dirs.), Women's Econ. Devel. Coun. Democrat. Episcopalian. Avocations: attending theatre and concerts, internat. traveling, studyof foreign cultures and languages, collecting antiques, vintage collectibles. Home and Office: 8341 White Flag Ln Ste 2010 Huntsville AL 35802-3459

SHAFFER, ANITA MOHRLAND, counselor; b. Racine, Wis., Apr. 5, 1939; d. Milton Arthur and Gudrun Amanda (Sundvoll) Stoffel. BS magna cum laude, U. Wis.-Madison, 1961; MEd, U. Wash., 1966; postgrad. Ariz. State U., 1971-76. Cert. in elem. edn., social sci. secondary edn., spl edn., Tex., Ariz.; lic. profl. counselor, Tex.; diplomate Internat. Acad. Behavioral Medicine, Counseling and Psychotherapy. Tchr. Racine Unified Dist. 1, 1961-63, Edmonds Sch. Dist. 15, Alderwood Manor, Wash., 1963-70; tchr. Ariz. Dept. Corrections, Phoenix, 1971-77; tchr. spl. edn. Pasadena Ind. Sch. Dist. (Tex.); 1977-78, spl. edn. counselor, 1978-90, elem. counselor, 1990—. Mem. Am. Counseling Assn., Am. Sch. Counselor Assn., Tex. Counseling Assn., Internat. Platform Assn., NAFE, Mus. Fine Arts Houston (patron), Beta Sigma Phi, Pi Lambda Theta. Home: 260 El Dorado Blvd H 801 Webster TX 77598 Office: Pasadena Ind Sch Dist 1515 Cherrybrook Ln Pasadena TX 77502-4048

SHAFFER, DAVID ELLSWORTH, marketing executive; b. Rio de Janeiro, Aug. 4, 1947; s. Ellsworth Walter and Faith Franklin (Bridges) S. BA in Biology, Westminster Coll., 1969; B in Internat. Mgmt., Am. Grad. Sch. Internat. Mgmt., Glendale, Ariz., 1970, M in Internat. Mgmt., 1972; PhD in Internat. Bus., U. Beverly Hills, 1986. Dir. prodn. Ric-Wil France, Paris, 1970-71; territory sales mgr. Dome Labs. div. Miles, West Haven, Conn., 1972-76; internat. factory rep. Ditch Witch Internat., Perry, Okla., 1976-79, internat. mktg. rep., 1979-81, sr. internat. mktg. rep., 1981-86, internat. sales mgr., 1986-92, internat. mktg. mgr., 1992-93, area mgr. continental Europe, 1993-94, sr. internat. market specialist, 1994—. Mem. Small Bus. Exporters Assn. (bd. dirs.), Okla. Dist. Export Coun., Okla. City Internat. Trade Assn., Tulsa World Trade Assn., Perry C. of C., Westminster Coll. Alumni Assn. (v.p. 1988-90, pres. elect 1990-92, pres. 1992-94), Phi Delta Theta, Elks. Republican. Episcopalian. Office: Ditch Witch Internat PO Box 66 1959 W Ditch Witch Rd Perry OK 73077-0066

SHAFFER, DEBORAH, nurse; b. Tampa, Fla., Jan. 20, 1954; d. Frank Solomon and Mary Louise (Swann) Shaffer; children: Danny, Dionne. LPN, Suwanee-Hamilton Nursing Sch., Live Oak, Fla., 1984; student, Hillsborough CC, 1992—. LPN, Fla. Nursing experience various hosps. and nursing homes, 10 yrs. Author poems, songs and short stories. Active Neighborhood Crime Watch, Parents Without Ptnrs., The Spring, Literacy Vols. Am.; ESL tutor First Bapt. Ch.; activities instr. A.D.C. Osborne Ctr.

SHAFFER, HUBERT ADAMS, JR., radiologist; b. Beckley, W.Va., Dec. 17, 1939; m. Ann Sleeth, June 18, 1961; children: Kendall, Daniel, David. AB, W.Va. U., 1961, MD, 1965. Diplomate Nat. Bd. Med. Examiners. Resident in diagnostic radiology U. Va., Charlottesville, 1969-72, fellow, instr. of radiology, 1972-73, asst. prof., 1973-79, assoc. prof., 1979-87, prof., 1987—, prof. of internal medicine, 1993—; radiologist U. Va. Hosps., Charlottesville, 1973—, dir. digital fluorography, 1981-86, acting dir. divsn. diagnosis U. Va. Health Scis. Ctr., 1989-92, dir. divsn. imaging and diagnosis, 1992-93, dir. divsn. abdominal imaging, 1993-94, co-dir. divsn. thoraco-abdominal imaging, 1994—. Manuscript reviewer Jour. Urology, 1988—, Clin. Imaging, 1990—, Investigative Radiology, 1991-94, Acad. Radiology, 1994—; contbr. articles and revs. to profl. jours. and chpts. to books. Webelos den leader Boy Scouts Am., Ivy, Va., 1977-78, asst. scoutmaster troop 79, Crozet, Va., 1978-92, mem. troop com., 1993—, advancement chmn., 1993—; Sunday sch. tchr. 1st United Meth. Ch., Charlottesville, 1973—, usher, 1973—, mem. adminstrv. bd., 1985-88, 95—, mem. endowment fund com., 1993—; bd. dirs. West Leight Owners Assn., 1981-83. Maj. U.S. Army. Decorated Expert Field Med. Badge, Cert. of Achievement. Fellow Am. Coll. Radiology; mem. AMA, Albemarle County Med. Soc., Am. Roentgen Ray Soc., Assn. Univ. Radiologists, Med. Soc. Va., Radiol. Soc. N.Am., Soc. Gastrointestinal Radiologists, Alpha Epsilon Delta. Office: U Va Dept Radiology PO Box 170 Charlottesville VA 22908-0170

SHAFFER, MARGARET MINOR, retired library director; b. New Orleans, Sept. 20, 1940; d. Milhado Lee and Margaret Minor (Krumbhaar) S. BS, Nicholls State U., Thibodaux, La., 1962; MLS, La. State U., 1965. Asst. dir. Terrebonne Parish Pub. Libr., Houma, La., 1965-72, dir., 1973-95; ret., 1995. Named Woman of Yr., Houma Bus. and Profl. Women's Club, 1981. Mem. ALA, La. Libr. Assn. (chmn. pub. libr. com. 1986-87), Southeastern Libr. Assn. Democrat. Episcopalian. Home: 1726 Highway 311 Schriever LA 70395-3240

SHAFFER, PETER THOMAS BARNUM, consultant; b. McKeesport, Pa., Oct. 24, 1929; s. Charles Holmes and Anne Barbara (Brubaker) S.; m. Suzanne Chesney, Aug. 25, 1962; children: Tanya Anne Shaffer Onori, Scott Peter. BS, MIT, 1951; PhD, Pa. State U., 1955; postdoctoral, Baylor U., 1974, U. N.H., 1974. Sr. engr. E I duPont de Nemours & Co., Niagara Falls, N.Y., 1955-58; sr. rsch. assoc. Carborundum, Niagara Falls, 1958-81; v.p., co-founder Advanced Refractory Techs., Buffalo, 1981-90; v.p. tech. Tech. Ceramics Labs., Alpharetta, Ga., 1985-94; cons. Cumming, Ga., 1994—; pres. Hartstoffe, Buffalo; pres., v.p. Heany Hartstoffe, Scottsdale, N.Y.; mem. Internat. Com. on Silicon Carbide, 1966; mem. materials tech. adv. com. U.S. Dept. Commerce, 1987-94. Contbr. articles to profl. jours. Recipient 6 Indsl. Rsch. IR-100 awards, N.Y., 1963, 64, 65, 74, 80, 87, Advanced Tech. award Inventors Clubs Am., 1990. Mem. ASTM, NRA (life), Am. Ceramic Soc., Am. Chem. Soc., Am. Soc. Materials, Izaac Walton League, Nat. Wildlife Fedn., Ducks Unltd., Trout Unltd. (chpt. pres., state coun., state chmn., nat. dir.), Am. Soc. Metals, Nat. Inst. Ceramic Engrs., Sigma Xi. Home and Office: 3225 Chimney Cove Dr Cumming GA 30131-7711

SHAFFER, RICHARD PAUL, business owner, retired career military officer; b. Ft. Worth, Oct. 12, 1949; s. Clinton Ollis and Sylvia (Katz) S. AA in Bus., Coll. of the Mainland, 1975; BBA in Bus., Sam Houston State U., Huntsville, Tex., 1975, MBA in Bus., 1976. Pers. technician U.S. Govt., Houston, 1968-75; pers. recruiter M.D. Anderson Cancer Hosp., Houston, 1976-79; acctg. auditor State of Tex., Galveston, 1979-82; owner, fin. planner Co. Benefits, Galveston, 1982—; owner Shaffer & Assocs. Real Estate, Galveston, 1982—. Mem. Rep. Party. Master sgt. USAFR, 1967-87. Mem. Nat. Guard Assn. of Tex., Guardian Life Ins. Co. of Am. Methodist. Home: 743 Marlin Bayou Vista Hitchcock TX 77563-2611 Office: Co Benefits 743 Marlin St Hitchcock TX 77563-2611

SHAFFER, SHEILA WEEKES, mathematics educator; b. Syracuse, N.Y., Oct. 20, 1957; d. Carroll Watson and Reina Lou (Yonkers) Judd; m. Jason Craig Shaffer, June 4, 1983 (div. Sept. 1994). BA, SUNY, Albany, 1979, MS, 1983. Cert. tchr. English/Math., N.Y.; cert. advanced profl. cert. in English and Math, Md. English tchr. Cortland (N.Y.) HS, 1979-81; English tchr. Prince George's County, Upper Marlboro, Md., 1984-86, math. tchr., 1986-87; math. tchr./coord. Prince George's County, 1990-95; math./English tchr. Camden HS, St. Mary's, Ga., 1988-90; math tchr. Frederick County,

Va., 1995-96, Prince George's County, Upper Marlboro, Md., 1996—; mem. SAT Com., The Coll. Bd., N.Y.C., 1993-96. Mem. Nat. Coun. Tchrs. Math. Office: Potomac High Sch 5211 Boydell Ave Oxon Hill MD 20745

SHAFFNER, RANDOLPH PRESTON, small business owner, educator, writer; b. Winston-Salem, N.C., Jan. 17, 1940; s. Emil Nathaniel and Anna Jackson (Preston) S.; m. Margaret Farmer Rhodes; children: Eric Randolph, Edward David, Joseph Andrew, Thomas Matthew, Jackson Rhodes. Student, Davidson Coll., 1958-60; BA in English with honors in writing, U. N.C., 1962; MA in Comparative Lit., 1969, PhD, 1973. Surveyor's lineman Joyce Mapping Co., Winston-Salem, 1955-58, 62; counselor, scoutmaster Camp Sequoyah, Weaverville, N.C., 1959; track repairman Alaska R.R., Anchorage, 1960; case handler Emard Packing Co., Anchorage, 1960, AYR Canneries, Seldovia, Alaska, 1961; tchr. U.S. Peace Corps, Chiengrai, Thailand, 1963-65, St. Christopher's Sch., Richmond, Va., 1969-71; instr. U. N.C., 1968-69, 71-73; asst. prof. Fairfield U., Conn., 1973-78, Western Carolina U., 1984, 87, Continuing Edn. program World Masterpieces, Highlands, N.C., 1987-89; moderator Highlands lecture series Western Carolina U., 1989-92; editor John F. Blair Pub., Winston-Salem, 1966-68; bookseller, owner Cyrano's Bookshop, Highlands, N.C., 1978—; asst. to dean Sch. Libr. Scis. U. N.C., Chapel Hill, 1973-74; literary mag. adv., mem. various subcoms. Dept. Eng. Fairfield Univ., 1973-78. Recipient God and Country award, 1955, Outstanding Pres. and Trustee award Hudson Libr. and Bascom-Louise Gallery, 1990. Author: Apprenticeship Novel, 1984, Tree Ordinance for Town of Highlands, 1987, Good Reading Material, Mostly Bound and New: The Hudson Library 1884-1994, 1994, (with others) Nineteenth Century Literature Criticism, Vol. 21, 1989; contbr. poetry to N.C. Poetry Soc. anthology Here's to The Land, 1992; contbr. short stories to mags. Lectr. with Alexander String Quartet, Words & Music, 1989, 92, 94, for Western Carolina U. Highlands lectr. series, 1991, 92, 93. Chmn. ARC Disaster Svcs., Fairfield, 1974-78, Zoning Bd. of Adjustment, Highlands, 1981-83, 85-90; pres., bd. trustees Hudson Libr., Inc., Highlands, 1987-90, chmn. libr. com., 1995—; trustee Hudson Libr., Bascom-Louise Art Gallery, 1987-90, 95—, Highlands Land Trust, Inc., 1995-96; bd. dirs. Highlands Cultural Art Ctr., 1987; fundraising com. Highlands Permament Endowment Scholarships, 1987-89; vice chmn. bd. missions Greenfield Hill Congl. Ch., Fairfield, Conn., 1977, chmn. scholarship com., 1975-77; bd. dirs. ARC, Fairfield, 1974-78; chaperon Am. Inst. for Fgn. Study, Grenoble, France, 1970. Goethe Inst. scholar, German Embassy, Munich, Fed. Rep. Germany, 1965, Univ. Besançon, France, 1965. Mem. Internat. Comparative Lit. Assn., Am. Comparative Lit. Assn., Writers' Workshop, N.C. Poetry Soc., Am. Acad. Poets, Am. Booksellers Assn., Southeastern Booksellers Assn., Highlands Merchants Assn. (chmn. fin. com., treas. 1984-87, chmn. tree com. and beautification com. 1984-89), Highlands Biol. Found. (exec. com. 1986—, bd. trustees 1981—, bd. dirs. 1981—, environ. protection com. 1986—, fund raising com. 1986, treas. 1990—, adv. com. on Nature Ctr. 1992—), Highlands C. of C., Clan Morrison Soc., Nat. Peace Corps Assn., Trail Hikers Am., Lambda Iota Tau (founder, faculty moderator Delta Omicron Ch. 1975-80), Rotary (Outstanding Vol. award, 1989). Democrat. Moravian. Avocations: construction, reading, travel, hiking, camping. Home: Hickory St PO Box 765 Highlands NC 28741-0765 Office: Cyrano's Bookshop Main St Highlands NC 28741

SHAFT, TERESA MARIE, data processing educator; b. Ridgecrest, Calif., Aug. 10, 1961; d. Fred Lee Shaft and Elinor Ann (Riesbeck) Finch; m. Mark Phillip Sharfman, May 19, 1985. BSBA, U. Ariz., 1982; PhD, Pa. State U., 1991. Software engr. Bell Tech. Ops., Tucson, 1982-84; asst. prof. MIS U. Tulsa, Okla., 1989—. Contbr. articles to profl. jours. Mem. AAUW, AAUP, Decision Sci. Inst., Assoc. Info. Systems, INFORMS. Office: U Tulsa 600 S College Tulsa OK 74104

SHAH, NANDLAL CHIMANLAL, physiatrist; b. Sadra, Gujarat, India, July 3, 1933; came to U.S., 1969; s. Chimanlal D. and Dahiben C. (Shah) S.; m. Indira N. Shah, May 15, 1990; children: Sandip N., Tushar N. Student, M.G. Sci. Inst., Ahmedabad, India, 1952; MB, BS, B.J. Med. Coll., Ahmedabad, India, 1957. Diplomate Am. Bd. Phys. Medicine and Rehab., Am. Bd. Quality Assurance and Utilization Review Physicians. Intern Yonkers (N.Y.) Gen. Hosp., 1970; resident in internal medicine St. Barnabas Hosp., Bronx, N.Y., 1971; resident in phys. medicine and rehab. Albert Einstein Coll. Medicine, Bronx, 1971-74; staff physiatrist, dir. med. svcs. Inst. Phys. Medicine and Rehab., Peoria, Ill., 1974-79; med. dir. Thomas Rehab. Hosp., Asheville, N.C., 1979-81; staff physiatrist phys. medicine and rehab. Charlotte (N.C.) Inst. Rehab. (formerly Charlotte Rehab. Hosp.), 1981; pvt. practice Carolina Rehab. Clinic, Charlotte, 1981—. Mem. Masons. Hindu. Office: Carolina Rehab Clinic 230 Baldwin Ave Charlotte NC 28204-3110

SHAH, NARENDRA KESHAVLAL, radiologist; b. Ahmedabad, India, Nov. 8, 1934; came to U.S., 1969; s. Keshavlal S. and Kamilaben K. Shah; m. Hansa Shah, Mar. 1, 1963; children: Malav, Darshini. MB BS, B.J. Med. Coll., Ahmedabad, 1961. Diplomate Am. Bd. Radiology. Rotating intern Gujarat State, India, 1960; resident in internal medicine V.S. Hosp., 1961, resident in radiology, 1962; resident in radiation therapy Velindre Hosp., Cardiff, Wales, U.K., 1963-64, 65-70; pvt. practice, Athens, Ga., 1975—. Fellow Royal Coll. Radiologists, Royal Soc. Medicine (hon.); mem. Am. Soc. Therapeutic Radiology, Am. Soc. Clin. Oncology, Crawford W. Long Soc., Med. Assn. Ga. Jainist. Office: East Ga Radiation Oncology Ctr 220 Hawthorne Park Athens GA 30606-2148

SHAH, SUDHIR VITHALBHAI, nephrologist, educator, researcher; b. Nairobi, Kenya, July 18, 1947; came to U.S., 1972; s. Vithal Ambalal and Champa (Shah) S. MB BS, Bombay Hosp., 1971. Diplomate Am. Bd. Internal Medicine, Am. Bd. Nephrology. Intern St. Louis City Hosp., 1972; resident Henry Ford Hosp., Detroit, 1973-75, fellow in nephrology, 1975-77; fellow in physiology Mayo Clinic, Rochester, Minn., 1977-79; asst. prof. medicine Tulane U. Sch. Medicine, New Orleans, 1979-81, assoc. prof., 1981-86, prof., 1986—; mem. ad hoc com. on grant rev. NIH, Bethesda, Md., 1990-94; dir. divsn. Nephrology U. Ark. for Med. Scis., Little Rock, 1990. Mem. editorial bd. Am. Jour. Physiology, 1989-91, Seminars in Nephrology, 1989—; contbr. articles to profl. jours. Established investigator Am. Heart Assn., 1982-87; NIH grantee, 1981—;. Fellow Am. Coll. Physicians; mem. Am. Soc. Nephrology, Am. Fedn. for Clin. Rsch., Internat. Soc. Nephrology, Am. Heart Assn. (kidney coun.), Am. Soc. Renal Metabolism and Biochemistry, Am. Soc. Clin. Investigation, Nat. Kidney Found. Office: U Ark for Med Scis 4301 W Markham Slot # 501 Little Rock AR 72205

SHAHAN, J. MICHAEL, academic administrator; b. Aug. 5, 1949; m. Bridget Gotte Shahan; stepchildren: Travis, Stephen. BA in History, U. Okla., 1971; MA in Am. History, Vanderbilt U., 1973, PhD in Am. History, 1981. Instr. history Lamar U., Port Arthur, Tex., 1977-81, asst. prof. history, 1981-87, head dept. liberal arts, 1985-87, assoc. prof. history, 1987—, v.p. acad. affairs, 1987-94; interim pres. Lamar U., Orange, Tex., 1994-95, pres., 1995—. past bd. dirs., treas. Caplad Ctr. Comm. Disorders; former deacon, elder Presbyn. Ch. of the Covenant, Port Arthur. Mem. Am. Assn. Cmty. Colls. (bd. dirs.), Greater Orange Area C. of C. (bd. dirs. 1995-96, 96—), Port Arthur Hist. Soc. (bd. dirs.), North Port Arthur Rotary Club (bd. dirs. 1990-95, pres. 1993-94). Home: 4500 Briarwood Ln Port Arthur TX 77642 Office: Office of Pres 410 W Front St Orange TX 77630-5899

SHAHEEN, NASEEB, English literature educator; b. Chgo., June 24, 1931; s. Azeez and Saleemeh (Balluteen) S. BA, Am. Univ. Beirut, Lebanon, 1962; MA, UCLA, 1966, PhD, 1969. Univ. prof. U. Memphis, 1969—. Author: Biblical References in The Faerie Queen, 1976, Ramallah: Its History and Its Genealogies, 1982, Biblical References in Shakespeare's Tragedies, 1987, Biblical References in Shakespeare's History Plays, 1989, Pictorial History of Ramallah, 1992, Biblical References in Shakespeare's Comedies, 1993; contbr. over 30 articles, revs. to profl. jours. Woodrow Wilson Found. fellow, 1968-69. Mem. MLA. Office: Univ of Memphis Dept English Memphis TN 38152

SHAHIED, ISHAK I., biochemistry educator. BA, Ea. Nazarene Coll., Quincy, Mass., 1959; MS, U. Tenn., 1964; PhD, Colo. State U., 1973. Chem. analyst Cornell U. Med. Coll., N.Y.C., 1959-60; chemist Hunt Foods (Wesson Oil), Bayonne, N.J., 1960-61, Johnson & Johnson, New Brunswick, N.J., 1961-62, Schering Corp., Union, N.J., 1962-63, Stokely-Van Camp, Indpls., 1965; sr. rsch. chemist Aerospace Med. Rsch. Lab. USAF, Ohio, 1973-74; researcher U. Mo., Kansas City, 1975-77, prof. biochemistry, 1986-89; prof. biochemistry, chmn. dept. St. George's U. Sch. Medicine, Grenada, West Indies, 1977-86; prof. biochemistry, head biochemist Life Coll., Marietta, Ga., 1989—; taught at Cleve. Chiropractic Coll., Kansas City, Mo., 1976-77, 86-89. Author: Biochemistry of Foods and the Biocatalysts, 1977, (textbook) Physiology, 1980. Named Hon. fellow Truman Libr. Inst.; recipient Best Instr. award, 1984. Mem. N.Y. Acad. Sci.

SHAIKUN, MICHAEL GARY, lawyer; b. Ky., Mar. 17, 1942; s. Leon J. and Cleo (Taub) S.; m. Phyllis Miriam Cohen, Aug. 21, 1964; children: Benjamin, Stephanie, Alissa. BS in Econs. with highest honors, U. Pa., 1963; JD, Harvard U., 1966. Bar: Ky. 1966, U.S. Dist. Ct. (we. dist.) Ky. 1966. Assoc. Greenebaum, Doll & McDonald PLLC, Louisville, 1966-69; mem. Greenebaum, Doll & McDonald PLLC, 1970—. Contbr. articles to profl. jours. Bd. dirs. Jewish Community Fedn. Louisville, 1971—, past pres.; chmn. Found. for Planned Giving, Jewish Community Fedn., Louisville; vice-chmn. fin. safe place svcs. YMCA. Mem. ABA, Ky. Bar Assn., Louisville Bar Assn. Democrat. Jewish. Home: 5907 Burlington Ave Louisville KY 40222-6118 Office: Greenebaum Doll & McDonald PLLC 3300 National City Tower Louisville KY 40202

SHAKER, WILLIAM H., marketing professional, public policy reformer; b. Downey, Calif., Apr. 22, 1938; s. Elmer S. and Marylee (Watts) S.; m. Joanna L. Shaker, Jan. 28, 1966; children: Catherine Patricia, Marylee, Marcus, Matthew. BS in Engring., U. So. Calif., 1964; MS in Engring., U. Mich., 1969. Registered profl. engr., Calif. Exec. Dow Chem. Co., Midland, Mich., 1966-78; v.p. Nat. Legal Ctr. for the Pub. Interest, Washington, 1979; exec. v.p. Nat. Tax Limitation Com., Washington, 1980-86; pres. Am. Coun. for Health Care Reform, Arlington, Va., 1982—, Heart to Heart Found., Arlington, Va., 1992—, Washington Mktg. Group, Arlington, Va., 1987—, Health PAC, Arlington, Va., 1994—. Author: Health Care Reform, 1994, also legislation and govt. publs.; editor: Electric Power Reform, 1979; contbr. articles to profl. jours. Founder, chmn. Taxpayers United, Mich., 1972-84. Mem. Govtl. Rsch. Assn. (most effective presentation of govtl. rsch. award 1973), Direct Mktg. Assn. (echo awards 1982-95, maxi awards 1995), Pub. Rels. Soc. (silver anvil 1979), Am. Conservative Union (health care reform award 1995). Republican. Lutheran. Office: Washington Mktg Group 5155 N 37th St Arlington VA 22207

SHAKLAN, ALLEN YALE, broadcast executive; b. Newark, July 10, 1945; s. David George and Esther (Sweet) S.; m. Marlene Sokoloff, July 11, 1968; children: Steven, Daniel. AB, Rutgers U., Newark, 1967, JD, 1969; LLM, NYU, 1974. Bar: N.Y., D.C. Atty. FTC, N.Y.C., 1969-71, CBS, N.Y.C., 1971-84; v.p., asst. to pres. CBS TV, N.Y.C., 1984-86, v.p. programming, news adminstrn. and sta. services, 1986-88; v.p., gen. mgr. Sta. WFOR-TV, Miami, Fla., 1989—. Mem. Nat Assn. TV Programming Execs., Fla. Assn. Broadcasters. Office: Sta WFOR-TV 8900 NW 18th Ter Miami FL 33172-2623

SHAKLEE, TONI SUE, university administrator; b. Enid, Okla., July 31, 1952; d. James Lee and Ramona Jane (Ballard) S.; m. William Jarrell Focht, May 12, 1990. BA in Polit. Sci. magna cum laude, Southwestern Okla. State U., 1974; postgrad., Phillips U., 1978-79; MA in Polit. Sci., Okla. State U., 1985, PhD in Environ. Scis., 1994. Sec.-receptionist Enid Bd. Trade/Okla. Grain and Feed Assn., 1974-76; sports photographer Enid News and Eagle, Enid Pub. Co., 1979-81; acting dir. info. svcs. and publs. Phillips U., Enid, 1979, dir. News Bur., sports info. dir., 1976-80, dir. info. svcs., sports info. dir., 1981-82; office mgr. radiation therapy/oncology dept. Bass Bapt. Meml. Hosp., 1982; publs. editor agrl. info. divsn. agr. Okla. State U., Stillwater, 1982-84, coord. rsch. support svcs. Coll. Arts and Scis., 1984-91, mgr. rsch. support svcs., 1992—; staff scientist Sci. Applications Internat. Corp., Columbus, Ohio, 1991-95. Mem. NAFE, Assn. Women in Sci., Nat. Coun. Univ. Rsch. Adminstrs., Soc. Rsch. Adminstrs., Assn. Univ. Tech. Mgrs., Am. Soc. Pub. Adminstrn., Nat. Assn. Environ. Profls., Okla. Acad. Scis., Soc. Environ. Scientists, Nat. Press Photographers Assn., Phi Alpha Theta, Phi Kappa Phi. Office: Okla State U 212 Life Scis E Stillwater OK 74078

SHALHOUP, JUDY LYNN, marketing communications executive; b. Charleston, W.Va., Oct. 25, 1940; s. George Ferris and Mary Margaret (Moses) S.; BA, Morris Harvey Coll., Charleston, 1967; MS, W.Va. U., 1970. With Union Carbide Corp., 1960-92, publicity mgr. plastics, N.Y.C., 1971-73, coatings materials div. advt. mgr., 1973-82, mgr. mktg. comm. splty. chems. div., 1982-85; mgr. mktg. comm., solvents and coatings materials div., 1982-92; pres. GMJC Assocs., 1992—. v.p., gen. mgr. Fruit Bowl, Charleston, 1975-78. Recipient Best Teller award Bus. Profl. Advt. Assn., 1978-84, 86-87, Pro-Com. award, 1991, Excellence in Bus.-to-Bus. Advt. award, 1989, Objectives and Results Advt. award Am. Bus. Press, 1978, Clio Advt. Recognition award, 1978-86, Clio award, 1984, Andy award, 1983, 84, Nutmegger award, 1985 . Mem. Telefood Assn., Internat. Platform Assn., Assn. Nat. Advt., Inc., SSPC, AAAS, Nat. Paint and Coatings Assn. (comm. com.), Fedn. Socs. Coatings Tech., Bus. Profl. Advt. Assn. (Star awards for excellence 1989-90, Procom award 1990).

SHALLCROSS, WILLIAM CHARLES, pharmacist; b. Paterson, N.J., Feb. 20, 1954; s. Walter William and Doris Jean (Dewis) S.; m. Maureen Margaret Quilty, June 22, 1980; children: Dewis Anne, William Ezekiel. BS in Animal Sci., Iowa State U., 1976; BS, Phila. Coll. Pharmacy & Sci., 1980. Pharmacist Reses Pharmacy, Pleasantville, N.J., 1980-85; clin. pharmacist Naples Cmty. Hosp., Naples, Fla., 1985—; cons. Harringtons Pharmacy, Naples, 1991—, Marco Island Urgent Care, Marco Island, Fla., 1993—, Chelaton Therapy & Wellness Ctr., Naples, 1995—. Cons. Hospice Naples. Mem. Am. Soc. Hospital Pharmacists, So. Golf Soc. Hosp. Pharmacists. Republican. Home: 3581 3rd Ave SW Naples FL 34117

SHAMIS, EDWARD ANTHONY, JR., lawyer; b. Pensacola, Fla., Dec. 12, 1949; s. Edward Anthony Sr. and Mona Kathryn (McLauglin) S.; m. Elizabeth Handley, Jan. 24, 1971; children: Ashley Vera, Edward Anthony III. BS, La. State U., 1972, JD, 1974. Bar: La. 1974, U.S. Dist. Ct. (ea. dist.) La. 1975, U.S. Tax Ct. 1981, U.S. Ct. Appeals (5th cir.) 1982, U.S. Supreme Ct. 1983. Pvt. practice law Slidell, 1974—. Bd. dirs. Pope John High Sch., Slidell, 1988-90, Children's Wish Endowment Fund, Inc. (formerly Northshore Children's Endowment Fund) 1991—; mem., pres. St. Tammany Assn. for Children with Learning Disabilities, Slidell, 1976-81; chmn. Slidell Bd. Zoning Adjustments, 1976-81; past mem. Boys Club. Mem. ATLA, La. Bar Assn. (hos. of dels. 1985-86, 88-89, 89-90, 94-97), St. Tammany Bar Assn., Slidell Bar Assn. (pres. 1978-79), La. Trial Lawyers Assn. (pres.'s adv. coun. 1980-81, 84-85, 89-90, 95-96, St. Tam. par ethics com., spl. counsel to Slidell City Counsel 1984—), Rotary. Republican. Roman Catholic. Home: 32809 CC Rd Slidell LA 70460-9653 Office: 486 Brownswitch Rd Slidell LA 70458-1102

SHANAHAN, ELIZABETH ANNE, art educator; b. High Point, N.C., Apr. 5, 1950; d. Joe Thomas and Nancy Elizabeth (Moran) Gibson; m. Robert James Shanahan, Aug. 31, 1969 (div. Mar. 1987); children: Kimberly Marie Shanahan Conlon, Brigette Susanne. Student, Forsyth Tech. Coll., 1974-83, Tri-County Tech. Coll., 1989, Inst. of Children's Lit., 1989. Owner cleaning bus. Winston-Salem, N.C., 1985-86, 87; instr. Anderson (S.C.) Arts Coun., 1987—, Tri-County Tech. Coll., Pendleton, S.C., 1987—. Artist Wild Geese, 1985 (Best in Show). Active Libr. of Congress, 1994. Mem. Anderson Art Assn. (con. 1987—), Met. Arts Coun. (Upstate Visual Arts divsn.), Triad Art Assn. (pres. Kernersville, N.C. chpt. 1984-85), Nat. Mus. Women in Arts (charter), Libr. of Congress (charter). Home: 7 Woodbridge Ct Anderson SC 29621-2260 Office: Tri County Tech Coll PO Box 587 Pendleton SC 29670-0587

SHANDLES, IRA DAVID, podiatrist; b. Phila., Feb. 27, 1949; s. Samuel Aaron and Sara (Brooks) S.; divorced; children: Martine, Neil; m. Elizabeth Jacobs, Aug. 1, 1993; 1 child, Aleah. BA, Temple U., 1971; DPM, Pa. Coll. Podiatric Medicine, 1977; postgrad., U. Pa. Sports Medicine Ctr., 1977-79. Diplomate Am. Bd. Podiatric Surgery, Am. Bd. Podiatric Orthopedics and Primary Podiatric Medicine; lic. podiatrist, N.Y., Fla., Pa. Resident in podiatric surgery Oxford Hosp., Phila., 1977-79; asst. instr. pediatric orthopedics Pa. Coll. Podiatric Medicine, Phila., 1977-78; cons. Binghamton (N.Y.) Gen. Hosp. Sports Medicine Ctr., 1979-83; pvt. practice podiatric medicine Binghamton, 1979-83, Tampa, Fla., 1983—; podiatric cons. Tampa Gen. Hosp. Sports Medicine Ctr., 1985—; clin. faculty podiatric residency program Tampa Vets. Hosp., 1985—; staff privileges United Health Svcs., Inc. Binghamton, 1980-83; Tampa Outpatient Surgical Facility, Tampa Gen. Hosp., Centurion Community Hosp., Univ. Community Hosp., Tampa; Humana Hosp., Brandon, Fla. 1986—; cons. Bull Run, U. South Fla., 1986, Fla.'s Sunshine State Games, 1986, Dow Corning Corp. 1987—, Diapulse Corp. Am., 1988—, Edward T. White Hosp., 1992—, Bayfront Med. Ctr., 1992—, St. Petersburg, Chmn. Dept. Podiatric Surgery Univ. Hosp., Tampa, 1992—; speaker to Binghamton Civic Orgns., TV, newspaper interviewee, Binghamton, 1979-83; mem. faculty John H. Weed Meml. Seminars, 1995—, Ontario Soc. Chiropodists, 1993; cons., lectr. U.S. Army Rsch. Inst. Envrion. Medicine, Natick, Mass., 1991-94; cons., clin. faculty mem. locomotor biomechanics program Edward White Hosp., St. Petersburg, 1985—; mem. clin. faculty podiatric residency program Tampa VA Hosp., 1985—; cons. Sports Medicine Ctr. Tampa Gen. Hosp., 1983—; pvt. practice, Tampa. Contbr. articles to profl. jours. Lectr. Hillsborough County Pub. Schs. Sch. Enrichment Resource Vols. Edn. series, 1987—, Edward T. White Hosp., 1992—. Fellow Am. Coll. Foot Surgeons (Outstanding Paper award 1977), Am. Coll. Foot and Ankle Surgery; mem. Hillsborough County Podiatric Med. Assn., Am. Podiatric Med. Assn. Jewish.

SHANDS, JACK L., human resource executive, lawyer; b. Cardwell, Mo., Dec. 1, 1943; s. Gideon Jackson and Cora Lee (Sutherland) S.; m. Barbara Jean Franks, Oct. 19, 1962; children: Freida Davette, Jackie L. II, James, Barbara. Bar: Tenn. 1976, U.S. Dist. Ct. (we. dist.) Tenn. 1976; qualified mediator and arbitrator Am. Arbitration Assn. Various positions, 1962-72; elec. foreman Haines Electric Co., Memphis, 1972-75; asst. bus. mgr. I.B.E.W. Local Union #474, Memphis, 1975-82; mgr. indsl. rels. Sanyo Mfg. Corp., Forrest City, Ark., 1982-86, dir. indsl. rels., 1986-87, dir. human resources, 1987-89; dir. human resources Sanyo Mfg. Corp., San Diego, 1989-90, exec. dir. adminstrn. & human resources, 1990-91, gen. counsel, 1991-92; atty. and arbitrator Memphis, 1992-93; mgr. labor rels. Johnson Controls World Svcs. Inc., Cape Canaveral, Fla., 1993-95; mgr. human resources Ky. W.Va. Gas Co., Prestonsburg, Ky., 1995, Quebecor Printing Memphis Inc., Memphis, 1995—; labor cons. in field. Mem. exec. com., 1st v.p. Shelby County Dem. Party, Memphis, 1982-83; bd. dirs. Arthritis Found., Memphis, 1982. Recipient Patterson award Southern States Apprenticeship Conf., 1970. Mem. Am. Mgmt. Assn., Am. Soc. for Personnel Adminstrn., Rotary, Moose. Home: 4715 Harvest Knoll Ln Memphis TN 38125 Office: Quebecor Printing Memphis 828 E Holmes Rd Memphis TN 38116-8240

SHANE, JOHN MARDER, endocrinologist; b. Kansas City, Mo., Oct. 5, 1942; s. Henry Kamsler and Ruth (Marder) S.; m. Eileen Goodart, June 18, 1967; children: Robert M., Edward G. BS, U. Okla., 1964, MD, 1967. Diplomate Am. Bd. Ob-Gyn., Am. Bd. Reproductive Endocrinology. Resident Harvard Med. Sch., Boston, 1970-73, fellowship, 1973-75, instr., 1970-75, asst. prof., 1975-78; pvt. practice Tulsa, 1978—; lectr., cons. Tutorial Svcs. Internat., England, 1984—; bd. dirs. St. Francies G.I.F.T. Lab., Tulsa; cons. to preimplantation genetics project Chapman Genetics Inst., Children's Med. Ctr., Tulsa. Author: CIBA Symposium Infertility: Diagnosis and Treatment; contbr. articles to profl. jours. and publs. Mem. Tulsa Garden Ctr., 1988—; bd. dirs. Temple Israel, Tulsa, 1985-86, cited in The Best Doctor's in Am.:Ctrl. Region. Captain USAF, 1967-69. Recipient Annual award Boston Obstet. Soc., 1977. Mem. ACS, Tulsa Gynecol. Soc. (past pres. 1986-87), Soc. Reproductive Endocrinologists, Tulsa bonsai Soc. (bd. dirs. 1988—), Am. Coll. Ob-Gyn. (v.p. 1971-92, pres. New England Jr. divsn. 1972-73), Am. Bonsai Soc. (nat. bd. dirs.), Chanie des Rotisseurs (l'Ordre Mondial, Tulsa v.p.), Southside Rotary of Tulsa (bd. dirs., pres. elect), Nat. Arboretum (nat. bd. dirs.). Republican. Jewish. Office: 1705 E 19th St Ste 703 Tulsa OK 74104-5418

SHANE, ROBERT SAMUEL, chemical engineer, consultant; b. Chgo., Dec. 8, 1910; s. Jacob and Selma (Shayne) S.; m. Jeanne Felice Lazarus, Aug. 21, 1936; children: Stephen H., Susan R., Jacqueline G. SB, U. Chgo., 1930, PhD, 1933. Plant supt. Amecco Chems., Rochester, N.Y., 1941-42; plant chemist Bausch & Lomb Optical Co., Rochester, 1942-46; project supr. Wyandotte (Mich.) Chems. Corp., 1952-54; assoc. dir. rsch. Davis & Geck div. Am. Cyanamid, Danbury, Conn., 1954-55; mgr. chem., ceramics, powder metals Westinghouse Atomic Power, Forest Hills, Pa., 1955-57; nucleonics specialist Bell Aircraft Co., Niagara Falls, N.Y., 1958-59; mgr. parts, materials, process engring. GE, Valley Forge, Pa., 1959-69; staff cons. Nat. Materials Adv. Bd., Washington, 1969-80; prin. Shane Assocs., Stuart, Fla., 1980-96; cons. in field; editor material engring. Marcel Dekker, Inc., N.Y.C., 1983—. Author, editor: Space Radiation Effects on Materials, 1962, Predictive Testing, 1972, Materials and Processes, 1985; author: Technology Transfer & Innovation, 1982; editor: Testing for Prediction of Material Performance, 1972; contbr. articles to profl. jours. Adult leader Boy Scouts Am.; organizer Literacy Coun., Ardmore, Pa., 1988. Recipient Joseph Stewart award Am. Chem. Soc., 1987, medal Swedish Royal Acad. Engring., 1972; named to space tech. hall of fame NASA, 1995. Fellow ASTM (award of merit 1973, F-15 com. on consumer product stds.), AIChE; mem. Am. Chem. Soc. (emeritus), Am. Soc. for Metals Internat. (life), Sigma Xi. Home and Office: 1904 NW 22nd St Stuart FL 34994-9270

SHANFIELD, STEPHEN B., medical educator, physician; b. Toronto, Ont., Can., Aug. 14, 1939; s. Joseph P. and Mildred Lenore (Neiman) S.; m. Carmen Lynn Kight, Aug. 15, 1971 (div. Mar. 1990); 1 child, Jason Gabriel. BA, UCLA, 1961; MD, U. So. Calif., 1965. Intern Montefiore Hosp. and Med. Ctr., N.Y.C., 1965-66; resident in psychiatry Sch. of Medicine Yale U., New Haven, 1966-69; maj. USAF, 1969-79; staff physician Wilford Hall USAF Med. Ctr., San Antonio, Tex., 1969-71; from asst. prof. to prof. Coll. Medicine U. Ariz., Tucson, 1973-85; prof. Health Scis. Ctr. U. Tex., San Antonio, 1985—. Contbr. articles to prof. jours. Fellow Am. Psychiat. Assn., Am. Coll. Psychiatrists; mem. Group for Advancement of Psychiatry, Assn. of Academic Psychiatry (treas. 1990-91). Home: 221 Losoya St Apt 3B San Antonio TX 78205-2675 Office: U Tex Dept Psychiatry 7703 Floyd Curl Dr San Antonio TX 78284-7792

SHANG, CHARLES YULIN, medical physicist; b. Shanghai, May 6, 1956; came to U.S., 1987; s. Jian and Ming Shang; m. Monica Jinhong Meng, Aug. 1, 1985; children: Stephen, Michael. MD, 2nd Med. Coll., Shanghai, China, 1983; postdoctoral cert., Chgo. Med. Sch., North Chgo., Ill., 1988; MS in Radiation, Health/Med. Physics, U. Pitts., 1990. Diplomate in Radiological Physics, Am. Bd. Radiology. Resident 301 Gen. Hosp., Beijing, China, 1983-85; radiologist 301 Gen. Hosp., Beijing, 1985-87; vis. radiologist Evanston (Ill.) Univ. Hosp., 1988, Allegheny Gen. Hosp., Pitts., 1988-89; grad. student rschr. Presbyn. Univ. Hosp., Pitts., 1989-90; med. physicist St. Mary's Hosp., Waterbury, Conn., 1991-93; sr. med. physicist Boca Raton (Fla.) Comty. Hosp., 1993—. Contbr. articles to profl. jours. including Radiology, Neurosurgery, Annals N.Y. Acad. Scis., IEEE Transactions on Biomed. Engring. Recipient grad. scholarship U. Pitts., 1989-90. Mem. Am. Assn. Physicists in Medicine, Am. Coll. Radiology. Home: 9340 Lake Serena Dr Boca Raton FL 33496 Office: Boca Raton Cmty Hosp Lynn Regional Cancer Ctr 16313 Military Trl Delray Beach FL 33484-6628

SHANK, MARILYN SUE, special education educator; b. Charleston, W.Va., May 20, 1953; d. Joseph Thomas and Lenah Mae (Casto) S. BA in Elem. Edn., Asbury Coll., 1974; MS In Pers. Svcs., Bob Jones U., 1978; MA in Spl. Edn., W.Va. Coll. Grad. Studies, 1982; PhD in Spl. Edn., U. Kans. Cert. elem. and specific learning disabilities tchr., W.Va. Tchr. Rochester (Mich.) Hills Christian Sch., 1974-75, Cross Lanes (W.Va.) Christian Sch., 1975-84; instr. Bob Jones U., Greenville, S.C., 1984-88; relief child care worker Davis Child Care Shelter, South Charleston, W.Va., 1988; rsch. cons. Kaye Cons. Svcs., Overland Park, Kans., 1989, Beach Ctr. on Families with Disabilities, Lawrence, Kans., 1990-91; asst. prof. U. South Ala., Mobile, 1991—; presenter in field. Co-author: (textbook) Exceptional Lives: Special Education in Today's Schools, 1995; contbr. articles to profl. jours. Mem. Coun. for Exceptional Children, Coun. for Learning Disabilities, Learning Disabilities Assn., Soc. Children's Book Writers and Illustrators, Delta Found. Home: 813 Schaub Ave Mobile AL 36609-5155 Office: U South Ala Dept Spl Edn Ilb # 215 Mobile AL 36688

SHANK, THOMAS JEFFREY, computer animator; b. Huntington, W.Va., Nov. 19, 1963; s. Thomas Joseph Jr. and Mary Ellen (DeFoe) S. BBA in Mktg., Marshall U., 1988; postgrad. in computer art and design, Ringling Sch. Art and Design, Sarasota, Fla., 1989. 3D computer animator Video

Technics, Atlanta, 1989-90, dir. animation, 1990-91; dir. animation Health Sci. Media, Atlanta, 1991—. Recipient 2d pl. award U.S. Internat. Film and Video Festival, 1993, Silver medal N.Y. Festival, 1996, CINE Golden Eagle award, 1993, 94, 95, 96. Home: 3777 Wintercrest Ct Atlanta GA 30340-4439 Office: Health Sci Media 990 Hammond Dr NE Ste 660 Atlanta GA 30328-5529

SHANKS, JUDITH WEIL, editor; b. Montgomery, Ala., Nov. 2, 1941; d. Roman Lee and Charlotte (Alexander) Weil; m. Hershel Shanks, Feb. 20, 1966; children: Elizabeth Jeannette, Julia Emily. BA in Econs., Wellesley Coll., 1963; MBA, Trinity Coll., 1980. Econs. asst. Export-Import Bank, Washington, 1963-68; cons. econs. and social sci., 1968-76; researcher Time-Life Books, Alexandria, Va., 1976-80, prin. researcher, 1980-83, illustrations editor, 1983, adminstrv. editor, 1984-95, dir. editl. adminstrn., 1996. Vol. dinner program for homeless women, Mentors, Inc., vol. mentor with Mentors, Inc.; bd. dirs. Anne Frank House, for formerly homeless women. Mem. Garden Writers Am., Internat. Alliance, Washington Alliance Bus. Women, Leadership Greater Washington, Washington Wellesley Club (career caucus). Democrat. Jewish. Home: 5208 38th St NW Washington DC 20015-1812

SHANKS, KATHRYN MARY, health care administrator; b. Glens Falls, N.Y., Aug. 4, 1950; d. John Anthony and Lenita (Combs) S. BS summa cum laude, Spring Hill Coll., 1972; MPA, Auburn U., 1976. Program evaluator Mobile Mental Health, Ala., 1972-73; dir. spl. projects Ala. Dept. Mental Health, Montgomery, 1973-76; dir. adminstrn. S.W. Ala. Mental Health/Mental Retardation, Andulusia, Ala., 1976-78; adminstr. Mobile County Health Dept., 1978-82; exec. dir. Coastal Family Health Ctr., Biloxi, Miss., 1982-95; cons. med. group practice, 1995—; ptnr. Shanks & Allen, Mobile, 1979—; healthcare consulting pvt. practice, 1995—; cons. S.W. Health Agy., Tylertown, Miss., 1984-86; preceptor Sch. Nursing, U. So. Miss., Hattiesburg, 1983, 84; advisor Headstart Program, Gulfport, Miss., 1984-95; LPN Program, Gulf Coast C.C., 1984-95; lectr. Auburn U., Montgomery, 1977-78. Bd. dirs. Mobile Cmty. Action Agy., 1979-81, Moore Cmty. House; mem. S.W. Ala. Regional Goals Forum, Mobile, 1971-72, Cardiac Rehab. Study Com., Biloxi, Miss., 1983-84, Mothers and Babies Coalition, Jackson, Miss., 1983-95, Gulf Coast Coalition Human Svcs., Biloxi, Miss., 1983-95; exec. dir. Year for Miss., 1993-94. Spring Hill Coll. Pres.'s scholar, 1972. Mem. Miss. Primary Health Care Assn. (pres.), Med. Group Mgmt. Assn., Biloxi C. of C., ACLU, Soc. for Advancement of Ambulatory Care, Spring Hills Alumni Assn. Avocations: tennis, home restoration, golf.

SHANNON, GEORGE WARD, JR., museum director, anthropologist, archaeologist; b. Landstuhl, Germany, Sept. 25, 1954; s. George Ward Sr. and Frances Ada (Terrell) S.; m. Faye Joy Grimsby; children: Benjamin (dec.), George Ward III. BA in Anthropology, U. Alaska, 1976; MA in Anthropology, Fla. Atlantic U., 1979; PhD in Anthropology, Mich. State U., 1987. Exec. dir. Northlake Mus. & Nature Ctr., Mandeville, La., 1988-89; curator La. State Mus., New Orleans, 1988-89; br. dir. La. State Mus., Shreveport, 1989-91; exec. dir., CAO La. State Exhibit Mus., Shreveport, 1991—. Mem. Rotary. Presbyterian.

SHANNON, ISABELLE LOUISE, education director; b. Newton, Mass., Sept. 5, 1934; d. Clarence Edward and Evelyn Marie (Peters) Overlock; m. Albert M. Shannon, Dec. 20, 1970 (div. 1982); children: Clare Louise Lord, William Christopher Lord. BA in French, Wheaton (Ill.) Coll., 1956; MA in French Lit., Boston U., 1970; PhD in Comparative and Internat. Edn., Mich. State U., East Lansing, 1977. Cert. French tchr., instrnl. supr., Va., French tchr., Mass. Tchr. French Belmont (Mass.) High Sch., 1966-70, East Lansing Pub. Schs., 1973-77; outreach dir. Can. Studies Ctr. Duke U., Durham, N.C., 1977-79; prof., dir. secondary edn. Va. Wesleyan Coll., Norfolk, 1979—; presenter in field; reviewer Longman Pubs., N.Y.C., 1987—; evaluator, tchr. edn. programs Va. Dept. Edn., 1985-87. Host, program cons. Options in Edn., WHRV-FM, Norfolk, 1991-95; contbr. articles to profl. jours. Mem. adminstrv. bd. Cmty. United Meth. Ch., Virginia Beach, Va., 1985-92, chair, 1988, chair staff parish com., 1995—; mem. Va. Symphony League, Norfolk, 1986-89; bd. dirs. Norfolk Sister Cities, 1987-92. Mem. ASCD, Assn. Tchr. Educators, Va. Assn. Colls. Tchr. Edn. (exec. bd. 1985-86, 90-94, pres.-elect 1992-94), Am. Assn. Coll. Tchr. Edn. (chief instl. rep. 1992—). Office: Va Wesleyan Coll Wesleyan Dr Norfolk VA 23502

SHANNON, JOE, JR., lawyer; b. Fort Worth, Nov. 9, 1940; s. Joe and Juanita Elizabeth (Milliorn) S.; children: Kelley Jane, Joseph Patrick, Shelley Carol; m. Monica Walsh, June 17, 1993. BA, U. Tex., 1962, LLB, 1963. Bar: Tex. 1963, U.S. Supreme Ct. 1977, U.S. Dist. Ct. (no. dist.) Tex. 1970, U.S. Ct. Appeals (5th cir.) 1977; cert. family law Tex. Bd. Legal Specialization, matrimonial arbitrator. Ptnr. Shannon & Shannon, Fort Worth, 1963-72; adminstrv. asst. to speaker, Tex. Ho. of Reps., Austin, 1970; chief criminal div. Tarrant County Dist. Atty., Ft. Worth, 1972-78; pvt. practice, Fort Worth, 1978-86; ptnr. Law, Snakard & Gambill, Ft. Worth, 1986-90. Mem. Tex. Ho. of Reps., 1964-70. Fellow Tex. Bar Found., Am. Acad. Matrimonial Lawyers (cert.); mem. ABA, State Bar of Tex. (adv. com. family law, state bd. legal specialization, dist. grievance com. 1973-76, chmn. 1975-76, 95—, sec. 2d ct. Appeals adv. com., 1995—), North Tex. Family Law Specialists Assn., Tex. Acad. Family Law Specialists, Tarrant County Bar Assn., Tarrant County Family Law Bar Assn., Phi Alpha Delta, Masons, Shriners. Office: 2610 Bank One Tower Fort Worth TX 76102

SHANNON, LARRY REDDING, administrative assistant; b. St. Joseph, Mo., Apr. 5, 1949; s. Charles R. Jr. and Dorothy May (Dunham) Redding. Student, U. Tex., Arlington, 1967-69. Announcer Sta. KVIL, Dallas, 1968, Sta. KFJZ, Fort Worth and Dallas, 1968-78; pvt. practice pub. rels. and advt., Ft. Worth, 1978-85; pvt. practice pub. rels., advt. and mgmt., N.Y.C., 1985-86; adminstrv. asst. former U.S. Ho. of Reps. spkr. Jim Wright, Ft. Worth, 1986—. Democrat. Office: #9A 10 819 Taylor St Fort Worth TX 76102-6114

SHANNON, MARY KAY, museum administrator; b. Fort Stockton, Tex., July 9, 1954; d. Narvel R. Shannon and Bobby Louise (Walker) Wells. BS in Edn., S.W. Tex. State U., 1977; postgrad., La. State U., 1978, U. Tex., El Paso, 1979, Sul Ross State U., 1981. 1st grade tchr. Kiddie Korner Pvt. Sch., Dallas, 1977; classroom tchr. El Paso Pub. Schs., 1978-81; curator Annie Riggs Meml. Mus. Fort Stockton Hist. Soc., 1981-90; adminstrv. dir. Fort Stockton Hist. Soc., 1990-95; asst. supt. Magoffin Home State Hist. Site, 1995—. Named Outstanding Commn. Mem. Pecos County Hist. Commn., 1984, Outstanding Young Citizen Fort Stockton Jaycees, 1987, one of Five Outstanding Young Texans Tex. Jaycees, 1987, Outstanding Young Woman Tex., 1988. Mem. Am. Assn. Mus., Am. Assn. for State and Local History, Nat. Trust for Historic Preservation, Mountain-Plains Mus. Assn., Tex. Assn. Mus. Office: 1120 Magoffin Ave El Paso TX 79901

SHANNON, MARY LOU, adult health nursing educator; b. Memphis, Apr. 4, 1938; d. Sidney Richmond Shannon and Lucille (Gwaltney) Cloud. BSN, U. Tenn., 1959; MA, Columbia U., 1963, MEd, 1964, EdD, 1972. Staff nurse City of Memphis Hosps., 1959-60, instr. Sch. Nursing, 1960-62; asst. prof. U. Tenn., Memphis, 1964-70, assoc. prof., 1970-73, prof., 1973-89; prof., chair adult health dept. Sch. Nursing U. Tex., Galveston, 1989—; bd. dirs. Nat. Pressure Ulcer Adv. Panel, Buffalo, 1987-96; vis. prof. U. Alta., Edmonton, Can., 1982; mem. project adv. bd. RAND, Santa Monica, Calif., 1994. Contbr. chpts. to books in field and to periodicals; mem. editl. bd. Advances in Wound Care, 1987—. Trustee Nurses Edn. Funds, N.Y.C., 1972-86. Mem. ANA, Nat. League Nursing (bd. of rev. 1983-86), Orthopedic Nurses Assn., So. Nursing Rsch. Soc., Am. Assn. for History of Nursing. Office: U Tex Sch Nursing 301 University Blvd Galveston TX 77550-2708

SHANNON, TIMOTHY MAYZE, industrial designer, consultant; b. Atlanta, May 4, 1948; s. Otha Mayze and Selma Almead (Godbee) S.; m. Claudia L. Holmes, Apr. 4, 1987. BS, Ga. Tech. U., 1976. Product designer Leggett & Paltt, Inc., Atlanta, 1976-80; design mgr. Miller, Zell, Inc., Atlanta, 1980-85; v.p. design and engring. The Display Works, Inc., Kennesaw, Ga., 1985-87; pres. Shannon Assocs., Inc., Kennesaw, Ga., 1987—. Mem. Industry Designers Soc. Am., Soc. Plastic Engrs. Office: Shannon Assocs PO Box 1225 Kennesaw GA 30144-8225

SHAPARD, SANDRA GALES, poetess; b. Oklahoma City, Okla., Jan. 12, 1943; d. Theodore Nicholas and Gertrude W. (Schwarz) G.; m. Edwin Jenning Shapard, July 12, 1969; children: Nicole, Nathan, Ericka. BS, Spring Hill Coll., 1964; MA, U. Okla., 1967. Spl. events dir. Ackerman Assocs., Inc., Oklahoma City, Okla., 1966-67; assoc. prof. journalism Okla. City Univ., 1967-68; career woman advisor Complete Woman Mag., Chgo., 1982—; columnist Women Today Mag., Chgo., 1983-84; editor Okla. Tennis Publs., Okla. City, 1986—; guest speaker Jr. Leagues throughout U.S., 1978—. Author: (poetry) Woman Sounds, 1977, Night Flight 35, 1979, Summer Woman, 1984, Minor Miracles, 1995; inventor: designed and patented a wine cooler glass. Mem. Jr. League Okla. City (editor newsletter 1979-80, bd. dirs. 1979-83, publicity chairwoman, 1992-93), Okla. Publs. Assn. (bd. dirs. 1966-69), Kappa Alpha Theta Alumnae (bd. dirs. 1984-95, pres., 1990, Woman of Yr. 1996), Kappa Alpha Theta Mothers Club at Okla. U. (pres. 1992). Republican. Roman Catholic. Home and Office: 109 Lake Aluma Dr Oklahoma City OK 73121

SHAPIRA, EMMANUEL, clinical geneticist, biochemical geneticist, educator; b. Kovno, Lithuania, Nov. 22, 1933. MD, Hebrew U., Jerusalem, 1959; PhD in Immunochemistry, Weizmann Inst. Sci., Rehovot, Israel, 1968. Diplomate Am. Bd. Clin. Genetics, Am. Bd. Clin. Biochem. Genetics. Intern Kaplan Hosp., Rehovot, 1958-59, resident in pediatrics, 1962-66; with Tulane U. Med. Ctr., New Orleans; assoc. prof. pediatrics Med. Sch. Northwestern U., New Orleans, 1973; prof. pediatrics and pathology Med. Sch. Tulane U., 1978-83, prof. pediatrics and biochemistry Med. Sch., 1984, dir. human genetics program Hayward Genetics Ctr. Sch. Medicine, 1984—. Mem. AAAS, AMA, Assn. Am. Physicians, Am. Coll. Med. Genetics, Am. Pediatric Soc., Am. Soc. Human Genetics, Am. Soc. Pediatric Rsch., La. State Med. Soc., N.Y. Acad. Sci., Midwestern Soc. Pediatric Rsch., Southern Soc. Pediatric Rsch., Israel Immunol. Soc., European Soc. Pediatric Rsch., Internat. Soc. Newborn Screening, Soc. Inherited Metabolic Disease (bd. dirs.). Office: Tulane U Sch Med Human Genetics Prog 1430 Tulane Ave New Orleans LA 70112-2699

SHAPIRO, DAVID HOWARD, surgeon; b. Newark, Apr. 20, 1939; s. Nathan and Theresa Marie (Brown) S.; m. Jean R. Vetter, Aug. 16, 1979; children: Seth, Adam, Corey. AB, Williams Coll., 1961; MD, Tufts U., 1965. Diplomate Am. Bd. Surgery, Am. Bd. Med. Examiners. Intern in surgery Boston City Hosp., 1965-66, resident in surgery, 1966-67; resident in ob/gyn Yale-New Haven Hosp., 1967-68, resident, chief resident, 1968-71; from asst. clin. prof. surgery to clin. prof. surgery Univ. South Fla. Coll. Medicine, Tampa, 1973—; pvt. practice surgery Clearwater, Fla., 1973—. Cons. editor Jour. Fla. Med. Assn., 1988-81. Pres. bd. dirs. Pasco County subdiv. West Coast Regional Health Planning Commn., 1973; v.p. bd. trustees Fla. West Coast Regional Health Planning Commn., 1973; bd. dirs. Family Svcs. Pinellas County, 1984, Suncoast Internat. Adoptions, 1982-84; trustee St. Paul's Sch., chmn. strategic long-range planning com.; bd. dirs. Pinellas Regional Health Planning Commn., 1973-76; apptd. Fla. Cancer Control Rsch. Adv. Bd., 1988—; found. trustee Hospice Care, Inc., 1991; trustee, exec. com., quality assurance com., mktg. com. Morton Plant Hosp.; bd. dirs., med. adv. Pasco County div. Am. Cancer Soc., 1973, edn. com. Fla. div., 1978, colo-rectal task force, 1978, bd. dirs. Pinellas div., 1973-86, chmn. profl. edn. com., Fla. profl. edn. com., 1979, com. on rsch., 1978-80, bd. dirs., 1979-80. Maj. USAMC, 1971-73. Fellow Am. Coll. Surgeons (sec.-treas. Fla. chpt. 1980-82, pres.-elect 1982-84, pres. 1984-86, mem. various coms.), Southeastern Surg. Conf.; mem. AMA, Soc. for Laser Medicine and Surgery, Am. Soc. Bariatric Surgery, Soc. Clin. Vascular Surgery, Fla. Vascular Soc., Fla. Soc. Clin. Oncology, Fla. Surg. Assn., Fla. Med. Assn., Tampa Bay Med. Soc. (steering com., sec. 1993), Pinellas County Med. Soc. (bd. govs. 1983, chmn. coms.), Pinellas County Med. Assn., Tampa Bay Surg. Soc. (founding sec.), U South Fla. Soc. Clin. Profs. (founding pres.), Sigma Xi. Office: 1260 S Greenwood Ave Clearwater FL 34616-4172

SHAPIRO, DAVID L., lawyer; b. Corsicana, Tex., May 19, 1936; s. Harry and Alice (Laibovitz) S. BA, U. Tex., 1967; JD, St. Mary's U., 1970. Bar: Tex. 1970, U.S. Dist. Ct. (we. dist.) Tex. 1972, U.S. Supreme Ct. 1975, U.S. Ct. Appeals (5th cir.) 1981. Assoc. Law Office Jim S. Phelps, Houston, 1971; pvt. practice Austin, 1972—; spl. counsel com. human resources Tex. Ho. Reps., Austin, 1973-74; counsel subcom. health svcs. Tex. Senate, Austin, 1983-87. With U.S. Army, 1959-61. Mem. State Bar Tex. (chmn. lawyer referral svc. com. 1980-82, adminstrn. of justice com. 1990-93, contbr. Media Law Handbook supplement 1986), Travis County Bar Assn. (sec.-treas. 1977-78, dir. 1979, pres. family law sect. 1980-81), Coll. of State Bar of Tex., Austin Criminal Def. Lawyers Assn. Democrat. Home: 920 E 40th St #106 Austin TX 78751-4821

SHAPIRO, EDWARD MURAY, dermatologist; b. Denver, Oct. 6, 1924; s. Isador Benjamin and Sara (Berezin) S.; student U. Colo., 1941-43; m. Ruth Young, Oct. 14, 1944; children: Adrian Michael, Stefanie Ann; m. Dorothy Rosmarin, July 22, 1990. AB with honors, U. Tex., 1948, MD, 1952. Intern, Jefferson Coll. Medicine Hosp., Phila., 1952-53; resident in dermatology U. Tex. Med. Br., Galveston, 1953-55; resident in dermatology Henry Ford Hosp., Detroit, 1955-56, asso. in dermatology div. dermatology, 1956-57; clin. instr. dermatology Baylor U. Coll. Medicine, Houston, 1957-68, assoc. clin. prof., 1968—; staff Jefferson Davis Hosp., Houston, 1958—; active staff Pasadena Bayshore Hosp., 1962—, Southmore Hosp., Pasadena, 1958—. Served with USAAF, 1943-46. Henry J. N. Taub research grantee, 1958-60; diplomate Am. Bd. Dermatology. Fellow Am. Acad. Dermatology; mem. AMA, Tex. Med. Assn., Tex. Dermatol. Soc. (pres.-elect 1988, pres. 1989-90), South Cen. Dermatol. Assn. (bd. dirs. 1987-88), Harris County Med. Assn. (pres. S.E. br. 1968-69), Houston Dermatology Assn., Houston Art League, Gulf Coast Art Soc., Am. Physicians Art Assn. (v.p. 1993). Jewish. Clubs: B'nai B'rith, Rotary Internat. (Paul Harris fellow 1995). Contbr. articles in field to med. jours. Home: 2506 Potomac Dr Houston TX 77057-4548 Office: 1020 Pasadena Blvd Pasadena TX 77506-4700

SHAPIRO, LEE TOBEY, planetarium administrator, astronomer; b. Chgo., Dec. 12, 1943; s. Sydney Harold and Ruth Iva (Levin) S.; m. Linda Susan Goldman, Aug. 16, 1970; children: Steven Robert, Aaron Edward. BS in Physics, Carnegie Inst. Tech., 1966; MS in Astronomy, Northwestern U., 1968, PhD, 1974. Lectr. Adler Planetarium, Chgo., 1967-74; asst. prof. astronomy Mich. State U., East Lansing, 1974-79, assoc. prof., 1979-82; bd. dirs. Abrams Planetarium, 1974-82, Morehead Planetarium U. N.C.-Chapel Hill, 1982—, adj. assoc. prof., 1983—; vis. prof. Duke U., Durham, N.C., summers 1987-89, 93-94, 96. Fellow Royal Astron. Soc.; mem. Am. Astron. Soc., Am. Assn. Mus., Astronomical Soc. of the Pacific, Internat. Planetarium Soc., Great Lakes Planetarium Assn. (pres. 1980). Jewish. Office: Morehead Planetarium # 3480 U of NC Chapel Hill NC 27599-3480

SHAPIRO, MARCIA HASKEL, speech and language pathologist; b. N.Y.C., Nov. 6, 1949; d. Ben and Edna Haskel; m. Louis Shapiro, Aug. 1, 1981. BA, Hunter Coll., 1982; MA, NYU, 1983; MA in Speech Pathology, U. Cen. Fla., 1991. Cert. deaf educator, Fla. Tchr. deaf Pub. Sch. 47, N.Y.C., 1983-84; speech pathologist St. Francis Sch. for the Deaf, Bklyn., 1984-86, Seminole County Schs., 1986-87, Lake County Schs., 1987-89, Orange County Schs., Orlando, Fla., 1989-91, West Volusia Meml. Hosp., Deland, Fla., 1991-93, Orlando Regional Med. Ctr., 1993, Sand Lake Hosp., 1993—; staff head swallowing dept. Leesburg Regional Med. Ctr., 1994; dir. speech pathology Fla. Hosp., Waterman, 1994—. Mem. ASHA, AFTRA, EQITY, Annals of Deaf, CAID, Alexander Graham Bell Assn. for Deaf.

SHAPIRO, MAURICE MANDEL, astrophysicist; b. Jerusalem, Israel, Nov. 13, 1915; came to U.S., 1921; s. Asher and Miriam R. (Grunbaum) S.; m. Inez Weinfeld, Feb. 8, 1942 (dec. Oct. 1964); children: Joel Nevin, Elana Shapiro Ashley Naktin, Raquel Tamar Shapiro Kislinger. B.S., U. Chgo., 1936, M.S., 1940, Ph.D., 1942. Instr. physics and math. Chgo. City Colls., 1937-41; chmn. dept. phys. and biol. scis. Austin Coll., 1938-41; instr. math. Gary Coll., 1942; physicist Dept. Navy, 1942-44; lectr. physics and math. George Washington U., 1943-44; group leader, mem. coordinating council of lab. Los Alamos Sci. Lab., U. Calif., 1944-46; sr. physicist, lectr. Oak Ridge Nat. Lab., Union Carbon and Carbide Corp., 1946-49; cons. div. nuc. energy for propulsion aircraft Fairchild Engine & Aircraft Corp., 1948-49; head cosmic ray br. nucleonics div. U.S. Naval Research Lab., Washington, 1949-65, supt. nucleonics div., 1953-65, chief scientist Lab. for Cosmic Ray Physics, 1965-82, apptd. to chair of cosmic ray physics, 1966-82, chief scientist emeritus, 1982—; lectr. U. Md., 1949-50, 52—, assoc. prof., 1950-51, vis. prof. physics and astronomy, 1986—; vis. prof. physics and astronomy U. Iowa, 1981-84; vis. prof. astrophysics U. Bonn, 1982-84; vis. scientist Max Planck Inst. für Astrophysik, W. Ger., 1984-85; cons. Argonne Nat. Lab., 1949; cons. panel on cosmic rays U.S. nat. com. IGY; lectr. physics and engring. Nuclear Products-Erco div. ACF Industries, Inc., 1956-58; lectr. E. Fermi Internat. Sch. Physics, Varenna, Italy, 1962; vis. prof. Weizmann Inst. Sci., Rehovoth, Israel, 1962-63, Inst. Math. Scis., Madras, India, 1971; Inst. Astronomy and Geophysics Nat. U. Mex., 1976; vis. prof. physics and astronomy Northwestern U., Evanston, Ill., 1978; cons. space rsch. in astronomy Space Sci. Bd., Nat. Acad. Scis., 1965; cons. Office Space Scis., NASA, 1965-66, 89; prin. investigator Gemini S-9 Cosmic Ray Expts., NASA, 1964-69, Skylab, 1967-76, Long Duration Exposure Facility, 1977—; mem. Groupe de Travail de Biologie Spatiale, Council of Europe, 1970—; mem. steering com. DUMAND Consortium, 1976—, mem. exec. com., 1979-82, mem. sci. adv. com., 1982—; lectr. Summer Space Inst., Deutsche Physikalische Gesellschaft, 1972; dir. Internat. Sch. Cosmic-Ray Astrophysics, Ettore Majorana Centre Sci. Culture, Erice, Italy, 1977—, also sr. corr., 1977—; chmn. U.S. IGY com. on interdisciplinary research, mem. nuclear emulsion panel space sci. bd.; Nat. Acad. Scis., 1959—; chief U.S. rep., steering com. Internat. Coop. Emulsion Flights for Cosmic Ray Research; cons. CREI Atomics, 1959—; vis. com. Bartol Research Found., Franklin Inst., 1967-74; mem. U.S. organizing com. 13th and 19th Internat. Confs. on Cosmic Rays; mem. sci. adv. com. Internat. Confs. on Nuclear Photography and Solid State Detectors, 1966—; mem. Com. of Honor for Einstein Centennial, Acad. Naz. Lincei, 1977; mem. Internat. Organizing com. Tex. Symposia on Relativistic Astrophysics, 1976—; Regents lectr. U. Calif. Riverside, 1985; Edison lectr. Naval Rsch. Lab award, 1990; Victor Hess Meml. lectr., Rome, 1995. Mem. editorial bd. Astrophysics and Space Sci., 1968-75; assoc. editor: Phys. Rev. Letters, 1977-84; editor (NATO) ASI Series on Cosmic-Ray Astrophysics; contbr. to Am. Inst. Handbook of Physics, various encys. Mem. exec. bd. Cong. Beth Chai, Washington, 1987—; trustee Nat. Capital Astronomers, Washington, 1989—; mem. internat. panel Chernobyl World Lab., 1988. Recipient Disting. Civilian Svc. awrad Dept. Navy, 1967, medal of honor Soc. for Encouragement au Progrés, 1978, publs. award Naval Rsch. Lab., 1970, 74, 76, Dir.'s Spl. award, 1974, Sr. U.S. Scientist award Alexander von Humboldt Found., 1982, Profl. Achievement citation U. Chgo., 1992. Fellow Am. Phys. Soc. (chmn. organizing com. div. cosmic physics, chmn. 1971-72, com. on publs. 1977-79), AAAS, Washington Acad. Scis. (past com. chmn., Disting. Career in Scis. award, 1993); mem. Am. Astron. Soc. (exec. com. div. high-energy astrophysics 1978—, chmn. 1982), Philos. Soc. Washington (past pres.), Am. Technion Soc. (Washington bd.), Assn. Los Alamos Scientists (past chmn.), Assn. Oak Ridge Engrs. and Scientists (past chmn.), Fedn. Am. Scientists (past mem. exec. com., nat. council), Internat. Astron. Union (organizing com. commn. on high-energy astrophysics), Internat. Conf. on Cosmic Rays (Victor Hess Meml. lectr., 1995), Phi Beta Kappa, Sigma Xi (Edison lectr. 1990). Club: Cosmos (Washington). Office: 205 S Yoakum Pky Ste 1514 Alexandria VA 22304-3838

SHAPIRO, MICHAEL EDWARD, museum administrator, curator, art historian; b. N.Y.C., Nov. 15, 1949; s. Edward Aaron and Sylvia (Fishman) S.; m. Elizabeth Harvey, 1977; 2 children. BA, Hamilton Coll., 1972; MA, Williams Coll., 1976, Harvard U., 1978; PhD, Harvard U., 1980. Asst. prof. dept. art history Duke U., Durham, N.C., 1980-84; curator 19th-20th century art St. Louis Art Mus., 1984-92, chief curator, 1987-92; dir. Los Angeles County Mus. Art, 1992-93; dir. mus. programs, chief curator High Mus. Art, Atlanta, 1994-95, dep. dir., chief curator, 1996—. Author: Bronze Casting and American Sculpture, 1985; contbg. author: Frederic Remington: The Masterworks, 1988, George Caleb Bingham, 1990; mng. curator, editor Rings: Five Passions in World Art, 1996.

SHAPIRO, NELSON HIRSH, lawyer; b. Washington, Feb. 3, 1928; s. Arthur and Anna (Zenitz) S.; m. Helen Lenora Sykes, June 27, 1948; children—Ronald Evan, Mitchell Wayne, Jeffrey Mark, Julie Beth. B.E.E., Johns Hopkins U., 1948; J.D., George Washington U., 1952. Bar: D.C. 1952, Va. 1981. Patent examiner U.S. Patent Office, 1948-50; patent advisor U.S. Signal Corps, 1950-52; mem. Shapiro & Shapiro, Arlington, Va., 1952—. Mem. ABA, Am. Patent Law Assn., Bar Assn. D.C., Order of Coif, Tau Beta Pi. Patentee; contbr. articles to legal publs. and Ency. of Patent Practice and Invention Management, 1964. Home: 7001 Old Cabin Ln Rockville MD 20852-4531 Office: Shapiro & Shapiro 1100 Wilson Blvd Ste 1701 Arlington VA 22209-2297

SHAPIRO, ROBERT ALAN, retail executive; b. Denver, Dec. 24, 1946; s. George and Ruth Bearnice (Horn) S.; m. Jan Laurelle Tilker, Nov. 8, 1980; children: Aaron Phillip, Michael Samuel. BA, U. Denver, 1968; student, Northwestern U. Law Sch, 1968-70. V.p. Draper and Kramer, Inc., Chgo., 1970-73; asst. v.p. Urban Investment & Devel. Co., Chgo., 1973-75; dir. real estate The Limited, Columbus, Ohio, 1975-78; pres. Robert A. Shapiro & Assocs., Chgo., 1978-85; sr. v.p., corp. ops. asst. sec. County Seat Stores, Inc., Dallas, 1985—; lectr. Northwestern U., Evanston, Ill., Ohio State U., Columbus, 1976-78; mem. retail adv. bd. Shopping Ctr. Bus. mag.; originator Old Farmer's Almanac Gen. Stores. Mem. Internat. Coun. Shopping Ctrs. (tenant com. 1975-78), Nat. Retail Fedn. (splty. store task force com.). Jewish. Office: County Seat Stores 17950 Preston Rd Dallas TX 75252-5793

SHAPIRO, STEPHEN RICHARD, retired air force officer, physician; b. Bklyn., Dec. 30, 1934; s. George Daniel and Bertha Brinna (Bazerman) S.; m. Myrna Farber, May 28, 1960; children: David C., Robert S., Marc E. BA, Bklyn. Coll., 1956; MD, SUNY Downstate Med. Ctr., 1960. Diplomate Am. Bd. Internal Medicine, Am. Bd. Allergy and Immunology, Am. Bd. Med. Mgmt. Commd. 2nd lt. USAF, 1960, advanced through grades to brig. gen., 1987; intern, then resident and fellow Walter Reed Gen. Hosp., Washington, 1960-65; asst. chief allergy Wilford Hall USAF Med. Ctr., San Antonio, 1965-73; chief clin. svc. Ramstein (Germany) Clinic, 1973-74; chief divsn. clin. medicine Hdqrs. USAFE/SG, Ramstein, 1974-76; comdr. USAF Hosp. RAF, Upper Heyford, Eng., 1976-80; dep. surgeon Hdqrs. AFSC/SG, Andrews AFB, Md., 1980-82; surgeon Hdqrs. AFRES/SG, Robins AFB, Ga., 1982-84; command surgeon Hdqrs. AFSC/SG, Andrews AFB, Md., 1984-87; comdr. Malcolm Grow USAF Med. Ctr., Andrews AFB, 1987-89; command surgeon Hdqrs. AFLC/SG, Wright-Patterson AFB, Ohio, 1989-92, Hdqrs. AFMC, 1991-92; chief of staff VA Health Care Ctr., El Paso, Tex., 1992—. Fellow Aerospace Med. Assn. (assoc.); mem. Am. Coll. Physician Execs., Am. Acad. Allergy and Immunology, Air Force Soc. Flight Surgeons, Air Force Soc. Physicians, Alpha Omega Alpha. Jewish. Office: 5001 N Piedras St El Paso TX 79930-4211

SHARETT, ALAN RICHARD, lawyer, environmental litigator, mediator, and arbitrator, law educator; b. Hammond, Ind., Apr. 15, 1943; s. Henry S. and Frances (Givel) Smulevitz; children: Lauren Ruth, Charles Daniel; m. Cherie Ann Vick, Oct. 15, 1993. Student Ind. U., 1962-65; J.D., DePaul U., 1968; advanced postgrad. legal edn. U. Mich. and U. Chgo., 1970-71. Bar: N.Y. 1975, Ind. 1969, U.S. Ct. Appeals (2d cir.) 1975, U.S. Ct. Appeals (7th cir.) 1974, U.S. Supreme Ct. 1973. Assoc. Call, Call, Borns & Theodoros, Gary, Ind., 1969-71; judge protem Gary City Ct., 1970-71; environ. dist. atty. 31st Jud. Cir., Lake County, Ind., 1971-75; counsel Dunes Nat. Lakeshore Group, 1971-75; mem. Cohan, Cohan & Smulevitz, 1971-75; town atty., Independence Hill, Ind., 1974-75; judge pro tem Superior Ct., Lake County, Ind., 1971-75; professorial dir. NYU Pub. Liability Inst., N.Y.C., 1975-76; speaker, guest lectr., adj. faculty ATLA, Purdue U., N.Y. U., Ind. U., De Paul U., Valparaiso U., St. Joseph Coll., U. Miami; Coll. paralegal instr., 1970-89; adj. faculty prof. constl. law Union Inst., Miami, Cin., 1990-92; adj. prof. environ. litigation and alternative dispute resolution Ward Stone Coll., Miami, 1994; guest prof. internat. environ. law Dept. Internat. and Comparative Law, U. Miami, 1992—; mem. adv. panel, seminar speaker on internat. issues Interamerican Dialogue on Water Mgmt., 1993; spkr. on environ. transactions and litigation North Dade County Fla. Bar Assn., 1995—; seminar spkr. on environ. politics U. Miami Dept. Environ. Sci., 1995—; gen. counsel Marjory Stoneman Douglas Friends of Everglades, 1992-93; asst. atty. gen., chair fed. and constnl. practice litigation group, N.Y. State, N.Y.C., 1976-78; pvt. practice, Flushing, N.Y., 1980-82, Miami Beach, Fla., 1988—, lead trial counsel, chmn. lawyers panel for No. Ind., ACLU, 1969-71; liaison trial counsel Lake County and Ind. State Health Depts. and Atty. Gen., 1971-75; mem. Nat. Dist. Attys. Assn., 1972-75, mem. environ. protection com; pres. ESI Group, Nat. Environ. Responsibility Cons, Inc.; spkr. in field. Editor in chief DePaul U. The Summons,

1967-68; mem. staff DePaul Law Rev., 1968; jud. clerkship Superior Ct. 31st Ind. Jud. Cir., 1971-73; contbr. articles to profl. jours. Mem. coalition Fla. Save Our Everglades Program. Recipient Honors award in forensic litigation Law-Sci. Acad. Am., 1967. Mem. ABA (nat. article editor law student div. 1967-68, nat. com. environ. litigation, com. fed. procedure, com. toxic torts, hazardous substances and environ. law, com. energy resources law, com. internat. environ. law, com. internat. litigation, environ. interest group, sect. natural resources, energy and environ. law, judge negotiation competition championship round, law student divsn., midyear meeting 1995, sect. sci. and tech., nat. toxic and hazardous substances and environ. law com., sect. tort and ins. practice, corp. gen. counsel com., non-profit orgns. com., media law and defamation torts com., tort and hazardous substances and environ. law com.), Am. Arbitration Assn., Soc. Profls. in Dispute Resolution, Assn. Bar of City of N.Y., N.Y. County Lawyers Assn. (com. on fed. cts. 1977-82), Am. Judicature Soc., ATLA (nat. coms. toxic, environ. and pharm. torts, environ. litigation), Environ. Law Inst., Am. Immigration Lawyers Assn., Ill. State Bar Assn. (staff editor 1967-68), N.Y. State Bar Assn. (environ. law sect., family law sect.), Ind. State Bar Assn. (environ. law sect., internat. law sect., trial practice sect.), Nat. Fla. Assn. Environ. Profls., Greater Miami C. of C. (coms. on environ. awareness, environ. econs., biomedical exch., planning and zoning growth mgmt., internat. econ. devel., bus. and industry econ. devel., govtl. affairs, ins., internat. banking, Europe/Pacific rim), AAAS (physics, math., astronomy), Am. Acad. Poets. Office: ESI Group Nat Environ Responsibility Cons Inc 6421 Cow Pen Rd Ste M 107 Miami Lakes FL 33014-6655

SHARFMAN, MARC IRWIN, neurologist; b. Chgo., May 1, 1961; s. Sheldon Marvin Sharfman and Frances June (Harris) Fisher; m. Cindy Joy Karlin, June 12, 1988; 1 child, David Scott. BS in Biology, U. Ill., 1983; MD, U. Health Sci./Chgo. Med. Sch., 1987. Diplomate Nat. Bd. Med. Examiners; cert. Am. Bd. Psychiatry and Neurology. Intern Northwestern Meml. Hosp., Chgo., 1987-88, resident neurology, 1988-89; resident neurology U. Mass. Med. Ctr., Worcester, 1989-91; pvt. practice headache specialist Fla., 1991—; clin. asst. prof. dept. neurology U. South Fla. Coll. Medicine, Tampa, 1991-92; courtesy clin. instr. dept. medicine U. Fla. Coll. Medicine, Gainesville, 1994-96; staff mem. Orlando (Fla.) Regional Med. Ctr., 1992—, Fla. Hosp., Orlando, 1992—, Winter Park (Fla.) Meml. Hosp., 1992—, Morton Plant Hosp., Clearwater, Fla., 1992-93; assoc. dir. Headache Mgmt. Ctr., Inc., Winter Park, 1992-93; dir. Headache and Neurol. Treatment Inst., Winter Park, 1993—; presenter and lectr. in field. Mem. AMA, Am. Assn. Study Headache, Nat. Headache Found., Internat. Headache Soc., Alpha Omega Alpha. Office: 1936 Lee Rd Ste 137 Winter Park FL 32789-7201

SHARICK, MERLE DAYTON, JR., mortgage insurance company executive; b. Bloomington, Ill, May 5, 1946; s. Merle Dayton and Joyce Madeline (Reed) S.; m. Cheryl Jean Easterday, Dec. 28, 1966; children: Amber Dawn, Cami Nicole. BA, Southwestern Coll., Winfield, Kans., 1968; MS in Edn., U. Kans., 1970. Tchr., coach Kans. High Schs., Lawrence, Hutchinson, 1968-73; asst. prin., prin. Kans. High Schs., Buhler, Inman, Leoti, 1973-77; auctioneer, real estate salesman R.E.I.B., Inc., Hutchinson, Kans., 1977-78; account exec. Mortgage Guaranty Ins. Co., Hutchinson, 1978-81; regional sales mgr. Mortgage Guaranty Ins. Co., Shawnee Mission, Kans., 1981-83, Houston, 1983-86; div. risk mgr. Mortgage Guaranty Ins. Co., Atlanta, 1986-90; regional dir. Mortgage Guaranty Ins. Co., Charlotte, N.C., 1990-93; v.p., mgr. risk mgmt. Republic Mortgage Ins. Co., Winston-Salem, N.C., 1993—; sports editor Winfield (Kans.) Daily Couier, 1966-68; grad. asst. U. Kans., Lawrence, 1968-70; owner, operator Riverside Home Style Laundry, South Hutchinson, Kans., 1975-79, founder, owner, The Sport Shack, Hutchinson, Kans., 1977-79; guest speaker various orgns. Active in Rep. support groups, Houston, Atlanta, 1983—. Fellow Inst. for Devel. Ednl. Adminstrs.; mem. Nat. Assn. Rev. Appraisers and Mortgage Underwriters (bd. dirs. 1989-93, Ark. Traveler award 1995), Mortgage Bankers Am., Ga. Mortgage Bankers, Mortgage Bankers Carolinas, N.C. Alliance Cmty. Fin. Instns., S.C. League Savs. Instns., Fla. Mortgage Bankers, Tex. Mortgage Bankers, Charlotte Mortgage Bankers, The Housing Roundtable, The Piedmont Club. Baptist.

SHARMA, MAHENDRA KUMAR, chemist; b. Etah, India, Oct. 15, 1948; came to U.S., 1981; s. Makhan Lal and Shree (Devi) S.; m. Rama Sharma, Dec. 6, 1978; children: Amol, Anuj. BS in Chemistry, Agra U., India, 1968, MS in Phys. Chemistry, 1970, PhD in Colloid and Surface Sci., 1975. Grad. rsch. asst. Agra U., 1971-75, rsch. scientist, assoc., 1975-79; vis. rsch. assoc. Basel (Switzerland) U., 1979-81; rsch. assoc. U. Fla., Gainesville, 1981-83, asst. rsch. prof., scientist, 1983-85; sr. rsch. chemist, scientist Eastman Kodak Co., Kingsport, Tenn., 1986-91, prin. rsch. chemist, scientist, 1991—. Author 5 books; editor: Surface Phenomena and Fine Particles in Water-Based Coatings and Printing Technology, 1991, Surface Phenomena and Additives in Water-Based Coatings and Printing Technology, 1991, Particles Technology and Surface Phenomena in Minerals and Petroleum, 1991; contbr. over 50 articles to profl. jours. Mem. Am. Chem. Soc., Fine Particle Soc. (mem. exec. coun., bd. dirs. 1989-93), Hindi Literary Assn. Home: 2600 Brighton Ct Kingsport TN 37660-4762 Office: Eastman Chem Co PO Box 1972 Kingsport TN 37662-1972

SHARMA, RASHMI, toxicologist, researcher; b. Mathura, India, Aug. 10, 1960; came to U.S., 1989; d. Ghanshiam Nath and Gomati (Ramnathji) S. BSc, U. Allahabad, India, 1979, MSc, 1981, PhD, 1989. Rsch. assoc. U. Miss., Jackson, 1989-91; postdoctoral fellow U. Tex. Med. Br., Galveston, 1991—; attendee workshops and meetings Congress Zoology, Gwalior (India) U., 1983, Meerut (India) U., 1985, Indian Sci. Congress Assn., Lucknow (India), 1984, Delhi U., 1985, Bangalore (Karnataka) India, 1986, USA Internat. Conf., Stanford (Calif.) U., 1987, Young Scientist Workshop on Environ. Nematology, U. Allahabad, India, 1987, South Ctrl. Soc. Toxicology, Oxford (Miss.) U., 1989, Nat. Ctr. for Toxicol. Rsch., Jefferson, Ark., 1990, Miss. Acad. Sci., Biloxi, 1990, Jackson, Miss., 1991, Soc. Toxicology, Dallas, 1991, New Orleans, 1993, Am. Assn. Cancer Rsch., San Diego, 1992, Orlando, Fla., 1993, San Francisco, 1994, Toronto, Can., 1995. Contbr. articles to profl. jours. Fellow Coun. Sci. and Indsl. Rsch., Govt. of India, 1984-87; grantee NIH, 1989-91. Mem. AAAS, Am. Assn. for Cancer Rsch. Home: 515 1st St Apt 335 Galveston TX 77550-5743 Office: U Tex Med Br 7 138 MRB Rt J-67 Galveston TX 77555-1067

SHARON, THOMAS E., science company executive. CEO Electromagnetic Scis., Inc., Norcross, Ga. Office: Electromagnetic Sciences Inc. PO Box 7700 Norcross GA 30091*

SHARP, DIANA LEIGH MILLER, psychologist, educator; b. Tucson, June 7, 1963; d. Dean Markey and Alice Juanita (Falk) Miller; m. William Allen Sharp, Oct. 4, 1957. BA in Psychology, Dickinson Coll., 1985; PhD in Cognitive Psychology, Vanderbilt U., 1989. Barbara S. Wallston postdoctoral rsch. fellow Vanderbilt U., Nashville, 1989-90, lectr. in psychology Coll. of Arts and Scis., 1991; rsch. assoc. Learning Tech. Ctr., Nashville, 1990-93, sr. rsch. assoc., 1993—. Cons. reviewer Developmental Psychology, Memory and Cognition, Psychol. Bull.; cons. reviewer books for Oxford Univ. Press; contbr. articles to profl. jours. Elem. tchr. Westminster Presbyn. Ch. Office of Spl. Edn./Dept. of Edn. grantee, 1993-95, NIMH grantee, 1991-95. mem. ASCD, Am. Ednl. Rsch. Assn., Internat. Reading Assn., Consortium for Sch. Networking. Office: Learning Technology Ctr Box 45 Peabody Nashville TN 37203

SHARP, DOUGLAS ANDREW, secondary school educator; b. Austin, Tex., July 19, 1945; s. Jack Weston and Jean Ernestine (Beeman) S.; m. Marylin Gene Martin, Jan. 20, 1977. BA in Math., Tex. A&M U., 1967, MS in Math., 1970, postgrad., 1969-71; EdD, La Salle U., Mandville, La., 1993. Teaching fellow dept. math. Tex. A&M U., College Station, 1967-71; chmn. math. dept., asst. coach/coach athletics dept. Southfield Sch., Shreveport, La., 1972-73; coach athletics dept. St. John's Sch., Houston, 1975, chmn. math. dept., 1981-93, master teaching chair math., 1987-89; disting. vis. lectr. U. Houston, 1989-90, adj. prof., 1990. Contbr. articles to profl. jours. Recipient Excellence in Teaching award Fin. Dept. U. Houston, 1993, Outstanding Tchr. award Tandy Technol. Scholars, 1993-94. Mem. Am. Math. Soc., Am. Soc. Composer, Authors and Pubs., Am. Statistical Assn., Math. Assn. Am. (Edyth May Sliffe award 1991), Calculus and Elem. Analysis Tchrs. Houston, Nat. Coun. Tchrs.Math. Office: St John's Sch 2401 Claremont St Houston TX 77019-5811

SHARP, ELAINE CECILE, obstetrician, gynecologist; b. Hoven, S.D., Feb. 19, 1952; d. Lewis Ralph and Bernadette Teresa (Bastien) Arbach; m. Walton H. Sharp, Oct. 26, 1979 (div.); m. Shane Daigle, Nov. 1991; 1 child, Sean Patrick Daigle. BA, No. State U., 1974, BS, 1976; MD, U. Tex., Houston, 1985. Diplomate Am. Bd. Ob-Gyn. Pvt. practice Pensacola, Fla., 1989—; speaker, chmn. Body Talk, Milton, Fla., 1989—. Mem. Am. Med. Womens' Assn., Am. Diabetes Assn., Am. Bus. Womens' Assn., Am. Coll. Ob-Gyn, Soc. Laparoendoscopic Surgeons, Fla. Ob-Gyn Soc., Exec. Club (asst. chmn. cancer com.). Republic. Roman Catholic. Office: PO Box 17062 Pensacola FL 32522-7062 also: Elaine Sharp MD PA 1717 N E St # 436 Pensacola FL 32501-6339

SHARP, HOWARD ROGER EMLYN, civil engineer; b. Bolton, Lancashire, U.K., Jan. 28, 1946; s. David Henry and Enid Catherine (Williams) S.; m. Kathlyn Smith, July 10, 1974 (div. 1983); 1 child, Anastasia Emily. BSc, Portsmouth Coll., U.K., 1969; MA, U. North Fla., 1985. Registered profl. engr., Fla. Project mgr. Frederic R. Harris, Ft. Lauderdale, Fla., 1977-82; div. chief City of Jacksonville, Fla., 1982-89; dep. dir. engring. Jacksonville Transp. Authority, 1989—. Contbr. to book of proceedings: Major Development and Transportation Projects, 1990. Mem. Instn. of Civil Engrs., Fla. Engring. Soc., Inst. of Transp. Engrs., Instn. of Hwys. and Transp. Episcopalian. Home: 4631 Empire Ave Jacksonville FL 32207-2192 Office: Jacksonville Transp Auth 100 N Myrtle Ave Jacksonville FL 32204-1310

SHARP, JOHN, state railroad commissioner; b. July 28, 1950. B.A., Tex. A&M U.; M.P.A., Southwest Tex. State U. Mem. Tex. Ho. of Reps., 1979-82, mem. econ. devel., intergovtl. relations, and health and human resources coms.; mem. Tex. Senate, 1982-86; elected to Tex. R.R. Commn., 1986, chmn. of the Commn., 1986—; mem. Sunset Adv. Com. Democrat. Office: Tex RR Commn PO Box 12967 Austin TX 78711-2967 also: 111 W 17th St Austin TX 78701-1334*

SHARP, JOHN ERBIN, criminal justice educator; b. Taylor, Tex., Jan. 6, 1935; s. James Pinkney and Ida Maude (Carter) S.; m. Kathleen Loretta Marx-Sharp, Nov. 19, 1960; children: Lance David, Theresa Marie, John Vincent, Moira Eileen. BA in History/Govt., U. Tex., 1961; MA in Police Sci. and Adminstrn., Sam Houston State U., 1974; MA in Pub. Mgmt., U. Houston-Clear Lake, 1984. Cert. law enforcement instr. Mgr. Sharp Furniture Co., Bastrop, Tex., 1958-62; welfare agt. Tex. Dept. Pub. Welfare, Granbury, 1962-63; instr. law enforcement and security Coll. of Mainland, 1975-77; instr. criminal justice and arson investigation program Houston Community Coll. System, 1977—; pres. Tex. Assn. Criminal Justice Educators, 1992-95; co-chair Tex. Criminal Justice Educators Planning Com., 1986-88; mem. criminal justice curriculum study com. Tex. Coord. Bd. Colls. and Univs., Austin, 1982-84; criminal justice program course cons. Tex. Edn. Agy.; mem. Task Force on Community Coll. Criminal Justice Edn., Law Enforcement Asst. Adminstrn., Washington, 1979-81; co-chmn. com. on acad. goals for Houston Ind. Sch. Dist. Magnet High Sch. for Law Enforcement and Criminal Justice. With USAF Res., ret. Mem. AAUP, Am. Soc. Criminology, Acad. Criminal Justice Scis., Community Coll. Criminal Justice Educators Tex., Tex. Jr. Coll. Tchrs. Assn. Democrat. Methodist. Office: Houston Community Coll 1215 Holman St Houston TX 77004

SHARP, JOHN LEWIS, oil industry executive, geologist; b. Warren, Ark., Nov. 1, 1959; s. Billy Ray and Jerry Lynn (Lewis) S.; m. Kyoung Sun Kim, June 20, 1981; 1 child, Alex Lewis. BS in Geology with high hons., U. Ark., Fayetteville, 1981, MS in Geology, 1983. Exploration geologist Marathon Oil Co., Houston, 1983-88; ops. geologist Marathon Petroleum Korea, Ltd., Houston, 1988-90; sr. geologist ArkLa Exploration Co., Houston, 1990-93; geol. cons. Houston, 1993; exploration mgr. Transfuel Resources, Inc., Houston, 1993-94, v.p. exploration, 1994-95; co-owner Praxis resources LLC, Houston, 1996—. Mem. Am. Assn. Petroleum Geologists (cert. petroleum geologist), Houston Geolog. Soc. Republican. Office: Praxis Resources LLC 10700 Richmond Ste 100 Houston TX 77042

SHARP, JOHN MALCOLM, JR., geology educator; b. St. Paul, Mar. 11, 1944. BGeoE, U. Minn., 1967; MS, PhD., U. Ill., 1974. Civil engring. officer USAF, 1967-71; with geology dept. U. Mo., Columbia, 1974-82; Chevron Centennial prof. geology U. Tex., Austin, 1982—. Alexander von Humbolt fellow 1981-83. Fellow Geol. Soc. Am. (O.E. Meinzer award 1979); mem. Phi Kappa Phi, Sigma Xi, Tau Beta Pi. Office: U Tex Dept Geol Scis Austin TX 78712-1101

SHARP, RICHARD L., retail company executive; b. Washington, Apr. 12, 1947. Student, U. Va., 1965-66, Coll. of William and Mary, 1968-70. Programmer Group Health Inc., Washington, 1970-75; founder, pres. Applied Systems Corp., Washington, 1975-81; with Circuit City Stores, Inc., Richmond, Va., 1982—, exec. v.p., 1982-84, pres., 1984-86, pres., CEO, 1986-94, chmn. pres., CEO, 1994—; bd. dirs. Flextronics Internat., James River Corp. With USAF, 1967-70. Office: Circuit City Stores Inc 9950 Mayland Dr Richmond VA 23233-1464

SHARP, RONALD ARVELL, sociology educator; b. Vivian, La., Sept. 29, 1941; s. Walter Arvell and Virginia (Refield-King) S.; m. Imelda Idalia Pena, Sept. 16, 1967; children: Ronald Arvell II, Donald Allen. BS in Edn., Cameron U., 1976; BA in Sociology, SUNY, Albany, 1977; MEd in Counseling Psychology, U. Okla., 1978; PhD in Sociology, Clayton U., 1985. Ret. U.S. Army, 1960-82; radiologic technologist VA Hosp., Temple, Tex., 1983-84; vets. counselor Vets. Outreach Program, San Antonio, Tex., 1982-83; dir. personnel & mktg. Heran Pharms., San Antonio, Tex., 1988-91; prof. sociology Ctrl. Tech. Coll., Killeen, 1991-95; instr. sociology Tex. State Tech. Coll., Waco, 1995-96, Academia Assocs., 1996—; part-time instr. Ctrl. Tex. Coll., 1980-82, City Coll. Chgo., 1981, Big Bend C.C., Mannheim, Germany, 1981-82; instr. Acad. Health Scis., 1977-79. Contbr. articles to profl. jours. Coach Youth Soccer Orgns., San Antonio and Mannheim, 1976-82. Nat. Coll. Radiology Technologists fellow, 1968. Mem. AAUP, Am. Sociol. Assn., Soc. Applied Sociology, La. Archeol. Soc., Choctaw Nation of Okla., Okla. Anthrop. Soc., Okla. Hist. Soc., La. Archeol. Conservancy, Caddoan Hist. Soc., Okla. Archeol. Survey, Order of Alhambra, KC, Masons, Soc. for the Study of Social Problems, Psi Beta (chpt. sponsor), Alpha Kappa Delta, Psi Chi, Sigma Eta Sigma (nat. dir.). Roman Catholic. Home: 9310 Oak Hills Dr Temple TX 76502-5272 Office: Academia Assocs Waco TX 76705

SHARP, VERNON HIBBETT, psychiatrist; b. Nashville, Apr. 6, 1932; s. Vernon Hibbett Sr. and Sarah McDonald (Robinson) S.; m. Valeria Nell Parker Storms, Aug. 17, 1956 (div. July 1975); children: Mark, Christopher, Daniel; m. Alix Ingrid Weiss, Nov. 17, 1979; 1 child, Monica Elena. BA, Vanderbilt U., 1953, MD, 1957. Diplomate Am. Bd. Psychiatry and Neurology. Intern internal medicine Washington U., St. Louis, 1957-58; resident psychiatry Yale U., New Haven, 1958-61; asst. prof. dept. psychiatry Cornell U. Med. Ctr., N.Y.C., 1963-66, SUNY, Downstate Med. Ctr., Bklyn., 1966-69; pvt. practice adults, adolescents and families Scarsdale, N.Y., 1969-83; pvt. practice Nashville, 1983-93; clin. asst. prof. psychiatry Vanderbilt U. Sch. Medicine, Nashville, 1983-86, clin. assoc. prof., 1986—; chief dept. psychiatry St. Thomas Hosp., Nashville, 1985-87; dir. family treatment tng. program Vanderbilt Med. Sch., Nashville, 1990—; founding mem. bd. dirs. Ctr. for Family, Nashville, 1985-93; vis. lectr. adolescent psychiatry Columbia U. Sch. Social Work, 1979-81; asst. attending psychiatrist Cornell U. Med. Coll., 1982-83; adj. assoc. prof. human resources Peabody Coll., Vanderbilt U., 1994-95; mem. attending staff various hosps. Contbr. articles to profl. jours. Lt. comdr. USN, 1961-63. Recipient Career Tchr. award NIMH, Downstate Med. Ctr., Bklyn., 1967-69. Mem. Am. Psychiat. Assn., Soc. for Adolescent Psychiatry, Am. Assn. Marriage and Family Therapy, Am. Family Therapy Acad., Coffee House Club (pres. 1985). Democrat. Episcopalian. Home and Office: 215 Leonard Ave Nashville TN 37205-2425

SHARP, WILLIAM WHEELER, geologist; b. Shreveport, La., Oct. 9, 1923; s. William Wheeler and Jennie V. (Benson) S.; m. Rubylin Slaughter, 1958; children: Staci Lynn, Kimberly Cecile; 1 child from previous marriage, John E. BS in Geology, U. Tex., Austin, 1950, MA, 1951. Lic. pvt. pilot. Geol. Socony-Vacuum, Caracas, Venezuela, 1951-53; surface geol. chief Creole, 1953-57; dist. devel. geologist, supr. exploration, devel., and unitization of 132 multi-pay oil and gas fields, expert geol. witness, coll. recruiter, research assoc. ARCO, 1957-85; discovered oil and gas at Bayou Boullion, Bayou Sale, Jeanerette, La.; petroleum exploration in Alaska, Aus., Can., U.S. and S.A. Contbr. articles to profl. jours. Past dir. and chmn. U.S. Tennis Assn. Tournaments, 12th Nat. Boys Tournament; pres. Lafayette Tennis Adv. Com., 1972; past dir. Jr. Achievememt and United Fund Programs. Served as sgt. USAF, 1943-46, PTO. Winner and finalist more than 75 amateur tennis tournaments including Confederate Oil Invitational, Gulf Coast Oilmen's Tournament, So. Oilmen's Tournament, Tex.-Ark.-La. Oilmen's Tournament; named Hon. Citizen of New Orleans, 1971, recipient Key to New Orleans. Mem. Dallas Geol. Soc., Lafayette Geol. Soc. (bd. dirs. 1973-74), Am. Assn. Petroleum Geologists (co-author Best of SEG conv. 1982), VFW, Am. Legion, Appaloosa Horse Club. Republican. Methodist. Avocations: sports, music, reading history. Home: 7312 Mimosa Ln Dallas TX 75230-5446

SHARPE, AUBREY DEAN, college administrator; b. Miami, Fla., Oct. 4, 1944; s. William Gibson and Ila-Mae (Albritton) S.; m. Linda Lee Rush, Dec. 22, 1973. BA, E. Tex. Bapt. U., 1967; MDiv, Southwestern Bapt. Theol. Sem., Ft. Worth, 1970; MA, southwestern Bapt. Theol. Sem., Ft. Worth, 1972; EdD, U. No. Tex., 1993. Assoc. pastor edn. Trinity Bapt. Ch., Ft. Worth, Tex., 1970-72; minister edn. Polytechnic Bapt. Ch., Ft. Worth, Tex., 1972-73; dean community svcs. Tarrant County Jr. Coll., Ft. Worth, Tex., 1973-84; religion inst. Tarrant County Jr. Coll., Ft. Worth, 1976-78; nat. dir. tng. Presbyn. Ministers Fund, Phila., 1984-89; v.p. The Pat Petersen Collection, Ft. Worth, 1984-91; owner ADS Investments, Ft. Worth, 1984—; dean continuing studies, Regional Tng. and Devel. Complex Tyler (Tex.) Jr. Coll., 1989—. Pres. Ft. Worth Boys Club, 1979; allocations chmn. United Way Tarrant County, Ft. Worth, 1981-87, Sr. Citizens, Inc., Ft. Worth, 1985-86, Tyler Metro YMCA, 1992-93; bd. dirs. United Way Tyler and Smith County, 1991-96, v.p. allocations/funding, trainer for loaned exec. program, 1991-95, Pacesetter Campaign chair 1996; adv. bd. North Tex. Small Bus. Devel. Ctr., 1995-96. Recipient Nat. Sales Achievement award Nat. Assn. Life Underwriters, 1987, Nat. Sales Leader award 1987; recipient Achievers award Presbyn. Ministers Fund, 1987, Vol. Svc. Award, United Way of Tarrant County, 1987. Mem. ASTD (pres.-elect 1991, pres. 1992-93), Tex. Assn. Community Svcs. and Continuing Edn., Tex. Jr. Coll. Tchrs. Assn., Nat. Coun. for Community Svcs./Continuing Edn., Tex. Adminstrs. Continuing Edn., Tyler Area C. of C., Phi Delta Kappa. Republican. Baptist. Home: 503 Towne Oaks Dr Tyler TX 75701-9536 Office: Tyler Jr Coll Regional Training Complex 1530 S SW Loop # 323 Tyler TX 75701

SHARPE, JAMES SHELBY, lawyer; b. Ft. Worth, Sept. 11, 1940; s. James Henry and Wanzel (Vanderbilt) S.; m. Martha Moudy Holland, June 9, 1962; children: Marthanne Freeman, Caren Roark, Stephen. BA, U. Tex., 1962, JD, 1965. Bar: Tex. 1965, U.S. Dist. Ct. (no. dist.) Tex. 1966, U.S. Dist. Ct. (ea. dist.) Tex. 1993, U.S. Ct. Appeals (5th and 6th cirs.) 1982, U.S. Ct. Appeals (fed. cir.) 1983, U.S. Ct. Appeals (10th cir.) 1992, U.S. Supreme Ct. 1972. Briefing atty. for chief justice Supreme Ct. of Tex., Austin, 1965-66; ptnr. Brown, Herman, Scott, Dean & Miles, Ft. Worth, 1966-84, Gandy Michener Swindle Whitaker & Pratt, Ft. Worth, 1984-87; shareholder Sharpe & Tillman, Ft. Worth, 1988—; adj. prof. polit. sci. Tex. Christian U., Ft. Worth, 1969-79, Dallas Bapt. U., 1987, 1992-94; gen. counsel U.S.A. Radio Network, Internat. Christian Media, Denton Pub. Co. Pres. Ft. Worth-Tarrant County Jr. Bar, 1969-70, bd. dirs., 1968, sec., 1968, v.p., 1968-69; head marshal USA-USSR Track and Field Championships, Ft. Worth, USA-USSR Jr. Track and Field Championships, Austin, Tex., Relays, Austin, 1963—, NCAA Nat. Track and Field Championships, 1976, 80, 85, 92, 95, S.W. Conf. Indoor Track and Field Championships, 1987-96, Olympic Festival, San Antonio, 1993, Colorado Springs, 1995; 12 time head marshal S.W. Conf. Track and Field Championships. USA/Mobil Track Championship, 1994, 95; USA Nat. Jr. Track Championship, 1994, 95. Mem. ABA, State Bar of Tex. (dist. 7-A grievance com. 1983-85, com. adminstrn. of justice 1985-92, com. on ct. rules 1992—, chmn. 1992-93, 93-94). Baptist. Home: 8304 Crosswind Dr Fort Worth TX 76179-3003 Office: Sharpe & Tillman 500 Throckmorton St Ste 2400 Fort Worth TX 76102-3811

SHARPE, JUDITH A., mental health nurse, administrator, psychiatric clinical specialist; b. Grand Rapids, Mich., July 6, 1946; d. Romeo J. and Santina (Borgia) Viventi; 1 child, Joseph P. Sharpe. Diploma with highest honors, Holy Cross Sch. Nursing, South Bend, Ind., 1968; BA magna cum laude, San Francisco State U., 1974; MA in Psychology with highest honors, U. of the Pacific, 1976. DON Allendale (Mich.) Nursing Home; clin. supr. Butler Hosp., Providence; nursing clin. coord. Loudon Hosp. Ctr., Leesburg, Va., chem. dependency program coord.; clin. specialist, pvt. practice; adv. coun. mem. Biomed. Ethics Coun. Diabetes, Lic. Practical Nurses Students Comms.; cons., educator in field. Recipient Loudoun County Outstanding Woman of the Yr. award, 1993.

SHARPE, KATHRYN MOYE, psychologist; b. Barnesville, Ga., Nov. 27, 1922; d. Herbert Johnston and Henri Lucile (Winter) Moye; m. William Herschel Sharpe, Mar. 2, 1946; children: William Herschel Jr., Mark Stephens. AB, Piedmont Coll., Demorest, Ga., 1942; MA, U. N.C., 1947; PhD, U. S.C., 1975. Tchr., guidance counselor Charleston (S.C.) Pub. Schs., 1947-66; prof. sociology, chmn. dept. Bapt. Coll. at Charleston, 1966-88, prof. emeritus, 1988—; pvt. practice psychology, Charleston, 1975—. Kathryn Moye Sharpe scholarship given in her honor Bapt. Coll. at Charleston, 1988. Fellow Am. Assn. for Marriage and Family Therapy (approved supr., pres. S.C. div. 1975-77). Congregationalist. Home and Office: 6 Cavalier Ave Charleston SC 29407-7702

SHARPE, MITCHELL RAYMOND, science writer; b. Knoxville, Tenn., Dec. 22, 1924; s. Mitchell Raymond and Katie Grace (Hill) S.; m. Virginia Ruth Lowry, 1952 (div.); children: Rebecca, Rachel, David. BS, Auburn U., 1948, MA, 1954; postgrad., Emory U., 1955, U.S. Army Command and Gen. Staff Coll., 1967. Supervisory tech. writer U.S. Army Missile Command, Redstone Arsenal, Ala., 1955-60; tech. writer, historian Marshall Space Flight Ctr., Huntsville, Ala., 1960-74; cons. U.S. Space and Rocket Ctr., Huntsville, 1970—, Nat. Air and Space Mus., Washington, 1965-80, Coupole d'Helfaut-Wizernes, Arques, France, 1989—, Gemeindererwaltung Peenemuende His-tech., Informationzentrum, Peenemuende, Germany, 1991—. Author: It Is I, Seagull, Valentina Tereshkova, First Woman in Space, 1975, Living in Space, The Astronaut and His Environment, 1969, Yuri Gagarin, First Man in Space, 1969, Satellites and Probes, The Development of Unmanned Space Flight, 1970; co-author: Applied Astronautics, An Introduction to Space Flight, 1963, Basic Astronautics, An Introduction to Space Science, Engineering, and Medicine, 1962, Dividends from Space, 1974, The Rocket Team, 1979, 82, 92; also articles. With U.S. Army, World War II, Korean War; col. USAR ret. Recipient Goddard Essay award Nat. Space Club, 1969, 75, Gold medal Tsiolkovsky Hist. Mus., Kaluga, USSR, 1973. Fellow Brit. Interplanetary Soc.; mem. AIAA (sr., tech. com. on history), Internat. Acad. Astronautics (corr., history com. 1985—), Soc. for History of Tech., Nat. Assn. Sci. Writers, Nat. Geog. Soc. Home and Office: 7302 Chadwell Rd SW Huntsville AL 35802-1718

SHARPE, ROCHELLE PHYLLIS, journalist; b. Gary, Ind., Apr. 27, 1956; d. Norman Nathaniel and Shirley (Kaplan) S. BA, Yale U., 1978. Reporter Concord (N.H.) Monitor, 1979-81; statehouse rep. Wilmington News Jour., Dover, Del., 1981-85; statehouse corr. Gannett News Svc., Albany, N.Y., 1985; nat. reporter Gannett News Svc., Washington, 1986-93; staff reporter social issues The Wall St. Jour., Washington, 1993—. Contbr. articles to profl. jours. Recipient Pulitzer prize for series in child abuse, Columbia U., 1991. Home: 2500 Q St NW Apt 315 Washington DC 20007-4360 Office: Wall St Jour Washington Bur 1025 Connecticut Ave NW Ste 800 Washington DC 20036-5405

SHARPLES, FRANCES ELLEN, zoologist, researcher; b. Bklyn., Feb. 5, 1950; d. Frank and Ingrid (Beuthien) S. BA, Barnard Coll., 1972; MA, U. Calif., Davis, 1974, PhD, 1978. Rsch. assoc. Environ. Impacts Program Oak Ridge (Tenn.) Nat. Lab., 1978-82, rsch. assoc. program planning & analysis office, 1982-84, rsch. staff mem. Hazardous Waste Remedial Actions program, 1985-87, R&D group leader environ. compliance group, 1987-92, R&D sect. head environ. analyses sect. Environ. Scis. Divsn., 1992-96; legis. asst. Energy & Natural Resources Senator Albert Gore, Jr., Washington, 1984-85; cons. Ctr. Pub. Issues Biotech. Md. Biotech. Inst. U. Md., 1989-90; mem. EPA Environ. Biology peer review panel, 1989-91; cons. UN Indsl. Devel. Orgn./WHO/UN Environ. Program Working Group biotech. safety, 1986-88; organizer, transcript editor hearing on antibiotic resistance U.S. Ho.

Reps., 1984; mem. recombinant DNA adv. com. NIH, 1984-87; environ. sci. & engring. fellow EPA, Washington, 1981. Bd. dirs. Recording for Blind & Dyslexic, Oak Ridge, Tenn., 1993-96. Fellow AAAS (com. sci., engring. & pub. policy 1990-96, Environ. Sci. & Engring. fellow 1981, Congl. Sci. & Engring. fellow 1984); mem. Am. Inst. Biol. Scis., Assn. Women Sci. (awards com. East Tenn. chpt. 1985-86, pres. 1986-87), Ecol. Soc. Am. (pub. affairs com. 1986-88), Sigma Xi (nominations com. Oak Ridge chpt. 1987-88, pres. 1989-90, rsch. grantee 1977). Office: Oak Ridge Nat Lab Environ Scis Divsn Bldg 1505 MS 6036 PO Box 2008 Oak Ridge TN 37831-6036

SHARPLESS, MARY REBECCA, historian; b. Waco, Tex., Oct. 14, 1958; d. Garland Lester and Mary Helen (Frierson) S.; m. Joe A. Jimenez, May 26, 1979 (div. Dec. 1985); m. Thomas Lee Charlton, Dec. 31, 1988. BA, Baylor U., 1978, MA, 1983; PhD, Emory U., 1993. Assoc. dir. Baylor Inst. Oral History, Waco, Tex., 1979-87, interim dir. Program for Regional Studies, 1990-93, dir. Inst. Oral History, 1993—; exec. sec. Oral History Assn., Waco, TX, 1995—. Editor: The Past Meets the Present: Essays on Oral History, 1987, The Texas Blackland Prairie, 1993. Treas. Brookview Neighborhood Assn., Waco, 1993-95, pres. 1996-97. Mem. Am. Studies Assn., Am. Studies Assn. Tex., Orgn. Am. Historians, So. Assn. Women Historians, So. Hist. Assn., Tex. Oral History Assn. (sec.-treas. 1982-87), Tex. State Hist. Assn., Oral History Assn. (exec. coun. 1986-89), Phi Beta Kappa. Democrat. Baptist. Home: 2915 Sanger Ave Waco TX 76707-3381 Office: Baylor U Inst Oral History PO Box 97271 Waco TX 76798-7271

SHARPSTEIN, RICHARD ALAN, lawyer; b. Boston, Oct. 20, 1950; s. Sidney Joseph and Marilyn (Weitzman) S.; m. Janice Burton, Oct. 20, 1979; children: Jessica Ashley, Katherine Erin, Michael Burton. BA, Tulane U., 1972, JD, 1975. Bar: U.S. Supreme Ct. 1976, Fla. 1976, U.S. Dist. Ct. (no. dist., so. dist., mid. dist.) Fla. 1976, U.S. Ct. Appeals (5th cir.) 1976, U.S. Ct. Appeals (11th cir.) 1980, U.S. Ct. Appeals (3d cir.) 1982, U.S. Ct. Appeals (4th cir.) 1983. Atty. Fla. Bar Assn., Miami, 1976—; asst. state atty. Dade County, Miami, 1976-79; ptnr., pres. Sharpstein & Sharpstein, P.A., Miami, 1982—; of counsel Kluger Peretz Kaplan & Berlin, P.A., Miami. Mem. bd. editors Money Laundering Alert. Fellow Am. Bd. of Criminal Lawyers; mem. ABA, Acad. Fla. Trial Lawyers, Fla. Criminal Def. Attys. Assn. (v.p. 1985-86, pres. 1986-87, bd. dirs. 1986-92), Am. Inns of Covrt, Omicron Delta Kappa. Home: 12650 SW 104th Ave Miami FL 33176-4705 Office: Sharpstein & Sharpstein PA 201 S Biscayne Blvd Ste 2380 Miami FL 33131-4329

SHARRER, GEORGE TERRY, museum curator; b. Balt., Dec. 30, 1944; s. George Jacob and Alease May (Bell) S.; m. Patricia Rose Duggan; children: Nicholas Burnham, Alexander Quinton. BA, U. Md., 1966, MA, 1968, PhD, 1975. Curator of medicine The Smithsonian Instn., Washington, 1969—; vis. prof. history Mont. State U., Bozeman, 1982-83; trustee Immune Deficiency Found. Trustee Land Between the Lakes Assn., Golden Pond, Ky., 1983—. Mem. Assn. for Living Hist. Farms and Agrl. Mus. (editor newsletter 1975—), Agrl. History Soc. (editorial bd. 1985—). Home: 17601 Coachman Dr Hamilton VA 22068-9518 Office: Mus Am History Smithsonian Instn Washington DC 20560

SHATWELL, SHERITA RHEA, psychotherapist, psychiatric services director; b. Tulsa; d. Lloyd Bert BeBout and Mereta Lenore (Stephens) Waymire; m. Levon Marion Shatwell, Nov. 12, 1968. BA in Psychology, U. Tulsa, 1989; MS in Psychology, Northea. State U., Tahlequah, Okla., 1991; postgrad., U. Tulsa. CEO, co-owner Shatwell Inc., Tulsa, 1974-93; psychotherapist geropsychiat. in-patient and day units Horizon Mental Health Svcs., Tulsa, 1991, program dir., 1991-92; v.p. SES, Inc., 1993—; v.p. SES, Inc., Owasso, Okla., 1974—; pvt. practice psychotherapy, Tulsa, 1991—. Mem. NAFE, Okla. Assn. Counseling and Devel., Okla. Assn. Aging and Devel., Bus. and Profl. Women, Psi Chi. Office: SES Inc PO Box 75 Owasso OK 74055-0075

SHAUGHNESSY, MARIE KANEKO, artist, business executive; b. Detroit, Sept. 14, 1924; d. Eishiro and Kiyo (Yoshida) Kaneko; m. John Thomas Shaughnessy, Sept. 23, 1959. Assocs. in Liberal Arts, Keisen Women's Coll., Tokyo, 1944. Ops. mgr. Webco Alaska, Inc., Anchorage, 1970-88; ptnr. Webco Partnership, Anchorage, 1983—, also bd. dirs.; faculty The Art League Sch., Alexandria, Va. Paintings include Lilacs, 1984, Blooms, 1985, The Fence, 1986 (Purchase award 1986). Bd. dirs. Alaska Artists Guild, 1971-87; commr. Mcpl. Anchorage Fine Arts Commn., 1983-87; organizing com. Japanese Soc. Alaska, 1987. Recipient arts affiliates award Anchorage C. of C., 1975, 78, 84, Univ. Artists award Alaska Pacific U., 1986, Am. Juror's Choice award Sumi-E Soc. Am., 1994, Ikebana Internat. award, 1994, Dorothy Klein Meml. award, 1995. Mem. AAUW, Potomac Valley Watercolorists (bd. dirs., awards 1989, 91, Spl. award 1995), Va. Watercolor Soc. (pres.), Sumi-E Soc. Am. (past pres., bd. dirs., Nat. Capital Area chpt. award 1990, 91, 92, 94, Purchase award 1993), Vienna Art Soc. (bd. dirs. 1995-96), Alaska Watercolor Soc. (charter and life, Grumbacher Silver medal 1989), McLean Arts Club (1st pl. award 1991), Nat. League Am. Penwomen (Grumbacher gold medal award excellence 1993), Potomac Valley Watercolorists (bd. dirs. 1995-95). Republican. Episcopalian.

SHAVER, DAVID CORYDON, obstetrician, gynecologist; b. Newport, Ark., Apr. 19, 1950; s. Edwin C. and Wanda (Pollard) S.; m. Lizabeth L. Stout (div.); children: Aaron, Daniel, Joseph, Timothy; m. Susan K. McDonald, Apr. 3, 1993. BA, Hendrix Coll., 1972; MD, U. Ark., 1976. Dipomate Am. Bd. Ob-Gyn., Am. Bd. Maternal/Fetal Medicine. Resident U. Tenn. Sch. of Medicine, Memphis, 1978-81, fellow maternal/fetal medicine, 1981-83, asst. prof., 1983-90, assoc. prof., 1990-93; dir. maternal/fetal medicine Presbyn. Hosp., Charlotte, N.C., 1993—. Editor: (book) Clinical Manual of Obstetrics, 1993; contbr. numerous articles to profl. jours. Fellow Am. Coll. Ob-Gyn.; mem. Soc. of Perinatal Obstetrics, Am. Inst. of Ultrasound Medicine. Office: Charlote Perinatal Assocs 1718 E 4th St Ste 604 Charlotte NC 28204-3260

SHAVER, EDWARDS BOONE, telephone company executive; b. Louisville, Nov. 24, 1948; s. John Mebane and Martha Perkins (Boone) S.; m. Sherry Lynn Spicer, 1992; children: Katherine Leigh, Martha Boone, Edwards Boone, Jr. B.S. in Indsl. Mgmt., Ga. Inst. Tech., 1970; M.B.A., Ga. State U., 1984. Supr. traffic staff So. Bell, Savannah, Ga., 1975-76, mgr., Valdosta, Ga., 1976-77, Dublin, Ga., 1977-78, Savannah, 1978-79, ops. mgr., Atlanta, 1980-85, ops. mgr. labor relations and benefits, 1985-89, dir corp. and external affairs, 1989—; asst. mgr. AT&T, Basking Ridge, N.J., 1979-80; advisor dir. Northside Bank, 1989; mem. adv. bd. Honey Creek Elem. Sch., 1993-94. Life Enrichment Svcs., 100 Black Men of Dekalb County, 1993; mem. bd. dirs. Dunwoody Rotary, 1994-95. Bd. dirs. DeKalb unit Am. Cancer Soc., Atlanta, 1983-90, v.p., 1984-85, pres. elect, 1985-86, pres., 1986-87, chmn., bd. dirs, 1989-90, bd. dir. Ga. div. Am. Cancer Soc., 1989-92; bd. dirs. Dekalb unit Am. Heart Assn., exec. v.p., 1990-91, pres., 1991-93, chmn. 1994; bd. dirs. The Tommy Nobis Ctr., 1987-90, gen. chmn. 4th ann. Tommy Nobis Ctr./Rotary Charity Golf Tournament, 1988, gen. chmn. 5th ann., 1989; bd. dirs. Atlanta Affordable Housing Found., 1990-92, Our House, Inc., 1991-93; sect. chmn. Atlanta Council for Battered Women, 1987; div. chmn. Met. United Way, Atlanta, 1982, sect. chmn., 1985, campaign vice chmn., 1991; pres. Parkside Homes Assn., Roswell, Ga., 1981, Riverside Landing Home Owners Assn., 1988; chmn. Laurens County Christmas Seal Drive, Dublin, 1978; bd. dirs. North Fulton YMCA, 1986-90, vice chmn., 1988-89, chmn., 1989-90; chmn. Corp. & Found. Com., 1993-94; trustee Dekalb Med. Ctr. Found, 1991—; bd. dirs. Met. Atlanta YMCA, 1987-88; citizen rep. student tribunal Fulton County Sch. Bd.; mem. Leadership Dekalb, 1990-91; team capt. Execs. for Egleston Children's Hosp., 1991, 92, 93, 94. Named Vol. of Yr., North Metro YMCA, 1990. Mem. Am. Mgmt. Assn., North Fulton C. of C. (bd. dirs.) Dekalb County C. of C. (bd. dirs. 1990—, chmn. legis. affairs com. 1990-91, vice chmn. membership 1992, bus. advocacy, 1993, 94). Republican. Methodist. Club: Horseshoe Bend Country. Lodges: Rotary, Elks. Home: 535 Burridge Trl Alpharetta GA 30202-5211 Office: So Bell 528-2310 Parklake Dr Atlanta GA 30345

SHAVER, JENISE WHITTEN, dietitian; b. San Antonio, Tex., Aug. 10, 1957; d. Lacey Rorier and Joann Cunningham Whitten; m. John Borroum Shaver, July 11, 1980; children: Benjamin Borroum, Elizabeth Marie. BS, U. Tex. Austin, 1980. Registered dietician; lic. dietician, Okla., Tex. Regional cons. dietician ARA Living Ctrs., San Antonio, 1981-83; clin./adminstrv. dietitian Manor Care Ctrs., San Antonio, 1988-92, San Pedro Manor, San Antonio, 1988-92, Camlu Care Ctr., San Antonio, 1988-92, Nutrition Cons. San Antonio, 1988-92; pvt. practice cons. Oklahoma City, 1992—; cons. sports nutrition/wellness St. Anthony North, Oklahoma City; cons. cmty. wellness promotions Pratt Foods Inc., Edmond, Okla., 1995-96; preceptor Food Svc. Mgrs., San Antonio, 1988-92. Contbr. articles to profl. jours. Speaker Am. Cancer Soc., San Antonio, 1985, 88; speaker, vol. Am. Heart Assn., San Antonio, 1988-92; chmn. Neighborhood Network, San Antonio, 1988-90. Recipient Mary E. Gearing scholar U. Tex., 1978. Mem. Am. Dietetic Assn., Okla. Dietetic Assn., Oklahoma City Dist. Dietetic Assn., San Antonio Dist. Dietetic Assn. (sec. 1988-89, historian 1991-93), Jr. League Oklahoma City, Jr. League San Antonio. Republican. Roman Catholic. Home: 13933 Sterlington Edmond OK 73013-7032

SHAVER, MARTHA EILEEN, secondary school teacher; b. Charleston, Dec. 5, 1946; d. Louis James and Louise Edith (Rapp) Gross; m. Roger Lee Shaver, May 4, 1968. BA in Bus. Edn., Glenville State Coll., 1968; M in Vocat. Tech. Edn., Marshall U., 1976. Bus. tchr. Newburg (W. Va.) H.S., 1968-69, Wirt County H.S., Elizabeth, W. Va., 1969—. Mem. W. Va. Computer Tech. task force, 1990; chmn. Wirt County Computer Tech. team, Elizabeth, W. Va., 1994-95. Recipient Nat. Educator award Milken Family Found., 1995-96, Alumni Achievement award Glenville State Alumni Assn., 1996, Presdl. Citation award Glenville State Coll. pres., 1996. Mem. Am. Vocat. Assn., Am. Fedn. Tchrs., Nat. Bus. Edn.Assn., So. Bus. Edn.Assn., W. Va. Bus. Edn. Assn., Internat. Soc. Bus. Educators, W. Va. Future Bus. Leaders Am. (state exec. com.), W. Va. Fedn. Women (membership com. 1995—), Woman's Club Elizabeth (W. Va.) (festivals and camp, officer, trustee 1995—, auditor 1996—). Republican. Home: PO Box 251 Elizabeth WV 26143 Office: Wirt County H S Mulberry St Elizabeth WV 26143

SHAW, ANGUS ROBERTSON, III, minister; b. Charlotte, N.C., Oct. 7, 1932; s. Angus Robertson Jr. and Claudia (Morrison) S.; m. Carolyn Farmer, Aug. 14, 1965; children: Karen, Rob. BA, Bob Jones U., 1955; MDiv, Columbia Theol. Sem., 1958, DMin, 1989; DD (hon.), King Coll., 1965. Asst. pastor 1st Presbyn. Ch., Pulaski, Va., 1956-62; pastor Seagle Meml. Ch., Pulaski, 1956-62, Royal Oak Ch., Marion, Va., 1962-69; sr. pastor 1st Presbyn. Ch., Dothan, Ala., 1969-78, Johnson City, Tenn., 1978—; chmn. bd. Salvation Army, Johnson City, Tenn., 1986, Contact Teleministries, Johnson City, 1987-88. Trustee Lees-McRae Coll., Banner Elk, N.C., 1979-84; chmn. ch., coll. coun. Montreat (N.C.)-Anderson Coll., 1980; chmn. ann. fund King Coll., Briston, Tenn., 1985-86; bd. trustees Tusculum Coll., 1993—, chair coun. on ch. rels., 1992, chair Ptnrs. in Ministry Drive, 1996; bd. dirs. United Way, 1991—. Mem. Watauga Mental Health Assn. (bd. dirs. 1990-96, chair 1992-93), Kiwanis (pres. 1990-91), Soc. Theta Pi. Home: 1013 Somerset Dr Johnson City TN 37604-2919 Office: 1st Presbyn Ch 105 S Boone St Johnson City TN 37604-6262

SHAW, GLORIA DORIS, art educator; b. Huntington, W.Va., Nov. 10, 1928; d. Charles Bert and Theodosia Doris (Shimer) Haley; m. Arthur Shaw, July 13, 1954 (dec. Aug. 1985); children: Deirdra E. Franz, Stewart N. Student, SUNY, 1969-70, Art Students League, N.Y.C., 1969-70, 74; BA, SUNY, N.Y.C., 1980; postgrad., U. Tenn., 1982, Nat Kaz, Pietrasanta, Italy, 1992. Sculptor replicator Am. Mus. Natural History, N.Y.C., 1976-77; adj. prof. sculpture Fla. Keys C.C., Key West, 1983—; prof. TV art history Fla. Keys C.C., 1989—; host moderator Channel 5 TV, Fla. Keys, 1982—; presenter Humanities Studies and Art History Channel 19 TV, 1995—. Sculptor (portrait) Jimmy Carter, Carter Meml. Libr., 1976, Tennessee Williams, Tennessee Williams Fine Arts Ctr., 1982, UNICEF, 1978-79, (series) Fla. Panther and Audubon Wall Relief, 1985, (bust) AIDS Meml., 1990; one woman shows include Bank Street Coll., 1979, Hollywood Mus. of Art, 1985, Islander Gallery, 1983, Martello Mus., 1984, Greenpeace, 1987; exhibited in group shows at Montoya, West Palm Beach, Fla., 1989, N.Y.C. Bd. of Edn. Tour of Schs., 1979, Earthworks East, N.Y., 1987, Man and Sci., 1978, Cuban Club, Key West, Fla., 1991, Leda Bruce Gallery, Big Pine, 1992, Kaz, Pietrasanta, Italy, 1992, Fla. Keys C.C. Gallery, 1993, Tennessee Williams Fine Arts Ctr., Key West, 1993, Internat. Woman's Show, Fla. Keys, 1994, Joy Gallery, 1994, 95, 96, Baron Gallery, Girls of Mauritania to UNICEF, 1996; designer Windows at Greenpeace Bldg., Key West, 1985-88. Recipient Children and Other Endangered Species award Thomas Cultural Ctr., 1980, Purchase award Cuban C. of C., 1982, Sierra Club, 1983, Blue Ribbon, Martello Towers Art and Hist. Soc., 1985, Red Ribbon, South Fla. Sculptors, 1986, Endangered Species award Greenpeace, 1986. Mem. Nat. Sculpture Soc. of N.Y.C., Internat. Sculpture Ctr., Art Students League of N.Y.C. (life), Art and Hist. Soc. Democrat.

SHAW, JAMES, computer systems analyst; b. Salt Lake City, June 26, 1944; s. James Irvin and Cleo Lea (Bell) S. Student, San Antonio Coll., 1962-64; BA in History, St. Mary's U., San Antonio, 1966. With VA Automation Ctr., Austin, Tex., 1967—, sr. computer programmer analyst, 1984-87, supervisory computer programmer analyst, 1987-88, computer systems analyst, 1988-94, sr. computer systems analyst, 1994—; conversion team manual to computerized acctg. VA, 1974-76; participant conversion computerized acctg. sys. to database, 1984-88; participant complete replacement of VA computerized acctg. sys., 1989-95. Active Smithsonian Institution, Planned Parenthood, Met. Mus. Art, Austin Mus. Art. Mem. Am. Assn. Individual Investors. Democrat. Home: 11500 Jollyville Rd Apt 1312 Austin TX 78759-4070 Office: VA Automation Ctr 1615 Woodward St Austin TX 78772-0001

SHAW, JULIUS C., SR., carpet manufacturing company executive; b. 1929. Student, Ga. Inst. Tech. Supt. Crown Cotton Mills Inc., 1950-57; with Rocky Creek Mills, 1957-63; v.p., gen. mgr. Dan River Carpets, Danville, Va., 1965-67; pres. Sabre Carpets Inc. (merged into Shaw Industries), Dalton, Ga., 1967—; now chmn. Emeritus, dir. Shaw Industries, Dalton, Ga. Office: Shaw Industries Inc PO Box 2128 Dalton GA 30722*

SHAW, LAURIE JO, grant project director; b. Morris, Minn., Feb. 23, 1956; d. Edgar Allen and Dorothy Ruth (Harms) S.; m. Grant William Carlson, July 23, 1983 (div. Feb. 1986). Tchr. aide degree, Hutchinson Area Vocat. Tech., Minn., 1975; audio visual prodn., Hutchinson (Minn.) AVTI, 1976; BA in Psychology, S.W. State U., 1982; MA in Counseling, N.Mex. State U., 1987. Libr. tech. S.W. State U., Marshall, Minn., 1976-84; student svcs. coord. Mohave C.C., Bullhead City, Ariz., 1987-91; counselor, instr. Prestonsburg C.C., Pikeville, Ky., 1992-93; project dir. So. W.Va. C.C., Williamson, 1993—. Mem. AAUW (v.p. 1990-92), Nat. Assn. Student Pers. Adminstrs., Ky. Assn. Student Fin. Aid Adminstrs., Bus. and Profl. Women (pres. 1990-91, Young Career Woman award 1989), W.Va. Assn. Edn. Opportunity Program Pers., Mid.-East Assn. Edn. Opportunity Program Pers. Democrat. Methodist. Office: So WV Community Coll Armory Dr Williamson WV 25661

SHAW, LEANDER JERRY, JR., state supreme court justice; b. Salem, Va., Sept. 6, 1930; s. Leander J. and Margaret S.; m. Vidya B. Lye. BA, W.Va. State Coll., 1952, LLD (hon.), 1986; JD, Howard U., 1957; PhD (hon.) in Pub. Affairs, Fla. Internat. U., 1990; LLD (hon.), Nova Law Sch., 1991, Washington & Lee Law Sch., 1991. Asst. prof. law Fla. A&M U., 1957-60; sole practice Jacksonville, Fla., 1960-69, 72-74; asst. pub. defender Fla., 1965-69; asst. state's atty. Fla., 1969-72; judge Fla. Indsl. Relations Commn., 1974-79, Fla. Ct. Appeals (1st dist.), 1979-83; justice Fla. Supreme Ct., Tallahassee, 1983—, chief justice, 1990-92. Office: Fla Supreme Ct Supreme Ct Bldg Tallahassee FL 32399

SHAW, MARY ANN, psychologist; b. Dallas, July 5, 1937; d. Leon V. and Mabel (Bartlett) S.; B.S., U. Tex., 1959; M.Ed., U. Houston, 1966, Ed.D., 1973. Diplomate Profl. Acad. Custody Evaluators. Tchr. educable mentally retarded Spring Branch, Tex., 1959-64; vocat. counselor, Houston, 1964-66; psychometrist pvt. psychol. clinic, Houston, 1966-70; coord. rsch. Tex. Edn. Agency grant project, 1970-72; dir. psychol. svcs. Tex. Scottish Rite Hosp. for Crippled Children, Dallas, 1972-82; dir. Dean Evaluation Ctr., Dallas, 1982-84; pvt. practice, 1982—; mem. clin. staff U. Tex. Health Sci. Ctr.; mem. Allied Health Profl. Staff, Green Oaks; cons. Children's Med. Ctr., Dallas, pvt. and pub. schs. Mem. APA, Am. Profl. Soc. on Abuse of Children (diplomate), Am. Coll. Forensic Examiners, Tex. Psychol. Assn., Mental Health Assn. Greater Dallas, Dallas Psychol. Assn., Soc. Pediat. Psychology, Soc. Personality Assessment Assn. Author: What Do I Do When, Because I Said So, Your Anxious Child; contbr. article to profl. jour.; research in field.

SHAW, MARY TODD, artist, art educator; b. Gadsden, Ala., Feb. 9, 1921; d. Oscar E. and Jennie (Harris) T.; m. Edward H. Shaw; children: Barbara Shaw Brinson, George N. BCA, Atlanta Coll. Art, 1942; BFA, U. N.C., 1974; postgrad., Ga. Inst. Tech., U. N.C., Greensboro. Draftsman So. Bell, Atlanta, 1941-42, U.S. Warfare, Atlanta, 1942-43; comml. artist Maurice Coleman & Assocs., Atlanta; instr. art Mint Mus., Charlotte, N.C., 1966-76, Spirit Square, Charlotte, 1976-93. One person shows include Mint Mus., Charlotte, N.C., 1967, Herman Art Gallery, Statesville, N.C., 1972, Queens Coll., Charlotte, 1973, Harold Decker Gallery, Norfolk, Va., 1973, The Arts Works, Statesville, N.C., 1978, Spirit Sq., Charlotte, 1977, 81, Lancaster (S.C.) Gallery, 1983, Queen's Coll. Paul Klapper Art Libr., Flushing, N.Y., Secca, Winston Salem, N.C., 1982, Milliken Gallery, Spartanburg, S.C., 1986, Upstairs Gallery, Tryon, N.C., 1988, Asheville (N.C.) Mus. Art, 1990, The Waterworks, Salisbury, N.C., 1991, Mus. York County, 1994, Wingate U., 1996; group exhbns. include Nat. Acad., N.Y.C., Atlanta Art Inst., Winston-Salem Gallery of Fine Arts, Richmond Mus., Collectors' Gallery, Washington, Riverside Mus., N.Y.C., Museo de Bella Artes, Buenos Aires, Winston-Salem, Art and Sci. Mus., Statesville, Columbia (S.C.) Mus. Art, Columbus (Ga.) Mus. Art, Birmingham (Ala.) Mus. Art, Dulin Gallery of Art, Knoxville, Mint Mus. Art, Charlotte, Atlier-Galerie, Dijon, France, Pallazzo Ducale, Venezia, Italy, Mark Milliken Gallery, others. Recipient Henri Bendel award Nat. Acad., N.Y., 1961, 1st prize Drake House Pub. Co., Charlotte, 1971, Purchase award U. N.C., 1973, Charlotte Open Exhbn., 1980, Best in Show award Spring Fest, Charlotte, 1986, numerous others; fellow Yaddo, 1980, 81, Va. Ctr. for Arts, Sweet Briar, 1984, 86, 93, Tyrone Guthrie Found., 1986, Banff Ctr. for Arts, Can., 1987, Atlantic Ctr. for Arts, 1983, others. Mem. Tri-State Sculptors Assn., So. Graphics Assn. Home: 6611 Burlwood Rd Charlotte NC 28211-5607

SHAW, MICHAEL JOSEPH, automotive executive; b. Fort Wayne, Ind., Aug. 30, 1946; s. Robert Brons and Eva (Fernandez) S.; m. Nancy Merrill James, June 21, 1969; children: Michael Joseph Jr., Eleanor Merrill, Robert Richardson. BBA, Tex. A&M U., 1968; MBA, Lamar Tech. U., 1970. With sales dept. David Taylor Buick, Beaumont, Tex., 1969-70; sales mgr. Tommy Vaughn Motors, Houston, 1972; gen. sales mgr. Boggus Motors, McAllen, Tex., 1973; owner, pres. Tradewinds Ford, Corpus Christi, Tex., 1973-88, Tradewinds Subaru, Corpus Christi, 1984-88, Tradewinds Chrysler Imports, Corpus Christi, 1985-88, Tradewinds Suzuki, Corpus Christi, 1987-88, Tradewinds Mgmt. Group, Corpus Christi, 1987-88; v.p., gen. mgr. David Taylor Cadillac, Houston, 1989—; bd. dirs. Subaru Nat. Dealer Coun., San Antonio, 1985-88, Suzuki Nat. Advt. Coun., Atlanta, 1987-88, Ford Dealer Advt. Coun., Houston. Bd. dirs. Task Force on Edn., Austin, 1988. 1st lt. U.S. Army, 1970-72. Mem. Tex. Automobile Dealers Assn., Houston Automobile Dealers Assn., Rotary. Episcopalian. Home: PO Box 687 Fulshear TX 77441-0687 Office: David Taylor Cadillac Co 9120 Southwest Fwy Houston TX 77074-1512

SHAW, R. PRESTON, physician, psychiatrist, educator; b. Lubbock, Tex., Mar. 31, 1928; s. Earnie Whitfield and Euna Irene (Heald) S.; m. Gwen Ellen Grose, June 24, 1956; 1 child, Wendelin Autumn. BA in Chemistry, Tex. Tech. U., 1949; MD, U. Tex., Galveston, 1956. Diplomate in psychiatry and forensic psychiatry Am. Bd. Psychiatry and Neurology. Med. and surg. intern St. Joseph's Hosp., Ft. Worth, Tex., 1956-57; resident in psychiatry Austin (Tex.) Psychiatry Program, 1959-62; pvt. practice Midland, Tex., 1962-72; staff psychiatrist Austin State Hosp., 1972-76; fellow in forensic psychiatry U. Va., Charlottesville, 1976-77; pvt. practice Lubbock, 1977—; clin. assoc. prof. dept. psychiatry Tex. Tech. U. Sch. Medicine, Lubbock, 1977—; chief dept. psychiatry Meth. Hosp., Lubbock, 1978-79, St. Mary's Plains Hosp., Lubbock, 1978-79. Capt. USAF, 1957-59. Fellow Am. Psychiat. Assn. (life); mem. Nat. Soc. SAR, Tex. Soc. SAR, Tex. Tech. chpt. SAR (v.p. 1989-90, pres. 1990-93). Methodist. Office: 3515 22nd St Lubbock TX 79410-1307

SHAW, ROBERT E., carpeting company executive; b. Cartersville, GA, 1931. Pres., chief exec. officer Star Finishing Co. Inc. (merged into Shaw Industries Inc.), Dalton, Ga., until 1969; now pres., chief exec. officer Shaw Industries Inc., Dalton, Ga., 1969—, also bd. dirs., 1969—. Office: Shaw Industries Inc 616 E Walnut Ave Dalton GA 30721-4409*

SHAW, ROBERT WILSON, chemist; b. York, Pa., Jan. 27, 1942; s. Robert Wilson and Harriet Katharine (Thompson) S.; m. Barbara Joanne Ramsay, June 14, 1969; 1 child, Susan Maureen. BA in Chemistry cum laude, Williams Coll., 1964; PhD in Phys. Chemistry, U. Wash., 1970; postgrad., Duke U., 1977. Postdoctoral fellow dept. chemistry Princeton (N.J.) U., 1970-72; rsch. assoc. Radiation Ctr., Oreg. State U., Corvallis, 1972-73; vis. asst. prof. U. Oreg., Eugene, 1973-75; postdoctoral fellow Duke U., Durham, N.C., 1975-77; rsch. chemist and physicist EPA, Research Triangle Park, N.C., 1977-83; chief phys. chemistry and surface sci. U.S. Army Rsch. Office, Research Triangle Park, 1983—, assoc. dir. divsn. chem. & biol. scis., 1988-95, dir., 1995—, U.S. sr. exec. svc., 1995—; bd. dirs. Am. Inks & Coatings, Valley Forge, Pa. Contbr. articles to profl. jours. Recipient sci. and technol. achievement award EPA, 1981, 83-85, silver medal, 1983. Mem. Am. Chem. Soc., Am. Inst. Physics, Fedn. Am. Scientists, Phi Beta Kappa, Sigma Xi. Home: 3811 Northampton Rd Durham NC 27707-5083 Office: US Army Rsch Office PO Box 12211 Durham NC 27709-2211

SHAW, STEPHEN LYNN, geoscientist; b. San Angelo, Tex., May 28, 1949; s. Joe William and Verda D. (Tankersley) S.; m. Nancy Berry Keeling; children: Katherine Lynn, William Keeling. BS in Geology, U. Tex., Austin, 1971, MA in Geology, 1974. Cert. profl. geol. scientist Am. Inst. Profl. Geologists. Ground water hydrologist William F. Guyton & Assocs., Austin, 1973-79; exploration geologist Superior Oil, Midland, Tex., 1979-81, exploration supr., 1981; exploration geologist Buckeye Energy, Midland, Tex., 1981-82, Conquest Exploration, Midland, Tex., 1982-86; adj. geology instr. U. Tex. Permian Basin, Odessa, 1983-84; petroleum geologist Meridian Oil, Midland, 1986-93, regional geoscientist, 1993—. Contbr. articles to Tex. Jour. Sci., West Tex. Geol. Soc. Bull. Bd. dirs. Permian Basin Grad. Ctr., Midland, 1986-87, Midland Energy Libr., 1990—, West Tex. Geology Found., Midland, 1992-95, Midland Habitat for Humanity, 1994—; vestry mem. St. Nicholas Episcopal Ch., Midland, 1990-92. Mem. Am. Assn. Petroleum Geologists (cert., vice-chmn. elect ho. of dels. 1995—, del.), Geol. Soc. Am., West Tex. Geol. Soc. (pres.), Nat. Ground Water Assn., Midland Lee Football Booster Club (pres., v.p., adviser). Episcopalian. Home: 3513 Stanolind Midland TX 79707 Office: Meridian Oil 3300 N A St Bldg 6 Midland TX 79705

SHAW, STEPHEN RAGSDALE, trust investment executive; b. N.Y.C., Jan. 16, 1945; s. Harry Lee and Marie (Ragsdale) S.; m. Mary James Baskervill, June 9, 1969; children: Lee Berkeley, Stephen Stovall. BA in History, Coll. of William and Mary, 1969; postgrad., N.Y. Inst. of Fin., 1971; MBA in Fin., Loyola U., 1983. Sales rep. Lehigh Portland Cement Co., Allentown, Pa., 1969-71; account exec. W.E. Hutton & Co., Balt., 1971-74; asst. v.p. Union Trust Co., Balt., 1974-80; v.p. Mercantile Safe Deposit & Trust Co., Balt., 1980-83; v.p., sr. investment officer Wilmington Trust of Fla., N.A., Stuart, 1983-95; v.p. Wilmington Trust, FSB, Stuart, 1995—. Bd. dirs., treas. Second Sight Taping Studio, Inc., Jenson Beach, Fla., 1989-92. With USMCR, 1967-73. Fellow Assn. for Investment Mgmt. and Rsch. Republican. Episcopalian. Home: 152 SE Harbor Point Dr Stuart FL 34996-1348 Office: Wilmington Trust FSB 800 SE Monterey Commons Blvd Stuart FL 34996-9999

SHAW, SUSAN KIME, secondary school educator, administrator; b. Greensboro, N.C., Mar. 12, 1945; d. James Roland and Vivian Thelma (Sullivan) S. BA in English, Greensboro Coll., 1967; MEd in English, U. Va., 1971. Cert. speech, gifted edn., English and social studies tchr., Va. English tchr., dept. chair Prince William County Schools, Manassas, Va., 1967-77; English tchr. and supervisor Manassas City Schools, 1977—; mem. Gifted and Talented Adv. Bd., Manassas, 1993—. Active Manassas PTA, 1990-96. Recipient Agnes Meyer Outstanding Educator award Washington Post, 1987. Mem. NEA, ASCD, AAUW (officer 1986—), Va. Edn. Assn., Manassas Ed. Assn., Phi Beta Kappa. Presbyterian. Home: 8233 Wycliffe Ct Manassas VA 20109 Office: Grace E Metz Jr HS 9700 Fairview Ave Manassas VA 22111

SHAW, TALBERT O., university president. BD, Andrews U., 1963; MA, U. Chgo., 1968, PhD, 1973. Dean of students Oakwood Coll., Huntsville,

Ala., 1965-71; dean Howard U., Washington, 1971-76; dean Coll. Arts and Scis. Morgan State U., Balt., 1976-87; pres. Shaw U., Raleigh, N.C., 1987—. Office: Shaw U 118 E South St Raleigh NC 27601-2341

SHAW, VIRGINIA RUTH, clinical psychologist; b. Salina, Kans., Dec. 10, 1952; d. Lawrence Eugene and Gladys (Wilbur) S.; m. Joseph Eugene Scuro Jr., July 14, 1990. BA magna cum laude, Kans. Wesleyan U., 1973; MA, Wichita State U., 1975; PhD, U. Southern Miss., 1984. Diplomate Am. Bd. Med. Psychotherapists (fellow). Rsch. fellow Wichita (Kans.) State U., 1973-75; rsch. fellow, teaching fellow U. So. Miss., 1978-79, 80-81; staff psychologist Big Spring (Tex.) State Hosp., 1976-78; predoctoral clin. psychology intern U. Okla. Health Scis. Ctr., Oklahoma City, 1981-82; postdoctoral fellow in neuropsychology Neuropsychiat. Inst., UCLA, 1982-83; rsch. psychologist, neuropsychologist L.A. VA Med. Ctr. Wadsworth Div., 1983-84; clin. neuropsychologist Patton (Calif.) State Hosp., 1984-85; clin. neuropsychologist Brentwood div. LA VA Med. Ctr., 1985; clinical, neuropsychologist Timberlawn Psychiatric Hosp., Dallas, 1985-87, Dallas Rehab. Inst., 1987-93; cons. clin. neuropsychology Dallas area hosps., Willowbrook Hosp., Waxahachie, Tex., Cedars Hosp., Waxahachie, 1988-96; clin. psychologist Maui child and adolescent mental health team State of Hawaii Dept. Health, 1996—; presenter profl. meetings, 1975—. Contbr. articles to profl. jours. Mem. Dallas Mayor's Com. for Employment of the Disabled (cert. appreciation), 1987, 500 Inc., Dallas, 1988-96. Remiatte Meml. scholar Kans. Wesleyan U., 1970-73; recipient Nat. Disting. Svc. Registry award in rehab., 1989, Early Career Contbns. to Clin. Neuropsychology award candidate Nat. Acad. Neuropsychology, 1993, 94. Mem. AAUW (v.p. programs Maui chpt. 1996), APA Divsn. 35/Psychology of Women (student rsch. prize com. 1996), Internat. Neuropsychol. Soc., Nat. Head Injury Found., Assn. for Women in Psychology, Tex. Head Injury Found., Dallas Head Injury Found. (Vol. award, cert. appreciation 1991), Am. Congress Rehab. Medicine, Nat. Rehab. Assn., Nat. Acad. Neuropsychology (membership com. 1991-94, rsch. consortium 1991—, co-chair poster program com. 1994, 95). Office: 444 Hana Hwy Ste 202 Kahului HI 96732-2315

SHAW-RICE, JUDI, internist, health facility administrator; b. Mandeville, W.I., Jamaica, Aug. 21, 1965; came to U.S., 1981; d. Michael and Gloria Scott (Jacobs) Shaw; m. Tommy Rice, Jr., Dec. 19, 1992. BA cum laude, Knox Coll., Galesburg, Ill., 1985; MD, Med. U. S.C., 1989; postgrad., U. Tex. Health Sci. Ctr. Diplomate Am. Bd. Internal medicine; lic. physician, Tex. Resident in internal medicine Baylor Coll. Medicine, Houston, 1989-92; pvt. practice Sugarland, Tex., 1993—; founder Southwest Travel & Immunization Ctr., Houston, 1994—; mem. utilization rev. and quality assurance com. West Houston Hosp., 1994-95, Ft Bend Hosp., 1993-94; mem. ethics com. West Houston Hosp, 1995—. Mem. Harris County Interdisciplinary Drug Edn. Alliance Program, 1992—; mem. choir Brookhollow Ch.; mem. fundraising and scholarship coms. Jamaican Assn. Greater Houston, 1994—. Pilot scholar, 1981-89. Mem. AMA, ACP, Am. Coll. Preventive Medicine, Tex. Med. Assn., Harris County Med. Soc. (com. on preventive health), Am. Pub. Health Assn., Am. Med. Women's Assn., Ft. Bend County C. of C., Mortar Bd. Presbyterian. Office: 1111 Hwy 6 Ste 160 Sugar Land TX 77478

SHE, (SHING) SIXING, development engineer; b. Chang Chun, Jilin, China, May 2, 1963; Came to U.S., 1985; s. Baoyu She and Shunhua Shi. BS, Peking U., 1985; MS, U. Tenn., 1988, postgrad., 1985-90. Rsch. asst. U. Tenn., Knoxville, 1988-90; devel. engr. Columbus McKinnon Corp., Damascus, Va., 1990-95; finite element engr. Hartzell Propeller Inc., Puqua, Ohio, 1996—. Home: 90 Maryville Ln #241 Piqua OH 45356 Office: Hartzell Propeller Inc One Propeller Pl Piqua OH 45356-2634

SHEA, ANNE JOAN, fashion editor; b. Beacon, N.Y., Dec. 29, 1907; d. Patrick Henry and Mary Loretta (Walsh) S. AB in Liberal Arts, Syracuse (N.Y.) U., 1929. Fashion editor The Bride's Mag., N.Y.C., 1952-63; dir. fashion promotion Angelo Bridals, N.Y.C., 1964-65; asst. to N.Y. mgr. Nat. Home Fashions League, 1965; freelance sec. to mgr. Union League Club of N.Y., 1963, 65; fashion cons. to pub. rels. dir. French Lace Inst., Paris, 1965-67; freelance fashion cons., stylist, 1966-70. Bd. dirs. Dag Hammerskjold Fund; mem. mobile blood bank unit ARC; vol. Svcs. for Children, Bide-A-Wee Home, Fairchild Tropical Gardens, Miami Heart Inst. Aux., Am. Mus. Natural History. Mem. Women in Communications, Fashion Group (bd. dirs. Fashion Critics award), Syracuse U. Alumni Assn., AAUW, Am. Assn. Ret. Persons, English Speaking Union, Internat. Platform Assn., Lucy Stone League, Smithsonian Assocs., Theta Phi Alpha. Home: 4735 NW 7th Ct Lantana FL 33462

SHEA, BRENT MACK, social science educator; b. Oneida, N.Y., June 3, 1946; s. Mack Evered and Alice May (Meeker) S. BA, SUNY, Binghamton, 1968, MA, 1972, PhD, 1977. Vis. instr. Harpur Coll. SUNY, Binghamton, 1975-76, resident dir. Coll.-in-the-Woods, 1976-78, rsch. assoc., 1977-78; asst. prof. Sweet Briar (Va.) Coll., 1978-84, assoc. prof., 1984-92, prof., 1992—, chmn. dept. anthropology and sociology, 1986-90, 96—; vis. fellow Yale U., New Haven, 1984-85; sci. collaboratore Centro studi per l'Evoluzione Umana, Rome, Italy, 1990—; vis. scholar Summer Inst. for Survey Rsch. U. Mich., 1991; consulting prof. Emile Durkheim Inst., George Town, B.W.I., 1989-92; sec. of faculty Sweet Briar Coll., 1991-92; presenter, rschr. in field. Co-editor, contbg. author: Social Psychiatary Across Cultures, 1995; editor conf. procs. Work and Mental Health, 1996; contbr. articles to profl. jours., chpts. to books. Sweet Briar faculty fellow Yale U., 1984-85, Centro studi per l'Evoluzione Umana Rome, 1992-93, NIMH postdoctoral rsch. fellow Instn. for Social and Policy Studies, Yale U., 1985-86; Regents scholar Harpur Coll. SUNY, 1964-68. Mem. AAUP (chpt. pres. 1996—), Internat. Sociol. Assn. (v.p. exec. bd. 1994—, mental health and illness rsch. com.), Ius Primi Viri Internat. Assn. Rome (vice chmn. bd. govs. 1994—), Ea. Ednl. Rsch. Assn. (dir. rsch. ethics 1979-83, bd. dirs. 1979-85, gen. sec. 1983-85), Va. Sociol. Assn. (pres., mem. exec. com. 1980-81). Home: PO Box 1 Sweet Briar VA 24595-0001 Office: Sweet Briar Coll Dept Anthropology and Sociology Sweet Briar VA 24595

SHEA, THOMAS CHARLES, physician, educator; b. Phila., Sept. 17, 1952; s. Thomas M. and Grace V. (Taylor) S.; m. Katharine Marie Dressler Shea, June 27, 1981; children: Margaret, Joseph. BA in Psychology, U. N.C., 1974, MD, 1978. Internship U. N.C., Chapel Hill; residency Beth Israel Hosp.; fellow/instr. in medicine Beth Israel Hosp., Boston, 1982-88, Dana-Farber Cancer Inst., Boston, 1982-88, Harvard Med. Sch., Boston, 1982-88; asst. prof. medicine U. Calif., San Diego, 1988-92; assoc. prof. medicine U. N.C., Chapel Hill, 1992—. Office: Univ NC CB 7305 Chapel Hill NC 27599

SHEAFFER, WILLIAM JAY, lawyer; b. Carlisle, Pa., Jan. 18, 1948; s. Raymond Jay and Barbara Jean (Bell) S.; m. Carol Ann Madison, Jan. 5, 1974. BA cum laude, U. Cen. Fla., 1975; JD, Nova U., 1978. Bar: Fla. 1978, U.S. Dist. Ct. (mid. dist.) Fla. 1979, U.S. Dist. Ct. (so. and no. dists.) Fla. 1981, U.S. Ct. Appeals (5th and 11th cirs.) 1981, U.S. Supreme Ct. 1983. Atty. State of Fla., Orlando, 1978-79; pvt. practice, Orlando, 1979—; apptd. to merit selection panel to consider U.S. Magistrate Judge Applicants, 1995—. Served to ensign class 4 USN, 1967-71. Mem. ABA, NACDL, Fla. Bar Assn. (cert. criminal trial specialist, vice chmn. 9th judicial cir. grievance com.), Orange County Bar Assn. (Guardian Ad Litem of Yr. 1994, award of excellence 1995), Fed. Bar Assns., Fla. Assn. Criminal Def. Lawyers Inc., Fed. Trial Lawyers Assn., Am. Inns of Ct. (ctrl. Fla. master), Tiger Bay Club, Citrus Club. Republican. Office: 609 E Central Blvd Orlando FL 32801-2916

SHEAHAN, MELODY ANN, transportation executive; b. Cin., Aug. 5, 1959; d. Earl Sterling and Willie Catherine (Stonestreet) McCoy. AS in Mech. Enging. Tech., U. Cin., 1979; postgrad., U. North Fla., 1987-89, Fla. C.C., 1988-91; BA in Mgmt./Fin., Marshall U., 1996. Enging. tech. Chessie System R.R., Huntington, W.Va., 1979-81, asst. supr. motor vehicles, 1981-86; staff asst. CSX Transp., Jacksonville, Fla., 1986, engr. system material, 1986-91, mgr. work equipment, budget and planning, 1991-94; mgr. work equipment stds., specifications and tng., 1994—. Named one of Outstanding Young Women of Am., 1985, Woman of Yr. Am. Coun. R.R. Women, 1992. Mem. Am. Coun. R.R. Women (sec. 1984-86, 1st v.p. 1986-88, pres. 1988-90), Am. R.R. Enging. Assn., U. Cin. Alumni Assn., Marshall U. Alumni Assn., Order of Eastern Star. Home: 8986 Kings Charter Dr Mechanicsville VA 23116-5193 Office: CSX Transp 1 Csx Rd Richmond VA 23230-3349

SHEALY, Y. FULMER, medicinal and organic chemist; b. Chapin, S.C., Feb. 26, 1923; s. L. Yoder and L. Essie (Fulmer) S.; m. Elaine Curtis, Oct. 5, 1950; children: Robin T., Nancy G., Priscilla B. BS, U. S.C., 1943; PhD, U. Ill., 1949. Chemist Office of Sci. R&D, 1943-45; postdoctoral fellow U. Minn., Mpls., 1949-50; rsch. chemist Upjohn Co., Kalamazoo, 1950-56; asst. prof. U. S.C., 1956-57; sr. chemist So. Rsch. Inst., Birmingham, 1957-59, sect. head, 1959-66, head medicinal chem. div., 1966-90, disting. scientist, 1990—; speaker 12th Internat. Cancer Congress, 3d Internat. Conf. on Prevention of Cancer. Named to Hall of Fame, Chapin, S.C. U.S. and fgn. Patentee for medicinal agents; pioneer in carbocyclic analogs of purine and pyrimidine nucleosides including carbodine, 2'-CDG and aristeromycin; synthesized anti-cancer drugs dacarbazine, clomesone and BCTIC; synthesized antifungal and antibacterial agents including the first monocyclic 1,2,5-Selenadiazoles and triazenylimidazole esters; synthesized antiviral and anticancer agents including MCTIC and MTIC (which laid the foundations for mitozolomide and temozolomide) and chloroethylnitrosocarbamates; synthesized cancer chemopreventative retinoids such as retinoylamino acids, retinyl ethers and 4-oxoretinoic acid derivatives. Contbr. more than 130 articles to profl. jours.; awarded 19 patents. Fellow AAAS; mem. Am. Chem. Soc., Am. Assn. Cancer Rsch., Internat. Soc. Nutrition and Cancer, N.Y. Acad. Scis., Internat. AIDS Soc., Am. Pharm. Assn., Internat. Soc. Antiviral Rsch., European Retinoid Rsch. Group, Sigma Xi, Phi Beta Kappa, Phi Lambda Upsilon, Pi Mu Epsilon, Alpha Chi Sigma. Office: So Rsch Inst 2000 9th Ave S Birmingham AL 35205-2708

SHEAN, TIMOTHY JOSEPH, manufacturing company executive; b. Norfolk, Va., Sept. 19, 1945; s. Hobart Philip and Rita Regina (Perez) S.; m. Adriana Bergo, July 12, 1970; children: Jonathan Michael, Arianne Marie. BSME, U. Notre Dame, 1967; postgrad., U. Va. Sales engr. Shean Equipment Co., Syracuse, N.Y., 1967-69; application engr. Gen. Electric Co., Schenectady, 1970-71, prodn. control supr., 1972-75, process devel. engr., 1975-78, project mgr., 1978-80, mgr. facilities and engring., 1980-83; plant mgr. Hughes Tool Co., Bristol, Va., 1983-85; mgr. mfg. Sandvik Rock Tools, Inc., Bristol, 1985-89, gen. mgr., 1989-92, v.p., 1992—. Sr. patrolman Nat. Ski Patrol Sys., Wilminton, Vt., 1970-80; instr., trainer first aid ARC, Schenectady, 1975-78, vice chmn. disaster svcs., 1976-77; mem. sch. bd. Schalmont Ctrl. Sch. Dist., Schenectady, 1979-82; cmty. involvement com. Bristol Sch. Dist., 1990; chmn. Literacy Acad. Bristol, 1991-92; chmn. fin. coun. St. Anne's Cath. Ch., 1992-96; mem. Va. Attorney Gens. Commn., 1995-96, Commn. on Future S.W. Va., 1995—; mem. bd. visitors Va. Intermont Coll., 1996—; bd. fellows Intermont Coll., 1995—. Named Outstanding Young Man of Am., U.S. Jaycees, 1979. Mem. soc. Mfg. Engrs., soc. Plastics Engrs., Nat. Mining Assn. (chmn. resins gorup 1989—, tech. com. 1990—), Va. Coal Coun. (bd. dirs. 1993—), Bristol C. of C. (chmn. Legis. com. 1993, vice-chmn. govtl. affairs 1994, bd. dirs. 1994—), Pres. Club. Roman Catholic. Home: 16 Kingsbridge St Bristol TN 37620-2924 Office: Sandvik Rock Tools Inc PO Box 639 Bristol VA 24203-0639

SHEARER, CHARLES LIVINGSTON, academic administrator; b. Louisville, Ky., Nov. 23, 1942; s. Guy Cooper and Kathryn (Aufenkamp) S.; m. Susan Pulling Shearer, Nov. 30, 1968; children: Todd A., Mark G., Scott B. BS, U. Ky., 1964, MA, 1967; MA, Mich. State U., 1973, PhD, 1981. Instr. Henderson (Ky.) Community Coll., 1967-69; asst. prof. Ferris State Coll., Big Rapids, Mich., 1969-71; grad. asst. Mich. State U., East Lansing, 1971-73; dir. mgmt. program Albion (Mich.) Coll., 1973-75, dir. ops., 1975-79; v.p. fin. Transylvania U., Lexington, Ky., 1979-83, pres., 1983—; bd. dirs. Ky. Utilities, Lexington. Bd. dirs. Lexington Philharmonic Soc., 1983-89; mem. adv. bd. Salvation Army, Lexington, 1983-87; mem. Henry Clay Meml. Found., Lexington, 1983-89. Capt. U.S. Army Nat. Guard, 1966-76. Named One of Outstanding Young Men in Am., 1978. Mem. Am. Econs. Assn., Lexington C. of C. (bd. dirs. 1985—). Mem. Christian Ch. (Disciples of Christ). Lodge: Rotary.

SHEARER, KENNETH DECKER, JR., library science educator; b. Far Rockaway, N.Y., July 9, 1937; s. Kenneth Decker and Doris Louse (Bronson) S.; m. Ann Frances Martin, Nov. 29, 1963; Christopher, Timothy, Conan. AB, Amherst Coll., 1959; MLS, Rutgers U., 1963, PhD, 1963. Libr. Detroit Pub. Libr., 1963-68; asst. prof. libr. sci. U. N.C., Chapel Hill, 1968-74; prof. N.C. Ctrl. U., Durham, 1974—; mem. bd. Pub. Libr. Assn., Chgo, 1978-88, editor Pub. Librs. (jour.) 1978-88. Co-editor (with Josey) Politics and the Support of Libraries, 1990; editor: (books) Collection and Use of Pub. Statistics, 1976, Guiding the Reader to the Next Book, 1996; contbr. numerous articles to profl. jours. Mem. bd. dirs. Friends of Chapel Hill Libr., 1976-77, Friends of Durham Libr., 1979-80. Mem. Am. Libr. Assn. (numerous coms. 1963—), Durham County Libr. Assn. (pres. 1975-76), Assn. for Libr. and Info. Scis. Edn. (chmn. bylaws com. 1995-97), N.C. Libr. Assn., Southeastern Libr. Assn., Beta Phi Mu. Home: 1205 Le Clair Chapel Hill NC 27514 Office: NC Ctrl U Sch Libr & Info Scis Fayetteville St Durham NC 27707

SHEARER, MICHELE SLUSSER, acute care nurse practitioner; b. Shamokin, Pa., Jan. 26, 1959; d. Joseph Edmond and Allegra Marqueen (Tyson) Slusser; m. James E. Shearer, Aug. 1, 1981; 3 children. BS, U. S.C., Columbia, 1979; BSN, Med. U. S.C., 1982; MSN, U. Pitts., 1988; cert. acute care nurse practitioner, VSC, 1995. Cert. CCRN, ACLS. Staff nurse ICU-CCU Roper Hosp., Charleston, S.C., 1982-84; staff nurse CCU Allegheny Gen. Hosp., Pitts., 1984; cardiology nurse clincian Cardiologists Ltd., Pitts., 1984-86; clin. coord. CNS cardiac surgery Montefiore Hosp., Pitts., 1986-89; clin. instr. CCU Cape Fear Valley Med. Ctr., Fayetteville, N.C., 1990, staff nurse CCU, 1990-94; staff RN cardiac rehab. Cape Fear Valley Med. Ctr., Fayetteville, 1994-95; instr. ADN program Fayetteville Tech. C.C., 1991-92; mem. adj. faculty East Carolina U., 1993-96. Recipient Am. Lung Assn. Community Svc. award. Mem. AACN, Assn. Clin. Nurse Specialists, Coun. Asoc. Degree Nursing, Am. Heart Assn., Sigma Theta Tau, Kappa Kappa Gamma, Jr. League Fayetteville. Home: 227 Grey Fox Ln Fayetteville NC 28303-5003

SHEARER, ROSS STERLING, consultant, retired government official; b. Houston, Mar. 25, 1911; s. Thomas William and Hannah (Hutton) S.; m. Elizabeth Ann Rees, Apr. 16, 1938; children—Ross Sterling, Jr., Rees Rucker. Student George Washington U., 1928-31, U. Tex., 1931-34; LL.B., South Tex. Sch. of Law, 1937. Bar: Tex. 1937, U.S. Supreme Ct. 1951. With Tex. Employment Commn., Austin, 1936-41; adminstrv. analyst Social Security Bd., Washington, 1941-42; prin. budget examiner Bur. Budget, Exec. Office of Pres., Washington, 1942-51; acting adminstr. and asst. adminstr. Econ. Stblzn. Agy., Washington, 1951-53; asst. dir. orgn. and personnel Atomic Energy Commn., Washington, 1953-61; planning officer U.S. Dept. Commerce, Washington, 1961-63; dir. fin. and mgmt. services, asst. manpower adminstr. U.S. Dept. Labor, Washington, 1963-74; cons., Arlington, Va., 1975—; sec. Pres.'s Nat. Labor Mgmt. Conf., 1945-46; cons. Ind. U., Bloomington for pub. service tng. at Thammasat U., Bangkok, Thailand, 1959; mem. Fgn. Service Selection Bds., Washington, 1965, 68; clk. Com. for Cts. of Justice, Ho. of Dels., Va. Gen. Assembly, Richmond, 1975-79; cons., field rep. Nat. Council Sr. Citizens, Washington, 1975-81. Trustee U. Richmond, 1951-55; investigator appropriations com. U.S. Ho. of Reps., Washington, 1963; bd. dirs., com. mem. Nat. Capital Area United Way, 1967—; chmn. Arlington United Way, 1969-71; treas. For Love of Children, Washington, 1974-80. Mem. Am. Polit. Sci. Assn., State Bar Tex., Kappa Sigma. Democrat. Baptist. Club: Washington Golf and Country (Arlington). Home: 3125 N Abingdon St Arlington VA 22207-4211

SHEARER, WILLIAM THOMAS, pediatrician, educator; b. Detroit, Aug. 23, 1937. BS, U. Detroit, 1960; PhD, Wayne State U., 1966; MD, Washington U., St. Louis, 1970. Diplomate Am. Bd. Pediatrics, Am. Bd. Allergy and Immunology (chmn. 1994-95, dir. 1990-95, chair nominations com., clin. immunology soc.), Nat. Bd. Med. Examiners; cert. in diagnostic lab. immunology. Post-doctoral fellow in biochemistry dept. chem. Indiana U., Bloomington, 1966-67; intern in pediatrics St. Louis Children's Hosp., 1970-71, resident in immunology in pediatrics, 1971-72, dir. divsn. allergy and immunology, 1974-78; fellow in immunology in pediatrics Barnes Hosp., Washington U., St. Louis, 1972-74; spl. USPHA sci. rsch. fellow in medicine dept. medicine Washington U., 1972-74, assoc. prof., 1978, prof., 1978; prof. pediat., microbiology, immunology Baylor Coll. Medicine, Houston, 1978—, dir. AIDS rsch. ctr., 1991—; head sect. allergy & immunology Tex. Children's Hosp., Houston, 1978—; mem. ACTU Cmty. Adv. Bd., Tex. Children's Hosp., Houston, 1991—; chmn. pediat. core com. pediat. AIDS clin. trial group Nat. Inst. Allergy and Infectious Diseases NIH, Bethesda, Md., 1989—, ad hoc reviewer, 1991, mem. therapeutics subcom. AIDS rsch. adv. com., 1993—, chmn. pediat. AIDS clin. trial group immunology com., 1994—, mem. pediat. AIDS clin. trials group exec. com., 1991-95, mem. spl. rev. com. persons affected by chronic granulomatous disease, 1992; site visitor Gen. Clin. rsch. Ctr., NIH, Bethesda, 1993, vice chmn. pediat. AIDS clin. trials group exec. com., 1996—; chmn. study population/patient mgmt. com. Clin. Ctrs. for the Study of Pediat. Lung and Heart Complications of HIV Infection Nat. Heart, Lung and Blood Inst. NIH, Bethesda, 1989—, mem. AIDS ad hoc work group, 1991; dir. pediat. HIV/AIDS Clin. Rsch. Ctr., Houston, 1988—; chmn. exec. com. clin. trial intravenous gammaglobulin in HIV infected children Nat. Inst. Child and Health and Human Devel., Bethesda, 1989—; dir. Am. Bd. Allergy and Immunology, 1990-95, chair, 1994-95; vice-chair Pediatrics AIDS Clin. Trials Group Exec. com., 1996—. Editor: Pediatric Asthma, Allergy, and Immunology, 1989; editl. bd. Jour. of Allergy and Clin. Immunology, 1993—, Clin. and Diagnostic Lab. Immunology, 1994—; editor Pediatric Allergy and Immunology, 1995—, Allergy and Immunology Tng. Program Dir.; guest editor Seminar Pediatric Infectious Disease, 1990; contbr. intro.: Allergy: Principles and Practice, 1992; contbr. articles to profl. jours. including New Eng. Jour. Medicine. AIDS cons. Houston Ind. Sch. Dist., 1986—; med. adv. Spring Branch Ind. Sch. Dist., Houston, 1987—; chmn. community HIV/AIDS adv. group Tex. Med. Ctr., 1991—. Recipient faculty rsch. award Am. Cancer Soc., 1977-79, Myrtle Wreath award Hadassah, 1985, spl. recognition award Am. Acad. Allergy and Immunology, 1994; rsch. scholar Cystic Fibrosis Found., 1974-77; grantee NIH, 1988—. Mem. Am. Soc. Clin. Investigation, Am. Acad. Pediats. (mem. exec. com. sect. allergy and immunology 1991—), Tex. Allergy Soc. (exec. com. 1990—, Tex. Allergy and Immunology Soc. (chmn. nat. issues com. 1992-96, pres. 1994-96), Am. Acad. allergy and Immunology (chmn. clin. and lab. immunology com. 1994-96, chmn. tng. program dirs. nat. issues subcom. 1994-96), Am. Acad. Allergy, Asthma and Immunology (assoc. chmn. for planning of 1997-98 internat. meetings, profl. ednl. coun.), Clin. Immunology Soc. (chair Am. Bd. Allergy and Immunology nominations com. 1994-96). Office: Tex Childrens Hosp A/I Svc 6621 Fannin St MC 1-3291 Houston TX 77030-2303

SHEARIN, BETTY SPURLOCK, retired educational administrator; b. Salem, Va., Nov. 7, 1931; d. Thomas Shirley and Willie Ann (Borden) Spurlock; m. Alexander Moore Shearin Jr. (dec.), June 1 1957; 1 child, Victoria Louise. BS, Va. State U., 1954. Mem. staff Benedict Coll., Columbia, S.C., 1957-94; acting pres. Benedict Coll., 1984-85, v.p. adminstrn., 1986-87, coord. archives, telecommunications, 1987-88, spl. asst. to v.p. bus. affairs, 1988-90; cons., 1990-94; vol. coord. Richland County Pub. Libr., Columbia, 1991-95. Bd. dirs. Benedict Coll. Fed. Credit Union, 1974-79, 84-91; asst. sec. bd. trustees Benedict Coll., 1976-85, sec., 1985-86; sec. Colonial Park Comty. Home Assn., Columbia, 1988—; vol. Friends Richland County Pub. Libr., 1991—; mem. S.C. State Mus. Mem. NAFE, Assn. Records Mgrs. and Adminstrs. (sec. bd. dirs. 1983-85), Assn. Vol. Adminstrs. S.C. Assn. Vol. Adminstrs. (historian), Alpha Kappa Alpha. Democrat. Episcopalian. Home: 4116 Grand St Columbia SC 29203-6656

SHEARON, FORREST BEDFORD, humanities educator; b. Bolivar, Tenn., Sept. 7, 1934; s. George W. and Carrie Mae (Shinault) S.; m. Jeannette Brooks, June 5, 1955 (div. 1972); children: Angelia J. Shearon Schulte, Michael F.; m. Lynn Britton, June 11, 1981. AB in History, Union U., 1956; postgrad., Northwestern U., 1962-63; MA in English, U. Louisville, 1965, PhD in English, 1973. English tchr. Halls (Tenn.) High Sch., 1956-58, Pleasure Ridge Park High Sch., Louisville, 1958-62, 63-65; asst. prof. English Ky. So. Coll., Louisville, 1965-68; instr. English U. Louisville, 1969-73; asst. prof., assoc. prof., prof. humanities Ea. Ky. U., Richmond, 1973—. Contbr. articles to profl. jours. Recipient Outstanding Grad. Student award U. Louisville, 1973; Ford Found. fellow, 1962-63, NEH fellow, 1979; Fulbright-Hays grantee, 1987. Mem. MLA, So. Humanities Coun. (co-chair 1995-96, sec. 1989—), Ky. Philological Assn. (exec. sec. 1983-84), South Atlantic MLA, South Asian Lit. Assn., Phi Kappa Phi. Democrat. Presbyterian. Home: 305 Summit St Richmond KY 40475-2133 Office: Ea Ky U Dept Humanities Case Annex 368 Richmond KY 40475-3140

SHECHTER, ODED, physician; b. Ramat-gan, Israel, Aug. 11, 1948; came to U.S., 1959; s. Samuel Isaac and Shoshana (Storch) S.; m. Ruth Greenblatt; children: Ezri, Benli Moshe, Ari, Erika Orli. BS, CUNY, 1970, MA, 1972; MD, U Paris, 1980. Diplomate Am. Bd. Internal Medicine, Am. Bd. Geriatric Medicine. Intern N.Y.C.; resident Winthrop U., Mineola, N.Y., 1980-82; sr. medical resident Mt. Sinai Med. Ctr, Miami Beach, Fla., 1982-83; cons. internist, medical dir. Lauderdale Med. Ctr., Ft. Lauderdale, Fla., 1984-86; pvt. practice internal medicine Sunrise, Fla., 1986—. Mem. Am. Soc. Internal Medicine. Office: 3080 NW 60th Ave Fort Lauderdale FL 33313-1203

SHEEHAN, MICHAEL JARBOE, archbishop; b. Wichita, Kans., July 9, 1939; s. John Edward and Mildred (Jarboe) S. MST, Gregorian U., Rome, 1965; D of Canon Law, Lateran U., Rome, 1971. Ordained priest Roman Cath. Ch., 1964. Asst. gen. sec. Nat. Coun. Cath. Bishops, Washington, 1971-76; rector Holy Trinity Sem., Dallas, 1976-82; pastor Immaculate Conception Ch., Grand Prairie, Tex., 1982-83; bishop Diocese of Lubbock, Tex., 1983-93; archbishop Archdiocese of Santa Fe, Albuquerqe, N.Mex., 1993—; past chmn. Am. Bd. Cath. Missions, 1989-91; trustee Cath. Relief Svcs., 1992—. Contbr. articles to New Cath. Ency. Trustee St. Mary Hosp., Lubbock, 1983-89; bd. dirs. Tex. Conf. of Chs. Mem. Serra Club (chaplain 1983-93). Office: Archdiocese of Santa Fe 4000 Saint Josephs Pl NW Albuquerque NM 87120-1714

SHEETS, MARTHA LOUISE, civic activist; b. Toledo, Mar. 25, 1923; d. Ira Elmo and Nellie Gertrude Merrill; m. Ted Charles Sheets, Dec. 21, 1946; children: Thomas Merrill, Susan Ruth, Laura Louise, Charles Ira. B in Edn., U. Toledo, 1945. speaker in field. Charter mem., trustee, sec.-treas., v.p., pres. Citizens for Metroparks, Inc.; commr. Met. Park Dist. Bd., 1976; mem. Gov.'s Commn. Restoration of State Capitol Bldg., Nashville, 1986; historian designer show houses Chattanooga Symphony and Opera Guild, 1981-93; appointee City Commn. to Greenway Adv. Bd., 1989, re-appointed, 1992-93; active numerous civic orgns. including garden clubs and ch. groups; active Save Outdoor Sculpture project Tenn. State Mus. and Smithsonian Inst., 1992-93; mem. com. Hamilton County (Tenn.) Bicentennial, 1996. Mem. AAUW (chmn. 75th birthday luncheon 1982, grantee Ednl. Found prog.), ASME (chmn., pres. Northwest Ohio sect. women's aux.), Jr. Coterie Club (founding pres.), Zonta Internat. Svc. Club, Little Theatre Assocs. (past pres.), Murray Hills Garden Club (pres. 1991-92, 92-93), Tenn. Fedn. Garden Clubs (dist. hist. preservation chmn. 1981-85, state hist. preservation chmn. 1987-89, dist. III hist. preservation chmn. 1992-94), Chattanooga Coun. Garden Clubs (awards chmn., hist. preservation chmn. 1992-94), PEO.

SHEFFEL, DONALD DAVID, neurosurgeon; b. N.Y.C., Nov. 9, 1928; s. Joseph and Ethel (Homansky) S.; m. Sheila Alice Moffat; children: Jeffrey, Scott, Elissa. BA, Duke U., 1948; MD, U. Leiden, Netherlands, 1954. Diplomate Am. Bd. Neurol. Surgery. Resident in pathology U. Miami, 1956; resident in neurosurgery U. Tex., Galveston, 1958-63; NIH fellow in neurosurgery Harvard Med. Sch. and Mass. Gen. Hosp., Boston, 1962; neurosurgeon in pvt. practice Hollywood, Fla., 1963-86; asst. prof. U. Miami, 1964-66, clin. assoc. prof., 1966—; chief div. neurosurgery Meml. Hosp., Hollywood, 1986—; asst. prof. U. N.Mex., Albuquerque, 1974-75; past chmn. Joint Coun. of STae Neurosurg. Socs., 1992-94. Contbr. chpts.: The Development and Neurotrauma Systems and Centers, 1993; speaker in field. Site visitor Pa. Trauma Found. Lt. USN, 1956-58. Mem. AMA, Am. Assn. Neurol. Surgeons (bd. dirs. 1994—), Congress Neurol. Surgeons (exec. com. 1992-94), So. Neursurg. Soc., Fla. Neurosurg. Soc., Singleton Surg. Soc. Office: Meml Hosp Div Neurosurgery 1150 N 35th Ave Ste 300 Hollywood FL 33021-5428

SHEFFIELD, GLORIA CAROL, elementary education educator; b. Eastman, Ga., Aug. 5, 1951; d. Dewey and Geneva (Cartwright) S. BS in Elem. Edn., Ga. So. U., Statesboro, 1972; M in Elem. Edn., Ga. Southwestern U., Americus, 1973; postgrad., Brewton Parker Coll., 1983, 86, 89-90.

Tchr. Dodge County Bd. Edn., Eastman, Ga., 1973-79, 82-83, Baker Acad., Hawkinsville, Ga., 1979-82, 84-85; tchr. Pulaski County Bd. Edn., Hawkinsville, 1985—, computer instr., coord., 1990—. Sec. Chauncey Elem. Parent-Tchr. Orgn. Named Tchr. of Yr., Pulaski Elem., 1988, 91. Mem. NEA, Ga. Assn. Educators, Delta Kappa Gamma (Alpha Phi chpt.). Baptist. Home: RR 1 Box 61 Chauncey GA 31011-8900 Office: Pulaski County Bd Edn Broadstreet Hawkinsville GA 31036

SHEFFIELD, HENRY LEE, fire chief; b. Lakeland, Fla., Nov. 15, 1954; s. Marlin Robert and Elizabeth Ann (Carlton) S.; m. Joyce Ann Dollar, Nov. 23, 1972; children: Christopher, Jennifer. AS, Polk C.C., 1982; BA, Eckerd Coll., 1992. Cert. exec. fire officer Nat. Fire Acad. Fire chief Braden River Fire Dist., Bradenton, Fla., 1983-95; chmn. Fire Svcs. Adv. Bd. Manatee Vocat. Tech. Ctr., Bradenton, 1985-87. Emergency hurricane responder Braden River Fire Dist., Dade County, 1992, Fla. Divsn. Forestry, N.W. Fla., 1995. Manatee County Fire Chiefs' Assn. (pres. 1995-96). Republican. Office: Braden River Fire Dist 8800 State Rd 70 E Bradenton FL 34202

SHEFFIELD, NANCY Y., secondary school educator; b. Ozark, Ala., June 5, 1946; d. Lionel and Sara Nell (Covington) Young; children: Timothy William-Conan Young, Deborah Lynn. BA in Lit., Fla. Presbyn. Coll., 1968; postgrad., Ga. Southwestern U., 1975-82; MS in English Edn., Fla. State U., 1989. Cert. tchr. in gifted edn., Ga. Lang. arts tchr. Graham (N.C.) High Sch., 1968-69, Early County High Sch., Blakely, Ga., 1974-77; gifted resource tchr. Early County Elem. Sch., Blakely, 1977-79; tchr. of the gifted Early County Middle Sch., Blakely, 1979-85; tchr. lang. arts, TV prodn., gifted Bay High Sch., Panama City, Fla., 1985—; adj. prof. lang. arts Gulf Coast C.C., Panama City, 1988—; mem. dist. improvement team Bay Dist. Schs., 1995—; sponsor Quill and Scroll Bay High Sch., 1986—; cons. Fla. Dept. Edn., 1990. Editor: Alive Home Newsletter, 1994—. Diocesan pres. Daus. of the King Episc. Diocese Ctrl. Gulf Coast, 1994—; chpt. pres. Daus. of the King-St. Andrews Episc., Panama City, 1992—, vestry mem., 1996—. Mem. Bay Lang. Arts Coun. (pres., v.p. 1993-95), Nat. Coun. Tchrs. English (com. on tracking/grouping in lang. arts 1991—), Assn. Bay County Educators (exec. bd. 1995—, sr. bldg. rep. 1988—), Fla. Teaching Profession (messenger 1996—), NEA, Fla. Coun. Tchrs. English (del., presenter, Cert. of Merit 1990). Home: 213 San Gabriel St Panama City Beach FL 32413 Office: Bay High Sch 1200 Harrison Ave Panama City FL 32401-2433

SHEFFIELD, SUE, nursing educator; b. Silsbee, Tex., Apr. 9, 1953; d. Floyd and Earline (Crawford) McKee; m. Wayne Sheffield, Sept. 2, 1977; children: Kyle, Beau, Chris. BSN, Tex. Woman's U., 1975. Charge nurse, supr. 3-11 shift Silsbee Dr's. Hosp.; staff nurse Spring Br. Meml. Hosp., Houston; nurse Eustace (Tex.) Ind. Sch. Dist. Home: PO Box 647 Kemp TX 75143-0647

SHEFFIELD, WALTER JERVIS, lawyer; b. Petersburg, Va., Mar. 20, 1946; s. John Courtney and Betty Lou (Loftis) S.; m. Susan Jarrett Moore, May 4, 1968 (div. June 1980); children: John Courtney II, Walter Alexander; m. Christina Meredith Shipp, Jan. 23, 1982; 1 child, Margaret Ashbrooke. BA magna cum laude, Old Dominion U., 1971; JD, Emory U., 1973; LLM in taxation, NYU, 1974. Bar: Va. 1975, U.S. Dist. Ct. (ea. dist.) Va. 1975, U.S. Ct. Appeals (4th cir.) 1975, U.S. Ct. Claims 1975, U.S. Tax Ct. 1975, U.S. Supreme Ct. 1979. Asst. to Sec. of Commonwealth, Office of Gov. Commonwealth of Va., Richmond, 1974-75; assoc. Cox, Woodbridge, Smith, Scott & VanLear, Fredericksburg, Va., 1975-76; city atty. City of Fredericksburg, 1976-86; pres. Sheffield & Bricken, Fredericksburg, 1979-91; pvt. practice Walter J. Sheffield, Atty., 1976-79, 91—; chmn. Va. State Bd. Surface Mining Rev., 1989-93; vice mayor City of Fredericksburg, 1988-92, chmn. fin. com., 1988-92; chmn. Rappahannock regional jail bd., 1988-90; constrn. dispute arbitrator Am. Arbitration Assn., 1985—; mem. legis. and effective govt. coms. Va. Mcpl. League. Bd. dirs. 7th Dist. Dem. Com., 1985-89; mem. State Dem. Ctrl. Com., 1985-89; legal counsel, dir. Fredericksburg Area Mus. and Cultural Ctr., Inc., 1988—, Mary Washington Hosp. Found., 1989-91; trustee, chmn. adminstrv. bd. Fredericksburg United Meth. Ch.; mem. com. on instl. relationships Va. Ann. Conf. United Meth. Ch.; pres. Fredericksburg Civil War Roundtable, 1996—. 1st lt. Quartermaster Corps, U.S. Army, 1966-69. Recipient Disting. Svc. award Fredericksburg Jaycees, 1978. Mem. Fredericksburg Area Bar Assn. (chmn. elect 1996), Fredericksburg Area C. of C., Va. Assn. Def. Attys., Phi Alpha Theta, Phi Delta Phi (magister 1972-73). Club: Fredericksburg Country. Home: 1314 Sophia St Fredericksburg VA 22401-3742 Office: PO Box 7818 Fredericksburg VA 22404-7818

SHEFMAN, MARGA R., real estate educator; b. Jersey City, N.J., Oct. 4, 1943; d. Gustav Roy Drenowatz and Evangeline (Wilson); m. Lee David Shefman, Dec. 22, 1963 (div. 1978); children: David Ben, Lenore Rae. Lic. real estate agent, Tex. Real estate sales K.L. McGuirt Co. Realtors, Houston, 1966-78; bus. develop. Realty World So. Tex., Houston, 1978-80; tng. dir. Deanie Owens/Better Homes & Gardens, San Antonio, Tex., 1980-83; owner, pres. Shefman Assoc. Realtors, San Antonio, 1983-86; tng. mgr. NPC Homes, San Antonio, 1986, Guy Chipman Co. Realtors, San Antonio, 1986-91; tng. dir. Bill Milburn Co., Austin, Tex., 1991, Austin Bd. of Realtors, 1991—; lead instr. San Antonio Bd. of Realtors, 1981-91, mem. chair program com. 1989-91; mem., bd. dirs. Homeowners Warranty Coun., San Antonio, 1986-91; mem. ad hoc com. Tex. Real Estate Comm., Austin, 1996. Contbr. articles to profl. jours., courses for mandatory continuing edn. V.p., bd. dirs. Jewish Cmty. North, Houston, 1977-79; mem. adv. bd. Austin Cmty. Coll., 1995, U. of Tex. Quality Ctr., Austin, 1993-95. Recipient Nat. Business Develop. Director award Realty World Internat., Annahale, Va., 1979. Mem. Nat. Assn. of Realtors (best edn. programming award 1994), Am. Soc. of Assn. Execs. (best education program award 1995), Tex. Assn. of Realtors, Tes. Real Estate Tchrs. Assn. (dir. 1993, bd. dirs.), Austin Bd. of Realtors (staff mgr. 1992), Real Estate Educators Assn. Republican. Jewish. Home: 3200 Funston St Austin TX 78703 Office: Austin Bd of Realtors 4106 Medical Pkwy Austin TX 78756

SHEFTMAN, HOWARD STEPHEN, lawyer; b. Columbia, S.C., May 20, 1949; s. Nathan and Rena Mae (Kantor) S.; m. Sylvia Elaine Williams, Nov. 30, 1974; children: Amanda Elaine, Emily Catherine. BS in Bus. Adminstrn., U. S.C., 1971, JD, 1974. Bar: S.C. 1974, U.S. Dist. Ct. 1975, U.S. Ct. Appeals (4th cir.) 1982. Assoc. Kirkland, Taylor & Wilson, West Columbia, S.C., 1974-75; ptnr. Sheftman, Oswald & Holland, West Columbia, 1975-77, Finkel, Altman & Bailey, LLC, Columbia, 1977—. Mem. S.C. Bar Assn. (practice and procedure com. 1978—), S.C. Trial Lawyers Assn. (chmn. domestic rels. sect. 1982-83, bd. govs. 1987-93, 94—), Richland Bar Assn., Met. Sertoma Club (pres. 1986-87). Jewish. Office: Finkel Altman & Bailey PO Box 1799 Columbia SC 29202-1799

SHEHEEN, FRED ROUKOS, education agency administrator; b. Camden, S.C., July 7, 1936; s. Austin M. and Lucile (Roukos) S.; m. Rose Maria Serio, Nov. 26, 1966; children: Maria, Vincent, Margaret Rose. AB Polit. Sci., Duke U., 1958; postgrad., Harvard U., 1990; LLD (hon.), Claflin Coll., 1990; HHD, Lander Coll., 1992; AA honoris causa, Tech. Coll. Lowcountry, Beaufort, S.C., 1992. Bureau chief Charlotte (N.C.) Observer, Rock Hill, Columbia, S.C., 1958-63; press sec. to Gov. Donald Russell, Columbia, 1963-65; exec. asst. to Sen. Donald Russell, Washington, 1965-66; asst. to dir. S.C. State Devel. Bd., Columbia, 1967-68; v.p. & sec., pres. & publisher Banner Publishers Inc., Chronicle Publishers Inc., N.C., S.C., 1968-76; founder, pres., prin. owner Camden (S.C.) Co., 1976-87; commr. of higher edn. S.C. Commn. on Higher Edn., Columbia, 1987—; bd. dirs. S.C. Rsch. Authority, Columbia, 1983-86; mem. S.C. Commn. Human Affairs, 1971-72, S.C. Commn. Higher Edn., 1971-75, 79-86, (chmn. 1983-86), Edn. Improvement Act Selection com., 1983-86, Commn. Future S.C., Columbia, 1987-89. Contbr. chpt. to book, article to profl. jour. Pres. Kershaw County Mental Health Assn., Camden, S.C., 1971, 76; mem. S.C. Tuition Grants Commn., 1988—, Nat. Edn. Goals Panel task force Collegiate Attainment and Assessment, 1988—, S.C. Edn. Goals Panel, 1992—, So. Regional Coun. Coll. Bd., 1993—; adv. bd. Master Pub. Adminstrn. program U. S.C. Coll. Charleston, 1992—; trustee Springdale Sch., Camden, 1976-84, Boyland-Haven-Mather Acad., Camden, 1976-83, S.C. Gov's. Sch. Sci. and Mathematics, 1987—; bd. dirs. Kershaw County Cancer Soc. Recipient Sertoma Svc. to Mankind award Sertoma club, 1973; named Educator of Yr. S.C. Tech. Edn. Assn., 1990. Mem. State Higher Edn. Exec. Officers (exec. com. 1990—, Nat. Ctr. Edn. Statistics Network adv. com. 1990—), S.C. Agy. Dir's. Orgn. (pres. 1992). Roman Catholic. Home: 2107 Washington Ln Camden SC 29020-1723 Office: SC Commn Higher Edn 1333 Main St Ste 200 Columbia SC 29201-3201

SHEIN, JAY LESING, financial planner; b. Chgo., Jan. 27, 1951; s. Garrett Melchior and Evelyn (Blitt) Hamm; m. Val Margaret Rich, Dec. 14, 1984; children: Melissa Loree, Blair Charles, Christina Anne, Allison Marie, Lindsay Gayle. Student, Broward C.C., Davie, Fla., 1969-71; CFP, Coll. for Fin. Planning, Denver, 1990; MS in Taxation and Fin., LaSalle U., 1994, PhD, 1994. Tech. technician Broward County Sch. Bd., Ft. Lauderdale, Fla., 1973-76; owner, mgr. Bus. and Tax Consulting Firm, Ft. Lauderdale, 1976-83; dist. mgr. United Group and Group One, Ft. Lauderdale, 1983-84; from account exec. to v.p. Compass Fin. Group, Inc., Lighthouse Point, Fla., 1984-90; pres. Compass Fin. Group, Inc., Lighthouse Point, 1990—; adv. bd. devel. coun., mem. Highlands Christian Acad., Pompano Beach, Fla., 1992—; adj. prof. Nova Southeastern U. Grad. Sch. Bus., LaSalle U.; mem. adj. faculty Rollins Coll., 1996. Contbr. articles to newspapers and pubs. in field. Mem. Estate Planning Coun. of Broward County. Mem. Inst. CFP, Nat. Assn. Life Underwriters, Practising Law Inst. (assoc.), South Fla. Soc. of Inst. of CFPs (pres.-elect 1996, pres. 1997, edn. chmn. 1994, dir. ethics 1993-94), Broward County Assn. Life Underwriters (v.p. 1992-94), Greater Ft. Lauderdale Tax Coun., Marine Industries of South Fla. Republican. Baptist. Office: Compass Fin Group Inc 3050 N Federal Hwy Ste 208 Lighthouse Point FL 33064-6866

SHEINFELD, MYRON M., lawyer, educator; b. Mass., Mar. 18, 1930; s. Robert and Sadye (Rosenberg) S.; m. Christina Trzcinski, Mar. 30, 1985; children: Scott, Tom. BA, Tulane U., 1951; JD, U. Mich., 1954. Bar: Mich. 1954, Tex. 1956. Researcher Legis. Research Inst. U. Mich., 1954; asst. U.S. atty. So. Dist. Tex., 1958-60; law clk. U.S. Dist. Judge, 1960-61; ptnr. Strickland, Gordon & Sheinfeld, Houston, 1961-68, Shareholder, Sheinfeld, Maley & Kay, P.C., Houston, 1968—; adj. prof. law U. Tex.; mem. Nat. Bankruptcy Conf.; chmn. Tex. Bankruptcy Adv. Commn.; bd. dirs. Nabors Industries, Third Ave. Value Fund, Inc., Am. Coll. Bankruptcy. Bd. editors Practical Lawyer; contbr. articles to profl. jours. With JAG U.S. Army, 1955-58. Fellow Am. Coll. Bankruptcy; mem. State Bar Tex., Houston Ctr. Club (bd. dirs.), Ramada Tejas Club, Phi Beta Kappa, Phi Sigma Alpha. Office: Sheinfeld Maley & Kay PC 1001 Fannin St Ste 3700 Houston TX 77002

SHELBY, JAMES STANFORD, cardiovascular surgeon; b. Ringgold, La., June 15, 1934; s. Jesse Audrey and Mable (Martin) S.; BS in Liberal Arts La. Tech. U., 1956; MD, La. State U., 1958; m. Susan Rainey, July 15, 1967; children: Bryan Christian, Christopher Linden. Intern, Charity Hosp. La., New Orleans, 1958-59, resident surgery and thoracic surgery, 1959-65; fellow cardiovascular surgery Baylor U. Coll. Medicine, Houston, 1965-66; practice medicine specializing in cardiovascular surgery, Shreveport, La., 1967—; mem. staff Schumpert Med. Ctr., Highland Hosp., Willis-Knighton Med. Ctr.; assoc. prof. surgery La. State U. Sch. Medicine, Shreveport, 1967—. With M.C., AUS, 1961-62. Diplomate Am. Bd. Surgery, Am. Bd. Thoracic Surgery. Recipient Tower of Medallion award La. Tech. U., 1982. Mem. Am. Coll. Cardiology, AMA, Soc. Thoracic Surgeons, Am. Heart Assn., Southeastern Surg. Congress, So. Thoracic Surg. Assn. Home: 6003 E Ridge Dr Shreveport LA 71106-2425 Office: 3300 Virginia Ave Ste 7B Shreveport LA 71103-3941

SHELBY, RICHARD CRAIG, senator, former congressman; b. Birmingham, Ala., May 6, 1934; s. O.H. and Alice L. (Skinner) S.; m. Annette Nevin, June 11, 1960; children: Richard Craig, Claude Nevin. AB, U. Ala., 1957, LLB, 1963. Bar: Ala. 1961, D.C. 1979. Law clk. Supreme Ct. of Ala., 1961-62; practice law Tuscaloosa, Ala., 1963-79; prosecutor City of Tuscaloosa, 1964-70; spl. asst. atty. gen. State of Ala., 1969-70; U.S. magistrate No. Dist. of Ala., 1966-70; mem. Ala. State Senate, 1970-78, 96th-99th Congresses from 7th Ala. dist., 1979-87; mem. energy and commerce com., mem. vets. affairs com., U.S. senator from Ala., 1987—, mem. com. on appropriations, com. on banking, housing, and urban affairs, select com. on intelligence, spl. com. on aging. Active Boy Scouts Am.; pres. Tuscaloosa County Mental Health Assn., 1969-70; bd. govs. Nat. Legis. Conf., 1975-78. Mem. ABA, Ala. Bar Assn., Tuscaloosa County Bar Assn., D.C. Bar Assn., Exch. Club. Republican. Presbyterian. Home: 1414 High Forest Dr N Tuscaloosa AL 35406-2152 Office: US Senate 110 Hart Senate Bldg Washington DC 20510

SHELDON, ELI HOWARD, minister; b. Monroe, Mich., May 25, 1937; s. Clarence O. and Orean Lavon (Longdon) S.; m. Freida Orene Townsend, Feb. 17, 1962; children: Stefanie Ann, Todd Howard. BA, Dallas Bapt. U., 1970; MDiv, Southwestern Bapt. Theol. Sem., 1973, D. Ministry, 1976. Ordained to ministry So. Bapt. Conv., 1971. Minister Plain View Bapt. Ch., Chalk Mountain, Tex., 1969-70, Eastside Bapt. Ch., Marietta, Okla., 1970-73, 1st Bapt. Ch., Roosevelt, Okla., 1974-77, Crown Heights Bapt. Ch., Oklahoma City, 1978—; bd. dirs. Bapt. Gen. Convention Okla., Oklahoma City; adj. prof. Okla. Bapt. U., Shawnee, 1986—. Editor, writer, artist Crown Heights Comics; contbr. articles to newspapers and mags. Chaplain Lions Club, Roosevelt, 1974-77; chmn. Bi-Centennial Com., Roosevelt, 1975-76. Mem. Capital Bapt. Assn. (chmn. continuing edn. com. 1982—, mem. exec. bd. 1978—), Cowboy Hall of Fame (life). Home: 5732 NW 46th St Oklahoma City OK 73122-5101 Office: Crown Heights Bapt Ch 4802 N Western Ave Oklahoma City OK 73118-5215

SHELDON, JEFFREY ANDREW, college official; b. Northampton, Mass., Sept. 1, 1959; s. Wallace J. and Marilyn M. S. BS, Springfield (Mass.) Coll., 1981; postgrad., U. Va., 1981-83; EdM in Adminstrn., Harvard U., 1990. Mem. sci. faculty, chmn. dept. The Forman Sch., Litchfield, Conn., 1984-89; fin. mgr. and adminstrn. The Clin.-Devel. Inst., Belmont, Mass., 1989-90; owner, dir. Island Tutorials, Hilton Head Island, S.C., 1990-93; dir. instl. advancement Tech. Coll. of Lowcountry, Beaufort, S.C., 1993—; mgmt. team Acad. C.C. Leadership Advancement Innovation & Modeling (ACCLAIM), 1995—; presenter in field. Bd. dirs. Beaufort Chamber Orch. Guild, 1994-96, 2d v.p.; mem. Leadership Hilton Head, 1994, Nat. Coun. for Resource Devel., Beaufort County Human Svcs. Coun., 1996; v.p. bd. dirs. Hilton Head Choral Soc., 1992-93, tenor, 1991—; mem. core curriculum task force Beaufort 2000, 1992-93; candidate for Beaufort County Bd. Edn., Hilton Head, 1992, 94; bd. dirs. YMCA, Beaufort County, 1995; active ACCLAIM Project, Beaufort County, 1993—. Klingenstein Summer Inst. fellow Columbia U., 1988. Mem. Paris Island Masters Swim Team, Greater Beaufort C. of C. (govt. rels. com., edn. com.). Republican. Presbyterian. Home: 809 Scotts St Beaufort SC 29902 Office: Tech Coll Lowcountry 921 Ribaut Rd Beaufort SC 29902-5430

SHELDON, NANCY WAY, environmental management consultant; b. Bryn Mawr, Pa., Nov. 10, 1944; d. John Harold and Elizabeth Semple (Hoff) W.; m. Robert Charles Sheldon, June 15, 1968. BA, Wellesley Coll., 1966; MA, Columbia U., 1968, M in Philosophy, 1972. Cert. hazardous materials mgr., environ. auditor, Calif.; registered environ. profl., environ. assessor, Calif. Mgmt. cons. ABT Assocs., Cambridge, Mass., 1969-70; mgmt. cons. Harbridge House, Inc., 1970-79, L.A., 1977-79, v.p., 1977-79; mgmt. cons., pres. Resource Assessment, Inc., 1979—. Author: Social and Economic Benefits of Public Transit, 1973. Contbr. articles to profl. jours. Columbia U. fellow, 1966-68; recipient Nat. Achievement award Nat. Assn. Women Geographers, 1966. Mem. DAR, Nat. Environ. Health Assn., Air and Waste Mgmt. Assn., Nat. Ground Water Assn., Water Pollution Control Fedn., Water Environment Fedn., Fla. Pollution Control Assn., Grad. Faculties Alumni Assn. Columbia U. Office: Resource Assessment Inc 1192 Kittiwake Cir Sanibel FL 33957-3606

SHELET, DAWN ARDELLE, financial analyst; b. Lac La Biche, Alberta, Can., Feb. 23, 1954; d. Laura Myrtle (Gould) Thacher; m. Paul Buettiker, Aug. 30, 1983. Student, McMaster U., Hamilton, Ontario, Can., 1976-78, B of Commerce (with honours), 1986; MBA, U. Miami, 1988. Mktg. rsch. asst. U. Miami Mktg. Dept., Coral Gables, Fla., 1986-87; fin. mgmt. intern Am. Express TRS Inc., Latin Am. Hdqrs., Coral Gables, Fla., 1987; internat. law rsch. asst. U. Miami Bus. Law Dept., Coral Gables, 1987-88; fin. analyst mktg. Eastern Air Lines Hdqrs., Miami, 1988-89; fin. planning systems analyst Am. Airlines Hdqrs., Dallas, 1989-90, fin. analyst internat., 1990-93, sr. bus. analyst, 1993—. Fund raising coord. United Way, Dallas-Ft. Worth Airport, 1989, 90, 91, 93, 94. Recipient U. Miami Grad. scholarship, 1986, 87, 88, Fees scholarship McMaster U., 1977; named to Dean's Honours list McMaster U., 1976, 77, 84, 85, 86. Mem. AMR Mgmt. Club (sec. 1991, treas. 1990-91, dir. 1992-93, v.p. 1994-95), Internat. Bus. Assn. (treas. 1986-87), Beta Gamma Sigma.

SHELEY, SUSAN CUMMINGS, journalism educator, rancher; b. Baytown, Tex., Dec. 5, 1957; d. John Kay and Florence (Teten) Cummings; m. Thomas Scott Sheley, Dec. 18, 1993; 1 child, Scott Austin. BA in Journalism, U. Houston, 1980, MA in Humanities, 1984; postgrad., U. Tex. Reporter, editor The Baytown Sun, 1979-82; student pubs. adminstr. Lee Coll., Baytown, 1982—, chmn. visual and performing arts, 1994—; rancher, Baytown. Bd. dirs. Big Bros. and Sisters, Baytown. Recipient Excellence in Edn. award Lee Coll. and Exxon Edn. Found., 1989. Mem. Soc. Profl. Journalists, Tex. C.C. Journalism Assn., Tex. Intercollegiate Press Assn., Coll. Media Advisors, Tex. Jr. Coll. Tchg. Assn., Jaycees (Baytown chpt. pres. 1993-94, Outstanding Young Baytonian 1993). Democrat. Episcopalian. Home: 201 N 4th St Baytown TX 77520 Office: Lee College PO Box 818 Baytown TX 77522

SHELL, LOUIS CALVIN, lawyer; b. Dinwiddie County, Va., Dec. 8, 1925; s. Roger LaFayette and Susie Ann (Hill) S.; m. Barbara Marie Pamplin, Aug. 5, 1950; children—Pamela Shell Baskervill, Patricia Shell Caulkins. B.A., U. Va., 1946, LL.B., 1947. Bar: Va. 1947. Assoc. White, Hamilton, Wyche & Shell and predecessor White, Hamilton & Wyche, Petersburg, Va., 1948-50, ptnr., 1950—, now chief trial counsel. Chmn. Petersburg Electoral Bd., 1952, vice mayor city council, 1957-60; trustee Petersburg Dist. United Methodist Ch. Named Outstanding Young Man, Petersburg Jr. C. of C., 1956. Fellow Am. Coll. Trial Lawyers; mem. ABA, Va. State Bar Assn., Petersburg Bar Assn., Am. Judicature Soc., Va. State Bar (council 1972-75). Democrat. Club: Kiwanis (Petersburg). Home: 10813 Lakeview Dr Petersburg VA 23805-7152 Office: White Hamilton Wyche & Shell 20 E Tabb St Petersburg VA 23803-4541

SHELL, OWEN G., JR., banker; b. Greenville, S.C., June 19, 1936; s. Owen and Katherine S.; m. Mary Ruth Trammell, Aug. 9, 1980; children: Katherine Sloan, Mary Carroll, Robert Owen, James Walker. B.S., U. S.C., 1960; post grad., Stonier Grad. Sch. Banking, 1971; grad., Advanced Mgmt. Program, Harvard U., 1979. Tech. supt. Deering-Milliken, Inc., 1962-63; v.p. Citizens & So. Nat. Bank S.C., Columbia, 1968-71; sr. v.p. Citizens & So. Nat. Bank S.C., 1971-74, exec. v.p., 1974-79; pres., dir., chief exec. officer First Am. Nat. Bank, Nashville, 1979-86; vice chmn. bd., dir. First Am. Corp., 1979-86; chmn., pres., chief exec. officer Sovran Bank/Tenn., Nashville, 1986-91; pres. Nations Bank of Tenn. (formerly Sovran Bank), Nashville, 1992—; chmn. NationsBank of Ky.; dir. Nashville br. Fed. Res. Bank of Atlanta. Adv. bd. INROADS/Nashville; active Leadership Nashville, Tenn. Performing Arts Found., Mid. Tenn. coun. Boy Scouts Am., Vanderbilt U. Owen Grad. Sch. Mgmt.; trustee Met. Nashville Pub. Edn.; bd. dirs. Tenn. Bus. Roundtable, Tenn. Tomorrow. Mem. Assn. Res. City Bankers, Nashville Area C. of C., Kappa Alpha, Omicron Delta Kappa. Presbyterian. Clubs: Rotary, Cumberland, Belle Meade Country. Home: 4412 Chickering Ln Nashville TN 37215-4915

SHELL, ROBERT EDWARD LEE, photographer, writer; b. Roanoke, Va., Dec. 3, 1946; s. James Ralph and Mary (Terry) S.; m. Darlene Bridget. Student, Va. Poly. Inst. and State U., 1965-68, Elkins Inst., 1972, Nat. Camera Inst., 1973. Staff SMithsonian Inst., Washington, 1968-72; photographer Sta. WBRA-Pub. TV, Roanoke, 1972-74; owner Camera, Inc., Salem, Va., 1974-76; photographer, technician Gentry Studios, Blacksburg, Va., 1976-81; tech. editor Shutterbug Mag., Patch Communications, Radford, Va., 1984-91; editor Shutterbug Mag., Patch Communications, Titusville, Fla., 1991—, tech. editor, 1984-91, editor, 1991—; U.S. corr. Asahi Camera, Tokyo, 1986—, Color Foto, Munich, 1989—, Photo Answers, U.K.; pub. PIC Mag., U.K., 1994—. Author: Photography with Canon EOS System, 1990, Hasselblad Camera System Guide, 1991, Mamiya Camera System Guide, 1992, Photo Business Careers, 1992, Canon Compendium, 1994, Metz Flash System Handbook, 1994, Olympus IS System Handbook, 1994, Canon Rebel Handbook, 1994; tech. editor numerous publs; contbr. articles to profl. jours. Smithsonian Inst. grantee, Washington, 1968. Mem. Photo Mktg. Assn. Internat., German Photographers Soc., Megapress. Home and Office: Bob Shell Photography 1601 Grove Ave Radford VA 24141-1624

SHELLEY, BRYAN KEITH, English language educator; b. Willston, N.D., Feb. 25, 1949; s. Keith Gorman and Mildred Lenore (Wilson) S. BA in English cum laude, Bryan Coll., Dayton, Tenn., 1971; M Litt in English, Middlebury (Vt.) Coll., 1981; DPhil, Oxford U., 1986. Summer instr. creative writing Blue Ridge Tech. Inst., Hendersonville, N.C., 1972; tchg. asst. Appalachian State U., 1971-73; reporter, sports editor Laurens (S.C.) County Advertiser, 1973-75; instr. composition, lit. and speech Bryan Coll., Dayton, 1975-76; assoc. prof. English Campbell U., Buies Creek, N.C., 1989—; vis. asst. prof. English Wheaton (Ill.) Coll., 1989. Author: Shelley and Scripture: The Interpreting Angel, 1994. Mem. MLA, Nat. Assn. Scholars, Keats-Shelley Assn. Am., C.S. Lewis Soc., Oxford (life), Friends of Dove Cottage (life). Home: 20 Country Rd Hendersonville NC 28791 Office: Campbell Univ Dept English Buies Creek NC 27506

SHELNUTT, JOHN MARK, lawyer; b. Gainesville, Ga., Jan. 19, 1963; s. Dumas Broughton and Georgia Texana (Ruff) S.; m. Leila Christine Ricketson, June 24, 1989; children: John Mark Jr., Sarah. AA, Emory U., 1983, BA, 1985, JD, 1988. Bar: Ga. 1988, U.S. Dist. Ct. (mid. dist.) Ga. 1994. Asst. dist. atty. Dist. Atty.-Dougherty Jud. Cir., Albany, Ga., 1988, Dist. Atty.-Chattahoochee Jud. Cir., Columbus, Ga., 1989-94; ptnr. Berry and Shelnutt, Columbus, 1994—; faculty basic litigation course Prosecuting Atty.'s Coun., Forsyth, Ga., 1992—. Mem. ABA, State Bar Ga., Columbus Bar Assn., Ga. Trial Lawyers Assn., Ga. Assn. Criminal Def. Lawyers. Methodist. Home: 6451 S Branch Ct Columbus GA 31909 Office: Berry & Shelnutt 1024 2nd Ave Columbus GA 31901-2406

SHELTON, BETTY CLARE, organization executive; b. S. Range, Mich., Mar. 8, 1940; d. Robert R. Salo and Rauha O. Liimatainen; m. Charles E. Shelton, Aug. 31, 1959 (div. May 1982); children: Kimberly, Taylor, Christine. BA, U. Ky., 1984. Sec. City of Garden City, Garden City, Mich., 1958-62; sec. Ford Motor Co., Dearborn, Mich., 1962-67, Plymouth, Mich., 1970-71; sec. Whirlpool Corp., Danville, Ky., 1975-77; coun. field dir. Girl Scouts U.S.A., Miami, Fla., 1982-88, coun. adult devel. dir., 1988-94, dir. vol. svcs., 1994—; mem. faculty continuing edn. Fla. Internat. U., mem. alumni bd., 1989-95. Photograph exhibited by Photogroup of Miami, Inc., Coral Gables. Instr. Girl Scouts U.S. Miami, 1988—, hostess, coun. asst., co-dir. Girl Scouts Nat. Conv., Miami Beach, 1990; vol. first aid instr. ARC, Miami, 1989—; active Dirs. of Vols. in Agys., 1988—, exec. bd., 1994—, v.p., 1995—, tri-county conf. com. 1996, treas. 1994-95; bd. dirs. Waters Edge Assn., 1994-96, v.p., 1994-95, pres., 1995-96. Mem. Am. Assoc. of U. Women. Home: 100 Edgewater Dr Apt 310 Miami FL 33133-6939 Office: Girl Scout Coun Tropical 11347 SW 160th St Miami FL 33157-2703

SHELTON, CHARLES BASCOM, III, investment banker; b. Atlanta, Oct. 14, 1941; s. Charles Bascom Jr. and Elizabeth (Colley) S.; m. Deborah Jackson, July 3, 1965; children: Lara Elizabeth, Ashley Howell. BS, U. N.C., 1963; MBA, U. Pa., 1970. Assoc. McKinsey & Co., Cleve., 1970-74; asst. to treas. Aladdin Industries, Nashville, 1974-75, London, 1975-76, Nashville, 1976-77; mng. dir. Robinson-Humphrey Co., Atlanta, 1977—; bd. dirs. The Robinson/Humphrey Co., Northside Hosp, The Baylor Sch., 1992—. Lt. comdr. USN, 1963-70. Mem. Soc. Internat. Bus. Fellows, Piedmont Driving Club (Atlanta), Buckhead Club, East Lake Golf Club, Cullasaja Club, Golf Club of Ga., Beta Gamma Sigma. Republican. Episcopalian. Avocations: golf, hunting, travel. Home: 1766 W Paces Ferry Rd NW Atlanta GA 30327-2448 Office: The Robinson-Humphrey Co Inc 3333 Peachtree Rd NE Atlanta GA 30326-1070

SHELTON, GARY RICHARD, administrative law judge; b. Batesville, Ark., June 17, 1947; s. Glenn Ray and Polly Jean (Pankey) S.; m. Linda Kay Cook, 1972 (div. 1977); m. Angela Nolley Jones, Jan. 19, 1980. BA, Ark. Coll., 1970; JD, U. Ark., 1974. Bar: Ark. 1974. Law clk. to presiding justice Ark. Supreme Ct., Little Rock, 1974-75; exec. dir. Ark. Workers' Compensation Commn., Little Rock, 1975-76, adminstrv. law judge, 1976-87, chief adminstrv. law judge, 1987-95, also spl. commr., bd. dirs.; law judge, chief legal advisor Ark. Workers' Compensation Commn., 1991—; chief adminstrn. law judge, spl. counsel to the commn. Ark. Workers' Compensation Commn., Litte Rock, 1994-95; U.S. Adminstrv. Law Judge Office of Hearings & Appeals, Social Security Adminstrn., Little Rock, 1995—; lectr. in field; chmn. Gov.'s Task Force for Workers' Compensation Reform, 1994—; chair Gov.'s Task Force for ongoing rev. of Workers' Compensation System, 1994. Recipient Cert. of Recognition, Gov. of Ark., 1987, Nat. Jud. Coll., 1983, Certificate of Appreciation, Greater Little Rock Legal Sec.'s Assn., 1992. Mem. Ark. Bar Assn. (workers compensation sect., Cert. of Recognition 1990), So. Assn. Workers Compensation Adminstrs., Internat. Assn. Indsl. Bds. and Commns., Ark. Trial Lawyers (adv. mem. joint legislation ad hoc study com. Workers Compensation Reform 1992-93, mem. youth apprenticeship adv. com. 1992—, Cert. of Appreciation 1992), Phi Alpha Delta. Methodist. Home: 5 Wellington Ct Little Rock AR 72227-3848 Office: Office of Hearings/Appeals Social Security Adminstrn 700 W Capitol Little Rock AR 72201

SHELTON, JAMES KEITH, journalism educator; b. Altus, Okla., Oct. 28, 1932; s. Willis Oscar and Theodosia Agnes (Rupert) S.; m. Deborah Kennedy Evans, Dec. 26, 1953; children: Leslie Lynn, Lawrence Evans. BA, Midwestern State U., 1954; MA, U. North Tex., 1972. Reporter Lawton (Okla.) Constn., 1954; wire editor Wichita Falls (Tex.) Record-News, 1956-59; city hall reporter, polit. writer Dallas Times Herald, 1959-65; mng. editor, exec. editor Denton (Tex.) Record-Chronicle, 1965-69, 79-88; faculty mem., dir. pub. info. U. North Tex., Denton, 1969-79, journalist-in-residence, 1988—. Author: What Journalists Should Know About Business, 1993. Mem. Supreme Ct. Task Force on Jud. Ethics, Austin, 1992-94. with U.S. Army, 1954-56. Mem. Soc. Profl. Journalists, Freedom on Info. Found. of Tex., Inc. (sec., bd. dirs.). Democrat. Methodist. Home: 621 Grove St Denton TX 76201-7323 Office: Univ North Tex Box 5278 NT Denton TX 76203

SHELTON, JAMES LEE, bank executive, rancher; b. Vinita, Okla., Apr. 14, 1950; s. W.L. and Melbadene (Armstrong) S.; m. Sara Elizabeth Snedden, Oct. 25, 1976; children: Thomas Craig, Elizabeth Lee, William Michael, Mary Katherine. BS in Agr., Okla. State U., 1972; postgrad., So. Meth. U., 1985. Various to exec. v.p. Okla. State Bank, Vinita, 1974—. Pres. Vinita Pub. Schs. Bd. Edn., 1989—; mem. Okla. Long Range Capital Planning Commn., 1992—, Okla. Ag 2000 Commn., 1991. Mem. Okla. Bankers Assn., Okla. Agr. Leadership Alumni (bd. dirs. 1990—), Home of Hope, Inc. (bd. dirs. 1989—), Okla. Holistic Resource Mgmt., Vinita Community Found., In.c (vice chair 1992—), Lions (pres. Vinita Club 1984). Democrat. Presbyterian. Home: PO Box 494 Vinita OK 74301-0494 Office: Okla State Bank Vinita OK 74301

SHELTON, JAMMI M., municipal official; b. Frankfort, Fed. Republic of Germany, May 1, 1947; came to U.S., 1952; d. Fredrick George and Magda (von Tiermann) S. BA, U. Ky., 1969, MA, 1974, BS, 1977. Planning technician Dept. Long Range Planning, Lexington, Ky., 1977-80; environ. planner Dept. Planning/Zoning, Harrisburg, Pa., 1980-81; landscape supr. Am. Nurseries, Lexington, 1981-83; planning/zoning dir. Bourbon County Planning/Zoning, Paris, Ky., 1983-84; landscape supr. Lexington Country Club, 1984-85; planner II Beaufort (S.C.) County Joint Planning Commn., 1985-87; sr. landscape architect T.J. Scangarello Assocs., Medford, 1987; sr. planner III City of St. Petersburg, Fla., 1987—. Recipient grad. assistantship U. Ky., Lexington, 1972-74. Mem. Am. Planning Assn. Democrat. Office: St Petersburg Planning Dept Mcpl Svcs Ctr 1 4th St N Saint Petersburg FL 33701

SHELTON, MALCOLM WENDELL, biblical studies educator; b. Eckmansville, Ohio, Aug. 26, 1919; s. Charles Edward and Mary Ina (Suffron) S.; m. Muriel Payne Moore, Aug. 9, 1987. BS in Edn., Olivet Nazarene Coll., 1951, BTh, 1952; M in Religion, Pasadena Nazarene Coll., 1952; BD, Nazarene Theol. Sem., Kansas City, 1954, MDiv, 1972; MS in Edn., Cen. Mo. State U., 1965; D in Ministry, Philips U. Grad. Sem., 1977; postgrad., U. Kans., 1966-67, Hebrew U., Jerusalem, 1979, 81, Wheaton Coll., 1982. Prof. old testament So. Nazarene U., Bethany, Okla., 1967-85, Mid-Am. Bible Coll., Oklahoma City, 1985—; tchr. various pub. schs., Kansas City, Mo., 1954-65. Staff sgt. U.S. Army, 1941-45. Mem. Soc. Bibl. Lit., Am. Sch. Oriental Rsch., Brit. Sch. Archaeology, Wesleyan Theol. Soc., Evang. Theol. Soc., Am. Rsch. Ctr. in Egypt. Republican. Home: 6404 NW 35th St Bethany OK 73008-4136 Office: Mid-Am Bible Coll 3500 SW 119th St Oklahoma City OK 73170-4500

SHELTON, MURIEL MOORE, religious education administrator; b. Freeport, N.Y., May 29, 1921; d. Samuel Talbott and Agnes Jerolean (Trigg) Payne; m. Ernest William Moore, May 29, 1944 (dec. Apr. 2, 1978); children: Diana Moore Williams, David E. Moore, Cathi Moore Mount, Douglas L. Moore; m. Malcolm Wendell Shelton, Aug. 9, 1987. AB, Eastern Nazarene Coll., 1942; MusM, U. Tex., 1966. Cert. educator gen. and choral music, English, Tex., Tenn., Ark., Kans. Music dir. Coll. Ave. United Meth. Ch., Manhattan, Kans., 1969-71, Cen. United Meth. Ch., Lawrence, Kans., 1971-75, First United Meth. Ch., Horton, Kans., 1975-78; dir. Christian edn. St. Mark's United Meth. Ch., Bethany, Okla., 1980—; chmn. bd. dirs. Northwest Food Pantry, Oklahoma City, 1987-88; rep. St. mark's United Meth. Ch. Labor Link Ctr., 1989—; lectr. in field. Contbr. articles to quar. mags.; author: Song of Joy, 1985, Promises of Good, 1989, Healing in His Wings, 1992. Mem. Christian Educators' Fellowship. Home: 6404 NW 35th St Bethany OK 73008-4136 Office: St Mark's United Meth Ch 8140 NW 36th St Bethany OK 73008-3526

SHELTON, PATRICIA ANN ATNIP, elementary education educator; b. Taunton, Mass., Aug. 23, 1943; d. James Edward and Geneva Winnie Atnip; m. Joe Howard Shelton, Nov. 17, 1962; children: Gary Don, Jeffrey Lyn. BS, Tex. Woman's U., 1965, MEd, 1972, postgrad., 1976—; postgrad., U. North Tex., Denton, 1976—. Cert. elem. tchr., music tchr., high sch. English and reading tchr, Tex.; cert. in mid-mgmt., cert. in learning resources endorsement, Tex. Tchr. music Grapevine (Tex.) Ind. Sch. Dist., 1965-67; tchr. reading and history Lake Dallas (Tex.) Ind. Sch. Dist., 1968; elem. tchr. Keller (Tex.) Ind. Sch. Dist., 1969-73, Sanger (Tex.) Ind. Sch. Dist., 1973—. Mem. NEA, ASCD, Nat. Mid. Sch. Assn. (sec. 1982—), Phi Delta Kappa, Delta Kappa Gamma. Baptist. Home: 138 Terrace Rd Sanger TX 76266-9300 Office: Sanger Mid Sch 7th And Peach Sanger TX 76266-9300

SHELTON, PATRICIA COOK, staff development specialist; b. Marion, Ohio, Nov. 5, 1946; d. Lowell Donald and Betty Jane (Key) Cook; m. C. Kelly Shelton, June 29, 1969 (div. Sept. 1988); children: Christopher Kelly, Elizabeth Anne. BS in Edn., Ohio State U., 1968; MS in Reading Edn., Bowling Green (Ohio) State U., 1980; EdS in Adminstrn. and Supervision, U. Ctrl. Fla., 1986, EdD in Edn. Leadership, 1991. Cert. tchr. K-12, Fla. Tchr. Pleasant Local Schs., Marion, Ohio, 1969-79, Coral Springs (Fla.) Mid. Sch., 1979-80, St. Andrews Cath. Sch., Coral Springs, 1980-81, Coral Springs Christian Sch., 1981-82; reading specialist, tchr. Palm Bay H.S., Melbourne, Fla., 1982-86; staff devel. specialist Brevard County Schs., Melbourne, Fla., 1986—; adj. instr. Fla. Inst. of Tech., Melbourne, 1994—, Rollins Coll., Melbourne, 1994—; adj. prof. Nova Southwestern U., Ft. Lauderdale, Fla., 1991-96; sch. improvement cons. Gadsden County Schs., Havana, Fla., 1995-96, Okaloosa County Schs., 1995-96, Sumter County Schs., Wildwood, Fla., 1993-95; instr. Tchr. Edn. Inst., Winter Park, Fla., 1993—. Editor (with others) Teacher Education Centers-The Greatest Show on Earth, 1988; developer (with others) System-Oriented, School-Aimed Model for Staff Development, 1994. Mem. ASCD, Nat. Staff Devel. Coun., Fla. Reading Assn., Delta Kappa Gamma (parliamentarian 1989-96, scholarship 1991), Phi Delta Kappa, Kappa Delta Pi, Phi Kappa Phi. Republican. Episcopalian. Home: 550 Norwood Ct Satellite Beach FL 32937 Office: Brevard County Schs 2700 Judge Fran Jamieson Way Viera FL 32940

SHELTON, ROBERT WARREN, marketing executive; b. Albuquerque, Apr. 26, 1943; s. Eugene and Rusty M. (Jentsch) S.; children: Elise Straus, Samantha; m. Ginger Lee Rapp, Feb. 14, 1984. BBA in Mktg., St. Mary's U., San Antonio, 1969; postgrad., Ga. State U., 1972-73, postgrad. in fin. and internat. bus., 1973. Field mgr. Ford Motor Co., Atlanta, 1969-78; dir. fleet ops. Rollins, Inc., Atlanta, 1978-81; v.p. sales and ops. Lease Plan U.S.A., Atlanta, 1981-85; v.p. mktg. Spencer Services, Inc., Roswell, Ga., 1985-87; v.p. FX-10 Corp., 1987-88; pres. Shiloh Capital Corp., 1989—; pres. Victory Svcs., Inc., 1998—, Shiloh Capital Corp., 1989, Interactive Telenet USA, Inc., 1994, The Phone Co., Inc., 1993. Mem. Lost Forest Civic Assn. (pres. 1980-81). Mem. Nat. Assn. Fleet Adminstrs., Am. Fleet and Leasing Assn., NRA. Republican. Christian. Office: 1201 Peachtree St NE Atlanta GA 30361-3500

SHELTON, RONALD ALPHONSO, librarian, archivist; b. Richmond, Va., Oct. 6, 1953; s. Gary Gilbert and Ethel Elizabeth (Wright) Chapman. BA in History, Va. State U., 1977; MSLS, Atlanta U., 1978; MDiv, Va. Union U., 1985. Sales counselor Best Products Co., Richmond, 1978, 80—; tchr.'s aide Richmond Pub. Schs., 1979; children's libr. Richmond Pub. Libr., 1979-80; pub. svc. libr., archivist Va. Union U., Richmond, 1985—. Mem. Crusade for Voters, Richmond, 1994—, Bapt. Gen. Conv. Va., 1985—; deacon Sharon Bapt. Ch., Richmond. Recipient Martin Luther King Day award Sharon Bapt. Ch., Richmond, 1995. Mem. Va. Libr. Assn. (ethnic libr. forum 1987), Archival Roundtable Forum, Alpha Phi Alpha. Democrat. Home: 1000 N 26th St Richmond VA 23223 Office: Va Union U 1500 N Lombardy St Richmond VA 23220

SHEMESH, GARETH ELI, physiatrist, critical care physician; b. Mpls., June 4, 1958; s. Alvin and Rita (Fortin) S. BA in German and Natural Sci., St. John's U., 1979; MS in Biology, Loyola U., Chgo., 1981; MD, St. George's U., 1985. Diplomate Am. Bd. Internal Medicine, Am. Bd. Phys. Medicine and Rehab.; cert. ACLS. Intern in internal medicine Muhlenberg Regional Med. Ctr., Plainfield, N.J., 1986-87; resident in internal medicine, 1986-89; resident in phys. medicine and rehab. Jewish Hosp.-Washington U., St. Louis, 1989-92; med. technician Knollwood Clinic, Mpls., 1973-75; ind. med. examiner Vis. Physicians, Inc., Madison, N.J., 1975-78, Portamedics, Inc., East Brunswick, N.J., 1975-76; sci. writer Nutra-Dyn Corp., Dana Point, Calif., 1983; house physician Neuman Med. Ctr., Phila., 1988-89, Meth. Hosp., Phila., 1988-89; critical care physician St. Joseph Health Ctr., St. Charles, Mo., 1990—, De Paul Health Ctr., Bridgeton, Mo., 1991-92; pvt. practice as physiatrist Peninsula Med. Assocs., Bradenton, Fla., 1992-95; pvt. practice physiatrist with Yechiel Kleen, MD Denver, 1995—; dir. rehab. Greenbriar Nursing Ctr., Bradenton, 1994-95. Grad. fellow Loyola U., 1979-81. Fellow Am. Acad. Phys. Medicine and Rehab.; mem. AMA (Physician's Recognition award 1989), ACP (assoc.), Am. Acad. Electrodiagnostic Medicine (assoc.), Am. Soc. Regional Anesthesia, Am. Acad. Pain Mgmt. (diplomate). Office: 55 Madison St Ste 235 Denver CO 80206-5420

SHEMWELL, MARY ANNE, physical education educator; b. Shreveport, La., Mar. 16, 1942; d. James Dee Jr. and Frances (Oden) Youngblood; divorced; children: Dee Wade, Charles James. BS, Centenary Coll., 1965; postgrad., La. Poly. Inst. Phys. edn. tchr. Midway Jr. High Sch., Shreveport, 1965-69; adapted phys. edn. specialist Caddo Parish Pub. Schs., 1982—; phys. edn. tchr. for track and field events for physically handicapped State of La. Mem. Rep. Women's Orgn., 1989—; coach United Cerebral Palsy of La.; treas. Rep. Profl. Women's Club, 1993-94. Named G.U.M.B.O. coach of Yr. State of La., 1994. Mem. Coun. Exceptional Children (membership chmn. 1990-91, recipient Outstanding Educator award 1987), La. Assn. Health, Phys. Edn. and Recreation, La. Fedn. Tchrs., Jr. League of Shreveport, Cotillion Club, Plantation Club. Republican. Methodist. Home: 4431 Fern Ave Shreveport LA 71105-3103

SHENEFELT, PHILIP DAVID, dermatologist; b. Colfax, Wash., July 31, 1943; s. Roy David and Florence Vanita (Cagle) S.; m. Debrah Ann Levenson; children: Elizabeth, Sara, Shaina. BS with honors, U. Wis.-Madison, 1966, MD, 1970, MS in Adminstrv. Medicine, 1984. Intern U.S. Naval Hosp., Bethesda, Md., 1970-71; general practice Oregon (Wis.) Clinic, 1975; resident in dermatology U. Wis. Hosp., Madison, 1975-78, staff, 1978-87; asst. prof. dermatology sect. Dept. Internal Medicine U. South Fla., 1987—; chief dermatology sect. VA Hosp., Bay Pines, Fla., 1987-89, asst. chief, Tampa, 1988—; dermatologist Univ. Health Svc., U. Wis.-Madison, 1978-87, VA Hosp., Madison, 1982-85. Served to lt. comdr. USN, 1969-74; capt. USNR (ret.). Kellogg fellow, 1980-82. Mem. AMA, Am. Acad. Dermatology, Fla. Dermatol. Soc., Fla. West Coast Dermatol. Soc., Am. Coll. Physician Execs. Episcopalian. Home: 15919 Notting Hill Dr Lutz FL 33549-6147 Office: U South Fla Internal Medicine / Dermatology 12901 Bruce B Downs Blvd # 19 Tampa FL 33612-4742

SHENEFIELD, JOHN HALE, lawyer; b. Toledo, Jan. 23, 1939; s. Hale Thurel and Norma (Bird) S.; m. Judy Simmons, June 16, 1984; children: Stephen Hale, Christopher Newcomb. AB, Harvard U., 1960, LLB, 1965. Bar: Va. 1966, D.C. 1966. Assoc. Hunton & Williams, Richmond, Va., 1965-77; dep. asst. atty. gen. antitrust div. Dept. Justice, Washington, 1977; asst. atty. gen. Dept. Justice, 1977-79, assoc. atty. gen., 1979-81; assoc. Milbank, Tweed, Hadley & McCloy, 1981-86, Morgan, Lewis & Bockius, Washington, 1986—; assoc. prof. law U. Richmond, 1975; prof. law Georgetown Law Ctr., 1981-83; chmn. Nat. Commn. for Rev. Antitrust Law and Procedures, 1978-79. Co-author The Antitrust Laws - A Primer, 2d edit., 1996; contbr. articles on law to profl. jours. Sec. Va. Dem. Com., 1970-72, treas., 1976-77; chmn. Richmond Dem. Party, 1975-77; bd. govs. St. Albans Sch., 1983-90, chmn. 1988-90; mem. chpt. Washington Cathedral, 1988—; pres. Nat. Cathedral Assn., 1993-96; chmn. Va. Racing Commn., 1989—. 2d lt. U.S. Army, 1961-62; to capt. Res., 1965. Mem. ABA, Va. Bar Assn. Home: 220 Carrwood Rd Great Falls VA 22066-3721 Office: Morgan Lewis & Bockius 1800 M St NW Ste 6 Washington DC 20036-5802

SHEPARD, JANIE RAY (J. R. SHEPARD), software development executive; b. Montebello, Calif., Feb. 23, 1954; d. George Allen and Ada Janette (Barrow) Ray; 1 child, April Lynn. Grad. high sch., Albany, Ga., 1972. Adminstrv. asst. to pres. FRC Office Products, Jacksonville, Fla., 1979-82; adminstrv. asst. to v.p. comml. lending Stockton Savs., Dallas, 1983-84; exec. sec. to v.p. ops. Metromedia Long Distance, Ft. Lauderdale, Fla., 1985-87; owner, pres. RaceCom, Inc., Ormond Beach, Fla., 1986—, ALAdvt., Ormond Beach, 1986—. Developer computer text file editing system and computer artificial intelligence; developer optical character recognition neural network software. Active Jacksonville and Dallas areas Girl Scouts U.S., 1980-96, Citrus Coun., 1996—; vol. co-chair Jazz Matazz, 1992-94, adv. coord., 1995, 96; chair Home for the Holidays Parade, City of Ormond Beach, 1995, 96. Mem. Ormond Beach C. of C. Democrat. Methodist. Home: 10 Cypress View Trl Ormond Beach FL 32174-8295 Office: RaceCom Inc PO Box 730955 Ormond Beach FL 32173

SHEPARD, RAYMOND GUY, purchasing executive; b. Chicago Heights, Ill., June 10, 1942; s. Ewing Hugh and Anna (Luden) S.; m. Barbara Ellen Shepard, July 13, 1948; children: Gregory, Lauren. Student, So. Ill. U., 1964-68. Cost acct. Midland Screw, Chgo., 1968-71; purchasing agt. Harris Hub Co., Harvey, Ill., 1971-79; dir. purchasing Marvel Metal Co., Chgo., 1979-81; ptnr. Ather-Shepard Software Co., Columbus, Miss., 1986-88; divisional purchasing mgr. Ceco Bldgs. Divsn., Columbus, 1981-87; purchasing dir. Troxel Co., Moscow, Tenn., 1988—; del. mem. to Russia UN Indsl. Devel. Assn., N.Y.C., 1989, China The Citizen Amb. Program, Spokane, Wash., 1994. Author: (computer software) Real Estate Automation, 1990, Sales Automation, 1992. Tchr. Jr. Achievement, Moscow, 1990-91; bd. mem. ticket and seating Columbus Concert Assn., 1981-83, treas., 1983-86, v.p. membership drive, 1986-88; mem. pres. coun. So. Ill. U. Found., 1993-94. Recipient Humanitarian Svc. award Markham (Ill.) Sheltered Workshop, 1973, Community Svc. award Columbus Concert Assn., 1988, Capt. of Industry award Collierville (Tenn.) C. of C., 1989. Mem. Kiwanis (activities chmn. 1984-88), Civitan (activities chmn. 1981-84). Home: 1210 Cotton Hill Ln Collierville TN 38017-3238

SHEPARD, WILLIAM STEVE, JR., acoustics consultant; b. Columbus, Ind., Feb. 25, 1967; s. W. Steve and Betty J. (kelsey) S.; m. Naomi Alford, Aug. 14, 1966; 1 child, Julia. BSME, Ga. Inst. of Tech., 1989, MSME, 1993, postgrad. in mech. engring., 1993—. Audio salesman Ideal Acoustics, Starkville, Miss., 1983-87; test engr. Gen. Dynamics, Fort Worth, Tex., 1989-91; design engr. Ga. Tech., Atlanta, 1991; acoustical cons. Atlanta, 1995. Contbr. articles to profl. jours. Mem. ASME, Acoustical Soc. of Am., Tau Beta Pi. Baptist. Home: 3074 E Spring Hill Rd Smyrna GA 30080 Office: Ga Inst of Tech North Ave PC 0405 Atlanta GA 30332

SHEPARD TOWLES, STACEY ANN, legislative affairs administrator; b. Monterey, Calif., Aug. 23, 1969; d. Arthur Bishop Shepard and Sharon Kaye (Fitch) Iwanski; m. Thomas Berrigan Towles, May 25, 1996. BS, Ariz. State U., 1991; MA, Georgetown U., 1995. Intern U.S. Senate-Sen. John McCain, 1989, 91; exec. asst. U.S. Senate-Sen. Steve Symms, Washington, 1991; dep. press sec., 1992; legis. asst. AAI Corp. Washington Office, Arlington, Va., 1992-95, program devel. specialist, 1995; mgr. legis. affairs, 1996—. Mem. Women in Govt. Rels., Nat. Security Indsl. Assn., Am. Def. Preparedness Assn., Am. League of Lobbyists, Am. Pub. Transit Assn. (assoc.), Ariz. State U. Alumni (D.C. chpt.), St. Catherine's Soc., Delta Delta Delta (alumna Washington chpt.). Home: 9 Carriage House Cir Alexandria VA 22304

SHEPHARD, BRUCE DENNIS, obstetrician, educator, medical writer; b. San Francisco, Apr. 21, 1944; s. Richard G. and Madelyn (Rogers) S.; m. Carroll Anne Swanson; children: Christopher, Carleton, Elizabeth. BA in History, U. Calif., Berkeley, 1966; MD, U. Calif., San Francisco, 1970. Diplomate Am. Bd. Obstetrics and Gynecology. Intern Jackson Meml. Hosp.-U. Miami (Fla.), 1970-71, resident in ob-gyn., 1971-74; obstetrician Tampa (Fla.) Ob-Gyn Assocs., 1976-94; clin. assoc. prof. obstetrics U. So. Fla. Sch. Medicine, Tampa, 1976—; bd. dirs. Ctr. of Excellence, 1983-90, Humana Women's Hosp., Tampa, Fla., 1983-90, Gulf Coast Health Systems Agy., 1980-83; mem. midwifery adv. com. Fla. Dept. Health and Human Resources, Tallahassee, 1982-86. Author: (with Carroll Shephard) The Complete Guide to Women's Health, 1982; prin., writer, spokesperson (series of TV commls.) The Healthy Woman (Gold Link award 1987); mem. med. adv. bd. Baby Talk mag., 1995—; contbr. articles to profl. jours. and women's mags. Served as maj. USAF, 1974-76. Mem. AMA, Am. Coll. Obstetricians and Gynecologists (patient edn. com. 1984-86, John McCain fellow 1981), Am. Med. Writers Assn., Acad. Radio and TV Health Communicators, Phi Beta Kappa. Democrat. Lutheran. Home: 4201 Carrollwood Village Dr Tampa FL 33624-4609 Office: 4302 N Habana Ave Ste 300 Tampa FL 33607-6316

SHEPHARD, CHARLES CLINTON, real estate executive; b. Westport, Conn., May 25, 1929; s. J. Clinton and Gail Fleming (English) S.; m. June Stalls, June 19, 1956; children: Gail Paige, Susan Arlen, Richard Clinton. B in Landscape Arch., U. Fla., 1954, M in City Planning, 1956. Lic. real estate broker; registered landscape architect. Pres. Kendree and Shepherd, Phila., 1958-72; regional pres. Robino-Ladd Co., Palm Beach, Fla., 1972-75; v.p. Hovnanian Co., Lake Worth, Fla., 1975-78; pres. Gamina Co., Lake Worth, 1978-92, Charles Shepherd, Ent., Palm Beach, 1992—; chmn. Whitpain Planning Commn., Blue Bell, Pa., 1967-72; mem. land use adv. bd. Palm Beach County, 1989-91. Contbr. articles to profl. jours. Mem. Palm Beach County Task Force, 1984, Downtown Devel. Authority, Lake Worth, 1985-88, chmn., 1988. 1st lt. arty. U.S. Army, 1952-54. Mem. Am. Soc. Planners, Home Builders Assn. Home: 216 Monterey Rd Palm Beach FL 33480-3228

SHEPHERD, DONALD RAY, pathologist; b. Pampa, Tex., Sept. 7, 1935; s. Ray Browden and Lillie Lorene (Moore) S.; BS cum laude, Austin Coll., 1958; MD, U. Tex., Dallas, 1962; m. Elizabeth Day Poole, June 6, 1958; children: Lisa, Stephanie, Leslie, Don Poole. Intern, Univ. Hosp., Little Rock, 1962-63; gen. practice medicine, Bay City, Tex., 1965-66; resident in pathology Hermann Hosp., Houston, 1966-68, Baylor U. Med. Center, Dallas, 1968-70; asst. pathologist Harris Hosp., Ft. Worth, 1970-71; chief pathology, dir. labs. Leggett Meml. Hosp. (name now Cleve. Reg. Med. Ctr.), Cleveland, Tex., 1982—, chief of staff, 1989-92; pathologist, pres. Donald R. Shepherd M.D., P.A., Conroe, 1973—; pres. Profl. Labs., Inc., Houston, 1973-82. Bd. dirs. Am. Cancer Soc. Served as capt. M.C., U.S. Army, 1963-65. Decorated Army Commendation medal; diplomate Am. Bd. Pathology; Am. Cancer Soc. grantee, 1970-71. Fellow Coll. Am. Pathologists, Am. Soc. Clin. Pathologists; mem. Tex. Soc. Pathologists (del.), Tex. Med. Assn., Montgomery County Med. Soc., Phi Chi. Republican. Presbyterian. Home: 2007 Timber Ln Conroe TX 77301 Office: 704 Longmire Rd Conroe TX 77304-1850

SHEPHERD, ELIZABETH POOLE, health science facility administrator; b. Bulape, Kasai, Zaire, Mar. 16, 1937; (parents Am. citizens); d. Mark Keller and Sara Amelia (Day) Poole; m. Donald Ray Shepherd, June 6, 1958; children: Lisa, Stephanie, Leslie, Don Poole. BA magna cum laude, Austin Coll., 1958. Cert. secondary and elem. tchr., Tex. Tchr. Thomas Jefferson High Sch., Dallas, 1958, Edward H. Cary Jr. High Sch., Dallas, 1959-60; bus. mgr. Donald R. Shepherd, M.D., P.A., Conroe, Tex., 1972—; bus. mgr., co-owner Profl. Labs, Inc., Houston, 1975-82. Brownie leader Girl Scouts Am., 1967-69; dist. chmn. San Jacinto council Boy Scouts Am., Conroe, 1977; pres. Women of Ch. First Presbyn. Ch., Conroe, 1973-74, Montgomery County Med. Soc., Conroe, 1974-75; bd. dirs. ARC, Conroe, 1970-80; bd. dirs., officer Med. Ctr. Hosp. Vols., Conroe, 1978-81. Mem. AAUW, Alpha Chi, Alpha Delta. Republican. Presbyn. Home: 2007 Timber Lane Conroe TX 77301

SHEPHERD, ROBERT EDWIN, public administrator; b. Deep Gap, N.C., Sept. 29, 1940; s. Charles Thomas and Mary Pearl (McNeill) S.; m. Brenda Frances Lawrence; children: Robert Edwin, Eric Lawrence. BS, N.C. State U., Raleigh, 1962; MS, Kans. State U., Manhattan, 1964. Economist USDA, Washington, 1963-64, agrl. economist, 1966-69; dir. devel. planning and rsch. Econ. Devel. Coun. N.E. Pa., Wilkes-Barre, 1969-73; exec. dir. Land-of-Sky Regional Coun., Asheville, N.C., 1973—; outside dir. Clyde Savs. Bank, Asheville; chmn. Alliance of Bus. Leaders and Educators, Cullowhee, N.C., 1993—; pres. Devel. Dist. of Appalachia, Washington, 1982-83; chmn. N.C. Regional Coun. Dirs. Assn., Raleigh, 1980. Pres. We. N.C. Assoc. Communities, Cullowhee; v.p., bd. dirs. Givens Estates United Meth. Retirement Community, Asheville, 1991. Served to 1st lt., intelligence U.S. Army, 1964-66. Recipient Fed. Co-chmn.'s award Appalachian Regional Commn., 1991. Methodist. Home: 923 Sand Hill Rd Asheville NC 28806-1018 Office: Land-of-Sky Regional Coun 25 Heritage Dr Asheville NC 28806-1914

SHEPHERD, ROBERT PATRICK, lawyer; b. Clarksburg, W.Va., June 2, 1955; s. Richard Lee and Patricia Ann (McConlogue) S.; m. Susan Lynn Kuebler, Mar. 31, 1984; children: Patrick Ryan, Sara Caitlin, Emily Anne. BBA, U. Notre Dame, 1977; JD, DePaul U., 1980. Bar: Ill. 1980, U.S. Dist. Ct. (no. dist.) Ill. 1980, Tenn. 1984, U.S. Dist. Ct. (mid. dist.) Tenn. 1988. Asst. gen. counsel Heinold Commodities, Inc., Chgo., 1980-83; gen. counsel, ptnr. J.C. Bradford & Co., Nashville, 1987—; mem. compliance adv. com. N.Y. Stock Exch., 1987-94, arbitrator; panelist Commodities Law Inst., 1982-84, N.Y. Inst. Fin., 1989, law and compliance Securities Industry Assn., 1990, 91; mem. compliance and legal divsn. exec. com. SEC, 1996—; arbitrator Nat. Assn. Securities Dealers; mem. Futures Commn. Mcht. Adv. Com. Nat. Futures Assn. Active Nashville's Table, 1987—, United Way Mid. Tenn.; mem. Cathedral of the Incarnation Parish. Mem. Am. Corp. Counsel Assn., Nat. Futures Assn. (ctrl. region bus. conduct com. 1986-89), Nashville Bar Assn., Notre Dame Alumni Assn. Greater Nashville, Richland Country Club. Home: 5913 Robert E Lee Dr Nashville TN 37215-5236 Office: JC Bradford & Co 330 Commerce St Nashville TN 37201-1805

SHEPHERD, SAMUEL CLAUDE, JR., history educator; b. Alexandria, Va., June 30, 1948; s. Samuel Claude and Violet Dawn (Hampton) S.; m. Julienne Louise Wood, Sept. 2, 1978. BA, U. Del., 1970; MA, U. Wis., 1972, PhD, 1980. Asst. prof. Centenary Coll., Shreveport, La., 1980-86, assoc. prof., chmn. dept. history and polit. sci., 1986-92, prof. history, 1992—; grants panelist NEH, 1987-90, 92-95, La. Endowment for the Humanities, 1990-93; summer faculty U. Richmond, Va., 1974, 75. Contbr. articles to profl. jours. Sec. ch. coun. First Luth. Ch., Shreveport, 1985-86, v.p., 1986-89; mem. Mayor's Com. on Bicentennials, Shreveport, 1987-92, Cmty. Found. of Shreveport-Bossier, 1989—. Mellon Summer Faculty fellow, 1984, Centenary Alumni Faculty Rsch. fellow, 1988, NEH Summer Seminar fellow, 1992; La. Endowment for Humanities Libr. Reading Program scholar, 1991-92. Mem. Orgn. Am. Historians (life), So. Hist. Assn. (life, membership com. 1992), La. Hist. Assn. (life, bd. dirs. 1994—), North La. Hist. Assn. (bd. dirs. 1986—, pres. 1993-95), Va. Hist. Soc., Phi Alpha Theta (Alpha Alpha Omega chpt. advisor). Office: Centenary College Dept of History 2911 Centenary Blvd Shreveport LA 71134

SHEPHERD, STEVEN STEWART, auditor, consultant; b. Pauls Valley, Okla., Aug. 7, 1956; s. Lloyd Thomas and Barbara Lou (Garton) S.; m. Dawn Rachelle Godwin, Aug. 22, 1981; children: Shane, Lauren. BBA, U. Tex., 1981, MBA, 1990. Internal auditor Ark-La Gas Co., Shreveport, La., 1982-84; sr. constrn. auditor Cen. & S.W. Svcs., Inc., Dallas, 1984-87; constrn. audit supr. City of Ft. Worth, 1987—; cons. Constrn. Mgmt. Svcs.,

Arlington, Tex., 1990—, Eagle Tax Svcs., Arlington, 1990—; mem. adv. com. for acctg. program Tarrant County Jr. Coll., 1995-97; mem. internal audit adv. bd. U. North Tex., 1993-96. Contbr. articles to profl. jours. Mem. allocation com. Tarrant County United Way, Ft. Worth, 1991; bd. dirs. Charlotte Anderson Elem. Sch. PTA, Mansfield, Tex., 1990-91. Mem. Inst. Internal Auditors (bd. govs. Ft. Worth chpt. 1990—, sec. 1990-91, treas. 1991-92, v.p. 1992-93, pres. 1993-94), Mansfield Youth Baseball Assn. (bd. dirs. 1993-95), Delta Upsilon (bd. dirs. 1991-96, sec. 1994-95). Republican. Mem. Ch. of Christ.

SHEPPARD, DEBORAH CODY, hearing handicapped educator, clinician; b. Atlanta, Aug. 4, 1959; d. Jack Benar and Wilma (Shoffner) Cody; m. Kenneth Louis Sheppard, Nov. 14, 1987. BA in Speech Correction, Columbia (S.C.) Coll., 1981; MS in Edn. of Hearing Handicapped, U. Tenn., 1983; EdS in Spl. Edn. and Early Childhood, U. S.C., 1991. Cert. speech pathologist, S.C., cert. early childhood edn. tchr., cert. in hearing handicapped, S.C. Speech/lang. clinician Dist. 60 of Abbeville, S.C., 1981-82, Dist. of Pickens (S.C.) County, 1984-85; tchr. hearing handicapped Dist. 50 of Greenwood, S.C., 1985-88; speech/lang. clinician Saluda (S.C.) Dist. 1, 1989-91; tchr. hearing impaired Millbrook Elem. Sch., Aiken, S.C., 1991—; tchr. Am. sign lang. Saluda Dist. 1, 1989-91, 91—. Recipient grants, 1993-94, 94-95, 95-96. Mem. Coun. for Exceptional Children, S.C. Speech/Lang./Hearing Assn., Upper Savannah Speech/Lang. Consortium. Baptist. Home: 301 Chime Bell Church Rd Aiken SC 29803-9365 Office: Millbrook Elem Sch Aiken SC 29803

SHEPPARD, KATHRYN ANNE, pediatrics nurse, educator; b. Mobile, Ala., June 17, 1957; d. Lee and Jeanette (O'Gwynn) Jackson; m. Byron Edward Sheppard, Aug. 16, 1975; children: Jennifer, Jenelle. Student, U. South Ala., 1975-83; BSN, Mobile Coll., 1985; MS in Nursing, U. South Ala., 1985. Cert. CPR, med.-surg. nurse. Staff nurse Mobile Infirmary Med. Ctr., 1988-95; instr. nursing U. Mobile, 1987—. Sunday sch. tchr. Woodridge Bapt. Ch., Mobile. Mem. ANA, Sigma Theta Tau.

SHEPPARD, LOUIS CLARKE, biomedical engineering educator; b. Pine Bluff, Ark., May 28, 1933; s. Ellis Allen and Louise (Clarke) S.; m. Nancy Louise Mayer, Feb. 8, 1958; children: David, Susan, Lisa. BS in Chem. Engring., U. Ark., 1957; PhD in Elec. Engring., U. London, 1976. Registered profl. engr., Ala., Tex. Devel. staff supr. Diamond Alkali Co., Deer Park, Tex., 1957-63; staff engr. IBM, Rochester, Minn., 1963-66; assoc. prof. surgery dept. U. Ala.-Birmingham, 1966-88, sr. scientist Cystic Fibrosis Research Ctr., 1981-87, prof., chmn. biomed. engring. dept., 1979-88; prof. phsiology and biophysics, asst. v.p. rsch. U. Tex., Galveston, 1988-90, assoc. v.p. rsch., 1990-92, assoc. v.p. bioengring. and biotech., 1992—, prof. biomed. engring., Austin; adj. prof. elec. engring. U. Houston; mem. med. adv. bd. Hewlett Packard, 1980-84; cons. IMED Corp., 1982-83, Oximetrix, 1982, 86-88, MiniMed, 1986-88; mem. sci. adv. bd. JJMI, 1992-94; dir. FBK Internat.; pres. S.E.A. Corp., 1984-94; mem. editorial bd. Med. Progress Through Tech., 1984-94, Springer-Verlag, Berlin; cons. Nat. Heart, Lung and Blood Inst. Bd. dirs. Birmingham Met. Devel. Bd. Served with AUS, 1958-66. Recipient Ayerton Premium award IEE (U.K.), 1984. Recipient Disting. Alumnus citation, U. Ark., 1987, Lifetime Achievement award M.D. Buyline, 1987. Fellow IEEE, Am. Inst. for Med. and Biol. Engring., Am. Coll. Med. Informatics; mem. Brit. Computer Soc., Biomed. Engring. Soc. (dir.), IEEE, Am. Inst. Chem. Engrs., Am. Med. Informatics Assn., Univ. Space Rsch. Assn. (bd. dirs. 1995—), Acad. Med. Arts and Scis., Blue Key, Sigma Xi, Tau Beta Pi, Alpha Pi Mu, Eta Kappa Nu, Theta Tau. Clubs: St. Andrews Soc. of Middle South, The Houstonian, The Yacht. Contbr. abstracts, chpts. to books, editorials; patentee method and system for estimation of arterial pressure. Home: 5 E Broad Oaks Ln Houston TX 77056-1218 Office: U Tex Med Br 626 Jennie Sealy Hosp Galveston TX 77555-0455

SHEPPE, JOSEPH ANDREW, surgeon; b. Huntington, W.Va., Sept. 24, 1953; m. Kathy Chapman; children: Sheree Nicole, Natalee Marie, Brittany Lee. BS summa cum laude in Chemistry and Zoology, Marshall U., 1975; MD, W.Va. U., 1979. Diplomate Am. Bd. Surgery, Am. Bd. Colon and Rectal Surgery. Intern in gen. surgery Charleston (W.Va.) Area Med. Ctr., 1979-84; fellow in colon and rectal surgery William Beaumont Army Med. Ctr., Royal Oak, Mich., 1984-85; pvt. practice Columbia, S.C., 1985—; physician Bapt. Med. Ctr., Columbia, Providence Hosp., Columbia, Richland Meml. Hosp., Columbia, Lexington Med. Ctr., West Columbia, S.C.; clin. instr. in gen./colorectal surgery U. S.C. Med. Sch. Mem. ACS, Am. Soc. Colon and Rectal Surgery, S.C. Med. Soc., Columbia Med. Soc. Home: 204 Leaning Tree Rd Columbia SC 29223-3009 Office: 1333 Taylor St Ste 4-a Columbia SC 29201-2923

SHER, LEOPOLD ZANGWILL, lawyer; b. New Orleans, May 1, 1953; s. Joseph and Rachel (Israelowiec) S.; m. Karen Baumgarten, June 7, 1975; children: Rose Sarah, Samantha Jill. BA, Tulane U., 1974, JD, 1976. Bar: La., U.S. Dist. Ct. (ea. dist.) La., U.S. Ct. Appeals (5th cir.), U.S. Supreme Ct. Dir. McGlinchey Stafford Lang, New Orleans, 1976—. Mem. Leman-Stern Young Leadership Tng., New Orleans, 1980, Met. Area Com. Young Leadership Tng./Leadership Forum, New Orleans, 1982; chmn. Preservation Action Tax Task Force, La., 1985-86. Mem. ABA (chmn. real estate fin. subcom. of comml. fin. svcs. com. of bus. law sect., mem. supervisory coun. Group H, real property sect.), Anglo-Am. Real Property Inst., Am. Coll. Comml. Fin. Lawyer, Am. Land Title Assn. (lenders counsel group), Am. Coll. Real Estate Lawyers (chmn. title ins. com.), La. Bar Assn. Democrat. Jewish. Home: 5500 Marcia Ave New Orleans LA 70124-1055 Office: McGlinchey Stafford Lang 643 Magazine St New Orleans LA 70130-3405

SHERIDAN, ANDREW JAMES, III, ophthalmologist; b. Washington, Aug. 19, 1944; s. Andrew J. and Mildred (Stohlman) S.; m. Carol Dinkelacker, Oct. 23, 1971; children: Elizabeth, Margaret. AB, Villanova U., 1966; MD, Georgetown U., 1970. Diplomate Am. Bd. Ophthalmology. Intern Nassau County Med. Ctr., N.Y., 1970-71, resident in ophthalmology, 1973-76; practice medicine specializing in ophthalmology Eye Assocs., Arlington, Va., 1976—; chief of ophthalmology Arlington Hosp., 1980-84, 90-95; clin. instr. ophthalmology Georgetown U., 1982—. Bd. dirs. Va. Med. Polit. Action Com., 1985-89, Polit. Action Com. for Ophthalmology in Va., 1985—, chmn, 1991-94. Lt. comdr. USPHS, 1971-73; pres. Georgetown Clin. Soc., 1987-88. Fellow ACS, Am. Acad. Ophthalmology; mem. AMA, Med. Soc. Va., Arlington County Med. Soc. (exec. bd., sec. 1994, v.p. 1995, pres.-elect 1996, pres. 1997), No. Va. Acad. Ophthalmology (v.p. 1988-90, pres. 1990-92, bd. dirs.), Brent Soc. Republican. Roman Catholic. Office: Eye Assocs 1715 N George Mason Dr Ste 206 Arlington VA 22205-3609

SHERIDAN, DIANE FRANCES, public policy facilitator; b. Wilmington, Del., Mar. 12, 1945; d. Robert Kooch and Eileen Elizabeth (Forrest) Bupp; m. Mark MacDonald Sheridan III, Dec. 7, 1968; 1 child, Elizabeth Anne. BA in English, U. Del., 1967. Tchr. English Newark (Del.) Sch. Dist., 1967-68, Lumberton (Tex.) Ind. Sch. Dist., 1969-71, Crown Point (Ind.) Sch. Dist., 1972-75; sr. assoc. The Keystone (Colo.) Ctr., 1986—; environ. policy facilitator Taylor Lake Village, Tex., 1986—; chair Keystone Siting Process Local Rev. Com. 1st v.p. LWV, Washington, 1992-94, sec. treas. voters edn. fund, sec. treas. Nat. LWV, 1994-96, bd. dirs. 1996-98; pres. LWV of Tex., 1987-91, chair edn. fund, 1987-91, bd. dirs., 1983-87; pres. LWV of the Bay Area, 1981-83; mem. adv. com. Ctr. for Global Studies of Houston Advanced Rsch. Ctr., The Woodlands, Tex., 1991—, Ctr. for Conflict Analysis and Mgmt., bd. advisors Environ. Inst.; mem. U. Houston-Clear Lake Devel. Adv. Coun., 1989-95; mem. Bay Area Cmty. Awareness and Emergency Response Local Emergency Planning Com., 1988-92; active Tex. House-Senate Select Com. on Urban Affairs Regional Flooding Task Force, 1979-80, Congressman Mike Andrews Environ. Task Force, 1983-85, Gov.'s Task Force on Hazardous Waste Mgmt., 1984-85; dir. local PTAs, 1981-91; coord. Tex. Roundtable on Hazardous Waste, 1982-87; sec., v.p. Tex. Environ. Coalition, 1983-85; co-chair Tex. Risk Commn. Project, 1986-89; mem. Leadership Tex., Class of 1988. Mem. LWV (bd. dirs. Washington chpt. 1996—, trustee nat. fund), Soc. for Profls. in Dispute Resolution, Internat. Assn. for Pub. Participation Practitioners, Mortarboard, Pi Sigma Alpha, Kappa Delta Pi.

SHERIDAN, RICHARD COLLINS, chemist, educator, historian; b. Trotwood, Ohio, Aug. 19, 1929; s. Max M. Sheridan and Melville Williamson; m. Carol Sue Moore, Dec. 7, 1957; children: Vicki, Susan, Laura, Jennifer. BS, Murray (Ky.) State Coll., 1956; MS, U. Ky., 1961; postgrad., U. North Ala., 1965-83, Shoals C.C., Muscle Shoals, Ala., 1990-93. Chemical operator Pennsalt, Calvert City, Ky., 1953; chemist B.F. Goodrich Chem. Co., Louisville, 1956-58; rsch. chemist TVA Nat. Fertilizer Devel. Ctr., Muscle Shoals, Ala., 1960-88; mem. salary policy panel Tennessee Valley Authority, Knoxville, 1976-77, coord. historic collection, 1990-93; adj. prof. chemistry U. North Ala., 1989-94. Author: Deshler Female Inst., 1986; editor Jour. of Muscle Shoals History, 1980-82, 92-96; columnist Times Daily newspaper, Florence, Ala., 1992-96; contbr. over 30 articles to profl. jours.; patentee in field. Pres. Tenn. Valley Hist. Soc., 1967-69; election poll clk., Colbert County, Ala., 1988-96; mem. libr. bd., Sheffield, Ala., 1989-95. With U.S. Army, 1951-53, Germany. Recipient Disting. Svc. award Ala. Hist. Commn., 1982. Mem. Am. Chem. Soc. (councilor 1981-84, 93-96, Outstanding mem. 1976, 95), Ala. Acad. of Sci. (v.p. 1969-70), Ala. Baptist Hist. Commn. (treas. 1988-92), Ala. Hist. Assn., Ky. Hist. Soc., Am. Legion (Veteran of Yr. 1994). Republican. Baptist. Home: 105 Terrace St Sheffield AL 35660

SHERIF, S. A., mechanical engineering educator; b. Alexandria, Egypt, June 25, 1952; came to U.S., 1978; s. Ahmed and Ietedal H. (Monib) S.; m. Azza A. Shamseldin, Feb. 6, 1977; children: Ahmed S., Mohammad S. BSME (hon.), Alexandria U., 1975, MSME, 1978; PhD in Mech. Engring., Iowa State U., 1985. Tchg. asst. mech. engring. Alexandria U., 1975-78; tchg. assoc. mech. and environtl. engring. U. Calif., Santa Barbara, 1978-79; rsch. asst. mech. engring. Iowa State U., Ames, 1979-84; asst. prof. No. Ill. U., Dekalb, 1984-87, mem. grad. faculty, 1985-87; mem. grad. faculty U. Miami, Coral Gables, Fla., 1987-91, asst. prof. civil, archtl. and mech. engring., 1987-91; assoc. prof. mech. engring. U. Fla., Gainesville, 1991—, mem. doctoral rsch. faculty, 1992—; cons. Solar Reactor Techs., Inc., Miami, Fla., 1988-91, Dade Power Corp., Miami, 1988-91, Ind. Energy Sys., Miami, 1988-91, Carey Dwyer Eckhart Mason Spring & Beckham, P.A. Law Offices, Miami, 1988-89, Michael G. Widoff, P.A., Attys. at Law, Ft. Lauderdale, Fla., 1989-93, Law Offices Pomeroy and Betts, Ft. Lauderdale, 1991-92, Ctr. for Indoor Air Rsch., 1994—; cons. Fla. Power and Light Co., 1996—; cons. U. Roorkee, 1994-95; adj. faculty cons. Kennedy Western U., Thousand Oaks, Calif., 1994—; resident assoc. Argonne (Ill.) Nat. Lab., Tech. Transfer Ctr., summer 1992; faculty fellow NASA Kennedy Space Ctr., Cape Caneveral, Fla., summer 1993; rsch. assoc. summer faculty rsch. program Air Force Office Sci. Rsch., Arnold Engring. Devel. Ctr., Arnold AFB, Tenn., 1994; faculty fellow NASA Marhsall Space Flight Ctr., Huntsville, Ala., 1996; reviewer 23 internal jours., 90 conf. procs. and several pub. cos. and rsch. svc. orgns. Co-editor: Industrial and Agricultural Applications of Fluid Mechanics, 1989, The Heuristics of Thermal Anemometry, 1990, Heat and Mass Transfer in Frost and Ice, Packed Beds, and Environmental Discharges, 1990, Industrial Applications of Fluid Mechanics, 1990, rev. edit., 1991, Mixed Convection and Environmental Flows, 1990, Measurement and Modeling of Environmental Flows, 1992, Industrial and Environment Applications of Fluid Mechanics, 1992, Thermal Anemometry-1993, 1993, Heat Transfer in Turbulent Flows-1993, 1993, Developments in Electroheological Flows and Measurement Uncertainty-1994, 1994, Heat, Mass and Momentum Transfer in Environmental Flows, 1995, Thermal Anemometry, 1996, Fluid Measurement Uncertainty Applications, 1996; contbr. numerous articles to profl. jours. NASA ambassador, 1996—; mem. environ. awareness adv. com., Dade County Pub. Schs., 1989-91, lab. dir. cmty. lab. rsch. program, 1989-91, also faculty liaison design svcs. dept.; active Com. for Nat. Inst. for Environ., 1992—; mem. senate U. Fla., 1994-95, mem. OUTREACH Spkrs. program, 1996—. Mem. ASME (mem. coord. group fluid measurements, fluids engring. divsn. 1987—, vice chmn. 1990-92, chmn. 1992-94, fluids engring. divsn. adv. bd. 1994—, honors and awards com. 1994—, mem. fluid mechs. tech. com. 1990—, fluid mech. com. 1987-90, environ. heat transfer com. heat transfer divsn. 1987—, mem. fluid applications and systems tech. com. 1990—, systems analysis tech. com. advanced energy sys. divsn., 1989—, newsletter editor advanced energy sys. divsn. 1995—, fundamentals and theory tech. com. solar energy divsn. 1990—, chmn. CGFM nominating com. 1992-94, mem. 1994—, chmn. profl. devel. com. Rock River Valley sect. 1987, tech. activities operating com. Gator sect. 1994-96, MFFCC subcom. 1 on uncertainties in flow measurements 1995-97), ASHRAE (mem. heat transfer fluid flow com. 1988-92, 93-97, corr. mem. 1992-93, mem. thermodynamics and psychrometrics com. 1988-92, 96—, corr. mem. 1992-96, vice chmn. 1990-92, mem. liquid to refrigerant heat exchangers com. 1989-93, 96—, sec. 1990-92, chmn. standards project com. on measurement of moist air properties 1989-95), AIAA (sr.), AIChE, Internat. Assn. Hydrogen Energy, Internat. Solar Energy Soc., Am. Solar Energy Soc., Internat. Energy Soc. (mem. sci. coun.), Assn. Energy Engrs. (sr.), European Assn. Laser Anemometry (ASME/FED rep., mem. steering com.), Internat. Inst. Refrigeration (U.S. nat. com.), ABI (hon. mem. rsch. bd. adv. 1994—), Sigma Xi. Moslem. Home: 3301 SW 13th St Apt W-302 Gainesville FL 32608 Office: U Fla Dept Mech Engring 228 MEB Gainesville FL 32611-6300

SHERIFF, JIMMY DON, accounting educator, academic dean; b. Greenville, S.C., Dec. 8, 1940; s. James Donald and Gladys Ellie (Chapman) S.; BA, So. Wesleyan U., 1964; MBA, U. Ga., 1970, PhD, 1976; m. Gwen Anne Campbell, Aug. 31, 1969. Acct., Maremont Corp., Greenville, 1965-68; instr. U. Ga., Athens, 1970-73; asst. prof. Presbyn. Coll., Clinton, S.C., 1973-74; prof. Clemson (S.C.) U., 1974-87, assoc. dean, dir. rsch., 1987-92, acting dean, 1992-93, sr. assoc. dean, 1993—; U.S. rep. Network Internat. Bus. Schs. Chmn. Pickens County Aeros. Commn., 1980-91; founding pres. Pickens County Property Owners Assn. 1st lt. U.S. Army, 1964; brig. gen. USNG ret. Decorated U.S. Legion of Merit, Order of the Palmetto; named to Officer Candidate Sch. Hall of Fame. Mem. Inst. Mgmt. Accts. (Most Valuable Mem. 1978, dir. 1975—, pres. Anderson area 1979-80, nat. dir. 1984-86), Am. Acctg. Assn. (doctoral consortium fellow 1972), Soc. Rsch. Adminstrs., Nat. Coun. Rsch. Adminstrs., Acad. Sci., Acad. Acctg. Historians, Nat. Coun. Govtl. Acctg., S.C. Assn. Acctg. Instrs. (pres. 1974-75), So. Wesleyan U. Alumni Assn. (pres. 1970-72, Alumnus of Yr. 1994), 228th Brigade Assn. (pres.), Pickens County Hist. Soc., Pickens County Property Owners Assn. (founding pres.), Am. Legion, Beta Gamma Sigma, Beta Alpha Psi, Sigma Iota Epsilon, Delta Sigma Pi. Baptist. Clubs: University (pres. 1985-86), Commerce (Greenville). Lodges: Lions (pres.), Masons, Rotary, Shriners, Am. Legion. Author: Attitudes Toward Current Values, 1976. Republican. Home: 988 Old Shirley Rd Central SC 29630-9337 Office: Clemson U Coll Bus & Public Affairs Dean's Office 165 Sirrine Hall Clemson SC 29634-1301

SHERK, GEORGE WILLIAM, lawyer; b. Washington, Mo., June 23, 1949; s. George William Sr. and Lorraine Martha (Meyer) S. AA, St. Louis Community Coll., 1970; BA, Colo. State U., 1972, MA, 1974; JD, U. Denver, 1978. Bar: Am. Samoa 1978, Colo. 1979, U.S. Dist. Ct. Colo. 1979, U.S. Ct. Claims 1984, U.S. Supreme Ct. 1985. Cons. office of legis. counsel Govt. of Am. Samoa, Pago Pago, 1978-79; atty. advisor western area power adminstrn. U.S. Dept. Energy, Colo., 1979-80; pvt. practice law Denver, 1980-82; staff assoc. Nat. Conf. State Legis., Denver, 1980-82; spl. asst. office of water policy U.S. Dept. Interior, Washington, 1982-83; atty. land and natural resources div. U.S. Dept. Justice, Washington, 1984-90; of counsel Will & Muys, Washington, 1990-93; pvt. practice Alexandria, Va., 1993—; vis. scholar U. Wyo. Coll. Law, 1993; vis. prof. Ga. State U. Coll. Law, 1994-95, Ga. State U. Policy Rsch. Ctr., 1995-96; lectr. various colls. and univs.; mem. assoc. faculty Va. Inst. Marine Sci., Coll. of William and Mary, Gloucester Pt., Va., 1989-94. Author, co-author or editor numerous books and articles on water law and alternative energy law; book review editor Rivers: Studies in the Science, Environmental Policy and Law of Instream Flow, 1989—. Mem. ABA, ASCE, Water Environ. Fedn., State Bar Colo. Democrat. Presbyterian. Home and Office: PO Box 19703 Alexandria VA 22320-0703

SHERLOCK, LYNN, critical care, emergency nurse; b. Sewickley, Pa., Dec. 2, 1945; d. William Patrick and Carol Louise (Wolfe) Sherlock. Diploma, Presbyn.-U. Sch. Nursing, Pitts., 1966; BA, Fairmont (W.Va.) State Coll., 1988; postgrad., W.Va. U. RN, Pa., W.Va.; CCRN; cert. emergency nurse; cert. ACLS, BLS, ABLS, ACLS instr., Trauma Nurse Care Provider. Head nurse Harrisburg (Pa.) Hosp.; charge nurse Graham Med. Ctr., Newville, Pa.; triage nurse United Hosp. Ctr., Clarksburg, W.Va.; mem. credential com. on clin. ladder, com. chairperson and edn. dir. in field. Mem. AACN, Emergency Nurses Assn. (cert.). Home: PO Box 8268 Clarksburg WV 26302-8268

SHERMAN, BEATRICE ETTINGER, business executive; b. N.Y.C., May 29, 1919; d. Max and Stella (Schrager) Ettinger; m. Herbert Jacob Howard, Feb. 15, 1942 (dec. 1971); children: Robert David Howard, Carolyn Howard Smith; m. Ernest John Sherman, Dec. 29, 1974. Student, Gulf Park Jr. Coll., Gulfport, Miss., 1934-35, Shimer Jr. Coll., Mt. Carroll, Ill., 1936-38; BA, U. Miami, Fla., 1940; postgrad. Harvard U., 1940, Paris-Am. Acad., Paris, 1972, Alliance Française, Paris, 1973. Corp. sec., dir. Save Electric Corp., Toledo, 1940-67, Verd-A-Ray Corp., Toledo, 1944-67, Penetray Corp., Toledo, 1962-67; ptnr. Stella Assocs., Newark, 1960-80, BHS Ptnrs., Miami, 1983—; pres. Besman Inc., Coral Gables, Fla., 1975—, All Am. Mobile Tel. Co., Coral Gables, 1986—, Besman Hospitality, Coral Gables, 1993—, Archer House, Gainesville, Fla., 1994. Vol. worker Jewish Welfare Fedn., Toledo, 1942-69; nat. speaker United Jewish Appeal; mem. womens div. Greater Miami Jewish Fedn., 1969—, trustee, 1986-95; adv. bd. Miami Bell South; active Miami advertiser adv. bd. Bell South Advt. and Pub. Co. Recipient Lion of Judah award Greater Miami Jewish Fedn., 1986. Mem. Assn. Telemessaging Svcs. Internat., Pioneers of Miami Beach, Biltmore Club (Coral Gables, Fla.). Home: 5108 SW 72nd Ave Miami FL 33155-5530 Office: Besman Inc 2355 Salzedo St Ste 308 Coral Gables FL 33134-5061

SHERMAN, EDWARD FRANCIS, law educator; b. El Paso, Tex., July 5, 1937; s. Raphael Eugene and Mary (Stedmond) S.; m. Alice Theresa Hammer, Feb. 23, 1963; children—Edward F. Jr., Paul. AB, Georgetown U., 1959; MA, U. Tex.-El Paso, 1962, 67; LLB, Harvard U., 1962. SJD, 1981. Bar: Tex. 1962, Ind. 1976. Aide to gov. Nev., state govt. fellow, Carson City, 1962; law clk. to U.S. dist. judge Western dist. Tex., El Paso, 1963; ptnr. firm Mayfield, Broaddus & Perrenot, El Paso, 1963-65; teaching fellow Harvard Law Sch., Cambridge, Mass., 1967-69; prof. Ind. U. Sch. Law, Bloomington, 1969-77; Fulbright prof. Trinity Coll., Dublin, 1973-74; vis. prof. U. London, 1989, U. London, 1989, Chuo U., Tokyo, 1995; Edward Clark Centennial prof. law, U. Tex., Austin, 1977—; counsel Tex. County Jail Litigation, 1978-85; bd. dirs., officer Travis County Dispute Resolution Ctr., Austin, 1985-88; chmn. bd. dirs. Tex. Resource Ctr., 1989-95, Tex. Ctr. Pub. Policy Dispute Resolution, 1993—; mem. arbitrator panel, course dir. Internat. Ctrs. for Arbitration. Capt. U.S. Army, 1965-67, lt. col. Res., 1970-90. Fulbright lectr. in law Trinity Coll., Dublin, Ireland, 1973-74. Fellow Tex. Bar Found.; mem. ABA (reporter ABA civil justice improvements project 1993, offer of judgement task force, 1995), Am. Arbitration Assn. (arbitrator panel), AAUP (gen. counsel 1986-88), Am. Law Inst., Tex. State Bar Assn. (alternative dispute resolution com. 1985—, chair Pattern Jury Charge Com. 1983-94), Tex. Civil Liberties Union (gen. counsel 1985-91). Co-author: The Military in American Society, 1979, Complex Litigation, 1985, 2d edit., 1992, Processes of Dispute Resolution, 1989, 2d edit., 1996, Civil Procedure: A Modern Approach, 1989, 2nd edit., 1995, Rau & Sherman's Texas ADR and Arbitration Statutes, 1994. Home: 2622 Woolridge Dr Austin TX 78703-2538 Office: U Tex Sch Law 727 E 26th St Austin TX 78705-3224

SHERMAN, HENRY THOMAS, retired physician; b. Donalsonville, Ga., Aug. 11, 1908; s. David Brady and Erin (Jones) S.; m. Jennie Ruth Morgan, Jan. 26, 1943; children: Henry Thomas Jr., Erin Mercer Sherman Wright, Mercer Lancaster. BS, Emory U., 1930; MD, Cornell U., 1934, postgrad., 1946-47; postgrad., Columbia U., 1947, NYU, 1947, Edinburgh (Scotland) Postgrad. bd. for Medicine, 1947, U. Pa., 1950. Intern Bellevue Hosp., N.Y.C., 1935-36; surgeon SS Ft. Townsend, Furness Lines, 1937; admitting physician St. Joseph's Hosp., Richmond, Va., 1937; pvt. practice gen. medicine Cairo, Ga., 1937-42; chief surgeon SS Marine Tiger U.S. Line, 1948; shore duty physician Grace Line, N.Y.C., 1948; chief of medicine Williamson (W.Va.) Meml. Hosp., 1948-49; pvt. practice internal medicine Valdosta, Ga., 1949-75; ret., 1975; mem. staff Little Griffin Owens Saunders Hosp., Pineview Gen. Hosp., Valdosta, 1955-71, South Ga. Med. Ctr., 1971-75. Capt. Med. Corps, U.S. Army, 1942-46, PTO. Mem. AMA, So. Med. Assn., Bockus Internat. Soc. Gastroenterology, Sigma Alpha Epsilon. Baptist. Home: 604 Georgia Ave Valdosta GA 31602-2431

SHERMAN, MALCOLM CHARLES, business consultant; b. Boston, Aug. 19, 1931; s. Benjamin and Kay (Sheff) S.; m. Jill Barbara Tawil, Dec. 6, 1970; children: Isaac, Martin. JD, Boston U., 1955. Registered profl. engr., Calif.; bar: Mass. 1955. Contract mgr. Curtiss-Wright, Quehanna, Pa., 1956-58, Litton Industries, L.A., 1958-64; program mgr. Hughes Aircraft Co., L.A., 1964-68; v.p. devel. Planning Rsch. Corp., L.A., 1971-74; sr. v.p. Info. Gen., L.A., 1968-69; pres., CEO, Meridian Group Internat., L.A., 1974-83; pres. KDT Systems, L.A., 1983-89; exec. cons. Rockwell Internat., L.A., 1989-91; bus. cons. El Segundo, Calif., 1991—; adj. prof. U. So. Calif., L.A., 1965-77, UCLA, 1965-77; lectr. NSF, Bangkok, 1989; cons. Asian-Am. Enterprise, L.A., 1992—. Contbr. articles to profl. publs. Recipient recognition and appreciation award Samsung Industries, Republic of Korea, 1989, NRC, 1990, Office Sci. Tech., Thailand, 1990. Mem. L.A. Execs. Club (v.p. 1983-84). Office: 17 Waldrup Ter Fletcher NC 28732-8428

SHERMAN, MARY ANGUS, public library administrator; b. Lawton, Okla., Jan. 3, 1937; d. Donald Adelbert and Mabel (Felkner) Angus; m. Donald Neil Sherman, Feb. 8, 1958; children: Elizabeth, Donald Neil II. BS in Home Econs., U. Okla., 1958, MLS, 1969. Br. head Pioneer Libr. System, Purcell, Okla., 1966-76; regional libr. Pioneer Libr. System, Norman, Okla., 1976-78, asst. dir., 1978-80, dir., 1987—. Named one of Distinguished Alumni Sch. Home Econs., U. Okla., 1980. Mem. ALA (councilor 1988-96, planning and budget assembly 1990-91, internat. rels. com. 1992-96), Pub. Libr. Assn. (divsn. of ALA, pres. pub. policy for pub. librs. sect. 1995-96), AAUW (pres. Okla. chpt. 1975-77, nat. bd. dirs. 1983-87, S.W. ctrl. region dir. 1983-85, v.p. nat. membership 1985-87, Woman of the Yr. Purcell chpt. 1982), Okla. Libr. Assn. (pres. 1982-83, interlibrary cooperation com. 1993-95, chair 1994-95, Disting. Svc. award 1986), Norman C. of C. (bd. dirs. 1988-96, pres. 1994-95), Rotary (program chair 1991-92, bd. dirs. 1993—, pres. 1995-96. Paul Harris fellow), Norman Assistance League Club (cmty. assoc.), Norman, Okla. Sister City Com. 1994—, Delta Gamma Mothers (pres. 1978-79), Kappa Alpha Theta (pres. Alpha Omicron House Corp. 1984-87, nat. dir. house corps. 1987-88), Beta Phi Mu, Phi Beta Kappa. Democrat. Methodist. Office: Pioneer Libr System 225 N Webster Ave Norman OK 73069-7133

SHERMAN, RICHARD ALLEN, lawyer; b. Atlanta, Mar. 16, 1946; s. Robert Hiram and Olivia Mae (Latham) S.; m. Mary Margaret Sawyer, June 23, 1973 (div. June 1994); children: Richard A. Jr., Jill Mary, James Warren; m. Catherine Agnes Oakley, May 4, 1996. BA, Tulane U., 1968, JD, 1972. Bar: Fla. 1974, La. 1973, U.S. Ct. Appeals (5th cir.) 1978, U.S. Ct. Appeals (11th cir.) 1981, U.S. Supreme Ct. 1981. Ptnr., head appellate divsn. Wicker, Smith, Blomqvist, Davant, Tutan, O'Hara, McCoy et al, Miami, 1973-83; pvt. practice Ft. Lauderdale, Fla., 1983—, practice limited to handling appeals in Fla. Active Rep. Nat. Com. Mem. ABA (vice-chmn. U.S. Ct. Appeals 5th cir. com. 1981), Fla. Bar Assn. (appellate rules com. 1979-81), Dade County Bar Assn. (chmn. appellate cts. com. 1982-83), Mensa, Pres. Club, Lauderdale Yacht Club, Upper Keys Sailing Club (bd. dirs.). Office: 1777 S Andrews Ave Ste 302 Fort Lauderdale FL 33316-2517

SHERMAN, RON, photographer; b. Cleve., May 10, 1942; s. Hyman B. and Sheryl D. Sherman; m. Myra LeBell, Aug. 16, 1969; children: Scott Neal, Jonathan Harris, Hannah Beth. BFA in illustrative photography, Rochester Inst. Tech., 1964; MA in photographic commn., Syracuse U., 1971. Staff photographer Gannett Newspapers (Democrat, Chronicle and Times Union), Rochester, N.Y., 1961-64, U. Fla., Gainesville, 1964-66; photo-officer, military intelligence unit U.S. Army-Signal Corps, Vietnam, 1967-68; staff photographer Milw. Journal, Wis., 1969; photographer Syracuse U., Syracuse, N.Y., 1969-71; prin. Ron Sherman Photographer, Atlanta, 1971—, Computer Aided Photography, Inc., Atlanta, 1991—; adv. comml. photography Gwinett Tech. Inst., Lawrenceville, Ga., 1983—; cons. ABC TV, Alcoa, AT&T, CBS Sports, The Coca-Cola Co., Eastman Kodak, Ford Motor Co., IBM, TRW, Atlanta Com. for the Olympic Games, BellSouth, Southern Bell, Atlanta Gas Light Co., Nat. Hockey League, Sonat, Gen. Mills, Ga. Power, Southern Co., Phoenix Comms. Photographer; pub. in Life, Time, Newsweek, Inside Sports, Bus. Week, Forbes, Reader's Digest, Ford Times, America Illustrated, Med. World News, N.Y. Times, U. S. News and World Report, Venture; pub. works in Atlanta calendar, 1994, 95, 96, 97; Atlanta photos used to illustrate Peter Max's Super Bowl XXVIII poster; (hard cover books) Greater North Fulton and Atlanta, A Vision for the New Millenium. 1st Lt. U.S. Army 1968-69, Vietnam. Mem. Nat. Press

Photographers Assn., Am. Soc. Media Photographers (pres. Atlanta chpt. 1980-81). Office: PO Box 2268 Roswell GA 30077

SHERRICK, DANIEL NOAH, real estate broker; b. Greenup, Ill., Mar. 28, 1929; s. Conrad Donovan and Helen Lorene (Neeley) S.; m. Dora Ann Moore, Aug. 11, 1957; children: Renata Ann Sherrick McBride, Sherrie Dee Sherrick Sierra. B.S. in Edn., Eastern Ill. U., Charleston, 1956. Owner Midwest Ins. Agy., Greenup, 1956-60; supt. agys. Midwest Life Ins. Co., Lincoln, Nebr., 1960-62; asst. v.p. Gulf Life Ins. Co., Jacksonville, Fla., 1962-71; pres. Bank of Carbondale, Ill., 1971-74, Prescription Learning Corp., Springfield, Ill., 1974-76; exec. v.p. Imperial Industries, Inc., Miami Lakes, Fla., 1976-88, pres., chief exec. officer, 1988-90; broker, salesman Coldwell Banker Residential Real Estate, 1990-91, 93—; pres., bd. dirs. Palmer State Bank, Taylorville, Ill., 1991-93; broker-salesman Coldwell Banker Hunter Realty, 1993—. Pres. Alderman Park Civic Assn., Jacksonville, 1968, Heritage Hills Home Owners Assn., Carbondale, 1973. With USAF, 1948-52. Mem. Am. Legion, Greater Sebring C. of C., VFW, Internat. Torch Club, Masons, Elks. Presbyterian. Home: 6228 Aquavista Dr Sebring FL 33870-7409 Office: Coldwell Banker Hunter Realty 2617 Us Highway 27 S Sebring FL 33870-2127

SHERRILL, SABRINA RAWLINSON, healthcare administrator; b. Montgomery, Ala., June 3, 1957. BSN, U. Ala., 1979, MS in Nursing, 1981; MBA, La. State U., 1991. RN, Miss.; cert. advanced nursing adminstrn. Staff nurse intermediate coronary care unit Westgate Hosp., Denton, Tex., 1979; staff nurse ICU South Highlands Hosp., Birmingham, Ala., 1980; staff critical care units and emergency rm. Sacred Heart Hosp., Pensacola, Fla., 1981-82, cardiac rehab. clin. nurse specialist, 1982-83; dept. head intensive coronary care unit Bapt. Hosp., Pensacola, 1983-86; nursing adminstrv. supr. Baton Rouge Gen. Hosp., 1986-87; instr. Sch. of Nursing Our Lady of the Lake Regional Med. Ctr., Baton Rouge, 1987-91; dir. clin. svcs. Vol. Hosps. Am., Baton Rouge, 1991-95; dir. Health Choice & Integrity HMO, Jackson, Miss., 1995—. Contbr. articles to profl. publs. Profl. advisor Mended Hearts, Pensacola, 1983. Mem. Am. Soc. Risk Mgrs., Am. Coll. Healthcare, Sigma Theta Tau, Omicron Delta Kappa. Home: 5893 Kristen Dr Jackson MS 39211-2831

SHERRINGTON, PAUL WILLIAM, marketing communications executive; b. Champaign, Ill., Oct. 7, 1949; s. P. William and Quirine (Kinate) S.; m. Nancy Sherrington; children: Gregg, Sally. BS in Communications, U. Tenn., 1971. Staff writer News Palladium, Benton Harbor, Mich., 1971-72; copywriter Retail Credit Co., Atlanta, 1972-75; asst. advt. dir. Equifax Inc., Atlanta, 1975-79, mgr. advt., 1979-83; mgr. communications Equifax, Atlanta, 1983-88, dir., advt. and sales promotion, 1988-93, asst. v.p. mktg. comm., 1993-95; dir. sales and mktg. Fernbank Mus. Natural History, 1996—. Author (book) What Communicators Must Know About Service Marketing, 1991; co-author (book) Business-to-Business Advertising, 1991. Bd. dirs. Atlanta Arthritis Found., 1991-95. Recipient Addy award, 1985-86. Mem. Bus. Mktg. Assn. (chmn. 1988, 95-96, vice chmn. 1987, 94-95, internat. bd. dirs. 1984-88, 93-96, pres. Atlant chpt. 1983-84, 92-93, Atlanta bd. dirs. 1980-84, 91-93, Peach award 1986-88, 95). Republican. Roman Catholic. Home: 1920 Barnes Mill Rd Marietta GA 30062 Office: Fernbank 767 Clifton Rd Atlanta GA 30307

SHERWOOD, ARLENE GAIL, federal agency administrator; b. Euclid, Ohio, July 28, 1956; d. Robert S. and Madolyn A. (King) Lough; m. Theodore Eckert II, May 14, 1983 (div. Oct. 1985); m. Julius Sherwood, Feb. 1993. BS in Law Enforcement, U. No. Ala., 1978. Cert. social worker. Probation, parole officer Tenn. Dept. Corrections, Columbia, 1978-83; child protection svc. specialist II Tex. Dept. Human Svcs., Killeen, 1984-86; child protective svcs. specialist IV, Tex. Dept. Human Svcs., Gatesville, 1988-90; coord. employees assistance project Associated Counseling Svcs., Harker Heights, Tex., 1986-88; case mgr. Dept. of Justice, Fed. Bur. of Prisons, Danbury, Conn., 1990-95; sr. case mgr. FCI, Beckley, W.Va., 1995—. Bd. dirs. Truancy Bd. Pulaski, Tenn., 1978-84, Truancy Bd., Lawrenceburg, Tenn., 1978-84, Multidisciplinary Child Abuse Rev. Team, Columbia, Tenn., 1979-84. Mem. Am. Correctional Assn., Tenn. State Employees Assn., NAFE. Lutheran. Office: FCI Beckley PO Box 1280 Beaver WV 25813

SHERWOOD, KENNETH WESLEY, information systems executive, consultant; b. Denver, Nov. 15, 1943; s. Richard Wesley Sherwood and Mary Ellen (Sorling) McClure; m. Virginia Kay Betts, June 24, 1966; children: Jeremy James, Pamela Ann. BS summa cum laude, Met. State Coll., Denver, 1971. Missile mechanic helper Martin Marietta, Littleton, Colo., 1963-64, electronics technician, 1964, communications ctr. operator, 1968-69; systems rep. Burroughs Corp., Denver, 1971-76; systems supr. Burroughs Corp., Las Vegas, Nev., 1976-79; dept. mgr. Burroughs Corp., Atlanta, 1979-83, mgr. support ctr., 1983-85; sr. mgr. profl. svcs. UNISYS, Atlanta, 1985—; cons. in pers. computer and check processing fields. Sgt. U.S. Army, 1964-68, Tokyo. Methodist. Home: 5271 Lanford Springs Ct SW Lilburn GA 30247-6551 Office: UNISYS 5550A Peachtree Pky Norcross GA 30092-2533

SHERWOOD, RHONDA GRIFFIN, fashion and costume designer; b. Pampa, Tex., July 26, 1953; d. Riley Russell and Lola Christina (Apperson) Griffin; m. Mark Lawson Sherwood; 1 child, Elizabeth Lynn. BA in Speech and Drama magna cum laude, Trinity U., San Antonio, 1975. Escrow sec. Am. Title Co., Dallas, 1977-79; legal asst. Blalack & Williams, P.C., Dallas, 1979-91; fashion and costume designer Sherwood Sew Faire, 1991-94; info. svcs. coord. Towers Perrin, Dallas, 1995—. Writer, performer: Pictures of First Baptist Ch., 1986, The Easter Story, 1987-91, 94, Living Christmas, 1987-90, Christmas Puzzle N.W. Bapt. Ch., 1995, Mobberly Baptist Church-50th Anniversary Pageant-A Dramatic Church History, and numerous short subjects. Mem. choir First Baptist Ch., Richardson, Tex., 1977-95, prin. viola, 1983—, chmn. drama com., 1985-94, mem. handbell choir, 1979—; coll. dept. dir., 1990-95. Mem. Alpha Chi, Alpha Lambda Delta, Alpha Psi Omega. Home: 1611 Barclay Dr Richardson TX 75081-2001 Office: Towers Perrin 12377 Merit # 1200 Dallas TX 75251

SHETTY, SHANKARA RAMA, packaging technologist, food packaging consultant; b. Kaup, India, Nov. 19, 1941; s. Rama and Seetha Shetty; m. Shakila; children: Ameet, Priya. BSc in Chemistry with honors, U. Bombay, 1963, BScTech. in Food Technology, 1965, MSTech. in Food Technology, 1968; MBA, Bloomsburg State Coll., 1978. Asst. dir. R & D Indian Inst. Packaging, Bombay, India, 1968-75; coord. packaging and promotions Borden, Inc., Columbus, Ohio, 1975-80; nat. mgr. PQA Frito-Lay, Inc., Dallas, 1980-83; rsch. scientist Beatrice, Inc., Chgo., 1983-88; packaging mgr. Rich SeaPak Corp., St. Simons Island, Ga., 1988—. Patentee in field. Mem. Inst. Packaging Profls., Microwave Power Inst., Inst. Food Technologists, Inst. Plastic Engrs. Home: 109 Saint Clair Dr Saint Simons GA 31522-1034 Office: Rich Seapak Corp PO Box 20670 Saint Simons GA 31522-0270

SHEVIS, JAMES MURDOCH, journalist; b. Brattleboro, Vt., Oct. 2, 1929; s. James Allan and Frances (Ritchie) S.; divorced; children: Heidi Shevis Clark, Holly Shevis Markwood, Andrew. BA in English, U. Mass., 1951; M in Liberal Studies, Georgetown U., 1977; postgrad., Am. U., 1975-83. Bur. mgr. UPI, Lubbock Tex., Springfield, Mass., 1964-65; mng. editor Airline Pilot, Washington, 1985-86, Courier, Fairfax County, Va., 1986-88; editor N.Am. Newspaper Alliance, N.Y.C., 1965-67, Newhouse Nat. News Svc., Washington, 1967-68, AFL-CIO News, Washington, 1972-85; writer, reporter Worcester (Mass.) Telegram & Gazette, 1961-63, UPI, Dallas, 1963, Reuters and Bur. Nat. Affairs, Washington, 1968-69; sr. writer, reporter, editor USIA, Washington, 1988-9; lectr. writing George Mason U., Fairfax, 1987—; lectr. feature writing USDA Grad. Sch., Washington. Columnist The Observer, 1990-91; contbr. articles to profl. jours. Mem. Soc. Environ. Journalists (charter), Soc. Profl. Journalists, Nat. Assn. Govt. Communicators, Nat. Press Club, Washington Ind. Writers, Freelance Cons. Assn. (v.p.), Tree Action. Home: 2857 Viking Dr Herndon VA 20171-2422

SHEVY, ALLEN EARL, JR., publishing executive; b. Mar. 23, 1959; s. Allen Earl Shevy Sr. and Myra Lee (Cone) Muller. Sales rep. Police Benevolent Assn., Tampa, Fla., 1974-79, Fox and Fink Inc., Tampa, 1979-85; pub. World of Fandom Mag., Tampa, 1985—; sales and mktg. rep. Fla. Spl. Olympics, 1979-85, U. South Fla. Basketball, 1979-85, U. South Fla. Baseball, 1979-85, U. South Fla. Soccer, 1979-85, U. South Fla. Volleyball, 1979-85, U. South Fla. Student Calendar of Events, 1979-85, Internat. Motor Sports Assn., 1979-85, Sports Car Off Road Events, 1979-85, Gasperilla Distance Classic, 1979-85, Saint Pete Grand Prix, 1979-85, Bucaneer Mag., 1989-93; pub. Rat Fink Comics, 1989-91, Comic Collectors Guide, 1989-91. Office: World of Fandom Mag PO Box 9421 Tampa FL 33674-9421

SHI, FENG SHENG, mathematician; b. Shanghai, China, Sept. 28, 1935; came to U.S., 1990; s. Jing Long and Xu Wenzheng Shi; m. Dorothy Shi, May 30, 1992. Degree of engr., 1957. Prof. math. and physics U. Industry, Shanghai, 1961-64; ship designer Govt. of China, Shanghai, 1964; rschr., business liaison Hong Kong of U.S.A. Liaison for Bus. Investment; owner, editor Pendulum Math. Jour. in Libr. of Congress; trustee, founder, dir. Chinese Math. Students Orgn., Miami, Fla., 1993—; dir. Chinese Internat. Math. Students Orgn., 1994—. Author: (math. solutions) Exist, 1991 (Libr. of Congress), Solving the Fermat Problem and Goldbach's Conjecture, 1993. Recipient Son of Yr. award Son's & Daughter's Found., 1990. Mem. All Nations (trustee, bd. dirs. 1990-93, Internat. Man of Yr. 1991). Home and Office: 1000 8th St N Saint Petersburg FL 33701-1510

SHI, MING ZHENG, history educator; b. Beijing, Nov. 3, 1963; came to U.S., 1986; s. Pinglin Shi and Shuqin Xu. BA in Internat. Studies, Peking U., Beijing, 1986; MA in Am. History, U. Conn., 1988; MPhil in Chinese History, Columbia U., 1990, PhD in Chinese History, 1993. Translator press and culture sect. U.S. Embassy, Beijing, 1984-85; rschr. N.Y. Chinatown history project Chinatown History Mus., N.Y.C., 1988-89; lectr. dept. history Peking U., Beijing, 1990, U. Conn., Stamford, 1992; tchg. fellow dept. East Asian Langs. and Cultures Columbia U., N.Y.C., 1992; postdoctoral fellow Ctr. for Chinese Studies U. Calif., Berkeley, 1993-94; asst. prof. dept. history U. Houston, Houston, 1992—. Author: Remaking Beijing: Urban Development and Social Change in the 20th Century, 1995; contbr. articles to profl. jours. Traveling fellow Columbia U., 1990-91, Whiting Doctoral Dissertation fellow Mrs. Giles Whiting Found., 1991-92. Mem. Am. Hist. Assn., Assn. for Asian Studies, Urban History Assn., Asia Soc. Houston (bd. dirs.), Assn. of Chinese Historians in the U.S., Chinese Bus. History Rsch. Group, Beijing History Rsch. Group (China), Pub. Works Hist. Soc. Office: Dept History U Houston Houston TX 77204-3785

SHI, XIANGRONG, physiologist; b. Shanghai, China, July 24, 1953; arrived in U.S., 1983; m. Qi Wen Tao, Dec. 11, 1982; 1 child, Tracy. PhD, Yale U., 1989. Postdoctoral assoc. J.B. Pierce Found. Lab., New Haven, 1989-90; sci. assoc. U. North Tex. Health Scis. Ctr., Ft. Worth, 1990-91, rsch. asst. prof., 1991-94, asst. prof., 1994—. Active Am. Heart Assn. Mem. Am. Physiology Soc., Am. Coll. Sports Medicine. Office: U North Tex Health Sci Ctr 3500 Camp Bowie Blvd Fort Worth TX 76107-2644

SHICKMAN, BARRY LOUIS, physician, obstetrician, gynecologist; b. Phila., May 29, 1939; s. Charles Bernard and Adele (Levy) S.; m. Merle Sandra Rachlin, May 30, 1965 (dec. June 1973); 1 child, Joel Nathan; m. Dora Ann Moore, Mar. 13, 1994. BA, Franklin & Marshall Coll., 1961; MD, U. Pa., 1965. Diplomate Am. Bd. Ob-Gyn. Intern U. Rochester (N.Y.) Strong Meml. Hsop., 1965-66; resident Kaiser FOund. Hosp., Oakland, Calif., 1968-71; ob-gyn. physician Berkeley (Calif.) Health Dept., 1971, Charles R. Drew Med. Ctr., East Palo Alto, Calif., 1971-76, Health Alliance of No. Calif., San Jose, 1976-79, Pacific Med. Clinic, Saratoga, Calif., 1979-83, City of Houston Health Dept., 1983-93, Riverwalk Ob-Gyn. Assocs., San Antonio, 1993-94; cons. Clinica Sierra Vista, Lamont, Calif., 1972-81. Capt. U.S. Army, 1966-68. Mem. Tex. Med. Assn., Bexar County Med. Assn. Republican. Jewish. Home: 4302 Fir Valley Dr Kingwood TX 77345-1362

SHIELDS, EDGAR THOMSON, JR., American literature educator; b. Chagrin Falls, Ohio, Dec. 29, 1958; s. Edgar Thomson Sr. and Grace Anne (Daschbach) S.; m. Claire Lee Sikoryak, July 15, 1989. BA in English, Bucknell U., 1982; MA in English, Western Ky. U., 1984; PhD in English, U. Tenn., 1990. Grad. teaching asst. dept. English Western Ky. U., Bowling Green, 1982-84; grad. teaching assoc. dept. English U. Tenn., Knoxville, 1984-89; asst. prof. dept. English East Carolina U., Greenville, N.C., 1985-89; assoc. prof. dept. English East Caroline U., Greenville, N.C., 1989—; dir. Roanoke Colonies Rsch. Office East Carolina U., Greenville, 1993—. Editor Roanoke Colonies Rsch. Newsletter, 1993—. Mem. MLA, Soc. Early Americanists, Hakluyt Soc., Am. Lit. Assn., Soc. for Study of So. Lit., N.C. Lit. and Hist. Assn., South Atlantic MLA. Home: 611 Old 2nd St Washington NC 27889-5157 Office: East Carolina U Roanoke Colonies Rsch Off Dept English Greenville NC 27858-4353

SHIELDS, PAUL KEITH, psychotherapist, management consultant; b. Tulsa, Mar. 1, 1949; s. Vester Earl and Ruby Belle (Myers) S.; m. Sydney Lynn Brown, Apr. 9, 1983; children: Michael Barrett, Sarah Elizabeth. BS in Psychology, Tulsa U., 1975, MA in Counseling, 1976, EdD in Counseling Psychology, 1984. Lic. marriage and family therapist. Clin. intern Tulsa Psychiat. Ctr., 1976-77; oncology social worker St. Francis Med. Ctr., Tulsa, 1978-80; social svcs. dir. St. John Med. Ctr. Hospice Program, Tulsa, 1980-82; clin. dir. Countryview Psychiatric Hosp., Broken Arrow, OK, 1984-86; program dir. Green Country Counseling Ctr., Tulsa, 1986-88; organizational mgmt. cons., psychotherapist Dr. Paul K. Shields, Inc., Tulsa, 1989-94; area v.p. Midland Psychiat. Assocs., 1994—; cons. in field. Contbr. various articles to profl. jours. With USAF, 1969-73. Mem. APA, Am. Assn. and Family Therapists (clin.), Nat. Bd. for Cert. Counselors, Am. Group Psychotherapy Assn., Nat. Assn. Alcoholism and Drug Abuse, Okla. Drug and Alcohol Profl. Counselors Assn. Republican. Office: 6104 E 32nd St Ste 212 Tulsa OK 74135

SHIELDS, RANA COLLEEN, special education educator; b. Midland, Tex., Oct. 2, 1951; d. Robert Campbell and Edith Sue (Alexander) S.; m. Micheal Leggett; children: Daniel Robert Tilly, Casey Michelle Leggett; 1 stepchild, Laurie Ayn Leggett. B of Journalism, U. Tex., 1974; JD magna cum laude, South Tex. U., 1984; MEd in Spl. Edn., S.W. Tex. State U., 1993. Bar: Tex., 1985; cert. generic spl. edn., reading, Tex. City editor Huntsville (Tex.) Item, 1976-78; asst. county atty. Travis County Atty.'s Office, Austin, Tex., 1986-87; tchr. spl. edn. Liberty Hill (Tex.) H.S., 1990-91, Tex. Sch. for the Blind, Austin, 1991-93; grad. rsch. asst. in spl. edn. U. Tex., Austin, spring 1994, tchg. asst. spl. edn., 1995-96. Asst. casenotes editor: South Tex. Law Jour., 1983. Recipient 1st Pl. Spot News Photography award AP Mng. Editors, 1978, Am. Jurisprudence awards, 1979, 82, 83; named Outstanding Sophomore Journalist, Women in Comm., 1971; Univ. fellow, 1996-97. Mem. Assn. Tex. Profl. Educators, Kappa Delta Pi, Phi Kappa Phi.

SHIELDS, THEODOSIA T., librarian; b. Timmonsville, S.C., Dec. 22, 1955; d. Theron Elford and Ruth (Ward) S.; 1 child, Rakisha Nicolen Ballen.; BS, S.C. State, 1977; MS in Libr. Sci., Atlanta U., 1978; PhD, U. Pitts., 1991. Reference and info. specialist S.C. State Libr., Orangeburg, 1978-84, govt. documents libr., 1987-89, asst. coord. collection devel., 1989-90; grad. asst. U. Pitts., 1984-86; libr. supr. We. Psychiat. Inst. Libr., Pitts., 1986; libr. dir. Florence (S.C.)-Darlington Tech., 1990-92; u. libr. Dillard U., New Orleans, 1993—. Mem. ALA (mem. Black caucus), Assn. Colls. and Rsch. Librs., La. Libr. Assn. Methodist. Office: Dillard U 2601 Gentilly Ave New Orleans LA 70122

SHIFLETT, MARY ELLEN, library media specialist; b. Thibodaux, La., May 1, 1944; d. Edward Joseph and Estelle Amelie (Ayo) Hebert; m. Ron Landry, Aug. 14, 1965 (div.); children: C. Benton Landry, Lauryn Elizabeth Landry; m. Lee Shiflett, June 16, 1990. BS, La. State U., 1965, MLIS, 1988. Libr. media specialist Archbishop Chapelle H.S., Metairie, La., 1988-91, J.B. Martin Mid. Sch., Paradis, La., 1991—. Co-author: (bibliography) On Account of Sex, 1991. Mem. ALA, Am. Assn. Sch. Librs., La. Assn. Sch. Librs. (1st v.p. 1993-94, pres., 1994-95). Home: 5 Country Club Dr LaPlace LA 70068 Office: JB Martin Mid Sch 434 South St Paradis LA 70080

SHIFLETT, ORVIN LEE, librarian, educator; b. Melbourne, Fla., Aug. 1, 1947; s. James Winfield and Elsie Mae (Davis) S.; m. Mary Ellen Landry, June 16, 1990; children: Benton, Lauryn. BA, U. Fla., 1969; MLS, Rutgers U., 1971; PhD, Fla. State U., 1979. Instr. U. Wis., LaCrosse, 1971-76, asst. prof., 1976-78; asst. prof. La. State U., Baton Rouge, 1979-83, assoc. prof., 1983-94, prof., 1994—. Author: Louis Shores, 1996, Bookman's Guide to Americana, 1991, Origins of American Academic Librarianship, 1981; contbr. articles to profl. jours. Mem. ALA (chair libr. history round table 1984), La. Libr. Assn. (chair govt. documents round table 1986), Assn. for Libr. and Info. Sci. Edn. Home: # 5 Country Club La Place LA 70068 Office: La State U Sch Libr and Info Sci Baton Rouge LA 70803

SHILEY, ANDREA GAIL, secondary school educator; b. Lewistown, Pa., July 27, 1956; d. Robert Banks and Marjorie Katheryn (Shearer) Henry; m. Richard C. Shiley, m. May 13, 1978 (dec. June 1996); 1 child, Evan Andrew. BS in Music Edn., Indiana U. of Pa., 1978; Jr. High Sci. Cert., Brevard Community Coll., Melbourne, Fla. Choral dir./tchr. S.W. Jr. High Sch., Brevard County Sch. Dist., Palm Bay, Fla., 1988—. Contbr. articles to profl. jours. Named Stone Middle Sch. tchr. of the Yr., 1984-85. Mem. ASCD, AAUW, Music Educators Nat. Conf., Fla. Music Educators Assn. (bd. dirs.), Fla. Vocal Assn., Brevard Fedn. Tchrs., Am. Fedn. Tchrs., Tri-M (Fla. chmn.), Nat. Tri-M Adv. Com. Home: 1721 Rangoon Rd NW Palm Bay FL 32907-6940

SHILLING, ROY BRYANT, JR., academic administrator; b. Enville, Okla., Apr. 7, 1931; s. Roy Bryant and Lila M. (Prestage) S.; m. Margaret Riddle, Oct. 16, 1952; children: Roy Bryant III, Nancy Gale. BA, McMurry U., 1951, HHD, 1982; BD, So. Meth. U., 1957; MS, Ind. U., 1966, PhD, 1967. Presdl. asst. McMurry U., Abilene, Tex., 1959-61; asst. to pres. Tenn. Wesleyan Coll., 1961-64; asst. in devel. Ball State U., 1964-65; rsch. assoc. Ind. U., 1965-67; dir. planning and rsch. Baldwin Wallace Coll., 1967-68; exec. v.p. Southwestern U., 1968-69, pres., 1981—; pres. Hendrix Coll., 1969-81; mem. Nat. Commn. on United Meth. Higher Edn., 1975-77. Mem. Ark. Arts and Humanities Coun., 1970-76, chmn., 1974-75; bd. dirs. Ark. Children's Hosp., 1981; mem. bd. higher edn. and ministry United Meth. Ch., 1972-80, mem. univ. senate, 1980-88, v.p. 1983-84, pres., 1984-88; chmn. Gulf dist. Rhodes Scholarship Selection Com., 1992, Ark. chmn., 1973-74, Tex. chmn., 1985-91; mem. Young Pres. Orgn., 1975-81; mem. bd. visitors Air U., 1991-94. With U.S. Army, 1952-54. Recipient Disting. Alumnus award McMurry U., 1980, Perkins Disting. Alumnus award So. Meth. U., 1987, Owen B. Sherrill award for leadership in econ. devel. Georgetown, 1988; named one of Top 100 Most Effective Coll. Pres. in Nation, Bowling Green State U./Exxon Edn. Found., 1988. Mem. North Ctrl. Assn. Colls. and Schs. (vice chmn., chmn. elect 1980-81), Nat. Assn Schs. and Colls. of United Meth. Ch. (v.p. 1975-76, pres. 1976-77), Nat. Coun. Ind. Colls. and Univs. (bd. dirs. 1984-88), So. U. Conf. (exec. com. 1974-78), 79-86, sec.-treas. 1979-86, v.p. 1991-92, pres. 1992-93), Am. Coun. Edn. (bd. dirs. 1989-91), Inst. for Humanities (bd. dirs. Salado, Tex. chpt. 1985-91, mem. internat. com. advs. 1994), Philos Soc. Tex., Rotary, Masons, Alpha Chi, Phi Delta Kappa. Office: Southwestern U Office Pres Georgetown TX 78626

SHILLINGBURG, HERBERT THOMPSON, JR., dental educator; b. Ganado, Ariz., Mar. 21, 1938; s. Herbert Thompson and Stefi Marie (Schuster) S.; m. Constance Joanne Murphy, June 11, 1960; children: Lisa Grace, Leslie Susan, Lara Stephanie. Student U. N.Mex., 1955-58, 65-66; DDS, U. So. Calif., 1962. Gen. practice dentistry, Albuquerque, 1964-67; asst. prof. fixed prosthodontics sect. UCLA Sch. Dentistry, 1967-70, chmn. 1970-72; chmn. dept. fixed prosthodontics U. Okla. Coll. Dentistry, Oklahoma City, 1972—, David Ross Boyd Disting. prof., 1983; cons. VA Hosp., Muskogee, Okla., 1975-84, Oklahoma City, 1977-93, U.S. Army Dental Activity, Ft. Knox, Ky., 1980-94. Author: (also in Japanese, German, Greek, Spanish, Italian, French, Portuguese and Polish) Preparations for Cast Gold Restorations, 1974; Fundamentals of Fixed Prosthodontics, 1976, 2d edit., 1981; Guide to Occlusal Waxing, 1979, 2d edit., 1984; Restoration of the Endodontically Treated Tooth, 1984, Fundamentals of Tooth Preparations for Cast Metal and Porcelain Restorations, 1987; co-editor Quintessence of Dental Technology, 1984-88; sect. editor Quintessence Internat., 1988—; mem. editl. coun. Jour. Prosthetic Dentistry. Served to capt. U.S. Army, 1962-64. Recipient award for Teaching Excellence, UCLA Sch. Dentistry, 1969, 72, 73, U. Okla. Coll. Dentistry, 1976, 78, 82, 87, 93, 94, 1st prize Am. Med. Writers Assn., 1988, La Médaille de la Ville de Paris (échelon Argent), 1990; named O U Assocs. Disting. Lectr., 1989. Fellow Am. Coll. Dentists; mem. ADA, Acad. Operative Dentistry, Am. Acad. Fixed Prosthodontics, Am. Acad. Restorative Dentistry, Am. Coll. Prosthodontists (hon.), Okla. State Dental Assn., Internat. Assn. Dental Rsch., Omicron Kappa Upsilon. Republican. Episcopalian. Avocations: travel, photography. Home: 1312 Brixton Rd Edmond OK 73034-3314 Office: U Okla Coll Dentistry PO Box 26901 # U Oklahoma City OK 73190

SHIM, EUNSHIL, nutritionist, educator, business owner, consultant; b. Pusan, Kyungsang, Republic of Korea, July 10, 1952; came to U.S., 1969; d. Myungwon and Haeran (Kim) S.; m. W.E. Gene Holder, Aug. 16, 1986; children: Michael-Saejong, Michelle-Yumi. B in Dietetics, Mich. State U., 1975; M in Advanced Human Nutrition, U. Fla., 1979. Lic. dietitian, Fla. Dietary interviewer U. Fla., Gainesville, 1979; sr. dietitian Sunland Ctr., Gainesville, 1979-82; asst. prof. U. Fla., 1983-87; dietitian cons. Nutrition Assocs. of Jacksonville, Fla., 1987-88; owner, nutrition cons. Nutrition Profls., Inc., 1991—; adj. instr. U. Fla., 1981-82; vol. dietitian VA Med. Ctr., Gainesville, 1979; acting project dir. NIH Rsch. Grant, Gainesville, 1985-87; gov. apptd. mem. Long Term Care Ombudsmen Coun., 1987-89; instr. Fla. Community Coll. at Jacksonville, 1990—; pres. Nutrition Profls., Inc., Jacksonville, 1991—; cons. in field. Elder Presbyn. Ch.; chmn. Kids' Cafe adv. com. of N.E. Fla. Second Harvest Food Bank, 1996—. Named one of Outstanding Young Women Am., 1986; Fla. Dietetic Assn. scholar, 1979; recipient Univ. Affiliated Facility Traineeship award U. Miami, 1978. Mem. Am. Assn. Mental Deficiency, Am. Dietetic Assn. (exhibit chair gerontol. nutritionists group 1989-90, area coord. 1990-92, chair-elect 1992-93, chmn. 1993-94, health care reform media coord. Jacksonville area, 1994—), Fla. Dietetic Assn. 9chmn. dist. pres. 1986-87, awards com. 1987-88, chmn. scholarship com. 1988-89, chair bylaws com. 1990-91, chair nutrition svcs. payment system, 1992-93), Jacksonville Dietetic Assn. (bylaws com. chmn. 1987-88, 89-90, 90-91, legis. com. chmn. 1995-96), Gainesville Dist. Dietetic Assn. (edn. com. chmn. 1982-83, sec. 1983-84, mem. com. chmn. 1984-85, pres. 1985-86, ex-officio and nominating com. chmn. 1986-87), Mandarin Jr. Women's Club (newsletter editor, pub. rels. com. chair 1989-90). Home: 9967 Larkdale Ct Jacksonville FL 32257-6005 Office: PO Box 57134 Jacksonville FL 32241-7134

SHIMASAKI, CRAIG DAVID, research scientist; b. Stockton, Calif., Sept. 11, 1956; s. S. Jack and Betty Lou Shimasaki; m. Verna Joyce, Dec. 9, 1978; children: Alyssa, Lori. BS, U. Calif. Davis, 1983; PhD, U. Tulsa, 1995. Cert. pharmacy technician, Calif. Rsch. assoc. Genentech, Inc., San Francisco, 1983-87; from head biochemistry dept. to exec. dir. rsch. Symex, Corp., Tulsa, 1987-93; exec. dir. rsch. Zymetx, Inc., Oklahoma City, 1993-95, v.p. rsch., 1995—. Inventor in field. Children's ch. worship leader Victory Christian Ch., Oklahoma City, 1994-96. Home: 4204 NW 146th Terr Oklahoma City OK 73134 Office: ZymeTx Inc Ste 100 800 Research Pkwy Oklahoma City OK 73104

SHIMBERG, ELAINE FANTLE, writer; b. Yankton, S.D., Feb. 26, 1937; d. Karl S. and Alfreda (Edelson) Fantle; BS, Northwestern U., 1958; m. Mandell Shimberg, Oct. 1, 1961; children: Karen, Scott, Betsy, Andrew, Michael. Freelance writer, 1961—; co-hostess WFLA-TV talk show Women's Point of View, Tampa, Fla., 1976-81; tchr. Writing for Publication and Profit, Hillsborough Community Coll., Tampa 1980-82. Mem. public info. com. Fla. div. Am. Cancer Soc., 1974-89; bd. dirs. United Way, 1986-89. Mem. Am. Soc. Journalists and Authors, Am. Med. Writers Assn., Athena Soc., Fla. Medical Assn. (coun. ethical and judicial affairs, 1993—). Author: How to be A Successful Housewife/Writer, 1979; Two for the Money: A Woman's Guide to a Double Career Marriage, 1981; contbg. author: The Complete Guide to Writing Non-Fiction, 1983, Teenage Drinking and Driving: A Deadly Duo, 1984, Coping with Kids and Vacation, 1986, Relief From Irritable Bowel Syndrome, 1988, Strokes: What Families Should Know, 1990, Depression: What Families Should Know, 1992, Gifts of Time, 1993, Living with Tourette Syndrome, 1995, How to Get Out of the Hospital Alive, 1997; contbr. articles to various mags. Office: 611 W Bay St Tampa FL 33606-2703

SHIMER, DANIEL LEWIS, corporate executive; b. San Angelo, Tex., July 30, 1944; s. Lewis V. and Mary A. (Slick) S.; married. BS in Acctg. and Mktg., Ind. U., 1972; postgrad., Loyola U., New Orleans, 1977. CPA. Sr. acct. Peat, Marwick, Mitchell & Co., Indpls., 1973-75; asst. treas. LTV Corp., Dallas, 1975-79; v.p. fin. Stoller Chem. Co., Houston, 1979-81; v.p., CFO Petro-Silver, Inc., Denver, 1981-83; v.p., treas. FoxMeyer Corp., Denver, 1983-86; v.p., treas., sec. CoastAmerica Corp., Denver, 1986-88;

exec. v.p. Bard & Co., Denver, 1989-90; pres. nat accounts divsn. I Can't Believe It's Yogurt/ Brice Foods, Inc., Dallas, 1991-93; exec. v.p., CFO COREStaff Inc., Houston, 1994-96; pres. Shimer Capital Ptnrs., Inc., Dallas, 1996—. Mem. AICPA, Nat. Assn. Corp. Treas. Methodist. Home: 11 Duncannon Ct Dallas TX 75225-1809

SHIMKETS, LAWRENCE JOSEPH, JR., microbiology educator; b. Pitts., May 16, 1952; s. Lawrence Joseph and Dorothy Marie (Ehlinger) S.; m. Diane Jean Schoettle, July 19, 1980. BS, Fla. State U., 1974; PhD, U. Minn., 1980. NIH postdoctoral fellow Stanford (Calif.) U., 1980-82; asst. prof. U. Ga., Athens, 1982-88, assoc. prof. microbiology, 1988-93, prof., 1993—, head dept. microbiology, 1997—. Named Presdl. Young Investigator, NSF, 1984-89. Mem. Am. Soc. Microbiology, Sigma Xi. Home: RR 1 Box 56 Arnoldsville GA 30619-9602 Office: U Ga Dept Microbiology Athens GA 30602

SHIMMIN, MARGARET ANN, women's health nurse; b. Forbes, N.D., Oct. 26, 1941; d. George Robert and Reba Aleda (Strain) S. Diploma in Nursing, St. Luke's Hosp. Sch. Nursing, Fargo, N.D., 1962; BSW, U. West Fla., 1978; cert. ob-gyn nurse practitioner, U. Ala., Birmingham, 1983, MPH, 1986. Lic. nurse, Fla., N.D., Ala. Head nurse, emergency room St. Luke's Hosps., Fargo, 1962-67; charge nurse, labor and delivery, perinatal nurse educator Sacred Heart Hosp., Pensacola, Fla., 1970-82; ARNP Escambia County Pub. Health Unit, Pensacola, 1983-89; cmty. health nursing cons. Dist. 1 Health and Rehab. Svcs., Pensacola, 1989—. Capt. nurse corps U.S. Army, 1967-70, Japan. Mem. NAACOG (cert. maternal-gynecol.-neonatal nursing 1978, ob-gyn nurse practitioner 1983), Fla. Nurses' Assn., ANA, N.W. Fla. ARNP (past sec./treas.), Fla. Perinatal Assn., Nat. Perinatal Assn., Healthy Mothers/Healthy Babies Coalition, Fla. Pub. Health Assn., U. West Fla. Alumni Assn., U. Ala. at Birmingham Sch. of Public Health Alumni Assn., Phi Alpha. Republican. Presbyterian. Home: 8570 Olympia Rd Pensacola FL 32514-8029 Office: Dist 1 HRS 160 Governmental Ctr Pensacola FL 32501

SHIMP, ROBERT EVERETT, JR., academic administrator, historian; b. Phila., Mar. 1, 1942; s. Robert Everett Sr. and Vivian (Myrtetus) S.; m. Marilyn Hopkins, Aug. 3, 1963; children: Gregory, Cecily, Jennifer. BA, Thiel Coll., 1964; MA, Ohio State U., 1965, PhD, 1970. Instr. history Ohio Wesleyan U., Delaware, Ohio, 1968-70, asst. prof., 1970-76, assoc. prof., 1976-82, prof. history, 1982-84, dir. off campus program, 1979-84; acad. dean Ky. Wesleyan Coll., Owensboro, 1984-88; provost, v.p. for acad. affairs Millikin U., Decatur, Ill., 1988-93; pres. McMurry U., Abilene, Tex., 1993—; vis. assoc. prof. Ohio State U., Columbus, summer 1978, Coll. of V.I., St. Croix, fall 1982; mem. Inst. for Ednl. Mgmt. Harvard U., 1985; reader and table leader European history AP, Princeton, N.J. 1976-83; dir. Newberry Libr. Program in the Humanities, Chgo., 1976-77. Contbr. articles to profl. jours. Mem. Leadership Owensboro, 1986-87; capt. drives United Way, Owensboro and Delaware, 1981-85, bd. dirs., Decatur and Abilene; trustee for Sears Retirement Systems and Abilene Higher Edn. Authority; bd. dirs. Abilene C. of C. Fellow Ohio State U., 1968, Newberry Libr., Chgo., 1976-77. Mem. Ohio Acad. History, Conf. on Brit. Studies. Democrat. Methodist. Office: McMurry U Office of Pres PO Box 98 Abilene TX 79604-0098

SHINN, GEORGE, owner NBA franchise; b. Kannapolis, N.C.. Owner The Charlotte (N.C.) Hornets, Charlotte Knights Baseball. Recipient Horatio Alger award, 1975. Mem. Charlotte C. of C. (bd. dirs.). Office: Charlotte Hornets 100 Hive Dr Charlotte NC 28217

SHINN, SUSA JANE, medical/surgical nurse; b. Marion, Ind., Apr. 9, 1940; d. Frederick Maurice and Marguerite (White) S. Diploma, Parkview Meth. Sch. Nursing, Ft. Wayne, Ind., 1961; BS, Tex. Woman's U., 1983. Cert. operating rm. nurse, cardiovascular nurse specialist. Physicians asst. Ft. Wayne; supr. operating rm. and recovery room Med. Ctr. Del Oro Hosp., Houston; supr., asst. Meth. Hosp., Houston, mgr. operating rm.; head nurse oper. rm. Meth. Hosp. Mem. ANA, NAFE, Tex. Nurses Assn., Assn. Oper. Rm. Nurses, Fedn. Houston Profl. Women, Parkview Meth. Sch. Nursing Alumni Assn., Tex. Woman's U. Alumni Assn., Zool. Soc. Houston, Houston Mus. Natural Sci., Mus. Fine Arts. Methodist. Home: 3211 Elmridge St Houston TX 77025-4311

SHIPLEY, ALDEN PEVERLY, broadcaster, broadcasting executive; b. Phila., Nov. 27, 1946; s. Alden Peverly and Selma Nadine (Smith) S.; m. Rose Marie Welsh, Dec. 27, 1969. Account exec. Sta. WAKY Radio/Multimedia Broadcast, Louisville, 1974-78; sales mgr. Sta. WGAC/Beasley Broadcast, Augusta, Ga., 1978-80; regional sales mgr. Stas. WVCG-WYOR/Insilco Broadcast, Coral Gables, Fla., 1980-83; gen. mgr. Sta. WMAD Radio, Madison, Wis., 1983-84; gen. sales mgr. Sta. WKAT Radio-Hernstadt Broadcast, Miami Beach, Fla., 1984-85; cons. Advanced Broadcast Mgmt., Washington, 1983-85; v.p. ops. Network Media Comm., N.Y.C., 1985-86; founder, owner, dir. Automated Broadcast Cons., Inc., Miami Beach, 1986—. Co-author software Automated Cable Billing Sys.; prodr. TV programs Dance TV, Miss Robins Dance Class, World's Greatest Dancers. With USNR, 1965-67. Republican. Roman Catholic. Home: 5401 Collins Ave Apt 516 Miami FL 33140-2532 Office: Automated Broadcast Cons 1440 Kennedy Causeway 5401 Collins Ave Miami FL 33140-2573

SHIPLEY, GEORGE CORLESS, political consultant; b. Houston, May 26, 1947; s. George Hale and Florence (Corless) S.; m. Donna West, June 2, 1972; children: George West Shipley, Andrew Corless Shipley. BA in Fgn. Affairs, U. Va., 1969; PhD, U. Tex., 1977; grad. study, Harvard U., 1968. Teaching asst. U. Tex., Austin, 1970-73; rsch. asst. U. Tex., 1971; spl. asst. U.S. Sen. Lloyd Bentsen, Austin, 1973-77; faculty mem. U. Tex. Govt. Dept., Austin, 1977-78; ptnr. Henson, Hopkins & Shipley, Austin, 1978-80; pres., CEO Shipley & Assocs., Inc., Austin, 1980—; vis. faculty LBJ Sch. Pub. Affairs, U. Tex. Contbr. articles to profl. jours. Communications dir. Gore for Pres., 1987-88; cons. Dem. Congl. Campaign Com., 1983-86. Named Congl. fellow Am. Polit. Sci. Assn., 1973, U. Tex. fellow, 1972. Mem. Dem. Leadership Coun., Congl. Fellows Assn., Internat. Assn. Polit. Cons., Am. Assn. Polit. Cons., Am. Polit. Sci. Assn., U. Va. Alumni Assn., Friends of LBJ Libr., Va. Club of N.Y.C. Democrat. Episcopalian. Office: Shipley & Assocs Inc 919 Congress Ave Ste 750 Austin TX 78701-2444

SHIPMAN, ROSS LOVELACE, petroleum executive; b. Jackson, Miss., Nov. 20, 1926; s. William Smylie and Jeanette Scott (Lovelace) S.; m. Lois Pegrim, June 6, 1948; 1 dau., Smylie Shipman Anderson. BA, U. Miss., 1950. Registered profl. geologist, Ark, chartered geologist, U.K. Geologist Humble Oil & Refining Co., West Tex., 1950-55; petroleum cons., Midland, Tex., 1955-60, Corpus Christi, Tex., 1960-67; asst. exec. dir. Am. Geol. Inst., Washington, 1967-71; assoc. dir. U. Tex. Marine Sci. Inst., Austin, 1971-79; assoc. v.p. for research U. Tex., Austin, 1979-85; pres., chief exec. officer Live Oak Energy, Inc., 1985-86; prin. Petroleum Investments/Worldwide, 1975—; dir. Indsl. Assocs. program Coll. Nat. Scis. U. Tex., Austin, 1986-89; mem. Tex. Coastal and Marine Council, 1979-85; U.S.-Mexico Boundary Water Study Program, 1978— ; del. Argonne Univs. Assn., Chgo., 1982. Author numerous geol. reports and studies, 1955—; editor, pub. The AGI Report newsletter, 1968-70; editor Profl. Geologist, 1975-76. Served with U.S. Army, 1944-46; PTO. Fellow Geol. Soc. London; mem. Am. Inst. Profl. Geologists (cert. profl. geologist, Tex. pres. 1974, nat. editor 1975-76), Soc. Ind. Profl. Earth Scientists, Tex. Soc. SAR (pres.), Soc. of Mayflower Descendents (San Antonio colony), Petroleum Club of San Antonio, Jamestowne Soc. (lt. gov. San Antonio co.), Sons of Confederate Vets. (comdr. Hood's Tex. Brigage Camp). Episcopalian. Research on petroleum and mineral exploration and enhanced oil recovery devel., internat. water devel. Home: 1911 E Lawndale Dr San Antonio TX 78209-2043

SHIRCLIFF, JAMES VANDERBURGH, communications executive; b. Vincennes, Ind., Dec. 11, 1938; s. Thomas Maxwell and Martha Bayard (Somes) S.; AB, Brown U., 1961; postgrad. U. Va., 1963-64; m. Sally Anne Hoing, June 20, 1964; children: Thomas, Susan, Anne, Catherine, Caroline. Asst. gen. mgr. Pepsi Cola Allied Bottlers, Inc., Lynchburg, Va., 1964-65; gen. mgr. First Colony Canners, Inc., Lynchburg, 1965-66; v.p., divisional coord. Pepsi Cola Allied Bottlers, Inc., Lynchburg, 1966-68, v.p., dir. personnel, 1968-70; v.p., gen. mgr. GCC Beverages, Inc., Lynchburg, 1970-74, group v.p. Va., 1974-75; corp. v.p. Gen. Cinema Corp., Beverage Div., Lynchburg, 1976-77; owner/mgr. WLLL-AM, WGOL-FM, Lynchburg, 1977-86; pres. Jamarbo Corp., 1977-88; chmn. bd. SignWaves, Inc., presdl. interchange exec., 1975-76; exec. dir. Nat. Indsl. Energy Coun., Dept. Commerce, Washington, 1975-76. V.p. JOBS, Lynchburg, 1970; dir. Cen. Va. Health Planning Coun., 1974-75; mem. Govs. Indsl. Energy Adv. Coun., 1976—; dir. Piedmont coun., Boy Scouts Am., 1972-73; mem. City of Lynchburg Keep Lynchburg Beautiful Commn., 1974-75, chmn. emergency planning bd., 1974-75, chmn. overall econ. planning coun., 1977-88; bd. dirs. Lynchburg Broadway Theatre, 1973-75, Acad. Music, 1973-74, United Fund, Lynchburg, 1966-67, Cen. Va. Industries, 1971-72, Va. Pub. Telecommunications Coun.; former trustee Culver Ednl. Found.; chmn. campaign United Way, 1982, pres., 1983; chmn. Citizens for a Clean Lynchburg; campaign chmn. United Way of Ctrl. Va., dir. 1996; chmn. Arts Coun. Cen. Va., 1990-93; mem. nat. adv. coun. U.S. Small Bus. Adminstrn., 1990-93; past trustee Va. Episc. Sch.; past mem. pres.' coun. Randolph-Macon Women's Coll., Cen. Va. Community Coll. Found. Bd.; past mem. Va-Israel Commn.; dir. Lynchburg Hist. Found., 1996—. Lt. (j.g.), USN, 1961-63. Recipient Cloyd Meml. award for outstanding svc., Greater Lynchburg C. of C., 1975; Va. Soft Drink Assn. citation, 1970, 73, 74; NCCJ Brotherhood Citation; Pub. Svc. award Radio-TV Commn. of So. Bapt. Conv., NCCJ State Adv. Bd., Exec. Com. Swensen's Owners Coun., 1988. Va. C. of C. (dir. 1976-79), Greater Lynchburg C. of C. (dir., v.p. 1973-74, chmn. community appearance task force 1977-79), Va. Soft Drink Assn. (pres. 1973-74), Va. Pepsi Cola Bottlers Assn. (pres. 1970-73), Nat., Va. (dir. 1974, pres. 1985-86) assns. broadcasters, Lynchburg Advt. Club (v.p.), Va. AP Broadcasters Assn. (pres.), Lynchburg Fine Arts Ctr. (pres.), Culver Academies Alumni Assn. (pres.), Culver Cum Laude Soc. (award 1996, hon.), Mensa, Commonwealth Club, Oakwood Country Club, Piedmont Club, Navy League, The Pavane Club, Lynchburg Sports Club, Knight Sovereign Military Order Malta Fedn. Assn., Rotary (past pres., Paul Harris fellow 1982, dist. gov. 1986-87). Roman Catholic. Home: 3525 Otter View Pl Lynchburg VA 24503-3035 Address: Box 10486 Lynchburg VA 24506-0486

SHIREK, JOHN RICHARD, retired savings and loan executive; b. Bismarck, N.D., Feb. 5, 1926; s. James Max and Anna Agatha (Lala) S.; student U. Minn., 1944-46; BS with honors, Rollins Coll., 1978; m. Ruth Martha Lietz, Sept. 22, 1950; children: Barbara Jo (Mrs. James A. Fowler), Jon Richard, Kenneth Edward. Sports editor Bismarck (N.D.) Tribune, 1943-44; with Gate City Savs. and Loan Assn., Fargo, N.D., 1947-65, v.p., dir., 1960-65; exec. v.p., dir. 1st Fed. Savs. and Loan Assn., Melbourne, Fla., 1966-70; pres., dir. 1st Fed. Savs. and Loan Assn., Cocoa, Fla., 1970-82; exec. v.p., dir. The First, F.A. (formerly 1st Fed. Savs. and Loan Assn. of Orlando), 1982-91; interim pres. Freedom Savs. and Loan Assn., Tampa, Fla., 1987-88; trustee Savs. & Loan Found., Inc., 1980-84; dir. Fin. Trans. Systems, Inc., Magnolia Svcs. Corp., 1st Cocoa Corp., Magnolia Realty Co., 1982-91. Chmn., dir. United Fund, Fargo, N.D., 1962-65; dir., exec. bd. mem. Boy Scouts Am., 1960-70, mem. adv. bd. cen. Fla. coun., 1983-85, 91—, exec. bd., 1985-91, v.p. long-range planning, 1989-91; bd. assocs. Fla. Inst. Tech., founding pres., 1968; moderator St. Johns Presbytery, 1979, chmn. advisory coun., 1980-81; chair local arrangements com., 1993. Gen. Assembly Presbyn. Ch.; moderator Synod of Fla., 1983, Cen. Fla. Presbytery, 1991, coordinating coun., 1992; mem. adv. bd. Brevard Art Ctr. and Mus., 1980-82; bd. dirs., founding chmn. devel. coun. Holmes Regional Med. Ctr., Melbourne, 1981-84; bd. dirs. Orlando Regional Med. Ctr. Found., 1982-85, Jr. Achievement Cen. Fla., 1989-91; mem. fin. com. Mayor's Task Force on Housing, 1983-84; chmn. spl. com. on Nat. Council Chs./World Council Chs. rels. Presbyn. Ch. in U.S.A., 1983-86; pres. Ecumenical Ctr. Inc., Orlando, 1985-91; chmn. Fla. adv. com. Ctr. Theol. Studies Columbia Theol. Sem., 1991—. Lt. (j.g.) USNR, World War II. Mem. Fla. Savs. and Loan League (past dir.), Fla. Savs. and Loan Svcs. (past dir.), Savs. and Loan Found. (state membership chmn. 1976), Fla. Savs. and Loan Polit. Action Com. (dir. 1976-82), U.S. Savs. and Loan League (chmn. advt. and pub. rels. com. 1969-70, dir. S.E. conf., 1975-80), Downtown Melbourne Assn. (past pres.), Cocoa Rotary (pres. 1979), Rio Pinar Country Club, Masons, Shriners, Elks, Beta Theta Pi, Omicron Delta Epsilon. Republican. Home: PO Box 568831 Orlando FL 32856-8831

SHIRES, GEORGE THOMAS, surgeon, educator; b. Waco, Tex., Nov. 22, 1925; s. George Thomas and Donna Mae (Smith) S.; m. Robbie Jo Martin, Nov. 27, 1948; children: Donna Blain, George Thomas III, Jo Ellen. MD, U. Tex., Dallas, 1948. Diplomate Am. Bd. Surgery (dir. 1968-74, chmn. 1972-74). Intern Mass. Meml. Hosp., Boston, 1948-49; resident Parkland Meml. Hosp., Dallas, 1950-53; mem. faculty U. Tex. Southwestern Med. Sch. at Dallas, 1953-74, assoc. prof. surgery, acting chmn. dept., 1960-61, prof., chmn. dept., 1961-74; surgeon in chief surg. services Parkland Meml. Hosp., 1960-74; prof., chmn. dept. surgery U. Wash. Sch. Medicine, Seattle, 1974-75; chief of service Harborview Med. Center, Seattle, Univ. Hosp., Seattle, 1974-75; chmn. dept. surgery N.Y. Hosp.-Cornell Univ. Med. Coll., 1975-91; dean and provost for med. affairs Cornell U. Med. Coll., 1987-91; prof., chmn. surgery Tex. Tech. U., Lubbock, 1991-95, Canizaro disting. prof. surgery, 1995—; cons. Surgeon Gen., U.S. Army, 1965-75, Jamaica Hosp., 1978-91, Inst. Medicine Nat. Acad. Scis., 1975—; mem. com. metabolism and trauma Nat. Acad. Scis.-NRC, 1964-71, com. trauma, 1964-71; mem. rsch. program evaluation com., reviewer clin. investigation applications career devel. program VA, 1972-76; mem. gen. med. rsch. program projects com. NIH, 1965-69; mem. Surgery A study sect., 1970-74, chmn., 1976-78; mem. Nat. Adv. Gen. Med. Scis. Coun., 1980-84; cons. editl. bd. Jour. Trauma, 1968—. Mem. editl. bd. Year Book Med. Publs., 1970-92, Annals of Surgery, 1972—, Surg. Techniques Illustrated: An International Comparative Text, 1974-75, Am. Jour. Surgery, 1968—, Contemporary Surgery, 1973-89; assoc. editor-in-chief Infections in Surgery, 1981; mem. editl. coun. Jour. Clin. Surgery, 1980-82; editor Surgery, Gynecology and Obstetrics, 1982-93. Lt. M.C. USNR, 1949-50, 53-55. Life Ins. Med. Rsch. fellow, 1947. Mem. ACS (bd. regents 1971-82, chmn. bd. regents 1978-80, pres. 1981-82), AMA, Dallas Soc. Gen. Surgeons (pres.-elect, pres. 1972-74), Am. Assn. Surgery Trauma, Am. Surg. Assn. (sec. 1969-74, pres. 1980), Digestive Disease Found. (founding mem.), Halsted Soc., Internat. Soc. Burn Injuries, Internat. Surg. Soc. (sec. 1978-81, v.p. 1982-83, pres. U.S. chpt. 1984-85), Pan-Am. Med. Assn. (surgery council 1971—), Pan Pacific Surg. Assn., Soc. Clin. Surgery, Soc. Surgery Alimentary Tract, Soc. Surg. Chairmen (pres. 1972-74), Soc. Univ. Surgeons (chmn. publs. com. 1969-71), So. Surg. Assn., Surg. Biology Club (sec. 1968-70), Western Surg. Assn., Allen O. Whipple Surg. Soc., James IV Assn. Surgeons (bd. dirs. 1980-81, sec. 1981-87, pres. 1987-91), Alpha Omega Alpha, Alpha Pi Alpha, Phi Beta Pi. Office: Tex Tech U Med Coll Lubbock TX 79430

SHIRK, PAUL DAVID, research physiologist; b. Waterloo, Iowa, June 7, 1948; s. Joseph Gerald and Darlene Ann (Bolton) S.; m. Lynna Kay Lehew, Dec. 29, 1975; children: Heather Elaine, Bryce David. BA, U. No. Iowa, 1970; MS, Tex. A & M U., 1975, PhD, 1978. Rsch. asst. dept. biochemistry U. Iowa, Iowa City, 1970-72; grad. rsch. asst. dept. biochemistry Tex. A & M U., College Station, 1972-75, grad. rsch. asst. dept. biology, 1976-78; rsch. assoc. dept. biology U. Oreg., Eugene, 1978-79, NIH postdoctoral fellow dept. biology, 1979-81; asst. prof. dept. zoology Oreg. State U., Corvallis, 1981-84; rsch. physiologist USDA, ARS, Insect Attractants Behavior & Basic Biology Lab., Gainesville, Fla., 1984—. Editl. bd.: Archives of Insect Biochemistry and Physiology, 1991—; contbr. articles to profl. jours. NIH postdoctoral nat. rsch. awardee, 1979-81; grantee Med. Rsch. Found. Oreg., 1982-83, USDA/Competitive Rsch. Grants Program, 1986-88, USDA/ARS, 1986-88, 91-93, U.S.-Israel Binat. Agrl. R&D Fund, 1987-90. Mem. Am. Soc. for Cell Biology, Soc. for Developmental Biology, Sigma Xi. Office: USDA ARS 1700 SW 23rd Dr Gainesville FL 32608-1069

SHIRLEY, CHARLES WILLIAM, farm owner; b. Norfolk, Va., Jan. 28, 1954; s. Norris Winfred and Margorie Elizabeth (Whedbee) S.; m. Carol Ruth Montgomery, May 21, 1977; children: Sarah Ruth, Daniel Talmadge. Student, U. S.C., 1972-74; BS in Bus. and Journalism, Old Dominion U., 1977, cert. profl. fin. planner, 1986; cert. land use planner, Va. Polytech. Inst., 1987. assoc. agt. Nationwide Ins. Ptnr. N.W. Shirley Farms, Virginia Beach, Va., 1977-88; owner C.W. Shirley Farms, Chesapeake, Va., 1982—; dealer Northrup King, Chesapeake, Va., 1985-94; assoc. agt. Nationwide Ins., 1995—. Contbr. articles to newspapers and mags., 1985—. Planning commr. City of Chesapeake, 1986-94; chmn. Planning Commn., 1991-92; mem. Chesapeake Growth Commn., 1993; chmn. Virginia Beach Young Farmers Com., 1983-95; cmn. food com. S.E. Young Farmer's Tractor Pull, 1984; bd. dirs. Chesapeake Crime Line, 1985-93. Recipient Young Farmer award and Discussion Meet award Va. Farm Bur., 1984; named Young Farmer of Yr., Virginia Beach Jaycees, 1984; winner Va. corn yield contest, 1993. Mem. Nat. Assn. Profl. Fin. Planners, Va. Soybean Assn. (mem. com. chmn. 1991-92, v.p. 1992-93, pres. 1994, Young Leader Va. 1990), Virginia Beach Farm Bur. (v.p. 1990-92), Chesapeake Farm Bur. (v.p. 1994-95, pres. 1995), Creeds Ruritan Club (sec. 1987), Nat. Corn Growers Assn. (Va. Corn Contest winner 1993), Va. Small Grain Assn., Va. Citizen's Planners Assn., Va. Soybean Bd. Baptist. Home: 2420 Carolina Rd Chesapeake VA 23322-1428 Office: CW Shirley Farms 2424 Carolina Rd Chesapeake VA 23322-1428

SHIRLEY, GEORGE MILTON, JR., chemicals executive; b. Beaumont, Tex., Sept. 23, 1939; s. George Milton Sr. and Ava Pearl (Patty) S.; m. Anne Himmelheber, Dec. 26, 1960; children: Merrie P. Robertson, Ransome L. BS in Sociology, Lamar U., 1976. Sr. process operator Mobil Chem. Co., Beaumont, 1961-76; safety rep. Oxirane Chem. Co., Channelview, Tex., 1976-79; safety engr. Corpus Christi (Tex.) Petrochem. Co., 1979-80; loss prevention engr. Arabian Am. Oil Co., Yanbu Industrial City, Saudi Arabia, 1980-86; pres., chief exec. officer GMS Assocs., Houston, 1986-88; safety dir. Vista Chem. Co., Westlake, La., 1988-91; mgr. safety Yemen Hunt Oil Co., Sana'a, Republic of Yemen, 1991; pres., CEO GMS Assocs., Sulphur, La., 1991—. Mem. Calcasieu Parish Com. Awareness Emergency Response Com., 1988-91, La. Emergency Preparedness Assn., 1988-91; bd. dirs. Calcasieu Cameron ARC, Lake Charles, La., 1988-89. Mem. Am. Soc. Safety Engrs. (profl., sect. chmn. 1984-85, 91), World Safety Orgn. (cert. safety and security dir., cert. safety mgr.), S.W. La. Safety Engrs. Republican.

SHIVEL, GAIL LAUREN, English language educator; b. Fort Lauderdale, Fla., Mar. 29, 1969; d. James Walter and Mabel Ruth (Buchanan) S.; BS in Comm., U. Miami, 1990. Ad coord. Kridel & Assocs., Coral Gables, Fla., 1990-91; pub. affairs writer Miami (Fla.)-Dade C.C., 1991-93; account supr. Wragg & Casas Pub. Rels., Miami, 1993-96; lectr. U. Miami Sch. Comm., Coral Gables, 1996—; writing lectr. Miami-Dade C.C., 1992—; tchg. asst. Fla. Internat. U., Miami, 1996—. Mem. MLA, Pub. Rels. Soc. Am., Nat. Press Club (first place short story contest 1994), Ambs. Mercy Found., Mencken Soc. Democrat. Office: 5783 SW 40th St # 221 Miami FL 33155

SHOAF, CHON REGAN, federal agency health sciences administrator; b. Lexington, N.C., June 14, 1948; s. Irlo Norfleet and Jeanette (Michael) S.; children: Chon Regan II, JoAnna Dale. AB in Chemistry and Zoology, U. N.C., 1970, PhD in Biochemistry, 1980. Rsch. technician III U. N.C., Chapel Hill, 1970-73, rsch. assoc. dept. biochemistry and nutrition, 1979-81; Nat. Rsch. Svc. Award fellow lab. pharmacology Nat. Inst. Environ. Health Scis., Research Triangle Park, 1981-84; rsch. assoc. dept. pharmacology Duke U. Med. Ctr., Durham, N.C., 1984-88; cons. Menzel Assocs., Hillsborough, N.C., 1984-88; prin. Menzel-Shoaf, Inc., Durham, 1989-90; chief hazardous pollutant assessment br. U.S. EPA, Research Triangle Park, 1990—. Contbr. over 64 articles, abstracts, and monographs to profl. jours., chpts. to books. Elks scholar, 1966; scholar U. N.C., 1966-70; grantee Eastman Pharms, 1987. Mem. Nat. Soc. for Risk Analysis, Soc. Toxicology, Soc. for Risk Analysis, N.C. Soc. Toxicology. Democrat. Baptist. Home: 8021 Old Nc 86 Chapel Hill NC 27516-5142 Office: US EPA ECAO (MD-52) Durham NC 27711

SHOAF, KRISTIN ELIZABETH, foreign language educator; b. Richmond, Va., July 16, 1971; d. H. Kenneth and Anne (Saunders) S. Student, U. Valencia, Spain, 1991-92; BA in Spanish, Mary Washington Coll., 1993; MA in Spanish, U. Ga., 1995, postgrad., 1995—. Spanish tutor Mary Washington Coll., Fredericksburg, Va., 1989-91; resident advisor at the Govs. Spanish Acad. Va. Dept. Edn., Richmond, Va., summers 91-92; intern transcribing bibliographies of Spanish authors Libr. of Congress-Hispanic Studies Divsn., Washington, 1992-93; tchg. asst. U. Ga., Athens, 1993—; interpreter The Olympics, Atlanta, summer 1996; Spanish tutor U. Ga., Athens, 1996—; presenter in field. Vol. Humane Soc. for Animals, Fredericksburg, Va., 1990-91; vol. blood donor ARC, Athens. Mem. MLA, South Atlantic MLA, L.Am. Studies Assn., Sigma Delta Pi. Presbyterian. Office: Univ Ga 109 Moore Coll Athens GA 30602

SHOCKEY, THOMAS EDWARD, real estate executive, engineer; b. San Antonio, Aug. 17, 1926; s. Verlie Draper and Margaret Ruth (Shuford) S.; BS (Davidson fellow Tau Beta Pi), Tex. A&M U., 1950; postgrad. St. Mary's U., 1964, San Antonio Coll., 1972, Pacific Western U., 1981; m. Jacqueline McPherson, June 4, 1949; children: Cheryl Ann, Jocelyn Marie, Valerie Jean. With Petty Geophys. Survey, 1947-49, J.E. Ingram Equipment Co., 1950-51; co-owner, archtl. engr., realtor Moffett Lumber Co., Inc., San Antonio, 1952-76; cons. gen. contracting, gen. real estate, 1944—, retailer wholesale bldg. material, 1951—, v.p., 1959—; real estate counselor, appraiser, 1972—; real estate appraiser Gill Appraisal Svc., San Antonio, 1977—; comml. loan appraiser, underwriter, analyst Gill Savs. Assn., Gill Cos., San Antonio, 1979; chief appraiser, underwriter, architect, engr., insp. Gill Cos., 1981, v.p., 1981-87, ret., 1987; v.p. La Hacienda Savs. Assn., 1988-91, ret., 1991. Fire chief Mico Vol. Fire Dept., 1993-95. With inf. Signal Corps, U.S. Army, 1944-46; ETO. Mem. San Antonio C. of C., Nat. Lumber Dealers, Nat. Home Builders, Nat. Real Estate Bd., Nat. Inst. Real Estate Brokers, Internat. Soc. Real Estate Appraisers, Tex. Assn. Real Estate Insps., Real Estate Appraisers Tex., Nat. Assn. Rev. Appraisers and Mortgage Underwriters, Internat. Inst. Valuers, Internat. Platform Assn. Home: 126 County Road 2620 Mico TX 78056-5213

SHOCKLEY, CAROL FRANCES, psychologist, psychotherapist; b. Atlanta, Nov. 24, 1948; d. Robert Thomas and Frances Lavada (Scrivner) S. BA, Ga. State U., 1974, MEd, 1976; PhD, U. Ga., 1990. Cert. in gerontology; Diplomate Am. Bd. Forensic Examiners. Counselor Rape Crisis Ctr., Atlanta, 1979-80; emergency mental health clinician Gwinnett Med. Ctr., Lawrenceville, Ga., 1980-86; psychotherapist Fla. Mental Health Inst., Tampa, 1987-89, Tampa Bay Acad., Riverview, Fla., 1990-91; sr. psychologist State of Fla. Dept. of Corrections, Bushnell, 1991-92; ind. practice psychology Brunswick, Ga., 1992—; mem. Adv. Bd. for Mental Health/Mental Retardation, 1992-94. Author: (with others) Relapse Prevention with Sex Offenders, 1989. Vol. Ga. Mental Health Inst., Atlanta, 1972; leader Alzheimer's Disease Support Group, Athens, Ga., 1984; vol. therapist Reminiscence Group for Elderly, Athens, 1984-85. Recipient Meritorious Svc. award Beta Gamma Sigma, 1975. Mem. Am. Psychol. Assn., Ga. Psychol. Assn., Sigma Phi Omega, Psi Chi. Office: 14 Saint Andrews Ct Brunswick GA 31520-6764

SHOCKLEY, MARTIN STAPLES, retired English studies educator, writer; b. Stuart, Va., Mar. 24, 1908; s. John Calvin and Lelia Harwood (Staples) S.; m. Eliza Coffin Taylor, June 5, 1936; children: Ellen Taylor, John Staples. BA, U. Richmond, 1928; AM, Duke U., 1932; PhD, U. N.C., 1938. Asst. prof. The Citadel, Charleston, S.C., 1935-38, U. Okla., Norman, 1938-44; assoc. prof. Carleton Coll., Northfield, Minn., 1944-46; prof. Evansville (Ind.) Coll., 1946-50; prof. U. North Tex., Denton, 1950-74, prof. emeritus, 1974—. Author: Reading and Writing, 1955, Southwest Writers Anthology, 1967, The Richmond Stage, 1784-1812, 1977, Last Roundup, 1994. Mem. Poetry Soc. Tex. (pres. 1950-60), Tex. Conf. Coll. Tchrs. English (pres. 1955), Tex. Assn. Univ. Profs. (pres. 1960), Tex. Folklore Soc. (pres. 1962), Am. Studies Assn. Tex. (pres. 1965), Tex. Inst. Letters (sec.-treas. 1964-75). Democrat. Episcopalian. Home: 2315 Willowwood St Denton TX 76205-7420

SHOCKLEY, ROBERT KENNETH, medical researcher; b. Spartanburg, S.C., Oct. 31, 1949; m. JoEllen Dorand, Aug. 12, 1972; 1 child, Stephen Douglas. BS in Biology, U. S.C., 1971; MS in Microbiology, Clemson U., 1975; PhD in Microbiology, U. Tex. Health Scis. Ctr., Dallas, 1980; postdoctorate, U. Ga., 1980-82. Postdoctoral rsch. assoc. dept. microbiology U. Ga., Athens, 1980-82; microbiologist, prin. investigator VA Med. Ctr., Augusta, Ga., 1982-86; asst. rsch. prof. dept. medicine Med. Coll. Ga., Augusta, 1983-85, asst. prof., 1985-86; sr. scientist rsch. and devel. Murex Corp., Norcross, Ga., 1986-87, project mgr. R&D, 1987-88, dir. infectious diseases, R&D, 1988-92, dir. regulatory affairs and responsible head, 1990—, dir. R&D, 1992-94; dir. sci. and tech. affairs, 1994—. Contbr. articles to profl. jours. Participant career day Pinckneyville Mid. Sch., 1993; asst. leader, adult vol. troop 403 Boy Scouts Am., Doraville, Ga., 1992—. Grantee Shering Co., 1985-86, Bristol Meyers Co., 1984-86, Hoffman-LaRoche, Inc., 1982-84, VA, 1984-86. Mem. Am. Soc. Microbiology, Sigma Xi. Office: Murex Corp 30-75 Northwoods Cir Norcross GA 30071-1542

SHOEMAKER, EDWARD CONNIE, librarian; b. Nowata, Okla., July 20, 1943; s. Virgil and Virginia Bell (Huey) S. AA, Northeastern A&M Coll., 1963; BA, Okla. State U., 1967; MLS, U. Okla., 1976. Supr. tech. svcs. Okla. Hist. Soc., Oklahoma City, 1980-88, dir. libr. resources divsn., 1988—. Vol. Cleveland County Family "Y", Norman, 1987—. Petty officer 3d class USN, 1967-69. Vol. of Yr., Cleveland County Family "Y", 1992. Mem. Okla. Libr. Assn., Sch. of Libr. & Info. Sci. of U. Okla., Vol. Cmty. Cleveland County "Y". Democrat. Home: PO Box 2513 Norman OK 73070-2513 Office: Okla Hist Soc 2100 N Lincoln Blvd Oklahoma City OK 73105-4915

SHOEMAKER, M. WESLEY, history educator; b. Pa., May 3, 1935; s. Warry Henry and Mary Elizabeth (Bochert) S.; m. Mary Charlotte Alexich, July 2, 1962. BA, Waynesburg Coll., 1957; MA, Syracuse U., 1973, PhD, 1979. Internat. affairs specialist European Bur., U.S. Dept. State, Washington, 1962-64; 3d sec. U.S. Embassy, Kingston, Jamaica, 1964-66; 2d sec. U.S. Embassy, Bonn, Germany, 1966-67, U.S. Consulate Gen., Stuttgart, Germany, 1967-68; teaching asst. Syracuse (N.Y.) U., 1970; asst. prof. Lynchburg (Va.) Coll., 1971-79, assoc. prof., 1980-90, prof. history, 1990—, chair internat. rels. program, 1986-96, chair history dept., 1988-91; chair campus life policies com. Lynchburg Coll., 1989-90, chair ednl. policies com., 1994-95, assoc. dean, 1996—. Author: Soviet Union and Eastern Europe, annually 1983—, Russia, CIS and East Europe, 1992, 93, 94, 95, 96. With U.S. Army, 1958-61. Recipient Syracuse U. fellowship Syracuse (N.Y.) U., 1957, univ. fellowship lang., 1968-70, NDEA, 1970. Mem. Internat. Studies Assn., Ctrl. European History Assn., Va. Assn. Polit. Scientists, Va. Assn. Asian Scholars. Republican. Home: RR 4 Box 570 Forest VA 24551-9221 Office: Lynchburg College History Dept Lynchburg VA 24501

SHOEMAKER, SANDRA KAYE, aerospace executive; b. Dallas, July 13, 1954; d. Vondyl Claud and Billie Juanita (Pritchett) Willis; m. Carl Vernon Shoemaker, Aug. 16, 1975; children: Regan Amanda, Ryan Adam. BBA, Baylor U., 1975. Fin. coord. Tex. A&M U., College Station, 1975-77; from engrng. planner to mgr. adminstrv. support Gen. Dynamics Corp., Ft. Worth, 1977-90; dir. engrng. adminstrn. Lockheed Ft. Worth Co., 1990-94, dir. rsch. & engrng. svcs. & process support, 1994-96, dir. labs. and tech. support, 1996—. Republican. Baptist. Home: 5100 Dewdrop Ln Fort Worth TX 76123-1931 Office: Lockheed Ft Worth Co PO Box 748 Fort Worth TX 76101-0748

SHOEMAKER, WILLIAM EDWARD, financial executive; b. Charleston, W.Va., Sept. 17, 1945; s. Robert Edward and Janet Elizabeth (Hoglund) S. BBA, U. Notre Dame, 1967. Assoc. buyer Proctor & Gamble, Cin., 1971; gen. mgr. Eastwind Inc., Anchorage, 1972-73; pres., operator Golden Horn Lodge, Inc., Bristol Bay, Alaska, 1973-79; treas. Hawley Resource Group, Inc., Anchorage, 1979-88; treas., chief fin. officer Golden Zone Resources, Inc., Campbell, Calif., 1988-90; ptnr. Resort Mgmt. Corp., Anchorage, 1987-90; pres. Discovery Holdings, Inc., Ft. Lauderdale, Fla., 1991—; bd. dirs. Pacific Art & Design Cons., Inc. Bd. dirs. Anchorage Econ. Devel. Corp., 1988-90. Served to lt. (j.g.) USN, 1967-71. Mem. Quarter Deck Club (Anchorage). Republican. Home: 2301 Solar Plaza Dr Fort Lauderdale FL 33301 Office: Discovery Holdings Inc Ste 173 2400 E Las Olas Blvd Fort Lauderdale FL 33301

SHOENFELT, CATHERINE RUTH, marketing executive; b. Dallas, Dec. 9, 1954; d. Marion Justus and Nell (Harden) S. B of Music Edn., U. Tex., San Antonio, 1980. Tchr. music Viva Musica, San Antonio, 1980-81, Northside Ind. Sch. Dist., San Antonio, 1981-84; mktg. mgr. Austin Pathology Assocs., Tex., 1984-86; dir. mktg. Nat. Lab. Svcs., Inc., Austin, 1987; clin. sales rep. Roche Biomed. Labs., Inc., 1987-88; sales rep. Milex So., 1989-91, sales rep., Medi-U.S.A.-Sales, 1991-93; rehab. coord., sales rep., Therma-Care, 1993-94; area mgr. Healthtronix Med. Equipment, Dallas, 1994-95, owner, pres. CRS Med. Sales, Houston, 1995—. Singer Chamber Choralet Symphony, San Antonio, 1982; vol. Symphony Designer Showplace, Austin, 1986-87, Healthfest-Pathology Booth, Austin, 1986. Mem. NAFE, Blair County Genealogy Soc. Club. (Altoona, Pa.). Republican. Lutheran. Avocations: music, tennis, reading, needlework, swimming. Home: 18307 Elmdon Dr Houston TX 77084-3266 Office: CRS Med Sales 18307 Elmdon Dr Houston TX 77084

SHOENIGHT, PAULINE ALOISE SOUERS (ALOISE TRACY), author; b. Bridgeport, Ill., Nov. 20, 1914; d. William Fitch and Carrie (Milhouse) Souers; m. James Richard Tracy, Sept. 18, 1946 (dec. Aug. 1972); m. 2nd, Hurley F. Shoenight, June 25, 1976. BEd, Eastern Ill. U., 1937 . Mem. hon. bd. advs. Am. Biog. Inst; active Nat. Arbor Day Found. Mem. Nat. Ret. Tchrs. Assn., Eastern Ill. Alumni Assn. (life), PEO Sisterhood, Am. Bible Soc., Am. Poets Fellowship Soc. (hon. life mem.), Pleasure Island Sr. Citizens Club (charter), Ill. Poetry Soc. (charter), Ala. State Poetry Soc., Acad. Am. Poets, Baldwin Heritage Mus. Assn. (charter life), Friends of U. Mo. Libraries (life), Friends of Foley Library, 1000 Club. Republican. Baptist. Club: Bible-A-Month. Author: His Handiwork, 1954, Memory is a Poet, 1964, The Silken Web, 1965, A Merry Heart, 1966, In Two or Three Tomorrows, 1968, All Flesh Is Grass, 1971, Beyond The Edge, 1973. Address: 7425 Riverwood Dr W Foley AL 36535-4075

SHOFFIT, RICHARD CALVIN, martial arts educator; b. Fort Worth, Tex., July 14, 1949; s. Cyrus Dean and Nathalee Dale (Henry) S. BS, North Tex. State U., 1974. cert. instr.; 1st degree black belt Kobudo, Iai-Do, Kendo, Jukido Jujitsu, 4th degree black belt Karate Shin-Toshi, 5th degree black belt Song Moo Kwan Tae Kwon Do, 6th degree black belt Moo Duk Kwan Tae Twon Do. Owner Denton (Tex.) Acad. of Martial Arts, 1986—; substitute tchr. Denton Ind. Sch. Dist., 1990—. Editor: Texas Tae Kwon Do Federation Instructors Manual, 1980; author: National Karate Shin-Toshi Association Reference Manual, 1993. Recipient First pl. So. Kuk Sool Won Sem., 1984, 5th pl. World Kuk Sool Won Assn., 1979. Mem. Internat. Martial Arts Fedn., Nat. Arnis Assn., Seishin-kai Budo Union, Tex. Tae Kwon Do Fedn., So. U.S. Kendo & Iai-do Fedn., U.S. Tai Kwon Do Assn., World Tae Kwon Do Fedn. Office: Denton Acad Martial Arts 612 Hercules Ln Denton TX 76201-8067

SHOKOUH-AMIRI, M. HOSEIN, transplant surgeon, educator; b. Tehran, Iran, Mar. 21, 1948; Danish citizen; s. Manouchehr and Saadat (Fathi) S.; m. Firouze Pouresmaeil, June 18, 1973; children: Ziba, Amir, Solomon. Gen. diploma, Pahlavi High Sch., Iran, 1966; MD, Pahlavi U. Med. Sch., Iran, 1976; postgrad., Copenhagen U., 1988—. Diplomate gen. surgery, Nat. Bd. Health, Denmark, in gastrointestinal and hepato-pancreato-biliary surgery; lic. surg. Tenn., Iran (Ministry Health), European Common Market Countries, Nat. Bd. Health, Denmark, cert. in gastroenterol. surg. and gen. surg.; cert. Edn. Comsn. Fgn. Med. Grads. Intern dept. ob-gyn. Saadi Hosp., U. Pahlavi, Shiraz, Iran, 1974-75, dept. pediatrics, 1975, dept. internal medicine, 1975-76, dept. surgery, 1976, resident in surgery, 1979-80; resident dept. radiology Kommunehospital, Copenhagen, Denmark, 1980-81, resident gen. surgery, 1981-84; resident in surgery Rigshospitalet, U. Copenhagen, 1984-88; instr. surgery, dept. surg. gastroenterology Herlev Hosp., U. Copenhagen, 1989; instr. surgery, dept. urology and kidney transplantation Aarhus (Denmark) Kommunehospital, U. Aarhus; fellow transplantation U. Tenn., Memphis, 1990-91; asst. prof. surgery William F. Bowld Hosp., U. Tenn., 1992—; dir. edn. Iranian Nat. Blood Transfusion Svc., Shiraz, 1978-79; clin. lectr. surgery U. Aarhus, 1990-91; past co-chmn. Danish Transplantation Soc.; mem. outpatient svcs. and ARA com. UT Bowld Hosp., 1993—, spl. care units com., 1993—, organ, tissue and eye donation com., 1993—; rschr., speaker and invited lectr. in field. Author: Clinical Transplantation, 1994; author and editor: (with others) Essentials of Experimental Surgery: Gastroenterology, 1994; contbr. numerous articles to profl. jours., chpts. to books. Lt. dept. surgery Iranian Air Force, 1976-78. Recipient 10,000 DKR prize Danish Soc. Gastroenterology, 1989; grantee U. Tenn. Med. Group, 1993. Mem. World Assn. Hepato-Pancreato-Biliary Surgery, Scandinavian Soc. Laser Therapy, Am. Soc. Transplant Surgeons, Am. Diabetes Assn., Danish Surg. Soc., Danish Hepatology Soc., Southeastern Surg. Congress, Internat. Pancreas and Islet Transplant Assn., Internat. Liver Transplant Soc. Home: 8825 Classic Dr Memphis TN 38125-8840 Office: U Tenn Dept Surgery 956 Court Ave Ste C208 Memphis TN 38103-2814

SHOMER, ENID, poet, fiction writer; b. Washington. BA, Wellesley Coll.; MA, U. Miami, Fla. Faculty Antioch Writers Workshop, Yellow Springs, Ohio, 1988-91; writer-in-residence The Thurber House, Columbus, Ohio, 1994. Author: Imaginary Men (Iowa Short Fiction award 1992, So. Rev. Fiction award 1994), This Close to the Earth, 1992, Stalking the Florida Panther, 1988. State of Fla. Lit. fellow, 1985, 91, NEA Creative fellow inlit. 1989, 96. Office: care Roberta Pryor Inc 24 W 55th St New York NY 10019

SHOMETTE, C.D., protective services official; b. Lockhart, Tex., Jan. 11, 1939; s. Wesley and Nettie Belle (Mealer) S.; m. Donna Marie Dixson, Dec. 5, 1995. BA in Econs., St. Mary's U., 1967; MA in English, U. N. Tex., 1993, postgrad. in English, 1996—. Officer San Antonio Police Dept., 1962-66; criminal investigator IRS, Dallas, 1969-78, Dept. of Transp., Ft. Worth, 1982; asst. spl. agent in charge Dept. Vet. Affairs, Dallas, 1982-95; EEO investigator Dept. Vet. Affairs, Washington, 1995—. Author, editor: The Critical Response to Tom Wolfe, 1993. Served in U.S. Army, 1962-64. Mem. MLA, Fed. Law Enforcement Officers Assn. Home: 735 S Guadalupe Lockhart TX 78644

SHONS, ALAN RANCE, plastic surgeon, educator; b. Freeport, Ill., Jan. 10, 1938; s. Ferral Caldwell and Margaret (Zimmerman) S.; AB, Dartmouth Coll., 1960; MD, Case Western Res. U., 1965; PhD in Surgery, U. Minn., 1976; m. Mary Ella Misamore, Aug. 5, 1961; children: Lesley, Susan. Intern, U. Hosp., Cleve., 1965-66, resident in surgery, 1966-67; research fellow transplantation immunology U. Minn., 1969-72; resident in surgery U. Minn. Hosp., 1972-74; resident in plastic surgery NYU, 1974-76; asst. prof. plastic surgery U. Minn., Mpls., 1976-79, assoc. prof., 1979-84, prof., 1984; dir. div. plastic and reconstructive surgery U. Minn. Hosp., St. Paul Ramsey Hosp., Mpls. VA Hosp., 1976-84; cons. plastic surgery St. Louis Park Med. Center, 1980-84; prof. surgery Case Western Res. U., Cleve., 1984-93; dir. div. plastic and reconstructive surgery Univ. Hosps. Cleve., 1984-92; prof. surgery U. South Fla., H. Lee. Moffitt Cancer Ctr. and Rsch. Inst., Tampa, 1993—. Author: (with G.L. Adams and G.A. Brocone) Head and Neck Cancer, 1986; (with R. Jensen) Plastic Surgery Review, 1993. Served to capt. USAF, 1967-69. Diplomate Am. Bd. Surgery, Am. Bd. Plastic Surgery. Fellow ACS (chmn. Minn. com. on trauma 1978-84); mem. Am. Soc. Plastic and Reconstructive Surgeons, Am. Assn. Plastic Surgeons, Minn. Acad. Plastic Surgeons (pres. 1981-82), AMA, Soc. Head and Neck Surgeons, Am. Assn. Surgery Trauma, Transplantation Soc., Plastic Surgery Research Council, Am. Soc. Aesthetic Plastic Surgery, Am. Soc. Maxillofacial Surgeons, Am. Assn. Immunologists, Soc. Exptl. Pathology, Am. Burn Assn., Am. Cleft Palate Assn., Am. Soc. Craniofacial Surgery, Assn. Acad. Surgery, Central Surg. Assn., Fla. Soc. Plastic & Reconstructive Surgeons, Tampa Bay Soc. Plastic & Reconstructive Surgeons, Sigma Xi. Office: H Lee Moffitt Cancer Ctr & Rsch Inst 12902 Magnolia Dr Tampa FL 33612-9416

SHOOP, GLENN POWELL, investment consultant; b. Gracemont, Okla., Sept. 1, 1920; s. Roy Alonzo and Myrtle Nancy (Goodfellow) S.; m. Louise Wilhelmina Vollmer, Mar. 19, 1943; children: Merilou Love, Paul, Nancy Caver. Student, U. Okla., 1938-42. Pilot Braniff Internat. Airways, Dallas, 1946-80; cons. bd. dirs. Braniff Inc., 1984-88. Bd. dirs. 1st Bapt. Ch. Dallas, 1950-96; mem. devel. bd. Golden Gate Bapt. Sem., San Francisco, Southwestern Bapt. Sem., Fort Worth. Maj. USAF, 1942-46. Republican.

SHOOSTER, FRANK MALLORY, lawyer; b. Chester, Pa., Feb. 22, 1954; s. Herman and Dorothy (Schluger) S.; m. Gerryl Susan Abrams, July 18, 1986. BA in Philosophy and Poli. Sci., Antioch Coll., 1977; postgrad., U. Chgo., 1978; JD, U. Miami, 1982. Bar: Fla. 1982, U.S. Dist. Ct. (so. dist.) Fla. 1984; bd. cert. civil trial law Fla. Bar, 1992. Instr. philosophy Antioch Coll., Yellow Springs, Ohio, 1974; rsch. aide U.S. Libr. Congress, Washington, 1975-76; legis. aide select com. on small bus. U.S. Senate, Washington, 1975-76; legis. aide to Senators Thomas McIntyre and William D. Hathaway, 1976; now mng. ptnr. Frank Mallory Shooster P.A., Ft. Lauderdale; cert. mediator Fla. Supreme Ct., 1991. Guest columnist Miami Herald, 1988. Atty. conservation com. Audubon Soc. Broward County, FT. Lauderdale, 1983-85; at-large rep. Environ Leaders Coun., 1983-86. Mem. ABA, ACLU, Assn. Trial Lawyers Am., Acad. Fla. Trial Lawyers (jour. columnist 1991, 92), Broward County Trial Lawyers Assn. Democrat. Office: 777 S State Road 7 Margate FL 33068-2823

SHORES, JANIE LEDLOW, state supreme court justice; b. Georgiana, Ala., Apr. 30, 1932; d. John Wesley and Willie (Scott) Ledlow; m. James L. Shores, Jr., May 12, 1962; 1 child, Laura Scott. J.D., U. Ala., Tuscaloosa, 1959; LLM, U. Va., 1992. Bar: Ala. 1959. Pvt. practice Selma, 1959; mem. legal dept. Liberty Nat. Life Ins. Co., Birmingham, Ala., 1962-66; assoc. prof. law Cumberland Sch. Law, Samford U., Birmingham, 1966-74; assoc. justice Supreme Ct. Ala., 1975—; legal adviser Ala. Constn. Revision Commn., 1973; mem. Nat. Adv. Coun. State Ct. Planning, 1976—. Contbr. articles to legal jours. Mem. bd. dirs. State Justice Inst., 1995—. Mem. Am. Bar Assn., Am. Judicature Soc., Farrah Order Jurisprudence. Democrat. Episcopalian. Office: Ala Supreme Ct 300 Dexter Ave Montgomery AL 36104-3741

SHORNEY, MARGO KAY, art gallery owner; b. Great Falls, Mont., July 5, 1930; d. Angus Vaughn McIver and Loneta Eileen Kuhn; m. James Thomas Shorney, Apr. 17, 1954; 1 child, Blair Angus. Student, Coll. Edn., Great Falls, Mont., 1948-50, U. Denver, 1950-53. Owner, dir. Shorney Gallery Fine Art, Oklahoma City, 1976—; pres. Mont. Inst. Arts, Great Falls, 1953-54, Okla. Art Gallery Owners Assn., Oklahoma City, 1981-83; lectr. Norman (Okla.) Art League, 1987-91; judge fine arts Ponca City (Okla.) 12th Ann. Fine Arts, 1986, Edmond (Okla.) Art Assn. Expo 1995, Fine Arts Festival 22nd Ann., 1996; appraiser Globe Life, Oklahoma City, Ponca City Juried Art Assn. 22nd Ann. Fine Arts. Works exhibited in group shows, various orgns., 1953-90. Mentor South Oklahoma City Coll., 1990; active Okla. Mus. Art, 1973-78. Mem. Nat. Assn. Women Bus. Owners, Okla. Sculpture Soc. (charter), Okla. Art Guild (bd. dirs. 1979-82, lectr. 1981, 82, 83, 92). Republican. Episcopalian. Office: Shorney Gallery Fine Arts 6616 N Olie Ave Oklahoma City OK 73116-7318

SHORT, BETSY ANN, elementary education educator; b. Macon, Ga., Mar. 18, 1958; d. Garland Brooks Jr. and Mary Eleanor (Jordan) Turner; m. Lynn Robin Short, July 21, 1984. BS in Early Childhood Edn., Ga. Coll., Milledgeville, 1981, M in Early Childhood Edn., 1993, EdS, 1995. Cert. elem. tchr. and tchr. support specialist, Ga. Tchr. 3d grade Stockbridge (Ga.) Elem. Sch., 1983-84, tchr. kindergarten, 1984-93; tchr. augmented spl. instructional assistance Locust Grove (Ga.) Elem. Sch., 1993—. Author: Spinning Yarns, 1995; mem. editl. adv. bd. Ga. Jour. Reading; contbr. articles to profl. jours.; artist oil painting/pen and ink drawing. Mem. Profl. Assn. of Ga. Educators, Ga. Coun. Tchrs. Maths., Ga. Coun. Internat. Reading Assn., Ga. Coun. Social Studies, Ga. Sci. Tchrs. Assn., Henry Heritage Reading Coun. Baptist. Office: Locust Grove Elem 1727 Griffin Rd Locust Grove GA 30248

SHORT, DONALD WAYNE, city official; b. Richmond, Ky., Feb. 3, 1948; s. Earl F. and Zetta P. (Moore) S.; m. Lynda Nations, Dec. 27, 1976; children: David, Ashley. Student, Ea. Ky. U., 1966-67. Ins. rep. Nat. Life and Accident, Nashville, 1972-74; wastewater supt. Lexington-Fayete County Govt., Lexington, Ky., 1974-87, Georgetown (Ky.) Water and Sewer, 1987-94, City of Nicholasville, Ky., 1994—. Reviewer (book) Preliminary Treatment for Wastewater Facilities, 1993. With USN, 1968-72. Mem. Ky. Water/Wastewater Operators Assn. (pres. 1985-87), Water Environ. Fedn. (William D. Hatfield award 1985), Rotary (sec. 1992-94). Republican. Home: 100 Hickory Hill Rd Nicholasville KY 40356 Office: City of Nicholasville PO Box 450 Nicholasville KY 40340-0450

SHORT, EARL DE GREY, JR., psychiatrist, consultant; b. Talladega, Ala., Jan. 11, 1933; s. Earl de Grey and Adeline Eugenia (McWilliams) S.; m. Martha Burt Rossiter, Oct. 12, 1963; children: Earl D III, Philip A., Catherine E., William R. BS, The Citadel, 1956; MD, Med. U. S.C., Charleston, 1959. Commd. 2d lt. USAR, 1956; entered active duty U.S. Army, 1961, advanced through grades to col., 1976; battalion surgeon 4th Armored BN, 8th Inf. div., Germany, 1961-62; resident psychiatry Walter Reed Army Med. Ctr., Washington, 1962-65; chief dept. psychiatry U.S. Army Hosp., Ft. Polk, La., 1965-68, U.S. Walson Army Hosp., Ft. Dix, N.J., 1968-70; student Command and Gen. Staff Coll., Ft. Leavenworth, Kans., 1970-71; divsn. surgeon, comdr. 2d Med. Bn., 2d Infantry divsn., Korea, 1971-72; chief psychiatry svc. Brooke Army Med. Ctr., Ft. Sam Houston, Tex., 1972-80; ret. U.S. Army, 1980; psychiatrist Mecklenburg County Mental Health Ctr., Charlotte, N.C., 1980-86; ret. Mecklenburg County, 1993; psychiatrist Carolinas Medical Ctr. Ctr. for Mental Health, Charlotte, N.C., 1986—; pvt. practice Carolinas Med. Group, Psychiat. and Psychol. Assocs., 1992—; psychiat. cons. Mecklenburg County, Charlotte, 1987—, Amethyst, Charlotte, 1993-95. Founder Philip Alexander Short Meml. Scholarship Fund, Wingate (N.C.) Coll., 1988, Short Endowment Fund, Wingate Coll., 1991, Philip Alexander Short Meml. Fund, Elon Homes for Children, Elon Coll., N.C., 1989. Decorated Meritorious Svc. medal with 1 oak leaf cluster, U.S. Army, 1972, 80, Army Commendation medal with 1 oak leaf cluster, U.S. Army, 1968, 70; recipient All Am. award The Citadel, 1956. Mem. AMA, Am. Psychiat. Assn., N.C. Med. Soc., N.C. Psychiat. Assn., Charlotte Psychiat. Soc., Assn. Mil. Surgeons, Mecklenburg County Med. Soc., Ret. Officers Assn., Am. Legion, VFW, Sons Am. Revolution, Nat. Assn. for Uniformed Svcs. Republican. Presbyterian. Office: PO Box 18773 Charlotte NC 28218-0773

SHORT, EDGAR DEAN, sales executive, environmental scientist; b. El Reno, Okla., Feb. 21, 1949; s. Johnny Short and Jewel Loraine (McBride) Dewberry; Carrie Loucille Thornton, Aug. 4, 1990 (div. Mar. 10, 1995); stepchildren: Christi, Joshua. BS in Biology, Animal Sci., State U. Okla., Goodwill, 1972; MS in Zoology, U. Ark., 1976. Environ. scientist, engr. environ divsn. Ark. Hwy. and Trans. Dept., Little Rock, 1977-80; chief ecologist environ. divsn. Ark. Dept. Pollution Control and Ecology, Little Rock, 1980-81; owner, mgr. convenience outlet, package store, 1981-89; profl. sales specialist, sales counselor, pub. rels.; cons. State of Ark. Named Salesman of the Yr. Hot Springs (Ark.) Chrysler, 1991, Salesman of Yr. Lindel Timble Cadilac, 1994, 95. Mem. Nat. Audubon Soc., Nat. Wildlife Fedn. (water conservationist of yr. award 1981), Ark. Wildlife Fedn., Southwestern Assn. Naturalists (life), Sigma Xi (life), Lambda Sigma Tau. Democrat. Presbyterian. Home: 119 Spencer Hot Springs National Park AR 71901

SHORT, JAMES FEREBEE, investment advisor, financial consultant; b. Norfolk, Va., Feb. 23, 1968; s. Richard Turner IV and Florence King (Timolat) S. Grad., Woodberry Forest Sch.; BA, Coll. of William and Mary, 1990; MBA, U. Ga., 1996. Fin. cons. Br. Banking & Trust Co., Investment Mgmt., Raleigh, N.C., 1996—; sec., bd. dirs. Va. Coalition, Inc., Virginia Beach., Timolat Inc., 1986-90. Del. Va. State Rep. Conv., Salem, 1992, Richmond, 1993, Va. 2d Congrl. Dist., Virginia Beach, 1992; mem. Assn. Investment Mgmt. and Rsch.; bd. dirs. Ocean Pines Condominium Assn., Virginia Beach, 1991, 92; campaign aide John Chichester's Lt. Gubernatorial campaign, Norfolk, Va., 1985, mem. Gubernatorial Adv. Com., 1992-93; varsity baseball coach Cape Henry Collegiate Sch., Virginia Beach, 1991; vol. Am. Health Assn., Am. Cancer Soc., Westminster Canterbury Retirement Home, Surfrider Found. Mem. Nat. Assn. Security dealers, Am. Stock Exch., Pacific Stock Exch., Chgo. Bd. Options and Exch., U. Ga. Grad. Bus. Assn., Norfolk Cardinals, Virginia Beach Breakers Baseball Teams, Princess Anne Country Club, The Revelers (bd. govs., v.p.), Theta Delta Chi. Republican. Episcopalian. Office: Branch Banking & Trust PO Box 29575 Raleigh NC 27626-0575

SHORT, LINDA MATTHEWS, reading educator; b. Winston-Salem, N.C., Mar. 25, 1949; d. Edwin Kohl and Nannie Mae (Bowen) Matthews; m. James Coy Short, June 18, 1972. BS, Appalachian State U., 1971, MA, 1981. Cert. elem. edn. tchr. Tchr. Mount Airy City Schs., Mount Airy, N.C., 1971-72, 88—, Surry County Schs., Dobson, N.C., 1972-88; mem. Mt. Airy City Schs. Adv. Bd., 1994-95. Pres.-elect Foothills Reading Coun., 1992-93; active Mt. Airy Women's Club, 1970s, Mt. Airy Jaycettes, 1970s. Mem. Foothills Reading Coun. (pres. 1993-96), N.C. Reading Assn. (area dir. 1995-96), N.C. Assn. Educators (treas. 1992-94), Internat. Reading Assn., Mt. Airy N.C. Assn. Educators (treas. 1992-94). Democrat. Baptist. Home: 107 Brentwood Dr Mount Airy NC 27030 Office: BH Tharrington Elem Sch 315 Culbert St Mount Airy NC 27030

SHORT, LOUISE JOY, epidemiologist; b. Boston, June 16, 1960; d. Morris Irving and Minna (Wingersky) S.; m. Joel Lee Axler, Feb. 25, 1990; 2 children. BA in History and Sci. magna cum laude, Harvard U., 1982; postgrad., Johns Hopkins U., 1984-85; MD, Tufts U., 1987; MSc in Cmty. Medicine, Mt. Sinai Sch. Medicine, 1992. Diplomate Am. Bd. Internal Medicine, Nat. Bd. Med. Examiners, Am. Bd. Preventive Medicine, subspecialty occupational and environ. medicine. Resident in internal medicine Yale-New Haven (Conn.) Hosp., 1987-90; resident in occupational and environ. medicine/preventive medicine Mt. Sinai Med. Ctr., N.Y.C., 1990-92; med. epidemiologist HIV infections br., hosp. infections program Nat. Ctr. Infectious Diseases Ctrs. for Disease Control and Prevention, Pub. Health Svcs., Dept. Health and Human Svcs., Atlanta, 1992—; health and safety cons. United Fedn. Tchrs., N.Y.C., 1991-92; health educator White Lung Assn. N.J., Newark, 1990-92; mem. adv. bd. devel. AIDS in the Workplace curriculum Hunter Coll., 1990; mem. infectious diseases com. N.Y. Coun. Occupational Safety and Health, 1990-92; participant AIDS longitudinal clinic Yale-New Haven Hosp., 1989-90; internat. health elective Parirenyatwa Hosp. U. Zimbabwe, Africa, 1989-90; speaker, rschr., presenter abstracts in field. Isobel L. Briggs scholar, 1982, Rock Sleyster Meml. fellow psychiatry, 1986, Temkin fellow, 1984-85,. Mem. ACP, APHA, Am. Coll. Occupl. Medicine. Office: Ctrs for Disease Control and Prevention MS E-68 1600 Clifton Rd Atlanta GA 30333

SHORT, SALLIE LEE, physical plant service worker; b. Knoxville, Tenn., Feb. 17, 1932; d. John J. and Louise Maude (Robertson) Bassett; children: Jacqueline, Carita, Paulette, Shelia, Marilyn, Regina, Panthea, Greta, Michael (dec.). Legal sec. Earl Rossin, Atty., Cleve., 1952-53; nursing technician Meharry Med. Hosp., Nashville, 1958-64; inspector May Hosiery Mill Corp., Nashville, 1964-81; trustee sick leave bank Nashville State Tech. Inst., 1993—. Author poems. Campaign worker Dem. Party, Nashville, 1975-80; mem. com. on Svc. to Persons with Disabilities and Ams. with Disabilities Act. Roman Catholic. Home: 4113 Meadow Hill Dr Nashville TN 37218 Office: Nashville State Tech Inst 120 White Bridge Rd Nashville TN 37209-4515

SHORTAL, TERENCE MICHAEL, systems company executive; b. St. Louis, Oct. 13, 1937; s. Harold Leo and Catherine Margaret S.; BS in Elec. Engring., U. Mo., 1961; MS, U.S. Naval Postgrad. Sch., 1966; grad. program execs., Carnegie-Mellon U., 1979; m. Linda Margaret Elias, May 29, 1965; children: Jennifer (Mrs. Clay Morris Westbrook), Bradley Alexander. Commd. ensign U.S. Navy, 1961, advanced through grades to capt., 1980; service in Vietnam; asst. officer in charge Engring. Duty Officer Sch., Vallejo, Calif., 1974-77; ship engring. mgr. AEGIS shipbldg. project Naval Sea Systems Command, Washington, 1977-79, tech. dir. DDGX Project, 1979-81; ret., 1981; v.p., dir. Kastle Systems Inc., 1981—. Trustee Cathedral Choral Soc., Washington, 1983—, pres., 1986-88; mem. of vestry St. John's Episcopal Ch., McLean, Va., 1982-85; bd. dirs. Langley Sch., McLean, 1984-94, pres., 1986-88. Decorated Meritorious Service medal (2), Navy Commendation medal (2). Mem. Am. Soc. Naval Engrs. (Flagship Sect. award 1979), IEEE (br. award 1961), Tower Club, Gridiron Club (Washington), Nat. Press Club (Washington), Sigma Xi, Phi Kappa Theta. Home: 858 Canal Dr Mc Lean VA 22102-1408 Office: 1501 Wilson Blvd Arlington VA 22209-2403

SHORTELL, ANNABELLE PETERSEN, family nurse practitioner; b. Barnegrat, N.J., Nov. 14, 1924; d. Robert Charles and Mary Inman (Peterson) Petersen; m. Nicholas Emmett Shortell, Nov. 22, 1945 (dec. June 1992); children: Michael James, Susan Catherine, Nicholas Richard, Catherine Anne, Patricia Lynn. Diploma, Monmouth Meml. Hosp., 1946; cert. family nurse practitioner, Frontier Sch. Midwifery, Hyden, Ky., 1973. Cert. family nurse practitioner; lic. nurse practitioner with prescriptive privileges, Va. Nurse Va. Health Dept., Virginia Beach, 1968-71; family nurse practitioner Va. Health Dept., New Castle, 1973-87, 93—, Va. State Health Dept., Alleghany Dist., 1987-90, Va. Health Dept., Pennington Gap, Va., 1990-93, James Madison U., Harrisonburg, Va., 1994—. Bd. dirs. Am. Cancer Soc., Craig County, 1974-93; mem. planning com. Craig County Planning Commn., New Castle, 1978-93; pres. Craig County Cancer Unit, New Castle, 1983-84. Mem. Va. Health Dept. Nurses (continuing edn. com., judge ann. nurse practitioner award 1991—, dist. award as outstanding nurse practitioner for excellence 1990). Home: 1915 Creekside Ct Mc Gaheysville VA 22840

SHORTER, NINETTE, writer; b. Louisville, Sept. 5, 1958; d. Robert David and Doris Louise (Miller) S. BBA in Mktg. cum laude, Belmont U., 1991. Sec. Brown-Forman Corp., Louisville, 1978-87; mktg. asst. World Class Brands, Ltd., Nashville, 1987-90; mktg. assoc. Capital Holding Corp., Louisville, 1991-93; freelance copywriter, journalist Louisville, 1993—. Mem. Louisville Graphic Design Assn. (100 award 1993, 94, 95). Office: 1928 Roanoke Ave Louisville KY 40205-1416

SHORTRIDGE, JUDY BETH, lawyer; b. Johnson City, Tenn., Feb. 17, 1954; d. George Edd and Anna Louise (Salmon) Copenhaver; m. Michael L. Shortridge, July 27, 1984; children: Sarah Elizabeth, Alexander Blake. BA, Va. Poly. Inst. and State U., 1976; MEd, U. Va., 1982; JD, U. Tenn., 1989. Bar: Va. 1990, U.S. Dist. Ct. (we. dist.) Va. 1990. Tchr. Stafford County (Va.) Sch. System, 1976-84, Wise County (Va.) Sch. System, 1984-86; ptnr. Shortridge & Shortridge, P.C., Norton, Va., 1990—. Recipient Am. Jurisprudence award U. Tenn., 1989. Mem. Va. Bar Assn., Wise County Bar Assn., Nat. Orgn. Social Security Claimants Reps. Home: 325 Oakwood Ave SE Wise VA 24293-5470 Office: Shortridge & Shortridge PC 18 Seventh St Ste 300 Norton VA 24273

SHOSKY, JOHN EDWIN, communications consultant, speechwriter; b. Colorado Springs, Colo., Nov. 1, 1955; s. Alexander Matthew and Barbara Marie (Middelkamp) S. BA in Polic. Sci., Colo. Coll., 1979; MA in Philosophy, U. Wyo., 1987; PhD in Philosophy, Am. U., 1992. Dep. dir. Media and Sports Commns. White House Conf. for Drug Free Am., Washington, 1987-88; sr. policy analyst White House Office Pub. Affairs, 1988; cons. to sec. HHS, Washington, 1984-87, 88-91, cons. to Surgeon Gen., 1991-92; cons. to office of Nat. Drug Control Policy Exec. Office of the Pres., Washington, 1992-93; pres., sr. writer Roncalli Comm., 1991—; speech writer for govt. ofcls., corp. execs., profl. athletes, congressmen, senators; lectr. in philosophy Am. U., 1987-96, asst. prof., 1996—; lectr. No. Va. C.C., 1993-95; adj. prof. philosophy George Mason U., 1990-94. Contbr. numerous articles to acad. and profl. jours., trade publs., newsletters, regional and nat. newspapers. Mem. Nat. Assn. Advancement Sci., N.Y. Acad. Sci., Hume Assn., Russell Assn., Mind Assn., Colo. Coll. D.C. Alumni Assn., U. Wyo. Alumni Assn., Washington Philosophy Club. Republican. Roman Catholic. Home: 1806 Rollins Dr Alexandria VA 22307-1613

SHOTWELL, SHEILA MURRAY, medical/surgical nurse; b. Alamance County, Dec. 27, 1963; d. Homer Banks and Betty Jane (Robertson) Murray; m. Tony Allen Shotwell, July 30, 1988; children: Brent Allen, Emily Beth. Diploma, Watt's Sch. Nursing, 1985. RN, N.C. Staff nurse Durham (N.C.) County Gen. Hosp., 1985-91; home health nurse Home Care Providers, Burlington, N.C., 1992—. Mem. Watt's Alumni Assn. Office: 730 Hermitage Rd Burlington NC 27216

SHOUP, JAMES RAYMOND, computer systems consultant; b. McKees Rocks, Pa., Apr. 9, 1932; s. Jacob Daniel and Violet May Shoup; student U. Md., 1953-54, U. Miami, 1957-58, Palm Beach Jr. Coll., 1964-68; AA, Fla. Jr. Coll., 1978, AS, 1980; m. Caren Michelle Gagner, Nov. 20, 1988; children: Emily Ruth, Rhonda Lou, Richard Eugene, Sean Jason, Amy Marisa, Rodney Warren. With Fla. Power and Light Co., Delray Beach 1954-68; pres. JSE Corp., 1954-68; fin. cons. area bus., 1954-68; with FAA, 1968-72; with sales and mgmt. depts. Montgomery Ward Co., 1972-75; project mgr. JR Shoup & Assocs., Jacksonville, Fla., 1975-78; v.p. R & D JP Computing Co., Jacksonville Beach, 1981-86, Alken Computer Systems Co., Flower Mound, Tex., 1979-82; with U.S. Postal Svc., Jacksonville, 1975—; systems instr. microcomputer sci. Duval County Community Schs., Jacksonville, 1980-84; cons. on EDP acctg. applications analysis and EDP systems engring., 1976—; fin. cons., 1967—. Author manuals on computer applications in indsl. and transp. mgmt., 1975-84. Asst. chief, pres., dir. Tri-Cmty. Fire Dept., 1955-57; Sunday sch. tchr., deacon, treas., elder, local Presbyn. chs., 1955-80, chmn. pulpit com., 1990; pub. rels. officer N.B. Forrest High Sch. Band Parents Assn., 1973-79; mem. Rep. Presdl. Task Force. With USAF, 1950-54. Mem. EDP Auditors Assn., Jacksonville C. of C. (com. of 100-1982), Mensa. Designer Alken computers, disk patch for tiny Pascal, system 8000 computers, IMAS and IMASNET acctg. systems for microcomputers, MIC series computers; oil painter represented in pvt. collections, Fla. Home and Office: 1832 Lane Ave N Jacksonville FL 32254-1526

SHOUSHA, ANNETTE GENTRY, critical care nurse; b. Nashville, May 25, 1936; d. Thurman and Laura (Pugh) Gentry; m. Alfred Shousha, May 29, 1959; children: Mark André, Anne, Mary, Melanie. Diploma, St. Thomas Hosp., Nashville, 1957; student, Belmont Coll., Nashville, 1958, No. State U., Aberdeen, S.D., 1973; BSN, S.D. State U., 1985. Cert. coronary care. Instr. med. nursing Nashville Gen. Hosp., 1958-59, ob-gyn. nurse, 1959-60; insvc. educator Tri County Hosp., Ft. Oglethorpe, Ga., 1960-61; clin. mgr., office nurse Britton, S.D., 1962-90; med. nursing Nashville VA Hosp., 1990-92, gastrointestinal nurse, 1992-94, critical care nurse ICU, 1994-95. Contbr. essays to S.D. Jour. Medicine. Del., S.D. Dem. Conv. Recipient Gov.'s Recognition award for outstanding vol. svc. Mem. ANA, AMA Aux. (state pres.), Nat. Hospice Assn., Nurses Orgn. VA, Donelson/Hermitage C. of C. Home: 2809 Lealto Ct Nashville TN 37214-1813

SHOWALTER, JOSIAH THOMAS, JR., lawyer; s. Josiah T. and Nancy B. (Bartlett) S. BA in History, Va. Tech., 1984; JD, Stetson U., 1987. Bar: Va., Fla. Mng. atty. Stone, Harrison, Turk & Showalter, P.C., Radford, Va., 1991—. Pres., bd. dirs. New River Valley Legal Aid Soc., Christiansburg, Va., 1993-96; bd. dirs. Warm Hearth, Inc., Blacksburg, Va., 1994-96; Rep. candidate for Commonwealth's Atty., Montgomery County, Va., 1995. Mem. Christiansburg-Blacksburg Rotary (bd. dirs. 1989—), Masons. Presbyterian. Home: PO Box 714 Christiansburg VA 24073 Office: Stone Harrison Turk & Showalter PC PO Box 2968 Radford VA 24143

SHOWALTER-KEEFE, JEAN, data processing executive; b. Louisville, Mar. 11, 1938; d. William Joseph and Phyllis Rose (Reis) Showalter; m. James Washburn Keefe, Dec. 6, 1980. BA, Spalding U., 1963, MS in Edn. Adminstrn., 1969. Cert. tchr., Ky. Tchr., asst. prin. Louisville Cath. Schs., 1958-71; cons. and various editorial positions Harcourt Brace Jovanovich Co., Chgo. and N.Y.C., 1972-82; dir. editorial Ednl. Challenges, Alexandria, Va., 1982-83; mgr. project to cons. Xerox Corp., Leesburg, Va., 1983-88, mgr. systems edn., 1988-89; curriculum devel. mgr. corp. edn. and tng. Xerox Corp. Hdqrs., Stamford, Conn., 1989-94; mem. bd. Belcastle Cluster Assocs., Reston, Va., 1994—, pres. bd., 1995—, 1995—, mgmt. and sys. cons., 1995—; mem. adv. bd. Have a Heart Homes for Abused Children, 1991-93; instr. Sales Exec. Club N.Y., 1974-79; cons., Houston, 1980-83. Moderator Jr. Achievement, Louisville, 1968-70; cons. Future Bus. Leaders Am., Dade County, Fla. 1983. Named Outstanding Young Educator Louisville Jaycees, 1968. Mem. Nat. Assn. Female Execs., Am. Soc. Tng. and Devel., Am. Mgmt. Assn. Home and Office: 1419 Belcastle Ct Reston VA 22094-1245

SHOWERY, CHARLES GEORGE, JR., financial services company executive, consultant; b. El Paso, Tex., Sept. 28, 1951; s. Charles George and Mildred Marie (Romeu) S.; 1 child, Raelene Marie. Degree in med. microbiology, U. Tex., El Paso, 1976. Lab. mgr. Glass-Columbia Med., Conn., 1976-82; agt. Transamerica Life Cos., L.A., 1982-84; pres. Chico Enterprises, El Paso, 1984—; instr. Life Underwriters Tng. Coun., L.A., 1982. Author: It's a Great Career But, 1974, (booklet) M.D. vs. M.T., 1974. Mem. Nat. Assn. Life Underwriters. Democrat. Roman Catholic. Office: Chico Enterprises PO Box 220217 El Paso TX 79913-2217

SHOWS, CLARENCE OLIVER, dentist; b. nr. Brantley, Ala., Oct. 17, 1920; s. John Oliver and Cora (Nichols) S.; student Wis. State Coll., 1946-47; DDS, Northwestern U., 1951; : Toni Cherie, Kristin Clare Shows Ball, Bradley Scott, Gregory Norman, Jeffery Ryan. Individual practice dentistry, Valparaiso, Fla., 1951-53, Pensacola, 1953—. Mem. Pensacola Art Assn.; past pres. Escambia County unit Am. Cancer Soc., now bd. dirs. Fla. unit, also hon. life mem.; mem. Eagle Scout Bd. Rev., Escambia County; sec. Gulf Breeze Vol. Fire Dept. Served with USCG, 1939-46. Fellow Royal Soc. Health, Internat. Coll. Dentists, Internat. Acad. Gen. Dentistry, Am. Coll. Dentists; mem. Am. AAAS, ADA, Acad. Gen. Dentistry (master, past pres. Fla. unit), Internat. Orthodontic Assn., Internat. Acad. Preventive Medicine, Am. Orthodontic Soc., Gulf Breeze C. of C. (past pres.), Fla. Soc. Dentistry for Children (past pres.), Acad. Gen. Dentistry, Am. Profl. Practice Assn., L.D. Pankey Dental Found., Fedn. Dental Internat., Am. Assn. Clin. Hypnosis, Northwestern U. Alumni Assn., Navy League (life), G.V. Black Soc. (life), Pensacola Jr. Coll. Found. (life), Psi Omega. Presbyterian (elder). Clubs: Masons, Shriners, Jesters, Elks; Pensacola (past pres.), Exchange. Home: 519 Navy Cove Blvd Gulf Breeze FL 32561-4025 Office: PO Box 51 Gulf Breeze FL 32562-0051

SHRADER, LYNNE ANN, secondary school educator, coach; b. Concord, Mass., May 13, 1955; d. Arthur E. Jr. and Helen Louise (Eaton) Fay; m. John Neal Shrader, Nov. 11, 1978; children: Kristen Michelle, Michael Aaron. BS in Phys. Edn. and Health, Fla. So. Coll., 1978; postgrad., U. Tex., 1984, Augusta (Ga.) Coll., 1989—. Cert. middle level sci., life phys. edn. and health tchr., Tex., health and phys. edn. tchr. (K-12), Ga. Tchr. sci. Copperas Cove (Tex.) Jr. High Sch., 1982-83; tchr., coach Manor Mid. Sch., Killeen, Tex., 1983-85; tchr. phys. edn. John Milledge Elem. Sch., Augusta, Ga., 1985-86, Blythe (Ga.) Elem. Sch., 1986-88, Terrace Manor Elem. Sch., 1988-90; tchr. phys. edn., health, coach, dept. chair Lakeside Mid. Sch., Evans, Ga., 1990—; recreation specialist Frankfurt (Germany) Mil. Comty. Recreation Svcs., 1978-80, Richmond County Recreation and Parks Dept., Augusta, 1986-91; dir. Spl. Edn. Summer Camp Free-To-Be-Me, 1995. Mem. exec. com. Lakeside Mid. Sch. Booster Club, 1990-93; pres. Lakeside Mid. Sch. Parent-Tchr.-Student Orgn., 1992-93. Recipient outstanding vol. award Hershey (Pa.) Track and Field Orgn., 1989, Tchr. of Month award Lakeside Mid. Sch., 1991. Mem. AAHPERD, Profl. Assn. Ga. Educators (bldg. rep. 1991-94). Republican. Congregationalist. Home: 432 Halifax Dr Martinez GA 30907-3349 Office: Lakeside Mid Sch 527 Blue Ridge Dr Evans GA 30809-9202

SHREFFLER, GENEVIEVE, author; b. Kansas City, Kans., July 27, 1925; g. Raymond S. Gripkey and Genevieve Ruth O'Brien; m. S. Gordon Shreffler, Apr. 9, 1971; children: Steven Paul, Deborah Lynn, Rebekah Helena. BS in Polit. Sci., U. Ctrl. Okla., now postgrad. Designer Braille dress patterns Colorado Springs, Colo., 1966-69; pub. rels. dir. Okla. Women's Polit. Caucus, 1971-72; legis. intern Okla. State Legislature, 1976-77; ctrl. and ea. European specialist Internat. Trade Svcs., Oklahoma City, 1993—. Author: At the Edge, 1989; editor: Legends of Poland, 1990. Bd. dirs. Oklahoma City chpt. UN, 1988-89; founder, past pres. Polish-Am. Refugee Resettlement and Edn. Com., 1984—; active Freedoms Found. Valley Forge, Oklahoma City, 1990—; ex-officio mem. Ctrl. European Resettlement and Edn. Com., 1980-84, pres., 1984—; mem. Oklahoma City mayor's steering com. Internat. Sister City Program, 1993—; mem. internat. rels. commn. City of Scottsdale, Ariz., 1995—. Decorated Golden Cross of Merit (Poland), officer's cross Order of Poland Restituta; recipient Svc. award Rotary Internat. Club, 1984, Nat. Honor medal DAR, 1991. Mem. AAUW, Am. Bus. Women's Assn., Nat. Fedn. Press Women (Communicator of Achievement award Oklahoma City chpt.), European Acad. Arts, Scis. and Humanities (corr.), Alpha Chi. Home: 9815 N 100th Pl Scottsdale AZ 85258-4812

SHRINER, ROBERT DALE, economist, management consultant; b. Hobart, Okla., Nov. 28, 1937; s. William Dale and Mildred Ellen (Goodson) S.; m. Nancy Lee Thompson, June 6, 1961; 1 child, Leslie Annette. BA, U. Okla., 1965, MA, 1967; PhD, Ind. U., 1974. Asst. to chief ops. Gen. Dynamics Astronautics, Altus, Okla., 1961-63; dir. Wyo. tech. asst. program U. Wyoming, 1966-69; research assoc. Ind. U. Bur. Bus. Research, 1969-71; asst. prof. Ind. U. Sch. Pub. and Environ. Affairs, 1972-77; assoc. dir. resource devel. internship program Council of State Govt., 1970-72; dir. aerospace research application ctr. Ind. U., 1972-76; mng. assoc., sr. economist Booz Allen & Hamilton, Washington, 1977-79; dir. Washington ops. Chase Econometrics, Washington, 1979-82; mng. ptnr. Shriner-Midland Co., Washington, 1982—; cons. Aerospace Industries Assocs., Assn. for Mfg. Tech., Nat. Endowment for Arts, Nat. Restaurant Assn., Presdl. Commn. on Social Security, U.S. Cath. Conf., YMCA of U.S.; also cons. to various major corps. and nat. assns. Editor, pub. Managing Technology and Change, 1972-75, 86-89; creator computer programs, 1982, 91; contbr. articles to profl. jours. Pres. grad. students assn. U. Okla., Norman, 1965-66; chmn. Rocky Mountain Tech. Svcs. Coun., Wyo., 1967-69; sci. advisor Wyo. Gov., 1968-69; vice-chmn. YMCA Fairfax County, Va., 1978-82; bd. dirs. YMCA of Metro Washington, 1982-89, treas., 1986-89; exec. com. Gettysburg Coll. Parents Coun., 1985-89. With USAF, 1957-61. Recipient Disting. Svc. award YMCA Metro Washington, 1985, 91. Mem. AAAS, Nat. Assn. Bus. Economists, Am. Mgmt. Assn., Am. Econs. Assn., Va. Advanced Tech. Assn. (v.p. programs, 1986-89). Club: Nat. Economists. Lodge: Rotary (pres. 1976-77). Office: Shriner-Midland Co 6432 Quincy Pl Falls Church VA 22042-3117

SHROPSHIRE, GROVER CRAIG, oil company executive; b. Georgetown, Ky., Dec. 5, 1921; s. Grover and Mattie Craig (Burrier) S.; m. Eloise Adams Brown, Aug., 1951 (dec. Oct. 1985); m. Phyllis Ann Cox, Dec. 5, 1988. BS, U.S. Naval Acad., 1944; MBA, Washington U. St. Louis, 1963. Exec. Ashland (Ky.) Oil Co., 1947-80; owner Farmer, Georgetown, Ky., 1980—. Trustee Midway (Ky.) Coll, 1981-94, Headley-Whitney Mus., Lexington, Ky., 1982-93, Internat. Mus. of the Horse, Lexington, 1994—. Mem. Rotary. Episcopalian. Home: 1661 Paynes Depot Rd Georgetown KY 40324-9138

SHROYER, PATRICIA FAYE, real estate broker; b. Hollidaysburg, Pa., Mar. 24, 1938; d. John Jacob and Mabel Kathryn (Lafferty) S.; m. Joseph Fletcher Walls, III, June 18, 1960 (div. Apr. 1964). Student Pa. State U., 1960; BA, Temple U., 1967; postgrad. Drexel U., 1968, U. Minn., 1970, Tallahassee (Fla.) C.C., 1975, Fla. A&M U., 1976; real estate broker, Tex., Real Estate Sales, Fla.; enrolled agt. IRS. Tax shelter specialist Travelers Ins. Co., Balt., 1977; equity sales supr. Lincoln Nat. Sales Corp., Camp Hill, Pa., 1978; sales cons. U.S. Home, Inc., Houston, 1979-81; sales cons. Stuckey Home, Inc., Houston, 1981, Pre-paid Legal Services, Inc.; fin. planning cons., Houston, 1982—; data processing cons., polit. candidates, 1981—. Bus. and Profl. Women's scholar, 1975. Mem. Data Processing Mgmt. Assn., Nat. Assn. Enrolled Agts., Mensa. Home: 15214 Seahorse Dr Houston TX 77062-3611

SHRYOCK, CARMEN LAWSON, home health nurse, educator; b. Moss Landing, Calif., Apr. 20, 1937; d. Neal A. and Thelma G. (Wallace) Lawson; children: L. Denise Rasmus, Dennis D., Darin W., Daryl N. Diploma, St. Anthony's Sch. Nursing, Oklahoma City, 1958; BS in Edn. summa cum laude, Black Hills State U., Spearfish, S.D., 1973; MEd, U. Cen. Okla., 1986. Cert. CPR, first aid instr. Chmn., instr. med. assist. program Draughon Coll., Oklahoma City, asst. dir. edn.; pvt. duty nurse Geriatric Home Health Care, Edmond, Okla.; instr. allied health careers Eastern Okla. County Area VoTech Ctr., Choctaw; dir. Ernest Wolfe Adult Day Care Tng. Facility Eastern Okla. County Area Vocat. Ctr., Choctaw; nurse cons. geriatric day care; instr. health sci. tech. Vol. ARC; mem. Edmond Assn. for Retarded Citizens, Inc. Fullbright scholar. Mem. Am. Vocat. Assn., Okla. Vocat. Assn., Okla. Health Occupations, Edn. Tchrs. Assn., Kappa Delta Pi. Home: 1010 S Kelly Edmond OK 73003

SHUB, HARVEY ALLEN, surgeon; b. Bklyn., Oct. 28, 1942; s. Irving and Sara (Levin) S.; m. Susan Jayne Smith, Dec. 26, 1970; children: Carolyn, Todd. Student, NYU, 1960-61, 1964-65; BS in Zoology, Physics, U. Miami, 1964; MD, U. Rome, Italy, 1971. Diplomate Am. Bd. Colon and Rectal Surgery. Intern, Beth Israel Med. Ctr., N.Y.C., 1971-72, resident in surgery, 1972-76; fellow in colon and rectal surgery, Muhlenberg Hosp., Plainfield, N.J., 1976-77; practice medicine specializing in colon and rectal surgery, Orlando, Fla., 1977—; chmn. dept. surgery Fla. Hosp., 1988-89; pres. Med. Staff Fla. Hosp., 1992-93; asst. consulting prof. dept. surgery Duke U., 1995; mem. staff Winter Park Meml. Hosp., Orlando Regional Med. Ctr., Columbia Park Hosp., South Seminole Community Hosp.; clin. asst. prof. dept. family medicine U. South Fla., Tampa, 1982—. Chmn. pub. edn. com. Am. Cancer Soc. Orange County 1982—. Served to capt. M.C., USAR, 1971-77. Recipient Physician's Recognition award, AMA, 1976, 79, 81, 83, 87, 91, 94. Fellow ACS, Am. Soc. Colon and Rectal Surgeons, Internat. Coll. Surgeons, Southeastern Surg. Congress, Internat. Soc. Univ. Colon and Rectal Surgeons, Am. Soc. for Laser Medicine and Surgery; mem. AMA, So. Med. Assn., Fla. Med. Assn. (council splty. medicine), Orange County Med. Assn., Piedmont Soc. Colon and Rectal Surgeons, Orange County Ostomy Assn. (med. adviser), Fla. Soc. Colon and Rectal Surgeons (sec.-treas. 1980-82, pres. 1983-84, sec.- treas. 1996—), Am. Soc. Gastrointestinal Endoscopy, Internat. Soc. Univ. Colon and Rectal Surgeons, Am. Soc. Laser Medicine and Surgery, Soc. Am. Gastrointestinal Endoscopic Surgeons. Consulting editor Jour. Fla. Med. Assn.; contbr. articles to profl. jours. Home: 1224 Roxboro Rd Longwood FL 32750-6815 Office: 308 Groveland St Orlando FL 32804-4019

SHUCK, EDWIN HAYWOOD, III, surgeon; b. Chattanooga, Tenn., 1948. MD, Washington U., St. Louis, 1973. Diplomate Am. Bd. Surgery, Am. Bd. Colon and Rectal Surgery. Intern Tulane U. Hosps., New Orleans, 1973-74, resident, 1974-78; fellow in colon and rectal surgery Carle Clinic, Urbana, Ill., 1978-79; now with Meml. Hosp., Chattanooga, Tenn.; asst. prof. clin. surgery U. Tenn. Fellow ACS, Am. Soc. Colon and Rectal Surgery. Office: Colon & Rectal Surg Assoc Memorial Med Bldg W 721 Glenwood Dr Ste 473 Chattanooga TN 37404-1106

SHUEY, JUDITH LEWIS, counselor; b. Atlanta, Oct. 2, 1946; d. Oliver McCutchen and Hazel Kyle (Jones) Lewis; m. Theodore G. Jr. Shuey, June 21, 1969 (div. 1986); children: Ellen Lewis, Theodore G. III. BA in Econ., Bridgewater Coll., 1968; student, U. Va., 1969-71; MEd, James Madison U., 1990. Cert. fin. planner. Tchr. Augusta County Schs., Staunton, Va., 1968-70; sec.-treas. Cabinet Craft Va., Inc., Richmond, 1977-80; choir master Christ Luth. Ch., Staunton, 1982-88; career counselor Staunton City Schs., 1987-90; trainer student assistance programs Va. Dept. Edn., Broadway, 1991—; cons. on PULSAR to gov. of Va., 1990—; cons. interagy. comm. City of Petersburg; creater Student Assistance Program (winner state and local awards); speaker ann. conf. W.Va. Edn. Assn., 1992. Bd. dirs. Christ Luth. Ch., Staunton, 19185-88, 90—, Staunton CADRE, 1988—; bd. irs. Staunton Youth Commn. Recipient Citation for substance abuse prevention, Va. Atty. Gen. Mary Sue Terry, Richmond, 1990. Mem. NEA, Va. Edn. Assn. (presenter state instrn. conf. 1990), Va. Career Devel. Assn. (bd. dirs.), Staunton Mental Health Assn. (bd. dirs. 1989—), Va. Counselors Assn. Democrat. Home: 504 Rainbow Dr Staunton VA 24401-2141

SHUFORD, DAVID WILSON, aerospace engineer; b. Hickory, N.C., June 6, 1948; s. Gordon Eric and Vera Barber (Shuford) S.; m. Bessie Elizabeth Bollinger, June 13, 1970; children: Melissa Renae, Jonathan David. BS in Aerospace Engring., N.C. State U., Raleigh, 1970; postgrad., U. Ala., Huntsville, 1972-78, M in Adminstrv. Sci., 1980. Sr. engr. Northrop Svcs., Inc., Huntsville, 1973-76; program mgr., project engr. SCI Systems, Inc., Huntsville, 1976-80; project mgr., sr. engr. Avco Electronics, Huntsville, 1980-82; sr. staff engr. CAS, Inc., Huntsville, 1982—. Mem. Leadership Huntsville, 1987—; lay chmn. Prince of Peace Luth. Ch., Huntsville, 1984-85, 86-89, pres., 1993-95; treas. Ala. conf. Evang. Luth. Ch. in Am., 1988-90; treas. Ala. PTA, Montgomery, 1993—; candidate for Huntsville City Schs. Bd. Edn., 1996. Recipient Highest Acad. Achievement award U. Ala., Huntsville, 1981. Mem. Armed Forces Comms.-Electronics Assn., Ala. Congress of Parents and Tchrs. (hon. life). Home: 4700 Wellington Point Huntsville AL 35816 Office: CAS Inc 650 Discovery Dr NW Huntsville AL 35806-2802

SHUFORD, HARLEY FERGUSON, JR., furniture manufacturing executive; b. Norfolk, Va., Oct. 7, 1937; s. Harley Ferguson Sr. and Nancy (Pope) S.; m. Helgi Kuuskraa; children: Linda, David. BA, U. N.C., 1959. Engr. Century Furniture Co., Hickory, N.C., 1959-60, mgr. data processing, 1960-63, v.p. mfg., 1964-67, pres., 1967-95; chmn. Shuford Industries, Inc., Hickory, 1994—; bd. dirs. 1st Union Bank N.C., Charlotte. Trustee Catawba Meml. Hosp., Hickory, 1971-77, chmn., 1977-81; bd. dirs. U. N.C. Sys., Chapel Hill, 1975-83; bd. dirs. N.C. Citizens Bus. and Industry, Raleigh, 1982-95; chmn. N.C. Arts Coun., Raleigh, 1985-93. Mem. Am. Furniture Mfrs. Assn. (bd. dirs. 1968-92, pres., chmn. 1980-82), Catawba County C. of C. (pres. 1976), Phi Beta Kappa. Republican. Mem. United Ch. of Christ. Office: Shuford Industries PO Box 608 Hickory NC 28603-0608

SHUGAN, STEVEN MARK, marketing educator; b. Chgo., Apr. 21, 1952; s. David Lester and Charlotte Rose Shugan; m. Irene H. Ginter, Dec. 16, 1973; children: Adam Joshua, Elliot Hillel, Ross Isaac, Henry Andrew. BS in Chemistry, So. Ill. U., 1973, MBA, 1974; PhD in Managerial Econs. and Decision Scis., Northwestern U., 1978. Lectr. Grad. Sch. Mgmt., Northwestern U., Evanston, Ill., 1975-76; asst. prof. bus. adminstrn. Grad. Sch. Mgmt., U. Rochester, N.Y., 1977-79; asst. prof. mktg. Grad. Sch. Bus., U. Chgo., 1979-82, assoc. prof., 1982-87, prof., 1987-92; Russ Berrie eminent scholar, prof. mktg. U. Fla., Gainesville, 1991—; chmn., organizer sessions numerous nat. confs., 1979—; cons. various cos., 1976—; chmn. Mktg. Sci. Conf., 1983-96. Fellow Northwestern U., 1978. Mem. Am. Mktg. Assn., Ops. Rsch. Soc. Am., Assn. for Consumer Rsch., Inst. Mgmt. Scis. (pres. coll. mktg.), Am. Statis. Assn. Office: U Fla 209 Bryan Hall Gainesville FL 32611-2014

SHUGART, JILL, school system administrator; b. Dallas, July 15, 1940; d. Claude Ernest and Allie Merle (Hamilton) S. BA, Baylor U., 1962; MA, Tex. Woman's U., 1972, PhD, 1980. Middle sch. English tchr. Garland (Tex.) Ind. Sch. Dist., 1962-63, high sch. social studies tchr., 1963-76, high sch. asst. prin., 1976-79, dir. communications, 1979-82, asst. supt., 1982-85, supt., 1985—; mem. legis. coun. U. Interscholastic League, Tex., 1989—; chmn. Dist. III music com., Tex., 1989-98; adj. prof. Tex. Women's U., Denton, 1983; chmn. Region X ESC Adv. Coun., rep. to commr.'s supt.'s com., 1993-95. Gen. chmn. Boy Scouts Am. Scouting Night, Dallas, 1988-89; chmn. City of Garland Comty. Rels. Coun., 1992; sec. Tex. Sch. Alliance, 1992-96; life mem. Tex. PTA; pres. Garland br. Am. Heart Assn., 1990-91; co-chmn. sustaining dr. Garland YMCA, 1995-96. Recipient Lamar award for excellence Masons, Award of Distinction, Tex. Ret. Tchrs. Assn.; named Top 100 Educators to Watch, Executive Educator mag., 1985, Finalist as Outstanding Tex. Sch. Supt., 1990, Woman of Distinction, Soroptomist Club; Paul Harris fellow. Mem. Am. Assn. Sch. Adminstrs. (suburban sch. com. 1990-93), Tex. Assn. Sch. Adminstrs., Tex. Assn. for Supr. Curriculum Devel., Garland Adminstr. Assn. (pres. 1978-79), Nat. Tex. PTA. Republican. Baptist. Office: Garland Ind Sch Dist 720 Stadium Dr Garland TX 75040-4616

SHUGRUE, MARTIN ROGER, JR., airline executive; b. Providence, Aug. 31, 1940; s. Martin Roger and Dorothy Elizabeth (Campbell) S.; BA in Econs., Providence Coll., 1962; PhD in Bus. Adminstrn. (hon.), 1987, Centanary Coll., 1991; m. Marianne Zaalberg van Zelst, Mar. 9, 1979; children: Catherine, Michael, Marijke, Martijn. Pilot, flight engr. Pan Am. World Airways, N.Y.C., 1968-70, dir. performance measurements, 1970-72, dir. orgn. planning, 1972-74, staff v.p. corp. personnel, 1974-77, mng. dir. Eastern Central U.S., Washington, 1977-78, mng. dir. U.K. and Western Europe, London, 1978-80, v.p. indsl. relations, N.Y.C., 1980, v.p. personnel, 1980-81, sr. v.p. adminstrn., 1981-82, sr. v.p. mktg., 1982-84, chief oper. officer, 1984-88, pres. and CEO, 1996—; vice chmn. Pan-Am. Corp., 1984-88; pres. Continental Airlines Inc., 1988-89; pres. Martin R. Shugrue & Assocs., 1989-90; trustee Eastern Airlines, 1990-95; pres., CEO New Pan-Am. World Airways, 1995—; bd. dirs. Bus. Council for Internat. Understanding; chmn. Govt. Affairs Council of Travel and Tourism Industry; mem. U.S. Senate Adv. Com. for Travel and Tourism; nat. chmn. Travel Industry Assn., 1988-89. Mem. pres.'s council Providence Coll; bd. dirs. City of Houston Conv. and Visitors Bur.; mem. Ireland/U.S. Coun. for Commerce and Industry; dir. Enterprise Fla.; bd. dirs. Cooperation Ireland. Capt. USNR, 1968-89, ret. Mem. USO (bd. govs.), Am. Soc. Travel Agts. (mem. exec. adv. bd.), Travel Industry Assn. Am. (bd. dirs.), Airline Orgn. Planning and Adminstrn. Assn. (founding), Air Transport Assn. (bd. dirs.), Res. Officers Assn., Assn. for Naval Aviation, Navy League, U.S. C. of C., Westminster C. of C., Greater Miami C. of C. (trustee), Wings Club, Sky Club, Union League (N.Y.C.), Am. Club (London), Briar Club, Patterson Club (Conn.), Army and Navy Club (Washington). Home: 3260 Del Monte Dr Houston TX 77019-3218 Office: Eastern Air Lines Inc Miami Internat Airport Miami FL 33148

SHULA, DON FRANCIS, professional football coach; b. Grand River, OH, Jan. 4, 1930; s. Dan and Mary (Miller) S.; children: David, Donna, Sharon, Anne, Michael; m. Mary Anne Shula. B.S., John Carroll U., Cleve., 1951, H.H.D. (hon.), 1972; M.A., Case Western Res. U., 1953; Sc.D. (hon.), Biscayne Coll., 1974. Profl. football player Cleve. Browns, 1951-52, Balt. Colts, 1953-56, Washington Redskins, 1957; asst. coach U. Va., 1958, U. Ky., 1959, Detroit Lions, 1960-62; head coach Baltimore Colts, 1963-69, Miami (Fla.) Dolphins, 1970—. Author: The Winning Edge, 1972, (with Ken Blanchard)

Everyone's A Coach, 1995. Fla. crusade chmn. Nat. Cancer Soc., 1975; co-chmn. Jerry Lewis March Against Dystrophy, 1975; nat. bd. dirs. Jesuit Program for Living and Learning, 1976; mem. nat. sports com. Multiple Schlerosis Soc., Muscular Dystrophy Assn.; bd. dirs. Heart Assn. Greater Miami; hon. chmn. Belen Jesuit Intercultural Fund Campaign To Build Schs.; established Don Shula Found., breast cancer rsch., 1991—; sponsor Don Shula Scholarship, 1978—. Coached 6 Superbowl teams, winning teams 1972, 73; recipient Coach of Yr. awards 1964, 66, 70, 71, 72, Coach of decade Profl. Football Hall of Fame, 1980, Pro Football's All-Time Winningest Coach, 1994, Brotherhood award Fla. region NCCJ, 1977, Light of Flames Leadership award Barry Coll., 1977, Concern award Cedars Med. Ctr., 1992, Solheim Lifetime Achievement award, 1992, Jim Thorpe award, 1993, Sportsman of Yr. Sports Illustrated, 1993, Horrigan award Pro Football Writers, 1994, Horatio Alger award, 1995; named Balt. Colts Silver Anniversary Coach, 1977. Roman Catholic. Office: Miami Dolphins 7500 SW 30th St Davie FL 33314-1020

SHULER, GEORGE NIXON, JR., social worker, writer; b. Houston, Apr. 17, 1952; s. George Sr. and Anna Isabel (Huebner) S.; m. Lois Laverne Byram, June 16, 1979. BA, U. Tex., 1977; MSW, U. Houston, 1992. Lic. Master Social Worker, Tex. Mgr. Law Book Co. of Tex., San Antonio, 1973-74; mgr. store Elliot Garner Enterprises, San Antonio, 1974-77; child protective services specialist Karnes County (Tex.) Child Welfare, Karnes City, 1978-80, Atascosa County Child Welfare, Jourdanton, Tex., 1980, Bexar County Child Welfare, San Antonio, 1980-84; supr. child protective services Brazoria County Child Welfare, Angleton, Tex., 1984-86; child protective services specialist Harris County Child Welfare, Houston, 1986-92; respite specialist Galveston County Children's Protective Svcs., Texas City, 1993-95; clin. social worker Social Work Dept./Army Family Advocacy Program, Ft. Hood, Tex., 1995—. Columnist Leon Valley Leader newspaper, San Antonio, 1981-87; contbr. articles to profl. pubs. Dir. state exec. com. Tex. State Employees Union, Austin, 1983-84; del. ctrl. labor coun. AFL-CIO, San Antonio, 1981-84, Tex. Dem. Conf., 1974, 76, 78, 82, 84, 86, 90, 92, 96; campaign aide Dem. Com. Bexar County, San Antonio, 1974; campaign mgr. Jon Roland for U.S. Congress, San Antonio, 1974; chmn. resolutions com. Brazoria County Dem. Conv., Angleton, 1986; mem. rules com. Galveston County Dem. Conv., 1994; mem. exec. bd. North Galveston County Dems., 1994-95; lay min. Ch. of Subgenius of Gulf Coast, 1986-95, hierarchy candidate, 1990, initiate, 1993; min. Universal Life Ch., 1994—. Recipient Service award Tex. State Employees Union, 1984. Mem. Masons (Master Mason Tex. City Lodge #1118), AF & AM, Scottish Rite, Galveston Scottish Rite Bodies, Shriners (Noble, El Mina Shrine Temple, AAONMS, Galveston 1995—). Home: 713 Ridge Copperas Cove TX 76522 Office: Social Work Dept Bldg 307-A Fort Hood TX 76544

SHULL, STEVEN A., political science educator, researcher, author; b. Indpls., July 8, 1943; s.Arthur G. and Mildred (Neher) S.; children: Theodore, Amanda. BS, Manchester Coll., 1965; MA, Ball State U., 1968, Ohio State U., 1973; PhD, Ohio State U., 1974. Firefighter Bureau of Land Mgmt., Shoshone, Idaho, 1964, 66; social sci. tchr. High Sch., 1965-67; instr. polit. sci. Milikin U., 1969; legislative intern Ohio State Senate, 1970-71; grad. rsch. assoc. Ohio State U., 1971-73; budget analyst, adminstrv. asst. Ohio Senate Minority Leader, 1973-74; asst. prof. polit. sci. U. New Orleans, 1974-78, assoc. prof., 1978-83, prof., 1983-89, rsch. prof., 1989—; instr. Am. Fgn. Policy, Dem. Govts. of Europe, Innsbruck, Austria, 1980; Fulbright sr. scholar, instr. Am. govt. and U.S.-USSR mil. rels. Chinese U. Hong Kong, 1985. Author or editor 12 books including: Interrelated Concepts in Policiy Research, 1977, Presidential Policy-Making: An Analysis, 1979, Domestic Policy Formation: Presidential-Congressional Partnership?, 1983, The President and Civil Rights Policy: Leadership and Change, 1989, The Two Presidencies: A Quarter Century Assessment, 1991, A Kinder, Gentler Racism: The Reagan-Bush Civil Rights Legacy, 1993, (with others) Congress and The President: Studies in Public Policy, 1976, The Presidency and Public Policy Making, 1985, Economics and Politics of Industrial Policy, 1986; mem. 3 jour. editorial bds.; sr. editor: (book series) Politics and Policy in American Institutions; contbr. numerous articles to profl. jours. Mem. adv. bd. Plaza Shopping Ctr.; steering com. Excel '94. Recipient Univ. Alumni Career Achievement award for excellence in rsch., others. Mem. Am. Polit. Sci. Assn. (nom. com. pres. rsch. group 1985-86, steering com. 1986-89, chmn. Neustadt award com. 1986-87, publs. com. 1996-97), Southwest Polit. Sci. Assn. (exec. coun. 1983-85, Best Paper award com. 1986-87, 92-93, program com. and sect. chmn. 1993), Midwest Polit. Sci. Assn. (conv. program com. and sect. chmn. 1989), So. Polit. Sci. Assn. (conv. program com. and sect. chmn. 1983), Policy Studies Orgn., Ctr. for Study of the Presidency. Home: 5840 Kensington Blvd New Orleans LA 70127-2809 Office: Dept Polit Sci U New Orleans New Orleans LA 70148

SHULMAN, LEE PHILIP, medical educator; b. N.Y.C., Oct. 20, 1957; s. Abraham and Dorothy Eda (Bertash) S.; m. Laura A. Friend, July 12, 1981; children: Rebecca Ariel, Andrew James. BA, Cornell U., 1979, MD, 1983. Diplomate Nat. Bd. Med. Examiners, Am. Bd. Med. Genetics, Am. Bd. Ob-Gyn. Clin. assoc. Cornell U., N.Y.C., 1984-86, sr. clin. assoc., 1986-87; fellow in ob/gyn-reproductive genetics U. Tenn., Memphis, 1987-89, instr. reproductive genetics, 1989-90, asst. prof. ob-gyn., 1990-94, assoc. prof., dir. divsn. reproductive genetics, 1994—; disting. vis. prof. Artemesia Med. Ctr., Rome, 1993. Assoc. editor Adolescent and Pediatric Gynecology, 1993—; contbr. articles to profl. jours., chpts. to books. bd. dirs., chair ritual com. Beth Shalom Synagogue, Memphis, 1990—; baseball, basketball and soccer coach Jewish Community Ctr., Memphis, 1992—. fellow TSI, England, 1994; Ark. Traveler citation State of Ark., 1993; named James H. Becker Disting. Alumnus Lectr., Cornell U., 1993. Mem. Am. Soc. Human Genetics, Am. Fertility Soc., North Am. Soc. Pediatric and Adolescent Gynecology (program dir. 1994—), Soc. Perinatal Obstetricians, Assn. Profs. Gynecology and Obstetrics, Soc. Advancement of Contraception, Masons (chaplain 1992-93, jr. warden 1993-94). Republican. Jewish. Home: 1446 Tuscany Way Germantown TN 38138-1824 Office: U Tenn 853 Jefferson Ave Rm E-102 Memphis TN 38103-2807

SHULMISTER, M(ORRIS) ROSS, lawyer; b. Atlanta, Jan. 6, 1940; s. Morris and Kathryn Sybella (Baker) S.; m. Benita Vee Rosin, Dec. 16, 1974. BEE, U. Fla., 1962, JD, 1973. Bar: Fla. 1973, U.S. Dist. Ct. (so. dist.) Fla. 1974, U.S. Dist. Ct. (mid. dist.) Fla. 1985, U.S. Ct. Appeals (5th and 11th cirs.) 1981. Pvt. practice Ft. Lauderdale, Fla.; spl. master for code enforcement, Pompano Beach, Fla., 1991-92. Mem. Broward County Consumer Protection Bd., 1983—; chmn. Charter Review Bd., Pompano Beach, Fla., 1994—; mem. South Pompano Civic Assn., 1989—, v.p., 1989, pres., 1992—. Mem. ABA, Fla. Bar (mem. constrn. law subcom., civil trial cert. 1984), Broward County Bar Assn., Broward County Trial Lawyers Assn., Am. Arbitration Assn. (arbitrator). Office: 3081 E Commercial Blvd Fort Lauderdale FL 33308-4329

SHULTS, ROBERT LEE, real estate executive, airline executive; b. Helena, Ark., Feb. 23, 1936; s. Albert and Mary S.; m. Belinda Housley, Aug. 21, 1965; children: Catherine Ann, Robert L. BS in Acctg. magna cum laude, U. Ark.-Fayetteville, 1961. CPA, Ark. Mgr., Arthur Andersen & Co., Memphis, 1961-70; exec. v.p. Allied Tel. Co., Little Rock, 1970-80; chmn. bd. Scheduled Skyways, Inc., Little Rock, 1980-88, chmn. bd., chief exec. officer, Fin. Ctr. Corp., Little Rock, 1980—, cons. Alltel Corp., Little Rock, 1980-90; chmn. bd., chief exec. Ranch Prop Inc., 1989—; chmn. bd. dir., chief exec. Fin. Ctr. Devel. Co., Air Midwest Inc.; past chmn. bd. Regional Airline Assn., Washington, 1984; chmn. bd. gov. advisory bc. Telecom and Info Tech., 1996. Pres. bd. dirs. Ark. Children's Hosp., 1994—; bd. dirs., treas. Am. Cancer Soc., Ark., 1976-91, bd. dirs., Ark. Arts Ctr., 1996, Inst. Pub. Utilities, Mich. State U., 1976-80; chmn. bd. trustees Trinity Cathedral, 1982-92, Fifty for Future Little Rock. With USMC, 1956-58. Recipient Pres.'s citation, U.S. Ind. Tel. Assn., 1978, 80. Mem. AICPA, Mo. Bd. Accts., Tenn. Bd. Accts., Met. Little Rock C. of C., Little Rock Club, The Capital Club, Summit Club, Little Rock Country Club, Rotary (bd. dirs. 1988-90). Episcopalian. Office: Fin Ctr Corp PO Box 56350 Little Rock AR 72215-6350

SHULTS, THOMAS DANIEL, lawyer; b. Massena, N.Y., Apr. 18, 1955; s. Robert Daniel and Beverly Jean (Stowell) S.; m. Deborah Lynn Barmore, Nov. 17, 1979; children: Daniel, Timothy. BS, Fla. State U., 1977; JD, Washburn U., 1982. Bar: Fla. 1983, U.S. Dist. Ct. (mid. and so. dists.) Fla. 1984, U.S. Tax Ct. 1985, U.S. Ct. Appeals (11th cir.) 1985; cert. mediator Fla. Supreme Ct., mediator U.S. Dist. Ct. Asst. state atty. State of Fla. State's Atty. Office, Orlando, 1983-84; litigation assoc. Abel, Band, Brown, et al, Sarasota, Fla., 1984-87; ptnr. Shults & Pomeroy, P.A., Sarasota, 1988-94, Thomas D. Shults, P.A., Sarasota, 1995—; adj. prof. Manatee C.C., Bradenton, Fla., 1994-95; mem. individual rights com. Fla. Bar, 1987-88; chmn. pub. edn. com. Sarasota Bar, 1991-92; mem. counsel of attys. Am. Subcontractors Assn., Sarasota, 1990-96; pres. Sarasota Cmty. Mental Health Resource Ctr., 1996. Contbr. articles to profl. publs. Capt. U.S. Army, 1977-86. Mem. Order of Barristers, Sarasota Inn of Ct. Office: Thomas D Shults PA 1800 2nd St Ste 790 Sarasota FL 34236-5900

SHULTZ, RONALD EUGENE, computer specialist; b. Muncy, Pa., Sept. 30, 1952; s. Harold Clyde Jacob Jr. and Darlis Louise (Diehl) S.; m. Karen Louise Weaver, Dec. 24, 1970; children: Michelle Louise Shultz Hall, Barron Jarman Shultz. BRE, Piedmont Bible Coll., Winston-Salem, N.C., 1982. Ordained to ministry So. Bapt. Ch., 1985. Unit adminstr. Dept. of Army, Clemson, S.C., 1987-89; contract specialist VA Med. Ctr., Columbia, S.C., 1989-90; asst. chief, Purchase & Contract VA Med. Ctr., Dallas, 1990-92, computer specialist, 1992—; mem. hosp. info. steering com. VA Med. Ctr., Dallas, 1992—; freelance writer. Author: Metamorphosis, 1994. Bd. dirs., sec.-treas. Centro Para Desa Rollo de la Communidad, Dallas. Staff Sgt. USAF, 1970-. Mem. NRA, Non-Commd. Officers Assn. (life), So. League of Dallas (charter bd. dirs., chaplain), Single Action Shooting Soc., Order of Ky. Cols. Republican. Home: 4641 Lasater Rd Box 208 Mesquite TX 75181-3452

SHUMAKER, JOHN WILLIAM, academic administrator; b. Pitts., Aug. 21, 1942; s. Thomas E. Shumaker and Sara Jane (Giffn) Cobun; children: Timothy, Brian. BA, U. Pitts., 1964; MA, U. Pa., 1966, PhD, 1969; LLD hon., Briarwood Coll., 1989; EdD (hon.), Kyung Hee U., 1992. Asst. assoc. prof. classics Ohio State U., Columbus, 1969-77, asst. dean Coll. Humanities, 1971-72, acting chmn. dept. classics, 1972-73, assoc. dean Coll. Humanities, 1973-77; dean Coll. Humanities and Fine Art SUNY, Albany, 1977-83, v.p. rsch. and ednl. devel., 1983-85, v.p. academic planning and devel., 1985-87; pres. Ctrl. Conn. State U., New Britain, 1987-95, U. Louisville, 1995—; exec. dir. Capital Dist. Humanities Program, Albany, 1978-83; trustee, chmn. Conn. Inst. for the ARts in Edn., New Britain, 1988-91; trustee Nat. Commn. for Coop. Edn., Boston, 1987—, exec. com. 1993—. Bd. dirs. New Britain Gen. Hosp., 1988—, Hartford chpt. ARC, 1988-91, A.W. Stanley Found., New Britain, 1988-93, Fleet Bank Adv. Bd., 1993—, World Affairs Coun., Hartford, Conn., 1994—, New Britain Found. for Pub. Giving, 1994—. Mem. Internat. Assn. Univ. Pres. (exec. com. 1987—, vice chmn. N.Am. coun. 1990—), Internat. Assembly Coop. Edn., Am. Assn. State Colls. and Univs. (com. on internat. programs 1987-88, com. state reps. 1988-89, com. diversity 1993—), New Eng. Bd. Higher Edn. (bd. govs. 1990—), New Britain C. of C. (bd. dirs. 1988-89), Phi Beta Kappa. Office: Cen Conn State U 1615 Stanley St New Britain CT 06053-2439

SHUMAN, MARJORIE D. (GOULD) MURPHY, retired English language educator; b. Manchester, N.H., Nov. 16, 1916; d. LeRoy Boardman and Florence Emily (King) Gould; m. Howard Rogers Murphy, June 17, 1950 (dec. Sept. 1980); children: Arthur Gilbert Murphy, Katherine Rogers Murphy (dec.), Jennifer Davis Murphy; m. Edwin H. Shuman, May 4, 1991. AB, Colby Coll., Waterville, Maine, 1937; MA in Tchg., Radcliffe Coll., Cambridge, Mass., 1942. Instr. English and psychology Lasell Jr. Coll., Auburndale, Mass., 1941-44; staff asst. ARC, Italy & Germany, 1944-46; instr. English U. Conn. Ft. Trumball, New London, 1946-48; asst. to registrar Colby Coll., 1948-49; instr. English U. N.H., 1949-51, Hofstra U., Hempstead, N.Y., 1956, Hartwick Coll., Oneonta, N.Y., 1970-73; tutor Coll. Writing Ctr. SUNY, Oneonta, 1981-88; Editor children's page The Daily Star, Oneonta, 1979-81; contbr. poetry Nat. Poetry Inst., 1995, The Boston Herald, 1933; reporter Clay County Leader, Orange Park, Fla., 1995—. Bd. dirs. League of Women Voters, Oneonta, 1978, 86. Democrat. Protestant. Home: PO Box 305 Penney Farms FL 32079 Home (summer): PO Box 102 West Oneonta NY 13861

SHUMATE, CHARLES RAYMOND, oncology and general surgeon; b. Tuscaloosa, Ala., Apr. 14, 1958; s. Frank Allen and Mary Jane (Tennant) S.; m. Mary Pamela Sims, Dec. 17, 1983; children: Clayton Addison, Allyson Blair. BS, U. Ala., Tuscaloosa, 1980; MD, U. Ala., Birmingham, 1984. Diplomate Nat. Bd. Med. Examiners, Am. Bd. Surgery. Intern U. Louisville, 1984-85, resident, 1985-89; fellow M.D. Anderson Cancer Ctr., Houston, 1989-91; asst. prof. surgery U. Ala., Birmingham, 1991-95; sr. scientist Comprehensive Cancer Ctr., Birmingham, 1991-95. Mem. breast team Am. Cancer Soc. Fellow ACS (Best Paper award Ky. chpt. 1988); mem. AMA, So. Med. Assn., Birmingham Surg. Soc., Southeastern Surg. Congress, Soc. Surg. Oncology, Hiram C. Polk Jr. Surg. Soc., Ala. Breast and Cervical Cancer Detection Com., Phi Beta Kappa. Office: Surg Assocs Ste G-2 2018 Brookwood Medical Ctr Dr Birmingham AL 35209-6870

SHUMATE, GLORIA JONES, retired educational administrator; b. Meridian, Miss., Jan. 8, 1927; d. Thomas Marvin and Flora E. (Suggs) Jones; m. Jack B. Shumate, Nov. 19, 1946; children: Jack B. Jr., Thomas Edward. BS, Miss. State U., 1960; MA, U. South Fla., 1969, postgrad. in vocat. edn., 1970-72. Cert. guidance counselor, psychology and social studies specialist, Fla. High sch. tchr. Lauderdale County Schs., Meridian, 1952-56; tchr. vocat. edn. Manpower Devel. and Tng., St. Petersburg, Fla., 1964-69; counselor City Ctr. for Learning St. Petersburg Vocat.-Tech. Inst., 1969-70, registrar, 1970-72, asst. dir., 1972-80, exec. dir., 1980-85; dir. vocat.-tech.-adult edn. ops. Pinellas County Schs., Largo, Fla., 1985-89; chmn. Fla. Equity Council, 1980-81; mem. Fla. Adv. Council on Vocat. Edn., 1980-85, Fla. Job Tng. Coordinating Council, 1983-84. Named Outstanding Educator Pinellas Suncoast C. of C., 1980. Mem. Nat. Council Local Adminstrs., Am. Vocat. Assn., Fla. Vocat. Assn., So. Assn. Colls. and Schs. (standards com. 1975-81), Phi Delta Kappa, Kappa Delta Pi. Democrat. Baptist. Home: 900 63rd St S Saint Petersburg FL 33707-3016

SHUMICK, DIANA LYNN, computer executive; b. Canton, Ohio, Feb. 10, 1951; d. Frank A. and Mary J. (Mari) S.; 1 child, Tina Elyse. Student, Walsh Coll., 1969-70, Ohio U., 1970-71, Kent State U., 1971-77. Data entry clk. Ohio Power Co., Canton, 1969-70; clk. City of Canton Police Dept., 1971-73; system engr. IBM, Canton, 1973-81; adv. market support rep. IBM, Dallas, 1981-89; system engr. mgr. IBM, Madison, Wis., 1989-93; mktg. customer satisfaction mgr. IBM, Research Triangle Park, N.C., 1993; HelpCenter mgr. desktop and consumer sys. supporter IBM Personal Computer Co., Research Triangle Park, 1993-96; call ctr. brand ops. mgr. IBM PC Co., Research Triangle Park, 1996—. Author: Technical Coordinator Guidelines, 1984. Pres., bd. dirs. Big Bros. and Sisters of Denton (Tex.) County, 1989, v.p., 1988, sec., 1987; mem. St. Philip Parish Coun., Lewisville, Tex., 1988-89, Western Stark County Red Cross, Canton, 1980; v.p. Parents Without Ptnrs., Madison, 1991; founding bd. mem. Single Parents Network, 1991; vol. ARC, 1985—; mem. bd. dirs. Rape Crisis Ctr. Dane County, sec., 1990-91; vol. Paint-A-Thon, Dane County, 1990, Badger State Games Challenge, 1992, Cystic Fibrosis Found. Gt. Strides, 1992, 93, 94, 95, 96, Cystic Fibrosis Found. Mother's Day Tea, 1991, 92, 93, 94, 95, 96, Cystic Fibrosis Found. Golf Classic, 1995, 96; bd. dirs. Carolina's chpt. Fibrosis Carolina, 1996.

SHUMSKY, NEIL LARRY, historian, educator; b. Dayton, Ohio, May 28, 1944; s. Charles and Selma Marjorie (Hurwitz) S.; m. Marcia Sydney Green, July 29, 1966; children: Eric Alan, Michael David. AB, UCLA, 1966; PhD, U. Calif., Berkeley, 1972. Asst. prof. history Va. Poly. Inst. and State U., Blacksburg, 1972-78, assoc. prof., 1978—. Author: The Evolution of Political Protest, 1992; editor: Urban America, 1983, (book series, 8 vols.) American Cities, 1995. Grantee Fulbright Found., 1990-91, U.S. Dept. Edn., 1990, 92, 93, NSF, 1988. Mem. AAUP, Urban History Assn., Orgn. Am. Historians. Democrat. Jewish. Home: 2307 Terra Bella St Blacksburg VA 24060 Office: Va Poly Inst and State Univ Dept History Blacksburg VA 24061

SHUMWAY, CHARLES RICHARD, agricultural economics educator; b. Mesa, Ariz., Jan. 20, 1943; S. Charles Richard and Gladus Edna (Rolph) S. m. Janet Louise Bain, June 11, 1964; children: Shelly, Sharon, Richard, Randall, Jesse, Jodi. BS in Agrl. Econs., U. Calif., Davis, 1965, MS in Agrl. Econs., 1967, PhD in Agrl. Econs., 1969. Agrl. economist USDA, Davis, 1967-69; asst. prof. econs. N.C. State U., 1971-74; assoc. prof. agrl. econs. Tex. A&M U., College Station, 1974-80, prof. agrl. econs., 1980—, assoc. head for acad. programs agrl. econ., 1991-94; vis. scholar dept. econs. Harvard U., 1980-81; pres. Western Agrl. Econs. Assn., 1989-90. Co-editor: Western Jour. of Agrl. Econs., 1986-88; assoc. editor: Am. Jour. Agrl. Econs., 1994—; contbr. articles to profl. jours. Stake pres. Latter Day Saint Ch., College Station, Tex., 1990—. Capt. U.S. Army, 1969-71. Recipient Nat. Def. Edn. Act fellowship, 1965-67, Outstanding Pub. Rsch. award Am. Agrl. Econ. Assn., 1971, Outstanding Pub. Rsch. award Western Agrl. Econ. Assn., 1971, Quality Rsch. Discovery award Am. Agrl. Econ. Assn., 1984, Publ. of Enduring Quality award Am. Agrl. Econ. Assn., 1995. Office: Tex A&M Univ Agrl Econs Dept College Station TX 77843-2124

SHUPE, STEPHEN PAUL, electronics engineer; b. South Bend, Ind., Feb. 22, 1960; s. Arvil Mitchell Shupe and Elwanda Reece; m. Tammy Darlene Justice Brown, Dec. 31, 1978 (div. Feb. 1987); 1 child, Eric Randall; m. Effie May Hensley, June 6, 1991; 1 child, Rachel Darlene. BS, East Tenn. State U., 1995, postgrad. Supr. Nuclear Fuels Inc., Erwin, Tenn., 1980-88; technician Texas Instruments, Johnson City, Tenn., 1990-92; computer rep. Prodigy, Gray, Tenn., 1995—. Sgt. U.S. Army, 1986-90.

SHURBAJI, M. SALAH, pathologist; b. Cairo, Apr. 18, 1957; came to U.S., 1984; s. Muhammad B. and Salma Shurbaji; m. Hilda Touma, 1984; 2 children. BS with distinction, Am. U. Beirut, 1979, MS, 1981, MD with distinction, 1984. Diplomate Am. Bd. Pathology; lic. physician Md., Tenn., Mich. Intern Am. U. Beirut Med. Ctr., 1983-84; resident pathology Johns Hopkins Hosp., Balt., 1984-87, resident dept. lab. medicine, 1987-89; clin. fellow dept. pathology Johns Hopkins U. Sch. Medicine, Balt., 1984-89, rsch. fellow dept. pathology, 1989-90; asst. prof. pathology East Tenn. State U., Johnson City, 1990-94, assoc. prof. pathology, 1994—; staff pathologist Univ. Physicians Practice Group, Johnson City, 1990—; staff pathologist Vets. Affairs Med. Ctr., Johnson City, 1990—, acting chief pathology and lab. medicine svc., 1993-94, chief pathology and lab. medicine svc., 1994—. Contbr. articles to profl. jours. Recipient John Abi Hashem Pediatric award Am. U. Beirut, 1982. Fellow Am. Soc. Clin. Pathologists, Coll. Am. Pathologists; mem. AAAS, A.P. Stout Soc. Surg. Pathologists, Am. Soc. Cytology, U.S. and Can. Acad. Pathology, Papanicolaou Soc. Cytopathology, Internat. Soc. Urologic Pathology, Sigma Xi, Alpha Omega Alpha. Office: E Tenn State U Coll Medicine Dept Pathology PO Box 70568 Johnson City TN 37614-0568

SHURN, PETER JOSEPH, III, lawyer; b. Queens, N.Y., Aug. 30, 1946; s. Peter J. Jr. and Vivienne M. (Tagliarino) S.; m. Ingrid Kelbert; children: Steven Douglas, Vanessa Leigh, David Michael. BSEE magna cum laude, Poly. Inst. Bklyn., 1974; JD magna cum laude, New Eng. Sch. Law, 1977; LLM in Patent and Trade Regulation Law, George Washington U., 1981. Bar: N.C., 1977, Va., 1979, Tex., 1982. Research scientist GTE Labs., 1965-77; sole practice, Raleigh, N.C., 1977-78; asso. Burns, Doane, Swecker & Mathis, Alexandria, Va., 1978-80; tech. advisor to judge U.S. Ct. Appeals (fed. cir.), 1980-81; ptnr. Arnold, White & Durkee, Houston, 1981—; adj. prof. South Tex. Coll. Law, 1984-88; invited mem. nat. panel neutrals Am. Arbitration Assn., 1993—. With U.S. Army, 1966-68. Mem. ABA, Houston Bar Assn., Am. Patent Law Assn. (Robert C. Watson award 1981), Houston Patent Law Assn., Assn. Trial Lawyers Am., IEEE, Tex. Trial Lawyers Assn., Sigma Xi. Contbr. articles to legal jours. Office: Arnold White & Durkee 750 Bering Dr Ste 400 Houston TX 77057-2132

SHUSTER, JOHN A., civil engineer; b. Santa Fe, Jan. 18, 1939; s. William H. and Selma (Dingee) S.; m. Carol Habberley, July 1958 (div. Feb. 1960); m. Susan Handy, Aug. 20, 1962 (div. May 1992); children: David Brian, Karen. Student, U. N.Mex., 1961-63; BCE, U. Alaska, 1965; MCE, Stanford U., 1966. Registered profl. engr., Alaska, Calif., R.I., Mass., Va., Wash., Wis., Md., Del. Project engr. Woodward Clyde Assocs., Oakland, Calif., 1966-67, sr. project engr., 1969-72, resident project engr. Soil Cons. of S.E. Asia, Bangkok, Thailand, 1967-69; v.p. engrng. Am. Drilling Co., Providence, 1972-74, also bd. dirs.; exec. v.p. Terrafreeze Corp., Lorton, Va., 1974-79, also bd. dirs.; pres. Geocentric Engrng. Corp., Newington, Va., 1979-89; ind. profl. engr. Internat. Cons. Practice, Mason Neck, Va., 1989-91; pres. Geofreeze, Inc., Mason Neck, Va., 1991—; vis. lectr. on constrn. ground freezing and related techs., numerous univs. and profl. assns., 1975-88; bd. dirs. Geofreeze Corp., Lorton. Contbr. numerous tech. papers to internat. confs. Bd. dirs. Harbor View Civic Assn., Lorton, 1974-79; sect. dir. Operation Zap The Blackstone, Providence, 1972. Served with U.S. Army, 1957-61. Mem. ASCE, Internat. Soc. Soil Mechanics and Founds., Engrng. Inst. Can., Am. Underground Space Assn. (charter), Deep Founds. Inst., Nat. Rsch. Coun. Transp. Rsch. Bd., Internat. Organizing Com. for Ground Freezing (internat. contractors rep.), Harbor View Recreation Club (bd. dirs. 1977-80). Democrat. Unitarian.

SHUSTERMAN, NATHAN, life underwriter, financial consultant; b. Montreal, Que., Can., Aug. 27, 1927; came to U.S., 1950; s. Aaron and Annie (Nulman) S.; m. Norma Thalblum, Jan. 1950; children: Mark D., Claudia S. Student, Sir George Williams Coll., Montreal, 1944-47; grad. N.Y. Inst. Fin. CLU, chartered fin. cons. Retailing mgr. Jefferson Stores, Miami, Fla., 1950-65; gen. agt. Protective Life Ins. Co., Miami, 1965—, chmn. emeritus field adv. coun., past pres. Protective Club; fin. and estate planning cons.; pres. Am. Fin. Counseling Corp., Miami; instr. in estate and tax planning Am. Coll., Bryn Mawr, Pa., 1972—, U. Miami, Coral Gables, Fla., 1972—; registered rep. Pro Equity Services Inc. Mem. North Dade- South Broward Estate Planning Council. Named Man of Yr., Gen. Agts. and Mgrs. Assn., Miami, 1965-67. Mem. Million Dollar Round Table (life), Top of Table, Assn. Advanced Life Underwriting, Am. Soc. CLU's and Chartered Fin. Cons. (past pres. Miami chpt.), Nat. Assn. Life Underwriters (Nat. Sales Achievement award, Nat. Quality award), Fla. Assn. Life Underwriters, Miami Assn. Life Underwriters, Internat. Assn. Fin. Planners, Am. Soc. Pension Actuaries (assoc.), Internat. Platform Assn. Club: Optimists (pres. 1971) (North Miami Beach, Fla.). Lodges: Masons, Shriners, B'nai B'rith (pres. 1950) (Miami). Home: 2320 NE 196th St Miami FL 33180-2132 Office: Am Fin Counseling Corp 16121 NE 18th Ave Miami FL 33162-4749

SHUTE, MELODIE ANN, museum director; b. Ft. Worth, Apr. 17, 1947; d. James Roy and Annie Jo (Causseaux) S.; m. Robert Schmid, Aug. 31, 1968 (div. 1973). BA, Tex. Tech. U., 1969, postgrad. Art tchr. Lubbock (Tex.) H.S., 1969-73, Aspen (Colo.) Sch., 1973-77; educator Hillsborough County Schs., Tampa, Fla., 1978-81; sales rep. Jarvis Corp., Tampa, 1981-82; sales exec. Centel Bus. Sys., Tampa, 1982-86; account exec. Tel Plus, Tampa, 1986-88; supr. corp. comm. Siemens Info. Sys., Boca Raton, Fla., 1988-89; mgr. pub. rels. Siemens Pvt. Comm. Sys., Boca Raton, 1989-93; dir. comm. Boca Raton Mus. Art, 1993-95; dir. mktg. Morikami Mus. & Japanese Gardens, Delray Beach, Fla., 1995—. Mem. Greater Boca Raton C. of C., Palm Beach County Cultural Coun. and Attractions Assn. Christian. Home: 21655 Altamira Ave Boca Raton FL 33433-7547 Office: Morikami Mus 4000 Morikami Park Rd Delray Beach FL 33446-2305

SHUTT, HOWARD STEVEN, journalist; b. Lorain, Ohio, Aug. 27, 1958; s. Jack Shutt; m. Judy blanch Roark, Sept. 3, 1976 (div. Dec. 1996); children: Adam, Amy. Author: Lake Hole Cave, 1995. Recipient Golden Poet award World of Poetry, 1987. Home: PO Box 364 Mountain City TN 37683

SHYERS, LARRY EDWARD, mental health counselor, educator; b. Middletown, Ohio, Aug. 16, 1948; s. Edward and Ruth Evelyn (Davis) S.; m. Linda Faye Shearon, July 31, 1970; children: Jami Lynn, Karen Lindsey. BA, David Lipscomb Coll., Nashville, 1970; MA, Stetson U., DeLand, Fla., 1973; MEd, U. Cen. Fla., 1981; PhD U. Fla., 1992. Lic. mental health counselor, Fla.; nat. cert. counselor; ordained to ministry non-denominational Ch. of Christ, 1969. Minister Ch. of Christ, Ocala, Fla., 1970-75, Mt. Dora, Fla., 1975-80; tchr. Christian Home and Bible Sch., Mt. Dora, 1970-77, dir. guidance, 1977-86; pvt. practice individual and family counseling, Mount Dora, Fla., 1980—; appointed to state regulatory bd. for clin. social work, marriage, family therapy, mental health counseling, 1987-95, vice-chmn., 1987-88, chmn., 1989-95, legis. liaison, 1988-95; adj. prof. Nova U., 1986—, U. Cen. Fla., 1988—, psychology St. Leo Coll., 1985—, Rollins Coll., 1991—, Reformed Theol. Sem., 1995—; adj. instr. Lake Sumter C.C., 1989—, Stetson U., 1990—, Rollins Coll., 1991—; mem. individual manpower tng. system bd. Vocat.-Tech. Sch., Eustis, 1984-87; mem. adv. bd. U.S. Achievement Bd., 1983—; cons. in field. Dir. edn. Mt. Dora Ch. of Christ, 1983-86. Mem. Fla. Mental Health Counselors Assn. (chmn. award and profl. devel. coms. 1985, chmn. govt. relations com., pres. 1986-87), ACA (govt. rels. com. 1990-95, publs. rev. com. 1991—), Am. Mental Health Counselors Assn. (govt. rels. com. 1987-90, chmn. 1988-90, publs. com. 1991—, PP&L com. 1992-95), Am. Orthopsychiat. Assn., Am. Assn. Christian Counselors, Internat. Assn. Marriage and Family Counselors, Assn. of Assessment in Counseling, Am. Assn. Profl. Hypnotherapists, Lake Sumter Assn. for Counseling and Devel. (Pres. 1987-88), Mount Dora C. of C. (mem. youth com. 1984), Kappa Delta Pi, Pi Lambda Theta, Chi Sigma Iota. Republican. Lodge: Kiwanis. Avocations: amateur radio, target shooting. Office: 3900 Lake Center Dr Ste 5 Mount Dora FL 32757-2203

SIBERT, LUTHER LEWREN, health services administrator; b. Frederick, Md., Nov. 3, 1950; s. Luther Lewren and Anna Ruth (Grove) S.; m. Sharon Dunbar, Aug. 21, 1971. BS in Biology and Chemistry, Dickinson Coll., Carlisle, Pa., 1972; MS in Health Svcs. Adminstrn., Coll. St. Francis, Joliet, Ill., 1992. Profl. rep. Burroughs Wellcome Co., Research Triangle Park, N.C., 1972-95, med. ctr. rep., 1976-85, exec. med. ctr. rep., 1985-92, sr. exec. med. ctr., 1992-93, product mgr. HIV, oncology, biotech., 1993-95, regional acctg. mgr. managed health care, 1995; HIV/oncology rep. Glaxo Wellcome, Research Triangle Park, 1995—; bd. advisor Dickinson Coll., Carlisle, Pa., 1991—, alumni admissions program, 1985-92. Pres., bd. mem. Pebble Creek Home Owners, Tampa, 1975-80, Villas of Clearwater (Fla.) Beach Condo Assn., 1984-94. Mem. Am. Soc. Microbiology. Democrat. Methodist.

SIBLEY, JAMES MALCOLM, retired lawyer; b. Atlanta, Aug. 5, 1919; s. John Adams and Nettie Whitaker (Cone) S.; m. Karen Norris, Apr. 6, 1942; children: Karen Mariea, James Malcolm Jr., Jack Norris, Elsa Alexandria Victoria, Quintus Whitaker. A.B., Princeton U., 1941; student, Woodrow Wilson Sch. Law, 1942, Harvard Law Sch., 1945-46. Bar: Ga. 1942. Assoc. King & Spalding, Atlanta, 1942-47, ptnr., 1947-91; bd. dirs. Rock-Tenn. Co., Summit Industries, Inc.; dir. emeritus Life Ins. Co. of Ga.; exec. com., mem. pub. affairs com. Coca-Cola Co., 1979-91; chmn. exec. com. John H. Harland Co., 1963-91; chmn. exec. com., mem. compensation com. Trust Co. of Ga., 1975-92; mem. exec. com., mem. compensation com. SunTrust Banks, Inc., 1985-92. Trustee Joseph B. Whitehead Found., Lettie Pate Evans Found., Emory U., A.G. Rhodes Home, Inc., Robert W. Woodruff Found., Inc. (formerly Trebor Found.), John H. and Wilhelmina D. Harland Charitable Found., Inc.; bd. dirs. Callaway Gardens Found. With USAF, 1942-45. Mem. ABA, Ga. Bar Assn., Atlanta Bar Assn., Am. Coll. Probate Counsel, Am. Bar Found., Am. Law Inst. Episcopalian. Clubs: Piedmont Driving, Commerce. Home: 63 Peachtree Circle Atlanta GA 30309-3556 also: King & Spalding 191 Peachtree St NE Atlanta GA 30303-1763

SIBLEY, RICHARD CARL, real estate executive; b. Cumberland, Md., Nov. 15, 1951; s. Paul Howard and Evelyn Alberta (Carter) S.; m. Jean Virginia Cover, May 23, 1976; children: Pamela Jean, Patrick Ryan. AA in Forest Technology, Allegany Community Coll., 1973; BS in Geography, Frostburg State U., 1976. Draftsman, engrng. aide City of Cumberland, 1974-77; rsch. analyst-site engr. Chessie System (named changed to CSX), Balt., 1977-79, rsch. analyst-conveyancer, 1979-80, rep., 1980-82, asst. mgr., 1982-84, mgr. sales and leasing, 1984-86; dir., sr. dir. CSX Realty, Balt. and Jacksonville, Fla., 1986-90; asst. v.p. CSX Real Property Inc., Jacksonville, 1990—. Fed. Hwy. Adminstrn. scholar, 1975-76. Mem. Internat. Assn. Corp. Real Estate Execs., Internat. Right of Way Assn., Urban Land Inst. Office: CSX Real Property Inc 6757 Southpoint Dr S Ste 100 Jacksonville FL 32216-6177

SICHEWSKI, VERNON ROGER, physician; b. Winnipeg, Man., Can., Dec. 10, 1942; came to U.S., 1980; s. Nicholas and Helen (Sabanski) S. BS, U. Man., 1963; MD, Cairo U., 1979. Diploamte Am. Bd. Emergency Medicine. Resident Charity Hosp. La., New Orleans, 1980-83, Bellevue Hosp., N.Y.C., 1980-83; pvt. practice Broward Gen. Med. Ctr., Ft. Lauderdale, Fla., 1983-86, Trauma Care Assocs., North Miami, Fla., 1986—; flight physician Nat. Jets, Ft. Lauderdale, 1986—; attending physician trauma unit Jackson Meml. Hosp. U. Miami, 1989—. Flight lt. RCAF, 1963-74. Fellow Am. Coll. Emergency Physicians; mem. AMA, So. Med. Assn. Republican. Roman Catholic. Home: 1108-2841 N Ocean Blvd Fort Lauderdale FL 33308 Office: Trauma Care Assocs 1175 NE 125th St Ste 612 Miami FL 33161-5013

SIDDAYAO, CORAZÓN MORALES, economist, educator, energy consultant; b. Manila, July 26, 1932; came to U.S., 1968; d. Crispulo S. and Catalina T. (Morales) S. Cert. in elem. teaching, Philippine Normal Coll., 1951; BBA, U. East, Manila, 1962; MA in Econs., George Washington U., 1971, MPhil and PhD, 1975. Cert. Inst. de Francais, 1989. Tchr. pub. schs. Manila, 1951-53; exec. asst. multinational oil corps., 1953-68; asst. pensions officer IMF, Washington, 1968-71; cons. economist Washington, 1971-75; rsch. assoc. Policy Studies in Sci. and Tech. George Washington U., Washington, 1971-72, teaching fellow dept. econs., 1972-75; natural gas specialist U.S. Fed. Energy Adminstrn., Washington, 1974-75; sr. rsch. economist, assoc. prof. Inst. S.E.A. Studies, Singapore, 1975-78; sr. rsch. fellow energy/economist East-West Ctr., 1978-81, project dir. energy and industrialization, 1981-86; vis. fellow London Sch. Econ., 1984-85; sr. energy economist in charge energy program Econ. Devel. Inst., World Bank, Washington, 1986-94, ret., 1994; affiliate prof. econs. U. Hawaii, 1979—; vis. prof. econs. U. Philippines, intermittently, 1989—; co-dir. UPecon Inst. of Resource Studies, 1995—; vis. prof. U. Montpelier, France, 1992, 1995-96; cons. internat. orgns. and govts., 1995—; spkr. at confs. and symposia. Author or co-author: Increasing the Supply of Medical Personnel, 1973, The Offshore Petroleum Resources of Southeast Asia: Some Potential Conflicts and Related Economic Factors, 1978, Round Table Discussion on Asian and Multinational Corporations, 1978, The Supply of Petroleum Resources in Southeast Asia: Economic Implications of Evolving Property Rights Arrangements, 1980, Critical Energy Issues in Asia and the Pacific: The Next Twenty Years, 1982, Criteria for Energy Pricing Policy, 1985, Energy Demand and Economic Growth, 1986; editor: Energy Policy and Planning series, 1990-92, Energy Investments and the Environment, 1993; co-editor: Investissements Energetiques et Environnement, 1993; co-editor: (series) Energy Projecy Analysis for the CIS Countries (Russian), 1993, Politique d'Efficacité de l'Énergie et Environnement, Expérience pratiques, 1994, Matérial Pedagogique sur la Politique d'Efficacité de l'Energie et Environnement, 1994; contbr. chpts. to books, articles to profl. jours. Grantee in field. Mem. Am. Econ. Assn., Internat. Assn. Energy Economists (charter), Alliance Francaise, Omicron Delta Epsilon. Roman Catholic.

SIDDIQUI, FAROOQ AHMAD, medical educator; b. Unnao, India, Jan. 1, 1951; came to U.S., 1976; s. Siddique Ahmad and Humra (Ahmad) S.; m. Yasmeen Siddiqui, June 24, 1979; children: Tazeen, Sanna. BS in Biology, M.U. Aligarh, India, 1969; MS in Biochemistry, M.U., Aligarh, India, 1971, MPhil in Biochemistry, 1972, PhD in Biochemistry, 1975. Sr. rsch. fellow in biochemistry Patel Chest Inst., Delhi, 1975-76; cancer rsch. affiliate Dept. Exptl. Therapeutics Roswell Park Meml. Inst., Buffalo, N.Y., 1976-79; vis. assoc. in biology McGill U., Montreal, Que., Can., 1979-80; rsch. assoc. biochemistry Georgetown U., Washington, 1980-81; rsch. assoc. medicine Divsn. Hematology U. Miami, 1981-83, rsch. instr. medicine Divsn. Hematology, 1983-85, rsch. asst. prof. medicine Divsn. Hematology/Oncology, 1985-94, rsch. assoc. prof. medicine divsn. hematology/oncology, 1994—; sci. presenter at nat. and internat. meetings. Contbr. articles to profl. jours. Mem. coun. on thrombosis Am. Heart Assn. Co-Prin. Investigator grantee NIH, 1988-93; fellow Coun. Sci. and Indsl. Rsch., New Delhi, 1971-72, Indian Coun. Med. Rsch., 1972-75. Mem. Soc. Biol. Chemists (India), Sigma Xi. Home: 13324 SW 115th Pl Miami FL 33176-4493 Office: U Miami/Va Med Ctr #R-151 Rm 2A122 1201 NW 16th St Miami FL 33125-1624

SIDEBOTTOM, WILLIAM GEORGE, communications executive; b. Greeley, Colo., July 21, 1948; s. William Carroll and Florence Elaine (Krusenstjerna) S.; m. Rosemary Russell, May 16, 1981; children: Faith Ann, William Jeremiah. BS in Bgmt. cum laude, U. West Fla., 1975; MA in Pub. Policy magna cum laude, Regent U., 1985. Mgr. Mgmt. Recruiters, Internat., Pensacola, Fla., 1976-79; div. mgr. Mgmt. Recruiters, Internat., Virginia Beach, Va., 1979-81; dir. communications Rock Ch., Virginia Beach, 1981-83; dir. devel., v.p. comm. Nat. Freedom Inst., Chesapeake, Va., 1983-86; pres. William G. Sidebottom & Assocs., 1986—. Author: Who Owns the Children, 1985; sr. editor: The Perspective Papers, 1985, Essential Lectures, 1985. Cons. Coral Ridge Ministries, 1990—, Am. Ctr. for Law and Justice, 1990—, Christian Advocates Serving Evangelism, 1995—, Regent U., 1992—. Mem. Phi Kappa Phi, Pi Kappa Delta. Presbyterian. Office: PO Box 377 Lyndhurst VA 22952-0377

SIEBENTHALL, CURTIS ALAN, counselor, consultant, psychology educator; b. Odessa, Tex., June 30, 1929; s. Curtis Arnold and Norma T. (Henry) S.; m. Jane Madden, July 26, 1958; children: Rebecca Ann, David Alan. BS, Midwestern State U., 1951, MEd, 1955; EdD, U. North Tex., 1972. Civilian instr. USAF, Sheppard Air Force Base, Tex., 1951-53; chemist Phillips Petroleum, Phillips, Tex., 1953; math. tchr. Wichita Falls (Tex.) High Sch., 1953-55, counselor, 1955-65; dir. counseling Wichita Falls Ind. Sch. Dist., 1966-69; jr. high counselor Denton (Tex.) Ind. Sch. Dist., 1970-72; counselor, prof. psychology and math. Tarrant County Jr. Coll., Ft. Worth, 1972—; pvt. practice counselor Ft. Worth and Bedford, Tex., 1976-91; cons. Loma Rubber Queen, Ft. Worth, 1985-86, Profiles Internat., Bedford, 1976-87, Profit Tech., N.Y.C., 1986-87, U.S. Profiles, Ft. Worth, 1987—. Contbr. articles to profl. jours. Mem. ACA, Tex. Assn. for Counseling and Devel., Biofeedback Soc. Tex., Jr. Coll. Students Pers. Assn. Tex., Tex. Counselor Assn., Lions Internat. (v.p. Wichita Falls chpt. 1967, pres. 1968). Southern Baptist. Office: Siebenthall Assoc PO Box 751 Hurst TX 76053-0751

SIEDLE, ROBERT DOUGLAS, management consultant; b. Canton, Ohio, Aug. 8; m. Beverly Rose Scholl, Mar. 18, 1972 (div. Oct. 1983). BA in Econs., Hiram Coll., 1956; profl. cert. edn., Kent State/Western Res. Univs., 1963. Tchr., prin. Ohio secondary schs., 1957-65; salesman, area rep. visual products divsn. 3M Co., 1966-68; mgr. market devel. and tng. AV divsn. Bell & Howell, 1968-69; Chgo. br. mgr. info. systems divsn. Am. Std., 1969-72; mgr. edn. systems divsn. Audiotronics Corp., 1972-76; gen. mgr. Niles Entertainment/Wardway Films, 1977-80; pres. The Ultimate Image, Lakeland, Fla., 1985—. Producer: (films) New Dimensions in Learning II, 1969, District 65: The Exceptional Child, 1969, Career Exploration: Health, 1976, The Wide World of Work, 1976; author: Multisensory Learning: A Training Guide, 1973, Alphabet Zoo, 1973, City of Boston Young Adult Alternate Career Program, 1974, The Quick Job Hunt Guide, 1991; author, producer, dir.: (multimedia rd. show) "Rap" With Students, 1975; producer, editor: (film) Stampin' Ground, 1977; author poetry appearing in books and mags., 1983—; appeared on nat. radio and TV programs in U.S. and Can. Named Internat. Man of Yr., Internat. Biog. Ctr., Cambridge, Eng , 1992-93, recipient Internat. Order of Merit, 1993. Fellow Internat. Biog. Assn. (life), Am. Biog. Inst. (Man of Yr. and Most Admired Man of Decade 1993, Platinum Record award 1996, 500 Leadership Influence award 1996, Golden Record of Achievement 1996, Presdl. Seal of Honor 1996); mem. Am. Biog. Inst. Rsch. Assn. (dep. gov. life), U.S. Naval Aviation Mus. (life), U.S. Naval Inst. (life), Navy League of U.S. (life), World Future Soc., Internat. Platform Assn., Sun 'n Fun Air Mus. (life), Am. Air Mus. in Britain (founding mem.), Aircraft Owners and Pilots Assn., Aircraft Owners and Pilots Assn. Safety Found., Exptl. Aircraft Assn., Warbirds of Am., Soaring Soc. Am., Great Lakes Hist. Soc. (life), Navy League U.S. (life), Air Force Assn. Baptist. Office: The Ultimate Image PO Box 91388 Lakeland FL 33804-1388

SIEFKIN, WILLIAM CHARLES, international growth investor, consultant, publisher, writer; b. Glendale, Calif., Jan. 15, 1946; s. Ernest Roosevelt and Violet May (Richardson) S.; m. Deborah Sue Olinger, Dec. 21, 1971; children: Barbra Anne, Katherine Marie, William Andrew. BBA, Calif. Polytech. U., San Luis Obispo, 1968; postgrad., U. Del., 1985; MS in Applied Tech. Tng. and Devel., U. North Tex., 1996. Tech. rep. photo products dept. DuPont Co., Houston and San Antonio, 1968-71; sr. tech. rep. photo products dept. DuPont Co., Louisville, 1971-73; sr. export sales rep. photo products dept. internat. ops. div. DuPont Co., Wilmington, Del., 1973-74, internat. planning mgr. photo systems and electronics dept., 1979-85, mktg. mgr. imaging systems dept., 1985-87, mgr. sales devel. corp. plans dept., 1987-91; dir. sales devel. Du Pont Corp. Plans, 1991-92; tech. sales mgr. internat. dept. Du Pont de Nemours Co., Tokyo, 1974-79; pres., bd. dirs., chief cons. Webmaster Montchanin Corp., Denton, Tex., 1981—; v.p. customer growth Etheridge Printing Co., Dallas, 1992-93; realtor Ebby Halliday Realtors, Dallas, 1994; regional field trainer GTE Directories Sales Corp., Dallas-Ft. Worth Airport, 1994—; mem. adv. bd. Calif. Poly. State U. Sch. Graphic Comm. Author numerous articles and books in field. Life mem. Rep. Nat. Com., Washington, 1985; dir., mem. exec. com. Jr. Achievement Del., Wilmington, 1986; mem. Dover Symphony, Brandywine Pops Orch. Recipient Bronze Nat. Leadership award Jr. Achievement, 1985, Silver award, 1990; named Honored Alumni of Yr., Calif. Poly. U. Sch. Bus., 1984. Mem. Antique Automobile Club Am. (life), Mensa, Mercedes-Benz Club Am., Hon. Order Ky. Cols., Assn. Quality and Participation. Republican. Methodist. Home: 1412 Gatewood Dr Denton TX 76205-8068 Office: GTE Directories Sales Corp 5601 Executive Dr Irving TX 75038-2508

SIEGAL, GENE PHILIP, pathology educator; b. Bronx, N.Y., Nov. 16, 1948; s. Murray H. and Evelyne (Philips) S.; m. Sandra Helene Meyerowitz, Aug. 3, 1972; children: Gail Deborah, Rebecca Stacey. BA, Adelphi U., Garden City, N.Y., 1970; MD, U. Louisville, 1974; PhD, U. Minn., 1979; cert. in hosp. mgmt., U. N.C., 1988. Diplomate Nat. Bd. Med. Examiners, Am. Bd. Pathology. Intern, resident, rsch. fellow Mayo Clinic Found., Rochester, Minn., 1974-79; rsch. assoc. Lab. Pathophysiology, Nat. Cancer Inst., NIH, Bethesda, Md., 1979-81; fellow surg. pathology U. Minn., Mpls., 1981-82; asst. prof. pathology U. N.C., Chapel Hill, 1982-88, assoc. prof. pathology, 1988-90; mem. Lineberger Comprehensive Cancer Ctr., Chapel Hill, 1983-90; prof. pathology U. Ala., Birmingham, 1990—, sr. scientist/group leader breast, ovary, prostate program, 1990—, prof. cell biology, prof. surgery, 1991—; mem. Children's Cancer Study Group, 1987-90, Pediatric Oncology Group, 1990—. Co-editor: Molecular Antibodies in Diagnostic Immunohistochemistry, 1988; assoc. editor Archives of Pathology and Lab. Medicine, 1989-90; mem. editl. bd. Yearbook of Pathology, 1983-91, Archives of Pathology and Laboratory Medicine, 1990-91, Am. Jour. Clin. Pathology, 1990—, Modern Pathology, 1996—. With USPHS, 1979-81. Clin. fellow Am. Cancer Soc., Chapel Hill, 1981-82, jr. faculty fellow, 1983-86, Jefferson-Pilot fellow in acad. medicine, U. N.C., Chapel Hill, 1985-86. Fellow Coll. Am. Pathologists (inspector 1990—), Royal Soc. Medicine (London); mem. AMA, AAAS, Internat. Skeletal Soc., AOA, Am. Soc. for Investigative Pathology, U.S. and Can. Acad. Pathology (abstract rev. bd. 1989-91), A.P. Stout Surg. Pathologists (nominating com.), Metastasis Rsch. Soc., Am. Assn. Cancer Rsch., Assn. Dirs. Anatomic and Surg. Pathology, Sigma Xi (pres. U. N.C. chpt. 1989-90). Democrat. Jewish. Office: Univ Ala Dept Pathology 506 Kracke Birmingham AL 35233

SIEGEL, CHARLES ERIC, curator of birds; b. Chgo., July 25, 1958; s. Norm D. and Marley R. Siegel; m. Julie Ann Jamison, Jan. 21, 1996; 1 child, Lee Alice Jamison. BS in Ecology, Ethology and Evolution, U. Ill., 1980, MS in Biology, 1985; postgrad. in wildlife sci., Tex. A&M U., 1989. Grad. rsch. asst. U. Ill., Urbana, 1980-81, grad. tchg. asst., 1981-84; zookeeper Brookfield (Ill.) Zoo, 1979-82; asst. dir. Henson Robinson Zoo, Springfield, Ill., 1985-86; rsch. zoologist Dallas Zoo, 1986-88, asst. curator of birds, 1988-91, curator of birds, 1991—; bd. mem. North Tex. Birds of Prey Ctr., Dallas, 1990—; pres. Amazon Conservation Fund, Dallas, 1992-93. Contbr. articles to profl. jours. Grantee Dallas Zool. Soc., 1987; recipient innovative project award City of Dallas, 1992; Zimmer meml. scholar Inst. Profl. Edn., Chgo., 1993. Fellow Assn. Zoos and Aquaria; mem. N.Am. Ornithological Soc., Bird Interest Group Tex. (co-founder), Sigma Xi, Phi Kappa Phi, Gamma Sigma Delta. Office: Dallas Zoo 621 E Clarendon Dallas TX 75203

SIEGEL, JEFF, writer; b. Columbus, Ohio, May 10, 1958; s. Harold S. and Phyllis (Bahr) S.; m. Lynne Kleinpeter, Dec. 31, 1983. BS in Journalism, Northwestern U., Evanston, Ill., 1979. Freelance writer Dallas, 1981—; copy editor, reporter Dallas Times Herald, Dallas, 1985-89; co-owner Advocate Community Newspapers, Dallas, 1991—. Author: Casablanca Companion, 1992, The American Fictional Detective: 150 Years of Gumshoes, Snoops and Private Eyes, 1993; contbr. articles to profl. jours. and newspapers. Mem. Mystery Writers of Am., Soc. Profl. Journalists. Home: PO Box 140863 Dallas TX 75214-0863

SIEGEL, JEROME SEYMOUR, cardiologist; b. Memphis, Oct. 2, 1937; married; 2 children. Grad., Southwestern U., 1958; MD, U. Tenn., 1961. Intern U. Chgo. Hosps. and Clinics, 1961-62; commd. 2d lt. USAF, 1962, advanced through grades to lt. col., 1970, ret., 1970; resident in internal medicine and cardiovascular disease USAF Hosp., Lackland AFB, Tex., 1964-67; clin. asst. prof. medicine U. Tenn. Coll. Medicine, 1970-88, clin. asst. prof., 1988—; mem. jr. stafff Bapt. Meml. Hosp., Memphis, 1970-72, assoc. staff, 1972-75, active staff, 1975—, med. dir. ICU-CCU, 1982-90; cons. staff Meth. Hosp., Memphis, 1970—, St. Francis Hosp., Memphis, 1975—, St. Joseph Hosp., Memphis, 1970—; mem. active staff City of Memphis Hosp., 1970-82, cons. staff, 1982—; pvt. practice, Memphis, 1970—; instr. ACLS. Contbr. articles to profl. jours. Fellow ACP, Memphis Acad. Internal Medicine, Coun. Clin. Cardiology Am. Heart Assn., Am. Coll. Cardiology (assoc.); mem. Memphis and Shelby County Med. Soc., Memphis Heart Assn., Mid-South Med. Assn., Tenn. Med. Assn., Tenn. Soc. Internal Medicine, Am. Soc. Internal Medicine, Am. Physicians Fellowship, So. Med. Assn., AMA, Memphis Cardiovascular Soc., Beta Sigma Rho, Phi Delta Epsilon. Home: 6624 Westminster Rd Memphis TN 38120-3447

SIEGEL, JOY HAYES, banker, writer, educator, entrepreneur; b. Portland, Maine; d. Erwin Roland and Doris (Hazelton) Hayes; m. Frederick W. Siegel; 1 child, Christopher Erik. BA magna cum laude, U. Louisville, MBA; postgrad., East Tenn. State U., U. Fla.; student, Am. Acad. Dramatic Arts, N.Y.C., Acad. Radio-TV Broadcasting, Cleve. Inst. Tech. With Mid-Am. Bancorp and Bank of Louisville, Nat. City Bank, Ky., Ohio, S.E. Bank, Fla., Hamilton Bank, Tenn., Key Bank, Maine, Bankers Trust, N.Y.C.; sr. v.p. corp. credit Bank of Louisville; instr. fin., econs. and mgmt. U. Louisville; founder Joy's Creations, Hayes Boarding Stables, The Believings Power Press, YouCanDoIt! Western Apparel. Author textbooks on credit analysis, motivational books for children; creator, editor The Brilliant Banker. Active Focus Louisville, Boy Scouts Am. With U.S. Army, Vietnam. Mem. Robert Morris Assocs. (bd. dirs.), Bus. and Profl. Women (River City mem. state fin. com., state bd. dirs.), U. Louisville Women (bd. dirs.), Ky. Soc. Mayflower Descs. (bd. dirs.), Belle of Louisville (hon. capt.), Hon. Order Ky.Cols., Filson Club, Jefferson Club, Doe Valley Country Club, We.-English Retailers Assn., Oxford Hills C. of C., Nat. Assn. Women Bus. Owners, N. Am. Horsemen's Assn. Office: Bank of Louisville 322 Kenwood Hill Rd Louisville KY 40214-3562

SIEGEL, LAWRENCE IVER, real estate development company executive; b. Cleve., Aug. 19, 1925; s. Edward I. and Mary (Mentz) S.; BBA, Western Res. U., 1949, LLB, 1952; m. Joyce Reske, Nov. 4, 1950; children—Leslie, Diane, Frederick, Edward. Pres., Lawrence I. Siegel Co., Baton Rouge, 1980—; chmn. bd. Lisscorp. Inc. Bd. dirs. Tara High Sch. Backers, Baton Rouge, Community Concerts Assn., New Orleans; Cub Scout master, 1967-68. Served with inf. U.S. Army, 1943-46; ETO, PTO. Col. on Staff of gov. La. Decorated Combat Inf. Badge Bronze Star. Mem Internat. Council Shopping Centers, Mortgage Bankers Assn. Am., Am. Bankers Assn., U.S. C. of C., Baton Rouge C. of C. Club: Kiwanis. Home: 7844-A Jefferson Place Blvd Baton Rouge LA 70809 Office: 10455 Jefferson Hwy Baton Rouge LA 70809-2732

SIEGEL, MARK JORDAN, lawyer; b. Dallas, Feb. 22, 1949; s. Jack H. and Zelda (Sikora) S. BS in Psychology, North Tex. State U., 1972; JD, South Tex. Coll. Law, 1977. Bar: Tex. 1977, U.S. Dist. Ct. (no. dist.) Tex, 1980, U.S. Ct. Appeals (11th and 5th cirs.) 1982, U.S. Supreme Ct. 1982. Pvt. practice, Dallas, 1977-87; mem. bd. dirs. Scotch Corp., Dallas. Sponser Civil Justice Found. Mem. N. Dallas 40. Named one of Outstanding Young Men Am., 1985, 86. Mem. Tex. Trial Lawyers Assn., Dallas Trial Lawyers Assn., Assn. Trial Lawyers Am., Nat. Bd. Trial Advocacy (cert. civil trial specialist), Tex. Bd. Legal Specialization (cert. civil trial law). Office: 3607 Fairmount St Dallas TX 75219-4710

SIEGEL, MARY ANN GARVIN, volunteer; b. Louisville, Apr. 3, 1944; d. Samuel Hughes and Ann Wendell (Smith) Garvin; m. Charles Holladay Siegel, Sept. 2, 1967; children: Emily Hughes, Charles Holladay, Jr., Margaret Shafer. BA, Conn. Coll., 1966. Photographic rschr. Time Inc., N.Y.C., 1966-67, Nat. Geographic Soc., Washington, 1967-68; cmty. vol., activist in edn., religion and other non-profit agys. and orgns. Ga., N.C., Conn.; Leadership Atlanta, 1993-94, exec. com. program, 1995-96. Trustee Conn. Coll., New London, 1985-90; chair Friends of Spelman Coll., Atlanta, 1990-92; active Atlanta/Fulton County adv. bd. United Way Met. Atlanta, 1994-96; Olympic Envoy to Republic of Nauru, Atlanta Com. Olympic Games, 1994-96; formerly active adv. bd. N.C. Outward Bound Sch., Asheville. Recipient Agnes Berkeley Leahy award Conn. Coll. Alumni Assn., 1991. Democrat. Episcopalian.

SIEGEL, RANDY, public relations executive; b. Atlanta, Aug. 29, 1955; s. R.A. and Marion (Kasten) S.; m. Jill F., May 18, 1981. BBA in Mktg., U. Ga., 1978. Assoc. exec. dir. Kidney Found., Atlanta, 1978-83; acct. supr. Cohn & Wolfe, Atlanta, 1983-86; dir. communications Canada Dry and Sunkist, Atlanta, 1986; v.p. A. Brown-Olmstead Assocs., 1986-88; exec. v.p., gen. mgr., ptnr. Fleishman-Hillard, Atlanta, 1988—; cons. in field. Contbr. articles to profl. jours. Adv. bd. Mus. Am. Folk Art, N.Y.C., 1988—, High Mus. Art, 1993—, Nat. Kidney Found., N.Y.C., 1988-93, Berry Coll., Rome, Ga., 1988-91; dir. Nat. Kidney Found. Ga., 1986-93. Recipient Vol. award Nat. Kidney Found. Ga., 1988. Mem. Pub. Rels. Soc. Am., Leadership Atlanta 1992, Piedmont Driving Club. Republican. Episcopalian. Home: 162 Rumson Rd NE Atlanta GA 30305-3112 Office: Fleishman-Hillard 233 Peachtree St NE Ste 1250 Atlanta GA 30303-1507

SIEGEL, ROBERT JAMES, communications executive; b. N.Y.C., Feb. 26, 1929; s. Hiram and Regina (Goldstein) S. ; m. Gonnie McClung, Jan. 8, 1953; children: William Laird, Richard Joseph. BS in Econs., Marietta Coll., 1950. With copy desk N.Y. Times, 1951-53; assoc. editor Lorain (Ohio) Jour., 1953-56; reporter Cleve. Press, 1956-61; with IBM, Armonk, N.Y., 1961—, data processing div. press rels. mgr., corp. info. mgr., corp. pub. affairs mgr., 1979—, dir. info., dir. internal communications, 1988-89; mng. dir. advt. and mktg. communications Metaphor, Inc., Atlanta, 1989-90; pres. Siegel Assocs., Communications Cons., Bal Harbour, Fla., 1991—. Mayor Key Colony Beach, Fla., 1995—. Mem. Nat. Press Club, Overseas Press Club, Deadline Club of N.Y., Sigma Delta Chi. Office: PO Box 510022 City Hall Key Colony Beach FL 33051 Home: PO Box 510022 Key Colony Beach FL 33051

SIEGELMAN, DON EUGENE, state official; b. Mobil, Ala., Feb. 24, 1946; m. Lori Allen; c. Dana, Joseph. B.A., U. Ala.; J.D., Georgetown U., 1972; postgrad., Oxford U., Eng., 1972-73. Bar: Ala. 1972. Sec. of state State of Ala., Montgomery, 1979-87, atty. gen., 1987-94; lt. gov. State of Ala., 1996—. Office: Office of Lt Gov 11 Union St Montgomery AL 36130

SIEGFELDT, DENISE VANASSE, management educator; b. Newport News, Va., Dec. 27, 1957; d. Alan Richard and Mary Ann (Saunders) Vanasse; married, June 1985 (div. Nov. 1992); 1 child, Amber Marie. BS in Psychology, Old Dominion, 1978, MS in Edn., 1980, PhD in Mgmt., 1991. Cert. nat. counselor, 1983. Vocat. evaluator Penninsuls Vocat. Assessment Ctr., Hampton, Va., 1980-81, assessment counselor, 1981-83; assessment counselor Job Tgn. Svcs., Hampton, Va., 1983-86; instr., Grad. Sch. Pub. Adminstrn. Langley AFB, Golden Gate U., Langley, Va., 1989-90; asst. prof. Atlantic Region, Norfolk Naval Base, Troy State U., Norfolk, Va., 1991-92; co-dir. rsch. and devel. Inst. Acad. Coaching and Counseling, Norfolk, Va., 1992-93; prof. mgmt. Fla. Inst. Tech., Fort Eustis, Va., 1993; asst. prof.dept. mgmt. Hampton U., Hampton, Va., 1993—. Contbr. to profl. jours. V.p. Francis Asbury Elem. Sch. PTA, 1993—. Post Doctoral Rsch. fellow NASA/Langley Rsch. Ctr., 1992, 93, 94. Mem. Am. Soc. Pub. Adminstrn., Va. Peninsula C. of C., Pi Alpha Alpha, Psi Chi. Home: 475 Stockton St Hampton VA 23669-1348 Office: Hampton U Rsch & Devel Office Hampton VA 23661

SIEMONT, KATHLEEN O., lawyer; b. San Mateo, Calif., Jan. 9, 1970; d. Joseph and June Siemont. AA, Skyline Coll., 1990; BA in English Lit., Calif. State U. Chico, 1992; JD, George Washington U., 1996, MPH, 1996. Intern Office Atty. Gen. State of Calif., Sacramento, 1992; intern Office Dist. Atty., Oroville, Calif., 1992-93; clk. legal rsch. Calif. State U., Chico, 1994-95. Contbr. articles to profl. jours. Vol. Whitman-Walker Med. Clinic, Washington, 1996—. Mem. ABA (Health Law Forum), Nat. Lawyers Assn., Golden Key Nat. Honor Soc.

SIENKIEWICZ, RAYMOND JEROME, army officer; b. Travis AFB, Calif., Dec. 4, 1952; s. Henry Vincent and Elizabeth Eloise (Elston) S.; m.

Sook Park, May 27, 1983; 1 child, Raymond Matthew. BS in Chemistry, Tex. A&M U., 1975, BA in Russian, 1976; MS in Bus. Adminstrn., Boston U., Heidelberg, Germany, 1983. Commd. 2d lt. U.S. Army, 1975, advanced through grades to maj., 1987; platoon leader 1st Cavalry Divsn., Ft. Hood, Tex., 1976-80; ops. officer 3rd Armored Divsn., Buedingen, Germany, 1980-81; co. comdr. 3rd Armored Divsn., Hanau, Germany, 1981-83; R&D officer U.S. Army Chem. Sch., Ft. McClellan, Ala., 1984-87; left active duty U.S. Army, 1987; material specialist U.S. Army Chem. Sch., Ft. McClellan, Ala., 1987-90; mil. analyst 7th Army Tng. Ctr., Hohenfels, Germany, 1990-93; test and evaluation specialist U.S. Army Chem. Sch., Ft. McClellan, Ala., 1993—. Pres. Parish Coun. St. Michael's Parish, Hohenfels, 1992-93. Mem. Assn. U.S. Army, U.S. Army Armor Assn., KC. Roman Catholic. Home: 1205 Delwood Dr SW Jacksonville AL 36265-3393 Office: US Army Chem Sch ATZN-CM-CS Fort McClellan AL 36205-5020

SIEWERT, EDGAR ALLEN, retired military non-commissioned officer; b. Slayton, Minn., Nov. 9, 1927; s. Albert William and Matilda Ernestine (Zahn) S.; m. Irene Phyllis Zevenbergen, Apr. 6, 1950; 1 child, Kevin Lee. Grad., Sgt. Maj. Acad., 1974, El Paso (Tex.) Community Coll., 1978. Lic. real estate agent; cert. pilot, airframe mechanic. Electrician USS Philippine Sea USN, 1945-48; aircraft mechanic Sevedy & Sornsen Aviation, Worthington, Minn., 1948-51; tank platoon sgt. U.S. Army, Ft. Rucker, Ala., 1951-52; aircraft electrician Douglas Aircraft, Tulsa, Okla., 1952-56; self-employed Tulsa, Okla., 1956-61; adminstrn. and supply technician Okla. Nat. Guard, Claremore, 1961-72; ops., tng. and readiness specialist Okla. Nat. Guard, Tulsa, 1972-76; tng. technician Okla. Nat. Guard, Oklahoma City, 1976-87, ret., 1987; state command sgt. maj., 1976-78; comdt. Okla. Nat. Guard Non-Commd. Officers Acad., Oklahoma City, 1978-83; chief ops. sgt. Okla. Mil. Dept., Oklahoma City, 1983-87; sgt. maj. acad. selection bd. Nat. Guard Bur., Edgewood Arsenal, Md., 1979. Scout master Boy Scouts Am., Tulsa, 1962-65; vol. various orgns., 1989—. Mem. Okla. Real Estate Investors Assn., Nat. Guard Assn. (bd. dirs.), Nat. Guard Enlisted Assn. (pres., v.p. 1976-78), Nat. Guard Assn. Okla. (bd. dirs. 1976-77, 83-84), 45th Infantry Div. Assn., USS Philippine Sea Assn., Dale Carnegie Alumni Assn. (pres. 1956-57). Republican. Presbyterian. Home: 1313 SW 106th Pl Oklahoma City OK 73170-4213

SIGDESTAD, CURTIS PAUL, radiobiology educator; b. St. Paul, Feb. 15, 1938; s. Daniel John and Myrtle O. (Nellermoe) S.; m. K. M. Schneider, Sept. 10, 1966; children: Kristen Lee, Jennifer Ann. BA, Concordia Coll., 1963; MS, N.D. State U., 1965; PhD, U. Iowa, 1968. Postdoctoral fellow Allegheny Gen. Hosp., Pitts., 1968-70; asst. prof. radiology U. Louisville Sch. Medicine, 1970-73, head radiobiology sect., 1970—, assoc. prof. radiology, 1973-81, prof. radiation oncology, 1981—; assoc. in pharmacology U. Louisville Health Sci. Ctr., 1973—, assoc. in oncology, 1975—; cons. UAB Med. Ctr., Birmingham, Ala., 1972, Osler Inst., Terre Haute, Ind., 1989-93; vis. assoc. prof. MD Anderson Tumor Inst., Houston, 1977-78; vis. scientist Argonne (Ill.) Nat. Lab., 1985-86. Contbr. numerous articles to sci. publs. With USNR, 1957-66. Rsch. grantee U.S. Army, 1971-88, USPHS, 1972-75. Mem. Am. Soc. Therapeutic Radiology, Am. Assn. for Cancer Rsch., Internat. Soc. for Radiation Rsch., Radiation Rsch. Soc., Cell Kinetic Soc. Office: U Louisville Brown Cancer Ctr 529 S Jackson St Louisville KY 40202-3229

SIGETY, CHARLES BIRGE, investment company executive; b. N.Y.C., Sept. 30, 1952; s. Charles Edward and Katharine Kinne (Snell) S.; m. Elizabeth Ross Pennington, Nov. 27, 1976; children: Austin Douglas, Katharine Colyer, Alexander Birge. BA in English Lit., Bates Coll., 1975. Lic. nursing home adminstr. Adminstr. in tng. Florence Nightingale Nursing Home, N.Y.C., 1972, asst. dir. facility ops., 1975, dir. facility ops., 1975-78, assoc. adminstr., 1978-81, exec. dir., 1981-82; pres., CEO Profl. Med. Products, Inc., Greenwood, S.C., 1982-96; dir. Upper Savannah Internat. Trade Assn., Greenwood, S.C., 1993-94; pres. Upper Savannah Internat. Trade Assn., Greenwood, 1993; CEO Bison Investments, Inc., Tampa, Fla., 1996—; mem. Liberty Mutual Ins. Cos. S.C. Adv. Bd., 1986-96; mem. adv. bd. Nations Bank's S.C., 1984-96, County Bank, Greenwood, 1981; bd. dirs. Profl. Med. Products, Inc.; vice chmn. Upper Savannah Bus. Group on Health Care, Greenwood, 1982-87; mem. S.C. Bus. Roundtable for The Initiative for Work Force Excellence, Columbia, 1988-92; dir., mem. exec. com. OSTEO Am., Inc., 1993-96; bd. dir. Help for Incontinent People, 1993-96. Bd. visitors Med. U. S.C., 1988. Mem. Young Pres. Orgn., Am. Coll. of Health Care Adminstrs., Health Industry Mfrs. Assn. (official rep. 1982-96), Upper Savannah Internat. Trade Assn. (pres. 1993). Republican. Presbyterian. Office: Bison Investments Inc 3225 S MacDill Ave #236 Tampa FL 33629

SIGETY, CHARLES EDWARD, lawyer, family business consultant; b. N.Y.C., Oct. 10, 1922; s. Charles and Anna (Toth) S.; m. Katharine K. Snell, July 17, 1948; children: Charles, Katharine, Robert, Cornelius, Elizabeth. BS, Columbia U., 1944; MBA, Harvard U., 1947; LLB, Yale U., 1951; LHD (hon.), Cazenovia Coll., 1994. Bar: N.Y. 1952, D.C. 1958. With Bankers Trust Co., 1939-42; instr. adminstrv. engring. Pratt Inst., 1948; instr. econs. Yale U., 1948-50; vis. lectr. acctg. Sch. Gen. Studies Columbia U., N.Y.C., 1948-50, 52; rapporteur com. fed. taxation for U.S. coun. Internat. C. of C., 1952-53; asst. to com. fed. taxation Am. Inst. Accts., 1950-53; with Compton Advt. Agy., N.Y.C., 1954; vis. lectr. law Yale U., 1952; pvt. practice law N.Y.C., 1952-67; pres., dir. Video Vittles, Inc., N.Y.C., 1953-67; dep. commr. FHA, 1955-57; of counsel Javits and Javits, 1959-60; 1st asst. atty. gen. N.Y., 1958-59; dir., mem. exec. com. Gotham Bank, N.Y.C., 1961-63; dir. N.Y. State Housing Fin. Agy., 1962-63; chmn. Met. Ski Slopes, Inc., N.Y.C., 1962-65; pres., exec. adminstr. Florence Nightingale Health Ctr., N.Y.C., 1965-85; chmn. bd. Profl. Med. Products, Inc., Greenwood, S.C., 1982-96; dir. Schaerer AG, Wabern, Switzerland, 1982-88; professorial lectr. Sch. Architecture, Pratt Inst., N.Y.C., 1962-66; mem. Sigety Assocs., cons. in housing mortgage financing and urban renewal, 1957-67; ho. cons. Govt. of Peru, 1956; mem. missions to Hungary, Poland, Fed. Republic Germany, Malta, Czechoslovakia, Russia, Israel, Overseas Pvt. Investment Corp., 1990-92; owner, operator Peppermill Farms, Pipersville, Pa., 1956—. Bd. dirs., sec., v.p., treas. Nat. Coun. Health Ctrs., 1969-85; bd. dirs. Am.-Hungarian Found., 1974-76, Pritikin Rsch. Found., 1991—, Stratford Arms Condo Assn., 1992-93, Global LEadership Inst., 1993—; trustee Cazenovia (N.Y.) Coll., 1981-95; del. White House Conf. on Aging, 1971, White House Conf. on Mgmt. Tng. and Market Econs. Edn. in Ctrl. and Ea. Europe, 1991; bd. visitors Lander Coll., U. S.C., Greenwood, 1982-84; mem. fin. com. World Games, Santa Clara, 1981, London, 1985, Karlsruhe, 1989, The Hague, 1993, Confrerie des Chevaliers du Tastevin, Confrerie de la Chaine des Rotisseurs, Wine and Food Soc., Wednesday 10. Recipient President's medal Cazenovia Coll., 1990, George Washington laureate Am. Hungarian Found., 1996; Baker scholar Harvard U., 1947. Mem. Harvard Bus. Sch. Assn. (exec. coun. 1966-69, area chmn. 1967-69), Townsend Harris Alumni Assn. (bd. dirs. 1993—), Yale Club (N.Y.C.), Harvard Bus. Sch. Club (N.Y.C., pres. 1964-65, chmn. 1965-66, bd. dirs. 1964-70), Harvard Club (N.Y.C.), Met. Club (Washington), Alpha Kappa Psi, Phi Delta Phi. Presbyterian. Office: 2600 S Ocean Blvd Boca Raton FL 33432

SIGHTLER, DEBRA H., community health nurse; b. Pensacola, Fla., June 15, 1954; d. Dewey C. and Lizzie (Scofield) Henderson; m. Ricky Sightler, Apr. 14, 1976; 1 child, Heather. BSN, Troy State U., 1979. Staff nurse Andalusia (Ala.) Hosp., 1979-80; home health nurse Wiregrass Home Health Agy., Opp, Ala., 1980-84; pub. health nurse Covington County Health Dept., Andalusia, 1984-88; nurse reviewer div. long term care, rehab. Alabanu Dept. Pub. Health, Montgomery, Ala., 1988-90; quality assurance nurse home base svcs. div. Ala. Dept Pub. Health, Montgomery, 1990-95; nursing cons. for paraprofl. devel., 1995—; cons. Bur. of Home and Cmty. Svcs. Mem. ASNA, Ala. Pub. Health Assn., Troy State U. Sch. Nursing Alumni Assn. Home: RR 1 Box 208 Andalusia AL 36420-9745

SIGLER, LOIS OLIVER, retired secondary school educator; b. Piney Flats, Tenn., Sept. 8, 1923; d. Willie Campbell and Lillie (Brown) Oliver; m. William Virgil Sigler Jr., Aug. 25, 1962; 1 child, William Oliver. BS, East Tenn. State U., 1944; MS, U. Tenn., 1952; postgrad., Memphis State U., U. Tenn. Home econs. tchr. Buchanan (Va.) pub. schs., 1944-46; area supr. home econs. edn. and sch. lunch prog. State Dept. Edn., Commonwealth of Va., 1946-54; asst. nat. advisor Future Homemakers of Am./New Homemakers of Am., HEW, Washington, 1954-56; nat. advisor Future Homemakers of Am./New Homemakers of Am., HEW, 1956-63; family living coord. Ohio State Dept. and Columbus (Ohio) Pub. Schs., Columbus Met. Housing Authority, 1963; tchr. Millington (Tenn.) High Sch., 1966-92; ret., 1992. Mem. Pres. Kennedy's Food for Peace Coun., Pres. Eisenhower's Adv. Com. on Youth Fitness. Named Tenn. Home Econs. Tchr. of Yr., 1975, Woman of Yr., 1991, Twentieth Century award for achievement, 1991. Mem. NEA, Am. Home Econs. Assn., Tenn. Home Econs. Assn., Am. Voc. Assn., Tenn. Voc. Assn., Nat. Voc. Home Econs. Tchrs. Assn., Tenn. Voc. Home Econs. Tchrs. Assn. (hon. 1992, past sec.-treas., Outstanding Svc. award 1986), W. Tenn. Home Econs. Edn. Assn. (past sec.), Tenn. Edn. Assn. (bd. dirs. 1977-80), W. Tenn. Edn. Assn., Shelby County Edn. Assn. (past sch. rep.), Greater Memphis State U., Inc., Future Homemakers Am. (nat. hon. 1956, state hon. 1991, master advisor award 1988, advisor mentor 1991), Omicron Nu, Pi Lambda Theta. Home: 4785 Rolling Meadows Dr Memphis TN 38128-4868

SIGMAN, KENNETH MARTIN, gastroenterologist, educator; b. Cleve., Jan. 19, 1953; s. Ralph M. and Mildred Sigman; m. Mary M. Matyac, Apr. 26, 1981; children: Heather Michelle, Kyle Matthew. BA, Miami U., Oxford, Ohio, 1975; MD, Ohio State U., 1980. Diplomate Am. Bd. Internal Medicine and Gastroenterology. Resident in internal medicine Ohio State U. Hosp., Columbus, 1980-83, fellow in gastroenterology, 1984-86; pvt. practice Asheboro, N.C., 1986-91; asst. prof. medicine gastroenterology div. U. Ala., Birmingham, 1991-95, chief biliary endoscopy, 1991-95. Mem. ACP, Am. Gastrointestinal Assn., Am. Soc. Gastrointestinal Endoscopy, Am. Coll. Gastroenterology. Office: Birmingham Gastroent Assocs 880 Montclair Rd Ste 579 Birmingham AL 35213-1980

SIGMAR, LUCIA ANNE STRETCHER, English language educator, administrator; b. Waynesville, N.C., Oct. 24, 1959; d. Robert Hatfield and Amelia Joyce (Simpson) S.; m. Axel Michael Sigmar, Aug. 17, 1991. BA in French and English, Delta State U., 1981; MA in English, U. So. Miss., 1986; PhD in English, U. Tenn., 1995. Cert. tchr., Miss. English instr. Roane State C.C., Harriman, Tenn., 1987-89, dir. writing ctr., 1989-91; cons. corp. comm. and tech. writing, 1996—. Recipient Star Tchr. award, Miss. Econ. Coun., 1983-84. Mem. S. Atlantic Modern Lang. Assn., Nat. Coun. Tchrs. of English, Lambda Iota Tau. Office: PO Box 1892 Stafford TX 77497

SIGMON, DANIEL RAY, foundation administrator; b. Orangeburg, S.C., Sept. 15, 1949; s. Carment Ray and Freida Marion (Stoudenmire) S.; m. Cheryl Mahaffey, Dec. 31, 1976; children: Ashley W. Truluck, Elizabeth Wakefield, Caroline Christine. BE, U. S.C., 1971, MA, 1992. Tchr. Calhoun County Sch. Dist., St. Matthews, S.C., 1971-72; hist. sites supt. S.C. Dept. Parks, Recreation & Tourism, Columbia, S.C., 1972-73; staff historian S.C. Dept. Parks, Recreation & Tourism, 1973-85; exec. dir. Hist. Camden (S.C.), 1985-87; dir. Alexander Homesite & History Mus., Charlotte, N.C., 1987-88; exec. dir. Hist. Columbia Found., Columbia, 1988—. Author: Huntington Beach State Park; A Visitor's Guide, 1984, Hampton Plantation; Visitor's Guide, 1983; editor: A Guide to Historic Sites in Camden, S.C., 1985. Mem. Columbia Action Coun., 1989—, Cultural Coun. Richland and Lexington County, Columbia, 1989—; bd. dirs. Sunrise Found., 1992—; mem. county commn. Palmetto Project Discovery '92, 1991-92. Mem. Nat. Trust Hist. Preservation, Am. Assn. State and Local History, S.C. Confedn. Local Hist. Socs. (exec. coun. 1991—), S.C. Fedn. Mus. (pres. 1994-96), Palmetto Trust Hist. Preservation (exec. com. 1991—). Methodist. Office: Hist Columbia Found 1601 Richland St Columbia SC 29201-2633

SIGUA, GILBERT C., environmental specialist; b. San Pablo, Isabela, Philippines, Oct. 14, 1957; s. Basilio M. and Angelina C. (Castaneda) S.; m. Celia F. Avellanoza, Aug. 20, 1983; children: Gerald Christian, Christine Gicelle. BS in Agr. cum laude, Ctrl. Luzon State U., Nueva Ecija, Philippines, 1978; MS in Soil Chemistry, U. Ark., 1983; PhD in Environ. Soil Chemistry, La. State U., 1990. Cert. profl. soil scientist. Instr. Ctrl. Luzon State U., Nueva Ecija, 1978-83, asst. prof., 1983-86; rsch. asst. La. State U., Baton Rouge, 1986-90, postdoctoral rsch. assoc., 1990-92; rsch. soil scientist Agrl. Rsch. Svc.-USDA, Beltsville, Md., 1992-94; environ. specialist St. Johns River Water Mgmt. Dist., Palatka, Fla., 1994—. Contbr. articles to profl. jours. Pub. rels. officer Filipino-Am. Student Assn., La. State U., 1987-88. Recipient Agrl. Rsch. Svc./USDA Spl. Rsch. Achievement award, 1993; U.S. AID grantee, 1981-83; Rotary Found. fellow, 1986-90. Mem. Soil Sci. Soc. Am., Agronomy Soc. Am., Am. Registry of Cert. Profl. in Agronomy, Crops and Soils, Estuarine Rsch. Fedn., Gamma Sigma Delta. Roman Catholic. Home: 3531 NW 65th Ln Gainesville FL 32653-8824 Office: Saint Johns River Water Mgmt Environ Scis Divsn PO Box 1429 Palatka FL 32178-1429

SIKES, RUTH COX, investment representative; b. Macon, Ga., Sept. 29, 1952; d. Z. Sweeney and Louise (Cox) S.; m. Eugene W. Dabbs, IV, Apr. 1978 (div. 1981); m. Dennis L. Crow, July 1994. BA, Emory U., 1974; MSW, Tulane U., 1975. CLU; chartered fin. cons. Social worker Brawner Psychiat. Inst., Atlanta, 1976-77, Griffin (Ga.) Hosp., 1977-78, Personnel Growth Ctr., Griffin, 1978-79; agt., rep. Equitable Fin. Cos., Griffin, 1979-92, master agt., dist. asst., 1979-92; S.E. regional dir. ins. sales Waddell & Reed Inc., Atlanta, 1992-93; divsn. mgr. Waddell & Reed Inc., Marietta, Ga., 1993-94; dist. mgr. Waddell & Reed Inc., Atlanta, 1994-95; investment rep. Edward Jones Investments, Atlanta, 1995—. Mem. Am. Soc. CLU and ChFC (Atlanta chpt.), Women's Life Underwriters Confedn. (Atlanta chpt., pres.-elect, pres. 1995-96), Atlanta Women's Network, Atlanta Women in Bus., Women's Bus. Exch., Buckhead Bus. Assn., Atlanta C. of C. Republican. Office: Edward Jones Investments Ste 112 Tuxedo Atrium 3833 Rosell Rd Atlanta GA 30342

SIKIVIE, PIERRE, physics educator; b. Sint Truiden, Belgium, Oct. 29, 1949; came to U.S. 1970; s. Armand and Claire (Roebroeck) S.; m. Cynthia L. Chennault, July 2, 1980; children: Paul Justin, Michael Chennault. Licencie en Sciences, U. Liege, Belgium, 1970; MS in Physics, Yale U., 1972, PhD in Physics, 1975. Rsch. assoc. dept. physics and astronomy U. Md., College Park, 1975-77; rsch. assoc. SLAC Theory Group, Stanford, Calif., 1977-79; sr. fellow CERN Theory Group, Geneva, Switzerland, 1979-81; asst. prof. physics and math. U. Fla., Gainesville, 1981-83, asst. prof. physics, 1983-84, assoc. prof. physics, 1984-88, prof. physics, 1988—; lectr. in field. Contbr. numerous articles to profl. jours. Fellow Am. Phys. Soc.; mem. AAAS. Home: 3130 NW 31st St Gainesville FL 32605-2163 Office: Univ of Fla Dept Physics Gainesville FL 32611

SIKORA, EUGENE STANLEY, engineer; b. Duquesne, Pa., July 21, 1924; s. Adam Joseph and Helen (Pietrowska) S.; m. Corinne Mary Coliane, Sept. 7, 1946; children: Karyn Ann, Leslie Ann. Student Okla. Bapt. U., 1943-44; BS in Indsl. Engring., U. Pitts., 1949; C.E., Carnegie Inst. Tech., 1951. Bridge design engr. Gannett, Fleming, Corddry & Carpenter, Pitts., 1949-50; structural designer Rust Engring. Co., Pitts., 1950-51, chief field engr., 1951-52, asst. project engr.; project engr. Frank E. Murphy & Assos., Bartow, Fla., 1952-55; v.p. Wellman-Lord Engring. Co., Lakeland, Fla., 1955-61; pres. Gulf Design Co., Lakeland, 1961-74, chmn. Lakeland Constrn., 1974-85; pres. Witcher Creek Coal Co., Belle, W.Va., 1979-84; ptnr. Gulf Atlantic Mgmt. Assocs., Lakeland; chmn. Horizon Constrn. & Devel. Inc., 1974—; v.p. The Badger Co., Cambridge, Mass.; pres. Sebco Resources Gold Mining Corp., Fairbanks, Alaska, 1974-84. Bd. dirs. Polk County Mus. Art. USAAF, 1943-45. Mem. Nat. Soc. Profl. Engrs., Am. Inst. Mining, Metall. and Petroleum Engrs., Am. Mgmt. Assn., Am. Inst. Chem. Engrs., Am. Inst. Indsl. Engrs., Fla. Engring. Soc., Lakeland C. of C. (dir.). Democrat. Episcopalian. Home: 1400 Seville Pl Lakeland FL 33803-2353 Office: 3115 Providence Rd Lakeland FL 33805-2338

SILAGI, BARBARA WEIBLER, corporate administrator; b. Chgo., June 26, 1930; d. Carleton Thomas and Catherine Josephine (Wolph) Weibler; m. Joseph Edward Sturgulewski (Sturgus), Feb. 12, 1953 (div. Aug. 1954); 1 child, Mariann Catherine; m. John Louis Silagi, Jr., July 2, 1960 (div. July 1968). BM in Edn., Northwestern U., 1958; MS in Edn., No. Ill. U., 1965. Cert. K-14 supervisory teaching, spl. edn. tchr., airline transport pilot, FAA dispatcher. Elem. sch. tchr. St. Mary's Sch., Chgo., 1947-49, Kingman, Ariz., 1949-52; legal sec. Judge Edward J. Mahoney, Quincy, Ill., 1954-55; elem. sch. tchr. C.M. Bardwell Sch., Aurora, Ill., 1955-76; flight instr. flight schs. Chgo., Aurora and Frankfort, Ill., Clinton, Iowa, 1970-77; aircraft dispatcher Transcontinental Airlines, Zantop Internat. Airlines, Ypsilanti, Mich., 1977-81; airline pilot Mannion Air Charter, Ypsilanti, 1977-80; head night auditor Howard Johnson, Quality Inn, Travelodge, BestWestern, others, Ocala, Fla., Silver Springs, Fla., 1983-87; sec.-treas. Diamond Design Svcs., Inc., Ocklawaha, Fla., 1985—; pub. Forest Shopper, Springs Shopper, Belle Shopper. Author: Dispatch Training, 1989; editor tng. manuals, 1977-85. Violist Chgo. Suburban Symphony, Naperville, Ill., 1956-60; contralto Palestrina A capella Choir, Aurora, Ill., 1956-60; life mem. Ill. PTA, Aurora, 1974—; apptd. vice chmn. adv. bd. Dunnellon Airport and Indsl. Park, 1992. Recipient 1st place Suburban Aviation Assn., Chgo., 1975, 5th place Illi-Nines Air Derby, Chgo., Moline, Ill., 1973, 2d place Leg prize Powder Puff Derby, McLean to Lincoln, Nebr., 1971; Eckstein scholar Northwestern U., 1952. Mem. AAUW (life), NEA (life), Ill. Edn. Assn., Ninety Nines Internat. (life), Illi-Nines Air Derby (handicap chmn. 1972-76, air marking chmn. 99's Chgo. chpt. 1972-76, corr. sec. Chgo. chpt. 1976-77, 1st pl. achievement awards 1972-78), Ocala Orchid Soc. (sec.), Lake Wier Garden Club, Pi Lambda Theta (charter, life, rsch. chmn. Beta Delta chpt. 1962-63). Roman Catholic. Home: RR 2 Box 1837-A Ocklawaha FL 32179-8757 also: 6385 SE 158th Ct Ocklawaha FL 32179 Office: Diamond Design Svcs Inc PO Box 186 Ocklawaha FL 32183

SILAS, CECIL JESSE, retired petroleum company executive; b. Miami, Fla., Apr. 15, 1932; s. David Edward and Hilda Videll (Carver) S.; m. Theodosea Hejda, Nov. 27, 1965; children: Karla, Peter, Michael, James. BSChemE, Ga. Inst. Tech., Atlanta, 1953. With Phillips Petroleum Co., Bartlesville, Okla., 1953-94; pres. Europe-Africa, Brussels and London Phillips Petroleum Co., 1968-74; mng. dir. natural resource group Europe/Africa Phillips Petroleum Co., London, 1974-76; v.p. gas and gas liquids div. natural resources group Phillips Petroleum Co., Bartlesville, 1976-78, sr. v.p. natural resources group, 1978-80, exec. v.p. exploration and prodn., minerals, gas and gas liquids, 1980-82, pres., chief operating officer, 1982-85, chmn., CEO, 1985-94; bd. dirs. Milliken & Co., Ascent Entertainment. Bd. dirs. Jr. Achievement, Reader's digest Assocs., Inc., bd. dirs. of Halliburton Co. COMSAT Corp, Boys/Girls Clubs Am., Atlanta, parton councillor Atlantic Coun. of the U.S.; bd. dirs. Ethics Resource Ctr., Inc., Okla. Found. for Excellence; trustee Frank Phillips Found.; active Trilateral Commn. Served to 1st lt. Chem. Corps, AUS, 1954-56. Decorated comdr. Order St. Olaf (Norway); inducted into Ga. Inst. Tech. Athletic Hall of Fame, 1959, recipient Former Scholar-Athlete Total Person award, 1988; inducted into Okla. Bus. Hall of Fame, 1989; named CEO of Yr., Internat. TV Assn., 1987. Mem. Am. Petroleum Inst., U.S. C. of C. (past chmn. bd. dirs.), 25 Yr. Club, Phi Delta Theta. Office: PO Box 2127 Bartlesville OK 74005-2127

SILBERMAN, WARREN STEVEN, internist; b. Phila., Jan. 5, 1950; s. Seymour Albert and Ruth (Thurm) S.; m. Yvonne Lesley Kingston, Apr. 27, 1985; children: Suzanne, Jenna, Carly. AA, C.C. Phila., 1969; BA, Temple U., 1971; DO, Coll. Osteo. Medicine Surgery, 1974; MPH, U. Tex. Health Sci. Ctr., 1991. Commd. capt. U.S. Army, 1983, advanced through grades to col., 1995; intern Lancaster (Pa.) Osteo. Hosp., 1974-75; resident Community Gen. Osteo. Hosp., Harrisburg, Pa., 1975-78; pvt. practice Ariz. Clin. Internists Ltd., Phoenix, 1978-81, Ctrl. Ariz. Med. Assocs., Mesa, 1981-85; staff internist Noble Army Hosp., Ft. McClellan, Ala., 1985-88; chief dept. medicine U.S. Army Aeromed. Ctr., Ft. Rucker, Ala., 1988-90, dep. comdr. for clin. svcs., 1992-95; resident in aerospace/preventive medicine USAF Sch. Aerospace Medicine, Brooks AFB, Tex., 1991-92; commdr. USA MEDDAC, Ft. Huachuca, Ariz., 1995—; mem. staff Phoenix Gen. Hosp., 1978-83, staff sec., 1981-82, treas. dept. internal medicine, 1981-82; mem. staff Scottsdale (Ariz.) Community Hosp., 1978-82, chmn. dept. internal medicine, 1981; mem. staff Community Hosp. Phoenix, 1978-82, Mesa (Ariz.) Gen. Hosp., 1978-85; lectr. in field. Contbr. articles to profl. jours. Decorated Army Commendation medal, Army Achievement medal; named one of Outstanding Young Men Am., 1983. Fellow Am. Coll. Osteo. Internists, Aerospace Medicine Assn. (assoc.); mem. Am. Osteo. Assn., Assn. Mil. Osteo. Physicians and Surgeons, Army Aviation Assn. Am., Aerospace Med. Assn., Soc. U.S. Army Flight Surgeons, Internat. Assn. Mil. Flight Surgeon Pilots (assoc.). Home: 1476 Grierson Fort Huachuca AZ 85613 Office: Raymond W Bliss Cmty Hosp Fort Huachuca AZ 85613

SILCOX, TINSLEY EDWARD, fine arts library director, choral conductor; b. Bristol, Tenn., July 26, 1956; s. Roncie Taylor and June Carolyn (Trivette) S.; m. Barbara Ann Saffold, May 14, 1988; children: Janet Elaine, Michael Westmoreland. MusB, Carson-Newman Coll., 1978; MusM, U. Tenn., 1980, MLS and Info. Sci., 1987. Acting head Music Libr. U. Tenn., Knoxville, 1986-88; music libr., blues archivist U. Miss., Oxford, 1989-92; dir. Hamon Arts Libr. So. Meth. U., Dallas, 1992—, dir. SMU univ. choir, 1993—; dir. music North Park Presbyn. Ch., Dallas, 1995—; mem. libr. adv. bd. Dallas Mus. Art, 1992—. Editor: Plot Locator, 1991; composer (radio drama) Mr. Immith's Dog, 1986; mem. editorial bd. Fontes Artis Musicae, 1993—. Recipient Award of Appreciation Nat. Black Music Found., 1991. Mem. ALA, Am. Choral Dirs. Assn., Internat. Music Libr. Assn., Pi Kappa Lambda. Episcopalian. Home: 809 Bristol Ct Richardson TX 75080-6913 Office: So Meth Univ Hamon Arts Library Dallas TX 75275

SILER, EUGENE EDWARD, JR., federal judge; b. Williamsburg, Ky., Oct. 19, 1936; s. Eugene Edward and Lowell (Jones) S.; m. Christy Dyanne Minnich, Oct. 18, 1969; children—Eugene Edward, Adam Troy. B.A. cum laude, Vanderbilt U., 1958; LL.B., U. Va., 1963; LL.M., Georgetown U., 1964. Bar: Ky. 1963, Va. 1963, D.C. 1963. Individual practice law Williamsburg, 1964-65; atty. Whitley County, Ky., 1965-70; U.S. atty. Eastern Dist. Ky., Lexington, 1970-75; judge U.S. Dist. Ct., Eastern and Western Dists., Ky., 1975-91; chief judge Eastern Dist., Ky., 1984-91; judge U.S. Ct. Appeals (6th cir.), 1991—. Campaign co-chmn. Congressman Tim L. Carter, 1966, 5th Congl. Dist.; campaign co-chmn. U.S. Senator J.S. Cooper, 1966; trustee Cumberland Coll., Williamsburg, 1965-73, 80-88; 1st v.p. Ky. Bapt. Convention, 1986-87; bd. dirs. Bapt. Healthcare Systems Inc., 1990—. Served with USN, 1958-60, with Res. 1960-83. E. Barrett Prettyman fellow, 1963-64; recipient medal Freedom's Found., 1968. Mem. FBA, Ky. Bar Assn. (Judge of Yr. award 1992), D.C. Bar Assn., Va. State Bar. Republican. Baptist. Home: PO Box 129 Williamsburg KY 40769-0129 Office: US Ct Appeals 1380 W 5th St Ste 200 London KY 40741-1615

SILER, SUSAN REEDER, communications educator; b. Knoxville, Tenn., May 31, 1940; d. Claude S. Jr. and Mary Frances (Cook) Reeder; m. Theodore Paul Siler Jr., Sept. 3, 1960; children: Mary Siler Walker, Theodore Paul III. BS in Communications and Journalism, U. Tenn., Knoxville, 1988, MS, 1994. 2d grade tchr. Lawton (Okla.) Pub. Schs., 1961-62, substitute tchr., 1963-64; with By Design, 1987-88; English tutor, 1991-95; adj. instr. comm. U. Tenn., 1994—, U. Tenn., Pellissippi State Tech. C.C., Knoxville, Tenn.; bd. dirs. Hlen Ross McNabb Mental Health Ctr., Knoxville. Tutor Episc. Ch. Ascension, Knoxville, 1990—; instr. United Meth. Ch., Knoxville, 1985-92; chmn. Dogwood Arts Festival, Knoxville, 1980-85; chmn., mem. Bd. Govs. of East Tenn. Presentation Soc., 1988-96; chmn., sec. bd. dirs. YWCA, Knoxville, 1982-88; Knoxville Jr. League, 1979-95; bd. dirs. Knoxville Women's Ctr., 1993-94; spl. events chmn. St. Mary's Med. Ctr. Found., 1986-89; Pres. Knoxville area Literacy Assn., 1989-92, tutor Episcopal Ch. Literacy program, Knoxville, 1990-95. Mem. Internat. Mass Comm. Assn., Soc. Profl. Journalists, Am. Journalism Historians Assn., Assn. for Edn. in Journalism and Mass Comms., Kappa Tau Alpha, Golden Key. Home: 717 Kenesaw Ave Knoxville TN 37919

SILFEN, ROBERTA DAWN, school system administrator; b. Bklyn.; m. Arthur Morris Silfen; children: Frederick, Richard. BA, CUNY, 1953; MA, U. Hawaii, 1970; MS, Troy State U., Montgomery, Ala., 1971; MA, U. Tex., San Antonio, 1983; EdD, Tex. A&M U., 1991. Cert. mid.-mgmt., supt., Tex. Tchr. Pearl Harbor Kai Elem. Sch., Honolulu, 1968-71, Montgomery Pub. Schs., 1971-76; tchr. East Cen. Ind. Sch. Dist., San Antonio, 1976-78, adminstr., 1978-95; cons. in reading Thinking, Learning Ctr., San Antonio; practicum adviser Nova Southeastern U., Ft. Lauderdale, Fla., 1992—; spkr. in field. Author: Practical Guide to Teaching Adult Learning, 5 Minute Classroom Manager: Behavior Management in a Nutshell, also articles. Exec. dir. Wildlife Care Ctr., Ft. Lauderdale, Fla., 1995—. Named Hon. 1st Lady, Gov. State of Ala.; Fulbright scholar; grantee U.S. Dept. Edn., 1979, 82, 89, 92, 93. Mem. ASCD, Internat. Reading Assn., Fulbright Alumni Assn., Phi Delta Kappa. Home: 3880 Queens Way Boca Raton FL 33434-3309 Office: 3200 SW 4th Ave Fort Lauderdale FL 33315-3019

SILL, GERALD DE SCHRENCK, hotel executive; b. Czechoslovakia, Dec. 11, 1917; s. Edward and Margaret (Baroness von Schrenck-Notzing) S.; BS, Budapest Tech. U., 1942; m. Maria Countess Draskovich, May 11, 1946; children: Susan, Gabrielle. Came to U.S., 1948, naturalized, 1953. With econs. div. U.S. Hdqrs., Vienna, Austria, 1945-48; exec. hotel positions N.Y.C., 1948-52; managerial positions with Hilton Hotel Corp., 1953-61; exec. v.p. Houston Internat. Hotels, Inc., 1961-72, pres., chief exec. officer, 1972-84, chmn. bd., 1984-86; v.p., bd. dirs. 1986-88; chmn. emeritus, adv. dir. Preferred Hotels Worldwide; pres., CEO GdSS Mgmt. and Consulting Inc., Houston. Mem. Am. Arbitration Assn. (panel arbitrators), River Oaks Country Club (Houston). Home: 2227 Pelham Dr Houston TX 77019-3530

SILLARS, STUART JOHN, English literature educator, writer; b. Loughton, Essex, Eng., Jan. 5, 1951; came to U.S., 1994; s. Duncan Melbourne and Lillian Alma (Strevens) S.; (div.); 1 child, Laurence. BA in English and Music, U. Exeter, Eng., 1972; MA in English, Univ. Coll. of Wales, Aberystwyth, 1976; PhD, U. Amsterdam, 1993. Lectr. in English S.E. Essex 6th-Form Coll., Eng., 1972-75, Aberystwyth (Wales) Coll. Further Edn., 1976-83; lectr. in English bd. continuing edn. U. Cambridge, Eng., 1983-93; prof., coord. dept. English U. of the Incarnate Word, San Antonio, 1994—; tutor in English The Open Univ., Cambridge, 1983-93; dir. studies summer programs U. Cambridge, 1983—; cons. Macmillan Pubs., Eng., 1989—; course leader in field; creator distance learning courses for profl. exams. Assn. Storekeepers in Purchasing and Supply, Nigerian and Ghanaian Inst. Bankers, Chartered Inst. Bankers, Chartered Inst. Bankers Hong Kong, Assn. Acctg. Technicians, Assn. Bus. Execs., Inst. Credit Mgmt., Assn. Brit. Dispensing Opticians. Author: Spelling Rules OK!, 1984, reprinted, 1991, rev. edit., 1992, Australian edit., 1992, Grammar Rules OK!, 1985, rev. edit., 1991, Developing New Products: Practical Science in Business, 1985, Your Own Place, 1986, Correspondence Rules OK!, 1986, reprinted, 1991, Computer Literacy Themes and Skills, 1986, Working in TV and Video, 1986, Times English Guides: Spelling, 1987, Times English Guides: Grammar, 1987, Women in the First World War, 1987, Art and Survival in First World War Britain, 1987, Success in Communication, 1988, rev. edit., 1992, The Welfare State, 1988, Getting Through: Communication for Young People at Work, 1990, A-Level English, 1990, rev. edit., 1992, (with Barbara and George Keith) English: A and AS Level, 1991, Talking Rules OK!, 1991, Spelling Rules OK Basic, 1992, Work Challenge, 1992, Caring for People: A Workbook for Care Workers, 1992, 2d edit., 1993, British Romantic Art and the Second World War, 1992, GCE O-Level English Revision Guide, Paper 1119, 1993, Paper 1120, 1993, Visualisation in English Popular Fiction 1860-1960: Graphic Narratives, Fictional Images, 1995; contbr. numerous chpts. to books, articles to profl. jours. Fellow Royal Soc. Arts (London); mem. MLA. Anglican. Office: U of Incarnate Word 4301 Broadway San Antonio TX 78209

SILLMAN, ADRIENNE PATITEAUX, educational specialist, consultant; b. Newark, Nov. 30, 1937; d. Emanuel Harlan and Muriel (Sternick) Patiteaux; divorced; children: Keith Brett Darrell, Marc Scott. BEd, U. Miami, 1961, postgrad., 1962-63; MS in Early Childhood Edn., Nova U., 1974, cert. elem. adminstrn. and supervision, 1975, EdD, 1982. Cert. in early childhood edn., elem. edn., specific learning disabilities, elem. adminstrn. and supervision, Fla. Tchr. Dade County Pub. Sch. Sys., Miami, Fla., 1961-71; master tchr. Norwood Elem. Sch. Dade County Pub. Sch. Sys., Miami, 1971-73, team coord. Norwood Elem. Sch., 1973-74, acting prin. Norwood Elem. Sch., 1974, adminstrv. asst. to prin. Norwood Elem. Sch., 1974-76; ednl. specialist Hollywood, Fla., 1973—; adminstrv. asst. to prin. Fulford Elem. Sch. Hollywood, 1976-78; adj. prof. undergrad. program Nova U., Ft. Lauderdale, Fla., 1976, adj. instr. grad. program, 1984—; mem. steering com., participant Differentiated Staffing Project, Fla. Network of U.S. Office of Edn., Sch. Pers. Utilization Project, 1970-72; supervising tchr. internship program Fla. State U., Fla. Atlantic U., 1970-73, cons. Dade County Pub. Schs., Miami, 1971, mem. rev. com. RS/VP Reading Program field testing, 1976-77; cons. to pvt. schs., 1973—; presenter workshops in field. Author: Individualized Reading Instruction—A Handbook for Classroom Teachers, 1974, Preschool Language Development Handbook, 1981. Active Congl. Citizen Coun., State of Fla. Guardian Ad Litem Program. Mem. CEC, Assn. for Children and Adults with Learning Disabilities, Orton Dyslexia Soc., Nat. Coun. for Spl. Edn. (U.K.). Office: # 204 3816 Hollywood Blvd Hollywood FL 33021

SILLS, SALLIE ALEXANDER, elementary school educator; b. Ocala, Fla., Feb. 16, 1916; d. Joe and Marie (Jefferson) Alexander; m. Mell Sills, Sept. 16, 1936 (dec. 1980). AA, Bethune Cookman Coll., 1936, BS, 1948. Elem. tchr. Marion County Sch. Systems, 1936-46, elem. prin., 1938-47; tchr. 1st grade Gadsden County Schs., Quincy, Fla., 26 years. Contbr. poetry to anthologies. Mem. Vol. Tchrs. Group, Ocala, Fla., 1977—; tchr. 1st aid Am. Red. Cross, Quincy, 1964-66; dir. St. John Rhythm Band, Quincy, 1959-77; chmn. program com. St. John Bapt. Ch., Ocala, 1978-79, Mt. Moriah Bapt. Ch., Quincy, 1977-79; chmn. welfare and health Sojourner Truth Club, Ocala, 1988—. Mem. Marion County Ret. Tchrs. Assn. (Area 3 leader 1977—), Am. Assn. Ret. Persons, Nat. Ret. Tchrs. Assn., Nat. Assn. for Female Execs., Am. Legion. Democrat. Baptist. Home: 815 W Silver Springs Pl Ocala FL 34475-6562

SILVA, ALAN AUGUSTINE, retired international ecomonic development; b. Fall River, Mass., June 21, 1950; s. Augustine and Lucille (Mello) S. BS in Fgn. svc., Georgetown U., 1972; MPA, Harvard U., 1981. Capital devel. officer USAID, Dhaka, Bangladesh, 1974-76, Lisbon, Portugal, 1976-80; regional project devel. officer USAID, Harare, Zimbabwe, 1984-84; AID rep. USAID, Maputo, Mozambique, 1984-87; dep. dir. AID mission USAID, Lima, 1987-92; dep. dir. Caribbean affairs USAID, Washington, 1990-92; city adminstr. Exec. Office of the Mayor, Fall River, Mass., 1981-84; dir. emergency/human assistance NIS Bur. Agy. for Internat. Devel., Washington, 1992-94, dir. social sectors devel. ENI Bur., 1994-96; ret. Mem. Am. Soc. Pub. Adminstrn., Nat. Assn. Ret. Fed. Employees, Am. Fgn. Svc. Assn. Democrat. Roman Catholic. Home: PO Box 10671 Arlington VA 22210-1671

SILVA, DAVID JAMES, linguistics educator; b. Somerville, Mass., Nov. 7, 1964; s. Ilidio Mendonca and Maria Alice Silva. AB magna cum laude, Harvard U., 1986; MA, Cornell U., 1989, PhD, 1992. Asst. prof. linguistics Syracuse (N.Y.) U., 1992-93, U. Tex., Arlington, 1993—. Author monograph The Phonetics and Phonoloy of Stop Lenition in Korean, 1992. Fulbright fellow, 1989-90. Mem. Internat. Cir. Korean Linguistics (editor newsletter 1988—), Linguistic Soc. Am. (chair com. 1986—). Democrat. Episcopalian. Office: U Tex Arlington Linguistics Box 19559 Arlington TX 76019-0559

SILVA, DONNA STEEDLE, coffee service company official; b. Riverside, N.J., Dec. 12, 1957; d. William Edward and SHirley Elaine (Klingler) Steedle; m. Eldon Joseph Silva, Nov. 25, 1988; children: Adele Genevieve, Mary Arthemise. Student, Rider Coll., 1975-77; student, Rutgers U., 1984. Cashier and office clerk Pantry-Pride Grocery Stores, Inc., Delran, N.J., 1975-79; account rep. P.F. Collier, Inc., Delran, N.J., 1979-81, customer svc. supr., 1981, asst. v.p. of ops., nat. sales svc. ctr., 1982-83, payroll dept. mgr., nat. sales svc. ctr., 1983-85, regional sales mgr., ednl. svcs. div., 1985-86, dir. adminstrn., ednl. svcs. div., 1986-88, v.p. adminstrn., ednl. svcs. div., 1988-90; dir. ops. The New Grolier Interstate, Inc., White Plains, N.Y., 1981-82; dir. customer svc. Standard Coffee Svc. Co., New Orleans, 1990-94; cust. svc. supr. Intralox, Ind., Harahan, La., 1995; dir. ops. Parker, Murray and Assocs., 1996—. Vol. Contemporary Arts Ctr., New Orleans, 1985—. Mem. NAFE. Republican. Roman Catholic. Office: Standard Coffee Svc Co 640 Magazine St New Orleans LA 70130-3406

SILVER, ARCHIE AARON, psychiatry educator, psychiatry director; b. Hoboken, N.J., Jan. 29, 1917; s. Samuel and Esther (Lesser) S.; m. Mary Louise Berkovitz, June 27, 1943; children: Frederick M., Robert A. BS in Biology cum laude, NYU, 1936, MD, 1940. Diplomate in psychiatry, child psychiatry Am. Bd. Psychiatry and Neurology; lic. MD, N.Y., Fla. Intern Kings County Hosp., Bklyn., 1940-42; asst. resident Bellevue Hosp., N.Y.C., 1946, jr. psychiatrist, 1948-49; sr. psychiatrist, psychiatrist in charge children's sect. Bellevue Hosp., NYC, 1949-60, from asst. attending to attending psychiatrist, 1950-79; fellow in neuropsychiatry NYU Coll. Medicine, N.Y.C., 1946-68, from asst. clin. prof. to prof. clin. psychiatry, 1947-79; pvt. practice psychiatrist NYC, 1947-79; dir. preventive psychiatry learning disorders unit NYU-Bellevue Med. Ctr., 1960-79; prof., dir. child and adolescent psychiatry U. South Fla. Coll. Medicine, Tampa, 1979—; adj. prof. clin. psychiatry NYU Coll. Medicine, NYC, 1979—; cons. Supreme Ct. State of N.Y., 1960-79, N.Y.C. Patrolmen's Benevolent Assn., 1972-82; peer reviewer Am. Jour. Psychiatry, Jour. Hosp. and Cmty. Psychiatry, Jour. Neuropsychology and Clin. Neuroscis., N.Y. State Jour. Medicine; mem. initial rev. group NIMH Divsn. Psychiatry Edn. Br., NIMH Psychopharmacology Rsch. Br., adv. panel neurol. and psychiat. disease U.S. Pharmacopoeia, 1975-80, 80-85, faculty senate U. South Fla., 1988-91, search coms. for chairpersons pathology, biochemistry, pharmacology, Roskamp Chair for Biol. Rsch. in Psychiatry, Rank and Tenure Com. dept. psychiatry, chairperson, 1988—, curriculum com. 1987—. Author: Search, Teach, 2d edit., 1981, Disorders of Learning in Childhood, 1990; editor: Bridges to Tomorrow, 1981; contbr. over 140 articles to profl. jours., encys., confs., symposia, books revs., chpts. to books. Mem. initial group Profl. Adv. Com. Children's TV NEtwork, N.Y. State Interdepartmental Com. on Learning Problems, 1973-74, N.Y.C. Dept. Hosps. Com. on Psychiat. Svcs. for Children, 1963-64, Com. on Children and Adolscence N.Y. Soc. Clin. Psychiatry, 1961-63, 75, children's com. Cmty. Mental Health Bd. Dist. VI, 1980—, Purchase of Svc. Com. Fla. Dept. Health and Rehab. Svcs., Tampa, 1980-86, steering com. Fla. State Network for Severly Disturbed Children, 1982-84, Fla. State Task Force for Svc. Plans for Autistic Children, 1987-88, Child and Parent Com. Bd. Edn., Tampa, 1990-93, steering com. Edn. for Handicapped Children, Bd. Edn., Children's Med. Svcs., Tallahassee, Fla., 1985-90; examiner certification in child psychiatry Am. Bd. Psychiatry and Neurology, panel for psychiatrists N.Y.C. Bd. Edn.; chmn. Nat. Interdisciplinary Com. on Reading Problems Ford Found., and Ctr. Applied Linguistics, 1968-74. With USPHS, 1942-46. Recipient Wilfred C. Hulse award N.Y. Coun. Child Psychiatry, 1972, NYU Med. Sch. Svc. award NYU Med. Sch. Alumni Assn., 1985, cert. appreciation State of Fla. Health and Rehab. Svcs., 1987, Assn. Children and Adults with Learning Disabilities, 1987, Alumni Leadership award NYU Coll. Medicine, 1992, Outstanding Contbn. award Tampa Bay Coun. Child and Adolescent Psychiatry, 1993; named Psychiatrist of Yr. Tampa Mag., 1982, Outstanding Profl. in Field of Mental Health Hillsborough County Mental Health Assn., 1985; grantee Field Found., 1961-63, Carnegie Corp. N.Y., 1964-68, N.Y. Cmty. Trust, 1969, Ritter Found., 1970, N.Y.C. Dept. Mental Health and Mental Retardation Svcs., 1969-78, Ford Found., 1970-72, U.S. Office Edn. Divsn. Handicapped, 1976-79, 79-82, Found. Children with Learning Disabilities, 1983-84, Fla. State Dept. Edn., Fla. Diagnostic and Learning Resources Sys., 1984-87, Bd. Edn. Hillsborough County, 1983-93, Smokeless Tobacco Rsch. Coun., Inc., 1992-95, Nat. Inst. Neurol. Disease and Stroke, 1994—. Fellow Am. Psychiat. Assn. (life) (conf. on psychiat. inpatient treatment of children 1956, peer reviewer Jour. Am. Psychiat. Assn.), Am. Acad. Child and Adolescent Psychiatry (life) (com. on psychiat. facilities for children 1973-75, com. on rsch. Am. Acad. Child Psychiatry, steering com. Project Prevention 1987, Founders' Meml. Lecture 1987, Irving Philips Meml. award 1994), N.Y. Acad. Medicine, N.Y. Acad. Scis., Orton Soc., Phi Beta Kappa, Beta Lambda Sigma, Psi Chi. Home: 13906 Hayward Pl Tampa FL 33624 Office: U South Fla Child & Adolescent Psychiatry Dept 3515 E Fletcher Ave Tampa FL 33613

SILVER, BARRY MORRIS, lawyer, lay preacher; b. Mt. Vernon, N.Y., Nov. 18, 1956; s. Samuel Manuel and Elaine Martha (Shapiro) S. BA, Fla. Atlantic U., 1979; JD, Nova U., 1983. Bar: Fla. 1983. Law clk. to presiding justice 4th Dist. Ct. Appeals, West Palm Beach, Fla., 1982-83; sole practice Boca Raton, 1986—; tchr. Hebrew and religion Temple Beth El, Boca Raton, 1979-84; tchr. bilingual edn. Palm Beach County Schs., Delray Beach, Fla., 1981-83; ind. lay preacher, pub. speaker, Boca Raton, 1980—; lectr. law, Boca Raton, 1985—; faculty Palm Beach Jr. Coll., Boca Raton, 1990—; atty. NOW, South Palm Beach County; mem. Fla. Ho. Reps., 1997-98. Vol. Haitian Refugee Ctr., Miami, 1982; mem. Temple Sinai; mem. Fla. Action for Animals. Mem. Fla. Bar Assn., Palm Beach County Bar Assn., Sierra, South Fla. Greens. Democrat. Jewish. Home: 6024 Glendale Dr Boca Raton FL 33433-3838 Office: 7777 Glades Rd Ste 210 Boca Raton FL 33434-4150

SILVER, GEORGE, metal trading and processing company executive; b. Warren, Ohio, Dec. 17, 1918; s. Jacob and Sophie (Bradlyn) S.; m. Irene Miller, Aug. 5, 1945. Student U. Ala., 1938; BA, Ohio U., 1940, postgrad. law sch. Ohio State U., 1940-41; grad. Adj. Gen. Sch., 1944. Pres., Riverside Indsl. Materials, Bettendorf, Iowa, 1947-70, Metalpel subs. Continental Telephone Co., Bettendorf, 1970-71, Riverside Industries Inc., Bettendorf, 1971—; pres. Scott Resources Inc., Davenport, Iowa; v.p. Durbin Midwest, Davenport, 1987-90; mktg. dir. NAMCO Internat., Miami; cons. Waste Mgmt.-non Ferrous Mktg., 1990—, Snyer Steel Casting, Iowa, Riverside Products, Ill., 1992-93; founder Iowa Steel Mills (name changed to North Star Steel), Cargill and Wilton; mktg. dir. NAMCO Environ. Svcs. Corp., Miami, Fla., 1995—; bd. dirs. NAMCO Trading Co., Miami; cons. metal trading Cricket Club, Miami. Contbr. articles to profl. jours. Mem. Nat. UN Day Com., 1975-83. Served to capt. AC, USAF, 1941-46, 50-51, Korea. Named to Hon. Order Ky. Cols., 1991. Mem. Nat. Assn. Recycling Industries (co-chmn. nat. planning com., bd. dirs.), Copper Club, Paper Stock Inst. Am. (mem. exec. com.), Bur. Internat. de la Recuperation (chmn. adv. com.), Inter Global Trading Group (chmn. bd. dirs.), Mining Club N.Y.C., Outing Club, Hatchet Men's Chowder and Protective Assn., Copper Club, Jockey Club Miami, Williams Island Club, Rock Island Arsenal Officer's Club, Chemist Club (N.Y.C.), Crow Valley Country Club, Elks, Phi Sigma Delta. Republican. Jewish.

SILVER, PAUL ROBERT, marketing executive, consultant; b. Balt., Mar. 15, 1931; s. Harry and Frieda (Rosengarten) S.; m. Natalie Nessa Nechamkin, May 17, 1957; children; Geri Ellen, Steven Marc, Lawrence Alan. BA, U. Md., 1949; BS, U. Balt., 1958; postgrad., Eckerd Coll., 1984. Pres., CEO Sterling Prodns. Inc., Balt., 1950-51; advt. mgr. Hecht Co., Washington, 1951-53; pres., CEO Artists & Models, Inc., Washington and Balt., 1974-76, The Charles Agy. Inc., Washington and Balt., 1955-80, The Golden Triangle Agy., Clearwater, Fla., 1980-82; COO Bridgman Assocs. Inc., Annapolis, Md., 1985-86; dir. promotions Internat. Beverage Expn., Washington, 1986; pres., CEO Prasco Inc., Tampa, Fla., 1982—; cons. Lewis and Ptnrs., Inc., San Francisco, Corp. Vision, Inc., L.A., Computer Response, Inc., Balt., Themes and Schemes, Inc., Dunedin, Fla., San Diego, 1984—, J&B Mgmt. Co., 1991, Alberee Products, Inc., 1992; v.p. Coupon Am., Bel Air, Md., 1987-88; dir. mktg. Miles Homes, Inc., Cheshire, Conn., 1993; CEO Universal Industries, Inc., 1994—; ptnr. Drakeford & Drakeford, PA, 1995-96; v.p. Chapman Security Inc., 1995—. Active in Radio Free Asia, 1972, Pinellas County Heart Savers, Clearwater, 1981; campaign mgr. for candidates for Balt. City Coun., U.S. Senate and U.S. Congress, 1968, 88, Fla. Commr. Agr., 1990. With U.S. Army, 1953-55, 72. Democrat. Jewish. Office: Prasco Inc PO Box 24461 Tampa FL 33623-4461

SILVERBERG, HOWARD J. (HANK SILVERBERG), broadcast journalist; b. N.Y., Nov. 23, 1954; s. Sidney and Ruth (Lippy) S.; m. Jody M. Lander, May 30, 1982; children: Anna, Samantha. BA in Polit. Sci., Fairleigh Dickinson U., 1976; MA in Comm., Am. U., 1977. Instr. Poughkeepsie (N.Y.) D.C. C.C., 1990; anchor WHPN Radio, Hyde Park, N.Y., 1977-78; anchor reporter WCTC Radio, New Brunswick, N.J., 1978-84; news dir. WGHQ Radio, Kingston, N.Y., 1984-90, WBNR Radio, Poughkeepsie, 1990-92; corr. Standard News, Washington, 1992—. Mem. Radio and TV News Dirs. Assn. Jewish. Home: 15109 Colder Ln Woodbridge VA 22193-1620

SILVERMAN, GARY WILLIAM, financial planner; b. L.A., Nov. 30, 1957; s. Albert and Anna Marie (Robinson) S.; m. Joanne Marie Robinson, Aug. 29, 1976. BS summa cum laude Psychology/Counseling, Miami (Fla.) Christian Coll., 1987; MBA, U. Dallas, 1992. CFP. Tng. supr. Tex. Utilities, Glen Rose, Tex., 1982-92; registered rep. Waddell & Reed, Ft. Worth, 1990-94; tng. dir. Howmet Refurbishment, Wichita Falls, Tex., 1992-94; owner, fin. planner Personal Money Planning, Wichita Falls, 1993—. Grad. Leadership Wichita Falls, 1993; loaned exec. Wichita Falls United Way, 1993; instr. ARC, 1983—; Wichita Falls Gold Coast ambassador; mem. Pvt. Industry Coun., Job. Svc. Employer Com., Mayor's Com. on the Status of Women; columnist Wichita Women mag. Mem. Inst. Cert. Fin. Planners, Registry Cert. Fin. Planners, Internat. Assn. Fin. Planning, S.W. Wichita Falls Rotary, Sigma Iota Epsilon. Office: Personal Money Planning 4245 Kemp Blvd Ste 818 Wichita Falls TX 76308-2824

SILVERMAN, MARC H., real estate developer, business owner; b. Phila., Oct. 24, 1938; s. Meyer H. and Mary Jane (Schloss) S.; m. Mattye Bukatman, Dec. 28, 1965; children: M. David, Shara, Lorin. BA, Ohio Wesleyan, 1961. Sales rep. then owner, mgr. Schloss Outdoor Adv., Charlotte, N.C., 1962-86; gen. ptnr. MHS Holding Ltd., Charlotte, N.C., 1987—; dir. city/region Ctrl. Carolina Bank, Charlotte, 1989—. Dir., past co-chmn. bldg. fund Temple Beth, Charlotte, 1975—; park commr. Charlotte Parks and Recreation; v.p., dir., dir. devel. Mint Mus., Charlotte, 1988-94; dir. Sta. WTVI, Charlotte, 1993-96. With USAR. Mem. Ballantyne Country Club (dir.). Office: MHS Holdings Ltd 6707-C Fairview Rd Charlotte NC 28210

SILVERSTEIN, BARRY, cable company executive; b. 1933. With CCX, Inc. divsn. Phoenix II, Charlotte, N.C., CEO, 1986-88, 91, chmn. bd., 1986-88, 91—; prin. owner, chmn. bd. or bd. dirs. Coaxial Comm. Inc. and subs., Coaxial Comm. Ctrl. Ohio Inc., Coaxial Comm. So. Ohio Inc. Office: CCX Inc 1901 Richmond Rd Charlotte NC 28211

SILVERSTEIN, BURTON VICTOR, cardiologist; b. Durham, N.C., May 7, 1945; s. Jacob Morris and Beatrice Deborah (Grodner) S.; m. Janet H. Fisher, Aug. 18, 1968; children: Craig Daryl, Todd Alan. AB in Chemistry, U. Rochester, 1966; MD, U. Pa., 1970. Diplomate Am. Bd. Internal Medicine, Am. Bd. Cardiovascular Disease, Nat. Bd. Med. Examiners. Intern Hosp. of U. Pa., Phila., 1970-71, jr. asst. resident medicine, 1971-72, sr. asst. resident medicine, 1974-75; cardiology fellow Duke U. Med. Ctr., Durham, N.C., 1975-77; clin. asst. prof. medicine U. Fla., Gainesville, 1978—; assoc. dir. cardiovascular lab. Alachua Gen. Hosp., Gainesville, 1978—, attending physician, 1979—; pvt. practice Cardiology Assocs. of Gainesville, 1978—; assoc. in medicine Duke U. Med. Ctr., 1977-78; dir. non-invasive lab. Vet.'s Hosp., Durham, 1977-78; clin. asst. prof. medicine U. Fla., Gainesville, 1979—; clin. instr. medicine Duke U. Med. Ctr., 1975-77. Mem. edn. com. Fla. Heart Assn., 1979-82. Maj. USAF, 1972-74. Fellow Am. Coll. Cardiology, Soc. Cardiac Angiography and Interventions, Am. Soc. Cardiovascular Interventionalists; mem. Am. Heart Assn., Fla. Heart Assn., Fla. Med. Soc., Alachua County Med. Soc. Office: Cardiology Assocs 1026 SW 2nd Ave Gainesville FL 32601-6166

SILVERSTEIN, VICTORIA, retired sales executive; b. Bklyn., May 7, 1927; d. Meyer and Rose (Granoff) K.; divorced; children: Gary Mark Silvers, Arleen Renée Kazeck. Student, Queens C.C., 1975, Daytona (Fla.) C.C., 1995-96. Sec. bus. Jon Paul Perfumes, N.Y.C., 1960-75; troubleshooter N.Y. Life, Floral Park, N.Y., 1975-80; owner Candy Story, Bayside, N.Y., 1980-81; office worker, troubleshooter various offices, N.Y.C., 1981-89; perfume salesperson Palm Coast, Fla., 1990-95; perfume salesperson Rubyat Cosmetic Co., N.Y.C., 1960-96. Author: (handbook for children) Safe With ABC's, 1994, (fairy tales) Vickie Silvers Fairy Tales, 1995; inventor Cane-Take adaptor adjustable cane, 1993; exhibited art in 3 art shows. Home: 1 Blaine Ct Palm Coast FL 32137

SIMCIC, KENNETH JOSEPH, career officer, endocrinologist; b. Pitts., Oct. 19, 1956; s. Nicholas Francis and Margaret (Krotec) S.; m. Mary Margaret Welsh, June 12, 1982; children: Natalie Marie, Jacqueline Marie, Lauren Elizabeth. BS in Biology, Duquesne U., 1977; MD, Temple U. Med. Sch., 1982. Cert. Am. Bd. Internal Medicine, 1985, Am. Bd. Endocrinology and Metabolism, 1989, Nat. Bd. Med. Examiners, 1983. Commd. 2d lt. U.S. Army, 1982, advanced through grades to lt. col., 1994; intern internal medicine Fitzsimmons Army Med. Ctr., Aurora, Colo., 1982-83, resident internal medicine, 1983-85; asst. clin. prof. Tex. Tech. U. Sch. Medicine, El Paso, 1990-95, assoc. prof. medicine, 1995—; presenter in field. Contbr. articles to profl. jours. Active Focus on Family. Fitzsimmons Army Med. Ctr. Endocrinology fellow, 1987-89; recipient Intern' award for Best Attending Physician/Dept. Medicine William Beaumont Army Med. Ctr., 1990. Fellow ACP; mem. Endocrine Soc., Soc. Uniformed Endocrinologists, Omicron Delta Kappa, Phi Kappa Phi. Republican. Roman Catholic. Office: William Beaumont Army Med Ctr Endocrinology Clinic El Paso TX 79920-5001

SIMIEN, CLYDE RAY, lawyer; b. Opelousas, La., Jan. 9, 1960; s. Vincent Jr. and Mercedes Simien; m. Margo St. Julien. BSBA, U. Southwestern La., 1982; postgrad., La. State U., 1985; JD, So. U. La., 1986. Bar: La. 1986. Counselor spl. svcs. dept. U. Southwestern La., 1982-84; law clerk Hon. Ron Gomez, House of Reps., La., 1984, Bur. Legis., Senate, La., 1984-85, L.D. Sledge, Atty.-at-law, 1985-86, Sixteenth Judicial Dist. Ct., 1986—; ptnr. Simien & Miniex, Attys.-at-law, Lafayette, La., 1987—; asst. adj. prof. criminal justice Coll. of Arts and Humanities, U. Southwestern La.; asst. dist. atty. Parishes of St. Martin, Iberia, and St. Mary. Mem. ABA, La. Trial Lawyers Assn., La. State Bar Assn., Am. Trial Lawyers Assn., La. Soc. Ind. Accountants, Nat. Soc. Pub. Accountants, Nat. Dist. Attys. Assn., U. Southwestern La. Debate Team, U. Southwestern La. Alumni Assn. Office: Simien & Miniex APLC 104 Rue Iberville Lafayette LA 70508-3102

SIMMONDS, WARREN L., podiatrist; b. Bklyn., Oct. 29, 1932; s. Harold E. and Mildred I. (Siegel) S.; m. Norma J. Coffman, Mar. 20, 1955 (dec. Mar. 5, 1990); 1 child, Garey; m. Karen L. Kaminsky, June 11, 1995. BA, Vanderbilt U., 1954; D.P.M., N.Y. Coll. Podiatric Medicine, 1960. Podiatrist pvt. practice N.Y.C., 1961-1980, Miami Beach, Fla, 1981—; instr. N.Y. Coll. Podiatric Medicine, 1961-68; mem. adv. bd. Barry U. Sch. of Podiatric Medicine, 1988—, adv. bd. Podiatric Risk Mgmt. Soc. Fla. chpt. 1988—; meem. Nat. Bd. Podiatric Med. Examiners; pres. Am. Fedn Podiatric Med. Bds. 1993-95; chmn.exam. com. 1991-92, vice chmn. bd. 1991-93, chmn. of bd., 1992-93. Assoc. editor Footprints, 1987-94; lectr. on foot care to sports groups, sr. citizen groups. and to basic radiologic technologists. Pres. Baseball Booster Club Miami Beach Sr. H.S., 1977-85; pres. Miami Beach Baseball Booster Club, 1987-88, 91-94; adminstr. and coach Youth Baseball, Miami Beach, 1970-83; vol. cmty. health fairs, March of Dimes. Fellow Am. Soc. Podiatric Medicine (sec. 1988—, exec. dir. 1994—, treas. 1994—, bd. trustees 1987-90, Disting. Svc. award 1994). Am. Coll. Podiatric Radiologists, Acad. Ambulatory Foot Surgeons.; mem. Am. Podiatric Med. Assn., Fla. Podiatric Med. Assn. (alt. del. to Am. Podiatric Med. Assn. 1980-83, del. 84-88, chmn. licensing and regulation com. 1985-88, state bd. liaison 1983-88. unlic. practitioners com. 1983-88, mem. peer rev. com. 1982-83, budget com. 1985), Dade County Podiatric Med. Assn. (pres. 1972-73, Outstanding Podiatrist 1981, Podiatrist of Yr. 1985)., Am. Soc. of Sports Medicine (assoc.). Office: 7331 Collins Ave Miami Beach FL 33141-2711

SIMMONS, BARRY WILLIAM, university official, consultant; b. Farmville, Va., June 26, 1950; s. William Luther Simmons and Mary Ellen (Roberts) Williams; m. Janie McCulley, June 10, 1972; children: Marysue H.R. and Barry Jr. AB, Elon Coll., 1973; MEd, U. N.C., 1984, EdD, 1987. Dir. fin. aid Elon Coll., Elon College, N.C., 1973-82, coord. admissions and fin. aid depts., 1982-84; coord. U. N.C., Greensboro, 1987-88; asst. v.p. student enrollment St. Paul's Coll., Lawrenceville, Va., 1988-91; dir. acad. campus fin. sect. Counseling Ctr. Va. Commonwealth U.-Med. Coll. Va., Richmond, 1993—; mem. state regional adv. panel Coll. Bd., 1981-82, Am. Coll. Testing, 1975-82; mem. nat. adv. bd. Nat. Coll. Svcs. Ltd. Capt. United Way, Alamance County, N.C., 1976; chartering officer Elon Coll. Vol. Fire Dept., Inc., 1976. Named one of Outstanding Young Men in Am., 1982. Mem. So. Assn. Student Fin. Aid Adminstrs., Va. Assn. Student Fin. Aid Adminstrs. (quality assurance commn.), So. Gerontol. Soc., Va. State Coun. Higher Edn. (work study task force Richmond chpt. 1988-91), Am. Theatre Organ Soc. (nat. curator 1976-80), Pi Kappa Phi (Outstanding Svc. award 1981). Home: 1465 Bauers Rd Baskerville VA 23915-9707

SIMMONS, BRADFORD RENA, university coach; b. Morgan City, La., July 14, 1971; s. Bevis and Bertha Elizabeth (Harris) S. BS, Ga. So. U., Statesboro, 1993; MPA, Ga. So. U., 1996. Cert. tchr., Ga. Bd. Edn. Asst. cross-country coach Ga. So. U., 1993-94, head cross-country coach, 1994—. Intern The White House, Washington, 1994, Bulloch County (Ga.) Govt., Statesboro, 1995; vol. 1996 Olympic Games, Atlanta. Named Acad. All-Conf. Trans Am. Athletic Conf., 1991; named to acad. honor roll, So. Conf., 1991, 92. Mem. Pi Alpha Alpha (pres. 1995-96). Democrat. Presbyterian. Home: 477 Atlanta Hwy SE Winder GA 30680 Office: Georgia Southern Athletics Landrum Box 8082 Statesboro GA 30460

SIMMONS, BRYAN PAUL, physician, researcher; b. Lexington, Ky., Oct. 21, 1949; m. Barbara Simmons; children: Rebecca, Ryan. BS in Math.

magna cum laude, Duke U., 1972; MD, Vanderbilt U., 1976. Diplomate Am. Bd. Internal Medicine, Nat. Bd. Med. Examiners. Intern in internal medicine Pa. State U., Hershey, 1976-77, resident in internal medicine, 1977-79; fellow in infectious diseases Sch. Medicine Emory U., Atlanta, 1982-84; med. dir. infection control Meth. Hosps. of Memphis, 1984—, mem. faculty internal medicine residency program, 1984—, sr. leadership coun., 1990—, mem. continuous quality improvement coun., 1991—, chmn. physician computer automation com., 1992; from clin. instr. to clin. asst. prof. medicine U. Tenn., Memphis, 1985-93, clin. assoc. prof. medicine, 1993—; med. dir. quality mgmt. Meth. Health Sys., Tenn. and Miss., 1984-93; participant symposium on chem. germicides in health care field Assn. Practitioners of Infection Control, 1987; cons. Joint Commn. on Accreditation of Healthcare Orgn., 1987; ofcl. rep. Shelby County Adv. Com. on AIDS, Memphis and Shelby County Med. Soc., 1988-89; mem. workgroup to derive med. rev. criteria Agy. for Healthcare Policy and Rsch., USPHS, 1992-93; speaker numerous confs. Author: (with others) Hospital Infections, 2d edit., 1986, How to Achieve Quality and Accreditation in an Infection Control Program, 2d edit., 1992, Hospital Epidemiology and Infection Control, A Practical Handbook for Hospital Epidemiologists; sect. co-editor: Infection Control and Hosp. Epidemiology, 1992—; contbr. articles to profl. jours. Fellow ACP, Infectious Disease Soc. Am.; mem. AMA, Soc. for Hosp. Epidemiology Am. (nat. gov. bd. councilor 1986-88, severity illness working group 1987-88, chmn. nat. nominations com. 1988, edn. com. 1989—, chmn. quality mgmt. com. 1991—, com. for revision of JCAHO manual on infection control 1991, v.p. 1993, pres. elect 1994, pres. 1995, ann. meeting planning com. 1993—), Epidemic Intelligence Svc. Alumni Assn., Assn. Practitioners of Infection Control (nat. guidelines com. 1987-88, liaison Am. Hosp. Assn. 1987), Tenn. med. Assn. (infectious disease com. 1993—), Infectious Diseases Soc. Tenn. (founding, constn. and bylaws com. 1990, sec./treas. 1990-93), Memphis and Shelby County Med. Soc. (rep. to Shelby County adv. com. AIDS), Duke Club Memphis (pres. 1989-94). Office: Meth Hosps of Memphis Drs Bldg 188 S Bellevue Blvd Ste 408 Memphis TN 38104-3429

SIMMONS, CECELIA E., quality improvement, infection control and employee health nurse; b. Norfolk, Va., Aug. 20, 1949; d. Oscar Y. Jr. and Evelyn C. (Hermann) McClannan; m. Richard P. Simmons Jr., June 28, 1970; children: Robin Lea, Paul David. Diploma in nursing, Norfolk Gen. Hosp., 1970; degree in nursing, St. Phillips Coll., San Antonio, 1986, San Antonio Coll., 1988; postgrad., U. Tex. Health Sci. Ctr., San Antonio. Cert. in infection control. Home health specialist Luth. Gen. Hosp., San Antonio; oncology nurse San Antonio Tumor and Blood Clinic, San Antonio; dir. medicare dept. Personal Touch Home Care, San Antonio; infection control-employee health nurse, outpatient coord. Warm Springs Rehab. Hosp., San Antonio; quality improvement coord., infection control coord. Cancer Therapy and Rsch. Ctr., San Antonio, occupational health nurse. Mem. Oncology Nurses Soc., Assn. Practitioners Infection Control (chpt. pres.), Assn. of Occupational Health Nurses, Tex. Soc. of Infection Control Practitioners, Tex. Hosp. Assn., Assn. Profls. in Healthcare Quality. Home: 6315 Willow Hill St San Antonio TX 78247-1116

SIMMONS, CHARLES BEDFORD, JR., lawyer; b. Greenville, S.C., Dec. 4, 1956; s. Charles Bedford and Mary Margaret (Mason) S.; children: Charles B. III, Elizabeth S., Mason W. AA magna cum laude, Spartanburg Meth. Coll., 1977; BS magna cum laude, E. Tenn. State U., 1979; JD, U. S.C., 1982. Bar: S.C. 1982, U.S. Dist. Ct. S.C. 1983, U.S. Ct. Appeals (4th cir.) 1986. Law clk. to presiding justice S.C. Cir. Ct., Greenville, 1982-83; with Carter Law Firm, Greenville, 1983-86; ptnr. Wilkins, Nelson, Kittredge & Simmons, Greenville, 1986-89; civil ct. judge Greenville, 1989—; mem. bench-bar com. S.C. Supreme Ct., 1992—. Mem. adv. com. paralegal program Greenville Tech. Coll., 1989—, chmn., 1990-91; mem. Friends of 200 Adv. Bd., 1991—. Named Big Brother of Yr., Big Bros.-Bis Sisters, 1988; recipient Svc. to Manking award Rotary Club, 1989, Outstanding Young Disting. Svc. award Greenville Jaycees, 1990-91. Mem. S.C. Bar Assn. (young lawyer liason 1985—, named Outstanding Young Lawyer of Yr. 1989), Greenville Bar Assn., Assn. Trial Lawyers Am., S.C. Trial Lawyers Assn., Greenville Young Lawyers (pres. 1988—), Gamma Beta Phi, Pi Gamma Mu, Phi Delta Phi. Republican. Presbyterian. Clubs: Greenville City, Textile (v.p. 1985—), Revelers (Greenville). Home: 11 W Hillcrest Dr Greenville SC 29609-4615 Office: Ste 207 County Courthouse Greenville SC 29601

SIMMONS, CHARLES EDWARD PHILLIP, history educator; b. Boston, Mar. 11, 1936; s. Charles L. and Isabella C. (Young) S.; m. Margret L. Simmons; children: Paul, Susan, Carol, Katherine, Damon, Andrea, Alexia. BA, Seattle U., 1960; MA, Drake U., 1960; PhD, Wash. State U., 1966. Chmn. history dept. Braldey U., Peoria, Ill., 1966-70; dean of arts, humanities Moorhead (Minn.) State U., 1970-73; acad. v.p. U. Evansville, Ind., 1973-77; pres. Lake Erie Coll., Painesville, Ohio, 1977-84; dir. Coll. Mgmt. Cons., Wilmington, Del., 1984-85; prof. Midland (Tex.) Coll., 1985—; cons. higher edn. devel. Judson Coll., 1975, Tenn. Wesleyan U., 1975, Philander Smith Coll., 1977, Wilmington Coll., 1979, Antioch Presdl. Commn. Fiscal and Acad. Policies, 1977-79; vice chmn. Higher Edn. Policy: ACE Energy Commn., 1979, chmn., 1984, chmn. energy task for fin., 1982-84, subcom. mem. on edn., 1982-84. Contbr. articles to profl. jours. Lay reader Trinity Ch., 1985, Eucharistic min., 1989; tutor Casa de Amigos Children's Tutor, 1985—; bd. dirs. Casa de Amigos, 1987—; participant Outward Bound, Colo. mountains, 1989. Sgt. U.S. Army, 1949-54. Recipient Nat. Short Story award, Faculty Rsch. grant Bradley U., Postdoctoral award Dalhousie U., Can., 1968, Faculty fellowship Hamline U., 1969, Outstanding Teaching award Midland Coll., 1989-90, Liberty Bell award, 1989; named vis. fellow Dalhousie U. N.S., Can., 1965-66, Outstanding Alum, 1984; named to Am. Coun. non Edn. Acad. Deans, 1971, Am. Coun. on Edn. Inst. for Pres., 1977; Piper prof. Piffer Found., 1993. Mem. Plaza Club. Home: 2301 Country Club Dr Midland TX 79701-5663

SIMMONS, DAVID JEFFREY, real estate executive; b. Greenville, S.C., Oct. 12, 1961; s. Wilbur Bernard and Grace (Duncan) S.; m. Georgie Ann Lollis, June 8, 1985. BS in Fin. and Mgmt., U. S.C., 1983. Lic. real estate broker, S.C. V.p. W.B. Simmons and Co., Greenville, 1983—; pres. Simmons Realty and Devel., Greenville, 1983—; v.p. Greenville Turf and Tractor, 1987-94, Foothills Turf and Tractor, Easley, S.C., 1987-94; pres., chief exec. officer Simmons Chevrolet-Geo Inc., Pendleton, S.C., 1989-92. Active March of Dimes, Greenville. Mem. NRA, Nat. Assn. Realtors, S.C. Assn. Realtors, Aircraft Owners and Pilots Assn. Republican. Baptist. Clubs: Poinsett, Commerce (Greenville). Office: PO Box 1315 Greenville SC 29602-1315

SIMMONS, FRANKIE WHEELER, primary school educator; b. Swainsboro, Ga., July 29, 1956; d. Joseph Harville and Betty (Price) Wheeler; children: Jessica Brooke, Wes. AA, E. Ga. Coll., 1976; BS, Ul Ga., 1977; MEd, Ga. Coll., 1988; EdS, Ga. So. U., 1989. Cert. elem. tchr., Ga. 1st grade tchr. Adrian (Ga.) Sch., 1977-78; 1st and 2d grade tchr. Vidalia (Ga.) City Schs., 1978-80; 1st grade tchr. Swainsboro Primary Sch., 1983-85, pre-1st grade tchr., 1988-91, tchr. 1st grade, 1991—; kindergarten tchr. Swainsboro Elem. Sch., 1985-88. Mem. NEA, Ga. Assn. Educators, Phi Kappa Phi, Gamma Beta Phi. Home: 339 S College St Metter GA 30439 Office: Emanuel County Let's Start Lead Tchr Pre K Ctr 220 Jefferson St Swainsboro GA 30401

SIMMONS, GARY M., small business owner, writer; b. Chgo., Dec. 21, 1961; s. Larry Franklin S. and Carol T. Berry. Student, W. Ky. Tech., 1982-83. Respiratory therapist Loures Hosp., Paducah, Ky., 1982-96; owner Pets Plus, Sympsonia, Ky., 1990-91; retail mgr. Dippin' Dots Inc., Paducah, Ky., 1991-95; owner Pen, Inc., Paducah, 1995—. Author: Nature's Impressions, 1995. Mem. Club Theatrical Arts (pres. 1981-82). Home: 2912 Fisher Rd Paducah KY 42086

SIMMONS, JESSE DONALD, JR., government acquisition manager; b. Birmingham, Ala., Nov. 9, 1946; s. Jesse Donald and Sara Rowena (Godwin) S.; m. Thelesa Susan Eubanks, Aug. 30, 1969; children: Sonya Thelesa, Krista Leigh. B of Elec. Engring., Auburn U., 1969, MS, 1971; MBA, U. West Fla., 1982. Quality/reliability engr. Tex. Instruments, Dallas, 1973-75; quality assurance engr. Rockwell Internat., Richardson, Tex., 1975-76; electronics engr. USACEEIA USA, Ft. Ritchie, Md., 1976-78, NAVELEX USN, Washington, 1978-79; prodn. engr. AD/PMD USAF, Eglin AFB, Fla., 1979-82; dir. mfg. MSD/YMD USAF, Eglin AFB, 1982-89; chief mfg. ASD/MYEM USAF, Eglin AFB, 1989-92; divsn. chief mfg. and supportability ASC/YAE USAF, Eglin AFB, 1992-94; staff specialist OUSD (A&T)/TWP(AW) Pentagon, Washington, 1994-95; chief engr. ASC/VXG, Eglin AFB, 1995-96, ASC/WMR, Eglin AFB, 1996—. Lt. U.S. Army, 1970-72. Mem. IEEE. Home: 630 Overbrook Dr Fort Walton Beach FL 32547-3548 Office: ASC/YAE Eglin AFB FL 32542

SIMMONS, LORNA WOMACK, elementary school educator; b. Enid, Okla., Dec. 25, 1954; d. Doyle Alex and Ruth Phyllis (Wiens) Nunneley; m. Daniel Bruce Womack, June 7, 1975 (widowed Jan. 1981); children: Zachary Womack, Travis Womack, Shawn Simmons, Shayla Simmons; m. H. Lynn Simmons, Feb. 14, 1982. BS cum laude, U. Tex., 1977. Spl. edn. tchr. Sand Springs (Okla.) I.S.D., 1977-78; pvt. therapist Alphabetic Phonics, Big Spring, Tex., 1981-87; dyslexia cons. Big Spring (Tex.) I.S.D., 1987-88; chpt. I tchr. Forsan I.S.D., Big Spring, Tex., 1988-91; cons. Classroom Phonics, Big Spring, Tex., 1991—. Author: Classroom Phonics, 1989, Classroom Phonics II, 1991, Classroom Phonics Spelling, 1991, Classroom Phonics Kid Cards, 1994, Classroom Phonics Comprehension Tests, 1994, Saxon Phonics K, 1996, Saxon Phonics 1, 1996, Saxon Phonics 2, 1996. Mem. Assn. Tex. Profl. Educators. Republican. Mem. Ch. of God. Home: 3200 Wasson Dr Big Spring TX 79720-7302

SIMMONS, MICHAEL ANTHONY, dean; m. Margaret Clare Martindale; children: Kristen Ann, Jeffrey Michael, Jennifer Clare Roe, Jason Davis. AB cum laude, Harvard Coll., 1963, MD, 1967. Diplomate Am. Bd. Pediatrics, Am. Bd. Neonatal-Perinatal Medicine. Intern Harriet Lane Svc., Johns Hopkins Hosp., Balt., 1967-68, asst. resident, 1968-69, sr. asst. resident, 1969; chief resident Dept. Pediatrics, U. Colo. Med. Ctr., Denver, 1971-72, rsch. fellow in perinatal medicine, 1972-74, clin. instr. in pediatrics, 1974-77, assoc. prof. pediatrics, 1977; assoc. prof. pediatrics and obstetrics Johns Hopkins U. Sch. Medicine, Balt., 1977-83; prof., chmn. dept. pediatrics U. Utah Sch. of Medicine, Salt Lake City, 1983-94; prof. pediatrics, dean U. N.C. at Chapel Hill Sch. Medicine, 1994—; adj. prof. dept. obstetrics and gynecology U. Utah Sch. of Medicine, Salt Lake City, 1984-94; co-dir. newborn svcs. U. Colo. Med. Ctr., Denver, 1974-77, Johns Hopkins Hosp., 1977-83; mem. staff Denver Gen. Hosp., 1976-77, Denver Children's Hosp., 1976-77; vice chmn. clin. affairs dept. pediatrics Johns Hopkins Hosp., 1981-83; chief of pediatrics U. Utah Med. Ctr., Salt Lake City, 1983-94; med. dir. Primary Children's Med. Ctr., 1983-94; bd. dirs. Triangle Univs. Licensing Consortium, U. N.C. Hosps. Contbr. numerous articles to profl. jours. Fellow Am. Acad. of Pediatrics (excellence in pediatric rsch. com. 1991—, coun. on govt. affairs 1992—); mem. Perinatal Rsch. Soc. (coun. 1982-84, pres.-elect 1985-87, pres. 1989), Western Soc. for Pediatric Rsch. (coun. 1985-86, pres.-elect 1987, pres. 1988), Soc. for Pediatric Rsch., Am. Bd. Pediatrics (sub-bd. of neonatal-perinatal medicine 1983-89, chmn. 1984-88). Office: U NC Sch of Medicine Chapel Hill NC 27599-7000

SIMMONS, RANDALL ALLEN, small business owner, consultant; b. Dallas, July 22, 1956; s. Robert A. and Helen F. (Bennett) S. BS, U. Tex., Arlington, 1980; MEd, U. Tex., 1984. Owner DataVisions, El Paso, 1987—; cons. Lazer Ventures, El Paso, 1988—, DataVisions of Tex., Houston, 1995—. Programmer computer software, 1984—. Mem. El Paso-Juarez Attitudinal Healing (bd. dirs., treas. 1995—). Office: Lazer Ventures 4551 Sun Valley El Paso TX 79924

SIMMONS, ROBERT DANIEL, clergyman, machinist; b. Strasburg, Va., Dec. 21, 1921; s. Marion Harvey and Winifred Rebecca (Baker) S.; m. Lois Marie French, Dec. 28, 1955; children: Andrew Kirk, Mary Esther Simmons Lauderman, Rebecca Alice Simmons DeBolt. BA, Hampden Sydney Coll., 1950; MDiv, Union Theol. Sem., 1953; ThM, Princeton Theol. Sem., 1957. Ordained to ministry Presbyterian Ch., 1953. Slasher operator Am. Viscose Corp., Front Royal, Va., 1940-41; clergyman Warm Springs (Va.) Presbyn. Ch., 1953-62, Neshanic (N.J.) Reformed Ch., 1956-57, Manokin Presbyn. Ch., Princess Anne, Md., 1962-67, Bethel Presbyn. Ch., Waverly, W.Va., 1976-91, St. Marys (W.Va.) Presbyn. Ch., 1967-91, Hughes River Presbyn. Ch., Cairo, W.Va., 1995—; moderator Parkersburg Presbytery, W.Va., 1974; commr. Presbyn. Gen. Assembly, 1962, 74, 82; stated supply pastor Hughes River Presbyn. Ch., Cairo, W.Va., 1995—. Author: The Christian Marriage, 1962, Blueprint for Living, 1994, Prayers for Daily Need, 1996. Charter mem., v.p. Pleasants County Commn. on Aging, St. Marys, 1974-91; donor ARC, 1968-91. With U.S. Navy, 1946-47. Recipient Clergyman of Yr. award W.Va. Kiwanis, 1983-84, State Min. of Yr. award W.Va. Soil Conservation Com., 1978, Safety award Nat. Found. for Hwy. Safety, 1968. Mem. W.Va. Ministerial Assn. (pres. Pleasants County 1970-91), Greater Marietta Ministerial Assn., W.Va. Hist. Soc. (pres. Pleasants County 1973-91), Masons (Worshipful master 1958-59, 50 Yr. Mem. award 1995). Home and Office: Simmons Theol Libr 100 Water St Williamstown WV 26187

SIMMONS, S. DALLAS, university president; b. Ahoskie, N.C., Jan. 28, 1940; s. Yvonne Martin; m. Mary A. Simmons, Feb. 10, 1963; children: S. Dallas Jr., Kristie Lynn. BS, N.C. Cen. U., 1962, MS, 1967; PhD, Duke U., 1977. Asst. prof. bus. adminstrn. N.C. Cen. U., Durham, 1967-71, asst. to chancellor, 1971-77, vice chancellor for univ. relations, 1977-81; pres. St. Paul's Coll., Lawrenceville, Va., 1981-85, Va. Union Univ., Richmond, 1985—; faculty cons. IBM, Research Triangle Park, N.C., 1968-71; cons. for edn. devel. officers Nat. Lab. for Higher Edn., Durham, 1972-73; staff asst. to Pres., White House Advance Office, Washington, 1975-76; univ. fed. liaison officer Moton Coll. Service Bur., Washington, 1972-80; mem. competency testing commn. N.C. Bd. Edn., 1977-81; bd. dirs., mem. loan com., mem. planning com. Pace Am. Bank, Lawrenceville, 1984-85. Bd. dirs. N.C. Mus. Life and Sci., Durham, 1972-75, Volunteer Services Bur, Inc., Durham, 1972-77, Va. Poly. Inst. and State U., 1982-83; mem. Durham Civic/Conv. Ctr. Commn., 1972-73, U.S./Zululand Ednl. Found., 1985; trustee, mem. exec. and pers. com. N.C. Cen. U., 1983-85; active various coms. United Negro Coll. Fund; mem. exec. bd. John B. McLendon Found., Inc., 1985. Named one of Outstanding Young Men Am., 1972, Citizen of Yr. Omega Psi Phi, 1983-84, Bus. Assoc. of Yr. Am. Bus. Women's Assn., 1984. Mem. Assn. Episc. Colls. (pres.-elect), Cen. Intercollegiate Athletic Assn. (exec. com. 1981—, bd. dirs. 1981—), Nat. Assn. for Equal Opportunity in Higher Edn. (bd. dirs., chmn. leadership awards com. 1984-85), Am. Mgmt. Assn., Data Processing Mgmt. Assn. (cen. Carolina chpt.), Am. Assn. Sch. Adminstrs., Am. Assn. Univ. Adminstrs., Kappa Alpha Psi (Kappa of Month Dec. 1981), Sigma Pi Phi (alpha beta boulé). African Methodist Episcopalian. Club: Downtown. Lodges: Masons (32 degree), Shriners, Kiwanis, Optimists. Home: 1200 W Graham Rd Richmond VA 23220-1409 Office: Va Union U 1500 N Lombardy St Richmond VA 23220-1711

SIMMONS, SHARON DIANNE, elementary education educator; b. Woodruff, S.C., Apr. 5, 1961; d. James Madison and Lucy Nell (Carlton) Crow; m. Wayne Roy Simmons, Mar. 29, 1986; children: Zachary, Luke. BA in Elem. Edn., U. S.C., 1983, M of Elem. Edn., 1987. Tchr. 3d grade M.S. Bailey Elem. Sch., Clinton, S.C., 1984-85, tchr. 4th grade, 1985-86; tchr. 5th grade Eastside Elem. Sch., Clinton, S.C., 1986-88, tchr. 4th & 5th grades, 1988-90, 91-92, tchr. 5th grade, 1990-91, tchr. 4th grade, 1993-95, tchr. 3rd grade, 1995—; pilot tchr. authentic assessment Eastside Elem. Sch., 1992—, mem. sch. libr. com., 1993—, tchr. chair 4th grade, 1993-94, tchr. grad. course authentic assessment, 1996. Pres. libr. coun. Spartanburg-Woodruff (S.C.) Br. Libr., 1993-95, v.p., 1995—. Recipient Ambassador award The Edn. Ctr., 1993-94. Mem. S.C. Math. Tchrs. Assn., Sch. Improvement Coun. Baptist. Home: 651 Parsons Rd Woodruff SC 29388-8700 Office: Eastside Elem Sch 103 Old Colony Rd Clinton SC 29325-9317

SIMMONS, SUSAN ANNETTE, production management and statistics educator; b. Pascagoula, Miss., Apr. 12, 1947; d. Emmitt Leroy and Margie Marie (Coker) S. BS, Miss. State Coll. for Women, 1969; MBA, Miss. State U., 1970; PhD, U. Miss., 1976. Asst. prof. Eastern Ky. U., 1976-78, U. Southwestern La., Lafayette, 1978-80; assoc. prof. U. Iowa, Iowa City, 1980-83; assoc. prof. Sam Houston State U., Huntsville, Tex., 1983-90; prof. The Citadel, Charleston, S.C., 1990—. Contbr. articles to profl. jours. Editor Jour. Bus. Strategies, 1985-87; mem. bd. editors Jour. Econs. and Fin., 1979—. Mem. Nat. Decision Scis. Inst., Am. Econs. Assn., Western Econ. Assn., SE Decision Scis. Inst. (v.p. student liaison 1978-79, sec. 1979-81, 91-92, coun. 1981-83, placement dir. 1989-90, v.p. pub. 1993-94, mem. coun. 1994-96), Phi Kappa Phi, Omicron Delta Epsilon, Kappa Epsilon (assoc.). Baptist. Office: The Citadel Dept of Bus Adminstrn Charleston SC 29409

SIMMONS, WARREN HATHAWAY, JR., retired retail executive; b. Indpls., May 10, 1927; s. Warren Hathaway and Jane (Jillson) S.; m. Nancy Lynn Sullivan; 1 child, Warren Hathaway III. AB in English, Princeton U., 1948. From mgr. tour ops. to supr. employees svcs. NBC, 1949-53; various positions in pers., labor rels. and store ops. Bamberger's, a divsn. of R.H. Macy and Co., Inc., 1953-63; v.p., dir. pers. and labor rels. Bamberger's divsn. R.H. Macy and Co., Inc., 1963-65, sr. v.p., dir., 1965-70, sr. v.p. pers. and indsl. rels., 1970-83, cons., 1983-89; ltd. practice in human resource cons. and project mgmt. Princeton, N.J., 1983-87. Mem. Plainfield Planning Bd. and Traffic/Parking Commn.; mem., former chmn. and life gov. Muhlenberg Regional Med. Ctr.; life trustee Muhlenberg Found.; trustee, former chmn. Huntington Found.; mem., former chmn. bd. Nat. Captioning Inst., Vienna, Va.; trustee Rider U., Lawrenceville, N.J., Wardlaw/Hartridge Sch., Plainfield, Princeton/Blairstown Ctr., Prospect Found., Princeton; past trustee McCarter Theatre Co., Princeton, 1981-88, N.J. Symphony Orch., United Way of Essex and Union County, Mental Health Assn. Essex County, Robert Treat coun. Boys Scouts Am.; trustee, past pres. Friends of Pub. Broadcasting in N.H.; commr. Pub. Broadcasting Authority in N.J; trustee David Larence Found. for Mental Health, Naples. With USN, 1945-46. Mem. Am. Mgmt. Assn. (human resources coun.), U.S. C. of C., (bus. adv. com. on white collar crime), Pub. Employees Rels. Commn. Naples, Fla. Home: 3 Sabre Cay Naples FL 33940

SIMMS, ALBERT EGERTON, minister, retirement communities consultant; b. Raleigh, N.C., Jan. 24, 1918; s. Robert Nirwana and Virginia Adelaide (Egerton) S.; m. Helen Frances Canaday, Jan. 1, 1941; children: Albert Egerton Jr., Mary Helen, David Ernest. BA, Wake Forest U., 1938; postgrad., So. Bapt. Theol. Sem., Louisville, 1939-40, Va. Poly. Inst. & State U., 1976. Lic. nursing home adminstr. Pastor Wendell Bapt. Ch., Wendell, N.C., 1937-39; pastor Bear Swamp Bapt. Ch., Littleton, N.C., 1941-46, Littleton Bapt. Ch., 1943-46, Calvary Bapt. Ch., Newport News, Va., 1946-60, Rivermont Ave Bapt. Ch., Lynchburg, Va., 1960-74; adminstr. Lakewood Manor Retirement Community, Richmond, Va., 1974-83; interim adminstr. Springmoor Retirement Community, Raleigh, 1985; ind. cons. to retirement communities Va., N.C., 1982—. Contbr. articles in Religious Herald, Christian Herald. Bd. dirs. So. Bapt. Home Mission, Atlanta, 1984-92; vice chair customer adv. coun. U.S. Postal Svc., Richmond, 1989—; vol. rsch. asst. Bapt. Hist. Soc., Richmond, 1993—; campaign solicitor United Way, Newport News, Lynchburg and Richmond. Mem. Va. Assn. Non-Profit Homes for Aging (sec. 1979-81, bd. dirs. 1976-81, hon. life mem.), Richmond Bapt. Assn. (exec. com. 1986-89), Exec. Club Newport News, Rotary, Kiwanis. Home and Office: Apt C-211 1900 Lauderdale Dr Richmond VA 23233-3917

SIMMS, ALICE JANE, secondary school educator; b. Wilson, N.C., Mar. 3, 1951; d. William Wiley and Alice Jane (Greene) S. BA, Randolph-Macon Woman's Coll., 1973; MA, U. Colo., 1978. Tchr. math. Amherst (Va.) County High Sch., 1973-76, Linkhorne Mid. Sch., Lynchburg, Va., 1979-83, E.C. Glass High Sch., Lynchburg, 1983-88; instr. math. Cen. Va. Govs. Sch., Lynchburg, 1988—. Mem. Nat. Coun. Tchrs. Math., Nat. Consortium of Specialized Secondary Schs. of Math., Sci. and Tech., Delta Kappa Gamma. Home: RR 4 Box 182C Lynchburg VA 24503-9723 Office: Cen Va Govs Sch Sci & Tech 3020 Wards Ferry Rd Lynchburg VA 24502-2451

SIMMS, FRANCES BELL, elementary education educator; b. Salisbury, N.C., July 29, 1936; d. William Taft and Anne Elmira (Sink) Bell; m. Howard Homer Simms, June 24, 1966 (dec. Oct. 1993); 1 child, Shannon Lara. AB in English, U. N.C., 1958; MEd, U. Fla., 1962; postgrad., Boston U., 1963—, U. Va.; Queen's Coll., Cambridge, U.K. Playroom attendant dept. neurology Children's Hosp., Boston, 1958-60; reading clinician Mills Ctr., Inc., Ft. Lauderdale, Fla., 1960-61; reading/lang. arts tchr. Arlington (Va.) Pub. Schs., 1962—; adv. bd. mem. ad hoc com. Edn. Tech., Arlington, 1965-67; reading instr. Va. Poly. Inst. and State U., Arlington, 1974; prodr., dir. Barcroft Newsbag-CATV, Arlington, 1982—; chair self-study Elem. Sch., Arlington, 1987, 93; adv. bd. Reading is Fundamental of No. Va., Arlington, 1988—. Lay leader, choir mem. Cherrydale Meth. Ch., Arlington, 1976—; laborer Christmas in April, Arlington, 1990—; tutor, vol. instr. Henderson Hall Marine Corps, Arlington, 1990—; organizer, instr. Better Beginnings, Arlington, 1994—, The Reading Connection, P.R., 1994—. Recipient Literacy award, Margaret McNamara award Reading is Fundamental of No. Va., 1994-95. Mem. Va. State Reading Assn. (mem. conf. coms.), Arlington Edn. Assn. (contbg. editor newsletter 1967-69), Greater Washington Reading Coun. (com. chairperson 1962—, Tchr. of Yr. 1995-96), Delta Kappa Gamma (Alpha Omicron former news writer, v.p., program chairperson, news editor). Home: 6110 23rd St N Arlington VA 22205-3414

SIMMS, JACK, journalism educator; b. Corvallis, Oreg., Nov. 22, 1926; s. Bennett T. and Lillian Elizabeth (LaLonde) S.; m. Lassie Jo Rounds; children: John M., Jane Simms Love. BA, Auburn U., 1949; M in Journalism, La. State U., 1951. Newsman, editor AP, Atlanta, 1951-58; corr. in charge AP, Tampa, Fla., 1958-61; chief of bur. AP, Louisville, 1961-65; bur. chief AP, Boston, 1965-71; dep. gen. sports editor AP, N.Y.C., 1971-74; prof., head dept. Journalism Auburn (Ala.) U., 1974-92, emeritus prof. journalism, 1992—; Pres., bd. mem. Auburn-Opelika Touchdown Club, 1981, 78-80, Auburn Cotillion Club, 1984-85, v.p. 1983-84; chmn. Selection Com., Sigma Delta Chi Soc. Profl. Journalists, 1963; v.p. Ky. chpt.; treas. Boston Cmty. Media Com. of race Rels., 1966-70; elector New England Journalism Hall of Fame, 1966-71; exec. com. Ala. Sportswriter Hall of Fame; v.p., program chmn. Auburn U. faculty Club, 1977-79, bd. mem. 1990-94. Author: Ted Williams, 1972, (with Hanchey E. Logue Jr.) Auburn, A Pictorial History of the Loveliest Village, 1981, rev. edit., 1996. Cpl. USMC, 1944-46. Recipient Outstanding Alumni award Omicron Delta Kappa, 1967, Student Govt. Assn. award Tchr. of Yr., Coll. Liberal Arts, Auburn U., 1989, Student Govt. Assn. award Tchr. of Yr., School Arts and Scis., Auburn U., 1981. Home: 208 Willow Creek Rd Auburn AL 36830-4118 Office: Auburn U Journalism Dept 312 Tichnor Hall Auburn AL 36849

SIMMS, LOIS AVERETTA, retired secondary education educator, musician; b. Charleston, S.C., May 27, 1919; d. Jasper Simeon and Anna Inez (Ferguson) S. BA, Johnson C. Smith U., 1941; MA, Howard U., 1954. Cert. English and social studies educator, S.C. Directive tchr. Avery Normal Inst., Charleston, 1941-42; tchr. English and French Laing H.S., Mt. Pleasant, S.C., 1942-44; tchr. English and math. Henry P. Archer Sch., Charleston, 1944-45; tchr. social studies and English Burke H.S., Charleston, 1945-52; tchr. English Avery H.S., Charleston, 1952-54, Burke H.S., Charleston, 1954-73; tchr. English and history Charleston H.S., 1973-76; ret., 1976; co-adviser Dramatic Club, Burke H.S., 1945-46, trainer section of chorus, 1945-47, chief advisor 1961 Bulldog Yearbook, 1960-61; advisor Crochet Club, Avery H.S., 1952-54, Charleston H.S., 1973-76. Author: Growing Up Presbyterian: Life in Presbyterian Colleges and Churches, 1991, Profiles of African American Females in Low Country of South Carolina, 1992, A Chalk and Chalkboard Career in Carolina, 1995, A History of Zion, Olivet, and Zion-Olivet Churches 1850-1985, 1989; editor The Scroll newsletter, 1984-94. Sec. exec. bd. YWCA of Greater Charleston, 1950s; mem. YWCA, S.C. Hist. Soc., S.C. ETV Endowment. Recipient plaque Zion-Olivet Presbyn. Ch., 1987, C.L. Campbell award Presbyn. Ch., 1988, plaque Staff of The Scroll, 1990. Mem. NAACP, Charleston County Ret. Educators Assn. Unit 2, Pres.'s Club (plaque 1991), Avery Inst. Afro-Am. History and Culture (editor The Bull. 1990-96, Cert.), S.C. Soc. Home: 28 Jasper St Charleston SC 29403

SIMMS, ROBERT D., state supreme court justice; b. Tulsa, Feb. 6, 1926; s. Matthew Scott and Bessie L. (Moore) S.; m. Patricia C., Feb. 16, 1950; 1 son, Robert D. Student, Milligan Coll., Phillips U.; LLB, U. Tulsa. Bar: Okla. 1950. Pvt. practice law Sand Springs, Okla., from 1950; asst. county atty. Tulsa County, 1953-54; chief prosecutor County Atty.'s Office, 1955-58, county atty., 1958-62; judge Okla. Dist. Ct., Dist. 14, 1962-71, Okla. Ct. Criminal Appeals, 1971-72; justice Okla. Supreme Ct., 1972—; mem. Okla. Crime Commn. Mem. Gov.'s Spl. Com. on Drug Abuse, 1970; sponsor and coach Pee-Wee Baseball. Served with USN, 1943-46. Mem. Tulsa County Bar Assn., Okla. Bar Assn. (chmn. dist. atty. sect. 1959). Office: Okla Supreme Ct State Capital Bldg Rm 1 Oklahoma City OK 73105*

SIMON, CHARLES G., chemist; b. West Palm Beach, Fla., Aug. 18, 1954; m. Diane Cosner; children: Mark David, Mathew Albert. BS in Chemistry,

Jacksonville U., 1976; MS in Environ./Analytical Chemistry, U. S.C., 1979; PhD in Exptl. Phys. Chemistry, U. Fla., 1988. Cert. Radon Measurement Specialist HRS, Fla. Analytical chemsit, indsl. hygienist SCM/PCR Inc., Gainesville, Fla., 1979-80; analytical, environ. rsch. chemist Nat. Coun. Paper Industry for Air and Steam Improvement Inc., Gainesville, 1980-85; grad. rsch. asst. U. Fla., Gainesville, 1986-88; rsch. scientist McDonnell Ctr. Space Scis. Washington U., St. Louis, 1989-91; rsch. scientist, mgr. tech. programs Inst. Space Sci. and Tech., Inc., Gainesville, 1991-93; corp. mgr. Air Consulting and Engring., Inc., Gainesville, 1993—; v.p. Precision Analytical Labs., Inc., Gainesville; chmn. LDEF meteoroid and debris spl. investigation group Microcrator Com.; dir. IMPACT Consortium; mem. space environment and effects tech. working group NASA. Contbr. articles to profl. jours. Mem. AIAA, Am. Chem. Soc., Am. Vacuum Soc., Am. Phys. Soc., Hypervelocity Impact Soc. Office: Air Consulting & Engring 2106 NW 67th Pl Gainesville FL 32653-1667

SIMON, H(UEY) PAUL, lawyer; b. Lafayette, La., Oct. 19, 1923; s. Jules and Ida (Rogere) S.; m. Carolyn Perkins, Aug. 6, 1949; 1 child, John Clark. B.S., U. Southwestern La., 1943; J.D., Tulane U., 1947. Bar: La. 1947; CPA, La. 1947. Pvt. practice New Orleans, 1947—; asst. prof. advanced acctg. and taxation U. Southwestern La., 1944-45; staff acct. Haskins & Sells (now Deloitte & Touche), New Orleans, 1945-53, prin., 1953-57; ptnr. law firm Deutsch, Kerrigan & Stiles, 1957-79; sr. founding ptnr. law firm Simon, Peragine, Smith & Redfearn, 1979—; mem. bd. adv. editors Tulane Law Rev., 1992—; mem. New Orleans Bd. Trade. Author: Community Property and Liability for Funeral Expenses of Deceased Spouse, 1946, Income Tax Deductibility of Attorney's Fees in Action in Boundary, 1946, Fair Labor Standards Act and Employee's Waiver of Liquidated Damages, 1946, Louisiana Income Tax Law, 1956, Changes Effected by the Louisiana Trust Code, 1965, Gifts to Minors and the Parent's Obligation of Support, 1968; co-author: Deductions—Business or Hobby, 1975, Role of Attorney in IRS Tax Return Examination, 1978; assoc. editor: The Louisiana CPA, 1956-60; mem. bd. editors Tulane Law Rev., 1945-46, adv. bd. editors, 1992—; estates, gifts and trusts editor The Tax Times, 1986-87. Bd. dirs., mem. fin. com. World Trade Ctr., 1985-86; mem. New Orleans Met. Crime Commn., Coun. for a Better La., New Orleans Met. Area Com., Bur. Govtl. Rsch., Pub. Affairs Rsch. Coun.; co-chmn. NYU Tax Conf., New Orleans, 1976; mem. dean's coun. Tulane U. Law Sch. Fellow Am. Coll. Tax Counsel; mem. ABA (com. ct. procedure tax sect. 1958—), AICPA, La. Bar Assn. (com. on legis. and adminstrv. practice 1966-70), New Orleans Bar Assn., Internat. Bar Assn. (com. on securities issues and trading 1970-88), Am. Judicature Soc., Soc. La. CPAs, New Orleans Assn. Notaries, Tulane U. Alumni Assn., New Orleans C. of C. (coun. 1952-66), Tulane Tax Inst. (program com. 1960—), Internat. House (bd. dirs. 1976-79, 82-85), Internat. Platform Assn., City Energy Club, Press Club, New Orleans Country Club, Phi Delta Phi (past pres. New Orleans chpt.), Sigma Pi Alpha. Roman Catholic. Home: 6075 Canal Blvd New Orleans LA 70124-2936 Office: 30th Fl Energy Ctr New Orleans LA 70163

SIMON, THEODORE RONALD, physician, medical educator; b. Hartford, Conn., Feb. 2, 1949; s. Theologos Lingos and Lillian (Faix) S.; m. Marcia Anyzeski, Apr. 5, 1974; children: Jacob T., Theodore H., Mark G. BA cum laude, Trinity Coll., Hartford, 1970; MD, Yale U., 1975. Diplomate Am. Bd. Nuclear Medicine, Diplomate Nat. Bd. Med. Examiners; lic. Calif., Tex. Intern in surgery Strong Meml. Hosp., Rochester, N.Y., 1975-76; resident in diagnostic radiology U. Calif., San Francisco, 1976-78; resident in nuclear medicine Yale-New Haven Hosp., Conn., 1978-80, chief resident, 1979-80; asst. prof. nuclear medicine U. Tex. Southwestern Med. Ctr., Dallas, 1980-88, assoc. prof., 1990—; cons. nuclear medicine St. Paul's Hosp., Dallas, 1981-88; cons. internal medicine Presbyn. Hosp., Dallas, 1981-88, 90, Med. City Hosp., Dallas, 1989—; cons. nuclear medicine VA Med. Ctr., Dallas, 1981-82, chief nuclear medicine svc., 1982-88; nat. dep. dir. nuclear medicine VA, 1985-88; dep. chief nuclear medicine NIH, Bethesda, Md., 1988-90; mem. del. Taiwan Atomic Energy, U.S. State Dept., 1990. Mem. editorial bd. Jour. History of Med. and Allied Scis., 1974-75; contbr. articles to Internat. Jour. Radiol. Applications, Jour. Nuclear Medicine, Am. Jour. Cardiology, Clin. Nuclear Medicine, Circulation, Yale Jour. Biol. Medicine, Radiology, Surg. Radiology, and others. Pres. Christ Lutheran Ch., University Park, Tex. Mem. Soc. Nuclear Medicine (treas. correlative imaging coun. 1988-90, mem. exec. com 1988—). Home and Office: 4429 Southern Ave Dallas TX 75205-2622

SIMONAITIS, RICHARD AMBROSE, chemist; b. Chgo., Dec. 7, 1930; s. George Peter and Sofija Constance (Woijkiewicz) S.; m. Vera Sandra Hall, Sept. 17, 1960; children: Steven, Rachel, Laura. Student Loyola U., Chgo., 1948-50; BS, U. Ill., 1952; postgrad. Ohio State U., 1952-55, MS, 1957, PhD, 1962. Chemist, Aerojet-Gen. Corp., Nimbus, Calif., 1962-64; rsch. chemist, Gulf Oil Corp., Merriam, Kans., 1964-66; analytical chemist, Gen. Electric Co., Liverpool, N.Y., 1966-69; rsch. chemist, Agrl. Rsch. Svc., U.S. Dept. Agr., Savannah, Ga., 1970—; abstractor, Chem. Abstracts, 1965-85. Bd. dirs. Savannah coun. Girl Scouts U.S.A., 1978-84, exec. com., 1980-84, neighborhood chmn., Oleander Neighborhood, 1980-89; booth chmn., Night in Old Savannah Ethnic Festival, 1977-91; usher, Nativity of Our Lord Ch., 1974—, capt. ushers, 1977—, sec., Men's Club, 1976, Sunday sch. tchr., 1977-81; bd. dirs., Savannah Young People's Theater, 1980-85, treas., 1983-85; bd. dirs., Savannah Theatre Co., 1990-94, treas., 1991-95, house mgr., 1986—. With U.S. Army, 1955-56. Mem. Am. Chem. Soc. (exec. com. 1979-83, disting. contbn. plaque, 1978, cert. recognition Chem. Abstract Service 1975, sec., treas., 1979, chmn. elect., 1980, chmn., 1981, counselor, 1981), Entomol. Soc. Am., Rsch. Soc. Am., Ga. Entomol. Soc., Assn. Ofcl. Analytical Chemists, ASTM, Chem. Analysts Central N.Y., Wilmington Island Pleasure and Improvement Assn. (treas. 1975—), Tybee Light Power Squadron, KC, Sigma Xi, Phi Lambda Upsilon. Roman Catholic. Contbr. numerous articles to sci. jours. Office: USDA Agrl Rsch Svc PO Box 22909 3401 Edwin Ave Savannah GA 31405-1607

SIMONDS, MARIE CELESTE, architect; b. Miami, Fla., Mar. 30, 1947; d. Hinton Joseph and Frances Olivia (Burnett) Baker; m. Albert Rhett Simonds, Jr., Oct. 9, 1974; children: Caroline Lamar, Frances Rhett. BA, U. Pa., 1968; BArch, U. Md., 1973. Registered architect, Va. Architect Harry Weese & Assocs., Washington, 1973-75; pvt. practice Alexandria, Va., 1976—. Com. chmn. Jr. Friends Alexandria YWCA, 1974-78; mem. Jr. League Washington, 1978—. NSF grantee, 1972; recipient Design award No. Va. Chpt. AIA, 1990. Mem. AIA (scholar 1971, Design award No. Va. 1990), Va. Soc. AIA, West River Sailing Club (Galesville, Md.), Belle Haven Country Club (Alexandria). Episcopalian. Home and Office: 624 S Lee St Alexandria VA 22314-3820

SIMONS, CHARLES EARL, JR., federal judge; b. Johnston, S.C., Aug. 17, 1916; s. Charles Earl Sr. and Frances (Rhoden) S.; m. Jean Knapp, Oct. 18, 1941 (dec. 1991); children: Charles Earl III, Paul Knapp, Richard Brewster, Jean Brewster Smith; m. Gail Shaw, Feb. 27, 1993. AB, U. S.C., 1937, LLB cum laude, 1939. Bar: S.C. 1939. Ptnr. Lybrand & Simons, Aiken, S.C., 1939-50, Thurmond, Lybrand and Simons, Aiken, 1950-54, Lybrand, Simons & Rich, Aiken, 1950-54, 1954-64; mem. S.C. Ho. of Reps., 1942, 47-48, 61-64; mem. ways and means com., 1947-48, 61-64; judge U.S. Dist. Ct. S.C., Aiken, 1964—, chief judge, 1980-86; sr. status U.S. Dist. Ct., 1987—; mem. S.C. Constl. Revision Com., 1948, Bd. Discipline and Grievance, S.C. Bar, 1958-61, Ethics Adv. Panel, 1981-87; jud. rep. 4th cir. Jud. Conf. U.S., 1973-79; chmn. subcom. on fed. jurisdiction of Com. on Ct. Adminstrn., 1986-87. Mem. Chief Met. Dist. Judges Conf., 1980-89, chmn., 1986-89; bd. dirs. S.C. Athletic Hall of Fame; mem. Jud. Conf. Commn. on Jud. Br., 1988-92. With USN, World War II. Recipient Algernon Sidney Sullivan award, 1937, 64. Mem ABA, S.C. Bar Assn. (com. mem.), Am. Law Inst., Am. Legion, U. S.C. Alumni Assn. (past pres. 1964), S.C. Golf Assn., Aiken Bus. Men's Club (past pres.), Palmetto Golf Club (pres. 1994—), Rotary. Baptist. Home: PO Box 2185 Aiken SC 29802-2185 Office: US Dist Ct SC Charles E Simons Jr Fed Courthouse PO Box 2185 Aiken SC 29802-2185

SIMONS, DONA, artist; b. Bryn Athyn, Pa., Aug. 10, 1953; d. Keneth Alden and Reta Isabel (Evens) S.; m. John Louis Vigo, May 17, 1986. Student, Phila. Coll. Art, 1974, Moore Coll. Art, 1976, Pa. Acad. Fine Arts, 1977-79. One-woman shows include Frank Tanzer Gallery, Boston, 1975, The Curaçao Mus., Netherlands Antilles, 1991, The Curaçao Seaquarium, Netherlands Antilles, 1991, Sylvia Schmidt Gallery, New Orleans, 1992; exhibited in group shows at Berg Gallery, Jenkintown, Pa., 1973, United Artisans Gallery, Chalfont, Pa., 1974, 75, Arthur Roger Gallery, New Orleans, La., 1980, Arts Coun. New Orleans C. of C., 1980, Acad. Gallery, New Orleans Acad. Fine Arts, La., 1982, Am. Italian Renaissance Found., New Orleans, 1985, Found. Prince Pierre de Monaco, Monaco, 1985, The Rittenhouse Galleries, Phila., 1993, 94, Sylvia Schmidt Gallery, New Orleans, 1993, 94, 95, 96; commn. portrait of Manuel Piar, Curaçao, Netherlands Antilles, 1990. Office: Sylvia Schmidt Gallery 400 Julia St # A New Orleans LA 70130-3606

SIMONS, ELWYN LAVERNE, physical anthropologist, primatologist, paleontologist, educator; b. Lawrence, Kans., July 14, 1930; s. Verne Franklin and Verna Irene (Cuddeback) S.; m. Friderun Annursel Ankel, Dec. 2, 1972; children: Cornelia Verna Mathilde, Verne Franklin Herbert; 1 child by previous marriage: David Brenton. B.S. in Biology, Rice U., 1953; M.A., Princeton U., 1955, Ph.D. in Paleobiology, 1956; D.Phil., Oxford (Eng.) U., 1959; M.A. (hon.), Yale U., 1967; DSc, Oxford U., 1995. Demonstrator, exhibitor Oxford U., 1956-58; lectr. geology Princeton (N.J.) U., 1958-59; asst. prof. zoology U. Pa., Phila., 1959-61; vis. assoc. prof. geology, curator vertebrate paleontology Yale U., New Haven, Conn., 1960-61, head divsn. vert. paleontology, 1961-77, prof. paleontology, 1967; prof. geology, curator charge div. vertebrate paleontology Peabody Mus., 1965-77; prof. biol. anthropology, anatomy Duke U., Durham, N.C., 1977-82, James B. Duke prof., 1982—, prof. zoology, dir. Duke Primate Center, 1977-91, sci. dir., 1991—; dir. Paleontol. Expdns. Egypt, 1961-68, 77-96, No. India, 1968-69; rsch. expdns. for fossil mammals, Wyo., 1960-96, Iran, 1970, Spain, 1971, Madagascar, 1986, 87-94; Barbour-Schramm Meml. lectr. U. Nebr., 1974; David French lectr. Claremont Colls., 1974; traveling lectr. French Bur. Fgn. Affairs, 1976; bd. dirs. Ctr. Tropical Conservation, N.C., Malagasy Fauna Group. Author: Primate Evolution: An Introduction To Man's Place In Nature, 1972; co-editor: Macmillan Series in Physical Anthropology; A Simons Family History in England and America, 1975; contbr. numerous articles to profl. publs. Recipient Annadale Meml. medal Asiatic Soc. Bengal, 1973, Sr. U.S. Scientist award Alexander von Humboldt Found., Fed. Republic Germany, 1975; named hon. citizen Fayum province of Egypt., 1981; Gen. George Marshall scholar Oxford U., 1956-59; Richard C. Hunt Meml. fellow Wenner-Gren Found., 1965. Mem. AAAS, Am. Philos. Soc., Nat. Acad. Scis., Soc. Vertebrate Paleontology, Am. Soc. Naturalists, Inst. Human Paleontology, Am. Assn. Zool. Parks and Aquariums (primate specialist group, advisor prosimian taxon group), Assn. Phys. Anthropology, Geol. Soc. Am., Soc. Study Human Biology, Soc. Study Evolution, Am. Soc. Zoologists, Internat. Assn. Human Biologists, Madagascar Fauna Group (bd. dirs.), Sigma Xi. Democrat. Office: Duke Primate Ctr 3705 Erwin Rd Durham NC 27705-5015

SIMONS-OPARAH, TANYA, library administrator; b. Jamaica, N.Y., Jan. 9, 1947; d. Herbert John and Olga May Louise (Giscome) Simons; m. Victor A. Oparah, Dec. 25, 1981; children: Chiaka, Ola, David, Teddy, Chineyre. AAS, Bronx C.C., 1971; BS, Hunter Coll., 1973, MS, 1975. Adminstrv. libr. Broward County Libr., Ft. Lauderdale, Fla., 1977-83, staff devel. officer, 1983-89, asst. dir. for outreach svcs., 1989—; mem. adv. bd. human devel. resource Fla. Internat. U. Ctr. for Mgmt., Miami, 1986; mem. adv. bd. Broward Ctr. for the Performing Arts, Ft. Lauderdale, 1994-96. Pres., CEO Sistrunk Hist. Festival, Broward County, 1988-95; v.p. Friends of Children, Lauderdale Lakes, Fla., 1995-96; mem. Sisterhood of African Women, Lauderhill, Fla., 1993-96. Recipient Achievement award Nat. Assn. Counties, 1989, 96, Unsung Hero award South Fla. Mag., 1993, Leadership awrd Phi Delta Kappa, 1993, Role Model award UN Chpt., Broward County, 1994. Office: Broward County Libr 100 S Andrews Ave Fort Lauderdale FL 33301

SIMONTON, GAIL MAUREEN, lawyer; b. Ripley, Tenn., July 5, 1951; d. William Christopher and Elizabeth Jane (Butler) S. Student Centre Coll., Danville, Ky., 1969-71, Alliance Francaise, 1971, Institut Americain U., Avignon, France, 1971-72; BA, U. Tenn.-Martin, 1975; JD, U. Tenn.-Knoxville, 1977. Bar: Tenn. 1978. Law clk. to judge Tenn. Ct. Criminal Appeals, Covington, 1977-79; assoc. firm Thomason, Crawford & Hendrix, Memphis, 1979-82; asst. sec., staff atty. Guardsmark, Inc., Memphis, 1982-85; exec. dir., gen. counsel Nat. Assn. Security Cos., Inc., Memphis, 1985—. Mem. ABA, Am. Soc. Indsl. Security, Am. Soc. Assn. Execs., Security Cos. Organized Legis. Action (sec. 1989-96), Nat. Assn. Security and Investigative Regulators (assoc. dir.-at-large 1996—). Office: Nat Assn Security Cos Inc 2670 Union Ave Ste 710 Memphis TN 38112-4428

SIMPSON, ALLAN BOYD, real estate company executive; b. Lakeland, Fla., Nov. 24, 1948; s. Alfred Forsythe and Ruth Jeanette (Coker) S.; l child, Lauren Leigh. B in Indsl. Ingring., Ga. Inst. Tech., 1970; MBA, U. Pa., 1972. Cert. rev. appraiser; lic. realtor, Ga. Dir. mortgage banking Ackerman & Co., Atlanta, 1972-73; v.p. B.F. Saul & Co., Atlanta, 1973-79; pres. L.J. Hooker, Atlanta, 1979-88; also bd. dirs. Hooker/Barnes, Atlanta; bd. dirs. Hooker Holdings (USA), Inc., Century Ins. Co., Hooker Internat. Devels. Ltd., Hooker Internat. Fin. BV, Charter Credit Corp. Ltd., Simpson Spring, Inc., Strategic Land, Inc., Dunwoody Retail, Inc.; bd. dirs., treas. Midtown Bus. Assn., 1979-88; chmn., CEO The Simpson Orgn., Inc., Coker Capital Corp., 1989—. Bd. dirs. YES Atlanta, 1991—, Atlanta Coll. Art, Theatrical Outfit. Mem. Am. Inst. Indsl. Engrs., MBA Execs. Assn., Bldg. Owners and Mgrs. Assn., Nat. Assn. Realtors, U.S. C. of C., Atlanta C. of C., Internat. Coun. of Shopping Ctrs., Urban Land Inst., Nat. Assn. of Office and Indsl. Pks., Cherokee Town and Country Club, Big Canoe Club, Amelia Island Club. Democrat. Methodist. Home: 1847 Homestead Ave NE Atlanta GA 30306-3163 Office: 600 W Peachtree St NW Atlanta GA 30308

SIMPSON, BERRY DON, petroleum engineer; b. Big Spring, Tex., June 23, 1956; s. Deane and Lenelle (Haynes) S.; m. Cynthia Deanna Richardson, July 28, 1979; children: Byron, Katherine. AAS, N.Mex. Jr. Coll., Hobbs, 1978; BS in Petroleum Engring., U. Okla., 1979. Registered profl. engr., Tex., 1986. Engr. Amerada Hess Corp., Brownfield, Tex., 1979-82; dist. engr. Amerada Hess Corp., Midland, Tex., 1982-94; ind. petroleum engr. Midland, 1994—. Mem. Midland Parks and Recreation Commn., 1993-95, Midland City Coun. Dist. 4, 1995—. Mem. Soc. Petroleum Engrs., Daybreak Rotary Club (bd. dirs. 1990-92, pres. 1992-93, newsletter editor 1991-94, Permian Basin Road Runners Club (pres. 1988-91, editor 1988-94). Republican. Baptist. Home: 3003 Whittle Way Midland TX 79707-5273 Office: PO Box 2744 Midland TX 79702-2744

SIMPSON, BILL KEMPTON, JR., retail executive; b. Hardwick, Vt., June 23, 1954; s. Willard K. and Winnifred Ada (Kennedy) S.; m. Debra Ann Schmader, Aug. 30, 1975; children: Andrew Kyle, Steven Michael, Matthew Alan. BS, Auburn U., 1976. Mgr. trainee Bealls Dept. Stores, Inc., various location, Fla., 1976-77, asst. mgr. stores, 1978-79; warehouse mgr. Bealls Dept. Stores, Inc., 1979-81; store mgr. Bealls Dept. Stores, Inc., Bradenton, 1981-83, dist. mgr., 1983-85, dir. traffic and distbn. ctr. ops., 1985-93, divisional v.p. traffic and distbn., 1993—. Home: PO Box 14804 Bradenton FL 34280-4804 Office: Bealls Inc PO Box N Bradenton FL 34206

SIMPSON, CHARLES R., III, judge; b. Cleve., July 8, 1945; s. Charles Ralph and Anne Marie (Markel) S.; married; 3 children. BA, U. Louisville, 1967, JD, 1970. Bar: Ky. 1970, U.S. Dist. Ct. (we. dist.) Ky. 1971, U.S. Cir. Ct. (6th cir.) 1985. With Rubin, Trautwein & Mays, Louisville, 1971-75, Levin, Yussman & Simpson, Louisville, 1975-77; judge U.S. Dist. Ct. (we. dist.) Ky., Louisville, 1986—; pvt. practice Louisville, 1977-86; part-time staff counsel Jefferson County Judge/Exec., 1978-84; adminstr. Jefferson County Alcoholic Beverage Control, 1983-84; city clk. City of Rolling Fields, 1985-86. Roman Catholic. Office: We Dist Ct Ky 247 US Courthouse 601 W Broadway Louisville KY 40202-2238*

SIMPSON, CHARLES REAGAN, retired judge; b. Danville, Ill., June 16, 1921; s. Frank and Mamie (Moreland) S.; m. Ruth V. Thomason, June 5, 1948. B.A. with highest honors, U. Ill., 1944, J.D. with high honors, 1945; LL.M., Harvard U., 1950. Bar: Ill. 1945. Practiced in Champaign, Ill., 1946-49; atty. OPS, 1951-52; with legislation and regulations div. Office Chief Counsel, IRS, 1952-65, dir. office, 1964-65; judge U.S. Tax Ct., 1965-88, ret., 1988; Teaching fellow Harvard Law Sch., 1950-51. Chmn. Champaign County chpt. Nat. Found. Infantile Paralysis, 1947-49; Mem. Ill. Gen. Assembly from 24th Dist., 1947-50. Recipient Justice Tom C. Clark award Fed. Bar Assn., 1964. Mem. ABA, Am. Law Inst., Am. Judicature Soc., Phi Beta Kappa, Order of Coif, Phi Kappa Phi. Office: US Tax Ct 400 2nd St NW Washington DC 20217-0001

SIMPSON, DANIEL REID, lawyer; b. Glen Alpine, N.C., Feb. 20, 1927; s. James R. and Margaret Ethel (Newton) S.; m. Mary Alice Leonard, Feb. 25, 1930; children: Mary Simpson Beyer, Ethel B. Simpson Todd, James R. II. BS, Wake Forest U., 1949, LLB, 1951. Bar: N.C. 1951, U.S. Dist. Ct. (we. dist.) N.C. 1951, U.S. Ct. Appeals (4th and 5th cirs.) 1980. Dir. First Union Nat. Bank, Morganton, N.C. Mem. N.C. Ho. of Reps., 1959-65; now mem. N.C. Senate, mem. N.C. Joint Legis. Edn. Oversight Com.; mem. oversight com. N.C. Dept. of Corrections; hon. mem. bd. dirs. N.C. Restaurant Assns.; del. Rep. Nat. Conv., 1968, 76, mem. N.C. Rep. Exec. Com. Served with AUS, 1943-45, PTO. Mem. N.C. Bar Assn., Burke County Bar Assn. Baptist. Club: Masons. Home: Box 2358 Nebo NC 28761 Office: Simpson Aycock PA 204 E Mcdowell St Morganton NC 28655-3545 also: PO Box 1329 Morganton NC 28680-1329

SIMPSON, DENNIS ARDEN, lighting contracting company executive; b. Monroe, N.C., July 10, 1944; s. Arden L. and Lola M. Simpson; children from previous marriage: Anthony Dennis, Legare Catherine; m. Peggy Lee Kay, Oct. 22, 1983; 1 child, Andrew Dennis. AB in Econs., U. N.C., 1967. Trainee Jordan Marsh, Miami, Fla., 1966-67; with planning dept. Burlington Industries, Reidsville, N.C., 1967-69; with scheduling dept. Burlington Industries, N.Y.C., 1969-71; ops. mgr. Unifi/Summerfield, Rocky Mt., N.C., 1971-75; pres., CEO East Industries, Rocky Mt., 1974-88, Dennis A. Simpson, Inc., Rocky Mt., 1988—. Mem. Illuminating Engring. Soc., Assn. Energy Engrs., Benvenue Country Club. Republican. Baptist. Office: 1114 Instrument Dr PO Box 8526 Rocky Mount NC 27804

SIMPSON, ELIZABETH ANN, reading and language arts educator; b. Collins, Miss., Oct. 20, 1940; d. Clyde C. and Edna L. (Lewis) McRaney; m. Arthur Thomas Simpson, Dec. 15, 1962; children: Lisa Bukovnik, Art, Cindy Simpson-Scharff, Sheri Lucas. BS, U. So. Miss., 1978, MEd, 1982. Tchr. Biloxi (Miss.) Pub. Schs., 1978—; conv. presenter Miss. Coun. Tchrs. of English, Jackson, 1992. Leader Girl Scouts Am., San Antonio, 1970, Biloxi, 1975; Sunday sch. tchr. Episcopal Ch. of the Redeemer, Biloxi, 1978. Fellow South Miss. Writing Project, 1991, 92. Mem. Internat. Reading Assn., Nat. Coun. Tchrs. of English, Nat. Coun. Tchrs. of Math., Miss. Reading Assn. (sec. Gulf Coast chpt. 1986), Phi Delta Kappa, Phi Kappa Phi. Home: 347 Saint Mary Blvd Biloxi MS 39531-3419 Office: Beauvoir Elem Sch 2003 Lawrence St Biloxi MS 39531-4106

SIMPSON, H. RICHARD (DICK SIMPSON), retailer; b. Akron, Ohio, Oct. 10, 1930; s. Bert M. and Violet K. (Mathias) S.; m. Joan Rose Marshall, Mar. 22, 1970; children: Carla Sue, Barry Nelson, Richard Drew, Catherine, Irene Elizabeth, Student, U. Akron, 1949-50; BS, U. Md., 1955. Mgr. Tex. Gen. Motors Corp., Detroit, 1959-62; pres. Friendly Pontiac, Friendly Toyota, Derrick Chrysler, Simpson Oil Corp., Corp. S., Dick Tiger Homes, Austin, 1962-85. Served to lt. col. USAF, 1953-75; Korea. Decorated D.F.C., Air Medal. Mem. Soc. Automotive Engrs., Res. Officers Assn. Methodist. Clubs: Horseshoe Bay Yacht, Horseshoe Bay Country. Lodges: Rotary, Masons. Office: PO Box 8186 Marble Falls TX 78657-9206

SIMPSON, JACK BENJAMIN, medical technologist, business executive; b. Tompkinsville, Ky., Oct. 30, 1937; s. Benjamin Harrison and Verda Mae (Woods) S.; student Western Ky. U., 1954-57; grad. Norton Infirmary Sch. Med. Tech., 1958; m. Winona Clara Walden, Mar. 21, 1957; children: Janet Lazann, Richard Benjamin, Randall Walden, Angela Elizabeth. Asst. chief med. technologist Jackson County Hosp., Seymour, Ind., 1958-61; chief med. technologist, bus. mgr. Mershon Med. Labs., Indpls., 1962-66; founder, dir., officer Am. Monitor Corp., Indpls., 1966-77; founder, pres., dir. Global Data, Inc., Ft. Lauderdale, Fla., 1986—; mng. partner Astroland Enterprises, Indpls., 1968—, 106th St. Assocs., Indpls., 1969-72, Keystones Ltd., Indpls., 1970-82 Delray Rd. Assoc., Ltd., Indpls., 1970-71, Allisonville Assocs. Ltd., Indpls., 1970-82, Grandview Assocs. Ltd., 1977—, Rucker Assocs., Ltd., Indpls., 1974—; mng. ptnr. Raintree Assocs., Ltd., Indpls., 1978—, Westgate Assocs., Ltd., Indpls., 1978—; pres., dir. Topps Constrn. Co., Inc., Bradenton, Fla., 1973-91, Acrouest Corp., Asheville, N.C., 1980—; dir. Indpls. Broadcasting, Inc.; founder, bd. dirs. Bank of Bradenton, 1986-92. Mem. Am. Soc. Med. Technologists (cert.), Indpls. Soc. Med. Technologists, Ind. Soc. Med. Technologists, Am. Soc. Clin. Pathologists, Royal Soc. Health (London), Internat. Platform Assn., Am. Mus. Natural History. Republican. Baptist. Clubs: Columbia of Indpls.; Harbor Beach Surf, Fishing of Am., Marina Bay (Fort Lauderdale, Fla.). Lodge: Elks.

SIMPSON, JEROME DEAN, librarian; b. Edmond, Okla., Sept. 25, 1934; s. John Butler and Selma Teresa (Bohlken) S.; m. Kathryn Dale Powers Flobeck, Aug. 17, 1956 (div. Aug. 1970); children: Donald Richard, Jason Bateman. BA in Edn., Cen. State Coll., Edmond, 1956; MLS, U. Okla., 1963. Ref. libr. Cen. State Coll., 1963-65; circulation libr. U. N.Mex., Albuquerque, 1965-68; rsch. libr. U. Ill., Champaign/Urbana, 1968-69; southwest history libr. N.Mex. State Libr., Santa Fe, 1969-72; sr. libr. Libr. for the Blind, Oklahoma City, 1977-91. Editor: newsletter/Libr. for the Blind, Oklahoma City, 1987-91; contbr. articles to profl. jours. Bd. dirs. Common Cause, Oklahoma City, 1992-93, Okla. Homeless Network, Oklahoma City, 1993-96, Downtown Outreach Com., Oklahoma City, 1989-91; southwest regional coord. Unitarian-Universalist Svc. Com., Cambridge, Mass., 1994—. With U.S. Army, 1957-59, Korea. Fellow U. Ill., Champaign/Urbana, 1968-69; named Outstanding Mem. of Yr., 1st Unitarian Ch., Oklahoma City, 1994. Mem. Okla. Libr. Assn., N.Mex. Libr. Assn. Democratic Socialists. Home: 1606 NW 31st Apt 236 Oklahoma City OK 73118

SIMPSON, JERRY HOWARD, JR., travel company executive; b. Providence, Dec. 11, 1925; s. Jerry Howard Simpson Sr. and Malta Faye (Atkins) Kelly; m. Charlotte Ann Bauserman, June 7, 1947 (div. Feb. 1963); children: Mary Ellen Lehman Jampole, Charles Frederick; m. Jane Coral Augustine, Sept. 4, 1973. Student, Moravian Coll. for Men, 1947-48, Emory & Henry Coll., 1948-50; BA, U. N.C., 1950. Seaman Merchant Marine, 1943-44; writer, dir., producer WSJS-TV, Winston-Salem, N.C., 1962-64; journalist, editor various newspapers and mags., 1965-75; founder, pres., dir. Bike Tour France, Charlotte, N.C., 1975—. Author: Torn Land, 1970, Annals of the Orient, 1987, Cycling France, 1992, Reflections on the French Recolution, 1994, Winter in Paris, 1994, Mille Pensées Impolies Fléches de Ma Cellule, 1996; translator: The Gardens of Villandry (Robert Carvallo), 1986. Sgt. USMC, 1944-46; master sgt. U.S. Army, 1951-58. Decorated Bronze Star; recipient Franco-Am. Friendship medal City of Blois, France, 1984, Tanvier medal J. Tanvier found., 1987. Home and Office: 5523 Wedgewood Dr Charlotte NC 28210-2432

SIMPSON, JOHN AROL, retired government executive, physicist; b. Toronto, Ont., Can., Mar. 30, 1923; came to U.S., 1926; naturalized, 1938; s. Henry George and Verna Lavinia (Green) S.; m. Arlene Badel, Feb. 11, 1948; 1 child, George Badel. BS, Lehigh U., 1946, MS, 1948, PhD, 1951. Rsch. physicist Nat. Bur. Standards, Washington, 1948-62, supervisory physicist, 1962-69, dep. chief optical physics div., 1969-75, chief mechanics div., 1975-78; dir. Ctr. for Mfg. Engring. Nat. Bur. Standards, Gaithersburg, Md., 1978-91; dir. Mfg. Engring. Lab., Nat. Inst. Standards and Tech., Gaithersburg, 1991—; ret. Contbr. articles on electron optics to profl. jours. With U.S. Army, 1943-46. Recipient Silver medal Dept. Commerce, 1964, Gold medal, 1975; Allen V. Austin Measurement Sci. award, 1984; Disting. Exec. award Sr. Exec. Svc., 1985, Am. Machinist award, 1986. Fellow Am. Phys. Soc.; mem. NAE, Sigma Xi. Home: 312 Riley St Falls Church VA 22046-3310

SIMPSON, JOHN NOEL, healthcare administrator; b. Durham, N.C., Feb. 27, 1936; s. William Hays and Lucile (McNab) S.; A.B., Duke U., 1957; M.H.A., Med. Coll. Va., 1959; m. Virginia Marshall, June 27, 1959; children: John Noel, William M. Asst. adminstr. Riverside Health Sys., Newport News, Va., 1962-65, assoc. adminstr., 1965-70; assoc. adminstr. Richmond (Va.) Meml. Hosp., 1970-74, sr. v.p., adminstr., 1974-77, exec. v.p., 1977-80, pres., 1980-85; pres. Health Corp. Va., 1985—; preceptor Sch. Health Adminstrn., Duke U. and Med. Coll. Va., Washington U., St. Louis; bd. dirs. Sun Health, Inc./Sun Alliance, 1979-92, vice chmn., 1984, chmn., 1985-87; vice-chmn. Med./Bus. Coalition, 1981-83; participant Leadership Met. Richmond; bd. dirs. Ctrl. Va. Health Sys. Agy., 1980-84, Richmond chpt.

ARC, 1980-83; mem. Va. Bd. Med. Assistance, 1980-84; mem. joint subcom. studying Va.'s med. malpractice laws divsn. legal svcs. Gen. Assembly of Comm. of Va., 1984; chmn. Va. Health Network, 1989-91; chmn. Hanover Bus. Coun., 1994-95; mem. Gov.'s Regional Econ. Devel. Adv. Coun., 1994-95. Served with Med. Service Corps, U.S. Army, 1959-62. Fellow Am. Coll. Healthcare Execs. (Council of Regents 1976-82, Edgar C. Hayhow award 1976, bd. govs. 1990-94, regents award sr. exec. level 1995); mem. Am. Hosp. Assn. (chmn. RPBIII 1994—, del. 1989-93, mem. bd. trustees 1994—, Va. Hosp. Assn. (dir. 1974—, chmn.-elect, chmn. 1984-85), Va. Ins. Reciprocal (chmn. 1977-79), Met. Richmond C. of C. (bd. dirs.). Republican. Presbyterian. Home: 9127 Carterham Rd Richmond VA 23229-7752 Office: Health Corp of Va 1300 Westwood Ave Richmond VA 23227-4612

SIMPSON, MARILYN JEAN, artist; b. Birmingham, Ala., Aug. 24, 1929; d. Homer Kyle and Ellen (Allan) Parker; student U. Ala., Art Students League N.Y., San Miguel, Mex., Robert Brackman Sch., Conn., Am. U., Avignon, France, Rome and Florence, Italy; children—Carol Leann, Charles Boyd. Dir., Acad. Fine Arts, Ft. Walton Beach, Fla., 1974-77; Marilyn Simpson Sch. Fine Art, Ft. Walton Beach, 1962-73, Artists Workshop, Ft. Walton Beach, 1982—; exhbns. include: Kotter Gallery, Nat. Arts Club, Lever House, Paula Insel Gallery (all N.Y.C.), Destin (Fla.) Gallery Fine Art, Pastel Soc. West Coast (exhbn. Calif. 1994, Pres. award). Recipient award Am. Artist Profl. League, 1975, Golden Egg Gallery award, Golden Centaur award, 1982, Vol. of the Yr. award Pensacola. Mem. Am. Artists Profl. League, Pastel Soc. of Southwest (recipient Dick Blick award, exhbn. Dallas), Pastel Soc. of No. Fla. (founder, pres., Best in Show cash award 1994), Pastel Soc. of Am. (exhbn. N.Y., recipient Artspace Cash award 1994, signature mem.), Internat. Assn. Pastel Socs. (coord., v.p.), Allied Artists Am. (assoc.), Acad. Italia. (recipient Gold medal, hon. degree, 1979). Address: 2991 W Highway 98 Mary Esther FL 32569-2336

SIMPSON, MURRAY, engineer, consultant; b. N.Y.C., July 27, 1921; s. George and Sonia (Vernov) S.; m. Ethel Gladstein, June 29, 1947; children: Anne Simpson Everett, David, Mindy, Jonathan. BEE, CCNY, 1942; MEE, Polytech. Inst. of N.Y., 1952. Engr. Internat. Tel.&Tel., N.Y.C., 1942-44; sr. engr. Raytheon Co., Waltham, Mass., 1946-48; sect. mgr. Fairchild Guided Missles div., Farmingdale, N.Y., 1948-50; v.p. Maxson Elec. Co., N.Y.C., 1950-62; pres. SEDCO Systems Inc. subs. Raytheon Co., Melville, N.Y., 1963-86; cons. M. Simpson Assocs., West Hempstead, N.Y., 1986—; former chmn. bd. dirs. Radyne Corp. Contbr. articles to profl. jours. former bd. dirs. United Way of L.I., N.Y., 1984-87. Served to lt. (j.g.) USNR, 1944-46, PTO. Fellow IEEE (chmn. L.I. sect. 1963-64); mem. Anchorage Yacht Club, Inverrary Country Club. Clubs: Anchorage Yacht, Inverrary Country.

SIMPSON, WENDELL PHILLIPS, chartered financial consultant; b. New Orleans, Dec. 1, 1927; s. Wendell Howard Simpson and Margaret (Scruggs) Patten; m. Pamela Lamar Brown, July 28, 1956; children: Wendell P. III, James R., Richard A. Student, Cornell U., 1945-46, 47-50. ChFC; CLU. Agy. interline mgr. TACA Internat. Airlines, New Orleans, 1952-54; v.p. internat. Raybestos-Manhattan Inc., N.Y.C., 1954-69; v.p. Industria Americana Inc., L.A., 1969-73; prin. Wendell P. Simpson & Assocs., L.A., 1973-78; pres. Deferred Benefits, Inc., Pasadena, Calif., 1978-81, Personal Fin. Planning Inc., San Marino, Calif., 1981-86; prin. Personal Fin. Planning Inc., Livingston, Tex., 1986—; mem. Western Pension Conf., L.A., 1978-83, Estate Planning Coun., Pasadena, 1984-86. Chmn. Conf. of Neighborhood Assn. Pres., Scarsdale, N.Y., 1969; sec. Rep. Town Com., Scarsdale, 1969; bd. dirs. Christian Businessmens Com., Pasadena, 1985; scoutmaster Boy Scouts Am., San Marino, Calif., 1975-78; chmn. Pasadena chpt. ARC, 1985-86. Col. USAF Res., 1950—. Republican. Episcopalian. Home: 101 Rainbow Dr # 209 Livingston TX 77351-9330

SIMS, ALBERT MAURICE, marketing professional; b. N.Y.C., Jan. 22, 1930; s. Samuel Lee and Jennie (Rosenberg) S.; m. Estelle Deiner-Sims, Nov. 15, 1963 (div. June 1985). Diploma in Physics, Adelphi Coll., 1960; postgrad., Bklyn. Coll., 1968-72. Analytic engr. Stratos Divsn. Fairchild, Bayshore, N.Y., 1954-60; program mgr. EDO Corp., College Point, N.Y., 1960-76; mktg. mgr. Sperry, Great Neck, N.Y., 1976-85; dir. programs devel. PRC, McLean, Va., 1986-95; dir. bus. devel. Grumman Data Systems, Herndon, Va., 1986-95; v.p. programs Info. Tech. Solutions, Reston, Va., 1995—; v.p. mktg. EPI, Fairfax, Va., 1989-96; cons. Naval Studies Bd., D.C., 1982-83; adv. bd. SDS, Fairfax, 1990—; pres. Performance Engring., Fairfax, 1980—. Editor: Patron mag., 1956-50. Lobbyist PEI, Fairfax, 1980-95; campaigner fgn. aid issues, 1992-94; mem. U.S. Congl. adv. bd., D.C., 1982. Mem. Armed Forces Comms./Electronics Assn., Navy League, Nat. Def. Transp. Assn., Assn. of Old Crows.

SIMS, BENNETT JONES, minister, educator; b. Greenfield, Mass., Aug. 9, 1920; s. Lewis Raymond and Sarah Cosette (Jones) S.; children: Laura (Mrs. John P. Boucher), Grayson, David. AB, Baker U., 1943, LHD (hon.), 1985; postgrad., Princeton Theol. Sem., 1946-47; B.D., Va. Theol. Sem., 1949, D.D., 1966; D.D., U. of South, 1972; Merrill fellow, Harvard U., 1964-65; postgrad., Cath. U., 1969-71. Ordained to ministry Episc. Ch. as deacon, 1949, priest, 1950. Rector Ch. of Redeemer, Balt., 1951-64; dir. continuing edn. Va. Theol. Sem., 1966-72; bishop of Atlanta, 1972-83; vis. prof. theology Emory U., Atlanta, 1980-88, pres. Inst. for Servant Leadership, 1988—; priest-in-charge St. Alban's Ch., Tokyo, 1962, 69. Trustee U. of South. With USNR, 1943-46. Named Young Man of Yr. Balt. C. of C., 1953; Disting. Alumnus of Yr., Baker U., 1972. Office: Inst Servant Leadership Hendersonville NC 28793

SIMS, DAVID BRYSON, JR., engineer; b. Memphis, Aug. 12, 1947; s. David Bryson and Ruth (Gnuse) S.; m. Carole Braddock (dec.), Nov. 21, 1970; children: Jennifer Braddock, David Bryson III. BSChemE, U. Tenn., 1969; MS Mech. Engring., U. Memphis, 1972, MS Civil Engring., 1974. Registered profl. engr., Ga., Mi., Va., Kans., N.C., Tenn., S.C., La., Ohio, Ind., Fla., Md. Engr. DuPont, Memphis, 1969-73; cons. engr. Elles, Reaves, Fanning & Oakley, Memphis, 1973-75; engr. W.R. Grace, Memphis, 1975-79; engring. mgr. W.R. Grace, Wilmington, N.C., 1979-85; prin. David Sims & Assocs., Wilmington, 1985—; trustee Cape Fear Acad., Wilmington, 1987-92; part-time instr. Cape Fear C.C., Wilmington, 1981-86. Bd. dirs., pres. Bradley Creek Boatominium, Wilmington, 1990—. Mem. NSPE, ASHRAE, AIChE (sec. 1972, pres. 1973), Nat. Fire Protection Assn. Republican. Presbyterian. Home: 2721 Shandy Ln Wilmington NC 28409-2042 Office: David Sims & Assocs 108 N Kerr Ave Ste K-1 Wilmington NC 28405-3444

SIMS, DAVID SUTHERN, university maintenance official; b. Louisville, July 16, 1965; s. O. Suthern and Mary (Horn) S.; m. Sabrina Abrams, Dec. 5, 1988; 1 child, David Suthern, Jr. AS in Phys. Edn. magna cum laude, Wingate (N.C.) Coll., 1983, BS in Parks and Recreation Adminstrn., 1984. With Horn's Farm, Inc., Wawbeek, Ala., 1984-85, Tift Coll., Forsyth, Ga., 1985-86; dir. phys. plant Tift Coll. of Mercer U., 1986-87, Mercer U., Atlanta, 1987—; facilities mgmt. cons. St. Judes Rehab. Ctr., Atlanta, 1989. Recipient Disting. Svc. Citation, Tift Coll., 1985-87. Mem. Assn. Phys. Plant Adminstrs. (award for excellence in facilities mgmt. 1989, grad. Inst. Facilities Mgmt. program 1990), Ga. Assn. Phys. Plant Adminstrs. (bd. dirs. 1990—, 1st v.p. 1994—, Pres.'s Outstanding Svc. award 1992), Southeastern Assn. Phys. Plant Adminstrs. (bd. dirs. 1994—, v.p. at large). Democrat. Baptist. Office: Mercer U Phys Plant Dept 3001 Mercer University Dr Atlanta GA 30341-4115

SIMS, FRED WILLIAM, SR., orthodontist; b. Weatherford, Okla., Feb. 4, 1915; s. Fred E. and Lodine H. (Strong) S.; m. Helen L. Abbe; children: Fred W. Jr., Sandra Jean Sims Reeve. BS, Kans. State U., 1939; DDS, Baylor U., 1955; MS, U. Tenn., 1956. Pvt. practice orthodontics Tulsa, 1956-89; ret., 1989; mem. Found. Orthodontic Research; v.p. Okla. Dental Found. Research and Edn., 1971-72, pres., 1973-74, bd. dirs., 1961—. Served as maj. USAF, 1941-46, ETO. Fellow Internat. Coll. Dentists, Am. Coll. Dentists; mem. ADA (life), Okla. Dental Assn. (life, Okla. Man in Dentistry award 1974), Am. Assn. Orthodontists, Southwestern Soc. Orthodontists (life), Oaks Country Club (Tulsa), Rotary (charter mem. Southside club Tulsa), Masons (32 degrees), Blue Key, Beta Theta Pi, Psi Omega. Republican. Home: 2927 E 75th St Tulsa OK 74136-5642

SIMS, GREGORY EVANS, electronics distribution company executive; b. Sharon, Pa., Jan. 17, 1946; s. George Joseph Jr. and Georgiana (Kennedy) S.; children: Jeffrey Joseph, Forrest Evans. A in Engring., U. Tex., 1966. Tech. rep. NCR Corp., Houston, 1966-76, sales account rep., 1977-78; dir. mktg. Kent Electronics, Houston, 1978-82; v.p. Kent Electronics, Houston, Tex., 1982-91; founder and v.p. Kent Datacomm, Houston, 1988-90, region v.p., 1994. Mem. Sales and Mktg. Execs. Office: Kent Electronics 7433 Harwin Dr Houston TX 77036-2015

SIMS, JANETTE ELIZABETH LOWMAN, educational director; b. Lincolnton, N.C., July 21, 1934; d. Lee Hobson and Myrtle Elizabeth (Travis) Lowman; m. Mickey Ray Sims, Feb. 2, 1951; children: Carol Lee Sims Walden, Rickey Ray. BS, Lenoir-Rhyne Coll., 1968; MAT, U. N.C., 1973; EdD, U. N.C., Greensboro, 1989. N.C. "G" tchg. cert; cert. devel. edn. specialist. Quality control supr. Kiser Roth Hosiery, Inc., Maiden, N.C., 1959-63; 9th grade phys. sci. and math. tchr. Cherryville (N.C.) Jr. H.S., 1968; phys. sci., chemistry and astronomy tchr. Maiden (N.C.) H.S., 1968-75; dir. studies lab. coord. Catawba Valley C.C., Hickory, N.C., 1975-79; physics, chemistry, math. and computer sci. instr. Catawba Valley C.C., Hickory, 1979-90, dir. developmental studies and learning assistance ctr., 1990—; trustee Catawba County Assn. for Spl. Edn., Conover, 1978-79, Catawba Valley Found., Hickory, 1993—, chair, 1996; apprentice program instr. Meredith/Burda Corp., Newton, N.C., 1979-88. Coun. mem., choir mem., tchr. Faith Luth. Ch., Conover, 1980—. Mem. NEA, N.C. Assn. Educators (local unit pres.), Nat. Assn. Developmental Educators, N.C. Assn. Developmental Educators (regional chair 1990), Atlantic Assn. Physics Tchrs. (chair nominations com. 1992), N.C. Math. Assn. Two-Yr. Colls. (chairperson devel. math. com. 1991-93, sec. 1996-97), Am. Legion Aux., Delta Kappa Gamma. Home: 300 Parlier Ave Conover NC 28613-9312 Office: Catawba Valley CC 2550 Us Highway 70 SE Hickory NC 28602-8302

SIMS, JUDY, software company executive; b. 1953. BBA in Acctg., Tex. Tech. U., 1974. CPA. Staff acct. Coopers & Lybrand, Dallas, 1974-76; auditor Grant Thornton, Dallas, 1976-85; co-founder, owner Software Spectrum, 1983—. Office: Software Spectrum 2140 Merritt Dr Garland TX 75041-6135*

SIMS, KONSTANZE OLEVIA, social worker; b. Dallas, Dec. 20, 1944; d. Kenneth Winn and Odie Lee (Wells) S. Student, U. Dallas, 1963-64; BA, U. Tex., Arlington, 1968; MEd, U. North Tex., 1972. Sec. Stillman Coll. Regional Campaign Fund, Dallas, 1969; employment interviewer Zale Corp., Dallas, 1969-71; sch. counselor Bishop Dunne High Sch, Dallas, 1973-78; dir. guidance Notre Dame High Sch., Wichita Falls, Tex., 1978-81; taxpayer svc. rep. IRS, Dallas, 1981-83, acct. analyst, 1983-88; freelance Dallas, 1989-90; social worker Tex. Dept. Human Svcs., Dallas, 1991-96, Tex. Workforce Commn., 1996—. Reader, North Tex. Taping & Radio for the Blind, Dallas, 1991—; mem. choir St. Peter the Apostle Cath. Ch.; mem. Whale Adoption Project; mem. Union Chorale. Mem. AAUW, Am. Counseling Assn., Nat. Specialty Merchandising Assn., Am. Multicultural Counseling Assn., Am. Bible Tchrs. Assn., Tex. Counseling Assn., Tex. Multicultural Counseling Assn., Assn. Rsch. and Enlightenment, Inc., Assn. for Spiritual, Ethical, and Religious Values in Counseling, U. Tex Arlington Alumni Assn., U. North Tex. Alumni Assn. Office: Tex Workforce Commn 4533 Ross Ave Dallas TX 75204-8417

SIMS, LYNN LEE, historian, educator; b. Washington, Sept. 23, 1937; s. Lynn Boyd and Audrey (Jacobs) S.; m. Sharon Obitts, Sept. 10, 1960; children: Devyn, David, Dayle, Danelle. BA, Wheaton Coll., 1960; MA, Kans. State U., 1963; PhD, NYU, 1975. Prof. history The Kings Coll., Briarcliff Manor, N.Y., 1963-74; U.S. mil. historian Command & Gen. Staff Coll., Ft. Leavenworth, Kans., 1974-76; city historian Richmond, Va., 1976-80; historian Richmond, 1980-82; command historian Dept. Def., Ft. Lee, Va., 1982—; adj. faculty Va. Commonwealth U., Richmond,1976—; cons. faculty Command & Gen. Staff Coll., Ft. Leavenworth, 1974-84. Author: Combined Arms Action, 1939, 1976, They Have Seen the Elephant, 1985, First 40 Years of LOGEX, 1987, Operation Strong Wind, 1994; contbr. articles to mil. jours.; reviewer mil. books. Mem. state com. to select Va. history book for pub. schs., Richmond, 1980, conduct battlefield tours. Lt. col. USAR. Mem. NRA, Conf. Faith and History, Vintage Chevrolet Club Am. Presbyterian. Home: 9157 Graff Ct Mechanicsville VA 23116-2692 Office: CASCOM 3901 A Ave Ste 100 Fort Lee VA 23801-1807

SIMS, REBECCA GIBBS, accountant, certified fraud examiner; b. Houston, Mar. 13, 1951; d. Shelton P. Gibbs and Elizabeth Gill Bisby; m. Morris Raymond Sims (div. 1977); children: Diana Elizabeth, Aaron Redding. BFA, U. Houston, 1977. Cert. fraud examiner. V.p. Lexley U.S.A., Inc., Houston and Mexico City, 1977-81; acct. self-employed, Houston, 1982-87, journalist/investigator, 1987—, fin. fraud investigator, 1991—; mng. ptnr. Boynton & Assocs., 1996—. Editor, rschr.: Maria, CIA and George Bush, 1992; screenwriter; journalist Bilanz mag., Switzerland, 1989-91; author article. Childbirth instr. Houston Orgn. Parent Edn., Houston, 1974-77. Mem. Investigative Reporters and Editors, Nat. Writers Union, Mensa. Democrat. Office: 440 Louisiana Ste 1720 Houston TX 77002

SIMS, ROBERT MCNEILL, retired educational administrator, soccer coach; b. Birmingham, Ala., Mar. 25, 1928; s. Edwin Webb and Margaret Pauline (McNeill) S.; m. Marie Ficklen Newton; children: Robert Clayton, Kevin McNeill, Boyce Griffin. BS, Birmingham-So. Coll., 1950; MA, U. Ala., 1951; postgrad. U. N.C., U. Denver, Hope Coll., Emory U. Chemistry tchr. Riverside Mil. Acad., Gainesville, Ga., 1951-52, 54-57, Tuscaloosa (Ala.) High Sch., 1952-54; chmn. sci. dept. Westminster Sch., Atlanta, 1957-89, head soccer coach, 1958-92, dir. admissions & fin. aid, 1987-93; sci. cons. Coll. Bd.; mem. ACS Adv. Test Com., 1966—, chmn., 1986-90; soccer coord. Ga. High Sch. Assn., 1966-93; mem. soccer rules com. Nat. Fedn. State High Sch. Assns., 1970-76, 83-87; coach 1st nat. All-Star soccer game, West Point, N.Y., 1984. Mem. choir Peachtree Rd. United Meth. Ch., 1957—, mem. adminstrv. bd., 1978-89; mem. adminstrv. bd. Northside YMCA, 1976—. Mem. test com. Secondary Schs. Admissions Testing Bd., 1989-91. Named Atlanta STAR Tchr., 1963, 68, Nat. Tchr.-of-Yr., DuPont award, 1968, Outstanding Educator, Oglethorpe U., 1976, Nat. Soccer Coach-of-Yr., High Sch. Athletic Coaches Assn., 1975, Southeast Soccer Coach of Yr., Nat. Soccer Coaches Assn., 1981, 83, Ga. High Sch. Soccer Coach of Yr., Ga. Athletic Coaches Assn., 1983; named to Westminster Athletic Hall of Fame, 1994. Mem. AAAS, Am. Chem. Soc. (chmn. Ga. sect. 1970), Am. Inst. Chemists (chmn. Ga. sect. 1972), Atlanta Amateur Soccer League (pres. 1982-83), Nat. Soccer Coaches Assn. Am., Pine Hills Civic Club. Democrat. Home: 3068 W Roxboro Rd NE Atlanta GA 30324-2922

SIMS, SAMUEL RICHARD FARRELL, electronic engineer; b. Charleston, S.C., Dec. 17, 1952; s. Samuel Elmore and O'Leta (Lipscomb) S.; m. Terri Sue Hendry, Oct. 23, 1976; children: Julie Elizabeth, Samuel Richard, Christopher John. BS in Engring., U. Ala., Huntsville, 1974, MS in Engring., 1978, PhD in Elec. and Computer Engring., 1989. Electronic engr. U.S. Army Missile Command, Redstone Arsenal, Ala., 1971—. Contbr. articles to profl. jours.; patentee in field. Mem. U. Ala. Coll. Engring. Alumni Assn. (alumni steering com. 1992—). Home: 2005 Woodmore Dr Huntsville AL 35803

SIMS, THOMAS AUBURN, retired shipbuilding company executive; b. Little Rock, Miss., Oct. 20, 1925; s. Thomas Alexander and Evie Jane (Riche) S.; m. Ruby Pearl Graham, Oct. 6, 1946; children: Gloria Jean, Judy Ann, Janet Lea. AA, East Central Jr. Coll., 1948; BS, U. Md., 1957; MBA, Babson Coll., 1962. Commd. 2d lt. U.S. Army, 1949, advanced through grades to lt. col., retired, 1967; asst. to purchasing agt. Ingalls Shipbuilding, Inc., Pascagoula, Miss., 1968-69, purchasing mgr., 1970-77, dir. procurement, 1978-93. Mem. Gov. of Miss. Minority Adv. Bd., Jackson, 1972-75; bd. dirs. Miss. Minority Supplier Devel. Coun., Jackson, 1980-93; deacon, Sunday sch. tchr. 1st Bapt. Ch., Ocean Springs, Miss., 1972—. With USN, 1943-46, PTO. Mem. Nat. Contract Mgmt. Assn. (bd. dirs. 1980-82, mem. coun. fellows 1993), Retired Officers Assn. Home: 6309 Prado Rd Ocean Springs MS 39564-2210

SINANIAN, LORIS R., financial consultant, deacon; b. N.Y.C., Oct. 23, 1931; s. John and Araksi (Ozanian) S.; m. Peggy Gavin, July 18, 1959; children: Arlene, Linda, Claire, Stephen. B of Mech. Engring., NYU, 1952; grad. bus., UCLA, 1967. Ordained permanent deacon Roman Cath. Ch., 1989. Dir. reentry systems TRW Systems Group, Redondo Beach, Calif., 1963-72; v.p. devel., v.p. mktg. Nat. Distbn. Svcs. (subs. Eastern Airlines), Atlanta, 1972-73; exec. v.p. Credit Data of Southeast (now TRW Credit Data), Atlanta, 1973-80; pres. LRS Assocs., Atlanta, 1980-84; fin. cons. The Robinson-Humphrey Co., Atlanta, 1984—; founder-pres. and exec. dir. Faith Enrichment Inst., Atlanta, 1987—, Cath. Family Forum, Atlanta, 1992—; dir. Formation, Archdiocese of Atlanta 1994, Fellowship of Cath. Scholars, 1994. Contbr. (newspaper) The Money Manager, Ga., 1985—. V.p. United Reps. Calif., 1964-71; mem. Rep. Ctrl. Com., 1966-68; formation dir. Archdiocese of Atlanta, asst. vicar for deacons, 1995—; spiritual dir. Ga. Cath. Home Educators, Atlanta chpt. Caths. United for Faith, 1994—; chaplain Ga. chpt. Cath. League for Religious and Civil Rights, 1994—. Lt. USAF, 1952-54. Home: 90 River Court Pky NW Atlanta GA 30328-1141 also: Archdiocese Atlanta 680 W Peachtree St Atlanta GA 30308

SINCLAIR, CAROL, educational specialist; b. Manchester, Ga., Mar. 25, 1942. BA, LaGrange (Ga.) Coll., 1964; MEd, Ga. Southwestern Coll., 1976. Tchr. English Macon County High Sch., Montezuma, Ga., 1972-74; tchr. English and drama Riviera Jr. High Sch., Miami, Fla., 1978-79; instr. Tallahassee C.C., 1981-83, part-time instr., 1980-85; program specialit Fla. Dept. Edn., Tallahassee, 1986-90; adminstrv. asst. Morse Diesel Internat., Tallahassee, 1991—; grad. tchg. asst. Fla. State U., Tallahassee, 1985-89; ednl. specialist Life Skills Found., Tallahassee, 1993—. Dir., promoter theatrical prodns. Killearn United Meth. Ch., 1988-93, pub. speaker, publicity chmn. Home: 1951 N Meridian Rd Apt 80 Tallahassee FL 32303-5246

SINCLAIR, JAMES LEWIS, research microbiologist; b. Salina, Kans., Aug. 12, 1949; m. Martha Jean Walker, Sept. 8, 1979; children: Michael, Anne. BS with distinction, Colo. State U., 1971, PhD, 1980. Microbiologist Bur. of Water Works, City of Portland, Oreg., 1980; postdoctoral assoc. Dept. Agronomy, Cornell U., Ithaca, N.Y., 1980-84, rsch. assoc., 1984-88; rsch. microbiologist Mantech Environ., Rsch. Svcs. Corp., Ada, Okla., 1988—. Contbr. articles to profl. jours. Grantee Westinghouse Savannah River Co., 1992. Mem. Am. Soc. for Microbiology, Soc. of Protozoologists. Home: 524 E 13th St Ada OK 74820-6610 Office: ManTech Environ Rsch Svcs Robert S Kerr Lab PO Box 1198 Ada OK 74821-1198

SINCLAIR, JULIE MOORES WILLIAMS, consulting law librarian; b. Montgomery, Ala., May 2, 1954; d. Benjamin Buford and Marilyn Moores (Simpson) Williams; m. Winfield James Sinclair, Dec. 16, 1978. BA, U. of South, 1976; MLS, U. Ala., Tuscaloosa, 1977; JD, Washington U., St. Louis, 1987. Bar: Ala. 1989, U.S. Dist. Ct. (no. dist.) Ala. 1989. Serials libr. Ala. Dept. Archives and History, Montgomery, 1977; cataloguing libr. Ala. Pub. Libr. Svc., Montgomery, 1978; league libr. Ala. League Municipalities, Montgomery, 1978-84; asst. libr. Mo. Ct. Appeals, St. Louis, 1984-86, law clk., 1987-88; cons. Law Libr. Cons., Birmingham, Ala., 1988—. Contbr. numerous articles to profl. jours. Mem. exec. com. Jefferson County Women's Polit. Caucus, 1988—. Mem. Ala. Bar Assn., Ala. Libr. Assn., Am. Assn. Law Librs., Law Libr. Assn. Ala. (charter, v.p. 1992-93, pres. 1993-94), Ala. Fedn. Bus. and Profl. Women (sec. 1993-94, 2d v.p. 1994-95, 1st v.p. 1995-96), Order of Gownsmen, Phi Alpha Theta. Episcopalian. Office: Law Libr Cons 956 Montclair Rd Ste 218 Birmingham AL 35213-1215

SINE, RICHARD, editor, writor, consultant; b. Morgantown, W.Va., Mar. 2, 1943; s. Jack L. and Anne (Levinson) S.; m. Beverly P. August, Mar. 18, 1967; children: Jack L. II, James E., Suzanne G. BA, Lehigh U., 1965; postgrad., Edinboro State Coll., 1965-66, Union Coll., Schenectady, N.Y., 1967-68. Accredited, Pub. Rels. Soc. Am. Spanish tchr. Eisenhower H.S., Russell, Pa., 1965-67; city editor Times-Mirror & Observer, Warren, Pa., 1965-67; news dir. Union Coll., 1967-69; dir. pub. rels. Beloit (Wis.) Coll., 1969-74; pres. P.S. Comm., Inc., Beloit, 1974-76; editor, dir. edn. Am. Philatelic Soc., State Coll., Pa., 1976-85; editor Scott Pub. Co., Sidney, Ohio, 1985; editl. dir. Scott Pub. Co., Sidney, 1985-93; owner Envision, 1992-94; exec. editor Novus Debut Inc., Charlotte, N.C., 1994—; stamp columnist, N.Y. Times, N.Y.C., 1984-85. Author 2 correspondence courses, 1982 (disting. study course 1982), 1983, CD-ROM Ency. U.S. Postage Stamps, 1992. Home: 100 Poplar St Fort Mill SC 29715-1824 Office: Novus Debut Inc 10725 John Price Rd Charlotte NC 28273

SING, WILLIAM BENDER, lawyer; b. Houston, Oct. 16, 1947; s. William Bender Sr. and Alice Irene (Detmers) S.; m. Doris Anne Spradley, Sept. 1, 1967; children: Erin Elaine, Emily Elizabeth. BS cum laude, U. Houston, 1968, JD magna cum laude, 1971. Bar: Tex. 1971. Assoc. Fulbright & Jaworski, LLP, Houston, 1973-80, ptnr., 1980—. Elder, trustee St. Andrew's Presbyn. Ch., Houston; past pres., bd. dirs. St. Andrew's Presbyn. Sch., Houston; past pres. Houston C.C. Place Civic Assn. 1st lt. U.S. Army, 1971-73. Mem. ABA, Tex. Bar Assn., Houston Bar Assn., Order of the Barons Law Honor Soc., Phi Delta Phi, Phi Kappa Phi, Omicron Delta Epsilon. Presbyterian. Office: Fulbright & Jaworski LLP 1301 Mckinney St Houston TX 77010

SINGER, ARMAND EDWARDS, foreign language educator; b. Detroit, Nov. 30, 1914; s. Elvin Satori Singer and Fredericka Elizabeth (Edwards) Singer Goetz; m. Mary Rebecca White, Aug. 8, 1940; 1 child, Fredericka Ann Hill. A.B., Amherst Coll., 1935; M.A., Duke U., 1939, Ph.D., 1944; diplôme, U. Paris, 1939; postgrad., Ind. U., summer 1964. Teaching fellow in sci. Amherst Coll., 1935-36; instr. French and Spanish, part-time Duke, 1938-40; teaching fellow Romance langs. W.Va. U., Morgantown, 1940-41, instr., 1941-47, asst. prof., 1947-55, assoc. prof., 1955-60, prof., 1960-80, prof. emeritus, 1980—, chmn. program for humanities, 1963-72, chmn. dept. integrated studies, 1963, acting chmn. dept. religion and program for humanities, 1973, dir. ann. colloquium on modern lit., 1976-80, 85-86, 96. Author: A Bibliography of the Don Juan Theme: Versions and Criticism, 1954, The Don Juan Theme, Versions and Criticism: An Annotated Bibliography, 1965, Paul Bourget, 1975, The Don Juan Theme: A Bibliography of Versions, Analogues, Uses, and Adaptations, 1993, The Armand E. Singer Tibet, 1809-1975, 1995, (with J.F. Stasny) Anthology of Readings: Humanities I, 1966, Anthology of Readings: Humanities II, 1967; editor: (with Jürgen E. Schlunk) Martin Walser: International Perspectives, 1987; editor W.Va. U. Philol. Papers, 1948-50, 53-55, editor-in-chief, 1951-52, 55—, 1001 Horny Limericks by Ward Marden, 1996; editor, contbr. Essays on the Literature of Mountaineering, 1982; contbr. numerous articles to profl. and philatelic jours. Bd. dirs. Community Concert Assn., Morgantown, 1959-60, Humanities Found. W.Va., 1981-87. Recipient 4th Ann. Humanities award W.Va. Humanities Coun., 1990. Mem. MLA (internat. bibliography com. 1956-59, nat. del. assembly 1975-78), So. Atlantic MLA (exec. com. 1971-74), Am. Assn. Tchrs. Spanish and Portuguese, Am. Philatelic Soc., Nepal and Tibet Philatelic Study Circle, Nepal Philatelic Soc., Collectors Club of N.Y., Phi Beta Kappa. Republican. Home: 248 Grandview Ave Morgantown WV 26505-6925

SINGER, DONNA LEA, writer, editor, educator; b. Wilmington, Del., Oct. 6, 1944; d. Marshall Richard and Sara Emma (Eppihimer) S. BA in English cum laude, Gettysburg Coll., 1966; postgrad., Montclair State Coll., 1972-73, U. Birmingham, Eng., 1977; M of Letters, Drew U., 1985. Asst. to dir. student activities Fairleigh Dickinson U., Madison, N.J., 1966-68; tchr., drama coach Morris Hills High Sch., Rockaway, N.J., 1968-84; free-lance editor Basic Books, Inc., N.Y.C., 1983-86; adj. instr. Fairleigh Dickinson U., Madison, 1986-87; free-lance writer, editor Visual Edn. Corp., Princeton, N.J., 1988—, Fact's on File, Bantam, Random House, Fodor's Travel Books, N.Y.C., 1990—, John Wiley & Sons, N.Y.C., 1990—; co-founder, co-dir. Traveling Hist. Troupe, Rockaway, 1976-78; tour leader Am. Leadership Study Groups, 1976, 78, 82; theatre studies participant Royal Shakespeare Co., Stratford, Eng., 1978, 79, 81; docent, lectr. acting co. Hist. Spanish Point, Osprey, Fla., 1989—. Contbg. author: (poetry) Chasing Rainbows, 1987, An American Heritage, 1994, (biographies) Past and Promise: Lives of New Jersey Women, 1990, American Cultural Leaders, 1993. Big sister Big Bros./Big Sisters, Sarasota, Fla., 1990—. Mem. Internat. Women's Writing Guild, Gulf Coast Writers Forum, Met. Mus. Art, Royal Shakespeare Company Assocs.

SINGER, IGOR, cardiologist, electrophysiologist; b. Australia, July 13, 1952; came to U.S., 1984; s. Ivan and Draginja (Remeljan) S.; m. Sylvia Ann Novacek, June 12, 1978; children: Justin, Jessica, Christina. B. Medicine, B. Surgery, U. NSW, 1976. Diplomate Am. Bd. Internal Medicine, Am. Bd. Cardiology, Am. Bd. Electrophysiology. Chief electrophysiology pacing, prof. medicine U. Louisville, 1987—; reviewer Pacing and Electrophysiology, N.Y.C., Circulation, 1990—. Editor: Clinical Manual of Electrophysiology, 1993, Implantable Cardioverter Defibrillator, 1994; mem. edit. bd. Louisville Medicine, 1989-91, Interventional Electrophysiology, 1996; contbr. articles to profl. jours. Fellow ACP, Am. Coll. Cardiology, Am. Coll. Angiology, Royal Australian Coll. Physicians; mem. N.Am. Soc. Pacing and Electrophysiology, Am. Fedn. Clin. Rsch., Australian Soc. Cardiology, N.Y. Acad. Sci. Office: University Hosp U Louisville 530 S Jackson St Louisville KY 40202-1675

SINGER, MERLE ELLIOT, rabbi; b. Duluth, Minn., May 11, 1939; s. Samuel and Brenda (Naymark) S.; m. Myra Golden, Aug. 29, 1965; children: Jonathan, Jeremy, Michael, Mark. AB, U. Cin., 1961; BHL, M.A.H.L., Hebrew Union Coll., Cin., 1966; DHL, Gwynedd-Mercy Coll., 1978; DD (hon.), 1991. Ordained rabbi. Rabbi Temple Sinai, Washington, 1966-71, Reform Congregation Beth Or, Phila., 1971-78; sr. rabbi Temple Beth El, Boca Raton, Fla., 1978—; adj. prof. history, Judaic studies Fla. Atlantic U., Boca Raton,1978-79; adj. prof. Judaic studies Gwynedd Mercy Coll., Phila., 1975-78; instr. I.M. Wise div. Gratz Coll., Phila., 1971-76; chaplain Boca Raton Police Dept.; rabbinic and com. Camp Coleman, Union Am. Hebrew Congregations, Cleveland, Ga., 1978—. Sponsor inter-faith and Holocaust seminars for the Sisters of Mercy, facuty and students of Gwynedd Mercy Coll., 1978; Jewish student affairs advisor Phila. Coll. of Textiles and Scis., 1976-77, Villanova U., 1976-77; Rabbinic bd. overseers Hebrew Union Coll., 1985—; campaign v.p. United Way of South Palm Beach County, 1986-87, pres., 1987-88; mem. adv. bd. Mae Volen Sr. Ctr., Boca Raton, 1981; clergy advisor Planned Parenthood of Palm Beach County, Inc., Boca Raton; bd. dirs. Edn. Found. Palm Beach County, Inc., 1986-88, Florence Fuller Child Devel. Ctr., Boca Raton, Am. Jewish Com., 1995—; past pres. Religious Leadres Assn. Boca Raton; mem. ethics com. Boca Raton Cmty. Hosp., 1992—; invitee Pres.'s Ann. Prayer Breakfast, Washington, 1996. Recipient nat. award for outstanding svc. Domestic Policy Assn./Nat. Issues Forum, 1985-86, Ben Gurion award for Israel bonds State of Israel, 1975, 85, Torch of Liberty Humanitarian award Anti-Defamation League, 1981, Cmty. Svc. award Boca Raton News, 1982, So Far award Boy Scouts Am., 1987, B'nai Avraham award Am. Jewish Com., 1991, citation Jewish Chautauqua Soc., 1993, Silver Medallion Brotherhood award NCCJ, 1992, Cmty. Svc. award Boys Town Jerusalem, 1993; named to Four Chaplains Legion of Honor, Phila., 1981; named Minister of Day, State of Fla., 1993; Merle E. Singer Day proclaimed in his honor, City of Boca Raton, 1991, 96. Mem. South Palm Beach Bd. of Rabbis, Palm Beach Bd. of Rabbis (past. pres.), Union of Am. Hebrew Congregations (com. for winning the unaffiliated), Assn. Reform Zionists Am. (bd. dirs. 1983—), S.E. Ctrl. Conf. Am. Rabbis (pres. 1995—), Ctrl. Conf. Am. Rabbis (com. on relief, subvention and solicitation, nat. bd. 1995—), Israel Bonds (nat. rabbinic cabinet), Hebrew Union Coll. Inst. of Religion (presidents alumni assn. 1984—), Synagogue Coun. Am. (nat. bd. govs.). Office: Temple Beth El 333 SW 4th Ave Boca Raton FL 33432-5709

SINGH, BALWANT, secondary education educator; b. Lyall Pur, Punjab, Pakistan, Aug. 5, 1932; naturalized U.S. citizen, 1969; s. Jowinder and Amar (Kaur) S.; m. Mohinder Kaur Sangha, June 14, 1964; children: Gurminder Jit (dec.), Ravinder Jit, Davinder Jit. BA, Punjab U., 1963, B of Teaching, 1964, MA, 1967; EdS, Delta State U., 1975; PhD, U. So. Miss., 1977. With Doaba Khalsa Higher Secondary Sch., Jullundur, India, 1964-65, Nat. H.S., Lambra, Punjab, India, 1965-67, G.G.N. Khalsa Coll., Ludhiana, India, 1967-69, J.F.K. H.S., Mound Bayou, Miss., 1970-71, I.T. Montgomery Elem. Sch., Mound Bayou, 1971-76, USM Children's Lab., Hattiesburg, Miss., 1976-77, U. S.C., Spartanburg, 1977-78, Moss Point (Miss.) Sch. System, 1978—. Guest editor Bolivar Commercial, 1972-75; editor series on India, Miss. Delta, 1973-75; contbr. articles to profl. jours. Elector for Pres. Clinton, Miss., 1996; del. Dem. Conv., Chgo., 1996; mem. steering com. to reelect Pres. Clinton; active Jackson County Dem. Ctrl. Com., Dem. State Exec. Com., 1988-92, 92-96. Mem. Internat. Platform Assn., Internat. Reading Assn., Internat. Cultural Soc., Miss. Reading Assn., NEA, Nat. Coun. Tchrs. English, Nat. Coun. Tchrs. Math., ASCD, Am. Heart Assn., March of Dimes, Nat. Wildlife Fedn., Nat. Guard Assn., Nat. Geog. Soc., Am. Legion, VFW, the Sikh Soc. of South, Sikh Coun. N.Am., Pacific Coast Khalsa Divan Soc., U. So. Miss. Alumni Assn., Delta State U. Alumni Assn., Phi Delta Kappa, Kappa Delta Phi. Democrat. Home: 5111 Old Mobile Ave Pascagoula MS 39581

SINGH, NIRBHAY NAND, psychology educator, researcher; b. Suva, Fiji, Jan. 27, 1952; arrived in New Zealand, 1970; s. Shiri Ram and Janki Kumari (Singh) S.; m. Judy Daya, May 17, 1973; children: Ashvind Nand, Subhashi Devi. Ph.D., U. Auckland, New Zealand, 1979. Sr. clin. psychologist, head psychology dept. Mangere Hosp. and Tng. Sch., Auckland, 1976-81; assoc. in clin. psychology U. Auckland, 1977-80; lectr. psychology U. Canterbury, Christchurch, New Zealand, 1981-82, sr. lectr. psychology, 1983-87; sr. rsch. scientist Ednl. Rsch. and Svcs. Ctr., De Kalb, Ill., 1987-89; prof. psychiatry and pediatrics Med. Coll. of Va., Richmond, 1989—; dir. Commonwealth Inst. for Child and Family Studies, Richmond, 1989—; clin. prof. of psychology Va. Commonwealth U., 1994—; cons. Project MESH, U. Otago, Dunedin, New Zealand, 1982-87, external examiner, diploma in edn., 1982-87; cons. Kimberley Hosp. and Tng. Sch., Levin, N.Z., 1984-87; cons. adv. com. tng. officers Dept. Health, Wellington, 1984-87; cons. curriculum adv. com. Vol. Welfare Agy. Tng. Bd., Wellington, 1984-87; cons. spl. edn. adv. com. Christchurch Tchrs.' Coll., 1986-87; expert cons. Dept. Justice, Washington, 1988—. Co-author: I Can Cook. Editor: Mental Retardation in New Zealand: Research and Policy Issues, 1983; Mental Retardation in New Zealand: Provisions, Services and Research, 1985; Exceptional Children in New Zealand, 1987, Psychopharmacology of the Developmental Disabilities, 1988, Perspective on the Use of Non-aversive and Aversive Interventions for Persons With Developmental Disabilities, 1990, The Regular Education Initiative, 1991, Learning Disabilities: Nature Theory and Treatment, 1992, Self-Injury: Analysis, Assessment and Treatment, 1992; editor-in-chief Jour. of Behavioral Edn., Jour. of Child and Family Studies, SED Quar.; contbr. chpts. to books; editorial bd. numerous jours. Winifred Gimblett scholar 1974; Med. Rsch. Coun. postgrad. scholar, 1975-76; Erskine fellow U. Canterbury, 1984. Fellow APA, APS, Behavior Therapy and Research Soc.; mem. Am. Assn. Mental Deficiency, Assn. Severely Handicapped, Assn. Child Psychology and Psychiatry, Assn. Advancement Behavior Therapy, Soc. Advancement Behavior Analysis, Psychonomic Soc., N.Y. Acad. Scis. Avocations: squash, racquetball. Office: Med Coll Va Dept Psychiatry PO Box 980489 Richmond VA 23298-0489

SINGLETARY, ALVIN D., lawyer; b. New Orleans, Sept. 27, 1942; s. Alvin E. and Alice (Pastoret) S.; m. Judy Louise Singletary, Dec. 3, 1983; children: Kimberly Dawn, Shane David, Kelly Diane. B.A., La. State U., 1964; J.D., Loyola U., New Orleans, 1969. Bar: La. 1969, U.S. Dist. Ct. (ea. dist.) La. 1972, U.S. Ct. Appeals (5th cir.) 1972, U.S. Supreme Ct. 1978, U.S. Ct. Appeals (11th cir.) 1981, U.S. Ct. Internat. Trade 1981, U.S. Ct. Customs and Patent Appeals 1982. Instr. Delgado Coll., New Orleans, 1976-77; sole practice, Slidell, La., 1970—; spl. asst. dist. atty. 22d Judicial Dist. Ct. Parish of St. Tammany, State of La.; sec.-treas. St. Tammany Pub. Trust Fin. Authority, Slidell, 1978—; Councilman-at-large City of Slidell, 1978—, interim mayor, 1985; mem. Democratic State Central Com., 1978-82; del. La. Constl. Conv., 1972-73; chmn. sustaining membership enrollment Cypress dist. Boy Scouts Am., 1989—; chmn. Together We Build Program First Baptist Ch. of Slidell, La.; treas. Slidell Centennial Commn.; bd. dirs. St. Tammany Coun. on Aging. Mem. Delta Theta Phi. Baptist. Lodge: Lions. Office: PO Box 1158 Slidell LA 70459-1158

SINGLETARY, JULIE B., home healthcare administrator, pediatrics nurse; b. Denver, Mar. 4, 1959; d. Dewey Elroy Jr. and Mary Elizabeth (Mays) Brunner; m. Harold Kelzo Singletary, Jan. 21, 1984; children: Amanda, Jessica. BSN, Valdosta State U., 1982. RN, Ga. Staff RN John Archibold Meml. Hosp., Thomasville, Ga., 1982-83, Med. Ctr. Ctrl. Ga., Macon, 1983-84, Kennestone Hosp., Marietta, Ga., 1984; staff/charge RN Gwinnett Med. Ctr., Lawrenceville, Ga., 1984-88; staff RN Primedical Urgent Care, Norcross, Ga., 1988, Egleston Children's Hosp., Atlanta, 1988-89, Pediatric Svcs. of Am., Norcross, 1989, Kid's Med. Club, Atlanta, 1987-93; staff RN, case mgr. Hand In Hand Home Health, Cumming, Ga., 1993-95; patient and care coord. Extended Cmty. Home Health of Atlanta, 1995—. Mem. Home Health Care Nurses Assn., Sigma Theta Tau, Kappa Delta. Republican. Baptist. Home: 1725 Lawrenceville Suwanee Rd Lawrenceville GA 30243-3587 Office: Extended Cmty Home Health Atlanta 4151 Memorial Dr Ste 223A Decatur GA 30032-1515

SINGLETARY, RUSSELL PRESSLEY, journalist; b. Charleston, S.C., Feb. 25, 1971; s. Wiggins Ellison and Gertrude Celeste (Cross) S. BA in History and French magna cum laude, Wofford Coll., 1993. Pub. rels. asst. S.C. Pub. Svc. Authority, Moncks Corner, 1993-95; staff writer Summerville (S.C.) Jour. Scene, 1995—. State del. Student Forum of Meth. Ch. in Am., Tulsa, 1992. Mem. Soc. Profl. Journalists, Friendship Men's Club, Phi Beta Kappa, Blue Key. Methodist.

SINGLETON, AUDREY BARNES, elementary education educator; b. Savannah, Ga., Aug. 9, 1947; d. Elmer Sr. and Estella (Johnson) Barnes; m. Marion Singleton, Feb. 10, 1973; children: Lisa Monique, Lori Michele. BS, Savannah State Coll., 1969, MEd, 1977, cert. in gifted edn., 1980. Tchr. Savannah-Chatham County Bd. Edn., 1969—. Named Tchr. of the Yr., Windsor Forest, 1994-95. Mem. NEA, Ga. Assn. Educators, Chatham Assn. Educators (bldg. rep. 1979-89, Bat Team award 1984), Internat. Reading Assn., Phi Delta Kappa, Alpha Kappa Alpha (Sisterhood award 1989). Democrat. Methodist. Home: 610 Sugar Bush Cir Savannah GA 31406-4434

SINGLETON, JOHN VIRGIL, JR., retired federal judge, lawyer; b. Kaufman, Tex., Mar. 20, 1918; s. John Virgil Sr. and Jennie (Shelton) S.; m. Jane Guilford Tully, Apr. 18, 1953 (dec. Apr. 1991); m. Sylvia Gregg, May 13, 1991. BA, U. Tex., LLB, 1942. Bar: Tex. 1942. Assoc., gen. counsel Houston Harris County Ship Channel Navigation Dist. Fulbright, Crooker, Freeman & Bates, 1946-54; ptnr. Bates, Riggs & Singleton, 1954-56, Bell & Singleton, 1957-61, Barrow, Bland, Rehmet & Singleton, 1962-66; judge U.S. Dist. Ct. (so. dist.) Tex., 1966-92, chief judge, 1979-88, sr. judge, 1988-92; pres. Houston Jr. Bar Assn., 1952-53; co-chmn. 5th cir. dist. judges divsn. Jud. Conf., 1969, chmn., 1970, rep. from 5th cir. Jud Conf. U.S., 1980-83, also chmn. legis. com.; mem. Fifth Cir. Jud. Coun., 1984—; bd. dirs. TransAmerican Waste Industries, Inc. Mem. Tex. Depository Bd., 1963-66; co-chmn. Harris County Lyndon B. Johnson for Pres. Com., 1960-61; del.-at-large Dem. Nat. Conv., 1956, 60, 64; regional coord. 7-state area Dem. Nat. Com., Lyndon B. Johnson-Hubert Humphrey Campaign for Pres., 1964; mem. exec. com., Tex. Dem. Com., 1962-65, chmn. fin. com. 1964-66; former bd. dirs. Houston Speech and Hearing Ctr.; trustee Houston Legal Found., Retina Rsch. Found.; mem. chancellor's coun. U. Tex.; mem. exec. com. Lombardi Awards Trophy; mem. tex. Longhorn Edn. Found.; sponsor Found. for Tex. Excellence; oversight com. renovation Meml. Park Golf Course, 1995. Named to Waxahachie High Sch. Hall of Fame. Mem. ABA (liaison rep. to spl. com. evaluation disciplinary enforcement, litigation sect. ad hoc com. on tng. for spl. masters, jury comprehension com.), Fed. Judges Assn. (bd. dirs. 1974—, mem. exec. com.), Houston Bar Assn. (v.p. 1956-57, editor Houston Lawyer 1954-55, chmn. unauthorized practice law com. 1961-62), Tex. Bar Found. (charter mem. fellows), Tex. Bar Assn. (dist. dir.), State Bar Tex. (adminstrn. justice com., chmn. unauthorized practice of law com., 1961-62, chmn. grievance com. 22d dist. 1965-66, bd. dirs. 1966, fed. jud. liaison to state bd. dirs. 1984-85, pres. state bar task force Thurgood Marshall Sch. Law, 1986—, charter mem. fellows Tex. Bar Found.), U. Tex. Ex-Students Assn. (life mem., pres. Houston chpt. 1961-62, mem. exec. com., chmn. scholarship com., at large mem. 1969-80), Rotary, Cowboys (foreman, straw boss), Am. Judicature Soc., Order of Coif (Houston chpt. 1989—), Delta Tau Delta (pres. 1940-41), Phi Alpha Delta, Lakeside Country Club (Houston, past sec., bd. dirs.). Episcopalian. Office: 314 N Post Oak Ln Houston TX 77024

SINGLETON, LAVERNA, community health nurse; b. Friend, Nebr., Nov. 14, 1940; d. Lester and Frances Anna M. (O'Dea) S. Diploma, St. Elizabeth Hosp., Lincoln, Nebr., 1961; BAAS, Midwestern State U., Wichita Falls, Tex., 1988, MA in Pub. Adminstrn., 1990. Quality control coord. Bethania Regional Health Care Ctr., Wichita Falls, head nurse, orthopedics, 1969-77, asst. dir. nursing, 1977-90; regional rev. mgr. Tex. Peer Rev. Orgn., Tex. Med. Found., Dallas, 1991-93; quality mgmt. mgr. Vis. Nurse Assn. Tex., Dallas, 1993-96; dir. QA Compliance Conss. for the Home Care Industry, Garland, Tex., 1996—. Mem. NLN, Tex. League Nursing, Tex. Orgn. Nurse Execs., Pi Sigma Alpha.

SINGLETON, PATRICIA MOORE, librarian; b. Montgomery, Ala.; d. Claude J. and Hattie P. (Gardner) Moore; m. Strafford Singleton, Aug. 31, 1968; 1 child, Strafford IV. BS, Ala. State U., 1962; MS in LS, Atlanta U., 1966; MS in Edn., Troy State U., 1975. Libr. S.W. Elem. Sch., Devereux, Ga., 1962-64, Drake H.S., Auburn, Ala., 1964-65; tchr. Booker T. Washington Sch., Montgomery, 1966-67; ref. libr./instr. Ala. State U., Montgomery, 1967-76, head ref. libr., asst. prof. libr. media, 1976-82, coord. pub. svcs., asst. prof. libr. media, 1982—, interim libr. dir., 1992-93. Contbr. chpt. to book. Andrew W. Mellon Found./Assn. Coll. and Rsch. Librs. fellow, 1975-76. Mem. ALA, Assn. Coll. and Rsch. Librs., Ala. Libr. Assn., Ala. Assn. Coll. and Rsch. Librs., Delta Sigma Theta. Office: Ala State U Library 915 S Jackson St Montgomery AL 36101-0271

SINGLETON, STELLA WOOD, educator and habilitation assistant; b. Moore County, N.C., Nov. 3, 1948; d. Jay and Thelma A. Wood; m. Tommy Singleton, Dec. 21, 1968; children: Jennifer, Mike. Diploma, Hamlet Hosp. Sch. Nursing, Hamlet, N.C., 1975; postgrad., Appalachian State U., Boone, N.C., 1990—. RN, N.C. Dir. Hospice of Boone (N.C.) Area, 1982-83; Hospice dir. Hospice of Avery County, Newland, N.C., 1983-85; DON Toe River Health Dist., Newland, N.C., 1983-84; mental health nurse II New River Mental Health, Newland, N.C., 1977-82, 85-95; beauty cons. Mary Kay Cosmetics, 1986—; habilitation asst. Devl. Disabilities Svcs., Boone, N.C., 1995—; instr. Mayland C.C., Spruce Pine, N.C. Co-facilitator Avery County Alzheimer's Support Group, group facilitator Cancer Support Group Svc.; rehab. chmn. Am. Cancer Soc. Recipient Gov's. award for administrv. vol. Mem. N.C. Biofeedback Soc. Home: PO Box 483 Crossnore NC 28616-0483 Office: Devel Disabilities Svcs 404 Oak Summit Boone NC 28607 also: Mayland CC PO Box 547 Spruce Pine NC 28777

SINGSTOCK, DAVID JOHN, military officer; b. Oshkosh, Wis., July 19, 1940; s. Arnold William and Viola Rufine (Gerdener) S.; children: Susan, Brian, Elissa, Timothy. BS with distinction, Maine Maritime Acad., 1964; student, U.S. Merchant Marine Acad., 1959-62; BSBA with distinction, George Washington U., 1973, MS, 1975. Lic. profl. marine engr. Commd. ensign USN, 1964, advanced through grades to comdr., 1984, various sea assignments including combat duty in Vietnam, 1964-69; engr. officer USS Harold J. Ellison USN, Norfolk, Va., 1969-71, ADP fin. mgr. Cinclantflt, 1971-73; planning and quality assurance officer supr. shipbuilding USN, Portsmouth, Va., 1973-76; prodn./repair officer supr. shipbuilding USN, Bath, Maine, 1976-79; ship maintenance mgr. chief naval ops. USN, Washington, 1980-83, dir. fleet modernization program space/naval warfare systems command, 1983-86, program mgr. USS Stark restoration naval sea systems command, 1986-88, tech. dir. dep. asst. sec. Navy for internat. programs, 1988-93; sr. tech. advisor Royal Saudi Naval Forces Ops. Desert Shield and Desert Storm, 1990-91; sr. naval tech. mem. to Sec. of Def. chartered delegation of sr. U.S. ofcls., Saudi Arabia, 1991; retired U.S. Navy, 1993. Asst. scoutmaster Boy Scouts Am., Dumfries, Va., 1985-90; coach Youth Soccer, Maine, Va., 1976-84; active local property owners civic orgns., Va., Maine, 1970—; instr. ARC, Seattle, 1967-68. Decorated Navy Commendation medal, Navy Achievement medal, Vietnamese Cross of Gallantry, Meritorious Svc. Medal, Joint Svc. Commendation medal, Bronze Star, Purple Heart; recipient Cert. of Appreciation and Gratitude, Comdr. of Saudi Arabian Armed Forces. Mem. Am. Soc. Naval Engrs. (dep. com. chmn., speaker 1988), Nat. Contract Mgmt. Assn. (cert. contracts mgr.), Ret. Officers Assn., Nat. Eagle Scout Assn., Mason (32 degree), Scottish Rite, Shriner. Presbyterian. Home: 1125 Portner Rd Alexandria VA 22314-1314 Office: Vitro Corp Ste ML 100 2361 Jefferson Davis Hwy Arlington VA 22202

SINISTRE, JEAN PAUL, television producer, journalist; b. El Paso, Tex., July 10, 1938; s. Enrico Carlo and Cathrina Elizabeth (St. Croix) S.; m. Ruth Lenore Morgan, Jan. 11, 1968. BSc, U. Nev., Las Vegas, 1970; AAS, Greenville Coll., 1973. Columnist Conroe (Tex.) Morning News, 1974, Rings Around Tex., Houston, 1974-77; entertainment editor Montgomery County News, Willis and Conroe, Tex., 1977-85; tv prodr. Moonchild TV Prodns., Cleveland, Tex., 1985-90; tv prodr., dir. Entertainment Unltd., Crocket and Willis, Tex., 1990—; bd. dirs. Nat. Boxing Assn., Hollywood, Fla. TV prodr. European Country Music Assn. TV Network, 1996—. Staff sgt. U.S. Army, 1967-70, Vietnam. Recipient Broadcasting/Prodr. award Can. Music Prodrs., Montreal, Can., 1995. Mem. Soc. Profl. Journalists (directory com. 1992—), Tex. Music Industry, Country Music Assn. Republican. Roman Catholic. Office: Moonchild TV Prodns PO Box 1467 Willis TX 77378

SINK, ADELAIDE ALEXANDER, banker; b. Mt. Airy, N.C., June 5, 1948; d. Kester Andrew and Adelaide (Bunker) S.; m. William Howard McBride, Jr., July 10, 1986; children: William Albert, Cheryle Alexander. BS, Wake Forest U., 1970. Tchr. Meth. Girls High Sch., Freetown, Sierra Leone, 1970-71, Am. Sch. of Liberia, Monrovia, 1971-72; v.p. NCNB, Charlotte, N.C., 1974-81; sr. v.p. NCNB, N.Y.C., 1981-84, Miami, Fla., 1984-89; exec. v.p. Nations Bank, Tampa, Fla., 1989-93; pres. Nations Bank of Fla., 1993—. Campaign chair United Way of Hillsborough County, Tampa, 1993; trustee Wake Forest U., 1992-96; mem. Govt. Accountability to the People Commn., Tallahassee; chair Hillsborough Edn. Found., 1994-96. Recipient Disting. Alumnus award Wake Forest U., 1993. Mem. Fla. Women's Alliance (chair 1995-96), Leadership Fla., Fla. Coun. 100, So. Growth Policies Bd., Fla. Taxwatch, Bus./Higher Edn. Partnership. Democrat. Presbyterian. Home: PO Box 219 Thonotosassa FL 33592-0219 Office: Nations Bank PO Box 31590 Tampa FL 33631-3590

SINK, DEBORAH J., nursing educator; b. Charlotte, N.C., Sept. 6, 1953; d. Robert W. and Carolyn (Sides) Jones; m. Edwin M. Sink, June 8, 1974; children: Cary, Christy, Jan, David. BSN, U. N.C., Greensboro, 1975, MEd, 1996; postgrad., Columbia Internat. Sem., 1981-83. RN, N.C., S.C. Neonatal nurse Richland County Hosp., Columbia, S.C., 1981-83, Lexington County Hosp., Columbia, 1985-92; nurse educator Women's Hosp., Greensboro, N.C., 1992—; asst. developer Adam's Farm Ch., Greensboro, 1992—, pres. women's club, 1993-95. Author: James: an Inductive Approach, 1991. Cons., speaker Assn. Reformed Presbyns., 1992—, Presbyn. Ch. Am., 1983-92; pres. PTA Lonnie B. Nelson Sch., Columbia, 1992; bd. mem. Jamestown Middle Sch., Greensboro, 1993-95; active Focus on Family, N.C., S.C., 1981-96. Mem. Adam's Farm Club, Columbia Country Club. Republican. Office: Adam's Farm Ch 5113 Mackey Rd Jamestown NC 27282

SINKHORN, MARY JEAN, real estate executive; b. Athens, Ga., May 19, 1941; d. Howard J. and Helen (Fields) Pickelsimer; m. Michael J. Gordon, Aug. 21, 1965 (div. 1985); children: Michael J. Jr., Mitzi J.; m. Walt P. Sinkhorn, Mar. 28, 1986. Degree, Lakeland Bus. Coll., 1960. Lic. realtor, Pa., Fla. Legal sec. C.A. Boswell, Sr., et al., Attys., Bartow, Fla., 1960-69; owner, operator Gordon and Whitaker Interiors, Phila., 1977-1978; assoc. realtor Fox and Lazo, Haverford, Pa., 1979-83; dir. real estate services The Polo Group, Inc., Tampa, Fla., 1984—. V.p. Tampa Jr. Woman's Club, 1971; treas. Bartow Jr. Woman's Club, 1966; sec. Bartow Jaycettes, 1967; vol. Fla. Soc. for Prevention of Blindness, 1971. Mem. Women's Council Realtors (civic project chmn. 1986), Tampa Bd. Realtors, Edn. and Realtor Assn. (com. main line bd. realtors 1979-83). Office: The Polo Group Inc 12966 N Dale Mabry Hwy Tampa FL 33618-2806

SINNAMON, WALTER BRUCE, college administrator, biology educator; b. Phila., Dec. 27, 1947; m. Carol Sinnamon; 1 child, Michel. BS in Zoology, Houghton Coll., 1969; postgrad., SUNY, Geneseo, 1975-77; PhD in Zoology, Clemson U., 1985. Cert. tchr. biology, chemistry, phys. sci., gen. sci., N.Y. Sci. instr. Houghton (N.Y.) Acad., 1969-77, bus. mgr., 1973-77; grad. teaching asst. dept. zoology Clemson (S.C.) U., 1977-82; asst. prof. So. Wesleyan U., 1982-85, assoc. prof., 1985-90, prof. biology, 1990—, spl. asst. to the pres. for instl. effectiveness, 1993—; mem. adv. bd. S.C. Higher Edn. Assessment Network, 1993—, chair spl. interest groups com., 1993—; mem. adv. bd. Anderson-Oconee-Pickens Sci. and Math. Hub, 1993—, vice-chair adv. bd., 1995—; grant writer Sigma Xi, 1980, U.S. Dept. Edn., Washington, 1990, Cannon Found., Kannapolis, N.C., 1991, JanIrve Found., Asheville, N.C., 1991, NSF, Washington, 1991, Consortium for Advancement of Pvt. Higher Edn. Contbr. articles to profl. jours. Mem. Soc. for Coll. and Univ. Planning, Am. Assn. Instl. Rsch., S.C. Assn. Instl. Rsch., Affiliation Christian Biologists, Human Anatomy and Physiology Soc., Am. Soc. Zoologists, Internat. Fedn. Comparative Endocrinol. Socs., Am. Sci. Affiliation, Am. Soc. Microbiology, Nat. Arbor Day Soc., Gideons Internat., Wycliff Assocs., Sigma Xi. Home: 423 Pin Du Lac Dr Central SC 29630-9435 Office: So Wesleyan U PO Box 407 Central SC 29630-0407

SINNINGER, DWIGHT VIRGIL, research engineer; b. Bourbon, Ind., Dec. 29, 1901; s. Norman E. and Myra (Huff) S.; student Armour Inst., 1928, U. Chgo., 1942, Northwestern U., 1943; m. Coyla Annetta Annis, Mar. 1, 1929; m. Charlotte M. Lenz, Jan. 21, 1983. Registered profl. engr., Ill. Electronics rsch. engr. Johnson Labs., Chgo., 1935-42; chief engr. Pathfinder Radio Corp., 1943-44, Rowe Engring. Corp., 1945-48, Hupp Electronics Co. div. Hupp Corp., 1948-61; dir. rsch. Pioneer Electric & Research Corp., Forest Park, Ill., 1961-65, Senn Custom, Inc., Forest Park and San Antonio, 1967—. Patentee in field. Mem. IEEE. Address: PO Box 982 Kerrville TX 78029-0982

SINTON, CHRISTOPHER MICHAEL, neurophysiologist, educator; b. Beckenham, Kent, Eng., Sept. 10, 1946; came to U.S., 1983; s. Leslie George and Evelyn Mabel (Burn) S. BA, Cambridge U., Eng., 1968, MA, 1977; BSc, London U., 1978; PhD, U. Lyon, France, 1981. Rsch. fellow U. Lyon, 1980-83; rsch. assoc. Princeton (N.J.) U., 1983-84; sr. scientist Ciba-Geigy Corp., Summit, N.J., 1984-88; dir. electrophysiology Neurogen Corp., Branford, Conn., 1988-94; asst. prof. U. Tex. Southwestern Med. Ctr., Dallas, 1994—; rsch. asst. prof. medicine NYU, N.y.C., 1986-94. Contbr. 40 articles to profl. jours. Med. Rsch. Coun. vis. scholar, France, 1983. Mem. N.Y. Acad. Scis., Soc. Neurosci., European Neurosci. Assn., European Sleep Rsch. Soc., Sleep Rsch. Soc. Office: U Tex SW Med Ctr Dept Psychiatry 5323 Harry Hines Blvd Dallas TX 75235-9070

SIPE, HERBERT JAMES, JR., chemistry educator; b. Lewistown, Pa., Aug. 17, 1940; s. Herbert James and Esther Louise (Bossinger) S. BS, Juniata Coll., 1962; PhD, U. Wis., 1969. Asst. prof. chemistry Hampden Sydney (Va.) Coll., 1968-72, assoc. prof., 1973-80, prof., 1981-93, Spalding prof., 1993—, chmn. dept., 1972-74, 76-80, 81-82, 86-87; rsch. assoc. chemistry dept. U. Ala., Tuscaloosa, 1980-81; rsch. chemist lab. molecular biophysics Nat. Inst. Environ. Health Sci., Research Triangle Park, N.C., 1987-88. Contbr. articles to profl. jours. Recipient Cabell Disting. Tchr. award Hampden Sydney Coll., 1990; grantee NSF, 1971-73, 77-78, 84-85, 88, 92. Mem. AAAS, AAUP, Am. Chem. Soc., Va. Acad. Sci., Internat. Electron Paramagnetic Resonance Soc. (charter), Sigma Xi, Omicron Delta Kappa, Alpha Chi Sigma (dist. counselor Piedmont-Appalachia dist. 1975-78, nat. chmn. house adv. com. 1981-86, mem. Ednl. Found. 1981—). Democrat. Home: Hillside Hmpden Sydney VA 23943 Office: Hampden Sydney Coll Dept Chemistry Hampden Sydney VA 23943

SIPES, JAMES LAMOYNE, landscape architect, educator; b. Elizabethtown, Ky., Jan. 28, 1957; s. William L. and Betty Jean (Miller) S.; m. Kimberly A. Blevins, Feb. 5, 1983; children: Matthew, Sara, Ally. BS in Landscape Architecture, U. Ky., 1982; M in Landscape Architecture, Iowa State U., 1984. Registered landscape architect, Tex. Teaching asst. U. Ky., Lexington, 1981-82; planning intern Lexington-Fayette Govt., 1982-83; teaching asst. Iowa State U., Ames, 1983-84; landscape architect Nat. Park Svc., Gunnison, Colo., 1984-85, Schrickel, Rollins Assocs., Arlington, Tex., 1985-88, U.S. Forest Svc., Dillon, Mont., 1989; computer graphic cons. Video Perspectives, Inc., Louisville, 1990; lectr. U. Idaho, Moscow, 1989-93; assoc. prof. landscape architecture Wash. State U., Pullman, 1988-94; dir. U. Okla., Norman, 1995—; cons. Computer Graphics and Simulations, Salt Lake City, 1993-94; mem. adv. bd. Cmty. Childcare Ctr., Pullman, 1992—. Computer editor Landscape Architecture Mag., Washington, 1994—; producer Animated World, PBS, 1994—; contbr. articles to profl. jours. Mem. Pullman Civic Trust, 1993-94. Recipient Cert. of Appreciation, Soil Conservation Svc., 1992, Cert. of Appreciation, U.S. Forest Svc., 1990. Mem. Am. Soc. Landscape Architects (Honor award 1984, 94, Tex. Design award 1992), Coun. Educators in Landscape Architecture, Nat. Computer Graphics Assn., Pacific N.W. Recreation Consortium, Gamma Sigma Delta, Phi Kappa Phi. Office: U Okla Landscape Architecture Dept Landscape Architecture Norman OK 73019

SIRGO, HENRY BARBIER, political science educator; b. New Orleans, s. George Louis and Noemie Germaine (Barbier) S. B.A., U. New Orleans, 1972; M.S., Fla. State U., 1973, Ph.D., 1976. Asst. prof. McNeese State U., Lake Charles, La., 1976-82 , assoc. prof. polit. sci., 1982-91, prof. polit. sci., 1991—. Mem. editl. bd. Southeastern Polit. Rev., 1995—; contbr. articles to profl. jours. Def. resource person LWV, Lake Charles, 1983; regulation resource person Council Better La., 1977, U.S. constn. bicentennial com. Grantee NEH, 1982, 86, Harry S. Truman Library, 1984, NSF, 1978, 79, 96; Shearman fellow, 1987, 90. Mem. Am. Polit. Sci. Assn., La. Polit. Assn. (pres. 1984-85), Southwest Assn. Prelaw Advisors, Southwestern Social Sci. Assn., Ark. Polit. Sci. Assn., Ctr. Study of the Presidency, Pi Sigma Alpha. Democrat. Roman Catholic. Avocations: scuba, weightlifting, running, bicycling. Office: McNeese State U Dept Social Scis Lake Charles LA 70609

SISISKY, NORMAN, congressman, soft drink bottler; b. Balt., June 9, 1927; m. Rhoda Brown, June 12, 1949; children: Mark B., Terry R., Richard L., Stuart J. BS in Bus. Adminstrn., Va. Commonwealth U., 1949; LLD (hon.), Va. State U. Pres., owner Pepsi-Cola Bottling Co. of Petersburg, Inc.; pres., dir. Lee Distbg. Co., Inc., Petersburg, Rhonor Corp., Petersburg; pres. Belfield Land, Inc., Petersburg; mem. Va. Gen. Assembly, Richmond, 1974-82, 98th-104th Congresses from 4th Va. dist., Washington, 1983—; mem. Ho. nat. security com., ranking mem. mil. readiness subcom., subcom. mil. procurement, panel on morale, welfare & recreation, Ho. small bus. com., subcom. procurement, exports & bus. opportunities; dir. Bank of Va., Richmond; vice-chair defense and security com. North Atlantic Assembly. Pres. Appomattox Indls. Devel. Corp.; bd. visitors Va. State U.; commr. Petersburg Hosp. Authority; trustee Va. State Coll. Found.; bd. dirs. Southside Va. Emergency Crew and Community Resource Devel. Bd. Served with USN 1945-46. Recipient Nat. Security Leadership award, Peace Through Stregnth Victory award, Douglas MacArthur award, Watchdog Treasury award, Thomas Jefferson award, 1994 Achievement award Va. Jaycees, Spirit of Enterprise U.S. C. of C., Small Bus. award Nat. Fedn. Ind. Bus. Mem. Nat. Soft Drink Assn. (chmn. bd. 1981-82), Petersburg C. of C. (v.p.). Democrat. Jewish. Club: Moose. Office: US Ho of Reps 2371 Rayburn Bldg Washington DC 20515-0005*

SISK, EILEEN VICTORIA, journalist; b. Henderson, Nev., Nov. 8, 1952; d. Hugh Albert and Susan Apathy (Shellenbarger) S.; m. Richard James Adams, Dec. 28, 1974 (div. Mar. 1979); m. Stephen Rudolph Tetreault, Aug. 29, 1981 (div. Oct. 1993); children: Jeffrey Hugh Tetreault, Douglas Gerard Tetreault. BA in Comm., Calif. State U., Fullerton, 1979. Feature writing intern L.A. Times, 1977-78; pub. info. asst. Orange County Transit Dist., Garden Grove, Calif., 1978; copy editor Las Vegas Rev. Jour., 1978-79, Sunday editor, 1979-81; copy editor U.S. C. of C., Washington, 1981-83; copy editor The Washington Post, 1982-86, design editor, 1987—; writer, N.Y.C., 1975—. Vol. NOW, Washington, 1981, Gloucester County Pub. Schs., 1992—. Recipient 4 Merit awards Calif. Photographers Pro Show, 1978. Mem. Soc. Profl. Journalists (profl. devel. com. 1986-92), Soc. Newspaper Design (4 Awards of Excellence 1990, 92), No. Va. Country Western Dance Assn. Office: Charlotte Sheedy Lit Agy 41 King St New York NY 10014-4949

SISK, ZENOBIA ANN, secondary school educator; b. Johnson City, Tenn., Sept. 5, 1938; d. Lone L. and Alberta (Garrett) S. AB, Milligan Coll., 1960; postgrad., East Tenn. State U., 1961-62. Tchr. chemistry, biology Washington College (Tenn.) Acad., 1962-71; tchr. chemistry, physics, biology David Crockett High Sch., Jonesborough, Tenn., 1971—. Mem. Am. Chem. Soc., Am. Inst. Chemists, NEA, Tenn. Edn. Assn., Washington County Edn. Assn. (bd. dirs.), DAR, Delta Kappa Gamma (2d v.p., sec.). Republican. Baptist. Home: RR 8 Box 41 Mountain View Dr Johnson City TN 37601-9449 Office: Washington County Bd Edn College St Jonesborough TN 37659

SISLEY, NINA MAE, physician, public health officer; b. Jacksonville, Fla., Aug. 19, 1924; d. Leonard Percy and Verna (Martin) S.; m. George W. Fischer, May 16, 1962 (dec. 1990). BA, Tex. State Coll. for Women, 1944; MD, U. Tex., Galveston, 1950; MPH, U. Mich., 1963. Intern City of Detroit Receiving Hosp., 1950-51; resident in gen. practice St. Mary's Infirmary, Galveston, Tex., 1951-52; sch. physician Galveston Ind. Sch. Dist., 1953-56; dir. med. svcs. San Antonio Health Dept., 1960-63, acting dir., 1963-64; resident in pub. health Tex. Dept. Pub. Health, San Antonio, 1963-65; dir. community health svcs. Corpus Christi-Nueces County (Tex.) Health Dept., 1964-67; dir. Corpus Christi-Nueces County (Tex.) Dept. Pub. Health, 1987—; dir. Tb control region 5 Tex. Dept. Health, Corpus Christi, 1967-73; dir. pub. health region 11 Tex. Dept. Health, Rosenberg, 1978-87; chief chronic illness control City of Houston Health Dept., 1973-78; lectr. Incarnate Word Coll., San Antonio, 1963-64; adj. prof. U. Tex. Sch. Pub. Health, Houston, 1980—; guest lectr. Corpus Christi State U., 1987—; pvt. practice Galveston, Stockdale, Hereford and Borger, Tex., 1952-59; mem. adv. bd. N.W. Cmty. Adv. Coun., North Bay Longterm Health Adv. Coun. Bd. dirs. Coastal Bend chpt. ARC, Corpus Christi, 1990-94, pres., 1990-91; bd. dirs. United Way-Coastal Bend, Coastal Bend Coalition on AIDS, 1988-94, Coastal Bend chpt. Am. Diabetes Assn., 1990—; mem. Nueces County Child Fatality Rev. Com. Fellow Am. Coll. Preventive Medicine; mem. AMA, APHA, Tex. Med. Assn., Nueces County Med. Soc. (pres.-elect 1996—), Tex. Assn. Pub. Health Physicians, Tex. Pub. Health Assn. (pres. 1991-92). Episcopalian. Home: 62 Rock Creek Dr Corpus Christi TX 78412-4214 Office: Corpus Christi-Nueces County Dept Health 1702 Horne Rd Corpus Christi TX 78416-1902

SISSOM, LEIGHTON ESTEN, engineering educator, dean, consultant; b. Manchester, Tenn., Aug. 26, 1934; s. Willie Esten and Bertha Sarah (Davis) S.; m. Evelyn Janelle Lee, June 13, 1953; children: Terry Lee, Denny Leighton. B.S., Middle Tenn. State Coll., 1956; B.S. in Mech. Engring., Tenn. Technol. U., 1962; M.S. in Mech. Engring., Ga. Inst. Tech., 1964, Ph.D., 1965. Diplomate Nat. Acad. Forensic Engrs.; registered profl. engr., Tenn. Draftsman Westinghouse Electric Corp., Tullahoma, 1953-57; mech. designer ARO, Inc., Tullahoma, 1957-58; instr. mech. engring. Tenn. Technol. U., Cookeville, 1958-62, chmn. dept. mech. engring., 1965-79, dean engring., 1979-88, dean of engring. emeritus, 1988—; prin. cons. Sissom & Assocs., Cookeville, Tenn., 1962—; bd. dirs. Accreditation Bd. Engring. and Tech., N.Y.C., 1978-86, treas., 1982-86. Author: (with Donald R. Pitts) Elements of Transport Phenomena, 1972, Heat Transfer, 1977, 1,000 Solved Problems in Heat Transfer, 1991; contbr. An Attorney's Guide to Engineering, 1986; contbr. articles to various publs. Fellow ASME (sr. v.p. 1982-86, gov. 1986-88, Golden medallion), Am. Soc. Engring. Edn. (bd. dirs. 1984-87, pres. 1991-92), Accreditation Bd. Engring. and Tech.; mem. NSPE, Soc. Automotive Engrs., Nat. Engring. Deans Coun. (chmn. 1984-87), Order of the Engr. (chmn. bd. govs. 1994-96), Tau Beta Pi (v.p. 1986-89, councillor 1986-89). Home and Office: 1151 Shipley Church Rd Cookeville TN 38501-7730

SISSON, JEAN CRALLE, middle school educator; b. Village, Va., Nov. 16, 1941; d. Willard Andrew and Carolyn (Headley) Cralle; m. James B. Sisson, June 20, 1964 (div. Oct. 1994); 1 child, Kimberly Carol. BS in Elem. Edn., Longwood Coll., 1964; MA in Adminstrn. and Supervision, Va. Commonwealth U., 1979. Tchr. 2nd grade Tappahannock (Va.) Elem. Sch., 1964-67; tchr. 2nd and 4th grades Farnham (Va.) Elem. Sch., 1967-71; tchr. 6th grade Callao (Va.) Elem. Sch., 1971-81; tchr. 6th and 7th grades Northumberland Mid. Sch., Heathsville, Va., 1981—; sr. mem. Supt. Adv. Com., Heathsville, 1986-93. Author: My Survival, 1994; author of children's books, short stories and poetry. Lifetime mem. Gibeon Bapt. Ch., Village, Va., 1942—. Mem. NEA, ASCD, People for Ethical Treatment of Animals, Aerobics & Fitness Assn. Am., Va. Mid. Sch. Assn., Exercise Safety Assn., Nat. Coun. of English Tchrs., Nat. Wildlife Fedn. Republican. Home: RR 1 Box 39A Callao VA 22435-9706 Office: Northumberland Mid Sch PO Box 100 Heathsville VA 22473-0100

SISSON, JERRY ALLAN, lawyer; b. Memphis, Oct. 13, 1956; s. Thomas E. and Jewel O. (Hipps) S.; m. Debra Elaine Martin, Aug. 13, 1977; children: Jennifer Elaine, Elizabeth Diane, Meredith Lydia, Allan Martin. BBA, Memphis State U., 1977, JD, 1979. Tenn. 1980, U.S. Dist. Ct. (we. dist.) Tenn. 1980, U.S. Supreme Ct. 1992; cert. property mgr. Ptnr. Sisson & Sisson, Memphis, 1980—. Mem. Firewise Found. Named one of Outstanding Young Men Am., 1981. Mem. Tenn. Bar Assn., Memphis-Shelby County Bar Assn., Inst. Real Estate Mgmt., Memphis Jaycees (legal counsel 1985, v.p. community action 1986-87, v.p. individual devel. 1987-88, pres. 1988-89). Republican. Mem. Ch. Christ. Home: 7919 Birnam Wood Cove Germantown TN 38138 Office: Sisson & Sisson 2171 Judicial Dr # 215 Germantown TN 38138-3869

SISSON, ROBERT F., photographer, writer, lecturer, educator; b. Glen Ridge, N.J., May 30, 1923; s. Horace R. and Frances A. S.; m. Patricia Matthews, Oct. 15, 1978; 1 son by previous marriage, Robert F.H.; 1 stepson, James A. Matthews. With Nat. Geographic Soc., Washington, 1942-88, chief nat. sci. photographer, 1981-88; free-lance photographer, 1988—; lectr. in field; mem. nature staff Sarastoa Mag., 1989; owner Macro/Nature Workshops, Englewood, Fla. Photographer one-man shows, Nat. Geog. Soc., Washington, 1974, Washington Press Club, 1976, Berkshire (Mass.) Mus., 1976, Brooks Inst., Santa Barbara, Calif., 1980, U. Miami, 1993, Sea Ctr., Santa Barbara, Calif., 1993, Corcoran Gallery of Art's Spl. World Tour, 1988, permanent collections, Mus. Art, N.Y.C. Recipient 1st prize for color photograph White House News Photographers Assn., 1961; recipient Canadian Natural Sci. award, 1967, Louis Schmidt award, 1991. Fellow Biol. Photographers Assn.; mem. Biol. Photog. Assn. (awards for color prints 1967), Nat. Audubon Soc., Nat. Geog. Soc., Nat. Wildlife Fedn., Soc. Photog. Scientists and Engrs., N.Y. Acad. Scis., Sigma Delta Chi. Office: Macro/Nature Photography PO Box 1649 Englewood FL 34295-1649

SITTERLY, CONNIE SUE, management training specialist, author, consultant, speaker; b. Fairfax, Okla., Oct. 9, 1953; d. Claude O. and Virda (Smith) S. AA, Frank Phillips Coll., 1973; BS, West Tex. State U., 1975, MA, 1978; EdD, Tex. Woman's U., 1991. Instr. Frank Phillips Coll., Borger, Tex., 1978-83; owner, founder Mgmt. Tng. Specialists, Ft. Worth, 1983—; asst. prof. Amarillo (Tex.) Coll., 1980-85; assoc. adj. prof. Tex. Woman's U., Denton, 1986—; speaker, author and cons. in field. Co-author: A Woman's Place: Management, 1988; author: The Woman Manager, 1993, The Female Enterpreneur, 1993; contbr. more than 350 articles to newspapers and profl. jours. Mem. ASTD, Am. Soc. Quality Control, Am. Bus. Women's Assn., Human Resources Assn. Home: 6816 Brants Ln Fort Worth TX 76116-7902 Office: Mgmt Tng Specialists Ste D 5320 Camp Bowie Blvd Fort Worth TX 76107

SITTIG, DEAN FORREST, medical informatician and biomedical engineer; b. Bellefonte, Pa., Mar. 2, 1961; s. Forrest Mark and Elizabeth Rachel (Stark) S.; m. JoAnn Kaalaas, July 4, 1989; 1 child, Rachel Kaalaas. BS, Pa. State U., 1982, MS, 1984; PhD, U. Utah, 1988. Assoc. rsch. scientist Yale U., New Haven, Conn., 1988-89, asst. prof., 1990-91; asst. prof. Vanderbilt U., Nashville, 1992-95; chief med. info. arch. on U.S. Univs.-Saudi project King Faisal Hosp. and Rsch. Ctr., Riyadh, Saudi Arabia, 1995-96; corp. mgr. info. systems Ptnrs. Healthcare Inc., Boston, 1996—; grant reviewer Nat. Libr. Medicine, Washington, 1994. Contbr. articles and revs. to profl. jours. and chpts. to books; assoc. editor: Internat. Jour. Clin. Monitoring and Computing, 1993. Recipient Martin Epstein award Symposium Computer Applications Med. Care, 1987, FIRST award Nat. Libr. Medicine, 1991; grantee Whitaker Found., 1989, Hewlett Packard Co., 1991. Fellow Am. Coll. Med. Informatics; mem. IEEE, Soc. for Computers in Critical Care Pulmonary Medicine (sec.-treas. 1993), Am. Med. Informatics Assn. (jour. asst. editor 1993-95). Home: 25 Boynton Rd Medford MA 02155-2930 Office: Brigham & Women's Hosp Dept Info Svcs Boston MA 02115

SIVER, CHESTER ASA, manufacturing executive; b. Kenosha, Wis., June 13, 1912; s. Frank Arch and Maud Ethel (Brooks) S.; m. Margaret Louise Rogers, Dec. 19, 1937; children: Roger Brooks, Frank Allen, Stanley Thomas. BS, U.S. Naval Acad., 1934; MS, MIT, 1935; postgrad., Harvard Bus. Sch., 1945. Registered profl. engr., N.Y. Engr. Linde Air Products Divsn. Union Carbide & Carbon Co., Tonawanda, N.Y., 1935-47; adminstrv. engr. Am. Machine and Foundry, Bklyn., 1947-50; mgr. engring. Liquid Carbonic Corp., Chgo., 1950-53; v.p., gen. mgr. control divsn. Black, Sivalls & Bryson, Inc., Kansas City, Mo., 1953-57; mgr. engring. Edward Valve Divsn. Rockwell Internat., East Chicago, Ind., 1958-60; mgr. mktg. Chapman Valve Co., Indian Orchard, Mass., 1961-62; program mgr. United Technols., Windsor, Conn., 1962-65; chmn., CEO, pres. Conval, Inc., Somers, Conn., 1967—. Patentee in field. Comdr. USNR, 1934-57, active duty, 1940-45. Mem. ASME, Instrument Soc. Am., Valve Mfrs. Assn. Home: 1 Seaside Ln Apt 503 Belleair FL 34616 Office: Conval Inc 265 Field Rd Somers CT 06071

SIVERD, ROBERT JOSEPH, lawyer; b. Newark, July 27, 1948; s. Clifford David and Elizabeth Ann (Klink) S.; m. Bonita Marie Shulock, Jan. 8, 1972; children: Robert J. Jr., Veronica Leigh. AB in French, Georgetown U., 1970; JD, 1973; postgrad. LaSorbonne, Paris, 1969. Bar: N.Y. 1974, U.S. Dist. Ct. (so. and ea. dists.) N.Y. 1974, U.S. Ct. Appeals (2nd cir.) 1974, U.S. Supreme Ct. 1980, U.S. Dist. Ct. (ea. dist.) Pa. 1984, U.S. Ct. Appeals (3rd cir.) 1984, (6th cir.) 1985, Ohio 1991, Ky. 1992. Assoc. Donovan Leisure Newton & Irvine, N.Y.C., 1973-83; staff v.p., litigation counsel Am. Fin. Group, Inc., Greenwich, Conn., 1983-86, v.p. litigation counsel, 1986-87, v.p. assoc. gen. counsel, Cin., 1987-92; sr. v.p., gen. counsel and sec. Gen. Cable Corp., 1992-94, exec. v.p., gen. counsel and sec., 1994—. Mem. ABA, Cin. Bar Assn., Assn. of Bar of City of N.Y., Ky. Bar Assn. Republican. Office: Gen Cable Corp 4 Tesseneer Dr Newport KY 41076-9753

SIZEMORE, CHRISTINE WICK, English language educator; b. Washington, Nov. 17, 1945; d. Paul Myron and Christine (Gawne) Wick; m. Michael M. Sizemore, June 1, 1968; children: Christine Corsaut, James Gawne. BA, Carnegie Inst. Tech., 1967; MA, U. Pa., 1968, PhD, 1972. Asst. prof. Ga. State U., 1972-78, Spelman Coll., 1978-84; assoc. prof. Spelman Coll., 1984-92, prof., 1992—; part-time instr. Ga. State U., 1971-72; vis. prof. Emory U., 1976. Author: A Female Vision of the City: London in the Novels of Five British Women, 1989; contbr. articles to profl. jours. Grantee Bush Found., 1988, United Negro Coll. Fund, 1986. Mem. MLA (women's caucus), South Atlantic MLA (treas. women's caucus 1987-89, nominating com. workshop I 1981-83, chair 1980, sec. 1979), Nat. Women's Studies Assn., Southeastern Renaissance Soc. Democrat. Presbyterian. Home: 860 Peachtree Battle Cir NW Atlanta GA 30327-1320 Office: Spelman Coll PO Box 273 Atlanta GA 30301-0273

SIZEMORE, DEBORAH LIGHTFOOT, writer, editor; b. Lamesa, Tex., Mar. 18, 1956; d. Glenn Billy and Francis Earlene (Cable) Lightfoot; m. O.E. Gene Sizemore, June 19, 1981. BS in Agrl. Journalism summa cum laude, Tex. A&M U., 1977. Writer, Tex. Agrl. Extension, College Station, 1976-77; copy editor Abilene (Tex.) Reporter-News, 1978; customer svc. rep. Motheral Printing Co., Ft. Worth, 1978-79; prodn. coord. Graphic Arts, Inc., Ft. Worth, 1980-81; writer, editor, Crowley, Tex., 1981—; freelance writer, editor Boy Scouts Am., Irving, Tex., 1981—. Author: Your Future With The BSA, 1989, The LH7 Ranch, 1991, Trail Fever, 1992; co-author: (with Simon W. Freese) A Century in The Works, 1994; contbg. writer New Handbook of Texas, 1996; contbg. editor Dairymen's Digest, Arlington, Tex., 1981-89, 95—, Longhorn Scene, Ft. Worth, 1982-84, Lone Star Horse Report, Ft. Worth, 1985-86; assoc. editor Boys' Life mag., Boy Scouts Am., Irving, 1995; writer, photographer Harvest Times, Dallas, 1983-84; Simbrah World, Ft. Worth, 1985-87; contbr. photographs to mags.; contbr. articles mags. Women's issues chmn., v.p. membership, pub. info. officer, newsletter editor, yearbook editor AAUW of Tarrant County, 1981-86, 90-92. Recipient Sr. Merit award in Agrl. Journalism, Tex. A&M U., 1978, Thomas S. Gathright Acad. Excellence award, 1976, Cert. of Merit, Livestock Publs Coun., 1984, 86, 2d place Nonfiction Book award Tex.-Wide Writers' Competition, 1988, 89, 2d Place Feature Story Dairy Coop. Comm. Competition Nat. Milk Producers Fedn., 1989, Publication awards San Antonio Conservation Soc., 1993; vice chmn. devel. com. Friends of Ft. Worth Pub. Libr., 1991-93, bd. mem., 1994—, v.p. 1995—. Mem. Nat. Writers Assn., Authors Guild, Soc. Children's Book Writers and Illustrators (publicity dir. North Ctrl. Tex. chpt. 1991-92, program dir. 1994-95), Freelance Writers Network, Phi Kappa Phi, Gamma Sigma Delta. Office: 19 Frazier Ln Crowley TX 76036

SIZEMORE, DOUGLAS M., state commerce and insurance commissioner; b. Johnson City, Tenn.; m. Faye Sizemore; 3 children. BS in BA, E. Tenn. State U. From staff to exec. positions various indsl. orgns., Johnson City, Tenn.; ins. agt. Johnson City, Tenn., 1959-60; pres. Johnson City Ins. Co., 1960-95; commr. Dept. Commerce and Ins., Nashville, Tenn., 1995—. Mem. Johnson City Indsl. Devel. Bd., E. Tenn. State U. Found; past pres. Johnson City Jaycees, Johnson City-Washington County C. of C. Mem. Johnson City Kiwanis Club. Office: State of Tenn Dept Commerce and Ins 500 James Robertson Pkwy Nashville TN 37219-1204

SIZEMORE, ROBERT CARLEN, immunologist, educator; b. Lexington, Ky., Sept. 30, 1951; s. Dewey and Juanita (Peel) S.; m. Katherine Killelea, Sept. 29, 1990; children: Katherine Peel, Robert Carlen Jr. BS, U. Ky., 1973, MS, 1975; PhD, U. Louisville, 1982. Postdoctoral rsch. assoc. U. Miss. Med. Ctr., Jackson, 1982-84; dir. immunology IMREG, Inc., New Orleans, 1984-94; adj. asst. prof. Tulane U. Sch. Medicine, New Orleans, 1985-94, asst. prof., 1994—. Patentee in field; contbr. articles and poems to profl. jours. Recipient Project award U. Louisville, 1978, Grad. Dean's Citation U. Louisville, 1983; named Outstanding Young Men of Am., 1984. Mem. Am. Assn. Immunologists, Internat. AIDS Soc., Am. Soc. Tropical Medicine & Hygiene, Internat. Soc. Devel. & Comparative Immunology, Fedn. Am. Scientists, AAAS. Home: 4401 Copernicus St New Orleans LA 70131-3615

SKAGFIELD, HILMAR SIGURDSSON, business executive; b. Skagafjörd, Iceland, July 25, 1923; came to U.S., 1950; s. Sigurd and Louisa (Alberts) S.; m. Kristin Gudmunds; children: Louisa, Hilda Ann, Hilmar Olafur. Student, Fla. State U., 1950-52. Pvt. practice mgmt. cons. Tallahassee, 1954-65; founder, pres. Skandia Industries div. Skagfield Corp., Tallahassee, 1965—. Consul of Iceland, 1980-85, consul gen. of Iceland for Fla., 1985—; pres. Apalachee Mental Health, Tallahassee, 1984-86, 95-96, Goodwill Industries, Tallahassee, 1986-87. Recipient Knights' Cross of the Falcon for pub. svc. Iceland Govt., 1996. Mem. Tallahassee C. of C. (v.p. 1972-83, Industry Hall of Fame 1981), Tallahassee Jaycees (various awards), Fla. Consular Corps (pres.), Icelandic-Am. C. of C. (bd. dirs. 1985), Capital City Country Club, Gov.'s Club, Kiwanis (local chpt. pres. 1962, lt. gov. 1963, Legion of Honor award Kiwanis Internat. 1987). Lutheran. Home: 425 Glenview Dr Tallahassee FL 32303-5207 Office: Skandia Industries 270 Crossway Rd PO Box 809 Tallahassee FL 32302

SKAGGS, ARLINE DOTSON, elementary school educator; b. Houston, Sept. 10, 1935; d. Gordon Alonzo and Fannie Mae (O'Kelley) Dotson; m. May 24, 1958 (div. Dec. 1969); children: Fred Mack, Ray Gordon. BS, U. Houston, 1957. Recreation leader VA Hosp., Houston, 1957-59; 4th and 5th grade tchr. Houston Ind. Sch. Dist., 1967-91; ret., 1991—; sponsor Number Sense, 1975-87, Sci. Fair, 1984-85. Auditor PTA, 1985, 87, 88; treas. Mt. Olive Luth. Sch. PTO, 1967-68; pres. Gulfgate Lioness Club, 1966-67; mem. Delphian Soc., 1965, Ch. of Houston Bread Distbn. program, 1990-91; treas. Houston Night Chpt. Women's Aglow, 1982; tchr. Children's Ch., 1972, 83, 84; prayer ptnr. Trinity Broadcasting Network, 1989-90, Christian Broadcasting Network, 1982-83; Braves scorekeeper Braes Bayou Little League, 1969-71; mem. United Way Funding Com., Salvation Army, Star of Hope & United Svcs. Orgn., 1974-76. Winning sponsor Citywide Math. Competition, Houston Ind. Sch. Dist., 1982, N.E. Area Math. Competition, 1976, 78, 79, 81, 82, 83, Lockhart Math. Contest, 1987. Mem. NEA (del. 1974), Houston Tchrs. Assn. (sch. rep. 1968-77, exec. bd. 1972-74, dir. N.E. area 1972-74, by-laws chmn. 1976), Tex. State Tchrs. Assn. (life, del. convs. 1968-75). Home: 4437 Vivian St Bellaire TX 77401-5630

SKAGGS, JAMES B., executive. Pres. Tracor, Inc., Austin, Tex. Address: 6500 Tracor Ln Austin TX 78725-2006

SKAGGS, KAREN GAYLE, elementary school educator; b. Campbellsville, Ky., Sept. 29, 1956; d. E. Edward and Mary Virginia (Kearney) Davis; m. Stephen Douglas Skaggs, July 30, 1976. BA in English, French and Journalism, Campbellsville Coll., 1977, elem. edn. endorsement 1-8, 1989; MA in Secondary Edn. and Psychology, Western Ky. U., 1980, reading specialist degree, 1986, rank 1 in edn., 1990. Cert. secondary tchr., Ky. Tchr. English, French, journalism Taylor County Bd. Edn., Campbellsville, 1978-81; adult edn. tchr. Taylor County Bd. Edn., 1981-89; elem. tchr. Campbellsville Bd. Edn., 1989—. Mem. Campbellsville Site Based Coun., 1993—. Recipient Outstanding Tchr. award State Dept. of Edn. Mem. NEA, Internat. Reading Assn., Ky. Edn. Assn., Campbellsville Edn. Assn. (v.p.), Taylor County Lit. Coun. (pres.), Taylor County Bus. and Profl. Women's Club (chmn. young careerist com. 1987-88, Outstanding Young Career Woman award 1987, Tchr. of Yr. award 1993, Excellence in Tchg. award 1994). Democrat. Baptist. Home: 901 S Columbia Ave Campbellsville KY 42718-2410

SKAGGS, KATHY CHERYL, lawyer; b. Campbellsville, Ky., Mar. 21, 1956; d. Charles Wilson and Naida Frances (Beams) S.; m. Dorman Gibson, Oct. 25, 1974 (div. Feb. 1984); children: Jacob Lee, Nathan Louis; m. Russell Turner, Dec. 13, 1985 (div. Aug. 1989). BA, Western Ky. U., 1978; JD, NYU, 1981. Bar: Tenn. 1981, U.S. Dist. Ct. (mid. dist.) Tenn. 1982. Reginald Heber Smith fellow Legal Svcs. Mid. Tenn., Gallatin, 1981-83, staff atty., 1983-85, mng. atty., 1985-89; dir. community programs Vanderbilt U. Ctr. for Health Svcs., Nashville, 1989-94; pvt. practice Gallatin, Tenn., 1994-96; exec. dir. Appalachian Comty. Fund, 1996—. Co-author: Understanding Economics for Local ORganizing, 1985; editor: Tennessee Domestic Violence Bench Book, 1996. Pres., founder Sumner County Coalition Against Domestic Violence, Gallatin, 1983-85; chairperson, founder Tenn. Task Force on Family Violence, Nashville, 1985-87; Tenn. rep. Nat. Coalition Agsinst Domestic Violence, Washington, 1985-86; founder Coalition in Def. of Battered Women, 1991—. Named Outstanding Young Woman of Am., 1986; recipient Sui Juris award Tenn. Task Force Against Domestic Violence, 1992. Office: 517 Union Ave Ste 206 Knoxville TN 37902-2129

SKAGGS, MERTON MELVIN, JR., environmental engineer; b. Kerrville, Tex., Nov. 16, 1953; s. Merton Melvin and Peggy LaNell (Dechert) S.; m. Susan Marie Frawley, Aug. 9, 1980; children: Alan, Marie, Bridget. B-SChemE, Tex. A&M U., 1976; MS in Biology, U. Houston, Clear Lake City, Tex., 1979. Registered profl. engr., Tex. Process engr. Diamond Shamrock Chems. Co., Pasadena, Tex., 1976-78, environ. engr., 1979-80, sr. environ. engr., 1981-84; ctrl. ops. mgr. Maxus Energy Corp., Dallas, 1985-91, gen. mgr. environ. affairs, 1991-96; pres. Chem. Land Holdings, Inc., Dallas, 1994—, Maxus Agrl. Chems., Inc., Dallas, 1994-96. Mem. DeSoto (Tex.) Playground Assn., 1988; coach Odyssey of the Mind, Southlake, Tex., 1993-95. Mem. AIChE, Soc. Petroleum Engrs. (chmn. environ. study group 1993-96, sect. treas. 1996-97), Water Environ. Federation, Air and Waste Assn. Methodist. Home: 600 Llano Ct Southlake TX 76092-4817 Office: Chemical Land Holdings Inc 717 N Harwood St Dallas TX 75201-6538

SKAMBIS, CHRISTOPHER CHARLES, JR., lawyer; b. Painesville, Ohio, Jan. 21, 1953; s. Christopher Charles and Anne (haritos) S.; m. Susan Elaine Adrianson, Dec. 18, 1976; children: Adrianne Elaine, Christopher Roy. Student, U. Pa., 1970-72; BA, U. Conn., 1972-74; JD, Ohio State U. Coll. Law, Columbus, 1975-78. Bar: Fla. 1978, Fla. Supreme Ct., 1978, U.S. Dist. Ct. (ctrl. dist.), 1979, U.S. Ct. Appeals (5th and 11th cir.) 1981, U.S. Supreme Ct. 1989. Assoc. VandenBerg, Gay & Burke, Orlando, Fla., 1978-81, ptnr., 1982; ptnr. VandenBurg, Gay, Burke, Wilson & Arkin, Orlando, Fla., 1982-85, Foley & Lardner, Orlando, Fla., 1985-96, Moran & Shams PA, Orlando, Fla., 1996—; mem. Orange County Bar Assn., Orlando, Fla., 1978, Fla. Bar 9D Grievance Commn., Orlando, Fla., 1989; arbitrator Fla. Bar 9th Cir. Fee Arbitration Commn., Orlando, Fla., 1987; co-chair Federal and State Trial Practice Co., Orlando, Fla., 1992—. Mem. Am. Judicature Soc., ABA. Office: Moran & Shams PA PO Box 472 111 N Orange Ave Ste 1200 Orlando FL 32802-2193 Office: 111 N Orange Ave Ste 900 Orlando FL 32801-2399

SKEEN, DAVID RAY, computer systems administrator; b. Bucklin, Kans., July 12, 1942; s. Claude E. and Velma A. (Birney) S.; BA in Math., Emporia State U., 1964; MS, Am. U., 1972, cert. in Computer Systems, 1973; grad. Fed. Exec. Inst., 1983, Naval War Coll., 1984; postgrad. George Washington U., 1989—; m. Carol J. Stimpert, Aug. 23, 1964; children: Jeffrey Kent, Timothy Sean, Kimberly Dawn. Cert. office automation profl. Computer systems analyst to comdr.-in-chief U.S. Naval Forces-Europe, London, 1967-70; computer systems analyst Naval Command Systems Support Activity, Washington, 1970-73; dir. data processing Office Naval Rsch., U.S. Navy Dept., Arlington, Va., 1973-78, dir. mgmt. info. systems Naval Civilian Pers. Command, Washington, 1978-80; dep. dir. manpower, pers. tng. automated systems Dept. Naval Mil. Pers. Command, Washington, 1980-85; dir. manpower, personnel & tng. info. resource mgmt. div. Chief Naval Ops., 1985-91; assoc. dir. Office of IRM, USDA, Washington, 1992—; lectr. Inst.

Sci. and Pub. Affairs, 1973-76; cons. Electronic Data Processing Career Devel. Programs, 1975—; detailed to Pres.'s Reorgn. Project for Automated Data Processing, 1978, Spl. Navy IRM Studies, SECNAV, 1991 and USDA/ Office of Mgmt. and Budget IRM, 1993, Pres.'s Fed. Automated Data Processing Users Group, Washington, 1978-80; assoc. prof. Sch. Engring. and Applied Sci., George Washington U. Served with USN, 1964-67, capt. Res. ret. Recipient Outstanding Performance award Interagy. Com. Data Processing, 1976. Mem. Sr. Exec. Assn., Am. Mgmt. Assn., Assn. Computing Machinery, Data Processing Mgmt. Assn., Naval Res. Assn., Navy League. Contbr. articles to profl. jours. Home: 2426 Garnett Dr Alexandria VA 22311-4907

SKEETERS, MARTHA C., historian, educator; b. Longview, Tex., Oct. 18, 1946; d. Laborn Leon and Ava Ellein (Tullos) S.; m. João Rego Cruz, Aug. 17, 1980; 1 child, Amy Elizabeth Skeeters-Behrens. BA, U. North Tex., 1969, MA, 1973; PhD, U. Tex. at Austin, 1984. World history tchr. Marshall (Tex.) High Sch., 1972-74; adj. instr. Austin (Tex.) C.C., 1976, Houston C.C., 1979-80, Rose State Coll., Midwest City, Okla., 1983; vis. asst. prof. Phillips U., Enid, Okla., 1984-85; historian U.S. Govt. Tinker AFB, Midwest City, 1986; vis. asst. prof. Okla. State U., Stillwater, 1987-88; student advisor Okla. City C.C., 1993-94; vis. asst. prof., adj. asst. prof. U. Okla., Norman, 1989-91, 91-94; asst. prof. Austin Coll., Sherman, Tex., 1994-96; evaluator NEH Applications for Grants, 1991. Author: Community and Clergy/ Bristol and the Reformation, 1530-1570, 1993; contbr. articles to profl. jours. Organizer, facilitator Focus: Central America, Unitarian-Universalist Svc. Com., 1989; participating scholar Okla. Found. for Humanities, Stillwater Pub. Libr., 1989. Recipient Mellon Seminar in History grant Rice U., 1985, Outstanding Centennial Alumna award U. North Tex., 1990, NEH Travel grant, 1990. Mem. AAUW (rep. state planning com. Lobby Day), Am. Hist. Assn., Sixteenth Century Studies Soc., North Am. Conf. on Brit. Studies, Women in Hist. Profession (coord. com.). Home: RR 1 Box 117b-4 Norman OK 73072-9722 also: 700 S FM 1417 Sherman TX 75092

SKELLEY, DEAN SUTHERLAND, clinical laboratory administrator; b. Melrose, Mass., Mar. 27, 1938; s. Robert Henry and Roberta Jane (Morse) S.; m. Eleanor Bachofen, Dec. 21, 1966; children: Caroline, Rachel, Jonathan, Susanna. BS, Bates Coll., 1960; MS, Ohio State U., 1966, PhD, 1968. Asst. prof. Coll. Vet. Medicine Ohio State U., Columbus, 1968-70; asst. prof. ob-gyn. Baylor Coll. Medicine, Houston, 1970-76; clin. biochemist Meml. Hosp., Houston, 1976-83; dir. ops. Severance Refence Lab., San Antonio, 1983-84; v.p. ops. Cone Biotech., Inc., Seguin, Tex., 1984-86; dir. product devel. MCLAS Techs. Inc., San Antonio, 1986-87; pres. Tech. and Profl. Svcs., Inc., San Antonio, 1987—; tech. dir. Lab Corp Am. (formerly, Nat. Health Labs., Inc.), San Antonio, 1989—; pres. Tech. and Profl. Svcs., Inc., San Antonio, 1973—. Elder, Presbyn. Ch., San Antonio, 1994; mem. admissions com. Bates Coll., Lewiston, Maine, 1990—. Served with U.S. Army, 1961-63. Democrat. Mem. United Ch. of Christ. Home: 16330 Hidden View St San Antonio TX 78232-2812

SKELLEY, GEORGE CALVIN, animal science educator; b. Boise City, Okla., Jan. 28, 1937; s. Geroge C. and Cahterine B. (May) S.; m. Aletha C. Brown, June 22, 1958; children: Mary L. S. Tripp, Martha A. S. Blanton. BS, Okla. Panhandle State U., 1958; MS, U. Ky., 1960, PhD, 1963. Rsch. asst. U. Ky., Lexington, 1958-62; asst. prof. Clemson (S.C.) U., 1962-66, assoc. prof., 1966-72, prof., 1972-95, prof. animal sci., chair dept., 1995—; adv. bd. S.C. Assn. Meat Processors, Columbia, 1962—, Block and Bridle Club, Clemson, 1962—, hon. mem. 1977. Contbr. articles to profl. jours. Active Clemson United Meth. Ch. Mem. Am. Meat Sci. Assn. (mem. and chmn. coms., Disting. tchr. 1991), Am. Soc. Animal Sci. (mem. coms.), Inst. Food Tech. (mem. coms.), Clemson Fellowship Club (mem. and chmn. coms.), Gamma Sigma Delta. Republican. Home: 112 Knight Cir Clemson SC 29631 Office: Clemson U Animal Vet Sci Dp B108 P&A Bldg Clemson SC 29634-0361

SKELTON, BYRON GEORGE, federal judge; b. Florence, Tex., Sept. 1, 1905; s. Clarence Edgar and Avis (Bowmer) S.; m. Ruth Alice Thomas, Nov. 28, 1931; children: Sue, Sandra. Student, Baylor U., 1923-24; AB, U. Tex., 1927, MA, 1928, LLB, 1931. Bar: Tex. 1931, Circuit Ct. Appeals 1937, U.S. Supreme Ct. 1946, FCC 1950, Tax Ct. U.S 1952, U.S. Treasury Dept 1952, ICC 1953. Practice of law Temple, Tex., 1931-66; partner Saulsbury & Skelton, 1934-42, Saulsbury, Skelton, Everton, Bowmer & Courtney, 1944-55, Skelton, Bowmer & Courtney, 1955-66; judge U.S. Ct. Claims, Washington, 1966-77; sr. fed. judge U.S. Ct. Claims, 1977-82, U.S. Ct. Appeals (fed. cir.), Washington, 1982—; county atty., Bell County, Tex., 1934-38; spl. asst. U.S. amb. to Argentina, 1942-45; city atty., Temple, 1945-60; dir. First Nat. Bank of Temple. Dem. nat. committeeman for Tex., 1956-64; del. Dem. Nat. Conv., 1948, 56, 60, 64; del. Tex. Dem. Conv., 1946, 48, 50, 52, 54, 56, 58, 60, 62, 64, vice chmn., 1948, 58; chmn. Dem. Adv. Coun. of Tex., 1955-57; former pres. Temple YMCA; pres. Temple Indsl. Found., 1966. Appointed Ky. Col. and Adm. in Tex. Navy, 1959; recipient Legion of Honor DeMolay, 1980, Temple Outstanding Citizen award, 1984. Mem. ABA, State Bar Tex., Bell-Lampasas and Mills Counties Bar Assn. (past pres.), Am. Law Inst., Am. Judicature Soc., Temple C. of C. (past pres., dir.), Ex-Students' Assn. U. Tex. (past pres., mem. exec.coun.), Gen. Soc. Mayflower Descs., Masons (past worshipful master), Shriners, Kiwanis (past pres.), Phi Beta Kappa, Pi Sigma Alpha, Sigma Delta Pi, Delta Theta Phi. Democrat. Methodist. Home: 1101 Dakota Dr Temple TX 76504-4905 Office: US Ct Appeals 305 Fed Bldg Temple TX 76501

SKELTON, DOROTHY GENEVA SIMMONS (MRS. JOHN WILLIAM SKELTON), art educator; b. Woodland, Calif.; d. Jack Elijah and Helen Anna (Siebe) Simmons; BA, U. Calif., 1940, MA, 1943; m. John William Skelton, July 16, 1941. Sr. rsch. analyst War Dept., Gen. Staff, M.I. Div. G-2, Pentagon, Washington, 1944-45; vol. rschr. monuments, fine arts and archives sect. Restitution Br., Office Mil. Govt. for Hesse, Wiesbaden, German, 1947-48; vol. art tchr. German children in Bad Nauheim, Germany, 1947-48; art educator, lectr. Dayton (Ohio) Art Inst., 1955; art educator Lincoln Sch., Dayton, 1956-60; instr. art and art edn. U. Va. Sch. Continuing Edn., Charlottesville, 1962-75; rschr. genealogy, exhibited in group shows, Calif., Colo., Ohio, Washington and Va.; represented in permanent collections Madison Hall, Charlottesville, Madison (Va.) Ctr. Recipient Hon. Black Belt Karate Sch. of Culpeper, Va., 1992. Vol. art cons.; bd. dirs. Va. Rappahannock-Rapidan Vol. Emergency Med. Svcs. Coun., 1978—. Mem. Nat. League Am. Pen Women, AAUW, Am. Assn. Museums, Coll. Art Assn. Am., Inst. for Study of Art in Edn., Dayton Soc. Painters and Sculptors, Nat. Soc. Arts and Letters (life), Va. Mus. Fine Arts, Cal. Alumni Assn., Air Force Officers Wives Club. Republican. Methodist. Club: Army Navy Country. Chief collaborator: John Skelton of Georgia, 1969; author: The Squire Simmons Family, 1746-1986, 1986. Address: Lotos Lakes Brightwood VA 22715

SKELTON, GORDON WILLIAM, data processing executive, educator; b. Vicksburg, Miss., Oct. 31, 1949; s. Alan Gordon and Martha Hope (Butcher) S.; m. Sandra Lea Champion, May 1974 (div. 1981); m. Janet Elaine Johnson, Feb. 14, 1986; 1 stepchild, Brian Quarles. BA, McMurry Coll., 1974; MA, U. So. Miss., 1975, postgrad., 1975-77, MS, 1987; postgrad., U. South Africa, 1994—. Cert. in data processing. Systems analyst Criminal Justice Planning Commn., Jackson, Miss., 1978-80; cord. Miss. Statis. Analysis Ctr., Jackson, 1980-83; data processing mgr. Dept. Adminstrn. Fed.-State Programs, Jackson, 1983-84; mgr. pub. tech. So. Ctr. Rsch. and Innovation, Hattiesburg, Miss., 1985-87; internal cons. Sec. of State, State of Miss., Jackson, 1987; system support mgr. CENTEC, Jackson, 1987-88; instr. dept. computer sci. Belhaven Coll., Jackson, 1988—; v.p. info. svcs. Miss. Valley Title Ins. Co., Jackson, 1988—. Author: (with others) Trends in Ergonomics/Human Factors, 1986. Treas. Singles and Doubles Sunday Sch. Class, Jackson, 1989, 91. With U.S. Army, 1970-73, Vietnam. Recipient Cert. of Appreciation, U.S. Dept. Justice/Bur. Justice Stats., 1982. Mem. IEEE Computer Soc., Data Processing Mgmt. Assn. (chpt. pres. 1991, 92, program chair 1990), Assn. Computing Machinery, Am. Soc. Quality Control. Presbyterian. Office: Miss Valley Title Ins Co 315 Tombigbee St Jackson MS 39201-4605

SKELTON, HELEN ROGERS, retired auditor; b. Bloomington, Tex., Sept. 23, 1917; d. Marshall Raymond and Clara Eva (Kennemer) Rogers; m. Clarance Carlton Skelton, Aug. 2, 1935; children: Doris Annette Skelton Swanson, Donald Melvin. Grad. high sch., Burkeville, Tex., 1935. Bookkeeper Am. Nat. Bank, Beaumont, Tex., 1944-56; auditor, payroll clerk Tex. Highway Dept., Austin, Dallas, 1956-76; genealogist The Rogers Clan, Tex., 1975—. Author, editor: (with Clarance Carlton Skelton) Rogers/Skelton Allied Families, 1987. Mem. Internat. Porcelain Arts, DAR, Colonial Dames XVIIC, Am. Colonists, Huguenot Soc., Magna Charta Dames, Sons & Daus of Pilgrims, UDC, Soverign Colonial Soc. Ams. of Royal Descent, Colonial Order of the Crown, Soc. of Most Noble Order of the Garter. Home: PO Box 340 Hwy 87 N Burkeville TX 75932 Office: The Rogers Clan PO Box 340 Hwy 87 N Burkeville TX 75932

SKELTON, JANICE KENMORE, retired secondary school educator; b. Royston, Ga., Oct. 15, 1918; d. Homer Lee and Gladys Mae (Griffin) Kenmore; m. Thomas Asa Skelton Jr., Dec. 28, 1940; children: Fran Skelton Boggs, Thomas A. III, Sara Skelton Simmons. Student, Piedmont Coll., 1935-37; student, Ga. So. U., 1938-39; BS, Tift Coll., 1962. Elem. tchr. Hart County Schs., Hartwell, Ga., 1937-40; elem. tchr. Madison County Schs., Danielsville, Ga., 1940-41, Griffin-Spalding County Schs., Griffin, Ga., 1955-63; elem. prin. Griffin-Spalding County Schs., 1959-63, jr. high math. tchr., 1963-80; math tutor Literacy PLUS Program, Griffin, 1986—; researcher geneal. info. Flint River Regional Libr., 1987-88, 90. Sec. Spalding County Bicentennial of Constn. Commn., Griffin, 1987-91; publicity chmn. Griffin-Spalding County Older Ams. Coun., 1988-91, sec., 1992-93, mem. organizing task force, 1986-88; vol. Griffin-Spalding County Schs., Spalding Regional Hosp., Salvation Army; historian First Presbyn. Ch., 1991-92, 94, 95, moderator, Presbyn. Women, 1993-94, sec., 1995—; active Spalding County Elder Coun. Named Woman of Achievement Bus. & Profl. Women, 1983. Mem. AAUW (pres., publicity chmn. Griffin br. 1985-91, 92-95), Am. Assn. Ret. Persons (local coord. tax-aide program 1991—), Griffin-Spalding County Ret. Tchrs. (pres. 1981-84, 89-90, 92-96, Cmty. Svc. award 1988, 92), Ga. Ret. Tchrs. Assn. (awards and recognition com. 1988-90, 95—, chmn. 1990-93), Griffin Hist. and Preservation Soc., Griffin Woman's Club (publicity chair 1992-96, sch. chmn. 1992-94, rec. sec. 1994-96), United Daus. Confederacy (3d v.p. Ga. divsn. 1986-90, 92-94, pres. James S. Boynton chpt. Griffin 1982-88, 89-90, 91-92, 2d v.p. and registrar 1990-91, 92-93, treas. 1994-96), DAR (regent Pulaski chpt. 1987-91, 95—, records sec. 1991-95), Alpha Delta Kappa (publicity chmn. 1986-91, 92-94, membership chair 1994-96). Democrat. Presbyterian. Home: 1325 Hillwood Ave Griffin GA 30223-2126

SKELTON, JOHN GOSS, JR., psychologist; b. Columbus, Ga.; s. John Goss and Willie Mae (Langford) S.; B.A., Emory U., 1950; M.Ed., Our Lady of Lake U., 1964; Ph.D., Tex. Tech. U., 1967. Positions with advt. agy., newspaper, trade assn., 1950-63; staff psychologist San Antonio State Hosp., 1963-65; resident in clin. psychology U. Tex. Med. Br., Galveston, 1966-67; dir., clin. psychologist Psychol. Services Clinic, Harlingen, Tex., 1967-68; clin. psychologist Santa Rosa Med. Center, San Antonio, 1968-71; pvt. practice clin. psychology San Antonio, 1971—; chmn. dept. psychology Park North Gen. Hosp., San Antonio, 1971-83; clin. asst. prof. U. Tex. Health Sci. Center, San Antonio, 1971-78; cons. S.W. Ind. Sch. Dist. San Antonio, 1974—, Parkside Lodge Ctr., San Antonio; instr. Our Lady of Lake U., San Antonio, summers 1968-71, Tex. Tech U., summer 1967. Pres., Vis. Nurses Assn. Bexar County, 1976-77; bd. dirs. Halfway House San Antonio, 1964-65, Mental Health Assn. Bexar County, 1969-75; dir. steering com. San Antonio Area Crisis Center, 1971-74. Served with USN, 1945-46. Vocat. Rehab. fellow, 1965-67. Mem. Am. Psychol. Assn., Bexar County Psychol. Assn. (pres. 1970-71), Biofeedback Soc. Tex., Tex. Psychol. Assn., Soc. Behavioral Medicine, San Antonio Mus. Assn. Episcopalian. Office: Ste 100 4402 Vance Jackson Rd San Antonio TX 78230

SKELTON, WILLIAM PAUL, III, medical educator; b. Spartanburg, S.C., Nov. 5, 1956; married: children: William Paul IV, James Andrew, Michelle Nadine. BS in Zoology summa cum laude, Clemson U., 1979; MD, Med. U. S.C., 1983. Diplomate Nat Bd. Med. Examiners, Am. Bd. Internal Medicine. Resident internal medicine U. S.C. Sch. Medicine, 1983-86; from asst. to prof. internal medicine U. So. Fla. Coll. Medicine, Tampa, 1986-96, prof. internal medicine, 1996—; ambulatory care staff physician James A. Haley Vets. Hosp., Tampa, 1986-92, asst. chief of staff, 1992-95, acting chief of staff, 1992-93; coll. medicine admissions interviewer U. So. Fla., Tampa, 1987—; adv. bd. Internat. Inst. Prisoners of War, N.Y.C., 1990—. Editorial adv. bd. Internal Medicine for the Specialist, 1987—; reviewer Annals of Internal Medicine, 1992—; contbr. articles to profl. jours. Vol. examiner N. Tampa Rams and Tampa Eagles Football and Cheerleader physicals, 1986—; mem. Greater Tampa Bay Imperial and National chpts. Am. Ex-POWs, 1987—; v.p. Tampa N.E. Camp of Gideons Internat., 1991-92; Sunday sch. tchr. First Bapt. Ch., Tample Terrace, Fla., 1991—; life mem. nat. and state chpt. Am. Defenders of Bataan & Corregidor, 1992—; assoc. mem. Mil. Order of Purple Heart, 1993—. Grantee Sandoz Pharm. Co., 1991, 94. Fellow Am. Coll. Physicians; mem. AMA (Physician's Recognition award 1986—), S.C. Med. Assn. Home: 11313 E Queensway Dr Tampa FL 33617-2421

SKERIS, ROBERT ALEXANDER, theology educator; b. Sheboygan, Wis., May 11, 1935; s. Alex F. and Eugenia Teresa (Cizauskas) S. ThD, U. Bonn, Germany, 1975. Ordained Roman Catholic priest, 1961. Dir. hymnology sect. Internat. Inst. for Hymnol. and Ethnomusicol. Studies, Maria Laach, Germany, 1978-86; prefetto della casa Pontifical Inst. Sacred Music, Rome, 1986-90; prof. chmn. theology dept. Christendom Coll., Front Royal, Va., 1990—. Author: Chroma Theou, 1976, Divini Cultus Studium, 1990; editor: Crux et Cithara, 1983, Cum Angelis Canere, 1990. Decorated Ordem Nacional dos Bandeirantes, Ordem Mater (Brazil) ; knight Republic of Austria; knight Holy Sepulchre. Mem. Consociatio Internat. Musical Sacrae (counselor 1978-90), Am. Musicol. Soc., Ch. Music Assn. Am. (gen. sec. 1970-72, v.p. 1972-76, dir. 1977—), Cath. Ch. Music Assocs. (pres. 1976—). Home and Office: Christendom Coll Dept Theology 2101 Shenandoah Shores Rd Front Royal VA 22630-5103

SKERPAN, ELIZABETH PENLEY, English language educator; b. Ravenna, Ohio, Oct. 11, 1955; d. Alfred Andrew and Ruth Elizabeth (Penley) S.; m. Kenneth John Winkle, July 24, 1976 (div. June 1987). AB magna cum laude, Miami U., 1976; MA, U. Wis., 1977, PhD, 1983. Substitute instr. Madison Area Tech. Coll., 1983; asst. prof. English S.W. Tex. State U., 1983-90, assoc. prof. English, 1990—; asst. to curator of rare books Meml. Libr., U. Wis., Madison, 1979; lectr. in field. Editor South-Ctrl. Renaissance Assn. newsletter, 1990-92; contbg. editor Renaissance and Renascences in Western Lit., 1979-81; author: The Rhetoric of Politics in the English Revolution, 1642-1660, 1992; contbr. articles to profl. jours. Mem. MLA, Nat. Coun. Tchrs. English, Renaissance Soc. Am., South-Ctrl. Renaissance Assn. (exec. bd. 1987-90), Tex. AAUP (del. spring conv. 1985), Tex. State Tchrs. Assn. (assn. del. to state conv. 1993, 94), Tex. Faculty Assn. (exec. com. 1993—), Phi Beta Kappa, Phi Kappa Phi. Democrat. Office: English Dept SW Tex State U 601 University Dr San Marcos TX 78666-4684

SKILLAN, MARK, internist; b. Phila., Jan. 4, 1949; s. Nelson D. and Jacqueline (B.) S.; m. Eulavia F. Smith, June 22, 1974 (div. June 1975); 1 child, Ru-Paula; m. Jo-Bertha, June 19, 1976; stepchildren: Hannah, Buffy, Albert Jr., Quinton, Pearl. BA, Lehigh U., 1970; MD, U. Ala., 1981. Diplomate Am. Bd. Internal Medicine, 1984. Commd. 2d. lt. U.S. Army, 1967, advanced through grades to lt. col., retired, 1977; internist pvt. practice, 1984—; cons. in field. Inventor in field. Mem. ACLU, Atlanta, 1990-96. Mem. Save the Whales. Home: PO Box 191293 Atlanta GA 31119-1293

SKILLERN, FRANK FLETCHER, law educator; b. Sept. 26, 1942; s. Will T. and Vera Catherine (Ryberg) S.; m. Susan Schlaefer, Sept. 3, 1966; children: Nathan Edward, Leah Catherine. AB, U. Chgo., 1964; JD, U. Denver, 1966; LLM, U. Mich., 1969. Bar: Colo. 1967, Tex. 1978. Pvt. practice law Denver, 1967; gen. atty. Maritime Adminstrn., Washington, 1967-68; asst. prof. law Ohio No. U., 1969-71; asst. prof. law Tex. Tech U., Lubbock, 1971-73, assoc. prof. law, 1973-75, prof. law, 1975—; vis. prof. U. Tex. Law Sch., summer 1979, U. Ark. Law Sch., 1979-80, U. Tulsa Coll. Law, 1981-82; cons. and speaker in field. Author: Environmental Protection: The Legal Framework, 1981, 2d edit. published as Environmental Protection Deskbook, 1995, Regulation of Water and Sewer Utilities, 1989, Texas Water Law, Vol. I, 1988, rev. edit., 1992, Vol. II, 1991; contbr. chpts. to Powell on Real Property, Zoning and Land Use Controls, others; author cong. procs. and numerous articles. Mem. ABA (mem. publs. com. Sect. Natural Resources Law 1984—, vice chair internat. environ. law com. Sect. Natural Resources Law 1987). Office: Tex Tech U Sch Law PO Box 40004 Lubbock TX 79409-0004

SKILLMAN, ERNEST EDWARD, JR., real estate sales and management executive; b. New Orleans, Oct. 3, 1937; s. Ernest Edward and Helen Cecilia (Klein) S. BA, La. State U., 1960, postgrad. in law, 1960-61; postgrad., Southeastern La. U., 1973. intelligence work for USN, 1960—. Engaged in real estate mgmt. Baton Rouge, 1964—, sales, 1969—. Sustaining mem. Republican Nat. Com., 1976—, life mem., 1980—, mem. congressional com., 1978—; mem. pres.'s club Democratic Nat. Com., 1979—; mem. Rep. Presdl. Task Force; mem. Jackson (La.) Assembly; Served with USN, 1961-64; Vietnam. Mem. La. Mem. Aviation Mus. Assn. (charter life), Feliciana C. of C., Res. Officers Assn. (life), Mil. Order World Wars (life), Am. Contract Bridge League (sr. master), U.S. Naval Inst. (life), Navy League U.S. (life), Am. Legion, Submarine Force Library and Mus. Assn. (life), Amvets (cmdr. 1985-87, pres. Foss-Landry Post #2 1985-87), Grad. Realtors Inst., Army and Navy Club, Rep. Senatorial Club (Washington), Camelot Club (Baton Rouge), Kiwanis, Sigma Chi (life). Roman Catholic. Home: 753 Kenilworth Pky Baton Rouge LA 70808-5716 Office: 4150 Perkins Rd Baton Rouge LA 70808-3027

SKILLRUD, HAROLD CLAYTON, minister; b. St. Cloud, Minn., June 29, 1928; s. Harold and Amanda Skillrud; m. Lois Dickhart, June 8, 1951; children: David, Janet, John. BA magna cum laude, Gustavus Adolphus Coll., 1950; MDiv magna cum laude, Augustana Theol. Sem., Rock Island, Ill., 1954; STM, Luth. Sch. Theology, Chgo., 1969; DD (hon.), Augustana Coll., 1978, Newberry Coll., 1988. Ordained to ministry Evang. Luth. Ch. in Am., 1954. Supply pastor Saron Luth. Ch., Big Lake, Minn., 1950-51; mem. staff 1st Luth. Ch., Rock Island, Ill., 1951-52; intern, organizer new mission Faith Luth. Ch., Syosset, N.Y., 1952-53; sr. pastor St. John's Luth. Ch., Bloomington, Ill., 1954-79, Luth. Ch. of the Redeemer, Atlanta, 1979-87; bishop Southeastern Synod Evang. Luth. Ch. in Am., Atlanta, 1987-95, regional rep. bd. pensions, 1995—; del. to various convs. Luth. Ch. in Am., Luth. World Fedn. in Helsinki, 1963, mem. bd. publ., 1976-84, pastor-evangelist Evang. Outreach Emphasis program, 1977-79, mem. exec. bd. Ill. synod, 1977-79, pres. bd. publ., 1980-84, leader stewardship cluster Southeastern synod, 1983, mem. exec. bd. Southeastern synod, 1984-87; mem. exec. coun., Luth. Ch. in Am., 1984-87; mem. task force on new ch. design Commn. on New Luth. Ch., task force on ch. pub. house, 1985; del. constituting conv. Evang. Luth. Ch. in Am., 1987, del. assemblies Evang. Luth. Ch. in Am., 1989, 91, 93, 95; mem. commn. on clergy confidentiality Luth. Coun. in USA, 1987; co-chair USA Luth.- Roman Cath. Dialogue; mem. Task Force on Theol. Edn. Author: LSTC: Decade of Decision, 1969; co-editor Scripture and Tradition, Lutherans and Catholics in Dialogue, 1995; mem. edtl. bd. Partners mag., 1978-80; contbr. articles and sermons to religious jours. Former bd. dirs. Augustana Theol. Sem.; bd. dirs. Augustana Coll., 1969-77, chmn. bd., 1976-77; bd. dirs. Kessler Reformation Collection, Newberry Coll., Luth. World Relief, Augsburg Fortress; chmn. bd. dirs. Luth. Sch. Theology, Chgo., 1962-69; mem. Leadership Atlanta, 1980-81, United Way, Atlanta, 1980-81; mem. Bishop's Commn. on Econ. Justice, 1985-86; pres. bd. dirs. Atlanta Samaritan House, 1986-87. Recipient Alumni award Luth. Sch. Theology, Chgo., 1976, award Leadership Atlanta, 1981, The Rev. John Bachman award, Luth. Theol. Sem., Columbia, S.C., 1996. Mem. Luth. Sch. Theology Alumni Assn. (pres. 1975-77), Conf. of Bishops, Kiwanis (pres. Midtown chpt. 1984-85). Home: 368 E Wesley Rd NE Atlanta GA 30305-3824*

SKINNER, EDWARD FOLLAND, retired thoracic surgeon; b. Hamilton, Ont., Can., Sept. 26, 1909; s. Edward Blake and Addie Maude (Large) S.; m. Helen Love Draper, Nov. 27, 1935 (dec. 1980); children: Wendy Skinner Templeton, Terri Skinner Chadwick, Edward D.; m. Lois Ellis Walker, May 29, 1984; children: James H. Kelley Jr., Anne W. Strand, William C. Walker Jr., Frances Walker McCampbell. BS, Detroit City Coll., now Wayne State U., 1931; B Medicine, Detroit Coll. Medicine, now Wayne State U., 1935; MD, Detroit Coll. Medicine, 1936. Diplomate Am. Bd. Thoracic Surgery. Intern St. Mary's Hosp., Detroit, 1935-36; chief resident St. Mary's Hosp., Saginaw, Mich., 1936-37; resident Herman Kiefer Hosp., Detroit, 1937-39, 42-45; resident in thoracic surgery No. Mich. Tuberculosis Sanatorium, Gaylord, 1939-41; pvt. practice Memphis, 1945-72; ret., 1972; asst. prof. surgery, U. Tenn. Med. Sch., Memphis, 1951-72; instr., Bapt. Meml. Hosp. Sch. Nursing, 1945-72, St. Joseph's Hosp. Sch. Nursing, 1945-72; cons., USPHS, Memphis, 1946-72. Author: Your Health, Wealth, and Happiness, 1994; contbr. numerous articles to med. jours. Fellow Am. Coll. Chest Physicians, AMA; mem. Am. Assn. Thoracic Surgery, Soc. Thoracic Surgeons, Memphis Surg. Assn., Mid-South Writers Assn. (pres. 1986-89), Writers Guild (founder Memphis sect.), Memphis Thoracic Soc., Forrest City Country Club. Presbyterian. Home: 165 Picardy St Memphis TN 38111-1925

SKINNER, JAMES LISTER, III, English language educator; b. Emory, Ga., Sept. 24, 1938; s. James Lister and Josephine Norvell (Fry) S.; m. Ramona Ann York Skinner, Apr. 2, 1961; 1 child, James Lister Skinner IV. AB in English, N. Ga. Coll., Dahlonega, 1960; MA in English, U. Ark., Fayetteville, 1962; PhD in English, 1965. Comdr. Headquarters and Headquarters Battery 28th Artillery Group, Selfridge AFB, Mich., 1964-65; assoc. prof. English Presbyterian Coll., Clinton, S.C., 1965-70; prof. English, 1970-92, Charles A. Dana prof. English, 1992—, chmn. The Russell Program, 1986—; co-chmn. English dept. Presbyn. Coll., 1996—; NDEA fellow U. Ark., Fayetteville, 1960-63; NEH summer fellow Yale U., New Haven, Conn., 1976; hon. vis. fellow Leicester (Eng.) U., 1983; sec. Presbyterian Coll. Faculty, Clinton, S.C., 1995—. Editor: The Autobiography of Henry Merrell: Industrial Missionary to the South, 1991; co-editor: The Death of a Confederate, 1996. 1st lt. U.S. Army, 1963-65. Recipient Commendation medal U.S. Army, 1965; named Presbyterian Prof. of Yr. Presbyterian Coll., Clinton, S.C., 1991, State Prof. of Yr. Coun. for Advancement and Support of Edn., 1991, Gov's. Prof. of Yr., Gov. of S.C., Columbia, 1991. Mem. Phi Beta Kappa, Omicron Delta Kappa, Alpha Psi Omega, Phi Alpha Theta. Democrat. Presbyterian. Home: 108 E Maple Clinton SC 29325 Office: Presbyterian Coll Broad St Clinton SC 29325

SKINNER, JOHN VERNON, retail credit executive; b. Merryville, La., Aug. 21, 1938; s. Vernon and Margaret (Kleinpeter) S.; m. Gail Grinnell, Sept. 1, 1960 (div. Sept. 1981); children: Sondra Skinner Keefer, Sherrin Skinner Mitzner, Stacey Skinner Schaefer, Jonathan; m. B. Jean Kevane, Nov. 1, 1983. Student, U. Houston, 1957-60. Cert. consumer credit exec. Mgr. collections, asst. mgr. Sears Roebuck & Co., Fitchburg, Mass., 1963-64; mgr. credit Torrington, Conn., 1964-65; mgr. collection/authorization Hartford, Conn., 1965-67; mgr. group collection Albany, N.Y., 1967-68; supr. credit field Boston, 1968; mgr. credit ctr. Balt., 1968-73, Washington, 1973-84; pres. Jewelers Fin. Svcs., Inc. sub. Zale Corp., Irving, Tex., 1984-96; pres., CEO Jewelers Fin. Svcs., Inc., Irving, Tex., 1987-96; sr. v.p. Zale Corp., 1984-96, exec. mgmt. com., 1993-96; officer, bd. dirs. Consumer Credit Counseling and Edn. Svc., Washington and Balt., 1968-84, pres., 1978-84, vice chmn., 1989; mem. governing bd. dirs. Credit Rsch. Ctr., Purdue U., 1985—, chmn., 1990-91. Contbr. numerous articles to profl. jours. Bd. dirs. Better Bus. Bur. of Met. Dallas, Inc., 1994-96. Recipient Disting. Svc. award Interant. Consumer Credit Assn., 1982, award of Excellence Assoc. Credit Burs., 1991. Mem. Fed. Reserve (mem. consumer adv. coun. 1992-94), Consumer Credit Assn. (pres. Greater Washington chpt. 1963-84, bd. dirs.), Internat. Credit Assn. (officer, bd. dirs. dist. XII chpt. 1975-84, bd. dirs., mem. exec. com. St. Louis chpt. 1980—, pres. dist. XII chpt. 1981, v.p. St. Louis chpt. 1985—, chmn. 1989-91, Outstanding Mem. award 1979, Greater Washington Outstanding Mem. award 1979, Svc. award 1985, Merit award 1988, Pinnacle award 1991), Nat. Found. for Consumer Credit (trustee, officer 1980-92, mem. exec. com. 1980-92, bd. dirs. 1980—, v.p., 1985—, chmn. 1991-92, Chmn.'s award 1982, Harry E. Fuller award 1985, Linkwilder award 1987), Nat. Retail Fedn. CMD divsn. (chmn. 1991-92, bd. dirs. 1985—), Nat. Retail Mchts. Assn. (bd. dirs. 1985—, sec., treas. 1989). Republican. Methodist. Home: 525 Ranch Trail #143 Irving TX 75063

SKINNER, MICHAEL HAVEN, pharmacologist, educator; b. Woodbury, N.J., Jan. 25, 1952; s. David Haven and Marilyn Joan (Michael) S.; m. Jennifer Tabora Anderson, May 3, 1989; children: Haven Blake, Miles Alden. BS in Biochemistry cum laude, UCLA, 1974; PharmD, U. Calif., San

Francisco, 1978; MD, Cebu Inst. Medicine, 1983. Resident Grant Hosp., Chgo., 1983-86; postdoctoral fellow in clin. pharmacology Stanford (Calif.) U. Med. Ctr., 1986-89; asst. prof. divsn. clin. pharmacology U. Tex. Health Sci. Ctr., San Antonio, 1989—; staff hosp. pharmacist Kaiser Hosp., Oakland, Calif., 1978-79. Contbr. articles and abstracts to profl. jours. Recipient F.I.R.S.T. award NIH, 1993. Mem. ACP, Am. Soc. for Clin. Pharmacology and Therapeutics (historian), Am. Fedn. for Clin. Rsch., Tex. Assn. Clin. Pharmacology (pres.-elect), Rho Chi.

SKINNER, SAMUEL BALLOU, III, physics educator, researcher; b. Russellville, S.C., Sept. 24, 1936; s. Samuel Ballou Jr. and Mary (Timmons) S.; m. Beverly Corinne Jones, Dec. 21, 1958; children: Teresa Lynn, Curtis Ballou, Mary Angela. BS, Clemson U., 1958; MA in Teaching, U. N.C., 1963, PhD, 1970. Sci. tchr. Franklin (Tenn.) High Sch., 1959-60, Irmo (S.C.) High Sch., 1960-62; asst. prof. physics St. Andrews Presbyn. Coll., Laurinburg, N.C., 1964-67; assoc. prof. physics Columbia (S.C.) Coll., 1970-72; prof. physics S.C. Coastal Carolina U., Conway, S.C., 1972—; dir. acad. affairs U. S.C. Coastal Carolina U., Conway, 1972-74; advisor Gov.'s Nuclear Adv. Coun., Columbia, 1977-80, S.C. Joint Legis. Com. on Energy, Columbia, 1980-85; U.S.A. rep. Internat. Symposium on Nuclear Waste, Vienna, Austria, 1980; researcher in current aerospace problems, nuclear radiation physics and crit. thinking devel.; project counselor Space Life Sci. Tng. Program, Kennedy Space Ctr., 1990. Author: Education and Psychology, 1973, Energy and Society, 1981; contbr. articles to profl. jours. Pres. Horry County Am. Cancer Soc., Conway, 1974-75, Horry County Literacy Coun., 1989-93; mem. Horry County Assessment Appeals Bd., 1981-91. Recipient fellowships NASA (6), 1987-93, Dept. Energy (5), 1972-86, USAF, 1985; grantee Dept. Energy, 1984; physics edn. del. to Vietnam, Citizen Amb. Program, 1993; participant Institut Teknologi MARA Mucia Program, Malaysia, 1993-94. Mem. Am. Assn. Physics Tchrs., Am. Assn. Higher Edn., S.C. Acad. Sci., U. S.C. Coastal Carolina Athletic Club (bd. dirs.), Lions (pres. Conway Club 1977-78). Presbyterian. Home: 126 Citadel Dr Conway SC 29526-8870 Office: Coastal Carolina U Physics Dept Conway SC 29526

SKINNER, WALTER WINSTON, journalist, minister; b. Newnan, Ga., Mar. 28, 1959; s. Walter Winston Sr. and Sara Jane (Trammell) S.; m. Deborah Lynn Strickland, Sept. 8, 1979; children: Sara Irene Skinner, Jane Golden Skinner. ABJ, U. Ga., 1980. Editor, publ. The Lee County Ledger, Leesburg, Ga., 1980-83; asst. news editor Newnan Times-Herald, Newnan, 1982—; pastor Mt. Zion Bapt. Ch., Alvaton, Ga., 1986—. Author Duty Patience and Endurance, 1977 (Louise Calhoun Barfield Local History Writing award 1977, Harris County Day award 1977), Wherein God Dwells, 1988. Chmn. Erskine Caldwell Mus., Moreland, Ga., 1992—; vol. fund drive Am. Heart Assn., Alvaton, 1993. Recipient Ga. Press Assn. awards, 1985, 92. Mem. Moreland Cmty. Hist. Soc., Meriwether County Hist. Soc., Soc. Profl. Journalists, Bapt. Bivocat. Pastor's Assn. (Outstanding Town and Country award 1992), Ga. Bapt. Hist. Soc., Ga. Bapt. Hist. Commn., Newnan Civitan Club (sgt. at arms, 1994-95, chaplain 1995-96, pres.-elect 1996—). Democrat. Home: 60 Temple Ave Newnan GA 30263-2023 Office: The Newnan Times-Herald PO Box 1052 Newnan GA 30264-1052

SKLAR, JUDITH ROSENBERG, editor, copywriter; b. Balt., Sept. 2, 1943; d. Abraham Issac and Sylvia Mayta (Rabinowitz) Rosenberg; m. Sheldon Manuel Sklar, Jan. 26, 1964 (div. June 1988); children: Craig Michael, Joshua David. Student, Armstrong Jr. Coll., 1962-63. Copywriter Albert Steiger Co., 1974, Forbes & Wallace, 1974-76, Castner-Knott Co., Sta. WBYQ-WMAK, 1978, WRDW-TV, 1979-80, Scarbrough's Dept. Store, 1982-85, Sta. WEZL, 1987-90; copywriter, editor Good Dog! mag., 1991—; mng. editor Good Communications, 1994—; spl. events/promotion mgmt. various events and shows including Charleston Chili Cookoff, Sta. WEZL Oyster Roast, Miller Beer Country Music Roundup, Suzuki Car Giveaway, concerts for Loretta Lynn, Conway Twitty, George Jones, Hank Williams, Jr., others, also cooking fairs, Christmas parades, car dealership remote promotions, autograph parties, fashion shows; freelance copywriter WBUB, 1990-91, Advance Advt. Agy., 1981. Voiceovers: Air South Airlines, Citadel Mall, Ann's Vogue Dress Shop, AAA Rentals, Conann Homes, Dorchester Brick, Centex Nissan, Texas Copier, Back in a Flash Photo Shop, others; actor: (films) D.O.A., Whatever Became of Lola Price?, (mini-series) Queen, White Squall, also commls. and indsl. shorts; writer/prodr. St. Joseph Hospice and Home Health Care slide presentation, 1980-81 (1st prize Greater Augusta (Ga.) Advt. Club competition, 1st pl. Ga. Hosp. Assn. competition). Democrat. Jewish. Office: Good Dog! Mag PO Box 10069 Austin TX 78766-1069

SKLAVER, NEAL LAWRENCE, internist; b. Conn., Sept. 1942; married, 3 children. BA in Polit. Sci. cum laude, Williams Coll., 1964; MD, U. Pa., 1968. Diplomate Am. Bd. Med. Examiners, Am. B. Internal Medicine; lic. Tex. Intern Presbyn.-St. Luke's Hosp., Chgo., 1968-69, resident internal medicine, 1969-70, instr. U. Ill. Sch. Medicine, 1970-71, chief med. resident, 1971-72; instr. Rush Med. Coll., Chgo., 1971-72; pct. practice internal medicine Dallas, 1974—; adj. clin. instr. Southwestern Med. Sch.; attending physician internal medicine Presbyn. Hosp. of Dallas, affiliate Baylor U. Med. Ctr., courtesy attending staff Parkland Meml. Hosp., Med. City of Dallas; mem. emergency rm. com. Baylor U. Med. Ctr., 1980-82, human rsch. com. Presbyn. Hosp., 1982-83. V.p. Jewish Family Svc., Dallas, 1991-93. Maj. U.S. Army Med. Corps, 1972-74. Fellow ACP; mem. AMA, Tex. Med. Soc., Dallas County Med. Soc., Am. Soc. Internal Medicine, Am. Assn. for Study of Headache, Nat. Headache Found. Office: 5461 La Sierra Dr Dallas TX 75231-4107

SKLENAR, HERBERT ANTHONY, industrial products manufacturing company executive; b. Omaha, June 7, 1931; s. Michael Joseph and Alice Madeline (Spicka) S.; m. Eleanor Lydia Vincenz, Sept. 15, 1956; children: Susan A., Patricia I. BSBA summa cum laude, U. Omaha, 1952; MBA, Harvard U., 1954; LLD (hon.), Birmingham-So. Coll., 1996. CPA, W.Va. V.p., comptr. Parkersburg-Aetna Corp., W.Va., 1956-63; v.p., dir. Marmac Corp, Parkersburg, 1963-66; mgr. fin. control Boise-Cascade Corp., Idaho, 1966-67; exec. v.p. fin. and adminstrn., sec. Cudahy Co., Phoenix, 1967-72; chmn. bd. dirs., CEO Vulcan Materials Co., Birmingham, Ala., 1972—; bd. dirs. Amsouth Bancorp., Birmingham, Protective Life Corp., Birmingham., Temple-Inland, Inc., Diboll, Tex. Author: (with others) The Automatic Factory: A Critical Examination, 1955. Trustee So. Rsch. Inst., Leadership Birmingham, Leadership Ala.; chmn. bd. trustees Birmingham-So. Coll. Recipient Alumni Achievement award U. Nebr.-Omaha, 1977, cert. merit W.Va. Soc. CPAs, Elizah Watts Sells award AICPA, 1965, Brotherhood award NCCJ, 1993. Mem. Shoal Creek Club, Birmingham Country Club, The Club, Univ. Club N.Y.C., Chgo. Club, Delta Sigma Pi (Leadership award 1952), Omicron Delta Kappa, Phi Kappa Phi, Phi Eta Sigma. Republican. Presbyterian. Home: 2809 Shook Hill Cir Birmingham AL 35223-2618 Office: Vulcan Materials Co 1 Metroplex Dr Birmingham AL 35209-6805

SKLENCAR, MARY, nurse; b. Milw., July 14, 1951; d. Raymond A. and Helen M. (Wagner) S. BS, U. Ill., 1973; ADN, William Rainey Harper Coll., 1985; MSN, George Mason U. RN, Ill., Va. With The Toadstool Cards & Gifts, Buffalo Grove, Ill., 1980-88; staff nurse ICU, critical care unit Jefferson Hosp., Alexandria, Va., 1986-91; head nurse The Washington Home, 1991—; rsch. assoc. Dr. Joanne Lynn Gerontol. Inst., George Washington U.; clin. rschr. Dartmouth Coll.; adj. faculty sch. nursing U. Va.; adult nurse practitioner George Washington U., Washington, 1995—. Scholar State of Ill., 1st Cath. Slovak Womens' Assn., Village of Arlington Heights Jr. Women's League, Fairfax Hosp. Assn.; recipient Svc. award Fairfax City. Mem. AACN, Am. Heart Assn. (BLSIT), Lit. Coun. No. Va.

SKLENKA, STEPHEN DOUGLAS, marine corps officer; b. Miami, Fla., June 16, 1966; s. Ronald Julian and Jacqueline Mary (Haynen) S.; m. Loriann Elizabeth Winter, Feb. 25, 1995. BS, U.S. Naval Acad., 1988; postgrad., Am. Mil. U., Manassas, Va., 1996—. Commd. 2d lt. USMC, 1988, advanced through grades to capt., 1993; logistics, ops. and exec. positions various locations, 1988-94; comdg. officer bravo co. and beach and terminal ops. co. 1st Landing SPT Bn., Camp Pendleton, Calif., 1994-95; student Amphibious Warfare Sch., Quantico, Va., 1995-96; instr. Basic Officer Course, Quantico, 1996—. Decorated Navy Commendation medal with V, Navy Commendation medal, Navy Achievement medal. Mem. Marine Corps Assn., Marine Corps. Hist. Soc. Republican. Roman Catholic. Home: A6 Quarters Quantico VA 22134

SKOLNICK, S. HAROLD, lawyer; b. Woonsocket, R.I., June 17, 1915; s. David and Elsie (Silberman) S.; m. Shirley Marshall. A.B. cum laude, Amherst Coll., 1936; J.D., Boston U., 1940. Bar: R.I. 1940, D.C. 1947, U.S. Supreme Ct. 1946, Fla. 1952, U.S. Dist. Ct. (so. dist.) Fla. 1953, U.S. Ct. Appeals (5th cir.) 1960, U.S. Ct. Appeals (11th cir.) 1981. Atty., Dept. War, Washington, 1940-42; asst. gen. counsel, asst. chief legal dept. Office Chief Ordnance, Dept. Army, Washington, 1947-50; assoc. Francis I. McCanna, Providence, 1951-52; ptnr. French & Skolnick, Miami, 1953-60; sole practice, Miami, 1961—. Trustee Beth David Congregation. Served to lt. col. U.S. Army, 1942-47. Mem. ABA, R.I. Bar Assn., D.C. Bar Assn., Dade County Bar Assn., Am. Judicature Soc., Am. Def. Preparedness Assn., Estate Planning Council of Greater Miami. Clubs: Mason, Shriners. Home and Office: 6521 SW 122nd St Miami FL 33156-5550

SKOLROOD, ROBERT KENNETH, lawyer; b. Stockton, Ill., May 17, 1928; s. Myron Clifford and Lola Mae (Lincicum) S.; m. Marilyn Jean Riegel, June 18, 1955; children: Cynthia, Mark, Kent, Richard. BA, Ohio Wesleyan U., 1952; JD, U. Chgo., 1957. Bar: Ill. 1957, Okla. 1981, D.C. 1987, U.S. Supreme Ct., 1982, Va. 1985, U.S. Dist. Ct. (no. dist.) Ill. 1959, U.S. Ct. Appeals (7th cir.) 1970, U.S. Dist. Ct. (no. dist.) Okla. 1982, U.S. Ct. Appeals (10th cir.) 1983, Va. 1985, U.S. Dist. Ct. Nebr. 1985, U.S. Dist. Ct. (so. dist.) Ala. 1986, U.S. Dist. Ct. (so. dist.) N.Y. 1986, U.S. Dist. Ct. (ea. and we. dists.) Va. 1986, U.S. Ct. Appeals (2nd, 4th, 6th, 7th, 8th 1oth and 11th cirs.) 1986, U.S. Dist. Ct. D.C. 1987, Ptnr. Reno, Zahm, Folgate, Skolrood, Lindberg & Powell, Rockford, Ill., 1957-80; prof. O.W. Coburn Sch. Law, Oral Roberts U., Tulsa, 1980-81, gen. counsel, 1980-84; exec. dir., gen. counsel Nat. Legal Found., Virginia Beach, Va., 1984-95; with Law Firm of Scogins & Skolrood, Roanoke, Va., 1995—. Contbr. articles to legal jours.; lead counsel on several major constitutional cases. Pres., John Ericsson Rep. Club, 1964; trustee No. Ill. conf. United Meth. Ch., 1957-74, chmn., 1972-74; pres. Ill. Home and Aid Soc.; mem. Evangelical Free Ch. Served with U.S. Army, 1952-54, Korea. Fellow Am. Coll. Trial Lawyers; mem. Ill. Bar Assn., Okla. Bar Assn., Va., Bar Assn., Dist of Columbia Bar Assn, ATLA, Va. Trial Lawyers Assn., Tex. Trial Lawyers Assn., Ill. Trial Lawyers Assn., Okla. Trial Lawyers Assn., Christian Educators Assn. Internat. (bd. reference), Kappa Delta Pi, Pi Sigma Kappa. Home: 5217 Dresden Ln Roanoke VA 24012 Office: Law Firm Scogins & Skolrood 3243 Electric Rd Ste 1A Roanoke VA 24018

SKROBOT, GARRETT LEE, space system engineer; b. Myrtle Beach, S.C., Jan. 28, 1962; s. Frederick Joseph and Betty Lou (Anderson) S.; m. Yvette Rae Glover, May 26, 1990; 1 child, Brianna Leenee. AS in Pre-Engring. cum laude, Roane State Community Coll., 1986; BSEE, U. Tenn., 1988; MS in Space System Engring., Fla. Inst. Tech., 1993. Asst. to chief pharmacist VA Outpatient Clinic-Pharmacy, Knoxville, Tenn., 1985-88; sales person Clone World, Knoxville, 1986-87; data processor First Pharmacy Mgmt., Knoxville, 1987-88; svc. planner engr. Fla. Power & Light, Sanford, 1988-89; elec. system engr. Gen. Dynamics Space System, Cocoa Beach, Fla., 1989-92, instrumentation system engr., 1992-94; design engr. Gen. Dynamics Svc. Co., Cape Canaveral, Fla., 1992; payload mission integrater Gen. Dynamics Svc. Co., Cape Canaveral, 1994—; founder, pres., mem. nat. exec. bd. Students for Exploration and Devel. of Space, U. Tenn., 1988, advisor Fla. chpts. 1993 (Exceptional Svc. award 1988, Disting. Svc. award 1990); treas. Student Govt. Assn., 1986 (Outstanding Leadership award 1986). With USMC, 1980-84. Recipient Cert. of Appreciation, Gamma Beta Phi, 1986. Mem. IEEE (treas. Region 3 Southeastern Conv. 1988). Home: 6785 Caliph Ave Port Saint John FL 32927-8312 Office: Gen Dynamics Space System PO Box 320999 Cocoa Beach FL 32932-0999

SKUBE, MICHAEL, journalist, critic; b. Springfield, Ill.; 1 child, Noah. Degree in polit. sci., La. State U. Former tchr. math and sci. La.; formerly with U.S. Customs Svc., Miami, Fla.; book reviewer Miami Herald, from 1974; Raleigh (N.C.) bur. chief Winston-Salem (N.C.) Jour., 1978-82; editorial writer The News and Observer, Raleigh, 1982-86, became book editor, 1986; columnist, critic Atlanta Jour. and Constn., 1987—. Recipient Pulitzer Prize for criticism, 1989, Disting. Writing award for commentary and column writing Am. Soc. Newspaper Editors, 1989, 1st Pl. award for columns N.C. Press Assn. Office: Atlanta Jour and Constn 72 Marietta St NW Atlanta GA 30303-2804

SKUP, DAVID ALAN, insurance company executive; b. Balt., Nov. 9, 1952; s. Murray and Elaine Betty (Goldberg) S.; m. Joan Elaine Earnest, Sept. 1, 1973; chidren: Brian Murray, Robert Ryan. BS, Fla. State U., 1974. Mgr. Deloitte Haskins & Sells, Jacksonville, Fla., 1974-84; v.p. Ind. Ins. Group, Inc., Jacksonville, 1984—. Commr. allocations United Way N.E. Fla., Jacksonville, 1987. Mem. AICPA, Ins. Acctg. and Sys. Assn. (bd. dirs. 1987—, pres. 1988-89), Inst. Internal Auditors (bd. dirs. 1984-86, pres. 1988—), Fla. Inst. CPAs, Fla. State U. Alumni Bd. (pres. Jacksonville chpt. 1986), Fla. State U. Bus. Sch. Alumni Bd., Pres.'s Club, San Jose Country Club, Tournament Players. Home: 9156 Paisley Ct Jacksonville FL 32257-8021 Office: Ind Ins Group Inc 1 Independent Dr Jacksonville FL 32276-0001

SKURKA, KATHLEEN, sculptor, educator; b. Pitts., Pa., Jan. 23, 1947; d. Cornelius Albert and Ruby Nell (Spencer) S. BFA, U. Ala., Tuscaloosa, 1969, MA, 1970, MFA, 1971. Asst. prof. art Ala. State U., Montgomery, 1971—; pottery instr. Montgomery Sch. Fine Arts, 1989-90, Armory Learning Arts Ctr., Montgomery, 1990—. Exhibited sculpture in one-person exhbn. Other-Worldly Creatures and Forms, 1988, Sculpture in Black and White, 1989, Odd Icons, 1992, Ala. City Invitational, 1992, 93, El Dorado Gallery, Colorado Springs, Colo., 1992, Gallery La Luz, N.Mex., 1992, South Bend (Ind.) Regional Mus. Art, 1992, Catskill Arts Soc., Hurleyville, N.Y., 1992, Jacksonville (Ala.) State U., 1994. Recipient 1st pl. award and Best Media ward Roswell Fine Arts LEague, N.MEx. Miniatrue Art Soc., 1992, Ala. Originality award, 1993, 3d pl. award Women Artists Exhbn., Ala., 1993. Mem. Internat. Sculpture Ctr., Ala. Craftsman Assn., Artifice Rex, Women's Caucus Art. Roman Catholic. Home: PO Box 6085 Montgomery AL 36106-0085

SKURNICK, SAM, stockbroker, investment manager; b. Bklyn., Dec. 1, 1915; s. Philip and Fanny (Bornstein) S.; m. Myrna Gordon Skurnick, Feb. 24, 1963; 1 child, Michelle. BA, Bklyn. Coll., 1938. Registered prin. in securities. Meteorologist U.S. Army Signal Corps, Ft. Monmouth, N.J., 1940-52; registered rep. Bache and Co., N.Y.C., 1952-72; mem. N.Y. Stock Exch., N.Y.C., 1972—; pres. Sam Skurnick, N.Y. Stock Exch., 1972—. Patentee meteorol. telemetering system. With Air Corps U.S. Army, 1938-40. Home: 300 SE 5th Ave Apt 6030 Boca Raton FL 33432-5048

SLACK, KAREN KERSHNER, advertising agency executive; b. Port Arthur, Tex., Aug. 28, 1951; d. Hugh Cleveland and Eleanor Lucille (Beaty) Kershner; BJ, U. Tex., Austin, 1973; m. Jim Slack, Jr., May 12, 1979; children: Megan, James Ryan. Pub. rels. dir. Lakeway Co., Austin, 1973-74; account coord., copywriter Point Comm., Inc., Houston, 1974-76; account exec., then v.p. Rochelle Mktg. Co., Inc., Houston, 1976-80; pres., owner Comm. Plus, Houston, 1980—; ptnr. The Agy. Tool Box Workshops, 1989—; mem. comm. adv. com. Houston United Way, 1980—; chmn. steering com. Houston Festival, 1979—; bd. dirs. S.W. YMCA, 1990-96, pres., bd. mgrs., 1993-95; exec. com.; vol. pub. schs., 1992—. Mem. Houston Advt. Fedn., Houston Prodn. Mgrs. Assn., Soc. Mktg. Profls., Houston Bus. Forum, Am. Mktg. Assn. (named Marketer of the Year, 1992), Tex. Exec. Women, Am. Hosp. Assn., West Univ. Rotary (charter). Home: 4063 Dumbarton St Houston TX 77025-2313 Office: 3730 Kirby Dr Ste 1150 Houston TX 77098-3927

SLATE, JOANNE TALBOTT, mental health counselor; b. Peoria, Ill., July 17, 1931; d. Coral Edward and Cleo (Kirkwood) Talbott; m. Marston G. Slate, Aug. 2, 1958 (dec. Sept. 1964); children: Larry, Claudia, Dennis, Stan, Harry. Student, U. So. Calif.; BA, Bradley U., 1953, MA in Psychology, 1955; MA in Counseling, St. Mary's U., San Antonio, 1979. Lic. profl. counselor. Adoption counselor Crittenton Home, Peoria, 1953-55, Cath. Charities, Houston, 1960-61; dir. post-adoption svcs. Meth. Mission Home, San Antonio, 1979-88, Tex. Cradle Soc., San Antonio, 1988—; dir. Post Adoption Ctr. of the S.W., San Antonio, 1988—; mem. adv. bd. ICAN-Child Abuse Prevention, San Antonio, 1989—. Mem. AACD, Am. Mental Health Counselors, Tex. Psychol. Assn., Tex. Assn. Counseling and Devel., Tex. Mental Health Com. (sec. 1981), Tex. Assn. Post Adoption Profls. (founder 1987). Home: PO Box 40343 San Antonio TX 78229-1343 Office: Post Adoption Ctr 8600 Wurzbach Rd Ste 1110 San Antonio TX 78240-4334

SLATER, A. DAVID, surgeon, educator; b. N.Y.C., Oct. 2, 1949; s. Irwin Holzman and Virginia (Hall) S.; m. Gail Poust, Aug. 14, 1971; 1 child, William David. BA cum laude, Vanderbilt U., 1971, MD, 1975. Diplomate Am. Bd. Surgery, Am. Bd. Thoracic Surgery. Intern U. Mich. Hosps., Ann Arbor, 1975-76, resident in gen. surgery, 1976-81, resident in thoracic surgery, 1981-83; surgeon Drs. Pearce, Gibson, Weichert, Bethea and Slater, New Orleans, 1983-84, Diagnostic Clinic, Largo, Fla., 1984-85; instr. divsn. thoracic and cardiovascular surgery U. Louisville, 1985-86, asst. prof. divsn. thoracic and cardiovascular surgery, 1986-91, assoc. prof. divsn. thoracic and cardiovascular surgery, 1991—; asst. clin. prof. surgery La. State U., New Orleans, 1983-84; chief thoracic and cardiovascular surgery U. Louisville Hosp.; mem. surg. evaluation com. Humana Hosp.- U., ad hoc endoscopy com.; mem. rsch. com. Heart and Lung Inst. Jewish Hosp.; apptd. various hosps.; lectr. in field. Author: (with others) The Clinical Manual of Electrophysiology, 1993; contbr. articles to profl. jours.; patentee interferon in cardiac transplantation. Student Rsch. fellow Vanderbilt U., 1974; Rsch. grantee Sol Strauss Fund, AMA, Genentech, Inc., Jewish Hosp., Heart and Lung Inst., Abiomed, Inc., Medtronic, Inc., Cadwell, Inc., CPI, Inc., others. Mem. ACS, Am. Coll. Cardiology, Am. Coll. Chest Physicians, Am. Coll. Emergency Physicians, Internat. Soc. Heart Transplantation, N. Am. Soc. Pacing and Electrophysiology, So. Thoracic Surg. Assn., So. Surg. Assn., Soc. Thoracic Surgeons, Ky. Med. Assn., Jefferson County Med. Soc., Louisville Surg. Soc., Frederick Coller Surg. Soc., John Alexander Soc., Skull and Bones Hon. Premed. Soc. (pres.), Phi Beta Kappa, Alpha Omega Alpha. Office: U Louisville Dept Surgery Louisville KY 40292

SLATER, CHARLES JAMES, construction company executive; b. Munich, Feb. 16, 1949; s. Robert Marsh and Mary Elizabeth (James) S.; m. Pamela S. Senning, Sept. 17, 1974 (div. Apr. 1992); children: Mary Katherine, Robert Charles; m. Kristie J. Alexander, May 11, 1992. BA in Polit. Sci., U. Tenn., 1974. Safety mgr. Daniel Internat. Co., Kingsport, Tenn., 1981-83; safety and med. mgr. Daniel Internat. Co., Georgetown, S.C., 1983-84; risk mgmt. mgr. Yeargin Inc., Kingsport, 1985-88, Omaha, 1990; resident engr. Yeargin Inc., Frankfort, Ind., 1991, Florence, S.C., 1991; safety and risk mgmt. dir. Harbert-Yeargin Inc., Greenville, S.C., 1992-96; safety and health mgr. Fluor-Daniel Inc., Seaford, Del., 1996—; bd. advisors Assoc. Bldrs. and Contractors/Nat. Safety Coun., Washington, 1993—. Pres. Tenn. Vol. Firefighters Assn., Sullivan County, 1987-89, Kingsport Area Safety Coun., 1989. Mem. Am. Inst. Constructors (chpt. pres. 1993-94), Am. Soc. Safety Engrs., Nat. Safety Mgmt. Soc., Constrn. Industry Coop. Alliance (instr. 1992), Safety Dirs. League (charter), Constrn. Specifications Inst. Episcopalian. Home: PO Box 361 Seaford DE 19973-0361 Office: Fluor-Daniel Inc 500 Woodland Rd Seaford DE 19973

SLATER, JAMES GREGORY, primary education educator; b. Bklyn., Feb. 29, 1960; s. Jesse James Kearse and Dorothy Hellen (Ransom) Jennings; m. Kimberly Cheryl Singleton, Sept. 5, 1986; 1 child, Frederick Darnell. AA, St. Louis C.C., 1990; BS in Elem. Edn., U. Mo., 1992; student, George Mason Univ., 1994—. Cert. primary tchr., Va., Mo. Sgt. USMC, 1981-89; computer instr. Ferguson Florissant Sch. Dist., St. Louis, 1990-92; computer tchr. Boulder (Colo.) County Pub. Schs., 1993; math. tchr. Arlington (Va.) Pub. Schs., 1993—; track coach, mem. staff devel. com. Arlington Pub. Sch., 1993—. Youth coord. Calvary Bapt. Ch., St. Louis, 1989-92; trustee Calvary Missionary Bapt. Ch., 1989—; sound room technician Mt. Olive Bapt. Ch., 1993—. Recipient Navy Achievement medal USMC, 1988. Mem. Nat. Ednl. Assn., Nat. Counsel Tchrs. Math., Va. Ednl. Assn. Democrat. Home: 13705 Northbourne Dr Centreville VA 22020 Office: Kenmore Middle Sch 200 S Carlin Springs Rd Arlington VA 22204

SLATER, JOAN ELIZABETH, secondary education educator; b. Paterson, N.J., Aug. 27, 1947; d. Anthony Joseph and Emma (Liguori) Nicola; m. Francis Graham Slater, Nov. 16, 1974; children: David, Kristin, Kylie. BA in English, Montclair State Coll., 1968, MA in English, 1971. Cert. English, speech and theater arts tchr., N.J., Tex. Tchr. Anthony Wayne Jr. High Sch., Wayne, N.J., 1968-70, Wayne Valley High Sch., Wayne, N.J., 1970-74, Strack Intermediate Sch., Klein, Tex., 1987—; cons. Tex. Assessment Acad. Skills, Houston Post Newspaper, 1994—; adv. bd. Tex. Edn. Assn., winter 1993; sch. dist. rep. Southern Assn. Colls. and Schs., 1993; editor, advisor Pawprints Lit. Mag., 1989—. Co-author: Klein Curriculum for the Gifted and Talented, 1992-93. Com. chairperson Klein After-Prom Extravaganza, 1994-95; parent supporter Challenge Soccer Club, Klein, 1993—; mem. Klein H.S. Girls Soccer Team Bd., 1995-96. Mem. North Harris County Coun. Tchrs. English (sec. 1992-95), Klein Edn. Assn., Nat. Coun. Tchrs. English, Tex. Mid. Sch. Assn., Internat. Reading Assn., Greater Houston Area Reading Coun., Nat. Charity League. Home: 6018 Spring Oak Holw Spring TX 77379-8833 Office: Strack Intermediate Sch 18027 Kuykendahl Rd Klein TX 77379-8116

SLATER, KRISTIE, construction company executive; b. Rock Springs, Wyo., Nov. 14, 1957; d. Fredrick Earl and Shirley Joan (McWilliams) Alexander; m. C. James Slater, May 11, 1992. A in Bus. Adminstrn., Salt Lake City Coll., 1978. EMT, Wyo. Cost engr., material coord. Project Constrn. Corp., LaBarge, Wyo., 1985; cost engr., scheduler Flour Daniel Constrn. Co., Salt Lake City, 1985-86, Bibby Edible Oils, Liverpool, Eng., 1986-87; cost engr., safety technician Sunvic, Inc./I.S.T.S., Inc., Augusta, Ga., 1987-88; cost engr. Brown & Root, Inc., Ashdown, Ark., 1988-89, Wickliffe, Ky., 1989; sr. cost engr. Brown & Root, Inc., Pasadena, Tex., 1989-90, LaPorte, Tex., 1990-91; project controls mgr. Yeargin Inc., Thousand Oaks, Calif., 1991-92; corp. controls mgr. Suitt Constrn. Co., Greenville, S.C., 1993-95; site scheduler, planner Fluor Daniel Constrn. Co., Seaford, Del., 1996—. Pres. 4-H State Coun., Laramie, Wyo., 1976; mem. com. Houston Livestock Show and Rodeo. Mem. LDS Ch. Office: Fluor Daniel Inc Box 361 Seaford DE 19973

SLATER, THOMAS GLASCOCK, JR., lawyer; b. Washington, Mar. 15, 1944; s. Thomas G. and Hylton R. S.; m. Scott Newell Brent, Aug. 31, 1996; children: Thomas Glascock, Tacie Holden, Andrew Fletcher. B.A., Va. Mil. Inst., 1966; LL.B., U. Va., 1969. Bar: Va. 1969, U.S. Dist. Ct. (ea. dist.) Va. 1970, U.S. Dist Ct. (we. dist.) Va. 1979, U.S. Ct. Appeals (4th cir.) 1975, U.S. Ct. Appeals D.C. 1980, U.S. Supreme Ct. 1981. Assoc. Hunton & Williams, Richmond, Va., 1969-76, ptnr., 1976—; lectr. Pres. VMI Found. Fellow ABA, Va. Law Found.; mem. 4th Cir. Jud. Conf., Va. Bar Assn., Va. State Bar Coun. (exec. com.), D.C. Bar Assn., Richmond Bar Assn. (pres. 1989-90), Va. Mil. Inst. Alumni Assn. (past pres.). Office: Hunton & Williams Riverfrnt Plaza East Tower 951 E Byrd St Richmond VA 23219-4040

SLATER, WILLIAM THOMAS, dean, communications researcher; b. Pitts., Oct. 31, 1942; s. William E. and Margaret Ruth (Briggs) S. BA, Tufts U., 1971; AM, Harvard U., 1972; MA, Stanford U., 1973, PhD, 1977. Reporter, editor, Afro-Am. newspaper, 1959-61; reporter Newark News, 1961-62; news dir. Sta. WABQ, Cleve., 1962-64; reporter, anchor Sta. WBZ-TV-AM, Boston, 1964-69; asst. to Gov. of Mass., 1969-71; asst. prof. U. Wash., Seattle, 1973-75; asst. prof. U. So. Calif., L.A., 1975-77; assoc. prof., head div. broadcasting U. Cin., 1977-79; prof., head dept. radio-TV, U. Ariz., Tucson, 1979-83; dean Sch. Fine Arts, Eastern Wash. U., Cheney, 1983-86; v.p. univ. rels. Oreg. State U., Corvallis, 1986-88; pres. Charter Oak Coll., Farmington, CT., 1988-89; v.p. Inst. Adv., U. Md., Princess Anne, 1989-90; v.p. adv. and pub. svcs. Western Ill. U., Macomb, 1990-94; dean Sch. Journalism W.Va. U., Morgantown, 1994—; cons. broadcasting and edn. planning. Mem. Phi Beta Kappa. Author: Aspen Handbook on Communication, 1972, 2d edit., 1975; contbr. articles to profl. jours.

SLATON, JOSEPH GUILFORD, social worker; b. N.Y.C., Sept. 29, 1951; s. Joseph Slachta and Hilda Elizabeth (Sims) S.; 1 child, Nicholas Michael. BS, E. Carolina U., 1974; MSW, U. N.C., 1977. Cert. pub. mgr. Cottage parent supr. N.C. Div. Youth Svcs., Rocky Mount, 1974-75; juvenile evaluation counselor N.C. Div. Youth Svcs., Rocky Mount and Butner, N.C., 1975-77; social worker Murdoch Ctr., N.C. Dept. Human Resources, Butner, 1977-78; facility survey cons., mental retardation profl. N.C. Div. Facility Svcs., Raleigh, 1978-81, facility survey cons. long-term care programs, 1981-83, program mgr. health care facilities br., 1983-87, human svcs. planner cert. of need program, 1987-94; sr. analyst, 1994—; asst. Scoutmaster BSA Troop 300, speaker in field. Author: Guide for the Newly Active Democrat, 1996. Mem. N.C. Rehab. Task Force, Raleigh, 1988-90; chmn. subcom. N.C. Mental Retardation Task Force, Raleigh, 1982-83; active N.C. Regional Strategic Planning Task Force, Raleigh, 1982-83; active N.C. Regional Strategic Planning Task Force on Mental Retardation, 1982; mem. allocations panel Wake County United Way, Raleigh, 1984-95; mem. planning com. Wake County Ptnrs. Program—Sta. WRAL-TV, Raleigh, 1980, coord. Auction Day, 1981, mem. exec. planning com., 1982; campaign mgr., vol. coord., treas. rep. for N.C. Ho. Reps. Mem. NASW (legis. policy com.), Acad. Cert. Social Workers, Triangle Health Execs.' Forum. Episcopalian. Office: NC Div Facility Svcs PO Box 29530 Raleigh NC 27626-0530

SLATTERY, EDWARD J., bishop; b. Chgo., Aug. 11, 1940. Student, St. Mary of the Lake Sem., Mundelein, Ill., Loyola U., Chgo. Ordained priest Roman Cath. Ch., 1966. Ordained priest Chgo., 1966; v.p. Cath. Ch. Ext. Soc., 1971-76, pres., 1976-94; ordained bishop Diocese of Tulsa, 1994—. Office: Diocese of Tulsa Chancery Office PO Box 2009 Tulsa OK 74101-2009*

SLATTON, RALPH DAVID, printmaking educator; b. Trumann, Ark., Mar. 19, 1952; s. Ralph George and Nobuko (Nozaki) S. BFA, Ark. State U., 1981, MA, 1986; MFA, U. Iowa, 1990. Asst. prof. E. Tenn. State U., Johnson City, 1980—. Exhibited in group shows at Elizabeth Slocumb Galleries, E. Tenn. State U., Johnson City, 1991, Rike Ctr. Gallery, U. Dayton, Ohio, 1991, The Carnegie ARt Ctr., 1991, 92, U. Wis., Madison, 1991, Fine ARts Ctr. Art Gallery, Ark. State U., Jonesboro, 1994, and others; represented in permanent collections The Found. of the Arts, Jonesboro, The Meth. Hosp., Jonesboro, Ark. State U., U. Iowa Print Archives, Iowa City, Taiwan Mus. Art, Ino-cho Paper Mus., Kochi-shi, Japan, and others. Sgt. U.S. Army, 1972-75. Artist grantee U. Iowa Art ASsn., 1988, R&D grantee E. Tenn. State U., 1991. Mem. Md. Printmakers, The Print Club Albany, The Print Consortium, Asociacion Difusora Obra Graficia. Office: E Tenn State U Dept Art Box 70708 Johnson City TN 37614-0708

SLAUGHTER, EDWARD RATLIFF, JR., lawyer; b. Raleigh, N.C., Sept. 15, 1931; s. Edward Ratliff and Mary McBee (Hoke) S.; m. Anne Limbosch, July 25, 1957; children: Anne-Marie, Hoke, Bryan. A.B., Princeton U., 1953; postgrad. (Rotary Found. fellow), U. Brussels, 1955-56; LL.B., U. Va., 1959. Bar: Va. 1959, D.C. 1981. Assoc. firm McGuire, Woods & Battle (now McGuire, Woods, Battle & Boothe) and predecessors, Charlottesville, Va., 1959-64; ptnr. McGuire, Woods & Battle and predecessors, 1964-79, head dept. litigation, 1964-79; spl. asst. for litigation to atty. gen. U.S., 1979-81; ptnr. firm Whitman & Ransom, Washington, 1981-84; prin. Slaughter & Redinger, P.C., Charlottesville, 1984-95, Slaughter, Izakowitz, Clarke & Nunley, P.C., 1995-96, Woods, Rogers & Hazlegrove, P.L.C., 1996—; vis. lectr. trial advocacy U. Va., 1970-77, Va. procedure, 1986-91; disting. lectr. U. Tunis, 1996. Chmn. Albemarle County (Va.) Dem. Com., 1969-73; pres. Charlottesville-Albemarle United Way, 1972; commr. accounts Albemarle County, 1986—; trustee Lime Kiln Arts, Inc., 1992—. Served with USNR, 1953-55. Fellow Am. Bar Found., Am. Coll. Trial Lawyers; mem. Am. Bar Assn., D.C. Bar, Charlottesville-Albemarle Bar Assn. (pres. 1976-77), Va. Bar Assn. (pres. 1978), Va. State Bar (bd. govs. internat. practice sect. 1992—), Va. Trial Lawyers Assn., Thomas Jefferson Inn Ct. (pres. 1995-96). Club: Boar's Head Sports, Farmington Country. Home: 111 Falcon Dr Charlottesville VA 22901-2035 Office: Woods Rogers & Hazlegrove PLC PO Box 2964 250 W Main St Ste 300 Charlottesville VA 22902-2964

SLAUGHTER, FREEMAN CLUFF, retired dentist; b. Estes, Miss., Dec. 30, 1926; s. William Cluff and Vay (Fox) S.; student Wake Forest Coll., 1944; student Emory U., 1946-47, DDS, 1951; m. Genevieve Anne Parks, July 30, 1948; children: Mary Anne, Thomas Freeman, James Hugh. Practice gen. dentistry, Kannapolis, N.C., 1951-89; ret.; mem. N.C. Bd. Dental Examiners, 1966-75, pres., 1968-69, sec.-treas., 1971-74; chief dental staff Cabarrus Meml. Hosp., Concord, N.C., 1965-66, 75; mem. N.C. Adv. Com. for Edn. Dental Aux. Personnel-N.C. State Bd. Edn., 1967-70; adviser dental asst. program Rowan Tech. Inst., 1974-76; Duke Med. Ctr. Davison Century Club. Trustee N.C. Symphony Soc., 1962-68, pres. Kannapolis chpt., 1961; mem. Cabarrus County Bd. Health, 1977-83, chmn., 1981-83, acting health dir., 1981; vice chmn. Kannapolis Charter Commn., 1983-84; mem. City Council Kannapolis, 1984-85; Mayor protem, Kannapolis, 1984-85; active Boy Scouts Am., Eagle scout with silver palm. Served with USN, 1944-46, WW II. ETO, MTO. Recipient Kannapolis Citizen of Yr. award, 1982; lic. real estate broker. Fellow Am. Coll. Dentists; mem. Am. Legion, Kannapolis Jr. C. of C. (v.p. 1952), Toastmasters Internat. (pres. Kannapolis 1963-64), ADA (life), Am. Assn. Dental Examiners (Dentist Citizen of Year 1975; v.p. 1977-79), So. Conf. Dental Deans and Examiners (v.p. 1969), N.C. Dental Soc. (resolution of commendation 1975), N.C. Dental Soc. Anesthesiology (pres. 1964), Southeastern Acad. Prosthodontics, So. Acad. Oral Surgery, Am. Soc. Dentistry for Children (pres. N.C. unit 1957), Internat. Assn. Dental Research, Cabarrus County Dental Soc. (pres. 1953-54, 63-64, 69), N.C. Assn. Professions (dir. 1976-80), Omicron Kappa Upsilon, Alpha Epsilon Upsilon. Clubs: Masons, Shriners, Kannapolis Music (pres. 1962-63), Rotary (dir. 1977-80).

SLAUGHTER, GLORIA JEAN, elementary education educator; b. Norfolk, Va., Nov. 20, 1940; d. Cloyce Miner and Mary Leatrice (McClure) McClurkin; m. John Wilson Slaughter, June 4, 1961; children: Hugh Leland, Lara Lee. BS, U. South Ala., 1972; MEd, Ga. State U., 1984. First grade tchr. Ocean Gate (N.J.) Elem., 1968-70, Old Shell Rd. Sch., Mobile, Ala., 1972-80; second grade tchr. Columbia Elem., Decatur, Ga., 1980—. Participant DeKalb Neighborhood Leadership Inst., Decatur, 1986; exec. com. Dem. Party, Decatur, 1990—; mem. Up and Out of Poverty, Atlanta, 1990-94, Jobs With Peace, Atlanta, 1981-89; bd. mem. WRFG Radio. Mem. Orgn. DeKalb Educators (pres. 1984-86, pub. rels. 1986—), Ga. Assn. Educators (governing bd. 1991-94, resolution com. 1992-94). Methodist. Home: 567 Raven Springs Tr Stone Mountain GA 30087 Office: Columbia Elem 3230 Columbia Woods Dr Decatur GA 30032

SLAUGHTER, PHILLIP HOWARD, computer company executive; b. Ft. Worth, Jan. 6, 1948; s. Howard Biles and Ella Louise (Humphrey) S.; m. Virginia Hurst, Jan. 1970 (div. Dec. 1972); 1 child, Mallory Lynn; m. Sharon Wills, Apr. 1975 (dec. May 1987); m. Linda Neilson, Nov. 1987 (div. Aug. 1992); children: Leah Elizabeth, William Geer. BS in Physics and Math., Tex. Christ. U., 1970; postgrad. in computer sci., U. Ala., Huntsville, 1970-87. Acct. exec. Merrill Lynch, Pierce Ferner & Smith, Huntsville, 1971-73; programmer SCI Systems, Huntsville, 1973-74; programmer, analyst Teledyne Brown Engring., Huntsville, 1974-75; sr. scientist McDonnell Douglas Astronautics, Huntsville, 1975-77; programming mgr. Essex Corp., Huntsville, 1977-79; sr. cons. Analysts Internat. Corp., Huntsville, 1979-81; founder, cons. Systems Solutions, Inc., Huntsville, 1981—, chmn., 1982—, also bd. dirs. Contbr. articles to profl. jours. Mem. Mensa (founder, pres. North Ala. group 1972-75, 82-83), Pi Mu Epsilon, Sigma Pi Sigma. Republican. Methodist. Home and Office: Sys Solutions Inc 23 Glen Wood Dr Jackson TN 38305-1722

SLAUGHTER, TED DAVID, public relations executive, health care executive; b. Beaumont, Tex., Dec. 14, 1963; s. Ted Harper and Carolyn Ann (Caldwell) S.; m. Deborah Sue Hesseltine, July 1, 1989; 1 child, Ted James. BS in Comm., Lamar U., 1992. Journalist KJAC TV Channel 4, Port Arthur, Tex., 1983-84, KBMT TV Channel 12, Beaumont, 1985-91, KFDM TV Channel 6, Beaumont, 1991-93; dir. cmty. edn. Managed Home Health Care, Beaumont, 1993-95; field mgmt. First Am. Health Care, Beaumont, 1995—; photographer television features, outdoor hunting features, 1988. City coun., City of Vidor, Tex., 1994-95; Operation Blue Santa, Orange County (Tex.) Sheriff Dept., 1989; Leadership S.E. Tex., Beaumont, 1994-95. Mem. Am. Cancer Soc., Tex. Pub. Rels. Assn., Team Cities Tex. Republican. Southern Baptist. Office: City of Vidor 170 N Main Vidor TX 77662

SLAUGHTER, THOMAS EDWIN, family services agency executive; b. Lyons, N.Y., Sept. 26, 1949; s. I.W. and Doris Leona (McQueen) S.; m. Joan Elizabeth Guttery, July 4, 1969; children: Justin Daryl, Elizabeth Nicole. Student, David Lipscomb U., Nashville, 1967-69; BS in Social Wk., U. N.C., Greensboro, 1988; MSW, U. N.C., chapel Hill, 1992. Lic. gen. contr., N.C. Retail sales assoc. Belk, Melbourne, Fla., 1965-67; title clk. Dept. Revenue, State of Tenn., Nashville, 1967-69; pub. rels., order processing supr. TEMCO, Inc., Nashville, 1969-72; v.p. mktg. Frost-Arnett Co., Nashville, 1972-79; adminstrv. dir. AGAPE, Inc., Nashville, 1979-82; treas., dir. mktg. BJ Enterprises & Svcs., Inc., Portland, Tenn., 1990—; exec. dir. AGAPE of N.C., Inc., Greensboro, 1982—; instrument rated pvt. pilot FAA, Washington, 1991—; cert. instr. Active Parenting Today, Atlanta, 1993—. Author: Carolina Christian, 1996. Youth minister/assoc. minister Scottsboro Ch. of Christ, Nashville, 1969-72; minister/family counselor Corinth Ch. of Christ, Portland, Tenn., 1972-82; dir. edn. Friendly Ave. Ch. of Christ, Greensboro, 1984—; coord. symposium on needs of children Human Svcs. Inst., Greensboro, 1988; foster parent Dept. Social Svcs., Greensboro and Nashville, 1979—; sgt.-at-arms Tenn. Gen. Assembly, Nashville, 1972. Mem. NASW, Christian Adoption Resource Exch., N.C. Coalition of Pvt. Adoption Agencies. Republican. Office: AGAPE of NC Inc 302 College Rd Greensboro NC 27410

SLAVEN, BETTYE DEJON, psychotherapist; b. New Orleans, Sept. 27, 1946; d. Edward William and Bettye (Ray) DeJ.; m. Richard W. Slaven, Nov. 28, 1968; children: Kelly DeJon Slaven, Richard Daniel. BA, Tex. Tech U., 1969; MA, U. Houston, 1974; postgrad. N. Tex. State U., 1974-76. Lic. counselor, Tex., marriage and family therapist, Tex. Tchr. Richardson Ind. Sch. Dist., Tex., 1970-71, 73-74, Somerville Pub. Schs., Mass., 1971-72, Trinity Episcopal Sch., New Orleans, 1972-73; with Goals for Dallas-Devel., 1975—; pvt. practice psychotherapy, Dallas, 1979—; therapist family crisis intervention Dallas Ind. Sch. Dist., 1986-94. Bd. dirs. Way Back House-Vol. Psychol. Assistance, 1979—, Freedom Rides Found, bylaws com., 1987—, Foster Child Advocate Services, 1987—, sec. 1989-90, v.p., pers. chmn., 1990—; founder, project chmn. Women's Way Back House, 1979; project chairman, bd. dirs. Interfaith Housing Coalition, 1987-88; pres. living bible class Highland Park Meth. Ch., Dallas, 1982, 90-91, mem. adminstrv. bd., 1986, also bd. dirs.; adv. bd.; bd. dirs. Dallas County Mental Health Assn., 1989, Dallas Coun. Alcoholism, 1989-90; mem. Communities Found. Tex. Networking, 1986—, Letot task force, 1986, nominating com. Camp Fire Girls Inc., 1987-90; city chmn. Dallas Area Rapid Transit, 1983; pub. affairs chmn. Jr. League Dallas, 1984, resch. and devel. chmn., 1985-86, cmty. v.p., 1986-87, exec. and pub. rels. coms., 1986-87, grantee sr. mentor program at N. Dallas H.S., 1995-96; chmn. Camp Task Force for Chronically Ill Children, 1986-87, Spl. Camps for Spl. Kids, 1987-88, bd. dirs. 1988-89, adv. bd., 1989-92; pres. McCulloch Middle Sch. PTA, 1987—; chmn. Career Day Highland High Sch. PTA, 1990, coll. night chair, 1991; assoc. Pathways to Prevention, 1989-91; pers. chmn. bd. dirs. Foster Child Advocates Svcs., 1989-93; bd. dirs. Dallas Mental Health Assn., 1990-95; co-chmn. Jr. Symphony Ball, 1993; bldg. coord. Safe Haven grant, 1995-96. Recipient Lenz award cmty. agy. liaison Susan G. Komen luncheon com., 1996; named one of Outstanding Young Women in Am., 1980, Leadership Dallas, 1996. Avocations: sailing, swimming, reading.

SLAVIN, ALEXANDRA NADAL, artistic director, educator; b. Port-au-Prince, Haiti, Oct. 26, 1943; came to U.S., 1946; d. Pierre E. and Marie Therese (Clerié) Nadal; m. Eugene Slavin, Dec. 24, 1967; 1 child, Nicholas V. Grad. high sch., Chgo. Dancer Ballet Russe de Monte Carlo, N.Y.C., 1960-61, Chgo. Opera Ballet and N.Y.C. Opera Ballet, 1961-64, Am. Ballet Theatre, N.Y.C., 1965-66, Ballet de Monte Carlo, 1966-67, The Royal Winnipeg (Can.) Ballet, 1967-72; artistic dir. Ballet Austin, Tex., 1972-89; owner, dir. The Slavin Nadal Sch. Ballet, Austin, 1989—. Recipient Achievement in the Arts award Austin chpt. YWCA, 1987. Roman Catholic. Office: Slavin-Nadal Sch Ballet 5521 Burnet Rd Austin TX 78756-1603

SLAVIN, HILARY BERNARD, psychologist, neuropsychologist; b. Bklyn., Aug. 22, 1948; s. Louis and Betty (Fleischer) S.; m. Maria Pico, June 18, 1989; 1 child, Lauren Chloe. B.A., Bklyn. Coll., 1969; M.A., Clark U., 1974; Psy.D., Fla. Inst. Tech., 1983. Lic. psychologist, Ga. Staff psychologist Taunton Community Mental Health Program, Mass., 1976-79; clin. child psychologist Taunton Area Assocs. for Human Services, 1979-80; psychologist trainee Brevard County Mental Health Ctr., Melbourne, Fla., 1981; clin. psychology intern Atlanta VA Med. Ctr., 1982-83; psychologist Ga. Mental Health Inst., Atlanta, 1983-86; pvt. practice clin. psychology, Atlanta, 1984—. Clark U. fellow, 1969-70, 71-73. Mem. Nat. Acad. Neuropsychology, Southeastern Psychol. Assn., Ga. Psychol. Assn., Am. Psychol. Assn., Internat. Neuropsychol. Soc. Jewish. Avocations: photography, hiking, reading. Home: 1089 Mountain Creek Trl NW Atlanta GA 30328-3565 Office: 3111 Paces Mill Rd NW Ste 200C Atlanta GA 30339-5704

SLAY, JACK, JR., English language educator; b. Oxford, Miss., Mar. 28, 1961; s. Jack C. Sr. and Theresa (McCormack) S.; m. Lori Kirk, July 25, 1987; children: Jack Kirk, Justin Perry. BA, Miss. State U., Starkville, 1983, MA, 1985; PhD, U. Tenn., Knoxville, 1990. Instr. English U. Tenn., Knoxville, 1990-92; asst. prof. English LaGrange (Ga.) Coll., 1992—. Author: Ian McEwan, 1996; author short stories; contbr. articles to profl. jours. Democrat. Roman Catholic. Home: 313 Park Ave Lagrange GA 30240 Office: LaGrange Coll Dept English 601 Broad St Lagrange GA 30240

SLAYDON, JEANNE MILLER, secondary school educator; b. Kansas City, Mo.; d. Sanderson Staley and Bea Amelia (Hoeger) Miller; m. George S. Wolbert; children: Kathleen Amelia Slaydon Mayer, Dianne Louise Slaydon Springer. BA, Tex. Christian U.; MEd, U. Houston. Pvt. tutor Midland and Houston, Tex.; elem. tchr. Midland Ind. Sch. Dist.; tchr. sec. social studies Spring Branch Ind. Sch. Dist., Houston, chmn. Social Studies dept., dist. Social Studies coord., 1977-91; pvt. practice social studies cons. Houston, 1991—; cons. So. Assn. Colls. and Univs., 1978—; mem. Tex. State Task Force on Restructuring Social Studies, Grade 1 to 12, 1991-92. Author: (econs. curriculum) Confluent Economic Education, 1979; cons. (textbook) World History, 1982. Mem. Tex. Citizen Bee, Local Close Up, 1985-91; coord. Congl. Dist. 7 Bicentennial Commn.; spkr. Inst. Internat. Edn., Network for Zero Population Growth. Mem. AAUW, Social Studies Suprs. Assn., Inst. for Internat. Edn., Spring Br. Coun. for Social Studies (treas 1970-73, pres. 1983), Tex. Coun. for Social Studies (v.p. 1986, pres. 1988), Tex. Assn. Advancement of History (bd. dirs.), Tex. State Hist. Assn., Tex Alliance Geog. Edn., Houston Friends of Geography, Houston Geog. Soc., Nat. Coun. Social Studies, Nat. Coun. Geog. Edn., Alpha Delta Kappa, Alpha Gamma, Phi Delta Kappa (chpt. sec. 1991-93). Congregationalist.

SLEDD, JAMES HINTON, English language educator; b. Atlanta, Dec. 5, 1914; s. Andrew and Annie Florence (Candler) S.; m. Joan Webb, July 16, 1939; children: Andrew, Robert, James Jr., John, Ann. B.A., Emory U., 1936; BA (Rhodes scholar), Oxford U., 1939; Ph.D., U. Tex., 1947; postdoctoral studies, U. Mich., 1948, U. Chgo., 1951. Instr. English U. Chgo., 1945-46, asst. prof., 1948-55, asso. prof., 1955-56; asst. prof. Duke, 1946-48; asso. prof. U. Calif. at Berkeley, 1956-59; vis. prof. U. Ceylon, 1959-60; prof. Northwestern U., Evanston, Ill., 1960-64; prof. U. Tex., Austin, 1964-85, prof. emeritus, 1985—; vis. prof. U. Mich., summer 1956, U. London, 1963, U. Wash., summer 1963, Mont. State U., summer, 1967, U. Nev.-Reno, 1986, others. Author editor of books; contbr. articles to profl. jours. Guggenheim fellow, 1953-54; Ford Found. grantee, 1950-51; Rockefeller Found. grantee, 1952-53. Mem. Linguistic Soc., Nat. Council Tchrs. English, Am. Dialect Soc., Internat. Assn. Univ. Profs. English. Methodist. Home: PO Box 5311 Austin TX 78763-5311 Office: Dept English Univ Texas Austin TX 78712

SLEDGE, C. LINDEN, oil company executive; b. Pearsall, Tex., Apr. 25, 1929; s. Clarence Williamson and Lillian Claire (Manford) S.; m. Ellanore Josephine Barnes, May 10, 1952 (div. 1976); m. Jon Ann Rice, Sept. 2, 1979; children: Scott L., Susan L., John T., Linda C. BBA, U. Tex., 1956, LLD (hon.), 1973. Chmn., CEO Frost Nat. Bank, San Antonio, 1956-85; pres. Azrock Industries, San Antonio, 1986-92; chmn., CEO Linden-David Co., San Antonio, 1992—; bd. dirs. Frost Bank, Cullen-Frost Bankers, San Antonio, Cullen Bank, Dallas. Pres. Alamo chpt. Boy Scouts Am.; trustee Trinity U., San Antonio, 1976—. Capt. USAF, 1951-54. Mem. Tex. Bankers Assn. (bd. dirs.), Greater San Antonio C. of C. (chmn. 1975), Order of Alamo, Town Club, Cavaliers, German Club. Republican. Episcopalian.

SLEDGE, TERRY LYNN, minister; b. Ponca City, Okla., Jan. 6, 1951; s. Orville Eugene and Ophelia Ann (Tullis) S.; m. Patricia Louise Humble, May 25, 1972; children: Tara Lynn, Patrick Todd. A of Divinity, Southwestern Bapt. Theol. Sem., 1990. Ordained to ministry So. Bapt. Conv., 1972. Pastor 1st Bapt. Ch., Ripley, Okla., 1972-74; assoc. pastor Trinity Bapt. Ch., Seminole, Okla., 1974; pastor Longwood Bapt. Ch., Ponca City, Okla., 1974-76; 1st Bapt. Ch. Fittstown, Okla., 1976-81, Victory Park Bapt. Ch., McAlester, 1981—; trustee Okla. Bapt. U., Shawnee, Okla., 1985-88. Coord. McAlester News Capitol Religious Article, 1984—; adminstr. Victory Park soup Kitch, McAlester, 1987—; location supr. Operation Oasis of Bapt. Conv., McAlester, 1991; bd. dirs. Okla. Commn. on Children and Youth. Mem. Bapt. Gen. Conv. (mem. resolution com. 1987, credentials com. 1988). Republican. Home: 639 E Harrison Ave Mcalester OK 74501-4213 Office: Victory Park Bapt Ch 601 E Harrison Ave Mcalester OK 74501-4213

SLEEMAN, WILLIAM CLIFFORD, JR., aerospace technologist; b. Birmingham, Ala., June 29, 1923; s. William Clifford and Olive Mae (Watson) S.; student Birmingham-So. Coll., 1940-42; B.S. in Aero. Engring., U. Ala., 1944; m. Mary Frances Mikell, Apr. 12, 1947; children: William Clifford III, Richard McDonald, Melanie Frances. Aero. engr. NACA/NASA Langley Rsch. Center, Hampton, Va., 1944-52, aero. rsch. engr., 1952-62, aerospace engr., 1962-67, aerospace technologist, 1967-81, head flexible wing sect., 1967-73, ret., 1981, disting. rsch. assoc., 1981—. Singer in prin. roles, chorus Peninsula Civic Opera Co., Newport News, Va. 1955-65. Choir dir. Hidenwood Presbyterian Ch., Newport News, 1956-76, elder, 1967-75, 79-82. Recipient Achievements awards NASA, 1968-70. Assoc. fellow Am. Inst. Aeros. and Astronautics; mem. Engrs.' Club of Va. Peninsula (treas. 1963-64). Club: Warwick Yacht and Country (Newport News). Contbr. articles to profl. jours. Home: 207 Mistletoe Dr Newport News VA 23606-3609 Office: NASA Langley Rsch Ctr Hampton VA 23665

SLEMMONS, DAVID ROBERT, librarian; b. Berkeley, Calif., Dec. 20, 1948; s. David Burton and Ruth Marilyn (Evans) S.; children: Michael, Mabry. BA, U. Nev., 1971; postgrad., U. Alaska, 1975-76; MFA, U. Okla., 1988, MLIS, 1988. Spl. svc. rep. Bechtel, Alaska, 1974-75; actor Art Inc., Oklahoma City, Okla., 1979; spl. places ops. supr. Census Bur., L.A., 1980; artist-in-residence, dir. Kiroli Arts and L.A. Legend, West Monroe, L.A., 1980; instr. Ouachita Par. Schs., Monroe, 1980-81; prodr. dir., program dir., air talent Sta. KMLB-KWEZ, Monroe, 1982-85; morning anchor, prodn. dir. Sta. KGOU, Norman, 1987-89; artistic dir. Street Players Theatre, Norman, 1988-89; libr. Okla. Libr. for Blind, Oklahoma City, 1989—. Author: Head, 1995; dir. (play) Frankenstein, 1989, playwright (play) Daedalus, 1970. Founder Outlaw Poets, Okla.; dir. Medieval Fair, Okla., 1979; mem. Friends for Dem. Reform. With U.S. Army, 1971-73. Mem. Amnesty Internat., Sierra Club, Students for a Dem. Soc. Home: Box 2425 Norman OK 73070 Office: Okla Libr for the Blind and Physically Handicapped 300 NE 18th St Oklahoma City OK 73105

SLEVIN, JOHN THOMAS, neurologist, educator; b. Parkersburg, W.Va., Dec. 15, 1948; s. John Marshal and Mary Belle (Kysor) S.; m. Barbara Jeanne Nyere, June 26, 1971. BA in Biology, Johns Hopkins U., 1970; MD, W.Va. U., 1975. Intern W.Va. U. Hosp., Morgantown, 1975-76; resident in neurology U. Va. Hosp., Charlottesville, 1976-79; fellow in neuropharmacology Johns Hopkins U., Balt., 1979-81; asst. prof. neurology U. Ky. Med. Ctr., 1981-86, assoc. prof., 1986-93, prof. neurology and pharmacology, 1993—; assoc. Sanders-Brown Ctr. on Aging U. Ky. Med. Ctr., 1981—; mem. grad. faculty U. Ky., 1986—; staff neurologist U. Ky. Hosp., 1981—, VA Med. Ctr., Lexington, Ky., 1981—; neurol. cons. Woodrow Wilson Rehab. Ctr., Fishersville, Va., 1979-81; med. cons. Montebello State Ctr., Balt., 1979-81; assoc. med. staff divsn. maternal and child health Commonwealth of Ky., Frankfort, 1982—, mem. med. rev. bd., 1985—; examiner Am. Bd. Psychiatry and Neurology. Contbr. articles to profl. jours. Med. advisor Parkinson's Disease Support Group Lexington, 1991—. Grantee NIA, NINDS, VA. Fellow Am. Acad. Neurology; mem. AAAS, Soc. for Neurosci. (pres. Bluegrass chpt. 1990-93), Internat. Soc. for Neurochemistry, Am. Soc. for Pharmacology and Exptl. Therapeutics, Am. Soc. for Neurologic Investigation, Internat. Brain Rsch. Orgn., Am. Neurol. Assn., Sigma Xi. Home: 2293 Abbeywood Rd Lexington KY 40515-1112 Office: U Ky/Chandler Med Ctr Dept Neurology Rm L445 Ky Clinic Lexington KY 40536-0284

SLICKER, FREDERICK KENT, lawyer; b. Tulsa, Aug. 21, 1943; s. James Floyd and Lucille Geneva (Nordling) S.; children: Laura, Kipp. BA, U. Kans., 1965, JD with highest distinction, 1968; LLM, Harvard U., 1973. Bar: Kans. 1968, U.S. Ct. Mil. Appeals 1968, Tex. 1973, U.S. Supreme Ct. 1972, Okla. 1980. Assoc. Jackson, Walker, Winstead, Cantwell & Miller, Dallas, 1973-76; assoc. Worsham, Forsythe & Sampels, 1977-80, ptnr., 1980; assoc. Hall, Estill, Hardwick, Gable, Collingsworth & Nelson, Tulsa, 1980-81, mem., 1982-86; ptnr. Baker, Hoster, McSpadden, Clark, Rasure & Slicker, Tulsa, 1986-91; pvt. practice, Tulsa, 1991-92; shareholder Sneed Lang Adams & Barnett, Tulsa, 1992-95; pvt. practice law Tulsa, 1995—. Author: A Practical Guide to Church Bond Financing, 1985. Chmn./vice-chmn. admnstrv. bd. 1st United Meth. Ch., Tulsa, 1990-94, chmn./vice-chmn. fin. com., treas., 1990-94; active Promise Keepers. Capt. U.S. Army, 1965-72. Mem. ABA, Okla. Bar Assn., Order of Coif. Republican. Home: 5211 S Harvard Apt D Tulsa OK 74135 Office: 4444 E 66th Ste 200 Tulsa OK 74136

SLIDER, GARY JAY, technician; b. Paden City, W.Va., Feb. 9, 1951; s. William Ralph and Phyllis Lee (Weaver) S.; m. Wendy Jean Wilkin, Dec. 2, 1978; children: Gary J. II, Belinda, Laura, Sara, Charlie. EMT. Diploma Lethal Force Inst., Concord, N.H., 1993. Mech. technician Miles Inc., New Martinsville, W.Va., 1972—. Pres. Child Help of Wetzel County, New Martinsville, 1987-89. With U.S. Army, 1970-72. Mem. Am. Soc. Law Enforcement Trainers, Inst. Advanced Conservative Studies. Republican. Roman Catholic. Home: HC 61 Box 24 New Martinsville WV 26155-9784 Office: Miles Inc PO Box 500 New Martinsville WV 26155-0500

SLIDER, RUSSELL LOGAN, dean; b. Atlanta, Aug. 30, 1957; s. Earl Ring and Gertrude (Williams) S.; m. Sandra Pounds, Nov. 12, 1989; 1 child, Reid Logan. BA in Psychology, U. Ga., 1980; MEd in Psychometry, Ga. State U., 1993, EdS in Sch. Psychology, 1995. Dir. devel. Woodward Acad., Atlanta, 1981-85, dean of students, 1986-91, dean of admissions, 1992—; internat. ednl. found. dir. Tau Kappa Epsilon, Indpls., 1988-95; mem. vis. com. So. Assn. Schs. and Colls., 1994—. Pres. Hist. Coll. Park (Ga.) Neighborhood Assn., 1993-95, bd. dirs., 1995—; city councilman, mayor pro tem, College Park. Recipient triangle award Tau Kappa Epsilon, 1991. Mem. Atlanta Area Assn. Ind. Schs. (pres. 1995—). Baptist. Home: 1950 Walker Ave College Park GA 30337 Office: Woodward Acad PO Box 87190 Atlanta GA 30337

SLIPMAN, (SAMUEL) RONALD, hospital administrator; b. New Orleans, Aug. 24, 1939; s. Jake and Esther (Steinman) S.; m. Carole Marie Green, July 1, 1961 (div. Feb. 1982); children: Susan Rachel, Lawrence Jay; m. Marilyn Morais, Feb. 5, 1983 (dec. June 1985); m. Lelia Ruth Foster, Jan. 12, 1986; children: Ronald Andrew, Brian Edward. BS, Tulane U., 1961; cert. in supervision techniques, La. State U., 1984; postgrad., NE La. U., 1978-79, 80-81. Design progress estimator Boeing Co., New Orleans, 1964-66; interviewer Tex. Employment Commn., Tyler and Lufkin, 1977-78; pers. technician State of La., Baton Rouge, 1961-62, 63-64, 73-75, 81; rsch. statistician La. Ins. Commn., Baton Rouge, 1967-68; labor market analyst La. Dept. Labor, Baton Rouge, 1969-70, 77; pers. dir. Royal Orleans Hotel, New Orleans, 1966-67; mgmt. analyst for quality assurance Earl K. Long Hosp., Baton Rouge, 1981-84, dir. ancillary svcs., 1984-86; mgmt. analyst, spl. asst. to dir. for total quality mgmt. Dept. Vets. Affairs Med. Ctr., Alexandria, La., 1987-88, 89-90; mgmt. cons., 1990—. Mem. adminstrv. bd. 1st United Ch., chmn. presch. bd.; cubmaster pack 10 Boy Scouts Am., 1993-94, 96—, asst. cubmaster, 1994-96. Mem. La. Soc. Hosp. Pharmacists, Ctrl. La. Soc. for Human Resource Mgmt., S.W. La. Bridge Assn. (pres., bd. dirs.). Republican. Methodist. Home and Office: Rt 2 105 Fox Fire Ln Alexandria LA 71302-8638

SLIVKA, MICHAEL ANDREW, lawyer; b. Ambridge, Pa., Jan. 14, 1955; s. Andrew and Veronica (Yanko) S.; m. Maritza Caldas, Aug. 1, 1991. AB in Psychology, Cornell U., 1977; JD, U. Miami, 1980. Bar: Fla. 1980, U.S. Dist. Ct. (so. dist.) Fla. 1981, U.S. Ct. Appeals (5th cir.) 1981, U.S. Ct. Appeals (11th cir.) 1981. Pvt. practice, Ft. Lauderdale, Fla., 1990—. Precinct capt., exec. com. Broward County Rep. Party, 1991-92; v.p. West

Broward Rep. Club, 1991-92; sec. North Dade/South Broward Estate Planning Coun., 1991-92. Recipient Albert C. Murphy scholar Cornell U., 1973. Mem. Fla. Bar Assn. (young lawyers sect., mem. collection forms com. 1983-85, bicentennial com. 1987), Bankruptcy Bar Assn., Assn. for Objective Law, Weston Area Jaycees (past sec.). Republican. Home: 10827 Charleston Pl Cooper City FL 33026-4908 Office: Barnett Bank Bldg 9000 Sheridan St Ste 114 Pembroke Pines FL 33024

SLIWA, STEVEN MARK, engineering executive, academic administrator. BS in Engring., Princeton (N.J.) U., 1977; MEng, George Washington U., 1978; Phd in Engring., Stanford U., 1983, M in Bus. Mgmt., 1989. Program mgr. controls and human factors div. NASA, Washington; dep. div. chief guidance and control div. NASA/Langley Rsch. Ctr., Hampton, Va.; v.p. product devel. Integrated Systems, Inc., Santa Clara, Calif., 1989—; pres. Embry-Riddle Aero. U., Dayton Beach, Fla., 1991—; chmn. nat. flying qualities strategic planning and flight systems planning coms. Nat. Aerospace Plane Tech. Maturation Plan; owner Sliwa Enterprises, Inc.; tchr. grad. level engring. in automatic controls for flight vehicles George Washington U., 1987, 88. NASA fellow. Fellow AIAA (chmn. guidance, navigation and control tech. com., past adv. bd. Jour. of Guidance). Office: Embry-Riddle Aero U Office of President 600 S Clyde Morris Blvd Daytona Beach FL 32114-3966*

SLJIVICH, MILAN, allergist; b. Asuncion, Paraguay, Mar. 2, 1963; came to U.S., 1989; s. Mile and Mara (Keserich) S.; m. Maria Eugenia Gomez, Apr. 11, 1986; children: mara, Milan, Michaela, Murielle. BS, Colegio Internacional, Asuncion, 1980; MD, U. Asuncion, 1986. Diplomate Am. Bd. Internal Medicine. Intern Hosp. de Clinicas, Asuncion, 1987; intern in medicine Cleve. Clin., 1989-92; fellow in allergy & immunology Baylor Coll. Medicine, Houston, 1992—. Mem. Am. Coll. Physicians, Am. Acad. Allergy & Immunology, Clin. Immunology Soc. Office: Baylor Coll Medicine 6565 Fannin MS F-501 Houston TX 77030

SLOAN, DONNIE ROBERT, JR., lawyer; b. Nashville, July 24, 1946; s. Donnie R. Sr. and Mary Catharine (Willis) S. BS in Indsl. Engring., Ga. Inst. Tech, 1968; JD cum laude, U. Ga., 1971; LLM, Harvard U., 1975. Bar: Ga. 1971, U.S. Dist. Ct. (no. dist.) Ga. 1971, U.S. Ct. Appeals (11th cir.). Atty. Southwire Co., Carrollton, Ga., 1971-74; assoc., ptnr. Hyatt & Rhoads, P.C., Atlanta, 1975-89; pvt. practice, 1989—; instr. legal research U. Ga., Athens, 1970-71; instr. music law Ga. State U., Atlanta, 1976. Mem. editorial bd. Ga. Law Rev., 1969-71. Treas. Ga. Wheelchair Athletic Assn., Atlanta, 1981-84; pres., treas. Dixie Wheelchair Athletic Assn., Atlanta, 1984-87. Recipient Appreciation award Ga. Wheelchair Sports and Recreation Assn., 1979; named to Outstanding Young Men Am., 1981, Dixie Wheelchair Athletic Assn. Hall of Fame, 1990. Mem. Am. Judicature Soc., Phi Kappa Phi, Alpha Phi Mu, Ga. Tech. Club, Harvard Club. Presbyterian. Home: 410 Shoni Ln Woodstock GA 30189-5121 Office: 6325 Amherst Ct Ste 100 Norcross GA 30092

SLOAN, HAROLD DAVID, chemical engineering consultant; b. Olney, Tex., Jan. 4, 1949; s. James Robert Jr. and Laura Faye (Riddle) S.; m. Barbara Ellen Wilson, Dec. 17, 1970 (div. 1982); m. Maureen Ann Moriarity, Mar. 17, 1983; children: Christa Lauren, Elizabeth Michele. BSChemE, Tex. Tech U., 1972. Registered profl. engr., Tex. Field engr. Halliburton Svcs., Corpus Christi, Tex., 1972-73; mgr. tech. svc. Engelhard Corp., Houston, 1987-90; systems engr., process engr., then process mgr. M.W. Kellogg Co., Houston, 1973-87, sr. product tech. cons., 1990-94, refining product tech. mgr., 1994-95; product dir. Rose, 1995—. Contbr. articles to tech. jours. and mags. Pres. Sagemeadow Civic Club, Houston, 1978; v.p. West Harris County Mcpl. Utility Dist. 10, Houston, 1985; Sunday sch. tchr. Met. Bapt. Ch., Houston, 1992—. Mem. AIChE, Tex. Soc. Profl. Engrs. (pres. Sam Houston chpt. 1980, Outstanding Young Engr. award 1978), NRA (life), Tex. State Rifle Assn., Nat. Petroleum Refiners Assn. (co. rep.), Am. Petroleum Inst. (co. rep.), Sigma Xi. Home: 16631 Avenfield Rd Tomball TX 77375-9034 Office: MW Kellogg Co 601 Jefferson St Houston TX 77002

SLOAN, JOHN JOSEPH, III, sociology educator; b. Detroit, May 3, 1956; s. John Joseph Jr. and Christine Anne S. BS in Criminal Justice, Ea. Mich. U., 1980, MS in Sociology, 1982; PhD in Sociology, Purdue U., 1987. Rsch. assoc. dept. sociology Ea. Mich. U., 1980-82, rsch. asst. Inst. for Study of Children and Families, 1982-84; grad. instr. dept. sociology/anthropology Purdue U., West Lafayette, Ind., 1985-87, vis. asst. prof., 1987-88; asst. to assoc. prof. dept. criminal justice U. Ala., Birmingham, 1988—, acting dir. grad. program dept. criminal justice, 1989-90, dir. grad. program, 1994—; adj. asst. to assoc. prof. dept. criminal justice U. Ala., Tuscaloosa, 1990—; lectr. in field. Co-editor: Campus Crime: Legal, Social, and Policy Perspectives, 1995; contbr. articles to profl. jours.; editorial bd. Criminal Justice and Behavior, 1992—; jour. referee Am. Jour. of Police, 1991—, Justice Quar., 1992—, Jour. Criminal Justice, 1991—, Criminal Justice and Behavior, 1992—; manuscript reviewer Prentice Hall, Coll. Textbook Div., 1991—. Fellow Mich. State Supreme Ct. Adminstrs. Office, 1980, Nat. Inst. Justice, 1986, Chgo. Housing Authority Police, 1992. Mem. Acad. Criminal Justice Scis. (police sect. election com. 1992), Am. Soc. Criminology, Am. Sociol. Assn., Law and Soc. Assn., So. Criminal Justice Assn. Office: Univ of Ala Dept Criminal Justice 901 15th St S Birmingham AL 35205-3406

SLOAN, LARUE LOVE, English language and literature educator; b. Freer, Tex., Oct. 19, 1947; d. Homer Stewart and Naomi LaRue (Newman) Love; m. Gary Glenven Sloan, May 30, 1969; children: Joseph Benjamin, Laura Melissa, Leah Rebecca. BA, East Tex. State U., 1968, MA, 1970; PhD, Tex. Tech. U., 1973. Instr. Grambling (La.) State U., 1974-78; instr. La. Tech. U., Ruston, 1981-82, cons., 1983; instr. N.E. La. U., Monroe, 1984-91, asst. prof., 1991—; cons. Nat. Fedn. of the Blind, Ruston, 1982-84. Contbr. articles to profl. jours. Bd. dirs. Ruston Cmty. Theatre, 1985-91, pres., 1989-90. Mem. South Ctrl. MLA, Philol. Assn. La., North Ctrl. La. Arts Coun. (bd. dirs. 1989—), South Ctrl. Conf. Christianity and Lit., South Ctrl. Renaissance Conf. Office: NE La U 900 University Ave Monroe LA 71203-3636

SLOAN, MACEO KENNEDY, lawyer, investment executive; b. Phila., Oct. 18, 1949; s. Maceo Archibald and Charlotte (Kennedy) S.; m. Melva Iona Wilder, July 3, 1971; children: Maceo S., Malia K. BA, Morehouse Coll., 1971; MBA with honors, Ga. State U., 1973; JD with honors, N.C. Cen. U., 1979. CFA. Investment analyst N.C. Mut. Life Ins. Co., Durham, 1973-77, asst. to treas., 1977-78, asst. v.p., 1978-83, treas., 1983-85, v.p., treas., 1985-86; pres. NCM Devel. Group subs. N.C. Mut. Life Ins. Co., Durham, 1985-86; of counsel Moore & Van Allen, Durham, 1985-86; pres., CEO NCM Capital Mgmt. Group, Inc., Durham, 1986-91, chmn., pres., CEO, 1991—; chmn., pres., CEO Sloan Fin. Group, Inc., Durham, N.C., 1991—; adj. vis. prof. N.C. Ctrl. U., Durham, 1978-86, workshop rev. leader Study Seminar for Fin. Analysts, Windsor, Ont., Can., 1980—; bd. dirs. Mechanics & Farmers Bank, Durham, 1979—, chmn. trust com., 1979-93; networking leader Black Enterprise mag., 1987—; bd. trustees Coll. Retirement Equities Fund, 1991—, ERISA Adv. Coun. U.S. Dept. Labor, 1991-93; bd. dirs. News and Observer Pub. Co. Bd. dirs. United Way, Durham, 1980-87, Urban Ministries, Durham, 1983-88, Internat. Found. Edn. and Self Help, 1993—, N.C. Air Cargo Airport Authority, 1993—; bd. visitors N.C. Ctrl. U. Sch. Law, Durham, 1979-86, U. N.C., Chapel Hill, 1990—. Recipient Outstanding Svc. award Better Bus. Bur., 1980, Freedom Guard award Durham Jaycees, 1982, Outstanding Leadership award United Way Durham, 1984, Resolution in Appreciation Durham City Coun., 1983. Fellow Life Mgmt. Inst.; mem. ABA, Fin. Analysts Fedn., N.C. Soc. Fin. Analysts (v.p. 1977-78), N.C. State Bar Assn., Durham C. of C., Nat. Investment Mgrs. Assn. (founder, chmn.), Nat. Assn. Securities Profls., Treyburn Country Club (Durham), Univ. Club (Durham), The George Town (Washington). Democrat. Baptist. Home: 24000 S Lowell Rd Bahama NC 27503-9693 Office: Sloan Fin Group Inc 103 W Main St Fl 4 Durham NC 27701-3638

SLOAN, MARY JEAN, retired media specialist; b. Lakeland, Fla., Nov. 29, 1927; d. Marion Wilder and Elba (Jinks) Sloan. BS, Peabody Coll., Nashville, 1949; MLS, Atlanta U., 1978, S.L.S., 1980. Cert. libr. media specialist. Music dir. Pinecrest Sch., Tampa, Fla., 1949-50, Polk County Schs., Bartow, Fla., 1950-54; pvt. music tchr. Lakeland, 1954-58; tchr. Clayton County Schs., Jonesboro Ga., 1958-59; media specialist Eastualley Sch., Marietta, Ga., 1959-89, retired, 1989; coord. conf. Ga. Library Media Dept., Jekyll Island, 1982-83, sec., Atlanta, 1982-83, com. chmn. ethnic conf., Atlanta, 1978, pres., 1984-85, state pres., 1985-86; program chmn. Ga. Media Orgns. Conf, Jekyll Island, 1988. Contbr. to bibliographies. Recipient Walter Bell award Ga. Assn. Instructional Tech., 1988, Disting. Svc. award, 1991. Mem. ALA (del. 1984, 85, 90), NEA, Southeastern Library Assn., Am. Assn. Sch. Librarians, Soc. for Sch. Librarians, Internat., Ga. Assn. Educators (polit. action com. 1983), Beta Phi Mu, Phi Delta Kappa. Republican. Methodist. Home: 797 Yorkshire Rd NE Atlanta GA 30306-3264 Office: Eastvalley Elem Sch 2570 Lower Roswell Rd Marietta GA 30068-3635

SLOAN, NANCY MARIE, artist; b. Duncan, Okla., Oct. 10, 1946; d. Laymon Edison and Frances Mae (Jones) S. AA, U. S.C., 1979; BA, U. Okla., 1981, M in Human Rels., 1983. Inventory staff Stephens County Hist. Mus., Duncan; legal asst. Neimeyer's Law Firm, Oklahoma City, Legal Aid Western Okla., Oklahoma City; interviewer Okla. State Employment Sec., Norman; gift shop cashier Okla. U. Mus. of Art. With USN, 1975-79. Scholar Arts and Humanities Coun., Okla., 1992, 95. Mem. Federated Music Club (treas. 1994—), Duncan Art Guild (historian 1996—), Duncan Arts and Humanities (chairperson arts explosion 1996, co-chairperson fall fest gallery 1996—). Democrat. Roman Catholic. Home: PO Box 1962 Duncan OK 73534

SLOAN, REBA FAYE, dietitian, consultant; b. South Bend, Ind., Feb. 5, 1955; d. Kenneth and Ruby Faye (Long) Lewis; m. Gilbert Kevin Sloan, May 22, 1976. BS, Harding U., 1976; MPH, Loma Linda U., 1989; Cert. Tng. in Child/Adolescent Obesity, U. Calif., San Francisco. Registered dietitian; lic. dietitian and nutritionist; cert. advanced clin. tng. adolescent obesity. Dietetic intern Vanderbilt U. Med. Ctr., Nashville, 1978, rsch. dietitian, 1979-80; therapeutic dietitian Bapt. Hosp., Nashville, 1981-85; staff dietitian Nautilus Total Fitness Ctrs., Nashville, 1983-86; cons. dietitian Nashville Met. Govt., 1986-95, Bapt. Hosp. Ctr. for Health Promotion, Nashville, 1987-91, Parkwest Eating Disorder Clinic, Nashville, 1989-91; nutrition therapist, pvt. practice Nashville, Tenn., 1992—; adj. prof. Vanderbilt U., 1995; nutrition cons. The Nashville Striders, 1979-81; cons. nutritionist; mem. Vanderbilt U. Eating Disorder Com. Vol. Belmont Ch. Ministries, Nashville, 1981—; speaker Am. Heart Assn., Nashville, 1990—. Recipient cert. of appreciation Am. Heart Assn., 1990; Leaders fellow YMCA. Mem. Am. Dietetic Assn., Sports and Cardiovascular Nutritionists, Cons. Nutritionists, Am. Coll. Sports Medicine, Am. Running and Fitness Assn., Nashville Dist. Dietetic Assn. (contbr. diet manual 1984), Nat. Assn. for Chrisian Recovery, Alpha Chi. Home: 1817 Shackleford Rd Nashville TN 37215-3525 Office: 121 21st Ave N Ste 208 Nashville TN 37203-5213

SLOAN, TINA RYE, elementary school educator; b. Guin, Ala., Sept. 21, 1963; d. James Washington and Mary Lee (Box) Rye; m. Clayton Dawson Sloan, June 5, 1993. BS in Edn., U. Montevallo, 1985, Edn. Specialist, 1992; MA in Edn., U. North Ala., 1988. Tutor U. Montevallo, Ala., 1983-84; tchr. Lamar County Schs., Detroit, Ala., 1985-88; adult basic edn. instr. Lamar County Schs., Detroit, 1989-90, Decatur (Ala.) City Schs.; tchr. Sulligent (Ala.) Elem. Sch., 1988-93, Somerville Rd. Elem. Sch., Decatur, 1993—; adj. prof. Athens (Ala.) State Coll., 1995—. Named to Outstanding Young Women of Am. Mem. NEA, Ala. Edn. Assn., Decatur Edn. Assn., Phi Kappa Phi, Kappa Delta Pi (Katherine Vickery award), Omicron Delta Kappa, Alpha Delta Kappa (historian). Home: 891 Higdon Rd SW Hartselle AL 35640 Office: Somerville Road Elem Sch 891 Higdon Rd SW Hartselle AL 35640

SLOAND, ELAINE MARIE, hematologist; b. Buffalo, Feb. 14, 1953; d. Anthony and Muriel (Kieffer) S.; m. Robert Chiarello, June 21, 1979. BA, Canisius Coll., 1975; MD, U. Rochester, 1979. Intern Deaconess Hosp., Boston, 1979-80, resident in internal medicine, 1980-82, hematology fellow, 1982-84; assoc. physician Peter Bent Brigham Hosp., Boston, 1984-86; with dept. transfusion medicine NIH, Bethesda, 1986-88; asst. to dir. Nat. Heart, Lung and Blood Inst., Bethesda, 1988—. Home: 1600 N Oak St Apt 1820 Arlington VA 22209-2770

SLOANE, ARLENE L., rehabilitation nurse, specialist; b. Phila., Sept. 7, 1936; d. Sidney Ted and Adele (Kaizen) Loupus; m. Bernard L. Sloane, June 23, 1956; children: Marc, David, Karen, Cynthia. BSN cum laude, Am. U., 1976. Cert. ins. rehab. specialist. Cert. case mgr., supr. World Wide Rehab., Clinton, Md.; rehab. nurse, cons. Upjohn Health Program, Greenbelt, Md.; pres. MOKC Rehab. Resources, Reston, Va. Mem. NARPPS, Assn. Rehab. Nurse, Sigma Theta Tau.

SLOAT, ROBERT STUART, academic consultant; b. N.Y.C., Dec. 16, 1935; s. Bernard Howard and Pauline (Schwartz) S.; m. Beth Sharon Perlmutter, June 21, 1959; children: Alison Stacy, Erika Sydney, Vanessa Dawn. BA, Adelphi Coll., 1957; MS in Edn., Hofstra Coll., 1959; PhD, U. Tex., 1969. Cert. secondary, spl. edn. and gifted thr., adminstr. Asst. edn. svcs. dir. Mitchell AFB, Hempstead, N.Y., 1960-61; pub. sch. tchr. Lawrence High Sch., Cedarhurst, N.Y., 1961-63; assoc. dir. admissions Hofstra U., Hempstead, 1963-66; doctoral fellow U. Tex., Austin, 1966-69; assoc. prof. exceptional edn. Fla. Atlantic U., Boca Raton, 1969-76, acting head exceptional edn., 1976-77; dir. Sch. Spl. Edn., Rehab. U. No. Colo., Greeley, 1977-82, dir. Kephart Child Study Ctr., 1982-83, prof. emeritus human rehab. svcs., 1983—; pvt. sch. cons. Matlock Acad., West Palm Beach, Fla., 1983-87; assoc. prof. edn. Tex. Woman's U., Denton, 1987-93; dir. assessment svcs. Daytona Beach (Fla.) C.C., 1993; cons., ind. contractor Dallas, 1994-96; team leader Dept. Edn., Dallas, 1996—; cons. Amarillo (Tex.) Coll., 1990-91; manuscript reviewer Merrill Pub. Co., 1989-91; grant cons. U. North Fla., 1987; sex. discrimination cons. Va. Poly. Inst., 1987. Mem. editorial bd. Educating Able Learners, Gifted Students Inst., 1990-93; contbr. articles to profl. jours. Mem. Addison (Tex.) Edn. Steering Com., 1990-91. With USAR, 1954-59. Recipient Award of Excellence Mental Health Assn. of Palm Beach County, 1985. Mem. Dallas UN Assn. (bd. dirs., parliamentarian 1992-93, newsletter photography editor), Nat. Network of Learning Disabled Adults, Attention Deficit Hyperactive Assn. Tex. (profl. adv. bd.), Therapeutic Learning Ctrs. N.J. (profl. adv. bd.), UNIFEM.

SLOCUM, DONALD HILLMAN, product development executive; b. Flushing, N.Y., Jan. 6, 1930; s. John G. and Frances H. S.; m. June Manning, Sept. 22, 1952 (dec. 1976); children: Richard, Mark, Carol; m. Barbara M. Ruane, Nov. 1, 1986. BS, Davis and Elkins Coll., 1951; MS, U. Vt., 1956; PhD, Ohio State U., 1958; LLD, Fla. Tech. Inst., 1968; MBA, Rider Coll., 1971; ScD, Norton U., 1972; Dr. Profl. Studies, Pace U., 1974. Rsch. chem. Charles Pfizer, Inc., Bklyn., 1954; rsch. scientist Procter & Gamble, Cin., 1958-68; mgr. product devel. E.I. DuPont de Nemours & Co., Wilmington, Del., 1960-68; dir. new ventures N.L. Industries, N.Y.C., 1968-71; dir. fin. planning Hoffmann LaRoche, Nutley, N.J., 1971-74; v.p. Curtiss-Wright Corp., Woodridge, N.J., 1974-78; sr. v.p. Masonite-USG, Chgo., 1978-85; pres. Doner-Viking Corp., Madison, N.J., 1985-87, Woodtec, Inc. subs. Masco, Taylor, Mich., 1987-96, Versitec Industries, 1996—. Author: New Venture Methodology, 1974; contbr. articles to tech. and bus. publs.; patentee in field. Lt. U.S. Army, 1951-54, Korea, Col. Res., ret. Home and Office: Versitec Industries 61 Chimney Ridge Dr Morristown NJ 07960-4722 Office: SRA 3400 Bee Ridge Rd Sarasota FL 34239-7223

SLOCUM, GEORGE SIGMAN, energy company executive; b. East Orange, N.J., Sept. 9, 1940. B.A., Cornell U., 1962, M.B.A., 1967. Mgmt. trainee Richardson-Merrell, Inc., 1962; v.p. Citibank N.A., 1967-78; v.p. fin. Transco Energy Co., Houston, 1978-80, sr. v.p., 1980-81, exec. v.p., CFO, dir., 1981-84, pres., COO, dir., 1984-87, pres., CEO, dir., 1987-92. Bd. dirs. Houston Hospice, Soc. for Performing Arts, Houston; trustee Boy Scouts Am., Cornell U.; mem. alumni adv. coun. Cornell U. Grad. Sch. Mgmt. Served with U.S. Army, 1963-65. Mem. Am. Gas Assn., Nat. Petroleum Coun. Home: 10776 Bridlewood St Houston TX 77024-5413 Office: Cayuga Lake Farm 3533 R and 90 Aurora NY 13026

SLOCUM, R.C., university athletic coach. Asst. football coach Tex. A&M U. Aggies, 1972-80, 82-89, U. So. Calif., 1981; head football coach Tex. A&M U. Aggies, 1989—. Office: Texas A&M Univ Athletics Dept College Station TX 77843-1228

SLOMAN, MARVIN SHERK, lawyer; b. Fort Worth, Apr. 17, 1925; s. Richard Jack and Lucy Janette (Sherk) S.; m. Margaret Jane Dinwiddie, Apr. 11, 1953; children: Lucy Carter, Richard Dinwiddie. AB, U. Tex., 1948, LLB with honors, 1950. Bar: Tex. 1950, N.Y. 1951. Assoc., Sullivan & Cromwell, N.Y.C., 1950-56, Carrington, Coleman, Sloman & Blumenthal, Dallas, 1956-60, ptnr., 1960—. Fellow ABA, Tex. Bar Found.; mem. State Bar Tex. (chmn. sect. corp., banking and bus. law 1969-70, appelate practice and advocacy sect. 1992-93), Bar Assn. 5th Fed. Cir. (pres. 1984-85, bd. govs. 1984-87), Dallas Bar Assn. (chmn. com. on judiciary 1979), Assn. Bar City of N.Y., Am. Law Inst. Clubs: City (bd. dirs. 1970-87). Office: Carrington Coleman Sloman & Blumenthal 200 Crescent Ct Ste 1500 Dallas TX 75201-7839

SLONAKER, CELESTER LEE, principal; b. Richmond, Va., Sept. 13, 1943; s. Troy Kent and Betty Lee (Ferguson) S.; m. Carol Preston Laws, Aug. 1, 1970; children: Allen Terrell, Sarah Lindsey. B Music Edn., Va. Commonwealth U., Richmond, 1965, MA, 1972. Music tchr. Chesterfield County (Va.)-Elem. and High Sch., 1965-71; asst. prin. Chesterfield County-Crestwood, 1971-75, prin., 1975-81; prin. Chesterfield County-Greenfield, 1981-90, Chesterfield County-Woolridge, 1990-92; dir. elem. edn. Instrn. Div. Ctr., Richmond, 1992—; organist/choirmaster Meth. Ch., Richmond, 1962-69, St. Andrew's Episcopal Ch., Richmond, 1969—; cellist Richmond Community Orch., 1955-73. Group leader Community Orgns., Richmond, 1970-85; chmn. sch. bd. Episcopal Parochial Sch., Richmond, 1975-85; bd. mem. Richmond Ballet, 1983-89. Recipient Sch. Community award County Coun. PTA, Chesterfield County, 1983. Mem. ASCD, Nat. Assn. Elem. Prins., Va. Assn. Elem. Prins., Chesterfield Assn. Elem. Prins. (pres. 1985). Office: Instrn Div Ctr 2318 Mcrae Rd Richmond VA 23235-3028

SLONE, JIM, nurse; b. Ft. Meade, Md., Aug. 19, 1960; s. John Houston Sr. and Bobbie Rae (Brannon) Slone; m. Vicki Stokes, June 16, 1984; children: Bobbie Rebecca, Jessica Anne. BS in Forest Resources, U. Ga., 1984; ADN, Harford C.C., 1995. Nurse Harford Meml. Hosp., Havre de Grace, Md., 1994-95, Columbia Clearwater (Fla.) Cmty. Hosp., 1995—. Loetell nursing scholar, 1995, Barbara Brandon Nursing award, 1995, pres. award, HCC, 1995. Mem. Nat. Eagle Scout Assn., Phi Theta Kappa (pres. 1994-95). Republican. Baptist. Home: 1429 Pinebrook Dr Clearwater FL 34615

SLONIM, GILVEN M., educational foundation administrator, educator, former naval officer; b. St. Paul, Sept. 29, 1913; s. Samuel Jacob and Susie (Goodman) S.; m. Louise Reynolds, Mar. 5, 1946 (div. Oct. 1960); m. Frances Dim Resnick, May 17, 1961 (dec. Nov. 1994); children: Richard Gilven, David Reynolds, Patricia Slonim Gordon. BS, U.S. Naval Acad., 1936; PhD, Walden U., 1987. Commd. ensign USN, 1936, advanced through grades to capt., 1955, with spl. intelligence to commdr. third fleet, fifth fleet, 1942-45; interpreter for arrangements of Japanese surrender USS Missouri, Tokyo, 1945; ret. USN, 1965; dir. univ. rels. L.I. U., Greenvale, N.Y., 1965-66; spl. asst. to pres. Navy League of the U.S., Washington, 1968-70; exec. dir., v.p. Oceanic Ednl. Found., Washington, 1970-80, pres., 1980—; dir. instr. oceanic edn. program U. Va., Fairfax, 1971-73, introduced new multidiscipline of oceanic edn. in classroom, 1971; advisor Wilson Ctr. Smithsonian Instn., Washington, 1980, NEH U. Calif., San Diego, 1973; cons. Am. Enterprise Inst. for Pub. Policy, Washington, 1972-73, Fed. Maritime Commn., Washington, 1971-73; mem. adv. bd. TV documentary Blue Revolution, Annapolis, Md., 1982-90; speaker in field. Author: Toward a Philosophy of the Seas, 1973; contbg. author to various books; contbr. articles to profl. jours. Decorated Legion of Merit with oak leaf cluster, Bronze Star with oak leaf cluster. Mem. Naval Order of the U.S., Navy League of U.S. (John Paul Jones award), Mil. Order of World Wars, Smithsonian Instn. (assoc.), Nat. Geographic Soc., Naval Intelligence Profls., U.S. Naval Inst. Office: The Oceanic Ednl Found 3710 Whispering Ln Falls Church VA 22041-1122

SLOOP, GREGORY TODD, clergyman; b. Kannapolis, N.C., Jan. 25, 1962; s. Guy Lorraine and Ava Geraldine (York) S.; m. Lisa Halleen Pait, Sept. 20, 1986; children: Hannah Elizabeth, Meghan Rebekah, Matthew David. BS, Davidson Coll., 1984; MDiv, Ch. of God Sch. Theology, 1996. Ordained to ministry Chs. of God, 1987. Minister music Lane St. Ch. of God, Kannapolis, N.C., 1982-86, youth pastor, 1987-89; intern Eastway Ch. of God, Charlotte, N.C., 1986-87; youth pastor/asst. prin. White Oak Ch. of God/Christian Acad., Newport, N.C., 1989-90; youth pastor Yorkwood Ch. of God, Gastonia, N.C., 1990-91; pastor Yadkinville (N.C.) Ch. of God, 1991-94, East Shelby (N.C.) Ch. of God, 1994-96, South Concord (N.C.) Ch. of God, 1996—; mem. We. N.C. State Youth Bd., 1992-96. Editor Solid Rock Teen Newsletter, 1990-91. Mem. Nat. Youth Leader's Assn., Western N.C. Youth Leader's Assn. (adv. bd. 1990-91). Home and Office: 701 Union Cemetery Rd SW Concord NC 28027

SLOTKIN, ALAN R., English language educator; b. Bklyn., Nov. 7, 1943; s. Mark and Lee (Tuckman) S. AB, U. Miami, 1965; MA, U. S.C., 1969, PhD, 1970. Asst. prof. Tenn. Tech. U., Cookeville, 1970-76, assoc. prof., 1976-81, prof. English, 1982—. Editor Tenn. Linguistics Jour., 1982-92. Author: The Language of Stephen Crane's "Bowery Tales", 1993; contbr. articles to profl. jours. NDEA fellow, 1965, NSF fellow, 1967-70. Mem. S.E. Conf. Linguistics, South Atlantic Modern Language Assn., Linguistic Soc. Am., Am. Dialect Soc. (mem. com. usage 1983-91, new words com. 1988-91, editor Usage Newsletter 1996—), Tenn. Conf. Linguistics (sec., treas. 1982-93), Linguistic Assn. Can. and U.S., Amici Linguarum. Democrat. Avocations: stamp collecting, travel, photography. Home: 2108 Clearview Dr Cookeville TN 38506-5930 Office: Tenn Tech U English Dept Box 5053 Cookeville TN 38505

SLOVENSKY, DEBORAH WILBANKS, secondary education educator; b. Birmingham, Ala., Nov. 9, 1951; d. Euel Wilburn and Mildred Louise (Canoles) Wilbanks; m. Ron R. Slovensky, Aug. 3, 1973; children: Adam R., Andrew T. BS in English, U. Montevallo, 1985. Cert. tchr. secondary lang. arts. Enrichment tchr. Birmingham City Schs./Glen Iris, Birmingham, Ala., 1985-86, Shelby County Schs./Riverchase Middle Sch., Columbiana, Ala., 1986-89; lang. arts tchr. 7th grade Hoover (Ala.) City Schs. - Simmons Middle Sch., 1989-91, enrichment tchr., 1991-96, lang. arts 7th grade tchr., 1996—; governing bd. mem. Inservice and Rsch. Ctr., U. Montevallo, 1994—; presenter Ala. Insvc. Annual Conf., Huntsville, 1995; dist. curriculum facilitator for lang. arts Hoover City Schs., 1993-95. Faculty rep. to nominating com. PTA for Simmons Middle Sch., 1994; co-capt.-mini-parish St. Peter's Cath. Ch., Hoover, 1993-95; mem. St. Peter's Cath. Ch., Hoover. Recipient Outstanding Alumna in Secondary Edn. U. Montevallo, 1996; grantee Hoover Found., 1996. Mem. ASCD, Nat. Coun. of Tchrs. of English. Democrat. Roman Catholic. Home: 1813 Napier Dr Hoover AL 35226 Office: Hoover City Schs Simmons Middle Sch 1575 Patton Chapel Rd Hoover AL 35226-2257

SLOWEN, WARREN THOMAS, lawyer; b. New Haven, Conn., Mar. 7, 1943; s. Warren Thomas and Amanda Vivian (Remor) S. BA, U. Conn., 1965; JD, Mercer U., Macon, Ga., 1972. Bar: Ga. 1973, U.S. Dist. Ct. (middle and no. dist.) Ga. 1974. Assoc. McCurdy & Candler, Attys., Decatur, Ga., 1973; pvt. practice law Clayton, Ga., 1973—; technician Dept. Biophysics, Yale Univ., 1960-61; city atty. City of Tiger, Ga., 1987—; cons. in field; judge Rabun Superior Ct., Pro Hac Vice, 1990; arbitrator Mt. Jud. Cir., Ga., 1990. Lt. col. Aide de Camp Gov.'s Staff, Gov. of Ga., 1983. Spl. agt. U.S. Army Intelligence, 1966-68. Mem. ABA, Rabun County Bar Assn. (v.p. 1977), Mt. Jud. Cir. Bar Assn., Phi Alpha Delta. Democrat. Methodist. Home: Bridge Creek Rd Tiger GA 30576 Office: W Thomas Slowen PO Box 892 Clayton GA 30525-0892

SLOWIK, RICHARD ANDREW, air force officer; b. Detroit, Sept. 9, 1939; s. Louis Stanley and Mary Jean (Zaucha) S. BS, USAF Acad., 1963; BS in Bus. Adminstrn., No. Mich. U., 1967; LLB, LaSalle Extension U., 1969; MBA, Fla. Tech. U., 1972; MS in Adminstrn., Ga. Coll., 1979; MA, Georgetown U., 1983; postgrad. cert., Va. Polytech. Inst. and State U., 1986. Commd. 1st lt. U.S. Air Force, 1963, advanced through grades to lt. col.; pilot Craig AFB, Ala., 1963-64, Sawyer AFB, Mich., 1964-68; forward air contr. Pacific Air Forces, South Vietnam, 1968-69; pilot SAC, McCoy AFB, Fla., 1969-71; asst. prof. aerospace studies Va. Poly. Inst. and State U., Blacksburg, 1972-76; br. chief current ops. br. Robins AFB, Ga., 1976-80; asst. dep. chief ops. group Hdqrs. Air Force, Pentagon, Washington, 1980-82; Western Hemisphere and Pacific Area desk officer Nat. Mil. Command

Center, Pentagon, Washington, 1982-83; mil. rep. Ops. Ctr., Dept. State, Washington, 1983-85; ops. officer 97th Bombardment Wing, Blytheville AFB, Ark., 1985-87, chief base ops. and trg. div., 97th Combat Support Group, Blythville AFB, 1987-88, chief airfield mgmt. div. Eaker AFB, Ark., 1988-91, free-lance writer, 1991—. Group ops. officer CAP, Marquette, Mich., 1967-68, Orlando, Fla., 1970-72, sr. programs officer, Blacksburg, 1972-76, Warner Robins, Ga., 1976-80, wing plans and programs officer, Washington, 1980—. Decorated Defense Meritorious Service Medal, 10 Air medals, 3 Air Force Meritorious Service medals, 2 Commendation medals, Cross of Gallantry with Palm, Presdl. Legion of Merit, others; recipient Presdl. Legion of Merit, Presdl. Medal of Merit (3), Presdl. Achievement award (3). Mem. Acad. of Mgmt., Air Force Assn., Cato Inst., Heritage Found., Mil. Order World Wars, Am. Def. Preparedness Assn., Am. Security Council, Order of Daedalians. Roman Catholic. Home and Office: 1708 N Broadway St Blytheville AR 72315-1313

SLUNG, HILTON B., surgeon; b. Louisville, May 10, 1950. MD, U. Louisville, 1976. Diplomate Am. Bd. Surgery, Am. Bd. Colon and Rectal Surgery. Intern Georgetown U. Hosp., Washington, 1976-77, resident in gen. surgery, 1977-79; resident in gen. surgery Marshall U. Hosp., Huntington, 1980-82; fellow in colon and rectal surgery Grant Hosp., Columbus, Ohio, 1983-84; mem. staff Jewish Hosp., Louisville, 1984—, Suburban Hosp., 1984—; mem. courtesy staff Bapt. East Hosp., 1984—, Audubon Hosp., 1984—; clin. instr. surgery U. Louisville. Fellow ACS; mem. Am. Soc. Colon and Rectal Surgery, So. Med. Assn., Jefferson County Med. Soc. Office: Doctors Office Bldg 250 E Liberty St Ste 610 Louisville KY 40202-1536

SLYE, CARROLL JAMES, instructional supervisor; b. Harrisonburg, Va., July 23, 1953; s. Junior Lee and Phyllis Ann (Dovel) S.; 1 child, Kelsey Alexandra. BS, James Madison U., 1979, MEd, 1991. Collegiate profl. lic. Classroom tchr., coach Rockingham County Schs., Harrisonburg, Va., 1980-91; asst. prin. H.S. Rockingham County Schs., Harrisonburg, 1991-95, gen. supr., 1995—; mem. com. on tchr. edn. Ea. Mennonite U., Harrisonburg, 1995—. Named Educator of the Yr., Elkton (Va.) Lions Club, 1990, Elkton (Va.) Combined PTA, 1991. Mem. ASCD, Va. H.S. Coaches Assn., Phi Kappa Delta. Home: Rt 2 Box 739 McGaheysville VA 22840 Office: Rockingham County Schs 304 County Office Bldg Harrisonburg VA 22801

SMAIL, LESLIE ANNE, librarian; b. Pitts., July 25, 1958; d. Laurence Mitchell and Nancy (Fried) S. BA, Christopher Newport Coll., 1980; MSLS, Cath. U., 1982. Libr. intern Tng. and Doctrine Command, Ft. Monroe, Va., 1982-84; libr. Ft. Story (Va.) Libr., 1985—. Mem. Diamond Springs Civic League, Virginia Beach, Va., 1989—. Recipient Exceptional Performance award U.S. Army, Ft. Eustis, Va., 1985-96, Comdr.'s award for civilian svc., 1995; Outstanding Program Mgr. TRADOC, Ft. Monroe, 1988, 89. Mem. Va. Libr. Assn., Sigma Tau Delta. Office: Fort Story Libr Bldg T-530 Fort Story VA 23459-5067

SMAILI, AHMAD, mechanical engineering educator; b. Gaza, Lebanon, Nov. 4, 1955; came to U.S., 1976; s. Abdulkarim and Fatme (Mourad) S.; m. Maha Hazime, Aug. 10, 1989; children: Layla, Ali. BS, Tenn. Technol. U., 1979, MS, 1981, PhD, 1986. Asst. prof. Miss. State U., Starkville, 1987-91; asst. prof. Tenn. Technol. U., Cookeville, 1991-95, assoc. prof., 1995—; cons. Waste Policy Inst., Washington, 1992, U. Tenn. Space Inst., Tullahoma, 1993-94, Marine Gears, Greenville, Miss., 1990-91, Geka Thermal Sys., Atlanta, 1994—. Contbr. articles to profl. jours. Co-chmn. Cookeville Refugee Support Com., 1993—. Named Outstanding Faculty Mem., Student Assn. Miss. State U., 1989; recipient Kinslow Rsch. award Tenn. Technol. U., 1996. Mem. ASME (faculty advisor), Am. Soc. Engring. Edn., Pi Tau Sigma (Purple Shaft Trophy 1989, 90), N.Y. Acad. Scis., Tau Beta Pi. Muslim. Home: 799 W Oak Dr Apt D-1 Cookeville TN 38501 Office: Tenn Technol U W 10th St Box 5014 Cookeville TN 38505

SMAISTRLA, JEAN ANN, family therapist; b. South Gate, Calif., Oct. 12, 1936; d. Benjamin J. and Janet (Pollock) Craig; m. Charles J. Smaistrla, July 12, 1958; children: Amy Jean, Ben, John. BBA in Mktg., Lamar U., 1958; elec. edn. cert. Tex. Wesleyan Coll., 1963; MEd in Counseling, Tex. Christian U., 1975. Lic. profl. counselor. Tchr. Houston Ind. Schs., 1958-61, Arlington Ind. Schs., Tex., 1961-72; counselor, therapist Arlington Counseling and Cons. Ctr., 1983-85; family therapist Willow Creek Adolescent Ctr., Arlington, 1985-86, dir. edn., 1986-90; therapist, Bob Caprenter PhD and Assoc., 1987-89; pvt. practice Triage Therapist Kaiser Permanente, Ft. Worth, 1989—; owner, founder, chmn. bd. Adolescent Svcs. Arlington, 1981—, founder, owner Mindtime, 1988-90; triage counselor Kaiser Permanente, Ft. Worth, 1991—; cons. Charles J. Smaistrla, D.D.S., Arlington, 1978-85. Vice chmn. bd. Arlington Cmty. Hosp., 1981-85, Willow Creek Adolescent Ctr., 1984-90. Life mem. PTA; bd. dirs. Arlington Art Assn., 1981-85, S. Arlington Med. Ctr., 1987, Ctr. for Well-Being, 1985; chmn. clin. svcs. Parenting Ctr. for Tarrant County, Ft. Worth, 1992—, v.p., 1994-95, pres.-elect, 1994-96, pres. bd., 1996—. Mem. Am. Assn. Marriage and Family Therapy (assoc.), Tarrant County Assn. Marriage and Family Therapy, North Central Tex. Assn. Counseling and Devel., Am. Assn. Counseling and Devel., Alpha Delta Pi. Republican. Roman Catholic. Clubs: Jr. League Arlington, Arlington Women's. Avocations: Sailing; sewing; doll collecting.

SMALBEIN, DOROTHY ANN, guidance counselor; b. Rochester, N.Y.; d. Karl Taylor and Virginia (Woodcock) Howard; m. June 27, 1954 (div.); children: William Paul, John Allen. Student, St. Lawrence U., Canton, N.Y., 1952-54; BA, U. Cen. Fla., 1971, MEd in Counseling, 1978. Guidance counselor Pine Trail Elem. Sch., Volusia County Sch. Bd., Fla., 1978—. Recipient Outstanding Svc. award, Volusia County Counselors, 1979. Mem. AACD, Fla. Sch. Counselors Assn., Fla. Assn. for Counseling and Devel. (conv. presenter 1981-88), Volusia Assn. for Counseling and Devel. (sunshine chmn. 1980-81, treas. 1988-90), Volusia County Elementary Counselors Assn. (chmn. 1981-82), Jr. League, Pi Beta Phi. Methodist. Office: Pine Trail Elem Sch 300 Airport Rd Ormond Beach FL 32174-2917

SMALL, LINDA JUANITA BOND, nursing administrator; b. Sunbury, N.C., Feb. 28, 1951; d. James Tommie and Mildred Vernice (Howell) Bond; m. Julius Alexander Small, Dec. 30, 1972; children: Julius Alexander II, Jamein Bond. BSN, N.C. Cen. U., Durham, 1973, MA, 1989. Nurse, charge nurse med.-surg. Lincoln Hosp., Durham; charge nurse ob-gyn. Durham County Gen. Hosp., Durham, nursing adminstr.; nurse mgr.; clin. dir. nursing Durham County Gen. Hosp., Durham, asst. to v.p. nursing; asst. v.p. nursing Durham Regional Hosp., Durham County Hosp. Corp., interim v.p. nursing, sr. dir. nursing ops.; adminstrv. dir. patient svcs. Mem. ANA, Am. Orgn. Nurse Execs., N.C. Nurses Assn., Am. Coll. Healthcare Execs., N.C. Orgn. Nurse Execs., Chi Eta Phi.

SMALL, MELVIN D., physician, educator; b. Somerville, Mass., May 22, 1925; s. Sidney J. and Ida (Gelbsman) S.; m. Judith Nogee, Dec. 23, 1962; children: Michael Dorian, Michele. AB, U. Wis., 1953; MD, Duke U., 1959; studied under Dr. Gregory Pincus, Worcester Found. Exptl. Biol. and Medicine, 1950-53; studied under Prof. Brian Abel-Smith, London Sch. Econs, 1986-90. Lic. physician, Fla., Md., D.C., Va. Intern Georgetown U. Med. Ctr., Washington, 1959-60, resident, 1960-61; chief gastrointestinal rsch. Georgetown U. Med. Ctr., 1961-64, instr. medicine, 1961-66, asst. prof. medicine, 1966-67, asst. clin. prof. medicine, 1967-81, 93—; chief gastroenterology sect. Georgetown divsn. D.C. Gen. Hosp., 1964-68; cons. Children's Hosp., Washington, 1962-66; active staff Fairfax (Va.) Hosp., 1961-73, Commonwealth Drs. Hosp., Fairfax, 1969-74, Arlington (Va.) Hosp., 1961-85, Circle Terr. Hosp., Alexandria, 1965-85, Mt. Vernon Hosp., Alexandria, 1976-85; hon. staff mem. Alexandria Hosp., 1985-89, 92—; attending physician D.C. Gen. Hosp., 1961-68, Georgetown U. Hosp., 1961-81, 93—, Mt. Sinai Hosp., Miami Beach, Fla., 1992—; chief animal experimentation Cancer rsch. under Dr. Sidney Farber Children's Med. Ctr., Boston, 1948-50; rsch. asst. Boston U. Sch. Medicine, 1956-57; chmn. dept. medicine Alexandria Hosp., 1964-85; founder, chmn., No. Va. Consortium for Continuing Med. Edn., 1974-86, chmn. emeritus, 1986; lectr. in field. Author publs. in field. Trustee Jefferson Meml. Hosp., 1965-74, mem. founding group, 1965, chmn. pharmacy com., 1965-76, co-chmn. tissue com., 1965-74; nominated candidate for Palm Beach (Fla.) Town Coun., 1995-96. Rsch. fellow under Norman Zamcheck Mallory Inst. Pathology, Boston, 1953-59, Gastroenterology rsch. under Franz Ingelfinger, Evans Meml. Hosp., Boston, AEC, 1951-53. Mem. AMA, Am. Coll. Gastroenterology, ACP, Am. Gastroent. Assn., Am. Inst. Nutrition, Am. Physiol. Soc., Am. Soc. Gastrointestinal Endoscopy, D.C. Med. Soc., Med. Soc. Va. (chmn. commn. on continuing med. edn. 1978-81), Alexandria Med. Soc. (v.p. 1979-80), Royal Soc. Medicine, Fla. Med. Soc., Palm Beach County Med. Soc. Home: 47 Saint George Pl Palm Beach Gardens FL 33418

SMALL, NATALIE SETTIMELLI, pediatric mental health counselor; b. Quincy, Mass., June 2, 1933; d. Joseph Peter and Edmea Natalie (Bagnaschi) Settimelli; m. Parker Adams Small, Jr., Aug. 26, 1956; children: Parker Adams III, Peter McMichael, Carla Edmea. BA, Tufts U., 1955; MA, EdS, U. Fla., 1976; PhD, 1987. Cert. child life specialist. Pediatric counselor U. Fla. Coll. Medicine, Gainesville, 1976-80; pediatric counselor Shands Hosp.-U. Fla., Gainesville, 1980-87, supr. child life dept. patient and family resources, 1987—; adminstrv. liaison for self-dir. work teams, mem. faculty Ctr. for Coop. Learning for Health and Sci. Edn., Gainesville, 1988—, assoc. dir., 1996; cons. and lectr. in field. Author: Parents Know Best, 1991; co-author team packs series for teaching at risk adolescent health edn. and coop. learning. Bd. dirs. Ronald McDonald House, Gainesville, 1980—, mem. exec. com., 1991—; bd. dirs. Gainesville Assn. Creative Arts, 1994—; mem. health profl. adv. com. March of Dimes, Gainesville, 1986—, HIV prevention planning partnership, 1995. Boston Stewart Club scholar, Florence, Italy, 1955; grantee Jessie Ball Du Pont Fund, 1978, Children's Miracle Network, 1990, 92, 93, 94, 95; recipient Caring and Sharing award Ronald McDonald House, 1995. Mem. ACA, Nat. Bd. Cert. Counselors, Am. Assn. Mental Health Counselors, Assn. for the Care of Children's Health, Fla. Assn. Child Life Profls., Child Life Coun. Roman Catholic. Home: 3454 NW 12th Ave Gainesville FL 32605-4811 Office: Shands Hosp Patient and Family Resources PO Box 100306 Gainesville FL 32610

SMALL, REBECCA ELAINE, accountant; b. Meridian, Tex., Apr. 5, 1946; d. James Milford and Rosa Lee Elaine (Berry) Allen; m. Jay Austin Small, Sept. 16, 1964 (div.); children: Lashawn Renee, Jay Austin Jr.; m. Jerry Leon Cooper, Dec. 10, 1983 (div. Sept. 1985). Student Okla. Sch. Bus. and Banking, 1972; BS in Acctg. magna cum laude, Cen. State U., Edmond, Okla., 1977, MA in Exptl. Psychology summa cum laude, 1989; postgrad., U. Okla., 1991—. Staff acct. Robert A. Mosley, CPA, Moore, Okla., 1972-74, Robert Stewart, CPA, Edmond, 1974-75, Lowder & Co., Oklahoma City, 1975-81; pvt. practice acctg., Oklahoma City, 1981—. Fellow Nat. Inst. Mental Health, NIH; recipient Rsch. award Dept. Psychology Cent. State U., 1988. Mem. AICPA, Okla. Woman's Bus. Orgn. (chmn. 1982), Okla. Soc. CPAs, Am. Woman's Soc. CPAs, Nat. Assn. Accts. (hon.), Soc. of Neurosci., Alpha Lambda Delta, Alpha Chi, Psi Chi. Democrat. Avocations: writing poetry, horticulture, bicycling.

SMALL, ROBERT COLEMAN, JR., English language educator; b. Washington, Dec. 2, 1936; s. Robert Coleman and Edna Eleanor (McCrea) S. BA, U. Va., 1958, MA, 1960, EdD, 1970. Tchr. English Waynesboro (Va.) Pub. Schs., 1960-61, Charlottesville (Va.) Pub. Schs., 1961-68; instr. English U. Va., Charlottesville, 1968-70; asst. prof. English edn. Va. Tech., Blacksburg, 1970-74; assoc. prof. Va. Poly. Inst. and State U., Blacksburg, 1974-80, prof., 1980-90, assoc. dean, 1975-84; dean Coll. Edn. Radford (Va.) U.; chmn. Conf. on English Edn., Urbana, Ill., 1988-90, Assembly on Lit. for Adolescents, Urbana, 1982-83. Author: A Casebook for Teaching English, 1988; editor: Literature for Adolescents, 1973, Va. English Bull., 1987-90, Books for You, 1982, ALAN Rev., 1990—, Guidelines for the Preparation of Teachers of the English Language Arts, 1996; contbr. articles to profl. jours. and chpts. to books. Recipient Alan award for disting. contbns. to field of young adult lit., 1995. Mem. Nat. Coun. Tchrs. English (exec. com. 1988-90, chair standing com. on tchr. preparation and cert. 1993-96), Internat. Reading Assn. (chmn. spl. interest group on adolescent lit. 1992-94, joint task force with Nat. Coun. Tchrs. of English on intellectual freedom 1991-93), Phi Delta Kappa. Office: Radford U Office Of Dean Coll Ed Radford VA 24142

SMALL, WILFRED THOMAS, surgeon, educator; b. Boston, June 13, 1920; s. Fred Wentworth and Isabelle (Scott) S.; BS, Bowdoin Coll., 1943; MD, Tufts U., 1946; m. Muriel Yoe Gratton, Sept. 25, 1948; children: Wilfred Thomas, Richard Gratton, James Stewart, John Wentworth. Diplomate Am. Bd. Surgery. Intern surg. svc. The Boston Children's Hosp., 1946-47, then research fellow; assoc. in surgery Peter Bent Brigham Hosp., Harvard U., 1949-50; resident, chief resident in surgery New Eng. Med. Ctr., Tufts U., 1950-53; practice medicine specializing in surgery, Worcester, Mass., 1953-88; assoc. prof. surgery U. Mass., from 1973, now prof. surgery; mem. staff Meml. Hosp., 1953-88, chief div. surgery, 1973-81; instr. Harvard U., 1949-50, Tufts U., 1952-60. Active Worcester Art Mus., Worcester County Music Assn.; sec. bd. dirs. Indian River UN Assn. Served to lt. (j.g.) USN, 1947-49. Fellow ACS (pres. Mass. chpt. 1979); mem. AMA, New Eng. Surg. Soc., New Eng. Cancer Soc., Soc. Surgery Alimentary Tract, Mass., Pan Am. Med. Socs., Am. Trauma Soc., Indian River Hosp. Assn. (bd. dirs.), Vis. Nurses Assn. (bd. dirs.), Worcester Econs. Club (past pres.), Worcester Council on Fgn. Rels., Tatnuck Country Club, Sakonnet Golf Club, Riomar Golf Club (Vero Beach, Fla.). Episcopalian. Contbr. articles to profl. jours. Home: 16 Warrens Point Rd Little Compton RI 02837-1433

SMALLEY, ARTHUR LOUIS, JR., engineering and construction company executive; b. Houston, Jan. 25, 1921; s. Arthur L. and Ebby (Curry) S.; m. Ruth Evelyn Britton, Mar. 18, 1946; children: Arthur Louis III, Tom Edward. BSChemE, U. Tex., Austin, 1942. Registered profl. engr., Tex. Dir. engring. Celanese Chem. Co., Houston, 1964-72; mktg. exec. Fish Engring. Co., Houston, 1972-74; pres. Matthew Hall & Co., Inc., Houston, 1974-87; cons. Davy McKee Corp., Houston, 1987-95; exec. v.p. Offshore Gas Devels. Ltd., San Marino, Calif., 1995—; dir. Walter Internat., 1991. Life mem. Houston Livestock and Rodeo; mem. Engring. Found. Adv. Coun. U. Tex. Recipient Silver Beaver award Boy Scouts Am., 1963; named Disting. Engring. Grad., U. Tex., 1987. Mem. Am. Inst. Chem. Engrs., Am. Petroleum Inst., Pres. Assn., Petroleum Club (Houston), Chemists Club of N.Y., Oriental Club (London), Houston Club, Traveler's Century Club, Rotary. Republican. Episcopalian. Mem. internat. adv. bd. Ency. Chem. Processing and Design. Home: 438 Hunterwood Dr Houston TX 77024-6936 Office: 7887 Katy Freeway Houston TX 77024

SMALLMAN, JOSEPH DEMPSTER, financial consultant, qualified plans coordinator; b. Knoxville, Tenn., Dec. 2, 1955; s. Joseph Monroe and Ann Gordon (Dempster) S.; m. Merry Joyce Daffer, Dec. 4, 1975 (div. May 1984); children: Amber Kristen, Morgan Lee. BSBA, U. Tenn., 1987; MPhil in Fin. Economics, London Sch. Economics, 1992. Sales assoc. Century 21 AID Realty, Aurora, Colo., 1978-82; pres. Mortgage Brokers Inc., Knoxville, 1982-84; exec. mgr. Australia & New Zealand Banking Group, London, 1990-91; mng. dir. Morgan Brown Ayres & Co. Inc., Knoxville, 1991; fin. cons. Smith Barney, Knoxville, Tenn., 1991—; cons. in field, London, 1987-89, Salomon Bros., London, 1987, Household Fin. Corp., London, 1987; lectr. Cambridge (Eng.) U., 1989. Author: Securitisation, 1990; author working papers. Recipient Postgrad. Studentship, London Sch. Econs., 1988. Mem. Bd. of Realtors, Golden Key Club, Phi Kappa Phi, Beta Gamma Sigma (v.p. U. Tenn. Knoxville 1986). Republican. Episcopalian. Office: Shearson Barney Ste P-190 1111 N Shore Dr Knoxville TN 37919

SMART, EDITH MERRILL, civic worker; b. N.Y.C., Sept. 10, 1929; d. Edwin Katte and Helen Phelps (Stokes) Merrill; student Smith Coll., 1947-49, Barnard Coll., 1949-50; m. S. Bruce Smart, Jr., Sept. 10, 1949; children—Edith Minturn Smart Moore, William Candler, Charlotte Merrill Smart Rogan, Priscilla Smart Schwarzenbach. Tchr. elem. schs., Gibson Island, Md., 1959-60; guide, instr. Mill River Wetlands Com., Fairfield, Conn., 1967-85; treas. Near and Far Aid Assn., Fairfield, 1970-75, v.p., 1975-77, pres., 1977-79; pres. Nature Ctr. of Environ. Activities, Westport, Conn., chmn., 1981-85; trustee Fairfield Univ., 1987-93; leader No. Cook County council Girl Scouts U.S.A., Kenilworth, Ill., 1962-64; chmn. Southport-Westport Antiques Show, 1974-76; trustee Conn. chpt. Nature Conservancy, 1981-91, Va. chpt., 1992—; guide Nat. Acquarium, 1985-90; dir. Piedmont Child Devel. Ctr., 1994—; vestryman St. Timothy's Ch., Fairfield, 1976-79. Republican. Episcopalian. Clubs: Sasqua Garden (Fairfield), Upperville Garden, Middleburg Tennis, MFH The Fairfax Hunt. Home: 20561 Trappe Rd Upperville VA 20184-9708

SMEAL, PAUL LESTER, retired horticulture educator; b. Clearfield, Pa., June 11, 1932; s. Walter Vernon and Agatha (Cowder) S.; m. Gladys Matilda Smeal, July 17, 1954; children: Lester Alan, Gwen Hope, Tracy Gay. BS, Pa. State U., 1954; MS, U. Md., 1958, PhD, 1961. Asst. prof. horticulture Va. Poly. Inst. and State U., Blacksburg, 1960-61, assoc. prof., 1961-67, prof., 1967-92, prof. emeritus, 1993—; pres. faculty senate Va. Poly. Inst. and State U., 1984-86. Advisor Alpha Zeta, 1984-86. Recipient Quill and Trowel Comm. award Garden Writers Assn. Am., 1986, 87, Disting. Svc. award Nat. Assn. Country Agrl. Agts., 1987, L.C. Chadwick Teaching award Am. Assn. Nurserymen, 1988, Nursery Ext. award Am. Assn. Nurserymen, 1990. Fellow Am. Soc. Hort. Sci. (mem. pub. affairs com. 1979-82, chmn. ad hoc com 1984-86, pres. so. region 1978-79, sec.-treas. 1989—, others, Carl S. Bittner Extension award 1984, Henry M. Covington Extension award 1991); mem. Internat. Plant Propagator's Soc. (chmn. rsch. com. ea. region 1987-90, bd. dirs. 1991, 2d v.p. 1991, v.p. 1992, pres. 1993), Va. Nurserymen's Assn. (hon.). Republican. Lutheran. Home: 1107 Kentwood Dr Blacksburg VA 24060-5656

SMELTZ, EDWARD J., engineer; b. Willard, Ohio, Nov. 26, 1952; s. Harold Munroe and Marvel Arneta (Swander) S.; m. Mary Ruth Huffman, Oct. 15, 1977; children: Keith, Jeremy, Kendra. BA in Physics, Otterbein Coll., 1975. Assembly line worker Midwest Inds., Willard, Ohio, 1972-76; telephone maintenance CXS Corp., Willard, Ohio, 1976-82; technician Motorola, Ft. Worth, 1982-84, board test engr., 1984-87, system adminstr., 1987-90, 94—, lead engr. Fastco lab., 1990-94, system designer, 1984—. Active Cmty. Cleanup, Recycling, Ft. Worth, 1992-94, Watauga, Tex., 1986-92,. Mem. IEEE, Nat. Model Railroading Assn.

SMELTZER, DEBRA JEAN, botanist; b. Camden, Ark., Oct. 13, 1953; d. William Dewey and Frankie Jean (Braswell) S.; m. James Richard Ziesler, Sept. 1, 1984. Cert. in interior design, Bauder Fashion Coll., Arlington, Tex., 1973; BA in Botany, U. Tex., 1985. Biol. rsch. asst. U.S. Dept. Interior, Everglades Nat. Park, Fla., 1980; biologist, surveyor Great Lakes Dredge and Dock, Miami Beach, Fla., 1981-82, 1984; biologist, surveyor, drafter Great Lakes Dredge and Dock, Port Everglades, Fla., 1984; biologist, lab. tech. J.B. Reark and Assocs., Miami, 1982-84; fisheries biologist Kathryn Chandler and Assocs., Alexandria, Va., 1981-84; pres. Greensleeves, Inc., Miami and San Juan, P.R., 1985—, San Juan, P.R., 1991-95; v.p. G.D.S., Inc., Miami, 1995—; bd. govs. Nat. Coun. for Interior Hort. Cert., Columbus, Ohio, 1989-92; licensee Interior Landscape Internat. Corp., Dade, Monroe, Caribbean, 1990-92. Active Fairchild Tropical Gardens, Miami, Ch. of the Little Flower. Recipient Best Project award Interiorscape Mag., 1989, State Award of Excellence Fla. Nurserymen and Growers Assn., 1989. Mem. Associated Landscape Contractors Am. (award of Distinction 1989, 91, 92 [2], Grand award 1990), South Fla. Interior Landscape Assn. (ednl. com. 1987-89, bd. dirs. 1986-87, author newsletter articles 1986-89, founder 1986), South Fla. Hort. Soc., Inc., South Fla. Tex. Execs., Coral Gables C. of C. (trustee coun.). Democrat.

SMETHERAM, HERBERT EDWIN, government official; b. Seattle, Sept. 9, 1934; s. Francis Edwin and Grace Elizabeth (Warner) S.; m. Beverly Joan Heckert, Sept. 7, 1963; children: Alice, Helen, Charles. BA, U. Wash., 1956; diploma, Naval Intelligence Sch., 1962; MA, U. Md., 1971; diploma in Swedish, U.S. Fgn. Svc. Inst., 1978; MBA, Rollins Coll., 1991. Ensign USN, 1956, advanced through grades to capt., 1976; comdr. USS Lind (DD-703), 1971-73; attache to Sweden USN, Stockholm, 1978-81; comdr. Naval Adminstrn. Command, Orlando, Fla., 1981-84; ret. USN, 1984; strategic planner electronics, info. and missiles group Martin Marietta Corp., Orlando, 1985-93; exec. dir. re-use com. Naval Tng. Ctr., Orlando, 1993—, mem. retention com., 1991-93. Mem. ARC Ctrl. Fla.; mem. steering com. U.S. Congressman McCollum for Re-election; mem. U.S. Senator Hawkins Naval Acad. Nominating Com., Orlando, 1982-86, Fla. Gov.'s Def. Reinvestment Task Force, 1992-93; mem. Ctrl. Fla. coun. USO, Orlando, 1981-93, pres., 1991-93. Decorated Royal Order of North Star (Sweden). Mem. AIAA, SAR, Electronics Industry Assn. (requirements com. 1985-93), Nat. Assn. Installation Developers (southeast regional dir. 1996—, treas. 1996—), Ret. Officers Assn., Navy League, Fla. Tennis Assn., Army Navy Country Club, Orlando Tennis Ctr., Royal Tennis Club Stockholm, Delta Kappa Epsilon. Republican. Episcopalian. Home: 3985 Lake Mira Dr Orlando FL 32817-1643

SMIALOWICZ, RALPH JOSEPH, immunotoxicologist; b. Montclair, N.J., Apr. 20, 1946; s. Sylvester Ralph and Helen Theresa S.; m. Susan Ray, Oct. 27, 1973; 1 child, Amy Bargess Smialowicz. BA in Biology, Seton Hall U., 1968; MS in Biology, St. John's U., 1970; PhD in Bacteriology and Immunology, U. N.C., 1974. Grad. teaching asst. Dept. Biology St. John's U., Jamaica, N.Y., 1968-70; NIH predoctoral trainee Dept. Bacteriology and Immunology U. N.C., Chapel Hill, 1970-74; rsch. microbiologist U.S. EPA, Research Triangle Park, N.C., 1974-80; chief immunobiology sect. cellular biophysics br. EBD, HERL, U.S. EPA, Research Triangle Park, 1980-83; chief immunology sect. perinatal toxicology br. DCTD, HERL, U.S. EPA, Research Triangle Park, 1983-88; immunotoxicology br. ETD, HERL, U.S. EPA, Research Triangle Park, 1989—; adj. assoc. prof. Toxicology U. N.C., 1990—. Mem. editl. bd. Bioelectromagnetics, 1981-85, Jour. Toxicology and Environ. Health, 1986—, Toxicology (immunotoxicology sect.), 1993; ad hoc reviewer several sci. jours.; editor book; author book chpts., reports; contbr. articles to profl. jours. Mem. AAAS, Am. Soc. for Microbiology, Soc. of Toxicology, Am. Assn. of Immunologists. Office: US EPA MD-92 Durham NC 27711

SMIDDY, WILLIAM EARL, ophthalmologist; b. Boston, Dec. 4, 1957; s. Earl Raymond Jr. and Helen Maye (Putkisto) S.; m. Julie Therese Fradel, Dec. 27, 1978; children: Robert, Matthew, Rebecca, Susan, Andrew, Samuel, Clara. BS, Johns Hopkins U., 1980, MD, 1983. Diplomate Am. Bd. Ophthalmology. Intern Mercy Hosp., Balt., 1983-84; resident Johns Hopkins U., Balt., 1984-87, fellow, 1987, asst., 1987-88, instr., 1988-89; assoc. prof. ophthalmology U. Miami, Fla., 1989—. Author 1 book, 8 book chpts. and 110 articles. Served to capt. M.C., U.S. Army, 1984-92. Home: 9840 SW 60th Ct Miami FL 33156-1908 Office: Bascom Palmer/U Miami PO Box 016880 Miami FL 33101-6880

SMILES, RONALD, management educator; b. Sunderland, Eng., June 15, 1933; s. Andrew and Margaret (Turns) S.; m. Evelyn Lorraine Webster, Apr. 12, 1959 (div. June 1981); children: Tracy Lynn, Scott Webster, Wendy Louise; m. Linda Janet Miller, June 23, 1990. Assoc. in Bus. Adminstrn., U. Pa., 1968; BSBA, Phila. Coll. Textiles & Sci., 1969; PhD, Calif. Western U., 1977; MA, U. Tex., Arlington, 1985, PhD, 1987. V.p. Liquid Dynamics Corp., Southampton, Pa., 1968-71; pres., gen. mgr. Internat. Election Systems Corp., Burlington, N.J., 1971-76; plant mgr. Rack Engring. Co., Connellsville, Pa., 1977-80; v.p. Ft. Worth (Tex.) Houdaille, 1980-85; chmn. grad. sch. bus. Dallas Bapt. U., 1987-92, prof., 1987—, assoc. dean Coll. Bus., 1996—. Author: Impact on Legislation of Competition in the Voting Machine Industry, 1978, A Study of Japanese Targeting Practices and U.S. Machine Tool Industry Responses, 1985, Occupational Accident Statistics: An Evaluation of Injury and Illness Incidence Rates, 1987. Mem. Burlington County (N.J.) Selective Svc. Bd., 1974-76. Served with Royal Arty., 1951-53. Mem. Greater Connellsville C. of C. (v.p. 1979-80), Night Watch Honor Soc., Sigma Kappa Phi, Alpha Delta Epsilon (award 1968). Home: 2818 Timber Hill Dr Grapevine TX 76051-6432 Office: Dallas Bapt Univ Off Dean Coll Bus Dallas TX 75211

SMILEY, JAMES DONALD, rheumatology educator; b. Lubbock, Tex., Dec. 6, 1930; s. James Neil and Imogene (Perrin) S.; m. Helen Olivia Hood, Jan. 19, 1957; children: Barbara Ellen, Lynn Estelle, James Neil II, Cameron Perrin, David Christian. BS, Tex. Tech. U., 1948-52; MD, Johns Hopkins U., 1956. Diplomate Am. Bd. Internal Medicine, Am. Bd. Rheumatology. Intern then resident Columbia Prebyn. Hosp., N.Y.C., 1956-58; rsch. assoc. NIH, Bethesda, Md., 1958-60; from instr. to full prof. internal medicine U. Tex. Southwestern Med. Ctr. Dallas, 1960—; chief rheumatology Presbyn. Hosp., Dallas, 1977—; adv. com. arthritis and analgesic drugs U.S. FDA, Washington, 1983-84. Assoc. editor Jour. Clin. Investigation, 1972-77; contbr. 43 articles to profl. jours. Councillor Midwinter Conf. Immunologists, Asilomar, Calif., 1969-72; mem. test com. in rheumatology Am. Bd. Internal Medicine, Phila., 1970-72. With USPHS, 1958-60. Recipient Russell Cecil award Arthritis Found., 1972. Fellow ACP, Am. Coll. Rheumatology (nat. program chmn. 1969); mem. AMA, Nat. Soc. Clin. Rheumatologists (pres. 1987-89), Tex. Rheumatism Assn. (pres. 1976), Ctrl. Rheumatism Assn. (pres. 1977-78). Mem. Ch. of Christ. Office: Presbyn Hosp 8200 Walnut Hill Ln Dallas TX 75231-4402

SMILEY, LOGAN HENRY, journalist, public concern consultant; b. Atlanta, Feb. 1, 1926; s. Logan Smiley and Gladys (McCullum) Butcher. BA in Cinema, U. So. Calif., 1950; MS in Journalism, U. Calif., L.A., 1953. Pub. rels. dir. L.A. Open Golf Tournament, 1953-54; producer, dir., co-founder Bishop's Co., Westwood, Calif., 1953-55; producer ABC-TV, Hollywood, Calif., 1957-58; asst. producer Marlon Brando Prodns., Paramount Pictures, Hollywood, Calif., 1957-58, Paris, 1959-60; cons. L.A. C. of C., 1953-56, United Artists Corp., L.A., 1958-60, Russell Birdwell, Pub. Rels., N.Y.C. and London, 1960-64; pres. Pub. Concern Films, Ft. Lauderdale, Fla., 1990—, Nat. Comm. Assocs., Miami, also Jalapa, Mex., 1948—. Writer, columnist San Antonio Light, 1948-50; editor Art Direction Mag., 1968-70, Group Travel Mag., 1970-71; editor, assoc. pub. CLIO Mag., 1968-74, Musical Am. Mag., 1964-66; editor, designer New Spirit Mag. of Social Svc., 1978-80. Mem. Fla. press corps Jimmy Carter for Pres., Atlanta, 1976; chmn. So. Fla. Jerry Brown for Pres., Miami, 1992. With USNR, 1943-45. Recipient Barnett Peace prize Southwestern U., 1944, scholarship S.W. State Tchrs. Coll., 1943, 1st place award Tex. Secondary Sch. System, 1943. Democrat. Home: 18301 NE 11th Ave Miami FL 33179-4606 Office: Nat Comms Assn PO Box 630715 Miami FL 33163

SMILLIE, THOMSON JOHN, opera producer; b. Glasgow, Scotland, Sept. 29, 1942; s. John Baird and Mary (Thomson) S.; m. Anne Ivy Pringle, July 14, 1965; children: Jane, Jonathan, Julia, David. MA, Glasgow U., 1963. Dir. pub. rels. Scottish Opera, 1966-78; artistic dir. Wexford Festival, Ireland, 1973-78; gen. mgr. Opera Co., Boston, 1978-80; gen. dir. Ky. Opera, Louisville, 1981—. Contbr. articles to various publs. Home: 4701 Kitty Hawk Way Louisville KY 40207-1752*

SMITH, AL JACKSON, JR., environmental engineer, lawyer; b. Meridian, Miss., Aug. 26, 1935; s. Al Jackson and Katherine (Felker) S.; m. Patricia Scruggs, Dec. 20, 1957; children: Johnny, Vicki, Katherine. BSCE, Miss. State U., 1958; MS in Environ. Engring., Vanderbilt U., 1969; JD, Atlanta Coll. Law, 1977; LLM, Woodrow Wilson Coll., 1980. Bar: Ga. 1979, U.S. Dist. Ct. (no. dist.) Ga. 1979, U.S. Ct. Appeals (11th cir.). Engr. City of Vicksburg, Miss., 1964-66; dir. br. emergency Region IV EPA, Atlanta, 1966-86, dep. dir. div. water, 1986-90; counsel Hurt, Richardson, Todd, Garner and Caddenhead, Atlanta, 1990-93, McRae Secrest & Fox, Atlanta, 1993; pvt. cons., 1994-95; dir. engring. Kiber Environ. Svcs., Inc., Atlanta, 1995—; solicitor City of Stockbridge, Ga., 1984-87; lectr. Nat. Emergency Tng. Ctr., Emmitsburg, Md. 1980—; city judge Locust Grove, Ga., 1988—. Author: Managing Hazardous Substance Accidents, 1981; Oil Pollution Control, 1973; contbg. author: Hazardous Materials Handbook, 1982; contbr. articles to profl. jours. Served to capt. USAR, 1958-70. Mem. Internat. Assn. Chiefs Police, Ga. Bar Assn., N.C. Assn. Fire Chiefs. Baptist. Home: 1550 S Ola Rd Locust Grove GA 30248-9472

SMITH, ALMA DAVIS, elementary education educator; b. Washington, June 27, 1951; d. Wyatt Deeble and Martha Elizabeth (Lingenfelter) Davis; m. Perry James Smith, Jan. 1, 1979; children: Lauren, Hunter. BS, James Madison U., 1973; MEd, U. Va., 1978. Cert. elem. tchr. and prin., Va. Tchr. Robert E. Lee Elem. Sch., Spotsylvania, Va., 1973-79, Conehurst Elem. Sch., Salem, Va., 1979, Hopkins Rd. Elem. Sch., Richmond, Va., 1980-87; tchr. Reams Rd. Elem. Sch., Richmond, Va., 1987-95, asst. prin. summer sch., 1990; tchr. Crestwood Elem. Sch., Richmond, Va., 1995—. Bd. mem. PTA, 1994-95, life mem., 1995. Mem. NEA, Spotsylvania Edn. Assn. (numerous chair positions), Chesterfield Edn. Assn. Home: 2811 Ellesmere Dr Midlothian VA 23113-3800

SMITH, ANN HAMILL, retired religion educator; b. Lumberton, N.C., Oct. 12, 1929; d. Walter Franklin and Mabel Willey (Braswell) Hamill; (div.); children: Leslie Wade Smith Hodeen, Courtney Drake Smith Johnson. BSEE, Old Dominion U., 1973; Edn. for Ministry degree, U. South, 1986; postgrad., Loyola U., New Orleans, 1986-89. Sunday sch. tchr. Christ Ch., Poughkeepsie, N.Y., 1957-60; E.C.W. pres. Christ Ch., Poughkeepsie, 1958-59; asst. Christ Ch. Nursery, Poughkeepsie, 1959-60; asst. parish sec. Christ and St. Luke's Ch., Norfolk, Va., 1970; mgr. Picnic in the Yard St. Paul's Ch., Norfolk, 1982-83; min. Christian edn. St. Andrew's Ch., Newport News, Va., 1985-90; spiritual dir. Virginia Beach, Va., 1990—. Author: (meditations) Our Church Times, 1988-91. Bd. dirs. Christ Ch. Day Sch., Poughkeepsie, 1960-65; mentor Edn. for Ministry, Virginia Beach, 1994—. Democrat.

SMITH, ANNE P., historical society director. Dir. Ga. Hist. Soc. Office: Ga Hist Soc 501 Whitaker St Savannah GA 31401-4830

SMITH, ARTHUR, English language educator. BA in English Lit., San Francisco State U., 1970, MA in English Lit. and Creative Writing, 1971; PhD in English Lit., U. Houston, 1986. Tchg. fellow dept. English U. Houston, 1979-83; instr. dept. English Houston Bapt. U., 1984-86; asst. prof. dept. English U. Tenn., Knoxville, 1986-92, assoc. prof., 1992—. Author: Elegy on Independence Day, 1985 (Norma Farber 1st Book award 1985, Agnes Lynch Starrett Poetry prize 1984), Orders of Affection, 1996; contbr. poetry to anthologies, articles to profl. publs. Adv. mem. Lit. Panel Tenn. Arts Commn., 1991-94; profl. staff The Sandhills Writer's Conf., Augusta, Ga., 1988. Mem. MLA, Poetry Soc. Am. (judge Ruth Lake Meml. award 1989), South Atlantic MLA, South Ctrl. MLA. Office: U Tenn English Dept Knoxville TN 37996-0430

SMITH, ARTHUR MORGAN, public relations executive; b. Bklyn., Nov. 10, 1948; s. Arthur Wallace Smith and Virginia Veronica O'Brian; m. Sidonie Madeleine Faust, Mar. 26, 1994. BA, Tulane U., 1970. Dir. pub. rels. Bauerlein, Inc., New Orleans; dir., v.p. mktg. and pub. rels. Vols. Am., New Orleans, 1989-91. Editor, pub. (mag.) Spirit. Cons., vol. Contemporary Arts Ctr., New Orleans, 1989—. Mem. C. G. Jung Soc. (bd. dirs. 1988-92). Democrat. Roman Catholic. Home: 1321 Louisiana Ave New Orleans LA 70115-2434 Office: Vols of Am 3939 N Causeway Blvd Metairie LA 70002-1777

SMITH, ASHTON CARPENTER, minister; b. Richmond, Va., Nov. 26, 1957; s. Ashton Vivian and Mary Louise (Carpenter) S.; m. Lori Jean McConaghy, June 15, 1985. BS, Va. Commonwealth U., 1980; MDiv, Southeastern Sem., 1985; D in Ministry, Luther Rice Sem., 1992. Ordained to ministry So. Bapt. Conv., 1982. Youth dir. Pine St. Bapt. Ch., Richmond, Va., 1979; youth pastor Living Clay Bapt. Ch., Henderson, N.C., 1982; pastor Ashland (Va.) Bapt. Ch., 1983-84, Glebe Landing Bapt. Ch., Laneview, Va., 1984-87, Bethel Bapt. Ch., Fredericksburg, Va., 1987-93, Virginia Beach (Va.) Bapt. Ch., 1993—; sec.-treas. Mid-Tidewater Pastors' Conf., Laneview, 1985-86, pres. 1986-87. Asst. editor Bapt. Banner, 1993—. Carmel Bapt. Ch., Ruther Glen, Va. scholar, 1984. Mem. Fredericksburg Bapt. Mins.' Conf. (v.p. 1991—), Fredericksburg Bapt. Christian Life Com. Home: 2155 Hedgelawn Way Virginia Beach VA 23454-5826 Office: Virginia Beach Bapt Ch 2301 Newstead Dr Virginia Beach VA 23454

SMITH, BARBARA HERRNSTEIN, English language and literature educator, writer; b. N.Y.C., Aug. 6, 1932; m. Richard J. Herrnstein, May 1951 (div. 1961); m. Thomas H. Smith, Feb. 1964 (div. 1974); children: Julia, Deirdre. BA summa cum laude, Brandeis U., 1954, MA, 1955, PhD in English and Am. Lit., 1965. Mem. faculty divsn. lit. and langs. Bennington Coll., 1961-73, chmn. divsn. lit. and langs., 1967-68, 71-72; vis. lectr. comm. U. Pa., 1973-74, prof. English and comm., 1974-80, Univ. prof., 1980-87; Braxton Craven prof. comparative lit. and English Duke U., Durham, N.C., 1987—; coord. com. establish grad. program comparative lit. U. Pa., 1976-79, mem. adminstrv. com. grad. program comparative lit. and lit. theory, 1979-87, mem. acad. adv. coun. to dean, 1979-81, mem. SAS provost's coun., 1979-81, dir. ctr. cultural studies, 1979-85, chmn. grad. program comparative lit. and lit. theory, 1981-84; mem. faculty sch. criticism and theory U. Calif., Irvine, summer 1977; vis. scholar Princeton U., 1980; mem. bd. overseers' vis. com. Harvard U., 1981-87; mem. Delegation Profs. Comparative Lit. to People's Republic of China, 1983; mem. external rev. coms. Franklin and Marshall Coll., U. Minn., Glassboro State Coll., Ga. Inst. Tech., 1985-86; dir. summer seminar coll. tchrs. NEH, 1985; mem. various coms. Duke U., 1987—, mem. program sci., tech. and human values, 1987, bd. advisors Duke U. Press, 1987-90, acting dir. grad. studies grad. program lit., 1989, dir. ctr. interdisciplinary studies sci. and cultural theory, 1991—; mem. faculty sch. criticism and theory Dartmouth Coll., summer 1989; Northrop Frye chair lit. theory U. Toronto, 1990; mem. Delegation Profs. LIt. and Linguistics to USSR, 1990; cons. in field; guest lectr. in field. Author: Poetic Closure: A Study of How Poems End, 1968 (Christian Gauss award 1968, Explicator award 1968), On the Margins of Discourse: The Relation of Literature to Language, 1978, Contingencies of Value: Alternative Perspectives for Critical Theory, 1988, Belief and Resistance: Dynamics of Contemporary Intellectual Controversy, 1997; editor: Discussions of Shakespeare's Sonnets, 1964, Shakespeare's Sonnets, 1969; co-editor: The Politics of Liberal Education, 1991 (Critic's Choice award Am. Ednl. Studies Assn. 1992), Mathematics, Science and Postclassical Theory, 1996; mem. editl. bd. Critical Inquiry, 1975—, Publication-MLA, 1977-79, Poetics Today, 1979—, South Atlantic Quar., 1987—, Ency. Americana, 1992—, Ency. of Aesthetics, 1994—; mem. bd. internat. editors PTL: A Jour. for Descriptive Poetics and Theory of Literature, 1975-79; contbr. articles to profl. jours. Grantee Huber Found., 1966-72, Ford Found., 1966-72; fellow NEH, 1970-71, Guggenheim fellow, 1977-78, Humanities fellow Rockefeller Found., 1981, fellow Ctr. Advanced Study Behavioral Scis., 1985-86, Nat. Ctr. Humanities, fall 1992, Shelby Cullom Davis Ctr. Hist. Studies Princeton U., spring 1993; resident fellow Bellagio Inst., Rockefeller Found., 1995; scholar N.Y. State, 1950-51. Mem. AAAS, MLA (mem. exec. com. poetry divsn. 1976-78, mem. exec. com. divsn. philos. approaches lit. 1980-84, mem. com. rsch. activities 1983-84, pres. 1988), Am. Comparative Lit. Assn., Internat. Assn. Philosophy & Lit., Acad. Lit. Studies, Soc. Critical Exch. (pres. 1987-89), English Inst. (mem. supervising com. 1978-80, trustee 1986-93), Phi Beta Kappa. Office: Duke U Box 90015 325 Allen Bldg Durham NC 27708

SMITH, BARNEY OVEYETTE, JR., lawyer; b. Mobile, Ala., July 29, 1952; s. Barney O. Sr. and Delores (Long) S.; m. Rita Ward, May 31, 1975; children: Barney O. III, Berkley Lauren. BA, Furman U., 1973; JD, U. S.C., 1976. Bar: S.C. 1976, U.S. Dist. Ct. S.C. 1976, U.S. Ct. Appeals (4th cir.) 1981, U.S. Supreme Ct. 1981. Ptnr. Parham & Smith, Greenville, S.C., 1976—. Fellow Nat. Bd. Trial Advocates, So. Trial Lawyers Assn.; mem. ABA, Am. Bd. Trial Advocates, Assn. Trial Lawyers Am. (sustaining), S.C. Trial Lawyers Assn. (bd. dirs. 1984—, pres. elect 1986-87, pres. 1987-88). Democrat. Home: 6 Rugosa Way Greer SC 29650-4417 Office: Parham & Smith Falls Pl 531 S Main St Ste 200 Greenville SC 29601-2557

SMITH, BARRY ALAN, hotel executive; b. L.A., Sept. 1, 1945; s. Joel Herman and Daphne Peggy (Wigsten) S.; m. Gayle Swift, Feb. 21, 1970. BBA, U. Houston, 1968. Cert. hotel adminstr., mgr. cmty. assn. Front office mgr. Warwick Hotel, Houston, 1966-73; asst. mgr. Hyatt Regency Hotel, Houston, 1973-75; exec. asst. mgr. Whitehall Hotel, Houston, 1975-77; resident mgr. Stouffer's Greenway Plaza Hotel, Houston, 1977-79, Registry Hotel, Dallas, 1979-81; mng. dir. NortPark Inn and Conv. Ctr., Dallas, 1981-84; dir. ops. Bradford Hotels, Austin, Tex., 1984; v.p. ops. Landmark Hotels, Inc., Dallas, 1984-86; gen. mgr. Midland (Tex.) Hilton, 1986-91; pres. 117 Wall St. Corp., 1989-91; gen. mgr. Austin (Tex.) Crest Hotel, 1991-92, Austin (Tex.) Cambridge Tower, 1992—. Mem. Tex. Hotel/Motel Assn. (bd. dirs. 1987-91), Cmty. Assn. Inst., Mobile Hotel Assn. (pres. 1985-86), Midland Hotel Assn. (pres., v.p. 1986-88), Mobile C. of C. (bd. dirs. 1985), Midland C. of C. (adv. bd. 1987-91), Austin Conv. and Visitors Bur. (adv. bd. 1991-92), Rotary. Republican. Methodist. Home: 8001 Spandera Cv Austin TX 78759-8722

SMITH, BARRY MERTON, financial planner, consultant; b. Dunedin, Fla., Oct. 18, 1943; s. Ollie Morris and Leila Elizabeth (Crisman) S.; m. Susan Gay Stewart, Aug. 13, 1977; children: Jason, Justin, Joshua. Student, U. Fla., 1961-65, St. Petersburg Jr. Coll., 1963; BS in Agr., U. Fla., 1971; postgrad., U. Ctrl. Fla., 1980-83. CFP. Loan svc. rep. Columbia (S.C.) Bank for Coops., 1972; v.p. Apopka (Fla.) Growers Supply Inc., 1972-78, V-J Growers Supply Inc., Apopka, 1978-81, Estimation, Inc., Timonium, Md., 1981, Benbow Industries, Apopka, 1982; ptnr. Billy H. Wells and Assocs., Sanford, Fla., 1982-85; dist. mgr. The Equitable Life of N.Y., Orlando, Fla., 1982-85; v.p. CFS Securities Corp., Longwood, Fla., 1985-90, pres., CEO, 1991—. Capt. U.S. Army, 1966-70, Vietnam. Mem. Internat. Assn. for Fin. Planners (bd. dirs. ctrl. Fla. chpt. 1989-91), Inst. CFPs, Fla. Foliage Assn. (bd. dirs. 1978, treas. 1979-80, Sertoma Club (v.p. 1978-79). Office: CFG Securities Corp 2180 State Road 434 W Ste 1150 Longwood FL 32779-5008

SMITH, BARRY SAMUEL, physiatrist; b. Windber, Pa., Jan. 15, 1947. MD, Thomas Jefferson U., 1969. Diplomate Am. Bd. Phys. Medicine and Rehab. Intern Reading (Pa.) Hosp., 1969-70; resident in phys. medicine and rehab. Inst. Phys. Med. Rehab., Louisville, 1970-73; now with Baylor U. Med. Ctr., Dallas, chief in phys. medicine and rehab. Mem. AMA, Am. Acad. Pediats., Am. Coll. Rehab. Medicine, Am. Acad. Phys. Medicine and Rehab., Am. Acad. Emergency Medicine. Office: Baylor U Med Ctr Dept Phys Medicine and Rehab 3500 Gaston Ave Dallas TX 75246-2045

SMITH, BERT KRUGER, mental health services professional, consultant; b. Wichita Falls, Tex., Nov. 18, 1915; d. Sam and Fania (Feldman) Kruger; m. Sidney Stewart Smith, Jan. 19, 1936; children: Sheldon Stuart, Jared Burt (dec.), Randy Smith Huke. BJ, U. Mo., 1936; MA, U. Tex., 1949; DHL (hon.), U. Mo., 1985. Soc. and entertainment editor Wichita Falls Post, 1936-37; freelance writer Juneau, Alaska, 1937; assoc. pub. Coleman Daily Dem. Voice, 1950-51; assoc. editor Jr. Coll. Jour., Austin, Tex., 1952-55; spl. cons., exec. Hogg Found. for Mental Health, Austin, 1952—; chmn. bd. Austin Groups for the Elderly, 1985—. Author: No Language But A Cry, 1964, Your Non-Learning Child, 1968, A Teaspoon of Honey, 1970, Insights for Uptights, 1970, Aging in America, 1973, The Pursuit of Dignity, 1977, Looking Forward, 1983; contbr. numerous articles to profl. jours. Bert Kruger Smith professorship Sch. Social Work U. Tex., 1982; recipient Disting. Svc. award City of Austin, 1988, Cert. of Appreciation, Tex. Dept. Human Svcs., 1989, Ann Bert Smith award Sr.'s Respite Svc., 1989, S.W. Found. Founders' Spirit award, 1990, Tex. Leadership award Ann. Tex. Joint Conf. on Aging, 1992, Tex. Leadership award Tex. Dept. on Aging, 1992; named to Tex. Women's Hall of Fame, 1988. Mem. Women in Comm. (Lifetime Achievement award 1994), Am. Fedn. for Aging Rsch., Adult Svc. Coun. (bd. dirs. 1970—, Family Elder Care Guardian Angel award 1996), Family Eldercare (bd. dirs. 1979—), Authors Guild, Nat. Assn. Sci. Writers, Hadassah, B'nai B'rith Women, Delta Kappa Gamma (hon). Jewish. Home: 5818 Westslope Dr Austin TX 78731-3633 Office: Hogg Found Mental Health PO Box 7998 Austin TX 78713-7998 also: U Tex Austin Austin TX 78713

SMITH, BETSY KEISER, telecommunications company executive; b. Washington, July 31, 1960; d. Henry Bruce and Jessie (Weeks) Keiser; m. Patrick C. Smith, June 2, 1984; 1 child, Alexander Keiser Smith. BA in Fine Arts and Art History, U. Mich., 1984. Account rep. Adam A. Weschler Galleries, Inc., Washington, 1984-85; mgr. customer service Presdl. Airways, Inc., Washington, 1986; merchandise mgr. Burdines Inc., Boynton Beach, Fla., 1986-87; sr. account exec. Cellular One Co., West Palm Beach, Fla., 1987—; cons. Fed. Publs. Inc., Washington, 1981-83, U.S. Telemktg. Inc., Atlanta, 1986—, Lion Internat., London, 1985—, Inst. Paralegal Tng., Phila., 1986—. Mem. DAR, U. Mich. Alumni Assn. (sec.-bd. dirs. Palm Beach chpt.), U. Mich. Alumni Club, Stuart Corinthian Yacht Club. Home: # A47 709 Harbour Point Dr North Palm Beach FL 33410 Office: Cellular One Co 250 S Australian Ave West Palm Beach FL 33401-5010

SMITH, BETTY ROBINSON, elementary education educator; b. Athens, Ga., Jan. 31, 1941; d. Willie Martin and Leila Mary Robinson; m. Freddie Smith; children: Natalie Yvonne, Rewa Patrice. BSEd, Tuskegee (Ala.) Inst., 1964; MS, Nova U., Ft. Lauderdale, Fla., 1979; Cert. Early Childhood, U. S. Fla. Head tchr. in headstart program Perkins Elem. Sch., St. Petersburg, Fla., 1965; tchr. Orange Grove Elem. Sch., Tampa, Fla., 1967-68, Largo Ctrl. Elem. Sch., Tampa, Fla., 1970-71, North Shore Elem. Sch., St. Petersburg, Fla., 1971—; head tchr. Early Success Program; active Appreciate Cultures Program for sch. improvement plan Pinellas County; chair Multicultural Club; organizer ann. Elem. workshop. Dir. youth choir, active community and religious roles; mem. mass choir Mt. Zion Progressive Baptist Ch.; organizer 55 Club; head multicultural com. North Shore Elem. Sch. Mem. PCTA, Zeta Gamma Zta, PPEP (rep. for Pinellas County, Fla.). Home: 4301 Cortez Way S Saint Petersburg FL 33712-4024 Office: North Shore Elem Sch 3500 Oak St NE Saint Petersburg FL 33704-1538

SMITH, BEVERLY ANN EVANS, performance management consultant; b. Massillon, Ohio, Apr. 12, 1948; d. Louie Edward and Willa (Dumas) Evans; m. Stephen John Smith, Aug. 1971; children: Brian Stephen, Stacy Nicole. MEd, Kent State U., 1973; BS in Edn., Bowling Green State U., 1970; diploma exch. edn. program, Babson Coll., 1987. Tchr. Garfield High Sch., Akron, Ohio, 1971-72; fin. aids officer, Upward Bound dir. Kent (Ohio) State U., 1971-76; dean student affairs Ga. State U., Atlanta, 1971-76; varied mgmt. positions So. Bell, Atlanta, 1976-84; dist. mgr. AT&T, Atlanta, 1984-96; cons. in field. Bd. dirs., chmn. United Way, Cobb County, Ga., 1991; bd. dirs. Girls Inc., Cobb County, Women for a Meaningful Summit, Washington, 1988-90; appointee Ga. Clean and Beautiful Commn., Atlanta, 1984-88; mem. Leadership Cobb, 1988—, mem. governing bd., 1993—; cert. Stephen (lay) min. Episc. Ch., 1991—. Named Cobb County Ga. Woman of Yr. in Bus., Marietta (Ga.) Girls Club, 1984, Outstanding Young Profl., Washington, D.C. Bus. Exch., Outstanding Sr. Woman, Bowling Green State U., 1970, Outstanding Freshman Woman, 1967, recipient Disting. Svc. award, 1970; named one of Outstanding Young Women of Am., 1971, 80. Mem. Omicron Delta Kappa, Delta Sigma Theta (1st v.p. local chpt. 1986-88, nat. exec. dir. 1988-90). Home: 1152 Clarendon Dr Marietta GA 30068-2161

SMITH, BRADLEY KIRK, town manager; b. Mt. Airy, N.C., Nov. 3, 1959; s. Charles Richrd and Blanche Yvonne (Boyd) S. BS in Polit. Sci., N.C. State U., 1983, MPA, 1990. Town mgr. Town of Madison, N.C., 1990—. Capt. U.S. Army, 1983-87. Mem. Internat. City/County Mgmt. Assn., Am. Soc. Pub. Adminstrn., N.C. City/County Mgmt. Assn. Democrat. Methodist. Home: 522 W Hunter St Madison NC 27025-1806 Office: Town of Madison 120 N Market St Madison NC 27025-1949

SMITH, BRIAN C., newscaster; b. New Kensington, Pa., Jan. 11, 1966; s. Vernon Carl and Eleanor Hope (Gallagher) S.; m. Joanna Marie Bennett, Oct. 9, 1993. BA in Broadcast Journalism, Lock Haven U., 1991; MA in Mass Comm., Okla. State U., 1995. Evening personality, weekend news anchor Radio Sta. WANB, Waynesburg, Pa., 1991-94; technologist specialist NASA Aerospace Edn. Svs. program, Stillwater, Okla., 1994—; beat reporter Radio Sta. WBPZ and WSNU, Lock Haven, Pa., 1990-91; reporter, overnight operator Radio Sta. WJPA and WYTK, Washington, Pa., 1988-92; sound designer Lakeview Theatre, Morgantown, W.Va., 1993; asst. sound designer Flat Rock (N.C.) Playhouse, 1992. Author: NASA Aerospace Educational Services Program, Home page; Mem. editl. bd. Communicating Effectively, 3d edit., 1992. County chmn. Patriot Party, Green County, Pa., 1993; bd. dirs. World Bible Quiz Assn., 1989-93, sec., 1990. Recipient Outstanding Svc. award Theta Zeta Cast or Alpha Psi Omega, 1991. Mem. Soc. for Profl. Journalists, Phi Kappa Phi, Sigma Tau Delta.

SMITH, BRIAN DAVID, lawyer, educator; b. Fayetteville, Ark., Oct. 29, 1953; s. Samuel Charles and Janelle (McCaskill) S.; children: Garrett Walker, Brian Austin, Marshall David. JD, La. State U., 1977. Bar: La. 1978, U.S. Dist. Ct. (we. dist.) La. 1979, U.S. Tax Ct. 1980, U.S. Ct. Appeals (5th cir.) 1980, U.S. Supreme Ct. 1990, Tex. 1993. Law clk. to presiding justice 1st Jud. Cir. Ct. La., Shreveport, La., 1978-79; assoc. Nelson, Hammons & Johnson, Shreveport, 1979-84, Lunn, Irion, Johnson, Salley & Carlisle, Shreveport, 1984—; instr. legal asst. cirriculum La. State U., Shreveport, 1984-87. Mem. ABA, La. Bar Assn., La. Assn. Def. Counsel, State Bar Tex., Mensa, Shreveport Country Club. Methodist. Home: 901 Monrovia St Shreveport LA 71106-1127 Office: Lunn Irion Johnson Salley & Carlisle PO Box 1534 Shreveport LA 71165-1534

SMITH, BROOKE ELLEN, lawyer; b. Geneva, Ill., Nov. 24, 1956; d. Dale Corwin and Imogene (Henderson) S.; m. Russell W. Ault, June 24, 1988; 1 child, Blair Elizabeth Ault. AB, U. Mo., 1977; JD, Harvard U., 1980. Bar: D.C. 1980, Tex. 1982, U.S. Ct. Appeals (5th cir.) 1982, U.S. Dist. Ct. (so. dist.) Tex. 1982, U.S. Dist. Ct. (we. dist.) Tex. 1984; cert. in bus. bankruptcy law Tex. Bd. legal Specialization. Law clk. to judge U.S. Bankruptcy Ct., Houston, 1980-81; assoc. Ross, Banks, May, Cron & Cavin, Houston, 1981-86, Baker, Brown, Sharman & Parker, Houston, 1986-89, Leonard, Hurt, Terry & Blinn, Houston, 1989—; co-host legal issues talk show Sta. KQQK-FM, Houston, 1988; mediator Tex. Bankruptcy Forum on Lexis Counsel Connect; spkr. in field. Author: Bankruptcy Strategies for Lenders, 2nd edit., 1993. Mem. ABA, Houston Bar Assn., Am. Bankruptcy Inst., State Bar Tex. (bankruptcy com., cert. in bus. bankruptcy law Bd. Legal Specialization 1989), Gulf Coast Mensa (bd. dirs. 1988). Office: Leonard Hurt & Parvin 1221 Mckinney St Ste 2775 Houston TX 77010-2011

SMITH, BRUCE MACKENZIE, journalist, writer, publisher; b. Binghamton, N.Y., Aug. 13, 1952; s. Robert Leland and Elizabeth MacKenzie (Geddes) S.; m. Angela Louise Razzano, Mar. 19, 1977; children: Justin MacKenzie, Mackenzie Alexis, Devon Richard. BA in Comm., Elizabethtown Coll., 1974; MA in Journalism, U. S.C., 1979. Reporter, announcer Sta. WGAL-AM-FM, Lancaster, Pa., 1974-76; news dir. Sta. WCSS-AM-FM, Amsterdam, N.Y., 1976-78; grad. asst., news dir. Sta. WLTR-S.C. Ednl. Radio Network, Columbia, 1978-79; S.C. broadcast editor AP, Columbia, 1979-83, Charleston corr., 1983—; adj. prof. comm. Coll. Charleston, S.C., 1996—; adj. prof. broadcast journalism Benedict Coll., Columbia, 1981-82; lectr. to local high schs. and colls. in field, 1983—. Author: Charleston Christmas Storybook, 4 vols., 1991-94, Sideways to the Sun, 1991, The Silver Locket, 1994, Flowers in Winter, 1995, Saints and Vagabonds, 1996; editor Will O' The Wisp: Mr. Bowen's Days Along the Ashley, 1995; contbr. numerous articles and short stories to publs. Pub. reader creative works, Charleston, 1989—; mem. yearbook editl. bd. PTA Whiteside Elem., Mt. Pleasant, 1992-94; coach Mt. Pleasant Youth Basketball, 1993, Hungryneck Youth Soccer, 1993-96; active Mt. Pleasant Presbyn. Ch. Winner Charleston Lit. Arts competition Charleston Cultural Affairs Office, 1991; recipient Cert. of Merit, Writer's Digest Pub. Awards, 1996. Mem. Soc. profl. Journalists (v.p. Lowcountry chpt. 1985, pres. 1989-90, Outstanding Contbns. to Journalism award 1992), S.E. Regional Cov. Planning Com., Charleston Media Club (founder). Office: Broad St Ste 303 Charleston SC 29401-1824

SMITH, BRUCE WILLIAM, safety engineer; b. Louisville, Ky., July 23, 1932; s. Roy Sylvester and Anna Lois (Levine) S.; m. Barbara Ruth Lischin, Oct. 13, 1951; children: Carl Wayne, Joyce Leslie, Nancy Florence. Student, U. Cin., 1953-58, Miami U., Oxford, Ohio, 1950-52. Registered profl. engr., Ohio. Materials testing spec. Gen. Electric AE, Cin., 1952-56, systems engr., 1956-79, facitities engr., 1979-83, safety engr., 1983-91; ret. Gen. Electric AE, 1991; consulting engr. Exec. Resource Assocs., Inc., Cape Coral, Fla., 1991—. Paramedic, Community Medic Res., No. Hamilton County, 1975-84; asst. fire chief Springdale (Ohio) Vol. Fire Dept., 1956-84; councilman, Springdale, 1960-62; mem. Springdale Charter Comm., 1962. Recipient physics scholarship, Ohio Acad. Sci., 1950. Mem. Am. Soc. Safety Engrs., Nat. Fire Protection Assn. Home: 919 SE 26th Ter Cape Coral FL 33904-2919

SMITH, CAREY DANIEL, acoustician, undersea warfare technologist; b. Kenedy, Tex., July 10, 1932; s. Ernest Edwin and Nancy Margaret (Willoughby) S.; m. Fannie Belle Walker, Sept. 18, 1954; children: Daniel Carey, Bryan Owen, Ernest Price, Sara Elizabeth Babyak. BS in Math. and Physics, U. Tex., 1959. Rsch. physicist Def. Rsch. Lab./U. Tex., Austin, 1958-64; electro-acoustic engr. Bur. Ships, Washington, 1964-66; dir. sonar tech. office Naval Sea Sys. Command, Washington, 1966-79, dir. Undersea Warfare Tech. Office, 1979-86; sr. cons. U.S. Navy/Sec. of Def., Washington, 1987—; fgn. liaison specialist in undersea warfare as collatoral duty USN, 1966-86; chmn. sonar tech. panel Tech. Coop. Program of multiple allied nations, 1972-86; tech. advisor undersea warfare div. Am. Def. Preparedness Assn., 1976-86. Chair deacons McLean (Va.) Bapt. Ch., 1988-89; chair band Parents, McLean H.S., 1979-80, chair Sports Boosters, 1977-78. With USN, 1951-56. Decorated Legion of Honor (France); recipient Disting. Civilian Svc. award Sec. Navy, 1979, also Brit., Can., French, Japanese, and New Zealand navies commendations, 1985-86. Fellow Acoustical Soc. Am. Home and Office: 1638 Dinneen Dr Mc Lean VA 22101-4646

SMITH, CARL JENNINGS, professional designer, educator; b. Akron, Ohio, Jan. 30, 1941; s. Walter Richard and Alvah Josephine (Jennings) S.; m.

Stephanie Jo Musser, Feb. 6, 1970; 1 child, Alyssa Caroline. BA, U. Akron, 1966; MA, Kent State U., 1972; grad., Mcpl. Elected Officials Inst., Columbia, S.C. Instr. Kent (Ohio) State U., 1971-72, Charleston (S.C.) City Schs., 1972-73, 74-78; art cons. S.C. State Arts Com., Columbia, 1973-74; instr. Coll. of Charleston, S.C., 1975-76; tchr. Trident Acad., Mt. Pleasant, S.C., 1978-83; designer, small bus. owner C. Jennings Smith, Sullivan's Island, S.C., 1975—. Illustrator: (cookbook) Gourmet Gifts from Your Kitchen, 1974. Mem. bd. of adjustment Town of Sullivan's Island, 1980-87, Town Coun. Town of Sullivan's Island, 1987—; chmn., organizer Disaster Preparedness Team, Sullivan's Island, 1990—; chmn. beach erosion task force com., Town of Sullivan's Island, Coast Guard neighborhood adv. coun.; involved in aiding evacuation from island during Hurricane Hugo and very active in various reconstruction projects for the town. 2d lt. U.S. Army, 1959-64. His painting purchased by S.C. Arts Commn. for state's permanent collection, 1975. Mem. Am. Inst. Bldg. Design, Constrn. Specs. Inst., Carolina Art Assn, Nat. Trust for Hist. Preservation, S.C. Hist. Soc., S.C. Wildlife Fedn., S.C. Coastal Conservation League, E. Cooper Outboard Motor Club, Phi Delta Theta. Office: C Jennings Smith PO Box 250 Sullivans Island SC 29482

SMITH, CARL MICHAEL, lawyer; b. Oklahoma City, Oct. 11, 1944; s. Carl W. Jr. and Nina (Furr) S.; m. Sharon Kay Lewis, June 5, 1971. BA, U. Okla., 1966, JD, 1969. Bar: Okla. 1969, U.S. Dist. Ct. (we., no. and ea. dists.) Okla. 1971, U.S. Ct. Appeals (10th cir.) 1976, U.S. Supreme Ct. 1976. Mem. firm Lawrence, Smith & Harmon, Oklahoma City, 1977-80; pres. Red Rock Exploration, Inc., Oklahoma City, 1980-83; mem. firm Lawrence & Ellis, P.A., Oklahoma City, 1983—. Mem. Blue Ribbon Commn. on Natural Gas, Oklahoma City, 1982; chmn. Okla. Polit. Action Com., Oklahoma City, 1986-90; mem. Okla. Legis. Interim Task Force on Environ. Regulation, Oklahoma City, 1991-92; sec. Okla. Energy Resources Bd., 1992-94; mem. Okla. Sec. of Energy, 1995—. Capt. U.S. Army, 1969-71, Vietnam. Mem. Okla. Ind. Petroleum Assn. (pres. 1994-95). Office: Lawrence & Ellis PA 600 Union Plz 3030 NW Expressway St Oklahoma City OK 73112-5466

SMITH, CARSON EUGENE, university administrator; b. Louisville, Dec. 23, 1947; s. Fred Eugene and Louise Bernadine (Carson) S.; m. Gleneva McCowan, Dec. 26, 1965; children: Mark, Shanna, Angela, Andrew. MA in Polit. Sci., U. Ky., 1972; BA in History/Polit. Sci., Ky. State U., 1965. Devel. specialist Ky. State Govt., Frankfort, 1972-73, policy advisor higher edn., 1973-74; coord. for fin. planning Coun. on Higher Edn., Frankfort, 1974-77; asst. budget dir. U. Ky., Lexington, 1977-80; asst. dir. of budgets U. Mo., Columbia, 1980-83; v.p., bus. affairs Ky. State U., Frankfort, 1983-90, exec. dir. OPM, 1993—; dir. bus. and fin. Iowa State Bd. of Regents, Des Moines, 1991-92; mem. Nat. HBCU Conf., Hampton, Va., 1995-96, Adv. Planning Coun., 1986-90, NACUBO Facilities Com., 1986-90, Task Force on Higher Edn., Frankfort, 1995-96, Formula Funding Com., Frankfort, 1995-96. Mem. budget com. Western Hills H.S., Frankfort, 1994-96, facilities com., 1994—. Capt. USAF, 1966-70. Mem. Nat. Assn. of Coll. and Univ. Bus. Officers, So. Assn. of Coll. and Univ. Bus. Officers. Baptist. Home: 169 Bellemeade Dr Frankfort KY 40601 Office: Ky State U East Main St Frankfort KY 40601

SMITH, CHARLES CLARENCE, JR., physician, medical educator; b. Fonde, Ky., Sept. 27, 1930; s. Charles Clarence Sr. and Clytie (Morgan) S.; m. Rosemary Sledge, June 19, 1955; children: Charles C. Smith III, Mark Glendeaux, Cynthia Daphne, Stephanie Smith Altobellis. BA, Georgetown Coll., 1951, LLD (hon.), 1987; MD, U. Louisville, 1955. Diplomate Am. Bd. Internal Medicine. Intern U. Hosp. and Hillman Clinic, Birmingham, Ala., 1955-56; resident U. Louisville Hosps., 1958-61, chief resident, 1960-61; medicine instr. U. Louisville, 1961-63, clin. instr. medicine, 1963-66, asst. clin. prof. medicine, 1968-78, assoc. clin. prof. medicine, 1978-85, clin. prof. medicine, 1985—; dir. med. edn. Jewish Hosp., 1961-63; mem. adv. bd. dirs. U. Louisville Hosp., 1996—; dir. med. edn. Jewish Hosp., 1961-63; sec. med. staff Meth. Evang. Hosp., Louisville, 1966-67, chief of medicine, 1969-72, pres. med. staff, 1974-75, trustee, 1974-79, found. trustee, 1979-85; pres. Louisville Area Consortium for Continuing Med. Edn., 1979—. Sci. editor Ky. Med. Jour., 1967-74. Trustee Ky. Health Care Access Found., 1984-86; mem. gov.'s com. on medicaid reform Commonwealth of Ky., 1985-89; bd. dirs., exec. com. Ky. Blue Cross-Blue Shield, 1985-93, chmn. provider adv. com., 1985-93, vice chmn., bd. dirs., 1990-93, long-range planning com., 1989-93; mem. gov. bd. dirs. Alliant Health Sys., 1989-90; bd. dirs. Assoc. Group, Ind. Blue Cross and Blue Shield, 1993—. Recipient Outstanding Alumnus award Georgetown Coll., 1973, Disting. Alumnus award U. Louisville, 1993. Fellow ACP (health professions subcom. 1986-87, exec. com. 1988-90, bd. govs. 1986-90, masterships and hon. fellowships com. 1989-91, Physician Laureate 1991, mem. clin. efficacy assessment project 1987-90); mem. AMA, Jefferson County Med. Soc. (pres. 1975-76), Ky. Med. Assn. (v.p. 1982-83, pres. 1984-85, chmn. trends in med. edn. 1982-87, sci. works com. 1982-83, chmn. publs. com. 1983-87), Louisville Soc. Internists (pres. 1979-80), Innominate Soc. Med. History (pres. 1980-81), Alpha Omega Alpha, Phi Kapp. Republican. Home: 2109 Starmont Rd Louisville KY 40207 Office: 201 Abraham Flexner Way Louisville KY 40202-1817

SMITH, CHARLES E., company executive; b. 1930. Supr. cost acct. Page Comms. Engrs. Inc., Washington, 1957-62; acctg. sys. mgr. Leasco Sys. and Rsch. Corp., Bethesda, Md., 1968; v.p. Ringling Bros., Barnum & Bailey, Vienna, Va., 1968—; clk. FBI, Washington. Office: Ringling Bros Barnum & Bailey 8607 Westwood Center Dr Vienna VA 22182

SMITH, CHARLES EDWARD, state agency administrator; b. White County, Tenn., May 19, 1939; s. Cecil Edward and Christine (Newsome) S.; m. Shawna Lea Hickerson, Dec. 15, 1962; children: Chip, Tandy. B.S. in Journalism, U. Tenn., 1961; M.A. in English, George Peabody Coll., Nashville, 1966, Ph.D. in Higher Edn., 1976. Editor Sparta Expositor, Tenn., 1961-63; mng. editor Putnam County Herald-Cookeville Citizen, Cookeville, Tenn., 1963-64; asst. news editor Nashville Tennessean, 1964-67; news bur. dir. U. Tenn., Knoxville, 1967-68, pub. relations dir., 1968-70, exec. asst. to chancellor, 1971-73; exec. asst. to pres. U. Tenn. System, Knoxville, 1973-75; chancellor U. Tenn., Nashville, 1975-79; v.p. pub. service U. Tenn. System; editor Nashville Banner, 1979-80; chancellor U.Tenn.-Martin, 1980-85; v.p. adminstrn. state-wide system U. Tenn.-Knoxville, 1985-87; commr. edn. State of Tenn., Nashville, 1987-93; chancellor Tenn. Bd. Regents, Nashville, 1994—; trustee Am. Coll. Testing Bd., Iowa City, 1987-93; mem. So. Regional Edn. Bd., 1989-95, exec. com., 1991-95, vice chmn., 1994-95. Contbr. articles to profl. jours. Mem. Peabody Coll. Alumni Bd., 1994—. Recipient Single Best Editorial award Tenn. Press Assn., 1962, Peabody Coll. Disting. Alumnus award, 1993; named Fulbright fellow, 1980, One of Nation's Top 100 Coll. Educators, Bowling Green State U., 1985. Mem. Phi Kappa Phi. Democrat. Mem. Ch. of Christ. Home: 6340 Chickering Cir Nashville TN 37215-5301 Office: Tenn Bd Regents 1415 Murfreesboro Pike Ste 350 Nashville TN 37217-2829

SMITH, CHARLES EDWIN, computer science educator, consultant; b. Columbia, Mo., Apr. 15, 1950; s. William Walter and Nelletha Pearl (Lavendar) S.; m. Mary L. Davis, July 27, 1991. AA, Edison C.C., Ft. Myers, Fla., 1971; BS, Troy State U., 1979; MA, Webster U., St. Louis, 1989. Cert. computing profl. Enlisted USAF, Tyndall AFB, Fla., 1975-79; advanced through grades to maj. USAF; commd. 2d lt. USAF, Scott AFB, Ill., 1979; maj. USAFR, 1989—; adj. instr. Manatee C.C., Venice, Fla., 1989-90, Edison C.C., Punta Gorda, Fla., 1989-92; prof. computer sci. Edison C.C., 1992—; cons. Charles E. Smith Consulting, North Port, Fla., 1989-91. Assoc. mem. Charlotte County Econs. Devel. Coun., Port Charlotte, Fla., 1992—. Mem. Fla. Assn. C.C.s, Bass Anglers Sportsman's Soc. Republican. Office: Edison C C 2511 Vasco St Punta Gorda FL 33950-2807

SMITH, CHARLES L., personal care home administrator; b. Clarksville, Tenn., June 19, 1946; s. Charles Ed and Robbie Louise (DeFriese) S.; m. Patricia Rhea Yardley Sept. 6th, 1995; children: Matthew S., Sarah Ruth. BA in Edn., Belmont U., 1969; MA in Edn., So. Sem., Louisville, 1986. Assoc. Tenn. Bapt. Music Dept., Brentwood, 1965-71; min. music and edn. Haywood Hills Bapt. Ch., Nashville, 1971-73; pres. Revelation Media Svcs., Nashville, 1973-76; health educator Planned Parenthood, Nashville, 1977-79; assoc. min. 1st Bapt. Ch., Lewisburg, Tenn., 1979-82; media prodr. So. Sem. 1982-86; organist 1st Christian Ch., Jeffersonville, Ind., 1987-88; mental health tech. coord. Jefferson Hosp., Jeffersonville, 1988-93; adminstr. Parr's Rest, Inc., Louisville, 1993—; music dir. Vanderbilt U., Nashville, 1969-73; v.p. Tenn. Bapt. Ch. Music Assn., Nashville, 1970; founding pres. Omicron Rho/Phi Mu Alpha, Nashville, 1966-69. Pres. Field Elem. PTA, Louisville, 1990, Media Ministry Workshop, So. Sem., 1984-86; coach Crescent Hills Athletic Assn., Louisville, 1984-86; sec./treas. Marshall County Ministerial Assn., Lewisburg, 1981-82; music dir. North Oldham Bapt. Ch., 1990—. Office: Parr's Rest Inc 969 Cherokee Rd Louisville KY 40204

SMITH, CHARLES WILLIAM, engineering educator; b. Christiansburg, Va., Jan. 1, 1926; s. Robert Floyd and Ollie (Surface) S.; m. Doris Graham Burton, Sept. 9, 1950; children: Terry Jane Kelley, David Bryan. BSCE, Va. Poly. Inst., 1947, MS in Applied Mechanics, 1949. Registered profl. engr., Va. Isntr. Va. Poly. Inst. and State U., Blacksburg, 1947-48, asst. prof., 1949-52, assoc. prof., 1953-57, prof. engring., 1958-81, alumni disting. prof., 1982-92, alumni disting. prof. emeritus, 1992—; advanced grad. engring. tng. program GE Co., Lynchburg, Va., 1962; grad. tng. program Western Elec.-Bell Labs., Winston-Salem, N.C., 1963, 64; bd. dirs. Local Water Authority, Blacksburg, 1975—. Author: (with others) Experimental Techniques in Fracture Mechanics, Vol. 2, 1973, Inelastic Behavior of Composite Materials, 1975, Mechanics of Fracture, Vol. 6, 1981, Handbook of Experimental Stress Analysis, 1986, Experimental Techniques in Fracture, Vol. 3, 1993; editor: Fracture Mechanics, Vol. 11, co-editor, Vol. 17; regional editor: Jour. of Theoretical and Applied Fracture Mechanics, 1984—; guest editor: (jour.) Optics and Lasers in Engineering, 1991; contbr. articles to profl. jours. Recipient Scientific Achievement award NASA Langley Rsch. Ctr., 1986, Dan H. Pletta award for engring. educator of yr. Va. Consortium Engring. Schs., 1991. Fellow Soc. Experimental Mechanics (numerous coms., M.M. Frocht award for oustanding educator in experimental mechanics 1983, William M. Murray medal for contbns. to experimental mechanics, 1993, B.J. Lazan award for rsch. in experimental mechanics, 1995), Am. Acad. Mechanics; mem. ASTM, ASME, NSPE (many coms. 1950-70), Am. Soc. Engring. Edn. (chmn. nominating com. 1971), Soc. Engring. Sci. (organizing com. 1977-81 annual meetings co-chmn. 1984), Internat. Assn. Structural Mechanics in Reactor Tech. Methodist. Office: Va Poly Inst and State Univ ESM-VPISU-0219 Blacksburg VA 24061

SMITH, CLODUS RAY, academic administrator; b. Blanchard, Okla., May 15, 1928; s. William Thomas and Rachel (Hale) S.; m. Pauline R. Chaat; children: Martha Lynn, William Paul, Paula Diane. Assoc. degree, Cameron State Coll., 1948; BS in Agrl. Edn., Okla. A & M Coll., 1950; MS in Vocat. Edn., Okla. State U., 1955; EdD in Vocat. Edn., Cornell U., 1960. Grad. asst. Cornell U., 1957-59; asst. prof. U. Md., 1959-62, assoc. prof., 1962-63, dir. Summer Sch., 1963-72, adminstrv. dean, 1972-73; spl. asst. to pres. Cleve. State U., 1973-74, v.p. for univ. rels., 1974-83; pres. Rio Grande Coll. and Rio Grande Community Coll., Ohio, 1983-86, Lake Erie Coll., Painesville, Ohio, 1986-92, Okla. Ind. Coll. Found., Oklahoma City, 1993—, Okla. Assn. Ind. Colls. and Univs., 1993—; cons. NEA, Naval Weapons Lab., Dehlgren, Va.; researcher Personal and Profl. Satisfactions; contract investigator Nat. Endowment for Humanities; dir. Human Resources and Community Devel., Prince George's County, Md. Author: Planning and Paying for College, 1958, Rural Recreation for Profit, 1971, A Strategy for University Relations, 1975, State Relations for the 1980 Decade, 1982. Amb. Natural Resources, Ohio, 1984, chmn. dept.; founder N.Am. Assn. of Summer Schs., 1979. Recipient Rsch. award Nat. Project in Agrl. Communications, 1959, Edn. award Prince George's C. of C., 1971. Mem. Am. Assn. U. Adminstrs., Am. Assn. for Higher Edn., Nat. Soc. for Study Edn., Coun. for Support and Advancement Edn., Am. Alumni Coun., Al Koran Hunter's Club, Shriners. Methodist. Home: 6617 115th St Oklahoma City OK 73162 Office: Okla Ind Coll Found 114 E Sheridan Ave Ste 101 Oklahoma City OK 73104-2418

SMITH, CONSTANCE LEWIS, secondary school educator; b. Macon, Ga., May 29, 1936; d. Isiah and Anna (Duncan) Lewis; m. Willie S. Smith, Dec. 2, 1956; children: Glenda Smith Hubbard, Kristen Y. MA, Ft. Valley (Ga.) State Coll., 1981. Cert. early childhood edn. tchr., Ga. Tchr. pub. schs., Macon, 1971—. Mem. NEA, Ga. Assn. Educators, Bibb County Assn. Educators, Delta Sigma Theta. Roman Catholic. Home: 3703 Greenbriar Rd Macon GA 31204-4255

SMITH, COURTLAND CLEMENT, JR., actuarial consultant; b. N.Y.C., Feb. 3, 1927; s. Clement Courtland and Rachel Leah (Ornstein) S.; m. Lila Rita Rubin, Nov. 7, 1953 (div. Apr. 1973); children: David, Jonathan, Nancy, Valerie; m. Judith Anne Austin, June 2, 1973. AB, Yale U., 1949. CLU. Actuarial clk. Met. Life Ins. Co., N.Y.C., 1954-62, asst. actuary, 1969-74; asst. actuary N.A. Reassurance Co., N.Y.C., 1962-69; sr. v.p. Cologne Life Reins. Co., Stamford, Conn., 1974-83; pvt. practice cons. actuary Stamford, 1983-90; v.p. Winterthur Life Re Ins. Co., Dallas, 1990-94; ret., 1994. Editor: Actuarial Rsch. Clearing House, 1976-80. With U.S. Army, 1945-46. Fellow Soc. Actuaries; mem. Am. Acad. Actuaries, Internat. Actuarial Assn. Home and Office: 4224 High Star Ln Dallas TX 75287-6624

SMITH, DANI ALLRED, sociologist, educator; b. Natchez, Miss., Dec. 12, 1955; d. Paul Hollis and Mary Frances (Byrd) Allred; m. Ronald Bassel Smith, Aug. 9, 1980. BS in Social Sci., Lee Coll., 1977; MA in Sociology, U. Miss., 1980; postgrad., U. Tenn., 1989—. Staff writer Natchez Dem., 1977; secondary tchr. Natchez Pub. Schs., 1977-78; instr. sociology U. Miss., 1980-81, 82, rsch. assoc., instr. mgmt. info. systems, 1982-87; secondary tchr. Coffeeville (Miss.) Schs., 1981-82; asst. prof. sociology Lee Coll., Cleveland, Tenn., 1988-96; instr. sociology Fisk U., Nashville, 1996—; workshop speaker Ch. of God Prison Conf., Cleveland, 1993, 94, 95; speaker Bradley County Law Enforcement Tng. Assn., Cleveland, 1992; advisor Lee Collegian, 1988-93. Contbr. articles to profl. jours. and newspapers. Advisor Sociology Club, 1988-96, Alpha Kappa Delta, 1992-96, Soc. for Law and Justice, 1995-96. Mellon Appalachian fellow, 1993-94; named one of Outstanding Young Women Am., 1981. Mem. Am. Sociol. Assn., So. Sociol. Assn., Christian Sociol. Assn., Am. Soc. Criminology, Am. Mus. Natural History, Gt. Smoky Mountains Natural History Assn., Am. Hiking Soc., Smithsonian Assocs., Phi Kappa Phi, Alpha Chi, Alpha Kappa Delta. Home: 430 20th St NE Cleveland TN 37311-3949 Office: Fisk U 1000 17th Ave N Nashville TN 37208-3051

SMITH, DANNY LEON, sales executive; b. Springsdale, Ark., Nov. 4, 1958; s. Gene Leroy and Reba Lea (Quick) S. BS in Pharmacy, U. Ark., Little Rock, 1982. Cert. pharmacist. Pharmacist Petty's Drug, Little Rock, 1982-84, Consumer's Pharmacy div. Petty Drug Co., Fayetteville, Ark., 1984-88; pharm. sales rep. Eli Lilly & Co., Pine Bluff, Ark., 1988—; mgr. Economy Drugstore, Huntsville, Ark., 1994—; developer North Park Med. Pk., 1994—; cons. pharmacist Beaumont Nursing Home, Little Rock, 1982-84, Convalescence Ctr., Conway, Ark., 1982-84, Washington County Health Dept., Fayetteville, 1984-85. Recipient Lemmon Drug Co. Outstanding Sr. Pharmacy Student award, 1982. Mem. Ark. Pharmacist Assn., Springdale C. of C. Republican. Home: PO Box 6191 Springdale AR 72766-6191

SMITH, DAVID CARR, organic chemist; b. Ft. Wayne, Ind., Aug. 9, 1944; s. James Nolan and Kathryn Ellen (Mefford) S.; m. Dolores Joan Kurz, July 9, 1966; children: David James, Daniel Paul. BS in Chemistry, Clarkson Coll., 1969, PhD in Chemistry, 1975. Postdoctoral fellow Utah State U., Logan, 1974-75, U. S.C., Columbia, 1975-77; sr. rsch. chemist Ash Stevens Inc., Detroit, 1977-80; group leader Sterling Organics, Rensselaer, N.Y., 1980-84; mgr. bus. devel. Sterling Organics, N.Y.C., 1984-85; mgr. pharm. technology John Brown Inc., Stamford, Conn., 1985-93; sr. project mgr. Lockwood Greene Engrs., Inc., Atlanta, 1993—. Contbr. articles to profl. jours. Mem. AAAS, Am. Chem. Soc., Licensing Exec. Soc., Internat. Soc. Pharm. Engrs., Parenteral Drug Assn., Regulatory Affairs Profls. Soc. (cert.), Sigma Xi. Office: Lockwood Greene Engrs Inc 250 Williams St NW Atlanta GA 30303-1032

SMITH, DAVID CLAIBORNE, construction company executive; b. Burlington, N.C., Sept. 23, 1953; s. Claiborne Pendleton and Betty Jane (Hancock) S.; m. Elizabeth Marjorie Collins, Aug. 19, 1954. Student, Va. Polytech. Inst., 1972-74, Va. Polytech. Inst., 1977-78. Sail cons. Bacon and Assocs., Annapolis, Md., 1974-77; project acct. Hardin Constrn. Group, Wilmington, N.C., 1978-79; field engr. Hardin Constrn. Group, Tulsa, 1979-83; asst. supt. Hardin Constrn. Group, Stamford, Conn., 1983-84, Charlottesville, Va., 1984-85, Ft. Wayne, Ind., 1985, Charlotte, N.C., 1985-86, Myrtle Beach, S.C., 1986-87, San Antonio, 1987-88, Stone Mountain, Ga., 1988-89; supt. Hardin Constrn. Group, St. Croix, V.I., U.S.V.I., 1989-90; supt. Hardin Constrn. Group, Atlanta, 1990—, dir. quality enhancement, 1995—. Elder Chestnut Mountain Presbyn. Ch.; bd. dirs. Presbyn. Evangelistic Fellowship. Presbyterian. Home: 5609 Monk Dr Oakwood GA 30566-3026

SMITH, DAVID DOYLE, international management consultant, consulting engineer; b. Newport, Tenn., Aug. 17, 1956; s. Doyle E. and Lena Maude (Clemmons) S.; m. Judith Ann Craig, Nov. 1, 1991; 1 child, Adam Gabriel; stepchildren: Christine, James. BSEE, U. Tenn., 1981. Registered profl. engr., Tenn., Ga. Engring. apprentice E.I. DuPont, Brevard, N.C., 1976; field engr. IBM Corp., Knoxville, Tenn., 1977-79; rsch. asst. Office of Naval Rsch. U. Tenn., Knoxville, 1980-81; systems test engr. Tex. Instruments, Inc., Johnson City, Tenn., 1981-82, product engr., 1982-83, product mgr., 1983-87; missile design engr., supr. Tex. Instruments, Inc., Lewisville, Tex., 1987-89; sr. systems engr. U.S. Data Corp., Richardson, Tex., 1989-90; lead cons. Keane, Inc., Atlanta, 1991-94; mgr., mgmt. cons. Ernst & Young LLP, Atlanta, 1994—; lectr. Tech. Inst., 1983-86; developer RTU Sys. for oil and gas, water, and electric utilities, 1990-92. Co-author profl. papers. Mem. IEEE, NSPE, Am. Prodn. and Inventory Control Socs. Home: 1080 Allenbrook Ln Roswell GA 30075-2983 Office: Ernst & Young LLP 600 Peachtree St Atlanta GA 30308-2215

SMITH, DAVID EDWARD, business executive; b. Battle Creek, Mich., Sept. 16, 1939; s. Hebdin Leslie and Dureatha Rosella (Stephens) S.; m. Margaret Eugenia Clark, June 13, 1964; 1 child, Wendy Leigh. Student, Kellogg Community Coll., 1957-58; BS in Mech. Engring., Mich State U., 1962; MS in Real Estate Investing (hon.), Meta U., Salt Lake City, 1992. Engr., scientist Douglas Aircraft Co., Santa Monica, Calif., 1962-63, McDonnell Douglas Astronautics Co., Cape Kennedy, Fla., 1963-78; broker salesman Cape Kennedy Realty, Inc., Cape Canaveral, Fla., 1978-87; pres., founder Cash Flow Seminars, Merritt Island, Fla., 1979—, Cash Flow Systems, Inc., Merritt Island, Fla., 1983—; prof. fin. Meta U., Salt Lake City, 1992—; lectr. fin. convs. and orgns. including Fed. GSA, Pub. Bldg. Svc., Am. League of Savs., Fin. Instns. Mktg. Assn., Acad. Real Estate, Am. Congress Real Estate; prof. fin. Meta U., 1992—; distbr. Hewlett Packard Copr., 1985-88; dir. comml. investment div. CKBOR, Merritt Island, 1978-79; adv. bd., lectr. Fin. Freedom Report, Nat. Inst. Fin. Planning, both Salt Lake City, 1985—; instr. Fla. real Estate Commn., La. Real Estate Commn., Fla. Bd. Accountancy, Am. Inst. Real Estate Appraisers. Author: Turbo-Diesel, The Time Value of Money, Creative Financing Techniques; contbr. numerous fin. articles to jours. and mags. Mem. Fla. Real Estate Exchangors, Internat. Platform Assn. Republican. Office: Cash Flow Seminars PO Box 540634 Merritt Island FL 32954-0634

SMITH, DAVID KINGMAN, retired oil company executive, consultant; b. Malone, N.Y., June 5, 1928; s. Ernest DeAlton and Louisa Kingman (Bolster) S.; m. Lois Louise Wing, June 13, 1959; children: Mara Louise, David Andrew. BS in Engring., Princeton U., 1952. Registered profl. engr., Tex. Civil engr., supt. Raymond Internat. Inc., N.Y.C., 1952-55, asst. v.p., 1970-71, v.p., 1971-74; group v.p. Raymond Internat. Inc., Houston, 1974-80; mgr. Raymond-Brown and Root, Maracaibo, Venezuela, 1955-70; sr. engring. assoc. Exxon Prodn. Rsch. Co., Houston, 1980-81, supr., 1982-95; cons. project mgmt., 1995—. Pres. Yorkshire Civic Assn., Houston, 1979-80, trustee, 1985—. With U.S. Army, 1946-48, PTO. Mem. ASCE, NSPE, Soc. Petroleum Engrs. (continuing edn. com. Gulf Coast chmn. 1989-93, treas. 1987-88, nat. continuing edn. com. 1991-93, dir. Gulf Coast sect. 1994-95), Tex. Soc. Profl. Engrs., Men's Garden Club Houston, Am. Legion, Princeton Alumni Assn. (dir. Houston sect.), Cen Ners In Square Dance Club (pres. 1996—). Republican. Methodist. Home: 611 W Forest Dr Houston TX 77079-6915

SMITH, DAVID YARNELL, financial consultant; b. Chattanooga, Apr. 9, 1963; s. Eugene Scott and Johnathan (Yarnell) S.; m. Donna Kathryn Swisher, July 1, 1989. BS in Bus. Adminstrn. with honors, U. Tenn., 1985; MBA, Ga. State U., 1989. Comml. banking officer, comml. bus. devel. coord., then asst. v.p. and asst. mgr. Trust Co. Bank, Atlanta, 1985-89; asst. v.p. Bank of Am., Nat. Trust & Savings Assn., Atlanta, 1989-91; fin. cons., mgr. Petty & Landis, CPAs, Chattanooga, 1991—. Mem. Omicron Delta Kappa, Alpha Gamma Rho, Delta Sigma Pi. Office: Petty & Landis Krystal Bldg Ste 700 Chattanooga TN 37402

SMITH, DEAN EDWARDS, university basketball coach; b. Emporia, Kans., Feb. 28, 1931; s. Alfred Dillon and Vesta Marie (Edwards) S.; m. Linnea Weblemoe, May 21, 1976; children: Sharon, Sandy, Scott, Kristen, Kelly. B.S. in Math. and Phys. Edn., U. Kans., 1953. Asst. basketball coach U.S. Air Force Acad., 1955-58; asst. basketball coach U. N.C., 1958-61, head basketball coach, 1961—; mem. U.S. and Canadian Basketball Rules Com., 1967-73; U.S. basketball coach Olympics, Montreal, Que., Can., 1976; lectr. basketball clinics, Germany, Italy. Served with USAF, 1954-58. Named Coach of Year Atlantic Coast Conf., 1967, 1968, 1971, 1976, 1977, 79, Nat. Basketball Coach of Year, 1977, Nat. Coach of Yr. U.S. Basketball Writers, 1979, Naismith Basketball Hall of Fame, 1982. Mem. Nat. Assn. Basketball Coaches (Nat. Basketball Coach of Year 1976, dir. 1972—, pres. 1981-82), Fellowship Christian Athletes (dir. 1965-70). Baptist. Office: U NC Office Basketball Coach PO Box 2126 Chapel Hill NC 27515-2126

SMITH, DEBORAH S., maternal and women's health nurse; b. Seneca, S.C., Aug. 25, 1957; d. Charles Robert and Emmy Lou (Jones) S.; m. Michael E. Smith, Aug. 12, 1977; children: Ashley Leigh, Jennifer Michelle, Lindsey Elizabeth. ADN, Clemson U., 1977. RN, S.C. Office nurse Dr. Perry B. Deloach, Clemson, S.C., 1986; nurse St. Francis Community Hosp., Greenville, S.C., 1977-78; nursing supr. Oconee Meml. Hosp., Seneca, 1983-85; new mother educator Pediatric Assocs., P.A., Seneca; prenatal educator for an ob-gyn. physician Seneca, 1992-95; newborn nursery nurse, labor and delivery nurse Oconee Meml. Hosp., Seneca, 1979-83; labor and delivery nurse Bapt. Med. Ctr., Easley, S.C., 1995—.

SMITH, DEBRA ANN, advertising executive; b. Oklahoma City, Jan. 6, 1954; d. Wesley Irons and Lorene Margaret (Price) Dryden; m. Tommy Allen Smith, June 24, 1978; children: Andrew Thomas, Michael Dryden. Student, Ctrl. State U., 1990. Dir. Okla. Blood Inst., Oklahoma City, 1978-83; ind. contractor Jimco Advt., Oklahoma City, 1987-91; owner Smith Advt., Oklahoma City, 1991—. Bd. dirs. March of Dimes, 1989-93. Mem. Am. Mktg. Assn. (bd. dirs. 1994—), Okla. Soc. Assn. Execs., Ctrl. Okla. Home Builders. Office: Smith Advt 1800 E Memorial Rd Ste 105 Oklahoma City OK 73131-1837

SMITH, DENNIS A., insurance company executive; married; 3 children. Degrees in Polit. Sci. and Civil Engring., N.C. State U., 1972; postgrad., Harvard U., Ga. State U., U. Va. Casualty adjuster Crawford & Co., Greensboro, N.C., 1972-80, v.p., midwest regional mgr., 1980-86, sr. v.p., 1986-91; pres. internat. divsn. Graham Miller Crawford & Co., London, 1991-92; pres., COO claims svcs. bus. unit Crawford & Co., Atlanta, 1992-94, pres., COO, chmn. internat. ops., 1994-95, chmn., CEO, 1995—. Office: Crawford & Co 5620 Glenridge Dr NE Atlanta GA 30342

SMITH, DENTYE M., library media specialist; b. Atlanta, July 21, 1936; d. William Harry and Gladys Magdalene (Bruce) S. AB, Spelman Coll., 1958; MLM, Ga. State U., 1975. Cert. Libr., media specialist. Tchr. English Atlanta Pub. Schs., 1961-82, supr. tchr., 1968-69, tchr. journalism, 1975-80, libr. media specialist, 1982-94; media specialist West Fulton High Sch., 1982-92, West Fulton Mid. Sch., 1992, Booker T. Washington Comprehensive High Sch., Atlanta, 1992-94; leader jur. gt. books Archer and West Fulton high schs.; coord. Atlanta Pub. Schs. reading cert., program West Fulton H.S.; vol. liaison Atlanta-Fulton Pub. Libr., 1987-94, local arrangements com. Atlanta Libr. Assn., 1990-91; seminar presenter in field; coord. study skills seminars Morris Brown Coll.'s Summer Upward Bound Program, 1993, 94, 95; mem. High Mus. of Art, Atlanta, Atlanta Hist. Soc., Ga. Pub. TV. Contbr. articles to profl. jours. Named to Acad. Hall of Fame, Atlanta Pub. Schs., 1990; recipient Tchr. of Yr. award West Fulton H.S., Atlanta, 1974, acad. achievement incentive program award in media APS, 1990. Mem. ALA, NEA, Nat. Ret. Tchrs. Assn., Nat. Coun. Tchrs. English, Am. Assn. Sch. Librs., Soc. Sch. Librs. Internat., Ga. Assn. Educators, Atlanta

Assn. Educators, Ga. Libr. Assn., Ga. Libr. Media Assn., Nat. Alumnae Assn. Apelman Coll., Ga. State U. Alumni Assn., Nat. Trust Hist. Preservation, Ga. Trust Hist. Preservation, Atlanta Ret. Tchrs. Assn., Atlanta Hist. Assn., Ga. Ret. Tchrs. Assn., the Smithsonian Assocs., Libr. of Congress Assocs.

SMITH, DON EDWARD, JR., army officer, pilot; b. Sullivan, Mo., Sept. 8, 1968; s. Don E. Smith and Emily Linda (Schaper) Swint; m. Kristi L. Carter, Dec. 19, 1992; 1 child, Taylor Nikole. BA, Ouachita Bapt. U., 1991. Assoc. Sam's Club, Little Rock, 1990-91; commd. 2d lt. U.S. Army, 1991, advanced through grades to capt., 1995; platoon leader U.S. Army, Ft. Campbell, Ky., 1992-93, ops. staff officer, 1993-95; assigned to advanced officers course U.S. Army, Ft. Rucker, Ala., 1995-96, assigned to maintenance mgrs. course, 1996; assigned to Korea as avionics platoon leader U.S. Army, 1996-97. Mem. Aircraft Owners and Pilots Assn., Assn. U.S. Army, Army Aviation Assn. Am. Republican. Baptist. Home: 123 Cave Creek Rd Beebe AR 72012

SMITH, DON NOEL, academic administrator; b. Big Rock, Va., Aug. 12, 1937; s. Arthur Lionel Cecil and Drucie (Mullens) S.; m. Mona May Green Smith, Jan. 17, 1967; children: Emily Claire, Garrett Julian. BA, Bera Coll., 1962; MA, Ohio U., 1963; PhD, U. Mich., 1970. Instr. Ohio U., Athens, 1963-64; lectr. U. Md., Abroad, 1964-67; asst. prof. U. Wis., Madison, 1970-71; assoc. prof. Frostburg (Md.) State U., 1971-73, prof., 1973-87, English dept. head, 1972-80, dean Sch. Arts and Humanities, 1980-87; dean/provost for acad. affairs U. Houston, Victoria, Tex., 1987-93, provost, v.p. acad. affairs, 1995—; v.p., dean faculties West Ga. Coll., Carrollton, 1993-95; pres. S. Atlantic Assn. Depts. English, 1977-78; mem. Md. Humanities Coun., Balt., 1977-81; presenter profl. assns., 1970-95. Author short stories and poems, 1964-70; contbr. articles to profl. jours. Bd. dirs. Victoria Symphony, Carrollton Rotary; chair edn. divsn. United Way, Victoria. Fellow, grantee NEH, Washington, 1976, 77, 78, Mellon Found., 1981. Mem. Phi Kappa Phi, Phi Delta Kappa, Beta Gamma Sigma. Home: 409 Bloomingdale Victoria TX 77901 Office: Univ Houston-Victoria 2506 E Red River Victoria TX 77901

SMITH, DONALD EVERETT, city official; b. East Tallassee, Ala., May 25, 1945; s. Frankie (Smith) Kelly; m. Yvonne Haygood, Oct. 7, 1970; children: DaSharn, Sia, Donielle. BS in Child Devel., N.C. A&T State U., 1978, MS in Adult Edn. Adminstrn., 1987. Tchr. Head Start, Ala. Coun. Human Rels., Auburn, 1967-70; field svcs. and demonstration pre-sch. coord. Learning Inst. of N.C., Greensboro, 1970-75; ednl. tng. specialist Ctr. for Action Based Leadership Experiences, Greensboro, 1975-79; dir. Project Headstart Macon County Bd. Edn., Tuskegee, Ala., 1979-81; mgmt. tng. specialist N.C. A&T State U., Greensboro, 1981-83; pers. tng. specialist City of Greensboro, 1983-86, tng. dir., 1986-93, mgr. staffing and diversity, 1993—; cons. Project Head Start, region IV, HHS, Atlanta, 1979—, U. N.C. Fellows Program, Chapel Hill, 1991—; co-founder, cons. We Are One project. Mem. Community Unity Coun. Greensboro C. of C., 1976-77. Mem. Internat. Pers. Mgmt. Assn., N.C. Local Govt. Trainers Consortium. Office: City of Greensboro Phill McDonald Plz Greensboro NC 27402-3136

SMITH, DONALD RAY, magazine dealer; b. Louisville, Dec. 12, 1934; s. Henry Bland and Margaret Frances (Corbett) S. Ed. pvt. schs., Louisville. Clerk Huber & Huber Motor Express, Louisville, 1951-52, Retail Credit Co., Louisville, 1952-53, Louisville & Nashville R.R., Louisville, 1953-65; owner, appraiser, cons. Don Smith's Nat. Geog. Mags., Louisville, 1969—. Author: Nat. Geog. Mag. for Collectors, 1975, 2d edit., 1978, 3d rev. edit., 1985, 4th rev. edit., 1988, 5th rev. edit., 1992, 6th rev. edit., 1996, Gone With the Wagons, 1980; composer song My Dreams Desire Another Way, 1968, poem Calico Waltz, 1986, Beyond Repast, 1986, The Essence of Darkness, 1986, The Dominant Submissive, 1987, Agony's Prelude, 1987, The Unmoving Distance, 1988; price guide booklet for collectors of Nat. Geog. Mag.; also numerous pamphlets and articles on colecting mags. Democrat. Roman Catholic. Home and Office: 3930 Rankin St Louisville KY 40214-1748

SMITH, DONALD RAYMOND, librarian; b. Highland, Ill., Sept. 25, 1946; s. Raymond Stanley and Gladys Loraine (Martin) S.; m. Elaine Marie Neudecker, Apr. 12, 1969; 1 child, Benjamin Christopher. BA, Southern Ill. U., 1968, MA, 1972, MS, 1978; MLS, U. Mo., 1976. Acad. adv. So. Ill. U., Edwardsville, 1970-73, libr. instr., 1973-78, edn. libr., 1978-82; assoc. dir. pub. svc. and collection devel. U. Tulsa, 1982-88, assoc. dir. gen. svcs., 1988-93; dir. libr. N.E. La. U., Monroe, La., 1993-96; dean info. svcs. N.E. La. U., Monroe, 1996—; cons. Hayner Pub. Libr., Alton, Ill., 1977-82, Tulsa City County Libr., 1984; cons. facilitator Tulsa Area Libr. Coop., 1987-88, 90; collection evaulator Okla. Jr. Coll., Tulsa, 1984. Author: Newspaper Indexing Handbook, 1981; editor and compiler newspaper index, 1976-77. Cataloger Our Lady Queen of Peace Sch., Belleville, Ill., 1979-82; campaign worker Dem. Party, Belleville, 1972; chair bd. dirs. Tulsa Area Libr. Coop., 1991-93. With U.S. Army, 1969-70. Recipient Millicent C. Palmer award Friends of Lovejoy Library, So. Ill. U., 1974, H.W. Wilson scholar, 1974, Higher Edn. Coordinating Act grantee Ill. State Library, 1980-81, Workshop award U. Okla. Sch. Library Sci., 1984. Mem. ALA, Assn. Coll. and Rsch. Librs., Libr. Adminstrn. and Mgmt. Assn., Okla. Libr. Assn. (chmn. continuing edn. com. 1985-86, chmn. adminstrn. roundtable 1989-90, chair automation roundtable 1991-92), La. Libr. Assn. (sec. scholarship trust 1994—), La. Assn. Coll. & Rsch. Librs., Southeastern Libr. Assn., La. Acad. Libr. Info. Network Consortium (at-large exec. bd. mem. 1994-96), Trailblazer Libr. Dirs. Bd., NOTIS Users Group, OCLC Users Coun. Roman Catholic. Home: PO Box 15062 Monroe LA 71207-5062 Office: Sandel Libr NE La Library Monroe LA 71209-0720

SMITH, DONNA TRATNYEK, flight nurse, pediatric specialist nurse; b. Tacoma, Wash., May 29, 1965; d. Joseph Paul and Barbara Ann (Wirth) T. BSN, U. Pitts. Cert. in neonatal resuscitation, PALS, BTLS, BLS, ACLS; cert. EMT. Staff nurse, urology surgery Duke U. Med. Ctr., Durham, N.C., staff nurse, neonatal ICU, 1989-92, flight nurse on Duke Life Flight, 1992—. Mem. Nat. Assn. Neonatal Nurses, NFNA, AACN.

SMITH, DORIS CORINNE KEMP, retired nurse; b. Bogalusa, La., Nov. 22, 1919; d. Milton Jones and Maude Maria (Fortenberry) Kemp; m. Joseph William Smith, Oct. 13, 1940 (dec.). BS in Nursing, U. Colo., 1957, MS in Nursing Adminstrn., 1958. RN, Colo. Head nurse Chgo. Bridge & Iron Co., Morgan City, La., 1941-45, Shannon Hosp., San Angelo, Tex., 1945-50; dir. nursing Yoakum County Hosp., Denver City, Tex., 1951-52; hosp. supr. Med. Arts Hosp., Odessa, Tex., 1952-55; dir. insvc. edn. St. Anthony Hosp., Denver, 1961-66; coord. Sch. Vocat. Nursing, Kiamichi Area Vocat.-Tech. Nursing Sch., Wilburton, Okla., 1969-77; supr. non-ambulatory unit Lubbock (Tex.) State Sch., 1978-85, ret., 1985; mem. steering com. Western Interstate Commn. on Higher Edn. for Nurses, Denver, 1963-65; mem. curriculum and materials com. Okla. Bd. Vocat.-Tech. Edn., Stillwater, 1971-76; mem. Invitational Conf. To Plan Nursing for Future, Oklahoma City, 1976-77; mem. survey team to appraise Sch. of Vocat.-Tech. Edn. Schs. for Okla. Dept. Vocat.-Tech. Edn., 1975-76. Author, editor: Survey of Functions Expected of the General Duty Nurse, State of Colorado, 1958; co-editor: Curriculum Guides; contbr. numerous articles to profl. jours. Recipient citation of merit Okla. State U., 1976; named Woman of Yr. Sunrise chpt. Am. Bus. Women's Assn., 1994-95. Mem. AAAS, ANA (program co-chair 1996—), AAUW (life), Nat. League for Nursing, Tex. League for Nursing, Tex. Nurses Assn., Dist. 18 Nurses Assn., Tex. Employees Assn. (v.p. 1984-85), U. Colo. Alumni Assn., Am. Bus. Women's Assn. (pres. Lubbock chpt. 1986-87, rec. sec. 1989-90, edn. chair 1994-95, hospitality chair 1995-96), Bus. and Profl. Women's Assn. (sec. 1992-95), Chancellor's Club U. Colo., Pi Lambda Theta (sec. local chpt. 1957-58). Republican. Home: 2103 55th St Lubbock TX 79412-2612

SMITH, DOROTHY BRAND, retired librarian; b. Beaumont, Tex., Oct. 4, 1922; d. Robert and Lula (Jones) Brand; m. William E. Smith, June 15, 1941; children: Wilson B., Lurinda. BS in Social Sci., Lamar U., 1954; MLS, U., Tex., 1971. Tchr., Beaumont Ind. Sch. Dist., 1954-62; tchr. Austin (Tex.) Ind. Sch. Dist., 1962-66; libr. Galindo Elem. Sch., Austin, 1966-94; ret., 1994; cons. Edn. Svc. Ctr., Austin, 1974, 83; workshop leader Austin Ind. Schs., 1980; China del. Citizen Amb. Program People Internat., 1993. Author: Texas in Children's Books, a Bibliography, 1974. Recipient Siddle Joe Johnson award Children's Roundtable of Tex. Library Assn., 1984. Mem. ALA, AAUW, Tex. Libr. Assn. (life), Tex. State Tchrs. Assn. (life), Delta Kappa Gamma, Phi Delta Kappa. Presbyterian. Home: 6108 Mountainclimb Dr Austin TX 78731-3824

SMITH, DOROTHY GALE BATTON, oncological nurse; b. Minden, La., Nov. 30, 1945; d. James B. and Dorothy Alice (Shurtleff) Batton; m. Luis H. Rodriguez, Aug. 29, 1969 (div. Aug. 1976); 1 child, Rachel B.; m. Harold E. Smith, Mar. 20, 1982. BSN, N.E. La. State U., 1967; MSN, U. Colo., Denver, 1969. RN, Tex. Staff nurse U. Tex. M.D. Anderson Cancer Ctr., Houston, 1967-68, program dir. entero-therapy, 1974-83, nurse specialist entero-therapy and sex rehab., 1983-88, dir. nursing edn., 1988-93; asst. prof. Northwestern La. U., Shreveport, 1993-95; clin. coord. nursing svcs. Cheyenne Mountain Rehab., Colorado Springs, Colo., 1995—; asst. prof. Tex. Woman's U., Houston, 1969-71; assoc. prof. U. Ark., Little Rock, 1971-72; pres. Tex. Med. Ctr. Edn. Consortium, Houston, 1992, co-chair Golden Jubilee Quality of Life series, 1990-91. Editor Sexual Rehabilitation of Genito-urinary Oncology Patient, 1981, Ostomy Care and the Cancer Patient, 1986, Dimensions in Oncology Nursing, 1987-92, Jour. Entero Therapy Nursing, 1990-93; mem. rev. bd. RN mag., 1989—. Pres. Sunday School class, Meth. Ch., Houston, 1984-85; team mom softball, Houston, 1985-87, volleyball St. Agnes High Sch., 1989-91; vol. Tex. Spl. Olympics, 1992. Recipient Brown Found. Oncology award, Houston, 1985, Mara Mogensen Flaherty award Oncology Nursing Soc., 1991. Fellow Am. Acad. Nursing; mem. ANA, Internat. Assn. Entero Therapy (bd. mem. 1991-93, editor 1990-93, manuscript award 1989, 90), Tex. Med. Ctr. Ednl. Consortium (pres. 1992), Golden Jubilee Quality of Life Series (co-chair 1990-91), Am. Med. Writers Assn. (book award 1982), Am. Sex Educators and Counselors, Tex. Nurses Assn. Republican. Methodist. Office: Cheyenne Mountain Rehab 101 N Cascade Ave Ste 200 Colorado Springs CO 80903-1413

SMITH, DOROTHY LOUISE, pharmacy consultant, author; b. Regina, Sask., Can., Apr. 29, 1946; d. William Edward and Edna Irene (Libby) S. BS in Pharmacy, U. Saskatchewan, 1968; PharmD, U. Cin., 1972. Asst. prof. pharmacy U. B.C., Can., 1972-74; assoc. prof. clin. pharmacy U. Toronto, Ont., Can., 1974-80; coord. ambulatory pharmacy care Sunnybrook Med. Ctr., Toronto, 1974-79; dir. clin. affairs Am. Pharm. Assn., Washington, 1980-83; pres. Consumer Health Info. Corp., McLean, Va., 1983—; assoc. clin. prof. Sch. Pharmacy, Med. Coll. Va., 1991—; adj. assoc. prof. community and family medicine Georgetown U., Washington, 1983—. Author several books in field; contbr. articles to profl. jours. Mem. nat. bd. advisors Coll. Pharmacy, Ariz., 1987—. Fellow Am. Coll. Clin. Pharmacy, Am. Coll. Apothecaries; mem. Am. Soc. Hosp. Pharmacists, Am. Pharm. Assn. (chmn. policy com. on pub. affairs), Internat. Order Job's Daughters, Rotary. Presbyterian. Office: Consumer Health Info Corp 8300 Greensboro Dr Ste 1220 Mc Lean VA 22102-3604

SMITH, EDWARD JUDE, biologist; b. Serabu, Sierra Leone, Oct. 31, 1961; s. Karimu and Yemah (Brewah) S.; m. Gilceria Estandien Pimentel, Oct. 9, 1991; children: Dehmeh, Ngeindaloh. BSc, U. Sierra Leone, 1984; MSc, Oreg. State U., 1989, PhD, 1991. Rsch. asst. Oreg. State U., Corvallis, Oreg., 1987-91; postdoctoral rsch. assoc. Iowa State U., Ames, 1991-92; asst. prof. Tuskegee (Ala.) U., 1992—. Contbr. articles to profl. jours. Sec. Pace, Auburn, Ala., 1994. Mem. Am. Soc. Genetics, USDA (sec. 1994, pres. 1995). Roman Catholic. Home: 827 Cahaba Dr Auburn AL 36830 Office: Tuskegee U 109 Milbank Hall Tuskegee AL 36088

SMITH, EDWARD W.L., psychology educator, psychotherapist; b. South Bend, Ind., Sept. 13, 1942; s. Edward Howard and Luvina Adeline (Braland) S.; m. Lynda Lee Glore, June 19, 1965; children: Sandnes Lyn, Edward Shannon. Student, Grand View Coll., 1959-61; BA, Drake U., 1963; MS, U. Ky., 1966, PhD, 1969. Lic. psychologist, Ga. Mem. faculty psychology dept. Ga. State U., Atlanta, 1969-76; pvt. practice psychology Atlanta, 1976-94; prof. psychology, coord. clin. tng. Ga. So. U., Statesboro, 1994. Author: The Body in Psychotherapy, 1985, Sexual Aliveness, 1987; editor: The Growing Edge of Gestalt Therapy, 1976, Gestalt Voices, 1992; mem. editl. bd. Voices, 1976—, Pimgrimage, 1976-84, Jour. of Couples Therapy, 1988—. NDEA fellow, 1963-66. Fellow APA, Ga. Psychol. Assn.; mem. Am. Acad. Psychotherapists (chair tng. 1990-92), Internat. Soc. for Study of Symbols (pres. 1971-73), Phi Beta Kappa, Psi Chi. Office: Ga So U Dept Psychology Landrum Box 8041 Statesboro GA 30460-8041

SMITH, ELAINE CAMPBELL, editor, author; b. Fayetteville, Ark.; d. J.C. and O.I. (Rutherford) C.; m. Rodney P. Smith Jr.; children: Melissa Elaine, Rodney P. III. BA, Fla. State U., 1970, MA, 1997. Sr. editor Snap Mag., Tallahassee, Fla., 1989-92; editl. asst. Jour. Am. Statis. Assn.-Theory and Methods, Tallahassee, 1993—. Author: Fantasy Lover, 1984, A Wish Too Soon, 1985; contbr. stories to mags. Mem. Modern Lang. Assn. Home: 5587 WW Kelly Rd Tallahassee FL 32311

SMITH, ELIZABETH HEGEMAN, mental health therapist, hypnotherapist; b. Mineola, N.Y., Oct. 5, 1942; d. Andrew Burt and Ruth Eliza (Velsor) Hegeman; m. Lloyd W. Smith, June 11, 1966; children: Warren Willits, Lisa Velsor. BA, Adelphi U., 1964; MEd, Temple U., 1969. Cert. tchr., Pa.; registered hypnotherapist. Tchr. health, phys. edn. Friends Acad., Locust Valley, N.Y., 1964-66, Darby (Pa.)-Colwyn Schs., 1966-70; pvt. practice mental health therapy Wallingford, Pa., 1980-85, Charlotte, N.C., 1985—; cons. Dynamic Health Systems, Charlotte, 1989—. Mem. LWV, Wallingford, 1976-85; pres., editor Taxpayers for Quality Edn., Wallingford, 1976-85; chmn. Raintree Archtl. Rev. Com., Charlotte, 1989-91, com. mem., 1987-88; treas. Raintree Homeowners Assn. Mem. Am. Guild Hypnotherapists, Raintree Homeowners Assn. (treas. 1993-95, pres. 1995-96); Village of Raintree and the Southeast Coalition of Neighborhoods (pres. 1996—). Mem. Soc. of Friends. Home and Office: 3609 Windbluff Dr Charlotte NC 28277-9897

SMITH, ELIZABETH HULL, small business owner; b. Nuremburg, Fed. Republic Germany, Apr. 4, 1956; d. James Wells and Margaret Sue (Lewis) Hull; m. Keith Scott, Aug. 27, 1983; 1 child, Margaret Ann. BS in Therapeutic Recreation, U. Mo., 1978, postgrad., 1981; BSN, U. Colo., 1990, MS in Health Adminstrn., 1993, MBA, 1993. Recreational therapist Crittenton Ctr., Kans. City, 1979-81; med. auditor Claim Cons., Inc., Massapequa, N.Y., 1983-88; recreation socialization planner Sussex County Welfare Bd., Sussex, 1983-87; owner, pres., med. auditor Med. Audit, Inc., Denver and Dallas, Colo.; charter mem. Douglas County Bus. & Profl. Women. Bd. dirs. Children's Diabetes Found.; treas. Am. Diabetes Assn., 1991-93; mem. Dallas Children's Med. Aux., Dallas Symphony Orch. League. Merit scholar Colo., 1989, Rose Med. Ctr. Nursing scholar, 1989. Mem. DAR, Jr. League Dallas, Denver Ctr. Alliance (bd. dirs. 1990—), Am. Diabetes Assn. Aux. (treas. 1991-93), Children's Diabetes Guild (bd. dirs.), Assn. Hosp. Internal Auditors, Hosp. Fin. Mgmt. Assn., Pi Beta Phi. Home: 4437 Druid Ln Dallas TX 75205-1030

SMITH, ELIZABETH SHELTON, art educator; b. Washington, Feb. 12, 1924; d. Benjamin Warren and Sarah Priscilla (Harrell) Shelton; m. John Edwin Smith, Aug. 16, 1947 (dec. July 1992); children: Shelley Hobson, Dale Henslee, John Edwin Jr.; m. Headley Morris Cox Jr., Dec. 30, 1994. BA in Art, Meredith Coll., 1946; MEd in Supervision and Adminstrn., Clemson U., 1974. Youth dir. St. John's Bapt. Ch., Charlotte, N.C., 1946-47; art tchr. Raleigh (N.C.) Pub. Schs., 1947-49, East Mecklenberg H.S., Charlotte, 1968-69, D. W. Daniel H.S., Central, S.C., 1970-86; art instr. U. S.C., Columbia, 1966-68; adj. prof. Clemson (S.C.) U., 1991-93; artist-in-residence edn. program S.C. Arts Commn., Columbia, 1991—. Exhibited in numerous one and two person shows and in group exhibits, 1946—. Vol. worker, editor newsletter Pickens County Habitat for Humanity, Clemson, 1981—; vol. art tchr. St. Andrew's Elem. Sch., Columbia, 1962-68. Named S.C. Tchr. of Yr., S.C. Dept. Edn. and Ency. Britannica, 1976, Citizen of Yr. Clemson Rotary Club, 1979, Disting. Alumna award Meredith Coll., 1996. Mem. S.C. Art Edn. Assn. (pres. 1978, Lifetime Svc. award 1990, Lifetime Achievement in Art Edn. award 1995), Nat. Art Edn. Assn. (ret. art educator affiliate, pres. 1994, Disting. Svc. award 1995), S.C. Watercolor Soc., Upstate Visual Artists (Best in Show award). Baptist. Home: 1604 Six Mile Hwy Central SC 29630-9483

SMITH, ELOUISE BEARD, restaurant owner; b. Richmond, Tex., Jan. 8, 1920; d. Lee Roy and Ruby Myrtle (Foy) Beard; m. Omar Smith, Nov. 27, 1940 (dec. July 1981); children: Mary Jean Smith Cherry, Terry Omar, Don Alan. Student, Tex. Womens U., 1937-39. Sec. First Nat. Bank, Rosenberg, Tex., 1939-41; owner Smith Dairy Queen, Bryan, Tex., 1947—. Author: The Haunted House, 1986; editor The College Widow, 1986. Omar and Elouise Beard Smith chair named in her honor Tex. A&M U., College Station, 1983, Elouise Beard Smith Human Performance Labs. named in her honor Tex. A&M U., 1984. Mem. AAUW. Republican. Baptist. Home: 411 Crescent Dr Bryan TX 77801-3712 Office: Metro Ctr 3833 S Texas Ave Bryan TX 77802-4039

SMITH, ELTON EDWARD, clergyman, religious studies educator; b. N.Y.C., Nov. 9, 1915; s. Elton Herbert Sherow and Christine (Conway) S.; m. Esther Greenwell, Oct. 17, 1942; children: Elton Greenwell, Esther Smith Shaw, Stephen Lloyd. BS, NYU, 1939; BDiv, Andover Newton Theol. Sem., 1940; MST, Harvard U., 1940; PhD, Syracuse U., 1961; DD (hon.), Berkeley Div. & Linfield Coll., 1960. Ordained min. Am. Bapt. Conv., 1940. Pastor various chs. in Mass., N.Y., Oreg., 1940-61; prof. Brit. lit. and the Bible U. South Fla., Tampa, 1961—, Askounes-Ashford Disting. faculty scholar, 1988; Legis. Gt. Tchr. Bible U. South Fla., Tampa, 1990; disting. prof. British lit. U. South Fla., 1994—; vis. lectr. U. Paris, 1982, U. London, 1983; sr. Fulbright lectr. U. Algiers, 1969-70, Mohammed Univ., Rabat, Morocco, 1974-75; outside reader, cons. MLA, CLIO, Victorian Studies, U. Fla. Press, Case Western Res. U. Press, Harcourt Brace Jovanovich; Bible lectr. to over 50 chs. and colls. Author: The Two Voices: A Tennyson Study, 1964, (with E.M.G. Smith) William Godwin, 1965, Louis MacNeice, 1970, The Angry Young Men of the Thirties: Day Lewis, MacNeice, Spender, Auden, 1975, Charles Reade, 1976; contbr. articles to profl. jours. Named Disting. Prof. U. South Fla., 1994. Mem. MLA, AAUP, South Atlantic MLA, Southeastern Nineteenth-Century Studies, Conf. on Christianity and Lit. Home: 14714 Oak Vine Dr Lutz FL 33549-3229 Office: U South Fla English Dept Tampa FL 33620

SMITH, EMMITT J., III, professional football player; b. Pensacola, Fla., May 15, 1969; s. Emmitt Jr. and Mary Smith. Student, U. Fla. With Dallas Cowboys, 1990—; player Pro-Bowl, 1990-92, NFC Championship game, 1992, 93, Super Bowl XXVII, 1992, Super Bowl XXVIII, 1993; owner Emmitt Inc. Recipient MVP award for season, 1993, MVP award for Super Bowl, 1993; named Running Back, Sporting News Coll. All-Am. team, 1989, Offensive Rookie of Yr., 1990, Running Back, Sporting News NFL All-Pro team, 1992, 93, NFL Player of Yr., Sporting News, 1993; named to Pro-Bowl, 1993, 95. Office: Dallas Cowboys One Cowboys Pky Irving TX 75063*

SMITH, EUGENIA SEWELL, funeral home executive; b. Albany, Ky., Oct. 24, 1922; d. Leo Matheny and Marjorie (Warinner) Sewell; m. James Frederick Smith, June 25, 1948; 1 child, Bryson Sewell (dec.). Student Berea Coll., 1937-41, Bowling Green Coll. Commerce, 1944-45. Owner, operator Sewell Funeral Home, Albany, 1977—; bd. dir. Citizens Bank of Albany, Ky., 1989—. Sec. Albany Woman's Club, 1950-54; den mother Cub Scouts, Boy Scouts Am., 1958-62; pres. Clinton County Homemakers, Albany, 1968-70, Modern Homemakers, 1992-94; mission action chmn. Missionary Baptist Ch., 1965-91; v.p. Modern Homemakers Club of Albany, 1990-92. Democrat. Lodge: Demolay Mother's (pres. Albany club 1966-67), Order Eastern Star (former assoc. conductress, former Martha and Esther). Home: RR 5 Box 104 Burkesville Rd Albany KY 42602-9310 Office: Sewell Funeral Home 115 Cross St Albany KY 42602

SMITH, EVANS LANSING, English language educator; b. Balt., Aug. 23, 1950; s. Henry Evans and Jane Lansing (Moller) S.; m. Michelle Ruppert, Oct. 21, 1984; children: Anita, Carly, Angela. BA in English, Williams Coll., 1973; MA in Creative Writing, Antioch Internat., 1977; MA in English, Claremont Grad. Sch., 1980, PhD in English, 1986. Prof. English Franklin Coll., Lugano, Switzerland, 1986-88, Anne Arundel C.C., Arnold, Md., 1988-90; assoc. prof. English Midwestern State U., Wichita Falls, Tex., 1990—; lectr. in field. Contbr. 4 books and 12 articles to profl. publs. Office: Midwestern State U English Dept 3400 Taft Blvd Wichita Falls TX 76308-2036

SMITH, EVELYN ELAINE, language educator; b. Waco, Tex., July 25, 1952; d. Walstein Bennett and Evelyn Daugherty (Box) S. BA, Baylor U., 1974, MA, 1979, PhD, 1995. Cert. secondary tchr., Tex. Grad. asst. Baylor U., Waco, Tex., 1975, proofreader, 1980, rsch. assoc., 1981-86; reporter Killeen (Tex.) Daily Herald, 1981; writing tchr. Waco (Tex.) Ind. Sch. Dist., 1989-90; grad. asst. Tex. Christian U., Ft. Worth, 1992-93; adj. prof. English McLennan C.C., Waco, Tex., 1993-94; adj. instr. English Tex. State Tech. Coll., Waco, 1993-94, 96—; instr. English Hill Coll., Hillsboro, Tex., 1997. Contbr. articles to profl. jours. Bd. dirs., newsletter editor Historic Waco Found., 1981-85, sec., exec., mem. nominating coms., 1994-96. Mem. Am. Studies Assn. Tex., Nat. Conf. Tchrs. English, Conf. Coll. Composition and Comm., MLA, S. Ctrl. Modern Lang. Assn. Democrat. Mem. So. Bapt. Ch. Home: 5848 Mt Rockwood Waco TX 76710 Office: Tex State Tech Coll Dept English 3801 Campus Dr Waco TX 76705 also: Hill Coll Humanities PO Box 619 Hillsboro TX 76645

SMITH, FORREST ALLEN, business owner, graphic artist; b. Memphis, Dec. 10, 1946; s. Forrest Nubern and Dorothy Allene (Escue) S.; m. Lynda Carol Shaddix, May 28, 1966; 1 child, Leigh Michelle. Student, U. Memphis. Profl. camera operator Mercury Printing Co., Memphis, 1966, 73; shift supr. Holiday Press, Olive Branch, Miss., 1973-80; pre-press dept. mgr. Lithograph Printing & Pub., Memphis, 1980-93; founder, owner, ops. mgr. Family Graphics, Memphis, 1993—. Author: They Call Me Good Luck Charley, 1983. Activities chmn. Frayser Jaycees, Memphis, 1967-76; Boy Scouts dist. rep. Boy Scouts Am., Memphis Chickasaw Coun., 1968-76; dist. vol. Republican Com. in Southeast Memphis, 1990-96; dist. vol. Nat. Diabetes Assn., Memphis, 1995-96. Recipient Silver Beaver award Boy Scouts Am. Chickasaw Coun., 1972, Jaycees of Month award Frayser Jaycees, 1972, 74. Mem. Nat. Assn. Desktop Pubs. Republican. Baptist. Home and Office: Family Graphics 4579 Tracy Lynn Dr Memphis TN 38125

SMITH, FRED DEMPSEY, JR., lawyer; b. Mt. Airy, N.C., June 2, 1947; s. Fred Dempsey and Agnes Maybelle (Smith) S.; children: Emily Hope, Jenny Noel, Davis Sheffney. BA, U. Richmond, 1969; JD, U. Va., 1972. Bar: Va. 1976, U.S. Dist. Ct. (we. dist.) Va. 1977, U.S. Ct. Appeals 1980, U.S. Supreme Ct. 1981, U.S. Dist. Ct. (ea. dist.) Va. 1987. Prosecutor Henry County Commonwealth's Atty's. Office, Martinsville, Va., 1972-77; pvt. practice law Martinsville, 1977, 80-82, 85-87, 89—; ptnr. Gendron, Kirby & Smith, Martinsville, 1977-80; pres. Hartley & Smith, P.C., Martinsville, 1983-85; ptnr. Minor & Smith, Richmond, Va., 1987-88; mem. civil trial adv. Nat. Bd. Trial Advocacy. Contbr. article and seminar materials to legal publs. Mem. Henry County Dem. Com., 1975-76, candidate Va. Gen. Assembly, 1977; active Piedmont Regional Mental Health & Mental Retardation, Martinsville, 1975-83. Capt. JAGC, USAR, 1972-77. Recipient Appreciationcert. Gov. Va., 1971. Mem. ABA, Va. State Bar Assn., Assn. Trial Lawyers, Va. Trial Lawyers Assn. (bd. govs. 1983-90, mem. continuing legal edn. com. 1986-87, publ. com. 1984-85, amicus curiae 1988-90, chmn. ann. conv. 1990), Martinsville & Henry County Bar Assn. (v.p., pres. 1986-87). Mem. Disciples of Christ. Office: Young Haskins Mann Gregory PO Box 72 Martinsville VA 24114

SMITH, FREDERICK WALLACE, transportation company executive; b. Marks, Miss., Aug. 11, 1944; s. Frederick Smith; m. Diane Avis. Grad., Yale U., 1966. Cert. comml. pilot. Owner Ark Aviation, 1969-71; founder, pres. Fed. Express Corp., Memphis, 1971—, chmn. bd., pres, CEO, 1975—. Served with USMC, 1966-70. Office: Fed Express Corp 2005 Corporate Ave PO Box 727 Memphis TN 38132

SMITH, GARY LEE, process and design engineer; b. Roanoke, Va., Nov. 9, 1959; s. John Thomas Jr. and Anna Mae (Sult) S. AS in Edn., Bus. Adminstrn., Sci., Va. Western C. C., 1980; BS in Chemistry & BA in Philosophy, Roanoke Coll., 1982; postgrad., Calif. Coast U. Environ. lab. technician Centec Corp. Analytical Svcs. Div., Salem, Va., 1979-81; environ. chemist Centec Corp. Analytical Svcs. Div., 1985; process ops. engr. IT&T Electro Optical Products Div., Roanoke, 1985-87; environ. chemist Environ. Options Inc., Rocky Mount, Va., 1987-88; sr. rsch. & devel. engr. Ni-Tec Optic Elec. Corp., Garland, Tex., 1988-91; sr. process engr. Silicon Materials Svc./Air Products, Garland, Tex., 1991-95; prin. design engr. Ball Aerospace - NASA - Goddard S.F.C., Boulder, Colo., 1995—. Trauma med. tech.

Roanoke Life Saving Crew, Inc., 1973-79; woodland search & rescue Civil Air Patrol, Roanoke, 1971-73. With U.S. Army Med. Corps., 1982-84. Recipient Freshman Chemistry & Physics award Chem. Rubber Co., 1980. Mem. Electrochem. Soc., Am. Inst. Physics, Am. Geophys. Union (life mem.), Am. Chem. Soc., NRA, Am. Vacuum Soc. Republican. Home: 1606 S Coffman Longmont CO 80501

SMITH, GEORGANNE MORRIS, nursing administrator, nursing educator, psychiatric-mental health consultant; b. Dayton, Ohio, Dec. 23, 1939; d. Arthur McKinley and Fannie Thelma (Shroyer) Morris; children: Heather Lee, Kimberly Reneé. BSN, Ohio State U., 1963; postgrad., Wright State U., 1983-85; MS in Nursing Svc. Adminstrn., U. So. Miss., 1989. Cert. psychiat.-mental health nurse ANA. Several med. positions, 1960-75; asst. dir. insvc. edn. Grandview Hosp., Dayton, Ohio, 1975-79; asst. dir. nursing svc. Kettering (Ohio) Convalescent Ctr., 1979; PSRO nurse reviewer long-term care Region II Med. Rev. Corp., Dayton, 1979-81; psychiat. nurse VA Med. Ctr., Dayton, 1981-85; chem. dependency nurse Gulf Oak Hosp., Biloxi, Miss., 1987-88; psychiat.-mental health nurse cons., contract home health nurse Quality Home Health Care, Biloxi, 1988-90; clin. instr. Miss. Gulf Coast Community Coll., Gulfport, 1989-90; contract home health nurse Coastal Plains Pub. Health Dist. IX, Miss. State Dept Health, Gulfport, 1989-90; dir. quality assurance/edn. Profl. Home Health Agy., Biloxi, 1990; dir. nursing Sand Hill Hosp., Gulfport, 1990—; adj. clin. faculty William Carey Coll., Gulfport, 1990, night shift charge nurse med.-surg. and psychiatry Biloxi Regional Med. Ctr., 1992-95; vol. regional liaison officer peer assistance program Ohio Nurses Assn., 1983-85, La. Nurses' Network Impaired Profls. La. State Nurses Assn., 1990. Vol. divsn. probation Harrison County Family Ct., 1990-92, ARC Disaster Health Svcs., 1994—, Keesler AFB Health Promotion Program, 1995-96, ARC Blood Svc., 1996. Mem. ANA, Miss. Nurses Assn., Ohio Nurses Assn., Ohio State U. Sch. Nursing Alumni Assn., Sigma Theta Tau, Gamma Beta Phi. Home: 2434 W Shore Dr Biloxi MS 39532-3022

SMITH, GEORGE LOUIS, research scientist; b. Raleigh, N.C., Jan. 7, 1938; s. Louis Norman and Viola Ruth (Rogerson) S.; m. Olivia Parrilee, June 25, 1960; children: Joni Lynn, Diann Patsy, Laurie Ruth. BS in Aero. Engring., Va. Poly. Inst. & State U., 1960, MS in Aerospace Engring., 1963, PhD in Aerospace Engring., 1968. Rsch. scientist, engr. Langley Rsch. Ctr. NASA, Hampton, Va., 1960—; internat. scanner radiation sci. working group Centre Nationale Etudes Spatiale, Paris, 1995—; investigator Earth Radiation Budget Sci. Team, Goddard Space Flight Ctr., Beltsville, Md., 1975-83, Earth Radiation Budget Experiment Sci. Team, Langley Rsch. Ctr., Hampton, 1979-92, Clouds and Earth Radiation Energy Sci. Team, Langley Rsch. Ctr., Hampton, 1990—. Contbr. numerous rsch. articles to profl. jours. Mem. Am. Meteorol. Soc., Am. Geophysical Union, Yorktown (Va.) Rotary Club.

SMITH, GEORGE ROBERT, JR., family physician; b. Caswell County, N.C., Jan. 14, 1927; s. George Robert and Louise (Jones) S.; m. Mildred Hodges; children: George Robert III, Julia A., Mary B., Linda L. BS, U. N.C., 1951; MD, Harvard U., Boston, 1953. Diplomate Am. Bd. Family Physicians (Award of Merit). Intern, resident Med. Coll. Va., Richmond, 1953-55; founder, owner Alleghany Clinic Inc., Shawsville, Va., 1955-94; physician Lewis Gale Clinic/Shawsville Family Practice Ctr., 1994—; pres., chmn. bd. Va. Health Quality Ctr., Richmond, 1993—; bd. dirs. Premier Bank Shares, Bluefield, Va.; chmn. bd. dirs. Premier Trust Co., Bluefield, 1996—; founder, chmn., pres. Meadowbrook, Inc., 1962-86, bd. dirs., 1962—. Pres. Shawsville Raritan Club, 1960—; bd. visitors Radford (Va.) U., 1992-96. With USN, 1944-45. Mem. AMA, Med. Soc. Va. (del. 1962—), Am. Acad. Family Physicians (pres. 1977-78), Va. Acad. Family Physicians, Masons, Shriner. Methodist. Home: 4330 Pair-o-Docs Ln Shawsville VA 24162 Office: Shawsville Family Practice Ctr PO Box 467 Shawsville VA 24162

SMITH, GEORGE THORNEWELL, retired state supreme court justice; b. Camilla, Ga., Oct. 15, 1916; s. George C. and Rosa (Gray) S.; m. Eloise Taylor, Sept. 1, 1943 (dec.). Grad., Abraham Baldwin Agrl. Coll., 1940; LLB, U. Ga., 1948. Bar: Ga. 1947. Assoc. Cain & Smith, Cairo, Ga., 1947-71; city atty. Cairo, 1949-58; atty. Grady County, 1950-59; solicitor Cairo City Ct., 1951-59; mem. Ga. Ho. of Reps., 1959-67, speaker of the house, 1963-67; lt. gov. State of Ga., 1967-71; city atty. East Point, Ga., 1973-76; judge Ga. Ct. Appeals, 1976-81; justice Ga. Supreme Ct., Atlanta, 1981-91, presiding justice, 1990-91; of counsel Barnes, Browning Tanksley and Casurella, Marietta, Ga., 1992—; past mem. exec. com. Nat. Conf. Appellate Judges; vice chmn. Nat. Conf. Lt. Govs. Trustee Nat. Arthritis Found. Lt. comdr. USN, 1940-45. Only person in the state's history to serve in an elective capacity in all 3 brs. of govt. Mem. State Bar Ga., Cobb County Bar Assn., Lawyers Club Atlanta, Am. Legion, VFW, Moose, Kiwanis. Office: Barnes Browning Tanksley and Casurella 166 Anderson St Ste 225 Marietta GA 30060-1984

SMITH, GERALDINE FIELD, medical/surgical nurse; b. Talequah, Okla., Dec. 11, 1955; d. Crosslin Field and Glenna E. (Foster) S. BSN, Okla. U., 1982. Staff nurse med./surg. floor Gallup Pub. health Svc., Indian Med. Ctr., Gallup, N.Mex., 1982-83; staff nurse/med./surg./emergency rm. W.W. Hastings Hosp., Talequah, 1983-84; patient instr. W.W. Hastings Hosp., 1983-94, med. quality assurance asst., 1988—. Mem. ANA, Am. Diabetes Assn., Epilepsy Found. Am., Okla. Nurses Assn.

SMITH, GERI GARRETT, nurse educator; b. Brownsville, Tenn., Nov. 21, 1948; d. F.G. and Willie Mae (Morris) Garrett; m. Lu Smith, Dec. 20, 1967 (dec.); children: Taylor, Alexandra, Amber; m. Tom Jeanes, July 16, 1984; children: Zachary, Garrett. BSN, U. Tenn., Memphis, 1987; MSN, U. Memphis, 1989; MS, Memphis State U., 1978; BS, U. Tenn., Martin, 1970. RN, Tenn.; NCAST instr.; cert. tchr., Fla., Tenn., Tex. Tchr. Aldine Schs., Houston, 1972-74, 1972-74; tchr. Shelby County Schs., Memphis, 1977-85; sch. nurse Memphis Shelby County Health Dept., Memphis, 1987-89, nurse supr. new mothers program, 1989-94; asst. prof. Sch. Nursing Union U., 1993—. Mem. NAACOG, ICEA, Tenn. Nurses Assn., Tenn. Pub. Health Assn., Sigma Theta Tau. Home: 70 Grassland Dr Jackson TN 38305

SMITH, GRANT WARREN, II, university administrator, physical sciences educator; b. Kansas City, Mo., Jan. 21, 1941; m. Constance M. Krambeer, 1962; 1 child, Grant Warren III. BA, Grinnell Coll., 1962; PhD, Cornell U., 1966, postgrad., 1967. Asst. prof. chemistry Cornell U., Ithaca, N.Y., 1966-68, vis. prof., Am. Council on Edn. fellow, 1973-74; assoc. prof. U. Alaska, Fairbanks, 1968-77, prof., 1977-78, head dept. chemistry and chem. engring., 1968-73, acting head dept. gen. sci., 1972-73; pres. univ. assembly U. Alaska System, 1976-77; prof. phys. scis., dean Sch. Scis. and Techs. U. Houston, Clear Lake, 1979-84; prof. chemistry Southeastern La. U., Hammond, 1984-95, honors prof. arts and scis., 1995—, v.p. for acad. affairs, 1984-86, pres., 1986—. Bd. dirs. Houston Area Research Ctr., 1982-83; violinist, pres. exec. bd. Clear Lake Symphony, 1980-84. NIH fellow, 1963-66, DuPont fellow, 1967. Fellow Royal Soc. Chemistry (London, chartered chemist), Explorers Club; mem. Am. Assn. Higher Edn., Am. Assn. Univ. Adminstrs. (bd. dirs. 1982-85, 86-88, v.p. 1988-90), AAAS, Am. Chem. Soc., Internat. Assn. Univ. Pres., Soc. Econ. Botany, Am. Soc. Pharmacognosy, Ethnopharmacology Soc., Soc. of Ethnobiology, Nat. Speleological Soc., Am. Spelean History Assn., Arctic Inst. N.Am., Hammond C. of C. (bd. dirs. 1988-90), Rotary, Sigma Xi, Phi Kappa Phi, Beta Gamma Sigma, Phi Eta Sigma. Office: Southeastern La U # 942 Hammond LA 70402

SMITH, GREGORY MARSHALL, sports editor, communications executive; b. Somerville, Mass., Apr. 25, 1967; s. Eric Ronald and Gail Frances (Wheaton) S. BA in Journalism, Prairie View (Tex.) A&M U., 1989. Cert. paralegal PCDI, Tex. Telemarketer BBC Group, Bedford, Tex., 1984-85; mng. editor Prairie View (Tex.) Panther, 1986-87; editor-in-chief Prarie View (Tex.) Panther, 1987-89; sports writer Bryan-Coll. Sta. Eagle, Bryan, Tex., 1988-89; profl. bodyguard Asset Protection Team, Oakton, Va., 1993-94; exec. security specialist Nat. Bodyguard Assn., Dallas, 1994; pres. Tangent Comm. Corp., Fort Worth, 1993—; sport editor supr. ON TV, Arlington, Tex., 1994—. editor news column Time Out for Sports, 1994-96; columnist The In Between Side, 1983-85; author: (book short stories) Crawl, 1996, The Root Faith Hope & Charity, 1996; editor Internet Web Site The Ultimate Sports Weekend, 1996. Recipient Cmty. Svc. award Prairie View, Tex., 1989. Mem. Soc. Profl. Journalists. Episcopalian. Home: 4129 Staghorn Cir N Fort Worth TX 76137

SMITH, GREGORY STUART, lawyer; b. Wilmington, Del., Feb. 24, 1959; s. William Channing and Barbara (Verne) S. BA with honors, Wake Forest U., 1981; JD with honors, U. N.C., 1985. Jud. clk. Hon. Eugene A. Gordon, Greensboro, N.C., 1985-86; assoc. King & Spalding, Atlanta, 1986-90; atty. Fed. Defender Program, Atlanta, 1990—. Mem. ABA (ho. dels., criminal justice sect., exec. coun.), NACDL, Am. Judicature Soc., Ga. State Bar, Atlanta Bar Assn. (treas.), Atlanta Coun. Young Lawyers (past pres.), Atlanta Vol. Lawyers Found. (past pres.), Leadership Ga. Democrat. Episcopalian. Home: 1930 Dellwood Dr NW Atlanta GA 30309-1257 Office: Fed Defender Program 101 Marietta St NW Ste 3512 Atlanta GA 30303-2711

SMITH, HAROLD ALLEN, educational administrator, researcher, educator; b. Franklin, La., Nov. 28, 1944; s. Bernie Lloyd and Lily Madge (Thompson) S.; m. Pheny Shang Fen Zhou, May 27, 1985. MusB in Edn., Delta State U., 1966; MDiv, New Orleans Bapt. Theol. Sem., 1977; MEd, Ariz. State U., 1984; EdD, Miss. State U., 1989. Educator Matthews/Doniphan (Mo.) Schs., 1966-70, Phoenix Pub. Schs., 1970-71; pvt. sch. educator John Curtis Schs., New Orleans, 1974-77; founder, dir. Chattanooga Assn. for Resettlement, 1977-83; adult educator Phoenix Union High Sch. Dist., 1983-84; vis. prof. Cen. Fgn. Expert Bur., Beijing, People's Republic of China, 1984-86; dir. China study program Miss. State U., 1986-90, editor Internat. Newsletter, 1987-89, program coord. Asian Studies Ctr., 1990-92; editor Miss. Meets Asia, 1990-92; program coord. ESL Ctr., 1991-92; prof. Shenandoah U., 1993—; cons. AMG Internat., Chattanooga, 1977-79, Chattanooga Area Literacy Movement, 1979-83; vis. prof. Georgetown U., 1992—, Notre Dame Seishin Coll. (Japan), 1993. Author: Education and Culture in China, 1988, Mississippi Agriculture and World Hunger, 1988; editor: International Experience and Relationships, 1988, International Student Handbook, 1991, AMTESOL Newsletter, 1991-92, AMTESOL Jour., 1991-92; contbr. numerous articles to profl. jours. Bd. dirs. Chattanooga Area Literacy Movement, 1979-83, Maricopa Refugee Com., Phoenix, 1983-84. With U.S. Army, 1971-74. Mem. NAFSA: Assn. Internat. Educators, Tchrs. of English to Speakers of Other Langs., Japan Assn. Of Lang. Tchrs., Washington Area Tchrs. of English to Speakers of Other Langs., Ala.-Miss. Tchrs. of English to Speakers of Other Langs., Assn. Tchr. Educators, Mid-South Edn. Rsch. Assn., Assn. Multicultural Counseling and Devel., Assn. Comparative and Internat. Edn. (also So. and Western orgns.), Ea. Ednl. Rsch. Assn., Kiwanis (bd. dirs. breakfast club Starkville, Miss. chpt. 1988-89), Phi Delta Kappa. Republican. Baptist. Office: Shenandoah U 1460 University Dr Winchester VA 22601-5100

SMITH, HARRISON HARVEY, journalism consultant; b. Wilkes-Barre, Pa., Oct. 24, 1915; s. Ernest Gray and Marjorie (Harvey) S.; m. Joanne Christopher, June 7, 1940 (div.); children: Barbara DeWitt, Marjorie Harvey, Susan C.; m. Margaret Simons, July 18, 1947 (dec. May 1978); children: Rosanne Jameson, Elizabeth Simons; m. Dorothy Wright Welborn, June 22, 1989. Diploma in lit., Wyoming (Pa.) Sem., 1936; postgrad., Northwestern U., 1937-38. Asst. to pub. Wilkes-Barre Times-Leader, 1938-39, v.p., asst. sec., 1939-46, pres., 1946-79; editor Wilkes-Barre Record, 1962-72; newspaper cons. Key Biscayne, Fla., 1979—; dir. emeritus 1st Ea. Bank Wilkes-Barre; pres. Pa. AP, 1953. Chmn. Wyoming Valley ARC, 1954-55; v.p. bd. dirs. Wilkes-Barre Gen. Hosp., 1954-76. With U.S. Army, 1945-46, Korea. Mem. Am. Soc. Newspaper Editors, Nat. Conf. Editl. Writers, Soc. Profl. Journalists, Pa. Newspaper Pubs. Assn. (exec. com. 1954-62), Wyoming Valley Hist. Soc. (pres. 1971-74), Newcomen Soc., Am. Legion, VFW, Poor Richard Club (Phila.), Mirador Club (Geneva), Westmoreland Club, Sankaty Head Golf and Beach Club (Nantucket Island, Mass.), Country Club Coral Gables, Key Biscayne Yacht Club, Masons (33d degree). Republican. Presbyterian. Home and Office: 177 Ocean Lane Dr Apt 811 Key Biscayne FL 33149-1427 also: 10 Lyons Ln PO Box 180 Siasconset MA 02564-0180

SMITH, HARRY DELANO, educational administrator; b. Florence, Ala., June 10, 1954; s. Cornelius Everett and Nadine (Olive) S.; m. Wanda Joy Skipworth, Nov. 23, 1978; children: Benjamin Delano, Rebekah Joy. BS, U. North Ala., 1975, MA, 1977, EdS, 1983; EdD, U. Ala., Tuscaloosa, 1989. Cert. class AA supr.-prin., Ala. Exec. dir. Christian Student Ctr., Florence, 1980-83; head dept. math. Mars Hill Bible Sch., Florence, 1983-87; tchr. math. and physics Muscle Shoals (Ala.) High Sch., 1975-80, asst. prin., 1987-88, prin., 1989—; farmer, Killen, Ala., 1974-80; tchr. summer sch. Sheffield (Ala.) High Sch., 1977-78; dir. scholars program Muscle Shoals Schs., 1987-88; asst. prin. Avalon Mid. Sch., Muscle Shoals, 1987-88, prin., 1988-89; math. cons. Cartersville (Ga.) City Schs., 1991-92; curriculum cons. Eufaula (Ala.) High Sch., 1991-92; co-chmn. Ala. Learner Outcomes Com., Montgomery, 1991-92; dist. judge All-State Acad. Team, Athens, Ala., 1991-92; coach Ala. Mathcounts team NSPE, Birmingham, 1985. Dir. music and edn. Shoals Ch. of Christ, 1992. Named Outstanding Young Educator, No. Dist. Ala. Jaycees, 1987; Beeson fellow Samford U., 1987. Mem. ASCD, Nat. Assn. Secondary Sch. Prins., Am. Assn. Sch. Adminstrs., Ala. Coun. Sch. Adminstrs. and Suprs., Ala. Assn. Secondary Sch. Prins., Kappa Delta Pi, Phi Kappa Phi. Home: 1403 Brookford Pl Muscle Shoals AL 35661-2670 Office: Muscle Shoals High Sch 100 E Trojan Dr Muscle Shoals AL 35661-3173*

SMITH, HAZEL GWYNN, elementary school educator; b. Jackson, Miss., Aug. 25, 1945; d. Clarence Elwin and Hazel Elizabeth (Weber) Speed; m. David J. Smith, Apr. 21, 1978; stepchildren: David J. Jr., Jamie Elaine. BS in Edn., Miss. Coll., 1969; MA, Western Ky. U., 1973; Ed. specialist, Ga. So. U., 1995. Cert. tchr., Ga. Tchr. Hinds County Sch. System, Clinton, Miss., 1969-70, Clinton (Miss.) Separate Sch. Dist., 1970-71, Glynn County Sch. System, Brunswick, Ga., 1973-80, Liberty County Sch. System, Hinesville, Ga., 1980—. Named Tchr. of the Yr., Liberty Elem. Sch., 1991-92. Mem. NEA, DAR, Phi Delta Kappa, Alpha Delta Kappa. Home: 55 Gum Dr Midway GA 31320-9658

SMITH, HOWARD BRECKINRIDGE, art, design educator; b. Lexington, Va., May 8, 1953; s. Oliver Wendell and Mildred Louise (Markham) S.; m. Karen Stephanie, June 6, 1992. BA, Averett Coll., 1980; MFA, U. N.C., Greensboro, 1982. Exhibit design tech. N.C. Zool. Park, Asheboro, N.C., 1983-88; asst. prof. art Campbell U., Buies Creek, N.C., 1988—. N.C. Arts Coun. fellow, Raleigh, 1989-90. Mem. Coll. Art Assn. Democrat. Home: 208 Round About Rd Holly Springs NC 27540 Office: Campbell Univ Art Dept Buies Creek NC 27506

SMITH, HOWARD EDWARD, chemistry educator; b. San Francisco, Aug. 1, 1925; s. Charles Augustus and Gertrude Bernadette (Higgins) S.; m. Louise Meier, Nov. 18, 1960; children: David Charles, Marie-Louise, Erika Bernadette. BS, U. Calif., Berkeley, 1951; MS, Stanford U., 1954, PhD, 1957. Asst. rsch. chemist Calif. Rsch. Corp., Richmond, 1951-52; rsch. assoc. Stanford U., 1956; USPHS postdoctoral fellow Wayne State U., Detroit, 1956-58, Swiss Fed. Inst. Tech., Zurich, 1958-59; asst. prof. chemistry Vanderbilt U., Nashville, 1959-63, assoc. prof. chemistry, 1963-71, prof. chemistry, 1971-93, prof. chemistry emeritus, 1993—. Contbr. articles to profl. jours. Grantee NSF, NIH. Fellow AAAS; mem. Am. Chem. Soc. (chmn. Nashville sect. 1971), Royal Soc. Chemistry, Tenn. Acad. Sci., Sigma Xi, Phi Lambda Upsilon. Democrat. Roman Catholic. Home: 3610 Trimble Rd Nashville TN 37215-3246

SMITH, HOWARD THOMPSON, business executive; b. Camden, Ark., Apr. 30, 1937; s. Howard Thompson and Pauline Virginia (Rogers) S.; m. Ann Monroe; children: Paul R., Elizabeth M. BS, Tulane U., 1960; postgrad. studies, La. State U., 1961-63; EPBA, Columbia U., 1978. Dir. planning Ethyl Corp., Baton Rouge, La., 1970-76; exec. v.p., gen. mgr. William Bonnell Co. subs. Ethyl Corp., Newman, Ga., 1976-81; pres. Steelcraft, Cin., 1981-84; v.p., group exec. Am. Standard, Cin., 1984-89; sr. v.p. Am. Standard, N.Y.C., 1989—, also bd. dirs., 1989—; pres., CEO The Trane Co., N.Y.C., 1989-94; mng. ptnr. Septa Assocs., 1994—; pres. Thompson Smith Found., 1993—; chmn. bd. dirs. Trinity Mother Francis Health Sys., 1996—. Bd. dirs. Salvation Army, 1988—, Tex. Rsch. League, Austin, 1989, U. Tex., Tyler, 1990—, Mother Francis Hosp. Found., 1991—; chmn. bd. dirs. East Tex. Communities Found., 1993—; elder, trustee 1st Presbyn. Ch.; trustee U. Tex., Tyler, East Tex. Pres. Found., Union Theol. Sem., 1994—. Mem. Tex. Assn. Taxpayers (dir.), Smith County C. of C. (bd. dirs. 1988-91), Tyler Petroleum Club, Hollytree Country Club, Willowbrook Country Club. Republican. Presbyterian. Home: 6110 Covey Ln Tyler TX 75703-4507 Office: The Trane Co PO Box 9010 Tyler TX 75711-9010

SMITH, HOWARD WELLINGTON, education educator, dean; b. Granby, Mo., Jan. 19, 1929; s. Howard W. and Margaret L. (Sanderson) S.; m. Margaret E. Bell, Mar. 1, 1953; 1 child, Christopher Alan. BS, S.W. Mo. State U., 1954; MEd, U. Mo., 1955, EdD, 1959. Tchr. Newton County (Mo.) Pub. Schs., 1948-51; instr. U. Mo., Columbia, 1955-59; asst. prof. So. Meth. U., Dallas, 1959-61; from asst. to full prof. U. North Tex., Denton, 1961-95; assoc. dean Coll. Edn. U. North Tex., 1972-76, assoc. v.p. acad. affairs, 1976-79, v.p. acad. affairs, 1979-82, interim dean, 1994—; interim chancellor U. North Tex. Coll. Osteo. Medicine, Denton and Ft. Worth, 1981; sr. cons. Am. Assn. State Colls. and Univs., Washington, 1982; cons. Srinakharinwirot U., Thailand, 1986, Tex. Instrnl. Edn. Consortium, Austin, 1992, sr. author Operation Manual Al Akhawayn U., 1993; vis. prof. Shanxi Ednl. Coll. Taiyuan, China, 1993. Contbr. articles to ednl. jours. Prin. investigator Micro Tchg. Lab., 1967-69. With USAF, 1951-53. Democrat. Presbyterian. Office: U North Tex Coll Edn Po Box 13857 UNT Denton TX 76203

SMITH, IVAN HURON, architect; b. Danville, Ind., Jan. 25, 1907; s. Calvin Wesley and Irma (Huron) S.; m. Sara Butler, Aug. 18, 1972; 1 child by previous marriage, Norma Smith Benton. Student, Ga. Inst. Tech., 1926; B.Arch., U. Fla., 1929. With Ivan H. Smith (architect), 1936-41; partner Reynolds, Smith & Hills (architects and engrs.), Jacksonville, Fla., 1941-70; chmn. bd. emeritus Reynolds, Smith & Hills (Architects, Engrs., Planners, Inc.), Jacksonville, Tampa, Orlando, Merritt Island and Ft. Lauderdale, Fla., 1971-77; sec. Jacksonville Bldg. Code Adv. Bd., 1951-68; mem. Duval County Govt. Study Commn., 1966-67; chmn. Jacksonville Constrn. Trades Qualification Bd., 1971. Important works include City Hall, Jacksonville, Duval County Ct. House, Jacksonville, Baptist Hosp, Jacksonville, Engring. Bldg, Nuclear Sci. Bldg, Fla. Field Stadium at, U. Fla.; dormitories Council Bldg, Jacksonville U.; fed. bldgs., Jacksonville, Gainesville, Fla., So. Bell Telephone bldgs; Internat. Airport, Tampa, Fla.; (with Edward Durell Stone) Fla. State Capitol Center. Mem. council Jacksonville U., 1958-76; pres. Jacksonville Humane Soc., 1956-59; bd. dirs. Jacksonville-Duval Safety Council. Served with USNR, 1943-45. Recipient U. Fla. Disting. Alumnus award, 1981, Jacksonville U. Order of the Dolphin, 1985; Paul Harris fellow, 1980. Fellow AIA (Outstanding Service award Fla. region 1965, chpt. pres. 1942, 56); mem. Fla. Assn. Architects (dir. 1957, Gold medal 1981), Jacksonville C. of C. (dir. 1957-59), Beta Theta Pi, Phi Kappa Phi, Sigma Tau. Clubs: Gargoyle (U. Fla.); River (Jacksonville), Univ. (Jacksonville), San Jose Country (Jacksonville), Epping Forest Yacht (Jacksonville), Rotary (Jacksonville, Paul Harris fellow 1980). Home: 6000 San Jose Blvd # 201 Jacksonville FL 32217-2381 Office: 4651 Salisbury Rd Jacksonville FL 32256-6107

SMITH, J. THOMAS, psychotherapist; b. Detroit, Feb. 19, 1947; s. Louis Edward and Marjorie Ursula (Martin) S. BS, Windsor U., 1974; PhD, Acad. of Universal Truth, Seattle, 1981; JD, City U., L.A., 1983; MA, Norwich U., 1988; BS, U. State of N.Y., 1988; PhD, U. San Jose (Costa Rica), 1995. Lic. profl. counselor, Ga., Tex., marriage and family therapist; cert. addictions counselor; registered hypnotherapist; lic. chem. dependency counselor, Tex.; internat. cert. alcohol and other drug abuse counselor; cert. clin. mental health counselor. Air personality Sta. KDAY Radio, L.A., 1975-77, KPVU Radio, Houston, 1993—, Sta. KMJQ Radio, Houston, 1977-87, 94—; asst. campus dir., instr. Houston Community Coll., 1982-87; program dir. Cultural Health Network, Inc., Houston, 1986-89; dean City U. Sch. of Law, L.A., 1989-90; program dir. Urban Health Network, Inc., Atlanta, 1990-91; minister 1st Ch. of Religious Sci., Atlanta, 1990-91; instr. Altanta Met. Coll., 1990-91; broadcaster Sta. WSTR Radio, Atlanta, 1990-91; psychotherapist J. Thomas Smith & Assocs., Atlanta, 1990—; cons. Coalesce, Atlanta, 1990-91; affiliated staff Spring Shadows Glen, Houston, 1990—; program dir. HCA/Spring Br. Med. Ctr. John Lucas Treatment and Recovery Ctr., Houston, 1991-93; dir. counseling and multicultural svcs. Prairie View (Tex.), A&M U., 1993—; instr. Tex. Southern U. Sch. of Cont. Edn., 1993—. Author: Mind Science Primer, 1986; contbr. artilces to publs. Com mem. March of Dimes, Houston, 1985-87; fundraiser Lukemia Soc., Houston, 1983; life mem. NAACP, Houston, 1988. Mem. Am. Counseling Assn., Am. Assn. Clin. Mental Health Counselors, Tex. Assn. of Alcoholism and Drug Abuse Counselors, Nat. Assn. Alcohol and Drug Abuse Counselors, United Clergy of Religious Sci., SAG, AFTRA, Assn. Multicultural Counseling Devel., Internat. New Thought Alliance (life), Nat. Bd. Cert. Counselors, Nat. Com. Mental Health Counselor Training (bd. govs. 1995-96), Nat. Assn. Athletes Against Drugs (bd. dirs. 1994-96). Home: PO Box 681113 Houston TX 77268-1113 Office: Thomas Smith & Assocs World Famous Presentations 3845 FM 1960 W Ste 285 Houston TX 77068

SMITH, JACK WAYNE, family practice physician; b. Staunton, Va., May 27, 1952; s. Jack Maynard and Betty Jean (Fortney) S.; m. Sharon Lorraine Bennett, Nov. 20, 1973; children: David Allen, Jonathan Edward. BA, U. Va., 1974, MD, 1978. Diplomate Am. Bd. Family Practice. Resident U.S. Naval Hosp., Charleston, S.C., 1978-81; staff physician U.S. Naval Hosp., Guam, 1981-84, Orlando, 1984-87; sr. med. officer USS Missouri, Long Beach, Calif., 1987-89; dir. clin. svcs. U.S. Naval Hosp., Millington, Tenn., 1989-92; group surgeon 2D Force Svc. Support Group, Camp Lejeune, N.C., 1992-95; exec. officer U.S. Naval Hosp., Corpus Christi, Tex., 1995—; bd. dirs. Uniformed Svcs. Acad. Family Physicians, Richmond, Va., 1988-92; surgeon Joint Task Force 160, Guantanamo Bay, Cuba, 1994. Com. mem Troop 255 Boy Scouts Am., Bartlett, Tenn., 1989-92, asst. scoutmaster Troop 20, Jacksonville, N.C., 1994-95. Decorated def. superior svc. medal U.S. Joint Chiefs of Staff, 1994. Fellow Am. Acad. Family Physicians; mem. AMA, Am. Coll. Physician Execs., Assn. Mil. Surgeons U.S.

SMITH, JAMES BONNER, lawyer; b. Dallas, Jan. 11, 1950; s. B.J. and Mary Louise (Landrum) S.; m. Shelly Smith, May 1, 1977; children: Bonny Leigh, Robyn Paige, Brooke Alyn. BS, Midwestern U., 1972; JD, Tex. Tech U., 1977. Bar: Tex. 1977. Law clk. Wichita County Dist. Atty.'s Office, Wichita Falls, Tex., 1975, Vickers, Moreau & Huckaby, Wichita Falls, 1976, Hance, Thompson & Thomas, Lubbock, Tex., 1976; asst. city atty. City of Lubbock, 1977-78; asst. criminal dist. atty. Lubbock County, 1978-79; assoc. firm Wicks & Lee, 1979-80; pvt. practice, Lubbock, 1980-82; ptnr. Freeman, McNeely & Smith, Lubbock, 1982-84; ptnr. McNeely & Smith, Lubbock, 1984-90; pvt. practice, 1990—; instr. law Continuing Edn. div. Tex. Tech Univ., Lubbock, 1986-91; instr. health law and bus. law Wayland Bapt. U., Lubbock Center, 1987—; mem. pres. coun. Wayland Bapt. U., Lubbock, 1990—, Tex. Tech U., 1991-93. Mem. Leadership Lubbock, 1986-87, Lubbock City-County Librs. Bd., 1992— vice chmn., 1995— Rotary Cerebral Palsy Ctr. Bd., Sch. Medicine Health Sci. Ctr., Tex. Tech U., 1989-92. Served to lt. col. USAFR, 1973—. Mem. Tex. Bar Assn., ABA, Nat. Mil. Intelligence Assn., Lubbock County Bar Assn., West Tex. Bankruptcy Bar Assn., Tex. Assn. Bank Counsel, Tex. Hosp. Assn., Air Force Assn., Am. Bus. Club (v.p. 1985-86, dir. 1989-90), Lubbock C. of C., Tau Kappa Epsilon (chmn. bd. trustees Tex. Tech Univ. chpt. 1976—, sec., treas. housing corp. 1986—, nat. real estate adv. group 1986), Res. Officers Assn. U.S. (chpt. pres. 1981), Southwest Hunter Jumper Assn. (bd. dirs. 1992—, v.p., 1995, pres. 1996—), Mackenzie Meadows Hunter Jumper Horse Club (pres. 1992—), Order of Daedalians, Lions, Rotary (chmn. classification com. 1987-91, dir., Lubbock Vollyball Assn., 1996—, Coach, LCAA and T-Ball, 1993, Tribal chief Indian Campers, 1987—, chmn. membership devel. com. 1990-92). Home: 8708 Richmond Ave Lubbock TX 79424-4209 Office: 5220 80th St Lubbock TX 79424

SMITH, JAMES EARLIE, JR., accountant; b. Petersburg, Va., Nov. 25, 1945; s. Dorothy Mae (Brown) Crews; m. Sandra Kim Oh, Mar. 23, 1967 (div. 1981); children: Ricky Young Smith; m. Joanne Hamlin, May 17, 1986. BS in Acctg., BS in Fin., Kans. State U., 1985. Enlisted U.S. Army, 1964, advanced through grades to Master Sgt., 1983, retired, 1984; asst. bank examiner Fed. Deposit Ins. Corp., San Francisco, 1986-92; regional rep. Grant Thornton CPA Inc., San Antonio, 1992; loan acctg. officer Broadway Nat. Bank, San Antonio, 1992-93; staff acct. USAA Fed. Savs. Bank, San Antonio, 1993; chief internal control and analysis Def. Acctg. Office, Ft. Polk, La., 1993; rsch. acct. Grant Thornton CPA Inc., San Antonio, 1993-94; fin. instn. analyst Smith Fin. Instn. Svcs., Universal City, Tex., 1995—. Author: Finance Procedures Handbook for Military Leaders, 1983. Mem.

San Antonio Choral Soc., 1993—. Decorated Army Meritorious Svc. medal with 1st oak leaf cluster. Mem. Inst. Mgmt. Accts., San Antonio Area Bankers Compliance Assn., Greater San Antonio C. of C., Black Profl. Leadership Network, San Antonio Choral Soc. (bd. dirs. 1995—), Phi Beta Sigma. United Methodist. Home and Office: 13438 Forum Rd Universal City TX 78148-2801

SMITH, JAMES LEE, aerospace engineer, educator; b. Lester, Ala., Jan. 23, 1957; s. Bobby Ray and Geraldine (Mason) S.; m. Peggy Ruth Greene, Oct. 27, 1984; children: Anah Rebekah, Jacob Andrew. BS, U. North Ala., 1979; MS, U. Tenn., 1982; DEng, Southeastern Inst. Tech., Huntsville, Ala., 1986; M of Bibl. Studies, Bethany Theol. Sem., Dothan, Ala., 1988; MDiv, New Orleans Bapt. Theol. Sem., 1991. Cert. engr.-in-tng., Tenn.; ordained to ministry So. Bapt. Ch., 1989; cert. radiographer. Aerospace engr. NASA, Huntsville, 1982-91; missionary tchr. physics Morrison Acad., Taichung, Taiwan, 1991-92; sr. engr. AMTEC Corp., Huntsville, 1992-93; sr. pastor Rocky Br. Bapt. Ch., Woodland, Ala., 1993-94; aerospace engr. Dept. of Def., Huntsville, 1994—; pres. H.O.P.E. Ministries, Inc., Florence, Ala., 1995—; dean undergrad. studies Andrew Jackson U., Huntsville, 1995—; missionary evangelist, 1988—. Author: (poetry) Poems, Prose, and Praise, 1995, (children's book) Gibe-Up the Frog, 1995; writer (Christian songs) Will He Find Me Faithful Collection, 1995; contbr. articles to profl. jours. Youth basketball coach Anderson (Ala.) Jr. H.S., 1983-88; youth basketball coach N.W. Christian Acad., Florence, 1994—, space flight lectr., 1994-95. Recipient Coach of Yr. award So. Intercollegiate Athletic Conf., 1981, Coach's award N.W. Christian Acad., 1995-96. Republican. Home: Rt 5 Box 109 Florence AL 35630

SMITH, JAMES RANDOLPH, JR., lawyer; b. Martinsville, Va., Mar. 7, 1945; s. James Randolph and Ruth (Boykin) S. BA, Randolph-Macon Coll., 1967; LLB, U. Va., 1970. Bar: Va. 1970, U.S. Dist. Ct. (we. dist.) Va. 1972, U.S. Supreme Ct. 1973, U.S. Ct. Appeals (4th cir.) 1976. Law clk. to judge U.S. Dist. Ct., Wilmington, Del., 1970-71; asst. commonwealth atty. City of Martinsville, 1971-81, commonwealth atty. 1981—; ptnr. Smith & Penn, P.C., Martinsville, 1981-86; instr. New River Criminal Justice Acad., 1980—. Vice chmn. Martinsville Rep. Com., 1986-90, chmn., 1990-94; chmn. bd. dirs. Broad Street Christian Ch., 1996. Mem. Martinsville-Henry County Bar Assn. (v.p. 1983-84, pres. 1984-85), Am. Judicature Soc., Nat. Dist. Attys. Assn., Va. Assn. Comm. Attys. (bd. dirs. 1992-96, coun. 1996—), Rotary (pres. 1993-94), Phi Delta Phi. Mem. Disciples of Christ Ch. Home: 817 Mulberry Rd Martinsville VA 24112-4414 Office: 55 W Church St PO Box 1311 Martinsville VA 24114-1311

SMITH, JAMES W., JR., judge; b. Louisville, Miss., Oct. 28, 1943. BS, U. So. Miss., 1965; JD, Jackson Sch. Law, 1972; MEd with honors, Miss. Coll., 1973. Bar: Miss. 1972, U.S. Dist. Ct. (no. and so. dists.) Miss. 1973, U.S. Ct. Appeals (5th cir.) 1974. Pvt. practice Pearl, 1972-78, Brandon, 1979-80; prosecuting atty. City of Pearl, 1973-80; dist. atty. 20th Jud. Dist., 1977-82; judge Rankin County, 1982-92; Supreme Ct. justice Cen. Dist., 1993—; instr. courtroom procedure and testifying Miss. Law Enforcement Tng. Acad., 1980-91. With U.S. Army, 1966-69. Named Wildlife Conservationist of Yr. Rankin County, 1988. Mem. ABA, NRA, Miss. State Bar Assn., Rankin County Bar Assn., Nat. Wildlife Fedn., Nat. Wild Turkey Fedn. Office: Carroll Gartin Justice Bldg PO Box 117 Jackson MS 39201

SMITH, JAMESETTA DELORISE, author; b. Chgo., Jan. 26, 1942; d. James Gilbert and Ora Mae (Roberts) Howell; m. Leroy Smith, June 2, 1962; children: Leroy, Darryll Keith. Student, Oxford Bus. Coll., Chgo., 1961-62. Office clerk Justice of the Peace, Gary, Ind., 1966-69; bookkeeper, office mgr. Jones Electric, Gary, Ind., 1971-85. Author: How Strong is Strong, 1988; contbr. articles to profl. jours., newspapers. Treas., bd. dirs. N.W. Ind. Lupus Found., Gary, 1988-92; co-founder, pres. Ark. chpt. Lupus Found., 1993—, mem., race organizer, 1995; facilitator Gary Meth. Hosp. for Lupus Found., 1991-92; pastor's aide Bible study leader Greater St. Paul Bapt. Ch., 1995, sec. ch. food com., 1994, ch. trustee, 1994; Bible enrichment instr., 1996—; pastor's aide sec. Clark Rd. M.B. Ch., 1990-92. Named Vol. of Yr., Ark. chpt. Lupus Found., 1995. Mem. Jones Electric Gary Ind. (Sec. 1986). Democratic. Baptist.

SMITH, JANET, librarian; b. Magee, Miss., Apr. 1, 1949; d. Ralph and Sarah Myrle (Delk) Easterling; m. Richard Brinson Smith, Aug. 21, 1970; 1 child, Brandy Smith Persons. Assoc. degree, Jones Jr. Coll., 1968; BS, U. So. Miss., 1970, MLS, 1978. High sch. libr. Petal (Miss.) High Sch., 1970-71; br. libr. Lucedale (Miss.)-George County Pub. Libr., 1971—. Editor: Who Married Whom Covington County, 1991. Mem. adv. com. Lucedale Tree Bd., 1989-96; mem. adv. bd. George County Ext., Lucedale, 1985-96; fin. dir. Miss. Shakespeare in the Park, 1994-96. Mem. ALA, Pub. Libr. Assn., Libr. Adminstrn. and Mgmt. Assn. (John Cotton Dana Pub. Rels. award 1991), Miss. Libr. Assn. Democrat. Baptist. Home: PO Box 266 Lucedale MS 39452 Office: Jackson George Reg Libr System 3214 Pascagoula St Pascagoula MS 39567-4217

SMITH, JANI MARIE, special education educator; b. Holyoke, Mass., Oct. 14, 1947; d. Gail Homer and Lucille M. (Smith) Wagar; m. David William Smith, June 14, 1970; children: Cassandra Ann, Shani Marie. BS cum laude, Old Dominion U., 1970; MEd, Sul Ross U., 1975. Cert. secondary and spl. edn. tchr.-learning disabilities, hist. and social sci. tchr., secondary prin., secondary supr., supr. spl. edn., Va., Fla., Tex. Tchr. social studies Waynesboro (Va.) High Sch., 1970-72; tchr. learning disabilities Coahoma (Tex.) High Sch., 1973-77, So. Wayne High Sch., Dudley, N.C., 1978-84; tchr. reading Wayne Community Coll., Goldsboro, N.C., 1978-79; tchr. learning disabilities Leavenworth (Kans.) Pub. Schs., 1984-85; dept. chmn., tchr. learning disabilities Ferguson High Sch., Newport News, Va., 1985-90; tchr. learning disabled Jinks Mid. Sch., Panama City, Fla., 1990-93; ESE cons. Jinks Middle Sch., Panama City, Fla., 1993-94; staffing specialist Bay Dist. Schs., 1994—; adj. prof. George Washington U., Hampton, Va., 1988-90, U. West Fla., 1993—. Vol. ARC, 1973-77, AFT Dial a Tchr., Hampton, 1987-90; Sunday sch. tchr. Emmanuel Episcopal Ch., Hampton, 1987-90; pes. Capt. John Smith Elem. Sch. PTA, Hampton, 1987-89. Mem. NEA, Coun. for Exceptional Children, Tyndall AFB Officers Wives Club, 4484th Test Squadron Support Group, Delta Kappa Gamma, Beta Sigma Phi, Pi Beta Phi. Republican. Home: 1718 Country Club Dr Lynn Haven FL 32444-1982 Office: Bay District Schools 311 Balboa Ave Panama City FL 32402

SMITH, JANICE SELF, family nurse practitioner; b. Marietta, Ga., Nov. 8, 1942; d. Robert Dewey and Dovia Evelyn (Seay) Self; m. Charles William Smith, Nov. 9, 1963; children: Scott, Stephanie, Suzanne. Diploma, Piedmont Hosp. Sch. Nursing, 1963; Cert. Family Nurse Practitioner, Ga. State U., 1981; BSN, West Ga. Coll., 1994. RN, Ga.; cert. family nurse practitioner, Ga. Staff nurse Gordon Hosp., Calhoun, Ga., 1963-69; pub. health nurse Gordon County Health Dept., Calhoun, Ga., 1977-80; family nurse practitioner Gordon Primary Care Unit, Calhoun, Ga., 1982—; rep. health dept. Child ABuse Coun., Calhoun, 1986; led effort to implement Good Touch-Bad Touch program, Calhoun, 1986. Chmn. pub. edn. Am. Cancer Soc., Calhoun, 1971, bd. chmn., 1973, chmn. patient svcs., 1974-79; sec. commn. on missions 1st United Meth. Ch., Calhoun, 1994. Named Gord County Vol. of the Yr., 1979; Ingram scholar West Ga. Coll., 1994. Mem. ANA, Ga. Pub. Health Assn. (sec. nursing sect. 1994-95, vice chair nursing sect. 1995-96, chair nursing sect. 1996—), Ga. Nurses Assn. (treas. 1995-96), Nurses Honor Soc. West Ga. Coll. Methodist. Home: 141 Derby Ln Calhoun GA 30701-2023 Office: Gordon County Health Dept 310 N River St Calhoun GA 30701

SMITH, JANNA HOGAN, nursing administrator, surgical nurse; b. Tyler, Tex., Sept. 6, 1949; d. David Walker (dec.) and Callie Jewel (White) Hogan; m. Ronald Garth Smith, May 24, 1969; 1 child, Holly Marie. Diploma, Med. Ctr. Hosp. Sch. Vocat. Nursing, 1973, operating room technologist diploma, 1973; AAS in Nursing, Tyler (Tex.) Jr. Coll., 1985. Lic. vocat. Nurse, Tex.; RN, Tex.; cert. surg. technologist. Vocat. nurse, surg. technologist various hosps., Tex., 1974-78, Good Shepherd Hosp., Longview, Tex., 1979-80, Mother Francis Hosp., Tyler, 1981; vocat. nurse, surg. technologist Med. Ctr. Hosp., Tyler, 1980-83, staff nurse, 1985; staff nurse operating room Woman's Hosp. Tex., Houston, 1985; profl. sales rep., ter. mgr. McNeil Consumer Products Co., Ft. Washington, Pa., 1986-87; profl. sales rep. CIBA-Geigy Pharms., Summit, N.J., 1987-89; supr. operating room, nurse mgr. Bay Area Surgicare Ctr., Webster, Tex., 1989—; clin. rsch. monitor CIBA-Geigy Pharm. Co., Summit, N.J.; dir. bd. dirs. Tyler Health Facilities Develop. Corp., 1996—. Mem. Assn. Operating Room Nurses (cert.), Am. Bus. Women's Assn. Home: 526 W Houston St Tyler TX 75702-8044

SMITH, JEANNE HAWKINS, critical care nurse; b. Atlanta, Dec. 6, 1956; d. Frank Edward Hawkins and Marcelle Cox Watkins; m. Michael G. Smith, Apr. 19, 1986; children: Cristen Michelle, Michael Shane, Lindsay Nicole, Mathew Austin. BSN, Emory U., 1978. RN, Ga.; CCRN. Staff nurse, then head nurse urology unit Emory U. Hosp., Atlanta, 1978-82; staff nurse, asst. nurse mgr. surg ICU, cardiovasc. ICU, CCU Ga. Bapt. Med. Ctr., Atlanta, 1985-96. Mem. AACN. Home: 703 Rockingham Ct Woodstock GA 30189-2300

SMITH, JEARLD VAN, secondary education educator, realtor; b. Colorado City, Tex., Jan. 5, 1952; s. Jearld and Ione (Conner) S.; m. Barbara Gay Siegfried, Oct. 1, 1989. AA, Western Tex. Coll., 1972; BA, U. Tex. Permian Basin, Odessa, 1974; MS, Tex. Tech U., 1982. Cert. secondary tchr., Tex.; lic. Realtor, Tex. Contractor, realtor Snyder (Tex.) Builder's Supply, 1974-88; tchr. Midland (Tex.) Lee H.S., 1986-87; instr. South Plains Coll., Levelland, Tex., 1983-87; parole officer Tex. Bd. of Pardons & Parole, Austin, 1989; instr. Tarrant County Jr. Coll., Ft. Worth, 1990—; tchr. Lake Worth H.S., Ft. Worth, 1991-96; tchr. honors IB program Wyatt H.S., Ft. Worth Ind. Sch. Dist., 1996—. Del. Dem. State Conv., Austin, 1972, San Antonio, 1974, Rep. State Conv., San Antonio, 1996; candidate Rep. Party of Tex., Ft. Worth, 1996. Mem. Assn. of Tex. Profl. Educators, Tex. Cmty. Colls. Assn.

SMITH, JEFF SCOTT, trauma, critical care nurse; b. Pasadena, Calif., July 24, 1952; s. Carl F. and Arlene L. (Pfeiffer) S.; m. Kathleen B. Staker, Feb. 10, 1990, 1 child, Allison Diann. BS, Abilene Christian U., 1974; ADN, Arapahoe Community Coll., 1984. CEN; cert. ACLS, Am. Heart Assn. Charge nurse ICU Humana Hosp., Abilene, Tex., 1984-85, dir. shift oper., 1985-87, staff nurse emergency rm., 1987-90; charge nurse ICU Humana Hosp., Aurora, Colo., 1990-91; charge nurse emergency rm. Humana Hosp., Abilene, Tex., 1991-94; trauma coord. Abilene (Tex.) Regional Med. Ctr., 1994—. Mem. Emergency Nurse's Assn. (cert. trauma nurse core course instr.), Tex. Trauma Coord.'s Forum. Home: 8041 Scooter Ct Abilene TX 79606-5439 Office: Abilene Regional Med Ctr 6250 Us Highway 83 Abilene TX 79606-5215

SMITH, JEFFREY ALAN, occupational medicine physician, toxicologist; b. Plainfield, N.J., Dec. 13, 1953; s. John Oliver and Regina Delores (Rudnicki) S. BSChemE with high honors, N.C. State U., 1974; MD with honors, U. N.C., 1979; MS in Toxicology, W.Va. U., 1990. Environ. engr. U.S. EPA, Durham, N.C., 1974-75; mem. staff, cons. PEDCo Environ., Inc., Durham, 1975-80; dir. environ. health PEDCo Environ., Inc., Cin., 1981-82; intern New Hanover Meml. Hosp., Wilmington, N.C., 1980-81; ind. contractor various urgent care ctrs. Cin., 1982-84; dir. Marion (Ohio) Correctional Inst., F.C. Smith Clinic, Inc., 1984-88; resident W.Va. U., Morgantown, 1988-91; med. officer Nat. Inst. Occupational Safety and Health, Morgantown, 1991; dir. occupational medicine Concord (N.C.) Family Medicine/Monroe Urgent Care, 1991-95. Co-author: Environmental Assessment of the Domestic Industries, 1976, Dioxins, 1980. Mem. Am. Coll. Occupation and Environ. Medicine, Am. Conf. Govt. Indsl. Hygienists, Am. Coll. Physician Execs., N.C. Med. Soc., So. Med. Assn., Phi Kappa Phi, Alpha Omega Alpha. Home: 1511 Lake Dr Monroe NC 28112-9415

SMITH, JEFFREY EUGENE, public relations executive; b. Columbus, Ohio, Sept. 30, 1947; s. Jay Birney and Norma (Lee) S. BA in Journalism, Ohio State U., 1969; MS in Comm., Ohio U., 1971. Assoc. dir. alumni affairs Case Western Res. U., Cleve., 1971-73; reporter Sta. WTVN-TV (ABC affiliate), Columbus, Ohio, 1973-74; comm. specialist Ohio Edn. Assn., Columbus, 1974-78; pub. affairs officer Can. Consulate Gen., Atlanta, 1978-88; dir. pub. rels. Life Coll., Marietta, Ga., 1988—. Contbr. articles to newspapers and mags. Founding mem., bd. dirs. Ctr. for Puppetry Arts, Atlanta, 1978-89, Atlanta Internat. Mus., 1988—; mem. adv.bd. Cobb County Ext. Svc., 1993—, chmn., 1995-96; mem. Leadership Cobb, 1990-91. Recipient award Edn. Press Assn., 1975. Mem. Pub. Rels. Soc. Am., Coun. for Advancement and Support of Edn., Condominium Assn. (pres. 1987-89), Ga. Ednl. Advancement Coun., Olmstead Soc. Atlanta, Atlanta Press Club, Cobb C. of C., English Speaking Union, Kappa Tau Alpha, Phi Delta Kappa, Sigma Delta Chi. Office: Life Coll 1269 Barclay Cir Marietta GA 30060-2903

SMITH, JERRALYN RENÉE, trade association executive; b. Houston, Oct. 8, 1957; d. Gerald Harris and Rita Faye (Minsky) S. BS with honors, U. Tex., 1979. Lic. interior designer, Tex. Design assoc./urban planner J.T. Dunkin & Assocs., Dallas, 1980-83; interior designer/store planner Sanger Harris/Federated Stores, Dallas, 1983-85; project designer/space planner Crescent Interior Planning Group divsn. Rosewood, Dallas, 1985-86; prin., designer and cons. J.R. Smith & Assocs., Dallas, 1986-92; with Internat. Assn. Elec. Insps., Richardson, Tex., 1992—, dir. comm. and mktg., 1996—, also mng. editor IAEI News. Mng. editor IAEI News, 1992—. Vol. Habitat for Humanity, Dallas, 1995-96; race dir. Kidsport Triathlon, ARC, Dallas, 1989, chair, 1990-91, exec. com. for youth svcs., 1990-92; newsletter editor, vol. trainer Inner City outings Sierra Club, Dallas, 1992-94. Recipient Vol. Appreciation award ARC, Dallas, 1991. Mem. Internat. Assn. Bus. Communicators (media coord. Dallas 1995-96). Office: Internat Assn Electrical Inspectors 901 Waterfall Way #602 Richardson TX 75080-7702

SMITH, JERRY DON, food service executive; b. Cin., June 21, 1940; s. Clarence E. and Victoria Lynn (Roberts) S.; m. Vicki Ann Speer, Mar. 7, 1959; children: Jeffrey, Kimberly. BS in Econs., U. Cin., 1967; postgrad., U. Chgo., 1967-68, Ill. Cen. Coll., 1978. Fin. analyst IBM Corp., Chgo., 1967-70, mgr. adminstrn., 1970-75; mgr. systems mktg. IBM Corp., Peoria, 1975-81; owner, operator McDonald's Restaurants, Dallas, 1981—; pres. JVS Enterprises Inc., 1982—, JVS Mgmt. Co., Inc., 1985—; instr. Ill. Cen. Coll., 1975-76; cons. Small Bus. Devel. Ctr., Dallas, 1990-91; bd. dirs. Dallas-Ft. Worth Advt. Assn., 1992-93; speaker in field; v.p. North Tex. Advt. Assn., 1995-96. Bd. dirs. Interfaith Job Search Coun., Dallas, 1990-91, Hillcrest Bapt. Ch., Dallas, 1990-91; facilator Restart, Inc., Dallas, 1989-91; bd. dirs. Ministry to Men Found., Memphis, 1996; mem. Rep. Presdl. Task Force, Washington, 1984-85. Mem. North Tex. Advt. Assn. (v.p. 1995-96), North Tex. Speakers Assn., Oak Cliff C. of C., U.S. C. of C. Home: 1655 Nob Hill Dr Duncanville TX 75137-3739 Office: JVS Enterprises PO Box 210889 Dallas TX 75211-0889

SMITH, JERRY EDWIN, federal judge; b. Del Rio, Tex., Nov. 7, 1946; s. Lemuel Edwin and Ruth Irene (Henderson) S.; m. Mary Jane Blackburn, June 4, 1977; children: Clark, Ruth Ann, J.J. BA, Yale U., 1969, JD, 1972. Bar: Tex. 1972. Law clk. to judge U.S. Dist. Ct. (no. dist.) Tex., Lubbock, 1972-73; assoc. then ptnr. Fulbright & Jaworski, Houston, 1973-84; city atty. City of Houston, 1984-88; cir. judge U.S. Ct. Appeals (5th cir.), Houston, 1988—. Chmn. Harris County Rep. Party, Houston, 1977-78; committeeman State Rep. Exec. Com., Tex., 1976-88. Mem. State Bar Tex., Houston Bar Assn. Methodist. Home: PO Box 130608 Houston TX 77219-0608 Office: US Ct Appeals 12621 US Courthouse 515 Rusk St Houston TX 77002-2698*

SMITH, JOHN DRAKE, JR., lawyer; b. Richmond, Va., Mar. 17, 1950; s. John Drake Sr. and Louise (Riley) S. BS in Commerce, U. Va., 1973; JD, U. Richmond, 1981; career prosecutor course, Nat. Coll. Dist. Attys., 1988. Bar: Va., 1981, U.S. Dist. Ct. (ea. dist.) Va., 1981, U.S. Ct. Appeals (4th cir.) 1981, U.S. Bankruptcy Ct. (ea. dist.) Va., 1981. Engr. Ins. Svcs. Office, Richmond, 1973-78; assoc. Purcell, Cherry, Kerns & Abady, Richmond, 1982-85; pvt. practice Richmond, 1985-86; asst. commonwealth atty. City of Richmond, 1986-89, Spotsylvania County, Va., 1990-95; pvt. practice Fredericksburg, Va., 1995—. Named Class Champion So. Road Racing Series, 1986, 88, Amelia Kart Track, 1986, Summit Point Raceway, 1987, 90, 91, 95, King George Speedway, 1990, one of Outstanding Young Men of Am., 1984, 85, 86. Mem. Va. Bar Assn., World Karting Assn. (Nat. Class Champion 1975, 76, World Class Champion 1992), Woodbridge Kart Club (v.p. 1992, 96, pres. 1993), Delta Theta Phi. Methodist. Home: 808 1/2 Caroline St Fredericksburg VA 22401-5806 Office: Ste 401 904 Princess Anne St Fredericksburg VA 22401

SMITH, JOHN HERBERT, career officer; b. Chillicothe, Ohio, Feb. 16, 1957; s. Herbert Arvin and Virginia Mae (Marchand) S.; m. Wanda Ann Brewer, June 16, 1979; children: Melissa Christine, Stephanie Diane, Craig Mathew, Tyler Jordan. BS in Computer & Info. Sci., Ohio State U., 1979; master tng. specialist, Trident Training Facility, 1986. Cert. for supervision, operation and maintenance of naval nuclear power plants. Ensign USN, 1979, advanced through grades to lt. comdr., 1989; ret., 1994; trainee, student Nuclear Power Sch., Orlando, Fla., 1979; watch officer Nuclear Power Tng. Unit, Balston Spa, N.Y., 1979-80; div. officer USS Benjamin Franklin, Kittery, Maine, 1980-82; head quality assurance and DC instructors Trident Tng. Facility, Bremerton, Wash., 1982-85; chief engr. USS Spadefish, Norfolk, Va., 1986-89; chief policy br., programs divsn. U.S. Spl. Ops. Cmd., MacDill AFB, Fla., 1989-94; mgr. info. sys. Precision Sys. Inc., St. Petersburg, Fla., 1995—. Pres. coun. of ministry Bangor Sub Base Chapel, Bremerton, 1984-86; pres. United Meth. Men, St. Paul's Ch., Chesapeake, Va., 1988-89; coach Brandon (Fla.) Area Youth Soccer League, 1990—; referee U.S. Soccer Fedn., 1995—. Decorated Navy Achievement medal, Joint Svc. Achievement medal, Def. Svc. medal, Joint Svc. Commendation medal. Mem. Mil. Ops. Rsch. Soc., U.S. Naval Inst., Triangle Frat. (chpt. v.p.). Home: 625 Ephrata Dr Brandon FL 33511-7908 Office: Precision Sys Inc 11800 30th Ct N Saint Petersburg FL 33716-1846

SMITH, JOHN HOLMES, IV, trucking terminal manager, sales representative; b. Nashville, Oct. 13, 1949; s. John Holmes III and Elizabeth Howard (Neel) S.; m. Carol Anne Rubin, July 15, 1972 (div. Sept. 1992); children: Jennifer Alison, Andrew Oliver. BA in History, Vanderbilt U., 1974. So. div. trainee Roadway Express, Inc., New Orleans, 1974; dispatcher Roadway Express, Inc., Batesville, Ark., 1974-75, Jonesboro, Ark., 1975-78; terminal mgr. Roadway Express, Inc., Monticello, Ark., 1978-93, group terminal mgr., 1993—. Co-founder S.E. Ark. Quality Initiative, 1992; mem. Gov.'s State-wide Quality Task Force, 1994—; com. chmn. cub scouts Boy Scouts Am., Monticello, 1989-92; state committeeman Rep. Party Ark., Little Rock, 1987-93; chmn. Drew County Rep. Party, 1993—; pres. Internat. Visitors Com., Monticello, 1993—; bd. dirs. Ark. Coun. Internat. Visitors, Little Rock, 1992—; deacon, chmn. bd. dirs. First Presbyn. Ch., Monticello, 1983, elder, clk., 1989. Named one of Outstanding Young Men of Am., 1983. Mem. Rotary (pres. 1994-95, Paul Harris fellow 1989), Monticello Music Club, Ducks Unltd., Drew County C. of C., Monticello Art League. Home: PO Box 492 Monticello AR 71655-0492 Office: Roadway Express Inc 424 N Conley St Monticello AR 71655-4506

SMITH, JOHN KENNETH, oil company executive, retired; b. Liberty, Tex., Feb. 3, 1928; s. Lonnie Phillip and Wordnia Laura (Ashmore) S.; m. Mary Catherine Smith (dec. Dec. 16, 1993); children: Catherine Lorraine, Joel Kenneth, Gary Phillip, Phillip Wayne. BS in Mech. Engring., Tex. A&M U., 1949. Petroleum engr. Sun Oil Co., Beaumont, Tex., 1949-57, sr. petroleum engr., 1957-62; rep. to Fed. Power Commn. Sun Oil Co., Washington, 1962-70, asst. dir. govt. rels., 1970-82; dir. govt. rels. Sun Exploration and Prodn. Co., Dallas, 1982-86; ret., 1986; bd. dirs. Atrion Corp., Florence, Ala. Mem. Soc. Petroleum Engrs., Timberlane Golf and Country Club. Republican. Methodist.

SMITH, JOHN MARVIN, III, surgeon, educator; b. San Antonio, July 31, 1947; s. John M. and Jane (Jordan) S.; m. Jill Jones, Aug. 1, 1981. MD, Tulane U., 1972. Diplomate Am. Bd. Surgery, Am. Bd. Thoracic Surgery. Intern, U. Tex. Southwest Med. Sch., Dallas, 1972-73; resident in surgery U. Tex., San Antonio, 1973-77, resident in thoracic and cardiovascular surgery Tex. Heart Inst., Houston, 1977-79; practice medicine specializing in cardiovascular and thoracic surgery, San Antonio, 1979—; mem. Staff Bapt. Med. Ctr., S.W. Tex. Meth. Hosp., Santa Rosa Med. Center, Met. Hosp., Nix Meml. Hosp.; clin. prof. surgery U. Tex. Health Sci. Ctr., San Antonio, 1979—. Contbr. articles to profl. jours. Bd. mgrs. Bexar County Hosp. Dist.; chmn. bd. dirs. Tex. Ranger Assn., San Antonio Med. Found., Meth. Hosp. Found. Internat. Affairs Coun. Served to maj. USAF, 1979-81. Fellow Am. Coll. Cardiology, ACP, ACS; mem. AMA, Tex. Med. Assn., Bexar County Med. Soc., Denton A. Cooley Cardiovascular Surg. Soc., Cooley Hands, J. Bradley Aust Surg. Soc., Soc. Air Force Clin. Surgeons, San Antonio Surg. Soc., San Antonio Cardiology Soc., Soc. of Thoracic Surgeons, Tex. Surgical Soc., Tulane Med. Alumni Assn. (bd. dirs.), Tex. Hist. Soc., Sigma Alpha Epsilon, Nu Sigma Nu. Episcopalian. Clubs: Tex. Cavaliers, San Antonio Country, The Argyle, Giraud, Order Alamo, German, Christmas Cotillion, Rolling Rock Club, Sons Republic Tex., San Antonio Gun. Home: 204 Zambrano Rd San Antonio TX 78209-5459 Office: 4330 Medical Dr Ste 300 San Antonio TX 78229-3326

SMITH, JOHN MICHAEL, lawyer; b. Summit, N.J., Sept. 23, 1959; s. Paul Harry and Mary (Konieczny) S. BA in Polit. Sci., Ursinus Coll., Collegeville, Pa., 1981; JD, Del. Law Sch., Wilmington, 1985; LLM in Environ. Law, George Washington U., Washington, 1995. Bar: Pa. 1985, U.S. Ct. Military Appeals 1986. Asst. staff judge adv. 4th Combat Support Group, Seymour Johnson AFB, N.C., 1986-87, 343d Combat Support Group, Eielson AFB, AK, 1987-88; area def. counsel USAF Judiciary, Eielson AFB, AK, 1988-90; asst. staff judge adv. Headquarters 7th Air Force, Osan AFB, Rep. of Korea, 1990-91; dep. staff judge adv. 438th Airlift Wing, McGuire AFB, N.J., 1991-94, Air Force Environ. Law & Litigation Divsn., Arlington, Va., 1995—; Mem. Pa. Bar Assn., 1985-88. Recipient Air Force Commendation medal USAF, 1987, 90, 91, Air Force Achievement medal USAF, 1992, Air Force Meritorious Svc. medal, 1995. Roman Catholic. Home: Apt 203 1201 Braddock Pl Alexandria VA 22314 Office: AFL/JACE Ste 629 1501 Wilson Blvd Arlington VA 22209-2403

SMITH, JOHN ROSCOE, glass artist; b. Hollywood, Fla., Mar. 13, 1952; s. David Roscoe and Marie (DiFatta) S. AA, Broward C.C., 1976; BA, Fla. Atlantic U., 1978. Freelance wash oil artist Hallandale, Fla., 1967—; freelance jewelry artist Hallandale, 1971—; glass artist Crystal Rainbow Glass, Dania, Fla., 1990—; instr. seminars Art Glass Supplier Assn., Orlando, Fla., 1993, 95, 96, World Glass Craft Festival, Newark, 1994, 95, 96, World Glass Craft Festival, Orlando, 1996, Las Vegas, 1996, 97. Author: Something's Fishy, 1993, (book and video) Hot and Wired, 1993, Rainforest, 1994, Stargazing, 1995; co-author: Image is Everything, 1996; artist stained glass and glassblowing. Mem. Art Glass Guild Artists (founding mem.). Home: 819 NE 8th St Hallandale FL 33009-2624 Office: Crystal Rainbow Glass Studio # 2B 1300 Stirling Rd Dania FL 33004-3537

SMITH, JONATHAN KENNON THOMPSON, retired academic administrator, volunteer, genealogist; b. Benton County, Tenn., May 8, 1939; s. Herschel Kennon and Dorothy (McGrady) S. BS, George Peabody Coll., 1960; MA, Memphis State U., 1962. Cert. tchr. and sch. adminstr., Tenn. Tchr. Shelby County Sch. System, Memphis, 1962-75, adminstr., curriculum coord., 1975-77, 78-91, ret., 1991. Copyright (30) history and genealogy. Historian Benton County, 1973-83, historian emeritus, 1983—; vol. Jackson/Madison County (Tenn.) Pub. Libr. Recipient Mayor's Key to City, Bartlett, Tenn., 1991. Democrat. Unitarian-Universalist. Home: 2313 Williamsburg Village Dr Jackson TN 38305-5103 also: PO Box 2767 Jackson TN 38302-2767

SMITH, JONATHAN RICHARDSON, English language educator; b. Alexandria, Va., Nov. 5, 1963; s. Charles Alphonso and Anne Vaughan (Sutton) S.; m. Gail Katherine Schroeder, Aug. 20, 1988. BA in Philosophy, Yale U., 1985; MA in English, MEd in English Edn., U. Va., 1989, PhD in English, 1994. Lectr. dept. English U. Wis., Madison, 1994-95; asst. prof. Miss. State U., 1995—. Contbr. articles to profl. jours. Mem. MLA, Nat. Coun. Tchrs. English, Assn. for Study of Lit. and the Environment, Am. Soc. for Environ. History, SOc. for Study of So. Lit., Nat. Speleological Soc. (chmn. libr. com. 1995—). Home: PO Box 3801 Mississsippi State MS 39762 Office: Miss State U Dept English Drawer E Mississippi State MS 39762

SMITH, JOSEPH PHILIP, lawyer; b. Jackson, Tenn., June 14, 1944; s. William Benjamin and Virginia Marie (Carey) S.; m. Deborah J. Smith, Dec. 22, 1972; 1 child, Virginia Louise. BA, U. Miss., 1967, JD, 1975; MEd, U. So. Miss., 1977; postgrad., U. Memphis, 1994—. Bar: Miss. 1975, Tex. 1979, N. Mex. 1991, Colo. 1991, Tenn. 1995, U.S. Dist. Ct. (no. dist.) Miss.

1975, U.S. Dist. Ct. (no. dist.) Tex. 1982, U.S. Dist. Ct. N.Mex. 1993, U.S. Dist. Ct. Colo. 1993, U.S. Ct. Appeals (10th cir.) 1993. Tchr. math. Marks (Miss.) Jr. H.S., 1971-73; tchr., asst. prin. Biloxi (Miss.) City Schs., 1975-78; oil and gas landman Modling & Assocs., 1978-79; assoc., then ptnr. Byrnes, Myers, Adair, Campbell & Sinex, Houston, 1979-85; farmer Quitman County, Miss., 1988-90; pvt. practice Marks, Miss., Memphis, Raton, N.Mex., 1985—. Mem. Archdiocese of Santa Fe Sch. Bd., 1991-92. Capt. USAF, 1967-71. Mem. ABA, Colo. Bar Assn., Miss. Pub. Defender Assn. (treas. 1988-90), Rotary (pres., sec. Marks club 1985-90, mem. Raton club 1990-91). Republican. Roman Catholic. Home: 674 St Augustine Sq Memphis TN 38104

SMITH, JUDITH DAY, early childhood educator; b. Birmingham, Ala., Feb. 7, 1949; d. Robert Henry and Margaret Ann (Moulton) Day; m. Richard Monroe Smith, Aug. 22, 1970; 1 child, Wendy Elaine. BA in English, Jacksonville State U., 1971, MS in Edn., 1978. Cert. early childhood edn., elem. edn., lay speaker United Meth. Ch. Kindergarten tchr., dir. St. Mark United Meth. Ch., Anniston, Ala., 1973-78; kindergarten tchr. The Donoho Sch., Anniston, 1978-79, 1st grade tchr., 1979-80, 2nd grade tchr., 1980—, lower sch. ann. advisor, 1987-94, primary dept. head, 1993—; Wee Deliver post office advisor, 1994—; applicant Tchr.-in-Space NASA, Washington, 1984-85; conducted primary tchrs.' seminar, Kenya, 1996. Mem. Anniston Mus. Nat. History, Mus. League; vol. Boy Scouts Am. Recipient Golden Apple award Ala. Power and WJSU-TV, 1994; nominee Outstanding Educator for 1996, Women Committed to Excellence, sponsored by Cottaquilla Coun. of Girl Scouts. Mem. Internat. Platform Assn., Ala. Coun. Tchrs. of English, Environ. Edn. Assn. of Ala., Alpha Delta Kappa. Republican. Methodist. Home: 3905 Cloverdale Rd Anniston AL 36207-7014 Office: The Donoho Sch 2501 Henry Rd Anniston AL 36207-6341

SMITH, JULIA AMELIA, English language educator; b. San Antonio, Tex., Dec. 25, 1935; d. George Leon and Julia E. (Garcia) S. BA, Our Lady of the Lake, San Antonio, Tex., 1956; MA, U. Tex., 1958; postgrad., Harvard U., 1961; PhD, U. Tex, 1969. Elem. tchr. San Antonio (Tex.) Sch. Dist., 1956-57; instr. Laredo (Tex.) Jr. Coll., 1959-68; asst. prof. English, Tex. A&M U., Kingsville, 1969-72; assoc. prof. Tex. A&I U., Kingsville, 1972-78, prof., 1978—, chmn. dept., 1977-83. Contbr. articles to profl. jours. Organist St. Martin's Ch., Kingsville, Tex. Mem. Modern Language Assn., Nat. Council of Tchrs of English, Conf. of Coll. Tchrs. of English, Tex. Coll English Assn., Music Club of Kingsville, Audubon Soc., Delta Kappa Gamma, Kappa Nu. Democrat. Roman Catholic. Office: Tex A&M PO Box 162 Kingsville TX 78364-0162

SMITH, KAREN COLE, sociologist, educator; b. Jamaica, N.Y., Mar. 30, 1956; d. William Charles and Naomi Janice (Daniels) Cole; m. James Leroy Smith, July 14, 1979; children: Michelle Denise, Brittany Ranay Alexis. BA, Bethune-Cookman Coll., 1977; MA, Ohio State U., 1978; PhD, U. Fla., 1989. Prof. Bethune-Cookman Coll., Daytona Beach, Fla., 1978-82; faculty Santa Fe C.C., Gainesville, Fla., 1986—, chairperson, 1995—. Bd. dirs. Girls Club, Gainesville, 1995—, Vol. Action Agy., Gainesville, 1996, Leadership Gainesville, 1995—; coun. mem. Cmty. Involvement Coun., Tallahassee, Fla., 1993-95; vol. Gainesville Police Dept., Multicultural Task Force. Mem. Nat. Assn. Women in Cmty. Colls., The Links Inc. (youth svcs. coord. 1996), The Visionaires (chaplain, youth coord. 1995—), Alpha Kappa Alpha. Democrat. Baptist. Office: Santa Fe CC 3000 NW 83rd St Gainesville FL 32606-6210

SMITH, LARRY GLENN, retired state judge; b. Montgomery, Ala., Aug. 6, 1924; s. Alonzo Nathan and Louise (Norman) S.; m. Mary Emmalyn Murphree, Feb. 28, 1948; children: Cynthia Lynn Smith Ramirez, Larry Glenn Jr., Celia Dell Smith Rudolph. Student, U. Ala., Tuscaloosa, 1942-43, 46-48; LLB, U. Fla., 1949. Bar: Fla. 1949. Pvt. practice, Panama City, Fla., 1949-53; assoc. Mathis & Mathis, Panama City, 1953-57; asst. state's atty. Office State's Atty. for 14th Cir., Panama City, 1953-57; rsch. asst. Fla. Supreme Ct., Tallahassee, 1958-60; ptnr. Baker, Baker & Smith, Orlando, Fla., 1960-64, Isler, Welch, Smith, Higby & Brown, Panama City, 1964-72; judge cir. ct. Fla. 14th Jud. Cir., Panama City, 1973-79; judge Fla. 1st Dist. Ct. Appeal, Tallahassee, 1979-94; ret., 1994; chief judge Fla. 1st Dist. Ct. Appeal, Tallahassee, 1987-89; ret., 1994; sr. judge State of Fla.; Mem. Fla. Bd. Bar Examiners, Tallahassee, 1967-72, Fla. Ct. Edn. Coun., Tallahassee, 1979-81, 86-91, Fla. Bench and Bar Commn., Tallahassee, 1990-91; pres. Fla. Conf. of Dist. Ct. Appeals Judges, Tallahassee, 1986-87. Mem. Panama City Airport Authority, 1952-55; past pres. Bay County Libr. Assn., Panama City. Lt. (j.g.) USNR, 1943-45. Mem. ABA, Fla. Bar, Tallahassee Bar Assn., Am. Judicature Soc. Home: 4115 W 17th St Panama City FL 32401-1122

SMITH, LARRY KEITH, newspaper publisher, editor, educator; b. Hickory, N.C., Apr. 3, 1939; s. David Lee and Edna Gertrude (Poovey) S.; m. Julia Bonham Smith, Oct. 1, 1960; children: Cynthia Smith Card, Amy Smith Strange, Leslie Smith Bohannon, Lara Smith Edwards, Heather Smith Packard. BA in Journalism, U. N.C., 1961; MA, U. Tenn., Knoxville, 1996. Assoc. editor The Leaksville (N.C.) News, 1963-64; editor The Herald Advocate, Wauchula, Fla., 1964-69; publisher, editor La Follette (Tenn.) Press, Advance Sentinel, Jeccico, Tenn., 1969—, The Town Crier, Lake City, Tenn., 1975—. Mem. Nat. Newspaper Assn. (numerous writing awards), Tenn. Press Assn. (pres. 1977-78, numerous writing awards), Tenn. Press Assn. Found. (pres. 1995—), Tenn. Press Svc. (v.p. 1984-85), S. Campbell County Rotary Club (pres. 1973-74, 80-81), Campbell County C. of C. (pres. 1970-71). Baptist. Office: La Follette Press PO Box 1261 La Follette TN 37766

SMITH, LARRY R., pediatrician, allergist, immunologist; b. Savannah, Ga., Jan. 16, 1950. MD, Med. Coll. Ga., 1976. Diplomate Am. Bd. Pediat., Am. Bd. Allergy and Immunology. Resident in pediat. Lloyd Noland Hosp., Fairfield, 1976-79; fellow in allergy and immunology Med. Coll. Ga., Augusta, 1982-84; pvt. practice. Mem. AMA, Am. Acad. Allergy and Immunology, Am. Coll. Allergy and Immunology. Office: South Georgia Allergy Clinic 2305 Robinhood Rd Albany GA 31707-3271*

SMITH, LARRY STEVEN, financial analyst, farmer, accountant; b. Jasper, Tenn., Sept. 30, 1950; s. Samuel Lester and Stella Mae (Barnes) S. BA in Econs., U. Ala., Tuscaloosa, 1972, MBA, 1975. Laborer Lester Smith Farms, Scottsboro, Ala., 1975-76; acct. Ala. Hwy. Dept., Montgomery, 1976-77, Ala. State Agy. for Social Security, Montgomery, 1977-78; acct., analyst Ala. Pub. Svc. Commn., Montgomery, 1978-79, utilities analyst II, 1980-81, supr., 1981-89, chmn. computer oversight com., 1988-91, supr. tariff sect. Telecommunications div., 1989—; sales assoc. Jack Hendrix Real Estate, Montgomery, 1979-80; interim dir. telecomm. divsn. Ala. Pub. Svc. Commn., 1993, mem. Telecomm. Task Force, 1996—. Mem. Montgomery Jaycees, 1978-81, bd. dirs., 1979, 80; bd. dirs. Ala. Jr. Miss. , Montgomery, 1979-81; mem. Ala. Reps., 1983—. Nat. Grad. Coun. Fellowship grantee, 1973. Mem. N.Am. Limousin Found., Nat. Audubon Soc., Wilderness Soc., Environ. Def. Fund, Am. Assn. of Ind. Investors, Amnesty Internat., Nat. Wildlife Fedn, Sierra Club. Baptist. Home: 1600 Cobblestone Ct Montgomery AL 36117-1702 Office: Ala Pub Svc Commn PO Box 991 Montgomery AL 36101-0991

SMITH, LARRY WAYNE, medical/surgical nurse; b. Washington, N.C., Jan. 2, 1962; s. Larry Grey and Norma D. Wilson. Grad. lic. practical nurse, Craven Community Coll., 1984, AAS, 1989. RN; cert. BCLS, ACLS, PALS. Patient care asst. Craven Regional Med. Ctr., New Bern, N.C., 1980-84, lic. practical nurse surg. unit, 1984-89, nurse in surg. unit, 1989, nurse in hosp. homecare, 1989, neurology nurse, 1989-90, staff nurse ICU, 1990-94; staff nurse ICU Naval Hosp., Camp Lejeune, N.C., 1991—. Home: PO Box 4004 Emerald Isle NC 28594-4004 Office: Craven Regional Med Ctr 2000 Neuse Blvd New Bern NC 28560-3449

SMITH, LAWRENCE LEIGHTON, conductor; b. Portland, Oreg., Apr. 8, 1936; s. Lawrence Keller and Bonita Evelyn (Wood) S.; children by previous marriage: Kevin, Laura, Gregory; stepchildren: Kristine, John. B.S. cum laude, Portland State Coll., 1956; grad. magna cum laude, Mannes Coll. Music, N.Y.C., 1959; Ph D (Hon.), Ind. U, 1992; D (hon.), U. Louisville, Ind. State U. Mem. faculty Mannes Coll. Music, 1959-62; prof. piano Boston U., 1963-64; asst. condr. Met. Opera, 1964-67; mem. faculty Curtis Inst., Phila., 1968-69, Calif. Inst. Arts, 1970-72, U. Tex., 1962-63; prin. guest condr. Phoenix Symphony, 1970-73; music dir., condr. Austin (Tex.) Symphony, 1971-72, Oreg. Symphony, Portland, 1973-80; pres., music dir. San Antonio Symphony, 1980-85; music dir., condr. Louisville Orch., 1983-95, condr. laureate, 1995-97; prin. guest condr. N.J. Symphony Orch., 1997—; faculty mem. Yale U., 1994—; guest condr. N.Y. Philharm., L.A. Philharm., Tulsa Philharm., Winnipeg (Man., Can.) Orch., Minn. Orch., Cin. Symphony, St. Louis Symphony, Moscow Philharm., Tokyo Philharm. Recipient 1st prize Met. Internat. Condrs. competition, 1964, Ditson Condrs. award Columbia U., 1988. Mem. Am. Fedn. Musicians, Mensa. Buddhist.

SMITH, LELAND WRIGHTMAN, retired military officer; b. Joplin, Ark., Feb. 2, 1914; m. Helen Doernenburg. BA, George Washington U., 1956, MA, 1958. Commd. 2d lt. USMCR, 1940; advanced through grades to maj., 1940-52; acct. VA, Washington, 1952-60; chief fin. mgmt. officer Nat. Ctrs. for Disease Control USPHS, Atlanta, 1960-70; commanding officer Marine Air Res., Washington and Atlanta, 1952-66; brig. gen., flag rank USMC, 1966-70. mem., vice chmn. Ark. Gov.'s Rural Health Com., Little Rock, 1978-79, Western Ark. Health Systems Agy., Russellville, 1980-88; mem., pres. Ozark Guidance Ctr., Harrison, Ark., 1968-82; past treas. Newton County Med. Ctr., 1972-83; lay leader, del. ann. conf., lay spkr. Jasper United Meth. Ch., 1980-91; lay leader Fayetteville Dist. United Meth. Ch., 1982-84; past Newton County rep. Comprehensive Health Planning Coun., 1971-73, N.W. Ark. Econ. Devel. Dist.; past Newton County rep., 1971-74, bd. dirs., pres. Ozark Regional Mental Health Ctr., 1984-85; past chair Newton County bldg. and equipment fund drive Claude Parish Radiation Therapy Inst., Harrison, Ark., 1990; bd. dirs. PARTI Found., 1991-94; charter mem. bd. dirs. Deer Vol. Fire Assn., 1988-92, coord. comm., active FCC licensing, installation and maintenance of radio repeater, 1988; past coord. Newton County Emergency Comm., Am. Radio Relay League, 1936—; charter, life mem. Friends of Libr., Newton County, 1990; v.p. Newton County Hist. Soc., 1975-82; bd. dirs. Boone County Hist. and Railroad Soc., 1993—. Decorated Bronze Star with Combat V, USMC, 1945; recipient Legion of Merit award USMC, San Diego, 1970. Fellow Radio Club of Am. (bd. dirs. 1986-87); mem. Marine Corps Res. Officers Assn. (nat. pres. 1966-67, Non Sibi Patria Roll of Honor 1968), Quarter Century Wireless Assn. (nat. pres. 1984-88, Roll of Honor 1988), Old Old Timers Club (nat. pres. 1994—), Masons (worshipful master 1947—, chaplain, numerous offices), Shriners, Am. Legion (comdr. Jasper Campbell-Edgmon). Home: 10 Hawthorn Dr Harrison AR 72601

SMITH, LEONARD, JR., medical/surgical and oncology nurse; b. Ft. Lauderdale, Fla., Aug. 17, 1955; s. Leonard and Ruthe Mae (Taylor) S.; m. Koreen Andrea Smith, Dec. 31, 1989; children: Jessica, Sara Marie, Marcus Alan. BS in Biology and Chemistry, Jacksonville U., 1977; postgrad., Fla. Atlantic U., 1978-82, U. fla., 1984-87; AS in Nursing, Broward Community Coll., Ft. Lauderdale, 1990; cert. in theol. studies, Knox Theol. Sem., 1994. RN, Fla., BLS. Physician asst. trained East Broward Med. Ctr., Pompano, Fla., 1987-88; mental health technician, counselor CPR-Ft. Lauderdale, 1988-90; nurse med.-surg. and oncology units Broward Gen. Med. Ctr., Ft. Lauderdale, 1990—; nurse mgr. Ft. Lauderdale (Fla.) Hosp., 1992—; cmty. health nurse Staff Builders Profl. Nursing, Ft. Lauderdale, 1991-94; RN Broward County Hospice, North Lauderdale, Fla., 1994—; community health nurse Staff Builders Profl. Nursing, Ft. Lauderdale, 1991—. Mem. AANC (cert. med.-surg. nursing). Democrat. Presbyterian.

SMITH, LINDA ANN, dietitian, consultant; b. Tyler, Tex., Jan. 26, 1950; d. John Franklin Fields and Bertha Areba Colby-Fields; m. Billy Ray Smith, Jr., May 1, 1975 (div. Aug. 1983); children: Angela Dawn, Amanda Rae. AA, Tyler (Tex.) Jr. Coll., 1970; BS, Tex. Woman's U., 1972, MS, 1973. Lic. dietitian; profl. sanitarian, tchr. Instr. Blinn Coll., Brenham, Tex., 1973-75; dietitian Mother Frances Hosp., Tyler, 1975-76; nutritionist III Tex. Dept. of Health, Tyler, 1976-81; dietitian Beverly Enterprises, Tyler, 1981-82; cons. dietitian various nursing homes, E. Tex., 1982—. Trustee Troup (Tex.) Sch. Bd., 1992-95, sec. 194-95. Mem. E. Tex. Dietetic Assn. (pres. 1975-76, Young Dietitian of the Yr. 1976), Tex. Dietetic Assn., Am. Dietetic Assn. Republican. Roman Catholic. Home: PO Box 665 Troup TX 75789-0665

SMITH, LISA E., guidance counselor; b. Bronx, N.Y., May 6, 1969; d. Frank C. and Jacquelyn S. (Satterfield) S. BS, Iona Coll., 1992; MS, Coll. New Rochelle, 1993. Cert. guidance and counseling, N.Y., Va. Guidance counselor Culpeper (Va.) County Schs., 1993—. Mem. Am. Vocat. Assn., Va. Sch. Counselors Assn., Am. Counselors Assn., Nat. Tech. Prep Network, Va. Admissions Coun. in Black C.C.s, Nat. Alliance of Black Sch. Educators. Democrat. Presbyterian. Home: 10705 Live Oak Ct Fredericksburg VA 22407 Office: Culpeper County HS 14240 Achievement Dr Culpeper VA 22701

SMITH, LISA WHITE, sociologist; b. Knoxville, July 20, 1960; d. Roger Kreis White and Mary Ann (Hall) Scruggs; m. Clifford Hirst, Dec. 17, 1983 (div. May 1989); children: Nichole, Andrea; m. Walker O. Smith, July 19, 1991; 1 child, Walker T. BA, U. Tenn., 1993, MA, 1996. Various archtl. positions various cos., Tenn./Fla., 1979-91; tchg. asst. U. Tenn., Knoxville, 1993-96; educator coord. East Tenn. Holocaust Conf., Knoxville, 1995. Mem. U.S. Holocaust Meml. Mus. Mem. Soc. for Study of Social Problems, So. Sociol. Soc. Democrat. Home: 9013 Straw Flower Dr Knoxville TN 37922 Office: U Tenn Dept Sociology 901 McClung Tower Knoxville TN 37996

SMITH, LOIS ANN (L.A.), foundation administrator, consultant; b. Chattanooga, Nov. 30, 1944; d. W. and Rose C. (Tucker) Hicks; divorced; 1 child, Tony A. Student, Lemoyne-Owen Coll., 1962-64; BA in Sociology and Bus. Adminstrn., Howard U., 1976, postgrad., 1977-78. Cert. notary pub., Md., Ga. Field underwriter, sales trainer N.Y. Life Ins. Co., Franklin Life Ins. Co., 1979-82; pres., gen. mgr. Lotona Enterprises, Inc., Washington, 1979-85; mktg. coord. Montgomery County Dept. Transp., Md., 1985-87; fund raising and tng. cons. Princess Ann & Co., Washington, 1987-91; grant/contract adminstr. coll. medicine Howard U., NIH, Washington, 1991-92; founder, exec. dir. Good News & Give Aways, Inc., Tucker, Ga., 1989—; pub. speaker Princess Ann & Co., Md., Ga., 1970-94, seminar presenter, 1985-94; freelance writer, 1975—; counselor in various fields, 1977—. Author: The Most Precious Moments, 1973, Let's Consider, A Sociological View of Employment, 1976, (play) A Reversible Oreo, 1974; pub., editor newsletter Good News & Give Aways, Inc., 1989-93; author, speaker (audio cassette tapes) I Care . . . , 1989, 90. Speaker, soloist various ednl., religious and civic orgns., 1960—; coord. Up the Hill Gang, 1979—; treas. Faith Cmty. Bapt. Ch., 1986-87; pub. speaker, vol. Dekalb Responds/ Dekalb Econ. Opportunity Authority, Decatur, Ga., 1993-94. Recipient Disting. Svc. award Sta. WNOO, 1979. Mem. Ga. Coll. Counselors Assn., Bus. & Profl. Women's Club (charter, editor newsletter 1980-82, Woman of Yr. honoree 1980), Kappa Delta Pi, Phi Beta Lambda. Office: Good News & Give Aways Inc PO Box 1911 Tucker GA 30085-1911

SMITH, LOIS COLSTON, secondary school educator; b. Edgewater, Ala., Aug. 3, 1919; d. Roy Minnie and Rebecca (Hayes) Colston; children: Linnie Ree Colston Carter, Lois Louise Colston Smith, Jessie Mae Colston Smith, Johnniza Colston Purifoy, Johnny Colston, Dorothy Dean Colston Cottingham, Lillian Dolly B. Colston Tarver. BS, A&M U., 1939; MA, N.Y.U., 1957. Vocat. Home Econ. Edn. 3rd and 4th grade tchr. Sulligent, Ala., 1957-61; elem. prin. Millport, Ala., 1962-67; 11th grade sci. and social studies tchr. Vernon, Ala., 1967-70; 7th-9th grade gen. vocat. home econ. tchr. Tuscaloosa, Ala., 1970-80, 7th grade gen. and voca. home econ. tchr., 1980-92; ret., 1995. Chmn. Voters registration, Tuscaloosa, Ala., 1980; troop leader Girl Scouts Am., Tuscaloosa, Ala., 1967-92; mem. bd. dirs. Shelter State Community Coll. Wellness Coun., 1993. Recipient Tombigbee Girl Scout 15 yr. svc. pin, Cert. Appreciation, Valuable Svc. award, Girl Scouts; named Zeta of Yr., Beta Eta Zeta chpt., Stillman Coll., 1983, Golden Cert. of Appreciation and Admiration Ala. A&M U., Huntsville, 1993. Mem. Ala. Edn. Assn., NEA, Order of Eastern Star, Ala. Vocat. Assn., AAUW, Beta Eta Zeta. Democrat. Baptist. Home: 3238 18th Pl Tuscaloosa AL 35401-4102

SMITH, LUCY ANSELMO, mental health nurse; b. Bklyn., Jan. 23, 1951; d. Anthony J. and Victoria (Farash) Anselmo; m. Glenn Frederick Smith, July 20, 1973; 1 child, Katherine Avena Smith. BSN, SUNY, Buffalo, 1973, MS, 1977. Cert. clin. specialist in adult psychiat./mental health nursing. Program dir. emergency svcs. Buffalo Gen. Hosp., 1977-80; psychiat. clin. specialist-adult svcs. Westbrook Hosp., Richmonmd, 1981-86; dir. staff devel. and nurse recruitment Psychiat. Inst. Richmond, Va., 1987; coord. crisis and referral svcs. MCC Behavioral Care, Richmond, 1987-92, sr. therapist, 1992-95; pvt. psychotherapist Richmond, 1995—. Contbr. articles to profl. jours. Named one of Outstanding Young Women of Am., 1984. Mem. Va. Nurses Assn. (chmn. coun. clin. specialists 1986-87, commr. on profl. practice 1988-90). Home: 2420 Hampden Row Rockville VA 23146-2137

SMITH, MARCIA JEAN, accountant, tax specialist, financial consultant; b. Kansas City, Mo., Oct. 19, 1947; d. Eugene Hubert and Marcella Juanita (Greene) S. Student, U. Nebr., 1965-67; BA, Jersey City State Coll., 1971; MBA in Taxation, Golden Gate U., 1976, postgrad., 1976-77; MS in Acctg., Pace U., 1982; Cert. of completion, Cours Commerciaux de Geneve, 1985-86. Legal intern Port Authority, N.Y., N.J., N.Y.C., 1972; legis. aide to Senator Harrison A. Williams Washington, 1973; tax accountant Bechtel Corp., San Francisco, 1974-77; sr. tax accountant Equitable Life Assurance Soc. U.S., N.Y.C., 1977, sec., 1977-79; tax sr. Arthur Andersen & Co., N.Y.C., 1979-82; pres. M.J. Smith Co., N.Y.C., 1983-85; prin. owner MJS Cons. Svcs. Internat. Tax Cons., Boston, Mass., 1988-93; gen. auditor dept. fin. Fulton County Govt., Atlanta, 1993-95; auditor State of Georgia, Dept. Med. Assistance, 1995—; cons. U.N., specialized agys., Geneva, 1985-87; asst. sec. Equico Lessors, Inc., Mpls., 1977-78, Equitable Gen. Ins. Group, Ft. Worth, 1977-79, Heritage Life Infield Assurance Co., Toronto, Ont., Can., 1978-79, Informatics, Inc., L.A., 1978-79; sec. Equico Capital Corp., N.Y.C. 1977-79, Equico Personal Credit, Inc., Colorado Springs, Colo., 1978-79, Equico Securites, Inc., N.Y.C., 1977-79, Equitable Environ. Health, Inc., Woodbury, N.Y., 1977-79; tax cons., real estate salesperson. Spl. advisor U.S. Congl. Adv. Bd.; human rights chmn. YWCA, Lincoln, Nebr., 1966-67; mem. Atlanta Women's Network. Spl. advisor U.S. Congl. Adv. Bd.; human rights chmn. YWCA, Lincoln, Nebr., 1966-67; mem. Atlanta Women's Network. Mem. AAAS, AAUW, NAA (Swiss Romande chpt.), Am. Mgmt. Assn., Nat. Soc. Pub. Accts., Inst. Mgmt. Accts., Am. Acctg. Assn., Internat. Assn. Fin. Planners, Internat. Fin. Mgmt. Assn., Am. Women's Club of Geneva, Nat. Assn. Women Bus. Owners, Am. Assn. Individual Investors, Inst. Internal Auditors, N.Y. Acad. Scis., Nat. Hist. Soc., Nat. Assn. Tax Practitioners, Assn. Managerial Economists, Postal Commemorative Soc., Am. Mus. Natural Nistory, Nat. Trust Historic Preservation, Ga. Govt. Fin. Officers Assn., Internat. Tax Inst., Ga. Soc. CPAs, Ill. CPA Soc., Assn. Cert. Fraud Examiners, Assn. Govt. Accts., Am. Econs. Assn., UN Assn. USA, EDP Auditors Assn., Mass. Soc. Ind. Accts., Acad. Legal Studies in Bus., Am. Bus. Law Assn., Internat. Platform Assn., U.S. Senatorial Club. Office: State of Ga Dept Med Assist Ste 502 1430 W Peachtree St NW Atlanta GA 30309-2936

SMITH, MARGARET BRAND, insurance executive, lawyer; b. Chattanooga, Okla., June 29, 1911; d. William August and Flora May (Davis) Brand; m. Harry Eben Smith, July 24, 1937 (dec. 1970). LLB, Jefferson Sch. Law, Dallas. Pvt. practice, also ins. cos. atty. Dallas, 1937-57; exec. v.p. Union Bankers Ins. Co., Dallas, 1957-62, pres., chief exec. officer, 1962-68, vice chair, 1968-73; pres., chief exec. officer United Gen. Ins. Co., Dallas, 1973-76; chmn. bd. Dallas Gen. Life Ins. Co., Dallas, 1980—. Pres. Dallas Girl Scouts, 1952; bd. dirs., pres. Presbyn. Children's Home, Waxahachie, Tex., 1970-76; elder North Park Presbyn. Ch., Dallas, 1972-76. Recipient Top Hat award Nat. Assn. Bus. and Profl. Women, Chgo., 1963, Award of Excellence Dallas Bus. and Profl. Women, 1964, Mature Woman award Altrusa Club, 1965, Woman of Awareness B'nai B'rith, 1965, Outstanding Svc. award North Dallas Bus. and Profl. Women, 1969. Mem. State Bar of Tex., Dallas Bar Assn. Republican. Presbyterian.

SMITH, MARGARET DILL, academic administrator; b. Elkton, Ky., Mar. 9, 1949; d. Sidney B. and Elizabeth (Jett) Dill; m. Dan Smith, Aug. 25, 1968; 1 child, Lauren Marie. BS, Austin Peay State U., 1970, MA in English, 1974; PhD, Vanderbilt U., 1981. Instr. lang. arts U. Ky. Hopkinsville C.C., 1971-72; coord. Ft. Campbell programs U. Ky. Hopkinsville Community Coll., 1971-78, coord. testing programs, 1976-80, coord. off-campus programs, 1976-83, coord. continuing edn. and community svcs., 1978-91; v.p. acad. affairs Bainbridge (Ga.) Coll., 1991—; mem. steering com. Nat. Conf. for Minority Success in Community Colls., 1990—. Co-editor: Community Colleges: Pathway to Kentucky's Future, 1989; contbr. articles to profl. publs. Advisor Hopkinsville Econ. Devel. Coun., 1986-90; charter exec. dir. Leadership Hopkinsville-Christian County, 1985; trustee Jennie Stuart Med. Ctr., Hopkinsville, 1990-91; founder, advisor Christian County Literacy Coun., Hopkinsville, 1986-91. Named Outstanding Young Educator in Ky., Ky. Jaycees, 1984. Mem. ASTD, Ky. Assn. Continuing Edn. (pres. 1986, Outstanding Mem. 1987), Am. Assn. Adult and Continuing Edn. (chmn. com. 1984-87, Spl. Recognition award 1984), Am. Coun. on Edn. (Ga. chpt. nat. identification program, mem. steering com. for women coll. adminstrs. 1992—), Am. Assn. Women Community Colls. (Ga. chpt., pres. 1994—), Ky. Literacy Commn., Pennyroyal Arts Coun. (pres. 1988), Bainbridge-Decatur County Arts Coun. (bd. dirs. 1992—, pres. 1994), Bainbridge-Decatur County C. of C. (bd. dirs.), Hopkinsville-Christian C. of C., Bainbridge Rotary (bd. dirs. 1994—). Home: RR 5 Box 1435 Bainbridge GA 31717-9323 Office: Bainbridge Coll PO Box 953 Bainbridge GA 31717-0953

SMITH, MARGARET GRETEL, park ranger; b. Nürnburg, Germany, Nov. 14, 1968; d. Charles Edward and Margaret (Hampton) Burnett; m. Thomas Edward Smith, Feb. 9, 1996. BA in Elem. and Environ. Edn., Shippensburg (Pa.) U., 1991; M.Park and Recreation, Western Ky. U., 1995. Park ranger Carlsbad (N.Mex.) Caverns Nat. Park, summers 1988-90, Eisenhower Nat. Hist. Site, Gettysburg, Pa., winters 1989-91, Assateaque Island Nat. Seashore, Berlin, Md., summer 1991, Mammoth Cave (Ky.) Nat. Park, 1991—, Grand Canyon (Ariz.) Nat. Park, summer 1992. Mem. Assn. of Nat. Park Rangers, Ky. Assn. for Environ. Edn. Roman Catholic. Office: Mammoth Cave National Park Mammoth Cave KY 42259

SMITH, MARGHERITA, writer, editor; b. Chgo., May 24, 1922; d. Henry Christian and Alicia (Koke) Steinhoff; m. Rufus Zartman Smith, June 26, 1943; children: Matthew Benjamin, Timothy Rufus. AB, Ill. Coll., 1943. Proofreader Editorial Experts, Inc., Alexandria, Va., 1974; mgr. proofreading div. Editorial Experts, Inc., Alexandria, 1978-79, mgr. publs. div., 1979-81, asst. to pres., 1980-81; freelance editor, cons. Annandale, Va., 1981—; instr. proofreading and copy editing, George Washington U., Washington, 1978-82; presenter workshops on proofreading for various profl. orgns., 1981—. Author: (as Peggy Smith) Simplified Proofreading, 1980, Proofreading Manual and Reference Guide, 1981, Proofreading Workbook, 1981, The Proof Is In the Reading: A Comprehensive Guide to Staffing and Management of Typographic Proofreading, 1986, Mark My Words: Instructions and Practice in Proofreading, 1987, rev. edit., 1993, Letter Perfect: A Guide to Practical Proofreading, 1995; contbr. articles to revs. to various publs. Recipient Best Instrnl. Reporting award Newsletter Assn. Am., 1980, Disting. Achievement award for excellence in ednl. journalism Ednl. Press Assn. Am., 1981, Disting. Citizen award Ill. Coll., 1992. Home and Office: 9120 Belvoir Woods Pky # 110 Fort Belvoir VA 22060-2722

SMITH, MARILYN LYNNE, small business owner; b. Atlanta, Oct. 15, 1944; d. Odis Madre and Anne Katherine (Luetje) S.; m. Robert H. Jackson, Aug. 21, 1965 (div. 1970); m. William Howard Gamble, July 31, 1970 (div. 1980); children: John Robert Jackson, Benjamin Lewis Gamble. Student, Ga. State U., Atlanta, 1962-65. Bookkeeper Haas, Holland et al, Atlanta, 1963-69; office/bus. mgr. Dr. W. H. Gamble, Jr., Atlanta, 1970-73; placement councillor Amcell div. Norrell, Atlanta, 1973-74; bus. mgr. Dr. W. H. Gamble, Jr., Atlanta, 1974-79; owner Atlanta Document Svc., 1980—; co-owner Atlanta Med. Documents, 1991—. Sponsor Explorer Scout Post, Tucker, Ga., 1987. Named Counsellor of the Yr., Norrell Southeastern Corp., 1974. Mem. Ga. Assn. Personnel Cons. (treas. 1982-84), Women's Commerce Club. Republican. Baptist. Office: Atlanta Document Svcs 1750 Peachtree St NW Atlanta GA 30309-2333

SMITH, MARK EUGENE, architectural engineering service company executive; b. Wareham, Mass., Apr. 1, 1951; s. Mark Alvin and Evelyn Marie (Somers) S.; m. Brigid Ann Murray, Oct. 17, 1979; children: Hugh Talmidge, Patrick Morgan. Student, Western Carolina U., 1970-71; AS, New England Inst. Tech., 1981; student, Boston U., 1982. Owner Marks Motor Co.,

Wareham, 1965-69; dir. satellite communications Home Oil Co., Wareham, 1968-82; chief designer HF Scientific Instrument, Ft. Myers, Fla., 1981-83; chief designer HVE Keltron Corp., Waltham, Mass., 1984-85; chief exec. officer Home Svcs., Ft. Myers, 1985—; cons. Underwood & Assocs., Cape Coral, Fla., 1981-89, Shaban Mfg. Co., Ft. Myers, 1982-83; chief designer Keltron Corp., Waltham, 1984-85. Co-author: The Art of Custom Painting, 1978. With USMC, 1969-72. Named Advanced Designer, Metalflake Design Group, Springfield, Mass., 1977. Mem. Soc. Mech. Engrs., Soc. Automotive Engrs., Am. Inst. for Design and Drafting (nat. drafting award 1981). Republican. Office: Gen Capitol PO Box 2044 Fremont NC 27830-1244

SMITH, MARY HOWARD HARDING, business consultant; b. Washington, Jan. 24, 1944; d. John Edward Harding and Sonja (Karlow) Harding Mulroney. AB, Duke U., 1965; MPA, Cen. Mich. U., 1975. With U.S. Army, 1968-91; dir. program mgmt. systems devel. agy. U.S. Army, Washington, 1987-91, dep. dir. program analysis and evaluation, 1987-91; dep. dir. def. info. Office Sec. Def., Arlington, Va., 1991-94; pres. Enterprise Opportunities, Inc., Arlington, Va., 1994—. Contbr. numerous articles to profl. jours. Bd. dirs. Army Family Action Symposiu, Washington, 1982. Mem. Am. Soc. Mil. Comptrollers, NAFE. Home and Office: 1805 24th St S Arlington VA 22202-1534

SMITH, MARY LOU, librarian; b. Huntington, Ind., Mar. 8, 1927; d. Harry Martin and Birtha (Fox) Bowers; m. Donald Eugene Smith, Oct. 2, 1948; children: Larry Wayne, Samuel Lee, Lynn Ellen Smith Worch, Michael Ray. BS in Edn., Huntington Coll., 1971; MS in Edn., Ball State U., 1973, MLS, 1973. Cert. tchr.; cert. libr.; cert. audio visual. Profl. musician Ft. Wayne (Ind.) Civic Symphony, 1942-45, Philharmonic Orch., Ft. Wayne, 1945-57, Civic Symphony, Chgo., 1947-49; owner M.L. Smith Reed Co., Huntington, Ind., 1950-65; libr., audio-visual specialist Huntington Sch. Systems, 1971-75; libr. Huntington Coll., 1975-77, Warsaw (Ind.) High Sch., 1978-85, Pub. Libr., Port Isabel, Tex., 1994-95; area coord. Am. Inst. Fgn. Study, Greenwich, Conn., 1978-85. Head ladies dept. YMCA, Huntington, 1966-70; bd. dirs., sec.-treas. Outdoor Resorts, Port Isabel, 1986-92; swimming instr. ARC, 1966-69; mem. Rosary Sodality, Huntington. Mem. AAUW, Ind. Sch. Libr. Assn. (sec. 1973-75), Ind. Sch. Libr. Assn., Ind. Ret. Tchrs. Assn., Altrusa Internat. (editor Warsaw chpt. 1983-86), Sigma Phi Gamma. Roman Catholic. Home: 950 S Garcia St Unit 53 Port Isabel TX 78578-4010 Home (summer): 901 Evergreen Ave Huntington IN 46750-4026

SMITH, MARY LYNN, electrical engineer; b. Miami, Fla., Feb. 20, 1965; d. Charles Dibrell and Marylin May (Peterson) S. BEE, Ga. Inst. Tech., 1988; MSEE, Santa Clara U., 1994. Engr. trainee NASA, Kennedy Space Ctr., Fla., 1983-87; mem. tech. staff Watkins-Johnson Co., San Jose, 1988-95; assoc. staff antenna engr. Scientific Atlanta, Inc., 1995—; lectr. and author in field. Recipient Cert. of Appreciation for participation in space shuttle Challenger's accident investigation, NASA, 1986. Mem. IEEE, Microwave Theory and Techniques Soc., Antenna and Propagation Soc. (local arrangements chair local chpt. IEEE MTT/APS), Assn. Old Crows. Republican. Methodist. Office: Scientific Atlanta Inc Instrumentation Group 3845 Pleasantdale Rd Atlanta GA 30340-4205

SMITH, MAURY DRANE, lawyer; b. Samson, Ala., Feb. 2, 1927; s. Abb Jackson and Rose Drane (Sellers) S.; m. Lucile West Martin, Aug. 15, 1953; children: Martha Smith Vandervoort, Sally Smith Legg, Maury D. Smith, Jr. BS, U. Ala., 1950, LLB, JD, 1952. Bar: Ala., 1952; U.S. Dist. Ct. (mid., no. and so. dists.) Ala. 1953; U.S. Ct. Appeals, 1957, U.S. Supreme Ct., 1957. Asst. atty. gen. State of Ala., Montgomery, 1952-55; asst. dist. atty. Montgomery County, 1955-63; ptnr. Balch & Bingham, Montgomery, 1955—; chmn. lawyers adv. com. Mid. Dist. Ala., Montgomery, 1990—; mem. U.S. Ct. of Appeals 11th cir. adv. com. on rules, Montgomery, 1990—, U.S. Dist. Ct. Mid. Dist. civil justice reform act adv. com., Montgomery, 1991—. Pres. Montgomery Area United Way, Ala., 1987; mem. Leadership Montgomery, 1994. Fellow Am. Coll. Trial Lawyers, Am. Bar Found.; mem. Univ. Ala. System (bd. trustees 1991—), Ala. Law Inst. (mem. coun.), ABA (mem. litigation sect.), Montgomery County Bar Assn. (pres. 1976), Montgomery Area C. of C. (pres. 1984), Ala. State Bar (chmn. jud. bldg. task force 1987-94). Home: 2426 Midfield Dr Montgomery AL 36111-1529 Office: Balch & Bingham 2 Dexter Ave PO Box 78 Montgomery AL 36101

SMITH, MICAH PEARCE, JR., advertising executive; b. Norman, Okla., Nov. 13, 1916; s. Micah Pearce and Julia Maud (Beeler) S.; m. Viola Sarajane Hatfield, June 1, 1946 (dec. Apr. 1986); children: Julia Annette, Carla Marie. Student U. Okla., 1936-41, corr. student, 1941-78. Dir. advt. Clinton Daily News (Okla.), 1946-53; dir. advt. Great Bend Daily Tribune (Kans.), 1953-55; ptnr., exec. v.p., gen. mgr. Indsl. Printing Inc., Oklahoma City, 1956-57; dir. advt. Daily Ardmoreite, Ardmore, Okla., 1958; dir. advt. Norman Transcript (Okla.), 1959-60; editor, pub. North Star, Oklahoma City, 1961; ptnr., exec. v.p. Gelders, Holderby & Smith, Inc., Oklahoma City, 1961-73; founder, editor Chickasaw Times, Norman, 1970-78; fuels allocation officer State of Okla., 1973-80; chmn., pres., mgr. Media Mktg. Assocs., Inc., Oklahoma City, 1981-95, ret., 1995. Author: An Account of an Indian Territory Pioneer, 1992, Biography of a Century: Old Church, Chronicles of a 100 Year Old Church; columnist syndicated newspaper column; author, editor Genealogy of Smith, Pearce, Groom, Cecil et al; contbg. author Sec. Ruling Council of Chickasaw Indian Tribe, Ada, Okla., 1971-79; coord. gov. campaign State of Okla., 1969-70; deacon, trustee, elder Presbyn. Ch.; mem. U. Okla. Found. Mem. Advt. Mgrs. Assn. (pres.), Am. Assn. Advt. Agy., Soc. Profl. Journalists, Okla. Hist. Soc. Home and Office: 1525 Melrose Dr Norman OK 73069-5366

SMITH, MICHAEL, retired university chancellor; b. St. Joseph, Mo., Jan. 30, 1941; s. Walton Joseph and Margaret Dorothy (Chubb) S.; m. Connie Stanton, Oct. 27, 1965; children: Jeffrey, Timothy. AD, Mo. Western Community Coll., 1960; BS, N.E. Mo. State U., 1967; PhD, U. Nebr., 1975. Ins. investigator Retail Credit Co., St. Joseph, Mo., 1963-65; instr. Havana (Ill.) High Sch., 1967-68, West Bend (Iowa) High Sch., 1968-70, U. Nebr., 1972-75; asst. prof. English Albany (Ga.) Jr. Coll., 1975-78; chmn. arts and scis., dir. internat. programs U. Minn., Crookston, 1978-80; chief exec. officer, coll. dean N.D. State U., Bottineau, 1980-87; provost, dean of faculty Richard Bland Coll., Coll. William and Mary, 1987-89; chancellor La. State U., Eunice, 1989-95; commr. North Cen. Assn. Colls. and Schs., 1984-87, accreditation cons./evaluator, 1982-87. With U.S. Army, 1960-63.

SMITH, MICHAEL BRADLEY, French language educator, translator; b. Hot Springs, Ark., June 14, 1940; s. Bradley Smith and Adele (Godchaux) Dawson; m. Helen Paula Kaplan, Dec. 16, 1979. PhD, U. Calif., San Diego, 1979. Assoc. prof. French Berry Coll., Rome, Ga., 1983—. Co-editor: Ontology and Alterity in Merleau-Ponty Aesthetics Reader, 1990; translator The Mystic Fable, 1992, Outsdie the Subject, 1993, In the Time of the Nations, 1994, Proper Names/On Maurice Blanchot, 1996. Mem. Merleau-Ponty Cir., Levinas. Office: Berry Coll Dept French Mount Berry GA 30149

SMITH, MICHAEL JOSEPH, composer, pianist, lecturer; b. Tiline, Ky., Aug. 13, 1938; s. Marvin Gilford and Bobbie Bell (Vinson) S.; m. Kerstin Alli-Maria Andersson, May 1973; children: Tanja Michaelsdotter, Kassandra Michaelsdotter; m. Wei Wei, 1994; children: Symington Wei, Remington Wei. Student, New Eng. Conservatory Music, Julliard Sch. Pres., bd. dirs. World Music (U.S.A.), Inc., Atlanta, 1993—; composer-in-residence, Ga., 1980, 88-90; lectr., performer Agnes Scott Coll., Atlanta, Bowdoin Coll., Maine, Royal Opera, Stockholm, Ctrl. Conservatory Music, Beijing and Xian, China; rschr. IBM Corp. Scandinavia and Roland Synthesizer Corp., 1986—. Performed 1st European concert tour, 1970; on concert tours of jazz and contemporary ensembles in Western Europe and U.S., from 1972; composer 10 major ballet works, scores for major films and TV projects, 560 works for various ensembles; commns. include Moscow Philharm., Tbilisi Chamber Orch., various European ensembles, ballet cos.; performances include Atlanta Olympics, 1996, Bolshoi Theatre, Moscow, Leningrad U., Royal Swedish Opera, Stockholm, Lincoln Ctr., N.Y.C., Carnegie Hall, N.Y.C., Philharm. Hall, Berlin, stadiums in Shanghai, Guanzhou, Yunan and Hong Kong; numerous recs., from 1970. With USN, 1955-59. Mem. Swedish Composers Soc., Internat. Soc. Contemporary Music. Home and Office: PO Box 81107 Conyers GA 30208-9107

SMITH, MICHAEL WILLIAM, construction and consulting company executive; b. Chgo., Aug. 1, 1944; s. John Joseph and Maryann (Poczatko) S.; m. June Dolores Wieciech, Sept. 9, 1967; 1 child, Michael William. Student, Wright Coll., Chgo., 1962-63, Amondsen Coll., Chgo., 1963-65. Comm. engr. Automatic Elec. Co., Northlake, Ill., 1968-70; asst. engr. elec. design Pioneer Svc. & Engrng., Chgo., 1970-72, start-up engr. Kewaunee Nuclear Power Plant, 1972-73; design leader Fluor Power, Chgo., 1973-75; project mgr. Fluor Nederland BV, Harlem, Netherlands, 1975-77; project leader Fluor Engrs., Houston, 1977-79; project engr. Texamation, LaPorte, Tex., 1980-82; cons., project mgr. Shell Devel. Co., Houston, 1985—; pres. ASCI-All Side Constrn. Inc., Houston, 1978—; instr. Houston Community Coll., 1978. Awarded Outstanding Paper, ISA Internat. Program ICC-Computer, 1991. Mem. NRA (life), Aircraft Owners and Pilots Assn., Instrument Soc. Am. (sr.), Am. Radio Relay League (life), Confederate Air Force (col.), West Tex. Wing, West Houston Squadron, Traron 1, Lone Star Flight Mus. Home: 19810 Skycountry Ln Houston TX 77094-3017 Office: ASCI All Side Constrn Inc 19810 Skycountry Ln Houston TX 77094-3017

SMITH, MICHAEL WILLIAM, English language educator; b. Wheeling, W.Va., Dec. 4, 1963; s. Carl William and Catherine Russel (Keith) S. BS, Va. Poly. Inst., 1987, MA, 1989; PhD, Fla. State U., 1995. Instr. English Va. Poly. Inst., Blacksburg, Va., 1987-89, Fla. State U., Tallahassee, 1991—; judge World's Best Short Story Contest, Tallahassee, 1995, Sherman Anderson Essay Award, 1988. Editor: (jour.) Nomad, 1991-96; author: Body Politics: Journal of AIDS Terrorist, 1996; contbr. poetry to anthologies. Mem. MLA, Internat. Assn. Philosophy and Lit. Office: PO Box 211 Willis VA 24380

SMITH, MYRON GEORGE, former government official, consultant; b. Terrebonne, Minn., June 9, 1920; s. Adrian G. and Marie E. (Crompe) S.; m. Louise J. Hennessey, May 22, 1944 (div. 1973); children: Michael, Thomas, John, Patricia, Dennis; m. Nguyen Anh My, Aug. 30, 1975; children: Yvette, Bryan. BS in Agrl. Econs. and Soil Sci., U. Minn., 1946. Soil scientist USDA, 1946-50, agrl. ext. advisor, 1950-58; owner No. Ill. Agrl. Svc., 1958-62; with U.S. AID, Dept. State, 1962-84; agrl. sales advisor U.S. AID, Dept. State, India, 1962-66; asst. dir. crop prodn. Vietnam U.S. AID, Dept. State, 1966-70, chief agrl. divsn. Indonesia, 1970-73; assoc. dir. U.S. AID, Dept. State, Vietnam, 1974-75; chief agrl. divsn. Mali U.S. AID, Dept. State, 1976-81, chief agrl. project mgr. West Africa, 1981-84; agrl. cons. U.S. AID, Dept. State, Zaire, 1988-90, Indonesia, 1993-94; assoc. prof. U. Ark., 1985. 1st lt. USAAF, 1941-45. Decorated Purple Heart, Air medal with 6 oak leaf clusters, D.F.C., Am. Campaign medal, WW II Victory medal, European-African-Middle Eastern Campaign medals with 4 oak leaf clusters, Agr. medal 2d class, Vietnam, 1969, Agr. medal 1st class, Vietnam, 1970, Labor medal 1st class, Vietnam, 1970, Economy medal 2d class, Vietnam, 1970. Mem. Am. Fgn. Service Assn. Home and Office: 309 N Manchester St Arlington VA 22203

SMITH, NAN SHELLEY, art educator, sculptor; b. Phila., Nov. 10, 1952; d. Frank Smith and Rosalyn Schaeffer. BFA, Temple U., 1974; MFA, Ohio State U., 1977. Grad. teaching assoc. Ohio State U., Columbus, 1974-77; vis. instr. U. Ill., Champaign, 1977-79; assoc. prof. U. Fla., Gainesville, 1979-96, prof. 1996—, coord. Ceramics Program, 1979—, co-chmn. vis. artists com., 1981-86, 96—, chmn. publicity com., 1983-85. One woman shows include Valencia Community Coll. North Gallery, Orlando, Fla., 1985, The McQuade Gallery, North Andover, Mass., 1984, The Shillard-Smith Gallery, Clearwater-Belleair, Fla., 1983, The Sampson Gallery, Deland, Fla., 1983, The University Gallery, Gainesville, Fla., 1981; exhibited in group shows at The Contemporary Arts Ctr., New Orleans, 1994, San Angelo (Tex.) Mus. Fine Art, 1994, 96, Jacksonville (Fla.) Art Mus., 1994, Lill St. Gallery, Chgo., 1994, The Samuel P. Harn Mus. Art, Gainesville, 1995, Kennedy-Douglass Ctr Arts, Florence, Ala., 1995, Laband Gallery-Loyola Marymount U., L.A., 1995. Grantee Edith Fergus Material Fund, 1977, Ford Found., 1977, U. Ill. Ford Found. Faculty, 1977-1978, U. Fla. Grad. Faculty Research, 1980, 1983-84, U. Fla. Faculty Devel., 1986-87; Individual Artists fellow Dept. of State and Fine Arts Council Fla., 1980-81, 91-92; So. Arts Fedn./ NEA fellow in sculpture, 1993-94. Mem. Internat. Sculpture Ctr., Nat. Council Edn. Ceramic Arts. Democrat. Jewish. Clubs: Internat., Folk Dance. Home: 2310 NW 142nd Ave Gainesville FL 32609-4022 Office: Dept Art U Fla 302 FAC Gainesville FL 32611

SMITH, OWEN FRANKLIN, architect; b. Benson, N.C., Nov. 26, 1917; s. Robert Franklin and Myrtle Irene Smith; m. Dorothy Kate Hellen, Aug. 4, 1940; children: Owen Franklin Jr., Sidney David. BS in Archtl. Engrng., N.C. State Coll., 1939. Registered architect, N.C. Mgr. millworks divsn. Star Mfg. Co., Inc., Benson, N.C., 1938-41; archtl. draftsman Thomas W. Cooper, Architect, Raleigh, N.C., 1941-42; contract engr. Farm Security Adminstrn., Raleigh, 1942; estimator, expediter HSB&FJ Constrn. Co., Winston-Salem, N.C., 1943; archtl. draftsman W.H. Deitrich, Architect, Raleigh, 1944-45; architect Raleigh, 1946—. Recipient Excellence in Arch. and Engring., Design of N.C. Farm Bur. Fedn. Prestressed Concrete Inst., 1971, Merit award N.C. Dept. of Pub. Instrn., 1993. Mem. Raleigh Civitan Club (pres. 1991-92). Home: 122 Perquimans Dr Raleigh NC 27609-6938 Office: Owen F Smith Architect 419 N Boylan Ave Raleigh NC 27603-1211

SMITH, PAMELA RODGERS, elementary education educator; b. Hartselle, Ala., Feb. 21, 1961; d. Jesse Gene and Zella Lurline (Brown) Rodgers; m. Jeffrey Neal Smith, July 21, 1990. Student, Calhoun C.C., Decatur, Ala., 1979-82; BS in Early Childhood and Elem. Edn., Athens (Ala.) State Coll., 1984; M in Early Childhood Edn., U. Ala., Birmingham, 1990, AA cert., 1992. Day care tchr. Little Red Schoolhouse, Hartselle, 1977-84; tchr. kindergarten Neel (Ala.) Elem. Sch., 1985-86, Crestline Elem. Sch., Hartselle, 1987-95, Barkley Bridge Elem. Sch., Hartselle, 1995—; cons. whole lang. workshop No. Ala. Tchr. Exch., 1991—. Mem. NEA, Ala. Edn. Assn., Hartselle Edn. Assn., Internat. Reading Assn., Ala. Reading Assn., Tenn. Valley Reading Assn., Constructivist Math. Network, Whole Lang. Network, Civitan (sec. Hartselle 1992-93, 93—), Kappa Kappa Iota. Democrat. Baptist. Home: 709 Frost St SW Hartselle AL 35640-2703

SMITH, PAT EVERETT, chemical company executive; b. San Diego, July 17, 1930; s. Jack and Eva (Coffman) S.; m. Sept. 16, 1961. BS in Chemistry, UCLA, 1954. Chemist Lever Bros., Los Angeles, 1959-64; dir. rsch. and devel. Cee Bee Chem. Co., Los Angeles, 1964-69; material and process engr. Gary Aircraft Corp., San Antonio, 1969-71; v.p., owner Eldorado Chem. Co., San Antonio, 1969—. Inventor U.S. Patent Process for Biochemical Reactions, 1975. Election judge City of Hill Country Village, Tex. 1983. With U.S. Army, 1955-59. Recipient Smalley award Am. Oil Chemists' Soc. 1961. Mem. Nat. Assn. Corrosion Engrs., Am. Soc. Test Methods, Soc. Automotive Engrs., Soc. for the Advancement of Material and Process Engrs., Aircraft Owners and Pilots Assn., Tech. Assn. of Pulp and Paper Engrs., Harp & Shamrock Soc. Office: Eldorado Chem Co PO Box 34837 San Antonio TX 78265-4837

SMITH, PATRICIA JACQULINE, marketing executive; b. Orange, N.J., June 13, 1944; d. Michael Joseph and Helen Francis (Costello) S. BS, U. Md., 1967. Field dir. Colgate Palmolive Co., N.Y.C., 1967-71; account exec. Foote Cone & Belding, N.Y.C., 1971-72; dir. regional sales, dir. ARA Services, Inc., Phila., 1973-76; dir. federally funded programs Ogden Food Service, Boston, 1976-79; v.p. Smith Tool Co., Manesquan, N.J., 1979-84; chmn., CEO Hygolet Metro, Inc., New Canaan, Conn., 1984-87; mktg. cons. Smith Mktg. Svcs., La Jolla, Calif., 1988-94; pres. Tea for Two Inc., Laguna Beach, Calif., 1995—; ptnr. La Jolla Playhouse. Bd. dirs., treas. Big Sister League, San Diego; mem. exec. com. Multiple Sclerosis Brunch Soc.; ptnr. La Jolla Playhouse. Mem. Women in Sales, Nat. Assn. Profl. Saleswomen, Bus. and Profl. Women's Club (N.Y.), Victorian Tea Soc., The Discovery Mus., Women's Club Laguna Beach, AAUW, Laguna Beach C. of C. Republican. Home: PO Box 4994 Laguna Beach CA 92652

SMITH, PAUL EDMUND, JR., philosophy and religion educator; b. Northampton, Mass., Feb. 6, 1927; s. Paul Edmund and Mary Jane (Murphy) S.; B.A., U. Mass., 1948; postgrad. Harvard U., 1948-49; M.A., Boston U., 1957; B.D., Columbia Theol. Sem., 1957, M.Div., 1971; postgrad. U. N.C., 1967-68. Instr. Latin and French, Chester (Vt.) High Sch., 1949-53, Loris (S.C.) High Sch., 1953-54; lectr. history U. Ga., Albany, 1957-59; instr. Latin, Rocky Mount (Va.) High Sch., 1959-61; minister Henderson Presbyn. Ch., Albany, 1957-59, Rocky Mount (Va.) Presbyn. Ch., 1959-64; asst. prof. religion Ferrum (Va.) Coll., 1961-68; vis. lectr. history John Tyler C.C., Chester, Va., 1968-69; instr. philosophy and religion Richard Bland Coll., Petersburg, Va., 1968-71, asst. prof., 1971-76, asso. prof., 1976—, chmn. dept., 1971—. Mem. Am. Hist. Assn., Presbytery of the Peaks. Democrat. Presbyterian. Office: Richard Bland Coll Commerce Hall Petersburg VA 23805

SMITH, PAUL FREDERICK, plant physiologist, consultant; b. Copeland, Kans., Dec. 17, 1916; s. Frederick Eugene and Susie Irene (Wikoff) S.; m. Marjorie Haselwood, July 6, 1940; children: Gary Lynn, Carol Jeanne. BS, U. Okla., 1938, MS, 1940; PhD, U. Calif., 1944. Asst. plant physiologist USDA, Salinas, Calif., 1943-45, Orlando, Fla., 1946-50; assoc. physiologist USDA, 1950-55, plant physiologist, 1956-61, prin. physiologist, 1962-71, head physiologist, 1971-75, hort. cons., 1975—. Contbr. chpts. to books and articles to profl. publs. With USN, 1945-46. Fellow Am. Soc. Hort. Sci.; mem. Fla. Hort. Soc. (hon. life, Presdl. Gold medal 1970). Home and Office: 2695 Ashville St Orlando FL 32818-9018

SMITH, PAUL LOWELL, realtor, minister; b. Fairfield, Ala., July 5, 1940; m. Janet E. Lindsay, Jan. 23, 1964; children: Janine Smith Shelby, Paul L. Jr., Scott Lyndsay, Andrew Hamilton. BA, Samford U., 1962; ThM, New Orleans Bapt. Sem., 1965, ThD, 1972. Pastor Fulton (Ala.) Bapt. Ch., 1962-66, Ruth (Miss.) Bapt. Ch., 1968-70, Ethel (Miss.) Bapt. Ch., 1970-72, First Bapt. Ch., Citronelle, Ala., 1972-74; pres. Paul Lowell Smith Evangelistic Ministries, 1974-91, Smitty Realty, Inc., Saraland, Ala., 1975—, MTS Investment Corp., Saraland, Ala., 1989-91, 95—, Foley Plantation, Inc., 1994—; cons. land devel. Mcht.'s Nat. Bank, Mobile, Ala., 1985-86. Author: Greek Mystery Religions, 1971; contbr. articles on real estate investments and devels. Pres. Citronelle Youth Football League, 1982; master ceremonies Citronelle Oil Bowl Pageant, 1982; auctioneer various charities, Mobile, 1980-94; fgn. mission bd. So. Bapt. Conv.; evangelist for crusades in Ecuador, Antigua, Guyana. Home: 10801 Celeste Rd Saraland AL 36571-9705 Office: Smitty Realty Inc PO Box 683 Saraland AL 36571-0683

SMITH, PAUL WINSTON, petroleum geologist; b. Norman, Okla., Dec. 11, 1959; s. Earl Winston and Mona Margaret (Wicker) S.; m. Bridget Ann Bright, Dec. 10, 1983; 1 child, Daniel Winston. BS in Geology, U. Okla., 1982, MS, 1992. Geol. asst. Siskon Corp., Reno, Nev., 1978-80; from geologist to pres. Norex Corp., Norman, 1980-93; sr. geologist Dwight's Energydata, Oklahoma City, 1993—; bd. dirs. Gold Hill Corp., Norman, Norex Corp. Contbg. author: Oklahoma Geologic Survey Symposium on the Viola and Simpson Groups in the Mid Continent, 1995; contbr. articles to profl. jours. Asst. scoutmaster Boy Scouts Am., Norman, 1988-92. Mem. Am. Assn. Petroleum Geologists, Oklahoma City Geol. Soc. (grantee 1991). Home: 4304 Upper Lakes Dr Norman OK 73072 Office: Dwights Energydata 4350 Will Rogers Pkwy Oklahoma City OK 73108

SMITH, PENNY, middle school educator; b. Dayton, Ohio, Sept. 28, 1940; d. Sidney North and Helen (Elliott) Correll; m. Mark Richard Smith, June 21, 1980 (dec. Nov. 1994); children: Adam Mark, Erica North. BS in Edn., Taylor U., 1963; MEd, Bowling Green State U., 1966. Cert. tchr., N.C., Fla., Hawaii, Ind. 3d grade tchr. East Auburn (Ind.) Elem. Sch., 1963-66, Skycrest Elem. Sch., Clearwater, Fla., 1972-73; 1st grade tchr. John Wilson Elem. Sch., Honolulu, 1966-67; 4th grade tchr. Harrison-McKinney Elem. Sch., Auburn, Ind., 1967-71; 4th-6th grade tchr. Prospect Elem. Sch., Monroe, N.C., 1973-75; 6th grade tchr. Parkwood Mid. Sch., Monroe, 1975-96, advisor yearbook, cheerleaders, outward bound; internat. studies Soviet Union, 1988. Speaker Am. Cancer Soc., Charlotte, N.C.; actor Calvary Ch., Charlotte; singer/dancer Sweet Adelines, Charlotte. Recipient award Terry Sanford Orgn., 1980, Outstanding Young Educator award Auburn Jaycees, 1964; named Union County Tchr. of Yr., 1976, Parkwood Middle Sch. Tchr. of Yr., 1992; Fulbright scholar, India, 1992. Mem. NEA, N.C. Coun. Social Studies, Assn. English Tchrs., Assn. Classroom Tchrs., Assn. N.C. Educators. Republican. Home: 7722 Riverside Dr Apt 201D Tulsa OK 74136

SMITH, PETER, chemist, educator, consultant; b. Sale, Cheshire, Eng., Sept. 7, 1924; came to U.S., 1951; s. Peter and Winifred Emma (Jenkins) S.; m. Hilary Joan Hewitt Roe, 1951; children: Helen Andrews Winifred, Eric Peter, Richard Harry, Gillian Carol. B.A. Queens' Coll., Cambridge U., 1946, M.A., 1949, Ph.D., 1953. Jr. sci. officer Royal Aircraft Establishment, Farnborough, Hampshire, Eng., 1943-46; demonstrator chemistry dept. Leeds U., Yorkshire, England, 1950-51; postdoctoral research fellow in chemistry Harvard U., Cambridge, Mass., 1951-54; asst. prof. chemistry Purdue U., West Lafayette, Ind., 1954-59; asst. prof. chemistry Duke U., Durham, N.C., 1959-61, assoc. prof., 1961-70, prof., 1970-95, prof. emeritus chemistry, 1995—. Contbg. author: chem. research jours. Fulbright post-doctoral scholar Fulbright Commn., Harvard U., 1951-53. Mem. Am. Chem. Soc., Royal Soc. Chemistry, Am. Phys. Soc., Sigma Xi, Phi Lambda Upsilon, Alpha Chi Sigma. Home: 2711 Circle Dr Durham NC 27705-5726 Office: Dept Chemistry Paul M Gross Chem Lab PO Box 90346 Durham NC 27708-0346

SMITH, PHILIP WAYNE, writer, communications company executive; b. Fayetteville, Tenn., Sept. 2, 1945; s. Clyde Wilson and Chastain (Finch) S.; m. Susan Jones, June 22, 1968; 1 child, Alan Wayne. Student, U. So. Miss., 1963-64, Athens Coll., 1964-65, 69-70. Reporter The Huntsville (Ala.) Times, 1964-66, The Elk Valley Times, Fayetteville, 1969-70; edn. reporter The Huntsville Times, 1970-71; Washington corr. The Huntsville Times, Washington, 1971-76; White House corr. Newhouse News Svc., Washington, 1977-80, Pentagon corr., 1981-84; writer Huntsville, 1984—; pres. P.S. Comms., Huntsville, 1994—; pub. rels. cons. Teledyne Brown Engring., Huntsville, 1984—; safety film producer VECO, Inc., Prudhoe Bay, Alaska, 1991. Co-author: Protecting the President, 1985 (Lit. Guild alt. selection 1986); screenwriter Our Land Too, 1987, Chemicals in War, 1989, Security: Everyone's Job, 1990, Face to Face Prospecting, 1992, Investigating Child Abuse, 1992, Lead Generation, 1993, Telephone Prospecting, 1993, Delayed Enlistment Program Management, 1993, Recruiter Sales Presentation, 1994, Duties and Responsibilities of Recruiting Station Commanders, 1994, Training Future Leaders, 1994, Rehabilitative Training Instructor Program, 1994, U.S. Army Program Executive Office for Tactical Missiles, 1995, Training: The Army Advantage, 1995, National Environmental Policy Act Compliance, 1996, Operations of the M21 Remote Sensing Chemical Agent Alarm, 1996. Sgt. USMC, 1966-69, Vietnam. Decorated Navy Achievement medal with combat V; named for Reporting Without Deadline, Ala. Press Assn., 1972, News Feature Writing, Ala. AP, 1975. Mem. Tenn. Screenwriting Assn., VFW. Democrat. Episcopalian. Home and Office: 8007 Hickory Hill Ln SE Huntsville AL 35802-3252

SMITH, PHILLIP CARL, marine and ship pilot, rancher; b. Wewahitchka, Fla., Aug. 12, 1941; s. Ottis Benjamin and Bessie (Kemp) S.; m. Belle Melancon, Feb. 28, 1966; children: Debra Kay, Phillip Carl Jr. Diploma, Wewahitchka High Sch., 1959. Commd. radar observer, unltd. 1st class pilot lic. for Sabine Waterway and tributaries, Tex. From deckhand to capt. Sabine Towing Co., Groves, Tex., 1959-64; ship pilot, ptnr./owner Sabine Pilots, Groves, Tex., 1965—; rancher Tex., 1979—; rander, owner Red S Ranch, Kirbyville, Tex., 1979—, God's Little Acres Ranch; cons. in field, 1965—; expert witness maritime ct. cases, Beaumont, Tex. Elder LDS Ch., Port Arthur, Tex., 1973—. With U.S. Army, 1962-67. Mem. Masons (32 degree). Home: 324 Farm Dr Bridge City TX 77611-2723

SMITH, PRESTON, minister; b. Kinston, N.C., Jan. 1, 1946; s. Herman and Minnie Alberta (Houston) S.; m. Judy Noble, Aug. 17, 1968; children: Amanda L., Charles P., Jason C. BA in Religion, Campbell Coll., 1973; MDiv in Pastoral Care, S.E. Sem., 1978; postgrad., East Carolina U., 1994. Ordained to ministry Free Will Bapt. Ch., 1968; bd. cert. chaplain. Pastor Welcome Home Ch., Beaufort, N.C., 1968-71, Rains Crossroads, Princeton, N.C., 1972-76, Piney Grove, Kenly, N.C., 1976-78; res. chaplain U. N.C. Hosp., Chapel Hill, 1978-80, fellow in pastoral care, 1980-81; dir. of pastoral care Nash Gen. Hosp., Rocky Mount, N.C., 1981—; employee assistance coord. Nash Health Care Sys., Rocky Mount, 1994—; cons. for ch. conflict Presbyn. Chs., Rocky Mount, N.C., 1984-87, N.C. Chaplains Assn., 1986—; bioethics bd. Nash Health Care Sys., 1994; bd. dirs. Down East Christian Ins., 1996. Editor REPLINE, 1992—, N.C. Chaplains Assn. Newsletter, 1986-88. Bd. dirs. Kiwanis, Rocky Mount, 1988-90; mem. United Way, Rocky Mount. Mem. N.C. Chaplains Assn. (pres. v.p., sec. exec. com. 1986—, Outstanding Leadership award 1994), Coll. of Chaplains (state rep.

1991-96, chair mem. svc. coun., bd. dirs. 1996). Democrat. Baptist. Home: 100 N Applewood Ct Rocky Mount NC 27803 Office: Nash Health Care Sys Inc 2460 Curtis Ellis Dr Rocky Mount NC 27804

SMITH, PRESTON EARL, corporate executive; b. Canton, S.D., Dec. 17, 1944; s. Eugene Benjamin and Flavia (Ertz) S.; children: Janine Marie, Stephanie Ann, Flavia Ann. Buyer J.C. Penney's, Dayton, Ohio, 1966-69; with Montgomery County, Dayton, 1969-75; securities profl. GM Corp., Dayton, 1975-88; founder Buckey Radiant Barrier, Dayton, 1988-92, Quantum Internat., Pullayup, Wash., 1992-96, Tech 2000 Inc, Roswell, Ga., 1996—. Inducted into the U.S. Space Found. Hall of Fame, Colo., 1996; nominated to U.S. Space Tech. Hall of Fame NASA, 1995, One of 50 Cos. using NASA Tech. in the U.S., included in NASA Spinoff Book, 1993, 95. Mem. ASTM, Nat. Assn. Radiant Barrier Tech. (v.p., founder), Dayton Engrs. Club (Pres.'s award for excellence as outstanding new mem. 1991). Office: Tech 2000 Inc 770 Old Roswell Pl Ste J200 Roswell GA 30076

SMITH, R. J., JR., oil company executive; b. Big Spring, Tex., Sept. 9, 1930; s. R. J. and Myrtle (O'Quinn) S.; m. Sarah Sue Holmes, Sept. 8, 1950 (div. 1962); children: Molly Smith Frank, Cassie Smith Roop; m. 2d, Sandra Ann Schroeder, Jan. 21, 1971. Student, Abilene Christian U., 1948-50, So. Methodist U., 1951-52, Goethe U., Frankfurt, Germany, 1953-54; LL.D., Northwood U., 1983. Aero. engr. Chance-Vought Aircraft, Dallas, 1951-52; ind. oil operator, Dallas, 1960-62; ops. chief Leland Fikes, Dallas, 1963-66; owner, operator Texon Petroleum Corp (sold to Exxon USA 1983), Dallas, 1967-83; owner, pres. Cheyenne Petroleum Corp., Dallas, 1967—, Texan Petroleum Corp., Dallas, 1985—; pres., CEO Lehndorff Minerals, 1989—. Bd. dirs. Effie and Wofford Cain Found., Dallas, 1979—, Friends Dallas Police, U. Tex. Southwestern Med. Ctr. Fund, So. Meth. U. John Tower Ctr. Polit. Studies; chmn. bd. govs. Northwood U., Tex., trustee, West Palm Beach, Fla., Midland, Mich. and Dallas, 1968—; Tex. del. at large Rep. Nat. Conv., 1996; dir. Bob Dole for Pres. Com., Tex. Mem. Ind. Producers Assn. Am., Tex. Ind. Producers and Royalty Owners, Mid-Continent Producers Assn., N.Mex. Ind. Producers Assn. Republican. Clubs: Preston Trail Golf, Dallas Gun, Crescent, Montaigne, Bent Tree Country (all Tex.); Del Mar Turf (Calif.). Office: Texan Petroleum Corp 2626 Cole Ave Suite 603 LB 63 Dallas TX 75204

SMITH, R. MARK, English language educator; b. Tulsa, Apr. 23, 1960; s. William Leonard and Patsy Virginia (Peterson) S.; m. Shiela Renee Pate, July 20, 1985; children: Trevor Paul, Brittany Renee. BA in Journalism, N.E. La. U., 1982; MA in English, S.W. La. U., 1987, PhD in English, 1992. Teaching asst. S.W. La. U., Lafayette, 1987-92, instr. English, 1992-93; asst. prof. English Valdosta (Ga.) State U., 1993—; tech. writer La. Productivity Ctr., Lafayette, 1991-93. Named Outstanding Young Men of Am., 1989. Mem. Modern Lang. Assn., Coll. Conf. Composition and Comm., Phi Kappa Phi, Tau Kappa Epsilon. Baptist.

SMITH, R. RUCKER, superior court judge; b. Americus, Ga., Oct. 15, 1953; s. Herschel Atticas and Mary Ann Smith; m. Jincy Blair, May 23, 1986 (div. May 1993); children: Madison Blair, James Wilder Rucker, Mason Elizabeth. BA, U. Fla., 1976; LLD, Emory U., 1979. Bar: Ga. 1979, U.S. Dist. Ct. (no. dist.) Ga. 1979, (mid. dist.) Ga. 1982, U.S. Ct. Appeals (5th cir.) 1980, (11th cir.) 1981, U.S. Tax Ct. 1982. Pvt. practice Atlanta, 1979-81; asst. dist. atty. Southwestern Jud. Cir., Americus, 1981-83, chief asst. dist. atty., 1983-92, judge superior cts., 1993—. Mem. rules com. Ga. State Dem. Com., Atlanta, 1990—; past pres. Sumter Hist. Soc., 1991, Sumter County Coun on Child Abuse, 1992. Named Outstanding Young Man of Yr., Sumter County Jaycees, 1984. Mem. Kiwanis. Methodist. Home: PO Box 501 Americus GA 31709-0501 Office: Office of Superior Cts PO Box 748 Americus GA 31709-0748

SMITH, RALPH, artist; b. San Francisco, July 12, 1919; s. Joseph Jacob and Anna (Holecek) S.; m. Francis Ferne Sierth, Aug. 15, 1942; children: Peter Joseph, Beverly Christine. Student, Art Ctr. L.A., 1940, Oakland Arts/Crafts, 1946, Am. U., 1962-67. Aircraft mechanic Naval Repair Stas., Alameda, Calif., 1945-56; aircraft engrng. technician Dept. Navy, Washington, 1956-74; artist, tchr. Ralph Smith Workshops, Annandale, Va., 1974—; juror awards 100th Ann. Art Exhbn., Nat. League of Am. Pen Women, Washington, 1996. With USN, 1941-43. Mem. Midwest Watercolor Soc., Va. Watercolor Soc., Acad. Artists Assn. Republican. Roman Catholic. Home and Office: 7114 Cindy Ln Annandale VA 22003-5812

SMITH, RANDOLPH RELIHAN, plastic surgeon; b. Augusta, Ga., Apr. 13, 1944; s. Lester Vernon and Maxine (Relihan) S.; m. Becky Jo Hardy; children: Katherine, Randolph, Rececca, Michael. BS, Clemson U., 1966; M.D., Coll. Ga., 1970. Intern Bowman Gray Sch. Medicine, Winston-Salem, N.C., 1970-71; resident in surgery and otolaryngology Duke U., Durham, N.C., 1971-75; resident in plastic and reconstructive surgery Med. Coll. Ga., 1975-77; Christine Kleinert fellow in hand surgery U. Louisville, 1977; attending physician Univ. Hosp., Augusta, Ga., 1977—; asst. clin. prof. plastic surgery Med. Coll. Ga., 1978—; pres. med. staff Univ. Hosp., Augusta. Bd. dirs. Ga. Bank and Trust Co. of Augusta, Richmond County Hosp. Authority; vestryman St. Paul's Ch.; trustee Univ. Health, Inc. Served to maj. M.C., U.S. Army, 1971-77. Diplomate Am. Bd. Otolaryngology, Am. Bd. Plastic Surgery. Fellow ACS, Am. Acad. Otolaryngology; mem. Am. Soc. Plastic and Reconstructive Surgeons, Am. Soc. Aesthetic Plastic Surgery, Ga. Soc. Plastic and Reconstructive Surgeons, Southeastern Soc. Plastic and Reconstructive Surgeons. Episcopalian. Clubs: Exchange (bd. dirs.), Augusta Symphony League. Contbr. articles in field to profl. jours. Office: Univ Hosp Med Ctr 811 13th St Bldg # 3 Ste 28 Augusta GA 30901

SMITH, REBECCA BEACH, federal judge; b. 1949. BA, Coll. William and Mary, 1971; postgrad., U. Va., 1971-73; JD, Coll. William and Mary, 1979. Assoc. Wilcox & Savage, 1980-85; U.S. magistrate Ea. Dist. Va., 1985-89; dist. judge U.S. Dist. Ct. (ea. dist.) Va., Norfolk, 1989—; exec. editor Law Review, 1978-79. Active Chrysler Mus. Norfolk, Jean Outland Chrysler Libr. Assocs., Va. Opera Assn., Friends of the Zoo, Friends of Norfolk Pub. Libr., Ch. of the Good Shepherd. John Marshall Soc. fellow; recipient Acad. Achievement and Leadership award St. George Tucker Soc.; named one of Outstanding Women of Am., 1979. Mem. ABA, Va. State Bar Assn., Fed. Bar Assn. Supreme Ct. Hist. Soc., Fourth Cir. Judicial Conf., The Harbor Club, Order of Coif., Phi Beta Kappa. Office: US Dist Ct US Courthouse 600 Granby St Ste 358 Norfolk VA 23510-1915*

SMITH, REBECCA GODWIN, English language educator; b. Wilson, N.C., Aug. 2, 1954; d. Charlie Thurman and Beatrice Rae (Holland) Godwin; 1 child from previous marriage, Christopher Jerry Hodge; m. Blane Eston Smith, Dec. 20, 1980; 1 child, Alden Blane. BA in English, Barton Coll., 1979; MA in English, N.C. State U., 1983; PhD in English, U. N.C., 1993. Cert. tchr., N.C. English tchr. North Johnston H.S., Kenly, N.C., 1979-80; tchg. asst. dept. English N.C. State U., Raleigh, 1980-83, lectr. dept. English, 1983-86; assoc. prof. English Barton Coll., Wilson, N.C., 1986—; chair faculty assembly Barton Coll., 1995-96; co-dir. coastal plains writing project N.C. Writing Project, Greenville, 1991-96. Contbr. articles, rev. to profl. publs. Spkr. Wilson (N.C.) Book Clubs, 1992, 93, 94; judge County Sch. Speech Contests, Wilson, 1993, 94, 95, 96. Mem. AAUP, Nat. Coun. Tchrs. English, N.C. English Tchrs. Assn., N.C.-Va. Coll. English Assn., Faculty Forum Barton Coll. (v.p. 1993-94, pres. 1994-95). Democrat. Presbyterian.

SMITH, RICHARD JOSEPH, history educator; b. Sacramento, Oct. 30, 1944; s. Joseph Benjamin and Margaret Elaine (Stoddard) S.; m. Alice Ellen Weisenberger, July 1, 1967; 1 child, Tyler Stoddard. BA, U. Calif., Davis, 1966, MA, 1968, PhD, 1972. Lectr. Chinese U. Hong Kong, 1972-73, U. Calif., 1972-73; asst. prof. history Rice U., Houston, 1973-78, assoc. prof., 1978-83, prof., 1983—, Minnie Stevens Piper prof., 1987, Sarofim Disting. Teaching prof., 1993—; adj. prof. U. Tex., Austin, 1983—; cons. FBI, CIA, Washington, 1985—, NEH, Washington, 1983—, various mus., Houston, Boston, N.Y.C., 1987—. Author: Mercenaries and Mandarins, 1978, Traditional Chinese Culture, 1978, China's Cultural Heritage, 1983, 2d edit., 1994, Fortune-Tellers and Philosophers, 1991, Robert Hart and China's Early Modernization, 1991, Chinese Almanacs, 1993, Cosmology, Ontology and Human Efficacy, 1993, H.B. Morse: Customs Commissioner and Historian of China, 1995, Chinese Maps, 1996. adj. mem. Houston Mus. Fine Arts, 1986—; guest curator Children's Mus., Houston, 1987-89, 91—; pres. Tex. Found. for China Studies, Houston, 1988-93. Mem. Assn. for Asian Studies (pres. S.W. conf. 1990-91), Asia Soc. (bd. dirs. Houston Ctr. 1976—), Nat. Com. on U.S.-China Rels., Houston-Taipei Soc. (bd. dirs. 1990—), Phi Kappa Phi. Democrat. Home: 2403 Goldsmith St Houston TX 77030-1813 Office: Rice U Dept History MS-42 6100 Main St Houston TX 77005-1892

SMITH, RICK MONTGOMERY, physician, consultant; b. Milw., May 31, 1953; s. Robert Ross and Barbara Jane (Kirkpatrick) S.; m. Karen Lynn Hanson, Feb. 14, 1978; children: Christopher Montgomery, Brook Patrick, Kelley Grant, Kacee Lynn. AA, Polk C.C., Winter Haven, Fla., 1974; BS, Nat. Coll. Chiropractic, 1976, D in Chiropractics, 1977. Chiropractor Smith Clinic of Chiropractic, Winter Haven, 1978—; cons. Kats Mgmt. Svcs., Lincoln, Nebr., 1989—; cons. bd. dirs. Kats Mgmt./Chiro Am., Inc., Lincoln, 1989—; cons., 3 star mgr. Body Wise Internat., 1993—; nat. lectr. on health and nutrition, weight management and anti-aging. Author, editor: manual Chiro America Dr. Manual, 1988; contbr. articles to profl. jours. Mem. Polk County Chiropractic Soc. (pres. 1989, 90), Am. Chiropractic Assn., Fla. Chiropractic Assn., Coun. on Orthopedics, Coun. on Radiol. Imaging, Kiwanis (pres. Winter Haven chpt. 1986-87). Republican. Baptist. Office: Smith Clinic Chiropractic 1550 6th St SE Winter Haven FL 33880-4507

SMITH, ROBERT CARLISLE, department administrator, welding educator; b. St. Albans, W.Va., Sept. 2, 1939; s. Clarence Mack (stepfather) and Artimitia (Blake) Smith Fowler; m. Janet Lee Koehn, Dec. 28, 1958; children: Teresa Lynn, Stephen Carlisle. BA, Glenville State U., 1984; MSc, Marshall U., 1994. Cert. welding inspector, non-destructive tester. Br. mgr. Va. Welding, Charleston, W.Va., 1963-76; prin. Weld Inspection and Cons., St. Albans, W.Va., 1976-94; QA mgr. Kanawha Mfg., Charleston, 1988-94; dept. head, welding instr. W.Va. U., Parkersburg, 1981-94. Lt. ROTC 1957-71; commiteeman Rep. Party, Kanawha County, 1968-69; former Sun. sch. tchr. Highlawn Baptist Ch.; presenter Nat. Educators Workshop NASA, Langley Space Flight Ctr., 1993. Recipient Disting. West Virginian award Gov. W.Va., 1968. Mem. Am. Welding Soc. (chmn. 1971-72, program chairperson 1989-90, educator of yr. 1990, 92), Am. Soc. Non-Destructive Testing (membership recruiter 1988), W.Va. Edn. Assn., W.Va. C.C. Assn. Protestant. Home: 2302 S Walnut Dr Saint Albans WV 25177-3947

SMITH, ROBERT EARL, space scientist; b. Indpls., Sept. 13, 1923; s. Harold Bennett and Bernice (McCaslin) S.; m. Elizabeth Lee Usak, Jan. 3, 1947 (dec. 1984); children: Stephanie Lee, Robert Michael, Cynthia Ann, Kelly Andrew; m. Lyla Lee Lewellen, July 1, 1988. B.S., Fla. State U., 1959, M.S., 1960; M.S., U. Mich., 1969, Ph.D., 1974. Enlisted U.S. Army Air Force, 1943-44; advanced through grades to maj. U.S. Air Force, 1955; airway traffic controller Berlin, Germany, 1945; staff weather reconnaissance officer 9th Air Force, 1956; ret., 1963; project scientist Atmospheric Cloud Physics Lab.; dep. chief atmospheric scis. div. NASA/Marshall Space Flight Ctr., Ala., 1963-86; sr. scientific cons. Univs. Space Rsch. Assn., Huntsville, Ala., 1986-87; sr. computer cons. Computer Scis. Corp., Huntsville, 1987-89; chief space sci. and applications div. FWG Assocs., Inc., Huntsville, 1989-92; NASA program mgr. Physitron, Inc., Huntsville, 1992-96; sr. computer scientist Computer Scis. Corp., Huntsville, 1996—. Mem. AIAA, Pi Mu Epsilon, Sigma Phi Epsilon. Home: 125 Westbury Dr SW Huntsville AL 35802-1619 Office: NASA/MSFC Huntsville AL 35812

SMITH, ROBERT ERVIN, mathematics and computer science educator; b. Starkville, Miss., Apr. 8, 1948; s. Jackson Eliot and Bonnie (Addy) S. AA, East Central Community Coll., Decatur, Miss., 1968; BS, Miss. State U., 1970; postgrad., Auburn U., 1972; postgrad, Ga. Inst. Tech., 1973, U. Okla., 1975-76; MEd, Miss. State U., 1976; PhD, U. Miss., 1990. Cert. math., chemistry, biology, gen sci. tchr., adminstr., computer sci. Instr. math. Pascagoula (Miss.) City Schs., 1970-72; indsl. rep. Mid-Miss. Devel. Dist., Newton, 1973-76; instr. math. Newton County Schs., Decatur, Miss., 1977-79; civilian civil engrng. technician U.S. Army Corps, 1979-82; instr. math. U. So. Miss., Natchez, 1982-86; tchr. math. and computer sci. Copiah-Lincoln Community Coll., Natchez, 1982—; tchr. math. and physics Cathedral High Sch., Natchez, 1985-90; physics instr. Trinity Episcopal H.S., Natchez, 1996—; mem. absentee com. Copiah-Lincoln Community Coll., Natchez, Miss., 1982—, curriculum com., 1982-86, jud. rev. com., 1983-91, Institutional Effectiveness com., 1993—; chmn. Miss. Lamplighters Inst., 1996; vocat. craft com. East Cen. Community Coll., Decatur, Miss., 1974-75, bus. mgr. student newspaper, 1967-68; state v.p. Student Miss. Edn. Assn., 1968-69, state pres., 1969-70; faculty advisor Student Govt. Assn., Natchez, 1982-91; researcher Star Schs. Project, 1988-89; speaker liaison Natchez Lit. Celebration, 1990-92; lectr. Mem. So. Indsl. Devel. Coun., 1973-76; bd. dirs. Miss. Indsl. Devel. Coun., Jackson, 1976. Named to East Cen. Community Coll. Hall of Fame, 1968. Mem. Miss. Assn. Devel. Educators, Miss. Jr. and Community Coll. Faculty Assn., Miss. Ret. Pub. Employees Assn., Nat. Cath. Ednl. Assn., U.S. Distance Learning Assn., Math. Assn. Am., Lions, Phi Theta Kappa (advisor), Kappa Delta Pi, Phi Kappa Phi. Methodist. Home: 100 Woodville Dr Natchez MS 39120 Office: Copiah-Lincoln Community Coll Natchez Campus Natchez MS 39120

SMITH, ROBERT F., JR., civil engineer; b. Oneida, N.Y., Apr. 17, 1949; s. Robert F. and Lucy (Rice) S.; m. Lane K. McDonald, Nov. 21, 1984 (div. 1989); children: Sean Michael, Kevin Robert. BCE, Clarkson U., 1971. Registered profl. engr., N.Y., Ky. Asst. city engr. City of Oneida, 1971-78; chief stormwater mgmt. engr. Met. Sewer Dist., Louisville, 1978—. V.p. United Way, Oneida, 1976-77. Named Ky. Col., 1982. Mem. Nat. Soc. Profl. Engrs. (southeast region v.p. 1996—, chmn. profl. engrs. in govt., 1993-94), Ky. Soc. Profl. Engrs. (v.p. 1989-91, D.V. Terrell award 1990, Disting. Engr. 1983, 88), ASCE (chpt. pres. 1984, Zone II Govt. Civil Engr. of Yr. 1989), Am. Pub. Works Assn. Democrat. Roman Catholic. Office: Met Sewer Dist 700 W Liberty St Louisville KY 40203-1911

SMITH, ROBERT FRANCIS, transportation executive; b. Chgo., Oct. 5, 1943; s. Rudolph Louis and Marie Josephine (Klug) S.; m. Lea Reynolds, June 19, 1993; children: Wolfgang Sebastian, Dietrich Gustav, James Jeffrey, John Curtis, Edward Bradley, Michele, Lacy D., Angela B. BS, W. Tex. State U., 1972, MS, 1974, MPA, 1978. CPA, registered med. technologist. Staff technician St. Anthony's Hosp., Amarillo, Tex., 1966-72, staff med. technologist, 1972-73, blood bank supr., 1973-78; staff acct. Cornell and Co., Amarillo, Tex., 1978-80, sr. acct., 1980-81, ptnr., 1982-87; treas., bd. dirs. Jack B. Kelley, Inc., Amarillo, Tex., 1988—; bd. dirs. W. Tex. State U. Found. Patron Amarillo Little Theatre; treas., com. chair Downtown Lions; mem. St. Joseph's Sch. Bd., 1984-94, Mid. Sch. Coun., Diocese of Amarillo, 1986-88, hwy. com. Amarillo C. of C. Served to sgt. USAF, 1964-68. Mem. Am. Inst. CPAs, Tex. Soc. CPAs, Panhandle Chpt. Tex. CPAs (com. chair 1981-95), Sierra Club (dir. 1986-96), Toastmasters (Toastmaster of the Yr. 1987, Parliamentarian 1988, Disting. Toastmaster 1986, dist. gov. 1990—), Beta Beta Beta. Office: Jack B Kelley Inc 8101 W 34th Ave Amarillo TX 79121-9680

SMITH, ROBERT KEITH, information technology analyst; b. Ashland, Ky., Dec. 30, 1955; s. Robert French and Neva Lee (Stapleton) S.; m. Rebecca Slone, July 30, 1994; children: Jonathan Wesley, Robert Charles. BS in Police Adminstrn., Ea. Ky. U., 1977; MS in Sys. Mgmt., U. So. Calif., 1983. Commd. 2d lt., 1977; advanced through grades to lt. col. U.S. Army, 1989; internat. def. cons. TRW Sys. Overseas, Inc., Saudi Arabia, 1993-95; sr. info. tech. analyst, project mgr. Columbia Gas. Transmission, Inc., Charleston, W.Va., 1995—. With U.S. Army Res., 1993—. Mem. Am. Mgmt. Assn., Soc. Logistics Engrs., Inst. Indsl. Engrs., Project Mgmt. Inst. Republican. Baptist. Home: 2250 Circle Dr Milton WV 25541-1004 Office: Columbia Gas Transmission PO Box 1273 Charleston WV 25325-1273

SMITH, ROBERT LEE, marketing researcher; b. Houghton, Mich., Aug. 21, 1955; s. Ben Eric and Gertrude Rumaine (Palmer) S.; m. Barbara Elizabeth Prussak, Dec. 27, 1977; children: Jacalyn Kate, Robert Logan. BS in Wood and Fiber Utilization, Mich. Tech. U., 1977; MBA, U. Wis., Oshkosh, 1989; PhD in Forest Products Mktg., Va. Tech. U., 1994. Laborer All-Wood Inc., Baraga, Mich., 1973-77; dir. quality control St. Regis Paper Co., Cass Lake, Minn., 1977-79, mgr. prodn., 1979-83; sales rep. Wheeler Consol., Mpls., 1983-85; mktg. rep. Wheeler Consol., Stevens Point, Wis., 1985-91; asst. prof., ext. specialist Forest Products Mktg. Va. Tech. U., Blacksburg, 1994—. USDA fellow U.S. Forest Svc., 1991-93, grantee, 1992; scholar Va. Tech. U., 1991-93, leadership scholar, 1993. Mem. Forest Products Rsch. Soc., Soc. Wood Sci. and Forest Products, Inst. Mgmt. Sci., Toastmasters (Christiansburg chpt.), Xi Sigma Pi. Methodist. Home: 380 Tanglewood Dr Christiansburg VA 24073-4816 Office: Rm 210 Cheatham Hall Va Tech U Blacksburg VA 24061-0323

SMITH, ROBERT MASON, university dean; b. Fort Sill, Okla., May 5, 1945; s. Arnold Mason and Lillyan (Scott) S.; m. Ramona Lynne Stukey, June 15, 1968; children: David, Angela. BA, Wichita State U., 1967; MA, Ohio U., 1968; PhD, Temple U., 1976. Debate coach Princeton U. (N.J.), 1971-73, Wichita (Kans.) State U., 1973-87, assoc. dean Coll. Liberal Arts and Scis., 1977-87; dean coll. arts and scis. U. Tenn., Martin, 1987—, dir. Gov. Sch. for Humanities, 1996spl. asst. U.S. Dept. HHS, Washington, 1980-81; cons. in field; chmn. corp. communication bd. Ea. Airlines, Miami, Fla., 1984-86. Mem. State Behavorial Sci. Regulatory Bd., Topeka, 1985-87; trustee Leadership Kans., Topeka, 1986-87; founder, bd. dirs. WestStar Regional Tenn. Leadership Program, 1989—. Recipient Excellence in Tchg. award Coun. for Advancement and Support of Edn., 1984, Crystal Apple award for outstanding tchg., 1995, Nat. Assn. for Cmty. Leadership award for disting. leadership, 1995, HHS fellow, 1980. Mem. Kans. Speech Communication Assn. (Outstanding Coll. Speech Tchr. award 1977, pres. 1978), Assn. for Communication Adminstrn. (pres. 1988), Tenn. Coun. Colls. Arts & Scis. (pres. 1989-90), Tenn. Speech Comm. Assn. (pres. 1993-94), Phi Kappa Phi, Phi Eta Sigma, Beta Theta Pi, Phi Theta Kappa, Rotary. Baptist. Home: 168 Weldon Dr Martin TN 38237-1322 Office: U Tenn Coll Arts & Scis Martin TN 38238

SMITH, ROBERT POWELL, foundation executive, former ambassador; b. Joplin, Mo., Mar. 5, 1929; s. Powell Augusta and Estella (Farris) S.; m. Alice Irene Rountree, Aug. 22, 1953; children: Michael Bryan, Steven Powell, Karen Louise, David Robert. B.A., Tex. Christian U., 1954, M.A., 1955. Fgn. svc. officer Dept. State, 1955-81; press officer Washington, 1955; vice-consul Lahore, West Pakistan, 1956-58; 2d sec. Beirut, Lebanon, 1959-61; consul and prin. officer Enugu, Nigeria, 1962-65; officer-in-charge Ghanaian Affairs, 1966; officer-in-charge Nigerian Affairs, dep. dir. Office West African Affairs, 1967-69; dep. chief of mission, counselor of embassy Pretoria, South Africa, 1970-74; ambassador to Malta, 1974-76, Ghana, 1976-79, Liberia, 1979-81. Pres. Africa Wildlife Leadership Found., 1981-85. Served with USMCR, 1946-49, 50-52. Decorated Air medal.; recipient Meritorious Honor award State Dept., 1967. Mem. Am. Fgn. Service Assn. Baptist.

SMITH, ROBIN ALBERTSON, public relations executive; b. Panama Canal Zone, Panama, Mar. 18, 1962; came to U.S., 1963; d. Norman and Ellen (Frantz) Albertson. BA in English, Environ. Politics and Polit. Sci. cum laude, Appalachian State U., 1982; MA in English, U. N.C., Charlotte, 1990. V.p. comm. Bissell Cos., Charlotte, 1984-90; pres. Robin A. Smith Comm., Inc., Charlotte, 1991-96; v.p. investor rels and corp. comm. Sykes Enterprises, Inc., Tampa, Fla., 1996—; com. clk. Va. State Gen. Assembly, Richmond, 1993. Author: A Presidential Visit to the Park, Insider's Guide to Charlotte, 1994; pub., editor-in-chief SouthPark Update Mag., 1984-90; mem. editorial adv. bd. Charlotte Real Estate Rev., Charlotte Mag.; copywriter various profl. mags. Vice chmn. bd. dirs. Jr. Achievement, Charlotte, 1994—; chmn. pub. affairs bond campaign City of Charlotte/Mecklenburg County, 1991, 93; pres. alumni coun. Appalachian State U. Boone, N.C., 1991—, chmn. McKinney alumni ctr., 1992—, mem. chancellor's adv. coun.; pres. Charlotte chpt. Am. diabetes Assn., 1994—; immediate past mem. alumni bd. govs. U. N.C., Charlotte; appointee Cable Adv. Commn., Mayor's Adv. Coun. Cmty. Policing; immediate past mem. com. bd. United Way; immediate past mem. bd. advisors Keep N.C. Clean and Beutiful; chmn. N.C. Blumenthal Program; bd. visitors Mercy Hosp. Found.; bd. dirs. Alexander Children's Ctr.; former bd. dirs. Young Affiliates Mint Mus. Mem. DAR, Pub. Rels. Soc. Am., Rotary, Friends of Wine, City Club, Gamma Beta Phi. Republican. Presbyterian. Office: 100 N Tampa St Ste 3900 Tampa FL 33602

SMITH, ROBIN GREGORY, radiation oncologist; b. Little Rock, Apr. 12, 1955; s. Harold Van and Kay Jean (Ritler) S. BA, Hendrix Coll., 1977; MD, U. Ark., Little Rock, 1988. Diplomate Am. Bd. Radiology. Transitional intern U. Ark., 1988-89; resident in radiationoncology Hahnemann U., Phila., 1989-90; assoc. in radiation oncology Emory U., Atlanta, 1991-93, resident, 1993-96; pvt. practice, Atlanta, 1996. Contbr. articles and abstracts to med. jours.; inventor methods to improve vascular transplants. Vol. physician Olympic Games, Atlanta, 1996. McGuire med. scholar, 1986. Mem. Am. Coll. Radiology, Am. Coll. Radiation Oncology, Radiol. Soc. N.Am. (roentgen resident rsch. award), Med. Assn. Ga., Med. Assn. Atlanta, Alpha Omega Alpha. Office: One Hospital Dr Ste 100 Huntsville AL 35801

SMITH, ROBYN DOYAL, elementary and middle school educator; b. Atlanta, July 12, 1947; d. Buna Eugene and Robyn (Wall) Doyal; m. William Franklin Smith Jr., June 14, 1970; 1 child, William McBrayer. BS in Elem. Edn., Tift Coll., Forsyth, Ga., 1969; MEd, Mercer U., 1973. Tchr. Suder Elem. Sch., Jonesboro, Ga., 1969-73, Mundy's Mill Jr. High Sch., Jonesboro, 1973-82, Pointe South Mid. Sch., Jonesboro, 1982—; owner, mgr. Personalized Imprinting Svc., Fayetteville, Ga.; instr. Rightway Driver Improvement, Fayetteville, 1985—; adj. faculty Mercer U., 1994. Nominee Honor Tchr. award Atlanta Jour./Constitution, 1987, 96, Ga. Law Educator of Yr. nominee, 1991; recipient Clayton County Tchr. of Yr. award, 1987, Ga. Law Tchr. of Yr. award, 1992, Nat. Law Educator of Yr., 1993. Mem. NEA, Ga. Assn. Educators, Clayton County Assn. Educators, Risk Reduction Instrs., Ga. Law Consortium. Presbyterian. Home: 165 Essex Cir Fayetteville GA 30215 Office: Pointe South Middle Sch 626 Flint Jonesboro GA 30236-3415

SMITH, RODNEY WIKE, engineering company executive; b. Havre de Grace, Md., July 29, 1944; s. Marshall Thomas and Ellen Nora (Wike) S.; B.S., Va. Poly. Inst. and State U., 1972; m. Mary Katherine Trent, Dec. 20, 1967; children: Scott Walker, Craig Duncan. Project engr. Hercules, Inc., Radford, Va., 1967-72; planning engr. Va. state Water Control Bd., Richmond, 1972; project mgr. Cen. Shenandoah Planning Dist. Commn., Staunton, 1972-76; v.p., br. office mgr. Patton, Harris, Rust & Assocs., Bridgewater, Va., 1976-82, prin. in charge office Buchanan, W.Va., 1980-82; sr. v.p. Copper & Smith, P.C., Harrisonburg, Va., 1982-88; pres. R.W. Smith & Assocs., P.C., Verona, Va., 1988-95; with Va. Sports Tech. Inc., 1995—. Apptd. to Va. Resources Authority Citizens Adv. Comm., 1987—. Contbr. articles to profl. jours.; 3 patents in field. Registered profl. engr., Va., W.Va., N.C., Md. Named Exec. of Yr., Profl. Secs. Internat.; Copper and Smith listed among fastest growing pvt. cos. by Inc. mag., 1987. Mem. Nat. Soc. Profl. Engrs., Water Pollution Control Fedn. Republican. Lutheran. Home: RR 5 Box 128 E Staunton VA 24401-9805 Office: PO Box 187 Verona VA 24482-0187

SMITH, ROGER KEITH, insurance agent; b. Hazard, Ky., Mar. 31, 1962; s. Homer and Ruth (Hampton) S.; m. Carla Slone, June 5, 1982. AA in Bus. Mgmt., U. Ky., Hazard, 1981. CLU; ChFC; LUTCF; lic. life, health, property, casualty, Ky. Heavy equipment operator Golden Oak Mining Co., Isom, Ky., 1981-84; debit agt. Commonwealth Life Ins. Co., Louisville, 1984-90, spl. agent, then account rep., 1990-96; guest speaker Southeast C.C., Whitesburg, Ky., 1990-92. Mem. exec. com. Letcher County Dems., 1996—. Recipient Guest Speaker award Big Sandy Assn. Life Underwriters, Prestonburg, Ky., 1992. Fellow Life Underwriters Tng. Coun.; mem. Nat. Assn. Life Underwriters (Nat. Quality award 1989-92, Nat. Sales Achievement award 1992), Big Sandy Assn. Life Underwriters (chmn. comty. svc. 1994-96, bd. dirs. 1994—, sec., treas. 1996—), U.S. Jr. C. of C. (mgmt. devel. c.p. 1992-93, Key Man award, Most Outstanding Mgmt. Devel. v.p. 1992-93), Am. Soc. CLUs and ChFCs, Jaycees (pres. Letcher area 1993-94, regional dir. Ky. 1994-95), Letcher County C. of C. (v.p., chmn. tourism com., pres. 1995-96), Alpha Beta Gamma. Home: HC 71 Box 800 Jeremiah KY 41826-9722

SMITH, RONALD AUBREY, theology educator; b. Pecos, Tex., Jan. 9, 1937; s. Aubrey William and Godie Jane (Richie) S.; m. Patricia Ann Hetzel, Sept. 14, 1958; children: Wayne Edward, Brian Lee, Linda Gay Flinsbaugh, Craig Fredrick. BA in Sociology, U. Calif., Berkeley, 1959; BD in Theology, Golden Gate Bapt. Theol. Sem., Mill Valley, Calif., 1962; PhD in Religion, Baylor U., 1972. Ordained to ministry Bapt. Ch., 1962. Pastor First Bapt.

Ch., Newman, Calif., 1962-64, Pittsburg (Calif.) Bapt. Ch., 1964-66; instr. Bible and sociology McLennan C.C., Waco, Tex., 1966-68, instr. religion, chair humanities, 1968-72, instr. religion, dir. divsn. humanities, fine arts and comm., 1972-73, dean of instrn., 1973-79; v.p. for acad. affairs, prof. theology Hardin-Simmons U., Abilene, Tex., 1979-87, exec. v.p., provost, prof. theology, 1987-92, dir. instnl. rsch., 1992-95, prof., 1992—; mem., sometime chmn. adminstrv. coun. Abilene Intercollegiate Sch. Nursing, 1980-92; trustee Abilene Libr. Consortium, 1990-92; cons. Higher Edn. Task Force, Abilene, 1990; testified before Congl.Reauthorization hearing NEH, Dallas, 1989. Chmn. Abilene Com. for the Humanities, Abilene, 1987-88; bd. dirs. Abilene Edn. coun./Abilene C. of C., 1991-92. Mem. Am. Acad. Religion, Nat. Assn. Bapt. Profs. of Religion (pres. southwest region), Deans Conf. Assn. So. Baptist Colls. of Schs. (past pres.), Conf. Acad. Deans of So. States (past pres.), Tex. Assn. Acad. Deans and V.Ps. (past pres.). Office: Hardin-Simmons U Box 16235 2200 Hickory Abilene TX 79698

SMITH, RONALD EHLBERT, lawyer, referral-based distributor; b. Atlanta, Apr. 30, 1947; s. Frank Marion and Frances Jane (Canida) S.; m. Annemarie Krumholz, Dec. 26, 1969; children: Michele, Erika, Damian. BME, Stetson U., 1970; postgrad., Hochschule Fuer Musik, Frankfurt, Fed. Republic Germany, 1971-74; Masters in German Lit., Germany & Middlebury Coll., 1975; JD, Nova U., 1981. Bar: Fla. 1982, U.S. Dist. Ct. (mid. dist.) Fla. 1983, U.S. Ct. Appeals (11th cir.) 1990, Ga. 1994, U.S. Dist. Ct. (no. dist.) Ga. 1994. Asst. state atty. 10th Jud. Cir. Ct., Bartow, Fla., 1982-85; pvt. practice Lakeland, Fla., 1985-94, Atlanta, 1994—; rsch. asst. 10th Jud. Cir. Ct., Bartow, 1981-82; instr. Broward County C.C., Ft. Lauderdale, Fla., 1976-79, 91-94, pub. and pvt. schs., Broward County, Offenbach, Fed. Republic Germany, 1971-78; instr. Polk C.C. and Police Acad., Winter Haven, Fla., 1981-94; adj. prof. English, Ga. State U., 1996—. Tchr., drama dir. Disciples I and II, United Meth. Ch., Lakeland, 1980-94, Glenn Meml. United Meth. Ch., Atlanta, 1994—; Billy Graham counseling supr., 1994—. Freedom Bridge fellow German Acad. Exch. Svc., Mainz, 1974-75. Mem. ABA, Christian Legal Soc., Ga. Trial Lawyers Assn., Lakeland Bar Assn., Atlanta Bar Assn., Nat. Orgn. Soc. Sect. Claimant Rep., Ga. Assn. Criminal Def. Lawyers, Kiwanis. Democrat.

SMITH, ROWENA MARCUS, artist, educator; b. Bethel, Vt., June 6, 1923; d. Bertram Franklin and Frances Sarah (Frank) M.; m. Benjamin Smith, Sept. 27, 1947; children: Mark, Neal, Pamela. BFA in Indsl. Design, Syracuse U., 1943; MS in Edn., MS in Art Edn., Hofstra U., 1966; MS in Counselor Edn., MS in Art Edn., 1976; studied with Miles Batt, Rex Brandt, , Joan Irving, Charles Reid, Barbara Nechis and Fran Larsen, 1980-90. Cert. tchr. K-12, N.Y., Fla.; cert. guidance counselor C.C. Designer Queens, N.Y., 1960; owner, operator design studio Boston, 1960; supr. video tape techniques, dir. Upward Bound Hofstra U., Hempstead, N.Y., 1969-79; instr. watercolor workshop Broward ARt Guild, Everglades, Fla., 1984; tchr. watercolor/drawing workshop Fano, Denmark, 1987; tchr. watercolor painting Broward Art Guild, 1983—; tchr. Flamingo Bot. Gardens, 1987—; tchr. figurative workshops Mex. Inst. Art, Cancun, 1988-89; tchr. mixed media Charlotte Maloney Workshops, 1995, 96; coord. masters degree program creative arts therapy Hofstra U., 1974-75; juror selection and awards Broward, Date and Palm Beach County Art Exhbns., 1986—. Exhibited in group shows at Gold Coast Watercolor Soc., Miami Watercolor Soc. Ann., 1984, 87 (1st Pl. award 1984), Broward Art Guild, 1985, Automatic Data Processing, Roseland, N.J., 1985, Palm Beach Watercolor Soc. Showcase, 1985, Lighthouse Gallery, Festival of Arts, 1985, Goldcoast Watercolor Soc., 1985, Palm Beach Watercolor Soc. Ann., 1985, Stephanie Ropar Gallery, Frostberg (Md.) State Coll., 1985, Shardin Art Gallery, Pa. Soc. Watercolor Painters 7th Ann., Kutztown, 1985, Hockady Ctr. Arts, Kalispil, Mont., 1985, Adirondacks Nat. Exhbn. Am. Watercolors, Old Forge, N.Y., 1985-86, Broward C.C., 1985, 86, 88 (Judges Recognition award 1985, 86, 1st Pl. Abstract award 1988), Nabisco Brands USA Figurative Exhbn., East Hanover, N.J., 1986, Newbury Gallery, Boston, 1986, Center St. Gallery, Winter Park, Fla., 1986, McPherson (Kans.) Coll., 1986, Nat. Assn. Women Artists, N.Y.C., 1986-93, Palm Beach Watercolor Soc. Ann., 1986, 87 (Best in Show award 1986, Dick Blick award 1987), Riverside (Calif.) Mus., 1986-88, Edgewood Coll., 1987, Catherine Lorillard Wolfe Art Club, N.Y., 1987, River Rd. Nat. Watercolor Exhbn., Baton Rouge, La., 1987, Panama Art Assn., Panama City, Fla., 1987, Coral Springs Artist Guild, 1987, Lever House, N.Y.C., 1988, Niagara Frontier Watercolor Soc., 1988, Matrix Gallery Satellite, Roseville, Calif., 1988, Columbia (Mo.) Coll., 1988, Tri-County Visual Arts Ctr., 1988, 89 (Best in Show award 1988), Watercolor Art Soc. Houston, 1988, North Platt Valley Art Guild, Scottsbluff, Nebr., 1988-89, Mus. Art & Sci., Macon, Ga., 1989, Nat. League Am. Penwomen, 1989, (Best in Show award, 1st Pl. award), Brea (Calif.) Cultural Ctr., 1989, Hiram Coll., Ohio, 1989, Longview (Tex.) Mus. Art, 1989, Rocky Mountain Nat. Water Media Exhbn., Golden, Colo, 1989, Fine Arts Mus. of the South, Mobile, Ala., 1989, Salmagund Open, N.Y.C., 1989, Islip Mus. Art, East Islip, N.Y., 1989, Carefully Chosen Gallery, Miami Beach, 1989, Watercolor U.S.A., 1990, Sansker Kendra Mus., Ahmedbab, India, 1989-91, Jehinger Art Gallery; represented in permanent collections B.I.S. Engring., Ltd., Quebec, Can., Broward County Libr. Found., Charles J. Calitri Assocs., Inc., Ednl. Assocs., Inc., Floyd L. Wray Meml. Found., Mark A. Smith, P.C., Nutrition Connection, Inc., S.C.B. Investments, Inc., NAWA Collection, Broward C.C., Burleigh & Smith, P.C., Coral Spring Libr., Fla. Atlantic U., Levine Engring. Co., Montana Tucker Restaurants, Inc., Osrow Products, Inc., Rutgers U. Recipient numerous awards for exhibitions. Mem. Associated Artists Am., Boca Raton Mus. Art, Broward Art Guild, Nat. Assn. Women Artists, Nat. League Am. PEN Women, 2/3 The Artists Orgn., Nat. Watercolor Soc., Norton Gallery Art, Palm Beach Watercolor Soc., Profl. Artists Guild, Woman's Caucus Art; signature mem. Gold Coast Watercolor Soc., Miami Watercolor Soc., Midwest Watercolor Soc., Nat. Soc. Artists, North Coast Collage Soc., Watercolor West; mem. Alpha Xi Alpha. Home and Studio: 5313 Bayberry Ln Tamarac FL 33319-3124

SMITH, RUBY LUCILLE, librarian; b. Nobob, Ky., Sept. 19, 1917; d. James Ira and Myrtie Olive (Crabtree) Jones; AB, Western Ky. State Tchrs. Coll., 1943, MA, 1966; m. Kenneth Cornelius Smith, Dec. 25, 1946; children: Kenneth Cornelius, Corma Ann. Tchr. rural schs., Barren County, Ky., 1941-42; tchr. secondary sch. English, libr. Temple Hill Consol. Sch., Glasgow, Ky., 1943-47, 49-51, 53-56, sch. libr., 1956-83. Sec. Barren County Cancer Soc., 1968-70, Barren County Fair Bd., 1969-70; leader 4-H Club, 1957-72, mem. council Barren County; coord. AARP tax-aide program, 1985-88, assoc. dist. dir., 1988—. Trustee Mary Wood Weldon Meml. Libr., 1964—; trustee Barren County Pub. Libr., 1969—, sec., 1969—; instr. 55 Alive Mature Driving AARP, 1993—. Mem. NEA (life), Ky. Edn. Assn., Ky. Sch. Media Assn. (sec. 1970-71), 3d Dist. Libr. Assn. (pres. 1944, 66), Barren County Edn. Assn. (pres. 1960-62, treas. 1979-80), 3d Dist. Ret. Tchrs. Assn. (pres. 1991-92), Ky. Ret. Tchrs Assn. (v.p. 1992-93, pres.-elect 1993, pres. 1994-95), Ky. Audio Visual Assn., Glasgow-Barren County Ret. Tchrs. Assn. (pres. 1984-86, 96-97, sec. 1989, treas. 1990), Ky. Libr. Trustee Assn. (bd. dirs. 1985—, pres. 1986-88, 93-94, dir. Barren River region 1985—), Barren County Rep. Women's Club, Monroe Assn. Woman's Missionary Union (dir. 1968-72, 79-83 Monroe Assn. Bapts. (libr. dir. 1972-88, sec. 1985—), Ky. Libr. Assn., Delta Kappa Gamma (pres. Delta chpt. 1996—). Home: 54 E Nobob Rd Summer Shade KY 42166-8405

SMITH, SAMUEL DAVID, pediatric surgeon, educator; b. Magnolia, Ark., Aug. 20, 1955; s. Samuel Denny and Nancy Jane (Rogers) S.; m. Nancy Gail Marbury, June 2, 1985. MD, U. Ark., Little Rock, 1980. Cert. gen. surgery, pediatric surgery, surgery-critical care Am. Bd. Surgery. Surg. intern U. Ark. for Med. Scis., 1980-81, resident gen. surgery, 1981-82; resident pediatric surgery Children's Hosp. Med. Ctr., Boston, 1983-84; sr. resident gen. surgery U. Ark. for Med. Scis., 1983-85, chief resident gen. surgery, 1984-85; fellow pediatric surgery Children's Hosp. of Pitts., 1985-87, pediatric surg. critical care fellow, 1987-88; asst. prof. pediatric surgery U. Pitts., 1988-92; pediatric surgeon, dir. nutritional support svc. Children's Hosp. Pitts., 1988-92; chief pediatric surgery Ark. Children's Hosp., Little Rock, 1992—. Contbr. chpts. to med. books. Recipient Resident of Yr. award 1984-85 Med. Student Coun., U. Ark. for Med. Sci., 1985. Fellow ACS, Am. Acad. Pediatrics; mem. Surg. Infection Soc., Am. Pediatric Surgery Assn. Office: Ark Children's Hosp Dept Pediatric Surgery 800 Marshall St Little Rock AR 72202-3510

SMITH, SARA ELIZABETH CUSHING, English language educator, writer; b. Richmond, Va., July 7, 1950; d. William Routledge and Sara Margie (Williams) Cushing; m. Bertram Smith, May 18, 1991; stepchildren: David, Susan, Leona, Bernice. BA, Duke U., 1972; MS, SUNY, Cortland, 1978. Cert. tchr. secondary English, N.Y. Adminstrv. asst. Duke Players/Duke Univ., Durham, N.C., 1970-72; substitute tchr. Maine-Endwell and Union Endicott Schs., Endicott and Endwell, N.Y., 1972-73; tchr. English and drama John F. Kennedy High Sch., Richmond, Va., 1973-75; project coord. Alekna Constrn., Endicott, 1975-77; tchr. English Vestal (N.Y.) Sr. High Sch., 1977-78, Greene (N.Y.) Jr.-Sr. High Sch., 1978-88; writer, editor, writing cons., 1981—; instr. English, computer lab. mgr., weekend coord. coll. Piedmont Tech. Coll., Greenwood, S.C., 1988—; rental agt. Drucker and Falk, Richmond, 1974-75; liaison/amb. to Lander Coll., Greenwood, 1990-91, co-chmn. Praxis Conf., 1990-91. Author: (textbook) You, Too, Can Writer, 1990, 3d edit., 1996. Recipient summer seminar stipend NEH, Atlanta, 1984. Mem. South Atlantic MLA, Greene Tchrs. Assn. (pres. 1983-85, mem. negotiating team 1984-86), S.C. Tech. educators Assn., Phi Theta Kappa (hon.). Home: 109 Carriage Ct Greenwood SC 29646-9427 Office: Piedmont Tech Coll Emerald Rd/Drawer 1467 Greenwood SC 29648

SMITH, SARAH ESTELLE, elementary education educator; b. Apalachicola, Fla., May 10, 1954; d. Buford Jones and Ellen (Moses) Sansbury; m. Bobby Ray Smith, Apr. 1, 1982 (div. Dec. 1994); children: Sharon Marie, Michael Terry. AA, Gulf Coast Coll., Panama City, Fla., 1977; BA, U. West Fla., Pensacola, 1980. Cert. tchr. elem. edn. and early childhood. Tchr. Springfield Elem. Sch., Panama City, Fla., 1981-86, chpt. 1 tchr., 1986-92, tchr. 4th, 5th grade, 1991-92; chpt. 1 tchr. Tommy Smith Elem. Sch., Panama City, Fla., 1991-94; chpt. 1 resource tchr. Bay Dist. Office, Panama City, 1994—; kindergarten grade chmn. Springfield Elem. Sch., Panama City, Fla., 1983-84, peer tchr., 1986, 90, 92; trainer Bay County Parent Involvement, 1993-94; facilitator supplementary staff development Springfield Elem. Paraprofls., 1994-96; Bay Dist. Title I Take Home Computer trainer Springfield and Patterson Elem. Schs., 1995-96, Waller Elem., 1996-97; workshop trainer Title I Tchrs. as Cons. Mem. Parent Edn. Network, Tampa, 1985; mem. FTP-NEA, local br., Panama City, 1981—, polit. action com., 1989-90. Named Tchr. of the Yr., Springfield Elem. Sch., 1991. Mem. Internat. Reading Assn., Assn. Children with Learning Disabilities, Fla. Assn. Computer Edn., Bay County Reading Assn. (exec. bd. chairperson for social com. 1994-95), Bay County computer Assn., Assn. Bay County Educators, Sunshine Social Club. Democrat. Baptist. Home: 4507 Crestbrook Dr Panama City FL 32404-5208 Office: Bay County Chpt 1 Bay Dist Office 1311 Balboa Ave Panama City FL 32401-2080

SMITH, SCOTT CLYBOURN, media company executive; b. Evanston, Ill., Sept. 13, 1950; s. E. Sawyer and Jerolanne (Jones) S.; m. Martha Reilly, June 22, 1974; children—Carolyn Baldwin, Thomas Clybourn. B.A., Yale U., 1973; M.Mgmt., Northwestern U., 1976. Comml. banking officer No. Trust Co., Chgo., 1973-77; fin. planning mgr. Tribune Co., Chgo., 1977-79, asst. treas., 1979-81, treas., 1981-82, v.p., treas., 1982-84, v.p. fin., 1984-89, sr. v.p., chief fin. officer, 1989-91, sr. v.p. for devel., 1991-93; pres., CEO, pub. Sun Sentinel Co., Ft. Lauderdale, Fla., 1993—. Bd. dirs. United Way of Broward County, Broward Workshop, Broward C.C. Found., Boys and Girls Club of Broward, Mus. of Discovery and Sci., Econ. Coun. Palm Beach. Episcopalian. Clubs: Glen View (Golf, Ill.), Lauderdale Yacht Club, Fort Lauderdale Country Club. Office: Sun Sentinel 200 E Las Olas Blvd Fort Lauderdale FL 33301-2248

SMITH, SCOTTIE GOODMAN, reporter; b. Stillwater, Okla., June 2, 1971; d. James Franklin and Melinda Graves (Holloway) Goodman; m. Leslie Thomas Smith, Jr., Oct. 28, 1995. BA in Broadcast Journalism, Tex. Tech. U., 1994. Reporter, prodr. KAMC 28 TV, Lubbock, Tex., 1994; stringer Fayetteville (N.C.) Observer Times, 1995; announcer WFLB radio, Fayetteville, N.C., 1995; news dir. WZKB radio, Wallace, N.C., 1995; prodr. WWAY 3 TV, Wilmington, N.C., 1995-96; reporter/fill-in anchor WWAY 3 TV, Whiteville, N.C., 1996—; mem. media adv. bds., Whiteville, N.C., 1996; spkr. in field. Mem. Soc. Profl. Journalists, Radio and TV News Dirs. Assn. Mem. United Methodist Ch. Home: 109 S Morehead St Elizabethtown NC 28337 Office: WWAY 102 Washington St Whiteville NC 28337

SMITH, SHEILA, secondary education educator; b. Kosciusko, Miss., June 3, 1954; d. Sammuel Hue and Ethal Lee (Riley) George. BS in Biology, Jackson State U., 1976, MS in Biology, 1979. Advanced placement tchr. Byram H.S., Jackson, 1979—; chair sci. dept. Byram H.S., Jackson, 1988—; mem. Sch. Discipline Com., Jackson, 1990—, State Textbook Com., Jackson, 1994. Mem. Byram PTA, 1979—. Recipient Outstanding Tchr. award Tandy Corp., 1993, Star Tchr. award ACT Bd.; Gov.'s fellow State Miss., AT&T, 1995, Woodrow Wilson Found. fellow, 1996. Mem. Nat. Biology Tchr. Assn., Miss. Biology Tchr. Assn., Miss. Sci. Tchr. Assn. Democrat. Baptist. Office: Terry High Sch 235 W Beasley Rd Terry MS 39170

SMITH, SHELLEY MERRIFIELD, writer, non-profit organization administrator; b. Louisville, Ky., Sept. 24, 1950; d. Lucien Lyne and LaVerne (Weare) S. BA with honors, Ind. U., 1972. Missionary to India, India, 1978—; founder, pres., dir. Kailashananda Mission of Am., Inc., Watkinsville, Ga., 1981—; behavioral therapist Kailashananda Mission Am., Inc., Lexington, Ky., 1981—, Colo., 1989—. Author: Mother Light, 1994, The Journey of Being, 1996; contbr. articles to profl. jours. Organizer, dir. Oconee County Alliance for Literacy, Watkinsville, 1992—; vol., dir. Oconee County Libr., 1990—, dir. literacy program, 1991—; active Oconee Adolescence Orgn., 1993—, Oconee County 2000 for Literacy, 1993—. Recipient award of recognition for outstanding vol. svc. Athens Regional Libr., 1993. Mem. Watkinsville C. of C. (mem. edn. com. 1992—). Roman Catholic. Home: 1500 Broadlands Dr Watkinsville GA 30677-2148

SMITH, SHELLY GERALD, JR., small business owner, author; b. Jackson, Miss., Dec. 19, 1949; s. Shelly Gerald and Lanell (Reed) S.; m. Robin Jeanette Atkinson, Dec. 18, 1978; 1 child, Alicia Lanell. AA, Hinds Jr. Coll., 1987. Owner Smith's Parts Svc., Utica, Miss. Author biography, 1992; contbr. articles to music mags., 1989—. Bd. dirs. Miss. chpt. Nat. Multiple Sclerosis Soc., 1973-78; custodian Blood Donor File, Utica, 1974—; vol. St. Jude Children's Rsch. Hosp., 1978—; pres. Multiple Sclerosis of Miss., Jackson, 1981-83, 93-96; mem. adv. coun. Hinds County Miss. Pub. Schs., 1992-94; vol. Toys for Tots, 1994—, area chmn., 1993—; chmn. steering com. Utica Area Habitat for Humanity, 1995—. Named Communicator of the Yr., Miss. Chpt. Cystic Fibrosis, 1986; inductee Blood Donor's Wall of Fame, Miss. Blood Svcs., 1994. Mem. Jaycees (state project chmn. 1974-79, dist. v.p. Miss Jaycees 1974-75, named State Chmn. of the Yr. 1979). Mem. Ch. Disciples of Christ.

SMITH, SHERWOOD HUBBARD, JR., utilities executive; b. Jacksonville, Fla., Sept. 1, 1934; s. Sherwood Hubbard and Catherine Gertrude (Milliken) S.; m. Eva Hackney Hargrave, July 20, 1957; children: Marlin Hamilton, Cameron Hargrave, Eva Hackney. AB, U. N.C., 1956, JD, 1960; D civil laws, St. Augustine's Coll., 1988; LDD, Campbell U., 1990; HHD, Francis Marion Coll., 1990. Bar: N.C. 1960. Assoc. Lassiter, Moore & Van Allen, Charlotte, 1960-62; ptnr. Joyner & Howison, Raleigh, 1963-65; assoc. gen. counsel Carolina Power & Light Co., Raleigh, 1965-70, sr. v.p., gen. counsel, 1971-74, exec. v.p., 1974-76, pres., 1976-92, chmn. bd., 1980—; chmn., former CEO and pres. Carolina Power & Light Co., Raleigh, N.C.; bd. dirs. Global TransPark Found., Inc., Hackney Bros., Inc., No. Telecom Ltd., Northwestern Mut. Life Inst. Co., Springs Industries, Wachovia Corp.; dir. Nuclear Energy Inst., 1994—; pres., dir. Global TransPark Authority; chmn. Am. Nuclear Energy Coun., 1980-83, Edison Electric Inst., 1985-86, Southeastern Elec. Reliability Coun., 1988-90, Nuclear Power Oversight Com., 1990-94. Mem. N.C. Coun. Mgmt. and Devel.; trustee Z Smith Reynolds Found., 1978—, Nat. Humanities Ctr.; bd. dirs. N.C. Citizens for Bus. and Industry, chmn., 1985-86; bd. dirs. Rsch. Triangle Found. of N.C.; mem. com. U.S. World Energy Conf.; bd. dirs. Microelectronics Ctr. of N.C., 1980—; mem. Pres.'s Coun. for Internat. Youth Exch., Kenan Inst. Pvt. Enterprise; trustee Com. Econ. Devel.; mem. Bus. Coun., 1991—, Bus. Roundtable; former bd. trustees, chmn. Rex Hosp. Recipient Nat. Humanitarian award Am. Lung Assn., 1993, Outstanding Leadership award in Mgmt. scis. Am. Soc. Mech. Engrs., 1983, A.E. Finley Disting. Svc. award Greater Raleigh C. of C., 1985. Mem. Elec. Power Rsch. Inst. (bd. dirs. 1984-89), Greater Raleigh C. of C. (pres. 1979), Am. Nuclear Soc., U.S. C. of C. (energy com.), Assn. Edison Illuminating Cos. (pres. 1990-91), Phi Beta Kappa. Home: 408 Drummond Dr Raleigh NC 27609-7006 Office: Carolina Power & Light Co PO Box 1551 411 Fayetteville Street Mall Raleigh NC 27602-1551

SMITH, SHIRLEY ANN NABORS, secondary school educator; b. Lake Creek, Tex., Dec. 9, 1938; d. Herbert Lee and Golden Ann (George) Nabors; m. Don G. Smith, Mar. 31, 1962. BS, East Tex. State U., 1960, MEd, 1962. Jr. high sch. English tchr. Mesquite (Tex.) Ind. Sch. Dist., 1960-61, 65-66; thcr. English, drama Chisum High Sch., Paris, Tex., 1966—. Mem. NEA, DAR, Tex. State Tchrs. Assn. (local v.p. 1990—), Nat. Coun. Tchrs. English, Tex. Joint Coun. Tchrs. English, Tex. Ednl. Theatre Assoc., Inc., Delta Kappa Gamma (1st v.p. 1990—). Democrat. Methodist. Home: RR 1 Box 79 Lake Creek TX 75450-9704

SMITH, STANLEY BERTRAM, clinical pathologist, allergist, immunologist, anatomic pathologist; b. Phila., 1929. MD, Washington U., St. Louis, 1956. Diplomate Am. Bd. Clin. Pathology, Am. Bd. Allergy and Immunology, Am. Bd. Anatomic Pathology. Intern Barnes Hosp., St. Louis, 1956-57; resident in pathology Jackson Meml. Hosp., 1957-62; fellow in immunology Sch. Medicine Yale U., New Haven, 1963-65; chief of Pathology Lab Miami (Fla.) Children's Hosp. Mem. AMA, ACP, Am. Coll. Allergy and Immunology, N.Y. Acad. Sci., Internat. Assn. Psychneuroendocrinology. Office: Miami Children's Hosp 3100 SW 62nd Ave Miami FL 33155

SMITH, STEVE ALLEN, nursing administrator; b. Birmingham, Ala., July 25, 1954; s. Perry Austin and Martha Nell (Mills) S.; children: Eric Braxton, Lindsey Allyson. BSN, U. Ala., 1978. RN, Ala. Utilization rev. coord. Brookwood Med. Ctr., Birmingham; staff nurse med. ICU Bessemer (Ala.) Carraway Med. Ctr.; quality assurance and utilization rev. coord. U. Ala. Hosps., Birmingham; mgr. adolescent svcs. Hill Crest Hosp., mgr. adolescnet residential treatment ctr. Home: 1457 4th St NW Birmingham AL 35215-6138

SMITH, STEVEN GARRY, philosopher, religious studies educator; b. Hollywood, Fla., July 28, 1953; m. Elise Lawton, Dec. 29, 1973; children: Matthew Clark, Katherine Simpson. BA in Religion, Fla. State U., 1972; postgrad., Iowa State U., 1974; MA in Religion, Vanderbilt U., 1978; PhD in Religion, Duke U., 1980. Asst. prof. philosophy and religion N.C. Wesleyan Coll., 1980-85; asst. prof. philosophy and religion Millsaps Coll., Jackson, Miss., 1985-89, assoc. prof. philosophy and religion, 1989-95, chair religion, 1992-95, prof. philosophy and religion, 1995—, chair pub. events com., 1992-95, mem. faculty coun. and chair excellence in edn. com., 1989-90, 91-93, planner, participant film studies program, 1987—; dir. Heritage of the West in World Perspective, 1996—. Author: The Argument to the Other: Reason Beyond Reason in the Thought of Karl Barth and Emmanuel Levinas, 1983, The Concept of the Spiritual: An Essay in First Philosophy, 1988, Gender Thinking, 1992; contbr. articles to profl. jours. Mem. instnl. rev. bd. dirs. U. Miss. Med. Ctr., 1987-91, alt., 1991-93. James B. Duke fellow Duke U., 1976-78, Millsaps Disting. prof., 1993-94. Mem. Am. Acad. Religion, Am. Philos. Assn. Office: Millsaps Coll Box 150390 Jackson MS 39210

SMITH, STEVEN LEE, lawyer, judge; b. San Antonio, Apr. 19, 1952; s. Bill Lee and Maxine Rose (Williams) S.; m. Rebecca Ann Brimmer, Aug. 5, 1978;children: William Christopher, Laura Charlotte. B in Music Edn. magna cum laude, Abilene Christian U., 1974; JD, U. Tex., 1977. Bar: Tex. 1977. U.S. Dist. Ct. (so. dist.) Tex. 1979, U.S. Dist. Ct. (we. dist.) Tex. 1980; cert. civil trial lawyer, Tex. Assoc. Dillon & Giesenschlag, Bryan, Tex., 1977-80, ptnr., 1980-84; ptnr. Dillon, Lewis, Elmore & Smith, Bryan, 1985-88, Hoelscher, Lipsey, Elmore and Smith, College Station, Tex., 1988-94; asst. mcpl. judge City of College Station, 1988-91, presiding mcpl. judge, 1992-95; judge Brazos County Ct. at Law # 1, Bryan, 1995—; mem. faculty Tex. Mcpl. Cts. Edn. Ctr. Mem. devel. bd. Abilene Christian U., 1982—, vis. com. Dept. Music, 1983-86; chmn. March of Dimes Brazos Valley Chpt., 1983-84; Leadership Brazos Devel. Program, Bryan/Coll. Sta. C. of C., 1984-85; pres. Meml. Student Ctr. Opera and Performing Arts Soc., College Station, 1985-86. Recipient Charles Plum Disting. Svc. award Tex. A&M U., 1986. Mem. ABA, Abilene Christian U. Alumni Bd., U. Tex. Law Sch. Alumni Assn. (dist. dir. 1986-89), U. Tex. Ex-Students Assn. Exec. Coun. (club rep. 1987-88), Optimists (pres. 1982-83). Mem. Ch. of Christ. Home: 3840 Cedar Ridge Dr College Station TX 77845-6275 Office: County Ct at Law # 1 300 E 26th St Ste 210 Bryan TX 77803-5360

SMITH, TAD RANDOLPH, lawyer; b. El Paso, Tex., July 20, 1928; s. Eugene Rufus and Dorothy (Derrick) S.; m. JoAnn Wilson, Aug. 24, 1949; children: Laura Bonsch, Derrick, Cameron Ann Compton. BBA, U. Tex. 1952, LLB, 1951. Bar: Tex. 1951; assoc. firm Kemp, Smith, Duncan & Hammond, P.C., El Paso, 1951, ptnr., 1952-81, CEO, 1975-95, shareholder, 1981—; bd. dirs. El Paso Indsl. Devel. Corp. Active United Way of El Paso; chmn. El Paso County Reps., 1958-61, Tex. Rep. State Exec. Com., 1961-62; alt. del. Rep. Nat. Conv., 1952, 62, del., 1964; dir. El Paso Electric Co., 1961-90, State Nat. Bank of El Paso, 1969-90, The Leavell Co., 1970-94; trustee Robert E. and Evelyn McKee Found. 1970-90, Property Trust of America, 1971-91; mem. devel. bd. U. Tex. El Paso, 1973-81, v.p., 1975, chmn. 1976; dinner treas. Nat. Jewish Hosp. and Research Ctr., 1977, chmn. 1978, presenter of honoree, 1985; bd. dirs. Southwestern Children's Home, El Paso, 1959-78, Nat. Conf. Christians and Jews, 1965-76, chmn. 1968-69, adv. dir. 1976—; trustee Hervey Found., 1990—, Lydia Patterson Inst., 1994—. Named Outstanding Young Man El Paso, El Paso Jaycees, 1961; recipient Humanitarian award El Paso chpt. NCCJ, 1983. Fellow Tex. Bar Found.; mem. ABA, Tex. Bar Assn., El Paso Bar Assn. (pres. 1971-72), El Paso C. of C. (dir. 1979-82), Sigma Chi. Republican. Methodist. Home: 5716 Mira Grande Dr El Paso TX 79912-2006 Office: Kemp Smith Duncan & Hammond 2000 Norwest Plz 221 N Kansas St El Paso TX 79901-1443

SMITH, TED JAY, III, mass communications educator; b. Dobbs Ferry, N.Y., Sept. 14, 1945; s. Ted Jay Jr. and Marie Glencora (Hershey) S.; m. Rosemary Tibbe, June 12, 1971. Student, U. Pitts., 1963-64; Student, U. So. Miss., 1968-69; BA with high honors, Mich. State U., 1971, MA, 1972, PhD, 1978. Commd. 2nd lt. USAF, 1971, advanced through grades to 1st lt., 1973, from electronics technician to electronics instr., 1965-70; airman edn. & commissioning program student USAF, E. Lansing, Mich., 1970-71; info officer USAF, 1971-74, resigned, 1974; grad. teaching/rsch. asst. Mich. State U., E. Lansing, 1974-77; asst. prof. SUNY, Albany, 1977-79; lectr. I, Warrnambool Inst. Advanced Edn., Warrnambool, Australia, 1979-82; asst. prof. U. Va., Charlottesville, 1982-87, dir. grad. studies, 1984-87; assoc. prof. Va. Commonwealth U., Richmond, 1987—, dir. grad. studies, 1990-94; sr. rsch. fellow Ctr. for Media & Pub. Affairs, 1996—; Bradley resident scholar Heritage Found., Washington, 1992-93; pres. Applied Anaytics, Inc., Richmond, Va., 1986—; sr. analyst Rowan & Blewitt, Inc., Washington, 1986-90; co-founder, sr. rsch. fellow Ctr. for Comm. Rsch., Warrnambool, 1982—; mem. policy adv. coun. VA Inst. for Pub. Policy, 1996—; mem. nat. adv. bd. Comm. Rsch. Corp., Washington, 1986-95, nat. adv. coun. The Media Inst., Washington, 1987—; faculty adviser FBI Nat. Acad., Quantico, Va., 1983-87; bd. dirs. Nat. Assn. Scholars, 1990—; mem. Main St. Commn., Rockford Inst., 1992—; educators adv. bd. Inst. for Pub. Rels. Rsch. & Edn., 1992—; co-founder Statis. Assessment Svc., 1993. Author: The Vanishing Economy, 1988, Moscow Meets Main Street, 1988; editor: Propaganda: A Pluralistic Perspective, 1989, Communication in Australia, 1983; co-editor: Communication and Government, 1986; co-editor human communication book series SUNY Press, Albany, 1987—; contbr. articles to profl. jours. Mem. The Nature Conservancy, Albany, 1977-79, Charlottesville, 1982—, Accuracy in Media, Washington, 1982—; contbg. mem. Va. Mus. Fine Arts, Richmond, 1987—. Grantee FBI, U. Va., Warrnambool Inst., Bradley Found., Raldolph Found., Scaife Found., Earhart Found. Mem. Am. Assn. for Pub. Opinion Rsch., Assn. for Edn. in Journalism and Mass Communication, Australian Communication Assn. (founding), Internat. Communication Assn., Anglican Guild of Scholars, Nat. Assn. Scholars (bd. dirs. 1990—), Pub. Rels. Soc. Am., Phila. Soc., Va. Assn. Scholars (founding bd. dirs., pres. 1990—), So. Speech Communication Assn., St. George Tucker Soc., Southern League, Va. Speech Communication Assn. (chair theory divsn. 1986-91, 1st v.p. 1991-94), Phi Kappa Phi, Kappa Tau Alpha. Republican. Anglican Catholic. Home: 4010 Sherbrook Rd Richmond VA 23235-1643 Office: Va Commonwealth U Sch Mass Communications 901 W Main St Richmond VA 23284-9014

SMITH, THELMA TINA HARRIETTE, gallery owner, artist; b. Folkston, Ga., May 5, 1938; d. Harry Charles and Malinda Estelle (Kennison) Causey;

m. Billy Wayne Smith, July 23, 1955; children: Sherry Yvonne, Susan Marie, Dennis Wayne, Chris Michael. Student, U. Tex., Arlington, 1968-70; studies with various art instrs. Gen. office worker Superior Ins. Corp., Dallas, 1956-57, Zanes-Ewalt Warehouse, Dallas, 1957-67; bookkeeper Atlas Match Co., Arlington, 1967-68; sr. acct. Automated Refrigerated Air Conditioner Mfg. Corp., Arlington, 1968-70; acct. Conn. Gen. Life Ins. Corp., Dallas, 1972-74; freelance artist Denton, Tex., 1974—; gallery owner, custom framer Tina Smith Studio-Gallery, Mabank, Tex., 1983—. Painting in pub. and pvt. collections in numerous states including N.Y., Fla., Ga. and N.D.; editor Cedar Creek Art Soc. Yearbook, 1983—. Treas. Cedar Creek Art Soc., 1987-88, 89—; mem. com. to establish state endorsed Arts Coun. for Cedar Creek Lake Area, Gun Barrel City, Tex. Recipient numerous watercolor and pastel awards Henderson County Art League, Cedar Creek Art Soc., Cmty. Svc. award Mayor Wilson Tippit, Gun Barrel City, Tex., 1986. Mem. Southwestern Watercolor Soc. (Dallas), Pastel Soc. of the S.W. (Dallas), Cedar Creek Art Soc. (Gun Barrel City) (v.p. 1983-86, treas.), Profl. Picture Framers Assn. Baptist. Office: Tina Smith Studio-Gallery 139 W Main St Gun Barrel City TX 75147

SMITH, THOMAS ARTHUR, banker; b. Frederick, Md., June 22, 1954; s. Jack A. and Mary Ann (Holter) S.; m. Katherine Sue Leamon, Nov. 8, 1986; 1 child, Kevin Thomas. BA, Catawba Coll., 1976; MS, Purdue U., 1978; MS in Indsl. Mgmt., Ga. Inst. Tech., 1980. CPA, Ga. Mgr. fin. services Oglethorpe Power Corp., Atlanta, 1979-82, mgr. fin. dept., 1983-86, v.p. fin., 1986-90; sr. v.p. Rural Utility Banking Group, CoBank, Atlanta, 1990—. Vol. YMCA, Salisbury, N.C., 1973-76, West Lafayette, Ind., 1977-78. Fellow Ga. Soc. CPAs; mem. AICPA. Republican. Club: Yellow Jacket (Atlanta). Office: CoBank 200 Galleria Pky NW Ste 1900 Atlanta GA 30339-5946

SMITH, THOMAS HUNTER, ophthalmologist, ophthalmic plastic and orbital surgeon; b. Silver Creek, Miss., Aug. 10, 1939; s. Hunter and Wincil (Barr) S.; m. Michele Ann Campbell, Feb. 27, 1982; 1 child, Thomas Hunter IV. BA, U. So. Miss., 1961; MD, Tulane U., 1967; BA in Latin Am. Studies, Tex. Christian U., 1987, MA in Latin Am. History, 1995. Diplomate Am. Bd. Ophthalmology. Intern Charity Hosp., New Orleans, 1967-68; resident in ophthalmology Tulane U., New Orleans, 1968-71; dir., sec. bd. dirs. Ophthalmology Assocs., Ft. Worth, 1971—; clin. prof. Tex. Tech. U. Med. Sch., Lubbock, 1979—; bd. examiners Am. Bd. Ophthalmology, 1983-90; guest lectr., invited speaker numerous schs., confs., symposia throughout N.Am., Ctrl. Am., South Am., Europe and India; hon. mem. ophthalmology dept. Santa Casa de São Paulo Med. Sch. Contbr. articles to profl. jours. Cons. ophthalmologist Helen Keller Internat.; deacon South Hills Christian Ch.; mem. Rocky Mountain Coun. Latin Am. Studies. Recipient Tex. Chpt. award Am. Assn. Workers for the Blind, 1978, Recognition award Lions Club Sight & Tissue Found., Cen. Am., 1977-79; named to Alumni Hall of Fame U. So. Miss., 1989. Fellow ACS, Am. Acad. Ophthalmology (bd. counsellors 1995—), Am. Acad. Facial Plastic and Reconstructive Surgery; mem. Tex. Med. Assn. (com. socio-econs.), Pan-Am. Assn. Ophthalmology (adminstr. 1988-93, bd. dirs. 1993—), Internat. Cos. Cryosurgery, Royal Soc. Medicine (affiliate), Tex. Soc. Ophthalmology and Otolaryngology, Peruvian Ophthalmol. Soc. (hon.), Santa Casa De São Paulo (hon. assoc.), Tex. Ophthalmol. Assn. (past mem. exec. coun., treas.), Tex. Med. Assn., Tarrant County Med. Soc., Byron Smith Ex Fellows Assn., Tarrant County Multiple Sclerosis Soc. (past pres.), Tarrant County Assn. for Blind, Tulane Med. Alumni Assn. (bd. dirs.), S.Am. Explorers Club, Colonial Country Club, Petroleum Club Ft. Worth, Sigma Xi, Omicron Delta Kappa. Mem. Disciples of Christ. Office: Ophthalmology Assocs 1201 Summit Ave Fort Worth TX 76102-4413

SMITH, TODD LAWRENCE, computer scientist; b. July 11, 1956; m. Dawn M. Simpson, Oct. 24, 1992. BS in Computer Sci. and Physics, Loyola Coll., 1978; MS in Ops. Rsch. & Mgmt. Sci., George Mason U., 1993. Comm. programmer Computer Data Systems, 1978-82; tech. staff TRW, Inc., Fairfax, Va., 1982-94; sr. engr. Washington Cons. Group, 1994-95; sr. software engr. Mitech, Inc., Rockville, Md., 1995—. Foreman, fed. jury duty Fed. Justice Ct., Alexandria, Va., 1991. Recipient Spl. Achievement plaque TRW Systems Integration Group, 1989. Mem. IEEE Computer Soc. Home: 11050 Camfield Ct # 101 Manassas VA 20109-7507

SMITH, TODD MALCOLM, political consultant; b. Hallettsville, Tex., Aug. 7, 1961; s. Jerome Malcolm and Mary Eugenia (Devall) S. BS in Criminal Justice, S.W. Tex. State U., 1983; postgrad. in Criminal Justice Adminstrn., Sam Houston State U., 1988—; cert., Fed. Law Enforce. Tng. Acad., 1987. Chief juvenile probation officer 25th Jud. Dist. Tex., 1983-84; field coord. Mac Sweeney for Congress, Victoria, Tex., 1984; dist. coord. U.S. Congress-14th Congl. Dist. Tex., 1984-85; chief dep. sheriff Lavaca County Sheriff's Dept. Tex., 1985-88; dir. ops. Clayton Williams for Gov. Com., Austin, Tex., 1988-90; pres. Property Valuation Advisors, San Marcos, Tex., 1991-93; gen. ptnr. Wm. A. Tryon and Todd M. Smith Polit. Cons. Group, Austin, 1991-93; prin. Smith & Assocs. Polit. Cons. Group, Austin, 1993—; coord. Lavaca County Crime Stoppers, Hallettsville, 1985-88; apptd. by Tex. Gov. to Tex. Crime Stoppers Commn. Regulatory Agy., 1986-90; mem., appointee Golden Crescent Regional Planning Commn., Victoria, 1986-88; investigator U.S. Customs Svcs., Op. Blue Lightning Narcotics Task Force, Tex. 1988-89. Mem. Young Reps. Tex., Austin, 1989—, candidate selection com. Assoc. Reps. Tex., Austin, 1991—, rep. senatorial dist. 18 State Rep. Exec. Com., 1992-94; pres. Tex. Citizens United; chmn. Taxpayers Def. Fund. 2d lt. Tex. State N.G., 1990-92. Recipient Outstanding Svc. award Tex. Crime Stoppers Adv. Coun., 1990, Outstanding Coord. award Lavaca County Crime Stoppers, 1988, Outstanding ROTC Cadet award Daus. of Founders and Patriots, 1982. Mem. Am. Soc. Polit. Cons., Masons. Republican. Episcopalian. Home: 421 W San Antonio St Apt L3 San Marcos TX 78666-5559 Office: 807 Brazos St #408 Austin TX 78701

SMITH, TROY ALVIN, aerospace research engineer; b. Sylvatus, Va., July 4, 1922; s. Wade Hampton and Augusta Mabel (Lindsey) S.; m. Grace Marie Peacock, Nov. 24, 1990. BCE, U. Va., 1948; MS in Engring., U. Mich., 1952, PhD, 1970. Registered profl. engr., Va., Ala. Structural engr. U.S. Army C.E., Norfolk, Va., Wilmington, N.C., Washington, 1948-59; chief structural engr. Brown Engring. Co., Inc., Huntsville, Ala., 1959-60; structural rsch. engr. U.S. Army Missile Command, Redstone Arsenal, Ala., 1960-63, aerospace engr., 1963-80, aerospace rsch. engr., 1980—. Contbr. articles to AIAA Jour. With USNR, 1942-46, PTO. Fellow Dept. Army, 1969. Mem. N.Y. Acad. Scis., Assn. U.S. Army, Elks, Sigma Xi. Home: 2406 Bonita Dr SW Huntsville AL 35801-3907 Office: US Army Missile Command Redstone Arsenal AL 35898

SMITH, TUCKER FREEMAN, publishing executive; b. Santa Monica, Calif., Nov. 28, 1967; s. Charles Philip and Robyn (Ryder) S. BA, Randolph-Macon Coll., 1989. Editl. asst. Tuff Stuff Pubs., Richmond, 1989-90, asst. editor, 1990-91, features editor, 1991-92, mng. editor, 1992-93; editor-in-chief Wizard Press, Congers, Va., 1993-95; pres., CEO Freeman Ink, Richmond, 1995—; judge Nat. Mag. awards, N.Y., 1995, Editl. Excellence awards, N.Y., 1996. Author: The Intimate Friends of a Young Poet, John Keats, 1989; editor: Collector's Sportslook, 1993-95, Fantasy League, 1995. Mem. Am. Soc. Mag. Editors, Soc. Profl. Journalists, BAsketball Writers Assn. Am., Internat. Sports Press Assn., Nat. Sportscaster and Sportswriters Assn., Omicron Delta Kappa, Sigma Alpha Epsilon (alumni adv. Va. Alpha chpt. 1989—, province archon province Gamma 1992-93). Office: Freeman Ink 204-B N Mulberry St Richmond VA 23220

SMITH, VERNON SORUIX, neonatologist, pediatrician, educator; b. Dacoma, Okla., June 10, 1938; s. Guy Edward and Helen Marie (Rexroat) S.; children: Michelle Marie, Brian Patrick, Carol Wannette, Juanita Ann, Russell Wayne. BSBA, Phillips U., 1964; MS in Physiology, U. Okla., 1970; DO, Kansas City Coll. Osteo. Medicine, 1974. Dir. subhuman primate rsch. U. Okla. Coll. Medicine, Oklahoma City, 1963-70; staff pediatrician Indian Health Svc., Pawnee, Okla., 1977-79; prof. pediatrics, dir. sr. program Okla. State U. Coll. Osteo. Medicine, Tulsa, 1978-82; staff physician Dept. Corrections, Tulsa, 1980-92; asst. clin. prof. pediatrics U. Okla. Tulsa Med. Coll., 1984—; asst. dir. Ea. Okla. Perinatal Ctr., St. Francis Hosp., Tulsa, 1984-87; dir. spl. care nusery Hillcrest Med. Ctr., Tulsa, 1987—, sect. chief pediatrics, 1993-95; dir. newborn ICU Tulsa Regional Med. Ctr., 1991—; owner Maverick Ranch, Hulbert, Okla.; speaker med. continuing edn. various orgns. Contbr. articles to profl. jours. Bd. mem. Faith United Meth. Ch., Tulsa, 1986-90; physician, missionary Nicaragua, 1990. Lt. commdr. U.S. Coast Guard, 1977-79. Fellow Am. Coll. Osteo. Pediatricians (dir. resident writing 1991); mem. Okla. Osteo. Assn., AM. Osteo. Assn., Cimarron Valley Osteo. Assn. Office: Neonatal Assocs Tulsa Inc 1120 S Utica Ave Tulsa OK 74104-4012

SMITH, VICKI LYNN, lawyer; b. Lebanon, Ind., Sept. 15, 1949; d. Hamer Dean and Betty Joan (Hill) S.; m. Denis Wayne Sloan, Aug. 18, 1967 (div. Jan. 1971); 1 child, Christopher Wayne; m. John Robert Sloop, Jan. 13, 1982. BS in Psychology, Purdue U., 1975; MS in Psychology, Fla. State U., 1979, JD with honors, 1981. Bar: Fla. 1981, U.S. Dist. Ct. (mid. dist.) Fla. 1982. Grad. asst. Fla. State U., Tallahassee, 1975-77, psychometrist, 1976-77; law clk. tax dept. Office Atty. Gen., Tallahassee, 1979-80; intern Office Pub. Defender, Tallahassee, 1980; asst. state's atty. Orange County, Orlando, Fla., 1981-84; ptnr. Sloop & Smith, P.A., Orlando, 1984-90; instr. Fla. Inst. for Legal Assts., Orlando, 1986-88; arbitrator U.S. Dist. Ct. (mid. dist.) Fla., 1987—; mem. Atty.'s Title Ins. Fund., spl. master, 1991—. Contbr. articles to profl. jours. Vol. Respond, 1985, Guardian Ad Litem, Habitat for Humanity; bd. dirs. Foxwood Cmty. Assn., 1988-89. Mem. ABA, Fla. Bar Assn. (real property com. 1985-87, corp. and banking com. 1986-87), Seminole County Bar Assn. (jud. poll com. 1987-88), Orange County Bar Assn. (legis. com. 1985-86, real property com. 1986-91, estate planning com. 1986—), Cen. Fla. Safety Coun., Am. Bus. Women's Assn. (pres. Nu Vista chpt. 1985-86, 88-89, v.p. 1987-89, chmn.program com. 1988-89), Phi Delta Phi, Psi Chi, Alpha Kappa Delta. Office: PO Box 447 Sanford FL 32772-0447

SMITH, VIRGINIA A., media consultant; b. Washington, Oct. 23, 1962; d. Kenneth Ross and Patricia Marcella (Maher) S. BBA, Va. Commonwealth U., 1986; postgrad., George Washington U., 1994—. Pub. rels. coord. Richmond Comedy Club, Va., 1987-90; media coord. Medalist Sports, Richmond, Va., 1991; event coord. ProServ, Washington, 1992; paralegal Law Resources, Washington, 1993-94; cons. MCI, McLean, Va., 1994—; cons., media rels. Va. Internat. Gold Cup, Middleburg, Va., 1993-94, Project Life Animal Rescue, Washington, 1994, media chairperson; cons., media rels. The President's Golf Cup, Washington, 1994, 96. Editor: Tour DuPont Mag., 1991. Vol. Octagon Club, Winchester, Va., 1980-81, Senatorial Campaigns, Richmond, 1988, Washington, 1994. Mem. Smithsonian, Nat. Assn. Female Execs. Republican. Roman Catholic. Home: 116 Stonewall Dr Winchester VA 22602

SMITH, VIRGINIA WARREN, artist, writer, educator; b. Atlanta, Mar. 7, 1947; d. Ralph Henry and Dorothy Jane (Kubler) S. AB in Philosophy, Ga. State U., 1976, M Visual Art in Art and Photography, 1978. dir. The Upstairs Artspace, Tryon, N.C., 1984-86; mng. editor Art Papers, Atlanta, 1986-88; art critic Atlanta (Ga.) Jour./Constn., Atlanta, 1987-92; adj. faculty Atlanta (Ga.) Coll. Art, 1991—, Ga. State U., Atlanta, 1991—. Author, photographer: Scoring in Heaven: Gravestones and Cemetery Art in the American Sunbelt States, 1991, Alaska: Trail Tails and Eccentric Detours, 1992; exhbns. include High Mus. Art, Atlanta, 1972, 78, 80, 81, 82, 84, 88, 89, Nexus Contemporary Art Ctr., Atlanta, 1986, 87, 91, Sandler Hudson Gallery, Atlanta, 1987, 89, 92, Jackson Fine Art, Atlanta, 1988, 91, 93, Aperture Found., N.Y.C., 1989, MS Found., N.Y.C., 1991, Albany (Ga.) Mus. Art, 1991, Montgomery (Ala.) Mus. Art, 1992, Bernice Steinbaum Gallery, N.Y.C., 1992, Wyndy MoreLead Gallery, New Orleans, 1991, 92, U.S. Info. Agy., Washington, 1994, Chatahouchee Valley Art Mus., Lagrange, Ga., 1994, others; works in permanent collections including Mus. Modern Art, N.Y.C., Mus. Fine Arts, Boston, High Mus. of Art, Atlanta, New Orleans Mus. Art, Harvard U., Rochester Inst. Tech., N.Y., U. N.Mex., Ctr. for Study of So. Culture U. Miss., Oxford, Miss., Columbia (S.C.) Mus. Art and Sci., Ringling Sch. Art, Sarasota, Fla., City of Atlanta, Franklin Furnace, N.Y.C. Bd. mem. Art Papers, Atlanta, 1983-88; adv. bd. memd. Arts Festival Atlanta, Ga., 1990-93. Mem. Coll. Art Assn., Soc. for Photog. Edn., Photography Forum of the High Mus. Art (v.p. 1994-95). Democrat. Home and Office: PO Box 1110 Columbus NC 28722

SMITH, VME (VERNA MAE EDOM SMITH), sociology educator, freelance writer, photographer; b. Marshfield, Wis., June 19, 1929; d. Clifton Cedric and Vilia Clarissa (Patefield) Edom; children: Teri Freas, Anthony Thomas. AB in Sociology, U. Mo., 1951; MA in Sociology, George Washington, 1965; PhD in Human Devel., U. Md., 1981. Tchr. Alcohol Safety Action Program Fairfax County, Va., 1973-75; instr. sociology No. Va. C.C., Manassas, 1975-77, asst. prof., 1977-81, assoc. prof., 1981-84, prof., 1984-94, prof. emerita, 1995; coord. coop. edn. No. Va. Community Coll., Manassas, 1983-89; Chancellor's Commonwealth prof. Manassas, 1991-93; freelance writer, editor and photographer, 1965—; co-dir. Clifton C. Edom Truth With a Camera (photography seminars); asst. producer history of photography program Sta. WETA-TV, Washington, 1965; rsch. and prodn. asst., photographer, publs. editor No. Va. Ednl. TV, Sta. WNVT, 1970-71; cons. migrant div. Md. Dept. Edn., Balt., summer 1977; researcher, photographer Roundabout presch. high sch. series on Am. Values Sta. WNVT, 1970-71. Author, photographer: Middleburg and Nearby, 1986; co-author: Small Town America, 1993; contbr. photography to various works including Visual Impact in Print (Hurley and McDougall), 1971, Looking Forward to a Career in Education (Moses), 1976, Child Growth and Development (Terry, Sorrentino and Flatter), 1979, Photojournalism (Edom), 1976, 80, Migrant Child Welfare, 1977, (Cavenaugh), Caring for Children, 1973 (5 publs. by L.B. Murphy), Dept. Health, Edn. and Welfare, Nat. Geog., 1961, Head Start Newsletter, 1973-74. Mem. ednl. adv. com. Head Start, Warrenton, Va. Recipient Emmy Ohio State Children's Programming award; Fulbright-Hays Rsch. grantee, 1993. Mem. Va. Assn. Coop. Edn. (com. mem.). Democrat.

SMITH, WADE KILGORE, physician, educator, researcher; b. Paterson, N.J., Sept. 7, 1939; s. Wade Sutherin and Helen Agnes (Kilgore) S.; m. Muriel Elizabeth Hagen, June 15, 1963; children: Karen Elizabeth, Deborah Anne. AB cum laude in Zoology-Chemistry, with honors in Zoology, Oberlin Coll., 1959; MD, Johns Hopkins U., 1963. Diplomate Nat. Bd. Med. Examiners, Am. Bd. Internal Medicine, Am. Bd. Hematology. Intern Mt. Sinai Hosp., N.Y.C., 1963-64, asst. resident, 1964, 67-68, chief resident and instr. in medicine, 1968-69, ednl. fellow and instr. in medicine, 1969; rsch. assoc. in immunology Duke U. Med. Ctr., Durham, N.C., 1970-71, instr. immunology, 1971-72, assoc. in medicine, divsn. hematology and oncology, assoc. immunology, 1972-75; asst. prof. medicine Med. Coll. Va./Va. Commonwealth U., Richmond, 1975-80, mem. cancer ctr., 1976—, assoc. prof. medicine, 1980—; dir. comprehensive cancer ctr. Hunter Holmes McGuire VA Med. Ctr., Richmond, 1987—; med. dir. hospice program McGuire VA Med. Ctr., Richmond, 1991—; guest investigator and asst. resident physician hosp. Rockefeller U., N.Y.C., 1969; cons. med. oncology McGuire VA Med. Ctr., 1980—, chief hematology-med. oncology sect., 1981-88, other coms.; acting chmn. divsn. med. oncology, dept. medicine Med. Coll. Va./Va. Commonwealth U., 1981, numerous other positions and coms.; vis. lectr. Tata Meml. Cancer Centre, Bombay, 1985, Mid-Atlantic Soc. Radiation Oncologists, Richmond, 1988. Contbr. numerous articles to profl. jours. Lectr. Berkeley Model Health Curriculum, Richmond Pub. Schs., 1976-84, I Can Cope program richmond area unit Am. Cancer Soc., 1991, 92, 93, 94, bd. dirs., 1979-83, chmn. profl. edn. com., 1980-83, v.p., 1981-82; lectr. Math. and Sci. Ctr., 1984, 85; mem. med. adv. bd. Richmond Met. Blood Ctr., 1986-93. Capt. med. Crops U.S. Army, 1965-66. Decorated Legion of Merit, U.S. Army, 1967; NIH, Nat. Cancer Inst. spl. fellowship, 1970-72; recipient Profl. Edn. award Va. divsn. Am. Cancer Soc., 1988. Fellow Internat. Soc. Hematology; mem. AAAS, Am. Assn. Clin. Histocompatibility and Immungenetics, Am. Chemical Soc. (divsn. med. chemistry), Am. Coll. Physicians, Am. Soc. Clin. Oncology, Am. Soc. Hematology, Mid-Atlantic Oncology Program, N.Y. Acad. Scis., Va. Soc. Hematology and Oncology, Tissue Culture Assn., Richmond Acad. Medicine, Johns Hopkins Med. and Surg. Assn., Richmond Blood Club, Sigma Xi (assoc.). Office: Med Coll Va Divsn Hematology/Oncology PO Box 980162 Richmond VA 23201-0162 also: Hunter Holmes McGuire VAMC Comprehensive Cancer Ctr 1201 Broad Rock Blvd Richmond VA 23249-0001

SMITH, WALTER S., JR., federal judge; b. Marlin, Tex., Oct. 26, 1940; s. Walter S. and Mary Elizabeth Smith; children—Debra Elizabeth, Susan Kay. BA, Baylor U., 1964, JD, 1966. Bar: Tex. Assoc. Dunnam & Dunnam, Waco, Tex., 1966-69; ptnr. Wallace & Smith, Waco, 1969-78, Haley & Fulbright, Waco, 1978-80; judge Tex. Dist. Ct., 1980-83; U.S. magistrate U.S. Dist. Ct. (we. dist.) Tex., 1983-84; judge U.S. Dist. Ct. (we. dist.) Tex., Waco, 1984—. Named Outstanding Young Lawyer of Yr., Waco-McLennan County Bar Assn., 1976. Office: US Dist Ct PO Box 1908 Waco TX 76703-1908*

SMITH, WAYNE CASON, organization executive, educator; b. Ackerly, Tex., July 17, 1934; s. William Wayne and Geraldyne Beatrice (Archer) S.; m. Connie Lee Nolen, May 21, 1960; children: Kimberly Diane, Jennifer Leigh. BA, Baylor U., 1956; MA, Tex. Tech U., 1967, EdD, 1990. Teacher Lamesa (Tex.) I.S.D., 1959-73, adminstr., 1973-90; coll. instr. Howard Coll., Lamesa, 1977—; exec. v.p. Lamesa C. of C., 1995—; adv. bd. Howard Coll., Lamesa, 1975—. Bd. dirs. Caprock Fed. Credit Union, 1973—; bd. trustees Dawson Co. Pub. Libr., 1963—; bd. mem. Tex. Divsn. Am. Cancer Soc., 1976—. With U.S. Army, 1956-58. Mem. Lamesa Lodge. Baptist. Home: 404 No 21st Pl Lamesa TX 79331 Office: Lamesa Chamber of Commerce 123 Main Lamesa TX 79331

SMITH, WENDELL PATRICK, language educator, writer; b. Toppenish, Wash., Mar. 5, 1965. BA English and Spanish, Vanderbilt U., 1987; MA Spanish Literature, U. Tex., 1995. Intern Harper's mag., N.Y.C., 1988; editl. researcher Rolling Stone mag., N.Y.C., 1989, Spy mag., N.Y.C., 1989-92; asst. instr. Spanish literature U. Tex., Austin, 1992—. Editor: Versus student mag., 1987; contbr. articles to Spy, Columbia Journalism Review; mem. editl. bd. Dactylus Jour. of Dept. Spanish and Portuguese U. Tex., Austin, 1996—. Office: U Tex Dept Spanish and Portuguese Batts Hall 110 Austin TX 78712-1155

SMITH, WILLIAM BARNEY, allergist; b. Memphis, Aug. 23, 1959; m. Carol Nix, 1985; children: Lauren Ashley, William Braden. BS magna cum laude, Memphis State U., 1980; MD, U. Tenn., 1985. Diplomate Am. Bd. Internal Medicine, Am. Bd. Allergy and Immunology; cert. Advanced Cardiac Life Support. Intern dept. internal medicine U. Tenn., Memphis, 1985-86, resident dept. internal medicine, 1986-88; fellow dept. allergy and immunology Vanderbilt U., Nashville, 1988-90, asst. clin. prof. dept. medicine, 1992—; pvt. practice Allergy and Asthma Assocs. of Mid. Tenn., Nashville, 1990—. Fellow Am. Coll. Allergy and Immunology; mem. ACP, Tenn. Med. Assn., Nashville Acad. Medicine, Alpha Epsilon Delta. Office: 300 20th Ave N Ste 100 Nashville TN 37203-2132 also: Ste 127-b 353 New Shackle Island Rd Hendersonville TN 37075

SMITH, WILLIAM GEORGE, writer/journalist; b. Ft. Wayne, Ind., Aug. 29, 1926; s. Fred alonzo and Esther Margaret (Jacobs) S.; children: Leslie Ann, Lisbeth Gail. BA cum laude, DePauw U., Greencastle, Ind., 1948. Reporter/corr. UP, Indpls., 1948-49; mng. editor The Sturgis (Mich.) Jour., 1949-50; reporter Wall St. Jour., Dallas, 1955-58; account exec. Butcher & Assocs., Shreveport, La., 1958-62; copywriter/pub. rels. dir. Olinkraft Inc., West Monroe, La., 1962-70; assoc. editor, co-founder Financial Trend, Dallas, 1970-75; media rels. mgr. E-Systems, Inc., Dallas, 1975-78; exec./mng. editor Tex. Bus. Mag., Dallas, 1978-88; freelance writer/journalist Dallas, 1988—; pub. rels. cons., Dallas, 1988—. Mem. Rep. State Ctrl. Com., La., 1963-69; dist. chmn. La. Rep. Party, 1964-67; bd. dirs. Shakespeare Festival of Dallas, 1982-89. Lt. col. (ret.) USAF, 1950-55, 61-62, USAFR, 1962-86. Decorated Air Medal; recipient Pacesetter award City of Monroe, La., 1967; named Outstanding Vol. world Cup '94, Dallas, 1994. Mem. Soc. Profl. Journalists (dir., treas. 1971—), Lions Club (dir., editor newsletter 1991—), Press Club of Dallas (dir., treas. 1970—). Home: 6025 Chalet Ct #3210 Dallas TX 75205-8672

SMITH, WILLIAM LESTER, sales executive; b. Benton, Tenn., Apr. 20, 1940; s. Rufus Lewis and Effie Mae (Stepp) S.; m. Rowena Dawson, July 10, 1965; children: Valerie, Bradford. BS, U. Tenn., Chattanooga, 1962; postgrad., Fla. Atlantic U., Boca Raton, 1967-70. Sales rep. Shell Oil Co., Miami, Fla., 1965-70; sales, mktg. mgr. Mobil Chem. Co., Covington, Ga., 1970-80; v.p. sales, mktg. Ball Corp. Plastics Div., Evansville, Ind., 1980-82; mfr.'s sales agt. Polymer Sales Inc, Conyers, Ga., 1982—. Capt. U.S. Army, 1962-64. Mem. Soc. Plastics Engrs. (treas., bd. dirs.1996—), Big Canoe Property Owners Assn. (bd. dirs., treas.). Methodist. Office: Polymer Sales Inc 992 E Freeway Dr Ste C PO Box 80924 Conyers GA 30208

SMITH, WILLIAM RANDOLPH (RANDY SMITH), health care management association executive; b. Spartanburg, S.C., July 23, 1948; s. Jesse Edward and Helen (Knox) S.; m. Donna Marie HAwthorne, July 18, 1970; children: Kirstin Leigh, Andrea Marie. BA, Furman U., 1970; MHA, Duke U., 1972. Exec. dir. Riverside Hosp., Wilmington, Del., 1974-79; assoc. exec. dir. Brookwood Med. Ctr., Brimingham, Ala., 1979-81, exec. dir., 1983-85; v.p. ops. Am. Med. Internat., Atlanta, 1981-89; interim chief fin. officer Am. Med. Internat., Beverly Hills, Calif., 1989-90; chief adminstrv. officer Am. Med. Internat., Dallas, 1990, exec. v.p. ops., 1990-95; exec. v.p. Tenet Health Corp, Dallas, 1995—; bd. dirs. EPIC Healthcare Group, Dallas, 1989-92. Bd. dirs. Ala. Symphony Assn., Birmingham, 1985, State of Ala. Ballet, Birmingham, 1983-85. Lt. U.S. Army, 1972-74. Mem. Fedn. Am. Health Systems (bd. dirs. 1989—, pres. 1993, chmn. 1994). Episcopalian. Office: Tenet Healthcare Inc Ste 200 14001 Dallas Pkwy Dallas TX 75240

SMITH, WILLIE TESREAU, JR., retired judge, lawyer; b. Sumter, S.C., Jan. 17, 1920; s. Willie T. and Mary (Moore) S. ; student Benedict Coll., 1937-40; AB, Johnson C. Smith U., 1947; LLB, S.C. State Coll., 1954, JD, 1976; m. Anna Marie Clark, June 9, 1955; 1 son, Willie Tesreau, III. Admitted to S.C. bar, 1954; began gen. practice, Greenville, 1954; past exec. dir. Legal Svcs. Agy. Greenville County, Inc.; state family ct. judge 13th Jud. Circuit S.C., 1977-91; ret. 1991. Mem. adv. bd. Greenville Tech. Edn. Ctr. Adult Edn. Program and Para-Legal Program, Greenville Tech. Coll. Found. Bd.; bd. visitors Presbyn. Coll., Clinton, S.C.; past bd. dirs. Greenville Urban League; past trustee Greenville County Sch. Dist. Served with AUS, 1942-45, USAF, 1949-52. Mem. Am., Nat. (jud. coun.), S.C., Greenville County bar assns., Southeastern Lawyers Assn., Nat. Coun. Juvenile and Family Ct. Judges, Am. Legion, Greater Greenville C. of C. (past dir.), Peace Ctr. for The Performing Arts (v.p.), Phillis Wheatley Assn. (dir.), NAACP, Omega Psi Phi, Delta Beta Boule, Sigma Pi Phi. Presbyterian (past chmn. bd. trustees Fairfield-McClelland Presbytery, past moderator Foothills Presbytery). Clubs: Masons, Shriners, Rotary. Home: 601 Jacobs Rd Greenville SC 29605-3318

SMITH, WILLIS BALLARD (MILTON SMITH), business owner; b. Princeton, Fla., Nov. 11, 1931; s. Lonnie Sidney and Artie (McLendon) S.; m. Betty Jean Wilson, Dec. 10, 1955. Student, Translyvania Bible Sch., 1951-55. Owner, founder Mobile Cross-Cut Shredding Unit, Melbourne, Fla., 1989—, All-In-One Property Maintenance Svcs., Fla. Mem. Internat. Platform Assn. Democrat. Home: PO Box 461 Melbourne FL 32902-0461 Office: Secure Document Shredding PO Box 461 Melbourne FL 32902-0461

SMITH, YOUNG MERRITT, JR., lawyer; b. Hickory, N.C., July 25, 1944; s. Young Merritt and Christine Ellen (White) S.; m. Louise Garner Price, Sept. 6, 1966 (div. Aug. 1974); 1 child, Patrick Adam; m. Charlie Mae Early, Nov. 19, 1977 (div. May 1985); m. Mary Gayle Jones, June 8, 1985; children: Mary Gaither, Jennifer Gayle. AB, U. N.C., 1966; JD, Duke U., 1969. Bar: N.C. 1969. Pres. The Litchfield Plantation Co., Pawleys Island, S.C., 1969-74, The Figure Eight Island Co., Wilmington, N.C., 1971-74; ptnr. Smith and Smith, Hickory, N.C., 1974—. Trustee Fund for Peace, N.Y.C., 1970-79, United Health Services N.C., Durham, 1971-73, N.C. Design Found., Raleigh, 1973-76. Mem. N.C. Bar Assn., Delta Kappa Epsilon. Democrat. Episcopalian. Office: Smith & Smith PO Box 1948 Hickory NC 28603-1948

SMITHER, EDWARD MURRAY, art consultant, appraiser; b. Huntsville, Tex., July 23, 1937; s. Douglas Laverne and Cova Estella (Galloway) S. BS in Journalism, Sam Houston State U., 1958; student, Atelier Chapman Kelley, Dallas, 1959-61. Mgr. Atelier Chapman Kelley, Dallas, 1964-70; co-owner Cranfill Gallery, Dallas, 1970-72; owner Smither Gallery, Dallas, 1972-75; co-owner Delahunty Gallery, Dallas, 1975-83; owner Murray Smither, Inc., Dallas, 1983—; co-curator Outside/In, Tex. Fine Arts Assn., Austin, 1993, G.B. Dealey Collection, Dallas Morning News, 1987—; advisor Artist's Eye Program, Kimbell Art Mus., Fort Worth, Tex., 1987-89.

Mem. Art in Pub. Places adv. com to City Coun., Dallas, 1982-89, Art Com. DART, Dallas Rapid Transit (Hampton Sta.), 1992-94. With U.S. Army, 1961-62. Home and Office: Murray Smither Inc 1934 Kessler Pkwy Dallas TX 75208

SMITH-LEINS, TERRI L., mathematics educator; b. Salina, Kans., Sept. 19, 1950; d. John W. and Myldred M. (Hays) Smith; m. Larry L. Leins, May 26, 1984. BS, Ft. Hays (Kans.) U., 1973, MS, 1976; AA, Stephen Coll., Columbia, Mo., 1970. Math tchr. Scott City (Kans.) Jr. H.S., Howard (Kans.) Schs.; instr. math. Westark C.C., Ft. Smith, Ark. Contbr. articles to profl. jours., chpts. to books. Mem. AADE, ASCD, Nat. Assn. Devel. Edn. (state sec. 1986-88, computer access com. 1980-85), Phi Delta Kappa (Kappan of Yr. 1985), Delta Kappa Gamma (state chairperson women in art 1993-95). Home: PO Box 3446 Fort Smith AR 72913-3446

SMOCK, DONALD JOE, governmental liaison, political consultant; b. Ponca City, Okla., Sept. 24, 1964; s. Joe Clellan and Ruth Esther Smock. BA in Polit. Sci., U. Ctrl. Okla., 1991, MA in Urban Affairs, 1993. Founder Smock Polit. Systems, Edmond, Okla., 1990—; rschr. The Nigh Inst. State Govt., Edmond, 1993-94; U. Ctrl. Okla. del. to Ctr. Study of Pres. Symposium, Washington, 1993; govt. liaison Elizey Electric Motor Co., 1994—. Charter founder Ronald Reagan Rep. Ctr., 1989; del. State of Okla. Rep. Presdl. Task Force, 1996; mem. Rep. Presdl. Trust, 1996. Recipient Okla. Rep. Blue Key award, 1984, Presdl. Commn., 1992, Merit cert. Rep. Nat. Com., 1990; named to Ronald Reagon Rep. Ctr. Presdl. Commemorative Honor Roll, 1991; by order of President George Bush flag dedicated in name Rotunda of U.S. Capitol, 1990. Mem. Tau Kappa Epsilon (Delta Nu colony inductee, chpt. advisor 1990-92, Fraternity for Life inductee, David Crain Leadership award 1986, Ed Howell Leadership award 1988-89, Red Carnation Ball dedicated in name 1989-90, 94, Top Alumnus 1990-91), Pi Sigma Alpha. Republican. Mem. Ch. of Christ. Home: PO Box 6323 Edmond OK 73083-6323

SMOCOVITIS, VASSILIKI BETTY, history educator; b. El Mansura, Egypt, Nov. 15, 1955; came to U.S., 1988; d. Dimitrios and Alexandra (Karabogias) S. BSc with honors, U. Western Ont., 1979; PhD, Cornell U., 1988. Asst. prof. dept. history U. Fla., Gainesville, 1988—; vis. asst. prof. Stanford (Calif.) U., 1990-92. Author: Unifying Biology: The Evolutionary Synthesis and Evolutionary Biology, 1996; mem. editl. bd. Sc. Epistemology, Mendel Newsletter, Isis. Mellon fellow Stanford U., 1990-92; rsch. grantee NSF, 1994-95. Mem. AAAS, History of Sci. Soc. (editl. bd. ISIS), Am. Bot. Soc., Soc. for Study of Evolution, Internat. Soc. for Study of History, Philosophy and Social Studies of Biology. Greek Orthodox. Office: U Fla Dept History 4131 Turlington Hall Gainesville FL 32611

SMOLAR, EDWARD NELSON, physician, consultant; b. Bklyn., Sept. 26, 1943; s. Harry and Diane (Orans) S.; m. Sharon Elaine Wechsler, June 24, 1973; children: Todd Devon, Gregory Fielding. BS in Biol. Scis. with honors, Union Coll., 1964; MD, Albert Einstein Coll. of Medicine, 1968; MBA with honors, Nova U., 1985, MS, 1990. Diplomate Am. Bd. Internal Medicine, Am. Bd. Endocrinology and Metabolism, Am. Bd. Geriatric Medicine, Nat. Bd. Med. Examiners; CLU, ChFC, CFP. Asst. instr. of medicine SUNY, Bklyn., 1973-75; clin. instr. of medicine N.Y. Med. Coll., 1974-79; physician pvt. practice, N.Y., 1975-80; asst. prof. of clin. medicine N.Y. Med. Coll., 1979-80; pvt. practice N.Y.C., 1975-80, Pompano Beach, 1980-84, Ft. Lauderdale, Fla., 1984—; clin. asst. prof. medicine U. Miami, Fla., 1982-89; adj. faculty Friedt Sch. Bus., Nova U., Ft. Lauderdale, Fla., 1987-88;. cons. Profl. Fin. Cons. Palm Beach, Inc., Boca Raton, Fla., 1988—. Contbr. articles to med. jours. Pres. Am. Diabetes Assn., 1980-81, bd. dirs., 1987—; mem. adv. bd. Hospice, Inc., 1985—. Surgeon USPHS, 1968-71, inactive res., 1971—. Fellow ACP, Am. Coll. Angiology, Am. Coll. Endocrinology, N.Y. Acad. Medicine (life), Royal Soc. Health, Royal Soc. Medicine; mem. Am. Acad. Polit. and Social Sci., Endocrine Soc., Am. Acad. Polit. Sci. (life), Assn. Mil. Surgeons U.S. (life), Am. Soc. CLUs and ChFCs, U.S. Naval Inst. (life). Republican. Jewish. Office: 5601 N Dixie Hwy Fort Lauderdale FL 33334-4148

SMOLIK, DEBBIE BOWMAN, consulting dietitian; b. San Antonio, Sept. 19, 1953; d. Leslie LeRoy and Edith Otillia (Huebner) Bowman; m. Jim Brian Smolik, Aug. 26, 1973; children: Kelly, Erica, Brittany, Tiffany. BS in Foods and Nutrition, Tex. A&I Kingsville, 1975. Registered, lic. dietition, Tex. Asst. dietition Doctors Hosp. (now Humana), Corpus Christi, 1976-79; asst. tothe dir. dept. nutrition Corpus Christi Ind. Sch. Dist., 1979-80; pvt. practice cons. Corpus Christi, 1980-84; cons. John's Community Hosp., Taylor, 1991—; cons. dietitian Richards Meml. Hosp., Rocdale, Tex., 92—; dir. dietary Physicians and Surgeons Hosp., Corpus Christi, 1980-82. Bd. dirs. Women's Symphony League, 1995-96, Westlake H.S. Hyline Drill Team; active Jr. Forum, 1987—, Women's Art Guild, Laguna Gloria Art Mus., 1990-91. Mem. Am. Dietetic Assn., Austin Dietetic Assn. Catholic.

SMOOK, JOHN T., manufacturing company executive; b. Detroit, Oct. 28, 1927; s. Theo and Mary (O'Donnell) S.; m. Hope van der Smissen, Jan. 21, 1951 (div.); children: Ted, Jim, Cindy, Pam, Pat, Jeannette; m. Barbara Quinn, Feb. 4, 1984. Student Westminster Coll., 1947-48, U. Utah, 1949-50. Founder, chief exec. officer Kosmo Corp., Glen Allen, Va., 1954—; founder, pres. Internat. Security Vault Systems Inc., Glen Allen, 1982—; sec. Mid-Atlantic Ins. Underwriters, Richmond, Va., 1981. Served with USN, 1946, U.S. Army, 1950-53. Mem. Va. Campground Owners Assn., Va. Mfg. Housing Assn., Richmond Ski Club, Underseas Explorers Club. Office: 14100 Washington Hwy Glen Allen VA 23060

SMOTHERS, JIMMY, editor, sportswriter; b. Geraldine, Ala., Jan. 4, 1933; s. John Ezra and Lois Olga (Taylor) S.; m. Mary Kay Brock, July 7, 1954; 1 child Jim Jr. Grad., Jacksonville State U., 1954. Sports editor Gadsden (Ala.) Times, 1960—. Contbr. articles to popular mags. With USNG, 1951-65. Recipient Helms award, more than 50 AP awards; nominated for Pulitzer prizes, 1963. Mem. Ala. Sports Writers Assn. (sec.-treas. 1971—), Baseball Writers Assn., Coll. Football Writers Assn., Jacksonville State U. Alumni Assn. (past. Alumnus of Yr.). Office: Gadsden Times PO Box 188 Gadsden AL 35999-3501

SMREKAR, PAMELA LOUISE, secondary education educator; b. Hutchinson, Minn., May 27; d. Robert L. and Ruth C. (Lambert) Allison; m. Joseph J. Smrekar, June 22, 1968; children: Allison, Ruth Anne, Jacob. BA in Journalism, Mass Comm., Pub. Rels., U. Minn., 1967; BS in Journalism Edn., Iowa State U., 1970. Cert. educator, Ga.; cert. journalist Nat. Journalism Edn. Assn. Editor Esterville (Iowa) Daily News, 1967-68; mktg. and pub. rels. staff Iowa State Ext. Svc., 1968-70; editor Wallace's Farmer Mag., Des Moines, Iowa, 1970-72; news editor Troup County Herald, 1980-81; secondary English and journalism tchr. Troup County, La Grange, Ga., 1983—; presenter in field. Sunday sch. tchr. St. Peter's Cath. Ch., La Grange; mem. St. Peter's Ch. Women; active PTO. Mem. Profl. Assn. Ga. Educators, Ga. Scholastic Press Assn., Journalism Edn. Assn., Ga. Tchrs. English, Ga. So. Regional Press Inst., Ga. Scholastic Journalism Dirs. Office: La Grange HS 516 N Greenwood Lagrange GA 30240

SMYERS, STEVE, golf course architect. Golf course architect Fairway Design Internat., Inc. Officež: Fairway Design Internat Inc 2000 E Edgewood Dr Ste 103 Lakeland FL 33803-3600

SMYSER, RICHARD DAVID, retired newspaper editor, retired secondary education educator; b. York, Pa., Aug. 19, 1923; s. Adam Milton and Miriam Olivia (Stein) S.; m. Mary Cochran Pigford, May 12, 1950; children: Lucy Pigford Smyser Tashman, Katherine Mary Smyser McAleer. BA, Pa. State Coll., 1944. Reporter Chester Pa. Times, 1946-49; mng. editor The Oak Ridger, Oak Ridge, Tenn., 1949-68; editor The Oak Ridger, 1968-88, founding editor, 1988—; Atwood prof. journalism U. Alaska, Anchorage, 1986-87; editor in residence, vis. prof. journalism U. Nebr., Lincoln, 1988-89; Meeman disting. prof. of journalism U. Tenn., Knoxville, 1991-93; vis. prof. journalism Pa. State U., State College, 1989-91; bd. dirs. Coun. for Advancement of Sci. Writing, 1982—, Scientist Inst. for Pub. Information, 1985—. Author: Oak Ridge: A Commemorative Portrait, 1992, (with others) Journalism Stories from the Real World, 1995, The Newspaper, 1981, Read All About It - 50 Years of Am. Soc. Newspaper Editors, 1974; contbr. articles to profl. jours. Bd. dirs. Friends of Oak Ridge Nat. Laboratory, 1993—. With US Army, 1943-45. Recipient Kilgore Counselor award DePauw U., Greencastle, Ind., 1973, Carol Burnett Lecture on Journalism Ethics award U. Hawaii, Honolulu, 1985, dist. alumnus Pa. State U., 1985. Mem. AP Mng. Editors Assn. (pres. 1973-74), Am. Soc. of Newspaper Editors (pres. 1984-85), Rotary Club (hon., vocational svcs. award Oak Ridge Rotary, 1988). Unitarian. Home: 104 Osage Rd Oak Ridge TN 37830 Office: The Oak Ridger PO Box 3446 Oak Ridge TN 37831

SNAPP, ELIZABETH, librarian, educator; b. Lubbock, Tex., Mar. 31, 1937; d. William James and Louise (Lanham) Mitchell; BA magna cum laude, North Tex. State U., Denton, 1968, MLS, 1969, MA, 1977; m. Harry Franklin Snapp, June 1, 1956. Asst. to archivist Archive of New Orleans Jazz, Tulane U., 1960-63; catalog librarian Tex. Woman's U., Denton, 1969-71, head acquisitions dept., 1971-74, coord. readers svcs., 1974-77, asst. to dean Grad. Sch., 1977-79, instr. libr. sci., 1977-88, acting Univ. libr., 1979-82, dir. librs., 1982—, univ. historian, 1995—; chair-elect Tex. Coun. State U. Librs., 1988-90, chmn., 1990-92; mem. adv. com. on libr. formula Coordinating Bd. Tex. Coll. and Univ. System, 1981-92; del. OCLC Nat. Users Council, 1985-87, mem. by-laws com., 1985-86, com. on less-than-full-svcs. networks, 1986-87; trustee AMIGOS Bibliographic Coun., Inc., 1994—, sec. bd. trustees, 1996—; project dir. NEH consultancy grant on devel. core curriculum for women's studies, 1981-82; chmn. Blue Ribbon com. 1986 Gov.'s Commn. for Women to select 150 outstanding women in Tex. history; project dir. math./sci. anthology project Tex. Found. Women's Resources. Co-sponsor Irish Lecture Series, Denton, 1968, 70, 73, 78. Sec. Denton County Dem. Caucus, 1970. Recipient Ann. Pioneer award Tex. Women's U., 1986. Mem. AAUP, ALA (standards com. 1983-85), Tex. Libr. Assn. (program com. 1978, Dist. VII chmn. 1985-86, archives and oral history com. 1990-92, co-chair program com. Tex. Libr Assn. Ann. Conf. 1994, mem. Tall Texan selection com. 1995-96, treas. exec. bd. 1996—), Tex. Hist. Commn. (judge for Farenbach History prize 1990-93), Women's Collecting Group (chmn. ad hoc com. 1984-86), AAUW (legis. br. chmn. 1973-74, br. v.p. 1975-76, br. pres. 1979-80, state historian 1986-88), AAUW Ednl. Found. (rsch. and awards panel 1990-94), So. Conf. Brit. Studies, Tex. Assn. Coll. Tchrs. (pres. Tex. Woman's U. chpt. 1976-77), Alliance Higher Edn. (chair coun. libr. dirs. 1993-95), Woman's Shakespeare Club (pres. 1967-69), Beta Phi Mu (pres. chpt. 1976-78; sec. nat. adv. assembly 1978-79, pres. 1979-80, nat. dir. 1981-83), Alpha Chi, Alpha Lambda Sigma (pres. 1970-71), Pi Delta Phi. Methodist. Club: Soroptimist Internat. (Denton) (pres. 1986-88). Asst. editor Tex. Academe, 1973-76; co-editor: Read All About Her! Texas Women's History: A Working Bibliography, 1995; contbg. author: Women in Special Collections, 1984, Special Collections, 1986; book reviewer Library Resources and Tech. Services, 1973—. Contbr. articles to profl. jours. Home: 1904 N Lake Trl Denton TX 76201-0602 Office: TWU Sta PO Box 424093 Denton TX 76204-2093

SNAPP, HARRY FRANKLIN, historian; b. Bryan, Tex., Oct. 15, 1930; s. H.F. and Ethel (Manning) S.; BA, Baylor U., 1952, MA, 1953; PhD, Tulane U., 1963; m. Elizabeth Mitchell, June 1, 1956. Instr., U. Coll. Tulane U., 1960-62; asst. prof. history Wofford Coll., 1963-64; asst. prof. history U. North Tex. (formerly North Tex. State U.), Denton, 1964-69, assoc. prof., 1969-94; dir. Tex. Rsch. Ctr. Biog. Study of Women, Denton, 1995—; pres., dir. Read All About Her Tex. Women's Biographic Ctr., Inc., 1995—. Editor Brit. Studies Mercury, 1970—, Tex. Academy, 1973-76; co-editor: Read All About Her! Texas Women's History: A Working Bibliography, 1995; author: (with others) West Texas Historical Association Year Book, 1994; contbr. articles to profl. jours. Mem. Friends of Winchester Cathedral, Am. Com. Irish Studies; mem. adv. com. on acad. freedom and tenure policy, coordinating bd. Tex. Coll. and Univ. System. Recipient North Tex. State U. Faculty Rsch. award, 1966, 67. Mem. AAUP (pres. North Tex. chpt. 1968-69, pres. Southwestern regional conf. 1971-72, pres. Tex. conf. 1974-76, nat. coun. 1976-86), So. Conf. Brit. Studies (sec.-treas. 1969-84), Am. Hist. Assn., Tex. State Hist. Assn., Hist. Assn. (London), Libr. Rsch. Round Table, Libr. History Round Table, Northamptonshire Record Soc., Butler Soc. (Ireland), Econ. History Soc., Ch. Hist. Soc., Tulane U. Alumni Assn., Alpha Chi, Lambda Chi Alpha. Methodist. Home: 1904 N Lake Trl Denton TX 76201-0602 Office: Read All About Her Tex Women's Biographic Ctr Inc PO Box 424053 TWU Sta Denton TX 76204-4053

SNAREY, JOHN ROBERT, psychologist, researcher, educator; b. New Brighton, Pa., Jan. 12, 1948; s. John Herbert and Esther Snarey; m. Carol Dunn Snarey, June 11, 1970; children: Johnny, Elizabeth. BS, Geneva Coll., 1969; MA, Wheaton (Ill.) Coll., 1973; EdD, Harvard U., 1982. Postdoctoral rsch. fellow dept. psychiatry Harvard U., Cambridge, Mass., 1982-84; assoc. rsch. psychologist Wellesley (Mass.) Coll., 1984-85; assoc. prof. human devel. Northwestern U., Evanston, Ill., 1985-87; prof. human devel. Emory U., Atlanta, 1987—. Author: How Fathers Care for the Next Generation, 1993; mem. editl. bd. Harvard Edn. Rev., 1979-81; mem. editl. adv. bd. Lawrence Erlbaum Assocs., 1988-90; contbr. numerous articles to profl. jours. Recipient Exemplary Dissertation award Nat. Coun. for the Social Studies, 1982, Kuhmerker Dissertation award Assn. for Moral Edn., 1983, Outstanding Human Devel. Rsch. award Am. Ednl. Rsch., 1988, James D. Moran Book award Assn. Family and Consumer Scis., 1994. Mem. APA, Am. Ednl. Rsch. Assn. (div. E exec. bd. 1990—, moral devel. and edn. spl. interest group co-chair 1994—), Assn. for Moral Edn. (exec. bd. 1986—), Soc. for Rsch. in Child Devel., Nat. Coun. on Family Rels. Home: 2165 Pine Forest Dr NE Atlanta GA 30345-4184

SNEAD, JOHN DAVID, business administration educator; b. Princeton, W.Va., Sept. 23, 1962; s. Buster Bryant and Regina Vee (Belcher) S.; m. Sheryl Lynn Shumaker, Aug. 17, 1985. BSBA, Bluefield (W.Va.) State Coll., 1985; MBA, Radford U., 1990; doctoral student, Va. Tech, 1992—. Spl. agt. Northwestern Mut. Life Ins., Princeton, W.Va., 1985-86; mktg. dir. One Valley Bank, Princeton, W.Va., 1986-89; instr. Bluefield (W.Va.) State Coll., 1989-93, asst. prof., 1993—. Bd. dirs. Princeton-Mercer County C. of C., Princeton, 1991-92. Mem. ASPA, Phi Eta Sigma, Pi Alpha Alpha, Phi Kappa Phi. Home: 1060 Hemlock Ln Princeton WV 24740-2032 Office: Bluefield State Coll 219 Rock St Bluefield WV 24701-2100

SNEATH, WILLIAM EMMET, development professional, retired naval officer; b. Chgo., Mar. 29, 1943; s. William Ewart and Florence Louise (Seymour) S.; m. Cheryl Maxine Davis, Dec. 19, 1964 (div.); children: Michael William, Dawn Christine; m. Frances Ann Catalano, Apr. 22, 1990. BS, Western Mich. U., 1965, MBA, 1976. Enlisted USN, 1964, commd. ensign, 1965, advanced through grades to capt., 1990; staff Readiness Command Region 6, Washington, 1989-90; ret. USN, 1990; devel. officer Randolph-Macon Acad., Front Royal, Va., 1991—; dir. mktg. Hour Photos, Manassas, Va., 1986—; owner BFS Enterprises, Front Royal, 1995—. Mem. Nat. Soc. Fundraising Execs., Assn. Luth. Devel. Execs., Photo Mktg. Assn., Internat. Naval Rsch. Orgn., U.S. Naval Inst. Republican. Lutheran. Office: Randolph-Macon Acad 201 W 3rd St Front Royal VA 22630-2657

SNEDEKER, SEDGWICK, lawyer; b. Bklyn., Apr. 11, 1909; s. Edwin Snedeker and Louise (Sedgwick) Atwater; m. Anne Carl Parke, June 28, 1940 (dec. 1961); children—Thomas S., William D., James P.; m. Elizabeth Gabrielle Naudin, Sept. 15, 1962; stepchildren—Nancy Seagren, Lynn (Mrs. Pascal Franchot Tone), John F. Grad. Princeton U., 1933; LL.B., Columbia U., 1936. Bar: N.Y. 1938, U.S. Supreme Ct. 1945, U.S. Dist. Ct. (ea. dist.) N.Y. 1938. Trial asst. Holmes, Bernstein & O'Dwyer, Bklyn., 1937-39; trial atty. Leo T. Kisam, N.Y.C., 1939-42; trial atty. Snedeker & Snedeker, Bklyn., 1942-45, ptnr., 1945-50; banking and real estate atty. Shearman & Sterling, N.Y.C., 1950-74; counsel, trustee Bklyn. Savs. Bank. Pres. Cold Springs Harbor Civic Assn., 1940-45; treas. Holland Soc. N.Y.C., 1965-70. Republican. Episcopalian. Clubs: Piping Rock Locust Valley, Huntington Country, Princeton (N.Y.); Everglades, Beach (Palm Beach, Fla.); Tiger Inn (N.J.). Avocations: golf; gardening. Home and Office: 369 S Lake Dr Palm Beach FL 33480-4571

SNEED, RAPHAEL CORCORAN, physiatrist, pediatrician; b. Selma, Ala., 1942. MD, U. Ala., 1968. Diplomate Am. Bd. Pediat., Am. Bd. Phys. Medicine and Rehab. Intern U. Ala. Hosp. Clinic, Birmingham, 1968-69, resident in pediat., 1969-71, resident in phys. medicine and rehab., 1981-83, fellow in phys. medicine and rehab., 1983-84; with Children's Rehab. Ctr. Miss. Med. Ctr., Jackson. Mem. Am. Acad. Pediat., Am. Acad. Phys. Medicine and Rehab. Office: U Miss Med Ctr Children's Rehab Ctr 2500 N State St Jackson MS 39216-4500

SNELLING, LONIE EUGENE, JR., minister; b. Laurinburg, N.C., Apr. 5, 1937; s. Lonie Eugene Sr. and Doris (Stevens) S.; m. Sally Still, Apr. 14, 1965; children: Cynthia Lyn, David Eugene. BA cum laude, Southeastern Bible Coll., Birmingham, Ala., 1960, Th.B. cum laude, 1961; MEd magna cum laude, Boston U., 1974; PhD, Columbia Pacific U., San Rafael, Calif., 1984. Minister music So. Bapt. Chs., Birmingham, 1957-61; youth evangelist Youth for Christ, Atlanta, 1962-63; enlisted U.S. Army, 1963, advanced through grades to capt., 1982; served in Vietnam; chaplain adminstr. U.S. Army, 1963-74; behavioral scientist Med. Service Corps, U.S. Army, various locations, 1974-83; dir. Royal Palm Bibl. Counseling Ctrs., Ft. Myers, Fla., 1983-86; pres. Royal Palm Ministries, Inc., Ft. Myers, 1986—; cons. in psychology and counseling Gulf Shore Bapt. Grad. Sch., Ft. Myers, 1983—, head dept. psychology and counseling; sem. prof. So. Bapt. extension dept. Decorated Legion of Merit. Fellow Nat. Assn. Nouthetic Counselors; mem. Nat. Judo and Karate Assn. Am., Am. Assn. Christian Counselors. Republican. Home: 5367 Colony Ct Cape Coral FL 33904-5878 Office: Royal Palm Ministries Inc 5235 Ramsey Way Ste 13 Fort Myers FL 33907-2125

SNIDER, ROBERT LARRY, management consultant; b. Muskogee, Okla., Aug. 10, 1932; s. George Robert and Kathryn (Smiser) S.; m. Gerlene Rose Tipton, Nov. 26, 1953; children: Melody Kathryn Porter, Rebecca Lee. B.S. in Indsl. Engring., U. Houston, 1955, postgrad., 1956; postgrad., Pomona Coll., 1960. Cert. mgmt. cons. Instr. U. Houston Coll. Engring., 1955-56; sr. indsl. engr. Sheffield Steel Corp., Houston, 1955-59, Kaiser Steel Co., Fontana, Calif., 1959-60; cons. Arthur Young & Co., Los Angeles, 1960-61; mgmt. analyst Iranian Oil Exploration & Producing Co., Masjidi-Suliman, Iran, 1961-62; cons., 1962-65; v.p. operating methods div. Booz, Allen & Hamilton, Inc., Dallas, 1965-67; chmn., CEO RLS Profl. Svcs., Houston, Tex., 1995—; prin., gen. cons. practice Peat Marwick Mitchell, CPAs, Houston, 1969-71; exec. v.p. mfg. Sterling Electronics Corp., Houston, 1971-72, pres., chief operating officer, 1972-77; pres., chief exec. officer Rapoca Energy Corp., Cin., 1977-79; mng. partner, cons. Coopers & Lybrand, Southwest, Houston, 1979-81; mng. dir. Southwest region Korn Ferry Internat., Houston, 1981-86; ptnr.-in-charge Houston Mgmt. Cons. Practice, 1986-91; ptnr. cons. Southwest Enterprise Coopers & Lybrand, Houston, 1991-92; ptnr S.W. Mfg. Consulting Process Improvement Group Coopers & Lybrand, Houston, Pakistan/Mid. Asia, 1992-93; internat. cons. ptnr. Coopers & Lybrand, Houston, 1993-95; mng. ptnr. RLS Profl. Svcs. LLC, 1995—. Past mem. bd. dirs., exec. com. Houston Jr. Achievement; pastchmn. bd. mem. found. bd.and adminstrv. bd. Chapel Wood Meth. Ch.; ret. exec. com., bd. dirs. Houston Grand Opera. With C.E. AUS, 1956. Recipient Outstandng Mil. Engr. award Soc. Mil Engrs., 1955; named Disting. Alumni, Cullen Coll. Engring., U. Houston, 1991. Mem. Soc. Mining Engrs., U. Houston Alumni Assn. (past bd. dirs., exec. com., past pres., chmn.), Houston club, Houstonian Club, Phi Theta Kappa, Phi Kappa Phi. Home: 11643 Greenbay St Houston TX 77024-6430 Office: RLS Profl Svcs 681 Tealwood Rd Montgomery TX 77356

SNIDER, RUTH ATKINSON, retired counselor; b. Louisville, Jan. 7, 1930; d. Ellis Orrell and Fanola Blanche (Miller) Atkinson; m. Arnold Wills Snider, Feb. 17, 1950; children: Yvonne Marie, Ray Wills, Mark Alan. Student, Centre Coll., 1947-48; BS, Spalding U., 1965, MEd, 1970; rank I, Western Ky. U., 1981. Cert. sch. psychometrist, sch. prin., supr. of instrn. Tchr. Shelby County (Ky.) Bd. Edn., 1949-50, Louisville Pub. Schs., 1956-57; tchr. Jefferson County Pub. Schs., Louisville, 1965-67, counselor, 1967-92; vol. co-chairperson for mentor program Spalding U., Louisville, 1991. Vol. Ky. Ctr. for Arts, 1989, 90, 91, Actors Theatre of Louisville, 193-94, 95, 96, Klondike Elem. Sch. Libr., 1994-95; pub. chair World Day of Prayer, 1996; sec. adv. com. Beechwood Bapt. Ch. Mem. ACA (del.), Am. Sch. Counselors Assn. (del. nat. conf.), Ky. Assn. Counseling and Devel., Ky. Sch. Counselors Assn. (conf. chairperson), Spalding Soc. (pres. 1995-96), Spalding Alumni Assn. (sec. 1994-96, Caritas award), Jefferson County Ret. Tchrs. Assn., Christian Women's Club. Home: 2428 Chattesworth Ln Louisville KY 40242-2849

SNIHUR, WILLIAM JOSEPH, JR., lawyer; b. Paterson, N.J., Mar. 7, 1959; s. William Joseph and Lynn (Aboyoun) S.; m. May Lydia Cain, Oct. 14, 1990; children: Ariel Rose, Alexander Charles. Student, Mt. St. Mary's Coll., L.A., 1978-79, UCLA, 1979; BBA, U. Miami, 1982, JD, 1985. Law intern U.S. Atty.'s Office, Miami, Fla., 1984-85; assoc. Litman, Muchnick, Wasserman & Hartman, Hollywood, Fla., 1986-91; ptnr. Cain & Snihur, North Miami Beach, Fla., 1992—; adj. prof. Barry U., Miami Shores, Fla., 1989—; adj. faculty Legal Career Inst., Ftl. Lauderdale, Fla., 1991. Mem. editl. bd. The Fla. Bar Jour. and News, 1990-94; co-editor: The Fla. Bar Jour., 1991; contbg. writer The Fla. Bar News, 1995. Mem. exec. com. Philharm. Orch. of Fla., Ft. Lauderdale, 1990-92, bd. govs., 1990-93, pres.'s coun., 1990-93, ann. fund campaign leadership, 1991-92, long range planning com., 1992; pres., founder Maestro Broward Philharm., Ft. Lauderdale, 1989-92, Maestro Dade Philharm., co-founder, dir. fin., 1989-90; steering com. WTMI/Philharm. Festival and Radiothon, 1990; bd. dirs. Vinnette Carroll Repertory Theatre, 1989-91; entourage mem. Broward Ctr. for Performing Arts, 1992-93. Recipient music scholarships Mt. St. Mary's Coll., Aspen Music Sch., Depaw U., honor scholarship U. Miami, Coral Gables, 1981, UCLA, 1979, others. Mem. ATLA (mem. com. 1990-91), The Fla. Bar (bus. law, gen. practice, real property, probate and trust law sects., benefits com. 1995—), Broward County Bar Assn. (United Way com. 1989-90, chmn. pub. com. 1991-93, editor Broward Barrister 1991-93, pro bono legal assistance Broward Lawyers Care), North Dade Bar (bd. dirs. 1993—). Office: Cain & Snihur 16300 NE 19th Ave Ste 224 North Miami Beach FL 33162

SNIVELY, STEPHEN WAYNE, lawyer; b. Danville, Ill., Apr. 27, 1949; s. Roberts Eyster and Margaret Louise Snively; m. Heather Lea Patten, Mar. 19, 1988; children: Toby, Ben, Madeline, Taylor. BA, U. Ill., 1971, JD, 1975. Bar: Ill. 1975, Fla. 1980. Assoc. Kavanagh, Scully, Sudow, White & Frederick, Peoria, Ill., 1975-80, Maguire, Voorhis & Wells, P.A., Orlando, Fla., 1980—; seminar speaker, 1987. Contbr. articles to profl. jours. Bd. dirs. Found. for Orange County Pub. Schs., Orlando, 1987—, officer, 1987-96, pres., 1993-94, chmn., 1994-96; bd. dirs. Found. for Hospice of Ctrl. Fla., Inc., 1995-96; treas., bd. dirs. HCF Found., Inc., 1996—. Mem. Fla. Bar (liaison to land surveyor com. 1982—), Orange County Ba Assn., Internat. Coun. Shopping Ctrs., Fla. C. of C. (Leadership Fla. 1991-92), Fla. Zool. Soc. (sec., bd. dirs. 1991—), Univ. Club, Citrus Club, Tiger Bay Club, Econs. Club Orlando, Phi Beta Kappa. Republican. Presbyterian. Office: Maguire Voorhis & Wells PA Two S Orange Ave Orlando FL 32801

SNODGRASS, CHRIS, English literature educator; b. Indpls., Apr. 28, 1947; s. Garrett A. and Violet Evelyn (Courtney) S.; m. Carol Lee Greene Ackerman, Aug. 1967 (div. Oct. 1972); 1 child, Shelley Anne; m. Lesley Church Horton, May 1974 (div. Jan. 1985). BA summa cum laude, Wabash Coll., Crawfordsville, Ind., 1969; MA, SUNY, Buffalo, 1972, PhD, 1974. Grad. asst. SUNY, Buffalo, 1969-72; interim asst. prof. U. Fla., Gainesville, 1973-74, asst. prof. English, 1974-78, assoc. prof., 1978-96, prof., 1996—; chief negotiator United Faculty of Fla., 1981-84, 93-95, collective bargaining cons., 1979-85, 90-95; collective bargaining cons. NEA, Washington, 1995; textbook cons. John Wiley & Sons, N.Y.C., 1979-83. Author: Aubrey Beardsley, Dandy of the Grotesque, 1995 (Outstanding Acad. Book of 1995 Choice Rev. Svc.); contbr. articles to Victorian Poetry, Victorian Inst. Jour., Victorian Studies, English Lit. in Transition, Arnoldian, others. Recipient Margaret Farber award Wabash Coll., 1968, Outstanding Achievement award U. Fla., 1990, Outstanding Tchr. award, 1994; Woodrow Wilson fellow, 1969. Mem. NEA, MLA, Eighteen Nineties Soc., Victorian Inst., Phi Beta Kappa. Home: 2405 NW 59th Terr Gainesville FL 32606 Office: U Fla Dept English 4008 Turlington Hall Gainesville FL 32611

SNOKE, JUDITH HOUTZ, English language educator; b. N.Y.C., Oct. 7, 1940; d. Philip and Fanny (Bokstein) Houtz; m. J. Arthur Snoke, June 7, 1964; children: Timur, Margaret Grace. BA, Stanford U., 1963; MAT, Harvard U., 1964. Tchr. social studies Hamden (Conn.) High Sch., 1964-69; ESL tchr. Middle East Tech. U., Ankara, Turkey, 1969-71, New River C.C., Dublin, Va., 1980-81; ESL tchr., program coord. Univ. Community Internat. Coun., Blacksburg, Va., 1984-92; dir. Va. Tech. Lang. Inst., Blacksburg, 1992—. Bd. dirs. Literacy Vols., New River Valley, 1985-93. Mem.

TESOL, LWV (bd. dirs. Montgomery County 1986—). Office: Va Tech Lang Inst Continuing Edn 0104 Blacksburg VA 24061

SNOW, JOHN WILLIAM, railroad executive; b. Toledo, Aug. 2, 1939; s. William Dean and Catharine (Howard) S.; m. Fredrica Wheeler, June 11, 1964 (div. 1973); children: Bradley, Ian; m. Carolyn Kalk, Aug. 31, 1973; 1 child, Christopher. B.A., U. Toledo, 1962; Ph.D., U. Va., 1965; LL.B., George Washington U., 1967. Asst. prof. econs. U. Md., College Park, 1965-67; assoc. Wheeler & Wheeler, Washington, 1967-72; asst. gen. counsel Dept. Transp., Washington, 1972-73, dep. asst. sec. for policy, plans and internat. affairs, 1973-74, asst. sec. for govtl. affairs, 1974-75, dep. under sec., 1975-76; adminstr. Nat. Hwy. Traffic Safety Adminstrn., Washington, 1976-77; v.p. govt. affairs Chessie System Inc., Washington, 1977-80; sr. v.p. corp. services CSX Corp., Richmond, Va., 1980-84, exec. v.p., 1984-85; pres., chief exec. officer Chessie System R.R.s, Balt., 1985-86, CSX Rail Transport, Jacksonville, Fla., 1986-87, CSX Transp., Jacksonville, Va., 1987-88; pres., chief operating officer CSX Corp., Richmond, Va., 1988-89, pres., chief exec. officer, 1989-91, chmn., pres., chief exec. officer, 1991—, also bd. dirs.; adj. prof. law George Washington U., 1972-75; vis. prof. econs. U. Va., Charlottesville, spring 1977; vis. fellow Am. Enterprises Inst., Washington, spring 1977; bd. dirs. NationsBank Corp., Bassett Furniture Industries Inc., USX Corp., Textron Inc., Circuit City Stores, Inc. Bd. trustees Johns Hopkins U. Mem. Va. State Bar. Episcopalian. Clubs: Chevy Chase, Metropolitan (Washington); Commonwealth, Country of Va. (Richmond).

SNOW, JULIE ANN, maternal-child nurse; b. Sidney, Nebr., Sept. 2, 1955; d. Anton A. and Emma A. (Schnell) Lutringer; m. Paul D. Snow, Dec. 11, 1981 (div.); 1 child, Rachel Elizabeth. BSN, Mt. Marty Coll., Yankton, S.D., 1976. RN. Staff nurse Bishop Clarkson Meml. Hosp., Omaha; asst. head nurse St. Paul Med. Ctr., Dallas; head nurse El Centro (Calif.) Regional Med. Ctr.; nurse mgr. Mercy Med. Ctr., Redding, Calif.; dir. women's ctr. Beaumont (Tex.) Regional Med. Ctr.; dir. maternal-child svcs. St. Johns Regional Med. Ctr., Joplin, Mo. Mem. adv. bd. S.E. Mo. br. March of Dimes, Women's Ctr. Mem. AWHONN (nat., S.E. Tex. sect.), Nat. Assn. Neonatal Nurses.

SNOW, RUTH DARR, radiologist educator; b. Columbia, S.C., Aug. 19, 1951; d. Robert Alexander and Dorcas Adina (Goodman) Darr; m. David Mowery Snow, June 24, 1988; children: Adam Christopher, Rachael Elizabeth. MusB, Converse Coll., 1972; MusM, U. S.C., 1975; MD, U. Ark., 1986. Diplomate Am. Bd. Radiology. Intern U. Ark., Little Rock, 1986-87; resident U. South Ala., Mobile, 1987-91, fellow in neuroradiology, 1991-93, assoc. prof. radiology and neurology, 1991—; chief MRI U. South Ala., Mobile, 1993—; chief neuroradiology U. South Ala., 1995—. Contbr. articles to profl. jours.; reviewer. Mem. AMA, Am. Soc. Neuroradiology (sr.), Am. Roentgen Ray Soc., Radiol. Soc. N.Am., So. Med. Soc., Southeastern Neuroradiol. Soc. Episcopalian. Home: 5532 Regency Oaks Dr N Mobile AL 36609-2214 Office: Univ South Ala 2451 Fillingim St Mobile AL 36617-2238

SNOW, SHARON ELIZABETH, rare books curator; b. Statesville, N.C., Jan. 29, 1958; d. Roger Franklin and Ulean (Hayes) S. BS in Math., Wake Forest U., 1980; MLS, U. N.C., 1988; postgrad. in religion, Wake Forest U., 1. Systems analyst First Union Nat. Bank, Charlotte, N.C., 1980; employee benefits analyst Booke & Co., Winston-Salem, N.C., 1981-84; asst. to curator of rare books Wake Forest U., Winston-Salem, 1984-89, curator of rare books, 1989-94, 95—; chaplain resident N.C. Bapt. Hosp., Winston-Salem, 1994-95; speaker Internat. Congress for Basic Trauma Life Support, Greensboro, N.C., 1995. Vol. chaplain N.C. Bapt. Hosp., Winston-Salem, 1993—, Forsyth Meml. Hosp., Winston-Salem, 1993—, Hospice of Forsyth County, Winston-Salem, 1993-94, Samaritan Ministries and Shelter, Winston-Salem, 1991-94. Travel, study grantee Wake Forest U., Oxford U., Eng., 1988. Mem. N.C. Libr. Assn. (chair spl. collections 1992-95). Democrat. Baptist. Home: 1248 Brookwood Dr Winston-Salem NC 27106 Office: Wake Forest Univ Box 7777 E Smith Reynolds Libr Winston Salem NC 27109

SNOW, THOMAS RUSSELL, technical writer; b. Danville, Va., Mar. 29, 1943; s. Richard Adam and Virgina (Cather) S.; m. Linda Gilchrist; two children. BS, Carnegie Mellon, 1965; PhD, Duke U., 1971. Postdoctoral asst. Baylor Coll. Medicine, Houston, 1971-73; asst. prof. Duke U., Durham, N.C., 1973-81; assoc. mem. Okla. Med. Rsch. Found., Oklahoma City, 1981-91; assoc. prof. U. South Fl., Tampa, 1991-95; tech. writer FMQAI, Tampa, 1995—; ad hoc study sect. NIH, Bethesda, 1975—. Contbr. chpts. to books and articles to profl. jours. Named NSF fellow, 1972. Office: FMQAI 1211 West Shore Blvd Tampa FL 33607

SNOWDEN, BERNICE RIVES, former construction company executive; b. Houston, Mar. 21, 1923; d. Charles Samuel and Annie Pearl (Rorex) Rives; grad. Smalley Comml. Coll., 1941; student U. Houston, 1965; m. Walter G. Snowden; 1 dau., Bernice Ann Ogden. With Houston Pipe Line Co., 1944-45; clk.-typist Charles G. Heyne & Co., Inc., Houston, 1951-53, payroll asst., 1953-56, sec. to pres., also office mgr., 1956-62, sec. to pres., also controller, 1962-70, sec.-treas., 1970-77, chief fin. officer, also dir. Mem. Women in Constrn., Nat. Assn. Women in Constrn. (past pres.), San Leon C. of C. Methodist. Club: Lord and Ladies Dance. Home: 6611 Kury Ln Houston TX 77008-5101

SNOWDEN, FRASER, philosophy educator; b. Atlanta, Nov. 23, 1940; s. Barnard E.B. and Aline (Fraser) S.; m. Dian Mary Deckbar, May 7, 1962; children: Dawn, Juliet, Michael. BA in Philosophy, Tulane U., 1965, MA in Philosophy, 1968, PhD, 1989. Grad. teaching asst. Coll. Arts and Scis., Tulane U., 1966-67, Newcomb Coll., 1967-68; instr. philosophy U. Southwestern La., 1968-70; asst. prof. philosophy Northwestern State U., Natchitoches, La., 1970-75, assoc. prof. philosophy, 1975-89; assoc. prof. philosophy La. Scholars' Coll., Northwestern State U., Natchitoches, La., 1989-92, prof. philosophy, 1992—; adj. philosophy tchr. La. Sch. Math. Sci. and Arts, 1984-90; bd. dirs. La. Endowment for the Humanities State La., 1983-90, vice chair 1986, chair 1986-88, exec. com. 1989-90. Co-editor: (with Harris) Bioethical Frontiers in Perinatal Intensive Care, 1985; author: (chpt.) Bioethical Challenges at the Dawn of Life: An Introduction, 1985; Contbr. to profl. jours. NEH grantee, 1992. Democrat. Home: 509 White Oak Ln Natchitoches LA 71457-6715 Office: The La Scholars Coll Northwestern State U College Ave Natchitoches LA 71497

SNOWDEN, RUTH O'DELL GILLESPIE, artist; b. Gary, W.Va., Apr. 16, 1926; d. Haynes Thornton and Blanche Beaula (Boling) Gillespie; m. Eugene Louis Snowden, Dec. 21, 1946; children: Wanda Snowden Ballard, Eugene III, Ronald, Marian Snowden Warren, Jeffry. RN, Natharith Coll., 1946; postgrad., Transylvania U., 1983-84, U. Ky., 1985-89. Painter, publicity chmn. Artist's Attic Inc., Lexington, Ky., 1988-89. Exhibited in group shows at U. Ky. Art Mus., Lexington, 1988, 5th Internat. Juried Exhibition Pastels, Nyack, N.Y., 1988, Small Paintings Nat., Ky. Highlands Mus., Ashland, 1988, The Appalachian Cen., U. Ky., 1988, Ft. Wayne (Ind.) Mus. Art, 1986, John Howard Sanden Nat. Artists Seminar, Washington, Nat. Artists' Seminar, Chgo., Huntington (W.Va.) Galleries, Nat. Nursing Art Exhibit, Meth. Med. Cen., Peoria, Ill., Chautauqua Art Assn. Galleries, N.Y., 1990, Central Bank gallery, Chatauqua, 1990, Pastel & Chisel Acad. Fine Arts, 1990, Opera House Gallery, 1990, Sacramento Fine Arts Ctr., 1990, Ariel Gallery, Soho, N.Y., 1990, 91, Sumi-e Soc. Am., Inc., 1993, Watercolor Soc. Ala., 1994; represented in the Director of American Portrait Artists, Am. Portrait Soc., Huntington Harbour, Calif.; numerous local and nat. shows; in pvt. collections. Recipient Assn. Alliance award Am. Frame Co., 1993, also various watercolor and oil painting awards. Mem. Oil Pastel Assn., Nyack, N.Y., Winchester Art Guild, Lexington Art League, Ky. Watercolor Assn. (Bluegrass regional dir. 1988, 89, 90, 91, 92), Ky. Guild Artists and Craftsmen, Inc., Berea, Northwest Pastel Soc., Seattle, Degas Pastel Soc., New Orleans. Home: 2800 Old Boonesboro Rd Winchester KY 40391-8805 Office: Artists Attic Inc Victorian Square 401 W Main St Lexington KY 40507-1646

SNYDER, CHARLES WILLIAM, lawyer; b. Boston, June 15, 1949; s. Benjamin and Fay (Backaler) S. BA, Boston U., 1971; MA, U. Va., 1973, PhD, 1979; JD, U. Ga., 1982. Bar: Ga. 1982, Mass. 1982, U.S. Dist. Ct. (so. dist.) Ga. 1983. Law clk. to judge Ga. Superior Ct., Savannah, 1983-84; atty. Fed. Election Commn., Washington, 1984-90; panelist Hofstra U. Conf. on Presdl. Studies, 1990. Author: Liberty and Morality, 1995; contbr. articles to profl. jours. Mem. Ga. Bar Assn., Ga. Trial Lawyers Assn., Order of Coif. Jewish. Office: Jones Boykin & Assocs 701 Abercorn St Savannah GA 31401-5801

SNYDER, JOSEPH JOHN, editor, author, lecturer, historian, consultant; b. Washington, Aug. 27, 1946; s. Joseph John and Amy Josephine (Hamilton) S.; m. Sally Hale Walker, July 4, 1973; children: Lauren Elizabeth, Brian Joseph Seth. BA in Anthropology, George Washington U., 1968; MA in Anthropology, U. N.Mex., 1973. With U.S. CSC, Washington, 1974-77; editor, writer U.S. Nat. Park Svc., Harpers Ferry, W.Va., 1977-81; cons. editor Early Man mag., Evanston, Ill., 1978-83; cons. editor Sea Power Mag., 1987—; freelance writer, 1981—; pres. Sta. at Shepherdstown Inc., 1992—; pres., chmn. bd. dirs., Atlantic & Pacific High Speed Railway, Inc., 1993—; lectr. Maya archaeology Norwegian-Caribbean Lines, Miami, Fla., 1982; cons. mus. design. Chmn. parks com. Neighborhood Planning Adv. Group, Croydon Park, Rockville, Md., 1980-81; bd. dirs. Agrl. R & D Orgn, 1985—; v.p., bd. dirs., Hagerstown (Md.) Roundhouse Mus., 1989-91; sec. bd. dirs. Hagerstown-Washington County Conv. and Visitors. Bur., 1993—. With U.S. Army, 1970-71, Vietnam. Decorated Bronze Star. Mem. Coun. Md. Archaeology, Hakluyt Soc., Am. Com. to Advance Study of Petroglyphs and Pictographs, Nat. Geog. Soc. (cons. 1987—), Nat. Ry. Hist. Soc. Cons. editor jour. Archaeoastronomy, 1987—; contbr. articles to popular mags. Democrat. Home: 2008 Ashley Dr Shepherdstown WV 25443

SNYDER, KATHLEEN LOUISE, community health nurse; b. Erie, Pa., July 29, 1949; d. Philip W. and Dolores E. (Messmer) Robinson; m. Gary L. Snyder, May 8, 1971; children: Aaron James, Andrea Jae. Diploma, Spencer Hosp. Sch. Nursing, 1970. Office nurse pediatrics dept. Dr. W.C. Wilhelm, Erie, 1979-83; staff nurse orthopedics unit Hamot Med. Ctr., Erie, 1984-86; ins. rehab. nurse Vocat. Rehab. Svcs., Erie, 1986-88; patient care coord. Great Lakes Home Health, Erie, 1989-95. Mem. Erie Ind. Coun. on Aging.

SNYDER, LOUIS D., cardiovascular physician; b. N.Y.C., Apr. 20, 1954; m. Barbara; children: Todd, Alexander, Jordan. BA, Brandeis U., 1976; MD, Johns Hopkins U., 1980, postgrad., 1983-86; Harvard U., 1986. Diplomate Am. Bd. Internal Medicine, Am. Bd. Cardiovascular Disease. Assoc. dir. New Oleans Heart Clinic, 1986-89; med. dir. The Cardiology Center, Delray Beach, Fla., 1989—. Fellow Am. Coll. Cardiology, Am. Coll. Physicians. Office: The Cardiology Ctr #560 16244 Military Trl Ste 560 Delray Beach FL 33484-6505

SNYDER, ROBERT EDWARD, American studies educator; b. Amsterdam, N.Y., Mar. 27, 1943; s. Richard Earl and Clara Mary (Trzaskos) S.; m. Joan Marie Unchur; children: Kristin Marie, Dylan Michael. BA, Union Coll., 1967, MA, 1971; PhD, Syracuse U., 1980. Univ. fellow Syracuse (N.Y.) U., 1977-80; asst. prof. U. South Fla., Tampa, 1980-84, assoc. prof., 1984-90, prof. dept. Am. studies, 1990—, dir. grad. program in Am. studies, 1984-90; humanities cons. PBS documentary Huey Long. Sr. author: Pioneer Commercial Photography, 1992; author: Cotton Crisis, 1984; contbr. on So. politics and popular culture to profl. jours. Recipient Gen. L. Kemper Williams prize Kemper Found., 1974, Robert L. Brown award La. Hist. Assn., 1975, Willie D. Halsell award Miss. Hist. Assn., 1978, Cert. of Commendation, Am. Assn. for State and Local History, 1993, D.B. McKay award Hillsborough County Hist. Soc., 1993; NEH grantee, 1986, So. Regional Edn. Bd. grantee, 1982, 86, 91. Mem. Am. Hist. Assn., Orgn. Am. Historians, So. Hist. Assn., Am. Studies Assn., Popular Culture Assn., Fla. Hist. Soc. (Charlton Tebeau award 1993). Roman Catholic. Home: 2401 Blind Pond Ave Lutz FL 33549-7508 Office: U South Fla Dept Am Studies 4202 E Fowler Ave # 107 Tampa FL 33620-9900

SNYDER, RUSSELL ROBERT, obstetrician, gynecologist, educator, pathologist; b. Munich, May 10, 1953; (parents Am. citizens); s. Rex lee and Anna A. Snyder; m. Cecilia Kay Melville, June 4, 1975; children: Holly Ann, Clifford Lee. BS, USAF Acad., 1975; MD, U. Tex., 1978. Diplomate Am. Bd. Ob-Gyn. (indefinite bd. examiner 1995—). Commd. 2d lt. USAF, 1975, advanced through grades to col., 1996; intern ob-gyn. Wilford Hall USAF Med. Ctr., Lackland AFB, Tex., 1978-79, resident in ob-gyn., 1979-82; fellow Armed Forces Inst. Pathology, Washington, 1984; chief outpatient svcs. Wilford Hall USAF Med. Ctr., Lackland AFB, Tex., 1984-87, chief gynecologic pathology, 1986—, chief gynecologic svcs., 1987—, chair dept. ob-gyn., 1994—; assoc. prof. dept. ob-gyn. F. Edward Hebert Sch. Medicine, Bethesda, Md., 1990—; spl. cons. to surgeon gen. on ob-gyn. and gynecol. pathology USAF, 1991—, dep. chief cons. on ob-gyn., 1993-95, chief cons. on ob-gyn., 1995—. Author: Magnesium Sulfate Pharmacokinetics, 1986 (Chmn.'s award best sci. paper 1986), Endometrioid Tumors of Ovary, 1986 (Fellows award); (chpt.) HPV infection during Pregnancy, 1990; contbr. articles to med. jours.; mem. editl. bd. Obstetrics and Gynecology, 1996—. Adult leader Boy Scouts Am., San Antonio, 1990—; instr. Advanced Trauma Life Support, San Antonio, 1992—; mem. Nat. Adolescent Health Promotion Network, 1991—; mem. exec. bd. Jacobs Inst. for Women, Washington, 1992-95. Bristol-Myers Co. grantee, 1991-92, Surgeon Gen. grantee, 1993. Fellow Am. Coll. Ob-Gyn (exec. bd., sci. program chmn. dist. 10 ann. mtg. 1988, vice dist. chmn. 1988-92, dist. sec.-treas. 1989-92, dist. chmn. 1992—, nat. jr. fellow advisor 1993—, govt. rels. com. 1994-95, exec. com. 1994-95, com. on indsl. exhibits 1995—, nominations com. 1996-98); mem. Soc. Air Force Clin. Surgeons (treas. 1990-94, program chair 1994, pres.-elect 1994-95, pres. 1995—), Assn. Profs. Gynecology and Obstetrics (editl. bd. Obstetrics & Gynceology 1996-99), Assn. Mil. Surgeons U.S. Methodist. Office: Dept Ob-Gyn (PSO) 2200 Bergquist Dr Ste 1 Lackland AFB TX 78236-5302

SNYDER, STANLEY OWEN, vascular surgeon; b. Owensboro, Ky., June 6, 1946; m. Suzanne Snyder; children: Stanley O. III, Jessica, Jeffrey, Andrew. BA, Centre Coll., 1968; MD, U. Louisville, 1972. Diplomate Am. Bd. Surgeons, Va. Bd. Med. Examiners. Intern Parkland Hosp., Dallas, 1972-73, resident, 1973-77; fellow in vascular surgery St. Thomas Hosp., Nashville, 1977-78; vascular surgeon Norfolk (Va.) Surg. Group, 1978—; assoc. clin. prof. surgery Vanderbilt Sch. Medicine, Nashville, 1995—; assoc. prof. surgery Ea. Va. Med. Sch., Norfolk, 1987—, asst. prof. surgery, 1980-87; mem. med. staff Sentara Norfolk Gen. Hosp., Sentara Leigh Hosp., Sentara Bayside Hosp., DePaul Med. Ctr., Va. Beach Gen. Hosp., Children's Hosp. of the King's Daus., Portsmouth Naval Hosp., Southampton Meml. Hosp., Northampton Accomack Hosp.; presenter in field. Mem. editorial bd. Vascular Forum, 1992—, Forum, 1993—; contbr. articles to profl. jours. Grantee Ea. Va. Med. Sch., 1986. Fellow ACS; mem. Va. Vascular Soc. (pres. 1986-87, founding mem., organizing com. 1985, pres.-elect 1985-86), AMA, Norfolk County Med. Soc., Seaboard Med. Assn., Med. Soc. Va., So. Assn. for Vascular Surgery, Internat. Soc. for Cardiovascular Surgery, So. Med. Assn., Va. Surg. Soc., Va. Vascular Soc., Wound Healing Soc., So. Surg. Assn., Soc. for Vascular Soc., Internat. Study for Endovascular Surgery, Alpha Omega Alpha. Office: Edwards-Eye Clinic 4230 Harding Rd Ste 705 Nashville TN 37205-2013

SNYDER, THOMAS DANIEL, retired electronics engineer, consultant; b. Phila., Aug. 30, 1925; s. Thomas Daniel and Edith May (Lees) S.; Asso. in Applied Sci. in Radio and TV Tech., Milw. Sch. Engring., 1951; m. Mary Ann Wilson, Aug. 28, 1954; children: Thomas Daniel, Ellen Mary, John W. Foreman Prime Mfg. Co., Milw., 1951; with engring. dept. No. Light Co., Milw., 1951-52; communications clk. fgn. service U.S. Dept. State, 1952-55; electronics engr. U.S. Dept. Def., Warrenton, Va., 1955-85; staff cons. Am. Elect. Labs. Cons. accoustics and magnetics govt. agys., 1964—; lectr. metric conversion; participant Solid States Application Conf., Fla. Atlanta U., 1971; participant profl. seminars Mass. Inst. Tech., 1962, 64, 66, Columbia, 1963, Pa. State U., 1967, U. Wis., 1969. Pres., PTA, Fairfax, Va., 1971, county rep., 1972. Served with USNR, 1943-46; PTO. Recipient Meritorious award for outstanding design in electronics equipment, U.S. Govt., 1969. Mem. AAAS, IEEE, Optical Soc. Am., Metric Assn., Am. Nat. Metric Coun., Am. Legion, Cath. War Vets. (adj. 1964-67). Roman Catholic. Contbr. articles to profl. jours. Patentee in field. Home: 4246 Worcester Dr Fairfax VA 22032-1140

SNYDER, WESLEY WARREN, interior space planner and designer; b. Chgo., June 4, 1935; s. Warren Elmore and Grace Elizabeth (Gray) S. BS in Gen. Speech, Northwestern U., Evanston, Ill., 1958; student, Chgo. Art Inst., 1964. Furniture sales trainee Heywood Wakefield Co., Chgo., 1960-62; med. space planner and designer V. Mueller & Co., Chgo., 1962-63; mgr. wholesale showroom Charles L. Orr, Inc., Chgo., 1963-68; owner, pres., prin. designer Cristies of Chgo., Inc., 1968-81; instr. interior design Ringling Sch. of Art and Design, Sarasota, Fla., 1981-82; div. mgr. Comml. Designs by Saba, Sarasota, 1983; sr. designer Lambert Interiors, Sarasota, 1983-84; sales rep. Wagner Office Furniture, Tampa, Fla., 1984-85; v.p. and design dir. Office Design and Supplies, Inc., Sarasota, 1985-87; pres. Cristies Design Group, Sarasota, 1988—, Cristies Collection, Sarasota, 1992-96; mem. Landmark Preservation Coun. of Ill., 1972-79, exec. v.p., 1974, mem. city house preservation fair founding com. City of Chgo., 1979; mem. Inst. Bus Designers, Chgo., 1973-84, pres. Chgo. Regional chpt., 1978-79, nat. trustee, 1979-81; vice chmn. Sarasota County Arts Coun., 1986-89; lectr. in field. Designer various bldgs., including Northwestern U., No. Ill. U., DeKalb, Ill. State U., Luth. Gen. Hosp., Des Plaines, Ill., Cen. Maloney, Arcadia, Fla., Sarasota Bank, Nokomis br. 1st Nat. Bank Venice, Fla., trust and ops. depts. 1st Nat. Bank Venice, Cafe Baci, Sarasota, Key West Fish House, Naples, Bermuda Bay Cafe, Osprey, Fla., 1st of Englewood Bank, Guaranty Bank & Trust Bd. Room, Ops. Ctr., Jacaranda, Marudianna Estate, Boca Grande, Fla., Sarasota Chamber Office, also residences, Long Boat, Siesta Keys, Anna Maria Island, Fla., Riverwoods, Ill.; contbr. articles to profl. jours. and local press. Mem. adv. bd. Inst. Psychiatry, Northwestern Meml. Hosp., 1975-81, Chrysalis Learning Ctr., 1977-80; active Oak Park Music Theatre, 1967-72, Am. Cancer Soc. Bid for Bachelors, 1987, Jail and Bail, 1991; mem. alumni steering com. Speech Sch., Northwestern U., 1970-81, Chorus of Keys, Soc. for Preservation Barbershop Quartet Singing in Am.; chmn. ann. show, 1984, 85, v.p. membership com., 1985; grad. Leadership Sarasota, 1986, co-chmn. alumni program steering com., 1989-91, chmn. Arts Day, 1986-90, mem. steering com., 1990. Recipient Past Pres.'s award Chgo. region Inst. Bus. Designers, 1981. Mem. AIA (affiliate 1983-89), Am. Soc. Interior Designers (mem. steering com. Fla. chpt. 1982-96, v.p. North Fla. chpt. 1985, 89-90, chmn. design resource show 1985-91, local chmn. 1986, 89-90, Presdl. citation 1986, Spl. Recognition award 1989-90, Svc. awards 1991—), Sarasota County C. of C. (chmn. amb. and consul program 1986-88, mem. bd. 1987-91, vice chair membership 1989, chmn. Sarasota AM-Monthly broadcast event), Northwestern Alumni of Chgo. (bd. dirs. 1978-79, newsletter editor), John Evans Club (Chgo.), Kiwanis (v.p. Sarasota Sunrise chpt., bd. dirs., program chmn. 1985-86, newsletter writer 1987-88, Spl. award 1985, Bell award 1986, Editors award 1987), Masons, Delta Tau Delta (mem. alumni house bd., Spl. Svc. award 1981). Republican. Home: 720 47th St Sarasota FL 34234-4524 Office: Christies Design Group Unit D 2 1748 Independence Blvd Ste D 2 Sarasota FL 34234-2151

SNYDERMAN, RALPH, medical educator, physician; b. Bklyn., Mar. 13, 1940; m. Judith Ann Krebs, Nov. 18, 1967; 1 child, Theodore Benjamin. B.S., Washington Coll., Chestertown, Md., 1961; M.D., SUNY-Bklyn., 1965. Diplomate Am. Bd. Internal Medicine, Am. Bd. Allergy and Immunology. Med. intern Duke U. Hosp., Durham, N.C., 1965-66, med. resident, 1966-67, asst. prof. medicine and immunology, 1972-74, assoc. prof., 1974-77, chief, div. rheumatology and immunology, 1975-87, prof. medicine and immunology, 1980-87, Frederic M. Hanes prof. medicine, prof. immunology, 1984-87, adj. prof. medicine, 1987-89; surgeon USPHS, NIH, Bethesda, Md., 1967-69; sr. staff fellow Nat. Inst. Dental Research, NIH, Bethesda, Md., 1969-70, sr. investigator immunology sect. lab. microbiology and immunology, 1970-72; chief, div. rheumatology Durham VA Hosp., Bethesda, Md., 1972-75; v.p. med. rsch. and devel. Genentech, Inc., South San Francisco, Calif., 1987-88, sr. v.p. med. rsch. and devel., 1988-89; chancellor for health affairs, dean Sch. Medicine Duke U., Durham, 1989—, James E. Duke prof. medicine, 1989—; CEO Duke U. Health System; adj. asst. prof. oral biology U. N.C. Sch. Dental Medicine, Chapel Hill, 1974-75; Howard Hughes med. investigator, Durham, 1972-77; dir. Lab Immune Effector Function, Howard Hughes Med. Inst., Durham, 1977-87; adj. prof. medicine U. Calif., San Francisco, 1987-89. Editor: Contemporary Topics in Immunobiology, 1979, Inflammation: Basic Concepts and Clinical Correlates, 1988, 2d edit., 1992; contbr. articles to profl. jours. Recipient McLaughlin award for inflammation rsch., 1978, Alexander von Humboldt award Fed. Republic Germany, 1985, award for lifetime achievements in inflammation rsch. Ciba-Geigy Morris Ziff, 1991, Bonnizinga award for excellence in leukocyte biology rsch., 1993, Disting. Alumni Achievement award SUNY Bklyn., 1995, Disting. Alumni citation Washington Coll., 1996, others. Mem. NAS, Inst. Medicine, Assn. Am. Physicians, Am. Assn. Immunologists, Am. Soc. Clin. Investigation, Am. Acad. Allergy, Am. Assn. Cancer Rsch., Soc. for Leukocyte Biology, Am. Fedn. Clin. Rsch., Am. Assn. Pathologists, Am. Soc. for Biochemistry and Molecular Biology, Assn. Acad. Health Ctrs., Am. Coll. Rheumatology, Am. Assn. for Med. Colls., Soc. for Med. Adminstrs., Sigma Xi. Office: Duke U Sch Medicine PO Box 3701 Durham NC 27710

SOBCZAK, PATRICK MICHAEL, educational association administrator; b. Toledo, Jan. 12, 1952; s. Daniel John and Julia Michaeline (Tarasewicz) S. BA in Psychology, St. Meinrad (Ind.) Coll., 1974; MS in Health Care Adminstrn., Trinity U., San Antonio, 1982; PhD in Health Svcs. Adminstrn., U. Ala., Birmingham, 1990. Health ins. claims investigator Equifax Svcs., Toledo, 1978-80; adminstrv. resident VA Med. Ctr., Dallas, 1981-82, health sys. specialist trainee, 1983-84; health sys. specialist VA Med. Ctr., Allen Park, Mich., 1984-85; asst. prof. Med. Univ. S.C., Charleston, 1991-95; pres. Accreditation Commn. Edn. Health Svc. Adminstrn., Arlington, Va., 1995—; mktg. rsch. assoc. dept. strategic planning, market devel. U. Ala. Hosp., Birmingham, 1989-90, staff asst. dept. health svc. adminstrn., 1990-91; acad. affairs dir., adminstrv. resident coord. dept. health adminstrn. policy, Med. Univ. S.C., 1992-93, accreditation coord., 1993-95, rsch. coord. Hollings Cancer Ctr., 1995; presenter in field. Contbr. articles to profl. jours. Mem. sub-com. criteria Alliance Smoke-Free S.C., 1992-93, reviewer, 1993-95; mem. coalition Smoke Free Lowcountry, 1992-94; cons. Singles Sunday Sch., 1994; Sunday sch. tchr. East Cooper Bapt. Ch., Mt. Pleasant, S.C., 1994-95. Syracuse U.-U. Ala. Birmingham scholar 1986. Fellow Accrediting Commn. Edn. Health Svcs. Adminstrn. (accreditation rev. com. 1994); mem. Am. Coll. Health Care Execs. (faculty assoc.), Assn. Univ. Programs in Health Adminstrn. Office: Accrediting Commn Edn Health Svc Adminstrn Ste 503 1911 N Fort Myer Dr Arlington VA 22209

SOBEN, ROBERT SIDNEY, computer scientist; b. Corpus Christi, Tex., Feb. 7, 1947; s. Sydney Robert and Rose Mary (Bailey) S.; 1 child, Dena Dianne. BS in Electrical Engring., La. Tech. U., 1973; MA in Communication, U. Okla., 1982; MS in Mgmt. Scis., Troy (Ala.) State U., 1988; PhD in Engring. Mgmt. Sci., LaSalle U., 1990. Digital computer sci. USAF Air Training Command, Keesler AFB, Miss., 1966-71; command pilot USAF, worldwide, 1971-82; NATO instr. pilot 80th Fighter Training Wing, Sheppard AFB, Tex., 1978-82; electro-optics br. chief Electronics Systems Test Div., Eglin AFB, Fla., 1982-84; mission ops. officer Deputate for Testing Engring., Eglin AFB, Fla., 1984-85, test support div. chief, 1985-93; sr. TQ analyst 46TW/OG-1 TQM in 46 OG, 1994-95; CEO ORCOM, Eglin AFB, 1985—; adj. asst. prof. Troy State U., Ft. Walton Beach, Fla., 1987—, St. Leo's Coll., Eglin AFB, 1988—. Author: Digital Computer Basics, 1970, Application of Expert Systems to Scientific and Technical Information Command, Control and Communication Management, 1990; author USAF tech. report Video Augmentation, 1984, tng. manual and system test engring., 1988, POGI for Quality Results, a mil. pub., 1995. Home: 214 Stebbins Ter Port Charlotte FL 33952

SOBLE, FRIEDA, research center administrator. Dir. Dallas Meml. Ctr. for Holocaust Studies. Office: Dallas Meml Ctr Holocaust Studies 7900 Northhaven Dallas TX 75230

SOBLE, JAMES BARRY, lawyer; b. Chgo., Apr. 14, 1942; s. Julius R. Soble and Bernyce (Morris) Rossuck; children—Debra, Jeffrey, Tony, Leslie; m. Ann S. Valenstein, June 29, 1980. B.A., Grinnell Coll., 1963; J.D., Northwestern U., 1966. Bar: Ill. 1966, Fla. 1974. Assoc. Deutsch & Peskin, Chgo., 1966-68; ptnr. Siegel & Soble, 1969-71 Peskin & Soble, 1972-73; exec. v.p., corp. counsel Millstream Corp., Sunrise, Fla., 1973-79; pvt. developer, Ft. Lauderdale, Fla., 1979-81; ptnr., shareholder Jacobs, Robbins, Gaynor, Hampp, Burns, Cole & Shasteen, P.A., St. Petersburg, Fla., 1981-83; ptnr. Taub & Williams, Tampa, Fla., 1984-88; ptnr. Honigman Miller Schwartz and Cohn, 1988—; lectr. Law Forum, Inc., 1982-84. Pres., bd. dirs. Gulf Coast Jewish Family Services of Pinellas County, 1984-88; bd. dirs. Better Bus. Bur. West Florida, Inc.; pres. Jewish Fedn. Pinellas County, 1989-91, 93-95; pres.-elect Menorah Manor, Inc., 1996—. Mem. ABA, Ill. Bar Assn., Hillsborough County Bar Assn. Jewish. Home: 2996 Sandpiper Pl

Clearwater FL 34622-3058 Office: Honigman Miller Scharwtz & Cohn 2700 SunTrust Fin Ctr 401 E Jackson St Tampa FL 33602

SOBOL-GIVEN, MARY VALERIE, hospital financial services administrator; b. East St. Louis, Ill., Apr. 24, 1967; d. John J. D. and Charlotte Ann (Kokotovich) Sobol; m. John Franklin Given II, May 26, 1989. BA, U. Miss., 1987. Night supr. fin. svc. dept. Bapt. Meml. Hosp., Oxford, Miss., 1987—; owner, operator The Basket Broker Co., Oxford, 1989—. Mem. Kappa Kappa Gamma. Republican. Roman Catholic.

SOBONG, LORETO CALIBO, nursing researcher; b. Oroquieta City, The Philippines, Feb. 7, 1931; naturalized citizen, 1982; d. Jeremias Emilio and Expectacion (Calibo) S. BSE, Misamis Jr. Coll., Oroquieta City, 1954; MA, Philippine Normal Coll., Manila, 1962; postgrad., U. Philippines, Diliman, 1969, 71; PhD, NYU, 1975. Elem. tchr. Bur. Pub. Schs., Molave, The Philippines, 1955-57; elem. tchr. Bur. Pub. Schs., Oroquieta, 1958-66, supr. gen. edn., 1966-72; rsch. asst. Pa. State U., University Park, 1974-76; data editor Ill. Office Edn., Springfield, 1977; with So. Ill. U., Springfield, 1978; rsch. asst. Baylor Coll. Medicine, Houston, 1978-80; dir. sorority house Delta Delta Delta, Morgantown, W.Va., 1982-83; rsch. assoc. W.Va. U. Sch. Nursing, Morgantown, 1982—; instr. Harvardian Colls., Oroquieta City, 1963-71. Contbr. articles to profl. jours. Bd. dirs. Misamis Occidental Pub. Sch. Tchrs. Assn., 1964-66, Misamis Occidental chpt. Boy Scouts of the Philippines, 1966-71, Misamis Occidental chpt. Girl Scouts of the Philippines, 1966-71, Misamis Occidental chpt. Philippine Nat. Red Cross, 1966-71. Philippine Bur. of Pub. Schs. scholar, 1961-62, Philippine Pub. Schs. Tchrs. Assn. scholar, 1971, Than and Luz Porter scholar NYU, 1972-75. Mem. APHA, Am. Ednl. Rsch. Assn. Republican. Presbyterian. Home: RR 4 Box 388E Morgantown WV 26505-9434 Office: WVa Univ Sch Nursing Health Scis Ctr South Morgantown WV 26506-9640

SOBSEY, MARK DAVID, public health educator, researcher; b. Lakewood, N.J., Sept. 5, 1943; s. Sol and Cynthia (Jassinowsky) S.; m. Linda Belans, Dec. 26, 1965 (div. Jan. 1980); children: Adam B., Leah J.; m. Edith M. Alfano, Aug. 17, 1982. BS in Biology, U. Pitts., 1965, MS in Hygiene, 1967; PhD, U. Calif., Berkeley, 1971. Postdoctoral fellow Baylor Coll. Medicine, Houston, 1971-72, instr., 1972-73, asst. prof., 1973-74; asst. prof. U. N.C., Chapel Hill, 1974-79, assoc. prof., 1979-84, prof., 1984—; vis. scientist NIAID/NIH, Bethesda, Md., 1982; mem. sci. adv. bd., drinking water com. U.S. EPA, Washington, 1988—. Contbr. chpts. to books, articles to profl. jours. Recipient Rsch. Career Devel. award Nat. Inst. Environ. Health Sci./NIH, 1977-82. Office: U NC CB #7400 Rosenau Hall Rm 107 Chapel Hill NC 27599

SOCKEY, FELICIA WILLENE, elementary school educator; b. Stigler, Okla., Sept. 17, 1957; d. Jessie Fredrick abd Genevieve Madeline (Garland) Venable; m. Leland L. Sockey. BS, Northeastern State U., Tahlequah, Okla., 1979; AS, Ea. State Coll., Wilburton, Okla., 1977. Cert. tchr., Okla. Elem. tchr. Pocola (Okla.) Pub. Schs. Active Pocola PTA. Mem. NEA, Okla. Edn. Assn., Internat. Soc. Poets, Pocola Classroom Tchrs. Assn.

SODERQUIST, LARRY DEAN, lawyer, educator, consultant; b. Ypsilanti, Mich., July 20, 1944; s. Hugo E. and Emma A. (Johanson) S.; m. Ann Mangelsdorf, June 15, 1968; children: Hans, Lars. BS, Ea. Mich. U., 1966; JD, Harvard U., 1969. Bar: N.Y. 1971, Tenn. 1981. Assoc. Milbank, Tweed, Hadley & McCloy, N.Y.C., 1971-76; assoc. prof. law U. Notre Dame, South Bend, Ind., 1976-80, prof. 1980-81; vis. prof. law Vanderbilt U. Law Sch., Nashville, 1980-81, prof. 1981—, dir. corp. and securities law inst. 1993—; of counsel Tuke Yopp & Sweeney; spl. master U.S. Dist. Ct. (no. dist.) Ohio, 1977. Capt. U.S. Army 1969-71. Decorated Army Commendation medal. Mem. ABA, Am. Law Inst. Presbyterian. Author: Corporations, 1979, 3d edit., 1991, Understanding Corporation Law, 1990, Understanding the Securities Laws, 3d edit., 1993, Securities Regulation, 3d edit., 1994, Law of Federal Estate and Gift Taxation: Code Commentary, 1978, Analysis, 1980, Investor's Rights Handbook, 1993; contbr. numerous articles to legal jours. Home: 421 Sunnyside Dr Nashville TN 37205-3413 Office: Vanderbilt U Sch Law 21st Ave S Nashville TN 37240

SOEBBING, JANICE BROMERT, occupational health nurse; b. Carroll, Iowa, Mar. 8, 1939; d. William A. and Levina J. (Schmitt) Bromert; m. Vincent J. Soebbing, July 2, 1960; children: Kevin, John, Linda, Dana, Charles. Diploma, St. Margaret's Hosp., Kansas City, Kans., 1960; BSN, Pittsburg (Kans.) State U., 1989. Cert. occupational health nurse. Staff nurse St. Margaret's Hosp.; charge nurse O'Connor Hosp., Santa Clara, Calif.; night charge nurse Jane Phillips Episcopal-Meml. Med. Ctr., Bartlesville, Okla.; supr. nursing Phillips Petroleum Co., Bartlesville. Mem. ANA, Okla. Nurses Assn., Am. Assn. Occupational Health Nurses, Tulsa Area Assn. Occupational Health Nurses.

SOHMER, SEYMOUR HANS, botanist; b. Bronx, N.Y., Feb. 27, 1941; s. Ralph and Tanya (Naidus) S.; m. Sara Rose Harrison, Aug. 5, 1967; children: Rebecca Rose, Rachel Adrienne. BS, CCNY, 1963; MS, U. Tenn., 1966; PhD, U. Hawaii, 1971. Chmn. dept. botany Bernice P. Bishop Mus., Honolulu, 1980-90, asst. dir. rsch. and scholarly studies, 1985-90; assoc. prof. U. Wis., La Crosse, 1975-79; instr. dept. botany U. Tenn., Knoxville, 1966; instr. dept. biology U. Wis., La Crosse, 1967-70, asst. prof., 1970-75, dir. herbarium, 1968-80; sr. biodiversity advisor Agy. Internat. Devel., Washington, 1990-93; dir. Botanical Rsch. Inst., Fort Worth, Tex., 1993—; participant Flora of Ceylon project, Smithsonian Instn., 1973, rsch. collaborator dept. botany, 1977; rsch. affiliate U. Hawaii, 1974, adj. prof. botany, 1980-91; staff assoc. div. environ. biology NSF, 1977-78, rsch. botanist office of forests, divsn. botany, Lae, Papua New Guinea, 1979; chmn. standing com. botany Pacific Sci. Assn., 1983; edn. com. Hawaii Bishop Rsch. Inst., 1989—; adj. prof. pharmacology U. North Tex. Health Sci. Ctr., 1994—; adj. prof. biology Tex. Christian Univ., 1995—. Author: Manual of the Flowering Plants of Hawaii, 1990; contbr. numerous papers to profl. publs. Smithsonian rsch. fellow, 1975; grantee NSF, 1979, 81, 83, 84, 86, 87, 88, 90, 93, 94, 95, William G. Irwin Charity Found., 1982, 85, Plant Collection Program Southeast Asia, 1986, Yoshinaga Found., 1986, Stanley Smith Horticultural Trust, 1987, Bors Found., 1993, 94, 95, 96, Richardson Found., 1994, numerous others. Mem. Am. Inst. Biol. Scis., Am. Soc. Plant Taxonomists, Assn. Tropical Biology, Assn. Pacific Systematists, Botan. Soc. Am., Sci. Soc. Escuela Agricola Panamerica, Hawaiian Botan. Soc., Internat. Assn. Plant Taxonomy, Lund Botan. Soc., Lyon Arboretum Assn., Pacific Sci. Assn., Sigma Xi. Office: Botanical Rsch Inst 509 Pecan St Fort Worth TX 76102-4060

SOHNI, YOUVRAJ ROOPLAL, microbiology educator, research scientist; b. Hyderabad, India, June 9, 1960; came to U.S., 1989; s. Rooplal C. and Anandi (Ramlal) S.; m. Rajani Srinivasan, Aug. 15, 1988. BS, Bombay U., 1981, MS, 1984, PhD, 1988. Rsch. asst. Bombay U., 1981-88; biotech. fellow Indian Inst. Sci., Bangalore, 1987-89; postdoctoral assoc. U. Ga., Athens, 1989-90; postdoctoral assoc. Ala. A&M U., Normal, 1991-93, asst. prof., 1993—. Contbr. articles to profl. jours. Scouts' patrol leader St. Andrew's High, Bombay, 1972-75; cmty. worker Nat. Svc. Sci., Bombay, 1979-81. Fellow Dept. Biotech., India, 1987-89; rsch. grantee Hazardous Substance Rsch. Ctr., EPA, 1995-96, Gt. Plains Rocky Mountain Hazardous Substance Rsch. Ctr., summer 1995. Mem. AAAS, Am. Soc. Microbiology. Home: 8225 Bailey Cove Huntsville AL 35802 Office: Ala A&M Univ Carter Hall Normal AL 35762

SOILEAU, KERRY MICHAEL, aerospace technologist, researcher; b. New Orleans, June 8, 1956; s. Donald and Heloise Marie (LeBourgeois) S. BS, U. Cen. Fla., 1976; MS, La. State U., 1980. Aerospace technologist Johnson Space Ctr., NASA, Houston, 1980—; trajectory officer, flight dynamics officer Space Shuttle Mission Control NASA. Contbr. articles to profl. jours.; presenter sci. papers to confs.; developer (computer program) GradePlus. Newscaster Houston Taping for the Blind, 1984-90. Office: NASA Jsc OF1 Houston TX 77058

SOJOURNER, MARTHA A., healthcare administrator; b. Charleston, S.C., Mar. 19, 1939; d. David Eugene Sr. and Evelyn (Marchant) Sojourner. Diploma, Orange Meml. Hosp. Sch Nursing, Orlando, Fla., 1960; BSN, Hampton Inst., 1976; MS, Med. Coll. Va., 1979. RN, Fla. Asst. dist. nurse dir. Portsmouth (Va.) Health Dept., dist. nurse dir.; dist. nurse mgr. Tidewater Health Dist., Portsmouth; divsn. dir., asst. dean health programs, dir. self-study Pasco-Hernando Community Coll., New Port Richey, Fla. Lt. Nurses Corps, USNR, 1966-70. Mem. Nat. Orgn. for Advancement Assoc. Degree Nursing, Fla. Nurses Assn., Fla. Assn. C.C.s, Sigma Theta Tau.

SOKOLNIKOV, NICHOLAS S. See HOMESLEY, HORACE EDWARD

SOLARES, ANDRES JOSE, civil engineer, human rights advocate; b. Havana, Cuba, Jan. 28, 1946; came to U.S., 1988; s. Andres and Iluminada (Teseiro) S.; m. Adriana Chavez, May 5, 1967; children: Andres, Odette, Daniel. BSc, Sch. Civil Engring., Havana, 1968; diploma with distinction, U. Wales, Cardiff, Great Britain, 1970; diploma with excellence, Escuela Nacional Direccion Economia, Havana, 1980, Escuela Junta Nacional Planificacion, Havana, 1980. Registered civil engr., Cuba. Civil engr. Ministry Constrn., Havana, 1968; lectr. sch. civil engring. U. Havana, 1967-72; PhD researcher dept. maritime transp. U. Wales, Cardiff, 1969-70, 71-72; v.p. Constrn. Enterprises, Havana, 1973-78; head dept. airport investment Ministry Transp., Havana, 1978-80; lectr. Ministry Higher Edn., Havana, 1980-81; project mgr. Calmaquip Engring. Corp., Miami, 1988-93; pres. Talmac, Inc., gen. contractor, 1993—; radio commentator C.I.D. Radio Sta., Miami, 1989, Radio Voluntad Democratica, Voice of PRC-Autentico, 1991; realty assoc. Ameriserv Realty. Author: Investigaciones de la Construccion, 1978; columnist: Actualidad Latinoamericana Revista Ahora mag., 1989; contbr. articles to newspapers and mags. in Cuba and U.S. Ex-Vice pres. Partido Revolucionario Cubano Autentico, Miami, 1988—; pres. Alianza de Presos Politicos Cubanos, Miami, 1989, Partido Revolucionario Cubano, Cuba, 1980-88; v.p. Comite Cubano de Derechor Humanos, Cuba, 1987-88; mem. Junta Patriotica Cubana, Miami, 1989-95; del. Nat. Assembly of the Cuban Unity, 1991; founder first Dem. Polit. Party in Cuba after, 1959 (Partido Revolucionario Cubano) and polit. prisoner, 1981-88; mem. Directive Bd. Human Rights, 1990. UNESCO fellow, 1969-70, 71-72; named Prisoner of Month Amnesty Internat., 1987; named to Orden Jose Marti, 1989; recipient diploma for patriotic activities Ex Club, 1988, plaque Govt. of El Salvador for his efforts on behalf of democracy, 1991. Mem. Colegio de Ingenieros Cubanos en el Exilio. Roman Catholic. Office: Calmaquip Engring Corp 7240 NW 12th St Miami FL 33126-1909

SOLASKI, PAUL EDWARD, retired fire protection specialist; b. Logan County, W.Va., Oct. 25, 1922; s. Joseph John and Lucy Jane (Jarrett) S.; m. Carolyn Landers, Sept. 30, 1950 (div. June 1981); children: Joseph, Paula. Student in indsl. engring., Va. Polytechnic Inst., 1939-42; BSBA, Memphis State Coll., 1951. Spl. risks insp. La. Rating & Fire Prevention Bur., New Orleans, 1954-63; fire protection engr. Kemper Ins. Group, Atlanta, 1963-68; housing insp. Metro. Dade County Housing Authority, Miami, Fla., 1969-72; safety specialist Great Am. Ins. Co., Atlanta, 1972-74; sr. fire protection specialist M&M Protection Cons., Atlanta, 1974-79; constrn. insp. U.S. Army C.E., Elberton, Ga., 1980-81; support svcs. clk. U.S. Dept. Edn., Atlanta, 1982-84; msg. ground safety technician USAFR, New Orleans, 1955-64. Cpl. U.S. Army Air Corps, 1943-46. Mem. Am. Soc. Safety Engrs., Soc. Fire Protection Engrs., Nat. Fire Protection Assn. all emeritus. Republican. Home: Unit E108 55 Pharr Rd NW Unit E108 Atlanta GA 30305-2151

SOLBERG, LAWRENCE ARTHUR, JR., hematologist, oncologist, medical educator; b. Eureka, Calif., Dec. 3, 1944; m. Kathy Williams, July 26, 1986; 1 child, Megan. AB in Biol. Scis., U. Calif., Berkeley, 1966, PhD in Physiology, 1971; MD, St. Louis U., 1975; postgrad., Mayo Grad. Sch. of Medicine, 1975-78, 78-80. Diplomate Am. Bd. Internal Medicine, Am. Bd. Hematology. Trainee dept. physiology-anatomy U. Calif., Berkeley, 1968-71; instr. physiology St. Louis U. Sch. of Medicine, 1972-75; staff hematologist-oncologist USAF Med. Ctr., Wright-Patterson AFB, Ohio, 1980-82; cons. divsn. hematology and internal medicine, asst. prof. medicine Mayo Clinic and Found., Rochester, Minn., 1983-91; chair divsn. hematology-oncology, dir. bone marrow transplantation program Mayo Clinic, Jacksonville, Fla., 1991—; assoc. prof. medicine Mayo Med. Sch., Rochester, 1991—; assoc. cons. divsn. hematology and internal medicine Mayo Clinic, 1980; mem. transfusion com. Mayo Clinic, Rochester, 1983-87, bone marrow transplant team, 1983-91, cancer ctr. rsch. com., 1987-91, utilization com., 1987-91, rsch. planning com., 1987-91, chair hematology rsch. com., 1987-91, dir. myelproliferative and myeldysplastic disease related study group, 1987-91; mem. instl. rev. bd. Mayo Found., 1987-89, info. sys. mgmt. com., 1990-94, chair task force on broad based comm., 1993-94, chair divsn. hematology-oncology Mayo Clinic, Jacksonville, 1991—; mem. info. sys. com., 1992-94, rsch. com., 1993-95; lectr. in field. Contbr. articles to profl. jours., chpts. to books. With USAFR, 1973-80, major USAFMC, 1980-82. Program Project grantee NIH, 1983-86, 86-91; grantee Schering-Plough Rsch., 1988-89, 1991—, Eagles Cancer Fund, 1988-90, Bristol-Myers Co., 1989-91, Genentech, 1991-94, scholar Mayo Found., 1982-83. Fellow ACP; mem. Ea. Coop. Oncology Group, North Ctrl. Cancer Treatment Group, Am. Fedn. Clin. Rsch., Am. Soc. Hematology, Internat. Soc. Exptl. Hematology, Fla. Soc. Clin. Oncology, Sigma Xi, Alpha Omega Alpha. Office: Mayo Clinic Jacksonville 4500 San Pablo Rd S Jacksonville FL 32224-1865

SOLÉ, PEDRO, chemical engineer; b. Guatemala, Guatemala, Sept. 4, 1936; came to U.S., 1974; s. Pedro Solé and Luisa Raquel (Castellanos) de Solé; m. Dorothy Tuteur, Mar. 19, 1961; children: Tania Dolores, Jeanne Marguerite, Pedro Ernesto. Degree chem. engring., San Carlos U., Guatemala, 1958; MChE, PhD in Chem. Engring., Polytech U., N.Y., 1965. Ops. mgr. Alimentos Kern de Guatemala, 1968-72; gen. dir. Riviana España S.A., Seville, Spain, 1972-74; plant mgr. Casera Foods Inc., San Juan, P.R., 1974-78; gen. mgr. processed bananas Tela RR Co., La Lima, Honduras, 1979-82; v.p. bus. devel. Numar Processed Foods Group, San José, Costa Rica, 1982-86; dir. tech. svcs. Chiquita Brands Inc., N.Y.C., 1986-89; v.p. quality assurance/control Chiquita Brands Internat., Inc., Cin., 1989-94, mgmt. cons., 1994—. Contbr. articles to profl. jours. Exch. scholar U.S. Dept. State, 1959-60, Food Tech. scholar, Karlsruhe (Fed. Republic Germany) U., 1966-67. Mem. Inst. Food Tech. (profl.), Am. Inst. Chem. Engrs. Roman Catholic. Home and Office: 9375 SW 154 Pl Miami FL 33196-1129

SOLER, JOSEPH MANUEL, emergency physician; b. Mar. 6, 1948; s. Jose Esteban and Angela (Alonso) S.; m. Susan Cooper, July 25, 1969; children: Joseph, Zachary, Kelly. BS in Chemistry, U. Miami, 1970, MD, 1975. Diplomate Nat. Bd. Med. Examiners, Am. Bd. Emergency Medicine; lic. physician, Fla., S.C., Pa. Resident in emergency medicine Pa. State U., Hershey, 1975-78; emergency physician Richland Meml. Hosp., Columbia, S.C., 1978-79; asst. med. dir. dept. emergency med. svcs. Bapt. Hosp., Miami, Fla., 1983-87; med. dir. divsn. of emergency medicine Columbia Blake Med. Ctr., Bradenton, Fla., 1989—; clin. asst. prof. medicine U. Miami; asst. med. dir. Met. Dade County Fire Dept., Miami, 1980-82, med. dir., 1982-87; chmn. emergency medicine com. South Fla. Emergency Med. Svcs. Coun., 1981, mem. trauma triage and protocol com., 1981; lectr. in field. Contbr. articles to profl. jours. Med. adv. bd. Emergency Med. Svcs. Dept., Miami-Dade C.C., 1982-86, fire sci. program med. adv. com., 1983-86; med. adv. com. Dade County Trauma Network, Miami, 1985. Mem. AMA, Am. Coll. Emergency Physicians (disaster mgmt. com. 1984-85), Fla. Coll. Emergency Physicians (chmn. edn. com. 1990-92), Christian Med. Soc., Fla. Med. Assn. (Med. Comms. award 1991), Univ. Assn. for emergency Medicine, Dade County Med. Assn. (community health com. 1984), Manatee County Med. Soc. (pub. health com. 1991, disaster planning com. 1991-92, editor newsletter Vocal Chords 1993). Home: 2416 Landings Cir Bradenton FL 34209-9772 Office: Columbia Blake Med Ctr 2020 59th St W Bradenton FL 34209-4604

SOLKOFF, JEROME IRA, lawyer, consultant, lecturer; b. Rochester, N.Y., Feb. 15, 1939; s. Samuel and Dorothy (Krovetz) S.; m. Doreen Hurwitz, Aug. 11, 1963; children: Scott Michael, Anne Lynn. BS, Sch. Indsl. and Labor Relations, Cornell U., 1961; JD, U. Buffalo, 1964. Bar: N.Y. 1965, Fla. 1974, U.S. Dist. Ct. (we. dist.) N.Y. 1965. Assoc. Nusbaum, Tarricone, Weltman, Bilgore & Silver, Rochester, N.Y., 1964-66, Mousaw, Vigdor, Reeves, Heilbronner & Kroll, Rochester, 1966-70; sr. mcpl. atty. Urban Renewal Agy., Rochester, 1970-73; sole practice, Rochester, 1970-73; chief legal counsel Arlen Realty Mgmt., Inc., Miami, Fla., 1973-75; assoc. Britton, Cohen, Kaufman, Benson & Schantz, Miami, 1975-76; chief legal counsel First Mortgage Investors, Miami Beach, Fla., 1976-79; ptnr. Cassel & Cassel, P.A., Miami, 1979-82; sole practice, Deerfield Beach, Fla., 1982—; lectr. on fgn. investment practices in U.S., Eng., 1981-88, Montreal, Que., Can., 1981, estate planning, 1982—, medicaid law and elder law, 1988—. Author: Fundamentals of Foreign Investing in American Real Estate and Businesses, 1981, Checklist of N.Y. Mortgage Foreclosure Procedures, 1970, History of Municipal Employee Unions, 1964, Practice Guide for Florida Elder Law, 1996. Bd. dirs. Jewish Community Ctrs. of South Broward, Fla., 1979-90, Broward Homebound Program, 1990—, NE Alzheimers Daycare Ctr., Inc., 1990-92, Broward Alzheimers Assn. Mem. ABA (sects. elder law founder and former chmn., real property, trust and probate law), Fla. Bar Assn. (sects. real property, trust and probate law, vice chmn. com. on the elderly 1987-91, lectr. estate planning for the aging and disabled 1989—, founder, chmn. elder law sect. 1992-93), Nat. Acad. Elder Law Attys. (Fla. coord.), Elder Law Attys.

SOLLARS, DAVID LINDSEY, economics educator; b. Wilmington, Ohio, Apr. 28, 1964; s. G. Robert Sollars and Lora Lee (Drake) De Weese; m. Patricia Colette Guzzi, Aug. 24, 1985; children: Lindsay Colette, Juliana Christine. BBA, Ohio U., 1986, MA, 1987; PhD, Fla. State U., 1991. Asst. prof. econs. Auburn U., Montgomery, Ala., 1991-95; asst. dean Sch. of Bus. Auburn U., Montgomery, 1994—; assoc. prof. econs. Auburn U., Montgomery, Ala., 1996—. Contbr. articles to profl. jours. Recipient award for teaching excellence Auburn U. Sch. Bus., 1994; Salvatori fellow The Heritage Found., 1994—. Mem. Am. Econ. Assn., So. Econs. Assn., Pub. Choice Soc. Roman Catholic. Office: Auburn U at Montgomery Sch Bus 7300 University Dr Montgomery AL 36117-3531

SOLLENBERGER, DONNA FITZPATRICK, hospital and clinics executive; b. Tuscola, Ill., Jan. 13, 1949; d. Vincent Norman and Marian Louise (Mumbower) Fitzpatrick; m. Kent T. Sollenberger, Dec. 30, 1982; children: Shannon, Blake, Bradley. Student, U. Kans., 1968-70; BA in English and Chemistry, U. Ill., Springfield, 1970, MA in English, 1974. With pub. info. office Ill. Dept. Transp., Springfield, 1974-75; exec. III, dir. pub. info., strategic planning/spl. programs Ill. Dept. Conservation, Springfield, 1975-76; prof. Lincoln Land C.C., Springfield, 1980-84; chief adminstrv. officer surgery So. Ill. U. Sch. Medicine, Springfield, 1976-80, 85-91; divsn. adminstr., chief adminstrv. officer divsn. surgery U. Tex. M.D. Anderson Cancer Ctr., Houston, 1991-93, v.p. for hosps. and clinics, 1993-96; exec. v.p., COO City of Hope Nat. Med. Ctr., Duarte, Calif., 1997—; bd. dirs. svc. corp. Greater Houston Hosp. Coun. Mem. Houston Fine Arts Mus. Recipient Conservation Merit award State of Ill., 1976; named one of Outstanding Young Women in Am., 1980. Mem. Am. Coll. Healthcare Execs., Am. Hosp. Assn., Acad. Practice Assembly (instnl. membership coord. 1992—), Assn. Acad. Surgery Adminstrs. (exec. com. 1992-94, mem.-at-large so. region 1992-93, membership chairperson 1993-94), Med. Group Mgmt. Assn., Houston Area Delta Gamma Alumnae Assn., Lawndale Art Assn. Home: 4547 Warwick Dr Sugarland TX 77479 Office: U Tex MD Anderson Cancer Ctr 1515 Holcombe Houston TX 77030

SOLLEY, MICHAEL WILLIAM, computer executive, educator; b. Kansas City, Mo., Dec. 6, 1957; s. Stanley William and Dorothy (Springer) S.; m. Anita Faith Barclay, May 26, 1979. BSEE, U. Ala., Huntsville., 1981. Computer analyst Halstead & Mitchell, Scottsboro, Ala., 1977-81; elec. engr. Sci. Applications, Huntsville, 1981-83; corp. v.p. NRC, Huntsville, 1983—; instr. U. Ala., Huntsville, 1980-90. Home: 105 Waterford Cir Madison AL 35758-7847 Office: NRC 4040 Memorial Pky SW Huntsville AL 35802-1396

SOLLID, FAYE EISING, volunteer; b. Milw., Aug. 31, 1913; d. George Walter and Jessie Belle (Davey) Eising; m. Erik Sollid, Aug. 1, 1936 (dec. Mar. 1977); 1 child, Jon Erik. BA in Journalism, U. Wis., 1936; postgrad., U. Denver, 1947. Asst. in basic communications U. Denver, 1947. Editor Am. Hindi cookbook for Am. Woman's Club New Delhi, 1956; mem. Clearwater (Fla.) Libr. Bd., 1981-89, liaison between Libr. Bd. and Friends of Libr. Bd., 1984-89; mem. Clearwater Beautification Com., 1989-92. Recipient Citation of Sincere Appreciation for pub. svc. as mem. libr. bd. 1981-89 Mayor City of Clearwater, 1989. Mem. AAUW, Internat. Graphoanalysis Soc., Nat. Mus. Women in Arts, Upper Pinellas African Violet Soc. (v.p. 1973-74, pres. 1974-75), Sovereign Colonial Soc. Ams. Royal Descent, Plantagenet Soc., Soc. Descs. Most Noble Order Garter, Order of Crown Charlemagne in U.S.A., Colonial Order of the Crown, Suncoast Magna Charta Dames (rec. sec. 1980-83), Nat. Soc. Colonial Dames XVII Century (v.p. 1983-85, 89-93).

SOLO, JOYCE R., volunteer; b. Buffalo, N.Y., Feb. 14, 1924; d. Jay Harry and Rose (Maisel) Rubenstein; m. Richard D. Solo, Jan. 6, 1946; children: Harry Jay Solo, Eleanor Solo, Sally Solo. BA, Wellesley Coll., 1945. Pres. LWV, Sarasota County, Fla., 1990-92; healthcare com. chair, 1988-90, 92—; sec. Sarasota County Health Care Coord. Adv. Coun., 1993-95; active Planned Approach to Cmty. Health/Healthy Sarasota 2000; chair sr. adv. com. Sarasota Meml. Hosp.; vol. Reach to Recovery Breast Cancer Task Force, Manatee County Am. Cancer Soc.; pres. Beth Israel Women Bd., Temple Beth Israel, numerous others health and civic orgn. activities.

SOLOMON, CHARLES FRANCIS, electronics educator; b. Newark, N.J., Feb. 1, 1932; s. Milton Casper and Anne Marie (Casgrove) S.; m. Alice Margret Morris, Feb. 5, 1955; children: Charles Michael, Theresa Marie, Elizabeth Ann, Thomas Francis. BS, Okla. State U., 1966; MEd, Tex. A&M U., 1971, PhD, 1984., 1969-83, 90—; Aircraft mech. electronics Spartan Sch. Aero., Tulsa, Okla., 1956-62; bldg. maintenance engr. student union Okla. State U., Stillwater, 1962-64, rsch. technician, 1964-66; assoc. prof. Tex. State Tech. Coll., Waco, 1966-69; program chair Tex. State Tech. Inst., Waco, 1969-83, master instr. electronics, 1983-90, program chmn., 1990-93, master instr. electronics tech. and elec. electronics core, 1993—; cons. in field. Author: Audio Circuit Analysis, 1976, (manual) Audio Circuits, 1976; contbr. articles to profl. jours.; reviewer book Introduction Electronic Devices and Circuits, 1989. Music dir. St. Joseph Catholic Ch., Bellmead, Tex., 1966-90. Airman 1st class USAF, 1951-55. Mem. Tex. Tech. Soc., Tex. Jr. Coll. Tchrs. Assn., Campus Colleague Computer Assn. (chmn. 1985—, chmn. instnl. effectiveness com. 1992-94), Waco Civic Chorus, KC (trustee 1958-90). Home: RR 4 Box 551 Waco TX 76705-9705 Office: Tex State Tech Coll Electronics Tech Dept 3801 Campus Dr Waco TX 76705

SOLOMON, ELDRA PEARL BROD, psychologist, educator, biologist, author; b. Phila., Apr. 9, 1940; d. Theodore and Freda Miriam (Warhaftig) Brod; m. Edwin Marshall Solomon, June 28, 1959 (div. Jan. 1985); children: Mical Kenneth, Amy Lynn, Belicia Efros. BS, U. Tampa, 1961; MS, U. Fla., 1963; MA, U. South Fla., 1987, PhD, 1989. Lic. psychologist. Adj. biology prof. Hillsborough Community Coll., Tampa, Fla., 1968-86; biopsychologist Ctr. for Rsch. in Behavioral Medicine, U. South Fla., Tampa, 1985-89; dir. rsch. Advanced Devel. Systems, Tampa, 1989-92; pvt. practice clin. psychologist Tampa, 1990—; clin. dir. Ctr. for Mental Health Edn., Assessment and Therapy, Tampa, Fla., 1992—; adj. prof., mem. grad. faculty U. South Fla., 1992—; expert witness, psychol. expert county and cir. cts., 1989—; health edn. cons. Advanced Devel. Sys., Tampa, 1985-92. Author: Human Anatomy and Physiology, 1990, The World of Biology, 5th edit., 1995, Biology, 4th edit., 1996; author: (with others) Health Psychology: Individual Differences and Stress, 1988, Why Kids Kill Parents: Child Abuse and Adolescent Homicide (Treatment chpt.); contbr. chpt. to book. Mem. APA, Am. Soc. Criminology, Fla. Psychol. Assn., Internat. Soc. for the Study of Dissociation (chairperson Tampa chpt., 1994-95). Democrat. Jewish. Office: Ctr Mental Health Edn Assessment & Therapy 2727 W Martin Luther King Blvd Tampa FL 33607-6383

SOLOMON, FRANK, retired counselor, consultant; b. Allendale, S.C., Mar. 14, 1933; s. Samuel and Bessie (McDuffie) S. Diploma, Allendale Tng. Sch., 1954; diploma in radio and TV, Denmark (S.C.) Tech. Coll., 1960; student, NYU, 1979, U. S.C., Allendale, 1993. Customer svc. and inventory control clk. Panasonic Co., N.Y.C. and Secaucus, N.J., computer operator, coord. consumer rels., 1965-85; dir. sports, suspension supr., athletic dir. Allendale Elem. and Mid. Schs., 1986-89; counselor Commn. Alcohol and Drugs, Allendale and Hampton, S.C., 1989-91, alcohol and drug prevention specialist, 1991-93; cons., seminar and workshop condr., 1993—. Author: A Hell of A Life, 1975, (play) Flat Street Sa'day Nite, 1985 (Audelco award 1985), (book and play) Fighting Two Wars, 1995, 96. Del. Nat. Dem. Conv., San Francisco, 1984; founder African Am. Culture Ctr., Allendale, 1988; bd. dirs., counselor Youth Outreach Ctr., Allendale; chmn. Allendale County Voter Registration Bd.; former cmty. newsletter editor St. Johns

Place Block Assn. With U.S. Army, 1956-58. Recipeint Brotherhood award N.Y.C. Police Dept. Youth Coun., Disting. Dedicated Svc. award St. Johns Block Assn., presdl. citation Nat. Assn. for Equal Opportunity in Higher Edn. Mem. NAACP. Episcopalian. Home: PO Box 395 Allendale SC 29810-0395

SOLÒMON, JEAN-PIERRE See **WYNNE, CAREY HOWARD, JR.**

SOLOMON, RISA GREENBERG, video software industry executive; b. N.Y.C., June 22, 1948; d. Nathan and Frances (Guttman) Greenberg; m. Philip Howard Solomon, June 21, 1970; children: Elycia Beth, Cynthia Gayle. BA, NYU, 1969, MA, 1970. Asst. editor Redbook Mag., N.Y.C., 1969-70; assoc. editor Greenwood Press, Westport, Conn., 1970-71; mng. editor Dushkin Pub., Guilford, Conn., 1971-72; freelance editor Yale U. Press, New Haven, Conn., 1972-75; v.p. ops. Videoland, Inc., Dallas, 1980-82; v.p. Video Software Dealers Assn., Cherry Hill, N.J. and Dallas, 1981-83; pres. Videodome Enterprises, Dallas, 1983—; cons. Home Recording Rights Coalition, Washington, 1983-84. Contbr. articles to video mags. Bd. dirs. Congregation Anshai Emet, Dallas, 1985-86. Mem. Video Software Dealers Assn. (founder, dir. 1981-82). Democrat. Jewish. Office: Videodome Enterprises 11420 St Michaels Dr Dallas TX 75230-2436

SOLOMON, ROBERT DOUGLAS, pathology educator; b. Delavan, Wis., Aug. 28, 1917; s. Lewis Jacob and Sara (Ludgin) S.; m. Helen Fisher, Apr. 4, 1943; children: Susan, Wendy, James, William. Student, MIT, 1934-36; BS in Biochemistry, U. Chgo., 1938; MD, Johns Hopkins U., 1942. Intern John's Hopkins Hosp., 1942-43; resident in pathology Michael Reese Hosp., 1947-49; lectr. U. Ill., Chgo., 1947-50; fellow NIH pathology U. Ill., 1949-50; asst. prof. U. Md., Balt., 1955-60; assoc. prof. U. So. Calif., L.A., 1960-70; chief of staff City of Hope Nat. Med. Ctr., 1966-67; prof. U. Mo., Kansas City, 1977-78, SUNY, Syracuse, 1968-78; chief of staff The Hosp., Sidney, N.Y., 1985-86; adj. prof. U. N.C., Wilmington, 1988—; cons. VA Hosp., Balt., 1955-60, Med. Svc. Lab., Wilmington, 1989-93. Co-author: Progress in Gerontological Research, 1967; contbr. papers and profl. jours. and rsch. in biochemistry, revascular of heart, carcinogenisis, cancer chemotherapy, atherogenesis, discovery of reversibility of atherosclerosis. V.p. Rotary, Duarte, Calif., 1967; v.p. and pres. Force for an Informed Electorate. Capt. Med. Corps, AUS, 1943-46, PTO. Grantee NIH, Fleischmann Found., Am. Heart Assn., Nat. Cancer Inst., 1958-70. Fellow ACP (pres. Md. chpt.); mem. Coll. Am. Pathologists (past pres. Md. chpt.), Am. Soc. Clin. Pathologists, Assn. Clin. Scientists, Am. Chem. Soc., Royal Soc. Medicine (London). Home: 113 S Belvedere Dr Hampstead NC 28443-2504

SOLOMON, SHIRL G., handwriting expert, researcher; b. Phila., Jan. 29, 1928; d. William and Fannie (Lobel) Goldhirsh; m. Jay Lewis Solomon, Sept. 29, 1967 9div. July 1974); children: Cindy Solomon Goldstein, Mark, Lori Solomon Hemmis. Studied with Herb Sugar, Phila., 1960-62; student, U. Pa., Pa. Acad. Fine Arts. Cert. document expert Handwriting Analysis Workshop Unltd. Caseworker Dept. Pub. Welfare State of Pa., Phila., 1959-63; pvt. practice as handwriting expert and analyst Pa., Fla., 1963—; document examiner, trained by Charlie Cole, 1976-82; rschr., speaker, workshop condr. in field. Author: How To Really Know Yourself Thru Your Handwriting, 1974, SCRYPTICS (Personality & Compatibility Testing), 1977, Knowing Your Child Thru His Handwriting & Drawings, 1978, Quest for the Ideal Mate, 1987; contbr. articles to profl. jours. Recipient Fla. Screenwriter's award Fla. Dept. Commerce, 1990. Mem. Am. Handwriting Analysis Found. (cert.), Nat. Assn. Document Examiners (editor jour. 1993—), Nat. Forensic Ctr., Coun. Graphological Socs. (former mem. jour. rsch. com.). Jewish.

SOLTOW, JAMES HAROLD, historian, researcher; b. Chgo., July 1, 1924; s. Lawrence Milton and Gladys Louise (Combs) S.; m. Martha-Jane Stough, Sep. 14, 1946. AB, Dickinson Coll., 1948; AM, U. Pa., 1949, PhD, 1954. Lectr. Hunter Coll., 1952-55; rsch. assoc. Colonial Williamsburg, N.Y.C., Va., 1955-56, Colonial Willaimsburg (Va.), 1955-56; instr. Russell Sage Coll., Troy, N.Y., 1956-58; from asst. prof. to prof. Mich. State U., East Lansing, 1959-85, prof. emeritus, 1985—; chmn. dept. history Mich. State U., 1970-75. Author: Origins of Small Business, 1965, Economic Role of Williamsburg, 1965; co-author: The Evolution of the American Economy, 1993; contbr. articles to profl. jours. Pvt. U.S. Army, 1943-46. Fulbright Rsch. fellow U. Louvain, Belgium, 1965-66, Bus. History fellow Harvard U. Grad. Sch. Bus. Adminstrn., 1958-59. Mem. Econ. History Assn., Bus. History Conf. (trustee 1980-83), Econ. Bus. Hist. Soc. (pres. 1982, chief editor 1978-84), S.C. Hist. Soc. Roman Catholic. Home and Office: PO Box 442 Isle Of Palms SC 29451-0442

SOLYMOSSY, JOSEPH MARTIN, nuclear engineer, military officer; b. Wegscheid, Fed. Republic Germany, Oct. 11, 1945; came to U.S., 1952; s. Martin Von and Marlie (Mailath) S.; Kathleen Hammond, Aug. 1968 (div. 1977); m. Linda Hatley, Oct. 29, 1977; stepchildren: Lawrence Dale, Michael, Michele, Richard. BSEE, U.S. Naval Acad., 1968. Lt. comdr. USN, 1968-78; mgr. field support Newport News (Va.) Indsl., 1978-81; mgr. Inst. Nuclear Power Ops., Atlanta, 1981—; dir. nuclear quality and assessment svcs. Northeast Utilities, 1993-95; tech. expert Internat. Atomic Energy Agy., Vienna, Austria 1985-87. Vol. March of Dimes, Marietta, Ga., 1983-85, Multiple Sclerosis, 1990—, ARC, 1989—, Spl. Olympics, 1994—. Capt. USNR, 1978-91, ret. Mem. Am. Soc. Nuclear Engrs., Naval Reserve Assn., Naval Acad. Alumni Assn. (treas. 1989-93), Navy League, Garden Club (pres. 1989-91). Republican. Mem. Ch. of Christ. Office: Inst Nuclear Power Ops 700 Galleria Pky NW Atlanta GA 30339-5943

SOMEREVE, MARGARET MARY, administrative assistant, political campaigner; b. N.Y.C., June 27, 1966; d. William John and Florence Susan (Gallagher) Somereve. BA, Angelo State U., 1988; MPA, U. Tex., Arlington, 1993. Asst. office mgr. Rep. Party of Dallas Co., 1988-89; campaign coord. Congressman Joe Barton Campaign, Ennis, Tex., 1989-91; regional coord. Tex. Pub. Policy Found., Dallas, 1991; adminstrv. intern City of Cedar Hill, Tex., 1992-94; adminstrv. asst. City of Richardson, Tex., 1994—. Vol. Sam Johnson for Congress, Dallas, 1992, Richardson Comty. Band, Johnson County Rep. Women, Cleburne, Tex., 1989-91, Cedar Hill's Ann. Hilltop Classic Bike Rally, 1992-94. Urban fellow North Cen. Tex. Coun. of Govts., Arlington, 1992-93. Mem. Urban Mgmt. Assts. of North Tex. Republican. Roman Catholic. Address: 2942 Ermine Way Farmers Branch TX 75234-4933

SOMERS, CLIFFORD LOUIS, lawyer; b. Portland, Maine, Dec. 27, 1940; s. Norman Louis and Adeline Wilhemina (Witzke) S.; m. Barbara Suzanne Berry, Aug. 1, 1961; children: Alan Mark, Penelope Lee. BA, U. Fla., Gainsville, 1965, JD, 1967. Bar: Fla. 1967, U.S. Ct. Mil. Appeals 1968, U.S. Dist. Ct. (mid. dist.) Fla. 1972; cert. civil trial lawyer, cert. mediator. Ptnr. Burton, Somers & Reynolds, Tampa, 1975-77, Miller, McKendree & Somers, Tampa, 1977-85, McKendree & Somers, Tampa, 1985-89, Somers and Morgan, Tampa, 1989-91, Somers and Assocs., Tampa, 1991—; instr. law U. Fla., Gainesville, 1967; sec., treas. Chester H. Ferguson-Morris S. White Inn, Am. Inns of Ct. 1987-89, pres.-elect, 1989-90, pres. 1990-91; chmn. Fla. Bar civil procedure rules com., 1991-92. Contbr. article to profl. jours. With U.S. Army, 1961-64, Vietnam; capt. JAG, U.S. Army, 1968-72, mil. judge, 1971-72. Mem. Fla. Bar Assn., Def. Rsch. Inst. (chmn. 2nd dist. area west coast 1985—), Am. Legion (comdr. Post 278, 1975), Brandon Vet.'s Post and Park (pres. 1985), Am. Bd. Trial Attys. (v.p. Tampa chpt. 1990-91). Home: 2805 W Terrace Dr Tampa FL 33609-4027 Office: Somers and Assocs 3242 Henderson Blvd Ste 301 Tampa FL 33609-3056

SOMERS, FRED LEONARD, JR., lawyer; b. Orange, N.J., July 5, 1936; A.B., U. Va., 1958, LL.B., 1961. Bar: Va. 1961, Mo. 1963, Ga. 1967, U.S. Tax Ct. 1971, U.S. Supreme Ct. 1978. Assoc. Lewis, Rice, Tucker, Allen & Chubb, St. Louis, 1962-65; asst. regional counsel AT&T, Atlanta, 1965-67; assoc. Kaler, Karish & Reuben, Atlanta, 1968; ptnr. Stack & O'Brien, Atlanta, 1968-70, Somers & Hodges and predecessors, Atlanta, 1970—.Mem. Citizens Adv. Park Com., DeKalb County, Ga., 1969, Citizens Bond Commn. DeKalb County, 1970; chmn. DeKalb County Charter Commn., 1970; vice chmn. DeKalb County Planning Commn., 1971-77; chmn., trustee Callanwolde Found., 1971-83; chmn. Oglethorpe Housing Devel. Authority, De Kalb County, 1974; bd. dirs., pres.Nat. Club Assn., 1982—; bd. govs. Ravinia Club, 1986—. Author: The Written management Contract: Comfort for the Club and the Manager, 1987, More About Private Club Buyouts, 1986, sources of Revenue for Clubs, 1989, Creative Funding for Capital Needs, 1989, A Prolegomenon To a Right of Private Association, 1988, Model Bylaws for the Private Club, 1996, Model Club Rules, 1990, How to Effectively Select a Club Operating Entity, 1990, After Portland, What Next?, 1990, Golf Course Development, 1991, Model Golf Rules - A Guide for Clubs, 1991, Changing Your Operating Entity, 1992, Let's Go Equity!, 1992, Open or Closed Door?, 1994, Golf Course Liability and Exposures: A Primer FOr Private Clubs, 1995. Mem. ABA, Atlanta Bar Assn. Home: 1015 Oakpointe Pl Atlanta GA 30338 Office: 2 Ravinia Dr Atlanta GA 30346-2104

SOMES, GRANT WILLIAM, statistician, biomedical researcher; b. Bloomington, Ind., Jan. 30, 1947; s. William Henry and Margaret Juanita (Sparks) S.; m. Brenda Sue Weddle, Sept. 2, 1967; children: Anthony William, Joshua Michael, Meghan Elizabeth. AB, Ind. U., 1968; PhD, U. Ky., 1975. Asst. prof. dept. community medicine U. Ky., Lexington, 1975-79; assoc. prof., dir. Biostats./Epidemiology Rsch. Lab. East Carolina U., Greenville, N.C., 1979-84; prof., chmn. dept. biostats. & epidemiology U. Tenn., Memphis, 1984—; cons. Community Health Mgmt. Info. System, Memphis, 1992—, Mid-South Found. for Med. Care, Memphis, 1992—. Contbr. 72 articles to profl. jours.; author 70 presented papers/abstracts. Coach Little League baseball, Lexington, 1976-79, Aydon, N.C., 1979-84. Recipient Outstanding Alumni award U. Ky., 1993. Mem. Am. Statis. Assn. (v.p. West Tenn. chpt. 1985-86), Biometric Soc., Sigma Xi, Pi Mu Epsilon.

SOMLYO, ANDREW PAUL, physiology, biophysics and cardiology educator; b. Budapest, Hungary; s. Anton and Clara Maria (Kiss) S.; m. Avril V. Russell, May 25, 1961; 1 child, Andrew Paul. BS, U. Ill., 1954, MS, 1956, MD, 1956; MS, Drexel Inst. Tech., Phila., 1963; MA (hon.), U. Pa., Phila., 1981. Asst. physician Columbia-Presbyn. Med. Ctr., N.Y.C., 1960-61; rsch. assoc. Presbyn. Hosp., Phila., 1961-67; asst. prof. pathology U. Pa., Phila., 1964-67, assoc. prof., 1967-71, prof., 1971-88, prof. physiology and pathology, 1973-88, dir. Pa. Muscle Inst., 1973-88; Charles Slaughter prof. molecular physiology-biol. physics U. Va., Charlottesville, 1988—, chmn. dept., 1988—, prof. cardiology, 1988—; cons. NIH; Brit. Heart Found. vis. prof. Hammersmith Hosp., London, Shanghai (China) Med. U.. Author: (with others) Vascular Neuroeffector Systems, 1971, The Handbook of Physiology, Vascular Smooth Muscle, 1981, Microprobe Analysis of Biological Systems, 1981, Recent Advances in Light and Optical Imaging in Biology and Medicine, 1986; editor: Jour. Muscle Research and Cell Motility; contbr. numerous articles to jours. including Biol. Chemistry, Jour. Physiology, Am. Heart Jour., Jour. Pediatrics, Jour. Cell Biology, Cell Calcium, others; mem. editl. bd. Blood Vessels, Am. Jour. Physiology, 1979-83, Magnesium: Experimental and Clinical Rsch., Jour. Structural Biology. Recipient The Louis and Artur Lucian award for rsch. in circulatory diseases, 1996. Mem. AAAS, Soc. Gen. Physiologists, Am. Physiol. Soc. Biophys. Soc., Electron Microscopy Soc., Microbeam Analysis Soc. (Presdl. Sci. award 1996), Am. Soc. for Cell Biology, Hungarian Physiol. Soc. (hon.), Microscopy Soc. Am. (Disting. Scientist award for biol. scis. 1994), Alpha Omega Alpha Med. Soc. (CIBA-GEIGY award for Hypertension Rsch. 1991). Office: U Va Sch Medicine Dept Molecular Phys/Biol Physics PO Box 10011 449 Jordan Hall Charlottesville VA 22906-0011

SOMMER, LEONARD SAMUEL, medical educator; b. Springfield, Mass., July 3, 1924; s. Nathan and Jennie S.; m. Anita Friedman, Dec. 22, 1963; children: Wayne, Wendy, Babette, Anne. BS, Yale U., 1944; MD, Columbia U., 1947. Diplomate Am. Bd. Internal Medicine, Am. Bd. Cardiovasc. Diseases. Intern Peter Bent Brigham Hosp., Boston, 1947-48, resident, 1948-49, 53-54; rsch. fellow Columbia Presbyn. Med. Ctr., N.Y.C., 1949-50, Hammersmith Hosp., London, 1952-53; fellow in cardiology, asst. in medicine Children's Hosp. Med. Ctr., Peter Bent Brigham Hosp., Boston, 1954-56; asst. prof. medicine and pediat. U. Miami-Jackson (Fla.) Meml. Med. Ctr., 1956-62, assoc. prof. medicine, pediat., 1962-74, prof. cardiology, 1974—; teaching fellow in medicine Harvard Med. Sch., Boston, 1948-49, 53-54, rsch. fellow, asst. in medicine, 1954-56; instr. cardiology Georgetown U., Washington, 1951-52; investigator Howard Hughes Med. Inst., Univ. Miami Sch. Medicine, 1956-59; cardiovasc. cons. Office Hearings and Appeals, Social Security Adminstrn., Miami, 1988—. Reviewer, editl. writer Annals Internal Medicine CHEST. Vol. vis. cardiologist Care-Medico, Kabul, Afghanistan, 1978; physician Fla. Leg., Tallahasse, 1981. With USPHS, 1950-52. Named Rotarian of Yr., Key Biscayne, Fla., 1985. Fellow ACP, Am. Coll. Cardiology, Am. Fedn. Clin. Rsch., Am. Heart Assn. (coun. clin. cardiology), Sigma Xi, Alpha Omega Alpha. Home: 1111 Crandon Blvd B 1101 Key Biscayne FL 33149 Office: Univ Miami Sch Medicine 1475 NW 12th Ave # 4004 Miami FL 33136-1002

SOMMERS, LAURIE KAY, folklorist, ethnomusicologist; b. Lansing, Mich., Jan. 18, 1955; d. Lawrence M. and Marjorie (Smith) Sommers; m. David William Winder, July 8, 1995. BMA, U. Mich., 1977; MA, Ind. U., 1980, PhD, 1986. Asst. historian Mich. History Divsn., Lansing, 1977-78; historian Commonwealth Assocs., Jackson, Mich., 1979-80; dir. Harmonie Folk Arts Project Ind. Divsn. State Parks, New Harmony, Ind., 1982; hist. preservation cons. East Lansing, Mich., 1984-86; Mich. program curator Smithsonian Office of Folklife Programs, Washington, 1987; folklife specialist Mich. State U. Mus., East Lansing, 1987-94, curator ethnomusicology and folklore, 1994-95; instr. music Valdosta (Ga.) State U., 1995—; cons. Mich. Humanities Coun. Roads Project, Lansing, 1991-92; field rschr. Dade County, Bur. Fla. Folklife, Miami, 1985, Nicaraguan Traditions, Hist. Mus. South Fla., Miami, 1991. Author: Fiesta, Fe y Cultura: Celebrations of Faith in Detroit's Colonia Mexicana, 1995; author: (book/CD) Beaver Island House Party, 1996; editor Anatomy of a Folklife Festival, 1994. Grantee Nat. Endowment Arts, 1991, Mich. Coun. for Arts and Cultural Affairs, 1994, Mich. Humanities Coun., 1991, 93, Lila Wallace-Reader's Digest Cmty. Folklife Program, 1994, Ga. Folklife Program, 1996. Mem. Am. Folklore Soc., Soc. for Ethnomusicology, Fla. Folklore Soc.

SOMMERS, MAXINE MARIE BRIDGET, writer, educator, publisher; b. Crystal Falls, Mich., May 7, 1932; d. Francis Ernest and Irene Catherine (Raher) Munns; m. Clemens Struve, June 10, 1952 (div. 1975); children: Stephen, Joseph; m. Norval Isom Sommers (dec. 1989). Student, Milw. Downer Coll. for Women, 1948-49, U. Tex. Med. Br., Galveston, 1949-50, St. Mary's Hosp., 1950-51. Owner, operator Pound Sterling Publ., 1982—, Pound Sterling Media Svc., 1983—. Author: A Texan on the Road Again to the Far East, 1992; author 28 books and mini-books on cuisine, and travel, also children's books. Pres. Corpus Christi Symphony Guild, 1967-69, Tex. Assn. Symphony Orchestras, 1969; bd. dirs. Corpus Christi Symphony Soc., 1975—, South Tex. Health Syss. Agy., 1982-85; bd. dirs., pvt. svc. trainer Tex. divsn. Am. Cancer Soc., 1974-94; pres. Tex. Coastal Bend Mental Health Assn., 1976-78. Recipient cert. of award Byliners Tex. Wide Writers, 1992, Bus. Assoc. Night award Am. Bus. Women's Assn., 1992, cert. merit Corpus Christi Symphony Guild, 1969, cert. recognition Tex. Women's Assn. Symphony Orchestras, 1969, various awards Am. Cancer Soc. Mem. Byliners, Austin Writers League, Internat. Platform Assn. Home: 4270 Ocean Dr Corpus Christi TX 78411-1283

SON, CHANG HYUN, mechanical engineer; b. Seoul, Korea, July 15, 1957; came to U.S. 1982; s. Kwang Ki and Bok Im (Kim) S.; m. Joon Hwa Lee, May 31, 1981; children: Eugene, Dale, Erin. BS, Kyung Hee U., Seoul, 1981; MS, U. S.C., 1985, PhD, 1989. Registered profl. engr., Ala. Rsch. asst. U. S.C., Columbia, 1984-89; rsch. engr. Westinghouse Savannah River Lab., Aiken, S.C., 1989; sr. specialist Boeing Aerospace, Huntsville, Ala., 1989—. Contbr. articles to profl. jours. Mem. ASME, AIAA, ASHRAE, Internat. Solar Energy Soc., Korean Scientists and Engrs. Assn.. (chpt. pres. 1989, 91). Home: 118 Progress Ln Madison AL 35758-1084 Office: Boeing Def and Space Group M/S JR-41 PO Box 240002 Huntsville AL 35824-6402

SONDAK, ARTHUR, management consultant; b. N.Y.C., Oct. 16, 1929; s. Louis and Eva (Dolin) S.; m. Sylvia Mayran, Jan. 17, 1953 (div. 1975); children: Janet, Steven, Donald. BBA, Baruch Coll., 1950, MBA, 1958. Employment mgr. Saks Fifth Ave, N.Y.C., 1954-57; wage and salary adminstr. Royal Typewriter Co., N.Y.C., 1957-61; employment mgr. Sperry Rand Corp., N.Y.C., 1961-62; compensation dir., region personnel mgr. Royal Typewriter Co., N.Y.C., 1962-66; mgr. personnel program planning MAI, N.Y.C., 1966-69; personnel dir. ITEl Corp., White Plains, N.Y., 1969-73; dir. personnel and adminstrn. MAI, N.Y.C., 1973-75; instr. Baruch Coll. Grad. Sch., N.Y.C., 1969-70; prin. Personnel Mgmt. Svcs., Delray Beach, Fla., 1975—. Editorial adv. bd. AMACOM, N.Y.C., 1986-96; contbr. articles to profl. jours. Adv. bd. Cmty./Advancement Resource Ctr., Middlesex Coll., Edison, 1985-90 (career guidance counselor). With USAF, 1950-54. Home and Office: 3240 NW 10 Pl Delray Beach FL 33445

SONDOCK, RUBY KLESS, retired judge; b. Houston, Apr. 26, 1926; d. Herman Lewis and Celia (Juran) Kless; m. Melvin Adolph Sondock, Apr. 22, 1944; children: Marcia Cohen, Sandra Marcus. AA, Cottey Coll., Nevada, Mo., 1944; BS, U. Houston, 1959, LLB, 1961. Bar: Tex. 1961, U.S. Supreme Ct. 1977. Pvt. practice, Houston, 1961-73, 89—; judge Harris County Ct. Domestic Rels. (312th Dist.), 1973-77, 234th Jud. Dist. Ct., Houston, 1977-82, 83-89; justice Tex. Supreme Ct., Austin, 1982; of counsel Weil Gotshal and Manges, 1989-93, Houston Ctr., 1993—. Mem. ABA, Tex. Bar Assn., Houston Bar Assn., Houston Assn. Women Lawyers, Order of Barons, Phi Theta Phi, Kappa Beta Pi, Phi Kappa Phi, Alpha Epsilon Pi. Office: 2650 Two Houston Ctr 909 Fannin Houston TX 77010

SONEGO, IAN G., state assistant attorney general; b. Louisville, May 27, 1954; s. Angelo and Zella Mae (Causey) S. BA in Polit. Sci. with high honors, U. Louisville, 1976, JD, 1979. Bar: Ky. 1979, U.S. Dist Ct. (ea. dist.) Ky. 1980, U.S. Dist. Ct. (we. dist.) Ky. 1989, U.S. Ct. Appeals (6th cir.) 1989, U.S. Supreme Ct. 1990. Asst. atty. Office Commonwealth's Atty. Pike County, Pikeville, Ky., 1980, sr. asst. atty., 1988-89; assoc. John Paul Runyon Law Firm, Pikeville, 1981-87; asst. atty. gen. Office Atty. Gen., Frankfort, Ky., 1989—; lectr. criminal law Ky. Bar Assn., Jenny Wiley Park, 1981, Ky. Prosecutors Confs., 1989, 93; mem. Atty. Gen.'s task force child sexual abuse, 1992-94. Contbg. editor Ky. Prosecuter Newsletter, 1991—. Recipient Kessleman award U. Louisville, 1975, Bd. Trustee award 1979. Outstanding Prosecutor award Ky. Atty. Mem. Ky. Commonwealth's Attys. Assn. (hon., lectr. 1987, 90, chmn. com. ethics 1984-86, bd. dirs. 1983-85, Outstanding Svc. award 1985, Spl. award 1987). Office: Office Atty Gen Criminal Appellate Divsn 1024 Capital Ctr Dr Frankfort KY 40601-8204

SONES, SHARI CAROLYN, counselor, educator; b. Warner Robins, Ga., May 3, 1966; d. Jon Chalmers and Eleanor Jean (Spaulding) Niemeyer. BS, Brenau Coll., 1988; MS, Ga. State U., 1991. Cert. Nat. Bd. for Cert. Counselors, Inc.; lic. profl. counselor. Asst. tchr. Hi Hope, Lawrenceville, Ga., 1988; counselor Anxiety Disorder Inst. Atlanta, 1991-94; pvt. practice Atlanta, Ga., 1994—; tchr. Oglethorpe U., Atlanta, 1993; clin. dir. Trauma and Abuse Resource Program, 1994—. Vol. group leader Ga. Counsel on Child Abuse, Atlanta, 1991-92. Mem. ACA, Nat. Assn. Alcoholism and Drug Abuse Counselors. Office: Anxiety Disorders Inst 1 Dunwoody Pk Ste 112 Atlanta GA 30338

SONIAT, KATHERINE, English language educator; b. Washington. Instr. English Va. Poly. Inst. and State U., Blacksburg, 1985-88; asst. prof. English Hollins Coll., 1989-91; assoc. prof. English Va. Poly. Inst. and State U., Blacksburg, 1991—; workshop presenter in field. Author: (poems) Notes of Departure, 1985, Winter Toys, 1989, Cracking Eggs, 1990, A Shared Life, 1993; contbr. numerous poems fo profl. publs. Recipient Poetry Soc. of Am. Consuelo Ford Hon. Mention, Ann Stanford award U. So. Calif., Middlebury Coll. Bread Loaf Writers Conf. fellowship and scholarship in poetry, 1985, 89, Camden Poetry prize Walt Whitman Ctr. for the Arts and Humanities, 1985, Va. prize for Poetry, 1989, Edwin Ford Piper award U. Iowa Press, 1993. Office: English Dept Va Poly Inst and State U Blacksburg VA 24061-0112

SONNIER, DAVID JOSEPH, wholesale distributing executive; b. Lafayette, La., Aug. 25, 1939; s. Fernand and Joyce Marie (Lester) S.; m. Ellen Christine Fusselman, July 18, 1964; 1 child, Carole Marie. BS, McNeese State U., 1962. Mgr. tng. program Coburn Supply Co., Lake Charles, La., 1957-62; mgr., v.p. Coburn Supply Co., Longview, Tex., 1964—. Lt. col. USAR, 1962-90, Tex. N.G., 1966-76. Mem. Wholesale Distbrs. Assn., Nat. Assn. Home Builders, Tex. Assn. Builders, East Tex. Builders Assn., East Tex. Plumbing, Heating, Cooling Contractors, Res. Officers Assn. Roman Catholic. Home: 5407 Forest Lake West PO Box 97 Judson TX 75660-0097 Office: Coburn Supply Co 310 W Methvin PO Box 2068 Longview TX 75606-2068

SONSTEGAARD, MILES HARRY, economics educator; b. Langdon, N.D., July 5, 1924; s. Samuel and Ida Minerva (Baker) S.; m. Loretta Joyce Seller, June 28, 1950; children: Barbara, Judith, Paul, Richard. BSc, U. N.D., 1950; MBA, U. Denver, 1951; PhD, U. Ore., 1958. CPA. Econ. statistician U. Ark., Fayetteville, 1954-57; economist United Gas Corp., Shreveport, La., 1957-64; sr. rsch. specialist U. Ark., Little Rock, 1964-69; assoc. prof. economics U. Ark., Fayetteville, 1969—; sr. rsch. assoc. U. Ark., 1979-75, 88—; prin. investigator for railroad feasibility study Mack-Blackwell Transp. Ctr., 1994, for waterside indsl. sites study, 1995-96. Mem. Nat. Acad. Scis. (internat. trade and transp. com. 1987-93, freight trans. and planning com. 1996—), Am. Econ. Assn., Transp. Rsch. Forum.

SOOKNE, HERMAN SOLOMON (HANK SOOKNE), retirement center senior executive; b. Far Rockaway, N.Y., June 30, 1932; s. Harry Martin Sookne and Sarah (Kopolov) Sterenstein; m. Joan Gilman, Apr. 12, 1954 (div. Apr. 9, 1971); children: Charles Michael, David Howard, Susan Frances; m. Polly Henry Johnson, Mar. 1972. Student, Georgetown U., 1949-50; BS in Bus. & Econs., NYU, 1953. Pres., owner Gilclan Bldg. Corp., Merrick, N.Y., 1955-68; divsn. mgr. Boise Cascade Bldg. Corp., Freehold, N.J., 1968-70; dir. property mgmt. and engring. Amprop, Inc., Miami, Fla., 1970-73; pres., CEO Bowman Property Investors, Dallas, 1973-79; gen. mgr. Fidinam, Inc., Houston, 1979-82; mktg. cons. Cooper Communities, Inc., Bella Vista, Ark., 1982-88; dir. mktg. and funds devel. Epworth Villa, Oklahoma City, 1988—. Scoutmaster Boy Scouts Am., L.I., N.Y., 1955-60; bd. dirs., pres. Copperchase Condo's Inc., Oklahoma City, 1991-95; trustee United Meth. Ch. of the Servant. With U.S. Army, 1953-55, Korea. Mem. Ark. Bd. Realtors, Nat. Soc. for Fund Raising Execs., Soc. for Advancement of Mgmt., Nat. Assn. Home Builders, Nat. Soc. Heat, Refrigeration & Air Conditioning Engrs; bd. trustees Methodist Ch. Republican. Methodist. Home: #152 11300 N Pennsylvania Ave Oklahoma City OK 73120-7774 Office: 14901 N Pennsylvania Ave Oklahoma City OK 73134-6071

SOOUDI, MATTHEW M., surgeon; b. Iran, Oct. 24, 1934; came to U.S., 1962; s. Yahya and Iran (Nicknejad) S.; m. Joyce J. Sooudi, Oct. 2, 1965; 2 children. MD, U. Iran, 1962. Diplomate Am. Bd. Surgery, Am. Bd. Colon and Rectal Surgery, Internat. Bd. Proctology. Intern. Bon Secours Hosp., Grosse Pointe, Mich., 1962-63; resident Grace Hosp., Detroit, 1963-67, Ferguson Clinic, Grand Rapids, Mich., 1967-68; pvt. practice St. Elizabeth Hosp., Tex., Beaumont (Tex.) Med. Hosp., Bapt. Hosp., Tex. Fellow ACS, Am. Soc. Colon and Rectal Surgeons, Internat. Assn. Proctologists; mem. AMA, Am. Assn. Phys. Surgeons, So. Med. Assn., Tex. Med. Assn., Tex. Soc. Colon and Rectal Surgeons. Office: 3210 Medical Center Dr Beaumont TX 77701-4627

SOOY, WILLIAM RAY, electrical engineer; b. Vineland, N.J., Jan. 12, 1951; s. Edward Leinau and Alice Elizabeth (Franklin) S.; m. Jean Marie Sooy, Sept. 17, 1976; children: Jennifer, Karen, Diana, Julia. BSEE, U. Miami, 1973, MS, 1977. Registered profl. engr., Fla. Engr. Fla. Power and Light, Miami, 1973-80, prin. engr., 1981-94, design engr. 1995—; engr. Harris Corp., Melbourne, Fla., 1980-81. Mem. IEEE (sr. mem.), Mensa, B-26 Marauder Hist. Soc., Eta Kappa Nu. Republican. Presbyterian. Home: 12735 Ellison Wilson Rd North Palm Beach FL 33408-2113 Office: Fla Power and Light PO Box 14000 North Palm Beach FL 33408

SOPER, HOWARD KENT, printing company executive; b. Balt., May 5, 1928; s. Paul Stuart and M. Ruth (Smith) S.; m. Mary Pate, Apr. 15, 1957, (div.); children: Matthew Howard, William P., Mary; m. Carroll R. Beale, Dec. 23, 1989. BS, U. Md., 1950; LLB, U. Balt., 1961. Asst. contr. chem. divsn. W.R. Grace & Co., Balt., 1957-63; exec. v.p., treas., gen. mgr. Blumenthal Export Co. Inc., 1962-83; v.p., dir. Blumenthal Mills Inc., Marion, S.C., 1970-93; exec. v.p., dir. Blumenthal Print Works Inc., New Orleans. Dir. Info. Coun. Americas, New Orleans, 1993—; chmn. Americanism Com., C. of C., New Orleans, 1980-83; pres. parents assn. Benjamin Franklin Sr. H.S., 1979-81. Capt. U.S. Army, 1951-57. Named Comdr., Mil. Order Fgn. Wars, 1995—. Mem. Sons of the Revolution (v.p.), Order Founders and Patriots (treas.), Gen. Soc. of Colonial Wars (sec. gen. 1992—), Agri-Bus. Coun. (pres.-elect 1994-95), Soc. of the Cinn., Round Table Club, Pickwick Club, New Orleans Lawn Tennis Club, World Trade Center Plimsoll Club. Episcopalian.

SORCI-THOMAS, MARY GAY, biomedical researcher, educator; b. New Orleans, Mar. 9, 1956; d. Leon Philip and Ethel Mae (Andrews) S.; m. Michael J. Thomas, June 9, 1979. BS, La. State U., 1979; PhD, Wake Forest U., 1984. Instr. Bowman Gray Sch. Medicine/Wake Forest U., Winston-Salem, N.C., 1987-88, asst. prof., 1988-94, assoc. in biochemistry, 1989—, assoc. prof. comparative medicine, 1994—; ad hoc reviewer NIH, 1992—. Contbr. articles to Jour. Lipid Rsch., Jour. Biol. Chemistry, Arteriosclerosis. Spl. fellow R.J. Reynolds Co., 1983-84; NIH NRSA postdoctoral fellow, 1984-86; established investigator Am. Heart Assn., 1994—. Mem. Am. Heart Assn. (arteriosclerosis coun., coord. N.C. affiliate 1992, rsch. rev. subcom. 1989-92, bd. dirs. 1992—, rsch. com. 1992-95, Louis N. Katz finalist in Basic Sci. Rsch., 1991, nutrition com. 1992-95, chair women and minorities com. 1994—), Am. Soc. Biochemists and Molecular Biols., Sigma Xi (chpt. treas. 1991-92, chpt. v.p. 1992-93, chpt. pres. 1993-94, NIH R29 awardee 1989-93). Office: Bowman Gray Sch Medicine Dept Comparative Medicine Medical Center Blvd Winston Salem NC 27157

SORENSEN, JACKI FAYE, choreographer, aerobic dance company executive; b. Oakland, Calif., Dec. 10, 1942; d. Roy C. and Juanita F. (Bullon) Mills; m. Neil A. Sorensen, Jan. 3, 1965. BA, U. Calif., 1964. Cert. tchr., Calif. Ptnr., Big Spring Sch. Dance, 1965; tchr. Pasadena Ave. Sch., Sacramento, 1968; founder, pres., choreographer Jacki's Inc., DeLand, Fla., 1990—; cons., lectr. on phys. fitness. Author: Aerobic Dancing, 1979, Jacki Sorensen's Aerobic Lifestyle Book, 1983; choreographer numerous dance exercises for records and videocassettes. Trustee Women's Sports Found. Recipient Diamond Pin award Am. Heart Assn., 1979, Individual Contbn. award Am. Assn. Fitness Dirs. in Bus. and Industry, 1981, Spl. Olympics Contbn. award, 1982, Contbn. to Women's Fitness award Pres.'s Coun. Phys. Fitness and Sports, 1982, Healthy Am. Fitness Leader award U.S. Jaycees, 1984, Lifetime Achievement award Internat. Dance Exercise Assn., 1985, New Horizons award Caldwell (N.J.) Coll., 1985, Legend of Aerobics award City Sports mag., 1985; Pres. Coun. award Calif. Womens' Leadership Conf., 1986, Hall of Fame award Club Industry mag., 1986, IDEA, 1992. Mem. AAHPERD, AFTRA, Am. Coll. Sports Medicine, Nat. Intramural and Recreation Assn. Office: Jacki's Inc PO Box 289 Deland FL 32721-0289

SORENSEN, JILL ANN, computer scientist; b. Mpls., Aug. 1, 1950; d. Chester Clayton Sorensen and Carol H. (Pennekamp) Bridges; m. Joseph C. Humeas, Sept. 3, 1981; children: Julie, Joseph III, Jesse. BS, Shepherd Coll., 1987; AAS, C.C. of Air Force, 1989; BS, Shepherd Coll., 1991. Dir. data mgmt. Shepherd Coll., Shepherdstown, W.Va., 1990-91; info. mgmt. AT&T, Oakton, Va., 1991-93; cons., lectr. Shepherd Coll., 1993—; cons. Sorenware, Shenandoah Junction, W.Va., 1992—. Bd. dirs. Shenandoah Women's Ctr., Martinsburg, W.Va., 1981-85. With W.Va. Air Nat. Guard, 1985-89. Lutheran. Home and office: PO Box 104 Shenandoah Junction WV 25442-0104

SORENSEN, JOHN FREDERICK, retired minister; b. Cadillac, Mich., Apr. 4, 1923; s. Neil Thomas and Helga S. (Anderson) S.; m. D. Marieta Moore, Mar. 16, 1944; children: Jack, Keith, Robert. BA, Mich. State U., 1957; MDiv, Garrett Theol. Sem., 1962; DD (hon.), Holy Trinity Coll., 1996. Ordained to ministry United Meth. Ch. as deacon, 1960, as elder, 1962. Pastor Mulliken (Mich.) United Meth. Ch., 1951-55, Upton Ave. United Meth. Ch., Battle Creek, Mich., 1955-64, Haven United Meth. Ch., Jackson, Mich., 1964-67, Ithaca (Mich.) United Meth. Ch., 1967-72, 1st United Meth. Ch., Lansing, Mich., 1972-78; assoc. pastor Community United Meth. Ch., Holiday, Fla., 1985-93; mem. various coms. for Conf. Dist., United Meth. Ch., 1962-85; summer exch. pastor to Loughton, Eng., 1975. Contbr. columns to newspapers, 1967-72. Founder Free Health Clinic. With USN, 1942-46. Recipient Spl. Tribute Gov. Mich., 1985, Ionia Hospice award, 1986; named Rural Pastor of Yr. United Meth. Ch., Mich., 1955, Amb., Ionia C. of C., 1983-85; commd. Ky. Col., 1995. Fellow Designate Acad. Parish Clergy (edn. coom. 1982-84, state sec. 1994-97), West Pasco Ministerial Assn. Shriners (past master 1972), Masons; mem. Fla. Naval Sailors Assn. (chaplain 1996-97), Polish Legion Am. (chaplain post 184 1996-97). Home: 4427 Pelorus Dr New Port Richey FL 34652-5810

SORENSEN, RICARDO UWE, pediatrics educator; b. Valdivia, Chile, May 13, 1939; came to U.S., 1976; s. Hans C. and Emmeli (Detjens) S.; m. Sally O. Bruch; children: Sonja, Cynthia, Monica. MD, U. Chile, Santiago, 1962, med. degree, 1964; postdoctoral, WHO, 1970. Diplomate Am. Bd. Pediatrics; lic. pediatrician, La. Rotating intern depts. pediatrics, medicine, surgery and obstertrics hosps. U. Chile Sch. Medicine, Santiago, 1963-64, clin. cons. immunologic disorders, 1968-74; resident dept. pediatrics Hosp. Calvo Mackenna/U. Chile Sch. Medicine, Santiago, 1964, staff pediatrician emergency ward, 1967-71, asst. prof. dept. pediatrics, 1971-74, assoc. prof., devel., head divsn. clin. immunology dept. pediatrics, 1974-76; DAAD pediatric immunology fellow dept. pediatrics Eppendorf U. Hosps., Hamburg, Germany, 1965; resident dept. pediatrics U. Bonn Hosps., Germany, 1966; devel., head divsn. immunopathology Instituto Bacteriologico de Chile, Santiago, 1968-73, devel., head dept. immunology, 1973-76; mem. staff divsn. allergy and immunology dept. pediatrics Case Western Res. U., Cleve., 1977-89, asst. prof. pediatrics, 1977-80, assoc. prof. pediatrics, 1980-89, asst. prof. exptl. pathology dept. pathology, 1979-85, assoc. prof. pathology Inst. Pathology, 1986-89, acting head divsn. immunology dept. pediatrics, 1982-84; prof. pediatrics, head divsn. allergy and immunology, co-dir. allergy-immunology tng. program Med. Ctr. La. State U., New Orleans, 1989—; dir. clin. immunology lab. Children's Hosp., New Orleans, 1991—; WHO fellow Ctrl. Lab. Netherlands Red Cross, Amsterdam, Hamburg, Germany, 1973; mem. bone marrow transplantation com. Rainbow Babies and Childrens Hosp., Case Western Res. U., 1978-84; dept. pediat. rep. to Gen. Clin. Rsch. Ctr., Med. Ctr. New Orleans, 1990—; invited lectr. in field. Contbr. over 100 articles and revs. to med. and profl. jours., chpts. to books. Mem. Am. Acad. Allergy Immunology, Am. Coll. Allergy and Immunology, Am. Assn. Immunologists, Assn. Med. Lab. Immunologists, Clin. Immunology Soc., Soc. for Pediatric Rsch., La. Allergy Soc., Sociedad Chilena de Immunologia (founder, first pres.), Sociedad Chilena de Alergia e Immunologia (hon.). Office: La State U Med Ctr Dept Pediatrics 1542 Tulane Ave New Orleans LA 70112-2822

SORRELL, ADRIAN LLOYD, education educator; b. Hondo, Tex., Mar. 3, 1955; s. Lloyd and Ruby (George) S.; m. Alva Justine Williams, Apr. 27, 1984; 1 child, Andrea Khalilah. BS, U. Tex., 1978, MEd, 1989, PhD, 1993. Resource tchr. Williams Elem. Sch., Austin, Tex., 1978-93; asst. prof. Prairie View A&M U., 1993—, coord. spl. edn., 1994—; rsch. aide U. Tex., summer 1988, teaching asst., 1991. Editorial asst. Intervention in Schooland Clinic, 1991, mem. editorial bd., 1994—. Mem. Coun. for Learning Disabilities, Coun. for Exceptional Children, Tex. Coun. for Exceptional Children (sec.), Nat. Black Child Devel. Insts., Tex. Assn. Coll. Tchrs., Longhorn Alumni Band (sec. 1979-80), Kappa Delta Pi. Democrat. Episcopalian. Home: 20202 Maple Village Dr Cypress TX 77429-5631

SORRELLS, FRANK DOUGLAS, mechanical engineer, consultant; b. Toccoa, Ga., May 14, 1931; s. Ralph Price and Ila B. (Freeman) S.; m. Alma M. West, June 19, 1954; 1 child, Desiree G. BSME, U. Tenn., 1957, MS, 1968. Registered profl. engr., Tenn. Chief engr. Formex Co., Greeneville, Tenn., 1960-67; exec. v.p. Charles Lee Assoc., Knoxville, Tenn., 1967-76; pvt. practice consulting engr. Knoxville, Tenn., 1976-78, 83-88; dir. engring. Cole Nat. Corp., Knoxville, Tenn., 1978-83; mgr. tech. transfer Valmet Paper Machinery div. Valmet-Enerdry, Knoxville, Tenn., 1988-93; pres. PEPE Software LLC, Knoxville, Tenn., 1996—; cons., Knoxville, 1976—; mem. Advanced Toroidal Facility Design Team, cons. Oak Ridge (Tenn.) Nat. Lab., 1984-85. Inventor, patentee of 8 patents and co-inventor, patentee of 14 patents in fields of filtration, web processing, plastic forming and lens processing. Staff sgt. USAF, 1950-54. Mem. NSPE, ASME (Energy Resources Rech. award 1987), Tenn. Soc. Profl. Engrs. Home and Office: 5516 Timbercrest Trl Knoxville TN 37909-1837

SORRELS, JAMES ROBERT, computer company executive; b. Russellville, Ark., Mar. 1, 1941; s. Wade Lafayette and Grace Evelyn (Spaulding) S.; m. Verdia Mason Hawn, July 13, 1963 (div. Mar. 1974); children: Robert Alan, James Mitchell; m. Betty Ponder, Nov. 30, 1985. Tech. sch., U.S. Govt.; BSEE, Cook's Inst. Cert. electronics technician; lic. pvt. pilot. Elec. tech. USAF, Alaska, 1959-67, FAA, Alaska, 1967-73; chief engr. KXLR KCAB, Little Rock, Ark., 1973-80; avionics foreman Royale Airlines, Shreveport, La., 1980-83; instr. Caddo Career Ctr., Shreveport, La., 1983-86; owner Polytronics, Shreveport, La., 1986—; test adminstr. Internat. Soc. Cert. Electronics Technicians, Ft. Worth, 1973—. Mem. Masons. Republican. Methodist. Home: 110 Oak Ridge Dr Shreveport LA 71106-7314 Office: Polytronics 8101 Kingston Rd Shreveport LA 71108

SORRELS, JOHN PAUL, psychology educator; b. Dallas, Nov. 11, 1950; s. Thomas T. and Laverna L. (Elam) S.; m. Cherry Marie Reever, Dec. 16, 1972; children: Michele, Julie. BA, Howard Payne U., 1972; MA, Tex. Woman's U., 1975, PhD, 1978. Lic. psychologist, Tex. Grad. teaching asst. Tex. Woman's U., Denton, 1975-77; staff therapist, instr. psychology Dallas Bapt. Coll., 1977-78; asst. prof. psychology Wayland Bapt. U., Plainveiw, Tex., 1979-83; prof. psychology Hardin-Simmons U., Abilene, Tex., 1983—, dir. grad. program in family psychology, 1984-94, dean grad. studies, 1993—; pres. dir. C.H. Love & Co., Abilene, 1985-91. Contbr. articles to profl. jours. Bd. dirs. Mend-A-Child, Abilene; community advisor Jr. League, Abilene. Abilene Community Found. grantee, 1987. Mem. APA, Am. Assn. Marriage and Family Therapy, Nat. Coun. Family Rels., Tex. Assn. Marriage and Family Therapy, So. Bapt. Assn. of Counseling and Family Ministry, Tex. Bapt. Assn. Family Ministry (pres. 1986-88, Presdl. award 1990), Mental Health Assn. (bd. dirs. 1990-91). Office: Hardin-Simmons Univ Box 16210 Abilene TX 79698

SORRELS, RANDALL OWEN, lawyer; b. Va., Dec. 11, 1962; s. Charles Vernon and Marjorie Elaine (Jones) S.; m. Cheryl Ann Casas, June 29, 1985; children: Ashley Michelle, Stephanie Leigh. BA in Polit. Sci.and Speech Comm. magna cum laude, Houston Bapt. U., 1984; JD magna cum laude, South Tex. Coll. Law, 1987. Bar: Tex. 1987, U.S. Dist. Ct. (so. dist.) Tex.; bd. cert. in civil trial law and personal injury trial law tex. Bd. Legal Specialization. Assoc. Fulbright & Jaworski, Houston, 1987-90; ptnr. Abraham, Watkins, Nichols, & Friend, Houston, 1990—. Fellow Houston Bar Found., Tex. Bar Found. (sustaining life mem.); mem. ABA, ATLA, State Bar Tex. (bd. dirs. 1994—, bd. advisor pattern jury charge commt. Vol. 1 1994—, Vol. 4, 1995—, chmn. profl. devel. com. 1996—, vice chair legis. com. 1996—), Tex. Trial Lawyers Assn. (sustaining life mem., bd. dirs.), Houston Trial Lawyers Assn. (bd. dirs., chmn. CLE com. 1993—), Houston Young Lawyers Assn., Tex. Young Lawyers Assn., Coll. of the State Bar of Tex., Assn. of Civil Trial and Appellate Specialists, Am. Inns of Ct., Million Dollar Advocates Forum. Home: 4524 Palmetto St Bellaire TX 77401-3710 Office: Abraham Watkins Nichols & Friend 800 Commerce St Houston TX 77002-1707

SOSSAMAN, WILLIAM LYNWOOD, lawyer; b. High Point, N.C., May 30, 1947; s. Robert Allison and Elizabeth Bryce (Hethcox) S.; m. Sandra Clare Ward, June 9, 1973; children: Joana Leslie, David Lynwood. AB, Davidson Coll., 1969; JD, Vanderbilt U., 1972. Bar: Fla. 1972, U.S. Ct. Mil. Appeals 1973, U.S. Dist. Ct. (mid. dist.) Fla. 1977, Tenn. 1978, U.S. Dist. Ct. (we. dist.) Tenn. 1979, U.S. Dist. Ct. (no. dist.) Miss. 1979, U.S. Dist. Ct. (ea. and we. dists.) Ark, 1980, U.S. Dist. Ct. (mid. dist.) Tenn. 1985, U.S. Dist. Ct. (ea. dist.) Mich. 1988, U.S. Ct. Appeals (6th and 8th cirs.) 1989, U.S. Ct. Appeals (11th cir.) 1991. Mktg. resch. analyst First Tenn. Bank, Memphis, 1967-70; assoc. Alley, Rock & Dinkel, Tampa, Orlando and Miami, Fla., 1972-73, Rock & Brown, Orlando, 1976-77, Young & Perl, Memphis, 1978-88; ptnr. Allen, Scruggs, Sossaman, & Thompson, Memphis, 1988—; asst. county atty. Shelby County Govt., Memphis, 1978-79; asst. city atty. City of Memphis, 1978-79. Author: Preventing Lawsuits for Wrongful Termination, 1995. N.Am. regional sec. Project Ams., Davidson, N.C., 1967-69. Capt. U.S. Army, 1973-76. Named Hon. City Councilman City of Memphis, 1982. Mem. ABA (labor and employment sect., litigation sect., EEO com.), Fla. Bar (labor and employment law sect.), Mgmt. Counsel Roundtable (chmn. 1986-87), Def. Rsch. Inst. (employment law com.), Tenn. Bar Assn. (labor law sect.), Memphis Bar Assn., The Justice Network (bd. dirs. 1990-93). Presbyterian. Home: 8411 Beaverwood Dr Germantown TN 38138-7641 Office: Allen Scruggs Sossaman & Thompson 813 Ridge Lake Blvd Ste 300 Memphis TN 38120-9409

SOTOMORA-VON AHN, RICARDO FEDERICO, pediatrician, educator; b. Guatemala City, Guatemala, Oct. 22, 1947; s. Ricardo and Evelyn (Von Ahn) S.; m. Eileen Marie Holcomb, May 9, 1990. M.D., San Carlos U., 1972; M.S. in Physiology, U. Minn., 1978; m. Victoria Monzon, Nov. 26, 1971; children—Marisol, Clarisa, Ricardo, III, Charlotte Marie. Rotating intern Gen. Hosp. Guatemala, 1971-72; pediatric intern U. Ark., 1972-73, resident, 1973-75; fellow in pediatric cardiology U. Minn., 1975-78; research assoc. in cardiovascular pathology United Hosps., St. Paul, 1976; fellow in neonatal-perinatal medicine St. Paul's Children's Hosp., 1977-78, U. Ark., 1981-82; instr. pediatrics U. Minn., 1978-79; pediatric cardiologist, unit cardiovascular surgery Roosevelt Hosp., Guatemala City, 1979-81; asst. prof. pediatrics (cardiology and neonatology), U. Ark., Little Rock, 1981-83; practice medicine specializing in pediatric cardiology-neonatology, 1983—. Diplomate Am. Bd. Pediatrics, Sub-Bd. Pediatric Cardiology, Neonatal-Perinatal Medicine. Fellow Am. Acad. Pediatrics, Am. Coll. Cardiology, Am. Coll. Chest Physicians, Am. Coll. Angiology; mem. AMA, AAAS, Ark. Med. Soc., N.Y. Acad. Scis., Am. Heart Assn., Soc. Pediatric Echocardiography, Guatemala Coll. Physicians and Surgeons, Central Ark. Pediatric Soc., So. Soc. Pediatric Research, Soc. Critical Care Medicine. Clubs: Pleasant Valley Country (Little Rock). Home: 25 River Ridge Cir Little Rock AR 72227 Office: # 5 Office Park Dr Ste 105 Little Rock AR 72211

SOTTONG, PHILIPP C., social services consultant, physician, writer, artist, publisher; b. Cattaraugus, N.Y., Mar. 16, 1920; s. Peter and Grace Marion (Wagner) S.; m. Mary Lou Head, 1944; children: Gary, Geoffrey, Lincoln. Grad., Hamilton Coll., 1941; MD, Rochester U., 1945. Diplomate Nat. Bd. Med. Examiners, Am. Bd. Psychiatry and Neurology. Intern U. Pittsburgh, 1945; fellowship in pathology U. Rochester, 1949, resident in psychiatry, 1949-51; staff mem. Erlanger Children's Meml. Hosp., 1959—; dir. Chatta Guidence Clinic, 1953-59; pvt. practice, 1959—; rep. Mental Health Execeptional Children Inst., 1955-56; staff psychiatrist Ala. Mental Health Program, 1967-70; cons. Orange Grove Sch, Family Svc., Dept. Voc. Rehab., Depts. Pub. Welfare, VA, Office Hearings and Appeals, John Hancock. Author: Year of Chance, 1989, BZ Art, 1992; 7 one man shows (watercolor); pub.: Songs of Sottongs. Democratic nominee Dist. 6 Tenn., 1972; chmn. Speakers for McGovern-Shriver Hamilton County, 1972; preservation and restoration Walnut Bridge. Lt. (j.g.) USNR, 1947-48. Honorary fellow and Commonwealth fellow in Anthropology Cornell U., 1951-53. Mem. AMA (life), Am. Psychiat. Assn. (life), Chattanooga and Hamilton County Med. Soc., Tenn. Med. Assn., Tenn. Watercolor Assn. Home and Office: 709 Parsons Ln Signal Mountain TN 37377-2703

SOUDER, ANNETTE DENISE, secondary education educator; b. Maysville, Ky., Apr. 26, 1969; d. Kenneth Allen and Cheryl Ann (Bierley) S. BA in Teaching Chemistry and Bus. Adminstrn., Transylvania U., 1991; postgrad., Miami U., Oxford, Ohio, 1995—. Project asst. Dragon Fly mag.; tchr. chemistry, chemcom, phys. sci., environ. issues We. Hills H.S., Frankfort, Ky., 1991-95, co-chair sci. dept., 1992-94; tchr. biology Gov.'s Scholars Program, 1994-96; mem. Energy, Environment and Policy Choices Inst., U. Okla./Close-up Found., Norman, Okla. and Washington, 1993, Wetlands Inst., U. Ky., Lexington, 1993; tchr. coord. Kentuckians Apply Math. and Sci., Georgetown (Ky.) Coll./Toyota Motor Mfg., 1993; presenter Nat. Gov.'s Sch. Conf., Atlanta, 1994. Recipient Sallie Mae 1st Yr. Nat. Tchr. award, 1992; named Hon. Commr. Agr., Ky., 1992, Ky. Colo., 1992; tchg. fellow Ky. Gov.'s Scholar's Program, 1992, Ky. Dept. Edn. grantee for devel. of model unit. Mem. Ky. Sci. Tchrs. Assn., Omnicron Delta Kappa. Democrat. Mem. Ch. of Christ. Home: 616 S College Ave # 104 Oxford OH 45056

SOUSER, GERARD ALLEN, JR., marketing professional; b. Pitts., Dec. 10, 1959; s. Gerard Allen and Jane (Lind) S.; m. Anne Marie Gillies, Sept. 29, 1984. BS in Resources Mgmt. with honors, U.S. Naval Acad., 1982; MBA, Chadwick U., 1992. Owner Souser Mktg. Group, Alexandria, Va., 1982—; program mgr. Betac Corp., Alexandria, Va., 1983—. Registration couple Worldwide Marriage Encounter, Arlington, 1992-94. 2d lt. USMC, 1978-83. Mem. Am. Soc. for Quality Control, Nat. Eagle Scout Assn. (Crossed Palms award 1976). Roman Catholic. Home and Office: 6315 Yosemite Dr Alexandria VA 22312-1141

SOUTH, LARRY GLENN, town manager; b. Jefferson, N.C., Aug. 28, 1956; s. Rufus Glenn and Vilena Ruthie (Elliott) S.; m. Anne Marie Littel Bowlin, Oct. 10, 1977 (div. Apr. 1991); children: Wendy Allison, Kimberly Anne; m. Sheila Marie Prater, Dec. 22, 1995. BBA, Appalachian State U., 1978; cert. county adminstr., U. N.C. Chapel Hill, 1984. Ins. agt. Farm Bur., West Jefferson, N.C., 1978-81; sales rep. Twin City Chevrolet, West Jefferson, 1981-83; mgr. County of Ashe, Jefferson, N.C., 1983-88; mgr. regional N.C. Dept. Environment Health and Natural Resources, Raleigh, 1988-90; mgr. County of Davie, Mocksville, N.C., 1990-92; owner South Distbns. Co., Mocksville, 1992—; mgr. Town of Hillsville, Va., 1993—; bd. dirs. Galax (Va.), Carroll, Grayson Chamber, Carroll County C. of C., Hillsville. Mem. Va. Local Govt. Mgrs. Assn., Appalachian State U. Local Govt. Mgrs., Hillsville Vol. Rescue Squad. Republican. Home: 411 Victory Ln Hillsville VA 24343 Office: Town of Hillsville 410 N Main St PO Box 545 Hillsville VA 24343

SOUTH, STEPHEN A., academic administrator. Pres. Knoxville (Tenn.) Bus. Coll. Office: Knoxville Bus Coll Office of the President 720 N 5th Ave Knoxville TN 37917-6721

SOUTHERLAND, THOMAS PAUL, retired university administrator; b. Bossier City, La., June 9, 1920; s. Dell and Mattie Catherine (De Costomel) S.; m. Maxine Carmen Aycock, Apr. 2, 1943; children: Judith Ann S. Kessler, Lisa Louise S. Allen. BS, Northwestern State U., 1943; MS, La. State U., 1949, EdD, 1962. Cert. tchr., adminstr., La. Math. tchr. Bolton High Sch., Alexandria, La., 1947-51; head coach, athletic dir. Pineville (La.) High Sch., 1952-53; prin. Cherokee Elem. Sch., Alexandria, 1953-57, Alexandria Jr. High Sch., 1957-62; asst. supt. instrn. Repides PArish, 1962-66; dean coll. edn. Northwestern State U., Natchitoches, La., 1966-75, dean grad. sch., 1975-78, v.p. acad. affairs, 1978-86, exec. v.p., 1984-86; chair La. Adv. Coun. Accreditation, 1966-75; bd. dirs. Progressive Savs. and Loan Assn., Natchitoches, v.p., 1976-78, vice chmn., 1978—. Contbr. articles to profl. jours. Active First United Meth. Ch., Natchitoches; bd. dirs. Attakapas coun. Boy Scouts Am., 1958-66, ARC, Alexandria, Rapides Health Bd., Natchitoches-Northwestern Symphony Soc., pres., 1975. With USNR, 1943-46. Mem. Am. Assn. Colls. for Tchr. Edn., La. Assn. Sch. Execs., La. Ednl. Rsch. Assn., Am. Assn. Collegiate Registrars and Admission Officers, Natchitoches Country Club, Mustic Krewe de Sainte Denis, Red Red Rose Club, Masons, Natchitoches C. of C. (past pres.), Rotary (past pres. Natchitoches chpt.), La. Outdoor Drama Assn., Phi Delta Kappa, Kappa Delta Pi, Phi Kappa Phi, Blue Key.

SOUTHERN, DAVID LYNN, healthcare facilities operating company executive, psychologist; b. Cushing, Okla., Nov. 17, 1950; s. Jack Clay and Ruby Lorain Southern; m. Claudia Parrish, June 14, 1975; children: Alison C., Jack C. BS in Psychology, Abilene Christian U., 1972, MS in Psychology, 1975. Cert. psychol. assoc., Tex.; qualified mental retardation profl. Staff psychologist Abilene (Tex.) State Sch., 1975-77; staff psychologist, mental retardation profl. ARA/South Park Devel. Ctr., Brownwood, Tex., 1977-79; pvt. cons. Rock House Inc., Stephensville, Tex., 1979-80; CEO So. Concepts, Inc., Granbury, Tex., 1980—, Community Living Concepts, Inc., Cleburne, Tex., 1981-84. City councilman City of Granbury, 1985-87, 88-94. Mem. APA, Am. Assn. Mental Retardation, Tex. Psychol. Assn., Tex. Assn. Mental Retardation (bd. dirs. 1988-92), Pvt. Providers Assn. (pres. 1993), Community Residential Svcs. Assn. (pres. 1991-92), Lake Granbury Kiwanis Club (pres. 1990-91), Lake Granbury C. of C. Office: So Concepts Inc PO Box 758 226 E Pearl St Granbury TX 76048-2211

SOUTHERN, LONNIE STEVEN, minister; b. San Diego, Sept. 6, 1947; s. Henry Benjamin and Juanita Hilda (Fishburn-Bandy) S.; m. Vicki Leona Musgrave, Aug. 18, 1968; children: Katherine Michelle, Jesse Ryan. BTh, N.W. Christian Coll., Eugene, Oreg., 1970; D of Ministry, Sch. Theology, Claremont, Calif., 1977. Ordained to ministry Christian Ch., 1974. Min. to youth Hillsboro (Oreg.) Christian Ch., 1967-69; assoc. min. Lebanon (Oreg.) Christian Ch., 1969-70; min. in tng. 1st Christian Ch., Pomona, Calif., 1970-74; assoc. min., pastor Sullivan (Ill.)-Allenville Christian Chs., 1974-76; sr. pastor South Bay Christian Ch., Redondo Beach, Calif., 1976-80; pastor Allenville (Ill.) Christian Ch., 1980-86; sr. min. 1st Christian Ch., Selma, Calif., 1986-88, Bethany Park Christian Ch., Rantoul, Ill., 1988-93, Fairfax (Va.) Christian Ch., 1993—; v.p. Sullivan Ministerial Assn., 1975, pres., 1982-83; chmn. Regional Christian Edn. Commn., Sullivan, 1983-86, Lakeland Cluster of Christian Chs., Sullivan, 1983-86, South San Joaquin Cluster of Christian Chs., Fresno, Calif., 1986-88; bd. dirs., mem. exec. com. So. Calif. Coun. of Chs., L.A., 1976-78; v.p., bd. dirs. All Peoples Cmty. Ctr., L.A., 1977-79, Coll. Christian Profl. Mins., Ill., Wis., 1988-90; pres. South Bay Interfaith Coun., Redondo Beach, 1979-80, Selma (Calif.) Ministerial Assn., 1987-88; regional bd. dirs. Christian Chs. of Ill. and Wis., 1983-86; dean East Prairie Cluster, Rantoul, 1989-91; v.p. Christian Ch. Capital Area Ministers Assn., 1994-95, pres. 1996—; cons. Pilgrimage Christian Ch. Inner City Ministry, 1993;. Mem. Redondo Beach Coord. Coun., 1976-79, Redondo Beach Mayor's Roundtable, 1977-80, Moultrie County Adult Youth Awareness Coun., Sullivan, 1981-86, Base Reuse adn Devel. Exec. Com., Rantoul, 1990-93; mem. exec. com. Save Chanute AFB, Rantoul, 1990. Maj. U.S. Army D.C. N.G. Decorated Army Achievement medal, Commendation medal, Nat. Def. medal, Res. Officer Achievement medal, Meritorious Svc. medal, 1993; named Best Sr. Officer, 1990; recipient Calif. Medal of Merit, D.C. N.G. Impact award, 1994. Mem. Rotary (Paul Harris fellow 1990). Home: 4903 Carriagepark Rd Fairfax VA 22032-2368 Office: Fairfax Christian Ch 10185 Main St Fairfax VA 22031-3414

SOUTHWORTH, DAVID LESLIE, company financial executive; b. Jamestown, N.Y., Oct. 7, 1947; s. Donald Lee and Eva Marzella (Bundy) S.; m. Hiroko Igarashi, May 15, 1971; 1 child, Cynthia K. AA in Langs., U. Md., London, 1977; AAS in Math., SUNY, Jamestown, 1967; BA in Bus. Fin., U. South Fla., 1981. Notary pub., Fla. Enlisted man USAF, 1967-78, 82-92; asst. contr. Tropical Garment Mfg. Co., Tampa, Fla., 1978-82; contr. GCA Chem. Corp., Bradenton, Fla., 1992-94; CFO, Cyclodextrin Techs. Devel., Inc., Gainesville, Fla., 1994—. Mem. Am. Assn. Profl. Bookeepers (assoc.). Home: 3142 NE 13th St Gainesville FL 32609

SOUTHWORTH, R. MORRISON, development counsel; b. Charlottesville, Va., Jan. 2, 1951; s. Richard Spencer Southworth and Geneva (James) Sutphin; m. Diana Page Dunbar, Sept. 21, 1981 (div. Aug. 1983). BA in Econs. and Bus., Emory and Henry Coll., 1975; postgrad., George Washington U., 1988; MEd in Instnl. Advancement, Vanderbilt U., 1991. Account exec. Clay Media, Charlottesville, 1979-82, Wilson and Peck Advt., Balt., 1982-84, WHRO Pub. Broadcasting, Norfolk, Va., 1985-86, Forrsberg Advt., Virginia Beach, Va., 1986-87; ind. fundraising cons. Virginia Beach, 1987-89; edn. libr. Vanderbilt U., Nashville, 1989-91; asst. dir. devel. Fisk U., Nashville, 1990-91; pvt. practice Philanthropy Group, Palmyra, Va., 1991—. Contbg. editor to regional publs.; profl. drummer, vocalist, actor, stand-up comedian. Vol. Fluvanna Soc. for Prevention Cruelty to Animals, Back Bay Nat. Wildlife Refuge; docent Va. Life Saving Mus., 1986-88; mem. Tenn. Hist. Soc., 1993—, Friends of Fluvanna Libr., 1989, 94—; rep. Vanderbilt U. Press for Va. Festival of the Book and So. Festival of the Books. Mem. Virginia Beach Writers (founding), Sigma Iota, Alpha Phi Omega. Republican. Methodist. Office: Ct Green PO Box 476 Palmyra VA 22963-0476

SOVDE-PENNELL, BARBARA ANN, sonographer; b. McPherson, Kans., Sept. 27, 1955; d. Benton Ellis and Mary Ann (Ball) Sovde; m. Paul Edwin Pennell, June 5, 1982; 1 child, Eric Louis. AA in Radiologic Tech., Hutchinson Community Jr. Coll., 1977; BS in Radiologic Tech., U. Okla., 1993. Registered diagnostic med. sonographer, radiological technol. Radiographer Hertzler Clinic, Halstead, Kans., 1977-78; radiographer Mercy Health Ctr., Okla. City, 1978-81, sonographer, supr. ultrasound dept., 1981-83; mobile sonographer Sun Med. Systems, Okla. City, 1983-84, Diagnostic Radiology, Edmond, Okla., 1984-87; prin., owner, pres. of corp. Ultrasound Unltd., Inc., Edmond, 1987—; part-time clin. specialist ultrasound Circadian Can. Ultrasound Equipment Co., 1991—. Active neighborhood recycling, Edmond, 1990—; mem. Greenpeace. Named Outstanding Leader in S.W. Nat. Allied Health Assn., 1981; recipient Outstanding Alumnus award U. Okla. Coll. Allied Health, 1990. Mem. Soc. Diagnostic Med. Sonographers (state rep. 1981-87, regional dir., bd. dirs. 1987-90), Okla. Sonographers Soc. (pres. 1982-84, steering com. 1984—). Democrat.

SOVENYHAZY, GABOR FERENC, surgeon; b. Budapest, Hungary, Apr. 7, 1947. MD, SUNY, 1975. Diplomate Am. Bd. of Colon and Rectal Surgeons. Intern Maimonides Med. Ctr., Bklyn., 1974-75, resident in gen. surgery, 1976-79; resident in colon and rectal surgery Grant Hosp., Columbus, 1979-80; pvt. practice, 1980—; hosp. appt. Spartanburg Gen. Hosp., S.C.; asst. prof. colon and rectal surgery U. S.C. Fellow ACS, Am. Soc. Colorectal Surgery, Piedmont Colorectal Assn., Am. Soc. Gastrointestinal Endoscopy; mem. Am. Soc. Colon and Rectal Surgeons. Office: 1776 Skylyn Dr Spartanburg SC 29307-1045

SOWDER, DONALD DILLARD, chemicals executive; b. Rocky Mt., Va., Mar. 28, 1937; s. Roman Dillard and Virginia (Dowdy) S.; m. Beverly Reid, Nov. 29, 1957; children: Reid Dillard, Susan Allison, Donald Stuart. BS, Va. Tech., 1959; cert. in sales mgmt., Columbia U., 1976, cert. in fin., 1984; diploma, U.S. Army Command & Gen. Staff Coll., 1978; cert. in mgmt., U. Va., 1993. Sales rep. Sealtest Foods, Norfolk, Va., 1962-64; med. sales rep. Lederle Labs. div. Am. Cyanamid Co., Norfolk, 1964-69; dist. sales mgr. Lederle Labs. div. Am. Cyanamid Co., Washington, 1969-74; nat. mgr. sales tng. Lederle Labs. div. Am. Cyanamid Co., Pearl River, N.Y., 1974-76; mgr. fed. govt. affairs Lederle Labs. div. Am. Cyanamid Co., Washington, 1976-81; nat. sales mgr. hosp. div. Lederle Labs. div. Am. Cyanamid Co., Wayne, N.J., 1981-85, nat. sales mgr. oncology div., 1985-88; dir. govt. sales Lederle Labs. div. Am. Cyanamid Co., Fairfax, Va., 1988-95; pharmaceutical mktg. cons., 1995—; instr. U.S. Army Command & Gen. Staff Coll., Washington, 1977-81; govt. sales advisor Nat. Wholesale Drug Assn., Alexandria, Va., 1991; mem. Health Industry Fed. Adv. Coun., 1994. Editorial reviewer Mil. Medicine, 1992—; contbr. articles to profl. jours. Bd. dirs. Shadow Walk Devel. Assn., 1990—. Col. USAR. Instr. of Yr. USAR, 1979. Mem. Assn. Mil. Surgeons U.S. (chmn. sustaining mems. 1980-81, lectr. 1989), Am. Soc. Hosp. Pharmacists, Res. Officers Assn., Va. Tech. Soc. Alumni Assn. (bd. dirs.), Mil. Dist. of Washington Officers Club System. Republican. Methodist. Home and Office: 10415 Dominion Valley Dr Fairfax VA 22039-2415

SOWELL, DAVID S., III, internist, insurance company executive; b. Cleburne, Tex., Jan. 31, 1941; s. David S. Jr. and Esther Marrimon (Smith) S.; m. Claudia Ida Chambers, July 13, 1963; children: Laura Dennis, Elizabeth Sowell. BS, Abilene Christian Coll., 1962; MD, U. Tex. Southwest Med. Sch., 1966. Diplomate Am. Bd. Internal Medicine. Pvt. practice Dallas, 1972-87; asst. med. dir. Blue Cross Blue Shield of Tex., Dallas, 1987-91, v.p. corp. med. dir., 1991—. Lt. cmdr., surgeon USPHS, 1967-69. Fellow ACP; mem. AMA, Tex. Med. Assn. Mem. Ch. of Christ. Office: PO Box 660058 Dallas TX 75266-0058

SOWERS, AMELIA BARNET, speech and language pathologist; b. Houston, Mar. 13, 1952; d. Albert Glenn and Helen June (Meador) Barnet; m. George Vernon Sowers Jr., Aug. 23, 1975; children: George Vernon III, Adam Glenn. BA, U. Houston, 1975, MA, 1993. Lic. and cert. speech-lang. pathologist, Tex. Speech-lang. pathologist Aldine Ind. Sch. Dist., Houston, 1976-78, Tomball (Tex.) Ind. Sch. Dist., 1978-83, Conroe (Tex.) Ind. Sch. Dist., 1984-96; pvt. practice, 1996—. Bd. dirs. Crighton Players. Mem. NEA, Am. Speech, Lang. and Hearing Assn., Tex. Speech and Hearing Assn., Tex. Tchrs. Assn., Houston Assn. Comm. Disorders, Montgomery County Performing Arts Soc. (com.). Methodist. Home and Office: 25 Village Hill Dr Conroe TX 77304

SOWERS, GEORGE FREDERICK, civil engineer; b. Cleve., Sept. 23, 1921; s. George Bloomer and Marie (Tyler) S.; m. Frances Adair Lott, Apr. 29, 1944; children—Carol Adair, Janet, Nancy, George. B.S. in Civil Engring, Case Inst. Tech., 1942; M.S. in Civil Engring, Harvard, 1947. Registered civil engr., Ohio, Ga., N.C., Fla., Tenn., Va., Ala., Ariz.; registered geologist, Ga. Pvt. practice engring. with G. B. Sowers, Cleve., 1939-42; hydraulic engr. TVA, 1942-44, U.S. Navy, 1944-46; co-founder Law Engring. Inc., Atlanta, 1947-66; cons. engr., sr. v.p. Law Cos. Group, Inc.; Regents prof. civil engring. Ga. Inst. Tech., 1966-88, Regents prof. emeritus, 1988—; lectr. in field; cons. Resources Devel. Center of South East Asia, Roorkee, India, 1959, AID, 1966, Nat. Power Co. Indonesia, Duke Power Co., Ga. Power Co. Author: Soil Laboratory Manual, 1955, Earth and Rockfill Dam Engineering, 1961, Introductory Soil Mechanics and Foundations, 1951, 4th edit., 1979; co-author: Foundation Engineering, 1961; contbr. 140 articles to profl. jours. Recipient, Richard R. Torrens award American Soc. of Civil Engineers, 1995. Fellow Geol. Soc. Am.; mem. ASCE (hon.), Seismol. Soc. Am., Earthquake Engring. Inst., U.S. Nat. Soc. Soil Mechanics, Internat. Soc. Soil Mechanics (v.p.), Ga. Acad. Sci., Nat. Acad. Engring., Sigma Xi, Tau Beta Pi, Beta Theta Pi, Tau Kappa Alpha, Theta Tau. Home: 3031 Westminster Cir NW Atlanta GA 30327-1641 Office: 114 Townpark Dr Kennesaw GA 30144-5561

SOWERS, WESLEY HOYT, lawyer, management consultant; b. Whiting, Ind., Aug. 26, 1905; s. Samuel Walter and Bertha E. (Spurrier) S.; m. Gladys Krueger, Jan. 21, 1929; children: Penny (Mrs. David Buxton), Wesley Hoyt. BS, Purdue U., 1926, MS, 1927; JD, DePaul U., 1941; grad., Advanced Mgmt. Program, Harvard, 1960. Bar: Ill. 1940; registered patent atty. and practitioner ICC. Chemist Shell Oil Co., East Chicago, Ind., 1927-29; sales engr. Nat. Lead Co., St. Louis, 1929-31; lab. supr. patent atty. Pure Oil Co., Chgo., 1932-42; v.p. Bay Chem. Co., New Orleans, 1942-50, Frontier Chem. Co., Wichita, Kans., 1950-57; pres. Frontier Chem. div. Vulcan Materials Co., 1957-65; exec. v.p., dir. Vulcan Materials Co., Birmingham, 1958-65; mgmt. counsel, 1965—; mem. health professions vis. com. Wichita State U. Patentee in field. Past chmn. Met. Planning Commn., Wichita and Sedgwick County, 1958; commr. Kans. Econ. Devel. Bd.; chmn. Kansas Com. for Constitutional Revision, Sedgwick County U.S. Savs. Bonds Sales; past chmn. Kans. Radio Free Europe; past mem. adv. com. Kans. Geol. Survey; mem. Kans. Senate, 1970-81; former mem. engring. adv. council Sch. Engring. and Architecture, Kans. State U.; regent, trustee Wichita State U., HCA/Wesley Med. Ctr., Wichita; bd. dirs. Health Systems Agy. of Southeast Kans., Bd. of Health Sedgwick County, Inst. Logopedics, Quivira council Boy Scouts Am., YMCA, Health Systems Agy. S.E. Kans.; past trustee Midwest Research Inst.; mem. adv. bd. Kans. U. Bus. Sch.; vis. com. Coll. Health Profession, Wichita State U.; chmn. Kans. Health Care Providers Malpractice Commn.; mem. Kans. Health Care Costs Commn., Kans. Health Coordinating Council, Wichita/Sedgwick County Bd. Health; mem. gov.'s adv. commn. Kans. Dept. Health and Environment. Mem. AAAS, Kans. C. of C. (past pres., past dir.), Wichita C. of C. (past pres. 1959, past dir., Uncommon Citizen award 1988), Kans. Assn. Commerce and Industry (past pres., dir.), Am. Chem. Soc., AAAS, Smithsonian Assocs., Soc. Chem. Industry, Ill. Bar Assn., Wichita Bar Assn., Phi Delta Theta. Lodge: Rotary. Home and Office: care Canterbury Assisted Liv Ctr 1402 NW 122nd St Oklahoma City OK 73114

SOZIO, MARQUITA LYNELLE, travel manager, educator; b. Tulsa, May 9, 1949; d. C.F. and Paula Joanne McClung; m. Michael Allen Sozio, Nov. 24, 1990; children: Michelle Ann, Nicole Marie. BA, Oklahoma City U., 1981, MA, 1982. Cert. travel cons., cruise cons. Dir. travel program Draughon Coll., Oklahoma City, 1984-89; prof. tourism and hospitality Niagara (N.Y.) U., 1989-91; dir. ednl. tng. Omega World Travel Corp., Fairfax, Va., 1991-93; dir. nat. tng. U.S. Travel Corp., Arlington, Va., 1993-94; dir. travel mgmt. program Richland Coll., Dallas, 1995—; instr. continuing edn. Oklahoma City U., 1987-89; cons. Irwin Mirror Press, Riverton, Ill. Mem. AAUP, Am. Soc. Travel Agts., Internat. Assn. Exposition Mgmt., Meeting Profls. Internat., Coun. on Hospitality, Restaurant and Instl. Edn., Inst. Cert. Travel Agts., Soc. Travel and Tourism Educators, Profl. Women in Travel, Phi Sigma Iota, Eta Sigma Delta. Office: Richland Coll 14800 Abrams Rd Dallas TX 75243

SPAETH, DAVID HOLLINGSWORTH, corporate planner, consultant; b. Phila., Oct. 25, 1924; s. Albert David and Agnes (Hollingsworth) S.; m. Juanita Louise Hart, Nov. 23, 1945 (div. Aug., 1971); m. Carole Lane Putnam, Mar. 12, 1972; stepchildren: Dona, Terri, Lisa. BS in Agr., U. Ky., 1953; MS in Agrl. Econs., Mich. State U., 1961, PhD in Agr. Econs., 1962. Counry analyst U.S. Dept. Agr., Washington, 1962; economist U.S. Dept. Agr., Taipei, 1964-65; mgr. econ. devel. divsn. Spindletop Rsch. Inc., Lexington, Ky., 1962-64, 65-69; cons. Lexington, Ky., 1969-72; cons. to dir. Gateway Area Devel. Dist., Owingsville, Ky., 1972-74; v.p. branch mgr., airports planning Tolbert, Cox & Assocs., Columbia, S.C., 1974-80; ret., 1980; cmty. devel. trainer Summer Inst. Linguistics, Papua New Guinea, 1983-93; regional asst. dir. Summer Inst. Linguistics, Alotau, Papua New Guinea, 1993-95; internat. coord. for field planning Summer Inst. Linguistics, Dallas, 1995; mem. Gov.'s small mines adv. com., State of Ky., Frankfort, 1963-64. Author: Program Planning: A Process Approach, 1991, Transactional Economics, 1993. Sgt. U.S. Army, 1942-46. Mem. Am. Assn. Agrl. Economists. Presbyterian. Home and Office: 7500 W Camp Wisdom Rd Dallas TX 75236

SPAGNOLO, SAMUEL VINCENT, internist, pulmonary specialist, educator; b. Pitts., Sept. 3, 1939; s. Vincent Anthony and Mary Grace (Culotta) S.; m. Lucy Aleta Weyandt, June 20, 1961 (div. Feb., 1992); children: Samuel, Brad, Gregg. BA, Washington & Jefferson Coll., 1961; MD, Temple U., 1965. Diplomate Am. Bd. Internal Medicine, Bd. of Pulmonary Disease; active lic. physician in Fla., Calif., Md., D.C.; inactive Pa., Mass. Sr. resident in medicine VA Med. Ctr., Boston, 1969-70, chief resident in medicine, 1970-71; Harvard Clin. and Rsch. fellow in pulmonary diseases Mass. Gen. Hosp., Boston, 1971-72; asst. chief med. svc. VA Med. Ctr., Washington, 1972-75, acting chief med. svc., 1975-76, chief pulmonary disease sect., 1976-94; instr. in medicine Boston U. Sch. of Medicine, Tufts u. Sch. Medicine, Boston, 1970-71; clin. and rsch. fellow in pulmonary diseases Harvard U. Sch. of Medicine, Mass. Gen. Hosp., Boston, 1971-72; clin. asst. prof. medicine Georgetown U., Washington, 1975-77; asst. prof. medicine George Washington U. Sch. of Medicine and Health Scis., Washington, 1972-75, assoc. prof., 1975-81, prof. medicine, 1981—, dir. divsn. pulmonary diseases and allergy, 1978-93; assoc. chmn. dept. medicine George Washington U. Med. Ctr., Washington, 1986-89; cons. in pulmonary diseases The Washington Hosp. Ctr., Washington, D.C., 1977—, Will Rogers Inst., White Plains, N.Y., 1980—, U.S. Dept. Labor, Washington, 1980—, Walter Reed Army Med. Ctr., Washington, 1987; rep. Am. Coll. Chest Physicians to Am. Registry Pathology, Washington, 1981-92; numerous radio tv appearances on Health Oriented Programs; invited lectr. in U.S., Russia, Jordan; chmn., mem. many coms. George Washington U. Sch. of Medicine, George Washington Med. Ctr., VA Med. Ctr., Washington; med. chest cons. in attempted assasination of former Pres. Regan. Author: (books): Clinical Assessment of Patients with Pulmonary Disease, 1986; co-author: (with A.E. Medinger) Handbook of Pulmonary Emergencies, 1986, (with others) Handbook of Pulmonary Drug Therapy, 1993, (with Witorsch, P.) Air Pollution and Lung Disease in Adults, 1994; contbr. numerous articles to profl jours. including Med. Clin. N. Am., Chest, So. Med. Jour., Am. Jour. Cardiology, Jour. Am. Med. Assn., Clin. Rsch., Am. Rev. Respiratory Disease, Am. Lung Assn. Bull., Clin. Notes on Respiratory Diseases, Jour. Nuclear Medicine, Drug Therapy; presented abstracts at over 13 profl. meetings; reviewer for Chest, Am. Review Respiratory Diseases. Lt. cmmdr. U.S. Pub. Health Svc., 1966-68. Decorated Cavaliere in Order of Merit, Republic of Italy, 1983; nominated for Golden Apple award by med. students Geo. Washington Sch. of Medicine, Phila., 1977; recipient cert. appreciation D.C. Lung Assn., 1983. Fellow Am. Coll. Physicians (coun. critical care 1983-85), Am. Coll. Chest Physicians (gov. D.C., coun. of govs. 1989-96); mem. Am. Thoracic Soc. (exec. com. D.C. chpt. 1978, 85, 89, mem. adv. com. tuberculosis control, 1978-84, pres. D.C. chpt. 1981-83), Nat. Assn. VA Physicians (sec. 1987-89, v.p. 1989-91, pres. 1992—), Internat. Lung Found. (pres. 1991—). Office: Geo Washington U 2150 Pennsylvania Ave NW Washington DC 20037

SPAHN, JAMES FRANCIS, marketing professional; b. Dubuque, Iowa, Oct. 4, 1957; s. Ervin Henry and Denise Marie (Shuhert) S.; m. Beverly Joan Burns, Oct. 22, 1983. Grad., Brown Inst. Tech., 1977. Lic. real estate commn.; cert. mktg. dir. Mktg. dir. The Cafaro Co., Dubuque, 1979-80, The Herring Marathon Group, Dallas, 1980-83, Dusco Property Mgmt., Inc., Lancaster, Pa., 1983-87, Jim Wilson and Assocs., Montgomery, Ala., 1987—. Co-author: Operating Shopping Centers, 1984. Mem. Cen. Bus. Dist. Revitalization Task Force, Savannah, Ga., 1984-86, Transit Task Force, Savannah, 1985-86; bd. dirs. Conv. and Vis. Bur., Savannah, 1986-87. Recipient Addy awards Dubuque Advt. Club, 1980. Mem. Internat. Coun. Shopping Ctrs. (Maxi award 1982, Maxi finalist 1987, 89, 90, 94), Savannah Advt. Club (bd. dirs. 1984-87), Birmingham Advt. Club (Addy awards 1983-87, 89). Roman Catholic. Home: 7375 Thomas Hall Dr Trussville AL 35173-1851 Office: Jim Wilson & Assocs Inc 3000 Riverchase Galleria Birmingham AL 35244-2315

SPAIN, JACK HOLLAND, JR., lawyer; b. Greenville, N.C., Jan. 24, 1939; s. Jack Holland and Lucy Marie (Hardee) S.; m. Mary Elizabeth Rhamstine, May 9, 1964; children: John Hardee, Sidney Holland. AB, U. N.C., 1960; JD, Harvard U., 1963. Bar: Va. 1964, U.S. Dist. Ct. (ea. dist.) Va. 1964. Assoc. Hunton & Williams, Richmond, Va., 1964-71; ptnr. Hunton & Williams, Richmond, 1971—. Bd. dirs. Maymount Found., Richmond, 1975—, pres., 1980-82; mem. bd. elders 2d Presbyn. Ch., Richmond, City Dem. Com., Richmond; spl. counsel Local Govt. Com., Va. Constl. Revision Com. Lt. comdr. USN. Mem. ABA (chmn. taxation com., local govt. sect.), Va. Bar Assn., Richmond Bar Assn., Am. Coll. Bond Lawyers, Harvard U. Law Sch. Assn. Va. (pres.), Downtown Club (Richmond), Harvard Club (N.Y.C.), Phi Beta Kappa, Phi Eta Sigma, Phi Alpha Theta. Office: Hunton & Williams River Front Pla E Twr 951 E Byrd St Richmond VA 23219-4040

SPAIN, NETTIE EDWARDS (MRS. FRANK E. SPAIN), civic worker; b. Alexandria, La., Oct. 9, 1918; d. John Henry and Sallie Tamson (Donald) Edwards; student Alexandria Bus. Coll., 1936-37, Birmingham-So. Coll., 1958-59, Nat. Tng. Inst., United Community Funds and Councils Am., 1965-66; m. Frank E. Spain, May 18, 1974. Reporter, Alexandria Daily Town Talk, 1942-45; staff writer Birmingham (Ala.) Post, 1945-49; pub. rels. dir. Community Chest, Birmingham, 1949-53; dir. info. services Pa. United Fund, Phila., 1953-55; asst. exec. dir. Ala. Assn. Mental Health, Birmingham, 1956-57; pub. rels. dir. United Appeal, Birmingham, 1958-68, asst. exec. dir., 1968-71; asst. to pres. for devel. U. Ala., Birmingham, 1971-74, acting dir., 1975. Mem. pub. rels. com. Ala. Heart Assn., Birmingham, 1972-75; bd. dirs. Kate Duncan Smith DAR Sch., Grant, Ala., 1981-82; bd. dirs. Children's Aid Soc., 1971-77, 79, v.p., 1976-77; bd. dirs. Jefferson-Shelby Lung Assn., 1972-75, Vol. Bur. Greater Birmingham, 1973-77, Hale County chpt. ARC, Hale County Library; advisor fin. Hale County Library Bd., 1988; adv. com. Jr. League, 1974-75; exec. com. Historic Hale County Preservation Soc.; hon. mem. president's council U. Ala., Birmingham; bd. dirs. Norton Center Continuing Edn., Birmingham-So. Coll., mem. Edward Lee Norton Bd. Advisers for Mgmt. and Profl. Edn., internat. progam com.; charter mem. bd. Birmingham Children's Theater. Recipient 1st Place awards Nat. Photos for Fedn., 1966-67; citation Pa. United Fund, 1955, citation for service Jefferson-Shelby Lung Assn., 1975, citation Ala. Heart Assn., 1974, Vol. Bur. Greater Birmingham, 1977; award of Merit, Ala. Hist. Commn., 1977, Disting. Svc. award, 1987; Rotary Found. Paul Harris fellow; Benjamin Franklin fellow Royal Soc. Arts, London, U.S.A.; citation Veritas Club, Gt. Am. Citizen of Greensboro, Ala., 1987. Mem. Nat. Pub. Rels. Council of Health and Welfare Services (bd. dir. 1967-69), Birmingham Women's Com. of 100, Pub. Rels. Council Ala. (hon. life), Order of Crown in Am., Ala. Hist. Soc., Nat. Soc. Colonial Dames Am., English Speaking Union, Nat. Trust for Historic Preservation, Met. Opera Guild, Guy E. Snavely Soc. (Birmingham-So. Coll.), Colonial Dames Am., DAR, First Families of Va., Burgess for Ala., Birmingham Astron. Soc. (hon.), Children's Aid Foundation (charter mem). Episcopalian. Clubs: Lakeview Country (Greensboro, Ala.), Mountain Brook Country, The Summit (Birmingham), The Club (Birmingham), Northriver Yacht (Tuscaloosa), Mountain Brook Club (Birmingham). Home: Medley PO Box 400 Greensboro AL 36744-0400

SPAIN, STEVE RANDALL, secondary school educator; b. South Boston, Va., May 16, 1968; s. Steve Randall Sr. and Gloria Gale (Adcock) S. Student, Campbell U., 1986-88; BA in English Edn., Longwood Coll., 1990, MA in English, 1992. Cert. tchr., Va. English instr., forensic coach Mecklenburg County Pub. Schs., Boydton, Va., 1992-93, libr., debate coach, 1994; adj. prof. English Southside Va. C.C., Alberta, 1992-93, Ctrl. Tex. Coll., Norfolk, Va., 1995—; English instr. Randolph-Macon Acad., Front Royal, Va., 1994-95; English instr., forensic judge Colonial Heights (Va.) City Schs., 1995—; forensic judge Va. H.S. League, Charlottesville, 1992-94. Contbr. poetry to profl. publs. All-Am. scholar USAA, 1990; Lee-Jackson Found. grantee, 1996. Mem. MLA, Nat. Coun. Tchrs. English, Nat. Adj. Faculty Guild, Mable Powell English Club (projects chair 1987), Lambda Iota Tau (pres. 1990, life mem.), Alpha Phi Omega (pub. rels. com. 1987-88, projects chair 1987, life mem.).

SPAIN, THOMAS B., retired state supreme court justice. Justice Ky. Supreme Ct, Frankfort, 1991-95; ret., 1995.

SPANGELO, BRYAN LEE, biochemist, chemistry educator; b. Great Falls, Mont., Oct. 17, 1954; s. Noel James and Dorothy Ethel (Gillis) S.; m. Erin Kathleen Eads, Jan. 20, 1977; children: Eric Noel, Seth Gordon. BS in Chemistry-Biology, Keene State Coll., 1980; PhD in Biochemistry, George Washington U., 1986. Traineeship dept. medicine U. Va. Health Scis. Ctr., Divsn. Endocrinology, 1985-86, fellowship, 1986-88, rsch. asst. prof. dept. medicine, 1988-91; asst. prof. dept. physiology Med. U. S.C., 1991-94; assoc. prof. dept. chemistry U. Nev., Las Vegas, 1994—; teaching asst. dept. biochemistry The George Washington U. Med. Ctr., Washington, 1985; adj. instr. dept. natural scis. Trident Tech. Coll., Charleston, 1993-94; ad hoc reviewer NIH, Divsn. Rsch. Grants, Endocrinology Study Sect.; mem. dissertation examining coms. Med. U. S.C. and George Washington U., 1992; mem. grad. program com. dept. physiology Med. U. S.C., 1992-94; others; lectr. and presenter in field. Mem. editorial bd. Progress in NeuroEndocrinImmunology, 1990-92, NeuroImmunoModulation, 1995—; ad hoc jour. reviewer Endocrinology, Immunology Today, Jour. Endocrinology, Life Scis., others; contbr. articles to profl. jours., chpts. to books. With U.S. Army, 1973-76. Recipient Nat. Rsch. Svc. award USPHS, 1985-86, Nat. Rsch. Svc. award Nat. Cancer Inst., NIH, 1986-88, Travel grants Endocrine Soc., 1986, 88, Fifth Internat. Congress on Prolactin, Kyoto, Japan, 1988; grantee FIDIA Pharm., Washington, 1987, 89, NIH, 1990-96, Cultural and Ednl. Bur. of Embassy of Arab Republic of Egypt, Washington, 1992. Mem. AAAS, Endocrine Soc. Methodist. Office: U Nev Las Vegas Dept Chem 4505 S Maryland Pkwy Las Vegas NV 89154-9900

SPANGENBERG, DOROTHY BRESLIN, biology educator; b. Galveston, Tex., Aug. 31, 1931; d. William Aloysius and Louise Margaret (Poole) Breslin; m. Ronald Wesley Spangenberg, May 31, 1958; 1 child, Laurel Jane. BA, U. Tex., 1956, MA, 1958, PhD, 1960. Rsch. assoc. U. Ark. Med. Cen., Little Rock, 1962-65; assoc. prof. Little Rock U., 1965-66; rsch. scholar Ind. U., 1966-69; assoc. prof. U. Louisville sch. Dentistry, 1970-72, vis. assoc. prof. U. Colo., Boulder, 1972-77; assoc. prof. Eastern Va. Med. Sch., Norfolk, 1977-82, rsch. prof., 1982—. Prin. investigator JellyFish-in-Space Experiments, 1991, 94. Grantee, NSF, 1964-66, NIH 1966-79, Child Health and Human Devel. 1966-76, U.S. Dept. Energy, 1977-82, NASA, 1984—. Mem. Am. Soc. Zoologists, AIBS, Am. Soc. Cell Biologists, Electron Microscopy Soc. Am., AAAS, Am. Soc. Gravity and Space Biology, Soc. for Invitro Biology, Sigma Xi. Episcopalian. Contbr. articles to profl. jours. Home: 6085 River Cres Norfolk VA 23505-4706 Office: Eastern Va Med Sch Norfolk VA 23501

SPANGLER, CLEMMIE DIXON, JR., academic administrator; b. Charlotte, N.C., Apr. 5, 1932; s. Clemmie Dixon and Veva C. (Yelton) S.; m. Meredith Jane Riggs, June 25, 1960; children: Anna Wildy, Abigail Riggs. BS, U. N.C., 1954; MBA, Harvard U., 1956; LHD (hon.), Queens Coll., 1985; LLD (hon.), Davidson Coll., 1986, Furman U., 1993. Pres. C.D. Spangler Constrn. Co., Charlotte, 1958-86, Golden Eagle Industries, Inc., 1968-86; chmn. bd. Bank of N.C., Raleigh, 1973-82; dir. NCNB Corp., 1983-86; chmn. N.C. Bd. Edn., 1982-86; pres. U. N.C., Chapel Hill, 1986—; bd. dirs. BellSouth Corp., Atlanta; chmn. bd. dirs. Nat. Gypsum Co., Charlotte. Past deacon Myers Park Bapt. Ch., vice-chmn. Charlotte-Mecklenburg Bd. Edn., Charlotte, 1972-76, So. Regional Edn. Bd., 1987—; past trustee Charlotte Nature Mus., Charlotte Symphony Orch., Crozer Theol. Sem.; past chmn. Charlotte adv. bd. Salvation Army; past bd. dirs. YMCA, Equitable Life Assurance Soc., Jefferson-Pilot Corp.; pres. bd. trustees Mint Mus. Art; bd. dirs. Union Theol. Sem., 1985-90, Assocs. Harvard Bus. Sch. With U.S. Army, 1956-58. Recipient Liberty Bell award Mecklenburg County Bar Assn., 1985, Alumni Achievement award Harvard Bus. Sch., 1988. Mem. Assn. Am. Univs., Bus. Higher Edn. Forum, Harvard Club (N.Y.C.), Univ. Club (N.Y.C.), Quail Hollow Country Club (Charlotte). Office: U NC Gen Adminstrn Office of President PO Box 2688 Chapel Hill NC 27515-2688

SPANGLER, DENNIS LEE, physician; b. Akron, Ohio, Nov. 8, 1947; s. Wesley Daniel and Florence Adele (Smith) S.; m. July 7, 1972; children: Mathew Brian, Adam Christopher. BS, U. Akron, 1969; MD, Ohio State Med. Sch., 1973. Diplomate Am. Bd. Pediatrics, Am. Bd. Allergy and Immunology. Intern U. Fla. Med. Sch., Gainesville, 1973-74; resident U. Fla. Med. Sch., 1974-75, fellow allergy and clin. immunology, 1975-77; pvt. practice Atlanta Allergy Clinic, P.A., 1977—; dir. chronic lung clinic Ga. Bur. Crippled Children; asst. clin. prof. pediatrics Med. Coll. of Ga. Past pres., bd. dirs. midwest branch Ga. Lung Assn., Atlanta, 1981-82, med. adv. com., 1978—; pres. Fla. Pediatric Alumni Assn., Gainesville, 1985-86. Fellow Am. Acad. Pediatrics, Am. Acad. Allergy and Immunology, Am. Coll. Allergy (therapeutics com. 1983-88, chmn. drug and anaplylaxis Com. 1988—, chmn. com. 1987—, Am. Assn. Cert. Allergists (bd. govs. 1988—); mem. Am. Thoracic Soc., Ga. Med. Assn., Cobb County Med. Soc., Southeastern Allergy Assn., Cherokee Country Club. Roman Catholic. Office: Atlanta Allergy Clinic 1965 N Park Pl NW Atlanta GA 30339-2001

SPANN, BAXTER, design company executive. V.p. Finger Dye Spann, Inc. Address: # 213 1001 S Dairy Ashford Houston TX 77077

SPANN, LAURA NASON, data processing executive; b. Columbus, Ga., Aug. 5, 1947; d. Albert Dewey and Edith Maureen (Miller) Nason; m. George William Spann, June 10,1967; children: Tanya Lynne, Stephen William. BA in Math., Ga. State Coll., Atlanta, 1969. Programmer, analyst Coastal States Life Insur. Co., Atlanta, 1969-71, Rollins, Inc., Atlanta, 1972-73, Computech. Systems, Inc., Atlanta, 1975-77; private practice systems programming cons. Atlanta, 1977-81; pres., prin. Exec. Data Systems, Inc., Atlanta, 1981—. Troop leader Girl Scouts U.S., Atlanta, 1982-90; den leader Boy Scouts Am., Atlanta, 1987-92. Mem. Alpha Lambda Delta. Office: Exec Data Systems Inc Bldg 27 1640 Powers Ferry Rd Ste 300 Marietta GA 30067-5485

SPANN, RONALD THOMAS, lawyer; b. Chgo., Aug. 27, 1949; s. Daniel Anthony and Lorraine Marie (Gervasio) S. Student Sophia U., Tokyo, 1969, St. Mary's Coll., Rome, 1970; AB, U. Notre Dame, 1971; postgrad. Fordham U., diploma internat. trade law U. Fla., Inst. State and Law, Warsaw, Poland, 1976, Trinity Coll., Cambridge U., 1976; JD, John Marshall Law Sch., Chgo., 1977. Bar: Ill. 1977, D.C. 1980, U.S. Dist. Ct. (no. dist.) Ill., U.S. Ct. Appeals (7th cir.), N.Y. 1984, Fla. 1984, U.S. Dist. Ct. (so. dist.) Fla., U.S. Supreme Ct., U.S. Ct. Appeals (11th cir.) Fla., 1985; lic. real estate and mortgage broker. Assoc. solicitor U.S. Dept. Labor; trial atty. EEOC; law clk. to chief judge U.S. Dist. Ct. (no. dist.) Ill.; lobbyist Trade Assn. Execs. Food Industry, Ill., D.C., Va., Baker & McKenzie, Chgo., 1972-74; ptnr. Newman & Spann, Chgo.; sr. ptnr. Spann & Assocs., P.A., Miami, Berk, Spann & Bernstein, Fort Lauderdale, Fla.; pres. Soc. Profls. In Dispute Resolutions; mediation dir. Fla. Mediation Svc., U.S. Mediation Assn., Am. Arbitration Assn.; dir. Christian Legal Svc., Fla. Acad. Cert. Mediators; prof. Internat. Career Inst.; Instr. Ednl. Seminars, Inc. Bd. dirs. Edgewater Community Council, Advs. for Human Rights; corr. Amnesty Internat., U.S.A.; co-founder AID-Ctr. One, Lamda Legal Def. and Edn. Fund, Inc. Recipient Real Estate Rehabilitator award Chgo. City Council, 1981, Internat. Disting. Leadership award. Mem. ABA (former chmn. internat. human rights com., draft Model "Whistleblower" and mcpl. civil rights codes, chmn. internat. human rights. com.), Chgo. Bar Assn., Fed. Bar Assn. (former bd. dirs. Chgo. chpt.), Assn. Trial Lawyers Am., Christian Legal Soc., Lawyers in Mensa, Fla. Bar Assn., Broward County Bar Assn., Nat. Assn. Realtors, Assn. Mortgage Bankers (former chair alt. dispute resolution com.), Soc. Profl. Dispute Resolution (chair Fla. chpt., pres.), Nat. Acad. of Certified Mediators. Home: PO Box 1799 Fort Lauderdale FL 33302-1799 Office: 1600 SE 17th St Fort Lauderdale FL 33316-1717

SPANNAGEL, ALAN WAYNE, physiologist; b. Harlingen, Tex., May 9, 1958; s. Billy Wayne and Ersel Lou (Jones) S.; m. Kathy Lynn Lang, 1980 (div. 1982); m. Maristella Partin, 1987 (div. 1988). BS in Marine Biology, Tex. A&M U., 1980; MS in Biology, U. Houston, Clear Lake City, 1985; postgrad., U. Tex. Health Sci. Ctr., San Antonio. Rsch. technician dept. surgery U. Tex. Med. Br., Galveston, 1981-85, rsch. assoc., 1985-87; grad.

rsch. asst. dept. physiology U. Tex. Health Sci. Ctr., San Antonio, 1987—; instr., lectr. Physiology for Occupl. Therapy Students, 1990-93; reviewer and cons. on Physiol. Studies. Contbr. articles to profl. sci. jours. Mem. Am. Pancreatic Assn. Home: 154 Barbara Bend Universal City TX 78148 Office: Univ Tex Health Sci Ctr Dept of Physiology 7703 Floyd Curl Dr San Antonio TX 78284

SPANNAUS, NANCY BRADEEN, political newspaper editor; b. Portland, Maine, Dec. 13, 1943; d. Donald William and Mary Louise (Towle) Bradeen; m. Edward Wise Spannaus, Aug. 24, 1968; children: Michael (dec.), Andrew. BA, Bryn Mawr Coll., 1965; MSW, Columbia U., 1967. Social worker City of New York, 1968-70; editor in-chief New Solidarity newspaper, Campaigner Publs., N.Y.C., 1974-87; editor-in-chief The New Federalist, Sterling, Va., 1987—; mem. editorial bd. Exec. Intelligence Rev., Washington. Co-author: The Political Economy of the American Revolution, 1977, 2d edit., 1996. Mem. exec com. Nat. Caucus of Labor Coms., 1971—; pres. U.S. br. Club of Life, 1982—; ind. candidate U.S. Senate from Va., 1990, ind. candidate for Gov. of Va., 1993; candidate for Dem. nomination to U.S. Senate from Va., 1994; founder Defeat that Son-of-a-Bush Com., 1994; candidate for Dem. nomination to U.S. Senate from Va., 1996; exec. dir. FDR-PAC. Office: The New Federalist PO Box 889 Leesburg VA 22075-0889

SPARKES, CHERYL FLOWERS, accountant; b. Texarkana, Ark., July 31, 1956; d. Charles Glendon and Mary Carolyn (Caldwell) Flowers; m. Jay Bedford Sparkes, July 14, 1984. BSBA, U. Ark., 1978. CPA, Tex., CMA. Staff acct. Ernst & Ernst, Dallas, 1978-80; sr. acct. Ernst & Whinney, Dallas, 1980-82, mgr., 1983-84, sr. mgr., 1984-89; sr. mgr. Ernst & Young, Dallas, 1989-94, fin. adv. svcs. regional dir. human resources, 1993-95, ptnr., cons. dispute resolution & litigation svcs., 1994-95; with Ernst & Young, N.Y.C., 1995—. Chmn. Nat. Edn. Com., 1996—; neighborhood capt. Am. Cancer Soc., Dallas, 1990-92; active Dallas Mus. Art, 1985-95, Jr. League Dallas, 1990-95. Mem. AICPA, Inst. Mgmt. Accts., Tex. Soc. CPAs, Delta Delta Delta. Home: 250 E 54th St Apt 9C New York NY 10022 Office: Ernst & Young LLP 787 7th Ave New York NY 10019

SPARKMAN, GLENDA KATHLEEN, librarian, educator; b. Rockwood, Tenn., Sept. 2, 1941; d. James Monroe and Nannie Mae (Ledford) Lawson; m. Clifford Gregory Anderson Jr., June 7, 1966 (dec. 1985); m. Mickey Max Sparkman, Jan. 1, 1987. BA, David Lipscomb U., Nashville, 1963; MLS, George Peabody Coll., 1965. Music librarian David Lipscomb U., Nashville, 1964-67; ref. librarian Ft. Lauderdale (Fla.) Pub. Libr., 1967-68; sch. librarian Phyllis Wheatley Sch., Childersburg, Ala., 1968-69; asst. librarian Harcum Jr. Coll., Bryn Mawr, Pa., 1969-70; head of processing ctr. and cataloger Lower Merion Libr. Assn., Bryn Mawr, Pa., 1970-80; ref. librarian Bala Cynwyd Libr., 1981-82; cataloger, acquisitions librarian Barry U., Miami Shores, Fla., 1982-83, head of tech. svcs., 1983-86; head catalog librarian, asst. prof. Baylor U., Waco, Tex., 1986-96; head preservation and spl. svcs., asst. prof. Baylor U., Waco, 1996—. Reviewer books for Libr. Jour., 1989—. Mem. Miami Shores Fine Arts Commn., 1984-86, Historic Waco Found., 1986—. Mem. ALA, Assn. of Coll. and Rsch. Librs., Assn. for Libr. Collections and Tech. Svcs., Tex. Libr. Assn. (Coll. and Univ. Librs. div.), AAUP, AAUW, Soc. Am. Archivists.

SPARKMAN, LILA GILLIS, healthcare facility administrator; b. Cumby, Tex., Feb. 24, 1930; d. William Paul and Cora (Caviness) Gillis; m. Alton C. Sparkman, July 26, 1947; children: Claudia, Vivian, Alan. BS summa cum laude in Social Work, East Tex. State U., 1978, MA, 1980; postgrad. U. Tex., Tyler, 1982; PhD in Clin. Sociology, U. N. Tex. Cert. social worker, mental retardation diagnostic and evaluation specialist, mental retardational profl. Prof. sociology Paris (Tex.) Jr. Coll., 1980; coordinator geriatric services Sabine Valley Regional Mental Health-Mental Retardation Ctr., Marshall, Tex., 1980-82, adminstr. Mental Retardation Residential Homes, Longview, Tex., 1983—; clin. dir. Hunt County Family Svcs. Ctr., Greenville, Tex., 1987; pvt. clin. practice, Winnsboro, Tex., 1989—; sec.-treas. KAM Well Service, New London, Tex., 1981—; social work cons. Forest Acres, Longview, 1983. Author: Comparison of Traditional and Non-traditional Female Students and Their Perceived Reasons for University Attendance, 1980 co-author: Day Care Centers for the Elderly: An Alternative, 1983. Mem. Am. Sociol. Assn., Nat. Assn. Social Workers, Mid South Sociol. Assn., Pub. Health Assn., Alpha Kappa Delta, Alpha Chi, Cap and Gown. Democrat. Methodist. Lodge: Rebekah. Home: PO Box 529 Winnsboro TX 75494-0529

SPARKMAN, MARY M., medical, surgical and rehabilitation nurse; b. Ft. Leavenworth, Kans., Jan. 8, 1949; d. Ancil Woodrow and Margaret Louise (Conners) Hopper; m. Paul Aus Sparkman, Oct. 5, 1989; children: Michelle Marie Bingham, Andrea Marlene Bingham. Student, Cameron U., Lawton, Okla., 1980-82; BSN with distinction, U. Okla., 1984. Cert. in chemotherapy, fetal monitoring, arterial blood gases, coronary care, CPR instr. Mem. crisis intervention team Gt. Plains Hosp., Lawton; charge nurse spinal cord unit O'Donoghue Rehab. Inst., Oklahoma City; clin. nurse Lawton Indian Hosp., USPHS; therapy coord. Infusion Svcs., Lawton, Okla.; clin. nurse, charge nurse Reynold's Army Community Hosp., Ft. Sill, Okla. With U.S. Army, 1970-73. Mem. Nat. League Nursing, Okla. Nurses Assn., Golden Key, Phi Kappa Phi. Office: PO Box 2094 Lawton OK 73502-2094

SPARKMAN, RICHARD DALE, lawyer, author; b. Daytona Beach, Fla., Oct. 14, 1940; s. Guy R. and Helen Erline (Easterly) S.; m. Gail Winston Carol Lindequist (div. 1989); children: Cassandra, Eric. AS, Daytona Beach C.C., 1964; BA in Polit. Sci., Fla. State U., 1966; postgrad., Stetson U., 1969; JD, Samford U., 1973. Bar: Fla., U.S. Supreme Ct. Asst. county atty. Collier County, Fla., 1973, 74; ptnr. Sparkman & Quinn, Naples, Fla., 1974—. Author: Failed Justice, 1996 (Edison award, 1996). Dem. candidate for U.S. Ho. of Reps., 1980. With U.S. Army, 1960-63. Mem. Exptl. Aircraft Assn. Office: Sparkman & Quinn 307 Airport Rd N Naples FL 33942

SPARKS, ASA HOWARD, psychotherapist, educator; b. Gordonsville, Tenn., Mar. 16, 1937; s. Asa Hill and Pansy V. Sparks; children: Libbie, Dean, Lori. AB, Trevecca Coll., Nashville, 1958; MDiv, Christian Theol. Inst., Charlotte, N.C., 1972; DD, Emmanuel Bible Coll., Nashville, 1975; MA, U. Ala., 1976, Cert. Advanced Studies, 1978; PhD, Columbia Pacific U., 1986. Speech tchr. Ala.; exec. dir. Crossroads Youth Ctr., Decatur, Ala., 1975-89; edn. specialist in counseling Ala. Dept. Edn., 1989—; pres. Voluntary Action Ctr., Decatur. Author: Illustrations from Science, 1969, God Says I'm OK, 1976, Hope for the Frogs, 1979, The Two Minute Lover, 1989; psychology columnist Decatur Daily and Montgomery Advertiser; editor The Toonerville Collector; contbr. articles to mags. and newspapers. Pres. Decatur Arts Coun.; chmn. Decatur Foster Grandparents Assn., 1979-81. Mem. NEA, ASCD, Internat. Legion of Intelligence (exec. dir. 1989-91), Ala. Speakers' Assn. (pres. 1987, Speaker of Yr. 1988), Decatur C. of C., Kappa Delta Pi. Home: 6045 Camelot Ct Montgomery AL 36117-2555 Office: Persons Office Bldg Ala Dept Edn PO Box 302101 Montgomery AL 36130

SPARKS, HUGH CULLEN, university official; b. Galveston, Tex., Sept. 3, 1946; s. Frank Hubert and Genevieve Elwyn (Clark) S.; m. Kay Rivers Sparks, Dec. 4, 1982; children: Steven J. Walla, Elise Sparks. Student, San Jacinto Coll., 1964-66; MusB with honors, U. Tex., Austin, 1969, MusM, 1971, PhD, 1984. Mng. performer Wilding Showband, Hollywood, Calif., 1973-75; owner Sparks Musical Svcs., Austin, 1970—, Ursa Major Prodns., Austin, 1975—; dir. ops. dept. music Dept. Music U. Tex., Austin, 1977-89, dir. devel. and pub. rels., 1989—; cons. Entertainment Industry, 1974—; tchr. assorted festivals and workshops, 1985—. Author: An Investigation of the Emphasis on New Music in Current College Curricula, 1971, Stylistic Development and Compositional Processes of Selected Solo Singer/Songwriters in Austin, Texas, 1984; (with others) Groves Dictionary of American Music, 1985. Mem. The Music Umbrella of Austin, Inc., 1982—, pres., 1985-86; mem. The Austin Chamber Music Ctr., Inc., 1987—, v.p., 1987-94, pres., 1994—; co-founder The Austin Folk Music Found., Inc., 1981. Rsch. grantee U. Tex., 1978, 80. Mem. Am. Fedn. Musicians, Phi Mu Alpha (pres. chpt. 1968), Phi Kappa Phi, Pi Kappa Lambda. Democrat. Home: 3810 Hidden Holw Austin TX 78731-1511 Office: U Tex Sch Music MRH 30832 Austin TX 78712

SPARKS, MEREDITH PLEASANT (MRS. WILLIAM J. SPARKS), lawyer; b. Palestine, Ill.; d. John L. and Laura (Bicknell) Pleasant; A.B. with distinction, Ind. U., 1927, A.M., 1928; Ph.D., U. Ill., 1936; J.D., Rutgers U., 1958; m. William J. Sparks, Dec. 31, 1930 (dec.); children—Ruth Sparks Foster, Katherine Sparks Crowl, Charles, John. Tchr. chemistry Rochester (Ind.) High Sch., 1928-29; chemist DuPont Co., Niagara Falls, N.Y., 1929-34, Northam Warren Co., N.Y.C., 1939; chem. patent agt. Am. Cyanamid Co., Bound Brook N.J., 1941-46; bars: Fla. 1958, U.S. Ct. Appeals (fed. cir.), U.S. Dist. Ct. (so. dist.) Fla., U.S. Supreme Ct.; patent agt., 1946-58; patent atty., 1958—; pres. Sparks Innovators, Inc., 1979-84. Recipient Disting. Alumni award Coll. Arts & Scis. Ind. U., 1987. Mem. AAUW (Phoenix award Miami chpt. 1990), ABA, Assn. Ind. U. Chemists (pres. 1950-51), Internat. Bar Assn., Fla. Bar Assn., Coral Gables Bar Assn., Am. Patent Law Assn., N.J. Patent Law Assn., South Fla. Patent Law Assn., Internat. Patent and Trademark Assn., Am. Chem. Soc., Nat. Assn. Women Lawyers (pres. 1981-82), U. Ill. Pres. Council (life, homecoming honoree 1984), Phi Beta Kappa, Sigma Xi, Kappa Delta. Club: Zonta, Riviera Country (Coral Gables). Contbr. articles to profl. jours. Patentee in field. Home: 5129 Granada Blvd Miami FL 33146-2028

SPARKS, SAM, federal judge; b. 1939. BA, U. Tex., 1961, LLB, 1963. Aide Rep. Homer Thornberry, 1963; law clk. to Hon. Homer Thornberry U.S. Dist. Ct. (we. dist.) Tex., 1963-65; assoc. to ptnr., shareholder Hardie, Grambling, Sims & Galatzan (and successor firms), El Paso, Tex., 1965-91; dist. judge U.S. Dist. Ct. (we. dist.) Tex., 1991—. Fellow Am. Coll. Trial Lawyers, Tex. Bar Found. (life); mem. Am. Bd. Trial Advocates (advocate), State Bar Tex. Office: US Dist Ct Judge 200 W Eighth St Ste 100 Austin TX 78701-2333

SPARKS, SHERMAN PAUL, osteopathic physician; b. Toledo, Jan. 23, 1909; s. Earnest Melvin and Nancy Jane (Keller) S.; m. Helen Mildred Barnes, Aug. 1, 1930 (div. July 1945); 1 child, James Earl; m. Billie June Wester, Feb. 20, 1946 (dec. Apr. 1959); children: Randal Paul, Robert Dale; m. Joyce Marie Sparks, Jan. 23, 1965 (dec.); 1 child, David Paul. BS, U. Ill., 1932, MS, 1938; DO, Kirksville Coll. Osteopathy and Surgery, 1945. Diplomate Am. Bd. Osteo. Medicine. Tchr. high schs., Kincaid, Pesotum, Mt. Olive, Ill., 1930-42; intern Sparks Hosp. and Clinic, Dallas, 1945-46; pvt. practice, Rockwall, Tex., 1946-95; part-time cons., sci. rschr., ret.; team physician Rockwall High Sch., 1946-78; med. examiner Am. Cancer Soc., Rockwall, 1946-76. Coord. CD, Rockwall, 1946-80; chmn. Rockwall Centennial Assn., 1954, Rockwall County Rep. Com., 1964-78; pres. Rockwall PTA, 1961. Recipient Spirit of Tex. award, TV sta., Dallas, 1985; named Hon. State Farmer, Future Farmer's Am., 1980. Mem. Am. Coll. Gen. Practitioners, Tex. Osteo. Med. Assn. (chmn. chmn. 1946-54, numerous offices), Rockwall C. of C. (pres. 1961), SAR (pres. Plano chpt. 1989), Masons, Psi Sigma Alpha, Alpha Phi Omega. Home: 1405 Ave L Galveston TX 77550

SPEAKER, SUSAN JANE, lawyer; b. Dallas, Dec. 25, 1946; d. William R. and Jane E. (Aldrich) Turner; m. David C. Speaker, Dec. 21, 1968; children: David Allen, Melissa. BA, U. Ark., 1970, JD, 1985. Bar: Okla. 1985, U.S. Dist. Ct. (no., ea. and we. dists.) Okla. 1985. Assoc. Hall, Estill, Hardwick, Gable, Golden & Nelson, P.C., Tulsa, 1985-91; atty. Resolution Trust Corp., 1991-92; shareholder Speaker & Matthews, P.C., 1992-96; atty. Comml. Fin. Svcs., Inc., Tulsa, 1996—. Editor U. Ark. Law Rev., 1983-85. Mem. ABA, Okla. Bar Assn., Tulsa Bar Assn., Assn. Trial Lawyers Am., Phi Beta Kappa, Delta Theta Phi.

SPEAKS, JOHN THOMAS, JR., cultural consultant; b. Oceanside, Calif., Apr. 27, 1945; s. John Thomas and Martha Vivien (Banks) S.; m. Linda Gail Cohn, July 20, 1968; children: John III, Jacob. BA, Harvard U., 1968. Pres. John Speaks and Assocs., Atlanta, 1968-74; v.p. Onyx Corp., Atlanta, 1974-78, pres., 1978-79; pres., chief exec. officer OCI Cos., Atlanta, 1979—. Bd. dirs. Nat. Orgn. Men Against Sexism, Pitts., 1983-88, chair, 1985-88; bd. dirs. Men Stopping Violence, Atlanta, 1988-90. Mem. Burns Club Atlanta, Friends of Zoo Atlanta, Nature Conservancy, Cultural Survival, Survival Internat. Democrat.

SPEAR, ANDREA ASHFORD, principal, educator; b. Peterboro, N.H., Apr. 26, 1947; d. Ernest Hartwell and Sylvia Inez (Sawyer) Ashford; divorced; children: William Ernest, Cara Lyn. BS in Music Edn., U. N.H., 1970; MS in Spl. Edn., Radford U., 1977. Cert. music, severely emotionally handicapped, edn. adminstrn. Tchr. emotionally disturbed Montgomery County Schs., Blacksburg, Va., 1977, Hampton (Va.) City Schs., 1977-79, Augusta County Schs., Fishersville, Va., 1979-80, Rockbridge County Schs., Lexington, Va., 1980-82; tchr. learning disabilities Montgomery County Schs., Blacksburg, 1982-83; tchr. emotionally disturbed Pulaski (Va.) County Schs., 1983-85; tchr. BEH Thompson Children's Home, Charlotte, N.C., 1985-87, prin., tchr. BEH, 1987-93; tchr. BEH Mt. Pleasant Middle Sch., Cabarrus County Schs., Concord, N.C., 1993-94; cognitive edn. specialist Charlotte (N.C.) Inst. Rehab., 1994—. Deacon Presbyn. Ch., Charlotte, 1987-90. Mem. ASCD, Coun. for Exceptional Children, Coun. for Children with Behavioral Disorders, Soc. for Cognitive Rehab. Republican. Home: 8123 H Tremaine Ct Charlotte NC 28227 Office: Charlotte Inst Rehab 1100 Blythe Blvd Charlotte NC 28203

SPEAR, HAROLD CHARLES, physician, thoracic/cardiovascular surgeon; b. N.Y.C., Sept. 29, 1923; s. Harold and Helen (Baker) S.; m. Suzanne Bowmall, June 10, 1947; children: Laurinda Spear Fort, Alison Spear Gómez, Harold C. III. BS, Yale U., 1944; MD, Harvard U., 1947. Diplomate Am. Bd. Surgery, Am. Bd. Thoracic Surgery. Intern St. Lukes/Roosevelt Hosp., N.Y.C., 1947-48; asst. resident in surgery Yale-New Haven (Conn.) Med. Ctr., 1948-50; fellow in surgery Mayo Clinic, Rochester, Minn., 1950-51; sr. asst. resident in surgery, Yale-New Haven Med. Ctr., 1953-54, chief resident in surgery, 1954-56; ptnr. thoracic surg. group Daughtry, Chesney, Spear, Gentsch, Larson, Traad and Wu, Miami, Fla., 1956-71; sr. ptnr. thoracic surg. group Spear, Wu and Lipman, Miami, Fla., 1971-90; med. dir. Vascular Lab. North Shore Med. Ctr., 1990—. Contbr. articles to books and profl. jours. Chmn. bd. trustees North Shore Med. Ctr., Miami, 1981-83. Capt. USAF, 1951-53. Fellow Am. Coll. Surgeons; mem. Am. Assn. Thoracic Surgeons (sr. mem.), Soc. Thoracic Surgeons (founding mem.), So. Thoracic Surg. Assn. (sr. mem.). Republican. Home: 5500 Collins Ave # 1104 Miami Beach FL 33140 Office: North Shore Med Ctr Vascular Lab 1100 NW 95th St Miami FL 33150-2038

SPEAR, SCOTT JAY, physician; b. Austin, Tex., Oct. 7, 1953; s. Irwin and Helen (Charney) S.; m. Helen Marie Durig, Nov. 13, 1982; children: Benjamin Ivan, Diana Clare, Philip Jacob. BA, U. Tex., 1975; MD, Baylor Coll. Medicine, 1978. Intern in pediatrics Brackenridge Hosp., Austin, 1979; resident in pediatrics U. Colo., Denver, 1979-81; pediatric sr. resident Children' Hosp., San Francisco, 1981-82; fellow in adolescent medicine U. Calif., San Francisco, 1982-84; staff physician Student Health Ctr., U. Tex., Austin, 1984-94; assoc. dir. clin. svcs. U. Health Svcs., U. Wis., Madison, 1994—; asst. prof. pediatrics U. Wis., Madison, 1995—; physician coord. for clin. rsch. and acad. liaison U. Tex. Student Health Ctr., Austin, 1991-94. Bd. dirs. Planned Parenthood of Austin, 1991-94, Austin/Travis County HIV Commn., 1991-94, Planned Parenthood of Wis., 1995—; mem. sex edn. task force Austin Ind. Sch. Dist., 1992. Fellow Am. Acad. Pediatrics; mem. Soc. for Adolescent Medicine, Am. Coll. Health Assn., Phi Beta Kappa. Office: Univ Health Svcs 1552 University Ave Madison WI 53705-4084

SPEARMAN, DAVID HAGOOD, veterinarian; b. Greenville, S.C., Nov. 16, 1932; s. David Ralph and Elizabeth (Hagood) S.; student Clemson Coll., 1950-52, BS, 1975; DVM, U. Ga., 1956; m. Patsy Lee Cordle, Dec. 18, 1954; children: Kathleen Elizabeth, David Hagood. With Cleveland Park Animal Hosp., Greenville, 1956-57; individual practice vet. medicine, Easley and Powdersville, S.C., 1957—. Mem. S.C. State Bd. Vet. Examiners, 1981-87, chmn. 1987, Pickens County Planning and Devel. Bd., 1972—; pres. Northside Parent-Tchr. Orgn., 1965-67; mem. adv. bd. vet. technicians program Tri-County Tech., 1975-76; mem. admissions com. Vet. Coll., U. Ga., 1975; mem. adv. com. Pre-Vet Club, Clemson U.; chmn. Easley Zoning Bd., 1980-83; mem. S.C. Bd. Vet. Examiners, 1982-89, chmn., 1987. Mem. AVMA (alt. del. 1992-95, S.C. del. 1996—), Blue Ridge Veterinary Med. Assn. (founder, pres., sec.), S.C. Assn. Veterinarians (pres. 1974-75, publicity chmn. 1975—, chmn. animal health technician com., Veterinarian of Yr. 1985), Am. Animal Hosp. Assn. (assoc.), S.C. Wildlife, Pickens County Horse, Cattle, and Fair Assn. (pres.), Jr. C. of C. (past officer, Key Man award 1959), Trout Unltd. (state dir.), Pickens County Foxhunters Assn., Clemson U. Tiger Lettermen Assn., Easley Boosters Club, Easley C. of C., World Wildlife Fund, Nat. Wildlife Fedn., Audubon Soc., Nature Conservancy, Internat. Platform Assn., Pickens County Hist. Soc., Lions (pres., internat. del. 1971, 73) Pendelton Farmers Soc., Alpha Psi, Alpha Zeta. Presbyterian (deacon, elder, youth leader 1972-74, chmn. orgn. com. 1973-75, 83-85, pulpit com.), Nursery Bldg. com., Avocations: photography, fly fishing. Home: Burdine Springs 505 Asbury Cir PO Box 327 Easley SC 29640-1343 Office: 6714 Calhoun Memorial Hwy Easley SC 29640

SPEARMAN, LIONEL, mechanical engineer; b. Fairfield, Calif., July 25, 1964; s. Lionel Sr. and Mattie (Applin) S. Student, U. Mo., Rolla, 1982-83; BSME, Tuskegee U., 1988; postgrad., U. S.C., 1990—. Clk., cashier Oniel's Market, St. Louis, 1978-82; rsch. asst. Tuskegee (Ala.) U./NASA, 1987-88; project engr. I Monsanto Co., Greenwood, S.C., 1988-90, project engr. II, 1990-92, polymer process engr., 1992-94, environ. and health redesign engr., 1994, process engr., 1994—; summer intern Monsanto Co., Greenwood, 1987, project team mem. high tenacity, 1990—. Author: (tech. manual) Humidity Study S.P.-LDI, 1987. Pres.-elect Immanuel Luth Men, Greenwood, 1989-90, pres. 1990-91, mem. ch. coun., 1992-95, chmn. svc. (outreach) com. 1994; head bus. advisor applied econs. Jr. Achievement, Ninety Six (S.C.) H.S., 1988—; charter mem. Luth. Men in Mission, 1989—; mem. com. on inclusiveness S.C. Synod, Evang. Luth. Ch. in Am.; mem. Nat. Rep. Senatorial Com.; bd. visitors Lander Coll., 1991-93; mem. founding steering com. Grenwood Mut. Ministries. Recipient Spl. Recognition award Greenwood Sch. Dist. 52, 1990, Appreciation award Ninety Six Jr. Achievement, 1990. Mem. ASME (assoc., exec. bd. Greenville chpt. 1989-90), Nat. Soc. Black Engrs. Alumni Extension (charter, vice-chmn. region II 1989-90, chair region II 1990—, Chairperson Yr. 1990-91), Smithsonian Assocs., Greenwood C. of C. (edn. com., Leadership Greenwood Class of 1990, chairperson Jr. Achievement steering com. 1991, bd. dirs. 1992—), Internat. Platform Assn., Kiwanis Internat. (program com. 1991), Toastmasters Internat., Omega Psi Phi (keeper records and seals, Epsilon Gamma Gamma chpt. 1991, outreach com., social actions com., chair long range planning com.). Republican. Office: Monsanto Co Hwy 246 PO Box 1057 Greenwood SC 29646

SPEARMAN, MAXIE ANN, financial analyst, administrator; b. Piedmont, S.C., Sept. 14, 1942; d. J. Mac and Margaret Cecille (Johnson) S. BS, U. S.C., 1965; postgrad., Ga. State U., 1985; student U. Ga. Acct. Shell Oil Co., Atlanta, 1965-66; internal auditor Sears, Roebuck & Co., Atlanta, 1966-67; acct. Econ. Opportunity Atlanta, Atlanta, 1967-68; acct. City of Atlanta, 1968-78, fin. analyst, 1978-89, sr. fin. analyst planner, 1989—; investment cons., Atlanta, Conyers, Ga., 1980—. Mem. Rep. Presdl. Task Force, 1985—, U.S. Senatorial Club, Rep. Nat. Com., 1988—, Ga. Rep. Party, 1990—, Atlanta Safety Com., 1985—, Mayor's Spl. Events Task Force, 1990—; charter founder Ronald Reagan Rep. Ctr., 1988; del.-at-large Rep. Platform Planning Com., 1992, 94. Recipient safety award Atlanta City Govt., 1990, Presdl. Commn. Exec. Com. of Republican Party award, 1992; Order of Merit award Nat. Rep. Senatorial Com., 1996. Mem. NAFE, Am. Mgmt. Assn., Ga. Assn. Med. Victims, Inc. (sec., treas. 1985—), Nat. Trust for Historic Preservation. Methodist. Home: 1280 Vineyard Dr SE Conyers GA 30208-2466 Office: 55 Trinity Ave SW Ste 1450 Atlanta GA 30303-3531

SPEARMAN, PATSY CORDLE, real estate broker; b. Richmond, Va., Aug. 23, 1934; d. Lee Pierce and Kathleen Jeanette (Munn) Cordle; m. David Hagood Spearman, Dec. 18, 1954; children: Kathleen Elizabeth, David Hagood. AA, Coll. William and Mary, Richmond, 1952; student, U. Ga., 1953-54; grad., Realtors Inst., 1979. Copywriter Cabell Eanes Advt. Agy., Richmond, 1952; clk. athletic dept. U. Ga., Athens, 1954-55; sec. Coll. Agriculture, 1955-56; real estate saleswoman Merrill Lynch/C. Dan Joyner & Co., Inc. (now The Prudential, 1990), Greenville, S.C., 1978—. Past pres. Women of Ch.; Presbyn. ch. Sunday sch. tchr. and youth leader. Recipient numerous awards for obtaining eye bank donors Lions Club and S.C. Eye Bank, Listing Agt. of Yr., 1985-87, 89, 90-93, Sales Agt. Yr., 1987, 90, 91, 92. Mem. Nat. Assn. Realtors (cert. residential specialist), Real Estate Securities and Syndication Inst., S.C. Assn. Realtors, Greenville Bd. Realtors, Pickens County Bd. Realtors (chmn. cmty. svcs. com., edn. com., membership com. chmn.), Women's Coun. of Realtors, Million Dollar Club (life, charter, Greenville and Pickens County), Am. Vet. M.A. Aux. (S.C. del. 1992-96), S.C. Vet. Aux. (treas. 1988-92), Internat. Platform Soc., Smithsonian Assocs., Nat. Wildlife Fedn. (life), World Wildlife Fedn., S.C. Wildlife Assn., Audubon Soc., Cousteau Soc., Smithsonian Inst., Better Homes (Easley) Club, Commerce Club Greenville (life), Greenville Little Theater, Easley Foothills Theatre, Nature Conservancy, Edisto Hist. Soc. Home: 505 Asbury Cir Easley SC 29640-1343 Office: PO Box 327 Easley SC 29641-0327

SPEARS, CARLETON BLAISE, lawyer; b. San Antonio, Feb. 28, 1958; s. Franklin Scott Sr. and JoAnn (Hyltin) S.; m. Karen Ruth Baldwin, July 18, 1981; children: Shelby Virginia Katherine, Joshua Caleb Blaise. BBA Petroleum Land Mgmt., U. Tex., Austin, 1980, JD, 1983. Bar: Tex. 1983, U.S. Dist. Ct. (we. dist.) Tex. 1987. Assoc. Brock & Kelfer, San Antonio, 1983-88; of counsel Martin, Shannon & Drought, San Antonio, 1988; state dist. judge 150th Jud. Dist., Bexar County, 1988-94; with Wright & Spears, PC, San Antonio, 1994-96; owner Carleton B. Spears, PC, San Antonio, 1996—; adj. prof. law St. Mary's Sch. Law, 1992-96. Bexar County del. Tex. State Dem. Conv., 1978, 86; commr., mem. exec. bd., coun. commr. Alamo area Boy Scouts Am., 1984—; bd. dirs., pres. Battered Women's Shelter of Bexar County, 1989—; adv. bd. Dispute Resolution Ctr. Bexar County, 1990-94; mem. Bexar Dem. Leadership Coun.; mem. San Antonio Livestock Exposition. Recipient Silver Beaver award Boy Scouts Am. Mem. ABA, Fed. Bar Assn. (bd. dirs. San Antonio chpt. 1988-94), State Bar Tex. (adminstrn. of rules of evidence com., Bar Found. and MCLE task force), San Antonio Bar Assn., World Affairs Coun., Nat. Speleological Soc. (mem. expdn. to Mex.), Alumnus Leadership San Antonio, San Antonio Jaycees (Disting. Svc. award Outstanding Young San Antonian 1991), Tex. Supreme Ct. Hist. Soc., Am. Judicature Soc., SAR, Rotary, Phi Alpha Delta. Methodist. Home: 742 Lost Cyn San Antonio TX 78258-4001

SPEARS, GAY HOLMES, music educator; b. Blytheville, Ark., Oct. 2, 1958; d. Louis Lee and Dona Jene (Bohannon) H.; m. Jared Tozier Spears, July 20, 1985. BMus, U. Tenn., 1981; MMus, Ark. State U., 1984; DMus, U. Memphis, 1993. Prof. music Williams Coll., Walnut Ridge, Ark., 1983—. Organist First United Meth. Ch., Paragould, Ark., 1988—; clinician Ark. State U. Piano Camp, Jonesboro, 1987, Ark. Baptist Conv., Little Rock, 1988-89. Mem. ASCAP, Music Tchrs. Nat. Assn. (adjudicator 1990—), Southeastern Composers League, Federated Music Clubs, Sigma Alpha Iota, Pi Kappa Lambda. Home: PO Box 2259 State University AR 72467

SPEARS, GEORGANN WIMBISH, marketing executive; b. Ft. Worth, Apr. 21, 1946; d. George Vardeman and Lela Ellon (Clifton) Wimbish; m. Richard Scarborough Spears, Dec. 31, 1981. BA in Govt. and History, Tex. Christian U., 1969. Cert. secondary govt. and history tchr., Tex. V.p., gen. mgr. Sports Today Mag., Arlington, Tex., 1982-83; editor corp. newsletter Amason Internat. Mktg., Dallas, 1983-85; supply mgr., dir. Am. Photocopy, Arlington, 1985-92; v.p. Mineral Wells (Tex.) Clay Products, Inc., 1993-96; v.p. mktg., chmn. bd. dirs. Educators Industries, Inc., Ft. Worth, 1993-95, chmn. bd., 1995—; v.p., vice chmn., bd. dirs. Superior Properties, Inc., 1995—. Features editor mag. Sports Today, 1982. Active Jewel Charity Ball, Ft. Worth, 1979—, Rep. Party of Tex., Austin, 1983—, PETA, 1992—; vol. ICU and CCU Arlington Meml. Hosp., 1983-86; vol. John Peter Smith Hosp., 1980-82. Mem. U. North Tex. Athletics (trustee 1994—), People for Ethical Treatment of Animals. Republican. Episcopalian. Home: 1909 Rockbrook Dr Arlington TX 76006-6615 Office: Educators Industries Inc 6633 Grapevine Hwy Fort Worth TX 76180-1523

SPEARS, JAE, state legislator; b. Latonia, Ky.; d. James and Sylvia (Fox) Marshall; m. Lawrence E. Spears; children: Katherine Spears Cooper, Marsha Spears-Duncan, Lawrence M., James W. Student, U. Ky. Reporter Cin. Post, Cin. Enquirer newspapers; rschr. Stas. WLW-WSAI, Cin.; tchr. Jiya Gakuen Sch., Japan; lectr. U.S. Mil. installations East Anglia, Eng.; del. State of W.Va., Charleston, 1974-80; mem. W.Va. Senate, Charleston, 1980-1993; mem. state visitors com. W.Va. Extension and Continuing Edn., Morgantown, 1977-91, W.Va. U. Sch. Medicine, 1992—. Chmn. adv bd. Sta. WNPB, 1992-94; congl. liaison Am. Pub. TV Stas. and Sta. WNPB-TV,

1992—; mem. coun. W.Va. Autism Task Force, Huntington, 1981-90; mem. W.Va. exec. bd. Literacy Vols. Am., 1986-90, 94—, pres., 1990-92; mem. Gov.'s State Literacy Coun., 1991—; bd. dirs. Found. Ind. Colls. W.Va., 1986—; mem. regional adv. com. W.Va. Gov.'s Task Force for Children, Youth and Family, 1989; mem. USS W.Va. Commn., 1989; mem. exec. com. W.Va. Employer Support Group for Guard and Res., 1989, mem. steering com., 1990—. Recipient Susan B. Anthony award NOW, 1982, nat. award Mil. Order Purple Heart, 1984, Edn. award Profl. Educators Assn. W.Va., 1986, Ann. award W.Va. Assn. Ret. Sch. Employees, 1985, Meritorious Service award W.Va. State Vets. Commn., 1984, Vets. Employment and Tng. Service award U.S. Dept. Labor, 1984, award W.Va. Vets. Council, 1984; named Admiral in N.C. Navy, Gov. of N.C., 1982, Hon. Brigadier Gen. W.Va. N.G., 1984. Mem. Bus. and Profl. Women (Woman of Yr. award 1978), Nat. League Am. Pen Women (Pen Woman of Yr. 1984), Nat. Order Women Legislators, DAR, VFW (aux.), Am. Legion (aux.), Delta Kappa Gamma, Alpha Xi Delta. Democrat. Home and Office: PO Box 2088 Elkins WV 26241-2088

SPEARS, JAMES GRADY, small business owner; b. Port Arthur, Tex., July 20, 1941; s. John Grady and Dorothy Nell (Haney) S. Grad. high sch., Port Arthur. Adminstr. Child Health & Devel. Studies, Oakland, Calif., 1962-69; sales mgr. Sunshine Biscuits Inc., Houston, 1969-75; owner, pres. S.W. Tookie Inc./Tookie's Restaurant, Seabrook, Tex., 1975—. Mem. Greater Houston Convention & Visitors Bur., Clear Lake Convention & Visitors Bur. With USN, 1959-62. Mem. Tex. Restaurant Assn., Houston Restaurant Assn., Seabrook Assn., Old Seabrook Assn. Republican. Roman Catholic. Home: 16310 Hickory Knoll Dr Houston TX 77059-5311 Office: SW Tookie Inc/Tookie's Restaurant 1202 Bayport Blvd Seabrook TX 77586-3406

SPEARS, KAREN LYNN, art educator; b. Dallas, Jan. 24, 1955; d. William Charles Spears. AA, U. Louisville, 1974, BA, 1979; MFA, So. Ill. U. Carbondale, 1984. Curatorial asst. Univ. Mus. So. Ill. U., Carbondale, 1982-83; instr. Spalding U., Louisville, 1984; instr. Internat. Ctr. U. Louisville, 1985, Jefferson C.C., Louisville, 1985-86; instr. art dept. U. Louisville, 1983-86; instr. Ky. Inst. European Studies, Murray, 1988, 90, 94; assoc. prof. Ea. Ky. U., Richmond, 1987—; artist-in-residence Brisons Veor, Cornwall, Eng., 1992; artist-tchr. Vermont Coll., Montpelier, 1993—; vis. artist Am. Acad. Rome, 1990-91; vis. artist-in-residence U. Ga. Studies Abroad, Cortona, Italy, 1987. Author: (artist's book) Looking, 1991; contbr. New Delta Rev., 1992; numerous regional, nat. and internat. exhibits. Mem. Coll. Art Assn., Founds. in Art, Theory and Edn. Office: Ea Ky U Dept Art 309 Campbell Richmond KY 40475

SPEARS, ROBERT FIELDS, lawyer; b. Tulsa, Aug. 1, 1943; s. James Ward and Berneice (Fields) S.; m. Jacquelyn Castle, May 10, 1961; children: Jeff, Sally. BBA, Tex. Tech. U., 1965; JD, U. Tex., 1968. Bar: Tex. 1968. Assoc. Rain, Harrell, Emery, Young & Doke, Dallas, 1968-73, ptnr., 1974-87; ptnr. Locke Purnell Rain Harrell, Dallas, 1987-91; gen. counsel Fin. Industries Corp., Austin, Tex., 1991-96; gen. counsel, sec. Lone Star Technologies, Inc., Dallas, 1996—. Pres. Sr. Citizens of Greater Dallas, 1988. Mem. ABA, Tex. Bar Assn., Dallas Bar Assn., Dallas Country Club, Phi Delta Phi. Republican. Baptist. Office: Lone Star Technologies Inc 5501 LBJ Freeway Ste 1200 Dallas TX 75240

SPECK, DAVID GEORGE, investment executive; b. N.Y.C., Sept. 12, 1945; s. George and Doris Jean (de Ford) S.; divorced; children: Elizabeth Doris, Jonathan Samuel; m. Marcia E. Neuhaus, Nov. 28, 1987. Student U. Va., 1963-65; BA, George Washington U., 1967, MA, 1968, EdD, 1973. Various adminstrv. and teaching positions George Washington U., Washington, 1967-76; exec. asst. to dir. Office Fed. Contract Compliance, U.S. Dept. Labor, Washington, 1976-77; ind. cons., Alexandria, Va., 1977-82; exec. v.p. investments Johnston, Lemon & Co., Inc., Washington and Alexandria, 1982-90; sr. v.p., investment officer Wheat, First Butcher Singer, 1990—; moderator weekly news analysis panel show on cable TV, 1982-86. Fin. columnist Alexandria Gazette, 1984-87. Mem. Va. Ho. of Dels., 1979-82; bd. dirs. Alexandria Hosp., 1982-91; trustee Robert S. Rixse Found., Alexandria, 1984—; mem. Alexandria City Coun., 1991-94. Republican. Jewish. Office: Wheat First Butcher Singer 101 N Union St # 220 Alexandria VA 22314-3217

SPECK, PATRICIA MCMURRY, family nurse practitioner; b. Memphis, Oct. 9, 1948; d. Lawrence Douglas and Eunice Lenore McMurry; m. Ronald Lee Speck, Dec. 8, 1967; 1 child, Jonathan Michael. BSN, U. Tenn., Memphis, 1982, MSN, 1985. RN, Tenn.; nat. cert. family nurse practitioner, nat. cert. pediatric nurse. Staff, chg. and triage nurse LeBonheur Children's Hosp., Memphis, 1982-85; nurse practitioner Memphis/Shelby County Health Dept., Memphis, 1984-93; sexual assault nurse examiner Memphis Sexual Assault Resource Ctr., 1984—, coord. nursing svcs., 1988—; nurse cons. Regional Med. Ctr. at Memphis, 1994-95; adj. faculty nursing U. Memphis, 1991—, clin. instr., 1994; adj. faculty U. Tenn., Memphis, 1986—, clin. instr., 1986-87, adj. faculty Coll. of Medicine, 1989—; lectr. in field. Contbr. articles and abstracts to profl. jours. Mem. Memphis/Shelby County Coun. on Child Sexual Abuse, 1985-94, Coun. on Family Violence, 1986-89, bd. dirs., 1987-88, mem. edn. com. 1988-89; mem. Habitat for Humanity, 1992-95; MSARC forensic rep. Shelby County Child Protection Team, 1992—; mem. Assistance for Impaired Nursing Students's Coun., Coll. Nursing, U. Tenn., Memphis, 1992—. Lt. USNR, 1990-93. Recipient Dorothy Hocker Nursing award, 1985; named Nurse Practitioner of the Yr., Syntex, 1989, Golden Eagle award, CINE, 1991, Ace award Nat. Acad. Cable Programming, 1991, Pub. Citizen of Yr. West Tenn. chpt. NASW, 1996; Tenn. Dept. Human Svcs. grantee, 1989-90, 90-91, 91-92. Mem. ASTM, ANA, Tenn. Nurses Assn. Forensic Nurse Coun., Tenn. Nurses Assn., Coun. on Advanced Practice, Am. Profl. Soc. on Abuse of Children, Internat. Assn. Forensic Nurses (regional rep. South Ctrl. 1992—), Coun. Sexual Assualt Nurse Examiners (chair task force for stds. of practice 1993—), Sigma Theta Tau (awards com. 1993-94, sec.-at-large Beta Theta chpt. 1994-96), Chi Beta Phi. Office: City of Memphis Sexual Assault Resource Ctr 1331 Union Ave Ste 1150 Memphis TN 38104

SPECTOR, LOUIS, retired federal judge, lawyer, arbitrator, consultant; b. Niagara Falls, N.Y., Apr. 4, 1918; s. Jacob and Gussie (Yochelson) S.; children: Gale Anne Spector Pasternack, Arthur George, James Aland. Student (N.Y. State scholar), Niagara U., 1936-37; LL.B. with honors, U. Buffalo (later State U. N.Y.), 1940. Bar: N.Y. bar 1940, D.C. bar 1972, U.S. Supreme Ct. bar 1971, U.S. Ct. Claims bar 1968. Asso. firm Saperston, McNaughton & Saperston, Buffalo, 1941-42; asst. chief legal div. U.S. Army C.E., Buffalo Dist., 1942-43; chief sect. claims appeals and litigation U.S. Army C.E. (Great Lakes Div.), Chgo., 1946; chief legal br. and real estate div. U.S. Army C.E. (Great Lakes Div.), Buffalo Dist., 1946-53; exec. dir. Buffalo Port Authority, 1953-54; mem. Bd. Contract Appeals, Washington, 1954-59; chmn. Army panel Armed Services Bd. Contract Appeals, Washington, 1959-62, Unified Armed Services Bd. Contract Appeals, 1962-68; trial judge U.S. Ct. Claims, Washington, 1968-82, judge, 1982-85; cons., arbitrator, mediator Falls Church, Va., 1985—; lectr., speaker, writer public contracts; Congressional appearances, 1953, 66, 69, 77. Contbr. articles to profl. publs. Served with C.E. U.S. Army, 1943-46. Recipient Freshman medal Niagara U., 1936, Sophomore medal, 1937. Fellow Am. Bar Found.; mem. ABA (chmn. sect. pub. contract law 1967-68); Fellow Nat. Contract Mgmt. Assn. (nat. bd. advisers 1967—); mem. ABA (ho. of dels. 1968-70), Fed. Bar Assn. (gen. editor jour. 1960-74, nat. chmn. com. govt. contracts and procurement law 1961-63, Distinguished Service award D.C. chpt. 1974), Lincoln Law Soc. (alumni pres. 1951). Club: Cosmos. Home: 6219 Beachway Dr Falls Church VA 22041-1425

SPECTOR, MICHAEL JOSEPH, agribusiness executive; b. N.Y.C., Feb. 13, 1947; s. Martin Wilson and Dorothy (Miller) S.; BS in Chemistry, Washington and Lee U., 1968; m. Margaret Dickson, Sept. 14, 1977. Research chemist Am. Viscose, Phila., 1968-69; pres. MJS Entertainment Corp., Miami, Fla., 1970-84, also MJS Internat., Inc.; ptnr. Old Town Key West Devel. Ltd. (Fla.), 1977—; mem. bd. dirs. Plz. Bank of Miami, Fla., 1979-84, founder; pres. MJS Entertainment of Can. Inc., Toronto, Ont., Margo Farms, MJS Prodns., Inc., N.Y.C.; chmn., pres., CEO Margo Nursery Farms, Inc., Dorado, P.R., 1981—, also bd. dirs.; bd. dirs. Goodwill Industries So. Fla., v.p. fin., 1980, bd. dirs. Plz. Bank of Miami. Served with AUS, 1969-70. Recipient Robert E. Lee rsch. grant Washington and Lee U., 1967-68. Mem. Nat. Assn. Record Merchandisers (dir. Nova div., chmn. one-stop distbn. com. 1982-83), Country Music Assn., Dorado Beach, Golf and Tennis Club, Bankers Club of San Juan. Patentee synthetic stretching process. Home: Hyatt Dorado Beach Box 8 Dorado PR 00646-0008

SPECTOR, MICHAEL PHILLIP, biomedical scientist, microbiologist; b. Phila., Aug. 19, 1959; s. Larry and Emma Spector. BSc in Biology, Phila. Coll. Pharmacy and Sci., 1981; PhD in Biomed. Scis.-Microbiology, Marshall U./W.Va. U., 1986. Asst. prof. dept. biomed. scis. Coll. Allied Health, U. South Ala., Mobile, 1988-93, assoc. prof., 1993—, mem. Grad. Faculty, 1989—; adj. asst. prof. dept. microbiology and immunology Coll. Medicine, U. South Ala., 1988—. Office: U South Ala UCOM6000 Dept Biomed Scis Mobile AL 36688

SPEER, CYNTHIA, clinical support specialist, nephrology nurse; b. Houston, Sept. 9, 1957; d. F.G. and Willie Ruth (Kroll) S. Lic. vocat. nurse, Navarro Jr. Coll., Corsicana, Tex., 1978; ADN, El Centro Coll., Dallas, 1981; paralegal cert., Video Tech. Inst., Arlington, Tex., 1987. RN, Tex. Staff nurse, shift head nurse Gen. Mexia (Tex.) Meml. Hosp., 1978-82; staff nurse dialysis unit Med. Arts Clinic, Corsicana, 1982-86; staff nurse Harris Hosp., Ft. Worth, 1986-94; med. legal asst. Shannon, Gracey, Ratliff & Miller, Ft. Worth, 1987-94; clin. support specialist Abbott Labs., Abbott Park, Ill., 1994—. Mem. Am. Nephrology Nurses Assn. (past program chmn.), Tex. Nurses Assn. Office: Abbott Labs 200 Abbott Park Rd Abbott Park IL 60064-3501

SPEER, GLENDA O'BRYANT, middle school educator; b. Uvalde, Tex., Mar. 30, 1956; d. Harvey Glen and Mary (Miller) O'Bryant; m. Weldon Michael Speer, July 12, 1975; children: Janena Lea, Jon Michael. BS, Sul Ross State U., Alpine, Tex., 1978; MA, U. Tex., San Antonio, 1984. Tchr. math. Jackson Middle Sch., San Antonio, 1978-82; tchr. math., computers Bradley Middle Sch., San Antonio, 1982-86, chmn. dept. math., 1986—; computer edn. tchr. trainer N.E. Ind. Sch. Dist., San Antonio, 1984—; acad. pentathlon coach Bradley Middle Sch., 1988-92; software reviewer Nat. Coun. Tchrs. Math., Reston, Va., 1994. Editor Math Matters newsletter, 1989—; writer curriculum guide: Computer Literacy Guide for Teachers, 1992. Black belt Karate and self-defense instr. Tang So Do Karate Assn., San Antonio, 1994—. Recipient Supt.'s award N.E. Ind. Sch. Dist., 1990, 92, 93, Red Apple Tchrs. award St. Mary's U., San Antonio, 1992. Mem. Nat. Coun. Tchrs. Math., Tex. Coun. Tchrs. Math., Bradley Middle Sch. PTA. Office: Bradley Middle Sch 14819 Heimer Rd San Antonio TX 78232-4528

SPEER, JOSEPH ENRIQUE, videographer, editor, producer; b. Albuquerque, Oct. 24, 1948; s. Henry Allan and Maria Adela (Tafoya) S. BA, N.Mex. State U., 1970. Ranch husbandry staff Circle A Ranch, Cuba, N.Mex., 1980-87; videographer Kameleon Video, Albuquerque, 1987-90; video maker Video Joe, Nashville, 1990-96; videographer, editor, prodr. Channel 23, Tenn. State U., Nashville; prodr. Ch. 27, Albuquerque, 1985-90, Ch. 19, Nashville, 1990-96; poetry host Beatlicks, Nashville, 1988-96; documentor of events Tenn. State U., 1990-96; spkr. in field. Editor (literary mag.) Kameleon, 1976-96, (newsletters) Beatlick's Poetry, 1988-96, Speer Presents, 1994-96. Staff writer The Meter, Tenn. State U., Nashville, 1996; vol. Cmty. Pub. Libr. Recipient Vol. Program award Pub. Libr., Nashville, 1992, The Xernona Clayton award-broadcasting Soc. of Profl. Journalists/Tenn. State U., Nashville, 1996. Mem. Tenn. Writers Alliance, Cmty. Access TV (prodr.), Soc. Profl. Journalists (membership coord.). Democrat. Home: 1016 Kipling Dr Nashville TN 37217

SPEER, MICHAEL EMERY, neonatologist, educator; b. San Diego, Oct. 2, 1942; s. Emery and Meryl Elizabeth (Winn) S.; m. Mary Elizabeth Swiler, Apr. 26, 1969; children: James A., Mark S. BS in Biology, Occidental Coll., L.A., 1964; MD, Baylor Coll. Medicine, 1968. Diplomaed Am. Bd. Pediatrics, Sub-Bd. Neonatal-Perinatal Medicine; lic. neonatologist, Calif., Tex. Intern Ben Taub Gen. Hosp. and Jefferson Davis Hosp., Houston, 1968-69; resident in pediatrics Baylor Affiliated Hosps., Houston, 1969-70, 72-73; fellow in infectiour disease Baylor Coll. Medicine, Houston, 1973-74, fellow in neonatology, 1974-76, instr. pediatrics, 1976, asst. prof. pediatrics, 1976-89, assoc. prof. pediatrics, 1990—; mem. staff Woman's Hosp. Tex., 1976—, dep. dir. neonatology, 1976-81; attending neonatologist Harris County Hosp., 1977—, Tex. Children's Hosp., 1977—; med. dir. quality and outcomes mgmt. dept. Tex. Children's Hosp., 1993—; attending neonatologist St. Luke's Episc. Hosp., 1977—, assoc. chief newborn and premature svc., 1994—; dir. neonatology svcs. Meth. Hosp., 1981—, dep. chief pediat. svcs., 1993—; clin. coord. health care practice and quality of care Tex. Children's Hosp. and Baylor Coll. Medicine, 1993—; chair quality mgmt. com. Baylor MedCare, Baylor Coll. Medicine, 1995—. Reviewer Jour. of Infectiour Disease, 1984—, Pediatric Rsch., 1987—, Pediatrics, 1990—, Hosp. Formulary, 1990—, Acta Paediatrica Scandinavica, 1991—; contbr. numerous articles and abstracts to publs. Mem.-at-large, dist. com. Golden Arrow dist. Sam Houston Area coun. Boy Scouts Am.; bd. dirs. Friends of Jesse H. Jones Libr., 1992—. Lt. comdr. USN, 1970-72, USNR, 1972-79. Mem. AMA, Am. Acad. Pediats. (mem. fetus, newborn com.), Tex. Med. Assn. (mem. coms., mem. coun. sci. affairs), Tex. Perinatal Assn. (exec. bd. 1991—, pres. 1994-95), Tex. Pediatric Soc. (mem. fetus, newborn com., chmn. dist. 1 1995—), Harris County Med. Soc. (exec. bd. 1988-94), Houston Pediatric Soc. (pres. 1990-91, exec. bd. 1984-95), Houston Acad. Medicine (trustee 1988-94, pres. 1994), Houston Acad. Medicine Meml. Edn. and Rsch. Found. (bd. dirs. 1990-94, pres. 1994), So. Soc. Pediatric Rsch., Medserv (bd. dirs. 1991—), Houston Acad. Medicine/Tex. Med. Ctr. Libr. (bd. dirs. 1993—, chmn. 1994, 95). Home: 6031 Fordham St Houston TX 77005-3125 Office: Baylor Coll Medicine 1 Baylor Plz Houston TX 77030-3411

SPEIER, KAREN RINARDO, psychologist; b. New Orleans, Aug. 19, 1947; d. William Joseph Rinardo and Shirley Eva (Spreen) Christensen; m. Joe Max Sobotka, Nov. 27, 1970 (div. 1972); m. Anthony Herman Speier, May 29, 1982; children: Anthony Herman III, Austin Clay. Student, Vanderbilt U., 1965-67; BA, La. State U., New Orleans, 1969; MS, U. New Orleans, 1974; PhD, La. State U., 1985. Lic. psychologist, La. Tchr. spl. edn. Huntsville (Ala.) Achievement Sch., 1970-72; instr. neurology La. State U. Med. Ctr., New Orleans, 1972-78; clin. assoc. Dawson Psychol. Assocs., Baton Rouge, 1979-81; tchr. asst. dept. psychology La. State U., Baton Rouge, 1979-81; psychol. examiner La. Sch. for Deaf, Baton Rouge, 1979-80; psychology intern VA Med. Ctr., Martinez, Calif., 1981-82; psychology extern East La. State Hosp., Jackson, 1982-83; clin. assoc. Baton Rouge Psychol. Assocs., 1983-86, pvt. practice clin. psychology, 1986—; sr. neuropsychologist Rehab. Hosp. of Baton Rouge, 1995-96; sec. bd. dirs. Baton Rouge Employment Devel. Svcs., 1987-89; mem. psychology cons. com. Meadow Wood Hosp., Baton Rouge, 1987-89; mem. psychology adv. com. Parkland Hosp., Baton Rouge, 1989-92; clin. neuropsychologist Baton Rouge Gen. Med. Ctr., 1996—. Contbr. articles to profl. publs. Mem. steering com. Baton Rouge Stepfamily Support Group, 1983-90; tchr. St. James Episcopal Sunday Sch., Baton Rouge, 1984-86, 90-91, 92—). Mem. Orton Dyslexia Soc. (bd. dirs., pres. La. br.), Nat. Head Injury Found., Agenda For Children, Baton Rouge Area Soc. Psychologists, La. Psychol. Assn., Am. Psychology Assn., Internat. Soc. Child Abuse and Neglect, Mental Health Assn. La. Office: Ctr Psychol Resources 4521 Jamestown Ave Ste 2 Baton Rouge LA 70808-3234

SPEILLER-MORRIS, JOYCE, English composition educator; b. Utica, N.Y., Nov. 11, 1945; d. Arnold Leonard Speiller and Sybil (Sall) McAdam; m. Joseph Raymond Morris, Mar. 17, 1984. BS, Syracuse U., 1968; MA, Columbia U., 1969. Cert. tchr., N.Y., Fla. Chmn. upper sch. social studies dept., tchr. grade 6 social studies and English Cathedral Heights Elem. Sch., N.Y.C., 1969-74; adj. prof. Broward Community Coll., Hollywood, Davie and Pompano, Fla., 1982-90, Biscayne Coll., Miami, Fla., 1983, Miami-Dade Community Coll., 1983, Nova U., Miami and Davie, 1983-84; adj. prof., semester lectr. U. Miami, Coral Gables, 1985—; master tchr. U. Miami, 1990, 92, 94, faculty fellow, 1990-94, mem. curriculum devel., 1991-94; contbr. presentation to Fla. Coll. English Assn., 1991-92, Wyo. Conf. English, 1991; guest spkr. in field of svc.-learning, 1992-94; cons. svc.-learning curriculum design, 1994; acad. advisor U. Miami, 1994, 95, 96. Reviewer textbook McGraw Hill, 1993; contbr. instr.'s manual of textbook, 1994; contbr. poetry to revs., articles to profl. jours. Founder, dir. Meet the Author program, Coral Gables, 1989—. Recipient V.P. award U. Miami, 1992, cert. recognition West Palm Beach, Fla., TV sta., 1992; grantee Fla. Office for Campus Vols., 1992, Dade Community Found., 1992. Mem. MLA, Nat. Soc. Experiential Edn., Fla. Coll. English Assn., Coll. English Assn., Nat. Coun. Tchrs. English, Fla. Chpt. of Tchrs. of English to Spkrs. of Other Langs. (spkr. conf. 1992), Am. Correctional Assn., Phi Delta Kappa, Phi Lambda Theta. Home: Tower 200 Apt 806 19101 Mystic Pointe Dr North Miami Beach FL 33180 Office: U Miami Office English Composition PO Box 248145 Coral Gables FL 33124-8145

SPEIRS, CAROL LUCILLE, nurse, naval officer; b. Plainfield, N.J., Apr. 20, 1942; d. Alexander Walker and Catherine Lucille (McGovern) S.; diploma St. Peters Med. Ctr. Sch. Nursing, New Brunswick, N.J., 1963; student, Seton Hall U., 1972, BSN, Pacific Lutheran U., Tacoma, Wash., 1987-88; BA, San Diego State U., 1976; MA, Webster Coll., 1980. Staff nurse Muhlenberg Hosp., Plainfield, N.J., 1963-64, Burdette Tomlin Meml. Hosp., Cape May Court House, N.J., 1964, 65, Georgetown U. Hosp., Washington, 1964-65; pvt. duty nurse, North Plainfield, N.J., 1965-66; staff nurse, charge nurse Raritan Valley Hosp., Greenbrook, N.J., 1966-72; commd. lt. (j.g.) U.S. Navy, 1973, advanced through grades to comdr., 1985; charge nurse Naval Regional Med. Center, San Diego, 1973-76, Iwakuni, Japan, 1977-78, Long Beach, Calif., 1978-83; charge nurse, Bremerton, Wash., 1983-86, patient care coord., 1986, Naval Hosp. Corpus Christi, head ambulatory care nursing dept., 1989-90, head inpatient nursing dept., 1991-92, head male surg. nursing dept. Naval Hosp/ Portsmouth, Va., 1992-94, ret. 1994. Mem. Founders Ball Com., City of Cypress (Calif.), 1981. Recipient Outstanding Cath. Young Adult award Diocese of Trenton, 1970. Mem. 2020 Com. of Stafford County Va., Nat. Assn. for Healthcare Quality, Am. Acad. Ambulatory Nursing, Sigma Theta Tau, Nat. Mus. Women in Arts. Republican. Roman Catholic. Home: 4317 Turnberry Dr Fredericksburg VA 22408-9547

SPELIOS, LISA GARONE, nurse, educator; b. L.I., N.Y., Sept. 27, 1961; d. Michael John and Gloria Josephine (Riggio) Garone; m. Louis G. Spelios, June 30, 1984; children: Gregory Louis, Zachary Michael, Jeremy Daniel. BS in Nursing, Fla. Internat. U., 1984. Operating rm. nurse Carroway Meth. Med. Ctr., Birmingham, Ala.; labor and delivery rm. nurse Brookwood Med. Ctr., Birmingham, med.-surg. nurse; tchr. Am. Med. Tng. Inst., Miami, Fla. Mem. Fla. Nurses Assn.

SPELLER-BROWN, BARBARA JEAN, pediatric nurse practitioner; b. Windsor, N.C., Feb. 8, 1958; d. Thomas Franklin and Esther Lee (Bond) Speller; m. Samuel Brown Jr., Nov. 16, 1985; children: Samuel, Shaun, Shea, Shanele. BSN, Howard U., 1981; MSN, U. Utah, 1993. Cert. pediatric nurse practitioner. Charge nurse Rosebud (S.D.) Indian Health Facility, 1981-82, Carl Albert Indian Health Facility, 1982-83; asst. head nurse Pitt County Meml. Hosp., Greenville, N.C., 1984-85; staff nurse St. Bernardine's Hosp., San Bernardino, Calif., 1986, San Bernardino Cmty. Hosp., 1986-87; staff nurse/charge nurse Gorgas Army Hosp., Republic of Panama, 1987-90; charge nurse Humana Hosp. Davis North, Layton, Utah, 1990-93; staff nurse Primary Children's Med. Ctr., Salt Lake City, Utah, 1990-93; pediatric nurse practitioner Cmty. Health Care Inc., Capital Heights, Md., 1994-95, Our Kids Ctr., Nashville, 1995—; clin. preceptor Community Health Care, Capitol Heights, 1995. Treas. Word of God Bapt. Ch. Nurses Guild, Washington, 1995, mem. parents assn., 1995. 1st lt. USPHS, 1981-83. Named Outstanding Young Woman Am. Delta Sigma Theta. Mem. ANA, Nat. Assn. Pediatric Nurse Practitioners and Assns., Am. Profl. Soc. on the Abuse of Children, Sigma Theta Tau, Phi Kappa Phi. Home: 705 Wabash Pl Nashville TN 37221

SPENCE, EDWARD LEE, publisher, historian, archaeologist; b. Munich, Germany, Nov. 6, 1947; s. Judson Cauthen and Mary Virginia (Truett) S.; m. Mary Tabb Gildea, Sept. 11, 1979 (div. Feb. 1981); 1 child, Matthew Lee. BA in Marine Archeology, U. S.C., 1967, postgrad., 1977; D of Marine Histories, Coll. of Marine Arts, 1972; PhD (hon.), Sea Rsch. Soc., 1976, Colombian Rsch. Inst., 1993. Pres. Shipwreck Cons., Sullivan's Island, S.C., 1976-94; marine archeology cons. Coll. Charleston, S.C., 1983-84; underwater archeologist Shipwrecks Inc., Munhall, Pa., 1985-87; archeol. dir. Ocean Enterprises, Ltd., Nassau, The Bahamas, 1986-87; underwater archeologist Freedom Marine Ltd., Vancouver, B.C., Can., 1988-89; pub., sr. editor Shipwreck Press Inc., Sullivan's Island, 1988-91; chief underwater archeology Old Providence Island, Colombia, 1992-94; pub., sr. editor Narwhal Press Inc., Miami, Fla., 1994—; curator Mus. Sunken Treasure, Cape Canaveral, Fla., 1980; mem. adv. bd. Contemporary U., U. S.C., Columbia, 1971; cons. Seahawk Deep Ocean Tech., Tampa, Fla., 1991—. Author: Shipwrecks of South Carolina and Georgia 1521-1865, 1985, Shipwrecks of the Civil War, 1994, Romance on the Confederate Coast, 1994, Treasures of the Confederate Coast: The Real Rhett Butler & Other Revelations, 1995, Shipwrecks, Pirates, and Privateers: Sunken Treasuers of the Upper South Carolina Coast, 1521-1865, 1995. Co-founder Hot Line, Charleston, 1971; mem. maritime subcom. S.C. Bi-Centennial Commn., Charleston, 1975-76; co-founder S.C. Underwater Archeol. Rsch. Coun., 1971. Grantee S.C. Com. for Humanities, 1983-84, NEH, 1983-84; Nat. Honors scholar U. Miami, 1966. Mem. Sea Rsch. Soc. (pres., pres. emeritus 1970—), Intertel, French Honor Soc. (alumnus), Mensa, Order of De Molay (alumnus, chaplain, historian), Tau Kappa Epsilon (alumnus), Mu Alpha Theta (alumnus). Republican. Home: 1750 I'on Ave Sullivan's Island SC 29482 Office: Narwhal Press Inc 1629 Meeting St Charleston SC 29405-9408

SPENCE, FAYE YVONNE, elementary school educator; b. Raleigh, N.C., Nov. 11, 1952; d. Quinton and Martha (Wilkes) S. BA, N.C. Cen. U., 1974, MEd, 1982. Remedial reading tchr. Marboro County Schs., Bennettsville, S.C.; instr. Vance Granville Community Coll., Warrenton, N.C.; tchr. Durham (N.C.) City Schs.; tchr. Warren County Schs., Warrenton, kindergarten tchr., tchr. grade 1, mentor tchr.; tchr. grades 4 and 5; presenter math. workshop grades K-6. Named Outstanding Math. Educator for Region 3, 1991; Teaching Excellence and Math. Team fellow, 1991—. Mem. NEA, ASCD, N.C. Assn. Educators (assn. rep. Warren County chpt., chairperson PACE), N.C. Tchrs. Math., N.C. Coun. Tchr. Educators. Home: 5921 Three Ponds Dr Holly Springs NC 27540 Office: RR 4 Box 463 Warrenton NC 27589-9116

SPENCE, FLOYD DAVIDSON, congressman; b. Columbia, S.C., Apr. 9, 1928; s. James Wilson and Addie (Lucas) S.; m. Deborah Williams, July 3, 1988; children from previous marriage: David, Zack, Benjamin, Caldwell. A.B., U. S.C., 1952, J.D., 1956. Bar: S.C. 1956. Former partner firm Callison and Spence, West Columbia, S.C.; mem. S.C. Ho. Reps., 1956-62; mem. S.C. Senate, 1966-70, minority leader, 1966-70, chmn. joint com. internal security, 1967-70; mem. 92nd-103rd Congresses from 2nd S.C. dist., Washington, D.C., 1971—; chmn. nat. security com. 104th Congress, mem. subcom. mil. procurement; ranking minority mem. Armed Svcs. com., 1992-94; mem. Ho. of Reps. com. on coms. 103d Congress; mem. Rep. policy com. 104th Congress; mem. Vietnam Era Vets in Congress. Editor S.C. Law Quarterly. Past chmn. Indian Waters Coun. S.C. Boy Scouts Am., 1965-66, exec. bd., 1963—; chmn. Lexington County Mental Health Assn., 1959; former mem. bd. visitors U.S. Naval Acad. Served as capt. USNR, ret. Recipient Watchdog of the Treasury award, Order of the Palmetto award. Mem. ABA, U.S. Supreme Ct. Bar Assn., Lexington County Bar Assn., Am. Legion, VFW, Res. Officers Assn., Navy League, Kappa Alpha Order, Phi Alpha Delta (former chief justice), Kappa Sigma Kappa, Omicron Delta Kappa. Lutheran. Office: US Ho Reps 2405 Rayburn House Office Bldg Washington DC 20515-4002

SPENCE, JEFFREY BENNETT, minister, religious association administrator; b. White Plains, N.Y., July 16, 1949; s. Edwin Bartlett and Jean (Fowler) S.; m. Laura Mary Walkiewicz, Jan. 19, 1974. BA in Religion and Am. History, Washington and Lee U., 1971; MDiv in Counseling and Group Dynamics, Drew U., 1974; DMin in Ethics, Va. Union U., 1993. Ordained to ministry United Ch. of Christ, 1974. Mgr. Band Box Records, Lexington, Va., 1969-71; asst. minister First Presbyn. Ch., Ossinig, N.Y., 1971-72, Ossinig Heights United Meth. Ch., 1972-73; assoc. pastor Armonk (N.Y.) United Meth. Ch., 1973-74; pastor Bethlehem United Ch. of Christ, Tenth Legion, Va., 1974-77, Schroon Lake (N.Y.) Community Ch., 1977-78; exec. dir. Kansas City (Mo.) region NCCJ, 1978-80; exec. dir. Va. region NCCJ, Richmond, 1980—. Active Urban League Bd., Richmond, Va., 1981-87; chaplain Chesterfield (Va.) County Police, 1989—, Henrico (Va.) County Police, 1980—; emergency svcs. panel seven United Way Svcs. Greater Richmond, 1990—. Recipient Meritorious Citizenship award Chesterfield

County Police, 1984, Spl. tribute Interfaith Coun. Richmond, 1991. Mem. Masons (32d degree), Shriners, Elks, Sigma Phi Epsilon (v.p. alumni bd. Washington and Lee U. chpt.). Democrat. Office: NCCJ Va Region 4912 W Broad St Ste 200 Richmond VA 23230-3126

SPENCE, MARJORIE A., medical/surgical nurse; b. Pitts., Mar. 2, 1950; d. James Milton and Euphemia Martha (Brenner) McDowell; m. James L. Spence, Dec. 15, 1979. BSN, U. Evansville, 1972; MS in Nursing, U. Fla., 1989. Lic. advanced RN practitioner, Fla. Staff/charge nurse Gainesville (Fla.) VA Med. Ctr.; staff/charge nurse, relief supr. Transylvania Community Hosp., Brevard, N.C.; asst. head nurse Nairobi (Kenya) Hosp.; head nurse surg. fl. Lake City (Fla.) VA Med. Ctr.; head nurse rehab. unit Gainesville VA Med. Ctr., occupational health nurse, 1992—. Lt. USN, 1975-80. Mem. ANA (mem. coun. for advanced nursing practice, cert. med./surg. nurse), Sigma Theta Tau, Alpha Tau Delta.

SPENCE, SUSAN BATEMAN, counselor; b. Atlanta, Mar. 4, 1947; d. Gregory Wendell and Anne (Chambless) Bateman; m. James E. Spence Jr., Mar. 30, 1985; children: Anna Lee, Katherine Ellen. AB, U. Ga., 1969; MEd, Ga. State U., 1977. Caseworker Richmond County Dept. Family and Children Svcs., Augusta, Ga., 1970-73; vocat. rehab. counselor State of Ga., Atlanta, 1973-77; prof. counselor North DeKalb Mental Health Ctr., Atlanta, 1981—. Mem. Ga. Mental Health Counselors Assn., Alpha Chi Omega (treas. Athens, Ga. chpt. 1967-68), Alpha Lambda Delta. Republican. Baptist. Home: 1105 Oxford Cres NE Atlanta GA 30319-1624 Office: North DeKalb Mental Health Ctr 3300 Northeast Expy NE Atlanta GA 30341-3941

SPENCER, ALBERT FRANKLIN, physical education and education educator; b. Pitts., Dec. 31, 1943; s. Albert Clair and Ann Mary (Kielbas) S. BS in Edn., Slippery Rock (Pa.) State. Coll., 1966; MS, Clarion (Pa.) State Coll., 1981; PhD in LS, Fla. State U., Tallahassee, 1985, PhD in Phys. Edn., 1992. Phys. edn. tchr., libr., coach St. John's Indian Sch., Komatke, Ariz., 1976-79, Duncan (Ariz.) H.S., 1977-79; tchr. math. and sci. Army and Navy Acad., Carlsbad, Calif., 1979-80; phys. edn. tchr., libr., coach Baboquivari H.S., Sells, Ariz., 1980-81; asst. men's intercoll. basketball coach Fla. State U., Tallahassee, 1981-83; asst. prof. phys. edn., dir. audiovisual svcs. St. Leo (Fla.) Coll., 1983-86; asst. prof. Atlanta U. and Emory U., Atlanta, 1986-87; assoc. prof. phys. edn./athletics, libr. dir., coach Ga. Mil. Coll., Milledgeville, 1987-90; asst. prof. edn. U. Nev., Las Vegas, 1991-94; asst. prof. phys. edn., dept. human performance/health scis. Rice U., Houston, 1994—; cons. ednl. tech. Atlanta Pub. Schs., 1986-87; profl. basketball scout Bertka Agy. and L.A. Lakers, 1985-91; deptl. dir. KMart, New Kensington, Pa., 1972-74; dir. athletics YMCA, Kittanning, Pa., 1969. Contbg. author: Twentieth-Century Young Adult Writers, 1994; contbr. articles and revs. to profl. jours. Fundraiser KC, Las Vegas; vol. coach for youth league St. Anthony Elem. Sch., San Antonio, Fla.; scoutmaster Boy Scouss Am., New Kensington. Mem. AAHPERD, ALA, Am. Libr. and Info. Sci. Educators, Fla. Assn. for Health, Phys. Edn., Recreation and Dance, Tex. Assn. for Health, Phys. Edn., Recreation and Dance, U.S. Phys. Edn. Assn., Tex. Faculty Assn., Beta Phi Mu, Omicron Delta Kappa. Roman Catholic. Office: Rice U Dept Human Perf/Hlth Svcs PO Box 1892 Houston TX 77251

SPENCER, ANNA LOU, state official; b. Muse, Okla., Apr. 28, 1939; d. Artie Preston and Birdie Elma (Williams) Cole; m. John Preston Seymour, Dec. 17, 1957 (div. 1966); children: Bryan Paul Seymour, Bradley Preston Seymour; m. Billy Morris Spencer, Aug. 18, 1967 (dec. Mar. 1992). AS, Paris (Tex.) Jr. Coll., 1980; BS in Computer Sci., East Tex. State U., 1982. Clk. Strickland Transp., Paris, 1967; sec. Champion Packages, Paris, 1967-69; bookkeeper-sec. Paris Ind. Sch. Dist., 1969-77, tchr., 1977-78; office mgr. Bill Spencer Allstate Ins., Paris, 1985-87; word processing operator Dept. Human Svcs. State of Tex., Paris, 1987, registration technician Dept. Human Svcs., 1987-89, key entry operator Dept. Human Svcs., 1989-90, automation supr. Dept. Hwys., 1990—; self-employed cons., 1985—. Author: The Davis and Other Family Lines, 1990, Lamar County Texas Marriages, 1977; co-author: Providence Baptist Church, 1983. Mem. animal adv. bd. City of Paris, 1990—; organist Lakeway Bapt. Ch., 1988—. Mem. Tex. Pub. Employee Assn., Lamar County Humane Assn. (bd. dirs., pres.), Doris Day Animal League, Paris Area Computer Users Club, Alpha Chi. Home: 1710 34th St NE Paris TX 75462-2904 Office: Tex Dept Hwys 1365 N Main St Paris TX 75460-2650

SPENCER, DEBORAH JOYCE, school psychologist, consultant; b. Little Rock, Dec. 19, 1950; d. Virgil Roach and Frances Merle (Schafer) Moncrief; m. William Robert Price, Jr., June 14, 1970 (div. Dec. 1979), 1 child, Robert Geoffrey; m. James Leigh Spencer, Nov. 18, 1981 (div. Sept. 1993); children: Alicia Joyce, Leslie Leigh. Student, Wesleyan Coll., Macon, Ga., 1968-69; BA in Psychology, Ga. State U., 1972, MEd in Sch. Psychology, 1973; EdD, Nova U., 1989. Lic. psychol. examiner, Ark.; nationally cert. sch. psychologist, Ga., Fla.; cert. sch. psychology specialist, Ark. Tchr. phys. edn. Immaculate Heart of Mary Sch., Atlanta, 1972-73; cons. sch. psychology West Ga. Coop. Ednl. Svcs. Agy., Newnan, Ga., 1973-76; dir., specialist in sch. psychology Hollander Learning Ctrs., Vero Beach, Ft. Pierce, Fla., 1976-80; psychol. examiner Psychol. Testing Svc., Pine Bluff, Ark., 1981-84; sch. psychologist North Little Rock (Ark.) Sch. Dist., 1984-94; lectr. alternative assessment methods multi-cultural populations U. Witwatersrand, Johannesburg, South Africa, 1994-95; sch. psychologist Forrest City (Ark.) Sch. Dist., 1996—; Ark. field coord. Psychol. Corp., 1986-88; lectr. ann. conv. Ark. Assn. for Counseling Guidance and Devel., 1986-89, 93, Ann. Ark. Even Start Presch. Parent Conf., 1994. Vol. cons. devel. program alternative learning strategies for learning disabled students Christ the King Cath. Sch., Little Rock, 1988—. Grantee Rockfeller Found., 1988-89. Mem. Assn. for Measurement and Evaluation in Guidance (chmn. standards com. 1985-86), Nat. Assn. Sch. Psychologists, Ark. Assn. Sch. Psychologists (pres.-elect 1986-87, pres. 1987-88, exec. bd.), Mortar Bd., Phi Kappa Phi, Psi Chi. Republican. Roman Catholic. Home: 210 Seaton # 34 Forrest City AR 72336 Office: Forrest City Sch Dist Forrest City AR 72336

SPENCER, EDGAR WINSTON, geology educator; b. Monticello, Ark., May 27, 1931; s. Terrel Ford and Allie Belle (Shelton) S.; m. Elizabeth Penn Humphries, Nov. 26, 1958; children: Elizabeth Shawn, Kristen Shannon. Student, Vanderbilt U., 1949-50; B.S., Washington and Lee U., 1953; Ph.D., Columbia U., 1957. Lectr. Hunter Coll., 1954-57; mem. faculty Washington and Lee U., 1957—, prof. geology, head dept., 1962-95, Ruth Parmly prof.; pres. Rockbridge Area Conservation Coun., 1978-79, 95-97; NSF sci. faculty fellow, New Zealand and Australia; dir. grant for humanities and pub. policy on land use planning Va. Found., 1975; dir. grant Petroleum Rsch. Fund, 1981-82; leader field trip Ctrl. Appalachian Mts. Internat. Geol. Congress, 1989. Author: Basic Concepts of Physical Geology, 1962, Basic Concepts of Historical Geology, 1962, Geology: A Survey of Earth Science, 1965, Introduction to the Structure of the Earth, 1969, 3d edit., 1988, The Dynamics of the Earth, 1972, Physical Geology, 1983, Geologic Maps, 1993. Recipient Va. Outstanding Faculty award Va. Coun. of Higher Edn., 1990. Fellow Geol. Soc. Am., AAAS; mem. Am. Assn. Petroleum Geologists (dir. field seminar on fold and thrust belts 1987, 88-91), Am. Inst. Profl. Geologists, Am. Geophys. Union, Nat. Assn. Geology Tchrs., Yellowstone-Bighorn Rsch. Assn., Phi Beta Kappa (hon.), Sigma Xi. Home: PO Box 1055 Lexington VA 24450-1055

SPENCER, FRANCIS MONTGOMERY JAMES, pharmacist; b. St. John's, Antigua, Mar. 11, 1943; came to U.S., 1974; s. Stanley M. and Sarah Jane Elizabeth (Spencer) James; m. Jean V. Cole, May 9, 1981; children: David, Frances, Weslie. BS in Pharmacy, Northeastern U., Boston, 1982. Registered pharmacist, Mass., N.H., Fla.; registered cons. pharmacist, pharmacy preceptor, Fla. Sr. dispensing druggist Holberton Hosp., Antigua, 1968-73, lectr. in pharmacy, 1970-73; pharmacist, intern Mount Auburn Hosp., Cambridge, Mass., 1978-82; staff pharmacist Centro-Asturiano Hosp., Tampa, Fla., 1986-90, Dr.'s Hosp., Tampa, Fla., 1991—; pharmacy mgr. Eckerd Drug Co., Tampa, Fla., 1983—; co-founder, pres., chief exec. officer Spenscott, Inc., Bronx, N.Y., 1989—; assoc. mem. Delta Search, Inc., Tampa, 1987—. Mem. profl. adv. panel Drug Topics mag., Oradell, N.J., 1987—. Fellow Am. Soc. Cons. Pharmacists (registered cons. Fla.), Internat. Biog Assn. (life, dept. dir. gen.); mem. AAAS, Fla. Pharmacy Assn., Am. Biog. Inst. Inc. (dep. gov., hon. mem. rsch. bd. advisors), N.Y. Acad. Scis., Am. Soc. Pharmacy Law, Mass. State Pharmacy Assn., N.H. Pharmacy Assn., Am. Coll. Heatlh Care Adminstrs. Methodist. Home: PO Box 245 Mango FL 33550-0245

SPENCER, JAMES R., federal judge; b. 1949. BA magna cum laude, Clark Coll., 1971; JD, Harvard U., 1974, MDiv, 1985. Staff atty. Atlanta Legal Aid Soc., 1974-75; asst. U.S. atty. Washington, 1978, U.S. Dist. Ct. (ea. dist.) Va., 1983; judge U.S. Dist. Ct. (ea. dist.) Va., Richmond, 1986—; adj. prof. law U. Va., 1987—. Capt. JAGC, U.S.Army, 1975-78, res. 1981-86. Mem. ABA, Nat. Bar Assn., State Bar Ga., D.C. Bar, Va. State Bar, Richmond Bar Assn., Washington Bar Assn., Old Dominion Bar Assn., Omega Psi Phi, Sigma Pi Phi. Office: US Courthouse 1000 East Main St Richmond VA 23219-3525

SPENCER, MARY MILLER, civic worker; b. Comanche, Tex., May 25, 1924; d. Aaron Gaynor and Alma (Grissom) Miller; 1 child, Mara Lynn. BS, U. North Tex., 1943. Cafeteria dir. Mercedes (Tex.) Pub. Schs., 1943-46; home economist coordinator All-Orange Dessert Contest, Fla. Citrus Commn., Lakeland, 1959-62, 64; tchr. purchasing sch. lunch dept. Fla. Dept. Edn., 1960. Clothing judge Polk County (Fla.) Youth Fair, 1951-68, Polk County Federated Women's Clubs, 1964-66; pres. Dixieland Elem. Sch. PTA, 1955-57, Polk County Council PTA's, 1958-60; chmn. public edn. com. Polk County unit Am. Cancer Soc., 1959-60, bd. dirs., 1962-70; charter mem., bd. dirs. Lakeland YMCA, 1962-72; sec. Greater Lakeland Community Nursing Council, 1965-72; trustee, vice chmn. Polk County Eye Clinic, Inc., 1962-64, pres., 1964-82; bd. dirs. Polk County Scholarship and Loan Fund, 1962-70; mem. exec. com. West Polk County (Fla.) Community Welfare Council, 1960-62, 65-68; mem. budget and audit com. Greater Lakeland United Fund, 1960-62, bd. dirs., 1967-70, residential chmn. fund drive, 1968; mem. adv. bd. Polk County Juvenile and Domestic Relations Ct., 1960-69; worker children's services div. family services Dept. Health and Rehab. Services, State of Fla., 1969-70, social worker, 1970-72, 74-82, social worker OFR unit, 1977-81, with other pers. svcs., 1981-82; supr. OFR unit 1982-83, pub. assistance specialist IV, 1984-89; with other pers. svcs. Emergency Fin. Assistance Housing Program, 1990-96. Mem. exec. com. Suncoast Health Council, 1968-71; mem. Polk County Home Econs. Adv. Com., 1965-71; sec. bd. dirs. Fla. West Coast Ednl. TV, 1960-81; bd. dirs. Lake Region United Way, Winter Haven, 1976-81; mem. Polk County Community Services Council, 1978-88. Mem. Nat. Welfare Fraud Assn., Fla. Congress Parents and Tchrs. (hon. life; pres. dist. 7 1961-63, chmn. pub. relations 1962-66), AAUW (pres. Lakeland br. 1960-61), Polk County Mental Health Assn., Fla. Health and Welfare Council, Fla. Health and Social Service Council, U. North Tex. Alumni Assn. Democrat. Methodist. Lodge: Order of Eastern Star. Home and Office: PO Box 2161 Lakeland FL 33806-2161

SPENCER, RICHARD THOMAS, III, healthcare industry executive; b. Oak Park, Ill., Mar. 18, 1936; s. Richard Thomas Jr. and Lois Anne (Pollock) S.; m. Andrea B. Schlickeiser, June 29, 1962; 1 child, Richard Thomas IV. BA, U. Mich., 1959; postgrad., U. Pa., 1976, Stanford U., 1984, Clemson U., 1985. Mktg. group Mobil Oil Co., Detroit, 1962; internat. trade specialist U.S. Dept. Commerce, Detroit, 1963-64; account exec. J. Walter Thompson Co., Detroit, 1965-66; sales mgr. Sarns Inc., Ann Arbor, Mich., 1967-69; v.p. mktg. Cordis Dow Corp., Miami, Fla., 1970-81; pres. mktg. div. Cordis Corp., Miami, Fla., 1982-87; pres., CEO Uni-Med Internat. Corp., Miami, Fla., 1988—; bd. dirs. World Med. Mfg. Corp., Sunrise, Fla.; cons. in field. Contbr. articles to profl. jours. With U.S. Army, 1959-61. Republican. Office: Uni-Med Internat Corp PO Box 331120 Miami FL 33233-1120

SPENCER, STEPHEN ROBERT, theology educator; b. Gowanda, N.Y., July 1, 1952; s. James William and Lorna Rae (Johnston) S.; m. H. Gaylynn Trueblood, Dec. 21, 1974. BA, Cedarville Coll., 1974; MDiv, Grand Rapids Bapt. Sem., 1978, ThM, 1981; PhD, Mich. State U., 1988. Assoc. prof. hist. & philosophical theology Grand Rapids (Mich.) Bapt. Sem., 1978-90, spl. asst. libr., 1979-86; prof. systematic & hist. theology Dallas Theol. Sem., 1990-96, prof. systematic theology, 1996—. Contbr. articles to profl. jours. and symposia and reference books. Mem. Am. Acad. Religion, Am. Soc. Ch. history, Soc. Christian Philosophers, Evang. Theol. Soc., 16th Century Studies Conf., Calvin Studies Soc. Independent. Home: 9009 Bryson Dr Dallas TX 75238-2930 Office: Dallas Theol Sem 3909 Swiss Ave Dallas TX 75204-6471

SPENCER, THOMAS MORRIS, community college president; b. Llano, Tex., July 25, 1941; s. Thomas Morris and Betty Lou Rachel (Bradham) S.; m. Gloria Lee Blakeley, Dec. 27, 1961; children: Thomas, Blake. BA, U. Tex., 1961; MA, Texas Tech. U., 1962; PhD, U. Tex., 1964. Chief instrnl. officer Mitchell Co., Statesville, N.C., 1964-66, Bee County Coll., Beeville, Tex., 1966-70; dir. compensatory edn. project Coordinating Bd. Tex. Colls. and Univs. System, Austin, Tex., 1970-72; asst. and assoc. dir. cmty. colls., assoc. and dep. dir. Ark. Dept. Higher Edn., Little Rock, 1972-90; pres. East Ark. Cmty. Coll., Forrest City, 1990-94, Garland County Cmty. Coll., Hot Springs, Ark., 1994—; chmn. Nat. Coun. State Dirs., 1979; chmn. Ark. Assn. Two-Yr. Colls., 1993. Dist. chmn. Boy Scouts Thunderbird Dist., North Little Rock, 1982-84; mem. Ark. Higher Edn. funding com., 1995—. Named Outstanding Alumnus South Plains (Tex.) Coll., 1987; recipient W.K. Kellogg Found. grant, U. Tex., 1962-64. Mem. Salvation Army Bd., Hot Springs Rotary Club, Hot Springs C. of C. (bd. mem. 1995—), Leadership Hot Springs, Phi Delta Kappa. Episcopalian. Office: Garland County Cmty Coll 101 College Dr Hot Springs AR 71913-9174

SPENCER, W. E., oil company executive; b. 1937. BS, U. Texas, 1960. Engr. California Oil Comp., 1960-65; Coastal Corp, Houston, TX, 1965—; sr. vp, explor. prod. Coastal Corp., Houston, TX, 1983—. Office: Coastal Corp 9 E Greenway Plz Houston TX 77046

SPENCER, W(ALTER) THOMAS, lawyer; b. Crawfordsville, Ind., Aug. 6, 1928; s. Walter White and Jean Anna (Springer) S.; m. Patricia Audrey Raia, Mar. 30, 1974; children: Thomas Alfred, Jamie Raia. Student Wabash Coll., Crawfordsville, 1946-47; AB, U. Miami-Coral Gables, 1950, JD, 1956. Bar: Fla. 1956, U.S. Dist. Ct. (so. dist.) Fla. 1957, U.S. Dist. Ct. (no. dist.) Fla. 1963, U.S. Ct. Appeals (11th cir.) 1981, U.S. Supreme Ct. 1984. Assoc., Dean, Adams & Fischer, Miami, 1957-63; ptnr. Spencer & Taylor (George), Miami, 1963-81, Spencer & Taylor (Arthur), Miami, 1981-90; cir. judge 11th Jud. Cir. Ct. Fla., 1990—; mem. Fla. Ho. Reps., 1963-66; mem. Fla. Senate, 1966-68. Served to lt. USNR, 1952-55. Mem. ABA, Dade County Bar Assn., Am. Judicature Soc., Am. Judges Assn. Democrat. Methodist. Club: Coral Gables Country (Coral Gables). Home: 4520 Santa Maria St Miami FL 33146-1131 Office: 418 Dade County Courthouse 73 W Flagler St Miami FL 33130-1731

SPENCER, WILLIAM H., farming executive; b. 1945. Pres. Spencer Farms, 1964—, Plants of Ruskin (Fla.) Inc., 1979—; v.p. DiMare Ruskin Inc., Ruskin, 1968—.

SPENCER, WINIFRED MAY, art educator; b. Tulsa, Oct. 7, 1938; d. Len and Madge (Scofield) S. BA in Comml. Art, U. Tulsa, 1961, Cert. in Tchg., 1962. Cert. comml. art, K-12 art, English/journalism tchr. Freelance comml. artist Tulsa, 1962-63; art/sci. educator Pleasant Porter Elem. Tulsa Pub. Schs., 1963-65, art educator, supervising tchr. Kendall Elem., 1965-70, art educator, team leader pilot program Bunche Elem., 1970-75, art educator Carnegie Elem., 1975-81, art educator, fine arts dept. chair Foster Jr. High, 1982-83, art educator, fine arts dept. chair Foster Mid. Sch., 1983—; judge Okla. Wildlife Arts Festival, Okla. Wildlife Assn., Tulsa, 1988; supervising tchr., tchr. tng. U. Tulsa, 1965-70, Northeastern State U., Tahlequah, Okla, 1965-70; pres. Tulsa Elem. Art Tchrs., Tulsa Pub. Schs., 1967-68, curriculum writing/curriculum cons., 1970-75, 91—; coord. summer arts/artists in the schs. program Tchr. Adv. Bd., Summer Arts Tulsa Arts and Humanities Coun., 1986-94. Exhibited in group shows at Tulsa City-County Ctrl. Libr., 1989, Philbrook Art Mus., 1993, 94. Mem. Rep. Nat. Com., 1994-96; art adv. PTA, Tulsa, 1970—; ch. leader Christian Sci. Ch., Tulsa, 1960—; mem. city of Tulsa goals for tomorrow task force on cultural affairs, 1995—. Invited U.S. China Joint Conf. on Edn., Citizen Amb. Program People to People Internat., 1992, U.S. Spain Joint Conf. on Edn., Citizen Amb. Program People to People Internat., 1995. Mem. AAUW, NEA, ASCD, Okla. Edn. Assn., Tulsa Classroom Tchrs. Assn., Okla. Mid. Level Edn. Assn. (del. 1994), Nat. Art Edn. Assn. (del. 1992, 94, 96), Okla. Art Edn. Assn. Home: 439 S Memorial Dr Tulsa OK 74112-2203 Office: Foster Mid Sch 12121 E 21st St Tulsa OK 74129-1801

SPENCER-CISEK, PATRICIA A., oncological nurse; b. Albany, N.Y., Mar. 16, 1961; d. Lawrence L. and Maria S. (McNerney) Spencer; m. Walter W. Cisek, May 30, 1987; children: Emily Anne, Christopher L. BSN, Boston Coll., 1983; MS in Nursing, Tex. Woman's U., 1988; adult nurse practitioner, U. Tex. Health Sci. Ctr., 1994. RN, Mass.; cert. med.-surg. clin. nurse specialist; cert. oncology nurse; cert. adult nurse practitioner. Primary nurse Beth Israel Hosp., Boston, 1983-84; clin. nurse M.D. Anderson Cancer Ctr., Houston, 1984-86; clin. nurse specialist oncology unit Marlborough (Mass.) Hosp., 1986-87, St. Vincent Hosp., Worcester, Mass., 1987-90, Dana Farber Cancer Inst., Boston, 1990-91, U. Tex. M.D. Anderson Cancer Ctr., Houston, 1991—; mgr. LifeCheq Cancer Prevention Program; presenter in field. Mem. Oncology Nursing Soc. (pres. Houston chpt. 1994-95), Sigma Theta Tau.

SPENCER-DAHLEM, ANITA JOYCE, medical, surgical and critical care nurse; b. Weirton, W.Va., Aug. 26, 1961; d. Carlas A. and Evelyn Faye (Miller) Spencer; m. Terry Dahlem. BS, Alderson-Broaddus Coll., Philippi, W.Va., 1984. Staff nurse, orthopedic unit Charleston (W.Va.) Area Med. Ctr., 1984-86; ICU staff nurse Ohio Valley Hosp., Steubenville, Ohio, 1986—; nurse on cardiac catheterization unit Ohio Valley Hosp., Steubenville, 1994—. Mem. Ohio Nurses Assn.

SPERATH, ALBERT FRANK, artist, museum director. Student, U.S. Armed Forces Inst., U. Hawaii, Ind. U. Pa.; BFA, Ohio U., 1973; MFA, U. Nebr., 1976; postgrad., U. Ky., 1978. Dir. traveling exhibition svc. Ky. Arts Commn., 1976-81; ind. curator, gallery cons., exhibition and lighting designer, 1981-83, 85-86; exhibit designer, chief preparator J. B. Speed Art Mus., Louisville, 1983-85; curator Ky. Art and Craft Found. Gallery, Louisville, 1986-90; dir. univ. galleries Murray (Ky.) State U., 1990—; gallery asst. Sheldon Meml. Art Gallery, U. Nebr., Lincoln, 1974-76; cons. Stuhr Mus., Grand Island, Nebr., 1976; judge, juror Ohio U., 1979, Murray State U., 1990, Henderson County Arts Coun., Ky., 1990, Ky. Dept. Arts, Frankfort, 1990, Artswatch, Louisville, 1990, Fiber Guild Lexington, 1990, Am. Craft Enterprises, New Paltz, N.Y., 1990, Paris-Henry County Arts Coun., 1991, Shakertown, 1993, Mid Cumberland Arts League, 1993, Mayfield Graves Gallery, 1993, Murray Art Guild., 1994; chmn. visual arts com., bd. dirs. Ky. Citizens for Arts., 1983-85, 92—; mem. panel Ky. Arts Coun., 1983, Ind. Arts Coun., 1991; mem. steering com. Ky. participation Year Am. Craft, 1992-93; co-chair Jackson Purchase Art and Craft Fair, 1993, Crossroads and Connections, 1993; conf. coord. Ky. Assn. Mus. Ann. Conf., Murray State U., 1994. One-person shows include Archetype Gallery, New Haven, Conn., 1974, Springfield Art and Hist. Soc., Vt., 1974, East St. Gallery, Grinnell, Iowa, 1975, Capital Gallery Contemporary Art, Frankfort, Ky., 1985; exhibited in group shows Byck Gallery, 1981, Louisville, Art Ctr. Assn., Louisville, 1981, Ky. Heritage Coun., 1982, Martha White Gallery, Louisville, 1983, Jackson Hall Gallery, 1986, J. B. SPeed ArtMus., 1986, Liberty Gallery, 1988, Swanson Cralle Gallery, 1990, Murray State U., 1991, Ashland Area Art Gallery, 1992, Murray State U., 1993, Ky. Art and Craft Found. Gallery, 1993; represented in permanent collections Hyatt Regency Hotel, Louisville, Stuhr Mus., Grand Island, Nebr., SUNY, Geneseo, numerous pvt. collections. Fundraiser various local and statewide concers. With USN, Vietnam. Recipient 2nd Place award Gallery in the Market, Omaha, 1973, Stuhr Mus., 1975, Merit award Sheldon Meml. Art Gallery, 1975; Al Smith Scupture fellow Ky. Arts Coun., 1994. Mem. Am. Assn. Mus., Assn. Coll. and Univ. Mus. and Galleries, Coll. Art Assn., Ky. Assn. Mus. Home: 930 Billy Paschall Rd Murray KY 42071-9319 Office: Murray State U Eagle Gallery PO Box 9 Murray KY 42071

SPERBER, MATTHEW ARNOLD, direct marketing company executive; b. N.Y.C., Dec. 17, 1938; s. Raymond and Sylvia (Pollock) S.; m. Jane L. Trautman; children: Sean S., Dawn E. BS in Architecture, CUNY, 1961. Mgr. advt. IBM, White Plains, N.Y., 1967-78; mgr. advt. and promotion Exxon Office Systems, Lionsville, Pa., 1979-81; dir. advt. and promotion Wang, Lowell, Mass., 1981-83; dir. mkgt. communication Datapoint, San Antonio, 1983-85; pres. Bus. to Bus. div. Harte Hanks Direct Mktg., San Antonio, 1985-88; pres. Internat. Direct Mktg., San Antonio, 1988—. Mgr. IBM Copier, 1970, QYX Electronic Typewriter, 1980; dir. Wang Personal Computer, 1982, Datapoint 32 Mini Computer, 1985. With U.S. Army, 1961-63. Mem. Am. Mktg. Assn. (exec.), Direct Mktg. Assn. (Best Indsl. Direct Mktg. award 1978). Republican. Home: 331 Country Wood Dr San Antonio TX 78216-1610 Office: Internat Direct Mktg 8045 Antoine Dr Ste 109 Houston TX 77088-4301

SPERO, MORTON BERTRAM, lawyer; b. N.Y.C., Dec. 6, 1920; s. Adolph and Julia (Strasburger) S.; m. Louise Thacker, May 1, 1943; children: Donald S., Carol S. Flynn. BA, U. Va., 1942, LLB, 1946. Bar: Va. 1946, U.S. Supreme Ct. 1961. Mem. legal staff NLRB, Washington, 1946-48; sole practice, Petersburg, Va., 1948-70; sr. ptnr. Spero & Levinson, Petersburg, 1970-75; sr. ptnr. Spero & Diehl, Petersburg, 1975-85; sole practice, Petersburg, 1985—; chmn. The Community Bank, Petersburg, 1976-79, dir., 1976-91. Chmn. United Fund Drive, 1960; pres. Dist. IV Petersburg Council Social Welfare, Southside Sheltered Workshop, 1965, pres. Congregation B'rith Achim, 1973. Served to lt. USNR, 1943-45. Recipient Outstanding Mem. award Petersburg chapt. B'nai B'rith, 1966; Svc. to Law Enforcement award Petersburg Police Dept., 1965. Fellow Am. Acad. Matrimonial Lawyers; mem. Va. Bar Assn., Petersburg Bar Assn. (pres. 1981-82), Va. State Bar (council 1981-84, chmn. criminal law sect. 1972, chmn. family law sect. 1979, bd. dirs. litigation sect. 1983-86, bd. dirs. gen. practice sect., 1984-86, Lifetime Achievement award for family law sect. 1995), Va. Trial Lawyers Assn. (v.p. 1972). Democratic. Jewish. Clubs: Civitan (hon.), Rotary. Lodge: Elks (exalted ruler 1968). Home: 9706 Bunker Ct Petersburg VA 23805-9125 Office: PO Box 870 20 E Tabb St Ste 103 Petersburg VA 23804

SPERRY, DAVID BARTOW, pediatric neurologist, physician; b. Boston, May 2, 1945; s. Marcy Leavenworth Jr. and Virginia Bartow (Kimball) S.; children: Melissa Ashly, Liza Alexandra, Joshua Hamilton. BA, Yale U., 1968; MD, Wayne State U., 1972. Pediatric internship Children's Meml. Hosp., Chgo., 1972-73; pediatric and neurology resident Northwestern U., Chgo., 1975; pediatric neurology resident U. N.C., Chapel Hill, 1977; staff pediatric neurologist Univ. Affiliated Ctr., Dallas, 1977-79; asst. prof. pediatrics and neurology Southwestern Med. Sch. and Children's Med. Ctr., Dallas, 1977—; pvt. practice pediatric neurology Dallas, 1979—. Mem. health adv. coun. Dallas Ind. Sch. Dist., 1978-84; trustee Shelton Sch., Dallas, 1986—. Mem. Am. Acad. Neurology, Tex. Med. Assn., Dallas County Med. Soc., Child Neurology Soc., Dallas Epilepsy Assn. (mem. profl. adv. bd. 1978—). Office: 12801 N Central Expy Ste 580 Dallas TX 75243-1724

SPERRY, KRIS LEE, forensic pathologist; b. Topeka, Dec. 21, 1954; s. Corwin Everett and Irene (Forney) S.; m. Laurie Diane Beardsley, Mar. 27, 1977; children: Shanna Lyn, Krista Suzanne, Bekkah Elizabeth, Benjamin Everett. BS, Pittsburg (Kans.) State U., 1975; MD, U. Kans., 1978. Diplomate in anatomic and clin. pathology and forensic pathology Am. Bd. Pathology. Intern Allentown (Pa.) Hosp., 1978-79; resident in pathology U. N.Mex. Sch. Medicine, Albuquerque, 1981-85; fellow in forensic pathology Office of Med. Examiner, Albuquerque, 1985, med. investigator, 1986-89; dep. chief med. examiner Fulton County Med. Examiner, Atlanta, 1990—; forensic med. cons., Atlanta, 1990—. Mem. bd. editors Am. Jour. Forensic Medicine and Pathology, 1989—. Bd. dirs. Tourette Syndrome Assn. Ga., Atlanta, 1993—. Served with USPHS, 1979-81. Fellow Am. Acad. Forensic Scis., Am. Soc. Clin. Pathologists; mem. Nat. Assn. Med. Examiners. Office: Fulton County Med Examiner 50 Coca Cola Pl SE Atlanta GA 30303-3043

SPERRY, PAUL, newspaper columnist; b. Colorado Springs, Colo., June 16, 1964; s. P.E. (Joe) Sperry and Nancy L. McKinnon Kelley; m. Amy K. Sumrall, June 27, 1992. BJ, U. Tex., 1986. Sr. staff writer Investor's Bus. Daily, L.A., 1987—. Republican. Office: Investors Business Daily 12655 Beatrice St Los Angeles CA 90066-7300

SPEZZANO, VINCENT EDWARD, newspaper publisher; b. Retsof, N.Y., Apr. 3, 1926; s. Frank and Lucy S.; m. Marjorie Elliott, Dec. 18, 1948;

children: Steve, Judy, Mark, Christine (dec.). BA in Journalism, Syracuse (N.Y.) U., 1950. Reporter Livingston Republican, Geneseo, N.Y., 1950-51, Lynchburg (Va.) News, 1951-54, St. Louis Globe-Democrat, 1954-55; polit. writer, then dir. public service and research Rochester (N.Y.) Times Union, 1955-68; dir. public service, then dir. promotion and public service Gannett Co., Inc., 1968-75; pres., publisher Cape Publs., Inc., Cocoa, Fla., 1975-84; chmn. Cape Publs., Inc., 1984-91; asst., then v.p. Gannett/South, Gannett Co., Inc., 1977-79; pres. Gannett Southeast Newspaper Group, Gannett Co., Inc., 1979-82; exec. v.p. USA Today, 1982-83, pres., 1983; sr. v.p. communications Gannett Co., 1983-84, bd. dirs.; pres., pub. Gannett Rochester Newspapers, 1984-90, chmn., 1990-91; pres. Gannett N.E. Div., 1984-86; past mem. journalism endowment adv. com. U. Fla.; bd. dirs. Marine Midland Bank. Editor handbook. Past trustee St. John Fisher Coll., Rochester; trustee Brevard Art Ctr. and Mus., Melbourne, Fla.; bd. dirs. Cape Canaveral Hosp., 1991—, Fla. Inst. Tech., 1991—, Astronauts Meml. Found., 1991—, vice-chmn., space camp adv. bd.; bd. vice-chmn. Rochester Conv. Bur., 1986-91; mem. Founder's Com. The Rochesterians, 1986—; mem. adv. bd. Space Pioneers, Inc. With A.C., USNR, 1944-46. Recipient News Writing award Va. Press Assn., 1953, Citizen of Yr. award Citizens Club Rochester, 1960, Disting. Svc. award for non-members Kiwanis Club, 1960, Pub. Svc. Reporting award Am. Polit. Sci. Assn., 1963; named NE Kiwanis Citizen of Yr., 1987, Boss of Yr. Coca Beach chpt. Nat. Secretaries Assn., 1977, Rochester Communicator of Yr., 1987, Rochester Citizen of Yr., 1987, Cavaliere (Knight) in Order of Merit Republic of Italy, 1994. Mem. Internat. Newspaper Promotion Assn. (pres. 1970-71, Silver Shovel award 1975), Am. Newspapers Pubs. Assn., So. Newspaper Pubs. Assn. Found. (chmn.), Fla. Press Assn. (bd. dir., pres. 1984), N.Y. Newspaper Pubs. Assn. (bd. dirs.), Cocoa Beach Area C. of C., Rochester Area C. of C. (bd. dir. 1985—, chmn. bd. 1989-90). Roman Catholic. Home: 855 S Atlantic Ave Cocoa Beach FL 32931-2424 Office: 1 Gannett Plz Melbourne FL 32940 also: Cape Pubs Inc PO Box 363000 Melbourne FL 32936

SPIEGEL, H. JAY, lawyer; b. Cleve., July 7, 1952; s. Martin and Thea (Lange) S. BS, Cornell U., 1974; JD, George Mason U., 1981. Bar: Va. 1981, U.S. Patent Office 1982, U.S. Ct. Appeals (fed. cir.) 1982, U.S. Dist. Ct. (ea. dist.) Va. 1982, U.S. Supreme Ct. 1984, D.C. 1986. Primary and asst. examiner U.S. Patent and Trademark Office, Arlington, Va., 1974-82; assoc. Sherman & Shalloway, Alexandria, Va., 1982-88, of counsel, 1988; pvt. practice Alexandria, 1988—; owner, pres. Premium Products, Inc., Alexandria, 1984—, Jumpstart. Patentee sporting goods and jewelry; inventor Toe-Tal Tee football tee. Mem. ABA, Patent and Trademark Office Soc., Licensing Execs. Soc., Fairfax Yacht Club. Office: H Jay Spiegel & Assocs PC 703 King St Alexandria VA 22314-3014

SPIEGEL, JOHN WILLIAM, banker; b. Indpls., Mar. 14, 1941; s. William Sordon and Elizabeth (Hall) S.; children: W. Robert, John F., Bradley H.; m. Elizabeth Devereux Morgan, Aug. 16, 1986; stepchildren: David P. Adams III, Morgan G. Adams, Devereux Socas. BA, Wabash Coll., 1963; MBA, Emory U., 1965; postgrad., Nova U., 1993-96. Rsch. assoc. IMEDE (Mgmt. Inst.), Lausanne, Switzerland, 1965-66; mgmt. trainee Trust Co. Bank, Atlanta, 1966-67, bond portfolio mgr., 1967-72; data processing mgr. Trust Co. Ga., Atlanta, 1972-78, treas., 1978-85; exec. v.p., chief fin. officer SunTrust Banks Inc., Atlanta, 1985—; mem. exec. com. CFO divsn. ABA, 1987-90, chair, 1989-90. Mem. exec. com., bd. dirs. Alliance Theatre, Atlanta, 1985-92, pres., 1989-91; bd. dirs. High Mus. Art, Atlanta, 1985—; pres. Young Audiences Atlanta Inc., 1981-84, bd. dirs., 1985, mem. adv. bd., 1986—; pres. bd. visitors Grady Meml. Hosp., Atlanta, 1983-90; v.p. exec. bd. Atlanta Area coun. Boy Scouts Am., 1983-92, treas., 1989-91, mem. adv. bd., 1992; mem. adv. coun. Ga. State U. Sch. Accountancy, 1981-85, chmn. curriculum subcom., 1983-84; mem. exec. com., trustee Morehouse Sch. Medicine, 1984-93, chmn. fin. com., 1987-90, chmn., 1990-92; mem. Leadership Atlanta, 1976—, trustee, 1990-94; trustee, mem. exe. com. Robert W. Woodruff Arts Ctr. Inc., 1976—, treas., 1976-83, chmn. fin. com., 1984-89, 93—; chmn. fin. com., bd. dirs. Schenck Sch., Atlanta, 1986-88; exec. vice chmn. bd. trustees Holy Innocents Episcopal Sch., Atlanta, 1976-79, bd. dirs., treas., 1987-90; bd. dirs. Atlanta Opera, 1986—, United Way Met. Atlanta, Inc., 1994—. mem. Emory U. Bd. Visitors, 1991-95; bd. dirs. Rock Tenn. Co., Sallie Mae, Conti Fin. Corp., Suburban Lodges Am., Inc.; former mem. taxation and payment syss. com. ABA, mem. exec. com. divsn., 1987, 90, chair, 1989-90; former isntr. Morehouse Coll. and Banking Schs. Episcopalian. Home: 3043 Nancy Creek Rd NW Atlanta GA 30327-1901 Office: SunTrust Banks Inc PO Box 4418 Atlanta GA 30302-4418

SPIELMAN, BARBARA HELEN NEW, editor, consultant; b. Canton, Ohio, June 28, 1929; d. Arthur Daniel and Helen Barbara (Rickenmann) New; m. David Vernon Spielman, Nov. 24, 1956; children: Daniel Bruce, Linda Barbara. BS in English and History Edn. cum laude, Miami U., Oxford, Ohio, 1951. Cert. tchr., Ohio, Tex. Tchr. Canton Pub. Schs., 1951-53; vets. aide U. Tex., Austin, 1954-57; copy editor, mng. editor U. Tex. Press, Austin, 1964-91; ret., 1991; editorial cons. Chicago Manual of Style, 13th edit., 1975, Amon Carter Mus., Ft. Worth, 1970—, Ctr. for Mex. Am. Studies, Austin, 1980, Archer M. Huntington Art Gallery, Austin, 1975—, 64 Beds Project for Homeless and Hungry, Austin, 1989—; mem. search com. for dir., U. Tex. Press, 1991. Troop leader Girl Scouts Am., Austin, 1970-73; officer PTA, Austin, 1964-73. Mem. Am. Assn. Univ. Presses, Smithsonian Instn., Nat. Geog. Soc., Althenoi, Seton Med. Ctr. Aux., Phi Beta Kappa, Kappa Delta Pi, Sigma Sigma Sigma. Democrat. Presbyterian. Home: 3301 Perry Ln Austin TX 78731-5330

SPIELMAN, DAVID VERNON, retired insurance, finance and publications consultant; b. Humboldt, Iowa, Dec. 23, 1929; s. Elmo Bruce and Leona Belle (Blake) S.; m. Barbara Helen New, Nov. 24, 1956; children: Daniel Bruce, Linda Barbara. BA, U. Tex., 1966. Publs. engr. IBM Mil. Products, Kingston, N.Y., 1957-58; engring. writer Convair Astronautics div. Gen Dynamics Corp., San Diego, 1958-59; tech. publs. mgr. Ling-Temco Vought, Inc., Garland, Tex., 1960-62; tech. writer Ken Cook Pubs.-Tex. Co., Richardson, Tex., 1963-64; asst. coordinator Kuwait program U. Tex., Austin, 1964-66; ednl. writer Tex. Edn. Agy., Austin, 1966-74; real estate broker Dave Spielman Rsch. Assocs., Austin, 1974—, ins. broker, 1974—; cons. Nat. Ctr. Vocat. Edn., Columbus, Ohio, 1974-75, Tex. State Auditor, Austin, 1976-77, U.S. Dept. Labor, Washington, 1975-78; interviewee Fortune Mag.; exec. dir. Tex. Labor Ctr., Inc., 1978—. Counselor Distributive Edn. Clubs Am. Student Conf. Tex., Brenham, 1972; competition judge Tex. Carpenter's Apprentices, 1973-74; chpt. pres. Tex. Pub. Employees Assn., Austin, 1969-70; mem. Dem. Nat. Conv., 1988. Served to sgt. maj. U.S. Army, 1952-53, with USNR 1947-49, with Tex. N.G. 1949-50, cpl. USAF 1950-52. Recipient Outstanding Vocat. Edn. Contributor, Tex. House and Senate. Mem. Acctg. Computer Machinery Assn. (newsletter editor 1958-59), Soc. Tech Writers and Editors (chpt. pres. 1960-61), Soc. Tech. Writers and Pubs. (chpt. pres. 1961-62), Soc. Tech. Communications (membership chmn. 1983-84), Tex. State Tchrs. Assn., Delta Pi (local sec., treas.). Democrat. Presbyterian. Lodges: Masons. Home and Office: 3301 Perry Ln Austin TX 78731-5330

SPIERS, ALEXANDER STEWART D., medical educator; b. Melbourne, Australia, Jan. 31, 1936; came to U.S., 1976; s. Alexander Donaldson and Joan (Patterson) S.; m. Margaret Overend, Dec. 20, 1960; children: Alexander, Ronald, Deborah, Gordon, James. MBBS, U. Melbourne, 1960, PhD, 1968, MD, 1975. Cert. in internal medicine, hematology and oncology. Sr. lectr. in medicine Hammersmith Hosp., London, 1970-75; assoc. prof. Boston U., 1976-80; prof. medicine Albany (N.Y.) Med. Coll., 1980-87, U. South Fla., Tampa, from 1987; ret., 1996. Editor: Chemotherapy and Urological Malignancy, 1982; contbr. numerous articles and papers to profl. jours. Trustee Leukemia Soc. Am., Albany, 1980-87, Tampa, 1987—, chmn. edn. com., 1988—. Lt. col. Royal Army M.C., 1987—. Recipient Territorial decoration Queen Elizabeth, 1981; traveling fellow The Nuffield Found., 1968. Fellow Royal Coll. Pathologists Australasia, Royal Soc. Medicine, ACP, Royal Australasian Coll. Physicians, Royal Coll. Physicians Edinburgh; mem. Brit. Officers Club New Eng., Treasure Island Tennis & Yacht Club. Presbyterian.

SPIERS, WILLIAM KESLER, JR., financial aid administrator; b. Jacksonville, Fla., Oct. 7, 1957; s. William Kesler Sr. and Willma Eva (Greene) S.; m. Terrie Lynn Williams, Aug. 6, 1983; children: Laura Elane, Sara Lynn. BM, Jacksonville U., 1979, BME, 1981, MAT, 1994. Dir. placement Jacksonville (Fla.) U., 1980-83, dir. student fin. assistance, 1983—; Adv. bd. mem. Commr. Fin. Aid, Tallahassee, 1988—; adv. com. mem. Terri Loan, Boston, 1990-92; bd. mem. Coll. Scholarship Svc. Region, Atlanta, 1988—. Mem. Mayor's Edn. Com., Jacksonville, 1989; mem. stewardship edn. com., Jacksonville Bapt. Assn., 1988, mem. budget com., 1991-94, mem. adminstrv. com., 1993-94. Mem. Nat. Assn. of Student Fin. Aid Adminstrs., So. Assn. of Student Fin. Aid Adminstrs. (exec. bd. mem. 1989-90), Fla. Assn. of Student Fin. Aid Adminstrs. (pres. 1989-90). Baptist. Home: 3770 Townsend Oak Ct Jacksonville FL 32277-2283 Office: Jacksonville U 2800 University Blvd W Jacksonville FL 32211-2117

SPIES, JACOB JOHN, health care executive; b. Sheboygan, Wis., Jan. 27, 1931; s. Jacob Alfred and Julia Effie (Wescott) S.; m. Donna Dolores Jerale, June 17, 1954; children: Gary, Joni, Shari. BBA, U. Wis., 1955. V.p. health care systems Wausau (Wis.) Ins. Cos., 1972-77, v.p. mgmt. systems, 1977-79; dep. dir. Health Policy Inst. Boston U., 1979-85; pres., chief exec. officer Co-Med. Inc., Columbus, Ohio, 1984-85; sr. v.p. PARTNERS Nat. Health Plans, Irving, Tex., 1985-90; chmn. PARTNERS Health Plans of Colo., Denver, 1986-90; prin. The Furst Group, Dallas, 1990—; pres., CEO Dallas/Ft. Worth Health Industry Coun., 1994—; bd. dirs. Integrated Healthcare Corp.; adv. bd. Healthcare Adminstrn.; chmn. Tex. Women's U. Co-author: A Corporations Experience with IPA-HMO, 1981, Health Care Cost Containment, 1983. Sgt. U.S. Army, 1952-54, Korea. Decorated Bronze Star, 1953. Mem. Group Health Assn. Am. (com. mem. 1988, 91), Am. Managed Care and Rev. Assn. (bd. dirs.), Nat. Assn. Employers on Health Care Actions (chmn.), North Tex. Med. Edn. Consortium (bd. trustees 1995—), LaCima Club, Denton Country Club. Episcopalian. Home: 1492 Rockgate Rd S Roanoke TX 76262-7899 Office: The Furst Group 5215 N O Connor Blvd Ste 975 Irving TX 75039-3713

SPIESICKE, MARGRIT HERMA, counselor; b. Hannover, L. Saxonia, Germany, Dec. 29, 1925; came to U.S. 1960; d. Louis Adolf Otto Fritz and Else Herma (Meier) Becker; m. Horst Guenther Spiesicke, Nov. 9, 1949; 1 child, Marc Anthony. Cert. English/German Interpreter, Hannover (Germany) Lang. Coll., 1947; AA with hons., Broward C.C., Hollywood, Fla., 1983; BA in Humanities, Fla. Internat. U., 1989; postgrad., Nova U., 1992—. State interpreter British Mil. Govt., Hannover, 1947-49; sec., office mgr. Townsend Co., Montreal, Can., 1950-60; sec., adminstrv. asst. Wometco Enterprises, Miami, 1960-85; adminstrv. sec. Barry U., Miami, 1985-88; med. sec. Broward Correctional Instn., Pembroke Pines, Fla., 1988-90, instl. counselor, 1990—. Vol. group counselor Mancy Figueredo, M.D., Miami, 1988-89. Mem. Phi Kappa Phi. Republican. Lutheran.

SPILLER, HART, microbiologist; b. Berlin, Dec. 1, 1939; came to U.S., 1979; s. Helmut and Erika (Hurt) S. Degree, Pedagogical Coll. Univ., 1962, FA Univ. Erlangen, 1972; PhD, FA Univ. Erlangen, 1975. Registered primary, secondary tchr., Australia. Head tchr. Evang. Lutheran Ch., Territory Papua, New Guinea, Australia, 1963-65; supr. English schs. New Guinea, 1966; postdoctoral rsch. assoc. U. Konstanz, West Germany, 1975-78; fellow U. Calif., Davis, 1979-80; adj. postdoctoral assoc. U. Fla., Gainesville, 1981-85; postdoctoral assoc. U. Fla., 1986-87; rsch. asst. prof. biology Fisk U., Nashville, 1989-94. Active Amnesty Internat., Konstanz, Davis, 1977-79; founder, referee commr. Gainesville Recreational Soccer, 1981-88; bd. dirs. Clergy & Laity Concerned, Nashville, 1990-94; scoutmaster troop 76 Boy Scouts Am., 1990-94, scout coord.; councillor Corinthian Bapt. Ch., Nashville, 1989-94, ch. councillor 1994—. Mem. Am. Soc. Plant Physiologists, Am. Soc. Microbiology. Office: Corinthian Bapt Ch 819 33rd Ave N Nashville TN 37209

SPILLIAS, KENNETH GEORGE, lawyer; b. Steubenville, Ohio, Nov. 8, 1949; s. George and Angeline (Bouyoucas) S.; m. Monica Mary Saumweber, May 10, 1975; children: Geoffrey David, Alicia Anne, Stephanie Marie. BA, Pa. State U., 1971; JD magna cum laude, U. Pitts., 1974. Bar: Pa. 1974, Fla. 1978, U.S. Supreme Ct. 1978, U.S. Ct. Appeals (2d, 3d, 4th, 5th, 6th cirs.) 1975, (11th cir.) 1981, U.S. Dist. Ct. (mid. dist.) Fla. 1979, U.S. Dist. Ct. (so. dist.) Fla. 1978. Trial atty. U.S. Dept. Justice, Washington, 1974-76; asst. dist. atty. Dist. Atty. of Allegheny County, Pitts., 1976-78; asst. atty. gen. Fla. Dept. Legal Affairs, West Palm Beach, Fla., 1978-79; ptnr. Spillias & Mitchell, West Palm Beach, 1979-82, Considine & Spillias, West Palm Beach, 1982-83, Schneider, Maxwell, Spillias et al, West Palm Beach, 1984-86, Wolf, Block, Schorr et al, West Palm Beach, 1986-88, Shapiro & Bregman, West Palm Beach, 1988-91; of counsel Greenberg, Traurig et al, West Palm Beach, 1991; pvt. practice West Palm Beach, 1991—; instr. bus. law Coll. of the Palm Beaches, West Palm Beach, 1980-81; CLE lectr. Palm Beach County Bar Assn., 1983—. County commr. Bd. County Commrs., Palm Beach County, 1982-86; co-founder, mem. Children's Svcs. Coun., Palm Beach County, 1986-91; steering com. Fla. Atlantic U. Inst. of Govt., Boca Raton, 1983-94; bd. dirs. The Literacy Coalition of P.B.C., West Palm Beach, 1990—, health and human svcs. Fla. Dist. IX, 1995—, Ctr. for Family Svc., West Palm Beach, 1992-96, Palm Beach County Coun. of Arts, 1985-86; mem. policy coun. Fla. Inst. Govt., Tallahassee, 1985-86; fund raising chmn. United Cerebral Palsey Telethon, West Palm Beach, 1984-85; judge Palm Beach Post Pathfinders Awards, 1992-96. Recipient Cmty. Svc. award Downtown Civitan Club, West Palm Beach, 1983, Man of the Day award United Cerebral Palsey, 1986, Spl. Honoree award Palm Beach County Child Advocacy Bd., 1986, Children's Trust award Exch. Club/Dick Webber Ctr. for Prevention Child Abuse, 1991, Up and Comers Award in Law, South Fla. Bus. Jour./Price Waterhouse, 1988, Achievement award Nat. Assn. Counties, 1986; named to Outstanding Young Men of Am., U.S. Jaycees, 1975, 84. Mem. ABA, Acad. Fla. Trial Laywers, Assn. Trial Lawyers Am. (judge student trial competition 1995-96), Allegheny County Bar Assn., Palm Beach County Bar Assn. (appellate practice com. 1990—), Order of the Coif. Home: 147 Gregory Rd West Palm Beach FL 33405 Office: 250 S Australian Ave Ste 1504 West Palm Beach FL 33401-5016

SPILLMAN, ROBERT DANIEL, information systems educator; b. Winston-Salem, N.C., June 8, 1952; s. Robert Marion and Hattie Kate (Landreth) S. BS, Gardner-Webb U., 1974; MS, U. N.C., Greensboro, 1978; PhD, Ohio State U., 1983, postdoctoral, 1983-84. Salesman Maranville Camperland, Winston-Salem, 1976-77; installment loan officer Northwestern Bank, Winston-Salem, 1974-76; adj. prof. High-Point (N.C.) U., 1980; mktg. edn. tchr. High-Point City Schs., 1978-80; asst. prof. computer-based info. systems Radford (Va.) U., 1984—. Contbr. articles to profl. jours. Mem. AAUP, Data Processing Mgmt. Assn. Republican. Baptist. Home: 60 Justin Ln Christiansburg VA 24073 Office: Radford Univ Whitt Hall Radford VA 24142

SPILMAN, ROBERT HENKEL, furniture company executive; b. Knoxville, Tenn., Sept. 27, 1927; s. Robert Redd and Lila (Henkel) S.; m. Martha Jane Bassett, Apr. 2, 1955; children: Robert Henkel Jr., Virginia Perrin, Vance Henkel. BS, N.C. State U., 1950. With Cannon Mills, 1950-57; with Bassett Table Co., Va., 1957-60; dir. Bassett Furniture Industries Inc., 1960—, exec. v.p., 1966, pres., 1966-89, CEO, 1979—, chmn., 1982—; bd. dirs. Pittston Co., Greenwich, Conn., Nations Bank Corp., Charlotte, Trinova Corp., Maumee, Ohio, Dominion Resources, Inc., Richmond, Va., Dominion Energy, Richmond, Va. Elec. & Power Co.; chmn. bd. dirs. Jefferson-Pilot Corp., Greensboro, N.C., Internat. Home Furnishing Ctr., High Point, N.C.; mem. adv. bd. Liberty Mut. Ins. Co. Trustee Va. Found. Ind. Colls., Darden Sch. Found., N.C. State U.; bd. dirs. Blue Ridge Airport Authority. Lt. U.S. Army, WWII and Korea. Recipient Best Chief Exec. Officer in Home Furnishing Industry award Wall Street Transcript, 1981, 82; named Humanitarian of Yr., City of Hope, 1982. Mem. Am. Furniture Mfrs. Assn. (James T. Ryan award 1984), Nat. Furniture Mfrs. Assn. (bd. dirs., past pres.), Furniture Factories Mktg. Assn. (past chmn., bd. dirs.), Va. Mfrs. Assn. (past dir. exec. com.), Bassett Country Club, Chatmoss Country Club, Hunting Hills Country Club, Brook Club, Commonwealth Club, Linville Golf Club, Waterfront Golf Club (Moneta, Va.), Grandfather Golf and Country Club (Linville, N.C.). Episcopalian. Office: Bassett Furniture Industries Inc PO Box 626 Bassett VA 24055-0626 Home: PO Box 874 Bassett VA 24055

SPINCIC, WESLEY JAMES, oil company executive, consultant; b. New Castle, Pa., Aug. 6, 1945; s. Edward and Mary Louise (Ferk) S.; m. Gayle Sharon Burnett, June 21, 1975; children: John Reginold, Sheri Diane. BS in Engring., U.S. Mil. Acad., 1967; postgrad. in bus., U. So. Calif., 1973. Account rep. Dupont Glore-Forgon, L.A., 1973-74; drilling engr. Mobil Oil Co., Dallas, 1974-77; drilling supt. Ranger Oil Co., Houston, 1977; drilling and engring. mgr. Kilroy Co. Tex., Houston, 1977-81;, 1981-95; bd. dirs. Humble (Tex.) Nat. Bank, Cheyenne Oil and Gas Co., Houston, Avanti Internat., Drillpro Inc., Avanti Cons., Inc. Organizer Kingwood (Tex.) Emergency Med. Assn., 1978. Capt. U.S. Army, 1967-73. Mem. Soc. Petroleum Engrs., Am. Petroleum Inst., Internat. Assn. Drilling Contractors, Tex. Ind. Producers and Royalty Owners Assn., Assn. West Point Alumni. Republican. Roman Catholic. Home: 4714 Breezy Point Kingwood TX 77345 Office: Ste 220 15600 John F Kennedy Blvd Houston TX 77032-2343

SPINDEL, WILLIAM, chemist, consultant; b. N.Y.C., Sept. 9, 1922; s. Joseph and Esther (Goldstein) S.; m. Sara Lew, 1942 (div. 1966); children: Robert Andrew, Lawrence Marshall; m. Louise Phyllis Hoodenpyl, July 30, 1967. B.A., Bklyn. Coll., 1944; M.A., Columbia U., 1947, Ph.D., 1950. Jr. scientist Los Alamos Lab, Manhattan Dist., 1944-45; instr. Poly. Inst., Bklyn., 1949-50; assoc. prof. State U. N.Y., 1950-54; rsch. assoc., vis. prof. Columbia, 1954-57, vis. prof., sr. lectr., 1962-74; assoc. prof., then prof. Rutgers U., 1957-64; prof., chmn. dept. chemistry Belfer Grad. Sch. Sci., Yeshiva U., 1964-74; exec. sec., office chemistry and chem. tech. NAS-NRC, 1974-81, also staff dir. bd. on chem. scis. and tech., prin. staff officer commn. phys. scis., math. and resources, 1982-90, sr. cons., 1990—; vis. Am. scientist, Yugoslavia, 1971-72. Contbr. articles to profl. jours. Served with AUS, 1943-46. Recipient prof. staff award NRC, 1985; Guggenheim fellow, 1961-62; Fulbright Research scholar, 1961-62. Fellow AAAS; mem. Am. Chem. Soc. Club: Cosmos. Home: 6503 Dearborn Dr Falls Church VA 22044-1116

SPINDLER, JUDITH TARLETON, elementary school educator; b. Dayton, Tenn., Mar. 4, 1932; d. Frank Willson and Julia Elizabeth (Venable) S. BS in Edn., Longwood Coll., 1953; MA in Edn., Va. Commonwealth U., 1976. Tchr. Oceana, King's Grant Sch., Virginia Beach, Va., 1953-66, Ginter Park Elem. Sch., Richmond, Va., 1966-67, Bon Air Elem. Sch., Chesterfield County, Va., 1967-87; ret., 1987. Charter mem. Web of Hope sponsored by ARC (Humanitarian award). Recipient 1st, 2nd and 3rd pl. awards various knitting competitions, Best in Show award rosette competition. Mem. NEA, Va. Edn. Assn., Knitting Guild Am. (qualified tchr.), The Kitty Gritty, Knit Wit Guild. Home: 4103 Hyde Park Dr Chester VA 23831-4826

SPINKS, JOHN LYNN, librarian; b. Ryan, Okla., July 19, 1957; s. L.L. and Barbara Faye (Cole) S. BA in English/History, Dallas Bapt. U., 1980; MLS, U. North Tex., 1987. Audio/visual libr. Mesquite (Tex.) Pub. Libr., 1987-92, 94—, reference libr., 1992-94. Mem. Tex. Libr. Assn., Alpha Chi (Tex. Alpha Nu chpt.). Baptist. Office: Mequite Pub Libr 300 W Grubb Dr Mesquite TX 75149-3429

SPINNER, ROBERT JAY, orthopedic surgeon; b. N.Y.C., Dec. 8, 1961; s. Morton and Paula (Lerner) S. SB, MIT, 1984; M of Studies, Oxford (Eng.) U., 1985; MD, Mayo Clinic, 1989. Rsch. fellow, Luce scholar Prince of Wales Hosp., Hong Kong, 1989-90; intern in surgery Duke Univ., Durham, N.C., 1990-91, jr. resident in surgery, 1991-92, resident in orthopaedic surgery, 1992-96; resident in neurosurgery Mayo Clinic, Rochester, Minn., 1996—. Recipient Davison Teaching award Duke U. Med. Sch., 1993, Schilling scholar Mayo Found., 1984-86, Goldner Rsch. award in Orthopaedic Surgery Duke U. Med. Ctr., 1996. Mem. Phi Beta Kappa, Sigma Xi, Alpha Chi Sigma.

SPIRNAK, JOSEPH PATRICK, physician; b. Cleve., Nov. 9, 1963; s. John Joseph and Mary Elizabeth (Mancos) S.; m. Catherine Aida Schaefer, Sept. 8, 1991; children: Joshua Ryan, Jonathan Robert. BS in Zoology, Miami U., 1985; MD, Case Western Res. U., 1989. Diplomate Am. Bd. Radiology. Commd. 2d lt. U.S. Army, 1989, advanced through grades to maj., 1994; intern in medicine Tripler Army Med. Ctr., Honolulu, 1989-90; resident in radiology Brooke Army Med. Ctr., San Antonio, 1990-94; staff radiologist Dwight David Eisenhower Army Med. Ctr., Augusta, Ga., 1994—. Author: (chpt.) Otolaryngology, 1995; contbr. articles to profl. jours. Mem. Am. Bd. Radiology, Am. Coll. Radiology, Radiologic Soc. N.Am. Home: 1151 Oakton Ct Evans GA 30809

SPIRO, ROBERT HARRY, JR., foundation and business executive, educator; b. Asheville, N.C., Dec. 5, 1920; s. Robert Harry and Eoline Peterson (Shaw) S.; m. Terrie C. Gay, May 17, 1980; children by previous marriage: Robert Timothy, Elizabeth Susan, James Monroe. BS, Wheaton (Ill.) Coll., 1941; postgrad. Navy Supply Sch., Harvard U., 1943; postgrad., U. N.C., 1945-46; PhD, U. Edinburgh, Scotland, 1950; student, Union Theol. Sem., summers 1951-53; postdoctoral, Duke U., summer 1956; ScD (hon.), Fla. Inst. Tech. Assoc. prof. King Coll., Bristol, Tenn., 1946-50; prof. history Miss. Coll., 1950-57; pres. Blue Ridge Assembly, Black Mountain, N.C., 1957-60; dean Coll. Liberal Arts Mercer U., prof. history, 1960-64; pres. Jacksonville U., Fla., 1964-79; under sec. of Army, 1980-81; cons. to bus., 1981-84, 86—; nat. exec. dir. Res. Officers Assn. U.S., 1984-86; chmn. RHS Imprinted Products Inc.; past bd. mgrs. Voyager Variable Annuity of Fla., 1972-79; v.p. Am. Sec. Coun. Found.; past pres. Fla. Assn. Colls. and Univs.; mem., past chmn. Ind. Colls. and Univs., 1964-79, chmn., 1967; sec.-treas. Assn. Urban Univs., 1968-76; past mem. Fla.-Columbia Ptnrs.; gen. chmn. Jacksonville Sesquicentennial Commn., 1970-72; mem. N.C. Tricentennial Commn., 1962—; past mem. adv. coun. Robert A. Taft Inst. Govt., Inst. Internat. Edn. Contbr. articles to profl. publs. and encys. Trustee Southwestern Bapt. Theol. Sem., 1968-78; mem. Fla.-Colombia Ptnrs.; chmn. bd. Bapt. Coll. and Sem., Washington. Lt. USNR, 1941-45; ret. rear adm. USNR, 1978. Decorated Palmes Academique (France); recipient Disting. Civilian Svc. award Dept. of Army, 1981. Mem. Navy League U.S. (former pres. Jacksonville coun.), Naval Res. Assn. (nat. adv. coun.), Res. Officers Assn., Ret. Officers Assn., Am. Legion, Kiwanis (pres. Georgetown, D.C. club 1991-92), Army-Navy Country Club (Arlington, Va.), Army and Navy Club (Washington), Phi Delta Kappa, Alpha Kappa Psi, Phi Alpha Theta, Phi Kappa Phi. Home: 105 Follin Ln SE Vienna VA 22180-4957

SPITZ, HUGO MAX, lawyer; b. Richmond, Va., Aug. 17, 1927, s. Jacob Gustav and Clara (Herzfeld) S.; m. Barbara Steinberg, June 22, 1952; children: Jack Gray, Jill Ann Levy, Sally Spitz. AA, U. Fla., 1948, BLaws, 1951, JD, 1967. Bar: Fla. 1951, S.C., 1955, U.S. Dist. Ct. (so. dist.) Fla. 1951, U.S. Dist. Ct. (ea. dist.) S.C. 1956, U.S. Ct. Appeals (4th cir.) 1957. Asst. atty. gen. State of Fla., Tallahassee, 1951; assoc. Williams, Salomon & Katz, Miami, Fla., 1951-54, Steinberg & Levkoff, Charleston, S.C., 1954-57; sr. ptnr. Steinberg, Spitz, Goldberg, Pearlman Holmes, White & O'Neill, Charleston, 1957—; lectr. S.C. Trial Lawyers Assn., Columbia, 1958—, S.C. U. Sch. Law, Columbia, 1975, S.C. Bar Assn., 1955—. Assoc. mcpl. judge Charleston, 1972-74, mcpl. judge, 1974-76; commr. Charleston County Substance Abuse Commn., 1976-79; bd. govs. S.C. Patient's Compensation Fund, Columbia, 1978—; adv. mem., atty. S.C. Legis. Coun. for Workers' Compensation; chmn. bd. dirs. Franklin C. Fetter Health Ctr., Charleston, 1977-78; mem. S.C. Appellate Def. Commn., 1985-86; founding sponsor Civil Justice Found., 1986—; bd. pres. Charleston Jewish Fedn., 1990-91, pres., 1991-92. Pres., Synagogue Emanu-El, 1969-71. With USN, 1945-46. Fellow S.C. Bar Assn., U. S.C. Ednl. Found; mem. ABA, Civil Justice Found., S.C. Law Inst., S.C. Trial Lawyers Assn. (founder and pres. 1985-86), S.C. Claimants' Attys. for Worker's Compensation (exec. com. 1986), S.C. Worker's Compensation Ednl. Assn. (bd. dirs. 1978—), S.C. Law Inst., Am. Judicature Soc., Assn. Trial Lawyers Am. (mem. pres. council 1986-87), Nat. Rehab. Assn., Nat. Orgn. Social Security Claimants' Reps. S.C. Bar (chmn. trial and appellate sect. 1982-83; ho. of dels. 1984-85), So. Assn. Workmen's Compensation Adminstrs., Nat. Inst. for Trial Advocacy (com. chmn. 1985). Democrat. Clubs: Hebrew Benevolent Soc. (pres. 1974-75, life), Jewish Community Ctr. (Charleston, v.p. 1972-74), Hebrew Orphan Soc. (life), B'nai B'rith, Elks (life). Home: 337 Confederate Cir Charleston SC 29407-7430 Office: PO Box 9 Charleston SC 29402-0009

SPITZER, JAN JOSEF, chemist; b. Czech Republic, Dec. 6, 1946; came to U.S., 1992; s. Leo and Anna (Prusova) S.; m. Bozena Hasonova, Dec. 28, 1970; children: Helen, Max, Wendy. Diploma, Tech. U. Prague, 1969; PhD in Chemistry, U. London, 1975. Asst. prof. U. Lethbridge (Alberta, Can.), 1979-84; sr. scientist Polysar Corp., Sarnia, Ontario, Can., 1985-87; with BASF Can. Inc., Sarnia, Ontario, Can., 1987-92; sr. scientist BASF Corp., Charlotte, N.C., 1992—. Contbr. over 30 articles to profl. jours. Natural Scis. and Engring. Rsch. Coun. Can. fellow, 1979-84. Mem. Am. Chem.

Soc., Adhesion Soc., Internat. Assn. Colloid and Surface Scientists. Office: BASF Corp 11501 Steele Creek Rd Charlotte NC 28273-3730

SPITZLI, DONALD HAWKES, JR., lawyer; b. Newark, Mar. 19, 1934; s. Donald Hawkes and Beatrice (Banister) S.; children: Donald Hawkes III, Peter Gilbert, Seth Armstrong. A.B., Dartmouth Coll., 1956; LL.B., U. Va. 1963. Bar: Va. 1963. Assoc. Willcox, Savage, Lawrence, Dickson & Spindle, Norfolk, Va., 1964-67; atty. Eastman Kodak Co., Rochester, 1967-68; assoc. Willcox, Savage, Lawrence, Dickson & Spindle, Norfolk, Va., 1968-70, ptnr., 1971-77; pres. Marine Hydraulics Internat., Inc., Chesapeake, Va., 1978-80; sole practice, Virginia Beach, Va., 1980—; Served to comdr. USNR, 1956-70. Episcopalian. Office: 448 Viking Dr Ste 170 Virginia Beach VA 23452

SPITZNAGEL, JOHN KEITH, periodontist, researcher; b. St. Louis, Feb. 22, 1951; s. John Keith and Anne Moulton (Sirch) S.; m. Susan Victoria Lipton, Jan. 2, 1981; children: Matthew, Katya. BS in Biology, U. N.C., 1977, DDS, 1982, cert. in Periodontology, 1992, PhD in Microbiology, 1994. Postdoctoral fellow Forsyth Dental Ctr., Boston, 1983-85; cons. in bioinformatics, 1984—; periodontic resident U. Tex. Health Sci. Ctr., San Antonio, 1985-91, dentist-scientist fellow, 1987-93; asst. prof. periodontology U. Tenn., Memphis, 1993—. Contbr. articles to profl. jours. Scout leader Boy Scouts Am., Chapel Hill, N.C., 1978-81, Memphis, 1995—. With USCG, 1971-75. Recipient Dentist Scientist award Nat. Inst. Dental Rsch., 1987. Mem. ADA, AAAS, Am. Acad. Periodontology, Am. Soc. for Microbiology, Internat. Assn. Dental Rsch., Delta Sigma Delta. Episcopalian. Office: U Tenn Coll of Dentistry 875 Union Ave Memphis TN 38103-3513

SPIVEY, HOWARD OLIN, biochemistry and physical chemistry educator; b. Gainesville, Fla., Dec. 10, 1931; s. Herman Everette and Havens Edna (Taylor) S.; m. Dorothy Eleanor Luke, June 19, 1959; children: Bruce Allen, Curt Olin, Diane Elizabeth. BS, U. Ky., 1954; PhD, Harvard U., 1962. Rsch. assoc. Rockefeller U., N.Y.C., 1962-64; NIH fellow MIT, Cambridge, Mass., 1964-65; asst. prof. U. Md., College Park, 1965-67; asst. prof. Okla. State U., Stillwater, 1967-69, assoc. prof., 1969-75, prof., 1975—. Contbr. articles to profl. jours. Grantee NIH, 1969-72, 75-78, 79-83, NSF, 1969-72, 86-89, 96-98, Am. Heart Assn., 1988-91. Mem. AAAS, Am. Chem. Soc., Am. Soc. for Biochemistry & Molecular Biology, Phi Beta Kappa. Home: 2222 W 11th St Stillwater OK 74074-5116 Office: Okla State U Dept Biochem Molec Biol 246 NRC Stillwater OK 74078-3035

SPIVEY, SUZAN BROOKS NISBET, association administrator, medical technologist; b. Princeton, Ky., Sept. 19, 1932; d. Dixon Franklin and Eva (Brooks) Nisbet; m. Herman Everette Spivey Jr., June 8, 1953; children: Eva Kathryn Spivey Bridges, Herman Everette III. Student, U. Louisville, 1950; BS, U. Ky., 1954; grad., Inst. Orgnl. Mgmt. U. Ga., 1990; postgrad., U. Ga., 1990—. Registered med. technologist. Med. technologist Madison (Wis.) Gen. Hosp., 1955-58, Fern Creek Clinic, Louisville, 1958-62; med. technologist, cons. Ga. Primary Health Care, Summerville, 1981—, Chattooga County Hosp., Summerville, 1983-86; grad. Inst. for Orgnl. Mgmt. U.S. Chamber U. Ga., 1990; pres. Chattooga County C. of C., Summerville, 1984—; advisor Inst. for Orgnl. Mgmt. U.S. Chamber U. Ga., 1991. Author: (newsletter) Essentials, 1985—; editor: (book) Becoming a Better Board Member, 1982; columnist You and Your Schs., 1973-80. Pres. memls., dir. Chattooga chpt. Ga. Dist. Field Svc. Am. Cancer Soc., mem., 1964—; mem. Chattooga Bd. Edn., 1972-80, Ga. Assn. Leadership Communities, 1989—, Tri-State Coun., 1989—, Chattanooga County 911 Com., 1996; bd. dir., advisor Chattooga County Parent/Child Ctr., 1972-92; bd. control N.W. Ga. Regional Edn. Svc. Agy., 1996; adminstrv. bd. Chattanooga Early Learning Ctr., 1996; bd. dirs. Lookout Mountain Pkwy. Assn., 1988—, Job Tng. Ptnrship. Act, Chattooga County, 1985-95, 7th Dist. Ga. Sch. Bds. Assn., Atlanta, 1974-80; pres. Bicentennial Com., Chattooga County, 1974-76; producer Hallelujah Players, Summerville, 1976-85; trustee Floyd Coll., 1988—; bd. dirs. Literacy Adv. Com. Walker Tech. Inst., 1991—; mem. 7th dist. Ga. Congl. Adv. Com. on Health Care Reform, 1994; adminstrv. bd. Chattooga Early Learning Ctr., 1996; active Chattooga County 911 Com., 1996. Recipient Excellence award Am. Cancer Soc., 1991; grantee Ga. Bd. Edn., 1990, 91, Ga. Gov.'s Commn., 1991. Mem. Am. Soc. Clin. Pathologists, So. Ind. Devel. Coun., Ga. Econ. Devel. Assn., Am. C. of C., Bus. and Profl. Women (Woman of Achievement award 1984), Ga. Assn. of Chamber Execs., Am. C. of C. Execs. Assn. Democrat. Presbyterian. Office: Chattooga County C of C 4 College Ave Summerville GA 30747-1722

SPLAVER, SARAH, psychologist; b. N.Y.C.; d. Morris and Rose (Farber) S. BA, Hunter Coll., N.Y.C.; MA, Columbia U; PhD, NYU, 1953. Cert. psychologist, N.Y. Psychologist N.Y.C., 1953—, writer, 1949—; guidance dir. Rhodes Preparatory Sch., N.Y.C., 1946-52; editor, publisher Occu-Press, N.Y.C., 1953-70; editorial cons. Socioguidrama Series, N.Y.C., 1953-73; pres. Cancer Counselor, Breast Diseases Assn. Am., N.Y.C., 1975-80, Cancer Hopefuls United for Mut. Support, 1980-87. Author: Your Career -- If You're Not Going to College, 1971, Your College Education -- How to Pay for It, 1968, Your Handicap -- Don't Let It Handicap You, 1974, Your Personality and You, 1965, You and Today's Troubled World, 1970, Nontraditional Careers for Women, 1973, Your Mind and Breast Diseases, 1978. Co-chmn. Mental Health Profls. Com., N.Y.C., 1976; exec. dir. Com. for Establishment of Breast Splty., 1989-92; bd. dirs. Herzl Hadassah, 1991—. Named Woman of the Yr. CHUMS, 1985, Outstanding Woman Woman's Day Mag. 1987, City Coun. Citation, Coun. of City of N.Y., 1985. Fellow APA, Internat. Coun. Psychologists, Am. Counseling Assn.; mem. Nat. Career Devel. Assn. (life), Am. Rehab. Counseling Assn., Authors Guild, Bermuda Club (pres.), Poetry Club. Jewish. Home and Office: 6350 NW 62nd St Apt 207 Fort Lauderdale FL 33319-6287

SPONHEIMER, JON M., food products executive. Owner Ga. Poultry Producers, 1979-90; pres. Caribbean Agr. Projects, Gulf Breeze, Fla., 1990—. Office: Caribbean Agr Projects 81 Smugglers Cove Gulf Breeze FL 32561

SPOONER, BERNARD MYRICK, religious organization administrator; b. Pine Hill, Ala., Oct. 15, 1934; s. Earl William and Lomie (Vick) S.; m. Patricia Ann Fowler, June 8, 1957; children: Myra Joan Spooner Bush, Jane Ann Spooner Carlisle. BS, Miss. Coll., 1957; MA, Southwestern Bapt. Theol. Sem., 1962, PhD, 1994. Min. edn. First Bapt. Ch., Ruston, La., 1962-65, Immanual Bapt. Ch., Tulsa, 1965-66; min. edn. and adminstrn. Travis Ave. Bapt. Ch., Ft. Worth, 1966-77; prof. adminstrn. New Orleans Bapt. Theol. Sem., 1977-79; dir. Sunday sch. discipleship div. Bapt. Gen. Conv. Tex., Dallas, 1979—; bd. dirs. The Sweet Shop, USA, Inc., Ft. Worth; ptnr. Center St. Properties, Ft. Worth, Tex., 1977—. Co-author: You Can Reach People Now, 1971, The People Challenge, 1985; contbr. articles to various publs. Chmn. Ch. ministry Rsch. Team, 1994-96; cons. ch. growth and adminstrn., 1975—. Capt. USMCR, 1957-60. Mem. So. Bapt. Religious Educators Assn. (v.p. 1975-76, chmn. bd. dirs. 1990-92, pres. elect 1996-97), Metro Bapt. Religious Educators Assn. (chmn. 1974), Tarrant Bapt. Religious Educators Assn. (pres. 1970), Southwestern Bapt. Religious Edn. Assn. (pres. 1976), State Sunday Sch. Dirs. Fellowship (pres. 1995-97). Home: 330 Spyglass Dr Coppell TX 75019-5429 Office: Bapt Gen Conv Tex 333 N Washington Ave Dallas TX 75246-1754

SPOONHOUR, JAMES MICHAEL, lawyer; b. San Antonio, Mar. 24, 1946; s. Robert W. and Marie C. (Schulze) S.; m. Terri Walker; children: Taylor, Erin, Whitney, Michael. BA, U. Nebr., 1968, MA, 1970; JD, Georgetown U., 1974. Bar: Fla. 1974, U.S. Dist. Ct. (mid. dist.) Fla. 1974. Assoc. Lowndes, Piersol, Drosdick & Doster, Orlando, Fla., 1974-76; asst. prof. law Loyola U., New Orleans, 1976-77; ptnr. Lowndes, Drosdick, Doster, Kantor & Reed, P.A., Orlando, 1977—. Contbr. to profl. publs. Bd. dirs. Vis. Nurse Assn., Orlando, 1979-89; chmn. sch. bd. The First Acad., Orlando, 1986-89. With USAF, 1970-72. Mem. ABA, Assn. Trial Lawyers Am., Fla. Bar, Orange County Bar Assn. Republican. Office: Lowndes Drosdick Doster Kantor & Reed PA 215 N Eola Dr Orlando FL 32801-2028

SPORE, RICHARD ROLAND, III, lawyer, educator; b. Memphis, May 28, 1962; s. Richard R. Jr. and Melba (Cullum) S.; m. Patricia Ann Witherspoon, Aug. 15, 1987; 1 child, Caroline Dare. BA, U. of the South, 1984; JD, U. Va., 1987; MBA, Christian Bros. U., 1992. Bar: Tenn. 1987. Assoc. Burch, Porter & Johnson, Memphis, 1987-94, ptnr., 1995—; adj. prof. bus. law Christian Bros. U., Memphis, 1992—; chmn. Tenn. Bus. Law Forum. Author: The Partnering Paradigm: An Entrepreneur's Guide to Strategic Alliances, 1994, Business Organizations in Tennessee, 1995. Mem. Pro Bono Panel for Sr. Citizens, Memphis, 1987—; chmn. small bus. coun. Memphis Area C. of C., 1993; pres. Sewanee Club of Memphis, 1989. Recipient Disting. Svc. award Pro Bono Panel for Sr. Citizens, 1992. Mem. ABA, Tenn. Bar Assn., Memphis Bar Assn. Republican. Methodist. Office: Burch Porter & Johnson 130 Court Ave Memphis TN 38103-2217

SPOTO, ANGELO PETER, JR., internist, allergist; b. Tampa, Fla., Mar. 25, 1933; s. Angelo Peter and Zillah Marie (Renfroe) S.; m. Carolyn Jeanette Barbee, Aug. 30, 1958; children: Keith Peter, Elizabeth Anne, Jacqueline Marie. AA, U. Fla., 1953; BS in Medicine, Duke U., 1956, MD, 1957. Diplomate Am. Bd. Internal Medicine, Am. Bd. Allergy and Immunology. Intern Duke U. Med. Ctr., Durham, 1957-58, fellow in medicine (allergy), 1958-59; resident in internal medicine USAF Hosp., Lackland AFB, Tex., 1960-62; resident in allergy Walter Reed Army Med. Ctr., Washington, 1962-63; staff allergist Watson Clinic LLP, Lakeland, Fla., 1966—; ptnr., 1968—; med. staff Lakeland Reg. Med. Ctr., 1966—; bd. dirs. Watson Clinic Found., 1984—, pres., 1984-93; clin. assoc. prof. medicine U. South Fla., Tampa, 1973-77; chmn. bd. dirs. Polk Internat., Inc., 1986—; bd. dirs. Am. Group Practice Corp., 1991-94, chmn., 1992-94. Contbr. articles to profl. jours. Ruling elder Presbyn. Ch., 1970—. Maj. USAF, 1959-66. Decorated Air Force Commendation medal. Fellow ACP, Am. Acad. Allergy, Am. Coll. Allergy; mem. AMA (alt. del. 1992), Polk County Med. Assn. (exec. com. 1971), Fla. Med. Assn., Fla. Allergy Soc. (pres. 1973-74, exec. com. 1972-78), Southeastern Allergy Assn., So. Med. Assn., Am. Group Practice Assn. (trustee 1985-94, pres. 1991-92), Assn. Cert. Allergists (bd. govs. 1971-75), Lakeland C. of C. (bd. dirs. 1987-89). Republican. Presbyterian. Home: 2515 Hollingsworth Hill Ave Lakeland FL 33803-3236 Office: Watson Clinic LLP 1600 Lakeland Hills Blvd Lakeland FL 33805-3019

SPRABARY, LARRY DREW, military analyst; b. Lewisville, Tex., Sept. 24, 1946; s. H. L. and Frankie Charlene (Lester) S.; m. Glenda Kay Baggett, Feb. 28, 1970; 1 child, Christopher Lain. BS in Mgmt., Embry-Riddle Aero. U., 1979; MS in Human Resources, U. Ctrl. Tex., 1990. Commd. 2d lt. U.S. Army, 1967, advanced through grades to maj., 1977; inspector gen. HQ U.S. Army Europe and 7th Army U.S. Army, Heidelberg, Germany, 1979-82; test officer Tng. and Doctrine Command U.S. Army, Ft. Hood, Tex., 1982-87; spl. asst. to CG Test and Experimentation Command U.S. Army, Ft. Hood, 1987-88; ret. U.S. Army, 1988; staff analyst BDM Corp., Killeen, Tex., 1988-89; mil. plans analyst Test and Experimentation Command, Ft. Hood, 1989-91, 1991—. Decorated Air medal, Bronze Star, Army Commendation medal, Meritorious Svc. medal; named U.S. Army Civilian Tester of Yr., 1993. Baptist. Office: Hdqs TEXCOM CSTE-TCC-A Fort Hood TX 76544-5065

SPRADLIN, CHARLES LEONARD, secondary school educator; b. Hogansville, Ga., Oct. 7, 1941; s. George Newport and Corrie Mae (Hay) S.; m. Sherry Dawn Norman, June 9, 1963; children: Corrie Christine, Charles Leonard Jr. Diploma in drafting and design, Troup Area Vocat.-Tech. Sch., 1972; student, Ga. State U., 1979-81. Cert. drafting tchr., Ga. Graphics supr. Chattahoochee-Flint Area Planning and Devel. Commn., LaGrange, Ga., 1972-79; tchr. drafting Meadows Coll. Bus., LaGrange, 1977-79, LaGrange H.S., 1979-91, Newnan (Ga.) H.S., 1991-96; student adviser vocat. edn. Callaway H.S., Hogansville, Ga., 1996—; student adviser Vocat. Indsl. Clubs Am., 1981-94. Minister of music local Bapt. ch. With USN, 1959-63. Mem. Am. Vocat. Assn., Ga. Vocat. Assn., Profl. Assn. Ga. Educators, Vocat. Indsl. Clubs Am. Baptist. Home: 10818 Hwy 100 Hogansville GA 30230-9614 Office: Callaway HS 221 Whitfield Rd Hogansville GA 30230

SPRAGENS, WILLIAM CLARK, public policy educator, consultant; b. Lebanon, Ky., Oct. 1, 1925; s. Thomas Eugene and Edna Grace (Clark) S.; m. Elaine Jean Dunham, June 14, 1964. AB in Journalism, U. Ky., 1947, MA, 1953; PhD, Mich. State U., 1966. Instr. U. Tenn., Knoxville, 1962-64; part-time instr. Mich. State U., East Lansing, 1964-65; asst. prof. Millikin U., Decatur, Ill., 1965-67, Wis. State U., Oshkosh, 1967-69; assoc. prof. Bowling Green (Ohio) State U., 1969-82, prof., 1982-86, prof. emeritus, 1986—; pres. Spragens and Daracs Assocs., Reston, Va., 1996—. Author: Electronic Magazines, 1995; editor-in-chief: Popular Images of American Presidents, 1988. Del. candidate McGovern for pres. campaign, Bowling Green, 1972; co-dir. Nat. Convs. Program, 1972, 76, 80, 84. Lyndon Baines Johnson Found. grantee, 1977, 78. Mem. World Affairs Coun. Washington, Am. Polit. Sci. Assn., Internat. Soc. for Polit. Sociology, Am. Soc. for Pub. Adminstrn. Democrat. Presbyterian. Home and Office: PO Box 410 Herndon VA 20172-0410

SPRAGUE, CHRISTOPHER BENTLEY, manufacturing executive; b. Detroit, July 24, 1945; s. G. Sidney and Ida E. (Zimmer) S.; m. Sandra Lynn Mallory, June 10, 1967; 1 child, Donald Christopher. BS, USAF Acad., 1967. Commd. 2d lt. USAF, 1967, advanced through grades to capt., resigned, 1974; maintenance supr. Schneider Transport, Green Bay, Wis., 1974; sales engr. MCC Powers, Overland Park, Kans., 1974-78, Fluid Components, Inc., Tulsa, 1978-80; application engring. supr. CenterLine, Tulsa, 1981, mgr. sales adminstrn., 1981-82, gen. product mgr., 1982-85, dir. mktg., 1985-90; mktg. Rust-Oleum CPS, Tulsa, 1990—. Mem. Bus. Mktg. Assn. (sec. Tulsa chpt.), Instrument Soc. Am. (membership chmn. Tulsa sect.), Rotary (sec. Sunrise club Tulsa 1991—). Republican. Home: 2408 W Ft Worth St Broken Arrow OK 74012-3515 Office: Rust-Oleum CPS 1326 W 37th Pl Tulsa OK 74107-5600

SPRAGUE, HEATHER M., oncology nurse, chart audit specialist; b. Biloxi, Miss., Apr. 5, 1961; d. Charles Laird and Joan Elizabeth (Frenier) Ferguson; m. Vance Glover Sprague, Jr., June 3, 1989. BSN, U. South Ala., 1984; student, U. So. Miss., 1980-81, Presbyn. Hosp. Sch. Nursing, Charlotte, N.C., 1982-83. Staff nurse neurosurgery step-down unit Miss. Bapt. Med. Ctr., Jackson, 1984-85; staff nurse orthopaedic-neurosurg. Gulf Coast Community Hosp., Biloxi, 1985-86, hospice nurse, 1986-88; office nurse oncology, chemotherapy Dr. James Clarkson, Biloxi, 1988-89; staff nurse oncology Meml. Hosp. at Gulfport (Miss.), 1989-90, chart audit specialist, 1989—; pres., bd. dirs. Meml. Fed. Credit Union; spkr. in field. Mem. Assn. Healthcare Internal Auditors. Home: 114 Camelia Dr Pass Christian MS 39571-4706

SPRAGUE, VANCE GLOVER, JR., oceanography executive, naval reserve officer; b. Bellefonte, Pa., Oct. 28, 1941; s. Vance Glover and Elaine L. (Tottingham) S.; m. Claire Lewis, Nov. 26, 1982 (dec. Oct. 1987); m. Heather Munro Ferguson, June 3, 1989. BS, Pa. State U., 1963; MS, Salve Regina U., 1983, Naval War Coll., 1983. Commd. ensign USN, 1963; lt. j.g. USS Towhee, Norfolk, Va., 1963-65; oceanographer Naval Oceanographic Office, D.C., 1965-77, sect. head, 1977-80; br. head Naval Oceanographic Office, Stennis Space Ctr., Miss., 1980-85, dir. Phys. Oceanography Div., 1985-93, mem. sr. ops. staff, 1993-94, dir. database dept., 1994—; exec. officer, naval oceanography res. unit Naval Air Sta., New Orleans, 1983-87, comdg. officer, 1987-89. Capt. USNR, 1987. Mem. U.S. Naval Inst., Am. Geophys. Union, Long Beach (Miss.) Yacht Club, Delta Chi. Home: 114 Camelia Dr Pass Christian MS 39571-4706 Office: Naval Oceanographic Office Stennis Space Center MS 39522

SPRAGUE, WILLIAM WALLACE, JR., retired food company executive; b. Savannah, Ga., Nov. 11, 1926; s. William Wallace and Mary (Crowther) S.; m. Elizabeth Louise Carr, Oct. 3, 1953; children: Courtney, Lauren Duane, William Wallace III, Elizabeth Louise. BSME, Yale U., 1950. With Savannah Foods & Industries, Inc., 1952-94, ret., 1994, sec., 1961-62, v.p., 1962-72, pres., chief exec. officer, 1972-92, chmn. bd. dirs., CEO, 1993-94, also bd. dirs.; bd. dirs., pres. Adeline Sugar Factory Co., Ltd., Savannah, Coastal Mgmt. Corp., Savannah. Trustee Savannah Bus. Group; chmn. emeritus Youth Futures Authority, Savannah. With USN, 1945-46. Named Sugar Man of Yr. and recipient Dyer Meml. award B.W. Dyer & Co., 1985; named Industrialist of Yr. Internat. Mgmt. Coun., 1988. Mem. World Sugar Rsch. Orgn. (chmn. 1982-85), The Sugar Assn. (bd. dirs.),Carolina Plantation Soc., St. Andrews Soc., Oglethorpe Club, Century Club (Savannah). Office: Savannah Foods & Industries PO Box 339 Savannah GA 31402-0339

SPRAKER, MARY KATHERINE, pediatric dermatologist; b. Madison, Wis., Feb. 15, 1948; d. Charles Lewis and Mary Ellen (Ames) S.; m. Gregory Neel Studdard; children: Henry Lawrence, Margaret Ellen, Mary Louise and Lydia Ann (triplets). BS, U. Wis., 1970, MD, 1974. Diplomate Am. Bd. Dermatology, Am. Bd. Pediat. Resident in pediat. Children's Hosp., Cin., 1974-77; resident in dermatology U. Oreg., Portland, 1978-81; assoc. prof. Emory U. Sch. Medicine, Atlanta, 1981—. Mem. Soc. Pediat. Dermatology (pres.). Home: 1389 Cornell Rd NE Atlanta GA 30306-3220 Office: Emory Clinic 1365 Clifton Rd NE Atlanta GA 30307-1013

SPRAY, PAUL E., surgeon; b. Wilkinsburg, Pa., Apr. 9, 1921; s. Lester E. and Phoebe Gertrude (Hull) S.; m. Mary Louise Conover, Nov. 28, 1943; children: David C., Thomas L., Mary Lynn (Mrs. Thomas Branham). BS, U. Pitts., 1942; MD, George Washington U., 1944; MS, U. Minn., 1950. Diplomate Am. Bd. Orthopedic Surgery. Intern U.S. Marine Hosp., S.I., 1944-45; resident Mayo Found., Rochester, Minn., 1945-46, 48-50; practice medicine specializing in orthopedic surgery Oak Ridge, Tenn., 1950—; mem. staff Oak Ridge Hosp., Park West Hosp., Knoxville, Harriman Hosp., Tenn.; vol. vis. cons. CARE Medico, Jordan, 1959, Nigeria, 1962, 65, Algeria, 1963, Afghanistan, 1970, Bangladesh, 1975, 77, 79, Peru, 1980, U. Ghana, 1982; AMA vol. physician, Vietnam, 1967, 72; vis. assoc. prof. U. Nairobi, 1973; mem. tchg. team Internat. Coll. Surgeons to Khartoum; vis. prof. orthop. surgery U. Khartoum, 1976; hon. prof. San Luis Gonzaga U., Ica, Peru; AmDoc vol. cons. U. Biafra Tchg. Hosp., 1969; vis. prof. Mayo Clinic, 1988; sec. orthops. overseas divsn. CARE Medico, 1971-76, sec. Medico adv. bd., 1974-76, vice chmn., 1976, chmn., 1977-79, v.p. CARE, Inc., 1977-79, pub. mem. CARE bd. dirs., 1980-90, mem. bd. overseers, 1991—; chmn. Orthops. Overseas, Inc., 1982-86, treas., 1986-88, emeritus mem., 1994; mem. U.S. organizing com. 1st Internat. Acad. Symposium on Orthops., Tianjin, China, 1983; mem. CUPP Internat. Adv. Coun., 1986—; invited guest spkr. Japan Orthop. Assn., 1994. Mem. editorial bd. Contemporary Orthopedics, 1984-96. V.p. Anderson County Health Coun., 1975, pres., 1976-77, hon. bd. dirs., 1991; pres. health commn. Coun. So. Mountains, 1958-65, sec., bd. dirs., 1965-66; Tenn. pres. UN Assn., 1966-67; vice-chmn. bd. Camelot Care Ctr., Tenn., 1979-82, chmn., 1982-86; chmn. bd. dirs. Camelot Found., 1986-87; hon. mem. World Orthopedic Concern, 1990; with del. to Vietnam People to People, 1993, citizen amb. to Vietnam, 1993; del. to Oak Ridge's Sister City, Obinsk, Russia, 1993; trustee Vietnam Am. Scholarship Fund, 1992-95. Recipient Svc. to Mankind award Sertoma, 1967, Humanitarian award Lions Club, 1968, Freedom Citation Sertoma, 1978, Amb. Goodwill Lions Club, award 1979, Medico Disting. Svc. award, 1990, 1st Ann. Vocat. Svc. award Oak Ridge Rotary, 1979, Tech. Communication award East Tenn. chpt. Soc. for Tech. Communication, 1983, Individual Achievement award Meth. Med. Ctr. of Oak Ridge, 1991, Humanitarian award Orthopaedics Overseas, 1992; Melvin Jones fellow Lions Club, 1993. Fellow ACS, Internat. Coll. Surgeons (Tenn. regent 1976-80, bd. councillors 1980-84, hon. chmn. bd. turstees 1981-83, trustee 1983-84, v.p. U.S. sect. 1982-83, mem. surg. teams com. 1983-90, Humanitarian award 1992); mem. AMA (Humanitarian Svc. award 1967, 72), Sociètè International Chirugie Orthopèdique et de Traumuatologie, So. Orthopedic Assn., Western Pacific Orthopedic Assn., Am. Fracture Assn., Am. Acad. Orthopedic Surgeons (mem. com. on injuries 1980-86), Tenn. Med. Assn. (com. on emergency med. svcs. 1978-88), Peru Acad. Surgery (corr.), Peruvian Soc. Orthopedic Surgery and Traumatology (corr.), Clin. Orthopedic Soc., Mid-Am. Orthopaedic Soc., Rotary Club (Oak Ridge chpt.). Home: 507 Delaware Ave Oak Ridge TN 37830-3902 Office: 160 W Tennessee Ave Ste C Oak Ridge TN 37830-6501

SPRAYBERRY, ROSLYN RAYE, secondary school educator; b. Newnan, Ga., June 29, 1942; d. Henry Ray and Grace (Bernhard) S. BA, Valdosta State Coll., 1964; MA in Teaching, Ga. State U., 1976, EdS in Spanish, 1988; EdD, Nova U., 1993. Cert. tchr., Ga. Tchr. history Griffin (Ga.) High Sch., 1964-65; tchr. 6th grade Beaverbrook Elem Sch., Griffin, 1965-66; tchr. Spanish, chair fgn. lang. dept. Forest Park (Ga.) High Sch., 1966-77; chair fgn. lang. dept. Spanish Forest Park (Ga.) High Sch., 1969-77; tchr. Spanish, chair fgn. lang. dept. Riverdale (Ga.) High Sch., 1977—; correlator Harcourt, Brace, Jovanovich, 1989; adv. bd. So. Conf. Lang. Teaching, 1992—; lectr. and speaker in field. Contbr. articles to The Ednl. Resource Info. Ctr. Clearinghouse on Langs. and Linguistics, Ctr. for Applied Linguistics, Washington; designed courses for the Gifted, Ga. Dept. of Edn. Cnvener Acad. Alliances-Atlanta II, Clayton County, Ga., 1982—; advisor, workshop leader Ga. Fgn. Lang. Camp, Atlanta, 1983; dir. Clayton County Fgn. Lang. Festival, 1990-91. Recipient STAR Tchr. award Ga. C. of C., 1982; Fulbright-Hays scholar, 1978; NEH grantee, 1977, 84. Mem. NEA, Am. Coun. Tchrs. Fgn. Langs., Am. Assn. Tchrs. Spanish and Portuguese, Ga. Assn. Educators, Fgn. Lang. Assn. Ga. (treas. 1977-85, assoc. editor jour. 1981-86, Tchr. of Yr. award 1976), Clayton County Edn. Assn., So. Conf. Lang. Teaching, KPS Leadership Specialists (co-founder 1993). Methodist. Home: 9261 Brave Ct Jonesboro GA 30236-5110

SPRENGER, THOMAS ROBERT, orthopedic surgeon; b. Seymour, Ind., Aug. 22, 1931; s. Robert D. and Margaret Sprenger; m. Justine Gambill Stinson, June 24, 1956; children: Rebecca Lee, Michael Thomas. BS, Marshall U., 1976; MD, Ind. U., 1956; grad. U.S. Army War Coll., 1975, U.S. Army Command and Gen. Staff Coll., 1970. Diplomate Am. Bd. Orthopedic Surgery. Intern St. Vincent's Hosp., Indpls., 1956-57; resident in orthopedic surgery Indpls. Gen. Hosp., 1957-58, Riley Children's Hosp. Ind. U., 1958-59, VA Hosp., New Orleans, 1959-60, Tampa Gen. Hosp., 1960; practice medicine specializing in orthopedic surgery, Bradenton, Fla., 1961—; orthopedic surgeon Pitts. Pirates, Bradenton, 1969-87; sr. attending orthopedic surgeon Manatee Meml. Hosp., Bradenton, 1961—, chief of staff, 1967; sr. attending orthopedic surgeon L.W. Blake Meml. Hosp., Bradenton, 1973—, trustee, 1971-83, sec. bd., 1970-80, vice chmn. bd., 1980-81, chmn. bd., 1982-84. Pres., Gulfcoast chpt. Nat. Arthritis Found., 1965, 82—; mem. Bd. Pub. Instrn. Manatee County, 1966-71, chmn., 1967-69; mem. exec. com. Bishop Mus. and Planetarium, 1967-69; founding mem. Health Systems Agy. Manatee County, 1968, mem., 1968-79. With BG Army NG, 1956-91, ret. Contbr. articles to profl. jours. Mem. Pres.'s Council, U. South Fla., 1981. Mem. Am. Acad. Orthopedic Surgeons, ACS, Internat. Coll. Surgeons, Assn. Mil. Surgeons U.S., Am. Fracture Assn., Orthopedics Letters Club, Fla. Orthopedics Letters Club, Fla. Orthopedic Soc. (chmn. membership 1982-86, pres. 1989-90), Fla. Med. Soc., So. Orthopedic Assn., AMA, So. Med. Assn., Manatee County Med. Soc., Eastern Orthopedic Assn., Soc. Med. Cons. to Armed Forces, N.G. Officers Assn. Fla. (pres. 1980-81), Army Res. Forces (policy com. 1989-91), Phi Eta Sigma, Alpha Epsilon Delta. Presbyterian. Home: 8221 Desoto Memorial Hwy Bradenton FL 34209-9790 Office: 2101 61st St W Bradenton FL 34209-5528

SPRIGLER, MELAINE LYNN, accountant, consultant; b. Louisville, Sept. 25, 1968; d. Meinrad Joseph and Beverly Jean (Prather) S. BS in Bus., Ind. U., New Albany, 1990; MBA, Regent U., Virginia Beach, Va., 1995. Staff acct. Blue & Co., CPAs, Inpls., 1990-91; acct., mgr. Christian Internat., Santa Rosa Beach, Fla., 1991—. Youth leader Christian Internat. Family Ch., Santa Rosa Beach, 1996. Scholar Am. Soc. Women Accts. Mem. Alpha Chi, Beta Alpha Psi, Phi Eta Sigma. Republican. Office: Christian Internat. PO Box 9000 Santa Rosa Beach FL 32459

SPRINGER, FRED GENE, manufacturing engineer, mechanical engineer; b. Kokomo, Ind., Mar. 27, 1951; s. Dick Melvin and Joan Lucille (McGibbon) S.; m. Linda Marie Ward, Aug. 18, 1973 (div. 1987); children: Justin Ryan, Lindsey Rachelle. BA, Anderson Coll., 1973; MBA, Western Mich. U., 1979. Indsl. engr. GM, 1969-89; prodn. engr. Carolina Assemblies, Myrtle Beach, S.C., 1990-93. Active Jaycees, Big Bros. Mem. Coin Operators Assn., Masons. Home: 4347 Brookdale Ln Conway SC 29526-5597

SPRINGER, HOMER LEE, JR., art educator; b. Martinsville, Va., Oct. 16, 1939; s. Homer L. and Christine (Fago) S.; m. Maryann D., July 17, 1966; 1 child, Brian Christopher. BFA, Va. Commonwealth U., 1962; MEd, Towson State U., 1967. Tchr. Va. Mus. Art, Richmond, 1959-62, Anne Arundel County Pub. Schs., Annapolis, Md., 1962-69; prof. art Longwood Coll., Farmville, Va., 1969—. One-man shows include numerous galleries Calif., Ala., Ark., Wash., Va., N.Y., N.J., Vt., Ga., N.C., S.C., Fla., Brazil, Spain, Slovakia, Italy, Britain, Hungary, Can.. Vol. Food for Needy, Farmville, 1980—, New Horizon Hospice, 1983—; bd. dirs. Waterworks Players, Farmville, 1986—. Recipient Outstanding Faculty award Longwood Coll., 1987, Tech. award State Theatre Prodn., 1988, 93; numerous awards in field. Methodist. Home: 1804 E 3rd St Farmville VA 23901-2906 Office: Longwood Coll Art Dept Pine St Farmville VA 23909

SPRINGER, WAYNE GILBERT, computer leasing executive; b. El Paso, Tex., Oct. 6, 1951; s. Wayne Gill and Constance A. (Courtney) S.; m. Dianne Louise Slaydon, Jan. 3, 1981; children: Courtney Lee, Carol Jeanne, Kent Slaydon. BS in Engring., U.S. Mil. Acad., 1973; MBA, So. Meth. U., Dallas, 1979, MSCE, 1980. Registered profl. engr. Commd. 2d lt. U.S. Army, C.E., 1973, advanced through grades to capt., 1977, resigned, 1978; grad. sch. instr. So. Meth. U., 1978-80; engr. Fluor Corp., Irvine, Calif. and Houston, 1980-82; coord. project devel. United Energy Resources, Houston, 1982-83; founder Computer Leasing Exch. Corp., Houston, 1983—; founder Computer Helpline, Houston, 1984—, Network Systems Tech. Corp., 1993—; pres., founder Laser Express Corp., 1991; pres. Atiwa Computing, Inc., 1995—; ptnr. Springer Cons., Houston and Whittier, Calif., 1980-86. Contbr. articles to profl. jours.; inventor mech. devices. Mem. Houston Conv. and Visitors coun., 1983—, First Congl. Ch. 1981—. Mem. MIT Enterprise Forum, West Point Alumni Assn., Houston C. of C., West Houston C. of C., Houston Club, Computer and Audio Visual Execs. Assn. (founder 1989), Mensa, Plaza Oaks Club. Office: Computer Leasing Exch Corp 1003 Wirt Rd Ste 100 Houston TX 77055-6862

SPRINGFIELD, STEPHEN RAY, architect; b. Waco, Tex., Nov. 22, 1952; s. Milford Ray and Dorothy Lee (Hicks) S. BS with honors, U. Tex., Arlington, 1975, MArch, 1981. Registered architect, Tex.; registered interior designer, Tex. Architect TGMA, Architects, Dallas, 1982-87, HKS, Architects, Dallas, 1987—; field researcher, draftsman Historic Am. Bldg. Survey, Libr. of Congress, Washington, 1975. Mem. Old Oak Cliff Conservation League, Dallas; officer E. Kessler Park Neighborhood Assn., Dallas. Mem. Am. Inst. Architects (Dallas chpt.), Tex. Soc. Architects. Office: HKS Architects 700 N Pearl St Ste 1100 Dallas TX 75201-2814

SPRINGFIELD, WILLIAM FRANCIS, pharmacist, consultant; b. Phila., Dec. 10, 1938; s. William F. and Katherine M. (Myers) S.; m. Marie H. Pyle, Sept. 5, 1959; children: William V., Brian G., Maria Michelle. Student, Temple U., 1956-57; BS, U. Tex., 1970. Lic. pharmacist, Tex., Nev., La. Prin. community/chain pharmacy practice El Paso, 1970-72; staff pharmacist Hotel Dieu Hosp., El Paso, 1972-74; dir. Vista Hills Med. Ctr., El Paso, 1974-78; instr. Coll. of Nursing U. Tex., El Paso, 1976-78; dir. U. Med. Ctr., Las Vegas, Nev., 1979-80; divisional dir. pharmacy ops. AMI Pharmacy Mgmt. Svcs. (corp. nat. pharmacy subs.), Houston, 1981-86; project mgr. new ops. Owen Healthcare, Inc., Houston, 1986-87, asst. dir. quality assurance, 1987-92, dir. cons. svcs., 1988—; proprietor The Kingwood Pharmacy Resource Group; mem. dean's adv. coun. Coll. Pharmacy, U. Houston; mem. Tex. Pharmacy Act Sunset Rev. Commn., 1992-93; presenter in field. Mem. task force on class C (instnl. pharmacy) rules Tex. State Bd. Pharmacy, 1994. With USAF, 1959-62. Fellow Am. Soc. Cons. Pharmacists (del. long term care profl. and tech. adv. com., presenter ann. meeting 1991, 92); mem. Am. Soc. Hosp. Pharmacists, Tex. Pharm. Assn. (vice-chmn. 1992-93, chmn. 1993—, bd. councilors sect. cons. pharamcists), Tex. Soc. Hosp. Pharmacists (chmn. task force drug wholesale licensing 1991-920, Lake Houston Pharm. Assn., Houston-Galveston Area Soc. Hosp. Pharmacists (coun. legal and pub. affairs 1989-90). Home: 2159 Little Cedar Dr Kingwood TX 77339-1714 Office: Owen Healthcare Inc 9800 Centre Pky Ste 1100 Houston TX 77036-8223

SPRINGMANN, DOUGLAS MANDEL, JR., sales and marketing executive, fund raising consultant; b. Alexandria, Va., Apr. 23, 1941; s. Douglas M. Sr. and Florence Collins Taylor Springmann; m. Lucille Goodstein (div.); children: Erin Michelle, Leigh Taylor Springmann Hassett; m. Sebastiana Gagliano, June 9, 1984. BA in Philosophy, Coll. of William and Mary, 1961-64; MA in Fundraising Mgmt., New Sch. for Social Rsch., 1984-86. Asst. field dir. ARC, Alexandria, 1964-65; sales rep. AT&T Long Lines, Washington, 1965-68; exec. dir. and regional mgr. ECPI, Inc., various cities, 1968-71; nat. recruiter NCS, Inc., Lowell, Mass., 1971-72, regional sales mgr., 1972-73; v.p. Goal Getters, Inc., N.Y.C., 1974-84; pres. Campus Resources, Inc., Williamsburg, Va., 1984—; Cons. in field. Author: Product Fundraising How To Book and Satire, 1988. Emergency duty officer ARC, Washington, 1965-68; chmn. Ch. Fundraising Task Force, Williamsburg, 1989. Recipient numerous sales and sales mgmt. awards. Mem. Nat. Assn. Product Fundraisers, Assn. for Computing Machinery (vice chpt. chmn.), Data Processing Mgmt. Assn. (membership chmn.), United Way Info. and Referral Svc. (mem. bd. dirs.), C. of C. (com. chmn., edn. com. chair, Christmas Parade com.), Masonic Lodge # 6. Office: Campus Resources Inc 120B Tewning Rd Williamsburg VA 23188-2640

SPRINGSTON, RAYMOND LEROY, computer science educator; b. Iola, Kans., Nov. 17, 1946; s. Charles Harrison and Doris Arlene (Ballard) S.; m. Renee Weills, Aug. 7, 1970. BS in Aero. Engring., Wichita State U., 1969; MDiv, Southwestern Bapt. Theol. Sem., 1976; MS in Computer Sci. Engring., U. Tex., Arlington, 1991, postgrad., 1992—. Tool designer Boeing Airplane Co., Wichita, Kans., 1966-67; field mechanic S.W. Dodge, Ft. Worth, 1977-79, Chambers Chrysler-Dodge, Irving, Tex., 1978-79, David McDavid Pontiac, Irving, Tex., 1979-82, Sewell Village Cadillac, Dallas, 1982-89; asst. instr. U. Tex., Arlington, 1989—. Contbr. articles to profl. jours. Capt. USAF, 1969-73. Mem. IEEE, Assn. Computing Machinery, North Tex. Assn. for Art Intelligence. Baptist. Home: 3621 Woodmoor Rd Fort Worth TX 76133-6335 Office: U Tex Dept Computer Sci Engring PO Box 19015 Arlington TX 76019

SPRINKLE, JOE MELVIN, religious studies educator; b. Oklahoma City, Aug. 18, 1953; s. Joseph Melvin and Verna (Palmer) S.; m. Christilee Sprinkle; children: Rebecca Nicole, Tamara Renee. BS in Indsl. Engring., U. Okla., 1976; MDiv summa cum laude, Trinity Evang. Divinity Sch., 1981; MPhil in Hebraic & Cognate Studies, Hebrew Union Coll., 1987, PhD in Hebraic & Cognate Studies, 1991. Indsl. engr. Fibercast Co., Sand Springs, Okla., 1976-80; instr. biblical Hebrew Temple Bible Coll., Cin., 1985-86; teaching asst., tutor Hebrew, Hebrew Union Coll.-Jewish Inst. Religion-Wright State U., Dayton, Ohio, 1985-86; instr. O.T. Toccoa Falls (Ga.) Coll., 1988-91, asst. prof. O.T., 1991-96, assoc. prof. O.T., 1996—; lay preacher No. Hills Chapel, Cin., 1982-88, 1st Meth. Ch., Toccoa, 1990-93; rsch. asst. Hebrew Coll., 1985-86; pastor Prospect United Meth. Ch., Toccoa, 1993-94. Author: The Book of the Covenant: A Literary Approach, 1994; contbr. articles to profl. publs. Samuel Sandmel scholar, 1982-83, Hebrew Union Coll. scholar, 1983-91; Toccoa Falls Faculty Scholar of Yr., 1993-94. Mem. Soc. Biblical Lit., Evang. Theol. Soc. Republican. Office: Toccoa Falls Coll PO Box 800236 Toccoa GA 30598-0236

SPRINKLE, SARAH DAWN, medical/surgical nurse, civic worker; b. Lynchburg, Va., Dec. 30, 1962; d. Paul Vernon and Barbara Ann (Jennings) S. BS in Nursing, U. Va., 1986. Staff nurse, neurology U. Va., Charlottesville, 1986, primary nurse II, urology and gen. surgery, 1986-88, primary nurse III, urology and gen. surgery, 1988-89, chmn. unit-based quality assurance com., 1987-89; vol. Free Clinic Ctrl. Va., Lynchburg, 1989-94, coord. vol., indigent patient program mgr., 1994—. Home: 1100 Weeping Willow Dr # H Lynchburg VA 24501-3958

SPROUL, LORETTA ANN SCHROEDER, elementary school educator, reading specialist; b. Milw., Oct. 25, 1938; d. Paul Frederick and M. Faye (Brown) Schroeder; m. Hugh Bell Sproul III, July 30, 1966; children: Mary-Faye AnnTeresa, Hugh Bell IV. BS, Mount Mary Coll., 1960; MS, U. Wis., 1966, James Madison U., 1978. Cert. elem. tchr., reading specialist. Tchr. Milw. Pub. Schs., 1960-62, 63-64, 1965-66, 67-68; tchr. Dept. Def. Overseas Sch., Fed. Republic Germany, 1962-63, Okinawa, 1964-65; tchr. Muscogee County Schs., Columbus, Ga., 1966-67, Ft. Bragg (N.C.) Schs., 1974-76; reading and math. specialist Staunton (Va.) Pub. Schs., 1976—; facilitator Summer Ednl. Experiences for Knowledge program Bessie Weller Sch., Staunton, Va., 1989—. Bd. dirs. Community Child Care, Staunton, 1984-87; den mother Cub Scouts Am., Staunton, 1978-79; troop leader Girl Scouts U.S., Staunton, 1977-78; founder Children's Libr. Program, Martin, Tenn., 1970-73; vol. Meals on Wheels, Staunton, 1983-88, ARC Hosp., 1973-74. Recipient Outstanding Young Woman of Am. award, 1970, Excellence in Edn. award Va. Polytechnic Inst., 1989. Mem. MADD, Nat. Edn. Assn., AAUW (named Outstanding Young Woman of Am. 1970), Va. Reading Assn., Nat. Coun. Tchrs. of Math., Alpha Delta Kappa (treas.). Roman Catholic. Home: 951 E Beverley St Staunton VA 24401-3502 Office: Bessie Weller Sch 600 Greenville Ave Staunton VA 24401

SPROUSE, EARLENE PENTECOST, educational diagnostician; b. Hopewell, Va., Apr. 23, 1939; d. Earl Paige and Sophia Marlene (Chairky) Pentecost; m. David Andrew Koren, July 3, 1957 (div. Jan. 1963); children: David Andrew Jr., Elysia Marlene, Merri Paige; m. Wayne Alexender Sprouse, Sept. 2, 1964; 1 child, Michael Wayne. AS, Paul D. Camp C.C., Franklin, Va., 1973; BS in Comm. Disorders, Old Dominion U., 1975, MEd in Spl. Edn., 1977. Tchg. cert. with endorsement in speech lang. pathology, learning disabilities and emotional disturbance, Va. Speech lang. pathologist Southampton County Schs., Va., 1975-76; learning disabled tchr. itinerant Franklin (Va.) City Pub. Schs., 1976-78, emotionally disturbed/learning disabled tchr., 1978-85, speech lang. pathologist, 1986-91, ednl. diagnostician, 1992—; com. mem. The Childrens Ctr., Franklin, 1986—, Early Childhood Coun., Franklin, 1992—; needs assessment com. Juvenile Domestic Rels. Ct., Franklin, 1993—; project leader curriculum guide Listening and Lang. Processing Skills, 1990-91. Com. mem. Dem. Com., Suffolk, Va., 1985-92, Family Fair, Franklin, 1993—. Recipient Excellence in Edn. award C. of C., Hampton Roads, Va., 1988-89; grantee Va. Edn. Assn., Richmond, 1994—, Project UNITE Dept. Edn., Richmond, 1994—. Mem. ASCD, Coun. for Exceptional Children (com. mem.), Speech and Hearing Assn. Va., Franklin City Edn. Assn. (pub. rels. com., pres. 1980, 91), Orton Dyslexia Soc. Presbyterian. Home: 319 Gray's Creek Ln Surry VA 23883 Office: Franklin City Pub Schs 800 W 2nd Ave Franklin VA 23851-2162

SPROUSE, JAMES DEAN, nurse, anesthetist; b. Rutherfordton, N.C., June 7, 1949; s. Charles Ernest and Melba (Callahan) S.; m. Cheryl Geddes, May 26, 1978; children: Samuel, Susan. BS in Biology, Lenoir Rhyne Coll., 1970, BS in Nursing, 1973; diploma anesthesia program, N.C. Bapt. Hosp., Winston-Salem, 1975; MBA, U. S.C., 1992. Registered nurse anesthetist. Chief nurse anesthetist Cannon Meml. Hosp., Banner Elk, N.C., 1975-77, Greensboro (N.C.) Hosp., 1977-84; staff nurse anesthetist Wesley Long Hosp., Greensboro, 1984-87; chief nurse anesthetist Wallace Thomson Hosp., Union, S.C., 1987-96; pres. Aneserv, Inc., Union, 1996—. Mem. S.C. State Bd. Nursing, Columbia, 1991-93; pres. Union County Divsn. Am. Heart Assn., 1995-96. Spindale Mills Found. scholar, 1966-70, N.C. Med. Care Commn. scholar N.C. Div. Human Resources, 1971-75; recipient Agatha Hodgins Award for Outstanding Student Nurse Anesthesist, 1975. Mem. Am. Assn. Nurse Anesthetists, S.C. Assn. Nurse Anesthetists, Union Country Club. Republican. Presbyterian. Home: 205 E South St Union SC 29379-2346 Office: Wallace Thomson Hosp 720 Lakeside Dr Ste L-5 Union SC 29379

SPROUSE, JAMES MARSHALL, retired federal judge; b. Williamson, W.Va., Dec. 3, 1923; s. James and Garnet (Lawson) S.; m. June Dolores Burt, Sept. 25, 1952; children: Tracy Sprouse Ferguson, Jeffrey Marshall, Andrew Michael, Sherry Lee Sprouse Shinholser, Shelly Lynn Sprouse Schneider. A.B., St. Bonaventure (N.Y.) U., 1947; LL.B., Columbia U., 1949; postgrad. in internat. law, U. Bordeaux, France, 1950. Bar: W.Va. Asst. atty. gen. State of Va., 1949; with W.Va. CIA, 1952-57; pvt. practice W.Va., 1957-72, 75-79; justice W.Va. Supreme Ct. Appeals, 1972-75; judge U.S. Ct. Appeals (4th cir.), Lewisburg, W.Va., 1979-92, sr. cir. judge, 1992-95; retired, 1995, pvt. practice, 1995—. Served with AUS, 1942-45. Fulbright scholar. Mem. Am. Bar Assn., W.Va. State Bar, W.Va. Bar Assn., W.Va. Trial Lawyers Assn., Kanawha County Bar Assn., VFW, Am. Legion. Democrat. Presbyterian. Clubs: Shriners, Aheppa. Office: PO Box 159 Union WV 24983

SPROUSE, SUSAN RAE MOORE, human resources specialist; b. Amsterdam, N.Y., Feb. 23, 1948; d. Charles Franklin and Alice Rae (Lawson) Moore; m. Richard D. Sprouse, May 5, 1973; children: Jennifer Lynn, Melinda Rae. BS, U. So. Miss., 1970, MBA, 1971. Spl. non-exempt employee rels. GE Co., Owensboro, Ky., 1972-74; from instr. entry level tng. to spl. profl. rels. and EEO GE Co., Chgo., 1974-78; from employee rels. clk. to material control specialist GE Co., Ft. Smith, Ark., 1978-82; employee rels. rep. Mason Chamberlain Inc., Stennis Space Ctr., Miss., 1982-90; human resource specialist Inst. for Naval Oceanography, Stennis Space Ctr., Miss., 1990-92; program coord. Ctr. for Ocean and Atmospheric Modeling, Stennis Space Ctr., Miss., 1992-95; human resources specialist Computer Scis. Corp., Stennis Space Ctr., Miss., 1995—; co. rep. Jr. Achievement, Owensboro, 1972-74. Libr., Am. flag chair DAR, Picayune, Miss., 1967-92; bd. dirs. Picayune On Stage, v.p., sec., 1982—. Named Outstanding Jr. Mem. DAR, Picayune, 1970; profiled in Picayune Item, 1988. Mem. Nat. Soc. Magna Charta Dames, Sigma Sigma Sigma, Phi Delta Rho. Republican. Church of Christ. Office: CSC Bldg 3205 Stennis Space Center MS 39529

SPROWL, DAVID CHARLES, brokerage house executive; b. Sherman, Tex., Aug. 12, 1940; s. Charlie Clay and Alice (Patterson) S.; m. Frankie Joyce Melton; children: James, Rebecca. BA, Austin Coll., 1963. Sr. v.p. A.G. Edwards & Sons, Inc., St. Louis, 1974—, also bd. dirs. Mem. City Council, Sherman, 1979, mayor, 1983; bd. dirs. Greater Texoma Utility Authority, Pottsboro, Tex., 1985. Served with USAF, 1966-70. Mem. Internat. Assn. Fin. Planners, Sherman Area C. of C. (bd. dirs. 1978), Am. Legion. Republican. Methodist. Lodges: Rotary, Elks, Masons. Home: PO Box 1222 Sherman TX 75091-1222 Office: AG Edwards & Sons Inc PO Box 1236 Sherman TX 75091-1236

SPRUCE, KENNETH LAWRENCE, political scientist, educator; b. Toledo, Mar. 6, 1956; s. George Jr. and Helen Estelle (Jordan) S.; 1 child, Sierra Monique. BA, U. Cin., 1980; MPA, U. Toledo, 1982; postgrad., Clark Atlanta U., 1991—. Intern policy analyst Nat. League Cities, Washington, 1980-81; journalist Toledo Jour. Newspaper, 1981-83; pers. specialist State of Ohio, Toledo, 1983-91; instr. Morris Brown Coll., Atlanta, 1992; asst. prof. Floyd Coll., Rome, Ga., 1993—; grad. tchg. asst. Clark Atlanta U., 1993-94; interviewer pub. opinion survey Math. Policy Rsch., Princeton, N.J., 1993. Contbr. articles to profl. jours. Fellow Ford Found., 1993. Mem. Am. Polit. Sci. Assn., Nat. Conf. Black Polit. Scientists. Democrat. Baptist. Home: 505 Amberlake Ln Acworth GA 30101 Office: Floyd Coll 3175 Cedartown Hwy SE Rome GA 30162

SPRUIELL, VANN, psychoanalyst, educator, editor, researcher; b. Leeds, Ala., Oct. 16, 1926; s. Vann Lindley and Zada (Morton) S.; m. Iris Taylor, Sept. 20, 1951 (div. Oct. 1966); children: Graham, Fain, Garth; m. Joyce Ellis, Feb. 11, 1967; stepchildren: Sidney Reavey, Catherine Ellis, Matson Ellis. BS, U. Ala., Tuscaloosa, 1948; MD, Harvard U., 1952. Resident Bellevue Hosp., N.Y.C., 1952-53, N.Y. Hosp., N.Y.C., 1953-55; fellow Tulane Sch. Medicine, New Orleans, 1955-57; pvt. practice New Orleans, 1957—; vis. rschr. Anna Freud Ctr., London, 1972-73; co-pub. JOURLIT and BOOKREV; pres. and founding mem. Psychoanalytic Archives CD-ROM Texts (PACT), New Orleans, 1993—; clin. prof. psychiatry La. State U. Sch. Medicine, Tulane U. Sch. Medicine; sec. Ctr. for Advanced Studies in Psychoanalysis, 1989—. Editl. bd. Psychoanalytic Quarterly, 1973—; N.Am. editor Internat. Jour. Psychoanalysis, London, 1988-93; mem. various other editl. bds.; contbr. articles to profl. jours. and books. Sgt. U.S. Army, 1944-46. Mem. Am. Psychoanalytic Assn. (sec. bd. on profl. stds. 1979-92), Wyvern Club. Home: 215 Iona St Metairie LA 70005-4137

SPRUILL, HOWARD VERNON, minister, college official; b. South Norfolk, Va., Dec. 27, 1919; s. Veron B. and Mabel E. (Kirby) S.; m. Daisy Lee Singleton, Dec. 11, 1943; 1 child, Ruth Elaine. BS, Valley Forge Christian Coll., 1977; MDiv, Luther Rice Sem., 1978, DMin, 1980. Ordained to ministry Assemblies of God, 1953. Auditor, U.S. Navy, Little Creek, Va., 1945-50; pastor Elk Garden, W.Va., 1950-52, Emporia, Va., 1952-57, Manassas, Va., 1957-69, dist. sec., treas., 1968-74; pastor, Silver Spring, Md., 1974-79; dist. supt. Potomac Dist. Council, Assemblies of God Ch., 1979-91; pres. Valley Forge Christian Coll., 1982; chmn. bd. regents, 1968-91; pres. Prince William County Ministerial Assn., 1966-68. Served with U.S. Army, 1937-45. Author: Deacon Servant to God and Man, 1980. Home: 5945 Windwood Dr Lakeland FL 33813-4805

SPRUILL, LOUISE ELAM, retired secondary educator; b. Mecklenburg County, Va., Aug. 17, 1918; d. William Llewellyn and Lillie Clayton (Puryear) Elam; m. Jacob Sipe Fleming, Aug. 12, 1941 (dec. Nov. 1957); 1 son, James Sipe Fleming; m. Edward Muse Spruill, Nov. 6, 1968; 1 stepdaughter, Florence Spruill Mackie. BA, East Carolina U., 1939, MA, 1961. cert. secondary tchr. Tchr. Washington County Bd. Edn., Plymouth, N.C., 1957-69; chmn. math. dept. Plymouth High Sch., 1965-69; treas. Washington County Hosp. Aux., 1991-93, v.p., 1993—. Mem. Plymouth City Coun., 1980-87; trustee Pettigrew Regional Libr., 1983-88; mem. Washington County Libr. Bd., 1983-92, chmn., 1985-88; mem. Bd. of Adjustments, Plymouth, 1989—; sec. Grace Ch., 1981-84, vestry, 1981-84, 95—. Named Outstanding Woman in Washington County, Washington County Coun. on Status of Women, 1988. Mem. N.C. Ret. Sch. Pers., Washington County Hist. Soc. (bd. dirs. 1987—), Fortnightly Lit. Club of Chase City, Va. (pres. 1978-79), Delta Kappa Gamma (v.p. chpt. 1968-70, corr. sec. chpt. 1986-88). Democrat. Episcopalian.

SPUNBERG, JEROME J., radiation oncologist; b. N.Y.C., June 20, 1952; s. Edward I. and Gizela S.; m. June M. Spunberg, Jan 4, 1976; children: Eric, Adam, Daniel. BA, Columbia U., 1973; MD, Harvard U., 1977. Diplomate Am. Bd. Radiology. Dir. radiation oncology JFK Comprehensive Cancer Ctr., Atlantis, Fla., 1985—. Office: JFK Cancer Ctr 170 Jfk Dr Lake Worth FL 33462-6607

SPURLOCK, CAROLYN L., educational administrator; b. Essex, N.C., Feb. 24, 1937; d. Vernon and Mary (Evans) Lynch; children: Emmett III, Jonathan. BA in Elem. Edn., Shaw U., 1956; MA, Columbia U., 1959, EdD, 1987. Tchr. Eastman Sch., Enfield, N.C., 1956-60, Mansfield Twp. Schs., Columbus, N.J., 1960-63, Englewood Cliffs (N.J.) Bd. of Edn., 1963-71; edn. specialist Bank St. Coll., N.Y.C., 1971-74; sch. dir. Holley Child Care Devel., Hackensack, N.J., 1974-78; edn. specialist Bergen County office N.J. Dept., Paramus, N.J., 1978-85; prin. Andover Regional Pub. Sch., Newton, N.J., 1985-91; prin. Richmond (Va.) Pub. Schs., 1991-96, team leader grant programs and curriculum, 1996—; cons. Head Start follow-through Bank St. Coll., N.Y.C., 1971-72; mem. adv. bd., cons. Plan for Social Excellence, Mt. Kisco, N.Y., 1996—. Author: (periodical) Individualized Reading, 1961. Mem. Zoning Bd. Andover Twp., Newton, 1990-94; trustee Sussex County C.C., Newton, 1991-94; mem. Hand Workshop, Richmond, 1996—. Mem. ASCD, NAESP. Home: 8202 Tyndale Rd Richmond VA 23227

SPURRIER, MICHELLE See WILLIAMS, KRISTINA

SQUADRITO, GIUSEPPE LUCIANO, research scientist, chemist, educator; b. Lima, Peru, Dec. 13, 1959; came to U.S., 1983, permanent resident, 1991; s. Juan Jose and Lima Elizabeth (Goyzueta) S. BS, Pontifical Cath. U. Peru, Lima, 1983; PhD, La. State U., 1988. Teaching asst. Pontifical Catholic U. Peru, 1982; teaching asst. La. State U., Baton Rouge, 1983-84, rsch. asst., 1985-88, mem. faculty Biodynamics Inst., 1989-91, adj. asst. prof., 1989-91, asst. prof. rsch., 1991—; rchr. in free radicals and oxidative biology; lectr. in field; cons. to chem. cos., 1988—. Contbr. numerous articles to profl. jours. Fulbright fellow, 1983-89; Nat. Coun. Sci. and Tech. grantee, Peru, 1989-91. Mem. Am. Chem. Soc., Peruvian Chem. Soc., Phi Lambda Upsilon. Office: La State U Biodynamics Inst 711 Choppin Hall Baton Rouge LA 70803

SQUARE, BRENDA BILLIPS, archivist, librarian; b. Great Lakes, Ill., Feb. 10, 1953; d. Manuel Joseph Billips and Evelyn (Martin) Wilson; m. Allen Lee Square, Apr. 1, 1972; children: Allen Lee Jr., Arlyn Siyan. BA in Polit. Sci., U. New Orleans, 1981; paralegal cert., Tulane U., 1984; MLS, La. State U., 1996. Spl. asst. to dir., adminstrv. supr. Tulane Law Libr., New Orleans, 1981-93; reference archivist, libr. Amistad Rsch. Ctr., New Orleans, 1994—. Chmn. bd. trustees Beecher Meml. United Ch. Christ, New Orleans, 1991-94. Mem. ALA, Acad. Cert. Archivists, Soc. Am. Archivists, Greater New Orleans Archivists, New Orleans Assn. Law Librs., Soc. Southwest Archivists. Office: Tulane U Amistad Rsch Ctr Tilton Hall New Orleans LA 70118

SQUIER, THOMAS KEITH, columnist, educator, writer, environmentalist; b. Cherokee, N.C., Dec. 2, 1948; s. Richard Keith and Helen Rebecca (Jones) S.; m. Frances Dellinger, May 24, 1989; children: Thomas K. Jr., Amanda, Davey, Austin, Jessica. AA Social Scis., Campbell U., 1979; Chartered Herbalist, Dominion Herbal Coll., 1985; M in Herbology, Emerson Coll., Montreal, Quebec, Can., 1987; D in Naturopathy, Clayton Sch., 1989; BA in Human Svcs., St. Andrews Presbyn. Coll., 1994. Notary pub., N.C.; wilderness emergency med. technician. Enlisted U.S. Army Spl. Forces, 1966; trainer in survival techniques various U.S. Spl. Forces, worldwide, 1966-93; pres. Botanico Ednl. Svcs., Aberdeen, N.C., 1989—; columnist The Pilot, Southern Pines, N.C., 1990—, Fayetteville (N.C.) Observer-Times, 1989—, Ft. Bragg Paraglide, 1990—, Red Springs (N.C.) Citizen, 1995—, Spring Lake News, 1991—; cons. to US Army Survival Sch., Ft. Bragg, 1983—, Indian Mus. of the Carolinas, Laurinburg, N.C., 1989—; contbg. editor The Wildfoods Forum, Virginia Beach, Va., 1991—; subject matter expert cons. to Natick Rsch., Devel. & Engring. labs in Forager computer program project, 1987-92. Author: Living Off the Land, 1989, the Wildfoods Cookbook, 1992, rev. 2d edit., 1994, The Wild and Free Foods Cookbook, 1996; scriptwriter, narrator: (video) Edible Wild Plants of N.Am. (Army Commendation medal); columnist various newspapers: Nature Notes, Things to Do, Living Off the Land, Looks at Books; numerous ann. speaking engagements on bot. and environ. subjects; svc. officer Hoke County N.C. Vets., 1995—. Mem. Moore County Commrs. Environ. Quality Adv. Com., 1990-95. Sgt. U.S. Army Spl. Forces, 1966-93. Recipient Lifesaver award Woodmen of the World, Aberdeen, N.C., 1988; named Conservationist of Yr., Fayetteville, N.C., 1984; named N.C. Hunter Safety Instr. of Yr., Ithaca Firearms, Fayetteville, 1984, Gov.'s Conservationist, Aberdeen, 1989, Conservationist, Cumberland Urban Recycling an Beautification, Fayetteville, 1991. Mem. NRA (life), Spl. Forces Assn. (life, chpt. I-XVIII, Chaplain 1979-83, 90-94), Am. Forestry Assn. (life), Am. Mensa, N.C. Herpetol. Soc., N.C. Recycling Assn., Outdoors Writers Assn. Am., Garden Writers Assn. Am., Putting People First, Southeastern Outdoor Press Assn., Disabled Am. Vets. (life), N.Y. Acad. Scis., St. Andrews Honor Soc., Chi Sigma Iota (pres. Pembroke State U. chpt. 1996). Democrat.

SQUIRES, JAMES RALPH, development company executive; b. Dillon, S.C., Jan. 2, 1940; s. William Guilford and Ruby Alice (Whittington) S.; m. Ann Newton, Apr. 17, 1965; children: Samuel Guilford, James Drew. Student public schs., Charlotte, N.C. With Squires Constrn. Co., 1959-62; pres. SBS Builders, Inc., Charlotte, 1968-70; pres. Ralph Squires Homes, Charlotte, 1970-88, Squires & Assos., Realtors, 1975-88, JRS Enterprises, Inc., 1976-88, Squires Enterprises, Inc., exec. com.Park Meridian Bank, 1994. Mem. Charlotte Tree Commn., 1977; bd. dirs. Athletic Found. U. N.C., Charlotte, 1979, Providence Day Sch., 1981-84, Better Bus. Bur., 1983, Dover Mortgage, MMAES Inn, Charlotte Symphony; appointee pub. mem. N.C. State Bar; pres. Metrolina Home Owners, 1982, bd. dirs., 1983; bd. govs. Polit. Action Com for Bldg. Industry; mem. bd. visitors Mercy Hosp., Charlotte, 1986; bd. dirs. Mercy Hosp Found., chmn. 1993—; chmn. new bldg. fund United Cerebral Palsy; mem. exec. coun. Boy Scouts Am. Mecklenburg County council, 1986; exec. coun. Muscular Dystrophy Assn., Charlotte, 1987, speaker of NC House appt. to N.C. Wildlife Resources Commn., 1995. Recipient Profile award N.C. Blue Cross/Blue Shield, 1974, Albert Gallatin merit cert., 1974; named Charlotte Builder of Yr., 1977. Mem. Charlotte Homebuilders Assn. (pres. 1974), N.C. Home Builders Assn. (v.p. 1975), Nat. Homebuilders Assn., Charlotte Bd. Realtors, Carolina Ambassadors, Safari Club Internat. (Carolina chpt.), Quail Hollow Country Club, Old North State Country Club, Brays Island Plantation. Republican. Baptist. Home: 8811 Winged Bourne Rd Charlotte NC 28210-5941

SRINIVASAN, GANESAN, molecular biologist, educator; b. Thanjavur, Tamil Nadu, India, June 11, 1958; came to the U.S., 1982; s. Srinivasan Subramaniam and Jayalakshmi Srinivasan; m. Chandra Rajagopalan, July 7, 1985. BS in Chemistry, U. Madras, India, 1978, MS in Biochemistry, 1981; PhD, U. Md., 1986. Jr. rsch. fellow Protein Rsch. Unit Loyola Coll., Madras, 1981-82; teaching asst. U. Md., Baltimore County, 1982-86; postdoctoral fellow U. Md., Balt., 1986-87; postdoctoral fellow U. Tex. Med. Br., Galveston, 1988-90, asst. prof., 1991—. Contbr. articles to profl. jours. Grantee Am. Heart Assn., 1991-93. Mem. Endocrine Soc., Sigma Xi. Hindu. Office: U Tex Med Br 607 Basic Science Bldg Galveston TX 77555

SRINIVASAN, S., computer science educator, consultant; b. Mayiladuturai, Tamilnadu, India, July 15, 1948; came to U.S., 1975; s. Ponnuswamy and Avayambal Subramanian; m. Lakshmi Hariharan, Dec. 10, 1980; children: Sowmya Priya, Harish Mayur. BSc, Madras (India) U., 1968; MSc, Annamalai U., Annamalainagar, India, 1970; MA, U. Pitts., 1975, PhD, 1981;

MS, U. Akron, 1985. Asst. prof. Annamalai U., Annamalainagar, 1970-74; teaching fellow U. Pitts., 1975-81; asst. prof. Carlow Coll., Pitts., 1981-82, U. Akron, 1982-84; assoc. prof. Austin Peay State U., Clarksville, Tenn., 1984-87, U. Louisville, 1987—; cons. IBM, Lexington, Ky., 1988, Vencor Corp., Louisville, 1993; conf. panelist. Editor: ACM Computing Revs., 1985—; contbr. revs. and papers to profl. jours. Coord. Hindu Temple Ky., Louisville, 1992-93. Mem. IEEE (sr. mem.), Assn. Computing Machinery (local arrangements chair for conf. 1989). Hindu. Office: Univ of Louisville Dept Cis College of Bus Louisville KY 40292

STAATS, THOMAS ELWYN, neuropsychologist; b. Marietta, Ohio; s. Percy Anderson and Julia (Bourmorck) S.; m. Debra R.; children: Lauren Malu, Kara Kristyn, Stacy Rhnea, Ronald Derek. B.A. cum laude, Emory U., 1970; M.A., U. Ala., 1972, Ph.D., 1974; postgrad. U. Tex., Tyler, 1992. Diplomate Am. Bd. Profl. Disability Cons.; lic. psychologist. Dir., chief psychologist Caddo Parish Diagnostic Ctr., Shreveport, La., 1974-81; exec. dir. Doctors Psychol. Ctr., Shreveport, 1979-91, Comprehensive Assessments, 1991—; cons. to Charter Forest Hosp., Shreveport Impairment and Disability Evaluation Ctr.; neuropsychol. cons. La. State U. Med. Ctr.; clin. assoc. prof. psychology La. State U., Shreveport, 1977—, clin. assoc. prof. psychiatry Sch. Medicine, 1980—; mem. faculty Am. Acad. Disability Evaluating Physicians. Author: Manual For the Stress Vector Analysis Test Series, 1983, The Doctors Guide to Instant Stress Relief, 1987; Stress Management and Relaxation Training System Handbook. Contbr. articles to profl. jours. and popular mags. Mem. Gov's. Com. of 1000, La., 1979. U. Ala. Grad. Research Council fellow, 1974; recipient AADEP award 1991. Fellow Am. Inst. Stress; mem. APA, Nat. Acad. Neuropsychology. Republican, Nat. Register of Health Svc. Providers in Psychology. Episcopalian. Avocations: scuba diving, gun collecting, camping, boating, stress, malingering and chronic pain research. Home: 10816 Sunrise Pointe Shreveport LA 71106 Office: Comprehensive Assessments Inc 1532 Irving Pl Shreveport LA 71101-4604

STABER, DOROTHEE BEATRICE, administrative assistant; b. Frankfurt am Main, Germany, Jan. 19, 1961; came to U.S., 1983; d. Rolf Joachim and Sibylle Dorothee (Grafin von Nostitz) Kundahl; m. Harley Joseph Staber; children: Marina Inez, Christopher Patrick. Student, Goethe U., Frankfurt, 1981-83; BBA, U. North Tex., 1987; postgrad., U. Dallas, 1990-93. Sales asst. Xerox Corp., Irving, Tex., 1987-88; asst. mgr. Pioneer Life Ins. Co., Irving, 1988-89; adminstrv. asst. Howard Hughes Med. Inst., Dallas, 1989—. Mem. Women's Advocacy Project, Beta Gamma Sigma. Office: Howard Hughes Med Inst 5323 Harry Hines Blvd Dallas TX 75235-7200

STABIN, MICHAEL GREGORY, health physicist; b. Miami, Fla., Aug. 29, 1957; s. Norman and Shirley (Trotter) S.; m. Judith Bettie Collins, Aug. 30, 1980; children: Laura, Daniel, Mark, Julia. BS in Environ. Engring., U. Fla., 1981, ME in Envirion. Engring., 1983; postgrad., U. Tenn., 1988—. Cert. health physicist, Am. Bd. Health Physics. Grad. asst. dept. environ. engring. U. Fla., Gainesville, 1980-83; scientist Radiation Internal Dose Info. Ctr. Oak Ridge (Tenn.) Associated Univs., 1983—; cons. health physicist Oak Ridge Nuclear Medicine, 1984-89; mem. ethics com. Oak Ridge Associated Univs., 1989-90, environ. safety and health oversight com., 1989-91; spl. task group Internat. Commn. on Radiol. Protection on Dose to Patients from Radiopharms., 1991—, Soc. Nuclear Medicine Med. Internal Radiation Dose Com., 1985-92, 91—, Am. Assn. Physicists in Medicine, 1988—. Assoc. editor Health Physics Jour., 1992—; contbr. articles to profl. jours. Active Anderson County (Tenn.) Jail Ministry, Evang. Free Ch., 1983—. Mem. Health Physics Soc. (pres. med. sect. 1981—), Soc. Nuclear Medicine, Sigma Xi, Tau Beta Pi. Office: Oak Ridge Assoc Univs Med Scis Divsn PO Box 117 Oak Ridge TN 37831-0117

STABLEIN, JOHN JOSEPH, III, physician; b. Galesburg, Ill., Nov. 26, 1951; s. John Joseph Jr. and Evelyn May (Haggerty) S.; m. Diane Catherine Jansen, June 6, 1976; children: David James, Kara Marie. Student, Loyola U., Chgo., 1969-72; MD, U. Ill., Chgo., 1976. Diplomate Am. Bd. Allergy and Immunology, Am. Bd. Internal Medicine. Intern, resident U. South Fla. Affiliated Hosps.; asst. prof. medicine U. South Fla., Tampa, 1981-86; pvt. practice Brandon, Fla., 1981—; chief of medicine Humana Hosp. Brandon, 1987-89. Mem. Hillsborough County Med. Assn. (sec. 1989-90), Fla. Allergy Soc. (pres. 1988-89). Office: 500 Vonderburg Dr Ste 103 East Tower Brandon FL 33511-5968

STABLER, JEFFREY CALVIN, lawyer, accountant; b. Rusk, Tex., Jan. 27, 1956; s. Robert Paul and C. Maxine (Thedford) S.; m. Teresa Dianne Morris, July 13, 1984 (div. Mar. 1989). BS in Acctg., Cameron U., 1978; JD, U. Okla., 1981. Bar: Okla. 1981, U.S. Tax Ct. 1983; CPA, Okla. Pvt. practice law Lawton, Okla., 1981—; prin. Liester & Stabler, Inc., CPAs, Lawton, 1981—. Treas. Ch. of Christ, Sullivan Village, 1991-92. Mem. ABA, Okla. Bar Assn., Comanche County Bar Assn., AICPA, Okla. Soc. CPAs, Am. Assn. Atty.-CPAs, Lawton C. of C., Kiwanis (treas. 1985-92), Phi Kappa Phi. Republican. Mem. Ch. of Christ. Home: 1614 NW 27th St Lawton OK 73505-3947 Office: Liester & Stabler Inc 2629 NW Cache Rd Ste 5 Lawton OK 73505-5265

STABLER, MASON WESLEY, mathematics educator; b. Atmore, Ala., May 3, 1956; s. Lee Wesley and Mabel (Blackburn) S.; m. Deborah G. Stabler; children: Angie, Brad, Misty. BS in Math., Livingston (Ala.) U., 1978; MEd in Adminstrn. and Supervision, Southeastern La. U., 1985; EdS in Curriculum and Instrn., U. West Fla., 1995. Profl. tchg. cert., Fla., Ala. Math instr., coach Monroe County H.S., Monroeville, Ala., Troup County H.S., LaGrange, Ga., Marion (Ala.) Mil. Inst., Cen. H.S., Baton Rouge; asst. football coach, math instr. Southeastern La. U., Hammond; math. and sci. instr., coach Ernest Ward H.S., Walnut Hill, Fla.; math. instr., head football coach Apalachicola (Fla.) H.S.; math. instr., coach Ft. Walton Beach (Fla.) H.S.; math. instr. Escambia County H.S., Atmore, Ala. Asst. baseball coach Babe Ruth League, Atmore, 1994, 95. Recipient Tandy Outstanding Tchr. award, 1994-95.

STACEY, DARLA SUE, financial control consultant; b. Torrance, Calif., Aug. 14, 1961; d. Vernon R.B. and Jackie Louise (Maxwell) Goodson; m. Donald Norman Stacey Jr., Oct. 25, 1980; children: Colt Thomas, Shawn William, Brandon Lee. Student, Okla. State U., 1979, Tulsa Jr. Coll., 1980. From sec. to jr. claim approver to sr. claims approver MetLife Ins. Co., Tulsa, 1980-83, from sr. sec. to sr. field adminstrn. clk., 1983-86, from jr. fin. control analyst to fin. control cons., 1986—. Active Park Lane Elem. PTA, Broken Arrow, Okla., 1989—. Named Miss Broken Arrow, City of Broken Arrow, 1978-79. Democrat. Office: MetLife 12902 E 51st Tulsa OK 74134

STACEY, NORMA ELAINE, farmer, civic worker; b. Roanoke, La., Sept. 13, 1925; d. August and Julie (Ravet) Trahan; m. Louis Brewer, June 10, 1949 (dec. 1978); children: Louis Timothy Brewer, John August Brewer; m. Truman Stacey, Feb. 2, 1980. BA, St. Mary's Dominican Coll., New Orleans, 1946. Acct. Cities Svc. Refining Corp., Lake Charles, La., 1946-49; sec. La. Tchrs. Retirement System, Baton Rouge, 1950-51; bus. mgr. Brewer Studios, Lake Charles, 1951-78; co-owner Ravet Estate, Bell City, La., 1958—, Trahan Farm, Lake Arthur, La., 1969—; co-owner Trahan Ins. Agy., Welsh, La., 1964-72, Trahan Estate, Fenton, La., 1969—. Mem. Lake Charles Messiah Chorus, 1946-52; choir singer Immaculate Conception Ch., 1946-52, chmn. landscaping com., 1975-82; chmn. scrapbook com., mem. ticket com. Lake Charles Community Concerts, 1955—; coordinator Art Assocs., Lake Charles, 1955-58; mem. ticket com. Lake Charles Symphony Auxiliary, 1957—, sec., 1960-61, treas., 1962-64; vol. librarian Landry Meml. High Sch., Lake Charles, 1963-68; active St. Patrick Hosp. Auxiliary, 1965—; sec. Gov. La.'s Program for Gifted Childern McNeese State U., Lake Charles, 1978-80; mem. scholarship com. McNeese State U. Found., 1979—; mem. com. on scouting, vol. sec. and receptionist, chmn. decorating com. Diocese of Lake Charles, 1980—, sec., 1980-84, 90—, mem. Companions of Honor, 1982—; mem. Cath. com. on scouting South Cen. Region, Lake Charles, 1981-88, regional sec., 1985-88; mem. emblems subcom. Nat. Cath. Com. on Scouting, Irving, Tex., 1981-88; mem.-at-large Calcasieu Area council Boy Scouts Am., Lake Charles, 1980—; bd. dirs. Lake Charles Symphony Soc., 1981-87, mem. pops com., 1981, membership co-chmn., 1982-83, chmn., 1983-84, program chmn., 1985-88, mem. endowment com., 1987; patron La. Choral Found., Lake Charles, 1982—. Recipient Nat. Honors award Am. Guild Piano Competitions, 1943-45, Bronze Pelican Emblem award Nat. Cath. Com. on Scouting, 1984; named to Scouting Roll of Honor, Diocese of Lake Charles, 1982; named Dame Equestrian Order of Holy Sepulchre of Jerusalem, 1982, Dame Comdr., 1987, Dame Comdr. with Star, 1992, Dame of Grace, Mil. and Hospitaller Order of St. Lazarus of Jerusalem, 1993, Dame of Merit, Sacred Mil. Constantinian Order of St. George, 1994. Mem. AAUW (treas. pre-sch. program 1954-58), NCCJ (corr. sec. local chpt. 1988-91, sec.), Am. Rose Soc., Lake Charles Rose Soc., Lake Charles Garden Club (treas. 1958-61, sec. 1962-64, chmn. telephone com. 1964-86, cert appreciation 1985), Les Etudientes Book Club, Pioneer Club, Serra Club of Lake Charles (sec. 1992-93). Democrat. Home and Office: 1802 2nd Ave Lake Charles LA 70601-6432

STACEY, PATRICK, account executive; b. Dallas, Mar. 17, 1963; s. James Henry and Virginia Clara (Ruskay) S.; m. Stephanie Diane Graham, Mar. 10, 1990. BA, Stephen F. Austin Coll., 1985. Prodn. asst. Sta. KLTV-TV, Tyler, Tex., 1985, pub. svc. dir., 1985-86, promotion mgr., 1986-89, mktg. and rsch. dir., 1989-91. Vol. Eisenhower Internat. Golf Classic, Tyler, 1986-91, Multiple Sclerosis Soc., Tyler, 1991; bd. dirs. Children's Village, 1988-91, D-Fy-It; chmn. bd. Smith Countychpt. Am. Heart Assn., 1994—, devel. chmn. 1992-93, comm. chmn. 1990. Mem. East Tex. Muscular Dystrophy Assn. (v.p. 1989-91), Tyler Area C. of C. (membership svcs. coun. chmn.). Republican. Roman Catholic. Home: 4301 Aberdeen Dr Tyler TX 75703-1913 Office: Sta KLTV-TV Loop 323 At Old Kilgor H Tyler TX 75701

STACEY, TRUMAN, journalist, consultant; b. Port Arthur, Tex., Dec. 8, 1916; s. James Harrison and Billie (Davis) S.; m. Dorothy Mary Piboin, May 25, 1963 (dec.); m. Norma Elaine Trahan, Feb. 2, 1980. B in Philosophy, U. Detroit, 1946, MA, 1954. Reporter Beaumont (Tex.) Enterprise, 1937-42, Oklahoma City Daily Oklahoman, 1943-44, Detroit Free Press, 1944-45; dir. pub. rels. U. Detroit, 1945-49; reporter Washington Times Herald, 1949-50; sports editor Lake Charles (La.) Am. Press, 1950-60, editor-in-chief, 1961-82; dir. communications Diocese Lake Charles, 1982-90, pres. Coun. of Cath. Men, 1990-92; pres. Cath. social svcs. bd. Cath. Social Svcs. Bd., 1992-96. Mem. adv. bd., various coms. Boy Scouts Am., 1971—, coun. exec. bd. 1974—, nat. coun. rep., 1981-88; mem. exec. bd. Nat. Cath. Com. Scouting, commr. Diocese Lake Charles com., 1981-82, various other positions; mem. adv. com. Calcasieu Parish (La.) Family Svc. Agy., 1979-82; coord. SW La. Citizens for Ednl. Freedom, 1968-70; organizer Coun. Devel. French in La., pres. SW La. chpt. 1971-80, state bd. dirs., 1980-91; bd. dirs. La. Coun. Music and Performing Arts, 1967-79, Calcasieu Citizens for Decency, 1967-69, Lake Charles Symphony Orch., 1967-69. Sgt. U.S. Army, 1942-43. Decorated Knight Comdr. Order St. Gregory the Great (Pope John Paul II), 1982, Chevalier Nat. Order of Merit (France), Knight Comdr. with Star Order Holy Sepulchre (Pope John Paul), 1989, Knight Grand cross, 1992, Knight of Grace, Sovereign Mil. and Hospitaller Order of Malta, 1993, Knight of Grace, Mil. and Hospitaller Order of St. Lazarus, 1993, Knight of Merit, Sacred Mil. Constantinian Order of St. george, 1994, Companion with Star, Most Sacred Order Orthodox Hospitallers, 1994; recipient St. George Emblem Nat. Cath. Com. Scouting, 1975, Golden Ad Altare Dei emblem, 1992, Order of Golden Bow, 1995, Silver Beaver award Boy Scouts Am., 1976, Merit award Sociedad Esanñola de La., 1978, Silver Antelope award Boy Scouts Am., 1979, george Washington medal of Honor Freedom Found., 1980, Faith and Freedom award Religious Heritage Am., Inc., 1980, Pilgrim's Shell award Latin Patriarch Jerusalem, 1988, Nat. Silver Merit medal Knights Peter Claver, 1992, Past State Deputies award La. Knights Columbus, 1994; named to La. Sports Writers Hall of Fame, 1982, Columbian Hall of Fame, 1987. Mem. NCCJ (Brotherhood award 1975), La. Sports Writers Assn. (pres. 1952-54), La. Press Assn. (bd. dirs. 1976-79), La.-Miss. AP Assn. (pres. 1962-63, Merit citation 30 Yrs. Community Svc. 1980), AP Mng. Editors Assn., Am. Soc. Newspaper Editors, Serra Internat. (dist. gov. 1974-75, various coms. 1972—, adv. coun. 1986—, Serran of Yr. Lake Charles 1979, 86, Harry O'Haire award 1987, Paul Zimmerman award 1987), Lake Charles C. of C. (Man of Yr. 1971). Home: 1802 2nd Ave Lake Charles LA 70601-6432

STACK, BEATRIZ DE GREIFF, lawyer; b. Medellin, Antioquia, Colombia, Feb. 3, 1939; came to U.S., 1967; d. Luis and Carolina (González) de Greiff; m. Norman L. Stack Jr., Dec. 18, 1972; children: Carolina M., Ingrid C. BS, Sch. Sacred Heart, Medellin, 1956; LLD, U. Pontificia Bolivariana, Medellin, 1961; cert. of attendance, Inst. Internat. Studies, Geneva, Switzerland, 1965; M in Comparative Law, George Washington U., 1974. Bar: Medellin 1963, Pa. 1983, Va. 1992. Trademarks examiner U.S. Patent and Trademark Office, Arlington, Va., 1977-78; legal researcher Land and Natural Resources div. U.S. Dept. Justice, Washington, 1980-86; legal officer FAO, Rome, 1986-89; legal counsel Pan Am. Health Orgn. Staff Assn., Washington, 1989-92; pvt. practice Mc Lean, Va., 1992—; city judge Caldas, Antioquia, 1989-92; city atty. City of Medellin, 1963; head polit. sci. inst. Antioquia State U., Medellin, 1965; instr. in lang. Peace Corps Vols., Mex., 1968; asst. exec. sec. Interam. Commn. Women, OAS, Washington, 1970; stats. asst. Pan Am. Health Orgn., Washington; cons. Inst. Internat. Law and Econ. Devel., Washington, 1974; ct. interpreter U.S. Magistrate Ct. Alexandria, Va.; legal cons. Mozambique, 1992. Sec. Cath. Daus. Am., Arlington, 1965-66; pres. Colombian Cultural Forum, 1991-94. Mem. Alumna Spanish Sacred Heart (v.p. 1990). Democrat. Roman Catholic.

STACKS, DON WINSLOW, communications educator; b. Kalamazoo, Mich., Nov. 8, 1949; s. Frederick Winslow and Margaret Ada (Wheat) S.; m. Merry Robin Hickson, Aug. 11, 1974; children: Stacy Leigh, Kathleen Marie, Merry Margaret. BA, No. Mich. U., 1971; MA, Auburn U., 1975; PhD, U. Fla., 1978. Grad. asst. Auburn (Ala.) U., 1974-75, U. Fla., Gainesvill, 1975-78; asst. prof. U. South Ala., Mobile, 1978-82, assoc. prof., 1982-85; assoc. prof. U. Ala., Tuscaloosa, 1982-90; prof. U. Miami, 1990—; sr. mem. Market Analysis Rsch., Mobile, 1982—; assoc. dir. Ctr. for Advancement of Modern Media, 1994-95, dir. advt. and pub. rels. program, 1996—; communication cons., 1974—. Co-author: NVC: Nonverbal Communication, 1985, revised edit., 1989, 93, Essentials of Communication Research, 1992, Introduction to Communication Theory, 1991, Effective Communication for Academic Chairs, 1992, An Integrative Approach to Communication Theory and Research, 1996; editor World Comm. Jour., 1991-96; contbr. articles to profl. jours. Arbitrator Better Bus. Bur., 1973—. Served with U.S. Army, 1971-74. U. So. Ala. Research Council grantee, 1978-85, U. Ala. Research Com. grantee, 1985. Mem. Internat. Comm. Assn., Internat. Listening Assn., Ala. Speech Comm. and Theatre Assn. (pres. 1982-83, editor newsletter 1984—), Speech Comm. Assn., World Comm. Assn., So. Speech Comm. Assn. (div. chair 1978), PRSA, Assn. for Edn. in Journalism and Mass Comm. (div. chair 1997). Presbyterian. Home: 11112 SW 127th Pl Miami FL 33186 Office: U Miami PO Box 248127 Miami FL 33124-8127

STACY, MITCHELL PAUL, writer; b. Dayton, Ohio, Dec. 23, 1960; s. James Edward Stacy and Bonnie Lee (Neff) Katschanow; m. Holly Ring, Aug. 8, 1987. BS in Journalism, Ohio U., 1984. Staff writer The Daily Jeffersonian, Cambridge, Ohio, 1984-86, The Jour., Lorain, Ohio, 1986-87, The Gainesville (Fla.)Sun, 1987-92, The Sarasota (Fla.) Herald Tribune, 1992-93; staff writer features The Gainesville (Fla.) Sun, 1993-95, local columnist, 1995-96, asst. metro editor, 1996—. local news columnist The Gainesville Sun, 1995-96, asst. metro editor, 1996—. Vol. baseball coach Little League, Gainesville (Fla.) Pks. and Recreation, 1989-91. Recipient First Place for feature writing UPI Ohio Newspaper Awards, 1985, First Place for enterprise reporting AP Ohio Newspapers Awards, 1987, N.Y. Times Chmns. award, 1988, 1991, 95, First Place for excellence in med. journalism Fla. Med. Assn., 1988, Second Place for pub. svc. Fla. Soc. Newspaper Editors, 1990, First Place for news reporting, 1990, Second Place awards for depth reporting and spot-news reporting, 1991, First Place for columns, 1995, 1st Place Commentary award Am. Assn. Sunday and Feature Editors, 1994. Mem. Fla. Press Club. Home: 6711 NW 30th Terr Gainesville FL 32653 Office: The Gainesville Sun PO Box 147147 Gainesville FL 32614-7147

STADDON, JOHN ERIC RAYNER, psychology, zoology, neurobiology educator; b. Grayshott, Hampshire, Eng.; came to U.S., 1960; s. Leonard John and Dulce Norine (Rayner) S.; m. Lucinda Paris. BSc, Univ. Coll., London, 1960; PhD, Harvard U., 1964. Asst. prof. psychology U. Toronto, Ont., Can., 1964-67; from asst. prof. to prof. Duke U., Durham, N.C., 1967-72, prof., 1972-83, J.B. Duke prof. psychology, prof. neurobiology and zoology, 1983—. Author: Adaptive Behavior and Learning, 1983, Behaviorism, 1993; editor: Behavioral Processes, 1979; cons. editor Behavior and Philosophy, 1993; assoc. editor Jour. Exptl. Analysis of behavior, 1979-82. Recipient von Humboldt prize, 1985. Fellow AAAS, N.Y. Acad. Scis., Soc. Exptl. Psychologists; mem. Phi Beta Kappa (hon.), Sigma Xi. Office: Duke U Dept Exptl Psychology PO Box 90086 Durham NC 27708-0086

STADLER, DONALD ARTHUR, management engineer; b. Youngstown, Ohio, Dec. 14, 1943; s. Donald Arthur and Phyllis Helena (Lee) S.; m. Patricia McDonald, July 15, 1978; children: Jennifer, Jason. AB, Marquette U., 1966. Mgmt. analyst State of Vt., Montpelier, 1970-72; adminstr. Vt. State Dept. Health, Burlington, 1972-73; v.p. Planned Performance Co. Inc., Turnersville, N.J., 1973-79; pres. Performance Mgmt. Systems Inc., Roanoke, Va., 1979-82; chief analyst Leonhardt-Sullivan & Assocs. Inc., Tequesta, Fla., 1982-86; pres. D.A. Stadler Assocs., Inc., Roanoke, 1986—; mktg. cons. Planned Performance Co. Inc., Turnersville, 1984-86. Served as sgt. U.S. Army, 1966-69. Mem. Mensa, Intertel. Roman Catholic. Club: Roanoke Rifle and Revolver. Home and Office: D A Stadler Assocs Inc 3918 St James Cir Roanoke VA 24018-2428

STAEGER, EARL, nurse; b. St. Louis, Apr. 17, 1947; s. Earl and Virginia (Tilton) S.; m. Carla Campbell; children: Brian, Kevin, Eric, Bruce. BA, S.W. Tex. State U., 1970. RN, Tex.; CCRN; cert. ACLS, advanced trauma life support. Staff nurse CCU Columbia East Hosp., El Paso, Tex. Mem. AACN. Home: 9112 Lait Dr El Paso TX 79925-5948

STAFFEL, PETER L., copy editor, writer, English educator; b. Washington, Feb. 2, 1949; s. Herman E. and Margaret Kathryn (Matsen) S.; m. Mary Elizabeth Halford, Dec. 18, 1980; children: Huw Magnus Matsen, Johanna Mary Kathryn. BA in English, U. N.C., 1971; MA in English, U. Idaho, 1977; BA in Classics, Edinburgh (Scotland) U., 1981; PhD in English, Tulane U., 1989. Instr. English U. Idaho, Moscow, 1982; instr. mgmt. comm. Freeman Sch. Bus., Tulane U., New Orleans, 1986-88; instr. English Tulane U., New Orleans, 1988-90; asst. prof. English Wheeling (W.Va.) Jesuit Coll., 1990-96; freelance copyeditor Wheeling, 1996—. Mem. vestry St. Matthew's Episcopal Ch., Wheeling, 1996—. Lt. (j.g.) USN, 1971-73. Mem. MLA, Am. Soc. for 18th Century Studies, East-Central Am. Soc. for 18th Century Studies. Home and Office: 1313 Valley View Wheeling WV 26003

STAFFELBACH, ANDRE, interior designer; b. Chur, Switzerland, July 24, 1939; came to U.S., 1962; s. Jacob and Anna (Della-Bella) S.; children from previous marriage: Anna Lisa, Deon Andre. Apprentice in Interior Design, Chur, 1955-59; Profl. Degree in Interior Architecture, Kunstgewerbeschule, Zurich, Switzerland, 1960-61. Interior architect Sporri Interiors, Zurich, 1960-62; interior designer E.R. Cole, N.Y.C., 1962-63, Town House Interiors, Chgo., 1963-65, Weston's, Dallas, 1965-66; pres. Staffelbach Designs, Dallas, 1966—; cons. Nat. Endowment Arts, Washington, 1976. Served with Swiss Army, 1959-62. Recipient Giants 100 award Interior Design Mag., 1983—; named to Interior Design Mag. Hall of Fame, 1988; fellow Internat. Interior Design Assn., Chgo., 1977. Mem. Internat. Interior Design Assn. (nat. pres. 1975-77, Disting. Merit award 1987), Nat. Coun. Interior Design Qualification (coun. 1981-83, nat. pres. 1984), Am. Soc. Interior Designers (Designer of Distinction 1995). Republican. Avocations: cycling, snow skiing. Author: Commercial Interiors International, 1986; contbr. articles to Interior Design Mag., Interiors Mag., Contract Mag., 1986. Home: 4300 Mcfarlin Blvd Dallas TX 75205-1629 Office: 2525 Carlisle St Dallas TX 75201-1301

STAFFORD, DAN R., small business consultant, marketing analyst; b. Hickory, N.C., June 22, 1953; s. Ray Winford and Rebecca Cecil (Chapman) S.; m. Becky Jo Clark, July 24, 1976; children: Jonathan Daniel, Joshua Seth. BA in Sociology, Appalachian State U., 1975; MBA, Western Carolina U., 1982. Small bus. cons., 1982—. Mem. Am. Mktg. Assn. Democrat. Mem. So. Baptist Ch. Home: 3535 Rolls Ave Fayetteville NC 28311-2423 Office: Cape Fear Bus Cons 114 1/2 Anderson St Fayetteville NC 28301

STAFFORD, JAMES POLK, JR., civil engineer; b. Oxford, Miss., Oct. 13, 1918; s. James Polk and Lottie Etoile (Smith) S.; B.S., Miss. State Coll., 1939; M.S., Iowa State Coll., 1940; m. Edna Earle Snyder, May 29, 1941; children—Jeanette Patricia, Pamela Anne, James Polk III. Registered profl. engr., Miss. Engr., Soil Conservation Service, U.S. Dept. Agr., 1940, 46; officer, U.S. Army Corps Engrs., 1941-45, civil engr. office engring. br., constrn. div. U.S. Army Engr. Dist., Vicksburg, Miss., 1947-62, resident engr. DeGray Dam, Dike and Powerhouse, 1963-72, chief constrn. div., U.S. Army Engr. dist., Vicksburg, 1973-86; ret., 1986. Pres. Vicksburg Community Chorus, 1975-76. Served with USAR, 1946-73. Recipient George Marshall Scholastic award Command and Gen. Staff Coll., 1963; Meritorious Service medal U.S. Army Reserve, 1973. Mem. Soc. Am. Mil. Engrs. (Goethals award 1974), ASCE, U.S. Com. on Large Dams. Methodist. Club: Lions. Home: 326 Mcauley Dr Vicksburg MS 39180-2842

STAFFORD, KENNETH VICTOR, SR., minister; b. Claremont, N.H., Dec. 30, 1926; s. Victor Ernest and Marion (Dodge) S.; m. Doreen Beverly Mossey, Apr. 12, 1947; children: Beverlee, Kenneth Jr., Marilee, Mark. Diploma in airframe/powerplant, Spartan Sch. Aeronautics, Tulsa, 1948, diploma in airport mgmt., 1949; B in Counseling, Valley Christian U., Fresno, Calif., 1981; M in Counseling, Valley Christian U., 1983. Ordained to ministry Christian Ch., 1978; cert. counselor, 1990. Pres. Jacob's Well, Tulsa, 1974-78; dir. spiritual life Christian Broadcasting Network, Virginia Beach, Va., 1978, assoc. dir. counseling, 1978-83, dir. counseling, 1984, counselor tng. dir., 1985-87; founder, pres. Bearers of Light Ministries, Chesapeake, Va., 1987—; elder New Life Christian Fellowship, Chesapeake, 1990—. Author: Basic 8, 1982, Handbook for Helping Others, 1986, The Biblical Family, 1990. Staff sgt. U.S. Army, 1945-46, PTO; staff sgt. USAF, 1950-51. Recipient First Line Mgmt. award Am. Mgmt. Assn., 1981, Supervising People award Batten, 1984. Office: Bearers of Light Ministries PO Box 2672 Chesapeake VA 23327-2672

STAFFORD, PATRICK MORGAN, biophysicist; b. Roanoke, Va., June 3, 1950; s. Jess Woodrum and Georgine Elna (Morgan) S.; m. Kristina Lee Troyer, July 10, 1976; children: Kathryn Lee, Jess Walter. BS in Physics, Va. Poly. Inst., 1972; M Med. Sci. in Medical Physics, Emory U., 1979; PhD in Biophysics, U. Tex., Houston, 1987. Diplomate Am. Bd. Radiology. Assoc. engr. Duke Power Co., Charlotte, N.C., 1973-78; rsch. scientist U. N.Mex., Los Alamos, 1979-81; asst. physicist U. Tex., Houston, 1981-87; asst. prof. U. Pa., Phila., 1987-91; v.p. Radiation Care, Inc., Atlanta, 1991-95, Oncology Therapies, Inc., 1995—; adj. prof. Ga. Inst. Tech., 1993—; lectr. in field. Author: Dynamic Treatment with Pions at Lampf, 1980, Critical Angle Dependance of CR-39, 1986, Real-Time Portal Imaging; jour. reviewer Medical Physics, Internat. Jour. Radiation Oncology, Biology and Physics. Active Atlanta Emory Symphony, 1978; deacon Crabapple Bapt. Ch., Alpharetta, Ga., 1992. Rosalie B. Hite fellow U. Tex., 1983. Mem. Am. Assn. Physicists in Medicine (radiation therapy com. 1989-92, liaison from ASTRO 1995—, continuing edn. com. 1995—), Am. Coll. Med. Physics (commn. on comm. 1991-94), Am. Coll. Radiology, Am. Soc. for Therapeutic Radiology and Oncology. Home: 430 Kensington Farms Dr Alpharetta GA 30201-3740 Office: Oncology Therapies Inc 1155 Hammond Dr NE Ste A Atlanta GA 30328-5332

STAFFORD, SARAH JANE, English language educator; b. Danville, Ky., July 1, 1967; d. Kenneth Myrl and Effie Aloese (Hatter) S. BS, Campbellsville Coll., 1989; MA, Ea. Ky. U., 1990; ABD, U. Ky., 1995. Grad. asst. in English tchg. Ea. Ky. U., Richmond, 1989-90; instr. English Campbellsville (Ky.) Coll., 1991, 93-95, asst. prof. English, 1995—; sec. faculty-staff recognition com. Campbellsville (Ky.) Coll., 1994-96, sec. profl. devel. com., 1995-96; sec. faculty Campbellsville (Ky.) U., 1996—; presenter in field. Pianist Mt. Olive Christian Church. Mem. MLA, Ky. Coun. Tchrs. English. Home: Rt 1 Box 115 Yosemite KY 42566 Office: Campbellsville Univ 200 W College St Campbellsville KY 42718

STAFFORD, THOMAS PATTEN, retired military officer, former astronaut; b. Weatherford, Okla., Sept. 17, 1930; m. Linda A. Dishman; children: Dionne, Karin. BS, U.S. Naval Acad., 1952; student, USAF Exptl. Flight Test Sch., 1958-59; DSc (hon.), Oklahoma City U., 1967; LLD (hon.), Western State U. Coll. Law, 1969, U. Cordoba, Argentina; D Communications (hon.), Emerson Coll., 1969; D Aero. Engring. (hon.), Embry-Riddle Aero. Inst., 1970; LHD (hon.), U. Okla., 1994; M of Humane Letters (hon.), Southwestern U., 1994; HHD (hon.), Oklahoma Christian U. Commd. 2d lt. USAF, 1952; advanced through grades to lt. gen.; chief performance br. Aerospace Research Pilot Sch., Edwards AFB, Calif.; with NASA, Houston, 1962-75; assigned Project Gemini, pilot Gemini VI, 1965, command pilot Gemini IX, 1966, comdr. Apollo X, 1969, chief astronaut office, 1969-71; dep. dir. flight crew operations, comdr. Apollo-Soyuz flight, 1975; comdr. Air Force Flight Test Ctr., Edwards AFB, 1975; lt. gen., dep. chief staff Research, Devel. and Aquisition, 1979; ret., 1979; chair The White House/NASA Com. to Independently Advise NASA How to Return to Moon and Explore Mars, 1990-91; chmn. bd. Omega Watch Co. Am.; dir. start F-117A Stealth Fighter, B-2 Stealth Bomber program, 1978; co-founder tech. cons. firm, Stafford, Burke, Hecker, Inc., Alexandria, Va.; adv. numerous govtl. agys. including NASA, Air Force Systems Command; defense advisor to Ronald Reagan during presdl. campaign; bd. dirs. numerous cos. Co-author: Pilot's Handbook for Performance Flight Testing, Aerodynamics Handbook for Performance Flight Testing. Decorated DFC with oak leaf cluster, D.S.M. (3), Disting. Flying Cross (2); recipient NASA Disting. Svc. medal (2), NASA Exceptional Svc. medal (2), Air Force Command Pilot Astronaut Wings; Chanute Flight award AIAA, 1976, VFW Nat. Space award, 1976; Gen. Thomas D. White USAF Space trophy Nat. Geog. Soc., 1976; Gold Space medal Fedn. Aeronautique Internationale, 1976, Laurel Award, Space/Missiles, Aviation Week & Space Tech., 1991, Congl. Space medal honor V.P. Dan Quayle, 1993, Rotary Nat. award Space Achievement, 1993, Goddard award Astronaut Hall of Fame, 1993, Pub. Svc. award NASA, 1994; co-recipient AIAA, 1966, Harmon Internat. Aviation trophy, 1966, Spl. Trustees award NATAS, 1969. Fellow Am. Astronautical Soc., Soc. Exptl. Test Pilots; mem. AIAA, AFTRA (hon. life). Address: 1006 Cameron St Alexandria VA 22314-2427

STAFFORD, WILL ELBERT, financial company executive; b. Milan, Tenn., Jan. 23, 1935; s. Ether and Eva (Welch) S.; m. Karen Roberts, Aug. 7, 1960; children: Suzanne Welch, William Scott. BS, Memphis State U., 1957, MA, 1958. Tchr. Shelby County Schs., Whitehaven, Tenn., 1957-59, Tucson Pub. Schs., 1959-6l, Broward County Schs., Ft. Lauderdale, Fla., 1961-62; sr. group rep. Conn. Gen. Life Ins. Co., Memphis, 1962-65; regional mgr. Prin. Fin. Group (formerly Bankers Life Co. Des Moines), Memphis, 1965—; chmn. mktg. coun. Prin. Fin. Group, Des Moines, 1990—. Chmn. ann. fund Memphis State U., 1981-82; mem. Greater Memphis State, Inc., 1955—, The Univ. Memphis Soc., Inc. Named Friend of Univ., Memphis State U., 1987. Mem. Nat. Assn. Life Underwriters, Tenn. Life Unf=derwriters Assn., Memphis Life Underwriters Assn., Greater Memphis Employee Benefits Coun. (bd. dirs. 1986-88), Mid-South Organic Network, SCV, Memphis State U. Alumni Assn. (pres. 1987), Memphis Slow Pitch Assn. (pres. 1971), Tenn. Pres. Trust, Am. Legion, Assn. Health Ins. Agts. (charter), The Columns Soc., Phi Delta Kappa, Omicron Delta Kappa, Kappa Alpha. Republican. Presbyterian. Home: 3267 Prince George St Memphis TN 38115-3017 Office: Prin Fin Group 5l00 Poplar Ave Ste 2400 Memphis TN 38105-4510

STAFFORD, WILLIAM HENRY, JR., federal judge; b. Masury, Ohio, May 11, 1931; s. William Henry and Frieda Gertrude (Nau) S.; m. Nancy Marie Helman, July 11, 1959; children: William Henry, Donald Helman, David Harrold. B.S., Temple U., 1953, LL.B., 1956; J.D., 1968. Bar: Fla. 1961, U.S. Ct. Appeals (5th cir.) 1969, U.S. Supreme Ct. 1970. Assoc. firm Robinson & Roark, Pensacola, 1961-64; individual practice law Pensacola, 1964-67, state atty., 1967-69, U.S. atty., 1969-75; U.S. dist. judge U.S. Dist. Ct. for No. Dist. Fla., Tallahassee, 1975—, U.S. dist. judge, chief judge, 1981-93, sr. judge, 1996—; instr. Pensacola Jr. Coll., 1964, 68; mem. judicial council U.S. Ct. Appeals (11th cir.), 1986-89; apptd. com. on intercircuit assignments, 1987-92, subcom. on fed. jurisdiction, 1983-87. Lt. (j.g.) USN, 1957-60. Mem. Fla. Bar (mem. numerous coms., bench/bar commn. 1991-92, bench/bar implementation commn. 1993), Dist. Judges Assn. 11th Cir. (pres. 1984-85), State Fed. Judicial Council Fla., Am. Inns of Ct., Tallahassee Bar Assn., Tallahassee Inn (pres. 1989-91), Masons, Shriners, Rotary, Sigma Phi Epsilon, Phi Delta Phi. Republican. Episcopalian. Office: US Dist Ct 110 E Park Ave Tallahassee FL 32301-7750

STAGG, CLYDE LAWRENCE, lawyer; b. St. Petersburg, Fla., May 22, 1935; s. Milton Gurr and Clyda Montese (Lawrence) S.; m. Betsy Barron, Aug. 22, 1959; children: Sharon, Brian, Lauren, Stephen. BSJ, U. Fla., 1956, LLB, 1959. Bar: Fla. 1959, U.S. Dist. Ct. (mid. dist.) Fla. 1959, U.S. Ct. Appeals (5th cir.) 1969, U.S. Supreme Ct. 1971, U.S. Ct. Appeals (11th cir.) 1987. Assoc. Shackleford, Farrior, Tampa, Fla., 1959-60; asst. solicitor Hillsborough County Solicitor's Office, Tampa, 1960-61; chief asst. state's atty. State's Atty.'s Office State Atty.'s Office, Tampa, 1963-64, asst. state's atty. State's Atty.'s Office, 1961-63; ptnr. Whitaker, Mann & Stagg, Tampa, Knight, Jones & Whitaker, Tampa, 1965-67, Holland & Knight, Tampa, 1968-74, 80-86, Stichter, Stagg, Hoyt, et al, Tampa, 1974-79, Stagg, Hardy, Ferguson, Murnaghan & Mathews P.A., Tampa, 1986-93, Akerman, Senterfitt & Eidson P.A., Tampa, 1993—; bd. dirs. Fla. Lawyers Mut. Inst. Co. Mem., sec. Hillsborough Area Regional Transit Authority, Tampa, 1979-85; mem., sec., vice chmn., chmn. Tampa Sports Authority, 1985-89; bd. dirs. United Way Greater Tampa, Inc., 1988-91; bd. dirs. S.W. Fla. Blood Bank, Tampa, 1989—, chmn., 1994-95; spl. counsel to U.S. Senator Bob Graham, 1988. Mem. ABA, Am. Bar Found., Fla. Bar, Hillsborough County Bar Assn. (pres. 1970-71), Fla. Bar Found., Am. Bd. Trial Advocates, Greater Tampa C. of C. (bd. dirs. 1988-91), Am. Inn Ct. (master emeritus of bench). Home: 3303 W San Nicholas St Tampa FL 33629-7034 Office: Akerman Senterfitt & Eidson PA PO Box 3273 Tampa FL 33601-3273

STAGG, EVELYN WHEELER, educator, state legislator; b. Waterbury, Vt., Sept. 30, 1916; d. Aiton Grover and Edythe (Boyce) Wheeler; m. David Stagg, May 15, 1942; children: Christie Stagg Austin, Bonnie, Carol Stagg Kevan. BA, Middlebury Coll., 1939; MA, U. Vt., 1971. Assoc. prof. Castleton State Coll., Vt., 1966-82; mem. Vt. Ho. of Reps., 1982-90, chmn. house edn. com., 1982-90, vice chmn. health and welfare com., 1985-86, mem. ways and means com., 1989-90; Commn. of the States, 1987-88; cons. communications projects, Bomoseen, Vt., 1982—. Contbr. articles to profl. jours. Chmn. Women's Legis. Caucus, 1984-88; pres., bd. dirs. Rutland Area Vis. Nurse Assn., 1969-75, 89-92; bd. dirs. Rutland Mental Health Assn., 1986-88; adv. bd. nursing Castleton State Coll.; vol. LUVS for abused children, 1992—; trustee pub. funds, 1990-95, Castle Libr., 1992-95; bd. civil authority, 1984-93; justice of peace Town of Castleton, 1984-93; mem. customer adv. coun. U.S. Postal Svc., Naples. Mem. Women's Caucus, Vt. Women's Polit. Caucus of Collier County, Nat. Women's Polit. Caucus, Inst. for Gen. Semantics, Internat. Soc. for Gen. Semantics, Am. Philatelic Soc., Democratic Women's Club of Collier County, Castleton Hist. Soc. Clubs: Women's, Rutland County Stamp. Avocations: stamp and coin collecting, sailing, skiing, traveling. Home: 222 Harbour Dr Naples FL 34103-4071 Office: Evelyn Stagg Literary Agy Naples FL 34103

STAGG, LOUIS CHARLES, English language and literature educator; b. New Orleans, Jan. 3, 1933; s. Louis Anatol and Gladys (Andrews) S.; BA in English, La. Coll., 1955; MA in English U. Ark., 1957, PhD in English, 1963; m. Mary Casner, June 5, 1959; children: Robert Charles, Helen Marie. Teaching asst. English U. Ark., 1955-59; asst. prof. William Jewell Coll., 1959-60; instr. Stephen F. Austin State U., 1960-62; asst. prof. Memphis State U. (name changed to U. Memphis), 1962-69, assoc. prof., 1969-77, prof. English language and literature 1977—, dir. grad. studies in English, 1985-88, dir. English Drama Players, 1968—, dir undergrad. advising for English, 1970-80, 88-91, chair policies and procedures com. for English, 1983-95, tenure and promotion com. for English, 1978-80, 82-86, 89—; chmn. acad. policies com. Memphis State U. Senate, 1981-82, 88-90, 93-94, 95-96, mem. exec. com. senate, 1987-91, 93-96, parliamentarian of senate, 1987-88, 90-91, 94-95, humanities rep. budget adv. com. dean coll. arts and scis., 1992-93, mem. steering com., chair of schedules, originator Alliance Creative Theatre, Edn. and Rsch. series, 1989, 90, 92, 94, 96; cons. NEH, 1975, 76, 78, Ohio State U. Press, summer 1985, 86, U. Jordan, Aman, 1985; chair policies and procedures subdivsn. Eng. Dept. so. assn. colls., schs. self study, mem. steering com., 1992-93; cons. Memphis State U. Learning Media-Ctrs. catalogue Shakespeare holdings, 1992-93, rev., 1993-94, 94-95. Mem. Memphis Oratorio Soc. Chorus, 1969-92, diction coach, 1987, Memphis Symphony Chorus, 1993—, Memphis in May Tattoo Chorus, 1993, Memphis in May Sunset Symphony Choir, 1996, Martin Luther King Tribute Concert Choir, 1995, 96. Recipient summer stipend NEH, 1967; Memphis State U. grantee, 1965; travel grantee to U.S. Library of Congress, summer 1971. Mem. MLA, So. Humanities Coun. (sec.-treas. 1974-76, exec. com. 1976-83, 94-96, chmn. coun. 1993-94, chmn. sect. humanities in pluralistic society 1984, ad hoc com. on crisis in teaching humanities 1977, chmn. local arrangements for convs. 1975, 94, chmn. sect. on Thomas Hardy, 1996), Tenn. Philol. Assn. (pres. 1976-77, exec. com. 1977, local arrangements chmn. 1965, 69, 75, 87, chmn. Shakespeare sect. 1996), Marlowe Soc. Am. (book reviewer 1984, 86, 87, 88, 93), Am. Soc. for Theatre Rsch., Samuel Beckett Soc., Conf. on Christianity and Lit., South Cen. Conf. on Christianity and Lit. Soc. for Study of Works of Harold Pinter (asst. constitution revision 1988, asst. with planning 1992, treas. 1994—, mem. exec. com. 1994—), Ark. Philol. Assn., Shakespeare Assn. Am. (local arrangements host com. 1985), Stratford-Upon-Avon Shakespeare Festival, Eng.; Eugene O'Neill Soc., Alliance for Creative Theatre, Edn. and Rsch. (chmn. schedules com., rep. for English, mem. steering com., originator of proposal 1986, 89, 90, 92, 94, 96), Internat. Shakespeare Assn., Am. Soc. Theatre Rsch., Internat. Soc. Theatre Rsch., Medieval and Renaissance Drama Soc., Renaissance Soc. Am., South Cen. Renaissance Conf. (chmn. nominations 1976, exec. com. 1978-80, program com. 1981-83, chmn. sect. Shakespeare 1981, 85, 95, 16th Century lit. 1982, chmn. local arrangements 1983, symposium on humanism 1984, chmn. Shakespeare on film and the teaching of Brit. Drama 1986, chmn. music in Shakespeare's plays 1987, chmn. sect. Thematic Approaches to Tudor/Stuart Drama 1988, chmn. sect. Medieval influences on Renaissance drama 1993, chmn. Shakespeare's Villains: Stage and Page 1995, Adaptations of Renaissance Drama, 1996, chmn. local arrangements for convention 1990, chmn. spl. session 1989, 95), South Cen. MLA (assoc. editor for English, South Cen. Bull. 1982-84, nominations com. 1985-86, 95-96, book reviewer South Cen. Rev. 1983, 85, 86, sec. English I.B. Renaissance, 1986, chair, 1987, sec. spl. sect. Renaissance Drama, 1988, chair Shakespeare's Tragi-comedies and tragi-comic romances, 1989, co-chair local arrangements 1980, 92, chair panel on renaissance drama criticism 1995), South Atlantic MLA, South Cen. Coll. English Assn. (sec.-treas. 1980-81, v.p. 1981-82, pres. 1982-83, exec. com. 1983-90, co-host 1982, com. constitution revision 1989), Coll. English Assn., Internat. Patristic Medieval and Renaissance Conf. (sect. chmn. Medieval drama 1977, chair Shakespeare session 1994, chair Renaissance drama section 1995, chmn. 17th century Brit. lit. sect. 1996), Am. Theatre Assn. (chmn. sect. combining Brit. lit. and theatre in teaching of drama 1983, chmn. Shakespeare sect. 1994), The Stratford Can. Shakespeare Festival, AAUP (sec. treas. Memphis State U. chap. 1982-86, v.p. 1986-88, pres. 1988-90), Phi Beta Kappa (pres. Memphis alumni assn. 1985-88, mem. spl. panel The Soc. and the New Scholarship at 37th triennial coun. 1994), Alpha Chi. Democrat. Episcopalian (lay reader 1969-86). Author: (with J. Lasley Dameron) Poe's Critical Vocabulary, 1966; author series: Index To The Figurative Language of John Webster's Tragedies, 1967, of Ben Jonson's Tragedies, 1967, of Thomas Heywood's Tragedies, 1967, of George Chapman's Tragedies, 1970, of John Marston's Tragedies, 1970, of Thomas Middleton's Tragedies, 1970, of Cyril Tourneur's Tragedies, 2d edit. all 7 under title Index to the Figurative Language of the Tragedies of Shakespeare's Chief 17th Century Contemporaries 1977), 3d edit., 1982; Index to the Figurative Language of the Tragedies of Shakespeare's Chief 16th Century Contemporaries, 1984; contbr. to Great Writers of the English Language: Dramatists, 1979, 87; circulation editor Interpretations, 1976-80; contbr. articles on English and American drama to profl. jours., publs. on Shakespeare, other lit. publs. Home: 5219 Mason Rd Memphis TN 38117-2104 Office: U Memphis Dept English Memphis TN 38152

STAGG, TOM, federal judge; b. Shreveport, La., Jan. 19, 1923; s. Thomas Eaton and Beulah (Meyer) S.; m. Margaret Mary O'Brien, Aug. 21, 1946; children: Julie, Margaret Mary. B.A., La. State U., 1943, J.D., 1949. Bar: La. 1949. With firm Hargrove, Guyton, Van Hook & Hargrove, Shreveport, 1949-53; pvt. practice law Shreveport, 1953-58; sr. ptnr. firm Stagg, Cady & Beard, Shreveport, 1958-74; judge U.S. Dist. Ct. (we. dist.) La., 1974-84, 91-92, chief judge, 1984-90, sr. judge, 1992—; Pres. Abe Meyer Corp., 1960-74, Stagg Investments, Inc., 1964-74; mng. partner Pierremont Mall Shopping Center, 1963-74; v.p. King Hardware Co., 1955-74; Mem. Shreveport Airport Authority, 1967-73, chmn., 1970-73; chmn. Gov.'s Tidelands Adv. Council, 1969-70; del. La. Constl. Conv., 1973-74; chmn. rules com., com. on exec. dept.; mem. Gov.'s Adv. Com on Offshore Revenues, 1972-74. Active Republican party, 1950-74, del. convs., 1956, 60, 64, 68, 72; mem. Nat. Com. for La., 1964-72, mem. exec. com., 1964-68; Pres. Shreveport Jr. C. of C., 1955-56; v.p. La. Jr. C. of C., 1956-57. Served to capt., inf. AUS, 1943-46, ETO. Decorated Bronze Star, Purple Heart with oak leaf cluster. Mem. Am., La., Shreveport bar assns., Photog. Soc. Am. Office: US Dist Ct 300 Fannin St Ste 4100 Shreveport LA 71101-3121

STAGGS, MICHELLE DENISE, flight nurse; b. Ft. Smith, Ark., Mar. 13, 1963; d. Jesse Boyd and Carolyn June (Hays) Staggs. BA in Biology, Hendrix Coll., 1985; BS in Nursing, U. Ark., 1987. RN, Ark.; CEN, CCRN; cert. trauma nurse course instr., trauma nurse specialist/instr; cert., nat. registered EMT instr. Staff nurse emergency dept. U. Hosp., Little Rock, 1987-89; flight nurse, orientation continuing edn. coord. Med. Flight Med-Flight, Bapt. Med. Ctr., Little Rock, 1989—; clin. faculty U. Ark. for Med. Scis., Coll. of Health Related Professions, Little Rock, 1989-90. Mem. AACN, Nat. Flight Nurses Assn., Emergency Nurses Assn. (chpt. sec., treas. 1989, pres.-elect 1990, pres. 1991, del. nat. assembly). Home: 16 Michael Dr Little Rock AR 72204-2334 Office: Bapt Med Ctr 9601 Interstate 630 Exit 7 Little Rock AR 72205-7202

STAGNER, SHIRLEY, oncological nurse practitioner; b. Lebanon, Tenn., July 26, 1946; d. Clark and Edith Faye (Grizzell) Bowling; 1 child, Sema. BSN, U. Tenn., 1970, MSN, 1985. RN, Tenn., N.Y. Pediatric nurse practitioner St. Jude Children's Rsch. Hosp., Memphis; dir. quality of life svcs., dir. cmty. affairs Memphis Cancer Ctr.; oncology nurse practitioner Maimonides Med. Ctr., Bklyn. Exec. producer Voyage to Byzantium, 1991. Mem. Leadership Memphis. Recipient Telly award, 1992. Mem. ANA, Tenn. Nurses Assn., U. Tenn. Coll. Nursing Alumni Assn. (pres. 1977-78), U. Tenn. Nat. Alumni Assn. (bd. dirs. 1979-80), Internat. Soc. Nurses in Cancer Care, Oncology Nursing Soc., Assn. Pediatric Oncology Nurses (charter mem., pres. 1979-80), Assn. Care of Children in Hosps., Sigma Theta Tau, Upsilon Tau.

STAHL, CHARLES J., IV, city manager; b. Phila., June 28, 1957; s. Charles J. III and Ellen (Baran) S.; m. Janet Leigh Oaks, Oct. 16, 1962; children: Victoria Leigh, Joseph Charles. BA, Ursinus Coll., 1979; M City Mgmt., East Tenn. State U., 1983. Budget/productivity dir. City of Johnson City, Tenn., 1984-88; asst. city mgr., treas. City of Bluefield, W.Va., 1988-94; city mgr. City of Elizabethton, Tenn., 1994—; adj. faculty mem. dept. polit. sci. East Tenn. State U., 1984-88; mem. Elizabethton/Carter County Econ. Devel. Com., 1994—. Mem. Elizabethton/Carter County Tourism Coun., 1995—; dir. Carter County Emergency Comms. Dist., Elizabethton, 1995—; mem. Carter County Bd. Health, Elizabethton, 1995—. Named to 40 under Forty, Bus. Jour., Blountville, Tenn., 1994. Mem. Internat. City/County Mgmt. Assn., Tenn. City Mgrs. Assn., rotary. Office: City of Elizabethton 136 S Sycamore St Elizabethton TN 37643-3328

STAHL, DAVID, orchestra and opera conductor; b. N.Y.C., Nov. 4, 1949; s. Frank L. and Edith (Cosmann) S.; m. Karen Doss Shehan, Feb. 25, 1989; children: Sonya Leonore, Byron David, Anna June. B.Mus., Queens Coll., 1972, M.A., 1974; studied with, Leonard Bernstein and Seiji Ozawa, Tanglewood, 1975, Gunther Schuller, Joseph Rosenstock, Walter Susskind, Max Rudolf; LLD, Coll. of Charleston. Carnegie Hall debut with Youth Symphony Orch. of N.Y., 1973; music dir., Doctors' Orchestral Soc., N.Y.C., 1973-76, asst. condr., N.Y. Philharm., 1976, assoc. condr., Cin. Symphony Orch., 1976-79, music dir. St. Louis Philharm., 1976-81, Charleston (S.C.) Symphony Orch., 1984—; guest condr., prin. guest condr., Staatstheater am Gartnerplatz, Munich, 1996—, NDR Orch., Hamburg, Germany, Pitts., Atlanta, Buffalo, St. Louis, Nat., Am., N.J., Dallas, Edmonton, Louisville, Toronto Syphony, Balt., Winnipeg, Indpls. Symphony orchs., Cin. Opera, Teatro Comunale di Genoa, Spoleto Festival USA, Israel Festival, Concertgebouw, Amsterdam, Stadtheater Mannheim, Staatstheatre Darmstadt, Staatsphilharmonie Rheinlandpfalz, Festival of Two Worlds, Spoleto, Italy, N.Y.C. Opera, Wash. Opera, Lake George Opera Festival, Omaha Opera, Dayton Opera, Mich. Opera Theatre, Montreal Opera, Tulsa Opera, Hawaii Opera Theatre, Teatro Massimo di Palermo, Orchestre Colonne, Long Beach Opera, Leonard Bernstein Festival, Holland, RAI Orchestra Rome, Seoul (Dem. Republic Korea) Philharm., Orchestra del Sodre, Montevideo, Uruguay; music dir.: Broadway and internat. tour. West Side Story, Porgy and Bess, Israel Fest. Recipient Gov.'s award for Excellence in the Arts, S.C. Order of Palmetto Exxon/Arts Endowment Condr. award, 1976-79, S.C. Verner award 1996. Mem. Am. Symphony Orch. League.

STAHL, DAVID EDWARD, trade association administrator; b. Chgo., Apr. 10, 1934; s. Archie Edward and Dorothy (Berning) S.; m. Carolyn Downs Stahl, June 23, 1956; children: Stephen, Michael, Kurt, Thomas. BS, Miami U., 1956. Exec. v.p. Republic Realty Mortgage Corp., Chgo., 1963-66; dep. mayor City of Chgo., 1966-70, city comptroller, 1971-73; exec. v.p. Urban Land Inst., Washington, 1973-76, Nat. Assn. Home Builders, Washington, 1977-84; pres. Nat. Forest Products Assn., Washington, 1984-87; exec. v.p. Urban Land Inst., Washington, 1987-92; exec. dir. Young Pres.'s Orgn., Irving, Tex., 1992-95; ret., 1995; del. 6th Ill. Constl. Conv., Springfield, 1970. Served to lt. USAF, 1956-59. Mem. Am. Soc. Assn. Execs., Econ. Club (Chgo.), Wayfarers Club, Annapolis Yacht Club, Ocean Reef Club, Lambda Alpha. Roman Catholic. Home: 529 Rock Bluff Austin TX 78734

STAHL, GAEL BERNARD, editor; b. Plainville, Kans., Sept. 6, 1939; s. Bernard Carl and Grace Eva (Bissett) S.; m. Susan Lee McMahon, Oct. 28, 1948. BS in Philosophy, Quincy U., 1963, BS in Theology, 1967; MS, Tenn. State U., 1971. Cath. priest, assoc. pastor Corpus Christi Parish, Chgo., 1967-69; cath. priest, chaplain St. Vincent Cath. Ch., Nashville, 1969-73; admissions counselor Tenn. State U., Nashville, 1971-79; writer, assoc. editor Tenn. Mcpl. League, Nashville, 1983-95, editor Tenn. Town and City, 1995—. Author: Peckerwood Pilgrimage, 1979-80; contbr. articles to profl. jours. Mem. Sherlock Holmes Soc. (pres., editor newsletters 1982—). Roman Catholic. Home: 1763 Needmore Rd Old Hickory TN 37138 Office: Tenn Mcpl League 226 Capitol Blvd Ste 710 Nashville TN 37219-1803

STAHL, JOEL SOL, plastic and chemical engineer; b. Youngstown, Ohio, June 10, 1918; s. John Charles and Anna (Nadler) S.; B. in Chem. Engring., Ohio State U., 1939; postgrad. Alexander Hamilton Inst., 1946-48; m. Jane Elizabeth Anglin, June 23, 1950; 1 child, John Arthur. With Ashland (Ky.) Oil, Inc., 1939-50, mgr. spl. products, 1946-50; pres. Cool Ray Co., Youngstown, 1950-51, Stahl Industries, Inc., Youngstown, 1951—; CEO Stahl Cos., Orlando, Fla., 1992—. Pres.' cabinet bd. dirs. Ohio State U. Found.; chair dean's exec. adv. bd. Coll. Engring. U. Cen. Fla.; gov.'s coun. for High Tech. and Industry for State Fla. Named Ky. col., 1967. Mem. Regional Export Expansion Council, Soc. Plastics Engr., Soc. Plastics Industry, The Plastics Acad., Internat. Platform Assn., Ohio Soc. N.Y., Citrus Club, Masons, Shriners, Rotary, Toastmasters (pres. 1949), S.C. Yacht Club, Circumnavigators. N.Y. Acad. Sci., Sweetwater Country Club, Varsity O Club, Tau Kappa Epsilon, Phi Eta Sigma, Phi Lambda Upsilon. Republican. Chrisitan Scientist. Patentee insulated core walls, plastic plumbing wall, housing in continous process, encasement asbestos, lead, plutonium and nuclear toxic waste storage depot. Contbr. articles to profl. jours. Home: 530 E Central Blvd Apt 1504 Orlando FL 32801-4306 Office: 20 Federal Plz W Ste 600 Youngstown OH 44503-1423

STAHL, MICHAEL LEN, professional speaker, actor, educator; b. Johnstown, Pa., Aug. 27, 1969; s. Leonard Earl and Dorrie May (Leukenga) S. BSBA in Mktg., Okla. State U., 1991. Sales rep. C.R. Anthony Co., Oklahoma City, 1985-87; advt. sales, mktg. rep. Varisty Ad Sales, Oklahoma City, 1987; prodn. asst. Mickey Mouse Club Disney Channel, Orlando, Fla., 1990; intern Walt Disney Co., Orlando, 1989, 91-92; actor Universal Studios, Orlando, 1992-95; dir. acting edn. Barbizon Modeling and Acting Sch., Orlando, 1996—; pres. Motivational Concepts, Orlando; cons. I.E.S./FABCOM, 1988, 91; ind. cons., 1988—; speaker in field. Author: A Reality of Grandeur, 1992; exec. editor Bus. Solutions Mag. Cameraman live broadcast First Bapt. Ch. Orlando. Horatio Alger scholar. Mem. Nat. Spkrs. Assn., Ctrl. Fla. Conv. Svc. Assn. (v.p.).

STAHL, O(SCAR) GLENN, writer, lecturer, former government official; b. Evansville, Ind., Apr. 30, 1910; s. Oscar and Mayme (Wittmer) S.; m. Marie Jane Rueter, June 26, 1934; children: Elaine Marie, Alan G. A.B., U. Evansville, 1931, LL.D., 1984; M.A., U. Wis., 1933; Ph.D., N.Y. U., 1936. Instr. govt. NYU, 1933-35; personnel officer TVA, 1935-41; with Fed. Security Agy. (later HEW), 1941-51; dir. personnel, 1948-51; with U.S. CSC (now OPM), 1951-69, dir. bur. policies and standards, 1955-69; adj. prof. public adminstrn. Am. U., 1949-69; part time prof. U. Tenn., 1939, Dept. Agr. Grad. Sch., 1941-49; vis. lectr. various univs., U.S. and abroad; lectr. Salzburg Seminar in Am. Studies, 1965; tech. assistance adviser to Venezuela UN, 1958-59, 72; U.S. rep. UN Conf., Ethiopia, 1964; Ford Found. cons. to, India, 1968-69, 71, Nepal, 1969, Pakistan, 1974; AID adviser, Pakistan, 1969, 71; U.S. rapporteur Internat. Congress Adminstrv. Scis., Dublin, 1968; U.S. rep. UN Seminar, Tashkent, Uzbekistan, 1969; spl. advisor to W. Ger., 1971; spl. cons. Public Adminstrn. Service-Govtl. Affairs Inst. and Internat. Personnel Mgmt. Assn., 1973-76; dir. Internat. Symposium on Public Personnel Adminstrn., Salzburg, 1973, 75; speaker Latin Am. Conf. on Civil Service Tng., Venezuela, 1982. Author: Training Career Public Servants for the City of New York, 1936, Public Personnel Administration, 8th edit, 1983, The Personnel Job of Government Managers, 1971, Frontier Mother, 1979, The Need for a Public Philosophy, 1987, Standing Up for Government, 1990; editor: Personnel Adminstrn, 1945-55, Improving Public Services, 1979, (with others) Police Personnel Administration, 1974; contbr. numerous articles to jours. Mem. Arlington County (Va.) Sch. Bd., 1948-50; pres. Arlington Com. to Preserve Public Schs., 1958-61. Recipient Disting. Service award CSC, 1960; Stockberger award Soc. Personnel Adminstrn., 1962; Career Service award Nat. Civil Service League, 1967; medal of Honor U. Evansville, 1981; hon. fellow Nat. Acad. Pub. Adminstrn., 1988. Mem. Am. Polit. Sci. Assn., Am. Soc. Public Adminstrn. (editorial bd. 1955-58), Internat. Inst. Adminstrv. Sci., Internat. Personnel Mgmt. Assn. (hon. life mem., exec. com. Public Personnel Assn. 1951-54, pres. 1965-66, Washington rep. 1971-73). Presbyterian. Home: 3600 N Piedmont St Arlington VA 22207-5333

STAHL, RAY EMERSON, writer; b. Latrobe, Pa., Mar. 24, 1917; s. Curtis E. and Josephine (King) S.; AB, Bethany Coll., 1938; MDiv, Butler U., 1943; EdM, U. Pitts. 1946; postgrad. St. Vincent Coll., 1939. Pitts. Sch. Accountancy, 1939-40, U. Ky., 1955; MA, Ohio State U., 1969; LittD, Bethany Coll., 1995; m. Faith Worrell, Aug. 25, 1941; children: Ellen Josephine Carpenter, Ray Emerson Jr. Ordained to ministry Disciples of Christ Ch., 1941; minister Brentwood Christian Ch., Pitts., 1943-46, First Christian Ch., Erwin, Tenn., 1946-50; exec. sec. in charge bus. adminstrn. and pub. relations Milligan Coll., Tenn., 1950-68; dir. pub. relations E. Tenn. State U., Johnson City, 1968-78. Bd. dirs. United Way, ARC, Am. Cancer Soc., Reece Mus., Tipton-Haynes Hist. Assn., Johnson City Symphony. Mem. Council for Advancement Small Colls. (chmn. pub. relations 1957-61), Pub. Relations Soc. Am. (accredited 1974—), East Tenn. Edn. Assn. (chmn. pub. relations 1968-76), Johnson City C. of C. (dir., ofcl. city historian 1986—), Washington County Tenn. Hist. Assn. (pres.), Kappa Alpha, Theta Phi, Kappa Tau Alpha. Republican. Mem. Christian Ch. (elder). Club: Kiwanis (sec.-treas. 1983-84, bd. dirs., Kiwanian of Yr. 1995). Author: How to Finance the Local Church, 1953, Six Decades of Progress, 1976, History of Tennessee-Virginia Energy Corporation, 1981, Money, Wealth, the Bible and You, 1983, Johnson City, Tennessee, A Pictorial History, 1983, rev. 2d edit., 1986, A Beacon to Health Care, 1989; contbr. articles to profl. jours. Home and Office: 2007 Sherwood Dr # D Johnson City TN 37601-3236

STAHL, RUTHANNE, legal administrator; b. Albuquerque, Dec. 3, 1939; d. Benjamin Byron and Newel Harriett (Webb) Crego; m. David Dale Stahl, Nov. 7, 1980; children: Ginger Le'Ann Davidson Wells, Lindsey Trey Davidson. Student, Colo. Woman's Coll., Denver, 1957-58, U. Denver, 1976-77, Ga. State U., 1979-80. Several mgmt. positions Pub. Service Co. N.Mex., 1965-74; mgr. regional credit and collection tng., field support JCPenney Co., Denver, 1975-80; dir. personnel and regional credit ops. JCPenney Co., Atlanta; project mgr. tng. and devel. corp. staff JCPenney Co., Dallas; corp. tng. dir. Peoples Gas System Inc., Tampa, Fla., 1980-81; dir. adminstrn. Schwall and Ruff Atty., Atlanta, 1982—; guest NBC TV Not For Women Only, 1979. Author: (tng. manual) Effective Collection, 1978. Mem. Loan Exec. Com., City of Atlanta. Mem. Assn. Legal Adminstrs., Legal Assts. Mgmt. Assn., Assn. Personnel Adminstrn., Atlanta Consumer Credit Assn., Nat. Assn. Female Execs., Pilot Club (dir. fin. 1972-

74). Republican. Presbyterian. Lodge: Daus. of Nile. Office: Schwall and Ruff Atty 1615 Peachtree St NE Atlanta GA 30309-2433

STAHR, REBECCA, interior designer; b. New Orleans, Aug. 30, 1951; d. John Harold and Helen Theresa (Falanga) Mutter; m. Garrett Miles Stahr, Sept. 10, 1988. BS in Merchandising, La. State U., 1973; BFA, Ga. State U., 1985. Buyer Rich's Dept. Store, Atlanta, 1973-81; account exec. Comml. Interior Design, Atlanta, 1981-86; prin. interior designer builder divsn. KBG Interiors, Atlanta, 1986-87; interior designer Rebecca, Inc., Marietta, Ga., 1987—; co-owner Design Strategies, Inc.; speaker design seminar Atlanta Symphony Showhouse, 1990. Design editor Peachtree mag., 1989-92; contbr. articles to various publs. and newspapers. Mem. exec. com. Ga. Coun. for Internat. Visitors, Atlanta, 1992-93; mem. internat. com. Festival of Trees, Atlanta, 1991-93; home delivery vol. Meals on Wheels, Roswell, Ga., 1993-95; co-chairperson Quality of Life event Am. Cancer Soc., Atlanta, 1991. Recipient awards for Best Kitchen, Best Furnishings, Best Interior Design, and Best of Show Street of Dreams, Atlanta, 1987. Mem. AIA (allied mem.), Am. Soc. Interior Designers (legis. task force 1990), Women Healthcare Execs., Nat. Coun. on Aging, Am. Soc. on Aging, Am. Assn. Homes for Aging, Nat. Inst. Srs. Housing, Ga. Coun. on Aging, Sr. Living Assn. Ga. Office: Rebecca PO Box 70952 Marietta GA 30007-0952

STAKER, ROBERT JACKSON, senior federal judge; b. Kermit, W.Va., Feb. 14, 1925; s. Frederick George and Nada (Frazier) S.; m. Sue Blankenship Poore, July 16, 1955; 1 child, Donald Seth; 1 stepson, John Timothy Poore. Student, Marshall U., Huntington, W.Va., W.Va. U., Morgantown, U. Ky., Lexington; LL.B, W.Va. U., 1952. Bar: W.Va. 1952. Practiced in Williamson, 1952-68; judge Mingo County Circuit Ct., Williamson, 1969-79; U.S. dist. judge So. Dist. W.Va., Huntington, 1979-95, sr. U.S. dist. judge, 1995—. Served with USN, 1943-46. Democrat. Presbyterian.

STALDER, RICHARD L., executive secretary; b. Pender, Nebr., Mar. 23, 1951; married; 2 children. BA in Econs., La. State U., 1973, MS in Econs., 1978. Correctional officer Juvenile Adjustment Ctr., La. Correctional Inst. Women, 1971-73; from tng. officer to asst. dir. tng. La. Dept. Corrections, 1974-75, adminstr. fed. programs, 1975-76, acting corrections budget officer, 1976, officer corrections budget, 1977-78, officer agri-bus. planning and mgmt., divsn. agri-bus., 1978; exec. v.p. Doles Ins. Agy. Inc., Plain Dealing, La., 1981-85; supt. La. Tng. Inst., Monroe, 1978-81; dep. warden Dixon Correctional Inst., 1985-87; warden David Wade Correctional Ctr., 1987-92; sec. La. Dept. Pub. Safety and Corrections, Baton Rouge, 1992—; mem. Gov.'s adv. bd. Juvenile Delinquency and Prevention, 1975-82; mem. La. Coun. Criminal Justice, 1978-81; mem. North Delta Law Enformcement Dist. Adv. Coun., 1979-81, sec. treas., 1980-81; pres. Bolinger Water System, 1982-85; participant law enforcement coord. com. we. dist. La., 1991-92, mid. dist., 1994—; mem. Commn. Accreditation Corrections; chmn. Gov.'s Prison Population, Sentencing Practices, and Alternative Sanctions Task Force; mem. Gov.'s Drug Policy Bd., La. Commn. Law Enforcement, state adv. coun. La. N.G. Youth Challange program, continuing revision com. La. Children's Code, Interagy. Coord. Coun. Adult Literacy, Retng., Continuing Edn., Interagy. Coun. Prevention Sex Offenders and Treatment of Sex Offenders, Law Enforcement Coord. Com. Ea. Dist. La., policy bd. La. Criminal Justice Info. System, La. Sentencing Commn.; participant law enforcement coord. com. we. dist. La., 1991-92, mid. dist., 1994—. Chmn. bd. deacons 1st Presbyn. Ch., 1982-84, 1984; vice chair Plain Dealing Chorale Soc., 1982-85; adv. bd. N.W. La. Vocat. Sch., 1989-92. Received award Merit Victims and Citizens Against Crime, award for Outstanding Performance Concurrent Resolution La. Legislator. Mem. Am. Correctional Assn., (commn. accreditation for corrections 1990—, standards com. 1994—, constn. and by-laws com. 1994—), Assn. State Correctional Adminstrs. (standards review com. 1993-94, chmn. 1994—, fed. and state relations ad hoc com. 1993-94, Am. Correctional Assn. ad hoc com. 1993—), So. States Correctional Assn., La. Correctional Assn., Correctional Accreditation Mgrs. Assn., Homer Lions Club (pres. 1990-91), Oakland Plantation Country Club (bd. dirs. 1982-85, 1st v.p. 1984-85), Plain Dealing Lions Club (pres. 1983-85), Omicron Delta Epsilon. Methodist. Office: La Dept Pub Safety and Corrections PO Box 94304 Baton Rouge LA 70804-9304

STALKER, SUZY WOOSTER, human resources executive; b. Atlanta, Oct. 12, 1948; d. George Edward Wooster and Mary Evelyn (Dayton) Schmidt; m. James Marion Stalker, Nov. 11, 1966; children: Marian Paige, Jason Alexander. Student, Ga. State U., 1981—. Tng. rep. Rich's, Atlanta, 1980-81, tng. supr., 1981-82, regional tng. coord., 1982-84, employee communications specialist, 1983-84; dir. human resources Home Fed. Savs. & Loan, Atlanta, 1984-85, v.p. human resources, 1985-88; v.p. pers. Gulf States Mortgage Co., Inc., Atlanta, 1988-96; sr. v.p. Citizens Mortgage Corp., 1996—. Editor Richbits, 1983-84. Leader Girl Scouts U.S., Austell, Ga., 1975-76; pres. Clarkdale Elem. PTA, Austell, 1975-76. Mem. Nat. Assn. for Female Execs., Inc., Ga. Exec. Women's Network. Avocations: sailing, cross-stitching, watercolors. Home: 4820 Glore Rd Mableton GA 30059-5506

STALL, DAVID KEITH, city manager; b. Glendale, Calif., Feb. 16, 1958; m. Linda L. Williams, 1980; children: Samantha, Lauren, Jacob. Grad. Pub. Exec. Inst., U. Tex., Austin, 1994. Police lt. City of Nassau Bay, Tex., 1978-92, city mgr., 1992—; instr. Houston Community Coll., 1988-90. Author: Radio Frequency Guide, 1990, Texas Radio Directory, 1993. City councilman City of El Lago, Tex., 1978-79. Mem. Internat. City Mgmt. Assn., Internat. Assn. Arson Investigators (police com. 1980—), Am. Radio Relay League (pub. info. officer 1989—). Office: City of Nassau Bay 1800 Nasa Rd 1 # One Houston TX 77058-3502

STALLINGS, ELIZABETH ARUNDELL, governmental library management analyst; b. Washington, Sept. 30, 1927; d. Charles Rogers and Alice Judson (Wright) Arundell; m. James Henry Stallings, Jr., 1949 (div. 1975); children: Robert George, Anne Louise, Thomas James. BA in English, Wellesley Coll., 1949; MSLS, Cath. U. Am., 1968. Adminstrv. asst., sec. Am. Fedn. Labor, Labor's League for Polit Edn., Washington, 1949-55; libr., adminstrv. libr. HUD, Washington, 1968-83, mgmt. analyst, tech. mgr. libr. contract, 1983—; treas. Fed. Interagy. Field Librs.' Workshop, Washington, 1977-83; treas. D.C. chpt. Spl. Librs. Assn., Washington, 1981-84, pres. urban affairs sect., 1981-82; HUD rep. Fed. Libr. and Info. Ctr. Com. and Fed. Libr. Network (FEDLINK) Washington, 1983—. Vol. mus. docent Jr. League Washington, 1949-68; vol. Reach-to-Recovery program Am. Cancer Soc., Washington, 1977-87; treas., bd. dirs. Stoneleigh Homeowners Assn., McLean, Va., 1982, 83; bd. dirs. McLean Project for the Arts, 1985—, treas., 1985-52, sec., 1993, mem. exec. bd., 1985-93. Mem. Washington Wellesley Club, Beta Phi Mu (pres. 1980-81). Episcopalian. Home: 8340 Greensboro Dr Apt 726 Mc Lean VA 22102-3545 Office: HUD Rm 5172 451 7th St SW Washington DC 20410-0001

STALLINGS, FRANK, JR., industrial engineer; b. Concord, N.C., Aug. 21, 1954; s. Frank and Theresa Ann (Iorlano) S. BS in Indsl. Engring., N.C. State U., 1976; MS in Adminstrn., George Washington U., 1979. Jr. indsl. engr. Naval Air Rework Facility, Norfolk, Va., 1974-75; indsl. engr. Babcock & Wilcox, Lynchburg, Va., 1977-79; sr. prin. engr. NCR Corp., Columbia, S.C., 1979-82; mgr. indsl. engring. Mars Electronics, Ltd., Reading, Eng., 1987-88; liaison between European/U.S. mfg. divs., sr. indsl. engr. M&M/MARS, Inc., Waco, Tex., 1982-84, mgr. quality assurance, 1984-87, mgr. indsl. engring., 1988-92;, 1991-96; inbound logistics mgr. M&M/MARS, Inc., Waco, Tex., 1996—. Coach Heart of Tex. Soccer League, Waco, 1985-87; Sunday sch. tchr. Columbus Ave. Bapt. Ch., Waco, 1988—, mem. Missions com., 1991—, Bapt. Youth leader, 1990—, mem. ch. singles coun., 1989-91; exec. mem. singles coun. Waco Bapt. Assn.; counselor Royal Ambs., 1990—; children's leader Bible Study Fellowship, 1995—. Mem. Inst. Indsl. Engrs. (sr.), Am. Soc. Quality Control, Am. Prodn. and Inventory Control Socl., Am. Radio Relay League, Radio Amateurs Civil Emergency Svcs., Amateur Radio Emergency Svcs., Ten-10 Internat. Amateur Radio Network, Waco Amateur TV Soc. (bd. dirs. 1995—). Republican. Home: 1241 Woodland West Dr Waco TX 76712-2437 Office: M&M/MARS Inc 1001 Texas Central Pkwy Waco TX 76712

STALLINGS, MICHAEL DEAN, retail executive; b. Champaign, Ill., Feb. 3, 1958; s. C. Dean and Shirley J. (Rushing) S. BA in Bus. Adminstrn., Bellarmine Coll., 1980. Owner MDS Contracting, Edgewood, Ky., 1980-82; gen. mgr. Ohio Energy Cons., Cin., 1982-84; nat. sales mgr. Laux Comm., Cin., 1984-87; no. sales mgr. Metroweb Inc., Erlanger, Ky., 1987-89; v.p. Miarko Inc., Florence, Ky., 1989—, Radial Access Inc., Cin., 1994—. Mem. Tri County Amateur Hockey Assn. (treas. 1990-92), No. Ky. Jr. Hockey Assn. (pres. 1991-93). Republican. Home: 3657 Oxford Ct Erlanger KY 41018-2674 Office: Miarko Inc PO Box 153 Florence KY 41022-0153

STALLINGS, NANCY ROOSEVELT, rehabilitation nurse; b. Commerce, Tex., Oct. 7, 1958; d. Paul Hamilton and Kathryn June (Jack) Roosevelt; m. Bradford Lee Stallings, Aug. 22, 1987; children: Nicholas Lee, Alex Jared. BS, East Tex. State U., 1980; ADN, Paris (Tex.) Jr. Coll., 1986. RN, Tex.; cert. in ACLS. Nurse ICU, St. Joseph Hosp., Paris, 1986-92, cardiac rehab. nurse, mgr., 1992—, hospice mgr., 1995, telemetry mgr., 1995-96; asst. dir. nurses Magnolia Home Health, Paris, 1996—. Mem. Am. Assn. Cardiovasc. and Pulmonary Rehab., Tex. Assn. Cardiovasc. and Pulmonary Rehab. Home: 2995 Hubbard St Paris TX 75460-6379

STALLINGS, PHYLLIS ANN, music educator; b. Little Rock, Feb. 24, 1944; d. Roy Edwin and Helen Lavern (Waters) Moseley; m. Paul Harold Stallings, Jan. 22, 1966; children: Kevin Scott, Michael Shane, Natasha Lynette, Clayton Lane. B in Music Edn., Ouachita Bapt. U., 1966; M in Music Edn., Ark. State U., 1971. Cert. vocal and band music tchr., Ark., Mo. Tchr. vocal music Glenwood (Ark.) Pub. Sch., 1966-67; tchr. elem. music DeSoto (Mo.) Pub. Sch., 1967-69; tchr. secondary music Richland Pub. Sch., Essex, Mo., 1969-71; tchr. elem. music Augusta (Ark.) Pub. Sch., 1971-82; tchr. vocal music Independence (Mo.) Christian Sch., 1982-87; tchr. secondary music Doniphan (Mo.) Region I Pub. Sch., 1988-91; vocal and band dir. grades K-12 Delaplaine (Ark.) H.S., 1992, Stanford (Ark.) H.S., 1992-93; band and choir dir. grades K-12 Delaplaine Schs., 1993-94; dir. K-12 vocal and band Southland C-9 Schs., Cardwell, Mo., 1994—; camp music dir. YWCA/Camp Burgess Glen, Cedar Mountain, N.C., summer 1964; interum minister of music First Bapt. Ch., Paragould, Ark., 1988-89. Active PTA. Am. Coll. Musicians scholar, 1962; acad. and music scholar. Mem. Music Educators Nat. Conf., Cen. Tchrs. Assn., Mo. Tchrs. Assn. Home: Sunset Hills Subdivsn 1700 Hillcrest Dr Paragould AR 72450-9115

STALLWORTH, ANNE NALL, writer, writing educator; b. Birmingham, Ala., Sept. 30, 1935; d. John Martin and Lida Lucille (Crump) Nall; m. Clarke J. Stallworth Jr., Mar. 23, 1925; children: Carole Anne Stallworth, Clarke J. Stallworth III. Student, Birmingham-So. Coll., 1952-53. Tchr. U. Ala., Birmingham; tchr. Birmingham. Author: This Time Next Year, 1972 (Best Fiction award), Where the Bright Lights Shine, 1977, Go, Go, Said the Bird, 1984 (movie rights pending); (short story) Waiting (McCall's mag.), 1976. All had fgn. publ. Editor Found. for Women's Health newsletter, Birmingham; publicity dir. Birmingham Music Club. Recipient Best Fiction award Ala. Libr., 1972. Home: 4316 Wilderness Rd Birmingham AL 35213-2411

STALLWORTH-BARRON, DORIS A. CARTER, librarian, educator; b. Ala., June 12, 1932; d. Henry Lee Carter and Hattie Belle Stallworth; m. George Stallworth, 1950 (dec.); children: Annette LaVerne, Vanzette Yvonne; m. Walter L. Barron, 1989. BS, Ala. State U., 1955; MLS, CUNY, 1968; postgrad., Columbia U., St. John's U., NYU. Cert. supr. and tchr. sch. libr. media, N.Y. Libr. media specialist N.Y.C. Bd. Edn.; head libr. Calhoun County High Sch., Hobson City, Ala.; cons. Libr. Unit, N.Y.C. Bd. Edn.; cons. evaluator So. Assn. Secondary Schs., Ala.; supr., adminstr., liason rep. Community Sch. Dist. #24 N.Y.C. Sch. System; previewer libr. media Preview Mag., 1971-73; mem. ednl. svcs. adv. coun. Sta. WNET, 1987-89; mem. coun. N.Y.C. Schs. Libr. System, 1987-90; turn-key tchr. trainer N.Y. State Dept. Edn., 1988; spl. guest speaker and lectr. Queens Coll., City U., Community Sch. Dist. #24, PTA, N.Y. City Sch. System, Libr. unit, 1980-90; curriculum writer libr. unit N.Y.C. Bd. Edn., 1985-86. Contbr. articles to ednl. publs. Mem. State of Ala. Dem. Exec. Com., 1994—; active A+ for Kids. Mem. NAFE, ALA, Am. Assn. Sch. Librs. (spl. guest speaker and lectr. for conv. 1987), Am. Sch. Libr.'s Assn., Nat. Assn. Black Pub. Adminstrs., N.Y. State Libr. Assn., N.Y.C. Sch. Librs. Assn., Nat. Forum for Black Pub. Adminstrs., N.Y. Coalition 100 Black Women, Lambda Kappa Mu Sorority, Inc., Alpha Kappa Alpha Sorority.

STALNAKER, PHIL A., lawyer; b. South Charleston, W.Va., Jan. 28, 1947; s. Darus K. and Nell Marie (Young) S.; 1 child, Justin. BA, U. Ky., 1969; JD, U. Louisville, 1975. Pvt. practice Pikeville, Ky., 1977—; city atty. City of Coal Run Village, Ky., 1988—; atty. Pikeville City Sch. Dist., 1987—. Mem. Kiwanis (pres. Pikeville club 1993—). Office: 101 Summit Dr Ste 302 Pikeville KY 41501-1580

STAMBAUGH, WILLIAM SCOTT, investor, economist; b. Carlisle, Pa., Aug. 1, 1936; s. William Myers Stambaugh and Hannah Kathryn (Jacobs) Wallin; m. Oksana Stambaugh; children: Kathryn Elizabeth, John William; stepchild: Arkadiy. Student, Pa. State U., 1953-54; BS in Mil. Sci., U.S. Mil. Acad., 1958; MA in Econs., Syracuse U., 1967; PhD in Econs., U. Md., 1982. Commd. 2d lt. USAF, 1958-60, advanced through grades to col., 1983; planning and programming officer USAF Hdqs., Pentagon, 1978-83, dir. programs Germany, Europe, 1983-85; dep. chief of staff USAF Hdqs., Germany, 1985-86; spl. asst. to asst. chief of staff studies and analysis USAF Hdqs., Pentagon, 1986-88; investor Arlington, Va., 1988—; mem. faculty Indsl. Coll. Armed Forces, Ft. McNair, 1975-78, Paper Network, Washington, 1991-94. Pres. Bethel Ch., Arlington, Va. 1990-94; commr. Environment and Energy Conservation Com., Arlington, 1991-96; del. Rep. Conv., Richmond, 1993, 94. Decorated Legion of Merit, Disting. Flying Cross, Svc. medals. Mem. Nat. Assn. Real Estate Investors, Nat. Def. U. Assn. (life), Assn. Indsl. Coll. Armed Forces (life), Air Force Assn. (life), West Point Soc. Washington, D.C. (life), Am. Econs. Assn. (life), Am. Def. Preparedness Assn. Home and Office: 511 N Manchester St Arlington VA 22203-1038

STAMM, ROBERT CALVIN, consulting engineer; b. Phila., July 2, 1925; s. William Calvin and Allis Patience (Gill) S.; student Columbia Coll., 1943, Wittenberg U., 1944; B.S.M.E., Columbia U., 1950; m. Esther Elizabeth Smith, Aug. 8, 1953. Project engr. Westvaco Corp., N.Y.C., 1950-56, mgr. design and constrn., 1956-59, engring. group mgr., 1959-69, chief engr., 1969-75, corp. mgr. energy and property conservation, 1975-76; v.p. Brown & Root, Inc., Houston, 1976-82; cons. engr., 1982—. Served with USAAF, 1944-46. Fellow TAPPI (past dir., exec. com.); mem. AAAS, ASME, N.Y. Acad. Scis., Res. Officers Assn., Phi Kappa Psi, Tau Beta Pi. Home and Office: 1643 W Belt Dr S Houston TX 77042-2965

STAMP, FREDERICK PFARR, JR., federal judge; b. Wheeling, W.Va., July 24, 1934; s. Frederick P. Sr. and Louise (Aul) S.; m. Joan A. Corson, Sept. 20, 1975; children: Frederick Andrew, Joan Elizabeth. BA, Washington and Lee U., 1956; LLB, U. Richmond, 1959. Bar: W.Va. 1959, Va. 1959, Pa. 1986, U.S. Supreme Ct. 1973, U.S. Ct. Appeals (4th cir.) 1962, U.S. Dist. Ct. (no. dist.) W.Va. 1960, U.S. Dist. Ct. (so. dist.) W.Va. 1975, U.S. Dist. Ct. (we. dist.) Pa., U.S. Tax Ct. 1973, W.Va. Supreme Ct. Appeals 1966, Va. Supreme Ct. Appeals 1959. Assoc., then ptnr. Schrader, Stamp, Byrd, Byrum & Companion and predecessor firms, Wheeling, 1960-90; judge U.S. Dist. Ct. (no. dist.) W.Va., Wheeling, 1990-94, apptd. chief judge, 1994—; mem. ho. of dels. W.Va. Legislature, Charleston, 1966-70. Mem. W.Va. Bd. Regents, Charleston, 1970-77; trustee Linsly Sch., Wheeling, 1977—. Fellow Am. Bar Found., Am. Coll. Trial Lawyers; mem. W.Va. Bar Assn. (pres. 1981-82), W.Va. Commn. on Uniform State Laws, Nat. Conf. Commrs. on Uniform State Laws.

STAMPS, GEORGE MORELAND, communications consultant, facsimile pioneer; b. Kuling, Jiangxi, China, June 15, 1924; came to U.S., 1926 (parents Am. citizens); s. Drew Fletcher and Elizabeth Camilla (Belk) S.; m. Helen Leone Paty, Nov. 29, 1946; children: Margaret Evalyn, Robert Fletcher, Thomas Paty, John Belk. BS magna cum laude, Wake Forest U., 1947; MA in Physics, Columbia U., 1949; postgrad., Poly. Inst. Bklyn., 1950-52. Instr. physics and math. SUNY Maritime Coll., Bronx, 1949-51; asst. chief engr., dir. tech. sales Hogan Labs. Inc., N.Y.C., 1951-59; chief engr., asst. to pres. mktg. Telautograph Corp., Los Angeles, 1960-62; program mgr. Magnafax Program Magnavox Co., Torrance, Calif., 1963-65; mgr indsl. mktg. Magnavox Co., Urbana, Ill., 1965-71, mgr. bus. devel., 1971-73; corp. mgr. bus. devel. Xerox Corp., Stamford, Conn., 1973-76; pres. GMS Consulting, Westport, Conn., 1976-86, Oxford, Ga., 1986—; expert witness on facsimile-visual scis. N.Y. Supreme Ct., 1982; chmn. numerous sci. and profl. confs. Contbr. over 35 articles on facsimile and telecommunication scis. to profl. jours. and govt. coms. Patentee in field. Del. Conn. Dem. Conv., Hartford, 1980; bd. dirs. Champaign-Urbana (Ill.) Symphony Orch., 1968-72, Newton County Red Cross, 1988-94; sec. Newton County Hist. Soc., 1991-93, v.p., 1993-95, pres., 1995-96; v.p. Friends of Newton County Porter Meml. Libr., 1988-91, pres., 1991-93. Decorated Air medal with two oak leaf clusters; named Friend of Newton County Libr., 1994. Mem. IEEE, Computer Soc. of IEEE, Comm. Soc. of IEEE (officer Ft. Wayne chpt. 1972-73), Geosci. and Remote Sensing Soc. of IEEE, Electronics Industries Assn. (chmn. comm. terminals and interfaces sect. 1963-73, founder TR-29 facsimile systems and equipment engring. com. 1961), Armed Forces Comm. and Electronics Assn., Am. Phys. Soc., Wake Forest U. Alumni Coun., Kiwanis (pres. Covington club 1993-94, lt. gov. 21st dist. 1996—), Phi Beta Kappa, Omicron Delta Kappa. Presbyterian. Home: 1280 Lake Stone Lea Dr PO Box 1299 Oxford GA 30267

STAMPS, LAURA ANNE, writer, artist, editor; b. Indpls., Apr. 2, 1957; d. James Oliver and Isabelle Anne (Holland) Smith; m. Carl Thomas Stamps, Jr., June 30, 1979. Student, Dalton (Ga.) Jr. Coll., 1977, Coll. of Charleston, S.C., 1979. Owner Emmanuel Pub., Columbia, S.C., 1985—; cons. Art Editions, Inc., Salt Lake City, 1992—. Author: How to Create the Life You Desire, 1995, How to Become a Prosperous Woman, 1995, (fiction) Tuning Out, 1996; editor The Artist's Forum, 1989-94, Laura's Letter for Women, 1996—. Mem. Acad. of Am. Poets (assoc.). Office: Emmanuel Publishing PO Box 212534 Columbia SC 29221-2534

STAMPS, THOMAS PATY, lawyer, consultant; b. Mineola, N.Y., May 10, 1952; s. George Moreland and Helen Leone (Paty) S.; children: Katherine Camilla, George Belk, Elizabeth Margaret, Carley Lynn; m. Diana Lynn Whittaker, Dec. 11, 1993. BA, U. Ill., 1973; postgrad., Emory U., 1975-76; JD, Wake Forest U., 1979. Bar: Ga. 1979, N.C. 1979. Pers. dir. Norman Jaspan, N.Y.C., 1973-74; assoc. Macey & Zusmann, Atlanta, 1979-81; prin. Zusmann, Small, Stamps & White PC, Atlanta, 1981-85; cons. GMS Cons., Oxford, Ga., 1975—; ptnr. Destin Enterprises, Atlanta, 1983-85. Author: Study of a Student, 1973, History of Coca-Cola, 1976; asst. editor Ga. Jour. So. Legal History, 1991-94. Chmn. Summer Law Inst., Atlanta, 1981-85; mem. Dem. Party Ga., Atlanta, 1983—; atty. Vol. Lawyers for Arts, Atlanta, 1981-94, Atlanta Vol. Lawyers Found.; panel mem. U.S. Bankruptcy Trustees No. Dist. Ga., 1982-89; mem. Bench and Bar Com., State Bar Ga., 1996-97; active High Mus. Art, 1986—, Atlanta Hist. Soc., Atlanta Bot. Gardens, Atlanta Symphony Orch., Ga. Trust Hist. Preservation, Ind.; sec. Friends of Woodrow Wilson, 1988—, chmn. dinner, 1990—; trustee Ga. Legal History Found., 1989—. Named to Honorable Order of Ky. Colonels; recipient Svc. award Inst. Continuing Legal Edn., Athens, Ga., 1981, 86. Mem. ABA, Atlanta Bar Assn. (com. chmn. 1981-85), N.C. Bar Assn., Lawyers Club, Phi Alpha Delta (justice, Atlanta 1982-83, emeritus 1983). Office: 7715 Jett Ferry Rd Atlanta GA 30350

STANBERRY, DOSI ELAINE, English literature educator, writer; b. Elk Park, N.C.; m. Earl Stanberry; 1 child, Anita St. Lawrence. Student in Bus. Edn., Steed Coll. Tech., 1956; BS in Bus. and English, East Tenn. State U., 1961, MA in Shakespearean Lit., 1962; EdD, East Tex. State U., 1975; postgrad., North Tex. State U., U. South Fla., NYU, Duke U., U. N.C. Prof. Manatee Jr. Coll., Bradenton, Fla., 1964-67, Dickinson State U., N.D., 1967-81; retired, 1981. Author: Poetic Heartstrings, Mountain Echoes, Love's Perplexing Obsession Experienced by Heinrich Heine and Percy Bysshe Shelley, Poetry from the Ancients to Moderns: A Critical Anthology, Finley Forest, Chapel Hill's Tree-lined Tuck, (plays) The Big Toe, The Funeral Factory; contbr. articles, poetry to jours., mags. Recipient Editor's Choice award Nat. Libr. Poetry, 1988, 95, Distinguished Professorof English Award, Dickinson State U., 1981; included in Best Poems of 1995. Mem. Acad. Am. Poets, N.C. Writers Network, N.C. Poetry Soc. (Carl Sandburg Poetry award 1988), Poetic Page, Writers Jour., Poets and Writers, Friday-Noon Poets, Delta Kappa Gamma. Home: Finley Forest 193 Summerwalk Cir Chapel Hill NC 27514-8642

STANDEL, RICHARD REYNOLD, JR., lawyer, communications executive; b. N.Y.C., Nov. 20, 1936; s. Richard Reynold and Antoinette (Pfinder) S.; m. Elizabeth Hughes, Dec. 5, 1963. AB, Columbia U., 1956, JD, 1959; LLM, NYU, 1972. Bar: N.Y. 1960, Colo. 1974, Tenn. 1978. Assoc. Wickes, Riddell, Bloomer, Jacobi & McGuire, N.Y.C., 1959-64; assoc. gen. counsel Manville Corp., Denver, 1964-71, dir. acquisitions and divestments, 1972-76; v.p., gen. counsel, sec. No. Telecom Inc., Nashville and Dallas, 1976—. Bd. dirs. Nashville Urban League, 1984-86. Ford Found. scholar, 1952-56; Columbia U. Law Sch. scholar, 1956-59. Mem. Tenn. Bus. Roundtable (bd. dirs. 1985-92), Richland Country Club. Presbyterian. Office: No Telecom Inc Dept 8473 MS C-1531 2221 Lakeside Blvd Richardson TX 75082-4399

STANFEL, LARRY EUGENE, business educator; b. Waukegan, Ill., Feb. 6, 1940; s. Paul P. and Lola C. Stanfel; m. Jane Ellen Yetter, Sept. 1, 1962; children: Kenneth, Larry, Christine, Rebecca. BS in Math., Ill. Inst. Tech., 1962; MS in Indsl. Engring. & Mgmt. Sci., Northwestern U., 1965, PhD, 1966. Asst. prof. indsl. engring. U. Fla., Gainesville, 1966-69; assoc. prof. mech. engring. Colo. State U., Fort Collins, 1969-72; prof. indsl. engring. U. Tex., Arlington, 1972-80; prof. mgmt. Clarkson Coll., Potsdam, N.Y., 1980-84; prof. quantitative bus. analysis La. State U., Baton Rouge, 1984-88; prof. mgmt. sci. U. Ala., Tuscaloosa, 1988—; cons. Def. Info. Systems Agy., Reston, Va., 1988-90, 92, 94, Bur. Land Mgmt., Denver, 1991, Esca Corp., Bellevue, Wash., 1981-85, U.S. Army, White Sands Missile Range, 1969, 72-73, 77. Author: Optimization Techniques, 1975, Analysis of Systems in Operations Research, 1975; contbr. articles to profl. jours. Fellow Royal Norwegian Coun. for Sci. and Engring., 1975-77, 94-95. Mem. Inst. for Mgmt. Sci., Ops. Rsch. Soc. Am., Internat. Info. Mgmt. Assn., Sigma Xi, Beta Gamma Sigma. Roman Catholic. Office: U Ala Mgs Dept Tuscaloosa AL 35487 Address: Myrdalskogen 288, 5095 Ulset Norway

STANFORD, JANE HERRING, business administration educator; b. Lockhart, Tex., Dec. 17, 1939; d. John William and Frances Argyra (Cheatham) H. Jr.; m. Rube Valton Stanford, Sept. 17, 1966; children: Steven Scott, Lisa Ann. BS in Secondary Edn., Texas A&M U., Kingsville, 1965; MS in Counseling, Texas A&M U., Corpus Christi, 1982; MBA, Texas A&M U., Kingsville, 1988; PhD in Orgn. Theory and Policy, U. North Tex., 1992. Cert. secondary sch. tchr., coun., Tex. English tchr. Robstown (Tex.) H.S., 1965-67; Bus. tchr. Miller H.S., Corpus Christi, 1967-78; owner, mgr. The Cottage, Portland, Tex., 1978-81; instr. Del Mar Coll., Corpus Christi, 1981-83, Bee County Coll., Beeville, Tex., 1984-88; tching. fellow U. North Tex., Denton, 1988-90; assoc. prof. bus. policy and internat. mgmt. Texas A&M U., Kingsville, 1990—, chair dept. mgmt. and marketing, 1994—; mem. grad. faculty Tex. A&M U., Kingsville, chair faculty senate, 1995-96, mem. exec. com. of senate, 1993-96; cons., internat. lectr. on strategic mgmt. within internat. context, workshop leader and participant in acad. issues for various groups, including S.W. Fedn. Adminstrv. Disciplines, Houston, 1992-95. Author: Building Competitiveness: U.S. Expatriate Management Strategies in Mexico, 1995; co-editor Tex. A&M U. System Internat. Bus. Newsletter, 1993; contbr. articles to profl. jours. Co-author Best Conf. Paper, Richard d. Irwin, Inc., Houston, 1991; grantee SBA for Women in Bus. Conf., 1993; nominated to S.W. Acad. of Mgmt. Doctoral Consortium, S.W. Fedn. Adminstrv. Disciplines, 1990; Tex. A&M U. Sys. Chancellor's fellow in leadership in higher edn. program, 1996-97. Mem. AAUP, Acad. Internat. Bus. (track chair 1994-95), Acad. Mgmt., So. Mgmt. Assn., S.W. Acad. Mgmt., S.W. Case Rsch. Assn. (track chair 1992), Exec. Women in Tex. Govt., Kappa Delta Pi (life), Delta Sigma Pi. Presbyterian. Home: 13526 Carlos Fifth Ct Corpus Christi TX 78418 Office: Texas A&M Univ Campus Box 187 Kingsville TX 78363

STANFORD, KAREN ANNE, state agency administrator; b. Rome, N.Y., Nov. 25, 1941; d. Clarence Erwin and Mary Irene (Diable) S.; m. Michael Joseph Minerva Sr., Aug. 3, 1963 (div. 1980); children: Elizabeth Anne Minerva, Michael Joseph Minerva Jr. BA in Polit. Sci., U. Fla., Gainesville, 1963; MSPA, Fla. State U., 1980, PhD in Pub. Adminstrn./Fin. Mgmt., 1989. Dir. state bd. League of Women Voters, Tallahassee, 1977-79; dir. pub. sector rsch., treas. The Osprey Co., Tallahassee, 1980-83; devel. mgr. alternative health plans Fla. Dept. Health and Rehab. Svcs., Tallahassee, 1984-87; asst. prof. Polit. Sci. U. Wyo., Laramie, 1989-93; exec. dir. Gov.'s Commn. Govt. Accountability to the People Exec. Office of the Gov., Tallahassee, 1993—. Contbr. articles to profl. jours. Mem. State Task Force on

AIDS Edn., Sheridan, Wyo., 1990-92, Leadership Fla. Class XV, Tallahassee, 1996-97. Mem. ASPA (co-chair state task force on govt. accountability), Assn. Budgeting and Fin. Mgmt. (exec. bd. dirs. 1992—, chair 1997), Phi Kappa Phi, Pi Alpha Alphaha, Pi Sigma Alpha. Office: GAP Commn Exec Office Gov 154 Holland Bldg Tallahassee FL 32399-0001

STANFORD, YVONNE MCCLINTON, librarian; b. Clarksdale, Miss.; d. Thomas Anthony, Sr. and Josephine (Hurley) McClinton; m. Otis Stanford; children: Sean Christopher, Otis, II. BS in English Edn., Delta State U., 1971; MLS, La. State U., 1974. English tchr. West Tallahatchie H.S., Webb, Miss., 1971-73; elem. libr. Booker T. Washington Elem. Sch., Clarksdale, 1974-86; adult edn. tchr. Clarksdale Pub. Schs., 1981-86; counselor coord. youth employment Coahoma Opportunities, summers 1984-86; h.s. libr. Coahoma County H.S., 1986-94; libr. dir. Coahoma Comm. Coll., 1994—. Leadership Clarksdale Grad., C. of C., 1992; food ministry vol. Coahoma Opportunities, Inc., Clarksdale, 1990—; alt. del. Miss. Dem. Party, Jackson, 1992; Youth Leadership Clarksdale, C. of C., 1993—. Recipient Notable Svc. award Am. Cancer Soc., Clarksdale, 1992, 93; fellow La. State U., Baton Rouge, 1973-74; named one of Outstanding Young Women of Am., 1981. Mem. ALA, NEA, Coahoma County Assn. Educators (bldg. rep. 1976—), Miss. Libr. Assn. (black caucus com. chair 1994—), Miss. Assn. Educators, Delta Sigma Theta (reporter 1988-90, arts and letters chmn. 1995—). Democrat. Baptist. Office: Coahoma Comm Coll 3240 Friars Point Rd Clarksdale MS 38614

STANG, LOUIS GEORGE, computer scientist; b. Portland, Oreg., Oct. 25, 1919; s. Louis George and Pearl Dolina Stang; m. Dorian Ruth Heintz, June 5, 1943; children: David James, Steven Cory, Mark Edward. BA, Reed Coll., 1941. Rsch. chemist Manhattan Project, 1943-45, Universal Oil Products, Riverside, Ill., 1945-47; divsn. head Brookhaven Nat. Lab., Upton, N.Y., 1947-82; owner Dorilou Assocs., Wellington, Fla., 1982—; cons. H.K. Ferguson Co., N.Y.C., 1955. Author: The Really Great News, 1995; editor, editor-in-chief: American Nuclear Society. Mem. Am. Chem. Soc. (emeritus), Phi Beta Kappa. Baptist. Home and Office: 13769 Exotica Ln Wellington FL 33414

STANHOPE, WILLIAM HENRY, lawyer; b. Chillicothe, Ohio, Aug. 17, 1951; s. William Wallace and Elizabeth C. Stanhope; m. Kristen A. Keirsey, July 26, 1976; children: Liesel, Sally, Kaitlyn. BA, Duke U., 1973; JD, Northwestern U. Law Sch., 1976. Bar: Minn. Supreme Ct. 1976, U.S. Dist. Ct. Minn. 1976, U.S. Dist. Ct. Ga. 1979, Ga. Supreme Ct. 1979, Ga. Ct. Appeals 1979. Assoc. Robins, Kaplan, Miller & Ciresi, Mpls., Atlanta, 1976-82; ptnr. Robins, Kaplan, Miller & Ciresi, Atlanta, 1982-91, mng. ptnr. SE Regional Office,, 1991—; instr. NITA, Raleigh, N.C., 1988, Emory U., Atlanta, 1990—. Contbr. articles to profl. jours. Mem. ABA, Assn. Trial Lawyers Am., Ga. State Bar Assn., Ga. Trial Lawyers Assn. Office: Robins Kaplan Miller & Ciresi 2600 One Atlantic Plz 950 E Paces Ferry Rd NE Atlanta GA 30326-1119

STANKEE, GLEN ALLEN, lawyer; b. Clinton, Iowa, Sept. 27, 1953; s. Glen Earl and Marilyn Jean (Clark) S.; m. Carol Ann Prowe, Feb. 19, 1984. BSBA, Drake U., 1975; MBA, Mich. State U., 1977; JD, U. Detroit, 1979; LLM in Taxation, U. Miami, 1983. Bar: Mich. 1980, U.S. Dist. Ct. (ea. dist.) Mich. 1980, U.S. Ct. Appeals (6th cir.) 1980, U.S. Tax Ct. 1980, Fla. 1981, U.S. Ct. Appeals (11th cir.) 1981, U.S. Dist. Ct. (so. dist.) Fla. 1982, U.S. Dist. Ct. (mid. dist.) 1984, U.S. Supreme Ct. 1987; CPA, Fla. Assoc. Raymond & Dillon P.C., Detroit, 1980-81; assoc. Raymond & Dillon P.C., West Palm Beach, Fla., 1981-85, prin., 1985-86; prin. Raymond & Dillon P.C., Ft. Lauderdale, Fla., 1987-93; ptnr. Ruden, McClosky, Smith, Schuster & Russell, P.A., Ft. Lauderdale, 1993—. Contbr. articles to profl. jours. Mem. ABA, Fed. Bar Assn., Fla. Bar Assn., Mich. Bar Assn., Am. Assn. Attys./CPA's, Am. Inst. CPA's, Fla. Inst. CPA's, Palm Beach County Bar Assn., South Fla. Republican. Office: Ruden McClosky Smith Schuster & Russell PA PO Box 1900 Fort Lauderdale FL 33302-1900

STANLEY, CLYDE VAUGHAN, III, librarian; b. Martinsville, Va., June 27, 1950; s. Clyde Vaughan S. Jr. and Patricia Meighan; m. Margaret Elizabeth Gillie, Sept. 23, 1989; children: Thomas Crockett, William Vaughan. BA in History, Davidson Coll., 1973; MA in History, Virginia Tech., 1975; MA in Librarianship, U. Chgo., 1984. Adj. faculty Blue Ridge C.C., Weyers Cave, Va., 1975-78; asst. libr. SUNY, Oswego, 1982-85, Spring Hill Coll., Mobile, Ala., 1985-86; assoc. exec. dir. Stratford Hall Plantation, Stratford, Va., 1986-92; spl. collections libr. Washington & Lee U., Lexington, Va., 1993—. Author: A Guide to the Manuscripts Collection of the James Graham Leyburn Library, 1995; contbr. articles to periodicals. Mem. ALA, Lexington (Va.) Rotary Club (bd. dirs. 1996—), Va. Libr. Assn., Soc. Am. Archivists, Mid-Atlantic Regional Archives Conf., Rockbridge Hist. Soc. (bd. dirs. 1995—). Home: 2054 Forest Ave Buena Vista VA 24416 Office: Washington & Lee U James G Leyburn Libr Lexington VA 24450

STANLEY, DAVID WAYNE, utilities executive; b. Ft. Lauderdale, Fla., Aug. 7, 1953; s. Palmer Wayne and Margaret Theresa (Linardy) S.; m. Rosemary Collins, June 18, 1983; children: Kristen, Jonathan, Michael. AA, Palm Beach Jr. Coll., Lake Worth, Fla., 1973; BS in Civil Engring., U. Fla., 1976; MBA, U. North Fla., 1983. Registered profl. engr., Fla.; cert. gen. contractor, Fla. Crew foreman Stuart (Fla.) Flooring, 1971-75, office mgr., 1975-76; engr. Jacksonville (Fla.) Electric Authority, 1976-78, civil engring. supr., 1978-81, divsn. chief power engring. plant, 1981-84, divsn. chief new fossil generation, 1984-85, divsn. chief major projects, 1985-88, divsn. chief project mgmt., 1988-96; v.p. power supply projects group Jacksonville (FLa.) Electric Authority, 1996—; project mgr. St. Johns River Power Pk., Jacksonville, 1984-85, St. John's River Coal Terminal, 1985-88; initial devel. mgr. quality improvement program Jacksonville Electric Authority, 1985-86, charter mem. ethics com., 1990-92. Group leader Indian princess program YMCA, Orange Park, Fla., 1991-92. Recipient Outstanding Engring. Achievement award NSPE, 1990, Cert. Engring. Excellence award Assn. Cons. Engrs., 1990, Honor award Cons. Engring. Coun., 1990. Roman Catholic. Office: Jacksonville Electric Authority 21 W Church St Jacksonville FL 32202-3155

STANLEY, JAMES GORDON, retired engineering marketing executive, writer; b. Birmingham, Ala., Feb. 13, 1925; s. Joseph Gordon and Amy I. (Crocker) S.; BS, U. Ala., 1949; m. children: Cynthia Ruth, Pamela Anne, Gordon Bruce, James Alan, Joseph Christopher; m. Patricia Ann Peuvion, 1969. Instr., Miss. State U. Extension, Jackson, 1956; tech. rep. S.E., Price Brothers Co., Dayton, 1957-59; project mgr., dept. mgr. Brown Engring. Co., Kennedy Space Ctr., Fla. and Huntsville, Ala., 1959-64; dir. engring., reliability Bendix Launch Support Div., 1964-67; mgr. reliability, systems engr. Dow Chem. Co., Kennedy Space Ctr., 1967-71, mgr. engring. mktg. Houston, 1971-73, contract rsch. mgr., Midland, Mich., 1973-80, sr. project mgr. Houston, 1980-93, assigned as project bus. mgr. Dow/Dept. Energy geothermal project, Lafayette, La., 1981-83; project engr. Merrell Dow Pharms., Cin., 1987-88; project mgr. Admiral Equipment Co., Akron, Ohio, 1988-89; geothermal project mgr. Magma Power Co., Calipatria, Calif., 1989-92, ret. 1993; free lance writer. Contbg. editor, energy columnist Nat. Def. Mag., 1979-84. Served to lt. (j.g.) USNR, 1943-66. Recipient Toulmin medal for best article Mil. Engr. Mag., 1980. Mem. Cocoa Beach C. of C., Am. Philatelic Soc., Elks, Phi Gamma Delta. Baptist. Home: 2947 Meadowgrass Ln Houston TX 77082-1850

STANLEY, MARJORIE THINES, financial educator; b. Ashland, Wis., Feb. 20, 1928; d. Harold Wallace and Ruth Helen (Melstrand) Thines; m. John Deane Stanley, Feb. 17, 1951 (div. 1976); children: John Harold, William Deane. BA, U. Wis., 1949; MA, Ind. U., 1950, PhD, 1953; MDiv, Seabury Western Theol. Sem., 1988. Instr. econs. U. Ark., 1953-54, asst. prof. econs. Bur. Bus. Rsch., 1954-55; adj. prof. econs. Tex. Christian U., Ft. Worth, 1964, 65-66, adj. prof. fin., 1966-72, assoc. prof. fin., 1972-82, chmn. dept. fin. and decision sci., 1983-86, prof. fin. M. J. Neeley Sch. Bus., 1982-94, emeritus prof. M.J. Neeley Sch. Bus., 1994—; vis. prof. fin., scholar in residence Inst. for Bus. Ethics, De Paul U., Chgo., 1986-87; lectr. in field; researcher Weltwirtschaft Archiv, Hamburg, Fed. Republic Germany, 1979; mem. U.S. Dept. Commerce Dist. Export Coun., 1977-81, chmn. fin. task force, 1977-79;. Author: The Irwin Guide to Investing in Emerging Markets, 1995; contbr. articles to profl. publs.; mem. editl. bd. Jour. Internat. Fin., 1988-92, Jour. Internat. Bus. Studies, 1981-83, Internat. Trade Jour., 1988-92; referee various publs. in field. Trustee St. Alban's Episcopal Sch., Arlington, Tex., 1970-81. Millis fellow, 1949-50, All-Univ. fellow Ind. U., 1950-51, 51-52; grantee Tex. Christian U. Rsch. Found., 1977-78, 78-80, Sid Richardson Found., 1977, 78, 79, 80, M. J. Neeley Sch. Bus., 1981-86; European Econ. Community grantee, Inst. European Studies and Exxon Edn. Found., 1983. Mem. Am. Fin. Assn., Fin. Mgmt. Assn., Acad. Internat. Bus. (S.W. regional chair 1981-84), Bus. Assn. Latin Am. Studies (exec. com. mem. at large 1992-93), Soc. for Bus. Ethics, Am. Econ. Assn., Southwestern Fin. Assn. (bd. dirs. 1985-87). Office: Tex Christian U Box 298530 Fort Worth TX 76129

STANLEY, MELINDA LOUISE, mental health nurse, oncology researcher; b. Tyler, Tex., July 13, 1971; d. Jerry Luther and Joyce Louise (Kinard) S. ADN, Tyler Jr. Coll., 1992; BSN magna cum laude, U. Tex., Tyler, 1995. RN, Tex. Staff nurse East Tex. Med. Ctr. Hosp., Tyler, 1991-92, Tyler Rehab. Hosp., 1993-96, East Tex. Med. Ctr. Behavioral Health, Tyler, 1996—; presenter, lectr. on cmty. cancer awareness, prevention of breast cancer, Tyler, 1994—. Mem. ANA, Tex. Nurses Assn., Profl. Women's Assn., U. Tex. Alumni Assn., Sigma Theta Tau (Alpha Chi Honor Soc.).

STANLEY, ROBERT WARREN, association executive; b. Washington, Oct. 26, 1941; s. Herbert Homer and Ida Virginia S. B.A., U. Md., 1963. Editorial asst. personnel services Washington Gas Light Co., 1963-68; asst. coordinator Project Interchange, NEA, Washington, 1968-70; advt. and promotions mgr., membership dir. Assn. Supervision and Curriculum Devel., Washington, 1970-71; exec. dir. Nat. Assn. Floor Covering Installers, Washington, 1971-74; exec. v.p. Nat. Glass Dealers Assn., Washington, 1974-82; v.p. Orgn. Mgmt. Services Internat., 1982-83; exec. dir. Nat. Assn. Dental Labs., 1983—; v.p., sec. Robwood Interiors/Desks etc., Leesburg, Va., 1991-94; v.p. Table Works Plus, Leesburg, 1994—; mem. nat. adv. coun. Am. Subcontractors Assn., 1974-82; bd. dirs. Glass and Metal Inst., 1974-82, Nat. Constrn. Employees Coun., 1975-82; chmn. Consumer Safety Glazing Com., 1974-75, sec.-treas., 1978-82; sec. Auto Glass Industry Com. Hwy. Safety, 1975-82; co-chmn. Constrn. Industry Nat. Legis. Conf., 1975-82; chmn. task force U.S. C. of C.-sponsored Insts. Orgn. Mgmt., 1978-79; bd. dirs., trustee advisor Am. Fund for Dental Health, 1983-95, bd. dirs. Oral Health Am., 1995—; advisor Nat. Found. for Dentistry for Handicapped, 1988—. Author booklets, articles in field. Served with USAR, 1965. Recipient cert. of merit Nat. Glass Dealers Assn., 1975, Spl. Leadership Achievement award Nat. Assn. Dental Labs., 1987, 88, Merit award , 1988. Mem. Am. Soc. Assn. Execs., Nat. Assn. Exposition Mgrs., Nat. Assn. Execs. Club, Greater Washington Soc. Assn. Execs., Found. for Internat. Meetings (founding mem., bd. dirs. 1972-76, exec. com. 1977-82). Democrat. Episcopalian. Clubs: Masons, Shriners. Home: 9303 Clanbrook Ct Fairfax VA 22031-1910 Office: 555 E Braddock Rd Alexandria VA 22314-2106

STANLEY, SHIRLEY DAVIS, artist; b. Mt. Vernon, N.Y., Dec. 5, 1929; d. Walter Thompson and Elsie Viola (Lumpp) Davis; m. Charles B. Coble Jr., June 11, 1951 (div. 1968); children: Jennifer Susan Farmer, Charles B. Coble III; m. Marvin M. Stanley, Dec. 18, 1983 (dec.). BA in Home Econs. and Gen. Sci., Greensboro Coll., 1951; grad., Real Estate Inst., 1962. Tchr. Dryher H.S., Columbia, S.C., 1951-52, Haw River (N.C.) Sch., 1954-56, Alexander Wilson Sch., Graham, N.C., 1957-58; guest essayist for news Mebane (N.C.) Enterprise, 1955-56; pres. Shirley, Inc., Burlington, N.C., 1962-94; artist, 1956—. One woman show Art Gallery Originals, Winston-Salem, 1976, Olive Garden Gallery, 21st Century Gallery, Williamsburg, Va., numerous galleries in Fla., N.C. Bd. dirs. Girl Scouts Am., Burlington, 1961; life mem. Rep. Inner Cir., Washington, 1990—; active Salvation Army; vol. fund raiser Physicians for Peace; com. mem. York County Rep. Party, 1995; vol. disaster & blood banks ARC, 1990—; founding mem. Am. Air Force Mus. Recipient Rep. Medal of Freedom, 1994. Mem. AAUW, Am. Watercolor Soc. (assoc.), Va. Watercolor Soc., Nat. Soc. Amateur Dancers, Sierra Club, Williamsburg Bibliophiles. Episcopalian. Home and Studio: 103 Little John Rd Williamsburg VA 23185-4907

STANLEY-CHAVIS, SANDRA ORNECIA, special education educator, consultant; b. Jersey City, July 6, 1950; d. McKinley and Thelma Louise (Newberry) S. BA, Ottawa (Kans.) U., 1972; MS in Edn., U. Kass., 1975, PhD (fellow), 1980; postgrad. St. George's U. Sch. Medicine, Grenada, W.I. Dir., head tchr. Salem Bapt. Nursery Sch., Jersey City, 1972-73; spl. ednl. instr. Joan Davis Sch. Spl. Edn., Kansas City, Mo., 1975-76; instructional media/materials trainee, then rsch. asst. U. Kans. Med. Ctr., 1976-79; rsch. asst. U. Kans., Lawrence, 1979; dir., coord. tng. and observation Juniper Gardens Children's project Bur. Child Rsch., U. Kans., Kansas City, 1979-82, rsch. assoc., 1980; psychol assoc., ednl. cons. family crisis unit Internat. Youth Orgn., 1988-93; ednl. cons. Renaissance Ctr., 1994; exec. dir. 2000 Friends, 1994; asst. prof. spl. edn., Albany (Ga.) State Coll., 1995—; pres. Dare to Dream, Inc.; lectr., speaker, cons. edn. and med. sci. Author papers and manuals in field. Past mem. adv. bd. Rainbows for All God's Children. Christian Community Health fellow; scholar Coll. Women, Inc., 1977; Easter Seal grantee, 1975; recipient various awards, plaques, certs. of recognition. Mem. Christian Med. and Dental Soc., The Coun. of Exceptional Children, Assn. for Supervision and Curriculum devel., Nat Coun. for Learing disability Am. Assn U. Women Women's Ednl. Network, past mem. Home: 2301 Beattie Rd Albany GA 31707-2105

STANO, CARL RANDOLPH (RANDY STANO), newspaper editor, art director, educator; b. Russellville, Ark., Apr. 1, 1948; s. Carl J. Stano and Martha Lee (Linton) Partain. AA, San Jacinto Coll., 1968; BS in Edn., U. Tex., Austin, 1971; MA, Syracuse U., 1979. Cert. tchr., Tex. Dir. student publs., tchr. A.N. McCallum High Sch., Austin, Tex., 1971-78; grad. asst. S.I. Newhouse Sch. Pub. Communications Syracuse (N.Y.) U., 1978-79; asst. editor, art dir. Kansas City (Mo.) Star Times, 1980-81; dir. graphic arts Democrat and Chronicle, Rochester, N.Y., 1981-85; dir. editorial art and design The Miami (Fla.) Herald, 1985-95; Knight prof. commn. U. Miami, Coral Gables, Fla., 1995—; assoc. dir. for the Advance Media Ctr. U. Miami, Coral Gables, 1996—; bd. dirs. PBC Internat. Publ.; instr. summer workshops U. Tex., Austin, U. Iowa, Ball State U., Columbia U., Tex. Tech U., U. Okla., U. Houston, N.Mex. State U., Syracuse U., Kans. State U., Ctrl. Mich. State U., Ouachita State Bapt. U., 1970—; instr., lectr. Syracuse U., 1980, 1982-83, St. John Fisher Coll., Rochester, 1983-85, U. Miami, 1985-95; instr. profl. seminars Poynter Inst. for Media Studies, So. Newpapers Pubs. Assn.; chmn. SND Quick Course, 1996. Newspaper redesigns Democrat and Chronicle, 1982, Olympian, Olympia, Wash., 1985, Sentinel Newspapers, East Brunswick, N.J., 1986, Jacksonville, N.C. Daily News,1988, El Nuevo Herald, 1987, Miami Herald, 1991, Daily Record, Dunn, N.C., 1996. Recipient numerous Tex. State H.S. awards, 1971-78, Edith Fox King Tchg. award Tex. Interscholastic League Press Conf., Austin, 1972, Tex. H.S. Jour. Tchr. of Yr. award, 1974, Lifetime Achievement award Am. Student Press Assn., 1989, Nat. Jour. Tchr. of Yr. award Newspaper Fund and Wall St. Jour., Princeton, N.J., 1974, mem. Pub. Svc. award team Miami Herald, 1993; mem. Pulitzer Prize reporting team Kansas City Times/Star, 1981; named to Nat. Scholastic Journalism Hall of Fame U. Okla., 1987, Gallery of Profls. S.I. Newhouse Sch. Pub. Commns. Syracuse U., 1994. Mem. Soc. Newspaper Design (contest chmn. 6th edit. 1985e, southeast chmn. 1985-89, competition chmn. 1987-90, sec. 1989, exec. bd. dirs. 1989-93, 2d v.p. 1990, 1st v.p. 1991, pres. 1992, immediate past pres. 1993, excellence awards 3d-17th edits., bronze award 1991, 92, 93, silver award 1983, 85, 89-95, gold award 1986, 89, 92, Best of Show, 1992), Fla. Soc. News Editors (illustration graphic award 1987, 88, 90-96, page design award 1988, 90-96, print mag. award 1989-92), Columbia Scholastic Press Advisors Assn. (Gold Key award 1980, five Trendsetter awards 1975-77), Nat. Scholastic Press Assn. (3 five-star/Pacemaker awards). Home: 4718 SW 67th Ave Apt 8B Miami FL 33155-6849 Office: U Miami Sch Comm 121C Merrick Bldg Coral Gables FL 33124-2030

STANSBURY, HARRY CASE, state commissioner. BS in Gen. Studies, La. State U., 1968; JD, Loyola U., New Orleans, 1971; student, Oxford (Eng.) U., 1985, Harvard U., 1988. Bar: La., N.Y., D.C., U.S. Supreme Ct., U.S. Ct. Appeals (1st-11th cirs., D.C. cir., fed. cir.), U.S. Ct. Mil. Appeals, U.S. Ct. Fed. Claims, U.S. Ct. Internat. Trade, U.S. Tax Ct., U.S. Dist. Ct. (ea., mid. and we. dists.) La., U.S. Dist. Ct. (ea., no., so. and we. dists.) N.Y., U.S. Dist. Ct. D.C. Staff atty. La. Securities Commn., New Orleans, 1971-75, dep. commr. securities, 1975—; mem. liaison com. fed. securities code project Am. Law Inst.-ABA, 1974-80; speaker, expert witness in field. Contbr. articles to profl. jours. Mem. ABA (sect. bus. law, sect. internat. law and practice, sect. legal edn. and admissions to bar, mem. subcom. derivative instruments fed. regulation securities com. 1993—), N.Am. Securities Adminstrs. Assn. (mem. registration exemption com. 1991—), La. State Bar Assn. (sect. corp. and bus. law, mem. internat. law com. 1991-92), N.Y. State Bar Assn. (banking, corp. and bus. law sect.), D.C. Bar Assn. (corp., fin. and securities law divsn.), Assn. of Bar of City of N.Y., Assn. of Bar of D.C., New Orleans Bar Assn. (vice chair corps. and bus. law com. 1992-94, chair 1994—), Fed. Bar Assn. (fin. instns. and economy sect.), Internat. Bar Assn. (sect. bus. law, mem. issues and trading in securities com. 1991—), La. State U. Alumni Assn., Loyola Law Alumni Assn., Harvard Law Sch. Assn., Am. Friends Rewley House, Supreme Ct. Hist. Soc. Office: La Office Securities 1100 Poydras St Ste 2250 New Orleans LA 70163-1100

STANSELL, AISZELEEN, secondary school educator; b. Tyler, Tex., July 1, 1939; d. Clarence and Laura (Ates) Williams; m. Ross Earl Stansell, June 5, 1965; 1 child: Melanie Denise. BA, Texas Coll., 1962; MS, East Tex. State U., 1975. Tchr Corsicana (Tex.) Ind. Sch. Dist., 1962-67; bookkeeper Tyler (Tex.) Bank and Trust Co., 1968-71; tchr. Whitehouse (Tex.) Ind. Sch. Dist., 1971—. Mem. NEA, Tex. State Tchrs. Assn., Tex. Classroom Tchrs. Assn., Nat. Coun. Tchrs. Math., Math. Assn. Am., Top Ladies of Distinction, Order The Eastern Star. Home: 18313 Fm Rd # 756 Whitehouse TX 75791

STANSELL, LELAND EDWIN, JR., lawyer, educator; b. Central, S.C., July 13, 1934; s. Leland Edwin and Hettie Katherine (Hollis) S.; children: James Leland, Susan. BS, Fla. So. Coll., 1957; LLB, U. Miami (Fla.), 1961, JD, 1968. Bar: Fla. 1961. Assoc. Wicker & Smith, Miami, 1961-62, ptnr., 1962-75; sole practice, Miami, 1975-87; ptnr. Stansell & Rice, 1987-94; pvt. practice, Leland E. Stansell, Jr. P.A., 1995—; chmn. Appellate Jud. Nominating Com., Dade County (Fla.), 1983-87; adv. coun. Am. Arbitration Assn., 1975-90. Served with U.S. Army, 1957. Mem. U. Miami Law Alumni Assn. (dir., officer, pres. 1968-69), Dade County Bar Assn. (dir. 1969-72, exec. com. 1974-75, pres. 1975-76), Fla. Bar (bd. govs. 1966-70, 70-80), ABA (house of dels. 1982-86), Fla. Criminal Def. Attys. Assn. (treas. 1964-66), Am. Judicature Soc., Am. Bd. Trial Advs., Internat. Assn. Def. Counsel, Fedn. Ins. Counsel, Miami Beach Rod and Reel Club (pres.), Coral Reef Yacht Club, Jockey Club, Bankers Club, Ocean Reef Yacht Club, Delta Theta Phi (pres. Miami alumni chpt. 1966, regional dir. 1968). Office: 19 W Flagler St Miami FL 33130

STANSELL, ROBIN LOWEL, aeronautical engineer, pilot; b. Clearwater, Fla., Apr. 12, 1946; s. William Theron and Iva Lorane (Pursley) S.; m. Bonnie Ree Oesch, Sept. 25, 1973. AA in Gen. Studies, Hartnell Coll., 1977; BS in Profl. Aeronautics, Embry Riddle U., 1990. Chief warrant officer U.S. Army, 1964; x-ray technician U.S. Army, Germany, 1965-68; helicopter pilot U.S. Army, Vietnam and Germany, 1969-73, U.S., Germany, 1975-89; helicopter pilot Petroleum Helicopters Inc., Lafayette, La., 1973; asst. mgr. Air Marine Inc., Patterson, La., 1974-75; engring. test pilot Rockwell Internat., Shreveport, La., 1989—. Mem. Shreveport Kennel Club (treas. 1991-92, 95—, pres. 1993-94). Republican. Home: PO Box 1053 Waskom TX 75692 Office: Rockwell Internat 6990 Challenger Dr Shreveport LA 71109

STANTON, DONALD SHELDON, academic administrator; b. Balt., June 8, 1932; s. Kenneth Gladstone and Dorothy Erma (Hettrick) S.; m. Barbara Mae Hoot, June 25, 1955; children: Dale Richard, Debra Carol, Diane Karen. AB, Western Md. Coll., 1953, LLD, 1981; MDiv magna cum laude, Wesley Theol. Sem., 1956; MA, Am. U., 1960; Ed.D., U. Va., 1965; L.H.D., Columbia Coll., 1979; Litt.D., Albion Coll., 1983. Ordained to ministry United Methodist Ch., 1956; pastor Balt. and Va. confs. United Meth. Ch., 1953-59; dir. Richmond (Va.) Area Wesley Found., 1959-63; chaplain, dean of students Greensboro Coll., 1963-65; chaplain Wofford Coll., 1965-69; dir. office coll. services United Meth. Div. Higher Edn., Nashville, 1969-75; v.p. for devel. Wesleyan Coll., 1975-78; pres. Adrian Coll., 1978-88, Oglethorpe U., Atlanta, 1988—; adminstr., prof. European internat. ednl. programs, summers 1960, 69-71, 73; chmn. pres.'s assn. Mich. Intercollegiate Athletic Assn., 1986-87; mem. exec. com. Mich. Colls. Found., 1985-88. Contbr. articles, revs. to profl. publs. in U.S., Japan, Argentina, chpts. to books; editor: Faculty Forum, 1972-74; bass-baritone soloist. Bd. dirs. Toledo (Ohio) Symphony, 1980-83, Lewanee County Jr. Achievement, 1980-83; chair bd. trustees U. Ctr. Ga., 1994-96; mem. exec. com. So. Collegiate Athletic Conf., 1995—; bd. dirs. Found. Ind. Higher Edn., 1996—. Adminstrn. bldg. at Adrian Coll. named in honor of Stanton and his wife, 1988. Mem. Am. Assn. Univ. Adminstrs. (bd. dirs. 1990-93), Ga. Assn. Colls. (pres. 1992), Soc. Wesley (Disting. Alumni Recognition award 1988), Ga. Found. for Ind. Colls. (vice chair 1992), Nat. Assn. Ind. Colls. and Univs. (past mem. pub. rels. com.), Commerce Club, Rotary, Omicron Delta Kappa, Order of Omega, Tau Kappa Epsilon, Psi Chi, Phi Eta Sigma. Home: 1571 Windsor Pky NE Atlanta GA 30319-2740 Office: Oglethorpe U Office of Pres 4484 Peachtree Rd NE Atlanta GA 30319-2737

STANTON, EDWARD F., Spanish language educator; b. Colorado Springs, Oct. 29, 1942; s. Edward F. and Rose E. (Sunseri) S.; children: Daniel, Carlos; m. Melissa A. McEuen. BA, UCLA, 1964, MA, 1969, PhD, 1972. Asst. prof. U. Ky., Lexington, 1972-78, assoc. prof., 1978-88, prof. Spanish, 1988—; vis. Fulbright scholar U.S. Govt., Argentina, Uruguay, 1990; vis. prof. summer program Universidad Complutense, Ronda, Spain, 1996. Author: Road of Stars to Santiago, 1994, Hemingway and Spain, 1989, The Tragic Myth, 1978. With U.S. Army, 1966-67. Mem. Hemingway Soc., Friends of Camino de Santiago. Office: Dept of Spanish U Ky Lexington KY 40506-0027

STANTON, GEORGE PATRICK, JR., lawyer; b. Fairmont, W.Va., Nov. 21, 1933; s. George Patrick and Wilma Roberta (Everson) S.; m. Shirley Jean Champ, Sept. 3, 1956; children—George Patrick, Edward Scott. B.S. in Bus. Adminstrn., Fairmont Coll., 1956; M.B.A. in Fin., U. Dayton, 1969; J.D., U. Balt., 1977. Bar: Md. 1978, U.S. Dist. Ct. Md. 1978, W.Va. 1979, U.S. Dist. Ct. (so. dist.) W.Va. 1979, U.S. Dist. Ct. (no. dist.) W.Va. 1980, U.S. Ct. Appeals (4th cir.) 1985. Auditor 1st Nat. Bank Fairmont, 1955-61; asst. cashier S.C. Nat. Bank, Columbia, 1961-64; sr. systems analyst Chase Manhattan Bank, N.Y.C., 1964-65; asst. v.p. Winters Nat. Bank, Dayton, Ohio, 1965-69, Md. Nat. Bank, Balt., 1969-74; v.p. Equitable Trust Co., Balt., 1974-79; gen. ptnr. Stanton & Stanton Attys. at Law, Fairmont, 1979—; staff sect. leader, mem. faculty Sch. for Bank Adminstrn. U. Wis.-Madison, 1978-89. Treas. Mountaineer Area council Boy Scouts Am., Fairmont, 1982-90; pres. Three Rivers Coal Festival, Inc., Fairmont, 1984-85, pres., 1985-86, bd. dirs. 1982-86; pres. Appalachian Coal Festival, 1985-86, bd. dirs. 1985—; mem. adv. bd. Inst. for Living, Fairmont, 1983-85; pres. Firemans' Civil Svc. Commn., Fairmont, W.Va., 1992—. Mem. ABA, Assn. Trial Lawyers Am., Comml. Law League Am., W.Va. State Bar Assn., Marion County Bar Assn., Md. State Bar Assn., W.Va. Trial Lawyers Assn., Marion County C. of C. (bd. dirs. 1983—), Fairmont State Coll. Alumni Assn. (bd. dirs. 1982—, pres. 1992-94). Club: Fairmont Field. Lodges: Rotary, Masons. Home: 2 W Hills Dr Fairmont WV 26554-5015 Office: Stanton & Stanton PO Box 968 Ste 707 Fairmont WV 26555-0968

STANTON, JACK PERSHING, chemical engineer; b. Chgo., Nov. 2, 1919; s. Joseph Patrick Stanton and Henriette (Fourestie) Berry; m. Virginia Gail Dudek Myers, Mar. 27, 1947; children: D. Larry, J. Terry, Maureen Lee. Student, U. Ill., 1939-43, Ill. Inst. Tech., 1944; student chem. engring., Ctrl. YMCA Coll., 1938. Registered profl. engr. Chem. engr. The Pure Oil Co., Northfield, Ill., 1943-47; asst. supt. The Pure Oil Co., Van, Tex., 1947-48; resident chemist The Pure Oil Co., Worland, Wyo., 1948-50; mgr. oil testing, cons. Comml. Testing and Engring., Chgo., 1950-52; chem. engr., product mgr. to mgr. new products application Nalco Chem. Co., Chgo., 1952-57; product mgr. corrosion control Visco div. Nalco Chem. Co., Houston, 1957-60; regional mgr. So. S.Am. Internat. divsn., Nalco Chem. Co., Buenos Aires, 1960-62; v.p. Oilwell Rsch. Co., Dallas, 1962-63; tech. dir. Cochrane Chem. Co., Wewoka, Okla., 1963-64; pres., cons. Am. Coordinated Technologists Inc., Houston, 1964-73; real estate investor R-Innovators, Houston, 1973-78, residential builder, 1978-93. Author: They Never Rise Again, 1991-92; inventor chem. applications, yacht design, constrn. techniques; contbr. articles to profl. jours. Pub. address speaker Houston Bd. Edn., 1993, United We Stand Am., 1993; founder Peoples' Activist Leaders' Soc. and Voters Vanguard, 1993-94. Mem. ASTM (com. chmn. Indsl., nat. vice chmn.). Home and Office: Voters Vanguard 2400 Ardilla Atascadero CA 93422

STANTON, JOHN JEFFREY, editor, broadcast journalist, government programs director, analyst; b. Wichita Falls, Tex., July 19, 1956; s. John Joseph Jr. and Joan (Marley) S.; m. Scylla Maria Silva, Jan. 6, 1981; 1 child, Damien Kristian. BS in Pub. Adminstrn. and Bus. Adminstrn., Nichols Coll., 1978; M in Pub. Adminstrn., U. Detroit, 1980. Rsch. asst. Am. Enterprise Inst., Washington, 1977; rep. aide R.I. Ho. of Reps., Providence, 1977-78; mng. editor Am. Politics, Washington, 1982, assoc. editor, 1983, corp. advisor, 1984, sr. editor, 1985-87; editor, govt. programs mgr. ENTEK, Alexandria, Va., 1988-90; govt. programs dir., cons. Tuckerman Group, Springfield, Va., 1991; comm. industry writer Arlington, Va., 1991—; program dir. TeleStrategies, McLean, Va., 1991-93; Washington corr., editorial bd. mem. Tech. Transfer Jour., 1994—; editor Tech. Transfer Newsletter; asst. to pres., info. transfer specialist Am. Def. Preparedness Assn., Arlington, 1994—; creator, co-host (radio programs) Power Breakfast, Sta. WNTR, Washington, 1987, Am. Politics Radio, 1987; frequent guest broadcast journalist Stas. WNTR, WAMU-NPR, Washington, WBAL, Balt. and Washington areas. Polit. campaign cons. to Glenn Tenney, 1992—; commr. Arlington Little League Baseball, 1993; mem. Arlington Edn. Adv. Com. Recipient Doers Honoree The Washington Times, 1988. Roman Catholic.

STANTON, JOHN WALKER, management educator, tour director, poet; b. Casablanca, Morocco, May 2, 1937; s. Willard Quincy and Madeleine Frances (O'Brien) S.; m. Rebecca Dearborn, Jan. 3, 1962; children: Willard, Madeleine, Abraham, Tara, Erin, Shannon, John. BA, U. So. Miss., 1961; MA, Ctrl. Mo. State U., 1966; JD, U. N.Mex., 1970; LLM, U. Miami, 1973; MPA, Harvard U., 1981. Lawyer various orgns., 1970-85; prof. City Coll. Seattle, 1986-91; prof. mgmt. Sch. Extended Studies, Park Coll., Luke AFB, Ariz., 1991—; vis. prof. La. State U., Shreveport, 1993-95; tour dir., U.S. and overseas, pvt. practice, 1988—. Author: Tomorrow Never Knows, 1995; contbr. articles to profl. jours. Dem. presdl. campaign advisor, Seattle, 1988. With USMC, 1954-57, USAF, 1963-67, Viet Nam. Decorated Bronze Star, USAF, 1967. Poetry selected for Best Poems of 1996. Mem. VFW, Air Commando Assn., Marine Corps Assn., Ret. Officers Assn., Anglican Ch. Am. Anglican. Home: PO Box 1714 Litchfield Park AZ 85340 Office: Park College Education Office Luke AFB AZ 85309

STANTON, ROBERT JOHN, JR., English language educator; b. Manhattan, N.Y., July 7, 1942; s. Robert John Stanton and Mary McGinty; m. Felicia Lena Giancola, Nov. 15, 1959; children: Robert III, Sharon. Instr. English Flagler Coll., St. Augustine, Fla., 1972-74; tchg. asst. U. Mass., Amherst, 1974-77, lectr. in Rhetoric, 1979-81; English tchr. Bishop Kenny H.S., Jacksonville, Fla., 1982-83, Duval County Pub. Schs., Jacksonville, 1984-87; asst. prof. English Jacksonville U., 1987-91, assoc. prof. English, 1992-96, chmn. divsn. humanities, 1993—. Author: Seventeen British Novelists, 1978, Gore Vidal, 1978, Truman Capote, 1980, Views From A Window: Conversations with Gore Vidal, 1980; co-author: Beneath Mad River Mansion, 1992, Noah's Orbella, 1994, The Devil's Rood, 1996. Mem. MLA, Nat. Assn. Tchrs. English, Fla. Assn. Depts. English (pres. 1996), Swift River (Mass.) Hist. Soc. Democrat. Home: 614 15th Ave South Jacksonville Beach FL 32250 Office: Jacksonville Univ Jacksonville FL 32211

STANTON, SYLVIA DOUCET, small business owner; b. New Orleans, Sept. 21, 1935; d. Clifton Leo Sr. and Maria Del Vel (Alfonso Swiber) Doucet; m. Robert Elmer Stanton, Jan. 3, 1953; children: Robert, Sylvia, Barbara, Richard, Laura, Cheri. Grad. high sch., New Orleans, 1952. Real estate agt. Century 21, Slidell, La., 1982-88; ptnr. Doucet's Jewelry, Slidell, 1969-82; owner Plantation Antiques, Slidell, 1974-88, Magnolia Plantation, Slidell, 1988—, Doucet-Stanton Ltd., Slidell, 1988—; appraiser jewelry, antiques, real estate, 1969—; artist, painter, 1950—. Founder Le cotillion, Slidell, 1975; founding chmn. Pres. Coun. of Le Cotillion, 1987. Recieved title of nobility Countess De Miron Del Vel, Greece, 1988. Mem. Ozone Camellia Club, Picayune Garden Club, Bayou Liberty Garden Club (sec. 1988—), Albuquerque Art League, World Trade Ctr., Inner Wheel (dist. chmn. 6840 1990-91, founding pres. Slidell 1989). Republican. Roman Catholic. Home: 110 Williamsburg Rd Picayune MS 39466-8415 Office: Doucet-Stanton Ltd 857 Brownswitch Rd Slidell LA 70458-3041 Also: Doucet-Stanton Mktg 110 Grand Hotel Ct Saint Thomas VI 00802

STAPLE, BRUCE WILLIAM, acoustical engineer; b. Bklyn., Aug. 31, 1935; s. Carl and Sylvia (Shapiro) S. Grad., RCA Inst., N.Y.C., 1957. Lab. technician Hazeltine Elec., Bayside, N.Y., 1953-55; group leader quality RCA Victor Studios, N.Y.C., 1956-61; pres., chief engr. Allegro Sound Studios, N.Y.C., 1961-71; engring. cons. N.Y.C., 1972-74; exec. dir. Elec. Lady Studios, N.Y.C., 1974-76; v.p., gen. mgr. Soundmixer/Sound One, N.Y.C., 1976-81; prin. staff acoustical engr. Motorola, Plantation, Fla., 1983—; acoustical cons., Ft. Lauderdale, Fla., 1982—. Author: Determining Speech Intelligibility of a Transceiver in a Customers Environment, 1993. With U.S. Army, 1958-60. Mem. IEEE, Audio Engring. Soc., Acoustical Soc. Am., Am. Loudspeaker Mfrs. Assn. Office: Motorola 8000 W Sunrise Blvd Plantation FL 33322-4104

STAPLES, STEVEN RAY, school system administrator, education educator; b. Ettrick, Va., Apr. 9, 1954; s. William Snead and Mildred Gertrude (Cummins) S.; m. Barbara Carol Blaha, July 26, 1980; children: Kelsey Paige, Audrey Rae. BA in History, Coll. William and Mary, 1976, MEd, 1983; EdD in Edn. Adminstrn., Va. Tech., 1990. Pub. sch. tchr. Prince George (Va.) County Schs., 1976-84, asst. prin. H.S., 1984-85; prin. H.S. Hopewell (Va.) City Schs., 1985-88; asst. supt. Montgomery County Schs., Christiansburg, Va., 1988-91; supt. schs. York County Schs., Yorktown, Va., 1991—; adj. prof. Coll. of William and Mary, Williamsburg, Va., 1994—. Bd. dirs. Am. Heart Assn., Newport News, Va., 1991—, Boy Scout Coun., Newport News, 1994—, Greater Peninsula United Way, Newport News, 1995—. Named Educator of Yr., Drug Abuse Resistance Edn. Va., Richmond, 1995, Va. Supt. of Yr., Va. Assn. Sch. Supts., Charlottesville, Va., 1996—, Region II Supt. of Yr., Va. Assn. Sch. Supts., Charlottesville, 1996—. Mem. ASCD, Newport News Reading Coun., Grafton Kiwanis Club (club chmn. 1991—), Phi Delta Kappa. Roman Catholic. Home: 304 Autumn Way Yorktown VA 23693 Office: York County Pub Schs 302 Dare Rd Yorktown VA 23692

STAPLETON, CLAUDIA ANN, city official; b. Memphis, July 14, 1947; m. Mark Phillip Stapleton, Sept. 18, 1985. Student, Tex. Tech. U., 1976-77; AS, Amarillo Coll., 1995; student, West Tex. A&M U., 1990—. Code enforcement officer City of Lubbock, Tex., 1975-85; owner, operator Claudia Stapleton Consulting, Amarillo, Tex., 1985—; code enforcement officer City of Amarillo, 1990—; cons. in field. Mem. NAFE, Nat. Elec. Sign Assn., Tex. Assn. Legal Secs., Tex. Heritage, Am. Bus. Women's Assn., Code Enforcement Assn. of Tex. (2d v.p.), Beta Sigma Phi. Republican. Methodist. Home: 3321 Lenwood Dr Amarillo TX 79109-3345 Office: City of Amarillo 509 E 7th Ave Amarillo TX 79101-2539

STAPLETON, JAMES EDWARD, sales executive; b. Terre Haute, Ind., Nov. 7, 1943; s. Edward Anthony and Mary Garnet (Von Der Haar) S.; m. Kathryn Lynn Nevin; children: Jamie, Julie, Gregory. Student, Ind. U., Indpls., 1965-66, Coll. of the Sequoias, Visalia, Calif., 1967-68. Adminstrv. supply technician 451st Field Depot, Indpls., 1972-76; maint. adminstrv. technician 123rd Area Maint. Army Res. Command, Ft. Benjamin Harrison, Ind., 1976-78; adminstrv. supply technician Dept. of the Army, Camp Atterbury, Ind., 1978-82; commodity mgr. Supply & Svcs., Berlin, 1982-85; supply sys. analyst Def. Gen. Supply Ctr., Richmond, Va., 1985-93; corp. account exec. fgn. sales Def. Supply Ctr., Richmond, 1993—; advisor in logistics Fgn. Mil. Liaison Officers, Richmond, 1986—. Com. mem. Boy Scouts Am., 1989—. With U.S. Army, 1962-65. Mem. Assn. of U.S. Army (ctrl. Va. chpt. v.p. for programs 1992-96, v.p. for membership 1988-92), Am. Def. Preparedness Assn., Masons, Scottish Rite Bodies. Republican. Baptist. Home: 6036 Statute St Chesterfield VA 23832 Office: DSCR-XB 8000 Jefferson Davis Hwy Richmond VA 23297-5763

STAPLETON, JOHN OWEN, lawyer; b. Montgomery, Ala., July 24, 1951; s. Max O. Stapleton and Margaret (Lois) Gardner; m. Andrea Carol White, Apr. 1973 (div. June 1975); 1 child, Stefanie Michele; m. Nancy Jean Corbett, Sept. 20, 1980; 1 child, Kellie Nichole. BS, U. of Montevallo, 1976; JD, Samford U., 1980. Bar: Fla. 1981, U.S. Dist. Ct. (no. dist.) Fla. 1981, U.S. Ct. Appeals (11th cir.) 1982, U.S. Ct. Appeals (Fed. cir.) 1985, U.S. Dist. Ct. (mid. and so. dist.) Fla. 1993. Assoc. Shimek & Sutherland P.A., Pensacola, Fla., 1981-83; sole practice Pensacola, 1984-91; asst. county atty. Escambia County, Fla., 1992-93, asst. county atty. labor and employment divsn., 1993—; Broward County, Fla. guardian ad litem program 1st Jud. Cir., 1984-88. Democrat. Office: 115 S Andrews Ave Ste 423 Fort Lauderdale FL 33301-1801

STARK, ELIZABETH ANN, home health nurse; b. Wharton, Tex., Apr. 14, 1952; d. Ardell William and Mary Elizabeth (Thomas) Staggs; 1 child, Candice Ann Petersen. BSN cum laude, N.E. La. U., 1989. RN, La.; cert. med.-surg. nurse, home health nurse, ANA. Co-owner, mgr. Staggs Auto Parts, West Monroe, La., 1973-89; weekend nursing supr. Richland Nursing Home, Delhi, La., 1990; PRN staff gyn. clinic Dr. James Truly M.D., West Monroe, 1991; PRN contract work/supplemental staffing Advantage Nursing Svcs., Shreveport, La., 1991-92; staff nurse/charge nurse med.-surg. diabetes unit Glenwood Regional Med. Ctr., West Monroe, 1989-90, charge nurse med.-surg., diabetes unit, 1990-93; case mgr., asst. clin. dir. AlphaCare Home Health Inc., Monroe, 1993-94; DON Med-Care Home Health Inc., Ruston, La., 1994-96; asst. DON Today's Home Health, Inc., Monroe, 1994—. Mem. Strauss Playhouse, Monroe Symphony Orch. Concert Series; flutist Twin City Concert Band; vol. ARC, Monroe, 1994-95. Mem. ANA, La. State Nurses Assn., Nat. Assn. Health Care Quality, Monroe Dist. Nurses Assn. ARC, Am. Diabetes Assn., Med.-Surg. Nurses Assn., Sigma Theta Tau (Lambda Mu chpt.). Home: 117 Davis Ln West Monroe LA 71291 Office: Todays Home Health 810 N 29th St Monroe LA 71201

STARK, NANCY LYNN, critical care nurse; b. Clinton, Ind., July 31, 1956; d. William and Martha Louise (Reed) Gray; m. Matthew Topping Stark, Aug. 4, 1979; children: Matthew Gray, Kyle Reed. BSN, Ind. State U., 1978; MS in Nursing, Ind. U., Indpls., 1985. RN, Ind., Ga. Staff nurse Union Hosp., Terre Haute, Ind., 1978-81, St. Vincent Hosp. and Health Care Ctr., Indpls., 1981-85; head nurse Med. Coll. Ga., Augusta, 1985-86, 91-93, nurse educator, 1986-91, clin. instr. Sch. Nursing, 1990—; acting dir. nursing, critical care divsn. Med. Coll. of Ga., 1992-93, DON critical care divsn., 1993—; cons. on dimensions of critical care nursing, 1989-94. Contbg. author: Nursing Theorists and Their Work, 1989. Mem. AACN (cert., pres. 1990-91), ANA, Am. Trauma Soc., Soc. of Critical Care Medicine, Sigma Theta Tau. Republican. Presbyterian. Home: 595 Country Place Ln Evans GA 30809-8590 Office: Med Coll Ga 15th St # 206 Augusta GA 30901-1014

STARK, NORMAN, secondary school educator; b. Bronx, N.Y., Sept. 15, 1940; s. Martin and Margaret (Neuman) S.; m. Betty Joanne Kelton, Sept. 4, 1994; 1 child, Michelle Allison. Student, Newark State Coll., Union, 1963-69. Creative writing tchr., acting tchr., singles forum tchr., film tchr. Plantation (Fla.) High Sch., 1988; Hoover Mid. Sch. and Palm Bay H.S., Melbourne, Fla., 1995. Editor West Palm Beach News, 1979; screenplay writer, actor. With U.S. Army, 1963-69. Home: 2732 Locksley Rd Melbourne FL 32935

STARKEY, ELIZABETH LARUFFA, accountant; b. Franklin, Ky., May 23, 1947; d. Albert A. and Alma L. (Duer) LaRuffa; m. Jerry L. Starkey, June 14, 1969; children: James, Jonathan. AA, Miami-Dade Jr. Coll., 1967; BS in Math., Fla. State U., 1969; MS in Acctg., U. Houston, 1984. Cert. public acct., math. tchr. Tchr. Dade County, Miami, Fla., 1969-75; mgr. Ernst & Young, Houston, 1984-90; prin. Starkey & Co., Houston, 1990—. Bd. dirs. Am. Cancer Soc., Houston, 1985-87, 90—, legacy and planned giving com., 1987—; mem. Planned Giving and Coun. Houston, Houston Estate and Fin. Forum. Mem. AICPAs, Tex. Soc. CPAs (Houston chpt.), Nat. Soc. Tax Profls., Beta Gamma Sigma, Beta Alpha Psi, Omicron Delta Kappa. Roman Catholic. Home: 4410 Merwin St Houston TX 77027-6714 Office: Starkey & Co Ste 358 3000 Weslayan St Houston TX 77027-5753

STARKEY, RUSSELL BRUCE, JR., utilities executive; b. Lumberport, W.Va., July 20, 1942; s. Russell Bruce and Dorotha Mable (Field) S.; m. Joan McClellan, May 27, 1966; children: Christine, Pamela, Joanne. BS, Miami U., Oxford, Ohio, 1964; grad. student U. New Haven, 1972-73, N.C. State U., 1974-75, U.S. Navy Schs., 1964-66, 68. Sr. engr., nuclear generation sect. Carolina Power & Light Co., Raleigh, N.C., 1973-74, sr. engr. ops. quality assurance, 1974, prin. engr., 1974-75, quality assurance supr. Brunswick Steam Electric Plant, Southport, N.C., 1975-76, supt. tech. and adminstrn., 1976, supt. ops. and maintenance, 1976-77, plant mgr. H.B. Robinson Steam Electric Plant, Hartsville, S.C., 1977-83, mgr. environ. services, Raleigh, 1984-85, mgr. nuclear safety and environ. services dept., 1985-88; exec. dir. nuc. prodn. Pub. Svc. Ind., Jeffersonville, 1983-84; mgr. Brunswick Nuclear Project Dept., 1988-89, v.p., 1989-92; v.p. Nuclear Svcs. Dept., 1992-93, cons., 1993-94; exec. v.p. energy mgmt. divsn. Hesco, Inc., 1994; dir. Indsl. Electrotech. Lab. Alternate Energy Corp., 1994—. Served with USN, 1964-73. Mem. Am. Nuclear Soc., Rotary. Home: PO Box 306 Wilsons Mills NC 27593-0306 Office: PO Box 8301 2401 Rsch Dr Raleigh NC 27695-8301

STARKS, CHARLES WILEY, minister; b. Bastian, Va., June 27, 1954; s. Clarence Eugene and Mattiline Mae (Compton) S. BA, Emory and Henry Coll., 1976; MDiv, Emory Univ., 1979, D of Ministry, 1988. Lic. to ministry, 1972; ordained to ministry United Meth. Ch. as deacon, 1977, as elder, 1981. Personnel recruiter and trainer A Christian Ministry in the Nat. Parks, N.Y.C., 1979-80; minister Meadowview United Meth. Ch., Meadowview, Va., 1980-84, Pleasant View United Meth. Ch., Abingdon, Va., 1984-93, First United Meth. Ch., Newport, Tenn., 1993—; adj. prof. of philosophy/religion Va. Highlands Community Coll., Abingdon, 1986-93; coord. Abingdon Dist. Youth, 1980-84; New Life Missioner, 1983—; apptd. counseling elder Holston Conf., supervising pastor, 1985—; mem. Abingdon Dist. Com. on Sueprintendency, 1985-93, Holston Conf. Bd. of Ordained Ministry exec. com., 1985-92, chmn. psychol. testing and assessment com., 1987-92, com. on the Episcopacy, 1990—, task force on conf. strategy and structure for ministry and mission, 1990-92; mem. alumni exec. com. Candler Sch. Theology. Vol. Big Bro., Washington County Big Bro./Big Sister Orgn., 1985-88; chmn. Washington County Office on Youth Svcs. Citizens Bd., 1988-90; mem. Washington County Commonwealth Alliance for Drug Rehab. and Edn., 1989-90, Washington County Multi-Discipline Bd., 1989-90, Washington County Fed. Emergency Mgmt. Authority Bd., 1987-93; mem. bio-med. ethics com. Johnston Meml. Hosp., 1991-93; bd. dirs. Holston Home for Children, 1993—. Named to Outstanding Young Men in Am., 1985; Chaplain of the Day U.S. Senate, Washington, 1989. Mem. United Meth. Assn. of Ch. Bus. Adminstrs., Kiwanis (religious affairs com. 1988), Mason, others. Home: 531 2nd St Newport TN 37821-4041 Office: First United Meth Ch PO Box 35 Newport TN 37821-0035

STARKS, KENNETH MAURICE, elementary school educator, poet; b. Atlanta, Jan. 26, 1970; s. Jerome Edward and Jessica Ruth (Tolbert) S. BA in Biology, Hampton (Va.) U., 1991; MS in Chemistry, Ga. Inst. Tech., 1994. Substitute tchr. Atlanta Pub. Schs., 1994—; Morehouse Sch. Medicine vis. scholar in residence fellow NIOSH, 1996—. Author: (poetry book) Natural Inspirations, 1995; inventor. NIH fellow, 1992-94; recipient Vol. Award Cert., Atlanta Pub. Schs., 1996. Mem. Ga. Writers, Inc., Masons. Home: 3546 Heritage Valley Rd SW Atlanta GA 30331

STARLING, LARRY EUGENE, auditor; b. Nashville, Aug. 15, 1954; s. Thomas Edward and Montoria (Dickson) S.; m. Deborah Denise Askins, Sept. 8, 1984; children: Ryan Thomas, Sean Michael. BS, Tenn. State U., 1979. Tax auditor III State Tenn., Nashville, 1979-83; tax analyst No. Telecom Inc., Nashville, 1983-90; state tax specialist Burlington Industries, Inc., Greensboro, N.C., 1990—. Office: Burlington Industries Inc 3330 W Friendly Ave Greensboro NC 27410-4806

STARNES, EARL MAXWELL, urban and regional planner, architect; b. Winter Haven, Fla., Sept. 14, 1926; s. Thomas Lowe and Kathryn Maxwell (Gates) S.; m. Dorothy Jean Prather, Aug. 21, 1949; children: Tom, Will, Janet, Patricia. Student, Fla. So. Coll., 1946-48; BArch cum laude, U. Fla., 1951; MS in Urban and Regional Planning, Fla. State U., 1973, PhD, 1977. Registered architect, Fla. Assoc. Courtney Stewart (Architect), Ft. Lauderdale, Fla., 1951-52, William Bigoney, Architect, Ft. Lauderdale, 1952-53, William T. Vaughn, Architect, Ft. Lauderdale, 1953, Alfred B. Parker, Architect, Miami, Fla., 1953-55, Rufus Nims, Architect, Miami, 1955-57; ptnr. Starnes & Rentscher, Architects, Miami, 1957-63, Starnes, Rentscher & Assocs., Architects, Miami, 1963-71; dir. div. mass transp. Fla. Dept. Transp., Tallahassee, 1971-72; dir. div. state planning Fla. Dept. Adminstrn., 1972-75; engaged in research and cons. service Tallahassee, 1975; prof., chmn. urban and regional planning Coll. Architecture U. Fla., Gainesville, 1976-88; prof. urban and regional plan coordination, doctorial studies Coll. of Architecture U. Fla., 1989-93, prof. emeritus, 1993—; instr. architecture U. Miami, 1953; adj. asst. prof. dept. urban and regional planning Coll. Social Scis., Fla. State U., 1971-74; mem. adv. panel B8-15, Nat. Coop. Hwy. Research Program, Transp. Research Bd., NRC-Nat. Acad. Scis., 1974—; mem. adv. bd. Pub. Tech., Inc., 1974—; mem. North Central Fla. Regional Planning Com., 1980-85, Fla. Substate Dist. Com., 1985-87; co-chmn. Joint Liaison Com. on Div. Responsibility for Urban Services, Dade County, Fla., 1965-71; chmn. joint policy com. U. Miami-Dade County Jackson Med. Center, 1966-71; chmn. Cape Fla. State Park Adv. Council, 1966-69, Dade County Landscape Ordinance Study Com., 1967-70, South Fla. Everglades Area Planning Council, 1969-71; vis. lectr. Calif. Poly. State U., San Luis Obispo, 1988-89; cons. Urban Planning Fla. and Caribbean. Prin. works include 1st Unitarian Ch., Miami; contbr. article on archtl. planning relationship Ency. Architecture Planning, 1987, chpt. to Growth Management, 1992, chpt. and preface (with Ivonne Audinal) to Rural Sustainability in America, 1996; contbr. chpts. to books, articles on land use and urban devel. policies, wetland protection and state planning to profl. jours. Active South Dade Mental Health Soc., 1967-68, Cape Fla. Acquisition Com., 1966, Dade County Downtown Govtl. Center Com., 1967-71, Miami Downtown Devel. Authority, 1970, Gov.'s Task Force on Resource Mgmt., 1971-72, Nat. Task Force on Natural Resources and Land Use Info. and Tech., 1973-74, Fla. Gov.'s Commn. on Property Rights, 1993-94; county commr. Dist. 7, Dade County, 1964-71; vice mayor, 1964, 68; mem. adv. com. Legis. Council Subcom. on Constrn. Industry Study, 1966-68; bd. dirs., chmn. retirement and compensation com. State Assn. County Commrs., 1968-71; mem. Alachua County Budget Study Com., 1978, Fla. Land Use Adv. Com. for Phosphate Lands, 1978-80, Suwanee River Water Mgmt. Bd., 1982-87, 91—, chmn. 1987-88; chmn. Fla. Inst. Phosphate Research, 1984-87; bd. dirs. 1000 Friends of Fla, 1986—. With USCG, 1944-46. Fellow AIA (urban design com. 1976-80); mem. Am. Inst. Cert. Planners, Nat. Inst. Bldg. Scis. (steering com. for rsch. 1979-80), Assn. Collegiate Schs. of Planning (bd. dirs. 1986-88), Gargoyle Soc., Phi Kappa Phi. Democrat. Unitarian. Office: PO Box 234 Cedar Key FL 32625-0234

STARR, CHARLES CHRISTOPHER, foundation executive, priest; b. Atlanta, Jan. 15, 1952; s. David Homer and Margaret Mary (Bussey) S.; m. C. Kathy Wright, Dec. 15, 1984; 1 child, Anna Katherine. BA in Philosophy, St. Mary's Coll., 1975; MDiv, St. Vincent de Paul, 1980. Ordained to ministry Roman Cath. Ch., 1980; ordained to ministry Episc. Ch., 1993. Assoc. pastor Sacred Heart Ch., Atlanta, 1980-82, Immaculate Heart of Mary, Atlanta, 1983, Cathedral Christ the King, Atlanta, 1983-84; vice chancellor Archdiocese of Atlanta, 1982-84; v.p. Lehfeldt and Assocs., 1985-89; dir. devel. Winship Cancer Ctr., 1989-91; exec. dir. Henry W. Grady Found., 1992-95; assoc. rector Ch. of Atonement, 1993-95; exec. dir. Nat. Kidney Found. of Ga., Atlanta, 1995—. Founding bd. dirs. Holy Trinity Night Shelter, Decatur, Ga., 1986; pres. Transition House, Atlanta, 1988-92. Mem. Nat. Soc. Fund Raising Execs. (cert., Ga. chpt. bd. dirs. 1992—), Ga. Hosp. Assn. (pres.-elect Soc. Devel. Profls. 1993—), Assn. for Healthcare Philanthropy (Ga. chpt. bd. dirs. 1991—). Home: 1726 Coventry Pl Decatur GA 30030-1005 Office: Nat Kidney Found of Ga 1655 Tullie Cir Ste 111 Atlanta GA 30329

STARR, DOUGLAS PERRET, journalism educator; b. New Orleans, Nov. 15, 1925; s. Ray William and Jeanne-Marie (Perret) S.; m. Mildred Marguerite Emory, Dec. 28, 1949; children: Michael Jeffrey, David Emory, Andrew Hampden, Jonathan Price, Patricia Mary. BA, La. State U., 1950; MA, Fla. State U., 1970, PhD, 1972. Reporter North Baton Rouge (La.) Jour., 1950, Opelousas (La.) Daily World, 1951-52; newsman AP, various cities, 1952-65; dir. pub. info. Fla. State Treas.-Ins. Commr.-State Fire Marshal, 1965-69, Fla. State Dept. Commerce, 1972-74; prof. journalism U. North Tex., Denton, 1974-86; prof., head journalism dept. Tex. A&M U., College Station, 1986-87, prof., 1987—; copy editor Ft. Worth Star-Telegram, 1975-79. Author: Guide to Reporting and Fine Writing, 1994, How To Handle Speechwriting Assignments, 1978, How To Write, Free-Lance Feature Writing for Magazines, How To Tackle the Job Market, 1976, The Supervisor's Role in Coast Guard Safety and Occupational Health Program, Vol. II, Safety and Occupational Health Manual, 1983; co-author: The Coast Guardsman's Manual, 8th edit., 1992; contbr. articles to profl. jours., mags., and newspapers. With USN, 1943-47, 50-51, comdr. USCGR, 1965-85. Fellow Pub. Rels. Soc. Am.; mem. Assn. for Edn. in Journalism and Mass Communication, Soc. Profl. Journalists (life), Friends of Pub. Rels. Student Soc. Am., Tex. Pub. Rels. Assn., Pub. Rels. Found. Tex., Internat. Assn. Bus. Communicators, New Orleans Geneal. Rsch. Soc., German-Acadian Coast Hist. and Geneal. Soc., USCG Ret. Res., Res. Officers Assn. (life), Nat. Eagle Scout Assn., MENSA, Kappa Tau Alpha. Democrat. Roman Catholic. Office: Tex A&M U Dept Journalism College Station TX 77843-4111

STARR, FREDERICK BROWN, furniture manufacturing executive; b. Westfield, Mass., Dec. 11, 1932; s. Frederick Rickaby and Virginia (Brown) S.; m. Sue Zook, June 1958; children: Jonathan, Curtis, Anne. BA in English, Trinity Coll., Hartford, Conn., 1955. Archtl. ceilings salesman Armstrong World Industries, Inc., Indpls., 1958-63, mktg. mgmt., Lancaster, Pa., 1963-73, v.p., gen. sales mgr. subs. co. Thomasville Furniture Industries, Inc., (N.C.), 1973-77, sr. v.p., gen. sales mgr., 1977-82, pres., CEO, 1982—, also dir.; bd. dirs. Furniture Libr., High Point, N.C. vice-chair U. N.C., Greensboro, 1985—, Reynolds House Mus., 1988—; pres. N.C. Shakespeare Theatre, 1987—; bd. dirs. Community Hosp., Thomasville, 1984—; chmn. TFI Found., Thomasville, 1984—. Served with U.S. Army, 1955-57. Mem. Internat. Home Furnishings Market Assn. (chmn. 1995—). Republican. Episcopalian. Home: 5506 E Rockingham Rd Greensboro NC 27407-7242 Office: Thomasville Furniture 401 E Main St Thomasville NC 27360-4152

STARR, IVAR MILES, lawyer; b. N.Y.C., Sept. 19, 1950; s. Charles S. Scholnicoff and Rosalie (Paletz) Starr. AA, Nassau Community Coll., 1970; BA, Queens Coll., 1972; JD, U. Miami, 1980. Bar: Fla. 1981, U.S. Dist. Ct. (so. dist.) Fla. 1981, N.Y. 1988. Rep. securities sales Aetna Variable Life Ins. Co., Garden City, N.Y., 1973-75; freelance real estate broker New Fairfield, Conn., 1973-79; assoc. Law Offices of Peter Lopez, Miami, Fla., 1981-82, Mills & London P.A., Miami, 1982; pvt. practice Miami, 1982—; lectr. Dade County (Fla.) Consumer Advs. Office, 1984-87; instr. paralegal courses Briarcliffe Coll., 1991. Candidate judge Dade County Ct., 1988. Recipient Outstanding Svc. award Miami Beach Bd. Realtors, 1986, 87, 88, 91, 92. Mem. N.Y. State Bar Assn., Fla. Bar Assn. (vol. bar liaison com. 1993-96), Miami Beach Bar Assn. (bd. dirs. 1984—, treas. 1991, v.p. 1993, pres.-elect 1995, pres. 1996), Miami Beach C. of C. (lectr. 1985-89), Better Bus. Bur. South Fla. (arbitrator 1984—, Cert. of Appreciation 1985), Queens Coll. Alumni in South Fla. (chmn. 1986-96), Internat. Toastmasters (so. divsn. gov. dist. 47 1993-94, Able Toastmaster Bronze 1992, Able Toastmaster Silver 1993, dist. 47 club specialist 1996—, Dist. 47 Enthusiasm award 1993-94, Disting. Toastmaster 1994). Home: 6450 Collins Ave Apt 1401 Miami FL 33141-4670 Office: 350 Lincoln Rd Ste 407 Miami FL 33139-3148

STARR, JOHN ROBERT, retired newspaper editor, political columnist; b. Lake Village, Ark., Dec. 29, 1927; s. John Philip and Thelma (Russell) S.; m. Norma Wilson, Nov. 14, 1948; children—John P., Linda Sharon, Robert Russell. B.A. in French, Southwestern U.-Memphis, 1952; postgrad., U. Tenn., 1977-78. Sports writer The Comml. Appeal, Memphis, 1952-57; newsman A.P., Little Rock, 1957-66, bur. chief, 1966-76; writer in residence U. Ark.-Little Rock, 1976-77; mng. editor Ark. Democrat, 1978-92. Author: Yellow Dogs and Dark Horses, 1987. Served with U.S. Army, 1946-47. Recipient Ark. Journalist award U. Ark., 1981. Home: 8 Daven Ct Little Rock AR 72209-2924 Office: Little Rock Newspapers Inc 121 E Capitol Ave Little Rock AR 72201-3819

STARR, ROBERT RUSSELL (RUSTY STARR), newspaper executive editor; b. Memphis, Apr. 19, 1955; s. John Robert and Norman Jeanette (Wilson) S.; m. Tracye Ann Flippo, Oct. 5, 1984; children: Brandon, Amanda, Daniel. BS in Journalism, Ark. State U., 1976. Writer, photographer Jonesboro (Arkansas) Sun, 1974-78; from copy editor to news editor Wilmington (N.C.) Star-News, 1978-83; mng. editor Times Daily,

Florence, Ala., 1983-86; exec. editor The Gadsden (Ala.) Times, 1986—; speaker Am. Press Inst., Reston, Va., 1993. Mem. Ala. AP Assn. (treas. 1987-88, v.p. 1989, prs. 1990), Ala. Press Assn. (contest chmn. 1993, Most Improved award 1984, 5 Gen. excellence awards 1983-86, 93, 3 Pub. Svc. awards 1987-92). Office: The Gadsden Times 401 Locust St Gadsden AL 35901-3737

STARTZMAN, SHIRLEY KAYLEEN, editor; b. Elwood, Ind., May 5, 1946; d. Hubert A. and Wilma Jean (Hutcheson) S.; divorced; children: Jill Carmen, Tracie, Kayleen Startzman Barker. AS in Bus., Vincennes U., 1982; BS in Journalism, Ball State U., Muncie, Ind., 1985, MA in Adult Edn., 1990. Reporter Lawrence (Ind.) & Suburban Jour., 1965-67; asst. editor Soldier Support Jour., Ft. Benjamin Harrison, Ind., 1980-84, editor in chief, 1984-87; instnl. sys. specialist Ctr. for Army Lessons Learned, 1987; edn. specialist Staff and Faculty Devel. Divsn., Ft. Benjamin Harrison, 1988-94; chief Staff and Faculty Devel. divsn. Soldier Support Ctr., Ft. Benjamin Harrison, 1994; editor-in-chief INSCOM Jour., Ft. Belvoir, Va., 1996; command info. officer Pub. Affairs Office U.S. Army Intelligence and Security Command, Fort Belvoir, Va., 1996—; coach varsity softball Mt. Vernon H.S., Fortville, Ind., 1988, 89; coach varsity softball Lapel (Ind.) H.S., 1991, asst. coach varsity softball, 1993, coach varsity softball, 1994—; coach jr. varsity softball Lawrence (Ind.) Ctrl. H.S., 1992. Active Triple H Softball Hamilton County, Inc., 1986-94. Mem. Ind. H.S. Athletic Assn. (referee 1973—), Nat. Softball Coaches Assn., Assn. U.S. Army. Home: 9244 Ashland Woods Ln # B-2 Lorton VA 22079-1801 Office: US Army Intelligence & Security Command IAPA Fort Belvoir VA 22060-5256

STATEN, DONNA KAY, elementary art educator; b. Temple, Tex., Apr. 17, 1958; d. Paul James and Doris Mary (Kleypas) Hoelscher; 1 child, Ryan. BS in Edn., U. Mary Hardin-Baylor, Belton, Tex., 1980. Cert. tchr. in art, elem. edn., health, phys. edn. and recreation, Tex. Art tchr. Meridith Magnet Sch., Temple, 1980-84; bank officer mktg. Tex. Am. Bank, Houston, 1985-88; self employed art tchr. and designer, Houston, 1989; tchr. ESL Aldine Ind. Sch. Dist., Houston, 1990; art tchr. Meridith Magnet Sch., 1991—; exec. dir. Visual Arts Friends of the Cultural Activities Ctr., Temple, 1993-95, Temple Sister Cities Corp., Temple, 1994—; chmn. fine arts team Meridith Campus, 1993—. Curator Internat. Children's Art Exhbn., 1996, art exhibit From Russia with Love, 1993—. Mem. The Contemporaries, Temple, 1994—; singer St. Luke's Ch. Choir, Temple, 1991—, mem. St. Luke's Women's Soc., 1993—; treas. Oaks Homeowners Assn., Temple, 1994—. Recipient honorable mention in Christmas Decorating Contest Women's Day mag., 1989, cert. of recognition Crayola/Binney & Smith, 1993-94, 95-96. Mem. ASCD, AAUW, Fine Arts Network, Internat. Soc. for Edn. Through Art, Nat. Art Assn., Tex. Classrm. Tchrs. Assn., Am. Craft Coun., Soc. Craft Designers, Tex. Computer Edn. Assn., Tex. Fine Arts Assn., Tex. Art Edn. Assn., Nat. Mus. of Women in the Arts, Cultural Activities Ctr., Temple Assn. for the Gifted, Electronic Media Interest Group, Tex. Alliance Edn. and the Arts., Friends of the Temple Libr. Roman Catholic. Home: 3927 River Oaks Cir Temple TX 76504-3566 Office: Meridith Magnet Sch 1717 E Avenue J Temple TX 76501-8414

STATMAN, JACKIE C., career consultant; b. Kingman, Kansas, June 15, 1936; d. Jack Carl and Dorothy E. (Kendall) Pulliam; m. Jerome Maurice Statman, Dec. 29, 1959; children: David Alan, Susan Gail. BA, U. Kans., 1958. Reg. music therapist Topeka State Hosp., Kans., 1958-59; caseworker Child Welfare, Pensacola, Fla., 1960-61; devel. rsch. tester The Children and Youth Project, Dallas, 1973-74; middle sch. counselor The Hockaday Sch., Dallas, 1981-84; career cons. Career Design Assocs., Inc., Garland, Tex., 1984-86; owner Career Focus Assocs., Plano, Tex., 1987—; pres. Assn. Women Entrepreneurs of Dallas, Inc., 1991-93; mem. career edn. adv. com. Plano Ind. Sch. Dist., 1993—. Author: (newspaper column) "Career Forum", 1991-92. Mem. Cmty. Svcs. Commn., City of Plano, 1993—; mem. Leadership Plano Alumnae Assn., 1990—; mem. bd. dirs. Mental Health Assn. in Tex., 1989-93; founding pres. Mental Health Assn. Collin County, 1988-90. Recipient Child Advocacy award Mental Health Assn. of Greater Dallas, 1985, Golden Rule award JC Penney Comp., Inc., 1986, Humanitarian Vo. of the Yr. award Vol. Ctr. Collin County, 1990. Mem. Am. Counseling Assn., Nat. Assn. Women Bus. Owners (mem. Dallas/Ft. Worth bd. dirs. 1992-93), Nat. Career Devel. Assn., Plano C. of C. Office: Career Focus Assocs 1700 Coit Rd Ste 220 Plano TX 75075-6138

STATMAN, JAN B., artist; b. N.Y.C., July 27; d. Saul Berliner and Sylvia Charlotte (Rose) Berliner; m. Max Statman; children: Charles Barry, Louis Craig, Sherry. BA in Art, Hunter Coll. Works in pvt. mus. collections, including Mus. of Contemporary Art, Saso Ferrato, Italy, Alto Aragon En Huesca, Spain, Longview (Tex.) Art Mus., various pvt. collections; one-woman shows include Milam Gallery, Dallas, Tex., Longview (Tex.) Art Mus., McAllen (Tex.) Internat. Mus., Craft Alliance, Shreveport, La., Kilgore (Tex.) Coll., Vandersen Gallery, N.Y.C., Guild Gallery, Houston; author: (book) Battered Woman's Survival Guide, 1990; contbr. articles to profl. jours. Mem. Longview Women's Commn., 1995—. Named to Outstanding Young Women of Am., 1976, Artist-in-Residence, Tex. Commn. on the Arts, Austin, 1986, 94; recipient various awards Tex. Press Women, 1972-90. Mem. Nat. Assn. Women Artists, Zonta. Home: 27 Country Place Longview TX 75605

STATON, CECIL POPE, JR., religious publisher; b. Greenville, S.C., Jan. 26, 1958; s. Cecil Pope and Shirley Ann (Hughes) ; m. Catherine Lynn Davidson, Aug. 23, 1986. BA, Furman U., 1980; MDiv, Southeastern Bapt. Theol. Sem., 1982, ThM, 1985; DPhil, U. Oxford 1988. Assoc. minister Washington Ave. Bapt. Ch., Greenville, S.C., 1977-79; pastor Maple Heights Bapt. Ch., Greenville, 1979-80, Trinity Bapt. Ch., Arcadia, N.C., 1983-85; prof. Christianity Brewton-Parker Coll., Mount Vernon, Ga., 1989-91; pub. Smyth & Helwys, Macon, Ga., 1990—, also bd. dirs.; pub. Mercer U. Press, Macon, 1991—; prof. Coll. Liberal Arts, Mercer U., 1991—. Editor: Interpreting Isaiah for Preaching and Teaching, 1991, Interpreting Hosea for Preaching and Teaching, 1993, Interpreting Amos for Preaching and Teaching, 1995; contbr. articles to profl. jours. Recipient Am. scholarship Regent's Park Coll., 1986-87, G. Henton Davies Prize in Hebrew, 1985, R.T. Daniel award in Old Testament, 1983, Baggott award Furman U., 1980. Mem. Soc. Biblical Lit., Am. Acad. Religion, Nat. Assn. Bapt. Profs. Religion. Home: 116 Waterford Pl Macon GA 31210-3073 Office: 6316 Peake Rd Macon GA 31210-3960

STATON, DAVID MICHAEL, government affairs consultant; b. Parkersburg, W.Va., Feb. 11, 1940; s. Ernest Rutherford and Delta Rachael (Gumm) S.; m. Lynn May Spencer, Mar. 20, 1965; children: Cynthia Lynn, David Michael Jr. Diploma, Parkersburg (W. Va.) High Sch., 1958; student, Concord Coll., Athens, W.Va., 1961-63. Salesman Norhwestern Mut. Life, Parkersburg, W.Va., 1964-67, Burroughs Corp., Parkersburg, Wilmington, Del., 1967-72; v.p. Kanawha Valley Bank (now One Valley Bank), Charleston, W.Va., 1972-80; rep. U.S. Ho. Reps. from 3d Dist. W.Va., Washington, 1981-83; pres. Mick Staton Assoc., Washington, 1983-91; exec. U.S. C. of C., Washington, 1984-90; exec. v.p. Delchamps Assocs., Washington, 1990-92; pres. Capitol Link, Reston, Va., 1992—. Contbr. Perspectives (Washington Close Up textbook) 1987, Human Events and Citizen's Voice. Explorer Post Adv., Jaycees; coach Kanawha Valley Midget Football League 1979-80; del. 1980 Rep. Nat. Conv. With W.Va. N.G., 1975-75, USAR. Recipient Guardian of Small Bus. award Nat. Fedn. Ind. Bus., Watchbog of the Treasury Golden Bulldog award 1981-82, Am. Security Coun. Leadership award 1982, Am. Conservative Union Conservative Conscience of the Congress award 1981, Fraternal Order of Police Appreciation award 1981. Mem. NRA, W.Va. U. Alumni Assn., Concord Coll. Alumni Assn., W.Va. Soc. of Washington, D.C. (pres. 1994-95). Republican. Methodist. Home: PO Box 170 Inwood WV 25428-0170 Office: Capitol Link 11490 Commerce Pk Dr #130 Reston VA 22091

STATON, JON TOM, judge; b. Hollis, Okla., Jan. 7, 1933; s. William Francis and Sarah Elizabeth (Clark) S.; m. Dorothy Carolyn Brown, Dec. 10, 1933; children: Kelsey, Kevin, Sarah Dee Staton Click. BS, Okla. Bapt. U., 1954; MEd, Okla. U., 1959, EdD, 1962; JD, Oklahoma City U., 1979. Bar: Okla. 1980, U.S. Ct. Appeals (10th cir.) 1981, U.S. Dist. Ct. (we. and ea. dists.) Okla. 1980, U.S. Dist. Ct. (no. dist.) Okla. 1989, U.S. Supreme Ct. 1984. Tchr., coach City Schs., Roswell, N.Mex., 1956-60; dir. gen. svcs. U. Okla., Norman, 1961-62; prof. Ctrl. Mo. U., Warrensburg, 1962; supt. schs. Mountain Grove (Mo.) Schs., 1963-67, Muskogee (Okla.) Schs., 1967-74; pvt. practice lawyer Muskogee, 1979-89, 91-93; assoc. dist. judge State of Okla., Hobart, 1989-91, Waurika, 1993—; vis. prof. Drury Coll., Springfield, Mo., 1966. With U.S. Army, 1954-56. Mem. Okla. Bar Assn., Am. Assn. Sch. Adminstrs., Phi Delta Kappa (Okla. pres. 1961-62). Democrat. Baptist. Home: 614 E Monroe St Waurika OK 73573-1442 Office: 220 N Main St Waurika OK 73573-2235

STAUFF, WILLIAM JAMES, facility director; b. Providence, Mar. 2, 1949; s. William A. and Charlotte A. (Thorpe) S.; m. Bertha Nichols, Jan. 22, 1972; children: William J., Heidi A., Anneliese C. BS in Bus. Adminstrn., Northeastern U., Boston, 1977; MBA, Suffolk U., 1983; postgrad., U. Va., 1992—; DST, Bethany Theol. Sem., Dothan, Ala., 1997. Process writer, indsl. engr. Rockwell Internat., Hopedale, Mass., 1972-77; bus. mgr., acct. Luth. Svc. Assn. New Eng., Framingham, Mass., 1977-80; mgr. acctg. and fin. Office Info. Tech. Harvard U., Cambridge, Mass., 1980-89; dir. bus. ops. facilities mgmt. U. Va., Charlottesville, Va., 1989—; pub. acctg. auditor Charles Murphy/Paul Haggerty, CPAs, Framingham, 1977-80. Mem. Assn. Higher Edn. Facilities Officers. Home: RR 2 Box 286A Staunton VA 24401-9539 Office: U Va 575 Alderman Rd Charlottesville VA 22903-2405

STAUFFER, LOUISE LEE, retired secondary school educator; b. Altoona, Pa., Mar. 31, 1915; d. William Thomas and Mary Hall (Schroyer) Lee; m. John Nissley Stauffer, Aug. 20, 1938 (dec. Sept. 1983); children: Thomas Michael, Nancy Kay, John Lee, Donald David. BA, Juniata Coll., 1936; postgrad., Columbia U., U. Pa., Pa. State U. Tchr. Latin, Middletown (Pa.) High Sch., 1936-41; tchr. English and Latin, Roosevelt Jr. High Sch., Springfield, Ohio, 1949-57; tchr. French, North High Sch., Springfield, 1957-63; ret., 1963. Mem. Moorings Property Owners Assn., Naples, Fla., 1983—; sec. King's Port, Inc., Naples, 1990-96, Emmanuel Luth. Ch., Naples, 1980—; bd. dirs., editor newsletter, membership chmn., rec. sec., corr. sec., parliamentarian Naples Comty. Hosp. Aux., 1985—. Mem. AAUW, Am. Assn. Ret. Persons, Women's League (Juniata Coll.), Founders Club (Juniata Coll.), Moorings Country Club.

STAUFFER, THOMAS MICHAEL, university president; b. Harrisburg, Pa., Dec. 5, 1941; s. John Nisley and Louis Lee Stauffer; m. Marion Walker, Aug. 26, 1966 (div. Dec. 1989); children: Amity Juliet, Courtney Amanda, Winston Thomas; m. Deborah Whisnand, May 16, 1993; 1 stepchild, Elizabeth Stinson. Student, Juniata Coll., 1959-61; BA cum laude, Wittenberg U., Ohio, 1963; Cert. in E. European Politics, Freie U. Berlin, 1964; MA, PhD, U. Denver, 1973. Asst. dean coll., asst. prof. polit. sci. Keene State Coll., 1968-72; dir. fellows in acad. adminstrn., office leadership devel. Am. Coun. Edn., 1972-78; v.p., dir. div. external relations Am. Council on Edn., Washington, 1978-82; pres. Golden Gate U., San Francisco, 1982—; exec. sec. Fedn. of Assn. of the Acad. Health Care Professions, 1975-80; chmn. task force on the future of Am. Coun. on Edn., 1978; exec. dir. Bus.-Higher Edn. Forum, 1978-81, Nat. Commn. on Higher Edn. Issues, 1980-81; pres., prof. pub. policy U. Houston, Clear Lake, 1982-91; pres., prof. pub. policy and internat. rels. Golden Gate U., 1992—; spl. asst. to adminstr. NASA, 1992; cons. NSF, Dept. State, Coun. for Internat. Exch. Scholars, Japan External Trade Orgn.; mem. commn. on credit and credentials, Am. Coun. Edn., Bay Area Internat. Forum; chair nat. bd. Challenger Ctr. for Space Sci. Edn., 1987-89, Ctr. for Advanced Space Studies, 1990-94; mem. dels. on higher edn. and econ. devel. to People's Republic of China, S.E. Asia, Japan, Rwanda, Sri Lanka, United Arab Emirates, 1978-94. Exec. editor Ednl. Record and Higher Edn. and Nat. Affairs, 1978-82; contbr. articles to profl. jours., newspapers, monographs, chpts. to books. Chmn. com. advanced tech. Tex. Econ. Devel., 1984, Houston Com. on Econ. Diversification Planning, 1984, Houston World Trade Ctr. Task Force, 1985, East Tex. 2000 Com. on Econ. Devel., S.E. Tex. Higher Edn. Coun., 1989, Clear Lake Area Econ. Devel. Found.; v.p. Inter-Am., U. Coun. for Econ. and Social Devel., Houston World Trade Assn.; vice chmn. Tex. Sci. and Tech. Coun., 1986; pres. St. John Hosp.; chmn. San Francisco Consortium on Higher Edn.; bd. dirs. Houston Hosp. Coun. Found., Tex. Coun. on Econ. Edn., Tex. Senate Space Industry Tech. Commn., Tex. Innovation Info. Network Sys., San Francisco C. of C.; vice-chair San Francisco World Trade Assn.; mem. steering com. Houston Econ. Devel. Coun., Calif. Ind. Edn. Coun., blue ribbon com. City Coll., Bay Area Coun., Industry Edn. Coun. of Calif.; chair San Francisco Mayor's Blue Ribbon Com. on Econ. Devel. Recipient Disting. Alumni award Grad. Sch. Internat. Studies U. Denver, 1989, Tex. Senate Resolution of Commendation, 1991; Am. Coun. on Edn. fellow in acad. adminstrn., 1972, Ford Found. and Social Sci. Found. fellow, 1963-68, sr. fellow Am. Leadership Forum. Mem. AAAS, Internat. Studies Assn. (co-chmn. ann. meeting 1978), Am. Hosp. Assn., Policy Studies Orgn., Internat. Assn. Univ. Pres., San Francisco Com. on Fgn. Rels., Oakland C. of C., San Francisco C. of C. (econ. devel. com., bd. dirs.), Commonwealth Club, San Francisco World Trade Club, City Club, Univ. Club San Francisco. Home: 1806 Green St San Francisco CA 94123-4922 Office: Golden Gate U Office of Pres 536 Mission St San Francisco CA 94105-2921

STAUFFER, TITUS, electrical engineer, writer, publisher; b. Port Trevorton, Pa., Sept. 5, 1958; s. Daniel B. and Rhoda (Eby) S.; m. Mary Dove, Nov. 25, 1989; 1 child, Byron Dove. BSEE, USAF Acad., 1982. Cadet USAF Acad., Colorado Springs, Colo., 1978-82; commd. 2d lt. USAF, 1982-83; elec. engr. Digital Equip. Corp., Colorado Springs, 1983-87, Compaq Computer, Houston, 1987—. Author: Bats in the Belfry, By Design, 1995 (nominated for Prometheus award), Freedom From Freedom Froms, 1996. Libertarian. Office: Free Voice Pub PO Box 692168 Houston TX 77269

STAUTH, ROBERT E., food service executive; b. 1945. Grad., Kans. State U.; student, Stanford U. Exec. Program, 1989. Joined Fleming Cos., Inc., Oklahoma City, 1977, various mgmt. positions, 1977-93, pres., COO, bd. dirs., 1993, CEO, 1993—, chmn.,CEO, 1994; bd. dirs. IGA, Inc. Adv. bd. Coll. Bus. Adminstrn., Okla. U., Kans. State U.; mem. Okla. State Fair Bd. Mem. Food Distbrs. Internat., Food Mktg. Inst. (exec. steering com. on efficient consumer response, industry rels. com.), Okla. State C. of C. (bd. dirs.), Okla. Bus. Roundtable (bd. dirs., state fair bd.). Office: Fleming Cos Inc PO Box 26647 6301 Waterford Blvd Oklahoma City OK 73126

STAVE, GREGG MARTIN, occupational health physician; b. Queens, N.Y., May 10, 1957; s. Howard Donald and Renee (Fine) S.; m. Christine Marie Hunt, Sept. 12, 1987; 1 child, Elise Adriana. SB in Life Scis., MIT, 1979; JD, Duke U., 1983, MD, 1984; MPH, U. N.C., 1990. Diplomate Am. Bd. Preventive Medicine, Am. Bd. Internal Medicine, Nat. Bd. Med. Examiners; lic. physician, N.C.; bar: N.C. 1984, D.C. 1984. Rsch. asst. MIT, Cambridge, Mass., 1976-77, 78-79; with Merck, Sharpe and Dohme, West Point, Pa., 1983; fellow in occupational medicine Duke U., Durham, N.C., 1985, 88-90; resident in internal medicine Med. Coll. Va., 1985-88; part-time emergency rm. physician McGuire VA Med. Ctr., Richmond, Va., 1986-88; cons. to occupational health and safety program Burroughs-Wellcome Co., Research Triangle Park, N.C., 1988-90; occupational physician Glaxo Inc., Research Triangle Park, N.C., 1990-91, assoc. dir. occupational health svcs., 1991—; cons. assoc. dept. community and family medicine Divsn. of Occupational and Environ. Medicine, Duke U. Med. Ctr., Durham, 1990—. Co-editor: (with P. Wald) Physical and Biological Hazards of the Workplace, 1994; contbr. articles to profl. jours. Recipient Jean Spencer-Felton award for Excellence in Scientific Writing, 1995. Fellow ACP, Am. Coll. Occupl. and Environ. Medicine, Am. Coll. Preventive Medicine; mem. AMA, Am. Pub. Health Assn., Am. Soc. Internal Medicine, Carolinas Occupl. Medicine Assn., D.C. Bar Assn., Durham/Orange County Med. Soc., N.C. Bar Assn., N.C. Med. Soc. (tobacco control task force). Office: Glaxo Wellcome Inc Five Moore Dr Research Triangle Park NC 27709

STAVEN, LELAND CARROLL, art educator; b. Milw., Dec. 17, 1933; s. Herbert Ernest and Leona Marion (Travnick) S.; m. Joyce Harlean Waddell Manget, July 27, 1957 (div. 1981); children: Karl Eric, Kurt Daniel, Heidi Beth; m. Laura L. Johnson, Apr. 3, 1990. BFA, U. Wis., Milw., 1956; MFA, Calif. Coll. Arts and Crafts, 1959. Chmn. art dept. Berry Coll., Rome, Ga., 1960-68, Mercer U., Atlanta, 1968-69; dir. Dalton Galleries, assoc. prof. art Agnes Scott Coll., Decatur, Ga., 1969-89; apptd. Ga. Commn. on the Arts, 1967-72. One-man or juried shows include Callenwolde Invitational, Ga. Artist's Show, Calif. Painter's and Sculptor's Exhbn., San Francisco Art Assn., Ctrl. South Festival of Arts, South Atlantic Artists Exhbn., High Mus. Art, Macon Mus. Art, Piedmont Art Show, Art Originals Gallery, Milw., Lucien Laubadt Gallery, San Francisco, numerous others. Recipient Purchase award 4th Ann. Callaway Gardens Show, Achievement award Appalachian Corrider: Exhbn. I, Purchase award Rome Art League, Purchase award Assn. Ga. Artists, 1st prize Rome Art League, 1st prize Contemporary Southern Art Exhbn., Judge's Choice award Jr. League DeKalb County, Award of Merit, Mattie M. Kelly Ctr. Fine and Performing Arts; chosen as 1 of 2 Ga. artists to Painter's Choice Exhbn., 3d place award for poem Midwest Poetry Rev., 1995. Mem. Ga. State Poetry Soc. Republican. Lutheran. Home: 31 View Dr SE Rome GA 30161-8911

STEADHAM, CHARLES VICTOR, JR., entertainment agent, producer, software developer; b. Camp LeJune, N.C., Oct. 22, 1944; s. Charles Victor Sr. and Mary Alice (Adams) S. AA, U. Fla., 1964. Profl. musician various show bands, 1967-75; owner, agt. Blade Agy., Gainesville, Fla., 1975—; pres. Blade Software, Inc., Gainesville, 1990—. Contbr. articles to profl. jours. Mem. Orlando/Orange County (Fla.) Conv. and Visitors Bur., 1986—, Jacksonville (Fla.) Tourist and Conv. Bur., 1986—; grad. Leadership Gainesville XV, 1988; bd. dirs. Gamble Rogers Meml. Found., 1992—, CrimeTrac, 1995—. Recipient C. Shaw Smith Founders award, 1988. Mem. Fla. C. of C., Country Music Assn. (assoc.), Nat. Assn. Campus Activities (assoc., bd. dirs. 1976-83, Founders award 1981, Entertainment Agy. of Yr. award 1983, 87), Am. Soc. Assn. Execs. (assoc.), Fla. Soc. Assn. Execs. (assoc.), Meeting Planners Internat. (assoc.). Democrat. Office: Blade Agy PO Box 1556 Gainesville FL 32602-1556

STEAGALD, THOMAS RAY, minister; b. Nashville, Jan. 4, 1955; s. Ray Lassister and Sadie Frances (Nall) S.; m. Wanda Jo O'Neal, May 22, 1983; children: Bethany Hope, Jacob Christopher. BA, Belmont Coll., 1976; MDiv, So. Bapt. Theol. Sem., 1980; DMin, Emory U., 1995. Ordained to ministry So. Bapt. Conv., 1976; ordained elder United Meth. Ch., 1988. Editor Sunday Sch. Bd. So. Bapt. Conv., Nashville, 1981-82; tchr. Rutledge Coll., Winston-Salem, N.C., 1984-85; pastor Forsyth-Stokes United Meth. Ch., Walnut Cove, N.C., 1985-88, Highlands (N.C.) United Meth. Ch., 1988-93, First United Meth. Ch., Marion, N.C., 1993-95, Marshville (N.C.) United Meth. Ch., 1995—; speaker Nat. Conf. on Preaching. Author: Devotionally Yours, Philippians, 1980, The Birth That Changed My Life, 1988; contbr.: Great Preaching, 1991; also articles and revs. to profl. jours. Bd. dirs. Macon County Hospice, Franklin, N.C., 1989-91. Home and Office: Marshville United Meth Ch PO Box 427 Marshville NC 28103

STEAGALL, HENRY BASCOM, II, retired state supreme court justice; b. Abbeville, Ala., Sept. 4, 1922; s. Orlando Marvin and Susan (Koonce) S.; m. Frances Rector; children: Henry, Susan Steagall Brown, Fred. BS, Auburn U.; JD, U. Ala. Exec. sec. to Gov. George Wallace, 1975-79; dir. state fin., 1983-86; assoc. judge Ala. Supreme Ct., Montgomery, 1986-95. Mem. ABA, Ala. Bar Assn. Methodist.

STEARLEY, MILDRED SUTCLIFFE VOLANDT, foundation executive; b. Ft. Myer, Va., Aug. 3, 1905; d. William Frederick and Mabel Emma (Sutcliffe) Volandt; student George Washington U., 1923-24, 25-28; m. Ralph F. Stearley, Sept. 19, 1931. Elementary tchr. Brent Sch., Baguio, Philippines, 1929-30; staff aide vol. services ARC, also acting chmn., Charlotte, N.C., 1943, staff asst., Washington, 1943-47, Gray Lady vol., Okinawa, 1950-53, Brazil, Ind., 1954; trustee Air Force Village Found., San Antonio, 1975-78, sec. bd., 1975-77; sustaining mem. Tex. Gov.'s Com.; mem. 300 com. Bexar County Republican Com. Recipient commendation ARC, Washington, 1943. Mem. Army Daus., Am. Legion Aux., Army-Navy Club Aux., P.E.O. (life), Am. Security Council (nat. adv. bd.), San Antonio Mus. Assn., Smithsonian Inst., Pi Beta Phi. Episcopalian. Clubs: Ladies Reading (hon. mem.) (Brazil, Ind.); Lackland Officers Wives, Bright Shawl (San Antonio). Home: 4917 Ravenswood Dr Apt 311 San Antonio TX 78227-4338

STEARNS, CLIFFORD BUNDY, congressman, business executive; b. Washington, DC, Apr. 16, 1941; s. Clifford Robert and Emily Elizabeth (Newlin) S.; m. Joan Bette Moore; children: Douglas Moore, Clifford Bundy Jr., Scott Newlin. BSEE, George Washington U., 1963. Mgr. Control Data Systems, Inc., L.A., 1967-69; sr. contract adminstr. CBS, Inc., Stamford, Conn., 1969; account exec. Kutola Advt. Agy., Greenwich, Conn., 1970-71, Images 70/Wilson Haight Welch, Inc., Greenwich, 1971-72; motel owner Hatfield, Mass., 1972-77; pres., motel mgr. Stearns House, Inc., Silver Springs, Fla., 1977-88; mem. 101st-103rd Congresses from 6th Fla. dist., 1989—; mem. banking, fin. and urban affairs com., vets. affairs com. 101st Congress from 6th Fla. dist., mem. energy and commerce com., subcoms. energy and power, commerce, consumer protection and competetiveness; 104th Congress, mem. commerce and vets. coms., subcoms. telecom. and fin., healthcare, energy and power; broker Silver Springs (Fla.) Real Estate, 1981-88. Trustee, vice chmn. Monroe Regional Hosp., Ocala, Fla., 1984-89; bd. dirs. Boys Club of Ocala, 1980-84; pres. Toastmaster Club L.A., 1962. Capt. USAF, 1963-67. Mem. Am. Hotel/Motel Assn., Fla. Hotel/Motel Assn., Am. Assn. Realtors, Fla. Assn. Realtors, Marion County Motel Assn. (pres. 1979), Marion C. of C. (bd. dirs. 1987—), Kiwanis (pres. Ocala club 1984). Republican. Presbyterian. Home: 2071 SE 54th Ter Ocala FL 34471-8702 Office: US Ho of Reps 332 Channing St NE Bldg Washington DC 20002-1028 Office: Ho of Reps 2352 Rayburn Office Bldg Washington DC 20515 also: 115 SE 25th Ave Ocala FL 34471-9179

STEARNS, FRANK WARREN, lawyer; b. Washington, July 20, 1949; s. Robert Maynard and Ermyntrude (Vaiden) S.; m. Judith Anne Ketcheson, Sept. 7, 1974; children: Frank W. Jr., Brian S., Joe G. BA, Washington & Lee, 1971; JD with honors, George Washington U., 1974. Bar: Washington DC 1975, Va. 1980, U.S. Supreme Ct. 1980, U.S. Dist. Ct. DC 1975, U.S. Ct. Appeals (DC cir.) 1975, U.S. Ct. Appeals (4th cir.) 1985. Law clk. Superior Ct. D.C., Washington, 1974-75; asst. corp. counsel Office of the Corp. Counsel, Washington, 1975-79; asst. county atty. County Atty's Office, Fairfax County, Va., 1979-80; mng. ptnr. Wilkes, Artis, Hedrick & Lane, Fairfax, Va., 1984—; bd. dirs. No. Va. Bldg. Industry Assn., 1987-94; trustee Greater Washington Bd. Trade, 1987—; chmn. tech. adv. com. NVBIA, Loudoun, Va., 1986-90. Commr. Arlington County Econ. Devel. Commn., Arlington, Va., 1987-91; mem. Coun. for Excellence in Govt., Washington, 1989—. Mem. Barristers, Counsellors. Office: Wilkes Artis Hedrick & Lane 11320 Random Hills Rd Ste 600 Fairfax VA 22030-6001

STEARNS, JOSEPH T., printing company supervisor; b. Berkely, Calif., Dec. 21, 1966; s. Edward Perry Rosa and Judy Kipp S.; m. Anne Marie Castillo, June 8, 1985; children: Vincent, Gregory, Rebekah, Monica, Nicole, Mariah. Grad., St. Rose H.S., 1984. Data entry clk. St. Martin de Porress, Coarsegold, Calif., 1983-84; bindery personal St. Martin de Porress, New Hope, Ky., 1985-86, main press operator, 1986-94, bindery supr., 1994-95, press supr., mgr., 1995—, plant supr., mem. print shop adv. bd., 1996—; Owner Stearns Mailers, New Haven, Ky., 1995—. Editor: Angelic Warfare youth mag., New Hope, Ky., 1983-85. Youth chmn. Rep. Party, Bardstown, Ky., 1995. Republican. Roman Catholic. Home: 166 N Main St New Haven KY 40051 Office: St Martin de Porress 3050 Gap Knob Rd New Hope KY 40052

STEARNS, STEWART WARREN, charitable association executive; b. Denver, Apr. 8, 1947; s. Vinton H. and Marjorie L. (Tedro) S.; BS, Ea. N.Mex. U., 1970; MA, No. Ill. U., 1973; postgrad. SUNY, Albany, 1974—; m. Marjorie L. Fuller, Jan. 25, 1969; children: Theresa Lyn, Gregory Robert. Mng. editor Studies in Linguistics, DeKalb, Ill., 1972-73; instr. No. Ill. U., DeKalb, 1972-73; cons. AID, Guatemala, 1973-74; instr. Skidmore Coll., Saratoga Springs, N.Y., 1975; OAS fellow, Guatemala, 1976-77; asst. dir. Chaves County Community Action Program, Roswell, N.Mex., 1977-78; exec. dir. United Way Chaves County, Roswell, 1978-83, Levi Strauss Found., 1983-85; exec. dir. Community Trust of Met. Tarrant County, 1985-88, Community Found. Sarasota County, 1989—. NDEA fellow, Dallas, 1970-71.

STEBBINS, L. KAY, communications executive; b. Little Rock, Sept. 2, 1960; d. Billy J. and Alma M. (Lindsey) Gaines; m. Robert Bruce Stebbins, Nov. 2, 1991; children: Laura Lindsey, Anna Caroline. BFA in Journalism, So. Meth. U., 1982. Press asst. Clinton for Gov. Campaign, Little Rock, 1982; press asst. Office of the Gov., Little Rock, 1983, asst. press sec., 1983-86; press sec. Clinton for Gov. Campaign, Little Rock, 1984, 86; comms. supr. Ark. Dept. Edn., Little Rock, 1987-88; pub. rels. account exec.

Cranford Johnson Robinson Woods, Little Rock, 1988-92, sr. pub. rels. account exec., 1992-94; nat. advance staff Clinton for Pres. Campaign, Little Rock, 1991, 92; dir. info. svcs. Ark. Indsl. Devel. Commn., Little Rock, 1994—. Campaign vol. Coulter for Lt. Gov., Little Rock, 1993; advance team Presdl. Inaugural Com., Washington, 1993; com. chmn. Gubernatorial Inaugural Com., Little Rock, 1990, 93; mem. Jr. League of Little Rock, 1993—; publicity chmn. Regional Coun. of Alumni and Parents, So. Meth. U., 1992—. Recipient Best of Show award Ark. Advt. Fedn., 1989; Outstanding Young Woman of Am. Mem. Pub. Rels. Soc. Am. (accredited, pres. Ark. chpt. 1994, bd. dirs. 1992—, bd. dirs. S.W. Dist. 1994, Prism awards 1991-94, Bronze Quill awards 1989, 90, 93, Pres.'s award 1991), Indsl. Developers of Ark., Alpha Delta Pi. Democrat. Episcopalian. Office: Ark Indsl Devel Commn #4C-300 One State Capitol Mall Little Rock AR 72201

STEBBINS, LEROY JOSEPH (LEE STEBBINS), not-for-profit organization executive; b. Hartford, Conn., Sept. 25, 1945; s. Leroy Joseph and Eleanor Ann (Joseph) S.; m. Marjorie Ann Gould, Oct. 5, 1973 (div.); children: Daniel Chapman, David Liam. BA, U. Conn., 1967. Asst. dir. community health and safety programs ARC, Farmington, Conn., 1971-75; exec. dir. ARC, Greenwich, Conn., 1975-80; asst. mgr. ARC, Farmington, 1980-83; mng. dir. Region III, Ea. Ops. Hdqrs., ARC, Alexandria, Va., 1983-92; exec. dir. Am. Speech-Lang.-Hearing Found., 1992-95; dir. chpt. svcs. Am. Soc. Tng. and Devel., 1995—; disaster fund raising specialist Ea. Field Office, ARC, 1978-83; faculty health and safety symposium Conn. Health Dept., Hartford, 1976. Mem. Gov.'s Adv. Com., Conn. Health Dept., 1973-76; campaign account exec. United Way of Capital Area, Hartford, 1982; select soccer coach Fairfax (Va.) Police Youth Club, 1986-90; asst. soccer coach Fairfax H.S.; vol. World Cup organizing com. World Cup USA '94. Republican. Roman Catholic. Home: 9280 Bailey Ln Fairfax VA 22031 Office: Am Soc Tng and Devel 1640 King St Fairfax VA 22031

STEBBINS, RICHARD HENDERSON, electronics engineer, peace officer, security consultant; b. Pittsburgh, Pa., Dec. 2, 1938; s. Earl Carlos and Esther Frances (Kusluch) S.; m. Rosemary Tanneberger, Aug. 12, 1984; children from previous marriage: Richard Earl, Susan Elizabeth. BSEE with high honors, U. Md., 1965; postgrad., Trinity U., 1973-74. cert. peace officer, Tex. Engring. tech. Nat. Security Agy., Ft. Meade, Md., 1960-65; design engr. Page Communications Engr., Washington, 1965-66, Electromechanical Rsch., Inc., College Park, Md., 1966-67, Honeywell, Inc., Annapolis, Md., 1967-68; electronics engr., intelligence rsch. specialist Fed. Civil Svc., San Antonio, 1968-91; pvt. cons. San Antonio, 1991—; comdr.'s advisor Air Force Cryptologic Support Ctr., San Antonio, 1988-91; deputy dir. countermeasures ops., intelligence rsch. specialist USAF HQ Electronic Security Command, San Antonio, 1981-88; mem. blue ribbon com. on ops. security & comm. security roles & relationships for command and svc. Author, lectr. in field; contbr. articles to profl. jours. With USN, 1956-59. Mem. NRA, Tau Beta Pi, Eta Kappa Nu, Phi Kappa Phi. Republican. Episcopalian. Home: 9602 Clear Falls San Antonio TX 78250-5067

STECHMANN, RICHARD HENRY, oil company executive; b. Bay St. Louis, Miss., Feb. 28, 1947; s. Theodore Godfrey and Edris Claire (Vairin) S.; m. Judith Leah Seals, July 26, 1969; children: Cynthia C., Jennifer L., James R., S. Patrick. AA in Pre-Engring., Pearl River Jr. Coll., 1967; BSME, U. Miss., Oxford, 1970. Engr., supr. Gulf Oil Corp., La. and Miss., 1970-83; unit mgr. Cirtonelle Unit, Cirtonelle, Ala., 1983—. Coach youth sports, Columbia, Miss., 1971, Satsuma, Ala., 1985; leader Boy Scouts Am., Homer, La., 1974-75; officer Bass Club, Homer, 1974-75; vol. Dan Davis Egg Roll, Cirtonelle, 1988-89. Mem. Soc. Petroleum Engrs. (various offices, including chmn. southeastern sect. 1970—), Groundwater Protection Coun. Roman Catholic. Home: 6005 Valencia Ave Satsuma AL 36572-2851 Office: Citronelle Unit 8055 Joy St PO Box 408 Citronelle AL 36522

STECKLEY, LINDA GOODRIDGE, university official; b. Lockport, N.Y., Apr. 1, 1942; d. James Edwin and Mary Elizabeth (Wright) Goodridge; m. William Mathew Steckley, Aug. 10, 1963 (div. 1979); children: Matthew, Adam; m. Peter André Weitzel, Jan. 10, 1981; stepchildren: Anthony, Philip, Mark. BA, Dickinson Coll., 1963; MBA, U. Miami, 1987. Tchr. jr. high sch. Dade County (Fla.) Schs., 1966-70; asst. to county commr. Met. Dade County, 1976-80; polit. coord. Pettigrew for U.S. Senate, Fla., 1980; dir. devel. U. Miami Sch. Bus., Coral Gables, Fla., 1980-87, asst. dean grad. program, 1987-89; dir. major gifts U. Miami, Coral Gables, Fla., 1989-90, interim v.p., 1990-91; asst. v.p. Sch. Medicine U. Miami, 1991-92; asst. dean Sch. Law NYU, N.Y.C., 1992-95; assoc. dean Sch. Law Duke U., Durham, N.C., 1995—; cons. U. W.I., Kingston, Jamaica, 1989—; bd. dirs. Soc. Laparoendoscopic Surgeons, 1991—. Contbg. author: Building Bridges: Fund Raising, 1992. Founder Sunshine Coop. Pre Schs., Miami, 1973; chmn., bd. dirs., trustee Transition, Inc., Miami, 1976-92. Named Alumna of Distinction, U. Miami Sch. Bus., 1992, Outstanding Woman in Bus., YWCA, Miami, 1992. Mem. Coun. for Advancement and Support Edn. Home: 3800 Chippenham Rd Durham NC 27707-5078 Office: Duke U Sch Law Science Dr and Towerview Rd Durham NC 27708

STEED, ETHEL LAVERNA WILLIAMS See WILLIAMS, ETHEL LAVERNA

STEEG, MOISE S., JR., lawyer; b. New Orleans, July 25, 1916; s. Moise S. and Carrie (Gutmann) S.; m. Marion B., Sept. 14, 1943 (dec.); children: Barbara Steeg Midlo, Marion, Robert M.; m. Melba Law, Nov. 29, 1969. LLB, Tulane U., 1937. Bar: La. 1937, U.S. Dist. Ct. (ea. dist.) La. 1939, U.S. Ct. Appeals (5th cir.) 1946, U.S. Supreme Ct. 1950, U.S. Ct. Appeals (11th cir.) 1981. Practice, New Orleans, 1937—; assoc. Rittenberg & Rittenberg, 1937-38; sole practice, 1938-46; founder Gertler & Steeg, 1946-48, Steeg & Morrison, 1948-50, Marcus & Steeg, 1950-54, Steeg & Shushan, 1954-71; sr. ptnr. Steeg & O'Connor, 1972—. Bd. dirs. Loyola U., chmn., 1979—, mem. search com. for dean Coll. Law; chmn., founder New Orleans Hist. Dist. and Landmarks Com.; bd. dirs. chmn. bd. New Orleans Mus. Art, 1980; bd. overseers Hebrew Union Coll.; bd. dirs. Delgado Jr. Coll., New Orleans Symphony; founder, dir. New Orleans Ednl. and Rsch. Corp.; bd. dirs. Louise Davis Sch. for Retarded Children, Touro Infirmary, 1963-69; mem. Ochsner Found. Hosp. Bd., 1985—; bd. visitors Trinity Episcopal Sch., 1989—; organizer, sec. New Orleans Bus. Counsel, 1986; pres. Temple Sinai, 1966-67; chmn. Anti-Defamation League, Jewish Community Ctr., chmn. Acquarium Drive, Acquarium of Ams.; local counsel Nat. Dem. Party, 1966. Served to capt. USAF, 1942-46. Recipient Brotherhood Award, NCCJ, 1980, Disting. Alumnus award Tulane Law Sch., 1991, Isidore Newman Sch., Svc. award Newcomb Coll. Soc., Cmty. Svc. award New Orleans Bar Assn. Mem. Paul Tulane Honor Soc. Home: One River Place 3 Poydras St New Orleans LA 70130-1665 Office: 201 Saint Charles Ave Ste 3201 New Orleans LA 70170-1000

STEELE, CURTIS EUGENE, art educator, graphic designer, photographer; b. Culver City, Calif., July 17, 1951; s. Donald E. and Barbara (L.) S.; m. Caryl Handy Beyer, June 30, 1977; 1 child, Elizabeth Allen. BFA, Calif. Coll. Arts and Crafts, Oakland, 1974; MA, Calif. State U., Chico, 1976; MFA, U. Memphis, 1983. Photo-technician Am. Analysis Corp., Oakland, 1974-75; graphic designer Butte Coll., Oroville, Calif., 1977-78; instr. Ark. State U., Jonesboro, 1978-82, assoc. prof. art, 1989-96, chair, dept. art, 1995—, prof., 1996—; co-owner Aesthetic Techs., Jonesboro, 1980—. Recipient Juror's award, Erector Sq. Gallery, New Haven, Conn., 1993, Purchase award, Ark. Artists Registry, 1992. Mem. AAUP, Coll. Art Assn. Am., Greater Jonesboro C. of C. Office: Arkansas State Univ Dept of Art PO Box 1920 State University AR 72467

STEELE, DAVIS TILLOU, mechanical engineer; b. Springfield, Mo., Jan. 10, 1923; s. Davis William and Aliene (Tillou) S.; B.S. in Mech. Engring., U. Mo., Rolla, 1950; m. Frances Eloise Van Schaick, Feb. 23, 1952; children—Michael, Cynthia, Janet, Dan. Engr. and weapons system mgr. Boeing Co., Wichita, Kans., also Seattle, 1954-63; systems support mgr. Bendix Systems Div., Ann Arbor, Mich., 1963-68; v.p. Am. Sentry N. Tex., Fort Worth, 1968-71; pres. Housing Engrs., Inc., Fort Worth, 1971—. With USN, 1943-46. Registered profl. engr., Tex. Mem. Am. Engring. Assn. (sec./treas., bd. dirs.), Internat. Conf. Bldg. Ofcls. (profl.). Clubs: Masons, Shriners. Office: 5217 Davis Blvd Ste D North Richland Hills TX 76180

STEELE, DONNA K., endocrinology nurse specialist, educator; b. Brewton, Ala., June 9, 1955; d. Jesse Coleman and Evelyn Cecilia (Hassett) Steele; m. Timothy Alan Ashby, Apr. 29, 1988; 1 child, Joseph Coleman Singley. Lic. practical nurse diploma, Hobson State Tech. Coll., Thomasville, Ala., 1981; ADN, Jefferson Davis Jr. Coll., Brewton, 1987; student, U. South Ala. RN, Fla., Ala.; cert. ACLS and PALS instr.; cert. NALS and nat. trauma and neonatal support nurse. Practical nurse Rush Hosp.-Butler, Ala.; on call staff nurse pediatrics, office nurse endocrinology Sacred Heart Hosp., Pensacola, Fla., charge nurse part-time; clin. instr. Jefferson Davis Jr. Coll. Mem. AACCN.

STEELE, HOWARD LOUCKS, government official; b. Pitts., Jan. 27, 1929; s. Howard Bennington and Ruby Alberta (Loucks) S.; B.S., Washington and Lee U., 1950; M.S., Pa. State U., 1952; Ph.D., U. Ky., 1962; m. Sally E. Funk, June 6, 1952 (div. 1977); children: John F., David A., Patricia A.; m. 2d, Jane R. Cornelius, July 30, 1977; 1 dau., Jennifer L. Sales mgr. Greenville (Pa.) Dairy Co., 1952-56; owner H.L. Steele Bulk Milk Hauling, Greenville, Pa., 1955-60; asst. prof. Clemson (S.C.) U., 1956-57, asso. prof., 1957-64; assoc. prof. Ohio State U., Columbus, 1964-71; with Fgn. Agrl. Svc./Internat. Cooperation and Devel. U.S. Dept. Agr., Washington, 1971—, project mgr. AID, Guatemala, 1976-77, Bolivia, 1977-80, Honduras, 1980-82, Sri Lanka, 1982-84, Bur. Latin Am. and Caribbean AID, Washington, 1984-88, office of the dir. tech. assistance div., 1988-90, with Office of the Dep. Adminstr., 1990—; instr. U. Md., College Park, 1974-76; vis. prof. U. Sao Paulo, Piracicaba, Brazil, 1964-66; partner Kingwood Acres Farm, Rockwood, Pa., 1966—. Recipient Nat. Forensic Union award; named One of Outstanding Young Men in U.S., U.S. Jaycees, 1965; cert. of merit Dept. Agr., 1975, 1992. Mem. Am. Agrl. Econs. Assn., Internat. Assn. Agrl. Economists, Internat. Agribus. Mgmt. Assn., Sons Am. Revolution, Gamma Sigma Delta, Sigma Nu. Lodges: Masons, Shriners. Author: Comercialização Agrícola; contbr. to Agriculture, Lincoln Library of Essential Information; contbr. articles to profl. jours. Home: 5204 Holden St Fairfax VA 22032-3418 Office: USDA/FAS/ICD 14th St and Independence Ave South Bldg Rm 3117 Washington DC 20250-1083

STEELE, JAMES EUGENE, secondary school educator; b. South Norfolk, Va.; s. James Edward and Blanche Eugenia (Munden) S.; BS in Music Edn., William & Mary Coll., Norfolk, 1961; MEd in Ednl. Adminstrn. and Supervision, Temple U., 1972; EdD in Ednl. Adminstrn., Nova U., 1976. Cert. tchr., Va. Piccoloist, Norfolk Symphony Orch., 1951-73; dir. choral music Hampton (Va.) City Schs., 1960-65, supr. music, 1965—. Dir. fine arts div. Hampton Assn. Arts Humanities, 1967—. Mem. NEA, Va. Edn. Assn., Hampton Edn. Assn., Va. Assn. Sch. Execs., Hampton Instructional Suprs. Assn., Tidewater Regional Suprs., Va. Assn. Sch. Curriculum Devel., Va. Music Suprs. Assn., Va. Music Educators Assn., Music Educators Nat. Conf., Va. Choral Dirs. Assn., Va. Band and Orch. Dirs. Assn., Va. String Tchrs. Assn. Guest flute soloist Music Tchrs. Assn. Great Britain, 1962. Home: PO Box 9325 Norfolk VA 23505-0325 Office: 1819 Nickerson Blvd Hampton VA 23663-1026

STEELE, KAREN MASON, medical educator; b. Aberdeen, Md., June 16, 1951; d. Ronnie L. and Joann (Bledsoe) Mason; m. Gustavo S.L. Appeltauer, June 7, 1969 (div. Jan. 1975); 1 child, Sarah Josie; m. Thomas F. Steele, May 14, 1977; 1 child, Lydia Anne; stepchildren: John Thomas, Christine Elizabeth. BA and BS summa cum laude, Northeast Mo. State U., 1974; DO, Kirksville Coll. Osteopathy, 1978. Intern Eastmoreland Gen. Hosp., Portland, 1979; resident Kirksville (Mo.) Coll. Osteo. Medicine, 1986; physician pvt. practice, Portland, 1979-81; clin. instr. Kirksville Coll. Osteopathic Medicine, 1981-86, asst. prof., 1987-90, assoc. prof., 1990-92; assoc. prof. W.Va. Sch. Osteopathic Medicine, Lewisburg, 1992—; OPP section chairperson 1996—; cons. and lectr. in field. Author: (videos) Hospital Osteopathic Manipulative Treatment: A Protocol, 1991, Introduction to Palpation, 1992, (book chpt.) Foundations for Osteopathic Medicine, 1996; contbr. articles to profl. jours. Mem. adv. bd. U.S. Dept. Edn. Fund for Improvement of Post-Secondary Edn., Kirksville, 1991-92. Regents scholar N.E. Mo. State U., 1969, Lawrence W. Mills scholar Kirksville Coll. Osteo. Medicine, 1974. Fellow Am. Acad. Osteopathy (bd. trustees/bd. govs. 1992—); mem. Am. Osteo. Assn., Cranial Acad. (bd. dirs. 1989-93, v.p. 1992-93). Republican. Methodist. Home: 219 Crowfield Cir Lewisburg WV 24901-1263 Office: WVa Sch Osteopathic Medicine 400 N Lee St Lewisburg WV 24901-1128

STEELE, RODNEY REDFEARN, judge; b. Selma, Ala., May 22, 1930; s. C. Parker and Miriam Lera (Redfearn) S.; m. Frances Marion Blair, Aug. 1, 1964; children: Marion Scott, Claudia Redfearn, Parker Blair. AB, U. Ala., 1950, MA, 1951; LLB, U. Mich., 1954. Bar: Ala. 1954, U.S. Dist. Ct. (mid. dist.) Ala. 1959, U.S. Ct. Appeals (5th cir., now 11th cir.) 1981. Law clk. Ala. Ct. Appeals, 1956-57; assoc. Knabe & Nachman, Montgomery, Ala., 1957-61; asst. U.S. atty. Dept. Justice, Montgomery, 1961-66; staff atty. So. Bell T&T Co., Atlanta, 1966-67; judge U.S. Bankruptcy Ct., Mid. dist. Ala., Montgomery, 1967—, chief judge, 1985—; adj. prof. Jones Law Sch. Served with U.S. Army, 1954-56, Korea. Mem. ABA, Ala. State Bar, Montgomery County Bar Assn. Democrat. Episcopalian. Office: US Bankruptcy Ct PO Box 1248 1 Court Sq Montgomery AL 36102-1248

STEELE, THOMAS MCKNIGHT, law librarian, law educator; b. Bartlesville, Okla., June 4, 1948; s. James Robert and Erma Blanche (McKnight) S.; m. Barbara Van Curen, Mar. 23, 1973 (div. 1985); children: James Robert, Ryan Thomas, David Christopher Joyce, Justin Daniel Joyce; m. Martha Bolling Swann, Apr. 1985 (div. 1990); m. LeAnn P. Joyce, Jan. 1995. BA in History, Okla. State U., 1969; MLS, U. Oreg., 1974; JD, U. Tex., 1977. Adminstrv. asst. Tarlton Law Libr. U. Tex., Austin, 1975-77; acting law librarian Underwood Law Libr. So. Meth. U., Dallas, 1977-78, asst. law librarian, 1978-79; assoc. prof. law, dir. Franklin Pierce Law Ctr., Concord, N.H., 1979-82; asst. prof., dir. U. Miss. Law Libr., University, 1982-85; assoc. prof., dir. Wake Forest U. Sch. Law Libr., Winston-Salem, N.C., 1985-91; prof., dir. Profl. Ctr. Libr. Wake Forest U., Winston-Salem, N.C., 1991; cons. in field; exec. dir. SCRIBES--Am. Soc. Writers on Legal Subjects, 1988—. Editor (newsletter) Scrivener, 1986-88; mng. editor Scribes Jour. Legal Writing, 1989—; editor Pub. Librs. and Pub. Laws, 1986-88; compiler bibliography IDEA, 1981-83, Jour. Air Law and Commerce, 1977-81; co-author: A Law Library Move: Planning Preparation and Execution, 1994. With U.S. Army. Mem. Am. Assn. Law Librs. Democrat. Baptist. Office: Wake Forest U Sch Law PO Box 7206 Winston Salem NC 27109-7206

STEELMAN, FRANK (SITLEY), lawyer; b. Watsonville, Calif., June 6, 1936; s. Frank S. Sr. and Blossom J. (Daugherty) S.; m. Diane Elaine Duke, June 27, 1960; children: Susan Butler, Robin Thurmond, Joan Bentley, David, Carol. BA, Baylor U., 1958, LLB, 1962. Spl. agt. IRS, Houston, 1962-64, atty. for estate tax, 1964-68; trust officer First City Nat. Bank, Houston, 1968-71; sr. v.p., trust officer First Bank & Trust, Bryan, Tex., 1971-73; assoc. Goode, Skrivanek & Steelman, College Station, Tex., 1973-74; pvt. practice Bryan, 1974—; vis. lectr. Tex. A&M U., College Station, 1974-75; mcpl. judge City of Bryan, 1986-88. Bd. dirs. Bryan Devel. Found., 1994—; mem. Bryan Zoning Bd. Adjustments, 1992-94; pres. Brazos Valley Estate Planning Coun., 1973-74, Am. Heart Assn., 1975-76; deacon, mem. ch. choir, Sunday sch. tchr. So. Bapt. Ch. Mem. Rotary (bd. dirs. Bryan club 1973-74). Office: 1810 Greenfield Plz Bryan TX 77802-3408

STEELMAN, JOSEPH FLAKE, history educator; b. Wilkesboro, N.C., Dec. 22, 1922; s. Joseph Sankey and Gertrude Lenore (Edmisten) S.; m. Lala Frances Carr, Aug. 30, 1947; children: Lala Carr, Joseph Flake. AB, U. N.C., 1943, MA, 1947, PhD, 1955. Instr. history U. N.C., Chapel Hill, 1947-52, Tex. A&M Coll., College Station, 1952-53, State U. N.Y., Cortland, 1953-54; prof. history East Carolina U., Greenville, N.C., 1955-85, prof. history, dir. grad. studies in history, 1969-85, prof. emeritus, 1985—. Author: North Carolina's Role in the Spanish-American War, 1975; author, editor: Essays in American History, 1964, Essays in Southern Biography, 1965, Studies in the History of the South, 1966; editor: Of Tarheel Towns, Shipbuilding, Reconstructionists and Alliancemen, 1981; contbr. to The Ency. of So. History, 1979, Collier's Ency., 1978; mem. editorial bd. N.C. Hist. Rev., Raleigh, 1969-80. Mem. Pub. Housing Commn., Greenville, 1961-69; mem. N.C. Hist. Hwys. Marker Commn., N.C. Dept. Cultural Resources, Raleigh, 1977-82. With U.S. Army, 1943-46, ETO. Mem. N.C. Lit. and Hist. Assn. (pres. 1970, Christopher Crittenden Meml. award 1996), Hist. Soc. N.C. (pres. 1976, R.D.W. Connor award 1966, 67, 70), Am. Hist. Assn., Orgn. Am. Historians, So. Hist. Assn., Orgn. Historians in N.C. (founding mem.), Phi Beta Kappa. Democrat. Presbyterian. Home: 1703 Knollwood Dr Greenville NC 27858

STEEN, JOHN WARREN, III, fundraising executive; b. Louisville, July 1, 1954; s. John Warren Jr. and Dorothy J. (Lipham) S.; m. Kathryn Ruth Dorr, June 19, 1982; children: John Warren IV, Bartlett David, Matthew Ryan, Sarah Kathryn. BA, Wake Forest U., 1976. Group mgr. pub. affairs Greater Winston-Salem C. of C., 1978-88; exec. dir. Greater Winston-Salem C. of C. Found., 1985-88; dir. devel. Bapt. Children's Homes of N.C., Thomasville, 1988—; pres. Bapt. Devel. Officers of N.C., 1992-93; conv. spkr. So. Bapt. Found. and Devel. Officers, Nashville, 1992-93. Contbr. articles to profl. jours. Deacon Ardmore Bapt. Ch., 1978—. Recipient award of Excellence Am. C. of C. Execs., 1985, Mgmt. award N.C. Assn. C. of C. Execs., 1986; named Fund Raiser of Yr., Bapt. Devel. Officers N.C., 1994. Mem. Reynolda Rotary Club, Thomasville Area C. of C. (chmn. investment task force 1992), Nat. Soc. Fund Raising Execs. (bd. dirs. Triad chpt. 1991-94), Deacon Club of Wake Forest U. (bd. dirs. 1992-94). Home: 3351 Kirklees Rd Winston Salem NC 27104-1753 Office: Bapt Children's Homes of NC PO Box 338 Thomasville NC 27360-4505

STEEN, WESLEY WILSON, former bankruptcy judge, lawyer; b. Abbeville, La., Feb. 15, 1946; s. John Wesley and Margaret (Chauvin) S.; m. Evelyn Finch, Aug. 29, 1970; children: Anna Frances, John Wesley, Lee Wilson. BA in English, U. Va., 1968; JD, La. State U., 1974. Bar: La. 1974, Tex. 1988. Assoc. Sanders, Downing, et al, Baton Rouge, 1974-77, ptnr., 1977-80; solo practice law, Baton Rouge, 1980-83; pres., atty. Steen, Rubin, et al, Baton Rouge, 1983-84; bankruptcy judge U.S. Bankruptcy Ct., Middle Dist. La., part time, 1983-84, full time, Baton Rouge, 1984-87; mem. Winstead, Sechrest & Minick, Houston, 1988—; mem. La. State Law Inst. Continuous Revision Com., La. Trust Code, 1980-87; mem. Baton Rouge Estate and Bus. Planning Council, 1980-87, State Bar Com. on Bar Admissions, Baton Rouge, 1981-85; adj. asst. prof. law La. State U., 1979-87, So. U. Law Sch., 1981; congl. page U.S. Ho. of Reps., 1963-64. Adv. editor Am. Bankruptcy Law Jour.; contbr. articles to profl. jours. Vestryman, St. James Episcopal Ch., 1980-83; bd. dirs., pres. Baton Rouge Symphony Assn., 1976-87, St. James Place, 1985-87, Cerebral Palsy Ctr., 1981, Baton Rouge Gallery, 1982. Fellow Am. Coll. Bankruptcy; mem. Baton Rouge Bar Assns., La. Bar Assn., Order of Coif, Omicron Delta Kappa. Republican. Episcopalian. Avocations: jogging, computers. Office: Winstead Sechrest & Minick 910 Travis St Ste 1700 Houston TX 77002-5807

STEERE, ANNE BULLIVANT, retired student advisor; b. Phila., July 27, 1921; d. Stuart Lodge and Elizabeth MacCuen (Smith) B.; m. Richard M. H. Harper Jr., Nov. 14, 1942 (div. Oct. 1967); children: Virginia Harper Kliever, Richard M. H. Harper III, Patricia Harper Flint, Stuart Lodge Harper, Lucy Steere, Grace Steere Johnson; m. Bruce Middleton Steere, July 5, 1968. BS in Sociology, So. Meth. U., 1978, M in Liberal Arts, 1985. Asst. to dir. Harvard Law Sch. Fund, Cambridge, Mass., 1958-68; advisor to older students So. Meth. U., Dallas, 1976-85. Contbr. articles to profl. jours. Trustee, Pine Manor Coll., Chestnut Hill, Mass., 1983—; bd. dirs. Planned Parenthood, Dallas, 1975-85. Mem. New Eng. Hist. and Geneal. Soc., Alpha Kappa Delta. Episcopalian. Clubs: Chilton (Boston); Jr. League. Avocations: reading, needlepoint, sailing. Home (winter): 1177 N Lake Way Palm Beach FL 33480-3245

STEFAN, CHARLES GORDON, retired foreign service officer and educator; b. Omaha, July 21, 1920; m. Gabrielle M. Patry, May 17, 1952; children: Adrienne, Susan. AA, Salinas (Calif.) Jr. Coll., 1940; BA, U. Calif., Berkeley, 1942; Indsl. Adminstr., Harvard U., 1943. Fgn. svc. officer U.S. Dept. State, 1947-75; part-time instr. Santa Fe C.C., Gainesville, Fla., 1979-90; ret., 1990; participant Santa Fe C.C.-VISTA Project, 1977-78; acad. assignments U.S. Dept. State Russian Inst., Columbia U., 1951-52, Nat. War Coll., 1963-64. Contbr. articles to profl. jours. Mem. citizens participation com. North Ctrl. Fla. Regional Planning Coun., Gainesville, 1976-86; mem. Alachua County Citizen Adv. Com. on Variable Rates for Solid Waste Collection, Gainesville, 1993-94. Capt. Counter Intelligence Corps., U.S. Army, 1942-47, Germany. Recipient Meritorious Svc. Increase award Dept. State, Am. Embassy, Asuncion, Paraguay, 1969. Mem. U. Calif. Berkeley Alumni Assn. (life), Harvard Bus. Sch. Alumni Assn., Diplomatic and Consular Officers Ret., Nat. War Coll. Alumni Assn., Am. Legion, Nat. CIC Assn., Phi Beta Kappa. Episcopalian. Home: 8012 SW 5th Ave Gainesville FL 32607-1544

STEFANSEN, PEGGY ANN, special education educator; b. Newton, Kans., Sept. 16, 1953; d. Manny E. and Marjorie M. (Covalt) Osburn; m. Todd Stefansen, June 9, 1976; 1 child, Tyler L. BA, Oral Roberts U., 1975; MA, Tulsa U., 1981. Cert. tchr. educable mentally handicapped, trainable mentally retarded, learning disabilities, elem. edn., Okla. Tchr. learning disabilities Prague (Okla.) Pub. Schs., Chandler (Okla.) Pub. Schs., Skiatook (Okla.) Pub. Schs.; tchr. Prague Pub. Schs. Mem. NEA, Learning Disabilities Assn., Okla. Edn. Assn., Okla. Reading Coun. Home: Rte 1 Box 22A Paden OK 74860 Office: Prague Elementary Nbu # 3504 Prague OK 74864-2031

STEGALL, MARBURY TAYLOR, psychiatric, mental health nurse; b. Madison, Wis., June 23, 1948; d. Eldon Gordon and Dorothy Elaine (Lanzendorf) Hall; m. Richard Steven Taylor, 1968 (div. 1973); m. Raymond Hance Stegall, June 1, 1982; 1 child, Eldon Gordon. AS, DeKalb C.C., Clarkston, Ga., 1973; BS, Ga. State U., Atlanta, 1976; MN, Emory U., 1978. RN, Ga.; cert. clin. specialist in adult psychiat. mental health nursing. Adult psychiat. mental health clin. nurse specialist Grady Health Sys., Atlanta, 1968—, Ctr. for Interpersonal Studies, P.A., Smyrna, Ga., 1981-84; pvt. practice psychotherapy Riverdale, Ga., 1981—; clin. instr. Clayton State Coll., Morrow, Ga., 1995—; temporary clin. instr. Ga. Bapt. Coll. Sch. Nursing, 1993, 94; peer reviewer mental health peer rev. sys. Am. Psychiat. Assn., Washington, 1986-90; spkr. in field. Asst. den leader North Atlanta dist. Boy Scouts Am., 1993-95, commr., 1994-95; mem. Inman Park Neighborhood Assn., Atlanta, 1980—, sec., 1982. NIMH tng. grantee Emory U., 1977-78. Mem. ANA (nominating com. coun. on psychiat.-mental health 1984-85), Ga. Nurses Assn. (del. ann. meeting 1994), Am. Psychiat. Nurses Assn., Metro Atlanta Advanced Practice Nurse Group (founding, pres. 1986-89), Am. Soc. Law, Medicine and Ethics, Emory U. Alumni Assn., Ga. State U. Alumni Assn., Sigma Theta Tau. Home: 62 Spruce St NE Atlanta GA 30307-2430 Office: Bldg 700 Ste D 8455 Georgia Hwy 85 Riverdale GA 30274

STEGER, EDWARD HERMAN, chemist; b. New Orleans, Dec. 11, 1936; s. Herman Christoph and Katherine (Walther) S.; m. Amy Patricia Duvall, July 29, 1960; children: David B., Sandra E. BS, Tulane U., 1958. Analytical chemist Atlantic Rsch. Corp., Gainesville, Va., 1960-64, head control lab., 1964—; presenter at profl. confs. Contbr. articles to Fine Particle Soc. Jour. Lt. USNR, 1958-60. Mem. Am. Chem. Soc., N.Y. Acad. Scis., Phi Beta Kappa, Phi Eta Sigma, Alpha Chi Sigma. Baptist. Home: 4311 Alta Vista Dr Fairfax VA 22030-5302 Office: Atlantic Rsch Corp 5945 Wellington Rd Gainesville VA 22065-1633

STEGER, MARTHA WESSELLS, public relations executive; b. Nassawadox, Va., Oct. 21, 1943; d. Wilson Henry and Margaret Hylda (Hart) Wessells; m. John Thomas Steger, July 9, 1966; children: Michael Hart, Kathryn Ann. AB in English cum laude, Coll. of William and Mary, 1966. Accredited pub. rels. profl. Tchr. high sch. English Williamsburg (Va.)-James City County Schs., 1966-69; freelance writer Richmond, Va., 1976-78; staff writer, assoc. editor Va. Life Style Mag., Richmond, 1978-79; sr. editor Richmond Life Style Mag., 1979-82; comms. mgr. Va. Divsn. Tourism, Richmond, 1982-84, dir. pub. rels., 1984-93, 95-96; dir. pub. rels. Va. Dept. Econ. Devel., Richmond, 1993-95, dir. promotion and media devel., 1995—. Author: Measuring the Impact of Public Relations in the Travel Industry, 1996; coord. editor New Va. Rev., 1984. Vestry mem. St. Barnabas' Episcopal Ch., Chesterfield County, 1985-88, 90-93, trustee, 1985-95. Recipient 1st place award in editing and pub. rels. Nat. Fedn. Press Women, 1985, 90, 92, 93, 95, Media award Richmond chpt. Am. Soc. Interior Designers, 1981, 1st place speechwriting Ctrl. Va., Internat. Assn. Bus. Communicators, 1995. Mem. Pub. Rels. Soc. Am. (bd. dirs. Old Dominion chpt. 1991-93), Soc. Am. Travel Writers (assoc. 1994—, sec. Atlantic Caribbean chpt.), Travel Industry Assn. Am. (press and pub. rels. com. 1994—), Soc. Profl. Journalists (bd. dirs. 1983-84, 95-96, treas. 1996—, sec. 1994-95), Nat. League Am. Pen Women (v.p. Richmond br. 1978-80, pres. Richmond br. 1980-82, 1st pl. award in writing and pub. rels. 1978, 80, 82), Va. Press Women, Inc. (bd. dirs. 1986-96, newsletter editor and 2d v.p. 1990-92, pres. 1992-94, 1st pl. awards in writing/editing and pub. rels. 1980, 81, 84, 85, 86, 87, 90, 92, 93, 94). Office: Va Corp Tourism 901 E Byrd St Richmond VA 23219

STEGER, WILLIAM MERRITT, federal judge; b. Dallas, Aug. 22, 1920; s. Merritt and Lottie (Reese) S.; m. Ann Hollandsworth, Feb. 14, 1948; 1 son, Merritt Reed (dec.). Student, Baylor U., 1938-41; LL.B., So. Meth. U., 1950. Bar: Tex. 1951. Pvt. practice Longview, 1951-53; apptd. U.S. dist. atty. Eastern Dist. Tex., 1953-59; mem. firm Wilson, Miller, Spivey & Steger, Tyler, Tex., 1959-70; U.S. dist. judge Ea. Dist. Tex. Tyler, 1970—. Republican candidate for gov. of Tex., 1960; for U.S. Ho. of Reps., 1962; mem. Tex. State Republican Exec. Com., 1966-69; chmn. Tex. State Republican Party, 1969-70. Pilot with ranks 2d lt. to capt. USAAF, 1942-47. Mem. ABA, State Bar Tex., Masons (32 degree, Shriner). Home: 801 Meadowcreek Dr Tyler TX 75703-3524 Office: US Courthouse PO Box 1109 Tyler TX 75710-1109

STEIB, JAMES TERRY, bishop; b. May 17, 1940. Ordained priest Roman Cath. Ch., 1967. Titular bishop Fallaba, 1983; aux. bishop St. Louis, 1983; consecrated bishop, 1984; bishop Diocese of Mempis, 1993—. Address: Diocese of Memphis PO Box 341669 Memphis TN 38134-1669

STEIDLEY, JUAN DWAYNE, lawyer, legislator; b. Claremore, Okla., Mar. 8, 1959; s. J.D. and Gwendolyn Ann (Barnes) S.; m. Teresa Ann Brim, Aug. 31, 1987. BA, Okla. State U., 1981; JD, Tulsa U., 1984. Bar: Okla. 1985. Atty. Williams and Marlar, Claremore, 1983—; bd. dirs. Claremore Regional Med. Ctr. Mem. Ho. of Rep. Okla. Ho. of Reps., Oklahoma City, 1986—. Mem. Claremore Optimist. Democrat. Methodist. Home: 205 N Chambers Trl Claremore OK 74017-3602 Office: Williams & Marlar PO Box 99 501 W 1st St Claremore OK 74018

STEIER, MICHAEL EDWARD, cardiac surgeon; b. N.Y.C., Mar. 22, 1942; s. Philip and Gertrude S.; m. Sheila Elaine Steier, June 9, 1963; children: Douglas, James, Lauren. BA, Long Island U., 1964; MD, Univ. Health Scis., Chgo., 1968. Gen. surgery resident St. Vincent's Hosp., N.Y.C., 1969-73; thoracic surgery resident Mayo Clinic, Rochester, Minn., 1973-75; cardiac surgeon S.W. Fla. Regional Med. Ctr., Ft. Myers, Fla., 1975—, Lee Meml. Hosp., Ft. Myers, 1975—, Cape Coral (Fla.) Hosp., 1977—; chief surgery, S.W. Fla. Regional Med. Ctr., Ft. Myers, 1980-82, pres. med. staff, 1982; cons. Naples Cmty. Hosp. Fellow Am. Coll. Surgeons, Am. Coll. Chest Physicians, Am. Coll. Cardiology; mem. Soc. for Thoracic Surgeons, N.Y. Acad. Scis., Explorers Club. Office: Cardiac Surgical Assocs SW Fla 2675 Winkler Ave Fort Myers FL 33901-9342

STEIN, ALLAN MARK, lawyer; b. Montreal, Quebec, Can., Oct. 18, 1951; came to U.S., 1977; s. Boris and Beatrice (Fishman) S. B in Commerce, Sir George Williams, 1972; BA, Loyola, Montreal, 1973; B in Civil Law, McGill U., 1976, LLB, 1977; JD, Nova U., 1979. Bar: Fla. 1979, U.S. Dist. Ct. (so. dist.) Fla. 1979, U.S. Ct. Appeals (5th cir.) 1980, U.S. Ct. Appeals (11th cir.) 1983, U.S. Dist. Ct. Ariz. 1993. Assoc. Law Offices of Paul Landy Beiley, Miami, Fla., 1980, Heitner & Rosenfeld, Miami, 1980-85, Rosenfeld & Stein, Miami, 1985-90, Rosenfeld, Stein & Sugarman, Miami, 1990-94, Rosenfeld & Stein P.A., Miami, 1994—. Mem. North Dade Bar Assn. (bd. dirs. 1985-90). Republican. Jewish. Office: 18260 NE 19th Ave Ste 202 Miami FL 33162-1632

STEIN, GORDON EDWARD, mental health and chemical dependency nurse; b. Phila., Dec. 14, 1953; s. Maurice and Charlotte Eveloff (Liss) Stein; m. Judy Poletti, June 30, 1982. ADN, Miami Dade Community Coll., 1985; BSW in Social Work, Fla. Internat. U., Miami, 1979. Cert. psychiat. and mental health nurse, chem. dependency, assoc. addiction profl.; cert. correctional health care profl. Substance abuse staff nurse Humana Hosp., Pompano Beach, Fla., 1986-88, Wellington Regional Med. Ctr., West Palm Beach, Fla., 1988-89; psychiat. unit staff nurse Bethesda Hosp., Boynton Beach, Fla., 1989-90; psychiat. nurse Prison Health Svcs., Pompano Beach, Fla., 1990-93; head nurse EMSA Correction Care, Ft. Lauderdale, Fla., 1993—. Mem. Fla. Nurses Assn., Nat. Consortium of Chem. Dependency Nurses, Fla. Internat. U. Alumni Assn.

STEIN, LOTTE C., mathematics educator; b. Bonn, Germany, Apr. 30, 1926; came to U.S., 1937; d. Theodor and Elsa (Levy) Wolf; m. Gilbert Bernard Stein, Sept. 4, 1950; children: Richard, Claude. PhB, U. Chgo., 1945, BS, 1947; MS, DePaul U., 1950. Instr. Morgan Park (Ill.) Jr. Coll., 1947-49, John Adams H.S., Ozone Park, N.Y., 1951-53, C.W. Post Coll., L.I. U., Greenvale, N.Y., 1967-73, Island Trees (N.Y.) Sch., 1973-76, Elisabeth Irwin Sch., N.Y.C., 1976-77, Nightingale Bamford Sch., N.Y.C., 1977-79, Friends Sem., N.Y.C., 1979-83; asst. prof. math. Barry U., Miami Shores, Fla., 1983—, parliamentarian, 1989-91; cons., Frontier Fabrics, N.Y.C., 1953-67. Parliamentarian Birchwood Civic Assn., 1960-65; asst. editor Hallandale (Fla.) United Citizens publ., 1984-86; chair Temple Sinai Srs., North Miami, Fla., 1987-90; active mcpl. polit. campaigns; pres. Hallandale Symphonic Pops Orch., 1991—. Mem. B'nai B'rith Women (treas. 1985-90), Nat. Coun. Jewish Women, Book Roundtable (chair 1994—). Home: 200 Golden Isles Dr Hallandale FL 33009 Office: Barry U 11300 NE 2nd Ave Miami FL 33161-6628

STEIN, MARK RODGER, allergist; b. Phila., Apr. 24, 1943; s. Eli and Norma Ruth (Berman) S.; m. Phyllis Mary Feinstein, Dec. 27, 1964; children: Amy Lynn, Philip Warren. BA, LaSalle Coll., Phila., 1964; MD, Jefferson Med. Coll., Phila., 1968. Diplomate Nat. Bd. Med. Examiners, Am. Bd. Internal Medicine, Am. Bd. Allergy and Immunology. Intern Abington (Pa.) Meml. Hosp., 1968-69; resident internal medicine Letterman Army Med. Ctr., San Francisco, 1972-75; fellow allergy and clin. immunology Fitzsimons Army Med. Ctr., Denver, 1975-77; pvt. practice West Palm Beach, Fla., 1979—; asst. prof. depts. medicine and pediat. Uniformed Svcs. U. Health Scis., Sch. Medicine, Bethesda, Md., 1978-79; clin. asst. prof. dept. internal medicine U. South Fla. Coll. Medicine, Tampa, 1979-83; clin. care cons. Clin. Ctr., NIH, Bethesda, 1978-79; mem. active staff, chief dept. allergy, Good Samaritan Hosp., West Palm Beach, St. Mary's Hosp., West Palm Beach, 1985—; mem. active staff Palm Beach Gardens Med. Ctr., Jupiter Med. Ctr. Contbr. articles to profl. jours. Trustee Am. Lung Assn., West Palm Beach, 1984-93, 95—. Fellow ACP, Am. Acad. Allergy, Asthma and Immunology, Am. Coll. Allergy, Asthma and Immunology (chmn. geriatric com. 1988-90), Am. Assn. Cert. Allergists; mem. Am. Thoracic Soc., Mil. Allergists, Fla. Med. Assn., Palm Beach County Med. Assn., Asthma and Allergy Found. Am., Fla. Allergy and Immunology Soc. (pres. 1987-88), Southeastern Allergy Assn., B'nai B'rith. Jewish. Office: 840 Us Highway 1 North Palm Beach FL 33408

STEIN, MICHAEL ALAN, cardiologist; b. Chgo., May 31, 1958; s. Harold Marc and Carlyne Mae (Skirow) S.; m. Ann Palmer Coe, June 9, 1984; children: Sara Elizabeth, David Benjamin. BA, Lawrence U., 1980; MD, U. Ill., 1984. Diplomate in internal medicine and cardiovascular diseases Am. Bd. Internal Medicine. Intern, resident in medicine U. Ill., Chgo., 1984-87; fellow in cardiology, then interventional cardiology U. Iowa, Iowa City, 1987-91; asst. prof. Emory U., Atlanta, 1991-95; med. dir. CCU Atlanta VA Med. Ctr., Decatur, Ga., 1991-95; med. dir. cardiac catheterization lab., Dunwoody Med. Ctr., Atlanta, 1994-95; staff cardiologist Cardiology Cons., Pensacola, Fla., 1995-96; staff cardiologist So. Med. Group, Key West, Fla., 1996—. Recipient clin. investigator award NIH, 1990-95. Fellow Am. Coll. Cardiology, Am. Heart Assn. (coun. clin. cardiology); mem. AAAS, Soc. for Cardiac Angiography & Interventions. Home: 7 Amaryllis Dr Key West FL 33040-6204 Office: 1111 12th St Key West FL 33040

STEIN, RONALD MARC, telecommunications executive; b. Paterson, N.J., Aug. 1, 1951; s. Herbert I. and Lila (Dutkuwitz) S.; m. Bonnie M. Gabriel, Apr. 10, 1983. BSEE, U. Fla., 1973. Design engr. Motorola, Inc., Plantation, Fla., 1973-77; account exec. Motorola, Inc., Ft. Lauderdale, 1977-79; reg. supr. Racal-Milgo Comm., Des Plaines, Ill., 1979-81; dir. sales/mktg. Innovative Electronics, Miami, Fla., 1981-82; product sales mgr Paradyne Corp., Largo, Fla., 1982-84; mgr. telecom. mktg. Paradyne Corp., 1984-87, dir. telephone industry mktg., 1987-88; pres. Innovative Bus. Corp., Boca Raton, Fla., 1988-89; reg. sales mgr. Netrix Corp., Atlanta, 1989-92; regional dir. VideoServer, Inc., Atlanta, 1992-94; v.p. sales and mktg. Clear Sight Comm., Atlanta, 1994—; lectr. in field. Mem. Walking Club Ga. (bd. dirs.). Office: AC&E Ltd 4920 Roswell Rd NE Ste 405 Atlanta GA 30342-2636

STEINBERG, EUGENE BARRY, optician, researcher, contact lens specialist, ophthalmic technician, writer; b. Bklyn., Sept. 16, 1953; s. Lester and Hannah (Bailowitz) S.; m. Ilene G. Richards, Oct. 22, 1977; children—Jessica Brittany, Melissa Heather, Richard Jeremy. A.A. with honors, U. Hartford, 1973; B.A. with honors in Psychology, SUNY-Binghamton, 1975; A. Applied Sci. in Ophthalmic Dispensing with honors, N.Y.C. Tech. Coll., 1979. Lic. dispensing optician, Ga., Va., N.Y.; lic. contact lens specialist, N.Y. Apprentice optician Am. Vision Ctr., Bklyn., 1977-78; mgr. Cohens Fashion Optical, Bklyn., 1978-79; chief contact lens fitter Digby Opticians, Atlanta, 1979-80; clin. research coordinator dept. ophthalmology Emory U. Eye Ctr. Prospective Eval. Radial Keratotomy Study Atlanta, 1980-86, ophthalmic technician Emory Eye Ctr., 1980-87; pres. Eye to Eye Vision Ctr., Inc., Marietta, Ga., 1986—. Contbr. articles to profl. jours. and books. Recipient Disting. Service award Nat. Eye Inst., 1983, Appreciation cert. Binghamton Psychiatric Ctr., 1975. Mem. Opticians Assn. Ga., Atlanta Lawn Tennis Assn., Cobb C. of C., Tau Phi Sigma. Democrat. Jewish. Avocations: guitarist, vocalist, recording artist. Office: Eye to Eye Vision Ctr 2100 Roswell Rd Ste 100D Marietta GA 30062-3879

STEINBERG, JAMES PAUL, infectious diseases physician, hospital administrator; b. Omaha, June 12, 1954; s. Maurice M. and Muriel Naomi (Frank) S.; m. Shari Chaya Wasser, May 22, 1994; children: Eva Rose, Jonathan Alexander. BA, Cornell U., 1976; MD, U. Nebr., 1979. Med. resident Emory U., Atlanta, 1979-83; infectious diseases fellow Northwestern U., Chgo., 1985-87, assoc. in medicine, 1987-89; asst. prof. medicine Emory U., Atlanta, 1989-96; hosp. epidemiologist Crawford Long Hosp., Atlanta, 1991—, assoc. chief of medicine, 1993—. Fellow Infectious Diseases Soc. Am.; mem. ACP, AAAS, Am. Soc. Microbiology, Soc. for Healthcare Epidemiology of Am., Infectious Diseases Soc. Ga. (pres. 1995—). Office: Crawford Long Hosp Divsn Infectious Diseases 20 Linden Ave Ste 101-G Atlanta GA 30308

STEINBERGER, EMIL, health facility executive, educator; b. Berlin, Dec. 20, 1928; came to U.S., 1948; s. Isaac and Itta S.; m. Anna Schneider, Dec. 24, 1950; children: Pauline, Inette. Student, U. Wroclaw, Poland, 1946, J.W. Goethe U., Germany, 1946-48, CCNY, 1949-50; MS in Anatomy and Endocrinology, U. Iowa, 1955, MD, 1955. Diplomate Am. Bd. Internal Medicine, Am. Bd. Endocrinology. Intern Detroit Receiving Hosp., 1955-56, resident in internal medicine, 1959-61; assoc., then chmn. dept. endocrinology and human reproduction Albert Einstein Med. Ctr., Phila., 1961-71; prof., chmn. dept. reproductive medicine and biology U. Tex., Houston, 1971-83, clin. prof. endocrinology, 1983—; Ashbel Smith prof. U. Tex. Health Sci. Ctr., Houston; pres. Tex. Inst. for Reproductive Medicine & Endocrinology, Houston, 1983—; grad. asst. dept. anatomy U. Iowa, 1950-55; sr. rsch. officer Nat. Navy Med. Ctr., Bethesda, Md., 1956-58, chief sect. of endocrinology, 1957-58; rsch. assoc. in endocrinology Wayne State U., Detroit, 1958-61; adj. physician Albert Einstein Med. Ctr., Phila., 1961-65, assoc. physician, 1965-68, attending physician, 1968-71, chief sect. of clin. endocrinology, 1968-71; asst. prof. internal medicine Temple U., Phila., 1967-69, assoc. prof., 1969-71; mem. numerous coms. U. Tex. Med. Sch., 1971-83; dir. Tex. Hormone Assay Lab., Inc., 1983—; CEO Tex. Found. for Reproductive Medicine, 1985—; vis. prof. Harvard U. Med. Sch., 1967, U. of Poznan Med. Sch., Poland, 1977, U. of Sapporo Med. Sch., Japan, 1979, U. of Chile, Santiago, 1982; cons. NIH, Bethesda, 1957—; cons., advisor, lectr. in field. Co-editor: Endocrinology, vols. 1, 2, and 3, 1979, Testicular Development, Structure and Function, 1980, Reproductive Medicine: Medical Therapy, 1989; mem. edit. bd. dirs. Jour. Clin. Endocrinology and Metabolism, 1970-75, Jour. of Andrology, 1978-82; contbr. articles to profl. jours., chpts. to textbooks; pub. papers; reviewer in field. Active rsch. com. Planned Parenthood of Houston, exec. bd. dirs. Infertility Awareness, Natural Family Planning Assn. of Houston. Recipient cert. of Appreciation, Xian Med. U., China, 1987; Postdoctoral fellow NSF, 1958. Fellow Am. Coll. Endocardiologists; mem. AMA, AAUP, Am. Assn. Anatomists, Am. Assn. Planned Parenthood Physicians, Am. Fertility Soc., Am. Soc. Andrology (charter, founding pres. 1975-76, pres. 1976-77, dir. postgrad. edn. 1977-79, chmn. ednl. com. 1978-79, com. future meetings 1978-79, pub. com. 1978-82, awards com. 1981, exec. coun. 1981-83, nominating com. 1982, chmn. com. continuing edn. and postgrad. courses 1982-83, Disting. Andrologist award 1987), Am. Assn. Clin. Endocrinologists (charter), Comite Internacional de Andrologia (charter, exec. coun. 1973-80, pub. com. 1973-80, fin. subcom. 1976-80, exec. coun. subcom. for new mems. 1979-81, membership com. 1979-82), Internat. Soc. Rsch. in Biology, World Population Soc., Tex. Med. Assn., N.Y. Acad. of Scis., Houston Gynecol. and Obstet. Soc., Harris County Med. Assn., Soc. for Study of Reproduction (charter, nominating com. 1967-70, membership com. 1968-70, chmn. 1969-70), Endocrine Soc., Sigma Xi.

STEINER, GEOFFREY BLAKE, lawyer; b. El Paso, Tex., Aug. 28, 1952; s. LeRoy Marshall Steiner and Rosemary (Thurman) Milligan; m. Maria del Rosario Serrano, Dec. 24, 1975 (div. Jan. 1988); children: Karen Alexander, Xavier Oliver; m. Rosemarie Sylvia Erb, May 5, 1990; 1 child, Geoffrey Blake Jr. AB, Washington U., St. Louis, 1978; JD, Samford U., 1981. Bar: Fla. 1983, U.S. Dist. Ct. (mid. dist.) Fla. 1983, U.S. Ct. Appeals (11th cir.) 1985. Asst. pub. defender Office Pub. Defender, 13th Jud. Cir., Tampa, Fla., 1982-84; assoc. Hamilton & Douglas, P.A., Tampa, 1984-86, Mulholland and Anderson, Tampa, 1986-87, Limberopolous, Steiner & Cardillo, Tampa, 1987-89; pres. Geoffrey B. Steiner, P.A., Tampa, 1989—. Co-author: Florida Rules of Juvenile Procedure Annotated, 1982. Mem. Fla. Bar (bd. cert. civil trial lawyer Bd. of Specialization and Certification), Hillsborough County Bar Assn., Assn. Trial Lawyers Am., Acad. Fla. Trial Lawyers, Hunter's Green Country Club, Masons (32d degree), Shriners, Delta Theta Phi, Beta Theta Pi. Methodist. Office: 2529 W Busch Blvd Ste 100 Tampa FL 33618-4514

STEINER, KENNETH KEITH, nursing administrator; b. Louisville, Mar. 10, 1955; s. Kenneth and Jo Ann (Brill) S.; m. Diane LaRue Wilson; children: Kenneth Jr., Michelle, Reneé. AB, Faulkner St. Jr. Coll., Bay Minette, Ala., 1979; BSN, Mobile Coll., 1982; MSN in Adminstrn., U. So. Ala., Mobile, 1996. Cert. BCLS, ACLS; cert. nurse adminstr. Commd. USN, 1982, advanced through grades to lt., 1987; staff nurse medicine Portsmouth (Va.) Naval Hosp., 1982-84, staff nurse surgery, 1984-85; staff nurse ICU Pensacola (Fla.) Naval Hosp., 1985-86, nurse mgr. surgery, 1986-88; nurse mgr. ICU Yokosuka (Japan) Naval Hosp., 1988-89, nurse mgr. med./surgical, 1989-91; ret.; nurse mgr. telemetry Mobile Infirmary Med. Ctr., Ala., 1991-93; nurse mgr. med./surg. USA Knollwood Park Hosp., Mobile, Ala., 1993-95; dir. med. svcs. and nursing info. sys. Thomas Hosp., Fairhope, Ala., 1995—; instr. trainer ACLS, BCLS Am. Heart Assn., Pensacola, Fla., 1986-93. Pres. Baldwin County Tee-Ball Assn., Robertsdale, Ala., 1986-87; asst. scout master Boy Scouts of Am. Yokosuka, Japan and Fairhope, Ala., 1986—; coach Yokosuka Tee Ball Assn., Japan, 1989-90. Mem. Ala. State Nurses Assn., Mobile County Nurses Assn. (program dir., treas.).

STEINGLASS, ROBERT CARY, public health administrator; b. N.Y.C., Mar. 11, 1950; s. Sam and Rose (Feldbrill) S.; m. Dolores Crudge, May 8, 1976; children: Barry, Aaron. BA, Williams Coll., 1971; MPH, Johns Hopkins U., 1978. Smallpox surveillance officer Peace Corps, Wollo, Ethiopia, 1973-74; midwest regional coord. Oxfam-Am., Milw., 1975-76; internat. health intern USPHS, Rockville, Md., 1977; project coord. CARE/MEDICO, Nueva Guinea, Nicaragua, 1978; tech. officer WHO, Sana'a, Yemen, 1978-82, Muscat, Oman, 1982-84, Kathmandu, Nepal, 1984-87; sr. tech. officer REACH/John Snow, Inc., Arlington, Va., 1987-91, tech. dir., 1992-94; immunization coord. Basics/John Snow, Inc., Arlington, 1994—; cons. WHO, Bhutan, 1988, Nairobi, Kenya, 1978; occasional lectr. Johns Hopkins U., Balt., 1988—. Contbr. articles to profl. jours. Decorated Order of the Bifurcated Needle, WHO, 1980. Mem. Am. Pub. Health Orgn., Nat. Coun. Internat. Health, Technet, Internat. Tetanus Soc. Home: 2464 Freetown Dr Reston VA 22091-2528 Office: John Snow Inc 1616 Fort Myer Dr Ste 11F Arlington VA 22209-3100

STEINHAUFF, DAVID MARK, geologist, environmental consultant; b. Bakersfield, Calif., May 20, 1958; s. Fredrick Paul and Sara Ann (Taylor) S. AA in Gen. Edn., Chabot Coll., 1978; BS in Anthropology, U. Calif., Davis, 1981; BS in Geology, Calif. State U., Sacramento, 1983; MS in Geology, Ohio State U., 1985; PhD in Geology, U. Tenn., 1993. Registered profl. geologist, Tenn. Paper mill 3d hand Inland Container Corp., Newark, Calif., 1982; field asst. Calif. Divsn. Mines and Geology, Sacramento, 1983; geologist, micropaleontologist Shell Oil, U.S.A., Houston, 1985; rsch. assoc. Byrd Polar Inst., Columbus, Ohio, 1983-85; geologist Exxon U.S.A., Houston, 1987, ABB Environ., Inc., Knoxville, 1992; grad. tchg. asst. U. Tenn., Knoxville, 1987-91, instr., risk assessment advisor, 1995—; hydrogeologist SciTek, Inc., Oak Ridge, Tenn., 1991-92; risk assessment team leader, project mgr. Oak Ridge Nat. Lab., 1993—. Contbr. articles to profl. jours. Ctr. of Excellence fellow U. Tenn., 1986. Mem. AAAS, Geol. Soc. Am. (instr. short course St. Louis 1989, session chmn. Jackson, Miss. 1996, grantee 1988), Am. Assn. Petroleum Geologists (grantee 1985), Soc. for Sedimentary Geology (leader field trip 1992), Soc. for Risk Analysis, East Tenn. Geol. Soc. (spkr. 1993, 96), Sigma Xi. Office: Oak Ridge Nat Lab 1060 Commerce Park Dr Knoxville TN 37830

STEINKE, JEFFREY JAY, oil and gas company executive, lawyer; b. Ridgefield, Conn., Dec. 23, 1950; s. Carl F. and Elaine D. Steinke. BS, U. Tulsa, 1972, JD, 1975. Bar: Okla. 1976, U.S. Ct. Mil. Appeals 1985, U.S. Ct. Appeals 1977, U.S. Supreme Ct. 1978. Ptnr. Butler, Steinke & Linger, Attys. at Law, Tulsa, 1976-83; owner, pres. Warrior Drilling and Exploration, Tulsa, 1981—; v.p. Metro. Resources Corp., Tulsa, 1992-94; owner, pres. WDE Oil, Inc., Tulsa, 1992—; bd. dirs. CLV Oil and Gas, Inc., Tulsa, Oklatex Properties, Inc., Tulsa. Precinct officer Tulsa County Rep. Com., 1992. Mem. NRA (life), Elks, Am. Legion. Presbyterian. Office: Metro Resources Corp PO Box 690713 Tulsa OK 74169-0713

STEINKULLER, JOAN SOMMERS, physician, educator; b. Weymouth, Mass., July 21, 1942; d. Waldo Stepler and Cordelia Lucille (Schmidt) Sommers; m. Paul G. Steinkuller, May 7, 1966; children: Anne-Marie, Paul, John. BA, George Washington U., 1964, MD, 1967. Diplomate Am. Bd. Pediats., Pediat. Emergency Medicine. Attending physician Student Health Ctr. George Washington U., Washington, 1976-77; staff physician USPHS, Galveston, Tex., 1977-80; med. dir. East Africa Women's League Immunization Team, Kenya, 1982-83; cons. Adventist Mission Hosp., Malawi, Africa, 1985-86; instr. pediatrics Baylor Coll. Medicine, Houston, 1987-88, asst. prof. pediatrics, 1988—; cons. Criss Cole Childrens Fund, Houston, 1993; med. cons. First Bapt. Ch., Houston. Editor: Pediatric Ambulatory Care Handbook, 1991, 95. Ch. nursery dir. First Bapt. Ch., Houston. Recipient Active Tchr. award Baylor Family Practice, 1990, Outstanding Tchr. award Baylor Coll. Medicine, 1992, 95. Mem. Christian Med. and Dental Soc., Alpha Omega Alpha. Home: 4130 N Braeswood Blvd Houston TX 77025-2906 Office: Ben Taub Hosp Pediats 1504 Taub Loop Houston TX 77030-1608

STEINSAPIR, JAIME, physician, researcher; b. Santiago, Chile, Dec. 15, 1950; came to U.S., 1984; s. Mendel and Rosa (Medvinsky) S. BS in Biology and Physics, U. Chile, 1971, MD, 1975; PhD in Endocrinology, Med. Coll. Ga., 1988. Rsch. asst. U. Chile, Santiago, 1969-75, rsch. fellow, 1975-80, asst. prof. physiology and biophysics, 1980-84; postdoctoral fellow dept. endocrinology Med. Coll. Ga., Augusta, 1984-89, asst. rsch. scientist dept. physiology and endocrinology, 1989-93, resident internal medicine dept. medicine, 1993-96; endocrinology fellow Harvard Med. Sch., Boston, 1996—; cons. div. sci. devel. U. Chile, Santiago, 1982, Biomed. Rsch. Grant Support, Med. Coll. Ga., Augusta, 1990-92, Vet. Health Svcs. and Rsch. Adminstr., Washington, 1992; vis. scientist U. N.C., Chapel Hill, 1992. Guest reviewer for sci. and profl. jours. Named Instnl. grant awardee U. Chile, Santiago, 1982, awardee of UN grant PNUD/UNESCO, Santiago, 1982-83; recipient Rsch. grant Am. Cancer Soc., Augusta, 1990-92, Nat. Rsch. Svc. award NIH, Washington, 1992-93. Mem. AMA, Am. Soc. Andrology, Soc. Biology Chile (dir. physiology sect. 1982-83), Endocrine Soc. Chile, Soc. for Study Reproduction, Endocrine Soc. USA. Jewish. Home: 16 Addington Rd Apt 52 Brookline MA 02146 Office: Thyroid Divsn Brigham and Women's Hosp Harvard Med Sch 75 Francis St Boston MA 02115

STELLER, ARTHUR WAYNE, educational administrator; b. Columbus, Ohio, Apr. 12, 1947; s. Fredrick and Bonnie Jean (Clark) S. BS, Ohio U., 1969, MA, 1970, PhD, 1973. Tchr., Athens (Ohio) City Schs., 1969-71; curriculum coord., tchr. Belpre (Ohio) City Schs., 1971-72; prin. elem. schs., head tchr. learning disabilities South-Western City Schs., Grove City, Ohio, 1972-76; dir. elem. edn. Beverly (Mass.) Pub. Schs., 1976-78; adj. prof. Lesley Coll., Cambridge, Mass., 1976-78; coord. spl. projects and systemwide planning Montgomery County Pub. Schs., Rockville, Md., 1978-80; asst. supt. Shaker Heights (Ohio), 1980-83; supt. schs. Mercer County Pub. Schools., Princeton, W. Va., 1983-85; supt. schs. Oklahoma City Pub Schs., 1985-92; supt. schs. Cobb County, Ga., 1992-93; dep. supt. Boston Pub. Schs., 1993-95, acting supt., 1995—; adj. faculty Harvard U., 1992-93. Author: Educational Planning for Educational Success, Effective Schools Research: Practice and Promise; editor: Effective Instructional Management; cons. editor, book rev. editor Jour. for Ednl. Pub. Rels.; mem. editl. bd. Jour. for Curriculum & Supervision; contbr. articles to profl. jours. Bd. govs. Kirkpatrick Ctr.; mem. Oklahoma City Com. for Econ. Devel.; founding bd. dirs. Oklahoma Alliance Against Drugs, Oklahoma Zool. Soc. Inc.; selected for Leadership Okla. City, 1986; bd. dirs. Leadership Okla. City, ARC; bd. dirs. Okla. Centennial Sports Inc.; mem. Oklahoma Acad. for State Goals, State Supt.'s Adv. Coun.; mem. clin. experiences adv. com. U. Okla. Coll. Edn.; trustee Arts Coun. Oklahoma City, Omniplex Sci. and Arts Mus., Oklahoma City Area Vocat.-Tech. Dist. 22 Found.; mem. Urban Ctr. Ednl. Adv. Bd., U.S. Dept. Edn. Urban Supt. Network, Coun. Great City Schs. Bd., Urban Edn. Clearing House Adv. com., U. Okla. Adminstrn. cert. program com., Cmty. Literacy Coun. Bd.; chmn. bd. dirs. Langston U.; chairperson United Way Greater Okla., Sch. Mgmt. Study Group, Okla. Reading Coun. (Okla. literacy coun. reading award 1989), Okla. City PTA; bd. dirs. Oklahoma County chpt. ARC, Jr. Achievement Greater Oklahoma City Bd., Oklahoma State Fair Bd., Horace Mann League Bd., Last Frontier Coun. Bd. Charles Kettering Found. IDEA fellow, 1976, 78, 80; Nat. Endowment Humanities fellow, Danforth Found., 1987-88; recipient Silver Beaver award Boy Scouts Am., 1990, Amb. award Horace Mann League, 1995. Mem. ASCD (exec. coun., pres.-elect 1993-94, pres. 1994-95), Nat. Orgn. Legal Problems in Edn., Nat. Policy Bd. Ednl. Adminstrn., Am. Assn. Sch. Adminstrs. (life, Leadership for Learning award, 1991, Coll. Bd. Advanced Placement Spl. Recognition award 1991), Nat. Assn. Elem. Sch. Prins. (life), Nat. Assn. Edn. Young Children (life), Nat. Sch. Pub. Rels. Assn. (Honor award 1991), Internat. Soc. Ednl. Planning, Nat. Soc. Study Edn., Nat. Planning Assn., Coun. Basic Edn., Am. Edn. Fin. Assn., Ohio Assn. Elem. Sch. Adminstrs., Buckeye Assn. Sch. Adminstrs., Ohio ASCD, Ohio U. Coll. Edn. (disting. alumnus award 1991), Okla. ASCD (Publ. award 1989), Okla. Assn. Sch. Adminstrs., Mass. Assn. Sch. Adminstrs., Mass. ASCD, Okla. Coalition for Pub. Edn., Okla. Commn. for Ednl. Leadership, Urban Area Supts. (Oklahoma br.), Ohio U. Alumni Assn. (nat. dir. 1975-78, pres. Cen. Ohio chpt. 1975-76, pres. Mass. chpt. 1976-78, life mem. trustee's acad.), World Future Soc. (life), Greater Oklahoma City C. of C. (exec. bd. dirs.), South Oklahoma City C. of C. (bd. dirs.), Oklahoma Heritage Assn., Heritage Hills Assn. (bd. dirs.), Victorian Soc. (New England chpt.), Nat. Eagle Scout Assn., Aerospace Found. (hon. bd. dirs.), Am. Bus. Card Club, Coca Cola Collectors Club, Internat. Club, Rotary (Boston), Mgmt. Consortium (bd. advisors), Tau Kappa Epsilon Alumni Assn. (regional officer Mass. 1976-78, named Alumni Nat. Hall of Fame 1986, Nat. Alumnus of Yr. 1993, Excellence in Edn. award 1993), Kappa Delta Pi (life, advisor Cen. Okla. chpt., nat. publs. com.), Phi Delta Kappa (life). Methodist. Home: 225 N Manor Ave Kingston NY 12401-2503

STELLING, HERBERT PUND, family physician; b. Augusta, Ga., Sept. 23, 1919; s. Frank Henry II and Rhetta Evers (Pund) S.; m. Ann Trumbo, June 11, 1949; children: Herbert II, Rebecca, Deborah, Rhetta, David. AB, Emory U., 1940; BD, Luth. Theol. So. Sem., 1943; MD, Med. Coll. Ga., 1951. Diplomate Am. Bd. Family Practice. Pastor Capon-North River Pastorate, W.Va., 1943-44; intern The Charity Hosp. of La., New Orleans, 1951-52; resident E.A. Conway Meml., Monroe, La., 1952-53; med. supt. Luth. Gen. Hosp. and Christian Health Ctr., India, 1953-59; pvt. practice Romney, W.Va., 1961-75; assoc. med. dir. Barre Family Health Ctr., U. Mass. Sch. Medicine, Worcester, Mass., 1975-78; assoc. prof. Wright State U. Sch. Medicine, 1978-88, prof. emeritus, 1988—. Author: Wellness, Anyone?; contbr. articles to profl. jours. Vol. New Horizons Christian Counselling Group, Longwood, Fla.; vol. health cons. Fresh Start Ministries, Orlando, Fla.; physician, locum tenens Indian Reservations with Poject USA and Med. Missionary, Dominican Republic; resources vol. Seminole County (Fla.) Med. Soc., 1993; spkr. in pub. schs.; substitute tchr. health, Azalea Park (Fla.) Elem. Sch., 1988. Lt. s.g. USN, 1944-46. Univ. scholar Rotary Club of Atlanta, 1938. Fellow Am. Acad. Family Physicians (life); mem. Seminole County Med. Soc., Family Practice Found., Phi Theta Kappa, Theta Chi Delta. Home: 1504 Cuthill Way Casselberry FL 32707-5142

STELLING, JOHN HENRY EDWARD, chemical engineer; b. Charleston, S.C., Oct. 3, 1952; s. John Henry Edward Jr. and Louise Ferguson (Myers) S.; divorced. BSChemE, Clemson U., 1974; MSChemE, U. Tenn., 1979. Registered profl. engr., N.C., S.C., Fla., Ga., Mass., Mich., Conn., N.Y., Tenn., Ky., Ind., Ala., Maine; NCEES, REA, Calif.; QEP. Summer tech. worker Tenn. Eastman Co., Kingsport, 1973; rsch. engr. Dow Chem. USA, Plaquemine, La., 1974-77; teaching asst. U. Tenn., Knoxville, 1978-79; staff engr. Radian Corp., Durham, N.C., 1979-83; dept. head Radian Corp., Research Triangle Park, N.C., 1985-95; prin. project mgr. Radian Internat. LLC, Research Triangle Park, N.C., 1996—; v.p. Radian Engring. Inc., Rochester, N.Y., 1990-94, CEO, 1994—; v.p. The Herbert Co., Charleston, 1983-86. Mem. AIChE, Nat. Water Well Assn., Air and Waste Mgmt. Assn., Sigma Xi, Tau Beta Pi, Phi Kappa Phi. Home: 1319 Arnette Ave Durham NC 27707-1601 Office: Radian Corp PO Box 13000 Durham NC 27709-3000

STELTZLEN, JANELLE HICKS, lawyer; b. Atlanta, Sept. 18, 1937; d. William Duard and Mary Evelyn (Emberry) Hicks; divorced; children: Gerald William III, Christa Diane. BS, Okla. State U., 1958; MS, Kans. State U., 1961; JD, U. Tulsa, 1981. Bar: Okla. 1981, U.S. Dist. Ct. (no., ea. and we. dists.) Okla. 1981, U.S. Tax Ct. 1982, U.S. Ct. Claims 1982, U.S. Ct. Appeals (10th cir.) 1983, U.S. Ct. Appeals (Fed. cir.) 1984, U.S. Supreme Ct. 1986; lic. real estate broker. Pvt. practice, Tulsa, 1981—; lectr. Coll. of DuPage, Glen Ellyn, Ill., 1976, Tulsa Jr. Coll., 1981-88; dietitian, Tulsa; res. dep. for Tulsa County Sheriff's Office. Christian counselor 1st United Meth. Ch., Tulsa, 1986—, coord. legal counseling ministry, 1985—, lay pastor, 1987—; mem. Tulsa County Bd. Equalization and Excise Tax Bd., 1989-90; mem. Leadership Tulsa XX, 1993—; recipient of Leadership Tulsa Paragon award, 1996; bd. dirs. Sister Cities Tulsa/San Luis Potosi, 1988—, South Peoria Neighborhood Connection Found., 1991—, pres., 1995-96; active Tulsa County Tax Oversight Com., 1994—, Tulsa Home Rule Charter Com., 1994—. Recipient Okla. Sr. Olympics medal. Mem. Okla. Bar Assn., Tulsa County Bar Assn., Vol. Lawyers Assn. (bd. dirs.), Am. Dietetic Assn., Tulsa Dist. Dietetic Assn., Kiwanis Internat., Mensa, DAR, Delta Zeta. Republican. Home: 6636 S Jamestown Pl Tulsa OK 74136-2615 Office: 1150 E 61st St Tulsa OK 74136-0523

STELZNER, PAUL BURKE, textile company executive; b. Iowa City, Iowa, Jan. 1, 1935; s. Glenn W. and Ruth (Schroder) S.; m. Martha Jane Schneeberger, Aug. 23, 1958; children: Martha Elizabeth Beuke and Barrie Jane Lubbering. BS, Muskingum Coll., 1960; postgrad., Akron U., 1961-65. Tech. dir. Buckeye Fabric Finishing Co., Coshocton, Ohio, 1963-74; sec., sales mgr. Excello Fabric Finishers Inc., Coshocton, 1966-74; gen. mgr. Mineral Fiber Mfg. Corp., Coshocton, 1974-76; v.p., gen. mgr. Kellwood Co. Recreation Group, 1976-85; v.p. Am. Recreation Products, Inc., New Haven, Mo., 1985-88; v.p., gen. mgr. John Boyle & Co., Statesville, N.C., 1989-93, pres., 1993—. Pres. Coshocton County Young Rep. Club, 1960-62; mem. Coshocton County Rep. Exec. Com., 1960-62; pres. Coshocton Park Bd., 1972-76; mem. Coshocton City Planning Commn., 1972-76; chmn. indsl. div. United Fund, 1973; dist. commr. St. Louis Council Boy Scouts Am., 1977-79, pres. Gateway Amica, 1986-87. Served with USN, 1953-57. Mem. ASTM, Indsl. Fabrics Assn. Internat. (assoc. dir. 1973-74, 82-88, 94—), Am. Assn. Textile Colorists and Chemists, Soc. Plastics Engrs. (sr.). Presbyterian. Home: 210 Brierwood Rd Statesville NC 28677-5408 Office: John Boyle & Co Inc Salisbury Rd Statesville NC 28677-5935

STEMPEL, JOHN DALLAS, international studies educator; b. Easton, Pa., July 26, 1938; s. John Emmert and Mary Roberts (Farmer) S.; m. Nancy A. Dean, Feb. 11, 1961 (div. Jan. 1990); m. Susan Hodgetts, May 18, 1991; children: Amy, Alix, Jill. AB cum laude, Princeton U., 1960; MA with distinction, U. Calif., Berkeley, 1963, PhD, 1965. Jr. officer U.S. Embassy U.S. Fgn. Svc., Conakry, Guinea, 1966; acting dep. chief mission U.S. Embassy U.S. Fgn. Svc., Bujumbura, Burundi, 1966-68; watch officer State Dept. Ops. Ctr. U.S. Fgn. Svc., Washington, 1968-70, staff asst. to dep. sec. state, 1968-69; Ghana desk officer U.S. Fgn. Svc., 1970-72; polit.-econ. officer U.S. Embassy U.S. Fgn. Svc., Lusaka, Zambia, 1972-74; from sr. internal polit. reporter to dep. chief sect. to acting polit. counselor U.S. Embassy U.S. Fgn. Svc., Tehran, Iran, 1975-79; diplomat-in-residence, mem. faculty U.S. Naval Acad., Annapolis, Md., 1979-81; dir. ops. ctr. Dept. State U.S. Fgn. Svc., Washington, 1981-83, dir. Office Near East and South Asian Affairs Bur. Internat. Security Affairs Dept. Def., 1983-84, spl. asst. Persian Gulf affairs, 1984-85; consul gen. U.S. Fgn. Svc., Madras, India, 1985-88; prof. internat. studies, assoc. dir. Patterson Sch. Diplomacy and Internat. Commerce U. Ky., Lexington, 1988-93, prof. internat. studies, dir. Patterson Sch. Diplomacy, 1993—; adj. prof. George Washington U., Washington, 1968-72, 80-85, Am. U., Washington, 1975; prof. Regional Coop. and Devel. Coll., Tehran, 1975-78; rsch. assoc. Mershon Ctr. Ohio State U., 1972. Author: Inside the Iranian Revolution, 1981; (monograph) Theory and Practice in Foreign Affairs: Why Two Worlds Seldom Meet, 1972; contbr. articles to profl. jours. With USN, 1960-61, lt. USNR, 1962-70. Mem. Internat. Studies Assn., U.S.-Pakistan Forum. Office: U Ky Patterson Sch Diplomacy Patterson St Rm 455 Lexington KY 40508-2826

STEMPLER, BENJ L., clinical social worker; b. N.Y.C.; s. Samuel and Ethel (Lesser) S.; m. Sharlene J. Poticha, July 4, 1991; 1 child, Danielle Elizabeth. BA, CCNY, 1968; MSW, Hunter Coll., 1975. Lic. social worker, Ga., N.Y., marriage and family therapist; cert. social worker, N.Y. Pvt. practice Atlanta; clin. social worker Jewish Family Svcs., Inc., Atlanta; supr. ongoing svcs. Clayton County Protective Svcs. Team, Morrow, GA.; caseworker N.Y.C. Bur. Child Welfare, Bronx, N.Y. Sr. editor: Social Group Work Today and Tomorrow; Moving from Theory to Training and Practice, 1996; contbr. articles to profl. jours. Mem. NASW, Acad. Cert. Social Workers, Am. Assn. Marriage and Family Therapists, Assn. for Advancement of Social Work with Groups (chair 14th Ann. Symposium), Ga. Aassn. for Advancement of Social Work with Groups (founding chpt. pres. 1992-96). Office: 1924 Cliff Valley Way NE # 202 Atlanta GA 30329-2464

STENGER, NANCY RENE, emergency room nurse; b. Bradenton, Fla., Apr. 2, 1962; d. Edward Joseph and Sue Carolyn (Sherbert) S. BSN, Med. Coll. Ga., 1985. RN, Ga.; CEN; cert. ACLS, BLS, BTLS and PALS; cert. TNCCP. Intermediate care nursery RN Med. Coll. Ga., Augusta, 1985-86; ICU nursery RN U. Hosp., Augusta, 1986-88, RN, emergency rm. staff nurse, 1988-91; RN, emergency rm. staff nurse East Ala. Med. Ctr., Opelika, 1991-92; RN staff nurse Ga. Bapt. Urgent Care, Fayetteville, 1992-93, Stockbridge, 1993-94; RN, emergency rm. staff nurse Peachtree Regional Hosp., Newnan, Ga., 1994—. Recipient scholarship Atlanta Aux. to AMA, 1984, first recipient Emergency Rm. Nurse of Quarter, Sterling Emergency Physicians, 1995. Roman Catholic. Home: 310 Everdale Rd Peachtree City GA 30269

STENNETT, WILLIAM MITCHELL, association executive; b. Russellville, Ala., July 9, 1948; s. William Eugene and Lynne (Mitchell) S.; m. Jamie Delois Reeder, Aug. 10, 1973; children: William Mitchell Jr., James Gordon. BS, Memphis State U., 1970. Br. mgr. ARA Coffee Systems, Memphis, 1972-73; sales mgr. So. Sentinel, Ripley, Miss., 1973-79; div. mgr. Community Devel. Found., Tupelo, Miss., 1979-85; indsl. developer Miss. Dept. Econ. Devel., Tupelo, 1985-86; exec. dir. Coahoma County C. of C., Clarksdale, Miss., 1986-90; pres., exec. dir. EDA of Jones County, Laurel, Miss., 1990—. Bd. dirs., officer Miss. Indsl. Devel. Council, Jackson, 1986—; trustee Multiple Sclerosis of Miss., Jackson, 1977—; treas. Big Ten Devel. Assn., Tupelo, 1980-85. Served with USMC, 1970-72. Recipient Key award Multiple Sclerosis of Miss., 1976, Gov.'s award State of Tenn., 1983. Mem. Miss. Devel. Assn. (bd. dirs.), Assn. for Excellence in Edn. (adv. bd.), So. Indsl. Devel. Coun., So. Growth Policies Bd. (support group), Miss. Assn. C. of C. Execs. (bd. dirs. 1987-88, mem. allied enterprises adv. bd.), Laurel Country Club, Univ. Club Jackson. Methodist. Office: EDA of Jones County PO Box 527 Laurel MS 39441-0527

STENSAAS, HARLAN STANLEY, journalism educator; b. Burbank, S.D., Sept. 17, 1932; s. Arne Julius and Amy Evelyn (Ross) S.; m. Vianne Schooler, Mar. 5, 1954; children: Starla Anne, Tamara Marie, Willa Kay, Kirsten C. BS in English and Journalism, Gen. Beadle State Tchrs. Coll., 1955; MS in Journalism, S.D. State Coll., 1960; postgrad., Wash. State U., 1970-74; PhD in Comm., U. So. Miss., 1986. Reporter, photographer The Daily Leader, Madison, S.D., 1953-55; asst. publicity dir. publicity S.D. Dept. Hwys., Pierre, 1957-58; tchr. English, journalism and speech high schs., 1955-56, 57-59; instr. journalism, dir. H.S. Press Assn. S.D. State Coll., Brookings, 1959-63; dir. pub. rels. and placement, asst. prof. journalism Dakota Wesleyan U., Mitchell, S.D., 1963-68; asst. prof. comm. Wash. State U., Pullman, 1968-75; asst. prof. journalism Ea. Ill. U., Charleston, 1975-78; asst. prof. journalism, newspaper and yearbook adviser Oral Roberts U., Tulsa, 1978-85; instr. journalism Sch. Comm. U. So. Miss., Hattiesburg, 1984-86; assoc. prof. dept. English and Journalism Mercer U., Macon, Ga., 1986-88; assoc. prof. Mass Comm. Inst. Mankato (Minn.) State U., 1988-90; prof., chmn. comm. Tarkio (Mo.) Coll., 1990-91; assoc. prof. dept. comm. Southeastern Okla. State U., 1991-94; vol. svc. English lang. People's Republic of China, 1994—; lectr., panelist workshops and confs. in field; mem. adv. bd. Victory Life Acad., Durant, Okla., 1992—; mem. faculty coun., com. on tech. Sch. Arts and Letters, S.E. Okla. State U., 1993-94; bd. publs. Mercer U., 1986-88; mem. undergrad. curriculum rev. com. U. So. Miss. Sch. Comm., 1985-86, mem. univ. publs. bd., 1984-86; judge Nat. Critical Svc. Associated Collegiate Press and Nat. Scholastic Press, 1965-81. Mem. editorial bd. Am. Journalism, 1986-91; contr. articles to profl. jours. Sec. acad. affairs com., rank and promotion com. Tarkio Coll., 1990-91; libr. liaison Mass Comm. Inst., Mankato State U., 1989-90; dir., sponsor workshops Ea. Ill. High Sch. Press Assn., 1977-78; regional publicity chmn. Wash. State Heart Assn., 1969-71; judge Sch. Bell awards MEA, 1989-90; libr. liaison Mass Communication Inst., Mankato State U., 1989-90; mem. judges panel high sch. writing contest Miss. Power & Light, 1985. Recipient recognition Tulsa Christian Fellowship, 1984. Mem. Am. Journalism Historians Assn. (newsletter editor, ex-officio bd.), Soc. Profl. Journalists, Soc. Collegiate Journalists, Kappa Tau Alpha, Phi Delta Kappa. Republican. Home: 1020 Timberline Rd Durant OK 74701-2317

STENSVAAG, JAMES THOMAS, public historian, educator; b. Marshalltown, Iowa, Aug. 11, 1947; s. Thomas Alfred and Mable Valentine (Thompson) S.; m. Paula Lindstrom, Nov. 27, 1973; children: Cristina, Anna, Erika. BA, St. Olaf Coll., 1969; MA, Iowa State U., 1975; PhD, U. N.Mex., 1978. Mng. editor N.Mex. Hist. Review, asst. prof. history U. N.Mex., Albuquerque, 1978-79; supervisory historian Air Force Nuclear Test Personnel Review, Brooks AFB, Tex., 1980-82; chief hist. programs and policy U.S. Army Tng. and Doctrine Command, Ft. Monroe, Va., 1982-94, chief historian, 1994—, 1995—; adj. prof. history Old Dominion U., Norfolk, Va., 1994—; consulting historian Hampton (Va.) 375th Anniversary Com., 1984-85; parish historian St. Paul's Luth Ch., Hampton, 1984—. Editor: Hampton: From Sea to the Stars, 1610-1985, 1985; contbr. articles to profl. jours. Pres., bd. dirs. Hampton Rds. Evang. Luths. in Min., 1989—. Capt. USAF, 1971-75. Recipient John F. Kennedy Dissertation fellowship U. N.Mex., 1978, Sec. of Army Rsch. and Study fellowship Dept. of Army, 1988-89. Mem. Orgn. Am. Historians, Nat. Coun. Pub. History, Soc. History in Fed. Govt. Home: 106 Willis Church Yard Hampton VA 23669-2025 Office: US Army TRADOC Mil History Office Fort Monroe VA 23651

STENZEL, THOMAS E., association administrator. Pres. United Fresh Fruit and Vegetable Assn., Alexandria, Va. Office: United Fresh Fruit and Vegetable Assn 727 N Washington St Alexandria VA 22314

STEPHEN, MICHAEL, psychologist. BA in Psychology, U. Okla., 1973; MS, Okla. State U., 1077, PhD in Counseling Psychology, 1986. Lic. psychologist. Dir. Cmty. Mental Health Clinic; pvt. practice, 1991—; mem. univ. faculty; lectr. in field. Author: Cherry Lane-A Woman's Story: The Power of Abuse; Sex, Love, and God; and Healing, The Mental States Examination for Beginning and Advanced Professionals, Hypoglycemia: A Disease of the Mind. Vol. child abuse prevention and related polit. issues. Fellow Christian Athletes Assn., Okla. Thoroughbred Assn.; mem. APA, Okla. Psychol. Assn. Home: Unit G 14309 N Pennsylvania Ave Oklahoma City OK 73134-6007

STEPHENS, BETSY BAIN, retired elementary school educator; b. Bessemer, Ala., Apr. 1, 1927; d. Herman Merritt and Lorene Burnice (Waldrop) Bain; m. Merton Von Stephens, June 23, 1947; children: Marc Von, Timothy Merton, Martha Katherine. Diploma, Wheeler Bus. Coll., Birmingham, Ala., 1945; B, U. Montevallo, 1949; MA, U. Ala., Birmingham, 1972. Tchr. Lee County Bd. Edn., Auburn, Ala., 1950-52, Jefferson County Bd. Edn., Birmingham, Ala., 1964-89. Mem. Soc. of Ala. Retirees, Nat. Coun. Tchrs. English, Jefferson County Ret. Tchrs. Assn., Ala. Ret. Tchrs. Assn., Bessemer Music Club, Alpha Delta Kappa. Home: 7373 Warrior River Rd Bessemer AL 35023-7019

STEPHENS, BRENDA WILSON, librarian; b. Durham, N.C., Oct. 22, 1952; d. Leroy Thomas and Lucy Mae (Umstead) Wilson; m. Gregory Frederick Stephens, Mar. 6, 1977; children: Seth, Sara. Student, Vincennes U., 1970-71; BA, Winston-Salem State U., 1974; MLS, N.C. Cen. U., 1981. Cert. pub. libr., N.C. From bookmobile coord. to county libr. Orange County Pub. Libr., Hillsborough, N.C., 1976-92; regional libr. dir. Orange County Pub. Libr., Hillsborough, 1992—. Sec. United Way of Greater Orange County, 1991-93. With U.S. Army, 1974-76. Mem. ALA, N.C. Libr. Assn. (chair adult sect. 1987-93, co-chair 1985-87, lit. com. 1983-85), N.C. Pub. Libr. Dirs. Assn. (officer), Kiwanis Club (pres. 1992-93), A.L. Stanback Mid. Sch. PTO (pres. 1991-92). Democrat. Baptist. Home: 5807 Craig Rd Durham NC 27712-1008 Office: Orange County Pub Libr 300 W Tryon St Hillsborough NC 27278-2449

STEPHENS, C. MICHAEL, service executive; b. Wichita Falls, Tex., Feb. 4, 1949; s. Wilbur Wesley and Mildred Ruth (Smith) S.; m. Janet Kay Speare, Dec. 28, 1971 (div. 1996); children: Kelley Michelle, Suzanne Janelle. BA, Okla. State U., 1971; postgrad., U. Okla., 1971-72. V.p. sales Arrowlite Industries, Tulsa, 1972-76; v.p., regional mgr. Top Value Motivation, Dayton, Ohio, 1976-86; v.p. S&H Citadel, Inc. (formerly S&H Motivation and Travel), Chgo., 1986-96; v.p., regional mgr. Meridian Enterprises Corp., St. Louis, 1996—. Recipient Presdl. Achievement award, 1986. Mem. Am. Mgmt. Assn., Motivation Masters Coun., Kappa Sigma, Cedar Ridge Country Club. Baptist.

STEPHENS, CARSON WADE, minister; b. San Angelo, Tex., Mar. 12, 1950; s. Allison Carson and Betty Jo Justice (Ellis) S.; m. Jeanette Martha Zett, June 19, 1971; children: Jennifer Hope, Bethany June. MusB, U. Tex., 1974; DMin, Drew U., 1991; postdoctoral, Tex. A&M U., 1996; postdoctoral fellow, U. Tex., Austin, 1996. Tchr. Manor (Tex.) Ind. Schs., 1970-73; minister Three Rivers (Tex.) Ch. of Christ, 1976-77, East Main Ch. of Christ, Holdenville, Okla., 1977-83, Sharpstown Ch. of Christ, Houston, 1983-86, Clear Lake Ch. of Christ, Houston, 1986—; intern dept. of univ. advancement and pub. rels. U. Tex., Houston, 1996; intern dept. univ. advancement and pub. rels. U. Tex.-Houston Health Sci. Ctr., 1996; guest lectr. Fred-Hardeman U., Henderson, Tenn., 1992, Pepperdine U., 1996. Author: Evangelization, 1991, In the Beginning, Vol. 1, 1992, Vol. 2, 1993. Bd. dirs. Edgar A. Smith YMCA, Houston, 1987—' mem. Mayor's Com. for Drug Prevention, Houston; active Pasadena Mcpl. Band, Pasadena Mcpl. Orch.; past pres. Summer Repertoire Theatre. Mem. Am. Acad. Ministry, Rotary (youth chair Space Ctr. chpt. 1988-89, bd. dirs. 1990, Presdl. award 1989, 90, chmn. drug awareness program, 1989, 992-93, 93-94, Paul Harris fellow 1993). Home: 1127 Peachford Ln Houston TX 77062-2228 Office: Clear Lake Ch of Christ 938 El Dorado Blvd Houston TX 77062-4020

STEPHENS, DARREL W., protective services official. Office: 1300 1st Ave N Saint Petersburg FL 33705-1509

STEPHENS, DOROTHY ANNE, English language educator; b. Atlanta, Jan. 11, 1958; d. Wesley Daniel and Dorothy Antoinette (Aiken) S. Double BA in English/Creative Writing, Northwestern U., Evanston, Ill., 1979; MA in English, U. Ill., 1983; PhD in English, U. Calif., Berkeley, 1992. Assoc. editor Lakeside Literar Rev., Evanston, 1977-77, 78-79; assoc. writer Ill. Legis. Investigating Commn., 1979-81; various non-acad. positions to coord. CETA Computer Instrn. U. Ill., Chgo., summer 1983; tchng. assoc. U. Calif., Berkeley, 1987-92; asst. prof. English/lit. U. Ark., Fayetteville, 1992—. Contbr. essays to profl. jours. and publs. Mem. AAUP, MLA, Renaissance Soc. Am., Shakespeare Assn. Am., Soc. for Study of Women in Renaissance, Spenser Soc. (Isabel MacCaffrey award and medal for disting. work in Spenserian studies 1992). Office: U Ark Dept English 333 Kimpel Hall Fayetteville AR 72701

STEPHENS, DOUGLAS KIMBLE, chemical engineer; b. Monticello, Ark., June 22, 1939; s. Vardeman King and Lila Belle (McMurtery) S.; m. Mary Joan John, Dec. 4, 1957; children: Kenneth R., David B. BSChemE, U. Ark., 1962. Registered profl. engr., Tex.; cert. safety profl. Sr. engr., safety supt. Monsanto Co., Alvin, Tex., 1967-73, mfg. supt., 1973-78; ptnr. Robert T. Bell & Assocs., Houston, 1978-80; v.p. Tech. Inspection Svcs., Inc., Houston, 1980-84, Bell & Stephens Labs., Inc., Houston, 1980-84; pres. Stephens Engring. Labs., Inc., Webster, Tex., 1984—; pres., CEO N.Am. Environ. Coalition, Inc., Webster, 1993—; project dir./chief engr. enviroGuard enviroFoam Project, 1994—. Contbr. articles to profl. publs. Capt. U.S. Army, 1962-67, Vietnam. Decorated Bronze Star, Air medal. Mem. ASTM (mem. coms., cons.), Am. Inst. Chem. Engrs. (sect. chmn. 1976-77), Am. Soc. Safety Engrs. (cons.), Tex. Soc. Profl. Engrs. (chpt. chmn. 1991-92, pres. 1990-91, Engr. of Yr. 1992), Nat. Assn. Corrosion Engrs. (mem. com. 1978-93, cons.), Nat. Assn. Environ. Profls., Am. Bd. Forensic Examiners. Methodist. Home: 1116 Deats Rd Dickinson TX 77539-4426 Office: 100 E Nasa Blvd Ste 203 Webster TX 77598-5330

STEPHENS, GEORGE MYERS, real estate market research consultant, real estate broker; b. Asheville, N.C., June 11, 1930; s. George Myers and Eleanor (Waddell) S.; m. Karin Holscher, July 28, 1956; children: George, Anthony, Annette. BA in Econs., U. N.C., 1952, M of Regional Planning, 1958. Planner N.C. Hwy. Commn., Raleigh, 1958-61; asst. to gov. State of N.C., Raleigh, 1961-65; dep. dir. Appalachian Regional Commn., Washington, 1965-66; owner, pres. Stephens Assocs., Raleigh, 1966—. Contbr. articles on planning to profl. jours. Bd. dirs. N.C. Symphony, Raleigh, 1987-94; pres. Raleigh Chamber Music Guild, 1985-86, Raleigh Cmty. Band, 1984-85, Friends of the Libr. N.C. State U., 1981-83. Lt. USN, 1952-56. Recipient Arts medal City of Raleigh Arts Commn., 1985. Mem. Urban Land Inst., Nat. Trust for Hist. Preservation, Am. Inst. Planners (bd. dir. N.C. sect. 1960-61). Republican. Episcopalian. Home: 3307 Glen Henry Dr Raleigh NC 27612-4350 Office: PO Box 10761 Raleigh NC 27605-0761

STEPHENS, (HOLMAN) HAROLD, lawyer; b. Enterprise, Ala., Nov. 29, 1954; s. Holman Harrison and Louise (Bass) S. BA, U. Ala., 1976, JD, 1980. Bar: Ala. 1980, U.S. Dist. Ct. (no. dist.) Ala. 1980, U.S. Ct. Appeals (5th and 11th cirs.) 1981. Asst. U.S. atty. U.S. Dist. Ct. (no. dist.) Ala., Birmingham, 1980-82; assoc. Lanier, Shaver & Herring, Huntsville, Ala., 1982-84; ptnr. Lanier, Shaver & Herring, Huntsville, 1985-88, Lanier, Ford, Shaver & Payne PC, Huntsville, 1988—; lectr. U. Ala., Huntsville, 1982-86, So. Jr. Coll., Huntsville, 1984-86. Bd. dirs. Huntsville-Madison County Mental Health Ctr., 1983-89, pres. 1987-88; bd. dirs. Big Bros./Big Sisters of N. Ala., Huntsville, 1983-87, Friends of Pub. Radio, Huntsville, 1984-86. Mem. ABA, Trial Attys. Am., Ala. Bar Assn., Huntsville-Madison (Ala.) County bar Assn. (v.p. young lawyers div. 1986-87, pres. 1987-88). Baptist. Home: 1502 Locust Cir SE Huntsville AL 35801-2005 Office: Lanier Ford Shaver & Payne PC PO Box 2087 Huntsville AL 35804-2087

STEPHENS, JAMES T., publishing executive; b. 1939; married. BA in Bus. Adminstrn., Yale U., 1961; MBA, Harvard U., 1964. With Ebsco Industries Inc., Birmingham, Ala., 1961—, asst. v.p., 1966-67, v.p., 1967-70, exec. v.p., from 1970, now pres., also bd. dirs. Office: Ebsco Industries Inc PO Box 1943 Top of Oak Mountain Hwy 280 Birmingham AL 35201

STEPHENS, JOSEPH H., III, financial planner; b. Shreveport, La., Jan. 19, 1954; s. Joseph H. and Sybil (Law) S. MusB, Sam Houston State U., 1976, MusM, 1978; MBA, U. Houston, 1982. CPA, Tex. Acct. Ernst & Whinney, Houston, 1980; v.p. fin. Am. Teleprocessing, Houston, 1980—. Vol. staff accompanist St. Martins Episc. Ch., Houston, 1986—; bd. dirs. Houston Entrepreneurs Forum (former pres.). Office: American Teleprocessing PO Box 79682 Houston TX 77279

STEPHENS, LAURENCE DAVID, JR., linguist, financial executive; b. Dallas, July 26, 1947; s. Laurence D. Sr. and Amy Belle (Schickram) S.; m. Susan Leigh Foutz, Apr. 16, 1988; 1 child, Laurence David III. MA, Stanford U., 1972, PhD, 1976. Vis. fellow Yale U., New Haven, Conn., summer 1979; rsch. fellow U. S.C., Columbia, 1980; asst. prof. U. N.C., Chapel Hill, 1982-88, assoc. prof., 1989—; CEO Stephens and Family Investments, Dallas, 1994—. Co-author: Two Studies in Latin Phonology, 1977, Language and Metre, 1984, The Prosody of Greek Speech, 1994; editor ann. vol. L'Année Philologique, 1987-92; contbr. over 70 articles to profl. jours. Mem. Univ. Pk. Cmty. League, Park Cities Hist. Soc., Nat. Trust for Hist. Preservation, Washington, 1989—, Dallas Opera Guild, 1992—, The Dallas Symphony Assn. Ann. Fund, Metro. Opera Guild, N.Y.C., 1992—. Recipient L'Année Philologique, NEH, 1987-89, 89-91, 91-93. Mem. Am. Inst. Archaeology, Am. Philol. Assn., Greek and Latin Linguistic Assn. (chmn. 1987-92), Linguistic Soc. Am., N.Y. Acad. Scis., Indogermanische Gesellschaft, Société Internationale de Bibliographie Classique, Sigma Xi. Home: 3319 Greenbrier Dr Dallas TX 75225-4818 Office: Univ NC Chapel Hill Dept Classics CB # 3145 212 Murphey Hall Chapel Hill NC 27599 Address: Stephens Family Mineral Properties and Investments 4020 Colgate Ave Dallas TX 75225-5425

STEPHENS, LAWRENCE WESLEY, engineering executive; b. Terrell, Tex., Nov. 1, 1949; s. Arlie Lawrence and Delia Bess (Welborn) S.; m. Nancy Emaly Morris, June 18, 1977; children: Michael Wesley, Rachel Emaly. BS in Aerospace Engring., U. Tex., Arlington, 1972, MS in Aerospace Engring., 1979. Various engring positions Flight Techs. LORAL Vought Systems, Dallas, 1974-83; engring. project mgr. various weapon system programs Loral Vought, 1983—; mem. industry adv. com. aerospace engring. dept. U. Tex., Arlington, 1986 89, chmn., 1990, assoc. dir. aviation edn. resource ctr., 1974-78; judge regional sci. fairs aerospace awards. Contbr. articles to profl. jours. Coach, umpire Little League Baseball, Arlington, 1973-76; advisor Jr. Achievement, Dallas County, 1979-81; mem. Friends of Irving (Tex.) Pub. Librs., 1988—; bd. dirs., pres. Park People of Irving, 1991-94; tournament commr. Irving Soccer Assn., 1990-93, v.p., 1990-92. Named oustanding alumnus U. Tex. Coll. Engring. Mag., 1983; recipient vol. appreciation award City of Irving Parks & Recreation Dept., 1991. Fellow AIAA (assoc., chmn. North Tex. sect. pub. affairs com. 1976-78, dir. tech. activities 1978-79, gen. chmn. 7th ann. tech. symposium 1979, chmn. edn. & student activities com. 1979-80, dir. membership devel. 1980-81, dir. sect. affairs 1981-82, chmn. sect. 1982-83, nat. pub. policy com. 1980-85, dep. dir. S.W. region pub. policy 1980-85, profl. mem. edn. com. 1983-86, nat. student activities com. 1984—, nat. nominating com. 1985, 86, student jour. adv. bd. 1985-92, dep. dir. honors and awards S.W. region 1985-90, nat. honors and awards com. 1985-92, dep. dir. edn. S.W. region, 1990—, Disting. Svc. award 1991, chmn. 40th S.W. region student paper competition 1992), Tau Beta Pi, Sigma Gamma Tau.

STEPHENS, MARTHA LOCKHART, art educator; b. Corpus Christi, Tex., Jan. 3, 1940; d. Hugh Rairdon and Amelia Virginia (McRee) Lockhart; m. David George Hmiel, June 10, 1961 (div. Oct. 1969); m. William Melvin Stephens Jr., June 2, 1971. BA in English Lit., Colo. Coll., 1961; MA in English Lit., U. Ariz., 1967; BFA in Drawing, U. Tex., San Antonio, 1989. Cert. tchr., Tex. English tchr. Colo., Ala., N.Y., Va. and Calif. pub. schs., 1961-68, San Antonio Ind. Sch. Dist., 1968-73; English tchr. North East Ind. Sch. Dist., San Antonio, 1973-82, level chmn. English, 1974-82, chmn. English lit. selection com., 1977, art and creative writing tchr., 1981-85, art tchr., head dept., 1986-94; presenter in field; cons., tour guide, presenter workshops San Antonio Mus. Art, 1983-86; cons., docent McNay Art Mus., San Antonio, 1987; mem. adv. bd. San Antonio Coun. Tchrs. English, 1980. One woman show Art Ctr. Gallery, 1988; two-person show Chapman Grad. Ctr., Trinity U., 1979; numerous group exhbns. including Tex. Soc. Sculptors, 1979, NOW Art Show, San Antonio, 1980, Alternate Space Gallery, San Antonio, 1983, United Bank of Austin, 1985, U. Tex., San Antonio,

1986, N.E. Ind. Sch. Dist., 1986, others; contbr. articles to profl. publs.; authorized biographer Dorothy Dehner. Sponsor/recipient Gold Crown award Columbia Sch. Press Assn., 1992, citation for excellence Scholastic Art and Writing Awards, 1992, State Champion award Tex. H.S. Press Assn., 1990, 91, 92. Mem. NEA, Tex. State Tchrs.' Assn. (pres. Tchrs. of English sect. region 10 1979), North East Tchrs.' Assn., Nat. Art Edn. Assn., Tex. Art Edn. Assn. (regional rep. 1989-93, Merit award 1986, rep. region V 1989-93, capt. region V 1991-93), San Antonio Art Edn. Assn. (pres. 1990-92, Svc. award 1993, adv. bd. 1988-93). Democrat. Episcopalian. Home: 10935 Whisper Valley St San Antonio TX 78230-3617

STEPHENS, MARY JUNE, secondary school educator; b. Chattanooga, Aug. 28, 1948; d. Howard L. and Mary June (Coletta) S. BA in Math., U. Tenn., Chattanooga, 1970; MEd in Math., West Ga. Coll., 1988. Tchr. math., chmn. dept. Lakeview-Ft. Oglethorpe (Ga.) High Sch., 1971—. Named Tchr. of Yr. and Star Tchr., Lakeview-Ft. Olgethorpe High Schs.; Presdl. award nominee for excellence in sci. and math. teaching, 1992. Mem. NEA, Nat. Coun. Tchrs. Math., Ga. Assn. Educators, Catoosa Edn. Assn., Pilot Club, Delta Kappa Gamma (2d v.p. Alpha Phi chpt. 1982-84, 1st v.p. 1984-86, pres. 1986-88, state fin. com. 1988-90), Gamma Lambda (charter). Roman Catholic. Home: 530 Greenfield Dr Rossville GA 30741-3044 Office: Lakeview Ft Oglethorpe HS 1101 Battlefield Pky Fort Oglethorpe GA 30742-3957

STEPHENS, OTIS HAMMOND, JR., political science educator; b. East Point, Ga., Sept. 20, 1936; s. Otis Hammond and Mary Margaret (Fisher) S.; m. Linda Duren, June 18, 1960 (dec. July 1988); children: Ann S. Henderson, Carol S. Frazier; m. Mary Torpey Ballard, Oct. 21, 1989. AB cum laude, U. Ga., 1957, MA, 1958; PhD, Johns Hopkins U., 1963; JD with high honors, U. Tenn., 1983. Bar: Tenn. 1984. Grad. rsch. asst. U. Ga., 1957-58; jr. instr. Johns Hopkins U., 1959-61; asst. prof. to prof. Ga. So. Coll., 1962-67; assoc. prof. U. Tenn., Knoxville, 1967-71, prof., 1971—, Lindsay young prof., 1981-82, alumni disting. svc. prof. polit. sci., 1983—, acting head dept., 1986-88; Russell Sage Found. resident in law and social sci. Harvard Law Sch., 1975-76; assoc. dean Coll. of Liberal Arts Univ. Tenn.; lectr. U.S. Govt. Mgmt. Devel. Ctr., 1972—; panel mem., chmn. various assns. Author: The Supreme Court and Confessions of Guilt, 1973; co-author: (with Gregory J. Rathjen) The Supreme Court and the Allocation of Constitutional Power, 1980; (with John M. Scheb, II) American Constitutional Law: Essays and Cases, 1988, American Constitutional Law, 1993; contbr. articles to profl. jours., chpts. to books. Pres. Nat. Accreditation Coun. for Agys. Serving the Blind and Visually Handicapped, 1979-83; pres. Am. Coun. of Blind, 1987-89; trustee Am. Found. for Blind, 1987—, exec. com., 1992; mem. Gov.'s Adv.Com. on Fair Employment Opportunity, State of Tenn., 1987-95. Ford Found. pub. affairs grantee, 1961, faculty rsch. grantee summers 1968, 69, 70, 74, 91; grad. fellow Am. Found. Blind, 1962, Johns Hopkins U., 1958-62, liberal arts fellow law and polit. sci. Harvard Law Sch., 1975-76; recipient Acad. Achievement award Recording for the Blind, Inc., 1962, Alumni Assn. Outstanding Teaching award U. Tenn., 1977, 84, Rsch. Incentive award Coll. Liberal Arts, U. Tenn., 1983-84. Mem. AAUP (pres. U. Tenn. chpt. 1985-86), ABA, Am. Polit. Sci. Assn. (exec. coun. pub. law sect. 1990-92), Tenn. Polit. Sci. Assn. (pres. 1991-92), So. Polit. Sci. Assn., Knoxville Bar Assn., Phi Beta Kappa (pres. Epsilon of Tenn. chpt. 1981-82), Golden Key, Order of Coif, Omicron Delta Kappa, Phi Kappa Phi, Pi Sigma Alpha. Home: 1141 Southgate Rd Knoxville TN 37919-7647 Office: U Tenn Dept Polit Sci 1001 McClung Tower Knoxville TN 37996

STEPHENS, PATRICIA ANN, marketing professional; b. Gulfport, Miss., Feb. 1, 1945; d. James Marshall and Edna Mathilda (Hogan) S. BA, St. Louis U., 1967; MA, Memphis State U., 1971. Lic. secondary educator speech, theatre, English, religion. Exec. v.p. Prodns. Unltd., Memphis, 1971-73; chairperson speech dept. Southaven (Miss.) High Sch., 1973-77; instr. speech N.W. Jr. Coll., Southaven, 1974-76; pub. rels. dir., instr. St. Agnes Acad., Memphis, 1977-78; religion and English instr. Memphis Cath. High Sch., 1978-82; resource tchr. communications Mobile (Ala.) City Schs., 1982-84; mktg. devel. specialist/mktg. mgr. Prime Health Ala., Mobile, 1984-85; mktg. mgr. Blue Cross Blue Shield Fla./Health Options, Lakeland and Orlando, Fla., 1986-92; ind. agt., 1992-94; nat. mktg. and svc. coord. Delta Care, PMI, Tampa, 1994—. Bd. mem. Red Balloon Players, Memphis, 1971-73, Downtown Dream Machine, Memphis, 1980-82, Cir. Playhouse/Playhouse on the Square, Memphis, 1980-82. Newspaper Fund fellow Wall St. Jour. Newspaper Fund, U. Oreg., 1968, writing fellow Greater Memphis Writing Project, Memphis State U., 1980, part-time masters fellow Memphis State U., 1981-82; recipient Pres.'s Club BCBSF/Health Options Sales Mgr. award Health Options of Polk County, 1987. Democrat. Roman Catholic. Home: 4128 Sunny Land Dr Lakeland FL 33813-3946 Office: Deltacare Delta Dental Ste 300 9501 Princess Palm Ave Tampa FL 33619

STEPHENS, ROBERT DAVID, environmental engineering executive; b. La Follette, Tenn., Nov. 8, 1949; s. Robert Oscar and Billie Jean (Maples) S.; m. Donna Jean Reece, July 11, 1970 (div. Apr. 1984). BA in Biology, Berea (Ky.) Coll., 1971; postgrad., U. Cin., 1973-74. Cert. environ. assessor, Fla.; registered environ. property assessor. Environ. specialist Ky. Dept. Health, Ludlow, 1971-74; project mgr. Pedco Environ. Specialists, Cin., 1974-77; environ. control mgr. Mobil Chem. Corp., Richmond, Va., 1978-84; v.p. Environ. Analysis Corp., Richmond, 1984-85; mgr. Environ. Rsch. and Tech. Group GSX Corp., Greensboro, N.C., 1985-86; mgr. regulatory affairs and community relations Internat. Tech. Corp., Knoxville, Tenn., 1986-88; mgr. environ. studies Internat. Tech. Corp., Tampa, Fla., 1988-90; gen. mgr. First Environment, Inc., Tampa, 1990-91; co-owner BRUDER STEPHENS, INC., Tampa, 1991—. Author reports in field. Co-founder Berea Community Theater, 1970. Mem. Fla. Bar Assn. (assoc., environ and land use sect.), Fla. Environ. Assessors Assn. (pres. 1996-97, bd. dirs.), Water Pollution Control Fedn., Va. Orchid Soc. (pres. 190-85, del. World Orchid Congress, Miami 1984), Ridge Orchid Soc. Republican. Home: PO Box 145 Mango FL 33550-0145 Office: 6902 E 7th Ave Ste 100 Tampa FL 33619-3378

STEPHENS, ROBERT F., state supreme court chief justice; b. Covington, Ky., Aug. 16, 1927. Student, Ind. U.; LL.B., U. Ky., 1951. Bar: Ky. 1951. Asst. atty. Fayette County, Ky., 1964-69; judge Fayette County, 1969-75; atty. gen. Ky. Frankfort, 1976-79; justice Supreme Ct. Ky., Frankfort, 1979—, chief justice, 1982—; pres. Conf. of chief justices, 1992-93; chmn. Nat. Ctr. for State Ct., 1992-93. Staff: Ky. Law Jour. Bd. dirs. Nat. Assn. Counties, 1973-75; 1st pres. Ky. Assn. Counties; 1st chmn. Bluegrass Area Devel. Dist.; chmn. Ky. Heart Assn. Fund Drive, 1976-78. Served with USN, World War II. Named Outstanding Judge of Ky. Ky. Bar Assn., 1986, Outstnding County Judge, 1972; recipient Herbert Harley award Am. Judicature Soc. Mem. Order of Coif. Democrat. Office: Ky Supreme Ct 231 Capital Bldg 700 Capital Ave Frankfort KY 40601*

STEPHENS, SIDNEY DEE, chemical manufacturing company executive; b. St. Joseph, Mo., Apr. 26, 1945; s. Lindsay Caldwell and Edith Mae (Thompson) S.; m. Ellen Marie Boeh, June 15, 1968 (div. 1973); m. Elizabeth Ann Harris, Sept. 22, 1973; 1 child, Laura Nicole. BS, Mo. Western State U., 1971; MA, U. Houston, 1980. Assoc. urban planner Met. Planning Commn., St. Joseph, Mo., 1967-71; prodn. acctg. assoc. Quaker Oats Co., St. Joseph, 1971-72, office mgr., pers. rep., Rosemont, Ill., 1972-73, employee and community rels. mgr., New Brunswick, N.J., 1973-75, Pasadena, Tex., 1975-80; site pers. mgr. ICI Americas, Inc., Pasadena, Tex., 1980-90, regional mgr. human resources agrl. products div., 1990-93; regional mgr. human resources Zeneca Inc., 1993—; pvt. practice mgmt. cons., Houston, 1981—. Contbr. articles to profl. jours. With USNR, 1963-65. Mem. Soc. for Human Resources Mgmt., Houston Pers. Assn. (community and govtl. affairs com. 1984-85, 85-86). Republican. Methodist. Home: 16446 Longvale Dr Houston TX 77059-5420 Office: Zeneca Inc 5757 Underwood Rd Pasadena TX 77507-1031

STEPHENS, STEVEN SCOTT, lawyer, educator; b. Washington, Aug. 19, 1957; s. Norval R. Stephens and Eileen White; m. Heidi M. Stephens, Aug. 1, 1987; children: Samantha Marie, Eric Robert. BA, U. Md., 1981; JD, U. Balt., 1984; LLM, George Washington U., 1986; MS, Johns Hopkins, 1992; MA, U. S. Fla., 1994. Bar: Md. 1985, D.C. 1986, Fla. 1988, U.S. Supreme Ct. 1993. Rsch. atty. U.S. Ct. Appeals, Balt., 1982-85; atty. Birrane, Harlan & Sharretts, Balt., 1985-88, Alpert, Josey & Grilli, Tampa, Fla., 1988-93; pvt. practice Tampa, 1993—; adj. prof. Stetson U. Coll. of Law, St. Petersburg, Fla., 1992—. Contbr. articles to profl. jours. Chmn. Fla. Statewide Nominating Commn. for Judges of Compensation Claims, 1995-96. Office: 707 N Franklin St Fl 4 Tampa FL 33602-4430

STEPHENS, SUZANNE HARDY, oncology nurse; b. Birmingham, Ala., Feb. 15, 1949; d. Harold Edward and Rhonda Faye (Brown) Hardy; m. Emmett John Boylan III, Sept. 6, 1969 (div. Apr. 1983); 1 child, Allison C.; m. Chris H. Stephens, July 14, 1984. BSN, U. Ala., Birmingham, 1979, MSN, 1982. Cert. oncology nurse. Staff nurse Huntsville (Ala.) Hosp., 1979-81; grad. teaching asst. U. Ala., Birmingham, 1981-82, clin. rsch. nurse, 1983-90; oncology nurse specialist U. ala., Huntsville, 1982-83; hospice relief nurse Hospice of Huntsville, 1979-83; oncology clin. nurse specialist St. Patrick Hosp., Lake Charles, La., 1990-94, hosp. relief nurse, 1991-94; clin. rsch. coord. Advanced Cancer Techs., Chattanooga, 1994-95; rsch. clin. nurse specialist Meml. Hosp., Chattanooga, 1995—; mem. speakers' bur. A.H. Robins Co., Richmond, Va., 1984-89, Purdue Frederick Co., Norwalk, Conn., 1987—; mem. prof. edn. com. Am. Cancer Soc., Lake Charles and Chattanooga, 1991—, mem. nursing com., 1991—; clin. preceptor McNeese State U., Lake Charles, 1992-94; clin. preceptor, mentor U. Tenn., Chattanooga, 1994—. Contbr. articles to profl. jours. Vol. spkr. Am. Cancer Soc., Lake Charles, 1991-94, co-facilitator cancer support group, 1992-94. NIH fellow, 1981. Mem. Oncology Nursing Soc. (Chattanooga chpt. pres. 1996—), Am. Soc. Clin. Oncology, Nat. League for Nursing, Sigma Theta Tau, Omicron Delta Kappa. Democrat. Home: 101 S St Marks Ave Chattanooga TN 37411

STEPHENS, WANDA BREWER, social services administrator, investor; b. Bolckow, Mo., Nov. 6, 1932; d. Perry Clark and Mary Carolyn (Fisher) Brewer; m. Lloyd Wesley Stephens, June 19, 1954; children: Ruth Ann, Susie Jo, John Allen, Donna Lynn. BS in home econs., U. Ark., 1954, MS, 1958. Cert. secondary edn. Home economics tchr. West Fork (Ark.) High Sch., 1954-58; pres. Devel. Child Care Assn., Fayetteville, Ark., 1971-74; pres., founding bd. Infant Devel. Ctr., Fayetteville, Ark., 1972-75, treas., 1975-81; edn. chmn., fin. com., admin. bd. Cen. United Meth. Ch., Fayetteville, Ark., 1976-79; pres. League of Women Voters, Fayetteville, Ark., 1979-83, Nat. Orgn. Women, Fayetteville, Ark., 1983-89; state legis. v.p. NOW, Fayetteville, 1985-90, 93-96; state pres. Nat. Orgn. Women Ark., Fayetteville, 1991-93; bd. sec., headstart, Econ. Opportunity Agy., Fayetteville, 1969-70; treas. Mama's Milk Investment Club, 1970-72. Co-author: Bylaws for Economic Opportunity Agy., 1969; co-editor: Washington County, Ark., 1982. Fundraiser United Fund, 1972-75; polit. organizer NOW, 1986; treas. Washington County Dem. Women, 1990-92; organizer/staff/fund Women's Libr., 1982-91; cons./organizer Ctrl. Child Care Ctr., 1977-78. Recipient Internat. 4-H Youth Exch., 1953-54, Infant Devel. Ctr. Founders Plaque Univ. Ark., 1987; named Lay Person of Yr., Ctrl. United Meth. Ch., 1977. Mem. Mental Health Assn. (Community Svc. award 1972), AAUW (pres. Fayetteville 1975-77, state treas. 1996—, Edn. Found. fellow 1984), ACLU (Susan B. Anthony award 1985), Ark. Women's Polit. Caucus (Uppity Woman award 1987, 92). Democrat. Methodist. Home: 1177 E Ridgeway Dr Fayetteville AR 72701-2612

STEPHENSON, CRAIG ALAN, assistant city manager; b. Parsons, Kans., Apr. 20, 1960; s. Tom and Mary (Kraus) S.; m. Rebecca Louise Jamison, Nov. 17, 1984; children: Amanda Louise, Andrea Leigh, Aaron Lynn, Austin Laine, Adam Luke. BA, Fort Hays State U., 1984, MS, 1987. Resident mgr. Fort Hays (Kans.) State U., 1981-82; resident dir. Doane Coll., Crete, Nebr., 1982-83; grad. asst. Fort Hays State U., 1984-85; asst. city mgr. City of Dodge City, Kans., 1985-88, City of Enid, Okla., 1988—; asst. football coach Doane Coll., 1982-83. Trustee Amigo's, Dallas, 1992—, St. Mary's Hosp., Enid, 1993—; dir. Keep Okla. Beautiful, Oklahoma City, 1993—. Named one of Outstanding Young Men Am., 1988; recipient Citizens Recognition award Okla. Libr. Assn., 1993. Mme. Internat. City Mgr.'s Assn., City Mgr.'s Assn. of Okla., Air Force Assn. Office: City of Enid 401 W Owen K Garriott Rd Enid OK 73701-5521

STEPHENSON, G. WARREN, wholesale distribution executive; b. Memphis, Dec. 9, 1944; s. Gillis Warren Sr. and Ethel M. (Howson) S.; m. Martha Ann Sawrie, July 26, 1976; 1 child, Boyd. BBA in Acctg., U. Ark., 1967. Pres. DSM, Inc. div. Ark. Modification Ctr., Inc., Little Rock, 1983-86, U.W.F., Inc., Little Rock, 1986-90; chmn. United Wholesale Florist, Inc., Little Rock, 1990—; bd. dirs. One Nat. Bankshares, Inc., Little Rock. Bd. dirs. Boy Scouts Am., Little Rock, 1991, pres. Quapaw area coun.; bd. trustees Lyon Coll. Mem. Young Pres. Orgn. (pres. 1986-87). Home: 68 Robinwood Dr Little Rock AR 72227-2224 Office: United Wholesale Florist 1616 Brookwood Dr Little Rock AR 72202-1704

STEPHENSON, JOSEPH ANDERSON, vocational school educator; b. Richmond, Va., Jan. 19, 1960; s. Joseph Anderson Sr. and Marie (Beverly) S.; m. Laura Flowers, Sept. 24, 1983; children: William Kieth, Andrea Marie. BS in Indsl. Arts Edn., Ea. Ky. U., 1982, MS in Indsl. Tech. Edn., 1989. Indsl. arts tchr. Monticello (Ky.) Ind. Bd. Edn., 1983-88; tech. edn. tchr. Clark County Bd. Edn., Winchester, Ky., 1988—. Bd. dirs. Wayne County Little Leauge, Monticello, 1986-87. Recipient Class Act award Sta. WTVQ, 1992, Golden Apple Achievement award Ashland Oil, 1993. Mem. NEA, Ky. Edn. Assn., Ky. Indsl. Edn. Assn. (Tchr. of Yr. 1991), Internat. Tech. Edn. Assn. (Tchr. Excellence award 1992), Lions (v.p. Monticello chpt. 1986-88, zone chmn. dist. 43-C 1988, pres. Winchester chpt. 1990-91). Democrat. Baptist. Home: 14 Village Dr Winchester KY 40391-1729 Office: Conkwright Middle Sch 360 Mount Sterling Rd Winchester KY 40391-1528

STEPHENSON, ROSCOE BOLAR, JR., state supreme court justice; b. Covington, Va., Feb. 22, 1922. A.B., Washington and Lee U., 1943, J.D., 1947, LL.D. (hon.), 1983. Bar: Va. 1947. Ptnr. Stephenson & Stephenson, Covington, 1947-52; commonwealth's atty. Alleghany County, Va., 1952-64; ptnr. Stephenson, Kostel, Watson, Carson and Snyder, Covington, 1964-73; judge 25th Jud. Cir. Ct. Commonwealth Va., Covington, 1973-81; justice Va. Supreme Ct., Richmond, 1981—. Recipient Covington Citizen of Yr. award, 1973; recipient Outstanding Alumni award Covington High Sch., 1973. Fellow Am. Coll. Trial Lawyers; mem. Va. State Bar (council 1969-73), Va. Bar Assn., Va. Trial Lawyers Assn., Order of Coif. Home: North Ridge Hot Springs VA 24445 Office: Va Supreme Ct 100 N 9th St Richmond VA 23219-2335 also: 214 W Main St Covington VA 24426-1543

STEPHENSON, SHELBY, poet, editor, educator, singer; b. Benson, N.C., June 14, 1938; s. William Paul Sr. and Maytle Samantha (Johnson) S.; m. Linda Letchworth Wilson, July 30, 1966; children: Jacob Winsor, Catherine. AB in English, U. N.C., 1960; MA in English, U. Pitts., 1967; PhD in English, U. Wis., 1974. Chmn. English dept. Campbell U., Buies Creek, N.C., 1974-78; prof. English U. N.C., Pembroke, 1978—; pres. N.C. Writers Conf., 1979. Author: Plankhouse, 1993; author of numerous poems; editor: Pembroke Mag., 1979—. Recipient Sam Ragan award St. Andrew's Presbyn. Coll., Laurinburg, N.C., 1989. Mem. Poetry Soc. Am., Acad. Am. Poets, Associated Writing Programs, Poets and Writers, South Atlantic MLA, N.C. Poetry Soc. (hon. life), Paul Green Found., Friends of Weymouth (pres. 1994-95), N.C.-Va. Coll. English Assn. (pres. 1987-88), N.C. Writers Network (pres. 1994-95), N.C. Literary and Hist. Assn. (pres. 1982). Home: 985 Sanders Rd Benson NC 27504

STEPKOSKI, ROBERT JOHN, automobile dealership executive; b. Floral Park, N.Y., Mar. 15, 1933; s. John Vincent and Mary Victoria (Rudnicki) S.; m. Caryl Diane Henderson, June 20, 1953; 1 child, Caryl Dale Stepkoski Yarley. 1000 hour cert., L.I. Drafting Sch., Freeport, N.Y., 1952; cert. in forms design, NYU, 1957; AAS, C.W. Post Coll., 1961; continuing edn. certs., Clemson U., 1981-82. Distbn. mapper and planner L.I. Lighting Co., Roslyn and Hicksville, 1952-57; records analyst L.I. Lighting Co., Hicksville, 1957-58; statis. analyst L.I. Lighting Co., Mineola, 1958-65, mgr. budget div., 1965-70, econ. analyst, 1970-71; sec.-treas., bus. mgr. Hunter Chevrolet Co., Hendersonville, N.C., 1971-85; compt., asst. sec., asst. treas. Hughes Chem. Corp., Fletcher, N.C., 1985-86; contr. Raleigh (N.C.) Toyota, 1986-87; dir. ops. Boyd Pontiac-Cadillac-Buick, Inc., Hendersonville, 1988-95; ret., 1995—. With U.S. Army, 1953-55. Mem. Hendersonville Country Club, Kiwanis (bd. dirs. Hendersonville 1976-79, fund raising treas. 1976-86, Outstanding Committeeman award 1976, Disting. Svc. award 1981, Outstanding Svc. award 1995). Home: 15 White Squirrel Ln Hendersonville NC 28739-8360

STEPP, KENNETH STEPHENSON, lawyer; b. Greenville, S.C., Sept. 8, 1947; s. James Marvin and Vivian Olivia (Pittman) S.; m. Ann Watts, July 20, 1969 (dec. Aug. 1984); children: Brian Stephen, Mark Gregory (dec.); m. Wilma Smith, June 3, 1988; 1 child, Carson Kenneth. BS in Indsl. Mgt., Clemson U., 1968; MS in Mgt., U.S. Naval Postgrad. Sch., 1970; JD, U. Ga., 1976. Bar: Ga. 1976, U.S. Dist. Ct. (mid. dist.) Ga. 1976, Fla. 1977, U.S. Ct. Appeals (5th cir.) 1978, U.S. Dist. Ct. (mid. dist.) Fla. 1979, Ky. 1991, U.S. Dist. Ct. (ea. dist.) Ky. 1991. Assoc. Law Office of H. Norwood Pearce, Columbus, Ga., 1976-77; ptnr. Hawkins, Fitt, Messner & Stepp, Columbus, 1977-78; pvt. practice law Inverness, Fla., 1979-83; sole shareholder Kenneth S. Stepp P.A., Inverness, 1984-85, 90-91; shareholder Stepp & Travis, P.A., Inverness, 1985-88, Stepp, Travis & Nelson, P.A., Inverness, 1988-90; prin. Kenneth S. Stepp, P.A., P.S.C., Inverness, 1991—; atty. City of Inverness, 1980; bd. dirs. Withlacoochee Area Legal Svcs., Inc., Ocala, Inverness, Brooksville and Bushnell, Fla., 1982-85. Candidate U.S. Congress, 1986, 88, State Commr. Edn., 1990, State Senate, 1996; mem. Citrus County Rep. Exec. Com., Inverness, 1988-91. Lt. (j.g.) USN, 1968-73. Mem. Ky. Bar Assn., Ga. Bar Assn., Fla. Bar Assn., Citrus County Bar Assn. Methodist. Home: 100 N Edinburgh Dr Inverness FL 34450-1744 Office: 305 N Apopka Ave Inverness FL 34450-4201

STERLING, DONALD EUGENE, civil engineer; b. Rootville, Pa., May 30, 1939; s. Blanche Marie (Phelps) Vanik; m. Janet Leigh Wotring, Apr. 23, 1983. A in Engring., Pa. State U., 1966; BSCE, W.Va. Inst. Tech., 1981; MS in Engring., W.Va. Coll. Grad. Studies, Charleston, 1987. Cert. engr. technician. Hwy. drafting technician W.Va. Dept. Transp., Charleston, 1965-67, hwy. engr. technician, 1967-82, design rev. engr., 1982-89, sr. rev. engr., 1989-94; civil engr. Woolpert Cons., Charleston, W.Va., 1994-96. Tutor Charleston Dist. Outreach Ministries, 1981-83, counselor Camp For Under Privileged Children, 1982; treas., v.p. Kanawha City Midget Football Team, 1978. Sgt. USAF, 1959-63, with Pa. Nat. Guard, 1956-59. Recipient certs. Appreciation Kanawha City Midget Football Team, 1978, Charleston Dist. Outreach Ministries, 1981-83. Mem. ASCE (W.Va. sect. pres. 1990-91, v.p. 1989-90; pres. Charleston Br. 1988-89, sec., treas. 1987-88; corr. mem. nat. com. on employment conditions 1989-91). Democrat. Methodist. Home: 821 Scenic Dr Charleston WV 25311-1522

STERMER, JO CAROL, electrical engineer; b. Lexington, Ky., Dec. 19, 1942; d. James Hisle Johnson and Jeanne Boyd (Adams) Johnson Nichols; m. Anthony E. Stermer, Dec. 27, 1966; children: James Anthony, Adam Thomas. BSEE, U. Ky., 1964. Gen. engr. U.S. Army Space & Strategic Def.Comman, Huntsville, Ala., 1987—. Presbyterian. Home: 7438 Logan Dr SW Huntsville AL 35802-2964 Office: Arrow Project Office SFAE-MD-ARW PO Box 1500 Huntsville AL 35807-3801

STERN, BARNEY JOEL, neurologist; b. N.Y.C., July 11, 1949; s. Leo and Henny (Cohnen) S.; m. Elyce Geller, Jan. 26, 1975; children: Rachel, Melissa, Jamie. BS, CUNY, 1970; MD, U. Rochester, 1974. Diplomate Am. Bd. Neurology. Intern Boston City Hosp., 1974-75, resident in internal medicine, 1975-76; resident neurology Strong Meml. Hosp., Rochester, N.Y., 1976-79; assoc. prof. neurology Johns Hopkins U., Balt., 1988; dir. divsn. neurology Sinai Hosp., Balt., 1990-94; chief clin. svcs. dept. neurology, prof. neurology Emory U., Atlanta, 1994—. Fellow Am. Acad. Neurology; mem. Am. Neurol. Assn. Office: Emory U Hosp Ste C296D 1364 CLifton Rd NE Atlanta GA 30322

STERN, DANIEL, author, executive, educator; b. N.Y.C., Jan. 18, 1928; s. Morris and Dora (Hochman) S.; m. Gloria Shapiro, Nov. 9, 1963; 1 son, Eric Branfman. Sr. v.p., mng. dir., mem. bd. mgmt. McCann-Erickson Advt., Inc., N.Y.C., 1964-69; v.p. advt. and publicity worldwide, also dir. Warner Bros., 1969-72; v.p., dir. mktg. Longchamps, Inc., N.Y.C., 1972-73; v.p., creative dir. Lubar-Southard, Inc., N.Y.C., 1973; fellow Ctr. for Humanities, Wesleyan U., 1969, vis. prof. letters and English, 1976-79; v.p. promotion East Coast CBS Entertainment, N.Y.C., 1979-86; pres. entertainment divsn. McCaffrey & McCall, Advt., N.Y.C., 1986; prof. English and creative writing U. Houston, 1992—, Cullen disting. prof. English, 1993—; dir. Humanities, 92nd St. YMHA, 1988. Author: Girl with Glass Heart, 1953, The Guests of Fame, 1955, Miss America, 1959, Who Shall Live, Who Shall Die, 1963 (Internat. Remembrance award for fiction Bergen Belsen Assn. 1973), After the War, 1967, The Suicide Academy, 1968, The Rose Rabbi, 1971, Final Cut, 1975, An Urban Affair, 1980, Twice Told Tales, 1989 (Richard and Hinda Rosenthal Fiction award AAAL 1990), Twice Upon a Time, 1992. With U.S. Army, 1946-47. Mem. PEN, Nat. Book Critics Circle, Author's League.

STERN, DONNA VIRGINIA, underwriter; b. Memphis, Aug. 25, 1963; d. Samuel Solly and Mary Estel (Jenkins) S. BA, U. Memphis, 1985. Substitute tchr. Met. City Schs., Nashville, 1986; data entry operator Lawyer's Title Ins. Corp., Memphis, 1986-91, compiler, 1991-92, underwriter, 1992—. Editor newspaper Greenscene, 1993; writer newsletter Tennes-Sierran, 1993—. Mem. Sierra Club (toxics chair Tenn. chpt. 1992—), vol. group sec. 1994—, toxics chair 1992—). Democrat. Roman Catholic. Home: 5862 Kesswood Ct Memphis TN 38119-5129 Office: Lawyer s Title Ins Corp 6363 Poplar Ave Ste 108 Memphis TN 38119-4801

STERN, DOUGLAS DONALD, retired foundry company executive; b. New London, Wis., Apr. 29, 1939; s. Sylvester S. and Gretchen W. S.; divorced; children: Randal, Richard, Robert, Russell; m. Joy J. Schmitzer, Aug. 13, 1988. BS in Bus. and Math., U. Wis.-Oshkosh, 1962. With Neenah Foundry (Wis.), 1962—, indsl. engr., 1962-65, dir. indsl. engring., 1965-73, gen. supt. Plant 3, 1973-83, plant mgr. Plant 2, 1983-88; mgr. ops. Navistar Foundry, Waukesha Plant, 1988-89; mgr. foundry div. U.S. Foundry, Fla., 1989-95, retired 1995; cons. FMC, Lenox; instr. Fox Valley Tech. Inst., Leach; dir. Dura Products. Coach. Neenah Baseball, 1976—, treas., 1976—; pres. Our Savior's Luth. Ch., 1971, treas. Found., 1983. Recipient Neenah Football Rocket award, 1981. Mem. Am. Foundrymen's Soc. (speaker's award 1976, pres. N.E. Wis. chpt.), Am. Inst. Indsl. Engrs. (past pres. and bd. dirs.), Nat. Foundry Assn. (indsl. engring. com.). Republican. Author student workbook: Operations Analysis, 1983. Home: 1263 Lakeshore Dr Lorida FL 33857-9747 Office: 7378 Widgeon Ln Larsen WI 54947-9637

STERN, HAROLD PATRICK, behavioral pediatrician; b. Tampa, Fla., Sept. 11, 1948; s. Harold Gustav and Kathaleen Mary (Sullivan) S.; m. Patricia Anne Greywitt, Apr. 11, 1969; children: Theresa, Thomas, Ginine, Michael, Stephen. BS magna cum laude, U. Notre Dame, 1970; MD, Case Western Res. U., 1974. Diplomate Am. Bd. Pediat. (assoc.). Resident in pediatrics Wilford Hall USAF Med. Ctr., San Antonio, 1974-75; pediatrician Hickam Clinic, Hickam AFB, Hawaii, 1975-78; fellow in child psychiatry Hanna Pavilion, Cleve., 1978-80; med. staff Case Western Res. U., Cleve., 1978-80; fellow in ambulatory pediatrics Cleve. Met. Gen. Hosp., 1980-81; asst. prof. dept. pediatrics U. Ark. for Med. Scis., Little Rock, 1981, asst. prof. dept. psychiatry and behavioral sci., 1982, dir. continuity practice for pediatric residency program, 1981-84, attending staff gen. pediatrics dept. pediatrics, 1981—; attending staff behavioral pediatrics dept. pediatrics Ark. Children's Hosp., U. Ark. for Med. Scis., Little Rock, 1986—; chief sect. behavioral pediatrics, est. sect. in pediatric dept. U. Ark. for Med. Scis., 1986—, tenured assoc. prof. pediatrics, 1988; mem. staff Univ. Hosp., Little Rock, 1981-89, Doctors Hosp., Little Rock, 1986-89, Bridgeway Hosp.; mem. staff North Little Rock, Ark., 1988-96, dir. inpatient behavioral pediatric unit, 1989-91; cons. in pediat. Ark. Rehab. Inst., Little Rock, 19875-93; cons. Parents and Tchrs. Against Violence in Edn., Danville, Calif., 1989—, Am. Bd. Pediat., 1989, Little Rock Sch. Dist., 1987, Gov.'s Task Force on Youth at Risk, 1987, Pulaski County Spl. Sch. Dist., 1985; spkr. in field. Author: A Wellness Prescription - How to Raise a Happy, Healthy Child, 1992; editor: Gen. Pediatric Residency Curriculum Outline, 1983, Pediatric Phys. Diagnosis Course, 1984; editorial cons. Clin. Pediatrics; weekly newspaper columnist Kids in Sports, Ark. Gazette and Pitts. Press, 1985-87; contbr. numerous articles to profl. jours. Bd. dirs., med. advisor Woodlawn Therapeutic Children's Ctr., 1982-87; mem. sch. bd. Our Lady of Good Counsel, 1983-84; coach children's sports programs YMCA, 1981—; hon. field counsel devel. disabilities svcs. Ark. Dept. Human Svcs., 1991; coach children's sports programs Little Rock Boys Clubs, 1981—, bd. dirs., chmn. program com., 1987—. Maj. M.C., USAF, 1973-78. Recipient physician recognition award AMA, 1977, 80, 83, 86, 89, 92, 95; Named Coach of Yr., Penick Boys Club, 1985; grantee Ark. Hwy. Safety Program, 1982, HHS, 1983-86, U. Ark. for Med. Scis., 1985-86, 88-90, Devel. Disabilities Planning Coun., 1988-89, Nat. Conf. To Abolish Corporal Punishment in Schs., 1990, Rorer Pharms., 1991. Mem. Am. Acad. Pediat., So. Assn. on Children Under Six, Soc. for Behavioral Pediat., Soc. for Neurosci., Am. Pediatric Soc., Sol Soc. Pediatric Rsch., Phi Beta Kappa. Office: U Ark for Med Sci 800 Marshall St Little Rock AR 72202-3510

STERN, JOANNE THRASHER, elementary school educator; b. Norfolk, Va., Oct. 18, 1932; d. Thomas Williams and Mary Ellen (LaRue) Thrasher; m. Milford Josiah Stern, Apr. 29, 1956; children: Milford J. III, Thomas Thrasher, William Byrd. BS, James Madison U., 1952; MEd, U. Va., 1963. Cert. elem. tchr. Tchr. 5th grade City of Chesapeake, 1952-54; Tchr. Va. Beach Pub. Schs., 1957-60; tchr. Norfolk (Va.) City Pub. Schs., 1966-68, Def. Dependent Schs., Fed. Republic Germany, 1985; tchr. English Madison Middle Sch., 1987-89; tchr. ESOL 1st grade, 1988-91; prin. Marietta Mischia Toussaint Louverture Elem. Sch., 1989—, 1st grade tchr.; tchr. English Nan Ping Tchrs. Coll., summer 1993. Organist 1st Bapt. Ch. of North Miami Beach (Fla.). Mem. AAUW, Women Leaders Round Table (life), Chesapeake Bay Bus. and Profl. Women, Kappa Delta Pi. Home: 920 NE 199th St Apt 309 Miami FL 33179-3085

STERN, ROBERT JAMES, geologist, educator; b. Sacramento, Feb. 2, 1951; s. Robert Joseph Stern and Esther Juanita Weigel; m. Melissa Byer Fenton, Nov. 1950; children: Ryan Robert, Rebecca Lynn, Alexis Byer. BS, U. Calif., Davis, 1974; PhD, U. Calif., San Diego, 1979. Rsch. fellow Carnegie Inst. Washington, 1979-82; from asst. to assoc. to prof. U. Tex., Dallas, 1982—. Mem. editl. bd. Geology, Geologische Rundschau, 1982—; contbr. articles to profl. jours. NSF grantee, 1982—, NASA grantee, 1987—. Mem. Am. Geophys. Union, Geol. Soc. Am. Home: 7612 Roundrock Rd Dallas TX 75248-5336 Office: U Tex Geosci Dept PO Box 830688 Dept Richardson TX 75083-0688

STERN, STEVEN ALAN, investment bank executive; b. Chgo., Dec. 5, 1943; s. Sidney J. and Leona (Bernstein) S.; m. Helena Kerner, July 12, 1975; children: Jeremy, Jessica. AB, Brandeis U., 1965; postgrad. Columbia U. Grad. Sch. Bus., 1965-66. CPCU, III. Trust officer, First Nat. Bank Chgo., 1966-69; ptnr., Equicon, Inc., Chgo., 1970-74; coordinator Singer for Mayor, Chgo., 1974-75; mgr. underwriting policy CNA Ins., Chgo., 1976-79; project dir. Gov.'s Blue Ribbon Panel, Denver, 1979-81; dir. capital budget State of Colo., Denver, 1981-82; exec. dir. Ctr. Bus. and Econ. Forecasting, U. Denver, 1982-85; v.p. pub. fin., Kirchner Moore Divsn., George K. Baum & Co., Denver, 1986-93; sr. v.p. pub. fin. Donaldson, Lufkin & Jenrette Securities Co., 1993-95, William R. Hough & Co., 1995—; sr. fin. cons. Greenville S.C. Auditorium Dist., 1994—, Met. Denver Major League Baseball Stadium Dist., 1989-92; mem. adv. task force to capital devel. com. Colo. Gen. Assembly, 1985-87, chmn. adv. task force subcom. on privatization, 1986-87; mem. adv. coun. Colo. Advanced Tech. Inst., 1986-90; guest lectr., 1982-93; adv. task forces on capital budgeting, transp. Denver C. of C., 1980-91. Spkr. ann. meetings Nat. Assn. State Mental Health Program Dirs., 1987-89, Nat. Assn. State Mental Retardation Program Dirs., 1987, Nat. Assn. State Alcohol and Drug Abuse Dirs., 1988; treas., bd. dirs Mental Health Resources Corp., Renaissance Ctr., 1993-94, Denver, chmn. fin. com., 1992-93, Mental Health Resources Ctr., Renaissance Ctr., 1993-94. Author: Colorado Capital Investment Budget, 1982; (with others) Colorado; Investing in the Future, 1981; editor: Techniques of Economic Research, 1981. Speaker, Adopt-A-Sch., Denver Pub. Schs., 1983, 86, Brandeis U. Alumni Admissions Coun., 1990-93, numerous other orgns.; participant Leadership Denver, 1983-84; sec.-treas. Colo. Student Obligation Bond Authority, 1984-86, also bd. dirs.; bd. dirs. Circus Arts Found., 1985-86; chmn. devel. com. Stanley Brit. Primary Sch., Denver, 1984; mem. Denver Baseball Commn., 1987-89; bd. dirs., chmn. corp. gifts Epilepsy Found. Chgo., 1977-79. Mem. Brandeis U. Alumni Assn., NAACP (life). Jewish. Office: William R Hough & Co 2502 Independence Dr Jacksonville FL 32250-2518

STERN, STEVEN NEAL, economics educator; b. N.Y.C., July 22, 1958; s. Henry Leon and Doris (Bloss) S.; m. Sandra Mae Lichtenstein, May 20, 1984; children: Doriana Rivka, Aaron Amit. BA, U. Pa., Phila., 1979, BS, 1979; PhD, Yale U., 1985. Lectr. Yale U., New Haven, 1984-85; asst. prof. U. Va., Charlottesville, 1985-90, assoc. prof., 1990-96, prof., 1996—; cons., Charlottesville, 1985—. Contbr. articles to profl. jours. Chmn. Social Devel. Commn., Charlottesville, 1992-93, chmn. Godsey-Stilfried Freedom Fund, Charlottesville, 1988-94, Charlottesville-Albemarle Children and Youth Task Force on Teenage Pregnancy Prevention; pres. Jefferson Area United Transp., 1994-95. NIH grantee, 1986-91, NIMH grantee, 1992—. Democrat. Jewish. Office: U Va Dept Econs Charlottesville VA 22901

STERN, WAYNE BRIAN, investment company executive, management consultant; b. New Rochelle, N.Y., Jan. 8, 1948; s. Edward A. Stern and Gertrude (Eger) Lurie; m. Yvonne Eva Segelbaum, Sept. 1, 1968; children: Tiffany Joy, Colette Avi. BS in Aerospace Engring., U. Md., 1970; MBA in Fin. and Internat. Bus., U. Wash., 1977. Structures design engr. Pratt & Whitney Aircraft, West Palm Beach, Fla., 1970-72; control system engr., system cost analyst, mgr. internat. market research Boeing Co., Seattle, 1973-77; group mgr., v.p. planning and devel. W.R. Grace & Co., N.Y.C. and Troy, Mich., 1977-81; v.p., gen. mgr. Compo Industries, Inc., Cartersville, Ga., 1981-85; pres. Stern & Co., Atlanta, 1985—. Recipient Outstanding Research award AIAA, 1970. Mem. Am. Mgmt. Assn., Assn. Corp. Growth, Tau Beta Pi, Sigma Gamma Tau (past v.p.), Pi Mu Epsilon, Omicron Delta Kappa, Beta Gamma Sigma. Republican. Jewish. Home and Office: 745 Old Campus Trl NE Atlanta GA 30328-1009

STERNAL, SANDRA GAUNT, nutrition services administrator; b. Chgo., Oct. 1, 1946; d. George A. and Beatrice Gaunt; m. Joseph F. Sternal; children: Chandra, Karn Ann, John, Joseph. BS in Dietetics and Instl. Mgmt., U. Wis., 1969. Adminstrv. dietitian Luth Hosp., LaCrosse, Wis., 1970-73; cons. State of Wis., Madison, 1973-76, specialist procurement, 1976-81; dir. dietetic svcs. SunHealth, Charlotte, N.C., 1981-85; dist. mgr. ARA, Hunt Valley, Md., 1985-87, Morrison's Health Care Inc., Atlanta, 1987—; adminstr. nutrition svcs. Jackson Meml. Hosp., Miami, Fla., 1994—. Mem. Am. Dietetic Assn., Fla. Dietetic Assn., Dietitians in Bus. and Comm. (sec. 1986-87). Republican. Methodist. Office: Jackson Meml Hosp 777 SW 158th Ter Pembroke Pines FL 33027

STETSON, DANIEL EVERETT, museum director; b. Oneida, N.Y., Jan. 3, 1956; s. Robert Everett and Barbara Elizabeth (Gray) S.; m. Catherine Marie Smith; children: Kellee, Natalie, Philip. BA in Art History, Potsdam Coll. Arts and Scis., 1978; MFA in Museology, Syracuse U., 1981. Teaching asst. fine arts dept. Potsdam (N.Y.) Coll. Arts and Scis., 1977-78; grad. asst. Syracuse (N.Y.) U. Art Collections, 1979-80; acting dir. Picker Art Gallery and Colgate U. Art Collections, Colgate U., Hamilton, N.Y., 1980-81; dir. Gallery of Art U. No. Iowa, Cedar Falls, 1981-87; dir. Davenport (Iowa) Mus. Art, 1987-91; exec. dir. Austin (Tex.) Mus. Art (formerly Laguna Gloria Art Mus.), 1991-96, founding exec. dir., 1994; exec. dir. Polk Mus. Art, Lakeland, Fla., 1996—; guest curator Joe and Emily Lowe Art Gallery, Syracuse U., 1980; mem. Inter Mus. Conservation Lab., Oberlin, 1987-91; mem. design adv. com. Iowa Capitol, Des Moines, 1989-91; panel cons. Arts Midwest/Affiliated States Art Assns. of Upper Midwest, Mpls., 1983, 88; bd. dirs. Iowa Arts Coalition, 1990-91; chair Tex. Commn. on the Arts Visual Arts Review Panel, 1994; mem. planning com. Tex. Assn. of Mus., 1994; mem. art in pub. pls. com. Austin Airport, 1995. Author/curator: (exhbn. catalog) José de Creeft (1884-1982), 1983, Contemporary Icons and Explorations, 1988, (exhbn. catalog) Philip Perlstein-Painting to Watercolors, 1983, Walter Dusenbery Classical Echoes, 1985, Jaune Quick-to-See Smith and George Longfish: Personal Symbols, 1986, Reuban Nakian: Leda and The Swan, 1983, Focus 1 Michael Boyd: Paintings, 1980, 89, Focus 2 Photo Image League, 1989, Focus 3 The Art of Haiti: A Sense of Wonder, 1989, Focus 6—Contemporary Devel. in Glass, 1990, Peter Dean: Landscapes of the Mind, 1981, Joseph Raffael, 1987, Born in Iowa-The Homecoming, 1986, Stieglitz and 40 Other Photographers—The Development of a Collection, 1991-92, New Works (Austin and Central Texas Artists), 1992, 94, Companions in Time: The Paintings of William Lester & Everett Spruce Catalogue Essay, 1993, Human Nature, Human Form Catalogue Essay, 1993, Sources and Collaborations: The Making of the Holocaust Project by Judy Chicago and Donald Woodman tour and catalog, 1994—. Bd. mem. arts coun. Cedar Arts Forum, Black Hawk County, Iowa, 1983-85; curriculum com. Leadership Investment for Tomorrow, Cedar Falls-Waterloo, Iowa, 1985-86; mem. adv. com. MBA Course of Study Styles and Strategies Non-Profit Orgns. St. Ambrose U., 1989-91, Austin BCA Arts Week Poster and Awards, 1993; mem. City of Austin Funding Process Rev. Com., 1992; Facilities Team Austin Comprehensive Arts Plan, 1991-93; mem. adv. panel Tex. Commn. Arts Visual Arts, 1993; field reviewer Inst. Mus. Svcs.-Gen. Operating Support Grant Field Reviewer, 1993; mem. arts com. Downtown Mgmt. Assn., 1995; mem. arts sub-com. Downtown Commn.; bd. dirs. Friends of the Libr., Lakeland, 1996—, quality improvement coun. Harrison Arts Ctr., Lakeland, 1996—. Fellow N.E. Mus. Conf., Rochester, N.Y., 1979; grantee Iowa Arts Coun., Tex. Commn. Arts, NEA advancement program grant phase I & II, 1993-95; recipient mus. scholarship Am. Law Inst. ABA, Atlanta, Phila., 1984, 93. Mem. Am. Assn. Mus., Midwest Mus. Conf., Iowa Mus. Assn. (chair steering com. exhbn. workshop 1984-86, legis. action com. and indemnification com. 1981-90, bd. dirs. 1983-85), Tex. Assn. Mus. (program com., resources sharing com., 1992-94, Art Mus. Affinity group) Davenport Rotary (cultural affairs com. 1987-91), S.W. Mus. Conf., Fla. Art Mus. Dirs. Assn., Fla. Assn. Museums. Home: 5564 Highlands Vista Cir Lakeland FL 33813-3306 Office: Polk Mus Art Gloria 800 E Palmetto Lakeland FL 33801 Office: Polk Mus Art 800 E Palmetto St Lakeland FL 33801-5529

STETTNER, JERALD W., retail drugs stores executive; b. Miami, Fla., Mar. 31, 1952; s. Richard A. and LeJean D. (Haberman) S.; m. Linda G. Day, Dec. 22, 1978; children: Kelly R., Jarrod M., Zachary A. BS in Behavioral Mgmt., Ga. Inst. Tech., 1974. Various mgmt. positions Eckerd Drug Co., Orlando, Fla., 1974-87; regional v.p. Eckerd Corp., Clearwater, Fla., 1987—. Mem. Ga. Tech. Alumni Assn., Phi Delta Theta. Home: 3979 Arlington Dr Palm Harbor FL 34685

STEVENS, CHERYL B., utility company executive; b. Portsmouth, Va., Aug. 24, 1953; d. Bernard Louis and Lola Anne (Winstead) Berry; m. Don Edward Stevens, Aug. 17, 1984. BS, East Carolina U., 1975. Bookkeeper The State Nat. Bank, Big Spring, Tex., 1976-79; home economist Tex. Elec. Svc. Co., Big Spring, 1979-80, customer rep., 1980-81; adminstrv. asst. Tex. Utilities, Big Spring, 1981-83, customer ops. supr., 1983-90; minority bus. devel. coord. Tex. Utilities, Dallas, 1990-91, minority bus. devel. mgr., 1991—, contracts mgr., 1996—. Bd. dirs. Dallas/Ft. Worth Minority Bus. Devel. Coun., 1995—, North Tex. Women's Bus. Coun., Dallas, 1995—, North Tex. Women's Bus. Ctr., Dallas, 1995—, Minority Bus. News, Dallas, 1991—, Women's Enterprise, Dallas, 1994—; mem. econ. devel. com. State Senator Royce West, Dallas, 1994—; exec. com. mem. Edison Elec. Minority Bus. Com., Washington, 1993—. Named Minority Bus. Advocate of the Yr. Dallas/Ft. Worth Minority Bus. Devel. Coun., 1992, Woman of Excellence, Women's Enterprise Mag., 1994, Advocate of the Yr. SBA, 1996; recipient Helping Hands award Minority Bus. News, 1993, Women Who Mean Bus. award Minority Bus. News U.S.A., 1992. Mem. Greater Dallas C. of C. (mem. women's bus. issues com. 1994—, grad. Leadership Dallas 1996). Office: Texas Utilities 1601 Bryan St Dallas TX 75201-3411

STEVENS, DANA NELSON, economist; b. Alexandria, Va., Apr. 19, 1945; s. Robert Carl and Jean (White) S.; m. Jessica Rostow, Aug. 28, 1978 (div. Jan. 1981); children: Jeremiah Nelson, Anna Lillian, Benjamin Amos; m. Mary Bane Snyder, June 18, 1981; 1 child Jon Austin. Student, London Sch. Econs., 1965-66; BA cum laude, Williams Coll., 1967; PhD, Stanford U., 1973. Lic. mortgage broker, Fla. Program analyst Office Mgmt. and Budget, 1968-70; asst. prof. econs. Ga. State U., Atlanta, 1972-76; asst. prof. econs. New Coll. USF, Sarasota, Fla., 1976-78, assoc. prof. econs., 1978-83; vis. prof. econs. Williams Coll., Williamstown, Mass., 1983-85; pres. Lusitanian Investment Co., S.A., Panama City, Panama, 1985-89; owner, dir. Austin Econs., Sarasota, 1989-94, Foster Stevens, LLC, Nashville, 1994—; chmn., CEO Takashi Corp., 1995—; adj. prof. U. Sarasota, 1992—; cons. Sarasota County Arts Coun., 1992-93; econ. advisor Sarasota C. of C., 1979-83, Wood-Gundy Investment Brokers, 1983; proposal reviewer NSF, 1980. Contbr. column to Investment Insights, 1983, Gulf Coast News, 1983, also articles, revs. to profl. publs.; author reports in field; editor A.I.S. Newsletter, 1979-81. Sec. Sarasota County Dem. Party, 1981-82, precinctman, 1980-82; del. Dem. Unity Conf., 1981; Dem. candidate for U.S. Ho. of Reps., 1982; bd. dirs. Asolo State Theater, 1981; mem. New Coll. Found. Devel. Coun., 1978-83; sec., pres. William Coll. Alumni Club, 1977-83; bd. dirs., v.p., then pres. Indian Beach Homeowners Assn., 1978-81; pres. Whispering Oaks Homeowners Assn., 1992-94, Sarasota 50-Yr. Vision Plan, 1992-93. Grantee Met. Life, 1978-80, STAR rsch., 1978-80. Mem. Am. Econ. Assn., Phi Beta Kappa. Home: PO Box 10296 Sarasota FL 34278-0296

STEVENS, DAVID MICHAEL, retired naval officer; b. Shawnee, Okla., Apr. 4, 1941; s. Thomas Mann and Sadie Lee (Downing) S.; m. Evelyn Kay Mannan, Mar. 27, 1964; children: Kirstin Anne, Thomas Michael, Tiffany Suzanne. BA in History and Govt., Okla. Bapt. U., 1963; MA in Counseling, Ball State U., 1971; postgrad., Royal Naval Coll., Greenwich, Eng., 1973-74; MA in Strategic Studies, Naval War Coll., Newport, R.I., 1990. Commd. ensign USN, 1964, advanced through grades to capt., 1987; instr. Air Anti-Submarine Squadron 41, San Diego, 1976-77; maintenance and ops officer air anti-submarine squadron 30 USS Forestall, Jacksonville, Fla., 1977-80; chief staff Air-Anti Submarine Wing 1, Jacksonville, 1980-82; comdg. officer tactical air control squadron 12 USS Belleau Wood, Coronado, Calif., 1982-84; navigator USS Lexington, Pensacola, Fla., 1984-86, USS Independence, Persian Gulf, 1985; exec. officer, comdg. officer Naval Sta. Roosevelt Roads, Ceiba, P.R., 1986-89; spl. asst. for nuclear affairs Supreme Allied Comdr.-Atlantic, NATO, Norfolk, Va., 1990-93; dir. WJCT Radio Reading Svc. for Blind, Jacksonville, 1993—; Mem. Armed Forces Disciplinary Control Bd., Jacksonville, 1979-82, Active Duty Comdr. Selection Bd., Washington, 1989. Mayor RAF Sta. Shepherds Grove, Stanfon-Suffolk, Eng., 1969. Decorated Air Gallantry Cross (Vietnam); Meritorious Svc. medal, Air medal, Navy Commendation medal, Def. Superior Svc. medal, others. Fellow Brit. Watch and Clockmakers Guild; mem. Nat. Assn. Watch and Clock Collectors, Ret. Officers Assn. Baptist. Home: 2583 Franklin Ct Orange Park FL 32073-6513

STEVENS, DENNIS MAX, audit director; b. Jersey City, Sept. 3, 1944; m. Susan Gail Brown, Mar. 15, 1969; children: Julie Ayn, Daniel Ross. BBA, Rutgers U., 1966; MA in Acctg., U. Mo., 1968. CPA, Mo. Staff Peat, Marwick, Mitchell and Co., St. Louis, 1968-80, ptnr., 1980-84; sr. v.p. and internal auditor Southwestern States Bankcard Assn., Dallas, 1985-86, sr. v.p. and chief fin. officer, 1986-89; corp. planner NCH Corp., Irving, Tex., 1989-95, dir. corp. audit, 1995—. Contr. articles to profl. jours. Served to 1st lt. U.S. Army, 1969-70. Mem. AICPAs (electronic data processing auditing standards com. 1979-84), Am. Mgt. Assn., Beta Gamma Sigma, Beta Alpha Psi. Home: 2325 Fountain Head Dr Plano TX 75023-6413 Office: NCH Corp 2727 Chemsearch Blvd Irving TX 75062-6454

STEVENS, DIANNE FARRIA, secondary school educator; m. David J. Stevens; children: Sharri, Angela. BS, Mars Hill (N.C.) Coll., 1975; M in Ednl. Bus., George Mason U., 1996. Cert. secondary tchr., Va. Coord. Coop. Office Edn., tchr. bus. edn. Prince William Schs., Manassas, Va., 1975—. Baptist. Office: Potomac Sr HS 16706 Jefferson Davis Hwy Dumfries VA 22026

STEVENS, DONALD KING, aeronautical engineer, consultant; b. Danville, Ill., Oct. 27, 1920; s. Douglas Franklin and Ida Harriet (King) S.; BS with high honors in Ceramic Engring., U. Ill., 1942; MS in Aeros. and Guided Missiles, U. So. Calif., 1949; grad. U.S. Army Command and Gen. Staff Coll., 1957, U.S. Army War Coll., 1962; m. Adele Carman de Werff, July 11, 1942; children: Charles August, Anne Louise, Alice Jeanne Stevens Kay. Served with Ill. State Geol. Survey, 1938-40; ceramic engr. Harbison-Walker Refractories Co., Pitts., 1945-46; commd. 2d lt. U.S. Army, 1942, advanced through grades to col., 1963; with Arty. Sch., Fort Bliss, Tex., 1949-52; supr. unit tng. and Nike missile firings, N.Mex., 1953-56; mem. Weapons Systems Evaluation Group, Office Sec. of Def., Washington, 1957-61; comdr. Niagara-Buffalo (N.Y.) Def., 31st Arty. Brigade, Lockport, N.Y., 1963-65; study dir. U.S.A. ballistic missile def. studies DEPEX and X-66 for Sec. Def., 1965-66; chief Air Def. and Nuclear br. War Plans div. 1965-67, chief strategic forces div. Office Dep. Chief Staff for Mil. Ops., 1967-69; chief spl. weapons plans, J5, U.S. European Command, Fed. Republic Germany, 1969-72, ret., 1972; guest lectr. U.S. Mil. Acad. 1958-59; cons. U.S. Army Concepts Analysis Agy., Bethesda, Md., 1973-95; cons. on strategy Lulejian & Assocs., Inc., 1974-75; cons. nuclear policy and plans to Office Asst. Sec. of Def., 1975-80, 84-93; cons. Sci. Applications, Inc., 1976-78; Asst. camp dir. Piankeshaw Area coun. Boy Scouts Am., 1937; mem. chancel choir, elder First Christian Ch., Falls Church, Va., 1957-61, 65-69, 72—; elder, trustee Presbyn. Ch., 1963-65. Decorated D.S.M., Legion of Merit, Bronze Star. Mem. Am. Ceramic Soc., Assn. U.S. Army, U. Ill. Alumni Assn., U. So. Calif. Alumni Assn., Keramos, Sigma Xi, Sigma Tau, Tau Beta Pi, Phi Kappa Phi, Alpha Phi Omega. Clubs: Niagara Falls Country; Ill. (Washington); Terrapin, Rotary. Contbr. articles to engring. jours.; pioneer in tactics and deployment plans for Army surface-to-air missiles. Address: 5916 5th St N Arlington VA 22203-1010

STEVENS, EARL PATRICK, minister; b. Vicksburg, Miss., Nov. 21, 1925; s. Elton Alva and Mary Elizabeth (Keathley) S.; m. Vonda Jean Tuttle, Aug. 7, 1949; children: Teresa Darlene, Deborah Lalene, Earl P. II, David Paul. BA, Abilene Christian U., 1949; BRE, Coll. of the Bible, 1966; MA, MRE, Nat. Christian U., 1968, ThM, 1969, PhD, ThD, 1969; DD (hon.), Ohio Christian Coll., 1968. Ordained to ministry Ch. of Christ, 1943; cert. neuropsychiat. technician. Minister Ch. of Christ, Olden, Tex., 1946-49, Barrackville, W.Va., 1949-62, Parkersburg, W.Va., 1962-66, St. Mary's, W.Va., 1966-77, Shinnston, W.Va., 1977-90, Fairmont, W.Va., 1990-96, Mt. Nebo, W.Va., 1990-96, Pleasant Valley, W.Va., 1996—; instr. Ohio Valley Coll., Parkersburg, 1964-66; prof. Nat. Christian U., Ft. Worth, 1968-78. Author: The Glory of Christ, 1963, Doctrinal Study of I Timothy, 1987, 100 Years Preaching, 1995, 17 other books. Served with USN, 1944-46. Named to Eagle Scout, Boy Scouts Am., 1942; recipient Golden Record award Word Records, 1968, Colin Anderson award Colin Anderson Ctr., 1968. Mem. So. Assn. Marriage Counselors, Am. Numismatic Assn. Democrat. Home and Office: 204 Russell St Fairmont WV 26554-1860

STEVENS, ELIZABETH, psychotherapist, consultant; b. Evanston, Ill., Jan. 11, 1950; d. Kenneth M. and C. Jane (Reynolds) S.; m. David W. Handy, Oct. 3, 1986. BA in Psychology, U. Fla., 1973; MA in Clin. Psychology, Kent State U., 1976. Lic. profl. counselor; lic. marriage and family therapist. Exec. dir. Genesis Women's Shelter, Dallas, 1986-87; dir. outpatient svcs. Green Oaks Hosp., Dallas, 1987-88; mgmt. cons. Houston, 1977—, pvt. practice, 1990—; founder Integrated Clin. Resources, Inc., The Stevens Co., healthcare cons., Humble, Tex., 1995—; cons., amb. St. Joseph Hosp., 1977—; co-founder N.E. Hospice, Med. Affiliates, Support N.E. Cancer Workers, Emergency Support Systems for Police, fire Dept. and Ambulance Svc.; founder Stevens Counseling Ctrs., The Psychoimmunology Ctr., Stevens, Lancaster and Assocs.; co-founder Associated Mental Health Group, Inc.; cons. to devel. utilization rev. Kelsey-Seybold Clinics, 1992—; cons. creating feasibility studies for venture capitalists; cons. devel. triage. Contbr. articles to profl. jours., mags., and newspapers. Vol. Mental Health Assn., Houston and Harris County, bd. dirs., 1988—, chair nominating com., membership com., sec. exec. com.; bd. advisors N.E. Hospice; mem. strategic planning team Sisters of Charity. Named Exceptional Vol. of Yr. Mental Health Assn., Speakers Bur. award. Mem. Walden Country Club. Office: 300 Main St Humble TX 77338

STEVENS, ELLIOTT WALKER, JR., allergist, pulmonologist; b. Wilmington, N.C., Sept. 11, 1940; s. E. Walker Sr. and Margaret Ardelle (Hester) S.; m. Blanche Bonner, July 10, 1965; children: Elliott W. III, Margaret Baker. AB in French, U. N.C., 1962, MD, 1966. Diplomate Am. Bd. Internal Medicine, Am. Bd. Allergy and Immunology, Am. Bd. Pulmonery Diseases. Intern U. N.C. Hosp., Chapel Hill, N.C., 1966-67; resident Duke U., Durham, N.C., 1969-70, fellow Allergy and pulmonary diseases, 1970-72; allergist and pulmonologist Greensboro Chest Disease and Allergy Associates, Greensboro, N.C., 1972—. Capt. USAF, 1967-69. Fellow Am. Coll. Allergy and Immunology, Am. Coll. Chest Physicians. Republican. Episcopalian. Home: 4 Round Hill Ct Greensboro NC 27408-3709 Office: Greensboro Chest Diseases & Allergy Assocs 1018 N Elm St Greensboro NC 27401-1424

STEVENS, GAIL LAVINE, community health nurse, educator; b. Glens Falls, N.Y., June 10, 1938; d. Paul E. and Doris E. (Shippey) Lavine; m. Gary R. Stevens, Apr. 1, 1961; children: Ginelle Tonia, Gavin Wesley, Gordon Rickard. BSN, Syracuse (N.Y.) U., 1961; MA, U. South Ala., 1975, MS in Nursing, 1989; EdD, U. So. Miss., 1979. Instr. nursing Providence Sch. Nursing, Mobile, Ala., 1961-63, Mobile Infirmary Sch. Nursing, 1963-75; asst. and assoc. prof. nursing Mobile Coll., 1975-89; prof. nursing U. Mobile, 1989—. Contbr. articles to profl. jours. Mem. ANA, Syracuse U. Nurses Alumni Assn., Sigma Theta Tau. Home: 2710 Palao Ct Mobile AL 36693-2722

STEVENS, HAL, food service manager; b. N.Y.C., Dec. 28, 1952; s. Maxwell and Helen (Bromberg) Smallheiser; m. Patricia Rochelle Parker, May 3, 1985; children: Haley Lynn, Seth Asher, Ethan Aaron. AA, Sullivan County C.C., Loch Sheldrake, N.Y., 1973; BA, SUNY, New Paltz, 1975; MBA, St. John's U., 1979. Merchandiser Sysco Food Svcs. of Houston, 1984-86, White Swan, Houston, 1986-87; product mgr. Sysco Corp., Houston, 1987-90; dir. merchandising Sysco Food Svcs. of Austin, Tex., 1990-92, Sysco Food Svcs. of Seattle, 1992-94; v.p. merchandising U.S. Foodsvc.-Davis Divsn., Oklahoma City, 1994—; guest lectr. Quaker Oats, Houston, 1987; regional trainer Sysco Corp., Houston, 1988. Bd. regents Liberty U., Lynchburg, Va., 1990—; patron Child Advocates, Inc., Houston, 1989; hon. advisor Shaolin Kung Fu Sch., Edmond, Okla., 1996.

STEVENS, JAMES M., food processing executive; b. 1947. With Nabisco, Bethlehem, Pa., 1968, Pepsi Cola Bottling Group, Purchase, N.Y., 1969-76; sr. v.p. Great Waters France Inc., Greenwich, Conn., 1977-81; with Premium Products Sales Corp., Greenwich, 1981-86; COO Coca Cola Enterprises, Atlanta, 1986-92; pres. Suntory Water Group Inc., Atlanta, 1992—. Office: Suntory Water Group Inc 280 Interstate North Pky NW Atlanta GA 30339-2409

STEVENS, JOHN FLOURNOY, priest; b. Des Moines, June 19, 1914; s. Ralph Stoddard and Jeanne Flournoy (Thompson) S.; m. Ruth Elizabeth Brown, Jan. 19, 1945 (div. 1976); children: John Bruce, Michael Paul, James Andrew; m. Betty Louise Sinkola, June 2, 1976. BS with distinction, U.S. Naval Acad., 1938; MDiv, Va. Theol. Sem., 1948; postgrad., Johns Hopkins, 1941-42. Ordained to ministry as priest, 1949. Assoc. rector to rector Episcopal Chs., 1948-64; dir. dept. Christian social rels. Episcopal Diocese of Tex., Houston, 1964-66; mem. staff exec. coun. Episcopal Ch., 1966-74; assoc. coord. Joint Urban Prog., 1966-67, assoc. dir. gen. conv. spl. prog., 1967-69, asst. to dep. for prog., 1969-70, adminstrv. officer, also sec. exec. council, 1971-74, coord. Gen. Conv., 1972-73; bus. and circulation mgr. Episcopal Ch. Pub. Co., 1974-75, dir. Joint Strategy and Action Com., 1975-77; ret.; asst. to pastor Wheeler Ave. Bapt. Ch., Houston, 1979-80, mem clergy staff, 1980—; non-stipendiary rector Ch. of Advent, Houston, 1980-86, non-stipendiary assoc. rector Ch. of Good Shepherd, Friendswood, 1987-89, Ch. of Advent, Houston, 1991-96; chaplain Episc. Women's Caucus, 1996—; interim exec. dir. Houston Met. Mins., 1981. Author: To Tell the Story, 1963, No Place to Go, 1964. Bd. dirs. Houston Civil Liberties Union, 1963-66. Comdr. USN, 1938-46. Decorated Bronze Star medal. Fellow Episcopal Sem. of the S.W., Coll. of Preachers; mem. Episc. Soc. Cultural and Racial Unity (sec. 1964-66), Washington Fedn. Chs. (dir. 1950-53, fin. com. 1953-56), NAACP (dir. Houston chpt. 1962-66). Democrat. Episcopalian.

STEVENS, JULIE ANN, peri-operative nurse; b. Normal, Ill., June 3, 1961; d. James E. and Janice J. (Richey) S. BSN with honors, Baylor U., 1984. RN, Tex.; cert. CNOR, CNRN. Nurse intern operating rm. Parkland Meml. Hosp., Dallas, 1984-85, staff nurse, 1985-89; charter employee, staff nurse Zale Lipshy U. Hosp. at Southwestern Med. Ctr., Dallas, 1989-92, clin. coord. neurosurgery, 1992-96; staff nurse Med. City Dallas Hosp., 1996—. Recipient Interlocking Circle of Caring award Delta Airlines, Dallas, 1986, Divisional Achievement award Zale Lipshy U. Hosp., 1994. Mem. Assn. Oper. Rm. Nurses, Am. Assn. Neurosci. Nurses, DAR, Internat. Order of Job's Daus (past Honored Queen). Methodist. Home: 1913 Bachman Ct Plano TX 75075-6162 Office: Med City Dallas Hosp 7777 Forest Lane Dallas TX 75230

STEVENS, KENNETH R., history educator; b. Columbus, Ind., Aug. 18, 1946; s. Raymond Austin and Dorothy Louise (Goodman) S.; m. Nancy

Richmond, Aug. 31, 1968; children: James, Sally. BA, Ind. U., 1968, MA, 1974, PhD, 1982. Rev. editl. asst. Am. Hist. Rev. Ind. U., Bloomington, 1976-78; editor Daniel Webster Papers Dartmouth Coll., Hanover, N.H., 1978-83; assoc. prof. Tex. Christian U., Ft. Worth, 1983—. Author: Border Diplomacy, 1989; editor: Diplomatic Papers of Daniel Webster 1, 1983, 2, 1987. Served in USN, 1969-73. Mem. Soc. History of Am. Fgn. Rels., Soc. History Early Am. Republic, So. Hist. Assn., Orgn. Am. Historians, Phi Alpha Theta. Home: 4417 Norwich Dr Fort Worth TX 76109 Office: Tex Christian U Reed Hall 302 Fort Worth TX 76129

STEVENS, MARK, banker; b. Chgo., May 24, 1947; s. Joseph K. and Phoebe (Copeland) S.; m. Joyce Sue Skinner, Aug. 22, 1970; children: Mark Benjamin, Katherine Joyce. BA, W.Va. U., 1969, JD, 1972. V.p. Continental Ill. Nat. Bank & Trust Co., Chgo., 1972-79, No. Trust Co., Chgo., 1979-81; pres., CEO, No. Trust Bank Fla. N.A., Sarasota, 1981-87, chmn., pres., CEO,, 1987—; exec. v.p. No. Trust Co. & No. Trust Corp., 1996—; pres. No. Trust Fla. Corp., Miami, 1987—; exec. v.p. No. Trust Corp. and No. Trust Co., 1996—. Trustee Ctr. Fine Arts, 1988-94, Rowson Everglades Sch., 1988-94, Miami Children's Hosp. Found., 1993—, South Fla. Performing Arts Ctr. Found., 1993—, U. Miami, 1994, Beacon Coun., 1990—; mem. U. Miami Citizens Bd., 1988-89, Young Pres.'s Orgn., 1988—; bd. dirs. Miami Coalition and Task Force, 1988—, New World Symphony, 1991—, Miami Heart Rsch. Inst.; charter mem. Coun. of 100 Fla. Internat. Univ. Found., 1990—; hon. bd. dirs. Audubon House; mem. adv. bd. Coll. Assistance Program, 1991—; bd. govs. Dade Community Found., 1991; mem. steering com. The Miami 2000, 1992; exec. com. Homes for South Fla.; adv. com. Local Initiatives Support Corp.; mem. Orange Bowl Com., 1994. Mem. Young Pres. Orgn., Riviera Country Club, Miami Club. Office: No Trust Bank Fla 700 Brickell Ave No Trust Bank Fla Bldg Miami FL 33131

STEVENS, RICHARD YATES, county official, lawyer; b. Raleigh, N.C., Dec. 12, 1948; s. Floyd L. and Luna (Yates) S.; m. Jere Ann Gilmore, Sept. 13, 1980; children: Charles Andrew, Katherine Elizabeth. BA in Polit. Sci., U. N.C., 1970, JD, 1974, M.Pub. Adminstrn., 1978. Bar: N.C. 1974. Asst. dean men U. N.C., Chapel Hill, 1970-71, asst. residence dir., 1971-75, asst. Office Student Affairs, 1973-75; sole practice, Chapel Hill, 1974-76; adminstrv. asst. City of Durham (N.C.), 1975-76, budget officer, 1976-78, dir. adminstrn., 1978-79, dir. fin. and program devel., 1979-80; asst. county mgr. Wake County (N.C.), 1980-84, county mgr., 1984—; adj. prof. polit. sci. N.C. State U., 1979-80, 92, 94; coord. N.C. State Govt. intern program Inst. Govt., summer 1971. Mem. bd. visitors U. N.C., Chapel Hill, 1991-95, bd. trustees, 1995—. Mem. Internat. City/County Mgmt. Assn., Am. Soc. Pub. Adminstrn., Nat. Assn. County Adminstrs. (bd. dirs. 1989-92), N.C. Bar, N.C. City-County Mgmt. Assn. (bd. dirs. 1991-92), N.C. Mus. Natural Scis. Soc. (bd. dirs. 1987-88, treas. 1988-89, pres.-elect 1989-90, pres. 1990-91), U. N.C. Pub. Adminstrn. Alumni Assn. (pres. 1977-79, dir. 1982-84), U. N.C. Gen. Alumni Assn. (dir. 1978-80, 83-84, 85-88, treas. 1988—, Disting. Svc. medal 1994), Carolina Club (vice chmn. 1993-94, chmn. 1994—). Home: 132 Lochwood Dr W Cary NC 27511-8301 Office: Wake County Office Bldg PO Box 550 Raleigh NC 27602-0550

STEVENS, WILLIAM JOHN, management consultant, former association executive; b. Dusseldorf, Germany, Aug. 23, 1915; arrived in U.S., 1923, naturalized, 1931; s. Peter and Margaret (Kaumanns) S.; student McCall Sch. Printing, 1933; student assn. mgmt. Northwestern U., 1947; grad. Chadwick Univ., 1993; m. Dorothy V. Santangini, Feb. 14, 1937 (dec.). With Ruttle, Shaw & Wetherill, Phila., 1931-34; partner New Era Printing Co., Phila., 1934-37; plant mgr. Marcus & Co., Phila., 1937-41; supt. Edward Stern & Co., Phila., 1941-46; exec. sec. Nat. Assn. Photo-Lithographers, N.Y.C., 1946-50, exec. v.p., 1961-64, pres., 1964-71; pres., COO NPEA Exhibits, Inc., 1971-80; owner Dorval Co., pub.; pres. Opinion-3 Graphic Arts Rsch. Agy.; exec. sec. Met. Lithographers Assn., N.Y.C., 1946-50; asst. to v.p. Miehle Co., N.Y.C., 1950-56, mgr. Phila. dist., 1956-61; cons. Sales Devel. Inst., Phila., 1960-89; mem. Am. Bd. Arbitration, 1962—; chmn. adv. commn. on graphic arts N.Y.C. Tech. Coll., 1972-95; bus. adminstr. St. Joseph's Parish, 1980-85. Named Industry Man of Yr. Nat. Assn. Photo-Lithographers, 1954, Man of Yr., N.Y. Litho Guild, 1962; recipient Presdl. Citation Office Price Adminstrn., 1946, Mktg. award North Am. Pub. Co., 1967, B'nai B'rith award, 1968, N.Y. Navigators award, 1969, N.Y. Printing Craftsman Achievement award, 1989; laureate N.Y. Printers Hall of Fame, 1980, NAPL-Soderstrom award, 1984, recipient Gold Founders medal N.Y.C. Tech. Coll., 1987. Mem. Am. Soc. Assn. Execs., Graphic Arts Assn. Execs. (pres. 1969), Nat. Assn. Litho Clubs (founder, pres. 1947, Industry award 1947, 79, sec. 1964-71), N.Y. Club Printing House Craftsmen, Gamma Epsilon Tau. Clubs: Phila. Litho (pres. 1945), N.Y. Litho (N.Y.C.). Mem. Writers Inst. Author: How To Prepare Copy for Offset Lithography, 1948, Building Construction and Floor Plans for Installing Web Offset Presses; under author: Basic Facts for Creating Effective Art/Design, Advertising, and Printing, 1996; columnist for daily press; contbr. editor articles to trade publs. Inventor Hiky-Picker, Quik-Match Color File for selection paint color samples, Stevens Foto Sizing System, Steve-O-Heat Printing Ink Dryer, "Travelr" security pocket, "Mar-Too-Nee" salad dressing. Home and Office: 4575 Barclay Cres Lake Worth FL 33463-6037

STEVENSON, BEN, artistic director; b. Portsmouth, Eng., Apr. 4, 1936; came to U.S., 1968; s. Benjamin John and Florence May (Gundry) S.; m. Joan Toastivine, Jan. 6, 1968. Grad., Arts Ednl. Sch., London, 1955. Dir. Houston Ballet Acad.; mem. dance panel Tex. Commn. Arts, 1977; guest tchr. Am. Ballet Theatre, Joffrey Ballet, Royal Ballet, London, Beijing Dance Acad. Dancer Theatre Arts Ballet, London, 1952-54, Sadler's Wells Theatre Ballet, 1955-56, Royal Ballet, 1956-60, London Festival Ballet, 1960-62; appearances in Wedding in Paris, 1954-55, Music Man, London, 1962-63, Half a Sixpence, also, Boys in Syracuse, London, 1964; prin. dancer, ballet master, London Festival Ballet, 1964-68; artistic dir. Harkness Ballet Youth Dancers, 1968-71, Chgo. Ballet, 1974-75, Houston Ballet, 1976—; co-dir. Nat. Ballet, Washington, 1971-74; prin. ballets choreographed include Three Faces of Eve, 1965, Cast Out, 1966, Sleeping Beauty (full length), 1967, 71, 76, 78, Fervor, 1968, Three Preludes, 1968, Forbidden, 1969, Cinderella (full length), 1969, 71, 73, 74, 76, Bartok Concerto, 1970, Nutcracker (full length), 1972, 76, Symphonetta, 1972, Courant, 1973, Swan Lake (full length), 1977, L, 1978, Britten Pas de Deux, 1979, Four Last Songs, 1979, Space City, 1980, Peer Gynt (full length), 1981, Zheng Ban Qiao, 1982, The Prince of Pagodas, 1986. Recipient 1st prize London Choreographic competitions, 1965, 66, 67, 1st prize modern ballet choreography Internat. Ballet Competition, Varna, Bulgaria, 1972, Gold medal for choreography Internat. Ballet Competition, 1982. Asso. mem. Royal Acad. Dancing (Adeline Genee Gold medal 1955). Office: Houston Ballet PO Box 130487 Houston TX 77219-0487

STEVENSON, DENISE L., business executive, banking consultant; b. Washington, Sept. 18, 1946; d. Pierre and Alice (Mardrus) D'Auga; m. Walter Henry Stevenson, Oct. 17, 1970 (div. Dec. 1990). AA, Montgomery Coll., 1967; BA in Econs./Bus. Mgmt., N.C. State U., 1983; Cert. in Mgmt. Fin. Women Internat., 1990. Cert. legal asst., Meredith Coll., 1989. Lic. ins. agt. Savs. counselor Perpetual Bldg. Assn. (now Crestar Bank) Washington, 1968-70; regional asst. v.p. 1st Fed. Savs. (now Centura Bank, Rocky Mount), 1971-83; pres., owner Diversified Learning Services, Raleigh, 1983—; pres., treas. Daily Life Svcs., Inc., Raleigh, 1994—; instr. Inst. Fin. Edn., Raleigh, 1983-89, Am. Inst. Banking, 1986. Mem. Am. Bus. Women's Assn. (woman of yr. award 1982), Fin. Women Internat. (cert. leader 1987, mem. of yr. award 1992, N.C. woman of yr. award 1992), Laurel Hills Women's Club (pres. 1974-75, Raleigh), Omicron Delta Epsilon. Avocation: fishing. Office: Diversified Learning Svcs PO Box 33231 Raleigh NC 27636-3231

STEVENSON, EARL, JR., civil engineer; b. Royston, Ga., May 8, 1921; s. Earl and Compton Helen (Randall) S.; B.S. in Civil Engrng., Ga. Inst. Tech., 1953; m. Sue Roberts, Apr. 25, 1956; children—Catherine Helen, David Earl. Engr., GSA, Atlanta, 1959-60; engr., pres. Miller, Stevenson & Steinichen, Inc., Atlanta, 1960—; sr. v.p. Stevenson & Palmer, Inc., Camilla, 1984—; dir. Identification & Security Products, Inc., Atlanta. Served with USAAF, 1944-45. Registered profl. engr., Ga., Ala., S.C., Miss. Mem. Ga. Soc. Profl. Engrs., Water Pollution Control Fedn. Methodist. Home: 3163 Laramie Dr NW Atlanta GA 30339-4335 Office: 2430 Herodian Way Smyrna GA 30080-2906

STEVENSON, EDWARD WARD, retired physician, surgeon, otolaryngologist; b. Chester, S.C., Jan. 9, 1926; s. Thomas M. and Annie Lou (Ward) S.; m. Dorothy Giles, Sept. 2, 1947; children: Sally Anne Stevenson Yeilding, Laura Stevenson Healey, Nancy Stevenson Schonberger (dec.), Molly Stevenson Walker. Degree, Duke U., 1945; MD, U. Md., Balt., 1949. Intern Bapt. Meml. Hosp., Memphis, 1949-50; resident Med. Coll. Va. Hosp., Richmond, 1953-55; fellow Ochsner Found. Hosp., New Orleans, 1955-56; staff otolaryngologist Ochsner Clinic, New Orleans, 1956-57; pvt. practice Birmingham, 1957-60, 65-94; instr., clin. asst. prof. surgery U. Ala., Birmingham, 1957-94; pvt. practice Decatur, Ala., 1960-65; ret., 1994; faculty Tulane U. Sch. Medicine, 1956-57; mem. staff Bapt. Med. Ctr.-Montclair, Birmingham. Contbr. articles to profl. jours. Bd. dirs. So. Mus. Flight, Birmingham, 1989-96. Mem. AMA, ACS, Am. Laryngol., Rhinol. and Otol. Soc. (sec.- treas. so. sect. 1990-93, v.p. so. sect. 1993-94), Am. Soc. Head and Neck Surgery, Am. Acad. Otolaryn., Am. Soc. Ophthal. and Otolaryn. Allergy, So. Med. Assn., Jefferson County Med. Soc., Am. Sleep Disorders Assn., Ala. Otolaryn. Soc. (founder, pres. 1971), Med. Assn. State Ala., Morgan County Med. Soc. (pres. 1969), Tri-State Otolaryn. Assembly (co-founder), Birmngham Otolaryn. Soc. (pres. 1984), Birmingham Aero Club (pres. 1996), Birmingham Downtown Rotary Club. Methodist. Home: 4249 Antietam Dr Birmingham AL 35213-3221

STEVENSON, MARY EVA BLUE, elementary education educator; b. Dillon, S.C., Nov. 20, 1928; d. Alex Adolphus and Artie Mishael (Carmichael) Blue; m Damon Stevenson, Feb. 22, 1951 (dec. Sept. 1984); children: Gwendolyn, Jean Stevenson Arzani, Mary Stevenson Miller, Martha Stevenson Jones, Michele. BA, Allen U., Columbia, S.C., 1950; MA, U. West Fla., Pensacola, 1977. Tchr. 1st grade Worth County Schs., Sylvester, Ga., 1956-57; substitute tchr. Dept. Def. Schs., Tachikawa, Japan, 1966-68; tchr. 1st grade Roswell (N.Mex.) Cath. Sch., 1968-69, Okaloosa County Sch. System, Ft. Walton Beach, Fla., 1970-93; ret., 1993; coord. Each One-Teach One Tutorial Program, Ft. Walton Beach, 1980—. Named Outstanding Model Mother, Progressive Comty. Orgn., Ft. Walton Beach, 1984, educator of Yr., Delta Sigma Theta, Okaloosa Alumni chpt., Ft. Walton Beach, 1987; recipient Willie Bankston award for comty. svcs. So. Christian Leadership Conf., 1996. Fellow Alpha Kappa Alpha (v.p., past parliamentarian, philackter Sigma Omicron Omega chpt.); mem. Okaloosa County Edn. Assn., Okaloosa County Reading Coun., Okaloosa County Black Educators, Order Ea. Star (assoc. matron 1983-94, worthy matron 1994—). Democrat. African Methodist Episcopal. Home: 226 Watson Dr NW Fort Walton Beach FL 32548-4270

STEVENSON, PAUL MICHAEL, physics educator, researcher; b. Denham, Eng., Oct. 10, 1954; came to U.S., 1983; s. Jeremy and Jean Helen (Jennings) S. BA, Cambridge (Eng.) U., 1976; PhD, Imperial Coll., London, 1979. Rsch. assoc. U. Wis., Madison, 1979-81, 1983-84; fellow European Orgn. for Nuclear Rsch., Geneva, 1981-83; sr. rsch. assoc. Rice U., Houston, 1984-86, asst. prof. physics, 1986-89, assoc. prof., 1989-93; prof. physics, 1993—. Contbr. articles to profl. jours.

STEVENSON, RAMONA SHRUM, library director; b. Advance, Mo., Aug. 12, 1938; d. Glendon E. and Ella Mary Anna (Dreyer) Shrum; m. William Edward Stevenson, Aug. 29, 1959; children: Marjorie Stevenson Welch, Gretchen Stevenson Campbell. BS, Lambuth U., 1979. Cert. tchr. Tenn. Tchr. Haywood County Schs., Brownsville, Tenn., 1978-88; libr. dir. Elma Ross Pub. Libr., Brownsville, 1988—. Pres. Haywood Country Women Reps., Newcomer's Club, 1975; bd. dirs. Haywood Lit. Vols.; chmn. mid-south dist. Luth. Women's Christian Growth Commn., 1987-88; pres. Concordia Luth. Ladies' Aux., 1993-95; pres. West Tenn. zone Luth. Women's Missionary League, 1994-96. Mem. Tenn. Libr. Assn. Office: Elma Ross Pub Libr Brownsville TN 38012

STEVENSON, RAY, health care investor; b. Marion, Ohio, July 25, 1937; s. Ray and Hazel (Emmelhainz) S.; children: Jeffrey Parker, Kirk Andrew; m. Ellyn Gareleck, Feb. 8, 1985. BS, Ohio State U., 1959, MBA, 1967. Asst. adminstr. Children's Hosp., Columbus, Ohio, 1963-67; adminstr. Martin Meml. Hosp., Mt. Vernon, Ohio, 1967-71; sr. v.p. Hosp. Affiliates, Nashville, 1971-77; exec. v.p. Charter Med. Corp., Macon, Ga., 1977-79, pres., 1979-85; pres. R.S. Operators Inc., Atlanta, 1985—, R.S. Investors Inc., Atlanta, 1985—; chmn. bd. Am. Med. Trust, 1990—; bd. dirs. Atlanta Filmworks, Inc. Past chmn., bd. dirs. numerous hosps. and health-related orgns. Mem. Am. Coll. Hosp. Adminstrs., Fedn. Am. Hosps. (bd. dirs. 1979-81), Nat. Assn. Psychiat. Hosps. Home: One NE Lagoon Island Ct Stuart FL 34996

STEVENSON, WILLIAM EDWARD, chemical engineer; b. Farmington, Mo., Apr. 21, 1938; s. Herbert Coleman and Mary Jeannetta (Harrington) S.; m. Ramona Ann Shrum, Aug. 29, 1959; children: Marjorie Ellene, Gretchen Faithe. BS in ChemE, Washington U., St. Louis, 1971. Lab tchnician Internat. Oil Burner, St. Louis, 1959-61; maintenance supt. Lever Brothers Co., St. Louis, 1961-74; mgr. hose dept. Haywood Co., Brownsville, Tenn., 1974-95, safety mgr., 1995—. Pres. Haywood County Band Boosters, 1981-83, Haywood County Edn. Task Force, 1985-86; chmn. Haywood County Indsl. Com., 1999-91, mem., 1994—; chmn. Haywood County Job Svc. Employers Com., 1991—, Haywood County Ptnrs. in Edn. Com., 1987-94, Haywood County Rep. Com., 1995—; pres. bd. elders Luth. Ch., 1987-90; chmn. bd. edn. Concordia Luth. Ch. and Sch., 1990-93; v.p. Haywood County Arts Coun., 1994, 95, pres., 1995-96; mem. distbn. com. United Way, 1996. Mem. Haywood County C. of C., Brownsville Rotary (pres. elect 1996). Home: 127 Hillcrest St Brownsville TN 38012-2702 Office: Haywood Co 751 Dupree St Brownsville TN 38012-1708

STEVENTON, ROBERT WESLEY, marketing executive; b. Allentown, Pa., Nov. 2, 1948; s. Robert Wesley and Catherine May (Feineur) S; m. Deborah Damon Barrett, Aug. 29, 1977; children: Calvin Nathaniel, Alexander MacAuley. BA, Pa. State U., 1970; MA, U. Minn., 1975; Cert. Resident, Cambridge U., Eng. Mktg. specialist U.S. Bur. of Census, Washington, 1975-77; mktg. mgr. Am. Chem. Soc., Washington, 1978-83; account exec. Kreitlow & Assocs., Silver Spring, Md., 1983-84; sr. account exec. Mktg. Gen., Inc., Washington, 1984-85; v.p. Mktg. Gen., Inc., Alexandria, Va., 1985-89, sr. v.p., 1989-94; pres. Mktg. Strategies, Unltd., McLean, Va., 1994—; dir. Interlink Corp., 1995—; advisor Euro Broadcasting Corp., 1996—; lectr. Direct Mktg. Assn., Washington, 1988-92, Coun. Engring. and Sci. Soc. Execs., N.Y.C., 1988—; gen. chmn. Direct Mktg. Days Conv. Com., Washington, 1988. Mem. com. econ. devel. bur. Greater Washington Bd. Trade, 1989-92, bus. mktg. com., 1993-94; vol. Christ House, Alexandria, Va., 1987—. With U.S. Army, 1970-73. Recipient Capital award Nat. Leadership Coun., 1992. Mem. Am. Soc. Assn. Execs. (membership com. 1989—), Am.-European Cmty. Assn., Direct Mktg. Assn. Washington (bd. dirs. 1983-85), Soc. for Assn. Mktg. Internat. (pres. 1991-94), Assn. Svcs. Group (chmn. bd. 1996), Order St. Etheldreda (officer 1993), Manorial Soc. Gt. Britain (life), Kappa Tau Alpha. Republican. Episcopalian. Office: Mktg Strategies Unltd 8400 Westpark Dr Ste 100 Mc Lean VA 22102-3522

STEWARD, JERRY WAYNE, air transportation executive, consultant; b. Tulia, Tex., Mar. 22, 1945; s. Joe M. and Mary Evelyn (Boggs) S.; m. Peggy L. Thomas, Nov. 18, 1978 (div. May 1993; children: Eric, Chalynda, Julie. AMT, Spartan Aeronautics, Tulsa, 1965. Designated Airworthiness Rep., U.S. FAA. Dir. quality control Braniff, Dallas, Orlando, Tex., Fla., 1966-90; dir. tech. svcs. Polaris Aircraft Leasing, San Francisco, 1990-94; cons. Roanoke, Tex., 1994—. With U.S. Army, 1966-69. Home and Office: 1820 Summer Ln Roanoke TX 76262-9129

STEWART, ALEXANDER CONSTANTINE, medical technologist; b. N.Y.C., Nov. 3, 1957; s. Dudley Constantine and Lillian Eunice (Mills) S.; m. Shirlene Denise Keys, June 22, 1985; children: Shechianh Faith, Akilah Danielle, Omari Joseph Constantine. Student, Herbert H. Lehman Coll., 1975-77; BS in Med. Tech., U. Kans., 1979; BTh, Northgate Bible Coll., 1989. Cert. med. technologist Am. Soc. Clin. Pathologists.$Dert. clin. lab. supr. Nat. Cert. Agy. Med. Lab. Pers. Chemistry technologist White Plains (N.Y.) Med. Ctr., 1979-89, Mt. Vernon (N.Y.) Hosp., 1987-89; chemistry supr. St. Agnes Hosp., White Plains, 1989-92, Westchester Sq. Med. Ctr., Bronx, N.Y., 1992-93; med. technologist Richland Meml. Hosp., Columbia, S.C., 1993—; instr. William Lee Bonner Sch. Bible & Theology, 1995—. Asst. historian Ch. of Our Lord Jesus Christ, 1989—; deacon Refuge Temple, Ch. of Our Lord Jesus Christ, 1993—, chmn. bd. trustees, 1993—. Mem. NAACP, Soc. Pentecostal Studies (editl. com. 1992-95), Pentecostal Hist. Soc. Democrat. Pentecostal. Home: 801 River Walk Way Irmo SC 29063-9375 also: Refuge Temple 4450 Argent Ct Columbia SC 29203 also: 4159 Grace Ave Bronx NY 10466-2015

STEWART, ANTHONY JOSEPH, investment consultant; b. Buffalo, Nov. 17, 1959; s. Chauncey William and Julia Mae (Cafarella) S.; m. Penelope Marie Sexton, July 22, 1983; children: Krystie Marie, Ashley May. Assoc. in Criminal Justice, Erie C.C., 1981; Assoc. in Computer Sci., Hawaii Pacific Coll., 1986. Supr., CFO Burns Security, Atlanta; pub. safety specialist City of Atlanta; broker, owner KMA Realty & Fin. Svcs., Jonesboro, Ga.; owner, operator Alliance Distbrs., Peachtree City, Ga.; regional mgr. Primerica Fin. Svcs., 1989; regional tng. dir. Excel Telecomms., Inc., 1994. Author: How To Save Money on any Loan, 1993. Rep. Rep. Party, Atlanta, 1992. Sgt. U.S. Army, 1983-86. Recipient Most Inspirational award Hearts of Youth, 1992, MVP award Riverdale Recreation, 1993, Presdl. Sports award Presdl. Coun., 1993. Mem. Nat. Assn. Securities Dealers, Ga. Real Estate Commn. (broker), KC (3d deg.). Office: KMA Realty & Fin Svcs Ste 503 256 Commerce Dr Peachtree City GA 30269

STEWART, BURCH BYRON, chemist, physicist; b. Chattanooga, May 7, 1929; s. Burch Dayton and Mary Elizabeth Stewart; m. Lois Mildred Speaker, June 20, 1955 (div. Mar. 1965); children: Leslie, Alyson, Kathryn; m. Shirley Elizabeth Westervelt, June 8, 1965; children: Steven, Neal, Daryl. BS in Analytical Chemistry, U. Tenn., 1955, MS in Physical Organic Chemistry, 1957, PhD in Physical Chemistry, 1959. Sr. engr. Western Electric, Princeton, N.J., 1959-60; rsch. chemist Allied Chem., Morristown, N.J., 1960-68; mgr., asst. dir. Ciba-Geigy, Ardsley, N.Y., 1968-73; dir. Applied Rsch. Labs., Miami, Fla., 1973-86; pres. Applied Consumer Svcs., Miami, 1986—; rsch. scientist Solar Reactor Corp., Miami, 1978-79; cons. BBS Assocs., Inc., Miami, 1978-81, Worth Engring., Hialeah, Fla., 1986—, All State Engring., 1986—. Inventor and patentee in field; contbr. articles to profl. jours. and encyclopedias. Vol. Askew For Pres., Miami, 1983; pres. Miami Unitarian Soc., 1984, pres. Friends of Physics, U. Miami, 1990-92, 95-97. With USN, 1950-52. Recipient Hon. Mentionship award Westinghouse Sci. Talent Search, Knoxville, 1955; AEC grantee U. Tenn., Knoxville, 1957. Mem. Am. Chem. Soc., Am. Soc. Testing Materials, Assn. Offl. Analytical Chemists, Sigma Xi. Office: Applied Consumer Svcs 9500 NW 77th Ave Ste 5 Hialeah FL 33016-2522

STEWART, CARL DENVER, principal; b. Tallassee, Ala., May 23, 1948; s. Marshall and Izora (Lykes) S.; m. Martha Sue Brooks, Feb. 17, 1970; children: Tonia, Tamala, Carlos, Carl Jr. A.A., Texas Southmost Coll., 1967; B.A., U Tex., 1970. Social studies tchr. Elmdre County Bd. of Edn., Millbrook, Ala., 1975-78; social studies tchr., coach Holtville H.S., Deatsville, Ala., 1978-85, Edward Bell H.S., Camp Hill, Ala., 1985-87; history tchr., coach Tallassee H.S., 1987-92, asst. principal, 1992—; mem. adv. bd. Tallassee Hosp., 1995-96. Author social studies course for Elmore County, Ala., 1984. Pres. NAACP, Tallapoosa County Br., 1990. Mem. NEA, Ala. Edn. Assn., Tallassee Edn. Assn. Methodist. Home: 74 Robert R Morton St Tallassee AL 36078 Office: Tallassee HS 502 Barnett Blvd Tallassee AL 36078-1250

STEWART, CARL E., federal judge; b. 1950. BA magna cum laude, Dillard U., 1971; JD, Loyola U., New Orleans, 1974. Atty. Piper & Brown, Shreveport, La., 1977-78; staff atty. La. Atty. Gen. Office, Shreveport, 1978-79; asst. U.S. atty. Office U.S. Atty. (we. dist.) La., Shreveport, 1979-83; prin. Stewart & Dixon, Shreveport, 1983-85; spl. asst. dist. atty., asst. prosecutor City of Shreveport, 1983-85; judge La. Dist. Ct., 1985-91, La. Ct. Appeals (2d cir.), 1991-94, U.S. Ct. Appeals (5th cir.), 1994—; adj. instr. dept. mgmt. and mktg. La. State U., Shreveport, 1982-85. Mem. chancellor's adv. bd. La. State U., Shreveport, 1983-89, chmn., 1988-89; mem. black achievers program steering com. YMCA, 1990; active NAACP, 1988—. Capt. JAGC, 1974-77, Tex. Mem. ABA, Nat. Bar Assn., Am. Inns. of Ct. (Harry Booth chpt. Shreveport), Black Lawyers Assn. Shreveport-Bossier, La. Conf. Ct. Appeal Judges, La. State Bar Assn. (bench/bar liaison com.), Omega Psi Phi (Rho Omega chpt.). Office: US Ct Appeals 5th Cir 300 Fannin St Ste 2299 Shreveport LA 71101

STEWART, CHARLES HENRY, JR., oil company executive; b. Houston, Mar. 25, 1929; s. Charles Henry and Gertrude Abby (Jordan) S.; m. Jean Donna Zienkiewicz, Feb. 21, 1953; children: Bill, Donna, Jennifer. BS in Petroleum Engring., U. Houston, 1957; BS in Math., So. Meth. U., 1963. Div. engr. Exxon USA, Tex. and La., 1957-62; sr. research engr. Shell Devel. Co., Houston and Dallas, 1963-72; sr. v.p. devel. H.J. Gruy & Assoc., Inc., Houston, 1972-84; v.p. engring. Swift Energy Co., Houston, 1984—. Office: Swift Energy Co 16825 Northchase Dr Ste 400 Houston TX 77060-6027 :

STEWART, CINDY KATHLEEN, school social worker, educator; b. Scottsburg, Ind., June 23, 1958; d. Gordon Lee and Velva Kathleen (Henry) S. BS in Social Work, Ball State U., 1980; MS in Social Work, U. Louisville, 1981; PhD in Human Svcs., Walden U., 1992. Cert. social worker, Ky., clin. social worker, Ind.; lic. sch. social worker, Ky., Ga., Fla.; diplomate Am. Bd. Examiners in Clin. Social Work. Therapist Washington County Guidance Ctr., Salem, Ind., 1981-83; psychiat. social worker Madison (Ind.) State Hosp., 1983-85; sch. social worker Bullitt County day treatment program Bullitt County Pub. Schs., Shepherdsville, Ky., 1985-92; sch. social worker Hillsborough County Schs., Tampa, Fla., 1992—; prof. social work Lindsey Wilson Coll., Shepherdsville, Ky., 1991, U. Ky., Louisville, 1988-92; psychiat. social work cons. Ind. Rehab. Svcs., Indpls., 1984-85; ; instr. adult edn. Jefferson County Pub. Schs., Louisville, 1989-92; pvt. practice Price Counseling Assocs., New Albany, Ind., 1990; workshop facilitator dropout prevention Ashland Oil Co., 1989—; mem. foster care rev. bd. Jefferson County, 1988-92. Vol. Planned Parenthood Assn., Louisville, 1988—; student sponsor ARC, Shepherdsville, 1989-92. Mem. NASW, Phi Delta Kappa, Alpha Kappa Delta. Baptist.

STEWART, CLAUDETTE SUZANNE, small business owner, author; b. East Orange, N.J., Jan. 23, 1948; d. Michel Fred and Helen Alberta (Margerum) Mautor; children: Shaun R., Michael B. BS, Rollins Coll., 1980. Bus. mgr. Wometco, Orlando, Fla., 1978-80; acctg. mgr. CNA, Orlando, 1980-81; fin. mgr. Martin Marietta Data Sys., Orlando, 1981-83; owner, operator Yellow Mountain Flower Farm, Leicester, N.C., 1983—; rschr., contbr. Lark Books, Asheville, N.C., 1988, 89, 91; rsch. writer Rodale Press, Emmaus, Pa., 1991. Author: Living with Potpourri, 1988, Everlasting Floral Gifts, 1990, Nature at Ground Level, 1993; author numerous poems. Vol. counselor Youth Programs, Inc., Orlando, 1981-83; vol. instr. Jr. Achievement, Orlando, 1981-83; vol. mountain search and rescue Asheville Area Rescue Squad, 1990-92; vol. Leicester Vol. Fire Dept., 1990—, Nat. Hug-A-Tree and Survive, 1996, N.C. Assn. Rescue and Emergency Med. Svcs., 1992—. Mem. N.C. Herb Assn. Office: Yellow Mountain Flower Farm 57 Davidson Gap Rd Leicester NC 28748

STEWART, DAVID LAWRENCE, gastroenterologist; b. Lancaster, Pa., May 29, 1949; s. Lawrence T. and Marion Adelaine (Bitting) S.; m. Janice Lynne Surprenant, Jan. 31, 1970 (div. 1986); children: Karen, Jodi, Elizabeth; m. Johnnie Faye Walker, Dec. 6, 1986; children: Sarah, Susan. BEE, Lehigh U., 1971; MD, Pa. State U., 1975. Diplomate Nat. Bd. Med. Examiners, Am. Bd. Internal Medicine. Intern USAF Med. Ctr., Keesler AFB, Miss., 1975-76, resident, 1976-78; fellow in gastroenterology Wilford Hall USAF Med. Ctr., Lackland AFB, Tex., 1978-80, staff gastroenterologist, 1980-81, asst. chief gastroenterology, 1981-83; pvt. practice Digestive Disease Ctr. Red River Valley, Paris, Tex., 1983—; mem. med. staff McCuistion Regional Med. Ctr., Paris, St. Joseph's Hosp. and Med. Ctr., Paris, Hopkins County Meml. Hosp., Sulphur Springs, Tex., Titus County Regional Hosp.; clin. instr. U. Tex. Health Sci. Ctr., San Antonio, 1978-79, clin. asst. prof., 1979-83; asst. prof. Uniformed Svcs. U. of Health Scis., Bethesda, md., 1980-83. Contbr. articles and abstracts to profl. jours. Active Calvary United Meth. Ch., Paris, Valley of Reading, PA Consistory; mem. adv. bd. Paris Regional Rehab. Ctr. Mem. AMA, ACP, Am. Gastroenterology Assn., Am. Soc. for Gastrointestinal Endoscopy, Tex. Soc. for Gastrointestinal Endoscopy, Tex. Med. Assn., Lamar-Delta County Med. Soc., Masons (Ephrata 665), Rajah Shrine, Eta Kappa Nu. Methodist. Office: Digestive Disease Ctr 2890 Lewis Ln Paris TX 75462-2008

STEWART, DAVID MARSHALL, librarian; b. Nashville, Aug. 1, 1916; s. David and Mary (Marshall) S.; m. Gladys Carroll, June 9, 1947; 1 son, James Marshall. B.A., Bethel Coll., 1938; B.S. in L.S, George Peabody Coll., 1939. Circulation asst. Vanderbilt U. Library, 1938-39; county librarian Ark. Library Commn., 1939-40; Tenn. supr. WPA library service projects, 1940-42; librarian Memphis State U., 1942-46; spl. asst. to chief card div. Library of Congress, Washington, 1947; librarian CIA, Washington, 1948-60; chief librarian Nashville Pub. Library, 1960-85; Instr. Peabody Library Sch., 1966-80. Bd. dirs. Council Community Agys., Nashville, Middle-East Tenn. Arthritis Found. (v.p. 1965), Friends Chamber Music Nashville, Travelers Aid Nashville. Served to lt. comdr. USNR, 1942-46. Mem. ALA, Tenn. Library Assn. (chmn. legislative com. 1961-65, v.p. 1965, pres. 1966, Honor award, 1983), Southeastern Library Assn., Pub. Library Assn. Am. (chmn. standards com. 1964-65, pres. 1966-67), Alumni Assn. Bethel Coll. (dir., Disting. Alumni award 1992). Democrat. Mem. Ch. of Christ. Clubs: Kiwanian. (Nashville), Coffee House (Nashville). Home: 6342 Torrington Rd Nashville TN 37205-3157

STEWART, DORATHY ANNE, retired meteorologist; b. Beech Grove, Ind., June 2, 1937; d. Thomas Edward and Dorathy Anne (Browne) S.; BS, U. Tampa, 1958; MS, Fla. State U., 1961, PhD, 1966. Tchr. math, sci., high sch., Live Oak, Fla., 1958-59; rsch. physicist U.S. Army Missile Command, Redstone Arsenal, Ala., 1966-89, meteorologist, 1989-93; ret., 1993. Mem. Am. Meteorol. Soc., Am. Geophys. Union, Ala. Acad. Scis., Sigma Xi. Contbr. articles to profl. jours. Home: PO Box 12067 Huntsville AL 35815-2067

STEWART, EILEEN ROSE, real estate broker; b. Indpls., Oct. 20, 1942; d. Burgess Charles and Flora Clara (Schott) S.; m. Richard Michael Grindle, Feb. 12, 1966 (div. 1977). BS, Ind. U., 1965, MS, 1972; postgrad., Walden U., Naples, Fla., 1995-96, Liberty Retreat Yoga Tng. Sch., Boulevard, Calif., 1996. Lic. real estate broker, Ind., Fla. Tchr. pub. schs. various locations, Ind., Fla., 1965-72; sales rep. UARCO Bus. Forms, Ft. Lauderdale, Fla., 1972-74; staff trainer Palm Beach County Comprehensive Employment Tng. Act program, West Palm Beach, Fla., 1975-77; pres. Untapped Resources, Inc., West Palm Beach, 1978-80; mgmt. cons. Profl. Mgmt. Assocs., Silver Spring, Md., 1980-82; sales rep. The St. George's Club, Washington, 1983-84; real estate broker Mascari Realty, Indpls., 1985-89; pres. Stewart Manor, Inc., Indpls., 1987-89; sales mgr. Charles Hotel Condominium, Miami Beach, Fla., 1990-92; sales assoc. Infinity Realty, Miami Beach, 1992-93, Real Estate Enterprises, 1993—; gen. mgr. Charles Hotel Condominiums, 1994—; cons. Planned Parenthood, West Palm Beach, 1976-78, Jim Stewart Tire Co., Indpls., 1985-89; chair adv. bd. Palm Beach County Displaced Homemakers Ctr., Lake Worth, 1977-78. Mem. Women's Bus. Initiative, Indpls. Bus. Network, Ind. Bed and Breakfast Assn. (cen. regional coord. 1989), NOW (past officer South Palm Beach County chpt., asst. state coord. Fla. sect. 1978, nat. bd. dirs. 1978-79, newsletter editor 1976-77), Women of Miami Beach (pres. 1993-95), Miami Beach Devel. Corp. (bd. dirs. 1994-95). Democrat. Home: 569 Cielo Vista Ct Greenwood IN 46143-1712

STEWART, FRED RAY, journalism educator; b. Ranger, Tex., Dec. 28, 1950; s. Montie R. Stewart and Irene (Norris) Burge; m. Vaunie L. Von Storch, June 23, 1987; children: Brent, Dheren, Ian. BA, U. Tex., Tyler, 1976; MA, Morehead (Ky.) State U., 1980. Editor Mt. Pleasant (Tex.) Daily Times, 1971-72, Tex. East Times Newspaper, Troup, 1974-75; sports editor Mid-Cities Daily News, Hurst, Tex., 1972-74; dir. pub. info. East Tex. State U., Texarkana, 1976-78; dir pub. info. Santa Maria (Calif.) High Sch. Dist., 1990-91; dir. news svcs. Morehead State U., 1978-81; head dept. jouranlism Yavapai Coll., Prescott, Ariz., 1981-85; asst. prof. No. Ariz. U., Flagstaff, 1985-90; head dept. journalism, instr. journalism, newspaper advisor Ohlone Coll., Fremont, Calif., 1991-93; instr. journalism, newspaper adv. Tex. A&M U., Commerce, Tex., 1993—; exec. dir. Rocky Mountain Collegiate Press Assn., Flagstaff, 1990. Editor sports mag., 1984-85; contbr. articles to mags. Coach Pop Warner Youth Football, Prescott, 1982-85, No. Ariz. Youth Football, Flagstaff, 1988-90; den leader Boy Scouts Am., Pleasanton, Calif., 1991. Recipient Outstanding Svc. award Kappa Tau Alpha, 1989. Mem. Journalism Assn. Calif. C.C.'s, Coll. Media Advisers, Phi Kappa Phi. Office: Tex A&M U Commerce East Tex Sta Commerce TX 75429

STEWART, GEORGE EDWARD, II, physician; b. Little Rock, July 9, 1955; s. George Edward and Hazel Elizabeth (Ross) S.; m. Patricia Marie Bengston, June 16, 1979; children: Laura Elizabeth Stewart, George Edward Stewart III, Robert Allen Stewart. BS in Chemistry, Lambuth Coll., Jackson, Tenn., 1977; BS in Pharmacy, U. Tenn., Memphis, 1979, MD, 1988. Diplomate Am. Bd. Allergy and Immunology, Am. Bd. Internal Medicine. Cert. ACLS. Intern Bapt. Meml. Hosp., U. Tenn., Memphis, 1988-89, resident in internal medicine, 1989-91; advanced subspecialty resident in allergy and immunology J.A. Haley VA Hosp., Tampa Gen. Hosp., U. South Fla., Tampa, 1991-93; advanced subspecialty resident U. South Fla., Tampa, 1993—; chief resident divsn. allergy and clin. immunology U. South Fla., 1992-93; faculty post grad. seminars and symposia. Contbr. articles to profl. jours. Vol. various cmty. projects Fla. Asthma and Allergy Found., Tampa, 1991-94. Participant tchrs. group meeting, Ocala, Fla., 1993. Co-winner Bapt. Meml. Hosp. clin. vignette competition, 1988. Mem. AMA, ACP, Am. Acad. Allergy and Immunology (fellow-in-tng., co-chairperson fellow-in-tng. com., 1992—), Am. Coll. Allergy and Immunology (fellow-in-tng.), Am. Coll. Chest Physicians (assoc.), Fla. Allergy and Immunology Soc. Methodist. Home: 1515 S.E. 27th Terrace Ocala FL 34471 Office: Allergy and Asthma Care of Fla 1800 SE 17th Street Off 300 Ocala FL 34471

STEWART, GEORGE RAY, librarian; b. Birmingham, Ala., Aug. 19, 1944; s. DeWitt and Ann (McCain) S.; m. Nancy Ann Norton, June 5, 1964; children: Steven Ray, Jeffery Alan. B.A., Samford U., Birmingham, 1966, M.A., 1967; M.A., Emory U., 1971. Mem. staff Birmingham Pub. Libr., 1960—, assoc. dir., 1970-76, dir., 1976-93; system dir., 1993—; part-time instr. Grad. Sch. Libr. Svc. U. Ala.; bd. dirs. Southeastern Library Network, Inc., 1986-88. Editor: Birmingham Pub. Library Press. Bd. dirs. Red Mountain Mus., 1972-79, Literacy Coun. Ctrl. Ala., 1990-94; bd. dirs. Indsl. Health Coun., Birmingham, 1972-85, sec., 1979-81, pres. bd. dirs. 1982, 83. Mem. ALA, Southeastern Libr. Assn. (treas. 1985-86, v.p. 1986-88, pres. 1989-90), Ala. Libr. Assn. (scholarship 1968, pres. 1976), Ala. Hist. Assn., Birmingham Hist. Assn. Office: Birmingham-Jefferson County Libr System 2100 Park Pl Birmingham AL 35203-2744

STEWART, GREGORY WALLACE, physician; b. Balt., July 8, 1961; s. Don Milton and Martha (Davis) S.; married (div.); 1 child, Lauren Elizabeth; m. Bonnie Marie Johnson, June 8, 1991; children: Tess Marie, Shaid Michael. BS in Biology, Chemistry and Para-Med. Sports Therapy, Houston Baptist U., 1982; MD, U. Tex. Med. Branch Sch. of Medicine, 1986. Diplomate Am. Bd. Physical Medicine and Rehab. Resident in physical medicine and rehab. La. State U./Charity Hosp. in New Orleans, 1986-90; instr. and asst. residency Sect. Phys. Medicine and Rehab. La. State U. Sch. Medicine in New Orleans, 1990-92; clin. asst. prof. Dept. Orthopaedics Tulane U. Sch. Medicine, 1990-95; asst. prof. and residency program dir. Sect. of Phys. Medicine La. State U. Sch. Medicine in New Orleans, 1992-95; assoc. prof. orthopedics Tulane U. Sch. Medicine, 1995—; team physician New Orleans Night Arena Football Team, 1991-92, Tulane U., 1990—, Hahnville H.S., 1987—; physician Ballet Hysell, New Orleans; coord. sports medicine St. Charles and Plaquemines Parish Sch. Dists.; assoc. coord. sports medicine St. Bernard and Orleans Parish Sch. Dists.; mem. adv. coun. La. Sports Medicine and Safety; mem. U.S. Olympic Track and Field Trials Sports Medicine Staff, 1992; mem. sports medicine organizing com. NCAA Track and Field Championships, 1993. Contbr. numerous articles to med. jours. mem., chmn. task force on disabling violence La. Adv. Coun. on Disability Prevention, 1990-93, mem. com. on prevention of secondary disabilties; med. cons. Weiss Rehab. Ctr.; chmn. divsn. of rehab. svcs. head injury tech. assistance com. State of La.; mem. adv. com. for phys. therapy asst. program Delgado C.C.; reviewer Medicine and Sci. in Sports and Exercise Jour. of Orthopaedic and Sports Physical Therapy; abstract reviewer Nat. Head Injury Found.; grant reviewer Nat. Inst. Disability Rsch. and Rehab. Recipient Study of Personal Care Attendants for Indigent Quadriplegics grant Am. Assn. of Spinal Cord Injury Psychologists and Social Workers, 1991-93, Rehab. Long Term Tng. -Rehab. Medicine grant Rehab. Svcs. Adminstrn., 1993-95, La. Disability Prevention Program grant Sports Injury Surveillance in La., 1993-94. Fellow Am. Coll. Sports Medicine; mem. AMA, Am. Acad. Phys. Medicine and Rehab., Am. Congress Rehab. Medicine, Nat. Athletic Trainers Assn., S.E. Athletic Trainers Assn., La. State Med. Soc., La. Athletic Trainers Assn., Orleans Parish Med. Soc., La. Sports Medicine Soc. (edn. chmn. 1994—). Home: 4905 Clearlake Dr Metairie LA 70006-1112 Office: Dept Orthopaedics SL32 1430 Tulane Ave New Orleans LA 70112-2699

STEWART, HARRIS BATES, JR., oceanographer; b. Auburn, N.Y., Sept. 19, 1922; s. Harris B. and Mildred (Woodruff) S.; m. Elise Bennett Cunningham, Feb. 21, 1959; children: Dorothy Cunningham, Harry Hasburgh; 2d m. Louise Conant Thompson, Dec. 22, 1988. Grad., Phillips Exeter Acad., 1941; AB, Princeton, 1948; MS, Scripps Instn. Oceanography, U. Calif., 1952, PhD, 1956. Hydrographic engr. U.S. Navy Hydrographic Office expdn. to, Persian Gulf, 1948-49; instr. Hotchkiss Sch., 1949-51; research asst. Scripps Instn. Oceanography, 1951-56; diving geologist, project mgr. Geol. Diving Cons., Inc., San Diego, 1953-57; chief oceanographer U.S. Coast & Geodetic Survey, 1957-65, dept. asst. dir., 1962-65; dir. Inst. Oceanography, Environmental Sci. Services Adminstrn., U.S. Dept. Commerce, 1965-69; dir. Atlantic Oceanographic and Meteorol. Labs., NOAA, 1969-78, cons., 1978-80; prof. marine sci., dir. Center for Marine Studies, Old Dominion U., Norfolk, Va., 1980-85; adj. prof. dept. oceanography Old Dominion U., 1986—; dir. S.E. Bank of Dadeland; chmn. Fla. Commn. Marine Sci. and Tech.; mem. exec. com., earth scis. div. Nat. Acad. Scis.; chmn. adv. bd. Nat. Oceanographic Data Center, 1965-66; chmn. survey panel interagy. com. oceanography Fed. Council Sci. and Tech., 1959-67; chmn. adv. com. underseas features U.S. Bd. Geog. Names, 1964-67; mem. sci. party No. Holiday Expdn., 1951; Capricorn Expdn., 1952-53; chief scientist Explorer Oceanographic Expdn., 1960, Pioneer Indian Ocean Expdn., 1964, Discoverer Expdn., 1968, NOAA-Carib Expdn., 1972, Researcher Expdn., 1975; mem. U.S. delegation Intergovtl. Oceanographic Commn., 1961-65; mem. Gov. Calif. Adv. Commn. Marine Resources; chmn. adv. council Dept. Geol. and Geophys. Scis. Princeton; v.p. Dade Marine Inst., 1976-77, pres., 1977-79; trustee, mem. exec. com. Assoc. Marine Insts.; mem. Fisheries Mgmt. Adv. Council Va. Marine Resources Commn., 1984-85; vice chmn. adv. council Univ. Nat. Oceanographic Lab. System, 1983-85; U.S. nat. assoc. to intergovtl. oceanographic commn. UNESCO program for Caribbean, 1964-89, vice chmn., 1974. Author: The Global Sea, 1963, Deep Challenge, 1966, The Id of the Squid, 1970, Challenger Sketchbook, 1972, No Dinosaurs on the Ark, 1988, Grungy George and Sloppy Sally, 1993, Injections of Hospital Humor, 1996. Bd. dirs. Vanguard Sch., Miami, 1974-76; trustee Metro Zoo, Miami, 1991—. Served as pilot USAAF, 1942-46, PTO. Decorated comendador Almirante Padilla (Colombia); recipient Meritorious award Dept. Commerce, 1960, Exceptional Service award, 1965. Fellow AAAS, Geol. Soc. Am., Nat. Tropical Bot. Gardens, Marine Tech. Soc. (v.p.); mem. Fla. Acad. Scis. (pres. 1978-79), Va. Acad. Sci., Am. Geophys. Union, Internat. Oceanographic Found. (v.p. 1974-80), Zool. Soc. Fla. (pres. 1970-73), Maine Hist. Soc., Marine Hist. Assn., Cape Ann Hist. Assn., Marine Coun. (Miami), Explorers Club (N.Y.), Prouts Neck (Maine) Yacht Club, Cosmos Club (D.C.), Club Pelican Bay (Naples, Fla.). Presbyterian. Home (summer): 11 Atlantic Dr Scarborough ME 04074-8667 Home (winter): 720 Shadow Lake Ln Naples FL 34108-8500

STEWART, J. DANIEL, air force development and test center administrator; b. Savannah, Ga., June 20, 1941; s. Benjamin F. and Bessie L. (Edenfield) S.; m. Rebecca M. Smith; children: Daniel, Laura. BS in Aero. Engring., Ga. Inst. Tech., 1963, MS in Aero. Engring., 1965, PhD in Aero. Engring., 1967; M. in Mgmt. Sci., Stanford U., 1979. Mem. tech. staff applied mechanics divsn. Aerospace Corp., El Segundo, Calif., 1967-74; br. chief tech. divsn. Air Force Rocket Propulsion Lab., Edwards AFB, Calif., 1974-78, asst. for R&D mgmt., 1979-81; divsn. chief Air Force Armament Divsn., Eglin AFB, Fla., 1981-83; dir. drone control program office 3246 Test Wing, Eglin AFB, Fla., 1983-85, joint dir. US/Allied munitions program office, 1985-86; tech. dir. rsch./devel./acquisitions Air Force Armament Divsn., Eglin AFB, Fla., 1986-88; asst. to comdr. Air Force Munitions Divsn., Eglin AFB, Fla., 1988-90; tech. dir. Air Force Devel. and Test Ctr., Eglin AFB, 1990-93, exec. dir., 1993—; mem. policy coun. Scientist and Engr. Career Program, Randolph AFB, Tex., 1994—, chmn. career devel. panel, 1994-96. Bd. dirs. Internat. Found. for Telemetering, Woodland Hills, Calif., 1991-95; mem. engring. adv. bd. U. Fla., Gainesville, 1988—; mem. citizens adv. com. U. West Fla., Pensacola, 1991—; mem. civilian exec. adv. bd. Air Force Materiel Command, 1990—, also former chmn.; mem. curricular adv. com. Def. Test and Evaluation Profl. Inst., 1991—. Recipient Presdl. Meritorious Rank award Pres. of U.S., 1993. Mem. Air Force Assn. (Lewis H. Brereton award 1994), Sr. Exec. Assn., Am. Def. Preparedness Assn., Internat. Test and Evaluation Assn. (Cross medal 1994), Assn. of Old Crows, Fed. Exec. Inst. Alumni, Gulf Coast Alliance for Tech. Transfer. Office: AFDTC CD 101 W D Ave Ste 123 Eglin AFB FL 32542-5490

STEWART, JAMES CAMP, architect; b. Talladega, Ala., Dec. 19, 1953; s. James Camp and Elizabeth Opal Lee (Jackson) S.; m. Kathy Ethel Griffin, Sept. 13, 1980; children: Rebecca Kathryn, James Griffin, Carolyn Elizabeth. B in Environ. Design, Auburn U., 1976, BArch, 1977. Registered arch. Space planner So. Bell, Atlanta, 1977-79; arch. Gary Coursey & Assoc., Atlanta, 1979-83, v.p., 1987-90; project arch. SIMA, Nairobi, Kenya, 1983-85; chief arch. RACO, Atlanta, 1985-87; pres., owner Jim Stewart & Assoc., Atlanta, 1990—. Bd. dirs. ACT, Uganda, 1994—. Recipient Design Excellence award for indsl. projects Fulton County C. of C., 1989. Mem. Rotary (sec. Roswell chpt. 1994-95, dir. internat. svcs. 1995), Atlanta Auburn Club (v.p. 1978). Republican. Presbyterian. Home: 4695 Westchester Ct Duluth GA 30136

STEWART, JAMES CHARLES, II, insurance agent; b. Spartanburg, S.C., Jan. 2, 1952; s. James Charles Sr. and Thelma (Robertson) S.; m. Nancy Eleanor Bates, Dec. 23, 1973; children: James Ryan, Matthew Daniel, Megan Eleanor. BS in Mktg., U. S.C., 1974; CLU, Am. Coll., Bryn Mawr, Pa., 1983. Mgr. I-26 Svc. Ctr., Woodruff, S.C., 1975; agt. Ind. Life Ins. Co., Jacksonville, Fla., 1975-84, N.Y. Life Ins. Co., N.Y.C., 1984—; pres. Ins. Group, Spartanburg, S.C., 1992—. Coach So. Spartanburg Youth Athletic Assn., Walnut Grove, S.C., 1984-88; treas. Roebuck (S.C.) Primary Sch. PTA, 1986-87, pres., 1987-88; asst. chief Hobbysville Vol. Fire Dept., Woodruff, 1978; treas. Cavins (S.C.) Dem. Precinct, 1978; v.p. Dorman H.S. (Spartanburg) All Sports Booster Club, 1995—. Named Hon. Constable, S.C. Gov. Jim Edwards, 1975, S.C. Gov. R.W. Riley, 1979, S.C. Gov. Carrol A. Campbell, 1987, S.C. Gov. David Beasley, 1995; named Divsn. Co-winner, Grand Strand Fishing Rodeo, Myrtle Beach, S.C., 1987. Mem. Spartanburg Life Underwriters Assn. (pres. 1988-89, Underwriter of Yr. 1990), Life Ins. Leaders S.C., Am. Soc. CLUs, Nat. Assn. Life Underwriters, Gentlemen's Actuarial Soc. S.C. (charter), S.C. Assn. Life Underwriters (LUPIC chmn. 1989-92), U. S.C. Alumni Assn., Gamecock Club, Masons (master chpt. 1983), Ruritan Club (charter, pres. 1988), Delta Sigma Pi, Sigma Pi Mu (various offices). Home: 8 Tims Creek Rd Roebuck SC 29376-3353 Office: NY Life Ins Co 251 Magnolia St Ste 5 Spartanburg SC 29306-2331

STEWART, JAMES KEVIN, judicial administrator, management technology consultant; b. Berkeley, Calif., Nov. 28, 1942; s. Berthold and Myrle (Minson) S.; m. Marise Rene Duff, Oct. 26, 1985; children: Daphne Brooks, Andrew MacLaren, James Kevin Spencer, Mary Elizabeth Ainsley. B.S., U. Oreg., 1964; M.P.A., Calif. State U.-Hayward, 1977; grad. cert., U. Va., 1978; grad., FBI Nat. Acad., 1978. Cmmdr. criminal investigation div. Oakland Police Dept., 1976-81; instr. San Jose (Calif.) State U., 1978-81; spl. asst. atty. gen. Dept. Justice, Washington, 1981-82; dir. Nat. Inst. Justice, Washington, 1982-90, Booz, Allen & Hamilton, Inc., McLean, Va., 1990—; guest lectr. U. Calif., Berkeley, Harvard, U.; steering com. global organized crime initiative Ctr. Strategic Internat. Studies, 1994; U.S. del. Couns. of Europe, Strasborg, France, 1984; advisor DOD/DOJ Ops. Other Than War and Law Enforcement, 1994; chmn. pun. safety conf. SPTE, 1992; advisor, chmn. Dept. Justice Nat. Conf. Law Enforcement Tech., 21st Century, Washington, 1993; bd. dirs. White House Fellows Found., 1990; mem. Internat. Law Enforcement Conf., Washington, 1995. Recipient O.W. Wilson award for outstanding contbns. to law enforcement, 1986, Ennis J. Olgiati award Nat. Assn. Pre-Trial Services Agys., 1987, Predl. citation AIA, 1987, Nat. Criminal Justice Service award Nat. Criminal Justice Assn., 1988, Outstanding Nat. Contbn. to Policing Spl. award Police Exec. Research Forum, 1988, August Vollmer award Am. Soc. Criminology, 1992; White House fellow, 1981-82. Mem. Internat. Assn. Chiefs of Police (dir. 1981-82), Police Mgmt. Assn. (founder, pres. 1979-81), White House Fellows Alumni, White House Fellows Found. (bd. dirs.), FBI Nat. Acad. Assn., Internat. Homicide Investigation Assn. (charter), Nat. Inst. Corrections (bd. dirs.), Soc. for Reform of Criminal Law (planning chmn. Police Powers and Citizens Rights Conf.), Coun. For Excellence In Govt. (prin.), Delta Upsilon. Republican. Episcopalian. Club: University (Washington). Home: 6427 Lakeview Dr Falls Church VA 22041-1330 Office: Booz Allen & Hamilton Inc 8283 Greensboro Dr Mc Lean VA 22102-3838

STEWART, JEFFREY BAYRD, lawyer; b. Chgo., Feb. 6, 1952; s. Bruce A. and Harriet B. Stewart. A.B. magna cum laude (Rufus Choate scholar), Dartmouth Coll., 1974; J.D., Emory U., 1978. Bar: Ga. 1978, U.S. Dist. Ct. (no. dist.) Ga., U.S. Ct. Appeals (5th and 11th dists.). Ptnr., chair corp. dept., Arnall Golden & Gregory, Atlanta, 1978—. Mem. editorial bd. Emory Law Jour., 1977-78. Mem. ABA, State Bar Ga. Home: 4110 Pine Heights Dr Atlanta GA 30324 Office: Arnall Golden & Gregory 1201 W Peachtree St Atlanta GA 30309-3450

STEWART, JENISE DORENE, sales executive; b. Toledo, Jan. 18, 1966; d. Richard C. and Beverly (Gilchrist) S. BA, Fisk U., 1990. Sales exec. The Tennessean, Nashville, 1990—. Coll. and youth counselor Schrader Lane Ch. of Christ, Nashville, 1995—; active Walter Kaitz Found.; leader Girl Scout Troop # 606. Mem. NAACP (Nashville chpt.), Nat. Assn. Black Journalists. Home: 3305 Lealand Ln Nashville TN 37207

STEWART, JOE J., manufacturing executive; b. 1938. BSChemE, Purdue U., 1959; MA, Kansas State U., 1961; PhD, N.C. State U., 1963; DEng (hon.), Purdue U., 1994. With Aerojet-Gen. Corp., 1966-72; with Babcock & Wilcox Co., New Orleans, 1972—, v.p., 1978; pres., COO Babcock & Wilcox Co., Barberton, Ohio, 1993; now pres. Babcock & Wilcox, govt. grp., Lynchburg, VA; v.p., group exec. McDermott Marine Constrn., European Ops., 1984-87.

STEWART, JOHN EZELL, educational and business consultant; b. Sand Springs, Okla., Aug. 26, 1929; m. Elsie Louise Fonville, June 18, 1954; children: Barry, Johnetta, Rhonda, Howard. BS in Vocat. Edn., Langston (Okla.) U., 1951; MS in Gen. Supervision, Calif. State U., L.A., 1964; grad. study, U. Rich., 1980, 82. Cert. collegiate profl. tchr. Staff supr. Norfolk State U.; acct. exec., v.p. Bus. Devel.; tchr., project mgr. L.A. City Unified Sch. Dist.; edn. specialist cons. Pepperdine U., L.A.; substitute tchr. Richmond City Pub. Schs.; founder, exec. dir. Va. Adolescent Adult Rehab. Agy.; founder, prin. John Ezell Stewart Sch.; grant adminstr. Steamer Co., 1991—; faculty chmn. Mary McLeod Bethune Middle Sch.; spl. projects dir. Tchr. Human rels. Workshops; pres. Pan Hellenic Coun.; founder Motivation for Success in Life Inst., 1996. Mem. Am. Fedn. Tchrs., United Tchrs. L.A., Omega Psi Phi. Democrat. Buddhist.

STEWART, JOHN GILMAN, government official; b. Bklyn., Feb. 15, 1935; s. F. Gilman and Winifred Ann (Link) S.; m. Nancy Potter, June 23, 1957; children—Michael Gilman, Cara Jane. BA, Colgate U., 1957; MA, U. Chgo., 1959, PhD, 1968. Asst. dir. Am. Polit. Sci. Assn., Washington, 1961-62; legis. asst. to Senator Hubert Humphrey, Washington, 1962-65; exec. asst. to v.p. Hubert Humphrey, Washington, 1965-69; dir. comms. Democratic Nat. Com., Washington, 1970-73; staff dir. energy subcom. Joint Econ. Com., U.S. Congress, 1974-77; staff dir. Sci. Tech. and Space Subcom., U.S. Senate, Washington, 1977-79; mgr. office of planning and budget, TVA, Knoxville, 1979-82, office corp. adminstrn. and planning, 1982-87; office of policy, planning and budget, 1987-89, v.p. valley resources, 1989-93; dir. Consortium of Rsch. Instns., Knoxville, Tenn., 1993-95; co-dir., Fulbright prof. Georgian-Am. Inst. Pub. Adminstrn., Tbilisi, Republic of Georgia, 1995—. cons. Joint Com. on Congl. Ops., U.S. Congress, Washington, 1973-75; mem. aerospace safety adv. panel NASA, Washington, 1980—. Author: One Last Chance, The Democratic Party, 1974-76, 1974. Contbr. articles on congl. leadership and polit. parties and civil rights to profl. jours. Bd. dirs. Knoxville Opera Co., 1982—. Fulbright prof. Republic of Georgia. Fellow Inst. Politics, Harvard U., Cambridge, Mass., 1966-67; recipient Disting. Alumnus award U. Chgo., 1973. Fellow Nat. Acad. Pub. Adminstrn.; mem. Am. Polit. Sci. Assn., Am. Soc. Pub. Adminstrn., Nat. Acad. Pub. Adminstrn. (Nat. Pub. Svc. award 1993), Nat. Mgmt. Assn. Democrat. Avocations: gardening, running.ng. Home: 6611 Ridge Rock Ln Knoxville TN 37909-2769

STEWART, JOHN MURRAY, banker; b. Summit, N.J., Apr. 2, 1943; s. Robert John Stewart and Mary Catherine (Grabhorn) Stewart Yoder; m. Sandra Meyers Frazier, Feb. 26, 1966; children: Jennifer Bricar, Catherine Dorothy. BA, U. Va., 1965; MBA, NYU, 1983. Trust officer, v.p. Bankers Trust Co., N.Y.C., 1965-82, Morgan Guaranty Trust Co., N.Y.C., 1982-83; mgr., pres., dir. Morgan Trust Co. Fla., Palm Beach, 1983-89; pres., dir. Bankers Trust Co. Fla., 1989-93; pres. pvt. capital group SunTrust Bank, Orlando, Fla., 1993-96; pres., dir. Harris Trust Co. Fla., West Palm Beach, 1996—. Campaign chmn. Palm Beach Cmty. Chest, 1985, 86; vestryman Bethesda By the Sea Ch., Palm Beach, 1986-89, 92-94, treas., 1986-87; treas. Cathedral Ch. of St. Luke, Orlando, 1996; bd. dirs. Orlando Opera Co., 1994-96. Mem. Fla. Bankers Assn. (chmn. trust bus. devel. com. 1989, planning commn., chmn. trust legis. com. 1990), N.Y. State Bankers Assn. (mem. trust bus. devel. com. 1978-82), N.Y. Yacht Club (N.Y.C.), Everglades Club (Palm Beach), Winter Park Racquet Club, Monmouth Boat Club (Red Bank, N.J.), Sailfish Club of Fla. (Palm Beach) (bd. govs. 1992-96), SAR (1st v.p. 1995, 96.

STEWART, JOSEPH, JR., political science educator, researcher; b. Chattanooga, June 22, 1951; s. Joseph Earl Sr. and Naomi Gertrude (Kennamer) S. AB Polit. Sci., U. Ga., 1970; MA Internat. Affairs, Fla. State U., 1971; PhD Polit. Sci., U. Houston, 1977. Tchr. government Jeff Davis (County) High Sch., 1971-72; instr. social scis. So. Ga. Coll., 1972-74, dir. Office Coop. Edn., 1973-74; teaching asst. U. Ga., 1974-75; lectr. U. Houston, 1975-77; asst. prof. polit. sci. Wichita State U., 1977-78; asst. prof. polit. sci. U. New Orleans, 1978-82, assoc. prof. polit. sci., 1982-84; assoc. prof. polit. sci. W.Va. U., 1984-89; assoc. prof. polit. sci. U. Tex., Dallas, 1989-92, prof., 1992-96; prof. polit. sci. U. N.Mex., Albuquerque, 1996—; disting. prof. polit. sci. San Diego State U., 1989; vis. scholar Inst. for Pub. Policy, U. N.Mex., 1995; invited speaker in field; panelist numerous profl. meetings. Author: (with James E. Anderson, David W. Brady, Charles S. Bullock, III) Public Policy and Politics in America, 1984, (with Kenneth J. Meier and Robert E. England) Race, Class, and Education: the Politics of Second-Generation Discrimination, 1989 (Bustavus Myers award 1991), (with Kenneth J. Meier) The Politics of Hispanic Education: Un Paso Pa'Lante y Dos Pa'tras, 1991 (Bustavus Myers award 1992), (with Paula D. McClain) Can We All Get Along? Racial and Ethnic Minorities in American Politics, 1995, (with James P. Lester) Public Policy: An Evolutionary Approach, 1996; contbr. articles to profl. jours., chpts. to books; rev. in field. Culpeper fellow Rice, 1981-83, hon. fellow U. Wis., 1987; grantee NSF, 1982-84; nat. assessment of ednl. progress scholar Ednl. Testing Svc., 1991-92. mem. Am. Ednl. Rsch. Assn., Am. Polit. Sci. Assn. (exec. coun. 1996-98, Kaufman award com. pub. adminstrn. 1992-93, best book award com. urban politics sect. 1992-93, exec. coun. urban politics sect. 1993-95, pub. policy sec. 1994—), Am. Soc. Pub. Adminstrn., Law and Soc. Assn., Midwest Polit. Sci. Assn. (mem. program com. 1993-94, exec. coun. 1994-97, race, ethnicity and politics sect. 1995—), Nat. Conf. Black Polit. Scis., Polit. Edn. Assn., So. Polit. Sci. Assn. (mem. com. on status of women 1986-87), Southwestern Polit. Sci. Assn. (program com. 1980-81, 89-90, best paper awards com. 1987-88, 88-89, chair Ted Robinson Meml. award com. 1989-90, v.p. and program chair 1990-91, pres. 1995-96), Western Polit. Sci. Assn., Western Social Sci. Assn. (program coord., pub. adminstrn. 1989-90). Democrat. Home: 57 Berta Dr Edgewood NM 87015-8003

STEWART, JOSEPH GRIER, lawyer; b. Tuscaloosa, Ala., July 24, 1941; s. Jesse Grier and Kyle Vann (Pruett) S.; m. Linda Louise Hogue, Mar. 2, 1963; children: Joseph Grier Jr., Robert Byars, James Vann. BS, U. Ala., Tuscaloosa, 1963, LLB, 1966. Bar: Ala. 1966, U.S. Dist. Ct. (no. dist.) Ala. 1968, U.S. Dist. Ct. (middle Dist.of Ala.), 1996, U.S. Tax Court. Ptnr. Burr & Forman, Birmingham, Ala., 1968—. Mem. ABA, Ala. State Bar, Birmingham Bar Assn. (chmn. com. 1989-90), Ala. Law Inst., Kiwanis, Birmingham Tip Off Club (pres. 1988-89). Methodist. Office: Burr & Forman 3100 S Trust Tower 420 20th St N Birmingham AL 35203-3204

STEWART, LYN VARN, critical care nurse; b. Charleston, S.C., July 3, 1957; d. Allen Hamilton and Merilyn (Windsor) Varn; m. James Milton Stewart Jr., May 26, 1979; children: Kevin James, Sean Allen. BA in History, Clemson U., 1979; ADN, U. S.C., 1983. Cert. BLS, ACLS. Staff RN med.-surg. units Piedmont Med. Ctr., Rock Hill, S.C., 1983-85, staff nurse progressive care unit, 1985-94, RN, asst. head nurse progressive care unit, 1991-92, preceptor coord., 1991-93, quality improvement rep. progressive care unit, 1991-92; office nurse, cardiac stress testing Carolinas Med. Group-Shiland, Rock Hill, 1995—; preceptor coord., quality improvement rep. progressive care unit Piedmont Med. Ctr., Rock Hill, 1991-92; office RN cardiac stress testing Carolinas Med. Group-Shiland, Rock Hill, 1995—. Bd. dirs. Westminster Christian Sch., Rock Hill., 1991-93, mem. yearbook staff, 1991-93, mem. PTO bd., 1992-93, coach Westminster Little Tigers soccer team, 1992-93, asst. coach Westminster Lions soccer team, 1992-93; bd. trustees Westminster Catawba Christian Sch., Rock Hill, 1993-94, mem. PTO bd., 1993-95, newsletter editor, 1992—, co-coord. sch. soccer program, 1992-95, asst. coach under-10 & under-12 soccer team, 1994—; sec. Westminster Catawba Christian Sch. Athletic Booster Club, 1994—; founding mem. Spirit Soccer League, Rock Hill, 1996—. Mem. S.C. Assn. Nurses Endorsing Transplantation. Home: 603 Greenbriar Ave Rock Hill SC 29730-3301

STEWART, LYNN BEARD, public relations executive; b. Shreveport, La., Nov. 1, 1949; d. Delma Olander and Bonnie Ernestine (Thrasher) Beard; m. Marshall Gattis Stewart, Nov. 28, 1970; children: James Marshall, Meredith Lynn. BA in Journalism magna cum laude, La. Tech. U., 1970; postgrad., La. State U., 1993—. X-ray file rm. clk. La. State U. Med. Ctr. Hosp., 1968; acting city editor The Ruston Daily Leader, 1969; instr. journalism La. Tech. U., 1970-71; copy editor, city desk asst. The Times, 1971-72, edn. writer, 1972-76, enterprise editor, 1976-79; asst. mng. editor The (Shreveport) Times, 1979-82; dir. info. svcs. La. State U., Shreveport, 1982-93; dir. pub. rels. Centenary Coll. La., Shreveport, 1994—; Bd. dirs., adminstrs., chair scholarship policy and procedures Shreveport Journalism Found., 1990, 91, 92, 93, 94, 95, 96, golf tournament fundraiser vols. chmn., 1990—. Mem. La. State U. in Shreveport 25th Anniversary Com., 1991-92; chair La. State U. in Shreveport Communi-Versity Day, 1991; bd. dirs., v.p. pub. rels., mem. exec. bd. Shreveport Opera, 1988-89, bd. dirs., 1986-92; mem. River Cities Network, 1987-92, 94—; mem. pub. rels. com. Shreveport Sesquicentennial, 1986; team capt. United Way Campaign, 1986; mem. planning com. FutureShape Shreveport, 1985-86; loaned exec. United Way, 1984; bd. dirs. South Highlands Elem. Magnet PTA, 1984; mem. YWCA N.W. La., bd. dirs., 1996—. Recipient Letter of Commendation Pulitzer Prize Com. on Pub. Svc., 1978, Woman of Achievement La. Press Women, 1979, Nat. Fedn. Press Women, 1980. Mem. Shreveport Journalism Found. (mng. dir.), Pub. Rels. Soc. Am. (bd. dirs. North La. chpt. 1991, 92—), La. Higher Edn. Pub. Rels. Assn. (treas. 1990-91, v.p. 1991-92, pres. 1992-93), Soc. Profl. Journalists (bd. dirs., program chair Shreveport profl. chpt. 1990, v.p. 1991, 92), Shreveport C. of C., Leadership Shreveport (bd. dirs. 1989-92), Nat. Fedn. Press Women, La. Press Women, Coun. for Advancement and Support of Edn., Literacy Vols. Am. (bd. dirs. 1994—). Methodist. Office: Centenary Coll 2911 Centenary Blvd Shreveport LA 71134-1188

STEWART, MARCUS J(EFFERSON), orthopedic surgeon, consultant, educator; b. Whiteville, Tenn., July 13, 1911; s. Marcus Jefferson and Mattie Sue (Crowder) S.; m. Mariette Solvay McDonald, Nov. 3, 1944; children—Mariette E. Stewart Rhodes, Jeanne M. Stewart Jemison, Lee Jurion Stewart Bowen. B.S. cum laude, Milligan Coll., 1933; M.D., U. Tenn., 1938, M.S. in Orthopedic Surgery, 1945. Diplomate Am. Bd. Orthopedic Surgery. (examiner 1952-70). Intern, City of Memphis Hosp., 1938-39; resident in orthopedic surgery Campbell Clinic, Memphis, 1939-41; postgrad. course in fractures U. London, 1942, course in prosthetics UCLA, 1954; clin. asst. dept. orthopedics, U. Tenn. Ctr. Health Scis., Memphis, 1947-49, clin. instr., 1949-51, clin. asst. prof., 1951-58, clin. assoc. prof., 1958-71, prof., 1971—, chmn. med. affairs com., trustee, 1975-81; chief orthopedic sect. VA Med. Ctr., Memphis, 1981—; mem. Council on Sports Medicine U.S. Olympic Com., 1978-84; mem. staff Campbell Clinic, Crippled Children's Hosp. Memphis, 1947-81; mem. staff Bapt. Meml. Hosp., 1947—, chief staff, 1963; mem. staff City of Memphis Hosp., 1947—, bd. dirs., 1971-78; mem. staff Meth. Hosp.; cons. to surgeon gen. U.S. Army, 1947—; active staff cons. LeBonheur Children's Hosp., Memphis, Crittenden Meml. Hosp., West Memphis, Ark.; chmn. Com. of Sports Medicine for Disabled Athletes, 1981—; mem. Pres.'s Com. for Employment of Physically Handicapped, 1959-72; chmn. Gov.'s Com. for Employment of Physically Handicapped, 1959, 1960. Vestryman, St. John's Episcopal Ch., 1966-68, 81-83, sr. warden, 1968; bd. dirs. Les Passees Rehab. Ctr., chmn., 1964-65; trustee U. Tenn., 1970-81, Memphis and Shelby County hosps., 1970-78, Hutchison Sch. for Girls, 1967-70; adv. bd. Am. Phys. Therapy Assn.; chmn. med. com. Memphis Sesquicentennial, 1969; dir. First Fed. Savs. and Loan Assn., 1965—. Served with M.C. U.S. Army, 1941-46; served to col. USAR, 1947-71. Decorated Legion of Merit. Recipient Disting. Alumnus award Milligan Coll., 1973, U. Tenn. Coll. Medicine, 1976; mem. U. Tenn. Pres.'s Club, 1970—, Milligan Coll. Pres.'s Club, 1972—. Fellow ACS (gov. 1962-64); mem. Am. Orthopedic Assn., Am. Assn. for Surgery of Trauma, Am. Acad. Orthopedic Surgeons (joint com. mil. affairs 1948-70, mem., chmn. coms.), AMA, Am. Orthopedic Foot Soc. (founding), Am. Orthopedic Soc. for Sports Medicine (founding pres. 1977-78), Contemporary Orthopedic Soc. (pres. 1959), Internat. Soc. Orthopedics and Traumatology, Am. Trauma Soc. (founding), Mid-Am. Orthopedic Assn. (founding), So. Med. Soc., Robert Jones Orthopedic Soc. (pres. 1960), Tenn. State Med. Soc., Tenn. State Orthopedic Soc. (pres. 1955), Clin. Orthopedic Soc. (pres. 1958), Memphis Orthopedic Soc. (founding pres. 1976), Brit. Orthopedic Assn. (guest), La. Orthopedic Assn. (hon.), S.C. Orthopedic Assn. (hon.), Memphis and Shelby County Med. Soc., Soc. of Med. Cons. to Armed Forces, U. Tenn. Med. Alumni Assn. (founder, past pres.), Willis C. Campbell Orthopedic Club (founder, pres. 1955, bd. dirs., found. pres. 1965-80), Alpha Omega Alpha. Republican. Clubs: Memphis Country, Rotary (v.p. Memphis 1981-82, pres. 1983-84). Panel mem., speaker, lectr. in field profl. confs.; vis. prof., invited lectr. profl. orgns. and hosps.; contbr. writings to profl. publs. Home: 3071 Southern Ave Memphis TN 38111-3220

STEWART, MARTHA MITCHELL, librarian; b. Troy, Ala., June 11, 1950; d. Willie L. and Mary Helen (Whitehurst) Mitchell; m. Ronald D. Stewart, Dec. 20, 1969 (div. May 1984); 1 child, Chet. BA, Troy State U., 1972; MLS, U. Ala., 1983. Libr. Troy (Ala.) State U. Libr., 1983-85, Troy State U./Montgomery Libr., 1985-87; librarian Air U. Libr., Montgomery, Ala., 1987—. Editor Air Univ. Libr. Index Mil. Periodicals, 1989—. Office: Air Univ Libr 600 Chennault Cir Maxwell AFB AL 36112-6424

STEWART, MICHAEL MCFADDEN, professional speaker; b. Eupora, Miss., Aug. 24, 1938; s. Judge Ernest and Billie Rivers (McFadden) S.; m. Barbara Ann Dickerson, June 2, 1962; children: Michael Jr., Mark Robert. BS, La. State U., 1961. Cert. speaking profl. Nat. Spkrs. Assn., 1996. Cons. E.K. Williams & Co., Birmingham, Ala., 1964-66, br. mgr., 1966-68; br. mgr. E.K. Williams & Co., Miami, Fla., 1968-69, Marcoin, Inc., Balt., 1969-73; dist. mgr. Marcoin, Inc., Falls Church, Va., 1973-74; v.p. Marcoin Western Ops., Inc., Houston, 1974-77; dir., v.p. Marcoin, Inc., Atlanta, 1977-85; ptnr. Cherokee/G & S Assocs., Atlanta, 1985-88; pres. Stewart & Stewart, Inc., Dunwoody, Ga., 1988—, The Sales Power Resource Group, Inc., Atlanta, 1991—; cons., speaker AMA, N.Y.C., Duffy-Vinet Inst., Langhorne, Pa., 1987-92, The Sullivan Group, Guilford, Conn., 1990-92; guest speaker SBA, Bell South Success Symposium Series, 1990-91. Author: How to Get Started with a Small Business Computer, 1984, Quality Customer Service, 1990, Using Your Financial Statements to Boost Your Bottom Line Profits, 1990, Computerizing Your Business, 1991, The Magic of Customer Service, 1991, Bring Home the Bacon, 1992, Customer Service Excellence: How to Implement a Corporate-wide Program, 1992, Strategic Relationship Selling, 1992, Transition into Sales Management, 1992, Sales Managememt Call Reluctance Workshop, 1992, Negotiating with Style, 1992, Meeting Today's Competitive Challenges, 1992, Creative Management in Tough Economic Times, 1993, Relationship Empowered Technical Selling, 1993, Consultative Relationship Selling, 1993, Customer-Centered Sales Management Leadership, 1993, Customer Centered Selling, 1993, Being Different in a Niche Market, 1993, Moving, Shaking and Prospecting, 1993, 50/250 The Smart Way, 1993, Customer-Centered Relationship Selling, 1994, Working Sucessfully with Others, 1994, Fundamentals of Quality Customer Service, 1994, Sales Are The Life-Blood Service is the Heart Beat, 1994, Customer-Centered Value Selling, 1994, Customer-Centered Sales Management, 1994, Make the Number by Selling Value, 1995, Hiring Smart, 1995, Customer-Centered Sales Management, 1995, Live the Spirit, 1996, Sell Value, Not Price, 1996; contbg. author: Chicken Soup for the Soul at Work, 1996; contbr. numerous articles to profl. jours. Fin. officer Atlanta Colts Youth Assn., 1979; vol. speaker Am. Cancer Soc., 1994—. Capt. U.S. Army, 1961-64. Recipient Silver award Carlson Learning Co., Mpls., 1990. Mem. ASTD, Ga. Speakers Assn. (pres.-elect, past dir., Mem. of Yr. 1996), Nat. Speakers Assn. (cert. speaking profl.), Dunwoody Country Club, Dunwoody Gridiron Club (pres. 1981), Lambda Chi Alpha. Episcopalian. Home: 490 Tavern Cir Atlanta GA 30350

STEWART, MURRAY BAKER, lawyer; b. Muskogee, Okla., May 16, 1931; s. Francis and Fannie Penelope (Murray) S.; m. Roseanna Furgason; children: Melinda, Jeffrey, Cheryl. BA, U. Okla., 1953, JD, 1955; postgrad. Georgetown U., 1958-59. Bar: Okla. 1955; CLU, chartered fin. cons. Judge adv. U.S. Army, 1955-59; ptnr. Stewart & Stewart, Tulsa and Muskogee, Okla., 1955, 62-72; asst. v.p. First Nat. Bank and Trust Co. of Tulsa, 1959-62, 77-78; mem. Hutchins, Stewart, Stewart & Elmore, Tulsa, 1972-77; atty., cons. advanced underwriting Met. Life Ins. Co., N.Y.C., 1978-94; assoc. Metlife Securities, Inc., SEC Registered Investment Advisors, 1984-94; cons., lectr. in field. Fellow Life Mgmt. Inst.; mem. Okla. Bar Assn., Tulsa Estate Planning Forum, Native Am. Bar Assn., Tulsa Employee Benefits Group. Contbr. articles to profl. jours; producer texts and videos on investment and bus. Office: PO Box 1000 Broken Arrow OK 74013-1000

STEWART, PAMELA L., lawyer; b. Bogalusa, La., Mar. 13, 1953; d. James Adrian and Patricia Lynn (Wood) Lloyd; m. Steven Bernard Stewart, Aug. 31, 1974 (div. July 1980); 1 child, Christopher. BA, U. New Orleans, 1986; JD, U. Houston, 1990. Intern La. Supreme Ct., New Orleans, 1984, Councilman Bryan Wagner, New Orleans, 1984-85; legal asst. Clann, Bell & Murphy, Houston, 1988-89, Tejas Gas Corp., Houston, 1989-90; atty. Law Offices of Pamela L. Stewart, Katy, Tex., 1991—. Bd. dirs. Alliance for Good Govt., New Orleans, 1983-84, Attention Deficit Hyperactivity Disorder Assn. Tex., 1989-90; vol. Houston Vol. Lawyers Program, Houston, 1992—. Innsbruck scholar, U. New Orleans, 1985. Fellow Inst. Politics; mem. ABA, Am. Bankruptcy Inst., Tax Freedom Inst., Nat. Assn. Consumer Bankruptcy Attys. (co-chair ethics com.), Houston Bar Assn., Houston Bankruptcy Conf., Nat. Assn. of Chpt. 13 Trustees (assoc.), Katy Bar Assn., Houston Assn. Debtors Attys. (pres.), Am. Acad. Estate Planning Attys. Methodist. Home: 22415 N Rebecca Burwell Ln Katy TX 77449-2908 Office: Law Offices of Pamela L Stewart Ste 219 One West Loop South Houston TX 77027

STEWART, PRISCILLA ANN MABIE, art historian, educator; b. Iowa City, Sept. 21, 1926; d. Edward Charles and Grace Frances (Chase) Mabie; m. Thomas Wilson Stewart, Aug. 28, 1949. BA, U. Iowa, 1948; MA, U. South Fla., 1971; EdS, Fla. Atlantic U., 1983. Coord. elem. art Manatee County (Fla.), 1953-59; prof. art history, intercultural humanities and photography Manatee C.C., Bradenton, Fla., 1959—; organizer, dir. Pelican Perch Wild Bird Hosp., Bradenton, 1953-85. Mem. AAUP, AAUW, Am. Assn. Women in C.Cs. Intertel Soc., Nat. Art Edn. Assn., Fla. Art Edn. Assn., Fla. Assn. C.Cs., Mensa, Sarasota-Manatee Phi Beta Kappa Assn. (pres. 1984-86), Phi Beta Kappa, Alpha Xi Delta, Phi Kappa Phi. Republican. Episcopalian. Home: 2705 Riverview Blvd W Bradenton FL 34205-4335 Office: Manatee Community Coll Dept Art and Humanities 5840 26th St W Bradenton FL 34207-3522

STEWART, REGE SZUTS, psychiatrist, educator; b. Budapest, Hungary, Apr. 26, 1941; came to U.S., 1956; m. Robert Malcolm Stewart, 1967; children: Charles, Sharon. BA, Houghton Coll., 1963; BS in Med. Scis., U. N.D., 1965; MD, Northwestern U., 1967. Diplomate Am. Bd. Psychiatry and Neurology, Nat. Bd. Med. Examiners. Intern Chgo. Wesley Meml. Hosp. and Northwestern Med. Ctr., 1967-69; clin. fellow in psychiatry Harvard Med. Sch., Boston, 1972-74; resident in psychiatry Mass. Gen. Hosp., Boston, 1972-75, clin. asst. in psychiatry dept. psychiatry, 1975-77; clin. teaching in consultation to psychiatry residents Parkland Meml. Hosp., Dallas, 1979-82, psychiat. cons. to neurology, neurosurgery, phys. medicine and rehab., transplantation and dialysis, 1979-82; asst. prof. psychiatry U. Tex. Southwestern Med. Ctr., Dallas, 1977-82, assoc. prof., 1982; cons. to dialysis ctrs. Dallas, 1977-85; svc. chief PGY III psychiatry residents Parkland Meml. Hosp., Dallas, 1982, dir. psychiatry outpatient clinic, 1982—; mem. utilization review com. Parkland Meml. Hosp., 1978-83, undergrad. edn. com., 1978, clin. svc. com., 1982, residency tng. com., 1982, pharmacy and therapeutics com., 1984; mem. quality assurance com. Zale-Lipshy U. Hosp., 1990; reviewer Hosp. and Cmty. Psychiatry, 1984; chairperson Mental Health and Mental Ratardation Peer Review Com., Dallas, 1987-88; mem. med. adv. com. Dallas County Mental Health and Mental Retardation, 1991—; speaker numerous orgns. and confs. in psychiat. field. Author 7 book chpts.; reviewer: Clinical Neurology for Psychiatrist, 1983; contbr. articles to profl. jours. Recipient grants Upjohn, 1983-86, 88-90, 92-93, CIBA-GEIGY, 1985-86, 87, 92—, Besselaar and Assocs., 1987, Wyeth-Ayerst, 1989-92, Hoffmann-La Roche, 1992-93. Fellow Am. Psychat. Assn. (program evaluator 1982-85, sci. program com. 1982-88, chairperson workshop subcom. 1986-88); mem. AMA, Tex. Med. Assn., Am. Coll. Psychiatrists, Am. Bd. Psychiatry and Neurology (examiner), Am. Med. Women's Assn., North Tex. Soc. Psychiat. Physicians (program com. 1981-82, bylaws com. 1983-85, fellowship com. 1986-88, chairperson program com. 1987-88, chairperson fellowship com. 1989-91, sec. 1990-91, v.p. 1991-92, pres. 1992-93), Dallas Area Women Psychiatrists (pres. 1980-81, Myesthenia Gravis Found. (Dallas-Ft. Worth chpt. med. adv. bd. 1982-84), Tex. Soc. Psychiat. Physicians (fellowship com. 1989-91, continuing med. edn. com. 1989—, vice chair fellowship com. 1989-91, sec. 1990-91, v.p. 1991-92, pres. 1992-93). Home: 3939 Hockaday Dr Dallas TX 75229-2725 Office: U Tex Southwestern Med Ctr Dallas Dept Psychiatry Dallas TX 75229

STEWART, RICHARD DOUGLAS, newspaper publisher; b. Raleigh, N.C., Sept. 21, 1949; s. Douglas Wade and June Marie (Russell) S.; m. Karen Elizabeth Brown, Aug. 18, 1973; children: Brian, Mark. BA in History, Atlantic Christian, 1971; MA in Journalism, U. S.C., 1975. Sports writer Wilson (N.C.) Daily Times, 1971-72; staff writer The Greensboro (N.C.) Record, 1973-81; editor, pub. Kenly (N.C.) News, 1981—; dir. Biblical Recorder, Raleigh, 1978-85. Chmn. Kenly Centennial Com., 1987. Named Citizen of Yr., Kenly C. of C., 1987; recipient Silver Beaver award Boy Scouts Am., 1996. Mem. N.C. Press Assn. (bd. dirs. 1987-88), N.C. Community Newspaper Assn. (pres. 1987-88), Eastern N.C. Press Assn. (pres. 1990-91), Nat. Newspaper Assn., Kenly Kiwanis Club (pres. 1989-90). Southern Baptist. Office: Kenly News PO Box 39 Kenly NC 27542-0039

STEWART, ROBERT HENRY, oceanographer, educator; b. York, Pa., Dec. 26, 1941; s. Robert Henry and Mildred June (Smith) S.; m. Hedvig Susan Bagdy, June 26, 1966 (div. Dec. 1976); 1 child, Alethea Ildico Stewart; m. Tracy Ann Bertolucci, July 19, 1986; children: Farrar Clee, Margaret Montgomery. BS, U. Tex., Arlington, 1963; PhD, U. Calif., San Diego, 1969. Asst. rsch. oceanographer Scripps Inst. Oceanography U. Calif., San Diego, 1969-78, assoc. rsch. oceanographer, 1978-79; assoc. rsch. oceanographer, assoc. adj. prof. Scripps Inst. Oceanography, U. Calif., San Diego, 1979-83, rsch. oceanographer, adj. prof., 1983-89; mem. tech. staff Jet Propulsion Lab., Calif. Inst. Tech., Pasadena, 1979-80, rsch. scientist, 1980-83, sr. rsch. scientist, 1983-89; prof. oceanography Tex. A&M U., College Station, 1989—; Topex/Poseidon project scientist Jet Propulsion Lab., 1980-88; mem. many NASA coms.; mem. coms. of Nat. Rsch. Coun., Nat. Acad. Scis.; mem. various internat. scientific coms.; cons. Univ. Corp. for Atmospheric Rsch. Author: Methods of Satellite Oceanography, 1985; editor: Radio Oceanography, 1978; contbr. articles to profl. jours. Trustee San Juan Capistrano Inst. Co-recipient Group Achievement award for Topex/Poseidon mission design NASA, 1993, NASA Pub. Svc. medal, 1994; U. Calif. Regents spl. fellow, 1963; NSF fellow, 1964. Mem. Am. Geophys. Union. Republican. Roman Catholic. Home: 8710 Appomattox Dr College Station TX 77845-5567 Office: Oceanography Dept Tex A&M U College Station TX 77843-3146

STEWART, ROBERT ROY, III, art director; b. Summerville, Ga., Feb. 8, 1953; s. Robert Roy and Lois (Wehunt) S. BS in Art, U. Montevallo, Ala., 1975. Artist, cameraman Midstate Advt., Montgomery, Ala., 1975-78; artist, cameraman Ala. Labels & Graphics, Birmingham, 1978-86, art dir., 1986-95; art dir. Label-Aid Sys., Inc., Madison, Ala., 1995—. Exhibited art and photographs at various juried shows and galleries, 1970-84. Home: 222 S Kyser Blvd # 134 Madison AL 35758-2309

STEWART, SALLY BEAL, pilot; b. Englewood, N.J., Apr. 10, 1955; d. Peter Coakley and Betty (Meyer) Van de Water. BS, Northwestern U., 1977. Lic. airline transport pilot, flight engr., flight instr., jumpmaster, skydiving. Sr. tech. rep. Xerox, Milw., 1979-81; flight instr. Capital Aviation, Milw., 1981-82; DC-3 pilot Air Charter/Mr. Douglas, De Leon Springs, Fla., 1982; capt. Mueller Pipeliners, New Berlin, Wis., 1982, Aero Taxi, Rockford, Ill., 1982; skydiver Hi Sky Promotions, Milw., 1980-82; capt., 1st officer Simmons Airlines, Marquette, Mich., 1983-84; capt. Am. Cen. Airlines, Dubuque, Iowa, 1984; first officer Boeing 747-400 Northwest Airlines, Mpls., 1984—; model John Casablancas, Berg Talent Agy., Tampa, Fla., 1991—. Pilot TV spl. Wide World of Sports, 1982; skydiver, interviewee TV spl./video Flight of the Dream Team, 1988. Holder world record for 60 woman freefall formation, Deland, Fla., 1986, world record for 120 person freefall formation, Quincy, Ill., 1986, world record for 144 person formation, Quincy, 1988. Mem. Air Line Pilots Assn., U.S. Parachute Assn. Home and Office: PO Box 7399-101 Breckenridge CO 80424

STEWART, SANDRA KAY, music educator; b. New Albany, Ind., Dec. 24, 1947; d. Dale F. and June V. (Martin) Byrne; m. William Lee Stewart, June 25, 1971. B Music Edn., Ind. U., 1969; MusM, Norfolk State U., 1992; D Mus. Arts, U. S.C., 1995. Cert. vocal music tchr., N.Y., Mo. Vocal music tchr., choral dir. Ritenour Sch. Dist., St. Louis, 1969-75, Sch. Dist. # 54, chgo., 1975-76, Waverly (N.Y.) Jr./Sr. H.S., 1977-78, Clarence (N.Y.) H.S., 1978-82; piano instr., show choir dir. Inst. Fine Arts, Reading, Pa., 1982-85; piano accompanist Berks Grand Opera Co., Reading, Pa., 1982-85, Va. Opera Co., Norfolk, 1986, U. S.C., Columbia, 1992-95, Jacksonville Masterworks Sr. Chorale, 1996—, Bolles Sr. H.S., 1996—, Pinewood Presbyn. Ch., 1996—; piano and music theory instr. Acad. of Music, Virginia Beach, Va., 1986-91; piano instr., choral dir. Jacksonville (Fla.) U., 1995—. Contbr. articles to profl. publs. Mem. Virginia Beach Pops Orch., 1989-91. Mem. AAUW (numerous offices 1975-95), Am. Choral Dirs. Assn., Coll. Music Soc., Nat. Piano Found., Music Educators Nat. Conf., Nat. Guild Piano Tchrs., Music Tchrs. Nat. Assn., Delius Assn. Fla., Phi Kappa Lambda, Mu Phi Epsilon. Home: 11657 Falling Leaf Trail Jacksonville FL 32258 Office: Jacksonville U University Blvd Jacksonville FL 32211

STEWART, SANDRA MARIE, juvenile court administrator; b. Tuscaloosa, Ala., Apr. 15, 1965; d. Wise Dale and Elizabeth Marie (Boyer) S. BA in Mass Communications, U. Ala., 1987, MS in Criminal Justice, 1991. Copy editor The Times, Gainesville, Ga., 1987; news editor Natchez (Miss.) Dem., 1987-89; grad. teaching asst. U. Ala., Tuscaloosa, 1990, grad. rsch. asst., 1990-91; officer mgr., student monitor Dept. Youth Svcs., Tuscaloosa, 1990-91; loss prevention specialist Macy's, Birmingham, Ala., 1991-92; restitution officer Tuscaloosa County Juvenile Ct., 1992-93, restitution coord., 1993—; rschr., investigator Veritas, Inc. Investigative and Security Svcs., Northport, Ala., 1990. Recipient Gould/Wysinger award Ala. Dept. of Justice, 1992, 93; recipient 1st place award Miss. Women's Press Assn., 1988, 2d place award Miss. Press Assn., 1988, Excellence in Svc. award Criminal Justice Student Assn., 1985. Mem. So. Assn. Criminal Justice, Soc. Profl. Journalists, Capstone Comms. Alumni, U. Ala. Alumni Assn., Tuscaloosa chpt. Pilot Club. Office: Tuscaloosa County Juvenile 6001 12th Ave E Tuscaloosa AL 35405-5163

STEWART, STEVEN ELTON, state agency administrator; b. Oklahoma City, July 12, 1952; s. Elton Alexander and Bonnie Kate (Elms) S.; m. Jana Richardson, Aug. 6, 1974; children: Stacey Anne, Scott Elton. BA in Edn., East Cen. U., 1976, MEd, 1978; M Sch. Adminstrn., Okla. U., 1983. Child-find coord. Region XIV Regional Edn. Svc. Ctr./Okla. Dept. Edn., 1976-78, psychometrist, 1978-80, asst. dir., 1980-82, adminstr., 1982—; mem. Spl. Svcs. cadre Okla. Dept. Edn., Oklahoma City, 1989-90; mem. State Regional Edn. Svc. Ctr. Leadership Team, 1991—; mem. Okla. Policies and Procedures Compliance Team, 1992—, RESC Eval. Team, 1995. Mem. Coun. Exceptional Children, Coun. Adminstrs. Spl. Edn., Learning Disabilities Assn., Okla. Coun. on Children and Youth. Democrat. Mem. Ch. of Christ. Office: Ada Regional Edn Svc Ctr 704 N Oak Ave Ada OK 74820-3267

STEWART, THOMAS WILSON, lawyer; b. Miami, Fla., Oct. 23, 1926; s. Thelmar Wilson and Katherine (Smith) S.; m. Priscilla Ann Mabie, Aug. 28, 1949. BS, Miami U., Oxford, Ohio, 1948; JD with distinction, State U. Iowa, 1951. Bar: Iowa 1951, Fla. 1952, U.S. Supreme Ct. 1969. Assoc. Daniel & Woodward, Bradenton, Fla., 1952-57; ptnr. Daniel, Woodward & Stewart, 1957-68, pvt. practice, Bradenton, 1968—; asst. prof. bus. law Fla. State U., Tallahassee, 1951-52. Chmn. Manatee County Republican Com., 1970-71; Fla. state Rep. committeeman, 1970-71. Served with USN, 1944-46. Mem. Manatee County Bar Assn. (pres. 1968-69), Fla. Bar Assn., Mensa, Intertel, Manatee County Hist. Soc., Alpha Tau Omega, Republican. Episcopalian. Author: Labor Laws of Iowa, 1951. Home: 2705 Riverview Blvd W Bradenton FL 34205-4335 Office: 406 13th St W Bradenton FL 34205-7533

STEWART, WESLEY HOLMGREEN, judge, lawyer; b. Dallas, Aug. 19, 1948; s. Wesley Gilbert and Angres Margaret (Schmitz) S. BA in Philosophy and Polit. Sci., Benedictine Coll., 1974; postgrad., So. Meth. U., 1974-75, 78-80. Bar: Tex. 1980, U.S. Dist. Ct. (no. dist.) Tex. 1981, U.S. Ct. Appeals (5th cir.) 1992, U.S. Dist. Ct. (we. dist.) Tex. 1992. Asst. dist. atty. county of Collin, McKinney, Tex., 1982-83; pvt. practice law Dallas, 1983-84, Denton, Tex., 1985-86; mcpl. judge Plano (Tex.) County, 1984; asst. dist. aty. County of Denton, 1984-85; judge County Ct. #3, Denton, 1986, County Ct. #1, Denton, 1987-90. Del. Rep. State Conv., Dallas, 1986, Houston, 1988, chair credentials com. Dist. 22 Conv., Denton, 1988—; congrl. caucas chmn. Rep. State Conv., 1988. Mem. Tex. Bar Assn., Denton County Bar Assn. Jewish. Home: 2212 Pembrooke Pl Denton TX 76205-8264 Office: 2212 Pembrooke Pl Denton TX 76205

STEWART, WILLIAM BARTLEY, software developer; b. Alexandria, La., June 13, 1962; s. William B. Sr. and Margaret Ellen (Robertson) S. BS in Computer Sci., La. Tech. U., 1985. System operator Procter & Gamble, Tioga, La., 1986; assoc. tech. specialist Computer Scis. Corp., Herndon, Va., 1987-90, programmer, analyst, 1990—. Nat. merit scholar Dresser Harbison-Walker Found., 1980. Mem. AAAS, Assn. for Computing Machinery (spl. interest group on artificial intelligence), Planetary Soc. Republican. Home: 11653 Stone View Sq Apt 1B Reston VA 22091-2922 Office: Computer Scis Corp 3001 Centreville Rd Herndon VA 22071-3709

STICE, DWAYNE LEE, broadcasting company executive; b. Paducah, Ky., Aug. 10, 1956; s. Freeman D. and Dorris Olive (Lee) S. AA, Paducah Community Coll., 1976; BS, Murray State U., 1977; MS, Southern Ill. U., 1983. Lic. funeral dir., Ky. Dir. Johnson-Lambert Funeral Home, Calvert City, Ky., 1974-81; gen. mgr. Paducah Area Transit System, 1980-92; pres. Sta. WCCK-FM, Stice Comm., Inc., Calvert City, 1990—; adj. bus. instr. Paducah Community Coll., 1979—, Lindsey Wilson Coll., Columbia, Ky., 1991. Contbr. articles to profl. jours. Bd. dirs. Lakeland Parish, Inc., Benton, Ky., Paducah Cmty. Concert Assn., Wesley Found., Murray State U.; mem. Calvert Area Devel. Assn., transp. com. Purchase Area Devel. Dist. Outstanding grantee Ky. Transp. Cabinet, 1985, 86. Mem. Ky. Pub. Transit Assn. (pres. 1988-91), Ky. Broadcasters Assn., Paducah Area C. of C. (chmn. higher edn. com. 1991), Marshall C. of C. (bd. dirs.), Paducah C.C. Alumni Assn. (pres. 1983), Hon. Order Ky. Cols., Travelers Protective Assn. (pres. Paducah chpt. 1989-90), Lions, Masons (master Calvert City 1984), Shriners, Order Ea. Star, Phi Kappa Phi, Phi Theta Kappa. Methodist. Home: 647 S Main St Calvert City KY 42029-8373 Office: Sta WCCK-FM 2 Aspen St Calvert City KY 42029-9304

STICHT, J. PAUL, retired food products and tobacco company executive; b. Clairton, Pa., 1917. BA, Grove City Coll., 1939; postgrad., U. Pitts. With U.S. Steel Corp., 1939-44; personnel dir. Trans World Airlines, 1944-48; v.p. Campbell Soup Co., 1947-57, pres. internat., 1957-60; exec. v.p. Federated Dept. Stores, Inc., 1960-65, vice chmn., 1965-67, pres., 1967-72; chmn. exec. com., COO R.J. Reynolds Industries, Inc., Winston-Salem, N.C., 1972-73, pres., CEO, 1978-79, chmn. bd., 1979-85; chmn. RJR Nabisco, Inc., Winston-Salem, 1987-89, acting chmn., CEO, 1989. Trustee Grove City Coll.; chmn. Caribbean/L.Am. Action; mem. bd. visitors

Bowman Gray Sch. Medicine, former chmn. bd. visitors; mem. bd. visitors Fuqua Sch. Bus. Duke U. Office: Castle Springs Corp 119 Brookstown Ave Winston Salem NC 27101-5245

STIEBER, ANDREI CAROL, surgeon; b. Bucharest, Romania, Apr. 11, 1952; s. Carol and Cleo Stieber; m. Laurie Anne Shapiro, Dec. 18, 1982; children: Alexandra Nicole, Jarrett David. BS, Mihai Viteazul Gymnasium, Bucharest, 1971; MD, State U., Milan, Italy, 1978. Diplomate Am. Bd. Surgery. Asst. prof. U. Pitts., 1987-92; assoc. prof. Emory U., Atlanta, 1992—. Author books and articles in field; designer surg. retractor: The Stieber Rib Grip, 1988. Fellow Am. Coll. Surgeons; mem. Am. Soc. Transplant Surgeons, Transplantation Soc., Assn. for Acad. Surgery, Internat. Microsurg. Soc. Office: Emory U Hosp Rm H 124 1364 Clifton Rd NE Atlanta GA 30322

STIEG, FRANK HENRY, III, plastic surgeon; b. Hamilton, Ohio, Mar. 12, 1950; s. Frank Henry Jr. and Edna Leone (Pottenger) S.; m. Sharon Jean Bushong, June 17, 1972; children: Shannon Elizabeth, Megan Lynette, Gretchen Michele. BS in Biology, Ohio State U., 1972, JD cum laude, 1974; MD, U. Cin., 1980. Diplomate Am. Bd. Plastic and Reconstructive Surgery, Am. Bd. Otolaryngology; bar: Ohio 1975. Rsch. assoc. Ohio State U., Columbus, 1974-75; pvt. practice in law Fairfield, Ohio, 1976-80; resident in gen. surgery U. Cin., 1980-81, resident in otolaryngology-head and neck surgery, 1981-85, resident in plastic and reconstructive surgery, 1985-87; pvt. practice Orlando, Fla., 1987-92, Winter Park, Fla., 1992—. Contbr. articles to profl. jours. Sunday sch. tchr. First United Meth. Ch., Winter Park; bd. dirs. Orlando Met. unit Am. Cancer Soc., 1989-96; vol. AMA-ABA Drug Awareness Program, 1992-96. With USAR, 1970-71. Fellow ACS, Am. Soc. Plastic and Reconstructive Surgeons, Am. Acad. Otolaryngology, Fla. Soc. Plastic and Reconstructive Surgeons; mem. AMA, Fla. Med. Assn., Orange County Med. Soc. (conv. del., bd. dirs.). Office: Plastic Surgery Specialists PA 851 W Morse Blvd Winter Park FL 32789-3708

STIFF, ROBERT MARTIN, newspaper editor; b. Detroit, Aug. 25, 1931; s. Martin L. and Gladys (Mathews) S.; m. Cindy Rose, Aug. 30, 1980; children: David Alan, Amy Anne, Kirsten Marie. BA in Radio and Journalism, Ohio State U., 1953. Reporter, bur. chief, city editor Painesville (Ohio) Telegraph, 1953-61; deskman, asst. city editor, sports editor, city editor, day editor, state editor, asst. mng. editor St. Petersburg (Fla.) Times, 1961-67; editor St. Petersburg Evening Ind., 1967-84; dir. St. Petersburg Times Pub. Co., 1969-84; exec. editor, v.p. Tallahassee Democrat, 1985-91; pres. Bob Stiff & Assocs., Tallahassee, 1991-95; exec. editor JMT Assocs., 1991-92, 95—; mng. editor About Florida, 1991-94; editor Lexington (N.C.) Dispatch, 1995—; dir. devel. and pub. rels. Fla. Taxwatch Inc., 1992-94; bd. dir. N.C. AP News Coun., 1995—. Bd. dirs. Cancer Svcs. Davidson County. Mem. AP Assn. Fla. (pres. 1970-71), Am. Soc. Newspaper Editors (dir. 1981-87), Am. Soc. Newspaper Editors Found. (bd. dirs., treas. 1986-90), Fla. Soc. Newspaper Editors (pres. 1975-76, dir. 1971-84, 90-93), Fla. Bar Found. (bd. dirs. 1990-92), AP Mng. Editors Assn., Sigma Delta Chi (pres. West Coast chpt. 1970-710, N.C. Press Assn., Nat. Coun. Editl. Writers, Lexington Kiwanis (bd. dirs. 1996—).

STIFF, RONALD DAVID, corporate banker; b. Louisville, Oct. 15, 1956; s. Joseph Elder and Monica Mary (Wheatley) S.; m. Lisa Ellen Horsley, June 4, 1983; 1 child, Graham David. BA in Acctg., Bellarmine Coll., 1980. CPA, Ky. Audit mgr. Ernst & Whinney CPAs, Louisville, 1980-84; sr. auditor Liberty Nat. Bank, Louisville, 1984-85; sr. audit mgr. Citizens Fidelity Bank, Louisville, 1986-91; regional audit dir. PNC Bank Corp., Louisville, 1992-95; corp. banker PNC Bank Kentucky, Inc., Louisville, 1996—; dir. fin. Am. Diabetes Assn., Louisville, 1992—. Mem. AICPA, Ky. Soc. CPAs, Bank Adminstrn. Inst. (pres. 1993-96). Home: 10101 Dorsey Hill Rd Louisville KY 40223-2957 Office: PNC Bank of Kentucky Inc 500 W Jefferson St Louisville KY 40296-0001

STILES, CHARLES MERRILL, physician; b. Mangum, Okla., Mar. 9, 1938; s. Charles Doyle and Millicent Cloe (Landrith) S.; m. Emily Carolyn Hogan, Aug. 22, 1958; children: Steven Merrill, Sherri Suzanne. BA, U. Kans., 1960; MD, U. Kans. Med. Ctr., 1964. Diplomate Am. Bd. Internal Medicine, sub-bd. Geriatric Medicine. Straight med. intern U. Kans. Med. Ctr., 1965, resident in internal medicine, 1966-67, fellow in cardiology, 1968; Staff dir. clinic Doctors Clinic, Galveston, Tex., 1970-76, pres., 1976-92; med.-legal cons. in pvt. practice pvt. practice, Houston, 1992—. Pres. Salvation Army, Galveston, 1976. Capt. USAF, 1968-70. Mem. AMA, Am. Coll. Cardiology, Tex. Med. Assn. Galveston Med. Assn., Phi Beta Kappa, Alpha Omega Alpha. Republican. Presbyterian.

STILES, MARY ANN, lawyer; b. Tampa, Fla., Nov. 16, 1944; d. Ralph A. and Bonnie (Smith) S. AA, Hills Community Coll., 1973; BS, Fla. State U., 1975; JD, Antioch Sch. Law, 1978. Bar: Fla. 1978. Legis. analyst Fla. Ho. of Reps., Tallahassee, 1973-74, 74-75; intern U.S. Senate, Washington, 1977; v.p., gen. counsel Associated Industries Fla., Tallahassee, 1978-81, gen. counsel, 1981-84, spl. counsel, 1986—; assoc. Deschler, Reed & Crichfield, Boca Raton, Fla., 1980-81; founding ptnr. Stiles, Taylor & Metzler, Tampa, Fla., 1982—; shareholder and dir. Stiles Taylor & Metzler, P.A., Six Stars Devel. Co. of Fla., Inc.; with 1st Trust, Inc.; shareholder First Comml. Bank of Tampa. Author: Workers' Copmenstaion Law Handbook, 1980-94 edit. Bd. dirs., sec. Hillsborough C.C. Found., Tampa, 1985-87, 94-96; bd. dirs. Hillsborough Area Regional Transit Authority, Tampa, 1986-89, Boys and Girls Club of Tampa, 1986—; mem. Bay Area chpt. Nat. Women's Polit. Caucus, 1993—, The Spring, 1992-93, What's My Chance, 1992-94; mem. Gov.'s Oversite Bd. on Workers' Compensation, 1989-90, Workers Comp. Rules Com., Fla. Bar, 1990-95, Workers Comp. Exec. Counsel Fla. Bar, 1990-95Jud. Nominating Commn. for Workers' Compensation Cts., 1990-93, trustee Hillsborough Cmty. Coll., 1994—, vice-chair, 1995-96, chair, 1996—. Mem. ABA, Fla. Bar Assn., Hillsborough County Bar Assn., Hillsborough Assn. Women Lawyers, Fla. Assn. Women Lawyers, Fla. Women's Alliance, Hillsborough County Seminole Boosters (past pres.). Democrat. Baptist. Club: Tiger Bay (Tampa, past pres., sec.). Office: 315 S Plant Ave Tampa FL 33606-2325 also: 111 N Orange Ave Ste 850 Orlando FL 32801-2381 also: 317 N Calhoun St Tallahassee FL 32301-7605 also: 200 E Las Olas Blvd Ste 1760 Fort Lauderdale FL 33301-2248

STILL, EUGENE FONTAINE, II, plastic surgeon, educator; b. Rocky Mount, N.C., Sept. 2, 1937; s. Eugene Fontaine and Eva Ruth (Stevens) S.; m. Frances Davis, Aug. 14, 1965; 1 child, Eugene Fontaine III. BA, Vanderbilt U., 1959; MD, U. Ark., 1966. Diplomate Am. Bd. Comseteic Surgery (examiner, trustee 1994—), Am. Bd. Plastic Surgery, Inc. Intern Univ. Hosp., Little Rock, 1966-67; resident in gen. surgery U. Tenn. Med. Ctr., Memphis, 1967-71; resident in plastic surgery U. Mo. Med. Ctr., Kansas City, 1971-73; instr. surgery U. Mo., Kansas City, 1972-73; sr. surgeon dept. plastic surgery Holt-Krock Clinic, Ft. Smith, Ark., 1973-87; asst. prof. surgery U. Ark., Little Rock, 1974—; chief surgery Sparks Regional Med. Cen., Ft. Smith, 1979; pres. Bd. Cert. Plastic Srugeons, Ft. Smith, 1979—; dir. Ark. Ctr. Plastic Surgery, Van Buren, 1984—; chief of surgery St. Edward Mercy Med. Ctr., Ft. Smith, Ark., 1989-93, Crawford Meml. Hosp., 1993, 94; chief staff St. Edward Mercy Med. Ctr., 1990, 91; bd. trustees Crawford Meml. Hosp., 1985-86, 95—, St. Edwards Mercy Med. Ctr., 1996—, Am. Bd. Cosmetic Surgery, 1994—, examiner, 1990-96. Served with U.S. Army, 1960-62. Merck Pharm. Co. scholar, 1966. Fellow ACS, Am. Acad. Cosmetic Surgery; mem. Am. Soc. Plastic Surgeons, Southeastern Soc. Plastic Surgeons, Ark. Soc. Plastic Surgeons (sec.-treas. 1983-85, pres.-elect 1986-88, co-founder, pres. 1988-93), Am. Soc. Lipo-suction Surgery, Am. Coll. Physician Execs., Am. Soc. Maxillofacial Surgeons, Ark. Med. Soc. (chmn. ins. com. 1984-90), Ft. Smith Town, Handscrabble County Club, Alpha Omega Alpha. Home: 10101 Highway 253 Fort Smith AR 72916-4118 Office: Plastic Surgery Specialists 2717 S 74th St Fort Smith AR 72903-5100

STILL, LISA STOTSBERY, lawyer; b. North Kingstown, R.I., Dec. 4, 1960; d. Lawrence Edward Stotsbery and Clarice Ann Dudley; m. July, 1992. AA with honors, Pensacola Jr. Coll., 1979; BA with honors, U. West Fla., 1981; JD, U. Fla., 1985. Bar: Fla. 1986, U.S. Dist. Ct. (mid. dist.) Fla. 1986, U.S. Ct. Appeals (11th cir.) 1987, U.S. Tax Ct. 1987, U.S. Supreme Ct. 1993. Tax specialist Coopers & Lybrand, Miami, Fla., 1986, Jacksonville, Fla., 1986-87; pvt. practice Jacksonville, 1987; trial atty. SBA, Jacksonville, 1987—; spl. asst. U.S. atty. No. and Mid. Dists. Fla., 1990—. Mem. ABA (com. enforcement creditors rights and bankruptcy 1990), FBA (treas. Jacksonville chpt. 1990-92, v.p. membership 1993, v.p. programs 1994, pres.-elect 1995, pres. 1995—), Fla. Bar (real property, probate and trust law sect., govt. lawyer sect. 1990-91, voluntary bar liaison com. 1996—, bus. law sect.). Home: 9920 Blakeford Mill Rd Jacksonville FL 32256 Office: SBA 7825 Baymeadows Way Ste 100B Jacksonville FL 32256-7504

STILLER, LISA ANN, biostatistician; b. New Orleans, Oct. 5, 1960; d. Oliver Theophile and Beverly May (Rodriguez) Prudhomme; m. Richard G. Franklin, Sept. 7, 1991 (dec. 1992); m. Alvin H. Stiller Jr., May 6, 1995. BS in Biology, U. New Orleans, 1982; MS in Biometry, La. State U. Med. Ctr., 1985. Rsch. assoc. biometry and genetics La. State U. Med. Ctr., New Orleans, 1983-85, rsch. assoc., 1985-88; assoc. statistician Boots Pharms. Inc., Shreveport, La., 1988-90; statistician T.E.A.M.S., Dallas, 1990-91; data analyst Tex. Heart Inst., Houston, 1991-92; biostatistician State of La., New Orleans, 1992-95; programmer Orkand-CDC-OSH, Atlanta, 1995—. Office: CDC-OSH Buford Hwy Atlanta GA 30247

STILLMAN, EVELYN, interior designer; b. N.Y.C., July 11, 1914; d. Herman and Sarina Berger; m. Murray Warren Stillman, Aug. 29, 1933; children: Stuart Bruce, Joyce. Student, Pratt Inst., Bklyn., 1935-37, Bklyn. Coll., 1930, NYU, 1932, New Sch., N.Y.C., 1934-36. Designer of interiors, art cons. Am. Soc. Interior Design, Boca Raton, Fla./N.Y., 1975—. Cons. designer fundraising events for underprivileged, Great Neck, N.Y., 1956-76. Home and Office: 19580 Bayview Rd Boca Raton FL 33434-5101

STIMPSON, RITCHIE PLES, retired air force officer; b. Black Mountain, N.C., Mar. 22, 1917; s. David Ples and Lydia Hinson Stimpson; m. Marjorie Spruce, May 3, 1942; children: Ritchie P. Jr., David Fleming. BS in Physics, Furman U., 1940. Commd. 2nd lt. U.S. Air Force, 1941, advanced through grades to col., 1953; squadron comdr. 13th Tactical Reconnaissance Squadron, 1942-44; dir. ops. 24 Composite Wing, Borinquen Field, P.R., 1946-47; liaison officer Armed Forces Spl. Weapons Project to Strategic Air Commd., Offutt AFB, Nebr., 1950-52; dir. plans and negotiations Joint U.S. Asst. Adv. Group, Madrid, Spain, 1957-59; staff officer Joint Chiefs Staff, Washington, 1960-61, Weapons System Evaluation Group/Office of Sec. of Def., 1964-67; comdt. Air Force ROTC detachment Auburn (Ala.) U., 1967-71; ret., 1971; owner Ritch Stimpson Co., Inc., College Station, Tex., 1975-82; ind. writer, Dallas, 1982-93. Author: The Protestant Church and Bible Disregard the Truth, 1989, "Is It True?" Answers to Questions About the Bible, 1992. Decorated Commendation medals (2), Identification Badge, Outstanding Unit award. Mem. Air Force Assn., Greater Dallas Ret. Officers Assn., Greater Dallas Ret. Officers Assn. Investment Club, Oakridge Country Club, Furman U. Paladin Club. Republican. Methodist. Home: 2729 Laurel Oaks Dr Garland TX 75044-6939

STINCHCOMB, JAMES DELWIN, criminologist, training consultant, educator, administrator; b. Pitts.; s. James A. and Kathryn (McBride) S.; m. Jeanne B. Stinchcomb, 1973; children: James W., David Alan, June E. BS, U. Pitts., 1952, MA, 1956; postgrad., Ind. U., 1957-59, Fla. State U., 1959-62. Patrol officer Louisville (Ky.) Police Dept., 1955-57; police instr. Fla. State U., Tallahassee, 1957-61; chmn. Police Adminstrn. Dept., St. Petersburg, Fla., 1961-62; staff asst. Police Task Force, Pres.'s Crime Commn., Washington, 1963-65; edn. dir. Internat. Assn. Chiefs of Police, Washington, 1964-69; cons. Law Enforcement Assistance Adminstrn., Washington, 1967-71; pub. order and policy office Urban Inst. & Univ. Rsch. Co., Washington, 1970-73; chmn., assoc. prof. Va. Commonwealth U., Richmond, 1973-81; dir. Sch. Justice and Safety Adminstrn., Miami, Fla., 1981-96; evaluator police and mil. tng. Am. Coun. Edn., Washington, 1967—; Criminal Justice series adv. Anderson Pub. Co., Cin.; prin. investigator Nat. Plannign Assn. NAt. Criminal Justice Manpower Study, Washington, 1975-77; expert witness in police tng.; cons. on driving simulators Contraves USA, Inc., 1990—. Author: Law Enforcement/Criminal Justice Career Opportunities, 6th edit., 1996; editor Criminal Justice Series. Served with U.S. Army, 1953-54. Grantee traffic safety ctr. Va. Commonwealth U., 1971-72, police tng. grantee, 1978-79, computer lab. grantee Fla. Dept., 1992-94. Mem. Internat. Assn. Chiefs of Police, Acad. Criminal Justice Scis., Am. Correctional Assn., Dade County Chiefs of Police Assn., Fla. Police Chiefs Assn., Nat. Sheriff's Assn., Pitts. Golden Panthers, Rotary. Presbyterian. Home: 3320 Simms St # J Hollywood FL 33021-3106 Office: Sch Justice & Safety Adm 11380 NW 27th Ave Miami FL 33167-3418

STINE, EARLE JOHN, JR., radiologist; b. Saginaw, Mich., Feb. 21, 1932; s. Earle John and Ione Genevieve (Best) S.; m. Bernita Evelyn Emerson, Aug. 27, 1954; children: Renee Evelyn, Mark Earle, John Emerson. AB, Albion Coll., 1954; MD, Wayne State U., 1958. Diplomate Am. Bd. Radiology, Am. Bd. Nuclear Radiology. Intern Bon Secours Hosp., Grosse Pointe, Mich., 1958-59, gen. surgery resident, 1959-61; pvt. practice medicine, Pigeon, Mich., 1961-62, Marcus, Iowa, 1962-65, Ida Grove, Iowa, 1965-75; resident radiology U. Iowa, Iowa City, 1975-78; staff radiologist St. Joseph Med. Ctr., Ponca City, Okla., 1978-80; med. dir. radiology Jackson County Meml. Hosp., Altus, Okla., 1980-95, med. missions Karaganda, Kazakstan, 1995—. Mem. AMA. Republican. Methodist. Avocations: loomweaving, oil painting, woodcarving. Home: 1213 Canterbury Altus OK 73521 Office: Diagnostic Imaging Cons 1133 E Maple PO Box 679 Altus OK 73522-0679

STINEMETZ, STEVEN DOUGLAS, lawyer; b. Marysville, Ohio, Nov. 23, 1957; s. Glenn Melvin and Lona Lee (Payne) S.; m. Carol Sue Bialecki, Aug. 16, 1980; children: Emily Katrina, Eric Douglas, Ellen Michelle. AB in European History, Harvard U., 1980, AM in Modern Russian History, 1983; JD, NYU, 1986. Bar: Tex. 1986, Ohio 1991, D.C. 1992. Assoc. Haynes and Boone, Dallas, 1986-90, Davis, Graham & Stubbs, Washington, 1990-92; sr. atty. Western Atlas Internat., Houston, 1992—; gen. counsel PetroAlliance Svcs. Co. Ltd., Houston, 1995—; bd. dirs. Tex. Kazakhstan Alliance, 1992—. Assoc., editor, book rev. editor NYU Jour. Internat. Law and Politics, 1984-86; contbr. articles to legal jours. Chmn. bus. com. Dallas Soviet Sister City Program, 1987-88. Harvard U. scholar, 1976-80. Mem. ABA (vice chmn. Sonreel, county coord. Azerbaijan), Tex. Bar Assn. (planning com. adv. internat, law conf. 1994). Home: 2022 Richland Ct Sugar Land TX 77478-4414 Office: PetroAlliance Svcs Co 10011 Meadowglen Ln Houston TX 77042-3115

STINGER, KENNETH FRANK, lawyer, professional association executive; b. Trenton, N.J., Apr. 12, 1941; s. Frank and Mary Elisabeth Stinger; m. Eloise V. Czarda, June 8, 1963; children: K. Clinton, Laura Louisa, Emily Elizabeth. BA, Rutgers U., 1963; LLB, George Washington U., 1966. Bar: D.C. 1967, U.S. Supreme Ct. Tax and labor issues mgr. Met. Washington Bd. Trade, 1964-67; exec. mgr. consumer affairs com. C. of C. of U.S.A., Washington, 1967-73; exec. mgr. Am. Movers Conf., Arlington, Va., 1973-76; dir. govt. affairs Am. Trucking Assn., Washington, 1976—; exec. sec. Coalition Against Regressive Taxation, Washington, 1986—; tchr. Practicing Law Inst., N.Y.C., 1976; mgr. Truck Operators Non-Partisan Com., Washington, 1978-89. Contbr. articles to profl. publs. Recipient Cert. of Appreciation, Practicing Law Inst., 1976. Mem. ABA, D.C. Bar Assn., Transp. Practitioners Assn. (editor Motor Carrier), Nat. Dem. Club, Capitol Hill Club, Pi Sigma Alpha. Episcopalian. Home: 8512 Braeburn Dr Annandale VA 22003-4414 Office: Am Trucking Assn 430 1st St SE Washington DC 20003-1826

STINNETTE, TIMOTHY EARL, minister; b. Lynchburg, Va., Sept. 29, 1956; s. Sherwood Earl and Barbara Ann (Wiley) S.; m. Jenifer D. Wills, June 5, 1982. BA in Religion, Carson-Newman Coll., 1978; MDiv, Southeastern Bapt. Theol. Sem., 1982; cert. in life basics, Mng. and Mktg. Inst., West Palm Beach, Fla., 1983. Ordained to ministry So. Bapt. Conv., 1984; lic. preacher. Edn. and youth min. Oak St. Bapt. Ch., Elizabethton, Tenn., 1978; youth min. Big Island (Va.) Bapt. Ch., 1979-80; missionary assoc., ch. planter apprentice Home Mission Bd., Atlanta, 1984-86; pastor Midway and Emmanuel Bapt. Chs., Amherst, Va., 1988-92, Midway Bapt. Ch., Amherst, Va., 1992-95; Gwathmey Bapt. Ch., Ashland, Va., 1995—; sales mgr. Kirby Project North Industries, San Diego, 1986-88. Recipient R.B. Park Fund Raising award Los Rancheros Kiwanis, 1986, Master Life, Master Builder and Continuing Witness Tng. award Sunday Sch. Bd., Nashville, 1986. Mem. Piedmont Bapt. Assn. (convenor population study group 1989, vice moderator 1990, moderator 1990-92, chmn. office search com. 1990), Dover Assn. (chmn. nominating com. 1996-2000), Pedlar Ruritan Club (chaplain 1989-95), Alpha Phi Omega (life, 1st v.p. 1977-78). Home: 905 S Center St Ashland VA 23005 Office: Gwathmey Baptist Ch PO Box 1478 Ashland VA 23005

STINO, FARID K.R., biostatistician, educator, researcher, consultant; b. Cairo, Sept. 1, 1943; came to U.S., 1988; s. Kamal Ramzi and Farida (Shenouda) S.; m. Zandra Hargrove, 1968; children: Ramzi, Farida, Karim, Magdi. BSc, Cairo U., 1964; MSc, U. Ga., 1968, PhD, 1971. Instr. Cairo U., 1964-66; rsch. asst., teaching asst. U. Ga., Athens, 1966-68, 68-71, postdoctoral fellow, 1971-72; asst. prof. Cairo U., 1972-77, assoc. prof., 1977-82, prof., 1982-88; prof. biostats. Fla. A&M U., Tallahassee, 1988—; pres. Stino Agroconsult, Giza, Egypt, 1977-78. V.p. Coptic Orthodox Ch., Tallahassee, 1990—. Mem. Am. Statistical Assn., Biometric Soc., Sigma Xi, Gamma Sigma Delta. Home: 6579 Montrose Trl Tallahassee FL 32308-1607 Office: Fla A&M U Coll Pharmacy Tallahassee FL 32307

STINSON, DONALD LEE, school administrator; b. Frisco City, Ala., Nov. 6, 1931; s. Chester G. and Dottie N. (Black) S.; m. Mary Grace Mitchell, June 6, 1954; children: Gina Jo, Sharon Renee Stinson Palmer. BA, Berry Coll., 1954; MS, Fla. State U., 1963. Cert. tchr. Fla., Ala. Tchr. Grady County Sch. Bd., Cairo, Ga., 1956-57; lab. technician St. Regis Paper Co., Pensacola, Fla., 1957-58; tchr., counselor Escambia Sch. Bd., Pensacola, Fla., 1958-67, sch. adminstr., 1967-92; sch. prin. Conecuh Sch. Bd., Evergreen, Ala., 1994—; mem., chmn. Pensacola Jr. Coll. Sch. of Nursing adv. bd., Pensacola, 1972-75, Cokesbury Children's Bd., Pensacola, 1976-81; bd. dirs. Edn. Credit Unont of N.W. Fla., Pensacola, 1985-90. With U.S. Army, 1954-56. Mem. ASCD, Coneeuh Children's Found. (bd. dirs. 1995-96), C. of C. Democrat. Methodist. Home: 2958 Swan Ln Pensacola FL 32504 Office: Evergreen City Sch 101 Perryman St Evergreen AL 36401-2933

STINSON, GEORGE ARTHUR, lawyer, former steel company executive; b. Camden, Ark., Feb. 11, 1915; s. John McCollum and Alice (Loving) S.; m. Betty Millsop, May 31, 1947; children: Thomas, Lauretta, Peter, Joel. A.B., Northwestern U., 1936; J.D., Columbia U., 1939; LL.D., U. W.Va., Bethany Coll., Theil Coll., Salem Coll. Bar: N.Y. 1939. Partner Cleary, Gottlieb, Friendly & Hamilton, N.Y.C., 1951-61; spl. asst. to atty. gen., acting asst. atty. gen. tax div. Dept. Justice, 1947-48; v.p., sec. Nat. Steel Corp. (now Nat. Intergroup, Inc.), Pitts., 1961-63; pres. Nat. Steel Corp., 1963-75, bd. dirs., 1963-86, CEO, 1966-80, chmn., 1972-81; dir. Birmingham Steel Co., Pathe Techs. Inc.; trustee emeritus Mut. Life Ins. Co. N.Y. Trustee emeritus U. Pitts.; mem. Presdl. Commn. on Internat. Trade and Investment Policy, 1970-71; chmn. U.S. Indsl. Payroll Savs. Com., 1976; trustee George C. Marshall Found. Served to lt. col. USAAF, 1941-45. Decorated Legion of Merit. Mem. Am. Iron and Steel Inst. (chmn. bd. 1969-71), Internat. Iron and Steel Inst. (bd. dirs., chmn. 1975-77), Am. Law Inst., Bus. Coun., Links Club (N.Y.C.), Duquesne Club (Pitts.), Laurel Valley Golf Club (Pitts.), Phi Beta Kappa. Home: Hunting Country Rd Tryon NC 28782

STINSON, ROBERT WAYNE, meat company executive; b. Pierson, Mich., Jan. 11, 1936; s. Thomas Levi and Esther Amy (Smith) S.; m. Altha Jane Irwin, Mar. 4, 1961; children: Robert W., Debra A. AS, Davenport Coll., 1970. Meat mgr. Kroger Co., Grand Rapids, Mich., 1963-70; asst. meat buyer Kroger Co., Detroit, 1970-71; meat merchandising Kroger Co., Ft. Wayne, Ind., 1971-73, Grand Rapids, 1973-75; meat plant procurement Kroger Co., Indpls., 1975-77; corp. office meat procurement Kroger Co., Cin., 1977-86, retired, 1986; v.p. nat. sales Grove Meat Co., 1986—. Mem. Am. Meat Inst. Home and Office: 254 Braeburn Cir Daytona Beach FL 32114

STINSON, STANLEY THOMAS, computer consultant; b. Dothan, Ala., Dec. 17, 1961; s. Leonis and Betty Lois (Harrison) S.; m. Sharin B. Clark, Aug. 25, 1984; children: Sarah Ashley, Amy Rebecca, Rachel Elizabeth, Thomas Clark. AS in Computer Sci., Enterprise State Jr. Coll., 1982; BSBA cum laude, Troy State U., 1984; MBA, Samford U., 1989. Fin. sys. engr. NCR Corp., Birmingham, Ala., 1984-87; sr. sys. specialist Systematics Inc., Birmingham, 1987-88, sys. engr., 1988-90, sr. sys. engr., 1990; consulting devel. analyst Systematics, Inc., Little Rock, 1990-92; sr. sys. engr. Systematics Fin. Svcs., Atlanta, 1992-93; sr. applications programmer/analyst Capital City Bank, Tallahassee, 1993-96; sys. cons. Consultec, Inc., Tallahassee, 1996—; co-founder HomePage Plus, 1996—. Conservative. Baptist. Home: 3009 Giles Pl Tallahassee FL 32308 Office: Consultec Inc 1801 Hermitage Blvd Ste 460 Tallahassee FL 32308

STIPANOVIC, ROBERT DOUGLAS, chemist, researcher; b. Houston, Oct. 28, 1939. BS, Loyola U., 1961; PhD, Rice U., 1966. Rsch. technician Stauffer Chem. Co., Houston, 1961; teaching asst. Rice U., Houston, 1961-62, rsch. asst., 1962-66; rsch. assoc. Stanford (Calif.) U., 1966-67; mem. grad. faculty Tex. A&M U., College Station, 1967—, asst. prof. chemistry, 1967-71; rsch. chemist Cotton Pathology Rsch. Unit USDA, College Station, 1971-87; rsch. leader USDA, College Station, 1987—; vis. rsch. scientist Agr. Can., Rsch. Ctr. London, Ont., 1985. Welch fellow Rice U., 1963-65, Grad. fellow, 1965-66. Mem. Sigma Xi. Home: 1103 Esther Blvd Bryan TX 77802-1924 Office: USDA Agrl Rsch Svc So Crops Rsch Lab 2765 F & B Rd College Station TX 77845-9593

STIPE, JOHN RYBURN, bank executive; b. Batesville, Ark., Oct. 14, 1930; s. Ryburn Irvin and Ethel (Martin) S.; m. Mary Ann Cato, Dec. 19, 1958; children: Richard M., Roger W. BS in Agrl., U. Ark., 1953. County agt. Ark. Corp. Extension Svc., Forrest City, 1954-58; credit officer Forrest City Prodn. Credit Assn., 1958-67, pres., 1967-86; pres. Forrest City Bank FSB, 1986—; mem. adv. coun. Ark. Gifted and Talented Children Assn., Little Rock, 1976-82; bd. dirs. Am. Inst. Coops., Washington, 1980-84, Ark. League Savs. Inst., Little Rock, 1988-92, vice chmn., 1994-95, chmn., 1995-96. Trustee East Ark. C.C., Forrest City, 1990—, Ouachita Bapt. U., Arkedelphia, Ark., 1995—; deacon, treas. bd. deacons 1st Bapt. Ch., 1972—. Capt. U.S. Army, 1946-67. Mem. Rotary (bd. dirs. Forrest City chpt.), Jaycees (Ark chpt nat dir. 1964, pres. Forrest City chpt. 1963). Democrat. Office: Forrest City Bank FSB PO Box 1935 Forrest City AR 72336-5935

STIRLING, DOUGLAS BLEECKER, JR., human resources specialist; b. Kennett Square, Pa., Nov. 30, 1959; s. Douglas Bleecker and Katherine Parsons (Eaton) S.; m. Jo Lynn Kenes, July 18, 1981. BA in Sociology, Oral Roberts U., 1981; cert. basic mgmt., U. Tulsa, 1987; MBA, Okla. State U., 1993, Sr. Profl. Human Resources, 1994. Cert. temporary staffing specialist. Data analyst MPSI, Inc., Tulsa, 1981-82, quality control coord., 1982-84, tech. writer, 1984-89, adminstrn. mgr., 1989-90, corp. communications mgr., 1990-91; human resources mgr. StairMaster Sports/Medical Products, Inc., Tulsa, 1991-93; mgr. br. Maxwell Staffing of Bristow, Inc., Bristow, Okla., 1993-96; human resources mgr., cons. The Maxwell Cos., Tulsa, 1996—; part-time computer graphics operator Mabee Ctr. Oral Roberts U., Tulsa, 1979—; owner franchise Subway sandwich store; adj. instr. Tulsa Jr. Coll., 1993-96. Tchr. Jr. Achievement, Tulsa, 1987-88; coach basketball Tulsa Jr. Athletic Assn., 1987; mem. Tulsa Sr. Men's Baseball League. Mem. Soc. Human Resource Mgmt., Indsl. Rels. Assn., Tulsa Area Human Resources Assn., Tulsa C. of C. (adopt-a-sch. com. 1989). Republican. Methodist. Home: 1221 N Aster Ave Broken Arrow OK 74012-8551 Office: 8221 E 63rd Pl Tulsa OK 74133

STIRLING, JO LYNN, special education educator; b. Harrisburg, Pa., July 6, 1960; d. Barry Lee and Audrey Rose (Shorter) Kenes; m. Douglas R. Bleecker Stirling, July 18, 1981. BS in Spl. Edn., Northeastern State U., Tahlequah, Okla., 1991. Technician MPSI Inc., Tulsa, 1981-91; trainable mentally handicapped tchr. Arrowhead Elem. Sch., Broken Arrow, 1991-93, Broken Arrow (Okla.) Sr. H.S., 1993—; camp counselor CEC Camp Mentally Retarded, Ft. Gibson, Okla., 1990; pre-intern I, Roy Clark Elem, Tulsa, 1988; pre-intern II, Union 7th Grade Ctr., Tulsa, 1990; intern tchr. Arrowhead Elem. Sch., North Intermediate High Sch., Broken Arrow, Okla., 1991. Part-owner Subway Sandwiches and Salads, Broken Arrow; corp. sec., treas. TreasureHeart, Inc. Mem. Coun. Exceptional Children, Student Okla. Edn. Assn., Rho Theta Sigma. Republican. Methodist. Home: 1221 N Aster Ave Broken Arrow OK 74012-8551

STITES, DARL KAY, marketing professional; b. Rockford, Ill., May 2, 1936; s. Darl Glen and Doris Pearl (McDanel) S.; m. Lila Jane Echtenkamp, Mar. 30, 1957; children: Kelly Lynn Gilliland, Kevin Leigh. BS, IIT, 1959;

MBA, U. So. Calif., L.A., 1973. Reliability engr. Sundstrand Aviation, Rockford, Ill., 1958-60; design engr. Ingersoll Milling Machine Co., Rockford, 1960-61; engring. writer, configuration mgmt. Gen. Dynamics/ Convair, San Diego, 1961-65; structres administr. Lockheed Ga. Co., Marietta, 1965-67; configuration mgmt. mgr. Hughes Aircraft Co., Culver City, Calif., 1967-76, mfg. project mgr., 1977-78, program mgr., 1978-84, dist. mktg. mgr., 1984-92; dir. mktg. Loral Fairchild, Syosset, N.Y., 1992-93, Miltope Corp., Hope Hull, Ala., 1994—. Scholarship Ingersoll Milling Machine Co., 1954-58. Mem. Assn. of U.S. Army, Am. Def. Preparedness Assn. (pres. 1987-88), Armed Forces Comm. and Electronics Assn., Navy League, Air Force Assn., Wynlakes Country Club, C. of C. (info. systems com. 1995-96). Republican. Home: 8143 Wynlakes Blvd Montgomery AL 36117 Office: Miltope Corp 500 Richardson Rd Hope Hull AL 36043-4022

STITH, CHERYL DIANE ADAMS, elementary school educator; b. Birmingham, Ala., Oct. 15, 1950; d. Mack Jones and Joan (Logan) Adams; m. Hugh P. Stith, III, Jan. 7, 1972; children: Jennifer Dawn, Kristy Michelle. BS cum laude, U. Ala., Birmingham, 1986, MA in Edn., 1992, EdS, 1994. Cert. ednl. specialist, Ala. Substitute tchr. Homewood City (Ala.) Schs., 1986-87; tchr. Robert C. Arthur Elem. Sch., Birmingham, 1987-95; instrnl. support specialist Edgewood Elem. Homewood City Schs., 1995—; mem. summer enrichment program U. Ala.-Birmingham, 1993; mem. State of Ala. Textbook Com., Montgomery, 1995; lectr. in field. Vol. Birmingham Soup Kitchens, 1988—, Habitat for Humanity, Birmingham, 1992—; spkr. Ala. Kidney Found., Birmingham, 1992—; vol. U. Ala.-Birmingham's Young Author's Conf., 1986-92; mem. Robert C. Arthur Elem. Sch. PTO. Named Tchr. of the Yr., Birmingham Pub. Schs., 1993-94, Outstanding Tchr., 1994; Beeson fellow Samford U. Writing Project, 1990; Ala. Ret. Tchrs. Found. scholar, 1994. Mem. NEA, Ala. Edn. Assn., Birmingham Edn. Assn., Internat. Reading Assn. (S.E. regional conf. presider and vol.), Ala. Reading Assn., Birmingham Reading Coun., Birmingham Tchrs. Applying Whole Lang., Nat. Coun. Tchrs. English, Phi Kappa Phi, Kappa Delta Pi. Methodist. Home: 1034 Greystone Ct Birmingham AL 35242

STOBBE, MICHAEL, reporter; b. Lexington, Ky., May 10, 1966; s. Edward Michael and Patricia Ann (Quealy) Stobbe. BS in Polit. Sci., Northwestern U., BA in Journalism, MA in Journalism, 1988; MA in Pub. Health, U. Mich., 1994. Reporter The Sun Herald, Biloxi, 1988-89; health and environment writer The Flint (Mich.) Journal, 1989-94; health and human svcs. writer The Fla. Times-Union, Jacksonville, 1994—. Case We. Res. U. fellow, Cleve., 1995; recipient award Mich. Emergency Mgrs. Assn., 1990, Internat. Assn. Firefighters award, 1990; hon. mention, best news story Miss. Press Assn., 1989. Office: The Fla Times-Union 1 Riverside Ave Jacksonville FL 32202-4904

STOCK, MARGOT THERESE, nurse, anthropologist, consultant, educator; b. Toronto, Ont., Can., Aug. 10, 1936; Arrived in US 1967.; d. Karl Dwight and Marguerite Anne (Lafitte) K.; m. Philip Anthony, Jan. 11, 1946; children: Dwight, Scott, Kayler, Travis & Anthony (twins) Sean. AAS, Suffolk County Com. Coll., Selden, N.Y., 1981; BS in Nursing, U. S. Fla., Ft. Myers, Fla., 1983; MS in Nursing, U. Tex., 1984; DPhil in Social Anthropology, U. Oxford, England, 1989. Nurse Sarasota Meml. Hosp., Fla., 1981-82, LW Blake Meml. Hosp., Bradenton, Fla., 1982-83, Med. Center Del Oro, Houston, 1983-85, Pitt County Meml. Hosp., Greenville, N.C.; asst. prof. E. Carolina U., Greenville, N.C., 1985-89; Cons. Gerontol. Nursing Network Greensboro N.C. Designer Game and Software (computer), Nursing Math Made Easy, Understanding Mgmt., Teaching Nursing Theory 1984; Author (with others) Book Clinical Pharmacology & Nursing 1987, Poetry Evolution Lycidas Jaso 1980-87. Mem. AAUW, Sigma Theta Tau, Sigma Kappa Found. (Houston Sigma Kappa award), Phi Theta Kappa (pres. 1981). Roman Catholic. Home: 118 Old London Rd Greenville NC 27834-8833 Office: East Carolina U Sch of Nursing Greenville NC 27858-4353

STOCK, STEPHEN MICHAEL, broadcast journalist; b. Colorado Springs, May 16, 1961; s. Ray Kesecker and Juanita Madeline (Keller) S.; m. Lynn Victoria Peithman, July 20, 1985; 1 child, Michael Stephen Ray. BA, U. N.C., 1983. From engring. tech. to gen. assignment reporter WDBJ-TV, Roanoke, Va., 1983-86; from investigative reporter to weekend anchor, producer WECT-TV, Wilmington, N.C., 1986-87; bur. chief Anderson, S.C. WYFF-TV, Greenville, S.C., 1987-91; bur. chief Ocala, Fla. WESH-TV, Orlando, 1991—; standby SE corr. NBC NewsChannel, 1995—; guest lectr. Marion County Sheriff's Office, Ocala, 1993—, U. Fla. Press Club, Gainesville, 1993—. Adv. bd. Jack Eckerd Youth Camp E-Kel-Etu, Silver Springs, Fla., 1996—; elder First Presbyn. Ch., Ocala, 1996—; founder Ocala/Marion County Town Mtg. on Violence, 1996; adv. bd. Fla. Envirothon, Ocala/ Silver Springs, 1993; mem. adv. bd. Ocala Habitat for Humanity. Named TV journalist of yr. RTNDA of Carolinas, 1989; recipient award for TV agrl. news coverage S.C. Agriculture Co., 1989. Mem. Ctrl. Fla. Press Club (best gen. news 1994, merit recognition for spot news 1995, Best Spot News award 1996, Best Investigative Report award 1996, Merit Gen. News award 1996), Soc. Profl. Journalists, Investigative Reporters and Editors Assn. Office: WESH-TV Bur Chief 7 E Silver Springs Blvd Ocala FL 34470-6614

STOCKARD, JOE LEE, public health service officer, consultant; b. Lees Summit, Mo., May 5, 1924; s. Joseph Frederick and Madge Lorraine (Jones) S.; m. Elsie Anne Chamberlain, Dec. 27, 1957. BS, Yale U., 1945; MD, U. Kans., 1948; MPH, Johns Hopkins U., 1961. Med. officer U.S. Army Med. Corps, Korea and Malaya, 1952-55; asst. prof. preventive medicine Sch. Medicine U. Md., Balt., 1955-58; dep. dir. Cholera Rsch. Lab., Dhaka, Bangladesh, 1960-63; advanced through grades to capt., epidemiologist USPHS, Washington, 1960-76, 64-67; chief preventive medicine sect. USAID, Saigon, Vietnam, 1965-68; assoc. dir. Office Internat. Health, Office of Surgeon Gen. USPHS, Washington, 1967-69; epidemiologist, med. officer Agy. for Internat. Devel., Washington, 1969-87; mem. expert adv. com. WHO, Ouagadougou, Burkina, Faso, 1987-92; mem. joint programme com. AID project officer Onchocerciasis Control Program, West Africa, 1975-87; med. officer AID Africa Bur., Washington, 1976-87; guest speaker prol. seminar on leptospirosis, 1956; organizer plague sect. meeting 8th Internat. Congress Tropical Medicine, 1969. Author: (with others) Communicable and Infectious Diseases, 1964; contbr. articles to U.S. Armed Forces Med. Jour., N.Y. Acad. Scis. Jour. Citizens rep. on regional water quality adv. com. Low County Coun. of Govts., 1996—. Recognized for support of onchocerciasis control in West Africa by Pres. Jerry Rawlings, Rep. of Ghana, 1986. Fellow Royal Soc. Tropical Medicine and Hygiene; mem. APHA, Am. Soc. Tropical Medicine and Hygiene, Retired Officers Assn. Office: 17 Angel Wing Dr Hilton Head Island SC 29926-1903

STOCKBAUER, ROGER LEWIS, physicist, educator; b. Victoria, Tex., Feb. 3, 1944; s. Fred Ferdinand and Elizabeth (Nitschman) S.; m. Catherine Pauline Jones, June 10, 1972; children: Robbin Renee, Kathryn Elizabeth, Marc Daniel. BA, Rice U., 1966; MS, U. Chgo., 1968, PhD, 1973. Rsch. assoc. U. Chgo., 1972-73; rsch. physicist Nat. Inst. Standards and Tech., Gaithersburg, Md., 1973-89; prof. physics La. State U., Baton Rouge, 1989—. Editor: High Tc Superconducting Thin Films, 1990; contbr. articles to profl. jours. Recipient Silver medal U.S. Dept. Commerce, 1983; NRC fellow, 1973-75. Fellow Am. Phys. Soc.; mem. AAAS, Am. Vacuum Soc., Materials Rsch. Soc., Sigma Xi. Office: La State U Dept Physics 202 Nicholson Hall Baton Rouge LA 70803

STOCKDALE, GAYLE SUE, wholesale florist, ornamental horticulturalist; b. Crawfordsville, Ind., July 3, 1955; d. Robert Lavern and Faye Louise (Ball) S. Student St. Joseph's Coll., 1973-74, Purdue U., 1974; BS in Tech. Horticulture, Eastern Ky. U., 1977. Reclamation foreman South East Coal Co., Irvine, Ky., 1977-79; asst. mgr., landscape designer Evergreen Garden Ctr., Lexington, Ky., 1979-80; asst. mgr., landscape designer, head grower South Trail Garden Ctr., Ft. Myers, Fla., 1980-82; floral designer Flowers by Jean, Cape Coral, Fla., 1982-83; floral designer, landscape designer Bev's Greenhouse, Owenton, Ky., 1983-84; co-owner Royalty Wholesale, Lexington, 1984-87, Imperial Flowers and Gifts, Lexington, 1988—. Contbr. poetry to anthologies. Sponsor Save the Children, Korea, 1986. Moose lodge scholar, 1973. Mem. NAFE. Democrat. Avocations: reading, movies, exercise, golf, racquetball. Office: Imperial Flowers & Gifts 393 Waller Ave Lexington KY 40504-2914

STOCKELL, ALBERT W., III, information systems analyst, accountant; b. Nashville, Jan. 24, 1945; s. Albert W. II and Sue (Morton) S. AS, Nashville State Tech. Inst., 1984. Acctg. clk. C.E., U.S. Army, Vicksburg, Miss., 1969-76; salesman C.Y. Hart Distbn. Co., Nashville, 1976-78; office supr. State of Tenn., Nashville, 1978-85, info. systems analyst, 1985—. With USMC, 1966-67, Vietnam; Chief USN, 1991, Persian Gulf. Mem. SAR, VFW, Am. Legion, Masons, Gamma Beta Phi. Home: 6410 Jocelyn Hollow Rd Nashville TN 37205-3522 Office: State of Tenn 15th Flr L and C Tower 401 Church St Nashville TN 37219-2213

STOCKER, ARTHUR FREDERICK, classics educator; b. Bethlehem, Pa., Jan. 24, 1914; s. Harry Emilius and Alice (Stratton) S.; m. Marian West, July 16, 1968. A.B. summa cum laude, Williams Coll., 1934; A.M., Harvard U., 1935, Ph.D., 1939. Instr. Greek Bates Coll., 1941-42; asst. prof. classics U. Va., 1946-52, assoc. prof., 1952-60, prof., 1960-84, prof. emeritus, 1984—, chmn. dept., 1955-63, 68-78, assoc. dean Grad. Sch. Arts and Scis., 1962-66; vis. asst. prof. classics U. Chgo., summer 1951. Editor: (with others) Servianorum in Vergilii Carmina Commentariorum Editio Harvardiana, Vol. II, 1946, Vol. III, 1965; assoc. editor: Classical Outlook. Served with USAAF, 1942-46; col. (ret.). Sheldon traveling fellow from Harvard, 1940-41. Mem. Va. Classical Assn. (pres. 1949-52), Mid. West and South Classical Assn. (pres. So. sect. 1960-62, pres. 1970-71), Nat. Huguenot Soc. (pres. gen. 1989-91), Am. Philol. Assn., Mediaeval Acad. Am., Poetry Soc. Va. (pres. 1966-69), S.A.R. (chpt. pres. 1972, 91), Huguenot Soc. Va. (pres. 1981-83), Raven Soc. (Raven award 1977), Phi Beta Kappa, Omicron Delta Kappa. Republican. Presbyterian (elder). Clubs: Masons, Internat. Torch, Colonnade (Charlottesville, Va.), Farmington Country (Charlottesville, Va.), Commonwealth (Richmond, Va.), Williams (N.Y.C.), Army and Navy (Washington). Home: 1434 Grove Rd Charlottesville VA 22901-3126

STOCKFORD, BARBARA LYNN, middle school educator; b. Birmingham, Ala., June 29, 1959; d. Charles James Stockford and Joyce Louise (Newell) Sundheim. BS, U. Maine, 1991, MEd, 1994. Cert. tchr. elem. edn. and reading K-12, Fla., Mass. Edn. technician III Pemetic Sch., Southwest Harbor, Maine, 1990; tchr. reading West Hernando Mid. Sch., Spring Hill, Fla., 1994—. Mem. Policy Adv. Com., Orono, 1993-94; bd. dirs. Ctrl. Maine Indian Assn., Bangor, 1992; pres. Hall Governing Bd., Orono, 1992—. Recipient Acad. Achievement award U. Maine, 1991, 93, Work Merit award, 1991, South Campus Leadership award, 1992. Mem. Nat. Reading Assn., Hernando County Tchrs. Assn., Kappa Delta Pi. Baha'i Faith. Home: 6379 Alderwood St Spring Hill FL 34606

STOCKINGER, JILL FAITH, librarian; b. Oceanside, N.Y., Mar. 18, 1951; d. Harold Louis and Sara (Gordon) Wattel; m. Max Stockinger, Sept. 6, 1984; 1 child, Kaolin Fire. BA with honors, U. Wis., 1975, MLS, 1984. Music cataloger Chgo. Pub. Libr., 1985-87, adult ref. libr. Edgewater br., 1987-88; head ref. dept. Port Arthur (Tex.) Pub. Libr., 1988-91, chief libr., 1991—. Bd. dirs. Children's Trust Fund Family Pride Coun., Port Arthur, 1996—, Inst. for the Healing of Racism, Port Arthur, 1994—; pres. Golden Triangle chpt. NOW, Jefferson County, Tex., 1994; mem. Martin Luther King Jr. Support Group of S.E. Tex., Port Arthur, 1996—. Recipient Cmty. Svc. award Martin Luther King Jr. Support Group of S.E. Tex., 1996, Edgewater C. of C., 1987. Mem. ALA, Phi Beta Mu. Jewish. Office: Port Arthur Public Library 3601 Cultural Center Dr Port Arthur TX 77642

STOCKMAN, STEPHEN E., congressman; b. Bloomfield Hills, Mich., Nov. 14, 1956; m. Patti Stockman. BS in Acctg., U. Houston, 1990. Acct., tech. McKee Environ. Health, Inc., 1991-93; mem. 104th Congress from 9th Tex. dist., 1995—. Republican. Office: US House Reps 417 Cannon House Office Bldg Washington DC 20515-4309

STOCKSTILL, JAMES WILLIAM, secondary school educator; b. Springfield, Mo., Aug. 28, 1945; s. Arley Ian and Elma Jean Stockstill; m. Vicki Bell, Aug. 20, 1966 (div. 1970); 1 child, Michelle LaDawn; m. Meredith Jeanine Spencer, Dec. 26, 1974; 1 child, Danielle. BS in Edn., S.W. Mo. State U., 1969. Head football coach, phys. edn. tchr. Golden City (Mo.) High Sch., 1969-70; coach, tchr. Mountain View (Mo.) High Sch., 1970-71; journeyman bricklayer Fort Lauderdale (Fla.) BMPI Union, 1971-74; masonry contractor Waynesville, N.C., 1974-86; masonry contractor, master stone and brick masonry contractor Hillsborough, N.C., 1986—; masonry instr. Orange High Sch., Hillsborough, 1986—; owner Athenian Lady Fitness Ctr., Waynesville, 1984-86; gymnastics instr. Canton (N.C.) YMCA, 1976-80; pres. Trade and Industry Adv. Coun., Hillsborough, 1988-90; rep. VICA Skill Contest Orange High Sch., 1986-88. Author: A Collection of Poems, 1992, 93. Mem. Com. to Increase and Diversify Tax Base, Hillsborough, 1992. Mem. AFT. Home: 2801 Canter Dr Hillsborough NC 27278-8853 Office: Orange High Sch 500 Orange High Rd Hillsborough NC 27278

STOCKTON, KIM WELCH, home health nurse, administrator; b. Tullahoma, Tenn., Mar. 31, 1953; d. James Barnett and Wilma E. (Blackburn) Welch; m. Paul Dale Stockton, Sept. 13, 1982; 1 child, Jason Dendy. ASN, Motlow State Community Coll., Tullahoma, 1976. Cert. emergency nurse, ACLS. Staff nurse, quality assurance profl. Elk Valley Profl. Affiliates/ Home Health Agy., Inc., Fayetteville, Tenn., 1984-87; dir. profl. svcs. Med. Ctr. Home Health, Murfreesboro, Tenn., 1987-88, adminstr., dir., 1988-90; adminstr. ABC Home Health Svcs., Inc., Tullahoma, 1990-91; dir. clin. svcs. So. Tenn. Home Care, Winchester, 1991-94; dir. quality assurance staff devel. Century Home Health Care, Shelbyville, Tenn., 1994-96; staff nurse pediatric PCU/CCU Harton Regional Med. Ctr., 1996—. Mem. Tenn. Assn. for Home Care (standards care com. 1989-90, 92-93, focus group 1993), Tenn. Nurses Assn., Home Health Care Nurses Assn. Home: 130 Deerfield Rd Normandy TN 37360-3144

STODDARD, M. ANITA, psychiatric nurse; b. Spartanburg, S.C., July 7, 1946; d. David Dupree and Maudie (Johnson) S. BSN, U. S.C., 1968; MSN, U. N.C., 1972. RN, S.C.; cert. clin. specialist in adult psychiatric and mental health nursing, lic. marriage and family therapist, S.C. Staff nurse in psychiatry S.C. Bapt. Hosp., Columbia, 1968; staff nurse Columbia Area Mental Health Ctr., 1968-70; dir. nursing Spartanburg Area Mental Health Ctr., 1972-87, asst. dir., 1987—; mem. summer faculty U. S.C. Sch. Nursing, Columbia, 1971-72; adj. faculty Mary Black Sch. Nursing, U. S.C., Spartanburg, 1980—; adv. bd. women's program Spartanburg Tech. Coll., 1987—; presenter at profl. meetings. Mem. Spartanburg Symphony Chorus, 1972—, Spartanburg County Emergency Preparedness, 1988—. Mem. ANA (local bd. dirs. 1987-92, pres. 1974-76, Excellence in Practice award 1990), Am. Assn. Marriage and Family Therapy, Sigma Theta Tau. Methodist. Office: Spartanburg Area Mental Health Ctr 149 E Wood St Spartanburg SC 29303-3085

STOESEN, ALEXANDER RUDOLPH, history educator; b. Austin, Tex., Apr. 9, 1932; s. Andrew Robert William and Laura Tomine (Thompson) S.; m. Carol Annette Cronk, Aug. 22, 1959; children: Robert Andrew, William Darden, Carolyn Anne. BA, The Citadel, 1954; MA, U. Rochester, 1958; PhD, U. N.C., 1965. Tchr. Washington Sq. Reading Ctr., N.Y.C., 1958-59; asst. prof. history Newberry (S.C.) Coll., 1964-66; from asst. to prof. history Guilford Coll., Greensboro, N.C., 1966—, chmn. dept. history, 1972-77, 82-84, 90-91; Lilly fellow Duke U., Durham, N.C., 1976-77; mem., past chair N.C. Hwy. Hist. Market Adv. Commn., Raleigh, 1986-91, 94—; v.p. So. Assn. Pre-Law Advisers, 1989-91, pres., 1991-93; mem. Pre-Law Advisers Nat. Coun., 1991-93, cons., 1993—. Author: Guilford College: On the Strength of 150 Years, 1987, Guilford County Since 1890, Part II of History of Guilford County, 1981, Guilford County: A Brief History, 1993; author: (with others) The North Carolina Experience, 1984, Encyclopedia of Southern History, 1979; contbr. articles to profl. jours. and reviews to newspapers. Mem. Greensboro Sit-Ins Twentieth Anniversary Com., 1979-80, Thirtieth Anniversary Com., 1989-90; chmn. bd. trustees Unitarian Ch. of Greensboro, 1979-81. 1st lt. U.S. Army, 1955-57, capt. USAR, 1969. Recipient Congl. Leadership award Thomas Jefferson dist. Unitarian-Universalist Assn., 1995, Appreciation award Guilford County Bd. of Pub. Health; grantee NEH, 1975, 82. Mem. Am. Hist. Assn., Hist. Soc. N.C. (coun. 1988-90, sec. 1990-96, mem. Hugh T. Lefler undergrad. history award com. 1983, chmn. 1984), N.C. Lit. and Hist. Assn. (mem. Mayflower Cup book prize com. 1987, 91), Southern Hist. Assn., Orgn. Am. Historians (chmn. mem. com., 1991—), Assn. of Citadel Men (life). Democrat. Home: 611 Candlewood Dr Greensboro NC 27403-1102 Office: Guilford Coll 5800 W Friendly Ave Greensboro NC 27410-4108

STOGNER, WILLIAM LOUIS, pharmaceutical company sales executive; b. Las Vegas, Nev., Oct. 24, 1957; s. James Stogner and Mary Louise (Bierley) Alberts; m. Jennifer Dawn Pruitt, July 11, 1985; 1 child Dana DeAnne. Student, Niagara U., Niagara Falls, N.Y., 1976. Retail salesman, warehouse mgr. McGrath & Durk, Inc., Niagara Falls, 1973-77; retail salesman, S&R mgr. Gill's Plumbing Supply, Inc., Niagara Falls, 1977-79; prin. H.B. Contractors, Niagara Falls, 1979-81; sales supr. Parmed Pharms., Inc., Niagara Falls, 1981-82; sales cons. Republic Drug Co., Buffalo, 1982; sr. v.p. Ea. divsn. Major Pharms., Ormond Beach, Fla., 1982-92; ptnr. Suncoast Investors, Ormond Beach, 1988—; dir., v.p. Expert-Med, Inc., Ormond Beach, 1992—. Mem. Cold & Adpipe Soc., 1991—; pres. Tuscany Trails Homeowners Assn., Inc., 1987-89; bd. dirs. The Trails Homeowners Assn., 1988-91. Named hon. mem. Ky. Colonials by Gov. Martha Layne Collins, 1985. Home: 9 Fox Run Trl Ormond Beach FL 32174

STOKER, HOWARD W., former education educator, educational administrator, consultant; b. Highland Park, Ill., July 20, 1925; s. Howard W. and Elsie (Holgate) S.; m. M. Annette Stoker, July 9, 1949; children: Joanne, Dianna, Patricia, Robert. EdB, Wis. State U., Whitewater, 1949; MA, State U. Iowa, 1950; PhD, Purdue U., 1957. H.S. tchr. Dixon (Ill.) Pub. Schs., 1950-55; prof. Fla. State U., Tallahassee, 1957-84; head instrnl. devel. and evaluation U. Tenn., Memphis, 1984-88; vis. prof. U. Tenn., Knoxville, 1988-89, rsch. prof. Coll. Edn., 1989-92; ednl. cons. H.W. Stoker, Inc., Knoxville, 1992—; sr. assoc. prof. Ednl. Testing Svc./So. Regional Office, Atlanta, 1979-80; test devel. cons. State of Tenn., 1989—; cons. in field. Editor Fla. Jour. Ednl. Rsch., 1974-83; contbr. chpts. to books and articles to profl. jours. With USN, 1944-46. Mem. Am. Edn. Rsch. Assn., Nat. Coun. on Measurement in Edn. (bd. mem.).

STOKES, ARCH YOW, lawyer, writer; b. Atlanta, Sept. 2, 1946; s. Mack B. and Rose Stokes; m. Maggie Mead; children: Jennifer Jean, Austin Christopher, Susannah Rose, Travis, Emmarose. BA, Emory U., 1967, JD, 1970. Bar: Ga. 1970, U.S. Dist. Ct. (no. dist.) Ga. 1970, U.S. Ct. Appeals (5th cir.) Ga. 1970, U.S. Ct. Mil. Appeals 1971, U.S. Ct. Appeals (9th cir.) Ga. 1980, (2d cir.) Ga. 1990, U.S. Supreme Ct. 1981, U.S. Dist. Ct. (no. dist.) Calif. 1981, U.S. Ct. Appeals (11th cir.) Calif. 1982, U.S. Ct. Appeals (7th cir.) Calif. 1986, U.S. Ct. Appeals (1st cir.) Calif. 1992, U.S. Ct. Appeals (8th cir.) Calif. 1991, U.S. Dist. Ct. (no. dist.) N.Y. 1991, U.S. Dist. Ct. (ea. dist.) Mich. 1986. Ptnr. Stokes & Murphy, Atlanta, 1970-92, San Diego, 1992—. Author: The Wage & Hour Handbook, 1978, The Equal Employment Opportunity Handbook, 1979, The Collective Bargaining Handbook, 1981. Mem. bd. visitors Emory Univ., Ga. State Univ.; student rels. com. Cecil B. Day Sch. of Hospitality Adminstrn. Capt. USMC, 1971-73. Recipient Hal Holbrook award Internat. Platform Assn., 1990. Mem. ABA, ATLA, Union Internat. des Avocats, Internat. Soc. Hospitality Cons., Confrérie de la Chaîne des Rôtissuers, Am. Hotel and Motel Assn. Office: Stokes & Murphy 4751 Best Rd Ste 350 Atlanta GA 30337-5610

STOKES, CHARLES EUGENE, JR., retired wool merchant; b. Temple, Tex., Oct. 11, 1926; s. Charles Eugene and Esther Annette (Lawlis) S. BBA, U. Tex., 1948; MA, U. Tex., El Paso, 1968; PhD, Tulane U., 1974. Apprentice, then asst. buyer Conant & Co., Inc., Boston, 1946-48; wool buyer and dir. Stokes & Co., Ltd., Puno, Peru, 1949-55; pres., treas. Stokes Bros., Inc., New Braunfels, Tex., 1955-59; mng. ptnr. Stokes Bros. & Co., Peru, Uruguay and San Antonio, 1959-94; owner Merino Ranch, Ft. McKavett, Tex., 1994—; wool mktg. and processing advisor Ministry Agr., La Paz, Bolivia, 1961-63. Fulbright fellow Tulane U., Bolivia and Brazil, 1970-71. Mem. Phi Alpha Theta. Republican. Episcopalian. Home and Office: Merino Ranch PO Box 7 Fort Mc Kavett TX 76841-0007

STOKES, GRACE HAMRICK, retired occupational health nurse; b. Ala., Mar. 15, 1933; d. Thomas Dewey and Minnie Rosalie (Tindle) Hamrick; m. Robert E. Stokes, Apr. 19, 1958; 1 child, Cynthia Grace Stokes Sayes. Diploma in nursing, Mercy Hosp.-Street Meml. Hosp., Vicksburg, Miss., 1954; student, La. State U., New Orleans, Tulane U., 1977-82. RN, La.; cert. Am. Bd. Occupational Health Nurses (chmn., treas., edn. chmn., exam. item writer). Occupational health nurse Am. Can Co., 1957-71; occupational health nurse southeastern region Gulf Oil Corp., New Orleans, 1972-74; occupational health nurse single nurse unit Shell Chem. Co., Norco, La., 1974-94; ret. Shell Chem. Co., 1994. Contbr. articles to nursing jours. Recipient Schering award; grantee, 1978. Mem. Am. Assn. Occupational Health Nurses, La. Assn. Occupational Health Nurses, Greater New Orleans Assn. Occuptional Health Nurses, Greater New Orleans Dist. Nurses Assn. (Great One Hundred Nurse award).

STOKES, LISA ODHAM, humanities educator; b. Brunswick, Ga., July 6, 1953; d. James Brailey and Annie Louise (Tyler) Odham; m. Brian Atwood Stokes, May 7, 1983 (div. July 1985); 1 child, Tyler Philip. BA summa cum laude, Emory U., 1974; MA in English, U. N.C., 1975; PhD in English, U. Fla., 1989. Adj. inst. of English Seminole C.C., Sanford, Fla., 1975-79, humanities instr., 1983—; reporter Orlando Weekly, Winter Park, Fla., 1995—. Contbg. author: Encyclopedia of Popular Culture, 1995; contbr. articles to profl. jours. Art Enrichment Program Devel. vol. Park Maitland Sch., 1993—; vol. Fla. Film Festival, Maitland, 1994; active San Antonio Women's Caucus for Art and the LWV, 1992. Named Outstanding Tchr. U. Md. Sch. of Edn., 1996, Humanities Networking Project Recognition Am. Assn. of Cmty. and Jr. Colls., 1991. Mem. MLA (ed. assembly person), Union of Dem. Intellectuals, Am. Culture Assn. of Am., Enzian Film Soc. Democrat. Office: Seminole CC F-118 100 Weldon Blvd Sanford FL 32773-6132

STOKES, MACK (MARION) BOYD, bishop; b. Wonsan, Korea, Dec. 21, 1911; came to U.S., 1929; s. Marion Boyd and Florence Pauline (Davis) S.; m. Ada Rose Yow, June 19, 1942; children: Marion Boyd III, Arch Yow, Elsie Pauline. Student, Seoul Fgn. High Sch., Korea; A.B., Asbury Coll., 1932; B.D., Duke, 1935; postgrad., Boston U. Sch. Theol., 1935-37, Harvard, 1936-37; Ph.D., Boston U., 1940; LL.D., Lambuth U., Jackson, Tenn., 1963; D.D., Millsaps Coll., 1974. Resident fellow systematic theology Boston U., 1936-38, Bowne fellow in philosophy, 1938-39; ordained to ministry Meth. Ch., deacon, 1938, elder, 1940; vis. prof. philosophy and religion Ill. Wesleyan U., 1940-41; prof. Christian doctrine Candler Sch. Theology, Emory U., 1941-56, asso. dean, Parker prof. systematic theology, 1956-72, chmn. exec. com. div. of religion of grad. sch., 1956-72; acting dean Candler Sch. Theology, Emory U. (Candler Sch.), 1968-69; bishop-in-residence Peachtree Rd. United Meth. Ch. Atlanta, 1988—; faculty mem. Inst. Theol. Studies, Oxford U., 1958; Del. Meth. Ecumenical Conf., 1947, 52, 61, 71, Holston, Gen. confs., S.E. Jurisdictional Conf., 1956, 60, 64, 68, 72; chmn. com. ministry Gen. Conf. Meth. Ch., 1960; nat. com. Nature Unity We Seek, 1956—; mem. gen. com. ecumenical affairs theol. study com. United Meth. Ch., 1968-72, com. on Cath.-Meth. relations, 1969—, bishop, 1972—. Author: Major Methodist Beliefs, 1956, rev. 15th edit., 1990, also Chinese transl., The Evangelism of Jesus, 1960, The Epic of Revelation, 1961, Our Methodist Heritage, 1963, Crencas Fundamentals Dos Methodistas, 1964, Study Guide on the Teachings of Jesus, 1970, The Bible and Modern Doubt, 1970, Major United Methodist Beliefs, 1971, Korean transl., 1977, rev. 16th edit., 1990, The Holy Spirit and Christian Experience, 1975, Korean transl., 1985, Twelve Dialogues on John's Gospel, 1975; Jesus, The Master-Evangel, 1978, Can God See the Inside of an Apple?, 1979, Questions Asked by United Methodists, Philippine transl., 1980; The Bible in the Wesleyan Heritage, 1981, Respuestas A Preguntas Que Hacen Los Metodistas Unidos, 1983, The Holy Spirit in the Wesleyan Heritage, 1985, Spanish translation, 1992, Korean translation, 1992, Scriptural Holiness for the United Methodist Christian, 1988, Talking with God: A Guide to Prayer, 1989, Theology for Preaching, 1994. Trustee Emory U., Millsaps Coll., Rust Coll., Wood Jr. Coll. Home: Peachtree House 306 2637 Peachtree Rd NE Atlanta GA 30305

STOKES, PAUL MASON, lawyer; b. Miami Beach, Fla., July 16, 1946; s. Walter Johnson and Juanita (Hemperley) S.; m. Carol Crocker, Sept. 12, 1970; children: Macon Lanford, Walter Ashley, Mary Juanita. BA, Duke U., 1968; JD, U. Chgo., 1971. Bar: Fla. 1971. Law clerk to hon. Milton Pollack U.S. Dist. Ct. (so. dist.) N.Y., N.Y.C., 1971-72; assoc. Smathers and Thompson, Miami, Fla., 1972-77, ptnr., 1977-88; ptnr. Kelley Drye &

Warren, Miami, 1988—; adj. prof. law U. Miami, Coral Gables, Fla., 1987—; pub. defender Miami Springs, Fla., 1974, City of Hialeah, Fla., 1974-75. Mem. Code Enforcement Bd. Miami Springs, 1990-92; trustee Trinity Internat. U., Deerfield, Ill., 1989—. Fellow Am. Coll. Trust and Estate Coun.; mem. Dade County Bar Assn. (probate and guardianship ct. com. 1988—, bd. dirs. 1989-92, 94—), Fla. Bar (cert. wills, trusts and estates). Democrat. Presbyterian. Office: Kelley Drye & Warren 201 S Biscayne Blvd Miami FL 33131-4332

STOKES, WILLIAM FINLEY, JR., insurance executive; b. Hendersonville, N.C., Apr. 24, 1938; s. William Finley and Sally Moore (Pippin) S.; m. Grace Galloway, May 19, 1962; children: William Finley III, Susan Galloway Kain. AB, Wofford Coll., Spartanburg, S.C., 1960. Casualty adjustor Crawford & Co., Charlotte, N.C., 1960-65; salesman Ayerst Labs., Asheville, N.C., 1965-69; v.p. Wachovia Ins. Agy. Inc., Asheville, 1969-76; regional v.p. Alexander & Alexander Inc., Asheville, 1976-80; pres. Morrow Ins. Agy. Inc., Hendersonville, N.C., 1980-94; chmn., CEO Morrow Inst. Agy. Inc., Hendersonville, N.C., 1994—, also bd. dirs.; pres. Blue Ridge Comty. Health Svcs., Inc., Hendersonville, 1991, Blue Ridge Comty. Health Svcs. Found., Inc., Hendersonville, 1994-95; pres. Blue Ridge Comty. Health Found.; bd. dirs. Blue ridge comm. Health Svcs.; sec. Comty. Found.; chmn. Aetna agts. adv. coun. N.C. and S.C. Aetna Life & Casualty, Charlotte, 1989—. Bd. dirs. Community Found. Henderson County, Hendersonville, 1989. With U.S. Army, 1961. Mem. Greater Hendersonville C. of C. (pres. 1987), Rotary Club (pres. 1983), Hendersonville Country Club (bd. dirs., green com. chmn. 1988—), Champion Hills Club (pres. 1991), Elks. Democrat. Methodist. Office: Morrow Ins Agy Inc PO Box 1109 Hendersonville NC 28793-1109

STOLBERG, MARY MARGARET, historian; b. Denver, Colo., Sept. 8, 1956; d. David Fox and Anne Stewart (Brand) S.; m. Lynn Doyle, Jan. 18, 1986. BA, U. Chgo., 1977; MA, U. Va., 1986, PhD, 1991. Reporter S.W. Times Record, Fort Smith, Ark., 1977-78, The Pitts. Press, 1978-84; lectr., asst. prof. Appalachian State U., Boone, N.C., 1990-93; ind. scholar Boone, N.C., 1993—. Author: Fighting Organized Crime, 1995, (Little Brown award 1995); also articles in Sat. Eve. Post, Jour. of Policy History. Mem. Am. Soc. for Legal History, Am. Hist. Assn., Orgn. of Am. Historians. Democrat. Episcopalian. Home: 150 Canterbury Ln Boone NC 28607 Agent: David Hendin Lit Enterprises PO Box 990 Nyack NJ 10960

STOLER, MARK HOWARD, pathologist, educator; b. Mar. 1, 1954; s. Leonard and Evelyn (Yellen) S.; m. Paula Maria Piccini, June 12, 1977; children: Leah Elizabeth, Abby Rebecca. BA magna cum laude in Biology, U. Rochester, 1976, MD, 1980. Diplomate Am. Bd. Pathology, Am. Bd. Cytopathology, Nat. Bd. Med. Examiners. Intern in medicine Rochester (N.Y.) Gen. Hosp., 1980; intern in pathology U. Rochester Med. Ctr., 1980-81, resident in pathology, 1981-83, chief resident, 1983-84, instr. pathology and lab. medicine, 1983-85, fellow in surgical pathology and cytopathology, 1984-85, asst. prof. pathology and lab. medicine, 1985-87, attending pathologist, 1985-89, asst. prof. pathology, lab. medicine and oncology, 1988-89; attending pathologist Cleve. Clinic Found., 1989-93; assoc. prof. pathology, attending pathologist U. Va. Health Scis. Ctr., Charlottesville, 1993—; dir. molecular pathology lab. Cleve. Clinic Found., 1989-93, dir. histology lab., 1990-92. Recipient Young Investigator award Acad. Clin. Lab. Physicians and Scientists, 1983. Fellow Coll. Am. Pathologists (molecular pathology com. 1989—, cell markers com. 1989—); mem. AAAS, AMA, Am. Soc. Investigative Pathology, Am. Soc. Cytology, Am. Soc. Clin. Pathologists (coun. spl. topics 1989—, 2d tier abstract rev. com. 1990—), Internat. Soc. Gynecol. Pathologists, Arthur Purdy Stout Soc. Surg. Pathologists, Phi Beta Kappa. Office: U Va Med Ctr Dept Pathology Box 214 Jefferson Park Ave Charlottesville VA 22908

STOLHANSKE, LINDA LOUISE, English language educator; b. Richland Center, Wis.; d. Sidney J. and Irene H. (Jamieson) Hanson; m. James G. Stolhanske, Aug. 8, 1964; children: Andrea Lynn, Erik James. BS, U. Wis.; MA, U. West Fla., 1992. Tchr. English Wauwatosa (Wis.) Sch. Sys., 1961-62, Edina (Minn.) Sch. Sys., 1962-66; substitute tchr. Hopkins (Minn.) Sch. Sys., 1970-76; pub. rels. asst. Fed. Reserve Bank of Minn., Minneapolis, 1976-87; tchg. asst. world history U. West Fla., 1989-92, instr. English, 1992—. Contbr. Emerald Coast Rev., 1990-91. Active Pensacola Symphony Orch. Guild, 1989—; West Fla. Literary Fedn., 1989—; coord. adult edn. class Trinity Presbyn. Ch., Pensacola, 1994—. Mem. AAUW (membership chair 1996-97), MLA, Nat. Coun. of Tchrs. of English, Conf. on Coll. Communication and Composition, Phi Kappa Phi, Delta Delta Delta Alumnae Assn. Republican. Presbyterian. Home: 7408 Camale Dr Pensacola FL 32504 Office: U West Fla Dept English 11000 University Pkwy Pensacola FL 32514-5756

STOLL, RICHARD EDMUND, retired manufacturing executive; b. Dayton, Ohio, Aug. 5, 1927; s. George Elmer and Mary Francis (Zimmerle) S.; m. Vera Mae Cohagen, Sept. 2, 1950; children: Richard Edmund, Linda Ann, Donna Gail. Student in mech. engring., MIT, 1945-47; MetE, Ohio State U., 1950. Registered profl. engr. Ill., Tex. Various staff and operating positions U.S. Steel Corp., Pitts., Chgo., Houston, 1952-78; gen. mgr. metall. services U.S. Steel Corp., Pitts., 1978-84, dir. quality mgmt. program and tech., 1984-85; corp. chief metallurgist Wheeling-Pitts. Steel Corp., Wheeling, W.Va., 1985-86, v.p., gen. mgr. flat rolled steel, 1986-87, v.p., gen. mgr., interim chief ops. officer, 1987-89, exec. v.p., 1989-91, ret., 1991; cons. McElrath & Assocs., Mpls., 1984. Contbr. articles to profl. jours.; patentee in field. Served with C.E., U.S. Army, 1950-52. Fellow Am. Soc. Metals (chmn. 1963); mem. Am. Iron and Steel Inst., Am. Inst. Mining and Metallurgy (Nat. Open Hearth award 1957, bd. dirs. 1961-68), Am. Inst. Steel Engrs., Am. Soc. Metals, Dolphin Head Golf Club. Republican. Roman Catholic. Home: 3 Kinglet Lagoon Rd Hilton Head Island SC 29926-2548

STOLLER, DAVID ALLEN, lawyer; b. Burlington, Iowa, Oct. 27, 1947; s. Richard L. and Marjorie E. (Thornton) S.; m. Nancy E. Leachman, July 14, 1973; children: Aaron J., Anne C., John D. BSBA, Drake U., 1970, JD, 1977. Bar: Iowa 1977, U.S. Dist. Ct. (so. dist.) Iowa 1978, (no. dist.) Iowa 1981, U.S. Ct. Appeals (8th cir.) 1981, N.C. 1985, U.S. Dist. Ct. (ea. dist.) N.C. 1985, U.S. Ct. Appeals (4th cir.) 1986; cert. mediator, N.C., 1996. Assoc. city atty. City of Des Moines, 1977-81; assoc. Connolly, O'Malley, Lillis, Hansen & Olson, Des Moines, 1981-85, Ward & Smith, New Bern, N.C., 1985-89; ptnr. Dunn, Dunn & Stoller, New Bern, 1990—. Bd. dirs. Episcopal Found. of Diocese of East Carolina, v.p. 1996—; bd. dirs. Thompson's Children's Home, Inc., Charlotte, N.C.; mem., sec. standing com. Episcopal Diocese of East Carolina. Eagle Scout Boy Scouts Am., 1964. Mem. ABA (torts and ins. practice, litigation, law office mgmt., dispute resolution sects.), Def. Rsch. Inst., N.C. Bar Assn. (litigation sect.), N.C. State Bar (councillor 1995—), 3rd Jud. Dist. Bar, Craven County Bar Assn., New Bern Golf and Country Club, Def. Rsch. Inst. Home: 2432 Tram Rd New Bern NC 28562-7370 Office: Dunn Dunn & Stoller 3230 Country Club Rd New Bern NC 28562-7304

STOLLER, ROGER EARL, materials scientist, researcher; b. Van Wert, Ohio, Nov. 10, 1951; s. Eugene Ernest and Minerva Ernestine (Guingrich) S.; m. Robin Suzanne Benn Stoller, Oct. 1, 1973. BS in Nuclear Engring., U. Calif., Santa Barbara, 1978; MS in Nuclear Engring., U. Wis., 1979; PhD in Chem. Engring., U. Calif., Santa Barbara, 1987. Assoc. engr. advanced reactor systems dept. GE, Sunnyvale, Calif., 1979-80; rsch. assoc. dept. chem. and nuclear engring. U. Calif., Santa Barbara, 1980-81, vis. rschr. dept. chem. and nuclear engring., 1990-91; sr. rsch. staff Metals and Ceramics divsn. Oak Ridge Nat. Lab., 1984—. Contbr. articles to profl. jours. Fellow U.S. DOE Magnetic Fusion Energy Fellowship Program, 1982-84; recipient ASTM Appreciation award, 1988, Significant Implication for DOE-Related Tech. award, 1990, ASTM Appreciation award, 1990. Fellow ASTM (award of merit, nuclear tech. and applications com. 1995); mem. ASM Internat., Am. Nuclear Soc., Tau Beta Pi. Office: Oak Ridge National Lab PO Box 2008 Oak Ridge TN 37831-2008

STONE, ANN E., health facility administrator; b. Bartow County, Ga., Oct. 27, 1943; d. Charles Matthew and Sarah Inez (Hilliard) Earwood; m. James Harold Stone, July 1, 1961; children: Sandy, Jennifer, Teresa. Assoc. with honors, Floyd Coll., 1982, BEd with honors, 1978. RN, Ga. Staff nurse Redmond Regional Med. Ctr., Rome, Ga., 1980-81, nurse ICU, 1981-86, nursing supr., 1986-92. Home: 731 Harmony Rd Aragon GA 30104-1155 Office: Redmond Regional Med Ctr 501 Redmond Rd Rome GA 30165-1415

STONE, ANTOINETTE A., outpatient coordinator; b. Blackwell, Okla., July 8, 1950; d. Chester Henry Albert and Roslie Angie (Anzalone) Peterson; m. William L. Stone, Nov. 4, 1967; children: Toni Marie Stone Hromas, William L. III. AAS, No. Okla. Coll., 1975; BSN, Northwestern Okla. U., 1991. RNC, EPSDT pediatrics; cert. aids counselor. Staff nurse Blackwell Regional Hosp., 1975; publ health nurse III, Kay County Health Dept., Blackwell; outpatient coord. Blackwell Regional Hosp. Mem. ANA, Okla. Nurses Assn., Okla. Pub. Health Assn., NAPNAP, Okla. Pub. Employee Assn., Bus. and Profl. Womens Organ. (pres., Woman of the Yr.). Home: 316 S 13th St Blackwell OK 74631-3156

STONE, DELORES BARROW, special education educator; b. Windsor, N.C., June 30, 1941; d. Lee Roy and Sybil Virginia (Howell) Barrow; 1 child, Michael Alan. BS, East Carolina U., 1963; MLS, U. N.C., 1979; postgrad., East Carolina U., 1990—. Cert. elem. tchr., N.C. Libr. Edenton-Chowan Bd. Edn., Edenton, N.C., 1968-74; elem. tchr. Albemarle Sch., Elizabeth City, N.C., 1974-76; tchr. remedial English, Currituck County Bd. Edn., Barco, N.C., 1976-78; resource tchr. Camden County Bd. Edn., Camden, N.C., 1978—; owner ceramic bus. Named Camden Tchr. of Yr., 1984. Mem. NEA, ASCD, N.C. Edn. Assn., Phi Delta Kappa. Home: 100 Morris Cir Edenton NC 27932-1438 Office: Grandy Primary Sch 174 N 343rd Camden NC 27921

STONE, EDWARD DURELL, JR., landscape architect and planner; b. Norwalk, Conn., Aug. 30, 1932; s. Edward Durell and Orlean (Vandiver) S.; m. Jacqueline Marty, Dec. 15, 1954 (div.); children: Edward D. III, Patricia Marty; m. Helen S. Eccelstone, Aug. 5, 1995. B.A. in Architecture, Yale U., 1954; M.Landscape Architecture, Harvard U., 1959. Pres. Edward D. Stone, Jr. & Assos. (P.A.), Ft. Lauderdale, Fla., 1960-89, chmn., 1989—; vis. critic, lectr. Tex. A&M U., Lawrence Inst. Tech., U. Ga.; chmn. Edward D. Stone Jr & Assocs., Ft. Lauderdale, Fka; vis. critic, lectr. U. Mich., U. Ill., U. Va., U. Tenn.; adj. prof. landscape architecture U. Miami, Fla.; cons. First Lady's Com. More Beautiful Capital, 1965-68, Fla. Gov.'s. Conf. Environ. Quality, 1968-69; mem. Commn. Fine Arts, Washington, 1971-85; Mem. vis. com. Harvard U. Sch. Design; guest lectr. Chautauqua Inst., 1989, Golf Course Europe '89, Wiesbaden, Fed. Republic Germany, 1st Internat. Resort Conf., Tokyo, 1989, Symposium on European Recreational and Leisure Devel., Opio, France, 1989. Landscape archtl. designer: Pepsico World Hdqrs, Purchase, N.Y., 1972, Bal Harbour Shops (Fla.), 1971, El Morro Resort, Puerto La Cruz, Venezuela, 1972—, Profl. Golf Assn. Hdqrs. Master Plan, Palm Beach, Fla., 1978-79, Grand Cypress Resort, Orlando, Fla., 1983, Carambola Beach and Golf Club, St. Croix, V.I., 1988, Ft. Lauderdale (Fla.) Beach Revitalization, 1989, Onagawa, Japan, 1989, Pont Royal, Aix-en-Provence, France, 1989, Treyburn, Durham N.C., 1984, Euro Disney, Marne la Vallee, France, 1990, Riverwalk, Ft. Lauderdale, FL, 1989, El Conquistador, P.R., 1990. V.p. Landscape Architecture Found.; bd. dirs. Fla. Trust for Hist. Preservation, 1985-88. Capt. USAF, 1954-57. Recipient Profl. Landscape Architecture award HUD, 1968, awards Am. Assn. Nurserymen, 1967, 69, 70, 71, 77, 83, 88, 90, 91, Fla. Nurserymen and Growers Assn., 1982, 83, 85, 86, 88, 90, 91, 92, Am. Resort and Residential Devel. Assn., 1984, 85, 88, 89, 90, 91, 92, Interior Landscape Assn., 1984, 85. Fellow Am. Soc. Landscape Architects (13 awards 1963-88, 8 awards Fla. chpt. 1981-89, awards N.C. chpt. 1987, 88, 89, 92, medal 1994). Office: Edward D Stone Jr & Assocs 1512 E Broward Blvd Ste 110 Fort Lauderdale FL 33301-2126

STONE, ELAINE MURRAY, author, composer, television producer; b. N.Y.C., Jan. 22, 1922; d. H. and Catherine (Fairbanks) Murray-Jacoby; m. F. Courtney Stone, May 30, 1944; children: Catherine Gladnick, Pamela Webb, Victoria. Student, Juilliard Sch. Music, 1939-41; BA, N.Y. Coll. Music, 1943; licentiate in organ, Trinity Coll. Music, London, 1947; student, U. Miami, 1952, Fla. Inst. Tech., 1963; PhD (hon.), World U., 1985. Organist, choir dir. St. Ingatius Episc. Ch., 1940-44; accompanist Strawbridge Ballet on Tour, N.Y.C., 1944; organist All Saints Episc. Ch., Ft. Lauderdale, 1951-54, St. John's Episc. Ch., Melbourne, Fla., 1956-59, First Christian Ch., Melbourne, 1962-63, United Ch. Christ, Melbourne, 1963-65, piano studio, Melbourne, 1955-70; editor-in-chief Cass Inc., 1970-71; dir. continuity radio Sta. WTAI, AM-FM, Melbourne, 1971-74; mem. sales staff Engle Realty Inc., Indialantic, Fla., 1975-78; v.p. pub. relations Consol. Cybertronics Inc., Cocoa Beach, Fla., 1969-70; writer, producer Countdown News, Sta. KXTX-TV, Dallas, 1978-80; assoc. producer Focus News, Dallas, 1980; host producer TV show, Focus on History, 1982-94, Epsic. Digest, 1984-90; judge Writer's Contest sponsored Brevard Cmty. Coll., 1987; v.p. Judges Fla. Space Coast Writer's Conf., 1985—, chmn., 1987. Author: The Taming of the Tongue, 1954, Love One Another, 1957, Menéndez de Avilés, 1968, Bedtime Bible Stories, Travel Fun, Sleepytime Tales, Improve Your Spelling for Better Grades, Improve Your Business Spelling, Tranquility Tapes, 1970, The Melbourne Bi-Centennial Book, 1976, Uganda: Fire and Blood, 1977, Tekla and the Lion, 1981 (1st Place award Nat. League Am. PEN Woman), Brevard County: From Cape of the Canes to Space Coast, 1988, Kizito, Boy Saint of Uganda, 1989 (2nd Place award Nat. League Am. PEN Woman 1990), Christopher Columbus: His World, His Faith., His Adventures, 1991 (1st Place award Nat. League Am. PEN Woman 1992), Elizabeth Bayley Seton: An American Saint, 1993 (3d Place award Nat. League Am. PEN Women 1994), Dimples The Dolphin, 1994 (1st Place award Fla. Space Coast Writer's Guild, 1994), Brevard at The Edge of Sea and Space, 1995, Carter G. Woodson Father of Black History, 1996, Maximilian Kolbe: Saint of Auschwitz, 1996; composer: Christopher Columbus Suite, 1992 (1st Place award PEN Women Music Awards 1992, 2d Place award 1993), Florida Suite for cello and piano, 1993; contbr. articles to nat. mags., newspapers including N.Y. Herald Tribune, Living Church, Christian Life; space corr. Religious News Service, Kennedy Space Ctr., 1962-78. Mem. exec. bd. Women's Assn., Brevard Symphony, 1967—; mem. heritage com. Melbourne Bicentennial Commn.; mem. Evangelism Commn. Episc. Diocese Cen. Fla., 1985-94; v.p. churchwomen group Holy Trinity Episcopal Ch., Melbourne, 1988-89, Stephen minister, 1988—, pres. churchwomen group, 1989—; bd. dirs. Fla. Space Coast Council Internat. Visitors, Fla. Space Coast Philharm., 1989—, Aid for the Arts, 1994. Recipient 1st place for piano Ashley Hall, 1935-39, S.C. State Music Contest, 1939, 1st place for piano composition Colonial Suite, Constitution Hall, Washington 1987, 88, 89, 3d place for vocal composition, 1989, honorable mention for article, 1989, 2nd place for piano composition, 1989, award lit. contest Fla. AAUW, 1989, 1st place award Fla. State PEN Women, 1990, 1st Place award Nat. Black History Essay Contest, 1990, Disting. Author of Yr. plaque Fla. Space Coast Writers Guild, 1992; numerous other awards. Mem. AAUW, ASCAP, Nat. League Am. PEN Women (1st place awards Tex. 1979, v.p. Dallas br. 1978-80, organizing pres. Cape Canaveral br. 1969, pres. 1988-90, 96—), Women Communications, DAR (Fla. state chmn. music 1962-63), Colonial Dames Am. (organizing pres. Melbourne chpt. 1994), Nat. Soc. DAR (organizing regent Rufus Fairbanks chpt. 1981-85, vice regent 1987—, historian 1989—), Children Am. Revolution (past N.Y. state chaplain), Am. Guild Organists (organizing warden Ft. Lauderdale), Space Pioneers, Fla. Press Episc. Home: 1945 Pineapple Ave Melbourne FL 32935-7656

STONE, FRANZ THEODORE, retired fabricated metal products manufacturing executive; b. Columbus, Ohio, May 11, 1907; s. Julius Frederick and Edna (Andress) S.; m. Katherine Devereux Jones, Feb. 23, 1935; children: Franz Theodore, Thomas Devereux Mackay, Raymond Courtney (dec.), Catherine Devereux Diebold. AB magna cum laude, Harvard U., 1929; hon. degrees, Canisius Coll., 1975, Ohio State U., 1976. Chmn. bd. Columbus McKinnon Corp., Amherst, N.Y., 1935-86. Chmn. emeritus Arts Council in Buffalo and Erie County, 1973-86; pres. Buffalo Philharmonic Orch. Soc., 1959-61, also life dir.; chmn. emeritus Studio Arena Theatre, Buffalo, 1968-86; Nat. Conf. of Christian and Jews Brother Sisterhood citation, 1986; First Arts award Arts Council and Greater Buffalo C. of C. Recipient Gold Key award Buffalo YMCA, 1966, Red Jacket award Buffalo & Erie County Hist. Soc., 1976, Disting. Citizen award SUNY, Buffalo, 1985, Conductor's award Buffalo Philharm. Orch., 1993. Mem. Gulfstream Bath & Tennis Club, Ocean Club of Fla., Boca Raton Country Club, Pundits Club, Buffalo Country Club, Buffalo Club, Saturn Club (Buffalo), The Little Club (Gulfstream). Home: 1171 N Ocean Blvd Apt 4CS Gulf Stream FL 33483

STONE, GARY EDWARD, municipal official; b. Honolulu, July 24, 1963; s. Joseph Edward and Carol M. (Trimm) S.; m. Kimberley Lee Ashmore, Dec. 23, 1988; children: Joseph Edward, Kristine Elizabeth. Student, Tex. A&M U., 1982-83; BS in Polit. Sci., U. Tex., Tyler, 1984, MS in Pub. Planning and Adminstrn., 1988. Planning intern City of Longview, 1984-85, traffic engring. tech., 1985-86, adminstrv. asst. to dir. utilities, 1986-88; asst. dir. utilities City of Galveston, 1988-92, dep. dir. pub. works dept., 1992-94; city mgr. City of Freeport, Tex., 1994—; mem. exec. com. Coastal Coord. Coun., Austin, 1992—; mem. adv. com. East San Jacinto Basin Group, Houston, 1991—; mem. adv. bd. dirs. Consumer Credit Counseling, Houston, 1989—. Co-chmn. Greater Longview United Way Campaign, 1987. Named Boss of Yr. Am. Bus. Women's Assn., 1987. Mem. Tex. City Mgrs. Assn., Am. Water Works Assn., Am. Pub. Works Assn., Tex. Mcpl. Utilities Assn. (membership chair 1993-94), Tex. Water Utilities Assn., Water Environment Fedn., Solid Waste Assn. N.Am. Office: City of Freeport 200 W 2d St Freeport TX 77541-5910

STONE, HUBERT DEAN, editor, journalist; b. Maryville, Tenn., Sept. 23, 1924; s. Archie Hubert and Annie (Cupp) S.; student Maryville Coll., 1942-43; B.A., U. Okla., 1949; m. Agnes Shirley, Sept. 12, 1953 (dec. Mar. 1973); 1 son, Neal Anson. Sunday editor Maryville-Alcoa Daily Times, 1949; mng. editor Maryville-Alcoa Times, 1949-78, editor, 1978—; v.p. Maryville-Alcoa Newspapers, Inc., 1960-90; pres. Stonecraft, 1954—. Photographer in field. Vice-chmn., chmn. Tenn. Great Smoky Mountains Park commn.; mem. State of Tenn. Hist. Commn.; co-chmn. 175th anniversary com. Maryville Coll.; mem. mayor's adv. com. City of Maryville; mem. air service adv. com. Knoxville Met. Airport Authority; bd. dirs. United Fund of Blount County, 1961-63, 74-76, vice chmn. campaign, 1971-72, chmn. campaign, 1973, v.p., 1974, pres., 1975; vice chmn. bd. dirs. Maryville Utilities Bd.; bd. dirs. Sam Houston Meml. Assn., Alcoa City Sch. Found., Blount County Hist. Trust, Nat. Hillbilly Homecoming Assn., Friendsville Acad., 1968-73, Alkiwan Crafts, Inc., 1970-73, Middle East Tenn. Regional Tourism Group; dir. Foothills Land Conservancy, Smoky Mountains Passion Play Assn., Blount County History Mus.; mem. adv. com. Blount County Alternative Center for Learning, Overlook Center, Inc., Sr. Citizens Home Assistance Svcs.; chmn. Blount County Long Range Planning for Sch. Facilities; mem. Blount County Bicentennial task force; mem. adv. bd. Harrison-Chilhowee Bapt. Acad, mem. Leadership Knoxville; co-founder, vice pres., pres. Leadership Blount County; founder, chmn. Townsend-in-the-Smokies Art Show/Sale, 1984—; mem. bd. govs. Maryville-Alcoa C.C. Orch. Soc; mem. State of Tenn. Hist. Commn.; trustee, pres. bd. trustees, deacon, chmn. evangelism, fin. & pers. coms. Bapt. Ch.; mem. Blount County Bicentennial com., State of Tenn. Hist. commn. Served from pvt. to staff sgt. AUS, 1943-45. Decorated Bronze Star; named Outstanding Sr. Man of Blount County, 1970, 77, Hon. Order Ky. Cols., Commonwealth of Ky.; recipient Pride of Tenn. award for vol. work, 1993, Outstanding Leadership award Maryville Ch. of Christ, First Tourism Pioneer award Smoky Mount. Vis. Bur. and Blount C. of C., 1994. Mem. VFW, Profl. Photographers of Am., Internat. Post Card Distbrs. Assn., Great Smoky Mountains Natural History Assn., State of Tenn. Hist. Commn., Ft. Loudoun Assn., Tenn. Jaycees (editor 1954-55, sec.-treas. 1955-56), Blount County Arts/ Crafts Guild, Jr. Chamber Internat. (senator) Maryville-Alcoa Jaycees (life mem., pres. 1953-54), Blount County (v.p. 1971, 76, pres. 1977), Townsend C. of C. (dir. 1969-71, 83-85, pres. 1983), Tenn. AP News Execs. Assn. (v.p. 1973, pres. 1974), AP Mng. Editors Assn., Tenn. Profl. Photographers Assn., Am. Legion, Foothills Pkwy. Assn. (v.p., pres.), Chilhowee Bapt. Assn. (chmn. history com.) U. Okla. Alumni Assn. (life mem., pres. East Tenn. chpt. 1954-55), Sigma Delta Chi (life, dir. E. Tenn. chpt.), Mason, Kiwanian (pres. Alcoa 1969-70); Club: Green Meadow Country. Contbr. articles to profl. publs. Home: 1510 Scenic Dr Maryville TN 37803-5634 Office: 307 W Harper Ave Maryville TN 37801-4723

STONE, JOHN AUSTIN, nuclear chemist; b. Paintsville, Ky., Nov. 30, 1935; s. James William and Christine (Austin) S.; m. Helen Reynolds, June 2, 1968; children: Tracye Victoria, Philip Austin, Suzanne Reynolds. BS in Chemistry, with highest honors, U. Louisville, 1955; PhD, U. Calif.-Berkeley, 1963. Research chemist Savannah River Lab., E.I. duPont de Nemours & Co., Aiken, S.C., 1963-68, staff chemist, 1968-74, research staff chemist, 1974-81, research assoc., 1981-89; mgr. edn. programs Westinghouse Savannah River Co., 1989-93; ind. cons., 1993—; cons. IAEA, Vienna, 1965, 86; traveling lectr. Oak Ridge Assoc. Univs., 1964-74, univ. relations coordinator, 1985-89; mem. indsl. adv. com. Sch. Engring. Tech., S.C. State U., 1989-92. Served with USCG, 1955-57. Recipient Best Paper award Am. Ceramic Soc., 1982. Mem. Am. Phys. Soc., Am. Chem. Soc., Materials Research Soc. (chmn. steering com. Nuclear Waste Symposium 1980-81, chmn. program com. 1984, editor procs. 1985), Am. Soc. for Engring. Edn. (sec.-treas., vice chmn., chmn. nuclear engring. div. 1989-92). Episcopalian. Assoc. editor Materials Letters mag., 1983-89. Contbr. articles and reports to profl. jours. Home: 2221 Morningside Dr Augusta GA 30904-3441

STONE, JOHN VINCENT, applied anthropologist, researcher; b. Monroe, Mich., Dec. 11, 1960; s. Stanley Vincent and Jeanne Ann (Aldrich) S.; m. Eileen Camilla D'Annunzio, May 14, 1988. BA in Cultural Anthropology, Mich. State U., 1983; MA in Applied Cultural Anthropology, U. South Fla., 1989, postgrad., 1993—. Rsch. asst. rsch. divsn. Mich. Office Econ. Devel., Lansing, 1982-83; asst. zoning analyst dept. planning Office Bldg. and Zoning City of Temple Terrace, Fla., 1984; rsch. analyst hazards mgmt. group energy divsn. Oak Ridge (Tenn.) Nat. Lab., 1985-86; rsch. cons. alcohol, drug abuse and mental health programs dist. VI Fla. Dept. Health and Rehab. Svcs., Tampa, 1986-88, asst. contract mgr. children's med. svc. program office dist. VI, 1988; community planner dept. planning and zoning County of Hillsborough, Fla., 1988; rsch. assoc. Inst. for Social Rsch. U. Mich., Ann Arbor, 1988-92, rsch. assoc. dept. anthropology, 1992—; adj. instr. anthropology U. Mich., Dearborn, 1996, Henry Ford C.C., Dearborn, 1996-97; writer grant proprsals; presenter papers in field. Contbr. articles to profl. jours.; contbg. editor Com. Anthropologists in Envion. Planning, 1990-92. State of Mich. scholar, 1979-83. Mem. Am. Anthrop. Assn., Soc. for Applied Anthropology, Com. Anthropologists in Environ. Planning, Inst. for Social Impact Assessment, Superior Land Conservance, Internat. Assn. Impact Assessment (chair internat. meeting 1987, coord. directory and networking coms. 1987-88), Ann Arbor Area Assn. Applied Anthropologists, Risk Assessment and Policy Assn. Home: 2886 Weatherly Dr Howell MI 48843 Office: U South Fla Dept Anthropology 4202 E Fowler Ave Unit 107 Tampa FL 33620-9900

STONE, KURT FRANKLIN, rabbi; b. Hollywood, Calif., Aug. 21, 1949; s. Henry Ellis and Alice Marcel (Kagan) S.; m. Judith Claire Braun, Dec. 24, 1981; 1 child, Ilana Chaya. BA, U. Calif., Santa Cruz, 1971; MA, Hebrew Union Coll., Cin., 1979. Ordained rabbi. Eagleton fellow Rutgers U., New Brunswick, N.J., 1972-73; rabbi Temple Beth Torah, Tamarac, Fla., 1983-90; founding rabbi Congregation Beth Chaverim, Coral Springs, Fla., 1990—. Editor: The American Jewish Woman, 1980; prin. author: As Their Land Is, 1977; author: The Congressional Minyan, 1997; author, actor (one man show) Sholem Aleichen, 1975—. Intern U.S. Senate, Washington, 1969; spl. asst. Calif. Gov.'s Office, Sacramento, 1977; dir. Sholem Aleichen Found., N.Y.C., 1995—, Crohns Coleitus Found., Boca Raton, Fla., 1993—; mem. Civilian Rev. Bd., Ft. Lauderdale, 1986—; mem. Ind. Rev. Bd., Cleve. Clinic, 1995—. Recipient Lion of Judah award B'nai B'rith, 1986. Mem. Ctrl. Conf. Am. Rabbis. Democrat. Jewish.

STONE, LAWRENCE MYNATT, publishing executive; b. Balt., June 24, 1945; s. David G. and Clara Ruth (Coxey) S.; m. Lois V. Smith, June 10, 1967; children: Bradley Michael, Geoffrey David. BA, U. Iowa, 1968. Prof. Northeastern Bible Coll., Essex Fells, N.J., 1968-69; missionary Africa Evangelical Fellowship, Ndola, Zambia, 1969-71; asst. to production mgr. Am. Bible Soc., N.Y.C., 1971-72; book club mgr. Iversen-Norman Assocs., N.Y.C., 1972-75; editorial v.p. Thomas Nelson Pubs., Nashville, 1976-85; pres. Rutledge Hill Press, Nashville, 1985—; book and libr. adv. com. U.S. Info. Agency, Washington, 1984-88; editor in field; ghost writer. Office: Rutledge Hill Press 211 7th Ave N Nashville TN 37219-1823

STONE, MARVIN JULES, physician, educator; b. Columbus, Ohio, Aug. 3, 1937; s. Roy J. and Lillian (Bedwinek) S.; m. Jill Feinstein, June 29, 1958; children: Nancy Lillian, Robert Howard. Student, Ohio State U., 1955-58; SM in Pathology, U. Chgo., 1962, MD with honors, 1963. Diplomate Am. Bd. Internal Medicine, (Hematology, Med. Oncology). Intern ward med.

svc. Barnes Hosp., St. Louis, 1963-64, asst. resident, 1964-65; clin. assoc. arthritis and rheumatism br. Nat. Inst. Arthritis and Metabolic Diseases, NIH, Bethesda, Md., 1965-68; resident in medicine, ACP scholar Parkland Meml. Hosp., Dallas, 1968-69; fellow in hematology-oncology, dept. internal medicine U. Tex. Southwestern Med. Sch., Dallas, 1969-70, instr. dept. internal medicine, 1970-71, asst. prof., 1971-73, assoc. prof., 1974-76, clin. prof., 1976—, chmn. bioethics com., 1979-81; mem. faculty and steering com. immunology grad. program, Grad. Sch. Biomed. Scis., U. Tex. Health Sci. Ctr., Dallas, 1975, adj. mem., 1976—; dir. Charles A. Sammons Cancer Ctr., chief oncology, dir. immunology, co-dir. divsn. hematology-oncology, attending physician Baylor U. Med. Ctr., Dallas, 1976—; v.p. med. staff Parkland Meml. Hosp., Dallas, 1982. Contbr. chpts. to books, articles to profl. jours. Chmn. com. patient-aid Greater Dallas/Ft. Worth chpt. Leukemia Soc. Am., 1971-76, chmn. med. adv. com., 1978-80, bd. dirs., 1971-80; mem. v.p. Dallas unit Am. Cancer Soc., 1977-78, pres., 1978-80; mem. adv. bd. Baylor U. Med. Ctr. Found. With USPHS, 1965-68. Named Outstanding Full Time Faculty Mem. Dept. Internal Medicine, Baylor U. Med. Ctr., 1978, 87. Fellow ACP (gov. No. Tex. 1993—); mem. AMA, Am. Assn. Immunologists, Am. Soc. Hematology, Internat. Soc. Hematology, Coun. Thrombosis, Am. Heart Assn. (established investigator 1970-75), Am. Soc. Clin. Oncology, Am. Osler Soc., Am. Assn. for Cancer Rsch., So. Soc. Clin. Investigation, Tex. Med. Assn., Dallas County Med. Soc., Clin. Immunology Soc., Phi Beta Kappa, Sigma Xi, Alpha Omega Alpha. Office: Baylor U Med Ctr Charles A Sammons Cancer Ctr 3500 Gaston Ave Dallas TX 75246-2045

STONE, MARVIN LAWRENCE, journalist, government official; b. Burlington, Vt., Feb. 26, 1924; s. Samuel and Anita (Abrams) S.; m. Sydell Magelaner, Nov. 20, 1949; children—Jamie Faith, Stacey Hope, Torren Magelaner. Student, Emory and Henry Coll., 1943, U. Vt., 1948; B.A., Marshall Coll., 1947; M.S., Columbia U., 1949; Litt.D., Marshall U., 1968; LL.D., Emory and Henry Coll., 1981; D.H.L., Elon Coll., 1982. Assignment reporter Huntington (W.Va.) Herald-Dispatch, 1941-43, 46-48; European corr. Internat. News Service, 1949-52, Far Eastern dir., 1952-58; Sloan Found. fellow in sci. Columbia U., 1958-59; cons. chief army research and devel., 1959-60; assoc. editor U.S. News & World Report mag., 1960-66, gen. editor, 1966-68, asso. exec. editor, 1969-70, sr. asso. exec. editor, 1971-72, exec. editor, 1973-76, v.p., editor-in-chief, 1976-85, chmn. bd., 1984-85; chmn. bd. Madana Realty Co., 1984-85; dep. dir. USIA, 1985-89; U.S. commr. gen. Seville '92' Expo, 1989-90; mem. adv. com. U.S. Patent Office, 1976-78; adj. fellow Coun. on Strategic and Internat. Studies, 1989-90; mem. adv. bd. Univ. Pubs., 1989-92, Corp. for Pub. Broadcasting program adv. bd., 1992; chmn., pres., Internat. Media Fund, 1990-95. Author: Man in Space. Trustee, v.p., bd. dirs. Washington Opera; chmn. bd. dirs. USN Meml. Found., 1981-82, vice chmn., 1983-94, bd. dirs., 1991-95; mem. nat. adv. bd. Am. U.; bd. dirs. Pub. Diplomacy Found., Am. News Women's Found., 1991. Lt. (j.g.) USNR, 1943-46. Recipient Columbia Journalism 50th Anniversary Honor award, 1963, Marshall U. Disting. Alumnus award, 1973, Nat. Disting. Alumnus award Am. Assn. State Colls. and Univs., 1977, Freedoms Found. award, 1978, 79, 80, 81, Legion of Honor Chapel of Four Chaplains, 1980, Am. Eagle award, 1983, Silver Gavel award ABA, 1983, Gold Mercury Internat. award, Rome, Nat. Communication award Boys Clubs Am., Gill Robb Wilson award U.S. Air Force Assn., Disting. Honor award USIA; named to Washington Journalists' Hall of Fame, 1990; Pulitzer traveling fellow, Columbia, Austria, 1950, Knight fellowship, 1995. Fellow Ctr. for Security and Internat. Studies (adj.); mem. White House Corrs. Assn., Am. Soc. Mag. Editors (exec. com. 1985), Nat. Press Club, Omicron Delta Kappa, Sigma Delta Chi. Clubs: Fgn. Corrs. of Japan (pres. 1956-57); Internat. (Washington), Cosmos (Washington), Caribao (Washington). Home: 6318 Crosswoods Circle Lake Barcroft Falls Church VA 22044

STONE, MARY ALICE, sales executive; b. Savannah, Ga., Oct. 27, 1940; d. Melvin Theodore and Alice May (Shaw) Pearson; m. Thomas Lanier Stone, Aug. 14, 1960; children: Mary Elizabeth (dec.), Thomas Lanier, Jr., Michael A., Vicki Lynn. Bookkeeper, Radix Microelectronics, Tustin, Calif., 1967-69; owner Smart Set Bookkeeping-Employment Agy., Santa Ana, Calif., 1969-72; cons. Princess House Products, Havelock, N.C., 1973-74, unit organizer, 1974-77, area organizer, New Bern, N.C. and Ga., 1977-82, sr. area organizer, Marietta, Ga., 1982-88, divisional organizer, 1989—. Philanthropic chmn. Cystic Fibrosis Found., Tustin, Calif., 1971-72; vol. Craven Cherry Point Child Devel. Ctr., Havelock, 1972, Spl. Olympics, Marietta, 1983-84; choir dir. Christ Episc. Ch., Havelock, 1973; cookie chmn. Craven Country Council Girl Scouts U.S.; active Mother's March of Dimes, 1989. Mem. NAFE, Am. Soc. Profl. Exec. Women, Beta Sigma Phi (Woman of Yr. Havelock chpt. 1973), Beta Sigma Phi Internat. (life, order of Rose Degree 1979). Avocations: Swimming; reading; dancing. Office: Princess House Products PO Box 965065 Marietta GA 30066-0002

STONE, MARY OVERSTREET, newspaper editor; b. Auburndale, Fla., Mar. 17, 1924; d. LeRoy Blan and Aldah (Myrick) O.; children: Lily Sue, Mary Lou. Student, Orange County Vocat. Sch., Orlando, Fla., 1954-55, Lock Haven Art Inst., Orlando, 1960, U. Tenn., Knoxville, 1979, 89, 90, Walters State C.C., 1983, 89, 90-91, Arrowmont Sch. of Arts/Crafts, 1987-87, Carson Newman Coll., 1995. Owner/operator alteration, drape, slipcover bus., Kissimmee, Fla., 1942-50; retail sales Hunt Bros., Herzbergs, 1950-60; with Martin Marietta Co., Orlando, 1960-70; tchr. adult edn. Monroe County Vocat. Tech., Madisonville, Tenn., 1976-77, Hiwassee Coll., Madisonville, Tenn., 1977-79; corr. The Mountain Press, Sevierville, Tenn., 1981-89, E. Tenn. Bus. Jour., Knoxville, 1981-89, UPI, Knoxville, 1988-90; editor, writer Experienced Living, Sevierville, 1989—; owner, macrame designer Mary's Macrame, Sevierville, 1970-90; owner Inspiration Press, 1993—. Author: Eclectic Verse Mostly Terse, 1993, Confidence, Courage, Spunk, Smoky Mountain Women, 1995, macrame instrn. books; contbr. articles to profl. jours. Mem. Sevier County Geriatric Screening Team, 1986—, Sevier County Coun. on Aging, 1988—, East Tenn. Human Resources Agy., 1994-96, Sevier County Comm. Health Coun., 1994—. Mem. DAR, LWV, Nat. League Am. Pen Women, Am. Assn. Ret. Persons (women's Initiative spokesperson 1991-95). Republican. Episcopalian. Home: 1870 Sunnydale Dr Sevierville TN 37862-6128 Office: Experienced Living PO Box 4810 Sevierville TN 37864-4810

STONE, MATTHEW PETER, lawyer; b. L.A., Sept. 21, 1961. BA in English, UCLA, 1985; JD, Loyola U., L.A., 1988. Bar: Calif. 1989, Ga. 1992, U.S. Dist. Ct. (ctrl. dist.) Calif. 1989, U.S. Dist. Ct. (no., mid. and so. dists.) Ga. 1992. Litigation assoc. Seligmann, Slyngstad & Wright, L.A., 1988-90, Musick, Peeler & Garrett, L.A., 1990-92; asst. atty. gen. Ga. Dept. of Law, Atlanta, 1992-95; litig. assoc. Casey, Gilson & Williams P.C., Atlanta, 1995—. Chmn. Law Day and Liberty Bell com. younger lawyers sect. State Bar of Ga., 1993—, co-chair Law Day com., 1995—, mem. instrastate moot ct. com. younger lawyers sect., 1994—; panel judge Ga. Intrastate Moot Ct. Competition, 1994—, ABA Nat. Appellate Advocacy Competition, S.E. Regional, 1994; chmn. Parks Project Hands on Atlanta Day, 1994; vol. Hands on Atlanta Day, 1993, 95; mem. ethical action com. Univ. Synagogue, L.A., 1990-92; participant Bet Tzedek Legal Svcs., L.A., 1986; participant, vol. Income Tax Assistance, L.A., 1988. Office: Casey Gilson Williams PC 211 Perimeter Ctr Pkwy Ste 1000 Atlanta GA 30346-9003

STONE, MINNIE STRANGE, retired automotive service company executive; b. Palatka, Fla., Mar. 10, 1919; d. James Arrious and Pansy (Thomas) Strange; student Massey Bus. Coll., 1938-39; m. Fred Albion Stone, Nov. 30, 1939; children: Fred Albion, James Thomas, Thomas Demere. Sec., bookkeeper Sears, Roebuck & Co., Jacksonville, Fla., 1939-41; fin. sec. U.S. Army, Macon, Ga., 1941, Atlanta, 1942; sec., bookkeeper Raleigh Spring & Brake Sv., Inc. (name changed to Stone Heavy Vehicle Specialist) (N.C.), 1953-84, sec.-treas. corp., 1960-84, dir., sec. Vol. Wake County Mental Health, 1970-80; pres. YWCA, Wake County, 1973-76, bd. dirs., 1966-76; bd. dirs. Urban Ministry Ctr. Raleigh, 1983-89, mem. adv. bd., 1989—; bd. trustees Bapt. Children's Homes N.C.; former mem. subcom. Gov. Coun. Older Adult Fitness. Mem. N.C. Mus. of History Assocs., N.C. Art Soc., Monthly Investors Club, Coley Forest Garden Club. Republican. Baptist. Home: 920 Runnymede Rd Raleigh NC 27607-3108

STONE, ROSS GLUCK, physician; b. Pottsville, Pa., May 14, 1951; s. Jerome M. and Alma (Gluck) S.; m. Wendy E. Reiner, March 21, 1987; children: Melissa, Logan. BA in Philosophy, Yale U., 1973; MD, Columbia U., 1977. Diplomate Am. Bd. Orthopaedic Surgery. Intern, resident Harvard U., 1977-79; resident, vis. clin. fellow Columbia U., 1979-83; pvt. practice Atlantis, Fla., 1983—; clin. fellow in surgery Harvard Med. Sch., 1978-79; expert med. advisor Fla. Dept. Labor & Employment, 1995-97; editl. adv. bd. Am. Jour. Pain Mgmt., 1992—; chmn. surg. rev. com. Palm Beach Regional Hosp., 1995, institnl. rev. com. John F. Kennedy Med. Ctr., 1995-96, divsn. ortho. surgery Columbia Hosp., 1994—. Contbr. articles to profl. jours.; invented tension headache reliever device. Recipient Physician's Choice award So. Med. Assn. 88th Assembly, 1994, Scientific Poster recognition So. Med. Assn. 88th Assembly, 1994, 89th Assembly, 1995, Sr. Resident award Eastern Ortho. Assn. 14th ann. meeting, 1983, Rsch. Manuscript award Assn. for the Advancement of Med. Instrumentation, 1996. Mem. Palm Beach County (Fla.) Med. Soc. (bd. dirs. 1995—, del. Fla. Med. Assn. 1995, legis. com. 1995-96, emergency med. svc. and disaster relief plan coms. 1994-95, pub. rels. com. 1995—, health and human svcs. com. 1994-95). Republican. Jewish. Office: 120 John F Kennedy Dr Ste 124 Lake Worth FL 33462-1146

STONE, SAUL, lawyer; b. New Orleans, Dec. 15, 1906; s. Lazard David and Laura (Singer) S.; m. Sara Berenson, Apr. 7, 1938; children—David L., Richard B., Harvey M., Carol R. Stone Wright. LL.B., Tulane U., 1929. Bar: La. 1929, U.S. Ct. Appeals (5th cir.) 1930, U.S. Supreme Ct. 1950. Asst. U.S. atty., Eastern Dist. La., 1933-37; founder, ptnr. Wisdom and Stone and successor firm, Stone, Pigman, Walther, Wittmann and Hutchinson, New Orleans, 1957—. Mem. New Orleans Bar Assn., La. Bar Assn., ABA, Am. Law Inst. Home: 3 Poydras St New Orleans LA 70130-1665

STONE, VOYE LYNNE, women's health nurse practitioner; b. Grandfield, Okla., Apr. 17, 1941; d. Clint Voy and Mattie Evelyn (Averyt) Wynn; m. Don Dale Stone, Dec. 19, 1964; children: Melinda Anne Stone Phelps, Tari Elisabeth. Student, Bapt. Hosp. Sch. Nursing, Oklahoma City, 1965; diploma in nursing, U. Okla., Oklahoma City, 1965; BS, St. Joseph's Coll., North Windham, Maine, 1985; grad. women health care nursing program, U. Tex., Dallas, 1990; MS, U. Okla., 1996. Cert. women's health nurse. Dietary cons. Frederick Meml. Hosp., 1967; pub. health nurse Dept. Health, State of Okla., Frederick, 1985; insvc. educator Frederick Meml. Hosp.; women's health nurse practitioner Dept. Health, State of Okla., Oklahoma City, 1990. Vol., unit pres. Am. Cancer Soc.; vol. ARC; pres. adv. coun. 4-H Club; pres. local PTA. Named one of Outstanding Young Women of Am., 1970. Mem. AWHONN, Am. Acad. Nurse Practitioners, ANA, Okla. State Nurses Assn., Okla. Pub. Health Assn., Okla. Mental Health Assn., PEO, Beta Sigma Phi (various offices, Girl of Yr. 1976, 77, 78). Home: RR 1 Box 121 Frederick OK 73542-9721

STONE, WILLIAM SAMUEL, financial advisor; b. N.Y.C., May 23, 1923; s. Lewis and Flora (Pearlman) S.; m. Helen Rosen, Dec. 28, 1947; children: Louise, Barbara, Alan. BSBA, U. Mo., 1947. Owner Stone's Stores, Canton, Miss., 1947-61; pres. Chamcraft Greeting Cards, Hallandale, Fla., 1962-71; v.p. investments Investments Prin. Securities, Miami, 1972—; vis. prof. U. Mo.; lectr. in internat. fin. Mem. Rep. Presdl. Task Force, Washington, 1989-90, North Miami Beach Charter Comm., 1978. Mem. Mensa (keynote speaker investment seminar), Internat. Platform Speakers Assn., Cert. Investment Club, Toastmaster, Lions (bd. dirs. installation com. 1989). Home: 18181 NE 31st Ct Apt 110 Miami FL 33160

STONEBRIDGE, PETER WILLIAM JOHN, telecommunications engineering executive; b. Tonbridge, Kent, Eng., July 10, 1952; came to U.S., 1979; s. William and Betty Grace (Stacey) S.; 1 child, Anthony Peter William. BSc in Electronics Engring. with honors, U. Surrey, Guildford, Eng., 1974. Student engr. Ferranti Digital Sys., Bracknell, Eng., 1972-73, design engr., 1974-76; cons. engr. Philips Data Sys., Apeldorn, Holland, 1976-79; engr. Solfan Sys., Mountain View, Calif., 1979; sr. engr. Advanced Micro Conductors, Santa Clara, Calif., 1979-81; mem. engring. group Rolm Inc., Santa Clara, Calif., 1981-83; engring. mgr. Packet Technologies, Cupertino, Calif., 1983-86; v.p. engring. Stratacom, Inc., San Jose, Calif., 1986-94; cons. Netedge Systems Inc., Raleigh, N.C., 1994—. Patentee in field.

STONEKING, JERRY EDWARD, dean; b. Cin., July 12, 1942; s. Charles E. and Esther H. (Holmeyer) S.; m. Linda Kaye Parnell, Dec. 30, 1967; children: Jennifer, Jeffrey. BS in Engring. Mechanics cum laude, Ga. Inst. Tech., 1965; MS in Theoretical and Applied Mechanics, U. Ill., 1966, PhD in Theoretical and Applied Mechanics, 1969. Registered profl. engr., Tenn. Grad. student instr. theoretical and applied mechanics dept. U. Ill., Urbana, 1969-70; asst. prof. dept. civil and environ. engring. Clarkson U., Potsdam, N.Y., 1970-74; asst. prof. dept. civil engring. and mechanics U. S.C., Columbia, 1974-75; assoc. prof. dept. engring. sci. and mechanics U. Tenn., Knoxville, 1975-78, prof., 1978-92, Internat. Bus. Machines prof., 1981-84, head dept. engring. sci. and mechanics, 1983-92, interim dean coll. engring., 1992-93, dean, 1993—; mem. various coms. U. Tenn., 1976—, mem. faculty senate, 1980-83, 94—, mem. Saturn core team, 1991—, mem. policy adv. bd., 1992—; cons., rschr. in field. Author: Hydraulics, 1975; editor: Developments in Theoretical & Applied Mechanics, 1980; reviewer Internat. Jour. Structures and Solids, Applied Mechanics Revs., Jour. Applied Mechanics, others, contbr. articles to profl. jours. Recipient Outstanding Teaching and Rsch. award IBM, 1981-84, Best Tech. Presentation award Tenn. Dental Assn., 1990; fellow NSF, 1965-69. Mem. ASME, ASCE, Am. Soc. Engring. Edn., Soc. Engring. Sci. (bd. dirs. 1990—), Southeastern Conf. Theoretical and Applied Mechanics (chmn. editorial com. 10th conf. 1979-80, organizer, conf. chmn. 10th conf. 1980, chmn. ops. com. 1987-88, mem. policy com. 1988—), Phi Kappa Phi, Sigma Xi, Tau Beta Pi. Office: U Tenn Coll Engring 124 Perkins Hall Knoxville TN 37996-2000

STONE-MILLER, REBECCA ROLLINS, art historian, educator, curator; b. Manchester, N.H., July 17, 1958; d. Albert Edward and Grace Holt (Woodbury) S.; m. Douglas Jay Miller, July 8, 1989; children: Dylan Reed, Rhiannon Sarah. BA in Art and Perception, U. Mich., 1979; MA in History of Art, Yale U., 1982, PhD in History of Art, 1987. Teaching asst. II and III Yale U., New Haven, 1981-84, acting instr. in history of art, 1984-85; resident assoc. Smithsonian Instn., Washington, 1986; asst. prof., rsch. assoc. Johns Hopkins U. and Dumbarton Oaks, Balt. and Washington, 1987-88; Mellon postdoctoral fellow, cons. curator Emory U.-Michael C. Carlos Mus., Atlanta, 1988-90, asst. prof., curator, 1990-96, assoc. prof., 1996—; docent tng. high sch. tchrs.' workshops Michael C. Carlos Mus., 1988—, collections com., 1991—, long range planning com. 1993, curatorial assts. and curator search coms., 1993; mem. Latin Am. and Caribbean studies program steering com., Emory U., 1988—, undergrad. Woodruff scholars selection com., 1991, 92, condr. seminars on writing syllabi, grading, 1992—, Phi Beta Kappa com., 1993, acad. standards com., 1993; guest curator Andean Textiles Mus. Fine Arts, Boston, 1988-92; cons. exhbn. Chgo. Art Inst. 1992. Author: (books) To Weave for the Sun: Andean Textiles in the Museum of Fine Arts, Boston, 1992, Art of the Andes, 1996; script dir. Blood in the City of Dreams, 1991; contbr. articles and papers to profl. jours. Univ. tuition fellow Yale U.,1980-84, jr. fellow pre-Columbian studies, Dumbarton Oaks, 1985-86, Emory-Mellon postdoctoral fellow in art history Emory U., 1988-90, dissertation rsch. grantee Yale U., 1983-85, univ. rsch. com. summer grantee Emory U., 1991. Mem. Archaeol. Inst. Am., Coll. Art Assn., Inst. Andean Studies, Phi Beta Kappa. Democrat. Office: Emory U Art History Dept Atlanta GA 30322

STONER, ROYAL CLINTON, rancher; b. Victoria, Tex., Apr. 25, 1918; s. Thomas Royal and Mamie Victoria S.; m. Robbie May Scrubbs, Dec. 28, 1958; children: Tom, Gil, Jamie. BBA, U. Tex., 1939. Mgr., owner Stoner Ranch, Uvalde, Tex., 1946—; judge, approved racing steward Am. Quarter Horse Assn., Amarillo, Tex.; judge Nat. Cutting Horse Assn., Ft. Worth, Tex. Author: Just Leaving Tracks, 1995. Dir. Uvalde County Farm Bur. Soil Conservation Dist., 1960-82; hist. commn. Uvalde County, 1982-95. Sgt., Air Corps, 1941-46, WWII. Home and Office: HCR 33 Box 630 Uvalde TX 78801

STONNINGTON, HENRY HERBERT, physician, medical executive, educator; b. Vienna, Austria, Feb. 12, 1927; came to U.S., 1969; m. Constance Mary Leigh Hamersley, Sept. 19, 1953. MB, BS, Melbourne U., Victoria, Australia, 1950; MS, U. Minn., 1972. Diplomate Am. Bd. Phys. Medicine and Rehab. Pvt. practice Sydney, N.S.W., Australia, 1955-65; clin. tchr. U. N.S.W., Sydney, 1965-69; resident in Phys. Medicine and Rehab. Mayo Clinic, Rochester, Minn., 1969-72, mem. staff, 1972-83; assoc. prof. Mayo Med. Sch., Rochester, 1975-83; chmn. dept rehab. medicine Med. Coll. Va., Va. Commonwealth U., Richmond, 1983-88, prof. rehab. medicine, 1983—, dir. rsch. tng. ctr., 1988-89; v.p. med. svcs. Sheltering Arms Hosp., Richmond, 1985-92; prof. and chmn. dept. phys. medicine and rehab. U. Mo., Columbia, 1992-94; med. dir. Meml. Rehab. Ctr., Savannah, Ga., 1994—. Editor Brain Injury, 1987—; contbr. articles to profl. jours. Recipient award Rsch. Tng. Ctr. Model Sys., Nat. Inst. Disability and Rehab. Rsch., Washington, 1987, 88. Fellow Australia Coll. Rehab. Medicine, Australasia Faculty Rehab. Medicine, Royal Coll. Physicians Edinburgh (Scotland), Am. Acad. Phys. Medicine and Rehab., Am. Coun. Rehab. Medicine, Am. Assn. Acad. Physicians. Office: Meml Rehab Ctr 4750 Waters Ave Ste 307 Savannah GA 31404-6268

STOOKSBURY, JAYNE MOYER, special education educator; b. Knoxville, Tenn., Dec. 7, 1951; d. James Robert and Thena Catherine (Harrington) Moyer; m. William Claude Stooksbury, Mar. 21, 1970; 1 child, William David. BS, U. Tenn., 1990, MS, 1993. Cert. tchr., Tenn. Pvt. practice as optician, 1972-81; lead tchr. Christian Life Day Care, Nashville, Tenn., 1987-88; rsch. asst. U. Tenn., Knoxville, 1990-92; cons. dept. spl. svcs. edn. U. Tenn. LRE for LIFE Project, Knoxville, 1992—; presenter to various profl. socs. and seminars, 1992—; mem. adv. bd. Tenn. Dept. Edn., 1993—. Named one of Outstanding Young Women Am., 1983. Fellow Nat. Optometric Assn., Nat. Contact Lens Assn.; mem. Assn. for Persons with Severe Handicaps, Optometric Assn. Am., Phi Lambda Theta. Democrat. Methodist. Home: 1105 Katherine Ave Knoxville TN 37921 Office: U Tenn LRE Project 600 Henley St Ste 312 Knoxville TN 37902-2900

STOOKSBURY, WILLIAM CLAUDE, minister; b. Knoxville, Tenn., June 6, 1947; s. William Claude and Vera Faye (Hudman) S.; m. Mary Jayne Moyer, Mar. 21, 1970; 1 child, William David. BS, U. Tenn., Chattanooga, 1980; MDiv, Vanderbilt U., 1987. Ordained to ministry Bapt. Ch., 1978. Min. of visitation 1st Bapt. Ch., Chattanooga, 1975-78; pastor Beacon Bapt. Ch., Rossville, Ga., 1978-80; asst. min. Ea. Pkwy. Bapt. Ch., Louisville, 1980-81; pastor 1st Bapt. Ch., Fisherville, Ky., 1981-84, Baker's Grove Bapt. Ch., Mt. Juliet, Tenn., 1984-86, Fairgarden United Meth. Ch., Sevierville, Tenn., 1988-92, Lonsdale United Meth. Ch., Knoxville, 1992—; design team urban ministry Holston Conf., Meth. Ch., Knoxville, 1992. Mem. search com. dean of human svcs. U. Tenn., Chattanooga, 1980; co-chair area II, Campbellsville Coll. Fund-raising, Ky., 1983; mem. steering com. Tenn. Alliance Strong Cmtys., Nashville, 1989—; charter mem. Ams. for Change, Washington, 1993—; mem. nat. steering com. Clinton/Gore '96 Campaign. Named one of Outstanding Young Men of Am., Outstanding Young Assn., 1982, Dyer scholarship Vanderbilt Div., 1986. Fellow Westar Inst.; mem. ACLU, Am. Acad. Religion, Long Run Bapt. Assn. (chair assn. message com. 1984, com. to study ordination 1982, exec. bd. dirs. 1981-84), People for the Am. Way, The Interfaith Alliance, Internat. Platform Assn. Democrat. Methodist. Home: 1105 Katherine Ave Knoxville TN 37921-2035 Office: Lonsdale United Meth Ch 3002 Galbraith St Knoxville TN 37921-2023

STOPHEL, JOHN CARROLL, lawyer, accountant; b. Bristol, Tenn., June 13, 1926; s. Oscar William Stophel and Cora Lee (Frye) Booher; m. Pauline Phipps, Aug. 7, 1946; children: Phyllis Stophel Bethea (dec.), Nathan Carroll. Student, Duke U., 1944-45; BSBA, Bob Jones U., 1949; MS in Acctg., U. Tenn., 1950; LLB, McKenzie Coll. Law, 1955; LHD (hon.), Tenn. Temple U., 1988. Bar: Ga. 1953, Tenn. 1955; CPA, Tenn. From staff acct., assoc., ptnr. to sr. ptnr. Stophel & Stophel P.C., Chattanooga, 1950—; church, civic and profl. orgns. speaker; pres. Tenn. State Bd. Accountancy, 1962-63; mem. Tenn. Tax Study Commn., 1966-67. Vice chmn., treas. Pub. Sch. Bible Study Com., 1970—; trustee Sunday Sch. Bd., So. Bapt. Conv., 1967-74; trustee Tenn. Bapt. Found., 1973-79, Bob Jones U., 1960-83; trustee U. Chattanooga Found., 1975—, vice chmn., 1983-87; deacon Brainerd Bapt. Ch., 1958—, chn., 1960-61, chmn. priorities study com., 1971-81, gen. dir.Sunday sch., 1960-68, dir. coll. and career Sunday sch. dept., 1968-83, trustee, sec. bd. dirs., 1961-85, chmn. budget planning com., 1981-83, chmn. nominating com., 1984-85, chmn. fin. com., 1989-90, tchr. adult men Sunday sch. class; bd. dirs. YMCA, 1974-88, Christian Legal Soc., 1979-92, Chattanooga-Hamilton County Bicentennial Commn., treas., 1973-76; mem. bd. assocs. Covenant Coll., 1977—; chmn. Chattanooga Venture Meml. Auditorium Com., 1985; mem. bd. reference Tenn. Temple U., 1986-94; bd. govs. Walden Club, 1990-93; bd. dirs. Leadership Ministries Worldwide, 1995—, Chattanooga Christian Cmty. Found., 1996—. Named Young Man of Yr., City of Chattanooga, 1960, Alumnus of Yr., Bob Jones U., 1970, Boss of Yr., Chattanooga Legal Sec.'s Assn., 1976; recipient Disting. Svc. award Bapt. Sunday Sch. Bd., 1974, Disting. Svc. award Chattanooga Kiwanis Club, 1993. Fellow Am. Bar Found. (life), Tenn. Bar Found. (founding), Chattanooga Bar Found. (founding), Am. Coll. Tax Counsel; mem. ABA (exempt orgns. com. tax sect., chmn. subcom. religious orgns. 1983-89), AICPA, Tenn. Bar Assn., Chattanooga Bar Assn. (pres. 1964-65, President's award 1990, Ralph Kelly Humanitarian award 1996), Tenn. Fed. Tax Inst. (bd. dirs., pres. 1973), Estate Planning Coun. (pres. 1961), Chattanooga C. of C. (pres. 1968), Rotary (pres. 1982-83). Republican. Office: Stophel & Stophel PC 500 Tallan Bldg Two Union Sq Chattanooga TN 37402-2571

STORCH, BARBARA JEAN COHEN, librarian; b. N.Y.C., Jan. 13, 1942; d. Isidore and Ruth (Goldman) Cohen; m. Fred Storch, May 24, 1964; children: Bruce F., Emily S. BA, Bklyn. Coll., 1962; MLS, L.I. Univ., 1981. Cataloger Nassau Libr. System, Uniondale, N.Y., 1981-87; head tech. svcs. West Palm Beach (Fla.) Pub. Libr., 1987-96, mgr. extension and tech. svcs., 1996—, interim libr. dir., 1996—. Pres. Nassau Libr. Sys. Employees Assn., Uniondale, 1986-87; mem. pers. issues and profl. concerns com. Nassau County (N.Y.) Libr. Assn., 1986-87; chair door prize com. BookFest of the Palm Beaches!, Palm Beach County, Fla., 1990' program co-chair auction com. Epilepsy Assn. for the Palm Beaches, bd. dirs., Epilepsy Svcs., of Southwest Fla. Mem. ALA (new mems. round table, local arrangements com. 1994 ann. conf.), , Palm Beach County Libr. Assn. (sec. 1989-90), Fla. Libr. Assn., Fla. Pub. Libr. Assn. (chair tech. svcs. divsn. 1989-90, chair tech. svcs. civ. 1st conf. program on preservation 1990). Democrat. Jewish. Home: PO Box 3773 Boca Raton FL 33427 Office: West Palm Beach Pub Libr 100 Clematis St West Palm Beach FL 33401-5511

STORCH, SAMUEL JAY, urologist; b. N.Y.C., June 5, 1952; s. Clifford and Doris Bernice (Schachne) S.; m. Robin Marie Dawson, Oct. 17, 1986; 1 child, Ariel. BA, U. Rochester, 1974; MD, Georgetown U., 1980. Diplomate Am. Bd. Urology, Nat. Bd. Med. Examiners. Resident in surgery Georgetown U., Washington, 1980-82; resident in urology Albert Einstein/Montefiore, Bronx, N.Y., 1982-85; urologist Moore Regional Hosp., Pinehurst, N.C., 1986—, Cape Fear Valley Med. Ctr., Fayetteville, N.C., 1991—, Montgomery Meml. Hosp., Troy, N.C., 1986—. Mem. Am. Assn. Boomers, N.C. chpt. Nature Conservancy. Fellow Am. Coll. Surgeons; mem. AMA, Am. Urol. Assn., Am. Fertility Soc., Am. Assn. Clin. Urologists, N.C. Med. Soc., Elks. Office: Mid South Urology Ctr 2 Memorial Dr Pinehurst NC 28374-8707

STORER, FRANCES NELL, artist, musician; b. Central City, Ky., June 17, 1917; d. Harry Franklin and Nola Belle (Stewart) S. Student, Ward Belmont Conservatory, Nashville, 1935-37, Cin. Conservatory, 1938-40, various art workshops. Tchr. Numerous art ctrs. and schs.; artist Railrowad Mag., 1965. Work has been exhibited in over 33 one-person shows, numerous group shows, travelling exhbn. Am. Water Color Soc., 1968. Named Woman of Yr. Times-Argos, Ctrl. Ky., 1962; profile in L.A. Revue Modern Mag., Paris, 1964. Mem. J.B. Speed Art Mus, MacDowell Music Club, Louisville Visual Arts Assn., Ky. Watercolor Soc., Am. Watercolor Soc. (signature). Republican. Presbyterian.

STOREY, BOBBY EUGENE, JR., electrical engineer, engineering consultant; b. Bainbridge, Md., Jan. 26, 1958; s. Bobby E. Sr. and Rebecca J. (Seagraves) S.; m. Lynn M. Miller, May 24, 1976 (div. June 1988); 1 child, Christopher David; m. Mary H. Freeman, Feb. 14, 1992. AA in Math., Gordon Jr. Coll., 1986; BS in Applied Physics, Ga. Inst. Tech., 1988, M in Applied Physics, 1989. Engr. instrumentation and controls Va. Power Co., Mineral, 1982-85; engr. electro optics GEC Avionics, Norcross, Ga., 1988; v.p. EnerSci Inc., Norcross, 1989-94; project engr. LXE, Inc., Norcross, 1988-94; pres. E & H Enterprises, Inc., Duluth, Ga., 1994-96; sr. program mgr. Sci. Atlanta, Inc., Norcross, Ga., 1995—. With USN, 1976-82. Mem. Internat. Orgn. Electrical and Electronic Engrs. Republican. Home: 2820 Bluebird Cir Duluth GA 30136-3908 Office: Sci Atlanta Inc 4386 Park Dr Norcross GA 30092

STOREY, JOANN, lawyer; b. Poughkeepsie, N.Y., Apr. 30, 1951; d. Neil George and Virginia Elizabeth (Spengler) MaGee; m. Boude Erwin Storey II, May 15, 1976; children: Matthew David, Mark Andrew. BS in Mgmt., Jacksonville U., Fla., 1973; JD summa cum laude, South Tex. Coll. Law, Houston, 1980. Bar: Tex. 1980, U.S. Dist. ct. (so. dist.) Tex. Assoc. Crain, Caton, James & Womble, Houston, 1980-84, Storey & Storey, Houston, 1984-85, Crain, Caton, James & Womble, Houston, 1985-87; mem. McFall & Sartwelle (formerly Cook, Davis & McFall), Houston, 1987-90; of counsel Womble & Spain, Houston, 1990—. Contbg. author: Texas Appellate Practice Manual, 1993. Mem. ABA, Bd. Cert.-Civil Appellate Law, Tex. Bd. Legal Specialization, Tex. Bar Assn., Houston Bar Assn. (chmn. appellate practice sect. 1990-91). Republican. Presbyterian. Home: 1327 Trace Dr Houston TX 77077-2213 Office: Womble & Spain 2500 Two Houston Ctr Houston TX 77010

STOREY, ROBERT C., financial planner; b. Detroit, Nov. 9, 1930; s. Clifton L. and Jane (Ormsby) S.; children: Michael, Robert Jr., Diane, Frank; m. Stephanie Trombley, Oct. 18, 1975. Student, Dearborn (Mich.) Jr. Coll., 1949-50, Wayne State U., 1950-51. Mgr. br. U.S. Leasing, Detroit, 1960-61; regional v.p. Equilease Corp., Detroit, 1962-69; founder, pres. Master Lease Corp., Detroit, 1969-83, Capital Resource Mgmt., Columbia, S.C., 1986-90, Network Leasing Sys. Am., Columbia, 1990—; dir., v.p., founder Long Creek Equestrian Ctr., Blythewood, S.C., 1983—. Contbr. articles to profl. jours. Mem. Equipment Leasing Assn. (dir., v.p. 1982-83), Columbia Country Club. Methodist. Office: Network Leasing Sys Am Inc 3031 Scotsman Dr Columbia SC 29223

STORKE, DWIGHT CLIFTON, JR., government official; b. Fredericksburg, Va., Sept. 6, 1939; s. Dwight Clifton and Shirley Williams (King) S.; m. Sylvia Hitch Clark, Oct. 25, 1963; children: Theresa Storke Marshall, David Wallace, John Benjamin. BS, Richmond Profl. Inst., 1962; MEd, Va. Commonwealth U., 1973; PhD with honor, Internat. Sem., Plymouth, Fla., 1990. Instr. Dept. Navy, Dahlgren, Va., 1963-71; interpreter Nat. Park Svc., Washington's Birthplace, Va., 1971-74, park ranger, 1974-87, instr., 1984-86; supt. Nat. Park Svc., Richmond, Va., 1987-89, Washington's Birthplace, 1989—; fed. firearms instr. Nat. Park Svc., Va., 1980—; with Mid-Atlantic Lab., King George, Va.; adj. instr. Nat. Park Svc. Tng. Acad., Grand Canyon, Ariz., 1972-75; mem. pers. mgmt. rev. bd. Nat. Park Svc., Phila., 1993—. Author: Communication Skills, 1975. Facility and program facilitator DAR, Westmoreland, Va., 1980—; capt. Va. State Guard, Fredericksburg, 1985—; dir. Shenandoah Valley Civil War Task Force, Va., 1993. Recipient Interpreter of Yr. award Mid-Atlantic region Nat. Park Svc., 1981, 82, Superior Performance award, 1986, Supt. of Yr. award Mid-Atlantic region, 1993, Meritorious Svc. award Dept. Interior, 1993. Mem. Va. Assn. Mus., No. Neck Va. Hist. Soc., Masons (master), Kappa Delta Pi. Baptist. Office: Mid-Atlantic Lab 14294 Big Timber Rd King George VA 22485

STORRS, BRUCE BRYSON, pediatric neurosurgeon; b. Syracuse, N.Y., Nov. 3, 1946; s. Bruce Dixson and Anna Margery (Bryson) S.; m. Kathleen Carrie Wiemolo, Sept. 12, 1962; children: Anna, Alison. BA, U. N.Mex., 1968, MD, 1972. Diplomate Am. Bd. Neurology. Resident in surgery Kaiser Hosp., Oakland, Calif., 1972-73, U. N.M., Albuquerque, 1973-74; resident in neurosurgery U. Utah, Salt Lake City, 1976-80; resident Hosp. for Sick Children, Toronto, Ont., Can., 1980-81; asst. prof. surgery and pediat. U. Utah, Salt Lake City, 1981-86, Northwestern U., Chgo., 1986-90; neurosurgeon Childrens Meml., Chgo., 1990; prof. surgery and pediat. Med. U. S.C., Charleston, 1990—; safety and performance com. NIH. Mem. editl. bd. Pediat. Neurosurgery, 1994—. Fellow ACS, Am. Acad. Pediat.; mem. Am. Soc. Pediat. Neurosurgeons (sec. 1996—), Am. Assn. Neurol. Surgeons. Office: Children's Hosp N M 2211 Lomas Blvd Albuquerque NM 87103

STORY, GARY, business executive; b. 1955. Grad., U. Mo., 1977. With Six Flags Corp., St. Louis, 1972-81; gen. gmr. Diversions dell Rein, Mex., 1981-83, Ulna Park, Sydney, Australia, 1983-84; pres., COO Premier Parks, Inc., Oklahoma City, Okla., 1984—. Office: Premier Parks Inc 11501 NE Expwy St Oklahoma City OK 73131

STORY, JAMES EDDLEMAN, lawyer; b. Calvert City, Ky., June 7, 1928; s. William Arthur and Estella (Harper) S.; m. Barbara Owens, Oct. 11, 1953; children: Paul, Margaret, Virginia Lee, Sara Jane, Betty Ann, James Arthur. BS, Murray State Coll., 1952; JD, U. Louisville, 1958. Bar: Ky. 1958. Tchr. Jefferson County Bd. Edn., Louisville, 1954-58; assoc. prof. U. Ky. C.C., Paducah, 1958-64; county atty. Lyon County, Eddyville, Ky., 1962-74; pub. defender Lyon County, Princeton, Ky., 1974-82; pvt. practive Eddyville, 1974—; atty. Lake Barkley Project, U.S. Army Corp Engrs., Cadiz, Ky., 1960-62. With U.S. Army, 1946-48. Mem. ATLA, Ky. Trial Lawyers Assn., Ky. Assn. Criminal Def. Lawyers, Ky. Bar Assn., Sierra Club, Wilderness Club, Kentuckians for the Commonwealth, Am. Legion, Lions. Office: PO Box 216 Eddyville KY 42038-0216

STORZ, JOHANNES, veterinary microbiologist, educator; b. Hardt, Germany, Apr. 29, 1931; came to U.S., 1958; s. Johannes and Theresia (Klausmann) S.; m. Hannelore Roeber, Aug. 8, 1959; children: Gisela Therese, J. Peter K., Heidi Ella. DMV, Vet. Coll., Hannover, Germany, 1958; PhD, U. Calif., Davis, 1961; Dr.honoris causae, U. Zurich, Switzerland, 1994. Diplomate Am. Coll. Vet. Microbiologists. Rsch. asst. Fed. Rsch. Ctr. Virology, Tubingen, Germany, 1957-58; lectr. U. Calif., Davis, 1958-61; asst. prof. vet. sci. Utah State U., Logan, 1961-63, assoc. prof., 1963-65; assoc. prof. vet. microbiology Colo. State U., Ft. Collins, 1965-67, prof., 1967-82; prof. and dept. head La. State U., Baton Rouge, 1982—; vis. prof. virology Justus Liebig U., Giessen, Germany, 1978-79, 90; cons. WHO, Geneva, Switzerland, 1970; pres. Workshop Human and Animal Chlamydial Infections, Buenos Aires, 1994. Author: Chlamydia and Chlamydia Ind. Disease, 1971. Mem. Internat. Rels. Commn., Baton Rouge, 1989-94; chmn. European Exhibits, Internat. Heritage Celebration, Baton Rouge, 1994. Recipient Norden Tchg. award Colo. State U., 1978, A.C. Clark Rsch. award, 1978, Rsch. award Am. Vet. Med. Assn., 1983, Svc. award Gamma Sigma Delta, Alexander Von Humboldt prize, 1978. Mem. Am. Soc. Microbiology (pres. south cen. br. 1994-96), Faculty Club. Republican. Roman Catholic. Home: 2942 Rene Beauregard Baton Rouge LA 70820 Office: La State Univ Sch Vet Medicine S Stadium Rd Baton Rouge LA 70803

STOUT, GARY, company executive. Pres. Gannett Offset. Office: Gannett Offset 6883 Commercial Dr Springfield VA 22159*

STOUT, JANIS PITTS, English language educator; b. Ft. Worth, May 4, 1939; d. Kenneth C. and Helean B. (Minshew) Pitts; m. Bob J. Stout, Aug. 27, 1956 (div. Aug., 1981); children: Douglas C., Alan K., Richard K., Steven C.; m. Loren D. Lutes, May 15, 1982; stepchildren: L. Daniel, David J., Laura Lutes Gomez, Rebekah Lutes Thomas. BA, Lamar St. U., 1966, MA, 1968; PhD, Rice U., 1973. Dir. grad. programs Rice U., Houston, 1977-1987; assoc. dean liberal arts Tex. A&M U, Coll. Station, 1987-94; English prof. Tex. A&M U, Coll. Station, 1987—, 1987—. Author: (novels) A Family Likeness, 1982, Eighteen Holes, 1984, Home Truth, 1992; (nonfiction) Sodoms In Eden: The City in American Fiction Before the Civil War, 1976,The Journey Narrative in American Literature: Patterns and Departures, 1983, Strategies of Reticence: Silence and Meaning in the Works of Jane Austen, Willa Cather, Katherine Anne Porter, and Joan Didion, 1990, Katherine Anne Porter: A sense of the Times, 1995; contbr. articles to profl. jours. Mem: Modern Lang. Assn, Western Lit. Assn., Soc. for the Study of So. Lit., Katherine Anne Porter Soc. (sec. 1994—), PEN, Phi Kappa Phi. Democrat. Presbyterian. Home: 2512 Twisted Oaks Bryan TX 77802 Office: Tex A & M Univ Dept of English College Station TX 77843-4227

STOUT, JOSEPHINE SINGERMAN, clinical psychologist; b. York, Pa.; d. Abraham and Sophie (Kauffman) Singerman; m. William Harvey Stout, Jan. 13, 1965 (dec. Oct. 1971); 1 child, Wendy Lynn Scher Thompson; m. Charles Robert Freeburg, June 15, 1974; stepchildren: Charles, Jennie, Eric. BA, NYU, 1949; MS, CCNY, 1959; PhD, Yeshiva U., 1966. cert. sch. psychologist, clin. psychologist. Cons. The Lenox Sch., N.Y.C., 1966-69; sr. psychologist Bellevue Hosp., N.Y.C., 1966-69; dir. clin. psychology So. Plains Guidance Ctr., Lubbock, Tex., 1969-70; cons. Lubbock Ind. Sch. Dist., 1970-75; dir. eating disorders program Univ. Med. Ctr., Lubbock, 1987-89; pvt. practice psychology N.Y.C., 1966-69, Lubbock, 1969—; adj. assoc. prof. Tex. Tech. U. Health Scis. Ctr., Lubbock. Mem. APA, Tex. Psychol. Assn., South Plains Assn. Psychologists. Office: 1901 University Ave Ste 503A Lubbock TX 79410-1556

STOUT, RICHARD ALAN, museum director; b. Lenoir City, Tenn., 1941; m. Linda Ellen Canipe; 1 child, Shane. Grad., Carson-Newman Coll., 1963; postgrad., N.C. State U., 1964. Former asst. dir. Schiele Mus., Gastonia, N.C., 1965-74, now exec. dir., from 1974; one of 17 dept. heads City of Gastonia; mem. faculty South Point Sr. High Sch., Belmont, N.C., 1963-64; former instr. art Dept. Adult and Continuing Edn. Gaston Coll. in Dallas, N.C.; bd. dirs. N.C. Museums Council, Gaston County Mus. Art and History, United Arts and Scis. Council of Gaston County. Numerous one-man shows throughout U.S.; contbr. over 700 articles on natural history to profl. jours. Cultural advisor Gaston County C. of C.; mem. Mayor's Blue Task Force; mem. adv. council and found. Look Up Gaston. Recipient Silver Cup for Notable Achievement in Mus. Profession N.C. Museums Council, 1978, also named Mus. Dir. of Yr., 1978, Catlin Peace Pipe award Am. Indian Lore Assn., Confederation of Adopted Indians of Am., 1981, Medal of Honor for Professionalism Carson-Newman Coll. Pres.'s Adv. Council and Bd. Alumni, 1985; recipient numerous Commendations Gastonia City Council, Gaston County C. of C., Bd. dirs. Schiele Mus. Mem. Watercolor Soc. of N.C. (past v.p.), Southern Watercolor Soc. (charter mem.). Office: Schiele Mus Natural History and Planetarium Inc PO Box 953 Gastonia NC 28053-0953

STOVALL, GERALD THOMAS, religious organization administrator; b. Dallas, Mar. 4, 1940; s. James Roy and Gladys Wilton (Moore) S.; m. Marcia Louise Hearn, May 27, 1967; children: Traci Lynn, Amy Reneé, Keith Roy. BS in Edn., U. North Tex., 1964; MRE, Southwestern Bapt. Theol. Sem., 1966. Min. of music Worth St. Bapt. Ch., Dallas, 1960-64; min. music and edn. Inglewood Bapt. Ch., Grand Prairie, Tex., 1964-67, Siloam Bapt. Ch., Marion, Ala., 1967-69; min. of youth N. Dallas Bapt. Ch., 1969-71; min. of music Emmanuel Bapt. Ch., Lafayette, La., 1971-75; dir. Bapt. Student Ctr. Nicholls State U., Thibodaux, La., 1975-79, U. New Orleans, 1979—; adj. instr. New Orleans Bapt. Theol. Sem.; bd. dirs. Morality in Media, New Orleans, 1989-91, Bapt Assn. Greater New Orleans, 1990-91, Fedn. Chs., New Orleans, 1991—; workshop and conf. leader in student ministry. Mem. Assn. So. Bapt. Campus Ministers, La. Chaplains Assn. (bd. dirs.). Office: Bapt Student Ctr 2222 Lakeshore Dr New Orleans LA 70122-3502

STOVALL, STEVEN AUSTIN, human resources administrator; b. Dallas, June 3, 1969; s. Billy F. and Joan (Holman) S.; m. Joy Littleton, Aug. 18, 1987. BBA, East Tex. State U., 1990, MBA, 1991. Pres. Stovall Group, Garland, Tex., 1990-96; human resources mgr. Oakwood Homes, Hillsboro, Tex., 1996—; bus. cons. various profl. orgns., Garland, 1990—. Author: American Business Terms Dictionary, 1994; editor newsletter Customer Svc. Report, 1991-96; contbr. articles to mags. and profl. jours., 1991—. Mem. Garland Postal Adv. Com., 1994; mem. adv. com. Richland Coll., Dallas, 1993. Mem. Soc. for Human Resources Mgmt. (cert. profl. in human resources), Nat. Forensic League (life), Tex. Restaurant Assn., Dallas Restaurant Assn. (mem. edn. com.), Beta Gamma Sigma (life), Alpha Chi (life). Methodist. Office: Oakwood Homes 1020 Industrial Loop Hillsboro TX 76645

STOVER, BRIAN ALLAN, advertising executive, marketing consultant; b. Syracuse, N.Y., Aug. 12, 1947; s. David Reuben and Helen Rose (Smith) S.; m. Fredda Ann Berkowitz, Oct. 12, 1980; children: Pamela Lynn, Amy Beth. BS in Mktg. and Advt., Syracuse U., 1968. Advt. producer Zayre Corp., Framingham, Mass., 1969-73; v.p. accounts Recruitment Advt. Inc., Boston, 1973-74; dir. advt. Superior Distbg. Co. Inc., Boston, 1974-76; pres. BGM Mktg., Inc., Syracuse, 1976-82, Oakmont Advt., Inc., Fayetteville, N.Y., 1982-87; pres., CEO Invincible Roofing Systems, Inc., Largo, Fla., 1987—; pres. Clark/Kent Cons., Inc., 1991—, Pub. Direct Svcs., Inc., 1992—, Invincible Mktg. Group, Seminole, Fla.; cons. GE, Syracuse, 1968, Contemporary Talent, Nashville, 1984—, Dread Beat Records, Nashville; advt. instr. Cen. Cities Bus. Inst., 1986; mktg. instr. Bd. Continuing Edn. Svcs., 1987. Author handbook Guide for Retail Advertising, 1974. Recipient Drummer award Cahners Pub. Co., 1975, 3 Telly awards, 1987, 5 Silver Microphone awards, 1987, 7 Merit awards Syracuse Ad Club, 1987. Mem. Constrn. Fin. Mgrs. Assn. (Tampa Bay chpt.), Seminole Lake Country Club. Jewish.

STOVER, CURTIS SYLVESTER, retired vocational school educator; b. Glenmore, Ohio, Dec. 18, 1933; s. Paul R. and Sarah J. (Jones) S.; m. Betty J. Christian, Oct. 3, 1953; children: Anita, Brenda, Linda, Curtis, Brian, Russell. BS, So. Ill. U., 1976; MS, Cen. State U., Edmond, Okla., 1989. Cert. secondary and vocat. tchr. Ill. Vocat. Ctr. Indsl. maintenance instr. Belleville Area Coll., Granite City, Ill., 1976-83; elec., mechanical, automated indsl. systems instr. Moore-Norman Area Votech Sch., Norman, Okla., 1983—; tng. cons. Nat. Steel Co., Granite City Steel Co., 1976-83. Author: Life & Other Illusions, 1995. Mem. Am. Vocat. Assn., Okla. Vocat. Assn., Nat. Assn. Trade and Indsl. Instrs. (sec-treas. 1989-92), Fluid Power Soc. Internat. (cert. fluid power mechanic instr., hydraulic technician instr., pneumatic technician instr.), Okla. Trade and Indsl. Assn. (chmn. indsl. maintenance tech. trade group), Vocat. Indsl. Clubs Am. (advisor, mem. tech. com. robotics workcell 1989-90), Masons, Aniad Shrine, Iota Lambda Sigma. Home: 808 N Stout Cir Moore OK 73170-1118 Office: Moore-Norman Votech Sch 4701 12th Ave NW Norman OK 73069-8308

STOVER, LYNN MARIE, nurse educator; b. Kittanning, Pa., June 23, 1967; d. Randolph John and Joan Patricia (Hillgrove) S. BSN, U. Ala., Birmingham, 1989, MSN, 1993, postgrad., 1995—. RN cert. pediatric nurse, ANCC. Nursing asst. U. Ala. Hosp., Birmingham, 1988-89; staff nurse III Children's Hosp. of Ala., Birmingham, 1989-93; grad. teaching asst. U. Ala., Birmingham, 1991-93; instr. nursing Capstone Coll. Nursing U. Ala., Tuscaloosa, 1993—; comty. infant care instr. DCH Regional Med. Ctr., Tuscaloosa, 1994—; faculty advisor U. Ala. Assn. Nursing Students, Tuscaloosa, 1994—; camp nurse Camp Winnataska, Pell City, Ala., 1992—; unit-level staff nurse orientation chmn. Children's Hosp. Ala., Birmingham, 1991-93. Contbr. articles to nursing jours. instr. religious edn. St. Francis Cath. Ch., Tuscaloosa, 1994—; vol. Crestwood Hosp., Huntsville, Ala., 1981-85, ARC, Huntsville and Birmingham, 1981-88; leader Girl Scouts Am., Birmingham, 1990-91. Recipient Best Student Paper award Ala. Acad. Sci., 1993; faculty summer rsch. grantee U. Ala., 1994. Mem. ANA, Nat. League Nursing (advocacy mem.), Nat. Student Nurse's Assn. (sustaining mem.), Ala. State Nurse's Assn. (treas. dist. III 1994-96, Outstanding New Mem. 1991), Sigma Theta Tau (Epsilon Omega chpt., publicity chmn., newsletter editor 1994—), Omicron Delta Kappa. Republican. Roman Catholic. Home: 4709 Cypress Creek Ave E # 106 Tuscaloosa AL 35405-4441 Office: U Ala Box 870358 Tuscaloosa AL 35487

STOW, WESTON LOGHRY, shipping company executive; b. Westover, Md., June 22, 1928; s. Phillip John and Villa Loghry (Emmett) S.; m. Jean Louise Bodio, Nov. 1952 (div. Jan. 1966); children: Weston James, Robert Louis. BS in Sociology, U. Md., 1972. Lic. master of oceans USCG; master mariner. Commd. lt. jr. grade USN, 1958, advanced through grades to comdr., 1970, ret., 1979; marine mgr. Marcona Ocean Industries, Ft. Lauderdale, Fla., 1979-83; capt. oceanographic ship Scripps Inst. Oceanography, San Diego, 1983; dir. marine ops. Clipper Cruise Line, St. Louis, 1983-85; pres. Stow Marine Svcs., Inc., Ft. Lauderdale, 1985-91, Sea Power Internat., Inc., Crystal River, Fla., 1991-94; cons., spl. asst. to chmn. Consolidated Minerals, Inc., Leesburg, Fla., 1994-95; ops. mgr. Sargeant Marine, Inc., Coral Springs, Fla., 1995—; cons., expert witness U.S. Fed. Dist. Ct. (so. dist.) Fla., West Palm Beach, Ft. Lauderdale, 1979—; mem. Calif. Maritime Agy. Continuing Adult Edn. Bd., U. Calif., Vallejo, 1976-79. Author: Guide to Excellence in Cruise Line Training, 1985. Vice chmn. Rep. Exec. Com., Citrus County, Fla., 1988-90; pres. North Suncoast Rep. Club, Citrus County, 1988-90; v.p. Woods n Waters Homeowners Assn., Crystal River, 1986-90; sr. warden St. Anne's Episs. Ch., Crystal River, 1988-90. Decorated Navy Commendation medals (2); recipient Meritorious Svc. medals (2) Pres. of U.S., 1972, 79. Mem. VFW (life), Ret. Officers Assn. (life), Masons (master mason, 32 degree), Shriner. Home: 9655 NW 26 Ct Coral Springs FL 33065 Office: Sargeant Marine Inc 3111 University Dr #1000 Coral Springs FL 33065

STOWE, CHARLES ROBINSON PEECHER, management consultant, educator, lawyer; b. Seattle, July 18, 1949; s. David Beecher and Edith Beecher (Andrade) S.; m. Laura Everett, Mar. 9, 1985. BA, Vanderbilt U., 1971; MBA, U. Dallas, 1975; JD, U. Houston, 1982, U. Warsaw; AbD, Warsaw U., Poland; Bar: Tex. 1982, U.S. Dist. Ct. (so. dist.) Tex., 1984, U.S. Tax Ct., 1984. Account exec. Engleman Co., pub. rels. and advt., Dallas, 1974-75; instr. Richland Coll., Dallas, spring 1976; acct. Arthur Andersen & Co., Dallas, 1976-78; part-time pub. rels. cons.; dir. Productive Capital Corp.; gen. ptnr. Productive Capital Assocs., 1975-81; pres. Stowe & Co., mgmt. cons., Dallas, 1978—; from asst. to assoc. prof. dept. gen. bus. and fin. Coll. Bus. Adminstrn., Sam Houston State U., 1982—, dir. Office Free Enterprise and Entrepreneurship, 1982—; adminstrv. intern, asst. to pres., spring 1985; summer fellow Tex. Coordinating Bd., 1988. Trustee, Stowe-Day Found., 1979-90; mem. nat. adv. bd. Young Am.'s Found., 1979—; vol. faculty State Bar Tex. Profl. Devl. Program, 1988—; vol., mediator Dispute Resolution Ctr. Montgomery County; mediator so. dist. U.S. Dist. Ct. Tex. 1993; team chief, U.S. Milit. liason Republic of Poland, 1994 . With USNR, 1971-74; capt. Res. Recipient Freedoms Found. award, 1969, Navy Achievement medal, 1973, Gold Star, 1985, Def. Meritorious Svc. medal, 1996, Navy Meritorious Svc. award, 1996; Price-Babson fellow Entrepreneurship Symposium, 1991. Mem. ABA, Am. Arbitration Assn., State Bar Tex. (vol. faculty profl. devel. program 1988-90, vice chair profl. efficiency and econ. rsch. com. 1993, chair law offcie mgmt. com. 1993-94), Walker County Bar Assn. (pres. 1987-88), Pub. Rels. Soc. Am., Tex. Assn. Realtors, U.S. Navy League, Naval Res. Assn., Res. Officers Assn., Sigma Iota Epsilon. Club: Dallas Vanderbilt (pres. 1977-78). Author: Bankruptcy I Micro-Mash Inc., 1989, rev. edit. 1995; co-author CPA review; editor Houston Jour. Internat. Law, 1981-82; contbr. articles to profl. jours. Office: PO Box 2144 Huntsville TX 77341-2144

STOWELL, JOHN CHARLES, chemistry educator; b. Passaic, N.J., Sept. 10, 1938; s. Charles and Daisy Clara (Hindle) S.; m. Jane Beverly Myers, Nov. 27, 1964 (div. 1985); children—Sandra, Alan. BS in Chemistry, Rutgers U., 1960; PhD in Chemistry, MIT, 1964. Rsch. specialist Minn. Mining and Mfg. Co., St. Paul, 1964-69; NIH postdoctoral fellow Ohio State U., Columbus, 1969-70; prof. chemistry U. New Orleans, 1970—. Author: Carbanions in Organic Synthesis, 1979, Intermediate Organic Chemistry, 2d edit., 1994. Contbr. articles to profl. jours. V.p. Grace Luth. Ch., New Orleans, 1984-88; mem. Symphony Chorus New Orleans, 1988-92. Mem. Am. Chem. Soc. Avocations: canoeing, sailing, microscopy, cooking, photography, art. Office: U New Orleans Dept Chemistry New Orleans LA 70148

STOWELL, PENELOPE MARY, nursing administrator, community health nurse; b. Warsaw, N.Y., Aug. 17, 1941; d. Charles Edward and Leona Cecelia (Hawkins) Powers; children: Scott Edward Stowell, Holly Jean Stowell. Diploma in nursing, U. Rochester, 1962; BSN, Fla. So. Coll. Coord. community edn. Mid Fla. Home Health Svcs., Inc., Winter Haven, 1989-90; asst. dir. nursing Meridian Nursing Ctr., Lakeland, Fla., 1990-94, dir. nursing, 1995-96; dir. nursing Lakeland (Fla.) Hills Ctr., 1996—.

STOY, JOSEPH FRANK, chemical engineer, consultant; b. Clifton, N.J., Apr. 10, 1926; s. Joseph and Mary (Sudol) S.; m. Mayfa Reep, June 1, 1952; children: Joseph III, Joanne, Jerrold. BSChemE, Washington U., 1950; postgrad., NYU, U. Houston, U. Cin., 1950-56. Lic. profl. engr. N.Y., N.J., La. Va. Tex., Utah, Ill., Wis., Ohio, Kans. With tech. sales dept. Belco Indsl. Co., Paterson, N.J., 1950-53; project engr. Chem. & Indsl., Cin., 1953-57; sr. project engr. Foster Wheeler, Livingston, N.J., 1957-64; project mgr. M.W. Kellogg, N.Y.C., 1964-69; asst. mgr. constrn. Chem. Constrn., N.Y.C., 1969-74; project dir. C.E. Lummus, The Hague, The Netherlands, 1974-81; dir. projects Petrochem. Industries, Kuwait, 1981-87. Contbr. (book) Project Management: Reference for Professionals, 1989. Mem. AIChE, Tau Beta Pi, Sigma Xi, Axe. Home: 6408 Dougherty Dr Charlotte NC 28213

STRADER, MELINDA ANN AMASON, nursing consultant; b. Amarillo, Tex., Apr. 13, 1955; d. Robert Daniel Amason and MaryLou Ivy Amason Jordan; m. Dan M. Strader, June 12, 1976; children: Aaron, Ashley. Diploma, Meth. Hosp., 1976. RN, Tex.; cert. in audiometric screening, CPR. Staff nurse nursery HCA Med. Ctr., Plano, Tex., 1982-83; pediatrics nurse for pvt. physician Plano, 1983-87; nurse auditor Blue Cross/Blue Shield, Dallas, 1987-90; nurse cons. Genex Svcs. (formerly Gen. Rehab.), Dallas, 1990-95; case mgmt. supr. S.W. divsn. Sullivan Health mgmt., Plano, 1995—, dir. S.W. region. Mem. ICMA, CMSA, Nat. Assn. Rehab. Profls. in Pvt. Sector, Tex. Assn. Rehab. Profls. in Pvt. Sector, Tex. Nurses Assn. Office: Sullivan Health Mgmt 5757 Alpha #615 Dallas TX 75240

STRADLEY, WILLIAM JACKSON, lawyer; b. Houston, Oct. 27, 1939; s. Samuel H. and Mary Stradley; m. Emmalee H. Stradley, Apr. 16, 1960; children—Lisa D., William M. B.S., U. Houston, 1964; J.D., 1967. Bar: Tex. 1967, U.S. Dist. Ct. (so. dist.) Tex. 1967, U.S. Ct. Appeals (5th cir.)1967, U.S. Supreme Ct. 1970. Cert. Civil Trial Law, Personal Injury Trial Law Tex. Bd. of Legal Specialization. of coun. Mithoff & Jacks, L.L.P. mem. faculty trial advocacy course Law Sch. U. Houston, 1982. Pres., Police Adv. Com. 1981-84, sec., 1980-81; bd. dirs. Houston Council Human Relations, 1982-84; mem. adminstrv. bd. St. Luke's United Meth. Ch.; co-chair fed. judiciary appointments com. State Bar Tex., 1991, mem. continuing legal edn. com., 1991, adminstrn. justice com., spl. com. professionalsm. Recipient Pub. Service award Houston Police Dept., 1984. Mem. Houston Bar Found. (charter), Am. Bd. Trial Advocates (pres., treas. 1980-82, v.p. 1983-84 Houston), State Bar of Tex. (chmn. grievance com.), Supreme Ct. Tex. (mem. profl. ethics com. 1984-94), Houston Trial Lawyers Assn. (bd. dirs. 1980-82, v.p. 1983-84, pres. 1985-86), Houston Bar Assn. (chmn. tort and compensation sect. 1980-81, chmn. continuing legal edn. com., com. on professionalism), Tex. Trial Lawyers Assn. (dir. emeritus, chmn. ethics com., by-laws com.), Assn. Trial Lawyers Am., Houston Club, Met. Racquet Club. Home: 64 E Broad Oaks Dr Houston TX 77056-1202 Office: 3450 One Allen Ctr Houston TX 77002

STRADLEY, WILLIAM LAMAR, agricultural publisher; b. Borger, Tex., Oct. 20, 1940; s. Forrest W. and Hettie J. (Nolan) S.; m. Jeanette Bell, Apr. 20, 1962; children: William Bradford II, Page Lamar. BJ, U. Tex., 1964; postgrad. Mktg. Mgmt., Northwestern U., 1973. Dir pub. info. Abilene (Tex.) Christian Coll., 1964-65; account supr. Fidelity Enterprises, Abilene, Dallas, 1965-67; group supr. Ford Tractor/Meldrum & Fewsmith, Detroit, 1967-71; account supr. Eli Lilly/Gardner Advt., St Louis, 1971; advt. mgr. agrl. and indsl. div. Internat. Harvester, Chgo., 1972-74; communications dir. Hesston (Kans.) Corp., 1974-76; membership dir. Agrl. Coun. Am., Washington, 1976-77; mktg. v.p. Farmer-Stockman Pub., Dallas, 1978; regional mgr. and trade rels. dir. Progressive Farmer, Memphis and Dallas, 1979-88, gen. mgr. mktg. svcs. div., 1988—, dir. advt., 1993—. Active in Christian activities. Mem. Nat. Agri-Mktg. Assn. (officer, dir. various chpts.), Agr. Coun. Am. (bd. dirs. 1972-74). Republican. Home: 1409 Angelina Bend Dr Denton TX 76205-8106 Office: Progressive Farmer 4809 Cole Ave Ste 300 Dallas TX 75205-3581

STRAHAN, HOWARD LAWSON, oil field exploration executive, retired; b. Lumberton, Miss., May 5, 1926; s. Carl Edward and Addye Mary (Lawson) S.; m. Frankie Sessums, Mar. 11, 1944 div. July 1986); children: Leslie Dale, Frankie Linda; m. Yanneth Rodriguez Zea, Aug. 6, 1987; children: Jamie Paola, Maria Camila. Student, La. State U., 1946-48. Owner Bengal Oil Corp., Baton Rouge, 1951-70; co-owner Golden Petroleum Corp., Dallas, 1977-81; owner Strahan Oil Field Cons., Mt. Sterling, Ill., 1982-84; ret., 1985; owner Tai-Pan Jewel's S.A., Baton Rouge, 1991—; v.p., reunion chmn. 2nd Marine Divsn. Assn., 1953. Author: Of Time's When Men Were Men, 1992. Charter mem. Rep. Nat. Task Force, 1982. With USMC, 1943-46. Recipient Presdl. Unit citations Pres. Roosevelt, Saipan-Okinawa, 1944-45. Fellow VFW. Baptist. Home: # 160 8508 Greenwell Spring Rd Baton Rouge LA 70814-2439

STRAHAN, JIMMIE ROSE, mathematics educator; b. Slate Springs, Miss., June 2, 1942; d. William Vance and Minnie Lee (Bridges) Earnest; m. Richard Denman Strahan, May 30, 1970. AA, Hinds Community Coll., 1961; BS, Miss. Coll., 1963; MCS, U. Miss., Oxford, 1968; EdD, U. Fla., 1980. Tchr. math. Gulfport (Miss.) High Sch., 1963-66, Murrah High Sch., Jackson, Miss., 1966-68; instr. Delta State U., Cleveland, Miss., 1968-75, asst. prof., 1975-79, asst. prof., acting chair, 1979-80, assoc. prof., chair dept., 1980-83, prof., chmn. dept., 1983—; author curriculum Dept. Edn. Miss., 1988; dir. Delta Math. Project; speaker Nat. Coun. Tchrs. Math., 1974, 76, 77, 79, 82, 86, 87, 91, 95, conv. chmn., 1993. Author (manual) Miss. Assn. Colls. Tchr. Edn., 1988. Democrat. Baptist. Home: 1611 Bellavista Rd Cleveland MS 38732-2910 Office: Delta State U PO Box 3242 Cleveland MS 38733

STRAIN, JAMES ROBERT, agricultural economist; b. Greencastle, Ind., Feb. 20, 1925; s. James Franklin and Gladys Ellen (Kersey) S.; m. Carroll Joyce Bagshaw, Jan. 25, 1953; children: Patricia Jean Strain Foster, Sharon Kay Strain Womack. BS in Dairy Mfg., Purdue U., 1950, MS in Agrl. Mktg., 1955; PhD in Agrl. Mktg., Oreg. State U., 1957. Asst. prof., ext. economist Iowa State U., Ames, 1957-62, assoc. prof., ext. economist, 1962-65, prof., ext. economist, 1965-76; prof., ext. economist U. Fla., Gainesville, 1976-90, prof. emeritus, 1990—; mem. U.S. Sec. of Agr. Fed. Order Study Com., Washington, 1960-62; sec. Midwest Milk Mktg. Conf., Ames, 1963, 72; chmn. Dairy Mktg. Adv. Com., 1964-70; mem. Milk Industry Found. Econ. & Mktg. Panel, Washington, 1968; chmn. Iowa Coop. Leadership Devel. Com., Ames, 1968-76; mem. Nat. Milk Producers Fedn. Class I Price Policy Com., Washington, 1969; mem. Dairy Market Study Com., 1969-70; mem. United Dairy Industry Assn. Adv. Com., Chgo., 1970-72; chmn. Standby Pool Com., 1972-73; conf. coord. Am. Inst. Coop., 1972. Co-author: Marketing Farm Products, 1976; contbr. articles to profl. jours. Baritone player Gainesville Comty. Band, 1978—, Santa Fe Brass Ensemble, 1994—; chmn. host com. Ann. Conv. Assn. Concert Bands, 1994-95. Recipient Spl. award for exceptional svc. to dairy industry Producers Creamery Co., Springfield, Mo., 1965, Disting. Svcs. award Assoc. Milk Producers, Inc., San Antonio, 1970, award for outstanding contbn. to coop. edn. Iowa Inst. Coop., Ames, 1972, Meritorious Svc. award Fla. Foliage Found., Apopka, 1987, Bus. and Arts award hon. mention Vol. Cmty. Svcs., 1995. Mem. Am. Assn. Agrl. Economists, Fla. Assn. County Agrl. Agts., Fla. Nurserymen and Growers Assn. (hon. Most Valuable Industry Person award 1989), Assn. Concert Bands, U. Fla. Athenaeum Club (sec. 1992, v.p. 1993, pres. 1994), Ext. Honor Soc., Alpha Zeta, Gamma Sigma Delta. Mem. Christian Ch. Home: 6001 NW 39th Ave Gainesville FL 32606-5862 Office: U Fla 1157 Mccarty Hall Gainesville FL 32611

STRAIN BYNUM, ROBIN MICHELLE, academic administrator; b. Hartselle, Ala., Aug. 21, 1957; d. W.L. and Mendy L. (McGregor) Strain; m. Kenneth Howard Bynum, Mar. 25, 1995; children: Wendy Dionne, Kayotris Kenyatta. BS, Tuskegee U., 1978, MEd, 1982. Tchr. Dothan (Ala.) City Sch. Sys., 1979-93; program devel. specialist Southeast Ala. Regional Insvc. Ctr Troy State U., 1993—; extended day coord. Cloverdale Elem. Sch., Dothan, 1987-93, asst. prin., 1988-93; ednl. cons. COMP Peabody Coll., Nashville, 1994—, State of Ala. Dept. Edn., Montgomery, 1994—, Peace Edn., Miami, 1995—, ASCD, Aurora, Colo., 1996. Mem. ASCD, Nat. Assn. Tchrs. of English, Nat. Staff Devel. Coun., Alpha Kappa Mu, Kappa Delta Pi, Phi Delta Kappa, Sigma Gamma Rho. Baptist. Office: Troy State U SE Ala Regional Insvc Ctr Continuing Edn Ctr Troy AL 36802

STRAIT, VIOLA EDWINA WASHINGTON, librarian; b. El Paso, Tex., Aug. 29, 1925; d. Leroy Wentworth and Viola Edwina (Wright) Washington; m. Freeman Adams, Mar. 6, 1943; 1 child, Norma Jean (Mrs. Louis Lee James); m. Clifford Moody, Jan. 8, 1950; 1 child, Viola Edwina III (Mrs. Paul M. Cunningham); m. Amos O. Strait, Dec. 9, 1972. Bus. cert., Tillotson Coll., 1946, BA, 1948; MS in Libr. Sci., U. So. Calif., 1954. Substitute tchr. El Paso Pub. Schs., 1948; sec., bookkeeper U.S.O.-YWCA, El Paso, 1948-50; libr. asst. Spl. Svcs. Libr., Ft. Bliss, Tex., 1950-53, libr., 1954-71; equal employment opportunity officer Ft. Bliss, 1971-72; dep. equal employment opportunity officer Long Beach (Calif.) Naval Shipyard, 1972-85; with Temp. Job Mart, Torrance, Calif., 1986-87; substitute tchr. Ysleta Ind. Sch. Dist., 1988-89; profl. libr. Eastwood Hts. Elem. Sch., 1989-90; sec. Shiloh Bapt. Ch., El Paso, 1991-92; br. mgr. El Paso Pub. Libr., 1992—. Sec. Sunday sch. Bapt. Ch., 1956-66, min. music, 1958-72, supr. young adult choir, 1966-72, pres. sr. choir, 1969-71; disc jockey Sta. KELP, El Paso, 1970-72; host radio show Sta. KTEP, U. Tex., El Paso, 1994—. Mem. ALA, Border Region Libr. Assn. (chmn. scholarship com. 1970), NAACP (sec. 1996), Alpha Kappa Alpha. Democrat. Baptist. Home: 1667 Nancy Lopez Ln El Paso TX 79936-5410 Office: El Paso Pub Libr Vets Park Br 5303 Salem Dr El Paso TX 79924-1801

STRAITON, T(HOMAS) HARMON, JR., librarian; b. Selma, Ala., June 28, 1941; s. Thomas Harmon and Marie (Khoeler) S. BS in Ornamental Horticulture, Auburn U., 1963; MLS, U. Ala., Tuscaloosa, 1979. Math. tchr. Tallassee (Ala.) City Schs., 1965-66, math., sci. tchr., 1966-68, head math. and sci. depts., 1968-78; head microforms and documents dept. Auburn (Ala.) U. Librs., 1980—; adj. faculty Grad. Sch. Libr. Svc., U. Ala., 1988, 90, 95, 96—; chmn. Govt. Documents Roundtable, Southeastern Libr. Assn., 1986-88; condr. numerous workshops, seminars, presentations include 1992-93, 96 Notis Users Group meetings. Contbr. numerous articles on microforms to fed. publs. and profl. jours. including The Ala. Librarian, Microform Rev.; pub.: Major Microform Sets Held by Alabama Libraries, 1988, Alabama's Major Microform Collections: The Enlarged and Revised Edition, 1991, Alabama's Major Microform Collections: The Electronic Edition, 1996. Group coord. United Way, 1981-83. Recipient Award of Excellence, Univ. Microfilm Internat., 1994. Mem. ALA (chmn. bylaws com. 1988-89, Govt. Documents Roundtable 1986-88, v.p. 1985-86, exec. coun. 1985-86), Ala. Libr. Assn. (numerous editl. and ednl. coms., rep. 1991—, chmn. handbook com. 1986-90, chmn. awards com. 1995—, bibliographic com. 1993—), Southeastern Libr. Assn. (Ala. rep., exec. bd. dirs., handbook com. 1995—, nominations com. 1995—), Alpha Zeta, Beta Phi Mu (Ala. chpt. Libr. of Yr. 1992), Gamma Sigma Delta, Pi Alpha Sigma. Democrat. Baptist. Home: PO Box 132 Auburn AL 36831-0132 Office: Microforms & Documents Dept Auburn U Librs Auburn AL 36849

STRAKE, GEORGE WILLIAM, JR., oil and gas industry executive; b. Houston, June 10, 1935; s. George William Sr. and Susan Kehoe S.; m. Frances Annette DeWalch, Jan. 10, 1959; children: George W. III, Stephen D., Michele S. Sommerfield, Melanie S. Meeks, Gregory P., Melissa A. BA, U. Notre Dame, 1957; MBA, Harvard U., 1961; LLD (hon.), Houston Bapt. U., 1982. Mgr. oil ops. G.W. Strake Co., Houston, 1961-69, prin., 1969—; founder, chmn. bd., CEO Strake Trading Group, Inc., Houston, 1988—. Sec. of State, Tex., 1979-81; state chmn., nat. com. mem. Rep. Party, Tex., 1983-88; alt. del. Rep. Nat. Conv., 1976, 92, del. 1984, 88; active Task Force on Pub. Edn., Tex., 1989—, Interstate Oil Compact Commn., Tex. Ind. Producers and Royalty Bd.; co-chmn. Houston econ. summit host com. Econ. Summit Industrialized Nations, Houston, 1990; bd. dirs. Boy Scouts of Am., Freedoms Found., Valley Forge, Pa., MacArthur Meml. Found., Norfolk, Va.; pres. Strake Found., 1993—; apptd. adv. coun. Coll. Arts and Scis., U. Notre Dame, 1996—. With USN, 1957-59. Recipient Mayors Proud Ptnrs. award Mayor of the City of Houston, 1990, Fr. John Cavanaugh award U. Notre Dame., 1993; named to Hall of Honor St. Thomas High Sch., 1992. Republican. Roman Catholic. Office: Strake Trading Group Inc 712 Main St Ste 3300 Houston TX 77002-3210

STRALEY, JOHN ADRIAN, urban planner; b. Franklin, Ind., Dec. 11, 1941; s. Mervyn John and Ruth (Mallow) S.; m. Margaret Bartlett Wilder, Dec. 27, 1969; children: Christopher Thomas, Miriam Elizabeth. BA, U. Chgo., 1964; M in City Planning, Ohio State U., 1969. Planner Pitts. Regional Planning Assn., 1969-71; from prin. planner to dir. Cmty. Planning and Devel. Dept., Tuscaloosa, Ala., 1971—; mem. campus master plan com. U. Ala., Tuscaloosa, 1983—. Pres. Univ. Place Sch. PTA, Tuscaloosa, 1979-80; scoutmaster Troop 7 Boy Scouts Am., Tuscaloosa, 1986-90. Mem. Am. Inst. Cert. Planners, Am. Planning Assn. (v.p. 1985-86, treas. 1984-85, editor The Ala. Planner 1981-84). Roman Catholic. Office: Cmty Planning and Devel 2201 Univ Blvd PO Box 2089 Tuscaloosa AL 35403

STRALEY, RUTH A. STEWART, federal agency administrator, small business owner; b. Tanner, W.Va., May 31, 1949; d. Robert Sherwood Sr. and Reta Virginia (Frymier) Stewart; m. Charles Edward Straley, Aug. 17, 1968. BS magna cum laude, U. Md., 1982. Sec. W.Va. U., Morgantown, 1968-70; certification asst. Prince Georges County Bd. Edn., Upper Marlboro, Md., 1970-71; clerical asst. Def. Intelligence Agy., Washington, 1971-72; budget asst. Naval Weather Svc. Command, Washington, 1972-76; budget analyst Navy Recruiting Exhibit Ctr., Washington, 1976-78, Navy Regional Data Automation Command, Washington, 1978-80; hdqrs. budget officer Naval Facilities Engring. Command, Alexandria, Va., 1980-83; fin. mgr. Naval Res. Readiness Command Region 8, Naval Air Sta., Jacksonville, Fla., 1983-93; owner, pres. Horizons Unltd. Planning Svcs., Orange Park, Fla., 1989—; comptr. Naval Pers. Support Activity Europe, Naples, Italy, 1993-94; comptroller U.S. Naval Sta., San Diego, 1994—. Treas. Eagle Bay Homeowners Assn., Orange Park, 1989-93. Named Woman of Yr., Fed. Women's Program, 1983. Mem. NAFE, Am. Soc. Mil. Comptrs. (sec. 1984-89, v.p. 1990-91, 95-96, pres. 1989-90, 91-93), Profl. Housing Mgmt. Assn. Republican. Methodist. Home: 432 C Ave Coronado CA 92118-1823 Office: Horizons Unltd Planning Svc PO Box 181611 Coronado CA 92178-1611

STRAND, MARY RUTH, paralegal assistant; b. Tacoma, Wash., June 3, 1962. BA in Comparative Lit. cum laude, Smith Coll., 1984; MA in German Lit., U. Minn., 1988, PhD, 1995; postgrad., Rollins Coll., 1996. Tchg. asst. in German U. Minn., Mpls., 1986-90, 92-93; prof. German St. Olaf Coll., Northfield, Minn., 1994-95; asst. paralegal So. Staffing, Tampa, Fla., 1996. Keyboard player, female vocalist Prince Band, Mpls., 1994-95, MTV Spl., Mpls., Tampa, 1995-96. Mellon Fund grantee Western European Area Studies Ctr., 1990. Mem. MLA, Am. Assn. Tchrs. German, German Studies Assn., Women in German, Phi Kappa Phi, Phi Beta Kappa.

STRANG, STEPHEN EDWARD, magazine editor, publisher; b. Springfield, Mo., Jan. 31, 1951; s. A. Edward and Amy Alice (Farley) S.; m. Joy Darlene Ferrell, Aug. 19, 1972; children: Cameron Edward, Chandler Stephen. BS in Journalism, U. Fla., Gainesville, 1973; LittD (hon.), Lee Coll., 1995. Reporter Orlando Sentinel Star, Fla., 1973-76; editor Charisma mag. Calvary Assembly, Winter Park, Fla., 1976-81; pres. Strang Comm. Co., Lake Mary, Fla., 1981—; owner Creation House Books, 1986, Christian Retailing mag., 1986. Founding editor Charisma mag., 1975, Ministries Today mag., 1983; founding pub. CharismaLife Learning Resources, 1990, New Man mag., 1994. Mem. steering com. N.Am. Renewal Svcs. Com., 1985—; trustee Internat. Charismatic Bible Ministries, 1986—; pres. Christian Life Missions, 1991—. Recipient First Place award Nat. Writing Championship, William Randolph Hearst Found., 1973, Alumnus of Distinction award U. Fla. Coll. of Journalism and Comm., 1994, Industry of Yr. award for Seminole County, Fla., Econ. Devel. Commn. of Mid-Fla., 1994. Mem. Internat. Pentecostal Press Assn., Christian Booksellers Assn., Fla. Mag. Assn. (pres. 1979-80), Evang. Christian Pubs. Assn., Evang. Press Assn. Republican. Mem. Assemblies of God. Office: Strang Comm Co 600 Rinehart Rd Lake Mary FL 32746-4872

STRANGE, CHARLTON BELL, III, internal medicine educator; b. Fairbanks, Alaska, Mar. 3, 1956; s. Charlton Bell Jr. and Carol Linda (Everett) S.; m. Pamela Elaine Neagley, June 18, 1983; children: Matthew Alexander, Robert Charlton. BS, Davidson Coll., 1978; MD, Med. Coll. Va., 1982. Diplomate Am. Bd. Internal Medicine, Am. Bd. Pulmonary Medicine, Am. Bd. Critical Care Medicine. Intern and resident in internal medicine Med. U. S.C., Charleston, 1982-85, fellow div. pulmonary and critical care medicine, 1986-87, instr. medicine div. pulmonary and critical care medicine, 1987-88, asst. prof., 1988-93, assoc. prof., 1993—, co-dir. med. ICU, 1990—, dir. Pulmonary Function Lab., 1991—; coord. Alpha-l-Antitrypsin Clin. Ctr., Nat. Heart, Lung and Blood Inst., 1990—; cons. to editl. bd. Am. Rev. Respiratory and Cirtical Care MEdicine, Jour. Am. Acad. Dermatology, Jour. Am. Coll. Cardiology, Thorax. Contbr. articles to med. jours., chpts. to books. Burroughs-Wellcome grantee, 1993. Fellow Am. Coll. Chest Physicians; mem. Am. Thoracic Soc., S.C. Thoracic Soc., Am. Fedn. for Clin. Rsch. Home: 17 Bull St Charleston SC 29401-1317 Office: Med U SC Pulmonary Medicine Unit 171 Ashley Ave Charleston SC 29425-0001

STRANGE, DOUGLAS HART MCKOY, civic worker; b. Wilmington, N.C., Mar. 16, 1929; d. Adair Morey and Katie Reston (Grainger) McKoy; student Hollins Coll., 1946-48; m. Robert Strange, July 16, 1949; children: Robert VI, John Allan, Elizabeth Adair, Katherine Grainger. Former fin. chmn. and provisional co-chmn. Knoxville Jr. League; former tchr. Bible class, vestrywoman, pres. ch. women Fox Chapel Episcopal Ch.; former chmn. Fox Chapel House Tour; former chmn. altar guild, mem. worship com. bd. dirs. ch. women, St. John's Episcopal Ch.; altar chmn. Episcopal Diocese of Tenn.; bd. dirs. Dulin Com., Dulin Gallery Art; invitation coordinator Heart Gala Ball, 1985; vol. crisis counselor Contact of Knoxville, Inc.; vol. Fish of Knox County. Recipient cert. of merit Pitts. Heart Fund, 1975, engraved plate Fox Chapel Episcopal Ch., 1976. Mem. Assn. Jr. Leagues Am., Nat. Soc. Colonial Dames Am. (asst. to editor and bus. mgr. newsletter, 1978-79), Knoxville Civic Opera. Republican. Clubs: Cherokee Garden, Nine-o-clock Cotillion, Cherokee Country. Home: 1400 Kenesaw Ave Apt 11G Knoxville TN 37919-7775

STRANGE, MARTHA, neonatologist; b. Bessemer, Ala., May 11, 1952; d. Robert M. and Ruth Strange. BS in Chemistry magna cum laude, U. Ala., Tuscaloosa, 1974; MD cum laude, U. Ala., Birmingham, 1978. Diplomate Nat. Bd. Med. Examiners; lic. physician, Ala. Intern The Children's Hosp., U. Ala. Med. Ctr., Birmingham, 1978-79, pediat. resident, 1979-81; pvt. practice newborn care Birmingham, 1981-82; fellow in neonatal-perinatal medicine U. Ala. Med. Ctr., Birmingham, 1982-84, asst. prof. pediat., 1984—; med. dir. neonatal ICU AMI Brookwood Med. Ctr., Birmingham, 1984—; med. staff Brookwood Hosp., U. Ala.-Birmingham, Children's Hosp., Princeton Hosp., St. Vincent's Hosp., Bapt. Montclair Hosp. Contbr. articles to profl. jours. Mem. women's adv. bd. Found. for Women's Health in Ala., Birmingham, 1988-90; med. advisor to bd. Svc. Guild Early Intervention Program, Birmingham, 1990—. Recipient citation of achievement Am. Med. Women's Assn., 1978. Mem. AMA, Am. Acad. Pediats. (chpt. com. on early childhood, adoption and dependent care 1990, chmn. 1990, com. on fetus and newborn 1994—), Jefferson County Med. Soc., Jefferson County Pediat. Soc., So. Perinatal Assn., So. Soc. Pediat. Rsch. (Young Investigator award 1984), Alpha Omega Alpha, Alpha Epsilon Delta, Phi Beta Kappa, Gamma Sigma Epsilon (Grand Alchemist 1973). Home: 2926 Smyer Rd Birmingham AL 35216 Office: Brookwood Neonatology Neonatal ICU 2010 Brookwood Med Ctr Dr Birmingham AL 35209

STRASSER, DALE CHRISTIAN, physiatrist; b. Oak Ridge, Tenn., Sept. 17, 1953. BA in Psychology cum laude, Vanderbilt U., 1976; MD, Northwestern U., 1984. Diplomate Nat. Bd. Med. Examiners, Am. Bd. Phys. Medicine and Rehab.; lic. physician, Ga., Ill. Resident in phys. medicine and rehab. Northwestern U./Rehab. Inst. of Chgo., 1984-88; Julius Frankel Found. fellow arthritis/orthopedic rehab. Rehab. Inst. of Chgo., 1988; fellow in geriatric medicine Northwestern U., Chgo., 1989-90; staff physiatrist Ctr. for Rehab. Medicine, The Emory Clinic, Atlanta, 1990—; chief rehab. svcs., med. dir. inpatient rehab. svcs. Wesley Woods Geriatric Hosp., Atlanta, 1992—, med. dir. comprehensive outpatient rehab., 1992, 96—; rsch. health scientist and co-med. dir. Atlanta VA Med. Ctr., Rehab. Rsch. and Devel. Ctr.; asst. prof. rehab. medicine Emory U. Sch. Medicine; lectr. in field. Contbr. articles and abstracts to profl. jours. Andrus Found. grantee, 1993—, VA Merit Rev. grantee, 1992-95, 96-99. Fellow Am. Acad. Phys. Medicine and Rehab.; mem. Am. Congress Rehab. Medicine, Am. Geriatrics Soc., Ga. Soc. Phys. Medicine and Rehab., Acad. Acad. Physiatrists, Assn. of Health Svcs. Rsch. Office: 1841 Clifton Rd NE Fl 2 Atlanta GA 30329-4049

STRASSER, JACK C., association professional; b. Hannibal, Mo., Aug. 4, 1934; s. Joseph Mast and Lois Elizabeth (Lucas) S.; m. Barbara Jean Patnoude, Apr. 21, 1957; children: Kimberly Ann and Karol Sue (twins). BA, Mich. State U., 1956; MA, Shippensburg U., Pa., 1975; grad., U.S. Army War Coll., 1975. Commd. pilot USAF; combat pilot S.E. Asia, 1966-67; advanced through grades to col. USAF, 1975; staff officer Hdqrs., Pacific Air Forces, Honolulu, 1967-71; spl. project officer Air Staff, Washington, 1971-73; staff officer Joint Chiefs of Staff, Washington, 1973-74; dir. mil. airlift command USAF, Scott AFB, Ill., 1975-80; adminstrv. mgr. Kassly, Bone, Becker, Dix & Tillery, Belleville, Ill., 1980-85; dir. adminstrn. Law, Snakard & Gambill, Fort Worth, Tex., 1985-89; assoc. dir. Tex. Workers Compensation Commn., 1990-95; pres. Metro Mgmt. Cons., Ft. Worth, 1995—. Decorated Legion of Merit, DFC, Bronze Star medal, Air Medals (9). Mem. U.S. Army War Coll. Found. (life), U.S. Army War Coll. Alumni Assn. (life), Ret. Officers Assn., Order of Daedalians, Lambda Chi Alpha. Republican. Presbyterian. Home: 1021 N Shady River Ct Fort Worth TX 76126-2900

STRASSMANN, DIANA LOUISE, economist; b. Washington, Aug. 8, 1955; d. Wolfgang Paul and Elizabeth Marsh (Fanck) S.; m. Jeffery Alan Smisek, June 18, 1983; children: Julian, Patrick, Jonathan (dec.). AB, Princeton U., 1977; MA, Harvard U., 1982, PhD, 1983. Instr. Wellesley (Mass.) Coll., 1982-83; asst. prof. Rice U., Houston, 1983-92, sr. rsch. fellow, 1992—. Editor: Feminist Economics, 1994—. Mem. Am. Econ. Assn., Internat. Assn. for Feminist Econs. (v.p. 1992—), Internat. Network Econ. Method, Nat. Coun. Rsch. on Women, Assn. Social Econs., Assn. Evolutionary Econs., Soc. for Advancement Socio-Econs., So. Econ. Assn. Office: Rice U Ctr Cultural Studies MS 18 6100 Main St Houston TX 77005-1892

STRATTON, JOHN CARYL, real estate executive; b. Chgo., July 11, 1920; s. John Frederick Otto and Dorothy Marjorie (Young) S.; BS cum laude, Princeton, 1949; MBA, U. New Haven, 1980; m. Lucille Waterhouse Hall, Mar. 13, 1974; children by previous marriage: Caryl Stratton Killing, John Caryl II, Susan Hall Levy, Evelyn Hall Brenton, Kenneth Hall. Chief liaison engr., Avco Mfg. Co., Stratford, Conn., 1950-55; pres. Yankee Engring. Svc., Roxbury Conn., 1955-65, Stratton Realty, Roxbury, 1965-85; dir. Auto Swage Products Inc.; lectr. U. Conn., 1968-74, Western Conn. State U., 1975-80; spl. adviser U.S. Congl. Adv. Bd. Chmn. Zoning Commn. Newtown, 1971-77; mem. Republican Nat. Com., Rep. Presdl. Task Force; corp. mem. Naples Community Hosp.; del.-at-large Rep. Party. Served with USAF, 1942-46, PTO. Decorated D.F.C., Air medal with oak leaf cluster; recipient Presdl. Achievement award, 1981. Mem. AIAA, Internat. Real Estate Fedn., Nat. Real Estate Exchange, Internat. Speakers Platform Assn., Newtown Bd. Realtors (pres. 1974, dir. 1975-79), New Milford Bd. Realtors, Conn. Assn. Realtors (v.p. 1981), Nat. Assns. Realtors, Internat. Real Estate Fedn., Realtors Nat. Mktg. Inst. (cert. real estate salesman, cert. real estate broker), Naples Bd. Realtors, Fla. Assn. Realtors Comml. Investment Realtors of Southwest Fla., Am. Assn. Individual Investors, mem. Conn. Soc of The Order of the Founders and Patriots of Anj, Nat. Soc. Sons Am. Revolution, Nat. Soc. of the Order of the Founders and Patriots of America, Inc., Hump Pilots Assn., (life) Fla. Sherrif's Assn., (hon., life), Internat. Arabian Horse Assn., Arabian Horse Club Conn., Mensa, Sigma Xi. Republican. Congregationalist. Clubs: N.Y. Athletic, Princeton. Address: 10490 Regent Cir Naples FL 33942-1570

STRAUGHAN, CAROL ANNETTE, human resource director; b. Oklahoma City, Apr. 29, 1935; d. Tom Henderson and Lou Abbot (Hannah) Sanders; m. Benjamin Earle Straughan (div.); children: Lara, Caris, B. Kent. Grad. high sch., Vaughn, N.Mex. Telephone operator Mountain Bell, Vaughn, N.Mex., 1952-53; asst. mgr. Vaughn Mercantile Co., 1963-65; correspondent Santa Rosa (N.Mex.) News., 1967-72; instr. Dale Carnegie Courses, El Paso, Tex., 1974-89; tng. dir. Ben E. Straughan & Assocs., El Paso, 1976-86; tng. dir. Whataburger of El Paso, 1987, human resource dir., 1987-91; sales mgr., trainer Indsl. Chem. Distributors, Inc., Macon, Ga., 1991-92, ind. distributor, 1992—; instr. adult continuing edn. U. Tex., El Paso, 1992—; lifestyles facilitator Jenny Craig Weight Ctrs., 1992-94; regional mgr. Clean Control Corp., Warner Robins, Ga., 1994-95; mem. adv. bd. Whataburger of El Paso, 1987-91; speaker El Paso Pub. Librs., Tex. Employment Com., Career Ctr. of El Paso. Seminar leader YMCA, El Paso, 1988, Stanton Elem. Sch.; mem. bus. adv. com. Torch of Hope, Inc., El Paso; career day presenter Thomas Manor Elem. Sch., El Paso, 1996. Mem. NAFE, ASTD (past pres. El Paso chpt. 1990, speaker 1987), Pod of the Pass, Chili Appreciation Soc. Internat. (area referee 1986-87), Order Ea. Star, Order Rainbow for Girls, Beta Sigma Phi. Republican. Methodist. Home: 3608 Buxton Ln El Paso TX 79927-6515

STRAUGHAN, WILLIAM THOMAS, engineering educator; b. Shreveport, La., Aug. 2, 1936; s. William Eugene and Sara Chloetilde (Harrell) S.; m. Rubie Ann Barnes, Aug. 20, 1957; children: Donna Ann, Sara Arlene, Eugene Thomas. BS, MIT, 1959; MS, U. Tex., 1986; PhD, Tex. Tech. U., 1990. Registered profl. engr., Fla., Ill., Iowa., La., Tex., Wash. Project engr. Gen. Dynamics Corp., Chgo., 1959-60; chief project, design engr. Gen. Foods Corp., Kankakee, Ill., 1960-64; mgr. plant engring. Standard Brands Inc., Clinton, Iowa, 1964-66; regional mgr. Air Products & Chems., Inc., Creighton, Pa., 1966-68; gen. mgr. Skyline Corp., Harrisburg, N.C., 1968-70; cons. Charlotte, N.C., 1970-72; dir. engring. and Fla. ops. Zimmer Homes Corp., Pompano Beach, 1972-73; v.p. engring. and mfg. Nobility Homes, Inc., Ocala, Fla., 1973-78, Moduline Internat., Inc., Lacey, Wash., 1978-85; rsch. engr. U. Tex., Austin, 1985-86; lectr., rschr. Tex. Tech. U., Lubbock, 1987-90; assoc. prof. U. New Orleans, 1990-92; asst. prof. dept. civil engring. La. Tech. U., Ruston, 1992—; cons. in field, Dubach, La., 1992—; condr. workshops in field; apptd. spokesman Mfrd. Housing Industry before U.S. Congress. Contbr. articles to profl. jours. Vol. engring. svcs. Lubbock Fire Safety House, 1990; judge sci. fair Ben Franklin H.S., New Orleans, 1990. Recipient T.L. James Svc. award La. Tech. U., 1994; grantee Urban Waste Mgmt. and Rsch. Ctr., New Orleans, 1991, Shell Devel. Co., 1993, La. Edn. Quality Support Fund, Insituform Techs., Inc., Trenchless Tech. Ctr., PABCO, Inc., InLiner USA, Inc., 1995, and numerous others. Mem. ASME (life), ASCE (Student chpt. Tchr. of Yr. award 1995), NSPE, Am. Soc. Engring. Edn., Phi Kappa Phi, Sigma Xi, Chi Epsilon. Home: 199 Sellers Rd Dubach LA 71235

STRAUSER, BEVERLY ANN, education educator; b. Dunkirk, N.Y., July 19, 1956; d. Henry Frank and Agnes Frances (Bielat) Rutkowski; m. Edward Britton Strauser, Oct. 9, 1982; children: Nicholas, Douglas, Thomas. BS, Regents Coll., Albany, N.Y., 1985; MS, SUNY, Fredonia, 1990. Cert. tchr. early childhood, bus. adminstrn., N.Y. Tchr. gifted edn. and computer literacy North Collins (N.Y.) Ctrl. Sch., 1986-87; tchr. pre-sch. St. Anthony's Sch., Fredonia, 1988-91; asst. prof. edn. Armstrong State Coll., Savannah, Ga., 1992—; cons. Jamestown (N.Y.) Cmty. Schs., 1989-91, Jewish Ednl. Allance, Savannah, 1991-92, Meth. Daysch. of Richmond Hill, Ga., 1992-93; presenter in field. Recipient Key award Jamestown Cmty. Schs., 1990. Mem. Nat. Assn. for the Edn. of Young Children, Ga. Assn. on Young Children (bd. dirs., sr. dist. rep. 1992-94), Internat. Reading Assn., Assn. Childhood Edn. Internat. Home: 264 Boyd Dr Richmond Hill GA 31324-9400 Office: Armstrong State Coll 11935 Abercorn St Savannah GA 31419-1909

STRAUSER, EDWARD B., psychologist, educator; b. Dunkirk, N.Y., June 6, 1953; s. Fredrick Edward and Lucille Ruth (Mayott) S.; m. Beverly Ann Rutkoswki; children: Nicholas, Douglas, Thomas. BS, SUNY, Fredonia, 1975; MS, Canisius Coll., 1980; EdD, SUNY, Buffalo, 1986. 4th-9th grade tchr. Pioneer Mid. Sch., Yorkshire, N.Y., 1977-82; sch. psychologist BOCES, Orchard Park, N.Y., 1982-91; asst. prof. Pembroke (N.C.) State U., 1987-88; asst. prof., then assoc. prof. Armstrong State Coll., Savannah, Ga., 1991—; cons. ACT/PEP Test Svc., Albany, N.Y., 1988, SUNY, Fredonia, 1988-89, Cleve. City Schs., 1992. Contbr. chpts. to books and articles to profl. jours. Mem. exec. bd. Erie County Spl. Olympics, Orchard Park, 1983-84; bd. dirs. N.Y. Assn. Sch. Psychologists, 1990. Recipient Citation of Appreciation for Profl. Contbn., Nat. Mid. Sch. Assn., 1988, Cmty. Svc. Operation Safe Place award, 1995. Mem. AAUP, Am. Assn. Tchg. and Curriculum, Nat. Assn. Sch. Psychologists, N.Y. State Tchrs. of Handicapped, Ga. Mid. Level Educators, Phi Delta Kappa. Home: 264 Boyd Dr Richmond Hill GA 31324-9400 Office: Armstrong State Coll 11935 Abercorn St Savannah GA 31419-1909

STRAUSER, ROBERT WAYNE, lawyer; b. Little Rock, Aug. 28, 1943; s. Christopher Columbus and Opal (Orr) S.; m. Atha Maxine Tubbs, June 26, 1971 (div. 1991); children: Robert Benjamin, Ann Kathleen. BA, Davidson (N.C.) Coll., 1965; postgrad., Vanderbilt U., Nashville, 1965-66; LLB, U. Tex., 1968. Bar: Tex. 1968, U.S. Ct. Mil. Appeals 1971. Staff atty. Tex. Legis. Coun., Austin, 1969-71; counsel Jud. Com., Tex. Ho. of Reps., Austin, 1971-73; chief counsel Jud. Com., Tex. Constl. Conv., Austin, 1974; exec. v.p. and legis. counsel Tex. Assn. Taxpayers, Austin, 1974-85; assoc. Baker & Botts, Austin, 1985-87; ptnr. Baker & Botts, 1988—. Assoc. editor Tex. Internat. Law Jour., 1968. Mem. Tex. Ho. Speakers Econ. Devel. Com.,

Austin, 1986-87; mem. Austin Coun. Fgn. Affairs, 1987—; dir. McDonald Obs. Bd. Visitors, 1988—; mem. adv. bd. Sch. of Social Work, U. Tex. Lyceum Assn., 1980-81, 84-88; mem. Dean's Roundtable, U. Tex. Law Sch.; elder Presbyn. Ch.; mem. exec. com. Austin Symphony Orch. Soc., 1985—, v.p., 1993-94. Capt. USNR, ret. Named Rising Star of Tex., Tex. Bus. Mag., 1983. Mem. State Bar of Tex. (coun. mem. tax sect.), Travis County Bar Assn., Headliners Club (Austin). Home: 3312 Gilbert St Austin TX 78703-2102 Office: Baker & Botts 1600 San Jacinto Blvd Austin TX 78701

STRAUSS, GORDON DARROW, psychiatrist, educator; b. L.A., Oct. 18, 1947; s. Donald Adler and Dorothy Marie (Richardson) S.; m. Gayle Elizabeth Patterson, May 30, 1969 (div. Mar., 1996); children: Matthew K., Adam P. BA, Stanford U., 1970; MD, NYU Sch. Medicine, 1974. Diplomate Am. Bd. Psychiatry & Neurology. Intern Harbor Gen. Hosp., Torrance, Calif., 1974-75; resident in psychiatry UCLA Neuropsychiat. Inst., 1975-78; from asst. prof. to assoc. prof. UCLA Dept. Psychiatry, 1978-92; prof. psychiatry U. Louisville, 1992—; dir. UCLA Ctr. for Study of Orgnl. Group Dynamics, 1988-92; cons. The Wellness Cmty., 1992—; sr. examiner Am. Bd. Psychiatry & Neurology, 1986—. Fellow Am. Psychiat. Assn.; mem. Am. Coll. Psychiatrists, Am. Assn. Dirs. Psychiat. Residency Tng. Office: U Louisville Dept Psychiatr 500 S Preston St Bldg A Louisville KY 40202-1702

STRAWN, FRANCES FREELAND, real estate executive; b. Waynesville, N.C., Nov. 18, 1946; d. Thomas M. and Jimmie (Smith) Freeland; m. David Updegraff Strawn, Aug. 30, 1974; children: Kirk, Trisha. AA, Brevard C.C., Cocoa, Fla., 1976; postgrad. U. Cen. Fla., 1976-77, Grad. Realtor Inst. Cert. real estate brokerage mgr., residential specialist. Acting sr. buyer Brevard County Purchasing Bd. of County Commns., Titusville, Fla., 1971-75; rsch. analyst Brevard C.C., Cocoa, 1977-78; realtor assoc., Orlando, Fla., 1979-82; realtor, broker, pres. Advance Am., Inc., Orlando, 1982-89; assoc. Ann Cross, Inc., Winter Park, Fla., 1988—. Contbr. articles to Fla. Realtor, 1993, Communique, 1994. Bd. dirs. Vol. Ctr. of Cen. Fla. (rec. sec. 1989), Cen. Fla. Zool. Pk., 1989-92; co-chmn, fundraiser Black Tie Walk on the Wild Side, 1992; program chmn. Young Rep. Women, Orlando, 1983; coord. Congressman Bill Nelson's Washington Internship Program; co-ticket chmn. Art and Architecture Orlando Regional Hosp.; mem. steering com. Fla. Heritage Homecoming, Orlando, 1987; sec. Mayor's Wife's Campaign Activities, Orlando, 1986-87; vice chmn. Horizon Exec. Bd., 1987-89, chmn., 1989; recording sec. Women's Bus. Edn. Council, 1988, mem. adv. bd., 1987, bd. dirs. 1988-90; active calendar com. Women's Resource Ctr., bd. dirs. 1989-90; lectr. Jr. Achievement., 1988-93; mem. steering com. scholarship dinner Crummer Bus. Coll. Rollins Coll., 1992. Mem. Orange County Bar Aux. (bd. dirs. 1986-88, corr. sec. 1987), Creative Bus. Ownership for Women (adv. bd. 1986-88, grievance vice chmn. 1989), Nat. Assn. Realtors, Orlando Bd. Realtors (grievance com. 1985-91), Orlando Area Bd. Realtors (membership com. 1980-84, profl. standards com. 1983-84, lectr. Success Series 1988—), Women's Coun. of Realtors, Women's Exec. Coun., Citrus Club (Orlando, social com. 1987-88, bd. dirs 1990-95). Episcopalian. Avocations: travel, needlepoint, canoe trips, skiing. Home: 105 NW Ivanhoe Blvd Orlando FL 32804-5958 Office: Ann Cross Inc 233 W Park Ave Winter Park FL 32789-4343

STRAWN, KAREN KAY IMMEL, editor, educator; b. Marietta, Ohio, Nov. 11, 1942; d. Warren Harding and Bessie Louise (McAdoo) Immel; m. Steven Rogers Strawn, Aug. 23, 1964 (dec. June 1994); children: Warren Harding Immel, Robert Elden Edmund (dec.), Rachel Elizabeth. BS in Edn., Miami U., Oxford, Ohio, 1964; cert. lang. and cultural studies, Am. Grad. Sch. Internat. Mgmt., Glendale, Ariz., 1967. Cert. tchr., Ohio, Md. Tchr. 6th grade Balt. County Bd. Edn., Towson, Md., 1964-65; tchr. 2nd grade Lake County Bd. Edn., Painesville, Ohio, 1965-66; contracted asst. spl. edn. dept. La. State Dept. Edn., Baton Rouge, 1976; editor le Baton Rouge Baton Rouge Geneal. & Hist. Soc., 1988—; editor various ch. and sch. orgns., Ohio, Ariz., S.C., Md., La., 1958—. Editor Wildcat News, 1982-87 (La. PTA Newsletter 1st pl. award 1985, 87). Pres. Relief Soc., Spartanburg, S.C., 1973, Baton Rouge, 1974-76, Primary Assn., Baton Rouge, 1989-90; leader, asst. leader Girl Scouts Am., Baton Rouge, 1986-94. Recipient Green Angel award Girl Scouts Am., Baton Rouge, 1989, Outstanding Leader award, 1990. Republican. Mem. Ch. of Jesus Christ of Latter-Day Saints. Home: 9458 High Point Rd Baton Rouge LA 70810 Office: Baton Rouge Geneal. & Hist Soc SE Sta PO Box 80565 Baton Rouge LA 70898-0565

STRAYHORN, RALPH NICHOLS, JR., lawyer; b. Durham, N.C., Feb. 16, 1923; Ralph Nichols and Annie Jane (Cooper) S.; m. Donleen Carol MacDonald, Sept. 10, 1949; children: Carol Strayhorn Rose, Ralph Nichols III. BS in Bus. Adminstrn., U. N.C., 1947, LLB/JD, 1950. Bar: N.C. 1950, U.S. Dist. Ct. (mid. and ea. dists.) N.C. 1950, U.S. Ct. Appeals (4th cir.) 1950. Assoc. Victor S. Bryant, Sr., Durham, 1950-55; ptnr. Bryant, Lipton, Strayhorn & Bryant, Durham, 1956-62; sr. ptnr. Newson, Graham, Strayhorn & Hedrick, Durham, 1962-78; gen. counsel Wachovia Corp., Wachovia Bank and Trust Co., N.A., Winston-Salem, N.C., 1978-88; of counsel Petree Stockton Winston-Salem, N.C., 1988—; mem. legal adv. com. to N.Y. Stock Exch., 1986-89; adv. dir. Wachovia Bank and Trust Co., Durham, 1973-78; chmn. bd. 1st Fed. Savs. & Loan Assn., Durham, 1976-78; mem. N.C. Gen. Assembly, 1959-61; bd. of visitors U. N.C., Wake Forest U. Law Sch. Lt. comdr. USNR, 1943-46. Fellow Am. Coll. Trial Lawyers, Am. Bar Found., Internat. Assn. Def. Counsel; mem. ABA, N.C. Bar Assn. (pres. 1971-72), Newcomen Soc. of U.S., 4th Jud. Conf. Episcopalian. Clubs: Old Town Club (Winston-Salem). Office: Petree Stockton 1001 W 4th St Winston Salem NC 27101-2410

STRECKER, DAVID EUGENE, lawyer; b. Carthage, Mo., Nov. 29, 1950; s. Eugene Albert and Erma Freida (Wood) S.; children: Charles David, Carrie Christina. BA, Westminster Coll., 1972; JD, Cornell U., 1975, M Indsl. Labor Relations, 1976. Bar: N.Y. 1976, U.S. Dist. Ct. (no. dist.) N.Y. 1976, Okla. 1981, U.S. Ct. Appeals (no. dist.) Okla. 1981, U.S. Ct. Appeals (10th cir.) 1982, U.S. Dist. Ct. (ea. dist.) Okla. 1984, U.S. Ct. Appeals (6th cir.) 1990, U.S. Supreme Ct. 1991. Assoc. Conner & Winters, Tulsa, 1980-85, ptnr., 1985-91; ptnr. Shipley, Inhofe & Strecker, Tulsa, 1991-95, Strecker & Assocs. P.C., Tulsa, 1995—; instr. paralegal program Tulsa Jr. Coll., 1985—, mem. adv. com., 1986-91; mem. Cornell Secondary Schs. Com., Tulsa, 1985—; adj. instr. labor rels. Okla. State U., 1995—; barrister Am. Inns of Ct. Bd. dirs., v.p. Tulsa Sr. Svcs., 1988-91; mem. pers. com. Philbrook Art Mus. Capt. JAGC, U.S. Army, 1976-80. Mem. ABA, Okla. Bar Assn. (chmn. labor sect. 1990-91), Tulsa County Bar Assn. (continuing legal edn. com. 1981—), Soc. for Human Resource Mgmt., Tulsa Area Human Resources Assn. (gen. counsel 1989—, v.p. 1994—), Kappa Alpha. Democrat. Episcopalian. Home: 1219 S Lawton Ave Tulsa OK 74127-9173 Office: Ste 412 601 S Boulder Tulsa OK 74103

STREETMAN, NANCY KATHERINE, cellist; b. Houston, Feb. 15, 1933; d. Sam and Christine (Norman) S. BS, U. Houston, 1953; Diploma, Juilliard Sch. Music, 1960; MA, Sarah Lawrence Coll., 1961. Instr. cello Manhattan Sch. Music, N.Y.C., 1967—, Manatee Community Coll., Bradenton, Fla., 1989—, Fla. W. Coast Symphony Youth Program, Sarasota, Fla., 1989—; instr. cello UN Internat. Sch., N.Y.C., 1967-84; free lance chamber musician various groups, N.Y.C. and on tour. Mem. Prospect Heights Neighborhood Assn. (pres. 1975-78), Bklyn. Mem. Sarasota/Manatee Amiga Computer Group (v.p. 1988—). Democrat. Home: 4346 Bryants Pond Ln Sarasota FL 34233-1900

STREIB, GORDON FRANKLIN, sociology educator; b. Rochester, N.Y., July 7, 1918; s. Edward Carl and Hattie Nellie (Molz) S.; m. Ruth Boyer, Nov. 27, 1943; children: Marshall, Carol, Lawrence, Nelson. BA, N. Ctrl. Coll., 1941; MSc, New Sch. for Social Rsch., 1947; PhD, Columbia U., 1954; LLD, U. Waterloo, Ont., Can., 1991. Lectr. Rutgers U., New Brunswick, N.J., 1947-48; instr. Cornell U., Ithaca, N.Y., 1949-53, asst. prof. sociology, 1953-56, assoc. prof., 1956-58, prof., 1958-75, chair dept. sociology, 1962-66, prof. emeritus, 1975—; grad. rsch. prof. U. Fla., Gainesville, 1975-89, grad. rsch. prof. emeritus, 1989—; cons. Ford Found., N.Y.C., Nat. Inst. on Aging, Bethesda, Md., NIMH, Bethesda, NSF, Washington. Sr. author: Retirement in American Society, 1971, Old Homes---New Families, 1984; editor: programs for Older Americans, 1981; contbr. articles to profl. jours. Rsch. Tng. fellow Social Sci. Rsch. Coun., 1950-51, post-doctoral fellow NIMH, 1971-72, Traveling fellow WHO, 1979. Fellow Am. Sociol. Assn. (disting. contbr. to sociology of aging 1984), Gerontol. Soc. Am. (Kleemeier award 1989). Home: 315 NW 28th Ter Gainesville FL 32607-2513 Office: U Fla Dept Sociology PO Box 117330 Gainesville FL 32611-7330

STREIBICH, RONALD LELAND, fundraising executive; b. Peoria, Ill., May 5, 1936; s. Leland Roy and Evelyn (Moffatt) S.; m. Donna Jane Matthews, Sept. 14, 1958 (div. Jan. 1980); children: John, James; m. Elinor Sue Gaines, Apr. 23, 1988. BA, Knox Coll., 1958. Regional pub. rels. dir. GE, Winston Salem, N.C., 1959-66; dir. devel. Northwestern U., Evanston, Ill., 1966-76; exec. v.p. Meth. Med. Found., Peoria, Ill., 1976-79; v.p. Knox Colll., Galesburg, Ill., 1979-82; exec. v.p. Meml. Hosp. Found., Houston, 1982-84; v.p. St. Louis Children's Hosp., 1984-88; asst. vice chancellor Tex. A&M U., College Station & Houston, 1988—. 1st lt. U.S. Army, 1958-59. Republican. Presbyterian. Home: 15710 Greencourt Dr Houston TX 77062-4706 Office: Tex A&M U 2121 W Holcombe Blvd Ste 1107 Houston TX 77030-3303

STREKOWSKI, LUCJAN, chemistry educator; b. Grabowo, Poland, June 21, 1945; came to U.S., 1981; s. Antoni and Janina (Chrapowicz) S.; m. Alewtina Smirnova, Oct. 14, 1967; children: Rafal, Anna. BS in Polymer Chemistry with distinction, Mendeleev Inst. Chemistry, Moscow, 1967; PhD in Organic Chemistry, Polish Acad. Scis., 1972; DSc in Chemistry, Adam Mickiewicz U., Poznan, Poland, 1976. Instr. organic chemistry Adam Mickiewicz U., Poznan, 1971-72, asst. prof. dept. chemistry, 1972-78, assoc. prof. dept. chemistry, 1978-81; rsch. assoc. dept. chemistry U. Fla., Gainesville, 1981-84; asst. prof. dept. chemistry Ga. State U., Atlanta, 1984-89, assoc. prof. dept. chemistry, 1989-96, prof. dept. chem., 1996—; vis. prof. U. Fla., Gainesville, 1979-80, 81, Australian Nat. U., 1980, U. Kans., Lawrence, 1972-73. Editor: Pyridine-Metal Complexes, Vol. 14, Part 6, 1985; contbr. more than 150 articles to profl. jours.; patentee in field. Recipient award Polish Ministry Sci., 1977, Polish Chem. Soc., 1973, Polish Acad. Scis., 1972, Ga. State U., 1993; grantee Am. Chem. Soc.-Petroleum Rsch. Fund, 1985—, Solvay Pharms., 1992-93, Nat. Diagnostics, 1991-93, NIAID/NIH, 1988—, Rohm and Hass Co., 1988, Am. Cancer Soc., 1987-89, Rsch. Corp., 1985-94, Milheim Found. Cancer Rsch., 1985-86, DuPont Co., 1996-97, numerous others. Mem. Am. Chem. Soc., Internat. Soc. Heterocyclic Chemistry, Internat. Acad. Scis. of Nature and Soc. (mem. presidium). Office: Ga State Univ Dept Chemistry Atlanta GA 30303

STRELAU, RENATE, historical researcher, artist; b. Berlin, Feb. 1, 1951; came to U.S., 1960; d. Werner Ernst and Gerda Gertrud (Bargel) S. BA, U. Calif., Berkeley, 1974; cert. Arabic lang. proficiency, Johns Hopkins U., 1976; MA, Am. U., 1985, MFA, 1991. Rsch. asst. Iranian Embassy, Washington, 1976-80. One-woman shows include Cafe Espresso, Berkeley, Calif., 1973, Riggs Bank, Arlington, Va., 1994-95; represented in permanent collections at C. Law Watkins Meml. Collection, Am. U. Mem. Am. Hist. Assn., Orgn. Am. Historians, Soc. for Historians Am. Fgn. Rels. (life). Home: 1021 Arlington Blvd Apt E-1041 Arlington VA 22209-2212

STRENGTH, ROBERT SAMUEL, manufacturing company executive; b. Tullos, La., May 14, 1929; s. Houston Orion and Gurcie Dean (Cousins) S.; BS in Indsl. Mgmt., Auburn U., 1956; m. Janis Lynette Grace, Sept. 12, 1954; children: Robert David (dec.), James Steven (dec.), Stewart Alan, James Houston (dec.). Engr., supr. plant safety Monsanto Co., 1956-74, engrng. stds. mgr. Corporate Fire Safety Center, St. Louis, 1974-78, mgr. product safety and acceptability Monsanto Polymer Products Co. (formerly Monsanto Plastics and Resins Co.), St. Louis, 1978-82, mgr. product safety, Monsanto Chem. Co., 1982-87; founder, pres. Product Safety Mgmt., Inc., 1987—. mem. com. on toxicity of materials used in rapid rail transit, NRC, 1984-87. Pres. Greenwood (S.C.) Citizens Safety Coun., 1966-68; U.S. del. Internat. Electrotech. Commn. With USAF, 1948-52. Recipient S. C. Outstanding Svc. to Safety award Nat. Safety Coun., 1968; registered profl. engr., Calif.; cert. safety profl. Mem. Am. Soc. Safety Engrs., Nat. Safety Coun. (pres. textile sect. 1966), So. Bldg. Code Congress, Internat. Conf. of Bldg. Ofcls., Bldg. Ofcls. and Code Adminstrs. Internat., Nat. Fire Protection Assn. (mem. code making panel 7 nat. electrical code), ASTM Fire Test Com. (chmn. fire hazard & risk assessment sub-com., mem. exec. com. fire test com.), Nat. Inst. Bldg. Scis., Plastic Pipe and Fittings Assn. ASHRAE, Soc. Plastics Ind. (past chmn. coordinating com. on fire safety 1985-87), Nat. Acad. Scis., Cherry Hills Country Club, Raintree Plantation Golf and Country Club, Tiger Point Country Club. Republican. Methodist. Editor textile sect. newsletter Nat. Safety Coun., 1961-62. Home and Office: 3371 Edgewater Dr Gulf Breeze FL 32561-3309

STREZISHAR, ANTHONY MICHAEL, corporate executive; b. Evanston, Ill., June 15, 1957; s. Jacob E. Strezishar and Elaine T. DeBacker; m. Sheryl A. Moneyhon, June 12, 1976; children: Michael S., Katherine A. Grad. high sch., Wheeling (Ill.) High Sch., 1975. Cert. termite and pest control technician. Mgr. U.S. Auto Glass, Chgo., 1976-87; v.p. of sales/mktg. Equalizer Industries, Inc., Round Rock, Tex., 1987-93; pres. P&K Industries, Inc., San Antonio, Tex., 1993-94; sales mgr. Tex. Mobile Glass, San Antonio, 1994-96; sales, inspector Sears Termite and Pest Control, 1996—; instr. Ford Glass Technician Sch., Dearborn, Mich., 1990-93. Precinct capt. Spl. Election, San Antonio, 1989; precinct capt. for David Swift, Tex. rep. 121. Mem. Tex. Glass Assn. (bd. dirs. 1988-93), Nat. Glass Assn. (master glass technician 1991-93). Office: Sears 10103 Broadway San Antonio TX 78247

STRIAR, BRIAN, literature educator; b. Bangor, Maine, Dec. 31, 1952. BA in Politics, English and Classics, Brandeis U., 1975; MA in Comparative Lit., U. Conn., 1981; PhD in English, Claremont (Calif.) Grad. Sch., 1984. Asst. prof. Marquette U., Milw., 1983-84; asst. prof. U. North Fla., Jacksonville, 1984-88, assoc. prof., 1988—; manuscript referee Pa. State Press, AMS Press. Contbr. articles on Horace, Ovid, Chaucer and Marlowe to profl. jours. Recipient rsch. fellowship Huntington Libr./NEH, 1989, Folger Shakespeare Libr., 1987, Clark Libr., 1985, So. Regional Edn. Bd., 1988, 89, summer stipend NEH, 1984. Mem. MLA, Renaissance Soc. Am., Shakespeare Assn. Am., Am. Philological Assn., Marlowe Soc. Am., Milton Soc. Am., Philological Assn. Pacific Coast, Am. Assn. Neo-Latin Studies. Office: English Dept Univ of North Fla 4567 Saint Johns Bluff Rd S Jacksonville FL 32224-2646

STRIBLIN, LORI ANN, critical care nurse, medicare coordinator, nursing educator; b. Valley, Ala., Sept. 23, 1962; d. James Author and Dorothy Jane (Cole) Burt; m. Thomas Edward Striblin, Oct. 26, 1984; children: Natalie Nicole, Crystal Danielle. AAS in Nursing, So. Union State Jr. Coll., Valley, Ala., 1992. RN, Ala.; cert. ACLS and BLS. Surg. staff nurse East Ala. Med. Ctr., Opelika, 1992-93, surg. charge nurse, 1993-95, critical care ICU staff nurse, 1993-95; RN case mgr. East Ala. Home Care, Opelika, 1995-96; staff devel. coord., medicare coord. Lanett (Ala.) Geriatric Ctr., 1996—; case mgr. Lanier Home Health Svcs., Valley, Ala., 1996—; clin. instr. educator So. Union C.C., Valley, 1994—. Mem. AACN, Ala. State Nurses Assn. Baptist. Home: 268 Lee Rd 913 Valley AL 36854-6655 Office: Lanier Home Health Svcs 14 Medical Park Valley AL 36854

STRICKLAND, DANIEL MICHAEL, reproductive endocrinologist, obstetrician; b. San Francisco, Sept. 19, 1944; s. Dan and Doris Elise (Schaffner) S.: m. Nola Karen Massie, June 10, 1967; children: Daniel Jr., Leslie, Bevin. BS, U. Ga., Athens, 1966; MS, A.F. Inst. of Tech., Dayton, Ohio, 1968; MD, Med. Coll. Ga., Augusta, 1976. Diplomate Am. Bd. Obstetrics and Gynecology, Cert. in Reproductive Endocrinology. Nuclear rsch. officer Air Force Weapons Lab, Albuquerque, N.Mex., 1967-73; chief, reproductive endrocrinology Wilford Hall USAF Med. Ctr., San Antonio, 1983-89, chief maternal child health, 1986-89, resident ob.-gyn., 1976-81; fellow reproductive endocrinology U. Tex. Southwestern Med. Sch., Dallas, 1981-83; chief reproductive endocrinology Dhahran (Saudi Arabia) Health Ctr., 1989-95; assoc. prof., U. Tex. Health Sci. Ctr., San Antonio, 1983-89. Contbr. articles to profl. jours.; inventor: Split Ring Marx Generator, 1974. Mem. Am. Soc. Reproductive Medicine, Soc. Reproductive Endocrinologists, Am. Coll. Obstetricians and Gynecologists, The Endocrine Soc., Sigma Xi, Sigma Delta Chi. Office: Reproductive Endocrinologists PC 903 15th St Augusta GA 30910

STRICKLAND, JIMMY RAY, librarian; b. Lubbock, Tex., Sept. 4, 1936; s. James Freeman and Florence Virginia (Ivy) S.; m. Peggy Joyce Thigpen, May 29, 1960; children: Randall Ray, Jimmy Jay, Terry Dale. BA, Hardin-Simmons U., 1959; MEd, Sul Ross State U., 1967; MSLS, East Tex. State U., 1972. Cert. secondary tchr., Tex., libr. Tchr. English Wilson (Tex.) Ind. Sch. Dist., 1959-60; tchr. English, coach Loraine (Tex.) Ind. Sch. Dist., 1962-63; tchr. English Kermit (Tex.) Ind. Sch. Dist., 1962-66, H.S. libr., 1966-78; audio-visual-periodicals libr. South Plains Coll., Levelland, Tex., 1978-80, dir. librs., 1980-89; dir. libr. svcs. Vernon (Tex.) Regional Jr. Coll., 1989—. Coach Lions Club Little League, San Antonio, 1961-62, Kermit Little League, 1973-77, Levelland Little League, 1981-85; cub master Cub Scouts Am., Kermit, 1969-74. Recipient State Advisors award Tex. Future Tchrs. Am., 1978. Mem. Tex. Libr. Assn., Tex. State Tchrs. Assn. (state exec. com. 1975-77, dist. v.p. 1977-78, local pres. 1994-96), Tex. Jr. Coll. Tchrs. Assn., Vernon Lions (dir. 1993-95). Baptist. Home: 2710 Highland Park Dr Vernon TX 76384-6741 Office: Vernon Regional Jr Coll 4400 College Dr Vernon TX 76384-4005

STRICKLAND, LYNDA MCKAY, special education educator; b. Waycross, Ga., Mar. 4, 1945; d. Archie Carl and Estelle (Sammons) McKay; m. Hubert Admas Strickland, Dec. 16, 1967 (div. Nov. 1978); children: Summer Lyn, Matthew Adam. BA, Valdosta State Coll., 1967, MEd, 1989. Cert. History, spl. edn. P-12 tchr., Ga. Tchr. Bacon County Jr. High Sch., Alma, Ga., 1979-83, Ware County Middle Sch., Waycross, 1983—; coord. spl. edn. Ware County Mid. Sch., Waycross, 1985—. Mem. Profl. Assn. Ga. Educators. Presbyterian. Home: 2580 Pennsylvania Ave Waycross GA 31503-8186 Office: Ware County Mid Sch Cherokee St Waycross GA 31501

STRICKLAND, MICHAEL LEE, engineering executive, school administrator; b. Nashville, Aug. 1, 1946; s. Grover Thomas and Azalee (Hubbard) S.; m. Ellen Marie Morris, Sept. 16, 1967; children: Angela Marie Strickland Slate, Jeffrey Lee. BSEE, Coop/Ga. Inst. Tech., 1969, postgrad., 1975-76. Engr. Lockheed-Ga. Co., Marietta, 1970-79; project mgr. Marconi Avionics, Inc., Atlanta, 1979-82; engrng. mgr. Hayes Microcomputer Prodns., Norcross, Ga., 1982-84; dir. engrng. Quadram Corp., Norcross, Ga., 1984-85; divsn. mgr. Cross Syss., Atlanta, 1986-88; dir. engrng. Micrometrics, Inc., Norcross, Ga., 1988—. Contbr. to (book) An Introduction to Analytical Methods in Fine Particle Technology, 1997; patentee in field. Vol. scientist Sci.-by-mail, Ga., 1993—; vice chmn., founding mem. bd. dirs. Cumberland Christian Acad., Marietta, Ga., 1989—; precinct worker Rep. Party, Cobb County, Ga., 1986-87; registered lobbyist Ga. State legislature, 1986-87. Operation Integrity fellow, 1996—. Mem. Soc. Photooptical Instrumentation Engrs., Optical Soc. Am., Mensa. Republican. Mem. So. Bapt. Ch. Home: 3305 Doyle Ln Marietta GA 30060 Office: Micromeritics Inc 1 Micromeritics Dr Norcross GA 30093

STRICKLAND, RENNARD JAMES, law educator, dean; b. St. Louis, Sept. 26, 1940; s. Ruel James and Adell (Tucker) S. BA, Northeastern State U., 1962; JD, U. Va., 1965, SJD, 1970; MA, U. Ark., 1966. Asst. prof. U. West Fla., 1970-71; assoc. prof. St. Mary's U., 1971-72; assoc. prof. U. Tulsa (Okla.), 1972-74, acting dean sch. Law, 1974-75; assoc. prof. U. Wash., Seattle, 1975-76; prof. U. Tulsa, 1975, rsch. prof. Law/History, supr. dir. Native Am. collection, 1976-85; dean, prof. Law So. Ill. U., 1985-88; prof. Law U. Wis., Madison, 1988-90, U. Okla., Norman, 1990-95; dean Oklahoma City U. Sch. Law, 1995—; vis. prof. St. Mary's U., summer 1973, U. N.Mex., fall 1976, summer 1975-79, Harvard Law Sch., fall 1980, U. W.Va., 1982, U. Fla., spring 1983, U. Kans., spring 1985, Ariz. State U., Tempe, 1988-89; scholar in residence Heard Mus. of Native Am. and Primitive Art, Phoenix, 1988-89; lectr. in field. Contbr. articles to profl. jours. ABA fellow in Legal History, 1970-71, Am. Coun. of Learned Socs. fellow, 1972; recipient Disting. Svc. award Creek Indian Nation, 1972, Award of Excellence Western Book Assn., 1982, Chmn.'s award Okla. Indian Affairs Commn., 1990. Mem. ABA (site inspector 1974—, affirmative action com. 1988-91, co-chmn. legal edn. and admission to the bar 1984-87), Assn. Am. Law Schs. (pres.-elect 1993, pres. 1994). Office: Oklahoma City Univ 2501 N Blackwelder Oklahoma City OK 73106

STRICKLAND, ROBERT LOUIS, business executive; b. Florence, S.C., Mar. 3, 1931; s. Franz M. and Hazel (Eaddy) S.; m. Elizabeth Ann Miller, Feb. 2, 1952; children: Cynthia Anne, Robert Edson. AB, U. N.C., 1952; MBA with distinction, Harvard U., 1957. With Lowe's Cos., Inc., North Wilkesboro, N.C., 1957—, sr. v.p., 1970-76, exec. v.p., 1976-78, chmn. bd., 1978—, chmn. exec. com., 1988—, mem. office of pres., 1970-78, also bd. dirs.; founder Sterling Advt., Ltd., 1966; v.p., mem. adminstrv. com. Lowe's Profit-Sharing Trust, 1961-87, chmn. ops. com., 1972-78; mgmt. com. Lowe's ESOP Plan, 1978—; bd. dirs. T. Rowe Price Assocs., Balt., Hannaford Bros., Portland; paenlist investor rels. field, 1972—; spkr., panelist employee stock ownership, 1978—; spkr. on investor rels., London, Edinburgh, Glasgow, Paris, Zurich, Frankfurt. Author: Lowe's Cybernetwork, 1969, Lowe's Living Legend, 1970, Ten Years of Growth, 1971, The Growth Continues, 1972, 73, 74, Lowe's Scoreboard, 1978, also articles. Mem. N.C. Ho. of Reps., 1962-64, Rep. Senatorial Inner Circle, 1980-95; exec. com. N.C. Rep. Com., 1963-73; trustee U. N.C., Chapel Hill, 1987-95, chmn. bd., 1991-93; dir., dep. chmn. Fed. Res. Bank of Richmond, 1996—; com. on bus. laws and the economy N.C., 1994—; dir. U.S. Coun. Better Bus. Burs., 1981-85; bd. dirs., v.p. Nat. Home Improvement Coun., 1972-76; bd. dirs. N.C. Sch. Arts Found., 1975-79, N.C. Bd. Natural and Econ. Resources, 1975-76; bd. dirs., govt. affairs com. Home Ctr. Inst.; trustee, sec. bd. Wilkes C.C., 1964-73; chmn., pres. bd. dirs. Do-It-Yourself Rsch. Inst., 1981-89; pres. Hardware Home Improvement Coun. City of Hope Nat. Med. Ctr., L.A., 1987-89. With USN, 1952-55, lt. Res. 1955-62. Named Wilkes County N.C. Young Man of Yr., Wilkes Jr. C. of C., 1962; recipient Bronze Oscar of Industry award Fin. World, 1969-74, 76-79, Silver Oscar of Industry award, 1970, 72-74, 76-79, Gold Oscar of Industry award as best of all industry, 1972, 87, Excellence award in corp. reporting Fin. Analysts Fedn., 1970, 72, 74, 81-82, cert. of Distinction Brand Names Found., 1970, Retailer of Yr. award, 1971, 73, Disting. Mcht. award, 1972, Spirit of Life award City of Hope, 1983, Free Enterprise Legend award Students Free Enterprise, 1994; named to Home Ctr. Hall of Fame, 1985. Mem. Nat. Assn. Over-Counter Cos. (bd. advisers 1973-77), Newcomen Soc., Employee Stock Ownership Assn. (pres. 1983-85, chmn. 1985-87), Twin City Club, Forsyth Country Club, Piedmont City Club, Hound Ears Club (Blowing Rock, N.C.), Elk River Club (Banner Elk, N.C.), Roaring Gap Club (N.C.), Ponte Vedra Inn and Club (Fla.), Scabbard and Blade, Phi Beta Kappa, Pi Kappa Alpha. Home: 226 N Stratford Rd Winston Salem NC 27104 Office: Lowes Cos Inc 604 Two Piedmont Plz Winston Salem NC 27104

STRICKLAND, SANDRA JEAN HEINRICH, nursing educator; b. Tucson, Sept. 18, 1943; d. Henry and Ada (Schmidt) Heinrich; BS, U. Tex. Sch. Nursing, 1965; MS in Nursing (fellow), U. Md., 1969; DrPH, U. Tex., 1978; m. William C. Strickland, Aug. 18, 1973; children: William Henry, Angela Lee. Clin. instr. U. Tex. Sch. Nursing, Galveston, 1965-66; staff nurse Hidalgo County Health Dept., Edinburg, Tex., 1966-67; supr. nursing Tex. Dept. Health Tb Control, Austin, 1969-70; instr. St. Luke's Hosp. Sch. Nursing, Houston, 1971-72, Tex. Women's U. Sch. Nursing, Houston and Dallas, 1972-73; dir. nursing Dallas City Health Dept., 1974-80; assoc. prof. community health nursing grad. program Tex. Woman's U., Dallas, 1980-87, U. Incarnate Word, 1987—; mem. profl. adv. com. Dallas Vis. Nurse Assn., 1978-83, Santa Rosa Home Health Agy., 1991-94; mem. health adv. bd. Dallas Ind. Sch. Dist., 1976-84; chmn. nursing and health services Dallas chpt. ARC, 1984-86, bd. dirs. San Antonio chpt., 1990; Tex. Lung Assn., 1991—, bd. dirs. San Antonio Chpt., Tex. Public Health Assn. fellow, 1977. Mem. APHA, Tex. Public Health Assn., Sigma Theta Tau. Methodist. Home: 508 US Highway 90 E Castroville TX 78009-5230

STRICKLAND, THOMAS JOSEPH, artist; b. Keyport, N.J., Dec. 27, 1932; s. Charles Edward and Clementine Maria (Grasso) S.; m. Ann DeBaun Browne, Apr. 28, 1992. Student, Newark Sch. Fine and Indsl. Arts, 1951-53, Am. Art Sch., 1956-59, Nat. Acad. Sch. Fine Arts with Robert Philipp, 1957-59. Judge local and nat. art shows; TV guest; instr. painting and pastels Grove House; lectr. Exhibited in one man shows at, Hollywood (Fla.) Art Mus., 1972-76, Elliott Mus., Stuart, Fla., 1974, others; exhibited in group shows at, Am. Artists Profl. League, N.Y.C., 1958, 61, Parke-Bernet Galleries, N.Y.C., 1959, 61, 64, Exposition Intercontinentale, Monaco, 1966-68, Salon Rouge du Casino Dieppe, 1967, 7e Grand Prix Internat. de Peinture de la Cote d'Azur, Cannes, 1971, Hollywood Art Mus., 1972-76, Art Guild of Boca Raton, 1973, Stagecoach Gallery, 1973, Am. Painters in Paris, 1975; represented in permanent collections, St. Vincent Coll., Elliott Mus., Martin County Hist. Soc., Hollywood Art Mus., Salem Coll., Winston-Salem, N.C., St. Hugh Catholic Ch., Fla.; (Recipient Digby Chandler prize

Knickerbocker Artists 1965, Best in Show Blue Dome Art Fellowship 1972, 1st Place, Fine Arts League, La Junta, Colo. 1973, Blue Ribbon award Cape Coral Nat. Art Show 1973, 1st prize Hollywood Art Mus. 1973, Charles Hawthorne Meml. award Nat. Arts Club Exhbn. 1977, 1st prize Miami Palette Club 1978, others.); Contbr. articles to profl. jours. With AUS, 1953-55. Mem. Blue Dome Art Fellowship, Pastel Soc. Am., Nat. Soc. Lit. and Arts, Grove House, Miami Palette Club. Roman Catholic. Home: 2595 Taluga Dr Miami FL 33133-2433

STRICKLER, HOWARD MARTIN, physician; b. New Haven, Conn., Oct. 26, 1950; s. Thomas David and Mildred Laing (Martin) S.; m. Susan Hunter, May 2, 1982; children: Hunter Gregory, Howard Martin Jr. BA, Berea Coll., 1975; MD, Univ. Louisville, 1979. Diplomate Am. Bd. Family Practice. Resident Anniston (Ala.) Family Practice Residency, 1979-82; pvt. practice Monteagle, Tenn., 1982-85; fellow in addictive diseases Willingway Hosp., Statesboro, Ga., 1985-86; faculty devel. fellow Univ. N.C., Chapel Hill, 1985-86; pvt. practice Birmingham, Ala., 1986-90; pres. Employers Drug Program Mgmt., Inc., Birmingham, 1990—; med. dir. Am. Health Svcs., Inc., 1993—; med. dir. Bradford Facilities, Birmingham, 1987-90, New Life Clinic, Bessemer, ala., Physicians Smoke Free Clinic, Birmingham, 1988-90, Am. Health Svcs., Inc., 1993—; chmn. dept. family practice and emergency medicine Bessemer Carraway Med. Ctr., 1993-95. With U.S. Army, 1969-72, Vietnam. Decorated Bronze Star, 1971, Vietnam Campaign medal, Vietnam Svc. medal 3 Stars, 1971. Fellow Am. Acad. Family Physicians; mem. Am. Soc. Addiction Medicine (cert.), Am. Coll. Occupl. and Environ. Medicine, Am. Assn. Med. Rev. Officers (cert.), Med. Assn. State of Ala., Am. Bd. Forensic Examiners, Phi Kappa Phi. Methodist. Home: 868 Tulip Poplar Dr Birmingham AL 35244-1633 Office: 616 9th St S Birmingham AL 35233-1113

STRICKLIN, JAMES THOMAS, II, sales executive; b. Mt. Pleasant, Tex., May 15, 1947; s. James Thomas and Alyce (Basinger) S.; m. Beverly Ann Wade, Mar. 31, 1973; children: James Thomas, Kelly Wade. BBA, Tex. Tech. U., 1973. Truck tire ctr. mgr. Montgomery Wards, Lubbock, Tex., 1973-78; dist. rep. Tennant Co., Oklahoma City, 1978-81; sr. dist. rep. Tennant Co., 1981-84, area mgr., 1984-91; dir. indsl. maintenance div. Westquip Co., Oklahoma City, 1991—; area mgr. Tennant Co., Mpls.; mem. sr. mktg. coun. Tennant Co., 1985-88; cons. on video for Firestone. With USAF, 1968-72. Named Salesman of the Yr., Tennant Co., 1980, 87, Urethane Sales lLeader, 1987, 88, others. Mem. Westbury Golf and Country Club (bd. dirs. 1989—), Lions. Republican. Mem. Christian Ch. Home: 9937 Sudbury Rd Yukon OK 73099-7958 Office: Westquip Co 1901 SE 22nd St Oklahoma City OK 73129-7515

STRIKAS, RAYMOND ALGIMANTAS, medical epidemiologist; b. Hamilton, Ont., Canada, Feb. 28, 1953; s. Vytautas L. and Jovita (Antanaitis) S.; m. Nancy A. Dalton, Feb. 19, 1983 (div.); 1 child, Ona Marie. BS in Biol. Scis., U. Ill., Chgo., 1974, MD, 1978. Diplomate in internal medicine and infectious diseases Am. Bd. Internal Medicine. Resident internal medicine VA Hines (Ill.) Med. Ctr., 1978-81; fellow infectious diseases VA Hines Med. Ctr., Loyola U. Med. Ctr., Maywood, Ill., 1981-83; Epidemic Intelligence Svc. officer Ctr. for Disease Control, Atlanta, 1983-85; chief Evaluation Clinic VA Med. Ctr., Decatur, Ga., 1985-89; med. epidemiologist Ctrs. for Disease Control and Prevention, Atlanta, 1989-94; dep. chief Adult Vaccine Preventable Diseases br. Ctrs. for Disease Control, Atlanta, 1994—; instr. Emory U. Sch. of Medicine, Atlanta, 1984-89. Contbr. articles to profl. jours. Exec. v.p. Lithuanian Scouts Assn., Chgo., 1979-85. Fellow Am. Coll. Physicians; mem. Am. Soc. Microbiology. Home: 1970 Six Branches Ln Roswell GA 30076 Office: Nat Immunization Prog E-61 Centers For Disease Co Atlanta GA 30333

STRINGER, DAVID LAWRENCE, air force officer; b. Arrington, Cambridgeshire, Eng., Dec. 24, 1952; s. William Lawrence and Diane (Des Islets) S.; m. Diane Larryne Pearce, Oct. 20, 1984; children: Katherine, Laura, James. BS in Fgn. Svc., Georgetown U., 1974; MA in History, U. Ala., 1987. Commd. 2d lt. USAF, 1974, advanced through grades to col., 1994; chief of maintenance 6200th Tactical Fighter Tng. Group, Clark Air Base, Philippines, 1978-79; air staff tng. officer Hdqrs. USAF, Washington, 1979-80; squadron maintenance officer 4477th Test & Evaluation Squadron, Nellis AFB, Nev., 1980-83; group quality assurance officer 86th Tactical Fighter Group, Ramstein Air Base, Germany, 1983-84; fighter avionics chief Hdqrs. USAF in Europe, Ramstein Air Base, Germany, 1984-86; comdr. 20th Aircraft Generation Squadron, Upper Heyford, Eng., 1987-89; chief joint and mobilization plans Hdqrs. USAF, Washington, 1989-92; chief prepositioning, chief programs divsn. U.S. Cen. Command, MacDill AFB, Fla., 1993-95; comdr. 31st Logistics Group, Aviano Air Base, Italy, 1995—; ROTC credit reviewer Georgetown U., Washington, 1973-74. Nat. Security fellow Harvard U., Cambridge, Mass., 1993. Mem. Air Force Assn., U.S. Naval Inst. Roman Catholic. Office: 31st Logistics Group Unit 6100 Box 225 APO AE 09601

STRINGER, JERRY RAY, magazine editor; b. Dallas, Oct. 24, 1941; s. Henry H. and Eleanor (Guess) S.; m. Chongrak Sriratanakorn, Dec. 18, 1971; children: Gary E. BS, East Tex. State U., 1964, MS, 1966. Commd. 2d lt. USAF, 1964; editl. project officer Air Univ. Rev., Maxwell AFB, Ala., 1966-69; base info. officer 631st Combat Support Group, Bangkok, Thailand, 1969-70; staff info. officer Dep. Chief of Staff for R&D, Pentagon, 1970-73; info. officer, editor Arctic Bull. mag. Office of Polar Programs, NSF, Washington, 1973-77; staff mem. air reservist mag. Air Force Res. Pub. Affairs, Bolling AFB, D.C., 1977-78; writer, editor Internal./Cmty. Rels. div. Air Force Systems Command, Bolling AFB, Washington, 1978-80; writer editor Comm. div. Office of Comptroller of Currency, Washington, 1980-82; writer, editor Air Force News Agy., Kelly AFB, Tex., 1982-83; mng. editor Airman Mag., Kelly AFB, Tex., 1983-89, exec. editor, 1989-96; editor, 1996—. Contbr. articles to profl. publs. Webelos leader Cub Scouts, San Antonio, 1984-86; asst. scoutmaster Boy Scouts Am., San Antonio, 1986-95. Col. Air Force Res., ret., 1996. Mem. Air Force Assn., Sigma Delta Chi. Home: 5615 Timberhurst San Antonio TX 78250-4148 Office: Airman Mag AFNEWS 203 Norton St Kelly A F B TX 78241-6104

STRINGFIELD, CHARLES DAVID, hospital administrator; b. Nashville, May 11, 1939; s. Ernest Jake Stringfield and Lucille (Lovelace) Birthright; m. Ruth Dvorak, Aug. 25, 1962; children—David Fisher, John Lovelace. B.A., Vanderbilt U., 1961; cert. tchr., George Peabody Coll., 1962, M.A. in Sch. Adminstrn., 1964; M.A. in Hosp. Adminstrn., Washington U., St. Louis, 1966. Tchr. Sch. Dist. No. 11, Colorado Springs, Colo., 1962-64; adminstrv. asst., adminstrv. resident Milwaukee County Instns., Milw., 1965-66; exec. dir. Tenn. Nursing Home Assn., Nashville, 1966-67; asst. dir. Tenn. Hosp. Assn., Nashville, 1966-68; adminstrv. dir. Bapt. Hosp., Inc., Nashville, 1968-70, exec. v.p., 1970-82, exec. v.p., chief exec. officer, 1981-82, pres., chief exec. officer, 1982—; pres. dedication of C. David Stringfield Bldg. to Bapt. Hosp.; mem. governing bd. Mid.-Tenn. Eye Bank Found.; bd. dirs. NationaBank/Ctrl. South, Nashville Health Care Mgmt. Found./Comprehensive Care Ctr., 1993. Author: Hospital Administrator - Physician Relationships. Recipient 1st Ann. Arthritis Foun. Tribute, 1989, C. David Stringfield Dedicatory plaque Bapt. Women's Pavillion East at Mid. Tenn. Med. Ctr., Disting. Svc. award Tenn. Secondary Sch. Athletic Assn., 1993; named one of Nashville's 100 Most Influential Leaders, SOURCEBOOK, 1991, 92, one of Nashville's 100 Most Powerful People, Bus. Nashville, 1994, 95, 96. Fellow Am. Coll. Hosp. Adminstrs.; mem. Am. Hosp. Assn., Am. Nursing Home Assn., Southeastern Hosp. Assn., Vol. Hosps. of Am. (bd. dirs.). Lodge: Kiwanis. Office: Bapt Hosp 2000 Church St Nashville TN 37236-0001

STRODE, JOSEPH ARLIN, lawyer; b. DeWitt, Ark., Mar. 5, 1946; s. Thomas Joseph and Nora (Richardson) S.; m. Carolyn Taylor, Feb. 9, 1969; children: Tanya Briana, William Joseph. BSEE with honors, U. Ark., 1969; JD, So. Meth. U., 1972. Bar: Ark. 1972. Design engr. Tex. Instruments Inc., Dallas, 1969-70, patent agt., 1970-72; assoc. Bridges, Young, Matthews, Drake, Pine Bluff, Ark., 1972-74, ptnr., 1975—. Chmn. Pine Bluff Airport Commn., 1993; bd. dirs. United Way Jefferson County, Pine Bluff, 1975-77, campaign chmn., 1983, pres., 1986, exec. com., 1983-87; bd. dirs. Leadership Pine Bluff, 1983-85. Mem. ABA, Ark. Bar Assn., Jefferson County Bar Assn. (pres. 1995), Pine Bluff C. of C. (dir. 1981-84, 94—), Ark. Wildlife Fed. (dir. 1979-81), Jefferson County Wildlife Assn. (dir. 1973-80, pres. 1974-76), Order of Coif, Tau Beta Pi, Eta Kappa Nu. Club: Kiwanis (lt. gov. Mo.-Ark. div. 1983-84, chmn. lt. govs. 1983-84). Home: 7600 Jay Lynn Ln Pine Bluff AR 71603-9387 Office: 315 E 8th Ave Pine Bluff AR 71601-5005

STRODE, STEVEN WAYNE, physician; b. Dallas, Jan. 4, 1949; s. Royall Maurice and Maida (Somerville) S.; m. Peggy Lee O'Neill, Sept. 21, 1974; children: Sean Wayne, Colleen Leigh. BS, So. Meth. U., 1969; MD, U. Tex. Southwestern Med. Sch., 1974. Intern U. Ark. for Med. Scis., Little Rock, 1974-75; resident in family practice U. Ark. for Med. Scis., Little Rock, 1974-77, chief resident in family medicine, 1976-77, assoc. prof. dept. family and community medicine, 1978—; med. dir. Rural Hosp. Program; dir. Telemedicine Programs; teaching fellow in family medicine U. Western Ont., London, Can., 1977; pvt. practice family medicine, Jacksonville, Ark., 1977, Sherwood, Ark., 1980-84. Diplomate Am. Bd. Family Practice. Fellow Am. Acad. Family Physicians; mem. Ark. Acad. Family Physicians (v.p., pres.), Soc. Tchrs. Family Medicine, Phi Beta Kappa, Phi Eta Sigma, Beta Beta Beta. Methodist. Home: 104 Charter Ct Sherwood AR 72120-5049 Office: U Ark Med Scis 4301 W Markham St Slot 599A Little Rock AR 72205

STRODEL, WILLIAM EDWARD, surgeon, medical educator; b. Sturgis, Mich., Sept. 16, 1947; s. William Edward and Margaret (Tate) S.; m. Melanie Lou Lobdell, Aug. 10, 1990; children: Amy, Matthew, Joshua, William, Forrest. BA, U. Mich., 1969, MD, 1973. Diplomate Am. Bd. Surgery (assoc. examiner 1994); lic. physician, Mich., Ky., Tex. Intern U. Mich. Affiliate Hosps., Ann Arbor, 1973-74, asst. resident, then resident, 1974-76, sr. resident, 1977-78, chief surg. resident, 1978-79; instr. sect. gen. surgery dept. surgery Med. Sch. U. Mich., Ann Arbor, 1979-81, asst. prof., 1981-84, assoc. prof., 1984-87; staff surgeon U. Mich. Med. Ctr., Ann Arbor, 1979-87, U.S. VA Hosp., Ann Arbor, 1979-87; prof., chief divsn. gen. surgery, assoc. chmn. dept. surgery U. Ky. Med. Ctr., Lexington, 1987-96, staff surgeon, 1987-96, W.O. Griffen endowed chair dept. surgery, 1991-967; Dr. Witten B. Russ prof., chmn. dept. surgery U. Tex. Health Scis. Ctr., San Antonio, 1996—; cons. surgeon U. Mich. Health Svc., 1979-82, Wayne County Gen. Hosp., Westland, Mich., 1979-85, U.S. VA Med. Ctr., San Antonio, 1996—; vis. prof. Temple U., Phila., 1984, Abington (Pa.) Meml. Hosp., 1984, 94, Loyola U., Maywood, Ill., 1987, U. Louisville, 1988, Shandong Med. U., Jinan, China, 1990, Mich. State U., Grand Rapids, 1990, Henry Ford Hosp., Detroit, 1991, Good Samaritan Hosp., Cin., 1991, Dartmouth-Hitchcock Med. Ctr., Hanover, N.H., 1991, Tripler Army Hosp., Honolulu, 1996, U. Hawaii, 1996, U. Tenn., Chattanooga, 1996, Sch. Medicine Dartmouth Coll., 1996; mem., then chmn. promotions com. U. Ky., 1988-92; mem. pathology rev. com., chmn. radiation medicine rev. U. Ky. Med. Ctr., 1987-88, mem. ICU com., mem. grad. edn. com., mem., then chmn. oper. rm. com., 1987-96; mem. physician's liaison coun. U. Mich., 1985-87, mem. coms., 1984-87; chmn. spl. study group/ambulatory surg. svcs. VA Med. Ctr., Ann Arbor, 1983, mem. various coms., 1980-84, co-dir. surg. ICU, 1980-82; preceptor U. Mich., 1979-87, mem. coms., 1979-87, participant faculty conf. on edn., 1982, dir. grad. surg. edn., 1983-87; mem. subcom. on practice guidelines for colorectal cancer screening Health Policy Bd. State of Ky., 1995; presenter numerous profl. confs. and symposia, most recently U. Hawaii, 1996, U. Tenn., Chattanooga, 1996, U. Tenn., 1996, Assn. Program Dirs. in Surgery, Phoenix, 1996, Dartmouth-Hitchcock Med. Ctr., 1996, Pan-Pacific Surg. Assn., Honolulu, 1996; presenter videotape ACS, 1982, 83, Southea. Surg. Congress, 1989. Co-author: Surgical Endoscopy, 1985, Surgical Education, 1986; contbr. more than 30 articles to books; reviewer Gastrointestinal Endoscopy, Digestive Disease Scis., Jour. Surg. Endoscopy, NIH, Jour. Surg. Rsch., Am. Jour. Gastroenterology, Surgery; contbr. more than 120 articles to profl. publs. Rsch. grantee or co-grantee various instns., most recently Markey Ctr., 1994, NIH, 1994-96. Fellow ACS (pres. Ky. chpt. 1995-96, mem. coun. 1993); mem. AMA, AAAS, Am. Assn. Endocrine Surgeons, Am. Coll. Gastroenterology, Am. Gastroenterology Assn. (mem. abstract selection com. esophageal, gastric and duodenal disorders sect. 1990-91), Am. Soc. Gastrointestinal Endoscopy, Assn. for Acad. Surgery, Soc. Am. Gastrointestinal Endoscopic Surgeons (bd. dirs. 1984-87), Assn. VA Surgeons, Soc. Critical Care Medicine, Soc. Univ. Surgeons, Ctrl. Surg. Assn. (mem. program com. 1991-94, chmn. 1993), Midwest Surg. Assn., Pancreas Club, Frederick A. Coller Surg. Soc. (mem. coun. 1987-90, mem. acad. fellowship com. 1993, scholar 1978), Pan-Pacific Surg. Assn., Ky. Soc. Gastrointestinal Endoscopy (pres. 1991-92), N.Y. Acad. Scis., Western Surg. Assn. (program com. 1995—), Soc. Surgery Alimentary Tract. Home: 118 Box Oak San Antonio TX 78230 Office: U Tex Health Sci Ctr Med 229 7703 Floyd Curl Dr San Antonio TX 78284

STRODL, PETER, educational administrator, educator; b. Bklyn., Apr. 28, 1943; s. Chester Arthur and Evine Strodl; m. Susan Marie Strodl, May 25, 1984; children: Jonathan P. Strodl, Jennifer Lynn, Briane M. Smillie. BA, Concordia U., 1967; MS in Edn., SUNY, New Paltz, 1970; EdD, NYU, 1980, postgrad., 1989-90. Elem. tchr. Smithtown & Monroe, Woodbury, N.Y., 1966-72; unit leader East Windsor Regional Sch. Dist., Highstown, N.J., 1972-74; prin. Dunkirk (N.Y.) Pub. Schs., 1975-78; prof. de formation de maitre Commn. Scolaire Crie, Valdor, Que., Can., 1979-82; prin. Luth. Sch. of Flushing, N.Y., 1982-86; adminstrv. asst. L.I. U., Bklyn., 1986-90; asst. prof. U. Hartford, West Hartford, 1990-93; pres., asst. prof. ednl. leadership U. So. Ala., Mobile, 1993—; bd. dirs. Martin Luther H.S., Maspeth, N.Y. Author: (with others) Educational Administration, 1993; contbr. articles to profl. jours. Mem. Am. Ednl. Rsch. Assn. (pres. 1970), Ea. Ednl. Rsch. Assn. (sec. 1986, bd. dirs. 1986-94), Phi Delta Kappa (Rsch. award 1996). Democrat. Lutheran. Home: 2211 Harrods Ct Mobile AL 36695 Office: U So Ala ILB/30 Mobile AL 36688

STROHBEHN, JOHN WALTER, engineering science educator; b. San Diego, Nov. 21, 1936; s. Walter William and Gertrude (Powell) S.; children from previous marriage: Jo, Kris, Carolyn; m. Barbara Ann Brungard, Aug. 30, 1980. BS, Stanford U., 1958, MS, 1959, PhD in Elec. Engring., 1964. Assoc. prof. engring. sci. Dartmouth Coll., Hanover, N.H., 1968-73, prof., 1973-94, assoc. dean, 1976-81, adj. prof. medicine, 1979-90, Sherman Fairchild prof., 1983-91, acting provost, 1987-89, provost, 1989-93; provost, prof. biomed. engring. Duke U., Durham, N.C., 1994—; disting. lectr. IEEE Antennas and Propagation Soc., 1979-82; vis. fellow Princeton (N.J.) U., 1993-94. Editor: Laser Propagation in the Clear Atmosphere, 1978; assoc. editor Trans. Ant and Propagation, 1969-71, Trans. Biomed. Engring., 1981-87; contbr. articles to profl. jours. Scoutmaster Boy Scouts Am., Norwich, Vt., 1971-73; bd. dirs. Norwich Recreation and Conservation Council. Fellow AAAS, IEEE, Optical Soc. Am., Am. Inst. Med. Biol. Engring. (founding); mem. Radiation Rsch. Soc., Bioelectromagnetics Soc. (bd. dirs. 1982-85), N.Am. Hyperthermia Group (pres. 1986). Home: 3806 Chippenham Rd Durham NC 27707 Office: Duke U Provost's Office 220 Allen Box 90005 Durham NC 27708

STROHM, RAYMOND WILLIAM, laboratory equipment company executive; b. Elgin, Ill., Sept. 14, 1924; s. Raympnd H. and Norma (Riggs) S.; BSBA, Northwestern U., 1948; m. Frances D. Plath, Sept. 1, 1946; children: Phillip A., David N., Meredith L., Ellen K. Pres., Pelam, Inc., Hinsdale, Ill., 1966-70, Gelman Instrument Co., Ann Arbor, Mich., 1971-74, Barnstead div. Sybron, Boston, 1974-78; group v.p. Sybron Corp., Rochester, N.Y., 1978-86; cons., pvt. investor, 1986—; bd. dirs. YSI Inc., Yellow Springs, Ohio, Promega Corp., Madison, Wis. Served with USAAC, 1942-46. Mem. Am. Chem. Soc., Northwestern Mgmt. Alumni Assn. Club, Bear's Paw Country Club.

STROHM, ROBERT FRANK, historian; b. Brownsville, Pa., May 2, 1946; s. William Henry and Elizabeth Carolyn (Wallace) S.; m. Jane Helen Bennett, Apr. 7, 1974; children: Robert Benjamin, Jane Elizabeth. BA in history and English, Davis & Elkins Coll., 1964-68; MLS, U. Pitts., 1975-76. Sr. assistant Coll. of William and Mary Libr., Williamsburg, Va., 1972-75; libr. Henrico County Pub. Librs., Richmond, Va., 1976-78, Va. Historical Soc., Richmond, 1978-81; asst. dir. Va. Historical Soc., 1981-88, assoc. dir., 1988—. Contbr. articles to profl. jours. Mem. Va. Assn. of Mus. (coun. mem.), Am. Assn. for State and Local History (state chair awards com.), Beta Phi Mu. Republican. Presbyterian. Home: 4665 Melody Rd Richmond VA 23234 Office: Va Hist Soc 428 N Boulevard Richmond VA 23220

STRONACH, CAREY ELLIOTT, physicist, educator; b. Boston, Aug. 8, 1940; s. Ralph Howard and Frances Burns (Maynard) S.; m. Joan Alice Louise Venner, Aug. 20, 1966; children: John Maynard, Howard Stanley. BS, U. Richmond, Va., 1961; MS, U. Va., 1963; PhD, Coll. William and Mary, Williamsburg, Va., 1975. Instr. physics Va. State U., Petersburg, 1965-66, asst. prof., 1966-71, 72-76, assoc. prof., 1976-78, 79-80, prof., 1980—, dir. Muon Spin Rotation Rsch. Program, 1977—, dir. Solid State Physics Rsch.Inst., 1983-87, radiation safety officer, 1983-87, dir. Superconducting Materials Rsch. Program, 1988—; dir. Galactic Cosmic Radiation Rsch. Program, 1993—; dir. U.S.- France Joint Muon Spin Rotation Rsch. Program, 1985-91; vis. assoc. prof. U. Alta., 1978-79; guest scientist Brookhaven Nat. Lab.; mem. organizing com. Internat. Symposium on the Electronic Structure and Properties of Hydrogen in Metals, 1982, Internat. Symposium on the Physics and Chemistry of Small Clusters, 1986, From Clusters to Crystals, 1991, The Sci. and Tech. of Atomically Engineered Materials, 1995; mem. sci. adv. com. European Workshop on the Spectroscopy of Subatomic Species in Non-Metallic Solids, 1985, govs. com on Superconducting Supercollider, 1987; TV physics lectr., 1991—. Contbr. 94 articles to publs. in field; playwright. Pres. Petersburg area chpt. Va. Coun. Human Rels., 1965-67; mem. Petersburg Commn. Community Rels. Affairs, 1974-77; corr. sec. Petersburg Dem. Com., 1974-77, mem., 1972-78, 79-85, vice chmn., 1981-85; mem. long-range transp. adv. com. City of Petersburg, 1994—. Fellow duPont Corp. 1961-63, NSF, 1971-72, NASA, 1976. Mem. AAAS, Am. Phys. Soc., Am. Assn. Physics Tchrs., AAUP (chpt. pres. 1968-70), Va. Acad. Sci. (sec. astronomy, math. and physics sect. 1983-84, chmn. 1984-85), Southeastern Univs. Rsch. Assn. (site selection com. 1980-81, materials sci. com. 1983-86, trustee 1983—, sci. and tech. com. 1986-88, rules com. 1988-92, edn. com. 1992-94, new projects com. 1994-95, CEBAF com. 1995—), High Speed Rail/Maglev Assn. (govt. rels. com. 1992—, Maglev Task Force, 1994—), Coun. Secular Humanism (assoc.), Los Alamos Meson Physics Facility Users' Group, Continuous Electron Beam Accelerator Facility User's Group, Tri-Univ. Meson Facility Users Group, Va. Computer Networking Com., 1983-86, N.Y. Acad. Scis., Phi Beta Kappa, Sigma Xi (chpt. sec. 1977-78, chpt. pres. 1980-84, 87-88), Sigma Pi Sigma, Pi Mu Epsilon. Achievements include development (with others) of low-energy muon beam line at the AGS of Brookhaven Nat. Lab.; research in pion-nucleus interactions, heavy-ion reactions, muon spin rotation studies of high-temperature superconductors and related materials, fullerenes, heavy-fermion materials, ferromagnetic metals, metal hydrides, fatigue in metals and other materials; participation in the establishment of the Southeastern Universities Research Association and the Thomas Jefferson National Accelerator facility; discovery of formation of muonium and muonated radicals in Buckminster-Fullerene; development of TV lecture series on physics. Home: 2241 Buckner St Petersburg VA 23805-2207 Office: Va State U Box 9325 Petersburg VA 23806

STRONG, B. JEAN, writer, publisher; b. Marion, Iowa, July 19, 1925; d. Walter Benjamin and Thelma Iris (Oliver) S. BA in Journalism, U. Iowa, 1951. Editor, mgr. Center Point (Iowa) Weekly, 1949-50; feature writer, photographer The Gazette, Cedar Rapids, Iowa, 1951-54; reporter, rschr. Time Inc./Life and Fortune mags., N.Y.C., 1954-62; freelance writer, pub. Jean Strong, Iowa Illustrated, Cedar Rapids, 1962-71; assoc. editor books divsn. Farm Jour., Phila., 1971-72; instr. newswriting Temple U., Phila., 1973; project dir. U.S. Ho. of Reps., Washington, 1973-75; rschr., media mgr. Time-Life Books, Alexandria, Va., 1978-86; writer and pub. self-employed, Washington, 1986-90, Bella Vista, Ark., 1990—; cons. Women's Job Corps Ctr., Clinton, Iowa, 1966-68; cons. contbr. Time-Life Books, 1966-68; mem. editorial adv. bd. The Weekly Vista, Bella Vista, 1993-94. Editor, pub. ann. periodical Iowa Illus., 1964-66; author, editor, pub. A Prairie Almanac 1839-1919, 1996. Mem. ctr. com., precinct organizer Linn County Reps., Cedar Rapids, 1964-68; youth chair Linn County ARC, 1968-69; chmn. residence com. YWCA, Cedar Rapids, 1968. Recipient Outstanding Sr. Woman of Yr. award Mortar Board/Omicron Delta Kappa, 1949; recipient 5 first awards Iowa Press Women, 1954, 1 in 1966. Mem. AAUW, Computer Club, Writers Group at Rogers. Home: 2 Pine St Bella Vista AR 72714-5728 Office: Prairie Almanac Pub PO Box 1312 Bentonville AR 72712-1312

STRONG, CARSON MCCARTY, medical ethics educator; b. Shreveport, La., Dec. 16, 1946; s. Ralph Charles and Bertha Raye (Hart) S.; m. Margaret Elizabeth Shindler, Mar. 12, 1977; children: Ardis Elizabeth, Tara Colleen. BS in Aeronautics and Astronautics, MIT, 1968; MA in Philosophy, U. Dayton, 1974; PhD in Philosophy, U. Pa., 1978. Asst. prof. Med. Ethics U. Tenn., Memphis, 1978-84; adj. asst. prof. Philosophy U. Tenn., Knoxville, 1979-84; assoc. prof. Med. Ethics U. Tenn., Memphis, 1984-93; adj. assoc. prof. Philosophy U. Tenn., Knoxville, 1984-88; prof. Med. Ethics U. Tenn., Memphis, 1993—; lectr. in field. Author: A Casebook of Medical Ethics, 1989; manuscript reviewer Jour. Med. Ethics, 1990—, Theoretical Medicine, 1990—, Jour. Clin. Ethics, 1993—, Oxford U. Press, 1994—, Politics and the Life Scis.; contbr. chpts. to books, articles to profl. jours. With USAF, 1969-73. U. Pa. Teaching fellow, 1974-75, 75-76, 76-77, Fritz Thyssen Stiftung Dissertation Rsch. grantee, 1977-78. Mem. Soc. for Health and Human Values, Soc. for Bioethics Consultation, The Am. Soc. of Law Medicine and Ethics, The Hastings Ctr. Office: U Tenn Dept Med Ethics 956 Court Ave Memphis TN 38103-2814

STRONG, CHARLES ROBERT, waste management administrator; b. Bklyn., Aug. 9, 1935; s. Charles Stanley and Ida May (Brower) S.; m. Melba Janice Cochran, July 8, 1961; children: William Charles, Colin Brower. BSME, Yale U., 1957. Registered profl. engr., Tex. Equipment engr. Remington Arms Co., Bridgeport, Conn., 1957-60; prodn. supr. Johnson & Johnson, Decatur, Ill., 1960; prodn. and maintenance dept. mgr. Johnson & Johnson, New Brunswick, N.J., 1961-66; maintenance supt. Johnson & Johnson, Chgo., 1966-70; from maintenance & engr. plant mgr. to facility engring. mgr Johnson & Johnson, Sherman, Tex., 1970-80; cons. engr. Acurex Solar Corp., Mountainview, Calif., 1980-83; tech. v.p. Young-Montenay, Inc., Sherman, Tex., 1983-85, Metro Energy Co., Miami, 1985-86; pres. Airko Svc. Co., Miami, 1986-87; v.p., adminstr. Montenay Power Corp., Miami, 1987—. Contbr. articles to profl. jours. Dir. Greater Texoma Utility Dist., Sherman, 1982-85; pres. Texoma Valley Coun. Boy Scouts Am., Sherman, 1980-82, Salvation Army, Sherman, 1983; chmn., bd. dirs. 1st United Meth. Ch., Sherman, 1982-84; bd. dirs. United Meth. Ch., Plantation, Fla. Recipient Silver Beaver award Boy Scouts Am., 1982. Mem. ASME, N.W. Dade Hialeah, Miami Springs C. of C. (bd. dirs., trustee 1995, 96), Rotary (program chmn. 1976-85). Republican. Methodist. Office: Montenay Power Corp 6990 NW 97th Ave Miami FL 33178-2500

STRONG, LEAH AUDREY, humanities educator; b. Buffalo, Mar. 14, 1922; d. Robert LeRoy and Dorothy Sinclair (Kennedy) S. AB, Allegheny Coll., 1943; MA, Cornell U., 1944; PhD, Syracuse U., 1953. Instr. Syracuse (N.Y.) U., 1947-52; asst. prof. Cedar Crest Coll., Allentown, Pa., 1953-61; prof. Am. studies Wesleyan Coll., Macon, Ga., 1961-87; Banks prof. emerita Wesleyan Coll., Macon, 1987—. Author: Joseph Hopkins Twichell: Mark Twain's Friend and Pastor, 1966; contbr. articles to profl. jours. Instr. communications USCG Aux., Washington, 1984—. Mem. South Atlantic MLA, Am. Studies Assn., Sarasota Manatee Cornell Club, USCG Aux. (nat. staff officer 1986-93). Home: 2925 Wood Pine Circle Sarasota FL 34231-6325

STRONG, THOMAS S., college director; b. Mobile, Ala., June 2, 1945; s. Charles William and Florence (Wilkes) S.; m. Pamela Sparks, Aug. 12, 1972; children: Christopher Thomas, Britt Charles. BS in Biology, U. Mobile, 1967; MA in Counseling, U. Ala., 1969, PhD in Adminstrn., 1971. Dir. rsch. Am. Sch. Found., Mexico City, 1970; asst. to dean Va. Poly. Inst. and State U., Blacksburg, 1971; dir. housing U. Ala., Tuscaloosa, 1971-74, asst. dean students, 1974-75, asst. dean, dir. housing and recreation, 1975-77, assoc. dean students, 1977-86, dir. student svcs., 1986—; cons. Henderson (Ark.) State Coll., 1976, Mobile Coll., 1985. Author: American School Looks to the Future, 1970; editor: Technology in Student Services, 1994. Chmn. long-range planning Black Warrior coun. Boy Scouts Am., Tuscaloosa, 1976-82, bd. dirs., 1974-91; pres. PTA, Huntingdon Elem. Sch., Northport, Ala., 1984-86, Easter Seal Soc., Tuscaloosa, 1982-84; coach water ski team U. Ala.; sr. water ski judge; deacon 1st Bapt. Ch., 1973—. Alcohol edn. grantee NCAA, Kans., 1992; drug edn. grantee U.S. Dept. Edn., Washington, 1993; vigil honor mem. Boy Scouts Am., 1976, recipient Siver Beaver award, 1977. Mem. Nat. Assn. Student Adminstrs., Am. Pers. Guidance Assn., Anderson Soc., Omicron Delta Kappa. Home: 15224 Westwinds Dr Northport AL 35475 Office: Univ Ala PO Box 870270 Tuscaloosa AL 35487

STRONGIN, ROBERT MICHAEL, organic chemist; b. Bklyn., Nov. 22, 1955; s. Murray and Dorothy (Bernstein) S. BA in Chemistry with honors,

Temple U., 1988; PhD in Organic Chemistry, U. Pa., 1995. Rsch. chemist FMC Corp., Princeton, N.J., 1988-90, SmithKline Beecham, King of Prussia, Pa., 1990; rsch. chemist dept. chemistry U. Pa., Phila., 1990-95; asst. prof. chemistry La. State U., Baton Rouge, La., 1995—; lectr. in field. Contbr. articles to profl. jours. Mem. AAAS, Am. Chem. Soc., Materials Rsch. Soc., Phi Lambda Upsilon. Home: 7782 LaSalle Ave B7 Baton Rouge LA 70806 Office: La State U Dept Chemistry Baton Rouge LA 70803

STROTHER, GARLAND, public library director; b. St. Joseph, La., June 3, 1938; s. Robert Lee and Georgia Alma (Mathews) S.; m. Elizabeth Robin Ashin, Sept. 15, 1984. BS, Mont. State U., 1960; BA, U. Nev., 1965, MA, 1967; MLS, La. State U., 1974. Cert. adminstrv. libr. Libr. assoc. U. Nev., Reno, 1970-73; asst. dir. St. Charles Parish Pub. Libr., Luling, La., 1974-81, dir., 1981—; mem. State Bd. Libr. Examiners, Baton Rouge, 1989—. Author poems in various periodicals. Bd. dirs. St. Charles Literacy Project, Luling, 1992—. With U.S. Army, 1960-63. Named del. White House Conf. Librs. and Info. Sci., Washington, 1991. Mem. ALA, La. Libr. Assn. (Mid-Career award 1990, 2d v.p. 1991-92), Rotary Club (bd. dirs., Rotarian of the Yr. award 1993), Beta Phi Mu. Office: St Charles Parish Pub Libr 105 Lakewood Dr Luling LA 70070-6115

STROUD, JOHN FRED, JR., state supreme court justice; b. Hope, Ark., Oct. 3, 1931; s. John Fred and Clarine (Steel) S.; m. Marietta Kimball, June 1, 1958; children: John Fred III, Ann Kimball, Tracy Steel. Student, Hendrix Coll., 1949-51; BA, U. Ark., 1959, LLB, 1960. Bar: Ark. 1959, Tex. 1988, U.S. Supreme Ct. 1963. Ptnr. Stroud & McClerkin, 1959-62; city atty. City of Texarkana (Ark.), 1961; legislative asst. to U.S. Senator John L. McClellan, 1962-63; ptnr. Smith, Stroud, McClerkin, Dunn & Nutter, 1963-79, 1981—; assoc. justice Ark. Supreme Ct., Little Rock, 1980; judge Ark. Ct. Appeals, Little Rock, 1996—. Chmn. Texarkana Airport Authority, 1966-67, Texarkana United Way Campaign, 1988; pres. Caddo area coun. Boy Scouts Am., 1971-73; former trustee Ark. Nature COnservancy; former bd. dirs. Ark. Cmty. Found.; former pres. Red River Valley Assn.; former commr. Red River Compact Commn.; past vice chmn. Ark. Water Code Study Commn.; chmn. bd., chmn. coun. ministries Meth. Ch. Lt. col. USAF, 1951-56, Res. ret. Recipient award of exceptional accomplishment Ark. State C. of C., 1972, 86, Silver Beaver and Disting. Eagle awards Boy Scouts Am.; named Outstanding Young Man of Texarkana, 1966, One of Five Outstanding Young Men of Ark., 1967, Outstanding Alumnus of U. Ark. Law Sch., 1980. Fellow Am. Bar Foun.; mem. ABA, Ark. Bar Assn. (chmn. exec. coun. 1979-80, pres. 1987-88), Four States Area Estate Planning Coun. (past chmn.), State Bar Tex., Miller County Bar Assn. (past pres.), Texarkana Bar Assn. (pres. 1982-83), Ark. Bar Found. (chmn. 1974-75), Am. Coll. Trust and Estate Counsel (chmn. Ark. chpt. 1986-91), S.W. Ark. Bar Assn., Texarkana C. of C. (pres. 1969, C.E. Palmer award 1979), Texarkana Country Club (pres. 1990-92), Rotary (pres. Texarkana 1965-66). Democrat. Office: Ark Ct Appeals 625 Marshall Little Rock AR 72201

STROUD, MATTHEW DAVID, foreign languages educator; b. Hillsboro, Tex., Oct. 4, 1950; s. Lowell and Augusta Louise (Wynn) S. BA with honors, U. Tex., 1971; AM, U. So. Calif., 1974, PhD, 1977. Asst. prof. Trinity U., San Antonio, 1977-83, assoc. prof., 1983-89, prof., 1989—, chmn. fgn. langs., 1984-87. Author: Fatal Union: A Pluralistic Approach to the Spanish Wife-Murder Comedias, 1990, The Play in the Mirror: Lacanian Perspectives on Spanish Baroque Theater, 1996; prin. editor introduction: After Its Kind: Approaches to the Comedia (James A. Parr) 1991; editor, translator opera prodr.: Celos Aun del Aire Matan (Calderon) 1981; contbr. numerous articles to profl. jours. Pres. Festival Calderon, San Antonio, 1983-84; bd. dirs. San Antonio Free Clinic, 1983-85. Mem. MLA, Am. Assn. Tchrs. Spanish and Portuguese, Assn. Internat. Hispanistas, Hispanic Soc. Am., Assn. Internat. Siglo de Oro, Assn. for Hispanic Classical Theatre (bd. dirs. 1984-93, 96—, treas., 1984-90), Phi Beta Kappa (pres. Trinity U. chpg. 1987-89, sec. San Antonio 1990—). Democrat. Office: Trinity U Dept Fgn Langs 715 Stadium Dr San Antonio TX 78212-3104

STROUD, REBECCA ANN, pediatrics nurse practitioner; b. Houston, Jan. 29, 1957; d. David Vinson and Hallie (Sims) S. BSN, Tex. Woman's U., 1979; MSN, U. Tex., Houston, 1992; postgrad., U. Tex. and Tex. Woman's U., 1992—, 1993. Staff nurse low risk nursery Hermann Hosp., Houston, 1979-80; staff nurse spl. care nursery Park Plaza Hosp., Houston, 1980-92, instr. infant care class, 1989-92; pediatric nurse practitioner Monmouth Pediatric Assocs., Houston, 1992-96, Kelsey-Seybold Clinic, 1996—. Mem. Tex. Nurse Practitioners, Nat. Assn. Pediatric Nurses Assocs. and Practitioners (cert.). Office: Kelsey-Seybold Clinic Med Towers Bldg 1709 Dryden Houston TX 77030

STROUD, SALLY DAWLEY, nursing educator, researcher; b. Ellensburg, Wash., Sept. 24, 1947; d. Lawrence Eugene and Theda Eva (Crowe) D.; m. Donald Lewis Stroud, June 26, 1970 (div. 1973). Diploma, U. Ala. Hosp. Sch. Nursing, 1968; BSN, Columbus Coll., 1977; MSN, Vanderbilt U., 1978; EdD, Auburn U., 1987; cert. adult nurse practitioner, Med. U. S.C., 1996. RN, S.C. Staff nurse U. Wash. Hosp., Seattle, 1968-70; staff nurse ICU Lee County Hosp., Opelika, Ala., 1970-77; critical care coord. East Ala. Med. Ctr., Opelika, 1978-80; mem. faculty Sch. Nursing Auburn (Ala.) U., 1980-87, Ga. State U., Atlanta, 1987-91; part-time staff nurse Emory U. Hosp., Atlanta, 1987-91; dir. of rsch. Houston Immunological Inst., 1991-93; mem. faculty Coll. of Nursing Med. Univ. S.C., Charleston, 1993—; expert witness, lectr., cons. in field. Contbr. articles to profl. jours. Mem. ANA, S.C. Nurses Assn., So. Nursing Rsch. Soc., Sigma Theta Tau (pres. local chpt. 1986-87, 89-91), Phi Kappa Phi, Omicron Delta Kappa. Roman Catholic. Home: 1133 Monaco Dr Mount Pleasant SC 29464-9061 Office: Med Univ S C Coll Nursing 171 Ashley Ave Charleston SC 29425-0001

STROUP, DAVID RICHARD, architect; b. Asheville, N.C., Dec. 4, 1954; s. H. B. and Louise (Pinkerton) S.; m. Sandra Barbee. B Envirion Design in Architecture, N.C. State U., 1977. Lic. architect, N.C., S.C., Ga. Estimator Stroup Sheet Metal Works Inc., Asheville, N.C., 1973-74; student sales mgr. Southwestern Co., Nashville, 1974-77; drafstman Brown, Edwards & Miller, Raleigh, N.C., 1977-78; assoc. architect Flour/Daniel Internat. Corp., Greenville, S.C., 1978-82; project architect Hiller & Hiller, Architects, Greenville, 1982-83, Neal, Prince & Browning, Architects, Greenville, 1983-85, Craig, Gaulden & Davis Architects, Greenville, 1985-90; corp. architect Milliken & Co., Spartanburg, S.C., 1990—. Recipient Masonry Design award S.C. Masonry Assn., Spartanburg, 1986. Mem. AIA (pres. Greenville 1990, young architect forum rep. S.C. 1991), Constrn. Specifications Inst., Optimist Club Greenville (charter mem., pres. 1985-86, bd. mem. 1985—, sec.-treas. 1991-92), S.C. Dist. Optimist Internat. (lt. gov. 1986-87, bd. mem. 1985-87, outstanding lt. gov. 1987). Republican. Baptist. Home: 106 Idonia Dr Taylors SC 29687-3879 Office: Milliken & Co 920 Milliken Rd Spartanburg SC 29303-4906

STROUPE, CYNTHIA KAY, secondary school counselor, educator; b. Cleve., Dec. 22, 1942; d. Fred Richard and Florence Crockett (Hart) S. BA in History, Queens Coll., 1964; MA in Guidance and Counseling, Rollins Coll., 1982. Cert. tchr., guidance and counseling, history, social sci., Fla. Clerical staff acctg. ops. office IBM Corp.-Cleve., 1964-66; tchr. Andrews Sch. for Girls, Willoughby, Ohio, 1966-67, North Iredell High Sch., Statesville, N.C., 1967-70; tchr. Winter Haven (Fla.) Sch., 1970-82, counselor, 1982-95; counselor Lake Region H.S., Eagle Lake, Fla., 1995—; mem. scholarship selection com. Polk C.C., Winter Haven, 1991—, Polk EDn. Found., Bartow, Fla., 1990—; dir., sec., pres. Polk County Scholarship Fund, Inc., Lakeland, Fla., 1983—. Sec. Rep. Women of Greater Polk, Winter Haven, 1991-93. Mem. NEA, Fla. Edn. Assn., Polk Edn. Assn, Fla. Counseling and Devel. Assn., So. Assn. Coll. Admissions Advisors, Delta Kappa Gamma (2d v.p. 1994-96, 1st v.p. 1996—). Presbyterian. Office: Lake Region High Sch 1995 Thunder Rd Eagle Lake FL 33839-3086

STROUSE, CHARLES E., journalist; b. St. Paul, Apr. 6, 1959; s. Lester and Joan (Segelbaum) S. BA, Brown U., 1982. Guide, diplomate U.S. State Dept., USSR, 1986-87; reporter City Bus., Mpls.l, 1988, The Miami Herald, 1988-95; Miami bur. chief The Sun Sentinel, Ft. Lauderdale, Fla., 1996—. Vol. Big Bros./Big Sisters, Miami, 1994—. Recipient awards Fla. Soc. Newspaper Editors, 1994, 95; co-recipient Pulitzer prize, 1993. Mem. Nat. Assn. Hispanic Journalists. Office: Sun Sentinel 8323 NW 12th St # 212 Miami FL

STROUT, STEVEN BRIAN, media executive, infosystems specialist; b. Wausau, Wis., Dec. 20, 1957; s. Frank Everett and Beverly Elaine Strout; m. Kristine Ann Emmons (div. Oct. 1984); 1 child, Jeremy; m. Jeanne Leone Rump, Apr. 8, 1988; 1 child, Jessica. BSBA, U. South Fla., 1980; AS in Data Processing, Polk C.C., 1982; MBA, Kennesaw State Coll., 1992. Instr. Polk C.C., Winter Haven, Fla., 1979-81; programmer Amax Chem., Lakeland, Fla., 1981-83; asst. controller Ledger Pub. Co., Inc., Lakeland, 1983-86; info. systems dir. Sun Pub. Co., Inc., Myrtle Beach, S.C., 1986-87; nat. installation mgr. Integrated Newspaper Systems, Overland Park, Kans., 1987-88; group mgmt. info. systems coord. The N.Y. Times Co., Atlanta, 1988-90, dir. info. tech., 1990—. Mem. Data Processing Mgmt. Assn., Electronic Data Processing Auditors Assn., Assn. Small Computer Users, Assn. Info. Systems Profls., Common Cause, Jaycees, Kiwanis (com. chmn. Lakeland chpt. 1986-88), Polk 3X Plus Users Group, Myrtle Beach Mgmt. Info. Systems Assn. (chartered, bd. dirs. 1986-87). Republican. Methodist. Office: The NY Times Co PO Box 490 Ocala FL 34478-0490

STROZESKI, MICHAEL WAYNE, director research; b. McKinney, Tex., Aug. 19, 1944; s. Edwin Guy and Margaret K. (Orr) Parchman; m. Sandra S. Samples, June 9, 1967. BS, U. North Tex., 1966, MEd, 1970, PhD, 1980. Cert. tchr. sci. secondary, prin., supt. Tchr. sci. Grapevine (Tex.) Ind. Sch. Dist., 1966-70; tchr. physics and biology Ft. Worth Country Day Sch., 1970-78; tchg. fellow U. North Tex., Denton, 1978-79; evaluator, exec. dir. planning, research and evaluation Garland (Tex.) Ind. Sch. Dist., 1979—; adv. mem. grad. program U. North Tex., Denton, 1985—; dir., CEO Strozeski Enterprises Consulting, Garland, 1985—. Bd. dirs. Garland YMCA. Mem. Am. Evaluation assn. (charter), Am. Edn. Rsch. Assn., Am. Assn. Sch. Adminstrs., Nat. Coun. on Measurement in Edn., Nat. Assn. Test Dirs. (pres. 1988), Garland Rotary Club (pres. 1993-94, Paul Harris fellow 1994). Home: PO Box 462306 Garland TX 75046-2306 Office: Garland Ind Sch Dist 720 Stadium Dr Garland TX 75046

STRUDLER, ROBERT JACOB, real estate development executive; b. N.Y.C., Sept. 22, 1942; m. Ruth Honigman, Aug. 29, 1965; children: Seth, Keith, Craig. BS in Indsl. and Labor Relations, Cornell U., 1964; LLB, Columbia U., 1967. Bar: N.Y. 1967, Fla. 1973. Assoc. firms in N.Y.C., 1967-71; v.p., chmn. operating com. U.S. Home Corp., Clearwater, Fla., 1972-76, v.p. legal affairs, 1976-77, v.p. ops., 1977-79; sr. v.p. ops. U.S. Home Corp., Houston, 1979-81, sr. v.p. acquisitions, 1981-84, pres., chief operating officer, 1984-86, chmn., chief exec. officer, 1986—. Pres., trustee Sch. for Young Children; mem. pres.' adv. coun. U. St. Thomas. Co-recipient Builder of Yr. award Profl. Builder Mag., 1994, Bronze award Wall Street, 1995. Mem. ABA, N.Y. State Bar Assn., Fla. Bar Assn., Cornell Real Estate Coun., Nat. Assn. Homebuilders (chmn. high prodn. coun. 1991-93). Home: 11110 Greenbay St Houston TX 77024-6729 Office: US Home Corp 1800 West Loop S Houston TX 77027-3210*

STRUHL, THEODORE ROOSEVELT, surgeon; b. N.Y.C., Jan. 5, 1917; s. Samuel and Florence (Kossoy) S.; m. Ruth Brand, Oct. 19, 1941; children: Karsten, Wendy. BA, NYU, 1936, MS, 1938; MD, N.Y. Med. Coll., 1942, MS in Surgery, 1947; grad. Julliard Conservatory of Music, 1933. Diplomate Am. Bd. Abdominal Surgery, Am. Bd. Surgery. Intern Queens Gen. Hosp., Jamaica, N.Y., 1942-43; resident VA Hosp. Newington, Conn., 1947-48, Cumberland Med. Ctr., Bklyn., 1948-51; practice medicine specializing in surgery, Miami, Fla., 1951—; mem. staff Mt. Sinai Med. Ctr., Miami Beach, Fla., Jackson Meml. Hosp., Cedars of Lebanon Health Care Ctr. Variety Children's Hosp., South Shore Hosp., Miami Beach, Victoria Hosp.; former instr. in anatomy L.I. Coll. Medicine, N.Y.; instr. in surgery, instr. in anatomy and surg. anatomy U. Miami; instr. in surg. anatomy and surgery Mt. Sinai Med. Ctr.; med. adviser ARC of Dade County, Fla.; chief med. examiner Miami Beach Boxing Commn.; chief med. adviser World Boxing Assn., U.S. Boxing Assn.; med. adviser World Martial Arts, Judo and Karate; mem. Am. Bd. Quality Assurance and Utilization Rev. Physicians; formerly instr. in diving medicine Underwater Demolition Team Sch., U.S. Navy, Key West, Fla.; lectr., instr. in scuba diving, diving medicine; lectr. on medicine and surgery, cancer, artificial respiration, anatomy, hypnosis, boxing, weight lifting, judo, skin and scuba diving, swimming, water skiing, small craft, wrestling, music. Active ARC, 1936—, now bd. dirs., chmn. safety services ARC of Dade County; instr./trainer in CPR, instr. in advanced cardiac life support Am. Heart Assn.; former mem. N.Y. div. Olympic Wrestling Com. Served to maj. M.C., U.S. Army, World War II; ETO. Contbr. articles to profl. and sports publs. Fellow ACS, Internat. Coll. Surgeons (vice-regent Fla.), Am. Coll. Angiology, Internat. Acad. Proctology; mem. AMA, So. Med. Assn., Fla. Med. Assn., Dade County Med. Assn., Israeli Med. Assn., Fla. Assn. Gen. Surgeons (charter), Med. Hypnosis Assn. Dade County (past pres.), Am. Coll. Angiology, Pan Am. Med. Assn., Am. Soc. Abdominal Surgeons, Am. Soc. Contemporary Medicine and Surgery, Med. Aspects of Atomic Explosion, Assn. Mil. Surgeons U.S., Am. Coll. Sports Medicine, Commodore Longfellow Soc., Miami Beach Power Squadron (charter), Am. Canoe Assn., Am. White Water Assn., Underwater Med. Soc., Photog. Soc. Am., Contin Hon. Soc. of N.Y. Med. Coll., Phi Delta Epsilon (past pres. chpt.). Democrat. Jewish. Avocations: judo (3rd degree black belt), karate (black belt, 4th degree). Home: 44 Star Island Dr Miami FL 33139-5146 Office: 1444 Biscayne Blvd Ste 304 Miami FL 33132-1423

STRUL, GENE M., communications executive, former television news director; b. Bklyn., Mar. 25, 1927; s. Joseph and Sally (Chartoff) S.; student journalism U. Miami (Fla.), 1945-47; m. Shirley Dolly Silber, Aug. 7, 1949 (dec.); children: Ricky, Gary, Eileen. News dir. Sta. WIOD AM-FM, Miami, 1947-56; assignment editor, producer Sta. WCKT-TV, Miami, 1956-57, news dir., 1957-79; dir. broadcast news Miami News, 1957; free-lance writer newspapers and mags.; cons. dept. comm. U. Miami, 1979, dir. public relations, 1979-80; v.p. Hernstadt Broadcasting Corp., 1980-81; dir. corp. comm. Burnup & Sims, 1981-90; dir. comm. Printing Industry of South Fla., 1990-92, Printing Assn. Fla., 1992—. Comm. dir. United Way of Dade County, 1981. Served with AUS, 1945. Recipient Peabody award, 1975; Preceptor award Broadcast Industry conf., San Francisco State U.; Abe Lincoln awards (2) So. Baptist Radio-TV Conf.; Nat. Headliners awards (5); led Sta. WSVN (formerly WCKT) to more than 200 awards for news, including 3 Peabody awards, Emmy award. Mem. Nat. Acad. Television Arts and Scis. (past gov. Miami chpt.), Radio-TV News Dirs. Assn., Fla. AP Broadcasters (past pres.), Greater Miami C. of C., Nat. Broadcast Editorial Assn., Sigma Delta Chi (2 nat. awards). Home: 145 SW 49th Ave Miami FL 33134-1228

STRUNZ, KIM CAROL, military officer; b. Caro, Mich., May 3, 1954; d. Herbert James and Geraldine (Elliott) S. AAS with honors, Delta Coll., 1974; BS with honors, Alma Coll., 1980; postgrad., Ctrl. Mich. U., 1978-80; MPA, U. Okla., 1989. Commd. 2d lt. U.S. Army, 1980, advanced through grades to maj.; telecomms. ctr. specialist 178th signal co. U.S. Army, Heidelberg, Germany, 1974-77; chief plans, ops., tng. and security med. dept. activity U.S. Army, Bremerhaven, Germany, 1980-82; ambulance platoon leader Co. C 47th med. bn. U.S. Army, Furth, Germany, 1982-83; exec. officer dental activity U.S. Army, Ft. Lee, Va., 1983-85; adjutant Kenner Army Cmty. Hosp. U.S. Army, Ft. Lee, 1985; comdr. med. co. 47th Field Hosp. U.S. Army, Ft. Sill, Okla., 1986-88; chief pers. svcs. divsn. 121st Evac. Hosp. 18th med. command U.S. Army, Seoul, Korea, 1988-89; chief mil. pers. br. William Beaumont Army Med. Ctr., El Paso, Tex., 1990-92, comdr. troop command, 1992-93; career planning officer U.S. Total Army Personnel Command, Alexandria, Va., 1993-95; pers. policy analyst Office of the Army Surgeon Gen., Falls Church, Va., 1995—. Contbr. rsch. articles to profl. jours. Vol. Therapeutic Horsemanship Assn., El Paso, Alexandria Hosp.; mem. Highland Presbyn. Ch. Softball Team, El Paso. Mem. Am. Soc. Pub. Adminstrn., Assn. U.S. Army, Army Women's Profl. Assn. Presbyterian. Home: 801 N Howard St Apt 306 Alexandria VA 22304-5460

STRUPP, HANS HERMANN, psychologist, educator; b. Frankfurt am Main, Germany, Aug. 25, 1921; came to U.S., 1939, naturalized, 1945; s. Josef and Anna (Metzger) S.; m. Lottie Metzger, Aug. 19, 1951; children: Karen, Barbara, John. AB with distinction, George Washington U., 1945, AM, 1947, PhD, 1954; MD (hon.), U. Ulm, Fed. Republic of Germany, 1986. Diplomate in clin. psychology Am. Bd. Profl. Psychology; lic. clin. psychologist, Tenn. Research psychologist Human Factors Ops. Research Labs., Dept. Air Force, Washington, 1949-54; supervisory research psychologist, personnel research br. Adj. Gen.'s Office, Dept. of Army, Washington, 1954-55; dir. psychotherapy research project Sch. Medicine, George Washington U., Washington, 1955-57; dir. psychol. services, dept. psychiatry U. N.C. Sch. Medicine, Chapel Hill, 1957-64; asso. prof. psychology U. N.C. Sch. Medicine, 1957-62, prof., 1962-66; prof. dept. psychology Vanderbilt U., Nashville, 1966-76, dir. clin. tng., dept. psychology, 1967-76, disting. prof., 1976-94, disting. prof. emeritus, Harvie Branscomb disting. prof., 1985-86; disting. prof. emeritus, 1994—. Mem. editorial adv. bd. Psychotherapy: Theory, Research and Practice, 1963—, Jour. Cons. and Clin. Psychology, 1964—, Jour. Nervous and Mental Disease, 1965—, Jour. Am. Acad. Psychoanalysis, 1972—, Jour. Contemporary Psychotherapy, 1972-86, Psychiatry Research, 1979-86, Jour. Profl. Psychology, 1976-89, others; contbr. chpts. to books, articles and revs. to profl. jours. Recipient Helen Sargent meml. prize Menninger Found., 1963; Alumni Achievement award George Washington U., 1972; Disting. Profl. Achievement award Am. Bd. Profl. Psychology, 1976, Disting. Profl. Contbns. to Knowledge award Am. Psychol. Assn., 1987; others. Fellow Am. Psychol. Assn. (mem. exec. council 1964, exec. bd. 1969-72, council of reps. 1970-73, chmn. com. on fellows div. psychotherapy 1970-74, pres. div. clin. psychology 1974-75, recipient Disting. Profl. Psychologist award 1973, Disting. Scientist award 1979), Tenn. Psychol. Assn., AAAS; mem. Eastern Psychol. Assn., Southeastern Psychol. Assn., Am. Psychopathol. Assn., Soc. for Psychotherapy Research (pres. 1972-73, Career Contbr. award 1986), Psychologists Interested in Advancement of Psychoanalysis, Phi Beta Kappa, Sigma Xi. Home: 4117 Dorman Dr Nashville TN 37215-2404 Office: Vanderbilt U Dept Psychology Nashville TN 37240

STRUPP, JACQUELINE VIRGINIA, small business specialist; b. Montevideo, Uruguay, July 24, 1963; d. Gunther and Silvia (Klemens) S.; children: Matias, Mercedes. BA with hons. cum laude, NYU, 1986. Customer svc. mgr. Games Mag./Mail Order, N.Y.C., 1984-86; treas., property mgr., asst. to chief exec. officer Hudson Properties, Lyndhurst, N.J., 1986-90; sales assoc. Bloomingdale's, Palm Beach Gardens, Fla., 1990-91, staff tng. supr. and pers. asst., 1991-92; legal asst., bookkeeper Gov.'s Bank and Bruce W. Keihner, Palm Beach, Fla., 1993; assoc. Ideas & Things, 1994—; freelance bus. mgr., 1993—, personal and bus. coach, 1993—; ind. ins. agt. specializing in health ins. for self-employed bus. owners.

STRUTH, RAYMOND JOHN, JR., dietitian; b. Pitts., Oct. 3, 1954; s. Raymond John and June (Pace) S.; m. Barbara Ann Wilde, Aug. 12, 1989; 1 child, Raymond John III. BS, Ind. U. Pa., 1977; MS in edn., U. S.C., 1987. Registered dietitian. Chief production svcs. B. William Beaumont Army Medical Ctrs., Ft. Bliss, Tex., 1978-81; chief clinical dietetics Reynolds Army Hosp., Ft. Sill, Okla., 1981-83, Bayne-Jones Army Hosp., Ft. Palk, La., 1983-84; chief production & svc. 121 Eval Hosp., Seoul, South Korea, 1984-86; training officer, nutrition Quartermasters Sch., Ft. Lee, Va., 1986-89; class I and food svc. officer G-4 V Corps., Frankfurt, Germany, 1989-91; dep. dir. nutrition care Fitzsimmons Army Medical Ctr., Aurora, Colo., 1992-94; chief nutrition care div. Moncriet Army Hosp., Ft. Jackson, S.C., 1994—; adv. com. diet tech. program Front Range Comm. Coll., 1993-94. Contbr. articles to profl. jours. With Army Med. Specialist Corps, 1977-96. Mem. Am. Diabetes Assn. (pres. 1993-94), Sports Cardiovascular Nutritionist, Assn. U.S. Army, Assn. of Military Surgeons U.S., Am. Diatetic Assn.

STUART, ALEXANDER JAMES, JR., executive; b. Ft. Monroe, Va., Jan. 19, 1912; s. Alexander J. and Flavia Sophronia S.; m. Miriam Lore Vannaman, Sept. 2, 1934 (dec. June 1982); children: Alexander J. III, Douglas V., Susan Elizabeth; m. Helen Wilson Powers, Aug. 26, 1994; children: Helen, George, James, Pauline, John, H. Brooks, Mary, Susan. BS, USMA, 1934; MS, M.I.T., 1939; MEd, U. Tex., 1971. Colonel U.S. Army, 1934-62; tchr. El Paso (Tex.) Pub. Schs., 1962-72, Radford Sch. for Girls, El Paso, 1974-75, Father Yermo Cath. Sch., El Paso, 1975; pres. Nat. Character LAB, Inc., El Paso, 1971-96. Inventor artillery signt, 1948; author, editor (newsletter) Crime Prevention Cmty. Newsletter 1962-96, (newsletter) Nat. Character Lab., Inc., 1971-96. Chmn. Crime Prevention Com., El Paso, 1972-96. Mem. Am. Ordnance Assn. (life), Am. Soc. of Criminology, Acad. of Criminal Justice Scis. Republican. Methodist. Home: 4635 Leeds Ave El Paso TX 79903 Office: Nat Character Lab Inc 4635 Leeds Ave El Paso TX 79903

STUART, DORIS TODD (DEE STUART), writer; b. Phila.; d. William Frederick and Helen Mercia (MacDougall) Todd; m. John Bruce Stuart, Jr., June 7, 1947; children: Barbara Ellen, John Bruce II. BA, Duke U., 1946; postgrad., U. Mo., Kansas City. Feature writer Phila. Suburban Publs., Phila. Bull. Sunday Mag.; assoc. editor This Month mag., Kansas City; weekly columnist Glad You Asked, Young America Today, Overland Park, Kans.; editor non-fiction Fine Arts Discovery Mag., Kansas City; mem. staff numerous writers conf. Author: Blood Ties, 1995, The Astonishing Armadillo, 1993, (for young readers) Bats: Mysterious Flyers of the Night, 1984; author hist. romance and suspense novels; works in anthologies including Writer's Handbook, 1973-74, Lippincott, 1978, Writer's Digest, 1978, Horrors, Horrors, Horrors, 1978, Shock Treatment, 1988, others; contbr. articles and short stories to nat. mags. Recipient award for Outstanding Children's Sci. Trade Book of the Yr., Nat. Assn. Sci. Tchrs. and Children's Book Coun., also award for best book for children or young people Tex. Inst. Letters, 1993. Mem. Mystery Writers of Am., Greater Dallas Writers Assn. (co-chair 1993, chair 1994), Friends of Richardson Libr., Bat Conservation Internat., Dallas Internat. Cultural and Social Cir., U. Tex.-Dallas Writers Conf., PEO.

STUART, FRANK ADELL, county official; b. Tahoka, Tex., Dec. 18, 1928; s. John Franklin and Mary Elizabeth (Reed) S.; m. Mary Louise Wheat Crelia, Feb. 2, 1962; children: Rita, Donna, Franklin, Burce, Susan, Mary, Chris. BBA, Tex. Tech U., 1979. Asst. cashier Am. State Bank, Lubbock, Tex., 1949-52, Citizen Nat. Bank, Lubbock, 1953-59; acct. in pvt. practice Lubbock, 1960-63; asst. mgr. Gibson Discount Ctr., Lubbock, 1964-77; tax. assessor and collector Lubbock County, Lubbock, 1979-94, ret., 1994. Served to col. Tex. State Guard, 1988—. Mem. Tax Assessor-Collectors Assn. Tex., Lubbock C. of C., Masons, YorkRite, Scottish Rite, Shriners, Yellow House Lodge, Daylight Lodge. Baptist. Home: 2704 57th St Lubbock TX 79413-5605

STUART, JAMES LESTER, JR., communications educator; b. Augusta, Ga., May 13, 1942; s. James Lester and Anna Louise (Hand) S.; m. Lois Jean Garland, Nov. 7, 1963; children: Mary Louise, James Lester III. BA, Southwest Tex. State U., 1990. In comms. USAF, 1961-81; instr. comms. Litton Data Command, Agoura, Calif., 1981-83, Litton Internat., Jeddah, Saudi Arabia, 1983-88; computer programming analyst U.S. Treasury Dept., Hyattsville, Md., 1991; comms. instr. Colsa Internat., Jeddah, 1992—. Home: 407 Laurel Hill Dr San Marcos TX 78666

STUART, JOAN MARTHA, fund raising executive; b. Huntington, N.Y., June 2, 1945; d. Ervin Wencil and Flora Janet (Applebaum) S. Student, Boston U., 1963-67. Cert. fund raiser. Prodn. asst. Random House, N.Y.C., 1968-69; book designer Simon & Schuster, N.Y.C., 1969-71; feature writer Palm Beach (Fla.) Post, 1971-72; co-founder, comm. dir. Stuart, Gleimer & Assocs., West Palm Beach, 1973-84, pres., 1982—; fin. devel. dir. YWCA Greater Atlanta, 1984-86, Ctr. for the Visually Impaired, Atlanta, 1986-90; ea. divsn. dir. City of Hope, 1990-94; devel. dir. Jewish Family Svcs., Atlanta, 1994—; adj. prof. Kennesaw Coll. Contbr. articles to profl. jours. Mem. crusade com. Am. Cancer Soc. Bd., 1981—; bd. dirs. Theatre Arts Co., 1980-81; cmty. svcs. chmn., bd. dirs. B'nai B'rith Women, 1980-82; chmn. publicity Leukemia Soc. Atlanta Polo Benefit, 1983; com. chmn. Atlanta Zool. Beastly Feast Benefit, 1984; mem. Atlanta Symphony Assocs.; chmn. Salute to Women of Achievement, 1987-90; founder, advisor Lauren's Run, 1992—. Recipient Nat. award B'nai B'rith Women, 1978, Regional award, 1979, cert. of merit Big Bros./Big Sisters, 1976. Mem. Nat. Soc. Fund Raising Execs. (cert.), Ga. Exec. Women's Network, Diabetes Assn. (bd. dirs. 1990—), Jerusalem House (bd. dirs. 1991-94), Parent to Parent (bd. dirs. 1993-95). Democrat. Jewish. Office: 4549 Chamblee Dunwoody Rd Atlanta GA 30338

STUART, JOHN THOMAS, III, banker; b. Dallas, Aug. 12, 1936; m. Barbara White; children: John Michael, Melissa Stuart Macatee. BBA, U. Tex., 1958; postgrad., So. Meth. U., 1969, Harvard U., 1978. With RepublicBank Dallas, 1961-87, pres., 1986-88; pres. 1st Republic Bank Dallas (merged with First Nat. Bank), 1987-88; pres., CEO, The Alpert Corp.,

Austin, Tex., 1988-90, Lakeway Co., Austin, 1988-90; exec. v.p., chief lending officer Guaranty Fed. Bank subs. Temple Inland Inc., Dallas, 1990—; pres. Dallas Clearing House Assn., 1985-86. Bd. dirs. Cotton Bowl Athletic Assn., pres., 1990-92, chmn., 1992-94; bd. dirs., mem. exec. com. Pub. Comm. Found. for North Tex.; bd. dirs. Head Start Greater Dallas, Inc., L&N Housing Corp., Florence Found.; pres. Dallas Assn. for Retarded Citizens, 1971-73; founder adv. coun., chmn. U. Tex. Sch. Bus., Arlington, 1971-72; former trustee and mem. bldg. com. Children's Med. Ctr., Dallas; chmn. Housing and Econ. Devel. Corp., 1982-86; numerous others. With U.S. Army, 1959-61, mem. Res. ret. Recipient Disting. Alumnus award U. Tex. Coll. Bus. Adminstrn., Austin, named to Bus. Hall of Fame, 1986; Compadre award adv. coun. U. Tex. Coll. Bus., Arlington; named hon. letterman U. Tex., Austin; John T. Stuart Centennial chmn. endowed at U. Tex., Austin. Mem. Littlefield Soc., U. Tex.-Austin Ex-Students Assn. (pres. 1979-91, v.p. membership 1990-91, exec. com., bd. advisors, Top Hand award), Coll. Bus. Century Club, Dallas Country Club, Harvard Club N.Y., Beta Gamma Sigma, Phi Eta Sigma, Delta Tau Delta. Home: 3325 Southwestern Blvd Dallas TX 75225-7654

STUART, JUANITA RYAN, recreation facility executive; b. Cullman, Ala., Aug. 9, 1937; d. Stacy Carlton and Unie Mae (Hopkins) Ryan; m. Roy A. Stuart, Dec. 20, 1962 (div. Sept. 1964); 1 child, Dean Trent. Student, Alverson Draughn, Cleve., 1955-56. Cert. club mgr. Asst. mgr. Vestavia (Ala.) Country Club, 1964-75, Indian Hills Country Club, Tuscaloosa, Ala., 1975-78; gen. mgr. Mountain Brook Club, Birmingham, Ala., 1978—. Chairperson Taste of Birmingham, 1981—. Recipient Deanie Vacalis award Ala. Restaurant and Food Svc. Assn., 1987, Who's Who of Birmingham award C. of C., 1989, 90. Mem. CMAA (Ala. chpt., pres., bd. dirs.), Ala. Restaurant Assn. (pres., bd. dirs., Restaurateur of Yr. 1987, Salut Au Restaurateur of Yr. 1987), Birmingham-Jefferson Restaurant Assn. (pres., bd. dirs.), Ala. Sheriff's Boys and Girls Ranch (bd. dirs.), U. Ala. Alumni Assn. (life). Republican. Baptist. Office: Mountain Brook Club 19 Beechwood Rd Birmingham AL 35213-3955

STUART, LILLIAN MARY, writer; b. Chgo., Nov. 7, 1914; d. Ira and Katherine (Tries) Daugherty; m. Robert Graham Stuart, Aug. 7, 1936 (dec. Sept. 1969); 1 child, Mary Leone. Asst. to pres. Weisberger Bros., South Bend, 1933-42; head TWX distbn. Davis-Monthan AFB, Tucson, 1946-48; artist and music tchr., 1945-55; interviewer-counselor Ariz. State Employment Commn., Tucson, 1955-70; residence dir. YWCA, Tucson, 1970-71; tax preparer Tucson, 1971-72; U.S. census taker U.S. Govt., N.Mex., 1976, 80; mng. Luna County Rep. Party, Deming, 1976; tchr. YWCA, Tucson, 1969, El Paso Coll. Bus., 1972; tutor math, English, 1981; travel lectr. various civic groups and clubs; radio reader Lighthouse for the Blind, El Paso, 1983-89; spkr. Internat. Women's Day Celebration, 1996. Contbr. stories to The Quarterly; author: (series of biographies) Lighthouse for the Blind; actress Studebaker Players, South Bend, 1936-42, South Bend Theatre, 1936-42, (film) Extreme Prejudice, 1986; writer Centennial Mus. at U. Tex., El Paso, 1992-95. Counselor, vol. Crisis Ctr., Deming, 1975-77. Recipient plaques and prizes for various pieces of writing. Mem. Mensa, Rosicrucians, Sisters in Crime. Episcopalian. Address: 2710 W Ashby Pl Apt 323 San Antonio TX 78201-5380

STUART, ROBERT KENNETH, internist, oncologist, hematologist, educator; b. Baton Rouge, July 6, 1948; s. Walter Bynum and Rita Bess (Kleinpeter) S.; m. Gail Elaine Wiscarz, June 12, 1971 (div. Dec. 1988); children: R. Morgan, Elaine C.; m. F. Charlene Gates, Nov. 2, 1991. BS, Georgetown U., 1970; MD, Johns Hopkins U., Balt., 1974. Diplomate Am. Bd. Internal Medicine. Resident in medicine Johns Hopkins Hosp., Balt., 1974-76, oncology fellow Oncology Ctr., 1976-78; rsch. fellow Sloan-Kettering Inst., N.Y.C., 1978-79; asst. prof. Johns Hopkins U., Balt., 1979-84, assoc. prof., 1984-85; prof. medicine Med. U. S.C., Charleston, 1985—; assoc. dir. Hollings Cancer Ctr., Charleston, 1993—. Bd. dirs. Aplastic Anemia Found., Balt., 1982-93, med. adv. bd., 1993—. Democrat. Roman Catholic. Office: Medical Univ of South Carolina 171 Ashley Ave Charleston SC 29425

STUART, WALTER BYNUM, IV, lawyer; b. Grosse Tete, La., Nov. 23, 1946; s. Walter Bynum III and Rita (Kleinpeter) S.; m. Lettice Lee Binnings May 18, 1968; children: Courtney Lyon, Walter Burke V. Student Fordham U., 1964-65; BA, Tulane U., 1968, JD, 1973. Bar: La. 1973, U.S. Dist. Ct. (ea. and we. dists.) La. 1974, U.S. Tax Ct. 1974, U.S. Supreme Ct. 1981, U.S. Dist Ct. (so. dist.) Colo. 1987, U.S. Dist. Ct. (so. dist.) Tex. 1989. Ptnr. Stone, Pigman, Walther, Wittman and Hutchinson, New Orleans, 1973-78, Singer Hutner Levine Seeman and Stuart, New Orleans, 1978-81, Gordon, Arata, McCollam and Stuart, New Orleans, 1981-88, Vinson & Elkins, Houston, 1988—; instr. Tulane U. Law Sch., 1978-82; mem. faculty Banking Sch. of the South; bd. dirs. Inst. Politics; mem. adv. bd. City Atty.'s Office, New Orleans, 1978-79. Bd. dirs., gen. counsel Houston Grand Opera, 1992—. Mem. ABA, La. Bar Assn., Tex. Assn. Bank Counsel (pres. 1994-95), La. Bankers Assn. (chmn. bank counsel com.). Office: Vinson & Elkins 2500 First City Tower 1001 Fannin St Houston TX 77002-6760

STUBBLEFIELD, DAVID EDWARD, marketing executive; b. Fayetteville, Ark., May 26, 1937; s. William Hugh and Evelyn (Robertson) S.; m. Suzanne Scudder, Dec. 27, 1958; children: David, Tracy Stubblefield McNair. BSBA, U. Ark., 1958. Asst. dir. transp. ABF Freight System Inc., Ft. Smith, Ark., 1963-65, dir. rsch. and planning, 1965-67; v.p., gen. mgr. Data Tronics Corp., Ft. Smith, 1967-70, pres., 1970-74; v.p., treas. Ark. Best Corp., Ft. Smith, 1974-79; sr. v.p. mktg. ABF Freight System Inc., Ft. Smith, Ark., 1979—; bd. dirs. So. Motor Freight Bur., Atlanta; mem. Coun. Logistics Mgmt. Pres. Ft. Smith Sch. Bd., 1976-77, Hardscrabble Country Club, 1978-79; bd. advisors U. Ark. Area Health Edn. Ctr.; elder Ind. Church. Capt. USAR, 1958-66. Mem. Nat. Freight Transp. Assn. (vice chmn. bus. advisory com. 1989—), Nat. Indsl. Transp. League (assoc.), Rotary (pres. 1975-76). Office: ABF Freight System Inc 1000 S 21st St Fort Smith AR 72901-4008

STUBBS, DAVID MANNING, radiology educator; b. Atlanta, July 23, 1941; s. Harry Manning and Lola Isabelle (Coleburn) S.; m. Karen Crysta Johnsen, Nov. 18, 1978; 1 child, Eric Johnsen. BA, Berry Coll., 1963; MD, Med. Coll. Ga., 1967. Staff radiologist New Hanover Meml. Hosp., Wilmington, N.C., 1973-80; chief radiology dept. Mem. Hosp., Bainbridge, Ga., 1980-87; staff radiologist Phoebe Putney Meml. Hosp., Albany, Ga., 1987-88; asst. prof. radiology Med. Coll. Ga., Augusta, 1988-93; assoc. prof. radiology Med. Coll. Ga., 1993—; chief emergency radiology sect. Med. Coll. Ga., 1989—, chief outpatient radiology sect., 1993—, chief gen. radiology, 1995—. Mem. AMA, Assn. Univ. Radiologists, Am. Coll. Radiology, Radiol. Soc. N.Am., Am. Inst. Ultrasound in Medicine, Am. Soc. Emergency Radiology, Assn. Mil. Surgeons U.S., Med. Assn. Ga., Ga. Radiol. Soc., Richmond County Med. Soc. Office: Med Coll Ga Dept Radiology Augusta GA 30912

STUBBS, FRANK HUNTER, organization executive, lawyer; b. Tokyo, June 11, 1958; s. Frank Hunter Jr. and Ikuko (Hayakawa) S. BS, Coll. William and Mary, 1981; MS, Ctrl. Mich. U., 1984; JD, U. Richmond, 1993; MPA, Harvard U., 1994. Bar: Va. Profl. rep. Merck & Co., West Point, Pa., 1988-90; lawyer Glasser and Glasser, P.L.C., Norfolk, Va., 1994-95; lawyer in pvt. practice Chesapeake, Va., 1995-96; lawyer Smith & Jensen, P.C., Richmond, 1996; exec. dir. Urban League of Hampton Roads, Norfolk, 1996—; dir. med. readiness 439th Aeromed. Evacuation Squadron, Air Force Res., Westover AFB, Mass., 1995—. Mng. editor Harvard Jour. World Affairs, 1993-94. Vol. atty. AIDS Legal Svcs. S.E. Va., Norfolk, 1995—, VA Med. Ctr. Palliative Care Unit, Hampton, Va., 1994—; homeless shelter vol. Richmond Daily Planet, 1990-93; vol. math. tutor Alpha Phi Omega Nat. Svc. Frat., Williamsburg, Va., 1978-81. Capt. U.S. Army, 1981-88. Decorated Bronze Star medal, Army Commendation medal, Air Force Commendation medal; recipient Am. Jurisprudence award, 1993. Mem. ABA, Va. State Bar, Nat. Health Lawyers Assn., Am. Acad. Med. Adminstrs. Office: Urban League Hampton Roads 840 Church St Ste I Norfolk VA 23510

STUCK, ROGER DEAN, electrical engineering educator; b. Ventura, Calif., Nov. 6, 1924; s. William Henry and Marian Grace (Ready) S.; m. Opal Christine Phillips, July 25, 1948; children: Dean, Phyllis, Sandra. BSEE, Calif. Inst. Tech., 1947; MSEE, N.C. State U., 1957. Elec. engr. Warren Wilson Coll., Swannanoa, N.C., 1947—, instr. elec. engring. physics, 1948-69, dean students, 1969-72, instr. physics, elec. engr., 1972-86. Author: (charts) The Periodic Table of Physical Concepts, 1977, The Periodic Table of Physical Concepts with Economic Concepts, 1980; (book) The Periodic Table of Physical Concepts Book of Definitions, 1980. Lt. (j.g.) USNR, 1942-46. Mem. Sigma Xi. Republican. Presbyterian. Home: 65 Green Forest Rd Swannanoa NC 28778-2246

STUCKEY, BARBARA KATHRYN, publishing executive, trainer, consultant; b. Elgin, Ill.; d. John Elery and Hazel Margaret (Howard) Fletcher; m. James Merit Stuckey (div.). BA, Mary Washington Coll.; postgrad., The Catholic U., American U., U. Va. Support and asst. editor The Am. Aviation Pub. Co., Washington, D.C.; secondary sch. instr. Alexandria, Arlington, Falls Ch. Pub. Schs., Va.; owner, pres. The Exact Word, Arlington, Va. Author: (software) WordPrint: First of its Kind Syntax/Context Checker, 1994; (book) Bold English, 1985, Handbook: Elements of Thought, 1988, Successful Writing, 1989, Advanced Successful Writing, and Executive Communications, 1989, Executive Communications, 1990, Elements of Writing, 1992; inventor ThoughtPrint technology; profl. dancer. Recipient Agnes Myer award The Washington Post, D.C., 1984, 85, one of Va.'s Most Exciting New High-tech. Cos., Ctr. for Innovative Tech., 1994. Mem. NAFE, Am. Fedn. TV and Radio Artists (union mem.), Am. Guild Musical Artists (union mem., exec. com., rep. Wash., N.Y.), Fed. Exec. Inst. Alumni Assn. Office: The Exact Word Preston King Sta PO Box 5553 Arlington VA 22205

STUCKEY, SCOTT SHERWOOD, magazine editor; b. Wichita Falls, Tex., May 17, 1956; s. Norman Sherwood and Joanne Corinne (Scott) S. Student, Washburn U., 1974-75, U. Ibero-Am., Mexico City, 1978; BA, Kans. State U., 1979; MA, U. Mo., 1982. Reporter McPherson (Kans.) Sectinel, 1979, Topeka Capital-Jour., 1980; assoc. editor Boy's Life mag., Irving, Tex., 1983-86, mng. editor, 1986-90, exec. editor, 1990-93, editor, 1993-95; mng. editor Nat. Geog. World mag., Washington, 1995—. Mem. Soc. Profl. Journalists, Phi Beta Kappa, Kappa Tau Alpha. Home: 4964 Cloister Dr North Bethesda MD 20852 Office: National Geographic World Mag 1145 17th St NW Washington DC 20036-4688

STUCKY, DON E., family physician; b. Sidney, Mont., Jan. 4, 1949; s. Glenn Elmer and Dorothy Dolphin (Bailey) S.; m. Janet Louise Maxwell, Apr. 1, 1973; children: Bennett Taylor, William Paul. AB, Stanford U., 1971; MD, U. Nebr., 1975. Diplomate Am. Acad. Family Physicians. Pvt. practice Tahlequah, Okla., 1978—; chief family practice USPHS, IHS and E. E. Hastings Hosp., Tahlequah, 1978—. With USPHS. Democrat. Methodist. Home: 508 Greenwood Dr Tahlequah OK 74464-5141

STUFANO, THOMAS JOSEPH, investigative firm executive; b. Newport, R.I., July 23, 1955; s. Thomas and Zoe Anne (Halsey) S.; m. Sheila Murphy Stufano, May 22, 1978 (div. July 1988); 1 child, Christine Anne; m. Rene Ellen Goldfarb, Nov. 10, 1994. BSc in Criminal Justice, Pacific Western U., 1988; PhD in Criminal Justice, Clayton U., 1992. Legis. rschr. Rhode Island Ho. of Reps., Providence, R.I., 1978-79; sub com. investigator U.S. Ho. of Reps., Washington, 1979-81; law enforcement staff rschr. State of Fla., 1981-88; intelligence officer U.S. Govt., Washington, 1988-95; CEO Diversified Intelligence Group, Colorado Springs, Colo., 1995—; COO Starlink Telecomm. Technologies, Colorado Springs, Colo., 1996; cons. crime commn. State of Fla., 1986-87, U.S. Govt., Washington, 1990-92, State of R.I., Providence, 1979-80. Contbr. articles to profl. jours. Mem. Rep. Senatorial Inner Circle, Washington, 1992—; instr. ARC, Fla., 1994—; mem. adv. bd. Nat. Civil Def., Washington, 1988—. Recipient 3 Presdl. Commendation Pres. of U.S., 1991, Commendation U.S. Ho. of Reps. and Senate, 1982, 91, Prime Minister Lady Margaret Thatcher, 1991, Citation R.I. Ho. of Reps., 1980, Gov. of Mass., 1980, Tenn., Fla., Ky., 1990. Mem. Air Force Assn., World Assn. of Investigators, Civil Air Patrol, Aircraft Owners and Pilots Assn., Profl. Assn. of Diving Instrs. (instr., Platnuim Diving award 1989), Order of Ky. Cols. Roman Catholic. Home: PO Box 852 131 Aspen Dr Woodland Park CO 80863 Office: Starlink Telecomm Technologies 3474 N University Ste 523 Sunrise FL 33351

STULC, JAROSLAV PETER, surgeon, educator; b. Teplitz, Czechoslovakia, Sept. 14, 1947; came to U.S., 1948; s. Jaroslav Pavel and Emilie Vanca Stulc; m. Diana Susan Minassian, Dec. 27, 189; children: Alexan Christopher, Evan Thomas. BA, Cornell Coll., Mt. Vernon, Iowa, 1969; MD, U. Iowa, 1973. Diplomate Am. Bd. Surgery. Intern SUNY, Syracuse, 1973-75; resident in surgery Georgetown U., Washington, 1975-80, instr. surgery, 1979-80; instr. surgery, fellow transplant surgery Loyola U., Chgo., 1980-83; fellow surg. oncology Roswell Park Cancer Inst., Buffalo, 1983-85, attending surgeon, 1985-90; asst. prof. surgery SUNY, Buffalo, 1988-91; chief surgery VA Hosp., Buffalo, 1990-91; attending surgeon Trover Clinic Found., Madisonville, Ky., 1991—; clin. faculty U. Louisville, 1991—; co-dir. Mahr Cancer Ctr., Madisonville, 1992—. Editor Ky. Med. Jour., Physician Focus; contbr. articles and abstracts to publs. Vis. lectr. outreach program Am. Cancer Soc., bd. dirs. Ky. chpt., 1993—. Capt. USNR, 1987—. Fellow ACS (cert. advanced trauma life support), Internat. Coll. Surgeons; mem. AMA, AAAS, Am. Soc. Gastrointestinal Endoscopy, Am. Soc. Abdominal Surgeons, Am. Soc. Clin. Oncology, Soc. Am. Gastrointestinal Surgeons, Nat. Surg. Adjuvant Breast and Bowel Protocl, Ea. Coop. Oncology Group, Iowa Jr. Acad. Sci., Chgo. Assn. Immunologists, Roswell Park Surg. Soc., Buffalo Surg. Soc., Acad. Surg. Rsch., Assn. Acad. Surgery, Adrian Kantrowitz Surg. Rsch. Soc., Tri Beta. Presbyterian. Home: 1200 College Dr Madisonville KY 42431-9182 Office: Trover Clinic Found 435 N Kentucky Ave Madisonville KY 42431-1768

STULTZ, PATRICIA ADKINS, health care risk administrator; b. Wayne, W. Va.; d. John B. and Gladys (Osburn) Adkins; m. Joseph L. Stultz; children: Debra, Tammy. AS, Marshall U., 1978, BS, 1982; MS in Nursing, Bellarmine Coll., Louisville, Ky., 1990. RN, W. Va. Staff nurse Huntington (W.Va.) Hosp., 1978-79; staff nurse St. Mary's Hosp., 1979-82, nursing supr., 1982-89, nursing quality care, 1989-94, dir. risk mgmt., 1994—. Mem. Nat. Assn. Health Care Quality (cert. profl., presenter 1992 conf.), W. Va. Assn. Health Care Quality, Am. Assn. Healthcare Risk Mgmt., W. Va. Assn. Healtcare Risk Mgmt., Sigma Theta Tau (Nu Alpha chpt.). Home: 110 Beuhring St Lavalette WV 25535 Office: St Mary's Hosp 2900 First Ave Huntington WV 25701

STULTZ, THOMAS JOSEPH, newspaper executive; b. Ironton, Ohio, July 28, 1951; s. Riley Frederick and Mary (Leslie) S.; m. Patricia Ann Conley, Dec. 18, 1971; children: Leslie Faye, Jessica Kristin. Student, Ohio U., 1969-71, Marshall U., 1971, U. N.C., Chapel Hill. Reporter Ashland (Ky.) Daily Ind., 1970-73, Orlando (Fla.) Sentinel, 1973; owner/pub. Greenup County Sentinel, Greenup, Ky., 1973-80; editor, writer Bob Jones U., Greenville, S.C., 1980; advt. dir. Daily Adv., Greenville, 1980-81; dir. cmty. publs. Anderson (S.C.) Ind. Mail, 1981-84; v.p., gen. mgr. Leader Newspapers, Inc., Charlotte, N.C., 1984-86; mktg. dir. Suburban Newspapers Greater St. Louis, 1986-88; v.p. Multimedia Newspaper Co., Greenville, 1988-96; pres. pub. divsn. Gray Comms. Sys., Inc., Albany, Ga., 1996—; pres., owner Internat. Employment Gazette, Greenville, 1989—. Deacon, tchr. Temple Bapt. Ch., Flatwoods, Ky., 1978-80. Republican. Home: 6 Titleist Ct Taylors SC 29687-6651 Office: Gray Comms Sys Inc PO Box 48 Albany GA 31701

STUMBO, JANET L., judge; b. Prestonsburg, Ky.; d. Charles and Doris Stanley S.; m. Ned Pillersdorf; children: Sarah, Nancee, Samantha. BA, Morehead State U., 1976; JD, U. Ky., 1980. Bar: Ky. 1980, W. Va. 1982. Staff atty. to Judge Harris S. Howard Ky. Ct. Appeals, 1980-82; asst. county atty. Floyd County, 1982-85; pvt. practice Turner, Hall & Stumbo, P.S.C., 1982-88; prosecutor Floyd Dist. Ct. and Juvenile Ct.; ptnr. Stumbo, DeRossett & Pillersdorf, 1989; judge Ct. Appeals, Ky., 1989-93, Supreme Ct. of Ky., 1993—. Named to Morehead State U. Alumni Assn. Hall of Fame, 1990; recipient Justice award Ky. Women Advocates, 1991, Outstanding Just award Ky. Women Advocates, 1995, Bull's Eye award Women in State Govt. Network, 1995. Office: Ky Supreme Ct Capital Bldg Rm 226 700 Capital Ave Frankfort KY 40601

STUMP, T(OMMY) DOUGLAS, lawyer, educator; b. Cushing, Okla., Jan. 7, 1957; s. Thomas Burl and Lindsey L. (Laffoon) S.; children: Kelli Jo and Matthew Douglas. BA in English, E. Ctrl. U., Ada, Okla., 1979; JD, Oklahoma City U., 1982. Bar: Okla. 1983, U.S. Dist. Ct. (we. dist.) Okla. 1983, U.S. Ct. Appeals (10th cir.) 1983, U.S. Dist. Ct. (ea. and no. dists.) Okla. 1986, U.S. Ct. Appeals (5th cir.) 1986, U.S. Supreme Ct. 1986. Founding atty. T. Douglas Stump & Assocs., Oklahoma City, 1990—; adj. prof. law Oklahoma City U., asst. project coord. Okla./Am. Immigration Lawyers Assn. Pro Bono Amnesty Appeals Project, 1987-89; mem. pro bono panel (immigration) Legal Aid of Western Okla.; lectr. various continuing legal edn. programs, immigration seminars, 1983-94. Author: Matrimonal Maladies and the Alien, 1983, General Information Concerning United States Immigration Laws, 1989, L-1 Intracompany Transfers, 1995, Employment Based Immigration Law, 1995. Bd. dirs. Lyric Theater, mem. exec. com., co-sponsor various prodns., 1992-95, Oklahoma City Econ. Roundtable, founder and provider Focus on Success Scholarship Fund, Drumright H.S., Oklahoma City, 1993—. Fellow Okla. Bar Found., mem. ABA (young lawyers divsn. del. 1988, 1989, exec. mem. young lawyers divsn. com. on immigration law), Am. Immigration Lawyers Assn. (Okla., Tex., N.M. chptrs., chmn. com. on nonimmigrant visas 1986-88, Oklahoma City sect. chmn. 1987-91, chmn. membership com. 1988-90, treas. 1991-92, vice chmn. 1992-93, chmn. legis. action com., Okla. City INS liaison 1995—), Okla. Bar Assn. (treas. 1988, sec. 1989, mem. com. on legal specialization 1987-91, mem. spl. com. on Unauthorized Practice of Law 1988-90, mem. house counsel sect. 1988—, mem. com. on legal ethics 1990-92, com. on civil procedure 1991-94, mem. solo and small firm task force 1993—, bd. dirs. young lawyers divsn. 1986-90, dir. com. on alien/refugee assistance 1986-89, chmn. com. on alien/refugee assistance 1986-90, Outstanding Dir. award 1987), Oklahoma County Bar Assn (mem. Law Day com. 1983-84, participant "Ask A Lawyer" programs 1986-91, dir. Young Lawyers Assn. 1987, mem. fee grievance com. 1990-91), Oklahoma City U. Law Sch. Alumni Assn. (bd. dirs. 1989-94, pres. 1992-94, Outstanding Law School Alumni award 1993). Republican. Office: 50 Penn Pl Ste 1320 Oklahoma City OK 73118

STURDEVANT, WAYNE ALAN, computer scientist, instructor; b. Portland, Oreg., Apr. 3, 1946; s. Hervey Sturdevant and Georgia (Rawls) Bright; m. Helen F. Radbury, Sept. 24, 1976; children: Wayne Alan Jr., Stephen Thomas, John Howard, Brian Alan, Daniel Robert. BS in Edn., So. Ill. U., 1980. With USAF, 1964-85; supt. USAF On-Job-Tng. Svc., 1978-82, chief, 1982-85; ret., 1985; lead engr. instl. tech. McDonnell Douglas Corp., St. Louis, 1985-88; mgr., instr. sys. design Southeastern Computer Cons., Inc., Austin, 1988—; developed advanced concepts in occupational edn. and computer-based tng. design, innovations in support of ISO 9000. Contbr. articles on mgmt. and tng. innovations in the work place to profl. jours. Active mem. Bishop LDS Ch., 1983-84, mem. stake presidency, 1990-96, mem. mission presidency, 1996—; mem. exec. bd. Boy Scouts Am., 1986—. Recognized for leadership in multi-nat. programs; recipient Citation of Honor Air Force Assn., 1980, Award of Merit Boy Scouts Am., 1996. Mem. Internat. Orgn. for Standardization, Am. Soc. for Quality Control. Republican. Home: 9214 Independence Loop Austin TX 78748-6312

STURGEON, CHARLES EDWIN, management consultant; b. Cherryvale, Kans., May 30, 1928; s. William Charles and Lucile Myrtle (Gill) S.; children by previous marriage: Carol Ann, John Randolph, Richard Steven; m. Karen B. Riggan, May 21, 1988. A.A., Independence Jr. Coll., 1948; B.S., U. Kans., 1951; postgrad., U. Tulsa Grad. Sch., 1953-56; grad., Advanced Mgmt. Program, Harvard Bus. Sch., 1977. Research engr. Stanoline Oil and Gas, Tulsa, 1953-56; production supr. Vulcan Materials Co., Wichita, Kans., 1956-62; maintenance supt. Vulcan Materials Co., 1962-64, mgr. tech. services, 1964-69; plant mgr. Vulcan Materials Co., Newark, N.J., 1970-71; gen. mktg. mgr., v.p. mktg. Vulcan Materials Co., Wichita, 1971-73; v.p. mfg. Vulcan Materials Co., Birmingham, Ala., 1974-77, pres. chem. div., 1977-87, pres., sr. v.p., 1987-90; prin. CESCO Cons. Co., Birmingham, 1990-96, Sturgeon Energy Co., Birmingham, 1996—. Adv. U. Kans. Sch. Chem. Engring. Served with U.S. Army, 1951-53. Mem. Am. Inst. Chem. Engrs., Nat. Mgmt. Assn., Chlorine Inst. (bd. dirs.), Chem. Mfg. Assn., Soc. Chem. Industries, Soc. of Materials, The Club Inc., Tau Theta Pi, Tau Beta Pi, Sigma Tau. Republican. Presbyterian.

STURGES, ROBERT STUART, English language educator; b. Bridgeport, Conn., Apr. 29, 1953; s. Clifford William and Barbara Alice (Mackey) S. BA, U. Bridgeport, 1974; MA, Brown U., 1976, PhD, 1979. Asst. prof. lit. MIT, Cambridge, Mass., 1980-81; asst. prof. English Wesleyan U., Middletown, Conn., 1981-88; asst. prof. English U. New Orleans, 1988-91, assoc. prof. English, 1991-96, prof. English, 1996—; mem. editorial bd. Arthuriana, Dallas, 1994—. Author: Medieval Interpretation, 1991; contbr. articles to profl. jours. ACLS grantee, 1982; Mellon Found. fellow, 1984-85, Wesleyan Ctr. Humanities Faculty fellow, 1984. Mem. Internat. Arthurian Soc., South Ctrl. Modern Lang. Assn., Southeastern Medieval Assn., MLA Lesbian and Gay Caucus. Democrat. Office: U New Orleans Dept English New Orleans LA 70148

STUTTS, GARY THOMAS, health facility administrator; b. Dyersburg, Tenn., Feb. 13, 1957; s. Wiley Thomas and Betty Jane (Weeks) S.; m. Amy Ayers, June 19, 1993; children: Andrew Thomas, Emily Lynn, Joseph Wayne. AS, Austin Peay State U., Clarksville, Tenn., 1982; BS, Coll. St. Francis, Joliet, Ill., 1991. RN, Tenn. Organ donor coord. Nashville Regional Organ Procurement Agy., 1984-85; staff nurse emergency unit Jesse Holman Jones Hosp., Springfield, Tenn., 1982-83; mem. nursing staff emergency dept. Jackson-Madison County Gen. Hosp., Jackson, Tenn., 1983-94; nursing instr. Tenn. Tech. Ctr. at Jackson, 1994-95; geriat. liaison psychiat. unit Bolivar (Tenn.) Gen. Hosp., 1995—; nurse preceptor Genentech, Inc.; mem. nursing practice adv. com. Tenn. Bd. Nursing. Home: 229 Farmington Dr Jackson TN 38305-3818

STUTZMAN, BETH ANN, middle school educator; b. Bellevue, Pa., Sept. 25, 1967; d. William Joseph and Roberta Elaine (Hustus) Poole; m. Richard Joe Stutzman, Dec. 12, 1987; children: Ryan Joseph, Brooklynn Elaine. BA, Southeastern U., Lakeland, Fla., 1989. Tchr. Sebring (Fla.) Mid. Sch., 1990-94; tchr., team leader Avon Park (Fla.) Mid. Sch., 1994—; tutor Fed. Migrant After Sch. tutorial Program, Sebring, Avon Park, 1990—. Project S.U.C.C.E.S.S. grantee, 1995. Mem. NEA. Republican. Pentecostal Assembly of God Ch. Home: 412 E Camphor St Avon Park FL 33825-4202

SU, KENDALL LING-CHIAO, engineering educator; b. Fujian, China, July 10, 1926; came to U.S., 1948; s. Ru-chen and Sui-hsiong (Wang) S.; m. Jennifer Gee-tsone Chang, Sept. 10, 1960; children: Adrienne, Jonathan. BEE, Xiamen U., Peoples Republic China, 1947; MEE, Ga. Inst. Tech, 1949; PhD, Ga. Inst. Tech., 1954. Jr. engr. Taiwan Power Co., Taipei, Republic China, 1947-48; asst. prof. Ga. Inst. Tech., Atlanta, 1954-59, assoc. prof., 1959-65, prof., 1965-70, Regents prof., 1970-94, Regents' prof. emeritus, 1994—; mem. tech. staff Bell Labs., Murray Hill, N.J., 1957. Author: Active Network Synthesis, 1965, Time-Domain Synthesis of Linear Networks, 1969, Fundamentals of Circuits, Electronics, and Signal Analysis, 1978, Handbook of Tables for Elliptic-Function Filters, 1990, Fundamentals of Circuit Analysis, 1993, Analog Filters, 1996; mem. sci. adv. com. Newton Graphic Sci. mag., 1987—. Fellow IEEE (life); mem. Sigma Xi (pres. Ga. Inst. Tech. chpt. 1968-69, 72-73, Faculty Rsch. award 1957), Phi Kappa Phi, Eta Kappa Nu. Methodist. Office: Ga Inst Tech Sch Elec & Comp Engring Atlanta GA 30332-0250

SU, NAN-YAO, entomology educator; b. Li-Kang, Pin-Tong, Taiwan, Apr. 2, 1951; came to U.S., 1978; s. Chong-Chin Su and Ho-Mei Su-Lin; m. Jill Halliburton, Nov. 26, 1983; children: Amanda May, Justin William. BS, Kyoto Inst. Tech, Kyoto, Japan, 1975, MS, 1977; PhD, U. Hawaii, 1982. Rsch. asst., entomology dept. U. Hawaii, Honolulu, 1978-81; asst. entomologist U. Hawaii, Honolulu, Hawaii, 1984; post dr. assoc., entomology dept. La. State U., Baton Rouge, 1982-83; asst. prof. U. Fla., Ft. Lauderdale, 1984-88, assoc. prof., 1988-94, prof., 1994—. Editor: Isoptera Newsletter; co-editor: Biology & Control of the Formosan sub. Termite, 1987; contbr. articles to profl. jours. Contbg. mem. Amnesty Internat, N.Y., 1987—, So. Poverty Law Ctr., Atlanta, 1989, Hand Gun Control, Inc., Washington, 1988. Recipient Distinguished Achievement award Orkin, Inc., Atlanta, 1990, 93, Individual Rsch. Achievement award U.S. Sec. Agrl., 1996. Mem. Entomological Soc. am., Internat. Union Study of Social Insects, Internat. Rsch. Group on Wood Preservation, Internat. Isoptera Soc. (chmn. orgn. com. 1990), Fla. Entomological Soc. (resolution com. 1986-88, Achievement award for Rsch., 1992), Hawaiian Entomological Soc., Ga. Entomological

Soc. Democrat. Office: U Fla Ft Lauderdale REC 3205 College Ave Fort Lauderdale FL 33314-7719

SU, TSUNG-CHOW JOE, engineering educator; b. Taipei, Taiwan, Republic of China, July 9, 1947; came to U.S., 1969; s. Chin-shui and Chen-ling (Shih) S.; m. Hui-Fang Angie Huang, Dec. 26, 1976; children: Julius Tsu-Li, Jonathan Tsu-Wei, Judith Tsu-Te, Jessica Tsu-Yun. BS, Nat. Taiwan U., 1968; MS in Aeronautics, Calif. Inst. Technology, 1970, AE, 1973; EngScD, Columbia U., 1974. Registered profl. engr., Fla., Tex. Rsch. teaching asst. Calif. Inst. Technology, Pasadena, 197-72; rsch. asst. Columbia U., N.Y.C., 1972-73; naval architect John J. McMullen Assoc., Inc., N.Y.C., 1974-75; asst. prof. civil engring. Tex. A&M U., College Station, Tex., 1976-82; assoc. prof. ocean engring. Fla. Atlantic U., Boca Raton, 1982-87, prof. ocean engring, 1987-92, prof. mech. engring., 1992—. Contbr. more than 80 articles and papers to profl. jours.; assoc. editor Jour. Engring. Mechs., 1991-94. Coord. Calif. Tech. Alumni Fund, South Fla. area, 1987-88. 2d lt. Chinese Army, 1968-69. Grantee in field. Fellow AIAA (assoc.); mem. ASME, ASCE (chmn. fluids com. 1992-94), Am. Acad. Mechanics, Calif. Tech. Alumni Assn., Royal Palm Improvement Assn. Home: 2150 Areca Palm Rd Boca Raton FL 33432-7994 Office: Fla Atlantic U Dept Mech Engring Boca Raton FL 33431

SUAREZ, CELIA CRISTINA, university official; b. Habana, Cuba, Dec. 5, 1943; came to U.S., 1960; d. Ramon Florencio and Sarah (Pino) S.; m. Nicolas L. Perez-Stable, Aug. 1975; widowed; 1 child, Nicolas A. BA in History, Cath. U. Am., 1965, MS in Libr. Sci., 1970; EdD in Cmty. Coll. Teaching, Fla. Internat. U., 1994. Asst. to libr. dir. to libr. dir. Fla. Atlantic U., Miami, 1970-72; reference libr. World U. Libr., Rio Piedras, P.R., 1973; libr. Miami Dade C.C., 1973-75; dir. libr. svcs., head libr. North Campus Miami-Dade C.C., 1975-81, assoc. dean for instrnl. support and learning resources, 1981—; papers presented at Fla. Libr. Assn., 1978, 81, Fla. Devel. Edn. Assn., 1978, Broward County Libr. Assn., 1978, Fla. Atlantic U., 1982, Libr. of Congress, Washington, 1985, Cuban Am. Nat. Coun., Miami, 1986, Channel 17 program, 1989, U.S. Postal Svc., Miami, 1990, Miami-Dade C.C., 1992, 93; adj. instr. Fla. State U., 1978, 85, InterAm. Ctr., 1989; chair resource Cooperation Standing Com. of Coll. Ctr. for Libr. Automation, 1995—. Contbr. articles to profl. jours. Exec. bd. dirs. Cuban Am. Nat. Coun.; bd. dirs. Cuban Cultural Forum, 1990, New Horizons Cmty. Mental Health Ctr., 1984; mem. Hispanic leadership devel. com. United Way, 1984-86; com. on implementation of Fla. Equity Act of 1985, Dade County Sch. Bd., 19845-86; minority and women procurement adv. com. City of Miami, 1987; mem. planning com. and del. selection com. Fla. Gov.'s Conf. on Librs. and Info. Svsc., 1989-90. Mem. Fla. Libr. Assn. (chair cmty. and jr. coll. caucus, 1979, bd. dirs. 1985-87, chair libr. adminstr. caucus 1988-89), Fla. Assn. C.C.'s (learning resources state-wide task force 1985-87), Dade County Libr. Assn., Fla. Devel. Edn. Assn. (pres., v.p. 1978-80), Greater Miami C. of C. (leadership Miami conf. participant 1982, task force on conf. 1983, bd. dirs. 1983-85, exec. com. 1985), Coalition of Hispanic Am. Women (chair ann. conf. 1983, bd. dirs. 1984, issues com. 1985-86). Office: Miami-Dade CC 11380 NW 27th Ave Miami FL 33167-3418

SUAREZ, GEORGE MICHAEL, urologist; b. Havana, Cuba, Apr. 21, 1955; came to U.S., 1955; s. Miguel Angel and Elena (Sanchez) S. BA, Heideberg U., 1976; MD, U. Dominica, Portsmouth, 1980, Rutgers U., 1980. Diplomate Am. Bd. Urology; lic. physician, Ind., Fla., La. Intern straight gen. surgery Columbus-Cuneo-Cabrini Med. Ctr., Northwestern U. Med. Sch., Chgo., 1980-81; resident gen. surgery Columbus-Cuneo-Cabrini Med. Ctr., Northwestern U. Med. Sch., 1981-82; urology rsch. fellow Tulane U. Sch. Medicine and Delta Regional Primate Ctr., New Orleans, 1982-83; resident, chief resident urology Tulane U. Sch. Medicine, New Orleans, 1983-87; attending urologist, dir. urodynamics lab. spinal cord unit VA Med. Ctr., Miami, Fla., 1987-90; attending urologist U. Miami Hosp. and Clinics, 1987-90, dir. Urodynamics Lab., Jackson Meml. Med. Ctr., 1987-90, dir. urology rehab. rsch. program Bantle Rehab. Rsch. Ctr., 1987—; attending urologist Jackson Meml. Hosp., Miami, 1987—; asst. prof. dept. urology U. Miami Sch. Medicine, 1987-90; cons. Sylvester Comprehensive Cancer Ctr., Miami, 1987—, Childrens Med. Svcs., Miami, 1987—, Avalon Technologies, Indpls., Mentor Corp., Santa Barbara, Calif., Cook Urol., Spence, Ind., Teknar Ultrasound, Inc., Santa Barbara, Schering Labs. N.J., Rorer Pharms., Ft. Washington, Pa.; attending urologist Doctors Hosp., Bat. Hosp., Childrens Hosp., South Miami Hosp., Larkin Hosp., Mercy Hosp., Victoria Hosp., West Gables Hosp., Cedars Med. Ctr., Kidney Stone Ctr. Contbr. articles to profl. jours. Founder, pres. For the Love of Life Found. Recipient Urology Rsch. award Touro Infirmary Hosp., New Orleans, 1983-84, award of excellence Video Urology, 1989. Mem. ACS, AMA, Am. Acad. Pediatrics, Am. Fertility Soc., Am. Med. Polit. Action Com., Am. Soc. Andrology,. Am. Urol. Assn., Colegio Interam. de Medicos y Cirujanos, Am. Confederation Urology, Cuban Am. Urol. Soc., Dade County Med. Assn., European Urologic Soc., Fla. Med. Assn., Fla. Urol. Soc., Internat. Continence Soc., Greater Miami Urol. Soc., N.Y. Acad. Scis., So. Med. Assn., World Med. Assn., Urodynamics Soc., Surg. Aid to Children of the World, Internat. Soc. Urology. Office: Miami Urologic Inst 7051 SW 62nd Ave Miami FL 33143-4701

SUAREZ, ROBERTO, retired newspaper publishing executive; b. Havana, Cuba; came to U.S., 1961; m. Pitucha Campuzano; children: 7 sons, 5 daughters. Student, Colegio de Belén, Cuba; grad., Villanova Coll., 1949. Various postions in real estate, constrn., fin. Havana, 1950-60; from part-time mailer to contr. The Herald's subs., 1962-72; contr. Knight Pub. Co., Charlotte, N.C., 1972-78; v.p., gen. mgr. The Miami (Fla.) Herald, 1978-86, pres., 1986—; pub. El Nuevo Herald Knight Ridder Pub. Co., 1986-96. Past pres. Art and Sci. Coun., Spirit Sq. Arts Ctr., Charleston; chair Kids Voting/Dade County; bd. dirs. United Way. Recipient Gold medal Knight-Ridder Pub. Co., 1989, Heritage award HIspanic Alliance, 1990, Leadership award ASPIRA, 1991, Marion Guastella award Asociacion de Publicitarios Latinoamericanos, 1993. Mem. Inter Am. Press Assn. (pres. exec. com.), N.C. Press Assn. (former treas.), Interam. Businessmen Assn.

SUAREZ, VIRGIL, writer; b. Havana, Cuba, Jan. 29, 1962; came to U.S., 1974; s. Virgilio Rafael Suarez and Oneida Lopez-Rodriguez; m. Delia Poey; 2 children. BA in Creative Writing, Calif. State U., 1984; MFA in Creative Writing, La. State U., 1987. Instr. La. State U., 1991-93; asst. prof. Fla. State U., Tallahassee, 1993-96, assoc. prof., 1996—; adj. instr. Miami Dade C.C., 1988, 89, Fla. Internat. U., 1989-91, U. Miami, 1989-91. Author: Latin Jazz, 1990, The Cutter, 1991, Welcome to the Oasis, 1992, Iguana Dreams: New Latino Fiction, 1992, 2d edit., 1993, Paper Dance, 1994, Havana Thursdays, 1995, Going Under: A Cuban-American Fable, 1996; contbr. articles to profl. publs. Mem. MLA, PEN, Cuban-Am. Tchrs. Assn., Associated Writers' Program. Office: Fla State U Dept English Williams Bldg Tallahassee FL 32306

SUBA, STEVEN ANTONIO, obstetrician, gynecologist; b. Columbia, Mo., July 4, 1957; s. Antonio Ronquillo and Sylvia Marie (Karl) S.; m. Brenda Charlene Crosby, Aug. 9, 1986; children: Bethany Caroline, Sarah Marie. BA in Biology, St. Mary's U., San Antonio, 1979; MD, Tex. Tech U., 1984. Diplomate Am. Bd. Ob.-Gyn. Resident ob-gyn. Tex. Tech. U., Lubbock, Tex., 1984-87; chief resident ob-gyn. John Peter Smith Hosp., Ft. Worth, 1987-88; pvt. practice ob-gyn. Ft. Worth, 1988—. Fellow Am. Coll. Ob.-Gyn., mem. AMA, Tex. Med. Assn. Office: 6100 Harris Pky Ste 245 Fort Worth TX 76132-4107

SUBER, MARGARET ADELE, controller; b. New Orleans, Mar. 18, 1917; d. Harvey and Marie Bridget (Babin) Pearson; m. Thomas Joseph Scullin, Jan. 1937 (div. Nov. 1945); 1 child, Thomas Joseph; m. Thomas James Bresnahan, Dec. 1945 (div. July 1957); m. John M. Suber, Sept. 1957 (div. May 1964). Owner, mgr. various restaurants and clubs New Orleans, 1934-56; office mgr. Hausmann's Jewelry, New Orleans, 1960-68; bus. adminstr. New Orleans Jewish Home, 1969-72; acct. United Acceptance Corp., Metairie, La., 1972-74; chief acct. Automotive Svcs., New Orleans, 1974-75; controller Davis Industries, Metairie, 1975-76, Stuart Homes, Inc., Marrero, La., 1976-81, Canal Gift Shop, Inc., New Orleans, 1981—. Hon. mem. Boys Town. Republican. Roman Catholic. Home: 3200 Garden Oaks Dr Apt 706 New Orleans LA 70114-6752

SUBLETT, JAMES LEE, allergist, immunologist, pediatrician; b. Campbellsville, Ky., 1948. MD, U. Louisville, 1975. Diplomate Am. Bd. Allergy and Immunology, Am. Bd. Pediat. Intern U. Louisville, 1975-76, resident in pediat., 1976-77, resident in allergy and immunology, 1977-79; with Kosair Childrens Hosp., Louisville; assoc. clin. prof. U. Louisville; sect. chief allergy and immunology dept. pediats. U. Louisville. Fellow Am. Acad. Allergy, Asthma, and Immunology, Am. Coll. Allergy, Asthma, and Immunology; mem. Am. Acad. Pediat., Ky. Med. Assn. Office: Allergy and Asthma Assocs 9800 Shelbyville Rd Ste 220 Louisville KY 40223-5440

SUBLETTE, JULIA WRIGHT, music educator, performer, adjudicator; b. Natural Bridge, Va., Sept. 13, 1929; d. Paul Thomas and Annie Belle (Watkins) Wright; m. Richard Ashmore Sublette, Oct. 18, 1952; children: C. Mark, Carey P., Sylvia S. Bennett, Wright D. BA in Music, Furman U., 1951; MusM, Cin. Conservatory, 1954; postgrad., Chautaugua Inst., N.Y., 1951-52; PhD, Fla. State U., 1993. Ind. piano tchr., 1953—; instr. music and humanities Okaloosa-Walton C.C., Niceville, Fla., 1978—; panelist Music Tchr. Nat. Conv., Milw., 1992; instr. art humanities Troy State U., Ala. Editor Fla. Music Tchr., 1991—; contbr. articles to profl. music jours. Mem. AAUW, Music Tchrs. Nat. Assn. (cert., chmn. so. divsn. jr. high sch. piano/instrumental contests 1986-88), Fla. State Music Tchrs. Assn., So. Assn. Women Historians, Southeastern Hist. Keyboard Soc., Friday Morning Music Club, Colonial Dames of 17th Century Am., Pi Kappa Lambda. Home: 217 Country Club Rd Shalimar FL 32579-2203

SUBRAMAN, MARY BELINDA (BELINDA SUBRAMAN), writer; b. Stateville, N.C., Sept. 6, 1953; d. Thomas Lee and Mary Louise (Elledge) Bumgarner; m. Ramnath Subramanion, Sept. 24, 1977; children: Anna, Sundari. MA in humanities, Calif. State U., 1990. Editor Vergin' Press, El Paso, Tex., 1983—; freelance writer El Paso, 1975—; featured reader Calif. State U., Long Beach, 1994; featured reader, com. head Border Voices Literary Festival, El Paso, 1994—. Author: Elephants & Angels, 1991; editor: The Gulf War: Many Perspectives, 1992, Earth Tones: Creative Perspectives on Ecological Issues, 1994, (magazine) GYPSY, 1984—. Home: 10708 Gay Brewer Dr El Paso TX 79935-2004 Office: Vergin' Press PO Box 370322 El Paso TX 79937

SUDDUTH, ALBERT SCOTT, JR., lawyer; b. Washington, Mar. 23, 1959; s. Albert Scott Sudduth and Gladys Virginia Heller; m. Mary Alice Rogers, Aug. 10, 1991. BA, U. Tex., 1982; JD, Cath. U. Am., 1989. Bar: Va. Mem. legis. staff U.S. Senator Lloyd Bentsen, Washington, 1981-84; mgr. strategic planning AT&T, N.Y.C., 1984-85; comm. dir. Am. Retail Fedn., Washington, 1986-89; chief of staff U.S. Congressman Pete Geren, Washington, 1990-92; asst. vice chancellor U. Tex. System, Austin. Mem. ABA, Va. Bar Assn. Office: The U of Tex System 201 W 6th St Austin TX 78701

SUDHIVORASETH, NIPHON, pediatrician, allergist, immunologist; b. Bangkok, Thailand, 1940. MD, Chulalongkorn Hosp. U., Bangkok, 1966. Diplomate Am. Bd. Pediatrics, Am. Bd. Allergy and Immunology. Intern Ch. Home Hosp., Balt., 1967-68; resident in pediatrics St. Lukes Hosp., N.Y.C., 1968-69, Beth Israel Hosp., N.Y.C., 1969-70; fellow in allergy Metro Hosp., N.Y. Med. Coll., N.Y.C., 1970-72; staff Marshall Meml. Hosp., Tex., 1978—; pvt. practice. Mem. AMA, Am. Acad. Allergy, Asthma, and Immunology, Am. Acad. Pediats., Am. Coll. Allergy and Immunology. Office: PO Box 2087 705 S Grove St Marshall TX 75670-5220

SUELTENFUSS, SISTER ELIZABETH ANNE, academic administrator; b. San Antonio, Apr. 14, 1921; d. Edward L. and Elizabeth (Amrein) S. BA in Botany and Zoology, Our Lady of Lake Coll., San Antonio, 1944; MS in Biology, U. Notre Dame, 1961, PhD, 1963. Joined Sisters of Divine Providence, Roman Catholic Ch., 1939; tchr. high schs. Okla. and La., 1942-49; mem. summer faculty Our Lady of Lake U. (formerly coll.), 1941-49, mem. full-time faculty, 1949-59, chmn. biology dept., 1963-73, pres., 1978—; mem. adminstrv. staff to superior gen. Congregation Divine Providence, 1973-77. Author articles in field. Bd. dirs. Am. Cancer Soc., San Antonio chpt. ARC, Mind Sci. Found., YWCA, Alamo Pub. Telecomm. Bd., S.W. Rsch. Found., I Have a Dream Found., Inst. Ednl. Leadership, Trim and Swim, San Antonio Edn. Partnership; bd. dirs., chmn. San Antonio Pub. Libr. Recipient Achievement and Leadership awards U. Notre Dame, 1979, Svc. to Community award, 1991, Headliner award Women in Comms., 1980, Good Neighbor award NCCJ, 1982, Brotherhood award, 1992, Today's Woman award San Antonio Light, 1982, Outstanding Women award San Antonio Express-News, 1983, Spirit of Am. Woman award J.C. Penney, 1992, Lifetime Achievement award, 1993, Svc. to Edn. awrd Ford Found., 1993; named to San Antonio Women's Hall of Fame, 1985. Mem. AAUP, AAUW, San Antonio 100 Tex. Women's Forum, San Antonio Women's C. of C., Hispanic Assn. Colls. and Univs., Greater San Antonio C. of C. (past vice chmn.), San Antonio Coun. Pres. (past pres.), San Antonio Women's Hall of Fame (past pres.). Home and Office: Our Lady of the Lake U Office of Pres 411 SW 24th St San Antonio TX 78207-4689

SUESS, JAMES FRANCIS, clinical psychologist; b. Evanston, Ill., Aug. 8, 1950; s. James Francis and Rae Love (Miller) S.; m. Linda Grace Powell, July 31, 1976; 1 child, Misty Lynne. BS, U. So. Miss., 1974, MS, 1978, PhD, 1982. Lic. psychologist, N.Y., Ala.; diplomate Am. Bd. Profl. Psychology, Am. Bd. Med. Psychotherapists, Profl. Assn. Custody Evaluators, Am. Coll. Forensic Examiners. Assoc. psychologist State of Miss., Ellisville, 1978-80; clin. psychologist SUNY Med. Sch./Erie County Med. Ctr., Buffalo, 1982-84, supervisiong clin. psychologist, 1984-87, assoc. dir., 1987—; dir. practica SUNY Med. Sch., 1982-90, faculty counsel, 1988—; cons. Buffalo Dept. Social Svcs., 1985—; mem. spkrs. bur. Erie Alliance for Mentally Ill, 1986—; vis. prof. U. Guadalajara Sch. Medicine, 1985—; clin. dir. Stickney Adolescent Ctr. Mobile Met. Hosp. Ctr., 1993—. Author: Annotated Bibliography of Sex Roles, 1972, Personality Disorder and Self Psychology, 1991; contbr. articles to refereed jours. including Perceptual and Motor Skills, Jour. Clin. and Consulting Psychology, Am. Annals of Deaf. With USAR, 1969-76. Fellow Am. Orthopsychiat. Assn., Soc. Personality Assessment; mem. Am. Psychol. Assn. Home: 407 Stillwood Ln Mobile AL 36608-5847 Office: Baycare Hosp Stickney Ctr 1504 Springhill Ave Mobile AL 36604-3207

SUGAR, MAX, physician, psychiatrist, medical educator; b. Toronto, June 5, 1925; came to U.S., 1948; m. Barbara Avera; children: Melissa, David, Roxanne, Michael. MD, U. Toronto, 1948. Diplomate Am. Bd. Psychiatry and Neurology, Am. Bd. Child Psychiatry, Am. Bd. Adolescent Psychiatry. Intern Touro Infirmary, New Orleans, 1948-49, resident in pathology, 1949-50; resident in psychiatry La. State U.-Charity Hosp., New Orleans, 1952-53, 55-57; fellow in child psychiatry Child Guidance Ctr. New Orleans Tulane U., New Orleans, 1962-64; pvt. practice New Orleans, 1957—; instr. La. State U., New Orleans, 1957-62, clin. asst. prof. psychiatry, 1962-64, clin. assoc. prof. psychiatry, 1964-74, dir. child adolescent psychiatry and group therapy, 1964-68, prof. clin. psychiatry, 1974—; unit dir. children's unit Coliseum Med. Ctr., New Orleans, 1983-85; clin. prof. psychiatry Tulane U., New Orleans, 1985—; dir. profl. edn. and psychiat. residency tng. Coliseum Med. Ctr., New Orleans, 1985-88, mem. at large exec com., 1986-87, mem. bylaws com., 1990-92; vis. physician Charity Hosp., New Orleans, 1957-67, sr. vis. physician, 1967-87; staff mem. DePaul Hosp., New Orleans, 1957—, chmn. program com., 1960; lectr. nursing staff and edn. faculty Touro Infirmary, New Orleans, 1957, staff mem., 1957-71, mem. nursing com., 1962-64; lectr., cons. psychotherapy VA Hosps., Gulfport and Tuskegee, 1958-59; staff mem. New Orleans Child Guidance Ctr., 1961-62, Children's Hosp., New Orleans, 1976-90, East Jefferson Gen. Hosp., Metairie, 1976—, Lakeside Hosp., Metairie, 1976—; spl. lectr. child psychiatry sch. social welfare La. State U., Baton Rouge, 1961-65; group psychotherapy cons. La. State Evaluation Ctr. Exceptional Children, New Orleans, 1962-64; instr., chmn. faculty La. Group Psychotherapy Inst., 1967—; med. advisor U.S. HEW, 1972—; lectr. Tulane U. Sch. Social Work, New Orleans, 1978—; cons. Evangeline Area Guidance Ctr., Lafayette, La., 1956-57, USPHS, New Orleans, 1957, Family Svc. Soc., 1967, Kingsley House, 1964-68, Crippled Children's Hosp., 1964-68, Shreveport Mental Health Ctr. NIMH Project, 1966-68, St. Elizabeth's Home for Girls, New Orleans, 1967-69, Orleans Neighborhood Ctrs., 1964-67, Jefferson Parish Juvenile Ct., 1973—, East Jefferson Hosp. Psychiatry Unit, Metairie, La., 1976-79, others; mem. rev. bd. Hosp. and Community Psychiatry, 1979—; rschr. in field. Author: (with others) Adolescence: Care and Counseling, 1967, Adolescents Grow in Groups, 1972, The Adolescent in Group and Family Therapy, 1975, When Schools Care, 1975, Female Adolescent Development, 1979, Responding to Adolescent Needs, 1980, Psychotherapy Handbook, 1980, New Directions for Mental Health Services, 1980, Prevention of Psychosocial Disorders in Infancy: Emerging Perspectives for the 80s, 1981, Group and Family Therapy, 1981, others; author: The Premature in Context, 1982; editor: The Adolescent in Group and Family Therapy, 1975, 2d edit., 1986, Female Adolescent Development, 1979, 2d edit., 1993, Responding to Adolescent Needs, 1980, Adolescent Parenthood, 1984, Adolescent Psychiatry, vol. 11, 1984, Atypical Adolescence and Sexuality, 1990; mem. editl. bd. Group Process, 1969-74, Adolescent Psychiatry, 1970—, Jour. Youth and Adolescence, 1977—, Jour. Adolescence, 1985-91, Adolescent and Pediatric Gynecology, 1986—, others; mem. rev. bd. Jour. Clin. Psychiatry, 1977-82, Am. Jour. Psychiatry, 1979-87; series editor Med. Aspects Human Sexuality, 1983-85, cons.-editor, 1985-91; book reviewer U. Chgo. Press, 1983—. Mem. Appeal Bd. Ea. La. Selective Svc. System, 1969-70. Lt. USNR, 1953-55. Fellow Am. Psychiat. Assn. (life), Am. Group Psychotherapy Assn. (life, inst. instr. 1965-69, bd. dirs. 1967-70, chmn., mem. various coms.), So. Psychiat. Assn., Am. Orthopsychiat. Assn. (life, mem. regional publicity com. 1967-71, mem. program com. 1971-74, chmn. study group adolescence 1986-88), Am. Acad. Child Psychiatry (mem. com. adolescence 1974-86, mem. infant psychiatry com. 1975-80), Am. Coll. Psychiatrists, Am. Soc. for Adolescent Psychiatry (life, program chmn. 1972-73, v.p. 1971-72, pres.-elect 1972-73, pres. 1973-74, Meritorious Achievement citation 1974), La. Psychiat. Assn. (coms. on childhood and adolescence, mental health planning, allied professiona 1962-64, nursing com. del. to Am. Psychiat. Assn. 1962, coord. com. 1972-73, v.p. 1986-87, nominating com. 1989-90, children's com. 1990—, women's issues com. 1990); mem. Am. Acad. Pediatrics (mem. work group children disasters 1992—), Am. Bd. Adolescent Psychiatry (mem. written exam com. 1991-95), Am. Acad. Psychiatry and Law, Am. Acad. Child and Adolescent Psychiatry, La. Group Psychotherapy Soc. (sec. 1961-62, chmn. program com. 1962-63, ann. inst. instr. 1962-70, pres. 1963-64, treas. 1964-65, chmn. tng. com. 1965-75, chmn. interregional group psychotherapy socs. meeting com. 1964-67), La. Assn. Infant Mental Health, La. Coun. Child Psychiatry (founding mem., program chmn. 1974-76), La. State Med. Soc., New Orleans Soc. Adolescent Psychiatry (founder, pres. 1968-71, pres. 1986-87), New Orleans Area Psychiat. Assn. (mem. exec. coun. 1982-85, pres.-elect 1985-86, pres. 1986-87), New Orleans Pediatric Soc., Orleans Parish Med. Soc. (del. to La. state med. soc. meeting 1988—, gov.-at-large 1990-96, mem. various coms.), Internat. Soc. Adolescent Psychiatry (founding mem. various coms., del. 1986—, convention mgr. 1994—), editor of monographs, treas. 1995. Home: 17 Rosa Park New Orleans LA 70115-5043 Office: 4740 S I 10 Service Rd W Metairie LA 70001-1234

SUGERMAN, HARVEY JAY, surgery educator; b. Pitts., Apr. 13, 1938; s. Samuel J. and Rose M. (Margolis) S.; m. Elizabeth Levine, Jan. 7, 1968; children: Kathryn, Andrew, David, Elizabeth. BS, Johns Hopkins U., 1959; MS, Thomas Jefferson U., 1962, MD, 1966. Intern medicine Hosp. U. Pa., Phila., 1966-67, resident surgery, 1967-72; pvt. practice surgery Allentown, Pa., 1975-78; asst. prof. surgery Med. Coll. Va., Va. Commonwealth U., Richmond, 1978-81; assoc. prof. surgery Med. Coll. Va., VCU, Richmond, 1981-85, prof. surgery, 1985—, David Hume professorship, 1989—, vice chmn. dept. surgery, 1991—. Co-editor: (textbook) Current Practice Surgery, 1993; contbr. articles to profl. jours. Lt. col. U.S. Army, 1972-75. Mem. Am. Surg. Assn., So. Surg. Assn., Soc. Univ. Surgeons, Surg. Infection Soc., Am. Assn. Surgery Trauma. Office: Med Coll Va PO Box 980519 Richmond VA 23298-0519

SUGG, HARRY LEE, JR., dentist; b. Memphis, June 29, 1940; s. Harry Lee Sugg and Marguerite (Stephens) Richardson; m. Claire Joyner, Dec. 19, 1965 (div. 1969); m. Kerry Jane Brown, Nov. 30, 1980. BS, Memphis State U., 1965; DDS, U. Tenn., Memphis, 1969. Rotating dental intern VA Hosp., Memphis, 1969-70; gen. practice dentistry Dallas, 1970—. Mem. ADA, Tex. Dental Soc., Dallas County Dental Soc. Republican. Mem. Bible Ch. Club: Mastermind Study (charter). address: 3940 W Wheatland Rd Dallas TX 75237-3468

SUGG, ROBERT PERKINS, former state supreme court justice; b. Eupora, Miss., Feb. 21, 1916; s. Amos Watson and Virgie Christian (Cooper) S.; m. Elizabeth Lorraine Carroll, June 23, 1940; children: Robert Perkins, Charles William, John David. Student, Wood Jr. Coll., 1933-34, Miss. State U., 1935-37, Jackson Sch. Law, 1939-40. Bar: Miss. Practice law, 1940-51, chancery judge, 1951-71; asso. justice Miss. Supreme Ct., 1971-83; county pros. atty. Webster County, Miss., 1949-50; spl. chancery judge Hinds, Scott and Jasper counties, Miss., 1989, sr. judge, 1990—; mem. adv. council Nat. Ctr. for State Cts., 1973-79. Bd. govs. Miss. Jud. Coll., 1973-80; literacy missions assoc. Home Mission Bd. of So. Bapt. Conv., 1983—. Served with USAAF, 1942-43. Named Outstanding Citizen, Eupora Jr. C. of C., 1970, Alumnus of Year, Wood Jr. Coll., 1973; recipient Service to Humanity award Miss. Coll., 1976, Literacy Missions Svc. award Home Mission Bd. of So. Bapt. Conv., 1995. Mem. Miss. State Bar, Am. Judicature Soc., CAP (Miss. Wing, squadron comdr. 1974-76), Am. Legion (post comdr. 1950). Democrat. Baptist (chmn. bd. deacons 1964). Home: 1067 Meadow Heights Dr Jackson MS 39206-6021

SUGGARS, CANDICE LOUISE, special education educator; b. Pitts., Jan. 16, 1949; d. Albert Abraham and Patricia Louise (Stepp) S. BS in Elem. Edn., W.Va. U., 1972; MS in Spl. Edn., Johns Hopkins U., 1979, Cert. Advanced Studies, 1986. Clin. supr./head tchr. The Kennedy Krieger Inst., Balt., 1974-80, inpatient coord., 1980-83, ednl. evaluator, 1980-85, spl. educator/pediatric rehab. team, 1985-86; spl. edn. cons. Charleston County (S.C.) Sch. Dist., 1986-90, spl. edn. pre-sch. tchr., 1990-95; pvt. tutor children with spl. needs and disabilities, Charleston, 1995—; spl. needs cons. U. S.C., 1996—; mem. adv. bd. S.C. Accelerated Schs. Project, Charleston, 1994-95. Contbg. author: Disadvantaged Pre-School Child, 1979, Leisure Education for the Handicapped Curriculum, 1984. Exhibitor ann. conv. S.C. State Sch. Bd. Assn., 1994. Mem. Coun. for Exceptional Children (hospitality chair 1987-89, publicity chair 1989-90), Nat. Assn. for Edn. of Young Children. Home: 29 Savage St Apt B Charleston SC 29401-2409

SUHM, MARY KATHERINE, municipal official; b. Beaumont, Tex., Jan. 3, 1947; d. James Hayden and Margaret Ann (Hodges) Moore; m. Victor C. Suhm, May 4, 1989; m. Robert Powell Tod, Aug., 24, 1968 (div. May 1983); children: Robert Gabriel Tod, Joshua Alton Tod. BS, Lamar U., Beaumont, 1968; MLS, U. North Tex., 1975, MBA, 1984. Biology tchr. Carrollton (Tex.) Independent Sch. Dist., 1968-69, Allen (Tex.) Independent Sch. Dist., 1969-70; dir. Allen Pub. Libr., 1972-78; mgr. branch librs. Dallas Pub. Libr., 1978-81, mgr. Urban Info., 1981-84; asst. to mayor City of Dallas, 1985-87, asst. to City Mgr., 1987-88, dir. of court svcs., 1988-90; exec. asst. dir. of Police Dallas Police Dept., 1990-93; asst. city mgr. City of Dallas, 1993—; sec., bd. dirs. City Employees Credit Union, Dallas, 1982-86. Facilitator Goals for Dallas, 1982; active Leadership Dallas, 1986, Vol. Ctr. Bd., 1987-90; mem. Cmty. Svcs. Bd. YMCA, 1990-94. Recipient Linda Keithley award for Women in Pub. Mgmt., 1995. Mem. Internat. City Mgmt. Assn. Office: City of Dallas 1500 Marilla 4/D/N Dallas TX 75201

SUHRER-ROUSSEL, LYNDA, psychology educator; b. Mobile, Ala., Mar. 24, 1954; d. Samuel Weimar and Henrietta (Smith) Suhrer; m. Lewis Garnet Roussel, Aug. 14, 1980. BS in Psychology magna cum laude, U. Southwestern La., 1984, MS in Psychology, 1987; PhD, La. State U., 1995. Teaching asst. U. Southwestern La., 1984-86, instr., 1986-87; instr. La. State U., 1987-89, 1989-90; coord. art program St. Francis House Adult Day Health Care, Baton Rouge, 1990-91; rsch. asst. La. State U., 1990-91, 1991-92, mem. faculty divsn. continuing edn., 1993-94, search com. divsn. continuing edn., 1994; sr. human resources intern Our Lady of the Lake Regional Med. Ctr., Baton Rouge, 1994; rsch. analyst Our Lady of the Lake Regional Medical Ctr., Baton Rouge, 1995—; performance mgmt. cons., 1996—. Mem. APA, Div. 20 Adult Devel. and Aging, Gerontol. Soc. Am., Baton Rouge Alzheimer's Assn. Office: Our Lady of the Lake Regional Med Ctr 5000 Hennesy Blvd Baton Rouge LA 70808-4394

SUKHOLUTSKAYA, MARA EMMANUILOVNA, secondary education educator; b. Karaganda, Kaz., USSR, Sept. 4, 1950; came to U.S., 1991.; d. Muniy Markovich Sukholutsky and Ekaterina Mikhailovna (Feldmer) S.; m. Igor E. Berdichevsky, June 5, 1974; children: Anna I. Berdichevskaya, Maria I. Berdichevskaya. BA, Linguistics U., Kiev, 1972, MA, 1972, DEd, 1989. Tchr. fgn. lang. Sch. # 97, Kiev, Ukraine, 1972-74, Sch. # 80, Kiev, 1974-87; dir. Fgn. Lang. Ctr., Kiev, 1990-91, asst. prof., 1987-91; vis. prof. East

Ctrl. Univ., Ada, Okla., 1991—; chair Human Diversity com., Ada, 1994—; mem. adv. com. on improvement of fgn. lang. tchg. Okla. Dept. Edn., 1995-96; chair East Ctrl. Internat. Students Recruitment and Retention com., Ada, 1993-94. Author: (tchg. guide) Method Guide for Teaching English, German and Spanish at Special Foreign Language Schools, 1990, Method Guide for Initial Teaching of English to Junior Graders, 1990, (instructional material) Speak and Read Essential Ukrainian, 1993; contbr. articles to profl. jours. Recipient Educator of Month award Rotary, Okla., 1996; U.S. Dept. Edn. grantee, 1996—. Mem. Advocates for Lang. Learning, Am. Coun. on the Tchg. of Fgn. Lang., Okla. Coun. Tchrs. Russian (pres. 1996—), Okla. Fgn. Lang. Assn. (bd. dirs. 1996—), Kiwanis (cert. for disting. svcs., Ada, 1992), Sigma Tau Delta. Home: 424 Stadium Dr N-15 Ada OK 74820 Office: East Central University Ada OK 74820

SULC, DWIGHT GEORGE, investment advisor; b. Oklahoma City, May 25, 1948; s. George Bennett and Hedvika (Kyzivat) S. BA, U. Tex., 1971; JD, Tuebingen U., Germany, 1979, LLD, 1983. Cert. securities and exch. commn., Paris, U.S. Investment advisor Paris, Berlin, London, 1974-83, Oklahoma City, 1984—; strategic planning advisor cmty. orgns., Oklahoma City, 1989. Author: A National Neighborhood Association System for America, 1991, Building A Volunteer Neighborhood Watch Patrol, A Civic Leadership Training Manual of the Council of Confederated Neighborhoods of America, 1996, Czechoslovak Society of Arts and Sciences World Congress, Brno: Strategic Management Design for the International Society of Arts Management and the Arts, 1996. Chmn. strategic planning com. Federally Employed Women Assn., Tinker AFB, 1990; founder The Coun. of Confederated Neighborhoods of Am. Inc., Oklahoma City, 1991, The Internat. Soc. for the Arts Management and the Arts, Praha, Czechoslovakia/London/Oklahoma City, 1994; pres. Mil. Park chpt. Coun. Confederated Neighborhoods of Am., 1992. Rsch. grantee Fulbright, Berlin, 1980, Brusselles, 1981. Mem. Nat. Assn. Parliamentarians (pres. 1994). Presbyterian. Home: 3321 N Virginia Ave Oklahoma City OK 73118-3044

SULEIMAN, AHMAD ABDUL-FATTAH, chemistry educator; b. Al-Ras, Tulkarm, Palestine, Mar. 8, 1948; came to U.S., 1971; s. Abdul-Fattah and Faddiyah (Hamdan) S.; m. Mai J. Hashem, July 17, 1978; children: Jamal, Omar. BSc, U. Houston, 1975; MS, Tex. So. U., Houston, 1978; PhD, U. New Orleans, 1983. Rsch. chemist Gulf South Rsch. Inst., 1980-81; rsch. chemist Universal Sensors, Inc., 1980-83, sr. rsch. chemist, 1986-92; rsch. and teaching asst. U. New Orleans, 1978-83, postdoctoral rsch. assoc., 1983-84; asst. prof. Tex. So. U., Houston, 1984-86; instr., sr. rsch. assoc. U. New Orleans, 1986-92; assoc. prof. So. U., Baton Rouge, 1992—; adj. assoc. prof. U. New Orleans, 1992—. Contbr. numerous articles to profl. jours., chpts. to books. Recipient Chem. Rubber Co. award; grantee NIH, 1992—, NASA, 1995—, USDA, 1990-92, NSF, 1989, others. Mem. Am. Chem. Soc. (div. analytical chemistry), Am. Assoc. for the Advancement of Sci., Air Pollution Control Assn., Phi Theta Kappa. Islamic. Office: Southern U Dept Chemistry Baton Rouge LA 70813

SULEYMANIAN, MIRIK, biophysicist; b. Chartar, Karabagh, Armenia, Jan. 20, 1948; s. Avanes and Gohar (Hakopian) S.; m. Nelia Agababian, Mar. 24, 1973; children: Hovanes, Gagik. Diploma, Yerevan (Armenia) State U., 1973; PhD, Inst. Exptl. Biology, Yerevan, 1981, DS, 1990. Rsch. worker Acad. Scis. Armenia, Yerevan, 1975-81, sr. rsch. worker, 1981-88, leading rsch. worker, 1988-92; rsch. assoc. dept. physiology Va. Commonwealth U., Richmond, 1992—. Contbr. over 50 articles to profl. jours. Fellow U. Bristol, Gt. Britain, 1978, rsch. fellow Limnological Inst., Tihany, Hungary, 1979, 83, dept. muscle physiology Ruhr U. Bochum, Germany, 1987-88. Mem. Biophys. Soc. U.S.A., Internat. Soc. Heart Rsch. Office: Va Commonwealth U Sanger Hall 1101 E Marshall Richmond VA 23298

SULFARO, JOYCE A., parochial school educator; b. Bklyn., Oct. 23, 1948; d. John Joseph and Mildred Ann (Credidio) Carvelli; m. Guy Sulfaro, Aug. 1, 1971; children: Jacqueline Amber, Kristin Lynn. BA, Molloy Coll., 1970; postgrad. Fla. Atlantic U., 1979-80; MS in Adminstrn. and Supervision, Nova U., 1982. Tutor reading Our Lady of Loretto, Rockville Centre, N.Y., 1969-70; tchr. lang. arts and math. Resurrection Sch., Bklyn., 1970-73; tchr. Annunciation Sch., Hollywood, Fla., 1976-80, prin., 1980-84; tchr. St. Thomas More Sch., 1984-88; writer English curriculum for Jr. High for Archdiocese of Miami, 1979. Author: (with M. Sue Timmins) The Basket, 1980. Travel coord./sec. Rego Park (N.Y.) Met. Youth Orgn., 1969-70. Mem. ASTD, Nat. Council Tchrs. Math., Fla. League Mid. Schs., Cath. Educators Guild Archdiocese of Miami, Nat. Cath. Ednl. Assn. (chair sch.-based com. 1988-91), Am. Mus. Natural History, Rocky Mt. Mental Health Assn. (bd. dirs. 1988-90), IBS Adv. Coun., Prins. and Asst. Prins. Assn. (sec. 1990-91, adminstr. vocat. adv. com. 1990-93, adminstr. media adv. com. 1990-94, sec. 1991-94), Nat. Assn. Secondary Sch. Prins. Home: 1104 Waterloo Ct Rocky Mount NC 27804-8432

SULIK, EDWIN (PETE SULIK), health care administrator; b. Bryan, Tex., Feb. 1, 1957; s. Edwin Peter and Bonny Jo (Robertson) S.; m. Kolleen Marie Stevens, Aug. 8, 1981; 1 child, Laine Sheridan. Student, Blinn Jr. Coll., 1977-78, U. Tex., 1977, Tex. A&M U., 1977-83; BBA, Ky. Western. U., 1990; MBA, Ky. Western U., 1994. Lic. long term care adminstr.; cert. preceptor. Sr. v.p. ops. Sherwood Health Care, Inc., Bryan, 1976-90, pres., 1990—; sec.-treas. Sherwood Health Care, Inc., Lubbock, Tex., 1987-89; pres. Sherwood Health Care, Inc., Bryan, 1990, Lubbock, 1990; pres., owner Brazos Mgmt. Health Care, Inc., Bryan, 1991; owner Sherwood Forest Children's Ctr., 1991; pres. Sherwood Gardens Adult Day Health Care, 1996. Mem. Lt. Gov. Bullock's Nursing Home Work Group, 1991-92; participant state debate with Lt. Gov. Hobby, Austin, Tex., 1987; mem. Legis. Oversight Com.; active St. Joseph Sch. Bd. Fellow Am. Coll. Health Care Adminstrs., Am. Health Care Assn., Tex. Health Care Assn. (bd. dirs. 1987-90, chair, chpt. pres. 1987-88, facility stds. com. 1987—, payment for svcs. com. 1987—, Medicare com. 1989—, Omnibus Budget Reconciliation Act of 1987 com. 1987—, patient admission screening and resident rev. com. 1989—, legis. com. 1987-89, co-chair budget and fin. com. 1990-91, automation com. 1990-91, pilot project site NHIC automation 1990-91, nursing home quality and case mix demonstration pilot project 1995—), Bryan Coll. C. of C. Inner Cir., Am. Assn. Ret. Persons (Medicare/Medicaid steering com.), Tex. A&M U. Century Club, KC, Elks. Republican. Roman Catholic. Home: PO Box 3553 Bryan TX 77805-3553 Office: Sherwood Health Care Inc 1401 Memorial Dr Bryan TX 77802-5218

SULLIVAN, BEN FRANK, JR., real estate broker; b. Brookesmith, Tex., Aug. 10, 1919; s. Ben Frank and Vera Scott (Hennigan) S.; m. Frances Louise Levisay, Dec. 28, 1946; children: Thomas James, Ben Charles, Harold Lyndon. Student, Tarleton State U., 1937-39; BS, Tex. A&M U., 1941. Commd. 2d lt. U.S. Army, 1942, advanced through grades to capt., 1943-46; capt. U.S. Army Res., 1946-53, ret., 1953; sales/mktg. Armour & Co., Ft. Worth, 1946; owner Grocery Bus., Bangs, Tex., 1946-48; postmaster U.S. Postal Svc., Bangs, 1947-66, rural mail carrier, 1966-75; owner/broker Sullivan Real Estate, Bangs, 1963—; owner Sullivan Ranch, Bangs, 1962—; owner oper. Oil & Gas Prodn. on Ranch, Bangs, 1974—; owner, mgr. Home Bldg. & Sales, Bangs, 1965-94. Sunday sch. tchr., ch. supt., chmn. ofcl. bd. Bangs United Meth. Ch.; trustee Brownwood Dist. Ctrl. Tex. Conf. United Meth. Ch., 1983—, also chmn. bd.; committeeman Meth. Home, Waco, 1982-83; mem. steering com. to form Brookesmith Water Corp., Brown County, Tex., 1971, bd. dirs., 1971-73. With U.S. Army, 1941-46. Decorated 2 bronze stars, WWII victory medal. Mem. Brown County C. of C. (bd. dirs. 1993-95), Am. Legion (comdr. post # 308 1949), Masons, Order of Ea. Star, Shriners, Lions (pres. 1963-64). Methodist.

SULLIVAN, CHARLES ROBERT, history educator; b. Washington, Sept. 16, 1954; s. Charles Brown Jr. and Joan Carol (Flanagan) S.; m. Roberta Reed Westcott; children: Sylvia Camille, Alan Burke. BA in History, George Mason U., 1978; MA in Modern and Early European History, Columbia U., 1982, MPhil in Modern and Early European History, 1983, PhD in Modern and Early European History, 1992. Preceptor Columbia U., N.Y.C., 1983-87; asst. prof. U. Dallas, Irving, Tex., 1988—; adj. lectr. NYU, 1984-85, 86-87; vis. prof. Reed Coll., Portland, Oreg., 1993-94. Asst. Editor Common Knowledge, 1992—. Columbia U. fellow, 1980-83, Honorary Pres. fellow Columbia U., 1983-84, Columbia U. Travelling fellow, 1985-86, Chamberlain fellow Columbia U., 1987-88; Coun. European Studies grantee 1984; King Haggar scholar U. Dallas, 1993. Mem. Am. Hist. Assn., Soc. French Hist. Studies, So. Hist. Assn., Southwest Social Sci. Assn. Home: 11752 Coral Hills Pl Dallas TX 75229-2508 Office: U Dallas Dept History 1845 E Northgate Dr Irving TX 75062

SULLIVAN, DANIEL EDMOND, fundraising executive; b. Alexandria, La., Jan. 22, 1946; s. Edmond James and Ruth (Morris) S.; m. Camille Lafleur Broussand, June 13, 1970; children: Daniel Edmond Jr., Parish Coughlin. Student, La. State U., 1964-67; BS, Northwestern State U., Natchitoches, La., 1968. Field underwriter N.Y. Life Ins. Co., New Orleans, 1968-70; asst. dir. Tulane U. Alumni Fund, New Orleans, 1970-71; assoc. dir. La. Civil Svc. League, New Orleans, 1971-73, exec. v.p., 1973—, also bd. govs., 1973—; bd. of gov. La. Orgn. for Jud. Excellence, 1992—, v.p., 1995—; mem. com. La. Joint Legis. Com., 1982—; mem. pub. adminstrn. tng. adv. com. U. New Orleans, 1983-90. Bd. dirs. Young Audiences New Orleans, 1974-78. Named Hon. Alumnus Tulane U., 1977. Mem. Nat. Soc. Fund Raising Execs. (cert.), Am. Arbitration Assn. (panel of arbitrators), Northwestern State U. Alumni Assn. (bd. dirs. 1974-84), New Orleans Lawn Tennis Club (bd. govs. 1978-80), Stratford Club. Republican. Roman Catholic. Home: 919 Short St New Orleans LA 70118-2730 Office: La Civil Svc League 810 Union St Ste 305 New Orleans LA 70112-1402

SULLIVAN, GREGORY PAUL, secondary education educator; b. Buffalo, June 13, 1957; s. Jerome Patrick and Gloria Mae (Struble) S.; m. Sarah Davis Houston, May 17, 1986; 1 child, Patrick Benjamin. BS in Indsl. Edn., State U. Coll., Oswego, N.Y., 1979; MA in Indsl. Edn., Ball State U., 1983. postgrad. collegiate profl. teaching cert. Grad. asst. mfg. lab. Ball State U., Muncie, Ind., 1982-83; tchr. tech. edn. John Rolfe Mid. Sch., Richmond, Va., 1979-86, Horton Mid. Sch., Pittsboro, N.C., 1986-88, Dunbar Mid. Sch., Lynchburg, Va., 1988-93; supr. career-tech. programs Lynchburg City Schs., 1993—; coord./judge regional and nat. mfg. contest Tech. Edn. and Collegiate Assn., 1988—; coord. Eisenhower Grant, 1991-92; presenter in field. Asst. dir. Camp Minnehaha, Minnehaha Springs, W.Va., 1979-88. Named Va. Tchr. of Yr., Va. Dept. Edn., 1993. Mem. Soc. Mfg. Engrs. (internat. edn. com. career guidance 1984, 91), Internat. Tech. Edn. Assn. (mem. editl. rev. bd. The Tech. Tchr., delphi com. critical issues and concerns tech. edn. 1992), Coun. Tech. Tchr. Edn. (student svcs. com. 1991), Va. Tech. Edn. Assn., Phi Delta Kappa, Epsilon Pi Tau, Kappa Delta Pi. Home: 724 Sanhill Dr Lynchburg VA 24502-4924 Office: Lynchburg City Schs 10th and Court Sts PO Box 1599 Lynchburg VA 24505-1599

SULLIVAN, HARRY TRUMAN, research scientist; b. Camden, Ala., Mar. 21, 1952; s. Ernest Curley and Luticia Ann (Aaron) B.; m. Sandra Carol Jackson, Nov. 13, 1976; 1 child, Asha Nicole. AA, So. Tech. Inst., Marietta, Ga., 1976; BS in Computer Sci., Ga. State U., 1989. Instrumentation technician Ga. Power Co., Baxley, 1976-78; electronic technician Micromeritics Instrument Corp., Atlanta, 1978-80, GEC Avionics, Inc., Atlanta, 1980-82; electronic technician II Ga. Inst. of Tech., Atlanta, 1982—. Mem. IEEE, Assn. for Computing Machinery.

SULLIVAN, JAMES LENOX, clergyman; b. Silver Creek, Miss., Mar. 12, 1910; s. James Washington and Mary Ellen (Dampeer) S.; m. Velma Scott, Oct. 22, 1935; children: Mary Beth (Mrs. Bob R. Taylor), Martha Lynn (Mrs. James M. Porch, Jr.), James David. B.A., Miss. Coll., 1932, D.D., 1948; Th.M., So. Bapt. Theol. Sem., 1935. Ordained to ministry of Baptist Ch., 1930; pastor Baptist Ch., Boston, Ky., 1932-33, Beaver Dam, Ky., 1933-38, Ripley, Tenn., 1938-40, Clinton, Miss., 1940-42; pastor First Bapt. Ch., Brookhaven, Miss., 1942-46, Belmont Heights, Nashville, 1946-50, Abilene, Tex., 1950-53; exec. sec., treas. Bapt. Sunday Sch. Bd., Nashville, 1953-73; pres. Bapt. Sunday Sch. Bd., 1973-75; exec. sec. Broadman Press, 1953-75, Convention Press, 1955-75; pres. So. Bapt. Conv., 1977. Author: Your Life and Your Church, 1950, John's Witness of Jesus, Memos for Christian Living, Reach Out, Rope of Sand with Strength of Steel, God Is My Record, Baptist Polity As I See It, Southern Baptist Polity at Work in a Church; also articles and manuals. Trustee Union U., Cumberland U., So. Bapt. Theol. Sem., Hardin-Simmons U., Midstate (Tenn.) Bapt. Hosp., Hendrick Meml. Hosp., Tex. Recipient E.Y. Mullins Denominational Service award, 1973; named Miss. Bapt. Clergyman of Century. Mem. Baptist World Alliance (exec. com. 1953-80, v.p. 1970-75). Clubs: Rotary (Ripley, Tenn.); Lions (Brookhaven, Miss.); Kiwanis (Abilene, Tex.).

SULLIVAN, JERRY STEPHEN, electronics company executive; b. Havre, Mont., July 17, 1945; s. Patrick Joseph and Evangeline (O'Neil) S.; m. Sharon Lee Horton, June 17, 1967; children: Garrett, Mindy, Darren. BS, U. Colo., 1967, MS, 1969, PhD, 1970; advanced mgmt. program, Harvard U. Bus. Sch., 1986. Tech. mgr. N.V. Philips Co., Eindhoven, The Netherlands, 1971-75; group dir. N.Am. Philips Corp., Briarcliff Manor, N.Y., 1975-80; dir. Tektronix, Beaverton, Oreg., 1981-83, div. gen. mgr., 1983-85, corp. dir., 1985-88; v.p. Microelectronics & Computer Tech. Corp., Austin, Tex., 1988-92; pres., CEO, Design Techs. Inc., Austin, 1992—; bd. dirs. Sherpa Corp., San Jose, Calif., MINC Corp., Colorado Springs, Colo., Savantage, Inc., Austin, Tex.; mem. adv. bd. Ctr. Integrated Sys., Stanford U., Palo Alto, Calif., 1982—. Mem. adv. com. Coll. Engring., U. Tex., Austin, 1989—, bd. dirs. Edn. Found., 1990—. Mem. IEEE, Am. Phys. Soc., Assn. Computing Machinery, Am. Mgmt. Assn., Nat. Assn. Corp. Dirs. Office: Design Techs Inc 107 Ranch Rd 620 S Austin TX 78734-3942

SULLIVAN, JOHN FRANCIS, military officer; b. Boston, May 8, 1953; s. John Francis and Margaret Ella (Hynds) S.; m. Kathleen Ann Olsen, June 28, 1980; chilren: Megan Kathleen, Kelly Jean. BS in Mgmt., USAF Acad., 1975; MS in Sys. Mgmt., U. So. Calif., 1985; grad., USMC Command and Staff Coll., Quantico, Va., 1989, USAF Squadron's Officers Sch., Montgomery, Ala., 1979. Commd. 2d lt. USAF, 1975, advanced through grades to lt. col., 1991; student navigator Mather AFB, Calif., 1975-77; weapons sys. officer 8th Fighter Wing USAF, Kunsan AFB, 1977-78; weapons sys. officer 347th Fighter Wing USAF, Moody AFB, Ga., 1978-80; weapons sys. officer 50th Fighter Wing USAF, Hahn AFB, Germany, 1980-81; student pilot 82nd Flying Tng. Wing USAF, Williams AFB, Ariz., 1981-82; pilot/flight comdr. 67th Fighter Sq. 18th Fighter Wing USAF, Kadena AFB, Japan, 1983-86; pilot/chief acads. 57th Fighter Weapons Wing USAF, Nellis AFB, Nev., 1986-88; pilot/asst. ops. officer 12th Fighter Squadron USAF, Kadena AFB, 1989-92; combat forces basing mgr. Hdqrs. USAF, Washington, 1992-95; asst. for congrl. matters Hdqrs./USAF, 1995—. Dir. Twin Oaks Farm Homeowners Assn., Woodbridge, Va., 1993-95. Decorated Nat. Order of Security Merit (Korea), Air Force Meritorious Svc. medal (3), Air Force Commendation medal, Air Force Achievement medal. Mem. USAF Acad. Assn. Grads., Air Force Acad. Soc. Washington, Air Force Assn., Order of Daedalians. Home: 2680 Maple Ridge Dr Woodbridge VA 22192-3824

SULLIVAN, JOHN JAMES, JR., sales executive; b. Huntsville, Ala., Dec. 16, 1938; s. John James and Alma Corinne (Gatlin) S.; m. Janice Irvin Laughter; children: John James III, Robert Laughter. BA, U. Ala., 1961. Various positions Thomasville (N.C.) Furniture, 1966-80, sales rep., 1980-82; sales rep. Chromcraft Furniture, Senatobia, Miss., 1982-93, Master Design, Greensboro, N.C., 1993—. 1st lt. USAF, 1962-66. Mem. High Point Furniture Club (v.p.), Va.-Carolinas Home Furnishings Reps. Assn. (pres. 1990), Internat. Home Furnishing Reps. Assn. (cert. 1986), Rotary. Presbyterian. Home and Office: 3805 Meredith Dr Greensboro NC 27408-3141

SULLIVAN, JOHN MAGRUDER, II, government affairs administrator; b. Hattiesburg, Miss., Sept. 23, 1959; s. Camillus Caruthers and Elizabeth Josephine (McLeod) S.; m. Stacy Lynn Robinson; children: John Magruder III, Caitlyn Caruthers. BS, U. So. Miss., 1983. Cert. Am. Planners. Corp. liaison Chevron, Hattiesburg, Miss., 1983-88; dir. Best Leasing, Jackson, Miss., 1988-89; state dir. Muscular Dystrophy Assn., Jackson, Miss., 1989-90; adminstr. govt. affairs Tri State Brick and Tile Co. Inc./Medlin & Assocs., Jackson, 1990-95; planner for bus. devel. divsn. City of Jackson, 1995-96; planner and developer, Ron Costas Properties, Exec. Office Devel., Jackson, 1996; owner Red Brick Farm Inc.; cons. in field. Author: Hattiesburg Statistical Summary, 1983. Mem. ARC Disaster Relief Vol., Hattiesburg, 1977-85. Mem. Nat. Assn. Equipment Lessors, Nat. Assn. Planners, MIss. Assn. Planners, First Families of Miss., Masons (Forest Hill), Pi Kappa Alpha. Republican. Episcopalian. Home: 1955 Douglas Dr Jackson MS 39211-6604 Office: PO Box 9543 Jackson MS 39286-9543

SULLIVAN, KENNETH JOSEPH, strategic and intelligence programs analyst; b. N.Y.C., Sept. 19, 1949; s. John Joseph Sullivan and Eileen Teresa (Hannaway) Klein; m. Nan Nivin, May 22, 1971; 1 child, Brian Patrick. BE in Chem. Engring., Stevens Inst. Tech., 1971; MS in Systems Mgmt., U. Southern Calif., 1978. Commd. 2d lt. U.S. Air Force, 1971; advanced through grades to lt. col., 1988; navigator 374th Tactical Airlift Wing, Clark Air Force Base, Philippines, 1973-74; navigator, tng. flight instr. 509th Bomb Wing, Pease Air Force Base, N.H., 1974-78, chief of plans br., mission dir. tanker task force, 1978-80; chief instr., navigator upgrade tng. 55th Strategic Reconnaissance Wing, Offutt Air Force Base, Nebr., 1980-83, chief airborne battle staff, 1983-84, chief, command and control tng., 1984-85; chief, combat ops. plans divsn. Strategic Air Command Hdqs., Offutt Air Force Base, Nebr., 1985-89; nuclear command and control system studies mgr. U.S. Nuclear Command Control System Support Staff, Falls Church, Va., 1989-90, chief, assessments br., 1990-94; ret., 1994; sr. analyst JAYCOR, McLean, Va., 1994—. Exec. sec. Homeowner's Assn. Papillion, Nebr., 1982; asst. cub master Boy Scouts Am., Nebr., 1985-86; soccer coach Youth Soccer League, Nebr., 1985-87; adv. bd. Woodridge PTA, Va., 1989-94. Decorated Air medal. Mem. Armed Forces Comm. and Electronics Assn. (office rep. 1990-93), Air Force Assn., Ret. Officers Assn., Stevens Inst. Tech. Alumni Assn. (class fund agt. 1982-94), Sigma Nu. Home: 12595 Cricket Ln Woodbridge VA 22192-5239 Office: JAYCOR 1410 Spring Hill Rd Mc Lean VA 22102

SULLIVAN, KEVIN LAWRENCE, broadcast executive; b. Ranson, W.Va., July 22, 1958; s. Arthur Lawrence and Florence (Cahill) S.; m. Sybil Lee Ann Banks, Aug. 21, 1993. BJ, U. Mo., 1980. Disc jockey Sta. KHDN, Hardin, Mont., 1974-76; disc jockey, comml. producer Sta. KWRT-KDBX, Booneville, Mo., 1977-79; news reporter Sta. KBIA, Columbia, Mo., 1978-79; reporter, anchor Sta. KOMU-TV, Columbia, 1978-80; asst. news dir. Sta. KQTV-TV, St. Joseph, Mo., 1980-83; news dir. Sta. WTVA-TV, Tupelo, Miss., 1983-86; assignments mgr. Sta. WALA-TV, Mobile, Ala., 1986-93; exec. producer Sta. WBRC-TV, Birmingham, Ala., 1993—; instr. U. Miss., Oxford, 1984-85. Mem. Civitan Club, Tupelo, 1984-85, Jaycees, Mobile, 1985-89, Press Club of Mobile (bd. dirs. 1990-92), Soc. Profl. Journalists, Tupelo, 1983-86. Newscast named AP Best Spot News, 1984, AP Best Newscast, 1983, UPI Best Newscast in Southeast, 1987, Ala. AP Broadcasters Best Newscast, 1993. Mem. Ala. AP Broadcasters Assn. (bd. dirs. 1993—), Poynter Inst. Roman Catholic. Office: Sta WBRC TV PO Box 6 Birmingham AL 35201-0006

SULLIVAN, (ELSIE) LEE, counselor; b. Atlanta, Nov. 16, 1951; d. Lewis and Alice (Morrow) S.; 1 child, Shae Sullivan; m. James McIntyre, Aug. 7, 1982 (div. May 1996); 1 child, Kaleem. Cert. Montessori educator, Assn. Montessori Internat., 1984; BS in Edn., Morris Brown Coll., 1986; MA in Counseling and Human Devel., Clark Atlanta U., 1992. Lic. ins. agt., Ga. Substitute tchr. Atlanta Bd. Edn., 1986-93; counselor, proctor Project Genesis, Kennesaw (Ga.) State Coll., Kennesaw State Coll., 1994-95; interim dir., asst. dir. Covered Bridge Montessori Sch., Smyrna, Ga., 1995—. Author: All Men Are Dogs Down on Getting Sex, 1994. Vol. Atlanta Project, Ga. Games, Big Bros.-Big Sisters Metro Atlanta. Baptist. Home: 1839 Boulderview Dr SE Atlanta GA 30316

SULLIVAN, LOUIS WADE, former secretary health and human services, physician; b. Atlanta, Nov. 3, 1933; s. Walter Wade and Lubirda Elizabeth (Priester) S.; m. Eve Williamson, Sept. 30, 1955; children: Paul, Shanta, Halsted. B.S. magna cum laude, Morehouse Coll., Atlanta, 1954; M.D. cum laude, Boston U., 1958. Diplomate: Am. Bd. Internal Medicine. Intern N.Y. Hosp.-Cornell Med. Ctr., N.Y.C., 1958-59, resident in internal medicine, 1959-60; fellow in pathology Mass. Gen. Hosp., Boston, 1960-61; rsch. fellow Thorndike Meml. Lab. Harvard Med. Sch., Boston, 1961-63; instr. medicine Harvard Med. Sch., 1963-64; asst. prof. medicine N.J. Coll. Medicine, 1964-66; co-dir. hematology Boston U. Med. Ctr., 1966; assoc. prof. medicine Boston U., 1968-74; dir. hematology Boston City Hosp., 1973-75; also prof. medicine and physiology Boston U., 1974-75; dean Sch. Medicine, Morehouse Coll., Atlanta, 1975-89, pres., until 1989, 1993—; sec. Dept. of Health and Human Svcs., Washington, 1989-93; non-exec. dir. GM, 1993—; mem. sickle cell anemia adv. com. NIH, 1974-75; ad hoc panel on blood diseases Nat. Heart, Lung Blood Disease Bur., 1973, Nat. Adv. Rsch. Coun., 1977; mem. med. adv. bd. Nat. Leukemia Assn., 1968-70, chmn., 1970; researcher suppression of hematopoiesis by ethanol, pernicious anemia in childhood, folates in human nutrition. John Hay Whitney Found. Opportunity fellow, 1960-61; recipient Honor medal Am. Cancer Soc., 1991. Mem. Am. Soc. Hematology, Am. Soc. Clin. Investigation, Inst. Medicine, Phi Beta Kappa, Alpha Omega Alpha. Episcopalian. Office: Morehouse Sch Medicine Office of the Pres 720 Westview Dr SW Atlanta GA 30310-1495•

SULLIVAN, MARY JEAN, elementary school educator; b. Cambridge, Mass., May 13, 1956; d. Joseph Leo and Jean Marie (Isaac) S. BA, Flagler Coll., 1978; postgrad., U. No. Fla., 1980—, Fla. State U., 1992, Okla. State U., 1992. Cert. elem. educator, Fla. Tchr. grade 2 St. Agnes Sch., St. Augustine, Fla., 1978-79; tchr. grades 1 through 5 Evelyn Hamblen Elem. Sch., St. Augustine, 1979-91; tchr. grade 5 Osceola Elem. Sch., St. Augustine, 1991—, chair math./ sci.; adv. Sci. Club; chairperson, St. John's County Tchr. Edn. Coun., 1985—, SACS Evaluation Team, Duval County Schs., 1988, 89, 90; rep. tchr. edn. coun.; sch. improvement co-chair, 1994-95; trainer coll. intern students; mem. St. John's County Accomplished Practices Acad., 1995, 96. Developer tchr. edn. coun. tng. handbook for State of Fla. Active PTO, past pres., Cub Scouts Am., past asst. program dir., Cathedral-Basilica Ch., United Child Care After Sch. Program, 1988-89; coord. summer recreation Evelyn Hamblen Sch., St. Augustine, 1987-90; dir. tournament Pam Driskell Meml. Paddle Tennis Scholarship Fund, 1986, 87, 88, 89. Grantee Fla. Coun. Elem. Edn., 1981-82, Summer Enhancement, 1988-89, Fla. Inst. Oceanography, 1994, St. John's County Horizon award minigrantee, 1994, 96, Fla. Assn. for Computer Edn., 1994, Fla. Humanities Coun., 1995; recipient Human Rels. award State of Fla., 1992, NEWEST award, 1992, award Geography Summer Inst., 1992; named Kiwanis Tchr. of Month, 1993. Mem. NEA, Nat. Sci. Tchrs. Assn., Fla. Teaching Profession, Fla. Assn. Staff Devel., Fla. Geographic Alliance, Fla. Assn. Computer Edn., St. John's Educator Assn., Fla. Assn. for Sci. Tchrs., ASCD. Office: Osceola Elem Sch 1605 Osceola Elem Sch Rd Saint Augustine FL 32095

SULLIVAN, MICHAEL DAVID, state supreme court justice; b. Hattiesburg, Miss., Dec. 2, 1938; s. Curran W. and Mittie (Chambers) S.; m. Catherine Ainsworth Carter; children: David Paul, Rachel Michel, Margaret Elizabeth, Sarah Catherine. BS, U. So. Miss., 1960; JD, Tulane U., 1966; LLM in Jud. Process, U. Va., 1988. Atty. Hattiesburg, Miss., 1967-75; chancellor Miss. Chancery Ct. Dist. 10, 1975-84; justice Miss. Supreme Ct., Jackson, 1984—. Office: Miss Supreme Ct PO Box 117 Jackson MS 39205-0117

SULLIVAN, NEIL MAXWELL, oil and gas company executive; b. McKeesport, Pa., May 25, 1942; s. Thomas James and Jane Mason (Ginn) S.; m. Holly Abolt; children: Margaret Blair, Mason Pedrick. BS, Dickinson Coll., 1970; MS, Tulane U., 1994; postgrad., U. S.C., 1992—. Exploration geologist Bass Enterprises, Midland, Tex., 1976-77; dist. geologist ATAPCO, Midland, 1977-78, Anadarko Prodn. Co., Midland, 1978-79, chief geologist, 1979-80, v.p. exploration, regional mgr., Houston, 1980-82; exploration ops. mgr. Valero Producing Co., San Antonio, 1982-85, v.p. exploration, New Orleans, 1985-87; pres. Bluebonnet Petroleum Co., New Orleans, 1987—; mem. Dept. Interior Outer Continental Shelf Com. adv. bd., 1985-87. Editor: Petroleum Exploration in Thrust Belts and Their Adjacent Forelands, 1976, Ancient Carbonate Reservoirs and Their Modern Analogs, 1977, Guadalupian Delaware Mountain Group of West Texas and Southeast New Mexico, 1979, Deep Water Sands in the Gulf Coast Region, 1988 , Offshore Louisiana Geology: An Onshore Exploration Model, 1988, Risk: Evaluation and Management, 1989, Volga-Ural Basin Analysis, 1993, Northern Marginal Zone of the Pricaspian Basin, 1996. Bd. dirs. Permian Basin Grad. Ctr., Midland, 1979; com. chmn. Mus. of S.W., Midland, 1978. Served with USAF, 1964-68. Mem. Geol. Soc. Am., Am. Assn. Petroleum Geologists (cert. petroleum geologist), New Orleans Geol. Soc. (chmn. continuing edn. com. 1987-89), South Tex. Geol. Soc. (nominating com. chmn. 1985), Soc. Econ. Paleontologists and Mineralogists (pres. Permian Basin sect. 1979), Am. Inst. Profl. Geologists (cert. profl. geologist). Lodge: Elks. Home: 10240 Garners Ferry Rd Eastover SC 29044

SULLIVAN, NEIL SAMUEL, physicist, researcher, educator; b. Wanganui, Wellington, N.Z., Jan. 18, 1942; came to U.S., 1983; s. Reynold Richard and Edna Mary (Alger) S.; m. Robyn Annette Dawson, Aug. 28, 1965; children: Raoul Samuel, Robert Alexander and David Charles (twins). BSc with 1st class honors, U. Otago, N.Z., 1964, MSc in Physics, 1965; PhD in Physics, Harvard U., 1972. Postdoctoral rsch. Centre d'Etudes Nucleaires, Saclay, France, 1972-74, rsch. physicist, 1974-82; prof. physics U. Fla., Gainesville, 1982—, chair physics dept., 1989—; co-prin. US Nat. High Magnetic Field Lab., 1991. Contbr. numerous articles on quantum solids and nuclear magnetism to profl. jours., 1971—. Recipient prix Saintour, College de France, Paris, 1978, prix LaCaze, Academie des Sciences, Paris, 1982; Fulbright exch. grantee, 1965; Frank Knox Meml. fellow Harvard U., Cambridge, Mass., 1965-67. Mem. AAAS, Am. Assn. Physics Tchrs., Inst. Physics, Societe Francaise de Physique, European Phys. Soc., Am. Phys. Soc. Current work: Investigation of fundamental properties of solid hydrogen and solid helium at very low temperatures; studies of molecular motions using nuclear magnetic resonance; orientational disorder in molecular crystals, cryogenic detectors for dark matter particles and other cosmological relics of big bang theory; discovery of quadrupole glass phase of solid hydrogen, anomalous nuclear spin-lattice relaxation of solid 3He at interfaces; development of NMR techniques to study molecular dynamics at very low temperatures, quantum diffusion in solid hydrogen; design of ultrasensitive low-noise cryogenic UHF detectors. Subspecialties: Condensed matter physics; Low temperature physics; High magnetic fields. Home: 4244 NW 76th Ter Gainesville FL 32606-4132

SULLIVAN, NELL INKLEBARGER, administrative secretary, counselor assistant; b. Charleston, Ark., Jan. 27, 1932; d. Hubert Huel and Maybelle (Heather) Inklebarger; m. J.W. Miller, June 10, 1950 (div. 1973); children: Allan Evan Miller, Sandy Miller Hays-Lusted, Elizabeth Kay Speer, Judith Lynelle Miller; m. Nathan Doyal Sullivan Sr., 1973. AA in Journalism, Westark Coll., Ft. Smith, Ark., 1986. Clk. U.S. Postal Svc., Lavaca, Ark., 1959-73; co-owner, operator, photographer Nell Miller Studio, Lavaca, 1960-75; office supr. U.S. Postal Svc., Ft. Smith, 1972-75; computer specialist Westark Coll., Ft. Smith, 1984-86, assoc. editor coll. newspaper, 1985-87; adminstrv. asst. BDM, Inc., Ft. Chaffee, Ark., 1987-89; counselor asst. Ark. Rehab. Svc., Ft. Smith, 1990-94. Recipient journalism scholarship Westark Coll., 1984-86. Mem. YWCA (bd. dirs. Ft. Smith 1986-93), Nat. Rehab. Assn., Ark. Rehab. Svcs., Ark. State Employees Assn., Nat. Assn. Rehab. Secs., 4-H Alumni Assn. (life), Phi Beta Lambda. Office: Ark Rehab Svc Essex Pl 1115 S Waldron Rd Ste 207 Fort Smith AR 72903-2588

SULLIVAN, PATRICIA G., maternal, child and women's health nursing educator; b. Denver, June 26, 1948; d. Dale F. and Wilma (Fritz) Greb; m. Michael T. Sullivan, Sept. 10, 1971; children: Nicholas O., Matthew Alexander, Adam Michael. BS, Loretto Heights Coll., 1971; MS, U. Colo., 1976. Cert. bereavement svcs. counselor. Clin. instr. Loretto Hts. Coll., 1977-81; instr. pathophysiology U. Denver, summers 1983, 84; coord. women's health edn. Swedish Med. Ctr., Englewood, Colo., 1985-86; coord. childbirth edn. Med. Ctr. Hosp., Odessa, Tex., 1986-88; instr. nursing Midland (Tex.) Coll., 1990—; cons. Mosby's Med. Nursing & Allied Health Dictionary. Reviewer: Basic Nursing and Practice 3rd edit. 1995. Counselor RTS Bereavement Svcs., 1996. Mem. AWHONN, Tex. Nurses Assn., Tex. Jr. Coll. Tchrs. Assn., Sigma Theta Tau. Home: 2803 Douglas Ave Midland TX 79701-3831 Office: Midland Coll 3600 N Garfield St # 213 Midland TX 79705-6329

SULLIVAN, PATRICIA JACKSON, parochial school educator, consultant; b. Chicago Heights, Ill., Dec. 22, 1951; d. Thomas Earl and Barbara Jean (George) Jackson; m. David Austin Sullivan, Dec. 18, 1971; children: Jason Austin, Kevin Austin. BS, U. S. Ala., 1973, MEd, 1986. Cert. tchr. State Ala. Dept. Edn. Tchr. Mobile County (Ala.) Sch. Sys., Mobile, 1973-76; tchr.'s aide Office of Cath. Schs., Mobile, 1982-83, tchr., 1983—; trainer Project Success Enrichment, Seattle, 1994-96; presenter in field. Mem. Nat. Cath. Edn. Assn., Assn. Supervision and Curriculum Devel. Roman Catholic. Home: 3532 Springwood Dr E Mobile AL 36608 Office: St Ignatius Sch 3650 Springhill Ave Mobile AL 36608-5703

SULLIVAN, PATRICK GERALD, JR., electronics engineer; b. Washington, July 9, 1952; s. Patrick Gerald Sullivan and Virginia Ann (Berry) Sullivan Jones; m. Mary Katherine Zavilla, June 25, 1983; 1 child, Julia Cecile. BS in Physics, Coll. of William and Mary, 1974; MS in Engring., George Washington U., 1976; diploma, Armed Forces Staff Coll., 1990, Naval War Coll., 1996. Electronics engr. EG and G, Rockville, Md., 1976-80, Def. Comms. Agy., Arlington, Va., 1980-91; electronics engr., tech. policy-counterproliferation analyst Office of Sec. of Def., Arlington, 1991—; presenter various symposia and seminars including SHAPE Tech. Tcr. Ann. Symposium, Am. Def. Preparedness Assn. Spl. Ops.-Low Intensity Conflict Conf., 5th Nat. Ops. Security Conf. Contbr. papers to various symposia and seminars. Parishioner, vol. Our Lady of Good Counsel Cath. Ch., Vienna, Va., 1959-87, St. Joseph's Cath. Ch., Herndon, Va., 1987—. Rsch. fellow Joint Inst. for Acoustic and Flight Scis., George Washington U., 1974-76. Mem. IEEE, Armed Forces Comm. and Electronics Assn., Price Club, Sigma Pi Sigma, Phi Mu Alpha Sinfonia. Home: 903 Barker Hill Rd Herndon VA 20170-3015 Office: Office of Sec of Def 400 Army Navy Dr # 300 Arlington VA 22202-2885

SULLIVAN, PATRICK RANEY, labor management consultant; b. Alexandria, La., Nov. 24, 1919; s. Robert Bailey and Katey Francis (Raney) S.; m. Rose Mary DeBenedetta, Nov. 23, 1940 (dec. Dec. 1989); children: Patrick Raney, Michael Robert. Commd. officer U.S. Navy, 1939-59; ins. supervisor Gulf Life Ins. Co., Orlando, 1959-66; from employee rels. supervisor to labor rels. officer USAF, Robbins AFB, GA, 1966-78; self-employed labor mgmt. cons. Pensacola, Fla., 1978—. Mem. NRA, Am. Arbitration Assn., Ret. Officer's Assn., Elks, K. of C. Republican. Roman Catholic.

SULLIVAN, PAUL WILLIAM, communications specialist; b. Brockton, Mass., Dec. 7, 1939; s. Augustus Henry and Pearl Irene (Chisholm) S.; children: Todd Andrew, Geoffrey Scott, Dustin Raymond; m. Frances Tina Brown, Jan. 23, 1989. BA cum laude, Yale U., 1961; MA, U. Fla., 1971; PhD, So. Ill. U., 1977. Gen. mgr. Chronicle Pub. Co., Stoughton, Mass., 1962-67; editor Easton Bull., N. Easton, Mass., 1963-70; pub., editor Associated Weekly Newspapers, Stoughton, 1967-70; instr. dept. mass comm. Moorhead (Minn.) State U., 1971-73; assoc. prof., chmn. dept. comm. U. Evansville, Ind., 1973-78; prof., chmn. dept. journalism Temple U., Phila., 1978-87; pvt. practice comm. cons., sales tng. cons. Indian Rocks Beach, Fla., 1986-92; pvt. practice comm. and fin. cons. Sullivan Comms., Indian Rocks Beach, 1992—; mng. gen. ptnr. Atlantis Adventure Ltd. Partnership, Largo, Fla., 1996—; mem. rev. panel Harry S Truman Scholarship Found., 1981-86. Author: The Modern Free Press Fair Trial Precedent, 1987, monograph News Piracy, 1978; co-author, editor: The Teaching of Graphic Arts, 1977, The Art of Consulting, 1989; contbr. articles to profl. jours. Mem. Gov.'s Commn. for Pa. Lottery, 1981. Mem. Assn. for Edn. in Journalism and Mass Communications, Soc. Profl. Journalists, Pa. Soc. Newspaper Editors (bd. dirs. 1980-87), Phila. Bar Assn. (media rels. com. 1982-87), ACLU. Office: PO Box 1049 Indian Rocks Beach FL 33785-1049

SULLIVAN, PENELOPE DIETZ, computer consulting and software development company executive; b. Roanoke, Va., Dec. 29, 1939; d. Joseph Budding and Katherine Dietz; m. Thomas F. Sullivan, Sept. 7, 1963 (div. Mar. 1975); children: Courtney, Todd; m. Paul B. Hill, Mar. 31, 1990. BA, Colby Coll., 1961. Claims examiner Blue Cross/Blue Shield of D.C., Washington, 1961-66; self employed maker slipcovers and upholstery Springfield, Va., 1966-75; ins. sales Met. Life Ins. Co., Arlington, Va., 1975-76, Med. Pers. Pool Inc., Alexandria, Va., 1976-77; mktg. rep. IBM Corp., Washington, 1977-88; program mgr. Advanced Workstations IBM Corp., Somers, N.Y., 1988-92; sales cons. IBM Open Sys., Washington, 1992-93; co-founder Open Sys. Assocs., Inc., Reston, Va., 1993—. Office: Open Sys Assocs Inc Ste 400 1801 Robert Fulton Dr Reston VA 22091-4347

SULLIVAN, RUTH WILKINS, museum curator, author; b. Boston, Nov. 20, 1926; children: Peter Dana Wilkins, Michael Paul Wilkins. AB, Wellesley Coll., 1948. Adminstrv. asst. Everson Mus. Art, Syracuse, N.Y., 1958-60, curator, 1960-66, editor of publs., 1960-70, curator of collections, 1966-70; cons. Mus. Am. China Trade, Milton, Mass., 1971; curator of edn. Kimbell Art Mus., Ft. Worth, 1971-82, rsch. curator, 1983—. Contbr. articles to profl. jours. Home: Unit 1 4500 Westridge Ave Fort Worth TX 76116-8246 Office: Kimbell Art Mus 3333 Camp Bowie Blvd Fort Worth TX 76107-2792

SULLIVAN, STEPHEN WENTWORTH, publisher; b. Atlanta, May 17, 1946; s. John Wentworth and Ruth (Delmar) S.; m. Janis Yezak, Aug. 9, 1969; children: Colleen, Anne. BS, East Tex. State U., 1969. Account exec. Corpus Christi (Tex.) Caller-Times, 1970-74, advt. dir., 1977-80, circulation and mktg. dir., 1980, gen. mgr., 1982-84, pres., 1984—, pub., 1987—; nat. advt. mgr. Harte-Hanks Communications, Dallas, 1974-77; pres. Harte-Hanks Communications, Inc., San Antonio, 1984-92; sr. v.p. Harte-Hanks Comm., San Antonio, 1992—; gen. mgr. San Angelo (Tex.) Standard-Times, 1980-82. Chmn. United Way of Coastal Bend, Corpus Christi, 1986, Area Econ. Devel. Corp., Corpus Christi, 1990; bd. dirs. Tex. State Aquarium, Corpus Christi, 1990, pres., 1992—. Mem. So. Newspaper Pub. Assn., Tex. Daily Newspapers Assn. (pres. 1990), Corpus Christi C. of C. (chmn. 1987), Corpus Christi Country Club, Corpus Christi Yacht Club. Roman Catholic. Home: 333 Cape May Dr Corpus Christi TX 78412-2637 Office: Corpus Christi Caller-Times PO Box 9136 820 N Lower Broadway Corpus Christi TX 78469-9136 also: Harte-Hanks Communications Harte-Hanks Tower 200 Concord Plaza Dr Ste 800 San Antonio TX 78216-6942

SULLIVAN, TERESA ANN, law and sociology educator, academic administrator; b. Kewanee, Ill., July 9, 1949; d. Gordon Hager and Mary Elizabeth (Finnegan) S.; m. H. Douglas Laycock, June 14, 1971; children: Joseph Peter, John Patrick. BA, Mich. State U., 1970; MA, U. Chgo., 1972, PhD, 1975. Asst. prof. sociology U. Tex., Austin, 1975-76, assoc. prof. sociology, 1981-87, dir. women's studies, 1985-87, prof. sociology, 1987—, prof. law, 1988—, assoc. dean grad. sch., 1989-90, 1992-95, chair dept. sociology, 1990-92, vice provost, 1994-95, v.p., grad. dean, 1995—; asst. prof. sociology U. Chgo., 1977-81; pres. Southwestern Sociol. Assn., 1988-89; mem. faculty adv. bd. Hogg Found. Mental Health, 1989-92; mem. sociology panel NSF, 1983-85. Author: Marginal Workers Marginal Jobs, 1978; co-author: As We Forgive Our Debtors, 1989 (Silver Gavel 1990), Social Organization of Work, 1990, 2d edit. 1995; contbr. articles and chpts. to profl. jours. Bd. dirs. Calvert Found., Chgo., 1978, CARA, Inc., Washington, 1985; mem. U.S. Census Bur. Adv. Com., 1989-95, chmn., 1991-92; mem. sociology panel NSF, 1983-85. Grantee NSF, 1983-96, U.S. Dept. Labor, 1983-85, Leadership Tex. 1994. Fellow AAAS (liaison to Population Assn. Am. 1989-91, chair sect. K 1996), Sociol. Rsch. Assn., Am. Sociol. Assn. (sec. 1995—, editor Rose Monograph Series 1988-92), Soc. Study of Social Problems (chair fin. com. 1986-87), Population Assn. Am. (bd. dirs. 1989-91, chair fin. com. 1990-91). Roman Catholic. Office: U Tex Office Grad Studies Main Bldg 101 Austin TX 78712

SULLIVAN, THOMAS PATRICK, lawyer; b. El Paso, Tex., May 20, 1956; s. Bernard Francis and Betty Jane (Treadway) S.; children: Rory, Riley, Ramey. BS, U. Tex., El Paso, 1978; JD, U. Houston, 1986. Bar: Tex. 1986, U.S. Dist. Ct. (so. dist.) Tex. 1988, U.S. Dist. Ct. (no. dist.) Tex. 1989, U.S. Ct. Appeals (5th cir.) 1989, U.S. Supreme Ct. 1993. In house counsel Ins. Corp. Am., Houston, 1987-88, 90-93; pvt. practice El Paso, 1988-89; asst. criminal dist. atty. Galveston County, Tex., 1994—. Mediator Houston Neighborhood Dispute Resolution Ctr., 1981. Recipient Am. Jurisprudence award in Remedies, 1984. Mem. Assn. 5th Fed. Cir., Tex. Dist. and County Attys. Assn., Phi Kappa Phi. Democrat. Lutheran. Home: 2908 Beluche Galveston TX 77551 Office: Galveston County Courthouse Galveston TX 77550

SULLIVAN, TIMOTHY JACKSON, law educator, academic administrator; b. Ravenna, Ohio, Apr. 15, 1944; s. Ernest Tulio and Margaret Elizabeth (Caris) S.; m. Anne Doubet Klare, Jan. 21, 1973. AB, Coll. William and Mary, 1966; JD, Harvard U., 1969; LLD (hon.), U. Aberdeen, Scotland, 1993. Asst. prof. law Coll. William and Mary, Williamsburg, Va., 1972-75, assoc. prof., 1975-78, prof., 1978-85, Bryan prof. law, dean, 1985-92, pres., 1992—; exec. asst. for policy Office of Gov. Charles S. Robb, Richmond, Va., 1982-85; atty. Freeman, Drapers' Co., London, 1992; vis. prof. law U. Va., Charlottesville, 1981; exec. dir. Gov.'s Commn. on Va.'s Future, Richmond, 1982-84; vice-chmn. Gov.'s Commn. on Fed. Spending, Richmond, 1986; mem. Gov.'s Fellows Selection Com., 1985-90, Gov.'s Commn. on Sexual Assault and Substance Abuse on the Coll. Campus (chmn. enforcement subcom.), 1991-92; counsel Commn. on Future of Va.'s Jud. System, 1987-89. Mem. Va. State Bd. Edn., Richmond, 1987-92; chair Gov.'s Task Force on Intercollegiate Athletics, 1992-93. Decorated Bronze Star. Fellow Am. Bar Fedn., Va. Bar Fedn.; mem. ABA, Va. State Bar, Va. Bar Assn., Bull and Bear Club, Phi Beta Kappa, Omicron Delta Kappa, Univ. Club (N.Y.C., Washington). Democrat. Home: Pres House Williamsburg VA 23185 Office: Coll William & Mary PO Box 8795 Williamsburg VA 23187-8795

SULLIVAN, TIMOTHY PATRICK, telecommunications company executive; b. Springfield, Ill., Mar. 4, 1942; s. Jeremiah Joseph and Genevieve Anastasia (Stapleton) S.; m. Kathleen Veronica Logue, May 4, 1974; children: Timothy Patrick Jr., Michael Sean, Shannon Kathleen, Jennifer Hillary, Thomas Brendan. BSEE, U. Notre Dame, 1964; postgrad., Syracuse U., 1966-67. Tech. mgr. IBM Corp., Poughkeepsie, N.Y., 1964-68, Hursley, Eng., 1968-69; middle mgr. IBM Corp., Poughkeepsie, San Jose, Calif. and Boulder, Colo., 1969-77; sr. mgr. IBM Corp., Research Triangle Park, N.C., 1977-81; corp. cons. IBM Corp., Armonk, N.Y., 1981-83; product mgr. IBM Corp., Research Triange Park, N.C., 1983-85; v.p., officer No. Telecom, Richardson, Tex., 1985-92; pres., CEO Connectware, Inc., 1993—; bd. dirs., chmn. Corp. for Open Systems, McLean, Va., 1992; exec. adv. coun. Nat. Communications Forum, Chgo., 1989-90; chmn. bd. Osinet Corp., 1991. Inventor storage subsystems in field, 1969-71; author: Captain, 1974; contbr. articles to profl. jours. Mem. adv. bd. Dallas Mus. of Art, 1988-92; mem. North Tex. Commn., Dallas, 1988-91. Mem. North Dallas C. of C., Richardson C. of C., Gleneagles Country Club, Prestonwood Country Club, Notre Dame Alumna Assn. Republican. Roman Catholic. Home: 5221 Corinthian Bay Dr Plano TX 75093 Office: 1301 E Arapaho Blvd Richardson TX 75081

SUMMERLIN, GERALD TERRY, JR., financial advisor; b. Wilson, Dec. 9, 1963; s. Gerald Terry and Carol (Morris) S. BA in Bus., U. N.C., Charlotte, 1986. Salesman Rockingham Office Machines, Eden, N.C., 1987-93; fin. advisor Am Express Fin Advisors, Reidsville, N.C., 1993—; owner Dino's Music Sch., Eden, 1992—. Named Top 30 Pres., N.C. Jaycees, 1992. Mem. Madison-Mayodan (N.C.) Jaycees (v.p. 1991, pres. 1992, chmn. bd. 1993), Best Friends (v.p. 1994, pres. 1995). Baptist. Office: Am Express Fin Advisors First Nat Bank Bldg 202 S Main Reidsville NC 27320

SUMMERLIN, GLENN WOOD, advertising executive; b. Dallas, Ga., Apr. 1, 1934; s. Glenn Wood and Flora (Barrett) S.; student Ga. Inst. Tech., 1951-52; BBA, Ga. State U., 1956, MBA, 1967; m. Anne Valley, Oct. 16, 1971; 1 child, Wade Hampton; children by previous marriage: Glenn Wood III, Edward Lee. Prodn. mgr. Fred Worrill Advt., Atlanta, 1956-65; v.p. sales Grizzard, Atlanta, 1965-74, pres., 1974-94, vice chmn., 1994—. Vice chmn. Polaris dist. Boy Scouts Am., 1967. Vice chmn. Ga. State U. Found., 1974; chmn. distributive edn. adv. com. DeKalb Coll., 1974-76; bd. founders Geo. M. Sparks Scholarship Fund; bd. dirs. Atlanta Humane Soc., 1971—, treas., 1973, 81-82, 84-86, asst. treas. for capital devel., 1987—; mem. steering com. to Honor Hank Aaron, 1982; lay rep. animal care com. Emory U., 1984-85; mem. adv. bd. Families in Action, 1985-86, Soc. Nonprofit Orgns.; bd. dirs. Travelers Aid Metro. Atlanta, 1989-90; mem. Atlanta Sr. Marketers Coun. 100; chmn.'s coun., mem. mktg. adv. com. Crow Canyon Archeol. Ctr., 1993-95. Recipient C.S. Bolen award So. Council Indsl. Editors, 1967; named Outstanding Young Man in DeKalb County, DeKalb Jaycees, 1967, Alumnus of Year, Ga. State U., 1973; recipient Direct Mail Spokesman award Direct Mktg. Assn., 1973. Mem. Mail Advt. Svc. Assn. (pres. N.Ga. chpt. 1959-60), Ga. Assn. Bus. Communicators (pres. 1966-67), Am. Mktg. Assn. (pres. Atlanta chpt. 1973-74), Ga. State U. Alumni Assn. (pres. 1971-72, dir. 1966-78), Sales and Mktg. Execs. Atlanta (dir. 1969-71), Ga. Bus. and Industry Assn. (bd. govs. 1974-76), Asso. Mail Advt. Agys. (pres. 1975-77), Nat. Soc. Fund Raising Execs. (bd. dirs. Ga. chpt. 1984, cert. 1983), Ga. Arms Collectors Assn. (dir. 1974-76, Pres.'s award 1973), Southeastern Antique Arms Collectors (charter; bd. dirs. 1978—), Assn. Am. Sword Collectors (charter), Mid-Am. Antique Arms Soc. (charter), Mensa, Soc. Animal Welfare Adminstrs., Travelers Aid of Atlanta (bd. dirs. 1989-90), Am. Humane Assn., Omicron Delta Kappa. Home: 1133 Ragley Hall Rd NE Atlanta GA 30319-2511 Office: Grizzard 1144 Mailing Ave SE Atlanta GA 30315-2500

SUMMERLIN, HARRY HOLLER, JR., family physician, educator; b. Laurinburg, N.C., Dec. 2, 1935; s. Harry Holler and Mary James (Taylor) S.; m. Joyce Eleanor Roberts, July 10, 1961; children: Rebecca Sue Summerlin Huntley, Daniel Davies Summerlin. Student, U. N.C., 1954-57; MD, Duke U., 1961. Diplomate Am. Bd. Family Practice. Intern Watts Hosp., Durham, N.C., 1961-63; pvt. practice Asheville, N.C., 1965-89; cons., developer family practice residency Mountain Area Health Edn. Ctr., Asheville, 1974-75, acting dir. family practice residency, 1975-76, dir., 1976-77, faculty preceptor, 1978-83, preceptor, 1983-89, clin. prof. family practice, 1989—; clin. prof. family practice U. N.C. Chapel Hill, Asheville, 1989—; physician in attendance Venereal Disease Clinic Buncombe County Health Dept., 1966-86. Contbr. articles to profl. jours. Mem. Coun. Tng. Team Boy Scouts Am., 1984—; bd. dirs. med. clinic Asheville Buncombe Christian Coop. Ministry, 1994—; active Grace Covenant Presbyn. Ch. Capt. USAF, 1963-65. Recipient Silver Beaver award Boy Scouts Am., 1987. Mem. N.C. Acad. Family Physicians, Buncombe County Med. Soc. Home: 26 Crockett Ave Asheville NC 28805-2321 Office: Mountain Area Health Edn Ctr Family Health Ctr 118 W T Weaver Blvd Asheville NC 28804

SUMMERS, AMY ELDER, neonatal nurse; b. Santa Monica, Calif., May 3, 1963; d. Paul E. and Nellie (Henderson) Elder; m. Rodrick A. Summers, Dec. 28, 1985; children: Sarah, Molly. BSN, W.Va. U., 1986. RN, W.Va.; cert. neonatal nurse. Staff nurse Fairfax Hosp., Falls Church, Va. Mem. Nat. Assn. Neonatal Nurses, Sigma Theta Tau.

SUMMERS, HUGH BLOOMER, JR., chemical engineer; b. Lake City, Fla., Aug. 5, 1921; s. Hugh Bloomer and Hazel A. (Flory) S.; B.Chem. Engring., U. Fla., 1943; m. Betty Jane Karstedt, Aug. 17, 1946; children—Hugh Bloomer, III, Carole Anne. Research chem. engr. Dept. Agr., Olustee, Fla., 1947-65; chem. engr. Union Camp Corp., Savannah, Ga., 1965-86. Served with USNR, 1943-46. Registered profl. engr., Ga. Am. Inst. Chem. Engrs., Am. Chem. Soc. Democrat. Methodist. Author reports; patentee in field. Home: 17 Biscayne Blvd Lake City FL 32025-6501

SUMMERS, JAMES BRANSON, lawyer; b. Memphis, Sept. 18, 1950; s. James Mouzon and Marie (Jackson) S.; m. Deborah Ann Lambert, May 8, 1981; children: James W., Sarah Elizabeth. Student, U. Va.; BS in Fin., U. Tenn., Knoxville, 1973; JD, Memphis State U., 1976. Bar: Tenn. 1976,. Assoc. Neely Green Fargarson Brooke, Memphis, 1976-85, ptnr., 1985—; cons. playground safety, Memphis, 1988—. Assoc. editor Memphis State U. Law Jour., 1974-76; author/editor newsletter Tenn. Commentary, 1989-93, Report From Counsel, 1994—. Mem. ABA, Tenn. Bar Assn., Memphis Bar Assn., Shelby County Bar Assn. (sec. bd. govs. 1978-79, chmn. press liaison com. 1979), Tenn. Trial Lawyers Assn., Tenn. Def. Lawyers Assn., Def. Rsch. Inst., Rotary Club Internat., Delta Theta Phi. Mem. Disciples of Christ Ch. Office: Neely Green Fargarson Brooke & Summers 65 Union Ave Memphis TN 38103-5127

SUMMERS, JOSEPH FRANK, author, publisher; b. Newnan, Ga., June 26, 1914; s. John Dawson and Anne (Blalock) S.; BA in Math., U. Houston, 1942; profl. cert. meteorology, UCLA, 1943, U. Chgo., 1943; postgrad., U. P.R., 1943-44; MA in Math., U. Tex. at Austin, 1947; postgrad. Rice U., 1947-49; m. Evie Margaret Mott, July 8, 1939 (dec. May 1989); children: John Randolph, Thomas Franklin, James Mott. With Texaco Inc., Houston, 1933-42, 49-79, mgr. data processing, 1957-67, asst. gen. mgr. computer svcs. dept., 1967-79, automation cons., 1979-83; pres. Word Lab Inc., Houston, 1983—; instr. math. AAC, Ellington Field, Tex., 1941-42, U. Tex. at Austin, 1946-47. Pres. Houston Esperanto Assn., 1934-39; vol. tutor Thousand Points of Light, 1991—. Capt. AAC, 1942-46. Rice U. fellow, 1947-49. Mem. Assn. Computing Machinery (pres. 1956-58), Nat. Assn. Accts. (past bd. dir.), Am. Petroleum Inst. (mem. data processing and computing com. 1955-59), Rice U. Hist. Soc., Rice U. Assocs., Esperanto League N.Am., Universal Esperanto Assn. Author: Mathematics for Bombadiers and Navigators, 1942, Wholly Holey Holy, An Adult American Spelling Book, 1984. Contbg. author: American Petroleum Institute Drilling and Production Practices.

SUMMERS, MARK STEVEN, publishing executive, lawyer; b. Dallas, Sept. 29, 1947; s. William Leon and Esther (Selitsky) S.; m. Mary Gayle Phegley, May 6, 1979; children: Leonard Aaron, Alexis Lauren, Elliot Samuel. BA, U. Tex., 1971, JD, 1975; postgrad., Columbia U., 1975-76. Bar: Tex. 1975, U.S. Ct. Appeals (2d cir.) 1975, U.S. Dist. Ct. (we. dist.) Tex. 1978, U.S. Ct. Appeals (5th cir.) 1981. Editor Matthew Bender & Co., N.Y.C., 1975-78; ptnr. McLeroy & Summers, Austin, Tex., 1978-80; counsel for enforcement Tex. Comptroller Pub. Accounts, Austin, 1980-85; assoc. Law Offices Baker & Price, Austin, 1985-88; counsel Knowles Law Book Pub., Ft. Worth, 1988-90; pres. Summers Press, Inc., Bedford, Tex., 1990—. Author: Employment in Texas, 1983, Bankruptcy Explained, 1989, CA Employer's Guide, 1990, PA Employer's Guide, 1991. Mem. State Bar Tex., Travis County Bar Assn., Austin Writer's League. Office: Summers Press Inc 6631 Browning Dr North Richland Hills TX 76180

SUMMERS, RICHARD LYLE, safety executive, consultant; b. Ottawa, Ont., Can., Aug. 20, 1938; s. Stanley Lyle and Audrey Ruth (Bell) S.; m. Patricia Ann Lengyell, Oct. 8, 1960; children: David Steven Lyle, Janet Frances Ann. LLB, LaSalle U., 1968; PhD, U. Beverly Hills, 1979. Vice prin., tchr. Hamilton Bd. Edn., 1968-70; dir. edn. Indsl. Accident Prevention Assn., Toronto, Ont., 1970-76; exec. dir. Univ. and Coll. Placement Assn., Toronto, 1976-78; assoc. dir. Internat. Safety Acad., Houston, 1978-81; exec. v.p. Internat. Safety Assocs., Houston, 1981-83; dir. so. ops. Figgie Internat.-Waite Hill Services, Houston, 1983-88; dir. product safety Snorkel-Economy, St. Joseph, Mo., 1988-91; v.p. Safety Rust Indsl., Mulberry, Fla., 1991—; safety exec. Waste Mgmt. Inc., Lakeland, Fla.; mem. bd. examiners Certified Hazard Control Mgmt. Bd., Alexandria, Va., 1981—. Contbr. numerous articles to profl. jours. Arbitrator Greater Houston Better Bus. Bur., Houton, 1985-88; cons. Alaska Gov.'s Adv. Coun., Anchorage, 1983-88. Recipient Award of Appreciation Alaska Adv. Council, Anchorage, 1986. Mem. Am. Soc. Safety Engrs. (cons. 1980—), Australian Safety Soc. (hon.), Nat. Safety Mgmt. Soc. Home: # 135 1625 Ariana St Lakeland FL 33803

SUMMERS, WILSON, IV, college dean; b. Louisville, Mar. 26, 1946; s. Wilson III and Marilyn (Merten) S.; m. Laurel Eileen Wheeler, Apr. 25, 1970; children: Jennifer Joan, Tamara Diane. BS, USAF Acad., 1969; MA, Chapman Coll., Orange, Calif., 1978; MS, Indsl. Coll. Armed Forcesa, 1995. Cert. profl. contract mgr. Commd. 2d lt. USAF, 1969, advanced through grades to lt. col., 1985, ret., 1989; navigator 2d Bomb Wing, Barksdale AFB, La., 1970-75; wing navigation officer 93d Bomb Wing, Castle AFB, Calif., 1975-80; edn.-with-industry staff Northrop Corp., Hawthorne, Calif., 1980-81; contracting officer Space divsn. USAF, El Segundo, Calif., 1981-82, dep. dir. contracts, 1982-84; chief engring., program support Air Force Plant Rep. Office, Redondo Beach, Calif., 1984-86; prof. Def. Sys. Mgmt. Coll., Ft. Belvoir, Va., 1986-88, dep. chmn., 1988-95, assoc. dean, 1995—; assoc. prof. Webster U., Washington, 1989—. Decorated Air medals (2); recipient Def. Meritorious Svc. medal Dept. Def., 1989. Fellow Nat. Contract Mgmt. Assn.; mem. Assn. grads. USAF Acad. Home: 9805 Viewcrest Dr Fairfax Station VA 22039 Office: Defense Systems Mgmt College 9820 Belvoir Rd Fort Belvoir VA 22060

SUMMERSELL, FRANCES SHARPLEY, organization worker; b. Birmingham, Ala.; d. Arthur Croft and Thomas O. (Stone) Sharpley; m. Charles Grayson Summersell, Nov. 10, 1934. Student U. Montevallo, Peabody Coll.; LHD (hon.) U. Ala., 1996. Ptnr., artist, writer Assoc. Educators, 1959—. Vice chmn. Ft. Morgan Hist. Commn., 1959-63; active DAR, Magna Charta Dames, U. Women's Club (pres. 1957-58), Daus. Am. Colonists (organizing regent Tuscaloosa 1956-63). Recipient Algernon Sidney Sullivan award U. Ala., 1994. Mem. Tuscaloosa County Preservation Soc. (trustee 1965-78, svc. award 1975), Birmingham-Jefferson Hist. Soc., Ala. Hist. Assn. (exec. bd. Ala. Review 1991—), XXXI Women's Hon. Soc., Omicron Delta Kappa, Iota Circle, Anderson Soc. Clubs: University (Tuscaloosa). Co-author: Alabama History Filmstrips, 1961; Florida History Filmstrips, 1963; Texas History Filmstrips, 1965-66; Ohio History Filmstrips, 1967 (Merit award Am. Assn. State and Local History 1968);

California History Filmstrips, 1968; Illinois History Filmstrips, 1970. Home: 1411 Caplewood Dr Tuscaloosa AL 35401-1131

SUMMERVILLE, JAMES MELVIN SMITH, editor; b. Dickson, Tenn., Oct. 27, 1947; s. Melvin Wesley and Alice Jane (Hagood) S.; m. Linda Molgaard Andersen, Oct. 24, 1986; children: Laurel Bizaillon, Leigh Bizaillon. BA, U. Tenn., 1969; MA, U. Iowa, 1972, Vanderbilt U., 1983. Rsch. analyst State of Tenn., Nashville, 1972-77; asst. to vice chancellor Vanderbilt U., Nashville, 1977-82; editor Am. Assn. State and Local History, Nashville, 1983-88; exec. dir. Tenn. Hist. Soc., Nashville, 1988-89; editor Vanderbilt U., Nashville, 1994—; monument com. mem. Battle of Nashville, Tenn. Hist. Commn., 1995—. Author: Educating Black Doctors: A History of Meharry Medical College, 1983, The Carmack-Cooper Shooting: Tennessee Politics Turns Violent, 1994; editor, pub. Tennessee History, 1995—. Chmn. Hillsboro-West End Neighborhood Assn., Nashville, 1982-83, 86-87. Mem. Nat. Coun. Pub. History, Nat. Coalition Ind. Scholars, Theodore Roosevelt Assn., Assn. Tenn. History (pres. 1990—), Tenn. Assn. Scholars (v.p. 1995—). Home: 2911 Woodlawn Dr Nashville TN 37215 Office: Vanderbilt Univ 21st Ave S at Edgehill Ave Nashville TN 37203

SUMMEY, STEVEN MICHAEL, advertising company executive; b. Abingdon, Va., Jan. 26, 1946; s. Lee Roy Summey and Jacqueline Forest (Tomlinson) Kiser; m. Linda Sue Rasnake, June 27, 1965 (div. 1977); 1 child, Steven Michael II; m. Linda Lee Hoff, July 29, 1978; children: Jason Lee, Matthew Lawrence. Student, Western Carolina U., 1964, U. N.C. Lab technician Northrop Corp., Asheville, N.C., 1965-67; pres. Summey Outdoor Advt., Asheville, 1967—; co-founder Ind. Advt. Coun., Washington, 1986. Designer outdoor advt. package; inventor in field. Spl. dep. Buncombe County Sheriffs Dept., Asheville, 1966—; mem. Peaks Soc. United Way; grad. Leadership Asheville Program. Mem. Nat. Assn. Realtors, Nat. Speakers Assn., Carolina Speakers Assn., N.C. Outdoor Advt. Assn., S.C. Outdoor Advt. Assn., N.C. Assn. Realtors, Asheville Bd. Realtors, Asheville Sales and Mktg. Execs., Outdoor Advt. Assn. of Am. (bd. dirs., exec. com.), C. of C., Coun. Ind. Bus. Owners (found., pres. 1987—), Internat. Platform Assn. Office: Summey Outdoor Advt 95 Underwood Rd Fletcher NC 28732-9690

SUMMITT, ROBERT LAYMAN, pediatrician, educator; b. Knoxville, Tenn., Dec. 23, 1932; s. Robert Luther and Mary Ruth (Layman) S.; m. Joyce Ann Sharp, Dec. 23, 1955; children: Robert Layman Jr., Susan Kelly Summitt Pridgen, John Blair. Student, Davidson Coll., 1950-51; MD, U. Tenn., 1955, MS in Pediatrics, 1962. Diplomate Am. Bd. Pediatrics, recert. in pediatrics, 1983, 92, Am. Bd. Med. Genetics (bd. dirs. 1985-89). Rotating intern U. Tenn. Meml. Research Ctr. and Hosp., Knoxville, 1956; asst. resident in pediatrics U. Tenn. Coll. Medicine and City of Memphis Hosp., 1959-60, chief resident, 1960-61; USPHS fellow in pediatric endocrinology U. Tenn. Coll. Medicine, Memphis, 1961-62; fellow in med. genetics U. Wis.-Madison, 1963; asst. prof. pediatrics, child devel. U. Tenn., Memphis, 1964-68, assoc. prof., 1968-71, prof. pediatrics and anatomy, 1971—, dean Coll. Medicine, 1981—, provost, 1988-91; cons. President's Commn. on Mental Retardation, 1979-80; CEO U. Tenn. Med. Group, 1983-93, chmn., 1983—; mem. Coun. on Grad. Med. Edn., 1990—. Lt. M.C., USN, 1957-59, rear admiral USNR, ret. 1992. NIH grantee, 1965—; recipient Alumni Pub. Service award U. Tenn. Alumni Assn., 1980-81, U. Tenn. Coll. Medicine Student Body Disting. Tchr. award, 1981-82, 82-83, 83-84, 84-85, 85-86, Outstanding Alumnus award U. Tenn. Coll. of Medicine, 1984. Fellow Am. Coll. Med. Genetics, Am. Acad. Pediatrics (Tenn. Pediatrician of Yr. Tenn. chpt. 1996); mem. AMA (rep. to accreditation coun. on grad. med. edn. 1995—), Tenn. Med. Assn., Memphis-Shelby County Med. Soc. (bd. dirs. 1994—), Am. Soc. Human Genetics, Soc. Pediatric Rsch., Coun. Deans of AAMC, Jour. Rev. Club (Memphis), Tenn. Pediatric Soc. (Tenn. Pediatrician of Yr. 1996). Office: U Tenn Coll Medicine 800 Madison Ave Memphis TN 38103-3400

SUMMITT, ROBERT MURRAY, circuit judge; b. Sweetwater, Tenn., Jan. 14, 1924; s. Murray Dyer and Vina Mae (Brakebill) S.; m. Florence Varnell, May 14, 1955; children: Virginia Anne Sharber, Robert M. Jr., Laura Stephens, Martin Dyer. JD, U. Tenn., 1949; postgrad., Nat. Jud. Coll., 1972, 79, 82, Am. Acad. Jud. Edn., 1974, 75, 76, 77, U. Tenn., 1978. Bar: Tenn. 1949, U.S. Supreme Ct. 1956. Pvt. practice Chattanooga, 1949-68; cir. judge Tenn. Jud. 1st Div. 11th Jud. Dist. Ct., Tenn., 1968—; served on Tenn. Supreme Ct., 1990; pres. Tenn. Jud. Conf., 1980, ec., v.p., exec. com. mem., 1980-84, past chmn. nominating com., continuing edn. com., past chmn.; mem. Tenn. Ct. of the Judiciary; past chmn. ad hoc fed. diversity com. National Conf. State Trial Judges, past chmn. task force on jud. support, past chairman State Jud. Assn., chmn. fin. and budget com., Tenn. rep. to nat. conf. Author: (with others) Tenn. Trial Judges Benchbook; contbr. articles to profl. jours. State chmn., nat. rep., Inner City com. chmn., Boy Scouts Am. (Silver Beaver award 1976); bd. dirs. Salvation Army; mem. Freedom's Found.; bd. dirs., trustee, past Sunday Sch. tchr. First Centenary United Meth. Ch. Decorated Red Cross of Constantine; recipient Nat. Heritage award Downtown Sertoma Club, 1984; named Young Man of Yr., Jaycees, 1959. Mem. ABA (past chmn. Nat. Conf. State Trial Judges 1991-92, mem. judicial adminstrn. divsn. coun., judicial coun. House of Dels.), Tenn. Bar Assn., Chattanooga Bar Assn. (bd. govs.), Am. Judicature Soc., Am. Judges Assn., Internat. Acad. Trial Judges, Silver Falcon Assn., Air Force Assn., Res. Officers Assn., Retired Res. Officers Assn., U. Tenn. Alumni Assn. Century Club, Order of the Arrow, City Farmers Club, Half-Century Club, SAR (chancellor), Mason, Royal Order Jesters, Royal Order Scotland, Eastern Star, Alhambra Temple, Rotary, Phi Delta Phi, Sigma Alpha Epsilon. Home: 957 Ravine Rd Signal Mountain TN 37377-3054 Office: 11th Jud Dist Hamilton County Courthouse Chattanooga TN 37402-1401

SUMNER, GORDON HEYWARD, foreign language educator; b. Ancon, Panama, May 21, 1945; came to U.S., 1945; s. Jack Shelton and Lucy Melvina (Alford) S. BA cum laude, Fla. State U., 1966, MA, 1976, PhD, 1979. Tchr. Spanish, French Pub. Sch. in Calif. and Fla., 1967-77; grad. teaching asst. Fla. State U., 1977-79; asst. prof. Spanish, French Ala. State U., Montgomery, 1983-88, assoc. prof., 1988—; vis. asst. prof. Ball State U., Muncie, Ind., 1979-80, S.D. State U., Brookings, 1980-83; translator U.S. Fed. Ct., Montgomery, Ala., 1990, 93; cons. Fulbright Sel. Evaluation of Candidates, Montgomery, 1993. Fulbright scholar, 1977; NDEA fellow, 1966-67. Mem. NEA, Am. Assn. Tchrs. Spanish, Ala. Edn. Com., Assn. Classical Hispanic Theater, Modern Lang. Assn., Phi Beta Kappa, Phi Kappa Phi, Sigma Delta Pi, Pi Delta Phi. Office: Ala State U 309 McGehee Hall Montgomery AL

SUMNER, JOHN HEALY, systems engineer; b. Oklahoma City, Aug. 15, 1937; s. John Hull and Violet Mary (Healy) S.; m. Mary Elizabeth Vaughan, Aug. 26, 1961; children: Timothy P., Susan M. BS, U. Tenn., 1959; MS, U. Colo., 1975; grad. with honors, U.S. Army Command/Gen. Staff, 1974. Commd. U.S. Army, 1959-79, advanced through grades to lt. col.; chief presdl. comm. support office Def. Comm. Agy., Arlington, Va., 1975-79; mem. tech. staff Mitre Corp., McLean, Va., 1979-80; program mgr. Horizons Tech., Inc., McLean, 1980-84, Vanguard Rsch., Inc., Fairfax, 1984-86; gen. mgr. Washington divsn. Vanguard rsch., Inc., Fairfax, 1986-89, v.p. plans, 1989—, corp. sec., 1984—, also bd. dirs.; bd. dirs. Pumpkin Vine, Ltd., Occoquan, Va. Author: Telecommunications in Industry and Society, 1975. Bd. dirs. Villas Assn., Nags Head, N.C., 1990-95; pres. Spartan Booster Club, West Springfield (Va.) H.S., 1981-82; del. Va. Rep. Conv., Norfolk, 1984. Decorated Bronze Star (3). Methodist. Home: 11502 Havenner Rd Fairfax Station VA 22039 Office: Vanguard Research Inc 10400 Eaton Pl #450 Fairfax VA 22030

SUMNER, LORENE KNOWLES HART, retired medical/surgical and rehabilitation nurse; b. Telfair County, Ga., June 26, 1925; d. William Ira and Lola Amanda (Selph) Knowles; m. George Allen Hart, June 1, 1943 (dec. June 1953); children: Elizabeth Ann, George Allen, Charles Burnon; m. Joseph Rouss Sumner, Feb. 15, 1970; stepchildren: Joseph Rouss Jr., William Albert, Marvin Edwin, Charles Blaine (dec.). Lic. Practical Nurse, Macon Area Vocat. Tech. Sch., 1968; cert. coronary care technician, Meml. Med. Ctr., Savannah, Ga., 1971; ADN, Mid. Ga. Coll., 1977; cert. in fetal monitoring, Coromoetric Med. Systems, Savannah, 1981. Lic. practical nurse, Ga.; RN, Ga.; cert. EMT, Ga. Nursing asst. Telfair County Hosp., McRae, Ga., 1953-66; practical nurse psychiat. unit College Street Hosp., Macon, Ga., 1968-70; obstet. supr. Dodge County Hosp., Eastman, Ga., 1980-81; staff nurse med.-surg. and drug rehab. units Carl Vinson VA Med. Ctr., Dublin, Ga., 1981-93, ret., 1993. Vol. nurse blood bank and cmty. disaster svcs. ARC, 1984—; vol. Salvation Army. Mem. ANA, Ga. Nurses Assn. Home: 130 Rollingwood Dr Dublin GA 31021-7112

SUMNER, ROBERT LESLIE, minister; b. Norwich, N.Y., Aug. 3, 1922; s. Clarence Larkin and Gladys Mae (Thompson) S. M. Orphina M. Mingori, Aug. 16, 1942; children: Richard Lee, Ralph Leslie, Ruth Lynn Sumner Purvis, Rita Louise Sumner Phipps, Ronald Lloyd. Grad., Bapt. Bible Sem., Johnson City, N.Y., 1943; DD (hon.), Bob Jones U., 1964; D Sacred Laws and Letters (hon.), Bethany Coll. and Sem., Dothan, Ala., 1985. Ordained to ministry Gen. Assn. Regular Bapt. Chs., 1944. Pastor Calvary Bapt. Ch., Pontiac, Ill., 1943-45; evangelist, 1945-47, 54-59, Calif. Heights Bapt. Ch., Long Beach, 1947-49, Morningside Bapt. Ch., Graham, Tex., 1949-54; dir. Bibl. Evangelism, Ingleside, Tex., 1959-62, 64-88, asst. dir., 1988—; pastor Temple Bapt. Ch., Portsmouth, Ohio, 1962-64; mem. coun. 14 Gen. Assn. Regular Bapt. Chs., Schaumburg, Ill., 1964-68. Author 32 books including: Man Sent From God, 1959, Hell is No Joke, 1959, Evangelism - The Church on Fire, 1960, Biblical Evangelism In Action!, 1966, Saved By Grace . . . For Service, 1979, Jesus Christ is God, 1983; founder, editor The Bibl. Evangelist, 1966-80, 82-89, editorial cons., 1989—; mng. editor The Sword of the Lord, 1980-82. Trustee Sword of the Lord Found., Murfreesboro, Tenn., 1954-82, Bibl. Evangelism, Ingleside, 1959—, Cedarville Coll., Ohio, 1962-87, trustee emeritus, 1987—; mem. cooperating bd. Bob Jones U., Greenville, S.C., 1962-77. Inducted into Fundamentalist Hall of Fame, San Francisco Theol. Sem., 1977. Home: 2928 Lovers Ln Ingleside TX 78362 Office: PO Box 940 Ingleside TX 78362-0940

SUMNEY, LARRY W., research company executive. Pres., CEO Semiconductor Rsch. Corp., Research Triangle Park, N.C. Address: Semiconductor Rsch Corp PO Box 12053 Research Triangle Park NC 27709*

SUMPTER, DENNIS RAY, lawyer, construction company executive; b. Lake Charles, La., Apr. 26, 1948; s. Griffin Ray and Winnie Marie (Vincent) S.; m. Brenda Sue Waite, June 8, 1968; children: Leslie, Stephanie. JD, La. State U., 1975; BA in Government, McNeese U., 1981. U.S. Dist. Ct. (we. dist.) La., U.S. Ct. Appeals (5th cir.). Atty. Sumpter Law Offices, Sumpter, La., 1976—; mayor City of Sulphur, La., 1978-90; judge ad hoc Sulphur City Ct., 1980; mem. La. Commn. for Law Enforcement, Baton Rouge, 1985-86; constrn. co. exec., 1988-94. Pres. La. Mcpl. Assn., State of La., 1985-86; vice chmn. bd. dirs. West Calcasieu Airport, Sulphur, 1986-92. SSgt. USAF, 1967-71, Vietnam. Mem. La. Bar Assn., La. Trial Lawyers, S.W. La. Bar Assn. (ethics com., 1978), S.W. La. Trial Lawyers, Nat. Coll. Advocacy Trial Advocate, La. High Sch. Rodeo Assn. (v.p., pres.). Office: 1003 S Huntington St Sulphur LA 70663-4837

SUMRALL, KENNETH IRVIN, religious organization administrator; b. Ellisville, Miss., Dec. 24, 1926; s. Irvin Earnest and Amber Beatrice (Bynum) S.; m. Wanda Ruth Till, Oct. 17, 1947; children: John, Elizabeth, Stanley, Marlene. BA, William Carey Coll., 1957; MS in Speech, U. So. Miss., 1959; M in Religious Edn., New Orleans Bapt. Theol. Sem., 1962; LLD (hon.), Internat. Theol. Sem., 1986. Agt. Penisular Life Ins. Co., Pensacola, Fla., 1949-51; pastor So. Bapt. Conv., Pensacola, 1954-64; pres., founder Liberty Ministries, Pensacola, 1964-90, Ch. Foundational Network, Pensacola, 1995—; pres., founder Globe Missionary Evangelism, Pensacola, 1971-90, Liberty Fellowships of Min. and Chs., Pensacola, 1975-94, Nat. Leadership Confs., Pensacola, 1978-88, The Secret Place, Pensacola, 1994-96. Author: Manifestation of the Sons of God, 1969, What's Your Question?, 1968, New Wine Bottles, 1975, From Glory to Glory, 1979, Organized Flexibility, 1984, Confidence: The Key to Overwhelming Victory, 1994; editor: Chit-Chat, 1992-96. With U.S. Army, 1945-47. Mem. Scenic Hills Golf Club. Republican. Home and Office: 4900 Forest Creek Dr Pace FL 32571

SUMRELL, GENE, research chemist; b. Apache, Ariz., Oct. 7, 1919; s. Joe B. and Dixie (Hughes) S. BA, Eastern N.Mex. U., 1942; BS, U. N.Mex., 1947, MS, 1948; PhD, U. Calif., Berkeley, 1951. Asst. prof. chemistry Eastern N.Mex. U., 1951-53; sr. rsch. chemist J. T. Baker Chem. Co., Phillipsburg, N.J., 1953-58; sr. organic chemist Southwest Rsch. Inst., San Antonio, 1958-59; project leader Food Machinery & Chem. Corp., Balt., 1959-61; rsch. sect. leader El Paso Natural Gas Products Co. (Tex.), 1961-64; project leader So. utilization research and devel. div. U.S. Dept. Agr., New Orleans, 1964-67, investigations head, 1967-73, rsch. leader Oil Seed and Food Lab., So. Regional Rsch. Ctr., 1973-84, collaborator, 1984— . Contbr. numerous papers to profl. jours. Served from pvt. to staff sgt. AUS, 1942-46. Mem. AAAS, Am. Chem. Soc., N.Y. Acad. Scis., Am. Inst. Chemists, Am. Oil Chemists Soc., Am. Assn. Textile Chemists and Colorists, Rsch. Soc. Am., Phi Kappa Phi, Sigma Xi. Achievements include patents in field. Home: PO Box 24037 New Orleans LA 70184-4037 Office: 1100 Robert E Lee Blvd New Orleans LA 70124-4305

SUMWALT, ROBERT LLEWELLYN, JR., construction company executive; b. Columbia, S.C., Dec. 29, 1927; s. Robert Llewellyn and Caroline M. (Causey) S.; BS in Civil Engring., U. S.C., 1949; MS in Civil Engring., M.I.T., 1950; m. Mary Joyce Mills, Mar. 8, 1952; children: Elizabeth Ladson, Robert Llewellyn III. Area engr. E. I. duPont de Nemours & Co., Camden, S.C., 1950-52; constrn. engr. Columbia City Sch. System, 1952-58; sr. v.p., dir. McCrory-Sumwalt Constrn. Co., Inc., Columbia, 1958-77; chmn. bd., treas., dir. Sumwalt-Mashburn Engring. & Constrn. Co., Inc., Columbia, 1977-79; chmn. bd., pres., dir., chief exec. officer Sumwalt Constrn. Co., Inc., Columbia, 1979—. Pres., Richland County unit Am. Cancer Soc., 1956; chmn. Carolina Carillon Ball, 1963; sect. chmn. United Community Svcs., 1957; div. chmn. constrn. div. United Way, 1973; bd. dirs. Am. Cancer Soc., S.C. chpt., 1957, Richland County unit ARC, 1955-56; mem. adv. bd. Salvation Army, 1982-84; bd. dirs. Columbia City Wachovia Nat. Bank. Served to comdr., C.E.C., USNR. Named Young Man of Yr. Columbia Jr. C. of C., 1958. Registered profl. engr., S.C. Mem. Carolinas Assn. Gen. Contractors Am., (chmn. bldg. div., dir. Carolinas br. 1977, v.p. 1986, sr. v.p. 1987, pres. Carolinas AGC 1988, nat. dir. AGC of Am. 1989, 90, mem. pub. rels. com.) Columbia Contractors Assn. (pres. 1969), S.C. Soc. Engrs., S.C. Soc. Profl. Engrs., Assn. U.S. Army, U. S.C. Assocs. (v.p. 1996), U. S.C. Alumni Assn. (circuit v.p. 1956), Sigma Alpha Epsilon, Phi Beta Kappa, Omicron Delta Kappa, Tau Beta Pi. Presbyn. (chmn. bd. deacons 1968, elder, chmn. adminstrn. com. 1987, 88, adv. bd. Heathwood Hall Sch., 1995-96), Kiwanian (pres. 1962), Forest Lake Country, Tip Off (pres. 1981-82), Drecher High Sch. Found. (pres. 1994-96), Tarantilla, Columbia Ball, Centurion (Columbia); Litchfield Country (Litchfield Beach, S.C.). Home: 1420 Belmont Dr Columbia SC 29205-1510 Office: PO Box 6576 Columbia SC 29260-6576

SUN, JI, research scientist; b. Changsha, Hunan, People's Republic China, Dec. 4, 1971; s. Ming and Hong-Yan (Zhou) S. BS cum laude, Morningside Coll., 1991; PhD, U. Md., 1996. Rsch. scientist Hunan Med. U., Changsha, People's Republic China, 1989-91, Chemistry Dept. Morningside Coll., Sioux City, 1991; tchr. asst. Biology Dept., U. Md., Balt., 1992-96, rsch. asst., 1992—; rsch. asst. Biology Dept. U. Tex., Dallas, 1996. Mem. editl. bd. Chinese Jour. Modern Medicine, 1996—; contbr. articles to profl. jours. Chmn. Student Govt., Hunan Med. U., 1989-91. Travel grant NSF, 1996. Mem. AAAS, Am. Philatelic Soc. Office: U Tex at Dallas Mail Sta FO 3.1 Molecular & Cell Biology Richardson TX 75083-0688

SUNDBERG, MARSHALL DAVID, biology educator; b. Apr. 18, 1949; m. Sara Jane Brooks, Aug. 1, 1977; children: Marshall Isaac, Adam, Emma. BA in Biology, Carleton Coll., 1971; MA in Botany, U. Minn., 1973, PhD in Botany, 1978. Lab. technician Carleton Coll., Minn., 1973-74; teaching asst. U. Minn., Mpls., 1974-76, rsch. asst., 1976-77; adj. asst. prof. Biology U. Wis., Eau Claire, 1978-85, mem. faculty summer sci. inst., 1982-85; instr. La. State U., Baton Rouge, 1985-88, asst. prof. Biology, 1988-91, coord. dept. Biology, 1988-93, assoc. prof. Biology, 1991—. Author: General Botany Laboratory Workbook, 5th revision, 1984, General Botany 1001 Laboratory Manual, 1986, General Botany 1002 Laboratory Manual, 1987, Biology 1002 Correspondence Study Guide, 1987, Boty 1202: General Botany Laboratory Manual, 1988, Biol 1208: Biology for Science Majors Laboratory Manual, 1988, 2d edit., 1989, Instructor's Manual for J. Mauseth, Introductory Botany, 1991; contbr. articles to profl. jours. Judge sci. fairs, La. schs., 1985—; coach Baton Rouge Soccer Assn., 1991—; asst. scoutmaster, Boy Scouts Am. Troop 5, 1991—. Brand fellow U. Minn., 1976-77, Faculty Grants scholar U. Wis., 1984-85. Fellow Linnaean Soc. London; mem. NSTA, AAAS, Am. Inst. Biol. Scis. (coun. mem. at large 1992-95), Assn. Biology Lab. Edn., Bot. Soc. Am. (chmn. teaching sect. 1985-86, workshop com. teaching sect. 1983-84, slide exchange/lab. exchange teaching sect. 1980-89, edn. com. 1991, 92, Charles H. Bessey award 1992), Internat. Soc. Plant Morphologists, Nat. Assn. Biology Tchrs., Soc. Econ. Botany, The Nature Conservancy, Sigma Xi (sec. 1982-84, v.p. 1984-85). Home: 2370 Tulip St Baton Rouge LA 70806-6646 Office: La State U Dept Plant Biology 502 Life Sci Bldg Baton Rouge LA 70803-1705

SUNDBERG, RICHARD JAY, chemistry educator; b. Sioux Rapids, Iowa, Jan. 6, 1938; s. Ernest Julius and Rosa Paulina Christina (Christensen) S.; m. Lorna Swift, 1962 children—Kelly, Jennifer. B.S., U. Iowa, 1959; Ph.D., U. Minn., 1962. Mem. faculty dept. chemistry U. Va., Charlottesville, 1964—, prof., 1974—. Author monograph: Chemistry of Indoles, 1970; author (with F. A. Carey) Advanced Organic Chemistry, 1990. Served to 1st lt. U.S. Army, 1962-64. Mem. Am. Chem. Soc., Internat. Soc. Heterocyclic Chemistry. Lutheran. Home: 2001 Greenbrier Dr Charlottesville VA 22901-2916 Office: U Va Dept Chemistry Mccormick Rd Charlottesville VA 22904

SUNDQUIST, DONALD KENNETH (DON SUNDQUIST), governor, former congressman, sales corporation executive; b. Moline, Ill., Mar. 15, 1936; s. Kenneth M. and Louise (Rohren) S.; m. Martha Swanson, Oct. 3, 1959; children: Tania, Andrea, Donald Kenneth. BA, Augustana Coll., 1957. Div. mgr. Josten's, Inc., 1961-72; exec. v.p. Graphic Sales of Am., Memphis, 1972, pres., 1973-82; mem. 98th-103rd Congresses from 7th Tenn. dist., Washington, 1983-94; gov. State of Tenn., Nashville, 1995—; vice chmn. bd. Bank of Germantown, Tenn. Past mem. White House Commn. Presdl. Scholars; past chmn. Jobs for High Sch. Grads. of Memphis; chmn. Congl. Steering Com. George Bush for Pres., 1988, 92; nat. campaign mgr. Howard Baker for Pres., 1979; dir. com. ops., alt. del. Republican Nat. Conv., 1980; chmn. Shelby County Rep. Party, 1975-77; alt. del. Rep. Nat. Conv., 1976; exec. com. Rep. Nat. Com., 1971-73; nat. chmn. Young Rep. Nat. Fedn., 1971-73; sec. Bedford County Election Commn., 1968-70; chmn. Tenn. Young Rep. Fedn., 1969-70; dir. Mid-South Coliseum, Am. Council Young Polit. Leaders, 1972-74, U.S. Youth Council, 1972-75; bd. govs. Charles Edison Meml. Youth Fund; nat. adv. bd. Distributive Edn. Clubs Am.; mem. U.S. del. study tour, People's Republic of China, 1978, study tour, USSR, 1975. Served with USN, 1957-59. Lutheran. Lodge: Kiwanis. Office: Office of Gov State Capitol Bldg Nashville TN 37243-0001

SUNDY, JOHN SARGENT, physician, immunologist; b. Atlanta, Oct. 7, 1961; s. Robert Mason and Arlene Lee (Sargent) S.; m. Cynthia Anne Fetzer, Nov. 24, 1984; children: Kristin Lee, Anna Katherine. BS, Bucknell U., Lewisburg, Pa., 1983; MD, PhD., Hahnemann U., Phila., 1991. Diplomate Am. Bd. Internal Medicine, Nat. Bd. Med. Examiners. Regional dir. Sigma Phi Epsilon, Richmond, Va., 1983-84; intern in internal medicine Duke U. Med. Ctr., Durham, N.C., 1991-92, jr. asst. resident, 1992-93, fellow in rheumatology, 1993-95, fellow in allergy/immunology, 1995-96, assoc. in medicine, 1996—. Recipient Allen & Hanbury's Respiratory Inst. Fellowship award, 1994. Mem. AMA, ACP, Am. Coll. Rheumatology, Am. Fedn. Clin. Rsch., Nat. Eagle Scout Assn. Office: Duke University Medical Center Box 3258 Durham NC 27710

SUPERFINE, RICHARD, physicist; b. Phila., Dec. 25, 1960; s. Joseph and Adele (Friedman) S.; m. Ellen S. Medearis, Sept. 20, 1986; children: Mary Rose Medearis, Clara Hope Medearis. BS in physics, Lehigh Univ., 1982; PhD in physics, Univ. Calif., 1991. Sr. tech. assoc. AT&T Bell Labs., Murray Hill, N.J., 1982-85; fellow Lawrence Berkeley Labs., Berkeley, Calif., 1992; asst. prof. Univ. N.C., Chapel Hill, 1992. Mem. Am. Physical Soc., Optical Soc. Am., Am. Assn. Physics Tchrs. Office: U N C Dept Physics & Astronomy Phillips Hall CB3255 Chapel Hill NC 27599

SUPERNEAU, DUANE WILLIAM, geneticist, physician; b. Ogden, Utah, Dec. 31, 1950; s. Richard Edwin and Mary Ellen Superneau; m. Connie A. Saltalamacchia, Apr. 21, 1978; children: Adam, Ashley, Allison. BA, Carroll Coll., 1973; MD, U. Wash., 1977. Asst. prof. dept. med. genetics U. So. Ala., Mobile, 1982-87, assoc. prof. dept. med. genetics, 1987-91; chief divsn. med. genetics Ochsner Clinic, New Orleans, 1991—; clin. asst. prof. dept. biometry and genetics La. State U., New Orleans, 1992—, clin. asst. prof. dept. pediatrics, 1994—. Bd. dirs. Assn. Retarded Citizens, 1991—, pres. 1994—; bd. dirs. Jefferson Parish Human Svcs. Authority, Jefferson Parish, La., 1992—. Roman Catholic. Office: Ochsner Clin Dept Pediat Pathology Ob-Gyn 1514 Jefferson Hwy New Orleans LA 70121-2429

SURBER, DAVID FRANCIS, public affairs consultant, syndicated TV producer, journalist; b. Covington, Ky.; s. Elbert and Dorothy Kathryn (Mills) S.; BA in Physics, Thomas More Coll., 1960; LLD (h.c.), London Inst. Applied Research, 1973. Owner, The P.R. Co., pub. affairs counseling, Covington, 1960—. Spl. corr. Am. newspapers to Vatican II, Rome, Italy, 1965. Mem. Bd. Adjustment (Zoning Appeals), Covington, 1964-84, chmn., 1971-84; chmn. Covington Environ. Commn., 1971-72, Commn. Strip Mining, 1967-68; mem. pub. interest adv. com. Ohio River Valley Water Sanitation Commn., 1976-82; mem. water quality adv. com. Ohio-Ky.-Ind. Regional Council Govts., 1975-82; mem. environ. adv. council City of Cin., 1981-84; apptd. by Sec. of Energy to Nat. Coal Coun., 1992, 1994—. Mem. rehab. com. Community Chest Greater Cin., 1972-78, mem. agy. admissions com., 1972-78, mem. priorities com., 1972-78. Pres. bd. dirs. Cathedral Found., 1968-70; trustee Montessori Learning Center, 1973-75, Bklyn. Spanish Youth Choir; founding mem. Mayor's Task Force on the Environment, Cin., 1972-73; Dem. candidate for U.S. Ho. Reps., 1972; mem. Ky. Nature Preserves Commn., 1976-79. Recipient Community Service award Thomas More Coll., 1975. Mem. AFTRA, Tri-State Air Com. (chmn. 1973-74), Izaak Walton League (pres. Ky. 1973, dir. Ky.; nat. dir.), ACLU, Mousquetaires d'Armagnac, Nat. Inst. Urban Wildlife (bd. dirs. 1987—). Producer: (weekly TV. series) Make Peace with Nature, WKRC-TV, Cin., 1973—, Strip Mining: Two Views, 1972; Energy: Where Will It Come From; How Much Will It Cost, 1975; Atomic Power for Ohio, 1976; A Conversation With The Vice President, 1976; The Bad Water, 1977, The Trans-Alaska Pipeline: A Closeup Report, 1977, Acid Rain: A World View, 1986-89, Energy Independence in the U.K., 1992, Unhappy Prospects: Acid Rain & Global Climate Change, 1995. Office: PO Box 15555 Covington KY 41015-0555

SURBER, REGINA BRAMMELL, early childhood education educator, administrator; b. Grayson, Ky., Apr. 3, 1952; d. Jack D. and Opal (Mullins) Brammell; m. Thomas Jerry Surber, Dec. 18, 1976; 1 child, Jerry David. BA in Elem. Edn., Berea Coll., 1974; MA in Early Childhood Edn., Ea. Ky. U., 1975; MA in Child Care Adminstrn., Nova U. Cert. K-8 grade tchr., ky., Tenn. Kindergarten tchr. Carter County Bd. Edn., Grayson, Ky.; presch. tchr. Oak Ridge Nursery Sch., Tenn.; elem. tchr. Anderson County Bd. Edn., Clinton, Tenn.; dir. daycare Roane State Community Coll., Harriman, Tenn., 1989-90; exec. dir. Knox Assn. on Young Children, Knoxville, Tenn., 1993—. Dir. weekday sch. programs 1st Meth. Ch., Oak Ridge, 1990-93. Mem. ASCD, Nat. Assn. for Edn. Young Children, Tenn. Assn. on Young Children, Anderson Area Assn. on Young Children (pres.).

SURFACE, JAMES LOUIS, SR., trust officer, lawyer; b. Roanoke, Va., May 20, 1941; s. Thomas James and Elizabeth (Abbott) S.; m. Judith Marcia Woodford, Aug. 11, 1962; children: Susanna Elizabeth, James Louis Jr. BA cum laude, Washington & Lee U., 1963, JD cum laude, 1965. Bar: W.Va. Assoc. Spilman, Thomas, Battle & Klostermeyer, Charleston, W.Va., 1965-71; trust officer Kanawha Valley Bank, N.A., Charleston, 1971-77; v.p., trust counsel Liberty Nat. Bank & Trust Co., Louisville, 1977-84; v.p., trust officer United Va. Bank, Richmond, 1984-85; v.p., sr. trust officer First Citizens Nat. Bank, Dyersburg, Tenn., 1985-93; sr. v.p., sr. trust officer SunTrust Bank Northeast Tenn., N.A., Johnson City, 1993—. mem. adminstrv. bd. First United Meth. Ch., Dyersburg, 1988-90, pres., bd. dirs. Cmty. Concert Assn., Dyersburg, 1988-93; treas., bd. dirs. Louisville-Jefferson County Youth Orch., Louisville, 1980-84; pres., bd. dirs. W.Va. Opera Theater, Inc., Charleston, 1972-77. Mem. ABA (chmn. subcom. on duties and responsibilities of successor trustee real property, probate and trust sect., Charleston 1974-75), W.Va. Bar Assn., Tenn. Bankers Assn. (treas. trust divsn. Nashville chpt. 1988-89, sec. 1989-90, v.p. 1990-91, pres. 1991-92), W.Va. Bankers Assn. (chmn. trust divsn. Charleston chpt. 1974-70), Rotary (bd. dirs. Dyersburg chpt. 1987-88), Friends of Music (bd. dirs.). Democrat. Home: 2 Queens Ct Johnson City TN 37604-3641

SURGNIER, DAVID HERAL, gas company executive; b. Feb. 8, 1949; s. Florida Belle (Hair) S.; m. Mar. 20, 1973 (div. Nov. 1988); children: Jonathan, Angela, Nicholas. BS in Math., U. Okla., 1971, BS in Petroleum Engring., 1972; MS in Petroleum Engring., U. Tex., 1982. Registered profl. engr., Tex., Okla. Petroleum engr. Can. and mid-continent region Atlantic Richfield, Plano, Tex., 1972-75; mgr. spl. projects Atlantic Richfield, Houston, 1975-82; ops. mgr. Westwind Prodn., Oklahoma City, 1982-85; completion specialist Tex. Iron Workers, Oklahoma City, 1985-86; pres. David H. Surgnier, Inc., Oklahoma City, 1986-88; tech. sales rep. mid-continent area CTC (Completion Tool Co.) Internat., Oklahoma City, 1988-90; Rocky Mountain regional mgr. CTC (Completion Tool Co.) Internat., Denver, 1990-92; CEO, Delta Gas Corp., Ada, Okla., 1992—; cons. Naval Oil Shale Res. 3, U.S. Dept. Energy, 1993. Inventor and patentee in field. Trustee, pub. rels. chmn. Okla. chpt. Nat. Multiple Sclerosis Soc.; voting mem. Choctaw Indian Tribe. Mem. NSPE, Soc. Profl. Well Log Analysts, Geol. Soc. Am., Oklahoma City Geol. Soc. Home and Office: RR 7 Box 488 Ada OK 74820-9145

SURGUY, MARIA TERESA, language educator; b. Chihuahua, Mexico, Mar. 26, 1922; came to U.S., 1929; d. Nicholas and Teresa Irene Perez; m. Bertram Dee Surguy, Dec. 22, 1949; children: Grace Irene, Robert Charles. BS, Tex. U., El Paso, 1943; MA in Spanish, U. Houston, 1972. Cert. med. technologist, Tex. Chemist W.F. Curlee Mfg. Co., Houston, 1945-51; tchr. biology Houston Ind. Sch. Dist., 1964-65; instr. Spanish U. Houston, 1969-73, North Harris County Coll., Houston, 1973—; mem. fgn. langs. coun. North Harris County Coll., cons. bi-lingual edn. Houston Ind. Sch. Dist., 1975. Mem. Tex. Fgn. Lang. Assn., Phi Kappa Phi.

SURLES, CAROL D., university president; b. Pensacola, Fla., Oct. 7, 1946; d. Elza Allen and Versy Lee Smith; divorced; children: Lisa Surles, Philip Surles. BA, Fisk U., 1968; MA, Chapman Coll., 1971; PhD, U. Mich., 1978. Personnel rep. U. Mich., Ann Arbor, 1973-78; vice chancellor-adminstrn. U. Mich., Flint, 1987-89; exec. asst. to pres., assoc. v.p. for human resources U. Ctrl. Fla., Orlando, 1978-87; v.p. acad. affairs Jackson State U., Miss., 1989-92; v.p. adminstrn. and bus. Calif. State U., Hayward, 1992-94; pres. Tex. Woman's U., Denton, Dallas, Houston, 1994—. Trustee Pub. Broadcasting Ch. 24, Orlando, 1985-87; bd. dirs. First State Bank, Denton, Tex., Tex.-N.Mex. Power Co., TNP-Enterprise. Recipient Outstanding Scholar's award Delta Tau Kappa, 1983. Mem. AAUW, Am. Assn. Colls. and Univs., Golden Key Honor Soc., Mortar Bd. Soc., Dallas Citizens' Coun., Dallas Women's Found., Coun. of Pres. (Austin, Tex.), Phi Kappa Phi, Alpha Kappa Alpha. Methodist.

SURPLUS, ROBERT WILBUR, music educator; b. Scranton, Pa., Sept. 1, 1923; s. Willard K. and Olive T. (Wrightson) S.; m. Jean Craig, June 25, 1976; children: Amy, Melanie. BS, Susquehanna U., 1945; MA, Columbia U., 1947, EdD, 1968. Music tchr. Mineola, N.Y., 1945-46, Butler, N.J., 1946-47; music supr. Red Lion, Pa., 1947-56; assoc. prof. Shippensburg (Pa.) State U., 1956-58; music tchr. Fox Lane Sch., Bedford, N.Y., 1958-59; instr. Columbia U., N.Y.C., 1959-61; asst. prof. U. Minn., Mpls., 1961-65; prof. music Ea. Ky. U., Richmond, 1965—; rsch. chmn., So. Div., Music Educators Nat. Conf., 1974-80, rsch. coun. mem., 1974-80; cons. Nat. Assn. Jr. Colls., 1973-75. Author: Follow the Leader, 1962, The Alphabet of Music, 1963, The Beat of the Drum, 1963, The Story of Musical Organizations, 1963; editor: A Guidebook for State Music Education Associations, 1985, Beyond the Classroom: Informing Others, 1987; contbr. articles to profl. jours. Bd. dirs. Ky. Citizens for Arts. Mem. Music Educators Nat. Conf. (pres. so. divsn. 1982-84), Ky. Music Educators Assn. (pres. 1971-73, Disting. Svc. award 1983), Ky. Alliance for Arts Edn. (pres. 1974-82).

SURWIT, RICHARD SAMUEL, psychology educator; b. Bklyn., Oct. 7, 1946; s. David and Ethel (Turetsky) S.; m. Sandra E. Cummings, May 23, 1982; children: Daniel Alan, Sarah Jeanne. AB, Earlham Coll., 1968; PhD, McGill U., Montreal, Que., Can., 1972; postgrad., Harvard U., Boston. Postdoctoral fellow Harvard Med. Sch., 1972-74, instr., 1974-76, asst. prof., 1976-77; assoc. prof. psychiatry Duke U. Med. Ctr., Durham, N.C., 1977-83, prof., 1980, 83—, vice chmn., 1993—; prof. psychology Duke U., 1991-96; CEO Healthware Corp., Chapel Hill, N.C., 1983—; pres., CEO Healthware Corp. Author: Fear and Learning To Cope, 1978, Behavioral Approaches to Cardiovascular Diseases, 1982. Recipient rsch. devel. award NIMH, 1980, rsch. scientist award NIMH, 1993. Fellow APA, Soc. Behavioral Medicine (pres. 1994), Acad. Behavioral Medicine. Home: 3804 Sweeten Creek Rd Chapel Hill NC 27514-9706 Office: Duke U Med Ctr PO Box 3842 Durham NC 27710

SUSMAN, KAREN HYMAN, lawyer; b. Austin, Tex., Oct. 26, 1942; d. Paul and Dorothy (Goudchaux) Hyman; m. Stephen D. Susman, Dec. 26, 1965; children: Stacy M., Harry P. BA, U. Tex., 1964; JD, U. Houston, 1981. Bar: Tex. 1981; bd. cert. in family law 1987. Tchr. high schs. Houston and Washington, 1964-68; realty broker Susman Realty, Houston, 1968-78; assoc. Saccomanno, Clegg, Martin & Kipple, Houston, 1981-83, Marian S. Rosen & Assocs., Houston, 1983-86; of counsel Webb & Zimmerman, Houston, 1986-89; pvt. practice, Houston, 1989—. Editor Internat. Law Jour., 1980-81. Bd. dirs. Downtown YWCA, Houston, 1969-74, pres., 1974; bd. dirs. Tex. Arts Alliance, Houston, 1975-78, Lawyers and Accts. for Arts, Houston, 1985—, Houston Symphony Soc., 1985-95, Houston Grand Opera, 1988—; bd. dirs. S.W. region Anti-Defamation League, 1983—, chmn.; mem. alumni bd. U. Tex., Houston, 1991—; mem. adv. bd. art dept. U. Houston, 1992—; bd. dirs. NCCJ, 1995—, Glassell Sch.; trustee Contemporary Arts Mus. Fellow Tex. Bar Found., Houston Bar Found.; mem. ABA (chmn. com. on individual and personal rights litigation sect. 1989-92), Tex. Mediation Assn., Tex. Bar Assn., Houston Bar Assn., Gulf Coast Family Law Specialists, Tex. Acad. Family Law Specialists, U. Houston Alumni Assn. (bd. dirs., v.p., sec. 1983-89), Houston Club, Phi Delta Phi. Home: 10 Shadder Way Houston TX 77019-1416 Office: 3040 Post Oak Blvd Ste 1300 Houston TX 77056-6560

SUSMAN, MORTON LEE, lawyer; b. Detroit, Aug. 6, 1934; s. Harry and Alma (Koslow) S.; m. Nina Meyers, May 1, 1958; 1 child, Mark Lee. BBA, So. Meth. U., 1956, JD, 1958. Bar: Tex. 1958, U.S. Dist. Ct. (so. dist.) Tex. 1961, U.S. Ct. Appeals (5th cir.) 1961, U.S. Supreme Ct. 1961, U.S. Ct. Appeals (11th cir.) 1981, D.C. 1988, U.S. Ct. Appeals (D.C. cir.) 1988, N.Y. 1990, Colo. 1996. Asst. U.S. atty., Houston, 1961-64, 1st asst. U.S. atty., 1965-66, U.S. atty., 1966-69; ptnr. Weil, Gotshal & Manges and predecessor firm Susman & Kessler, Houston, 1969—. Lt. USNR, 1958-61. Fellow Am. Coll. Trial Lawyers, Tex. Bar Found.; mem. ABA, Fed. Bar Assn. (dir., Younger Fed. Lawyer award 1968), Tex. Bar Assn., Houston Club, Houstonian Club, Crescent Club. Democrat. Jewish. Home: 3238 Ella Lee Ln Houston TX 77019-5924 Office: Weil Gotshal & Manges 700 Louisiana St Ste 1600 Houston TX 77002-2722

SUSSMAN, LEWIS ARTHUR, classics educator; b. N.Y.C., June 26, 1941; s. Maurice Charles and Esther (Kramer) S.; m. Carol G. Holloway, June 11, 1965. AB in Classics cum laude, Princeton U., 1964; PhD in Classics, U. N.C., 1969. Asst. prof. U. Calif., Irvine, 1969-76; prof. U. Fla., Gainesville, 1976—; chmn. classics dept. U. Calif., Irvine, 1972-75, classics dept. U. Fla., Gainesville, 1993—; vis. prof. Aegean Inst., Poros, Greece, 1982; mem. adv. coun. Am. Acad. in Rome, 1980—; teaching fellow U. N.C., 1968-69; chmn., state-wide rep. univ. welfare com. U. Calif., chmn. subcom. collective bargaining, 1973, chmn. Sch. Humanities undergrad. advising staff, 1971-72, vice chmn., sec. Irvine divsn. acad. senate, 1975-76; pres. U. Fla. br. United Faculty Fla., 1980-81; chmn. departmental self-evaluation com. U. Fla., 1981; cons. evaluating foreign lang. programs Broward County Bd. Edn., 1983, Dept. Agriculture and Consumer Svcs., State of Fla., 1983—; admission interviewer Princeton U., 1984-90; speaker in field. Author: The Elder Seneca, 1978, The Major Declamations Attributed to Quintilian, 1987, Calpurnius Flaccus: The Declamations, 1993; advt. editor Classical Jour., 1979-82; reviewer The Elder Seneca: Declamations, 1974, Classical Rhetoric and its Christian and Secular Tradition, 1980, Seneca the Elder, 1983; contbr. articles to profl. jours. Panelist Bus. and Humanities Conf., Fla. Endowment for Humanities, 1977; mem. exec. com. Alachua County Rep. Party, 1980; expert witness higher edn. com. Fla. Ho. of Reps., Tallahassee, 1980. Grantee U. Calif., 1971, 69-76, U. Fla., 1977, Deutscher Akademischer Austauschdienst, 1989. Mem. Am. Philological Assn., Am. Inst. Archaeology (v.p. U. Fla. chpt. 1985-86), Am. Classical League (methodology com. 1980-84), Classical Assn. Fla. (v.p. 1977-78), Classical Assn. Mid. West and South (sec., treas. 1977-78, com. for promotion Latin 1981, awards com. 1989-91, chmn. 1990-91, bd. dirs. 1991-93, v.p. so. sect. 1995-96). Home: 2930 NW 34th Pl Gainesville FL 32605-2149 Office: Univ Fla 3-C Dauer Hall Box 117435 Gainesville FL 32611

SUTEMEIER, ANNE MANCHESTER, occupational therapist; b. St. Louis, Sept. 28, 1949; d. Otis Hervey Jr. and Laura Jean (Heitkamp) Manchester; m. Robert Emile Sutemeier, Aug. 18, 1973; 1 child, Amy Elizabeth. BA, Denison U., 1972; cert. in occupational therapy, U. Pa., 1976. Lic. occupl. therapist, Ala., Fla., Tex. Occupl. therapist, student supr. Morton F. Plant Hosp., Clearwater, Fla., 1976-78; chief occupl. therapist Arlington (Va.) Hosp., 1978-81, Prince William Hosp., Manassas, Va., 1981-84; home health occupl. therapist San Antonio, 1984-85; part-time occupl. therapist Med. Ctr. Hosp., San Antonio, 1985-87; occupl. therapist Austin (Tex.) Ind. Sch. Dist., 1987-90; pvt. practice Maxwell Elem. Sch., Montgomery, Ala., 1990-95; coord. neonatal care, occupl. therapist Rehab. Assocs., Montgomery, 1991-95; clin. dir. NovaCare Outpatient Rehab., Pensacola, Fla., 1995-96; sr. occupl. therapist Rehab. Inst. West Fla., Pensacola, 1996—; cons. Ballwin County Schs., Fairhope, Ala., 1995. Docent Montgomery Mus. Fine Arts, 1990-92; chmn. art selection com. USAF Judge Advocate Gen. Sch., Maxwell AFB, Ala., 1992-94. Computer equipment grantee Advanced Micro Devices, 1988-89. Mem. Am. Occupl. Therapy Assn., Sensory Integration Internat., Pensacola Pediat. Spl. Interest Group.

SUTER, GEORGE AUGUST, management and marketing consultant; b. Zurich, Switzerland, July 22, 1934; came to U.S., 1972; s. Jakob G. and Ann (Hagi) S.; m. Annelise Grone, July 2, 1962 (div.); children: Jeannine H., Marcel D.; m. Elanore K. Kazusky, Feb. 14, 1981. Comml. Sci. degree, St. Michael Coll., Fribourg, Switzerland, 1954. V.p. mktg. Panteplast, Zurich, 1954-62; mktg. mgr. Semperit AG, Zurich, 1962-69; pres., chmn. bd. Suter Assocs., Inc., Zurich and Pitts., 1969-81; mgmt. cons., chmn., chief exec. officer Access Mgmt. Corp., Charlotte, N.C., 1981—; seminar leader U.S. Dept. Commerce, 1975, 77-79; presenter seminars to other orgns. Author: Jumping Import Barriers Alternative to Exporting, 1978, revised edit., 1984, You Open the Door, 1984, revised edit., 1992. Mem. internat. bus. adv. com. Piedmont C.C. Named hon. consul Switzerland, Berne, 1980, Swiss Parliament rep. abroad, 1993. Mem. Am. Mgmt. Assn., Charlotte Trade Assn., Charlotte C. of C. (internat. trade com. 1986-87, 90, 91, 92), Internat. Factoring Inst., Nat. Assn. Factoring Profls., Swiss Soc. (founding pres. 1986-89), Swiss-Am. C. of C., Space Roundtable, Nat. Home Builders Assn., German-Am. C. of C., Brit. Am. Bus. Assn. Office: Access Mgmt Corp PO Box 12059 Charlotte NC 28220-2059

SUTHERLAND, C(ARL) TOM, librarian; b. Atlanta, Mar. 6, 1938; s. Carl Thomas and Alma (Shaw) S.; m. Nancy Elizabeth Glen; children: Glen, Amy. AB, U. Ga., 1959; MLN, U. S.C., 1978. Commd. 2d lt. U.S. Army, 1959, advanced through grades to lt. col., 1979; libr. Augusta (Ga.) Coll., 1979, Med. Coll Ga., Augusta, 1980, DuPont-Savannah River Plant, Aiken, S.C., 1980-89, Westinghouse Savannah River Site, Aiken, 1989—. Author: (book chpt.) Insider's Guide to Library Automation, 1993. Pres. Summerville Neighborhood Assn., Augusta. Mem. Ctrl. Savannah River Area Libr. Assn. (pres. 1993-94), S.C. Libr. Assn. (pres. spl. libr. sect. 1993-94). Office: Westinghouse Savanna Riv St Library 773-A Aiken SC 29808

SUTHERLAND, SAM S(HELTON), III, marketing and technical communications specialist; b. Brazoria County, Tex., Feb. 10, 1951; s. Sam S. Jr. and Rosalie Joy (Ketchum) S.; m. Nancy Elizabeth O'Rourke, Mar. 17, 1979. BA with high honors in English and History, U. Tex., 1973; MA in English, Stephen F. Austin State U., Nacogdoches, Tex., 1975. Cert. bus. communicator. Tchr. Port Isabel (Tex.) High Sch., 1973-74; intern Stephen F. Austin State U., 1975-76; instr. S.W. Mo. State U., Springfield, 1976-79; writer, editor supr. comm. svcs. group McDonnell Douglas Astronautics Co., St. Louis, 1979-86; copywriter Fisher-Rosemount, Austin, Tex., 1986—; editor, cons. Delta Soft, Inc., Tyler, Tex., 1984-85. Author: (with C. Niederlander and D. Kvernes) Practical Writing: A Process Approach to Business and Technical Communication, 1986; consulting editor Practical Supervision, 1988-95. Eagle scout Boy Scouts of Am., 1966. Named Outstanding Young Educator Port Isabel Jaycees, 1974. Mem. Soc. Tech. Comm. (sr. mem. 1979—, copy editor Tech. Comm. 1982-86), Am. Mktg. Assn.

SUTTER, JOHN BEN, political consultant; b. Cameron, Tex., Mar. 30, 1953; s. Cornelius John and Neil Imogene (Williams) S.; m. J. Ramsey Sutter, Apr. 1, 1989. BA in Comm., Baylor U., 1975, MA in Polit. Sci., 1982. Press sec. Office of Congressman W.R. Poage, Washington, 1976-78, Olson for Congress, Waco, Tex., 1978; sales mgr. Suntex Comm., Waco, 1981-82; nat. sales mgr. Stevens Pub. Corp., Waco and N.Y., 1978-80; pres. sec. Andrews for Congress, Houston, 1980; pub. relations dir. Tex. Automobile Dealers Assn., Austin, 1980-81; adminstr., exec. asst. Office of Dist. Atty., Waco, 1982-88; dir. spl. projects Tex. Atty. Gen's. Office, Austin, 1988-89; pres. Sutter and Assocs., Austin, Tex., 1989—; polit. and media cons., Waco, 1982—. Pres. bd. dirs. Waco Rape Crisis Ctr., 1987-89; mem. Heart Assn. Bd., Waco, 1984-87, Goodwill bd. dirs., Waco, 1985-87, Corrections Concepts, Inc. Bd., Dallas, 1987—; candidate judge Mclennan County, Waco, 1986. Named one of Outstanding Young Men of Am., 1977. Mem. Am. Assn. Pub. Adminstrn., Am. Polit. Sci. Assn., Ctr. for Study of Presidency, McLennan County Peace Officers Assn., Criminal Justice Adv. Com., Tex. Dist. and County Attys. Assn,, Tex. Assn. Mediators. Democrat. Baptist.

SUTTER, JOHN RICHARD, manufacturer, investor; b. St. Louis, Jan. 18, 1937; s. Richard Anthony and Elizabeth Ann (Henby) S.; m. Mary Etta Trexler, Apr. 4, 1964 (div. Nov. 1983); children: John Henby, Mary Elizabeth, Sarah Katherine; m. Madeline Ann Traugott Stribling, June 5, 1984; 1 stepchild, William Stribling. BA, Princeton U., 1958; MBA, Columbia U., 1964. CPA, N.Y., Mo. Mgr. Price Waterhouse, N.Y.C., 1964-71; pres. John Sutter and Co., Inc., St. Louis, 1972-86, Handlan-Buck Co., St. Louis, 1975-88; investor, 1988—; pres. Pamlico Jack Group, Oriental, N.C., 1989—; pres. Sutter Mgmt. Corp., St. Louis, 1972-79. Mem. Chpt. Christ Ch. Cathedral, 1987-88. Mem. AICPAs, Mo. Soc. CPAs, Neuse Sailing Assn., Cape Lookout Power Squadron, Sailing Club of Oriental. Episcopalian. Clubs: Princeton, Oriental Dinghy. Home and Office: PO Box 481 410 Whittaker Point Rd Oriental NC 28571-0481

SUTTER, MADELINE ANN, landscape architect; b. Chgo., Oct. 13, 1941; d. William Charles Matthew Traugott and Antonette Florence Geller; m. Gray Carroll Stribling Jr., June 3, 1967 (div. Aug. 1982); 1 child, William Charles Matthew Stribling. BA, U. Wis., 1965; A of Horticulture, Meramec Coll., 1982. Sys. analyst McDonnell-Douglas Corp., St. Louis, 1965-67; mem. faculty Washington U., St. Louis, 1967-70; pres. Inside/Outside, Inc., St. Louis, 1971-89; v.p. Handlan-Buck Co., St. Louis, 1983-88; pres. Madeline Sutter, Oriental, N.C., 1989—; lectr. Pamlico C.C., Grantsboro, N.C., 1990-94; cons. Hist. Beaufort (N.C.) Preservation, 1993-95, Coalition for Comty. Conservation, Raleigh, N.C., 1995—. Author: (urban forest program) Trees for Oriental, 1992-96 (Tree City award 1996). Chmn. Tree Bd. of Oriental, 1992-96. Named Disting. Woman of N.C., N.C. Coun. for Women, 1996; grantee Trees for Oriental Phase I, II and II Am. the Beautiful, 1992, 94, 95, Phase III Small Bus. Adminstrn., 1995, Trees for Small Towns Urban and Comty. Forestry Grant Program, 1996. Mem. Am. Soc. Landscape Archs., Herb Soc. Am. (mem.-at-large 1971—), N.C. Soc. Landscape Archs., St. Louis Herb Soc. (pres., all offices 1967—), N.C. Urban Forest Coun. (mem. exec. bd., treas. 1992—), Neuse Sailing Assn., Sailing Club Oriental. Home and Office: Whittaker Point Rd PO Box 481 Oriental NC 28571

SUTTERFIELD, DEBORAH KAY, special education educator; b. Amarillo, Tex., Apr. 22, 1956; d. Gail DeWayne and Esther Jane (Rogge) Quine; m. Thomas Wayne Sutterfield, Dec. 6, 1980; 1 child, Tristan Thomas. AD, Amarillo Jr. Coll., 1976; BS, Tex. Woman's U., 1978. Cert. in spl. edn., elem. edn. Jr. high resource tchr. Dumas (Tex.) Ind. Schs., 1978-80; substitute tchr. Amarillo Ind. Schs., 1980-81, secondary multiple handicapped tchr., 1981-95, functional living instr., 1995—; pvt. tutor, Amarillo, 1988-94. Vol. Vol. Action Ctr., Amarillo, 1991-94; active Boy Scouts Am., 1989—. Mem. CEC, Tex. Assn. for Improvement of Reading, Assn. Tex. Profl. Educators, Tex. Learning Disabilities Assn., Tex. Soc. Augmentative and Alternate Comm., Children and Adults with Attention Deficit Disorders. Methodist. Home: 1909 Beech St Amarillo TX 79106-4505

SUTTLE, CURTIS, science educator. BSc in Zoology, U. B.C., 1978, PhD in Botany, 1987. Rsch. asst. U. B.C., Can., 1977; tech. U. B.C., 1978-79, Dept. Fisheries & Oceans, Can., 1979-80; teaching asst. U. B.C., 1984-86; rsch. collaborator Brookhaven Nat. Lab., 1987-88; rsch. scientist U. Tex., Austin, 1988-96, asst. prof., 1990-94, assoc. prof., 1994-96; assoc. prof. U. B.C., Vancouver, 1996—; adj. asst. prof. SUNY, Stony Brook, 1988-94, adj. lectr., 1987-88; vis. prof. Duke U., Durham, N.C., 1988, supr. grad. students and doctoral candidates, 1988—; vis. prof. U. Constance (Germany), 1995. Grantee Office of Naval Rsch., 1989-91, 91, 92-93, 93-96, Tex. Higher Edn. Coordinating Bd. Advanced Tech. Program, 1991-93, NSF, 1989-91, 90-93, 91, 94—, Tex. A&M, 1990-91, 91, 91-93, Dept. Fisheries and Oceans, 1981-84; fellow Natural Scis. Engring. Rsch. Coun. Can., 1982-84, 88, Coastal Marine scholar SUNY, 1987-88. Mem. Am. Soc. Microbiology, Am. Soc. Limnology and Oceanography (session chair 1993, convener 1991, invited participant 1991), Psychol. Soc. Am., Am. Soc. Virology, Assoc. Editor Limnology and Oceanography (editor advisor Aquatic Microbial Ecology 1995—). Office: U Tex Marine Sci Inst, U BC Oceanography, 6270 University Blvd, Vancouver, BC Canada V6T 124

SUTTLE, STEPHEN HUNGATE, lawyer; b. Uvalde, Tex., Mar. 17, 1940; s. Dorwin Wallace and Ann Elizabeth (Barrett) S.; m. Rosemary Williams Davison, Aug. 3, 1963; children: Michael Barrett, David Paull, John Stewart. BA, Washington and Lee U., 1962; LLB, U. Tex., 1965. Bar: Tex. 1965, U.S. Dist. Ct. (no. and we. dists.) Tex. 1965, U.S. Ct. Appeals (5th cir.) 1967, U.S. Supreme Ct. 1970. Law clk. to Hon. Leo Brewster U.S. Dist. Ct., (no. dist.) Tex., Ft. Worth, 1965-67; ptnr. McMahon, Surovik, Suttle, Buhrmann, Hicks & Gill, P.C., Abilene, Tex., 1970—. Pres. Abilene Boys Clubs, Inc., 1975-76; bd. dirs. Abilene Cmty. Theater, 1979-80, Abilene Fine Arts Mus., 1977-78. Fellow Am. Coll. Trial Lawyers, Tex. Bar Found.; mem. Tex. Assn. Def. Counsel, Defense Rsch. Inst., Tex. Young Lawyers Assn. (chmn. bd. dirs. 1973-76), Am. Judicature Soc. (bd. dirs. 1981-84), Abilene Bar Assn. (pres. 1987-88), Tex. Bar Assn. (mem. coms. various sects.), ABA (chmn. young lawyers sect., award of merit 1976). Democrat. Episcopalian. Club: Abilene Country. Home: 1405 Woodland Trl Abilene TX 79605-4705 Office: McMahon Surovik Suttle Buhrmann Hicks & Gill PC PO Box 3679 Abilene TX 79604-3679

SUTTLES, DONALD ROLAND, educator, business consultant; b. Coldsprings, Ky., Nov. 14, 1929; s. Noah Elseworth and Bertha Viola (Seward) S.; m. Phyllis JoAnn McMullen, Dec. 12, 1952; children—Daniel, Ruth, Jonathan, Donna, Joanna, Stephen. Student U. Md., 1949-50, U.S. Naval Acad., 1951-52; BBA, U. Cin., 1959; MBA, Xavier U., 1966; Ed.D., U. N.C.-Greensboro, 1977. CPA, N.C.; cert. mgmt. acct.; cert. internal auditor. With Procter & Gamble Co., Cin., 1952-73, supr., 1959-60, indsl. engr., 1960-63, cost engr., 1963-64, mgr. prodn. planning, 1965-68, asst. security coordinator, 1968-70, dept. mgr., 1970-73; dir. bus. affairs Piedmont Bible Coll., Winston-Salem, N.C., 1973-80, v.p. adminstrn., faculty, 1990—; assoc. prof. bus. Winston-Salem State U., 1978-87; prof. acctg. Catawba Coll., Salisbury, N.C., 1987-91; bus. cons. Deacon, trustee, tchr. Bible sch. Salem Bapt. Ch. Served with USAF, 1948-51. Mem. AICPA, N.C. Assn. CPAs, Inst. Mgmt. Acctg., Inst. Cert. Mgmt. Accts. Republican. Home: 2300 Denise Ln Winston Salem NC 27127-8764 Office: Piedmont Bible Coll 716 Franklin St Winston Salem NC 27101-5197

SUTTON, BEVERLY JEWELL, psychiatrist; b. Rockford, Mich., May 27, 1932; d. Beryl Dewey and Cora Belle (Potes) Jewell; m. Harry Eldon Sutton, July 7, 1962; children: Susan, Caroline. MD, U. Mich., 1957. Diplomate Am. Bd. Pediatrics, Am. Bd. Psychiatry and Neurology. Rotating intern St. Joseph Mercy Hosp., Ann Arbor, Mich., 1958; resident in child psychiatry Hawthorne Ctr., Northville, Mich., 1958-62; resident in pediatrics U. Hosp./U. Mich. Med. Ctr., Ann Arbor, 1959-61; resident in psychiatry Austin (Tex.) State Hosp., 1962-64, dir. children's svc., 1964-89, dir. psychitric residency program, 1989—, dir. tng. and rsch., 1993—; cons. in field. Contbr. articles to profl. jours. Active numerous civic orgns. Recipient Outstanding Achievement award, YWCA, 1989, Jackson Day award, Tex. Soc. Child and Adolescent Psychiatry, 1989, Showcase award, Tex. Dept. Mental Health/Mental Retardation,1990, Disting. Svc. award, Tex. Soc. Psychiatric Physicians, 1990. Fellow Am. Acad. Child and Adolescent Psychiatry, Am. Psychiatric Soc., Am. Pediatric Assn.; mem. Tex. Soc. Child and Adolescent Psychiatry (pres. 1979-80), Tex. Soc. Psychiatric Physicians, AMA, Tex. Med. Soc., Am. Genetics Soc. Office: Austin State Hospital 4110 Guadalupe St Austin TX 78751-4223

SUTTON, DONALD MACLEAR, JR., museum executive; b. Phila., Apr. 1948; s. Donald M. Sutton; m. Barbara Clement, May 30, 1974; children: Marian C., Donald M. III, John T. BA, Roanoke Coll., Salem, Va., 1976; MALS, Hollins Coll., 1992. Lic. postgrad. profl. teacher, Va. Asst. dir. Camp Wallawhatoola, Inc., Milboro Springs, Va., 1971-79; assoc. prin., tchr. Jefferson Alternative Sch., Roanoke, 1976-78, prin., 1978-80; adminstr. alternative edn. programs Roanoke City Pub. Schs., 1980-81, supr. ednl. systems, 1981-87; asst. to pres. Roanoke Coll., 1987-89; v.p. instnl. advancement Hargrave Mil. Acad., Chatham, Va., 1989-92; dir. instnl. advancement Va. Mus. Natural History, Martinsville, 1993—; exec. dir. Va. Mus. Natural History Found., Inc., 1993—; exec. sec., chmn. spl. projects com. Roanoke Valley Ednl. Consortium, 1981-89. Mem. long range planning com. Roanoke Valley United Way, 1987, campaign chmn. divsn. D, 1986; bd. dirs. Roanoke Valley Jr. Achievement, 1987-89, Woodlawn Acad., Chatham, 1989-95; v.p. Martinsville/Henry County Travel and Tourism Task Force, 1995; mem. Va. Planned Giving Study Group, 1995—. With USN, 1969-71. Recipient gold award Roanoke Valley United Way, 1982. Mem. Nat. Soc. Fund Raising Execs. (treas., bd. dirs.), Roanoke Regional C. of C. (Leadership Roanoke Valley Calss of 1984, steering com.), Kiwanis (chmn. social com. Salem 1987-89; mem. Martinsville chpt.), Kappa Alpha (pres. S.Z. Ammen Ct. of Honor 1987-95, Cert. of Svc. 1984, Cert. of Honor 1988, Province Comdr. 1980-85), Martinsville/Henry County C. of C. (pub. rels. com. 1995—). Home: PO Box 1003 Chatham VA 24531-1003 Office: Va Mus Natural History 1001 Douglas St Martinsville VA 24112-4717

SUTTON, DOROTHY MOSELEY, poet, literature educator; b. Todd County, Ky., Oct. 11, 1938; d. John Preston and Mary Agnes (Swope) Moseley; m. George William Sutton, Sept. 2, 1961; children: Mary Elizabeth, Dorothy Cassandra. BA, Georgetown Coll., 1960; MA, U. Miss., 1963; PhD, U. Ky., 1981. From asst. to assoc. prof. Ea. Ky. U., Richmond, 1978-92, prof. English, 1992—; poetry reading at coll. and other instns., 1976—; dir. creative writing conf. Ea. Ky. U., 1992—. Author numerous poems; contbr. to mags. and anthologies in U.S. and abroad; poetry editor Scripsit Lit. Mag. Recipient Grolier award, 1991, Tyrone Guthrie award, 1995; Robert Frost scholar Bread Loaf Writers Conf., 1988. Mem. Acad. of Am. Poets, Poetry Soc. Am., South Atlantic MLA, Ky. Poetry Soc. (pres. 1990), Associated Writing Programs. Democrat. Unitarian. Home: 115 Southland Dr Richmond KY 40475-2413 Office: Ea Ky Univ Dept English Richmond KY 40475

SUTTON, DOUGLAS HOYT, nurse; b. McHenry, Ill., Oct. 27, 1962; s. Hoyt Douglas Sutton and Barbara (Sutton) Hensley. Cert. in emergency med. tech., Polk Community Coll., Winter Haven, Fla., 1985; ADN, SUNY, Albany, 1990, BS in Nursing, 1991, BS in Psychology, 1993; MSN, U. Fla., 1995; postgrad., U. S. Fla., 1995—. Cert. adv. nursing adminstrn., rehab. reg. nurse. Nurse adminstr. Bartow (Fla.) Meml. Hosp., 1991-94; paramedic Polk County Emergency Med. Svcs., Bartow, Fla., 1984-88; edn. cons. Moore Pubs., 1990-94; dir. subacute skilled care programs Columbia Healthcare, Inc., Gainesville, 1995—. Mem. Am. Assn. Rehab. Nurses, Am. Coll. Healthcare Execs., Sigma Theta Tau. Home: 7200 SW 8th Ave S-121 Gainesville FL 32607

SUTTON, JESSE NOEL, minister; b. Gilmer, Tex., Jan. 18, 1926; s. Rufus Noel and Jessie Lola (Parnell) S.; m. Norma Dell Beard, Dec. 24, 1948;

children: Rhonda Cheryl Sutton Stege, Lola Celeste Sutton Bailey, Andrea Gay Sutton Holcek. Student, Hardin-Simmons U., 1946-48; cert., So. Tech. Inst., Dallas, 1950; B Sacred Music, So. Bapt. Theol. Sem., Ft. Worth, 1957. Ordained to ministry So. Bapt. Conv., 1979. Min. music, edn. and youth Hilltop Drive Bapt. Ch., Irving, Tex., 1955-56; min. music, edn. and youth 1st Bapt. Ch., Ranger, Tex., 1957-58, Freeport, Tex., 1958-65, Canyon, Tex., 1965-67; min. music, edn. and youth Trinity Bapt. Ch., Amarillo, Tex., 1967-74; min. music and edn. 1st Bapt. Ch., Van Buren, Ark., 1974-78; min. music 1st Bapt. Ch., Delhi, La., 1978-95; interim min. Holly Brook Bapt. Ch., Hawkins, Tex., 1995—; 2d v.p. Ark. Bapt. Religious Edn. Conf., 1975-76, 1st v.p., 1976-77, pres., 1977-78. Mem. Singing Men of Ark., 1974-78. With AUS, 1944-46, ETO, PTO. Mem. La. Singing Mins., Lions (pres. Delhi 1984-85). Republican. Address: PO Box 46 Quitman TX 75783

SUTTON, JOHN EWING, judge; b. San Angelo, Tex., Oct. 7, 1950; s. John F. Jr. and Nancy (Ewing) S.; m. Jean Ann Schofield, July 2, 1977; 1 son, Joshua Ewing; 1 stepson, Michael Brandon Ducote. BBA, U. Tex., 1973, JD, 1976. Bar: Tex. 1976, U.S. Tax Ct. 1977, U.S. Ct. Claims, 1977, U.S. Dist. Ct. (no. dist.) Tex. 1977, U.S. Ct. Appeals (5th cir.) 1978, U.S. Dist. Ct. (we. dist.) Tex. 1979, U.S. Supreme Ct. 1980; CPA, Tex. With Daugherty, Kuperman & Golden, Austin, 1975-76; tax specialist Peat, Marwick, Mitchell & Co., CPAs, Dallas, 1976-77; ptnr. Shannon, Porter, Johnson, Sutton, and Greendyke Attys. at Law, San Angelo, Tex., 1977-87; judge 119th Dist. Ct. of Tex., 1987—. Treas. Good Shepherd Episcopal Ch., San Angelo, 1979-81; co-chmn. profl. div. United Way, San Angelo, 1980-82; trustee Angelo State U. Found., 1987—, pres., 1988-91, 95—, v.p., 1992-94, sec.-treas., 1991-92. Mem. ABA, Tex. Bar Assn., Tom Green County Bar Assn. (sec.-treas. young lawyers 1977-78), AICPAs, Tex. Soc. CPAs (bd. dir. 1980-87, pres. San Angelo chpt. 1980-81, mem. state exec. com. 1981-82, 86-87, state sec. 1986-87, chmn. profl. ethics com. 1985-86, Young CPA of Yr. 1984-85), Concho Valley Estate Planning Council (v.p. 1979-80, also dir.). Office: Tom Green County Courthouse San Angelo TX 76903

SUTTON, JOHN SCHUHMANN, JR., company executive; b. Louisville, July 12, 1931; s. John Schuhmann and Ruth Evelyn (Roby) S.; m. Doris Jean Hornung, Dec. 12, 1953; children: Deborah Ann, Francis Eugene, Thomas Gerard. BA in Zoology, U. Louisville, 1953, MA in Math., 1965. Cert. purchasing mgr. Quality control technician Brown-Forman Corp., Louisville, 1956-64, mgr. quality control, 1964-80, asst. dir. purchasing, 1980-83, dir. purchasing, 1983-85, asst. v.p. purchasing, 1985-88, v.p. purchasing, 1988-91; cons. in field, 1991-95, ret., 1995; cons. in field. With U.S. Army, 1953-55. Mem. Am. Soc. Quality Control, Nat. Assn. Purchasing Mgrs., Purchasing Mgrs. Assn. Louisville, Jefferson Club. Democrat. Roman Catholic. Home: 8628 Birch Ct Louisville KY 40242-3461

SUTTON, KATHY BALLARD, middle school educator, band director; b. Birmingham, Ala., Jan. 28, 1954; d. Albert Eugene Ballard and Dorothy Lee (Thomas) Benson; m. Daniel John Sutton,Aug. 10, 1975. BS, U. Ala., 1976, MA, 1981. Band dir. Fayette (Ala.) Acad., 1976-77; tchr. Greene County Bd. of Edn., Eufaw, Ala., 1977; band dir. Hillcrest Jr.-Sr High Sch., Tuscaloosa, Ala., 1978-81, Hillcrest Secondary Sch., Tuscaloosa, Ala., 1981-92, Hillcrest Middle Sch., Tuscaloosa, Ala., 1992—. Band awards Superior rating, Contest of Champions, Northport, Ala., 1982, '85. '88-90, Dist. 5 ABA, Tuscaloosa, 1988, '90, 3rd Place Southeastern Championships, Orlando, 1991, Grand Champions Marching Auxiliaries, Jacksonville, Ala., 1991. Mem. AAUW, Ala. Bandmasters, Music Educators Nat. Conf., Delta Kappa Gamma. Republican. Methodist. Home: 5231 Orchard Ln Tuscaloosa AL 35405-5733 Office: Hillcrest Sch 300 Patriot Pky Tuscaloosa AL 35405-8606

SUTTON, LOUISE NIXON, retired mathematics educator; b. Hertford, N.C., Nov. 4, 1925; d. John Calhoun and Annie Mariah (McNair) Nixon. BS, N.C. A&T State U., 1946; MA, NYU, 1951, PhD, 1962. Cert. tchr. sci. and math., N.C. Tchr. math./sci. Willis Hare H.S., Pendleton, N.C., summer 1946; tchr. math. Dudley High Sch., Greensboro, N.C., 1946-47; instr. math. N.C. A&T State U., Greensboro, 1947-57; asst. prof. math. Del. State U., Dover, 1957-62; assoc. prof. to prof. and dept. head math. Elizabeth City (N.C.) State U., 1962-87, prof. emeritus, 1987—; adv. com. math. cert. Del. State Bd. Edn., Dover, 1961-62, adv. com. cert. in math. and sci., 1959-61. Bd. dirs. Peruimans County Indsl. devel. Corp., Hertford, 1967-72; NAACP rep. adv. com. N.C. Bd. Social Svcs., Raleigh, 1969-71; mem. fin. bd. Pearson St. YWCA, Greensboro, 1954-56; AME Zion rep. Com. on Christian Edn. of Exceptional Persons, Nat. Coun. Chs., N.Y.C., 1963-65, rep. 150th Anniversary Advance, Am. Bible Soc., 1964-66; bd. dirs. Divsn. Higher Edn., N.C. Assn. Educators, 1969-72; trustee St. Paul AME Zion Ch., 1972—. Recipient Disting. Tchr. award Elizabeth City (N.C.) State U. Gen. Alumni Assn., 1974, Tchr. of Yr., 1980, Woman of Yr. award NAUW, 1976. Mem. Nat. Coun. Tchrs. Math., NAACP, Order Ea. Star (grand assoc. dean 1993-95, worthy matron 1993-96), George Washington Carver Floral Club (pres. 1990—), Daus. of Isis, Delta Sigma Theta. Republican. Home: 5277 Holiday Island Durants Neck NC 27944

SUTTON, MARK F., association administrator. Exec. dir. Gas Processors Assn., Tulsa. Office: Gas Processors Assn 6526 E 60th St Tulsa OK 74145

SUTTON, PAUL EUGENE, II, lawyer; b. Richmond, Va., July 25, 1943; s. Paul Eugene I and Martha Florence (Fernandez) S.; m. Marie Carmaechal Williams, Dec. 24, 1964; children: Donna Maria, Travis Alan. AS, Fla. Jr. Coll., 1973; BA, U. Richmond, 1975, JD, 1980. Bar: Va. 1980, U.S. Supreme Ct. 1989. Legis. asst. Va. State Senate, Richmond, 1974-75; assoc. Esposito & Armstrong, Richmond, 1980; atty. GE, Lynchburg, Va., 1980-82; pvt. practice Virginia Beach, Va., 1982-84; pvt. practice law Norfolk, Va., 1986—. With USN, 1961-72. Decorated Nat. Def. Medal. Mem. ABA, Va. Bar Assn., Norfolk-Portsmouth Bar Assn., Assn. Trial Lawyers, Va. Trial Lawyers Assn., Nat. Assn. Criminal Def. Lawyers, Lions (pres. Norfolk chpt. 1993—). Baptist. Home and Office: 125 Saint Pauls Blvd Ste 530 Norfolk VA 23510-2708

SUTTON, SHARON JEAN, surgical nurse; b. Salisbury, N.C., Nov. 3, 1947; d. Archie Moody and Colleen (Bowers) S. ASN, St. Petersburg Jr. Coll., Clearwater, Fla., 1979; student, Clearwater Cmty. Hosp., 1990-91, St. Petersburg Jr. Coll., 1991. Cert. surg. asst.; RN. Flight nurse Fromhagen Aviation Air Ambulance, Clearwater, 1970-75; nurse mgr. Women's Med. Ctr., Clearwater, 1983—, operating rm. supr., 1991—. Mem. Assn. Oper. Rm. Nurses. Office: Womens Medical Ctr 1745 S Highland Ave Clearwater FL 34616-1852

SUTTON, WILLIAM W., university administrator, biology educator; b. Monticello, Miss., Dec. 15, 1930; s. Talmon Lawrence and Bessie (Lewis) S.; m. Leatrice, 1954; children—William W., Jr., Averell H., Sheryl Lynn, Alan D., Allison M., Gavin J. B.A., Dillard U., 1953; M.S., Howard U., 1959, Ph.D., 1965. Med. technician D.C. Gen. Hosp., Washington, 1955-59; instr. to prof. Dillard U., New Orleans, 1959-79; v.p. acad. affairs, provost, prof. biol. sci. Chgo. State U., 1979-85; v.p. edn. and student services, prof. biology Kans. State U., Manhattan, 1985-88; pres. Miss. Valley State U., Itta Bena, 1988—; chmn., cons. 16 Instnl. Health Sci. Consortium, N.C. and Va., 1974—; reader proposals U.S. Dept. Edn., Washington, 1983, 84, NRC, Washington, 1980, 82, 83; cons. Loyola U., New Orleans, 1982, NSF, Washington, 1974, 76, 78, 80; adv. bd. Deposit Guaranty Nat. Bank; bd. dirs. Blue Cross and Blue Shield of Miss. Contbr. articles to profl. jours. Deacon Chgo. United, 1980-82; trustee sta. WYES-TV, New Orleans, 1973-79; bd. dirs. Urban League of New Orleans, 1970-78, Meth. Hosp., 1975-79, NCCJ, New Orleans, 1968-79. Recipient Disting. Alumni award Dillard U., 1978, Disting. Achievement award, 1982; Presdl. citation Nat. Assn. for Equal Opportunity, 1979, 80; Silver Beaver award Boy Scouts Am., 1976; named Man of the Middle South Changing Middle South Mag., 1973. Mem. Am. Coun. on Edn., Nat. Inst. Sci. (pres. 1973-74), Soc. Protozoologists, Nat. Assn. Biology Tchrs., Rotary, Greenwood-Leflore C. of C. (bd. dirs. 1989-91), Sigma Xi, Beta, Beta Beta, Omega Psi Phi. Club: Rotary (Manhattan, Kans.). Home: 125 Washington Ave Itta Bena MS 38941 Office: Mississippi Valley State U Itta Bena MS 38941

SUYCOTT, MARK LELAND, naval flight officer; b. Riverside, Calif., Oct. 3, 1956; s. Morgan L. Suycott and Dixie L. (Drury) Bobbitt; m. Lisa Lyn Brammer, Oct. 1, 1983. BSCE, U. Mo., 1979; MS in Aero. Engring., Naval Postgrad. Sch., Monterey, Calif., 1987; test flight officer, U.S. Naval Test Pilot Sch., Patuxent River, Md., 1987; student, Def. Sys. Mgmt. Coll., Ft. Belvoir, Va., 1994. Commd. ensign USN, 1979, advanced through grades to comdr., 1995; aviation armament divsn. officer Fighter Squadron Thirty Three, Virginia Beach, Va., 1981-84; flight test project officer Pacific Missile Test Ctr., Point Mugu, Calif., 1987-89; air ops. officer Comdr. U.S. 7th Fleet, Yokosuka, Japan, 1989-91; ops./maintenance officer Fighter Squadron 11, San Diego, 1992-93; dep. asst. program mgr. Naval Air Sys. Command, Arlington, Va., 1994—. Decorated Meritorious Svc. medal, Navy Commendation medal (2), Navy Achievement medal; named Outstanding Grad. U.S. Naval Test Pilot Sch. Mem. AIAA (sr.), Soc. Flight Test Engrs., Assn. Naval Aviation, NAt. Eagle Scout Assn., Masons (master mason), Omicron Delta Kappa, Tau Beta Pi, Chi Epsilon, Alpha Phi Omega (life). Office: Naval Air Sys Command 1421 Jefferson Davis Hwy Arlington VA 22243-0001

SUZUKI, FUJIO, immunologist, educator, researcher; b. Chiba, Japan, June 25, 1946; came to U.S., 1980; s. Takeshi and Kimie Suzuki; m. Katsuko Eda, Oct. 4, 1969; children: Emi, Sumihiro. BA in English Lit., Tohoku-Gakuin U., Sendai, Japan, 1968; PhD in Bacteriology, Sch. Medicine Tohoku U., Sendai, 1975. Postdoctoral fellow U. Tex. Med. Br., Galveston, 1980-82, asst. prof., 1982-84, assoc. prof., 1987-91, prof., 1991—; mem. sci. staff Shriners Burns Inst., Galveston, 1987—. Contbr. articles to profl. jours. Pres. Japanese Alumni Assn. Galveston, 1990—. Recipient Nohagi Rsch. award Tohoku U., 1972, James W. McLaughlin award U. Tex. Med. Br., 1980, prize for disting. svc. in med. sci. Tohoku U. Alumni Assn., 1996. Mem. Am. Soc. Microbiology, Am. Assn. Cancer Rsch., Internat. Soc. Antiviral Rsch., Soc. Leukocyte Biology, N.Y. Acad. Scis., Soc. Japanese Virologists, Japanese Soc. Immunology, Japanese Cancer Assn., Japanese Bacteriol. Soc. Republican. Buddhist. Home: 7714 Chantilly Cir Galveston TX 77551-1629 Office: U Tex Med Br 200 University Blvd Rm 730 Galveston TX 77555

SUZUKI, GENGO, banker; b. Mino-Kamo City, Japan, Feb. 11, 1904; s. Seijiro Suzuki and Sumi Kani; grad. Taihoku Coll. Commerce, 1925; M.A. in Econs., U. Wis., 1927; m. Hide Motoda, Dec. 29, 1929 (dec. May 1975); children—Tsutomu, Sunao; m. 2d, Toshi Toki, July 7, 1976. Instr., then prof. econs. Taihoku Coll. Commerce, Taihoku, Taiwan, 1930-45; prof. econs. Taiwan Nat. U., 1945-48; dep. fin. commr. Ministry Fin., Japan, 1949-51, fin. commr., 1951-57; E.E. and M.P., fin. minister Japanese Embassy, Washington, 1957-60; exec. dir. IMF and IBRD, 1960-66; spl. asst. to minister fgn. affairs, minister fin., 1960-66; auditor Bank of Japan, Tokyo, 1966-70; chmn. Associated Japanese Bank (Internat.) Ltd., London, 1970-79, bd. counselor, 1979-87. Adv. bd. Mekong Com. ECAFE, UN, 1968-75; chief fin. mission on Ryukyus Island, 1968-69; vice chmn. Japanese com. bus. and industry adv. com. OECD, Paris, 1974-75; mem. European Atlantic Group, London, 1971-85. Mem. Internat. C. of C. (mem. council 1974-85, mem. commn. on ethical practices 1976-78). Trustee, Internat. Christian U., Tokyo, 1968-89, hon. trustee, 1989—; bd. govs., Atlantic Inst. for Internat. Affairs, Paris, 1972-88; councilor The Atlantic Council of U.S., 1986—; mem. joint com. on remunerations of exec. dirs. and their alternatives IMF-IBRD, 1977; trustee Rikkyo Sch. in Eng. Trust, Rudgwick, Eng., 1972-90; bd. dirs. Per Jacobsson Found., Washington, 1970—; trustee ICU Cambridge House (Eng.), 1981-90. Mem. Chevy Chase Club. Episcopalian. Home: 6301 Stevenson Ave Apt 717 Alexandria VA 22304-3516 also: 2-5-13 Nukui-Kitamachi, Koganei-Shi Tokyo 184, Japan

SVALDI, MYRTHIA MOORE, financial advisor; b. Norwalk, Conn., Mar. 13, 1961; d. George L. III and Tirsa A. (Kinney) Moore; m. Michael John Svaldi, Oct. 11, 1987; children: Jason, Brian. Degree in fin. and econs., Harvard U., 1983. Fin. analyst banking industry; fin. and sales mgr. U.S. duty free market and Latin Am. Porsche Design; corp. fin. cons. Cellular One; fin. and estate analysis, ins., investments, group benefits Charter Fin. and Ins. Group, Inc., Miami, Fla., fin. and estate analysis, ins. investments. Bd. dirs. Voices for Children; mem. planned giving com. Am. Cancer Soc. Mem. Mercy Hosp. Found., Internat. Assn. Fin. Planners, Miami Assn. Life Underwriters, C. of C. Office: Charter Fin & Ins Group Inc 6161 Blue Lagoon Dr Ste 300 Miami FL 33126-2047

SVENSON, ERNEST OLANDER, psychiatrist, psychoanalyst; b. Duluth, Minn., Oct. 16, 1923; s. Ernest G. and Mabel A. (Benson) S.; m. Raquel Lefevre, 1954 (div. 1965); children: Ernest E., Stuart K.; m. Shirley Zupancic, 1982. BS, Wayne State U., 1948, MD, 1952; BA, Augustana Coll., 1948. Diplomate Am. Bd. Psychiatry and Neurology. Intern Gorgas Hosp., C.Z., 1952-53, staff physician, 1953-54; resident Charity Hosp., New Orleans, 1954-57; psychoanalytic trainee New Orleans Psychoanalytic Inst., 1958-62; pvt. practice, 1958—; assoc. prof. psychiatry La. State U., 1962-80, clin. prof. psychiatry, 1980—; chmn. dept. psychiatry Touro Infirmary, 1973-76; mem. Gov.'s Adv. Com., Mental Health, 1971-72; cons. S.E. La. State Hosp., 1958-61; sr. vis. physician, Charity Hosp., 1965—; clin. prof. psychiatry Tulane U. Med. Sch., 1983—. Bd. dirs. New Orleans Area/Bayou River Health Systems Agy., 1978-82, exec. com., 1979-82, chmn. project rev. com., 1978-79; mem. Area Health Planning, 1971-82. Lt. (j.g.) USNR, 1942-46. Recipient Disting. Alumni award Augustana Coll., 1990. Fellow Am. Psychiatric Assn.; mem. AAAS, Am. Psychoanalytic Assn. (com. new tng. facilities 1988-92), Internat. Psychoanalytic Assn., La. Med. Assn., Am. Coll. Psychiatrists, New Orleans Mental Health Assn. (bd. dirs. 1975-77), New Orleans Area Psychiatry Assn. (pres. 1969-70), La. Psychiatric Assn. (pres. 1969-71), New Orleans Psychoanalytic Soc. (pres. 1971-73), New Orleans Psychoanalytic Inst. (sec.-treas. 1975, tng. supr. analyst 1972—, pres. 1983-85, chmn. edn. com. 1983-85), N.Y. Acad. Scis., Alpha Omega Alpha. Home: 123 Walnut St Apt 1001 New Orleans LA 70118-4846 Office: 1301 Antonine St New Orleans LA 70115-3601

SWACKER, FRANK WARREN, lawyer; b. N.Y.C., May 18, 1922. BA, Union Coll., Schnectady, 1947; JD, U. Va., 1949; LLM in Internat. Law, NYU, 1961. Bar: Va. 1948, N.Y. 1950, Ohio 1962, Wis. 1969, D.C. 1977, Fla. 1991, U.S. Ct. Internat. Trade 1978, U.S. Supreme Ct. 1952. Pvt. practice N.Y.C., 1949-54, 64-68, Washington, 1977-84, Clearwater, Fla., 1984—; atty. Caltex Petroleum Corp., N.Y.C., 1955-60, Marathon Oil Co., Ohio, 1961-63; internat. counsel Allis-Chalmers Corp., Milw., 1968-78; chmn., pres. firm, sr. mem. Swacker & Assocs., P.C., Largo, Fla., 1989-93; dir. ATM CardPay, Largo, Fla., 1993-94, Lasergate Sys., Inc., 1995—; spl. asst. dep. atty. gen. State of N.Y., 1950; govtl. adviser U.S., P.I., Algeria; lectr. Ohio No. U., 1962, N.Y. World Trade Inst., 1976. Co-author: World Trade Without Barriers: World Trade Organization and Dispute Resolution, 1995; co-editor, contbr. Bus. and Legal Aspects of Latin American Trade and Investment, 1977, Reference Manual on Doing Business with Latin America, 1979; contbr. articles to legal jours. Mem. internat. bus. adv. bd. U. So. Fla., 1993-94. Mem. ABA (lectr. 1978, internat. comml. arbitration com. 1991—), Nat. Law Inst., Am. Arbitration Assn. (panel experts), Clearwater Bar Assn.

SWAFFAR, DIANE SHOMIN, research scientist, pharmacology educator; b. Baden, Pa., June 20, 1951; d. Michael Joseph and Catherine (Asperger) Shomin; m. Daniel Monroe Swaffar, Sept. 13, 1978. BS in Pharmacy, Ohio No. U., 1973; PhD in Pharmacology and Toxicology, U. Utah, 1991. Lic. pharmacist, Ohio. Pharmacist Sun Drug, Butler, Pa., 1973-75, Economy Drug, Ambridge, Pa., 1975-77; pharmacist owner, mgr. Noles Drug Store, Roby, Tex., 1978-81, Lindenwald Pharmacy, Hamilton, Ohio, 1981-86; rsch. asst. U. Utah, Salt Lake City, 1987-91, co-dir. ctr. drug discovery, 1991-92, rsch. assoc., 1991-92; asst. prof. N.E. La. U., Monroe, 1992-96, assoc. prof., 1996—. Contbr. cancer rsch. articles to profl. jours. Grantee N.E. La. U. Rsch. Coun., 1995, NIH/NCI, 1994-97. Mem. Am. Assoc. Cancer Rsch., Am. Soc. Pharmacognosy (grantee 1994-95), Am. Chem. Soc., Am. Assoc. Coll. Pharm., Fifth Dist. Pharm. Assoc. (bd. dirs.), Sigma Xi. Roman Catholic. Office: NE Louisiana University 700 University Ave Monroe LA 71209

SWAFFORD, DOUGLAS RICHARD, corporate credit executive; b. Chattanooga, Aug. 19, 1951; s. Herbert Harding and Helen Margaret (Smith) S.; m. Lynn Romaine Wudarcki, Aug. 18, 1973 (div. Aug. 1977); 1 child, Douglas Richard Jr.; m. Carole P. Farmer, Oct. 6, 1989 (div. Apr. 1992). BSBA, U. Tenn., Chattanooga, 1982; postgrad., Stanford U., 1994. Asst. credit mgr. Hart's Automotive Parts Co., Chattanooga, 1972-74; dir. corp. credit Brock Candy Co., Chattanooga, 1974-95; credit mgr. Brentwood Svc. Group, Inc., Chattanooga, 1995-96; corp. credit mgr. Arnold Palmer Golf Co., Ooltewah, Tenn., 1996—; chmn. Nat. Food, Allied Lines & Meat Packers Credit Group, Nashville, 1989. Pres. Citizens Taxpayers Assn., 1989; mem. Leadership Chattanooga, Friends of the Libr., Chattanooga Nature Ctr., Hunter Mus. Art, Allied Arts Chattanooga; bd. dis. Chattanooga Regional History Mus.; mem. U. Tenn. at Chattanooga Alumni Coun. Mem. Nat. Assn. Credit Mgmt. (chmn. S.E. unit 1991-92, Credit Mgr. of Yr. award 1994), Chattanooga C. of C. (chmn. fed. issues com. 1988-89), Chattanooga Track Club, Civitans (pres. Chattanooga 1986, bd. dirs. Appalachian dist. 1988-90). Republican. Home: 8115 Mee Mee Rd Chattanooga TN 37421-2757

SWAIM, MARK WENDELL, molecular biologist, gastroenterologist; b. Winston-Salem, N.C., Dec. 4, 1960; s. Donnie Lee and Bernice Earline (Brown) S. BA summa cum laude, U. N.C., 1983; MD, Duke U., 1990, PhD with honors, 1990. Diplomate Am. Bd of Internal Medicine. Resident Dept. of Med. Duke U. Med. Ctr., Durham, N.C., 1990-93; fellow gastroenterology Duke U. Med. Ctr., 1993—. Contbr. articles to profl. jours. Recipient Med. Sci. Training Program fellow Nat. Inst. of Health, 1983-90, numerous acad. scholarships. Mem. Am. Coll. Physicians, Reticuleondothelial Soc., Alpha Omega Alpha, Phi Beta Kappa, Sigma Xi. Home: 231-A Bridgefield Pl Durham NC 27705 Office: Duke Univ Medical Ctr PO Box 3913 Durham NC 27710

SWAIN, BRIAN TODD, municipal official; b. Russellville, Ark., Aug. 21, 1966; s. Dallas Lynn and Nealia Jane (Fry) S.; m. Jovie Lynn Arbaugh, July 29, 1989. BA with high honors in Journalism, Ark. Tech. U., Russellville, 1988; MPA, U. Ark., 1992. Grad. asst. U. Ark., Fayetteville, 1988; adminstrv. intern City of Fayetteville, 1989-90, rsch./performance analyst, 1990-91, fin. analyst, 1991-92, asst. to the adminstrv. svcs. dir., 1992—. Mem. audit com. United Way of Fayetteville, 1992-95. Recipient Hugh T. Henry award U. Ark., 1992. Mem. ASPA., Govt. Fin. Officers Assn., Ark. Govt. Fin. Officers Assn., Lions. Democrat. Methodist. Home: 2172 Deer Creek Dr Fayetteville AR 72703 Office: City of Fayetteville 113 W Mountain St Fayetteville AR 72701

SWAIN, DIANE SCOTT, principal; b. Atlantic City, N.J., July 13, 1946; d. Letha Noble; m. Raymond L. Swain Jr., Dec. 26, 1970; 1 child, Sean Scott Swain. BS, Hampton U., 1968; MEd, Lynchburg Coll., 1978; postgrad., U. Va., 1987—. Tchr. Lynchburg (Va.) City Schs., 1968-86, instructional coord., 1986-87, asst. prin., 1987-89, elem. prin., 1989—. Bd. dirs. Cen. Va. Speech and Hearing Ctr., Va. Bapt. Hosp., Lynchburg, 1990—. Mem. Lynchburg Assn. Elem. Prins. (pres. 1991—), Jack and Jill Inc. (v.p. Lynchburg chpt. 1989-90), Delta Sigma Theta Inc. (pres. Lynchburg alumnae chpt. 1982-84). Baptist. Home: 115 Yorkshire Cir Lynchburg VA 24502-2756 Office: Sheffield Elem Sch 115 Kenwood Pl Lynchburg VA 24502-2119

SWAIN, DONALD CHRISTIE, retired university president, history educator; b. Des Moines, Oct. 14, 1931; s. G. Christie and Irene L. (Alsop) S.; m. Lavinia Kathryn Lesh, Mar. 5, 1955; children: Alan Christie, Cynthia Catherine. BA, U. Dubuque, 1953; MA in History, U. Calif., Berkeley, 1958, PhD, 1961; D (hon.), U. Louisville, 1995, Bellarmine Coll., 1995. Asst. rsch. historian U. Calif., Berkeley, 1961-63; mem. faculty U. Calif., Davis, 1963-81, prof. history, 1970-81, acad. asst. to chancellor, 1967-68, asst. vice chancellor acad. affairs, 1971, vice chancellor acad. affairs, 1972-75; acad. v.p. U. Calif. System, Berkeley, 1975-81; pres. U. Louisville, 1981-95, pres. emeritus, 1995—, prof. history, 1981-95; ret., 1995; bd. dirs. LGE Energy, PNC Pank, Ky. Author: Federal Conservation Policy, 1921-33, 1963, Wilderness Defender: Horace M. Albright and Conservation, 1970; co-editor: The Politics of American Science 1939 to the Present, 1965. Mem. bd. govs. J.B. Speed Art Mus.; mem. exec. com. Ky. Hist. Soc. Lt. (j.g.) USNR, 1953-56. Recipient William B. Hellestine award Wis. State Hist. Soc., 1967, Disting. Tchg. award U. Calif., Davis, 1972, Wilson Wyatt award U. Louisville Alumni Assn., 1995; named Louisvillian of Yr., 1995. Democrat. Presbyterian. Home: 2506 Belknap Beach Rd Prospect KY 40059 Office: U Louisville Alumni Ctr Louisville KY 40292

SWAMY-MRUTHINTI, SATYANARAYANA, biochemist, molecular biologist; b. Andhra Pradesh, Audhra Pradesh, India, Jan. 10, 1955; came to U.S., 1986; s. Anjaneyulu and Kamalamma (Vindamuri) Mruthinti; m. Shyamala Sarvepalli, May 2, 1980; children: Harshita, Navyata, Namrata. MS, M.S. U., Baroda, Gujarat, India, 1977, PhD, 1982. Teaching asst. M.S. U., 1977-78, lectr., 1982-88; Univ. Grants Commn. rsch. fellow New Delhi, 1978-82; travel fellow Internat. Soc. Devel. Biol., L.A., 1985; NIH rsch. grantee Med. Coll. Ga., Augusta, 1988-92, asst. prof., 1992—. Contbr. articles to Investigative Ophthalmology and Visual Sciences, Exptl. Eye Rsch., Current Eye Rsch., Biochemical and Biophysical Research Communications; also to books the Maillard Reaction in Aging, Diabetes and Nutrition, 1989, The Maillard Reaction in Food Processing, Human Nutrition and Physiology, 1990, Nonenzymatic Glycosylation and Browning of Protein Invivo and Invitro, 1992. V.P. Hindu Temple Soc., Augusta, 1989-90, v. chmn., bd. trustees, 1990—. Mem. AAAS, Assn. for Rsch. in Vision and Ophthalmology, Internat. Soc. for Eye Rsch., N.Y. Acad. Scis. Office: Med Coll Ga Dept Biochem & Moleculular Biology Augusta GA 30912

SWAN, GEORGE STEVEN, law educator; b. St. Louis. BA, Ohio State U., 1970; JD, U. Notre Dame, 1974; LLM, U. Toronto, 1976, SJD, 1983. Bar: Ohio 1974, U.S. Dist. Ct. (so. dist.) Ohio 1975, U.S. Supreme Ct. 1987, U.S. Ct. Appeals (6th and 11th cirs.) 1993, U.S. Ct. Appeals (10th cir.) 1994; CFP; registered investment advisor U.S. Securities and Exchange Commn., 1989, Sec. of State, N.C., 1990, CFP. Asst. atty. gen. state of Ohio, Columbus, 1974-75; jud. clk. Supreme Ct. Ohio, Columbus, 1976-78; asst. prof. Del. Law Sch., Wilmington, 1980-83, assoc. prof., 1983-84; prof. law St. Thomas U. Law Sch., Miami, Fla., 1984-88; jud. clk. U.S. Ct. Appeals 7th cir., Chgo., 1988-89; assoc. prof. N.C. Agrl. & Tech. State U., Greensboro, 1989-96; vis. prof. John Marshall Law Sch., Atlanta, 1996—. Contbr. articles to law jours. Mem. Ohio State Bar Assn., Internat. Assn. for Fin. Planning, Am. Polit. Sci. Assn., Inst. CFP's. Office: John Marshall Law Sch 1422 W Peachtree St NE Atlanta GA 30309

SWAN, JOYCE ANN, comptroller; b. San Antonio, June 11, 1964; d. Richard Bronaugh II and Carolyn Ann (Gerhardt) Harn; m. Jesse G. Swan, June 3, 1983 (div. Dec. 1992). BBA in Acctg., U. Tex., San Antonio, 1986. Bookkeeper Gerhardts Paint and Wallpaper Co., San Antonio, 1976-84, Ike Neumann & Assocs., San Antonio, 1983-86, Patrician Properties, San Antonio, 1984-86; gen. mgr. San Antonio Hermann Sons Home Assn., 1982-86; comptroller Courtesy Chevrolet Co., Phoenix, 1986-91; CFO various orgns., Phoenix, 1992; human resources/customer rels., fin. mgr. Buick Co., Phoenix, 1993; office mgr. World Car Mazda, New Braunfels, Tex., 1993-94; comptr. Moretti's Fine Jewelry, San Antonio, Tex., 1995—. Mem. auditor bd. evaluators Valley of Sun United Way, Phoenix, 1988—, Chandler (Ariz.) Planning and Zoning Commn., 1990-92, Valley Forward Assn.; treas. com. re-elect Coy Payne for mayor City of Chandler; precinct com. person dist. 30 Dem. Nat. Com., 1991—; state com. person Ariz. Dem. Com., 1991-92; cmty. adv. bd. KLRN Pub. TV, 1995—; mem. spkrs. bur. Am. Cancer Soc., 1996—. Mem. Inst. Mgmt. Accts. (bd. dirs. Scottsdale chpt. 1988-89, v.p. edn. 1989-90, pres. 1990-91, mem. nat. contr.'s coun., scholarship sect. com. 1991-92, chmn. nominating com. 1991-92, bd. dirs., employment dir. San Antonio chpt. 1994-96), Am. Soc. Women Accts. (com. Mesa East Valley chpt.), Am. Soc. Assn. Execs., Internat. Credit Assn. Greater Phoenix, Retail Fin. Execs. Ariz., Ariz. Cash Mgmt. Assn., Am. Inst. Individual Investors, Ariz. Automotive Accts. Assn. (founding pres., organizer 1991-92), Exec. Bus. and Profl. Women's Club (sec. Phoenix chpt. 1986-88, auditor 1986-87, 88-89, pres. 1991-92, Woman of Yr. award 1991), Friends of Libr., Alamo City Tall Club, U. Tex. at San Antonio Alumni Assn.

SWANN, MARY OLIVIA (LIBBY SWANN), special education educator; b. DeFuniak Springs, Fla., Dec. 22, 1954; d. Walter Oliver and Ossie Lee (Bobbitt) S. BA in Edn., Troy State U., 1976; MEd, Valdosta State Coll., 1984; EdS, Valdosta State U., 1994. Cert. special edn. tchr., dir., adminstr. and supr., Ga. Tchr. Richbourg Jr. High Sch., Crestview, Fla., 1976-77, Turner County Sch. Sys., Ashburn, Ga., 1977-80, 94-95; itinerant special edn. tchr. Tift County Schs., Tifton, Ga., 1980-88; tchr. spl. edn. Okapilco Elem. Sch., Moultrie, Ga., 1988-93; tchr. S.W. Ga. Psychoednl. Svcs., Moultrie, 1993-94, Burroughs-Molette Elem., Brunswick, Ga., 1995—; data collector State of Ga. Tchr. Performance Assessment Instrument, Moultrie,

Tifton, 1985-94; mem. Program for Exceptional Children Spl. Edn. Adv. Coun. Moultrie, 1989-92; cons. Colquitt County Schs. Staff Devel. Program, Moultrie, 1989-90; instr. reading Abraham Baldwin Agrl. Coll., Tifton, Ga., 1991-95; adj. faculty mem. dept. curriculum and instrn. Albany (Ga.) State Coll., 1995—; adj. faculty mem. dept. learning support Brunswick (Ga.) Coll., 1996—. Mem. First United Meth. Ch., Tifton, Ga., 1983—. Named Tchr. of the Yr., Okapilco Sch., 1990-91. Mem. Nat. Assn. Devel. Edn. (Ga. chpt.), Coun. for Exceptional Children (exec. bd. Colquitt County chpt. 1990, pres. 1991), Internat. Reading Assn. (Tift County chpt.), Profl. Assn. Ga. Educators, Troy State U. Alumni and Loyalty Assns., Valdosta State Coll. Alumni Assn., Baldwin Woman's Club, Phi Mu Alumnae Assn. (past pres. Tift chpt., treas. 1992-93), Alpha Delta Kappa. Home: PO Box 24402 Saint Simons Island GA 31522 Office: Burroughs-Molette Elem 1900 Lee St Brunswick GA 31520-6340

SWANSBURG, RUSSELL CHESTER, medical administrator educator; b. Cambridge, Mass., Aug. 6, 1928; s. William W. and Mary A. (Pierce) S.; m. Laurel Swansburg, Sept. 1951; children: Philip Wayne, Michael Gary, Richard Jeffrey. Diploma, N.S. Hosp. Sch. Nursing, 1950; BSN, Western Res. U., 1952; MA in Nursing Edn., Columbia U., 1961; PhD, U. Miss., 1984. CNAA. Asst. adminstr. U. of S. Ala. Med. Ctr., Mobile; v.p. U. South Ala., Mobile; prof. Auburn U., Montgomery, Ala., Med. Coll. of Ga., Augusta; mil. cons. USAF Surgeon Gen., 1972; sr. med. svc. cons., 1973-76; nurse cons. VA Med. Ctr., Tuskegee, Ala., 1987-88; mem. editl. adv. bd. Nursing Adminstrn. Manual. Author: Team Nursing: A Programmed Learning Experience, 1968, Inservice Education, 1968, The Measurement of Vital Signs, 1970, The Team Plan, 1971, Management of Patient Care Services, 1976, Strategic Career Planning and Development, 1984, The Nurse Manager's Guide to Financial Management, 1988, Management and Leadership for Nurse Managers, 1990, 2d edit. 1996, Introductory Management and Leadership for Clinical Nurses, 1993, Staff Development: A Component of Human Resource Development, 1994, Budgeting and Financial Management for Nurse Managers, 1996, (audiovisual course) Nurses & Patients: An Introduction to Nursing Management, 1980; contbr. articles to profl. publs. Bd. dirs. Air Force Village Found., Alzheimer's Care and Research Found. Col. USAF, 1956-76. Decorated Legion of Merit. Fellow AONE, Ala. Orgn. Nurse Exec's. (past state pres.); mem. Council Grad. Edn. Adminstrn. in Nursing (sec.), Ala. Acad. Sci., Sigma Xi, Phi Kappa Phi, Sigma Theta Tau. Home and Office: 4917 Ravenswood Dr Apt 1711 San Antonio TX 78227-4356

SWANSON, JAMES ROBERT, busines administration educator; b. Palatka, Fla., Mar. 9, 1934; s. Norman Linné Swanson and Bessie Gertrude (Kennedy) Dekle; m. Elizabeth Jane Eppele, June 6, 1956 (div. May 1967); children: James Robert Jr., Franklyn Alden, Stephen Morey; m. Lucille Agnes Wriglesworth, Mar. 30, 1971; 1 child, Lori Kathryn. BS in Edn., U. Fla., 1955, MEd, 1956; PhD, Fla. State U., 1970. Adminstr. MIS Fla. Dept. Edn., Tallahassee, 1967-76; dir. rsch. and tng. Fla. Dept. HRS, Tallahassee, 1976-77; cons. in computer sci. Tallahassee, 1977-81; dir. MIS Leon County Schs., Tallahassee, 1981-83; tchg. assoc. U. Fla., Gainesville, 1983-86; asst. prof. Embry-Riddle Aero U., Daytona Beach, Fla., 1986-89; rsch. cons. N.H. Coll. and Univ. Coun., Manchester, 1989-91; asst. prof. Lenoir-Rhyne Coll., Hickory, N.C., 1991-92; assoc. prof. bus. adminstrn. Embry-Riddle Aero U., Daytona Beach, 1992—. With U.S. Army, 1957-59. Mem. Fla. Ednl. Rsch. Assn. (pres. 1979—), Nat. Coun. on Measurement in Edn., Assn. for Computing Machinery, U. Fla. Nat. Alumni Assn., Kappa Delta Pi, Delta Mu Delta. Home: PO Box 528 Pierson FL 32180-0528 Office: Embry-Riddle Aeronautical University 600 S Clyde Morris Blvd Daytona Beach FL 32114-3966

SWANSON, LORNA ELLEN, physical therapist, athletic trainer, researcher; b. Bridgeport, Conn., July 22, 1954; d. Harold Carl and Marna Ellyn (French) S.; m. James M. Kelley, Oct. 16, 1993; 1 child, Ellen Elizabeth Kelley. BFA in Dance, So. Meth. U., 1975, MFA in Dance, 1978; BS in Phys. Therapy, U. Tex., Dallas, 1984; PhD in Exercise Sci., U. Tenn., 1994. Lic. phys. therapist, Tenn. Mem. faculty Brookhaven Coll., Dallas, 1982-84; staff therapist St. Mary's Med. Ctr., Knoxville, Tenn., 1984-85, Ft. Sanders Regional Med. Ctr., Knoxville, 1985-86, Knoxville Sports Therapy, 1991-92; program dir., mem. faculty Roane State C.C., Harriman, Tenn., 1987-92; clin. specialist Ft. Sanders Ctr. for Sports Medicine, Knoxville, 1992-93, mgr., 1994-96; clin. specialist Ft. Sanders Therapy Ctr. West, Knoxville, 1996-96; ballet Instr. East Tenn. Acad. performing Arts, 1996—; grad. asst. athletic dept. U. Tenn., Knoxville, 1989-91; reviewer Jour. Orthopedic and Sports Phys. Therapy, 1993, 94; adj. faculty Pellissippi State Tech. C.C., 1994.; instr. East Tenn. Acad. Performing Arts, 1995-96; speaker at state and nat. profl. confs. Contbr. chpt. to book and articles to profl. jours. Ballet mistress Victoria Bolen Dance Theatre, Knoxville, 1986-88; mem. bd. of trust Appalachian Ballet Co., 1995—. Helen B. Watson dissertation rsch. awardee U. Tenn. Mem. Am. Phys. Therapy Assn. (bd. content experts 1990-93), Tenn. Phys. Therapy Assn., Nat. Athletic Tng. Assn. (cert. athletic trainer), Tenn. Athletic Tng. Assn., Nat. Strength and Conditioning Assn. (cert. specialist), Neurodevel. Treatment Assn. (nominating com. 1987-89). Democrat. Lutheran. Office: Ft Sanders Therapy Ctr West Ste 204 200 Fort Sanders West Blvd Knoxville TN 37922-3357

SWANSON, MARSHALL SYMMES, writer and editor; b. N.Y.C., May 29, 1947; s. Irving Arthur and Eleanor Hall (Fletcher) S.; m. Brenda Gayle Ruff, Nov. 2, 1974 (div. Jan. 5, 1988). BA in Journalism, U. S.C., 1973. Pub. info. specialist S.C. Commn. on Alcohol and Drug Abuse, Columbia, 1974-77; staff writer Divsn. Univ. rels., U. S.C., Columbia, 1977-78, asst. dir. news, 1978-80, asst. dir. periodicals, 1981-90; sr. writer/editor, asst. dir. periodicals Divsn. Univ. Pubs., U. S.C., Columbia, 1990—. Contbr. articles to newspapers and mags.; guest reviewer The Carolina Reporter, 1992. Staff sgt. U.S. Army, 1967-70. Decorated Army Commendation medal, Vietnam Svc. medal, Nat. Def. Svc. medal. Mem. Coun. for Advancement and Support of Edn., S.C. Press Assn. Office: U SC Publs Office 701 Byrnes Bldg Columbia SC 29208

SWANSON, MICHAEL ALAN, sales and marketing executive; b. Ticonderoga, N.Y., Aug. 26, 1958; s. Vernon George and Evelyn Marie (Vigliotti) S.; m. Lynette Ann Vagush, Apr. 14, 1993; 1 child, Connor Michael. A in Bus. Mgmt., Hudson Valley C. C., Troy, N.Y., 1978; BA in Bus. Mgmt., SUNY, Utica, 1981. City dispatcher Roadway Express, Tonawanda, N.Y., 1983-84, sales rep., 1984-86; acct. exec. Ryder Truck Rental, Albany, 1986-87; acct. rep. Roadway Package Sys., Albany, 1987-89; N.J. geographic nat. acct. exec. Roadway Package Sys., Trenton, 1989-92, pharmaceutical specialist, nat. acct. exec., 1992-95; v.p. sales and mktg. Caliber Logistics Health Care (formerly Mediquik Express), Chapel Hill, N.C., 1995—, Caliber Systems Co. (formerly Roadway Svcs.), Chapel Hill, 1995—. Mem. Am. Mktg. Assn., Nat. Assn. Chain Drug Stores, Coun. Logistics Mgmt., Health and Personal Care Conf. Republican. Episcopalian. Home: 1104 Colehurst Crescent Apex NC 27502 Office: Caliber Logistics Health Care Inc 1717 Legion Rd Chapel Hill NC 27514

SWANSON, RALPH WILLIAM, aerospace executive, consultant, engineer; b. Mpls.; m. Virginia May Peoples (dec.); children: John W., Timothy R.; m. Patricia Anne Smith. BS in Aero. Engring., U. Minn., 1947; MS in Nuclear Engring., N.C. State U., 1954; PhD in Engring., Kennedy-Western U., 1989. Design engr. Los Alamos (N.Mex.) Sci. Lab., 1948-52; asst. prof. physics Air Force Inst. Tech., Wright Patterson AFB, Ohio, 1954-56; chief radiation div. armed forces spl. weapons project Pentagon, Washington, 1957-61; dep. chief staff plans and programs Air Force Eastern Test Range, Patrick AFB, Fla., 1961-64; dep. for programs and requirements Air Force Nat. Range Div., Patrick AFB, Fla., 1964-65; mgr. advanced programs IBM Corp., Kennedy Space Center, Fla., 1965-75; chief engr. Planning Rsch. Corp., Kennedy Space Center, 1975-79, dep. project mgr., gen. mgr., 1979-87; project mgr. Bamsi, Inc., Kennedy Space Center, 1987-93; freelance cons., Cocoa Beach, Fla., 1987—. Bd. dirs. Brevard Achievement Ctr., Rockledge, Fla., 1977—. Col. USAF, 1941-65, ETO and Korea, ret. Mem. Air Force Assn., Assn. AFIT Grads., MacIntosh Computer User Group, Masons, Shriners, Sigma Xi, Sigma Pi Sigma. Republican.

SWANSON, ROY JOEL, lawyer; b. Houston, Feb. 21, 1945; s. Roy J. and Daisy Lee (Peper) S.; m. Lynn Northway, Apr. 5, 1986; children: Emily Rebecca, Nell Cameron. BSChemE, U. Tex., 1967; MBA, Harvard U., 1972, JD, 1972. Bar: Tex. 1972. Assoc. Baker & Botts, Houston, 1972-80, ptnr., 1980—. Office: Baker & Botts 3000 One Shell Pla 910 Louisiana St Houston TX 77002

SWANSON, WALLACE MARTIN, lawyer; b. Fergus Falls, Minn., Aug. 22, 1941; s. Marvin Walter and Mary Louise (Lindsey) S.; m. Susan W. Swanson; children: Kristen Lindsey, Eric Munger. B.A. with honors, U. Minn., 1962; LL.B. with honors, So. Methodist U., 1965. Bar: Tex. 1965. Since practiced in Dallas; assoc. Coke & Coke, Dallas, 1965-70; ptnr. firm Johnson & Swanson, Dallas, 1970-88; prin. Wallace M. Swanson, P.C., Dallas, 1988—; chmn., CEO Ace Cash Express Inc., Irving, Tex., 1987-88, State St. Capital Corp., 1990—. Served with USNR, 1960-65. Mem. ABA, Tex. Bar Found., State Bar Tex. (securities com. 1972-86, chmn. 1978-80, coun. bus. law sect. 1980-86), Dallas Bar Assn., Crescent Club. Methodist. Address: 3816 Miramar Ave Dallas TX 75205-3126

SWARTLING, DANIEL JOSEPH, chemistry educator, researcher; b. Black Falls, Wis., Sept. 3, 1960; s. Ronald James Swartling and Jean Marie (Welda) Trester. BS, Winona State U., 1985; PhD, U. N.D., 1989. Rsch. asst. Purdue U., West Lafayette, Ind., 1989-90; rsch. assoc. U. Chgo., 1990-92; teaching fellow S. Meth. U., Dallas, 1992-94; asst. prof. chemistry Tenn. Tech. U., Cookeville, 1994—; cons. ARCH Rsch. Corp., Chgo., 1992—. Contbr. chpt. to book; contbr. articles to prof. jours. Mem. Am. Chem. Soc., Am. Scientific Glassblowers Soc., Am. Orchid Soc., Sigma Xi. Office: Tenn Tech U P O Box 5055 Cookeville TN 38505

SWARTWOUT, JOSEPH RODOLPH, obstetrics and gynecology educator, administrator; b. Pascagoula, Miss., June 17, 1925; s. Thomas Roswell and Marshall (Coleman) S.; m. Brandon C. Leftwich, Jan. 23, 1989. Student, Miss. Coll., 1943-44; MD, Tulane U., 1951. Intern Touro Infirmary, New Orleans, 1951-52; asst. in obstetrics and medicine Tulane U., 1952-53, instr., 1955-60; Nat. Found. fellow Harvard U., 1953-55; asst. in medicine Peter Bent Brigham Hosp., Boston, 1953-55; assoc. in obstetric rsch. Boston Lying-In-Hosp., 1953-55; asst. prof. U. Pitts., 1960-61; assoc. prof. Emory U., Atlanta, 1961-66; assoc. prof. ob-gyn. U. Chgo., 1967-80; chief ob-gyn. at Prime Health, also clin. assoc. prof. U. Kans. Sch. Medicine, 1978-80; prof. dept. ob-gyn. Mercer U. Sch. Medicine, Macon, Ga., 1980-95, prof. emeritus, 1995; dist. health dir. Dist. 5-2, Macon, Ga., 1996—; dist. dir. Ga. Divsn. Pub. Health, Macon, 1996—. Fellow Am. Coll. Obstetricians and Gynecologists, Am. Heart Assn. (coun. clin. cardiology), Am. Acad. Reproductive Medicine; mem. AAAS, AMA, APHA, Population Assn. Am., Med. Assn. Ga., Bibb County Med. Soc. Home: 1622 Peach Pkwy Fort Valley GA 31030

SWARTZ, CHRISTIAN LEFEVRE, lawyer; b. Mechanicsburg, Pa., Aug. 14, 1915; s. Christian Ira and Anna Frances (LeFevre) S.; m. Jean Althan Vanderbilt, Nov. 30, 1946 (div. 1964); children: Christian Arthur, James Vanderbilt, B.S., U. Pa., 1937; LL.B., Temple U., 1946; LL.M., George Washington U., 1950. Bar: Pa. 1947, D.C. 1947, U.S. Dist. Ct. D.C. 1947, U.S. Supreme Ct. 1955, U.S. Ct. Claims 1959, U.S. Ct. Appeals (D.C. cir.) 1959, U.S. Ct. Customs and Patent Appeals 1963. Assoc. James W. Batchelor Law Office, Washington, 1947-50, Julia B. Hopkins Law Office, 1950-51; asst. counsel facilities br. Naval Air Systems Command, Office of Gen. Counsel, Dept. Navy, Washington, 1951-72; sole practice, Washington, 1972—. Exhibited woodcarvings in numerous shows. Served to lt. USNR, 1941-46. Mem. Fed. Bar Assn., D.C. Bar Assn., Nat. Woodcarvers Assn., Internat. Platform Assn. (art com.), No. Va. Carvers Assn., Capitol Hill Club, Capital Yacht Club (Washington), Corinthian Yacht Club (Ridge, Md.). Republican. Episcopalian. Home and Office: 2354 Dunbar Ln Falls Church VA 22046-2333

SWARTZ, CONRAD MELTON, psychiatrist; b. Bklyn., Nov. 22, 1946; s. Louis Jules and Frances (Shaw) S.; m. Cynthia Anne Heise, June 22, 1975; children: Meryle, Sandor. B Engring., Cooper Union, 1966; MS, Calif. Inst. Tech., 1968; PhD in Chem. Engring., U. Minn., 1972, MD, 1974. Diplomate Am. Bd. Psychiatry and Neurology. Intern Northwestern Hosp., Mpls., 1974-75; resident in psychiatry U. Iowa Hosps. and Clinics, Iowa City, 1975-78, asst. prof. psychiatry, 1978-82; asst. prof. psychiatry U. Health Scis./Chgo. Med. Sch., North Chicago, Ill., 1982-83, assoc. prof. psychiatry and pharmacology, 1983-87, prof. psychiatry, 1987-91; assoc. chief of staff for edn. VA Med. Ctr., North Chicago, 1987-91; prof. psychiatry med. sch. U. Okla., Oklahoma City, 1991-92; prof. psychiatry East Carolina U., Greenville, N.C., 1992-96; dir. rsch., prof. psychiatry East Tenn. State U., Johnson City, Tenn., 1996—; cons. Somatics, Inc., Lake Bluff, Ill., 1984—. Contbr. articles on adverse health effects of male hypogonadism, hormone kinetics theory to profl. publs. Recipient clin. rsch. award Am. Acad. Clin. Psychiatrists, 1989, 90. Fellow Am. Psychiat. Assn., Am. Coll. Clin. Pharmacology; mem. Assn. Convulsive Therapy (pres. 1990-92), Endocrine Soc., Soc. Biol. Psychiatry, Tau Beta Pi. Home: PO Box 5621 Johnson City TN 37603-5621 Office: Dept Psychiatry 116 A Dept Psychiat Medicine VA Med Ctr Mountain Home TN 37684

SWARTZLANDER, EARL EUGENE, JR., engineering educator, former electronics company executive; b. San Antonio, Feb. 1, 1945; s. Earl Eugene and Jane (Nicholas) S.; m. Joan Vickery, June 9, 1968. BSEE, Purdue U., 1967; MSEE, U. Colo., 1969; PhD, U. So. Calif., 1972. Registered profl. engr., Ala., Calif., Colo., Tex. Devel. engr. Ball Bros. Rsch. Corp., Boulder, Colo., 1967-69; Hughes fellow, mem. tech. staff Hughes Aircraft Co., Culver City, Calif., 1969-73; mem. rsch. staff Tech. Svc. Co., Santa Monica, Calif., 1973-74; chief engr. Geophys. Systems Corp., Pasadena, Calif., 1974-75, staff engr. to sr. staff engr., 1975-79, project mgr., 1979-84, lab. mgr., 1985-87; dir. ind. R&D TRW Inc., Redondo Beach, Calif., 1987-90; Schlumberger Centennial prof. engring. dept. elec. and computer engring. U. Tex., Austin, 1990—; gen. chmn. Internat. Conf. Wafer Scale Integration, 1989, 11th Internat. Symposium on Computer Arithmetic, 1992, others; gen. chmn. Internat. Conf. Application Specific Array Processors, 1990, co-gen. chmn., 1994; chmn. 3d Internat. Conf. Parallel and Distributed Sys., Taiwan, 1993. Author: VLSI Signal Processing Systems, 1986; editor: Computer Design Development, 1976, Systolic Signal Processing Systems, 1987, Wafer Scale Integration, 1989, Computer Arithmetic Vol. 1 and 2, 1990, Application Specific Processors, 1996; editor-in-chief Jour. of VLSI Signal Processing, 1989-95, IEEE Transactions on Computers, 1991-94, IEEE Transactions on Signal Processing, 1995; editor: IEEE Transactions on Computers, 1982-86, IEEE Transactions on Parallel and Distributed Systems, 1989-90; hardware area editor ACM Computing Revs., 1985—; assoc. editor: IEEE Jour. Solid-State Circuits, 1984-88; contbr. more than 150 articles to profl. jours. and tech. conf. procs. Bd. dirs. Casiano Estates Homeowners Assn., Bel Air, Calif., 1976-78, pres., 1978-80; bd. dirs. Benedict Hills Estates Homeowners Assn., Beverly Hills, Calif., 1984—, pres., 1990-95. Recipient Disting. Engring. Alumnus award Purdue U., 1989, U. Colo., 1997, Outstanding Elec. Engr. award Purdue U., 1992, knight Imperial Russian Order St. John of Jerusalem (Knights of Malta), 1993. Fellow IEEE; mem. IEEE Computer Soc. (bd. govs. 1987-91, Golden Core mem. 1996), IEEE Signal Proc. Soc. (bd. govs. 1992-94), IEEE Solid-State Cirs. Coun. (sec. 1992-93, treas. 1994—), Eta Kappa Nu, Sigma Tau, Omicron Delta Kappa. Office: U Tex Austin Dept Elec Computer Engring Austin TX 78712

SWATZELL, MARILYN LOUISE, nurse; b. Johnson City, Tenn., July 31, 1942; d. Dallas Fred and Minnie Thelma (Clark) S. BS cum laude, East Tenn. State U., 1966, MS, 1967; BSN, U. Tenn., 1974. Chmn. pediatric nursing Meth. Hosp. Sch. Nursing, Memphis, 1978-80; head nurse Le Bonheur Children's Med. Ctr., Memphis, 1981-83; dir. maternal child nursing Jackson (Tenn.) Madison County Gen. Hosp., 1985-88; staff nurse Vanderbilt U. Hosp., Nashville, 1988-90; supr. Meth. Hosp. Lexington, Tenn., 1990—. Contbr. articles on care plans to profl. jours. Mem. ANA, Tenn. Nurses Assn., Tenn. Orgn. Nurse Execs. Home: 231 Law Ln Lexington TN 38351-6048

SWEARINGEN, DAVID CLARKE, physician, musician; b. Shreveport, La., Apr. 23, 1942; s. David C. and Alverne (Walker) S.; m. Marion Joan Adams; children: David, Joy. BS, Centenary Coll., 1963; MD, La. State U., 1967. Intern Confederate Meml. Med. Ctr., Shreveport, 1967-68, resident in ophthalmology, 1968-71; staff ophthalmologist U.S. Naval Hosp., Memphis, 1971-73; pvt. practice in ophthalmology Shreveport, 1973-78; jr. officer of deck USS Halsey CG23, 1979; comdr. med. corps, head dept. ophthalmology, chmn. utilization rev. com. ophthalmology, family practice resident instr. opthalmology U.S. Naval Hosp., Jacksonville, Fla., 1981-84; med. dir. Bio Blood Components, Shreveport, 1985-88; dir. phys. health support svcs. Ctrl. La. State Hosp., Pineville, La., 1991—, exec. hosp. and med. exec. com., chmn. infection control and pharmacy, therapeutics com.; chmn. infection control com., pharmacy and therapeutics com.; pres. Shreveport Eye and Ear Soc., 1973-74; med. cons. Cenla Chem. Dependency Coun., Pineville, 1989—, Work Tng. Facility, Pineville, 1989—. Prin. bassoonist Cenla Symphonic Band, Pineville, 1988—; mem. Jacksonville Fla. Concert Choral, 1978-81; vestry mem. St. Michaels Ch., Pineville; active Am. Mus. Natural History Assocs. Recipient AMA Physician Recognition award for Continuing Med. Edn. Mem. Internat. Platform Assn., So. Med. Assn., Nat. Parks and Conservation Assn., N.Y. Acad. Scis., La. Wildlife Fedn., Wilderness Soc., Nature Conservancy, Smithsonian Assocs., Cousteau Soc., Soc. Hist. Preservation, Environ. Def. Fund, Planetary Soc., Nat. Audubon Soc., Am. Legion, Alpha Epsilon Delta, Gamma Beta Gamma, Nu Sigma Nu. Republican. Epsicopalian. Home: 10 Azalea Rd Pineville LA 71360-8004 Office: Ctrl La State Hosp PO Box 5031 242 W Shamrock Ave Pineville LA 71360-6439

SWEENEY, NEAL JAMES, lawyer; b. Paterson, N.J., Nov. 1, 1957; s. Bernard Thomas and Mary Agnes (Keneally) S.; m. Mary Elizabeth Finocchiaro, Oct. 27, 1984; children: Daniel Fulton, Clare Kenneally, Moira Ann. BA in History and Polit Sci., Rutgers U., 1979; JD, George Washington U., 1982. Bar: Ga. 1982, U.S. Dist. Ct. (no. dist.) Ga. 1982, U.S. Dist. Ct. (no. dist.) Tex. 1982, U.S. Claims Ct. 1984, U.S. Ct. Appeals (5th cir.) 1987. Assoc. Smith, Currie & Hancock, Atlanta, 1982-87, ptnr., 1988—. Co-author: Construction Business Handbook, 1985, Holding Subcontractors to Their Bids, 1986, Subcontractor Default, 1987, The New AIA Design and Construction Documents, 1988, Proving and Pricing Claims, 1995, Fifty State Construction Lien and Bond Law, 1992; editor: Construction Subcontracting, 1991, Wiley Construction Law Update, 1992-97; notes editor G.W.U.J. Internat. Law and Econs., 1981-82. Mem. ABA (pub. contract law sect., forum com. on constrn. industry), Atlanta Bar Assn., Am. Arbitration Assn. (panel of arbitrators), Assoc. Gen. Contractors (contrace documents com.), Water Environment Fedn. (editorial adv. bd.). Roman Catholic. Home: 4385 Glengary Dr NE Atlanta GA 30342-3536 Office: Smith Currie & Hancock 233 Peachtree St NE Ste 2600 Atlanta GA 30303-1510

SWEENEY, ROBERT FRANCIS, marketing professional; b. Paterson, N.J., Nov. 22, 1937; s. Harry F. and Frances M. (Najieka) S.; m. Johanna Marie Dix, Aug. 2, 1958; children: Robert F. II, Christine L. Sweeney Ronan, Leslie K. Sweeney Fagan, Dawn M. Sweeney Childress, Mona C. Sweeney Butler, Nicole S. Sweeney Grisham. BS, U. Dayton, 1959; MS, U. So. Calif., 1975. Commd. 2d lt. U.S. Army, 1959, advanced through grades to lt. col., 1975, ret., 1980; procurement budget mgr. Office Dept. Chief Staff for R & D and Acquisition, Washington, 1977-78; exec. asst. army sci. bd. Office Asst. Sec. Army for R & D and Acquisition, Washington, 1978-80; sr. internat. mktg. analyst Boeing Vertol Helicopter Co., Phila., 1980-81; mgr. mktg. adminstrn. Honeywell Inc., McLean, Va., 1981-86; v.p., gen. mgr. Logic Unlimited Inc., Vienna, Va., 1986-87; army mktg. mgt. Hughes Flight Simulation Systems, Herndon, Va., 1987-89; v.p. govt. mktg. Lucas Aerospace Inc., Reston, Va., 1989—. Decorated D.F.C., Legion of Merit, Air medal, Commendation medal. Mem. AIAA, Army Aviation Assn. (pres. Phila. chpt. 1980-81), Am. Helicopter Soc., Assn. U.S. Army, Air Force Assn., Navy League, Aerospace Industries Assn. Roman Catholic. Home: 9312 Kilby Glen Dr Vienna VA 22182-1652 Office: Lucas Aerospace Inc 11180 Sunrise Valley Dr Reston VA 22091

SWEENY, RUTH EVANS, psychotherapist; b. Orange, N.J., Jan. 21, 1922; d. Edward Francis and Gertrude (Evans) S.; m. Richard Bender Perkins, Nov. 27, 1970; children: Alexandra E. Johnson, Evan Johnson, Craig E. Johnson, J. Randall Johnson. BA, Smith Coll., 1944; MEd, Rutgers, 1970, EdD, 1981. Lic. marriage and family therapist, N.C.; diplomate Acad. Cert. Clin. Mental Health Counselors. Asst. editor U.S. News and World Report, Washington, 1945-46; asst. dir. N.J. Heart Assn., Union, 1967-69; counselor St. Peter's Coll., Jersey City, N.J., 1970-76; dir. women's ctr. St. Peter's Coll., 1974-76; psychotherapist Neuse Ctr., Morehead City, N.C., 1980-88, pvt. practice, Pine Knoll Shores, N.C., 1983—. Pres. Mental Health Assn. Morris County, N.J., 1958-60, Carteret County Coun. for Women, 1982-84, cons., 1991—; dir. Domestic Violence Program Carteret County, 1984-88; fund raiser Habitat for Humanity Carteret County, 1991—; vice chmn. Mental Health Bd., N.J., 1967-70, chair pers. com., 1972-74; chair Beach Preservation Assn. of Pine Knoll Shores, Inc., 1995-96. Recipient Woman of Yr. award Coun. for Women Carteret County, 1987. Mem. APA, Am. Assn. for Sex Educators, Counselors and Therapists, Am. Assn. Marriage and Family Therapy (clin.), Am. Counseling Assn., N.C. Assn. for Marriage and Family Therapy (editor newsletter 1987-95), Bogue Banks Country Club, Pine Knoll Shores, Ladies Golf Assn. (pres.), Carteret County Coun. for Women. (hon.), Beach Preservation Assn. Pine Knoll Shores (chairperson). Democrat. Roman Catholic. Office: 115 Dogwood Cir Pine Knoll Shores NC 28512-6134

SWEET, CHARLES G., paralegal school administrator, dean; b. Lewiston, Maine, Aug. 5, 1918; s. Alfred H. and Gladys (Greenleaf) S.; m. Margaret Gibson, July 29, 1948 (div. 1966); children: David W., Barbara G.; m. Martha Gossard, Nov. 10, 1966. AB, Pa. State U., 1939; LLB, Harvard U., 1946. Bar: Pa. 1947, D.C. 1947. Practiced in Washington, Pa., 1947-64; pres. judge Washington County Ct. Common Pleas, Washington, 1964-84; pres., dean Paralegal Careers Inc., Tampa, Fla., 1985-93; pres. Pa. Conf. State Trial Judges, 1979-80; judge adv. Dale Mabry Post, Am. Legion, Tampa. Contbr. articles to profl. jours. Del. Dem. Nat. Conv., Chgo., 1952; regional dir. Pa. Young Dems., 1954-55; former mem. Pa. Commn. on Police and Corrections; past pres. Ctrl. Washington County United Fund, bd. dirs. Pa. United Fund, 1974-82, Fla. United Fund, Tampa, 1984-86. With USMC, 1941-46; lt. col. Res. ret. Recipient Robert Steward award Domestic Rels. Assn. Pa., 1980, Man of Yr. award Washington C. of C., 1983, award Coun. on Alcohol and Drug Abuse, 1983, law enforcement commendation medal SAR, 1983, cert. of svc. United Way Tampa, 1988. Mem. Am. Arbitration Assn. (panel arbitrators), Washington County Bar Assn. (pres. 1960-61), Am. Legion (dist. officer Fla. & Pa. 1954-93, nat. law enforcement com.). Episcopalian. Home: 2424 W Tampa Bay Blvd Tampa FL 33607 Office: 10913 N Dale Mabry Hwy Tampa FL 33618-4112

SWEET, JAMES BROOKS, oral and maxillofacial surgeon; b. Darlington, Pa., Mar. 28, 1934; s. Lufay Anderson and Margaret Jean (Brooks) S.; m. N. Gayle Laird, Oct. 11, 1958; children: James Brooks II, Laird Anderson, Bradley Stephen. BA, Lafayette Coll., 1956; DDS, U. Pitts., 1964, DMD, 1974; MS in Dentistry, NYU, 1975. Aviation flight officer USNR, 1957; advanced through grades to dir. USPHS; rotating intern USPHS Hosp., Staten Island, N.Y., 1964-65, resident oral and maxillofacial surgery, 1970-73; chief dept. dentistry Fed. Correctional Inst. Hosp., Ashland, Ky., 1965-67, Terminal Island, Calif., 1967-70; chief oral and maxillofacial surgery Clin. Ctr. NIH, Bethesda, Md., 1973-80; chief dept. dentistry and oral and maxillofacial surgery USPHS Hosp., Nassau Bay, Tex., 1980-81; ret. USPHS, 1981; assoc. prof. dept. oral and maxillofacial surgery Health Sci. Ctr. U. Tex., Houston, 1981-84; prof., 1984—; asst. clin. prof. med. br. U. Tex., Galveston, 1980-; assoc. attending physicianBen Taub Gen. Hosp., Houston, 1984-; cons. oral and maxillofacial surgery self study guides, Stoma Press, Seattle, 1983-; cons. VA Hosp., Houston, 1986-. Contbr. articles to profl. jours.; editorial reviewer: Annals of Internal Medicine, 1977-. Coach basketball Olney (Md.) Boys Club, 1975-80; mem. aim rev. Tex. area USCG, 1981-82. Lt. USNR, 1957-64. Fellow Am. Assn. Oral and Maxillofacial Surgeons; mem. Tex. Soc. Oral and Maxillofacial Surgeons, Houston Soc. Oral and Maxillofacial Surgeons, Am. Assn. Dental Schs., USPHS Profl. Assn., NIH Sailing Club, Omicron Kappa Upslion (pres. Mu Mu chpt. 1993-94). Presbyterian. Office: U Tex Health Sci Ctr 6516 John Freeman St Houston TX 77030-3402

SWEETLAND, ANNETTE FLORENCE (ANNIE SWEETLAND), special education educator; b. Dallas; d. George R. and Odessa (Donnhue) S.; children: George William Davison, James Erron Davison; m. Ralph J. Guinn. BS in Edn., U. Okla., 1988, MS in Edn., 1992. Tchr. multi-handicapped students Noble (Okla.) Pub. Sch., 1988-90; child-find S.E.A.R.C.H. coord. and preschool handicap tchr. Shawnee (Okla.) Pub. Sch., 1989-93; regional coord. Sooner Start Okla. Dept. Edn., Norman, 1993-94; case mgr.

II Developmental Disabilities Scv. Divsn./DHS, State of Okla., Oklahoma City, 1994-95; spl. educator Okla. Youth Ctr., 1995-96; tchr. El Reno Pub. Schs., Oklahoma City, 1996—; mgr. group home Able Group Homes, Norman, Okla., 1989-90; dir. returning adult program St. Gregory's Coll., Shawnee, 1990-91. Mem. ARC, ACA, Coun. for Exceptional Children, Okla. Edn. Assn.

SWENSON, JILL DIANNE, journalism educator; b. St. Paul, July 16, 1958; d. Robert Louis and Arlene Janice (Kling) S. BA, Lawrence U., 1980; MA, U. Chgo., 1981, PhD, 1989. Instr. masters program in social scis. U. Chgo., 1984-86; instr. dept. polit. sci. Roosevelt U., Chgo., 1986-87; vis. lectr. dept. human devel. U. Wis., Green Bay, 1987-88; asst. prof. Coll. Journalism and Mass Communication U. Ga., Athens, 1988-92; project adminstr. Rural Media Project, Athens, 1989-92; judge screening com. Peabody Awards, Athens, 1989-92. Co-curator TV retrospective; author book chpts.; contbr. articles to profl. jours.; author computer software. Advisor Student Peace Coalition, Athens, 1990-92; mem. steering com. Athens Peace Coalition, 1991-93. Lilly teaching fellow, 1990-91; grantee C-SPAN, 1991, Cox Ctr., 1990. Mem. Broadcast Edn. Assn. (conf. com. 1990-91), Assn. Educators in Journalism and Mass Comm. (judge competitive papers 1991, 94), Popular Culture Assn. Lutheran. Office: Sch Comm Dept TV-Radio Ithaca Coll Ithaca NY 14850-7253

SWENTKOFSKE, MARK FRANCIS, air force officer; b. Milw., Feb. 12, 1966; s. Marvin and Eleanor (Montville) S.; m. Virginia Gail Thompson, Dec. 21, 1991. BS, USAF Acad., 1989. Comd. 2d lt. USAF, 1989, advanced through grades through grades to capt.; officer in charge advanced systems 6 Tactical Intelligence Group, Osan AFB, Republic of Korea, 1990-91; site dir. Forward Deployed Intelligence Unit, King Khalid Mil. City, Saudi Arabia, 1991; officer in charge exploitation team Joint Analysis Ctr., Raf Molesworth, U.K., 1991-93; project mgr. 605 Test Squadron-Air Warfare Ctr., Eglin AFB, Fla., 1993-96; intelligence collection mgr. Joint Task Force Southwest Asia, Operation Southern Watch, 1995. Decorated Bronze Star, AJ Commendation medal Joint Svc., Achievment Medal , Arir Force Achievement Medal, Air Force Departmental Requirements Officer, 1996—. Mem. USAF Assn., Officers Club, USAF Mus. in Eng. (founder). Roman Catholic.

SWERLING, JACK BRUCE, lawyer; b. N.Y.C., May 30, 1946; s. Benjamin Fidel and Jeanette (Fidler) S.; m. Erika Andrea Helfer, Jan. 17, 1970; children: Bryan, Stephanie. BA, Clemson U., 1968; JD, U. S.C., 1973. Bar: S.C. 1973, U.S. Dist. Ct. S.C. 1973, U.S. Ct. Appeals (4th cir.) 1974, U.S. Supreme Ct. 1978. Ptnr. Law Firm of Isadore Lourie, Columbia, S.C., 1973-83, Swerling, Harpootlian & McCulloch, Columbia, 1983-92; pvt. practice Columbia, 1992—; mem. Pre-Trial Intervention Adv. Com., 1980-82; mem. adv. com. Child Victim Ct. Notebook div. Pub. Safety Programs, 1987; mem. S.C. Bd. Law Examiners, 1987-92; adj. prof. U. S.C. Sch. Law, Columbia, 1986—; clin. prof. dept. Neuropsychiatry Sch. Medicine, 1988—; mem. S.C. Supreme Ct. com. on model criminal jury instructions, chmn. bule ribbon task force criminal docketing com.; mem. legal com. NORML. Author: South Carolina Criminal Trial Notebook, 1991; contbr. articles to profl. jours. Co-pres. Jewish Community Ctr., Columbia, 1977; bd. dirs. Rape Crisis Network, Columbia, 1985, Animal Protection League, Columbia, 1986. Recipient Am. Jurisprudence award Am. Jurisprudence Ency., 1973. Fellow Am. Coll. Trial Lawyers, Am. Acad. Appellate Lawyers, Am. Bd. Criminal Lawyers, S.C. Bar Found.; mem. ABA, ATLA, Am. Judicature Soc., Nat. Assn. Criminal Def. Lawyers, S.C. Trial Lawyers Assn. (chmn. criminal law sect. 1979-82), S.C. Bar Assn. (chmn. criminal law sect. 1985-86), Richland County Bar Assn. (chmn. criminal law sect. 1988-89). Democrat. Jewish. Office: 1720 Main St Ste 301 Columbia SC 29201-2850

SWETMAN, GLENN ROBERT, English language educator, poet; b. Biloxi, Miss., May 20, 1936; s. Glenn Lyle and June (Read) S. BS, U. So. Miss., 1957, MA, 1959; PhD, Tulane U., 1966; m. Margarita Ortiz, Feb. 8, 1964 (div. 1979); children: Margarita June, Glenn Lyle Maximilian, Glenda Louise. Instr., U. So. Miss., 1957-58, asst. prof., 1964-66; instr. Ark. State U., 1958-59, McNeese U., 1959-61; instr. English, Univ. Coll. Tulane U., 1961-64, spl. asst. dept. elec. engring., 1961-64; assoc. prof. La. Inst. Tech., 1966-67; prof., head dept. langs. Nicholls State Coll., Thibodaux, La., 1967-69, head dept. English, 1969-71, prof., 1971-91, prof. emeritus, William Carey Coll., Gulfport, Miss., 1991—; writer in residence, prof. English William Carey Coll., Gulfport, Miss., 1991—. Ptnr., Breeland Pl., Biloxi, Miss., 1960—; stringer corr. Shreveport (La.) Times, 1966—; ptnr. Ormuba, Inc., 1975—; cons. tech. writing Union Carbide Corp., Am. Fedn. Tchrs. State v.p. Nat. Com. to Resist Attacks on Tenure, 1974—. Subdiv. coord. Rep. Party, Hattiesburg, Miss., 1964. With AUS, 1957. Recipient Poetry awards KQUE Haiku contest, 1964, Coll. Arts contest, L.A., 1966, Black Ship Festival, Yoqosuka, Japan, 1967; Green World Brief Forms award Green World Poetry Editors, 1965. Mem. MLA, S. Cen. MLA, So. Literary Festival Assn. (v.p. 1975-76, 82-83, pres. 1984-85), Coll. Writers Soc. La. (pres. 1971-72, exec. dir. 1983—), IEEE, Am. Assn. Engring. Edn., La. Poetry Soc. (pres. 1971-74, 1986—), Internat. Boswellian Inst., Nat. Fedn. State Poetry Socs. (2d v.p., nat. membership chmn. 1972-74, pres. 1976-77), Nat. Soc. Scholars and Educators (bd. dirs. 1982—, sec. exec. bd. 1986—, sec. bd. dirs. 1968—, sec. soc. 1989—), Am. Fedn. Tchrs. (chpt. pres. 1973-78), Nat. Fedn. State Poetry Socs. (1st v.p. 1975-76, exec. bd. 1972—), Phi Eta Sigma, Omicron Delta Kappa. Book reviewer Jackson (Miss.) State Times, 1961. Poems pub. in various publs. including Poet, Prairie Schooner, Trace, Ball State U. Forum, Film Quar., Poetry Australia, numerous others worldwide; (books of poems) Tunel de Amor, 1973, Deka #1, 1973, Deka #2, 1979, Shards, 1979, Concerning Carpenters, 1980, Son of Igor, 1980; A Range of Sonnets, 1981, Christmas, 1982, Poems of the Fantastic, 1990; contbr. articles (147) to encys.; cons. editor (poetry) Paon Press, 1974—, Scott-Foresman, 1975; editorial bd. Scholar and Educator, 1980—. Home: PO Box 146 Biloxi MS 39533-0146 Office: Nicholls State U Thibodaux LA 70310 also: William Carey Coll 1856 Beach Dr Gulfport MS 39507-1508

SWIFF, KELLY, small business owner, civic volunteer, author. Student, Cordon Bleu Cookery Sch., London, LaVarenne Cookery Sch., Paris, Burgundy, France. Model The Dialing for Dollars, Good Morning Houston; co-owner Creative Mfg. Inc.; now coord. Makk Family Charitable Exhbns.; dir. ops. La Colombe d'Or Hotel and Restaurant; chef participant Beaujolais Wine Festival; instr. self-esteem courses, modeling courses, culinary courses, gala fund-raising. Author: Music Theory with F, A & C, Harp Theory with F, A & C, Take A Look Inside Yourself, Gala Fund Raising Fundamentals; contbr. articles to profl. publs. Founder, chair Woodlands Literary Gala for South Montgomery County; founder, pres. South Montgomery County Libr. Guild; founder Savoir-Faire Etiquette Program, Houston Fire Mus. Gala; past pres., Argonauta Women's Group; founder Neartown Bicycle Tour benefitting Houston Police Dept.; trustee Houston Fire Mus., founding chairperson Houston Fire Mus. Gala.; founder Houston Fire Mus. Gala. Recipient Women of Distinction award; named Top 94 Citizen, People Scene mag. Office: 3410 Montrose Blvd Houston TX 77056

SWIFT, DORI HOSLEY, environmental engineer, consultant; b. Waco, Tex., Oct. 28, 1961; d. David Lee and Barbara Ann (Dobbs) Hosley; m. Andrew William Swift, Dec. 20, 1986; children: Lauren Nicole, Andrew Jonathan, Jacob Michael. BS, Auburn U., 1985, postgrad., 1985-86. Registered environ. mgr.; cert. environ. auditor. Environ. coord. Blount Energy Resource Corp., Montgomery, 1986-87; environ. engr. Malcolm Pirnie Engrs., Inc., Orlando, Fla., 1987-88, Gen. Dynamics, Cape Canaveral, Fla., 1988-89, 89-91, Rockwell Internat., Cape Canaveral, 1989, McDonnell Douglas, Titusville, Fla., 1991-93; sr. environ. engr. Lockheed Space Ops. Co., Kennedy Space Center, Fla., 1993—; cons. and speaker in field. Mem. Soc. Women Engrs. Republican. Mem. Assembly of God Church. Home: 6760 Bright Ave Cocoa FL 32927 Office: United Space Alliance Mail Code USK-142 John F Kennedy Space Ctr-NASA Kennedy Space Center FL 32899

SWIFT, JILL ANNE, industrial engineer, educator; b. Memphis, Nov. 12, 1959; d. Gary Green and Sharon (Willoughby) Brown; m. Fredrick Wallace Swift, June 12, 1987; children: Andrew, Samantha. BS, Memphis State U., 1981, MS, 1982; PhD, Okla. State U., 1987. Registered profl. engr., Fla.; cert. quality engr. Design engr. DuPont Co., Glasgow, Del., 1982-83; head dept. physics Coll. Boca Raton, Fla., 1983-87; asst. prof. indsl. engring. U. Miami, Coral Gables, Fla., 1987—; vis. scholar Air Force Inst. Tech., Wright-Patterson AFB, Ohio, 1988; cons. A.T. Kearney, Amman, Jordan, 1990; quality liaison U. Miami Inst. Study of Quality in Mfg. and Svc., 1988—; cons., spkr. in field. Author: Introduction to Modern Statistical Quality Control and Management, 1995, Principles of Total Quality Control, 1996; contbr. articles to profl. publs. Mem. IIE (chpt. dir. 1988-90, Christmas toy dr. coord. 1989, 90), Am. Soc. Engring. Edn., Am. Soc. Quality Control, Phi Kappa Phi, Alpha Pi Mu (faculty adviser 1988—), Tau Beta Pi. Republican. Office: Univ Miami 268 McArthur Bldg Coral Gables FL 33124

SWIFT, JOHN GOULDING, lawyer; b. Lake Charles, La., Nov. 12, 1955; s. Goulding William Jr. and Betty Jane (Richardson) S.; m. Jan Lynette Whitehead. BS, La. State U., 1977, JD, 1980. Bar: La. 1980, U.S. Dist. Ct. (we. dist.) La. 1982, U.S. Ct. Appeals (5th cir.) 1983, U.S. Dist. Ct. (mid. dist.) La. 1985, U.S. Dist. Ct. (ea. dist.) Tex. 1986, U.S. Dist. Ct. (ea. dist.) La. 1986, U.S. Ct. Appeals (4th cir.) 1992. Law clk. to presiding justice U.S. Dist. Ct. (we. dist.) La., Lake Charles, 1980-81; assoc. Davidson, Meaux, Sonnier, McElligott & Swift, Lafayette, La., 1981-85, ptnr., 1985-89, sr. ptnr., 1990—. Mem. Golf Coast Conservation Assn.; bd. dirs. Hidden Hills Cmty., Inc., 1987-93, pres., 1989-93; bd. dirs. Lafayette Parish unit Am. Cancer Soc., 1992—, pres., 1996-97, bd. dirs. La. divsn., 1995-96; youth dir., mem. adminstrv. bd. Meth. Ch., 1992-93, chair staff-parish rels. com., 1996, mem. adminstrv. bd., 1996, trustee, 1996. Mem. ABA, La. Bar Assn. (ho. of dels. 1996—), La. Def. Counsel, La. Bar Found., Assn. Def. Trial Attys., Lafayette Parish Bar Assn. (bd. dirs. 1988-95, pres. 1993-94), 15th Jud. Dist. Bar Assn. (pres. 1993-94), La. State U. Alumni Fedn., Ducks Unltd., Kiwanis (Acadiana chpt. 1989-95). Republican. Home: 104 Hidden Hills Lake Arnaudville LA 70512-9803 Office: Davidson Meaux Sonnier McElligott & Swift 810 S Buchanan St Lafayette LA 70501-6863

SWIGGETT, HAROLD E., writer, photographer; b. Moline, Kans., July 22, 1921; s. Otho Benjamin and Mildred (Spray) S.; ed. high sch.; m. Wilma Caroline Turner, Mar. 1, 1942; children: Gerald, Vernon. Staff photographer San Antonio Express-News, 1946-67, head dept., 1955-67; freelance writer/photographer San Antonio, 1947—, full-time, 1967—; ordained minister So. Baptist Ch. Served with USAAC, World War II. Recipient 10th ann. Outstanding Am. Handgunner award, 1982, Lifetime Cicero award, 1991, St. Gabriel Possenti medal, 1991; named to Am. Handgunner Hall of Fame, 1987, Anschutz/PSI Gun Writer of Yr., 1990, Handgun Hunter Hall of Fame, 1991. Mem. NRA (life), Wildlife Unltd. (pres. chpt. 1955-58), Outdoor writers Assn. Am. (dir. 1969-72), Tex. Outdoor Writers Assn. (pres. 1967-68), Ducks Unltd., Tex. Rifle Assn. (life), Internat. Handgun Metallic Silhouette Assn. (life), Game Conservation Internat. Republican. Contbg. author books game hunting, gun-oriented paperbacks; author: Hal Swiggett on North American Deer, 1980; sr. editor Harris Publs., Guns/Hunting, Tex. Fish & Game; editor: Handguns 95; contbg. editor Gun Digest, North Am. Hunter. Home: 539 Roslyn Ave San Antonio TX 78204-2456

SWILLER, RANDOLPH JACOB, internist; b. N.Y.C., Jan. 21, 1946; s. Abraham Irving and Helen (Emmer) S.; m. Florence Tena Davis, Sept. 3, 1967; children: Jeremy Adam, Rebecca Susan, Steven Eric. BA in Biology cum laude, Hofstra U., 1968; MD, Chgo. Med. Sch., 1972. Diplomate Am. Bd. Psychiatry and Neurology, Am. Bd. Med. Examiners. Intern Long Island Jewish-Hillside Med. Ctr., New Hyde Park, N.Y., 1972-73; psychiatric resident SUNY Downstate Med. Ctr., Bklyn., 1973-76; asst. attending psychiatrist Maimonides Med. Ctr., Bklyn., 1976-78; medical resident, mem. med. ethics com. Jewish Hosp. Med. Ctr. of Bklyn., 1978-80; fellow in hematology North Shore U. Hosp., Manhasset, N.Y., 1980-81; attending physician in internal medicine Fla. Med. Ctr., Lauderdale Lakes, 1982—, mem. med. utilization rev. com., 1986—, mem. credentials and qualifications com., 1990—; attending physician in internal medicine Coral Springs (Fla.) Med. Ctr., 1987—, mem. med. utilization rev. com., 1987-89. Mem. ACP, AMA, Am. Soc. Internal Medicine, Fla. Med. Assn., Broward County Med. Assn., Am. Psychiat. Assn. Democrat. Jewish. Office: 7710 NW 71st Ct Ste 304 Fort Lauderdale FL 33321-2932

SWING, MARCE, producer, publisher; b. Wichita, Kans., Dec. 3, 1943; d. Eldon Derry and Ruth (Biddle) S. Bus. mgr. Old Westport Med. Assn., Kansas City, Mo., 1972-73; dept. chmn., instr. Ft. Bragg (N.C.) Nursery and Kindergarten, 1965-66, Luth. Schs., Tex. Dist., Irving, 1966-68, Kansas City (Kans.) Sch. Dist. 500, 1973-78, Extension Dept. U. Calif., Northridge, 1979-82, Pima Coll., Tucson, 1983-84, Kinder Care, Lake Buena Vista, Fla., 1989-90; TV/motion picture exec. producer, dir., writer Swing Prodns., Orlando, Fla., 1989—; owner, pres. Swing Enterprises/Swing Prodns., Orlando, 1978—, Living for Edn., Inc., Orlando, 1994—; exec. mgmt., acctg. andmktg. cons. to major internat. corps.; lectr., seminar instr., guest speaker, anchorperson, moderator, panelist. Exec. producer, dir., writer, featured talent on-air live and taped programming for networks, network affiliates and cable, feature motion picture, TV series, mini series, 30 celebrity profiles, 36 documentaries, 14 televents, 45 pub. svc. spots, 30 minute infomat, 12-hour entertinment Christmas Eve project; developer entertainment informational, ednl. and indsl. TV programs and videos; contbr. articles to profl. jours. Corp. adminstr., TV exec. producer, dir., fundraiser nat. hdqrs. March of Dimes, White Plains, N.Y., 1984-86, Arthritis Found., Atlanta, 1985; ofcl. hostess Seattle World's Fair; mem. Nat. Task Force for Child Care, Nat. Task Force for Youth Suicide, Nat. Task Force for Child Abuse; mem. Ariz. Commn. on Arts. Recipient local, regional and nat. art and craft awards. Mem. NEA, NAFE, AAUW, Am. Mgmt. Assn., Nat. Assn. Women Artists, Profl. Assn. Producers and Dirs., Nat. Printmaker's Assn., Nat. Thespian Soc., Thousand Oaks Art Assn., Show of Hands Gallery, Nat. Youth Camps. Lutheran.

SWINK, JAMES, food products executive; b. 1950. Grad., Presbyn. Coll. With McCall Farms, Effingham, S.C., 1972-84; exec. v.p., gen. mgr. Young Pecan Shell Co., Inc., Florence, S.C., 1984—. Office: Young Pecan Co 1200 N Pecan St Florence SC 29501

SWINSON, SUE WHITLOW, secondary education educator; b. Rocky Mount, Va., Apr. 14, 1939; d. Homer P. and Etholene R. (Ramsey) Whitlow; m. Arthur Pitt Burgess, 1961 (div. 1975); 1 child, Robert A.; m. William Edward Swinson, Jr., Sept. 7, 1979. AB, Coll. of William & Mary, 1961; MEd, Ga. State U., 1978. Cert. lifetime profl. DT-5. Tchr. Latin Chesterfield (Va.) County Bd. Edn., 1961-62; Army tchr. USAF I, Augsburg, Germany, 1962-64; tchr. Latin Henrico County Bd. Edn., Richmond, Va., 1965-68; tchr. Latin, English, history DeKalb County Bd. Edn., Decatur, Ga., 1974-92; tchr. Latin and English Randolph County Bd. Edn., Cuthbert, Ga., 1992—; book selection com. DeKalb County Bd. Edn., Decatur, 1983-84. Co-author, editor quar. bull. The Georgia Classicist, 1985-86; co-author: (resource guide) Ga. Advanced Latin State Dept. Resource, 1992-93; co-author: (curriculum guide) Latin Curriculum Guides. Named Ga. Latin Tchr. of Yr., Ga. Classical Assn., 1986, 92, recipient Student-Tchr. Achievement Recognition award, 1991-92. Mem. Am. Classical League, Ga. Classical Assn. (co-editor state paper 1985-86), Fgn. Lang. Assn. of Ga., Profl. Assn. Ga. Educators. Republican. Methodist. Home: RR 2 Box 254-d Georgetown GA 31754-9579 Office: Randolph-Clay HS Rte 4 Box 279 Cuthbert GA 31740

SWOPE, RICHARD MCALLISTER, lawyer; b. West Chester, Pa., Apr. 19, 1940; s. Charles Seigel and Edna McPherson (McAllister) S.; m. Karen Diane Glass, Aug. 24, 1963 (div. 1972). BS in Edn., Bucknell U., 1962; LLB cum laude, Washington and Lee U., 1968. Bar: Va. 1968. Ptnr. Williams, Kelly & Greer, P.C., Norfolk, Va., 1973—; instr. Nat. Inst. Trial Advocacy, 1982-86. Mem. Virginia Beach Beautification Commn.; bd. dirs. Virginia Beach Orchestral Assn., 1982-88; v.p., bd. dirs. Swope Found., West Chester, Pa., 1961—; v.p. Swope Coll. Scholarship Found. Capt. USMC, 1962-65. Mem. ABA, Va. Assn. Def. Attys. (bd. dirs. 1975-78, 88-90), Va. State Bar Assn., Norfolk/Portsmouth Bar Assn., Virginia Beach Bar Assn., Internat. Assn. Def. Counsel, Local Govt. Attys. Assn. Va., Virginia Beach C. of C., Rotary (pres. 1982, Paul Harris fellow). Home: 936 Poquoson Cir Virginia Beach VA 23452-5635 Office: Williams Kelly & Greer PC 600 Crestar Bank Bldg Norfolk VA 23510

SWOPE, WILLIAM RICHARDS, retail executive, lawyer; b. Washington, Oct. 17, 1920; s. King and Mary Margaret (Richards) S.; m. Bobbie Wylie Stringfellow, June 17, 1944 (div. Sept. 1993); children: Robert Cromwell, William Richards Jr.; m. Dorothy S. Taylor, Feb. 3, 1994. AB, U. Ky., 1941; LLB, Harvard U., 1947. Bar: Ky. 1947. V.p., sales mgr. Stringfellow Lumber Co., Birmingham, Ala., 1951-58; pres., owner Swope Co., Inc., Birmingham, Ala., 1958—. Bd. deacons Ind. Presbyn. Ch., Birmingham, 1953-56, 61-64, 71-74. Maj. U.S. Army, 1942-45. Mem. ABA, N.Am. Wholesale Lumber Assn., Nat. Fedn. Ind. Bus., Order of the Crown, Ams. of Royal Descent, First Families of Va., SAR, Lincoln's Inn Soc., Birmingham Country Club, The Club, Lions (pres. 1957-58), Idle Hour Country Club (Lexington), Phi Delta Theta. Republican. Presbyterian. Office: PO Box 1447 Birmingham AL 35201-1447

SWORDS, HENRY LOGAN, II, retail executive; b. Ft. Worth, Oct. 5, 1948; s. H. Logan and Ruth C. (Riley) S.; m. Beverly Craig McFall, June 27, 1981; children: H. Logan III, Justin McFall, Jennifer Lauren. BA, Tex. Wesleyan Coll., 1971. Instr. Logan Swords Drum Studio, Ft. Worth, 1967-69; prin. Swords Drum Studio, Ft. Worth, 1969-73, Swords Music Co., Ft. Worth, 1973-85; pres. Swords Music Cos. Inc., Ft. Worth, 1985—. Actor: (extra, movie) Cotton Candy, 1978, Tough Enough, 1981, Dallas: The Early Years, 1985; drummer, leader Logan Swords & Co. Band. Met. chmn. Tex. Jaycees, Grand Prairie, 1982-83; arbitrator BBB, Ft. Worth, 1984-86, bd. dirs., 1986—, membership chmn., 1991, exec. com., 1993; campaign worker Tarrant County Com. to Re-elect Ronald Reagan, Ft. Worth, 1984. Recipient Pres. of Yr. Tex. Jaycees, Galveston, 1982. Mem. Nat. Fedn. Ind. Bus., Nat. Assn. Music Mchts., Sales and Mktg. Execs. Ft. Worth (v.p. programs, bd. dirs. 1988—, v.p. pub. rels. 1991, exec. v.p. 1993, pres. 1994-95), Ft. Worth Jaycees (life, pres. 1981-82, v.p. 1986-87, JCI senator 1991, area II dir. Tex. JCI Senate, pres., past pres. 1995-96, Outstanding Recruiter 1982). Episcopalian. Home: 13 Legend Rd Fort Worth TX 76132-1008 Office: Swords Music Cos Inc 4300 E Lancaster Ave Fort Worth TX 76103-3225

SYED, IBRAHIM BIJLI, medical physicist, educator, theologist; b. Bellary, India, Mar. 16, 1939; came to U.S., 1969, naturalized, 1975; s. Ahmed Bijli and Mumtaz Begum (Maniyar) S.; m. Sajida Shariff, Nov. 29, 1964; children: Mubin, Zafrin. BS with honors, Veerasaiva Coll., Bellary, U. Mysore, 1960; MS with honors and distinction, Central Coll., Bangalore, U. Mysore, 1962; diploma Radiol. Physics and Hosp. Physics, U. Bombay, 1964; DSc, Johns Hopkins U., 1972; PhD (hon.), Marquis Giuseppe Scicluna Internat. U., Malta, 1985. Cert. hazard control officer, 1980, internat. health care safety profl., 1980; Diplomate: Am. Bd. Radiology, Am. Bd. Health Physics. Lectr. physics Veerasaiva Coll., Bellary, U. Mysore, 1962-63; med. physicist, radiation safety officer Victoria Hosp., India, 1964-67, Bowring and Lady Curz on Hosp. and Post-grad Med. Rsch. Inst., Bangalore, India, 1964-67; cons. med. physicist, radiation safety officer ministry of Health, Govt. of Karnataka, India, 1964-67, Bangalore Nursing Home, India, 1964-67; med. physicist, radiation safety officer. Halifax (N.S., Can.) Infirmary, 1967-69; dir. med. physics, radiation safety officer Baystate Med. Ctr, Springfield, Mass., 1973-79, assoc. prof. Springfield Tech. Community Coll., also adj. prof. radiology Holyoke Community Coll. (Mass.), 1973-79; asst. clin. prof. nuclear medicine U. Conn. Sch. Medicine, Farmington, 1975-79; cons. med. physicist Mercy Hosp., Springfield, also Wing Meml. Hosp., Palmer, Mass., 1973-79; med. physicist, radiation safety officer VA Med. Ctr., Louisville, 1979—, exec. officer radiation safety com., 1979—; prof. medicine (med. physics, nuclear cardiology, endocrinology, metabolism and radionuclide studies) and nuclear medicine, U. Louisville Sch. Medicine, 1979—, dir. nuclear med. scis., 1980—; guest lectr. religious studies program U. Louisville, 1979—; vis. prof. Bangalore U., 1987-88, Gulbarga U., India, 1987-88; vis. scientist Bhabha Atomic Rsch. Ctr., Bombay, India; course dir. licensing for nuclear cardiologists U. Louisville, 1980—; mem. admissions com. nuclear medicine program U. Louisville, 1980—; guest, relief examiner Am. Bd. Radiology, 1991; examiner in radiological physics, Am. Bd. Radiology, 1995; mem. panel of examiners Am. Bd. Health Physics; PhD thesis examiner U. Delhi, Internat. Inst. for Advanced Study, Clayton, Mo., 1985—, Allahabad (India) U., 1996—; faculty mem. Med. Physicists of India Ann. Meeting, 1987; Internat. Atomic Energy Agy. tech. expert in nuclear medicine on mission to People's Republic of Bangladesh, 1986, to Guatamala, 1994; founder, pres. Islamic Rsch. Found. for Advancement of Knowledge, Louisville, 1988—; convener Internat. conf. on Islamic Renaissance: Action Plan for the 21st Century, Chgo., 1995; cons. Coun. Sci. and Indsl. Rsch., Govt. India, 1980—, cons. Am. Coun. Sci and Health, 1980—, cons. gastoenterology and urology div. FDA, HHS, 1988—, cons. radiopharmaceutical div., 1989—; cons. Govt. of India in nuclear medicine, diagnostic radiol. physics, therapeutic radiol. physics, and radiation safety, 1992; cons. radiological and medical nuclear physics Govt. of India, UN Devel. Program, 1992; convener Internat. Conf. on Islamic Renaissance, Chgo., 1995; guest spkr. Muslim Cmty. Ctr., Chgo., 1988—. Author: Radiation Safety for Allied Health Professionals, Radiation Safety Manual, 1979; contbg. editor Jour. of Islamic Food and Nutrition Coun. of Am., 1986—, health and sci. column Muslim Jour., 1989—; freelance writer Minaret Biweekly, N.Y.C., 1975—, AL'FURQAN Internat., Norcross, Ga., 1990, Message Internat., Jamaica, N.Y., 1990, Minaret Monthly Mag., L.A., 1995—; editor: Science and Technology for the Developing World, 1988; mem. editorial bd. Jour. Islamic Med. Assn., 1981—; regular contbr. President's Page; contbr. over 100 articles to sci. jours.; manuscript reviewer for Sci. and Med. Jours., 1973. Pres. Springfield Islamic Ctr., 1973-79, India Assn., Louisville, 1980-81; v.p. Islamic Cultural Assn., Louisville, 1979-80, trustee, 1980—, vice chmn. bd. trustees, 1980-84, chmn. bd. trustees, 1984-86; vice chmn., bd. trustees Islamic Cultural Assn. of Louisville, Inc., 1987-89; ordained minister for Islamic marriages, 1983—; vol. Muslim Chaplain to Ky. State Reformatory, LaGrange, Ky., 1989—, to VA Med. Ctr., Louisville, 1990—, Luther Luckett Correctional Instn., LaGrange, Ky., Roederer Correctional Complex, La Grange, Ea. Ky. Correctional Complex, West Liberty, 1995—, Ky. Correctional Instn. for Women, Pee Wee Valley, 1995—, Imam Friday Khutbah, Islamic Ctr. Louisville, St. Mary's Correctional Instn., Lebanon, Ky., 1990—; khatib Muslim Friday Prayers; legal advisor Islamic Cultural Assn. Louisville, 1986-87; notary pub. Commonwealth of Ky., 1983—; mem. speaker's bur. Louisville C. of C., 1980—, U. of Louisville, 1980—; chmn. Ky. state nat. alumni schs. com. Johns Hopkins U.; judge Ky. State Sci. Fair, 1985—; dir. Ctr. for Qur'an and Sci. Studies, 1988—; trustee India Community Found. Louisville, 1980—, chmn. bd., 1984—; trustee of Karnataka India Community Found. Louisville, Inc., 1988—; bd. dirs. Child Guidance Clinic, Springfield, 1973-79, Heritage Corp., Louisville, 1981—, others; active Am. Cancer Soc., Heart Fund; vol. Muslim chaplain Ky. State Regormatory, La Grange, Dept. of Vets. Affairs Med. Ctr., Louisville, 1990—. Recipient Disting. Community Service award India Community Found., 1982, Hind Rattan Jewel of India Title award Govt. India, 1994; WHO fellow, Govt. India scholar Bhabha Atomic Research Center, Bombay, 1963-64; USPHS fellow Johns Hopkins U., 1969-72. Fellow Inst. Physics (U.K.), Am. Inst. Chemists, Royal Soc. Health, Am. Coll. Radiology, Internat. Acad. Med. Physics; mem. Am. Coll. Nuclear Medicine, Health Physics Soc., Am. Assn. Physicists in Medicine, Soc. Nuclear Medicine (faculty mem. ann. meeting 1987, convenor internat. conf. 1995), Nat. Assn. Ams. of Asian Indian Descent (chmn. state pub. relations com. 1982—), Islamic Soc. N.Am., Islamic Soc. Balt. (founding mem.), Islamic Cultural Ctr., Louisville, Islamic Assn. Maritime Provinces Can., Halifax, N.S. (asst. sec. 1967-69), Health Physics Soc. (chmn. med. health physics com. 1989—, affirmative action com. 1984—), Am. Assn. Physicists in Medicine (mem. biol. effects com.), Assn. Muslim Scientists and Engr. N. Am. (program chm. annual conf. 1987, treas. 1987-88, sec. 1988—), AAUP, Soc. Nuclear Medicine India (life, faculty mem. ann. meeting 1987), Assn. Med. Physicists India (life), Med. and Biol. Physics div. of Can. Assn. Physicists, Hosp. Physicists Assn., N.Y. Acad. Scis., Islamic Assn. Maritime Provinces of Can., Ky. Med. Assn., Jefferson County Med. Soc. (assoc.), Sigma Xi. Islamic. Home: 7102 Shefford Ln Louisville KY 40242-2853 Office: 800 Zorn Ave Louisville KY 40206-1433

SYGULA, ANDRZEJ, chemist, researcher; b. Suloszowa, Krakow, Poland, Aug. 31, 1952; came to U.S. 1990; s. Wladyslaw Sygula and Krystyna Sygula-Morawiec; m. Renata Solska, Jan. 19, 1976; 1 child, Peter. MS in Chemistry, Jagiellonian U., Krakow, 1976, PhD in Chemistry, 1982. Asst. prof. Jagiellonian U., 1983-90; sr. rsch. assoc. La. State U., Baton Rouge, 1990-93, asst. prof., researcher, 1993—. Contbr. articles to profl. jours., books. Office: La State U Dept Chemistry Choppin Hall Baton Rouge LA 70803

SYKES, ALSTON LEROY, analytical chemist, musician; b. Chgo., Sept. 1, 1948; s. Leslie McKoy and Perline Alphonsine (Holden) S.; m. Elizabeth White, Feb. 10, 1973; children: Brian A., Kevin M. BS in Chemistry,

Campbell U., 1972. Cert. profl. chemist. Intern in chemistry N.C. State Bur. of Invest, Raleigh, 1970-72; chemist N.C. Dept. Natural Resources, Raleigh, 1972-77, Rsch. Triangle Inst., Research Triangle Park, N.C., 1977-80; sr. scientist TRW/Radian Corp., Research Triangle Park, N.C., 1980-88; corp. quality assurance mgr., lab. dir. Acurex Environ., Research Triangle Park, N.C., 1988-93; prin. scientist, mgr. Quanterra Environ. Svcs., Raleigh, 1994—; pres. Rsch. Triangle Environ. Tech., 1993—. Author (computer database) NIOSH Analytical Methods, 1986; contbr. articles to profl. jours. Mem. Am. Chem. Soc., Air and Waste Mgmt. Assn. Home: 8905 Jeanew Ct Raleigh NC 27613 Office: RTP Laboratories Inc 8100A Brownleigh Dr Raleigh NC 27612

SYKES, FREDERICK GEORGE (RICK SYKES), association administrator; b. Detroit, Oct. 31, 1941; s. Frederick George Sr. and Margaret Jane (Enochs) S.; m. Judy Lee Roarabaugh Martin, Sept. 17, 1960 (div. Mar. 1984); children: Vikki Lynn, Donna Marjorie, Debra Leigh, Lara Jane; m. Della Frances Crews, Mar. 23, 1985; children: Brianna DeLaine, Casey Lane. AS cum laude, Augusta Coll., 1982, BBA, 1985. Enlisted USN, 1959, advanced through grades to chief petty officer, 1971, resigned, 1973; ptnr., mgr. Trail Cities Relaty, Thomson, Ga., 1974-79; news anchor Sta. WJBF-TV, Augusta, Ga., 1980-85, 87-90; asst. v.p. Graybill & Assocs., Inc., Augusta, 1985-87; news anchor, asst. news dir. Sta. WRDW-TV, Augusta, 1990-92; co-founder, gen. mgr., exec. dir., mem. exec. com. Nat. Barrel Horse Assn., Augusta, 1992—. Named Best of Augusta TV News Personality, Augusta Mag., 1983, 84, 88, 90, 91. Mem. Am. Soc. Assn. Execs. Baptist. Office: Nat Barrel Horse Assn 1355 Reynolds St Augusta GA 30901

SYLVIA, MARGARET JOOST, librarian; b. La Grange, Tex., May 4, 1957; d. Milton and Annie Mae (Havemann) Joost; m. Victor Louis Sylvia, Jan. 7, 1979; 1 child, Jessica Liann. BS, Tex. A&M U., 1979; M in Libr. and Info. Sci., U. Tex., 1989; MS, St. Mary's U., 1996. Serials asst. supr. Tex. A&M U., College Station, 1981-83, evening cataloging supr., 1983-84, catalog maintenance dept. head, 1984-85, automated acquisition receiving dept. head, 1985-87; govt. documents asst. U. Tex., Austin, 1987-88; acquisition and collection devel. dept. head St. Mary's U., San Antonio, 1989-95, adj. prof. in pub. justice dept., 1995—, asst. dir. for tech. svcs., 1995—; Internet trainer Coun. of Rsch. and Acad. Librs., San Antonio, 1995. Contbr. articles to profl. jours. Com. mem. United Way, St. Mary's U., 1991-92. Mem. ALA, Tex. libr. Assn., Bexar Libr. Assn., Beta Phi Mu, Phi Kappa Phi, Psi Chi (v.p. local chpt. 1979). Office: Saint Marys Univ Acad Libr One Camino Santa Maria San Antonio TX 78228

SYMON-GUTIERREZ, PATRICIA PAULETTE, dietitian; b. Orange, N.J., Jan. 21, 1948; d. Michael and Aneilia (Jablonski) Symon; m. Alfonso Pelayo Gutierrez, Jan. 20, 1990. Dietetic cert., N.Y. Inst. Dietetics, 1967; BS in Dietetics, Ga. Coll., 1978; MS in Nutrition and Dietetics, Finch U. Health Scis., Chgo., 1996. Lic. dietitian, Fla. Staff dietitian Landmark Learning Ctr., Opa-Loka, Fla., 1982-86; food svc. dir., dietitian Palm Ct. Nursing and Rehab. Ctr., Wilton Manors, Fla., 1986-87; food svc. dir. Canteen Co.-Dade County Juvenile Ctr., Miami, Fla., 1987-88; food svc. dir., dietitian Manor Care-Boca Raton, Fla., 1988-90, Manor Care-Plantation, Fla., 1990-92; dir. dietary svcs., dietitian Menorah House, Boca Raton, 1992—. Mem. Am. Dietetic Assn., Phi Sigma, Phi Upsilon Omicron. Episcopalian. Home: 8991 Sunset Strip Sunrise FL 33322-3737

SYNEK, M., physics consultant, researcher; b. Prague, Czechoslovakia, Sept. 18, 1930; came to U.S., 1958, naturalized 1963; s. Frantisek and Anna (Kokrment) S.; children: Mary Rose, Thomas Robert. Student Indsl. Chemistry Tech. Sch., Prague, 1946-50; cert. in liberal arts, Prague, 1951; MS in Physics with distinction, Charles U., Prague, 1956; PhD in Physics, U. Chgo., 1963. Analytical chemist Indsl. Medicine Inst., Prague, 1950-51; rsch. physicist Acad. of Scis., Prague, 1956-58; from asst. to assoc. prof. De Paul U., Chgo., 1962-67; prof. Tex. Christian U., Ft. Worth, 1967-71; lectr., researcher U. Tex.-Austin, 1971-75; tenured faculty U. Tex.-San Antonio, 1975-95; sci. advisor Tex. Edn. Agy., Austin, 1971-73, U. Tex., 1971-73; advisor Student Physics Soc., active numerous univ. coms. Researcher in laser-crystal energy efficiency, laser fusion, space lasers, approximate estimate of the extra-terrestrial intelligence probability, nuclear age requiring free elections. Contbr. articles to sci. jours. Campaigner United Way, San Antonio, 1975-95. Judge Alamo Sci. Fair. Rsch. grantee Robert A. Welch Found., 1968-71, 76-83, 93-95. Fellow AAAS, Am. Phys. Soc. (life), Tex. Acad. Sci., Am. Inst. Chemists; mem. AAUP, Am. Assn. Physics Tchrs., Am. Mus. Natural History, Internat. Platform Assn., Internat. Soc. Poets (disting.), N.Y. Acad. Scis., Tex. Faculty Assn., Disabled Am. Vets., Commdrs. Club, Am. Chem. Soc., Czechoslovak Nat. Council (dist. sec. Chgo. 1961-63), Czechoslovak Soc. Arts and Scis. Am., San Antonio Astronomical Assn. (mem. world affairs coun.), Bexar County Czech Heritage Soc., Sigma Xi (life), Sigma Pi Sigma. Roman Catholic.

SYNNETT, ROBERT JOHN, construction company executive; b. Wappingers Falls, N.Y., Jan. 20, 1958; s. William Thomas and Joan Gertrude (Dahlem) S.; m. Therese Frances Quinn, Oct. 24, 1981; children: Robert William, Conor Denis, Joseph Peter. BA, U. S.C., 1981. Personnel, safety mgr. M.B. Kahn Constrn. Co., Inc., Columbia, S.C., 1981-84, personnel, safety dir., 1984-87, asst. v.p., corp. sec., 1987-89, v.p., asst. corp. sec., 1989-96. Vol. United Way of Midlands, Columbia, S.C., 1983-86. Mem. Am. Soc. Pers. Adminstrn., Columbia Pers. Assn. Assoc. Gen. Contractors of Am., Inc. (active Carolina br. safety com. 1988, S.C. legis. com. 1988-92), Am. Soc. Safety Engrs., S.C. Occupational Safety Coun. (bd. dirs. 1994—). Home: 109 Chillingham Ct Irmo SC 29063-2519 Office: M B Kahn Constrn Co Inc PO Box 1179 Columbia SC 29202-1179

SYNNOTT, MARCIA GRAHAM, history educator; b. Camden, N.J., July 4, 1939; d. Thomas Whitney and Beatrice Adelaide (Colby) S.; m. William Edwin Sharp, June 16, 1979; children: Willard William Sharp, Laurel Beth Sharp. AB, Radcliffe Coll., 1961; MA, Brown U., 1964; PhD, U. Mass., 1974. History tchr. MacDuffie Sch., Springfield, Mass., 1963-68; instr. U. S.C., Columbia, 1972-74, asst. prof., 1974-79, assoc. prof. history, 1979—, dir. grad. studies history dept., 1990-92. Author: The Half-Opened Door, 1979; contbr. essays to books. Fulbright scholar, 1988; Am. Coun. Learned Socs. grantee, 1981. Mem. Am. Hist. Assn., So. Hist. Assn., Orgn. Am. Historians (membership com. 1990-93), S.C. Hist. Assn. (pres. 1994-95), History of Edn. Soc. (mem. editl. bd. 1996—). Office: U SC Dept History Columbia SC 29208

SZAL, GRACE ROWAN, research scientist; b. Amsterdam, N.Y., July 17, 1962; d. David Anderson and Helen Marie (Bursese) R.; m. Timothy James Szal, Dec. 31, 1988; children: Matthew David, Alexander James. BA, Siena Coll., 1983; MA, Rutgers U., 1985, PhD, 1988. Rsch. asst., instr. Rutgers U., New Brunswick, N.J., 1983-88; postdoctoral rsch. fellow U. Pa., Phila., 1988-89, Tex. Coll. Osteo. Medicine, Fort Worth, 1989-90; postdoctoral rsch. fellow Tex. Christian U., Fort Worth, 1990-91, assoc. rsch. scientist, 1991—. Contbr. articles to profl. jours. Recipient Nat. Rsch. Svc. award Nat. Inst. Drug Abuse, 1988-91. Mem. Am. Psychol. Soc., Soc. for Neurosci. Office: Tex Christian U PO Box 298740 Fort Worth TX 76129

SZALKOWSKI, CHARLES CONRAD, lawyer; b. Amarillo, Tex., Apr. 14, 1948; s. Chester Casimer and Virginia Lee (Hess) S.; m. Jane Howe, Dec. 28, 1971; children: Jennifer Lee, Stephen Claude. BA, BS in Acctg., Rice U., 1971; MBA, JD, Harvard U., 1975. Bar: Tex. 1975. Assoc. Baker & Botts, L.L.P., Houston, 1975-82, ptnr., 1983—; speaker in field. Chmn. ann. fund campaign Rice U., Houston, 1991-93, chmn. fund coun., 1995-96; chmn. adminstrv. bd. St. Luke's United Meth. Ch., Houston, 1994; bd. dirs., DePelchin Children's Ctr., Houston, 1996—; adv. bd. Meth. Home, Waco, MIT Enterprise Forum of Tex., Houston, The Entrepreneurship Inst., Houston. Mem. ABA (fed. regulation of securities com.), Am. Law Inst., State Bar Tex. (chmn., vice chmn. bus. law sect. 1990-92), Houston Bar Assn. (chmn., vice chmn., corp. counsel sect. 1988-90), Harvard Law Sch. Assn. Tex. (pres. 1983-84), Tex. Bus. Law Found. (bd. dirs., exec. com. 1988—, vice chmn. 1995—), Assn. Rice U. Alumni (chmn. various coms. 1981-86), Assn. for Corp. Growth (adv. bd. Houston chpt.), Lincoln's Inn Soc., Houston Philos. Soc. Office: Baker & Botts LLP 1 Shell Plz 910 Louisiana St Houston TX 77002

SZANISZLO, PAUL JOSEPH, microbiology educator, fungal biologist; b. Medina, Ohio, June 9, 1939; s. Paul and Irene (Toth) S.; m. Susan Jane Twigg, Sept. 4, 1960; children: Jennifer (dec.), Christopher, Juli. BA, Ohio Wesleyan U., 1961; MA, U. N.C., 1964, PhD, 1967. Postdoctoral fellow Harvard U., Cambridge, Mass., 1967-68; asst. prof. U. Tex., Austin, 1968-74, assoc. prof., 1974-80, chmn. divsn. biol. scis., 1976-82, prof., 1980—; guest microbiologist NIH, Bethesda, Md., 1993; co-chmn. Gordon Rsch. Conf. Fungal Metabolism, 1986. Author: Fungal Dimorphism, 1985; editor Fems Microbiol Letters, 1992-94; contbr. articles to profl. jours. Mem. AAAS, Am. Soc. Microbiology (chair-elect divsn. F 1996), Med. Mycological Soc., Am. Internat. Soc. Human and Animal Mycology, Mycological Soc. Am. (editl. bd. Mycologia 1991-95), Am. Men and Women Sci.

SZCZEPANSKI, JAN, chemistry and physics educator, researcher; b. Michalowice, Lodz, Poland, Oct. 15, 1946; came to U.S., 1987; s. Wincenty and Helena (Szlaga) S.; m. Irena Wencel, Apr. 11, 1971; 1 child, Adam. MS in Physics, U. Gdansk, Poland, 1975, PhD in Physics, 1985. Rsch. asst. U. Gdansk, 1975-87; rsch. assoc. U. Fla., Gainesville, 1987-89, asst. prof., 1989-90, rsch. assoc., 1990-94, asst. scientist, 1995—. Author: (with others) Materials Chemistry at High Temperature, 1990; contbr. articles to profl. jours. Group leader Inst. Physics, Solidarity, Gdansk, 1989. Grantee Ministry of Sci., Poland, 1986, award, 1985. Mem. Am. Chem. Soc. Office: U Fla Dept Chemistry Gainesville FL 32611

SZILAGYI, JOHN ALEX, federal agency administrator; b. N.Y.C., Feb. 6, 1940; s. John Michael and Elizabeth (Wesselenyi) S.; m. Mary Ann Mazzola, Sept. 7, 1963 (dec.); 1 child, Sherry. BBA, Hofstra U., 1961. Tax auditor IRS, Bklyn., 1961-67; adminstrv. intern IRS, Washington, 1967-68, revenue agt., 1968-76, planning officer, 1976-79, chmn. deferred tax research programs, 1979-92; tax rsch. cons. Port St. Lucie, Fla., 1995—; drafted U.S. tax legislation enacted in 1986 requiring Social Security number of dependents to be listed on income tax returns; drafted U.S. tax legislation enacted in 1988 requiring taxpayer ID number of child care provider to be listed on income tax returns; interviewee for missing-children article, Forbes mag., 1990; interviewee for tax cheating on child care articles, N.Y. Times, 1991; interviewee for Is the IRS After You? article, Working Mother mag., 1991. Author: (books): Energy Credit Limitations, 1983, Recapture of Deduction on HUD Housing, 1984, Monitoring Age 65 Exemptions, 1987, Improper Zero Bracket Amount Deductions, 1988, Where Have All the Dependents Gone?, 1989, Whatever Happened to Child Care in 1989?; editor (books): State Income Tax Refund Study, 1982, Stock Sales Disclosed by Dividends, 1983, Recapture of New Residence Credit, 1983, Monitoring Individual Noncash Contributions, 1988. Republican. Presbyterian.

SZLEGIER, RACHEL ELLEN, elementary school educator; b. New Bedford, Mass., June 28, 1972; d. Leonard James and June Ellen (Place) S. BAA in Psychology and Elem. Edn., U. Miami, 1994, MMEd, 1995. Cert. elem. tchr., Fla. Photo lab. asst. U. Miami, Coral Gables, Fla., 1992-94; programs coord. South Dade YMCA, Miami, 1993-94; paraprofl. II Southe Pointe Elem. Sch., Miami Beach, Fla., 1994—; tutor After Sch. House, Miami, 1991-93; mem. student literacy corp U. Miami Sch. Edn., 1993-94; coach, tutor South Dade YMCA, 1992-94. Vol. Spl. Olympics Funday, Miami, 1991-94. Bowman Ashe scholar, 1990-94, Alumni Devel. scholar U. Miami Sch. Edn, 1993-94. Mem. Nat. Coun. Tchrs. Math., Internat. Reading Assn., Golden Key Honor Soc., Phi Kappa Phi, Psi Chi. Home: 935 10th St Miami Beach FL 33139

SZYMANSKI, DAVID MARK, marketing specialist, educator; b. Buffalo, Feb. 26, 1957; s. Eugene Edward and Rita Helen (Ginter) S.; m. Maria Helen Kondilis, May 27, 1979; children: Ashley Elizabeth, Matthew Dean, Jessica Rita. BA in Econs., U. N.C., Asheville, 1979; MA in Econs., Vanderbilt U., 1983; MBA in Mktg., U. Wis., 1983, PhD in Mktg., 1987. Research cons. Comptroller of the Treasury, Nashville, 1980-81; teaching asst. Vanderbilt U., Nashville, 1981-82; instr. mktg. U. Wis., Madison, 1986-87; prof. mktg. Texas A&M U., College Station, 1987—; cons. The Dryden Press, N.Y.C., 1988, West Pub., Inc., 1990. Mem. editl. rev. bd. Jour. Mktg., Advances in Competitiveness Rsch.; contbr. articles to profl. jours., papers to confs. Fellow Kasciuszko Found., 1980, Coll. Bus Adminstrn., Tex. A&M U., 1988. Mem. Am. Mktg. Assn., Assn. for Consumer Research, Acad. Mktg. Sci. Roman Catholic. Office: Tex A&M U Dept Mktg College Station TX 77843-4112

SZYMCZAK, EDWARD JOSEPH, mechanical engineer; b. Anderson, Tex., Sept. 28, 1938; s. Harold and Verna (Walkoviak) S.; m. Lorena Jane Sharp, Sept. 26, 1964; children: Denise, Lisa, Brian. Student, U. St. Thomas, 1958; BSME, Tex. A&M, 1961; MBA, U. Houston, 1970. Registered profl. engr., Tex. Engr. trainee to engring. mgr. Cameron Iron Works, Houston, 1961-90; dir. engring. ea. hemisphere Cooper Oil Tool Div./Cooper Industries, London, 1990-91; dir. engring. Cooper Oil Tool Div./Cooper Industries, Houston, 1991-95, Cameron div. Cooper Cameron Corp., Houston, 1995—; chmn. indsl. adv. bd. U. Southwestern La., Lafayette; councilor Tex. A&M U. Rsch. Found., College Station, 1994—; mem. mech. engring. adv. bd. U. Tenn., Knoxville, 1996—; mem. mech. engr. adv. bd. U. Tenn., Knoxville, 1996—. Patentee (8) on tool equipment. Mem. ASME, Tex. A&M Former Students Assn., Tex. A&M 12th Man Found., Tex. A&M Mech. Engring. Acad. Disting. Grads., Soc. Petroleum Engrs., Nat. Assn. Corrosion Engrs., Tau Beta Pi. Republican. Roman Catholic. Home: 4002 Cypress Hill Spring TX 77388

TABACCHI, PATRICIA, elementary education educator; b. Boston, May 22, 1974; d. Otavio and Mary (Hanlon) T. BA, Tex. Christian U., Ft. Worth, 1996; MSEd in Elem. Edn., U. Pa., 1996. Head of swimming program Willows Child Learning Ctr., Englewood, Colo., 1993-94; edn. dept. intern Kimbell Art Mus., Ft. Worth, 1995; art asst. Kinderplatz of Fine Arts, Inc., Ft. Worth, 1995-96. Child life vol. Cook's Children's Med. Ctr., Ft. Worth, 1994-96. Recipient Sr. scholarship in art and art history Tex. Christian U., 1996, deptartmental honors in art history, 1996, Tex. Christian U. scholarship, 1992-96. Roman Catholic. Home: 3478 E Jamison Ave Littleton CO 80122

TABB, WALLER CROCKETT, allergist, immunologist; b. Richmond, Va., 1935. MD, U. Va., 1959. Diplomate Am. Bd. Internal Medicine, Am. Bd. Allergy and Immunology. Intern U. Va. Hosp., Charlottesville, 1959-60, resident in internal medicine, 1964-66, fellow in allergy/immunology and pulmonary medicine, 1966-67; mem. staff Lakeland (Fla.) Regional Med. Ctr., 1967—; now pvt. practice Watson Clinic, Lakeland. Fellow ACP, Am. Acad. Allergy and Immunology, Am. Coll. Chest Physicians; mem. Alpha Omega Alpha. Office: Watson Clin 1600 Lakeland Hills Blvd Lakeland FL 33805-3019

TABBERT, RONDI JO, accountant; b. Dallas, Mar. 14, 1953; d. Jack H. and June F. (Williams) Russell; m. Marc F. Habern, Oct. 20, 1990. AA, Tarrant County Jr. Coll., 1975; BS in Bus., U. Tex.-Dallas, 1980; MBA, U. Dallas, 1984. CPA, Tex. Bookkeeper, Kelly-Moore Paint, Dallas, 1976-78; corp. acct. Gen. Portland, Dallas, 1978-80; chief acct. W.R. Grace & Co., Dallas, 1980-83; contr. Little & Assocs., Dallas, 1983-85; prin. Rondi J. Tabbert, CPA, Desoto, Tex., 1985—; acctg. instr., Cedar Valley Community Coll., 1987-90. Weeky fin. columnist De Soto Tribune, 1986-87. Bd. dirs., treas. Unity Ch. Duncanville, 1989-91; mem. adv. bd. DeSoto Cultutal Ctr., 1989-90. Mem. AICPA, Tex. Soc. CPAs (vice chmn. tax edn. com. 1988-89, chmn. 1989-90, communication coun. steering com. 1989-91, bd. dirs. Dallas chpt. 1989-90), Nat. Soc. Tax Profls., Dallas Soc. CPAs (tax edn. com. 1985-86, vice chmn. 1986-87, chmn. 1987-88), Am. Women's Soc. CPAs, Am. Bus. Women's Assn. (program com. 1986-87, program chmn. 1987-88), DeSoto C. of C. Home: 510 Shockley Ave De Soto TX 75115-3314 Office: 1666 N Hampton Rd Ste 101 De Soto TX 75115-2390

TABER, PATRICK E., computer programmer; b. Lawrence, Kans., June 4, 1972; s. Patrick E. and Shirley M. (Pruske) T. BS, Trinity U., San Antnonio, Tex., 1994. Tech. support/programmer Southwest Software, Austin, 1995—. Home: 7201 Hart Lne # 2071 Austin TX 78731

TABIBZADEH, SIAMAK SHOKRI, pathologist, educator; b. Sept. 7, 1952. MD summa cum laude, Tehran (Iran) U., 1970-77. Lic. N.Y., Calif., Conn., Fla. Rotating intern Tehran U. Hosps., 1976-77; resident in anatomic and clin. pathology Montefiore Med. Ctr., Bronx, 1978-82; fellow in immunopathology Elmhurst (N.Y.) Hosp., 1982-83; asst. attending pathologist Elmhurst Hosp., N.Y.C., 1983-91; attending in pathology Moffitt Cancer Ctr., Tampa, 1991—; instr. pathology Mt. Sinai Sch. Medicine, N.Y.C., 1983-85, asst. prof., 1985-91, assoc. prof., 1991—; ad hoc grant referee NIH; rsch. com. mem. Elmhurst Hosp., N.Y.C.; recruitment com., GI com., Moffitt Cancer Ctr., Tampa; search com. for chairperson U. South Fla., Tampa; dir. immunopathology lab. Elmhurst Hosp., 1983-91, immunopathology and electron microscopy, 1984-91. Jour. referee Hepatalogy, 1988—, Jour. Histochemistry and Cytochemistry, 1989—, Am. Jour. Pathology, 1990—, Endocrinology, 1991—, Human Reproduction, 1992—, Jour. Ob-Gyn., 1993—, Endocrine, 1993—, mem. editl. bd., 1995—; editor-in-chief Frontiers in Biosci.; contbr. articles to profl. jours.; developed 3 labs. in field. NIH grantee. Mem. Internat. Acad. Patholgy (U.S.-Can. div.), Histochem. Soc., N.Y. Acad. Soc., Harvey Soc. Office: Moffitt Cancer Ctr Dept Pathology 12902 Magnolia Dr Tampa FL 33612-9416

TABOR, CURTIS HAROLD, JR., library director; b. Atlanta, July 3, 1936; s. Curtis Harold and Gertrude Olive (Casey) T.; m. Dorothy May Corbin, June 30, 1957 (dec. June 1996); children: Timothy M., John M. AA, Fla. Coll., Temple Terrace, 1957; BA, Harding Coll., 1960; MA, Butler U., 1967; MDiv, Bapt. Missionary Assn. Theol. Sem., Jacksonville, Tex., 1974; MLS, Tex. Woman's U., 1977. Min. Ch. of Christ, Bowling Green, Ky., 1960-61, Hamilton, Ont., Can., 1961-64, Indpls., 1964-67, Nacogdoches, Tex., 1967-75, Dallas, 1976-77, Columbus, Miss., 1977-79, Tampa, Fla., 1993—; tchr. Gt. Lakes Christian Coll., Beamville, Ont., Can., 1961-64; bible chair Stephen F. Austin State U., Nacogdoches, 1967-75; prof., libr. Fla. Coll., Temple Terrace, 1979-85, libr. dir., 1985—; participated archaeol. excavations, Tell Gezer, Israel, 1969, Tell Lachish, Israel, 1980. Author: (with others) Resurrection, 1973, Biblical Authority, 1974, The Lord of Glory, 1980. Cub master Cub Scouts Am., Nacogdoches, 1970-75; pres. Nacogdoches Baseball Assn., 1974-75. Recipient scouters key Cub Scouts Am., 1975. Mem. ALA, Fla. Libr. Assn., Tampa Bay Libr. Consortium (treas. 1986-89), Eta Beta Rho, Beta Phi Mu. Republican. Mem. Ch. of Christ. Home: 12316 Kelly Ln Thonotosassa FL 33592-2754 Office: Fla Coll Libr 119 N Glen Arven Ave Tampa FL 33617-5527

TABOR, WILLIAM EUGENE, employment relations specialist, writer, poet; b. Bluefield, Sept. 27, 1952; s. Joseph Edmondsdon and Norma Ethel (Blankenship) T.; m. Zenith Myra Proffitt, June 30, 1976; children: William Eugene Jr., Robert Al. AS in Law Enforcement, Bluefield State Coll., W. Va.; BS in Criminal Justice Adminstrn., Bluefield State Coll. Machinist W. Va. Armature, Bluefield; police chief Town of Pocahantas, Va.; employment rels. mgr. State of W. Va., Princeton; pres. Criminal Justice Club, Bluefield, W. Va., 1981, 82. Mem. VFW (post cmmdr. 1978), DAV, Am. Legion. Home: PO Box 112 Boissevain VA 24606

TADLOCK, GERRY LEE, perioperative nursing educator; b. Akron, Ohio, Apr. 24, 1944; d. William Claude and Alta Olive (Blosser) T. Dimploma in nursing, Akron City Hosp., 1966; BA in Psychology, U. Akron, 1976, MSN, 1991. Staff nurse ob/gyn. Akron City Hosp., 1966-68, staff nurse clinics, 1967-71, coord. quality assurance, 1989-90; mem. faculty Idabelle Firestone Sch. Nursing, Akron, 1971-89; dir. nursing Braver Meml. Ambulatory Ctr., Akron, 1987-88; perioperative educator Columbia Regional Med. Ctr. at Bayonet Point, Hudson, Fla., 1990—. Sec. Med. Explorer Scouts, Akron, 1975-90. Explorer Scouts Am. scholar. Mem. Assn. Oper. Room Nurses, Akron City Hosp. Alumnae Assn. (historian), NAFE, Sigma Theta Tau. Republican. Home: 8262 Norbert St Spring Hill FL 34606-3140 Office: Columbia Regional Med Ctr at Bayonet Point 14000 Fivay Rd Hudson FL 34667-7103

TAFFET, GEORGE EFREM, geriatrician; b. N.Y.C., Jan. 13, 1958; s. Arthur and Elizabeth (Gropper) F.; m. Judy Ann Niolet, Sept. 21, 1986; children: Amy, Lori, Jason, Philip. BA in Math., Brown U., 1979, MD, 1982. Diplomate Am. Bd. Internal Medicine, Am. Bd. Geriatrics. Intern, resident Baylor Coll. of Medicine, Houston, 1982-85, fellow geriatrics, 1985-87, fellow cardiovascular, 1987-88, asst. prof., 1988—, dir. fellowship program, 1993—. Clin. investigator award Nat. Inst. on Aging, 1988. Mem. Am. Geriatrics Soc., Gerontol. Soc. Am., Internat. Soc. Heart Rsch., Am. Heart Assn. Basic Sci. Office: Huffington Ctr on Aging Baylor Coll Medicine Houston TX 77030-3498

TAGGE, JAMES FREDRICK, internist; b. Enid, Okla., July 10, 1920; s. Leonard Fredrick and Birdie (McKenzie) T.; m. Elizabeth Mae Stieg, July 24, 1947; children: Carol Adams, Fred Tagge, Dale Tagge, Bruce Tagge. BS, U. Okla., 1941; MD, Washington U., 1943. Diplomate Am. Bd. Internal Medicine. Intern Barnes Hosp., St. Louis, 1944, resident, 1944, 47-49; pvt. practice Enid, Okla., 1949-89; Chief of staff St. Mary's Hosp., Enid; chief of staff Bass Bapt. Hosp., Enid; trustee Bass Bapt. Hosp. Trustee St. Mary's Hosp., Enid; chmn. bd. of trustees Bass Bapt. Hosp., Enid. Capt. U.S. Army Med. Corps, 1945-47. Fellow ACP; mem. AMA, Am. Soc. Internal Medicine, Okla. Med. Assn., Rotary (pres. Enid club 1988). Republican. Baptist. Home: 1605 Tahlequah Pl Enid OK 73703-7018

TAHIR, ABE MAHMOUD, JR., art consultant; b. Greenwood, Miss., Feb. 18, 1931; s. Mahmoud and Mary (Ollie) T. BBA, U. Miss., 1953; MBA, George Washington U., 1960. Supply mgmt. specialist U.S. Gen. Svc. Adminstrn., Washington, 1958-64; advisor to Turkish govt. U.S. AID, Ankara, Turkey, 1964-66; owner, mgr. Tahir Gallery, Inc., New Orleans, 1966-86; art cons., 1987—; adj. curator prints and drawings New Orleans Mus. Art, 1991—. Author: Jacques Hnizdovsky-Woodcuts and Etchings, 1987. 1st lt. USAF, 1954-56. Mem. Delta Sigma Pi, Omicron Delta Kappa. Roman Catholic. Home and Office: PO Box 8805 Metairie LA 70011

TAHIR, MARY ELIZABETH, retail marketing and management consultant; b. Greenwood, Miss., Dec. 14, 1933; d. Mahmoud Ibrahim and Mary Constance (Ollie) T. Student, U. Miss., 1951-53. Cert. Profl. Cons., Acad, Profl. Cons. and Advisors. Mgmt. trainee Neiman-Marcus Co., Dallas, 1954-56; asst. buyer D.H. Holmes Co. Ltd., New Orleans, 1956-58, buyer, 1958-65, assoc. divisional mdse. mgr., 1965-67, divisional v.p., 1969-79, corp. v.p., gen. mdse. mgr., 1979-89; pres. Liz Tahir & Assocs., New Orleans, 1990—. Author: Mexico's Cosmetic and Fragrance Market: Past, Present and Future Opportunities, 1991, The Changing World of Mexican Retail Opportunities, 1991, Mexico: Window of Opportunity, 1991, Art of Negotiating, 1993, Negotiating More Profitable with Your Suppliers, Customers and Employees, 1994. Bd. dirs. Vieux Carre Property Owners Assn., New Orleans, 1990, YWCA, 1996—. Recipient Role Model award YWCA, 1990, Woman Bus. Owner of the Yr. award AWARE, 1996. Mem. Women's Profl. Coun. (chmn. New Choices 1989), World Trade Ctr., Fashion Group Internat. (Alpha award 1987-88, Lifetime Achievement award 1993), Nat. Spkrs. Assn., Am. Mktg. Assn. (bd. dirs. 1996—), Am. Assn. Profl. Cons., Am. Mgmt. Assn., Fgn. Rels. Assn. (bd. dirs. 1992—, pres. bd. dirs. 1994-96), Nat. Retail Fedn. Home: 817 Esplanade Ave New Orleans LA 70116-1940 Office: Liz Tahir & Assocs 201 Saint Charles Ave Ste 2500 New Orleans LA 70170-1000

TAI, CHONG-SOO STEPHEN, political scientist, educator; b. Seoul, Korea, Oct. 15, 1940; came to U.S., 1969, naturalized, 1983; s. Hyung-Kyoon and Ock-Hee (Park) T.; m. Susan Gillja Kang, Aug. 28, 1965; children: Hyounju, Elizabeth, Michael. BA, Yonsei U., Seoul, 1963; MA, Ill. State U., 1972; MA, Northwestern U., 1972, PhD, 1974. Lectr. Northwestern U., Evanston, Ill., 1974-75; asst. prof. U. Ark., Pine Bluff, 1976-80, assoc. prof. polit. sci., 1980-86 , prof. polit. sci., 1986—; great decisions coordinator Fgn. Policy Assn., Pine Bluff, 1977-84; cons. S.E. Ark. Planning Commn., Pine Bluff, 1979-80; active Southwestern Internat. Studies Consortium, Mex., 1986; vis. prof. polit. sci., Kyung Hee U., Korea, 1992-93. Contbr. articles to profl. jours. Bd. dirs. Korean Cmty. Assn. Little Rock, 1996—. Served with Korean AF, 1963-67. Grantee KOTN radio sta., 1978, Ark. Endowment for Humanities, 1979-80, NEH, 1980; Fulbright-Hays scholar, China, 1985. Fellow Internat. Ctr. for Asian Studies; mem. Am. Polit. Sci. Assn., Ark. Polit. Sci. Assn., Assn. for Asian Studies, Assn. Korean Polit. Studies N.Am. Roman Catholic. Avocation: golf. Home: 11324 Hickory Hill Rd Little Rock AR 72211-4368 Office: U Ark Pine Bluff 1200 N University Pine Bluff AR 71601

TAKEUCHI, HIROSHI, investment company executive, consultant; b. Okayama, Japan, Apr. 23, 1938; s. Buichi and Shigeko (Ueda) T.; m. Nobuko Hayashi, May 10, 1967; 1 child, Tsuruichi. Degree in lit., Osaka

U., 1962, degree in lang., 1962. Chief exports Mitsui Engr. & Shipbuilding Co., Tokyo, 1965-69, mgr. off-shore bus. devel., 1973-81; spl. rep. Mitsui Engring. & Shipbuilding Co., London, 1969-73; gen. mgr., exec. v.p. Mitsui Zosen (U.S.A.), Inc., Houston, 1981-90; exec. v.p., dir. Global Tech. Inc., Houston, 1990-93, Arlington, Va., 1993—; mktg. cons. Iben, Albuquerque, N.M., 1993—, Takt Internat., N.J., 1993—. Office: Global Tech Inc 1324 Park Garden Ln Reston VA 22094-2010

TALBERT, ROY, JR., history educator; b. Cheraw, S.C., Aug. 1, 1943; s. Roy and Betty Jean (Harper) T.; BA (Furman Scholar), Furman U., 1965; MA (NDEA fellow), Vanderbilt U., 1967, PhD, 1971; grad. Inst. Ednl. Mgmt., Harvard U., 1981; grad. Computer Literacy Inst., Pepperdine U., 1983; Jane Boyd Holbert, Oct. 24, 1986; children: Matthew, Rebecca Anne, Drew, Elizabeth. Sr. teaching fellow Vanderbilt U., Nashville, 1967-70; asst. prof. history Ferrum (Va.) Coll., 1974-76, dir. curriculum and programs, 1976-79; vice chancellor for acad. affairs Coastal Carolina U., Conway, 1979-84, assoc. prof. history, 1979-89, prof., 1989—, chmn. 1991—; producer, host The Public Eye, TV show, 1978-79; host Waccamaw Mag., TV show, 1983; project dir. numerous film, TV and pub. programming projects for community and civic groups, 1975-79. Served to capt. U.S. Army, 1970-72. Mem. So. Hist. Assn., Orgn. Am. Historians. Methodist. Author: FDR's Utopian: Arthur Morgan of the TVA, 1987, Negative Intelligence: The Army and the American Left, 1917-41, 1991, No Greater Legacy: The Centennial History of Willcox, McLeod, Buyck and Williams, 1995. Home: 106 Wofford Ln Conway SC 29526-8823 Office: Coastal Carolina Univ History Dept Conway SC 29526

TALBOT, ALFRED WAYNE, JR., human resources executive; b. El Paso, Tex., Feb. 28, 1950; s. Alfred Wayne and Dora Merle (Waldrep) T.; m. Josephine Marie White, Mar. 27, 1971; children: Malinda Hope, Carson Wayne. BA in Teaching, Sam Houston State U., 1972. Cert. secondary tchr., Tex.; cert. mediator for Tex. cts.; cert. master practitioner Neuro-Linguistic Programming; designated sr. profl. in human resources. Regional supr. Pizza Inn Inc., Dallas, 1972-86; gen. mgr. ops. J.R. Paden, Inc., Killeen, Tex., 1986-88; v.p. ops. KTH Corp., Austin, Tex., 1988-90; trainer Travis County Tax Office, Austin, Tex., 1990-91; dir. tng. Child Support divsn. Atty. Gen. of Tex., Austin, 1991-92, dir. orgn. devel., 1992-95; analyst fed. regulations, 1995—. Guest lectr. Career Resouce Ctr., Austin, 1990-93, Tarbiyyat Sch., Round Rock, Tex., 1993, curriculum com., 1993. Named Sr. Profl. in Human Resources, Soc. for Human Resources Mgmt. Home: 805 Norwell Ln Pflugerville TX 78660-2443 Office: Office of Atty Gen of Tex Child Support Divsn PO Box 12017 Austin TX 78711-2017

TALBOTT, MARY ANN BRITT, secondary education educator; b. Augusta, Ga., Nov. 29, 1945; d. Charles Hubert and Mary Ann (Day) Britt; m. Lonnie Loyd Talbott, Oct. 20, 1978. AB, U. Ga., 1967, EdS, 1981, Cert. in Adminstrn./Supervision, 1989; MEd, Augusta Coll., 1975. Cert. tchr. support specialist. Tchr. English Hilsman Jr. H.S., Athens, Ga., 1967-68; tchr. English, chmn. dept. Tubman Jr. H.S., Augusta, Ga., 1969-73, Aquinas H.S., Augusta, 1973-79; tchr. English Winder (Ga.)-Barrow H.S., 1979-82; tchr. remedial writing/reading/math, career planning, Latin Morrow (Ga.) H.S., 1982-91, tchr. English, 1982-93; tchr. English Brunswick (Ga.) H.S., 1993—, mem. discipline task force, 1995-96; instr. English Clayton State Coll., Morrow, 1991-92, Ga. Mil. Coll., Ft. Gordon, 1975-77; instr. staff devel. Clayton County Bd. Edn., Jonesboro, Ga., 1985-91. Elder Stockbridge (Ga.) Presbyn. Ch., 1989-92; active Am. Cancer Soc., Augusta Choral Soc., Athens Choral Soc.; mem. Evangel. Luth. Ch. Resurrection, Augusta, Ga., 1995—. Recipient Psi Achievment award, 1979-81. Mem. Delta Kappa Gamma (pres. 1978-80, chmn. music com. 1985-87, 89-91, chair Psi State Achievement Award Com. 1979-81, dist. dir. 1981-83, scholar 1980, 87, Golden Gift award 1984), Alpha Lambda Delta, Kappa Delta Sigma, Phi Delta Kappa (Tchr. of Yr. 1989). Lutheran. Home: PO Box 13163 Jekyll Island GA 31527-3163 Office: Brunswick High Sch Habersham St Brunswick GA 31520

TALIAFERRO, CECIL RAYNARD, college dean; b. Pitts., Feb. 3, 1942; s. Blair Leo and Dorothy Olene (Edmonson) T.; m. Colleen R. White-Taliaferro, June 18, 1994. BA, Va. Union U., 1966; MEd, U. Pitts., 1971, PhD, 1975; diploma in ednl. mgmt., Harvard U., 1990. Asst. prof. edn. Ind. U. Pa., 1984-88; v.p. acad. affairs Philander-Smith Coll., Little Rock, 1988-90; acad. dean Wiley Coll., Marshall, Tex., 1990-92; asst. dean instrn. Tex. State Tech. Coll., Marshall, 1992-95; dean ednl. support San Antonio Coll., 1995—; cons. Pro-Ed Cons. Co., Memphis, 1989-91; mem. edn. adv. bd. Urban League Ark., Little Rock, 1989-90. Active Leadership Marshall, 1992-95; bd. dirs. Am. Heart Assn. Tex., Marshall, 1994-95, Cities in Schs., Inc., Marshall, 1994-95, Boys and Girls Club Am., Marshall, 1994-95. Named one of Outstanding Young Men of Am., 1978; U.S. HEW fellow, Washington, 1966. Mem. Omega Psi Phi (editor to oracle). Democrat. Baptist. Home: 234 Tammy Dr San Antonio TX 78216 Office: San Antonio Coll 1300 San Pedro Ave San Antonio TX 78212

TALIAFERRO, HENRY BEAUFORD, JR., lawyer; b. Shawnee, Okla., Jan. 12, 1932; s. Henry Beauford Sr. and Laudys L. (Anthony) T.; m. Janet Stewart Myers, Nov. 23, 1955 (div. Feb. 1985); children: Sarah Stewart T. deLeon, Henry B. III, William N.; m. Patricia Ann Calloway, May 16, 1987. BA, U. Okla., 1954, JD, 1956. Bar: Okla. 1956, U.S. Supreme Ct. 1966, D.C. 1969, U.S. Claims Ct. 1970. Assoc. Monnet, Hayes & Bullis, Oklahoma CIty, 1956-59, ptnr., 1959-66; exec. dir. O.E.O. legal svcs. program Oklahoma County, 1966-67; dir. congl. rels., acting exec. dir. Pres.'s Nat. Adv. Commn. on Civil Disorders, Washington, 1967-68; assoc. solicitor for Indian Affairs Dept. of the Interior, Washington, 1968-69; pvt. practice law Washington, 1969-70; ptnr. Casey, Lane & Mittendorf, Washington, 1970-80; exec. v.p., gen. counsel The GHK Cos., Oklahoma City, 1980-83; of counsel Kerr, Irvine & Rhodes, Oklahoma City, 1987—; cons. O.E.O. Legal Svcs., 1966-67, Gas Pipeline Acquisitions & Mgmt., Oklahoma City, 1983-87; mem. Interstate Oil and Gas Compact Commn., 1980—, Okla. Commn. on Nat. Gas Policy, 1991—, Okla. Energy Resources Bd., 1994—. Author: (with others) Report of Presidents National Advisory Commission on Civil Disorders, 1968; contbr. articles to profl. jours. Candidate 5th dist. U.S. Ho. of Reps., Okla., 1966; mem. planning commn. Fairfax County, Va., 1973, platform com. Dem. Nat. Conv., San Francisco, 1984. Mem. ABA, Okla. Bar Assn., D.C. Bar Assn., Fed. Energy Bar Assn., Met. Club (Washington), Oklahoma City Golf and Country Club. Democrat. Episcopalian. Office: Kerr Irvine Rhodes & Ables 201 Robert S Kerr Ave Ste 600 Oklahoma City OK 73102-4202

TALIAFERRO, NANCY ELLEN TAYLOR, artist; b. Richmond, Va., Feb. 16, 1937; d. Samuel Beryl and Nancy Loomis (Brinton) Taylor; m. Charles Mitchell Taliaferro, July 3, 1958; children: Chester Parsons, Nancy Brinton. BFA, Va. Commonwealth U., 1959. Comml. artist, illustrator, 1959-63, drawings, pastel portraits, 1963—, oil paintings, 1978—. Exhbns. include The Chrysler Mus., Norfolk, Va., 1994, Du Pont Art Gallery, Washington and Lee U., Lexington, Va., 1993, Uptown Gallery, Richmond, 1992-96, The Art Gallery, Ashland, Va., 1992-96, Va. Gen. Assembly and State Capitol Bldgs., 1989, 91, 93, Jacob Javits Fed. Bldg., N.Y.C., 1986, Women's Resource Ctr., U. Richmond, 1985. Recipient award The Artists Mag., 1992. Mem. Nat. Assn. Women Artists (Medal of Honor 1995, Audrey Hope Shirk Meml. award 1995), Uptown Gallery (charter mem.), James River Art League, U. Painters. Republican. Methodist. Home: 6724 Forest Hill Ave Richmond VA 23225-1802 Studio: 8413 Forest Hill Ave Richmond VA 23235-3125

TALLANT, MARY KAY, school nurse; b. Shamrock, Tex., May 21, 1955; d. Billy Wayne and Kikue (Hanoka) Franklin; m. Randy Tallant, Feb. 7, 1986; children: Bobby Don, Chelsey Dawn. Liv. vocat. nurse, Frank Phillips Jr. Coll., Borger, Tex., 1978; diploma, NW Tex. Hosp. Sch. Nursing, Amarillo, 1981; AA, Clarendon (Tex.) Jr. Coll., 1985. Lic. practical nurse, Tex.; RN, Tex.; cert. in vision, hearing and spinal screening, Tex. Nurse labor and delivery room NW Tex. Hosp.; weekend charge nurse Shamrock Gen. Hosp.; coop. sch. nurse ind. sch. dists., Shamrock, Kelton, Briscoe, Samnorwood, Allison, Mobeetie, Tex.; Patient First Home Health, dir. nursing. mem., sec. S. Wheeler County Hosp. Bd. Mem. Tex. Sch. Nurse Assn. Home: 800 N Madden St Shamrock TX 79079-1836

TALLEY, BETTE SUE, elementary education educator; b. Fayette County, W.Va., Sept. 3, 1940; d. James Garland and Juanita H. (Butcher) Tilley; m. John D. Talley, Jr., June 26, 1959; children: John D. III, David Lee, Paul Chester. B in Religious Edn., Southeastern Bible Coll., Birmingham, 1963, BS, 1980; MEd, U. Ala., 1983; PhD, U. Ala., Tuscaloosa, 1988. Cert. tchr. Ala. Tchr. Trinity Christian Sch., Birmingham, 1980-83; from instr. to prof. Southeastern Bible Coll., 1983—; seminar leader various chs. Asst. editor elem. Bible curriculum Assn. Christian Schs. Internat., Colorado Springs, Colo., 1995. Mem. Coun. Exceptional Children, Assn. Christian Schs. Internat. (seminar leader 1985-95), Ala. Assn. Christian Edn. (judge in bible tchg. 1987-94), Kappa Delta Pi, Delta Epsilon Chi. Home: 3029 Dolly Ridge Dr Birmingham AL 35243 Office: Southeastern Bible Coll 3001 Highway 280 E Birmingham AL 35243-4181

TALLEY, LINDA JEAN, food scientist, dietitian; b. Hearne, Tex., July 15, 1948; d. Roy Wesley and Dorothy Louise (Allen) Dugger; m. Thomas James Talley, May 15, 1970; children: John Paul, Jo Ann. BS in Food Tech., Tex. A & M U., 1969, MS in Food Sci. and Tech., 1979, PhD in Food Sci. and Tech., 1981. Registered dietitian Am. Dietetic Assn.; registered sanitarian; lic. dietitian, Tex. Technician I soil and crop scis. dept. Tex. A & M U., College Station, 1969-72; technician I in horticulture scis. Tex. A&M U., College Station, 1977-78, grad. asst., 1978-81; quality assurance mgr. food products divsn. Southland Corp., Ft. Worth, 1972-73; pub. health inspector Ft. Worth Pub. Health Dept., 1973-74; dir. quality assurance plant sanitation and product devel. Kimbell Foods, Inc., Mfg. Divsn., Ft. Worth, 1974-75; profl. cons. Ft. Worth, 1975-76; v.p., cons. TALCO, Dallas, 1981-91; sr. food scientist Enersyst Devel. Ctr., Inc., Dallas, 1990—; presenter in field. Contbr. articles to profl. jours. Mem. Inst. Food Techs., Sigma Xi, Phi Tau Sigma. Home: 3706 Oak Ridge Dr Bryan TX 77802-3426 Office: Enersyst Devel Ctr 2051 Valley View Ln Dallas TX 75234-8920

TALLEY, RICHARD BATES, lawyer; b. Oklahoma City, Mar. 19, 1947; s. Olin Jack and Betty Lee (Bates) T.; m. Joan Walker, Sept. 15, 1992; children from a previous marriage: Richard Bates, Samuel Logan, Bradley Dale, Rachel Alexandra. BBA, Okla. U., 1969, JD, 1972. Bar: Okla. 1972, U.S. Dist. Ct. (we. dist.) Okla. 1972, U.S. Ct. Appeals (10th cir.) 1973, U.S. Dist. Ct. (no. dist.) Tex. 1987, U.S. Tax Ct. 1987.; CPA, Okla. Ptnr. Talley and Perrine, Norman, Okla., 1982—, Talley, Perrine, Smith & Farrar, Norman, Okla., 1985—; bd. dirs. Bacchus Enterprises, Inc., Norman, The Top of the Center, Inc. Mem. ABA, Okla. Bar Found., Okla. Bar Assn., Okla. Trial Lawyers Assn., Okla. Soc. CPAs, Cleve. County Bar Assn., Soc. CPAs. Democrat. Methodist. Home: 1819 Joe Taylor Cir Norman OK 73072-6650 Office: Talley and Perrine 219 E Main St Norman OK 73069-1304

TALLEY, RICHARD WOODROW, accountant; b. Birmingham, Ala., Sept. 10, 1941; s. Alton Woodrow and Alta O. (Tittle) T.; m. Anita Marcell Moses, Jan. 14, 1966; children: Richard Woodrow Jr., Leah Michelle. BS in Commerce and Bus. Adminstrn., U. Ala., 1984. CPA, Ala. Pres. Smither, Talley & Mauldin, Decatur, Ala., 1964—. Officer Boy Scouts Am., Decatur, Austin Band Boosters, Decatur, PTA, Decatur; mgr., coach Dixie Youth Baseball, Decatur; deacon Ch. of Christ. Served as sgt. USAR, 1964-70. Named Boss of Yr. Decatur Jaycees, 1980. Mem. AICPA, Ala. Soc. CPAs, Commerce Execs. Soc. U. Ala., Lions (sec. 1982-83, treas. 1985-86, sec.-treas. 1994-95). Home: 1266 Brandywine Ln SE Decatur AL 35601-4582 Office: Smither Talley & Mauldin PO Box 2067 Decatur AL 35602-2067

TALLEY, WILLIAM GILES, JR., container manufacturing company executive; b. Adel, Ga., Sept. 25, 1939; s. William Giles and Mary (McGlamry) T.; BSBA, U. S.C., 1961; m. Jacqueline Vickery, Apr. 14, 1962; children: William Giles, John Lindsey, Bronwyn Ashley. Mgmt. trainee Talley Veneer & Crate Co., Inc., Adel, 1961-62, plant mgr., salesman, Waynesboro, Ga., 1965-67; with Talley's Box Co., Leesburg, Fla., 1962-69, plant mgr., partner, 1967-69; gen. mgr. Growers Container Coop., Inc., Leesburg, 1969—; pres. Talley Acres, Inc., 1979—, pres. Talley Classic Woods, Inc., 1992—; bd. dirs. Sun Trust Bank Ctrl. Fla., N.A., Orlando, Fla. Past chmn. and bd. dirs. Leesburg Hosp. Assn. Served with USAAF, 1961. Mem. Leesburg C. of C. (dir.), Fla. Forestry Assn. (dir. 1977—), Elks, Kiwanis, Sigma Alpha Epsilon. Republican. Methodist. Home: 2206 Talley Court Rd Leesburg FL 34748-3177 Office: PO Box 490817 Leesburg FL 34749-0817

TALMADGE, JOHN MILLS, physician; b. San Marcos, Tex., Oct. 4, 1946; s. John Mills Sr. and Marjorie Nell (Beach) T.; m. Dana Maria Mancill, Apr. 24, 1976; children: Caitlin, Chelsea, Jeffrey. AB, Dartmouth Coll., 1969; MD with honors, Duke U., 1973. Diplomate Am. Bd. Psychiatry and Neurology. Asst. prof. Med. Sch. U. Tex., Houston, 1976-77; asst. clin. prof. Baylor U., Houston, 1977-82; faculty Tex. A&M Univ., College Station, Tex., 1984-90, SWT Univ., Tex., 1982-84; founder, chmn. bd., med. dir. The Sandstone Corp., College Station, Tex., 1984-90; med. dir. Charter Med., Nat. Med. Enterprises, Dallas, 1990-93, Horizon Recovery Svcs., Dallas, 1993—; faculty SW Health Sci. Ctr. U. (Dallas) Tex., 1992—; pvt. practice hosp., cmty. psychiatry Conroe, Tex., 1977-82, San Marcos, Tex., 1982-84, Bryan-College Station, Tex., 1984-90, Dallas, 1990—; med. dir. psychiat. svcs. Planned Behavioral Health Care, 1994—; tchr., lectr. Episc. Diosc. of Dallas, 1993—. Samuel E. Ziegler fellow, 1969-70, Mosher Inst. Def. Studies fellow, Tex. A&M U.; recipient Leadership Brazos award, 1988. Mem. AMA, APA, TMA, TSPP, ASAM, AAPAA. Home: 13626 Tanglewood Dr Dallas TX 75234-3842 Office: 14232 Marsh Ln Ste 442 Dallas TX 75234-3865

TAMAYO, RAQUEL, medical/surgical nurse; b. Havana, Cuba, Nov. 30, 1958; d. Francisco and Raquel (Naranjo) Suau; m. William Piferrer, Feb. 21, 1976 (div.); children: William, Andre; m. Julio H. Tamayo. AS, Miami Dade C.C., 1985. Cert. oper. rm. nurse, mgr.; ACLS, RNFA. Staff nurse cardiac catheterization lab. Bat. Hosp., 1995—. Contbr. articles to profl. jours. Mem. nat. adv. coun. on nurse tng. U.S. Dept. HHS, Washington; active Big Bros-Big Sisters Orgn. Mem. Assn. Oper. Rm. Nurses, Dade County Assn. Post Anesthesia Nurses, Phi Theta Kappa.

TAMBERRINO, FRANK MICHAEL, professional association executive; b. Wilmington, Del., May 3, 1955; s. Frank and Mary Pauline (Wilson) T.; m. Charlotte Jane Yates, June 4, 1982; children: F. Michael, Cara J. BA in Urban Affairs, Va. Poly. Inst. and State U., 1977, M in Urban Regional Planning, 1979. Grad. teaching asst. Va. Poly. Inst. and State U., Blacksburg, 1979; rsch. asst. R. Yearwood Enterprises, Blacksburg, 1979; sr. planner Pinellas County Planning Commn., Clearwater, Fla., 1979-83; exec. dir. com. of 100 Citrus County, Inverness, Fla., 1983-86; exec. dir. Citrus County Indsl. Devel. Authority, Crystal River, Fla., 1986-89; sr. v.p. econ. devel. Pensacola (Fla.) Area C. of C., 1990—; mem. practitioners adv. com. Fla. Dept. Commerce, 1988, 91-96, chmn., 1994-96; mem. adv. coun. Enterprise Fla. Practitioners, 1996—. Contbr. articles to profl. jours. Mem. Citrus County Extension Svc. Adv. Com., Inverness, 1987-89, Pvt. Industry Coun. Escambia County, 1995-96; bd. dirs. Crystal River chpt. Jr. Achivement, 1987, Com. of 100 Citrus County, 1987-88, USO Greater Pensacola, 1995—; mem. devel. bd. Escarosa Regional Workforce, 1996—. Recipient So. Practitioners award So. Bus. and Devel., 1995. Mem. Fla. Econ. Devel. Coun. (bd. dirs. 1988—, v.p. 1989, pres.-elect 1990, pres. 1991, Profl. or Yr. award 1994), So. Indsl. Devel. Coun. (state bd. dirs. 1989-90), Ducks Unltd. (chmn. Crystal River chpt. 1987-89), Rotary (pres. Inverness 1987-88, mem. Five Flags 1990—), Irish Politicians Club. Roman Catholic. Office: Pensacola Area C of C 117 W Garden St PO Box 550 Pensacola FL 32593

TAN, BOEN HIE, biochemist; b. Padangan, Java, Indonesia, Dec. 14, 1926; s. King Hoo and Bwan Nio (Oei) T. BS, U. Leyden, Holland, 1952, MS, 1955, ScD, 1962. Profl. nuclear medicine specialist. Fellow, asst. prof. U. Leyden, Holland, 1953-55, 62-64; fellow, rsch. assoc. Max Planck Inst., Gottingen, Germany, 1961-62, U. Minn., Mpls., 1955-61, 64-68, 1972-73; rsch. assoc. N.Y. Hosp., Cornell Med. Ctr., N.Y.C., 1968-72; rsch. assoc., prof. U. Groningen, Maastricht, Holland, 1973-81; rsch. assoc. U. South Ala., Mobile, 1982-92; analytical biochemist Ala. Dept. Environ. Mgmt., Montgomery, 1992—. Contbr. over 55 articles to profl. jours. Treas. "Aesculapius" Leyden U. Pharm. Student Assn., 1952-53. Mem. Nederlandse Vereniging voor Nucleaire Geneeskunde, Am. Assn. for Clin. Chemistry, FASEB, AAAS, Am. Chem. Soc. Home: PO Box 230451 Montgomery AL 36123-0451 Office: Ala Dept Environ Mgmt 1890 Dickinson Dr # A Montgomery AL 36109

TAN, DALI, secondary school educator; b. Shenyang, Liaoning, People's Republic of China, Aug. 19, 1958; came to U.S., 1987; d. Changming and Yong (Fu) T.; m. Jianming Gong, Jan. 13, 1987; 1 child, Wade. BA, Heilongjiang U., 1982; MA, Liaoning U., 1985; postgrad., U. Md., 1991—. Translator, interpreter, 1982—; tchr. Chinese St. Catherine's Sch., Richmond, Va., 1993—; project coord. Md. Summer Inst. for Tchrs. Chinese, U. Md., College Park, 1991-93. Contbr. articles to profl. publs. Mem. Am. Comparative Lit. Assn., Assn. Asian Studies, Nat. Women's Studies Assn., Internat. Soc. for Comparative Study of Civilizations. Home and Office: 6001 Grove Ave Richmond VA 23226-2603

TAN, PING, computer systems manager; b. Shenyang, Liaoning, China, Feb. 23, 1951; came to U.S., 1984; s. Yunhe and Wenguo (Zheng) T.; m. Cheping Cheng, May 25, 1987; 1 child, Xiao. BSEE, Dalian (China) Engring. Coll., 1976; MS in Computer Sci., Wayne State U., 1987; postgrad. computer and info scis., Nova Southwestern U., 1993—. Engr. Harbin (China) Electronic Equipment Factory, 1976-80; lectr. Heilongjang Engring. Inst., Harbin, China, 1980-84; sys. mgr., DBMS mgr. Bowman Gray Sch. of Medicine, Winston Salem, N.C., 1986—; rsch. assoc. Harbin Sci. and Tech. U., 1980-84; teaching asst. Wayne State U., Detroit, 1985-87. Contbr. articles to profl. jours. Mem. IEEE, Assn. Computing Machinery, Am. Fedn. for Clin. Rsch. Home: 651 Dover Dr Winston Salem NC 27104-1524 Office: Bowman Gray Sch Medicine Dept Cardiology Medical Center Blvd Winston Salem NC 27157

TANAS, KHALIL SALIBA, psychiatrist; b. Jaffa, Palestine, Israel, Aug. 11, 1944; came to U.S., 1972; s. Saliba Khalil and Evelyn Issa Tanas; m. Nelly Antoun, Oct. 16, 1971; children: Christopher, Anthony, Robin. AS, Bir-Zeit (Israel) U., 1965; BS, Am. U. Beirut, 1967, MD, 1972. Diplomate Am. Bd. Psychiatry and Neurology; lic. psychiatrist, N.C. Intern Am. U. Med. Ctr., Beirut, 1971-72; resident in psychiatry John Umstead Hosp., Butner, N.C., 1972-74, fellow in child psychiatry Children Psychiat. Inst., 1974-75; staff psychiatrist Cherry Hosp. Acute Admission Unit, Goldsboro, N.C., 1975-77; area clin. dir. Guilford County Area Mental Health Programs, Greensboro, N.C., 1977-78; adminstrv. dir. Greensboro Mental Health Ctr., 1977-78; dir. clin. svcs. John Umstead Hosp., Butner, 1978-85; forensic psychiatrist Dorothea Dix Hosp., Raleigh, N.C., 1985-87; dir. adult svcs. Broughton Hosp., Morganton, N.C., 1987-89, adolescent and child psychiatrist, 1989-90, dir. geropsychiatry divsn., 1990-91, interim dir. youth divsn., 1990-91; pvt. practice, 1988-93; mem. nat. program com. Inst. Hosp. and Cmty. Psychiatry, 1982-84; mem. active staff Grace Hosp., Morganton, 1989-91, cons. med. staff, 1991-93; mem. staff Franklin County and Granville County Mental Health Ctr., Forsyth County Mental Health Ctr., Neuse Clinic, Edgecombe-Nash Mental Health Ctr., Halifax County Mental Health Svcs., Guilford County Mental Health Ctr., Alamance-Caswell Mental Health Ctr., , Vance/Granville/Franklin/Warren County Mental Health Ctr., Cleveland County Mental Health, 1987-92; pres. med. staff Guilford County Area Program, 1977-78, John Umstead Hosp., Butner, N.C., 1978-81, Broughton Hosp., Morganton, 1989-90; chief resident psychiatry John Umstead Hosp., Butner, 1974-75; dir. residency tng., assoc. dir. John Umstead residency program Cherry Hosp., 1975-77; clin. instr. basic psychiatry John Umstead residency tng. program John Umstead Hosp., Butner, 1975-77; clin. asst. prof. psychiatry Med. Sch. East Carolina U., 1977-83; dir. residency tng. John Umstead/Duke U. combined programs, Butner, 1980-83; clin. asst. prof. Duke U. Med. Ctr., Durham, 1978-87; clin. asst. prof. psychiatry U. N.C., Chapel Hill, 1986—. Contbr. articles to profl. jours. Grantee McNeil Pharms., 1988-89, Sandoz Pharm. Corp., 1988-90. Fellow Am. Psychiat. Assn. (cert.).; mem. N.C. Psychiat. Assn., N.C. Med. Soc., Burke County Med. Soc., Am. Acad. Psychiatry. Democrat. Presbyterian. Office: Broughton Hosp 1000 S Sterling St Morganton NC 28655-3938

TANG, DE-CHU, molecular biologist, gene therapist, researcher; b. Taipei, Republic of China, June 21, 1951; came to U.S., 1979; PhD, Ind. U., 1989. Rsch. assoc. Baylor Coll. Medicine, Houston, 1988-90, Duke U., Durham, N.C., 1990-91; instr. U. Tex. Southwestern Med. Ctr., Dallas, 1991-94; asst. prof. U. Ala., Birmingham, 1994—. Office: U Ala Birmingham 1900 University Blvd THT 215 Birmingham AL 35294-0006

TANG, IRVING CHE-HONG, mathematician, educator; b. Macau, China, Dec. 29, 1931; came to U.S., 1948; s. Man-yan and Susie Wei-chun (Chung) T. BS, U. Calif., Berkeley, 1952; MS, U. Ill., 1953; DS, Washington U., St. Louis, 1965. Chartered engr., Brit. Engring. Coun. Design engr. Friden Calculators, San Leandro, Calif., 1955-56; staff engr. IBM Corp., San Jose, Calif., 1956-66; postdoctoral fellow U. Oslo, 1966-68; head math. dept. NSW Inst. Tech., Sydney, Australia, 1969-76, Hong Kong Poly., 1977-89; prof. math. Phillips U., Enid, Okla., 1989-91, Oklahoma City C.C., Rose State Coll., 1991-94, Okla. State U., Oklahoma City, 1994—. Contbr. articles to profl. jours. Fellow Brit. Computer Soc.; mem. Math. Assn. Am., Hong Kong Math. Soc. (pres. 1977-81), Sigma Xi, Tau Beta Pi, Eta Kappa Nu. Office: Okla State U Dept Math Dept Math 900 N Portland Oklahoma City OK 73107

TANGMAN, DARRELL GRANT, computer engineer; b. Chgo., Feb. 24, 2947; s. Donald Newton and Hulda Mae (Swanson) T. BS in mathematics, Mich. State U., 1969. Programmer Sperry Corp., Roseville, Minn., 1971-80; programming cons. Sperry Corp., 1980-85, Unisys Corp., Norcross, Ga., 1985-86; software cons. Nat. Advanced Sys., Norcross, 1987-88; software design engineer Nat. Sci. Ctr. Found., Augusta, Ga., 1989—; chief instr. Twin Cities Aikido Ctr., St. Paul, Minn., 1976-85; inst. Aikido Ctr. of Atlanta, Clarkston, Ga., 1985-88; chief instr. Augusta Aikido Club, 1989—; pres. Midwest Aikido Fedn., Chgo., 1983-85; bd. govs. U.S. Aikido Fedn., N.Y.C., 1983-85. Mem. IEEE, Assn. for Computing Machinery, U.S. Aikido Fedn. (Shidoin award 1988). Libertarian. Home: 217 Old Mill Rd Martinez GA 30907 Office: Nat Sci Ctr Found 159 Craig Sims Pkwy Augusta GA 30909

TANNEBAUM, SAMUEL HUGO, accountant; b. Oklahoma City, Aug. 15, 1933; s. Simon L. and Eva (Kapp) T.; B.B.A. with spl. distinction, U. Okla., 1955; m. Nita Mae Levy, June 12, 1955; children: Joel L., Marilyn J. Staff acct. Alford, Meroney & Co., Dallas, 1955-61; pvt. practice acctg., Dallas, 1961-63; partner Tannebaum & Bindler, CPAs, Dallas, 1963-67; mng. ptnr. Tannebaum, Bindler & Lewis, CPAs, Dallas, 1967-80, Tannebaum, Bindler & Co., CPAs, Dallas, 1980-84; pres. Tannebaum Bindler & Co., P.C., 1984-94; sr. exec. ptnr. Weaver & Tidwell, L.L.P., CPAs, Dallas, 1995—; dir. Nat. Ctr. Banks, Inc., 1983-86. Mem. adv. coun. Cmtys. Found. Tex., 1987—; bd. dirs. Dallas Home for Jewish Aged, 1973-76; trustee Temple Emanu-El, Dallas, 1976-83, treas., 1980-82, v.p., 1982-83; trustee Found. Jewish Fedn. Greater Dallas, 1987-96. Named C.P.A. of Yr., Dallas chpt. Tex. Soc. CPAs, 1976; CPA, Tex., Okla. Mem. AICPAs (coun. 1979-82, 95—, personal fin. specialist), Tex. Soc. CPAs (dir., past v.p., past chpt. pres.), Nat. Assn. Estate Planners (accredited estate planner), Nat. Assn. Estate Planning Couns. (dir. 1978-82, treas. 1982-83, v.p. 1983-84, pres. 1984-85), Dallas Estate Planning Coun. (past pres.), Brookhaven Country Club. Home: 5820 Meletio Ln Dallas TX 75230-2108 Office: 12221 Merit Dr Ste 1700 Dallas TX 75251

TANNENBAUM, SAMUEL VICTOR, philanthropic consultant; b. Washington, July 10, 1942; s. Henry Irving and Bertha (Fidel) T.; m. Rachel Jane Eichelman; 1 child, Lisa Beth. BA, CUNY, 1965, MPA, 1970. Cert. fund raising exec. Supr. N.Y.C. Dept. Social Svcs., N.Y.C., 1965-70; alumni coordinator CCNY Alumni Assn., N.Y.C., 1970-71; asst. exec. dir. Nat. Fedn. Temple Brotherhoods, N.Y.C., 1971-72; grants dir. Fedn. Employment and Guidance Svc., N.Y.C., 1972-81; fund raising assoc. Greater Miami (Fla.) Jewish Fedn., 1981-82; devel. dir. Am. Heart Assn., Miami, 1982-85, Covenant House/Fla., Fort Lauderdale, 1985-86; pres. Tannenbaum Assocs., Inc., Ft. Lauderdale, Fla., 1986—. Author Nat. Soc. of Fund Raising Execs. Jour., 1986; contbg. author: A Treasury of Successful Appeal Letters, 1985. Mem. Nat. Soc. Fund Raising Execs. South Fla. Chpt. (bd. dirs. 1985—, cert. chmn. and others).

TANNER, JOHN S., congressman, lawyer; b. Dyersburg, Tenn., Sept. 22, 1944; s. E.B. and Edith (Summers) T.; m. Betty Ann Portis, Sept. 2, 1967; children: Elizabeth Tanner Atkins, John Portis. BS, U. Tenn., 1966, JD, 1968. Bar: Tenn., 1968. Mem. Tenn. Ho. of Reps., 1976-88, 101st-104th Congresses from 8th Tenn. dist., Washington, 1988—; mem. Nat. Security Commn., Sci. Commn.; vice chmn. Cong. Sportsmen's Caucas. Active Obion County Cancer Soc.; bd. visitors USAF Acad.; founding mem. The Coalition; former chmn. bd. visitors U.S. Mil. Acad. Lt. USN, 1968-72; col.

Tenn. Army N.G., 1974—. Mem. Obion County C. of C., Obion County Bar Assn., Rotary. Democrat. Disciples of Christ. Office: US House of Reps 1127 Longworth House Washington DC 20515

TANNER, TERESA L., medical nurse; b. Lancaster, Pa., Nov. 21, 1968; d. Donald G. and Roxie B. Wood. AS, Odessa (Tex.) Coll., 1990, postgrad., 1990—. TN, Tex.; ACLS; advanced EKG cert. Former oncology/telemetry charge nurse; now staff nurse med. floor Akron (Ohio) City Hosp. Vol. ARC, Lancaster.

TANNER, WILLIAM E., English language educator. BA, U. Tex., 1964; MA, East Tex. State U., 1967; PhD, U. Tulsa, 1972. Instr. French East Tex. State U., 1968; grad. fellow U. Tulsa, 1969-71; project dir. Mayor's Office, Tulsa, 1971; asst. prof. Hendrix Coll., 1971-72; chmn. dept., assoc. prof. Tex. Coll., 1972-73; asst. prof. English Tex. Woman's U., 1973-79, from assoc. prof. to prof. English, 1979—. Author: Symposium in Rhetoric, 1974, 75, Retrospectives and Perspectives, 1978, Rhetoric and Change, 1982, Rhetoric of the Arts, 1983, A Writer's Plan, 1985, Rhetoric and Change, rev. edit., 1985, Echoing Voices, 1986, A Guide for Teachers of Basic Writrs, 1986, Out of Chaos, 1991, The Toulmin Method: Exploration and Controversy, 1991, The Arthurian Myth of Quest and Magic, 1993, Rhetorical Designs: A Teacher's Guide, 1994. Home: 3701 Turtle Creek Dallas TX 75219 Office: Tex Woman's U Dept English/Speech/Langs Denton TX 76204

TANOUS, HELENE MARY, radiologist, educator; b. Zanesville, Ohio, Oct. 22, 1939; d. Joseph and Rose Marie (Mokarzel) T.; m. John Camp, 1986 (dec. 1990). BA, Marymount Coll., 1961; MD, U. Tex., 1967. Diplomate Am. Bd. Radiology. Intern County Hosp., L.A., 1967-68; resident in radiology U. So. Calif. Hosp., L.A., 1969-71; pvt. practice medicine specializing in radiology, L.A., 1972-73; instr. radiology U. So. Calif. Med. Sch., L.A., 1971-72; asst. prof. diagnostic radiology Baylor Med. Sch., Houston, 1973-75; dir. med. student elective in diagnostic radiology Ben Taub Hosp., Houston, 1973-75; pvt. practice diagnostic radiology, Largo, Fla., 1975—; chief Radiology Diagnostic Clinic, Largo; asst. prof. diagnostic radiology U. South Fla. Med. Sch., 1980—; asst. prof., dir. of med. student edn. in diagnostic radiology U. Tex., Galveston, 1988-91. Pres., founder Children's Advs., Inc., 1977-85; bd. dirs. Fla. Endowment for Humanities, 1979-83. Decorated Chevalier des Palmes Academiques Govt. of France, 1988. Mem. AMA, So. Med. Assn., L'Alliance Francaise of Tampa (bd. dirs. 1984—, pres. 1985-87), Fedn. Alliances Francaises U.S.A. (bd. dirs. 1987-89). Home: 661 Bering Dr Houston TX 77057-2137

TANRIKORUR, TULU M., computer programmer, systems analyst; b. Istanbul, Turkey; s. Burhan and Guner T.; m. Pinar Turek. BS in Computer Sci., Math., Columbus Coll., 1988; MBA in MIS, Mercer U., 1992. Programmer, analyst Total System Svcs. Inc., Columbus, Ga., 1988-89, Equifax Mktg. Svcs. Inc., Atlanta, 1989-90; sr. programmer, analyst AGS Info. Svcs., Inc., Atlanta, 1990-93; systems engr. Am. Software, Inc., Atlanta, 1993—. Mem. Assn. Sys. Mgmt. Home: 691 Foxcroft Cir Marietta GA 30067-5501

TANZER, JED SAMUEL, lawyer, financial consultant; b. Arverne, N.Y., Nov. 16, 1947; s. David and Mildred (Bondy) T.; m. Sally Jane Ketcham, July 10, 1971. BS with honors in Social Sci., SUNY, Oneonta, 1970; JD cum laude, Syracuse U., 1978, MBA, 1978. Tchr., union grievance chmn. Cen. Sch. Dist., Windsor, N.Y., 1970-75; rsch. asst. Sch. Mgmt., Syracuse (N.Y.) U., 1977-78; admitted to N.Y. State bar, 1979, Fed. Dist. Ct. bar, 1979, U.S. Tax Ct. bar, 1979; sr. atty. Ayco/Am. Express Corp., Albany, N.Y., 1978-82, assoc. regional mgr., 1982-85, v.p., regional mgr., 1986-92, regional v.p., 1988-91, v.p. counseling, 1992-93; fin. cons., 1978-93; v.p. Sanford Bernstein Co., 1993—. Permanent teaching cert. N.Y. State; bd. dirs. Cobb Youth Chorus Ga., 1988-93, treas., 1988-93. Mem. ABA (com. state and local taxation 1981-82), N.Y. State Bar Assn., Justinian Law Soc., Beta Gamma Sigma, Kappa Delta Pi. Home: 10853 Egret Pointe Ln West Palm Beach FL 33412-1539

TANZER, LESTER, editor; b. N.Y.C., Aug. 3, 1929; s. Charles and Clara (Ente) T.; m. Marlene June Luckton, June 29, 1949; children—Stephen Drew, Jeffrey Marc, Andrew Wayne, M. David. A.B., Columbia U., 1951, M.S., Sch. Journalism, 1952. Reporter, Washington bur. Wall St. Jour., 1952-59; assoc. editor Changing Times mag., Washington, 1959-64; assoc. editor U.S. News & World Report, Washington, 1964-76, mng. editor, 1976-85; editor Cosmos Jour., 1990-93. Author: (with Stefan Ilok) Brotherhood of Silence, 1962; editor: The Kennedy Circle, 1961. Mem. Nat. Symphony Assn. Club: Cosmos. Home: 4859 30th St N Arlington VA 22207-2715

TAPLEY, PHILIP ALLEN, English language and literature educator; b. Blackwell, Okla., June 11, 1938; s. Robert G. Sr. and Valena M. (Simmons) T.; m. Mary Stringer, Aug. 10, 1974; children: Mary Margaret, Laura Katherine. BA, U. North Tex., 1960, MA, 1962; PhD, La. State U., 1974. Cert. secondary tchr., Tex. Teaching asst. U. North Tex., Denton, 1960-61; teaching asst. La. State U., Baton Rouge, 1961-65, 68-69, instr., 1965-68; asst. prof. La. Coll., Pineville, 1969-74, assoc. prof., 1974-80, acting chmn. dept. English, journalism and langs., 1980, prof. dept. English, journalism and langs., 1980—; maj. scholar, presenter La. Endowment for the Humanities, Alexandria, 1977—; vis. cons. Ctrl. La. Electric Co., Pineville, 1989-95. Author: A History of First United Methodist, 1976, 2d edit., 1989, (with others) Procs. of the Red River Symposium, 1987, 2d edit., 1991, Issues and Indentities in Literature, 1996; contbr. articles to profl. jours. Pres., Friends of Rapides Libr., Alexandria,1985-86, bd. dirs., 1996—; bd. dirs. Arna Bontemps Mus., 1995—. Mellon Found. fellow, 1982, 88, Ford Found. fellow, 1989. Mem. AAUP, South Ctrl. MLA (program chair so. lit. 1979), La. Folklore Soc. (pres. 1978-79), Hist. Assn. Ctrl. La. (pres. 1978-80, bd. dirs. 1978—), Phi Kappa Phi, Alpha Chi, Sigma Tau Delta, Omicron Delta Kappa. Democrat. Episcopalian. Home: 1721 Polk St Alexandria LA 71301-6334 Office: La Coll English Dept 1140 College Dr Pineville LA 71359-0001

TAPPERT, TARA LEIGH, art historian, archivist, researcher; b. Detroit, Jan. 9, 1950; d. Herman Henry and Carol Louise (Zannoth) T.; m. Clarke Foster Dilks, Oct. 18, 1975 (div. Apr. 9, 1980). BA in History, Hope College, 1973; MSLS in Libr. and Archives Adminstrn., Wayne State U., 1976; PhD in Am. Civilization, George Washington U., 1990. Law libr. U.S. Dist. Ct. (ea. dist.), Detroit, 1973-77, Sullivan & Cromwell, Washington, 1977-83; editor Am. Studies Internat. George Washington U., Washington, 1983-85; curatorial asst., researcher Nat. Mus. Am. Art, Washington, 1987; curatorial asst. Nat. Portrait Gallery, Washington, 1988-90, guest curator, 1990-96; curator exhbns. and collections Roanoke (Va.) Mus. Fine Arts, 1990; guest curator Borghi & Co., N.Y.C., 1991-93; rsch. assoc. Am. Craft Mus., N.Y.C., 1992-96; pvt. practice Roanoke, Va., 1990—; libr. cons. Nat. Press Club Libr., Washington, 1984-85; fine arts bibliographer Nat. Trust Brit. Libr., Cambridge, Mass., 1985-86; fine arts cons. Pa. Acad. Fine Arts, Phila., 1987; curatorial researcher, writer Detroit Inst. Arts, 1995. Author: (exhbn. catalogue) The Emmets: A Generation of Gifted Women, 1993, (exhbn. catalogue) Craft in the Machine Age: 1920-45, 1995, (exhbn. catalogue) Cecilia Beaux and the Art of Portraiture, 1995. Archivist, editor Roanoke Network for Profl. and Managerial Women, Roanoke, Va., 1992-93; founder women's reading group, Roanoke, 1995. Libr. Congress fellow George Washington U., 1985-86, Smithsonian pre-doctoral fellow, 1986-87, Beverly R. Robinson doctoral fellow Winterthur Mus., 1988. Mem. Am. Assn. Mus., Am. Studies Assn. (student 1985-87), Assn. Ind. Historians of Art, Coll. Art Assn., Mid-Atlantic Archives Conf. (local arrangements 1991), Women's Caucus for Art. Democrat. Mem. Soc. of Friends. Home and Office: 2408 Longview Ave SW #3-B Roanoke VA 24014

TARBOX, GURDON LUCIUS, JR., retired museum executive; b. Plainfield, N.J., Dec. 25, 1927; s. Gurdon Lucius and Lillie (Hodgson) T.; BS, Mich. State U., 1952; MS, Purdue U., 1954, D Pub. Svc. U. S.C., 1993; m. Milver Ann Johnson, Sept. 25, 1952; children—Janet Ellen LeGrand, Joyce Elaine Schumacher, Paul Edward, Lucia Ann. Asst. dir. Brookgreen Gardens, Murrells Inlet, S.C., 1954-59, trustee, 1959—, dir., 1963-94, pres., 1990—. Chmn. Georgetown County Mental Health Commn., 1964-66; mem. exec. council Confedn. S.C. Local Hist. Socs., 1976—; trustee S.C. Hall Fame, 1976—, S.C. Heritage Trust, 1981-86, S.C. Mansion Commn., 1986—. Served with AUS, 1946-48. Recipient Francis K. Hutchinson medal for svc. to conservation The Garden Club of Am., 1995. Mem. Soc. Am. Foresters, Am. Assn. Bot. Gardens and Arboreta (dir. 1971-74, sec.-treas. 1982, v.p. 1983, pres. 1985-86), Georgetown County Hist. Soc. (pres. 1970-74), Am., Royal hort. socs., Am. Assn. Mus. (council 1983), Southeastern Mus. Conf. (dir. 1977-80), S.C. Fedn. Museums (pres. 1974-76), Am. Assn. State and Local History, S.C. Confedn. Local Hist. Socs. Episcopalian. Lodge: Rotary (pres. 1979-80). Home: 641 Crooked Oak Dr Pawleys Island SC 29585

TARDONA, DANIEL RICHARD, ethologist, naturalist, writer, park ranger, educator; b. Bklyn., Nov. 9, 1953; s. Felix Carmine and Patricia Ann (Tynan) T.; m. Jayne Hardwick, Apr. 28, 1990. BA, Monmouth Coll., 1976; MA, Cen. Mich. U., 1981. Cert. sch. psychologist, N.J. Pediat. psychologist Montclair (N.J.) State Coll., 1982-83; radiation/hazardous substances safety asst. Cytogen Corp., Princeton, N.J., 1984-85; park naturalist Frozen Head State Natural Area, Wartburg, Tenn., 1986; park ranger Cape Hatteras Nat. Seashore, Manteo, N.C., 1987; park ranger Great Smoky Mtns. Nat. Pk., Gatlinburg, Tenn., 1987-90, asst. dist. supr., 1990-92; west dist. supr. Timucuan Ecological and Hist. Preserve, Jacksonville, Fla., 1992—. Mem. editorial review bd. Infant Mental Health Jour., 1982-85; guest reviewer Edn. and Treatment of Children, 1980, 81; contbr. articles to profl. jours. Mem. Am. Littoral Soc., 1992—, Fla. Audubon Soc., 1992—. Recipient Trustees scholar Rider Coll., 1983-84. Mem. Soc. for Conservation Biology, Animal Behavior Soc., Internat. Soc. Behavioral Ecology, Fauna and Flora Preservation Soc., Am. Ornithologists Union, Nat. Assn. Underwater Instrs. (openwater I scuba diver), Sigma Gamma Epsilon, Phi Delta Kappa, Psi Chi. Home and Office: Timucuan Ecol and Hist Preserve 12713 Fort Caroline Rd Jacksonville FL 32225-1240

TARLETON, BENNETT, arts administrator; b. Wadesboro, N.C., Apr. 9, 1943; s. Claude Bennett and Frances Brama (Covington) T.; m. Victoria Jane Smith, Jan. 29, 1977; children: Catherine Victoria, William Wiley. BA in English Honors, U. Mo., 1965; MA in Teaching, Harvard U., 1966; postgrad. U. Mo., 1969-71. Secondary English tchr. Great Neck Schs., N.Y., 1966-69; adminstrv. asst. U. Mo., Columbia, 1969-71; curriculum developer, coord. CEMREL, Inc., St. Louis, 1971-76; coordinator Nat. Aesthetic Edn. Learning Ctr., Kennedy Ctr., Washington, 1976-79; dir. Alliance for Arts Edn., Kennedy Ctr., Washington, 1979-82; exec. dir. Dance St. Louis, 1982-83, Tenn. Arts Commn., Nashville, 1984—; panelist NEA; arts edn. cons. U. Mich., Nat. Inventory Conf. on Learning Resources Related to East Asia, Very Spl. Arts, U. Va. Sch. Edn., Fla. Dept. State; arts cons. NEA, Young Audiences, Mo. Arts Council, Mississippi River Festival, Am. Film Festival, St. Louis Art Mus., Washington U. Film Arts Soc.; host Tenn. Arts, Sta. WDCN-TV; bd. dirs. The Children's House, 1988-90, Nat. Assembly of State Arts Agys. 1985-87, So. Arts Fedn., 1984—, Assn. Performing Arts Presenters, 1994—; chmn. So. Arts Fedn., 1992-94. Contbr. film reviews and criticism to profl. jours. Editor newsletter Alliance for Arts Education, 1980-82. Contbr. to Sta. KWMU-FM and Sta. WPLN-FM radio. Episcopalian. Club: Harvard (N.Y.C.). Home: 1405 Hampshire Pl Nashville TN 37221-3624 Office: Tenn Arts Commn 401 Charlotte Ave Nashville TN 37243-0780

TARLETON, HAROLD VERNON, editor; b. Wadesboro, N.C., Mar. 2, 1949; s. Harold Wilson and Martha Elizabeth (Roberson) T.; m. Virginia Kendall Witherington, Apr. 23, 1971; children: Tracy, Emilia, Adam. BA, U. N.C., 1971. Summer intern The Anson Record, Wadesboro, N.C., 1968, The Charlotte (N.C.) Observer, 1970; editor The Hamlet (N.C.) News, 1975-77, The Danville (Va.) Register, 1977-79; mng. editor The Wilson (N.C.) Daily Times, 1980-87, editor, 1987—; adj. lectr. Atlantic Christian Coll., Wilson, N.C., 1984-89; news analyst WUNC-TV, Research Triangle Pk., N.C., 1989-94; adj. instr. Barton Coll., Wilson, N.C., 1996; mem. pubs. bd. N.C. Synod Luth. Ch. in Am., Salisbury, 1986-88. Chmn. chpt. ARC, 1993-94. Lt. j.g. U.S. Coast Guard, 1972-75. Mem. N.C. Assoc. Press News Coun. (pres. 1991), N.C. Editl. Writers (pres. 1996—). Office: The Wilson Daily Times 2001 Downing St Wilson NC 27894

TARLETON, JESSE S., business educator; b. Upper Darby, Pa., Nov. 1, 1928; s. Leslie Sauren and Jessie Dorothy (Sommers) T.; m. Lavonne Catherine Olson, June 25, 1955; children: Lesley C., David T. BS in Chem. Engring., Pa. State U., 1952; PhD in Chem. Engring., Cornell U., 1958; MBA, Coll. William and Mary, 1970; postgrad., Am. Grad. Sch. Internat. Mgmt., (Thunderbird), 1974. Cert. planning commr., Va. Teaching asst. Sch. Chem. Engring. Cornell U., Ithaca, N.Y., 1952-53, 55-57; rsch. engr. E.I. duPont de Nemours, Wilmington, Del., 1957-59; various positions in prodn. and engring. to sr. engr. Dow Badische Co. formerly Dow Chem. Co., Williamsburg, Va., 1959-70; from asst. prof. to prof. bus. adminstrn. Coll. William and Mary, Williamsburg, Va., 1970—; spkr. in field. Contbr. chpts. to books, articles to profl. jours. City of Williamsburg rep. Richmond Rd. Transp. Study Group, 1992-94, Regional Issues Com., 1991-95; mem. City of Williamsburg Beautification Adv. Com., 1987-91; mem. City of Williamsburg Planning Commn., 1987-95; vice chair, 1994; mem. City of Williamsburg Indsl. Devel. Authority, 1996—. Standard Oil of Ind. fellow, 1953-55. Mem. AIChE, Acad. of Mgmt., Acad. Internat. Bus., Decision Scis. Inst., Am. Prodn. and Inventory Control Soc., James River Assn., Nat. Ry. Hist. Soc., Coalition for Quality Growth, Kiwanis Club of Williamsburg (sec. 1965-74, dir., com. chmn.), Colonial Road Runners, Phi Kappa Phi, Tau Beta Pi, Sigma Tau, Phi Lambda Upsilon Alpha Chi Sigma. Office: Coll William and Mary 314 Tyler Hall Williamsburg VA 23187

TARPLEY, JAMES DOUGLAS, journalism educator, magazine editor; b. Los Angeles, May 2, 1946; Cert. tchr., Mo. BS in Edn., SW Mo. U., 1968, MA in English, 1972; MA in Mass Comm., Cen. Mo. U., 1976; PhD in Journalism, So. Ill. U., 1983. Prof. journalism Evangel Coll., Springfield, Mo., 1976-87; chmn. Sch. of Journalism Regent U. (formerly Christian Broadcasting Network U.), Virginia Beach, Va., 1987—; guest lectr. Cen. Mo. U., S.W. Mo. U., So. Ill. U., U. Ohio summer journalism workshops, 1976—. Youth page editor Eldon Advertiser, 1972-76, mng. editor Home Free, 1988-90, High Adventure, 1983-87, Criminal Justice Management, 1978-81, editor Ranger News, 1979-81, design and layout editor Vision Mag., 1984-87; free-lance writer, contbr. biog. entries to profl. publs.; free-lance photographer; graphic artist, copywriter Disco-Fair advt. dept., 1964-68. Exec. com. Eldon PTA, 1971-74; youth dir. Eldon Assembly of God, 1968-75; Sunday sch. supt. Cen. Assembly of God, Springfield, Mo., 1978-82; mem. Sch. Effectiveness Evaluation Team Springfield Pub. Schs., 1985-86, 86-87. Recipient Mo. Journalism Tchr. Yr. award, 1976, Cert. of Merit Columbia U., 1984, Gold Medal of Merit Columbia U. Scholastic Press Assn., 1984; named Outstanding Grad., Dept. Mass Communication Cen. Mo. U. 1976; fellow U. Pa. and Freedom Found. project on press freedom, 1984, Nat. Newspaper Fund Fellow Dow Jones and U. Mo., 1975; named fellow of Scripps-Howard CCCU Washington D.C. Capstone proj., 1995. Mem. Assn. Christian Collegiate Media (nat. exec. dir. 1995—), Coll. Media Advisers (bd. dirs., chmn. various coms., pres. citation 1981, 84-89), Soc. Coll. Journalists (pres. 1992—, exec. dir. 1983-92, pres. citation 1981, 85, 87, 90), Assn. Christian Collegiate Media (exec. dir. 1995—), Assn. Edn. in Journalism and Mass Comm., Nat. Conf. Editl. Writers (com. scholarly rsch. 1985), Soc. Newspaper Design (edn. com. 1986-88), Broadcast Edn. Assn. (intern. com. 1984), Assn. Journalism Historials, Inst. Cert. Photographers, Mo. Tchrs. Assn., Evang. Press Assn., Pi Delta Kappa. Republican. Lodge: Kiwanis.

TART, DAVID EARL, dermatologist; b. Fayetteville, N.C., Oct. 22, 1948; s. Parlie D. and Evadine (Barefoot) T.; m. Patricia Diane Melvin, May 31, 1969; 1 child, Kimberly. AB in Chemistry, U. N.C., 1970, MD with honors, 1974. Diplomate Am. Bd. Dermatology, Am. Bd. Internal Medicine. Dermatologist Catawba Dermatology Assocs., Hickory, N.C., 1978—; chief of staff Frye Regional Med. Ctr., Hickory, 1994, bd. dirs.; assoc. clin. prof. U. N.C. Sch. Medicine, Chapel Hill, 1978-94. Bd. dirs., past pres. Am. Cancer Soc., Hickory, 1988—. Recipient Roche award U. N.C. Med. Sch., 1974. Fellow Am. Acad. Dermatology, Am. Coll. Cryo Surgery, Am. Soc. Dermatol. Surgery; mem. N.C. State Med. Soc. (del. 1987-93), N.C. Dermatology Assn. (pres. 1996), Catawba County Med. Soc. (pres. 1986). Office: Catawba Dermatology Assocs 220 18th Street Cir SE Hickory NC 28602-1361

TARTT, BLAKE, lawyer; b. Houston, Mar. 16, 1929; s. Herbert Blake and Bernice (Schwalm) T.; m. Barbara Jean Moore, Jan. 30, 1960; children: Blake III, Courtnay Elias. B.B.A., So. Methodist U., 1949, J.D. cum laude, 1959. Bar: Tex. 1959. Assoc. Fulbright & Jaworski, Houston, 1959-70; ptnr. Fulbright & Jaworski, 1970—; mem. Tex. Commn. on Jud. Conduct, 1996—. Bd. dirs. Mus. Fine Arts, Houston. Served to 1st lt. USAF, 1951-55, Korea. Decorated Air medal. Fellow Am. Bar Found. (chmn. fellows 1987), Tex. Bar Found. (chmn. bd. 1974-75, chmn. fellows 1978-79), Am. Coll. Trial Lawyers; mem. ABA (ho. of dels. 1976-81, 84, state del. 1990-93), Am. Bd. Trial Advocates (advocate), Houston Bar Found. (chmn., bd. dirs. 1992), Fed. Bar Assn., Internat. Assn. Def. Counsel, Am. Judicature Soc. (bd. dirs. 1984-88), So. Conf. Bar Pres. (pres. 1984), State Bar Tex. (dir. 1972-75, exec. com. 1975-76, pres. elect 1982-83, pres. 1983-84), Houston Bar Assn., Dallas Bar Assn., Am. Law Inst., Tex. Jud. Council, Citizens Commn. on the Tex. Judiciary, Houston Philosophical Soc., Coronado Club, Forest Club, Houston Club, Argyle Club (San Antonio), Reform Club (London), Delta Theta Phi, Alpha Tau Omega. Episcopalian. Office: Fulbright & Jaworski 1301 Mckinney St Houston TX 77010

TARVER, JOHN REED, historian; b. Natchitoches, La., Jan. 30, 1932; s. George F. and Lena Vivian (Dowden) T.; m. Annis Dowden, Sept. 18, 1959; children: John Mark, Annis Elizabeth. BA, La. State U., 1959; MA, Northwest State U., 1979; PhD, La. State U., 1985. Historia Ag Ctr. La. State U., Baton Rouge, 1979—. Editor: Dairy Science Research, 1984, Plantations Around the World, 1984, One World, One Institution, 1986, The Rice World, 1994, Plant Variety Development in Louisiana, 1995, An African Odessy, 1996, Louisiana Agriculture Mag., 1985—. Home: PO Box 20001 Baton Rouge LA 70894

TARVIN, ALBERT LEON, writer; b. Atlanta, Nov. 27, 1929; s. Wilter Cicel and Sara Alice (Westbrooks) T.; children: Valerie Susan Tarvin-Kibler, William Clay, William Walter; m. Christle Jean Holzman, July 6, 1991. BS, Utah State U., 1966; MS in Secondary Edn., U. So. Calif., 1969; MS in Pers. Mgmt., Troy State U., Montgomery, Ala., 1980; MS in Nat. Studies, Air War Coll., Montgomery, 1974. Enlisted USAF, 1948, advanced through grades to col.; comdr. 1956th Comm. Group USAF, Yokota AB, Japan, 1974-78; retired USAF, 1978; headmaster Lowndes Acad., Hanyeville, Ala., 1978-80; field engr. Westinghouse Electric Corp., Balt., 1980-90; instr. Bauder Coll., Ft. Lauderdale, Fla., 1984-91; tax cons. Gulf Breeze, Fla., 1988—; author, freelance writer, Gulf Breeze, 1984—. Author: Chelsea, Chelsea, 1994, 2d printing 1996, Chelsea, The Final Chapter, 1995, Twenty-One Divorcees, 1995, Run, Chelsea, Run, 1996, Till Death Do Us Part, 1996; writer Santa Rosa Sun, 1993-94. Decorated Legion of Merit. Mem. West Fla. Literary Fedn. Inc. (treas. 1992-94). Republican. Methodist. Home and Office: 6020 Mayberry Ln Milton FL 32570-8875

TASHIRO, PAUL YUKIO, Assyriology educator; b. Tokyo, Sept. 21, 1933; came to U.S., 1969; s. Ushitaro and Ko (Maeshima) T.; m. Eiko Kurata, Apr. 7, 1963; 1 child, Naomu Charles. BA in Philosophy summa cum laude, Oglethorpe U., 1972; MDiv in Pastoral Ministries, Asbury Theol. Sem., 1975; PhM Hebrew Bible-Ancient Near Ea Studies, Hebrew Union Coll., 1987, PhD, 1989. Ordained to ministry, Meth. Ch., 1975. Lectr. religion and philosophy Lindsey Wilson Coll., Columbia, Ky., 1987-89, assoc. prof. religion, 1989-90, prof. religion, 1990-91; assoc. prof. old testament and bibl. langs. Wesley Bibl. Sem., Jackson, Miss., 1991—; internat. mktg. cons., Corydon, Ky., 1985—; dir. internat. mktg. dept. Am. Indsl. Corp., Lawrence, Ind., 1987—; treas. GKK Automotive, Ltd., Farmington Hills, Mich., 1989—; lectr. Louisville, 1975—. Co-author: A Christian Beliefs Primer, 1989, Words of Faith, 1990. Julius and Hildegard Lewy fellowship, 1979-81, Ilse Hitchman fellowship, 1983-86, S.H. and H.R. Scheuer fellowship, 1980-81, Rose Skillman Interfaith fellowship, 1986-89. Mem. AAUP, Wesleyan Theol. Soc., Am. Oriental Soc., Am. Acad. Religion (midwest div. 1978—), Nat. Assn. of Profs. of Hebrew, Evang. Theol. Soc. (Deep South region 1991—), Inst. for Bibl. Rsch., Theta Phi. Republican. Home: 6007 Lake Trace Cir Jackson MS 39211-2804

TATE, CAROLYN E., art historian; b. Heidelberg, Germany, Sept. 21, 1952; d. Willie Lee and Eve (Kraft) T. BA, U. Tex., 1974, BFA, 1974, MA, 1980, PhD, 1986. Instr. Calif. State U., Northridge, 1982; vis. prof. Pre-Columbian UCLA, 1986, U. Iowa, Iowa City, 1987; assoc. curator Pre-Columbian Dallas Mus. Art, 1987-93; pres. New World Travel, Dallas, 1993; asst. prof. art history Tex. Tech. U., Lubbock, 1993—. Author: Yaxchilan: Design of a Maya Ceremonial City, 1992; writer, actor (video) Art of Ancient Americas, 1992; curator (exhbns.) Dallas Mus. Art, 1992, M.C. Carlos Mus., Atlanta, 1993, Royal Ont. Mus., 1994, Art. Mus., Princeton U., 1996, Houston Mus. Fine Arts, 1996. Grantee Fulbright-Hays, 1984-85, NEH, 1990, Getty Found., 1991, 92. Mem. Coll. Art Assn. Office: Tex Tech U Dept Art PO Box 42081 Lubbock TX 79409-2081

TATE, CURTIS E., management educator; b. Trezvant, Tenn., July 5, 1920; s. Curtis E. and Mary Kathryn (Haskins) T.; m. Evelyn Ruth Mann, Apr. 12, 1945 (div. May, 1969); m. Mary Jim Combs, Aug. 28, 1977; children: Curtis Emory, Milton Oglesby. Student, N. Ga. Coll., 1943-44, U. Ga., 1945-46; AB, Bethel Coll., 1946; MS, U. Tenn., 1952. Clk. Family Gen. Grocery, Trezevant, Tenn., 1938-42; clk. purchasing dept. P&G Defense Corp., Milan, Twnn., 1942; plant mgr. Keathley Pie Co., Memphis, 1946-50; instr. Furman U., Greenville, S.C., 1952-53; bus. mgr. Lander Coll., Greenwood, S.C., 1953-56; from asst. to assoc. prof. Coll. of Bus. Adminstrn. U. Ga., Athens, 1956-92; prof. emeritus Terry Coll. of Bus. U. Ga., Athens, 1991—; bd. dirs. Flexible Products, Inc., Marietta, Ga., 1968-76, Case Pub. Corp.; asst. dean fund raising, 1991—. Co-author: Successful Small Business Management, 1975, latest rev. edit., 1985, Complete Guide to Your Own Business, 1977, Dow-Jones-Irwin Business Papers, 1977, Bus. Policy: Administrative, Strategic and Constitigency Issues, 1983, 92, Managing for Profits, 1984, Small Business Management and Entrepreneurship, 1992; mem. adv. bd. Am. Jour. Case Rsch. With U.S. Army, 1942-45, ETO. Fellow N. Am. Case Rsch. Assn. (sec., v.p., bd. dirs., pres. so. casewriters, Outstandinc Case Contbr. 1992), Acad. Mgmt., Kiwanis, Sigma Iota Epsilon, Beta Gamma Sigma. Home and Office: 1640 Broadlands Dr Watkinsville GA 30677-2148

TATE, GAYLE BLAIR, art dealer, artist; b. Abilene, Tex., Apr. 3, 1944; s. Robert Warren and Rowena (Preston) T.; m. Hephzibah Meegaaoh, Jan. 12, 1970; children: Jai-Sua Robert, Stanley Myles, Song-Win Melissa. Student, U. Wyo.; BS, Fla. State U., 1967. Lic. auctioneer, N.C. Pres. Tate Galleries, Tallahassee-Tampa, Fla., 1972-83, Interarts, Inc., Tallahassee-Tampa, 1973-83, G.B. Tate & Sons, Black Mountain, N.C., 1986—. Exhibited in shows at Ken Allen Fine Art, Hendersonville, N.C., 1984-94, Beltexsan Galleries, Ft. Worth, 1992, Creighton Davis Galleries, Washington, 1993-94, Christie's, N.Y., Sotheby's, N.Y. Capt. USAF, 1967-72. Recipient 1st pl., 2d pl. and 3d pl. awards, Best of Show award Spring Show, Charlotte, N.C., 1992. Mem. S.E. Profl. Art Dealers Assn. (pres. 1980-83), The Seven Alliance (founder, pres. 1992—), Alpha Kappa Lambda. Home: PO Box 333 Black Mountain NC 28711-0333 Studio: 28 Hendersonville Rd Asheville NC 28803-2641

TATE, J. KENNETH, real estate executive; b. Miami Beach, Fla., Mar. 6, 1952; s. Stanley G. and Joanne M. (Greenwood) T.; m. Sandra L. Rolter, June 11, 1977; children: Jennifer, Stefanie, Jaclyn. B of Engring. cum laude, Vanderbilt U., 1974; MBA in Fin., Duke U., 1976. Cert. gen. contractor, Fla.; cert. community assn. mgr., Fla. Corp. banking officer S.E. Bank, 1976; v.p. Stanley Tate Builders, Inc., 1977—, High Point Delray Builders, Inc., 1977—, High Point Golf Course, Inc., 1982—, Tate Devel. Corp., 1986—; COO, receiver Property Mgmt. Owned Properties and Non-Owned Properties, 1986—; mem. Constrn. Industry Licensing Bd., State of Fla., 1990—. Mem. bd. advisors univ. sch. Nova U., 1991—. Mem. Nat. Assn. Home Builders, Builders Assn. South Fla. (bd. dirs. 1991—). Office: Tate Devel Corp 1175 NE 125th St Ste 102 North Miami FL 33161-5009

TATE, MANLEY SIDNEY, real estate broker; b. Victoria, Mich., July 30, 1919; s. John J. and Mary Magdalene (Klee) T.; m. Verna Louise Manier, Aug. 25, 1940 (dec. May 1985); 1 child, Manley A. BS, Ferris State U., 1939. Lic. real estate broker. Spl. rep. Standard Oil. Co. Ind., Saginaw, Mich., 1946-56, mgr. sales, 1956-57; mgr. regional merchandise Standard Oil. Co. Ind., Detroit, 1957-60; mgr. sales promotion Standard Oil. Co. Ind., Indpls., 1960-62; dist. mgr. Standard Oil. Co. Ind., Ft. Wayne, Ind., 1963-66; pvt. practice realty, appraiser Pompano Beach, Fla., 1967-80, Sarasota, Fla., 1980—; com. chmn. Pompano Beach Bd. Realtors, 1976, 78; lectr. Butler U., Indpls., 1962. Author: (play) What's In It For Me, 1960, (book) Marketing in Real Estate, 1978; contbr. articles to profl. jours. Served with USN, USN, 1944-46, PTO. Mem. Nat. Assn. Realtors, Fla. Assn. Realtors, Sarasota Bd.

Realtors, Sarasota C. of C., VFW. Democrat. Congregationalist. Clubs: Orchard Ridge Country (Ft. Wayne); Sunrise Country. Lodge: Masons. Office: PO Box 3845 Sarasota FL 34230-3845

TATE, RICHARD ALBERT, marketing research consultant; b. Athens, Mar. 1, 1951; s. Albert Mathis and Ina Mae (Bulloch) T.; m. Martha Russell Foster, Jan. 7, 1948; children: Katherine Olvia, Ashley Elizabeth, Erin Nicole. BS magna cum laude, U. Ga., 1973, MEd, 1974, PhD in Econ. Geography, 1980. Project mgr. USDA So. Piedmont Rsch. Ctr., Watkinsville, Ga., 1976-78, Harland Bartholomew & Assocs., Inc., Memphis, Tenn., 1978-82; mktg. rsch. analyst Ga. Power Co., Atlanta, 1982-86; v.p. Vanderveer Group, Inc., Atlanta, 1986-87; group mgr. Ga. Inst. Tech., Atlanta, 1987-91; divsn. mgr. mktg. rsch. svcs. A&C Enercom, Atlanta, 1991-94; pres. Guideline Rsch./Atlanta, Inc., Duluth, Ga., 1994—. Contbr. articles to profl. jours. Mem. Am. Mktg. Assn., Am. Planning Assn., Tech. Transfer Soc., Phi Kappa Phi, Kappa Delta Pi. Episcopalian. Home: 3297 Rememberance Ter Lawrenceville GA 30244-4815 Office: Guideline Rsch/ Atlanta Inc 3675 Crestwood Pky NW Ste 520 Duluth GA 30136-5054

TATE, SHARON SUE, special events and catering executive; b. Gainesville, Tex., Sept. 21, 1949; d. Lucien Harvey and Ollie Pauline (Insel) T. AA, Cooke County Coll., 1972; postgrad., U. North Tex., 1973-74, So. Meth. U., 1984. Credit collections cons. J.C. Penney, Dallas, 1978-80; exec. v.p. Orville McDonald Assocs., Dallas, 1980-86; conf. coord. Plaza Ams. Hotel, Dallas, 1986-92; spl. events and catering mgr. dani' Foods at the Dallas Mus. Art, 1992-95; pres. Orville McDonald Assocs., Dallas, 1995—. Republican. Home: 8780 Park Ln Apt 1017 Dallas TX 75231-5504 Office: Orville McDonald Assocs PO Box 823185 Dallas TX 75382-3185

TATE, STONEWALL SHEPHERD, lawyer; b. Memphis, Dec. 19, 1917; m. Janet Graf; children: Adele Shepherd, Shepherd Davis, Janet Reid Walker. BA, Southwestern at Memphis (now Rhodes Coll.), 1939; JD, U. Va., 1942; LLD (hon.), Samford U., 1979, Suffolk U., 1982, Capital U., 1989, Rhodes Coll., 1993. Bar: Va. 1941, Tenn. 1942. Mem. Martin, Tate, Morrow & Marston, P.C. (and predecessor firms), Memphis, 1947—; chmn. pres.'s coun. Rhodes Coll., 1995-96. trustee Rhodes Coll., 1967-77, 1980-84, sec. bd. trustees, 1969-77, 1980-84; pres. Episcopal Churchmen of Tenn., 1961-62; sec. standing com. Episcopal Diocese of Tenn., 1969-71; pres. Chickasaw Coun. Boy Scouts Am., 1967-78. With USNR, 1942-46; comdr. USNR; ret. Decorated Order of Cloud Banner (China); recipient Silver Beaver award Boy Scouts Am., 1963, Disting. Eagle Scout award, 1980, Disting. Svc. medal Rhodes Coll., 1978, Disting. Alumni award, 1991, Lawyers' Lawyer award Memphis Bar Assn., 1990; Memphis Rotary Club Civic Recognition award, 1983; Paul Harris fellow, 1985. Fellow Am. Bar Found., Am. Coll. Trust and Estate Counsel, Internat. Acad. Estate and Trust Law, Coll. Law Practice Mgmt. (hon.), Tenn. Bar Found., Memphis and Shelby County Bar Found.; mem. ABA (chmn. standing com. on profl. discipline 1973-76, chmn. standing com. on scope and correlation of work 1977, chmn. task force on lawyer advt. 1977, pres. ABA 1978-79, chmn. standing com. on lawyer competence 1986-96), Am. Judicature Soc. (past bd. dirs.), Am. Law Inst., Am. Arbitration Assn. (large complex case panel 1993—), Lawyer-Pilots Bar Assn., Tenn. Bar Assn. (pres. 1963-64), Memphis and Shelby County Bar Assn. (pres. 1959-60), Nat. Conf. Bar Pres. (pres. 1972-73), U.S. 6th Cir. Jud. Conf. (life), U. Va. Law Sch. Alumni Assn. (mem. exec. coun. 1974-77), Rhodes Coll. Alumni Assn. (pres. 1951-53), Order of Coif, Raven Soc., Rotary (pres. 1982-83, bd. dirs. 1974, 80-84, 89-90), Phi Beta Kappa, Omicron Delta Kappa, Phi Delta Phi, Sigma Alpha Epsilon (highest effort award N.Y.C. Alumni Assn. 1979). Office: Martin Tate Morrow & Marston PC Falls Bldg 22 N Front St Ste 1100 Memphis TN 38103-2109

TATE-JACKSON, PATRICIA, fundraiser; b. Marvell, Ark., Dec. 23, 1951; d. Oliver and Ozella (Donald) Scaife; m. John M. Tate Jr., June 3, 1971 (div. Apr. 1978); 1 child, Stacy Nicole Tate; m. Charles Edward Jackson, Dec. 31, 1981 (div. Aug. 1989); 1 child, Charles Edward Jackson Jr. BS in Acctg., U. Ark., Pine Bluff, 1981; postgrad., Ark. State U., U. Mo., St. Louis, U. Md. Sec. II U. Ark., Pine Bluff, 1978-79, adminstrv. asst., 1979-82, adminstrv. asst. I Office of Instnl. Advancement, 1982-85, program coord. Office of Instnl. Advancement, 1985-87, program coord., mgmt. project analyst Office Devel. U. Rels., 1987-92, dir. ann. fund dr. Office Devel. U. Rels., 1992-95; dir. devel. and u. rels., 1995—; clk. typist Resource Mgmt. Office U.S. Mil., Munich, 1977-78; clk. Ark. State U., Jonesboro, 1970-71; clk. typist Office Econ. Opportunity, Helena, Ark., 1971, Recreation Svc. Agy., Worms, Germany, 1972-74; clk. II U. Mo., St. Louis, 1975-76; nurse's aide Vets. Hosp. Ft. Roots, North Little Rock, Ark., 1970; mem. Title III Internal Evaluation Team, 1991-93; cons.-treas. U. Ark., Pine Bluff/Agrl., Mech. & Normal Alumni Bldg. Fund; co-advisor Ebony Queen Soc., U. Ark., Pine Bluff, 1979-80. Pres. Women's Missionary Soc., St. Bethel Bapt. Ch., 1990-95; asst. Sunday sch. instr., choir mem., youth counselor; campaign worker Sen. Jean C. Edwards, State Rep. Josetta Wilkins; past pres. Young Matrons Group, St. Bethel Bapt. Ch., past v.p. pastor's aide club; bd. dirs. Pine Bluff Comty. Concert Assn., 1992-96, sec., 1993-94; bd. dirs. cen. coun. PTA Pine Bluff Sch. Dist., 1994-95, treas., 1993-94, auditor, 1992-93; mem. Pine Bluff Planning Commn., 1995—; chair publicity/ad souvenir book Art Ctr., Pine Bluff, 1994; co-chairperson Ann. Chancellor's Benefit for Arts, 1989—, chair publicity/promotion sub-com.; chairperson logistic com. Nat. Heart Assn., 1991, participant phonathon, 1990; treas. Coll. Industry Cluster UAPB, 1990—, coord. Wiley Branton Civil Liberties Found., 1990—; active Leadership Pine Bluff; bd. dirs. Cornerstone, 1996—. Mem. Agrl., Mech. & Normal/U. Ark. Nat. Alumni Assn. (Jefferson County chpt.), Pine Bluff C. of C. (all civic night feasibility com. 1993-94), Nat. Assn. Fundraising Execs. (capt. recruitment team 1993—). Home: 2701 Avondale Dr Pine Bluff AR 71601-5500 Office: U Ark PO Box X 4067 Pine Bluff AR 71601

TATERA, JAMES FRANK, chemist, process analysis specialist; b. Milw., June 27, 1946; s. Harry Frank and Agnes Rose (Szymanowski) T.; m. Kaaren Marie Piekarski, Sept. 9, 1972; children: Patrick, Monica, David. BS in Chemistry, Math., U. Wis., Oshkosh, 1968; postgrad., U. Minn., 1968, 71-73; MBA, Cen. Mich. U., 1982. Cert. specialist in analytical tech. Teaching rsch. assoc. chemistry dept. U. Minn., Mpls., 1968, 71-73; analytical chemist Dow Corning Corp., Midland, Mich., 1973-76, scale up engr. new products commercialization, 1976-78, prodn. bldg. supt. prodn. dept., 1978-80; analytical systems specialist project and plant engring. Dow Corning Ltd., Barry, Wales, 1981-84; analytical systems supr. plant engring. & maintenance Dow Corning Corp., Carrollton, Ky., 1984-85, analytical systems specialist plant engring. and maintenance, 1985-87, sr. analytical and control specialist project engring., 1988-90, sr. analytical systems specialist strategic change program, 1991—; session developer, panelist, presenter in field; U.S. nat. com. Internat. Electrotech. Commn., Paris, 1993, Milan, 1994, Montreal, 1996, U.S. nat. com. tech. advisor subcom. 65D, 1993—. Contbr. articles to profl. jours. 1st lt. arty. U.S. Army, 1969-71. Decorated Bronze Star, Bronze Star with oak leaf cluster. Mem. Am. Chem. Soc. (rep. Vol. in Pub. Outreach program), Instrument Soc. Am. (dir.-elect analysis divsn. 1994—, chmn. SP 76 stds. com. 1991—, pres. N.E. Mich. sect. 1979-80, various sect. offices 1976-79), Air and Waste Mgmt. Assn. (optical sensing divsn. indsl. issues and applications com. on enhanced monitoring), Elks, Am. Legion, VFW, KC, Delta Sigma Phi, Phi Lambda Upsilon, Sigma Iota Epsilon. Roman Catholic. Home: 2038 Ridgewood Dr Madison IN 47250-2729 Office: Dow Corning Corp 4770 Hwy 42 E Mail Stop 32 Carrollton KY 41008

TATHAM, JULIE CAMPBELL, writer; b. N.Y.C., June 1, 1908; d. Archibald and Julia deFres (Sample) Campbell; student pvt. schs., N.Y.C.; m. Charles Tatham, Mar. 30, 1933; children—Charles III, Campbell. Author more than 30 juvenile books including: The Mongrel of Merryway Farm, 1952; The World Book of Dogs, 1953; To Nick from Jan, 1957; author Trixie Belden series, 1946—, Ginny Gordon series, 1946—; co-author Cherry Ames and Vicki Barr series, 1947—; author: The Old Testament Made Easy, 1985; many series books transl. into fgn. langs.; contbr. numerous mag. stories and articles to popular publs., 1935—; free-lance writer, 1935—; contbr. numerous articles to Christian Sci. publs., including Christian Sci. Monitor, 1960—. Address: 1202 S Washington St Apt 814 Alexandria VA 22314-4446

TATHAM, ROBERT HAINES, geophysicist; b. Merced, Calif., Dec. 10, 1943; s. Robert and Dorothy (Fitzgerald) T.; m. Henna E. Solomin, Aug. 29, 1970; children: Sarah, Rachel, Benjamin. BS in Physics, Calif. State U.-Northridge, 1967; MS in Applied Geophysics, U. Houston, 1970; PhD in Geophysics, Columbia U., 1975. Geophysicist, Texaco, Inc., Houston, 1967-71; spl. projects geophysicist, 1975-81; rsch. geophysicist Geosource, Houston, 1981-86; mgr. geophys. rsch. Texaco Inc., Houston, 1986—; adj. prof. U. Houston, 1988—. Contbr., instr. industry Continuing Edn. Ctr., Houston. Co-author: Multicomponent Seismology in Petroleum Exploration; contbr. articles to tech. jours. and books. Mem. IEEE, Soc. Exploration Geophysicists, European Assn. Exploration Geophysicists, Am. Assn. Petroleum Geologists, Am. Geophys. Union, Seismol. Soc. Am., Geophys. Soc. Houston (1st v.p.). Democrat. Jewish. Avocation: gardening. Home: 4526 Park Ct Bellaire TX 77401-3714 Office: Texaco Inc 3901 Briarpark Dr Houston TX 77042-5301

TATKON-COKER, ANDREA LAURA, nurse, business consultant; b. Queens, N.Y., Aug. 10, 1954; d. Marvin Daniel Tatkon and Marcha Prottas Flint; m. James E. Tatkon Coker, Aug. 27, 1982; children: Jonathan Louis, Sophia Laurel. BSN with honors, U. Maine, 1975; MSN, U. Md., 1980; MBA with honors, Nova U., 1989, postgrad., 1989—. RN, Mich., N.Y., Pa., Ala., U.K. Ctrl. Coun. for Nursing, Midwifery and Health Visiting. Pvt. practice cons. Gadsden, Ala.; RN, Wis., Iowa, Maine, Tex., Colo. Mem. APHA, ANA, Am. Acad. Mgmt. Assn., Med. Group Mgmt. Assn., Fin. Mgmt. Assn., Sigma Theta Tau.

TATOM, KENNETH DUKE, pharmacist; b. Dayton, Ohio, June 28, 1949; s. James William and Velma (Smith) T.; m. Susan Jean Wickham, Dec. 4, 1970; 1 child, Robert Allen. BS in Pharmacy, Ferris State Coll., 1972. Pharmacist Fidelity Prescriptions, Dayton, 1972-79, Eckerd Drugs, Palm Bay, Fla., 1979—; cons. pharmacy K & S Cons., Palm Bay, 1984—. Mem. Am. Pharm. Assn., Ohio State Pharm. Assn., Fla. Pharmacy Assn., Brevard County Pharmacist Assn. Home: 591 Minor Ave NE Melbourne FL 32907-2622 Office: Eckerd Drugs 4711 Babcock St NE Melbourne FL 32905-2805

TATSIS, GEORGE PETER, research laboratory administrative director; b. Charlotte, N.C., Dec. 7, 1958; s. Peter Demetrios and Antonia (Tzefos) T. BA, U. N.C., 1981; MS, U. N.C., Charlotte, 1989. Vol. Heineman Med. Rsch. Ctr., Charlotte, N.C., 1982; rsch. technician Heineman Med. Rsch. Ctr., Charlotte, 1982-85, rsch. assoc., 1985-87; adminstrv. dir. Laser and Applied Techs. Lab. div. Carolinas Med. Ctr., Charlotte, 1987—; dir. clin. rsch. Carolinas Heart Inst., Charlotte, 1993—; sec., treas. Assn. Biology Grad. Students, Charlotte, 1984-86. Contbr. articles to profl. jours. Tchr. Sunday sch., Charlotte, 1987—, ch. bd. dirs., 1992—, sec., 1992, v.p., 1993, 94, pres., 1995, 96. Mem. Am. Heart Assn., Am. Soc. for Laser Medicine and Surgery, Laser Inst. Am., Internat. Soc. for Optical Engring., Soc. for Rsch. Administrators, AAAS. Office: Carolinas Med Ctr Laser and Applied Techs Lab 1000 Blythe Blvd Charlotte NC 28203-5812

TATUM, JOHN ALLEN, JR., manufacturing company executive; b. Memphis, Oct. 6, 1936; s. John Allen and Lovie Parthenia (Thurmond) T.; m. Virginia Ann Tilson, July 23, 1955; children: Karen Ann, John Allen III, Susan Alynn. BS in geology, U. Houston, 1961, postgrad., 1963-65; postgrad., N.Mex. Inst. Mining and Tech., 1962. Pres. The Randolph Co., Houston, 1956—. Mem. Soc. Plastics Engrs., Soc. Mfg. Engrs. (sr.), Soc. for Advancement of Material and Process Engring., Am. Soc. Metals Internat., Am. Chem. Soc. (affiliate rubber divsn.), Energy Rubber Group. Office: The Randolph Company 1018 Rosine Houston TX 77019

TAUB, EDWARD, psychology researcher; b. Bklyn., Oct. 22, 1931; s. Samuel Hart and Ida Pearl (Kimmel) T.; m. Mildred Allen Taub, Aug. 13, 1959. BA, Bklyn. Coll., 1953; MA, Columbia U., 1959; PhD, NYU, 1969. Rsch. asst. Columbia U., N.Y.C., 1956, Dept. Exptl. Neurology, Jewish Chronic Disease Hosp., N.Y.C., 1957-60; rsch. assoc. Dept. Exptl. Neurology, Jewish Chronic Disease Hosp., 1960-68; dir. Behavioral Biology Ctr., Inst. for Behavioral Rsch., 1968-83; assoc. dir. Inst. for Behavioral Rsch., 1978-83; dir. Feedback Rsch. Ctr., Birmingham, Ala., 1984-91; prof. psychology U. Ala., Birmingham, 1986-95, sr. scientist ctr. for aging; guest prof. U. Konstanz, Germany, 1995-96, U. Jena, Germany, 1996—; asst. prof. dept. psychiatry Johns Hopkins U., Balt., 1972-82; vis. prof. grad. prog. dept. psychology CUNY, 1984-85; guest rechr. U. Tuebingen, U. Trier, U. Muenster, Humboldt U., Germany, 1993—. Contbr. articles to profl. jours.; co-inventor technnique of thermal biofeedback, 1970-71. Guggenheim Found. fellow, 1983-84; Pioneering Rsch. Contbn. award Assn. Applied Psychophysiol. and Biofeedback, 1989. Fellow AAAS, APA (exec. com. div. 6), Soc. for Behavioral Medicine, Am. Psychol. Soc. (charter); mem. Soc. for Neurosci., Biofeedback Soc. Am. (pres. 1978-79, Outstanding Rsch. Contbn. award 1988), Am. Physiol. Soc. (exec. com. neurosci. sect. 1988-91). Office: U Ala at Birmingham 201 Campbell Hall Birmingham AL 35294

TAVASSOLI, FATTANEH ABBAS-ZADEH, pathologist, consultant; b. Teheran, Iran, Mar. 30, 1949; came to U.S., 1963; d. Hossein Abbas-zadeh and Homa (Rassadi) T.; m. Bahman Jabbari, Dec. 30, 1975. BS in Chemistry, S.W. Mo. State Coll., 1968; MD, St. Louis U., 1972. Diplomate Am. Bd. Pathology. Intern, resident in pathology Barnes Hosp., St. Louis, 1972-75; fellow in gynecol. pathology St. John's Mercy Med. Ctr., St. Louis, 1975-76; from staff pathologist to vice chmn. Armed Forces Inst. Pathology, Washington, 1976-92; dir. gynecology and breast pathology, dir. rsch. Fairfax Hosp., Falls Church, Va., 1992-94, chmn. dept. gynecology and breast pathology, Armed Forces Inst. Pathology, 1994; adj. prof. pathology Uniformed Svcs. Sch. Health Scis., Bethesda, Md., 1987-92; cons. NIH, Bethesda, 1991—; clin. prof.. pathology George Washington U. Author: Pathology of the Breast, 1992, Expert Computer System: Breast Pathology, 1990; contbr. over 70 articles to profl. jours., chpts. to books. Mem. Am. Soc. Clin. Pathologists (coun. in anatomic pathology 1991-96, course dir.), Internat. Acad. Pathology, U.S.-Can. Acad. Pathology (former mem. abstract rev. com., moderator gynecol. subsplty., panel 1993-95), Internat. Soc. Gynecol. Pathologists (at-large), Arthur Purdy Scout Soc. Surg. Pathologists (bd. editors Modern Pathology, Human Pathology, Internat. Jour. Gynecol. Pathology, The Breast Jour.). Office: Dept Gynecologic & Breast Pathology Armed Forces Institute of Pathology Washington DC 20306

TAVEL, LINDA BENITEZ, educational facility administrator; b. San Antonio, Jan. 12, 1954; d. Charles Ortiz and Guadalupe (Lozano) B.; m. James Richard Tavel, May 21, 1983 (div.); children: Brendalyn, Analiza. Student, San Antonio Coll., 1975, S.W. Tex. State U., 1975-80. Licensed social worker assoc. Tex. State Bd. Social Workers, chem. dependency counseloer intern. Tex. Commn. Alcohol and Drug Abuse. Mental health worker, sr. mental health worker San Marcos (Tex.) Treatment Ctr., 1975-82; caseworker I Bexar County M.H.M.R., San Antonio, 1983-84, case mgr., 1984-90; chem. dependency counselor Mexican Am. Unity Coun., San Antonio, 1990-92, interim mental health, substance abuse programs mgr., 1992, program mgr., outpatient adv. program, 1992-94; child protective svcs. specialist State of Oreg. Children Svcs., Salem, 1994-95; pres., CEO Creative Learning Concepts, San Antonio, 1995—. Author: (workbook) Alcohol, Tobacco and Other Drugs Informational Workbook, 1995, Behavior, Attitude, Anger Management Workbook, 1995, (bi-cultural parenting workbook) El Gato Tecato, 1995, Alcohol and Drug Teachment Workbook, 1995. Vice-chmn. exec. bd. Hwys. and Hedges Outreach Inc., San Antonio, 1992-94; bd. dirs. Bexar County Detention Ministeries, San Antonio, 1992-94, match program State of Oreg. Marion County Hispanic Adv. Bd., Salem, 1994-95, Women at the Well House, San Antonio, 1995—. Democrat. Roman Catholic. Office: Creative Learning Concepts 2106 W Commerce San Antonio TX 78207

TAWADROS, AZMI MILAD, oral surgeon; b. Cairo, Egypt, Mar. 14, 1957; came to U.S., 1962; s. Milad A. and Sabah T.; m. Deborah Ann Hulderman, Apr. 16, 1988; children: Brianna, Alyssa. BS in Pharmacy, Purdue U., 1979; DDS, Indiana U., 1983; MD, Hahnemann U., 1990. Diplomate Am. Bd. Oral and Maxillofacial Surgery. Pharmacist Indpls., 1979-84; resident Emory U., Atlanta, 1984-85, Henry Ford Hosp., Detroit, 1985-88; pharmacist Phila., 1988-90; resident Ga. Baptist Med. Ctr., Atlanta, 1990-91; pvt. practice Acworth, Ga., 1991—. Mem. ADA, AMA, Northwest Dist. Dental Soc., Ga. Dental Assn. Home: 726 Creek Trl Kennesaw GA 30144-2132 Office: 5471 Bells Ferry Rd Ste 104 Acworth GA 30102-7520

TAWPASH, WILLIAM ROBERT, public relations executive; b. Orange, N.J., Dec. 9, 1962; s. William Jr. and Pamela (Fraizer) T.; m. Christine McCauley, May 20, 1989; children: Ryan, McCauley. Student, Word of Life, Schroonlake, N.Y., 1985-86, Northeastern Bible, Essex Fells, N.J., 1987-88. Waterfront dir. Word of Life Camps, Schroon Lake, 1986; clubs dir. Youth for Christ, Wayne, N.J., 1987-89; activities dir. Big Oak Ranch Children's Home, Gadsden, Ala., 1989-91, pub. rels. dir., 1991—; founder Coll. Outreach Ministries, Schroon Lake, 1985-86; retreat/camp speaker, Gadsden, 1986—. Active pub. rels. Road Svc. Ministries, Sussex, N.J., 1985, DC '88 Youth Congress, Washington, 1988; tour mem. Athletics in Action, South Am., 1987, Super Bowl XXVIII Event. Scholar United Meth. Ch., 1981. Home: 77 Highway 487 Vandiver AL 35176-7161 Office: Big Oak Ranch Inc 250 Jake Mintz Rd Gadsden AL 35905-8958

TAYLOE, EDWARD DICKINSON, II, portfolio manager; b. Norfolk, Va., May 21, 1942; s. Edward Thornton and Virginia Barron (Baird) T.; BS, East Carolina U., 1971; cert. N.Y. Inst. Fin., 1972; CFP, Coll. Fin. Planning, 1977; m. Louise Miller Fletcher, June 13, 1970; children—Michaux Stuart, Edward Thornton. Account exec. Thomson McKinnon Securities, Charlottesville, Va., 1971-81; investment officer Wheat First Securities, Kilmarnock, Va., 1981; trust officer Va. Nat. Bank (now Nations Bank Va., N.A.), Charlottesville, 1981-84, v.p., regional investment officer, 1984-94; v.p. Davenport Asset Mgmt., Davenport & Co. of Va., Inc., Charlottesville, 1994—; chmn. Indsl. Devel. Authority of City of Charlottesville, 1977-80. Trustee Miller Endowment Fund for U. Va., Blue Ridge Sch., Dyke, Va., 1986—; trustee, treas. Perry Found., 1988; bd. dirs., treas. Lee-Jackson Found.; mem. Cen. Va. Estate Planning Coun.; team capt. for various fund-raising orgns. Served with Spl. Forces, U.S. Army, 1967-68, as spl. agt., 1969; Vietnam. Decorated Bronze Star with V device, Army Commendation medal. Episcopalian. Clubs: Greencroft (dir. 1983-87 , pres. 1985-85), Stock and Bond. (dir. Charlottesville chpt. 1990), Young Men's Bus. (pres. Charlottesville and Albemarle County club 1976-77); Red Lands (pres. club 1980-81, 91-92) (Charlottesville), Farmington Country. Home: PO Box 351 Charlottesville VA 22902-0351 Office: PO Box 1481 Charlottesville VA 22902-1481

TAYLOR, ADAM DAVID, real estate executive; b. N.Y.C., Mar. 31, 1917; s. William and Anne (Bernstein) T.; m. Sylvia Park, Oct. 15, 1941 (div. Apr. 1963); children: Hillary, Jeremy; m. Edna Deutsch, Jan. 28, 1964. BCS, NYU, 1941. Pres. Dealers Supply, N.Y.C., 1955-63, Taylor Lumber Co., Inc., N.Y.C., 1936-63, Raje Realty, Inc., N.Y.C., 1955-63, Architects Svc. Ctr., Inc., N.Y.C., 1955-63, Bahama Properties, Inc., Miami, 1965-68; dir. sales Arlen Properties, Miami, 1968-72; owner Adam D. Taylor Real Estate, Miami, 1972—; mng. ptnr. Oak Plaza Assocs., Miami, 1985—, Plz. Ctr. Assocs., Miami, 1986—, Circle K, Ft. Myers, Fla., Kentucky Fried Chicken, Gainesville, Fla. Office: 12955 Biscayne Blvd Ste 304 Miami FL 33181-2022

TAYLOR, ALFRED RALEIGH, geologist; b. Eure, Gates County, N.C., July 7, 1928; s. Raleigh Jackson and Annie B. Taylor; m. Eugenia Dare Eure, Nov. 9, 1946; children: Patricia Dare, Teri Ann. BS in Geology, U. N.C., 1955. Cert. geologist Va. Geologist U.S. Geol. Survey, Worldwide, 1955-81, Minerals Mgmt. Svc., Reston, 1981-82, Bur. Land Mgmt., Reston and Washington, 1982-83; geol. cons. Somerset, Ky., 1984-87; sr. geologist Va. Divsn. of Mineral Resources, Cedar Bluff, Va., 1988-89; geol. cons. Cedar Bluff, 1989; supr. geologist Va. Divsn. Min. Resources, Dept. Mines, Minerals & Energy, Abingdon, Va., 1990—; adj. faculty in geology and geography Somerset C.C. of U. Ky., Somerset, 1968-77, 86-88. Contbr. over 50 articles and chpts. to books and profl. jours. S/sgt. USMC, PTO, ATO; lt. USNR. Recipient Antarctic Svc. medal, commendation U.S. Dept. Interior, 1961, citations U.S. Geol. Survey; Alfred Taylor Mountain in Antarctica named for him; named Ky. Col. Mem. Am. Assn. Petroleum Geologists, Am. Inst. Profl. Geologists (cert. prof. geologist), Geol. Soc. Washington, Geol. Soc. Ky., Fleet Res. Assn., VFW (life), Am. Legion, Naval Res. Assn., Sigma Gamma Epsilon. Office: Va Divsn Mineral Resources PO Box 144 Abingdon VA 24212-0144

TAYLOR, ANDREW LEX, endocrinologist, educator; b. Boston, Apr. 21, 1937; s. Fredrick Bayles and Cathleen Lex (Huckel) T.; m. Antoinette Rose Pugliese, Sept. 6, 1969; children: Joshua A., Noah A. AB, Amherst U., 1959; MD, Boston U., 1963. Intern Georgetown U. Hosp., Washington, 1963-64, resident, 1964-66; fellow U. Pitts., 1967-69, resident, 1969-70; asst. prof. U. Miami (Fla.) Sch. Medicine, 1970-76, assoc. prof., 1976-89, prof., 1989—; staff physician VA Med. Ctr., Jackson Hosp., Miami, 1970-93. Author: (book chpt.) Peptide Hormones: Effects and Mechanisms; contbr. articles and revs. to profl. jours. Capt. U.S. Army, 1965-67. Mem. Endocrine Soc., Am. Bd. Fed. Clin. Rsch. (councillor 1973-75). Democrat. Home: 10915 SW 63rd Ave Miami FL 33156-4030 Office: U Miami Dept Medicine D-26 PO Box 016760 Miami FL 33101-6760

TAYLOR, AUBREY ELMO, physiologist, educator; b. El Paso, Tex., June 4, 1933; s. Virgil T. and Mildred (Maher) T.; m. Mary Jane Davis, Apr. 4, 1953; children: Audrey Jane Hildebrand, Lenda Sue Brown, Mary Ann Smith. BA in Math. and Psychology, Tex. Christian U., 1960; PhD in Physiology, U. Miss., 1964; Postdoctoral fellow biophysics lab. Harvard U. Med. Sch., Boston, 1965-67; from asst. prof. to prof. dept. physiology U. Miss. Coll. Medicine, Jackson, 1967-77; prof., chmn. dept. physiology U. South Ala. Coll. Medicine, Mobile, 1977—, Louise Lenoir Locke eminent scholar; mem. pulmonary score com. Nat. Heart, Lung and Blood Inst., 1976; with Surgery and anesthesiology, 1979-82, and Manpower Com., 1985-95; chmn. RAP, 1983. Author 5 books; contbr. chpts. to books, 700 articles to profl. jours; assoc. editor Jour. Applied Physiology, 1984-94, Critical Care medicine, 1987—; mem. editorial bd. Circulation Rsch. Am. Jour. Physiology, Microvascular Rsch., Internat. Pathophysiology, Microcirculatory and Lymphatic Rsch., Microcirculation, Chinese Jour. of Physiology Jour. Biomed. Science, Jour. Biomed. Rsch., Am. Rev. Resp. and Critical Care. Served with U.S. Army, 1953-55. NIH grantee, 1967—; recipient Lederle Faculty award, 1967-70, Philip Dow award U. Ga., 1984, NIH Merit award, 1988—, Lucian award McGill U., 1988, John Whitney award U. Ark., 1990, Gelen award Intestinal Shock Soc., 1991; named Disting. Physiologist Am. Coll. Chest Physicians, 1994. Fellow AAAS, Am. Heart Assn. (circulation, coun., cardiopulmonary and critical care coun. 1977—, chmn. 1993—, chmn. So. regional rev. com. 1977-81, EIA Review Com. 1986-95, mem. pulmonary and devel. rev. com. 1987-95, chmn. grant/review com., 1994-95, chmn. med. student rsch. award com. 1992-94, nat. rsch. com. 1990-95, Dickson Richards award 1988, Bronze award Miss. AHA, 1976, Outstanding Alabaman AHA program 1993, sci. coun. achievement award, 1995, ACDP Svc. award, 1995), Royal Soc. Medicine, NAS (mem. com. for Internat. Union Physiol. Sci.); mem. Am. Physiol. Soc. (coun. 1984-87, chmn. membership com. 1985-87, pres. 1987-90, Wiggers award 1987, chmn. Perkins fellow com., 1996—), Microcirculatory Soc. (coun. 1977-81, pres. 1981-83, Landis award 1985), Ala. Acad. Scis. (State Rsch. award 1988), Internat. Lymphology Soc., N.Am. Soc. Lymphology (pres. 1988-90, recipient First Cecil Drinker award 1988), Internat. Pathophysiology Soc. (v.p. 1991—), N.Y. Acad. Scis., Biophys. Soc., Fedn. Am. Socs. for Exptl. Biology (bd. dirs. 1988-90), Am. Thoracic Soc., Alpha Omega Alpha, Sigma Xi. Democrat. Presbyterian. Current work: Cardio-pulmonary physiology; fluid balance, edema, microcirculation and capillary exchange of solute and water. Subspecialties: Physiology (medicine); Pulmonary medicine. Home: 11 Audubon Pl Mobile AL 36606-1907

TAYLOR, AUSTIN RANDALL, sales executive; b. Memphis, July 14, 1954; s. Guy Austin and Jeneva Ruth (Haase) T.; m. Patricia Carol Souchak, Nov. 7, 1981; children: Lauren Frances, Lisa Anne. BA in Life Scis., Rollins Coll., 1976. Video engr. Sta. WESH-TV, Orlando, Fla., 1976-77; sales rep. Motorola Comm., Orlando, 1977-78; sales rep. USV Labs., Tuckahoe, N.Y., 1978-81, mktg. cons., 1980-81; spl. tng. rep. Ortho Pharm. Corp., Raritan, N.J., 1981-87; territory mgr. Medtronic/Andover Med., Haverhill, Mass., 1987-89; area mgr. Bruel & Kjaer Instruments Inc., Marlborough, Mass., 1989-90; regional mgr. Medtronic/Andover Med., Haverhill, Mass., 1990—. Mem. Rep. Nat. Com., 1979—; reader, announcer Sta. WUSF Radio Reading Service, Tampa, Fla., 1983-87. Mem. Chaine des Rotisseurs, Tampa Yacht and Country Club, Omicron Delta Kappa, Sigma Phi Epsilon. Home: 1703 S Westshore Blvd Tampa FL 33629-5442

TAYLOR, BARBARA E., museum director. BA in History, Trinity Coll., 1974; MAT in Mus. Edn./Am. History, George Washington U., 1976. Tour scheduler Smithsonian Inst., Washington, 1974-75; curator Mint Mus. History, Charlotte, N.C., 1976-83; dir. Mus. Albemarle, Elizabeth City, N.C.,

1983-93; CEO Mus. of City of Mobile (Ala.), 1993—; grant reader Inst. Mus. Svcs., 1980, 81, 86; mem. at large N.C. Muss. Coun., 1981-83, 86-87, sec./treas., 1984-86, long range planning mem., 1986-87, chmn. spring meeting, 1987, membership com., 1991, archives and standing rules chair, 1992; mem. N.C. Quilt Symposium Bd., 1983-85; mem. at large Hist. Albemarle Tour, 1984-87, 91-93, pres., 1987-88. Editor: (manuscripts) On The Shores of The Pasquotank: An Architectural History of Elizabeth City ans Pasquotank County, 1989, (exhbn. catalog) A Taste of The Past: Early Foodways of The Albemarle Region, 1585-1830, 1991; author: (video) Experiment in History, 1978, Fanfaire, 1984. Mem. Am. Assn. State and Local History, Am. Assn. Muss., Nat. Trust Hist. Preservation, Ala. Muss. Assn., Mobile Area Muss. Assn. Office: Mus of the City of Mobile 355 Government St Mobile AL 36602-2315*

TAYLOR, CAROL, rehabilitation nurse; b. York, Pa., June 26, 1949; d. James Vincent and Arlene Catherine (Rosenzweig) Kavanagh; m. David Eugene Taylor, June 9, 1983; children: Shannon Kathleen Kaye, Kevin Christopher, David Jason, E. J. Meyer. RN diploma, E.J. Meyer Meml. Hosp. Sch. Nursing, Buffalo, 1970; student, SUNY, Buffalo, 1967-68, 72-73, U. South Miss., Gulfport, 1984; BSN, U. South Ala., Mobile, 1989; M of Health Sci., Tex. Wesleyan U., 1991. Cert. nurse anesthetist. Nurse operating rm. Biloxi (Miss.) Regional Med. Ctr.; nurse operating rm./recovery rm. Meml. Hosp., Gulfport, Miss.; charge nurse operating rm. Sacred Heart Hosp., Pensacola, Fla., 1987-88; staff nurse rehab. HCA West Fla. Regional Med Ctr. Rehab. Inst., Pensacola, 1989-90; nurse anesthetist Fitzsimons Army Med. Ctr., Aurora, Colo., 1993-95, Lyster Army Hosp., Ft. Rucker, Ala., 1995—. Capt. U.S. Army, 1990—. Mem. AANA. Home: 203 Lakeside Dr Enterprise AL 36330

TAYLOR, CAROLE JAN HUDSON, insurance company administrator; b. Port Arthur, Tex., May 17, 1949; d. Henry and Vivian Corine (Duncan) Hudson. BBA, Stephen F. Austin U., 1971. Claim rep. The Travelers Ins. Co., Houston, 1971-73, asst. supr., 1973-78, sr. rep., 1978-87, regional gen. adjuster, 1987-93, exec. gen. adjuster, 1993—. Author software program Business Interruption, 1988. Mem. Women for Reagan, Houston, 1983. Recipient cert. of achievement Am. Ednl. Inst., 1974, G.A.B. Bus. Interruption, 1988. Mem. NAFE, Ford's of 50's (treas. 1981-82). Republican. Baptist. Office: Travelers Ins Co 10800 Richmond Houston TX 77042

TAYLOR, CAROLYN A., women's health nurse, administrator; b. Fairfield, Ala., Feb. 18, 1947; d. David and Daisy Mae (Hill) Oden; m. Leslie H. Taylor, May 20, 1966; children: Tresha, Traci, Kelley. BSN, George Mason U., 1978, MS in Nursing, 1986. Staff nurse dept. of the Army, Ft. Belvoir, Va.; coord. family care Fairfax Hosp., Falls Church, Va., coord. labor and delivery; dir. maternal child health care Holy Cross Hosp., Silver Springs, Md. Mem. NAACOG. Home: 8619 Eagle Glen Ter Fairfax VA 22039-2679

TAYLOR, CHARLES H., congressman; b. Brevard, N.C., Jan. 3, 1941; m. Elizabeth Owen; 3 children. BA, Wake Forest U., 1963, JD, 1966. Mem. N.C. Ho. of Reps., Raleigh, 1967-73, minority leader, 1969-73; mem. N.C. Senate, Raleigh, 1973-75, minority leader, 1973-75; mem. 102nd-104th Congresses from 11th N.C. dist., Washington, 1991—; mem. appropriations subcoms. commerce, justice, state jud. and related agys., legis. com., subcom. on interior; tree farmer N.C. Baptist. Office: U S Ho of Reps 231 Cannon HOB Washington DC 20515 also: 22 S Pack Sq Ste 330 Asheville NC 28801-3524

TAYLOR, CLARENCE ALBERT, JR., housing coordinator, drug counselor; b. Charlottesville, Va., Nov. 23, 1950; s. Clarence A. and Mary E. (Washington) T. BS, Wilberforce (Ohio) U., 1974. G.E.D. instr. Dept. Labor Svcs., Topeka, 1978-80; youth svc. worker Youth Ctr., Topeka, 1981-86; coord. transitional living-employment Breakthrough House, Inc., Topeka, 1982-86; program mgr. N. W. Mental Health Ctr., Phila., 1986-89; employment counselor Offender Aid and Restoration, Charlottesville, Va., 1989; housing coord. Greene Co. Community Devel., Stanardsville, Va., 1991-94; housing coord., EEO officer Skyline Cmty. Action Program, Inc., Stanardsville, 1994—; trainee Horizon House, Phila., 1987-88, Med. Coll. of Pa., Phila., 1988. Named Outstanding Young Man Am., Jaycees of Am., 1978; first black hired in middle level mgmt. position in history of Greene County govt. Democrat. Baptist. Home: RR 33 Box 157 Quinque VA 22965 Office: Skyline Cmty Action Program PO Box 508 Stanardsville VA 22973-0508

TAYLOR, CLAUDE J., sales executive, consultant; b. Winston-Salem, N.C., Apr. 29, 1943; s. Claude V. and Jessie K. T.; m. Frances T. Denty, Dec. 22, 1962; children: Joseph Vinston, Jeffrey Alan, Marc David, Michael Edward. Student, U.S. Army Schs., 1961-62; AS in Aircraft Comms., Nat. Inst., 1966-68, AS in Indsl. Electronics, 1968-71; student, Palm Beach Jr. Coll., 1971-73. Inside salesman and office ops. Graybar Electric Co., West Palm Beach, Fla., 1964-66; mgr. Lewisville (N.C.) Shell Svc., 1966-67; salesman Joyce Foods, Inc., Lewisville, 1967-69; instrument tech. Pratt-Whitney Aircraft, West Palm Beach, 1969-73; tech. resp., instr., tech. mgr. Siemens Med. Systems, Iselin, N.J., 1973-87; salesman, mfr. rep. Ohmeda div. BOC, LIttleton, Colo., 1987-88; dist. sales mgr. Planmeca, Inc. and Planmed, Wood Dale, 1988-93; owner, pres. dental and medical sales Tech. Splty. Mktg., Jupiter, Fla., 1993—; cons. Instrumentarium Imaging, Inc., Milw., 1993—. With U.S. Army, 1961-64. Home: PO Box 1443 Jupiter FL 33468-1443 Office: Tech Splty 16220 128th Trl N Jupiter FL 33478-6527

TAYLOR, CLAUDIA ANN, psychotherapist, nurse; b. Knoxville, Tenn., May 22, 1946; d. Darlene M. Moore; m. Kendryl S. Taylor (div. 1974). RN, Grady Nursing Sch., 1966; BSN, Ga. State U., 1979, MEd, 1982. Acting head nurse Grady Meml. Hosp., Atlanta, 1966, psychiatric clin. coordinator, 1969—; instr. in counseling Barbara King Sch. of Ministry, Atlanta, 1982-83; workshop, seminar coordinator and facilitator Atlanta, 1977—; pvt. practice psychotherapist, cons. C. Ann Taylor & Assocs., Atlanta, 1983—; assoc. trainer, counselor The Inst. for Effective Living, Trinidad, 1983—; producer Relationships on Cable Atlanta, 1984—; founder, CEO Inst. for Psychotherapy and Rsch. for HIV-Positive Women and, 1994—; cons. Ga. Inst. Tech., Atlanta, 1985-87, Psychiatric Inst. Atlanta, 1986-87, AT&T, Atlanta, 1988, IRS, Atlanta, 1988. Bd. dirs. Community Friendship, Inc., Atlanta; group leader Dept. Offender Rehab., Atlanta, 1980. Lt. col. USAFR, 1976—. Mem. NAFE, ASTD, Assn. Black Psychologists (chmn. 1986-88), Mental Health Assn., Ga. Nurses Assn., Res. Officers Assn., Internat. Transactional Analysis Assn., Nat. Coun. Negro Women (chmn. Atlanta 1983—, award of appreciation 1985, 87), Delta Sigma Theta (award of appreciation 1986). Democrat. Home: 410 Mary Erna Dr Fairburn GA 30213-2720 Office: Peachtree Psychol Svcs 600 W Peachtree St NW Ste 1430 Atlanta GA 30308-3603

TAYLOR, DAVID NEIL, minister; b. Tampa, Fla., Feb. 15, 1954; s. O.L. Zack and Bessie Nell (Miley) T.; m. Laura Nanette Thompson, Oct. 29, 1977; children: Jonathan, Stephen, Christina. Student, U. So. Miss., 1972-75. Ordained to ministry Bapt. Ch., 1973. Youth pastor Ridgecrest Bapt. Ch., Hattiesburg, Miss., 1969-70; assoc. minister Big Level Bapt. Ch., Wiggins, Miss., 1971-74, Glendale United Meth. Ch., Hattiesburg, 1975; sr. pastor New Christian Fellowship, Port Gibson, Miss., 1976-83, Word of Life Ch., Auburn, 1983, The Storehouse Ch., Hattiesburg, 1984-94; founder, pres. David Taylor Ministries, 1976—; founder Youth Leadership Camps, 1979—, Nat. Intercessors Congress, 1981; officer, mem. exec. coun. Internat. Congress Local Chs., Washington, 1988—; vice chmn. Azusa Fellowship of Chs. and Ministries, 1993-94, bd. dirs., 1995-96. Pastor's coun. Ams. for Robertson, Miss. Chpt., 1987-88; state rep. Christian Coalition, 1991. Named to Outstanding Young Men of Am., 1986. Home: 1320 Grantham Rd Sumrall MS 39482-4028 Office: David Taylor Ministries PO Box 16256 Hattiesburg MS 39404-6256

TAYLOR, EDWARD REGINALD, food and beverage industry executive; b. Chgo., June 14, 1955; s. Edward John and Lanell (Green) T.; m. Janice Marie Scott, Aug. 29, 1992; 1 child, Desmond. AS in Sci., Thornton C.C., 1978; BA in Environ. Sci., Gov.'s State U., 1980; MS in Environ. Sci., McNeese State U., 1988. Lab. technician Vista Chem. Co. (formerly Conoco Chems. Co.), Hammond, Ind., 1976-80, lab. supr., 1980-84; safety inspector Vista Chem. Co. (formerly Conoco Chems. Co.), Westlake, La., 1984-85, environ. coord., 1985-88, sr. environ. coord., 1988-89; sr. environ. specialist Vista Chem. Co. (formerly Conoco Chems. Co.), Houston, 1989-90; sr. environ. engr. divsn. hdqrs. office Minute Maid Co. divsn. Coca-Cola Co., Houston, 1990-91; mgr. environ. affairs Coca-Cola Foods divsn. Coca-Cola Co., Houston, 1991-94, dir. environ. affairs, 1994—; mem. environ. and energy in the food industry conf. com. Engring. Found. Vol., instr. ARC, 1982-89, bd. dirs. Calcasieu-Cameron chpt. 1986-89; campaign mgr. Calcasieu Parish Policy Jury election, 1987; Minute Maid Mentor to local area schs.; mentor INROADS program. Named Houston Young Black Achiever, Human Enrichment of Life Program, Inc., 1992. Mem. Nat. Assn. Environ. Profls. (registered environ. profl.), Water Environ. Fedn., Air and Waste Mgmt. Assn., Nat. Soc. Black Engrs., Nat. Environ. Tng. Assn., Knights of Peter Claver (coun. rec. sec. 1987-90, Merit award 1988), St. Monica's Young Adult Club, Alpha Phi Alpha. Roman Catholic. Home: 7335 Athlone Dr Houston TX 77088-7422 Office: Minute Maid Co 2000 Saint James Pl Houston TX 77056-4125

TAYLOR, ELIZABETH JANE, investment consultant, real estate and international marketing executive; b. Tiffin, Ohio, Oct. 27, 1941; d. Albert Joseph Lucas and Mary Jane Siebenaller-Swander; m. Gaylen Lloyd Taylor, July 11, 1977. Student, Heidelberg Coll., 1961, Austin Community Coll., Tex., 1983-84; grad. Real Estate Edn. Ctr., 1984, Inst. Real Estate, 1988, Real Estate Inst., 1989, Tex. Realtors Inst., 1989; student Rockhurst Coll., 1991-92. Cons., Hypnosis Conn., Ohio, Tex. and Ariz., 1967—; dir. regional mktg. Sibrow, Inc., Ottawa, Can., 1981-83; realtor assoc. Alliance Sales, Austin, 1985-88; assoc. Broadway Comml. Investments, 1988-91; prin., Taylor & Assocs., Internat. Mktg. & Bus. Devel., Hong Kong, U.S., 1980—; tchr. mktg. and bus. develop., 1980-96. Author: profl. column Austin Women Mag., 1984-86; (poetry) Letters from Home, 1986, Best New Poets of 1986, American Poetry Anthology, vol. VI., #3, 1986. V.p. Am. Congress on Real Estate, 1982-83; arbitrator Better Bus. Bur., 1984-89, sr. arbitrator, Austin, Tex., 1989-95; mem. speakers bur. Austin Woman's Ctr., 1985-88; v.p. Austin World Affairs Coun., 1984-94; mem. adv. panel Austin Woman Mag., 1984-86. Nominated to Tex. Womens Hall of Fame, 1984. Mem. NAFE (network dir. 1980-88), Am. Biog. Inst. Rsch. (hon., bd. advisers 1988). Avocations: writing, behavior research. Home: 3926 E Cherokee St Phoenix AZ 85044

TAYLOR, ELLEN BORDEN BROADHURST, civic worker; b. Goldsboro, N.C., Jan. 18, 1913; d. Jack Johnson and Mabel Moran (Borden) Broadhurst; student Converse Coll., 1930-32; m. Marvin Edward Taylor, June 13, 1936; children: Marvin Edward, Jack Borden, William Lambert. Bd. govs. Elizabethan Garden, Manteo, N.C., 1964-74; mem. Gov. Robert Scott's Adv. Com. on Beautification, N.C., 1971-73; mem. ACE nat. action com. for environ. Nat. Coun. State Garden Clubs, 1973-75; bd. dirs. Keep N.C. Beautiful, 1973-85; mem. steering com., charter mem. bd. dirs. Keep Johnston County (N.C.) Beautiful, 1977-92; life judge roses Am. Rose Soc.; chmn. local com. that published jointly with N.C. Dept. Cultural Resources: An Inventory of Historic Architecture, Smithfield, N.C., 1977; co-chmn. local com. to survey and publish jointly with N.C. Div. Archives and History: Historical Resources of Johnston County, 1980-91; charter life mem. N.C. Mus. History Assocs., 1994; charter mem. founder's circle New Mus. History Bldg., Raleigh, 1994. Mem. Nat. Coun. State Garden Clubs (life; master judge flower shows), Johnston County Hist. Soc. (charter), Johnston County Arts Coun. (Spl. award for 1987 projects of Pub. Libr. Johnston County & Smithfield 1965-87), N.C. Geneal. Soc. (charter), Johnston County Geneal. Soc. (charter), Hist. Preservation Soc. N.C. (life), N.C. Art Soc. (life). Democrat. Episcopalian. Clubs: Smithfield (N.C.) Garden (charter; pres. 1969-71), Smithfield Woman's (v.p. 1976), DAR (organizing vice-regent chpt. 1976), Gen. Soc. Mayflower Descs. (life), Descs. of Richard Warren, Nat. Soc. New Eng. Women (charter mem. Carolina Capital chpt.), Colonial Dames Am. (life), Magna Charta Dames, Nat. Soc. Daus. of Founders and Patriots Am. Home: 616 Hancock St Smithfield NC 27577-4008

TAYLOR, GENE, congressman; b. New Orleans, La., Sept. 17, 1953; m. Margaret Gordon; children: Sarah, Emily, Gary. BA, Tulane U.; grad., U. So. Miss. Sales rep. Stone Container Corp.; U.S. senator from Miss., dist. 46, 1984-89; mem. 101st-104th Congresses from 5th Miss. dist., 1989—; mem. govt. reform & oversight com., ranking minority mem. merchant marine. With USCGR. Mem. Lions, Rotary, Kappa Sigma. Roman Catholic. Office: US House of Reps 2447 Rayburn Washington DC 20002-1025

TAYLOR, GREGORY EUGENE, optometrist; b. Maysville, Ky., Feb. 14, 1960; s. Eugene Ball and Janice Dean (McRoberts) T.; m. Cynthia Ann Stapleton, May 26, 1990. BA, Transylvania U., 1982; OD, So. Coll. Optometry, 1986. Optometrist Offices of Drs. Sherman & Taylor, Maysville, 1986—. Dep. dir. Mason County Disaster and Emergency Svcs. Named Ky. Col. Mem. Am. Optometric Assn., Ky. Optometric Assn., Greater Mason County Amateur Radio Assn. (pres. 1991-92), Limestone Jaycees (pres. 1993-96). Methodist. Office: Drs Sherman & Taylor 15 E 3rd St Maysville KY 41056-1148

TAYLOR, JAMES ALBERT, university administrator; b. Acushnet, Mass., Sept. 10, 1943; s. George Thomas and Gladys (Howarth) T.; m. Barbara Jean Bradley, Apr. 26, 1996; children: Derek James, Daryle Christopher, Katherine Eileen. BA in Edn., U. Fla., 1964, MEd, 1969; M in Health Adminstrn., Baylor U., 1977; EdD, George Washington U., Washington, 1981. Social studies tchr. Bayshore Jr. H.S., Bradenton, Fla., 1965-66; commd. 2d lt. U.S. Army, 1966, advanced through grades to lt. col., retired, 1986; assoc. dean Sch. of Allied Health Profls. St. Louis U., St. Louis, 1986-95; dir. Sch. of Allied Health Scis. N.E. La. U., Monroe, 1995—. Decorated Bronze Star U.S. Army, Vietnam, 1969, Legion of Merit U.S. Army, 1986. Episcopalian. Home: 634 Hwy 134 Monroe LA 71203 Office: NE La U Sch Allied Health Scis 700 University Ave Monroe LA 71209

TAYLOR, JAMES B., securities trader, financial planner; b. Kenosha, Wis., June 23, 1944; s. George R. and Virginia Dare (Scenters) T.; m. Rebecca Matthew, Feb. 14, 1983; children: Joseph F., Jennifer R., Jessica J. Cert., Ky. Bus. Coll., Lexington, 1969; student, U. Wis., 1970-72. Lic. NASD Securities Broker, Tex. Securities Exchange Commn. Lab. technician Allen-Bradley Co., Inc., Milw., 1962-65; mktg. Jaeger Ols, Inc., Milw., 1965-68; mktg., retail mgmt. G.W. Taylor Co., Inc., Williamson, W.Va., 1968-69; acct. RTE Corp., Waukesha, Wis., 1969-72; mktg. new product introduction Victor Comptometer, Milw., Chgo., 1972-76; account exec., personal fin. mgmt. Merrill Lynch Pierce Fenner & Smith, Houston, 1977-80, Rotan Mosle Inc. (merger with Paine Webber Corp.), Houston, 1980-84, Paine Webber Corp./Rotan Mosle Inc., Houston, 1984—; instr. investing and personal fin. mgmt., Merrill Lynch, Houston. 1976-80, Paine Webber, Houston, 1980—; internat. stockbroker. Author articles on personal investing and fin. mgmt. for bus. mags., profl. newsletters, and internat. newspapers; prin. works exhibited in numerous galleries including Art Cetera, Houston, Harris County Coll. Gallery, Houston, Wimberly (Tex.) Galleries; paintings and photographs represented in pvt. collections in Europe and the U.S.; contbr. photos to local newspapers. Parrish coun. Catholic Ch., Livingston, Tex., 1979, 80, 81; dir. Hispanic Arts Group, Houston, 1990-91; active election campaign Ronald Reagan, Jack Fields. Mem. Stockbroker Soc. Am., Visual Arts Alliance. Office: Paine Webber/Rotan Mosle Inc 16945 Northchase Dr Ste 100 Houston TX 77060-2131

TAYLOR, J(AMES) BENNETT, management consultant; b. Sarasota, Fla., June 15, 1943; s. Thurman Ralph and Lucille (Bennett) T.; 1 child, Kelly Christine; m. Charlene Kenney Taylor. BS in Advt., U. Fla., 1965. Dist. mgr. The Coca-Cola Co., Shreveport, La., 1966-68; allied product specialist Coca-Cola U.S.A., Dallas, 1968-70, dist. mgr., Cin., Indpls., 1970-75; v.p. Ott Rsch. and Devel., Miami, Fla., 1975-78; pres., CEO Exec. Group, Inc., Tampa, Fla., 1978—, Grand Central Corp., Tampa, 1992—. Named Fellow Outplacement Inst., 1995. Mem. Rotary. Home: 1111 N Bayshore Blvd F3 Clearwater FL 34619-3319

TAYLOR, JAMES DANIEL, beverage and chemical companies executive; b. Rahway, N.J., Nov. 21, 1928; s. James Daniel and Ella Sophie (Sneedse) T.; student Bates Coll., 1948, Sch. Fgn. Service, Georgetown U., 1949-51, U. Mex., summer 1949; MBA, Ateneo of Manila, 1964; postgrad. Bus. Sch., Harvard U., 1978-80; m. Teresa Frances Lavers, Dec. 18, 1965; children: Anita Teresa, Andrea Ella, Alex James. With Standard Vacuum Oil Co., Philippines, 1951-65; mktg. exec. Esso Standard Oil Co., C.Am., 1965-68; dir. mgmt. cons. Price Waterhouse Co., N.Y.C., Tampa, Fla., 1968-74; pres. Jim Taylor Corp., Orlando, Fla., 1974—, Brevard, Inc., 1987—; pres. Autochlor Suncoast, 1978—, also chmn. bd.; pres. Sarasota Beverage Co., 1980—, St. Petersburg (Fla.) Beverage Co., 1983—; mem. wholesale adv. bd. Schlitz Brewing Co; chmn. All Brands adv. bd., 1988; mem. Stroh's Strategy Bd. Contbr. articles to profl. jours. Mem. Mountainside (N.J.) Sch. Bd., 1971-72, Stroh Brewery Wholesale, 1987—; patron Rollins Coll., U. Central Fla.; mem. panel United Cerebral Palsy Found.; bd. dirs. Union County Sch. Bd., 1972; cons. Fla. Senate, 1974; Jaycee senator, 1969—. With U.S. Army, 1946-48. Recipient Inner Circle award Jos. Schlitz Brewing Co., 1978, 80, C.Am. award Govt. of Honduras, 1950, Golden Lion award Stroh Brewery, 1987. Mem. Am. Mgmt. Assn., Sales Execs. Club, Beer Industry Fla. (dir.), Econs. Club of Orlando (dir.), Boston Beer Co. (dir.), Georgetown U. Alumni Assn. (bd. govs. interviewing com. chmn. Fla., Pres.'s award), Stroh's Wholesalers Long-range Task Force, Winter Park Racquet Club (past pres.), University Club, Tar Boosters Club, Manila Polo Club, Interlachen Country Club. Republican. Episcopalian. Office: 133 Atlantic Dr Maitland FL 32751-3328

TAYLOR, JAMES FRANCIS, marketing professional; b. Detroit, Sept. 5, 1951; s. Harold James and Mary Frances (Law) T.; m. Janet Elizabeth Joss, May 21, 1977; children: Jonathan Harold, Jessica Frances, Jenna Leigh, Jeanette Mary. BA in Polit. Sci., Mich. State U., 1976; postgrad., Thomas Cooley Law Sch., 1979. Product mgr. Gen. Aluminum Products, Charlotte, Mich., 1975-77; sales mgr. Empire Metal Products, Columbus, Ohio, 1978; bus. mgr. Law Offices of Paul Martin, Lansing, Mich., 1978-79; dir. mktg. and sales Feather-Lite Mfg. Co., Troy, Mich., 1979-81; v.p. mktg. and sales Innovative Products Corp., Madison Heights, Mich., 1981-82; pres. J.F. Taylor Assocs., Inc., Durham, N.C., 1982—, Meadowcrest Group, Inc., 1989—; pres., bd. dirs. The Taylor-Grant-Joss Found., Durham, N.C.; corp. sec., bd. dirs. Unfinished Furniture Express, Inc., Durham, N.C., Unfinished Furniture Express of Charlotte, Inc., Unfinished Furniture Express of Raleigh, Inc., Unfinished Furniture Express of Roanoke, Va. Bd. dirs. Triangle Opera Theatre. Mem. Mfrs. Agts. Nat. Assn., Nat. Assn. Home Builders, Univ. Club Mich. State U., Hope Valley Country Club, Rotary, Carolina Club. Republican. Roman Catholic. Home: 4 Roswell Ct Durham NC 27707-5070 Office: Ste 410 3518 Westgate Dr Ste 410 Durham NC 27707

TAYLOR, JAMES MARION, II, automotive wholesale executive; b. Andalusia, Ala., Jan. 20, 1926; s. Marion Doby and Catherine (Hill) T.; m. Abbie Chapman Henderson, Mar. 22, 1947; children: Cathy, James III, Merrily, Abbie, John. Student, U.S. Merchant Marine Acad., 1944-46, Auburn U., 1946-47. Salesman Taylor Parts, Inc., Andalusia, 1947-49, salesman, dir., 1950, v.p., sales mgr., 1950-61, v.p., gen. mgr., 1961-62, pres., 1962-88, chmn., chief exec. officer, 1988-92; bd. dirs. Covington County Bank, Andalusia; chmn. Southern Nat., Andalusia, 1986—; mem. adv. bd. Shatterproof Glass Co., Detroit, 1968, AC-Delco, Detroit, 1966-67, Walker (Tenneco), Racine, Wis., 1985. Bd. dirs. Ala. Wildlife Fedn., Montgomery, 1974-77, pres., 1977-78; bd. dirs. Lurleen B. Wallace Jr. Coll. Found., Andalusia, 1986-89, Covington County Bd. Edn., Andalusia, 1960-74, City of Andalusia Downtown Devel. Authority, 1989-96, City of Andalusia Indsl. Devel. Bd., 1969-71. Mem. Nat. Assn. Wholesalers (bd. dirs. and 1st vice chmn. 1988-90, chmn.-elect 1991, chmn. 1992, treas. 1993-94), Automotive Hall of Fame (Midland, Mich. bd. dirs. 1986-94), Automotive Info. Coun. (bd. dirs. 1987-92), Andalusia C. of C. (bd. dirs. 1960-62, 89-92), Auburn Alumni Assn. (life), Kiwanis (pres. Andalusia club 1969-70), Am. Legion. Republican. Baptist. Home: 104 S Ridge Rd Andalusia AL 36420-4214 Office: Taylor Parts Inc PO Box 4008 Andalusia AL 36420

TAYLOR, JERRINE STEIFLE, retired business educator; b. Greensboro, N.C., Aug. 28, 1933; d. James Riley and Ruby Jerrine (Martin) Steifle; m. William C. Taylor, June 18, 1955; children: Deborah Ann Taylor Mayo, Cynthia Taylor, Laura Taylor Frischmann. BS in Secretarial Adminstrn., U. N.C., Greensboro, 1955. Cert. tchr., N.C. Tchr. Anne B. Snipes Sch., Wilmington, N.C., 1955-56, Ctrl. Jr. High Sch., Greensboro, 1956-58; instr. office adminstrn. Miller-Motte Bus. Coll., Wilmington, N.C., 1980-95, mem. adv. com., 1992-94. Precinct chmn. Rep. Party, Wilmington; past sec. Garden Coun. New Hanover County. Named N.C. Tchr. of Yr., Assn. Ind. Colls. and Schs., 1992. Mem. Profl. Secs. Internat., Collegiate Secs. Internat. (advisor 1992-95), N.C. Bus. Edn. Assn. Baptist. Home: 125 Partridge Rd Wilmington NC 28412-6819

TAYLOR, JOE WILLIAM, publishing executive, writer; b. Cin., Jan. 27, 1949; s. William Louis Taylor and Mary Louise Cox; m. Patricia Lou Willey, Dec. 12, 1982. BA in Philosophy, U. Ky., 1975; MA, Fla. State U., 1981, PhD, 1985. Pub. Swallow's Tale Press, Tallahassee, Fla., 1984—; dir. Livingston Press, U. West Ala., Livingston, 1992—; prof. U. West Ala., 1990—. Author: Oldcat & Ms. Puss: A Book of Days, 1996. Mem. MLA, Associated Writing Program, Pubs. of the South Assn. Home: Rt 2 Box 90-D Coatopa AL 35470

TAYLOR, JOHN RENFORD, JR., writer, business consultant; b. Lubbock, Tex., June 15, 1933; s. John Renford and Lucille (Grier) T.; m. Rosalie Fore, Oct. 1, 1977; children: Perry, Katherine, Michael, David. LLB, LaSalle Ext. U., Chgo., 1962; diploma in banking, So. Meth. U., 1972. Mgr. consumer loan dept. to v.p. and sr. comml. loan officer Frost Nat. Bank, San Antonio, 1966-74; pres., organizer, CEO and dir. Continental Nat. Bank, San Antonio, 1974-77; adminstrv. v.p. Walter Hall Banking Group, various locations, 1977-81; pre-opening pres., dir. North Ctrl. Nat. Bank, Austin, Tex., 1981-87; co-founder Taylor Gray Multi-media Pubs.; asst. prof. fin. U. Houston, Clear Lake, Tex., 1981; ind. businessman, venture capitalist, bus. cons., ind. comml. software developer; lectr. in field; cons. bus. editor Reston (Va.) Pub., divsn. Prentice-Hall, 1977-82. Author: How to Start and Succeed in a Business of Your Own, 1978, Consumer Lending, 1983, The President's Letter Book, 1987, How to Analyze Business Finances, 1992, Business Plans and Loan Applications That Work, 1993, Dollars at Your Feet -- How to Find and Sell Nature's Treasures, 1988; contbr. articles to profl. jours.; newspaper columnist: Across the Counter, Bay Area News, Houston, 1980. With USAF, 1952-55. Mem. Nat. Audubon Soc., Conchologists of Am., Intertel, Am. Mensa. Home: 12303 Beartrap Ln Austin TX 78729-7302

TAYLOR, JOSEPH CHRISTOPHER, audio systems electrical and controls engineer; b. Polkton, N.C., May 7, 1959; s. James Guy and Estell Rose (Wright) T.; m. Selena Renée Ray, May 7, 1983; children: Courtney Desireé, Emily Ashton. BSEE, Clemson U., 1983. Rep. service Neotek West, Los Angeles, 1983-84; engr. electronics AFPRO/TRW, Redondo Beach, Calif., 1983-84; engr. audio Premore Inc., North Hollywood, Calif., 1984-87; field engr. West Coast region Adams Smith, Burbank, Calif., 1987-88; facilities elec. engr. GE, Greenville, S.C., 1994—; co-owner Update Audio/Video Services, Clemson, S.C., 1983—. Baptist. Office: Update Audio/Video Svcs 201 Kelly Rd Clemson SC 29631-1638

TAYLOR, KAREN ANNETTE, mental health nurse; b. Kinston, N.C., Oct. 7, 1952; d. Emmett Green and Polly Ann (Taylor) Tyndall; m. Paul Othell Taylor Jr., June 24, 1979; 1 child, Clarissa Anne. AA, Lenoir C.C., Kinston, 1972; Diploma, Lenoir Meml. Hosp. Sch. of, Nursing, 1984; student, St. Joseph's Coll., Windham, Maine, 1993-94. RN, N.C. Staff nurse Lenoir Meml. Hosp., 1984-86; staff nurse, relief patient care dir. Brynn Marr Hosp., Jacksonville, N.C., 1987-90; staff nurse, quality assurance Naval Hosp., Camp Lejeune, N.C., 1990-92. Recipient Meritorious Unit Commendation Am. Fedn. of Govt. Employees, 1992. Baptist.

TAYLOR, KIMBERLY A., geriatrics nurse; b. Lynchburg, Va., Sept. 15, 1965; d. William Thomas and Shirley Anne (Beville) Arthur; m. Kevin J. Taylor, May 30, 1987; children: Kevin Jeffery Jr., Kara Lindsey. BSN, Lynchburg Coll., 1987. Nurse, instr. Campbell County Schs., Rustburg, Va.; staff and charge nurse, neurol. ICU Lynchburg Gen. Hosp.; nursing supr., care plan coord. Camelot Hall Nursing Home, Lynchburg; staff devel. coord., asst. dir. nursing Autumn Care of Altavista, Va.; health occupations dir. Amherst (Va.) County Pub. Schs. Home: 1108 7th St Altavista VA 24517-1416

TAYLOR, LESLI ANN, pediatric surgery educator; b. N.Y.C., Mar. 2, 1953; d. Charles Vincent Taylor and Valene Patricia (Blake) Garfield. BFA, Boston U., 1975; MD, Johns Hopkins U., 1981. Diplomate Am. Bd. Surgery. Surg. resident Beth Israel Hosp., Boston, 1981-88; rsch. fellow

Pediatric Rsch. Lab. Mass. Gen. Hosp., Boston, 1984-86; fellow pediatric surgery Children's Hosp. of Phila., Phila., 1988-90; asst. prof. pediatric surgery U. N.C., Chapel Hill, 1990—. Author: (booklet) Think Twice: The Medical Effects of Physical Punishment, 1985. Recipient Nat. Rsch. Svc. award NIH, 1984-86. Fellow Am. Coll. Surgeons; mem. AMA, Am. Acad. Pediatrics, Am. Pediat. Surg. Assn.

TAYLOR, LEWIS JEROME, JR., priest; b. Norfolk, Va., Feb. 22, 1923; s. Lewis Jerome and Roberta Page (Newton) T.; m. Pauline Rector Green, Nov. 24, 1945; children: Lewis J. III, Michael R., John B., Mary F., Joan E. BS in Engring., U.S. Naval Acad., 1944; MDiv, Seabury-Western Theol. Sem., Evanston, Ill., 1961; PhD in Religion, Duke U., 1972. Ordained priest Episcopal Ch., 1962. With George R. Green, Inc., White Post, Va., 1949-52, Travelers Ins. Co., Norfolk, 1956-58; chaplain Coll. William and Mary, Williamsburg, Va., 1961-63; rector St. Aidan's Episc. Ch., Virginia beach, Va., 1963-68; prof. theology St. Andrews Sem., Manila, The Philippines, 1971-76; rector Ch. of the Messiah, Chester, N.J., 1978-86; interim rector of various parishes Diocese of Southern Va., 1986-93; instnl. chaplain Indian Creek Correctional Ctr., Chesapeake, Va., 1993—; mem. dept. missions Diocese of Newark, 1965-68, commn. on ministry, Newark, 1979-82; dean Lay Sch. of Christian Studies, Newark, 1977-82; chmn. Commn. on Racism, southern Va., 1992-95. Author: In Search of Self: Life, Death, and Walker Percy, 1985; contbr. articles to profl. jours. Bd. dirs. Samaritan House, Virginia Beach, 1995—. Comdr. USN, 1944-49, 52-56; PTO. Trinity Inst. grantee, 1986. Mem. Rotary (pres. 1980-86). Democrat.

TAYLOR, MARSHA LOPEZ, secondary school educator; b. Richmond, Va., June 13, 1965; d. Louis James and Marlene Alice (Blanchard) Lopez; m. James Rodney Taylor, Oct. 18, 1986. BS in Mgmt. Sci., Averett Coll., 1986; MBA, W.Va. U., 1987. Cert. tchr. Va. Comptr. Schenker Internat., Phila., 1987-88; sales analyst Schenker Internat., Norfolk, Va., 1988-89, accounts receivable mgr., 1989-94; tchr., COE coord. Bassett (Va.) H.S., 1994—; cheerleading coach Bassett H.S., 1994—; aerobics instr. Bally's Health & Fitness, Virginia Beach, 1994. Aerobics instr. Martinsville YMCA, 1994—. Recipient Tchr. of Yr. Bassett Jaycees, 1996. Mem. NAFE, IDEA Exercise Assn., Youth Svcs. Commn. Methodist. Home: 430 Sandy River Rd Axton VA 24054 Office: Bassett High Sch 85 Riverside Dr Bassett VA 24055

TAYLOR, MARTHA ELLEN, private school educator; b. Denver, Apr. 25, 1952; d. James John and Adelina Elise (Collier) Fagan; m. Don Ware Taylor, Nov. 24, 1977 (dec. Jan. 1980); 1 child, Michelle. BA, Cath. U., 1974; MEd, North Tex. State, 1982; postgrad., U. North Tex., 1983-89. Tchr. Peace Corps, Sierra Leone, 1974-75, St. Bernard Sch., Dallas, 1975-76, St. Anthony Sch., Dallas, 1976-77, McDonald Mid. Sch., Mesquite, Tex., 1982-96, Eastfield Community Coll., Mesquite, 1986—, Jesuit Coll. Prep. Sch., Dallas, 1996—. Sunday sch. tchr. St. Patrick's Ch., Dallas, 1983-94, choir dir., 1989-94, bd. religious edn., 1989; choir St. Joseph's Ch., Richardson, 1995—. Mem. Coun. for Exceptional Children, Tex. Assn. for Gifted & Talented, Tex. Computer Edn. Assn., Tex. Coun. Tchrs. Math., Mesquite Edn. Assn., Phi Kappa Phi, Phi Delta Kappa. Roman Catholic. Home: 10645 Longmeadow Dr Dallas TX 75238-2828 Office: Mesquite Ind Sch Dist 2930 N Town East Blvd Mesquite TX 75150-3935

TAYLOR, MARY JANE, art educator, artist; b. Schenectady, N.Y., May 30, 1953; d. Robert Richard and Mary Jane (Thomson) Bender; m. George Richter Taylor, June 21, 1975; children: George Ryan, Rachel Marie. BFA, Valdosta (Ga.) State U., 1975; MEd, U. Ga., 1980, EdD, 1995. Cert. tchr., Ga. Tchr. art grades 9-12 Colquitt County Schs., Moultrie, Ga., 1975-76, Valdosta (Ga.) City Schs., 1976-78; tchr. art grades K-6 Clark County Schs., Athens, Ga., 1978-79; mem. faculty visual arts Brenau U., Gainesville, Ga., 1979—; mem. adj. faculty Ga. Mil. Coll., Valdosta, 1977-78; dir. visual arts Brenau U., 1980—, dir. gallery, 1979-90, acting chair fine arts, 1990-92, chair fine arts, 1993-94, dir. visual arts, assoc. prof., 1995—; mem. faculty art Elderhostel/Brenau U., Gainesville, 1980, 85; mem. adv. bd. Brenau Galleries, Interior Design, Bd., Gainesville, 1990—. One-woman show at Brenau U., 1988; exhibited in group show at Phila. Rug & Carpets, 1975 (1st place), Nat. Invitational Art Exhbn., 1992 (1st prize clay), Sautee Nacoochee Arts Ctr., 1994. Bd. dirs. Ga. Mountains Mus., Gainesville, 1995—, Quinlan Art Ctr., 1991-93; co-chair state conf. Nat. Art Honor Soc., 1992; mem. stds. com., juror 502 Gallery, Gainesville, 1993-94; coord. visual art Ga. Mountains Jubilee, Gainesville, 1983. Art and mus. program grantee Coca Cola Found., 1993-96. Mem. AAUP, Nat. Art Edn. Assn., Ga. Art Edn. Assn. (pres. Pioneer Dist. 1987-90, dir. spl. activities 1990-95, dir. higher edn. divsn. 1995—), Omicron Delta Kappa, Sigma Alpha Iota. Republican. Presbyterian. Home: 3581 Meadow Ln Gainesville GA 30506 Office: Brenau U 1 Centennial Cir Gainesville GA 30501

TAYLOR, MARY LEE, college administrator; b. Amarillo, Tex., Nov. 13, 1931; d. David Kelly and Bessie F. (Peck) McGehee; m. Lindsey Taylor, Sept. 13, 1950 (dec. Aug. 1985); children: Gary, Kent, Ronald. BS, W. Tex. State U., 1959; MEd, Tex. Tech U., 1975. Tchr. Mesquite (Tex.) Pub. Schs., 1961-63; resource tchr. Amarillo Pub. Schs., 1971-79, supr., 1979-80; reading instr. Amarillo Coll., 1981-88, asst. prof. reading, 1988-93, assoc. prof., 1994—; project dir. Tex. Edn. Agy., Austin, 1984-85, 85-86, Amarillo Coll., 1988-89. Mem. Tex. Assn. for Children with Learning Disabilities (meritorious svc. award 1985), Coll. Reading and Learning Assn. (spl. interest group leader 1987-89, cert. 1988, editor newsletter 1987-89), Am. Assn. Cmty. and Jr. Colls., North Plains Assn. for Learning Disabilities (pres. 1987-88, coord. accessibility svcs. 1993—), Tex. Assn. Developmental Educators (membership chmn. 1992-93), Assn. of Higher Edn. and Disabled Students. Office: Amarillo Coll PO Box 447 Amarillo TX 79178-0001

TAYLOR, MILDRED JUANITA, accountant; b. Delray Beach, Fla., Nov. 21, 1947; d. Le Roy and Lula Bell (Comb) Weiss; m. Ronald I. Taylor, Oct. 8, 1965 (div. July 1967); 1 child, Cheryl. BS in Acctg., Kingsenton Coll., 1969. Mgr. bldg. dept. City of Boca Raton, 1970-78; adminstr. constrn. dept. Arvida Corp., Boca Raton, Fla., 1978-80; cont. Seiko Time Corp., U.S.A., Boca Raton, 1978-88, Lytal & Reiter, West Palm Beach, Fla., 1988-91, Prime Mgmt., Boynton Beach, Fla., 1991-92; adminstr. contr. Lake Worth (Fla.) Animal Hosp., 1992—, Calusa Animal Hosp., Boca Raton, 1992—; controller Culligan Water, Delray Beach, 1993-94; pres., owner N. Taylor Enterprises Inc., Boynton Beach, Fla., 1994—. Mem. Orgn. Women Execs. Democrat. Baptist. Home: 96 Mayfair Ln Lake Worth FL 33462-7027 Office: N Taylor Enterprises Inc 96 Mayfair Ln Lake Worth FL 33462-7027

TAYLOR, NATHALEE BRITTON, nutritionist; b. Lubbock, Tex., June 8, 1941; d. Nathaniel E. and Dessie Pauline (Moss) Britton; children by previous marriage: Clay H., Bret N. Courtney. BS in Home Econs., Tex. Tech U., 1963. Home economist Pioneer Gas, Lubbock, Tex., 1963-65; dietician Tex. Tech U., Lubbock, 1966-71; home economist South Plains Electric Co-op., Lubbock, 1986; mgr. quality control Rip Griffins Enterprises, Lubbock, Tex., 1987; sales rep. Time Chem., Lubbock, 1987—; with Sentry, Lubbock; mktg. rep. Dodson Group Ins., Lubbock. Co-author: (cookbook) From Our House to Yours, 1975; columnist: Lubbock Lights mag.; presenter TV show Southwestern Cooking Sta. KTXT. Bd. dirs. Am. Heart Assn., Lubbock, 1985-87; mem. Home Economist in Bus. (pres. Lubbock chpt., 1985); culinary co-chmn. Lubbock C. of C. Arts Festival, 1982, 83, 84. Named Lincoln County Fair Queen. Mem. Tech. Home Ec Alumns (sec./treas.), Am. Home Econs. Assn. (v.p., sec./treas.), Soroptomist (v.p. Lubbock club). Democrat.

TAYLOR, PATRICIA KRAMER, nurse; b. Kempton, Germany, Nov. 20, 1948; came to U.S., 1950; d. Claude John and Dorothy Ruth (Carpenter) Kramer; m. Robert Lemuel Taylor Sr., Oct. 8, 1971; children: Robert Lemuel Jr., John Barden, William Russell. BSN, Duke U., 1971. RN, N.C.; cert. post anesthesia nurse; cert. ACLS, BLS Instr., PALS, TNCC. Staff nurse Duke U. Med. Ctr., Durham, N.C., 1971-73; office nurse Drs. Proctor, Gaddy & Johnston, Raleigh, N.C., 1973; clin. staff nurse Wake Med. Ctr., Raleigh, N.C., 1973-74, surg. staff nurse, 1974-78, staff nurse PACU, 1978—. Den. pack leader Boy Scouts Am., Knightdale, N.C., 1981-90; pres. Phillips H.S. PTA, 1994-95. Mem. Triangle Assn. Post Anesthesia Nurses, N.C. Assn. Post Anesthesia Nurses (treas. 1995—), Am. Soc. Post Anesthesia Nurses, N.C. Assn. Perianesthesia Nurses (treas. 1995-97). Home: PO Box 646 Knightdale NC 27545-0646 Office: Wake Med Ctr Post Anesthesia Care Unit PO Box 14465 Raleigh NC 27620-4465

TAYLOR, RAYMOND GEORGE, JR., educator; b. New Brighton, Pa., Mar. 2, 1939; s. Raymond George and Florence Lydia (Wood) T.; m. Christine Mary Morton, June 1, 1959; children: Raymond G., Leslie W. Taylor McCormick. BS in math., Bucknell Univ., 1959; BS in theology, Epsicopal Theol. Sch., 1962; MS, Univ. Pa., 1964, EdD, 1966; MPA, Pa. State Univ., 1976; MBA, Univ. So. Maine, 1985; PhD, Grad. Theol. Found., 1995. Dir. edn. Vanguard Schs., Haverford, Pa., 1970-74; curriculum dir. Phoenixville (Pa.) Sch. Dist., 1974-77; supt. schs. MSAD # 54, Skowhegan, Maine, 1977-80, Augusta (Maine) City Schs., 1980-86; prof. N.C. State Univ., Raleigh, 1986—; pres. OR/Ed Labs., Oriental, N.C., 1989—. Contbr. over 150 articles to profl. jours. Recipient grants Eurasia Found., 1994-96. Home: 652 Swan Point Rd Bayboro NC 28515 Office: N C State Univ Campus Box 7801 Raleigh NC 28515

TAYLOR, REBECCA ANNE, librarian; b. Gulfport, Miss.; d. William Marion and Irma Adair (Porter) T. AA, Miss. Gulf Coast Jr. Coll., Gulfport, Miss., 1972; BA, U. So. Miss., 1974; MLS, La. State U., 1975. Bookmobile children's libr. St. Charles Parish Libr., Luling, La., 1976-81; asst. dir. Jefferson David Parish Libr., Jennings, La., 1981-82; br. mgr. St. Tammany Parish Libr., Slidell, La., 1982—. Mem. ALA, La. Libr. Assn. Office: Saint Tammany Parish Libr 555 Robert Blvd Slidell LA 70458-1645

TAYLOR, RICHARD BERTROM, accountant; b. Cuthbert, Ga., Nov. 1, 1951; s. Wilburn Bertrom and Marjorie (Hixon) T.; m. Sherrie L. Lieber; children: Kenneth, Douglas. AS cum laude, Andrew Coll., 1971; BBA, U. Ga., 1973. CPA, Ga., Fla. Staff acct. Lester Witte & Co., Atlanta, 1973-79; mgr. Gross, Collins & Cress, P.C., Atlanta, 1979-84, ptnr., 1984—, also v.p. and bd. dirs. Bd. dirs. North Cobb Christian Sch., 1989-90. Mem. AICPAs, Ga. Soc. CPAs, Pinetree Country Club (bd. dirs. 1983-87, 91-93, treas. 1984-85, 91, v.p. 1986), Optimists (sec. 1982-84), Phi Kappa Phi, Beta Alpha Psi, Phi Theta Kappa. Methodist. Office: Gross Collins & Cress PC 2625 Cumberland Pky NW Ste 400 Atlanta GA 30339-3911

TAYLOR, ROBERT BETZ, healthcare administrator, military officer; b. Kingston, N.Y., Jan. 27, 1956; s. Joseph David and Elizabeth Jane (Betz) T.; m. Nancy Lynn Spiri, Sept. 4, 1982; children: Ryan C., Matthew J. BA in Biology, SUNY, Oswego, 1978; MS in Systems Mgmt., U. So. Calif., 1986. Enlisted USN, 1978; hosp. corpsman USN, various locations, 1978-87; commd. USN, 1987, advanced through grades to lt. comdr., 1989; sr. policy analyst Bur. Medicine and Surgery Naval Med. Commd. USN, Washington, 1987-90; dir. pub. rels. Naval Hosp. USN, Camp Lejeuene, N.C., 1990-93, dir. managed care program. Naval Hosp., 1992-94; managed care planner Tricare Region 3 Eisenhower Army Med. Ctr.; spl. lectr. George Washington U., Washington, 1986-90; guest lectr. NSHS, 1989-90; mem. adv. com. on ret. pers. SECNAV, 1989-90; mem. Sec. Def. Panel Mil. Health Svcs. System Reform, 1991; chmn. strategic planning task force BUMED, 1992; presenter in field. Coach West Carteret Little League, Cape Carteret, N.C., 1992-94; scoutmaster Cub Scouts, Boy Scouts Am., 1993. Republican. Roman Catholic. Home: 4611 Sheffield Dr Evans GA 30809-9133 Office: Eisenhower Army Med Ctr Fort Gordon GA 30905

TAYLOR, ROBERT JOHN, academic administrator; b. Camden, N.J., Dec. 3, 1946; s. Joseph John and Catherine Margaret (Williams) T.; m. Connie Gwen Brown, May 1, 1977. BA, Stetson U., 1969, MA, 1971. From dir. fin. aid to dir. student life Clayton State Coll., Morrow, Ga., 1971-96; asst. dir. devel. Operation Mobilization-USA, Tyrone, Ga., 1996—. Sec. bd. trustees Clayton County Libr., Jonesboro, Ga., 1980-92; newsletter editor, bd. dirs. Arts Clayton, Inc., Jonesboro, 1991-92; chmn. Clayton County Arts and Humanities Coun., 1980-82. Mem. Univ. Sys. Ga. Activities Dirs. (chmn. 1995-96, recorder 1992-95), Ga. Coll. Personnel Assn. (2-year coll. rep. 1980-82, newsletter editor 1982-83). Republican. Office: Operation Mobilization-USA 285 Lynnwood Ave Tyrone GA 30290

TAYLOR, RONALD DEAN, marketing and advertising educator; b. Fayetteville, Ark., Apr. 5, 1948; s. C. Paul and O. Joyce (Bindley) T.; m. Jan Erwin Cooper. BS, S.W. Mo. State U., 1973, MBA, 1975; PhD, U. North Tex., 1978. Asst. prof. So. Ill. U., Carbondale, 1978-84; prof. Miss. State U., Starkville, 1984—, assoc. dean Coll. Bus.; assoc. prof. S.W. Mo. State U., Springfield, 1986-87; cons. Zales, Dallas, 1977-79, Hawaiian Tropic, Murray, Ky., 1979-80, Miss. Power and Light, Jackson, 1985, Republic Express Airlines, Memphis, 1986. Contbr. articles to mktg. and bus. jours. Fellow Am. Mktg. Assn. (Outstanding Paper award 1986), Midwest Mktg. Assn. (treas. 1993-94, pres. 1996—, Outstanding Paper award 1986, 87), S.W. Mktg. Assn., Pi Sigma Epsilon; mem. So. Mktg. Assn. (pres. 1987-88), Allied So. Bus. Assn. (pres. 1987-88). Methodist. Home: 501 Colonial Cir Starkville MS 39759-4211 Office: Miss State U Dept Mktg PO Drawer N Mississippi State MS 39762

TAYLOR, ROSLYN DONNY, family practice physician; b. Columbia, S.C., Feb. 14, 1941; d. Otto Gary and Roslyn (Alfriend) Donny; children: Cynthia Gambill, Kevin Emory. BA, Emory U., 1963, MD, 1967. Diplomate Am. Bd. Family Practice. Intern USN, Jacksonville, Fla., 1967-68; resident in family practice Spartanburg (S.C.) Gen. Hosp., 1974-76; pvt. practice Green Cove Springs, Fla., 1968-70, Inman, S.C., 1976-78; student health physician U.S.C., Columbia, 1978-81; with faculty sch. med. U.S.C. Richland Meml. Hosp., 1979-87; vis. prof. family practice U. Utah, Salt Lake City, 1987-88, residency dir. family practice, 1988-94; assoc. prof. family medicine Mercer U. Sch. Medicine, Macon, Ga., 1990-94; assoc. dir. family practice residency Meml. Med. Ctr., Savannah, Ga., 1994—; med. dir. Woodrow Dormitory for Disabled U. S.C., 1984-86; attending physician pain therapy ctr. Richland Meml. Hosp., 1986-87. Rural physician fin. assistance com. State of Utah, 1990-94. Lt. comdr. USNR, 1967-68, 72-73. Named Physician of Yr. Mayor's Com. Employment of Handicapped, Columbia, 1984. Fellow Am. Acad. Family Physicians (Mead-Johnson awards com. 1985-87, commn. on continuing edn. 1988-94), Utah Acad. Family Physicians (alternate del. 1990-94, pres.-elect, pres. 1989-90),, Ga. Acad. Family Physicians (rsch. com., edn. com.); mem. AMA. Presbyterian. Office: Family Practice Ctr Dept Family Practice 1107 E 66th St Savannah GA 31404-5701

TAYLOR, SHAHANE RICHARDSON, JR., ophthalmologist; b. Greensboro, N.C., Sept. 5, 1928; s. Shahane Richardson and Mary Hoke (Hooker) T.; A.B., U. N.C., 1955, M.D., 1959; m. Betty Jane Teague, Aug. 2, 1952; children—Shahane R. III, Anne Teague, Mary Hooker. Intern, N.C. Meml. Hosp., Chapel Hill, 1959-60; resident in ophthalmology U. N.C.-McPherson Meml. Hosp., 1960-63; practice medicine specializing in ophthal. surgery, Greensboro, N.C., 1963—; staff ophthalmologist Wesley Long Hosp.; attending staff Moses Cone; cons. in ophthalmology N.C. State Employees Health Plan, Equicor Medicare, Title 19 program, Jeff-Pilot Life Ins. Co. Served to capt., M.I., U.S. Army, 1951-54. Diplomate Am. Bd. Ophthalmology. Mem. AMA, So. Med. Assn., N.C. Med. Soc. (exec. council 1979-85), Med. Assn. U. N.C. (pres. 1981), Guilford County Med. Soc. (pres. 1977), Med. Rev. N.C. (bd. dirs. 1986—), Am. Acad. Ophthalmology, N.Y. Acad. Scis., Pan Am. Ophthal. Soc., Soc. Eye Surgeons, Mensa, Quarter Century Wireless Assn., Intertel. Episcopalian. Clubs: Greensboro City, Whist, Greensboro Country, Greensboro City (dir.). Home: 2207 Carlisle Rd Greensboro NC 27408-5015 Office: 348 N Elm St Greensboro NC 27401-2141

TAYLOR, STEPHEN JOHN, scouting organization executive; b. Camden, N.J., Jan. 18, 1954; s. Frederick Joseph and Dolores (Harzer) T.; m. Cynthia Kaye McClanahan, June 1, 1976; children: C. Jason, Jared J., Alexander J. BA, Tenn. Wesleyan Coll., 1976; commission, Nat. Exec. Inst., Westlake, Tex., 1976-79. Paraprofl. Great Smoky Mountain coun. Boy Scouts Am., Knoxville, Tenn., 1975-76; dist. exec. Blue Ridge coun. Boy Scouts Am., Greenville, S.C., 1976-79; dist. exec. North Fla. coun. Boy Scouts Am., Jacksonville, 1979-84; asst. scout exec. Coastal Empire Coun. Boy Scouts Am., Savannah, Ga., 1984-90; scout exec. Attakapas coun. Boy Scouts Am., Alexandria, La., 1990-94; scout exec. Palmetto coun. Boy Scouts Am., Spartanburg, S.C., 1994—; mem. faculty All Hands Conf., Boy Scouts Am., Knoxville, 1982, Tarpon Springs, Fla., 1986, 94, Hot Springs, Ark., 1990, Savannah Pediatric Symposium, 1985; sr. advisor Scoutfest, Savannah, 1986-89; instr. Nat. Exec. Inst. II. Editor: Scouting for the Handicapped, 1985, Scouting for Exceptional Children, 1987. Loaned exec. United Way, Seneca, S.C., Gainesville, Fla. and Savannah, 1978-84, mem. cabinet, Alexandria, 1990-91; mem. exec. com. North Cen. Fla. March of Dimes, Gainesville, 1979-84. Recipient fellowship honor award, 1987, God and Svc. award, 1991, St. George award, 1994. Mem. Nat. Eagle Scout Assn. (life), Nat. Assn. Presbyn. Scouters, Rotary (career info. com., 4-way test chmn. Savannah 1984-90, Spartanburg 1994—), Skyuka Lodge, Ouxouiga Lodge, Tomo Chi Chi Lodge, Echockotee Lodge, Atta Kulla Kulla Lodge, LeKau Lodge, Sigma Phi Epsilon (nat. alumni com. 1988-90, faculty leadership conf. 1987-96, nat. elections task force 1993-94, nat. leadership com. 1990—, ambassador 1994—, Scott Key award 1976). Republican. Home: 109 Roswell Ter Spartanburg SC 29307-3738 Office: Palmetto Coun 420 S Church St Spartanburg SC 29306-5232

TAYLOR, STEVEN CRAIG, dentist; b. Anderson, S.C., Oct. 14, 1954; s. Ralph Barnes and L.O. (Pruitt) T.; m. Kathy Elizabeth Bumgarner, July 21, 1979; children: Kelly, Kristen. BS magna cum laude, U. Ga., 1976; DMD, Med. Coll. Ga., 1980. Diplomate Nat. Bd. Dental Examiners, Ga. Bd. Dentistry. Pvt. practice dentistry Monroe, Ga., 1980—. Mem. coun. City of Monroe, 1991-93; commr. Monroe Water, Light and Gas Commn., 1992-93, 95—. Mem. ADA, Ga. Dental Assn., Clarke County Dental Soc., Rotary (pres. 1993-94). Baptist. Home: PO Box 208 Monroe GA 30655-0208 Office: 303 S Broad St Monroe GA 30655-2119

TAYLOR, SYLVIA PINDLE, educational entrepreneur; b. Macon, Ga.; d. Arthur Jackson Sr. and Beatrice (Williams) Pindle; m. John Benjamin Taylor III, June 14, 1969 (div. 1976). BA, Spelman Coll., 1965; postgrad., Howard U., 1966-69, 72-73, Am. U., 1975, 76; MA, Fayetteville State U., 1987. Cert. tchr., N.C., adult counselor, D.C. Tchr. D.C. Pub. Schs., 1966-68; staff asst. U.S. Congresswoman Shirley Chisholm, Washington, 1970-72; adult counselor D.C. Skills Ctr. (Pub. Schs.), Washington, 1972-75; asst. to v.p. for student life Am. U., Washington, 1975-76; staff aide White House Press Office (Main), Washington, 1977-78; editorial asst. Assn. for the Study of Afro-Am. Life and History, Washington, 1980-82; adminstrv. asst. Operation Sickle Cell, Inc., Fayetteville, 1985-86; cert. substitute tchr. Cumberland County Pub. Sch., Fayetteville, 1987-90; owner, CEO, founder Nat. Coll. Svc., Inc., Fayetteville, 1987—; counselor Neighborhood Youth Corps, Inc. Washington, 1968-70; vol. cons. Conv. Planning, Inc., Washington, 1978, Ofield Dukes & Assocs., Inc., Washington, 1969-78, Nat. Urban League, Julius A. Thomas Vol. Soc., N.Y.C., 1979. Co-author: The Handbook of Information for International Students, 1976. Mem. NAACP, Fayetteville, 1987-89. Acad. scholar Coll. Entrance Exam. Bd., 1959, 61. Mem. ASCD, The Links Inc., Teen Involvement Project Inc., Alpha Kappa Alpha, Kappa Delta Pi, Alpha Kappa Mu. Episcopalian. Home and Office: Nat Coll Svc Inc PO Box 2056 3105 Mars Pl Fayetteville NC 28302-2056

TAYLOR, TERESA BROOKS, sociologist, educator; b. Kingsport, Tenn., May 4, 1967; d. Isaac D. and Virginia Mae (Brown) Brooks; m. Rodney Lee Taylor, May 15, 1993. BA, U. Tenn., Knoxville, 1989, MA, 1991. Grad. teaching asst. and assoc. dept. sociology U. Tenn., Knoxville, 1989-91; adj. faculty instr. sociology Pellissippi State Tech. C.C., Knoxville, 1992-93, East Tenn. State U., Johnson City, 1993—, N.E. State Tech. C.C., Blountville, 1993—; cmty. svc. vol.; presenter in field. Mem. Am. Sociol. Assn., So. Sociol. Soc., Mid-South Sociol. Assn. Home: 322 King Ave Church Hill TN 37642

TAYLOR, THOMAS, retired air force officer, security policy analyst; b. Sept. 17, 1945. BA in Internat. Affairs, Fla. State U., 1966; MSA in Pub. Adminstrn., George Washington U., 1977; postgrad., Indsl. Coll. Armed Forces, 1977, Air War Coll., 1989. Commd. 2d lt. USAF, 1967, advanced through grades to lt. col., 1990; with Allied Air Forces (NATO), 1981-83, inspector gen., 1983-86; mem. joint chiefs of staff Pentagon, Washington, 1986-90; with nuclear nonproliferation Dept. Energy, Washington. Home: 1713-B S Hayes St Arlington VA 22202

TAYLOR, THOMAS HUDSON, JR., import company executive; b. Somerville, Mass., June 8, 1920; s. Thomas Hudson and Virginia Gwendolyn (Wilson) T.; B.S. in Econs., Wharton Sch. Fin. and Commerce, U. Pa., 1947; m. Mary Jane Potter, Dec. 1, 1943; children—Thomas Hudson, III, James R., Jane, John E., Virginia. Acctg. exec. Collins & Aikman Corp., Phila., 1947-55, divisional controller automotive div., Albemarle, N.C., 1956-59, asst. dir. purchases, 1960-64; exec. v.p. Carolina Floral Imports, Inc., Gastonia, N.C., 1965-67, pres., treas., 1968—. County commr. Stanly County, Albemarle, N.C., 1962-66. Served to capt. USAAF, 1941-45. Decorated Air medal. Mem. Beta Theta Pi. Republican. Methodist. Clubs: Princeton, Gastonia City. Home: 4537 Forest Cove Dr Belmont NC 28012-8734 Office: PO Box 2201 Gastonia NC 28053-2201

TAYLOR, TIMOTHY GORDON, economics educator; b. Cin., Dec. 11, 1951; s. Jack G. and Ruth M. (Bengal) T.; m. Keri Hamacher, Dec. 30, 1978; children: Tracy S., Justin M. BA in Econs., U. Cin., 1975; PhD in Agrl. Econs., U. Fla., 1980. Econ. analyst U. Fla., Gainesville, 1980-81, asst. prof. econs., 1981-86, assoc. prof. econs., 1986-91, prof. econs., 1991—; cons. Orgn. Ea. Caribbean States, Rosseau, Dominica, 1992-93, Chemonics Internat., C.Am., 1993-94, Winrock Internat., Almaty, Kazakhstan, 1994. Contbr. articles, monograph to profl. publs., chpts. to books; author procs., papers, reports in field. Grantee USDA/Caribbean Basin Adv. Group, 1991-94, Orgn. Ea. Caribbean States, 1991-92, 93—, Am. Farm Bur. Fedn., 1991-92. Mem. So. Agrl. Econs. Assn. (Outstanding Rsch. award 1989), Econometric Soc., Am. Econ. Assn., Gamma Sigma Delta, Omicron Delta Epsilon. Home: 112 NW 101st Ct Gainesville FL 32607-6302 Office: U Fla Food and Resource Econs PO Box 240 Gainesville FL 32611-0240

TAYLOR, TOM ALLEN BRYAN, educational consulting firm executive; b. Houston, Mar. 29, 1944; s. Allen Davis and Pauleen Evelyn (Tucker) T.; m. Pamela Grace Dial, Apr. 13, 1968; children: Holly Rebecca Taylor Mayes, Bryan Jack Thomas. BS in Edn., U. Tex., 1969, MA in Comm., 1974. Speech instr., theatre dir. Temple (Tex.) Jr. Coll., 1974-76; internat. tour Tom Taylor as Woody Guthrie, 1976-81; advt. dir. Hydra-Fitness Industries, Belton, Tex., 1981-86; instr. speech and theatre U. Mary Hardin-Baylor, Belton, 1986-88; instr. English U. Mary Hardin Baylor, Belton, 1987-89; speech instr. Ctrl. Tex. Coll., Killeen, fall 1988, McLennan C.C., Waco, Tex., 1989-90; tchr. English Ellison H.S., Killeen, 1990-92; tchr. speech and theater dir. Killeen H.S., 1992-95; founder, pres. The Cairo Co. and His Handiwork Ministries, Belton, Tex., 1995—; mem. speech curriculum com. Tex. Edn. Agy., Austin, 1992-95; speech instr. U. Mary Hardin-Baylor, 1996—. Author: (children's books) Bernadette (The Worm), 1983, Mommy and Me, Beagle the Eagle, 1993, Brant the Ant, 1993, Tom Taylor's Poems for Children, Abaner, Al, Beagle and Brant, 1995, Tom Taylor's Poems for Children, Vol. II, If I Could Eat a Rainbow, 1995; (children's albums) Don't Ever Blow An Elephant's Nose, 1985, Ducklips, Worm Wings and Lots of Other Things, 1992, Abaner, Al, Beagle and Brant, 1993, Tom Taylor's Poems for Children, Vol. I, Abaner, Al, Beagle and Brant, 1995; (motivational/inspirational) Teachers Are, 1994, Get Outa Here, 1995; (instrnl. manual) Hydra-Fitness Training Manual, 1985. Active Hope for the Hungry, Belton, 1980—; bd. dirs. Table Rock Festival, Salado, Tex., 1992—; founder Ctrl. Tex. Tellers Guild. Recipient Best Prodn. award for Woody Guthrie, Artisan Awards of Chgo., 1978; named Best Actor for Woody Guthrie, Bay Area Theatre Critics, 1980. Mem. Tex. Storytelling Assn., Nat. Storytelling Assn., Internat. Platform Assn., Live Poets Soc., Tex. Classroom Tchrs. Assn., Tex. Ednl. Theatre Assn. Home: PO Box 2063 Belton TX 76513-2063

TAYLOR, VESTA FISK, real estate broker, educator; b. Ottawa County, Okla., July 15, 1917; d. Ira Sylvester and Judie Maude (Garman) Fisk; m. George E. Taylor, Aug. 17, 1957 (dec. Oct. 1963); stepchildren: Joyce, Jean, Luther. AA, Northeastern Okla. A&M, 1931; BA, N.E. State U., Tahlequah, Okla., 1937; MA, Okla. State U., 1942. Life cert. Spanish, English, history, elem. Tchr. rural sch. grades 1-4 Ottawa County, Okla., 1931-33; tchr. rural sch. grades 1-8 Ottawa County, 1933-38; tchr. H.S. Spanish, English Wyandotte, Okla., 1938-42; tchr. H.S. Spanish, English, math. Miami, Okla., 1942-57; tchr. H.S. Spanish Jacksonville, Ill., 1960-65; tchr. H.S. Spanish, English Miami, 1965-79; owner, broker First Lady Realty, Miami, 1979—; tchr. real estate for licensing N.E. Okla. Vocat.-Tech., Afton, 1980—; radio spellmaster weekly-county groups Coleman Theater Stage, 1954-57, radio program weekly 4-H, Miami, 1953-57. Author: (poem) The Country School, 1994. Sec. Ottawa County Senior's Ctr., 1993—; restoration com. Friends of Theater, 1993—; mem. Friends of the Libr. Named Outstanding Coach Ottawa County 4-H Clubs, Miami, 1955, 67, Outstanding Alumnus All Yrs. H.S. Reunion, Wyandotte, Okla.,

1992, Champion Speller N.E. Okla. Retirees, Oklahoma City, 1991. Mem. AAUW (pres. 1978-80, treas. 1994—), Ottawa County Ret. Educators (treas. 1990-94), Spanish Study Club (pres., instr. 1962-63), Miami Classroom Tchrs. (v.p. 1973-77), Tri-State Travel Club (purser 1989-95), Kappa Kappa Iota. Democrat. Baptist. Home: 821 Jefferson St Miami OK 74354-4910 Office: First Lady Realty 206 A St NW Miami OK 74354

TAYLOR, WASHINGTON THEOPHILUS, mathematics educator; b. Mobile, Ala., July 24, 1931; s. W. Howard and Iona (Fuller) T.; div.; children: Tara G. Taylor Marshall, Theolya RhoMayne Taylor Harris. BS, Ala. State U., 1953; MBS, U. Colo., 1960; EdD, Okla. State U., 1969. Tchr. Bd. of Sch. Commrs., Mobile, 1953-54, 56-59, 1985-86; prof. math. So. U., Baton Rouge, 1960-84; instr. math. U. South Ala., Moblie, 1986-87; assoc. prof. math. Ala. State U., Montgomery, 1987-92; instr. math. Bishop State Community Coll., Mobile, Ala., 1992—; cons. in field. Mem. Scotlandville Area Adv. Com., Baton Rouge, 1960-84, Ala. Dem. Com., Moblie, 1984—; bd. dirs. Com. to Elect St. Amant to Ho. or Reps., Baton Rouge, 1982, Citizens for Williams for City Coun., Prichard, Ala, 1984. Lt. col. USAR, ret. Fellow Internat. Paper Co., 1957, NSF, 1958-60, So. Fellowship Found., 1967-68; vis. fellow Ohio State U., 1972-73; Women's Federated Club scholar, 1949. Mem. NEA (life) Nat. Coun. Tchrs. Math., Comprehensive Health Ctr. N. Baton Rouge (bd. dirs. 1970-85), Ala. Mental Health Assn. (bd. dirs. 1990-92), Montgomery Mental Health Assn. (bd. dirs. 1987-92), Res. Officers Assn. (life), Mobile Area Mardi Gras Assn., Phi Delta Kappa, Alpha Phi Alpha (life), Pi Mu Epsilon. Home: 2150 Barlow St Mobile AL 36617-3104

TAYLOR, WATSON ROBBINS, JR., investment banker; b. Montgomery, Ala., Mar. 16, 1956; s. Watson Robbins and Ernestine (Jenkins) T.; m. Davis Anne Denson, July 12, 1980; children: Watson Robbins III, Caroline Davis, Davis Denson. BS, Auburn U., 1979, MBA, 1982. Ranch foreman Johnston & Sons, Letohatchee, Ala., 1975-76; estimator Standard Roofing Co., Montgomery, Ala., 1976-78; v.p. Standard Roofing Co., 1978-84; pres. Standard Roofing USA, Inc., Montgomery, 1984-93, Standard-Taylor Industries, 1990-93; ptnr. First Commerce Capital, Inc., Montgomery, 1993—; bd. dirs. Auburn U. Sch. Bus., Montgomery, Montgomery Acad. Fin. chmn. Ala. Rep. Com., Birmingham, 1989; trustee YMCA Endowment Found., Montgomery, 1989; bd. dirs. ARC, 1989, Montgomery coun. Boy Scouts Am., 1989. Mem. Montgomery Area C. of C. (bd. dirs. 1989-92), Ala. Alliance Bus. and Industry (bd. dirs. 1989-92), Rotary (past dir.), Young Pres.'s Assn. (Rebel chpt.), Montgomery Country Club. Episcopalian. Home: 3809 Colline Dr Montgomery AL 36106

TAYLOR, WESLEY ALAN, accountant, consultant; b. Johnson City, Tenn., Oct. 27, 1958; s. Wesley Wentworth and Charlotte Marie (Holly) T. BS in Acctg., U. Tenn., 1980. CPA, Tenn., Va.; registered rep. Nat. Assn. Securities Dealers; lic. pvt. pilot FAA. Staff acct. Wesley W. Taylor CPA, P.C., 1980-85; sr. acct. Blackburn, Childers & Stegall, CPAs, Elizabethton, Tenn., 1985-88; acct., mgr. BCS & Co., CPAs, Bristol, Tenn., 1988-89; pvt. practice, Elizabethton, 1989; tax sr. Brown, Edwards & Co., CPAs, Abingdon and Bristol, Va., 1989-91; pvt. practice Elizabethton, Tenn., 1991—. Auditor for various local Miss Am. preliminary pageants, 1985-96, local state fair pageant judge, 1992, local parade judge, 1994-95. Mem. AICPA, Johnson City Jaycees (pres., v.p., treas., Keyman of Yr., Jaycee of Yr., Presdl. award of excellence, others), Tenn. Jaycees (state sec.-treas.), Aircraft Owners and Pilots Assn. (pvt. pilot 1996—), Nat. Aeronautical Assn., Profl. Assn. Diving Instrs. (open water diver 1988). Republican. Home: 122 Mountain View Dr Apt 1 Johnson City TN 37601 Office: 308 E F St Elizabethton TN 37643-3270

TAYLOR, WILLIAM AL, church administrator; b. Danville, Va., Sept. 26, 1938; s. Preston Floyd and Helen Elizabeth (Doss) T.; m. Brenda Flo Owen, June 4, 1961; children: Fawnia Rae Ricks, Albert Todd, Athena Dawn Jarman. AA, Lee Coll., 1957; postgrad., U. Calif., Santa Barbara, 1980. Br. mgr. Ency. Britannica, Greensboro, N.C., 1960-62; divsn. trainer Ency. Britannica, Mpls., 1963; dist. mgr. Ency. Britannica, Omaha, 1964-72; adminstrv. asst. Forward in Faith Internat. Broadcast, Cleveland, Tenn., 1972-80; gen. mgr. Sta. WQNE-FM, Cleveland, 1980—; dir. stewardship Ch. of God Internat. Offices, Cleveland, 1980—; pres. Pathway Credit Union, Cleveland, 1985—, Vision Found., Cleveland, 1985—, exec. dir., 1979-80; chmn. Internat. Commn. on Prayer, Cleveland, 1986—. Author: Proving God, 1991, Days of Heaven on Earth, 1993, Stewardship Masterplanning, 1993. Pres. Clean Water Soc., Gastonia, N.C., 1974-75; speaker Citizens Against Legalized Liquor, Bradley County, Tenn., 1973, 75; advisor Mothers on March, Cleveland, 1976; active Nat. Conf. on Drug Abuse, Washington, 1978; master of ceremonies Nat. Religious Leaders Conf. on Alcohol and Drug Abuse, Indpls., 1979. Recipient Mass Communications award Ch. of God Media Ministries, 1980, Stephen award Ch. of God Lay Ministries, 1990. Mem. Nat. Assn. Evangelicals (bd. adminstrs. 1985—, chmn. stewardship commn. 1985-89), Christian Stewardship Assn. (bd. dirs. 1990-94). Office: Ch of God Dept Stewardship 2490 Keith St NW Cleveland TN 37311-1309

TAYLOR, WILLIAM DOUGLAS, college administrator; b. Johnson City, Tenn., Aug. 1, 1948; s. Ben Worley and Frances Nell (Joines) T.; m. Darby Ann O'Neil, Aug. 31, 1973; children: Ashley Elisabeth, Shelby O'Neil. BS, E. Tenn. State U., 1973, MA, 1974; PhD, U. Miss., 1982. Editor, spl. edn. tchr. S.C. Dept. Mental Retardation, Clinton, S.C., 1974-77; counselor U. Miss., Oxford, 1980-82, dir. student counseling ctr., 1982-84; chmn. counseling, developmental studies U. Ga., Athens, 1984-87; dir. career planning Carson-Newman Coll., Jefferson City, Tenn., 1987-90, dir. acad. advising, 1990-92; coord. acad. support Carson-Newman Coll., Jefferson City, 1992—. Author: College Study Skills, 1982, Home Growed Rebels: History of the 59th Tenn. Inf. REgiment, 1991. Sponsor Boy Scouts Explorer Troop, Jefferson City, 1988-90; mem. vestry, tchr. Episcopal Chs. in S.C., Miss., Tenn., 1975-89. With U.S. Army, 1969-72. Mem. So. Assn. Coll. Student Affairs, Tenn. Coll. Placement Coun., Coll. Placement Coun., 63rd Tenn. Inf. Regiment (re-enactor). Home: 819 W 2nd North St Morristown TN 37814-3817 Office: Carson-Newman Coll PO Box 2018 Jefferson City TN 37760

TAYLOR, WILLIAM FARNHAM, emergency physician; b. Port Chester, N.Y., Nov. 15, 1947; s. William Underhill and Evelyn Ruth (Farnham) T.; m. Barbara Kaser, Jan. 14, 1990. BA, Yale U., 1969; MD, Cornell U., 1973. Diplomate Am. Bd. Internal Medicine, Am. Bd. Emergency Medicine. Resident in internal medicine U. Wash., Seattle, 1973-78; med. dir. Pioneer Sq. Health Sta., Seattle, 1975-77; emergency physician Lakewood Hosp., Tacoma, 1975-90, med. dir. emergency dept., 1980-89; emergency physician Tacoma Gen. Hosp., 1978-90, Piedmont Emergency Medicine, Charlotte, N.C., 1990—. Mem. Alpha Omega Alpha. Office: Piedmont Emergency Med Assocs 1332 E Morehead St Ste 220 Charlotte NC 28204-2957

TAYLOR, WILLIAM L., executive. Chief adminstrv. officer, v.p. Universal Corp., Richmond, Va. Office: Universal Leaf Tobacco Co Hamilton St at Broad Box 25099 Richmond VA 23260*

TAYLOR, WOODROW MANNING, computer company executive, military officer; b. Kinston, N.C., June 14, 1941; s. Woodrow Wilson and Martha (Rogers) T.; m. Patricia Jane Phelps, Apr. 14, 1963; children: Hope Hathaway, Jennifer Peace, Woodrow Bryan. BS in Agrl. Econs., N.C. State U., 1963; MBA, Inter Am. U., 1968. B-52 Navigator 60th Bomb Squadron USAF, Ramey AFB, P.R., 1965-68; B-52 radar navigator 379th Bomb Wing USAF, Wurtsmith AFB, Mich., 1968-72; bomb navigator officer 8th AF USAF, Barksdale AFB, Ala., 1973-76; staff officer hqrs. SAC USAF, Offutt AFB, Nebr., 1976-79, div. chief hqrs. SAC, 1979-84; div. chief hqrs. USAF, Pentagon, Va., 1984-87; commdr. command & control systems ctr. USAF, Tinker AFB, Okla., 1987-91, vice commdr. comms. system ctr., 1991-92, commr. 654th CCSG, 1992-93. Prodn. chmn. Red Earth, Oklahoma City, 1989-97. Col. USAF, 1963-93. Mem. Air Force Assn., Armed Forces Comm. Electronic Assn. (pres. Oklahoma City chpt. 1995-96, dir. 1987-95). Democrat. Southern Baptist. Home: 1130 Whippoorwill Vis Choctaw OK 73020-7013 Office: BDM 5600 Liberty Pky Midwest City OK 73110-2835

TAYLOR, Z. LOWELL, environmental company executive; b. 1937. With U.S. Pipe & Foundry Co., Birmingham, Ala., 1969-70, Auburn (Ala.) U., 1970-75, Williams Environ. Mgmt. Inc., Stone Mountain, Ga., 1975-76, Frit Industries, Inc., Ozark, Ala., 1976-80, Jim Walter Resources Inc., Birmingham, Ala., 1980-87; pres. Williams Environ. Svcs., Stone Mountain, Ga., 1988—. Office: Williams Environ Svcs 2075 W Park Pl Ste E Stone Mountain GA 30087

TAYRIEN, DOROTHY PAULINE, retired nursing educator; b. Bartlesville, Okla., June 15, 1921; d. William Cyprian and Ida May (Bennett) Tayrien; student Bartlesville Coll. High Jr. Coll.; diploma in nursing St. John Hosp., Tulsa, 1945; BS, U. Colo., 1948; AM, U. Chgo., 1959; postgrad. U. S.C., 1980-81. Hosp. staff nurse Pawhuska City Hosp., 1945-48; tchg. fellow Vanderbilt U., 1948-49; instr. Sch. Nursing, U. Okla., Oklahoma City, 1948-50; instr. surg. nursing Fla. State U., Tallahassee, 1951-52; asst. prof. nursing fundamentals Northwestern State Coll., Natchitoches, La., 1950-51; asst. prof., dir. clin. edn. Monroe (La.) Div., 1952-54; asst. prof., asst. dean Sch. Nursing, Baylor U., Waco, Tex., 1954-55; asst. dir. nursing svc. Washington Meml. Hosp., Bartlesville, 1955-57; asst. prof. nursing fundamentals S.W. La. U., Lafayette, 1957-59; assoc. prof. med. surg. nursing E. Tenn. State U., Johnson City, 1960-65, So. Ill. U., Edwardsville, 1965-67, Forest Park Jr. Coll., St. Louis, 1967-68; prof., dir. assoc. degree nursing program Kankakee (Ill.) C.C., 1968-70; assoc. prof., dir. continuing edn. program Coll. Nursing, Med. U. S.C., Charleston, 1970-81; ret., 1981; dir. nursing Tallahassee chpt. ARC, 1951-52; cons. in nursing, Belleville (Ill.) Meml. Hosp., 1967-68; spkr. in field. Bd. dirs. Lewis & Clark C.C., Ill., 1968-70, Women and Children in Crisis, Bartlesville, 1986-90, La Quinta Preservation Found., 1986-91; active St. John Roman Cath. Ch. S.C. Regional Med. Program grantee, 1975-77. Mem. AAUW, Am. Assn. Ret. Persons, Allied Arts & Humanities Coun., Bartlesville Art Assn. Democrat. Contbr. articles to profl. jours.; initiated and established AAS Degree in Nursing Program, Kankakee (Ill.) C.C., 1968-70. Home: 6547 Clear Creek Loop Bartlesville OK 74006-8010

TAZEWELL, CALVERT WALKE (WILLIAM STONE DAWSON), retired military officer, publisher, author, historian, webmaster; b. Wilmington, Del., Apr. 13, 1917; s. Calvert W. and Sophie (Goode) T.; student Air Corps Tech. Sch., 1940, Air Tactical Sch., 1948, Sophia U., Tokyo, 1951, Air Command and Staff Sch., USAF Air U., 1952, Ind. U., 1956, Fisk U., 1964; m. Beverly Mae LaCour, Jan. 14, 1943 (div. Apr. 1959); children: Lyn Diane Hamilton, Patricia Marie Werner, Beverly Ann Innes; m. 2d, Belle Gordon, July 7, 1959 (div.); 1 child, William Bradford Dawson; m. 3d, Theresa Hoey, Feb. 20, 1976; adopted children: Valera Marie Strauser, Sabrina Maria; 7 stepchildren. Pvt., Va. NG, 1934-35; radio technician, San Antonio, 1936-37; pvt., USAC, 1937, m/sgt. weather observer and forecaster, 1941; commd. 2d lt. USAAF (by direct appointment while overseas), 1942, advanced through grades to lt. col. Airways and Air Comm. Svc.; comml. multi-engine pilot; comm. specialist on USAF meteorol. flight, flew over North Pole, 1947; during World War II developed and supervised for USAAF pioneer worldwide weather comm. system, which principles and techniques accepted by World Meteorol. Orgn. and Internat. Civil Aviation Orgn.; apptd. officer Regular Army, 1947; transferred to USAF, 1948; comdr. 1951st AAGS Squadron, Nagoya, Japan, 1950-51; dep. dir. plans and requirements Hdqrs. 1808th AACS Wing, Tokyo, 1951-52; comdr. 1300th Student Squadron, Great Falls, Mont., 1953-54, 818th AC & W Squadron, Randolph, Tex., 1955-56, Kangnung Air Base, Korea, 1957, Takaoyama Air. Sta., Japan, 1958; dir. comm.-electronics 314th Air div. Osan, Korea, 1956-57, Duluth Air Def. Sector, 1958-59; ret., 1959; civil def. coord. Dade County, Fla., 1961; organizer chmn. Met. Dade County Pub. Libr. Adv. Bd., 1963-64; instr. N.Y. U., 1962-63, Old Dominion U., 1964-65; microcomputer mktg. systems specialist, 1977-82; owner W.S. Dawson Co. Pubs.; amateur radio sta. operator, 1934—; amateur nutritionist, computerist; organizer and webmaster Hampton Rds. Ctrl. Libr., 1995. Author, editor 31 books including True Owners of the Soil, Moon Walk 1835, Genealogy of the Tazewell and Allied Families, Meet the Tazewells, Waller Scrapbook, Ye Hysterical History of Ye Norfolk Towne, The Goode Diary, Meet Marshall Marks, Greatness Lost?, Cittie of Ralegh. Trustee Assn. Preservation Va. Antiquities, 1967-69; bd. dirs. Boush-Tazewell-Waller House, Norfolk, 1982-83. Recipient awards Writers Digest, 1974, 75, Nat. Writers Club, 1976. Decorated Bronze Star. Mem. Norfolk Hist. Soc. (life mem., 1st pres., founder 1965), Va. History Fedn. (1st pres., founder 1967). Contbr. articles on nutrition, electronics and history to periodicals in U.S., Gt. Britain. Address: PO Box 62823 Virginia Beach VA 23466-2823

TCHERNESHOFF, LYNDON MARK, business development executive; b. Ft. Worth, July 26, 1956; s. Peter John and Rheta Nell (Thrasher) T.; m. Leila Marie Freeman, July 30, 1988. BSME, U. Ala., Huntsville, 1987. Engring. asst. U. Ala., Huntsville, 1977-84; test engr. U. Ala., 1984; cryogenic test engr. Ala. Cryogenic Engring. Inc., Huntsville, 1984-87; SRB devel. flight instrumentation test engr. Teledyne Brown Engring., Huntsville, 1987-88; Spacelab experiment integration engr. Teledyne Brown Engring., 1988-90; STS-42 lead systems engr. Teledyne Brown Engring., Huntsville, 1990-91; sales, engring. and quality assurance mgr. Communication Assocs., Inc., Anniston, Ala., 1991-93; robotics sales engr. Westinghouse-Remotec, Knoxville, Tenn., 1993-96; bus. devel. mgr. Northrop-Grumman-Remotec, Knoxville, 1996—. Mem. Internat. Assn. Bomb Technicians and Investigators, Assn. Unmanned Vehicle Systems, Pi Kappa Alpha. Republican. Baptist. Office: Northrup Grumman Corp REMOTEC 114 Union Valley Rd Oak Ridge TN 37830-8044

TCHORYK, ROBERT CHARLES, oil company administrator; b. Johnstown, Pa., Jan. 14, 1956; s. Wasyl and Mary (Rudy) T. BA, Washington and Jefferson Coll., 1977; M of Accountancy, Bowling Green St. U., 1979. Sr. joint venture acct. Cities Service Co., Houston, 1979-83; sr. internat. acct. Ashland Oil Co., Houston, 1983-85; sr. administrator Sedco Forex-Schlumberger, Dallas, 1985-86; fin. analyst Continental Airlines, Inc., Houston, 1986-87; internat. contracts specialist Marathon Oil Co., Houston, 1987—. Home: 1301 Wood Hollow Dr Apt 11104 Houston TX 77057-1639 Office: Marathon Oil Co 5555 San Felipe St Houston TX 77056-2725

TCHOUNWOU, PAUL BERNARD, environmental health specialist; b. Bangou, Cameroon, Aug. 14, 1960; came to U.S., 1985; s. Maurice and Christine (Kouanang) Seumo; m. Martha Namondo Mondoa, Aug. 3, 1990; children: Christine K., Hervey M. BSc, U. Yaounde, Cameroon, 1983, MSc, 1984; MS in Pub. Health, Tulane U., 1986, ScD, 1990. Cert. toxicologist Nat. Environ. Health Assn.; registered sanitarian La. State Bd. Examiners for Sanitarians. Tchg. asst. Tulane Sch. Pub. Health, New Orleans, 1988-90; med. rschr. Inst. Med. Rsch., Yaounde, 1991-94; asst. prof. Faculty Medicine, Yaounde, 1992-94; rsch. assoc. Xavier & Tulane Univs., New Orleans, 1994-96; assoc. prof., dir. environ. sci. PhD program Jackson State U., Jackson, 1996—; environ. health cons. Orstom & UNICEF, Yaounde, 1992-93, U.S. AID, Kaele, 1991-93; rsch. supr. Tulane Sch. Pub. Health, New Orleans, 1994—; tng. and rsch. fellow U.S. AID, Washington, 1985-90. Editl. bd. Internat. Jour. Environ. Toxicology and Water Quality, 1994—; contbr. articles to profl. jours. Grantee Internat. Devel. Rsch. Ctr., Ottowa, 1992-93. Mem. APHA, Water Environ. Fedn., Cameroon Bioscis. Soc., Cameroon Assn. Epidemiology, Nat. Environ. Health Assn., Delta Omega. Roman Catholic. Home: 1035 Lake Ave Apt 234 Metairie LA 70005 Office: Tulane U Med Ctr Dept Environ Health 1430 Tulane Ave New Orleans LA 70112

TEAGUE, BARBARA ANN, art educator; b. Star City, Ark., Feb. 5, 1938; d. Alfred Allen and Vera Margarette (Holloway) Ozment; m. Waymond L. Teague, Jan. 19, 1960; 1 child, Daniel Andrew. BSE, U. Ark., Monticello, 1960; MEd, U. Ark., 1964; PhD, U. North Tex., 1986. Cert. secondary tchr., Ark. Tchr. sci. Selma (Ark.) Pub. Schs., 1960-62, Warren (Ark.) Pub. Schs., 1962-63, U.S. Army Edn. Ctr., Ft. Carson, Colo., 1963-64; tchr. sci. and art Morrilton (Ark.) Pub. Schs., 1965-74; adj. art instr. Henderson State U., Mena, Ark., 1976-77; tchr. sci. and art Dardanelle (Ark.) Pub. Schs., 1980-87; adj. instr. art U. Ark., Little Rock, 1987; asst. prof. art U. Ark., Monticello, 1989-94, U. Cen. Ark., Conway, 1994-95; adj. instr. art East Tex. State U., Texarkana, 1988; cons. Ark. State Dept. of Edn., Little Rock, 1983—, Ark. Edn. TV Network, Conway, 1989. Author: (with others) Art Education: Administrator's Handbook, 1984, Arkansas Curriculum Guidelines, 1987; illustrator, artist logos and children's book; works represented in numerous one-woman shows and group exhibits, 1970—. Ark. State Dept. of Edn. grantee, 1985; assistantship U. North Tex., 1986. Mem. Ark. Art Educators (sec. 1988-90, v.p. 1990-92, pres. 1992—), Nat. Art Edn. Assn., Monticello Art League (v.p., bd. dirs. 1990-94), Mid-So. Watercolorists, Seark Concert Assn., Soc. Children's Book Writers and Illustrators, Texarkana Regional Arts & Humanities Ctr., Jaycettes (officer 1968-73), Phi Delta Kappa. Home: 295 Stone Rd Ashdown AR 71822-9803

TEAGUE, WAYNE, state agency administrator; b. Cullman, Ala., Nov. 19, 1927; s. Levi Wade and Floy Irene (McKelvey) T.; m. Eleanor Josephine Jones, June 5, 1949; children—Karen Jo, Dewey Wayne. B.S., Auburn U., 1950, M.S., 1953, Ed.D., 1962; LL.D., Troy State U., 1978. Tchr., coach, asst. prin. Heard High Sch., Franklin, Ga., 1950-55; prin. Marion County Elem. and High Sch., Buena Vista, Ga., 1955-56, Jonesboro (Ga.) Sr. High Sch., 1956-58, S.W. DeKalb High Sch., Decatur, Ga., 1958-63; coordinator field services Sch. Edn., dir. correspondence study, asso. prof. ednl. adminstrn. Auburn (Ala.) U., 1963-69; supt. Auburn City Schs., 1969-75; state supt. edn. Ala. Dept. Edn., 1975-95; ret. Served with USAAC, 1946. Methodist. Club: Masons.

TEAL, EDWIN EARL, retired engineering physicist, consultant; b. Dallas, May 10, 1914; s. Olin Allison and Azelia Clyde (Kidd) T.; m. Ruby Brown, Aug. 10, 1939; children: Barbara Teal Berry, Marilyn Teal Roberts. BA, Baylor U., 1935; MS, U. Mich., 1937. Mem. staff computer-seismic dept. Texaco, Inc., Houston, 1938-40, magnetometer operator, 1940-42; physicist Navy Underwater Sound Lab., New London, Conn., 1942-45, Texaco Geophys. Lab., Houston, 1945-47; physicist, chief engr. equipment dept. Bariod div. N.L. Industries, Houston, 1947-70; asst. to mgr. mfg. McCullough div. N.L. Industries, Houston, 1970-79; pvt. practice cons. physicist Houston, 1979-96; ret., 1996. Pres. Indsl. Mgmt. Club, Houston, 1963-64; area dir. Braeswood Pl. Homeowners Assn., Houston, 1981-83; advisor Jr. Achievement of Houston. Marston scholar Brown U., 1935-36. Mem. IEEE (life, chmn. Houston sect. 1976), Acoustical Soc. Am. (life), Sigma Pi Sigma. Baptist.

TEARE, JOHN RICHARD, JR., lawyer; b. Phila., Sept. 23, 1954; divorced; 1 child, John III; m. Gale Angela Waters, June 5, 1982; children: Angela, Stephanie. BS in Criminal Justice summa cum laude, Wilmington Coll., 1987; JD cum laude, U. Richmond, 1990. Bar: W.Va. 1990, U.S. Dist. Ct. (so. dist.) W.Va. 1990, (no. dist.) W.Va., 1996, U.S. Ct. Appeals (4th cir.) 1991, U.S. Dist. Ct. (no. dist.) W.Va. 1996. Sec. guard U. Del., Newark, 1973-76; police officer City of Dover (Del.), 1976-85; summer assoc. Hirschler Fleischer Weinberg Cox & Allen, Richmond, 1989; ptnr. Bowles Rice McDavid Graff & Love, Charleston, W.Va., 1990—; counsel Charleston Police Civil Svc. Commn. Cub scout leader Boy Scouts Am., Felton, Del., 1984-88, asst. scoutmaster, Richmond, 1988-89, Charleston, 1991—; chmn. pub. safety commn. Greater Charleston C. of C., 1991; sec. United Meth. Men, 1993; dir. Charleston Leadership Coun. on Pub. Safety, 1993—, chmn. police dept. resource task force, 1994—. Mem. ABA, W.Va. Bar Assn., Kanawha County Bar Assn., Def. Rsch. Inst., Def. Trial Counsel W.Va., Fraternal Order of Police, Nat. Eagle Scout Assn., McNeill Law Assn., Greater Charleston C. of C., Delta Epsilon Rho. United Methodist. Home: 1565 Virginia St E Charleston WV 25311-2416 Office: Bowles Rice McDavid Graff & Love PO Box 1386 Charleston WV 25325-1386

TEAS, ANDREW PARKER, association executive, political science educator; b. Houston, Jan. 31, 1962; s. Joseph Parker and Wanda (Wheeler) T.; m. Elaine Anne Elliott, Dec. 27, 1986; children: Robert Parker, Paul Elliott. BA, U. Tex., 1984, M Pub. Affairs, 1987. Legis. aide Tex. Ho. of Reps., Austin, 1983-89; dir. govt. affairs Houston Apt. Assn., 1989—; instr. govt. dept. Houston C.C., 1995—. Mem. pub. policy com. United Way Tex. Gulf Coast, Houston, 1996—. Mem. Am. Soc. Assn. Execs., Am. Mensa. Home: 2127 Jamara Ln Houston TX 77077 Office: Houston Apt Assn 10815 Fallstone Rd Houston TX 77099

TEAS, CHARLES BRYANT, physical education educator; b. Bellaire, Tex., July 18, 1938; s. Fred Augustus and Blanche (Bryant) T.; m. Karen Sue Keith, Oct. 20, 1962; children: Timothy Bryant, Tamara Annette. BS, Tex. A&M U., 1962; MEd, Sam Houston State U., 1968. Cert. health and phys. edn. tchr., Tex. Assoc. phys. dir. Longview (Tex.) YMCA, 1962-64; gymnastic specialist San Angelo (Tex.) Ind. Sch. Dist., 1964-67; fellow Sam Houston State U., Huntsville, 1967-68; prof. phys. edn. Del Mar Coll., Corpus Christi, Tex., 1968—. Recipient numerous awards for swimming and diving, including 1st Place Clown Diving award U.S. Masters Diving, 1974, 2d Place 1 Meter Diving award U.S. Masters Diving, 1974, 2d Place 3 Meter Diving award U.S. Masters Diving, 1974, 3d Place 3 Meter Diving award Masters Games, Toronto, Ont., Can., 1985. Mem. Tex. Assn. Health, Phys. Edn., Recreation and Dance (aquatics chmn. 1973, gymnastics chmn. 1975, 78), Am. Alliance Health, Phys. Edn. Recreation and Dance, Tex. Jr. Colls. of Tex., U.S. Gymnastics Fedn., Gymnastics Assn. Tex. (life). Home: 4421 Gaines St # 14 Corpus Christi TX 78412-2585 Office: Re/Max Metro Properties 5890 Everhart Rd Corpus Christi TX 78413

TEAS, CHARLOTTE ANN, editor; b. Russellville, Ala., Apr. 23, 1944; d. Aubry S. and Amy Eulalia Teas. BS in Edn., Samford U., 1967; M of Religious Edn., Southwestern Bapt. Theol. Sem., 1974. Therapeutic staff dietitian John Gaston Hosp., Memphis, 1968; tchr., nutrition resource tchr. Memphis City Schs., 1968-72; salesman, br. mgr. Electrolux Corp., Tenn., Tex. and Ala., 1972-74, 82-92; min. to children and singles, outreach dir. Bapt. chs., Tex., Ala. and Va., 1974-81, 91-92; editor Lad mag. Brotherhood Commn. of So. Bapt. Conv., Memphis, 1993—; mem. staff Ridgecrest (N.C.) Bapt. Assembly; freelance spkr., conf. leader Bapt. chs., Tex., Ala., Va., 1975—; freelance writer Bapt. Sunday Sch. Bd., Nashville, 1980; asst. team leader Calhoun Bapt. Assn., Calhoun County, Ala., 1987; mem. Ala. Bapt. Mission Friends Promotion Com., Montgomery, 1979-80; state-approved conf. leader So. Bapt. State Convs., Va., Ala., Tex., 1978-92; mem. child advocacy com. So. Bapt. Con., 1993—. Vol. Senator Jeremiah Denton, Anniston, Ala., 1981; sec. Citizen's Organized for Better Edn., Anniston, 1980; evaluator Tex. Day Care Licensing Revision Com., Ft. Worth, 1970s. Nat. Beta Club scholar, 1964. Mem. Bapt. Pub. Rels. Assn., Ed Press, Eta Epsilon (Svc. Girl award 1967, Miss Eta Epsilon 1967), Kappa Omicron Phi (Miss Kappa Omicron Phi 1967). Office: Brotherhood Commn 1548 Poplar Ave Memphis TN 38104-2432

TEAS, JOHN FREDERICK, small business owner; b. Bellaire, Tex., Oct. 10, 1934; s. Fred A. and Blanche (Bryant) T.; m. Patsy Tutt, 1967. Degree in horticulture, Tex. A&M U., 1957. Cert. nurseryman, Tex. With Teas Nursery Co., Inc., Bellaire, 1957—, v.p., since 1974; assoc. bd. dirs. Wesleyan Bank, Houston; tchr. plant identification Houston C.C. and U. Houston, 1991—. Mem. AAN (gov. region 2 1991), Am. Soc. Agriculture Cons., Tex. Soc. Landscape Architects (pres. 1975-77), Houston Landscape Nurserymen's Assn. (pres. 1974-75), Tex. Assn. Nurserymen (pres. region II 1978), SCV, Garden Ctrs. Am. (pres. 1986). Recipient Faith in God award Houston Jaycees, 1968. Mem. Am. Soc. Agriculture Cons., Tex. Soc. Landscape Architects (pres. 1975-77), Houston Landscape Nurserymen's Assn. (pres. 1974-75), Am. Assn. Nurserymen, Tex. Assn. Nurserymen (pres. region II 1978), SCV, Garden Ctrs. Am. (pres. 1986). Lodge: Rotary (bd. dirs. Houston chpt.). Home: 16 Town Oaks Pl Bellaire TX 77401-4237 Office: Teas Nursery Co Inc 4400 Bellaire Blvd Bellaire TX 77401-4306

TEDDER, DANIEL WILLIAM, chemical engineering educator; b. Orlando, Fla., Apr. 13, 1946; s. Daniel Webster and Adelaide Katheryn (Bruechert) T.; m. Wendy Elizabeth Widhelm, Aug. 3, 1968; children: Lisa Christine, Rachel Marie. Student, Kenyon Coll., 1964-67; B Chem. Engring. with highest honors, Ga. Inst. Tech., 1972; MS, U. Wis., 1973, PhD, 1975. Registered profl. engr., Tenn., Ga. Lab. technician Agrico Chem. Co., Pierce, Fla., 1965-67, Puritan Chem. Co., Atlanta, 1967-68; engr. Humble Oil and Refining Co., Baytown, Tex., summer 1972; staff engr. Oak Ridge (Tenn.) Nat. Lab., 1975-79; asst. prof. chem. engring. Ga. Inst. Tech., Atlanta, 1979-84, assoc. prof., 1984—; organizer symposia Emerging Techs. for Hazardous Waste Mgmt.; conf. presenter in field, 1977—; engring. cons. BCM Techs., Inc., Amherstberg, Ont., Can., 1985, Nat. Bur. Standards, U.S. Dept. Commerce, 1986—, Thermax Inc., Atlanta, 1987-88, Exxon R & D Lab., Baton Rouge, 1989—, Waste Policy Inst., Blacksburg, Va., 1992—, Geotech ChemNuclear, Golden, Colo., 1992—, Martin Marietta, Oak Ridge, 1992—, Resource Preservation Corp., Union City, Ga., 1992—; reviewer Jour. Phys. Chemistry, 1993—; others. Sr. series editor: Radioactive Waste Management Handbook; exec. editor Toxic and Hazardous Substance Control; assoc. editor Solvent Extraction and Ion Exchange; editor: (with F.G. Pohland) Emerging Technologies in Hazardous Waste Management, 1989, I, 1990, II, 1991, III, 1993, IV, 1994, V, 1995; contbr. numerous articles to profl. jours., chpts. to books. Mem. AIChE (pub. awareness com. Knoxville 1978-79), Am. Chem. Soc. (symposium chmn. I&EC divsn. 1989—), Am. Nuclear Soc., Water Pollution Control Fedn. Office: Ga Inst Tech Sch Chem Engring 778 Atlantic Dr Atlanta GA 30332-0100

TEDESCO, FRANCIS JOSEPH, university administrator; b. Derby, Conn., Mar. 8, 1944; s. Lena (Tufano) Tedesco; m. Luann Lee Ekern, Aug. 1, 1970; 1 child, Jennifer Nicole. BS cum laude, Fairfield U., 1965; MD cum laude, St. Louis U., 1969. Asst. instr. Hosp. of U. Pa., Phila., 1971-72; asst. prof. Washington U. Sch. Medicine, St. Louis, 1974-75; asst. prof. U. Miami (Fla.) Sch. Medicine, 1975-77, co-dir. clin. research, 1976-78, assoc. prof., 1977-78; assoc. prof. Med. Coll. Ga., Augusta, 1978-81, chief of gastroenterology dept., 1978-88, prof., 1981—, acting v.p. clin. activities, 1984, v.p. for clin. activities, 1984-88, Interim dean Sch. of Medicine, 1986-88, pres., 1988—; cons. Med.-Letter/AMA div. drugs, Dwight D. Eisenhower Army Med. Ctr., Ft. Gordon, Ga., VA Med. Ctr., Augusta, Walter Reed Army Med. Ctr., Washington; mem. gastroenterology spl. study sect. NIH, Washington, 1982—, mem. nat. digestive disease adv. bd., 1985-88, vice chmn., 1986-87, chmn., 1987-88. Contbr. numerous articles to profl. jours. Bd. dirs. Augusta Country Day Sch., 1981-83, Am. Cancer Soc., Augusta, 1985—, v.p., 1986—; bd. dirs., exec. com. Ga. Coalition for Health, 1995—; chmn. Gov.'s Health Strategies Coun., 1992—. Capt. N.G., 1970-72. Recipient Eddie Palmer award for gastrointestinal endoscopy, 1983, cert. of appreciation Am. Cancer Soc., 1986, Outstanding Faculty award Med. Coll. Ga. Sch. Medicine, 1988, Profl. Achievement award Fairfield U., 1993; Avalon Found. scholar St. Louis U., 1968-69, Paul Harris fellow Rotary, 1990. Fellow ACP, Am. Fedn. Clin. Investigation, Am. Gastroent. Assn., Am. Soc. Gastrointestinal Endoscopy (treas. 1981-84, pres.-elect 1984-85, pres. 1985-86, Rudolph Schindler award 1993); mem. Am. Coll. Gastroenterology, So. Soc. Clin. Investigation, Richmond County Med. Soc., Med. Assn. Ga. Roman Catholic. Home: 920 Milledge Rd Augusta GA 30912-7600 Office: Med Coll Ga Office Pres 1120 15th St Augusta GA 30912-0004

TEDFORD, BRUCE LEROY, physiologist, researcher; b. Little Rock, Sept. 9, 1954; s. Rufous Leroy and Elizabeth (Walicki) T.; m. Anice Kidd, June 7, 1975; children: Rebecca Ann, Samantha Rose. BS in Biology, U. Ark., Little Rock, 1976; MA in Zoology, UCLA, 1980; postgrad., U. Ark., Fayetteville, 1983; PhD in Physiology, La. State U., 1995. Rsch. assoc. Brain Rsch. Inst. UCLA, 1979-81, rsch. asst. dept. biology, 1979; tchr. sci and math. Am. Coop. Sch., La Paz, Bolivia, 1981-83; teaching asst., rsch. fellow La. State U., Baton Rouge, 1983-87, rsch. assoc. III dept. physiology, pharmacology and toxicology Sch. Vet. Medicine, 1987—; tutor dept. athletics La. State U., 1985; presenter numerous seminars. Contbr. articles, abstracts to profl. jours. Exec. bd. PTA Univ. Terrace Elem. Sch., 1984-87; v.p. men's fellowship Univ. United Meth. Ch., 1985-86, mem. exec. bd., 1989-91, properties com., 1989-91. Fellow La. State U Alumni Fedn. Mem. Am. Ornithologists' Union, Cooper Ornithol. Soc., Wilson Ornithol. Soc., Sch. Vet. Medicine Assocs. Orgn. (rep. dept. vet. physiology 1989—, rep. staff com. 1990-91). Office: La State U Sch Vet Medicine Dept Vet Physiology Baton Rouge LA 70803

TEEGARDEN, KENNETH LEROY, clergyman; b. Cushing, Okla., Dec. 22, 1921; s. Roy Albert and Eva B. (Swiggart) T.; m. Wanda Jean Strong, May 28, 1944; children: David Kent, Marshall Kirk. Student, Okla. State U., 1938-40; A.B., Phillips U., 1942, M.A., 1945, D.D., 1963; B.D., Tex. Christian U., 1949, D.D., 1976; D.D., Bethany Coll., 1974; LL.D., Lynchburg Coll., 1975; L.H.D., Culver-Stockton Coll., 1975. Ordained to ministry Christian Ch. (Disciples of Christ), 1940; pastor in Chandler, Okla., 1944-47, Texas City, Tex., 1947-48, Healdton, Okla., 1948-49, Vernon, Tex., 1949-55, Fort Smith, Ark., 1955-58; exec. minister Christian Ch. in, Ark., 1958-65; asst. to pres. Christian Ch. in U.S. and Can., Indpls., 1965-69; exec. minister Christian Ch. in Tex., 1969-73; gen. minister, pres. Christian Ch. in U.S. and Can., 1973-85; faculty Brite Div. Sch., Tex. Christian U., 1985-89; mem. governing bd. Nat. Council Chs., 1973-85; del. 5th Assembly of World Council Chs., Nairobi, Kenya, 1975, 6th Assembly, Vancouver, B.C., Can, 1983; rep. Nat. Council Chs. in Exchange of Ch. Leadership with Soviet Union, 1974. Author: We Call Ourselves Disciples, 1975. Named Disting. Alumnus Tex. Christian U., 1973, Phillips U., 1975; Outstanding Citizen Vernon, Tex., 1954. Home: 7013 Serrano Dr Fort Worth TX 76126-2317

TEEM, PAUL LLOYD, JR., savings and loan executive; b. Gastonia, N.C., Mar. 10, 1948; s. Paul Lloyd Sr. and Ruth Elaine (Bennett) T. BA, U. N.C., 1970; Cert., Inst. Fin. Edn., Chgo., 1984, Diploma, 1985, Degree of Distinction, 1989. Cert. tchr. N.C., cert. consumer credit exec.; lic. real estate broker. Exec. v.p., sec. Gaston Fed. Savs. and Loan Assn., Gastonia, N.C., 1983—; exec. v.p., sec., bd. dirs. Gaston Fin. Svcs., Inc., Gastonia, 1988—. Bd. dirs. Gastonia Mchts. Assn., Inc., 1981-83; lay reader Episcopal Ch. Decorated Order Purple Cross, Legion of Honor; named Ky. Col., 1995. Fellow Soc. Cert. Credit Execs.; mem. SAR, Sons of Confederate Vets., Mil. Order of Stars and Bars, Masons (32d degree, bd. dirs. 1981—, Disting. Svc. award 1987, Gold Honor award 1988, Active Legion of Honor 1989, Order of the Purple Cross of York 1990), Shriners, KT, Royal Order of Scotland, Hon. Order Ky. Cols., Phi Alpha Theta. Democrat. Home: 1208 Poston Cir Gastonia NC 28054-4634 Office: Gaston Fed Savs and Loan Assn 245 W Main Ave PO Box 2249 Gastonia NC 28053-2249

TEETER, DWIGHT LELAND, JR., journalism educator; b. L.A., Jan. 6, 1935; s. Dwight Leland and Ruth Elizabeth (Sauer) T.; m. Letitia Ruth Thoreson, July 7, 1956; children: Susan Letitia Hall, John Thoreson, William Weston. A.B. in Journalism, U. Calif.-Berkeley, 1956, M.J., 1959; Ph.D. in Mass Communications, U. Wis., 1966. Reporter Waterloo Daily Courier, Iowa, 1957-60; asst. prof. Iowa State U., Ames, 1964-66; asst. to assoc. prof. U. Wis., Madison, 1966-72; assoc.prof. to prof. U. Ky., Lexington, 1972-77, dir. journalism dept., 1975-77; prof. journalism, chmn. dept. journalism U. Tex., Austin, 1977-84, William P. Hobby Centennial prof. communication, 1983-87; prof., dept. mass communications U. Wis., Milw., 1987-91; dean, prof. Coll. Communications U. Tenn., Knoxville, 1991—; vis. assoc. prof. U. Wash., Seattle, 1969-70; treas. Journalism Council, Inc., N.Y.C., 1972-81. Author: (with Don R. Le Duc) Law of Mass Communications, 8th edit., 1995, (with Jean L. Folkerts) Voices of a Nation: A History of Media in the United States, 2d edit., 1994; contbr. articles to legal, hist., comm. jours. Chair Headliners Club of Tex. Media Contest, 1979-83; judge Tex. Bar Assn. Media Contest, 1981-85; mem. pub. affairs com. Tex. State Bar, 1985-87. Recipient Tex. Excellence in Teaching award Tex. Ex-Students' Assn., 1983, Harold L. Nelson award U. Wis., 1985. Mem. Assn. for Edn. in Journalism and Mass Comm. (chmn. prof. freedom and responsibility com. 1971-73, pres. 1985-86), Soc. Profl. Journalists (Disting. Tchr. award 1991), Phi Kappa Phi, Kappa Tau Alpha. Office: U Tenn Coll Comm Knoxville TN 37996

TEETS, CHARLES EDWARD, business consultant, lawyer; b. Terra Alta, W.Va., Feb. 11, 1947; s. Chester Carlton and Willye Katherine (Martin) T.; m. Judith Marlene Kildow, Dec. 19, 1970; children: Melissa Catherine, Brant Randolph. BS, Salisbury State Coll., 1973; MBA, So. Ill. U., 1980; JD, U Wis., 1994. Bar: Wis. 1994. Sr. cost acct. Perdue, Inc., Salisbury, Md., 1973-74; sect. chief acctg. terminal systems div. NCR, Millsboro, Del., 1974-76; contr. SPS Techs., Anasco, P.R., 1976-79; mgr. mfg. acctg. instrumentation div. Baxter Travenol Labs., Savage, Md., 1979-81; contr. Coated Abrasives N.Am. div. Standard Oil Co., Niagara Falls, N.Y., 1981-83; v.p., sec., treas. Carborundum Abrasives Co., Niagara Falls, 1983-86; v.p., CFO LeRoy (N.Y.) Industries, Inc., 1986-91; ind. cons., 1991—; mng. ptnr. Teets Kildow Internat., Dunedin, Fla., 1994—; adj. prof. Schiller Internat. U., 1995—, Hillsborough Coll., 1995—; lectr. Cash Mgmt. Inst., Holliston, Mass., 1983—; bus. guest, Beijing, China, 1986-87; mem. Korean trade mission Dept. Commerce, Washington, 1987; del. U.S./China Joint Session on Industry, Trade and Econ. Devel., Beijing, 1988; econ. and legal advisor Vietnam C. of C. and Industry, Hanoi, 1994. Sgt. U.S. Army, 1967-70, Vietnam. Recipient Wall St. Jour. award Dow Jones Co., 1973; Asia Found. grantee 1994. mem. ABA, State Bar of Wis., Nat. Assn. Accts., Am. C. of C. (Hong Kong chpt.), St. Petersburg Fla. C. of C., Beta Gamma Sigma. Republican. Methodist. Home: 95 Promenade Dr Ste 203 Dunedin FL 34698-8339

TEGENKAMP, GARY ELTON, lawyer; b. Dayton, Ohio, Nov. 27, 1946; s. Elmer Robert and Dorothy Ann (Hummerich) T.; m. June Evelyn Barber, Aug. 2, 1969; children: Emily Stratton, Andrew Elton. BA in Polit. Sci., U. South Fla., 1969; JD, Coll. William and Mary, 1972. Bar: Va. 1972, U.S. Dist. Ct. (we. and ea. dists.) Va. 1972, U.S. Ct. Appeals (4th cir.) 1973. Law clk. to presiding judge U.S. Dist. Ct. (we. dist.) Va., U.S. Ct. Appeals (4th cir.), Abingdon, Va., 1972-73; assoc. Hunter, Fox & Trabue, Roanoke, Va., 1973-77; ptnr. Fox, Wooten and Hart P.C., Roanoke, 1977-90, Wooten & Hart, P.C., Roanoke, Va., 1991-95; asst. city atty. Office of Roanoke City Atty., 1995—. Active United Way, Roanoke Valley, 1976; legal advisor Roanoke Jaycees, 1976-77. Mem. Va. Bar Assn. (constrn. and environ. sects.), Va. Assn. Def. Attys., Roanoke Bar Assn. (chmn. com. CLE 1983-86, 6th dist. ethics com. 1988-91), Local Govt. Attys. Va., Elks. United Methodist. Home: 2524 Stanley Ave SE Roanoke VA 24014-3332 Office: Office Roanoke City Atty 464 Municipal Bldg 215 Church Ave SW Roanoke VA 24011

TEGNELIA, ANTHONY G., controller; b. 1945. BSBA, Boston U., 1967, MBA, 1969. Various mgmt. and exec. positions Ryder System, Inc., 1977-88, controller, 1988-91, sr. v.p., controller, 1991—. Office: Ryder System Inc 3600 NW 82nd Ave Miami FL 33166-6623

TEITELBAUM, DANIEL JOSEPH, secondary education educator; b. Wilkes-Barre, Pa., Oct. 17, 1964; s. Carl and Marilynn Ann (Casse) T. Diploma in higher studies, U. Nancy II, France, 1985; BA in French and Polit. Sci., Bloomsburg U., 1986; MA in French Studies, Am. U., 1988. Tchr. French, Notre Dame Acad., Middleburg, Va., 1988-94, cross country coach, 1990-94, dean students, 1993-94; tchr. French, soccer coach Carolina Day Sch., Asheville, N.C., 1994—. Active St. Eugene's Parish, Asheville, 1995—. Grantee NEH, St. Michel de Montaigne, France, 1992; scholar Svc. Culturel France, St. Pierre Miquelon, 1996. Mem. Am. Assn. Tchrs. French, Fgn. Lang. Assn. N.C. Office: Carolina Day Sch 1345 Hendersonville Rd Asheville NC 28803

TEJA, AMYN SADRUDIN, chemical engineering educator, consultant; b. Zanzibar, Tanzania, May 11, 1946; came to U.S., 1980; s. Sadrudin N. and Amina (Dharsi) T.; m. Carole Rosina Thurlow, July 3, 1971; children: Kerima Amy, Adam Riaz. BSc in Engring., U. London, London, 1968; PhD, U. London, 1972. Intern Warren Springs Lab., Stevenage, Eng., summer 1966, Brit. Gas Corp., London, summer 1968; rsch. fellow in chem. engring. Loughborough (U.K.) U. Tech., 1971-74; chem. engring. lectr. Loughborough (Eng.) U. Tech., 1974-80; assoc. prof. chem. engring. Ga. Inst. Tech., Atlanta, 1980-83, prof., 1984-90, regents prof. Woodruff Sch. Mech. Engring., 1991—, regents prof. Sch. Chem. Engring., 1990—, dir. Fluid Properties Rsch. Inst., 1985—, co-dir. Specialty Separations Ctr., 1992—, assoc. dir. grad. studies, 1994—; vis. assoc. prof. chem. engring. U. Del., Newark, 1978-79, Ohio State U., 1980; cons. Laporte Chems., Eng., 1971, Mobil Rsch. and Devel. Co., N.J., 1979, Conoco Ltd., Humberside Refinery, Eng., 1980, Milliken Chem. Co., Spartanburg, S.C., 1981-83, Hoechst Celanese Corp., Corpus Christi, Tex., 1984, Charlotte, 1992. Philip Morris U.S.A., Richmond, Va., 1984-87, DuPont Co., 1988, Union Carbide Corp., South Charleston, W.Va., 1989—, Shell Oil Co., 1989-93; presenter in field, reviewer various jours. Editor: Chemical Engineering and the Environment, 1981; mem. editl. bd. Reports on the Progress of Applied Chemistry, 1972-76, Critical Reports on Applied Chemistry, 1976-80, Jour. Chem. and Engring. Data, 1991—, Chem. Engring. Rsch. Compendium, 1990—, Jour. Supercritical Fluids, 1990—; assoc. editor The Chem. Engring. Jour., 1973—; contbr. more than 170 articles to profl. jours. Recipient Hinchley medal Instn. Chem. Engrs., 1968, IBM Rsch. scholarship, 1968-71, Gas Coun. Rsch. scholarship, 1968-71, Brit. Coun. Younger Rsch. Workers award, 1977, Outstanding Tchr. award Omega Chi Epsilon, 1990. Mem. AIChE (pub. com. 1992—, jour. rev.), Am. Soc. Engring. Edn., Am. Chem. Soc., Sigma Xi (v.p. Ga. Tech. chpt. 1991-92. pres. 1992-93, Supr. Outstanding MS Thesis in Engring. 1984, 90, Supr. Outstanding PhD Thesis 1993, 96, Sustained Rsch. award 1987). Home: 1953 Huntington Hall Ct Atlanta GA 30338-5712 Office: Ga Inst Tech Dept Chem Engring Atlanta GA 30332-0100

TEJEDA, FRANK, congressman; b. San Antonio, Tex., Oct. 2, 1945; 3 children. BA in Government, St. Mary's U., 1970; JD, U. Calif., Berkeley, 1974; MPA, Harvard U., 1980; LLM, Yale U., 1989. Lawyer; mem. Tex. Ho. of Reps., 1977-87, Tex. State Senate from Dist. 19, 1987-93; mem. house armed svcs. com., mem. house vets. affairs com. 103rd-104th Congress from 28th Tex. dist., Washington, D.C., 1993—; chmn. com. judicial affairs Tex. Ho. Reps., 1983; chmn. sub-com. Urban Affairs Tex. Senate, 1991; mem. senate fin. com. Tex. Senate, 1991; mem. nat. security com., vets affairs com.; chmn. intergovernmental rels. com. urban affairs Tex. Senate, 1991. Maj. USMCR, Vietnam. Decorated Bronze Star, Purple Heart. Mem. Cath. War Vets., Marine Corps. League. Democrat. Roman Catholic.

TELEPAS, GEORGE PETER, lawyer; b. Kingston, N.Y., Nov. 20, 1935; s. Peter G. and Grace T.; m. Regina Tisiker, Sept. 6, 1969 (div.); m. Patricia Kilstofte, Apr. 30, 1995. B.S., U. Fla., 1960; J.D., U. Miami, 1965. Bar: Fla. 1965, Colo. 1986. Assoc., Preddy, Haddad, Kutner, & Hardy, 1966-67; assoc. Williams & Jabara, 1967-68; sole practice, Miami, Fla., 1968—. Mem. citizens bd. U. Miami. Served with USMC, 1954-56. Mem. ABA, Fla. Bar Assn., Colo. Bar Assn., Dade County Bar Assn., Assn. Trial Lawyers Am., Fla. Trial Lawyers Assn., Dade County Trial Lawyers Assn., Delta Theta Phi, Sigma Nu. Home and Office: 13645 Deering Bay Dr PH 164 Coral Gables FL 33158-2820

TELFORD, VAN QUINCY, pathologist; b. Naples, Tex., Oct. 6, 1934; s. John Quincy and Bertha (Van Hoosier) T.; m. Jane Ellis, Dec. 17, 1960; children: Ellis, Bradford. DVM, Tex. A&M U., 1958; MD, U. Tex., Dallas, 1965. Resident in pathology Parkland Meml. Hosp., Dallas, 1965-71; assoc. pathologist Hotel Dieu, El Paso, Tex., 1967-69; pathologist Presbyn. Hosp., Dallas, 1971-75, Richardson (Tex.) Med. Ctr., 1975-90, RHD Meml. Med. Ctr., 1996—; founding ptnr. Dallas Pathology Assocs., 1973—; cons. pathologist various hosps., 1975—; clin. prof. pathology S.W. Med. Sch., U. Tex., 1988—. Capt. Vet. Corps, USAF, 1958-60. Fellow Coll. Am. Pathologists (del.), Am. Soc. Clin. Pathologists; mem. Tex. Med. Assn. (past chmn. coun. on health facilities), Tex. Soc. Pathologists (past pres.). Home: 4 Kingsgate Ct Dallas TX 75225-2018

TELLEZ, GEORGE HENRY, safety professional, consultant; b. Bogotá, Colombia, June 24, 1951; came to U.S., 1954; s. Jorge Enrique and Nohemi (Rodriguez) T.; m. Nora Reyes, Aug. 24, 1974; children: Shantell, Sabrina. Student, CCNY, 1972-74, U. Cen. Fla., 1979-83. Cert. safety prof. Am. Bd. Cert. Safety Profls. Loss control rep. Hartford Ins. Group, Orlando, Fla., 1977-81, asst. loss control mgr., 1983-89; loss control cons. Comml. Union Ins. Co., Orlando, 1981-83; account engring. exec. Hartford Splty. Co., Dallas, 1989-91; loss control exec. Anco Ins. Houston, 1991-95; loss control mgr. Unicare Ins. Co., Houston, 1995—; instr. defensive driving Nat. Safety Coun., 1983-84. Chmn. health and safety Casselberry Elem. Sch. PTA, Orlando, 1986-87, coord. bicycle safety program, 1987; founding donor Lewisville (Tex.) Edn. Found., 1990-91. Mem. Am. Soc. Safety Engrs. (asst. regional v.p. region VIII 1986-87, v.p. Cen. Fla. chpt. 1985-86, pres. 1986-87, chmn. nominating com. 1988, chmn. welcome com. S.W. chpt. 1989-90, Pres. Club 1984-85, 86-88, 89-90, Pres. Cir. 1985-86, 91-92, Safety Profl. of Yr. award Cen. Fla. chpt. 1988). Office: Anco Ins Houston 16000 Barkers Point Ln Houston TX 77079-4023

TEMERLIN, LIENER, advertising agency executive; b. Ardmore, Okla., Mar. 27, 1928; s. Pincus and Julie (Kahn) T.; m. Karla Samuelsohn, July 23, 1950; children: Dana Temerlin Crawford, Lisa Temerlin Gottesman, Hayden Crawford, Sandy Gottesman. BFA, U. Okla., 1950. Assoc. editor Sponsor Mag., N.Y.C., 1950-51; copywriter Glenn Advt. Inc., Dallas, 1952-54, creative dir., 1954-70, chief oper. officer, 1970-74; pres. Glenn, Bozell & Jacobs, Inc., 1974-79; chmn. bd. dirs. Bozell & Jacobs Inc., 1979-86, Bozell, Jacobs, Kenyon & Eckhardt, Dallas, 1986-89; chmn. Bozell, 1989-92, Temerlin McClain, 1992—. Chmn. Winston Churchill Found. award dinner, 1986; chmn. Dallas Symphony Assn., 1986-88, pres., 1984-86, mem. bd. govs., 1982-84, pres. coun., 1989—; mem. Blair House Restoration Com., 1987-88; vice chmn. Am. Film Inst., 1992-93, bd. trustees, 1992—; bd. dirs. United Way of Met. Dallas Exec. Com., 1986-89, Dallas Bus. Com. for Arts, 1989, Dallas Citizen's Coun., 1984-86, 92; trustee Southwestern Med. Found., 1988—, bd. trustees, 1992—, So. Meth. U., trustee com. Univ. devel., 1988, exec. bd., 1990-91; trustee and chmn. of devel. com. Dallas Mus. Art, 1993-96; mem. steering com. Susan G. Komen Found., 1989-91, art acquisition com. Meyerson Symphony Ctr., 1989-92, exec. coun. Daytop/Dallas, 1989—; chmn. grand opening fortnight Morton H. Meyerson Symphony Ctr., 1989; mem. Madison Coun. Libr. Congress, Washington, 1991—; hon. chair 2d ann. rsch. dinner Am. Lung Assn. Tex. Recipient Bill D. Kerss award Dallas Advt. League, 1983, Brotherhood award NCCJ, 1984, Susan G. Komen Found. for Breast Cancer Rsch. Community award, 1989, James K. Wilson Silver Cup award, 1990, Linz award 1990, Silver Medal award Dallas Advt. League, 1991, Vol. Fundraiser of Yr. award Nat. Soc. Fundraising Execs., 1991, Best Man in Advt. award McCall's Mag., 1992; named Dallas Father of Yr., 1991. Office: 201 E Carpenter Fwy Irving TX 75062

TEMPLE, CARROLL GLENN, JR., medicinal chemist; b. Hickory, N.C., Mar. 7, 1932; s. Carroll Glenn Sr. and Cora Melissa (Stephens) T.; m. Leone Felton Newell, Apr. 21, 1956; children: Laura Felton, Sara Lisa. BS in Chemistry, Lenoir Rhyne Coll., 1954; MS in Chemistry, Birmingham-So. Coll., 1958; PhD in Organic Chemistry, U. N.C., 1962. Rsch. asst. dept. chemistry U. N.C., Chapel Hill, 1954, So. Rsch. Inst., Birmingham, Ala., 1955-59; mem. faculty U. Ala., Birmingham, 1962, Birmingham-So. Coll., 1964; head drug synthesis sect. organic chemistry dept. So. Rsch. Inst., Birmingham, 1966-80, head pharm. chemistry divsn., 1980-94, dir. organic chemistry dept., 1991-94, Disting. scientist, 1994—; formal presentations various meetings. Contbr. articles to profl. jours.; patentee in field. Ad hoc mem. Am. Cancer Soc., 1981, Nat. Cancer Inst., NIH, 1987. Recipient Disting. Alumnus award Lenoir-Rhyne Coll., 1983. Mem. Am. Chem. Soc. (chmn. Ala. sect. 1975, congl. counselor 1976-78, 78-80).

TEMPLE, ROBERT WINFIELD, chemical company executive; b. New Albany, Ind., Feb. 25, 1934; s. Edgar Winfield and Kathryn (Rady) T.; m. Katrina Voorhis, Jan. 4, 1954 (div. Oct. 1970); children: James V., Robert K., Jennifer Anne; m. Katharine Ann Stobbs, Apr. 29, 1977 (div. June 1985); children: Andrew, Philip; m. Angela J., Aug. 5, 1986; 1 child, Sarah Louise. BSChemE, BS in Indsl. Mgmt., MIT, 1955; postgrad., Chem. Engring. Sch. MIT, 1955, Sch. Bus. Adminstrn. NYU, 1955-58, Mgmt. Devel. Program, Columbia U., 1966. Dist. sales mgr. ACF Industries, 1955-59; sr. staff cons. Arthur D. Little, Inc., 1959-64; dir. planning and devel. Am. Cryogenics, Inc., Atlanta, 1964-69; v.p. Williams Bros. Co., Atlanta, 1969-70; pres. Lang Engring., Coral Gables, Fla., 1970-74; pres. Western Process Co., Geneva and Houston, 1974-87; head agribus., British-Am. Tobacco Co., London, 1988-91; pres. TMR-Viterra Internat., Ltd., 1989-92, CEO Gulfcrest Internat., 1987—; dir. World Congress on Super Conductivity, Global Econ. Action Inst. Conf. on African Devel.; dir. MIT Enterprise Forum (former chmn.). Spkr. on mgmt. and mktg. various seminars. Fellow Am. Inst. Chemists and Chem. Engrs.; mem. Am. Chem. Soc., Am. Mgmt. Assn., (seminar spkr.), Chem. Mktg. Rsch. Assn., Internat. Food Technologists (chmn. seminar on food irradiation 1995, presenter food irradiation as means of improved safety 1995), MIT Alumni Assn. (past regional pres., mem. adv. bd.), Am. Soc. Agrl. Cons., Houston Fresh Fruit & Vegetable Assn. (v.p.), Sigma Chi Alumni Assn. Presbyterian. Contrb. articles to profl. jours. Home: 14134 Bluebird Ln Houston TX 77079-6836 Office: Gulfcrest Internat PO Box 19435 Houston TX 77224-9435

TEMPLETON, GEORGE EARL, II, plant pathologist; b. Little Rock, June 27, 1931; s. George Earl and Gladys (Jones) T.; m. Bobbie Nell Moore, Aug. 31, 1958; children: George Earl, Gary Lee, Patricia Jan, Larry Ernest. BS, U. Ark., 1953, MS, 1954; PhD, U. Wis., 1958. Asst. prof. U. Ark., Fayetteville, 1958-62, assoc. prof., 1962-67, prof., 1967-85, univ. prof., 1985-91, disting. prof., 1991-96. 1st lt. Chem. Corp, 1954-56. Recipient Award of Excellence, Weed Sci. Soc. of Am., 1973, John White award for Agrl. Rsch., 1979, Disting. Rsch. award Ark. Alumni Assn., 1987, Burlington No. award U. Ark., 1988, Superior Sr. award USDA, 1990, Ruth Allen award Am. Phytopathol Soc., 1991. Fellow Am. Phytopathol. Soc.; mem. Weed Sci. Soc. of Am., Mycological Soc. of Am., Brit. Mycological Soc., Ark. Acad. Sci. (sec. 1964-69, pres. 1971-72). Methodist. Home: 2310 Winwood Dr Fayetteville AR 72703-4136 Office: U Ark Dept Plant Pathology P T SC 217 Fayetteville AR 72701-1202

TEMPLETON, RANDALL KEITH, insurance company executive; b. Jefferson City, Mo., June 4, 1957; s. William Glen and Betty Ann (Wood) T.; m. Barbara Jean Ensor, Dec. 29, 1979 (div. Apr. 1984); m. Kay Lynn Young, Aug. 17, 1985. BSBA, U. Mo., 1979, MBA, 1981. CPA, Tex., Mo.; cert. managerial acct., cert. profl. ins. agt. Staff acct. Laventhol & Horwath, CPA's, Houston, 1981-82, Saber Energy, Inc., Houston, 1982-84; sr. acct. Houston Lighting and Power, 1984-86; owner Templeton Ins. Agy., Spring, Tex., 1986—. Mem. Champions Forest Bapt. Ch., Houston; bd. dirs. Harris County Mcpl. Utility Dist. 19, 1987—, v.p., 1987-96, pres., 1996—; v.p., bd. dirs. Cypress Lakes Owners Assn., 1994—; precinct chmn. Harris County Rep. Party, 1994—. Life Underwriting Tng. Coun. fellow. Mem. AICPA, Inst. Mgmt. Accts., Nat. Assn. Profl. Ins. Agts., Nat. Assn. Life Underwriters, Cert. Profl. Ins. Agts. Soc., Nat. Fedn. Ind. Bus., Tex. Ins. Profls. (state treas. 1995-96, pres.-elect 1996—), U. Mo. Alumni Assn., Masons (lodge sec. 1989-90, jr. steward 1991-92, 96-97), KT, Shriners, Delta Sigma Pi, Beta Alpha Psi. Office: Templeton Ins Agy 1530 Spring Cypress # 101 Spring TX 77388

TEMPLETON, STEPHEN FARWELL, dermatopathologist, dermatologist; b. San Angelo, Tex., July 21, 1962; s. Stuart Edward and Katharine Elizabeth (Williams) T.; m. Elizabeth Patricia Freeman, June 7, 1986; children: Emma Elizabeth, Rachel Freeman, Julia Catherine. BS, U. of South, 1984; MD, U. Tex., Galveston, 1988. Diplomate Am. Bd. Dermatology. Resident in internal medicine U. N.C., Chapel Hill, 1988-89; resident in dermatology Emory U., Atlanta, 1989-92, fellow in dermatopathology, 1992-93, asst. prof. dermatology and pathology, 1993—. Author: Atlas of Dermatology, 1994, (chpts.) Cutaneous Medicine and Surgery, 1995. Vestry mem. Ch. of Jesus our Shepherd, Duluth, Ga., 1995-96. Fellow Am. Acad. Dermatology, Am. Soc. Dermatopathology; mem. Soc. Investigative Dermatology, Atlanta Dermatology Assn., Ga. Soc. Dermatologists. Office: Emory Univ Dept Dermatology Box 55 5001 Woodruff Meml Bldg Atlanta GA 30322

TENNANT, DONNA KAY, writer; b. Waynesburg, Pa., Nov. 28, 1949; d. Daniel Clay and Mary Aliff (Cole) T. BA in Philosophy, U. Rochester, 1971; MA in Art History, U. N.Mex., 1978. Art critic Houston Chronicle, 1979-81; assoc. editor Mus. Fine Arts, Houston, 1985-86; gallery mgr. Jeremy Stone Gallery, San Francisco, 1982-84, 89-91; adminstr. Houston Art Dealers Assn., 1987-89, 91—; editor Mus. and Arts Mag., Houston, 1993-94; mng. editor Houston Life Mag., 1994-95; sr. editor S.W. Art mag., Houston, 1996—. Freelance writer various local and nat. publs., 1978—.

TEPOEL, DONNA LEE FULLER, former education educator; b. Lewiston, Maine, Aug. 6, 1942; d. Francis Robinson and Gertrude Louise (Keene) Fuller; m. William Gagne, June 25, 1966 (div. 1972); m. Louis Dean TePoel, July 4, 1974; children: Jamie Lee, Sarah Louise. BS in Edn., Farmington State Tchrs. Coll., 1964; MA, U. Colo., 1973; EdD, U. No. Colo., 1980. Tchr. Westbrook (Maine) Sch. Dist., 1964-72, right to read dir., 1973-74; reading specialist Manning Jr. High Sch., Jefferson County, Colo., 1974-78; instr. Casper (Wyo.) Coll., 1978-79; instr. for extension classes U. Wyo, Gillette, 1982-83; asst. prof. edn. U. Mary, Bismarck, N.D., 1985-88; mem. consortium, rep. from Westbrook, New Eng. Consortium for Right to Read, 1973-74; presenter, staff Devel. Workshops, Greeley, Colo. Mem. Internat. Reading Assn., Delta Kappa Gamma, Phi Delta Kappa (life, membership chmn. 1986-88). Presbyterian. Home: 136 Ella Perry Addition Tazewell VA 24651-9636

TERAN, SISTER MARY INEZ, nun, educator; b. Austin, Tex., Nov. 15, 1924; d. Jose Julian and Petra (Meza) T. BA, Our Lady of the Lake U., 1960; MDE, Cath. U. Am., 1965. Joined Congregation Sisters of Divine Providence, Roman Cath. Ch., 1941. Coord. religious edn. Archdiocese San Antonio, 1966-71; dir. religious edn. Dolores Ch., Austin, 1971-74, St. Henry's Ch., San Antonio, 1974-78, St. Margaret Mary Ch., San Antonio, 1978-82, St. John Berchmans Ch., San Antonio, 1982-84, St. Cyril and Methodius Ch., Granger, Tex., 1986-88, Sacred Heart Ch., Von Ormy, Tex., 1988-94; vol. St. Jude Ch., San Antonio, Tex., 1994—. Mex.-Am. Cultural Ctr. scholar, San Antonio, 1985-86. Home: 515 SW 24th St San Antonio TX 78207-4619

TERIO, ANNE DOROUGH LINNEMANN, foreign service contracting officer, nurse; b. Lafayette, Ga., May 10, 1946; d. Calvin Cummins and Adelia (Park) Linnemann; m. James Donald Moore, Aug. 18, 1963 (div. July 1976); children: Marianne Lea Moore Elbertson, Christopher Cummins; m. Charles John Terio III, June 4, 1987; 1 stepchild, Christopher John. BA in History, U. N.C., Greensboro, 1971; AD in Nursing with honors, Prince George Coll., 1976. RN, Md., Va.; cert. secondary history tchr., N.C. Tchr. history Grimsley H.S., Greensboro, N.C., 1971-72; nurse Drs. Hoeck, Smith & Guarinello, Pediatricians, Clinton, Md., 1977-82; contract specialist Gen. Svcs. Adminstrn. real property contracts div., Washington, 1984-86; contract adminstr. Dept Navy Military Sealift Command M-104, Washington, 1986-88; contract specialist Dept. Transportation Maritime Adminstrn., Washington, 1988-92, U.S. AID, Rosslyn, Va., 1992-94; joined Fgn. Svc., 1994; contracting officer U.S. AID, Cairo, 1994—. Mem. Nat. Contract Mgmt. Assn., Beta Sigma Phi (numerous offices, Xi Gamma Gamma chpt., pres. 1992-93). Republican. Baptist. Home: Unit 64902 APO AE 09839-4902 Office: USAID Cairo Unit 64902 APO AE 09839-4902

TERLOUW, JOHN G., financial analyst; b. New Brunswick, N.J., May 14, 1945; s. John W. and Jane B. (van Kempen) T.; m. Janet A. Henry, Aug. 1, 1970; children: Janet R., Julie L., Joanne E., John G. Sr. BS in Acctg., Fla. State U., 1971. CPA, Fla. CFO Budget Luxury Inns of Am., Inc., Tallahassee, 1974-75; pres. Mgmt. Cons. Soc., Inc., Tallahassee, 1975-78; staff acct. Givens & Givens, CPA's, Tallahassee, 1979-80; CFO Tallahassee Food Systems Inc., 1980-83, Wenco of El Paso, Tex., 1983-84, Maxxima Corp., Tallahassee, 1984-85; pres. Creative Bu. Concepts, Inc., Tallahassee, 1985-90; sr. mgmt. analyst II Fla. Dept. of Profl. Regulation, Tallahassee, 1990-94, Fla. Agy. for Health Care Adminstrn., Tallahassee, 1994—. With USAF, 1965-69. Office: Fla Agy for Health Care Adminstrn 1940 N Monroe St Ste 60 Tallahassee FL 32399

TERRELL, CHARLES OLIVER, anesthesiologist; b. Quincy, Ill., Oct. 9, 1935; s. Hoydt Brooks and Ina Marie (Hamner) T.; m. Frances Ann Pfeiffer, Dec. 27, 1958; children: Charles Oliver Jr., Gregory Allen, Susan Marie. BS, U. Ill., Champaign, 1956; MD, U. Ill. Med. Ctr., Chgo., 1960. Diplomate Am. Bd. Anesthesiology. Rotating intern Tampa Gen. Hosp., Fla., 1960-61; staff anesthesiologist Med. Ctr. Clinic, Pensacola, Fla., 1965-82, chief anesthesiology, 1982—; resident in anesthesiology U. Tex., Galveston, Fla., 1963-65. Bd. dirs. United Meth. Ch., Pensacola, 1991-95. Mem. AMA, Fla. Med. Assn., Am. Soc. Anesthesia, Fla. Soc. Anesthesia, Soc. Cardiovascular Anesthesia, Soc. Regional Anesthesia, Internat. Anesthesia Rsch. Soc. Republican. Methodist. Home: 731 Tanglewood Dr Pensacola FL 32503-3230 Office: Med Ctr Clinic 8333 N Davis Hwy Pensacola FL 32514-6048

TERRELL, DAVID LEROY, author; b. Hinsdale, Ill., Dec. 25, 1946; s. LeRoy Terrell and Lena May (Beckner) Weston; m. Vickie Jeane Bartley, Jan. 21, 1968 (div. 1988); m. Linda Sue Ayers, Sept. 24, 1988. AAS, Sam's Tech. Inst., Indpls., 1967; BSEE, LaSalle U., 1995, MSEE, 1996. Cert. electronic technician. Electronics instr. ITT Tech. Inst., Indpls., 1972-77, 80-82, evening dean, 1982-83; dir. edn. ITT Tech. Inst., Tampa, 1983-84, 86-90; engring. mgr. Aircraft Electronics, Avon, Ind., 1977-80; sr. engr. TKC, Inc., Pinellas Park, Fla., 1984-86, 90-93; author Lutz, Fla., 1990-95; mgr. lab. ops. TKC, Inc., Pinellas Park, Fla., 1996—. Author: Digital Technology with Microprocessor, 1977, Microprocessor Technology, 1983, OPAMPS: Design, Application, Troubleshooting, 1992, Electronics into the Future, 1994. Staff sgt. USAF, 1968-72. Home and Office: Terrell Technologies Inc 1509 Newberger Rd Lutz FL 33549-4031

TERRELL, G. IRVIN, lawyer; b. Houston, Sept. 28, 1946; s. George I. and Adella (Weichert) T.; m. Karen Steenberg, Jan. 8, 1984; 1 child, Katharine. BA, U. Tex., 1968, JD, 1972. Bar: Tex., U.S. Supreme Ct., U.S. Ct. Appeals (5th cir.), U.S. Dist. Ct. (so. dist.) Tex. Assoc. Baker & Botts, Houston, 1972-79; ptnr. Baker & Botts, 1980—. Mem. ABA, Houston Bar Assn., Internat. Soc. Barristers. Office: Baker & Botts 3000 One Shell Pla 910 Louisiana St Houston TX 77002

TERRELL-MCDANIEL, ROBIN F., cardiac rehabilitation and critical care nurse; b. Charlton Heights, W.Va., May 9, 1961; d. Clarence E. Sr. and Dorothy Mae (Smith) T.; m. Charles Kevin McDaniel, Aug. 4, 1990. ADN, W.Va. Inst. Tech., 1982; BSN, W.Va. U., 1987. Emergency room charge nurse Montgomery (W.Va.) Gen. Hosp., 1982-87, nursing supr., 1987-88; coord. utilization rev. MedCert, Charleston, W.Va., 1988-89; vis. asst. prof. nursing W.Va. Inst. Tech., Montgomery, 1989-90; critical care nurse W.Va. Gen. Hosp., Montgomery, 1990—, cardiac rehab. nurse, 1995—. Mem. Am. Assn. Cardiovascular and Pulmonary Rehab. Home: PO Box 345 Pratt WV 25162-0345

TERRY, EDWARD DAVIS, Latin-American studies and literature educator; b. Eclectic, Ala., May 19, 1927; s. William Jefferson and Venola (Davis) T.; m. Nancy Joann Long, Jan. 20, 1956 (div. 1961); children: Susan Frances, Michael Edward; m. Marilyn Faye Landers, Apr. 5, 1963; children: Kathleen Faye, Edward Davis Jr. BS in Commerce and Bus. Adminstrn., U. Ala., 1949, MA in Spanish, 1953; PhD in Romance Langs., U. N.C., 1958. Acctg. clk. United Fruit Co., Tela, Honduras, 1949-50; asst. prof. Spanish So. Meth. U., Dallas, 1958-62, U. Tenn., Knoxville, 1962-64; assoc. prof. Spanish U. Ala., Tuscaloosa, 1964-70, prof. Spanish, 1970—, dir. Latin Am. studies program, 1966-72, dir. Alfredo Barrera Vasquez Ctr. for Yucatecan studies, 1986—. Editor: Artists and Writers in the Evolution of Latin America, 1969; editor, contbr. Yucatan: A World Apart, 1980; contbr. articles to profl. jours. Rotary Found. fellow, 1951, grad. fellow So. Fellowships Fund, 1955-56, 56-57; rsch. grantee Am. Philos. Soc., 1970. Home: 22 El Dorado E Tuscaloosa AL 35405-3514 Office: U Ala Dept Romance Langs & Classics Tuscaloosa AL 35487

TERRY, JAMES CROCKETT, school system administrator, mediator; b. Nevada City, Calif., Apr. 4, 1948; s. Seth Sprague and Crystal (Crockett) T.; m. Marsha Lynn Merrill, Apr. 24, 1988; children: Seth Roy, Max. BA, Allegheny Coll., 1971; MA, Sonoma State U., Rohnert Park, Calif., 1972; PhD, Saybrook Inst., San Francisco, 1978. CPA, Tex.; cert. sch. bus. ofcl., Tex. Rsch. asst. Inst. for Parapsychology, Durham, N.C., 1972-73, assoc. rschr., 1975; asst. rschr. div. parapsychology and psychophysics Maimonides Med. Ctr., Bklyn., 1973-75, dir. community mental health program, 1973-75; assoc. rschr. Mind Sci. Found., San Antonio, 1975-77; adminstr. resocialization program Dr. Paul Obert, Inez, Tex., 1977-80; divl. contr. Coca-Cola Co. S.W., San Antonio, 1978-81; asst. v.p. budgeting and mgmt. acctg. San Antonio Fed. Credit Union, 1981-86; dir. budgets, investments and fed. programs N.E. Ind. Sch. Dist., San Antonio, 1987-94, dir. internal auditing, 1994—; cons. Crockett Investments, San Antonio, 1980—, Mediation Svcs., Spring Branch, Tex., 1992—; instr. U. Tex., Austin, 1986-87, U. Tex., San Antonio, 1989-91. Contbr. articles to profl. jours. Mediator Bexar County Dispute Resolution Ctr., San Antonio, 1984—, mediator trainer, 1985—. Recipient Supt.'s award N.E. Ind. Sch. Dist., 1992, award for disting. budget GFOA, 1993-94; Parapsychology Found. grantee, 1974; Gardner Murphy Found. fellow, 1975. Mem. Parapsychology Assn., Tex. Soc. CPA's, San Antonio Soc. CPA's, Alamo Area Mediators Assn. (founding, treas. 1984—), Govt. Fin. Officers Assn., Tex. Assn. Sch. Bus. Ofcls., San Antonio Family Mediation Assn. (bd. dirs. 1989). Episcopalian. Home: PO Box 400 Spring Branch TX 78070-0400 Office: NE Ind Sch Dist 8961 Tesoro Dr San Antonio TX 78217-6225

TERRY, JOSEPH RAY, JR., lawyer; b. Vicksburg, Miss., Aug. 10, 1938; s. Joseph Ray Sr. and Alma Blanche (Smith) T.; m. Louise Caroline Beland, July 17, 1965; children: Kathleen A., Marie L., Bernard R. JD, Loyola U., 1965. Bar: D.C. 1966, Miss. 1968, U.S. Ct. Appeals (5th cir.) 1971, Ga. 1973, U.S. Dist. Ct. (no. and so. dists.) Ga. 1973, U.S. Ct. Appeals (D.C. cir.) 1973, U.S. Supreme Ct. 1973, U.S. Ct. Appeals (8th cir.) 1974, U.S. Dist. Ct. (we. dist.) Tenn. 1983, U.S. Ct. Appeals (6th cir.) 1989. Trial atty. civil rights div. U.S. Dept. Justice, Washington, 1966-69; assoc. regional counsel U.S. Dept. HUD, Atlanta, 1969-70; ptnr. Crosland, Myer, Rindskopf & Terry, Atlanta, 1974-76; regional counsel EEOC, Atlanta, 1970-73, supr. trial atty. Litigation Cen., 1976-79; regional atty. EEOC, Memphis, 1979-96; dep. gen. counsel EEOC, Washington, 1996—; part-time asst. atty. City of Atlanta, 1975-76; cons. Nat. Labor Rels. Bd., Memphis, 1981-82; adj. prof. law Emory U., 1971-75; vis. prof. law St. Louis U., 1973-74; acting program dir. EEOC, 1983, acting dist. dir., 1984-85; bd. dirs. Fed. Credit Union, 1984-91; mem. adv. com. to U.S. Dist. Ct. (we. dist.) Tenn., 1990-93, chair case mgmt. subcom. Author: (jour.) Eliminating the Plaintiff's Attorney in Equal Employment Litigation: A Shakespearean Tragedy, Labor Lawyer, 1989, Memphis and Race, The Commercial Appeal, 1987. Cons. Alaska Human Rights Commn., Anchorage, 1981; bd. dirs. Nat. Kidney Found. of West Tenn., Memphis, pres., 1984-85; bd. dirs. United Meth. Neighborhood Ctr., 1985-88; bd. dirs. St. Patrick's Parish Coun., Memphis, pres., 1986-88; mem. Leadership Memphis, 1988-96; mem. adv. com. U.S. Dist. Ct. (we. dist.) Tenn., 1990, fed. chmn. chmn. case mgmt. study com., 1991—. Named Honor Law Graduate U.S. Atty. Gen., 1965. Mem. ABA (EEOC liaison com. 1987-89), Fed. Bar Assn. (bd. dirs. 1988-89, v.p. West Tenn. chpt. 1991-92, pres. 1993-94, nat. coun. 1996—, named Younger Fed. Lawyer of Yr. 1973), Supreme Ct. Hist. Soc., Am. Judicature Soc., St. Thomas More Lawyers Guild, Salvation Army (bd. dirs. 1995-96). Roman Catholic. Home: 1560 Harbert Ave Memphis TN 38104-5033

TERRY, LINDA, social services professional; b. N.Y.C., Oct. 2, 1962; d. Richard Charles Williams, Sr. and Florence Douglas; m. Raymond Charles Terry, Sept. 15, 1991; children: James F. Eversley II, Alisha N. AAS, Onondaga C.C., Syracuse, N.Y., 1983; BS, SUNY, Albany, 1994. Med. specialist, adminstrv. asst. U.S. Army Res., Ft. Bragg, Ft. Benning, Ga., 1982-93; case mgr. Dept. Social Svcs., Fayetteville, N.C., 1988-90, Tacoma, Wash., 1990-92; self-sufficiency worker Dept. Social Svcs., Fairfax, Va., 1993—. Home: 6300 Betsy Ross Ct Centreville VA 20121

TERRY, LINDA STEWART, insurance agent; b. Collin County, Tex., Jan. 27, 1942; d. Jimmie and Myrtice (Higginbotham) Stewart. BS magna cum laude, Tex. Woman's U., 1982. Teller Collin County Nat. Bank, McKinney, Tex., 1960-69; dental asst. pvt. practice dental office, McKinney, 1969-76, McKinney Job Corps, 1976-78; dental asst., hygienist pvt. practice dental office, Plano, Tex., 1978-84; dental hygienist, adminstrv. asst. Dental Health Programs, Dallas, 1982-84; ins. agt. State Farm Ins., McKinney, 1984—. Author instructional manual, 1983. Mem. Jobs Svc. Employers Com., McKinney, 1992—; advisor McKinney Edn. Found., 1993-94. Mem. McKinney C. of C. (mem. Leadership McKinney 1992-94, bd. dirs. 1994—), Rotary (charter, sec. local club 1993-94, pres.-elect 1994-95, pres. 1995-96). Methodist. Office: State Farm Ins PO Box 1010 Mc Kinney TX 75070-1010

TERRY, REESE, engineering executive. Pres. Engring. Co., Webster, Tex. Office: 17448 Hwy 3 Webster TX 77598

TERRY, ROBERT MEREDITH, foreign language educator; b. Danville, Va., Dec. 16, 1939; s. Willard Terry and Martha Willeford; m. Anne Reynolds Beggarly, Jan. 30, 1965; children: Michael Reynolds, Christopher Robert, Meredith Anne. BA in French, Randolph-Macon Coll., Ashland, Va., 1962; PhD in Romance Langs., Duke U., Durham. N.C., 1966. Asst. prof. French U. Fla., Gainesville, Fla., 1966-68; assoc. prof. U. Richmond, Richmond, Va., 1968-83, prof., 1983—; pres. Am. Coun. on Tchg. Fgn. Langs., 1994. Co-author: Accent: Conversational French I, 1980, Vous Y Etes!, 1990, Intersections, 1991; editor Dimension, So. Conf. on Lang. Tchg., 1991—; assoc. editor ACTFL Foreign Language Education Series, 1994, 96; contbr. articles to profl. jours. Recipient Stephen A. Freeman award N.E. Conf. on Teaching Fgn. Lang., 1990, Robert J. Ludwig Nat. Fgn. Lang. Leadership award, 1995. Mem. Am. Coun. on Tchg. Fgn. Langs., Fgn. Lang. Assn. Va., Am. Assn. Tchrs. French, So. Conf. on Lang. Tchg., Pacific N.W. Coun. for Langs., Wis. Assn. Fgn. Lang. Tchrs. Home: 1504 Cloister Dr Richmond VA 23233 Office: Univ Richmond PO Box 25 28 Westhampton Way University Of Richmond VA 23173

TERRY, RONALD ANDERSON, bank holding company executive; b. Memphis, Dec. 5, 1930; s. John Burnett and Vernon (Lucas) T.; m. Wynoka W. Evans, May 21, 1989; children by previous marriage: Natalie Carol, Cynthia Leigh. B.S., Memphis State U., 1952; postgrad., So. Meth. U., 1961, Harvard U., 1970. Mgmt. trainee First Tenn. Bank, Memphis, 1957; pres. First Tenn. Nat. Corp., Memphis, 1971, chmn., 1973—; chmn. First Tenn. Bank N.A., Memphis, 1979-95, also bd. dirs.; bd. dirs. BellSouth Corp., AutoZone Inc., Delta Life Corp., Promus Hotel Corp., St. Jude Hosp., Blue Eagle Gold Ctrs., Inc., Home Account Network, Inc. Past pres. Boys Clubs Memphis, Future Memphis, Memphis Job Conf.; chmn. adv. com. Bapt. Meml. Hosp.; past Tenn. state chmn. Com. for Econ. Devel.; mem. adv. bd. Memphis Arts Coun. Lt. USN, 1953-57. Mem. Am. Bankers Assn. (treasury adv. com., bd. dirs., past chmn. govt. relations council), Assn. Res. City Bankers (dir., past chmn. govt. relations com. and pub. affairs com.), Assn. Bank Holding Cos. (legis. policy com., past pres. fed. adv. council), Econ. Club of Memphis (past pres.). Office: 6410 Poplar Ave Ste 375 Memphis TN 38119-4839

TERRY, STUART L(EE), plastics engineer; b. Chgo., Apr. 8, 1942; s. Gordon M. and Fredrica (Gordon) T.; m. Linda Jane Littenberg, Aug. 25, 1963 (div. 1974); m. Mary Ann Stames, Feb. 16, 1980; children: Robin D. Andrews, Mark R. Andrews, Marc L. Terry, Robin M. Terry. BSChemE, Cornell U., 1965, PhD, 1968; MS in Mgmt., Rensselear U., 1972. From sr. rsch. engr. to mgr. tech. acquisitions Monsanto Corp., Springfield, Mass., 1968-88; dir. tech. Sonoco Products Co., Hartsville, S.C., 1988—. Mem. Tech. Assn. of Pulp and Paper Industry, Soc. Plastics Engrs., Futures Soc. Office: Sonoco Products Co 1 N 2nd St Hartsville SC 29550-3300

TERWILLEGAR, JANE CUSACK, librarian, educator; b. Warsaw, N.Y., Nov. 7, 1935; d. James Scott and Estella B. (Ackerman) Cusack; m. Gordon H. Terwillegar, July 26, 1958 (div. Mar. 1989); children: Sarah Ann Terwillegar Smedley, Arne Matthew. BA, Elmira (N.Y.) Coll., 1957; MLS, SUNY, Geneseo, 1960; EdS, U. Ga., 1977. Cert. tchr., Fla. Instr. U. Ga., Athens, 1975-81; libr. Palm beach County Libr., West Palm Beach, Fla., 1981-83, Palm Beach County Schs., Royal Palm Beach, Fla., 1983-94; dist. libr. media svcs. specialist Palm Beach County Schs., West Palm Beach, 1994—; lectr. Sch. Libr. and Info. Sci., U. South Fla., Tampa, 1987—, Nova U., Ft. Lauderdale, Fla., 1995—; task force mem. SUNLINK project Fla. Dept. Edn., 1995—. Co-author: Commonsense Cataloging, 3d edit. 1983, 4th edit. 1990; reviewer Sch. Libr. Jour., 1986—; contbr. articles to profl. jours. Mem. ALA, AAUW, Am. Assn. Sch. Librs. (exec. bd. 1990-94), Assn. for Libr. Svc. to Children (Newbery com. 1988-89), Fla. Assn. Meda in Edn. (sec. 1988-89), Ednl. Media Assn. Fla. (pres. 1988), Delta Kappa Gamma, Phi Beta Kappa, Delta Kappa Phi, Phi Delta Kappa. Home: 911 Oak Harbour Dr Juno Beach FL 33408 Office: School Dist of Palm Beach County 1400 N Florida Mango Rd West Palm Beach FL 33409-5240

TESAR, DELBERT, machine systems and robotics educator, researcher, manufacturing consultant; b. Beaver Crossing, Nebr., Sept. 2, 1935; s. Louis and Clara (Capek) T.; m. Rogene Kresak, Feb. 1, 1957; children: Vim Lee, Aleta Anne, Landon Grady, Allison Jeanne. B.Sc. in Mech. Engring., U. Nebr., 1958, M.Sc., 1959; Ph.D., Ga. Tech. U., 1964. Assoc. prof. U. Fla., Gainesville, 1965-71, prof., 1972-83, grad. research prof., 1983-84, dir., founder Ctr. Intelligent Machines and Robotics, 1978-84; Curran chair in engring. U. Tex., Austin, 1985—; lectr. in field; mem. rev. panel Nat. Bur. Stds., Gaithersburg, Md., 1982-88; mem. sci. adv. bd. to Air Force, 1982-86; mem. standing com. NRC for Space Sta. (ISSA), 1992-95; interactor with Russian Acad. Sci. on sci. and tech. Author: (with others) Cam System Design, 1975. Patentee in field; contbr. articles to profl. jours.; assoc. editor 3 computer and mfg. jours. Expert witness house sci. and tech. com. U.S. Ho. of Reps., 1978-84. Fellow AAAS; mem. Fla. Engring. Soc. (Outstanding Tech. Achievement award 1982), ASME (machine design award 1987). Home: 8005 Two Cove Dr Austin TX 78730-3125 Office: U Tex Dept Mechanical Engineering Austin TX 78712-1063

TESAREK, DENNIS GEORGE, business consultant, writer, educator; b. Chgo., Jan. 2, 1935; s. George Joseph and Mary (Basl) T.; m. Caroline Arrena Myers, Jan. 1956 (div. Oct. 1968); children: William Paul, Dianne, Peter Bond; m. Kathleen Leigh Holm, Nov. 26, 1969; children: Philip Shawn, Leigh-Anne. BA in Math., U. Mo., 1956; postgrad., Systems Rsch. Inst., 1966, UCLA, 1984, Harvard U., 1985, MIT, 1986. Saleman Conn. Mut. Life Ins. Co., Dallas, 1959-61; systems engr. IBM, Phoenix, 1961-66; instr. IBM, L.A., 1966-68; mgr. IBM, Houston, 1968-74; industry mgr. IBM, White Plains, N.Y., 1974-76; project mgr. IBM, L.A., 1976-78; planning cons. IBM, Houston, 1978-84, cons. in bus. transformation, planning and gen. mgmt., 1984—; adj. prof. Ariz. State U., 1963-65; guest lectr. U. Houston, 1980, 81, 83, 87. Author: Distributed Information Systems Planning Methodology, 1982, Information Systems Management Effectiveness Assessment, 1983, Business Systems Planning for Competitive Advantage Methodology, 1986, Executive Strategy Session Methodology, 1987, Management Planning Session Methodology, 1987, Steps in Strategic Investment Methodology, 1989. Tutor Vols. in Pub. Schs., Houston Ind. Sch. Dist., 1972-74, 80-82. 1st lt. USMC, 1956-59. Republican. Mem. Christian Sci. Ch. Office: IBM Corp 2 Riverway Houston TX 77056-1912

TESAREK, WILLIAM PAUL, business consultant, writer, financial executive; b. Albuquerque, May 6, 1958; s. Dennis George and Caroline Arrena (Myers) T.; m. Nancy Anne Pence, May 12, 1984 (div. Feb. 1991); children: Michelle Marie, Allison Elaine. BS in Econs., U. Houston, 1986, MA in Econs., 1988, MBA in Fin., 1993, PhD, 1994. Instr. econs. U. Houston, 1987-88; sr. sales tax analyst Tex. State Comptroller, Austin, 1988-89; adj. prof. fin. U. Houston, 1989-93; sr. economist Asset Analysis & Mgmt., Houston, 1993; sr. fin. economist Asset Dynamics, Houston, 1993-94; owner The Tesarek Group, Houston, 1994—; cons. in strategic planning and process reengring. mgmt. Author: Housing Price and Regional Real Estate Cycles: Market Adjustments in Houston, 1991; Beyond Counting the Beans: How Chief Financial Executives Use Knowledge to Advance the Corporation, 1995. With USN, 1976-80. Econ. Honors. Soc. Achievement award, 1986. Mem. Am. Econs. Assn., Am. Fin. Assn., Western Econ. Assn., Tex. Econ. & Demographic Assn., Allied Soc. Sci. Assn., Houston Bus. Process Reengring. Share Group. Republican. Mem. Ch. of Christ. Home and Office: The Tesarek Grp 16011 Silver Valley Dr Houston TX 77084-2960

TESELLE, EUGENE ARTHUR, JR., religion educator; b. Ames, Iowa, Aug. 8, 1931; s. Eugene Arthur and Hildegarde (Flynn) TeS.; m. Sallie McFague, Sept. 12, 1959 (div. Oct. 1976); children: Elizabeth, John; m. Penelope Saunders, Mar. 4, 1978; children: William, James, Thomas. BA, U. Colo., 1952; BD, Princeton Theol. Sem., 1955; MA, Yale U., 1960, PhD, 1963. Commr. to gen. assembly Presbyn. Ch. in U.S.A., 1993; issues analyst Witherspoon Soc., 1987-93; chmn. global missions com. Presbytery Mid. Tenn., 1989-93. Author: Augustine, the Theologian, 1970, Augustine's Strategy as an Apologist, 1974, Christ in Context, 1975, Thomas Aquinas: Faith and Reason, 1988. Incorporator Belmont-Hillsboro Neighbors, Nashville, 1971, Consumer Coalition for Health, Nashville, 1980, Nashville Local, Dem. Socialists Am., 1983, Cen. Am. Solidarity Assn., Nashville, 1986. Presbyn. Grad. fellow, 1958, Rockefeller doctoral fellow, 1960, Kent fellow, 1961; recipient Thomas Jefferson award Vanderbilt U., 1996. Mem. Am. Acad. Religion, Am. Soc. Ch. History, Soc. for Values in Higher Edn., Workgroup on Constructive Christian Theology, Witherspoon Soc. (pres. 1995—), Phi Beta Kappa. Home: 2007 Linden Ave Nashville TN 37212-5021 Office: Vanderbilt U Divsn Sch Nashville TN 37240

TESH, VERNON LEWIS, biomedical researcher; b. Sunbury, Pa., Nov. 11, 1953; s. John Wade and Dorothy (McLaughlin) T.; m. Vickey Thayer, Mar. 22, 1980; children: Andrew Wade, Kirsten Leanne. BA in Biology, U. Va., 1976; PhD in Microbiology and Immunology, Emory U., 1988. Lab. tech. U. Va. Hosp., Charlottesville, 1976-79, supr. anaerobic labs., 1979-83; postdoctoral fellow Uniformed Svcs. U. Health Scis., Bethesda, Md., 1988-92; asst. prof. Tex. A&M U. Health Sci. Ctr., College Station, 1992—; faculty senator Tex. A&M U., 1994—. Contbr. articles to profl. jours. and chpts. to books. Grantee NIH, 1995—, Coun. for Tobacco Rsch., 1994—. Mem. Am. Soc. for Microbiology (editl. bd. Infection and Immunity 1994—, ICAAC Young Investigator award 1986), Sigma Xi. Methodist. Office: Tex A&M U Health Sci Ctr 407 Reynolds Med Bldg College Station TX 77843-1114

TETLIE, HAROLD, priest; b. Madison, Minn., Aug. 24, 1926; s. H. Ben and Anna (Mauland) T. BA cum laude, St. Olaf Coll., Northfield, Minn., 1951; MBA, U. Denver, 1956; postgrad., Cornell U., 1959-60; MDiv, Luther Sem., St. Paul, 1965. Ordained to ministry Am. Luth. Ch., 1965. Pastor Christ the King Chs. (Evang. Cath. Ch.), Alice, Tex., 1965—, congregation supr., 1969—; cir. parish priest, Nuevo Leon, Tamaulipas, Hidalgo, San Luis Potosi, Mex. Author numerous poems. Coord. Joint Action in Cmty. Svc., Inc., Alice, 1970—. Sgt. U.S. Army, 1945-46, PTO. Recipient Svc. to Mankind award Sertoma Club, Corpus Christi, Regional Vol. of Yr. award Joint Action in Cmty. Svc., 1991, Michael Madhusudan award for poem, Calcutta, 1996; Ky. Col., 1992. Mem. NEA (life), VFW, Am. Legion, 40 et 8, Family Motor Coach Assn., Sons of Norway, Order of Ky. Col., Internat. Platform Assn., Thousand Trails. Home and Office: Christ the King Chs PO Box 1607 Alice TX 78333-1607

TETLOW, LOUIS MULRY, clinical psychologist; b. New Orleans, Apr. 28, 1934; s. Joseph A. Sr. and Helen Mercedes (Mullen) T.; m. Elisabeth M. Tetlow, July 5, 1970; children: Tania, Maria (dec.) Sonia, Sarah. AB in Edn., Spring Hill Coll., 1959, MA in Philosophy cum laude, 1960; STL cum laude, St. Louis U., 1967; MA, Fordham U., 1970, PhD in Clin. Psychology, 1974. Lic. clin. psychologist, La. Staff psychologist Kingsbridge V.A. Hosp., Bronx, 1970-74; pvt. practice N.Y.C, La., Can., 1974—; asst. prof. psychology St. Thomas U., Fredericton, Can., 1974-76; assoc. prof. psychology Loyola U., New Orleans, 1978-84; asst. prof. La. State U. Sch. of Medicine, New Orleans, 1984-87; treatment and assessment supr. Jefferson Parish Juvenile Cts., 1987-88; chief psychologist La. State Penitentiary, Angola, La., 1989-90; prof. psychology Holy Cross Coll., New Orleans, 1992—; faculty senate Loyola U., 1980-82, chair fin. engring. com., 1982; pres. GSA Fordham U., 1968-69. Co-author: Partners in Service. Bd. dirs. Dystonia Med. Rsch. Found., L.A., 1993—; mem. Symphony Chorus of New Orleans, 1983—, Concert Choir of New Orleans. Mem. APA, La. Psychol. Assn. Democrat. Roman Catholic. Home: 16 Fontainebleau Dr New Orleans LA 70125 Office: Holy Cross Coll New Orleans LA 70131

TETOR, CAROL LYNN, business owner; b. Cin., Jan. 7, 1946; d. William E. and Ramona B. Stelzer; m. Walter Stephen Hood, Apr. 16, 1966 (div. Apr. 1970); m. Paul S. Tetor III, July 9, 1974; 1 child, Alexis. Cert. in dental assistance, Orlando Dental Soc., 1965; cert. in chiropractic assistance, Parker Rsch. Found., Ft. Worth, 1976. Dental asst. Orlando Dental Asst. Soc., 1964-76; chiropractic asst. Dr. Joel Grossman, Orlando, 1976-78; parimutuel clk. Sanford Orlando Kennel Club, 1976-80; owner Teet's Lounge & Package, Deland, Fla., 1980—; cons. Longaberger Co., Dresden, Ohio, 1989-94; substitute tchr. Volusia County Sch. Bd., Deland, 1992—; coord. Math. SuperStars program Orange City (Fla.) Elem. Sch., 1992-94. Mem. bd. adjustments Orange City, 1992-93; active Girl Scouts U.S., 1992-94; elected to Orange City Coun., 1993—. Home: 795 E Lansdowne Ave Orange City FL 32763-4329 Office: Teet's Lounge & Package 114 E Indiana Ave Deland FL 32724-4330

TEW, E. JAMES, JR., electronics company executive; b. Dallas, July 7, 1933; s. Elmer James and Bessie Fay (Bennett) T.; children: Teresa Annette, Linda Diane, Brian James. Student Arlington State Jr. Coll., 1955-57; B.B.A. in Indsl. Mgmt., So. Meth. U., 1969; M.S. in Quality Systems, U. Dallas, 1972, M.B.A. in Mgmt., 1975, EdD in Adult Edn., Nova U., 1986, postdoctoral, 1986, 89. Registered profl. engr., Calif. Mgr. quality assurance ops. Tex. Instruments Inc., Dallas, 1957—, chmn. corp. metric implementation com., co-chmn. credit com. Texins Credit Union; adj. faculty Richland Coll., Mountain View Coll. Precinct chmn., election judge, del. several county and state convs.; bus. computer info. systems adv. bd. U. North Tex., bd. dirs. ctr. for quality and productivity U. North Tex.; bd. examiners Malcolm Baldrige Nat. Quality award, U.S. Dept. Commerce, Nat. Inst. Standard and Tech., 1988, 89, 90, 91. With U.S. Army, 1953-55. Decorated Army Commendation medal with oak leaf cluster. Fellow Am. Soc. Quality Control (cert. as quality and reliability engr., chmn. Dallas-Ft. Worth sect. 1974-75). Fellow U.S. Metric Assn. (cert., chmn. cert. bd. 1986-87); mem.. U.S.Res. Officers Assn., Dallas C. of C. (chmn. world mfg. com. 1974-77, chmn. spl. task force career edn. adv. bd. 1973-74), Mensa, Sigma Iota Epsilon, Phi Delta Kappa. Baptist. Clubs: Texins Rod and Gun (pres. 1969-70), Texins Flying, Masons (32 degree). Contbr. articles to profl. jours. Home: 10235 Mapleridge Dr Dallas TX 75238-2256 Office: PO Box 660246 MS 3107 Dallas TX 75266

TEWKSBURY, RICHARD ALLAN, sociologist, educator; b. Fairview Park, Ohio, Nov. 30, 1963; s. Dale N. and Norma C. Tewksbury; m. Lisa J. Sutton, July 26, 1986. BA in Sociology and Psychology, Butler U., 1986; MA in Sociology, Ohio State U., 1988, PhD in Sociology, 1991. Asst. prof. Sch. of Justice Adminstrn., U. Louisville, 1992—. Editor Am. Jour. of Criminal Justice; contbr. articles to profl. jours. Dir. Health Edn. Columbus

AIDS Task Force, 1990; bd. dirs. Community Health Trust, Louisville, Ky., 1993-94; chmn. profl. edn. Jefferson County com. to Stop Child Sexual Abuse, Louisville; mem. AIDS material rev. com. Ky. Dept. Health, 1993-94. Mem. Am. Soc. Criminology, Acad. of Criminal Justice Sci., Am. Sociol. Assn., N. Ctrl. Sociol. Assn., Am. Correctional Assn., Ky. Coun. on Crime and Delinquency. Office: U Lousiville Sch Justice Adminstrn Louisville KY 40292

THACKER, SHANNON STEPHEN, financial advisor; b. Atlanta, July 5, 1956; s. Vincent Joseph and Rita (Wilkes) T.; m. Susan Robinson, Nov. 4, 1989; children: Shannon Stephanie, Stephen Phillip. BS in Corp. Fin., U. Ala., 1979. V.p. investments Prudential Securities, Houston, 1979-91, portfolio mgr., v.p., 1991—. Author newsletter Interesting Investing, 1991, 93. Elder Southwest Presbyn. Ch. Am., Houston. Mem. Internat. Platform Assn., Am. Assn. Mgmt. and Rsch. (affiliate), U. Ala. Alumni Assn., River Oaks Tennis Club. Republican. Office: Prudential Securities 1221 Mckinney St Fl 29 Houston TX 77010-2011

THAGARD, NORMAN E., astronaut, physician, engineer; b. Marianna, Fla., July 3, 1943; s. James E. Thagard and Mary F. Nicholson; m. Rex Kirby Johnson; children: Norman Gordon, James Robert, Daniel Cary. BS, Florida State U., 1965, MS, 1966; M.D., U. Texas Southwest Med. Sch., 1977. Intern, internal medicine Medical U. South Carolina, 1977-78; astronaut NASA, 1978—; mission specialist NASA Space Shuttle Challenger Flight STS-7, deployed satellites (ANIK C-2, PALAPA B-1), operated Remote Manipulator Sys., conducted experiments, 1983, NASA Spacelab-3 Mission STS-51 B, 1985, NASA Space Shuttle Atlantis Flight STS-30, deployed Magellan Venus exploration spacecraft, 1989; payload commander NASA Space Shuttle Discovery Flight STS-42, International Microgravity Lab.-1 module experiments, 1992; crew mem. Space Station MIR-18, 1995. Contbr. articles to profl. jours. With USMC, 1966-70, Capt. 1967-70, in Vietnam flew 163 combat missions. Decorated 11 Air medals, Navy Commednation medal with Combat V, Marine Corps E award, Vietnam Svc. medal, Vietnamese Cross of Gallantry with Palm. Mem. AIAA, Phi Kappa Phi. Office: Lyndon B Johnson Space Ctr NASA 2101 Nasa Rd 1 Houston TX 77058-3607

THAI, VAN ALBERT, design engineer. BSEE in Comm. Systems, Computer Hardware, Software, Stevens Inst. Tech., 1985. Elec. engr. E-Systems Melpar Divsn., Fairfax, Va., 1985-87; staff mem. Atlantic Aerospace Electronics Corp., Greenbelt, Md., 1987-88; sr. hardware designer Encore Computer Corp., Landover, Md., 1988-90; mem. tech. staff Am. Systems Corp., Chantilly, Va., 1990; contractor Smarthouse L.P., Upper Marlboro, Md., 1991, AT&T BL, Freehold, N.J., 1992, Telecommunications Techniques Corp., Germantown, Md., 1992-93; with TeleSystem Unternat. Corp., Rockville, Md., Plexsys Internat. Corp., McLean, Va. Home and Office: Product Design Consulting Vat and Assocs 13400 Marble Rock Dr Fairfax VA 22021-2400

THAKKER, ASHOK, aerospace engineering company executive; b. Bombay, Aug. 9, 1947; came to U.S., 1970; s. Bhagwandas P. and Champa (Lakhpatla) T.; m. Sarla A. Bhate, Dec. 30, 1975; 1 child, Amish. B of Engring., U. Bombay, 1970; MS, S.D. Tech. Inst., 1971; PhD, Va. Polytech. Inst. & State U., 1974; MBA, Fla. Inst. Tech., 1980. Registered profl. engr., Va., Fla.; cert. mfg. engr. Instr. Va. Poly. Inst., Blacksburg, 1972-74; engr. Alcoa Tech. Ctr., Alcoa Ctr., Pa., 1974-76, sr. engr., 1976-78; group leader Pratt and Whitney Aircraft, West Palm Beach, Fla., 1978-83; project mgr. U.S. govt. programs Rolls-Royce, Inc., Atlanta, 1983-85, mgr. materials rsch., 1985-86, sr. project mgr., 1986-88, sr. mgr. engring., 1988-94, dir. materiels, 1994—. Contbr. numerous articles to profl. jours. and tech. reports to coms. Chmn. Internat. Student Assn., Blacksburg, 1972-73; advisor Jr. Achievement Program, Palm Beach, Fla., 1982-83. R & D Sethna Scholarship award, 1970; recipient Best Paper award AIAA-Atlanta Symposium, 1987. Fellow Am. Soc. Materials Internat.; mem. ASTM (reviewer tech. papers, composites, fatigue and fracture coms.), Am. Soc. Materials (chpt. program chmn. 1982, internat. chpt. membership com. 1989, vice chmn., then chmn. Atlanta chpt. 1989, 90, nat. devel. coun. 1990-91, nat. govt. and pub. affairs com. 1992-94, advisor, profl. as resource for instruction in sci. and math. student outreach program 1992—, tech. awareness adv. com., edit. bd. Materials & Process Jour. 1993—), ASM Internat., Soc. Exptl. Mechanics (chpt. chmn. 1978, 81-82, chmn. fatigue com. 1984), Soc. Advancement Material and Process Engring., Soc. Mfg. Engrs. (com. mem., 1st vice chmn. Atlanta chpt. 1991-92, chmn. 1992-93, sr. internat. dir. 1992-93), Materials Rsch. Soc., Am. Ceramics Soc. (exec. com.), NASA Space Consortium (exec. com. 1992-93), Toastmasters, Lions, Sigma Xi, Vinings Club. Clubs: Toastmasters, Lions, Sigma Xi, Vinings (social com. 1992-93). Home: 2690 Spencer Trl Marietta GA 30062 Office: Rolls-Royce Inc 2849 Paces Ferry Rd NW Atlanta GA 30339-3769

THAMES, EARL GLENN, accounting educator; b. West Monroe, La., Sept. 13, 1925; s. Archie L. and Lila Belle (Drummond) T.; m. Barbara Ann Thomas Yeates, Aug. 17, 1966; children: Edwin Clifton Yeates III, William Thomas Yeates, Earl Glenn Thames Jr. BBA, U. Miss., 1948, MBA, 1950, PhD, 1964. CPA, Miss., La. Acct. Ford Motor Co., Memphis, 1950-55, Deloitte, Touche, CPA's, New Orleans, 1956-60; grad. asst. U. Miss., Oxford, 1961-64; prof. acctg. Northwestern State U., Natchitoches, La., 1964-87, chmn. dept. acctg., 1964-86; prof. acctg. Fred M. Hale Sch. Bus. East Tex. Bapt. U., Marshall, 1987—, interim dean, 1994-95; cons. in field. Author: Investors Guide to Accounting Statememts-Copyright, 1989, Essentials of Accounting-Copyright, 1995; contbr. articles to profl. jours. With inf. U.S. Army, 1943-45, ETO. Decorated Purple Heart. Mem. AICPA, Am. Acctg. Assn., La. Soc. CPAs, Am. Legion, U. Miss. Alumni Assn., Rotary. Republican. Methodist. Home: 711 Hancock Natchitoches LA 71457 Office: East Tex Bapt U Fred M Hale Sch Bus 1209 N Grove St Marshall TX 75670

THAMPI, MOHAN VARGHESE, environmental health and civil engineer; b. Kuching, Sarawak, Malaysia, Mar. 25, 1960; s. Padmanabha Ramachandran and Sosamma (Varghese) T. Gen. Cert. Edn., Cambridge U., 1976; B in Tech. with honors, Indian Inst. Tech., Kharagpur, India, 1983; MS in Engring., U. Tex., 1985; DSc (hon.), London Inst. Applied Rsch., 1992. Registered profl. engr., Tex., Fla., registered environ. mgr.; cert. safety tng. OSHA; cert. Nat. Coun. Examiners for Engrs. and Surveyors. Assoc. engr. Brown & Caldwell, Dallas, 1985-87; project mgr. Brown & Caldwell, Orlando, 1987-88, Stottler Stagg & Assocs., Cape Canaveral, Fla., 1988-91; sr. project engr. Chastain-Skillman, Inc., Lakeland, Fla., 1991-93; project mgr. Glace & Radcliffe, Inc., Winter Park, Fla., 1993-94; mgr. FDEP, West Palm Beach, Fla., 1995-96; project mgr. Collier County, Naples, Fla., 1996—, CCG-OCPM, Naples, Fla., 1996—. Author: Ultraviolet Disinfection Studies in a Teflon-Tube Reactor, 1985; contbr. articles to profl. jours. Active Rep. Pres.'s Citizens Adv. Commn., 1992. Recipient Cert. of Cont. Profl. Devel. award Fla. Engring. Soc., 1992. Mem. NSPE, ASCE (assoc.), Internat. Assn. Water Pollution Rsch. and Control, Am. Mensa, Am. Water Works Assn., Water Pollution Control Fedn. (com. for preparing design practice manuals 1989—), Internat. Freelance Photographers Assn., Internat. Platform Assn., Internat. Assn. Air Travel Couriers, Am. Mgmt. Assn., Am. Smokers Alliance, Smithsonian Instn., Nat. Geog. Soc., Nat. Registry Environ. Professionals, U. Tex. Ex-Students Assn., Wine Soc. Am., Nat. Family Opinion, Internat. Deep Purple Appreciation Soc., Wilson Ctr. Assocs., I.I.T. Kharagpur Tech. Found., NASA Tech Briefs Reader Opinion Panel, Chemical Engring. Jour. Product Rsch. Panel, Plant Engring. Editl. Quality Panel, Kharagpur Tech. Alumni Found., N.Am. Hunting Club, Knight Order of Templars (Jerusalem). Mar Thoma Syrian Christian. Office: OCPM 3301 E Yamiami Tr Naples FL 34111

THARP, DAVID MINTON, pharmacist; b. Nashville, Nov. 22, 1948; s. Robert Moore and Elizabeth Elaine (Pool) T.; m. Lynda Sue Broome (div. Mar. 1986); m. Carol Lynn Collins, Jan. 14, 1989. AS, South Ga. Jr. Coll., Douglas, 1969; BS in Pharmacy, U. Ga., 1972. Lic. registered pharmacist, Ga., Fla. Intern Dick & Meadows Pharmacy, Venice, Fla., 1972-73, pharmacist, 1973-76; pharmacist Gene's Prescription Shop, Pt. Charlotte, Fla., 1976-78; pharmacist, mgr. Gene's Prescription Shop, Punta Gorda, Fla., 1978-80; pharmacist F.P. May Drug Co., Quincy, Fla., 1980-83, Albertson's Pharmacy, Tallahassee, 1983-90; cons. pharmacist Fla. Dept. Health & Rehab. Svcs., Tallahassee, 1989-90; pharmacist Health Meds, Inc., Quincy, Fla., 1991-92, Big B Drugs #389, Tallahassee, 1992—. Delta Chi scholar, 1970-71. Mem. Am. Motorcyclist Assn. (life), Am. Pharm. Assn., Leon County Pharm. Assn., Tallahasee Trail Riders Club (pres. 1984-85, 89—, 1st v.p. 1986—, chmn. monthly events 1985, Rider of Yr. 1983, numerous awards), Fla. Trial Riders Club (area dir. 1985—, C-Open Enduro Class Champion 1985-86, Super Sr. B Enduro Class Champion, 1989-90). Republican. Baptist. Home: 1611 Redwood Dr Tallahassee FL 32301-2731 Office: Big B Drugs # 389 400 Capital Cir SE Tallahassee FL 32301-3802

THARP, KAREN ANN, insurance agent; b. Montpelier, Ohio, Sept. 24, 1944; d. Howard Wesley and Thelma (Myers) Skiles; children: Pamela Lyn Tharp Grasso, James Alan, Jennifer Ann. Grad. high sch., Edon, Ohio. Sales agt. Equitable Life, Delray Beach, Fla., 1978-79; owner, pres. Fin. Profiles, Inc., Coral Springs, Fla., 1980—. Mem. Nat. Assn. Life Underwriters, Million Dollar Round Table. Republican. Home: 12432 NW 17th Pl Coral Springs FL 33071-7892 Office: Fin Profiles Inc 10101A W Sample Rd Coral Springs FL 33065-3937

THATCHER, SAMUEL SELDEN, reproductive biologist, physician; b. Chattanooga, Dec. 31, 1949; s. Samuel Seldon and Lucille (Mays) T.; m. Helen Christine Walker, Apr. 4, 1987. BA, U. Tenn., 1972; PhD, MD, W.Va. U., 1981. Lectr. in anatomy W.Va. U., Morgantown, 1979-80; postdoctoral fellow Johns Hopkins Med. Inst., Balt., 1980-81; resident in ob-gyn. Yale-New Haven Hosp., 1981-85; lectr. reproductive medicine, med. dir. invitro program Edinburgh (Scotland) U., 1985-87; instr. div. reproductive endocrinology Yale U., New Haven, 1987-88; dir. reproductive endocrinology, assoc. prof. East Tenn. State U., Johnson City, 1988-95; dir. Ctr. for Applied Reproductive Sci., Johnson City, Tenn., 1996—. Fellow Am. Coll. Ob-Gyn. (subspecialty cert. in reproductive endocrinology); mem. Am. Fertility Soc., Soc. for the Study Reproduction, Soc. for the Study Fertility, European Soc. for Study Human Reproduction, Endocrine Soc., Am. Soc. Audiology. Office: 408 E State Of Franklin Rd Johnson City TN 37601

THAXTON, MARY LYNWOOD, psychologist; b. Detroit, Dec. 27, 1944; d. Osceola Alvin Jr. and Mary Phlegar (Penn) T. BA, Emory and Henry Coll., 1966; MLn, Emory U., 1967; AS, Ga. State U., 1978, MA, 1983, PhD, 1989. Reference libr. Coll. of William and Mary, Williamsburg, Va., 1967-71; reference libr., asst. prof. Ga. State U., Atlanta, 1971-77, social sci. bibliographer, assoc. prof., 1977-89; pvt. practice psychotherapy, gerontol cons., Tucker, Ga., 1989-91; gerontol. cons., psychotherapist in pvt. practice Marietta, Ga., 1991-95; Atlanta, 1996—. Editor bibliography: Metropolitan Atlanta Rapid Transit Authority, 1982, Community Mental Health Services to the Elderly, 1984 (Libr. award 1984); contbr. articles to profl. jours. Office: 1970 Cliff Valley Way NE Atlanta GA 30329-2428

THAYER, MARY NORENE, English language educator; b. Tuckerman, Ark., May 30, 1943; d. John Floie and Ethyl Lois (Kunkel) Runsick; m. Hugh MacDonald, Jr., 1963 (div. 1981); children: Melanie Fish, Melinda Hegarty, Hugh III; m. Nelson Kenneth Thayer, June 9, 1994. AA, Fla. Coll., 1963; BA, U. South Fla., 1967, MA, 1971, PhD, 1981. Prof. Fla. Coll., Temple Terrace, 1974—. Editor: Classical Voices, 1996. Mem. MLA, Assn. Literary Scholars & Critics, 19th Century Studies Assn., Southeastern Conf. on English in 2-Yr. Colls., Fla. Coll. English Assn. Republican. Ch. of Christ. Home: 3005 Kingsway Rd Thonotasassa FL 33592 Office: Fla Coll 119 Glen Arven Temple Terrace FL 33617

THEISEN, GEORGE I., manufacturing executive; b. N.Y.C., May 22, 1926; s. Svend I. and Olga (Sorensen) T.; m. Joan Lucille Gerold, Sept. 20, 1947; children: Claude, Lisbeth, Clifford, Susan, Eva-Marie. Student, NYU, 1942-43, 46, Pace Inst., 1947, 48. Founder, pres. T&S Brass & Bronze Works, Inc., N.Y.C., 1947-78, Greenville, S.C., 1978—; pres. GIT, Inc., Greenville, 1988—. Pres. PTA, East Norwich, N.Y., 1960; bd. dirs. Jr. Achievement, L.I., N.Y., 1974-76, Greenville, S.C., 1988, Greenville Tech. Found. Cpl. USMC, 1944-46, World War II. Decorated Purple Heart, Iwo Jima; recipient Humanitarian award Am. Jewish Com., 1976, 77. Mem. Am. Soc. Plumbing Engrs., Am. Soc. Sanitary Engrs., Nat. Assn. Food Equipment Mfrs., Plumbing Mfrs. Inst. (pres. 1976-78), Green Valley C. of C., Greenville C. of C. (pres. 1987-88). Republican. Methodist. Office: T&S Brass & Bronze Works Old Buncombe Rd Travelers Rest SC 29690

THEISEN, RUSSELL EUGENE, electrical engineer; b. Norfolk, Va., Aug. 3, 1937; s. Richard Roudolph and Pansie Mae (Garnette) T.; m. Mary Ann Asbury, May 30, 1962; children: Timothy Mark, Yvette Marie. BSEE, Old Dominion, 1962; MBA, Rollins Coll., 1973. Registered profl. engr., N.Y., Fla. Svc. mgr. Mastercraft Elect., Norfolk, 1955-62; design engr. IBM Corp., Endicott, N.Y., 1962-64; plant mgr. Compton Industries, Vestal, N.Y., 1964-66; sr. engr. Martin Marietta Aerospace, Orlando, Fla., 1966-74; sr. project engr. General Dynamics Corp., Longwood, Fla., 1974-76; sr. mem. profl. staff Martin Marietta Aerospace, Orlando, 1976-92; sr. system software analyst SCI Systems Inc., Huntsville, Ala., 1992—; mgr. Worldwide Document Mgmt. and Control Systems, 1996—; nat. dir. Halbert Genealogy, Bath, Ohio, 1987—; pres. Theisen Enterprises Inc., 1996—; cert. mgr., 1996, Nat. Mgmt. Assn.; Ala. chmn. Am. Enterprise Inst., High Teck Valley Coun. Nat. Mgmt. Assn., 1996-97; dir. Nat. Computer Conf., 1967-79, 83-85; POSIX Programming Language Standard IEEE 1986; 1094 Standard for Life Cycle Process 1989. Contbng. author: Reliability And Maintainibility, 1967; contbr. articles to profl. jours., Posix Prgmg. Language Standard IEEE, 1986; 1094 Standard for Life Cycle Process IEEE, 1989. Dir. Theisen Clan Theisen Genealogy Group, 1988-95, 96; dir. Fla. Libr. Adv. Bd., 1967-79; pres. Theisen Enterprises Inc., 1994—, profl., Nat Soc. for Profl. Engrs., 1963-76, bd. dirs. Am. Fedn. Info. Processing Soc., 1983-85. With USMC, 1953-65. Mem. IEEE (v.p. 1983-85, Fla. Coun. pres. 1987-89, sr.), Nat. Mgmt. Assn. (v.p. 1992-95, sr.), ACM (area chmn. 1987-89, sr.). Home: 3106 Heatherhill Dr Huntsville AL 35802-1140 Office: SCI Systems Inc 8600 Meml Pkwy Huntsville AL 35807-4001

THELEN, GIL, newspaper editor; b. Chgo.; s. Gilbert Carl and Violet (Okonn) T.; m. Carol Abernathy, July 1966 (div. Apr. 1978); children: Deborah Brooke, Todd Foster; m. Cynthia Jane Struby, Sept. 2, 1979; children: Matthew David, Jonathan Whitfield. BA, Duke U., 1960. Reporter Milw. Jour., 1960-61, AP, Washington, 1965-72; writer Consumer Reports, Mt. Vernon, N.Y., 1972-77; reporter Chgo. Daily News, 1977-78; asst. met. editor Charlotte (N.C.) Observer, 1978-82, met. editor, 1982-83, asst. mng. editor, 1983-87; editor The Sun News, Myrtle Beach, S.C., 1987-90; exec. editor The State, 1990—; adj. prof. U. S.C., Aiken, 1989—. Pres. Montgomery County Big Brothers, Bethesda, Md., 1967-69; co-founder Alpha Group, Myrtle Beach, S.C., 1989. Mem. Am. Soc. Newspaper Editors, S.C. Press Assn., Columbia Rotary Club, Leadership S.C., Leadership Columbia, Phi Beta Kappa, Omicron Delta Kappa. Methodist. Home: 128 Alexander Cir Columbia SC 29206-4956 Office: The State Newspaper 1401 Shop Rd Columbia SC 29201-4843

THEOBALD, ROBERT, futurist, writer, consultant; b. Madras, India, June 11, 1929; s. Raymond Walter and Irene (Pulleine) T.; m. Jeanne-Marie Scott, Dec. 8, 1951. BA in Econs., Cambridge U., 1951; MA in Econs., Cambridge U., Eng., 1952; postgrad., Harvard U., 1957-58. Adminstr. Orgn. European Econ. Coop., Paris, 1953-57; pvt. practice cons. N.Y.C., 1958-68; pres. Participation Pubs., Wickenburg, Ariz., 1973-89, New Orleans, 1989—; cons. Interactive Video Industry Assn., Nebr. State Dept. Banking, Ariz. Dept. Transp., U.S. Congl. Office Tech. Assessment, UN, Lewis and Clark Coll., State of Wis., Eastfield C.C., Dalls, Vols. Am.; presenter numerous seminars; speaker in field. Author: Free Men and Free Markets, 1963, An Alternative Future for America, 1968, The Economics of Abundance: A Non-Inflationary Future, 1970, The Rapids of Change, 1987 (New Options Book award 1987), Turning the Century, 1993, Reworking Success, 1996; co-author; The Triple Revolution, 1964, At The Crossroads, 1984; cons. to radio series Choice: The Imperative of Tomorrow. With Brit. Army, 1946-48. Can. Broadcasting Corp. Massey lectr., 1996. Home and Office: 509 Conti St New Orleans LA 70130-2232

THEODORIDIS, GEORGE CONSTANTIN, biomedical engineering educator, researcher; b. Braila, Romania, Dec. 3, 1935; came to U.S., 1959; s. Constantin George and Anastasia (Haritopoulos) T.; m. Lilly Kate Hyman, Sept. 20, 1975; 1 child, Alexander. BS in Mechanical and Elec. Engring., Nat. Tech. U. Athens, 1959; DSc, MIT, Cambridge, Mass., 1964. Rsch. assoc. MIT, Cambridge, Mass., 1964; sr. scientist Am. Sci. Engring., Cambridge, Mass., 1964-68; assoc. prof. in residence U. Calif., Berkeley, 1968-70; biomedical engring. U. Va., Charlottesville, 1970—; prof. elec. engring. U. Patras, Greece, 1976-83; cons. Food and Drug Adminstrn., Washington, 1975-76, Applied Physics Lab, Columbia, Md., 1978-79. Author: Applied Math, 1983; contbr. articles to profl. jours. Den leader Boy Scouts Am., Charlottesville, Va., 1984-85. Fulbright fellow U.S. Govt., MIT, 1959-60; Nato fellow NATO, MIT, 1961-64; Spl. fellow NIH, U. Calif., 1968-70; recipient teaching award GE, MIT, 1963. Mem. Inst. Elec. and Electronics Engrs., Sigma Xi. Greek Orthodox. Home: 1817 Fendall Ave Charlottesville VA 22903-1613 Office: U Va Dept Biomed Engring Box 377 Medical Ctr Charlottesville VA 22908

THERRIEN, FRANCOIS XAVIER, JR., business and tax consultant; b. Amesbury, Mass. June 6, 1928; s. Francis Xavier and Doris Alma (Cote) T.; BS, U.S. Mil. Acad., 1950; MS, U. Ariz., 1962; Cert. tax profl., tax advisor, enrolled agt., environ. inspector, bd. cert. bus. appraiser; m. Yoshiko Kashima, July 22, 1969; children: Francois Xavier, Norman, Sakura, Izumi. Commd. 2d lt., U.S. Army, 1950, advanced through grades to lt. col., 1965, ret., 1970; dist. dir. R. J. Carroll Assoc., Inc., Atlanta, 1970-71; with Treasure Lake, Atlanta, 1971; pres. Identiseal of Fla., Orlando, 1972-74; owner Yoshiko Enterprises, Winter Park, Fla., 1974-87, bd. dirs., pres., 1988—; instr. Seminole Community Coll., 1974-79; regional rep. H.D. Vest Investment Securities, Inc., Irving, Tex., 1989—. Decorated Army Commendation medals (2), Air medal, Bronze Star medal, Silver Star, Croix DeGuerre with palm. Mem. Nat. Assn. Enrolled Agts. Roman Catholic. Office: 2265 Lee Rd Ste 223 Winter Park FL 32789-1858

THIBAUDEAUX, MARY FRANCES, cultural organization administrator; b. Anaconda, Mont., Dec. 6, 1943; d. Frank Albert and Mary (May) T.; m. Alex W. Wells, Jr.; 1 child, Christopher. BA magna cum laude, U. Washington, Seattle, 1969. Therapist, counselor Thibaudeaux and Assocs., Atlanta, 1976-88; chmn. Vietnam Reconciliation Bus. Group, Atlanta, 1988—; cons. Ga. Vets. Leadership Program, Atlanta, 1994. Exec. prodr. (documentary) Vietnam: The Final Healing, 1991; co-author, editor (screenplay) Perfume River, 1995. Exchange dir. Friendship Force Internat., Atlanta, 1993-94. Named Ga. Outstanding Citizen, Ga. Sec. State, 1994. Mem. Atlanta Vets. Assn. (hon.). Home: 185 Softwood Cir Roswell GA 30076-2966

THIE, GENEVIEVE ANN, secondary school educator; b. Aledo, Ill., Sept. 4, 1939; d. Leroy James and Wilma Elizabeth (Wood) Robinson; m. Irvin Emil Thie, Sept. 9, 1977; children: Vyona Ann, Daryl Irvin. BA, Iowa State Tchrs. Coll., Cedar Falls, 1961; MA, U. No. Iowa, Cedar Falls, 1969. Tchr. Cedar Rapids (Iowa) Sch. Bd., 1961-64, New Hartford (Iowa) Sch. Bd., 1965-68, Holmes Jr. High Sch., Cedar Falls, 1968-77; tchr. East Bay High Sch. Hillsborough County Sch. Bd., Tampa, Fla., 1979-84, tchr. Armwood High Sch., 1984—. Editor Iowa Coun. Tchrs. Math. Jour., 1975-78. Mem. NEA, Nat. Coun. Tchrs. Math., Math. Assn. Am., Fla. Coun. Tchrs. Math., Hillsborough County Tchrs. Math., Phi Delta Kappa. Episcopalian. Home: 6311 Lake Sunrise Dr Ruskin FL 33572-2302 Office: Armwood H S 12000 E US Hwy 92 Seffner FL 33584-3418

THIEDE, RALF, English linguistics educator; b. Rhede, Germany, Dec. 8, 1957; arrived in U.S., 1981; s. Wilhelm and Evelyn (Welz) T.; m. Barbara Ann Shapiro, June 21, 1982; 1 child, Erik Henning. MA in English Lang., U. Mo., 1984, PhD, 1990. Grad. tchr. U. Mo., Columbia, Mo., 1981-86, 89-90; exchange faculty Nat. Kaohsiung Normal U., Kaohsiung, Taiwan, 1992-93; faculty U. N.C., Charlotte, N.C., 1990—. Translator (jour.) Peace Rsch. Inst. Bonn, 1989-95; contbr. articles to profl. jours. fellowship German Acad. Exchange Svc., 1978-79, teaching scholarship Taiwan Nat. Sci. Coun., 1992-93. Mem. Linguistic Soc. Am., Southeastern Conf. on Linguistics. Office: UNCC Dept English Fretwell Bldg Charlotte NC 28223

THIELE, HERBERT WILLIAM ALBERT, lawyer; b. Gananoque, Ont., Can., Apr. 14, 1953; s. Herbert and Bertha (Shields) T.; m. Kathi M. Brown, May 29, 1982; children: Herbert R. R., Eric W. R., Brian A. J., Kelly M. M., Kevin M. H., Karl S. H. BA, U. Notre Dame, 1975; JD, U. Fla., 1978. Bar: Fla. 1978, U.S. Dist. Ct. (so. dist. trial and gen. bars) Fla. 1979, U.S. Ct. Appeals (5th and 11th cirs.) 1981, U.S. Supreme Ct. 1982, U.S. Tax Ct. 1983, U.S. Dist. Ct. (no. dist.) Fla. 1991. Assoc. Law Offices of Roger G. Saberson, Delray Beach, Fla., 1979-81; asst. city atty. City of Delray Beach, 1979-81, city atty., 1981-90; county atty. Leon County, Tallahassee, Fla., 1990—. Bd. dirs. Delray Beach Mcpl. Employees Credit Union, 1985-88. Recipient award of recognition Stetson U. Law Rev., 1989, Ralph A. Marsicano award for Local Govt. Law, Fla. Bar, 1991. Mem. ABA (vice-chmn. urban, state and local govt. com. of gen. practice sect. 1991-95, mem. labor and employment law, litigation, govt. lawyers, gen. practice and trial practice com. sects.), ATLA, FBA, Fla. Bar (exec. coun. local govt. law sect. 1986-87, sec./treas. local govt. law sect. 1987-88, chmn.-elect 1988-89, chmn., 1989-90, immediate past chmn. 1990-91, ex-officio officer 1991—, trial, real property, gen. practice and labor and employment law sects., bar com. on individual rights and responsibilities 1986-90, long-range planning com. 1991-93), Tallahassee Bar Assn., Fla. Mcpl. Attys. Assn. (steering com. 1985-86, bd. dirs. 1980-89, sec./treas. 1989-90, Fla. Mcpl. Atty. of Yr. 1987), Fla. Assn. Policy Attys., Nat. Inst. Mcpl. Law Officers (pers. and labor law com., trial practices and litigation com., legal advocacy com., 11th cir. rep. 1989-90), Am. Soc. for Pub. Adminstrn., Fla. Pub. Employer Labor Rels. Assn., Fla. Assn. County Attys. (chmn. coun. county attys. 1990-91, bd. dirs. 1991-93, treas. 1993, sec. 1993-94, v.p. 1994-95, pres. 1995—, Recognition award 1994). Republican. Home: 318 Milestone Dr Tallahassee FL 32312-3574 Office: Office of Leon County Atty Leon County Courthouse Tallahassee FL 32301

THIELMAN, SAMUEL BARNETT, psychiatrist; b. Decatur, Ga., Feb. 17, 1955; m. Sara Wilson Thielman, 1980; children: Sam, Jacob, Fran, Daniel. BA magna cum laude, Wheaton (Ill.) Coll., 1977; MD, Duke U., 1980, AM, 1983, PhD, 1986. Diplomate Nat. Bd. Med. Examiners, Am. Bd. Psychiatry and Neurology, qualification in geriatric psychiatry; lic. physician, N.C. Resident psychiatry Duke U. Med. Ctr., 1981-84; fellow geropsychiatry Ctr. for Study of Aging and Human Devel., Duke U., 1985; asst. prof. psychiatry dept. psychiatry and health behavior Med. Coll. Ga., Augusta, 1986-88; clin. asst. prof. family medicine U. N.C., Chapel Hill, 1989—; pvt. practice psychiatry Asheville, N.C., 1988—; chmn. dept. psychiatry St. Joseph's Hosp., Asheville, N.C., 1992-96, med. dir. of psychiatry, 1993—. Contbr. articles and book revs. to profl. jours., chpts. to books. Grantee NIMH, 1987-88; tuition grantee Burroughs Wellcome Fund, 1981, Duke U. Dept. History, 1983. Mem. AMA, Am. Assn. History of Medicine (ethics com. 1991—), So. Psychiat. Assn. (chair young physician's com.), Am. Psychiat. Assn., N.C. Psychiat. Assn., Am. Assn. Geriatric Psychiatry, Am. Geriatrics Soc., Gerontol. Soc. Am., N.C. Med. Soc. Home: PO Box 789 Montreat NC 28757-0789 Office: 394 Merrimon Ave Asheville NC 28801-3609

THIER, ANNETTE, mortgage banking company executive. Student, Northwestern U., Met. State U. Adminstr. officer, asst. corp. sec. Unified Mortgage, Houston, 1988-90; dir. CHBP Unified Mortgage N/K/A, First Gibraltar Bank, Houston, 1990-91; pres. Mid South Mortgage Corp., Metairie, La., 1991-94; sr. v.p. mortgage banking Hibernia Mortgage Banking, New Orleans, Baton Rouge, 1994-95; writer, cons. Am. Home Mortgage Cons., Covington, La., 1995—. Dir. The CRA Group, New Orleans, Community Home Buyers Program, Affordable Housing Program, First Gibraltar Bank; active Paris Oaks Neighborhood Revitalization, Home Purchase Program Seminars, Habitat for Humanity Seminar, Houston, First Friday Forum Conf., San Antonio; speaker Tex. Housing Agy. Affordable Housing, Austin, Star-Telegram Conf. on Affordable Housing, Ft. Worth, Fed. Home Loan Bank Dallas Affordable Housing Program, Dallas; others. Recipient United Way Campaign award, Houston, First Friday Forum award, San Antonio. Mem. Nat. Assn. Real Estate Brokers, Nat. Assn. Realtors, St. Tammany Bd. Realtors, Combined New Orleans and Jefferson Bd. Realtors, Realtist Assn. La., Greater New Orleans Assn. Profl. Mortgage Women, Ft. Worth Met. Black C. of C. Home: 719 Saint Ann St New Orleans LA 70116-3169 Office: Am Home Mortgage Cons 74485 River Rd Covington LA 70435

THIERS, BRUCE HARRIS, dermatology educator. BA magna cum laude, Bklyn. Coll., 1970; MD, SUNY, Buffalo, 1974. Cert. Nat. Bd. Med. Examiners, Am. Bd. Dermatology. Intern in medicine SUNY, Buffalo, 1974-

75, resident in dermatology, 1975-78, asst. prof. dermatology, 1979-80; asst. prof. dermatology Med. U. S.C., Charleston, 1980-84, assoc. prof. dermatology, 1984-93, prof. dermatology, 1994—, faculty Sch. Grad. Studies, 1983—; attending physician dermatology Buffalo (N.Y.) Gen. Hosp., 1979-80, Erie County Med. Ctr., Buffalo, 1979-80, Med. U. S.C. Hosp., Charleston, 1980—; chief dermatology svc. VA Med. Ctr., Buffalo, 1979-80, Charleston, 1980—; vis. prof. UCLA Sch. Medicine, 1993, Mt. Sinai Sch. Medicine, N.Y.C., 1993, Albert Einstein Sch. Medicine, N.Y.C., 1993, U. Pitts. (Pa.) Sch. Medicine, 1991, others; various coms. Med. U. S.C. and Charleston VA Med. Ctr.; lectr. in field; others. Author of 10 books including Manifestazioni Dermatologiche in Corso di Neoplasie, 1992, others; editor (with R. Dobson) Year Book of Dermatology, 1980, 81, 82, (with J. Maize) Cutaneous T Cell Lymphoma and Related Disorders, 1985, (with R. Dobson) The Pathogenesis of Skin Disease, 1986, (with H. Ely), Dermatologic Therapy I, 1988, Dermatologic Therapy II, 1989, Current Concerns in Dermatology, 1993 (with G. Burg, H. Kerl) Cutaneous Lymphomas, 1994; assoc. editor: Jour. Am. Acad. Dermatology; sect. editor: Current Opinion in Dermatology; cons. editor: Dermatologic Clinics; editorial bd.: Exptl. Dermatology, Jour. European Acad. Dermatology and Venereology, Clin. Dermatology; reviewer: Jour. Investigative Dermatology, Archives Dermatology, Jour. Dermatologic Surgery and Oncology; contbr. chpts. to books and articles to profl. jours. Grantee Ortho Pharm. Corp., 1987-88, 88-90, Pfizer Inc., 1994-95, Ligand Pharms., 1996—, Bristol Myers-Squibb, 1996—. Mem. Am. Acad. Dermatology (com. on postgrad. courses, com. on curriculum devel., task force on therapeutic agts., task force on cost containment, coun. on sci. assembly), Am. Dermatologic Assn., Soc. for Investigative Dermatology, Dermatology Found. (membership subcom. devel. com.), S.C. Med. Assn., S.C. Derm. Assn. (sec.-treas.), Charleston County Med. Soc., Phi Beta Kappa, Alpha Omega Alpha. Office: Med Univ SC Dept Dermatology 171 Ashley Ave Charleston SC 29425-0001

THIGPEN, JAMES TATE, physician, oncology educator; b. Columbia, Miss., June 6, 1944; m. Louisa Berdie Kessler, June 14, 1969; children: Monroe Tate, James Howard, Samuel Calvin, Richard Allen, David Albert. BS, U. Miss., 1964, MD, 1969. Intern Strong Meml. Hosp., U. Rochester, N.Y., 1969-70; resident U. Miss. Sch. Medicine, 1970-71, fellow div. hematology/oncology dept. medicine, 1971-73, prof., dir. div. med. oncology dept. internal medicine, 1973—, also asst. prof. ob-gyn.; nat. med. del. from Miss. Am. Cancer Soc., 1983-85, mem. nat. pub. issues com., 1983-85; mem. cancer clin. investigations rev. com. Nat. Cancer Inst., 1990-95, chmn., 1993-95. Nat. bd. govs. ARC, 1981-87. Fellow ACP; mem. AMA, Miss. Med. Assn., Central Med. Soc., Jackson Acad. Medicine, Miss. Acad. Scis., SW Oncology Group, Gynecologic Oncology Group (group vice chmn. for sci 1988—), Am. Fedn. Clin. Rsch., Am. Assn. Cancer Edn., Am. Soc. Clin. Oncology, Am. Assn. Cancer Rsch., Am. Soc. Hematology, Soc. Gynecologic Oncologists, So. Assn. for Oncology (pres. 1988-90), Am. Radium Soc. Baptist (deacon 1978—, Sunday sch. tchr. 1979-85). Club: Optimist (internat. v.p. 1983-84, internat. pres. 1990-91). Home: 3601 Kings Hwy Jackson MS 39216-3322 Office: 2500 N State St Jackson MS 39216-4500

THIGPEN, RICHARD ELTON, JR., lawyer; b. Washington, Dec. 29, 1930; s. Richard Elton and Dorothy (Dotger) T.; m. Nancy H. Shand, Dec. 15, 1951; children: Susan B., Richard M. AB, Duke U., 1951; LLB, U. N.C., 1956. Bar: N.C., 1956, U.S. Ct. Appeals (4th cir.) 1960, U.S. Ct. Appeals (5th cir.) 1960, U.S. Ct. Appeals (10th cir.) 1974, U.S. Tax Ct. 1958, U.S. Ct. Claims 1978. Lawyer FTC, Washington, 1956-58, Thigpen & Hines, Charlotte, N.C., 1958-84, Moore & Van Allen, Charlotte, N.C., 1984-88, Poyner & Spruill, Charlotte, N.C., 1988-93; gen. counsel Richardson Sports, 1994—. Dir. Charlotte-Mecklenburg YMCA, 1964-88, Heineman Med. Rsch. Ctr., Charlotte, 1970—, Charlotte C. of C., 1982-85. Lt. USNR, 1951-53. Fellow Am. Bar Found., Am. Coll. Tax Counsel (regent 1989-95, vice chmn. 1992, chmn. 1993-94); mem. ABA, N.C. State Bar, N.C. Bar Assn. (pres. 1988-89, chmn. tax sect. 1976-80), Sports Lawyers Assn. (bd. dirs. 1995—). Home: 2518 Forest Dr Charlotte NC 28211-2110 Office: Richardson Sports 800 S Mint St Charlotte NC 28202-1502

THIND, GURDARSHAN S., medical educator; b. Lyallpore, Punjab, India, Oct. 17, 1940; came to U.S., 1963; s. S. Manmohan Singh and Sardarni Ajaib Kaur (Jawanda) T.; m. Rajinder Kaur Sekhon, June 25, 1967; children: Gurpreet K., Gurbir S. MB, BS, Punjab U., 1962; grad. diploma, U. Pa., 1965, MSc in Cardiology, 1966. Intern Rajindra Hosp. of Govt. Med. Coll., Patiala, India, 1962; intern U. Pa., 1963-64, cardiology fellow, 1964-67, resident in internal medicine, 1968-70; assoc. instr. in cardiology U. Pa., Phila., 1964-69, assoc. in medicine, 1970, asst. prof., 1970-72; asst. prof. Washington U., St. Louis, 1972-76; assoc. prof. U. Louisville, 1976-85, prof., 1985-95; clin. prof., 1995—; dir. hypertension sect. U. Louisville, 1976-95; lectr. univs. and sci. meetings in U.S. and ffgn. countries, 1965—. Contbr. over 130 articles to med. jours. Gen. sec. Sikh Study Circle Louisville, 1967-87; cons. Washington Sikh Ctr., 1988—; coord. Sikh Youth Camps, Silver Spring, Md., 1984—. Fellow ACP (life mem.), Am. Coll. Cardiology; mem. Am. Physiol. Soc., Am. Soc. Hypertension (founding), numerous others. Republican. Home: 17603 Popedale Rd Louisville KY 40245-4350 Office: 207 Sparks Ave Ste 104 Jeffersonville IN 47130

THISTLETHWAITE, MARK EDWARD, art history educator; b. Baton Rouge, La., Jan. 26, 1948; s. Lote and Aline (McQuiston) T.; m. Randall Eve Simpson, June 27, 1970; children: Benjamin, Caitlin. BA (hon.), U. Calif., Santa Barbara, 1970, MA in art, 1972; PhD in art history, U. Pa., 1977. Lectr. U. Pa., Phila., 1974, 75, Phila. Coll. Art, 1974, 75-6; asst. to full prof. Tex. Christian U., Ft. Worth, 1977—, Kay and Velma Kimbell Chair Art History, 1995—; cons. Getty Ctr. for Edn. in the Visual Arts, 1991; lectr. in field. Author: Painting in the Grand Manner: The Art of Peter F. Rothermel, 1995, William Tylee Ranney East of Mississippi, 1991, The Image of George Washington: Studies in Mid-Nineteenth-Century American History Painting, 1979; co-author: Grand Illusions: History Painting in America, 1988, American Paintings, Selections from the Amon Carter Museum, 1986; contbr. articles to profl. jours. Trustee Modern Art Mus., Ft. Worth, 1983—; com. mem. Dallas Mus. Art, 1983-84, 91-93; moderator Artists Eye Program Kimbell Art Mus., Ft. Worth, 1985-92; guest curator Brandywine River Mus., Chadds Ford, Pa., 1993-95; grant adv., evaluator Amon Carter Mus., Duke U. Art Mus. Recipient Chancellor's award Disting. Teaching, Tex. Christian U., 1990, Prof. of Yr. award, 1988; numerous grants. Mem. Coll. Art Assn., Midwest Art Hist. Soc. (bd. dirs. 1987-90), Am. Studies Assn., Am. Culture Assn. Office: Tex Christian U Dept Art & Art History TCU Box 298000 Fort Worth TX 76129

THOMA, RICHARD WILLIAM, chemical safety and waste management consultant; b. Milw., Dec. 7, 1921; s. Joseph Donath and Margaret Mary (Murphy) T.; A.A., U. Chgo., 1941; BS, U. Wis., Madison, 1947, MS in Biochemistry, 1949, PhD, 1951; m. Ida Mary Scharfschwerdt, Mar. 15, 1952; children: Adele, Richard W., Joseph O., John C. With E. R. Squibb & Sons, Inc., New Brunswick, N.J., 1951-82, sr. rsch. fellow, 1980-82; dir. process devel. New Brunswick Sci. Co., Inc., Edison, N.J., 1982-84; cons., 1984—. Commr. Somerset County Bd. Elections, 1981-84; mem. Bridgewater Town Coun., 1975-81, Environ. Commn., 1974-75, Sewerage Authority, 1975-76, Police Commn., 1977-81; chmn. Bridgewater Dem. Mcpl. Com., 1980-87; alderman St. Lucie Village, 1996—. Served with AUS, 1943-46. Mem. Am. Chem. Soc., Am. Soc. Safety Engrs., Nat. Safety Coun., Am. Soc. Microbiology, Am. Acad. Microbiology, N.Y. Acad. Scis., Am. Inst. Biol. Scis., Soc. Indsl. Microbiology, Soc. Gen. Microbiology (U.K.), St. Lucie County C. of C., Phi Beta Kappa, Sigma Xi, Phi Lambda Upsilon. Contbr. articles to sci. jours.; editor Industrial Microbiology, 1977; patentee microbiol. transformation of steroids. Home and Office: 3772 Outrigger Ct Fort Pierce FL 34946-1911

THOMAS, ADRIAN WESLEY, laboratory director; b. Edgefield, S.C., June 23, 1939; s. Hasting Adrian and Nancy Azalena (Bridges) T.; m. Martha Elizabeth McAllister, July 12, 1964; children: Wesley Adrian, Andrea Elizabeth. BS in Agrl. Engring., Clemson U., 1962, MS in Agrl. Engring., 1965; PhD, Colo. State U., 1972. Rsch. scientist USDA-Agrl. Rsch. Svc., Tifton, Ga., 1965-69, Fort Collins, Colo., 1969-72; rsch. leader USDA-Agrl. Rsch. Svc., Walkinsville, Ga., 1972-89; lab. dir. USDA-Agrl. Rsch. Svc., Tifton, 1989—; mem. acad. faculty Colo. State U. Ft. Collins, 1969-72; acad. faculty U. Ga., Athens, 1973—, grad. faculty, 1988—. Contbr. agrl. rsch. articles to profl. jours. With U.S. Army, 1962-63. Mem. Am. Soc. Agrl. Engrs., Am. Soc. Agronomy, Soil and Water Conservation Soc. Am., Soil Sci. Soc. Am., Sigma Xi, Alpha Epsilon, Gamma Sigma Delta, Phi Kappa Phi. Lutheran. Office: USDA Agrl Rsch Svc PO Box 946 Tifton GA 31793-0946

THOMAS, ANN VAN WYNEN, law educator; b. The Netherlands, May 27, 1919; came to U.S., 1921, naturalized, 1926; d. Cornelius and Cora Jacoba (Daansen) Van Wynen; m. A.J. Thomas Jr., Sept. 10, 1948. AB with distinction, U. Rochester, 1940; JD, U. Tex., 1943; post doctoral degree, So. Meth. U., 1952. U.S. fgn. svc. officer Johannesburg, South Africa, London, The Hague, The Netherlands, 1943-47; rsch. atty. Southwestern Legal Found., Sch. Law So. Meth. U., Dallas, 1952-67; asst. prof. polit. sci. Sch. Law So. Meth. U., 1968-73, assoc. prof., 1973-76, prof., 1976-85; prof. emeritus So. Meth. U. Sch. Law, 1985—. Author: Communism versus International Law, 1953, (with A.J. Thomas Jr.) International Treaties, 1950, Non-Intervention—The Law and its Import in the Americas, 1956, OAS: The Organization of American States, 1962, International Legal Aspects of Civil War in Spain, 1936-1939, 1967, Legal Limitations on Chemical and Biological Weapons, 1970, The Concept of Aggression, 1972, Presidential War Making Power: Constitutional and International Law Aspects, 1981, An International Rule of Law—Problems and Prospects, 1974. Chmn. time capsule com. Grayson County Commn. on Tex. Sesquicentennial, 1986-88; co-chmn. Grayson County Commn. on Bicentennial U.S. Constn., 1988-93; co-chmn. com. Grayson County Sesquicentennial, 1994—. Recipient Am. medal Nat. DAR Soc., 1992. Mem. Tex. Bar Assn., Am. Soc. Internat. Law, Grayson County Bar Assn. Home: Spaniel Hall RR 2, Box 444T Pottsboro TX 75076

THOMAS, ARCHIBALD JOHNS, III, lawyer; b. Jacksonville, Fla., Apr. 27, 1952; s. Archibald Johns and Jean (Snodgrass) T.; m. Martha Ann Marconi, Sept. 1, 1973. BA, U. So. Fla., 1973; JD, Stetson U., 1977. Bar: Fla. 1977, U.S. Dist. Ct. (mid. dist.) Fla. 1977, U.S. Ct. Appeals (11th cir.) 1981, U.S. Supreme Ct. 1981, U.S. Claims Ct. 1990. Law clk. to U.S. magistrate U.S. Dist. Ct., Tampa, Fla., 1977-78; 1st asst. fed. pub. defender U.S. dist. Ct., Jacksonville, 1978-84; sr. ptnr. Thomas & Skinner, P.A., Jacksonville, 1984-89; pvt. practice Jacksonville, 1990—. Mem. FBA (pres. 1982-83), Nat. Assn. Criminal Def. Lawyers, Nat. Employment Lawyers Assn. (co-chmn. Fla. chpt. 1992), Jacksonville Bar Assn. Democrat. Home: 708 Mccollum Cir Neptune Beach FL 32266-3789 Office: Riverplace Tower Ste 1640 Jacksonville FL 32207

THOMAS, BARBARA ANN, record company executive; b. Bklyn., Feb. 5, 1948; d. Wilfred Godfrey and Violet Rose (Howell) Swaby; m. Ronald L. Hannah (div.). Adminstrv. asst. Million Dollar Record Poll, College Park, Ga., 1985-86, Points East Records, College Park, 1986-87, Greer Booking Agy., Atlanta, 1986-87; pres. Gunsmoke Records, College Park, 1988—; v.p. Toroy Mercedes Records, 1994—; mgr. Jesse James, 1983—. Mem. NAFE, COPE, Blues Found., Atlanta Top Star Awards, Nat. Young Black Programmers (bd. dirs.), Nat. Club Owners, Promoters and Entertainment Assn. (bd. dirs. 1996). Democrat. Roman Catholic. Office: Gunsmoke Records 2523 Roosevelt Hwy Ste 3D Atlanta GA 30337-6243

THOMAS, BEVERLY IRENE, special education educator; b. Del Rio, Tex., Nov. 12, 1939; d. Clyde Louis and Eve Naomi (Avant) Whistler; m. James Henry Thomas, Jan. 28, 1972; children: Kenneth (dec.), Wade, Robert, Darcy, Betty Kay, James III, Debra, Brenda, Michael. BM summa cum laude, Sul Ross State U., 1972, MEd, 1976, MEd in Counseling, 1992, MEd in Mid. Mgmt., 1996. Cert. music, elem. edn., music edn., learning disabilities, spl. edn. generic, ednl. diagnosis, ednl. counseling, spl. edn. counseling and mid. mgmt. Edn. diagnostician West Tex. State Sch., Tex. Youth Commn. Mem. AAUW, ASCD, NEA, MENSA, Assn. for Children with Learning Disabilities (local sec. 1974), Tex. State Tchrs. Assn. (treas. 1991-94), Tex. Ednl. Diagnosticians Assn., Tex. Profl. Ednl. Diagnosticians, Reeves County Assn. of Children with Learning Disabilities, Nat. Coun. Tchrs. of Maths., Nat. Coun. Tchrs. English, Learning Disabilities Assn., Learning Disabilities Assoc., Tex., Coun. for Exceptional Children, Tex. Counseling Assn., Alpha Chi, Kappa Delta Pi. Home: 2410 S Eddy St Pecos TX 79772-7514

THOMAS, BILL, photojournalist; b. Elizabethtown, Ky., Nov. 11, 1934; s. William Roy and Elizabeth (Crabtree) T.; m. Joan McBroom (div. 1985); children: David, Dianne, Billy, Lisa, Alan. AB, Western Ky. U., 1958. Intelligence analyst U.S. Intelligence Corps, Balt. and Washington, 1958-59; staff writer United Press Internat., Louisville, 1959-62; travel editor Cinn. (Ohio) Enquirer, 1962-66; pvt. practice author/photojournalist Indpls., 1966-85, Lowell, Fla., 1985—; dir. Touch of Success Photo Seminars, Lowell, Fla. and Glendale, Ky. Author: The Swamp, 1976, American Rivers, 1978, The Island, 1980, Talkwing with the Animals, 1982, Wild Woodlands, For Love of a River, Summer of Discontent, Natural Washington, Natural Los Angeles. Maj. U.S. Army, 1958-60. Mem. Soc. Am. Travel Writers, Outdoor Writers Am., Am. Soc. Mag. Photographers, The Nature Conservancy, Sierra Club, Nat. Wildlife Refuge Assn. Home and Office: PO Box 194 Lowell FL 32663-0194

THOMAS, CAROLE DOLORES, gerontologist; b. Huntington, Ind., Dec. 20, 1937; d. James Robert and Gladys Agnes (Walraven) Williams; m. Norman Day Thomas, Sept. 1, 1962 (separated); children: Diane Thomas Laucirica, Mark Alexander. BA in Polit. Sci., U. Ill., 1960; MA in Gerontology, U. South Fla., 1982. Human svcs. analyst Dept. Health and Rehab. Svcs., Tampa, Fla., 1987-94, adult protective investigator, 1994—; mem. Adult Protection Team, Tampa, 1990—, Bradenton, Fla., 1990—, Long Term Care Ombudsman Coun., Tampa, 1989—. Mem. Fla. Orch. Guild, Tampa, 1985—; guardian ad litem 13th Jud. Cir., Tampa, 1991—; vol. Performing Arts Ctr., Tampa, 1992—. Home: 14314 Diplomat Dr Tampa FL 33613-3107 Office: Dept Health & Rehab Svcs 4000 W Martin Luther King Blvd Tampa FL 33614-7012

THOMAS, CARROLL MORGAN, petroleum consultant, business developer; b. Houston, Oct. 26, 1938; s. Carroll Lawhon and Evelyn Lucile (Sparks) T.; m. Georgia Lee Hall, Mar. 9, 1968; children: Brian Morgan, Christy Diane. BS in Geology, Tex. Tech. U., Lubbock, 1961, MS in Geology, 1964. Geologist Mobil Oil Corp., Midland, 1964-68, Ralph Lowe Estate, Midland, 1968-72, Am. Quasar Petroleum, Midland, 1972-73, Thomas, Harris & Anderson Petroleum Cons., Midland, 1973-78; fin. cons. Shearson Lehman Hutton, Midland, 1986-92; geologist Carroll M. Thomas Petroleum Cons., Midland, 1978—. Mayor City of Midland, 1986-92, bus. developer, 1992—; bd. dirs. Midland Energy Libr., 1984-88; chmn. Midland City Planning and Zoning Commn., 1974-75, mem., 1972-75; former mem. gov. body Permian Basin Regional Planning Commn.; conferee Midland Objectives for the 80s; city councilman, 1975-83; former bd. dirs. Langtry Village; bd. execs. Permian Basin Petroleum Mus., 1984-96; pres. Region IV Tex. Mcpl. League, 1990-91; mem. Forward Midland, 1989—; former pres. Cen. Divsn. Arthritis Found.; former dir. Boy's Club of Midland; former chmn. bus. sect. of fund dr. Am. Cancer Soc.; chmn. investment svc. divsn. United Way of Midland, 1994; mem. devel. bd. U. Tex. Permian Basin, 1989—; bd. dirs. Tex. Tech. Med. Found., 1994—; adv. coun. Tex. Tech. U. Health Scis. Ctr.-Odessa, 1994—; mem. deacon body, former chmn. membership com., former chmn. child care com. 1st Bapt. Ch.; campaign chmn. Ernest Angelo for Mayor, 1972; Midland County chmn. Citizens for Reagan, 1976; mem. fin. com. Reagan for Pres., 1980; former publicity chmn., former patronage chmn., former mem. candidate selection com. Midland County Rep. Party. Mem. West Tex. Geol. Soc. (hon. life, past pres., v.p., sec.), Am. Assn. Petroleum Geologists (past ho. of dels., past disting. lectr. com.), Soc. Econ. Paleonthologists and Mineralogists (past pres., v.p., treas. Permian Basin sect.), Midland County Young Reps. (former pres.), Midland C. of C. (chmn. transp. com., govtl. affairs com., former petroleum info. com.), Midland Jaycees (dir.), Rotary (pres., past v.p.). Republican. Baptist. Home: 913 Citation Midland TX 79705-1806

THOMAS, CHESTER WILEY, protective services official; b. Chgo., Dec. 17, 1940; s. Chester Wiley Sr. and Mary Katherine (Browne) T.; m. Ruby L. Keys, Mar. 15, 1962 (div. 1977); children: Rochelle, Kevin, Tamela; m. Regenia Fitz, Aug. 31, 1985; 1 child, Asia B. BA in Bus. Adminstrn., Columbia Coll., 1979; MA in Pub. Adminstrn., Webster U., 1980. Ordained to ministry Bapt. Ch., 1964. Security policeman USAF, 1959-81; classification specialist Dallas County Dept. Sheriff, 1982-83; parole case worker Tex. Dept. Pardons and Paroles, Grand Prairie, 1983-84; indsl. security rep. Dept. Defense, Dallas, 1984-89, chief indsl. security field office, 1989-91; dep. dir. indsl. security Dept. Defense, Irving, Tex., 1991—. Author: (manuscript) Defending America, 1967 (Freedoms Found. award 1967); author two poems. Pres. Glen Oaks Homeowners Assn., Dallas, 1988, v.p. 1991; vice-chairperson PTA, Mark Twain Elem. Sch., 1994, v.p., 1994-95, pres. 1995-96; chairperson Dallas-Ft. Worth Black Employee's Program Mgrs. Coun., pres. 1993-95. Home: 641 Misty Glen Ln Dallas TX 75232-1315

THOMAS, CLAYTON ALLEN, JR., telecommunications executive; b. Lynchburg, Va., May 18, 1962; s. Clayton Allen T. and Alice Thomas (Knight) McLaughlin. BA, U. Va., 1985. Mktg. asst. IBM, Charlottesville, Va., 1983-84; mgr. info. systems Commonwealth of Va., Richmond, 1985-86; account exec. Bell Atlantic, Roanoke, Va., 1986-90; regional account mgr. Bell Atlantic, Washington, 1990-92, mgr. corp. accounts, 1992-93; pres. Net2000 Group, Inc., McLean, Va., 1993—. Event organizer, fundraiser local chpt. Cystic Fibrosis, Washington, 1991-92. Mem. Telecommunications Mgrs. Capitol Area, U. Va. Alumni Assn., Pi Kappa Alpha. Republican. Office: Net2000 Group Inc 8614 Westwood Center Dr Ste 810 Vienna VA 22182-2233

THOMAS, CLEOPHUS, JR., lawyer; b. Sylacauga, Ala., June 20, 1956; s. Cleophus and Bernice (Cook) T.; m. Carla Ann Newbern, June 12, 1982; children: Cleophus Thomas III, Phillips Newbern, Caleb Spratling. BA, U. Ala., 1977, U. Oxford, 1980; JD, Harvard U., 1982. Bar: Ala. 1982. Law clk. to judge J. Foy Guin U.S. Dist. Ct., Birmingham, Ala., 1982-83; ptnr. Reid and Thomas, Attys.-at-Law, Anniston, Ala., 1983—; gen. counsel Booker T. Washington Ins. Co., Birmingham, Ala., 1992—; dir. AmSouth Bank Calhoun County, Anniston, Protective Investment Co., Birmingham. Mem. bd. contbrs. Birmingham News editorial page; contbr. book revs. to Anniston Star. Trustee U. Ala. System, Tuscaloosa, Birmingham, Huntsville, 1983—; mem. So. Regional Coun., Atlanta, 1993—; bd. dirs. Ala. Children's Hosp. Found., Birmingham, 1989, Kappa Alpha Psi Found., Phila., 1989. Recipient Betty Carr Svc. to Youth award Calhoun County (Ala.) YMCA, Anniston, 1987. Fellow Am. Bar Found.; mem. NCCJ (bd. dirs. 1993), Anniston Country Club, Heritage Club Huntsville, Newcomen Soc., Kappa Alpha Psi (Vice Polemarch 1974, Guy Levis Grant award 1976). Baptist. Home: 619 Hillyer High Rd Anniston AL 36207-6248 Office: Reid and Thomas Attys PO Box 2303 501 South Trust Bank Bldg Anniston AL 36202

THOMAS, COLIN GORDON, JR., surgeon, medical educator; b. Iowa City, July 25, 1918; s. Colin Gordon and Eloise Kinzer (Brainerd) T.; m. Shirley Forbes, Sept. 14, 1946; children: Karen, Barbara, James G., John F. B.S., U. Chgo., 1940, M.D., 1943. Diplomate Am. Bd. Surgery. Intern U. Iowa Hosp., 1943-44, resident surgery, 1944-45, 47-50; assoc. in surgery U. Iowa Med. Sch., 1950-51, asst. prof., 1951-52; mem. faculty U. N.C. Med. Sch., Chapel Hill, 1952—, prof. surgery, 1961—, Byah Thomason Doxey-Sanford Doxey prof. surgery, 1982—, chmn. dept., 1966-84, chief div. gen. surg., 1984-89, part-time prof., 1991—. Contbr. surg. texts, numerous articles to med. jours. Served to capt., M.C. AUS, 1945-47. Recipient Prof. award U. N.C. Sch. Medicine, 1964, Disting. Svc. award U. Chgo., 1982, Med. Alumni Disting. faculty award U. N.C., 1984; Berryhill lectr. U. N.C., 1989; recipient Fleming Fuller award U. N.C. Hosps., 1994. Mem. AMA, ACS (Disting. Leadership award N.C. chpt. 1990), AAUP, Am. Thyroid Assn., Am. Assn. Cancer Research, Am. Assn. Endocrine Surgeons (pres. 1989-90), Soc. Univ. Surgeons, So. Surg. Assn. (v.p. 1989-90), N.Y. Acad. Scis., Halsted Soc., Ga. Surg. Soc., Soc. Exptl. Biology and Medicine, Am. Surg. Assn., Womack Surg. Soc. (pres. 1981-83), Soc. Internationale de Chirurgie, Soc. Surgery Alimentary Tract, N.C. Surg. Assn., Internat. Assn. Endocrine Surgeons, Alpha Omega Alpha. Episcopalian (warden 1961-62). Home: 408 Morgan Creek Rd Chapel Hill NC 27514-4934

THOMAS, CYNTHIA GAIL, public policy research executive; b. Tulsa, Jan. 26, 1956; d. Jack Marcy and Dorothy (Bergfors) T. BS summa cum laude, U. Minn., 1978, MA, 1981. Analyst Met. Coun., St. Paul, 1978; rsch. analyst Common Cause Minn., St. Paul, 1979, lobbyist, 1980, rsch. cons., 1982; adminstr. NBC, N.Y.C., 1980; researcher Minn. State Sen., St. Paul, 1983-85, rsch. dir., 1985-86; owner Thomas Rsch., Dallas and Roseville, Minn., 1986—; pub. policy advisor Rep. Party, St. Paul, 1986—; commr. Roseville Planning Commn., 1991-95; sr. fellow Tex. Pub. Policy Found., 1996—. Contbr. articles to profl. publs. Vol. Little Bros. of Poor, Mpls., 1987-94, YWCA, St. Paul, 1989-90; mem. Tex. Pub. Policy Found.; softball coach Girls Age 10-12 team St. Paul, 1988. Mem. Greater Dallas C. of C., Nature Conservancy, Amnesty Internat., Fraser Ins. Republican. Home and Office: Thomas Rsch 1137 Meadow Creek Dr #271 Irving TX 75038

THOMAS, DANIEL HOLCOMBE, federal judge; b. Prattville, Ala., Aug. 25, 1906; s. Columbus Eugene and Augusta (Pratt) T.; m. Dorothy Quina, Sept. 26, 1936 (dec. 1977); children: Daniel H., Jr., Merrill Pratt; m. Catharine J. Miller, Oct. 25, 1979. LL.B., U. Ala., 1928. Bar: bar. Pvt. practice Mobile, Ala., 1929; asst. solicitor Mobile County; mem. firm Lyons, Chamberlain & Courtney, Mobile County, 1932-37, Lyons & Thomas, Mobile County, 1937-43, Lyons, Thomas & Pipes, Mobile County, 1946-51; judge U.S. Dist. Ct., Mobile, 1951—, now sr. judge. Mem. exec. bd. Mobile Area council Boy Scouts Am., 1963—, v.p., 1967-69, pres., 1973—, mem. nat. council, 1973—, Trustee dept. archieves and history, State of Ala. Served with USNR, 1943-45. Recipient Silver Beaver award Boy Scouts Am., 1970, Silver Antelope award, 1975. Methodist. Club: Mobile Country. Home: 13 Dogwood Cir Mobile AL 36608-2308 Office: US Dist Ct 459 US Courthouse Mobile AL 36602

THOMAS, DAVID LLOYD, accountant, consultant; b. Atlanta, May 10, 1942; s. Elbert Lamar and Evelyn Grace (Combs) T.; m. Mary Jo Ann Matney, June 25, 1966; children: Christine, Michael. BSBA, U.N.C., 1964. CPA, N.C. Auditor Price Waterhouse, N.Y.C., 1964, Atlanta, 1969-70; div. controller Dart Industries, Atlanta, 1971; contr. Ithaca Industries, Inc., Wilkesboro, N.C., 1971-82, sec.-treas., 1982-91, chief fin. officer, bd. dirs., 1983-91; prin. David L. Thomas, CPA, 1991—; CFO Wilkes Regional Med. Ctr., 1993—, v.p., 1996—; sec. Northwest Health Care, 1994-95. Bd. dirs., mem. Wilkes Art Gallery, 1985-91; bd. dirs. Wilkes Edn. Found., 1988-91, N.C. Citizen's For Bus. and Industry, 1989-92; mem. adv. bd. Wilkes C.C., 1989—, vice chair, 1994-96, chmn., 1996—. Capt. MSC, U.S. Army, 1965-68. Fellow N.C. Assn. CPA's (sec. Catawba Valley chpt. 1982-83); mem. AICPA, Inst. Mgmt. Accts., Healthcare Fin. Mgrs. Assn., Wilkesboro C. of C. (bd. dirs. 1979-81, 90-92, v.p. 1982, 86, 91, trustee found. 1983-90). Republican. Methodist. Home: 172 Walnut Pl Wilkesboro NC 28697-8775

THOMAS, DAVID RAYMOND, physician, educator; b. Jackson, Miss., Apr. 26, 1946; s. Raymond P. and Ella Margaret (Ballard) T.; m. Janice Lynn Nichols, June 30, 1967; children: Beth, Heather, Michael. BS, U. Miss., 1967, MD, 1971, residency, 1971-75; geriatric fellowship, Johns Hopkins Sch. of Med., 1987-88. Diplomate Am. Bd. Internal Medicine; diplomate Am. Bd. Geriatrics. Pvt. practice Starkville, Miss., 1975-80, Atlanta, 1980-81; asst. prof. Medicine U. of Miss. Sch. of Medicine, Jackson, 1981-88; visiting prof. Johns Hopkins Sch. of Medicine, Balt., 1987-88; assoc. prof. medicine Wake Forest U., Winston-Salem, N.C., 1990-93, U. Ala., Birmingham, 1993—; clin. instr. medicine U. Miss., Jackson, 1976-81; dir. Div. Geriatrics Gerontology, Jackson, 1988-89; clin. dir. sect. internal medicine and gerontology Wake Forest U., 1990-93; med. cons. Miss. State Bd. Health, Jackson, 1988—; bd. dirs. Miss. State Bd. Nursing Home Adminstrn., Jackson, 1988—; med. dir. Hosp.- based Home Care; mem. ombudsman com. Jefferson County Aging Group; bd. dirs. Nat. Pressure Ulcer Adv. Panel. Contbr. articles to profl. jours. Mem. faculty senate U. Miss., 1987-90; bd. dirs. Am. Cancer Soc. (Miss. chpt.), 1980. Named Univ. Scholar Montford B. Jones Found., 1965; recipient Faculty Fellow award, John A. Hartford Found., N.Y.C., 1987, Geriatric Edn. award, Geriatric Edn. Ctr., Jackson, 1988. Fellow Am. Coll. Physicians; mem. Am. Soc. Internal Medicine (nat. del. 1987), Miss. State Med. Assn. (del. 1986-89, environ. health com. 1986—), Am. Fed. Clin. Rsch., Gerontol. Soc. Am., Am. Geriatrics Assn., N.C. Med. Assn. (vice chmn. com. on aging 1991—). Office: U Ala Birmingham Divsn Gerontology 933 19th St S Ste 219 Birmingham AL 35205-3703

THOMAS, DOROTHY JEAN, counselor; b. Lynn, Mass., Mar. 6, 1931; d. James F. and Marion E. (White) Lynch; children: Alan J., Susan A. BA, Boston U., 1953, MEd, 1966; specialist, Nova U., 1985, EdD, 1990. Lic.

mental health counselor, fla.; lic. nat. cert. counselor; lic. nat. sch. counselor. 5th grade tchr. Vets. Meml. Sch., Saugus, Mass., 1954-55; 8th grade tchr. Saugus Jr. High Sch., 1955-56, 58-59; tchr. grades 3 & 5 Oakland Heights Elem. Sch., Fort Walton Beach, Fla., 1956-58; 3d grade tchr. North Saugus Elem. Sch., 1965; 5th grade tchr. Waybright Elem. Sch., Saugus, 1965-66, Nananja (Fla.) Elem. Sch., 1968-72; guidance counselor Pine Villa Elem. Sch., Nananja, 1972-77, William A. Chapman Elem. Sch., Nananja, 1977—; adj. Barry U., summers 1993, 94; presenter in field. Author: The Guidance Clinic, 1978, Yes, Parenting Is Fun, 1994. Adv. com. Family Counseling Svcs. Greater Miami, 1989-90. Grantee Citicorp Success Fund, 1988; recipient Career Edn. award Kiwanis Club Miami, 1980. Fellow AACD, Dade County Assn. for Counseling and Devel. (Counselor of Yr. 1990), Fla. Assn. for Counseling and Devel., Epsilon Tau Lambda. Congregationalist. Home: 11271 SW 175th St Miami FL 33157-3945 Office: William A Chapman Elem Sch 27190 SW 140th Ave Homestead FL 33032-8400

THOMAS, DWIGHT REMBERT, writer; b. Savannah, Ga., Dec. 8, 1944; s. Huguenin and Alma (Sanders) T. BA in English with honors, Emory U., 1967; PhD in Am. Lit., U. Pa., 1978. Fellow English dept. U. Pa., Phila., 1971-78; writer Savannah, 1979—; cons. Film Odyssey, Washington, 1988-89. Author: The Poe Log: A Documentary Life of Edgar Allan Poe, 1987. Dir. Edgar Allan Poe Mus., Richmond, Va., 1988—. With U.S. Army, 1969-71. Mem. MLA, Am. Med. Writers Assn., Mensa (treas. Savannah area 1985-88, local sec. 1989-90), Phi Beta Kappa. Roman Catholic. Home: 7 E Gordon St Savannah GA 31401-4925

THOMAS, ELLA COOPER, lawyer; b. Ft. Totten, N.Y.; d. Avery John and Ona Caroline (Gibson) C.; m. Robert Edward Lee Thomas, Nov. 22, 1938 (dec. Jan. 1985); 1 child, Robert Edward Lee Jr. Student, Vassar Coll., 1932-34, U. Hawaii, 1934-35, George Washington U., 1935-36; JD, George Washington U., 1940. Bar: U.S. Dist. Ct. D.C. 1942, U.S. Ct. Appeals (D.C. cir.) 1943, U.S. Supreme Ct. 1947, U.S. Tax Ct. 1973. Secret maps custodian U.S. Dist. Engrs., Honolulu, 1941-42; contbg. editor Labor Rels. Reporter, Washington, 1942; assoc. Smith, Ristig & Smith, Washington, 1942-45; law libr. George Washington Law Sch., Washington, 1946-53; reporter of decisions U.S. Tax Ct., Washington, 1953-75. Author: Law of Libel and Slander, 1949. Mem. Inter-Am. Bar Assn. (coun. mem. 1973—), D.C. Bar Assn.

THOMAS, ERIK ROBERT, linguistics educator; b. Columbus, Ohio, Dec. 29, 1965; s. Robert Bernie and Mary Rebecca (Conaway) T.; m. Barbara Ellen Hunter, July 28, 1995. AB, Duke U., 1988; MA, Tex. A&M U., 1989; PhD, U. Tex., 1995. Asst. prof. N.C. State U., Raleigh, 1995—. Contbr. articles to profl. jours. Nat. Merit scholar, 1984; Lechner fellow Tex. A&M U., 1988; Faculty R&D grantee N.C. State U., 1996. Mem. Am. Dialect Soc., Linguistic Soc. Am., Acoustical Soc. Am., Masons. Methodist. Office: Dept English NC State U Box 8105 Raleigh NC 27695-8105

THOMAS, GARNETT JETT, accountant; b. Farmington, Ky., July 27, 1920; s. Pinkney Madison and Ethel (Drinkard) T.; m. Katherine Gardner, Mar. 26, 1948 (dec. Sept. 1979); m. Nell Penton, May 23, 1981; stepchildren: Vernon Bice, Michael Bice, Gena Bice Amos. Student U. Notre Dame, 1943-44; BS, Lambuth U., 1947; MS, Miss. State U., 1949. Clk., acct. Ill. Cen. R.R., Paducah, Ky., 1941-42; mgr. Coll. Bookstore, Lambuth U., Jackson, Tenn., 1946-47; acct. Miss. Agrl. and Forestry Expt. Sta., Mississippi State, 1948-60, chief acct., 1960-75, adminstrv. officer and chief acct., 1975-85; mem. adv. bd. Nat. Bank of Commerce of Miss., 1974—; pres. Starkville (Miss.) PBR Corp., 1977-84; fin. adminstr. seed tech. research internat. programs, Brazil, India, Guatemala, Columbia, Thailand, Kenya, 1958-85; bd. dirs. Govt. Employees Credit Union, 1967-86, pres., 1969-73. Contbr. articles to profl. publs. Treas. Starkville Area Habitat for Humanity, Inc., 1989-93. Served with USN, 1942-46. Decorated Bronze Star with oak leaf cluster. Mem. Nat. Assn. Accts., Assn. Govt. Accts., Am. Assn. Accts., Acad. Acctg. Historians, So. Assn. Agrl. Scientists. Republican. Methodist. Lodge: Rotary (pres. 1959-60, dist. 682 gov. 1977-78, adv. com. to pres. 1979-80, dist. chmn. Poloplus). Home: 114 Grand Ridge Rd Starkville MS 39759-4112

THOMAS, GARY WAYNE, actor; b. Oklahoma City, Dec. 28, 1953; s. Wayne Saxon and Thelma (Hitchcock) T. BBA, U. Okla., 1976. Actor films including Dark Before Dawn, 1988, Rain Man, 1988, Born on the Fourth of July, 1989, JFK, 1991, Robin Hood-Men in Tights, 1993, The Flintstones, 1994, Wild Bill, 1994, Mel Brooks Dracula, 1995, Independence Day, 1996, (TV shows) The Nearly Quiet Orb, 1990, Winchester, 1989, A House of Shadows and Lies, 1992, Melrose Place, 1992, Long Shadows, 1994, Tracy Takes On..., 1995, (play) Feiffer's People, 1988. Mem. Actor's Fund Am. (life), Am. Film Inst., Screen Actors Guild. Democrat. Home: 1208 SW 78th Ter Oklahoma City OK 73139-2420

THOMAS, GEORGE, cardiologist; b. June 8, 1944; m.; 4 children. Student, Coll. Kottayam, India, 1960-61; BSc, St. Thomas Coll., Palai, India, 1964; MD, U. Kerala, India, 1969. Diplomate Am. Bd. Internal Medicine, Am. Bd. Cardiovascular Medicine; lic. cardiologist, Fla. Resident Med. Coll. Hosp., Kottayam, 1969-70; staff physician dept. medicine Holy Cross Hosp., Quilon, Kerala, 1970-73; intern South Balt. Gen. Hosp., 1974-76; cardiology fellow N.J. Coll. Medicine, Newark, 1976-78; courtesy staff dept. medicine and cardiology HCA Blake Hosp., Bradenton, Fla.; active staff dept. medicine sect. cardiology Manatee Meml. Hosp., Bradenton, Fla.; pvt. practice Bradenton, Fla., 1992—; Chmn. dept. medicine Manatee Meml. Hosp., Bradenton, 1988, chmn. coronary care com., dir. cardiology, 1984-89, exec. com. mem., 1989, sec.-treas. med. staff, 1990; co-dir. Manatee Heart Ctr., 1988—, vice-chief staff, 1991; bd. trustees Manatee Hosp. and Health Systems, 1991—, chief of staff, 1992. Bd. dirs. Manatee Community Cardiovascular Program, 1982. Fellow Am. Coll. Cardiology, Am. Coll. Chest Physicians; mem. ACP, AMA, Am. Heart Assn., Fla. Med. Assn. Manatee County Med. Soc. (bd. dirs. 1995, sec. 1996), Kerala Med. Grad. (pres. 1988-90, Disting. Svc. award 1978), Assn. Am. Physicians from India (treas. 1988-89, sec. 1989-90, v.p. 1991-92, pres. elect 1992, pres. 1993). Office: Bradenton Cardiology Ctr 203 3rd Ave E Bradenton FL 34208-1013

THOMAS, HAROLD EDWARD, saxophonist, producer, engineer, recording artist; b. Macon, Ga., May 31, 1954; s. Filmore Millard and Georgia Ella (Simmons) T.; 1 child, Harold E. Jr. Student, Ft. Valley (Ga.) State U., 1972-75. Prin. H.E.T. Aquarium Svc., Macon, 1982-87; pres. H.E.T. Enterprises, Inc., Macon, 1982; owner, engr. New Beginnings Sound Studio, Macon, 1982—; pres., CEO H.E.T. Records and Canbab Pub. Co., 1985—; owner, pres. Danger Zone, Macon, 1987—; mgr., performer with Danger Zone group. Recording artist gospel album, Changed, 1982, jazz album After Midnight, 1994. Active Greater Bellevue Bapt. Ch., Macon, dir. gospel choir, 1982, pres. gospel choir, 1982-84. Recipient Instrumental Praise Album of Yr. award Macon chpt. Gospel Music Work Shop, 1984. Mem. Kappa Alpha Psi. Home and Office: Danger Zone 2847 Bob O Link Dr Macon GA 31206-4847

THOMAS, JAMES ARTHUR, government official, electrical engineer; b. Meridian, Miss., Sept. 4, 1934; s. Walter James and Gladys Clarice (Harper) T.; m. Lily Juanita Purvis, Aug. 31, 1956; children: Karen Thomas Andrews, Chuck, Wendy Thomas Jones. BSEE, Miss. State U., 1962; MBA, Fla. State U., 1973. Sys. engr. NASA-Kennedy Space Ctr., Fla., 1962-74, engr. Orbiter project, 1974-82, engr. shuttle project, 1982-84; launch dir. of shuttle NASA-Kennedy Space Ctr., 1985-87, dir. safety, reliability and quality assurance, 1987-90, dep. ctr. dir., 1990—. Mem. Nat. Space Club, Rocket Pioneers Club. Baptist. Home: 355 Pine Blvd Merritt Island FL 32952 Office: NASA Kennedy Space Ctr Kennedy Space Center FL 32988

THOMAS, JAMES RAYMOND, accountant; b. Aberdeen, Wash., Jan. 22, 1947; s. Haywood and Ada Elnora (Gerhardt) T.; divorced; children: Ronald James, Wendy Gayle; m. Linda J. Jones, Mar. 23, 1991. AA, Wharton (Tex.) County Jr. Coll., 1967; BBA, U. Houston, 1970. CPA, Tex. Staff acct. Ernst & Young, Houston, 1970-71; acct. C&K Petroleum, Inc., Houston, 1972-73; contr. The Analysts, Inc., Houston, 1973; home builder Mountain Estates Constrn. Co., Cripple Creek, Colo., 1974-75; intermediate acct. Tenneco Realty, Inc., Houston, 1975-77; asst. contr. Weingarten Realty, Inc., Houston, 1977-78; pvt. practice Pearland, Tex., 1978-83; ptnr. Thomas Snyder MacAllister & Co., Pearland, 1983-86; pvt. practice Friendswood, Tex., 1986—. Contbr. articles to newspapers. Bd. dirs., treas. Tri-County YMCA, Pearland, sustaining mem., 1986—; amb. Pearland-Hobby C. of C., 1984-85, Friendswood C. of C., 1986—; mem. founding bd. dirs. Pearland Multi-Svcs. Ctr., United Way. Mem. AICPA, Tex. Soc. CPA's, Friendswood C. of C., Rotary (bd. dirs. Pearland 1983-86, pres. 1986-87, mem. dist. 589 com. 1986—, mem. team to teach free enterprise principles to Poland and Hungary chpts. 1991, 92, 93, Paul Harris Fellow 1987). Republican. Methodist. Home and Office: 903 Chesterwood Dr Pearland TX 77581-6772

THOMAS, JEAN-JACQUES ROBERT, Romance languages educator; b. Mirecourt, Vosges, France, Jan. 20, 1948; s. Jean-Robert and Yvonne Marie-Rose (Ladner) T.; m. Mary Lorene Hammial, Aug. 21, 1976; children: Dominick, Robert. Lic., U. Lille, France, 1968, M, 1969; diplome in lang. Orientales, U. Paris, France, 1972, PhD, 1972. Teaching asst. U. Paris, 1969-71, asst. researcher, 1971-72; lectr. U. Mich., 1972-75; asst. prof. Columbia U., N.Y.C., 1975-81; assoc. prof. Duke U., Durham, N.C., 1981-87, prof., 1989—, chmn. romance studies, 1989-94; pres. Educo, Paris, 1988-89, 95-96; dir. Institute French Studies U. Calif., Santa Barbara, 1991—; bd. dirs. Studies in Twenty-Century Lit., Lincoln, Nebr., Palmes Académiques, 1994. Author: Lire Leiris, 1972, La Langue la Poésie, 1987, La Langue Volée, 1988; co-author: Poétique Générative, 1978, Poética Generativa, 1983, 89; translator:Sémiotique de la Poésie, 1983; assoc. editor: Sub-Stance, 1975—, Poetics Today, 1980—. Grantee Rackham Found., 1973, IBM, 1984, Sloan Found., 1985. Mem. MLA (chmn. divsn. 1980-81, 86-87, 93-95), N.E. MLA (chmn. sect. 1982-83), Semiotic Soc. Am. Home: 26 Porchlight Ct Durham NC 27707-2442 Office: Duke U Dept Romance Studies Durham NC 27706

THOMAS, JIMMIE KAY, secondary education educator; b. Center, Tex., Sept. 8, 1954; d. James Powell and Peggy L. (Roberts) Daw; m. E.R. Thomas, Nov. 6, 1976; children: Jamie, Josh, Jenna. BS in Biology, Stephen F. Austin State U., 1990, MEd in Secondary Edn., 1993. Cert. tchr. Tex., La. Tchr. Marshall (Tex.) Ind. Sch. Dist., 1990, DeSoto Parish Schs., Logansport, La., 1991-94; chair sci. dept. DeSoto Parish Schs., Logansport, 1994—. Svc. rep. LAE Tchrs. Union, DeSoto Parish, 1994-96. Mem. Nat. Sci. Tchrs. Assn., La. Sci. Tchrs. Assn., La. Assn. Educators (svc. rep. 1996), Alpha Chi. Democrat. Office: Logansport High Sch La Hwy 5 Logansport LA 71049

THOMAS, JIMMY LYNN, financial executive; b. Mayfield, Ky., Aug. 3, 1941; s. Alben Stanley and Emma Laura (Alexander) T.; m. Kristin H. Kent, Oct. 1986; children: James Nelson, Carter Danforth. BS, U. Ky., 1963; MBA, Columbia U., 1964. Fin. analyst Ford Motor Co., Detroit, 1964-66; asst. treas. Joel Dean Assocs., N.Y.C., 1966-67; asst. contr. Trans World Airlines, N.Y.C., 1967-73; sr. v.p. fin. svcs., treas. Gannett Co., Inc., Arlington, Va., 1973—; bd. dirs. Marine Midland Bank, Rochester, Arkwright Boston Mut. Ins. Co.-Atlantic Region, Tremont Ptnrs., Brown Devel. Co., Newspaper Printing Corp., Pacific Media, Inc., Guam Publs., Gannett Supply Corp., Gannett Fla. Corp., Gannett Pacific Corp. With U.S. Army, 1966-72. Ashland Oil Co. scholar, 1959-63, McKinsey scholar 1964; Samuel Bronfman fellow, 1963-64. Mem. U. Ky. Alumni Assn., Columbia U. Alumni Assn., Fin. Execs. Inst., Inst. Newspaper Contrs. and Fin. Officers, Country Club of Rochester, Genessee Valley Club, Georgetown Club, Washington Golf and Country Club, Beta Gamma Sigma, Omicron Delta Kappa, Sigma Alpha Epsilon. Democrat. Mem. Christian Ch. (Disciples of Christ). Home: 100 Gibbon St Alexandria VA 22314-3836 Office: Gannett Co Inc 1100 Wilson Blvd Arlington VA 22234

THOMAS, JOHN CHARLES, lawyer, former state supreme court justice; b. Norfolk, Va., Sept. 18, 1950; s. John and Floretta V. (Sears) T.; m. Pearl Walden, Oct. 9, 1982; children: John Charles Jr., Ruby Virginia, Lewis LeGrant. B.A. in Am. Govt. with distinction, U. Va., 1972, J.D., 1975. Bar: Va. 1975, U.S. Dist. Ct. (ea. and we. dists.) 1976, U.S. Ct. Appeals (4th cir.) 1976, U.S. Supreme Ct. 1979, U.S. Ct. Appeals (D.C. cir.) 1980, U.S. Ct. Appeals (10th cir.) 1991, U.S. Ct. Appeals (11th cir.) 1992. Assoc. Hunton & Williams, Richmond, Va., 1975-82, ptnr., 1982-83, 89—; justice Supreme Ct. of Va., Richmond, 1983-89; mem. adv. con. on appellate rules U.S. Jud. Conf. Bd. dirs. U. Va. Law Sch. Found., Thomas Jefferson Meml. Foun. Master John Marshall Inn of Ct. (exec. com.); fellow Am. Bar Found., Va. Bar Found.; mem. Am. Arbitration Assn. (bd. dirs., exec. com.), Am. Acad. Appellate Lawyers, Va. State Bar, Va. Bar Assn., Bar Assn. City of Richmond, Old Dominion Bar Assn., Omega Psi Phi. Office: Hunton & Williams Riverfront Plz East Tower 951 E Byrd St Richmond VA 23219-4040

THOMAS, JOHN CLAYTON, public administration educator, academic official; b. Mpls.; s. Richard Leland and Constance Dorothy (Curtis) T.; m. Marilyn Gilbert, Dec. 27, 1985; children: Jason Elk, Bryan Elk. BA with honors, U. Minn., 1966, MA, 1967; PhD, Northwestern U., 1974. Urban affairs specialist U. Iowa, Iowa City, 1970-74; asst. prof. polit. sci. U. Cin., 1974-79, Tex. Christian U., Ft. Worth, 1979-81; assoc. prof. pub. adminstrn. U. Mo., Kansas City, 1981-87, prof. and dir. pub. adminstrn., 1987-93; prof. and chair pub. adminstrn. and urban studies Ga. State U., 1993—. Author: Between Citizen & City, 1986, Public Participation in Public Decisions, 1995; co-editor: Big City Politics in Transition, 1991; editor Am. Rev. Pub. Adminstrn., 1987—; assoc. editor Jour. Urban Affairs, 1987—; mem. editorial bd. Urban Affairs Quar., 1989-92. Advisor Mayor's Commn. Charter Reform, Kansas City, 1988. UKC Faculty fellow U. Mo., Kansas City, 1984. Mem. Am. Polit. Sci. Assn., Am. Soc. Pub. Adminstrn. (1994 program chair), Urban Affairs Assn. (chairperson 1990-92), Phi Beta Kappa. Office: Ga State Univ Pub Adminstrn Urban Studies Atlanta GA 30303

THOMAS, JOSEPH DOUGLAS, police forensic detective; b. Petersburg, Va., Jan. 23, 1958; s. George Lee and Virginia Eloise (Luck) T.; m. Deborah Lynn Washburn, Aug. 17, 1995. BS in Criminal Justice, U. Berkeley, Southfield, Mich., 1997. Chemical technician Lee Labs., Petersburg, Va., 1981-84; warehouse mgr. E.R. Carpenter Co., Richmond, Va., 1984-85; technician Chemlawn Co., Richmond, 1985-86; police officer, detective Petersburg (Va.) Bur. of Police, 1986—; police instr. Crater Criminal Justice Lab., Petersburg, Va., 1990—. Author: (book) Yesterday's Dreams, 1994; composer (song) The Clown, 1995. Pres., firefighter Ettrick Vol. Fire Dept., Chesterfield, Va., 1981-86. With U.S. Navy, 1981-86. Recipient Life Saving medal Petersburg Police, 1989, 93. Mem. Internat. Assn. for Identification, Va. Forensic Sci. Acad. Alumni Assn., Nat. Vet. Police Officers Assn. Office: Petersburg Bur of Police 37 E Tabb St Petersburg VA 23804

THOMAS, JOSEPH PAUL, psychiatrist; b. Bioloxi, Miss., Oct. 11, 1947; s. William Lloyd and Myrtis (Farmer) T.; m. Sandra Kay Elam, Dec. 20, 1973; children: Stephen Paul, Ashlie Lauren, Emily Grace. BA, U. Ala., Tuscaloosa, 1968; MA, U. Ala., 1971; MD, U. Ala., Birmingham, 1979. Diplomate Am. Bd. Psychiatry and Neurology with added qualification in geriat. psychiatry, addiction psychiatry, forensic psychiatry, Am. Bd. Adolescent Psychiatry; cert. Am. Soc. Addiction Medicine. Tchr. Gadsden (Ala.) Pub. Schs., 1968-69, Birmingham Bd. Edn., 1969-75, 80; resident Univ. Hosps., Birmingham, 1980; intern Mayo Grad. Sch. Medicine, Rochester, Minn., 1980-81; resident Johns Hopkins Hosp., Balt., 1981-84; psychiatrist The Thomas Clinic, P.C., Mobile, Ala., 1984, Neuropsychiatric Assocs. of South P.C., Mobile, 1984—. Fellow Am. Psychiat. Assn.; mem. Ala. Psychiat. Soc. (pres. 1993-94), Am. Acad. Psychaitry and Law, Med. Soc. Mobile County (bd. censors). Office: Neuropsychiat Assocs South PO Box 8309 Mobile AL 36689-0309

THOMAS, JOSEPH WINAND, lawyer; b. New Orleans, Aug. 2, 1940; s. Gerald Henry and Edith Louise (Winand) T., m. Claudette Condoll, Aug. 2, 1960 (div. Nov. 1985); children: Jeffery J., Anthony W.; m. Shawn B. Watkins, May 26, 1986 (div. June 1989); children: Adelle, Anne; m. Sandra J. Green, May 17, 1992; children: Winand, Elizabeth. BS, Loyola U., Chgo., 1967; JD, Loyola U., New Orleans, 1973; MBA, Tulane U., 1984. Bar: La. 1973, U.S. Dist. Ct. (ea. dist.) La. 1973, U.S. Ct. Appeals (5th cir.) 1973, U.S. Supreme Ct. 1976, D.C. 1980. Staff atty. New Orleans Legal Assistance Corp., 1973-74; asst. atty. gen. of La., 1974-80; pvt. practice law, New Orleans, 1980—. pres., bd. dir. New Orleans Legal Assistance Corp. Active NAACP, New Orleans, 1987-89; bd. dirs. Urban League, New Orleans. Mem. ABA, Louis Martinet Legal Soc., New Orleans Bar Assn., La. Bar Assn. Democrat. Roman Catholic. Office: 2 Canal St New Orleans LA 70130-1408

THOMAS, KEVIN ANTHONY, biomedical engineer; b. New Orleans, Oct. 22, 1959; s. James E. and Marian (Deffner) T.; m. Kathleen Liuzza, Oct. 22, 1982; children: Samuel Taylor, Philip Matthew. BS in Biomed. Engring. summa cum laude, Tulane U., 1981, MS in Biomed. Engring., 1983, PhD in Biomed. Engring., 1985. Pre-doctoral fellow/post-doctoral fellowship VA Med. Ctr., New Orleans, 1983-85; asst. prof. orthopedic surgery Tulane U. Sch. of Medicine, New Orleans, 1990-92; asst. prof. biomed. engring. Tulane U. Sch. Engring., New Orleans, 1990—; asst. prof. orthopedic surgery La. State U. Med. Ctr., New Orleans, 1991—, assoc. prof. orthopedic surgery, 1996—. Contbr. articles to profl. jours. Mem. Am. Soc. Biomechanics, Orthopaedic Rsch. Soc., Soc. for Biomaterials, Biomed. Engring. Soc., Sigma Xi, Tau Beta Pi. Office: La State U Med Ctr Dept of Orthopedic Surgery 2025 Gravier St Ste 400 New Orleans LA 70112

THOMAS, LAVON BULLOCK, interior designer; b. San Angelo, Tex., Oct. 6, 1929; d. J. T. and Ina (Malone) Bullock; m. W. Grant Thomas, June 9, 1956; children: Lorin Gwen Thomas Tavel, Lance Kevin. BS, Sam Houston State U., 1950; MEd, U. Houston, 1961. Tchr. Houston Ind. Sch., 1950-58; youth dir. St. Paul's Meth. Ch., Houston, 1958-60; designer Grant Thomas, Inc., Houston, 1960—, builder, 1994—; real estate broker Houston, 1975—. Unit pres. LWV, Houston, 1990, 91; v.p. Houston Assembly Delphian Chpts., Houston, 1992-93; bd. dirs. Panhellenic, Houston, 1993-94; active Houston UN Assn., 1994; Harris County Forest Landowners Assn. Recipient Cachet award for community svc. Women Helping Women, 1993. Mem. Nat. Assn. Realtors, Tes. Assn. Interior Designers, Tex. Ass. Realtors, Tex. Forestry Assn., Houston Assn. Realtors, Alph Chi Omega (pres. Beta Zeta Beta Chpt. 1994-96). Democrat. Methodist. Home: 15422 Mauna Loa Ln Houston TX 77040-1345

THOMAS, LEE DANIEL, lawyer; b. Scranton, Pa., Nov. 17, 1951; s. Darius Harris and Grace Louise (Johler) T.; m. Michele Rosita Rodriguez, May 5, 1978; children: Lee Marshall, Reece Daniel. BA, Lehigh U., 1973; JD, Loyola U., New Orleans, 1977. Bar: La. 1977, U.S. Dist. Ct. (ea. dist.) La. 1977, U.S. Ct. Appeals (5th cir.) 1987. Assoc. Weyman & Longenecker, New Orleans, 1977-80. Republican. Lutheran. Office: 3517 Canal St New Orleans LA 70119-6108

THOMAS, LEELAMMA KOSHY, women's health care nurse; b. Kerala, Kozhencherry, India, Feb. 10, 1936; naturalized Am. citizen, 1977; d. V.T. and Kunjamma (Koruth) Koshy; m. C.A. Thomas, Oct. 26, 1967; children: Linda Thomas Mathew, Lucie Thomas, John Thomas. BS in Nursing with honors, Coll. Nursing, Delhi, 1960; MA, Karnatak U., Dharwar Karnataka, Mysore, 1968. RN, Punjab, India, Tex.; RNC. PHN operational rsch. Nat. Tuberculosis Inst., Banglore, Mysore State, India, 1960-67; lectr. nursing Armed Forces Med. Coll., Maharstra State, India, 1971—; nurse labor and delivery U. Tex. Med. Br., nurse infant spl. care unit, nursing care coord. obgyn; head nurse U. Tex. Med. Br., Galveston, 1980-92, nurse clinician IV women and infants, 1993—; clin. instr. U. Tex. Sch. Nursing, Galveston, 1982—; presenter in field. Contbr. articles to profl. jours. Sunday sch. tchr. First Bapt. Ch., Galveston, Tex., 1982—. Recipient U. Tex. Med. Br. Maternal Health Coun. award, 1984; Am. Women's scholar. Mem. Sigma Theta Tau. Office: U Tex Med Br Ob-Gyn Nursing Svc Galveston TX 77550 also: U Tex Sch Nursing Galveston TX 77550

THOMAS, MARGARET LOUISE, rehabilitation nurse; b. Savannah, Ga., Nov. 27, 1953; d. Frederick William and Margaret Ann (Russell) T. AAS, County Coll. of Morris, 1982; BS, Kean Coll., 1988; BSN, Regents Coll. of N.Y. Cert. rehab. nurse, ACLS. Supr. Kessler Inst. for Rehab., West Orange, N.J.; staff nurse ICU Shepherd Spinal Ctr., Atlanta, 1988—. Recipient Pride in Heritage award DAV, 1981, 82, 86, 87, 89. Mem. Am. Assn. Spinal Cord Injured Nurses, Assn. Rehab. Nurses. Baptist. Home: 851 River Glen Pl Riverdale GA 30296-2784 Office: Shepherd Spinal Ctr 2020 Peachtree St NW Atlanta GA 30309-1402

THOMAS, MARK ELLIS, English language educator; b. Durham, N.C., May 4, 1955; s. Ellis Porter and Nancy Margaret (Cantrell) T.; m. Kimberley Sands, May 17, 1984. BA, N.C. State U., 1982; MA, Coll. William and Mary, 1984; MFA, U. N.C., Greensboro, 1986; PhD, U. Ill., 1992. Cert. secondary educator, N.C. Grad. teaching asst. U. N.C., Greensboro, 1983-86; grad. teaching asst. English dept. U. Ill., Urbana-Champaign, 1986-92, vis. instr., 1992-93; asst. prof. English Maryville (Tenn.) Coll., 1993-95; adj. instr. Roanoke State C.C., 1995—. Mem. MLA, Midwest Modern Lang. Assn., South Atlantic Modern Lang. Assn., Nat. Coun. Tchrs. English, Phi Kappa Phi, Kappa Delta Pi.

THOMAS, MARK VINCENT, periodontist; b. Louisville, Mar. 29, 1950; s. Charles Henry and Margie (Miller) T.; m. Betty Frances Owens, July 5, 1968; children: Anne Colette, Stephen Paul. DMD with distinction, U. Ky., 1979, cert. in periodontology, 1987. Diplomate Am. Bd. Periodontology. Gen. practice resident VA Hosp., Lexington, 1979-80; pvt. practice specializing in periodontology Lexington, 1980—; part-time asst. prof. dept. oral diagnosis/oral medicine Coll. of Dentistry U. Ky., 1980-84, dept. periodontics, 1987—; mem. adv. com. for dental hygiene tech., Lexington C.C., 1988—. Contbr. articles to profl. publs. With USN, 1968-72, Vietnam. Mem. ADA, ASDA, Ky. Dental Assn., Blue Grass Dental Soc., Am. Acad. Periodontology, So. Acad. Periodontology, Ky. Soc. Periodontists (past pres.), Sausalito Acad. Oral Rehab. (pres.), Blue Grass Dental Study Club (past pres.), Omicron Kappa Upsilon. Home and Office: 1529 Nicholasville Rd Ste 1 Lexington KY 40503

THOMAS, MICHAEL CHUMLEY, surgeon; b. Valley Creek, Tenn., Feb. 2, 1941. MD, U. Tenn., 1967. Diplomate Am. Bd. Colon and Rectal Surgery. Intern Meth. Hosp., Memphis, 1967-68; resident in gen. surgery Memphis VA Hosp./U. Tenn., 1968-72; surgeon Bapt. Meml. Hosp., Memphis; cons. in colon and rectal surgery U. Tenn. Fellow in colan and rectal surgery Schumpert Hosp./La. State U., Shreveport, 1979-80. Mem. ACS, AMA, Am. Soc. Colon and Rectal Surgery, Southeast Surg. Assn. Office: 6027 Walnut Grove Rd Ste 404 Memphis TN 38120-2129

THOMAS, MICHAEL I., engineering executive. V.p. engring., dir. R&D Great Dane Trailers Inc., Savannah, Ga. Office: Great Dane Trailers Inc PO Box 67 Savannah GA 31402

THOMAS, ORVILLE C., physician; b. Haynesville, La., Aug. 23, 1915; children—David, Diane, Cody. Pre-med. Student, Marian Mil. Inst., 1932-33, Tulane U., 1933; M.D., Tulane U., 1939. Diplomate Am. Bd. Pediatrics. Diplomate Am. Bd. Allergy and Immunology. Intern Shreveport Charity Hosp., La., 1939-40; asst. resident in pediatrics Children's Meml. Hosp., Chgo., 1946-47, resident in pediatrics, 1947, chief resident in pediatrics, 1948; active staff Tex. Children's Hosp., Houston, 1962—, fellow pediatric allergy, 1963-65, chief allergy sect., 1973-78; fellow in pediatric allergy Baylor Coll. Medicine, Houston, 1963-65; chief pediatrics Schumpert Meml. Hosp., Shreveport, La, 1958-61, chief of staff, 1958; sr. staff pediatrics Confederate Meml. Hosp., Shreveport, La, 1948-61; active staff Highland Hosp., Shreveport, La, 1948-61, North La. Hosp., Shreveport, La, 1948-61, Physicians and Surgeons Hosp., Shreveport, La, 1948-61, Ben Taub Gen. Hosp., Houston, 1962—, Hermann Hosp., Houston, 1966-69; hon. staff St. Luke's Hosp., Houston, 1962—; cons. staff Meth. Hosp., Houston, 1962—, St. Joseph Hosp., Houston, 1966—, Bellaire (Tex.) Gen. Hosp., 1966-86, Rosewood Gen. Hosp., Houston, 1967—, Meml. Bapt. Hosp., Houston, 1968—, Pasadena Bayshore Hosp., Pasadena, Tex., 1970—; instr. pediatrics Northwestern U. Sch. Medicine, Chgo., 1948; assoc. prof. pediatrics La. State U. Postgrad. Sch. Medicine, 1956-61; clin. instr. pediatrics Baylor Coll. Medicine, Houston, 1961-66, asst. clin. prof. pediatrics, 1966-76, assoc. clin. prof. pediatrics, 1977—; assoc. clin. prof. allergy and immunology U. Tex. Grad. Sch. Biomed. Scis., Houston, 1970—. Book reviewer: Venom Diseases; Aspects of Allergy and Applied Immunology. Contbr. articles to profl. jours. Served to maj. USMC AUS, 1942-46. Fellow Am. Coll. Allergy and Immunology (pediatrics com. 1964—, pres. 1978), Am. Acad. Allergy and Immunology, Am. Assn. Cert. Allergists (bd. govs. 1974, pres. 1979); mem. AMA, Am. Acad. Pediatrics, So. Med. Assn. (chmn. allergy sect. 1970-71), Tex. Allergy Research Found. Houston(research and edn. com. 1966-86, chmn. sci. adv. council 1973—), Tex. Pediatric Soc., Harris County Med. Soc., Tex. Med. Assn. (chmn. allergy sect. 1976-77), Am. Assn. for Inhalation Therapy (awards com. 1969-72, spl. edn. com. 1969-72), Greater Houston Allergy Soc. (pres. 1977), Joint Council of Allergy and Immunology, Internat. Assn. of Allergology and Clin. Immunology (U.S. rep. 1981-85). Home: 1111 Bering Dr Apt 704 Houston TX 77057-2320 Office: 6969 Brompton St Houston TX 77025-1611

THOMAS, PAMELLA DELORES, medical director, physician, educator; b. Wetmoreland, Jamaica, May 11, 1947; came to U.S., 1976; d. Wellesley Johnston and Hyacinth Ida Muir; m. Earl A. Thomas, Apr. 9, 1977; children: Ramogi O., Monifa J. MD, U. W.I., 1974; MPH, Med. Coll. Wis., 1990. Diplomate Am. Bd. Preventive Medicine in Occupational Medicine. Intern in surgery Brookdale Hosp., Bklyn., 1976-77, attending physician, 1979-83; resident in surgery Cath. Med. Ctr., Queens, N.Y., 1978-79; staff physician N.Y.C. Transit, Bklyn., 1983-86, asst. med. dir., 1986-89; med. dir. Lockheed Aeronautics, Marietta, Ga., 1989—; asst. adj. prof. Emory Sch. Pub. Health, 1992, chairperson residency adv. com. occupl. medicine program, 1995—. Bd. dirs. Am. Cancer Soc., Cobb County, Ga., 1989—; mem. Promina N.W. Hosp. Found., 1993—; dir. pub. rels. Cobb Med. Soc., 1993-96; v.p. bd. govs. Atlanta Wellness Alliance, 1993-95. Fellow Am. Coll. Preventive Medicine, Am. Coll. Occupational and Environ. Medicine (pres. Ga. chpt. 1996-97); mem. AMA, APHA, Am. Occupational Medicine Assn., Tchrs. Pub. Health Med. Assn. Ga., Am. Aerospace Med. Assn., Am. Coll. Physician Execs., Am. Coll. Legal Medicine. Office: Lockheed Aeronautics 86 S Cobb Dr # 0454 Marietta GA 30063-1000

THOMAS, PHILIP ROBINSON, management consulting company executive; b. Torquay, Devon, Eng., Dec. 9, 1934; s. Leslie Robinson and Margaret (Burridge) T.; came to U.S., 1963, naturalized, 1969; B.Sc., U. London, 1959, M.Sc., 1961, postgrad., 1961-64; m. Wayne Laverne Heirtzler, Apr. 6, 1973; children by previous marriage: Martin N.R., Stephen D. R. With Tex. Instruments Corp., 1961-72, ops. mgr., Dallas, 1963-72, Bedford, Eng., 1961-63; v.p., gen. mgr. MOS/LSI div. Gen. Instrument Co., N.Y.C., 1972-73; gen. mgr. MOS Products div. Fairchild Camera and Instrument Corp., Mountainview, Calif., 1973-75; v.p. Integrated Circuits div. RCA, Somerville, N.J., 1975-78; chmn. bd. dirs., CEO Thomas Group Inc., Dallas, 1978—; CEO, bd. dirs. Thomas Group Holding Co.; gen. ptnr. Celerity Investment Fund; speaker industry confs. Author: Competitiveness Through Total Cycle Time: An Overview for CEOs, 1989, Getting Competitive, 1990, Time Warrior, 1992, Quality Alone Is Not Enough, 1993, Survival at Nodulex, 1994; contbr. articles to profl. jours.; patentee semicondrs. Home: 3510 Turtle Creek Blvd Dallas TX 75219-5542 Office: Thomas Group Inc 5215 N O Connor Blvd Ste 2500 Irving TX 75039-3751

THOMAS, R. DALE, biologist, curator; b. Sevierville, Tenn., Nov. 12, 1936; s. James Edgar and Neva Elvira (Myers) T.; m. Barbara Ann Gilliam, May 31, 1959; children: Steven, Scott, Suzanne. BS in Biology, Carson-Newman Coll., Jefferson City, Tenn., 1958; BD in Theology and Greek, Southeastern Bapt. Sem., Wake Forest, N.C., 1962; PhD in Plant Taxonomy, U. Tenn., Knoxville, 1966. Summer forestry aide U.S. Forest Svc., Avery, Idaho, 1955-60; tchr. pub. schs. Hamblen County, Morristown, Tenn., 1962-63; teaching asst. U. Tenn., Knoxville, 1964-66; tchr. biology Northeast La. U., Monroe, 1966—, dir., curator Univ. Herbarium, 1968—. Author: Asteraceae of Louisiana, 1989, Monocots of Louisiana Checklist, 1993, 100 Woody Plants of Northern Louisiana, 1986, Checklist of Louisiana Plants, 1982; contbr. numerous articles to profl. jours. Botany dir. La. Acad. Scis., 1970-94; bd. dirs. Kalorama Nature Preserve, Collinston, La., 1992—. Recipient Outstanding Rschr. award Northeast La. U. Alumni Assn., 1985; named Conservationist of Yr., La. Assn. Garden Clubs, 1986. Mem. Internat. Assn. Plant Taxonomy, Am. Assn. Plant Taxonomists, Bot. Soc. Am., Soc. for Study of Econ. Botany, Southwestern Assn. Naturalists, Assn. Southeastern Biologists, Torrey Bot. Club, New Eng. Bot. Club, So. Appalachian Bot. Club, Sigma Xi, others. Republican. Baptist. Home: 403 Stevenson Dr Monroe LA 71203-2112 Office: NE La Univ Dept Biology 232 Stubbs Hall Monroe LA 71209-0502

THOMAS, RALPH UPTON, economic developer; b. Jackson, Tenn., Nov. 24, 1942; s. Guy Vernon and Audra Naomi (Upton) T.; m. Eva Marie Crouch, Aug. 7, 1965; children: Tacey Marie, Leah Bowman, Dana Farrington. BS, Union U., 1964; JD, Memphis State U., 1973. Indsl. economist State of Tenn., Jackson, 1964-66; v.p. econ. devel. Memphis Area C. of C., 1966-75; pres. San Antonio Econ. Devel. Found., 1975-79; exec. v.p. Greater Lafayette (La.) C. of C., 1979-88; pres. Palmetto Econ. Devel. Corp., Columbia, S.C., 1988—. Bd. dirs. Indian Waters Coun., Boy Scouts Am. Mem. Am. Econ. Assn. Coun. (bd. dirs. 1978), So. Indsl. Devel. Coun., S.C. Econ. Devel. Assn., Leadership S.C. Alumni Assn., Rotary. Democrat. Baptist. Office: Palmetto Econ Devel Corp 1201 Main St Ste 1710 Columbia SC 29201-3261

THOMAS, RICARDO D'WAYNE, financial advisor; b. New Orleans, May 12, 1966; s. Leroy Henderson and Muriel (Ellis) T. BBA in Fin., Loyola U., 1988. Accredited fin. counselor, registered fin. cons.; cert. div. planner; bd. cert. forensic examiner. Account exec. Pioneer Western Fin. Svc., Metairie, La., 1984-86, dist. v.p., 1986-87; pres., fin. cons. Thomas-Waddell & Assocs., Inc., Metairie, 1987—; instr. Delgado Community Coll., 1990. Louis J. Twomey acad. scholar, 1984. Mem. Internat. Assn. Fin. Planning, Assn. Fin. Counseling and Planning Edn., Assn. Family & Concilliation Cts., Internat. Assn. Registered Fin. Cons., Nat. Assn. Forensic Econs., Quantum Inst. Profl. Divorce Planning, Am. Coll. Forensic Examiners, Nat. Forensic Ctr., Delta Sigma Pi. Democrat. Baptist. Office: Thomas-Waddell & Assocs Inc 3000 Kingman St Ste 208 Metairie LA 70006-6633

THOMAS, RICHARD DALE, newspaper editor; b. Hogansville, Ga., Oct. 8, 1949; s. Benjamin J. Thomas and Marie (Phillips) Cook; m. Martha Yates, June 25, 1971; children: Richard J., Elizabeth L. BA, Mercer U., 1975. Pub. affairs coord. Sta. WMAZ-TV-AM, Macon, Ga., 1971-72; mng. editor Boca Raton (Fla.) News, 1977-81, editor, 1981-83; reporter The Macon Telegraph, 1973, city editor, 1973-76, asst. mng. editor, 1976-77, v.p., editor, 1983—. Pres. Goodwill Industries, Macon, 1988-89, Macon (Ga.) Arts Alliance, 1994-95; chmn. Kids Voting/Ga., Macon, 1992-94. Profl. Journalism fellow Stanford (Calif.) U., 1979-80. Mem. Am. Soc. Newspaper Editors, Ga. Press Assn. (bd. dirs. 1991-93, treas. 1995—). Roman Catholic. Home: 1132 Saint Andrews Dr Macon GA 31210-4776

THOMAS, ROBERT L., manufacturing company executive; b. Atlanta, Aug. 1, 1941; s. Orville Kermit Smith and Ina Evelyn (Farris) Peterson; m. Karen Degenhardt, Dec. 4, 1960 (div. Apr. 1978); children: John Harding, Gregory James, Kristen Ann; m. Mary Ellen Seaman, May 2, 1981; children: Lindsey Marian, Mark Gordon. BA in History, Queens Coll., 1969. Asst. buyer J.C. Penney Co. Inc., N.Y.C., 1964-70; sales mgr. Avon Products Inc., Atlanta, 1970-72; pres. Saul Bros. & Co. Inc., Atlanta, 1973—. Bd. dirs. Murphey Candler Little League, Atlanta, 1972, also bd. trustees; bd. dirs. Leukemia Soc., Atlanta, 1988—; mem. Dekalb County Exec. Com. Rep. Party, Atlanta, 1970-74; delegate State Convention Rep. Party, Atlanta, 1972. Mem. South East Textile and Apparel Mfrs., U.S. Polo Assn., Atlanta Polo Club, Gulfstream Polo Club (West Palm Beach), N.Y. Athletic Club (N.Y.C.), Country Club of the South (Alpharetta, Ga.). Republican. Roman Catholic. Home: 4095 Big Crk Overlook Alpharetta GA 30202-4213 Office: Saul Bros & Co Inc 6500 Peachtree Indsl Blvd Norcross GA 30071-1245

THOMAS, ROBERT LEE, financial services company executive, consultant; b. San Antonio, Dec. 29, 1938; s. Lawrence Grant and Mabel Louise (Carlson) T.; m. Terry Eileen Morgan, Dec. 14, 1972; 1 child, Evan Grant. Cert., Am. Coll., 1984, 85, cert. in fin. planning, 1990, cert. in health underwriting, 1991; postgrad., Northeastern U., 1991—. Cert. fin. planner, investment specialist; designated registered employee benefit cons. Various middle mgmt. positions Gen. Fin. Corp., Dallas, 1962-65; full charge mgmt. positions TransAm. Fin. Corp., Dallas, 1965-74; sr. agt. Am. Security Life, San Antonio, 1974-81; chmn., pres. Thomas Fin. Svcs., Inc., Dallas, 1981—; bd. dirs. Cherokee Children's Home; mem. adv. bd. Am. Security Life, 1977—; frequent guest on internat. and nat. radio and TV talk shows; host radio program, 1986—; nat. and internat. spkr. in field; initiator/tchr. fin. planning course for H.S. students. Mem. fin. profl. adv. panel Digest of Financial Planning Ideas mag., 1984; designer, creator Mortgage Pre-Payment System, 1990, Mortgage Management Software, 1990; author: Cost Cutter Mortgage Management Manual, 1990; creator Commercial Debt Expense Reduction System and Debt Cash Flow Analysis Software, 1991; columnist Jour. Shepherding group leader Meadowview Ch. Christ, Mesquite, Tex., 1983—, Bible class tchr., 1978—, deacon, 1987—; regular spokesman pub. svc. and promotional messages various civic orgns.; chmn. charity telethon Million Dollar Round Table; leader internat. missions ministry, Papau, New Guinea, 1989, S.E. Asia, 1990; team mem. for tribal contact, New Guinea, 1991-94, 95, 96; dir. Sr. Info. Svcs. of Ameritech, 1994—; bd. dirs. Cherokee Home for Children, 1994—; team leader group exploring un-charted region of South Pacific Island of New Guinea, 1995-96. Recipient Lone Star Leader award Tex. Assn. Life Underwriters, 1982—, Nat. Sales Achievement award, Nat. Quality award Nat. Assn. Life Underwriters, 1976—. Fellow Life Underwriting Tng. Coun.; mem. Dallas Estate Planning Coun., Dallas Assn. Life Underwriters (chmn. health com. 1979-80, president's cabinet 1989—, pub. rels. com. 1992—), Internat. Assn. Registered Fin. Planners, Internat. Assn. Fin Planning, Am. Soc. CLUs, Am. Inst. Cert. Fin. Planners, Am. Assn. Fin. Profls., Am. Health Ins. Assn., Investment Rsch. Inst., Million Dollar Round Table (life), Dallas Assn. Life Underwriters (mem. steering com. 1992—), Tex. Assn. Life Underwriters (nat. sales achievement award 1976—, nat. quality award 1976—), Am. Arbitration Assn (nat. arbitration panel, securities arbitrator 1989—), Better Bus. Bur. (sr. arbitrator nat. panel), Gen. Agts. and Mgmt. Assn. (yearling achievement 1975), Internat. Platform Assn., Internat. Assn. Registered Fin. Planners, Tex. Investment Mgmt. Coun., Aircraft Owners and Pilots Assn. Office: Thomas Fin Svcs Inc Ste 360 9330 Lyndon B Johnson Fwy Dallas TX 75243-3443

THOMAS, ROBERT LINDSAY, former congressman; b. Patterson, Ga., Nov. 20, 1943; s. James and Aline (Jones) T.; m. Nancy Newton; children: R. Lindsay, Ransom, Nell. BA in English, U. Ga., 1966. Banker C & S Bank, Savannah, Ga., 1966-67; investment banker Johnson, Lane, Space Smith & Co., Savannah, 1967-69, Varnedo, Chisholm & Skinner, Savannah, 1969-73; owner, operator farm Screven, Ga., 1973-82; mem. 98th-102d Congresses from 1st Ga. Dist., 1983-92; dir. govt. rels. Atlanta Com. Olympic Games, 1992-96; pres., CEO Ga. C. of C., Atlanta, 1996—. Recipient commendations and awards from numerous orgns. including Nat. Fedn. Ind. Businesses, Am. Farm Bur. Fedn., Forest Farmers Assn., Am. Security Coun. Democrat. Methodist. Address: PO Box 1996 Atlanta GA 30301-1996 Office: Ga C of C Ste 200 233 Peachtree St Atlanta GA 30303

THOMAS, ROBERT RAY, management consultant; b. Columbus, Ohio, Dec. 14, 1926; s. Robert Ray and Esther Susan (Wolfe) T.; BS in TV Engring., Am. Inst. of Tech., 1950; m. Ann Lee Estes, Nov. 24, 1973; children: Sandra Ann, Robert Ray; 1 child by previous marriage, Margo Lynne. Electronic engr. Oakton Engring. Co., Evanston, Ill., 1949-50, Stewart Warner Corp., Chgo., 1950-51, Gen. Transformer Co., Homewood, Ill., 1951-53; electronic sales engr. Electronic Components Inc., Chgo., 1953-54; gen. mgr. West Coast, Miller Calson Services, Los Angeles, 1954-55; sales engr. R. Edward Steem Co., Chgo., 1955-59; dist. sales mgr. Motorola Semiconductor div. Motorola, Inc., Chgo. and Dallas, 1959-61; pres., chmn. bd. Enterprises Ltd. Co., Inc., Dallas, 1961—, pres. subs. Robert R. Thomas Co., 1961—, Rep. Mgmt. & Mktg. Counselors, 1969—; pres. Press Insulator Co., 1978-92; co-founder CH&T Transformers Inc., 1983-85; owner, pres. Westwood Creations, Inc., 1986-89; co-founder, pres. Data MAXX Corp., 1994—. Served with USAAF, 1945-46. Named Boss of Year, Big D chpt. Am. Bus. Womens Assn., 1965, Super Salesman by Purchasing Mag., Oct. 1975. Mem. Mfrs. Electronic Reps. Assn. (dir. S.W. chpt. 1964-69, pres. S.W. chpt. 1968-69), Sales and Mktg. Execs. of Dallas pres. (1977-78), S.W. Found. for Free Enterprise in Dallas (pres. 1976-77), TESS (founder, pres.), Masons, Shriner. Baptist. Office: 4620 Sunbelt Dr Dallas TX 75248-1884

THOMAS, ROGER NELSON, pilot; b. Nashville, Sept. 5, 1946; s. Dan Anderson and Margaret Elizabeth (Glaze) T.; m. Nancy Rhyne, Mar. 31, 1973; children: Kevin Rhyne, Bonnie Lynn. BA in History, Jacksonville U., 1968, BS in Acctg., 1976; MBA, U. North Fla., 1980. Lic. pilot; lic. flight instr. Lt. commd. USN, 1966, advanced through grades to lt. commdr.; carrier and transport pilot, flight instr. USN, various locations, 1968-73, 78-88; v.p. bus. devel. Herlong Aviation Inc., Jacksonville, Fla., 1974-76; trust adminstr. Fla. Nat. Bank, Jacksonville, 1976-78; office and credit mgr. PYA Monarch Foods, Jacksonville, 1978; pilot, first officer US Air Express/Piedmont Airlines, Jacksonville, 1988-95; safety officer, instr. Jax Navy Flying Club; adj. instr. mktg. Embry-Riddle Aero. U., 1983, 85; security advisor Guam Internat. Airport, Agana, 1985-88; substitute tchr. Duval County Schs., Jacksonville, 1988—. Rescue pilot CAP, Jacksonville, 1963—, maj., 1970—, dept. commdr. ops., safety, aerospace edn. officer; lobbyist Jacksonville City Govt., 1990-93; mem. Jacksonville Maritime Mus.; mem. Camp Blauding Mus. and Hist. Assocs., Inc. Decorated Commdrs. Commendation for Hurricane Andrew Flights; recipient Search and Rescue Find award CAP, 1993, others. Mem. Naval Aviation Mus. Pensacola (founding mem.), Naval Inst., Naval League, U. North Fla. Grad. Bus. Club, Fla. Aviation Hist. Soc. Home: 2149 Holly Oaks River Dr Jacksonville FL 32225-4886 Office: HQ Fla Wing CAP 2700 Eagle Staff Ct Tampa FL 33621

THOMAS, SANDRA MARIE, training company executive; b. N.Y.C., Mar. 4, 1939; d. Dudley George and Helen Claire (Pitt) T. Student, Coll. of V.I., 1963-64, New Sch. for Social Rsch., N.Y.C., 1970-74, Art Students League, N.Y.C., 1974-76, Fordham U., 1980-82, N.Y.U., 1984-85. Mgr. Cutlass Shop, St. Thomas, V.I., 1964-67; rate analyst, in house trainer TWA, N.Y.C., 1968-85; seminar leader Big Body Work Shop, Orlando, Fla., 1986-87; pres., exec. dir. Leisure Learning Labs., Inc., Orlando, 1988-90; owner Skills Link, Orlando, 1992—; human resource devel. cons.; speaker, workshop leader on cultural diversity; coord. Frank Covino Portrait Painters workshops, 1993. Editor Orange County Dem., 1994; contbr. articles to profl. publs. Recipient awards for paintings. Mem. Am. Soc. for Tng. and Devel. (multi-cultural chair Cen. Fla. chpt. 1988-91), Fla. Freelance Writers Assn. Office: Skills Link 4524 Curry Ford Rd Ste 629 Orlando FL 32812-2799

THOMAS, WILLIAM CLARK, JR., internist, medical facility administrator; b. Bartow, Ga., Apr. 7, 1919; s. William Clark and Margaret (Smith) T.; m. Brenda Alfhild Wiltshire, Oct. 26, 1946; children: Sharron, Lynn, Clark, Valerie. BS, U. Fla., 1940; MD, Cornell U. Med. Coll., 1943. Diplomate Am. Bd. Internal Medicine. Med. house staff N.Y. Hosp., N.Y.C., 1944, 46-49; postdoctoral fellow Johns Hopkins Hosp., Balt., 1954-57; from asst. prof. to prof. U. Fla. Coll. Medicine, Gainesville, 1957-96, prof. emeritus, 1996—; from chief of medicine to chief of staff VA Med. Ctr., Gainesville, 1968-96. Author: Renal Calculi, 1976; contbr. numerous book chpts. over 100 articles to profl. jours. Mem. Alpha Omega Alpha, Phi Beta Kappa. Home: 2721 NW 5th Pl Gainesville FL 32607-2613 Office: VA Med Ctr Archer Rd Gainesville FL 32610

THOMASON, TOMMY GEORGE, journalism educator; b. Magnolia, Ark., Nov. 29, 1949; s. Harry Merle and Hazel Irene (Strange) T.; m. Deborah Lee Presley, Dec. 31, 1976; 1 child, Joshua Adam. BA, Ouachita U., 1971; MA, Tex. A&M U.-Commerce, 1973, EdD, 1984. Instr. journalism, dir. publs. So. Ark. U., Magnolia, 1973-76; asst. prof. journalism dept. Liberty U., Lynchburg, Va., 1979-81; dir. pub. rels. Dallas Bapt. U., 1982-84; assoc. prof. journalism dept. Tex. Christian U., Fort Worth, 1984—; copyeditor Growing Majority mag., Dallas, 1988; copyeditor and contbg. editor Aura Mag., Fort Worth, 1988-90; columnist Crossroads Newsmagazine, Mesquite, Tex., 1974-75; dir. sports info. Ouachita Bapt. U., 1970-71; sports writer Associated Press, Little Rock, 1969-70; dept. journalism advising coord., 1986-89, acting advising coord., 1991-92; premajor adviser Ctr. for Acad. Svcs., 1987-89; spkr. in field. Author: More Than A Writing Teacher: How to Become A Teacher Who Writes, 1993; contbr. numerous articles to profl. jours. Cons. Nat. Victim Ctr., Fort Worth; cons. various crime victim support groups. Grantee Gannett Found., 1985, Capital Cities/ABC/Fort Worth Star-Telegram, 1986, Sunny Von Bulow Nat. Victim Advocacy Ctr., 1987, Journalism Found. of Oklahoma City, 1989, Dallas Morning News, 1992, M.G. McNeill Found., 1994. Mem. Soc. of Profl. Journalists (coord., bd. dirs. Fort Worth Pro chpt. 1989-90), Associated Press Mng. Editors (fgn. news com.), Assn. for Edn. in Journalism and Mass Comm., S.W. Edn. Coun. for Journalism and Mass Comm., Internat. Inst. of Literacy Learning (v.p. pub. rels.). Republican. Baptist. Office: Tex Christian U PO Box 298060 Fort Worth TX 76129

THOMASSON, JOHN MELVIN, college administrator; b. Paducah, Ky., Feb. 3, 1950; s. Clois M. and Marijohn (Brigman) T.; m. Janice Elizabeth Hundley; children: Lauren Elizabeth, John Andrew. BS, Murray State U., 1972; MS, Nova U., 1978; postgrad. U. Ala. Tchr., athletic dir. Brevard County Schs., Titusville, Fla., 1972-78; sr. quality engr. Rockwell/McDonnell Douglas, Kennedy Space Center, Fla., 1979-92; dir. bus. ops. Med. Coll. Ga., Augusta, 1993—; mgmt. cons. Thomasson Cons. Group, Orlando, Fla., 1989—; ind. antique broker, Augusta, 1991—; keynote spkr. various profl. seminars and confs., U.S. and Can., 1989—. Author: Designing Management Models, 1992. Recipient numerous engring. and quality awards NASA, 1979-92. Mem. ASTD, Metro Augusta Quality Coun. (mem. steering com.).

THOMPSON, ALICE M. BROUSSARD, special education administrator; b. Opelousas, La., May 15, 1950; d. Melvin and Roseanna (Joseph) Broussard; m. Samuel Joe Thompson; 1 child, Tameka Rose Thompson. BS in Vocat. Home Econs., McNeese State U., 1973; MEd in Spl. Edn., U. Mo., St. Louis, 1993; cert. in mid-mgmt., Tex. So. U., 1993; completed studies, Harvard U., 1995. Food svc. supr. Parkland Meml. Hosp., Dallas, 1982-83; tchr. home econs. Milw. pub. Schs., 1984-85; tchr. career lab. Ft. Bend Ind. Sch., Sugarland, Tex., 1985-87; tchr. home econs. Epworth Pvt. Sch., Webster Grove, Mo., 1988-91; tchr. resource math. Ft. Bend Ind. Sch. Dist., Sugarland, 1991-92, coord. spl. edn., 1993—; cons. Inclusion, Tex., 1993; coord. Inclusion Adv. Bd., Sugarland, 1993—; mem. Inclusion Works Adv. Bd., Austin, 1994—. Mem. NAFE, ASCD, Coun. for Exceptional Children, Nat. Assn. Black Educators, Alpha Kappa Alpha (dean of pledges 1973). Home: 2811 Plantation Wood Ln Missouri City TX 77459-4253 Office: Ft Bend Ind Sch Dist PO Box 1004 Sugar Land TX 77487-1004

THOMPSON, ALLEN JOSEPH, construction executive, civil engineer; b. San Juan, P.R., May 14, 1937; s. Allen Lincoln and Antonia Bartolome (Martin) T.; m. Lucy Elizabeth Stoutenburgh, Oct. 4, 1957 (div. June 1982); children: Lucy An, Cristina Mae, Elizabeth Anne; m. Maria Josefina Moya, Oct. 1, 1987. BS in Civil Engring., The Citadel, 1956; postgrad., N.Y. Polytech. Inst., 1958-59, George Washington U., 1960-61. Registered profl. engr., D.C., Md., Miss., Fla., P.R. Civil engr. Raymond Internat., San Juan, 1956-58; structural designer Buell Engring., N.Y.C., 1958-59; civil engr. Norair Engring., Washington, 1959-62; constrn. mgr. Bechtel Corp., San Francisco, 1962-87; pres. Thompson Martin Assocs., Miami, Fla., 1987—, NCI Constrn., Miami, 1994—; cons. Bechtel Power Corp., San Francisco, 1987-90. Commr. Boy Scouts Am., Md., 1967. Mem. Am. Soc. Civil Engrs., Nat. Soc. Profl. Engrs. Republican. Roman Catholic. Home: 2333 Brickell Ave Apt 1716 Miami FL 33129-2414

THOMPSON, ARTHUR RAYMOND, marketing professional; b. Groveton, Tex., May 5, 1938; s. Charles Alton and Annie V. (Swor) T.; m. Alice Ann Church, Sept. 1, 1957; children: John Alton, Amy Lynn, Mark Alan. AA, Fla. Coll., 1960; postgrad., Fairmont (W.Va.) State U., 1961. Reporter aerospace UPI, Cape Canaveral, Fla., 1963-71; mgr. mktg. staff So. Bell Telephone and Telegraph, Ft. Lauderdale, 1971-91; ret., 1991; advisor radio and TV, Rep. Party of Fla., Ft. Lauderdale, 1967-71; v.p. ops. Fla. Broadcasting System, Ft. Lauderdale, 1968-70; chmn. bd. dirs. Rubicon Enterprises, Inc., Tampa, Fla., 1985—. Author: Republican Campaign Handbook, 1968, The Lord's Supper, 1987; co-author: Theophilus and the One True Church, 1991. Pres. high sch. adv. com. Broward County, Ft. Lauderdale, 1977-79; coord. communications for U.S. Tour of Pope John Paul II, 1987; bd. dirs. Truth and Freedom Ministry, Inc., 1987—. Named Hon. Blue Angel, 1964. Mem. Cape Canaveral Space Pioneers (charter mem. 1962). Home and Office: 146 Woodhaven Dr La Fayette GA 30728-4918

THOMPSON, BOBBY JOE, family physician; b. Edmond, Okla., Sept. 30, 1950; s. Charles H. and Florence (Kaiser) T.; m. Lynn M. Baird, Jan. 1, 1970; children: Trevor Wade, Jeremy Ryan. BS, Okla. Christian Coll., Oklahoma City, 1972; MS, Okla. State U., 1973; DO, Okla. Coll. Osteo. Medicine, 1979. Diplomate Am. Bd. Quality Assurance, Am. Coll. Gen. Practitioners. Instr. Okla. State U., Stillwater, 1973-74, Freed-Hardeman Coll., Henderson, Tenn., 1974-76; intern Okla. Osteo. Hosp., Tulsa, 1979-80; pvt. practice Clinton Family Clinic, Clinton, Okla., 1980—; med. examiner Custer County, Okla.; med. dir. Sinor Emergency Med. Svcs., Clinton. Physician advisor Okla. Found. Peer Rev. Mem. Am. Osteo. Assn., Okla. Asteo. Assn., Am. Osteo. Coll. Family Practitioners, Am. Bd. Quality Assurance and Utilization Review, Phi Kappa Phi. Sigma Sigma Phi. Mem. Ch. of Christ.

THOMPSON, CARLA JO HORN, mathematics educator; b. Oklahoma City, Feb. 10, 1951; d. Hubert Henry and Gilleen Cora (Hall) Horn; m. Michael J. Thompson, Aug. 4, 1973 (div. 1986); 1 child, Emily Jane. BS, U. Tulsa, 1972, MTA, 1973, EdD, 1980; postgrad. Okla. State U., 1975-77; dist. math. coord., Tulsa Pub. Schs., 1995-96. Tchr. math. Sapulpa (Okla.) pub. schs., 1973-79; research asst. U. Tulsa, 1979-80; asst. prof. math. and statistics Tulsa Jr. Coll., 1980—; research statistician Social & Edn. Research Assocs., Tulsa, 1987—; vis. adj. prof. U. Tulsa, 1989—, Univ. Ctr. at Tulsa, 1989—; reviewer Harcourt/Brace & Javonovich, Tulsa, 1988-89; cons. Little Brown Pubrs., Tulsa, 1984-86; evaluator Random House Pubrs., Tulsa, 1982-84. Contbr. articles to profl. jours.; author test manual: Basic Mathematics, 1989. Vol. Tulsa pub. schs., 1988—; co-leader Brownie troop Girl Scouts U.S., Tulsa, 1988—. Named Tchr. of the Yr., Sapulpa Pub Schs., 1979, Okla. Prof. of Yr., Carnegie Found., 1995. U. Tulsa grantee, 1980. Mem. Okla. Council Tchrs. Math. (coll. rep., exec. bd. 1983—), Am. Math. Assn. Two-Yr. Colls. (editorial bd. 1985—), Nat. Council Tchrs. Math., Phi Delta Kappa, Kappa Delta Pi. Democrat. Office: Tulsa Community College 3727 E Apache St Tulsa OK 74115-3150

THOMPSON, CHARLES OTIS, lighting designer; b. Dallas, Feb. 5, 1942; s. Truman Charles and Rose Bell (Cox) T.; children from previous marriage: Peter Mitchell, Carla Michelle; m. Frances Delores Hall, Nov. 23, 1977; children: Andrea S. Drew, Barry R. Drew. Degree in Archtl. Engring Tech., Tampa (Fla.) Tech. Inst., 1974. Elec. designer Capell & Clark, Columbia, S.C., 1974-75, Lyles, Bissett, Carlisle & Wolfe, Columbia, 1975-77, Wilbur Smith & Assocs., Columbia, 1977-78, Elec. Design Cons., Columbia, 1978-81; lighting cons. Cotangent Lighting Design, Columbia, 1981-84; sr. lighting designer Tectonics Engring. Cons., Columbia, 1984-87; prin., dir. design Charles Thompson Assocs., Columbia, 1987—; cons. S.C. Dept. Trade and Indsl. Edn., Columbia, 1981-84, Lighting Research and Edn. Fund, Atlanta, 1981-82. Designer archtl. lighting for St. Peter's Ch., Columbia, 1985 (Edwin F. Guth award 1986), Beaufort Tech. Coll. Learning Resource Ctr., 1987 (Edwin F. Guth award 1986), S.C. Senate Chamber, 1988, Forset Lake Country Club Ballroom, 1989 (Edwin F. Guth award 1990), S.C. Supreme Ct., 1990; patentee in field. With U.S. Army, 1959-62. Recipient 2 Internat. Illumination Design awards Illuminating Engring. Soc. N.Am., 1993, 96. Mem. Illuminating Engring. Soc. (sect. pres. 1980-82, 87-88, program chmn. 1979-80, steering com. Piedmont sect. 1981-82), Constrn. Specifications Inst. (Columbia chpt. membership chmn. 1990-92, pres. 1992-93), Quail Valley Swim and Racquet Club. Lutheran. Home: 109 Archers Ln Columbia SC 29212-1601 Office: Charles Thompson Assocs 2500C Devine St Columbia SC 29205-2408

THOMPSON, CLAUDE M., finance officer, pharmacy consultant; b. Maysville, Ga., Apr. 19, 1921; s. William Berry and Mary L. Indiana (Buffington) T.; m. Reba Watkins, May 5, 1946; children: Claudia, Cathy, David, Billy, Dickie. Student in bus. adminstrn., U. Houston, 1942; BS in Pharmacy, U. Ga., 1948. Registered pharmacist; cert. real estate broker, finance officer. Clin. coord. Hoffman-LaRoche, Inc., Atlanta, 1951-59; pres., owner Thompson's Pharmacy, Inc., Fayetteville and Peachtree, Ga., 1959-67; sales mgr. The Realty Group, Inc., Atlanta, 1967-71; v.p. The Howell-Thompson Inc, Atlanta, 1971-87; pres. First Madison Fin., Inc., Peachtree City, Ga., 1988—; cons. pharmacist Pharmacies, Inc., Atlanta, 1988-93; active United Mortgage Investment Corp. With USN, 1942-46, Korea. Mem. Internat. Alliance of Fin. Counselors, Ga. Pharm. Assn., Ga. Bd. Realtors, Elks, Flat Creek Country Club. Republican. Presbyterian. Office: First Madison Fin Inc 306 Willow Rd Ste 2306 Peachtree City GA 30269-1639

THOMPSON, CLEON F., JR., university administrator. BS in Biology, N.C. Cen. U., 1956, MS in Biology, 1958; PhD in Edn Adminstrn., Duke U., 1977. Vice-pres. student services and spl. programs U. N.C., to 1985; chancellor Winston-Salem State U., N.C., 1985—. Office: Winston Salem State U Office of Chancellor Winston Salem NC 27110

THOMPSON, CRAIG OWEN, author; b. L.A., Sept. 25, 1943; s. William Charles and Maxine Corinne (Townsend) T.; m. Janette Lynn Caniglia, Nov. 12, 1966; children: Kerri Louise Thompson Sullivan, Colleen Therese. AA in Theatre Arts, El Camino (Calif.) Coll., 1965; BA in Edn., No. Ariz. U., 1971, MA in Edn., 1973. Cert. life C.C.'s teaching and supervision credentials, Calif. Vol. Peace Corps, Sri Lanka, 1962-64; prodr., dir. Lucille Ball Studio Theater, Hollywood, Calif., 1966-69; post prodn. mgr. Delilu/Paramount TV, Hollywood, 1966-69; adminstrv. dir., instr. Navajo-Hawaii Cultural Exch., Navajo Reservation, Ariz., 1969-71; coord. coll. affairs Golden West Coll., Huntington Beach, Calif., 1971-74; dir. community svc. Shasta Coll., Redding, Calif., 1974-78; pres. Thompson-Hughes & Assocs., Redding, 1978-83; exec. dir. Warren Performing Arts Ctr., Indpls., 1983-90; exec. dir., CEO, Arts Coun. Grand Rapids, Mich., 1990-91; v.p. Coll. of W.Va., Beckley, 1991-92; pres. Brightwater Enterprises, Hurricane, W.Va., 1992—; cultural arts cons., Calif., Ariz., Ohio, Mich., W.Va., Ind., 1973—. Author: (anthology) Star Spangled Speakers, 1982, (novel) Secret Agenda, 1997. Pres. Western Alliance Arts Adminstrs., 1977-78; bd. dirs. Mich. Advs. for Arts, Lansing, 1990-91; mem. Concerned Citizens for Arts, Lansing, 1990-91; mem. arts festival com. Pan Am. Games, Indpls., 1986-88. Fellow Carnegie Inst., 1965. Mem. Washington Ind. Writers (bd. dirs. 1993-95), Kiwanis, The Crescent Rev. (bd. dirs. 1994-97). Roman Catholic.

THOMPSON, CRAIG WARREN, computer scientist, researcher; b. La Jolla, Calif., Aug. 3, 1949; s. Warren Charles and Dorothy Ann (Stanley) T.; m. Janet Ritter, Dec. 28, 1974; children: Jennifer, Kathryn. BA in Math., Stanford U., 1971; MA in Computer Sci., U. Tex., 1977, PhD, 1984. Instr. dept. computer sci. U. Tex., Austin, 1971-77, U. Tenn., Knoxville, 1977-81; with Tex. Instruments Inc., Dallas, 1981-95, sr. mem. tech. staff, 1985-88, mgr. database rsch., 1988-95, program mgr. ARPA-funded open object-oriented database rsch. project, 1990-95; pres. Object Svcs. and Cons., Inc., Dallas, 1995—; co-architect ARPA TRP Nat. Indsl. Info. Infrastructure Protocols Consortium, 1994—; organizer Workshop on Application Integration Architectures, 1993; chair OMG-Internet SIG. Editor: OMG Object Service Architecture, 1992. Mem. IEEE (sr.), Assn. for Computing Machinery. Baptist. Office: Object Svcs and Cons Inc 6316 Dykes Way Dallas TX 75230

THOMPSON, DAVID B., bishop. Ordained priest, 1950; consecrated bishop, 1989. Coadjutor bishop Diocese of Charleston, S.C., 1989-90, bishop, 1990—. Office: Bishop of Charleston 119 Broad St Charleston SC 29401

THOMPSON, DENISSE R., mathematics educator; b. Keesler AFB, Miss., Aug. 26, 1954. BA, BS, U. South Fla., 1976, MA, 1980; PhD, U. Chgo., 1992. Cert. tchr., Fla. Tchr. Hernando County Schs., Brooksville, Fla., 1977-82; instr. maths. Manatee C.C., Bradenton, Fla., 1982-87; asst. prof. U. South Fla., Tampa, 1991—; cons. in field. Author: Fundamental Skills of Mathematics, 1987, Advanced Algebra, 1990, 2d edit., 1996, (with others) Precalculus and Discrete Mathematics, 1992, Nat. Coun. Tchrs. of Math. Yearbook, 1991, 93, 94, 95. Recipient Carolyn Hoefer Meml. award Pi Lambda Theta, 1988. Mem. ASCD, Math. Assn. Am., Nat. Coun. Tchrs. Math., Nat. Coun. Suprs. Math., Assn. Women in Maths., Phi Delta Kappa, Phi Kappa Phi. Office: U South Fla College of Edn EDU208B Tampa FL 33620

THOMPSON, DENNIS SCOTT, psychiatrist; b. Detroit, June 18, 1943; s. Albert George and Mildred Marie (Mertens) T. BS, U. Mich., 1965; postgrad. Wayne State U., 1966; DO, Chgo. Coll. Osteo. Medicine, 1970. Cert. Am. Bd. Neurology and Psychiatry. Asst. prof., psychiatrist U. Ill. Med. Sch., Chgo., 1976-83, Chgo. Coll. Osteo. Medicine, 1983-84; med. dir. Hamilton Ctr., Terre Haute, Ind., 1984-87. Fellow Am. Acad. Child Psychiatry. Office: 401 SE Osceola St Ste 202 Stuart FL 34994-2503

THOMPSON, DIDI CASTLE (MARY BENNETT), writer, editor; b. Terre Haute, Ind., Feb. 7, 1918; d. Robert Langley Bennett and Marjorie Rose (Tyler) Castle; student U. Ill., Champaign, 1935-36, U. Ky., 1936-39; m. Jamie Campbell Thompson, Jr., June 24, 1939; children—Jamie III, Julia King Balko, Langley Stewart Ruede. News editor Glen-Echoes, Glencoe, Ill., 1930; columnist Ky. Kernel, U. Ky., Lexington, 1937-39; radio script writer Modern Am. Music, 1940-42; asst. pub. relations dir. Salem Coll., Winston-Salem, N.C., 1945; pub. relations chmn. Barrington (Ill.) Horse Show, 1959-67; staff writer, columnist Barrington Press Newspapers, 1958-84; editor ECHO, Defenders of the Fox River, Inc. newsletter, 1970-80; travel editor Barrington Press Newspapers, 1973-84; columnist The Daily Herald, Paddock Publs., 1984-86; columnist Rapid City (S.D.) Journal, 1990-95; free-lance writer, 1943—. Past bd. mem. Barrington chpt. Lyric Opera Guild Chgo., Barrington Sr. Center, Infant Welfare Soc. Chgo., Art Inst. Chgo., Barrington Assos.; elected trustee Village of Barrington Hills, 1969-73, health, pub. relations chmn., 1969-73; mem. Barrington Hills Plan Commn., 1986. Mem. Women in Communications (past dir.), Citizens for Conservation (past dir.), Barrington Countryside Assn. (past dir.), Barrington Hist. Soc., Spring Creek Basset Hounds Club, Barrington Hills Riding Club (past dir.), Pan Hellenic Council, DAR, Chgo. Press Club, Chi Omega. Episcopalian. Address: 1827 Princess Ct Naples FL 34110

THOMPSON, DOROTHEA WIDEMAN, educator; b. Meridian, Miss., Jan. 28, 1936; d. James Leonard and Newlyn Jones (Robinson) Wideman; m. Joseph Franklin Thompson, Mar. 5, 1955; children: Anne, Steven, Scott. BS, U. Ala., 1977, MA, 1978. Tchr. Tarrant Bd. of Edn., Birmingham, 1979-89, Jefferson County Bd. of Edn., Birmingham, 1989—. Bd. dirs. Day Care, Inc., Birmingham, 1972-75, Camp Fire, Birmingham, 1974-78. Recipient Disting Alumnae award U. Ala. Birmingham, 1993. Mem. Ala. Reading Assn. (pres. 1989), Birmingham Area Reading Coun. Republican. Episcopalian. Home: 3540 Overton Rd Birmingham AL 35223

THOMPSON, EDWARD IVINS BRAD, biological chemistry and genetics educator, molecular endocrinologist, department chairman; b. Burlington, Iowa, Dec. 20, 1933; s. Edward Bills and Lois Elizabeth (Bradbridge) T.; m. Lynn Taylor Parsons; children: Elizabeth Lynn, Edward Ernest Bradbridge. BA with distinction, Rice U., 1955; postgrad., Cambridge U., 1957-58; MD, Harvard U., 1960. Intern The Presbyn. Hosp., N.Y.C., 1960-61, asst. resident internal medicine, 1961-62; rsch. assoc. Nat. Inst. Mental Health, NIH, Bethesda, Md., 1962-64; rsch. scientist Nat. Inst. Arthritis and Metabolic Diseases, NIH, Bethesda, Md., 1964-68; rsch. scientist Lab of Biochemistry, Nat. Cancer Inst., NIH, Bethesda, Md., 1968-73, sect. chief, 1973-84; I.H. Kempner prof. U. Tex. Med. Br., Galveston, 1984, prof., chmn. dept. human biol. chemistry and genetics, 1984—, prof. internal medicine, 1984—; attending physician Nat. Naval Med. Ctr., Bethesda, 1978-80; chmn. hormones and cancer task force NIH, Bethesda, 1978-80; co-chmn. Gordon Research Conf., 1980; mem. adv. com. on Biochem. & Chem. Carcinogenesis, Am. Cancer Soc., 1982-86; mem. revision com. Endocrinology adv. panel U.S. Pharmacopoeial Conv., Inc., 1980-85; mem. council for clin. investigation and research awds., Am. Cancer Soc., 1989-93; bd. scientific overseers Pennington Nutrition Rsch. Ctr. La. State U., 1991—; Fulbright prof., Marburg, Germany. 1992-93. Co-editor Gene Expression and Carcinogenesis in Cultured Liver, 1975, Steroid Receptors and the Management of Cancer, 1979, DNA: Protein Interactions and Gene Regulation, other vols. in field; assoc. editor Cancer Rsch. jour., 1976-86; corr. editor Jour. Steroid Biochemistry, 1977-85; founding editor-in-chief Molecular Endocrinology Jour., 1985-92; contbr. over 200 sci. articles to profl. jours. Mem. troop com. Girl Scouts U.S., Rockville, Md., 1970-76; mem. PTA, Rockville, 1967-77, Wilderness Soc., Washington, 1964-75; initiator sci. edn. liaison program Galveston Pub. Schs., 1991; mem. pres.'s cabinet U. Tex. Med. Br. Served as med. dir. USPHS, 1962-84. Grantee NIH, Walls Rsch., Nat. Inst. Diabetes and Digestive and Kidney Diseases, Nat. Cancer Inst.; Am. Cancer Soc. scholar, 1992-93; Fulbright scholar. Mem. Am. Soc. Cell Biology, Am. Assn. Cancer Rsch., Am. Soc. Biol. Chemists, Endocrine Soc., Am. Soc. Microbiology, Am. Coll. Med. Genetics (affiliate), Tissue Culture Assn., S.W. Environ. Mutagen Soc., Rotary Internat., The Yacht Club, Racquet Club, Harvard Club, Pres.'s Clubs of Rice U. and U. Tex. Med. Br., Phi Beta Kappa, Alpha Omega Alpha. Office: U Tex Med Br Dept Human Biol Gene Galveston TX 77555

THOMPSON, EMERSON MCLEAN, JR., retired clergyman; b. Raleigh, N.C., Dec. 3, 1931; s. Emerson McLean and Grace (Neathery) T.; m. Catherine Traynham, June 9, 1956; children: Catherine Elizabeth, Emerson III, David Stuart. AB in English, Duke U., 1954; BD, Duke Divinity Sch., 1958. Ordained to ministry Meth. Ch. as deacon, 1956, as elder, 1958. Pastor Stantonsburg (N.C.) Meth. Ch., 1958-64, Scotland Neck (N.C.) Meth. Ch., 1964-70, McMannen United Meth. Ch., Durham, N.C., 1970-75, Grace United Meth. Ch., Wilmington, N.C., 1975-80, 1st United Meth. Ch., Roanoke Rapids, N.C., 1980-84; sr. minister 1st United Meth. Ch., Elizabeth City, N.C., 1984-90; dist. supt. Greenville (N.C.) Dist. United Meth. Ch., 1990-96; ret., 1996; trustee Meth. Coll., Fayetteville, N.C., 1977-85, Meth. Retirement Homes, Inc., 1986-96. Mem., chmn. bd. dirs. Migrant and Seasonal Farmworkers, Inc., Raleigh, N.C., 1977-83; mem. Rotary Internat., Wilmington, 1975-80, Roanoke Rapids, 1980-84, Elizabeth City, 1984-90, Greenville, 1994—. Home: 105 Kilby Dr Greenville NC 27858-6508

THOMPSON, ERIK, naval officer; b. Plattsmouth, Nebr., July 11, 1959; s. Jack Neal and Ingrid (Kringstad) T.; m. Mary Lou Pupke, May 12, 1979; children: Edward J., Kristine A. BS, U. State N.Y., Albany, 1984; postgrad., Naval War Coll., 1993; MS, Naval Postgrad. Sch., Monterey, Calif., 1995. Commd. ensign USN, 1986; supply officer USS Pollack, USS Guardfish, USS Alexandria, 1987-92; supply officer, spl. projects officer Spl. Boat Squadron TWO USN, 1992-94; ops. officer Assessments and Analysis divsn. FCSWA, 1995—. Asst. scoutmaster Boy Scouts Am., Virginia Beach, Va., and Monterey, Calif., 1991-95. Decorated Commendation medals. Mem. NRA (life). Republican. Baptist. Home: 37 Madole Rd Edgewood NM 87015 Office: Field Command Def Spl Weapons Kirtland AFB NM 87117

THOMPSON, FRED, senator; b. Sheffield, Ala., Aug. 19, 1942. BS, Memphis State U., 1964; JD, Vanderbilt U., 1967. Asst. U.S. atty. Mid. Tenn., 1969-72; min. counsel Senate Watergate Com., 1973-74; pvt. practice, 1975-94; spl. counsel senate fgn. rels. com. U.S. Intelligence and Fgn. Rels. Coms., 1980; spl. counsel Senate Intelligence Com., 1982; atty. Arent, Fox, Kintner, Plotkin & Kahn, 1991-94; U.S. senator from Tenn., 1994—. Appeared in 18 films including The Hunt for Red October, In the Line of Fire, Cape Fear, 1985-94. Office: US Senate 523 Dirksen Senate Bldg Washington DC 20510-4203

THOMPSON, GEORGE LEROY, mechanical engineer; b. Elwood, Nebr., Aug. 2, 1952; s. Leonard and Mary (Tillotson) T.; m. Linda Susan Philo, June 22, 1980; children: Samantha, Diana, David. BSME, U. Nebr., 1976; postgrad., U. No. Iowa, 1979-80. Registered profl. engr., Iowa, Ga. Design engr. Maytag Co., Newton, Iowa, 1977-79, Doerfer div. Container Corp. Am., Cedar Falls, Iowa, 1979-82; sr. mech. engr. Becton-Dickinson, Columbus, Nebr., 1982-85; sr. engr. Coca-Cola Co., Atlanta, 1985—. Co-inventor proportional flow control valve. Mem. Pi Tau Sigma. Republican. Methodist. Home: 2502 Meadow Glen Trl Snellville GA 30278-5631 Office: Coca Cola Co 1 Coca Cola Plz NW Ste 3A Atlanta GA 30313-2420

THOMPSON, GERARD MAURICE, import-export company executive, merchant banker; b. Glen Cove, N.Y., Jan. 8, 1945; s. Gerard Maurice Thompson and Rita (White) Mathews; m. Barbara Wilcox Thompson, June 13, 1970; children: Christopher G.A., Michael D.K. BA, Yale U., 1967. Asst. v.p. Merrill Lynch and Co., London, 1971-79; v.p. Smith Barney Harris Upham, Paris, London, 1979-84; exec. dir. DBL Trading Co., London, 1984-90; mng. dir. AIG Trading Corp., Greenwich, Conn., 1990-93; exec. v.p. Bariston, Inc., Toronto, Can., 1993-96; chmn., CEO Bariston, Inc., West Palm Beach, Fla., 1993-96; dir. Seaton Group Inc., Boca Raton, Fla.; pres. K-Pasa, Inc., Miami, Fla., 1996—; prin. Stoneridge Ptnrs., Southfield, Mass., 1990—. Sgt. U.S. Army, 1967-69. Mem. City of London Club, Yale Club of NYC. Office: K-Pasa Inc 10650 SW 186th Ln Miami FL 33157-6763

THOMPSON, GREGORY LEE, social sciences educator; b. Huntington Pk., Calif., June 14, 1946; s. Karl Windsor and Virginia Alice (Hanna) T. AB in Geography, U. Calif. at Davis, 1968; M of City Planning, U. Calif. Berkeley, 1970; PhD in Social Scis., U. Calif. at Irvine, 1987. Transp. planner City of Edmonton (Alberta) Transit System, 1970-72; transp. analyst Canadian Transport Commn., Ottawa, Ontario, 1972-73; transp. coord. City of Berkeley (Calif.) Planning Dept., 1973-74; sr. transp. planner San Diego County, 1974-77, Met. Transp. Devel. Bd., San Diego, 1977-80; sr. cons. Mass Transit, Calif. Assembly, Sacramento, 1980-81; doctoral cand. Sch. Social Sci., U. Calif. at Irvine, 1981-87; rsch. fellow Hagley Mus. & Libr., Wilmington, Del., 1987-88; asst. prof. Fla. State U., Tallahassee, 1988-94, assoc. prof., 1994—. Author: The Passenger Train in the Motor Age: California 1910-1941, 1993; contbr. articles to profl. jours. Organizer, pres. Citizens of Rail Calif., San Diego, 1976-80. Named Advanced Rsch. Fellow Andrew W. Mellon/NEH, 1987-88, Disting. Student Scholar Sch. Engring. U.Calif. at Irvine, 1983. Mem. Am. Planning Assn. (sect. dir. San Diego), Soc. for History of Technology, Econ. History Assn., Bus. History Assn., Planning History Assn., Am. Inst. Cert. Planners. Democrat. Home: 2635 Lucerne Dr Tallahassee FL 32303-2261 Office: Fla State U Dept Urban Regional Pl Tallahassee FL 32306

THOMPSON, GUY THOMAS, safety engineer; b. Chattanooga, Dec. 29, 1942; s. Thomas Nelson and Dorothy Leona (Dobbs) T.; m. Joy Ann Gray, July 22, 1966 (div. 1978); children: Jeffrey Leighton, Lydia Ann; m. Vicki Lynn Brogdon, Dec. 6, 1979; 1 child, Laura Lynn. BA in Engring. Electronic, Park Coll., Parkville, Mo., 1976; MS in Indsl. Safety, Middle Tenn. State U., 1989. Factory rep. Modern Maid Appliances, Chattanooga, 1966-68; biomed. tech. USAF, 1968-77, commd. 2d. lt., 1977, advanced through grades to capt., 1981, ret., 1987; tng. and safety coord. Murfreesboro (Tenn.) Area Vocat. Tech. Sch., 1987—; cons. Tenn. Elec. Coop. Assn., Nashville, 1987—, Tenn. Mcpl. Elec. Power Assn., Brentwood, 1987-92; dir. safety and loss control Okla. Assn. Electric Coops., 1992—. Author: Tech/Logistic Development Plans, 1978, Comprehensive Safety, 1988; copyright: Root Causes of Electric Contact Accidents and Electric Utility Safety Policy; inventor hyperbaric breathing apparatus. Coach Little League, Charleston, S.C., 1962-64, Girl's Softball League, Warner Robins, Ga., 1978-80, Girl's Softball, Tullahoma, Tenn., 1984-86. Mem. Am. Soc. Safety Engrs., Nat. Utility Tng. and Safety Edn. Assn. (coord. conf. 1989), Nat. Safety Coun., Tenn. Safety Congress (exec. com.), Am. Tech. Edn. Assn., Tri-County Bowling Assn. (pres. 1982-88), Arnold Engring. & Devel. Ctr. Golf Club (coun. 1984-88), Am. Legion, Phi Kappa Phi. Republican. Methodist. Home: 15089 N Oak Dr Choctaw OK 73020-7009 Office: Okla Assn Electric Coops PO Box 54309 Oklahoma City OK 73154-1309

THOMPSON, HAROLD JEROME, counselor, mental retardation professional; b. Oklahoma City, May 5, 1947; s. John Caldwell and Marian Louree (Cejda) T.; m. Donna Marie Steed, May 13, 1967 (div. Feb. 1977); children: Treva Marie, Derek Martin; m. Clydia Dee Nichols, Aug. 11, 1984 (div. Apr. 1993). BA, Langston U., 1983; MS, Northea. Okla. State U., 1985. Lic. profl. counselor; qualified mental retardation profl.; cert. behavior analyst. Sales rep. Jones-Newly Supply Co., Oklahoma City, 1969-72, Jones-Newby Supply Co., Tulsa, 1972-74; ins. sales agt. ind. brokers, Tulsa, 1974-77; sales rep. Empire Plumbing Supply, Tulsa, 1977-79, 81-82, Amfac Mech. Supply, Tulsa, 1979-81; chmn. citizens adv. bd. Tulsa Psychiat. Ctr., 1982-83; counselor Horizon Program Shadow Mountain Inst., Tulsa, 1983-90; psychologist Hissom Meml. Ctr., Sand Springs., Okla., 1985-91; pvt. practice Tulsa, 1990—; cons., vol. counselor to mentally retarded, Denver, 1987. With U.S. Army, 1966-68. Mem. Am. Assn. on Mental Deficiency, Nat. Assn. Masters in Philosophy. Republican. Roman Catholic. Office: Behavioral Solutions 7217 S Columbia Tulsa OK 74136

THOMPSON, HENRY LELON, JR., economist, educator; b. Ft. Payne, Ala., Dec. 21, 1947; s. Henry Lelon and Johnnie Vera (Richey) T.; m. Judy Waldrop Tidwell, 1967 (div. 1971); 1 child, Stacy Noel; m. Madeline Simos, Oct. 1, 1978; 1 child, Alexi Simos. BS, U. Houston, 1970, PhD, 1981. Asst. prof. U. Tenn., Knoxville, 1981-87; prof. econs. Auburn (Ala.) U., 1987—; cons. Bank Greece & Kuwait Inst. for Sci. Rsch., NASA. Author: International Economics, 1993, The Way the World Works, 1995; contbr. articles to profl. jours. Mem. Am. Econ. Assn., So. Econ. Assn., Western Econ. Assn., Southeastern Econ. Assn., Internat. Econs. and Fin. Soc. (treas. 1993—). Libertarian. Home: PO Box 1611 Auburn AL 36831-1611 Office: Auburn U Dept Econs Auburn AL 36849

THOMPSON, HUGH P, justice; b. Montezuma, Ga., July 7, 1943. Grad., Emory U., JD, 1969. Bar: Ga. 1970. Pvt. practice Milledgeville, Ga., 1970-71; judge Recorder's Ct. of Milledgeville, 1971-79, Baldwin County Ct., 1973-79; judge, chief judge Superior Ct. of Ga., 1979-94; justice Supreme Ct. of Ga., Atlanta, 1994—; instr. bus. law Ga. COll., 1971-72. Recipient Disting. Svc. award Baldwin County Jaycees, 1972; named Outstanding Young Man of Baldwin County, 1972. Mem. State Bar Ga., Jud. Coun. Ga., Ocmulgee Jud. Cir. Bar Assn. Office: Supreme Ct Ga State Judicial Bldg Atlanta GA 30334

THOMPSON, JAMES RICHARD, human resources management consultant; b. Marion, Ohio, June 6, 1933; s. Wallace Wait and Mabel Ann (Maloney) T.; m. Ann Bacon Hallett, Sept. 7, 1973; children: J. Matthew, Mark A. BS in Indsl. Mgmt., U. Dayton, 1956. Pers. asst. wage and salary Gen. Tel. Co. Ohio, Marion, 1957-59, pers. asst. communications and devel., 1959-61; mgmt. devel. adminstr. GTE Svc. Corp., N.Y.C., 1961-62, pers. mgr., 1962-66, pers. adminstr., 1966-67, dir. staffing coordination, Stamford, Conn., 1971-75; dir. pers. GTE Communications, Inc., N.Y.C., 1967-71; dir. labor rels. and compensation Gen. Tel. Co. S.W., San Angelo, Tex., 1975-78, v.p. human resources, 1978-88; asst. v.p. employee rels. and orgn. devel. GTE Tel. Ops., Irving, Tex., 1989-91; asst. v.p. human resources Compañia Dominicana de Teléfonos, Santo Domingo, Dominican Republic, 1991-93; pres. J.R. Thompson & Assocs., Colleyville, Tex., 1993—; v.p. human resources Universal Svc. Telephone Corp., Irving, 1995—. Mem. Dallas Pers. Assn., Soc. for Human Resources Mgmt., Ft. Worth C. of C. Republican. Home and Office: 3001 Glen Dale Dr Colleyville TX 76034-4645

THOMPSON, JEFFERY ELDERS, health care administrator, minister; b. Bremen, Ga., Feb. 21, 1951; s. Jack Elders and Jewell Dean (Hutto) T.; m. Pamela Jennette Watson, Aug. 26, 1972; children: Rebecca Lynn, Joshua Elders. BA, Auburn U., 1973; MDiv, So. Bapt. Theol. Sem., 1977, DMin, 1991. Ordained to ministry So. Bapt. Conv., 1977. Youth min. Calder Bapt. Ch., Beaumont, Tex., 1977-79, First Bapt. Ch., Florence, S.C., 1979-82; chaplain Ga. Regional Hosp., Augusta, Ga., 1982-84; dir. pastoral care East Ala. Med. Ctr., Opelika, 1984—. Pres. Hospice of Lee County, Opelika, 1986-87, bd. dirs., 1987-91; bd. dirs. Widowed Person Svc., Opelika; mem. Leadership Lee County, 1991; scoutmaster Boy Scouts Am., 1991-94, Explorer advisor, 1995—, mem. dist. com., 1994—. Fellow Coll. Chaplains; mem. Am. Assn. Pastoral Counselors (assoc.), Lions Club (chaplain Opelika club 1985, Outstanding Lion 1985, 1st v.p. 1994, pres. 1995-96). Office: East Ala Med Ctr 2000 Pepperell Pky Opelika AL 36801-5452

THOMPSON, JOANNE GUIMOND, pediatric nurse, educator; b. North Attleboro, Mass., June 10, 1945; d. Joseph R. and Peggy Lillian (Vest) G.; m. William Clark Thompson, Sept. 15, 1962; children: William Clark, Jeffrey Mark, Theresa Dawn. ASN, Fla. Jr. Coll., Jacksonville, 1981; BSN, Fla. Atlantic U., Boca Raton, 1993; postgrad., PFS U., Boynton Beach, Fla., 1995. RN, Fla.; cert. pediatric and adolescent nurse; lic. life ins. and variable annuities agt. Staff nurse pediatrics St. Vincent's Med. Ctr., Jacksonville, Fla., 1981; charge nurse adult Humana Hosp. of Palm Beaches, West Palm Beach, Fla., 1981-82; charge nurse pediatrics Boca Raton (Fla.) Cmty. Hosp., 1982-86; charge nurse pediatrics Wellington Regional Med. Ctr., West Palm Beach, 1986-88, pediatric and adult nurse mgr., 1988-89; sch. nurse and health instr. Jewish Cmty. Day Sch., West Palm Beach, 1991-93; nursing supr. Palms West Hosp., Loxahatchee, Fla., 1991-93, charge nurse pediatrics, 1989-96; agent Primerica Fin Svcs, Atlanta, 1995—; life ins., variable annuities agt. Primerica Fin. Svcs.; vol. child immunizer HRS, West Palm Beach, 1992-96; mem. Am. Cancer Nurse Bd., West Palm Beach, 1988-89; mem. health educator adv. bd. Palm Beach County Sch. Bd., West Palm Beach, 1991-93; owner A Legal-Med. Nurse Cons., 1995. Author numerous ednl. leaflets; contbr. articles to profl. jours. Mem. ANA (polit. action com. 1993-95), Fla. Nurses Assn. (2d v.p. Area 9 1995—). Democrat. Roman Catholic.

THOMPSON, JOHN ALBERT, JR., dermatologist; b. Austin, Tex., June 5, 1942; s. J. Albert Sr. and Elizabeth (Brady) T. BA, Georgetown U., 1963; MD, Bowman Gray Sch. Medicine, 1967; Dermatology Fellowship, U. N.C., 1971-73. Diplomate Am. Bd. Dermatology. Resident in internal medicine N.C. Baptist Hosp., Winston-Salem, N.C., 1967-69; resident in dermatology N.C. Meml. Hosp., Chapel Hill, N.C., 1971-73; pvt. practice Charlotte, N.C., 1974—; clin. prof. dermatology Dept. Dermatology, U. N.C. Sch. Medicine, Chapel Hill, 1974—. Author profl. papers. Lt. comdr. USNR, 1969-71, Vietnam. Mem. Am. Acad. Dermatology (chmn. subcom. for sch. health edn. 1976-79, task force--nat. health ins.), Carolinas-Va. Dermatology Assn. (adv. bd. council rep. 1976-79), Charlotte Dermatology Assn., Mecklenburg County Med. Soc., N.C. Med. Soc., North Am. Clin. Dermatology Soc. Southern Med. Assn., Southeastern Consortium for Continuing Dermatol. Edn. (steering com. 1983—), South Cen. Dermatol. Congress (organizing com. 1982-86), Am. Soc. Dermatol. Surgery, Am. Dermatol. Soc. Allergy and Immunology. Democrat. Episcopalian. Home: 2633 Richardson Dr Apt 8A Charlotte NC 28211-3346 Office: 2310 Randolph Rd Charlotte NC 28207-1526

THOMPSON, JOHN KENTON, energy company executive, natural gas engineer; b. McAllen, Tex., Sept. 25, 1947; s. Forrest Arnold and Virginia Lee (Womeldorf) T.; m. Mary Elizabeth White, June 18, 1971; children: Kathleen Ann, John Allen. BS in Natural Gas Engring., Tex. A&M U., Kingsville, 1971. Registered profl. engr., Tex. Gas engr. Sun Oil Co., Oklahoma City, 1972-75; mem. design mgmt. team Sun's First Cryogenic Turboexpander Plant, 1974; dist. gas engr. Sun E&P Co., McAllen, 1975-78; OBO plant engr./gas mktg. rep. Sun Gas Co., Dallas, 1978-86; mgr. OBO plants Oryx Energy Co., Dallas, 1986-92; mgr. joint venture plants/pipelines Mitchell Energy & Devel. Corp., The Woodlands, Tex., 1992—; class instr. Petroleum Ext. Svc.- U. Tex., 1995-96; session coord. USN/USMC Radio Svc. Net, Oklahoma City, 1974-75; session chmn. regional mtg. Gas Processors Assn., 1975; corp. ops. rep. to Spl. Revenue Project Phase III Sun Gas Co. divsn. Sun Oil Co., Del., 1989-91. Sect. leader, tchr. Custer Rd. United Meth. Ch., Plano, Tex., 1990; mem. com. Boy Scouts Am., Plano, 1989; co-chmn. edn. and family life com. St. Mark United Meth. Ch., McAllen, 1976; mem. adminstrv. bd. Woodlands (Tex.) Meth. Ch., 1994-96; event co-supr. Tri-Regional Games-Tex. Spl. Olympics, 1995-96; group rep. to United Way Campaign, 1995. Recipient Order of Arrow and Life Rand award Rio Grande coun. Boy Scouts Am., 1965. Mem. Am. Inst. Chem. Engrs., Woodlands Kiwanis (dir. 1993-94, v.p. 94-95, pres.-elect 1995-96, chmn. Key Club/Kiwanis Spl. Fund Event 1995). Republican. Home: 10 Gate Hill Dr The Woodlands TX 77381 Office: 2002 Timberloch Pl The Woodlands TX 77380

THOMPSON, JOHN MORGAN, neurological surgeon, educator; b. Tampa, Fla., Feb. 14, 1924; s. Robert Hamilton and Nannie Lee (Clewis) T.; m. Dorothy Georgene Kinne, June 21,1947; children: Lauralee Ann, John Tilynn. BS, Tulane U., 1946; MD, Johns Hopkins U., 1948. Diplomate Am. Bd. Neurol. Surgery. NRC fellow in neurophysiology John Hopkins U., Balt., 1948, 49; intern U. Mich. Hosp., Ann Arbor, 1949-50, resident, 1950-55; faculty dept. neurosurgery U. Mich. Med. Sch., Ann Arbor, 1955-56; practice neurosurgery Bayfront Med. Ctr./St. Anthony's Hosp., St. Petersburg, Fla., 1956—, All Children's Hosp., St. Petersburg, 1956—; mem. faculty U. So. Fla. Med. Sch., Tampa, 1971—, clin. prof. neurol. surgery, 1986—; cons. neurol. surgery U.S. VA Hosp., Tampa, 1975—. Editor: History Congress of Neurological Surgeons 1951-1991, 1991. Served to lt. M.C., USNR, 1950-52, Korea. Recipient Borden Rsch. award Johns Hopkins U., 1948; Henry Dennison fellow, 1946-48, NRC fellow, 1948-59. Mem. AMA, Congress Neurol. Surgeons (pres. 1969-70), Am. Assn. Neurol. Surgeons, Fla. Neurosrug. Soc., Pinellas County Med. Soc. (v.p. 1988-89), Phi Beta Kappa, Sigma Xi, Alpha Omega Alpha. Home: 2000 Blossom Way S Saint Petersburg FL 33712-6014

THOMPSON, JONATHAN SIMS, army officer; b. Ft. Benning, Ga., Nov. 19, 1947; s. Donald Frederick and Gene Elizabeth (Pierce) T.; m. Dinetha Lynn Richards, Aug. 26, 1979; children: Tracy A., Terry A., Jonathan S. II, Tiffany A. BSME, Tex. A&M U., 1970, M Indsl. Engring., 1978; M Bus. Mgmt., Ctrl. Mich. U., 1980; diploma in program mgmt., Def. Sys. Mgmt. Coll., 1987. Registered profl. engr., Tex. Commd. 2d. lt. U.S Army, 1971, advanced through grades to col.; engr. platoon leader 27th Engr. Battalion U.S Army, Ft. Bragg, N.C., 1971-72, staff engr. 5th Spl. Forces Group, 1973-74; engr. instr. Spl. Forces Sch. U.S Army, Ft. Bragg, 1974-75; co. comdr. 2d Engr. Battalion U.S Army, Camp Castle, Korea, 1976-77; project dir. Engr. Strategic Studies Ctr. U.S Army, Rockville, Md., 1978-81; plans and ops. officer 317th Engr. Battalion U.S Army, Eschborn, Germany, 1982-84; engr. staff officer Office of Chief of Staff U.S Army, Washington, 1985-87, ops. rsch. analyst Office of Sec. of Army, 1987-88; battalion comdr. 2d Engr. Battalion U.S Army, Camp Castle, 1989-90; dep. chief of staff Corps. of Engrs. U.S Army, Washington, 1991-92, exec. dir. Office of Chief of Engrs., 1992-93, fellow Ctr. Stratetic/Internat. Studies U.S. Army War Coll., 1993-94; brigade comdr. 20th Engr. Brigade U.S Army, Ft. Bragg, N.C., 1994—; sr. fellow U.S. Dept. State, 1996—. Editor: Peacetime Defensive Preparations in Europe, 1981 (deMarche award 1985); author govt. study, article in field. Adult leader, asst. scoutmaster Boy Scouts Am., Dale City, Va., 1990-92, chmn. troop advancement com., Ft. Bragg, 1994—; coun. rep. Recreation Ctr. Bd., Dale City, 1985-89. Decorated Legion of Merit with 2 oak leaf clusters; fellow in govt. affairs Coun. for Excellence in Govt., 1991-92. Fellow Soc. Am. Mil. Engrs. (nat. bd. dirs. 1990-92, post pres. 1994—); mem. NSPE, Army Navy Club, Shriners (life mem., Noble), Masons (Companion, Sir Knight). Presbyterian. Home: 9710 Dansk Ct Fairfax VA 22032 Office: 4000 Arlington Blvd Arlington VA 22204

THOMPSON, JUDITH KAY, realist painter; b. Kansas City, Kans., May 28, 1940; d. Dean Holmquist and Ethel Elisabeth (Rowan) T. Student, William Jewell Coll., 1958-60; BFA, Kansas City Art Inst., 1965; MFA, U. Cin., 1967. Grad. asst. undergrad. life drawing U. Cin., 1965-66, grad. instr., 1966-67; instr. drawing Cin. Art Mus., 1966; instr. undergrad.drawing St. Cloud (Minn.) State U., 1969; instr. painting and drawing Benedicta Arts Ctr., St. Benedict's Coll., Minn., 1969; front receptionist Am. Multi Cinema, Kansas City, 1977-78; sec. Lovaca Gas Gathering, Houston, 1978-93; sr. sec. Internat. Union Tex. Petroleum, Houston, 1979-93. One-person shows include Theatre L'Homme Dieu, Alexandria, Minn., 1968, St. Cloud State U., Headley Hall Art Gallery, 1970, Kiehle Visual Arts Ctr. Gallery, 1974, Country Gallery, Parkville, Mo., 1978; exhibited in group shows at Hermann Fine Arts Ctr., Marietta, Ohio, 1978, Meredith Long Gallery, Houston, 1979, Mus. Fine Arts, Glassel Sch. Art, Houston, 1982, represented at Country Gallery, Parkeville, Mo., Meredith Long Gallery, Houston, others. Mem. Nat. Assn. Women Artists (Goldie Paley award 1976). Home: 9337 Westwood Village Dr Houston TX 77036-8752

THOMPSON, LARRY JAMES, school system administrator; b. Savannah, Ga., May 14, 1948; s. James Howell and Dorothy (Hendley) T. BA, Armstrong State Coll., 1970; MAT, Tulane U., 1974; EdD, U. Ga., 1986. Cert. tchr., instrnl. supr., adminstr., Ga. Tchr. social studies Chatham County Bd. Edn., Savannah, 1970-71, 75-87, adminstrv. coord. social studies, 1987—. With USNR, 1971-73. Mem. Nat. Coun. Social Studies, Ga. Coun. Social Studies, Profl. Assn. Ga. Educators, Ga. Hist. Soc., Ga. Leadership Assn. for Social Scis., Nat. Trust for Hist. Preservation, Phi Delta Kappa. Home: 18 E Deerwood Savannah GA 31410-3171 Office: Chatham Bd of Edn 208 Bull St Savannah GA 31401-3901

THOMPSON, LARRY M., career officer; b. Clearwater, FL, Oct. 27, 1960; s. Charles E. and Barbara A. (Rau) T.; m. Laura Sue Reynolds, May 4, 1985; children: Stephen, Ryan. BA in History, U. South Fla., 1985; MA in Russian History, U. N.C., 1994; student, U.S. Army, 1996—. Commd. U.S. Army, 1985; advanced through grades to maj., 1996; co. comdr. 101st airborne divsn. air assault U.S. Army, Ft. Campbell, Ky., 1989-92; sr. fellow George C. Marshall European Ctr. for Security Studies, Garmisch, Germany, 1995-96. Decorated Bronze Star medal; recipient UN Observer Cert. Armed Forces of the Russian Fedn., 1996. Republican. Baptist. Home: 1106 Sunset Ln Tampa FL 33549 Office: US Army Command and Gen Staff Coll Fort Leavenworth KS 66027

THOMPSON, LEROY, JR., radio engineer, military reserve officer; b. Tulsa, July 7, 1913; s. LeRoy and Mary (McMurrain) T.; B.S. in Elec. Engring., Ala. Poly Inst., 1936; m. Ola Dell Tedder, Dec. 31, 1941; 1 son, Bartow McMurrain. Commd. 2d lt. U.S. Army Res., 1935, advanced through grades to col., 1963; signal officer CCC, 1936-40; radio engr. Officer Hdqrs. 4th C A., 1941; with signal sect. Hdqrs. Western Def. command and 4th Army, San Francisco, 1942, comdg. officer 234th Signal Ops. Co., 1942; asst. chief, chief signal corps ROTC U. Calif., Berkeley, 1942-43; radio engring. officer O.C. SigO War Dept., Washington, 1943; radio engring officer Hdqrs. 3105th Signal Service Co. Hdqrs. CBI, New Delhi, 1944; signal officer Hdqrs. Northern Combat Area Command, Burma, 1944; signal officer Hdqrs. OSS Det 101, Burma, 1945; signal officer Hdqrs. OSS, China, 1945, radio engr., tech. liaison officer, Central Intelligence Group, CIA, 1945-50; chief radio br. Hdqrs. FEC, Tokyo, 1950-53, chief radio engring br. Signal C Plant Engring. Agy., 1953-55; radio cons. to asst. dir. def. research and engring. communications, 1960-62; ret., 1973; pvt. research and devel. on communication and related problems, 1963—; owner Thompson Research Exptl. Devel. Lab. Lic. profl. radio engr., Ga. Mem. IEEE (life sr.), NRA, Vet. Wireless Operators Assn., Am. Radio Relay League, Mil. Order World Wars, Res. Officers Assn., Am. Motorcycle Assn., Nat. Wildlife Fedn. Baptist. Home: 6450 Overlook Dr Alexandria VA 22312-1327

THOMPSON, LINDA RUTH, psychology educator, university administrator; b. Wichita, Kans., Mar. 7, 1949; d. Earl Edmond and Ada Jean (Hatfield) Minor; m. Wesley Travis Thompson, Aug. 29, 1968; 1 child, Travis John. BA in Music, Harding Coll., 1972; MEd in Counselor Edn., U. Ark., 1976; EdD in Higher Edn., Memphis State U., 1993. Adj. instr. psychology/sociology Mich. Christian Coll., Rochester, 1977-78; counselor La. State U., Eunice, 1981-83, N.E. La. U., Monroe, 1983-85; dir. program for acad. success Harding U., Searcy, Ark., 1986-87, instr. psychology, 1986-88, dir. learning assistance programs, 1987-90, asst. prof., dir. student support svcs., 1990—; counselor, cons. Acad. Enhancement for Gifted and Talented in Summer programs Harding U., 1986—, mem. various coms., sponsor Dactylology Club, 1987—; field reader Upward Bound proposals U.S. Dept. Edn., 1992, 95; participant many ednl. seminars, insts. and workshops, 1986—; presenter profl. confs. Program chairperson Operation Stormwater, Pine Bluff, Ark., 1979-80; vol. MADD DAsh, Searcy, 1992; mem. Associated Women for Harding, 1986—, pres., 1989-90; active Coll. Ch. of Christ, tchr. kindergarten, 1986-89, interpreter for deaf, 1987—. Recipient Cert. of Merit, Am. Coll. Testing/Nat. Acad. Advising Assn. Recognition, 1988; named one of Outstanding Young Women of Am., 1982. Mem. Nat. Assn. for Devel. Edn. (co-chair nat. conf. 1996, mem. awards com. 1987-88, mem. publs. com. 1991-92), Ark. Assn. for Devel. Edn. (sec. 1987-88, pres.-elect 1989-91, pres. 1991-93, chair conf. 1990-91, editor newsletter 1988-90). Republican. Home: 1 Harding Dr Searcy AR 72143-5704 Office: Harding Univ Student Support Svcs PO Box 2235 Searcy AR 72149-2235

THOMPSON, MARCIA SLONE, choral director, educator; b. Ary, Ky., June 30, 1959; d. Ray and Wevena (Hall) Slone; m. Randall C. Thompson, Sept. 22, 1979; children: Tiffany, Ashley, Brittany, Alicia, Jessica, Matthew. B in Music Edn., Pikeville Coll., 1981; M in Secondary Edn., Morehead State U., 1985. Cert. Rank I supervision, music edn. tchr. with endorsement, grades K-12. Guitarist Slone Family Band, 1970-77; pvt. practice Hindman, Ky., 1977-93; band, choral dir. Pike County Bd. Edn., Pikeville, Ky., 1981-82, Floyd County Bd. Edn., Eastern, Ky., 1982-87; choral dir. Knott County Bd. Edn., Hindman, 1987—, Knott County Central High, Hindman, Ky, 1987—; piano instr. guitar instr., Upward Bound program Pikeville Coll., Hindman, 1977. Albums include Appalachian Bluegrass, 1972, Ramblin' Round with Slone Family, 1977; appeared on the Grand Ole Opry, 1976. Band conductor jr. high divsn. Pike County All-County Festival, Pikeville, 1981; music chair Red White Blue Festival, Martin, Ky., 1982; music judge Floyd County All-County Band, Prestonsburg, Ky., 1982-87; band dir. Ky. Derby Festival Parade, Louisville, 1985; piano accompanist choir 1st Bapt. Ch., Hindman, 1990-91, nursery asst., 1990-93, dir. youth choir, 1992, choral dir. music makers (children's music), 1994, Bapt. young women's hospitality officer, 1995, mem. sch. com.; performer Senator Benny Bailey Salute, Prestonsburg, 1991, Gingerbread Festival, Hindman, 1992-95; active Bapt. Young Women, 1993-95; cofounder Knott County Fine Arts Day Celebration, 1992—, hospitality officer Hindman Baptist Ch. Young Women's Group, 1995. Mem. Nat. Educators Assn., Am. Choral Dirs. Assn., Ky. Educators Assn., Ky. Music Educators. Democrat. Home: PO Box 15 Hindman KY 41822-0015 Office: Knott County Ctrl High Sch Hindman KY 41822

THOMPSON, MARGUERITE MYRTLE GRAMING (MRS. RALPH B. THOMPSON), librarian; b. Orangeburg, S.C., Apr. 23, 1912; d. Thomas Laurie and Rosa Lee (Stroman) Graming; m. Ralph B. Thompson, Sept. 17, 1949 (dec. Oct. 1960). BA in English cum laude, U. S.C., 1932, postgrad., 1937; BLS, Emory U., 1943. Tchr. English pub. high schs., S.C., 1932-43; libr. Rockingham (N.C.) High Sch., 1943-45, Randolph County (N.C.) Libr., Asheboro, 1945-48, Colleton County (S.C.) Libr., Walterboro, 1948-61; dir. Florence (S.C.) County Libr., 1961-78. Sec. com. community facilities, svcs. and instns. Florence County Resources Devel. Com., 1964-67; vice chmn. Florence County Coun. on Aging, 1968-70, exec. bd. 1968-82, bd. treas., 1973-75, bd. sec., 1976-77, bd. v.p., 1979; mem. Florence County Bicentennial Planning Com., 1975-76; mem. rels. and allocations com. United Way, 1979-80. Named Boss of Yr. Nat. Secs. Assn., 1971. Mem. ALA (coun. 1964-72), Southeastern Libr. Assn., S.C. Libr. Assn. (pres. 1960, chmn. assn. handbook revision com. 1967-69, 80, sect. co-chmn. com. standards for S.C. pub. libr. 1966-75, fed. rels. coord. 1972-73, planning com. 1976-78), Greater Florence C. of C. (women's div. chmn. 1969-70, bd. dirs. 1975-77), S.E. Regional Conf. Women in C. of C. (bd. dir. 1970-71), Florence Bus. and Profl. Women's Club (2d v.p. 1975-76, Career Woman of Yr. 1974, parliamentarian 1980-81, chmn. scholarship com. 1981-82), Delta Kappa Gamma (county chpt. charter pres. 1963-65, treas. 1966-70, chmn. com. on expansion 1977-80, 82-84, state chpt. chmn. state scholarship com. 1967-73, state 2d v.p. 1971-73, state 1st v.p. 1973-75, state pres. 1975-77, chmn. policy manual 1977-81, chmn. adv. coun. 1978-85, chmn. fin. com. 1981-83, parliamentarian 1987-91, adminstrv. bd. 1987—, chmn. nominations com. 1989-91, dir. S.E. Region 1978-80, coord. S.E. Regional Golden Anniversary Conf. 1979, internat. scholarship com. 1970-74, internat. exec. bd. 1975-77, 78-80, internat. adminstrv. bd. 1978-80, internat. constn. com. 1980-82, internat. achievement award com., 1986-88), Florence Literary Club (sec. 1964-66, 79-82, pres. 1970-72). Methodist (chmn. ch. libr. com. 1965-71, chmn. com. ch. history, 1968-69, sec. adminstrv. bd. 1979-82). Home: 1000 Live Oaks Dr SW # 8B Orangeburg SC 29115-9600

THOMPSON, MARY ANN, library assistant, publisher; b. Knoxville, Tenn., Mar. 16, 1937; d. Kenneth Calvin and Anna Margaret (Wade) Morris; m. John Arthur Thompson, July 9, 1960; children: Sean David, Kelly Morris Thompson Ringham. BA, U. Tenn., 1959. Libr. asst. Oak Ridge (Tenn.) Nat. Lab., Ctrl. Rsch. Libr., 1959-66, Fed. Res. Bank, Mpls. Libr., 1967, Richland County Pub. Libr., Columbia, S.C., 1978-81; libr. asst. II McDermott Libr., U. Tex. at Dallas, Richardson, 1984—. Author: Samuel Thompson of McMinn County, Tenn., 1993; co-author: Atchley Family History, 1965; editor (periodical) Collin County Geneal. Soc. newsletter, 1989—. Mem. com. mcpl. facilities com. Libr. Sub-com., Plano, Tex., 1990; vol. Vols. in Plano City Govt., 1995—. Mem. Nat. Soc. DAR, Daus. of Union Vets. of Civil War, 1861-1865. Republican. Episcopalian. Home: 2721 Knollwood Ct Plano TX 75075

THOMPSON, MATHEW JOHN, mechanical engineer; b. Elizabeth City County, Va., Sept. 10, 1922; s. Mathew John and Ella Mae (Kea) T.; m. Glenna Rae Howser, May 31, 1952; children: Mark Webster, Teresa Hope. BS in Mech. Engring., Va. Poly. and State U., 1950. Founder, chmn. Mathew J. Thompson III Cons. Engrs., Inc., Newport News, Va., 1954—. Bd. dirs., pres. YMCA, Newport News, 1984-93, Peninsula Pastoral Counseling Ctr., Newport News, 1995. Named Engr. of Yr., Engrs. Joint Coun. Va. Peninsula, 1987, Va. Soc. Profl. Engrs., 1987. Mem. Cons. Engrs. Coun. Va. (pres. 1974-75), Am. Coun. Cons. Engrs. Home: 419 Normandy Ln Newport News VA 23606 Office: 9308 Warwick Blvd Newport News VA 23601

THOMPSON, MICHAEL J., environmentalist; b. Plaquemine, La., Aug. 14, 1950; s. Pershing Joseph Thompson and Josephine (Stassi) Walker; m. Gail Theresa Hebert, Aug. 7, 1970 (div. Feb. 1988); children: Jesse, Letitia. Grad. high sch. Sr. environ. specialist The Geon Co., Louisville, 1970—. Office: The Geon Company PO Box 37240 Louisville KY 40233

THOMPSON, PATRICIA ANN, nursing assistant, writer; b. New Orleans, Oct. 14, 1951; d. Dave and Ethel (Bennett) Jackson; m. Edward Thompson, Aug. 21, 1971; children: Cleveland, Nicole, Crystal Thompson. Grad. high sch., New Orleans, 1970. Cert. nurse aide. Cook Airliner Restaurant, Gonzales, La., 1972-74; nurse aide/student Tuiro Infirmary Hosp., New Orleans, 1974; nurse aide East Ascension Gen. Hosp., Gonzales, 1974-79, Gillis Long Ctr. Hosp., Carville, La., 1979—. Author: Treasured Poems of America 93 Winter, 1993, Treasured Poems of America Summer, 1993, Wind in Night Sky, 1993 (editor's choice). Sgt.-at-arms Mt. Pilgrim Bapt. Ch., 1994. Mem. Internat. Soc. Poets (cert. 1993-94). Democrat. Home: PO Box 423 Geismar LA 70734-0423

THOMPSON, PAUL MICHAEL, lawyer; b. Dubuque, Iowa, Aug. 30, 1935; s. Frank W. and Genevieve (Cassutt) T.; m. Mary Jacqueline McManus, Jan. 30, 1960; children—Anne, Tricia, Paul, Tim, Jim. B.A. magna cum laude, Loras Coll., 1957; LL.B., Georgetown U., 1959. Bar: Iowa 1959, D.C. 1959, Va. 1966. Atty. appellate ct. br. NLRB, Washington, 1962-66; assoc. Hunton & Williams, Richmond, Va., 1966-71, ptnr., 1971—; adj. prof. The T.C. Williams Sch. Law, U. Richmond. Served with JAGC, USAF, 1960-62. Mem. ABA, Va. State Bar, Va. Bar Assn., Internat. Bar Assn. Roman Catholic. Club: Downtown (Richmond). Office: Hunton & Williams 951 E Byrd St Riverfront Pla E Tower Richmond VA 23219-4074

THOMPSON, RALPH GORDON, federal judge; b. Oklahoma City, Dec. 15, 1934; s. Lee Bennett and Elaine (Bizzell) T.; m. Barbara Irene Hencke, Sept. 5, 1964; children: Lisa, Elaine, Maria. BBA, U. Okla., 1956, JD, 1961. Bar: Okla. 1961. Ptnr. Thompson, Thompson, Harbour & Selph (and predecessors), Oklahoma City, 1961-75; judge U.S. Dist. Ct. for Western Dist. Okla., Oklahoma City, 1975—; chief judge U.S. Dist. Ct. (we. dist.) Okla., 1986-93; mem. Okla. Ho. of Reps., 1966-70, asst. minority floor leader, 1969-70; spl. justice Supreme Ct. Okla., 1970-71; tchr. Harvard Law Sch. Trial Advocacy Workshop, 1981—; apptd. by chief justice of U.S. to U.S. Fgn. Intelligence Surveillance Ct., 1990-97. Rep. nominee for lt. gov., Okla., 1970; chmn. bd. ARC, Oklahoma City, 1970-72; chmn., pres. Okla. Young Lawyers Conf., 1965; mem. bd. visitors U. Okla., 1975-78; pres. bd. dirs. St. John's Episcopal Sch., Oklahoma City. Lt. USAF, 1957-60, col. Res., ret. Decorated Legion of Merit; named Oklahoma City's Outstanding Young Man, Oklahoma City Jaycees, 1967, Outstanding Fed. Trial Judge, Okla Trial Lawyers Assn., 1980; recipient Regents Alumni award U. Okla., 1990, Disting. Svc. award, 1993; inducted Okla. Hall of Fame, 1995. Fellow Am. Bar Found.; mem. ABA, Fed. Bar Assn., Okla. Bar Assn. (chmn. sect. internat. law and gen. practice 1974-75), Oklahoma County Bar Assn. (Jud. Svc. award 1988), Jud. Conf. U.S. (com. on ct. adminstrn. 1981-89, com. on fed.-state jurisdiction 1988-91), U.S. Dist. Judges Assn. 105h Cir. (pres. 1992-94), Rotary (hon.), Order of Coif, Am. Inns of Ct. (pres. XXIII 1995-96), Phi Beta Kappa (pres. chpt. 1985-86, Phi Beta Kappa of Yr. 1991), Beta Theta Pi, Phi Alpha Delta. Episcopalian. Office: US Dist Ct 200 NW 4th St Oklahoma City OK 73102-3003

THOMPSON, RAYMOND EDWARD, lawyer; b. Miami, Fla., July 26, 1936; s. Roy Lavern and Caroline Magdaline (Dilg) T.; 1 child, Raymond Edward Jr. BBA, U. Miami, 1959; JD, Stetson U., 1962. Bar: Fla. 1962, U.S. Dist. Ct. (so. dist.) Fla. 1962, U.S. Supreme Ct. 1971. Assoc. Hunter and Paoli, Hollywood, Fla., 1962-63, Paoli and Paoli, Hollywood, 1963-67; pvt. practice Hollywood, 1967-81, Ocala, Fla., 1981-86; with Thompson & Burton, Ocala, 1981-86; gen. counsel South Broward Park Dist., Hollywood, 1968-76, Children's Home Soc., Ft. Lauderdale, Fla., 1970-75, Assn. for Retarded Citizens-Marion, Ocala, 1985-89. Pres., gen. counsel Assn. for Retarded Citizens-Marion, Ocala, 1985-89; gen. counsel South Broward Park Dist., Hollywood, 1968-76, Children's Home Soc., Ft. Lauderdale, 1970-75; pres. Children's Home Soc., Ft. Lauderdale, 1975; bd. dirs. Marion County Fair, Inc.,1989-90. Mem. ABA, Fla. Bar Assn., Marion County Bar Assn., Broward Amateur Radio Club (pres. 1971-72), Silver Springs Radio Club (bd. dirs. 1982-84, Outstanding Profl. Contbn. award 1982), Hollywood Jaycees (treas. 1971-72, Jaycee of the Yr. 1971-72, Kiwanis (sec. 1963-81). Office: 320 NW 3rd Ave Ocala FL 34475-8817

THOMPSON, RICHARD ARLEN, environmental scientist; b. El Dorado, Kans., June 25, 1934; s. George Hugh and Marion Katherine (Milbourn) T.; m. Sally Sue Thomason, Aug. 28, 1954; children: Mark Alan, Teri Lynn Thompson Lovell. BS, Okla. State U., 1963, MS, 1966. Enlisted individual USAF, 1956-63, advanced through grades to col., 1963-88; asst. project mgr. Kerr-McGee Corp., Oklahoma City, 1988-89, project mgr., 1989-95, environ. remediation mgr., 1995—. Mem. Air Force Assn., Soc. Am. Mil. Engrs. Home: 12429 Jersey Rd Midwest City OK 73130 Office: Kerr-McGee Chem Corp 123 Robert S Kerr Ave Oklahoma City OK 73102

THOMPSON, RICHARD VICTOR, JR., service executive; b. Ft. Lauderdale, Fl., Nov. 16, 1951; s. Richard Victor Thompson Sr. and Mary Frances (Barnett) Lariviere; m. Dana Luann Pavone, Mar. 25, 1983 (div. Dec. 1988); stepfather, Lionel Lariviere. Student, Wayne County Community Coll., 1977, Bates Flight Acad., Willow Run, Mich., 1978-80, Delta, Miami, Fl., 1987, Morris Sch. Real Estate, Ft. Pierce, Fl., 1989. Pres. Thompson Comml. Sweeping, Ft. Lauderdale, 1983-85, Travel With Us Inc. doing bus. as Around The World Corp., Ft. Lauderdale, 1985-88; mgr. Renown Aviation, Ft. Lauderdale, 1989-90; asst. mgr. Detroit Connection, 1990; pres. Full Blast Pressure Cleaning, Ft. Lauderdale, 1991-92; exec. Nu-Skin Internat., Ft. Lauderdale, 1992—. Com. organizer Save the Manatees, Ft. Lauderdale, 1980-87, Laud Rezoning Isles Com., Ft. Lauderdale, 1985, Gentle Giants & Manatees, Ft. Pierce, 1989; mem. advice coun. Manatee Info. Ft. Pierce and Ft. Lauderdale, 1989; pres. Ft. Pierce Manatee Com. (Gentle Giants). Mem. Am. Power Boat Assn., Miami. Democrat. Home and Office: 2637 Sugarloaf Ln Fort Lauderdale FL 33312-4635

THOMPSON, ROBERT JAYE, minister; b. Coffeyville, Kans., Nov. 4, 1951; s. Julis Levi and Verna Belle (Hardrick) T.; m. Carolyn Robinson, Aug. 23, 1971; children: Montie Shannon, Monica Shea, Marquis Shane, Marissa Seana, Terry Dwight, Mycal Shanton. AA in History, Coffeyville Community Jr. Coll, 1971; BA in History, Pittsburg (Kans.) State U., 1973; MDiv cum laude, Memphis Theol. Sem., 1991. Ordained to ministry Bapt. Ch., 1983. Pastor Sweet Home Bapt. Ch., Dardanelle, Ark., 1983-88; assoc. pastor Springdale Bapt. Ch., Memphis, 1988-92; instr. Tenn. Sch. of Religion, Memphis, 1989-92; asst. dean Regular Ark. Bapt. Home and Fgn. Mission Conv., 1994—; chaplain intern Federal Correctional Institution, Memphis, 1990; instr. Nat. Bapt. Congress of Christian Edn., 1994—, Greenfield Presbyn. Ch., Waterford, Miss., 1990-92, New Prospect Bapt. Ch., Russellville, Ark., 1992—; treas. Antioch Dist. Assn., Ft. Smith, Ark., 1987-88, youth min., 1987-89; sec. Ft. Smith Interdenominational Assn., 1984-88; sgt. Guardsmark, Inc., Memphis, 1989-92; program coord. Russellville Area Ministerial Assn., 1994; bd. dirs. Help Network; mem. steering com. Nat. Day of Prayer, Russellville, 1994-95. Dir. gen. Antioch Congress of Christian Edn., Ft. Smith, Ark., 1994—; treas. Antioch Dist. Assn., Ft. Smith, 1995—; pres.-elect Russellville Area Ministerial Assn., 1995, pres., 1996; chmn. Nat. Day of Prayer Russellville, 1995-96; block worker Am. Heart Assn., Memphis, 1991; student body pres. Memphis Theol. Sem., 1990-91; bd. dirs. Shelter of Sunshine, Russellville, 1996—; mem. Bd. of Adjustment, Russellville, 1996—; pres. Race Rels. Task Force, Russellville, 1995—. Recipient Benjamin E. Mays fellowship Fund for Theol. Edn., N.Y.C., 1990-91, Disting. Mil. Grad. Pittsburg State U., 1973. Mem. Memphis Bapt. Ministers Assn., Russellville Area Ministerial Assn. (pres. 1996), Downtown Rotary Club. Democrat. Home: 226 S Independence Ave Russellville AR 72801-4960

THOMPSON, STEVEN TERRY, city manager; b. Delhi, N.Y., May 2, 1955; s. Broadus Henry and Martha Jane Shirley (Pitts) T.; m. CHristine Salcedo Peralta, June 2, 1984; children: Darryl Salcedo, Ryan Christine. BA in Polit. Sci., Coll. of Charleston, 1977; MPA, U. S.C., 1980. Rsch. analyst, auditor State of S.C., Columbia, 1978-80; dir. of adminstrn. County of Richland, Columbia, 1980-82; asst. fin. dir. City of Aiken, S.C., 1982-83, asst. city mgr., 1983-91, city mgr., 1991—. Chmn. United Way Aiken County, 1989, 2d vice chmn., 1988, campaign chmn., 1987, 3d vice chmn., 1987, bd. dirs. 1986-89, chmn. govtl. divsn., 1983, 86; bd. dirs. Downtown Aiken Devel. Corp. Named one of Outstanding Young Men Am., 1989. Mem. Internat. City Mgmt. Assn., Greater Aiken C. of C. (v.p. for econ. devel. 1984), Kiwanis (pres. Aiken chpt. 1990-91, 1st v.p. 1989-90, 2d v.p. 1988-89, bd. dirs. 1986-87). Home: 126 Surrey Cir Aiken SC 29801-5138 Office: City of Aiken 214 Park Ave SW Aiken SC 29801-2404

THOMPSON, SUSAN ROBERTA, magazine publishing executive; b. Englewood, N.J., Mar. 14, 1949; d. Herbert Gustav and Sarah Jeanette (Black) Goeckel; m. Tommy Thompson, May 1, 1971; children: Jordan, Mark. BA in journalism, Ga. State U., 1979. Charter airline trip coord. Atlanta Skylarks, 1971-75; advt. exec. McDonald & Little Adv., Atlanta, 1980-84, Advantage Mktg., Atlanta, 1984-86; bus. owner, mag. pub. New South Pub., Atlanta, 1986—. Editor: Know Atlanta mag., 1989, Net News mag., 1992. Publicity mem. Gubernatorial campaign, Atlanta, 1989; publicity com. Decorator's Showhouse Atlanta Symphony Jr. Com., Atlanta, 1986-92. Mem. Ga. Mag. Assn. (pres. 1994-95), Metro Atlanta Relocation Coun. (pres. 1992), Atlanta C. of C., Greater Atlanta Home Builders Assn. (sales and mktg. coun., bd. dirs. 1988-93), Cob C. of C. Republican. Methodist. Home: 5071 Hampton Lake Dr Marietta GA 30068-4314 Office: New South Pub 7840 Roswell Rd Ste 328 Atlanta GA 30350-4889

THOMPSON, TIMOTHY CHARLES, research scientist; b. Indpls., Apr. 9, 1951; s. Charles Avery and Gladys Kathryn T.; m. Sang Hee Park, Feb. 9, 1988; 1 child, Benjamin Paul. AB, Ind. U., 1974; PhD, Colo. U., 1985; postdoctoral fellow, Imperial Cancer Rsch. Fund, London, 1988. Asst. prof. Dept. of Urology and Cell Biology Baylor Coll. of Medicine, Houston, 1988-92, dir. rsch. Scott Dept. of Urology, 1992—, assoc. prof. Dept. of Urology, Cell Biology and Radiology, 1992—; cons. reviewer for acad. jours. Cancer Rsch., 1991—; mem. pathology B study sect. NIH, Bethesda, Md., 1993—; cons. Oncor, Inc., Gaithersburg, Md., 1994—, UroCor, Inc., Oklahoma City, 1995—. Contbr. numerous articles to profl. jours. and chpts. to books. Adult class Sun. sch. tchr. Rice Temple Bapt. Ch., Houston, 1992—. Grantee NIH, 1989—. Mem. Soc. of Basic Urological Rsch. (program com. 1989—), CaP CURE (bd. sci. dir. 1993—), Metastasis Rsch. Soc., Keystone Symposia (co-organizer 1996 Symposium). Democrat. Office: Baylor Coll of Medicine One Baylor Plz Houston TX 77030

THOMPSON, VERDINE MAE, financial planner, tax preparer; b. Kilgore, Tex., Dec. 3, 1941; d. John Wesley and Verdine Mae (Brookes) Ford; m. James William Thompson, Jan. 25, 1963; 1 child, Susan Marie. Student, So. Meth. U., 1960-62; BA, Stephen F. Austin State U., 1964; MA, U. Tenn., 1975; grad. in credit union fin. counseling, Fla. Credit Union League, Tallahassee, 1987. CFP, Coll. for Fin. Planning, 1990. Tchr. Channelview (Tex.) Ind. Sch. Dist., 1968-69, Goose Creek Consol. Sch. Dist., Baytown, Tex., 1969-71, McMinn County Sch. Dist., Athens, Tenn., 1972-77; tax preparer H&R Block, Sweetwater, Tenn., 1978-86; mgr. APCO Employees Credit Union, Athens, 1978-92; fin. and tax planner, preparer Athens, 1986-91; fin. planner, tax preparer Verdine's Fin. Planning and Tax Svc., 1991—; developing support groups in East Tenn. for Tenn. Mental Health Consumers Assn., 1992-94. Organizer, leader Pendulum Depression Support Group, Athens, 1987-96; pres. bd. dirs. Dakoda Pl., a consumer-run drop-in ctr. for adults with mental illness, 1994-96; sch. sec. Trinity United Meth. Ch., Athens, 1985—, mem. handbell choir, 1983-92; mem. United Meth. Women, 1963—, mem. Ch. Stewardship Com., 1995—; mem., pres., treas. Contact Teleministries Bd., McMinn, Tenn., 1975-81; mem. Region III and Tenn. State Mental Health Planning Commns., 1994—; bd. dirs. Tenn. Mental Health Consumers Assn., 1994-96; mem. Consumer Adv. Bd. Tenn. State Office of Consumer Affairs, 1994—. Mem. IBCFP, ICFP, IAFP. Home and Office: 1110 Sioux St Athens TN 37303-3335

THOMPSON, VICTOR HAROLD, English language educator; b. Orange, N.J., Oct. 27, 1941; s. Harold Alonzo and Edith (Sivertsen) T.; m. Mary Macdonald, Aug. 26, 1967 (div. Jan. 1980); children: Inge Marie, Victor Alexander; m. Sharon Byrd, Sept. 1980. BA, Middlebury Coll., Vt., 1963; MA, Rutgers U., 1966, PhD, 1972. Instr. English U. Cin., 1966-70; asst. prof. English Thomas Nelson C.C., Hampton, Va., 1970-73, prof. English, 1973—, head, dept. English, 1988-92, divsn. chmn., 1993-94; coll. rep. Chancellor's Faculty Adv. Com., Richmond, Va., 1994—; chmn. planning com. English Discipline Conf. in Va. C.C. System, 1995-96; pres. Faculty Senate, 1994-95. Author: (book) Eudora Welty: A Reference Guide, 1976; contbr. articles to profl. jours. Trumpet player York River Band, Newport News, Va., 1995—, Peninsula Band, Newport News, 1995—; pres. Hilton Village Civic Club, Newport News, 1973-74; singer St. Paul's Luth. Ch., Hampton, Va., 1995—. Mem. Southeastern Conf. of English in the 2-Yr. Coll. Home: 18 Fort Worth St Hampton VA 23669-1108 Office: Thomas Nelson Comm Coll PO Box 9407 Hampton VA 23670

THOMPSON, WAYNE WRAY, historian; b. Wichita, Jan. 30, 1945; s. Clarence William and Elaine Maxine (Wray) T. m. Lillian Evelyn Hurlburt, June 28, 1969. BA, Union Coll., Schenectady, 1967; student, U. St. Andrews, Scotland, 1965-66; PhD, U. Calif., San Diego, 1975. Historian USAF, 1975—, Checkmate Air Campaign Planning Group, 1990-91; sr. hist. advisor Gulf War Air Power Survey, 1991-93. Contbr. Congress Investigates (Arthur M. Schlesinger Jr. and Roger Bruns, editors), 1975; editor Air Leadership, 1986; contbr. War in the Pacific (Bernard Nalty, editor), 1991. Served with AUS, 1971-72. Mem. Am. Hist. Assn., Orgn. Am. Historians, Air Force Hist. Found., Air Force Assn., Soc. Historians Am. Fgn. Rels., Soc. for Mil. History, U.S. Commn. on Mil. History, Inter-Univ. Seminar on Armed Forces, Assn. Asian Studies, Asia Soc., World History Assn., Phi Beta Kappa. Home: 9203 Saint Marks Pl Fairfax VA 22031-3045 Office: Hdqrs USAF History Washington DC 20332

THOMPSON, WILLIAM CARRINGTON, JR., federal agency administrator; b. Richmond, Va., Apr. 25, 1942; s. William Carrington and Margaret Sue (Colbert) T.; m. Marilyn Kaye Rush, July 31, 1969 (div. 1981); children: Tracy Robyn, William Carrington III; m. Diane Mavis Acuff, Mar. 25, 1983. BA in History, Va. Mil. Inst., 1964; JD, U. Va., 1967; MS in Mgmt., U. Ark., 1974. Bar: Va. Commd. 2d lt. USAF, 1967, advanced through grades to col., 1985; ret., 1994; adminstrv. law judge Social Security Adminstrn., Columbia, S.C., 1994—; dir., pres. Myrtle Beach (S.C.) AFB Fed. Credit Union, 1975-77; mem. supervisory com. Travis AFB (Calif.) Fed. Credit Union, 1978-81. Editor: A Comparative Analysis of Military Practice and Procedure and the ABA Standards of Criminal Practice and Procedure, 1978. Decorated Legion of Merit, Bronze Star. Office: SSA Office Hearings Appeals # 200 1927 Thurmond Mall Blvd Columbia SC 29201

THOMPSON, WILLIAM DENNISON, JR., aeronautical consultant; b. Chgo., Jan. 26, 1920; s. William Dennison and Bertha Helen (Lachnit) T.; m. Jeanne Ann Burkholder, Dec. 26, 1942; children: William III, Burk Blair, Constance Gail. BA in Aero. Engring., Purdue U., 1947. Draftsman/engr. Curtis-Wright Airplane Co., St. Louis, 1940-41; army air corps flight instr. Hawthorne Flying Svc., Orangeburg, S.C., 1942-45; flight instr. Purdue Aeronautics Corp., West Lafayette, Ind., 1946-47; engring. test pilot Cessna Aircraft Co., Wichita, Kans., 1947-53, mgr. flight test and aerodynamics, 1953-74; tech. cons. SIAI Marchetti, Sesto Calende, Italy, 1975-77; owner Thompson Aeronautical Cons., Sunriver, Oreg., 1978—; pres. Precise Flight, Inc., Bend, Oreg., 1980-83; owner Thompson Aero Products, Sunriver, 1984—; cons. for aerodynamics and aeronautics coms. NASA, 1969-73. Author: Cessna Wings for the World-The Single-Engine Development Story, 1991, Cessna Kings for the World--Development of the 300 Series Twins and Miscellaneous Prototypes, 1995; editor (booklets) Cessna Owners Manuals, 1953-74; co-inventor, patentee integrated spoiler/throttle assembly, 1984. Loaned exec. United Fund, Wichita, 1965; designated engring. rep., flight test pilot, flight analyst FAA, Seattle, Washington, 1980-93, Ft. Worth, 1994—. Fellow Soc. Exptl. Test Pilots (1st chmn. Wichita sect. 1962-63); mem. Soc. Automotive Engrs. (chmn. Wichita sect. 1970-71), Exptl. Aircraft Assn. Internat., Internat. 195 Club, Cardinal Club. Republican. Methodist. Home and Office: 2 Bridgeport Ln Bella Vista AR 72714-5309

THOMPSON, WILLIAM WEST, allergist, immunologist, pediatrician; b. Hallsboro, N.C., Apr. 6, 1921. MD, Duke U., 1947. Diplomate Am. Bd. Allergy and Immunology, Am. Bd. Pediatrics. Intern Mountainside Hosp., Montclair, 1947-48; resident in pediatrics Duke Hosp., Durham, N.C., 1948-49, Jefferson Davis Hosp., Houston, 1949-50; fellow in allergy Ark. Allergy Clinic, Little Rock, 1956-57; staff mem. Humana Hosp., Fort Walton Beach, Fla.; pvt. practice. Mem. AMA, Am. Acad. Allergy and Immunology, Am. Acad. Pediatrics, Am. Coll. Allergy and Immunology. Office: 906A Mar Walt Dr Fort Walton Beach FL 32547-6609

THOMPSON, WINFRED LEE, university president, lawyer; b. Little Rock, July 28, 1945; s. Vester Lee and Willow Mae (Mills) T.; m. Carmen Angeles Tiongson; children: Emily, Michael. BA, U. Ark., 1967; MA, U. Chgo., 1970, PhD, 1987; JD, George Washington U., 1978. Congl. aide U.S. Ho. of Reps., Washington, 1973-77; exec. asst. to asst. sec. labor U.S. Dept. Labor, Washington, 1977-78; atty. Hatfield and Thompson, Searcy, Ark., 1978-81; dir. devel. Ark. State U., Jonesboro, 1981-82, v.p. for planning and devel., 1982-84; v.p. for fin. and adminstrn. U. Ark. System, Fayetteville, 1984-85; vice chancellor for fin. and adminstrn. U. Ark, Fayetteville, 1985-87; pres. U. Cen. Ark., Conway, 1988—; bd. dirs. Ark. Sci. and Tech. Authority, Little Rock, 1984-89. Bd. dirs. Ark. Symphony Orch., 1991-94. 2d lt. USAR. Woodrow Wilson fellow U. Chgo., 1969-70. Mem. Phi Beta Kappa. Home: 140 Donaghey Ave Conway AR 72032-6252 Office: U Ctrl Ark Office of the President 201 Donaghey Ave Conway AR 72035

THOMPSON-STAFFORD, BETTY, secretary; b. Greene County, Mo., Aug. 20, 1925; d. William Joseph and Darthula Emeline (Gray) Thompson; m. Thomas Basil Stafford, Oct. 5, 1946; 1 child, Sondra Lynn Stafford. Student, Draughon's Coll., 1943-44, S.W. Mo. State U., 1944-46. Stenographer Bemis Bag Co., Memphis, 1957-67; sec. Clark Equipment Co., Memphis, 1975-80, Hyneman Co., Southaven, Miss., 1986-90, Magnolia Square Ptnrs., LP, Southaven, 1991—. Author: Poems - World War II, 1995. Sec., bd. dirs. Bemis Credit Union, Memphis, 1958-66; dist. mem. Nat. Libr. of Poetry, Owings Mills, Md., 1995—. Recipient Editor's Choice award Nat. Libr. of Poetry, 1996. Mem. Nat. Sec.'s Assn., Am. Cancer Soc., Beta Sigma Phi. Home: 4513 Tammy Ln Memphis TN 38116-2037 Office: 9105 Hwy 51 N Southaven MS 38671

THOMSON, FRANK EHRLICH, III, curator; b. Columbia, S.C., Apr. 28, 1952; s. Francis Ehrlich Thomson Jr. and Anne Elizabeth (Hallman) Harmon. BA, U. S.C., 1983; MFA, U. Fla., 1986. Lab. mgr. Carolina Custom Labs., Columbia, 1979-82; owner/photographer Columbia, 1982-84; curator/adminstr. Upstairs Artspace, Tryon, N.C., 1986-88; exec. dir. Wilkes Art Gallery, North Wilkesboro, N.C., 1988-89; art critic Asheville (N.C.) Citizen-Times, 1990—; art history instr. Mars Hill (N.C.) Coll., 1996—; curator Asheville Art Mus., 1990—. Author: (catalog) Dancing In a Sea of Light, 1995; editor: (catalog) An Architect & His Times: Richard Sharp Smith, 1995; author/editor: (catalog) Coming to Light, 1994. Mem. Asheville Bicentennial Steering Com., 1996-97. Mem. Am. Assn. Museums (curators com. 1990—), N.C. Museums Coun. (bd. dirs. 1995—), Southeastern Mus. Conf. (curators com. 1990—). Office: Asheville Art Museum 2 South Pack Sq Asheville NC 28801

THOMSON, JOHN CHRISTIAN, financial analyst, portfolio manager; b. Hattiesburg, Miss., Mar. 16, 1965; s. Richard Spotswood and Inez Christina (Heidelberg) T. Student, U. So. Miss., 1985, Mercer U., 1986; grad., Sch. Communication Arts, 1987. Producer, photographer Alternative Art Studios, Mpls., 1987-89; exec. producer, photographer Visual Art Studios, Hattiesburg, 1989-91; dir. Acme Toy Factory Inc., New Smyrna Beach, Fla., 1992—; CEO, portfolio mgr. Fin. Trust Svcs., New Smyrna Beach. Photos exhibited in galleries 1989, 90, Advt. Photographers of Am., Meteor Photo, Atlanta, 1991. Recipient 1st Pl. (state), Honorable Mention (nat.) Nat. Scholastic Art Assn., 1981, 1st Pl. Black & White, Civic Arts Coun., 1989, Cert. of Merit Nat. Fine Arts Video Competition, 1991, Addy award Greater Jackson Advt. Club, 1991. Mem. New Smyrna Yacht Club, Amnesty Internat. (leadership group 1989—). Republican. Episcopalian. Office: Fin Trust Svcs 702 Palmetto St New Smyrna Beach FL 32168

THOMSON, MABEL AMELIA, retired elementary school educator; b. Lancaster, Minn., Oct. 28, 1910; d. Ernest R. and Sophie Olinda (Rotert) Poore; m. Robert John Thomson, June 20, 1936; children: James Robert, William John. BS, U. Ill., 1933; MEd, Steven F. Austin Coll., Nacogdoches, Tex., 1959. Tchr. La Harpe (Ill.) Sch. Dist., 1930, Scotland (Ill.) Sch. Dist., 1934, Washburn (Ill.) Sch. Dist., 1935-36, Tyler (Tex.) Ind. Sch. Dist., 1959-76; ret., 1976; substitute tchr. Tyler (Tex.) Ind. Sch. Dist., 1976-86. Past pres. Woman's Soc. Christian Svc. of local Meth. Ch. Mem. AAUW (pres. Tyler chpt. 1947-48), Am. Childhood Edn. (pres. 1960-61), Alpha Delta Kappa (charter Tyler br.), Phi Mu (life). Republican. Methodist.

THOMSON, STUART MCGUIRE, JR., science educator; b. Rocky Mount, N.C., May 14, 1945; s. Stuart McGuire and Sarah Stilly (McLean) T.; m. Betty Jean Klapp, Mar. 8, 1986. BA in Psychology, N.C. State U., 1969, BS in Zoology, 1972; MS in Biology, East Carolina U., 1986. Cert. tchr., N.C. Tchr. sci. John Graham High Sch., Warrenton, N.C., 1968-70, Chesterfield (S.C.) High Sch., 1970-71, Pungo Christian Acad., Belhaven, N.C., 1989-91, Beaufort County C.C., Washington, N.C., 1986—; Hobgood (N.C.) Acad., 1995—; disability determination specialist N.C. Dept. Human Resources, Raleigh, 1973-79; mgr. computer div. Thomson TV Co., Washington, 1979-84; various part-time positions East Carolina U., Greenville, N.C., 1985-89. Contbr. articles to Alcohol and Jour. of the Elisha Mitchell Sci. Sco. Mem. AAAS, N.C. Acad. Sci., N.Y. Acad. Scis., Washington (N.C.) Community Band, Sigma Xi (assoc.). Presbyterian. Home: PO Box 401 Washington NC 27889-0401 Office: Beaufort County CC PO Box 1069 Washington NC 27889-1069

THON, PATRICIA FRANCES, pediatrics nurse, medical and surgical nurse; b. Portland, Oreg., Sept. 25, 1959; d. Anthony William and Catherine Mary (Scully) Brenneis; m. Eric Phillip Thon, Apr. 30, 1988. AS, Johnson County C.C., 1980; BSN, U. Kans., Kans. City, 1982; MA, Webster U., 1992; postgrad., Portland State U., 1977; grad., St. Louis U., 1994. Staff nurse in pediatrics and oncology St. Luke's Hosp., Kansas City, Mo., 1982-84; commd. nurse officer USAF, 1984, advanced through grades to maj., 1988; staff nurse USAF, Scott AFB, Ill., 1984-88; flight nurse USAF, Scott AFB, 1988-91, sr. staff nurse in pediatrics and orthopedics, 1992; head nurse, flight chief maternal/child health Pediatric Clinic, Altus AFB, Okla., 1994—. Office: 97 MDG/SGOB 301 N 1st St Altus AFB OK 73523-5005

THOPPIL, CECIL KOSHEY, pediatrician, educator; b. Trivandrum, India, Aug. 4, 1961; m. Jennifer Carrol Gallego, Apr. 25, 1992; children: Cecilia Ruth, Andrew Obed. Pre-degree, Mar Ivanios Coll., Trivandrum, Kerala, India, 1979; MB, BS, Med. Coll. Hosp., Trivandrum, 1984. Diplomate Am. Bd. Pediat.; cert. instr. neonatal advanced life support, pediat. advanced life support, BLS. Compulsory rotating internship Med. Coll. Hosp., Trivandrum, Kerala, India, 1985-86; postgrad. tng. pediatric medicine dept. child health S.A.T. Hosp., Trivandrum, Kerala, India, 1986-87; postdoctoral rsch. assoc. dept. perinatal pediatrics U. Tex. Med. Br., Galveston, 1987-89; pediatric internship Univ. Hosps. Cleve. Rainbow Babies and Children's Hosp., 1989-90; pediatric residency dept. pediatrics Scott & White Meml. Hosp./Tex. A&M U. Coll. Medicine, Temple, 1990-92; pediatrician Surry County Health Dept., Dobson, N.C., 1992-94, Med. Assocs. of Surry, Carolina Medicorp Inc., Mt. Airy, N.C., 1994—; physician cons. Surry County Sch. Health Adv. Coun., Surry Pre-sch. Interagy. Coun., Surry County Day Care Assn.; pediat. cons. Surry Smart Start Task Force. Contbr. articles to profl. jours. Provider for "Caring" Program; deacon Haymore Bapt. Ch. Recipient Father Kuncheria Goldmedal for First Rank in Loyola Sch. for Matriculation. Fellow Am. Acad. Pediat.; mem. AMA, N.C. Med. Soc., N.C. Pediat. Soc., Surry-Yadkin Med. Soc. Home: 860 Cross Creek Dr Mount Airy NC 27030-9229 Office: Med Assocs of Surry 865 W Lake Dr Mount Airy NC 27030

THORBECKE, WILLEM HENDRIK, economics educator; b. Berkeley, Calif., Aug. 9, 1958; s. Erik and Charla Jean (Westerbery) T.; m. Grace Mariko Taira, Mar. 12, 1989; 1 child, Mariko Louisette. BA, Cornell U., 1982; PhD, U. Calif., Berkeley, 1988. Researcher Yale U., New Haven, 1985-86; instr. U. Calif., Berkeley, 1986-88; prof. econs. George Mason U., Fairfax, Va., 1988—; rschr. Levy Econs. Inst., Annandale, N.Y., 1994-95; researcher Social Security Adminstrn., Washington, 1990-91; vis. scholar Cowles Found., New Haven, 1985-86. Contbr. articles to profl. jours. Assoc. Locke Inst., Fairfax, 1993-94. Grantee U.S. Dept. HHS, 1990, U.S. Dept. Edn., 1993. Mem. Am. Econ. Assn., Western Econ. Assn., Ea. Econ. Assn., Atlantic Econ. Edn. Home: 4420 Gilbertson Rd Fairfax VA 22032 Office: George Mason Dept Econs 4400 University Dr Fairfax VA 22030-4443

THORBURN, JAMES ALEXANDER, humanities educator; b. Martins Ferry, Ohio, Aug. 24, 1923; s. Charles David and Mary Edna (Ruble) T.; m. Lois McElroy, July 3, 1954; children: Alexander Maurice, Melissa Rachel; m. 2d, June Yingling O'Leary, Apr. 18, 1981. BA, Ohio State U., 1949, MA, 1951; postgrad., U. Mo., 1954-55; PhD, La. State U., 1977. Head English dept. high sch., Sheridan, Mich., 1951-52; instr. English, U. Mo., Columbia, 1952-55, Monmouth (Ill.) Coll., 1955-56, U. Tex., El Paso, 1956-60, U. Mo., St. Louis, 1960-61, La. State U., Baton Rouge, 1961-70; prof. Southeastern La. U., Hammond, 1970-89, ret., named prof. emeritus English and linguistics; testing and cert. examiner English Lang. Inst., U. Mich., 1969—; participant Southeastern Conf. on Linguistics; mem. Conf. Christianity and Lit. Contbg. author: Exercises in English, 1955, also poetry, short stories; book rev. editor: Experiment, 1958-87; editor: Innisfree, 1984-89. With F.A., AUS, 1943-46. Mem. MLA, Linguistic Assn. S.W., Avalon World Arts Acad., Linguistic Soc. Am., Am. Dialect Soc., La. Assn. for Coll. Composition, La. Retired Tchrs. Assn., Internat. Poetry Soc., Internat. Acad. Poets, Sociedad Nacional Hispánica, Sigma Delta Pi, Phi Kappa Phi (named emeritus life), Phi Mu Alpha Sinfonia. Republican. Presbyterian. Home: 602 Susan Dr Hammond LA 70403-3444 Office: Southeastern La U # 739 Hammond LA 70402

THORE, STEN ANDERS, economics and aerospace engineering educator; b. Stockholm, Apr. 22, 1930; came to U.S., 1978, naturalized, 1985; s. Eric and Elsa (Ostberg) T.; m. Margrethe Munck; children: Susanne, Alexander, Clementine. M. Commerce, U. Birmingham, Eng., 1954; Filosofie Doktor, U. Stockholm, 1961. Prof. econs. Norwegian Sch. Econs. and Bus. Adminstrn., Bergen, Norway, 1964-78; Gregory A. Kozmetsky Centennial fellow IC2 Inst., U. Tex., Austin, 1984—; instr. U. Tex., Austin, Washington, 1996—; vis. prof. Northwestern U., Carnegie-Mellon U., U. Va. Author: Economic Logistics, 1992, The Diversity, Complexity and Evolution of High Tech Capitalism, 1995; (with G.L. Thompson) Computational Economics, 1991; contbr. articles to profl. jours. Named Hon. Citizen, State of Tex., 1981. Mem. Inst. Mgmt. Scis. Econometric Soc. Home: 809 Electra St Austin TX 78734-4213 Office: U Tex Austin IC2 Inst 2815 San Gabriel St Austin TX 78705-3596

THORN, BRIAN EARL, retail company executive; b. Tucson, Oct. 30, 1955; s. Charles Walter and Jacquelyn Grace (Sloat) T.; m. Mary L. Ayala, Nov. 23, 1979 (div. 1981); m. Brenda Anne Benson, Dec. 28, 1983; 1 child, Justin. Student, U. Ariz. Loss prevention mgr. HRT Industries, Tucson, 1977-82; sales mgr. Circuit City, 1982-86; ops. mgr. Circuit City, Huntington Beach, Calif., 1986-87; divsn. mgr. Circuit City, 1987-90; store mgr. Barnes & Noble, Houston, 1992—; bd. dirs. Info.-Hwy. Internat., Inc.; mem. advt./mktg. com. Woodlands Corp. Mem. planning com. Edn. for Tomorrow Alliance. Mem. Woodlands C. of C. (bd. dirs., mem. exec. nominating com.), Woodlands Libr. Guild (bd. dirs.).

THORN, JAMES DOUGLAS, safety engineer; b. Tyler, Tex., May 20, 1959; s. Douglas Howard and Patricia Ann (Kolb) T. Student, U. of Mary, Manama, Bahrain, 1982, S.W. Tex. State U., 1984-86, La. State U., 1989, W.Va. Tech., 1991-92, Berlitz Sch. Langs., 1993. Cert. EMT, BTLS, ACLS, CPR instr., hazardous materials ops., hazardous waste ops., hazardous and indsl. waste mgmt. 3d officer Jackson Marine S.A., Manama, 1981; constrn. foreman Brown & Root S.A., Manama, 1982-83; barge officer Rezayat/Brown & Root E.C., Manama, 1983-84; safety insp. Brown & Root U.S.A., Carson, Calif., 1987-88; sr. safety insp. Brown & Root U.S.A., Taft, La., 1988-89; project safety mgr. Brown & Root Braun, Institute, W.Va., 1989-93; mgr. safety and health Brown & Root Braun, Phila., 1993-94; safety supt. Brown & Root, Carson, Calif., 1994; safety/security mgr. L.A. Export Terminal, 1995—; safety cons. Assn. Builders and Contractors, Charleston, W.Va., 1990-93, chmn. safety seminar, 1991-93; drill monitor Kanawha Valley Emergency Preparedness Coun., South Charleston, W.Va., 1990-93; v.p. Arco Contractors Safety Coun., Carson, 1995-96. Youth counsellor Neon League, St. Albans, W.Va., 1991; den leader cub scouts Boy Scouts Am., 1991-93; bd. dirs. NFL Booster Club Orange County, 1995—; v.p. Area Contractors Safety Coun., 1995—. Mem. Am. Soc. Safety Engrs., Nat. Assn. EMTs, Team 911, Great Wall of Tex. Soc., Angels Booster Club (bd. dirs. 1995—, 1st v.p. 1996—), Rams Booster Club (bd. dirs. 1995) now NFL Booster Club of Orange County (bd. dirs. 1996—). Office: Brown & Root PO Box 320 Long Beach CA 90801

THORNBURG, LEE ELLIS, film executive, director; b. Houston, Feb. 16, 1942; s. Richard Ellis and Lucyle (Comstock) T.; m. Jane Kaiser (div. 1981); children: Janette Mattas, Deanne Waddell; m. Patricia Ann Kirkham, June 16, 1987. Tech. svc. engr. Dresser Industries, Houston, 1970-76; pres. Lone Star Pictures Internat., Inc., Dallas, 1976—. Dir. films including Hollywood High Part II, 1981, 6-Pack, 1991; producer films including Kings of the Hill, 1976, Mr. Mean, 1978. Mem. Am. Film Market Assn. Republican. Methodist. Office: Lonestar Pictures Internat 8831 W Sunset Blvd Ste 204 Los Angeles CA 90069-2109

THORNE, B. MICHAEL, psychologist; b. Shreveport, La., Sept. 7, 1942; s. William Albert and Alice Jeanne (Mathis) T.; m. Wanda Yvonne Bourgeois, Feb. 1, 1964; children: Dean Keller, Erin Leigh. BA, La. State U., 1964, MA, 1967, PhD, 1969. Asst. prof. psychology La. State U., Baton Rouge, 1969-70; asst. prof. psychology Miss. State U., Mississippi State, 1970-72, assoc. prof., 1972-77, prof., 1978—. Author: Introductory Statistics for Psychology, 1980, Statistics for the Behavioral Sciences, 1989, 2d edit., 1996, Connections in the History and Systems of Psychology, 1996; co-author: Unit Mastery Workbook to Accompany Understanding Human Behavior, 1986. Mem. Psychonomic Soc., Am. Psychol. Soc., Sigma Xi, Phi Kappa Phi. Office: Miss State Univ PO Box 6161 Mississippi State MS 39762-6161

THORNE, GEORGE CLIFFORD, pediatrician, educator; b. El Paso, Tex., Feb. 1, 1921; s. Lansing Steven and Esther (Speer) T.; m. Betty Lang, Sept. 18, 1946; children: Barbara Jean, George Clifford, Julie Diane, Nancy Elizabeth. Student, U. Tex., El Paso, 1938, U. Tex., Austin, 1938-41; postgrad., Baylor U., 1941-42; MD, S.W. Med. Coll., 1944. Diplomate Am. Bd. Pediatrics. Fellow in pediatric pathology dept. pediatrics S.W. Med. Coll., 1945; intern in pediatrics coll. medicine Duke U., 1945-46; resident in pediatrics Cin. Children's Hosp./U. Cin. Coll. Medicine, 1946-48; clin. prof. pediatrics med. sch. U. Tex., Galveston; mem. staff Brackenridge Hosp., Austin, St. David's Community Hosp., Austin, Seton Med. Ctr., Austin; pvt. practice pediatrics Austin, 1948-91; pediatric cons. Tex. Rehab. Commn., 1991—; cons. disability determination div. Tex. State Health Dept., 1991—; participant White House Conf. on Child Health. Mem. bd. Austin Ind. Sch. Dist.; active Austin Pre-Sch. Hearing Clinic; mem. adv. bd. Cystic Fibrosis Found, Austin Community Coun.; mem. vestry Ch. of Good Shepherd. AOA S.W. Med. Coll. scholar. Fellow Am. Acad. Pediatrics; mem. AMA, So. Med. Assn., Tex. Med. Assn. (del.), Tex. Pediatric Soc., Travis County Med. Soc. (bd. dirs., v.p., bd. censors), Austin Pediatric Soc.

THORNHILL, GABRIEL FELDER, III, securities company executive; b. N.Y.C., Mar. 14, 1928; s. Gabriel Felder Jr. and Weta Acker (Ingram) T.; m. Mary Elizabeth Vick, Feb. 26, 1960; children: Gabriel Felder IV, Elizabeth, Mary Ann. BBA, U. Tex., 1948; postgrad. in banking, U. Pa., 1962. Ptnr. Dewar Robertson & Pancoast, Austin, Tex., 1953-68; exec. v.p. Hornblower & Weeks, Austin, 1968-74, Rotan Mosle, Austin, 1974-80, Fin. Svcs. Austin, 1980-88; pres. Thornhill Securities, Austin, 1988—; exec. v.p. FSA Inc., Austin, 1980-89; pres. FSA Capital, Austin, 1982-84; bd. dirs. Austin Trust Co. Vestryman Good Shepherd Episcopal Ch., Austin, 1967-69, mem. endowment fund com., 1988—; treas. Laguna Gloria Art Mus., Austin, 1963, bd. dirs. 1962-64; treas. Child and Family Svc., Austin, 1965, v.p., 1966; chmn. pacesetter div. United Way, Austin, 1967; bd. dirs. Child Guidance Ctr., Austin, 1973-75; mem. Austin Urban Renewal Bd., 1978-82; bd. dirs. Austin History Ctr., 1987-93, v.p., 1989; trustee Westminster Manor, Austin, 1985—, vice chmn., 1989, chmn., 1994. Sgt. U.S. Army, 1950-52, Korea. Mem. Investment Bankers Am. (fin. com. 1954-57), Austin Investment Assn. (founder, bd. dirs. 1963-69, v.p. 1963, pres. 1964), Allegro Club, Headliners Club, Westwood Country Club, Adms. Club (chmn. 1975), Coronet Club (pres. 1969), Tarry House (bd. dirs., v.p. 1989, pres. 1990-92). Home: 3233 Tarryhollow Dr Austin TX 78703-1638 Office: 100 Congress Ave Ste 790 Austin TX 78701-4042

THORNSBERRY, WILLIS LEE, JR., chemist; b. Sturgis, Ky., Aug. 10, 1940; s. Willis Lee and Jane (Hall) T.; m. Mary Elizabeth Gaswint, June 19, 1965; children: Brian, Michele. BS, Murray State U., 1963; MS, U. Ark., 1967; PhD, Tulane U., 1974. Rsch. chemist Freeport-McMoran Inc., Belle Chasse, La., 1967-74, sr. rsch. chemist, 1974-92; pres. Tech. Devel. Svcs. Inc., Harvey, La., 1992—. Contbr. articles to profl. jours. Coach, leader for youth groups Jefferson Parish Playgrounds, Gretna, La., 1970-84, Boy Scouts Am., Gretna, 1975-82. 1st lt. U.S. Army, 1963-65. Mem. Am. Chem. Soc. (sect. chmn. 1969-82), Sigma Xi (nominating com. 1967—). Democrat. Office: Tech Devel Svcs Inc 1024 N Main St Sturgis KY 42459-1245

THORNTON, ANNA VREE, pediatrics and medical-surgical nurse; b. Chgo., June 10, 1936; d. Edward and Elizabeth Vree; m. George Q. Thornton, June 19, 1982. BA in Edn. Psych., Barrington Coll., 1960; postgrad., NYU, 1960-62; ADN., Dutchess C.C., Poughkeepsie, N.Y., 1986. Tchr. Saugerties (N.Y.) Cen. Schs., 1960-64, Kingston (N.Y.) Consolidated Schs., 1964-66, 68-70; owner BeeVer House, Saugerties, 1970-76; ins. agt. Combined Life Ins. Co., Poughkeepsie, N.Y., 1976-82; staff nurse Putnam County Community Hosp., Carmel, N.Y., 1983-86; charge nurse Calloway County Community Hosp., Murray, Ky., 1986—; tchr. U.S. Peace Corps, Nigeria, 1966-68. Pres. Saugerties Busnessmen's Orgn., 1977. Baha'i'. Home: 4563 Kirksey Rd Kirksey KY 42054-9728 Office: Calloway County Comm Hosp 800 Poplar St Murray KY 42071-2566

THORNTON, BERETHA, plant biotechnologist; b. Demapolis, Ala., Sept. 24, 1964; d. Jessie and Louise (Brown) T. BS, Ala. Agr. and Mech. U., 1987, MS, 1993; cert. in radiation biology, Oak Ridge Assoc. U., 1995. Cert. profl. landscape designer, Ala. Grounds crew asst. Arnold Arboretum of Harvard U., Jamaica Plains, Mass., 1986; plant tissue culture lab. asst. Ala. A&M U., Normal, 1987-94; biol. sci. technician U.S. Forest Svc., Huntsville, Ala., 1994—; cons. on data analysis and exptl. design to grad. students, Normal, 1994—. Contbr. poetry to anthologies. Recipient Cert./Publ. for poetry World of Poetry, 1988, 89, 90, 91. Mem. Alpha Zeta (treas. 1991-93). Home: 143 Winchester Rd Huntsville AL 35811

THORNTON, DON RAY, gifted education educator, poet, artist; b. La., Dec. 15, 1936; s. Delmas Benson and Eutha (Cocherham) T.; m. Suzannah Smith, June 3, 1961; children: Kyla Katherine, Tribbey Bryan. BA, La. Technol. U., 1960; MA, La. State U., 1967; postgrad., U. Southwestern La., 1968. Cert. fine arts and gifted edn. tchr., La. Tchr. art Caddo Parish Schs., Vivian, La., 1960-64; mgr. arts and crafts and gallery Student Union, La. State U., Baton Rouge, 1964-67; instr. art U. Southwestern La., Lafayette, 1967-73, tchr. gifted and talented summer program, 1988, 93; artist-in-residence Coll. of Mainland, Texas City, Tex., 1973-76; dir. arts and crafts State Penal Instn., Petros, Tenn., 1976-77; tchr. indsl. arts Iberia Parish Schs., New Iberia, La., 1978-79, mid. sch. tchr., 1981-83; mid. sch. tchr. St. Martin Parish, St. Martinville, La., 1982-83, tchr. gifted, 1983-92; ednl. cons., 1968—; art cons. Headstart, Lafayette, 1968-69; set designer Houston Ballet, 1976; guest curator Natural History Mus., Lafayette, 1978-79. Author: Out Cry, 1960, Sounding, 1976, A Walk on Water, 1985, Mentor, 1993. Christa McAuliffe fellow U.S. Dept. Edn., 1992-93. Home and Office: 1504 Howard St New Iberia LA 70560-1054

THORNTON, J. RONALD, technology center director; b. Fayetteville, Tenn., Aug. 19, 1939; s. James Alanda and Thelma White (McGee) T.; m. Mary Beth Packard, June 14, 1964 (div. Apr. 1975); 1 child, Nancy Carole; m. Martha Klemann, Jan. 23, 1976 (div. Apr. 1982); 1 child, Trey; m. Bernice McKinney, Feb. 14, 1986; 1 child, Paul Leon. BS in Physics & Math., Berry Coll., 1961; MA in Physics, Wake Forest Coll., 1964; postgrad., U. Ala., 1965-66, Rollins Coll., 1970. Research physicist Brown Engring. Co., Huntsville, Ala., 1963-66; sr. staff engr. Martin Marietta Corp., Orlando, Fla., 1966-75; dep. dir. NASA, Washington, 1976-77; exec. asst. Congressman Louis Frey, Jr., Orlando, 1978; pres. Tens Tec, Inc., Orlando, 1978-79; dir. So. Tech. Applications Ctr. U. Fla., Gainesville, 1979—; bd. dirs., treas. North Fla. Tech. Innovation Ctr., 1994—; mem. light wave tech. com. Fla. High Tech. and Indsl. Coun., Tallahassee, 1986-93, NASA Tech. Transfer Exec. Com., Washington, 1987—, Javits Fellowship Bd., Washington, 1986-91, Gov.'s New Product Award Com., Tallahassee, 1988—, Fla. K-12 Math., Sci. and Computer Sci. Edn. Quality Improvement Adv. Coun., 1989-92, Fla. Sci. Edn. Improvement Adv. Com., 1991-92; bd. dirs. Fla.-NASA Bus. Incubation Ctr., mem. bd. dirs., Tech Transfer Soc., 1996. Pres. Orange County Young Rep. Club, Orlando, 1970-71; treas. Fla. Fedn. Young Reps., Orlando, 1971-72; chmn. Fla. Fedn. Young Reps., Orlando, 1972-74; pres. Gainesville Area Innovation Network, 1988-89. Named Engr. Exhibiting Tech. Excellence and Accomplishment cen. Fla. chpt. Fla. Engring. Soc., 1975, Achievement award NASA, 1977. Mem. IEEE, SME, Tech. Transfer Soc. (bd. dirs. 1996—), Nat. Assn. Mgmt. and Tech. Assistance Ctrs. (bd. dirs. 1988, pres. 1992), Gainesville Area C.

of C. Republican. Home: 17829 NW 20th Ave Newberry FL 32669-2143 Office: U Fla So Tech Applications Ctr 1 Progress Blvd Ste 24 Alachua FL 32615-9536

THORNTON, JOHN W., SR., lawyer; b. Toledo, July 3, 1928; s. Cletus Bernard and Mary Victoria (Carey) T.; m. Mary Feeley, Mar. 10, 1951; children: John, Jane Thornton Mastrucci, Deborah Thornton Hasty, Michael. AB magna cum laude, U. Notre Dame, 1950, LLB summa cum laude, 1956, JD, 1969. Bar: Fla. 1956, U.S. Dist. Ct. (so. dist.) Fla. 1956, U.S. Ct. Appeals (5th cir.) 1956, U.S. Ct. Appeals (11th cir.) 1982. Sole practice, Miami, Fla. Contbr. articles to legal jours. Served to lt. USN, 1950-53. Mem. Fla. Bar (chmn. continuing legal edn. program 1976-77, chmn. 1982-83), ABA (vice-chmn. practice and procedure com. 1969, 73, 76-81; vice-chmn. health ins. law com. 1972-73, chmn. 1974-76; chmn. Excess Surplus Lines and Re-ins. Law Commn., 1985-91; vice-chmn. program com. ann. meeting 1976; com. rules and procedure 1979-80), Internat. Assn. Ins. Counsel (chmn. med. malpractice com. 1975-90; def. counsel com. 1976-91; reins., excess and surplus lines com. 1980-91), Def. Rsch. Inst. (chmn. practice and procedure com. 1972-76; industry-wide litigation com. 1978-90), So. Def. Lawyers Assn., Dade County Def. Bar Assn., Fedn. Ins. Counsel (casualty ins. law com. 1972-91; med. malpractice com. 1974-87; excess surplus and reins. com. 1976-91; publs. com. 1976-87), Maritime Law Assn. U.S., Fla. Def. Lawyers Assn. (dir., chmn. legis. com. 1974-77), Broward County Bar Assn., Am. Judicature Soc. Roman Catholic. Clubs: Coral Gables, Ocean Reef (Key Largo, Fla.) Country, Riviera Country; Sapphire Valley (N.C.) Country.

THORNTON, MARK CHRISTOPHER, economist; b. Geneva, N.Y., June 7, 1960; s. Carroll Francis and Constance Katherine (Ryan) T. BS in Econs., St. Bonaventure U., Olean, N.Y., 1982; PhD in Econs., Auburn (Ala.) U., 1989. O.P. Alford asst. prof. econs. Ludwid von Mises Inst. and Auburn U., 1989—; acad. dir. Auburn C. Ctr. Ludwig Von Mises Inst., 1987—; con. Ekelund and Assocs., Auburn, 1986—. Author: The Economics of Prohibition, 1991; editor: Austrian Econ. Newsletter, 1984-92; contbr. articles to profl. jours. Constable Dist. 79 Lee County, Ala., 1988—; dist. rep. Ala. Libertarian Party, 1983-85, fin. chmn., 1987-89, vice chmn., 1985-86, chmn., 1996; U.S. congl. candidate 3d Dist., 1984; U.S. senate candidate, Ala., 1996. Office: Auburn U Dept Econs Coll Bus Auburn AL 36849

THORNTON, MARY ELIZABETH WELLS, critical care nurse, educator; b. McComb, Miss., Nov. 13, 1956; d. Wendell Randolph and Betty Lou (Carlisle) Wells; m. James Michael Thornton, June 4, 1977; 1 child, Benjamin Champ. BSN, William Carey Coll., Hattiesburg, Miss., 1976; MS, U. So. Miss., 1984. Cert. CPR instr., ACLS. Charge nurse, supr. Beacham Meml. Hosp., Magnolia, Miss.; dir. insvc. Franklin County Meml. Hosp., Meadville, Miss.; acting head nurse newborn intensive care and newborn nursery S.W. Miss. Regional Med. Ctr., McComb; instr. nursing S.W. Miss. Community Coll., Summit. Mem., acteens leader Mt Olive Baptist Ch. Mem. Miss. Ret. Pub. Employees Assn., Orgn. for Advancement Assoc. Degree Nursing, William Carey Coll. Alumni Assn., U. So. Miss. Alumni Assn., Sigma Theta Tau, Phi Kappa Phi.

THORNTON, PATRICIA WALKER, school development director; b. Rochester, N.Y., June 13, 1950; d. Jack L. and Ruth Marie (Hyde) Walker; m. Greg Thornton, June 15, 1974; children: Sarah Walker Thornton, Michael Walker Thornton. BA, Seton Hill Coll., 1972; MA in Comm., Ohio State U., 1973, postgrad., 1973-74; postgrad., Visual Studies Workshop, 1976, The New Sch., N.Y.C., 1979, Grantsmanship Ctr., 1980. Student teaching asst. comm. dept. Ohio State U., Columbus, 1973-74; instr. St. Thomas More Elem. Sch., Brighton, N.Y., 1975-76; instr. & asst. to devel. office, then alumni dir. St. Benedict's Prep. Sch., Newark, 1979-81; devel. dir. St. Vincent Acad., Newark, 1981-88, Montgomery (Ala.) Cath. H.S., 1988—. Active spl. events com., welcoming com., Ch. of the Holy Spirit, 1990—; dir. children's festival, 1st ann. Book Harvest, Friends of Auburn U. at Montgomery Libr., 1991; troop co-leader South Ctrl. Ala. coun. Girls Scouts U.S., 1990-92. Mem. Nat. Cath. Edn. Assn. Roman Catholic. Office: Montgomery Cath HS 5350 Vaughn Rd Montgomery AL 36116-1153

THORNTON, ROBERT DONALD, emeritus English language educator; b. West Somerville, Mass., Aug. 10, 1917; s. John William and Winifred (Harrington) T.; m. Grace Ellen Baker, May 22, 1943; children—Robert, David. B.A. with high distinction (Denison fellow, Caleb Winchester fellow), Wesleyan U., Middletown, Conn., 1939; M.A. in English, Western Res. U., 1940; M.A. in English (Univ. fellow), Harvard, 1942, Ph.D. (Dexter fellow), 1949. Instr. English Fenn Coll., Cleve., 1939-40, Worcester Acad., Mass., 1940-41; teaching fellow English Harvard U., 1941-42, 46-49; asst. prof. English U. Colo., Boulder, 1949-56; chmn. English St. Stephen's Episcopal Sch., Austin, Tex., 1956-57; assoc. prof. English U. S.C., Columbia, 1957-60; prof. English Kans. State U., Manhattan, 1960-68; prof. English, world lit., chmn. dept. SUNY-New Paltz, 1968-71, faculty research fellow, 1973; univ. exchange scholar SUNY Coll. New Paltz, 1974-82, emeritus prof. English, SUNY exchange scholar, 1982—. Author: A Manual for Reading Improvement, 1953, The Tuneful Flame, 1957, James Curie: The Entire Stranger and Robert Burns, 1963, Selected Poetry and Prose of Robert Burns, 1966, William Maxwell to Robert Burns, 1979, The American Legion in South Carolina, 1989, SNAFU, 1993; contbr. to Ency. World Lit. in Twentieth Century, Ency. Poetry and Poetics; cons. editor: The Robert Burns Song Book, 1996—. Served with USNR, 1942-46, PTO. Grantee Am. Philos. Soc., 1955-56, Am. Council Learned Socs., 1963; Guggenheim fellow, 1958-59. Mem. MLA, Modern Humanities Research Assn., AAUP, Am. Soc. Eighteenth-Century Studies, Internat. Soc. Eighteenth-Century Studies, Chi Psi. Republican. Episcopalian. Clubs: Folio, S.C. Harvard. Home: 504 State Rd Cheraw SC 29520-1600

THORNTON, WILLIAM EARL, physician, psychiatrist, psychoanalyst; b. Battle Creek, Mich., Apr. 29, 1938; s. Edward Leo and Frances Evelyn (McGinn) T.; m. Dareyth Y. O'Cleary, Dec. 24, 1981; children: William B., Ashley, Robert J., Kevin R., Marjorie F. BS, U. Mich., 1964; MD, Vanderbilt U., 1966. Resident in medicine U. Wis., Madison, 1966-67; resident in psychiatry Johns Hopkins U., Balt., 1967-70; asst. prof. psychiatry U. Chgo., 1971-73; assoc. prof. psychiatry U. Ill., Chgo., 1973-76; assoc. prof. psychiatry, family medicine Med. U. S.C., Charleston, 1976-79; asst. prof. psychiatry Johns Hopkins U., 1979-81; assoc. prof. family medicine, prof. psychiatry U. Nev., Reno, 1981-87; med. dir. Northshore Psychiat. Hosp., Slidell, La., 1987-93; pvt. practice Psychoanalytic Self Psychology, Slidell, La., 1993—; mem. Nev. State Physician Aid Com., 1982-88; FDA investigator for lithium carbonate, 1967-70, for methadone maintenance, 1970-71; spkr. in field. Author: Codependency, Sexuality and Depression, 1990; contbr. over 70 articles to profl. jours. Bd. dirs. Lupus Found. Am., Reno, 1984087, Chgo. Treatment Alternative to Street Crime, 1975-77; pres., bd. dirs. Chgo. Substance Abuse Svcs., 1975-77; bd. dirs. Northshore Psychiat. Hosp., 1988-93. Capt. U.S. Army, 1966-70. Recipient Physicians Recognition award AMA, 1969, 74, 76, 78. Fellow Acad. Psychosomatic Medicine (Convocation medal 1976); mem. Am. Acad. Psychoanalysis, Am. Soc. Physician Analysts, Johns Hopkins Med. and Surg. Soc., Am. Acad. Family Physicians, Am. Acad. Psychiatrists in Alcoholism and Addictions (founding mem.). Republican. Home: 117 Carina Cir Slidell LA 70458 Office: William Earl Thornton MD 2852 Carey Slidell LA 70458

THORPE, BETSY TUCKER, contracting company official; b. South Hill, Va., Jan. 14, 1956; d. Grattan Howard Jr. Tucker and Phyllis Freese (Draper) Haislip; m. Brady Bennett, Feb. 8, 1975 (div. 1980); 1 child, Jaime Elizabeth; m. Burton Walter Thorpe,Jr., Jan. 25, 1986 (div. 1989); 1 child, Brittney Leigh. BTech., U. North Fla., 1982. Cert. gen. contractor, Fla.; lic. real estate agt., Fla. Project engr. Blosam Contractors, Inc., St. Petersburg, Fla., 1982-84, Condel Constrn. Co., Jacksonville, Fla., 1984-85; asst. project mgr. McDevitt & Street Co., Jacksonville, 1985-86; owner, mgr. Tucker-Thorpe Gen. Contractors, Jacksonville, 1984-88; qualifying agt. Dynamic Land Devel., Inc., Jacksonville, 1987—; construction projects adminstr. Fla. Dept. of Corrections, Tallahasse, 1990—. N.E. Fla. Home Builders Assn. scholar, 1982. Republican. Episcopalian. Office: Fla Dept of Corrections 2601 Blairstone Rd Tallahassee FL 32399-6584

THORSTEINSSON, GUDNI, physiatrist; b. Vestmannaeyjar, Iceland, Aug. 5, 1941; came to U.S., 1971; s. Thorsteinn and Asdis Gudbjörg (Jesdottir) Einarsson; m. Elin Klein, Apr. 10, 1965; children: Arnar Karl, Asdis Thora. BS, Reykjavik (Iceland) Coll., 1961; candidatus med. et chirurg., U. Iceland, Reykjavik, 1968; MS, U. Minn., 1976. Diplomate Am. Bd. Phys. Medicine and Rehab. Dist physician Icelandic Govt., Djupivogur, 1970-71; resident dept. phys. medicine and rehab. Mayo Found., Rochester, Minn., 1972-75, mem. consulting staff, 1975-80; chair dept. Nat. Hosp., Reykjavik, 1980-81; dir. rehab. Mayo Clinic/St. Mary's Hosp., Rochester, 1981-85; dir. out-patient rehab. Mayo Clinic, Rochester, 1985-88, chair dept., 1987-91; chair dept. phys. medicine and rehab. Mayo Clinic, Jacksonville, Fla., 1991—; physiatrist cons. Mayo Clinic, Rochester, 81-91, Jacksonville, 1991—. Author: (with others) Therapeutic Electricity and Ultraviolet, 1983. Mem. AMA, Am. Acad. Phys. Medicine and Rehab., Am. Acad. Pain Medicine, Fla. Med. Assn., Fla. Soc. Phys. Medicine and Rehab. Office: Mayo Clinic Jacksonville 4500 San Pablo Rd S Jacksonville FL 32224-1865

THORUP, OSCAR ANDREAS, JR., internist, educator, researcher, administrator; b. Washington, Mar. 12, 1922; s. Oscar Andreas and Pattie Walter (Creecy) T.; m. Alleyn Barbara Turnbull, Sept. 17, 1944; children: Cathryn Lynn, Lisbeth Todd Thornton, Matthew Schuyler. BA, U. Va., 1944, MD, 1946. Diplomate Am. Bd. Internal Medicine. Intern Queen's Hosp., Honolulu, Hawaii, 1946-47; resident U. Va., Charlottesville, 1949-52; rsch. fellow U. N. Carolina, Chapel Hill, 1952-53; from instr. to asst. prof. U. Va., Charlottesville, 1953-59, assoc. prof., 1959-66, prof. of medicine, assoc. dean, 1974-89; prof., head dept. of medicine U. Ariz., Tucson, 1966-74; prof. seminar ethics/pub. policy Grad. Sch. Arts and Sci. U. Va., Charlottesville, 1980-88, prof. emeritus, 1990—; vis. rsch. assoc. Oxford (Eng.) U., Radcliffe Hosp., 1958-59, vis. rsch. prof., 1972; mem. planning team devel. U. Ariz. Med. Sch., Tucson, 1966-71; founding mem., mem. exec. com., pres. Soc. Med. Coll. Dirs. of Continuing Med. Edn., Charlottesville, 1975-89; co-dir. Program in Human Biology, Ethics and Soc., Charlottesville, 1977-89. Author: (with Leavell) Clinical Hematology, 1960 5th rev. edit., 1987; contbr. numerous articles to profl. jours. Bd. dirs., mem. exec. com., pres. Ariz. Health Planning Coun., Tucson, 1969-74; chmn. guidelines com. Tucson United Way Coun., 1971-77; bd. dirs., rep., chmn. suburban area coun. VA Health System Agy., Charlottesville, 1978-82; bd. dirs. VA Hosp. Assn., Richmond, Va., 1983-87. John and Mary Markle scholar, 1954-59; Commonwealth Found. fellow, 1959. Fellow Am. Clinical and Climatological Assn. (coun. 1984—), Coll. of Physicians; mem. Med. Soc. Va. (legis. com. 1984-89), Albemarle County Med. Soc. (pres. 1977-78), Am. Soc. Hematology, Am. Fedn. for Clin. Rsch. Home: 208 Colthurst Dr Charlottesville VA 22901-2038 Office: U Va Health Scis Ctr Jefferson Park Ave Charlottesville VA 22908

THOW, GEORGE BRUCE, surgeon; b. Toronto, Mar. 24, 1930; came to U.S., 1965; s. George and Helen Bruce (Smith) T.; m. Marion Bernice Perry, Sept. 7, 1956; children—Deborah, George, Helen, Catherine. M.D., U. Toronto, 1954. Diplomate Am. Bd. Gen. Surgery, Am. Bd. Colon and Rectal Surgery (pres. 1983-84, adv. coun. 1989—, sr. examiner 1989—). Intern Toronto East Gen. Hosp., 1954-55; gen. practice medicine Toronto, 1955-56; instr. anatomy U. Toronto; resident in gen. and colon and rectal surgery Mayo Postgrad. Sch. Medicine, Rochester, Minn., 1957-63; gen., colon and rectal surgeon Lockwood Clinic, Toronto, 1963-65; founder and dir. colon and rectal residency program U. Ill. Med. Sch. and Carle Found. Hosp., Urbana, 1974-85; dir. dept. colon and rectal surgery Carle Clinic Assocs., Urbana, Ill., 1974-85; clin. assoc. Sch. Basic Med. Scis., U. Ill., Urbana, 1973-77; clin. asst. prof. Coll. Medicine, U. Ill., Urbana-Champaign, 1975-78; clin. assoc. prof. Coll. Medicine, U. Ill., 1978-85; prof. clin. nutrition, dept. food sci. U. Ill., Urbana, 1981-85; practice medicine specializing in colon and rectal surgery Chattanooga, 1985—; vice chmn. Residency Rev. Bd. in Colon and Rectal Surgery, 1980-82; active Am. Bd. Med. Specialties, 1979-84; mem. interspecialty bd. AMA, Chgo., 1974-80. Assoc. editor Diseases of the Colon and Rectum Jour., 1978—; contbr. chpt. to book, numerous articles to profl. publs.; inventor Thow tube, Colovage operative irrigation tube. Cmty. coord. Urbana conv. Inter-Varsity Christian Fellowship, Ill., 1967-84. Recipient Med. Edn. award Carle Found., 1982. Fellow Royal Coll Surgeons (Can.) (cert. 1963), ACS (credentials com. 1980-82); mem. Priestley Surg. Soc., Mid-West Colon and Rectal Surg. Soc. (pres. 1985-86), Can. Assn. Gen. Surgeons, Am. Bd. of Colon and Rectal Surgery (chmn. exam. com.1980-83, pres. 1983-84, adv. coun. 1989), Soc. Surgery Alimentary Tract, Am. Cancer Soc. (pres. Champaign County unit 1975-77, Ill. Top Ten award 1973-74), United Ostomy Assn. (founding mem. Champaign-Urbana chpt.). Presbyterian. Home: 7142 Revere Cir Concord Highlands Chattanooga TN 37421-1205 Office: Univ Surg Assocs Inc Med Ctr Plz North 979 E 3d St Ste 300 Chattanooga TN 37403-2186

THRAILKILL, DANIEL B., lawyer; b. Fayetteville, Ark., Sept. 21, 1957. BSBA, U. Ark., 1979, J.D., 1981. Bar: Ark. 1982, Tex. 1988, U.S. Dist. Cts. (ea. and we. dists.) Ark. 1982, U.S. Ct. Appeals (8th cir.) 1983, U.S. Supreme Ct. 1985, U.S. Dist. Ct. (ea. dist.) Okla. 1995. Ptnr. Page & Thrailkill, Mena, Ark., 1981—; assoc. prof., lectr. Rich Mountain C.C.; assoc. justice Ark. Supreme Ct., 1996—; city atty. Cities of Mena and Hatfield. Recipient Appellate Advocacy award U. Ark. Sch. Law, 1981. Mem. ATLA, ABA, Nat. Dist. Attys. Assn., Ark. Bar Assn., Ark. Trial Lawyers Assn., Phi Alpha Delta. Methodist. Lodge: Lions. Home: 2011 Church Ave Mena AR 71953-2739 Office: Page & Thrailkill PO Drawer 30 Courthouse Sq W Mena AR 71953

THRASH, ARTIE YVONNE ADAMS, college foundation director; b. Joaquin, Tex., Oct. 29, 1939; d. Elton Herman and Gertrude (Bonner) Adams; m. Hollis Alvin Thrash, (div.); 1 child, Sheila Yvonne Thrash Moreland. BA, U. Houston, 1969, MA, 1970; PhD, La. State U., 1974. Tchr. Houston Ind. Sch. Dist., 1969, Galena Park (Tex.) Ind. Sch. Dist., 1970; instr. U. Houston, 1971; assoc. prof. Sam Houston State U., Huntsville, Tex., 1974-85, program head, 1981-83, asst. v.p., 1983-85; asst. to pres. Tex. Woman's U., Denton, 1985-89; interim exec. dir. Tex. Woman's U.-Houston Ctr., 1988-89; dir. instl. advancement Cooke County Coll., Gainesville, Tex., 1989-94; exec. dir. Cooke County Endowment Found. Inc., Gainesville, 1989-94; instnl. advancement office U. N. Tex., Denton, Tex., 1994-96; faculty U. Tex.-Tyler, 1996—; sec., bd. dirs. North Tex. Ednl. Network, Inc., Gainesville, 1990. Author: (books) Speaking up Successfully, 1985, Basic Skills of Effective Communication, 1985; contbr. articles to profl. jours. Mem. Speech Comm. Assn. So. Speech Comm. Assn., Tex. Speech Comm. Assn. (dist. chairperson 1975-79), Women's Club, Kiwanis, Phi Kappa Phi. Baptist. Home: 16329 CR 2202 Tyler TX 75707

THRASH, JOHN CURTIS, JR., petroleum engineer, executive; b. Harris County, Tex., Feb. 9, 1925; s. John Curtis and Alicia May (Lindsey) T.; m. Patricia Ruth Francis, Dec. 21, 1949; children: Denise S., John F., Allison E. BS in Petroleum Engring., U. Tex., 1947. Registered profl. engr., Tex. Prodn. engr. Tex. Co., Odessa, 1947-50; dist. engr. Forest Oil Corp., Odessa, Tex., 1950-55, Brit. Am. Oil Co., Dallas, Oklahoma City, 1955-63; cons. profl. engr. Bart De Coat & Assocs., Houston, 1963-65; v.p. Houston Pipe Line Co., Houston, 1965-81; pres. Thrash Oil and Gas Co., Houston, 1979-90, Togco Gas Storage Corp., Houston, 1985-90, Togco Natural Gas Storage Corp., Houston, 1991—. Contbr. articles to profl. jours. Chmn. Houston chpt. Am. Petroleum Inst., 1975-76. Lt. USNR, 1942-47, 51-54, Korea, World War II. Mem. Am. Petroleum Inst. (chmn. Houston chpt. 1975-76), Tex. Ind. Producers Assn., Ind. Producers Assn. of Am., Soc. Petroleum Engrs. Nat. Soc., Am. Gas Assn., Houston C. of C. (air and water conservation com.). Home: 3435 Westheimer Rd Apt 1500 Houston TX 77027-5347 Office: Togco Natural Gas Storage Corp 3131 W Alabama St Ste 500 Houston TX 77098-2031

THRASHER, BILLIE LEE, school counselor; b. Lewis County, Mo., Aug. 8, 1936; s. Noble Gale and Hazel Cindy (Ingle) T.; m. Beverly Carlene Smith, Dec. 5, 1938; children: Bonnie Lynn, Becky Leigh, Brian Lane. BS, N.E. Mo. State U., 1960, BS in Edn., 1966; MEd, U. Mo., 1969. Cert. tchr., Tenn., Mo. Design draftsman Nooter Corp., St. Louis, 1955-58; test engr. McDonnell-Douglas, St. Louis, 1960-67; tchr./counselor Fayette (Mo.) Pub. Schs., 1967-70; counselor Moberly (Mo.) Pub. Schs., 1970-79; farmer Fayette, 1967-82; owner Agri-Constrn. Co., Fayette, 1979-82; tchr./counselor Wayne County (Tenn.) Pub. Schs., 1982-96; ret.; appointee Strive Program, U. tenn./Oak Ridge Nat. Labs., 1988-89, Step Program, U. Ala.-Huntsville, NASA, 1995-96. Sec. South Ctrl. dist. Gov.'s Tchr. Study Coun., Tenn., 1987-88; pres. O'Fallon Jaycees, 1965-66, Fayette Jaycees, 1968-69; regional v.p. Mo. Jaycees, 1969-70; chmn. bd. dirs. Wayne Skills Orgn. for Handicapped Svcs., Waynesboro, Tenn., 1986-87. With USAF, 1961-62. Named to Outstanding Young Men of Am., 1971. Mem. Am. Vocat. Assn., Tenn. Vocat. Assn. (bd. dirs. 1995-96), Tenn. Vocat. Guidance Assn. (pres. 1989596), Am. Legion. Republican. Methodist. Home: PO Box 182 Collinwood TN 38450

THRASHER, JAMES PARKER, writer; b. Waltham, Mass., Jan. 15, 1932; s. Linus James and Doris Melissa (Parker) T.; B.S. in Indsl. Adminstrn., Yale U., 1953; children: Deborah Anne, Linda Carol, Anne Elizabeth. With U.S. Steel Corp., Cleve., 1953-60; cons. Booz, Allen & Hamilton Internat., London, 1960-65; mgmt. cons. McKinsey & Co., Inc., London, 1965-67; v.p. for Europe, Integrated Container Service, Inc., London, 1967-69, pres., chief exec. officer, N.Y.C., 1970-75; v.p., dir. Interway Corp., N.Y.C., 1969-75, pres., chief exec. officer, dir., 1975-79, Transam. Interway, Inc. subs. Transam. Corp., San Francisco, 1979-81. Author: A Crisis of Values, 1985. Home: 365 Lynn Cove Rd Asheville NC 28804-1914

THREADCRAFT, HAL LAW, III, pastor, counselor; b. Birmingham, Feb. 10, 1952; s. Hal L. Jr. and Helen Barbara (Foster) T.; m. Marion Lee Haygood, Aug. 18, 1973; children: Joshua, John Caleb, Anna. BSCE, U. Ala., 1975; ThM, Dallas Theol. Sem., 1979; MA, U. Ala., 1990, PhD, 1992. Lic. profl. counselor, Ala.; nat. cert. counselor. Min. Young Life, Dallas, 1975-79; prof. Evangelische Theologische Facultait, Heverlee, Belgium, 1979-83; preacher at large Christian Brethren, Alberta, Can., 1983-85; sr. pastor Grace Chapel, Halifax, N.S., Can., 1985-88; pvt. practice; adj. prof. Beeson Sch. Divinity; vis. lectr. U. Ala., 1992—. Author: Apostle Paul's Principles of Church Growth, 1980. Mem. ACA, Internat. Assn. Marriage and Family Counselors, U. Ala. Counseling and Devel. Assn. (pres. 1989-90), Kappa Delta Pi, Phi Kappa Phi, Chi Sigma Iota, Omicron Delta Kappa. Home: 1011 Berrington Cr Birmingham AL 35242

THRELKELD, MARY HELEN, accountant; b. East St. Louis, June 8, 1960; d. James John and Charlette Ann (Mongan) T. BBA, Tex. Christian U., 1982; MBA, U. Chgo., 1990. CPA. Software analyst Tandy Corp./Radio Shack, Ft. Worth, 1981-84; cons. supr. Coopers & Lybrand, Austin, Tex., 1985-88; cons. mgr. Coopers & Lybrand Europe, Brussels, Belgium, 1990-92; strategic analyst Software Spectrum, Inc., Garland, Tex., 1993-94, internat. acct., 1994—. Office: Software Spectrum 2140 Merritt Dr Garland TX 75041-6135

THRONE, GERALDINE GORNY, journalist; b. Newark, July 15, 1946; d. Norbert Richard and Genevieve Lucille (Raczynski) Gorny; m. Raymond Edgar Throne, Mar. 29, 1969; children: Michele, Ryan. BA, Syracuse U., 1968. Reporter Winter Park (Fla.) Sun Herald, 1976-79; reporter Orlando (Fla.) Sentinel, 1981-87, asst. metro editor, 1987-91, dep. bus. editor, 1991-95, mem. editl. bd., 1995—. Trustee First Unitarian Ch., Orlando, 1993-95. Fellow Knight Ctr. for Specialized Journalism, U. Md., 1993. Mem. Investigative Reporters and Editors. Office: Orlando Sentinel 633 N Orange Ave Orlando FL 32801

THUBRIKAR, MANO JUMDEO, medical scientist, educator; b. Nagpur, India, Aug. 27, 1947; came to U.S., 1970; s. Jumdeo and Varanasi (Burde) T.; m. Sudha M. Patekar, July 13, 1973; children: Vaishalee, Vishal. B in Engring., Nagpur U., 1969; MS, NYU, 1971, PhD, 1975. From instr. to assoc. prof. U. Va. Health Scis. Ctr., Charlottesville, 1975-91; assoc. dir. Heineman Med. Rsch. Ctr. Carolina Heart Inst., Charlotte, N.C., 1991—; adj. prof. U. N.C., Charlotte; cons. Meadox Med., Inc., St. Jude Med. Inc.; speaker internat. mtgs. in field, 1982—. Author: The Aortic Valve, 1989; contbr. chpts. in books and articles to profl. jours. Grantee NIH, 1975-81, Career Devel. award NIH 1980-85, 83-86, U. Va., 1982-83, 88-89, Meadox Med., Inc., 1985-86, St. Jude Med. Inc., 1988-89, AB Hassle Pharm. Co., 1988-89, 89-91, 91-95, Am. Heart Assn., 1992-94. Mem. IEEE, AAUP, Internat. Assn. Cardiac Biol. Implants, Am. Soc. Artificial Internal Organs, Biomed. Engring. Soc., Coun. on Arteriosclerosis, Diabetes Rsch. Ctr. U. Va. Home: 4703 Avonwood Ln Charlotte NC 28270-2558 Office: Carolina Med Ctr Heineman Rsch Lab 1000 Blythe Blvd Charlotte NC 28203-5812

THUN, MICHAEL JOHN, epidemiologist, cancer researcher; b. Reading, Pa., Sept. 29, 1944; s. Louis Reinhart and Cynthia (Cameron) T.; m. Patricia Lynne Moody, Dec. 22, 1974; children: Nicholas, Lupe, Haley. BA cum laude, Harvard Coll., 1970; MD, U. Pa., 1975; MS in Epidemiology, Harvard U., 1983. Diplomate Am. Bd. Occupational Medicine, Am. Bd. Preventive Medicine. Med. intern U. Fla., Gainesville, 1975-76, med. resident, 1976-77; med. officer N.J. State Health Dept., Trenton, 1978-80; Epidemic Intelligence Svc. officer Ctr. for Disease Control Nat. Inst. for Occupl. Safety & Health, Cin., 1980-82; supr. Ctr. for Disease Control, NIOSH, Cin., 1983-89; dir. analytic epidemiology Am. Cancer Soc., Atlanta, 1989—; clin. assoc. prof. epidemiology and biostats. div. epidemiology and biostats. Emory U. Sch. Pub. Health, 1990—, div. environ. and occupational health, 1992—. Assoc. editor: Teaching Epidemiology in Occupational Health, 1987; author chpts. in books; mem. editorial bd. Epidemiology; reviewer Am. Jour. Pub. Health, Am. Jour. Indsl. Medicine, Cancer, Environ. Rsch., Epidemiology, JAMA; contbr. articles to profl. jours. Capt. USPHS, 1980-89. Recipient Charles C. Shepard Sci. award, 1993, Alice Hamilton Sci. award, 1993. Mem. APHA, AAAS, Soc. for Epidemiologic Rsch., Physicians for Social Responsibility. Democrat. Home: 564 Ridgecrest Rd NE Atlanta GA 30307-1846 Office: Am Cancer Soc 1599 Clifton Rd NE Atlanta GA 30329-4250

THURBER, JAMES CAMERON, law enforcement officer, consultant, author; b. Boynton Beach, Fla., Oct. 3, 1965; s. John Cameron and JeanAnn (Bridgeman) T. AA, Palm Beach CC, 1986; BS in Criminology, Fla. State U., Tallahassee, 1988, MPA, 1991. Cert. Police Officer, EMT. EMT Atlantic Ambulance Svc., West Palm Beach, 1984-88, Bethesda Ambulance Svc., Boynton Beach, Fla., 1988-92; police officer Lake Worth (Fla.) Police Dept., 1992-94; law enforcement investigator Fla. Divsn. Ins. Fraud, 1994—; vol. aux. police officer Lake Worth Police Dept., 1985-92; cons. Fla. C. of C., Tallahassee, 1991, Fla. Div. Emergency Mgmt., Tallahassee, 1991; intern. Fed. Bureau of Prisons, Tallahassee, 1990, Fla. Dept. Law Enforcement, Pompano Beach, 1987. Contbr. articles to profl. jours. Mem. Lake Worth Pioneer Assn., West Palm Beach, 1965-94, Hist. Soc. Palm Beach County, 1993—; squadron emergency svcs. officer CAP, Lantana, Fla., 1983-89. Recipient Outstanding Academic Achievement award Fraternal Order of Police, Lake Worth, 1992. Mem. Am. Soc. Pub. Adminstrn., Lake Worth Scottish Rite, Masons (Boynton Lodge @ 236), Lambda Chi Alpha, Palm Beach County Seminole Boosters. Episcopalian. Office: Ste 704 1655 Palm Beach Lakes Blvd West Palm Beach FL 33401-2208

THURMAN, SUSAN SOMMERS, secondary education educator; b. Henderson, Ky., Oct. 21, 1949; d. Charles Herbert and Catherine Busby (Moss) Sommers; m. Michael Eugene Thurman, Dec. 27, 1981. BS, Ind. U., 1971; MA, U. Evansville, 1977; postgrad., Murray State U., 1980. Tchr. social studies Henderson County Middle Sch., 1971-77; tchr. Eng. Henderson County North Jr. H.S., 1977-87, Henderson County H.S., 1987—; adult edn. tchr. U. Ky., 1972-79; writing cluster leader Henderson County H.S., 1995—, KTIP mentor, 1995—. Co-author: Currents-Henderson's River Book, 1991; author: Dear Miz Jones; co-author: In the Beginning; editor Class Act, 1993—; author movie study guides. Bd. dirs., sec. Henderson Spl. Olympics, 1975-90; bd. dirs. Friends of Libr., Henderson, 1986—. Office: Class Act Inc PO Box 802 Henderson KY 42420-0802

THURMON, JACK JEWEL, financial services executive; b. Kilgore, Tex., Aug. 14, 1944; s. Merida Eldridge and Agnes (Jones) T.; BS in Indsl. Engring., So. Meth. U., 1967; MBA, Harvard U., 1969; m. Barbara Fern Henson, July 1, 1966; children: J. Gregory, J. Clarke, J. Douglas. Pres., Rimcor, Inc., Houston, 1969-72, Houston Mut. Agy., Inc., 1972-85, Jojoba Mgmt., Inc., Houston, 1982-88; sr. v.p. Crump Co. Houston, 1985-87; pres., chmn., CEO, Nardis, Inc. (formerly Strictly Petites, Inc.), Kilgore, Tex., 1987—; dir., sec./treas. East Tex. Regional Deve. Co.; trustee Kilgore Ind. Sch. Dist., 1987-90. Served with USAR, 1969-75. Republican. Home: 3000 Houston Kilgore TX 75662-3449 Office: 500 E Main St Kilgore TX 75662-5908

THURMON, THEODORE FRANCIS, medical educator; b. Baton Rouge, Oct. 20, 1937; s. Theodore Francis and Gertrude Wilhemena (Arnette) T.; m.

Virginia Ruth Strange, Sept. 1, 1961 (div. Oct. 1975); children: Penelope, Suzanna; m. Susonne Annette Ursin, Aug. 8, 1981 (div. Aug. 1992); children: Sarah Eileen, Amanda Aislinn; m. Suzanne Greenwood, Sept. 2, 1992. BS, La. State U., Baton Rouge, 1960; MD, La. State U., New Orleans, 1962. Diplomate Am. Bd. Pediatrics, Am. Bd. Med. Genetics. Commd. ensign USNR, 1957; transferred to USN, 1957, advanced through grades to lt. comdr., 1967; intern naval hosp. Pensacola, Fla., 1962-63; resident in pediatrics naval hosp. Phila., 1963-65, trainee in cytogenetics St. Christopher's Hosp., 1964-65; asst. cardiology naval hosp. St. Albans, N.Y., 1965-67; resigned USN, 1968; fellow in med. genetics Johns Hopkins Hosp., Balt., 1968-69; asst. prof. La. State U. Med. Ctr., New Orleans, 1969-72, assoc. prof., 1972-78, prof., 1978-86; prof. La. State U. Med. Ctr., Shreveport, 1986—. Author: Rare Genetic Diseases, 1974, Medical Genetics Primer, 1995; contbr. articles to med. jours. Active birth defects ctr. Nat. Found./March of Dimes, New Orleans, 1969-81, La. Bd. Regents, New Orleans, 1982, La. Dept. Health, New Orleans, 1984—, La. Cancer & Lung Trust Fund, New Orleans, 1985-86. Fellow Am. Coll. Med. Genetics, Am. Acad. Pediat.; mem. AAAS, Am. Genetic Assn., Am. Soc. Human Genetics, Am. Statis. Assn., Assn. Profs. Human or Med. Genetics, La. Med. Soc., N.Y. Acad. Scis. Home: 1732 Willow Point Dr Shreveport LA 71119-4108 Office: La State U Med Sch Pediat-Genetics 1501 Kings Hwy Shreveport LA 71103-4228

THURMOND, JOHN PETER, II, bank executive, rancher, archeologist; b. Elk City, Okla., Apr. 22, 1955; s. Arthur Leslie and Dorothea Jean (Lee) T.; m. Susan Ide Smith, June 7, 1979; children: Katherine Anne, Allison Lee, Patrick Andrew. BA, U. Tex., 1976, MA, 1979. Pres., chmn. First Nat. Bank of Leedey, Okla., 1984-92, Leedey Bancorporation, Inc., 1984-92, Thurmond Ranch, Inc., Cheyenne, Okla., 1982—; vice chmn. First Nat. Bank & Trust Co., Elk City, 1992—. Author: Archeology of the Cypress Basin, NE Texas, 1981, Late Paleoindian Utilization of the Dempsey Divide, 1990. Emergency med. technician, sec. Leedey Ambulance Svc., Inc., 1981-88. Recipient Hist. Preservation award Okla. Hist. Soc., 1991. Mem. Okla. Anthrop. Soc. (sec., treas. 1988—), Leedey C. of C. (pres. 1982-83), Geol. Soc. Am., Am. Quaternary Assn., Tex. Archeol. Soc., Plains Anthrop. Soc., Am. Quaternary Assn., Geol. Soc. Am., Okla. Cattlemen's Assn., Okla. Hist. Soc., Cum Laude Soc., Phi Beta Kappa, Phi Kappa Phi. Republican. Episcopalian.

THURMOND, STROM, senator; b. Edgefield, S.C., Dec. 5, 1902; s. John William and Eleanor Gertrude (Strom) T.; m. Jean Crouch, Nov. 7, 1947 (dec. Jan. 1960); m. Nancy Moore, Dec. 22, 1968; children: Nancy Moore (dec.), J. Strom, Jr., Juliana Gertrude, Paul Reynolds. B.S., Clemson Coll., 1923; 34 hon. degrees. Bar: S.C. 1930. Tchr. S.C. schs., 1923-29; city atty., county atty., supt. edn. Edgefield County, 1929-33; state senator, 1933-38, circuit judge, 1938-46, gov. of S.C., 1947-51; chmn. So. Govs. Conf., 1950; practiced in Alken, S.C., 1951-55; U.S. senator from S.C., 1955—, pres. pro tem 104th Congress; Del. Nat. Democratic Conv., 1932, 36, 48, 52, 56, 60; chmn. S.C. dels., armed svcs. com., Judiciary Subcom. on antitrust bus. rts. and competition; mem. Dem. Nat. Com., 1948, Vets. Affairs/Sen. Rep. Policy Com.; States Rights candidate for Pres. U.S., 1948; del. Nat. Republican Conv., 1968, 72, 76. Bd. dirs. Ga.-Carolina council Boy Scouts Am. Served with AUS; attached to 82d Airborne Div. for invasion 1942-46, Europe; maj. gen. Res. Decorated Legion of Merit with oak leaf cluster, Bronze Star with V, Purple Heart, Croix de Guerre France; Cross of Order of Crown Belgium; others; recipient Congl. Medal Honor Soc. Nat. Patriots award, 1974, Presdl. Medal of Freedom, 1993. Mem. S.C. (past v.p.), ABA, Clemson Coll. Alumni Assn. (past pres.), also numerous def., vets., civic, fraternal and farm orgns. Baptist. Office: US Senate 217 Russell Senate Office Bldg Washington DC 20510*

THWEATT, JOE MACK, computer science educator; b. Nashville, Apr. 3, 1939; s. Enoch Brown and Eloise (Turbeville) T.; m. Sandra Zapp, May 19, 1961; children: LeAnn Thweatt Harris, Shawn Thweatt Springer, Manly. BA, David Lipscomb U., 1961; MA, Mid. Tenn. State U., 1962, EdS, 1986; EdD, Tenn. State U., 1988. Cert. tchr. math., Tenn. Tchr. math. Hillwood High Sch., Nashville, 1962-64; tchr. math. and computer sci. Mid. Ten. State U., Murfreesboro, 1965—; cons. VA Hosp., Murfreesboro, Tenn., 1992-94. Co-author: Computer Science Lab Manual, 1994; author: (book sects.) Ency. Dictionary, 1963, 68. Recipient Tenn. Outstanding Achievement award Gov. Tenn., 1980; Nat. Champion Girl's Softball Coach, U.S. Slow Pitch Softball Assn., 1978, 79. Mem. Assn. Computing Machinery-Spl. Interest Group Computer Sci. Edn., Assn. Computing Machinery, Soc. Computer Simultion, Upsilon Pi Epsilon. Mem. Ch. of Christ. Office: Mid Tenn State U Dept Computer Sci Murfreesboro TN 37132

TIAN, GUOQIANG, economics educator; b. Wuhan, Hubei, China, Apr. 7, 1956; came to U.S., 1983; s. Zheng and Qunhua (Dai) T.; m. Yafei Lu, Jan. 18, 1982; children: Mary Humei, Robert Long. BA in Math., Huazhong (China) U. Sci. and Tech., 1980, MA in Math., 1982; PhD in Econs., U. Minn., 1987. Lectr. math. Huazhong U. Sci. and Tech., spring 1980, 82; rsch. asst., tchg. asst. U. Minn., Mpls., 1983-85, tchg. assoc. dept. econs., 1986; asst. prof. Tex. A&M U., College Station, 1987-90, assoc. prof., 1991-94, prof., 1995—; guest prof. Konstanz U., Germany, 1991; adj. prof. Wuhan Inst. Econs., 1993—, dept. econs. and fin. Wuhan U. Tech., 1993—, dept. social sci. Wuhan U. Hydraulic and Elec. Engring., 1993—, dept. quantitative econs. Huazhong U. Sci. and Tech., 1993—; invited participant Nat. Bur. Econ. Rsch.-NSF confs. on decentralization U. Rochester, N.Y., 1988, Calif. Inst. Tech., Pasadena, 1989, Northwestern U., Evanston, Ill., 1990, U. Ariz., Tucson, 1992, Toronto Univ., Can., 1994; invited participant other profl. confs., Chgo., Hong Kong, Minn.; pres. Assn. Chinese Profs. of Social Scis. in U.S. Author: (with Fan Zhang) book in A Series of Popular Economics Books for Institutional Transition in China, 1993; co-contbr. 2 chpts. to: Advances in Econometrics and Modeling, 1989; contbr. chpt. (with others) to: European Integration in the World Economy, 1992; contbr. many articles to profl. publs., including Econs. Letters, Rev. of Econ. Studies, Jour. Econ. Theory, Jour. Math. Analysis and Applications, Social Choice and Welfare, Jour. Math. Econs., Internat. Econ. Rev., Jour. Pub. Econs., Math. Ops. Rsch., others. Alfred P. Sloan doctoral dissertation fellow, 1986-87; nominee Presdl. Young Investigator award, 1989, 90; Interdisciplinary Rsch. Initiatives Enhancement Program rsch. grantee, 1993-94. Fellow Chinese Economists Soc. (hon., pres. 1991-92); mem. Am. Econ. Assn., Econometric Soc., Soc. for Promotion of Econ. Theory. Home: 3001 Durango St College Station TX 77845-6550 Office: Tex A&M U Dept Econs College Station TX 77843

TIBBO, HELEN RUTH, information and library science educator; b. Worcester, Mass., Apr. 22, 1955; d. Thomas M. and Frances H. Tibbo. BA in English, Bridgewater State Coll., 1977; MLS, Ind. U., 1983; MA in Am. Studies, U. Md., 1984, PhD in Info. and Libr. Sci., 1989. English tchr. grade 8 West Middle Sch., Whitman, Mass., 1977-78; English tchr. grades 7-8 North Jr. High Sch., Brockton, Mass., 1978-79, Sharon (Mass.) Jr. High Sch., 1979-82; adj. instr. U. Balt., 1986; adj. instr. U. Md., College Park, 1987, rsch./teaching asst., 1987-89; asst. prof. sch. info. and libr. sci. U. N.C., Chapel Hill, 1989-95, assoc. prof., 1995—, asst. dean, 1996—; reviewer for grants and contracts NEH, Washington, 1994—, Nat. Cancer Inst., Rockville, Md., 1994; ednl. cons. Nat. Archives and Records Adminstrn., Washington, 1993. Author: Abstracting, Information Retrieval and the Humanities, 1993; contbr. chpt.: Annual Review of Information Science and Technology, 1991; contbr. articles to profl. jours.; mem. editl. bd. Archives USA, 1994—. Rsch. grantee Nat. Libr. Medicine, 1995; recipient Excellence in Online Edn. award Dialog Info. Svcs., 1990. Mem. Soc. Am. Archivists (chair publ. bd. 1994-97, task force on future of Am. archivist 1996, Posner prize 1994), Am. Soc. for Info. Sci. (doctoral forum com. 1994-95), Assn. Libr. and Info. Sci. Educators (recruitment com. 1991-94), ALA (libr. rsch. roundtable steering com. 1995—), Mid-Atlantic Regional Archives Conf., Soc. N.C. Archivists. Democrat. Office: U NC Chapel Hill Sch Info Libr Sci 100 Manning Hall CB 3360 Chapel Hill NC 27599-3360

TIBLIER, FERNAND JOSEPH, JR., municipal engineering administrator; b. New Orleans, Mar. 11, 1960; s. Fernand Joseph and Dorothy May (Bosworth) T.; m. Janine Therese Cousineau, Sept. 1, 1990; children: Amanda, Christine. BA in Chemistry, Biology, Drury Coll., 1982; MS in Environ. Engring., U. Cen. Fla., 1986. Registered profl. engr., Fla. Rsch. asst. U. Cen. Fla., Orlando, 1983-86; asst. city engr., then acting city engr. City of Longwood, Fla., 1986-92, city engr., 1992-94, dir. pub. works, city engr., 1994—; mem. road impact fee com. Seminole County Citizen Adviser, Sanford, Fla., 1988-89; mem. water resources task force Seminole County Tech. Adviser, Sanford, 1992. Lector, youth minister Nativity Ch., Lake Mary, Fla., 1987—; team capt. City of Longwood March of Dimes, 1992. Mem. Am. Water Works Assn., Water Pollution Control Fedn., Community Leaders/Elected Ofcls. Seminole County, Longwood-Winter Springs C. of C. Republican. Roman Catholic. Home: 407 Parson Brown Way Longwood FL 32750-4020 Office: City of Longwood 180 E Warren Ave Longwood FL 32750-4266

TICE, DAVID ALLAN, forester, environmental consultant; b. Balt., Dec. 11, 1952; s. Richard Howard and Dorothy Eileen (Critchfield) T.; m. Vickie Denise Harris, Oct. 1, 1977; children: Elizabeth, Kathryn. BS, Va. Poly. Inst. and State U., 1974. Forester Va. Div. Forestry, Charlottesville, 1974-78; forester/planner Va. Div. Forestry, Salem, 1978-79; v.p. Mid-Atlantic Forestry Svcs., Inc., Charlottesville, 1979-87; pres. N. Am. Resource Mgmt., Inc., Charlottesville, 1987—; exec. dir. Bellevive Found., U.S.A., Charlottesville, 1989—; mem. faculty U. Va., Charlottesville, 1985-86, 93, 96, Piedmont Va. C.C. 1981-83; cons. in field; v. p. Am. Resources Group, 1982—. Contbr. articles to profl. jours.; developer computer info. sys.: Multiple Resource Inventory Analysis, 1987. Mem. Non-tidal Wetlands Roundtable, 1989, Albemarle County Planning Commn., 1996—; mem. Va. Task Force on Sustainable Devel., 1995; mem. Thomas Jefferson Sustainability Coun., 1994—; mem. adv. bd. Bellerive Found. U.S.A., 1987—; mem. Agrl. Adv. Com., Charlottesville. Named Young Forester of Yr., Va. Soc. Am. Foresters, 1981; recipient Forestry Best Mgmt. Practices award, 1989, numerous land mgmt. awards. Mem. Nature Conservancy (bd. dirs. 1979-92), Soc. Am. Foresters, Practicing Foresters Inst. (treas. 1987-89, trustee), Forest Resource Systems Inst. (bd. dirs. 1985-86), Nat. Woodland Owners Assn. (exec. com. 1984—), Va. Forestry Assn. (dir. 1989-92), Wildlife Soc., Nat. Urban Forest Coun., Va. Urban Forest Coun. (dir. 1992-93), Piedmont Environ. Coun. (dir. 1992-95). Methodist. Office: NAm Resource Mgmt PO Box 6777 Charlottesville VA 22906-6777

TICE, WILLIAM FLEET, JR., pastor; b. Rockford, Ill., Aug. 20, 1942; s. William Fleet and June Edna (Clark) T.; m. Martha Elizabeth Robertson, June 8, 1963; children: Elizabeth Ann, Belinda Sue, William Fleet III, Michael Meshell. BA in Religion, Ind. Wesleyan U., 1964; M in Pastoral Studies, Loyola U., New Orleans, 1992. Ordained to ministry Wesleyan Ch., 1966. Minister Sims (Ind.) Meth. Ch., 1963-64; asst. pastor 1st Wesleyan Ch., Waterloo, Iowa, 1964-66; minister, chaplain Oak Hills Wesleyan Ch./Mayo Clinic, Rochester, Minn., 1966-70; sr. pastor Wheaton (Ill.) Wesleyan Ch., 1970-73, 1st Wesleyan Ch., Bossier City, La., 1973—; pres. Rochester Ministerial Alliance, 1968-70, Bossier City Ministerial Alliance, 1975-78; dist. bd. advisors Delta Dist. Wesleyan Ch., Jackson, Miss., 1983—, dist. sec., 1987—; chaplain, cons. Bossier Med. Ctr. Hospice Program. Pres. Bossier City Kiwanis Club, 1976, Bossier City Clean City Com., 1987; trustee Bossier Med. Ctr., Bossier City, 1980; mem. human concerns com. Priorities for the Future, La., 1978. Mem. Kiwanis (founder South Bossier club 1982). Republican. Home: 125 Oaklawn Dr Bossier City LA 71112-9719 Office: 1st Wesleyan Ch 3200 Schuler Dr Bossier City LA 71112-5124

TICER, PATRICIA, state senator; m. Jack Ticer; 4 children. Grad., Sweet Briar Coll. Councilwoman City of Alexandria, Va., 1982-84, vice mayor, 1984-90, appointed mayor, 1991-92, mayor, 1992-95; state senator State of Va., 1995—, mem. agrl., conservation & natural resources com., transp. com., rehab. & social svcs. com., local govt. com., 1995—; chair COG Transp. Planning Bd., chmn. bd. dirs., 1994; mem. coordinating com. Woodrow Wilson Bridge; bd. dirs. No. Va. Transp. Commn., chmn., 1994; bd. dirs. Transp. Coordinating Coun. Founding mem. Early Childhood Devel. Commn., No. Va. Housing Coalition, Alexandria Commn. on the Arts; mem. Govs. Coun. on Child Care and Early Childhood Programs; mem. adv. coun. Alexandria Symphony Orch.; active No. Va. AIDS Mins. Mem. Nat. Assn. Regional Couns. (pres. 1994-95). Office: Rm 2007 Cith Hall 301 King St Alexandria VA 22314-3211

TICHENOR, FRED COOPER, JR., newspaper columnist; b. Shelbyville, Ky., Feb. 20, 1932; s. Fred Cooper S. and Mattye Lee (Stout) T.; m. Nancy Catherine Preso, Aug. 25, 1956 (div.); children: Frederick Woodson, David Lee; m. Jean Carol Stuecker, Aug. 11, 1989. BA in Philosophy, U. Louisville, 1957; postgrad. in psychiatry, Albert Einstein Coll. Medicine, 1991. Asst. mgr. Courier-Jour., Louisville, 1957-64; asst. v.p. Grolier Pubs., Chgo., 1964-71; syndicated newspaper columnist (Star Lore) Louisville, 1981—, TV Syndication, 1988—; bus. and personal cons., 1971—; organizer Moonbow Astrology Retreat, Cumberland Falls, Ky., 1974—, Cradle of Civilization Tour to Egypt, Greece, Eng., Mex., Peru, Bolivia, Honduras, 1979—; lectr. in U.S., Italy, France and U.S.S.R., 1980—. Councilman City of West Point, Ky., 1986-88; chmn. Planning and Zoning Commn., City of West Point, 1985-88; vice chmn. Salt River Area Coun. for the Arts, West Point, 1983-88; mem. Community Sch. Bd., West Point, 1986-88; sec. bd. dirs. Mead County Messenger, Brandenburg, Ky., 1985. With U.S. Army, 1951-53, Korea. Mem. Assn. for Psychol. Type. Republican. Office: Ste G 34-38 1169 Eastern Pky Louisville KY 40217-1417

TICHI, CECELIA, English language educator; b. Pitts., Apr. 10, 1942; d. James Francis Halbert and Mary Louise (Doherty) Tashman; m. William John Tichi, Sept. 8, 1967; children: Claire, Julia. BA, Pa. State U., 1964; MA, Johns Hopkins U., 1965; PhD, U. Calif., Davis, 1968. Asst. prof., English Boston U., 1968-75, assoc. prof., 1975-82, prof., 1982-87; prof., English Vanderbilt U., Nashville, 1987-90, William R. Kenan Jr. prof., English, 1991—; cons. Nat. Ctr. Humanities, Research Triangle Park, N.C., 1992—. Author: New World New Earth, 1979, Shifting Gears, 1987, Electronic Hearth, 1991, High Lonesome, 1994; editor: The Harper American Literature, 1986. Rsch. grantee Sci. Tech. Soc., NEH, 1986, summer seminar for coll. tchrs. grantee NEH, 1996. Mem. MLA, Am. Studies Assn. (pres. 1992-93). Home: 616 Hillwood Blvd Nashville TN 37205-1314 Office: Vanderbilt U Dept English Nashville TN 37235

TIDWELL, MARY ELLEN, risk/insurance coordinator; b. Liberty, S.C., June 25, 1940; d. William Robert and Ruby Irene (Trammell) Murphy; m. Howard Eugene Anderson, Sept. 8, 1956 (div. Jan. 1987); children: Howard Eugene Jr., Sterling Craig; m. Lear Tidwell, July 9, 1989. AS in Office Mgmt., Polk C.C., 1993. Sec. H. Lamar Stewart Ins. Agy, Frostproof, Fla., 1962-64; accounts payable clk. Ben Hill Griffin, Inc., Frostproof, 1964-65; agt. Bullard Ins. Agy., Inc., Lake Wales, Fla., 1966-79; risk/ins. coordinator Coca-Cola Foods, Auburndale, Fla., 1979—; dir. Fla. Girls State, Inc., Orlando, 1988-93. City chmn. March of Dimes, Frostproof, 1964; campaign worker Tom Wheeler for Sheriff, Winter Haven, Fla., 1988. Mem. Risk and Ins. Mgmt. Soc., Am. Legion, Order of Eastern Star. Democrat. Baptist. Office: Coca-Cola Foods PO Box 247 Auburndale FL 33823-0247

TIEDEMANN, ALBERT WILLIAM, JR., chemist; b. Balt., Nov. 7, 1924; s. Albert William and Catherine (Madigan) T.; m. Mary Therese Sellmayer, Apr. 6, 1953; children: Marie Therese, Donna Elise, Albert William III, David Lawrence. BS, Loyola Coll., Balt., 1947; MS, NYU, 1949; PhD, Georgetown U., 1958. Teaching fellow N.Y. U., 1947-50; instr. chemistry Mt. St. Agnes Coll., 1950-55; chief chemist Emerson Drug div. Warner Lambert Pharm. Co., Balt., 1955-60; analytical supr. Hercules Powder Co., Allegany Ballistics Lab., Cumberland, Md., 1960-68; tech. svc. supt. Hercules Inc., Radford, Va., 1968-72; dir. Va. Div. Consol. Labs., Richmond, 1972-78; vice-chmn. Va. Toxic Substances Adv. Council, 1978-92; dep. dir. for labs. Va. Dept. Gen. Svcs., 1978-92, cons. 1992—. Mem. sci. adv. com. Longwood Coll., 1983-90. Served to lt. (j.g.) USNR, 1943-46; capt. Res., 1946—. Fellow Am. Inst. Chemists; mem. Soc. Advancement Mgmt., chpt. v.p. 1983-84, chpt. pres. 1984-85), Am. Soc. Quality Control (chmn. Richmond sect. 1975-76, councilor biomed. div. 1978-80), U.S. Naval Inst., Naval Res. Assn. (dist. pres. 1954-57; nat. v.p. 1962-63, 65-69; nat. chmn. Navy Sabbath Program 1969-75; Nat. Meritorious Service award 1971, Twice a Citizen award 1978), Cen. Atlantic States Assn. Food & Drug Ofcls. (exec. bd. 1977-84, v.p. 1981-82, pres. 1982-83, CASA award 1986), Nat. Assn. Food & Drug Ofcls. (chmn. sci. and tech. com. 1981-85, sec.-treas. 1985-87), Internat. Assn. Ofcl. Analytical Chemists (editorial bd. 1986-88, bd. dirs. 1987-90), Analytical Lab. Mgrs. Assn., Royal Acad. Pharmacy (elected acad. fgn. mem. Barcelona, Spain 1989—). Home: 10511 Cherokee Rd Richmond VA 23235-1008

TIEDEMANN, RUTH ELIZABETH FULTON (SUNNYE TIEDEMANN), writer, educator; b. Knoxville, Tenn., Aug. 27, 1935; d. Frank Keene and Ruth Almeda (McConnell) Fulton; m. Herbert Allen Tiedemann, Sept. 3, 1955; children: Ruth Patten, Keene Fulton, Melvin John (dec.), Herbert Allen Jr. Student, U. Tenn., 1953-56; cert. in real estate, U. Md., 1976, cert. appraiser, 1977; student, U. Okla., 1983-84. Mgr. Corbin Co. Realtors, Bartlesville, Okla., 1977-80; legal document analyst Phillips Petroleum Co., Bartlesville, 1980-84; indexer, legal analyst, 1996; columnist Bartlesville Examiner-Enterprise, 1984-94, 96—; pres. Pens and Lens, Bartlesville, 1985—; book columnist The Bartlesville Times, 1994-95; contemporary books editor Rave Revs. Mag., N.Y.C., 1987-89; publicity dir. Okla. Mozart Internat. Festival, Bartlesville, 1988; adj. prof. Bartlesville Wesleyan Coll., 1990-96; tchr. creative writing Tri-County Vocat. Tech. Contbr. articles to comml. mags. and profl. jours. and newspapers. Co-founder Bartlesville Compassionate Friends, 1979—; developer libr. Creative Writing Contest. Mem. Women's Coun. Realtors, Okla. Writers Fedn. (Creative Writing award 1987, 89, 92, 93, 95), Nat. Book Critics Cir., Sisters in Crime, Bartlesville WordWeavers (pres. 1991-92), Tulsa Nightwriters, Okla. Ctr. for the Book (bd. dirs.), Delta Delta Delta. Republican. Presbyterian. Home: 1609 S Dewey Ave Bartlesville OK 74003-5820

TIEFEL, MARK GREGORY, real estate executive; b. Detroit, May 11, 1952; s. Paul Martin and Virginia May (Brenkert) T. BA, Kent State U., 1975; MBA, U. Pitts., 1996. Sales assoc. Innovent Mktg. Corp., Cleve., 1975-78; regional mktg. rep. M.G.I.C., Milw., 1978-83; gen. mgr. Great Lakes Securities, Columbus, Ohio, 1983-85; regional v.p. Sybedon, N.Y.C., 1985-87; v.p. Dover Asset Group, Newport Beach, Calif., 1987-91; sr. v.p. Gen. Capital Corp., Nashville, 1991-93; chmn. bd., dir. Resdl. Equity Corp., Cleve., 1984-92; cons. Mortgage Servicing Soc., Cleve., 1978-83. Officer Bedford (Ohio) Recreation Dept., 1982-87; mem. Youth for Christ, Cleve., 1991—; officer bus. for Jobs, 1991—. Mem. Bldg. Industry Assn., Am. Sailing Assn., Nat. Assn. Securities Dealers.

TIERNEY, MICHAEL JOHN, mathematics and computer science educator; b. St. Louis, Feb. 19, 1947; s. John Thomas and Alice Marie (Krieger) T.; m. Edith L. Echelmeyer, Nov. 21, 1975 (div. Sept. 1984); 1 child, John E.; m. Virginia Lee Christian, Apr. 6, 1985. BS, St. Louis U., 1969, MS, 1971, PhD, 1974; MS, U. Va., 1995. Prof. math. and actuarial sci. Maryville Coll., St. Louis, 1974-83; prof. math. and computer sci. Va. Mil. Inst., Lexington, 1983—; dept. chair, 1995—. Mem. AAUP, AAAS, Am. Math. Soc., Math. Assn. Am., Soc. Indsl. and AppliedMath., Assn. Computing Machinery, Sigma Xi. Presbyterian. Home: 819 Gwynne Ave Waynesboro VA 22980-3342 Office: Va Mil Inst Lexington VA 24450

TIESZEN, RALPH LELAND, SR., internist; b. Marion, S.D., Sept. 21, 1928; s. Bernard D. and Hulda J. (Thomas) T.; m. Florence Morrill Johnson, July 25, 1952; children: Ralph Leland Jr., Stuart Carl, Stephan Lee. Student, Freeman Jr. Coll., 1946-48; BS, Wheaton Coll., 1950; postgrad., U. S.D., 1950-52; MD, Loma Linda U., 1954. Diplomate Am. Bd. Internal Medicine, Am. Bd. Geriatric Medicine. Intern L.A. County Hosp., 1954-55, resident TB and Chest, 1955-56; commd. 2d lt. med. corps. USAF, 1956, advanced through grades to maj., 1964; chief medicine hosp. USAF, Eglin AFB, 1962-64; ret. USAF, 1979; resident in internal medicine Mayo Found., Rochester, Minn., 1957-60; mem. active staff dept. internal medicine Carraway Meth. Med. Ctr., Birmingham, 1964—, dir. resident program, 1968-72, trustee, 1972-77, pres. staff, 1973-75, exec. com., fin. com., 1974-77, dir. geriatrics, 1989—; pvt. practice Norwood Clinic, Inc., Birmingham, Ala., 1964—; asst. clin. prof. medicine Med. Coll. Ala., 1965-69, asst. clin. prof. dept. endocrinology, 1969-70, clin. assoc. prof. medicine, 1970-81, clin. prof. medicine, 1981—; med. dir. Community Hosp., 1989—; mem. faculty joint commn. accreditation hosps., 1974-78; exec. com. Birmingham Regional Health Systems Agy.; investigator numerous clin. trials. Contbr. articles to profl. jours. Chmn. Birmingham String Quartet, 1970-74; v.p. ticket sales Ala. Symphony Assn., 1979, exec. com.; sec. men's com. Ala. Symphony, 1986-88, pres. 1990-91. Gen. Med. Officer USAR, 197984, comdr. U.S. Army Hosp., Birmingham, 1984-88, col., chief profl. svcs. 5th med. group, Birmingham, 1988-92, ret., 1992. Mem. ACP, AMA, Am. Thoracic Soc. (sr.), Med. Assn. State Ala., Jefferson County Med. Soc. (past bd. censors, del. to state med. assn.), Birmingham Acad. Medicine (pres. 1987-88), Birmingham Internists Soc. (pres. 1972-73). Democrat. Office: Norwood Clinic Inc PO Box 830230 1528 26th St N Birmingham AL 35234-1911

TIETKE, WILHELM, gastroenterologist; b. Niengraben, Germany, Oct. 15, 1938; came to U.S., 1969, naturalized, 1979; s. Wilhelm and Frieda (Schmeding) T.; m. Imme Schmidt, Oct. 15, 1965; children: Cornelia, Isabel. MD, U Goettingen (West Germany), 1968. Diplomate Am. Bd. Internat. Medicine, Am. Bd. Gastroenterology. Intern Edward W. Sparrow Hosp., Lansing, Mich., 1970; resident in internal medicine Henry Ford Hosp., Detroit, 1971-73; fellow in gastroenterology, 1973-75; practice medicine specializing in gastroenterology, Huntsville, Ala., 1975—; mem. vol. faculty, cons. U. Ala., Huntsville, 1976; clin. assoc. prof. internal medicine, 1979—; v.p. Huntsville Gastroenterology Assocs., P.C., 1979—. Fellow Coll. Gastroenterology; mem. AMA, Ala. Med. Soc., Am. Coll. Physicians, Am. Soc. Gastrointestinal Endoscopy. Lutheran. Lodge: Rotary. Home: 2707 Westminister Way SE Huntsville AL 35801-2241 Office: 119 Longwood Dr Huntsville AL 35801-4205 also: PO Box 2169 Huntsville AL 35804-2169

TIGAR, MICHAEL EDWARD, lawyer, educator; b. Glendale, Calif., Jan. 18, 1941; s. Charles Henry and Margaret Elizabeth (Lang) T.; m. Pamet Ayer Jones, Sept. 21, 1961 (div. Mar. 1973); children: Jon Steven, Katherine Ayer; m. Amanda G. Birrell, Feb. 16, 1980 (div. Aug. 1996); 1 child, Elizabeth Torrey; m. Jane E. Blanksteen, Aug. 22, 1996. BA in Polit. Sci., U. Calif., Berkeley, 1962, JD, 1966. Bar: D.C. 1967, U.S. Ct. Appeals (2d, 4th, 5th, 6th, 7th, 8th, 9th, 10th and D.C. cirs.), U.S. Tax Ct., U.S. Supreme Ct. 1972, N.Y. 1993. Assoc. Williams & Connolly, Washington, 1966-69; editor-in-chief Selective Svc. Law Reporter, Washington, 1967-69; acting prof. law UCLA, 1969-71; pvt. practice law Grasse, France, 1972-74; assoc. William & Connolly, Washington, 1974, ptnr., 1975-77; ptnr. Tigar & Buffone, Washington, 1977-84; prof. law U. Tex., Austin, 1984-87, Joseph D. Jamail centennial chair in law, 1987—; of counsel Haddon, Morgan & Foreman, Denver, 1996—; reporter 5th Cir. Pattern Jury Instrns., Austin, 1988-90. Author: Practice Manual Selective Service Law Reporter, 1968, Law and the Rise of Capitalism, 1977, Federal Appeals: Jurisdiction and Practice, 2d edit., 1993, Examining Witnesses, 1993; contbr. articles to profl. jours. Mem. ABA (vice chair 1987-88, chair elect 1988-89, chair 1989-90 sect. litigation). Office: PO Box 160037 Austin TX 78716-0037

TIGH, MARK STEPHEN, telecommunications executive, engineering consultant; b. Salem, Mass., Apr. 26, 1948; s. Louis Mark II and Frances Winifred (Mitchell) T.; m. Theresa Ann Kirsher, Apr. 4, 1981; 1 child, Tanya Marcia; children: Tiffany Ann, Louis Mark III, William Sullivan. Student, Marist Coll., 1966; BS, Ga. Inst. Tech., 1966-67, 1972-76; student, West Ga. Coll., 1967, La. State U., Lafayette, 1977-78, Batelle Meml. Inst., 1981. Regional mgr. Wilson-Mankin Engrs., Atlanta, 1975-76; offshore engr. The Offshore Co., Venezuela, 1976-78; prin., CEO Mark Stephen Tigh Assocs., Atlanta, 1976-79; project engr. SP Comms., Burlingame, Calif., 1979-82; sr. engr. Aydin Systems Saudi Arabia, Riyadh, Saudi Arabia, 1982-85; v.p. Constrn. Surveillance Svcs., San Diego, 1985-87; sr. v.p. Transworld Consortium, Inc., San Francisco, 1987-92; sr. mgr. Bell South Internat., Atlanta, 1992—; wireless engring. cons. Royal Saudi Nat. Guard, Riyadh, 1982-86, U.S. Dept. Def., Washington, 1978—; bd. dirs. Transworld Consortium, Inc., San Francisco, Mango Internat., Inc., Sunnyvale, Calif. Author: Veet-A Nam-Ah, 1992; contbr. articles to profl. jours.; inventor of telecom equipment. Mem. San Mateo (Calif.) County Commn., 1985-92, Mott Twp. Police Res., Siskiyou County, Calif., 1982—. Sgt. USMC, 1967-72, Vietnam, maj. in Res. 1975-91. Named outstanding marine Leatherneck Mag., 1967; recipient Cross of Gallantry, 1st place design award Ga. Sheriff's Assn., 1975, 1st place cover shot Assn. Archtl. Photographers, 1981. Mem. AIA, USMC Ret. Officer's Assn., So. Bldg. Code Congress, USMC Force Recon Assn., Constrn. Specifications Inst., San Francisco C. of C., Engrs. Club. Roman Catholic. Home: 3855 Jettie Ct SW Lilburn GA 30247-2362 Office: Bell South Internat 1100 Peachtree St 11HO8 Atlanta GA 30309

TIJERINA, RAUL MARTIN, physics and mathematics educator; b. Brownsville, Tex., Dec. 10, 1962; s. Gregorio and Maria Olivia (Reyes) T. BS in Physics, U. North Tex., 1987; Cert. in Teaching, U. Tex., Brownsville, 1989. Cert. tchr., Tex. Math., physics tchr. U. Tex., Brownsville, 1988—; math., algebra tchr. Brownsville Ind. Sch. Dist., 1988—. Mem. Nat. Coun. Tchrs. Math., Math. Assn. Am., Am. Inst. Physics. Roman Catholic. Office: Perkins Mid Sch 4750 Austin Rd Brownsville TX 78521-5455

TILBE, LINDA MACLAUCHLAN, nursing administrator; b. Bangor, Maine, Mar. 1, 1950; d. John and Ruby Mae (Dorr) MacLauchlan; married; children: William, Robert, Grant. BSN, U. Maine, 1973; M in Healthcare Adminstrn., Quinnipiac Coll., 1988. RN, Conn., Fla. Ob-gyn. staff nurse Yale New Haven Hosp., 1973-79, med. ICU nurse, 1979-83, post anesthesia staff nurse, 1983-88; adminstrv. mgmt. intern Shirley Frank Found., New Haven, 1987-88; clin. nurse adminstr. pain mgmt. Yale U., New Haven, 1988-92; nurse mgr., arthritis and pain ctrs. North Broward Med. Ctr., 1992-95; clin. nurse supr. Pain Mgmt. Ctr. Doctors Hosp. Sarasota (Fla.), 1995—. Author: A Manual for Acute Postoperative Pain Management, 1992; author and editor: Acute Pain Mechanisms and Management, 1992; contbr. articles to profl. jours. Mem. Internat. Assn. Study of Pain, Am. Pain Soc., Am. Soc. Post Anesthesia Nurses, Am. Soc. Pain Mgmt. Nurses (founder), Conn. Soc. Post Anesthesia Nurses. Home: 5800 Milton Ave Sarasota FL 34243 Office: Doctors Hosp Sarasota Pain Mgmt Ctr 5741 Bee Ridge Rd Sarasota FL 34233-5064

TILGHMAN, CARL LEWIS, lawyer; b. Detroit, Aug. 3, 1944; s. Clifford Raymond and Alma (Gillikin) T.; m. Nancy Ann Huff, Aug. 21, 1965; children: Jason Andrew, Amanda Carol. Student, Beaufort H.S., 1962; BA, Wake Forest U., 1966, JD, 1969. Bar: N.C. 1969. Asst. U.S. atty. U.S. Dept. Justice, Raliegh, N.C., 1973-76; U.S. atty. U.S. Dist. Ct. (ea. dist.) N.C., Raleigh, 1976-77; sole practice Beaufort, N.C., 1977—. Vice chmn. Carteret County Commn., Beauford, 1984—, vice chm. 1984-88, re-elected 1988, chmn., 1988-92. Served to capt. JAGC, U.S. Army, 1969-73. Mem. N.C. Bar Assn., Carteret County Bar Assn. (pres. 1983-84), N.S. Acad. Trial Lawyers, mem. bd. dirs. N.C. Assn. County Commn., mem. bd. dirs. Coastal Regional Solid Waste Authority,(Chmn., 1991-92), mem. Neuse River Coun. of Gov.(pres. 1991-92),. Republican. Baptist. Home: RR 1 Box 214 Beaufort NC 28516-9801 Office: Attorney At Law PO Box 748 Beaufort NC 28516-0748*

TILGHMAN, RICHARD GRANVILLE, banker; b. Norfolk, Va., Sept. 18, 1940; s. Henry Granville and Frances (Fulghum) T.; m. Alice Creech, June 28, 1969; children—Elizabeth Arrington, Caroline Harrison. B.A., U. Va., 1963. Asst. cashier United Va. Bank-Seaboard Nat., Norfolk, Va., 1968-70, asst. v.p., 1970-72; pres., chief adminstrv. officer United Va. Bank, Richmond, 1978-80; asst. v.p. United Va. Mortgage Corp., Norfolk, Va., 1972, v.p., 1972-73, pres., chief exec. officer, 1974-76; pres., chief exec. officer United Va. Leasing Corp., Richmond, Va., 1973-74; sr. v.p. bank related United Va. Bankshares, Inc., Richmond, 1976-78, exec. v.p. corp. banking, 1980-84, vice chmn., 1984-85; pres., chief exec. officer United Va. Bankshares, Inc., now Crestar Fin. Corp., Richmond, 1985—, chmn., 1986—; bd. dirs. Chesapeake Corp., Richmond, 1986—; chmn. Va. Pub. Bldg. Authority, Richmond, 1982-87; prin. Va. Bus. Coun., 1987—; mem. Fed. Adv. Coun., 1994—. Chmn. bd. dirs. Richmond Symphony, 1984-85; bd. dirs., mem. gen. adv. coun. Sheltering Arms Hosp., Richmond, 1981-89; bd. dirs. Va. Free, 1989-90, Richmond Symphony Found., 1989-91, Va. Found. Ind. Colls., 1988—, Va. Literacy Found., 1986-89; bd. govs. St. Catherine's Sch., 1989-95; bd. dirs. Va. Mus. Found., 1986-92, trustee, 1994—; trustee Randolph Macon Coll., 1985-93, Richmond Renaissance, 1986—, Colonial Williamsburg Found., 1994—; co-chmn. NCCJ. 1st lt. U.S. Army, 1963-66. Mem. Bankers Rountable (dir. 1996—), Am. Bankers Assn., Va. Bankers Assn. (bd. dirs.). Episcopalian. Clubs: Commonwealth, Country of Va. Office: Crestar Fin Corp PO Box 26665 919 E Main St Richmond VA 23219-4625

TILLAR, THOMAS CATO, JR., university alumni relations administrator, consultant; b. Radford, Va., Sept. 9, 1947; s. Thomas Cato Sr. and Ruth (Wiemer) T. BS in Biology, Va. Poly. Inst., 1970, MA in Edn., 1973, EdD, 1978. Cert. fund raising executive. Program director Va. Poly. Inst., Blacksburg, 1970-73, coord. student programs, 1973-74, grad. teaching asst., 1974-75, dir. alumni svcs., 1975-78, dir. corp. foundn. prog., 1978-80, dir. ann. giving, 1980-90, dir. alumni rels., 1990-95, v.p. alumni rels., 1996—; cons. Colo. State U., Fort Collins, 1982, Va. Mil. Inst., Lexington, 1983, Datatel Minicomputer Co., Alexandria Va., 1985-86. Editor: (book) A Pictorial History of Virginia Tech, 1984. Mem. Nat. Soc. Fund Raising Execs., Coun. Advancement and Support of Edn., Rotary (pres. 1990-91), Pi Kappa Alpha (pres., trustee edn. found., Memphis, 1991-93). Republican. Presbyterian (elder). Home: 3010 Stradford Ln Blacksburg VA 24060-8176

TILLER, FRANK M., chemical engineering educator; b. Ky., Feb. 26, 1917; s. Frank McCorkill and Nellie Barker (Lawson) T.; m. Ann Wesley Quiggins, Dec. 20, 1941 (dec. July 1981); children: Fay Lee Tiller Bryan, Richard Bertrand; m. Martha Rowan Browder, Apr. 17, 1982. BSChemE, U. Louisville, 1937; MS, U. Cin., 1939, PhD, 1946; D honoris causa, U. Brazil, 1963, State U. Rio de Janeiro, 1967. Lab technician Charles R. Long Co., Paint Mfr., Louisville, 1934-35; chemist Durkee Famous Foods, Louisville, 1936, Colgate Palmolive Peet Co., Jeffersonville, Ind., 1937; civil engr. U.S. Engrs. Flood Control, Louisville, 1939; chem. engr. C.M. Hall Lamp Co., Detroit, 1940; teaching asst., instr. U. Cin., 1937-42; asst./assoc. prof. Vanderbilt U., Nashville, 1942-51; exec. dir. Gupton-Jones Coll. Mortuary Sci., Nashville, 1946-51; dean of engring., chmn. chem. engring., dir. rsch. Lamar U., Beaumont, Tex., 1951-55; dean engring., prof. chem. and electrical engring. U. Houston, 1955-63, dir. internat. affairs Ctr. Study Higher Edn. in Latin Am., 1963-72, M.D. Anderson prof. chem., civil and environ. engring., 1963—; vis. prof. Inst. de Oleos, Conselho Nac. de Petroleo, Rio de Janeiro, 1952, U. Ctrl. del Ecuador, U. de Guayquil, Ecuador, 1958, U. de Brasil, Rio de Janeiro, 1962-63, U. Coll., London, 1970, Rice U., Houston, 1973-74, Loughborough U., Eng., 1976, U. Fed do Rio de Janeiro, U. Fed. de Sergipe, Brazil, 1979, Nat. Taiwan U., Taipei, 1982, Nagoya (Japan) U., 1982-83, 86, CSIRO, Canberra, Australia, 1986. Author: Vector Analysis, 1964; founding editor Fluid/Particle Separation Jour., 1988-93; contbr. articles to profl. jours. Recipient Disting. Alumnus award U. Cin., 1969, Gold medal Filtration Soc. (U.K.), 1978, Dukler Disting. Faculty award U. Houston Engring. Alumni Assn., 1996. Fellow AIChE (Colburn award 1950, Presentation award 1952, 62, Best Paper award Suth Tex. sect. 1959, Founders award 1987); mem. Am. Soc. Engring. Edn., Am. Filtration and Separations Soc., Internat. Assn. Water Quality, Water Environment Fedn. Office: U Houston Dept Chem Engring Houston TX 77204-4792

TILLER, KATHLEEN BLANCHE (KAY), public relations consultant, photojournalist; b. Dallas, Nov. 11, 1925; d. Frank L. and Blanche Carrington (Hillyer) T. AA, Whitworth Coll., 1944; BJ, U. Tex., 1946. Reporter Laurel (Miss.) Leader Call, 1946; editor Winnsboro (Tex.) News, 1947-48, Seguin (Tex.) Gazette and others, 1970-72; account exec. Van Cronkhite & Maloy Pub. Rels., Dallas, 1973-74; dir. pub. rels. Crume & Assocs., Dallas, 1973-74; owner, pres. Kay Tiller Pub. Rels., Richardson, Tex., 1974—; freelance photojournalist. Contbr. articles and photographs to newspapers, mags. and books. Mem. Dallas County Hist. Commn., Dallas, 1977-83, 91-97; bd. dirs. Tex. Rose of Tralee. Mem. Pub. Rels. Soc. Am. (accredited, com. chmn. N. Tex. chpt. 1988-89), Am. Soc. Landscape Archs. (pub. rels. chmn. Tex. chpt. 1981-95, editor quar. newsletter 1981—), Women in Comm., Inc. (v.p. Dallas chpt. 1973-74, Matrix award 1975), Garden Writers Am., Tex. Golf Writers Assn., Press Club Tex. (bd. dirs. 1983-86, 90-92, dir. pub. rels. 1983-94), Irish Am. Soc. (bd. dirs. 1995—), Audubon Soc. (bd. dirs. 1994-97), Irish Am. Cultural Soc. Republican. Baptist. Home and Office: 625 Kirby Ln Richardson TX 75080-7690

TILLERY-TATE, JOHNNIE LEA, mental health and geriatrics nurse; b. San Angelo, Tex., Aug. 25, 1938; d. John A. and M. Inez (Balkum) Whittenberg; m. Leon Tillery, June 1, 1957; children: Valerie Joyce, Tanya Leann; m. Don Tate, Sept. 5, 1992. Student, Angelo State U., San Angelo, 1956; diploma, San Angelo Sch. Vocat. Nursing, 1979; ASN, Eastern N.Mex. U., 1984. Cert. mental health and gerontol. nurse. Staff nurse Sterling County Hosp., 1984-87, St. Johns Hosp., 1987, Sterling County Hosp., 1989; unit supr. San Angelo State Sch. Tex. Dept. Mental Health and Mental Retardation, 1987-93; investigator, surveyor Tex. Dept. Health, 1993; nurse, surveyor, qualified mental retardation profl. Tex. Dept. Human Svcs., 1993—; nurse supr. Riverside Manor. Mem. Tex. Pub. Employees Assn., Am. Assn. Mental Retardation (nursing div.). Home: 7593 Gladiolis San Angelo TX 76901

TILLEY, RICE M(ATTHEWS), JR., lawyer; b. Ft. Worth, June 21, 1936; s. Rice Matthews Sr. and Lucille Geyer (Kelly) T.; children: Marisa Lynn, Angela Ainsworth, Lisa Scott, Rice Matthews III; m. Sandra Cooper, May 13, 1994. BA, Washington & Lee U., 1958; JD, So. Meth. U., 1961; LLM in Taxation, NYU, 1962. Bar: Tex. 1961. Mem. Law, Snakard & Gambill, Ft. Worth, 1964—. Bd. dirs. Van Cliburn Found., Ft. Worth Ballet Assn., Ft. Worth Symphony Orch. Assn.; bd. trustees Tex. Wesleyan Univ.; pres. Ft. Worth Opera Assn. Mem. State Bar Tex. (chmn. real estate, probate and trust law sect.), Ft. Worth C. of C. (chmn. bd.), Century II Club (pres.), Leadership Ft. Worth (chmn. bd. dirs.), Exch. Club of Ft. Worth (pres.). Republican. Office: Law Snakard & Gambill 500 Throckmorton St Ste 3200 Fort Worth TX 76102-3819

TILLMAN, BARBARA NYLEVE, librarian; b. Kingsville, Tex., Aug. 8, 1940; d. Leslie Hallett and Lula Evelyn (Walker) Ballard; m. William Delmar Tillman, Sept. 22, 1962 (div. 1988); children: Andrea Clare Johnson, Kenneth Leslie. BA in sociology, psychology, Tex. Christian U., 1962. Extension dept. libr. Ft. Worth (Tex.) Pub. Libr., 1962-63; accounts payable bookkeeper Tex. Christian U., Ft. Worth, 1964-65; libr. periodicals Midland (Tex.) County Pub. Libr., 1978—. Home: 2508 Emerson Dr Midland TX 79705 Office: Midland County Pub Libr 301 W Missouri Midland TX 79701

TILLMAN, KAY HEIDT, real estate executive, commodity broker; b. Tampa, Fla., Jan. 24, 1945; d. Clarence Eugene and Doris (Tyson) Heidt; m. Thomas E. Barnes, Mar. 18, 1967 (div. 1972); children: Britton H., William H.; m. Herbert A. Tillman, Oct. 7, 1988. BA with honors, Rollins Coll., 1975, MS with honors, 1979. Lic. real estate sales person, Fla. Tchr. art Orange County Sch. Bd., Orlando, Fla., 1976-79; pres., owner Internat. Handcraft Ctr., Winter Garden, Fla., 1980-83, Decors Internat., Inc., Winter Garden, Fla., 1980-83, Mohamad & Barnes Investment Co., Orlando, Fla., 1983-89, Eagle Investment Properties, Orlando, 1985-89, Eagle-One Internat., Winter Garden, 1986—; pres., ptnr. Eagle Mktg. Group, Inc., Winter Garden, 1989—; cons. Nigerian Govt., Lagos, Nigeria, 1987-88, 93-94, Mid-East Investment Group, Orlando, Fla., 1986-89, 93-94. Pres. coun. Orlando C. of C., 1987-88; active recreation coun. Bapt. Ch., 1994; founder Loving Hands Outreach to Homeless, 1994. Miss. Fla., Am. Beauty Pageant, Long Beach, Calif., 1975. Mem. Orlando Bd. Realtors, Alpha Chi Omega (v.p. 1966). Republican. Baptist. Home: 215 Valencia Shores Dr Winter Garden FL 34787-2619 Office: Eagle One Internat PO Box 770397 Winter Garden FL 34777-0397

TILLMAN, KEVIN LAMAR, minister; b. Houston, Jan. 29, 1966; s. Lemuel Paul and Doris (Bennett) T.; m. Shawn Deneen Lloyd, May 12, 1989. BA, Oral Roberts U., 1996. Pres., CEO I.P.P. Records, Inc., Tulsa, Okla., 1987—. Evangelican. Home: 3164 S 76th E Ave Tulsa OK 74145-1241

TILLMAN, MASSIE MONROE, federal judge; b. Corpus Christi, Tex., Aug. 15, 1937; s. Clarence and Artie Lee (Stewart) T.; m. Karen Wright, July 2, 1993; children: Jeffrey Monroe, Holly. BBA, Baylor U., 1959, LLB, 1961. Bar: Tex. 1961, U.S. Dist. Ct. (no. dist.) Tex. 1961, U.S. Ct. Appeals (5th cir.) 1969, U.S. Supreme Ct. 1969; bd. cert. Personal Injury Trial Law, Tex. Ptnr. Herrick & Tillman, Ft. Worth, 1961-66; pvt. practice, Ft. Worth, 1966-70, 79-87; ptnr. Brown, Herman et al, Ft. Worth, 1970-78, Street, Swift et al, Ft. Worth, 1978-79; U.S. bankruptcy judge Ft. Worth divsn. No. Dist. Tex., 1987—. Author: Tillman's Trial Guide, 1970; Comments Editor/Case Notes Editor; mem. editl. bd. Baylor Law Rev., 1960-63. Fellow Am. Bd. Trial Advocates, Tex. Bar Found.; mem. Ft. Worth/Tarrant County Bar (bd. dirs. 1969-70, v.p. 1970-71), Assn. Trial Lawyers Am., Trial Attys.'s of Am., Nat. Conf. of Bankruptcy Judges, Am. Bankruptcy Inst. Republican. Baptist.

TIMBERLAKE, GREGORY ALAN, surgeon, educator; b. Washington, Dec. 7, 1949; m. Catherine Sue Burnley. BA, U. Va., 1972, MD, 1977. Diplomate Am. Bd. Surgery. Intern in surgery U. Va., Charlottsville, 1977; intern in basic surgery U.S. Naval Regional Med. Ctr., San Diego, 1977-78; resident in surgery U.S. NRMC, San Diego, 1979-83; fellow in trauma and critical care surgery Tulane U. Med. Ctr., New Orleans, 1985-86; assoc. prof. dept. surgery W.Va. U. Health Scis. Ctr., Morgantown, 1989-96; dir. Jon Michael Moore Trauma Ctr., Morgantown, 1989-94; dir. trauma svcs. Iowa Meth. Med. Ctr., Des Moines, 1996—. Author: Emergency Assessment and Treatment of Cervical Spine Injuries, 1988. Fellow ACS (com. on trauma), Am. Assn. for Surgery of Trauma, S.E. Surg. Congress; mem. AMA, ATLS (nat. faculty), Soc. for Critical Care Medicine, Assn. Mil. Surgeons U.S., Ea. Assn. for Surgery of Trauma, Internat. Assn. Trauma and Surg. Intensive Care, Internat. Soc. Surgery/Soc. Internat. le Chirargerie. Home: 19 Catalpa St Morgantown WV 26505-3677 Office: Iowa Meth Med Ctr Dept Surgery 1221 Pleasant St Ste 440 Des Moines IA 50309

TIMBERLAKE, RICHARD HENRY, JR., retired economics educator; b. Steubenville, Ohio, June 24, 1922; s. Richard Henry and Margaret Elizabeth (James) T.; m. Barbara Morehead Elder, June 6, 1945 (div. Jan. 1960); children: Richard Henry III, John William David, Megan Carol; m. Hildegard Maria Weber, May 28, 1960; children: Christopher Wolcott, Thomas Bernard. AB, Kenyon Coll., 1946; AM in Econs., Columbia U., 1950; PhD in Econs., U. Chgo., 1959. Instr. econs. Muhlenberg Coll., Allentown, Pa., 1948-51, Rensselaer Poly. Inst., Troy, N.Y., 1955-58; asst. prof. Norwich U., Northfield, Vt., 1953-55; assoc. prof. Fla. State U., Tallahassee, 1958-63; prof. banking and fin. U. Ga., Athens, 1964-85, prof. econs., 1985-90, prof. emeritus, 1990—; vis. prof. Tex. A&M U., 1973-74; rsch. cons. Fed. Res. Bank Richmond, Va., 1970-71; sr. fellow Inst. for Humane Studies, Palo Alto, Calif., summer 1983. Author: Money, Banking and Central Banking, 1965, Origins of Central Banking in the United States, 1978, Gold, Greenbacks and the Constitution, 1991, Monetary Policy in the United States: An Institutional and Intellectual History, 1993, (with Edward B. Selby) Money and Banking, 1972; bd. editors So. Econ. Jour., 1964-67; contbr. numerous articles and book revs. to profl. jours. Libertarian candidate for city-county commn., 1975, 92. 1st lt. USAAF, 1943-45, ETO. Recipient creative rsch. award U. Ga., 1980. Mem. So. Econ. Assn. (exec. com. 1966-68, v.p. 1971-72). Anglican Catholic. Office: U Ga Dept Econ Terry Coll Bus Athens GA 30602

TIMBERLAKE, STEPHEN GRANT, trust officer, bank officer; b. Pensacola, Fla., Dec. 18, 1958; s. David Winburn and Sylvia (Grant) T.; m. Nancy Ruth Snow, Aug. 7, 1982; children: Tiffany Rose, Sarah Elizabeth. BS, Troy State U., 1981; diploma, Fla. Trust Sch., 1985; diploma with high honors, Nat. Grad. Trust Sch., 1988. Loan adminstr. Troy (Ala.) Bank and Trust Co., 1978-82; trust adminstr. Fla. Nat. Bank, Pensacola, 1982-84; trust officer Fla. Nat. Bank, Ocala, 1984-86, First Union Nat. Bank, Jacksonville, Fla., 1986-87; asst. v.p., regional trust officer First Union Nat. Bank, Bradenton, Fla., 1987-88; v.p., regional trust officer First Union Nat. Bank, Tampa, Fla., 1988-89, Boca Raton, Fla., 1989-91; v.p., trust officer AmSouth Bank of Fla., Ft. Walton Beach, 1991-93; regional trust mgr. AmSouth Bank of Fla., Pensacola, 1993—. Loaned exec. Ocala United Way, 1986; bd. dirs. Pensacola Opera. Mem. NW Fla. Estate Planning Coun. (dir. 1994), Tampa Bay Estate Planning Coun., Gainesville Estate Planning Coun. (pres. 1986), Bradenton Estate Planning Coun., Greater Boca Raton Estate Planning Coun., Pensacola Jaycees (fin. dir. 1983-85), Pensacola Opera (dir. 1994), Navy League, Pensacola C. of C., Tau Kappa Epsilon. Republican. Methodist. Office: AmSouth Bank of Fla PO Box 12790 Pensacola FL 32575-2790

TIMM, JEFFREY THOMAS, chaplain, air force officer; b. Denver, Mar. 22, 1949; s. Paul A. and Louise (White) T.; m. Donna Faye Blanks, Sept. 7, 1974. BA, Tex. Christian U., 1971; M Div, Duke U., 1974; postgrad., U. Ark., 1974-76; PhD, Columbia Pacific U., 1980; cert. mgmt. Wichita State U., Kans., 1994. Ordained to ministry Christian Church (Disciples of Christ), 1973. Commd. capt. USAF, 1974, advanced through grades to lt. col., 1988; chaplain Little Rock AFB, 1974-76, Osan AB, Korea, 1976-77, Eglin AFB, Ft. Walton Beach, Fla., 1977-80, Luke AFB, Phoenix, 1980-82, Italy, 1982-85; sr. protestant chaplain Dover AFB, Del., 1985-88, sr. chaplain Mc ConnellAFB, Kans., 1988-94; assoc. min. St. Andrews UMC, 1984-85; min. discipleship and program Temple Terrace (Fla.) UMC, 1985—. Author: A Potpourri of Worship Resources, 1976, A Title, A Talk, and A Tool for Pastoral Pre-Marital Counselors, 1981, Living With Stress, 1985, Finishing Touches, 1994. Mem. Am. Assn. Christian Counselors (charter), Fla. Acad. Preachers (bd. dirs. 1995-96), Sigma Phi Epsilon. Home: 3018 Fallwood Glen Ct Falls Church VA 22044

TIMMCKE, ALAN EDWARD, physician and surgeon; b. Madison, Wis., July 7, 1949; s. Wesley Eugene Timmcke; m. Deborah Cameron Brosseau (div.); m. Teresa Ann Watkins, Dec. 31, 1977; children: Gretchen Kristine, Alan Edward Jr. BS, Dickinson Coll., 1971; MD with honors, Temple U., 1975. Diplomate Am. Bd. Surgery, Am. Bd. Colon and Rectal Surgery; lic. physician, Pa., Maine, Mo., La. Intern in surgery Nat. Naval Med. Ctr., Bethesda, Md., 1975-76, resident in gen. surgery, 1976-79; rsch. fellow in colon and rectal surgery Jewish Hosp./Washington U. Med. Ctr., St. Louis, 1985-86, clin. fellow in colon and rectal surgery, 1986-87; asst. in surgery Washington U. Sch. Medicine, St. Louis, 1985-87; staff colon and rectal surgeon Ochsner Clinic, New Orleans, 1987—; staff surgeon Nat. Naval Med. Ctr., Bethesda, 1979, Naval Regional Med. Ctr., Newport, R.I., 1979-82, dept. colon and rectal surgery Lahey Clinic Med. Ctr., Burlington, Mass., 1984-85; staff surgeon Rumford (Maine) Community Hosp., 1982-84, med. staff v.p., 1983-84; instr. surgery Uniformed Svcs. U. of Health Scis., Bethesda, 1978-79; lectr. in field. Contbr. articles and abstracts to profl. jours. Lt. comdr. M.C., USN, 1975-82. Recipient Harry E. Bacon Found. award for best original paper, 1987; NIH Summer Rsch. fellow, 1972. Fellow ACS, Am. Soc. Colon and Rectal Surgeons; mem. AMA, La. State Med. Soc., Jefferson Parish Med. Soc., So. Med. Assn., New Orleans Surg. Soc., Surg. Assn. of La., Internat. Soc. Univ. Colon and Rectal Surgeons, Soc. of Am. Gastrointestinal Endoscopic Surgeons, Am. Soc. Gastrointestinal Endoscopy, Alpha Omega Alpha. Office: Ochsner Clinic Dept Colon/Rectal Surgery 1514 Jefferson Hwy New Orleans LA 70121-2429

TIMMONS, GORDON DAVID, economics educator; b. Elbert, Tex., May 21, 1919; s. Walter James and Ella Mae (McCarson) T.; m. Jean Betty Kulhanek, Feb. 11, 1947; children: Kathy, Linda, Scott, Jim, Tamara, Dallas, Timothy, Kelly, Susanna. Student, U. Tex., 1937-40, U. Mont., 1961-64; BS, Utah State U., 1955; MS, Mont. State U., 1958. Enlisted USAF, 1939, advanced through grades to col., ret., 1961; instr. Columbia Basin Coll., Pasco, Wash., 1966-86; pres. Assn. Higher Edn., 1969-72. Decorated Legion of Merit, Croix de Guerre (France). Mem. Acad. Polit. Sci., N.W. Econ. Conf., Internat. Platform Assn. Democrat. Home and Office: PO Box 39-a Olney TX 76374-0039

TIMMS, RICHARD M., executive of fitness equipment company; b. 1941. Assoc. prof. U. Calif., San Diego, 1966-71; exec. Scripps Clinic & Rsch. Found., La Jolla, Calif., 1971-83; exec. Troxel Cycling & Fitness, Inc., San Diego, 1983-86, pres., 1986—. Office: Troxel Company Inc Hwy 57 W Moscow TN 38057

TIMOTHY, DAVID HARRY, biology educator; b. Pitts., June 9, 1928; s. David Edgar and Harriett P. (Stein) T.; m. Marian Claire Whiteley, Sept. 5, 1953; children: Marjory J., M. Elisabeth, David W. BS, Pa. State U., 1952, MS, 1955; PhD, U. Minn., 1956. Asst. geneticist Rockefeller Found., Bogota, Colombia, 1956-58; assoc. geneticist Rockefeller Found., Bogota, 1958-61; assoc. prof. N.C. State U., Raleigh, 1961-66, prof., 1966-93, prof. emeritus, 1993—; cons. to fgn. and U.S. govts., also U.S. and internat. sci. orgns.; mem. crop adv. com. on grasses USDA, 1983-87, mem. policy adv. com., sci. and edn. grants program, 1982-84, chief scientist Sci. and Edn. Competetive Rsch. Grants Office, 1985, 86; with Nat. Plant Genetic Resources Bd., 1984-91, vice chmn., 1991; bd. dirs., treas. Genetic Resources Comms. Sys., Inc., 1985-91, pres., 1991-93; mem. bd. on agr. NAS-NRC, work group on U.S. Nat. Plant Germplasm Sys., 1987-89. Co-author monographs, also author articles. With AUS, 1946-48, PTO. Grantee NSF, 1965, 78, Rockefeller Found., 1968, 69, Pioneer Hi-Bred Internat., 1982, 83. Fellow AAAS (electorate nominating com., sect. O, Agr. 1988-90), Am. Soc. Agronomy, Crop Sci. Soc. Am. (editl. bd. 1982-84, assoc. editor Crop Sci. 1982-84, Frank N. Meyer medal for plant genetic resources 1994). Home: 13 Furches St Raleigh NC 27607-7048

TIMPANY, ROBERT DANIEL, railroad executive; b. Panama, Ill., Feb. 24, 1919; s. Robert Gibson and Mary (Daily) T.; m. Margaret Jane Robey; children: Mary Suzanne, Robert Gibson. BS in Civil Engring., U. Ill., 1940. Registered profl. engr., Ill., Ind. Mining engr. Peabody Coal Co., Marion, Ill., 1940-41; asst. engr. N.Y. Central, Indpls., 1941-42; various positions to asst. gen. mgr. N.Y. Central, various locations, 1945-58; gen. mgr. N.Y. Central, Syracuse, N.Y., 1958-60, Cleve., 1960-63; asst. v.p., operating adminstr. N.Y. Central, N.Y.C., 1963-68; asst. v.p., operating adminstrn., asst. v.p. passenger svc. Penn Central, Phila., 1968-71; trustee Central R.R. N.J., Newark, 1971-79; pres., chief exec. officer, dir. Central Jersey Industries, Inc., Newark, 1979-84, vice-chmn., 1984-85. Capt. C.E., U.S. Army, 1942-45, PTO. Mem. Am. Rwy. Engring. Assn. (life), Am. Soc. Transp. and Logistics, Aronimink Golf Club (Newton Square, Pa.), Innisbrook (Tarpon Springs, Fla.), Masons, Kappa Delta Rho (Ordo Honorium award). Republican. Presbyterian. Home: Innisbrook PO 1088 Tarpon Springs FL 34688-1088

TIMS, RAMONA FAYE, medical/surgical nurse; b. Jackson, Tenn., Nov. 4, 1955; d. Willard Leon and Lois Ellen (Waldon) T. Assoc. Nursing, SUNY, Albany, 1987. LPN, RN; cert. BLS. Staff nurse neurol. ICU Jackson Madison County Gen. Hosp., 1976-88, clin. mgr., 1991—; nurse chemotherapy Jackson Clinic, P.A., 1988-91. Co-author: Oncology-Experience Counts. Republican. Baptist. Home: 43 Bemis Ln Jackson TN 38301

TIMS, ROBERT AUSTIN, data processing official, pilot; b. Seattle, Dec. 21, 1942; s. Robert Mitchell Tims and Winifred Eileen (Dorgan) Bristol; m. Jane Moore, June 6, 1980. Student, Pacific Union Coll., 1960-61, Alpha Aviation Sch., 1976-77, Ark. State U., 1995—. Lic. comml. and instrument pilot; cert. flight instr. Engring. technician Tex. Instruments, Inc., Ridgecrest, Calif., 1966-67, various projects, Conn., N.Y. and N.J., 1967-70; homesteader Leslie, Ark., 1970-77; chief pilot/flight instr. Sharp Aviation Co., Jonesboro, Ark., 1977-79; chief pilot Pizza Inn of Ark., Jonesboro, 1979-83; data processing mgr., chief pilot Realty Assocs. Brokerage, Inc., Jonesboro, 1983-91, microanalyst. 1991-94; pres., owner ABS Logic, Inc., computers and programming cons., Jonesboro, 1985—. Served with USN, 1962-66. Mem. CAP (squadron comdr. Jonesboro 1986-93), Am. Philatelic Soc., Data Processing Mgrs. Assn. Avocation: philately. Home and Office: 1616 Alonzo St Jonesboro AR 72401-4802

TINDELL, WILLIAM NORMAN, oil company executive, petroleum geologist; b. Calvin, Okla., Apr. 6, 1921; s. John Lawson and Nona Lou (Baldwin) T.; m. Mary Helen Cozart, Dec. 31, 1983. BS cum laude, U. Pitts., 1948, MS, 1950. Dist. mgr. Mayfair Minerals, Inc., Abilene, Tex., 1953-85; chmn. bd., chief exec. officer Westico Energy Co., Abilene, 1985-87. Chmn. Citizens for Better Govt., Abilene, 1974; pres. Goodfellows, Abilene, 1966; pres., bd. dirs. West Cen. Tex. Mcpl. Water Dist., Abilene, 1968-75. Mem. Abilene C. of C. (v.p., mem. exec. com., bd. dirs. 1984-85, Petroleum Industry award 1984), West Cen. Tex. Oil and Gas Assn. (pres. 1962-63, OilMan of Yr. 1983), Abilene Geol. Soc. (hon. life, pres. 1958), Am. Assn. Petroleum Geologists (mem. adv. council), Tex. Ind. Producers and Royalty Owners Assn. (v.p. 1963-64), Ind. Petroleum Assn. Am. (v.p. 1967-68). Republican. Episcopalian. Clubs: Petroleum (v.p.), Exchange (pres. 1965) (Abilene). Avocations: jogging, travel, reading. Home: 74 Fairway Oaks Blvd Abilene TX 79606-5102 Office: 1st Nat West Ste 224 Abilene TX 79601

TINER, DONNA TOWNSEND, nurse; b. Memphis, Dec. 14, 1947; d. Jack Edwin and Anne Coolidge (Burleigh) Townsend; m. Clinton William Matson, Aug. 30, 1969 (div. 1976); m. Dow David Tiner, Apr. 15, 1978; children: Jeffrey David, Cynthia Leigh, Catherine Renee. Grad., Bapt. Meml. Hosp. Sch. Nursing, Memphis, 1969. RN, Ark.; cert. ACLS. Nurse Bapt. Meml. Hosp., Memphis, 1969, 71-72, New Bern (N.C.) Surg. Assocs., 1970-71, Meml. Hosp., Little Rock, 1972-73, Bapt. Med. Ctr., Little Rock, 1974-87; practice nursing specializing in post-anesthesia care Little Rock, 1987-89; post-anesthesia care specialist Little Rock Surgery Ctr. (formerly Freeway Surgery Ctr.), 1989—. Instr., ARC, 1975—; leader Park Hill Bapt. Ch., 1986—. 1st. lt. U.S. Army Med. Unit 1976-79. Mem. Am. Soc. Post Anesthesia Nurses (chartered), Ark. Post Anesthesia Care Nurses, Alumnae

Assn. Bapt. Hosp. Sch. Nursing. Republican. Home: 12 Knights Bridge Rd North Little Rock AR 72120-6535

TINER, ELZA CHERYL, English language educator; b. Champaign, Ill., Jan. 27, 1952; d Jack Dalton and Marie (Rizzolo) T. BA with hons. in English, Seton Hall U., S. Orange, N.J., 1979; MA, U. Toronto, Ont., Can., 1980; MSL, Pontifical Inst. Mediaeval Stu, Toronto, 1985; PhD, U. Toronto, 1987. Sr. editl. asst. IEEE, N.Y.C., 1969-73; acctg. clk. Devenco, Inc., N.Y.C., 1973-79; rsch. asst. Records of Early English Drama project U. Toronto, 1981-87; tutor writing lab. Scarborough Coll. U. Toronto, 1986-87; asst. prof. N.Y. Inst. Tech., Old Westbury, N.Y., 1987-89; asst. prof. English Lynchburg (Va.) Coll., 1989-93, assoc. prof., 1993—, dir. writing ctr., 1989—; vis. lectr. expository writing Harvard U., spring 1993; vis. fellow Pontifical Inst. Medieval Studies, Toronto, 1995-96; sr. fellow Ctr. for Rsch. in Early Theatre, U. Toronto, summer 1995. Contbr. articles to profl. jours. AAUP rsch. grantee, 1988-89; Mednick Meml. fellow, Va. Found. Ind. Colls., 1990, 95. Mem. MLA, AAUW, Nat. Coun. Tchrs. English, Va. Assn. Tchrs. English, Writing Program Adminstrs., Medieval and Renaissance Drama Soc., Internat. Soc. for History of Rhetoric, Can. Soc. for History of Rhetoric, Discourse Analysis Rsch. Group. Office: Lynchburg Coll Dept English 1501 Lakeside Dr Lynchburg VA 24501-3113

TINER, STANLEY RAY, business communications executive, former editor; b. Springhill, La., Aug. 22, 1942; s. Elmer Ray and Nannie Lea (Randolph) T.; m. Veronica Jo Thibodeaux, Dec. 31, 1966; children—Mark Gerard, Jon Stuart, Heather Nicole. B.A., La. Tech. U., 1969. City editor Texarkana Daily News, 1969-70; mng. editor Minden (La.) Press-Herald, 1970-71; chief editorial writer Shreveport (La.) Times, 1972-74; editor Shreveport Jour., 1974-88; dir. pub. affairs Arkla Inc., 1988—. Bd. dirs. Shreveport chpt. NCCJ, 1981—, Assn. of Retarded Citizens, Caddo-Bossier, La. 1974-87; chmn. Holocaust Commemoration, Shreveport, 1987; bd. dirs. La. Assn. for Blind, 1988—; chmn. La. State Exhibit Mus., 1991—. Served as sgt. USMC, 1962-66, Vietnam. Recipient Frank Allen award La.-Miss. AP, 1976; Silver Gavel award ABA, 1977; Robert F. Kennedy award, 1978; Social Justice award Social Justice Com., Shreveport, 1981; Nieman fellow Harvard U., 1985-86; Liberty Bell award Shreveport Bar Assn., 1985; award of merit AIA. Mem. Interstate Natural Gas Assn. Am. (state rels. com. 1988—), Internat. Assn. Bus. Communicators, La. Assn. Bus. and Industry (bd. dirs. 1989—), Soc. Profl. Journalists (pres. 1974, bd. dirs. 3 yrs.), La. Press Assn. (bd. dirs. 1975-77). Democrat. Baptist. Office: Arkla Inc 525 Milam St Shreveport LA 71101-3539

TING, KWUN-LON, engineer, educator, consultant; b. Huwei, Taiwan, Oct. 1, 1948; s. Yin and Swei (Lin) T.; m. Rebecca Sun, May 10, 1975; children: Lilian, Daniel. BS, Nat. Taiwan U., Taipei, 1972; MS, Clemson U., 1977; PhD, Okla. State U., 1982. Instr. Army Ordinance Acad., Taiwan, 1972-74; mech. engr. Taiwan Polymer Chemicals Co., Taipei, 1974-75; rsch. asst. Clemson (S.C.) U., 1975-77; teaching asst. Okla. State U., Stillwater, 1977-80, rsch. assoc., 1980-82; asst. prof. Tenn. Tech. U., Cookeville, 1982-87, assoc. prof., 1987-92, prof., 1992—; co-dir. Nat. Conf. on Applied Mechanisms and Robotics, 1989, 91. Editor Jour. Applied Mechanisms & Robotics; contbr. articles to profl. jours. Recipient Kinslow Outstanding Engring. Rsch. award, 1992, B. Roth award, 1993; grantee NSF. Mem. ASME. Baptist. Office: Tenn Tech U PO Box 5014 Cookeville TN 38505

TING, ROBERT YEN-YING, physicist; b. Kwei-yang, China, Mar. 8, 1942; came to U.S. 1965; s. Chi-yung and Shou-feng (Yang) T.; m. Teresa Yen-chun Ting, June 3, 1967; children: Paul H., Peggy Y. BS, Nat. Taiwan U., 1964; MS, MIT, 1967; PhD, U. Calif., San Diego, 1971. Rsch. engr. U.S. Naval Rsch. Lab., Washington, 1971-77, supervisory engr., 1977-80; supervisory physicist U.S. Naval Rsch. Lab., Orlando, Fla., 1980—; prof. George Washington U., 1972-80. Contbr. over 100 articles in rheology, polymer and acoustics to profl. jours. Fellow Acoustical Soc. Am.; mem. Am. chem. Soc., Am. Ceramics Soc., Am. Inst. Chem. Engrs. Office: US Naval Rsch Lab PO Box 568337 Orlando FL 32856-8337

TINNER, FRANZISKA PAULA, social worker, artist, designer, educator; b. Zurich, Switzerland, Sept. 18, 1944; came to U.S., 1969; d. Siegfied Albin and Gertrude Emilie (Sigg) Maier; m. Rolf Christian Tinner, Dec. 19, 1976; 1 child, Eric Francis. Student, U. Del., 1973-74, Va. Commonwealth U., 1974; BFA, U. Tenn., 1984; BA of Arts, U. Ark., Little Rock, 1991, postgrad. Lic. real estate broker. Dominican nun Ilanz, Switzerland, 1961-67; waitress London, 1967-68; governess Bryn Mawr, Pa., 1969; saleswoman, 1970-90, model, 1983; artist, designer Made For You, Kerrville, Tex. and Milw., 1984—; realtor Century 21, Milw., 1987-91; intern Birch Community Ctr., 1992-93. Designer softsculptor doll Texas Cactus Blossom, 1984; author: (poem) The Gang (recorded by Nat. Libr. of Poetry), 1996. Ombudsman Action 10 Consumerline, Knoxville, Tenn., 1983-84; foster mother, Powhatan, Va., 1976-81; vol. ARC, Knoxville, 1979, Va. Home for Permanently Disabled, 1975; vol., counselor Youth For Understanding-Fgn. Exch., Powhatan, Va., 1975-77; tchr. pager/archiving host, mentor, area expert on Am. On Line; vol. Interactive Ednl. Svc. Recipient Art Display award U. Knoxville, 1983, Prof. Choice of Yr. award, 1983, Outstanding Achievemnt award TV Channel 10, Knoxville, 1984, 1st place award for paintings and crafts State Fair Va., Tenn., 1st place award Nat. Dollmakers, 1985, finalist Best of Coll. Photography, 1991, Achievement award Coll. Scholar af Am., 1991, Achievement cert. in technique of anger therapy, 1993, Achievement cert. in crisis response team tng., 1994; named One of Outstanding 1000 Women, 1995, Woman of Yr., 1995. Mem. NASW, NAFE, Milw. Bd. Realtors, Homemakers Club (pres. 1979-80), Newcomers Club, Bowlers Club (v.p.), Internat. Platform Assn.

TINNEY, RICHARD DALE, JR., mental health marketing administrator; b. Hudson, Mich., Jan. 29, 1956; s. Richard Dale and Nancy Ann (Rutledge) T.; m. Mary Lynn Keefer McMichael, Oct. 21, 1978 (div. Nov. 1985); children: Mariah Lynn, Megan Elise. BRE, Gt. Lakes Bible Coll., Lansing, Mich., 1978; student, Jefferson C.C., Louisville, 1979; MS in Family Studies, Abilene Christian U., 1984, M of Marriage and Family Therapy, 1984. Pvt. practice marriage and family therapist Abilene, Tex., 1984-87; adult counselor NOAH Project, Abilene, 1985-87; instr. depts. Psychology and Sociology McMurry Coll., Abilene, 1985-87; referral coord., staff trainer Woods Psychiat. Inst., Abilene, 1986-87; asst. dir. mktg. Meridell Achievement Ctr., Austin, 1987-89; co-owner Mesa Media, Austin, 1988-89; dir. profl. and community devel. Oak Grove Treatment Ctr., Burleson, Tex., 1989-92, staff devel. cons., 1990-92, dir. devel. and community rels., 1989-92; dir. referral devel. Devereux Psychiat. Residential Treatment Ctr. Tex., Victoria, 1992-96; project mgr. Devereaux Tex. Treatment Network, Victoria, Tex., 1996—; min. of youth and music Kenwood Hts. Christian Ch., Louisville, 1978-80; collections mgr., office clk. Walke Med. Assn. P.A., Abilene, 1981-84; area rep. Am. Intercultural Student Exch. Program, Abilene, 1983. Presenter cmty. workshops on stress mgmt. and motivation. Republican. Home: 2603 Woodmont Trl Fort Worth TX 76133-4444 Office: Devereux Psychiat Residential Treatment Ctr 120 David Wade Victoria TX 77902

TINSMAN, MARY ELIZABETH, special education educator; b. Milford, Del., Dec. 24, 1964; d. John Bailey Sr. and Jane (Carey) Roach; m. Howard Steven Tinsman, Oct. 28, 1989. BEd, U. Del., 1988. Cert. in elem., spl. edn., middle sch. math. Spl. edn. tchr. to learning disabled Laurel (Del.) Sch. Dist., 1988-89; spl. edn. tchr. to autistic Duval County Sch. Bd., Jacksonville, Fla., 1989-93; 3d grade magnet tchr. Pinedale Elem., Jacksonville, 1993-94; tchr. 4th grade Henry F. Kite Elem., Jacksonville, 1994—. Mem. NEA, Delta Kappa Gamma, Beta Pi. Home: 442 Moby Dick Dr S Jacksonville FL 32218-2894 Office: Henry F Kite Elem 9430 Lem Turner Rd Jacksonville FL 32208-1569

TIPPETTS, CHARLES SANFORD, JR., family practice physician, educator; b. Mpls., Aug. 24, 1925; s. Charles Sanford and Margaret Elizabeth (Griffith) T.; m. Marlon Hamer, June 8, 1954; children: Wendy, Caroline. AB, Princeton U., 1949; MD, Jefferson Med. Coll., 1954. Diplomate Nat. Bd. Med. Examiners, Am. Bd. Family Practice. Rotating intern Salem (Mass.) Hosp., 1954-55, asst. med. resident, 1955-56, mem. staff, 1956-87; asst. prof. community medicine Boston U. Sch. Medicine, 1987; mem. staff emeritus Salem Hosp., 1987—. With U.S. Army, 1944-46, ETO, World War II. Mem. Mass. Med. Soc., Ga. Med. Soc., Camden County Med. Soc. (pres. 1994). Home: 27 Marsh Creek Rd Amelia Island FL 32034-6414 Office: Willis Keene PC MD 130 N Gross Rd Kingsland GA 31548-9137

TIPPINS, SUSAN SMITH, elementary school educator, consultant; b. Jacksonville, Fla., Jan. 4, 1961; d. Arthur Thomas and kathleen May (Blake) Smith; m. John Malcolm Tippins Jr., Apr. 21, 1984; children: Matthew Scott, Paul Blake. AA, Fla. Jr. Coll., Jacksonville, 1980; BA in Edn., U. North Fla., 1983, MEd, 1993. Cert. tchr., Fla. 6th grade tchr. Duval County Sch. Sys., Jacksonville, 1984-87; 3rd grade tchr. Nassau County Sch. Sys., Callahan, Fla., 1987-88, tchr. specific learning disabilities, 1990-92, 1st grade tchr., 1992—, adminstrv. intern, 1995-96. Mem. ASCD, Internat. Reading Assn., Fla. Reading Assn., Fla. Assn. Computer Edn., Alpha Delta Kappa (pres. 1996), Kappa Delta Pi. Home: Rt 2 Box 1413 Bryceville FL 32009 Office: Callahan Elem Sch 100 Booth St S Callahan FL 32011-9542

TIPPY, MARGARET GRINDER, public affairs officer; b. Detroit, May 9, 1952; d. John Thomas and Laura Eileen (Marria) Grinder; m. John Darrell Tippy, Sr., May 20, 1977; 1 stepchild, John Darrell Jr. BA, Methodist Coll., Fayetteville, N.C., 1981. Soldier U.S. Army, 1975-78; sec. U.S. Army, Ft. Bragg, N.C., Europe, 1981-84; journalist, editor U.S. Army, Ft. Bragg, N.C., 1984-88, asst. chief media rels., 1988-89; pub. affairs officer Womack Army Med. Ctr., Ft. Bragg, N.C., 1989—; task force HealthCare 99, Fayetteville, 1993—, chair health promotion com., 1993; mem. Healthy Carolinians, 1994—; bd. dirs. Better Health of Cumberland County, N.C., 1995. Democrat. Office: Womack AMC Pub Affairs Office Fort Bragg NC 28307-5000

TIPTON, MARY DAVISON, banker; b. Atlanta, Jan. 11, 1947; d. W. Kay and M. Estelle (Reynolds) T. MA in History, Emory U., 1969, postgrad. in fin., 1978, MBA, 1986. Asst. bank examiner Fed. Res., Atlanta, 1969-72; credit officer 1st Nat. Bank, Atlanta, 1975-77; asst. treas. Bankers Trust, N.Y.C., 1979-81, asst. v.p., 1982; asst. v.p. Amro Bank, N.Y.C., 1983-84; fin. mgr. Reynolds Properties, 1984-86; cons. to Office of Gov. Ga., 1986—; independent fin. cons., 1987—. Author essay: The Analysis of Foreign Banks (Robert Morris Assocs. Contest Southeastern winner 1977), 1977. Vol. tutor adult literacy Martin Luther King Assn., Atlanta, 1975-79; sec. bd. dirs. North Ga. chpt. March of Dimes Birth Defects Found., 1988-90; co-chairperson silent auction to benefit juvenile Diabetes Found., 1991. Mem. Ga. Hunter Jumper Assn., Emory Alumni Club, Phi Beta Kappa, Phi Kappa Phi.

TIRAS, HERBERT GERALD, engineering executive; b. Houston, Aug. 11, 1924; s. Samuel Louis and Rose (Seibel) T.; m. Aileen Wilkenfeld, Dec. 14, 1955; children—Sheryle, Leslie. Student, Tex. A. and M. U., 1941-42; attended, Houston U., 1942-65, student, Nat. Defence U., 1986. Registered profl. engr., Calif. Cert. mfg. engr. in gen. mfg.; robotics; mfg. mgmt; gen. mgmt. Engr., Reed Roller Bit, Houston, 1942-60; pres. Tex. Truss, Houston, 1960-77; chief exec. officer Omnico, Houston, 1977—; Nat. Defense exec. res. resources officer, Region VI Fed. Emergency Mgmt. Agy., 1982—. Served to 1st lt. CAP, 1954-61. Mem. Machine Vision Assn., Nat. Defense U. Found., Am. Assn. Artificial Intelligence, Soc. Mfg. Engrs., Robot Inst. Am., Robotics Internat., Marine Tech. Soc., Coll. and Univ. Mfg. Ednl. Council (nat. dir.), Assn. of the Indsl. Coll. of the Armed Forces. Lodge: Masons, Shriners. Home: 9703 Runnymeade Dr Houston TX 77096-4219 Office: PO Box 2872 Houston TX 77252-2872

TIRYAKIAN, EDWARD ASHOD, sociology educator; b. Bronxville, N.Y., Aug. 6, 1929; s. Ashod Haroutioun and Keghinee (Agathon) T.; m. Josefina Cintron, Sept. 5, 1953; children: Edmund Carlos, Edwyn Ashod. BA summa cum laude, Princeton U., 1952; MA, Harvard U., 1954, PhD, 1956; PhD (hon.), U. Rene Descartes, Paris, 1987. Instr. Princeton U., 1956-57, asst. prof., 1957-62; lectr. Harvard U., 1962-65; assoc. prof. Duke U., Durham, N.C., 1965-67, prof., 1967—, chmn. dept. sociology and anthropology, 1969-72, dir. internat. studies, 1988-91; vis. lectr. U. Philippines, 1954-55, Bryn Mawr Coll., 1957-59; vis. scientist program Am. Sociol. Assn., 1967-70; vis. prof. Laval U., Quebec City, Que., Can., 1978, Inst. Polit. Studies, Paris, 1992, Free U., Berlin, 1996; summer seminar dir. NEH, 1978, 80, 93, 89, 91, 96; lectr. Kyoto Am. Studies Summer Seminar, 1985. Author: Sociologism and Existentialism, 1962; Editor: Sociological Theory, Values and Sociocultural Change: Essays in Honor of P.A. Sorokin, 1963, The Phenomenon of Sociology, 1971, On the Margin of the Visible: Sociology, the Esoteric, and the Occult, 1974, The Global Crisis: Sociological Analyses and Responses, 1984; co-editor: Theoretical Sociology: Perspectives and Developments, 1970; New Nationalisms of the Developed West, 1985. Recipient Fulbright rsch. award, 1955; Ford faculty rsch. fellow, 1971-72. Mem. Am. Sociol. Assn., African Studies Assn., Am. Soc. for Study Religion (council 1975-78, pres. 1981-84), Assn. Internationale des Sociologues de Langue Française (v.p. 1985-88, pres. 1988-92), Soc. for Phenomenology and Existential Philosophy, Phi Beta Kappa. Clubs: Princeton, Century Assn. (N.Y.C.). Home: 16 Pascal Way Durham NC 27705-4924

TISSUE, MIKE, medical educator, respiratory therapist; b. Garfield, Wash., Aug. 24, 1941; s. Altha Lester and Fern Adeline (Willard) T.; m. Marjorie Lena Atkinson, Feb. 24, 1961 (div. June 1991); children: Sue Tipton, Pam Kromholtz, Paul, Donna. AAS (4 degrees) with honors, Spokane (Wash.) C.C., 1985; BS in Respiratory Therapy cum laude, Loma Linda (Calif.) U., 1987; postgrad. in respiratory care, Ga. State U., 1995—. Registered Cardiovascular Technologist (invasive and non-invasive), Nat. Soc. Cardiopulmonary Technol./Cardiovascular Credentialing Internat.; Registered Respiratory Therapist, Pulmonary Function Technologist, Perinatal/Pediatric Specialist, NBRC; registered Respiratory Care Practitioner, Calif., Ga. Respiratory intern, Level III NICU Therapist Loma Linda (Calif.) U. Med. Ctr., 1985-87; educator, therapist Riyadh (Saudi Arabia) Armed Forces Hosp., 1987-91; dept. head respiratory care Security Forces Hosp., Riyadh, 1991-93; asst. prof., dir. clin. edn. respiratory therapy program Morehead (Ky.) State U., 1993-94; program dir. assoc. degree respiratory therapy Chattahoochee Tech. Inst., Marietta, Ga., 1994—; pres., founder Riyadh Cardiorespiratory Soc., 1988-93; rschr. Loma Linda U., 1987, Riyadh Armed Forces Hosp., 1988; instr. and affiliate faculty ACLS Wash. State Heart Assn., 1983-85, Calif. Heart Assn., 1985-87, Saudi Heart Assn., 1985-87, Ky. Heart Assn., 1993-94, Ga. affiliate, 1994—; instr. and affiliate faculty pediatric advanced life support Saudi Heart Assn., 1987-93; instr. and affiliate faculty basic life support/CPR Wash. State, 1974-85, Calif., 1985-87, Saudi Heart Assn., 1987-93, Ky. Heart Assn., 1993-94, Ga. affiliate, 1994—; cons. ARC, Tacoma, Wash., 1984, instr. advanced 1st aid, standard 1st aid, CPR, 1975—, Inland Empire Chpt., Spokane, Wash., 1975-94, San Bernardino/Redlands Svc. Ctr., Loma Linda, 1985-87, Am. Cmty. Svcs. U.S. Embassy, Riyadh, 1991-93, U.S. Mil. Operation Desert Storm, Riyadh, 1991-93, Ga. affiliate Cobb County chpt., Marietta, 1994—; instr. Freedom From Smoking Clinic Program Am. Lung Assn., Calif., 1985-87, Saudi Arabia, 1987-93, Smyrna, Ga., 1994—; mem. Instl. Effectiveness Com., Campus Computer Com. Chattahoochee Tech. Inst., 1994—. Contbr. articles to profl. jours. Bd. dirs. Am. Heart Assn., Spokane, 1976-83, chair fin. com., 1981-83; chair spkrs. bur. ARC, Inland Empire Chpt., Spokane, 1982-85, chair pub. rels., 1983-85; mem. Calif. affiliate San Bernardino Chpt., Loma Linda, 1985-87, Ga. affiliate Cobb County Chpt., Marietta, 1994—; chair programming and spkrs. bur. Am. Lung Assn., Smyrna, Ga., 1994—, chmn. bd. dirs., 1995—; sec. Cobb County Cmty. Coun., Marietta, 1995-96, spkr., 1995, v.p., 1996—; vol. Ga. Internat. Cultural Exch., 1995; registry exam. sr. proctor Cardiovascular Credentialing Internat./Nat. Bd. Cardiovascular Technologists, Riyadh, 1987-90; commr. Boy Scouts Am., Spokane, 1973-82, wood badge, 1977, commrs. key, 1977, scouters key, 1979. Named Citizen of Day KGA Radio, Spokane, 1983. Mem. AAUP (legislature com. Atlanta 1995—), Am. Assn. Respiratory Care (therapist driven protocol rev. com. 1994, ad hoc com. on patient-driven-protocol rev. com. 1996, ad hoc com. for sects. rev. 1995, 96), Ga. Soc. Respiratory Care (bd. dirs. 1994—, edn. com., smoking and health com.), Phi Delta Kappa (Alpha Nu chpt. Morehead, Ky. 1993-94, Kennesaw Mountain chpt. Atlanta 1994—, Pub. Rels. Com. 1995—). Roman Catholic. Home: 1565 Crider Rd SE Apt 12-B Marietta GA 30060-7430 Office: Chattahoochee Tech Inst Respiratory Therapy Program 980 S Cobb Dr SE Marietta GA 30060-3398

TITTSWORTH, CLAYTON (MAGNESS), lawyer; b. Tampa, Fla., Nov. 8, 1920. Student U. Tampa, 1939-42; LLB, Stetson Law Sch., 1951. Bar: Fla. 1951; ptnr. Tittsworth & Tittsworth, Tampa, 1951-65, Brandon, Fla., 1964-73; pvt. practice, Brandon, 1973-83; Tittsworth and Curry P.A., Brandon, 1983-87; pvt. practice, Brandon, 1983—. Mem. ABA, Fla. Bar Assn., Hillsborough County Bar Assn. Office: 1021 Hollyberry Ct Brandon FL 33511-7657

TKACZUK, NANCY ANNE, cardiovascular services administrator; b. Cambridge, Mass., Nov. 17, 1949; d. Ralph Aubrey and Eleanor Mae (Godding) Bedley; m. John Paul Tkaczuk, Apr. 9, 1977 (div. Apr. 1983); children: Timothy Aubrey, James Paul. AS in Social Svc., Endicott Coll., 1969; ADN, Clayton Coll., 1975. Coronary care nurse New England Meml. Hosp., Wakefield, Mass., 1975; cardiac cath lab nurse Saint Josephs Hosp., Atlanta, 1976-79; dir. cardiovascular svcs. Northside Hosp., Atlanta, 1979—; founder Mitral Valve Prolapse Support, Atlanta, 1986—; BCLS instr., trainer Am. Heart Assn., 1976—, instr. ACLS, 1990—, pub. spkr., 1975—. Author: Mitral Valve Prolapse, The Heart With A Different Beat, 1986. Mem. Am. Coll. Cardiovascular Adminstrs., Atlanta Health Care Alliance. Methodist. Home: 715 Cranberry Trail Roswell GA 30076 Office: Northside Hosp Cardiology Dept 1000 Johnson Ferry Rd NE Atlanta GA 30342

TLOU, JOSIAH S., education educator; b. Zimbabwe, Dec. 31, 1935; s. Litsila and Mothateho T.; m. Litha T., Sept. 3, 1959; children: Lee, Hla, Joy B., Leeto. BA, Luther Coll., 1968; MA, Ill. State U., 1969; EdD, U. Ill., 1976. Cons. curriculum Glencoe (Ill.) Pub. Schs.; specialist social studies USAID U. Botswana, Gaborone; assoc. prof. Va. Tech., Blacksburg; civic curriculum planner for U.S. AID project Harvard Inst. Internat. Devel./Creative Assocs. Internat., Malawi, 1996—; Cert. tchr., Zimbabwe. Contbr. articles to profl. jours. Recipient Disting. Svcs. award Luther Coll.; Luce-Bergeson rsch. grantee, African-Am., Scholars Coun. grantee, Creative Univ. Rsch. grantee, 1991-92, 94-95. Mem. ASCD, WCCI, Nat. Coun. Social Studies, ASA, AAPRDTW, Botswana Edn. Rsch. Assn., Phi Delta Kappa. Home: 108 Maywood St Blacksburg VA 24060-1315

TOAL, JEAN HOEFER, state supreme court justice, lawyer; b. Columbia, S.C., Aug. 11, 1943; d. Herbert W. and Lilla (Farrell) Hoefer; m. William Thomas Toal; children: Jean Hoefer, Lilla Patrick. BA in Philosophy, Agnes Scott Coll., 1965; JD, U. S.C., 1968; LHD (hon.), Coll. Charleston, 1991; LLD (hon.), Columbia Coll., 1992. Bar: S.C. Assoc. Haynsworth, Perry, Bryant, Marion & Johnstone, 1968-70; ptnr. Belser, Baker, Barwick, Ravenel, Toal & Bender, Columbia, 1970-88; assoc. justice S.C. Supreme Ct., 1988—; mem. S.C. Human Affairs Commn., 1972-74; mem. S.C. Ho. of Reps., 1975-88, chmn. house rules com., constitutional laws subcom. house judiciary com.; mem. parish coun. and lector St. Joseph's Cath. Ch.; chair S.C. Juvenile Justice Task Force, 1992-94; chair S.C. Rhodes Scholar Selection Com., 1994. Mng. editor S.C. Law Rev., 1967-68. Bd. visitors Clemson U., 1978; trustee Columbia Mus. Art. Named Legislator of Yr. Greenville News, Woman of Yr., U. S.C.; recipient Disting. Svc. award S.C. Mcpl. Assn., Univ. Notre Dame award, 1991, Algernon Sydney Sullivan award U. S.C., 1991. Mem. John Belton O'Neill Inn of Ct., Phi Beta Kappa, Mortar Bd., Order of the Coif. Office: Supreme Ct SC PO Box 12456 Columbia SC 29211-2456

TOALSTON, ARTHUR JOSEPH, JR., editor; b. Alliance, Ohio, Sept. 26, 1950; s. Arthur Joseph Sr. and L. Opal (Gerald) T.; m. Karen Ann Kendrick, June 4, 1986; 1 child, Kaeli. BS in Edn., Bowling Green (Ohio) State U., 1972; postgrad., Southwestern Bapt. Theol. Sem., 1983-84, Wesley Bibl. Sem., 1982-83, Presbyn. Sch. Christian Edn., 1985-86. Tchr. journalism and speech Findlay (Ohio) High Sch., 1972-74; staff writer The Courier, Findlay, summer 1973; regional editor The Rev.-Times, Fostoria, Ohio, 1974-76; staff writer The Middletown (Ohio) Jour., 1976-77; religion editor Jackson (Miss.) Daily News (now Clarion-Ledger), 1977-83; coord. Metroplex Rally for Decency, Am. Family Assn., Dallas-Ft. Worth, 1983; co-news dir. Southwestern Bapt. Theol. Sem., Ft. Worth, 1984; reporter Henrico County Line, Richmond, Va., 1988-90; secular news coord., staff writer Fgn. Mission Bd., So. Bapt. Conv., Richmond, 1985-91; editor Bapt. Press, Nashville, 1992. Corr. The Plain Dealer, Cleve., 1975-76, Nat. Courier, Plainfield, N.J., 1975-77, Religious News Svc., N.Y.C., 1979-83, Christianity Today, Carol Stream, Ill., 1980-85, USA Radio Network, 1993; author: The Amman Adventurer, 1990, Lamp Unto My Feet: 365 Christian Leaders Share the Scriptures That Have Guided Their Lives, 1997; contbr.; Victor Paul Wierwille and the Way, 1979. Recipient Sch. Bell award Ohio Sch. Bds. Assn., 1976-77. Mem. Religion Newswriters Assn. (assoc.), Bapt. Pub. Rels. Assn. (1st pl. writing awards 1986—). Baptist. Office: Bapt Press 901 Commerce St Ste 750 Nashville TN 37203-3629

TOBIAS, BENJAMIN ALAN, portfolio manager, financial planner; b. Bklyn., June 4, 1951; s. Joseph M. and Alma Ruth (Schneider) T.; m. Barbara Anne Biller, July 31, 1977; children: Daniel, Rachel. BBA, CUNY, 1973. CPA, N.Y., Fla.; cert. fin. planner, personal fin. specialist. Sr. acct. Deloitte & Touche, N.Y.C., Miami, 1973-79; pres. Benjamin A. Tobias, P.A. d/b/a Tobias Fin. Advisors, Pembroke Pines, Fla., 1980—; mem. adj. faculty Rollins Coll., 1996—. Author weekly newspaper column, Sun Newspapers, 1988-89. Named One of the Top 200 Advisors in U.S., Worth mag., 1996. Mem. AICPAs, Fla. Inst. CPAs (com. on personal and fin. planning 1989-90, 91), Gold Coast Soc. Cert. Fin. Planners (v.p. comm. 1989-90), South Fla. Cert. Fin. Planners (pres. 1992-93, chmn. 1993-94), Inst. Cert. Fin. Planners (mem. nat. com. 1994-95), Rotary (Pembroke Pines chpt., pres. 1986-87). Office: Tobias Fin Advisors 10081 Pines Blvd Ste E-1 Pembroke Pines FL 33024

TOBIN, JOSEPH RAPHAEL, medical educator; b. Rochester, N.Y., July 24, 1957; s. Joseph Lambert and Marjorie (Smith) T.; m. Mary Lou Voytko, Sept. 21, 1985. BA, SUNY, Buffalo, 1979; MD, SUNY, Syracuse, 1983. Asst. prof. Johns Hopkins, Balt., 1991-93; asst. prof. Bowman Gray Sch. of Medicine, Winston-Salem, N.C., 1993-95, assoc. prof., 1995—. Author: Textbook of Pediatric Intensive Care, 1994, 2nd edit., 1996; contbr. articles to Am. Jour. Physiology. Lt. comdr. USNR, 1988-93. Fellow Am. Acad. Pediat., Am. Coll. Critical Care Medicine; mem. Alpha Omega Alpha. Office: Bowman Gray Dept Anesthesia Medical Center Blvd Winston Salem NC 27157-1009

TOBIN, MARGARET ANN, cardiac medical critical care nurse; b. Oakland, Calif., Dec. 10, 1959; d. William Leroy Jones and Barbara Kay (Rains) Carter; m. Wesley Vernon Keene, June 21, 1977 (div. June 1984); m. James Edward Tobin, Aug. 15, 1985; 1 child, Nicholas William. ADN, Ctrl. Tex. Coll., 1983; BSN, U. Mary Harden Baylor, 1994; postgrad., Tex. A&M U., Corpus Christi, 1994—. RN, Tex.; cert. med.-surg. nurse ANCC; cert. BCLS instr., ACLS, ACLS instr. Grad. nurse surg. fl. Olin E. Teague VA Ctr., Temple, Tex., 1983-84, staff nurse cardiac med. ICU, 1984-95, nurse mgr. surg. ICU, 1995-96, nurse mgr. cardiac med. ICU, 1996, clin. instr., 1996—. Mem. Tar Wars Kids Against Tobacco, Temple, 1993—. Mem. AACN (pres.-elect 1993-94, pres. 1994-95), Sigma Theta Tau. Baptist. Home: 101 S 43rd St Temple TX 76504-3914

TOBIN, MARK STUART, internist, oncologist; b. N.Y.C., May 14, 1932; s. Chas. and Sophia T.; m. Rieva, Dec. 21, 1957; children: Jonathan, Chas., Pamela. BS, MIT, 1953; MD, Tufts U., 1957. Diplomate Am. Bd. Internal Medicine, Am. Bd. Oncology. Intern Maimonides Hosp., Bklyn., 1957-58, asst. med. resident, 1958-59; resident Bklyn. VA Hosp., 1959-60; fellowship in hematology Tufts/New Eng. Med. Ctr., Boston, 1960-62; instr. medicine N.Y. Med. Coll., N.Y.C., 1962-64; chief divsn. hematology/oncology Bklyn. Hosp., 1966-80; assoc. prof. medicine NYU Sch. Medicine, 1968-84; med. dir. cancer unit Med. Ctr. Hosp., Charlotte City, Fla., 1980-96. Contbr. articles to profl. jours. Office: Oncology Ctr 2400 Harbor Blvd Ste 18 Port Charlotte FL 33952

TOBIN, SHIRLEY ANN, elementary school educator; b. Elko, S.C., Aug. 29, 1953; d. Norman Hunter and Ruth Tobin. BS in Elementary Edn., Voorhees Coll., 1975; MEd, S.C. State Coll., 1981. Cert. tchr., S.C., APT observer, S.C. Tchr. 1st grade Blackville (S.C.) Pub. Schs., 1976—, homebound instr., 1979-84, coordinator drug and alcohol abuse program, 1987—; pper evaluator, tchr. evaluation com. Blackville (S.C.) Pub. Schs., 1989. Vol. tchr. Barnwell County Headstart, Blackville, 1967-69, Summer Sch. Program for Ch., Elko, 1983; del. Williston (S.C.) Dem. Party, 1984; co-chairperson St. Jude Children's Hosp. Bikeathon, 1985-87. Recipient Service award Cancer Drive, 1977, Cystic Fybrosis Drive, 1978, St. Jude Children's Hosp., Columbia, 1985-86. Mem. Nat. Tchrs. Assn. (faculty rep. 1982-85), S.C. Edn. Assn. (faculty rep. 1982-85, Cert. Appreciation 1982-85),

Blackville Edn. Assn. (faculty rep. 1982-85), AAUW (chmn. com. 1982-83), Council for Exceptional Children, Delta Sigma Theta (chmn. com. 1984—). Democrat. Baptist. Club: Please (sec. 1985-88) (Blackville). Home: PO Box 126 Elko SC 29826-0126 Office: Blackville Pub Schs PO Box 185 Blackville SC 29817-0185

TODD, IMO KELLAM, insurance association executive; b. Mobile, Ala., Dec. 26, 1943; d. Claude Moore and Minnie (Barth) Kellam; m. Jordan A.M. Todd, Sept. 29, 1962 (Div. 1972); 1 child, Shannon Elise. BA, Wesley U., 1963; BS, U. Montevallo, 1966; MBA, U. Ga., 1974. Exec. asst. Baumhauer-Croom Ins., Mobile, Ala., 1963-73; v.p. acct. exec. Haas & Dodd Ins., Atlanta, 1973-78; asst. prof. U. Ga., 1973-79; v.p. acct. exec. Fickling & Walker Ins. Agy., Atlanta, 1978-81; exec. v.p. Profl. Ins. Agts. Ga., Atlanta, 1981-93, Profl. Ins. Agts., Fla., 1991—; exec. v.p. Profl. Ins. Agts. Ala., 1991-96, S.C., 1992-96; dir. southeastern ins. conf. U. Greensboro, 1984-87; lectr. in field. Author: How to-of Education, 1984; editor monthly ins. mag.; contbr. articles to profl. mags. Campaign mgr. Cystic Fibrosis, Atlanta, 1975; chmn. annual fund raisers Spl. Olympics, 1983—. Named Speaker of Yr., Speakers Unltd., 1979, Atlanta's One in 100 Women, City of Atlanta, 1984, Cobb County Top 10 Women, 1991, Nat. Exec. of Yr., 1990. Mem. Am. Soc. Assn. Execs., Nat. Soc. Execs., U.S. Women's C. of C., Nat. Assn. Ins. Women (Ins. Woman of Yr. 1973-74, Exec. of Yr. 1989). Republican. Office: Assoc Profls of South Inc 3101 Roswell Rd Ste N-149 Marietta GA 30062-5594

TODD, JAMES DALE, federal judge; b. Scotts Hill, Tenn., May 20, 1943; s. James P. and Jeanette Grace (Duck) T.; m. Jeanie M. Todd, June 26, 1965; children: James Michael, Julie Diane. BS, Lambuth Coll., 1965; M Combined Scis., U. Miss., 1968; JD, Memphis State U., 1972. Bar: Tenn. 1972, U.S. Dist. Ct. (we. dist.) Tenn. 1972, U.S. Ct. Appeals (6th cir.) 1973, U.S. Supreme Ct. 1975. Tchr. sci., chmn. sci. dept. Lyman High Sch., Longwood, Fla., 1965-68, Memphis U. Sch., 1968-72; ptnr. Waldrop, Farmer, Todd & Breen, P.A., 1972-83; cir. judge div. II 26th Jud. Dist., Jackson, Tenn., 1983-85; judge U.S. Dist. Ct. (we. dist.) Tenn., Jackson, 1985—. Named Alumnus of Yr. Lambuth Coll. Alumni Assn., 1985. Fellow Tenn. Bar Found.; mem. Fed. Judges Assn., Fed. Bar Assn., Tenn. Bar Assn., Jackson Madison County Bar Assn. (pres. 1978-79). Methodist. Office: US Dist Ct 109 S Highland Ave Jackson TN 38301-6123

TODD, JAN THERESA, counselor; b. Mobile, Ala., Mar. 20, 1961; d. Joseph Thomas and Lessie Grey (Sullivan) T. BA, U. Tex., San Antonio, 1983, MA, 1992. Cert. profl. counselor; cert. provisional tchr. English tchr. Bandera (Tex.) High Sch.-Bandera (Tex.) Ind. Sch. Dist., 1987-91; counselor Yorktown (Tex.) High Sch.-Yorktown (Tex.) Ind. Sch. Dist., 1992-93, John F. Kennedy High Sch.-Edgewood Ind. Sch. Dist., San Antonio, 1993-95, Lackland Jr./Sr. H.S., San Antonio, 1995—. Mem. ACA, Tex. Counselors Assn., South Tex. Counselors Assn., Assn. Tex. Profl. Educators. Home: 9415 De Sapin San Antonio TX 78250-6308 Office: Lackland Jr/Sr High School Bldg 8265 2460 Bong Ave San Antonio TX 78236-1244

TODD, JOAN ABERNATHY, secondary school educator; b. Roanoke Rapids, N.C., June 14, 1947; d. Benjamin Cornelius and Mildred Lee (Davis) Abernathy; m. Douglas Felton Todd, Dec. 16, 1973 (dec. Aug. 1988); 1 child, Jason Douglas. BS, East Carolina U., Greenville, N.C., 1969. Cert. tchr., N.C. Tchr. Youngsville (N.C.) High Sch., 1969, Greensville County, Emporia, Va., 1969-72, N.W. High Sch., Littleton, N.C., 1972-82; tchr. home econs. Eastman Middle Sch., Enfield, N.C., 1982-96, Northwest H.S., Littleton, N.C., 1996—; instr. N.C. League of Middle Schs., Charlotte, 1990, Halifax C.C., Weldon, N.C., 1990-91; mentor tchr. Eastman Middle Sch., 1987-96; condr. workshops. Pres., treas. Sunshine Ext. Club, Roanoke Rapids, 1988-90, sec., 1995—; pres. Parents Without Ptnrs., Roanoke Rapids, 1992, Heritage Crafters, Halifax, 1992-96; vol. N.C. Coop. Ext. Mem. NEA (bldg. rep. 1980-94), N.C. Edn. Assn. (dist. 12 sec. 1995-96, Halifax County Edn. Assn. (sec. 1990-93, pres. 1994-95, 96-97), N.C. Home Econs. Assn., Delta Kappa Gamma (2d v.p. 1995-96, 1st v.p. 1996, pres. 1996—).

TODD, JOE LEE, historian; b. Bartlesville, Okla., Sept. 28, 1946; s. Harold Albert and Mildred Viola Todd. Student, Okla. State U., 1964-66; BA in Anthropology, U. Okla., 1974; postgrad. in Anthropology, U. Tex., Austin, 1979-81. Curator of collections Okla. Hist. Soc., Oklahoma City, 1971-76; dir. 45th Infantry div. mus., Oklahoma City, 1976-78; curator Ft. Hood (Tex.) Mus., 1978-82; oral historian, archivist Okla. Hist. Soc., Oklahoma City, 1982—; cons. Confederate Air Force, Midland, Tex., 1990—, Andersonville (Ga.) POW Ctr., 1991—. Author: Pipe-Tomahawks in the Oklahoma Historical Society, 1976, Native American Interveiws, oral histories, 1985, USS Oklahoma, 1990. Bd. dirs. Sacred Heart (Okla.) Indian Mission, 1989—. With U.S. Army, 1966-69, Okla. Nat. Guard, 1975-78, Tex. Nat. Guard, 1978-83, USAR, 1983—. Recipient Bronze Star U.S. Army, 1991, Humanitarian Svc. medal, 1992. Republican. Episcopalian. Office: Okla Hist Soc 2100 N Lincoln Blvd Oklahoma City OK 73105-4915

TODD, JOHN DICKERSON, III, special education administrator; b. Greenville, S.C., Mar. 24, 1952; s. John Dickerson Jr. and Mellicent (McWhorter) T.; m. Joan Shafer, Aug. 1, 1981; children: Emily Joan, Susan Mellicent, Anna Dickerson. BA in Sociology, Wofford Coll., 1974; MAT in Health/Phys. Edn., U. S.C., 1977, MA in Libr. and Info. Sci., 1996. Tchr., coach S.C. Sch. for Deaf and Blind, Spartanburg, 1979-90, dir. phys. edn., 1991, dir. media, libr. svcs., 1991—; track coach S.C. Sch. for Deaf and Blind, 1980-88, cross country coach, 1980-89 (coached 7 individual state champions); numerous nat. and internat. coaching positions U.S. Assn. Blind Athletes, 1980—. organizer Out of Sight Road Race, 1986—; founder and pres. S.C. Found. Disabled Athletes, 1990—; bd. dirs. YMCA, Spartanburg, 1991-93. Named Nat. Deaf Cross Country Coach of Yr., 1989, Outstanding Young Alumni, Wofford Coll., 1992. Mem. S.C. Assn. Blind Athletes (bd. dirs. 1980—, pres. 1984). Home: 820 Patch Dr Spartanburg SC 29302-3072 Office: SC Sch for Deaf and Blind 355 Cedar Springs Rd Spartanburg SC 29302-4699

TODD, KEITH, editor and publisher; b. Ilford, Essex, Eng., Jan. 23, 1958; came to U.S., 1979; s. George Eric and June (Smith) T. Dance dir. Fred Astaire Dance Studio, Miami, Fla., 1979-83; owner, dir. Dance City, Miami, 1983-90; pub., editor Dance Beat Inc, Miami, 1990—; adjudicator N.D.C.A., 1980—. Mem. NADTA, ISTD (assoc.). Office: Dance Beat Inc 12265 S Dixie Hwy Ste 909 Miami FL 33156

TODD, MARY PATRICIA, nursing administrator; b. Loogootee, Ind., Sept. 5, 1959; d. James Walter and Anna Margaret (Arvin) T.; m. Joe Linville, 1996; 1 child, B.J. BS in Social Work, St. Mary of the Woods Coll., 1982; AS in Nursing, Tenn. State U., 1989; postgrad., Vanderbilt U., 1995—. Cert. disaster nursing ARC. Comty. organizer Rogers Park Tenants Com., Chgo., 1984-85; dir. Nashville Comys. Orgn. for Progress, Nashville, 1986-87, Tenn. Coun. Sr. Citizens, Nashville, 1987-89; staff nurse Nashville VA Med. Ctr., Nashville, 1989-90; charge nurse Hartsville (Tenn.) Convalescent Ctr., 1990-94; quality assurance coord. ABC Home Health, Hartsville, 1992-93; adminstr. ABC Home Health, Lafayette, Tenn., 1994-95; charge nurse Trousdale Med. Ctr., Hartsville, Tenn., 1995—; presenter rural health conf. Meharry Med. Sch., Nashville, 1994; spkr. Tenn. rural Health Assn., 1995. Contbr., pub.: Love Passed On, 1991; contbr.: Photographic History of Martin County, 1993, Voices from the Hills, 1995; organizer, author: (diaster plan) Caring When it Counts, 1994. Bd. dirs., chair membership com. Mid. Cumberland Cmty. Health Agy., Nashville, 1992—; mem. Network, Washington, 1993—; organizer Trousdale County Cmty. Health Coun., Hartsville, 1992—; active Greenpeace, 1990-92; tchr. Confraternity of Christian Doctrine, Holy Family Cath. Ch., 1992, 94. Mem. ANA, Tenn. Nurses Assn., Tenn. Assn. for Home Care, Tenn. Rural Health Assn., Trousdale County C. of C., Amnesty Internat., Health Profls. Network, Rural Tenn. Women's Support Group (organizer 1994), Sigma Delta Tau. Democrat. Home: 314 Church St Apt 22 Hartsville TN 37074-1713 Office: Trousdale Medical Center 500 Church St #22 Hartsville TN 37074

TODD, RICHARD D. R., lawyer; b. Borger, Tex., July 17, 1962; s. William H. and Linda (Brumfield) T.; m. Lisa Ann McCown, Jan. 4, 1986; children: Richard Benjamin, Madison Claire. Student, Tex. Tech. U., Lubbock, 1984; BS in Health Care Adminstrn., Wayland Bapt. U., Plainview, Tex., 1988; JD magna cum laude, Oklahoma City U., 1991. Bar: Tex. 1992, Okla. 1992, U.S. Dist. Ct. (no. dist.) Tex. 1992, U.S. Dist. Ct. (we. dist.) Okla. 1992, U.S. Ct. Appeals (5th cir.) 1993, U.S. Supreme Ct. 1995. Paramedic/ops. mgr. Amarillo (Tex.) Med. Svcs., 1982-89; legal intern Lampkin, McCaffrey & Tawwater, Oklahoma City, 1990-92; pvt. practice Borger, Tex., 1992-95, Wichita Falls, Tex., 1995—; barrister Am. Inn of Ct., Oklahoma City, 1990-92. Percussionist First Bapt. Ch., Wichita Falls. Mem. ABA, Borger Bar Assn., State Bar Tex. (pro bono coll. 1994-95), Phi Delta Phi (vice magister 1991). Baptist. Office: 1417 9th St Wichita Falls TX 76301

TODD, ROBERT EDWARD, JR., purchasing manager; b. Cape Girardeau, Mo., July 30, 1956; s. Robert Edward and Mary Louise (Webb) T. BS in Commerce, U. Louisville, 1978. Cert. purchasing mgr. Purchasing officer Commonwealth of Ky., Frankfort, 1979-85; sr. buyer R.R. Donnelley & Sons Co., Danville, Ky., 1985-92; purchasing mgr. St. Ives, inc., Hollywood, Fla., 1992-96. Contbr. articles to profl. jours. Asst. scoutmaster, troop com. Boy Scouts Am., Louisville, Ky., 1974-85, Danville, Ky., 1985-92, Davie & Weston, Fla., 1992-94, dist. advancement chmn., Danville, 1988-92. Mem. Nat. Assn. Purchasing Mgrs. (chmn. profl. devel. 1993-94), Purchasing Mgmt. Asns. Louisville (chmn. coms. 1982-89, bd. dirs. 1989-91, 2d v.p. 1991-92). Roman Catholic. Home: 9256 Arborwood Cir Davie FL 33328-6770

TODD, SHIRLEY ANN, school system administrator; b. Botetourt County, Va., May 23, 1935; d. William Leonard and Margaret Judy (Simmons) Brown; m. Thomas Byron Todd, July 7, 1962 (dec. July 1977). B.S. in Edn., Madison Coll., 1956; M.Ed., U. Va., 1971. Cert. tchr., Va. Elem. tchr. Fairfax County Sch. Bd., Fairfax, Va., 1956-66, 8th grade history tchr., 1966-71, guidance counselor James F. Cooper Mid. Sch., McLean, Va., 1971-88, dir. guidance, 1988-96; chmn. mktg. Lake Anne Joint Venture, Falls Church, Va., 1979-82, mng. ptnr., 1980-82. Del. Fairfax County Republican Conv., 1985. Fellow Fairfax Edn. Assn. (mem. profl. rights and responsibilities commn. 1970-72, bd. dirs. 1968-70), Va. Edn. Assn. (mem. state com. on local assns. and urban affairs 1969-70), NEA, No. Va. Counselors Assn. (hospitality and social chmn., exec. bd. 1982-83), Va. Counselors Assn. (exec. com. 1987), Va. Sch. Counselors Assn., Am. Assn. for Counseling and Devel., Chantilly Nat. Golf and Country Club (v.p. social 1981-82, Centreville, Va.). Baptist. Avocations: golf, tennis. Home: 6543 Bay Tree Ct Falls Church VA 22041-1001

TODD, VIRGIL HOLCOMB, clergyman, religion educator; b. Jordonia, Tenn., June 22, 1921; s. George Thurman and Nellie Mai (Dutton) T.; m. Irene Rolman, Sept. 21, 1941; 1 child, Donald Edwin. BA, Bethel Coll., 1945; BD, Cumberland Presbyn. Sem., 1947; MA, Scarritt Coll., 1948; PhD, Vanderbilt U., 1956. Ordained to ministry Presbyn. Ch., 1944. Minister Cumberland Presbyn. Chs., Tenn. and Ky., 1943-52; assoc. prof. Bethel Coll., McKenzie, Tenn., 1952-54; prof. of Old Testament Memphis Theol. Sem., 1954—; interim minister Presbyn. chs. in Tenn., Ky. and Miss., 1952—; vice-moderator Gen. Assembly Cumberland Presbyn. Ch., 1984-85, moderator, 1985-86. Author: Prophet Without Portfolio (2d Isaiah), 1972, A New Look at an Old Prophet (Ezekiel), 1977, Biblical Eschatology, 1985. Active Shelby (County) United Neighbors, Memphis, 1973-74, United Way of Greater Memphis, 1974-82. Mem. Soc. Bibl. Lit., Memphis Ministers' Assn. Democrat. Lodge: Civitan (chaplain, bd. dirs. local chpt.). Office: Memphis Theol Sem 168 E Parkway S Memphis TN 38104-4340

TODD, WILLIAM H., JR., company executive; b. 1951. BSBA, Butler U., 1973; MBA, Heriott Watt U., Edinburgh, Scotland, 1988. Sales rep. Forwardair, Indpls., 1974-77; various position to gen. mgr. Atlantic Container Line, Indpls., Denver, Houston, South Plainfield, N.J., 1977-92; pres. Leschaco, Houston, 1992—. Office: Leschaco 8552 Katy Fwy Ste 223 Houston TX 77024

TOEDTE, SHARON LYNN SIMON, marketing professional; b. Coral Gables, Fla., Mar. 19, 1957; d. Gerald Tobias and Faye Marion (Fields) S.; m. Ross John Toedte, Sept. 6, 1987; 1 child, Blaire Simone, 1995. BA in Econs., Coll. William & Mary, 1978; MBA in Mktg., U. Tenn., 1987, postgrad. in sociology, 1994—. Asst. buyer Davison's, Atlanta, 1978-79, sales mgr., 1979-80; project dir. Leonard & Assocs., Atlanta, 1980-82; rsch. account exec. D'Arcy, MacManus, Masius, Atlanta, 1982-84; rsch. mgr. Whittle Communications, Knoxville, Tenn., 1984-87, rsch. dir., 1987-91; pres. SST Market Rsch. Designs, Knoxville, 1991—; spkr. mktg. classes U. Tenn., Knoxville, 1986—, instr., 1992—; adj. faculty Tenn. Wesleyan Coll., 1989-92. Active Knoxville Arts Coun., 1985—, Knoxville Mus. Art, 1985—, Knoxville Symphony Orch., 1987-90; contbr. Victor Ashe for Mayor, Knoxville, 1987. Mem. Am. Mktg. Assn. (v.p. programs 1988-89, v.p. cmty. edn. 1989-90, outreach 1990-92, spkr. 1989 Knoxville chpt., nominating com. chair 1992, co-chair CzechMate project, mem. mktg. rsch. coun. 1993-95, pres. elect 1993-94, pres. 1994-95, chair attitude rsch. conf. 1994). Jewish. Office: SST Market Rsch Designs 1400 Queensbridge Dr Knoxville TN 37922-6082

TOFTELAND, CURT L., producer, director; b. Martin, N.D., Apr. 30, 1952; s. Donald Morris and Jona Georgine (Goodman) T.; m. Marcia Tarbis, May 30, 1981; 1 child, Joshua Tarbis. BFA in Music, U. N.D., 1974; MFA, U. Minn., 1978. Actor Asolo Touring Theater, Sarasota, Fla., 1978-79; assoc. artistic dir. Stage One, Louisville, 1979-85; pres. Joshua Prodns., Louisville, 1985-89; producing dir. Ky. Shakespeare Festival, Louisville, 1989—; adj. faculty U. Louisville, 1987—, Ind. U. S.E., 1993—, Bellarmine Coll., 1994—; cons. Ky. Arts Coun., Frankfort, 1985—, Ky. Humanities Coun., Lexington, 1988, Very Spl. Arts Ky., Frankfort, 1987—. Playwright six plays. Al Smith fellow, 1988. Mem. Ky. Allinace for Arts in Edn., Ky. Citizens for the Arts, Actors' Equity Assn. Office: Ky Shakespeare Festival 1114 S 3rd St Louisville KY 40203-2902

TOGUT, TORIN DANA, lawyer; b. N.Y.C., Apr. 24, 1951; s. Benjamin Morris and Millicent (Friedman) T.; m. Emily Jane Greenberg, July 27, 1975 (dec. Oct. 1985); m. A. Teresa Romasco, Oct. 20, 1990. BS, Cornell U., 1973; JD, LaVerne U., 1976. Pvt. practice Decatur, Ga., 1977-84; atty. Ga. Legal Svcs. Program, Atlanta, 1984—; atty. trainer Advocacy Ctr., Inc., Tallahassee, 1990. Chair Citizens Adv. Coun. Brook Run, Atlanta, 1992-93; bd. dirs. Mental Health Assn. Ga., Atlanta, 1987-90, protection and advocacy com., 1986-87; mem. task force mentally ill State Bar Ga., 1988-89, task force forensic mental health svcs. Ga. Dept. Human resources, 1990; mem. human rights com. ARC/Ga., 1986-88; bd. dirs. GARAL, 1994-95. Named Prof. of Yr. by ARC/Ga., 1992. Mem. ABA, ACLU (bd. dirs. 1989—, co-chair legal com. 1988-90), North Fulton Bar Assn. Home: 9700 Loblolly Ln Roswell GA 30075-4316 Office: Ga Legal Svcs Program 161 Spring St NW Atlanta GA 30303-2000

TOIFEL, RONALD CHARLES, librarian; b. Mobile, Ala., June 4, 1933; s. Leopold Francis and Thelma Teresa (Eckert) T.; m. Peggy Suzanne White, Jan. 15, 1972; children: Ronald Charles Jr., Mark, Lance. BS, Miss. So. Coll., 1957; MS in Libr. Sci., La. State U., Baton Rouge, 1966; EdD in Higher Edn., Fla. State U., 1990. Head bookmobile divsn. Davis Ave. Br. Libr.; asst. head ref. dept., Internat. Trade Ctr. libr. Mobile Pub. Libr., 1966-68; asst. libr. dir. Gadsden (Ala.) Pub. Libr., 1968-69; libr. U. West Fla., Pensacola, 1969—. Contbr. articles to profl. jours. Mem. Bagdad Village Preervatoin Assn., Santa Rosa County Hist. Soc. With USAF, 1958-65. Mem. ALA (ednl. and behavioral scis. sect./bibliog. instrn. for edn. com., com. on problems of assessment and control of curriculum materials), Southeastern Libr. Assn., Online Svcs. Roundtable (sec.). Democrat. Home: PO Box 472 4561 Forsyth St Bagdad FL 32530 Office: University of West Florida John C Pace Libr 11000 University Pkwy Pensacola FL 32514-5732

TOLBERT, VINCENT TYSON, secondary education educator; b. Chgo., Jan. 1, 1968; s. Curtis DeRamus and Melva Lucille (Armstead) T. BS, Howard U., 1991, U. Ala., 1993; MA, Clark Atlanta U., 1995. Sci. tchr. Birmingham (Ala.) Pub. Schs., 1993, DeKalb County Schs., Scottdale, Ga., 1994—; dir. Ga. Power Shenandoah Environ. and Edn. Ctr., Newnan, Ga., 1994. DeWitt-Wallace fellow Reader's Digest Fund, 1994-95. Mem. ASCD, Ga. Assn. of Educators. Home: 4406 Treehills Pkwy Stone Mountain GA 30088 Office: DeKalb Alternative Sch 385 Glendale Rd Scottdale GA 30079

TOLER, ANN PATRICK, public relations executive; b. Washington, Oct. 7, 1948; d. William A. and Marie Violet (Tyer) Patrick; m. Ronald Aubrey Toler, July 4, 1970; 1 child, Bradley Neal. Student, East Carolina U., 1966-68; cert. bank mktg, U. Colo., 1989. Admiting clk. Beaufort County Hosp., Washington, N.C., 1966-69; receptionist then exec. sec. Flanders Filters, Washington, 1969-81; adminstrv. sec. Bank of Va., Richmond, 1981-85, personal svc. assoc., 1985-87; mktg. coord. Signet Bank, Richmond, 1987-89, mktg. officer, 1989-90, asst. v.p., 1990-93, regional pub. rels. exec., 1993-94, regional pub. rels. exec. Va. Cmty. Affairs, 1994—. Dir. tournament Signet Open Va., Richmond, 1986—; bd. dirs. Easter Seal Soc., Richmond, 1989—; co-chair spl. events com. United Way, Richmond, 1991, chair 1992 ; chair regional conf. Am. Heart Assn., Richmond, 1991; sec., bd. dirs. Christmas in Apr., Richmond; sec., bd. dirs. Christmas in April, Richmond, 1995-96, v.p., bd. dirs., 1996-97. Mem. Bank Mktg. Assn. Methodist. Office: Signet Bank Ste 200 800 E Main St Richmond VA 23219-2512

TOLER, RAY EDWARD, conductor, band director; b. Detroit, Feb. 1, 1942; s. Ralph Vivian and Neva Florence (Killough) T.; m. Catherine Virginia Hoff, Aug. 15, 1964; children: Ray Edward Jr., Eric Andrew, Bryan Alan. MusB, Tex. Christian U., 1964; MA summa cum laude, Trenton State Coll., 1975; grad., Air Command and Staff Coll., Maxwell AFB, Ala., 1982, Air War Coll, Maxwell AFB, Ala., 1984. Commd. 2d lt. USAF, 1968, advanced through grades to lt. col., 1984; trombonist 539th Air Force Band USAF, Lackland AFB, Tex., 1966-68; condr., comdr. Air Force Logistics Command Band Wright-Patterson AFB, Ohio, 1968-71; condr., comdr. 13th Air Force Band of the Pacific Clark AFB, The Philippines, 1971-73, Air Force Band of the East, McGuire AFB, N.J., 1973-75; condr., comdr. Mil. Airlift Command Band Scott AFB, Ill., 1975-78; condr., comdr. Air Force Band of the West, Lackland AFB, 1978-81, Band of the Air Force Res., Robins AFB, Ga., 1982-85; chief of bands and music USAF Pentagon, Washington, 1985-88; condr. USAF Band, Washington, 1985-88; ret. USAF, 1988; dir. bands Tex. A&M U., College Station, 1988—; trombonist Ft. Worth Symphony and Opera Co., 1963-65, Stan Kenton Orch. , L.A., 1965, Dallas Symphony Orch., 1965-66; band dir. Weatherford (Tex.) High Sch., 1964-66. Condr. rec. Music of the King, 1971; condr./prodr. rec. Music of West Africa, 1977, Ready Then, Ready Now, 1982, Concert Band Classics, 1983, Recall! Step-Off on Hullabaloo, 1990, Bands of Aggieland, 1993, Texas Aggie Band Centennial, 1994, Texas A&M Univ. Symphonic Band Live At TMEA, 1995; prodr. Comin' At 'Ya, 1984; condr./composer rec. In Concert, 1985; condr. rec. The Best of the Air Force Reserve, 1988. Deacon 1st Presbyn. Ch., Fairborn, Ohio, 1970; judge Miss Am. Scholarship Pageant, 1992, 94; bd. dirs. Woodcreek Homeowners assn., College Station, 1988-91; bd. dirs. Brazor Valley Symphony Orch., College Station, 1996. Mem. Nat. Assn. Mil. Marching Bands, John Philip Sousa Found. (bd. dirs.), Coll. Band Dirs. Nat. Assn., Tex. Bandmasters Assn., Tex. Music Educators Assn., World Assn. for Symphonic Bands and Ensembles, N.Am. Band Dirs. Coordinating Coun., Internat. Mil. Music Soc., Assn. Concert Bands, USAF Ret. Band Dirs. Soc., Kappa Kappa Psi, Phi Mu Alpha Sinfonia. Republican. Methodist. Office: Tex A&M U Adams Band Bldg College Station TX 77843

TOLES, THOMAS TAYLOR, newspaper editor; b. Marietta, Ga., Dec. 26, 1945; s. Thomas Taylor Sr. and Minnie Lee (Sentell) T. Student, U. Ga., 1963, Floyd Coll., 1986, U. Ala. Reporter Rome (Ga.) News-Tribune, 1963-67, city editor, 1973-78; mng. editor South Fulton Recorder, Fairburn, Ga., 1967-68; editor Douglas County Sentinel, Douglasville, 1968-73; press. asst. Congressman Larry McDonald, Washington, 1979-83; campaign mgr. Kathy McDonald Congressman, Marietta, Ga., 1983; news dir. WIYN Radio, Rome, 1985-86; editor The Summerville News, 1986-94, Rome News-Tribune, 1994—. Exec. dir. Larry McDonald Found., Marietta, 1985—; grad. Leadership Chattooga, 1990; former mem. Douglasville Recreation Authority, 1971-73; sec. N.W. Ga. Transp. com. 1991-94. Recipient Key Man award Douglas County C. of C., 1970, Oustanding Young Man award Douglas County Jaycees, 1970, Key to City of Wakkanai, Japan, 1984, Ga. Freedom of Info. award Ga. Press Assn., 1990, 93, 1st pl. feature writing, 1989, 91, Best editorial page, 1989, 92, Best local news, 1990, Best black and white news photo, 1992, First Community Svc., 1990, Second Bus. writing, 1990, Second Community Svc., 1990, Second Gen. Excellence, 1989, First Gen. Excellence, 1967, others. Mem. Ga. Press Assn. (chmn. continuing edn. com. 1991-92, chmn. pub. affairs com. 1995-96), Ga. Newspapers in Edn. Commn., Summerville-Trion Rotary (pres. 1992-93, mem. dist. long-range planning com. 1992-94, Rotarian of Yr. 1987-88, Outstanding Svc. to Rotary award 1991, Outstanding Rotary Pub. Info. award 1993, Outstanding Rotary Pres. award 1993), Ga. First Amendment Found. (bd. dirs. 1996—), Ga. Assn. Press Assn. (bd. dirs. 1996—). Mem. Ch. of Christ. Office: Rome News Tribune PO Box 1633 Rome GA 30162-1633

TOLFORD, FRANK STEFAN, bookseller; b. Bremen, Germany, June 30, 1949; came to U.S., 1955; s. Charles Lawrence and Marta Sophia Tolford. AA, St. Johns River Jr. Coll., Palatka, Fla., 1973; BA, U. North Fla., Jacksonville, 1976. Warehouse mgr. Smith & Royals Elec. Svc. Co., Jacksonville, 1977-80; gen. mgr. Chamblin Bookmine, Jacksonville, 1981—. Donor Fla.-Ga. Blood Alliance, Jacksonville, 1982—. Mem. Fla. Antiquarian Booksellers Assn. (v.p. 1990-91, pres. 1991-94). Republican. Episcopalian. Office: Chamblin Bookmine 4551 Roosevelt Blvd Jacksonville FL 32210

TOLLE, DONALD MACDAVID, computer scientist; b. Winter Haven, Fla., Apr. 21, 1947; s. Donald James and Mary Alice (McNeill) T.; m. Forough Danesh, May 29, 1988; children: Robert Cameron, Brooke Farah. AA in Liberal Arts, St. Petersburg (Fla.) Jr. Coll, 1967; BA in Math., U. South Fla., 1970, MA in Math., 1975; PhD in Computer Sci., U. N.C., 1981. Rsch. computer scientist Shell Devel. Co., Houston, 1981-89, rsch. mgr., 1989-93; project mgr. Shell Oil Co., Houston, 1993-95; mgr. applied technology investments Shell Svcs. Co., Houston, 1995—. Inventor syntactically self-structuring cellular computer; co-inventor seismic migration on multiprocessor computer. Recipient Morehead Found. fellowship U. N.C., 1975-79. Mem. IEEE, Assn. for Computing Machinery, Math. Assn. Am., Sigma Xi (mem. chpt. bd. dirs. 1992-94). Home: 4014 Bratton St Sugar Land TX 77479-2983 Office: Shell Oil Co 3737 Bellaire Blvd Houston TX 77025

TOLLETT, EILEEN RICE, professional association administrator; b. Little Rock, Mar. 28, 1947; d. Charles Jeptha and Mary Lois (Carroll) R.; m. Billy Eugene, Aug. 16, 1969; 1 child, Casey Elaine Tollett Collins. BS in Edn., U. Ctrl. Ark., 1969; M Liberal Arts, So. Meth. U., 1972; PhD, U. Tex., Dallas, 1981. Instr., dept. head McKinney (Tex.) Job Corps Ctr., 1970-75; owner, operator Tollett Typing & Cons., Allen, 1980-88; legal asst. Seeligson & Steinberg, Dallas, 1990-92; faculty assoc. U. Tex. Dallas, Richardson, 1992—; exec. adminstr. Am. Lit. Translators Assn., Richardson, Tex., 1992—. Editor: Translation Review: Annotated Books Received Suplement, 1994—; contbr. to profl. jours. Mem. Allen City Coun., 1976-78; bd. dirs. Allen Libr. Bd., Heard Natural Sci. Mus., McKinney, Tex., 1986-90; bd. dirs., pres. Caddo Camp and Edn. Ctr., McKinney, 1992-96. Named Woman of Yr., Am. Bus. Women's Assn., 1985. Democrat. Home: 404 Watson Dr Allen TX 75002 Office: Am Lit Translators Assn MC35 PO Box 830688 Richardson TX 75083-0688

TOLLETT, JAMES TERRELL, agriculture educator, department chair; b. Nashville, Ark., June 14, 1935; s. Vergil Elisa and Gladys Virginia (Sturgis) T.; m. Joann Latimer, Aug. 12, 1956; 1 child, Cheryl. AS in Agriculture, So. State Coll., 1955; BS, MS in Agriculture, U. Ark., 1957; PhD, U. Ill., 1961. Asst. prof. So. State Coll., Magnolia, Ark., 1961-62; sr. rsch. scientist Dow Chem. Co., Midland, Tex., 1962-85; prof. agr. No. Tex. C.C., Mt. Pleasant, Tex., 1985-90; prof., chair agr. So. Ark. U., Magnolia, 1990—; cons. Ark. Pork Coun., Russelville, 1990—. Patentee in field. Chair deacons First Bapt. Ch., Magnolia, Ark., 1995-96; mem. Magnolia 2000 City of Magnolia, 1991. Recipient Man of Agriculture Aubrey Pilgrim's award, 1989. Mem. Poultry Sci. (chair resolutions 1954-96), Animal Sci., Lion's Club (pres. svcs. 1996). Republican. Baptist. Home: 902 Sue Magnolia AR 71753 Office: So Ark U PO Box 1343SAU Magnolia AR 71753

TOLLEY, EDWARD DONALD, lawyer; b. San Antonio, Jan. 31, 1950; s. Lyle Oren and Mary Theresa Tolley; m. Beth Dekle Tolley; 1 child, Edward Spencer. BBA, U. Ga., 1971, MBA, 1974, JD, 1975. Bar: Ga. 1975, U.S. Dist. Ct. (5th cir.) 1976, U.S. Supreme Ct. 1978, U.S. Ct. Appeals (11th cir.) 1981. Ptnr. Cook, Noell, Tolley and Wiggins, Athens, Ga., 1975—; lectr. various colls., univs., civic and profl. groups. Mem. Family Counseling

Assn. of Athens, Inc., mem. Gov.'s Commn. on Criminal Sanctions and Correctional Facilities, 1988-90; past bd. dirs. Am. Cancer Soc.; pres. Clarke County Bd. Edn., 1992-93. Fellow Ga. Bar Found., Am. Bd. Criminal Lawyers (bd. dirs. 1987, pres.-elect 1995); mem. State Bar Ga. (chmn. law office and econ. com., bd. govs. 1985—, formal adv. opinion bd.), Ga. Trial Lawyers (v.p.), Ga. Assn. Criminal Def. Lawyers (pres. 1985, Indigent Def. award 1983, 88), Athens Bar Assn. (past pres.), Am. Judicature Soc., Fed. Bur. Assn. (treas. 1985, sec. 1983), Order of Barristers. Office: Cook Noell Tolley & Wiggins 304 E Washington St Athens GA 30601-2751

TOLLEY, GARY MAURICE, radiologist; b. Lesage, W.Va., Aug. 2, 1935; s. Eugene Franklin Tolley and Mary Virginia (Lunsford) Brandt; m. Wanda Gordon Chain, Aug. 23, 1957; children: Stephen Gregory, Mark Kevin, David Brian, Joseph Andrew. B.S., Marshall Coll., 1957, W.Va. U., 1959; M.D., Med. Coll. Va., 1961. Diplomate Am. Bd. Radiology, Am. Bd. Nuclear Medicine. Intern Charleston Meml. Hosp., W.Va., 1961-62; resident Ind. U. Med. Ctr., Indpls., 1965-68; staff radiologist Cabell-Huntington Hosp., St. Mary's Hosp., VA Hosp., 1968—; mem. staff sch. medicine Marshall U., clin. prof, 1985—, chmn. dept radiology , 1989-90, clin. prof., 1985—, prof., chmn. dept.radiology, 1989—; chief radiologyCabell-Huntington Hosp., 1983—, pres. staff, trustee, 1987-88; pres., trustee, 1987-88. Served with USN, 1962-65. Am. Cancer Soc. fellow, 1966-67; George Benedum Found. scholar, 1958. Del. Am. Coll. Nuclear Physicians; mem. AMA (Physician's Recognition award 1972, 75, 78, 81, 84, 87, 90), Am. Inst. Ultra Sound in Medicine, Pan Am. Med. Assn., W.Va. State Med. Assn., Cabell County Med. Assn. (pres. 1987), Am. Coll. Radiology, W.Va. State Radiologic Soc., Alpha Epsilon Delta. Home: 323 Woodland Dr Huntington WV 25705-3539 Office: Radiology Inc 1035 3rd Ave Huntington WV 25701-1567

TOLLEY, STEPHEN GREGORY, oceanographer; b. Huntington, W.Va., July 4, 1958; s. Gary Maurice and Wanda Gordon (Chain) T. BS, Marshall U., 1980; PhD, U. So. Fla., 1994, knight fellow, 1987-92. Rsch. asst. U. So. Fla., St. Petersburg, 1983-86; mgr., curator The Pier Aquarium, St. Petersburg, 1988-89; rsch. assoc. U. So. Fla., 1989-94, asst. prof., 1995—; cons. The Pier Aquarium, 1988, Natural History Mus., N.Y.C., 1988, Mote Marine Lab., Sarasota, Fla., 1985; treas. bd. dirs. Pier Aquarium, Inc., 1989-91. Judge Ann. State Sci. and Engring. Fair, 1990-96; sxhibit adv. St. Petersburg Hist. Mus., 1986. Mem. Am. Soc. Ichthyologists & Herpetologists, Am. Fisheries Soc., Ichthyological Soc. Japan, Oceanography Soc., Am. Inst. Fisheries Rsch. Biologists, Sigma Xi, Omicron Delta Kappa, Phi Kappa Phi. Office: U So Fla 140 7th Ave S Saint Petersburg FL 33701-5016

TOLLINGER, MELISSA LEE, geographer; b. West Chester, Pa., Oct. 6, 1962; d. Charles Jay and Jacquelyn Wells (Osmond) Barr; m. Michael James Tollinger, June 3, 1989. BS in Geography, Pa. State U., 1985; MA in Geography, East Carolina U., 1994. Cartographic/field technician Centre County, Bellefonte, Pa., 1985-87; cartographer Gannett-Fleming Engrs., Harrisburg, Pa., 1987-89; asst. city planner City of Roanoke Rapids (N.C.), 1989-91; instr. geography East Carolina U., Greenville, 1991—. Vol. park maintenance County Parks Commn., York, Pa., 1984; vol. waterway clean up The Big Sweep, Rocky Mount, N.C., 1990-92; vol. archaeological dig Tarboro Arts (N.C.) Coun., 1993; vol. ARC, Rocky Mount, 1994—. Mem. Assn. Am. Geographers, Gamma Theta Upsilon. Office: East Carolina U Dept Geography Greenville NC 27858

TOLLNER, ERNEST WILLIAM, agricultural engineering educator, agricultural radiology consultant; b. Maysville, Ky., July 14, 1949; s. Ernest Edward and Ruby Geneva (Henderson) T.; m. Caren Gayle Crane, Sept. 27, 1987. BS, U. Ky., 1972; PhD, Auburn (Ala.) U., 1981. Registered profl. engr., Ga. Rsch. specialist U. Ky., Lexington, 1972-74, rsch. engr., 1974-76; teaching asst. Tex. A&M U., College Station, 1976-77; rsch. specialist Auburn U., 1977-80; asst. prof. U. Ga., Griffin, 1980-85, assoc. prof., 1985-90, prof., 1990—; cons. Twiggs Corner Condominium Assn., Peachtree City, Ga., 1986-92, Masstock Dairies, Montezuma, Ga., 1988; mem. Ga. State Acad. Panel addressing stream sediment transport issues. Contbr. 60 articles to profl. jours. Treas. Condominium Assn., Peachtree City, 1988-91. Mem. Am. Soc. Agrl. Engrs., Am. Soc. Agronomy, Kiwanis. Home: 1010 Rogers Rd Bogart GA 30622-2723 Office: U Ga Dept Biology and Agrl Engring Driftmeir Engring Ctr Athens GA 30602

TOLO, KENNETH WILLIAM, public affairs educator, university administrator; b. Bemidji, Minn., Nov. 21, 1940; s. Modolf Wilhelm and Evelyn Irene (Larsen) T.; m. Roselyn JoAnn Solberg, June 27, 1964; children: Kristi, Julie. BA in Math, Concordia Coll., 1962; PhD in Math., U. Nebr., 1968; MA in Pub. Affairs, U. Minn., 1972; postgrad., Harvard U., 1974, Stanford U., 1987; postgrad. in Japanese, Dartmouth Coll., 1988. Asst. prof. dept. math. U. Tenn., Knoxville, 1968-70; assoc. prof. Lyndon Baines Johnson Sch. Pub. Affairs U. Tex., Austin, 1974-80, prof., 1980—, acting dean, 1975-76, assoc. v.p. acad. affairs, 1979-86, vice provost, 1986-90; dir. Office Policy Devel. and Coord. U.S. Dept. Commerce, Washington, 1976-77; com. on info. tech. Nat. Assn. State Univs. and Land Grant Colls., Washington, 1984—; cons., organizer Internat. Med. Benefits/Risk Found., Geneva, 1989-91; cons. Min. Rsch. and Tech., Indonesia, Jakarta, 1992, Nat. Performance Rev., White House, Washington, 1993; sr. advisor to Sec. U.S. Dept. Edn., Washington, 1994-96. Editor: Improving Drug Safety: A Joint Responsibility, 1991; author and editor numerous published reports. Deacon Gethsemane Luth. Ch., Austin, 1972—. Recipient Sec.'s medal U.S. Dept. Commerce, 1977; rsch. fellow German Marshall Fund U.S., 1981; grantee German Acad. Exchange, 1984-86, Aspen Inst. Berlin, 1988. Mem. AAAS, Assn. Pub. Policy Analysis & Mgmt., Policy Studies Assn., Austin C. of C. (internat. com. 1985—). Home: 2501 Porter St NW Apt 717 Washington DC 20008-1258 Office: U Tex Austin LBJ Sch Pub Affairs Drawer Y Univ Sta Austin TX 78713-7450

TOM, JAMES ROBERT, accountant; b. Odessa, Tex., Apr. 21, 1939; s. George Ellison and Mattie Inez (Zimmerman) T.; m. Frances Kay Mackey, Sept. 16, 1961; children: Susan Kay, James Robert Jr., Emily Christian. Student, Tex. A&M U., 1957; BBA in Acctg., Tex. Tech. U., 1961; postgrad., Colo. State U., 1961-62. CPA, Tex. Jr. acct. Peat, Marwick, Mitchell & Co., Midland, Tex., 1965; asst. trust officer First City Nat. Bank, Midland, 1966-67; sr. acct. Main Hurdman, Midland, 1967-68; v.p., trust officer First City Nat. Bank, Midland, 1969-72; pres. Gibson Mfg. Co., Midland, 1972-73; exec. v.p., chief exec. officer Teraco, Inc., Midland, 1974-75; fin. cons. Midland, 1975-76; acct., 1976—. Bd. dirs. Am. Heart Assn., Midland, 1966, Arthritis Found., Midland, 1971-72, 75, Midland County Livestock Assn., Midland, 1966-72, ARC, Midland, 1970-80, Boys Club, Midland, 1971-72. 1st lt. U.S. Army, 1963-65. Mem. AICPAs, Tex. Soc. CPAs, Permian Basin CPAs. Republican. Roman Catholic. Home: 3104 Humble Ave Midland TX 79705-8207 Office: 1010 W Texas Ave Midland TX 79701-6170

TOMASOVIC, STEPHEN PETER, oncologist; b. Bend, Ore., Jan. 5, 1947; s. Peter Alexander and Barbara Ann (Scott) T.; m. Barbara Jean Davis, Aug. 8, 1970. BS, Oreg. State U., 1969, MS, 1973; PhD, Colo. State U., 1977. From asst. prof. to prof. M.D. Anderson Cancer Ctr., Houston, 1981—; dep. chmn. tumor biology dept. M.D. Anderson Cancer Ctr., 1995; chmn. tumor biology, 1995—, adv. bd. Conquest Mag., Houston, 1993—; adv. com. Tex. Equine Rsch. Fund State Tex., College Station, 1992—; adv. coun. dist. scholars award North Harris Montgomery C.C., Houston, 1993—, biotech. adv. com., 1992—. Mem. AAAS, Am. Soc. Therapeutic Radiology and Oncology, N.Am. Hyperthermia Soc. (coun. 1990-92), Radiation Rsch. Soc. Office: MD Anderson Cancer Ctr 1515 Holcombe Blvd Houston TX 77030

TOMASULO, FRANK PETER, communications educator, writer; b. N.Y.C., Feb. 22, 1947; s. Anthony and Anne (Taiani) T.; m. Erica Fox. BA in Philosophy, Bklyn. Coll., 1967; MA in Cinema Studies, NYU, 1973; PhD in Film and TV Studies, UCLA, 1986. Dir. audio-visual unit Seafarers Internat. Union AFL-CIO, N.Y.C., 1973-74; instr. comm. arts St. John's U., Queens, N.Y., 1974-75; film/video dir. Medgar Evers Coll./CUNY, Bklyn., 1975-76; instr. dept. cinema Moorpark (Calif.) Coll., 1976-78; tchg. fellow dept. theatre arts UCLA, 1978-81; assoc. prof. dept. cinema Ithaca (N.Y.) Coll., 1981-91; vis. prof. U. Calif., Santa Cruz, 1989-90; prof. dept. comm. Ga. State U., Atlanta, 1991—; pres. Frank Films, L.A., 1976-80; head screenwriter Continental Cinema Industries, Inc., N.Y.C., 1974-75; presenter confs. in field; faculty advisor, supr. student film projects; mem. various coms. Ga. State U., 1991—, Ithaca Coll., 1981-91, UCLA, 1979-81, Moorpark Coll, 1977-78; co-organizer conf. Cornell U. and SUNY, Cortland, 1988; referee Am. Coun. Learned Socs., 1988, Stanford Humanities Ctr., 1989, Mellon Fellowship in Humanities, U. Pa., 1990, Fulbright Fellowship Com. Coun. for Internat. Exch. of Scholars U. Stockholm, 1991, John Simon Guggenheim Meml. Found., 1992, Nat. Endowment for Humanities, 1993; judge Ohio State U. Broadcasting Awards, 1985-91, Nicholl Screenwriting Awards Acad. Motion Picture Arts and Scis., 1987-88. Dir. 10 plays in N.Y. and L.A., 1973-78, (video) Neurotic Adolescents, 1974; screenwriter 8 feature-length scripts in L.A. and N.Y., 1974-91, Spin the Bottle, 1977; writer-dir. (short film) The Sky's In Love, 1991; cinematographer: (film) LAX, 1981 (several film festival awards); telescript writer (episodic TV) The Streets of San Francisco, 1975, Alice, 1977, Quincy, 1977, Three's Company, 1977; chief writer Jerry Lewis Muscular Dystrophy Telethon, Hollywood, Calif., 1976; contbr. numerous articles to prof. jours; editor: Jour. Film and Video, 1992-96, assoc. editor, 1987-92; manuscript reviewer, referee in field; mem. editl. adv. bd. Film Reader Series Am. Film Inst., 1987-89; conf. editor Quar. Rev. Film Studies, 1985-88; mem. adv. bd., editl. bd. On Film, L.A., 1980-86. Mem. Fulton County (Ga.) Arts Coun., 1994—; spl. advisor Atlanta Film Adv. Bd., Mayor's Office, 1993—; founding bd. dirs. and treas. Richard Leigh Walker Found. for Journalists, 1993—. Recipient Letter of Commendation Libr. of Congress Motion Picture Divsn., Washington, 1974; grantee Nat. Endowment for Humanities, U. Calif., Berkeley, 1989, N.Y. State Coun. on Arts, 1984-86, Nat. Mental Health Assn. Rsch. Found. of CUNY, 1975-76. Mem. Soc. for Cinema Studies (1st prize Scholarly Writing 1980, com. on tchg. 1994—, chair 1995—, mem. tenure and promotion/prof. stds. and practices com. 1991-93, chair 1987-91, task force on class 1993-95), Univ. Film and Video Assn. (bd. dirs.). Home: 1930 Lenox Rd NE Atlanta GA 30306 Office: Dept Comm Ga State U Atlanta GA 30303

TOMASULO, VIRGINIA MERRILLS, retired lawyer; b. Belleville, Ill., Feb. 10, 1919; d. Frederick Emerson and Mary Eckert (Turner) Merrills; m. Nicholas Angelo Tomasulo, Sept. 30, 1952; m. Harrison I. Anthes, March 5, 1988. BA, Wellesley Coll., 1940; LLB (now JD), Washington U., St. Louis, 1943. Bar: Mo. 1942, U.S. Ct. Appeals (D.C. cir.) 1958, Mich. 1974, U.S. Dist. Ct. (ea. dist.) Mo. 1943, U.S. Supreme Ct. 1954, U.S. Tax Ct. 1974, U.S. Ct. Appeals (6th cir.) 1976. Atty. Dept. of Agr., St. Louis and Washington, 1943-48, Office of Solicitor, Chief Counsel's Office, IRS, Washington and Detroit, 1949-75; assoc. Baker & Hostetler, Washington, 1977-82, ptnr., 1982-89, of counsel, 1989, ret., 1989. Sec., S.W. Day Care Assn., Washington, 1971-73. Mem. ABA, Mo. Bar, Fed. Bar, Village on the Green Residents Assn. (fin. com.), Wellesley Club (Ctrl. Fla.). Episcopalian. Home: 570 Village Pl Apt 300 Longwood FL 32779-6037

TOMASZEWSKI, CAROLE LOUISE, small business owner; b. Zanesville, Ohio, Dec. 13, 1940; d. Herbert W. and Edna M. (Wihfelt) Honaker; m. James Vincent Calhoun, Aug. 17, 1963 (div. 1979); children: James V. Calhoun Jr., Michael D. Calhoun; m. Robert John Tomaszewski, May 10, 1980. BFA, Ohio U., 1963. Cert. canine specialist. Tchr. Bellaire (Ohio) H.S., 1963, Toledo (Ohio) Pub. Schs., 1978, 79, Chesterfield County Schs., Va., 1980-89; owner Pet Pleasers, Inc., Richmond, Va., 1988—. Mem. Nat. Assn. Prof. Pet Sitters (bd. dirs. 1991-93, pres. 1993—, mentor, cons. 1993—), Heritage Commons Civic Assn. (v.p. 1988-89), Phi Mu. Republican. Home: 1700 Greenfield Dr Richmond VA 23235

TOMASZEWSKI, RICHARD PAUL, market representation specialist; b. Flushing, N.Y., Jan. 8, 1958; s. Francis Richard and Agatha Jean (Corsaro) T.; m. Joann L. Turone, Aug. 2, 1980; children: Elizabeth Jean, Annamaria Concetta. BA in Econs. and Polit. sci. cum laude, Union Coll., Schenectady, N.Y., 1980; MBA in Mktg., Fin., Syracuse U., 1982. Grad. asst. Syracuse (N.Y.) U., 1981; field ops. analyst Ford Motor Co., Charlotte, N.C., 1982-83; zone mgr. Ford Motor Co., Charlotte, 1983-93; market representation specialist Ford Motor Co., Atlanta, 1993—, nat. employee involvement rep. Atlanta region, 1994—. Mem. Ford Motor Co. Polit. Action Com., Atlanta, 1993. Recipient Tidmarsh scholarshp Union Coll., Schenectady, 1977. Mem. Union Coll. Alumni Assn., Syracuse U. Alumni Assn., U.S. Tennis Assn., Atlanta Lawn Tennis Assn., Omicron Delta Epsilon, Alpha Mu Alpha. Republican. Roman Catholic. Office: Ford Motor Co 1455 Lincoln Pky E Ste 530 Atlanta GA 30346-2209

TOMBAUGH, GEOFFREY CLARKE, neurobiologist; b. N.Y.C., Apr. 19, 1962; s. Richard Franklin and Sandra (Clarke) T. AB, Haverford Coll., 1984; PhD, Stanford U., 1992. Rsch. biologist Monsanto Co., St. Louis, 1984-86; rsch. assoc. Duke U., Durham, N.C., 1992—; wildlife biologist on retreat in Amazon rainforest, 1992. Contbr. numerous sci. articles to profl. jours. Vol. Habitat for Humanity, Chapel Hill, N.C., 1993. Recipient predoctoral fellowship NSF, Washington, 1987, post-doctoral fellowship Nat. Stroke Assn., Englewood, Colo., 1993. Mem. Soc. for Neuroscience, Internat. Brain Rsch. Orgn. Office: Duke Univ Med Ctr PO Box 3709 Durham NC 27710

TOMER, AARON, medical educator; b. Israel, Nov. 23, 1944; came to U.S., 1985; married; 3 children. BS with distinction, Hebrew U., Jerusalem, 1972; MS, Technion, Haifa, Israel, 1974, MD, 1980. Resident, fellow Sheba med. ctr. Tel Aviv U., 1980-85; postdoctoral fellow Scripps Clinic and Rsch. Found., La Jolla, Calif., 1985-89; asst. prof. sch. medicine Emory U., Atlanta, 1989—. Office: Emory U Divsn Hematology WMB Box AR Atlanta GA 30322

TOMER, MARK JOHN, manufacturing/research and development executive; b. Tulsa, Oct. 29, 1949; s. John Shaffer and Patricia Ann Tomer; m. Gloria Jane Gray, Apr. 12, 1985; 1 child, Evan G. Student, Okla. State U., 1967-70, U. Tulsa, 1975-80. Purchasing agt., gen. mgr., v.p. RST Svc. Mfg., Inc., Tulsa, 1975-85; pres. ENARDO Mfg. Co., Tulsa, 1985—. Bd. dirs. Tulsa Coun. on Alcoholism and Drug Abuse, 1987-90. Mem. Am. Petroleum Inst., Soc. Petroleum Engrs., Nat. Fire Protection Assn., Can. Standards Assn., Nat. Assn. Mfrs., U.S. C. of C., Met. Tulsa C. of C. Republican. Office: ENARDO Internat. Ltd. 6523 E Independence St Tulsa OK 74115-7861

TOMJANOVICH, RUDOLPH, professional athletic coach; b. Hamtramck, Mich., Nov. 24, 1948. Scout Houston Rockets, 1981-83, asst. coach, 1983-92, head coach, 1992—. Named to Sporting News All-Am. first team, 1970; coach NBA championship team, 1994-95. Office: Houston Rockets The Summit 10 Greenway Plz Houston TX 77046-3865*

TOMLIN, LINTON, court reporter; b. Pecos, Tex., July 26, 1953; d. John Frazier and Clara Mae (James) T. Reporter Tex. State Senate, Austin, 1975; sec., clk. Austin Bd. Realtors, 1975; reporter Austin Ct. Reporters, 1976, Waco (Tex.) Ct. Reporters, 1977; offcl. ct. reporter County Ct. at Law, Pecos, 1977-78; sec. Strauss, Jons & Parker Law Firm, Kerrville, Tex., 1979-81; offcl. ct. reporter 198th Jud. Dist. Ct., Kerrville, Tex., 1981—. Mem. Nat. Ct. Reporters Assn., Tex. Ct. Reporters Assn. Home: 208 Ball Dr Kerrville TX 78028 Office: Kerr County Ct House 700 Main St Kerrville TX 78028

TOMLINSON, CHARLES EDWIN, forestry consultant, writer; b. Denver, Sept. 11, 1932; s. Allen Robert and Ruth Eloise (Martin) T.; m. Mary Susanna Virtue, Dec. 17, 1955; children: Charles Allen, Vanessa Eloise Smyth, Stephan Roy. BS in Forestry, U. of the South, 1954. Registered forester, Ala., Miss. Forester Cherokee, Ala., 1958-64; forester, br. mgr. Resource Mgmt. Svc., Inc., Cherokee, 1964-72; owner, pres. Tomlinson & Assocs., Cherokee, 1972-83; pres. Forest Mgrs. and Cons., Inc., Cherokee, 1983-94, Tomlinson Group, Inc., Cherokee, 1994—, Tomlinson Forest, Inc., Cherokee, 1990—; mem., chmn., State of Ala. Bd. Registration for Foresters, Montgomery, 1979-85, cons. to bd., 1995—. Author: A View From My Stump, 1992; author essays: Alabama Forests; editor Registered Forester newsletter, 1996—. 1st lt. USAF, 1955-57. Mem. Ala. Forestry Coun., Ala. Forestry Assn. (bd. dirs.).

TOMLINSON, COLIN HENRY, engineer; b. Gravesend, Kent, England, Nov. 12, 1939; s. Harold and Gertrude (Smith) T.; m. Vicki Welch, Sept. 1962 (div.); children: Stephen John, Sandra; m. Irene Lilian, May 12, 1984. Diploma, London U., 1962. Design engr. Rochester Instruments, Crayford, Kent, Eng., 1969-80; chief engr. Rochester (N.Y.) Instruments, 1980-82, product mgr., 1982-86; direct mktg. profl. Brown Boveri, Allentown, Pa., 1986-92; internat. new market mgr. ABB Power T&D Co., Raleigh, N.C., 1992-96; gen. mgr. ABB Power T&D Co., Coral Springs, Fla., 1996—; AEI Design Engr., Woolwich, Eng., 1962-68; rediffusion engring. Design Engr., Kingston, Eng., 1968-69. Office: ABB Power T&D Co 4300 Coral Ridge Dr Coral Springs FL 33065-7617

TOMLINSON, IAN, software engineer; b. St. Johns, Antigua, Sept. 2, 1964; s. Lydia C. (Davis) Ross; m. Averil V. Archibald, Oct. 24, 1992; 1 child, Akil Ian. BA in Bus. Adminstrn., cert in data processing, U. V.I., 1988; MS in Info. Systems, Am. U., 1992; postgrad., George Mason U., 1994—. Database adminstrr., programmer V.I. Water and Power Auth., 1988-90; programmer, analyst, task leader Data Tree, Inc., 1990-92; sr. cons. Booz-Allen and Hamilton, Inc., 1992—; v.p. software engring. Omni Systems, Inc., 1993—. Joseph and Jenny Alexander scholar, 1983; Gail E. Boggs Data Processing scholar, 1987. Mem. Assn. for Computing Machinery. Office: Omni Sys Inc 1655 Fort Myer Dr Ste 700 Arlington VA 22209-3108

TOMLINSON, WILLIAM HOLMES, management educator, retired army officer, b. Thornton, Ark., Apr. 12, 1922; s. Hugh Oscar and Lucy Gray (Holmes) T.; m. Dorothy Payne, June 10, 1947 (dec.); children: Jane Axtell, Lucy Gray, William Payne; m. Florence Mood Smith, May 1, 1969 (div.); m. Suzanne Scollard Gill, Mar. 16, 1977. Student, Centenary Coll., 1938-39; BS, U.S. Mil. Acad., 1943; grad. Field Arty. Sch., 1951; grad. Air Command Staff Coll., 1958; MBA, U. Ala., 1960; MS in Internat. Affairs, George Washington U., 1966; grad. U.S. Army War Coll., 1966; grad. Indsl. Coll. Armed Forces, 1968; PhD in Bus. Adminstrn., Am. U., 1974; postgrad. 56th Advanced Mgmt. Program, Harvard U., 1968, 69; BAS, U. N. Fla., 1988. Commd. 2d lt. U.S. Army, 1943, advanced through grades to col., field arty., 1966; combat svc. in Leyte and Cebu, Philippines 246 Field Arty. Bn. American Divsn., 1945; aide de camp, comdg. gen. 8th U.S. Army, Japan, 1945-48, ops. officer 9th Divsn. Arty., Germany, 1954-56, Office of Undersec. Army, Pentagon, Washington, 1961-64; comdr. 2d Bn., 8th Arty. and 7th Div. Arty., UN Comd. S. Korea, 1964-65; faculty Indsl. Coll. Armed Forces, Ft. McNair, Washington, 1966-72, ret., 1973; faculty U. North Fla., Jacksonville, 1972—, prof. mgmt., 1993—; vis. prof. U. Glasgow, Scotland, fall 1987; vis. lectr. Moscow Linguistics U., Plekhanov Econ. U., Ulyanovsk U., Russia, fall 1993; mem. Nat. Def. Exec. Res., Fed. Emergency Mgmt. Agy., 1976—. Author: Assessment of the National Defense Executive Reserve; co-author: International Business, Theory and Practice; contbr. articles to profl. jours. and books. Exec. bd. Jacksonville Campus Ministry, 1991—. Decorated Bronze Star, Legion of Merit, Philippine Liberation medal, Japanese Occupation; recipient Freedom Found. award, 1967-71, Sr. Profl. in Human Resources, Teaching Incentive award State Univ. Sys., 1994-95. Mem. Soc. Human Resource Mgmt., Acad. Mgmt., Indsl. Rels. Rsch. Assn., Acad. Internat. Bus., European Internat. Bus. Assn., Internat. Trade and Fin. Assn., Exec. Svc. Corps. Bd., Co. Mil. Historians., Nat. Eagle Scout Assn., Northeast Fla. Employee Svcs. Assn. (charter pres. 1987-89), West Point Soc. N. Fla. (pres. 1976-77), Mil. Order Stars and Bars (comdr. 1980-90), Army Navy Club, Fla. Yacht Club, Mason, Shriner, Rotary, Beta Gamma Sigma (pres. 1988-89), Kappa Alpha. Presbyterian (elder). Home: 1890 Shadowlawn St Jacksonville FL 32205-9430 Office: U North Fla Dept Mgmt 4567 Saint Johns Bluff Rd S Jacksonville FL 32224-2646

TOMMEY, CHARLES ELDON, retired surgeon; b. Nashville, Ark., Jan. 13, 1922; s. William Robert and America Anna (Compton) T.; m. Clara Blair Newman, Aug. 28, 1948; children: Robert, Jean, Phillip, Dale, Scott. Student, Henderson State Tchrs. Coll., 1940-42; BSM, U. Ark. Sch. Medicine, 1944, MD, 1945. Diplomate Am. Bd. Surgery. Intern City Hosp., Columbus, Ga., 1945-46; surg. resident Bapt. Hosp., Little Rock, 1948-49, VA Hosp., Cleve., 1950-54; pvt. practice surgery El Dorado, Ark., 1954-95; ret., 1995; asst. clin. instr. surgery U. Ark. Coll. Medicine. Capt. U.S. Army Med. Corps, 1943-45, 46-48. Fellow ACS. Baptist. Home: 123 Glenridge Pky El Dorado AR 71730-3117

TOMPKINS, EDWARD DEAL, academic administrator; b. Vinton, Va., Aug. 12, 1946; s. Joseph Buford Sr. and Rebecca Louise (Johnston) T.; m. Lynn Parrish, June 26, 1993. BA, Randolph-Macon Coll., 1968. Owner, pres. Tompkins Hardware Co., Inc., Vinton, Va., 1974-79; realtor, asst. sales mgr. George Overby & Assoc., Inc., Roanoke, Va., 1979-81; dir. admissions So. Sem. Coll., Buena Vista, Va., 1983-85, dir. devel., 1985-87; dir. spl. gifts Mary Washington Coll., Fredericksburg, Va., 1987-89, v.p. coll. advancement, 1994-96; v.p. devel. Mary Washington Hosp. Found., Fredericksburg, 1989-94; dir. planned giving Randolph-Macon Coll., Ashland, Va., 1996—. Mem. adminstrv. bd. Fredericksburg United Meth. Ch. Mem. Coun. for Advancement and Support of Edn., Soc. Alumni Randolph-Macon Coll. (bd. dirs.). Home: PO Box 8075 Fredericksburg VA 22404-8075 Office: Randolph-Macon Coll PO Box 5005 Ashland VA 23005

TOMPKINS, JAMES RICHARD, special education educator; b. Camden, N.J., Jan. 17, 1935; s. Leo Joseph and Cecelia Nichols; children: Tim, Mark. BA cum laude, Mt. St. Mary's Coll., 1959; postgrad., U. Mich., 1960; MA, Niagara U., 1961; PhD, Cath. U., 1971. Coord. unit on edn. of emotionally disturbed Bur. Edn. Handicapped-USOE, Washington, 1966-71; asst. prof. U. N.C., Chapel Hill, 1971-72; exec. dir. N.C. Govs. Advocacy Commn., Raleigh, 1972-74; prof. spl. edn. Appalachian State U., Boone, N.C., 1974—; cons. edn. of disturbed children N.C. Dept. Human Resources. Contbr. articles to profl. jours. Mem. Coun. Exceptional Children, Coun. Children with Behavior Disorders, Coun. Career Devel., Give Youth a Chance Inc., Arts and Humanities for the Handicapped, N.C. Tchr. Preparation Programs for Emotionally Disturbed Children. Home: 117 Meadowbrook Ln Deep Gap NC 28618-9713

TOMPKINS, PATRICK, English language educator, writer; b. Phila., Nov. 6, 1963; s. Richard Joseph and Margaret (Kardish) T. BA in English, BA in Philosophy, Villanova U., 1986; MA in English, Iowa State U., 1988; MFA in Creative Writing, Va. Commonwealth U., 1990. Grad. asst. Iowa State U., Ames, 1986-88; grad. asst. Va. Commonwealth U., Richmond, 1988-90, adj. instr., 1990-92; dir. Acad. Mentors, Richmond, 1990-92; instr. S.W. Okla. State U., Weatherford, 1992-93; asst. prof. English, John Tyler C.C., Richmond, 1993—; participant profl. confs. Contbr. essays to mag. Mem. Conf. on Coll. Composition and Commn., Nat. Coun. Tchrs. English, Va. C.C. Sys. English Peer Group (planning com.). Office: John Tyler CC 13101 Jefferson Davis Hwy Chester VA 23831

TOMPKINS, RAYMOND EDGAR, lawyer; b. Oklahoma City, July 13, 1934; s. Charles Edgar and Eva Mae (Hodges) T.; m. Sue Anne Sharpe, June 10, 1963; children: Matthew Stephen, Christopher T., Katherine Anne. BS, Okla. State U., 1956; JD, U. Okla., 1963. Bar: Okla. 1963, U.S. Dist. Ct. (no. dist.) Okla. 1963, U.S. Dist. Ct. (we. dist.) Okla. 1964, U.S. Ct. Appeals (10th cir.) 1965, U.S. Supreme Ct. 1968, U.S. Dist. Ct. (ea. dist.) Okla. 1969, U.S. Ct. Appeals (9th cir.) 1981, U.S. Ct. Appeals (4th cir.) 1986. Adminstrv. asst. U.S. Congress, 1966-68; ptnr. Linn & Helms, Oklahoma City, 1980-90, Daughery, Bradford, Haught & Tompkins, P.C., Oklahoma City, 1990-94; shareholder Conner & Winters, P.C., Oklahoma City, 1994—. Chmn. bd. trustees Okla. Ann. Methodist Conf.; chmn. Okla. Bur. Investigation Commn.; gen. counsel Rep. State Com., Interstate Oil Compact. Maj. USAR. Recipient award of Honor Oklahoma City Bi-Centennial Commn., 1976. Master Am. Inns of Ct.; mem. ABA, Okla. County Bar Assn. (Pres.'s award 1988, chmn. bench & bar com. 1995—), Okla. Bar Assn. (Law Day award), Am. Judicature Soc., Assn. Atty.-Mediators (panel mem.), Blue Key, Lions (pres. Oklahoma City chpt.). Home: 329 NW 40th St Oklahoma City OK 73118-8419 Office: 211 N Robinson Ave Ste 1700 Oklahoma City OK 73102-6803

TOMSICK, ROBERT STANLEY, dermatologist; b. Cleve., Nov. 11, 1949; s. Stanley Frank and Ann (Skoda) T.; m. Madeline Andrysco, Dec. 21, 1975; 1 child, Robert Joseph. AB summa cum laude, Kenyon Coll., 1971; MD, U. N.C., 1976. Diplomate Nat. Bd. Med. Examiners, Am. Bd. Dermatology. Vis. house officer St. Thomas' Hosp., London, 1976; fellow in medicine Mayo Clinic, Rochester, Minn., 1976-77; resident in dermatology U. N.C., Chapel Hill, 1977-79, instr. dermatology Sch. of Medicine, 1980-81, asst. prof. dermatology, 1981-83; attending physician Ochsner Clinic, New Orleans, 1983-84; assoc. prof. dermatology U. N.C., Chapel Hill, 1984—. Contbr. articles to profl. jours. Morehead fellow in Medicine, 1971-76; recipient Pathology fellowship U. N.C., 1974, Chemosurgery fellowship U.

Miami, 1979-80. Fellow Am. Acad. Dermatology, Am. Coll. Micrographic Surgery and Oncology, Am. Soc. Dermatologic Soc.; mem. AMA, N.C. Med. Soc. Roman Catholic. Office: U NC Sch Medicine Dermatology Clinic CB 7715 Chapel Hill NC 27599-7715

TONER, MICHAEL F., journalist; b. LeMars, Iowa, Mar. 17, 1944; s. Francis F. and Mary Ann (Delaney) T.; m. Patricia L. Asleson, Aug. 28, 1966; children: Susan Michelle, Sharon Lynn. BA cum laude, U. Iowa, 1966; postgrad., U. Okla., Peru; MS cum laude, Northwestern U., 1967. Reporter UPI, Chgo., 1966-67; bur. chief Miami Herald, Key West, Fla., 1967-68, reporter, 1968-69, asst. city editor, 1970-72; sci./environ. writer Miami (Fla) Herald, 1973-84; sci. editor Atlanta Journal and Constitution, 1984-91, sci. writer, 1991—. Co-author: Florida by Paddle and Pack, 1979; contbr. articles to mags. Recipient Pulitzer Prize for explanatory journalism, 1993; Stanford U. profl. journalism fellow, 1973. Office: Atlanta Journal and Constn 72 Marietta St NW Atlanta GA 30303-2804

TONEY, KELLY LYNNE SMITH, violinist, educator; b. Tulsa, Sept. 23, 1959; d. Frederick Lloyd and Harriet Elizabeth (Powell) Smith; m. Gregory Ashby Toney, Jan. 3, 1987; 1 child, Claire. BM, Juilliard Sch., 1982, MusM, 1983. Soloist Gulf Coast Symphony Orchestra, Biloxi, Miss., 1983; 1st violinist, asst. concertmaster Singapore Symphony Orchestra, 1983-85; concertmaster, asst. concertmaster Singapore Symphony Chamber Orchestra & Recording Group, 1983-85; concertmaster, soloist La. Sinfonietta Chamber Orchestra, 1985—; first violinist Campanile String Quartet, Baton Rouge, 1986—; guest soloist La. State U. New Music Ensemble, New Orleans, La., 1986, N.Y.C., 1987, Baton Rouge, 1990; guest soloist Nicholls State U., Thibodaux, La., 1990, 92; recitalist Music Club of Baton Rouge, 1987—; rotating 1st violinist Valcour String Quartet, Baton Rouge, 1986-88; first violinist Baton Rouge Symphony Orchestra, 1986—; judge scholarship auditions Music Club of Baton Rouge, 1988—; judge string div. Solo and Ensemble Festival, Baton Rouge, 1988; judge violin All-Parish Orch. Audition, Baton Rouge, 1986-87, Student Div. Award la. Fedn. Music Clubs, Baton Rouge, 1986; state chair Crusade for Strings and Chamber Music, La. Fedn. Music Clubs, 1990-93; guest soloist La. United Meth. Ann. Conf., Shreveport, 1992. Mem. Downtown Devel. Dist., Baton Rouge, 1988—, Smithsonian Assocs., 1981—, Cherokee Indian Tribe, Capital Area Network, Baton Rouge, 1992-93. Recipient 2nd Place Student Div. award Nat. Fdn. Music Clubs, 1983, 1st Place Biennial Student award Dixie Dist. Fedn. Music Clubs, 1983, 1st. Place Student Div. award La. Fedn. Music Clubs, 1983, 2nd Place Young Artist award La. Fedn. Music Clubs, 1989. Mem. Music Tchrs. Nat. Assn., La. Music Tchrs. Assn. (state chair. string rally, 1992-94), Music Club Baton Rouge, Music Club Aux. Baton Rouge, Juilliard Sch. Alumni Club, Philharm. Club Baton Rouge. Methodist. Home and Office: 611 Chippenham Dr Baton Rouge LA 70808-5612

TONG, ALEX WAIMING, immunologist; b. Hong Kong, Apr. 8, 1952; came to U.S., 1970; s. Robert S. and Agnes M. (Cheng) T.; m. Susan J. Radtke, May 23, 1980 (div. Mar. 1988); 1 child, Nicole L.; m. S. Quay Mercer, May 13, 1995. BA in Biology, U. Oreg., 1973; PhD in Microbiology and Immunology, Oreg. Health Scis. U., 1980. Undergrad. teaching asst. biology dept. U. Oreg., Eugene, 1972-73; rsch. asst. dept. microbiology and immunology Oreg. Health Scis. U., Portland, 1975-80, teaching asst. Sch. Medicine, 1977-78, rsch. assoc. dept. micrology and immunology, 1981-82; postdoctoral fellow Surg. Rsch. Lab. Portland VA Med. Ctr., 1980-82; rsch. assoc. in immunology Charles A. Sammons Cancer Ctr., Baylor U. Med. Ctr., Dallas, 1982-86; assoc. dir. immunology lab. Baylor U. Med. Ctr., Dallas, Tex., 1986—; asst. prof. Inst. Biomed. Studies, Baylor U., Waco, 1988—; prin. investigator Nat. Cancer Inst., Bethesda, Md., 1994—; adj. faculty immunology grad. studies program U. Tex. Southwestern Med. Ctr., Dallas, 1982—. Contbr. articles to profl. jours. Tatar rsch. fellow Med. Rsch. Found. Oreg., Portland, 1981-83. Mem. Am. Assn. Immunologists, Am. Assn. Cancer Rsch., Am. Soc. Hematology, Clin. Immunology Soc., Japan Karate Assn. Dallas (dir.), Internat. Traditional Karate Fedn. (cert. coach 1990—, cert. referee 1988—), Am. Amateur Karate Fedn. (dir. S.W. region). Democrat. Office: Baylor U Med Ctr Cancer Immunology Rsch Lab 3500 Gaston Ave Dallas TX 75246-2045

TONG, LOUIS LIK-FU, information scientist; b. Kowloon, Hong Kong, June 15, 1962; came to U.S., 1980; naturalized, 1994; s. Yu-Tung and Chen (Yao) T. BS, U. Houston, 1985; M Libr. and Info. Sci., U. North Tex., 1992. Info. asst. Houston Acad. Medicine, Tex. Med. Ctr. Libr., Houston, 1990-93; rsch. libr. svcs. specialist, chair codes/regulations coms. Internat. Facility Mgmt. Assn., Houston, 1993—. Mem. ASHRAE, Am. Soc. Assn. Execs., Med. Libr. Assn. (minority scholar 1992), Spl. Librs. Assn. Republican. Home: PO Box 230453 Houston TX 77223-0453 Office: Internat Facility Mgmt Assn 1 E Greenway Plz Ste 1100 Houston TX 77046

TONG, PENGER, physicist; b. Jinzhou, Liaoning, China, Aug. 2, 1956; came to U.S., 1983; s. Zhong-Qi and Qiuying (Peng) T.; m. Jie Hu, Apr. 30, 1983; 1 child, Eric A. BSc in Physics, Northeast U. Tech., China, 1982; MSc in Physics, U. Pitts., 1984, PhD of Physics, 1988. Postdoctoral rsch. assoc. Exxon Rsch. and Engring. Co., N.J., 1988-90; asst. prof. dept. physics Okla. State U., Stillwater, 1990-95, assoc. prof., 1995—. Editor: (with P.L. Dubin) Colloid-Polymer Interactions, 1993; contbr. articles to profl. jours. Mem. Am. Phys. Soc. Office: Okla State U Dept Physics Stillwater OK 74078

TONGATE, DARREL EDWIN, accountant; b. Hopkinsville, Ky., Nov. 4, 1943; s. Forrest L. and Christine (Martin) Goodwin; m. Judy Jean Harrell, Dec. 20, 1964; children: Jean Rená, Scott Alan, John Edwin, Tammy Michelle. BS in Acctg., David Libscomb U., Nashville, 1965. CPA, Tenn., Ky. Staff acct. Smith & Smith, Nashville, 1965-67; asst. controller Nauta Line Houseboat Mfg. Co., Hendersonville, Tenn., 1968-70; acct., proprietor Darrel E. Tongate CPA, Madison, Tenn., 1971-73, Nashville, 1980-86; mng. ptnr. Tongate & Ryan, Nashville, 1974-76; CPA Tongate, Ryan, Connelly & Shaub, Nashville, 1977-80; dir.-in-charge James R. Meany & Assocs., Nashville, 1986-87; v.p. fin. Hydra Sports, Inc., Nashville, 1987-88; pres. Vision Boats, Inc., Old Hickory, Tenn., 1988-93; acct. Goodlettsville, Tenn., 1994—; exec. dir. Tenn. State Bd. Accountancy, Nashville, 1994—. Deacon Hendersonville Ch. of Christ, 1974-89, 91—, treas., 1974—. Fellow Tenn. Soc. CPAs (pres. 1990-91, treas. polit. action com. 1980-81, pres. polit. action com. 1986-87, sec. Nashville chpt. 1975-76, v.p. 1976-78, pres. 1978-79, bd. dirs. 1984-92), Nashville City Club, Kiwanis (bd. dirs. 1972-73). Home: 119 Cima Dr Goodlettsville TN 37072-2005

TONGATE, SCOTT ALAN, hospital assistant administrator and controller; b. Nashville, Aug. 22, 1968; s. Darrel Edwin and Judy Jean (Harrell) T.; m. Debra Ann Gutowski, Sept. 7, 1991; children: Zachary Alan, Andrew Blake. BS in Acctg., Tenn. Tech. U., 1991. Office mgr. Celina (Tenn.) Home Health, 1991-92; contr. Clay County Hosp., Celina, 1992-94; interim adminstr. PHC Home Health, Celina, 1993; asst. adminstr., contr. Carthage (Tenn.) Hosp., 1994—. Mem. Healthcare Fin. Mgmt. Assn. Office: Carthage Gen Hosp Hwy 70 N Carthage TN 37030

TONGUE, PAUL GRAHAM, financial executive; b. Phila., Dec. 30, 1932; s. George Paul and Florence Amelia (Kogel) T.; m. Marjorie Joan Meyers, May 26, 1954; children: Suzanne Marjorie, Douglas Paul. BS in Commerce, Drexel U., 1957; MBA, NYU, 1965. With Chase Manhattan Bank, N.Y.C., 1957-87; chmn. Plus Systems Inc., Denver, 1985; pres. Eppley-Tongue Assocs., Inc., Towson, Md., 1988—; exec. v.p. Veritas Venture Inc., Scotch Plains, N.J., 1990-91; cons. Prime Care Sys., Inc., Newport News, Va., 1995—; chmn. Plus Systems Inc., Denver, 1984-85. Pres. Our Saviour Luth. Ch., Manhasset, N.Y., 1984; bd. dirs. Nassau Symphony Orch. With U.S. Army, 1954-55. Mem. Ford's Colony Country Club.

TONRY, RICHARD ALVIN, lawyer, pecan farmer; b. New Orleans, June 25, 1935; s. Richard Gordon and Dolores Theresa (Kroger) T.; m. Joy Ann Willmouth, Feb. 3, 1950; children: Richard A., Tara Ann, Cullen Adair. BA magna cum laude, Spring Hill Coll., Mobile, Ala., 1961, M Philosophy summa cum laude, 1962; JD, Loyola U. of South, New Orleans, 1967. Bar: La. 1967, U.S. Dist. Ct. (ea. dist.) La. 1967, U.S. Ct. Appeals (5th cir.) 1972, U.S. Supreme Ct. 1972. Ptnr. McBride & Tonry, Arabi, La., 1967-73, Tonry & Mumphrey, Chalmette, La., 1973-80; mem. La. Ho. of Reps., 1976, U.S. Ho. Reps., Washington, 1977; ptnr. Tonry & Ginart, Chalmette, 1990—; pecan farmer, Lumberton, Miss., 1991—. Chmn. Heart Fund of St. Bernard, Chalmettee, 1971-73. Named Outstanding Young Man of St. Bernard, St. Bernard Jaycees, 1973. Mem. ABA, ATLA, La. Bar Assn. (ho. of dels. 1973-74), La. Trial Lawyers Assn. (bd. dirs. 1972-75). Democrat. Roman Catholic. Home: 1177 W Main Ave Lumberton MS 39455-8335

TOOKES, JAMES NELSON, real estate investment company executive; b. Tallahassee, Sept. 16, 1934; B.S., Fla. A&M U., 1955, M.Ed., 1956; m. Hortense Latricia James, June 22, 1958; 1 child, Gerald Ray. Tchr., Griffin Elem. Sch., Tallahassee, 1957-58, Douglas Elem. Sch., Wabasso, Fla., 1958-59; tchr. Barrow Hill Sch., Tallahassee, 1959-60, prin., 1960-67; summer sch. math. tchr. various sch. centers Leon County Dist., Tallahassee, 1960-65; prin. Pineview Elem. Sch., Tallahassee, 1967-73; pres. Geray Petroleum, Inc., Tallahassee, 1980—, J.N.T. Properties, Inc., Tallahassee, 1973-77; broker Tookes Realty, Tallahassee, 1973-85; adv. bd. Barnett Bank of Tallahassee, 1977-79. Bd. dirs. Marine State Bank, Tallahassee Youth Center, 1952-54, Tallahassee Meml. Regional Med. Center, 1977-82; chmn. div. United Fund campaign, 1962; trustee Tallahassee C.C., 1974-82, chmn. bd., 1976-77. Recipient Sch. Adminstr. Service award Pineview Elem. Sch. Student Coun., 1967-73; commendation award Bert Roger's Sch. Real Estate, 1973; Contbns. to Cmty. award Phi Beta Lambda, 1974; named 1 of 5 Most Outstanding Black Businessmen in State of Fla., Fla. A&M U. Sch. Bus. and Industry, 1974. Mem. Phi Delta Kappa, Kappa Alpha Psi (Man of Yr. 1973). Home: 925 E Magnolia Dr Apt 5C Tallahassee FL 32301 Office: JNT Properties Inc 3110 W Tennessee St Tallahassee FL 32304-2729

TOOLE, JAMES FRANCIS, medical educator; b. Atlanta, Mar. 22, 1925; s. Walter O'Brien and Helen (Whitehurst) T.; m. Patricia Anne Wooldridge, Oct. 25, 1952; children: William, Anne, James, Douglas Sean. BA, Princeton U., 1947; MD, Cornell U., 1949; LLB, LaSalle Extension U., 1962. Intern, then resident internal medicine and neurology U. Pa. Hosp., Nat. Hosp., London, Eng., 1953-58; mem. faculty U. Pa. Sch. Medicine, 1958-62; prof. neurology, chmn. dept. Bowman Gray Sch. Medicine Wake Forest U., 1962-83; vis. prof. neuroscis. U. Calif. at San Diego, 1969-70; vis. scholar Oxford U., 1989; mem. Nat. Bd. Med. Examiners, 1970-76; mem. task force arteriosclerosis Nat. Heart Lung & Blood Inst., 1970-81; chmn. 6th and 7th Princeton confs. cerebrovascular diseases; cons. epidemiology WHO, Japan, 1971, 73, 93, USSR, 1968, Ivory Coast, 1977, Japan, 1993; mem. Lasker Awards com., 1976-77; chmn. neuropharmacologic drugs com. FDA, 1979; co-chair Commn. on Presdl. Disability, 1994-97; cons. NASA, 1966. Author: Cerebrovascular Diseases, 4th edit., 1990; editor: Current Concepts in Cerebrovascular Disease, 1969-73, Jour. Neurol. Sci., 1990—; mem. editorial bd. Annals Internal Medicine, 1968-75, Stroke, 1972-91, Jour. AMA, 1975-77, Ann. Neurology, 1980-86, Jour. Neurol. Soc., 1990; mem. editorial bd. Jour. of Neurology, 1985-89. Pres. N.C. Heart Assn., 1976-77. Served with AUS, 1950-51; flight surgeon USNR, 1951-53. Decorated Bronze Star with V, Combat Med. badge. Fellow ACP (life), AAAS (life); mem. AMA, Am. Clin. and Climatol Assn. (life), Am. Heart Assn. (chmn. com. ethics 1970-75), Am. Physiol. Soc., Am. Neurol. Assn. (sec.-treas. 1978-82, pres. 1984-85, archivist, historian 1988—), World Fedn. Neurology (sec.-treas. 1982-89, mgmt. com. 1990—), Am. Acad. Neurology, Am. Soc. Neuroimaging (pres. 1992-94), Internat. Stroke Soc. (exec. com. 1989—, program chmn. 1992), Nat. Stroke Assn. (bd. dirs. 1993—, exec. com. 1994—, co-chmn. Commn. on U.S. Presdl. Disability 1994—); hon. mem. Assn. Brit. Neurologists, German Neurol. Soc., Austrian Soc. Neurology, Irish Neurol. Assn. Home: 1836 Virginia Rd Winston Salem NC 27104-2316

TOOLE, LINDA JERNIGAN, quality control technician, cosmetics company admininstrator; b. Smithfield, N.C., May 23, 1949; d. Jesse James Jernigan and Myrtle Irene Jernigan Brown; m. J.R. Toole; children: Rhonda Toole Griffin, Rodney, Scarlett. AAS, Johnston C.C., 1994. Cert. statis. process control technician. Line insp. GTE Sylvania, Smithfield, N.C., 1974-80; operator AP Parts, Goldsboro, N.C., 1982, insp., 1982-90, statis. process control tech., 1990-95; mng. dir. Luzier Personalized Cosmetics, Kansas City, Mo., 1990—; chief inspector B&M Machining and Fabrication, Smithfield, N.C., 1995—. Sunday sch. tchr. Yelverton Grove Ch., Smithfield, N.C., 1988—. Mem. Am. Soc. Quality Control, Phi Bata Lamba.

TOOMBS, KENNETH ELDRIDGE, librarian; b. Colonial Heights, Va., Aug. 25, 1928; s. Garnett Eldridge and Susie W. (Bryant) T.; m. Ada Teresa Hornsby, Aug. 29, 1949; children—Susan Elizabeth Shealy, Cheri Lynn Morris, Teresa Ann Heilman. A.A., Tenn. Wesleyan Coll., 1950; B.S., Tenn. Poly. Inst., 1951; M.A., U. Va., 1955; M.L.S., Rutgers U., 1956; student, La. State U., 1961-63. Reference asst. Alderman Library, U. Va., 1954-55; research asst. Grad. Sch . Library Sci., Rutgers U., 1955-56; mem. staff and faculty La. State U., 1956-63, asst. dir. charge pub. services, 1962-63; dir. libraries, prof. library sci. U. Southwestern La., 1963-67; dir. libraries U. S.C., Columbia, 1967—; bd. dirs. Southeastern Library Network, 1967-88; disting. dir. of librs. emeritus U. S.C., Columbia, 1988—; vice chmn. Southeastern Library Network, 1973-74, 83-84, chmn., 1974-75, treas., 1984-85; libr. cons. for bldgs. and adminstrn. for 60 colls. and univs. in past 30 yrs.; chmn. librarians sect. La. Coll. Conf., 1965-67; mem. Bd. La. Libr. Examiners, 1966-67; participant Libr. Mgmt. Inst., U. Wash., Seattle, 1969, Libr. Bldg. Problems Inst., UCLA, 1970. Contbr. articles to profl. jours.; editor: Bull. La. Library Assn, 1959-62; mng. editor: SW La. Jour, 1963-67; adv. bd.: Linguistic Atlas Am. Treas. Wesley Found.; v.p. Am. Field Services Internat. Scholarships; bd. dirs. U. S.C. Ednl. Found., 1975-82; Danforth assoc., 1967—; AIA/ALA Bldg. Awards Jury, 1987. Served to 1st lt. AUS, 1946-47, 51-53. Mem. ALA (life), La. Library Assn. (parliamentarian 1962-63, 66-67), Southeastern Library Assn. (Life mem., exec. bd. 1981-85, Rothrock award 1978), Southwestern Library Assn., S.C. Library Assn. (Life mem., pres. 1976, exec. bd. 1981-85), Assn. Southeastern Research Libraries (chmn. 1973-75, adv. com. to OCLC 1979-84), AAUP (sec.), La. Hist. Assn., La. Tchrs. Assn., Soc. Tympanuchus Cupido Pinnatus, South Caroliniana Soc., Nat. Library Bldg. Consultants List (chmn. 1981-84), Tenn. Squire, Omicron Delta Epsilon. Methodist. Clubs: Mason (Shriner), Kiwanis. Home: 16 Garden Springs Rd Columbia SC 29209-1716

TOOMBS, MARGARET STUTTS, speech and language pathologist; b. Houston, Sept. 20, 1948; d. Everette Junior and Lola Marie (Jaynes) Stutts. BA Speech Pathology/Audiology cum laude, U. Houston, 1976; MS in Lang. Scis., U. Tex., 1979. Cert. speech, lang. pathology ASHA, svc. provider City of Houston, Tex. Rehab. Commn.; lic. speech-lang. pathology, Tex. Cons., tchr. Intensive English Inst. U. Houston; pvt. practice cons./tng. Houston; dir. Accent on Communication, 1981—. Contbr. articles to profl. jours. Jack and Tina Bangs scholar; recipient Award for Continuing Edn. ASHA. Fellow Med. Ctr. del Oro-Speech Pathology; mem. ASTD (co-chair awards banquet), Am. Mktg. Assn. (chair networking event), Am. Speech and Hearing Assn., Tex. Speech Lang. Hearing Assn. (ins. task force), Houston Bus. Coun., Houston Assn. for Comm. Disorders, Houston Soc. Otolaryngology (assoc.), Orton Dyslexia Soc., U. Houston Alumni Assn., Sch. Comm. (bd. dirs.), Phi Kappa Phi. Home: 2211 Gardenia Dr Houston TX 77018

TOOMER, CLARENCE, library administrator; b. Asbury Park, N.J., June 12, 1952; s. Willie and Hazel (Markham) T. BA, Livingstone Coll., 1974; MLS, N.C. Ctrl. U., 1976; EdD, N.C. State U., 1993; Dr.Pedagogy (hon.), Teamer Sch. religion, Charlotte, N.C., 1979. Ref. libr. Johnson C. Smith U., Charlotte, 1979-80; dir. libr. svcs. Shaw U., Raleigh, 1980-88, Greensboro (N.C.) Coll., 1988-93, U. N.C.-Pembroke., 1993—. NEH grantee, 1985. Mem. ALA, NAACP, N.C. Libr. Assn. Republican. United Holy Ch. Home: 3055 Westminster Rd Lumberton NC 28358 Office: U NC at Pembroke Mary Livermore Library Faculty Row Pembroke NC 28372

TOOMEY, SHEILA CRAWFORD, education educator, consultant; b. Beckley, W.Va., Mar. 1, 1943; d. Roger and Ruth (Ashworth) Crawford; m. Lloyd E. Johnston, June 4, 1966 (dec. Dec. 1988); 1 child, Jacqueline De Vries; m. James E. Toomey, Feb. 10, 1989. BA, Tenn. Tech. U., 1963; MA in Christian Edn., Seabury Western Theol. Sem., 1965; MS in Curriculum and Instrn., U. Tenn., Martin, 1989; EdD in Instrn. and Curriculum Leadership, U. Memphis, 1994; postgrad., San Jose State U., U. Calif., Berkeley, U. Utah, Tex. Woman's U. Cert. tchr., Tenn; passed profl. in human resources profl. exam Soc. Human Resource Mgmt. Dir. Christian edn. St. Luke's Episcopal Ch., Rochester, Minn., 1965-66; elem. tchr. Santa Catalina Sch. Girls, 1967-69, Rowland-Hall St. Mark's Sch., Salt Lake City, 1968-69, Union City (Tenn.) Christian Sch., 1984-87; libr. Dept. Edn. U. Tenn. at Martin, 1987-89; rsch. asst. U. Memphis, 1989-92, adj. prof., 1996; prof., edn. dept. chair Lane Coll., Jackson, Tenn., 1992-94; reading tchr., drama club sponsor Ashland (Miss.) Mid. Sch., 1994-95; workshop presenter Jackson, Tenn., 1989—; ednl. cons. Delta Faucet of Tenn. divsn. Masco Corp., Jackson, 1995—; homebound tchr. Jackson-Madison County Schs., 1996—; adj. prof. Shelby State C.C., 1995, U. Memphis, 1996; mem. campus All Stars, Honda, Jackson, 1992-93. Contbr. articles to profl. jours. Mem. Am. Counseling Assn., Tenn. ASCD, Assn. for Case Method Rsch., DAR, Nat. Libr. Assn., Ch. and Synagogue Libr. Assn., AAUW, Order Eastern Star (worthy matron 1980-89), Sigma Tau Delta, Kappa Delta Pi. Anglican. Home: 137-2 Birchwood Ln Jackson TN 38305-2508 Office: 310 N Parkway Jackson TN 38305

TOOTHE, KAREN LEE, elementary and secondary school educator; b. Seattle, Dec. 13, 1957; d. Russell Minor and Donna Jean (Drolet) McGraw; m. Edward Frank Toothe, Aug. 6, 1983; 1 child, Kendall Erin. BA in Psychology with high honors, U. Fla., 1977, MEd in Emotional Handicaps and Learning Disabilities, 1979. Cert. behavior analysis Fla. Dept. Profl. Regulation. Alternative edn. self-contained tchr. grades 2 and 3 Gainesville Acad., Micanopy, Fla., 1979; emotional handicaps self-contained tchr. Ctr. Sch. Alternative Sch., Gainesville, Fla., 1979-80; learning disabilities resource tchr. grades 2 and 3 Galaxy Elem. Sch., Boynton Beach, Fla., 1980-81, learning disabilities self-contained tchr. grades 1-3, 1981, varying exceptionalities self-contained tchr. grades 3-5, 1981-83, chpt. one remedial reading tchr. grades 3 and 4, 1982-83; sec. and visual display unit operator Manpower, London, 1983-84; dir. sci./geography/social studies program Fairley House Sch., London, 1984-86, specific learning difficulties self-contained tchr. ages 8-12, dir. computing program, 1984-89; specific learning difficulties resource tchr. ages 8-16 Dyslexia Inst., Sutton Coldfield, Eng., 1990; behavior specialist, head Exceptional Student Edn. dept. Gateway High Sch., Kissimmee, Fla., 1990, behavior specialist, head ESE dept., 1991, resource compliance specialist, head ESE dept., 1991-93, tchr. summer youth tng. and enrichment program, 1993; tchr. summer youth tng. and enrichment program Osceola High Sch., Kissimmee, 1992; resource compliance specialist, program specialist for mentally handicapped, physically impaired, occupational and phys. therapy programs St. Cloud (Fla.) Mid. Sch., 1993-96, cmty.-based instrn., local augmentative/assistive tech. specialist, 1993-96; resource compliance specialist, program specialist physically impaired occupl. and phys. therapy programs, local augmentative/assistive tech. speciali st Hickory Tree Elem. Sch., 1996—; sch. rep. CREATE, Alachua County, Fla., 1979-80, Palm Beach County South Area Tchr. Edn. Ctr. Coun., 1980-83, chmn., 1982-83; mem. writing team Title IV-C Ednl. Improvement Grant, Palm Beach County, Fla., 1981; mem. math. curriculum writing team Palm Beach County (Fla.) Schs., 1983; mem., co-dir. Fairley House Rsch. Com., 1984-90; co-founder, dir. Rsch. Database, London, 1984-89; co-chmn. computer and behavior/social aspects writing teams Dyslexia Inst. Math., Staines, Eng., 1990; lectr., course tutor Brit. Dyslexia Assn., Crewe, Eng., 1990; mem. Vocat.-Exceptional Com., 1991-93; mem. Osceola Reading Coun., 1991—; mem. sch. adv. com. Gateway High Sch., 1991-93, St. Cloud Mid. Sch., 1993-96; presenter in field. Named Mid. Sch. Profl. of Yr. Osceola chpt. of Coun. Exceptional Children, 1995, 96. Mem. CEC (named local chpt. Mid. Sch. Profl. of Yr. 1995, 96), Fla. Soc. for Augmentative and Alt. Comm., Fla. Profl. Assn. Staffing Specialists, Phi Beta Kappa. Home: 2175 James Dr Saint Cloud FL 34771-8830 Office: Osceola Dist Schs 817 Bill Beck Blvd Kissimmee FL 34744-4492

TOOTHMAN, JOHN WILLIAM, lawyer; b. Bryn Mawr, Pa., Dec. 6, 1954; s. Nolan Ernest Toothman and Caroline Nell Reed Pawl; m. Elizabeth McGee; 1 child, William. BS ChemE with honors, U. Va., 1977, MS ChemE, 1979; JD cum laude, Harvard U., 1981. Bar: D.C. 1981, U.S. Dist. Ct. D.C. 1982, Va. 1987, U.S. Dist. Ct. (ea. dist.) Va. 1987, U.S. Claims Ct. 1987, U.S. Ct. Appeals (4th and fed. cir.) 1987, U.S. Supreme Ct. 1987, Md. 1990, U.S. Dist. Ct. Md. 1990, U.S. Bankruptcy Ct. (ea. dist.) Va. 1994. Assoc. Howrey & Simon, Washington, 1981-83, Akin, Gump, Strauss et al, Washington, 1983-84; trial atty. civil div. U.S. Dept. Justice, Washington, 1984-86; assoc. John Grad & Assocs., Alexandria, Va., 1986-88; ptnr. Grad, Toothman, Logan & Chabot, P.C., Alexandria, 1988-89, Shulman, Rogers, Gandal, Pordy & Ecker, P.A., Alexandria, 1989-93; founder The Devil's Advocate & John W. Toothman, P.C., 1993—; guest lectr. George Washington U. Law Sch., 1988; lectr. in field. Author: (with Douglas Danner) Danner & Toothman Trial Practice Checklists, 1989; contbr. articles to profl. jours. NSF fellow, 1977. Mem. ABA (Ross Essay award 1995), D.C. Bar Assn. (arbitrator), Am. Arbitration Assn. (arbitrator), Va. Bar (arbitrator), Am. Corp. Counsel Assn., Sigma Xi, Tau Beta Pi. Democrat. Address: Ste 250 400 N Columbus St Alexandria VA 22314

TOPE, DIANA RAY, library administrator; b. Jacksonville, Fla.; d. Laurie Graydon and Jane (Adams) R.; m. Stephen Lindsey Tope Jr., Sept. 6, 1958 (dec. July 1969); children: Melody Kim Tope Hainline, Jennifer Elyce Tope Stanton, Whitney Davison, Keri Adair Tope Turnbull. AB in English, Duke U., 1959; MLS, Emory U., 1971, Diploma Advanced Study in Librarianship, 1988; MEd, N.C. State U., 1979. Cert. pub. libr., N.C., Ga. Br. mgr. Rockingham Pub. Libr., Eden, N.C., 1971-73; coord. svcs. Sandhill Regional Libr. System, Rockingham, N.C., 1973-75; dir. Robeson County Pub. Libr., Lumberton, N.C., 1975-81, Cherokee Regional Libr., Lafayette, Ga., 1981-83; dept. dir. office pub. libr. svcs. Ga. Dept. Tech. and Adult Edn., Atlanta, 1983—. Assoc. editor: Robeson County: A Life of Quality, 1981; editor: Georgia Public Library Administrator's Sourcebook, 1989; contbr. articles to profl. jours. Mem. alumni interview com. Duke U., Atlanta, 1983—. Mem. ALA, Assn. Specialized and Coop. Libr. Agys. (bd. dirs. 1992-94), Southeastern Libr. Assn., Ga. Libr. Assn. (scholarship com.), Met. Atlanta Libr. Assn. Methodist. Office: Ga Dept Tech and Adult Edn Office Pub Libr Svcs 156 Trinity Ave SW Atlanta GA 30303-3692

TOPERZER, THOMAS RAYMOND, art museum director; b. Pitts., Aug. 12, 1939; s. Raymond Otto and Blodwyn (Roberts) T.; m. Carol Jane Reece, June 2, 1961; children: Scott Thomas, Max Otto. Student, West Liberty (W.Va.) State Coll., 1959, Sterling (Kans.) Coll., 1959-61; AB, Southwestern Coll., 1963; MFA, U. Nebr., 1970. Dir. Blanden Meml. Art Mus., Fort Dodge, Iowa, 1970-71, Rochester (Minn.) Art Ctr., 1971-72; curator univ. art gallery Ill. State U., Normal, 1972-73, asst. dir. univ. mus., 1972-73, dir. univ. art mus. and CVA art galleries, 1973-82; coordinator div. fine arts Bethel Coll., St. Paul, 1982-84; dir. Fred Jones Jr. Mus. Art, U. Okla., Norman, 1984—; arts cons. to various corps., Minn., Ill. and Okla., 1972—. Nelle Cochran Woods fellow U. Nebr., 1969-70. Mem. Assn. Coll. and U. Mus. and Galleries (mem. exec. com. 1986—), Am. Assn. Mus., Coll. Art Assn. Office: Fred Jones Jr Mus Art U Okla 410 W Boyd St Norman OK 73069-4851

TOPPING, EVA CATAFYGIOTU, writer, lecturer, educator; b. Fredericksburg, Va., Aug. 23, 1920; d. Themistocles John and Katherine (Polizou) Catafygiotu; m. Peter Topping, June 20, 1951; 1 child, John T. BA, Mary Washington Coll., 1941; MA in Classics, Radcliffe Coll., 1943; postgrad., U. Athens, 1950-51. trustee Greek Orthodox Ch. of Fredericksburg, 1990—; bd. dirs. Orthodox Christian Laity, Chgo., 1988-92, bd. advisors, 1992—; exec. coun. Ch. Women United, N.Y.C., 1981-85. Author: Sacred Stories from Byzantium, 1977, Holy Mothers of Orthodoxy, 1987, Saints and Sisterhood, 1990; contbg. editor: The Greek American, N.Y.C., 1991-94; contbr. articles to profl. jours. Exec. bd. Greek Am. Womens Network, N.Y.C., 1990-94; adv. com. Helen Z. Papanikolas Trust, Salt Lake City, 1989-94. Recipient Am. Hellenic Achievement award Hellenic Spirit Found., 1992, Lifetime Achievement award Am. Hellenic Inst., 1993; Fulbright scholar U.S. Ednl. Found., N.Y.C., 1950. Mem. NOW, Philoptochos Womens Soc., Orthodox Christian Assn. Medicine, Psychology and Religion, Peace Action, Greek Am. Womens Network, Phi Beta Kappa. Democrat. Greek Orthodox. Home: 1823 Rupert St Mc Lean VA 22101-5434

TORBERT, CLEMENT CLAY, JR., state supreme court justice; b. Opelika, Ala., Aug. 31, 1929; s. Clement Clay Sr. and Lynda (Meadows) T.; m. Gene Hurt, May 2, 1952; children: Mary Dixon, Gene Shealy, Clement Clay III. Student, U.S. Naval Acad., 1948-49; B.S., Auburn U., 1951; postgrad., U. Md., 1952; LL.B., U. Ala., 1954. Bar: Ala. 1954. Practiced in Opelika, 1954-77, city judge, 1954-58; partner firm Samford, Torbert, Denson & Horsley, 1959-74; chief justice Ala. Supreme Ct., 1977-89; ptnr. firm Maynard, Cooper & Gale, 1990—; past chmn. Ala. Jud. Study Commn.,

Jud. Coordination Com.; past pres. Conf. Chief Justices; supervisory bd. Ala. Law Enforcement Planning Agy., 1977-83; bd. dirs. Ala. Criminal Justice Info. Systems, Nat. Inst. for Dispute Resolution, First Nat. Bank Opelika, State Justice Inst., 1986-92; mem. panel of arbitrators Am. Arbitration Assn.; panelist-at-large Ctr. for Pub. Resources; held Leslie S. Wright Chair of Law, Cumberland Sch. Law, 1989, John Sparkman Chair, U. Ala. Sch. Law. Mem. Ala. Ho. of Reps., 1958-62, Ala. Senate, 1966-70, 74-77. Served to capt. USAF, 1952-53. Elected to Ala. Acad. of Honor, 1979; recipient Disting. Svc. award Nat. Ctr. for State Cts., 1989, 1989 award, Am. Judges Assn. Mem. Am. Judicature Soc., Farrah Law Soc., Phi Delta Phi, Phi Kappa Phi, Alpha Tau Omega. Methodist. Lodge: Kiwanis. Home: 611 Terracewood Dr Opelika AL 36801-3850 Office: One Commerce St Ste 302 Montgomery AL 36104

TORGUSON, MARLIN F., entertainment company executive; b. 1945. Owner, prin. Torgy's Inc., Glenwood, Minn., 1965—; with G M T Mgmt. Co., 1984-91; prin., v.p. Jackpot Junction Casino, Morton, Minn.; founder Mardi Gras Casino Corp., 1990—, Atlantic-Pacific Corp., 1990—, Bay St. Louis Casino Corp., 1992—, Biloxi Casino Corp., 1992—; chmn. bd., CEO Casino Magic Corp., 1992—. Office: Casino Magic Corp 711 Casino Magic Dr Bay Saint Louis MS 39520-1808*

TORNOS, CARMEN, surgical pathologist; b. Barcelona, Spain, Apr. 1, 1954; came to U.S., 1982; d. David and Angela (Salomo) Tornos; m. Roman Perez-Soler, Mar. 15, 1980; children: Paul, Christine. MD, U. Barcelona, 1977. Resident in hematology Ciudad Sanitaria Valle Hebron, Barcelona, 1978-82; resident in clin. and anat. pathology U. Tex. Med. Sch., Houston, 1985-89; postdoctoral fellow M.D. Anderson Cancer Ctr., Houston, 1982-83, fellow in surg. pathology, 1989-90, faculty assoc. in surg. pathology, 1990-91, asst. prof. surg. pathology, 1991-96, dir. fellowship in surg. pathology, 1995—, assoc. prof. pathology, 1996—. Office: MD Anderson Cancer Ctr 1515 Holcombe Blvd Box 85 Houston TX 77030

TORNOW, JOANNE SUSAN, molecular biologist, educator; b. Mpls., June 30, 1957; d. Joe Samuel and Rosaline Shirley (Stein) T.; m. George Michael Santangelo, July 15, 1989. BA in Biology, Rutgers U., 1979; PhD in Genetics, Yale U., 1983. Postdoctoral fellow U. Calif., Irvine, 1983-85; asst. rsch. biologist U. Calif., Santa Cruz, 1985-87; asst. prof. Portland (Oreg.) State U., 1987-89; asst. prof. rsch. U. So. Miss., Hattiesburg, 1989-91, asst. prof., 1991—. Contbr. articles to sci. and profl. jours. Mem. AAAS, Genetics Soc. Am., Miss. Acad. Scis., Phi Beta Kappa, Sigma Xi. Office: U So Miss SS Box 5018 Hattiesburg MS 39406

TORNQUIST, KRISTI MALINDA, librarian; b. Mpls., Feb. 16, 1958; d. Lowell W. and Barbara Jean (Friedlein) T. BA in Math. and English, U. Minn., Morris, 1980; MLS, U. Wis., 1982; PhD in Higher Edn. Adminstrn., U. Minn., 1992. Teaching asst. math. dept. U. Wis., Madison, 1980-82, intern, student asst. interlibr. loan dept., 1981-82; instr. math. dept. math. scis. U. Minn., Duluth, 1982-84; automation coord., reference libr. U. Wis., Stout, 1984-85; bibliog. instrn. and collection devel. libr. U. Wis., Superior, 1985-87, tech. svcs. and automation libr., 1988-89, instr. libr. sci. Coll. Edn., 1985-89; rsch. asst. mgmt. info. divsn. Office Pres. U. Minn., 1990-92; dir. libr. and info. svcs. So. Ark. U., Magnolia, 1992—; presenter in field. Author: (with others) Periodicals in College Libraries, 1987; contbr. articles to profl. jours. Active Magnolia Arts Coun., 1992—, bd. dirs., 1994—; mem. Golden Triangle FiberPark Coun., 1994—; bd. dirs. Ark. Humanities Coun., 1995—. Recipient Scholar of Coll. award U. Minn., Morris, 1980; Dept. Ednl. Policy and Adminstrn. scholar, 1989-90, Coll. Edn. Coffman Alumni scholar, 1989-90, U. Minn. Grad. Sch. fellow, 1989-90, U. Minn. dissertation fellow, 1991-92; grantee Ark. State Libr., 1993, Ark. Dept. Higher Edn., 1993-94, 94-95, U.S. Dept. Edn., 1993-95, Southwestern Bell Telephone, 1994. Mem. ALA (program officer student chpt.), Am. Ednl. Rsch. Assn., Ark. Libr. Assn. (vice chair new members roundtable 1993, chair 1994, mem. exec. bd. 1994, mem. membership com. 1994, coord. Ark. grass roots grant 1994), Assn. for Study Higher Edn., Assn. Coll. and Rsch. Librs., South Ark. Women's Network (charter, chair profl. devel. com. 1993-94), Magnolia/Columbia County C. of C. (chair telecom. com. 1994—), Lion's Club (bd. dirs. 1995—). Office: Southern Arkansas Univ SAU PO Box 1401 Magnolia AR 71753-5000

TORO, CARLOS HANS, insurance/financial products marketing executive; b. Lima, Peru, Jan. 20, 1943; s. Charlie Toro and Eufemia (Lopez); m. Liliana Irene Perez, Feb. 7, 1967; children: Michelle V., Hans C. Student Sch. Engring., Nev. So. U., 1964-67. Enlisted USAF, 1963, advanced through grades to staff sgt., resigned, 1972; regional dir. Am. Continental Life, Frankfurt, Germany, 1972-78, Continental Am. Securities, Ltd., Frankfurt, 1973-78; stockbroker Continental Am. Securities, Ltd., Phoenix, 1978-84; owner, ins. broker C.H. Toro Internat. Ltd., Phoenix, 1978—; officer Century Pacific Internat. Corp., Phoenix, 1984-90, pres., 1987-90. Mem. Miami (Fla.) C. of C. Republican. Roman Catholic. Office: CH Toro Internat Ltd 801 Brickell Ave Fl 9 Miami FL 33131-4945

TOROK, GEORGE DENNIS, history educator; b. Buffalo, Feb. 23, 1958; s. George D. and Dorothy I. (Moore) T. BA, SUNY, Buffalo, 1980, PhD, 1991. Asst. prof. history El Paso (Tex.) C.C., 1991—. Author: (exhibit catalog) Western N.Y.'s Hidden Past, 1993; contbg. author Photo-Pictorialists of Buffalo, 1981. Recipient Internationalizing the Curriculum Summer Teaching fellowship U. Ky., 1992, 93, Grad. Teaching citation SUNY Buffalo, 1990, N.Y. State Constitutional Bicentennial grant, 1988. Mem. Latin Am. Studies Assn., Soc. for Historians of the Early Am. Republic, Am. Hist. Assn., So. Hist. Assn. Office: El Paso CC PO Box 20500 El Paso TX 79998

TORRANCE, ELLIS PAUL, psychologist, educator; b. Milledgeville, Ga., Oct. 8, 1915; s. Ellis Watson and Jimmie Pearl (Ennis) T.; m. Jessie Pansy Nigh, Nov. 25, 1959 (dec. Nov. 1988). B.A., Mercer U., 1940; M.A., U. Minn., 1944; Ph.D., U. Mich., 1951. Tchr. Midway Vocational High Sch., Milledgeville, 1936-37; tchr., counselor Ga. Mil. Coll., 1937-40, prin., 1941-44; counselor student counseling bur. U. Minn., 1945; counselor counseling bur. Kans. State Coll., 1946-48, dir., 1949-51; dir. survival research field unit Stead AFB, Nev., 1951-57; dir. Bur. Ednl. Research, 1958-64; prof. ednl. psychology U. Minn., 1958-66; chmn., prof. dept. ednl. psychology U. Ga., 1966-78, Alumni Found. disting. prof., 1974-85; Alumni Found. disting. prof. emeritus, 1985—; advisor Torrance Ctr. for Creative Studies, U. Ga. Author: Torrance Tests of Creative Thinking, Thinking Creatively in Action and Movement, Style of Learning and Thinking, and Sounds and Images; contbr. articles to jours., mags., books. Trustee Creative Edn. Found.; founder Nat. Future Problem Solving Problem and Bowl, Nat. Scenario Writing Contest. Fellow Am. Psychol. Assn.; mem. Am. Ednl. Rsch. Assn., Am Soc. Group Psychotherapy and Psychodrama, Creative Edn. Leadership Coun., Nat. Assn. Gifted Children, Am. Creativity Assn., Phi Delta Kappa. Baptist. Home: 183 Cherokee Ave Athens GA 30606-4305

TORRENCE, BILLY HUBERT, minister; b. Lynchburg, Va., Aug. 29, 1949; s. Charles Hubert and Mabel (Pillow) T.; m. Linda P. Pool, Apr. 1, 1972; children: Joseph Scott, Susan Marie. Student, Cen. Va. Coll., Wesley Sem., Washington, 1990—. Local pastor Meth. Ch., Lynchburg, Va., 1990-93, Staunton, Va., 1993-95; Providence UMC, Danville Dist., Patrick Springs, Va., 1995—; bookkeeper Va. Dept. Hwys., 1992-93; foreman, crew leader Va. Dept. Transp., Lynchburg, 1987-90. With U.S. Army, 1968-72, Vietnam. Mem. Ruritan (zone gov. Peaks of Otter chpt. 1983, lt. dist. 1984-86, dist. gov. 1985, 87, Ruritan of Yr. 1984), Phi Theta Kappa. Home and Office: RR 2 Box 255 Patrick Springs VA 24133

TORRENCE, ROSETTA LENA, educational consultant; b. New Rochelle, N.Y., Nov. 3, 1948; d. Stanley Livinston and Evelyn Ann Phillips; m. John Wesley Torrence, Sept. 14, 1981. BA in Edn. cum laude, Bklyn. Coll., 1974. Instr. Dept. Def.-Kadena Air Base, Okinawa, Japan, 1984-86, Halifax C.C., Weldon, N.C., 1986-88; dir. The Ednl. Workshop, Richmond, Va., 1989—; ednl. cons. Philip Morris, USA (EDTC), Richmond, 1989—, Juvenile and Domestic Rels. Dist. Ct., Richmond, 1993—, Jack & Jill, Inc., Richmond, 1994—; dir. Sound-It-Out The Easy Way, Inc., 1995—. Author: (booklet, cassette) Sound-It-Out The Easy Way Pre-Phonics Program, 1989, (workbook, cassette) Sound-It-Out The Easy Way Pre-Phonics Workbook, 1993, Sound-It-Out The Easy Way: The Syllables Workbook, 1993, Sound-It-Out The Easy Way Phonics Readers, 1993. Spokesperson Concerned Business & Residents of South Side Community Group, Richmond, 1993. Baptist. Home and Office: The Ednl Workshop 1818 Stockton St Richmond VA 23224-3762

TORRES, HUGO R., financial analyst, international credit analyst, telecommunications analyst; b. Bogotá, Colombia, Nov. 29, 1963; arrived in U.S., 1979; s. Juan B. and Beatriz (Vanegas) T.; m. Michelle L. Hartman, Dec. 31, 1989; children: Brandon, Allison. BA in Bus. Adminstrn. and Econs., Hope Coll., 1988. Telecomm. analyst Metromedia Long Distance, East Rutherford, N.J., 1988-93; acct. analyst Cantor Fitzgerald Sec., N.Y.C., 1993-95; internat. credit analyst Whirlpool Corp., Miami, 1996—. Author: Ira Guia Hispana de Como Iniciar un Negocio, 1994. Co-founder, gen. sec., mem. Asocomercol, Jersey City, N.J., 1993-95; vol. CASA, Miami, 1995-96, Hispanic Orgn. of BC, Hackensack, N.J. Republican. Home: 12121 SW 94th St Miami FL 33186 Office: Whirlpool Fin Corp 6303 B Lagoon Dr Miami FL 33186

TORRES, ISRAEL, oral and maxillofacial surgeon; b. El Paso, Tex., Sept. 5, 1934; s. Francisco Mendoza and Manuela (Gallardo) T.; m. Karen Marie Hensley, Aug. 22, 1970; children: Michael, George Stanley, Dianna. BS, Tex. Western Coll., 1958; DDS, U. Tex.-Houston, 1963; postgrad. Health Sci. Ctr., Houston, 1963-66; diploma (hon.) XX Reunion de Provincia, Juarez, Chihuahua, Mexico, 1970, Ateneo Odontologica Mexicano, Valle de Bravo, Mexico, 1973, Colegio de Cirujanos Mexicanos, Juarez, 1975, 84. Cert. instr. Advanced Cardiac Life Support, 1986—. Diplomate Am. Bd. Oral and Maxillofacial Surgery. Resident in oral surgery Methodist Hosp., Houston, 1963-64, Ben Taub Hosp., Houston, 1964-65, Hermann Hosp., Houston, 1965-66; practice dentistry specializing in oral and maxillofacial surgery, El Paso, 1966—; mem. staff Sun Towers Hosp., chief oral and maxillofacial surgery, 1975, 76, 77, 93; gov. appointee Tex. State Bd. Dental Examiners, 1993-95; instr. pathology El Paso C.C., 1975-76; lectr. in field; OMS cons. Latuna Fed. Correct Inst. Author, editor: Magnificent Obsession: In Quest of High Mountain Game, 1990; contbg. author Asian Hunter, 1989; contbr. articles to Jour. Oral/Maxillofacial Surgery. Bd. dirs. Am. Cancer Soc., El Paso, 1971-73, El Paso Cancer Treatment Ctr., 1971-74; bd. dirs. West Tex. Health Systems Agy., 1980-82, chmn., 1981-82; med. adv. com. W. Tex. Council of Regional Health. Recipient Bowie Exes award, El Paso, 1982, Mexican Consul Gen. Award of Appreciation, 1986, Mexican Social Security Service Award of Appreciation, 1986. Fellow Am. Coll. Oral and Maxillofacial Surgeons, Am. Assn. Oral and Maxillofacial Surgeons, Internat. Assn. Oral and Maxillofacial Surgeons, Southwest Soc. Oral and Maxillofacial Surgeons, Acad. Internat. Dental Studies, Pan Am. Med. Assn., EPSDT (dental adv. and rev. com. 1985-86), Tex. Soc. Oral and Maxillofacial Surgeons, The Explorers Club; mem. El Paso Dist. Dental Soc. (pres. 1979), U. Tex. Dental Br. Alumni Assn. (life), Nat. Rifle Assn. (life), Tex. Rifle Assn. (life), Am. Found. for N.Am. Wild Sheep, Internat. Sheep Hunting Assn. Republican. Roman Catholic. Clubs: Anthony Rod and Gun, Grand Slam (life). Avocations: high mountain sheep hunting; outdoor activities. Home: 6632 Westside Dr El Paso TX 79932-2623 Office: 1201 E Schuster Ave Bldg 4A El Paso TX 79902-4646

TORRES, MILTON JOHN, industrial engineering educator; b. N.Y.C., July 28, 1931; s. Milton and Vitalia (Cabrera) T.; m. Dorothy Spaugh (div. Feb. 1971); children: Milton J. III, Geoffrey, Vicky L. Lopez; m. Dorothy Roberts. BS in Gen. Engring., U. Okla., 1963, M Aerospace Engring., 1964; DArts in Mech. Engring., U. Miami, 1989. Commd. 2d lt. USAF, 1954, advanced through grades to maj.; chief test control br. Ops. Directorate Air Force Ea. Test Range, Cape Kennedy, Fla., 1968-71; ret. USAF, 1971; indsl. engr., sr. indsl. engr. Pan Am. World Airways, Inc., Miami, Fla., 1972-73; plant supt. Am. Panel Corp., Miami, 1973-77; plant mgr. Dyplast of Fla., 1977-83; asst. prof. indsl. systems dept. Fla. Internat. U., 1983-87, rsch. scientist, lectr. dept. indsl. engring., 1987-94. Contbr. articles to profl. jours., patentee in field. Decorated DFC, Air medal (13), Air Force Meritorious Svc. medal, Air Force Commendation medal. Mem. Tau Beta Pi, Sigma Tau, Sigma Gamma Tau, Alpha Pi Mu. Home: 11200 SW 99th Ct Miami FL 33176-4123

TORRES OLIVER, JUAN FREMIOT, bishop; b. San German, P.R., Oct. 28, 1925; s. Luis N. and Amalia (Oliver) Torres. B.A., St. John's Seminary, 1944-50; M.A. Musicology, Catholic U., 1952; LL.B., U. of P.R., 1959; LL.M., St. John's U., 1964, LL.D., 1995. Ordained priest Roman Cath. Ch., 1950. Instr. Catholic U., Ponce, P.R., 1952-56; vice-chancellor Diocesan Curia, 1961-64; prof., assoc. dean Catholic U. Sch. of Law, Ponce, P.R., 1961-64; bishop of Ponce P.R., 1964—; grand chancellor Pontifical Cath. U. P.R., Ponce, 1964—; pres. P.R. Episcopal Conf. 1982-94; Grand Prior, P.R. lieutenancy of Equestrian Order of the Holy Sepulchre of Jerusalem, 1984—. Decorated Cross of Order Juan Pablo Duarte, Dominican Republic. mem. Academia de Artes y Ciencias; Phi Alpha Delta. Office: Final Glenview Garden Rio Chiquido Rd #504 Ponce PR 00731*

TORRETTA-GUAGLIARDO, JOANN, small business owner, image consultant, lecturer; b. Tampa, Fla., Dec. 29, 1931; d. Joseph N. and Elena M. (Saitta) Torretta; m. Joseph L. Guagliardo, Apr. 14, 1959; children: Paul Joseph, Gayle Ann. BS in Speech, Northwestern U., 1953; postgrad., Fashion Inst. Tech., N.Y.C., 1979-80, 85-86, 88-89, 91. Prodr. fashion shows, Tampa, N.Y.C., 1960—; fashion coord. Montgomery Ward Co., Tampa and Clearwater, Fla., 1970-83; dir., owner First Impressions Image Ctr. Inc., Tempa, 1983—; coord., prodr., hostess TV show NBC affiliate, 1953-56; freelance writer on fashion. Pres. Sword of Hope Guild, Am. Cancer Soc., Tampa Bay, 1985-86, chmn. income devel., 1990-91, bd. dirs. 1983-93. Recipient Vol. of Yr. award Am. Cancer Soc., 1989, People of Dedication award Salvation Army, Tampa Bay, 1990. Mem. AAUW (coord. fundraiser 1988, Rising to the Top award 1992), Fashion Group (membership chmn. Tampa Bay 1980—), Assn. Image cons. Internat. (regional bd. dirs. Tampa Bay 1988—), Northwestern U. Alumni Assn. (pres. Tampa Bay 1983-91), Rotary Anns (v.p. 1992-94, pres. 1995-97, Outstanding Mem. award 1989-92), Tampa Woman's Club (v.p. 1995-96, ways and means chmn.). Republican. Roman Catholic. Home: 566 Riviera Dr Tampa FL 33606-3808

TORREY, CLAUDIA OLIVIA, lawyer; b. Nashville, June 10, 1958; d. Claude Adolphus and Rubye Mayette (Prigmore) T. BA in Econ., Syracuse U., 1980; JD, N.Y. Law Sch., 1985. Bar: N.Y. State 1988. Legal intern Costello, Cooney & Fearon, Syracuse, N.Y., 1979; legal clk. First Am. Corp., Nashville, 1981; legal asst. James I. Meyerson, N.Y.C., 1982-85; jud. law clk. N.Y. State Supreme Ct., N.Y.C., 1985; interim project supr., legal asst. CUNY Ctrl. Office, 1985-86; legal asst. Rosenman & Colin Law Firm, N.Y.C., 1986-87; asst. counsel N.Y. State Legis., Albany, 1988-90; atty., cons. pvt. practice, Nashville, Cookeville, Tenn., 1991—; bd. mem. Children's Corner Day Care Ctr., Albany, N.Y., 1989-90. Ch. rep. FOCUS exec. coun. Westminster Presbyn. Ch., Albany, 1990; v.p. dormitory coun., flr. rep. Syracuse U., 1977-79. Mem. ABA (young lawyers divsn. liaison to ABA forum on health law 1994-96), N.Y. State Bar Assn., Alpha Kappa Alpha (Syracuse U. chpt. treas. 1977-78, pres. 1979). Home and Office: PO Box 150234 Nashville TN 37215-0234

TOTH, JAMES JOSEPH, power systems engineer; b. Perth Amboy, N.J.; s. James J. and Lucille J. Toth; m. Cynthia L. Camfield; children: Jennifer, James. BE with honor, Stevens Inst. Tech., Hoboken, N.J., 1976; ME, Rensselaer Poly. Inst., Troy, N.Y., 1977; student, Ga. Inst. Tech., 1977-82. Registered profl. engr., Ga., N.C., S.C., Va. Project engr. Westinghouse Elec. Corp., Pitts., 1982-84; power sys. engr. Westinghouse Elec. Corp., Atlanta, 1984-86; powersys. engr. GE Co., Charlotte, N.C., 1986-95; sr. power sys. engr. ABB Svc., Inc., Charlotte, 1995—. Contbr. articles to jour. IEEE. Sec. Newell Sch. Adv. Team, Charlotte, 1994; corr. sec. Reid Park PTA, Charlotte, 1994-95, pres., 1995-96. Faculty fellow Rensselaer Poly. Inst., 1976-77. Mem. IEEE, NSPE, GE Elfun Soc. Home: 7026 Leaves Ln Charlotte NC 28213-5746 Office: ABB Svc Inc 10820 H Independence Pt Pky Matthews NC 28105

TOTH, JUSTIN TYLER, lawyer; b. Phila., Dec. 1, 1967; s. Richard Eugene and Diana Lynn (Ives) T.; m. Kathleen Denise Weron, Dec. 3, 1994. BS in Polit. Sci. and Philosophy, U. Utah, 1989, JD, 1992. Bar: Tex. 1992. Atty./jud. clk. U.S. Dist. Ct., Salt Lake City, 1992-93; assoc. Weil, Gotshal & Manges, Houston, 1993—; adj. prof. U. Houston Law Ctr., 1996. Contbr. articles to profl. jours. Pro bono atty. Houston Juvenile Law Clinic, 1994-96, Houston Vol. Lawyers Referral, 1996; intern Office of Vice Pres. of U.S., Washington, 1987-88. Recipient Outstanding Pro Bono svc. award Weil, Gotshal & Manges, 1996; Willia H. Leary scholar, 1989-92. Mem. ABA, Houston bar Assn., Houston Young Lawyers Assn., Tex. Young Lawyers Assn. (com. on ethics), Pro Bono Coll. of State Bar Tex., Coll. of State Bar of Tex., U. Utah Alumni Assn. (chpt. pres. 1996), Phi Beta Kappa, Phi Kappa Phi. Republican. Home: 4848 Pin Oak Pk #1422 Houston TX 77081 Office: Weil Gotshal & Manges 700 Louisiana Houston TX 77002

TOTH, STEPHEN MICHAEL, electronics specialist; b. Columbus, Ohio, July 12, 1946; s. Stephen Charles and Marian June (Hamilton) T.; m. Loreen Ann Bromeling, May 6, 1965 (div. 1974); children: Kathleen Marie, Stephen Charles. Tech. degree, Gt. Lakes Naval Tng. Ctr., 1965; EE, Capitol Radio Engring. Inst., Washington, 1971. Cert. electronics technician, engring. technician. Navigational aids technician USN, Meridian, Miss., 1966-68; radar supr. USN, Sangley Point, Philippines, 1968-71; navigtional aids supr. USN, Lemoore, Calif., 1971-75; communications technician County of Tulare, Visalia, Calif., 1975-77, comm. supr., 1977-79; comm. technician Tidewater Comm. and Elec. Corp., Virginia Beach, Va., 1979-85; shop mgr. Tidewater Communications and Elec. Corp., Virginia Beach, Va., 1985—; communications cons. City of Virginia Beach, 1985-87; control system cons. USN, 1983, alarm system cons., 1986. Inventor security alarm system, 1971, portable telephone system, 1979; editor Chesapeake Bay Bugeye, 1985—. Asst. cub master Cub Scouts Am., Virginia Beach, 1980-85, sponsor, 1985—; dir. Tidewater Soap Box Derby, Inc., Virginia Beach, 1982-87 (nat. cert. of appreciation, 1983, 84). Mem. Nat. Assn. Bus. and Ednl. Radio, Am. Philatelic Soc., Smithsonian Inst. Republican. Lutheran. Club: Foresters (chief ranger, 1982-84, pub. relations officer 1987—, Forester of Yr., 1983). Home: 736 Lincoln Ave Virginia Beach VA 23452-4037 Office: Tidewater Comm Corp 216 N Witchduck Rd Virginia Beach VA 23462-6508

TOTTEN, ARTHUR IRVING, JR., retired metals company executive, consultant; b. Laurel, Del., Mar. 15, 1906; s. Arthur Irving and Lena Meade (Fowler) T.; m. Margaret Ross, Nov. 10, 1934 (dec. Mar. 1988); children: Margaret Totten Peters, Fitz-Randolph Fowler, Eleanor Totten Shumaker. BS in Chemistry, Union Coll., Schenectady, 1928. Rsch. chemist E.I. du Pont de Nemours & Co., Inc., Parlin, N.J., 1928-32; prodn. supt. E.I. du Pont de Nemours & Co., Inc., Parlin, 1932-37; rsch. chemist E.I. du Pont de Nemours & Co., Inc., Phila., 1937-42; dir. packaging rsch. Reynolds Metals Co., Richmond, Va., 1946-71; exec. v.p. rsch. Reynolds Rsch. Corp., Richmond, 1966-71; ret., 1971; cons. Nat. Inventors Coun., Washington, 1940-46; presenter in field, U.S., Can., Eng., France; pres. Rsch. & Devel. Assocs., N.Y.C., 1965-67, chmn. bd., 1967—. Contbr. numerous articles on packaging and paints to profl. jours. Pres. River Rd. Citizens Assn., 1949; head comml. divsn. Richmond chpt. ARC, 1954, bd. dirs., 1955-58; trustee Va. Inst. Sci. Rsch., 1970—; emeritus dir. Adult Care Svcs., Richmond, 1995—; pres. Westham Green Citizens Assn., 1982; sr. warden Episc. Ch., 1952, 60, 66. Lt. col. Chem. Warfare Svc., U.S. Army, 1942-46. Recipient cert. of appreciation U.S. Army Natick Lab., 1971, Humanitarian award Adult Devel. Ctr., 1992. Mem. Am. Inst. Chemists (life, past chpt. pres.), Rsch. and Devel. Assn. (life, past pres., cert. of appreciation, 1971), Packaging Inst. (pres. 1971, Profl. award 1968), N.Am. Packaging Inst. (pres. 1971), World Packaging Inst. (v.p. 1971), Inst. Food Tech. (Indsl. Achievement award 1978), Packaging Edn. Found. (Hall of Fame 1973), Country Club Va., Richmond Engrs. Club (past bd. dirs.), Soixante Plus, Masons, Sigma Phi. Home: 300 N Ridge Rd Apt 43 Richmond VA 23229-7452

TOTTEN, GLORIA JEAN (DOLLY TOTTEN), real estate executive, financial consultant; b. Port Huron, Mich., Sept. 23, 1943; d. Lewis Elmer and Inez Eugenia (Houston) King; m. Donald Ray Totten, Feb. 5, 1961 (div. Apr. 1981); children: D. Erik, Angela J. Totten Sales, Kymberly D. Totten DiVita. Student, Patricia Stevens Modeling Sch., Detroit, 1976-79, Gold Coast Sch., West Palm Beach, Fla., 1988; degree in mktg., St. Clair County Coll., Port Huron, Mich., 1979. Lic. real estate saleswoman, Fla., Mich. Demonstrator, saleswoman Hoover Co., 1969-75; instr., promoter Port Huron Sch. Bus., 1973-75; real estate borker Select Realty, Port Huron, 1979-81, Earn Keim Realty, Port Huron, 1981-83, Schweitzer's Better Homes and Gardens, Marysville, Mich., 1983-86, Coldwell Banker Property Concepts Corp., North Palm Beach, Fla., 1986-94; pres., broker, owner Dolly Totten Real Estate Inc., West Palm Beach, Fla., 1994—; model, instr. Patricia Stevens Modeling Sch., Troy, Mich., 1972-75; beauty cons. Mary Kay Cosmetics, 1982—. Grantee Mich. State U., 1972. Mem. Nat. Assn. Realtors, North Palm Beach Rd. Realtors, Million Dollar Club (Port Huron chpt.), Women's Coun. Realtors (co-founder Port Huron chpt.). Home and Office: 515 Evergreen Dr Lake Park FL 33403

TOTTEN, RANDOLPH FOWLER, lawyer; b. Washington, June 20, 1943; s. Arthur Irving and Margaret Holland (Ross) T.; m. Virginia Hunton, July 31, 1965; children—Louise, Fitz, Caroline. B.A., Yale U., 1965; LL.B., U. Va., 1968. Bar: Va. 1968. Law clk. to Justice Gordon, Va. Supreme Ct. Appeals, Richmond, 1968-69; from assoc. to ptnr. Hunton & Williams, Richmond., 1969—; dir. Mid-Atlantic Holdings, Inc. Chmn., Richmond Community High Sch., 1979-81; mem. exec. com. Christchurch Sch., 1982—; trustee Church Schs. Episcopal Diocese Va., 1974—, mem. standing com., 1984—. Mem. ABA, Va. Bar Assn. Clubs: Country of Va., Commonwealth. Bd. editors Va. Law Rev. Office: Hunton & Williams Riverfront Plz 951 E Byrd St Richmond VA 23219-4040

TOTTENHAM, TERRY OLIVER, lawyer; b. Dallas, June 5, 1944; s. Edwin Pier and Ruth Elizabeth (Paris) T.; m. Carolyn Sue Lewis, July 7, 1967; children: Leslie Jo, Dana Elizabeth, Jessica Leigh. Student, Blinn Jr. Coll., 1962-67; B.S. in Pharmacy with high honors, U. Tex.-Austin, 1967, J.D. with honors, 1970; LL.M., George Washington U., 1973. Bar: Tex. 1970, U.S. Ct. Mil. Appeals 1971. Assoc. firm Fulbright, Crooker & Jaworski, Houston, 1970; ptnr. Fulbright & Jaworski, Houston, 1978—; mem. faculty South Tex. Coll. Law, U. Houston; vis. prof. med. jurisprudence Baylor U.; vis. prof. health law Tex. Women's U.; adj. prof. law U. Tex. Sch. Law; speaker profl. groups. Author: Texas Medical Jurisprudence; editor: Patients Rights Handbook, 1980. Served to capt. USMC, 1971-75. Recipient Gene Cavin award, 1992; named Outstanding Young Lawyer Houston, 1981, Outstanding Young Lawyer Tex., 1981. Fellow Tex. Bar Found. (life, trustee 1986—); mem. Tex. Assn. Def. Counsel, Am. Soc. Law and Medicine, Am. Soc. Pharmacy Law, Tex. Ex-Students Assn. (life), ABA, Nat. Health Lawyers Assn., Am. Acad. Hosp. Attys. (bd. dirs. 1989—), State Bar Tex. (chmn. health law sect., chmn. litigation sect, bd. dirs. 1985-86, chmn. continuing legal edn. com., Cert. of Merit award 1989), Houston Young Lawyers Assn. (dir. 1975-77), Tex. Young Lawyers Assn. (chmn. bd. 1979-80). Democrat. Episcopalian. Home: 25 Cicero Ln Austin TX 78746-3206 Office: Fulbright & Jaworski 600 Congress Ave Ste 2400 Austin TX 78701-3248

TOUBY, KATHLEEN ANITA, lawyer; b. Miami Beach, Fla., Feb. 20, 1943; s. Harry and Kathleen Rebecca (Hamper) T.; m. Joseph Thomas Woodward; children: Mark Andrew, Judson David Touby. BS in Nursing, U. Fla., 1965, MRC in Rehab. Counseling, 1967; JD with honors, Nova U., 1977. Bar: Fla. 1978, D.C. 1978. Counselor, Jewish Vocat. Svc., Chgo., 1967-68; rehab. counselor Fla. Dept. Vocat. Rehab., Miami, 1968-70; spl. asst., asst. U.S. atty. U.S. Dept. Justice, Miami, 1978-80; assoc. firm Pyszka & Kessler, P.A., Miami, 1980-83; ptnr. firm Touby & Smith, P.A., Miami, Fla., 1983-89, Touby, Smith, DeMahy and Drake P.A., 1989-94, Touby & Woodward, P.A., 1994—; chmn. adv. exec. bd. Paralegal Edn. program Barry U., 1986-87; lectr. Food and Drug Law Inst., 1987-89, 91; lectr. environ. law Exec. Enterprises, 1987-88; lectr. trial techniques, Hispanic Nat. Bar Assn., St. Thomas Law Sch.; adj. prof. product liability Can. Govt., U.S. Trade and Mktg. Dept., 1989-95. Co-author (with Smith and O'Reilly) The Environmental Litigation Deskbook, 1989; contbr. articles to profl. jours.; Mem. ABA, Am. Inns of Ct., Dade County Bar Assn., Fed. Bar Assn. (bd. dirs. 1989—, v.p. 1991-92, pres.-elect So. Fla. chpt. 1992-93, pres. 1993-94), Dade County Bar Assn. (legal aid, pub. svcs. com. 1988), Phi Delta Phi (province pres. 1982-85, bd. dirs. 1985-87). Roman Catholic. Home: 450 Sabal Palm Rd Miami FL 33137 Office: Touby & Woodward PA 250 Bird Rd Ste 308 Miami FL 33146-1424

TOUCHY, DEBORAH K. P., lawyer, accountant; b. Pasadena, Tex., Dec. 9, 1957; d. Donald Carl and Bobbie Jo (Jackson) Putzka; m. Harry Roy Touchy, Jr., Feb. 23, 1980. BBA, Baylor U., 1979; JD, U. Houston, 1988. Bar: Tex. 1989; CPA, Tex.; cert. in estate planning and probate law Tex. Bd.

Legal Specialization. Sr. mgr. tax KMPG Peat Marwick, Houston, 1980-86; assoc. Fizer Beck Webster & Bentley, Houston, 1989-90; pvt. practice law and acctg. Houston, 1990—. Editor Houston Law Rev., 1988-89, Jr. League Houston, 1992—. Chmn. ticket sales incentives Chi Omega, Houston, 1985; active ticket sales Mus. Fine Arts, Houston, 1984; facilities chmn. Woodland Trails West Civic Orgn., Houston, 1982-83, Jr. League of Houston, 1993—; pres. Women Attys. in Tax & Probate, 1994-95. Mem. ABA (estate-probate sect. 1989—, vice chmn. commn. property com. 1994—), AICPA (taxation sect., estate and gift tax com. 1992-95), Tex. Soc. CPAs (bd. dirs. 1995—, chmn. tax inst. com. 1996-97, estate planning com. 1990-94, 96), Houston Chpg. CPAs (chmn. taxpayer edn. 1985-86, chmn. membership com. 1992-93, v.p. 1993-94, 96-97, chmn. tax forums 1994-95, long range planning com. 1995-96, treas.-elect 1997—), Houston Bar Assn. (estate-probate sect. 1989—), State Bar Tex. (estate-probate sect. 1989—, mem. elder law com. 1991—), Houston Estate and Fin. Forum, Baylor U. Women's Assn. (treas. 1993-94, chmn. fin. com. 1994-95, parliamentarian 1995-96, sec. 1996-97, pres. 1997—), Chief Justice-Advocates, Tex. Bd. Legal Specializations (cert. estate planning, probate law 1994), Order of Coif, Omicron Delta Kappa, Phi Delta Phi. Office: 2932 Plumb St Houston TX 77005-3058

TOULOUSE, MARK GENE, religion educator; b. Des Moines, Feb. 1, 1952; s. O. J. and Joan (VanDeventer) T.; m. Jeffica L. Smith, July 31, 1976; children: Joshua Aaron, Marcie JoAnn, Cara Lynn. BA, Howard Payne U., 1974; MDiv, Southwestern Bapt. Theol. Sem., 1977; PhD, U. Chgo., 1984. Instr. Ill. Benedictine Coll., Lisle, 1980-82, asst. prof., 1982-84; asst. prof. Grad. Sem., Phillips U., Enid, Okla., 1984-86; prof., assoc. dean Brite Div. Sch. Texas Christian U., Ft. Worth, 1986—. Author: The Transformation of John Foster Dulles, 1985, Joined in Discipleship: The Maturing of an American Religious Movement, 1992; co-editor: Makers of Christian Theology in America, 1997; contbr. articles to religious jours. Theol. scholar, rsch. award Assn. Theol. Schs., 1990-91. Mem. Am. Acad. Religion (jr. scholar S.W. region 1990-91), Am. Soc. Ch. History. Home: 4129 Alava Dr Fort Worth TX 76133-5462 Office: Brite Divinity Sch Texas Christian U TCU Box 298130 Fort Worth TX 76129

TOUMA, WALID RACHID, computer consultant; b. Kab-Elias, Bekaa, Lebanon, Apr. 2, 1965; came to U.S., 1983; s. Rachid Tanios and Laure Ibrahim (Layoun) T. BSEE with high honors, U. Tex., 1987, MS in Computer Engring., 1989, PhD in Computer Engring., 1992. Teaching asst. U. Tex., Austin, 1987-89, rsch. asst., 1990-92; tech. cons. Arnold, White & Durkee, Houston, 1988; mktg. strategy planner Tomacom, Middle East, 1992-93; vis. rsch. fellow IC2 Inst., Austin, 1993—; pres. Technologies & Computer Consultants, Austin, 1993—; dir. ASHTA Group Holding, SAL. Author: The Dynamics of the Computer Industry: Modeling the Supply of Workstations and Their Components, 1993. Recipient engring. scholarship U. Tex., 1985, 86, 87 (nat. dean's list 1986, honor roll 1984, 85, 86); named to Golden Key Honor Soc., 1985. Mem. IEEE. Home: 11th St Rabieh, North Metn Lebanon Office: Geocel Internat LLC 14850 Montfort Dr Ste 250 Dallas TX 75240 also: ASHTA Group Holding SAL, Dora Ct Bldg, Dora Lebanon

TOUR, JAMES MITCHELL, chemistry and biochemistry educator; b. 1959; m. Shireen Tour; children: Ambreen, Sabrina, Josiah, Beniah. BS in Chemistry cum laude, Syracuse U., 1981; PhD in Organic Chemistry, Purdue U., 1986. Postdoctoral fellow in organomettalic chemistry U. Wis., Madison, 1986-87; NIH postdoctoral fellow in organic chemistry Stanford (Calif.) U., 1987-88; asst. prof. dept. chemistry and biochemistry U. S.C., Columbia, 1988-92, assoc. prof., 1992-94, prof.; cons. Albemarle Corp., Baton Rouge, 1990—; IBM vis. lectr. polymer divsn. Almaden Rsch. Ctr., 1988. Contbr. articles to profl. jours.; patentee in field. Grad. fellow Celanese Corp., 1981-82, IBM, 1985-86; grantee Office Naval Rsch., 1989-92, NSF, 1991-96, Exxon Ednl. Found., 1994. Mem. Am. Chem. Soc. (assoc. dir. polymer div. material sci. secretariat 1991—). Office: U SC Dept Chemistry and Biochemistry 730 Main St Columbia SC 29201

TOURTELLOTTE, MILLS CHARLTON, mechanical and electrical engineer; b. Great Falls, Mont., Dec. 16, 1922; s. Nathaniel Mills and Frances Victoria (Charlton) T.; m. Dorothy Elsie Gray, Sept. 16, 1947 (dec. 1994); children: Jane Tourtellotte Collins, Kathryn Tourtellotte Bauman, Thomas; m. Linda M. Merritt, July 1, 1995. B.S., Ill. Inst. Tech., 1947, M.S., 1952. Registered profl. engr., Ill., Mich., Tex. Engr., Automatic Electric Co., Chgo., 1947-49, Inland Steel Co., East Chicago, Ind., 1952-56; sr. project engr. Gulf States Tube div. Quanex Corp., Rosenberg, Tex., 1956—; fallout shelter analyst Fed. Emergency Mgmt., Washington, 1970—. Contbr. papers to tech. lit. Patentee mech. and elec. devices. Election judge Ft. Bend County Republican Party, 1965; chmn. 4H Adult Leaders Assn., 1968; song leader, tenor in choir local Methodist Ch. Named Friend of 4H, Ft. Bend County Extension Service, 1968; named Eagle Scout, Order of the Arrow, Boys Scouts Am., 1937. Mem. Nat. Soc. Profl. Engrs., ASME (life), Tex. Soc. Profl. Engrs. (edn. chmn. 1969), Fluid Power Soc., Am. Soc. for Engring. Edn. (industry chmn. 1969), Assn. Iron and Steel Engrs. (life), VFW (life, quartermaster 1984), Am. Legion. Office: Quanex Corp Gulf State Tube div PO Box 952 Rosenberg TX 77471-0952

TOUS DE TORRES, LUZ M., banker; b. San Juan, P.R., Apr. 23, 1944; d. Rafael Tous Cortes and Iris Fernos; BBA magna cum laude, U. P.R., 1965; MBA summa cum laude, Interam. U., 1976, also P.R. Sch. Banking, 1976; m. Manuel A. de Torres, Jr., Feb. 17, 1967; children: Rosa Iris, Lara Sofia. With Banco Popular, San Juan, 1965—, sr. v.p., corp. real estate adminstrn., 1987—. Co-founder P.R. Indsl. Editors Assn., pres., 1970-72; dir. bank's blood program for ARC, 1972—, dir. bank's personnel donors program United Fund, 1981—; trustee BPPR Found., 1986-87; dir. Greater San Juan Com., 1993, Codefin. Recipient Outstanding Acad. Achievement award Interam. U., 1976. Mem. Soc. Human Resources Mgmt. (accredited profl. in human resources), Am. Mgmt. Assn., Internat. Assn. Bus. Communicators, Internat. Facility Mgmt. Assn. (cert. facility mgr.), Internat. Assn. Corp. Real Estate Execs., Bldg. Owners Mgmt. Assn., Urban Land Inst., MOMA (N.Y.), Mus. Contemporary Art, Corp. Devel. Hato Rey Fin. Ctr., Puerto Rico 2000. Office: PO Box 362708 San Juan PR 00936-2708

TOWBIN, JEFFREY ALLEN, pediatric cardiologist, educator; b. N.Y.C., Apr. 12, 1952; s. Eugene and Selma Faith (Rosenthal) T.; m. Patricia Lynn Srebnik, June 14, 1975; children: Jennifer Amy, Sara Elizabeth. BS, U. Cin., 1974, MS, 1977, MD, 1982. Cert. pediatrics. Biochemist EPA, Cin., 1976-77; pediatric intern Children's Hosp. Med. Ctr., Cin., 1982-83, resident pediatrics, 1983-85; fellow pediatric cardiology Baylor Coll. Medicine, Houston, 1985-89, asst. prof. pediatrics, 1989-93, assoc. prof. pediatrics, 1993—; bd. dirs. Am. Heart Assn., Tex. Affiliate, Houston (Tex.) Divsn.; reviewer Jour. Pediatrics, 1990—, Circulation, 1993—. Contbr. chpts. to books. Recipient Grant-in-Aid, Am. Heart Assn., 1989, 90, 91-93, Clinician Investigator award grant NIH, 1990—, Richard D. Rowe award Soc. Pediatric Rsch., 1991. Fellow Am. Acad. Pediatrics (Young Investigator award 1993); mem. AAAS, Am. Soc. Human Genetics, N.Y. Acad. Scis., Sudden Arrhythmia Death Syndromes Found. (sci. adv. bd., bd. mem.). Office: Baylor Coll Medicine Pediat Cardiology 1 Baylor Plz Rm 333E Houston TX 77030-3411

TOWER, ALTON G., JR., pharmacist; b. Buffalo, N.Y., Jan. 16, 1927; m. Nan R. Spinner, Aug. 15, 1953; children: Adrienne, Michele, Renee. BS in Pharmacy, U. Buffalo, 1953. Registered pharmacist. Pharmacist Woldmans Drug Store, Buffalo, 1946-53; med. svc. rep. Strasenburgh Lab., Rochester, N.Y., 1953-66; pharmacist, mgr. Eckerd Drugs, Clearwater, Fla., 1966—. Bd. dirs. Am. Cancer Soc. Pinellas County, Fla., 1976—, pres., 1988-89, Life Saver award, 1988, life mem., 1995—, dir. cmty. affairs Pinellas Pharmacist Soc.; charter mem. Smoke Free Class of 2000, Pinellas County, 1988—. Recipient Vol. of Yr. award Am. Cancer Soc. Pinellas County, 1987, Life Saver award Am. Cancer Soc. Pinellas County, 1988, James Beal award Pharmacist of the Yr., Fla. Pharm. Assn., 1992; named Hon. Life Mem., Am. Cancer Soc. Pinellas County Unit, 1995. Mem. Am. Pharm. Assn., Fla. Pharmacy Assn. (bd. dirs. 1981-85, speaker ho. of dels. 1986, R.Q. Richards award 1989, Bowl of Hygeia award 1990, Sid Simkowitz Involvement award 1991), Pinellas County Pharmacy Soc. (life; dir. 1968-73, 78-81, 89-91, pres. 1973, 88, Pharmacist of Yr. 1973). Office: Eckerds # 2332 Pinellas Park FL 34666

TOWERY, CURTIS KENT, lawyer; b. Hugoton, Kans., Jan. 29, 1954; s. Clyde D. and Jo June (Curtis) T. BA, Trinity U., 1976; JD, U. Okla., 1979; LLM in Taxation, Boston U., 1989. Mem. Curtis & Blanton, Pauls Valley, Okla., 1980-81; lawyer land and legal dept. Trigg Drilling Co., Oklahoma City, 1981-82; adminstrv. law judge Okla. Corp. Commn., Oklahoma City, 1982-85; counsel Curtis & Blanton, Pauls Valley, Okla., 1985-88; adminstrv. law judge Okla. Dept. Mines, Oklahoma City, 1985-88, assoc. gen. counsel, 1989-92; contracts and purchasing adminstr., atty. Okla. Turnpike Authority, Oklahoma City, 1992-93; asst. gen. counsel Okla. Corp. Commn., 1993—; bd. dirs. First Nat. Bank Pauls Valley, 1983-88. Assoc. bd. Okla. Mus. Art, 1985-88, Okla. Symphony Orch., 1987-92; assoc. bd. Ballet Okla., 1987-92, sec., 1990-91, v.p., 1988-89. Mem. ABA, Okla. Bar Assn., Am. Assn. Petroleum Landmen, Internat. Assn. Energy Economists, Men's Dinner Club, Faculty House, Rotary, Elks, Phi Alpha Delta, Sigma Nu. Democrat. Presbyterian. Home: PO Box 14891 Oklahoma City OK 73113-0891 Office: Jim Thorpe Bldg 2101 N Lincoln Blvd Oklahoma City OK 73105-4904

TOWNE, ALAN RAYMOND, neurologist, educator; b. Malden, Mass., July 9, 1948; s. Allen Newman and Carmelia (Foskin) T.; m. Elizabeth Ann Hull. BA, Hobart Coll., 1970; Cert. d'etudes in French Lit., U. d'Anger, France, 1972; MD with honors, U. Aix-Marseille, France, 1981. Diplomate Am. Bd. Psychiatry and Neurology; lic. MD, Va. Intern in neurology Hosp. Ste. Anne, Toulon, France, 1979-80; fellow in neuroimaging and neurophysiology U. Aix-Marseille, France, 1980-81; rotating intern Med. Coll. Va., Richmond, 1981-82, resident in neurology, chief resident in neurology, 1982-85, 84-85, fellow in neurophysiology, 1985-86, asst. prof. neurology dept. neurology, 1986-94, assoc. prof. neurology, 1994—, co-dir. clin. neurophysiology labs., 1994—, dir. ambulatory EEG svc. monitoring lab., 1988—, attending physician epilepsy monitoring unit, 1988—, dir. status epilepticus rsch. program, 1988—; chmn. dept. neurology residency recruitment program Med. Coll. of Va., 1989—; guest reviewer Epilepsia; guest lectr. in field. Contbr. articles to profl. publs. and chpts. to books. Usher com. Episcopal Ch. of the Redemmer, 1988—, spl. events com., 1992—; organizing com. Boy Scouts Am., Robert E. Lee Coun., 1992; com. chmn. Pack 811, Boy Scouts Am., 1992—. Grantee Abbott Labs., 1990, 92-93, 91-93, 92—, Burrough Wellcome, 1989-90, 90—, Janssen Rsch. Found., 1989-91, Merrell Dow Pharms. Inc., 1990-92, Marion Merrell Dow, 1991-92, 92—, Carter-Wallace Labs., 1992-93, 92—, Dainippon Pharm. Co., 1993—, NIH, 1987—. Mem. Am. Assn. for Study of Headache, Am. Acad. Neurology, Richmond Acad. Medicine, Am. Epilepsy Soc., Va. Neurol. Soc., Soc. for Neurosci., Am. Electroencephalographic Soc., Am. Acad. Clin. Neurophysiology. Episcopalian. Home: 10103 Cutter Dr Richmond VA 23235 Office: Va Commonwealth U Med Coll Va Dept Neurology Box 599 Richmond VA 23298

TOWNES, ANDREW W., JR., allergist, immunologist, pediatrician; b. Birmingham, Ala., 1922. MD, U. Va. Diplomate Am. Bd. Allergy and Immunology, Am. Bd. Pediatrics. Rotating intern U. Ala. Hosp./Vanderbilt U., 1948-49, 49-50; resident in pediatrics Va. Hosp., 1950-51; mem. sr. staff Orlando (Fla.) Regional Med. Ctr., 1951—. Vol. Coalition of the Homeless. Office: 414 N Mills Ave Orlando FL 32803

TOWNLEY, LINDA ROSE, financial analyst; b. Gainesville, Ga., Nov. 15, 1947; d. Herbert William and Bobbie (Talley) Goswick; children: Seth, Shelly, Audra. AS, Young Harris Coll., Ga., 1967; BS, North Ga. Coll., 1969. With Lockheed Aero. Sys. Corp., Marietta, Ga., 1969—, bus. mgmt. analyst, 1976—. Mayor City of Dawsonville, Ga., 1988-90; mem. Dawson County Sch. Bd.; bd. dirs. Ga. Mountains Area Planning Devel. Commn., 1988-90, Regional Planning Commn., Etowah Water and Sewer Authority, 1990—. Mem. Nat. Mgmt. Assn., Soc. Cost Estimating and Analysis (sec. bd. dirs.), Ga. Mcpl. Assn. (3d v.p., bd. dirs. 1989), Women in Govt. Club. Baptist. Home: 188 Stegall Pl Dawsonville GA 30534 Office: Lockheed Aero Sys Corp Zone 0095 86 S Cobb Dr # 8A Marietta GA 30063-1000

TOWNSEND, ALAN JEROME, biochemistry educator, pharmacology researcher; b. Decatur, Ga., June 16, 1952; s. Jerry Benson and Jean (Crump) T.; m. Teven Ann Harmon, Aug. 25, 1984; children: Kyle Garrett, Tyler Scott. AAS, St. Petersburg Jr. Coll., 1972; BS in Chemistry, U. South Fla., 1974; PhD, U. N.C., 1986. Clin. chemistry technologist Bayfront Med. Ctr., St. Petersburg, Fla., 1975-76; clin. chemistry technologist Meml. Hops., Chapel Hill, N.C., 1976-78, instrumentation specialist, 1978-79; fellow in biotech. Nat. Cancer Inst. NIH, 1986-90; assoc. prof. biochemistry Bowman-Gray Sch. Medicine, Winston-Salem, N.C., 1990—; cons. tech. transfer Oncor, Inc., Rockville, Md., 1990—, Terrapin Techs., San Francisco, 1993—; grant reviewer small bus. innovation and rsch. program Nat. Inst. Environ. Health Scis., 1991—. Reviewer Cancer Rsch., Biochemical Pharmacology, Molecular Pharmacology, Cancer Comm.; contbr. articles, abstracts to profl. jours. Grantee NIH Biomed. Rsch. Support, 1991-92, Leukemia Rsch. Found., 1991, 93, N.C. Biotech. Rsch. Ctr., 1991-92, NIH, 1992-94, 94-97. Mem. AAAS, Am. Soc. Biochemistry and Molecular Biology, Am. Assn. Cancer Rsch., Genotoxicity and Environmental Mutagenesis Soc. Democrat. Unitarian. Office: Bowman Gray Sch Medicine Medical Center Blvd Winston Salem NC 27157

TOWNSEND, CATHERINE ANNE MORGAN, information specialist; b. Mobile, Ala., June 6, 1944; d. Thomas Wendell and Catherine Light (Richmond) Morgan; m. Frank Covington Townsend, Dec. 18, 1966. BS in Edn., Auburn U., 1966; MLS, U. N.C., 1972; MEd, Clemson U., 1980; Specialist Libr. and Info. Sci., U. S.C., 1989. Asst. libr. Piedmont Tech. Coll., Greenwood, S.C., 1967-69; libr. Cen. Intermediate Sch., Greenwood, 1971-73, Cambridge Acad., Greenwood, 1973-89; media specialist McCormick (S.C.) Pub. Schs., 1989-94; humanities resource cons. Rural Edn. Alliance for Collaborative Humanities, 1990-93; chair Greenwood Cmty. Info. Network Task Force, 1993-95; CEO, owner Applied InterNet Solutions, Greenwood, S.C., 1995—; workshop cons. Polaris Grant-Seeking Workshops, 1994-95; Internet cons. Applied Internet Solutions, 1995—. Contbr. articles to profl. jours. Mem. S.C. Libr. Assn. (chmn. sch. libr. sect. 1981-82, 2d v.p. membership chair 1985-86, chmn. planning com. 1989-90), Assn. for Ednl. Comm. and Tech. of S.C. (rep. to state planning com. 1989, pres. 1986-87), regional bd. dirs. 1980-82). Home: 327 Callison Rd Ninety Six SC 29666-9590 Office: Applied InterNet Solutions Greenwood SC 29646

TOWNSEND, DAVID LEE, public relations executive; b. Wilmington, Del., Feb. 20, 1954; s. Carlos L. and Doris M. (Catts) T.; m. Lynn Rice, May 29, 1982; children: Paige, Alexander. BA, U. Del., 1976. Pub. rels. rep. Jim Walter Corp., Tampa, Fla., 1978-80, mgr. pub. rels., 1980-82, dir. pub. rels., 1982-83, v.p. pub. rels., 1983-88; v.p. pub. rels. Walter Industries, Inc., Tampa, 1988-94, v.p. human resources and pub. rels., 1994-96, v.p. adminstrn., 1996—. Selected Participant Leadership Tampa, 1982, Participant Leadership Tampa Bay, 1993. Recipient Tampa Bay Up and Comers award Price Waterhouse/Tampa Bay Bus. Jour., 1986. Mem. Pub. Rels. Soc. Am. (pres. Tampa Bay chpt. 1986), Nat. Investor Rels. Inst., Leadership Tampa Alumni, Com. 100, Greater Tampa C. of C. Office: Walter Industries Inc 1500 N Dale Mabry Hwy Tampa FL 33607-2551

TOWNSEND, FRANK MARION, pathology educator; b. Stamford, Tex., Oct. 29, 1914; s. Frank M. and Beatrice (House) T.; m. Gerda Eberlein, 1940 (dec. div. 1944); 1 son, Frank M.; m. Ann Graf, Aug. 25, 1951; 1 son, Robert N. Student, San Antonio Coll., 1931-32, U. Tex., 1932-34; MD, Tulane U., 1938. Diplomate: Am. Bd. Pathology. Intern Polyclinic Hosp., N.Y.C., 1939-40; commd. 1st lt. M.C., U.S. Army, 1940, advanced through grades to lt. col., 1946; resident instr. pathology Washington U., 1945-47; trans. to USAF, 1949, advanced through grades to col., 1956; instr. pathology Coll. Medicine, U. Nebr., 1947-48; asso. pathologist Scott and White Clinic, Temple, Tex., 1948-49; asso. prof. pathology Med. Br. U. Tex., Galveston, 1949-59; flight surgeon USAF, 1950-65; dir. labs. USAF Hosp. (now Wilford Hall USAF Hosp.), Lackland AFB, Tex., 1950-54; cons. pathology Office of Surgeon Gen. Hdqrs. USAF, Washington, 1954-63, chief cons. group Office of Surgeon Gen. Hdqrs., 1954-55; dep. dir. Armed Forces Inst. Pathology, Washington, 1955-59; dir. Armed Forces Inst. Pathology, 1959-63; vice comdr. aerospace med. divsn. Air Force Systems Command, 1963-65; ret., 1965; practice medicine specializing in pathology San Antonio, 1965—; dir. labs. San Antonio State Chest Hosp.; consulting pathologist Tex. Dept. Health hosps., 1965-72; clin. prof. pathology U. Tex. Med. Sch., San Antonio, 1969-72; prof., chmn. dept. pathology Health Sci. Ctr. U. Tex. Med. Sch., 1972-86, emeritus chmn., prof., 1986—; cons. U. Tex. Cancer Ctr.-M.D. Anderson Hosp., 1966-80, NASA, 1967-75; mem. adv. bd. cancer WHO, 1958-75; mem. Armed Forces Epidemiology Bd., 1983-91; bd. govs. Armed Forces Inst. Pathology, 1984-95. Mem. editorial bd. Tex. Med. Jour., 1978-86; contbr. articles to med. jours. Mem. adv. coun. Civil War Centennial Commn., 1960-65; bd. dirs. Alamo Area Sci. Fair, 1967-73. Decorated D.S.M., Legion of Merit; recipient Founders medal Assn. Mil. Surgeons, 1961. Recipient Comdr.'s award Armed Forces Epidemiol. Bd., 1990; F.M. Townsend Chair of Pathology endowed in his honor by faculty of Dept. Pathology, U. Tex. Health Sci. Ctr., 1987. Fellow ACP, Coll. Am. Pathologists (edn. advisor on accreditation, commr. lab. accreditation South Ctrl. States region 1971-84), Am. Soc. Clin. Pathologists (Ward Burdick award 1983), Aerospace Med. Assn. (H.G. Mosely award 1962); mem. AMA, AAAS, Tex. Med. Assn., Internat. Acad. Aviation and Space Medicine, Tex. Soc. Pathologists (Caldwell award 1971), Am. Assn. Pathologists, Internat. Acad. Pathology, Acad. Clin. Lab. Physicians and Scientists, Soc. Med. Cons. to Armed Forces, Torch Club. Home: PO Box 77 Harwood TX 78632-0077 Office: U Tex Health Sci Ctr Dept Pathology 7703 Floyd Curl Dr San Antonio TX 78284-7750

TOWNSEND, GAVIN EDWARD, art history educator; b. Santa Monica, Calif., June 16, 1956; s. Richard Edward and Ruth (Greene) T.; m. Bonnie Beth Bickford, Aug. 29, 1981; 1 child, Evan Edward. BA, Hamilton Coll., 1978; MA, U. Calif., Santa Barbara, 1981, PhD, 1986. Teaching asst. U. Calif., Santa Barbara, 1979-86, asst. curator Archtl. Drawing Collection, 1982-86; coord. Art Gallery U. Tenn., Chattanooga, 1986-93, asst. prof. dept. art, 1992—, assoc. prof., 1993—, asst. dir. Univ. Honors Program, 1992—. Contbr. articles to profl. jours. Chair Hist. Zoning Commn., Chattanooga, 1993—. Kress Found. fellow, 1982-83; N.Y. State Regents scholar, 1974-78. Mem. Soc. Archtl. Historians, Coll. Art Assn. Office: U Tenn Dept Art 615 Mccallie Ave Chattanooga TN 37403-2504

TOWNSEND, HEATHER MARIE, family nurse practitioner; b. Waukegan, Ill., Apr. 9, 1963; d. Henry Delano and Geneva May (Mitchell) Overby; m. Robert E. Townsend, Aug. 8, 1988; 1 child, Robert E. II. BSN magna cum laude, Columbus Coll., 1991; MSN summa cum laude, Emory U., 1995. RN, Ga.; cert. family nurse practitioner; cert. BLS, ACLS. Supr. Columbus (Ga.) Emergency Ctr., 1986-89; CCU nurse Doctors Hosp., Columbus, 1991-95; intern in internal medicine Martin Army Cmty. Hosp., Ft. Benning, Ga.; intern in family practice Hamilton (Ga.) Family Practice Ctr.; family nurse practitioner Cmty. Healthcare system Columbus Regional Healthcare System, 1995—; family nurse practitioner Opportunity Breakthrough, 1995—; preceptor coord. advisor Three Rivers Area Health Edn. Ctr., 1996—; sch. health advisor Talbot County, 1996—; cons. Nat. Student Nurses Assn., 1990-91, Alcohol and Drug Panel, Columbus, 1990. Active Concerned Citizens Columbus, 1989-91; chair Code 99 (Blue) Com., 1993-95. Recipient Spirit of Nursing award Army Nurse Corps, 1991, Nat. Health Svc. Core award, 1996—. Mem. ANA-PAC, Ga. Nurses Assn., Columbus Coll. Nursing Honor Soc., Sigma Theta Tau, Phi Kappa Phi, Phi Eta Sigma. Home: 2935 Hatcher Dr Columbus GA 31907-2157 Office: Columbus Regional Healthcare 707 Center St Columbus GA 31901-1547

TOWNSEND, HORRELL, III, obstetrician, gynecologist; b. Sikeston, Mo., Aug. 30, 1956; s. Horrell Henderson Jr. and Norma Nadine (Steward) T. BS in Biology, Southeast Mo. State U., 1977; DO, Kirksville Coll. Osteopathy, 1981. Intern then resident Normandy Osteo. Hosps., St. Louis, 1981-86; Staff physician Coastal Family Health Ctr., Gulfport, Miss., 1986-92; Locum Tenens physician Jackson & Coker, Denver, 1993; physician Mary Breckinridge Healthcare, Hyden, Ky., 1994—. Recipient Gold Medal award Hosp. Assn. Met. St. Louis, 1985. Mem. Am. Osteopathic Assn. Methodist. Office: Kate Ireland Womens Healthcare Ctr 100 Hosp Dr Hyden KY 41749

TOWNSEND, IRENE FOGLEMAN, accountant, tax specialist; b. Birmingham, Ala., May 29, 1932; d. James Woods and Virginia (Martin) Fogleman; m. Kenneth Ross Townsend, Mar. 18, 1951; children: Marietta Irene, Martha Shapard, Kenneth Ross Jr., Elizabeth Buchanan. BSBA, East Carolina U., 1980. CPA, N.C., Va. Acct. Norwood P. Whitehurst & Assocs., Greenville, N.C., 1981-86; asst. v.p. Tenet Healthcare Corp., Vienna, Va., 1995—. Fellow AICPA, N.C. Assn. CPAs, D.C. Inst. CPAs, Va. Soc. CPAs; mem. DAR, N.C. Soc. Daus. of Colonial Wars, Colonial Dames 17th Century. Democrat. Episcopalian (lay reader, chalice bearer). Home: 2521 Paxton St Lakeridge VA 22192-3414 Office: Tenet Healthcare Corp Ste 333 501 Church St NE Vienna VA 22180-4734

TOWNSEND, JAMES WILLIS, computer scientist; b. Evansville, Ind., Sept. 9, 1936; s. James Franklin and Elma Elizabeth (Galloway) T.; m. Leona Jean York, Apr. 20, 1958; 1 child, Eric Wayne. BS in Arts and Scis., Ball State U., 1962; PhD, Iowa State U., 1970. Rsch. technologist Neuromuscular div. Mead Johnson, Evansville, 1957-60; chief instr. Zoology dept. Iowa State U., Ames, 1965-67; asst. prof. Ind. State U., Evansville, 1967-72; cons. electron microscopy Mead Johnson Rsch. Ctr., Evansville, 1971-73; mgr. neurosci. Neurosci. Lab., Kans. State U., Manhattan, 1974-76; head electron microscopy Nat. Ctr. for Toxicology Rsch., Jefferson, Ark., 1976-82; dir. electron microscopy U. Ark. Med. Sci., Little Rock, 1982-87; dir. computer ops. pathology dept. Univ. Hosp., Little Rock, 1987—; workshop presenter Am. Soc. Clin. Pathology, 1980-81, Nat. Soc. Histotechnologists, 1984-88. With USAF, 1957. Contbr. articles to profl. jours.; reviewer Scanning Electron Microscopy, 1977-78. Nat. Def. fellowship NDEA, Iowa State U., 1962-65; recipient Chgo. Tribune award Chicago Tribune, 1955. Mem. Sigma Xi, Sigma Zeta. Baptist. Home: 4 Breeds Hill Ct Little Rock AR 72211-2514 Office: Univ Ark for Med Sci Dept Pathology Slot 517 4301 W Markham St Little Rock AR 72205-7101

TOWNSEND, JERRIE LYNNE, environmental services administrator; b. Pine Bluff, Ark., July 19, 1951; d. Charles Ray Sr. and Billie Jean (Morgan) Jones; m. Dennis Ewell Townsend, June 15, 1975 (dec. June 1980). BS, Ark. State U., 1973; MLIS, U. Okla., 1987. Cert. profl. sec. Sec. divsn. art Ark. State U., Jonesboro, 1973-74; adminstrv. sec. Steelship Corp., Pine Bluff, Ark., 1974; tchr. 5th grade Coleman Middle Sch., Pine Bluff, Ark., 1974-75; sec. I Mgmt. Devel. Ctr. U. Tulsa, Okla., 1975-76; sec. II City of Tulsa, 1976-78, adminstrv. sec., 1978-80; exec. sec. Hilti, Inc., Tulsa, 1980, statis. asst., 1980-82, sales promotion, mktg. analyst, 1982-87, mngr. sales planning, 1987-96; owner Townsend Environ. Solutions, Broken Arrow, Okla., 1996—. Mem. Citizens' Com. MTTA/City of Broken Arrow (Okla.) Bus Svc., 1977-79, Office Sci. Adv. Com. Tulsa Jr. Coll., 1980-83, Civic Ctr. Com., Broken Arrow, 1988-90, Broken Arrow City Coun., 1990—, Spl. Transp. Adv. Com., Tulsa, 1995-96; pres. Friends of Broken Arrow Libr., 1984-85; bd. dirs. Indian Nation Coun. Govts., Tulsa, 1992—; sec. bd. trustees Broken Arrow Cmty. Playhouse, 1992-94; vice mayor Broken Arrow, 1993—; v.p. Broken Arrow Hist. Soc., 1992-93, pres., 1994-95; libr. Broken Arrow Geneal. Soc., 1985, sec. 1992-94. Named Competent Toastmaster, Out-to-Lunch Toastmasters, Tulsa, 1985; elected to Broken Arrow Hall of Fame, 1996. Mem. Profl. Secs. Internat. (rec. sec. Tulsa chpt. 1979-80, pres. 1980-81, Outstanding Mem. of Yr. 1983). Democrat. Southern Baptist.

TOWNSEND, KENNETH ROSS, retired priest; b. Holly Grove, Ala., Oct. 31, 1927; s. James Ernest and Mary H. (Jordan) T.; m. Irene Fogleman, Mar. 18, 1951; children; Marietta, Martha, Kenneth Ross, Elizabeth. AB, Birmingham South Coll., 1956; postgrad., Union Theol. Sem., 1960-63; MDiv, Va. Theol. Sem., 1964. Ordained priest Episcopal Ch., 1965. Pastor meth. chs. N.C. and Va. Confs., 1954-63; priest Bath Priest Parish, Dinwiddie, Va., 1964-69, St. Paul's Ch., Vanceboro, N.C., 1969-89; ret., 1989; lectr. philosophy Richard Bland Coll. of Coll. William and Mary, Williamsburg, Va., 1966-68; del. to synod Province IV, 1973; mem. liturgical com. Episcopal Diocese of East Carolina, Wilmington, N.C., 1971-82, mem. prison commn., 1984. Writer, painter. With USNR, 1945-46. Mem. Delta Sigma Phi. Home: 2521 Paxton St Lake Ridge Woodbridge VA 22192

TOWNSEND, LINDA LADD, mental health nurse; b. Louisville, Apr. 26, 1948; d. Samuel Clyde and Mary Elizabeth (Denton) Ladd; m. Stanley Allen Oliver, June 7, 1970 (div. 1978); 1 child, Aaron; m. Warren Terry Townsend Jr., Jan. 1, 1979; children: Mark, Amy, Sarah. Student, Catherine Spalding Coll., 1966-67; BSN, Murray State U., 1970; MS in Psychiat./Mental Health Nursing, Tex. Woman's U., 1976. RN, Tex., Ky.; lic. advanced nurse practitioner, profl. counselor, marriage and family therapist, Tex.; cert. group psychotherapist. Charge nurse med. and pediatric units Murray (Ky.)-Calloway County Hosp., 1970-71; team leader surg./renal transplant unit VA Hosp., Nashville, 1971-73; team leader, charge nurse gen. med.-surg. unit Providence Hosp., Waco, Tex., 1973-74; outpatient therapist Mental Hygiene Clinic, Ft. Hood, Tex., 1975-76; outpatient nurse therapist Ctrl. Counties Ctr. for Mental Health/Mental Retardation, Copperas Cove & Lampasas, Tex., 1977-80; psychiat. nurse clin. specialist, marriage/family therapist Profl. Counseling Svc., Copperas Cove, 1979—; cons. Metroplex Hosp. and Pavilion, Killeen, Tex., 1980—. Founding mem. Family Outreach of Coryell County, Copperas Cove, 1986—, also past pres. and past sec.; founding mem. Partnership for a Drug and Violence-Free Copperas Cove; vol. music therapist Windcrest Nursing Ctr.; advocate Tex. Peer Assistance Program for Nurses; active Walk to Emmaus, 1993. Recipient Mary M. Roberts Writing award Am. Jour. of Nursing, 1970; named Mem. of Yr.-Vol., Family Outreach of Coryell County. Mem. ANA (cert. clin. specialist in adult psychiat. and mental health nursing, cert. clin. specialist in child and adolescent psychiat. and mental health nursing), AAUW (v.p. for membership, past bd. dirs., sec.-treas.), Tex. Nurses Assn., Am. Group Psychotherapy Assn. (cert.), Learning Disabilities Assn., Inst. for Humanities at Salado, Sigma Theta Tau. Democrat. Methodist. Home: RR 1 Box 253-E Kempner TX 76539-9502 Office: Profl Counseling Svc 806 E Avenue D Ste F Copperas Cove TX 76522-2231

TOWNSEND, MILES AVERILL, aerospace and mechanical engineering educator; b. Buffalo, N.Y., Apr. 16, 1935; s. Francis Devere and Sylvia (Wolpa) T.; children: Kathleen Townsend Hastings, Melissa, Stephen, Joel, Philip. BA, Stanford U., 1955; BS MechE, U. Mich., 1958; advanced cert., U. Ill., 1963, MS in Theoretical and Applied Mechanics, 1967; PhD, U. Wis., 1971. Registered profl. engr., Ill., Wis., Tenn., Ont. Project engr. Sundstrand, Rockford, Ill., 1959-63, Twin Disc Inc., Rockford, 1963-65, 67-68; sr. engr. Westinghouse Electric Corp., Sunnyvale, Calif., 1965-67; instr., fellow U. Wis., Madison, 1968-71; assoc. prof. U. Toronto, Ont., Can., 1971-74; prof. mech. engring. Vanderbilt U., Nashville, 1974-81; Wilson prof. mech. and aerospace engring. U. Va., Charlottesville, 1982—, chmn. dept., 1982-91; ptnr., v.p. Endev Ltd., Can. and U.S., 1972—; cons. in field. Contbr. numerous articles to profl. jours.; 7 patents in field. Recipient numerous research grants and contracts. Fellow ASME (mem. coun. on engring., productivity com., tech. editor Jour. Mech. Design); mem. AAAS, N.Y. Acad. Scis., Sigma Xi, Phi Kappa Phi, Pi Tau Sigma. Home: 221 Harvest Dr Charlottesville VA 22903-4850 Office: U Va Dept Mech and Aerospace Engring Thornton Hall Charlottesville VA 22903-2442

TOWNSEND, RICHARD MARVIN, government insurance executive, city manager, consultant; b. White Plains, N.Y., Dec. 28, 1933; s. Benjamin Richter and Frances (Mills) T.; m. Joanne Schwartz; children: Drue, Brent, Merric. BA, Cornell U., 1955, MPA with distinction, 1956. Adminstrv. aide, analyst City of Corpus Christi, Tex., 1956-58, budget and rsch. analyst, 1958-59, adminstrv. asst. III, 1959-60, asst. city mgr., 1960-67, city mgr., 1968-81; city mgr. City of Laredo, Tex., 1982-89; dep. dir. Tex. Mcpl. League Intergovtl. Risk Pool, Austin, 1990-91, exec. dir., 1991—; facilitator Future of a Region Conf., San Antonio, 1986. Contbr. articles to profl. jours. Mem. mobile home performance bd. State of Tex., Austin, 1971-76; bd. dirs. Legend Oaks Homeowners Assn., Austin, 1992—, United Way Bd., Laredo, 1984-89. Named one of Outstanding Young Men of Am., Corpus Christi Jr. C. of C., 1968. Mem. ASPA, Tex. City Mgmt. Assn. (pres. 1988), Internat. City Mgmt. Assn., Phi Kappa Phi. Home: 8008 Isaac Pryor Dr Austin TX 78749-1862 Office: 1821 Rutherford Ln Austin TX 78754

TOWNSEND, WILLIAM JACKSON, lawyer; b. Grayson, Ky., June 4, 1932; s. Robert Glenn and Lois Juanita (Jackson) T. BS, Wake Forest U., 1954; Student U. Ky., 1957, U. Louisville, 1958, U. N.C., 1960. Bar: N.C. 1965. Claims adjuster State Farm Ins. Co., 1963; sole practice, Fayetteville, N.C., 1965—; pub. adminstr. Robeson County, N.C., 1966; dir., treas. Colonial Foods, Inc., St. Paul, N.C., 1959—; tax atty. City of Lumberton, 1966-67 . Served as 1st lt. U.S. Army, 1954-56. Mem. N.C. Bar Assn., N.C. State Bar, Cumberland County Bar Assn., N.C. Bar Assn., Scabbard and Blade (pres.), Delta Theta Phi. Presbyterian. Club: Kiwanis (treas. Fayetteville 1973-82). Office: PO Box 584 2109 Elvira St 806 Fayetteville NC 28303

TOYNE, MARGUERITE CASTLES, management consultant, business executive; b. Batesburg, S.C., Jan. 7, 1942; d. Hal Ross and Myrtle (McKeown) Castles; children: Susanne Marguerite, Ross Brian. BA, U. S. Fla., 1970; M Bus. Edn., Ga. State U., 1971, PhD, 1974. Bookkeeper Erlangen (Fed. Republic Germany) Rod and Gun Club, 1964, Inmark, Inc., Kensington, Md., 1968; evening instr. DeKalb Tech. Sch., Clarkston, Ga., 1971; grad. instr. Ga. State U., Atlanta, 1972; instr. DeKalb Community Coll., Clarkston, 1974; mgmt. cons. Mescon, Inc., Atlanta, 1974-75; chair dept. bus. and econs., founder adv. bd. for dept. Columbia (S.C.) Coll., 1975-79; dir. mgmt., edn. and tng. programs Office Textile and Apparel, Dept. Commerce, Washington, 1979-82; sales support, nat. account exec. AT&T Info. Systems, 1982-85; pres. Bus. Resource Network, Atlanta, 1985—, The Toyne Group, 1990—; cons. orgn. design tng. programs, strategic planning for human resource devel.; planner, organizer, leader seminars, workshops for women in mgmt., 1975-78; cons. state and local govt., ednl. TV; leader presentations U.S.C., Columbia Coll., Ga. Vocat. Assn., Ga. Libr. Assn., others; speaker ann. mtg. Internat. Alliance, Emory U., ann. conf. Soc. for Info. Mgmt. Contbr. articles to profl. publs. V.p. liaison Am. Field Svc.; del. Internat. Community Conf., Cali, Colombia, 1978; mem. pub. ednl. workgroup task force S.C. Heart Assn., 1978—; mem. S.C. exec. com. Internat. Women's Yr., 1977; bd. dirs. Coun. on Battered Women, One Peachtree Battle Townhouses, Ga. Exec. Women's Network. Recipient awards S.C. Ednl. Resources Found., 1977, United Fund, others; named one of Outstanding Young Women Am., 1976; fellow NDEA, 1971-74, faculty forum fellow Exxon Corp., Houston, 1976; grantee AID, 1978. Mem. Columbia Sales and Mktg. Execs. (v.p. 1978-79, bd. dirs., fun raising com.), Ga. Exec. Women's Network (bd. dirs.), Am. Bus. Communication Assn. (nat. bus. practice and problems com. 1975), Am. Soc. Tng. and Devel., Data Processing Mgmt. Assn., Am. Mtg. Assn., Assn. Computing Machinery, Ptnrs. of the Ams., Bus. and Profl. Women's Assn., Coldstream Country Club (bd. govs.), Kappa Delta Pi, Delta Pi Epsilon. Home: One Peachtree Battle Ave NW Townhouse 14 Atlanta GA 30305-4109

TRACHTENBERG, DAVID, lawyer; b. Wurtsboro, N.Y., Apr. 4, 1925; s. Jacob and Frieda (Rossis) T.; m. Selma Harris, May 27, 1945; children: Carl Harris, Bruce Sheldon. BA summa cum laude, Hartwick Coll., 1944; MA, SUNY, Albany, 1947; EdD, NYU, 1973; JD with honors, U. Fla., 1982. Bar: Fla. 1983. Tchr. Latin and social studies Greenville (N.Y.) Cen. Sch., 1947-49; tchr. secondary social studies Middletown (N.Y.) High Sch., 1949-59, guidance counselor, 1959-61; dir. sch. improvement Enlarged City Sch. Dist. City of Middletown, 1961-64, dir. fed. programs, 1965-68, dir. instrn., 1968-70, asst. supt. instrn., 1970-80; asst. prof. edn. SUNY, New Paltz, 1964-65; staff atty. Fla. 4th Dist. Ct. Appeal, West Palm Beach, 1983-86, sr. staff atty., 1986-89, career staff atty., 1989-93. Co-author: The Nongraded School, 1965; rsch. editor U. Fla. Law Rev., 1981-82; contbr. articles to profl. publs. Bd. dirs. Regional Religious Sch., 1993—, Regional Cmty. Action Program, Orange County, N.Y., 1964-67, Temple Beth Tikvah, 1991—, v.p., 1993—; pres. Middletown Day Nursery Assn., 1978-79; rec. sec. Lake Worth (Fla.) Jewish Ctr., 1984-91. With U.S. Army, 1943-46, ETO. Decorated Bronze Star, Purple Heart. Mem. The Fla. Bar, Order of Coif, Phi Kappa Phi. Democrat.

TRACHTMAN, JERRY H., lawyer; b. Phila., Aug. 10, 1945. BSEE, Pa. State U., 1967; JD, U. Fla., 1976. Bar: Fla. 1976, U.S. Dist. Ct. (mid. dist.) Fla. 1978, U.S. Supreme Ct. 1980, U.S. Ct. Appeals (11th cir.) 1989; cert. aviation law. Elec. engr. N.Am. Aviation, Columbus, Ohio, 1967-68; Apollo spacecraft systems engr. N.Am. Aviation, Kennedy Space Ctr., Fla., 1968-71; Skylab project engr. Martin Marietta, Kennedy Space Ctr., 1971-74; pvt. practice Satellite Beach, Fla., 1976-80; atty., mng. ptnr. Trachtman and Henderson, P.A., Melbourne, Fla., 1980—; adj. prof. aviation law Fla. Inst. Tech., Melbourne, 1983-90; mem. adv. bd. Kaiser Coll., Melbourne, 1994—. Recipient Apollo achievement award NASA. Mem. ATLA, Fla. Bar Assn. (chmn. aviation law com. 1995, vice chmn. 1993-95), Lawyer-Pilots Bar Assn., NTSB Bar Assn. (founder 1984—), Acad. Fla. Trial Lawyers. Office: 1990 W New Haven Ave Ste 201 Melbourne FL 32904-3923

TRACY, ALOISE See **SHOENIGHT, PAULINE ALOISE SOUERS**

TRACY, BARBARA MARIE, lawyer; b. Mpls., Oct. 13, 1945; d. Thomas A. and Ruth C. (Roby) T. BA, U. Minn., 1971; JD, U. Okla., 1980. Bar: Okla. 1980, U.S. Dist. Ct. (we. dist.) Okla. 1980, U.S. Dist. Ct. (no. dist.) Tex. 1991, U.S. Supreme Ct. 1988, U.S. Dist. Ct. (ea. dist.) Tex. 1995. Assoc. Pierce, Couch, Hendrickson, Johnston & Baysinger, Oklahoma City, 1980-82; ptnr. Rizley & Tracy, Sayre, Okla., 1982-84; pvt. practice Oklahoma City, 1984-90; gen. atty. U.S. Army Corps Engrs., Ft. Worth, 1991—. Mem. citizens adv. bd. O'Donoghue Rehab. Inst., Oklahoma City. Mem. ABA, Okla. Bar Assn., Fed. Bar Assn., Internat. Tng. in Commn. (pres. Ace Club chpt.). Democrat. Roman Catholic. Office: 819 Taylor St Fort Worth TX 76102-6114

TRACY, J. DAVID, lawyer, educator; b. Ft. Worth, Jan. 1, 1946; s. Dennis Ford and Virginia Eloise (Hall) T.; m. Jeral Ann Wilson, June 3, 1967; children: Bradley Wilson, Jennifer Diann. BA with honors, U. Tex., Austin, 1968, JD, 1970; LLM, So. Meth. U., 1971. Bar: Tex. 1971, U.S. Tax Ct. 1971, U.S. Ct. Appeals (5th cir.) 1976, U.S. Supreme Ct. 1978; cert. in estate planning, probate and tax law Tex. Bd. Legal Specialization. ptnr., Tracy & Holland L.L.P., Fort Worth, Tex.; bd. dirs. Ft. Worth Conv. and Vis. Bur., sec., 1987-89; adj. prof. advanced corp. taxation So. Meth. U., 1975-77; lectr. continuing legal edn.; council mem. real estate, probate and trust law sect. State Bar Tex., 1983-87; newsletter editor 1987-89, chmn., 1991-92; mem. Coll. State Bar Tex., tax law adv. commn. Tex. Bd. Legal Specialization, 1987—. Mem. adv. bd. dirs. Tarrant County Conv. Ctr., 1983-89, chmn. 1986-87. Named Outstanding Young Lawyer of Tarrant County, Tarrant County Young Lawyers Assn., 1982. Fellow Am. Coll. Trust and Estate Counsel, Tex. Bar Found.; mem. ABA, Phi Delta Phi, Ft. Worth Club, Colonial Country Club. Contbr. articles to law jours. Presbyterian. Office: 306 W 7th St Ste 500 Fort Worth TX 76102-4982

TRACY, LOIS BARTLETT, painter; b. Jackson, Mich., Dec. 9, 1901; d. James Elwood and Nellie (Allen) Bartlett; m. Donald Lockwood Walker, Sept. 20, 1923 (div. Sept. 1931); 1 child, Donald Lockwood Walker; m. Harry Herbert Tracy, Sept. 21, 1931; 1 child, Nathan Bartlett. BA, Rollins Coll., 1929; MA, Mich. State, 1958. Head of art dept. Southeastern Community Coll. U. Ky., Edison Jr. Coll., Fla. One-woman shows include Studio Guild, N.Y.C., 1939-41, 41-43, Norlyst Gallery, N.Y.C., 1945-47, Charles E. Smith Gallery, Boston, 1949, Center St. Gallery, Boston, Burliuk Gallery, N.Y.C., 1952, Gallerie Internationale, N.Y.C., 1963, Fine Arts Mus., Greenville, S.C., Morse Mus. Art, Winter Park, Fla., Mus. Art, Clearwater, Fla., Wustun Mus., Racine, Wis., Fitchburg Art Mus., Mass., Gibbs Gallery, Charleston, S.C., Boise Art Mus., Idaho, Columbia Mus. Art, S.C., Worcester Art Ctr., Appleton, Wis., San Francisco Mus. Art, Syracuse Mus., Asheville Art Mus., N.C., Stork Gallery, Lynchburg, Va., Maryhill Mus. Fine Arts, Washington; represented in permanent collections Cornelle Mus. Art, Winter Park, Fla., 1994, Met. Mus. Art, N.Y.C., 1994, NAOAL Mus., Washington; represented in numerous pub. and pvt. collections; author: (books) Paintings, Principles and Practices, 1967, Adventuring in Art, 1989. State bd. mem LWV, Laconia, N.H.; active Dem. Nat. Com. Named Tchr. of Yr. Edison Coll., Ft. Myers, Fla.; recipient Award of Merit State of Fla, 1935, Most Creative Work of Art award Currier Mus., N.H., Gaisman Award Nat. Assn. Women Artists, Arvida award, Sarasota Art Assn., Watercolor prize Southeastern Annual High Mus., Atlanta, Norfolk Mus. Art., Pen & Brush, N.Y., Nat. Assn. Women Artists, Nat. Acad. Gallery, Sarasota Art Assn. Mem. LWV, Nat. Assn. Women Artists, Am. Assn. Univ. Women, Nat. League of Am. Pen Women, Fla. Artists Group, Artists Equity, Art Assn., Internat. Platform Assn. Democrat. Home: 580 Artist Ave Englewood FL 34223-2734

TRACY, PATRICIA ANN KOOP, secondary school educator; b. Chickasaw, Ala., Sept. 28, 1947; d. Augustus Galloway Koop and Mildred (Willingham) Koop Conlon; m. Charles Gerald Tracy, Jan. 24, 1970; children: Charles Gerald Jr., William Todd, Michael Patrick. BS in Edn., U. Ala., Tuscaloosa, 1970; postgrad., Ala. State U., Montgomery, 1988, Troy State U., 1989, U. Ala., Huntsville, 1989, Ala. State U., 1995, Auburn U., Montgomery, 1994. Cert. secondary sci. tchr. Tchr. sci. St. Bede Sch., Montgomery, Ala., 1986-90, coord. Sci. Fair, head dept. sci., 1986-90; libr., media specialist Our Lady Queen Mercy Sch., 1992-93, libr., media specialist, computer tchr., 1993-94, mem. libr. and media, earth sci. tchr., 1994—; established reading program for grades K-8 involving parents of K-2 and computers in grades 3-8; developed hands on approach in media with filmstrip, book tapes, computer games, and other games involving cognitive skills; sci. fair co-coord., 1994—. Mem. Ala. Edn. Assn., Nat. Cath. Edn. Assn., Ala. Sci. Tchrs. Assn., Montgomery Cath. H.S. PTO, Ala. Conservancy, Ala. Alumni Assn., Ala. Mus. Natural History, Wetumpka H.S. PTO, Alpha Xi Delta. Roman Catholic. Home: 2424 Trotters Trl Wetumpka AL 36092-8410 Office: 4435 Narrow Lane Rd Montgomery AL 36116-2953

TRACY, PHILIP R., computer company executive; b. 1940. JD, George Washington U., 1966. With FBI, Washington, 1966-69; atty. Steptoe & Johnson, Washington, 1966-69; with Burroughs Wellcome Co., Durham, N.C., 1974—, CEO, pres., 1989—. Office: Burroughs Wellcome Co 3030 W Cornwallis Rd Research Triangle Park NC 27709*

TRAKAS, WILLIAM SAMUEL, history educator; b. Laurens, S.C., Sept. 17, 1949; s. Samuel Nicholas and Callie Trakas; m. Kathryn Adams, Aug. 21, 1971; 1 child, Matthew. BA in French, Furman U., 1971; MA in History, U. Wis., 1972, PhD in History, 1979. Exec. dir. Laurens (S.C.) Arts Coun., 1976-79; adj. prof. Furman U., Greenville, S.C., 1979-80; asst. prof. Averett Coll., Danville, Va., 1980-85; assoc. prof. Averett Coll., Danville, 1985-90, prof., 1990—. Pres. Arts and Humanities Assn., Danville, 1981-84; dir. Danville (Va.) Concert Assn., 1982-94, Southside AIDS Venture, Danville, 1992-94; vestryman Ch. of the Epiphany, Danville, 1982-84, 87-93. Named Ford Found. scholar U. Wis., Madison, 1972-74, Fulbright scholar Fulbright Commn., Munich, Germany, 1974-75, Berlin Seminar award Coun. on Internat. Edn. Exch., Berlin, 1991, NYU Seminar award NEH, N.Y.C., 1993. Episcopalian. Office: Averett Coll 420 W Main St Danville VA 24541-3612

TRAMONTANA, EILEEN MARY, environmental educator, agricultural producer; b. Lake Worth, Fla., Oct. 24, 1957; d. Alexander Brendan and Maureen (Small) McCreery; m. Louis William Tramontana. BA, Barry U., Miami Shores, Fla., 1991. Libr. Lake Worth Pub. Libr., 1973-78; resource conservationist Palm Beach Soil and Water Consevation Dist., West Palm Beach, Fla., 1978-80; adminstrv. asst. Van Note-Harvey Assocs., Long Valley, N.J., 1980-84, Simmons & White, Inc., West Palm Beach, 1984-85; asst. adminstr., resource conservationist Palm Beach Soil and Water Conservation Dist., West Palm Beach, 1985-90; edn. coord. Suwannee River Water Mgmt. Dist., Live Oak, Fla., 1990—; facilitator Project WILD, Project Learning Tree, others; established more tha 20 outdoor classrooms. Author: Why the Grass is Greener over the Septic Tank, Weatherworks, Wetland Concepts Waterways, 1994. Past state bd. dirs. League of Environ. Edn. in Fla.; 4-H leader, 15 yrs. Recipient Nat. award for Conservation Edn., 1989, S.E. Regional award for Conservation Edn., 1989, State of Fla. award for conservation edn., 1988, 89, Golden LEEF award for environ. edn., 1996; grantee Fla. Adv. Coun. on Environ. Edn., SWIM, Coastal Zone Mgmt. Mem. NAFE, Nat. Wildlife Fedn., N.Am. Assn. Environ. Educators, Nat. Audubon Soc., League of Environ. Educators in Fla. Office: Suwannee River Water Mgmt Dist RR 3 Box 64 Live Oak FL 32060-9573

TRAN, BAO QUOC, lawyer; b. Saigon, Vietnam, Nov. 5, 1963; came to U.S., 1975; s. Chi V. and H Thi Tran. BSEE, Rice U., 1985; MBA, Columbia U., 1987; JD, U. Houston, 1993. Bar: Tex. 1993, U.S. Ct. Appeals (fed. cir.) 1994, U.S. Ct. Appeals (5th cir.) 1994, U.S. Patent and Trademark Office, 1994. Mgmt. cons. Lorne Weil, Inc., N.Y.C., 1987-90, Transworld Corp., Stafford, Tex., 1990-93; atty. Richards, Medlock & Andrews, Dallas, 1993-94; assoc. Pravel, Hewitt, Kimball & Krieger, Houston, 1995—. Contbr. articles to profl. jours. Mem. Internat. Trademark Assn. (mem. trademark usage com. 1994—), Assn. Computing Machinery (vice chmn. 1983-84), Eta Kappa Nu, Phi Delta Phi. Office: Pravel Hewitt Kimball & Krieger 1177 West Loop S Fl 10 Houston TX 77027

TRAN, HENRY BANG Q., social work case manager; b. Binh Dinh, Vietnam, Dec. 28, 1952; came to U.S., 1975; s. Mau Dinh and Ho Thi Tran; m. Thuhong T. Ngo; children: John, Michael, Robert, Richard, Jennifer. BA, Northeastern Ill. U., 1977, MA, 1978. Cert. social worker, real estate broker. Social worker Tex. Dept. Human Svcs., Houston, 1980-96; founder, pres. Texo Properties, Inc., Houston, 1984-85; pres. N.E.W.S. Properties, Houston, 1985—; case mgr. Tex. Workforce Commn., 1996—; instr. math. City Colls. Chgo., 1977, Vietnamese lang. U. Houston, 1985. V.p. Buddhist Assn. for Services of Humanity in Am., Houston, 1985—; pres. Quang Trung Mut. Assistance Assn., Houston, 1984—. Fellow U. Miami, 1979. Mem. Nat. Assn. Realtors, Tex. Pub. Employee Assn., Dalat U. Alumni Assn., Asia Soc., Houston Vietnam Lions Club (pres. 1991).

TRAN, LONG TRIEU, industrial engineer; b. Saigon, Vietnam, Oct. 10, 1956; came to U.S., 1973; s. Nguyen Dinh and Thiet Thi (Nguyen) T.; m. Khanh Thi-Hong Phan, Aug. 3, 1988. BS in Mech. Engring. with honors, U. Kans., 1976; MS in Mech. Engring., MIT, 1980; MBA in Bus. Adminstrn. with honors, U. Louisville, 1993. Cert. quality engr.; cert. mfg. engr.; cert. project mgmt. profl. Tchg. asst. U. Kans., 1975-76, U. Calif., Berkeley, 1977; rsch. asst. Lawrence Berkeley Labs., 1977, MIT, 1977-80; libr. staff Harvard U. Med. Sch. Libr., 1977-78; mem. staff New England Deaconess Hosp., Boston, 1978-80; prodn. programming engr. GE, Cleve., 1980-81; advanced mfg. engr. GE, Louisville, 1981-82, quality sys. engr., 1982-84, quality control engr., 1984-86, sr. quality info. equipment engr., 1986-89, sr. quality indsl. engr., 1990-94, sr. supplier tech. assistance engr., 1995-96, sr. advanced supplier quality engr., 1996—; exec. advisor Jr. Achievement Inc., Louisville, 1983-84; monitor/reader Rec. for the Blind, 1994—; fundraiser The Dream Factory Inc., 1994—. Vol. NCCJ, 1994—, Clothe-A-Child, 1993—, Dare-To-Care, 1994—, Ronald McDonald House, 1994—. Mem. AAAS, ASME, Am. Soc. Quality Control, Computer and Automated Sys. Assn. (charter), Robot Inst. Am., Robotics Internat. (charter), Soc. Mfg. Engrs. (sr.), Instrument Soc. Am. (sr.), Am. Mgmt. Assn., N.Y. Acad. Scis., Internat. Platform Assn., Indsl. Computing Soc. (founding), Project Mgmt. Inst., Nat. Pks. Conservation Assn., U.S. Libr. Congress Assocs. (founding), Sigma Xi, Pi Tau Sigma, Tau Beta Pi, Phi Kappa Phi, Beta Gamma Sigma. Republican. Home: 3423 Brookhollow Dr Louisville KY 40220-5009 Office: GE AP2-117 Louisville KY 40225

TRAN, QUI-PHIET, English language educator; b. Dalat, Vietnam, June 1, 1937; came to U.S., 1972; s. Qui-But and Anh Thi (Nguyen) T.; m. Ngan Thi Vo, Aug. 30, 1963; children: Hung Thuy, Long, Kien. BA, U. Hue, Vietnam, 1960; MA, U. Tex., 1974, PhD, 1977. Tchr. Vo Tanh H.S., Nhatrang, Vietnam, 1960-64, Petrus Ky. H.S., Saigon, Vietnam, 1964-65; English instr. U. Hue, 1965-72, U. Tex., Austin, 1977-78; document analyst Congrl. Info. Svcs., Inc., Washington, 1979-80; resourse specialist Arlington (Va.) County Pub. Schs., 1980-81; from asst. to assoc. prof. English Schreiner Coll., Kerrville, Tex., 1982-90, prof. English, 1990—; lectr. in Asian lang. and lit. George Mason U., Fairfax, Va., 1980-81; refugee resettlement cons. Ctr. for Applied Linguistics, Washington, 1980-81. Author: William Faulkner and The French New Novelists, 1990; contbr. articles and transl. to books and profl. jours. Grantee NEH, 1983, 89, Schreiner Coll., 1988, 92-94; Mellon Found. fellow Rice U., 1983, Rsch. fellow Am. Coun. Learned Soc., 1984. Mem. MLA, Assn. for Asian Am. Studies, Sigma Tau Delta (faculty sponsor, 1993—). Office: Schreiner Coll Highway 27 Kerrville TX 78028

TRANI, EUGENE PAUL, academic administrator, educator; b. Bklyn., Nov. 2, 1939; s. Frank Joseph and Rose Gertrude (Kelly) T.; m. Lois Elizabeth Quigley, June 2, 1962; children: Anne Chapman, Frank. BA in History with honors, U. Notre Dame, 1961; MA, Ind. U., 1963, PhD, 1966. Instr. history Ohio State U., Columbus, 1965-67; asst. prof. So. Ill. U., Carbondale, 1967-71, assoc. prof., 1971-75, prof., 1975-76; asst. v.p. acad. affairs, prof. U. Nebr., 1976-80; prof., vice chancellor acad. affairs U. Mo. Kansas City, 1980-86; prof., v.p. acad. affairs U. Wis. System, 1986-90; pres. Va. Commonwealth U., 1990—; pres., bd. dirs. Va. Biotechnology Rsch. Park, 1992—; vis. asst. prof. U. Wis. Milw., 1969; bd. dirs. Crestar Bank Richmond Met. Bd., Crestar Fin. Corp., Lawyers Title Corp., Innovative Tech. Authority; cons. various univ. presses, jours., govtl. agys.; advisor gov. La., Okla. State Regents Higher Edn.; mem. commn. Internat. Edn. Am. Coun. Higher Ed., 1991—; bd. gov. Ctr. Russian Am. Bus., Washington, 1993—; bd. advisors Inst. for U.S. Studies, I. London, 1993—; adv. coun. mem. Coun. on Grad. Studies and Rsch., U. Notre Dame, 1994—. Author, editor: Concerns of a Conservative Democrat, 1968, The Treaty of Portsmouth: An Adventure in American Diplomacy, 1969, The Secretaries of the Department of the Interior, 1849-69, 1975, (with David Wilson) The Presidency of Warren G. Harding, 3d edit., 1989; contbr. articles to profl. jours., newspapers; book reviewer. Permanent mem. Coun. Fgn. Rels., N.Y.C., 1979—; bd. dirs. Richmond Ballet, 1991—, NCCJ, Richmond, 1991—, Va. Spl. Olympics, 1991—, YMCA of Greater Richmond, 19926, Richmond Renaissance, 1992—, Met. Found., 1992-95; mem. U.S. Savs. Bond Vol. Com., chmn. higher edn. area, 1992, 93; adv. bd. Greater Richmond chpt. ARC, 1992—. Fellow Russian and East European Inst., 1964-65, Nat. Hist. Publs. Commn., 1969-70, Woodrow Wilson Internat. Ctr. Scholars, 1972-73, So. Ill. U. Sabbatical Leave, 1975-76, Coun. Internat. Exchange Scholars, 1981, U. Mo. Faculty, 1981; grantee U.S. Dept. Interior Rsch., 1965, 66, So. Ill. U. Office Rsch. and Projects, 1967-74, Am. Philos. Soc., 1968, 72, So. Ill U. Summer Rsch. 1970, 72, 75, Lilly Endowment, 1975-76, Sloan Commn. Govt. and Higher Edn., 1978, U.S. Info. Agy. Am. Participants Program, 1984, 85, 86, 88, 90; recipient Younger Humanist award NEH, 1972-73, Leadership and Achievement award Ctrl. Richmond Assn., 1992. Mem. Internat. Inst. Strategic Studies, Am. Assn. Advancement Slavic Studies, Orgn. Am. Historians, Soc. Historians Am. Fgn. Rels., Met. Richmond C. of C. (bd. dirs. 1991—), Va. Ctr. for Innovative Tech., Ctrl. Richmond Assn. (leadership award, 1992), Phi Kappa Phi. Roman Catholic. Office: Va Commonwealth U Box 842512 910 W Franklin St Richmond VA 23284-2512

TRANT, DOUGLAS ALLEN, lawyer; b. Pensacola, Fla., Nov. 14, 1951; s. David Amon and Annie Jacquetta (Sullivan) T.; m. Janis S. BA, Birmingham-So. Coll., 1973; MA, U. Toledo, 1974; JD, U. Tenn., 1977. Bar: Ala. 1978, U.S. Dist. Ct. (so. dist.) Ala. 1978, Tenn. 1980, U.S. Dist. Ct. (ea. dist.) Tenn. 1980, U.S. Supreme Ct. 1982, U.S. Ct. Appeals (6th cir.) 1984, U.S. Dist. Ct. (mid. dist.) Tenn. 1987, U.S. Ct. Appeals (4th cir.) 1995; cert. criminal trial specialist. Staff atty. Legal Svcs., Selma, Ala., 1977-78; staff atty., instr. legal clinic U. Tenn., Knoxville, 1978-80; ptnr. Trant & Stephens, Knoxville, 1980-88; pvt. practice law Knoxville, 1988—; cons. legal clinic U. Tenn., 1980-81. Author: Trial Manual for the Defense of Habitual Criminal Cases in Tennessee. Apptd. col. to staff of Gov. of Tenn.; chmn. Knox County Dem. Orgn. Recipient Cert. Appreciation Tenn. Gov. Lamar Alexander, Nashville, 1982. Mem. Knoxville Bar Assn., Nat. Assn. Criminal Def. Lawyers (trial advisor death penalty com. 1986—), Tenn. Assn. Criminal Def. Lawyers (lectr. 1983—, adv. bd. Death Penalty Def. Manual 1984—), Tenn. Bar Assn. Democrat. Office: Riverview Tower 900 S Gay St Ste 1502 Knoxville TN 37902-1858

TRAPHAN, BERNARD RICHARD, computer scientist, educator; b. Stamford, Conn., Feb. 7, 1967; s. Bernard Richard and Elizabeth (Biagiotti) T. BS in Computer Sci., Fla. State U., 1990, EdS in Coll. Teaching, 1991, MS in Computer Sci., MBA, 1993, postgrad., 1993—. Pres., CEO MicroSonic Software, Tallahassee, Fla., 1983—; teaching asst. dept. computer sci., rsch. asst. ednl. rsch. Fla. State U., Tallahassee, 1990-91; computer analyst Fla. Ho. of Reps., Tallahassee, 1990-91; fin. analyst Dept. of Air Force, Washington, 1992—; internat. pres. Student Advocate Assembly, Tallahassee, 1991—; chair Fla. Congress of Grad. Students, Tallahassee, 1993—. Contbr. articles to profl. publs. Candidate for sch. supt. Leon County Schs., Fla., 1992. Mem. Assn. Computing Machinery (vice-chair 1989-91), Mortar Bd., Mensa, Phi Beta Kappa, Phi Kappa Phi. Office: Student Advocate Assembly 619 S Woodward Ave Ste 20528 Tallahassee FL 32304-4339

TRAPIDO, EDWARD JAY, epidemiologist; b. N.Y.C., Sept. 14, 1952. BA in Psychology, SUNY, Stony Brook, 1973; MSPH in Parasitology, U. N.C., Chapel Hill, 1974; MSc in Epidemiology, Harvard Sch. Pub. Health, 1976, DSc in Epidemiology, 1981. Staff fellow Nat. Cancer Inst., Bethesda, Md., 1981-84; chief epidemiology and biostats. Sylvester Comprehensive Cancer Ctr., U. Miami Sch. Medicine, 1984-87, assoc. dir., 1987—, chief cancer control, 1993—, dir. PhD program in epidemiology, 1994—; dir. Fla. Cancer Data System, Miami, 1984—. Contbr. articles to profl. jours. Fla. dir. P.R. Cancer Info. Svc., Miami, 1992—, Components of Nat. Hispanic Leadership Initiative in Cancer, 1993—. Apptd. to Gov.'s Cancer Control Adv. Bd., Tallahassee, 1990, Exec. Com. Cancer Control Adv. Bd., Tampa, Fla., 1992. Mem. NOH (mem. study sect. 1993—), Am. Coll. Epidemiology, Hispanic Rsch. Network, COSSMHO/Nat. Hispanic Cancer Leadership (steering group 1992). Office: Sylvester Comprehensive Cancer Ctr PO Box 016960 D4-11 Miami FL 33101

TRAPP, E(DWARD) PHILIP, psychology educator; b. Akron, Ohio, Dec. 22, 1923; s. Philip Edward and Emily (Saul) T.; m. Myra Jane May, June 6, 1954 (dec. 1964); m. Jane Griffith, July 27, 1976. BS, Kent State U., 1947; MS, N.Mex. State U., 1948; PhD, Ohio State U., 1951. Lic. clin. psychologist, Ark. From asst. prof. to assoc. prof. psychology U. Ark., Fayetteville, 1951-59, prof., 1959-91, prof. emeritus, 1991—, dir. clin. doctoral program, 1959-71, chmn. dept. psychology, 1971-84; vis. prof. N. Mex. State U., Las Cruces, 1956-57, U. Wis., Madison, 1959, SUNY, Oswego, 1960. Editor: Readings on Exceptional Child, 1962-72; contbr. articles to profl. publs. Lt. USN, 1943-46. Recipient Disting. Teaching award U. Ark. Alumni Assn. Mem. APA, AAUP (local pres. 1958-60), Ark. Psychol. Assn. (pres. 1955-56 Disting. Svc. award 1985), Ark. Bd. Profl. Examiners (chmn. 1962-72). Home: 235 N Palmer Ave Fayetteville AR 72701-4800 Office: Univ Ark Dept Psychology Fayetteville AR 72701

TRASK, BENJAMIN HARRISON, librarian; b. Charleston, S.C., Oct. 12, 1956; s. Robert John and Virginia Lee (Forrest) T.; m. Susan La Paro, July 18, 1987; children: Alexander Anthony, Gwendolyn Virginia, Evan Hunter. BA, Va. Poly. Inst., 1978, MA, 1981; MSLS, U. N.C., 1987; post-grad., Christopher Newport U., 1980. Reference libr. Norfolk (Va.) Pub. Libr., 1987-88; libr. Mariners' Mus. Rsch. Libr., Newport News, Va., 1988-94, Newport News, 1994—; adj. lectr. Cath. U., Washington, 1989—; adj. instr. Tidewater C.C., Chesapeake, Va., 1988. Author: 9th Virginia Infantry, 1984, 16th Virginia Infantry, 1986, 61st Virginia Infantry, 1988; editor: A Pair of Blankets: War-time History in Letters to the Young People of the South, 1990; co-author: Grimes' Battery, Grand'y Battery, and Huger's Battery, Virginia Artillery, 1995; editor: Two Months in the Confederate States: An Englishman's Travels Through the South, 1996; contbr. articles to profl. jours. Vol. Ft. Monroe Casement Mus., Hampton, Va., 1978-79. 1st lt. USMCR, 1981-84. Mem. ALA, VLA, So. Hist. Assn., Williamsburg Bibliophiles (bd. advisors 1992-95, chmn. 1993-95), Phi Alpha Theta. Office: Mariners Mus 100 Museum Dr Newport News VA 23606-3759

TRAURIG, ROBERT HENRY, lawyer; b. Waterbury, Conn., June 9, 1925; s. Samuel and Lillian (Rosengarten) T.; m. Jacqueline Block; children: Madeline Traurig Sackel, Wendy. Student, U. Fla.; BBA, U. Miami, Fla., 1947, LLB, 1950. Bar: Fla. 1950, U.S. Dist. Ct. Fla. 1950. Ptnr. Greenberg, Traurig, Hoffman, Lipoff, Rosen & Quentel, P.A., Miami, 1967—. Pres. Greater Miami Opera, 1987-89. Lt. USNR, 1943-46, 51-52. Mem. Greater Miami C. of C. (chmn.). Democrat. Jewish. Office: Greenberg Traurig Hoffman 1221 Brickell Ave Miami FL 33131-3224*

TRAVIS, JON ERIC, education educator; s. Dean and Martha T.; m. Jacalyn Travis. BA, U. Iowa, 1971; MA, W.Va. U., 1974; EdD, Ariz. State U., 1992. Cert. secondary tchr., Ariz., community coll. tchr., Ariz. Asst. prof. theatre and comm. Henderson State U., Arkadelphia, Ark., 1985-88; intern Ariz. Dept. Edn., Phoenix, 1990; coord. staff devel. Maricopa C.C. Dist., Phoenix, 1990-91; grad. asst. Bur. Ednl. Rsch. and Svcs. Ariz. State U., Tempe, 1989-90, 91-92; intern Maricopa C.C. Dist., 1989-90, 91-92; asst. prof. secondary and higher edn., dir. for C.C. edn. Tex. A&M U.-Commerce, 1992—; adj. instr. Rio Salado C.C., Phoenix, 1989, 1992, Gateway C.C., Phoenix, 1991, Yavapai Coll., Prescott, Ariz., 1984; presenter in field. Contbr. articles to profl. jours. Grantee E. Tex. State U., 1992-93. Office: Tex A&M U Commerce Secondary and Higher Edn Commerce TX 75429

TRAVIS, NANCY, program director; b. Brownwood, Tex., Feb. 29, 1936; d. John Clyde and Annie (Bynum) Goosby; m. Floyd J. Travis (div. 1983); children: J. Barrett, Timothy Allen. BS, U. Tex., 1962; MS, U. So. Calif., 1976. Adminstr. U.S. Army Dept. Continuing Edn., Fed. Republic Germany, 1975-79; dir. Clear Creek County (Colo.) Dept. Community Edn., 1980-83, Dept. Social Svcs., Central City, Colo., 1980-82; program dir. Am. Ednl. Complex, Killeen, Tex., 1983-85; dir. mktg. Herring Marathon Group, Killeen, 1985-87; program dir. Am. Ednl. Complex Pacific Far East Campus, 1987-89; regional dir. Am. Heart Assn., 1989-92; dir. internat. intensive English program U. Mary Hardin Baylor, 1992—; lectr. and cons. in field; guest prof. Allen Coll., Japan, 1994, Ebino (Kyushu, Japan) Internat. Coll., 1996. Author: English Text, 1985; editor: Training in Communication Skills, 1985. Bd. dirs. Bluebonnet coun. Girl Scouts Am., Ctrl. Tex., 1986-87, Am. Heart Assn., 1986-87, regional dir., 1989—; mem. Dem. Ctrl. Com., Colo., 1982-83; advisor Ethiopian Ministry Social Welfare, Addis Ababa, 1971-74; chairperson Celebrate One World Cultural Activities Ctr., Temple, Tex., 1996. Recipient Comdrs.' award U.S. Army, 1987. Mem. Assn. Am. Bus. Women, Internat. Coun. Shopping Ctrs. (Merit award 1986), Mil. Educators and Counselors Assn., Rotary Internat. Sisters Cities Inc., Area Mental Health Assn. (bd. dirs.), Delta Kappa Gamma.

TRAVIS, PAUL NICHOLAS, international banker; b. N.Y.C., Jan. 11, 1949; s. Nicholas and Mary (Bondar) T.; m. Carol Ann Rush; children: Tanya Ann, Paul John. BA, Rutgers U., New Brunswick, N.J., 1971; M, Sch. Advanced Internat. Studies, Washington, 1973. Mgmt. trainee Marine Midland Bank, N.Y.C., 1973-74; asst. agt., credit Bank of Montreal, N.Y.C., 1974-76; rep. Bank of Montreal, Tokyo, 1976; dep. v.p. Algemene Bank-The Netherlands, N.Y.C., 1976-79; mgr. Banco Real S.A., N.Y.C., 1979-80; gen. mgr. Banco Real S.A., Houston, 1980-88; v.p. corp. fin., merger & acquisitions The Sumimoto Trust & Banking Co., Ltd. L.A. Agy., L.A., 1989-93; sr. v.p. and mktg. officer Riyad Bank, Houston, 1993—. Mem. Boys Club of N.Y., Alumni, 1974—. Mem. Western Coun. Internat. Banking, Houston Inter-Am. C. of C. (bd. dirs. 1987—), Boys Club N.Y. Alumni Assn., Assn. Energy Engrs. Republican.

TRAXLER, WILLIAM BYRD, JR., federal judge; b. Greenville, S.C., May 1, 1948; s. William Byrd and Bettie (Wooten) T.; m. Patricia Alford, Aug. 21, 1971; children: William Byrd III, James McCall. BA, Davidson Coll., 1970; JD, U. S.C., 1973. Assoc. William Byrd Traxler, Greenville, 1973-75; asst. solicitor 13th Jud. Ct., Greenville, 1975-78, dep. solicitor, 1978-81, solicitor, 1981-85, resident crct. judge, 1985-92; U.S. Dist. judge Dist. of S.C., Greenville, 1992—. Recipient Outstanding Svc. award Solicitors Assn., S.C., 1987, Leadership award Probation, Parole & Pardon Svcs., S.C., 1990. Office: US Dist Ct 300 E Washington St Greenville SC 29601-2800

TRAYANOVA, NATALIA ALEXANDROVA, biomedical engineering educator; b. Sofia, Bulgaria, Apr. 22, 1956; came to U.S., 1989; d. Alexander Atanasov Gydikov and Vera Dimitrova Ivanova; 1 child, Boyanna Atanasova. MS in Physics, Sofia U., 1979; PhD in Biophysics, Bulgarian Acad Scis., Sofia, 1986. Asst. prof. Ctrl. Lab. of Biophysics Bulgarian Acad. Scis., Sofia, 1986, 88-89; postdoctoral fellow dept. biomed. engring. Duke U., Durham, N.C., 1986-88, asst. rsch. prof. dept. biomed. engring., 1989-94; assoc. prof. dept. biomed. engring. Tulane U., New Orleans, 1995—; session chmn. 14th conf. IEEE/EMBS, Paris, 1992, World Congress on Med. Phys. and Biomed. Engring., Rio de Janeiro, 1994; organizer Biomed. Engring. electrophysiology seminar, Duke U., 1993, 94; lectr. Cray conf. on High Performance Computing Biomed. Rsch., Rsch. Triangle Park, N.C., 1992, IEEE/EMBS 13th Ann. Internat. Conf., Orlando, Fla., 1991, Internat. Meetings of BMES, Charlottesville, Va., 1991 and Tempe, Ariz., 1994. Rev. Annals of Biomed. Engring., IEEE Trans. Biomed. Engring., Jour. Math. Biology, Jour. Cardiac Electrophysiology; contbr. articles to profl. jours., presented papers at sci. confs. and meetings. Recipient Whitaker Found. award, 1992; U.S. NAS fellow, 1986-87. Mem. IEEE (sr.). Office: Tulane U Dept Biomed Engring New Orleans LA 70118

TRAYLOR, ANGELIKA, stained glass artist; b. Munich, Bavaria, Germany, Aug. 24, 1942; Came to U.S., 1959; d. Walther Artur Ferdinand and Berta Kreszentia (Boeck) Klau; m. Lindsay Montgomery Donaldson, June 10, 1959 (div. 1970); 1 child, Cameron Maria Greta; m. Samuel William Traylor III, June 12, 1970. Student, Pvt. Handelsschule Morawetz Jr. Coll., Munich, 1958. Freelance artist, 1980—. Works featured in profl. jours. including the Daylily Jour., 1987, Design Jour., South Korea, 1989, The Traveler's Guide to American Crafts, 1990, Florida Mag., 1991, Florida Today, 1993, Melbourne Times, 1994, The Orbiter, 1996, The Glass Collector's Digest, 1996. Recipient Fragile Art award Glass Art mag., 1982, 1st Yr. Exhibitor award Stained Glass Assn. Am., 1984, 2d pl. Non-figurative Composition award Vitraux des USA, 1985, Best of Show Stained Glass Assn. Am., 1989, 3d pl., 1989, Merit award George Plimpton All-Star Space Coast Art Open, 1994; named Hist. Woman of Brevard, Brevard Cultural Alliance, 1991, one of 200 Best Am. Craftsmen Early Am. Life mag., 1994, 95. Home and Office: 100 Poinciana Dr Indian Harbour Beach FL 32937-4437

TRAYLOR, SHIRLEY KINCAID, secondary school educator; b. Owenton, Ky., July 7, 1937; d. Ewell J. and Ethel (Harris) Kincaid; m. Robert Darryl Traylor, Jul. 28, 1956; children: Darryl Todd, Dana Lynn. BA, Northern Ky. Univ., 1973; MA, Georgetown Coll., 1980. Tchr. Owen County H.S., Owenton, Ky., 1975-95; retired, 1980; sponsor Beta Club, 1975-95. Baptist. Home: P O Box 52 New Liberty KY 40355 Office: Owen County H S Hwy 22 Owenton KY 40359

TREACY, GERALD BERNARD, lawyer; b. Newark, July 29, 1951; s. Gerald B. Sr. and Mabel L. (Nesbitt) T.; m. Joyce M. Biazzo, Apr. 6, 1974. BA summa cum laude, Rider Coll., 1973; JD, UCLA, 1981. Bar: Calif. 1981, Wash. 1982, D.C. 1995, Va. 1996. Tchr. English Arthur L. Johnson Regional High Sch., Clark, N.J., 1973-77; assoc. Gibson, Dunn & Crutcher, L.A., 1981-82; ptnr. Perkins Coie, Bellevue, Wash., 1982-94, McGuire Woods Battle & Boothe, McLean, Va., 1994-96; McGuire Woods Battle & Boothe, Bellevue, Wash.; ptnr. Egger, Betts, Sherwood, Austin & Treacy, Bellevue, Wash., 1996—; chmn. bd. dirs. estate planning adv. bd. U. Wash., Seattle, 1990-92; presenter TV Seminar, Where There's a Will, PBS affiliate. Author: Washington Guardianship Law, Administration and Litigation, 1988, supplemented, 1991, 2d edit., 1992, supplemented, 1993, Supporting Organizations, 1996. Mem. endowment fund com. United Way, Seattle, 1987-89, exec. com. Washington Planned Giving Coun., 1993—; bd. dirs., mem. adv. bd. ARC, Seattle, 1985-89, Arthritis Gift, 1987-89, Seattle Symphony, 1992—. Mem. Eastside King County Estate Planning Coun., Order of Coif. Office: Egger Betts Sherwood Austin & Treacy 500 108th Ave NE Ste 2300 Bellevue WA 98004-5500

TREACY, SANDRA JOANNE PRATT, art educator, artist; b. New Haven, Aug. 5, 1934; d. Willis Hadley Jr. and Gladys May (Gell) P.; m. Gillette van Nuyse, Aug. 27, 1955; 1 child, Jonathan Todd. BFA, R.I. Sch. Design, 1956; student, William Paterson Coll., 1973-74. Cert. elem. and secondary tchr., N.J. Tchr. art and music Pkwy. Christian Ch., Ft. Lauderdale, Fla., 1964-66; developer Pequannock Twp. Bd. of Edn., Pompton Plains, N.J., 1970-72, tchr. art, 1972-76; vol. art tchr. Person County Bd. of Edn., Roxboro, N.C., 1978-80, tchr. art, 1980-91; tchr. art So. Jr. High Sch., Roxboro, 1989-91, Woodland Elem. Sch., Roxboro, 1989-93; tchr. Helena Elem. Sch., Timberlake, N.C., 1991-93; tchr. elem. art Bethel Hill Sch., Roxboro, 1974-79, vol. art tchr., 1979-80; tchr. basic art, vol. all elem. schs. Person County, Roxboro, 1977-80; tchr. arts and crafts, summers 1981-882; tchr. art home sch. So. Mid. Sch., 1993—, Person H.S., 1993-94. Artist, illustrator. Mem. Roxboro EMTs, 1979-81; bd. dirs. Person County Art Coun., 1980--81, 93-95, pres., 1981-82; piano and organ choir accompanist Concord United Meth. Ch., 1981—; leader Morgan Trotters, 1992-94, asst. dir., 1993-96, bd. dirs.; mem. Roxboro Cmty. Choir, 1994—; coach, horseback riding for handicapped. Mem. NEA, Nat. Mus. of Women in the Arts (continuing charter), Smithsonian Assocs., N.C. Assn. Arts Edn., N.C. Assn. Educators, N.C. Art Soc. Mus. of Art, Internat. Platform Assn., Womans Club (tchr. Pompton Plains chpt. 1974-79), Person County Saddle Club (rec. sec. 1981-84), Puddingston Pony Club (dist. sec. 1974-75), Roxboro Garden Club (continuing, commr. 1980-82, pres. 1982-84, 87—, sec. 1993-94, v.p. 1993-95, pres. 1995—), Roxboro Woman's Club (arts dept.). Republican. Home: 1345 Kelly Brewer Rd Leasburg NC 27291-9720

TREADGOLD, WARREN TEMPLETON, history and literature educator; b. Oxford, Eng., Apr. 30, 1949; came to U.S., 1949; s. Donald Warren and Alva Adele (Granquist) T.; m. Irina Maria Andreescu, Sept. 25, 1982. AB, Harvard U., 1970, PhD, 1977. Lectr. in classics UCLA, 1977-78; rsch. fellow Alexander Von Humboldt Found., Munich, 1978-80; lectr. in history and classics Stanford (Calif.) U., 1980-82; asst. prof. history Hillsdale (Mich.) Coll., 1983-88; vis. asst. prof. history and classics U. Calif., Berkeley, 1986; asst. prof. history Fla. Internat. U., Miami, 1988-90, assoc. prof., 1990-91, prof., 1991—; vis. fellow All Souls Coll., Oxford, 1989; fellow Woodrow Wilson Ctr., Wash., 1996—. Author: The Nature of the Biblioteca of Photius, 1980, The Byzantine State Finances..., 1982, The Byzantine Revival, 1988, Byzantium and Its Army, 1995; editor: Renaissances Before the Renaissance, 1984; contbr. articles to profl. publs. NEH fellow, 1996-97. Mem. AAUP, Byzantine Studies Conf. (mem. governing bd. 1986-90), Am. Hist. Assn., Am. Philolog. Assn., Mediaeval Acad. Am., U.S. Nat. Com. for Byzantine Studies, Nat. Assn. Scholars, Dumbarton Oaks Alumni Assn. (sec. 1976-81). Office: Fla Internat U Dept History Miami FL 33199

TREADWAY, SUSAN MARIE, technical writer; b. West Palm Beach, Fla., June 14, 1951; d. Karl Paul and Margaret Elizabeth (Ross) Casseur; m. Oscar Gaines Owen, June 7, 1969 (div. 1979); 1 child, Angela (dec.); m. Ronald Jay Treadway, Nov. 22, 1980 (div. 1989); children: Cassandra Erin, Kimberly Dawn. Student, Craven Community Coll., Havelock, N.C., 1981, Mid. Ga. Tech. Inst., Warner Robins, 1987-89. NDI radiographer Space Sci. Services, Inc., Riviera Beach, Fla., 1968-69; with Hayes Internat. Corp., Napier Field, Ala., 1970-71; oper. room technician Flowers Hosp., Dothan, Ala., 1971-75; inventory programmer Barr Co., Niles, Ill., 1985-86; tech. writer Jana, Inc., Warner Robins, Ga., 1987-89; prodn. assoc. McDonnell Douglas, 1989; tech. writer HEBCO, Inc., Macon, Ga., 1989-94, C Sys., Inc., Dayton, Ohio, 1994-95; tech. data mgr. Advanced Testing Technologies, Inc., Robins AFB, Ga., 1995—. Author: Reflections of Feelings, 1980. Family services asst. coord. USAF, 1987. Sgt. USMC,1978-83. Mem. NAFE, Internat. Platform Assn., Assn. Old Crows. Presbyterian. Club: Mensa. Home: 217 Laverne Dr Warner Robins GA 31088-3729 Office: (WR-ALC) Warner Robins Air Logistics Ctr Robins AFB GA 31098

TREAT, JAMES J., accountant, business executive; b. Pittsfield, Mass., May 8, 1942; s. Orion F. and Gladdis A. (Whittsley) T.; m. Marcelle Joanne Felker, Sept. 8, 1967; children: James Matthew, Jessica Ann. BS, Butler U., 1965; student, U. New Haven, 1969-79, MIT, 1976. Cost acctg. mgr. Sperry Products, Inc., Danbury, Conn., 1969-70; chief acct. Automation Industries, Inc., Danbury, 1970-73, asst. controller, 1974-75, group controller, 1976-80; controller Nuclear Energy Services Inc., Danbury, 1975-76; gen. mgr. Conam Inspection, Midland, Tex., 1980-81; v.p. Conam Inspection, Longview, Tex., 1981-84; co-owner, v.p. Longview Inspection, Inc., 1984-90; pres., 1990-95; v.p. ops. Longview Holdings, Inc., 1995—; treas. Automation Fedn. Credit Union, Danbury, 1973-75, v.p., 1975-80. Inventor (with others) ultrasonic testing device, 1986. Fund raiser YMCA, Danbury, 1978, dir. regional YMCA, Danbury, 1978-79; fin. chmn. United Meth. Ch., Hallsville, Tex., 1984-85. Served with USN, 1965-69. Mem. Am. Welding Soc., Nat. Assn. Accts., Am. Soc. Nondestructive Testing, Nondestructive Mgmt. Assn.

TRECO-JONES, SHERYL LYNN, public relations professional; b. Winchester, Mass., Nov. 19, 1948; d. Richard Mitchell and Helen (Pleskus) T. BA in English, Beaver Coll., 1970. Assoc. editor nat. hdqrs. United Ch. of Christ, Phila., 1971-74; assoc. Ken Smith Pub. Relations, Atlanta, 1976-78; sr. pub. relations specialist Dept. Archives and History State of Ga., Atlanta, 1978-80; dir. pub. relations Scottish Rite Childrens' Hosp., Atlanta, 1980-85; account supr. Ketchum Pub. Relations, Atlanta, 1985-89; pres., owner Treco-Jones Pub. Rels. INc., Atlanta, 1989—; ptnr. The Health Care Group, 1992-94. Mem., 3d v.p. bd. dirs. N.W. Ga. Coun. Girl Scouts Am., Atlanta, 1986-91, rep. nat. roundup, 1965. Recipient Bronze award Southeastern Art Dirs., 1986, Golden ADDY-TV award AD Club, 1986, Champagne Edit. Gold Flame award Internat. Assn. Bus. Communicators, 1987, 90. Mem. Am. Hosp. Assn., Atlanta Women's Network (bd. dirs.), Pub. Rels. Soc. Am. (Silver Phoenix award 1988, 93, 96, Cert. of Excellence 1995, 96, com. chair 1990-91, bd. dirs. 1996—, chair edn. com. 1996), Atlanta C. of C. and Midtown Bus. Alliance, 1996 Leadership Midtown Class, Phi Sigma Tau. Democrat. Methodist. Home: 2663 Galahad Dr NE Atlanta GA 30345-3626 Office: 1800 Century Blvd Ste 1225 Atlanta GA 30345

TREHAN, RAJEEV R., psychiatrist, neurologist; b. Gorakhpur, India, June 19, 1955; came to U.S., 1981; s. Tej Ram and Mohni (Sahni) T. MB, BS, All India Inst. Med Scis., 1978, MD in Internal Medicine, 1981. Diplomate in psychiatry, neurology and geriatric psychiatry Am. Bd. Psychiatry and Neurology. Asst. prof. psychiatry Yale U., New Haven, 1985-89; resident neurologist U. So. Fla., Tampa, 1989-91; asst. prof. psychiatry and neurology U. So. Fla., 1991—; chief geriatric psychiatry J.A. Haley Veterans Hosp., Tampa, 1991—.

TREHARNE, GEORGE DAVID, small business owner; b. Wauseon, Ohio, Jan. 31, 1943; s. Samuel Richard and Marjorie I. (McGuffin) T.; m. Judith Arlene Nestler, June 27, 1964; children: Heather R., David Heath. BS in Bus., W.Va. U., 1964; MBA in Mgmt., Ohio U., 1968, postgrad., 1969. Adminstr. W.Va. Gov.'s Office Econ. Opportunity, Charleston, 1971-78; instr. Internat. Coll. of Cayman Island, W.I., 1978; pres. Treharne Inc., Parkersburg, W.Va., 1979—; exec. dir. W.Va. Cmty. Action Dirs. Assn., Parkersburg, 1989—; adj. instr. W.Va. U., Parkersburg, 1990; sec. Gt. Lakes Rural Comty. Assistance Network, Fremont, Ohio, 1990—; dir. Transitions Program, Parkersburg, 1991—; bd. dirs. Nat. Rural Comty. Assistance Program, W.Va. Rural Devel. Coun. Editor (newsletter) Rescue. Mem. Rotary. Office: W Va Cmty Action Dirs Assn PO Box 4007 North Parkersburg WV 26104

TREIBLE, KIRK, college president; b. Newton, N.J., Mar. 29, 1941; s. William Bryan and Grace Almond T.; BS, W.Va. Wesleyan Coll.; MBA, W.Va. U.; LLD, La Grange Coll.; m. Carol Ann Mosher, June 20, 1964; 1 son, Todd. Bus. mgr. Parkersburg (W.Va.) Community Coll., 1969-71; devel. officer W.Va. Wesleyan Coll., 1972-75, acting treas., 1975-77; v.p. fin. Southwestern U., Georgetown, Tex., 1977-88; pres. Andrew Coll. Cuthbert, Ga., 1988—; bd. dirs. Citizen Bank, Geogetown, Tex., 1978-88, 1st State Bank and Trust Co., Cuthbert, Ga., 1989—; cons. Nebr. Wesleyan U.; cons. So. Assn. Schs. and Colls. Bd. dirs. Georgetown Airport Authority, 1981-83; chmn. adminstrv. bd. First United Methodist Ch., 1983-85; mem. W.I.H. and Lula E. Pitts Found., Peed Scholarship Trust, United Meth. Ch. Served with USAF, 1966-69. Mem. Assn. Pvt. Colls. and Univs. Ga. (pres., dir.). Home: 408 N Lumpkin St Cuthbert GA 31740-1115 Office: Andrew Coll 413 College St Cuthbert GA 31740-1313

TREMPER, BOBBIE JO, special education educator; b. Fairbanks, Alaska, July 16, 1970; d. Bobby Joe and Dorothy Jean (Spence) Bates; m. Marc Randolph Tremper, May 4, 1996. BS, Mid. Tenn. State U., 1992. Tchr. Kinder Care Learning Ctr., Murfreesboro, Tenn., 1992-93, Tot's Landing Learning Ctr., Murfreesboro, 1993, Holly Tree, Nashville, 1994; nanny Mike and Carol Wierzba, Brentwood, Tenn., 1994-95; tchr. Inst. of Learning Rsch., Nashville, 1995-96; spl. edn. tchr. Glenn Middle Sch., 1996—. Office: Inst of Learning Rsch Glenn Middle Sch 322 Cleveland St Nashville TN 37027

TRENARY, CARLOS FRANCISCO, systems analyst, network manager; b. New Orleans, Feb. 4, 1949; s. Richard Arthur and Maria Juana (Jimenez) T.; children: Maggie, Jasmine. BS in Anthropology, Tulane U., 1986; MA in Anthropology, Vanderbilt U., 1993. Lab. ops. mgr. dept. physics and astronomy Tulane U., New Orleans, 1981-87; sci. apparatus mgr. dept. physics and astronomy Vanderbilt U., Nashville, 1987-95, sys. analyst, network mgr. Microcomputer Lab., 1995—. Mem. steering com. Mid. Tenn. Rainforest Action Group, Nashville, 1989-93. Democrat. Home: 719 Ashlawn Pl Nashville TN 37211-5881 Office: Microcomputer Lab Vanderbilt Hospital Nashville TN 37232

TRENKLER, MICHAEL, small business owner; b. Utica, N.Y., Dec. 31, 1960; s. Viktor Georg and Hildegard (Janocha) T. BS in Data Processing, Jones Coll., Jacksonville, Fla., 1989. Machinist Allprecise Tool & Mfg., Rochester, N.Y., 1980-84; salesman Radio Shack, Jacksonville, 1985-93; co-owner Imbiss Vending, Jacksonville, 1993—. Home and Office: 2114 Saye Dr Jacksonville FL 32225

TRENNEPOHL, GARY LEE, finance educator, consultant; b. Detroit, Dec. 6, 1946; s. Leo Donald and Wilma Mae (Tiensvold) T.; m. Sandra K. Yeager, June 9, 1968; children: Paige E., Adrienne A. BS, U. Tulsa, 1968; MBA, Utah State U., 1971; PhD, Tex. Tech U., 1976. Asst. prof. aero. studies Tex. Tech U., Lubbock, 1972-74; asst. prof. fin. Ariz. State U., Tempe, 1977-80, assoc. prof., 1980-82; prof. U. Mo., Columbia, 1982-86, dir. Sch. Bus., 1984-86; prof. fin., dept. head Tex. A&M U., College Station, 1986-91, assoc. dean Coll. Bus., 1991-93, Peters prof. fin., 1992—, exec. assoc. dean, 1994-95; dean Coll. Bus. Okla. State U., Stillwater, 1995—; mem. faculty Options Inst., Chgo. Bd. Options Exchange, 1987—. Author: An Introduction to Financial Management, 1984, Investment Management, 1993; assoc. editor Jour. Fin. Research, 1983-96, Rev. Bus. Studies, 1992—; contbr. chpts. Encyclopedia of Investments; contbr. articles to profl. jours. Capt. USAF, 1968-72. Decorated Commendation medal with oak leaf cluster, Vietnam Svc. medal. Mem. Fin. Mgmt. Assn. (v.p. program 1993, pres. 1993-94), So. Fin. Assn., Southwestern Fin. Assn. (bd. dirs. 1983-84, pres. 1986), Midwest Fin. Assn. (bd. dirs. 1985-89). Republican. Lutheran. Office: Okla State U 201 Business Bldg Stillwater OK 74078

TRENT, LUTHER E., airport executive, state agency executive. Dir. airports Okalhoma City Dept. Airports. Office: Will Rogers World Airport 7100 Terminal Dr Box 937 Oklahoma City OK 73159

TRENT, RICHARD O(WEN), financial executive; b. Ft. Worth, Nov. 13, 1920; m. Phoebe ann clark, 1947. Student U. Okla., 1940-47; grad. Inst. Life Ins. Mktg., So. Meth. U., 1948. Agt., Mass. Mut. Life Ins. Co., Oklahoma City, 1946-55; founder Mid-Am. Life Ins. Co., Oklahoma City, 1955, pres., chmn. bd., 1955-65, pres. Richard O. Trent and Assocs., Inc., Oklahoma City, 1965—, chmn. Sales, Mergers and Acquisitions-Worldwide, 1966—; dir. Okla. Mut. Investors, Inc.; past pres., chmn. bd. Liberty Investment Corp.; v.p., dir. Lee Realty Corp.; past v.p., dir. Cleary Petroleum Corp.; pres. Southwest Mut. Casualty Co. Lt. col. USAF ret., 1942-66, sr. pilot, 1946-53, command pilot, 1953-66. Decorated Air Medal, Purple Heart, D.F.C. Mem. Assn. Corp. Growth, Oklahoma City C. of C., YMCA, Okla. Econ. Club, Nat. Assn. Life Underwriters (life mem. Million Dollar Round Table), Am. Legion, Men's Dinner Club, Oklahoma City Golf and Country Club, Masons, Shriners, Jesters. Office: 7201 N Classen Blvd Ste 202 Oklahoma City OK 73116-7123

TRENT, ROBERT HAROLD, business educator; b. Norfolk, Va., Aug. 3, 1933; s. Floyd Murton and Myrtle Eugenia (White) T.; m. Joanne Bell, Aug. 17, 1951; 1 child, John Thomas. B.S., U. Richmond, 1963; Ph.D., U. N.C., 1968. Asst. prof. U. N.C., Chapel Hill, 1968-69; assoc. prof. commerce McIntire Sch. Commerce U. Va., Charlottesville, 1970-74, prof. commerce, 1975-84, Ralph A. Beeton prof. free enterprise, 1985-91; C. & P. Telephone Co. prof. commerce U. Va., Charlottesville, 1991—. Co-author: Marketing Decision Making, 1976, 4th edit., 1988; editor: Developments in Management Information Systems, 1974. Mem. Inst. Mgmt. Scis., Soc. Info. Mgmt., Assn. Comp. Machinery, Decision Scis. Inst., Beta Gamma Sigma, Omicron Delta Kappa. Office: U Va Monroe Hall Charlottesville VA 22903

TRENT, WARREN C., mechanical engineer; b. Boswell, Okla., Feb. 22, 1921; s. Clem and Fannie Edora (Greer) T.; m. Ruth Magdalene Potts, Apr. 2, 1948; 1 child, Paul Dudley. BSME, Okla. State U., 1943; MSME, Purdue U., 1948. Engr. Boeing Airplane Co., Seattle, 1943-45; instr. Okla. State U., Stillwater, 1946-47; rsch. engr. Kans. State U., Manhattan, 1948-51; mgr. sect. LTV Aerospace, Dallas, 1951-65; dir. engring. tech. McDonnell Douglas, St. Louis, 1965-77; owner Trent Assocs., Tyler, Tex., 1977-93; CEO Trent Techs., Inc., Tyler, 1993—; cons. Rockwell Internat., El Segundo, Calif., 1982-87; lectr. Navy Aviation Exec. Inst., Washington, 1973-76. Patentee in field. Arbitrator Better Bus. Bur., Tyler, 1985—. With USN, 1945-46. Fellow AIAA (assoc.); mem. ASHRAE, Tex. Profl. Engrs., Mo. Profl. Engrs. Republican. Baptist. Home: 1410 Woodlands Dr Tyler TX 75703-5718 Office: Trent Techs Inc 535 WSW Loop 323 Ste 301 Tyler TX 75701

TRETHEWEY, ERIC PETER, English language educator; b. Halifax, N.S., Can., Feb. 6, 1943; came to U.S., 1962; m. Katherine Soniat; 1 child, Natasha. BA with honors, Ky. State U., 1966; MA, U. New Orleans, 1970;

PhD, Tulane U., 1979. Teaching asst. U. New Orleans, 1969-70, Tulane U., New Orleans, 1970-74; instr. composition workshop Xavier U., New Orleans, 1976-77; instr. composition, lit. St. Joseph Sem. Coll., St. Benedict, La., 1977-80, asst. prof. drama, Brit. lit., 1984-85; asst. prof. lit., poetry, writing Hollins Coll., Roanoke, Va., 1985-88, assoc. prof., 1988-93, prof., 1993—, chairperson dept. English, 1989-91; dir. Nancy Thorp Nat. Poetry Contest, Hollins Coll., 1986-89; pres. English Grad. Orgn., Tulane U., 1972-73, judge Acad. Am. Poets competition, 1986-87; vis. asst. prof. lit., poetry, writing Tulane U., 1980-83, mem. adj. faculty, 1984-85; vis. asst. prof. lit. U. New Brunswick, Can., 1983-84; vis. writer-in-residence Cleve. State U., 1989; judge Artemis nat. poetry competition, 1986-87, G. Glenwood Clark Fiction prize Coll. William and Mary, 1990-91; presenter profl. confs. Author: (books of poetry) In The Traces, 1980, Dreaming of Rivers, 1984, Phrases After Noon, 1985, Evening Knowledge, 1991, The Long Road Home, 1994, (screenplay) The Home Waltz; contbr. articles, poems and revs. to profl. and lit. publs. Recipient awards, most recently Va. prize in Poetry, 2d prize, 1990, Cynthia Cahn/Anhinga prize for poetry, 1993; recent fellow, orgns. including Yaddo, Saratoga Springs, N.Y., 1989, Va. Ctr. for Creative Arts, 1990, Cabell, 1991, Aspen Inst., Wye, Md., 1993; recipient many other awards, honors, grants and fellows, 1970—. Mem. AAUP, MLA, Nat. Coun. Tchrs. of English, Associated Writing Programs (screening judge poetry award series 1986-87), Acad. Am. Poets (assoc.), Assn. for Study of Lit. and Environ., Poetry Soc. Am., South Atlantic MLA, Southea. Conf. for Can. Studies. Home: 5318 Catawba Creek Rd Catawba VA 24070-2004 Office: Hollins Coll Dept English Roanoke VA 24020

TRETTER, VINCENT JOSEPH, JR., chemical engineer, retired; b. Trinidad, Colo., June 15, 1940; s. Vincent Joseph and Lena (Oberto) T.; m. Lois Jane Outhier; children: Elizabeth, Christopher, Michael. AA, Pueblo (Colo.) Jr. Coll., 1960; BSChemE, U. Colo., 1962; MSChemE, U. Idaho, 1965. Process engr. 3M Co., Fairmout, Minn., 1962-63; rsch. engr. JM Huber, Borger, Tex., 1965-67; project engr., group leader Ga.-Pacific, Toledo, Oreg., 1967-69; corp. sr. environ. engr. Ga.-Pacific, Portland, Oreg., 1969-75, corp. chief engr. energy and environ., 1975-78; mgr. ea. regional environ. Ga.-Pacific, Atlanta, 1978-83; mgr. environ., health and safety Ga. Gulf, Plaquemine, La., 1983-94; chair air com. TAPPI, Atlanta, 1974-75; chair air com. Assn. Oreg. Ind., 1972-73; mem. environ. adv. com. Am. Plywood Assn., 1978-79. Contbr. articles to profl. jours; patentee in field. Pres. Ft. Vancouver Little League, Vancouver, Wash., 1977-78. Mem. AIChE, Air and Waste Mgmt. Assn., Multiple Sclerosis Soc. Republican. Catholic. Home: HC03 Box 1104 Marble Falls TX 78654-9999

TREVISANI, MICHAEL F., surgeon; b. Utica, N.Y., Mar. 25, 1958; s. Pasquale J. and Manuela Marie (Scarano) T.; m. Paula Josephine Wrazien, Oct. 8, 1988; 1 child Philip Hamilton. BA, Hamilton Coll., N.Y., 1980; MD, SUNY, Syracuse, 1984. Colon and rectal surgeon Associated Colon and Rectal Surgeons, Winter Park, Fla. Lector St. Peter Paul Ch., Goldenrod, Fla., 1993—. Fellow Am. Soc. Colon and Rectal Surgeons. Home: 2826 Kinloch Dr Orlando FL 32817-2669 Office: Associated Colon and Rectal Svcs 320 Edinburgh Dr Winter Park FL 32792-4157*

TREVOR, KIRK DAVID NIELL, orchestra conductor, cellist; b. London, Feb. 8, 1952. Student, Dartington Coll., 1968-69; grad. with distinction, Guildhall Sch. Music and Drama, 1974; student, N.C. Sch. Arts, 1975-77. Asst. condr. Guildhall Opera Sch., 1973-74; music dir. Youth Symphony of Carolinas, 1978-82; music dir., condr. Knoxville (Tenn.) Symphony Orch., 1984—; chief condr. Martinu Philharmonic Czech Rep., 1995—; assoc. condr. Charlotte (N.C.) Symphony Orch., 1978-82, Exxon Art Endowment and Dallas Symphony, 1982-85; former resident condr. Dallas Symphony; dir. music Indpls. Chamber Orch., 1988—; instr. U. Tenn., 1985—; guest condr. U.S., S.Am., USSR, Czech Republic, Poland, Romania, Switzerland; tchr. Condrs. Symphonic Workshop in Zlin, Czech Republic, 1991—, Artistic Dir. Recipient Libottom Meml. prize, 1972, Kappilis Condr. prize, 1974, Toussant prize, 1974; winner Am. Condrs. Program, 1990; Fulbright Exchange grantee U.K. and U.S. Dept. State, 1975, Am. Condrs. Program grantee, 1990. Mem. Condrs. Guild, Am. Symphony Orch. League. Office: Knoxville Symphony Orch 623 Market St Ste 600 Knoxville TN 37902-2243*

TREZZA, ALPHONSE FIORE, librarian, educator; b. Phila., Dec. 27, 1920; s. Vincent and Amalia (Ferrara) T.; m. Mildred Di Pietro, May 19, 1945; children: Carol Ann Trezza Johnston, Alphonse Fiore. B.S., U. Pa., 1948, M.S., 1950, postgrad.; librarian cert., Drexel Inst., 1949. Page Free Library, Phila., 1940-41, 45-48; library asst. Free Library, 1948-49; cataloger, asst. reference librarian Villanova U., 1949-50, instr., 1956-60; head circulation dept. U. Pa. Library, 1950-56; lectr. Drexel Inst. Sch. Library Sci., 1951-60; editor Cath. Library world, 1956-60; exec. sec. Cath. Library Assn., 1956-60; assoc. exec. dir. ALA, exec. sec. library adminstrn. div., 1960-67, assoc. dir. adminstrv. services, 1967-69; dir. Ill. State Library, Springfield, 1969-74; lectr. Grad. Sch. Library and Info. Sci., Cath. U., 1975-82; exec. dir. Nat. Commn. on Libraries and Info. Scis., Washington, 1974-80; dir. intergovt. library Cooperation Project Fed. Library Com./Library of Congress, Washington, 1980-82; assoc. prof. Sch. Library and Info. Studies Fla. State U., Tallahassee, 1982-87, prof., 1987-93, emeritus prof., 1993—; mem. Ill. Library LSCA TITLE I-II Adv. Commn., 1963-69; mem. network devel. com. Library of Congress, 1977-82; bd. visitors Sch. Library and Info. Sci., U. Pitts., 1977-80; cons. Becker & Hayes, Inc., 1980-84, King Research, Inc., 1981-82; mem. planning com and steering com. Fla. Gov.'s Conf. on Library and Info. Svcs., 1988-91. Nat. chmn. Cath. Book Week, 1954-56; pres. Joliet Diocesan Bd. Edn., 1966-68; Democratic committeeman, Lombard, Ill., 1961-69; auditor Borough of Norwood (Pa.), 1958-60. Served to 1st lt. USAAF, 1942-45. Decorated Air medal; recipient Ofcl. commendation White House Conf. on Libr. and Info. Svc., 1979. Mem. ALA (coun. 1973-82, 88-92, mem. exec. bd. 1974-79, chmn. stats. coordinating com. 1970-74, mem. pub. com. 1975-78, 81-83, 87-89, chmn. adv. com. interface, 1979-83, chmn. membership com. 1983-84, chmn. nominating com. 1988-89, mem. legis. com. 1989-91, adv. bd. ALA Yearbook 1976-91, Assn. Specialized and Coop. Library Agys. legis. com., 1987-89, ad hoc com. White House Conf. on Libr. and Info. Svcs. 1989-91, chmn. awards com. 1990-92, Exceptional Achievement award 1981, J.B. Lippincott award 1989), Cath. Library Assn. (life, adv. coun. 1960—), Ill. Library Assn. (chmn. legis.-library devel. com. 1964-69, mem. exec. bd., libr's. citation 1974), Fla. Library Assn. (bd. dirs. 1987-93, pres. 1991-92, intellectual freedom com., chmn. com. on Fla. Librs. publ., editor, publ. com., planning com., 1991, site com.), Continuing Libr. Edn. Network and Exchange (pres. 1982-83), Internat. Fedn. Library Assns. and Institutions (statistics standing com. 1976-85, planning com.), Coun. Nat. Library Assns. (chmn. 1959-61), Assn. Coll. and Research Librarians (pres. Phila. chpt. 1953-55), Drexel Inst. Library Sch. Alumni Assn. (pres. 1955-56, exec. bd. 1956-60, chmn. chief officers State Library Agys. 1973-74), Chgo. Library Club (pres. 1969), Assn. Library and Info. Sci. Edn. (govt. relation com. 1985-87), Drexel U. Alumni Assn. (Outstanding Alumnus award 1963), Kappa Phi Kappa (chpt. pres. 1948), Beta Phi Mu (hon.). Lodge: K.C. Office: Fla State U Sch Libr and Info Studies Tallahassee FL 32306

TRIBBLE, KEITH R., athletic and social events executive; b. Sept. 29, 1955; m. Terri Tribble; children, Carlyn, Kyle. BS in Pub. Rels. and Mktg., U. Fla., 1977. Sales trainee Celotex Corp., Chgo., 1977-78; asst. sales rep. Celotex Corp., Tampa, Fla., 1978-79, sr. sales rep., 1979-81; adminstrv. asst. to athletic dir. U. Fla. Athletic Assn., Gainesville, 1981-83, asst. athletic dir. spring sports, 1983-88, assoc. athletic dir., 1988-89; dir. event mgmt. Raycom Mgmt. Group, Inc., Charlotte, N.C., 1989-90; exec. dir. Sunshine Festival Football, Inc., Ft. Lauderdale, Fla., 1990-92; sr. assoc. athletic dir. U. Nev., Las Vegas, 1992-93; exec. dir. Fed. Express/Orange Bowl, Miami, Fla., 1993—; asst. football coach Morris Brown Coll., Atlanta, 1978-79; chmn. cheerleading bd. U. Fla., 1982-89, mem. Title XI com., 1984-89, mem. O'Connell Ctr. adv. bd., 1984-86; co-tournament dir. Southeastern Conf. Baseball Tournament, 1984; coord. Southeastern Conf. Tennis and Indoor Track and Field Championships, 1987; tournament dir. Southeastern Conf. Track Championships, 1989; mem. 1995 Superbowl Host Com. Active Beacon Coun., 1993-94; bd. dirs. Big Bros. & Sisters Gainesville, 1988, Big Bros. & Sisters Broward County, 1991, Boy Scouts Am., Broward County. Named one of 100 Black Men of South Fla., 1993—. Mem. Nat. Assn. Collegiate Dirs. Athletics, Nat. Urban League, Coll. Athletic Bus. Mgrs. Assn., Black Coaches Assn., Football Bowl Assn., Greater Miami C. of C. Baptist. Office: Orange Bowl Com 601 Brickell Key Dr Ste 206 Miami FL 33131-2652

TRICHEL, MARY LYDIA, middle school educator; b. Rosenberg, Tex., Feb. 2, 1957; d. Henry John and Henrietta (Jurek) Pavlicek; m. Keith Trichel, Aug. 8, 1981; children: Daniel, Nicholas. BS cum laude, Tex. A & M U., 1980. Cert. tchr., Tex. Social studies tchr. grades 6, 7 and 8 St. Francis de Sales, Houston, 1980-81; English tchr. grades 7 and 8 Dean Morgan Jr. High, Casper, Wyo., 1983-86; English and journalism tchr. grades 9 and 11 Tecumseh (Okla.) High Sch., 1987; English tchr. grade 6 Christa McAuliffe Middle Sch., Houston, 1988-92; tchr. Tex. history grade 7, journalism grade 8 Lake Olympia Middle Sch., Missouri City, Tex., 1991-92; tchr. social studies 6th grade Lake Olympia Mid. Sch. Ft. Bend Ind. Sch. Dist., 1993—. Recipient teaching awards. Mem. Nat. Coun. Tchrs. English, Nat. Coun. Tchrs. Social Studies, Am. Fedn. Tchrs. Home: 3707 Pin Oak Ct Missouri City TX 77459-7018

TRICK, ANN LOUISE, accountant; b. Jefferson Parish, La.; d. Claybourne and Avis Margaret (Middleton) Waldrop; m. Joseph Michael Trick, Dec. 28, 1982 (div.); children: Philip Michael, Justin Anthony, Kristen Alicia. BA, Tex. Tech. U., 1979; M of Profl. Acctg., U. Tex., Arlington, 1992. CPA, Tex. Acct. exec., office mgr. DBG & H, Dallas, 1979-80; bus. mgr. Creative Microsystems, Inc., Dayton, Ohio, 1980-81; office mgr. Sinclair & Rush, Inc., Arlington, 1981-83, Norand Corp., Arlington, 1983-84; sr. acct. Price Waterhouse, Ft. Worth, 1992-95; sr. fin. analyst Millers Insurance Group, Ft. Worth, 1995—. SERVA vol. Arlington Ind. Sch. Dist., 1990-91; den leader Cub Scout Pack 389, Arlington, 1992-93; mem. bd. fin. All Saints Luth. Ch. Recipient Scholarship Cert. of Merit, Inst. Cert. Mgmt. Accts., 1991; scholar Am. Women's Soc. CPAs, 1991, Mid Cities Assn. CPAs, 1991. Mem. Am. Soc. Women Accts., Tex. Soc. CPAs, Inst. Mgmt. Accts. (assoc. dir. acad. rels. 1991-92, dir. acad. rels. 1992-93), Beta Alpha Psi, Beta Gamma Sigma. Office: Millers Ins Group PO Box 2269 Fort Worth TX 76113-2269

TRICK, OTHO LEE, psychiatrist; b. Anderson, Ind., Aug. 4, 1931; s. Homer Forest and Merlie Juanita (Turner) T.; m. Melba Evelyn Heath, June 2, 1952 (div. Mar. 1973); children: David, Kevin, Cynthia Cooper, Brian; m. Reita A. Troum, June 2, 1974. Student, Anderson Coll., 1950-52; MD, Ind. U., Indpls., 1958. Diplomate Am. Bd. Psychiatry and Neurology; lic. physician, Ind., Mich., N.Mex., W.Va., Tex. Rotating intern Blodgett Meml. Hosp., Grand Rapids, Mich., 1958-59; gen. practice medicine surgery and obstetrics Durand, Mich., 1959-64; asst. resident, resident psychiatry Duke U. Med. Ctr., Durham, N.C., 1964-67; chief inpatient svc. VA Hosp., Albuquerque, 1967-68; dir. impatient program dept. behavioral med. and psychiatry W.Va. U. Sch. Medicine, Morgantown, 1968-73, dir. Charleston divsn. dept. behavioral med. and psychiatry, 1973-74; dir. Family Inst. S.W., Inc., Houston, 1974—; med. dir. utilization mgmt. Bellaire Gen. Hosp., Houston, 1992—; cons. surveyor Joint Commn. on Accreditation Healthcare orgns., Oakbrook Terrace, Ill., 1990—; quality healthcare cons.; psychiat. cons. Harris County Dept. Edn., Divsn. Psychol. Svcs., Houston, 1974-77; Harris County Med. Soc. liaision to Mental Health Mental Retardation Authority of Harris County, 1976-78; med. dir. utilization rev. program Sharpstown Gen. Hosp., Houston, 1987-91; mentor mentor program for rural hosps. Tex. Med. Assn., 1989-90; mem. active and courtesy staffs various hosps. Contbr. articles to profl. jours. Mem. Am. Psychiat. Assn. (coun. mem. W.Va. dist. br. 1971-74, chmn. continuing edn. com. 1972-74), Am. Soc. Quality Control, Tex. Med. Assn., Harris County Med. Soc. Home: 10002 Green Tree Rd Houston TX 77042-1228 Office: Family Inst Southwest 1202 Hawthorne St Houston TX 77006-3820

TRICKEY, SAMUEL BALDWIN, physics educator, researcher, university administrator; b. Detroit, Nov. 28, 1940; s. Samuel Miller and Betty Irene (Baldwin) T.; m. Lydia Hernandez Dec. 28, 1962 (div. June 1981); children: Matthew J., Phillip J.; m. Cynthia Karle, Aug. 13, 1983. BA in Physics, Rice U., 1962; MS, Tex. A&M U., 1966, PhD in Theoretical Physics, 1968. Rsch. scientist Mason & Hanger-Silas Mason Corp., 1962-64; asst. prof. physics U. Fla., Gainesville, 1968-73, assoc. prof., 1973-77, prof. physics and chemistry, 1979—, dir. J.C. Slater Meml. Computing Lab., 1981-93, dir. Computer and Communications Resources Coll. Liberal Arts and Scis., 1986-90, exec. dir. info. techs. and svcs. Office of Provost, 1991-96; prof. physics, chmn. physics and engring. physics Tex. Tech U., Lubbock, 1977-79; cons. Redstone Arsenal Ala., 1972-76; vis. rsch. scholar Mich. Tech. U., 1982-92; vis. scientist IBM Rsch. Ctr., San Jose, Calif., 1975-76; assoc. or dep. dir. Sanibel Symposia; cons. T div. Los Alamos Nat. Lab., 1984—, vis. scientist Max Planck Inst. für Astrophysik, Munich, 1985-94; internat. collaborator Technische U. München Lehrstedel für Theoretische Chemie, 1995—. Exec. v.p. U. Fla. chpt. United Faculty of Fla., 1981-83. Named Tchr. of Yr., Coll. Arts and Scis., U. Fla., 1973-74. Fellow Am. Phys. Soc.; mem. Am. Assn. Physics Tchrs., Nat. R.R. Hist. Soc., Gulf Atlantic Yacht Club, San Juan 21 Class Assn., S.W. R.R. Hist. Soc., Phi Kappa Phi, Sigma Xi, Sigma Pi Sigma. Democrat. Presbyterian. Contbr. articles to profl. jours. Home: 723 NW 19th St Gainesville FL 32603-1102 Office: Univ Fla Quantum Theory Project Williamson Hall Gainesville FL 32611

TRIFOLI-CUNNIFF, LAURA CATHERINE, psychologist, consultant; b. L.I., N.Y., June 8, 1958; d. Peter Nicholas and Susan Maria (Graziano) T.; m. John Kevin Cunniff, June 6, 1992; 1 child, James Peter. BA, Hofstra U., Uniondale, N.Y., 1980, MA, 1982, PhD, 1986. Founder, prin. Quality Cons., West Islip, N.Y., 1980-87; sr. tng. officer Norstar Bank, Garden City, N.Y., 1985-87; asst. v.p. mgmt. devel. First Boston Corp., N.Y.C., 1986-90; mgr. exec. devel. Merrill Lynch, N.Y.C., 1990-91; pres. The Exec. Process, 1991—; cons. Am. Mgmt. Assn., N.Y.C., 1981-83, AT&T, Basking Ridge, N.H., 1982-83, The First Boston Corp., 1991—, Goldman Sachs, 1991—, Merrill Lynch & Co., 1991—, Union Bank of Switzerland, 1991—, Sanford C. Bernstein & Co., 1992—, Alexander & Alexander, 1993—, S.G. Warburg, 1994; instr. dept. psychology Hofstra U., 1983-85. Author: Vietnam Veterans: Post Traumatic Stress and its Effects, 1986; contbr. articles to profl. publs. Shift coord. Islip Hotline, 1976-78; eucharistic min. Hofstra U. Cath. Soc., 1980-85, Good Samaritan Hosp., West Islip, N.Y., 1988—. Scholar, Hofstra U., 1978-81, fellow, 1980, 81. Mem. Am. Psychol. Assn., Am. Soc. Tng. and Devel., Nat. Psychol. Honor Soc., Internat. Platform Soc. Roman Catholic. Office: 2906 Bree Hill Rd Oakton VA 22124-1212

TRIGG, GLYN RAY, guidance counselor, educational administrator; b. Canton, Miss., Apr. 21, 1964; s. Bruce L. and Eunice W. (Davis) T. BS in Social and Rehabilitative Svcs., U. So. Miss., 1991. Alcohol-drug counselor, intervention-prevention counselor S.W. Miss. Mental Health, McComb, 1992-93; guidance counselor, tchr. phys. edn., coach Porter's Chapel Acad., Vicksburg, Miss., 1993-95, interim hedmaster, 1994—. Bell ringer Salvation Army, Vicksburg, 1993; organizer, activities chmn. Eagle Fest, Porter's Chapel Patron's Club, 1994. Named Jaycee of Month, Hattiesburg Jaycees, 1991, recipient cert. of merit, Jacke Eckerd svc. award. Mem. Jackson Jaycees (2d dir. 1990-92, Jaycee of Month 1992), Kiwanis (faculty advisor Key Club 1993-94). Baptist. Home: PO Box 821034 Vicksburg MS 39180 Office: Porter's Chapel Acad 3460 Porters Chapel Rd Vicksburg MS 39180-4594

TRIGONY, NICHOLAS D., broadcast executive; m. Rosemary McRory, 1967; children: Shannon, Sean. Grad., Syracuse U., 1961. Sales rep. John Blair and Co., Chgo., 1968-72; with ABC Radio, 1972-81; v.p., gen. mgr. Sta. WPLJ-FM ABC Radio, N.Y.C.; v.p., gen. mgr. Sta. KKK-AM/FM Viacom, 1981-86; from exec. v.p. radio to exec. v.p. broadcasting divsn. Cox Enterprises, 1986-90, pres. broadcasting divsn., 1990—; chmn. T.V. Operators Caucus; mem. T.V. bd. NAB; chmn. cable/telco entry task force NAB. Mem. Mayor's Entertainment Commn., Atlanta; bd. dirs. Link Counseling Ctr. 1st lt. U.S. Army. Mem. Assn. Maximum Svc. T.V. (bd. dirs., treas.). Address: Cox Broadcasting PO Box 105357 Atlanta GA 30348-5357*

TRIMBLE, BRIAN EDWARD, structural engineer; b. Sewickely, Pa., June 30, 1963; s. Ernest Cleveland and Mary Bernadette (Smith) T.; m. Jane Marie Stritzinger, May 2, 1987; children: Victoria Lynn, Rachel Nicole. B of Archtl. Engring., Pa. State U., 1986. Design engr. Glen-Gery Corp., Washington, 1986-88; sr. engr. tech. svcs. Brick Inst. Am., Reston, Va., 1988—. Author: Masonry: Components to Assemblages, 1990, Masonry: Design & Construction, Problems & Repair, 1993. Mem. ASCE, Constrn. Specifications Inst. (bd. dirs. 1991—), The Masonry Soc., Am. Soc. for Landscape Architects, Internat. Brick Collectors Assn. Office: Brick Inst Am 11490 Commerce Park Dr Reston VA 20191-1532

TRIMBLE, JAMES T., JR., federal judge; b. Bunkie, La., Sept. 13, 1932; s. James T. Sr. and Mabel (McNabb) T.; m. Murel Elise Biles, Aug. 18, 1956; children: Lise Ann Reed, Mary Olive Beacham, Martha McNabb Elliott, Sarah Palmer Trimble. Attended, U. Southwestern La. (formerly Southwestern La. Inst.), 1950-52; BA in Law, La. State U., 1955, JD, 1956. Bar: La. 1956. With Gist, Murchison & Gist (now Gist, Methvin, Hughes & Munsterman), 1959-78, Trimble, Percy, Smith, Wilson, Foote, Walker & Honeycutt, 1979-86; U.S. magistrate U.S. Dist. Ct. (we. dist.) La., 1986-91, judge, 1991—. Lt. USAF, 1956-59. Mem. Fed. Judges Assn., Southwest La. Bar Assn., La. Bar Assn., La. Bar Found. Office: 611 Broad St Ste 237 Lake Charles LA 70601-4380

TRIMBLE, VANCE HENRY, retired newspaper editor; b. Harrison, Ark., July 6, 1913; s. Guy L. and Josephine (Crump) T.; m. Elzene Miller, Jan. 9, 1932; 1 dau., Carol Ann. Student pub. schs., Wewoka, Okla. Cub reporter Okemah (Okla.) Daily Leader, 1928; worked various newspapers in Okmulgee, Muskogee, Tulsa and, Okla.; successively reporter, rewrite man, city editor Houston Press, 1939-50, mng. editor, 1950-55; news editor Scripps-Howard Newspaper Alliance, Washington, 1955-63; editor Ky. Post and Times-Star, Covington, 1963-79. Author: The Uncertain Miracle, 1974, Sam M. Walton, 1990, (biography) E.W. Scripps, 1992, Frederick Smith of Federal Express, 1993, An Empire Undone: Rise and Fall of Chris Whittle, 1995; co-author: Happy Chandler Autobiography, 1989; editor: Scripps-Howard Handbook, 1981. Trustee Scripps-Howard Found., 1974-79. Recipient Pulitzer prize for nat. reporting, 1960, Raymond Clapper award, 1960, Sigma Delta Chi award for disting. Washington correspondence, 1960, Frank Luther Mott award for journalism book rsch. U. Mo., 1993; named to Okla. Journalism Hall of Fame, 1974. Mem. Am. Soc. Newspaper Editors. Baptist. Clubs: Nat. Press (Washington); Press (Houston); Cincinnati, Ft. Mitchell Country. Home: 1013 Sunset Rd Covington KY 41011-1168

TRIMMIER, CHARLES STEPHEN, JR., lawyer; b. Chgo., June 25, 1943; s. Charles Stephen and Lucille E. (Anderson) T.; m. Rae Wade Trimmier, Aug. 19, 1966; children: Charles Stephen, Hallie Wade. B.A., U. Ala., Tuscaloosa, 1965, J.D., 1968. Bar: Ala. 1968. From assoc. to ptnr. Rives, Peterson, Pettus and Conway, Birmingham, Ala., 1968-77; pres. TrimmierLaw Firm, L.L.C., Birmingham, Mobile, Montgomery, Muscle Shoals, Dothan and Decatur, Ala., Orlando, Palm Beach and Panama City, Fla. 1977—; gen. counsel Nat. Assn. State Chartered Credit Union Suprs., Ala. Credit Union League, Fla. Credit Union League. Mem. ABA (bus. and banking law sect., credit union com.), Ala. Bar Assn., Birmingham Bar Assn., Comml. Law League, Ala. Law Inst., Shades Valley Jaycees (sec. 1973). Episcopalian. Editor-in-chief: Ala. Law Rev. 1968. Home: 3819 River View Cir Birmingham AL 35243-4801 Office: Trimmier Law Firm LLC PO Box 1885 Birmingham AL 35201-1885

TRINH, VICTOR, small business owner; b. Vientiane, Laos, Apr. 7, 1941; came to U.S., 1975; naturalized, 1981.; s. Thu and Mao (Nguyen) T.; m. Tuyet Mai Nguyen, Jan. 19, 1972; children: Nancy H., Wiliam Q. Grad. high sch., Vientiane. Electronic assembler Anilam Electronics, Miami, Fla., 1978-80; owner Kim-Do Food, Pitts., 1981-85, Jensen Food Mart, Houston, 1986—; pub. Vic Pub., Houston, 1993—. Author: Student Assignments Notebook, 1993.

TRIPLETT, GLOVER BROWN, agronomist, educator; b. Crawford, Miss., June 2, 1930; s. Glover Brown and Minnie Louise (Blake) T.; m. Imogene Crump, Feb. 24, 1950; 1 child, Dorinda. BS, Miss. State U., 1951, MS, 1955; PhD, Mich. State U., 1959. Agronomist Ohio Agrl. R & D Ctr., Wooster, 1959-82; agronomist, prof. Miss. State U., Mississippi State, 1983—. Editor: No Tillage Agriculture, 1986. 1st lt. U.S. Infantry, 1951-53, Korea. Mem. Am. Soc. Agronomy, Lions Internat. Home: 1102 Nottingham Rd Starkville MS 39759-4008 Office: Miss State Univ Dept Agriculture Mississippi State MS 39762

TRIPLETT, WILLIAM CARRYL, physician, researcher; b. St. Marys, W.Va., May 9, 1915; s. Harry Carryl and Glenna Olive (Dotson) T.; m. Jane Dinsmoor, June 11, 1940 (div. 1961); children: William C. II, Jan Frances; m. Josephine Vann (div.); children: Harriett, Amber, Charles; m. Kathleen Quigley. BA, W.Va. U., 1936; MD, U. Md., 1940. Intern Ohio Valley Gen. Hosp., Wheeling, W.Va., 1940; resident in internal medicine Berkley County Meml. Hosp., 1941-42; med. dir. Camp Wood (Tex.) Convalescent Ctr.; pvt. practice Corpus Christi, Tex., 1946-68, 72-88; dir. rsch. TRIAD Assocs. Inc., 1947—, ENA, 1968-92, Intercontinental Cardiac Rsch., 1984-92. Inventor and patentee in field. Bayfront adv. com. Corpus Christi, 1950-55; bay drilling com. Corpus Christi, 1954-56; environ. com., Tex., 1968-72; assoc. dir. Tex. Mil. Inst. Capt. USCG Aux., 1942-46. Named Man of Yr. Camp Wood/Nucces Canyon C. of C., 1990; 18 awards as editor Costal Bd. Medicine, Corpus Christi. Mem. AMA, Tex. Med. Assn., Corpus Christi Yacht Club (comdr. 1953). Anglican. Home and Office: TRIAD Assocs Inc PO Box 517 Camp Wood TX 78833-0517

TRIPP, KAREN BRYANT, lawyer; b. Rocky Mount, N.C., Sept. 2, 1955; d. Bryant and Katherine Rebecca (Watkins) Tripp; m. Robert Mark Burleson, June 25, 1977 (div. 1996). BA, U. N.C., 1976; JD, U. Ala., 1981. Bar: Tex. 1981, U.S. Dist. Ct. (so. dist.) Tex. 1982, U.S. Dist. Ct. (ea. dist.) Tex. 1991, U.S. Ct. Appeals (fed. cir.) 1983, U.S. Supreme Ct. 1994. Law clk. Tucker, Gray & Espy, Tuscaloosa, Ala., 1978-81, to presiding justice Ala. Supreme Ct., Montgomery, summer 1980; atty. Exxon Prodn. Rsch. Co., Houston, 1981-86, coord. tech. transfer, 1986-87; assoc. Arnold, White and Durkee, Attys. at Law, Houston, 1988-93, shareholder, 1994—; pres. Blake Barnett & Co., 1996—. Editor: Intellectual Property Law Review, 1995, 96; contbr. articles to profl. jours. Recipient Am. Jurisprudence award U. Ala., 1980, Dean's award, 1981. Mem. ABA (intellectual property law section, ethics com. 1992-95), Houston Bar Assn. (interprofl. rels. com. 1988-90), Houston Intellectual Property Lawyers Assn. (mem. outstanding inventor com. 1982-84, chmn. 1994-95, chmn. student edn. com. 1986, sec. 1987-88, chmn. awards com. 1988-89, chmn. program com. 1988-91, 95-96, treas. 1991-92, bd. dirs. 1992-94, nominations com. 1993, 96), Tex. Bar Assn. (antitrust law com. 1984-85, chmn. Internat. Law com. of Intellectual Property Law Sect. 1987-88, internat. transfer tech. com. 1983-84), Am. Intellectual Property Lawyers Assn. (mem. patent law com. 1995), Women in Tech. (founder), Phi Alpha Delta (clk. 1980). Democrat. Episcopalian. Office: Arnold White & Durkee PO Box 4433 Houston TX 77210-4433

TRIPP, LINDA LYNN, nutritition counselor; b. Patterson, Ga., Nov. 11, 1946; d. Bert L. and Jelain (Crews) Lynn; m. J. Randolph Tripp, Sept. 25, 1977. Student, South Ga. Coll., 1964-67, Pitt Community Coll., Greenville, N.C., 1977-78; cert. real estate broker, East Carolina U., 1979, BS, 1980, MA, 1981. Adminstr. State of N.C., Greenville, 1968-79; pres. Diet Instrn. and Eating Therapy Inc., Greenville, 1979—; co-owner, dir. AmeriCom Prodn. Group, Inc., 1989—; charter mem. Greenville Aquatics and Fitness Ctr.; chmn. bd. Am. Prodn. Group, Inc., Carolina Ct. Reporters. Contbr. articles to profl. jours. Vol. Pitt Community Coll., Greenville, 1984, Greenville Parks and Recreation, 1987; mem. St. Timothy's Episc. Ch., Greenville. Mem. Am. Pers. and Guidance Assn., N.C. Real Estate Commn., Diet Ctrs. of Carolinas, Ayden (N.C.) Country Club, Pi Omega Pi. Republican. Office: Carolina Ct Reporters Inc 102 Oakmont Profl Plz Greenville NC 27858

TRIPP, NORMAN DENSMORE, lawyer; b. Binghamton, N.Y., Apr. 11, 1938; s. Merritt Frederick and Eleonore Graves (Satterley) T.; m. Jane Grace Mighton, June 15, 1962; children—Jennifer, Norman, Christine, Michael. B.A., U. Miami, 1962; J.D. magna cum laude, Cleve. State U., 1967. Bar: Ohio, Fla. Chmn. Tripp, Scott, Conklin & Smith, P.A., Fort Lauderdale, Fla.; gen. counsel, dir. Alamo Rent A Car Inc., Fort Lauderdale; gen. counsel Cert. Tours (Delta Dream Vacations). Past mem. bd. adjustment City of Fort Lauderdale; mem. Ft. Lauderdale Downtown Devel. Authority; bd. of trustees State of Fla. Community Coll. System, U. Miami, Coral Gables, Fla. Mem. Am. Soc. Travel Agts., ABA, Broward County Bar Assn., Fla. Bar Assn. Clubs: Ocean Reef (Key Largo); Fort Lauderdale Yacht, Fort Lauderdale Country, Cat Key Club (Bahamas). Office: Tripp Scott Conklin & Smith PO Box 14245 Fort Lauderdale FL 33302-4245

TRIPPE, CHARLES WHITE, financial and development executive; b. N.Y.C., Jan. 30, 1935; s. Juan Terry and Elizabeth (Stettinius) T.; m. Pamela Reid; children: Charles Jr., James R., Elizabeth, Carie. BS in Engring., Yale U., 1957; MBA, Harvard U., 1959. V.p. fin. Intercontinental Hotels,

N.Y.C., 1962-66; v.p., treas. Pan Am, N.Y.C., 1966-69, v.p. planning, 1969-71; v.p. corp. devel. Pan Am., N.Y.C., 1971-77; v.p. planning Bell & Howell, Chgo., 1978-85; ptnr. and founder Trippe & Co., Greenwich, Conn., 1985—; founder, pres. AmPro Corp., 1988, Liberia Devel. Corp., The Liberia Co.; dir. Bermuda Properties, Ltd. Mem. Links Club (N.Y.C.), Round Hill Club (Greenwich), N.Y. Yacht Club, Orchard Is. Golf Club (Vero Beach, Fla.).

TRIPPLER, AARON KNOWLES, association executive; b. Canova, S.D., July 8, 1950; s. Knowles C. Trippler and Ines C. Matzke; m. Mary S. Dodge, Sept., 1990; children: Evan Knowles, Brennen Aaron. BSBA, Calif. Coast U., Santa Ana; postgrad., Dakota State Coll., Madison, S.D. Chief of staff Minn. State Senate IR Caucus, St. Paul, 1987-89; v.p. Communicating for Agr., Mpls., 1983-91; exec. dir. Health Care Solutions, Washington, 1991-92; dir. govt. affairs Am. Indsl. Hygiene Assn., Fairfax, Va., 1992—. Author: Analysis of Health Risk-Sharing Programs in U.S., 3 edits., 1987-91. Sgt. U.S. Army, 1970-73. Home: 20613 Belwood Ct Sterling VA 20165

TRITTEN, JAMES JOHN, national security educator; b. Yonkers, N.Y., Oct. 3, 1945; s. James Hanley and Jennie (Szucs) T.; m. Kathleen Tritten, (div. 1983); children: Kimberly, James John Jr.; m. Jasmine Clark, Dec. 29, 1990. BA in Internat. Studies, Am. U., 1971; MA in Internat. Affairs, Fla. State U., 1978; AM in Internat. Rels., U. So. Calif., L.A., 1982, PhD in Internat. Rels., 1984. Commd. officer USN, 1967, advanced through grades to commdr., 1981; joint strategic plans officer Office of the Chief of Naval Ops., Washington, 1984-85; asst. dir. net assessment Office of the Sec. of Def., Washington, 1985-86; chmn. dept. nat. security affairs Naval Postgrad. Sch., Monterey, Calif., 1986-89; ret. USN, 1989; assoc. prof. nat. security affairs Naval Postgrad. Sch., Monterey, 1989-93; spl. asst. to comdr. Naval Doctrine Command, Norfolk, Va., 1993-96; exercise and tng. dir. U.S. Atlantic Command Joint Tng., Analysis, Simulation Ctr., Suffolk, Va., 1996—; cons. Rand Corp., Santa Monica, Calif., 1982-84; with Nat. Security Rsch., Fairfax, Va., 1992, AmerInd, Alexandria, Va., 1996—. Author: Soviet Naval Forces and Nuclear Warfare, 1986, Our New National Security Strategy, 1992 (George Washington Honor medal 1991), A Doctrine Reader, 1996; contbr. chpts. to books and articles to profl. jours. Mem. Adv. Bd. on Alcohol Related Problems, Monterey County, Calif., 1987-90; bd., officer Leadership Monterey (Calif.) Peninsula, 1989-92, Carmel Valley (Calif.) Property Owners Assn., 1989-91; commr. Airport Land Use Commn., Monterey County, 1990-93, mem. Nat Eagle Scout Assn. Decorated Def. Superior Svc. medal Sec. Def., Washington, 1986, Meritorious Svc. medal Sec. Navy, Monterey, 1989, Navy Civilian Supr. Svc. medal, 1996; recipient Alfred Thayer Mahan award for literary achievement Navy League of U.S., Arlington, Va., 1986. Mem. Mil. Ops. Rsch. Soc. (v.p. 1990-91), U.S. Naval Inst. (Silver and Bronze medals), Pi Sigma Alpha, Pi Gamma Mu. Republican. Presbyterian. Office: US Atlantic Command Tng Analysis Simulation Ctr 116 Lakeview Pkwy Ste 2170 Suffolk VA 23435-2697

TRIVELPIECE, ALVIN WILLIAM, physicist, corporate executive; b. Stockton, Calif., Mar. 15, 1931; s. Alvin Stevens and Mae (Hughes) T.; m. Shirley Ann Ross, Mar. 23, 1953; children: Craig Evan, Steve Edward, Keith Eric. B.S., Calif. Poly. Coll., San Luis Obispo, 1953; M.S., Calif. Inst. Tech., 1955, Ph.D., 1958. Fulbright scholar Delft (Netherlands) U., 1958-59; asst. prof., then asso. prof. U. Calif. at Berkeley, 1959-66; prof. physics U. Md., 1966-76; on leave as asst. dir. for research div. controlled thermonuclear research AEC, Washington, 1973-75; v.p. Maxwell Labs. Inc., San Diego, 1976-78; corp. v.p. Sci. Applications, Inc., La Jolla, Calif., 1978-81; dir. Office of Energy Research, U.S. Dept. Energy, Washington, 1981-87; exec. officer AAAS, Washington, 1987-88; pres., dir. Oak Ridge (Tenn.) Nat. Lab., 1988—; v.p. Martin Marietta Energy Systems, 1989-95, Lockheed Martin Energy Systems, 1995—; pres. Lockheed Martin Energy Rsch. Corp., 1996—; head del. joint NAS and Soviet Acad. Scis. mtg. and conf. on energy and global ecol. problems, USSR, 1989; chmn. math. scis. ednl. bd. NAS, 1990-93, chmn. coordinating coun. for edn., 1990-93; chmn. coordinating coun. for edn. NRC, 1991-93, mem. Commn. on Phys. Scis., Math. and Applications, 1993—; bd. dirs. Bausch & Lomb, Inc., Rochester, N.Y.; mem. Tenn. Sci. and Tech. Adv. Commn., 1993-96, chmn., 1996—; adv. com. Federal Networking Coun., 1992-96. Author: Slow Wave Propagation in Plasma Wave Guides, 1966, Principles of Plasma Physics, 1973; also articles. Named Disting. Alumnus, Calif. Inst. Tech., Pasadena, Calif., 1987; recipient U.S. Sec. of Energy's Gold medal for Disting. Svc., 1986, Outstanding Engr. award IEEE Region 3, 1995; Guggenheim fellow, 1966. Fellow AAAS, IEEE (Outstanding Engr. award region 3 1995), Am. Phys. Soc.; mem. AAUP, NAE, Am. Nuclear Soc., Am. Assn. Physics Tchrs., Capital Hill Club, Nat. Press Club, Sigma Xi. Home: 8 Rivers Run Way Oak Ridge TN 37830-9004 Office: Oak Ridge Nat Lab Office of Dir PO Box 2008 Oak Ridge TN 37831-6255

TRIVETT, MARTHA STOVER, medical librarian; b. Greenville, S.C., Feb. 28, 1932; d. Charles Grattan and Mary Byrne (Simpson) Stover; m. Barclay Rexford Trivett, Sept. 22, 1956; children: Charles Rexford, Barbara Ellen, Mary Byrne. BA, Ga. State Coll. for Women, 1953; postgrad., East Tenn. State U., 1973-74; MS in Libr. Info. Sci., U. Tenn., 1984. Asst. chemist U. Tenn. Agr. Experiment Sta., Knoxville, 1953-54; analyst Union Carbide Nuclear Co., Oak Ridge, Tenn., 1954-58; admitting rep. Meml. Hosp./Johnson City Med. Ctr., Johnson City, Tenn., 1974-85; med. libr. Johnson City Med. Ctr., 1985—. Editor (coll. yearbook) SPECTRUM, 1953. Mem., treas. Annakusa Club, Kingston, Tenn., 1961-66, PTA, Johnson City, 1967-84, AAUW, Johnson City, 1986—; mem. Monday Club, Johnson City, 1968—. Mem. ALA, Med. Libr. Assn., Spl. Libr. Assn., Tri-Cities Health Scis. Libr. Consortium (pres. 1995). Presbyterian. Office: Johnson City Med Ctr 400 N State Of Franklin Rd Johnson City TN 37604-6035

TROCKI, LINDA KATHERINE, geoscientist, natural resource economist; b. Erie, Pa., Oct. 7, 1952; d. Bernard Joseph and Catherine Frances (Manczka) T. BS in Geology with highest honors, N.Mex. Inst. Mining and Tech., 1976; MS in Geochemistry, Pa. State U., 1983, PhD in Mineral Econs., 1985. Staff mem. Los Alamos (N.Mex.) Nat. Lab., 1976-78, 83-90; geologist Internat. Atomic Energy Agy., Vienna, Austria, 1978-80; grad. rsch. asst. Los Alamos (N.Mex.) Nat. Lab., 1981-83, dep. group leader, 1990-92, dep. program dir., 1992-93, program dir., 1993-95; asst. to pres. Chevron Petroleum Tech. Co., Houston, Tex., 1995—; spl. asst. to dep. sec. U.S. Dept. Energy, 1994-95; com. Global Found., Coral Gables, Fla., 1988—; mem. Chief of Naval Ops. Task Force on Energy, Alexandria, Va., 1990-91. Contbr. to profl. publs. Pres. Vista Encantada Neighborhood Assn., Santa Fe, 1988-89. Fellow East West Ctr., Honolulu, 1988. Mem. AAAS, Internat. Assn. Energy Economists, Mineral Econs. and Mgmt. Soc. (pres. 1994-95). Office: Chevron Petroleum Tech Co PO Box 42832 Houston TX 77242-2832

TROEDEL, LOWELL JEAN, anesthesiologist, nurse; b. Jamestown, N.Y., Apr. 28, 1937; d. Walter Stanley and Mary Jane (Lowers) Barker; (div. Dec. 1987); 1 child, Stephanie Liane. Diploma in nursing, Gowanda Sch. of Nursing, Helmuth, N.Y., 1958; cert. nurse anesthetist, S.W. Mo. Sch. Anesthesia, 1961; BS, St. Joseph's Coll., Windham, Maine, 1985. RN, N.Y., Tex. Asst. head nurse Gowanda State Hosp., Helmuth, 1958-59; evening supr. Osteo. Hosp., Springfield, Mo., 1960-61; staff anesthetist N.Y. Hosp. Cornell Med. Ctr., N.Y.C. and Manhattan, N.Y., 1961-63; instr. anesthesiology Project Hope, Ecuador, S. Am., 1963-64; staff anesthetist Jackson Meml. Hosp., Miami, Fla., 1965-66; contract anesthetist St. Anthony & N.W. Tex. Hosp., Amarillo, Tex., 1970-75; dir. dept. anesthesiology Cen. Plains Regional Hosp., Plainview, Tex., 1975-84; pvt. practice anesthetist Tex., 1984—; chairperson ann. sem. Ednl. Dist. IV, 1977-84. Capt. USAF, 1966-70. Mem. Am. Assn. Nurse Anesthetists, Tex. Assn. Nurse Anesthetists (pres. edn. dist. IV, 1977-84, govt. and pub. rels. coms. 1984-86), MENSA (sec. Amarillo chpt. 1972-75). Home: 2502 Itasca St Plainview TX 79072-1618

TROELSTRUP, GLENN CLARK, journalist; b. Hinsdale, Ill., July 3, 1930; s. Archibald William and Annabelle (Peterson) T.; divorced; children: Thang-Kim, Kenji-Erik. BJ with honors, U. Mo., 1957; MA in Journalism and East Asia, Columbia U., 1969. News editor Sta. KFRU, ABC, Columbia, Mo., 1955-57; reporter, subeditor Asahi Evening News, Tokyo, 1957-59; asst. to bur. chief NBC News, Tokyo, 1959-64; corr. U.S. News & World Report, Tokyo, Saigon, Singapore, 1962-67, Time-Life, Saigon, Vietnam, 1968; writer, reporter CBS News, N.Y.C., 1969-70; asst. editor Nucleonics Week, McGraw-Hill, N.Y.C., 1970-72; corr., assignment editor, prodr. ABC News, N.Y.C., 1972-73; reporter, subeditor Denver Post, 1973-78; regional dir. pub. affairs VA, Denver and Dallas, 1978-84; editor Commerce City (Colo.) Sentinel, 1986-88; staff editor Nat. Examiner, Boca Raton, Fla., 1989-94; advisor Internat. Mus. Cartoon Art. Author several books; contbr. numerous articles to mags. Staff sgt. USAF, 1950-57. Recipient reporting awards Denver Newspaper Guild, 1977, 78; scholar Kansas City Press Club, 1956; NDEA fellow, 1969, Ford fellow, 1968-69. Mem. Soc. Profl. Journalists (reporting awards 1982, 86, 87, 88), DAV, Japan-Am. Soc. South Fla. (bd. dirs.), Padmasambava Buddhist Ctr., Phi Kappa Psi, Omicron Delta Kappa. Buddhist. Home: 656 Eagle Dr Delray Beach FL 33444-1841

TROFATTER, KENNETH FRANK, obstetrician, gynecologist; b. Bklyn., Nov. 7, 1951; s. Kenneth Frank and Lorraine (Lewald) T.; m. Anna Michele Offutt, Nov. 6, 1992; 1 child, Maren Kendall; children from previous marriage: Peter Blair, Benjamin Cleland, Kenneth Parker. BS in Zoology, Duke U., 1973, PhD in Pathology, MD, 1979. Diplomate Am. Bd. Ob-Gyn. Intern and resident in ob-gyn. Duke U. Med. Ctr., Durham, N.C., 1979-83, fellow in maternal-fetal medicine, 1983-85, asst. prof., 1985-87; asst. prof. U. Tenn. Med. Ctr., Knoxville, 1987-89, assoc. prof., dir. reproductive immunology, 1989-93; prof., 1993—; dir. maternal-fetal medicine U. Tenn. Med. Ctr., 1990-94; dir. East Tenn. Regional Perinatal Program, 1990—; cons. Burroughs-Wellcome Corp., Rsch. Triangle Pk., N.C., 1985-87, Hoffman-LaRoche Labs., Nutley, N.J., 1988—, 3M Pharm., St. Paul, 1991—; mem. FDA Adv. Com. on Microbiol. Devices, Washington, 1989-92. Contbr. articles, chpts. to med. publs. Grantee Burroughs-Wellcome Corp., 1985-87, Hoffman-LaRoche Labs., 1987, 3M Pharmaceuticals, 1991—. Fellow Am. Coll. Ob.-Gyn.; mem. Soc. Perinatal Obstetricians, Tenn. Perinatal Assn., Am. Soc. for Immunology of Reproduction, AMA, So. Med. Assn., AAAS. Democrat. Methodist. Home: 713 Andover Blvd Knoxville TN 37922-1531 Office: U Tenn Med Ctr 1924 Alcoa Hwy Knoxville TN 37920-1511

TRONCOSO, CARLOS ALBERTO, surgeon; b. Roque Perez, Buenos Aires, Argentina, 1931. MD, Nat. U. La Plata, Argentina, 1957. Diplomate Am. Bd. Surgery, Am. Bd. Colon and Rectal Surgery. Intern St. Francis Hosp., Wichita, 1968-69; resident in gen. surgery ST. Francis Hosp., Wichita, 1969-72, Wichita VA Hosp., 1969-72; resident in colon and rectal surgery Ferguson-Droste Hosp., Grand Rapids, 1972-73; with Mercy Health Ctr., Oklahoma City; clin. asst. in surgery Okla. U. Mem. AMA, OCMA, OSMA. Office: 4200 W Memorial Rd Ste 303 Oklahoma City OK 73120-8305

TROOP, PAUL MELVIN, public relations executive, journalist; b. Jersey City, N.J., May 13, 1942; s. Bernard Lazarus and Ruth (Weiss) T.; m. Maxine Rubin, Dec. 6, 1970; 1 child, Wendy. BA, U. State of N.Y., 1980. Reporter L.I. Press, Jamaica, N.Y., 1965-66; political editor Suffolk Sun, Deer Park, N.Y., 1966-67; asst. news dir. L.I. Network News, Freeport, N.Y., 1967; asst. editor Am. Sch. & U., N.Y.C., 1967-68; acct. exec. Ruder & Finn, N.Y.C., 1969-70; mng. editor L.I. Comml. Rev., Syosset, N.Y., 1970; bus. writer Atlanta Jour., 1970-78; pres. Fin. Comm. Co., Atlanta, 1978—. Cpl. NJNG, 1965-71. Newspaper Fund scholar, 1961, Banking Sch. of the South fellow, 1975. Office: Fin Comm PO Box 29243 Atlanta GA 30359-0243

TROTT, EDWARD ASHLEY, reproductive endocrinologist; b. Apr. 6, 1961; s. Edward Wilbur and Patricia Dorothy (White) T.; m. Andrea Marie Steede, June 21, 1986; children: Kiley Edward, Kory Ashley. BS with honors, U. Calif., 1983; MD, Jefferson Med. Coll., 1990. Diplomate Nat. Bd. Med. Examiners. Intern Hahnemann U. Hosp., Phila., 1990-91; resident Med. Ctr. of Del., Newark, 1991-94; fellow, instr. Med. Coll. of Ga., Augusta, 1994—; cons. Univ. Hosp., Augusta, 1994-96; ad hoc reviewer Fertility and Sterility, Rochester, 1996; surg. skills instr. Med. Coll. of Ga., 1994-96. Author: Handbook for Primary Care in Ob/Gyn., 1996; contbr. articles to profl. jours. Recipient Tap Pharms. Resident award Tap Pharms., 1992. Mem. AMA, ACS, Nat. Med. Assn., Med. Assn. of Ga., Am. Soc. of Reproductive Medicine, Phi Beta Sigma, Phi Zeta Kappa. Methodist. Office: Med Coll of Ga 1120 15th St Augusta GA 30912

TROTT, WILLIAM MACNIDER, lawyer; b. Raleigh, N.C., July 30, 1946; s. Graham Foard and Cornelia (McKimmon) T.; m. Holly Wooten, Oct. 17, 1970 (div.); children: Hollister Wooten, James McKimmon; m. Jean Little, Aug. 11, 1984; children: Elizabeth Yost, William MacNider. AB, U. N.C., 1968, JD, 1971; LLM with highest honors, George Washington U., 1971. Bar: N.C. 1971, U.S. Dist. Ct. (ea., mid. and we. dists.) N.C. 1975, U.S. Supreme Ct. 1975. Assoc. Young, Moore and Henderson, Raleigh, 1975-78; ptnr., mem. Young, Moore & Henderson, Raleigh, 1978—; mem. N.C. Law Rev., 1969-71. Pres. Capital Area Soccer League, Raleigh, 1984-85; bd. dirs. N.C. Tennis Assn., Greensboro, 1987-94, N.C. Tennis Found., 1994—; mem. Wake County Pks. and Recreation Commn., Raleigh, 1988—, vice chmn., then chmn. Lt. JAGC, USNR, 1971-75. Morehead scholar U. N.C., 1964-68, Wettach scholar U. N.C. Law Sch., 1968-71. Mem. ABA, N.C. Bar Assn., Wake County Bar Assn., Execs. Club. Episcopalian. Office: Young Moore & Henderson PO Box 31627 Raleigh NC 27622-1627

TROTTER, DONALD WAYNE, publishing executive; b. York, Ala., Feb. 19, 1939; s. Israel Leonidas and Hazel (Jackson) T.; m. Gloria Lynn Gillenwater, Dec. 26, 1964; 1 child, Gregory Scott. BA, U. So. Miss., 1961. Mng. editor Herald-Courier, Bristol, Va., 1962-69; editor urban affairs Comml. Appeal, Memphis, 1969-77; editor Asheboro (N.C.) Courier-Tribune, 1977-83; editor, pub. County-Wide News Inc., Tecumseh, Okla., 1983—; editor, put Shawnee (Okla.) Sun, 1990—; instr. journalism U. So. Miss., Hattiesburg, 1963-64, Memphis State U., 1974-77. Trustee Mission Hill Meml. Hosp., Shawnee, 1990-91. Recipient Freedoms Found. award. Mem. Rotary, Tecumseh C. of C. (pres. 1991). Home: 412 S 9th St Tecumseh OK 74873-4023 Office: Shawnee Sun 114 N Broadway St Shawnee OK 74801-6916

TROTTER, IDE PEEBLES, financial planner, investment manager; b. Colombia, Mo., Oct. 27, 1932; s. Ide Peebles and Lena Ann (Breeze) T.; m. Luella Ruth Haupt, June 9, 1956; children: Ruth Elizabeth, Arrenia Ann, Catherine Suzanne. BS, Tex. A&M U., 1954; MA, Princeton U., 1957, PhD, 1960. Various tech. positions Exxon Research & Engring. Co., 1958-65; sect. head Exxon Research & Engring. Co., Baytown, Tex., 1965-67; advisor refining hdqrs. and corp. planning Exxon Co. USA, Houston, 1967-70; tech. supt. Exxon Co. USA, Billings, Mont., 1970-72; process supt. Exxon Co. USA, Billings, 1972-74; sr. advisor logistics Exxon Corp., N.Y.C., 1974-78; gen. mgr. logistics Esso Sekiyu, Tokyo, Japan, 1978-81; mgr. feedstock & energy Exxon Chem. Internat., Brussels, Belgium, 1981-86; dean Coll. Mgmt. & Free Enterprise Dallas Bapt. U., 1986-89, prof. fin., 1989-90; pres. Trotter Capital Mgmt. Inc., Duncanville, Tex., 1990—. Patentee in field. Chmn., bd. dirs. Met. Bapt. Ministries, N.Y.C., 1976-78. 1st lt. U.S. Army, 1960. NSF fellow, 1954; recipient Profl. Progress award Soc. Profl. Chemists & Engrs., 1964. Mem. Am. Inst. Chem. Engrs., Am. Chem. Soc., Am. Fin. Assn. Republican. Baptist. Home and Office: 1215 Rock Springs Rd Duncanville TX 75137-2839

TROTTY, WILLIE FRANCIS, university dean; b. Nacogdoches, Tex., Mar. 26, 1947; s. Luther Sr. and Hattie Marion (Anderson) T.; m. Sarah Ann Gamble, Dec. 21, 1974; children: Laurette Marion, Willette Francine, William Martin. BS in Biology and Polit. Sci., Stephen F. Austin State U., 1970, MS in Biology and Secondary Edn., 1972; PhD in Ednl. Adminstrn. and Indsl. Mgmt., Purdue U., 1977. Cert. biology and govt. tchr., prin., sch. supt., Tex. Asst. prof. edn. Prairie View (Tex.) A & M, 1977-79, asst. dir. tchr. certification, 1977-82, assoc. prof. edn., 1977-91, assoc. dean coll. edn., head dept. sch. svcs., 1988-90, dir. rsch. and sponsored projects, 1990—, dean Grad. Sch., 1991—; assoc. dir. So. Consortium Colls. and Tchr. Edn., 1977-79; chmn. self-study steering com. So. Assn. Colls., 1989-90; exec. com. Tex. Coun. Faculty Governance Orgns., 1990. Author: (with Louis Aikens) Theory into Practice: A Casebook for Students of School Administration, 1986; contbr. articles to profl. jours. Vice-chair adv. bd. Johnson-Phillip All Faiths Chapel, 1988—; mem. adv. com. Aldine Ind. Sch. Dist., 1991-92. Recipient Disting. Svc. award Houston Tchrs. Assn., 1974, Key Achiever award E.J. Campbell High Sch. Alumni Assn., 1992, Leadership award Prairie View A&M U., 1993. Mem. Nat. Coun. Univ. Rsch. Adminstrs., Tex. Profs. Ednl. Adminstrn., Tex. Assn. Sch. Adminstrs., Purdue U. Ednl. Adminstrn. Alumni Assn. (charter), Kiwanis (charter), Kappa Delta Pi, Phi Delta Kappa (treas., past pres., Disting. Svc. award 1974). Baptist. Home: 5926 Black Maple Ln Houston TX 77088-6617 Office: Prairie View A&M U PO Box 2355 Prairie View TX 77446-2355

TROUPE, MARILYN KAY, education educator; b. Tulsa, Sept. 30, 1945; d. Ernest Robinson and Lucille (Andrew) Troupe. BA in Social Sci., Langston U., Okla., 1967; MA in History, Okla. State U., 1976; EdD Okla. State U., 1993; Lic. in Cosmetology, Troupe's Beauty Sch., 1970. Cert. tchr. Okla., Tenn. Tchr. social studies Margaret Hudson Program, Tulsa, 1969-81, tutor Tulsa Indian Youth, 1971-72; instr. cosmetology McLain-Tulsa Pub. Schs., 1982-94; instrnl. devel. specialist Okla. Dept. Vocat. and Tech. Edn., Stillwater, 1987-94; asst. prof., coord. tchr. preparation program, chair divsn. liberal studies and edn. Lane Coll., Jackson, Tenn., 1995—; vis. lectr. Okla. State U., 1980-81; cons., lectr. cosmetology; bd. dirs., adv. bd. Stillwater Park & Recreation, Stillwater Community Relations and Fair Housing, 1991-94; bd. dirs Adult Day Care Center, 1990-94; v.p. Okla. Recreation and Park Soc., 1994; judge Okla. Sch. Sci. and Math., 1994; mem. Leadership Stillwater, 1990; vol. Special Olympics State Games, Meals on Wheels, United Way; mem. women's adv. coun. Jackson Regional Hosp. Roman Catholic Ch., Tulsa, 1985-86. Recipient numerous awards for profl. and civic contbns. including Woman of Yr., Zeta Phi Beta, 1985; Salute award Gov. Okla., 1985; Outstanding Community Service Cert., WomenFest, 1985. Mem. ASCD, Okla. Assn. Advancement of Black Ams. in Vocat. Edn. (Golden Torch award 1994), Vocat. Indsl. Clubs Am. (dist. advisor 1985-86, Appreciation award 1985), Am. Vocat. Assn., Okla. Vocat. Assn., Okla. State Beauty Culturalists League (pres. 1979-85, Outstanding Service award 1985), Nat. Assn. Bus. and Profl. Women's Club (charter mem., past pres.), Stillwater C. of C. (bd. dirs.), Langston Alumni Assn., Phi Alpha Theta, Theta Nu Sigma, Alpha Kappa Alpha (Soror of Yr. 1993), Iota Lambda Sigma, Phi Delta Kappa. Democrat. Roman Catholic. Clubs: Jackson Links, Cath. Daus. Am. Avocations: travel, reading, collecting antiques, volunteer work, shopping. Home: 18 Rachel Dr Apt 10 Jackson TN 38305-8605

TROUTMAN, GEORGE WILLIAM, geologist, geological consulting firm executive; b. Brandenburg, Ky., Aug. 8, 1949; s. George I. and Ellen G. (Parker) T.; m. Marcia Lyn Roseman, Aug. 14, 1971; children—Nancy, Anthony, Janet, David, Barbara, Jonathan. Student Murray State U., 1967-68; B.S. in Geology, Western Ky. U., 1974. Geophys. engr. Birdwell div. Seismograph Service Corp., Ohio, Pa., W.Va., 1974-77; geologist Consolidated Natural Gas, Clarksburg, W.Va., 1977-79; exploration geologist Mountain Fuel Supply Corp., Denver, 1979-80; regional exploration geologist Al-Aquitaine Exploration, Ltd., Denver, 1980-81; sr. staff geologist Resources Investment Corp., Denver, 1981-82; geol. mgr. Petro-Lewis Corp., MCR, Oklahoma City, 1982-84; pres., geologist Troutman Geol. & Assocs., Edmond, Okla., 1984—.Served with USN, 1968-70. Mem. Am. Assn. Petroleum Geologists (cert.), Soc. Profl. Well Log Analysts, Oklahoma City Geol. Soc. (exec. com. 1985-86, editor Shale Shaker Digest XI 1982-85, treas. 1987-88, v.p. 1988-89, pres.-elect 1996-97), Ardmore Geol. Soc., New Orleans Geol. Soc., Computer Oriented Geol. Soc., Geophysical Soc. of Oklahoma City. Republican. Mem. Ch. of Jesus Christ of Latter-day Saints. Office: Troutman Geological & Assocs Ste 100 4406 Karen Dr Edmond OK 73013-8124

TROUTT, DON RAY, radio executive; b. Oklahoma City, Dec. 5, 1948; m. Karen Antonelli; children: Stacy, Jeremy. BBA, Oklahoma U., 1972; MBA, Cen. State U., Okla., 1978; postgrad., Cen. State U., 1978-80. CPA, Okla. Sr. auditor Touche Ross and Co., Oklahoma City, 1973-77; v.p., contr. Sta. KOCO-TV, Oklahoma City, 1977-85; v.p., controller Gannett Radio Div., St. Louis, 1985-86; pres., gen. mgr. Sta. KCMO AM/FM, Kansas City, Mo., 1986-89; exec. v.p. Gannett Radio Div., 1989-92; pres., gen. mgr. KKBQ AM/FM, Houston, 1991—. Served to sgt. U.S. Army, 1970-72. Mem. AICPA, Houston Assn. Radio Broadcasters, Country Music Assn., Houston Livestock Show and Rodeo. Office: Sta KKBQ-FM 11 E Greenway Plz Ste 2022 Houston TX 77046-1104

TROWBRIDGE, JOHN PARKS, physician; b. Dinuba, Calif., Mar. 24, 1947; s. John Parks Sr. and Claire Dovie (Noroian) T.; m. Evelyn Anne Parker, Apr. 20, 1996; children: Sharla Tyann, Lyndi Kendyll. AB in Biol. Scis., Stanford U., 1970; MD, Case Western Res. U., 1976; postgrad., Fla. Inst. Tech., 1983-85. Diplomate in Preventive Medicine, Am. Bd. Chelation Therapy (examiner for bd. 1987—), Am. Bd. Biologic Reconstructive Therapy (examiner for bd. 1994—), Nat. Bd. Med. Examiners. Intern in gen. surgery Mt. Zion Hosp. & Med. Ctr., San Francisco, 1976-77; resident in urol. surgery U. Tex. Health Sci. Ctr., Houston, 1977-78; pvt. med. practice health recovery unit, pain relief unit Life Ctr. Houston, Humble, Tex., 1978—; chief corp. med. cons. Tex. Internat. Airlines, Houston, 1981-83; indsl. med. cons. to several heavy and light mfg. and svc. cos., Houston, 1979-84; immunology research asst. Stanford U. Med. Ctr., Stanford, Calif., 1967-70; night lab. supr. Kaiser Found. Hosp., Redwood City, Calif., 1971-72; advisor to bd. dirs. Am. Inst. Med. Preventics, Laguna Hills, Calif., 1988-90; featured lectr. profl. and civic orgns., U.S., 1983—; sr. aviation med. examiner FAA, 1983-96, rep. to Chelation Protocol Coun., 1996—. Co-author: The Yeast Syndrome, 1986, Chelation Therapy, 1985, 2d edit., 1990, Yeast Related Illnesses, 1987, Do What You Want to Do, 1996; contbr. Challenging Orthodoxy: America's Top Medical Preventives Speak Out, 1991; edit. adv. bd. mem. nat. health and wellness newsletters, and jours., 1990—; contbr. articles to profl. jours. Adv. bd. mem. Tex. Chamber Orchestra, Houston, 1979-80; med. dir. Humble unit Am. Cancer Soc., 1980-81; med. cons. personal fitness program Lake Houston YMCA, 1981-83. Nat. Merit scholar, 1965-69, Calif. State scholar, 1967-69; recipient Resolution of Commendation house of dels., 1974 Am. Podiatry Assn., Spl. Profl. Svc. Citation bd. trustees, 1976, Am. Podiatry Students Assn. Fellow Am. Acad. Neurol. and Orthopaedic Surgery, Am. Soc. for Laser Medicine and Surgery, Am. Coll. Advancement in Medicine (v.p. 1987-89, pres.-elect 1989-91); mem. AMA, Am. Coll. Preventive Medicine, Am. Preventive Med. Assn. (charter, bd. dirs. 1992—), Am. Acad. Environ. Medicine, Am. Soc. Gen. Laser Surgery, Nat. Health Fedn. (chmn. bd. govs. 1989), Am. Acad. Thermology, Am. Assn. Nutritional Cons., Am. Soc. Life Extension Physicians (founding), Am. Assn. Physicians and Surgeons, Tex. Med. Assn., Harris County Med. Soc., Houston Acad. Medicine, Aerospace Med. Assn., N.Y. Acad. Scis., Internat. Acad. Bariatric Medicine, Med. Acad. Rheumatoid Disease (med. adv. bd. 1995—), Huxley Inst. for Biosocial Rsch., Great Lakes Coll. Clin. Medicine (med. rsch. instnl. rev. bd., v.p. 1993-94, pres. 1994-95 program chair Advanced Tng. Seminar in Chelation Therapy 1996—), Soc. for Orthomolecular Medicine, Delta Chi. Office: Life Ctr Houston 9816 Memorial Blvd Ste 205 Humble TX 77338-4206

TROWER, JONATHAN K., management information systems educator; b. Bay City, Mich., Dec. 7, 1959; s. Guy W. and Derva E. (Dixon) T.; m. Debbie M. Shockey, Aug. 13, 1983; children: Jonathan David, John William Christopher, Marie Nicole. BA, Drury Coll., 1982; MBA, Baylor U., 1983; PhD, U. Minn., 1992. Lectr. Baylor U., Waco, Tex., 1983-87, asst. prof. mgmt. info. sys., 1991—; grad. teaching asst. U. Minn., Mpls., 1987-91; adj. instr. Hamline U., 1990-91; presenter in field. Author: Using Minitab for Introductory Statistical Analysis, 1989, Instructor's Guide to Management Information Systems, 4th edit., 1990, SPSS Manual to Business Statistics: Contemporary Decision Making, 1994, SAS Manual to Business Statistics: Contemporary Decision Making, 1994; contbr. articles to profl. jours. and revs. Grantee Index Summit Group, 1991, Baylor U., 1993. Mem. Inst. Mgmt. Sci., Assn. Computing Machinery (mem. spl. interest groups), S.W. Decision Scis. Inst. Office: Baylor U PO Box 98005 Waco TX 76798

TROXCLAIR, DEBRA ANN, gifted education educator; b. New Orleans, Jan. 29, 1953; d. Richard Joseph and Joyce Marie (Braud) Troxclair; divorced; 1 child, Christopher Richard Pinner. BA, U. New Orleans, 1976, MEd, 1989; postgrad., U. So. Miss., 1991—. Cert. edn. 4th grade tchr. Laurel Elem. Sch., New Orleans, 1977; 2d grade tchr. St. Frances Cabrini Elem., New Orleans, 1977-80; 1st grade tchr. St. Joseph Sch., Gretna, La., 1982-83; kindergarden tchr. Lake Castle Pvt. Sch., New Orleans, 1983-84; libr. St. Frances Cabrini, New Orleans, 1984-85; 3d grade tchr. Abney Elem. Sch., Slidell, La., 1985-89; gifted resource tchr. Little Oak Elem., Slidell, 1989—; instr. Delgado C.C., Slidell, 1991-94; cons. St. Tammany Parish Schs., Slidell, 1988-89, 90-91; presenter La. State Dept. Edn. Superconference, 1993, La. Assn. Gifted Students, 1993, Archdiocese of New Orleans Early Childhood Assn., 1996, U. So. Miss. Parenting Gifted Children Conf.,

1995. Elder Northminster Presbyn. Ch., Pearl River, La. Recipient Disting. Teaching awrd Northwestern State U., 1996; Grad. Student scholar U. So. Miss., 1995-96; La. Assn. for Gifted and Talented grantee, 1996. Mem. AAUW (newsletter editor Slidell br. 1985-86), CEC, Nat. Assn. for Gifted Children (conv. presenter 1993), Miss. Assn. for Gifted Children, Northshore Reading Coun., La. Assn. Gifted and Talented Students (grantee 1995-96), Phi Delta Kappa (pres. St. Tammany Parish 1991). Presbyterian. Office: Little Oak Elem 59241 Rebel Dr Slidell LA 70461-3713

TROXELL, RICHARD HAROLD, retired data processing company executive; b. Easton, Pa., Nov. 20, 1934; s. Raymond Robert and Mary Jane (Cooney) T.; m. Judy Caroline Gangewer; children: Viki, John, Tami, Danny. Student, Lafayette Coll., Easton, Pa., 1954-58; BLS magna cum laude, St. Edward's U., Austin, Tex., 1991; MBA, St. Edward's U., 1994. Engr. IBM Corp., Endicott/Owego, N.Y., 1963-66; mfg. mgr. IBM Corp., Owego, N.Y., 1966-70, mfg. engrng. mgr., 1970-75, environ. mgr., 1975-80; project mgr. mfg. engrng. IBM Corp., Austin, Tex., 1980-84, functional mgr. facilities, 1984-87, project mgr./engr., 1987-89, program mgr., 1989-93; instr. Austin C.C., 1993—; IBM Austin rep. I.P.C., 1981-84. Bd. dirs. Mcpl. Utility Dist., Round Rock, Tex., 1981-84;/ organizer Cos. Acting Responsibly for the Environment, Austin, 1986-89. Mem. ASTD, Alpha Sigma Lambda, Kappa Gamma Pi, Delta Mu Delta. Home: 2801 Carmel Dr Round Rock TX 78681-1601

TROYER, LISA LYNN, marketing and activities director; b. Washington, Mar. 26, 1964; d. Jarnot DeVere and Virginia Mae (Holmes) T. AA in Mktg. Mgmt., Prince George's Community Coll, 1985; B in Gen. Studies, U. Md., 1987; MS in Gerontology, Abilene Christian U., 1995; postgrad., U. Ark., 1995—. Staff asst. U.S. House Reps., Washington, 1987-88; adminstrv. coord. Nuclear Info. & Resource Svc., Washington, 1988-89; residential child devel. specialist Country Acres, Gilsum, N.H., 1989-90; program asst. NSF, Washington, 1990-92; mktg. and activities dir. Springvale Ter., Silver Spring, Md., 1992-93; grad. asst. Tex. Del. of the White House Conf. on Aging, 1994-95; mission team mem. S.E. Asia Global Campaign Project, summer 1994; grad. asst. to assoc. vice chancellor and dean of students U. Ark., Fayetteville, 1995—; bd. dirs. Employees Assn.; prin. rep. EEO Coun., Washington, 1991; sch. outreach vol. NSF Rep., Washington, 1991. Assoc. editor: Children of the American Revolution National Magazine, 1981-82, nat. pubs. chmn., 1982-83. bd. dirs. Prince George's County Chpt. ARC, Hyattsville, 1981-82; polit. intern Gary Hart's Pres. Campaign, 1983-84; del. Md. Young Democrats, Largo, 1984-85; pres. student program bd. Prince George's Community Coll., Largo, 1984-85, bd. trustees mem., 1985-86; active City's Human Resource League Com., Bowie, Md., 1987-89; coord. Laotian refugee camp rescue mission Ch. of Christ, Silver Spring, Md., 1989, youth coord.; vol. Silver Spring Soup Kitchen. Mem. AAUP, AAUW, NAFE, Nat. Assn. Student Personnel Adminstrs., Nat. Assn. Women in Edn., U. Md. Alumni Assn., Price George's C.C. Alumni Assn. (v.p. 1985-86, bd. dirs. 1985-91), Alpha Delta Pi Alumni Assn., Sigma Pi Omega. Democrat.

TRUAX, DENNIS DALE, civil engineering educator, consultant; b. Hagerstown, Md., July 25, 1953; s. Bernard James and Dorothy Hilda T.; m. Jeanie Ann Knable, Aug. 20, 1977. BS in Civil Engrng., Va. Poly. Inst. and State U., 1976; MS, Miss. State U., 1978, PhD, 1986. Registered profl. engr., Miss; cert. environ. engr. Asst. dep. constrn. mgr. Fairfax County, Va., 1972-74; design engr., Washington County, Md., 1976; instr. Miss. State U., Starkville, 1980-86, asst. prof. civil engrng., 1986-91, assoc. prof., 1991-96, prof., 1996—; environ. engrng. cons. Lay leader Aldersgate United Meth. Ch., Starkville, 1982-85, chmn. pastor/parish rels., 1985-86, chmn. coun. on ministries, 1986-90, chmn. adminstrv. bd., 1990-92, chmn. fin. com., 1992-94, chmn. bd. trustees, 1996—; adviser Triangle Fraternity, Starkville, Alumni Bd. Dirs. treas., 1989-96; bd. dirs. Meth. Student Ctr., Miss. State U., 1983-90, chmn. pastor/parish relations, 1984-86, v.p. bd., 1986, pres., 1987-89, treas., 1990-91; del. to Ann. Conf., Miss. Conf. United Meth. Ch., also vice chmn. com. on higher end.; active Starkville dist. lay coun.. Miss. State Herrin-Hess Prof., 1993-94, 94-95, 95-96; recipient Golden Key Outstanding Faculty award Golden Key Nat. Honor Soc., 1994, Miss. Outstanding Civil Engr. of Year ASCE Miss. sect., 1995; named Outstanding Young Man Am., U.S. Jaycees, 1983. Mem. ASCE (chair student svcs. com., 1995-96, vice chair 1996—, adv. student chpt. 1981-96, chair career guidance com. 1991-92, sec. 1990-91, Miss. sect. pres.-elect 1990-91, pres. 1991-92, chmn. student svc. com. 1995—, Outstanding Civil Engr. 1995), Am. Water Works Assn. (Miss. 41 chpt. scholarship bd. dirs. 1994—), Miss. Engrng. Soc. (pres., pres.-elect, region 3 v.p., bd. dirs., Tombigbee chpt. pres., chpt. pres.-elect, Engrng. educator 1995, Educator of the Year award, 1995), Nat. Soc. Profl. Engrs., Water Environ. Fedn. (rsch. com.), Sigma Xi (sec., pres.-elect, pres. Miss. State chpt.), Tau Beta Pi, Chi Epsilon. Democrat. Contbr. engrng. articles to profl. jours. Home: 1054 Southgate Dr Starkville MS 39759-8810 Office: Miss State U PO Box 9546 Mississippi State MS 39762-9546

TRUBEY, LILLIAN PRISCILLA, secondary education educator, retired; b. Hastings, Mich., Jan. 18, 1917; d. Leon George and Ethel Ada (Harlem) Tolhurst; m. Stanley Roger Trubey, Aug. 12, 1940 (dec. May 1965); children: Roger, Cornelia. BA, U. Mich., 1938, MA, 1942; MEd, Fla. Atlantic Univ., 1967; PhD, Fla. State U., 1972. Tchr. River Rouge (Mich.) H.S., 1938-41, South Broward H.S., Hollywood, Fla., 1951-69; tchr., head Eng. dept. Hollywood Hills H.S., 1969-84; tax preparer H&R Block, Ft. Lauderdale, 1985-92; tchr. Fla. State U., Tallahassee, 1970-71, Miami Dade Jr. Coll., Miami, Fla. 1971-72. Sec. Women's Rep. Club, Broward Co., 1947-49, v.p., 1950-51; sec. Victoria Park Civic Assn., Ft. Lauderdale, 1975-78. Mem. Genealogical Soc. Broward Co. (sec. 1991-93, pres. 1993-95, editor IMPRINTS, 1993), Retired Educators Broward Co., Ft. Lauderdale Bridge Club (dir. 1995), Guild Miniature Artisans, Delta Kappa Gamma. Episcopalian. Home: 1415 NE 4 Pl Fort Lauderdale FL 33301

TRUDNAK, STEPHEN JOSEPH, landscape architect; b. Nanticoke, Pa., Feb. 25, 1947; s. Stephen Adam and Marcella (Levulis) T.; m. Arden Batchelder Weill, Sept. 6, 1980. BS in Landscape Architecture, Pa. State U., 1970. Jr. landscape architect Kling Partnership, Phila., 1970-72; landscape architect firm Keith French Assocs., Washington, 1972-73; head dept. landscape architecture Linganore Center Design, Frederick, Md., 1973-74; head dept. landscape architecture Toups and Loiederman, Rockville, Md., 1974-76; project landscape architect Dade County Transit Improvement Program, Kaiser Transit Group, So. Calif. Rapid Transit Dist., Metro Rail Transit Cons.; v.p. Harry Weese & Assocs., Ltd., Miami, Fla., 1976-84; v.p. landscape architecture Canin Assocs., Orlando, Fla., 1984-87; dir. planning and design Bonita Bay Properties Inc., Bonita Springs, Fla., 1987-91; prin. Stephen J. Trudnak, P.A., Landscape Architecture and Land Planning, 1991—. V.p. bd. dirs. Koreshan State Hist. Site, 1989-94; mem. 'not for profit' com. Bonita Springs Cmty. Redevel. Agy., 1994—; v.p. Bonita Springs Mainstreet Program, 1996, pres., 1997. Fellow Am. Soc. Landscape Architects (pres. Fla. chpt. 1983, chpt. adv. bd. 1984-85, elections task force 1986, publs. task force 1987, trustee 1987-89, membership task force, chmn. 1989-90, nat. v.p. chpt. and mem. svcs. 1992-94, non-dues revenue task force 1994-95), Nat. Xeriscape Coun. (Fla. steering com.), Nat. Speleol. Soc. SCARAB; mem. Bonita Springs C. of C. (chair beautification com. 1991-92, 1994-95, bd. dirs. 1995—, v.p. edn. divsn. 1996—). Home: 554 104th Ave N Naples FL 33963-3225 Office: 3461 Bonita Bay Blvd Bonita Springs FL 34134-4384

TRUESDALE, GERALD LYNN, plastic and reconstructive surgeon; b. High Point, N.C., Aug. 3, 1949; s. Gonzales and Emma Dorothy (Allen) T.; m. Althea Ellen Sample, May 27, 1978; children: Gerard Lynn, Jessica Lynne. BS, Morehouse coll., 1971; MD, U. Chgo., 1975; LLD (hon.), A&T State U., 1995. Intern gen. surgery Emory U., 1975-78; resident gen. and plastic surgery Tulane Med. Ctr., 1978-82; pres. Greensboro (N.C.) Plastic Surg. Assocs. P.A., 1982—; bd. dirs. Greensboro Nat. Bank, 1989-92. Bd. dirs. N.C. A&T U. Found., Greensboro, 1988—, Natural Sci. Ctr., Greensboro, 1980—, N.C. A&T State Found., Greensboro Day Sch., Ctr. for Creative Leadership, Nat. Bank Greensboro; program chmn. Greensboro Men's Club, 1990; pres. Ea. Music Festival, 1992. Recipient Disting. Svc. award Morehouse Med. Sch., 1989, Bennett Coll., 1990, A&T State U., 1992; named Physician of Yr., Greensboro Med. Soc., 1992. Mem. AMA, NAACP (life, Greensboro chpt.), Greater Greensboro Med. Soc. (past pres.), Med. Splty. Jour. Club Greensboro, Beta Pi Phi, Sigma Pi Phi. Home: 502 Staunton Dr Greensboro NC 27410-6071 Office: Greensboro Plastic Surg Assocs PA 901 N Elm St Greensboro NC 27401-1512

TRUITT, JOHN H., insurance agency executive; b. Tallassee, Ala., Feb. 19, 1938; s. Woodrow Wilson and Nora Gladys (Taylor) T.; m. Gail Ward, Jan. 31, 1962: children: John Alan, Lee Anthony. LLB, Faulkner U., 1972. Asst. sec. Gulf Am. Fire & Casualty, Montgomery, Ala., 1962-70; mgr. product line Ins. Co. N.Am., Birmingham, Ala., 1970-74; mgr. Reliance Ins. co., Birmingham, 1974-75; sr. v.p. Molton, Allen & Williams, Birmingham, 1975-85; v.p. Krent-Truitt Ins. Agy., Birmingham, 1985-91; pres. Truitt Ins. Agy., Inc., Birmingham, 1991—; bd. dirs. Fire Mark Cir. Americus, Chamblee, Ga. Mem. Ind. Ins. Agts. Am., Ala. Ind. Ins. Agts., Birmingham Ind. Ins. Agts., The Club, Inc., C. of C., Sigma Delta Kappa (sec. 1969-70). Baptist. Office: Truitt Ins Agy Inc 3520 7th Ave S Birmingham AL 35222-3211

TRULOVE, HARRY DAVID, religious organization administrator; b. Rome, Ga., Jan. 13, 1927; s. Robert Don and Vida Nelson (Harris) T.; m. Carolyn Cecelia Goss, Jan. 16, 1949; children: Teresa Trulove Walker, James David, Timothy Goss. BA, Mercer U., 1948; MD, Southwestern Bapt. Theol. Sem., Ft. Worth, 1957. Ordained to Bapt. ministry, 1955. Asst. dept. mgr. J. C. Penney Co., Macon, Ga., 1948-49; dept. mgr. J. C. Penney Co., Dublin, Ga., 1949-50; ins. agt. Met. Life Ins., Macon, 1950-52; machinist Am. Mfg. Co., Ft. Worth, 1954, Chgo. Pneumatic Tool Co., Ft. Worth, 1955-57; pastor Leon Bapt. Ch., Okla., 1955-56, various chs., Tex., 1957-68; exec. dir. estate stewardship dept. Bapt. Gen. Conv. of Tex., Dallas, 1968-74; pres. Ark. Bapt. Found., Little Rock, 1974-94, pres. emeritus, 1994—; bd. dirs. Ark. State Coun. Econ. Edn., Little Rock, Christian Civic Found., Little Rock. Author: Financial Planning Workbook - A Better Tomorrow, 1970, 6th edit., 1982; contbr. articles to Home Life mag., Bapt. Program mag., Ch. Adminstrn. mag., weekly devotionals. Bd. dirs. Bapt. Gen. Conv. Texas, Dallas, 1963-68, Bapt. Meml. Geriatric Hosp., San Angelo, 1966-68. With USN, 1944-46. Named Bapt. Min. of Yr. by Williams Bapt. Coll., 1994. Mem. Assn. So. Bapt. Found. Execs. (sec., treas. 1975, pres. 1985), Kiwanis Internat. Home: 2308 Gunpowder Rd Little Rock AR 72227-3025 Office: Ark Bapt Found Superior Fed Bank 500 Broadway St Apt 402 Little Rock AR 72201-3343

TRULUCK, JAMES PAUL, JR., dentist, vintner; b. Florence, S.C., Feb. 6, 1933; s. James Paul and Catherine Lydia (Nesmith) TruL.; m. Kay Bowen (dec. Oct. 1981); children: James Paul III, David Bowen, Catherine Ann; m. Amelia Nickels Calhoun, Apr. 26, 1983; 1 child, George Calhoun. BS, Clemson (S.C.) U., 1954; DMD, U. Louisville, 1958. Pvt. practice Lake City, S.C., 1960—; founder, pres. TruLuck Vineyards & Winery, Lake City, 1976, Chateau TruLuck Natural Water Co., Lake City, 1990. Member bd. advisors Clemson U., 1978-84; mem. bd. visitors Coker Coll., Hartsville, S.C., 1978-84; pres., bd. dirs. Lions, Lake City, 1960-73; chmn. Greater Lake City Lake Commn., 1967-84. Capt. USAF, 1958-67. Recipient S.C. Bus. and Arts Partnership award S.C. State Arts Commn., 1988. Mem. ADA, Am. Assn. Vinters (bd. dirs. 1982-86), Am. Wine Soc. (nat. judge 1982-88), Am. Soc. Clin. Hypnosis (emeritus), Internat. Acad. Laser Dentistry (chartered), S.C. Dental Assn., Florence County Dental Assn., Soc. First Families of S.C. (exec. sec. 1991—), Descs. Colonial Govs. of Am., Descs. Magna Carta Barons Runnymede, Soc. Gem Cutters Am. Episcopalian. Home: 1036 Mccutcheon Rd Lake City SC 29560-5616 Office: 125 Epp St Lake City SC 29560-2449

TRULUCK, JOHN M., business executive; b. 1945. Grad., Coll. S.C., 1967. Owner John M. TruLuck Co., Lake City, S.C., 1968—. Office: 121 Carolina Ave Lake City SC 29560

TRUMAN, GARY TUCKER, photojournalist; b. Charleston, W.Va., June 1, 1950; s. Cecil Kenneth and Mary Alma (Tucker) T.; m. Grace Ann Hanley, Dec. 12, 1986; children: Joanna Mary, Hunter James. BS in Journalism, W.Va. U., 1972. Staff photographer W.Va. Newspaper Pub. Co., Morgantown, 1972-74; pub. info. officer W.Va. Air Pollution Control, Charleston, 1975-78; owner, operator Photo Comm., Charleston, 1977—; workshop presenter U.S. EPA, Washington, 1979; asst. instr. Smithsonian Instn., 1976, Documerica Project, U.S. EPA, 1975. Prin. works include assignment photography for Washington Post, New York Times, Newsweek, Business Week, Chicago Tribune, People and numerous others. Mem. Am. Soc. Mag. Photographers. Democrat. Office: Photo Communications Co PO Box 7144 Charleston WV 25356-0144

TRUNDLE, ROBERT CHRISTNER, JR., social sciences educator; b. Washington, July 7, 1943; s. Robert Christner and Dolores (Godek) T. BA, Ohio State U., 1972; MA, U. Toledo, 1974; PhD, U. Colo., Boulder, 1984. Instr. U. Colo., Colorado Springs, 1982-84; assoc. prof. N. Ky. U., Highland Heights, Ky., 1987—; adj. asst. prof. Regis Coll., Colorado Springs, 1982-86. Author: Ancient Greek Philosophy: Its Development and Relevance to our Time, 1994; (with R. Puligandla) Beyond Absurdity: The Philosophy of Albert Camus, 1986; contbr. articles to profl. jours. Lt. USAR, 1970-72. Postgrad. fellow Rice U., 1975. Mem. Sigma Xi, Phi Kappa Phi. Home: 8 Persimmon Grove Rd Alexandria KY 41001-1333 Office: No Ky U Dept Social Scis & Philosophy Highland Heights KY 41099

TRUNNELL, THOMAS NEWTON, dermatologist; b. Waterloo, Iowa, May 7, 1942; s. Thomas Lyle and Vivian (Dahl) T.; m. Patricia Rautiala, Aug. 2, 1974; children: Suzanne, Thomas, Sarah. AB cum laude, Princeton U., 1964; MD, U. Iowa, 1968. Diplomate Am. Bd. Dermatology. Intern U. So. Calif., L.A., 1969; resident NYU, 1972; pvt. practice dermatology Tampa, Fla., 1974—; asst. clin. prof. U. S. Fla., Tampa, 1975—; pres. Dermcorp., 1995, 96; pres. DermCorp, 1995—. Contbr. articles to profl. jours. Maj. USAF, 1972-74. Mem. AMA, Am. Acad. Dermatology, Am. Assn. Dermatol. Surgeons, Fla. Med. Assn., Fla. Soc. for Dermatol. Surgeons (pres. 1993), Fla. Dermatol. Soc., Hillsborough County Med. Assn., Cutaneous Therapy Soc., Ducks Unltd. (organizing com. North Tampa chpt. 1988—). Republican. United Methodist. Office: 13801 Bruce B Downs Blvd Tampa FL 33613-3946

TRUSCOTT, JUDITH FARREN, church education administrator; b. Parkersburg, W.Va., Mar. 20, 1939; d. Oran Bearl and Marjorie Elizabeth (Bergen) Farren; m. Frederick G. Truscott Jr., Aug. 25, 1961; children: Lisa Kay Truscott Wiggins, Tina Diane Truscott Strautman, Lynne Noelle Herron. BA, Marietta Coll., 1961; MA, U. West Fla., 1981. Cert. Christian educator, 1989. Dir. Christian edn. Grace Presbyn. Ch., Lakewood, Ohio, 1973-76, elder, 1973—; dir. Christian edn. 1st Presbyn. Ch., Pensacola, Fla., 1977-83, John Knox Presbyn. Kirk, Kansas City, Mo., 1983-91, Westover Hills Presbyn. Ch., Little Rock, 1991—; moderator, mem. Ecumenical Ch. Resource Ctr., Kansas City, 1986-91; cert. educator, advisor Heartland Presbytery, Kansas City, 1989-91, edn. cons., 1984-91; mem. Christian edn. com. Presbytery of Cleve.; cert. educator, adv. Ark. Presbytery, 1992; mem., moderator, adv. coun. Presbytery Resource Ctr., 1993—. Mem., treas. Presbytery PTA, Lakewood, 1966-70; mem., sec. PTA, Lakewood, 1970-76; mem. Ch. Women United Speaker's Bur., Cleve., 1970-76; mem. PTO, Pensacola, 1976-83, Girls Volleyball, Basketball Boosters, Shawnee, Kans., 1989-91; elder Presbyn. Ch., 1973. Mem. Mid-Cen. Assn. Presbyn. Ch. Educators (cabinet 1990-91), Heartland Presbyn. Assn. Christian Educators (steering com. 1984-88, cert. advocate 1989-91, Heartland Presbytery cert. educator advisor), Assn. Presbyn. Ch. Educators, Chi Omega Alumni Assn. Republican. Office: Westover Hills Presbyn Ch Little Rock AR 72207

TRUSTY, GREGG KENNETH, SR., public information director, magazine editor; b. Indpls., Sept. 29, 1944; s. Clay and Martha (Shepperd) T.; m. Betsy Lippincott, Jan. 31, 1970; 1 child, Gregg K. Jr. BS in Edn. Journalism, Ind. U., 1970. Mng. editor Courier Tribune, Bloomington, Ind., 1968-69; asst. publs. editor Western Elec., Indpls., 1969-70; head pub. rels. AT&T Shreveport (La.) Works, 1970-94; editor La. Youth Care Mag., Shreveport, La., 1982—; dir. pub. info. Caddo Parish Sheriff's Office, Shreveport, La., 1994—. Pres. River Oaks Homes Assn., Shreveport, 1982-87. Staff Sgt. Ind. Air Nat. Guard, 1963-69. Named Disting Toastmaster, Toastmasters Internat., 1975. Mem. Pub. Rels. Soc. Am. (chpt. pres 1980), Soc. Profl. Journalists (bd. dirs. 1969-75), Shreveport Journalism Found., (bd. dirs. 1984—, pres. 1987-95). Republican. Roman Catholic. Home: 10106 Los Altos Dr Shreveport LA 71115 Office: Caddo Parish Sheriff's Office 501 Texas Rm 101 Shreveport LA 71101

TRUTTY-COOHILL, PATRICIA, art historian, educator; b. Uniontown, Pa., Apr. 20, 1940; d. Joseph John and Agnes (Mardula) Trutty; m. Thomas Patrick Coohill; children: Joseph Coohill, Thomas Coohill Jr., Matthew Coohill. BA, U. Toronto, Ont., Can., 1962; MA, Pa. State U., 1966, PhD, 1982. From asst. to assoc. prof. Western Ky U., Bowling Green, 1980—. Author: Antonio Freiles Eminentia, 1986, The Drawings of Leonardo da Vinci and His Circle in AMerica, 1993; contbr. articles to art publs. Mem. Internat. Soc. for Phenomenology Aesthetics and the Fine Arts (sec. gen. 1995—), Coll. Art Assn., Renaissance Soc. Am., Raccolta Vingana (Italy). Democrat. Roman Catholic. Office: Western Ky U Dept Art Bowling Green KY 42101

TSAI, TSU-MIN, surgeon; b. Taipei, Taiwan, Dec. 15, 1936; arrived in U.S., 1976; m. Fu-Mei Tsai; children: Yi-Yi Tsai Chen, Ring-Ring Tsai Tien, Berlin Tsai. MD, Taiwan U., 1961. Diplomate Am. Bd. Orthopedic Surgeons with added qualifications in surgery of the hand. Intern Nat. Taiwan U. Hosp., China, 1961-62, resident in urology, surgery and orthopedics, 1964-70; intern U. Louisville, 1976-77, resident in orthopedics, 1977-79; Christine Kleinert fellow in hand surgery U. Louisville Affiliated Hosps., 1976; clin. prof. orthopaedic surg. Louisville Sch. Medicine, 1980—; presenter in field, including Oxmoor Ctr., Louisville, Shanghai, China, Dublin, Ireland, U. Ky., Lexington, Nara, Japan, Med. Coll. Ohio, Toledo, ASSH Ann. Meeting, Cin. (all 1994), Internat. Congress European Soc. Biomechs., Cologne, Germany, Chang Gung Meml. Hosp., Taipei, Taiwan, Shriner's Hosps. for Crippled Children, Lexington, Ky., IFSSH, Helsinki, Finland, French Surg. Soc., Paris, Harkess Soc., Nashville, Tenn., Hand Forum, Sea Island, Ga., 1st Internat. Workshop for Reconstructive Microsurgery, Inst. Plastic Surgery, Mexico City (all 1995), Mini symposium on Pediatric Hand and Microsurgery, Taipei, Taiwan, Internat. Soc. Reconstructive Microsurgery, Singapore, JSSH/ASSH Combined Meeting, Maui, Hawaii, European Congress Hand Surgery, Paris, Jap. Soc. Surgery of the Hand, Okinawa, Hiroshima (Japan) U. Hand Club, Keio U., Tokyo, Internat. Microsurg. Soc., Montreal, Que., Can. (all 1996); Disting. Vis. Prof. Divsn. Plastic and Reconstructive Surgery, Washington Hosp. Ctr., 1990, others. Contbr. articles to profl. jours. and publs. Fellow Am. Coll. Surgeons, Am. Acad. Orthopedic Surgeons; mem. Jefferson Count Med. Soc., Jefferson County Orthopaedic Soc., Ky. Orthopaedic Soc., Ky. Med. Soc., Ky. Pediat. Soc., AMA, Internat. Soc. Reconstructive Microsurgery, Am. Soc. Reconstructive Microsurgery, Western Pacific Orthopedic Assn., Am. Soc. Surgery of the Hand, Hand Forum, Clin. Orthopedic Soc., Japanese Orthopaedic Assn. SICOT Soc. Office: Kleinert Kutz & Assocs 225 Abraham Flexner Way Louisville KY 40202-1846

TSANG, WILLIAM XUE-TING, computer company executive; b. East Lansing, Mich., May 6, 1965; s. Paul Ja-Min and Helena Rosa (Lit) T.; m. Julia Tyler Perry, Sept. 9, 1989; 1 child, Sophia Wilkinson Rong-Xiu. BS in Physics and Applied Physics, Yale U., 1986; MBA in Mktg. and Fin., U. Chgo., 1990. Computational physicist Lawrence Livermore Nat. Lab., Livermore, Calif., 1986-88; mgr. sys. and mkt. rsch. Pfizer, Inc., N.Y.C., 1990-95; segment, product mgr. IBM Corp., Research Tri Park, N.C., 1995—. Mem. PDA Ind. Assn. (adv. bd. healthcare 1996—). Home: 104 Garden Gate Dr Chapel Hill NC 27516 Office: IBM Corp 3039 Cornwallis Rd Durham NC 27709

TSCHIDA, MIKE J., legislative aide; b. Cheverly, Md., May 17, 1968; s. Mike J. and Diane M. (De Sair) T. BA, The American Univ., 1991; MBA, Hawaii Pacific Univ., 1994. Chamber intern London C. of C., London, 1990; White House intern The White House, Washington, 1991; internat. market cons. Cable & Wireless, Inc., Vienna, Va., 1991; congressional intern Office U.S. Cong. Don Sundquist, Washington, 1992; legislative aide, rsch. specialist Hawaii State Senate, Honolulu, 1993—; campaign aide Pat Saike for Gov., Honolulu, 1993—. Fin. vol. Bush/Quale 92, Washington, 1992; active Young Rep. Young Rep. Hawaii, 1993-94. Recipient Cert. Accomplishment Colegio Mayor La Comlepcion, Valencia, Spain, 1991. Home: 4324 Columbia Pike Franklin TN 37064 Office: Hawaii State Senate Hemmeter Bldg 250 S Hotel St # 504 Honolulu HI 96813-2831

TSCHIRHART, JOHN HIPOLYTE, motion picture producer; b. San Antonio, Dec. 30, 1920; s. Arnold John and Lucie (Tissot) T.; m. Ngin Vo, Sept. 1, 1969 (div. 1972); 1 child, Lucy-Hoa. Grad., Radio-TV Arts Acad., Hollywood, Calif., 1948. Master of ceremony Spain, 1952-57; actor Hollywood, Calif., 1946-59; tchr. French Sang Lang. Sch., Washington, 1959-61; comm. advisor U.S. dept. State, 1963-71; prodr. Tschirhart Motion Pictures, Austin, Tex., 1984—; major retired; aviation cadet, commissioned 2nd lt., bombardier, b-17 305th Bombardment Group, 1941-46, psychological warfare officer, edn. officer, St. Louis. Mem. Rep. Club of Austin, 1987—. Maj., USAF, 41-46; ETO, with U.S. Army, 1971-83. Decorated Air medal, DFC, Medaille du Jubilé, Normandy Gov., 1995. Mem. Am. Club of Mallorca (1st pres. 1955-57), Toastmasters (area gov. 1971-83, area gov. hall of fame, 1975). Republican. Roman Catholic. Home: 9104 Gallant Fox Austin TX 78741 Office: Tschirhart Motion Pictures Apt 135 1300 S Pleasant Valley Austin TX 78741

TSCHUMY, FREDA COFFING, artist, educator; b. Danville, Ill., Mar. 18, 1939; d. Frederick Winfield and Minnie Isabelle (Buck) Coffing; m. William Edward Tschumy, Jr., June 17, 1967; 1 child, William Coffing. BA, Vassar Coll., 1961; postgrad., Art Students' League N.Y., 1961-63, Accademia di Belli Arti, Rome, 1963; MFA, U. Miami, 1990. Instr. art Miami (Fla.) Fine Arts Conservatory, 1968; instr. ceramics Grove House, Coconut Grove, Fla., summer 1970; instr. sculpture Upstairs Gallery, Miami Beach, 1971, Continuum Gallery, Miami Beach, 1972-73; instr. painting Barry Coll., Miami, fall 1974; instr. sculpture Met. Mus. Sch., Coral Gables, Fla., 1980-89, Bass Mus. Sch., Miami Beach, 1989-92; teaching asst. U. Miami, Coral Gables, 1988-90, lectr. sculpture, pres., 1991—; pres. founding mem. Continuum Gallery, Miami Beach, 1971-75, treas. 1975-83; treas. The Gallery at Mayfair, Coconut Grove, 1982-83, pres., 1983-84; artist in residence Hawaii Sch. for Girls, Honolulu, 1987; founding dir. Foundry Guild, U. Miami, Coral Gables, 1993—. Prin. works include sculptures at Dade Metrorail Univ. Sta., Melbourne (Fla.) Libr.; traveling exhbn. various colls., Miami. Mem. Tropical Audubon Soc., Miami, 1975—, Fla. Conservation Found., 1978—, Fla. Pub. Interest Rsch. Group, 1986—, Fla. Abortion Rights Action League, 1985—. Recipient Excellence award, Sculptors Fla. 1972, Fine Art Achievement award Binney & Smith, 1990; grantee Posey Found., 1989. Mem. Am. Foundryman's Soc., Womens Caucus Art (1st v.p. local chpt. 1981-86, bd. dirs. 1980-91, nat. bd. dirs. 1982-85), Internat. Sculpture Ctr. Studio: 3610 Bayview Rd Miami FL 33133-6503

TSE, DAVID, ophthalmologist, surgeon; b. Kwangtung, Peoples Republic of China, Aug. 25, 1950. MD, U. Miami, 1976. Diplomate Nat. Bd. Med. Examiners, Am. Bd. Ophthalmology. Intern in internal medicine U. So. Calif. Med. Ctr., L.A., 1976-77, resident in ophthalmology, 1978-81; fellow in oculoplastic, orbital surgery and oncology U. Iowa Hosp., Iowa City, 1981-82; assoc. prof. dept. ophthalmology U. Iowa, Iowa City, 1982-86; prof. Bascom Palmer Eye Inst. U. Miami Sch. Medicine, Fla., 1986—; attending physician, med. bd. dirs. Ann Bates Leach Eye Hosp.; attending physician Jackson Meml. Hosp., VA Hosp., Miami; lectr. in field; vis. prof. numerous univs. Author: Color Atlas of Ophthalmic Surgery, Oculoplastic Surgery, 1992; contbr. chpts. to 25 books; contbr. more than 60 articles to profl. jours. Recipient rsch. grant NIH, 1982-83, rsch. grant Coll. of Medicine, instnl. grant Am. Cancer Soc., 1983. Fellow ACS; mem. AMA, Am. Bd. Ophthalmology, Assn. Rsch. in Vision and Ophthalmology, Am. Soc. Ophthalmic and Reconstructive Plastic Surgery, Am. Acad. Ophthalmology, Am. Soc. Laser Medicine and Surgery. Office: 900 NW 17th St Miami FL 33136-1119

TSENG, HOWARD SHIH CHANG, business and economics educator, investment company executive; b. Tainan, Taiwan, Jan. 14, 1935; came to U.S., 1963; s. Picheng and Chaoliu (Wang) T.; m. Evelina M. Young, Dec. 25, 1965; 1 child, Elaine Evelina. BA, Nat. Taiwan U., Taipei, 1957, MA, 1963; PhD, U. Okla., 1972. Chief economist Cooperative Bank Taiwan, Taipei, 1959-61; dir. tax services Bur. Taxation, Govt. Taiwan, Republic China, Taipei, 1961-63; instr. U. Okla., Norman, 1968; asst. prof. Ga. So. U., Statosboro, 1968-71; prof. bus. and econs. Catawba Coll., Salisbury, N.C., 1971—; pres. Am. Prudential Investments, Salisbury, 1981-89; pres. Tsengs Investments, 1990—. Author: Investments, 1982; contbr. articles to profl. jours. Coordinator, supporter study mathematically precocious youth Johns

Hopkins U., Balt., 1982—; ptnr. World Vision, Calif., 1986-92. Academic research grantee Academia Sinica, Taipei, 1962; Ford Found. fellow, Taipei, 1963. Mem. AAUP, Ea. Econ. Assn., Am. Econ. Assn., Am. Assn. Individual Investors, Taiwan Investment (organizer 1986—), Taiwanese-Am. Assn. Greater Charlotte (pres. 1994-96), Nat. Travel Club. Home: 316 Bethel Dr Salisbury NC 28144-2808 Office: Catawba Coll W Innes St Salisbury NC 28144

TSIN, ANDREW TSANG CHEUNG, biochemistry educator; b. Hong Kong, July 19, 1950; came to U.S., 1979; s. Sai Nin and Chai Pong Tsin; m. Wendy L. Wickstrom, Jan. 20, 1979; 1 child, Cathy Mei. BS in Biology, Dalhousie U., Halifax, N.S., Can., 1973; MS in Zoology, U. Alberta, Edmonton, Alta., Can., 1976, PhD in Zoology, 1979; postgrad., Baylor Coll. Medicine, 1979-81. Prof. biochemistry and physiology U. Tex., San Antonio, 1990—; adj. prof. ophthalmology U. Tex. Health Sci. Ctr., San Antonio, 1990—; cons. Vision R & D, Lubbock, Tex., 1988-89, Alcon Lab., Ft. Worth, 1989-90, Tech. Inc., Dayton, Ohio, 1985-86; adminstrv. officer radiation and laser safety U. Tex., San Antonio, 1985-92, dir. divsn. life sci., 1994-95; sci. advisor, cons. NIH, Bethesda, Md., 1987-96, NSF, Washington, 1987-96. Contbr. articles to profl. jours. Named postgrad. scholar Nation Rsch. Coun. of Can., 1977-78, postdoctoral fellow Med. Rsch. Coun. Can., 1979-82, Alta. Heritage Found. Med. Rsch. fellow, 1981-82. Mem. AAAS, Am. Soc. Biochemistry and Molecular Biology, Assn. for Rsch. in Vision and Ophthalmology, Am. Physiol. Soc., Soc. for Neurosci. Office: U Tex San Antonio Divsn Life Scis San Antonio TX 78249

TUAN, CHRISTOPHER YOUNG-BEE, structural engineer, researcher; b. Taipei, Taiwan, Republic of China, Apr. 15, 1954; came to U.S., 1977; s. Chang-Yi and Hsiao-I (Chang) T.; m. Deborah Lynn Tollander, Nov. 25, 1989; children: Christopher Brandon, Sean Robert, Benjamin Alexander. BS, Nat. Taiwan U., Taipei City, 1977; MS, U. Wis., 1979, PhD, 1983. Registered profl. engr., Nebr., Tex. Assoc. prof. U. Nebr., Lincoln, 1983-89; sr. engr. Wilfred Baker Engring., Inc., San Antonio, 1989-91, Applied Rsch. Assocs., Inc., Panama City, Fla., 1991—; mem. solar dish rev. panel Sandia Nat. Lab., Albuquerque, 1987; cons. TELTECH, Inc., Mpls., 1990—. Contbr. articles to profl. jours. Mem. ASCE (mem. loading guide group 1985-88), Soc. Am. Mil. Engrs., Prestressed Concrete Inst. (seismic com. 1988), Sigma Xi, Chi Epsilon, Phi Kappa Phi. Home: 7709 Betty Louise Dr Panama City FL 32404

TUBB, JAMES CLARENCE, lawyer; b. Corsicana, Tex.; s. Cullen Louis and Sarah Elmore (Chapman) T.; m. Suzanne Alice Smith, Nov. 22, 1954; children: James Richard, Sara Elizabeth, Daniel Chapman. BA, So. Meth. U., 1951, JD, 1954. Bar: Tex. 1954, U.S. Dist. Ct. (no. dist.) Tex. 1955, U.S. Ct. Appeals (5th cir.) 1959, U.S. Supreme Ct. 1978; cert. comml. real estate specialist; lic. Tex. real estate broker; cert. mediator Dallas Bar Assn. With legal dept. Schlumberger Well Surveying Corp., Houston, 1954-55; claims atty. Franklin Am. Ins. Co., Dallas, 1957-58; ptnr. Vial, Hamilton, Koch, Tubb & Knox and predecessor firm Akin, Vial, Hamilton, Koch & Tubb, Dallas, 1958-84; dir., ptnr. Winstead, McGuire, Sechrest & Minick, Dallas, 1984-90; pvt. practice Dallas, 1990—; guest lectr. on real estate broker liability Real Estate Ctr., Tex. A&M U., 1987. Bd. dirs. Christian Concern Found., 1965-71, bd. deacons, 1972-78; ruling elder Highland Park Presbyn. Ch., Dallas, 1978-84, 88-91; mem. permanent jud. commn. Grace Presbytery, 1984-90; bd. dirs. Am. Diabetes Assn. Dallas County affiliate, 1991-95. 1st lt. JAGC, SAC, USAF, 1955-57, 1st lt. USAFR, ret. Recipient Outstanding Student award Student Bar Assn., 1954. Fellow Tex. Bar Found.; mem. ABA (chmn. comml. law com. gen. practice sect. 1982-84, real estate probate and trust law sect.), Tex. Bus. Law Found., Tex. Bar Assn., Am. Arbitration Assn. (comml. arbitration panelist), Soc. Profls. in Dispute Resolution, Dallas Country Club, Dallas County Rep. Men's Club (sec. 1978-79). Home: 3407 Haynie Ave Dallas TX 75205-1842 Office: 5956 Sherry Ln Ste 1000 Dallas TX 75225-8021

TUBBS, DAVID EUGENE, mechanical engineer, marketing professional; b. Springfield, Ill., Jan. 12, 1948; s. Eugene Lewellyn and Jacqueline Flo (Jones) T.; m. Linda Alyson Smith, Aug. 2, 1970; children: Corbin David, Cavan Scott. BSME, Ill. Inst. Tech., 1970; postgrad., Okla. State U., 1992. Registered profl. engr., Ill., Okla. Project engr. Sargent & Lundy, Chgo., 1970-82, bus. devel. mgr., 1982-83; mgr. power sales Yuba Heat Transfer Corp., Tulsa, 1983-85; with press products mktg. Nordam, Tulsa, 1985-86; dir. mktg. Brooks Aero. Svc. div. Nordam, Tulsa, 1986-91; mech. dept. mgr. The Benham Group, Tulsa, 1991-93; chief mech. engr. EDECO Engrs./Cons., Tulsa, 1993-94; mktg. support mgr. AGC Tech. Svcs. Inc., Tulsa, 1994—. Mem. ASME, Am. Welding Soc., Ill. Inst. Tech. Alumni Assn. (bd. dirs. 1977-80), Delta Tau Delta, Pi Tau Sigma. Republican. Club: Toastmasters. Home: 8313 E 60th St Apt 2322 Tulsa OK 74145 Office: AGC Tech Svcs Inc Ste 103 10810 E 45th St Tulsa OK 74146-3802

TUBESING, RICHARD LEE, library director; b. Kansas City, Mo., Nov. 25, 1937; s. Clarence and Letha (Thacker) T. BA, Yale U., 1959; MA, U. Chgo., 1969; MSL, Western Mich. U., 1972. Asst. to dir. U. Louisville, 1972-73; reference libr. Ga. Tech. Libr., Atlanta, 1973-76; head bus. and sci. Atlanta Pub. Libr., 1976-79; libr. dir. Lewis U., Romeoville, Ill., 1979-81; collection devel. coord. U. Toledo Libr., 1981-86; libr. dir. Coll. of the Southwest, Hobbs, N.Mex., 1986-89; libr. dir., dir. libr. sci. program Glenville (W.Va.) State Coll., 1989—. Author: Architectural Preservation, 1978, Architectural Preservation and Urban Renovation, 1982. Program coord. Lea County Archaeol. Soc., Hobbs, 1987-89. Lt. j.g. USNR, 1960-63. Mem. W.Va. Libr. Assn., Lea County Libr. Assn. (v.p. 1987-88, pres. 1988-89). Home: Rte 76 Box 17 Glenville WV 26351 Office: Glenville State Coll Robert F Kidd Libr Glenville WV 26351

TUCCI, STEVEN MICHAEL, health facility administrator, physician, recording industry executive; b. N.Y.C., Oct. 5, 1949; s. Louis Alexander and Nina Ida (Cerone) T.; m. Mari E. Koerner, Nov., 1974; children: Alexander, Michael, Lara. BS, Manhattan Coll., 1971; MS, SUNY, Brockport, 1977; PhD, Albany Med. Coll., 1978, MD, 1981. Diplomate Am. Coll. Phys. Medicine and Rehab., Am. Coll. Pain Mgmt.; cert. Nat. Bd. Med. Examiners. Rsch. fellow Birth Defects Inst. N.Y. State Dept. Health, 1976-81; instr. anatomy Albany (N.Y) Med. Coll., 1977-78, rsch. assoc. divns. endocrinology, 1978-81, asst. prof. anatomy, 1978-79, rsch. assoc. dept. anatomy, 1979-81; commd. officer student trainee, extern Nat. Inst. Neurol. and Communicative Disorders and Stroke/NIH, 1981; from intern to resident divsn. phys. medicine and rehabilitation George Washington Univ., 1981-84; staff fellowclin. ctr. dept. phys. medicine and rehabilitation NIH, 1983-84; mem. staff dept. medicine Commonwealth Hosp., Fairfax, Va., 1983-84; mem. med. staff Doctor's Hosp., Sarastota, Fla., 1984, med. dir. phys. medicine and rehab., 1989, med. dir., 1994—; founding med. dir. The Ctr. at Manatee Springs, Bradenton, Fla., 1985-86, The Rehab. Inst. Sarasota, Fla., 1986-88; med. dir. Fawcett Meml. Hosp., Port Charlotte, Fla., 1988—; med. dir. phys. medicine and rehab. Charlotte Community Rehab. Ctr., Port Charlotte, 1988; co-founder Sports, Pain and Rehab. Medicine Assocs., Sarasota and Port Charlotte, 1992; med. dir. Manatee Meml. Hosp., Bradenton, 1993—; pres., CEO Groove Tone Records, Sarasota, 1994—. Writer: (music) Take Me Down to the Ballgame, 1994, Spell on Me, 1994, On the Road to Nowhere, 1994; contbr. articles, papers to profl. jours. Mem. AMA, USTA, Am. Acad. Phys. Medicine and Rehab., Am. Coll. Sprots Medicine, Am. Congress Rehabilitative Medicine, Am. Soc. Pain Mgmt., Fla. Med. Assn., Fla. Soc. Phys. Medicine and Rehab., Major League Baseball Players Alumni Assn., Rep. Presdl. Task Force, Rep. Senatorial Inner Circle. Republican. Roman Catholic. Office: Sports and Rehab Medicine 3920 Bee Ridge Rd Sarasota FL 34233-1207

TUCCI, TONY M., lighting designer; b. Utica, N.Y., Jan. 29, 1944; s. Anthony and Amelia Tucci. BA, Syracuse U., 1965. resident lighting designer, tech. dir. Harkness Ballet of N.Y.; designer, cons. Ballet Internacional Caracas, 1975—. Lighting designer for prodns. for Royal Danish Ballet, (TV spl.) New World Ballet, (Scandinavian TV) Lucifer's Datter, Houston Ballet Co., Austin (Tex.) Ballet Co., Ft. Worth/Dallas Ballet Co., Monterey Ballet Co., Dallas Black Dance Theatre, Ballet Comtemporaneo de Caracas, Italy, also numerous stage prodns., including Van Cliburn Awards Ceremony, 1989, (pageants) Plymouth Park Bapt. Ch., Irving, Tex., First Bapt. Ch., Ft. Lauderdale, Fla.; 1996 Olympics dance lighting supr. Am. Ballet Theater, Alvin Alley Dance Theatre. Mem. Am. Massage Therapy Assn.

TUCK, MARY BETH, nutritionist, educator; b. Point, Tex., Dec. 9, 1930; d. Basil Barney and Daisy (Morris) Rabb; divorced; children: Karen, Kenny. BS, East Tex. State U., 1952, MEd, 1966; PhD, Tex. Woman's U., 1970. Lic. dietitian, Tex. Tchr. Longview (Tex.) Pub. Schs., 1952-64; instr. nutrition Stephen F. Austin U., Nacogdoches, Tex., 1966-69; assoc. prof. East Tex. State U., Commerce, Tex., 1970-96; ret., 1996; cons. Women, Infants and Children Program, Hunt County, Tex., 1989, East Tex. State U. Wellness Program, Commerce, 1989—, Selvaggi Med. Clinic, Commerce, 1989—; nutrition del. People to People Citizen Amb. Program, USSR, 1990; lectr. in field. Reviewer, editor textbooks; contbr. articles to profl. jours. Bd. dirs. Commerce div. Am. Heart Assn., 1994—; mem. Meth. Mission Work/Study Team, Israel, Palestine, Egypt, 1996. Recipient Gold Blazer award East Tex. State U. Alumni Assn., 1995. Mem. Am. Dietetic Assn., Tex. Dietetic Assn., Northeast Tex. Ret. Tchrs. Assn. (v.p. 1996—), Afflatus Culture Club (pres. 1988-91), Louise Drake Garden Club (v.p. 1991-92, pres. 1992-94), Commerce Area Alumni Assn. (1st v.p. 1993-94), Delta Kappa (sec. 1988-92, 94-96).

TUCKER, BOBBY GLENN, minister; b. Grand Saline, Tex., Sept. 11, 1954; s. Glen Burton and Edna LaFaye (Phillips) T. BS, Tex. A&M U., 1979; student, Southwestern Bapt. Theol., Seminary, Ft. Worth, 1980-83. Minister of music and youth First Missionary Bapt. Ch., Terrell, Tex., 1980; minister of youth Farley St. Bapt. Ch., Waxahachie, Tex., 1980-83; assoc. pastor First Bapt. Ch., Magnolia, Ark., 1983-86; youth ministry cons. Dept. Ch. Ministries Bapt. Missionary Assn. of Am., Waxahachie, 1986-87; exec. dir. Nat. Youth Dept. Bapt. Missionary Assn. of Am., Texarkana, Tex., 1987—; dir. Nat. Christian Youth Leadership Conf., Washington, 1984-87; trustee Found. for Christian Youth Leadership, 1983—; cons. to denominational curriculum com., 1987—. Named Outstanding Young Religious Leader, Jaycees, Magnolia, 1986, Outstanding Young Man of Am., 1976. Republican. Home: PO Box 871 College Station TX 77841-0871 Office: National Youth Dept PO Box 3376 Texarkana TX 75504-3376*

TUCKER, CHARLES RAY, metalworking company executive, sales and service engineer; b. Somerset, Ky., Jan. 18, 1950; s. Arthur William and Mildred Gladys (Taylor) T.; m. Charlotte Ann Wood, July 26, 1969; children: Shawn Dell, Ryan Scott. Student, U. Cin., 1968-70; grad. engring. program Cin. Milacron, 1970. Registered mech. engr., Ky., Miss. Asst. engring. lab mgr. Tecumseh Products Co., Somerset, Ky., 1971-76, engring. lab mgr., Tupelo, Miss., 1977-82; tech. sales mgr. Cin. Milacron, Grand Prairie, Tex., 1982-84; sales rep. E.F. Houghton & Co., Valley Forge, Pa., 1984—; lectr. in field. Mem. Somerset-Pulaski County Jaycees (bd. dirs. 1976). Republican. Baptist. Avocations: golf, fishing, hunting, traveling.

TUCKER, DEWEY DUANE, systems analyst; b. Burns, Oreg., Nov. 6, 1947; s. Dewey and Evelyn Evadine (Stewart) T.; m. Bertha Lorene Beach, Mar. 22, 1971; children: Tamera Reneé, Nicole Marie, Natasha Lynn. AS, Ricks Coll., Rexburg, Idaho, 1967; BS, Oreg. State U., 1971; MS, Naval Postgrad. Sch., Monterey, Calif., 1985. Distributor Oreg. Jour., Burns, 1959-63; clk. Richey's Supper Market, Burns, 1964-65; mailman U.S. Post Office, Burns, 1966-67; sawmill worker Hines (Oreg.) Lumber Co., 1965-67; mem. staff Sta. KOAC-AM/FM-TV, Corvallis, Oreg., 1969-71; commd. 2d lt. USMC, Washington, 1971; advanced through grades to lt. col. USMC, 1972-92; sr. systems analyst Potomac Systems Engring., Annandale, Va., 1992-95, Computing Technologies, Inc., Falls Church, Va., 1995—. Mem. Mil. Ops. Rsch. Soc., Marine Corps Assn. Republican. Home: 7879 Blue Gray Cir Manassas VA 20109-2825 Office: Computing Technologies Inc 3028 Javier Rd Ste 400 Fairfax VA 22031

TUCKER, EDWARD LLEWELLYN, English language educator; b. Crewe, Va., Nov. 19, 1921; s. Edward Llewellyn and Mary Frances (Graham) T. BA, Roanoke Coll., Salem, Va., 1946; MA, Columbia U., 1947; PhD, U. Ga., 1957. Instr. English Roanoke Coll., 1949-54; asst. prof. English U. Richmond, 1957-60, Va. Poly. Inst. and State U., Blacksburg, 1960-66; assoc. prof. English Va. Poly. Inst. and State U., 1966-86, prof. English, 1986—. Author: Richard Henry Wilde: His Life and Selected Poems, 1966, Vocabulary Power, 1968, The Shaping of Longfellow's John Endicott, 1985 (awarded emblem of Ctr. for Scholarly Edits. of MLA); contbr. articles to profl. jours. With U.S. Army, 1943-46; ETO. Mem. MLA, Soc. for Study of So. Lit., Sherwood Anderson Soc., Poe Studies Assn. Episcopalian. Home: 508 College View Dr Blacksburg VA 24060-3504 Office: Va Poly Inst and State U Dept English Blacksburg VA 24061

TUCKER, FRANCES LAUGHRIDGE, civic worker; b. Anderson, S.C., Dec. 4, 1916; d. John Franklin and Sallie V. (Cowart) Laughridge; m. Russell Hatch Tucker, Aug. 30, 1946 (dec. Aug. 1977); children—Russell Hatch, Pamela Tucker (dec.). Student U. Conn., 1970, Sacred Heart U., Fairfield, Conn., 1977, 79, Fairfield U., 1978, U. S.C., 1984. Sec. to atty., Asheville, N.C., 1935-37; sec. to gen. mgr. Ga. Talc Mining & Mfg., Asheville, 1937-42; sec. engring. dept. E.I. duPont de Nemours, Wilmington, Del., 1942-46. Chmn. radio com. D.C. chpt. ARC, 1947-48, bd. dirs., chmn. pub. rels. Westport-Weston Ct. chpt., 1968-73, mem. adv. coun. ARC Ct. Divsn., 1973-80, chmn. pub. rels., Hilton Head Island, S.C., 1981-84, 89-92, chmn. pub. rels. bloodmobile, Hilton Head Island, 1984-89; bd. dirs., mem. pub. relations com. United Fund, Westport-Weston, Conn., 1968-69, bd. dirs. Beaufort County chpt. ARC, 1982-87, 89-92; mem. media communications St. Luke's Episcopal Ch., Hilton Head Island, 1980-94, office vol., 1995—; with Hilton Head Hosp. Aux., 1984-89. Mem. Sea Pines Country Club. Home: 13 Willow Oak Rd Hilton Head Island SC 29928-5926

TUCKER, GARLAND SCOTT, III, investment banker; b. Raleigh, N.C., June 17, 1947; s. Garland Scott Jr. and Jean Smith (Barnes) T.; m. Greyson Conrad Shuff, Jan. 15, 1972; children—Greyson Carrington, Elizabeth Bradford. B.S. magna cum laude, Washington and Lee U., 1969; M.B.A., Harvard U., 1972. V.p. Tucker Furniture Co., Wilson, N.C., 1972-76; corp. fin. assoc. Investment Corp. of Va., Norfolk, 1976-78; v.p., to pres., chief exec. officer Carolina Securities Corp., Raleigh, N.C., 1978-88; v.p. corp. banking and fin. Chem. Bank, N.Y.C., 1988-90; pres. First Travelcorp., Inc., Raleigh, 1990—; ptnr. Chatham Ptnrs., Inc., 1996—. Mem. N.Y. Stock Exchange, 1983-88; mem. regional firms adv. com. N.Y. Stock Exchange, 1984-87. Dir. Raleigh Rescue Mission, 1980-83; vestry Christ Episcopal Ch., Raleigh, 1981-84; bd. advisors NCO Investors, N.Y.C, 1991—; trustee N.C. Mus. Art Found., 1990—, Chatham Hall Sch., Penick Episcopal Home for Aging, 1992—, Trinity Episc. Sem., Pitts., FOCUS, N.Y.C. Mem. Carolina Securities Corp. (bd. dirs. 1979-88), Securities Industry Assn. (bd. dirs. Mid-Atlantic region 1981-82, 84-88, regional firms com. 1983-86), Raleigh C. of C. (bd. dirs. 1984-86), Phi Beta Kappa. Republican. Clubs: Capital City, Carolina Country (Raleigh); Harvard of N.Y.C., Roaring Gap Club. Home: 2327 Lake Dr Raleigh NC 27609-7667 Office: First Travelcorp Inc 4513 Creedmoor Rd Raleigh NC 27612-3815

TUCKER, GARY W., psychiatric care nurse; b. Oct. 2, 1956; s. Clayton Wilson Jr. and Jewell (Shelton) T. ADN, Cleveland (Tenn.) State Community Coll., 1980; BSW, Lamar U., Beaumont, Tex., 1991; MPH, U. Tex. Sch. Pub. Health, 1996. CCRN, ACLS. Nurse, relief shift supr. Moccasin Bend Mental Health Inst., Chattanooga, 1980-81; staff nurse pediat. ICU Thompson Childrens', Chattanooga, 1981-83; nurse, cons. King Fahad Hosp., Riyadh, Saudi Arabia, 1983; staff nurse ICU/ CCU Beaumont Med.-Surg. Hosp., 1984-88; charge nurse CCU Bapt. Hosp. S.E. Tex., Beaumont, 1988—, staff nurse, hemodialysis, 1988—, cardio-vascular nurse educator, 1988—, cardiac rehab. coord., head edn., 1988—. mem. AACN, Southeast Tex. Cardiopulmonary Rehab. Profls., Alpha Delta Mu. Home: 601 22nd St Beaumont TX 77706-4915

TUCKER, HOWARD MCKELDIN, investment banker, consultant; b. Washington, Apr. 1, 1930; s. Howard Newell and Bessie Draper (McKeldin) T.; m. Julia Spencer Merrell, Feb. 1, 1952; children: Deborah, Mark, Alexander, H. David; m. Megan Evans, Aug. 17, 1979. BA, U. Va., 1954; MBA, NYU, 1956. CFA. Pension investment dept. J.P. Morgan & Co., N.Y.C., 1954-61; registered rep.-analyst Mackall & Coe, Washington, 1962-69; dir. internat. dept., analyst Legg Mason Wood Walker & Co., Washington, 1969-79; with Govt. Rsch. Corp./Nat. Jour., 1979-82, Potomac Asset Mgmt., 1982-91; ptnr., mng. dir. Capital Insights Group, Washington, 1992—; cons. County Natwest (Washington Analysis Corp.), 1985-90; bd. dirs. Monarch Enterprises, Inc., Uniflight, Inc., Sci. Mgmt. Assocs., Inc., Jeffrey Bigelow Assocs.; mem. task force on balance-of-payments U.S. Dept. Treasury, 1967—; co-organizer U.S.-Ger. Parliamentary Exchange, 1980-82; observer OECD, 1980-82; spl. overseas visitor Australian Govt., 1982. Author: Literature in Medicine; writer London Investment Jour.; contbr. articles to fin. jours. Trustee Nat. Cathedral Sch. for Girls, 1972-78; chmn. Missionary Devel. Fund Episcopal Diocese of D.C., 1974; vestryman Christ Episcopal Ch., Georgetown, 1962-65; mem. chpt. Washington Nat. Cathedral, 1966-72; del. Va. Republican Conv., 1968; dir. Washington Area Coun. Chs., 1962-65; co-dir. Andover-Exeter Washington Intern Program, 1976-86; patron West Europe program Woodrow Wilson Ctr., 1985-86. Served with USNR, 1950-56. Mem. Washington Soc. Investment Analysts, Nat. Economists Club, Cogswell Soc. Clubs: Naval and Mil. (London), Nat. Press, Georgetown Visitation Tennis, Saints and Sinners, Dumplings Yacht Club, Beta Theta Pi. Home: 4 Potomac Ct Alexandria VA 22314-3821 Office: Capital Insights Group 1700 K St NW Ste 1200 Washington DC 20006-3817

TUCKER, JOHN EDWARD, architect, consultant; b. Austin, Tex., Sept. 6, 1955; s. Oliver Truman and Jewel (Rogers) T.; m. Patricia Ann Holliman, Mar. 8, 1974; children: Jessica, Jathan, Joshua, Jolyna, Julie, Jaymes. BS in Architecture, U. Tex., Arlington, 1978. Project architect Oliver T. Tucker, Architect & Engr. Co., Irving, Tex., 1976-86; corp. pres. Ott: Tucker, Architects & Assocs., Inc., Irving, 1986-89; prin. Tucker, Architects & Assocs., Dallas, 1989-93, JPJ Architects, Inc., Dallas, 1993-95; facilities planning architect Dallas Pub. Schs., 1995—; cons. architect Dallas Ind. Sch. Dist., 1985-95, Hurst-Euless-Bedford Ind. Sch. Dist., 1994-95, Duncanville Ind. Sch. Dist., 1990-93. Prin. works include Bond Program Dallas Ind. Sch. Dist., 1985, 88, 92, ADA Facility Survey Campus Master Plan, Southwest Tex. State U., San Marcos, 1993, Bond Program Duncanville Ind. Sch. Dist., 1991. Active Boy Scouts Am. Mem. Nat. Eagle Scout Assn., Adopting Children Together (bd. dirs. 1995—). Office: Dallas Public Schs Facilities Planning 3701 S Lamar Box 100 Dallas TX 75215

TUCKER, N(IMROD) H(OLT), III, physician; b. Columbus, Ga., Nov. 22, 1947; s. Nimrod Holt Jr. and Sarah Elizabeth (King) T.; m. Kathryn Gail Waddle, June 6, 1976; children: Jennifer Leigh, Nimrod Holt IV. BS, Auburn (Ala.) U., 1969; MD, U. Ala., 1973. Diplomate Am. bd. Internal Medicine. Intern and resident ednl. program Jacksonville Hosp. U. Fla., 1973-76; pvt. practice Jacksonville, Fla., 1976—; mem. med. staff St. Vincent's Hosp., Jacksonville, 1976—; bd. dirs. Profl. Found. for Health Care, Tampa, Fla. Bd. dirs. Fla. Community Coll. Found., Jacksonville, 1986—, St. Vincent's Hosp. Heart and Lung Inst., 1989—. Mem. ACP (bd. dirs. Fla. chpt. 1988—), Fla. Soc. Internal Medicine (bd. dirs. 1988—), AMA, Fla. Med. Assn. (del. 1987, 89), Duval County Med. Soc. (bd. dirs., ex officio), Jacksonville C. of C., Timuquana Country Club, Fla. Yacht Club, River Club. Methodist. Office: 2149 Saint Johns Ave Jacksonville FL 32204-4418

TUCKER, PHYLLIS ANITA, sales representative, guidance counselor; b. Arkadelphia, Ark., July 26, 1952; d. Charles Wilson and Mary Katherine (Carter) T.; divorced. BS in Edn., Henderson State Coll., 1974, MEd, 1976. Teaching cert. for secondary social studies and guidance counseling. Social studies tchr. Monroe Acad., Wheatley, Ark., 1974-75; peer tutor Henderson State U., Arkadelphia, 1975-76; career orientation tchr. Heber Springs (Ark.) Mid. Sch., 1976-77; counselor Augusta (Ark.) Mid. Sch., 1977-78, Augusta H.S., 1978-86; vocat. special needs counselor White River Vocat.-Tech., Newport, Ark., 1986-87; guidance supr. Ark. Dept. Edn., Little Rock, 1987-89, ednl. supr., 1989-90; sales rep. Holt, Rinehart & Winston, Irving, Tex., 1990—. Chmn. Augusta Heart Fund Drive, 1979; bd. dirs. Saline County Chpt. Am. Cancer Soc., 1991. Named Young Career Woman of Yr. Augusta Bus. and Profl. Women, 1979. Mem. NAFE, Phi Delta Kappa. Republican. Methodist. Office: Holt Rinehart & Winston/HBJ 8551 Esters Blvd Irving TX 75063-2213

TUCKER, RANDOLPH WADSWORTH, engineering executive; b. Highland Pk., Ill., Dec. 3, 1949; s. Thomas Keith and Nancy Ellen (Jung) T.; m. Jean Marjorie Zenk, June 30, 1973 (div. 1991); 1 child, Nicholas Randolph; m. Lori Kaye Hicks, June 21, 1991. BS in Fire Protection Engring., Ill. Inst. Tech., 1972; M in Mgmt., Northwestern U., 1979. Registered profl. engr., Ill., Tex., Fla., La., Ga. With Ins. Svcs. Office of Ill., Chgo., 1972-74, bldg. insp., fire protection cons., 1972-74; with Rolf Jensen & Assocs., Inc., Deerfield, Ill., 1974—, cons. engr., 1974-77, mktg. mgr., 1977-81, mgr. Houston office, 1981-83, v.p. engring., mgr. Houston, 1983-89, v.p., tech. officer for Atlanta, Houston, N.Y.C., and Washington offices, 1989-90, sr. v.p., 1990-94, sr. v.p. internat. devel., 1994—; mem. adv. coun. Tex. State Fire Marshal, Austin, 1983-91; Dept. of Justice/Nat. Inst. Corrections cons. to Tex. Commn. on Jail Stds., 1993—. Editorial advisor Rusting Publs., N.Y.C., 1981—, Cahners Pub., 1993—; author articles in field. V.p. Juvenile Fire Setters Program, Houston, 1982-84; assoc. mem. Internat. Devel. Rsch. Coun., Urban Land Inst. Named one of Outstanding Young Men Am., U.S. Jaycees, 1981. Mem. AIA (profl. affiliate), Soc. Fire Protection Engrs. (chmn. nat. qualifications bd. 1985, pres. Houston chpt. 1983-84), Soc. Mktg. Profl. Svcs. (pres. Houston chpt. 1985, nat. pres. 1989-90), Nat. Fire Protection Assn., Internat. Conf. Bldg. Ofcls., Soc. Bldg. Code Cong. Internat., Inc., Bldg. Ofcls. Assn. Tex., Tex. Soc. Architects (profl. affiliate), Internat. Devel. Rsch. Coun., Houston C. of C. (vice chmn. fire protection com. 1983, govt. rels. com. 1984—), Aircraft Owners and Pilots Assn., Waller Country Club. Republican. Episcopalian. Office: Rolf Jensen & Assoc Inc 13831 Northwest Fwy Ste 330 Houston TX 77040-5215

TUCKER, ROY NELSON, mathematics educator, minister; b. LaGrange, Ga., Aug. 12, 1941; s. Henry Patrick Jr. and Katherine Irene (Irwin) T.; m. Sharon Elizabeth Knapp, May 10, 1974; children: Cheryl, Tina, David. PhD in Clin. Psychology, Ohio Christian U., 1967; MDiv, Southeastern Bapt. Theol. Sem., 1970; PhD in Psychology of Religion, Baylor U., 1978; MS in Math., Prairie View A&M U., 1983; MEd, Pan Am. U., 1987. Salesman, divsn. mgr. Sears, Roebuck & Co., Macon, Ga., 1962-66; learning lab coord. W.W. Holding Tech Inst., Raleigh, N.C., 1968-70; teaching asst. Baylor U., Waco, Tex., 1970-73; instr. Tex. State Tech. Inst., Waco, 1976-80, Blinn Coll., Bryan-College Sta., Tex., 1982-84, Tex. Southmost Coll., Brownsville, 1984-87, Embry-Riddle Aero. U., Beeville, Tex., 1988-89; assoc. prof. math./psychology Palo Alto Coll., San Antonio, 1988—. Author: Social Structures, 1978, Human Relations in Industry, 1979, A Time to Laugh, A Time to Cry, 1992, (play) The Innkeeper's Christmas, 1991. Pastor First Bapt. Ch., Jewell, Ga., 1965-67, Cmty. Bapt. Ch., Wake Forest, N.C., 1967-70, Marquez (Tex.) Bapt. Ch., 1975-79, Evang. U. C.C., Lyons, Tex., 1980-84, First Christian Ch., Aransas Pass, Tex., 1988-91, First Christian Ch., Devine, Tex., 1994—; pres. Boosters Assn., Waco, 1978-79; v.p. Family Abuse Ctr., Waco, 1978-79; pres. Faculty Senate Palo Alto Coll., 1995—; city councilman City of Hewitt, Tex., 1980. Maj. USAR, 1962-69. Mem. Tex. Faculty Assn., Tex. C.C. Tchrs. Assn., Masons. Republican. Home: 6208 Sawyer Rd San Antonio TX 78238-2205 Office: Palo Alto Coll 1400 W Villaret Blvd San Antonio TX 78224-2417

TUCKER, SHIRLEY ELIZABETH, music educator; b. Pensacola, Fla., Feb. 10, 1936; m. Lonnie Max Tucker, Feb. 19, 1954; children: Theresa, James Lonnie, Sharon Elizabeth. Bookkeeper Pensacola, St. Petersburg, Fla., 1963-87; substitute tchr. elem. schs., Pensacola, St. Petersburg; substitute tchr. elem. schs. New Orleans; singer, composer for ch. weddings, etc., 1952—. Author: But by the Grace of God, 1990, Love is Forgiving, 1997. Democrat. Baptist. Home: 72647 Country Club Dr Clearwater FL 34621

TUCKER, WILLIAM EDWARD, academic administrator, minister; b. Charlotte, N.C., June 22, 1932; s. Cecil Edward and Ethel Elizabeth (Godley) T.; m. Ruby Jean Jones, Apr. 8, 1955; children: Janet Sue, William Edward, Gordon Vance. BA, Barton Coll., Wilson, N.C., 1953, LLD (hon.), 1978; BD, Tex. Christian U., 1956; MA, Yale U., 1958, PhD, 1960; LHD (hon.), Chapman Coll., 1981; DH (hon.), Bethany Coll., 1982; DD (hon.), Austin Coll., 1985; LHD (hon.), Kentucky Wesleyan Coll., 1989. Ordained to ministry Disciples of Christ Ch., 1956; prof. Barton Coll., 1959-66, chmn. dept. religion and philosophy, 1961-66; mem. faculty Brite Div. Sch., Tex. Christian U., 1966-76, prof. ch. history, 1969-76, dean, 1971-76, chancellor, 1979—; pres. Bethany (W.Va.) Coll., 1976-79; dir. Justin Industries, Inc., Tandy Corp., Brown and Lupton Found.; mem. gen. bd. Christian Ch. (Disciples of Christ), 1971-74, 75-87, adminstrv. com., 1975-81, chmn. theol. edn. commn., 1972-73, mem. exec. com., chmn. bd. higher edn., 1975-77; dir. Christian Ch. Found., 1980-83; moderator Christian Ch. (Disciples of Christ), 1983-85. Author: J.H. Garrison and Disciples of Christ, 1964, (with others) Journey in Faith: A History of the Christian Church (Disciples of Christ), 1975; also articles. Bd. dirs. Ft. Worth Symphony Orch. Assn., 1980—, Van Cliburn Internat. Piano Competition, 1981—. Mem. Newcomen Soc. N.Am. Coll. Football Assn. (chmn. bd. 1993-96), Exch. Club, Phi Beta Kappa. Home: 2900 Simondale Dr Fort Worth TX 76109-1250 Office: Tex Christian U Office of Chancellor Fort Worth TX 76129

TUEL, STEPHEN MICHAEL, medical educator; b. Bainbridge, Md., Sept. 3, 1957; s. John King and Kay Yoko (Takayama) T. BS, Oral Roberts U., 1978; MS, U. Tex., 1980; MD, U. Tex., Houston, 1983. Diplomate Am. Bd. Phys. Medicine and Rehab. Med. dir. St. Joseph's Rehab. Hosp., Albuquerque, 1986-88; asst. prof., assoc. dir. phys. medicine and rehab. residency program U. Va., Charlottesville, 1989-91; asst. prof., dir. phys. medicine and rehab. fellowships Baylor Coll. of Medicine, Houston, 1992-95, assoc. prof., 1995—. Fellow Am. Acad. Phys. Medicine and Rehab., Assn. Acad. Physiatrists (chair undergrad. edn. com. 1994-95); mem. IEEE, Soc. Neurosci. Office: Baylor Coll of Medicine Dept Phys Medicine and Rehab 6550 Fannin St Ste 1421 4D Houston TX 77030-2717

TUERFF, JAMES RODRICK, insurance company executive; b. Gary, Ind., Jan. 17, 1941; m. Julie K. Luttinen; children: Brian J., Kevin A., Jeffrey J., Gregory S. BA in Econs., St. Joseph's Coll., 1963. CLU. Asst. v.p. Life and Casualty Ins. Co., Nashville, 1967-75; v.p. Commonwealth Life Ins. Co., Louisville, 1975-77; v.p. Am. Gen. Life Ins. Co., Houston, 1977-78, sr. v.p., exec. v.p., 1979-83; v.p. Am. Gen. Corp., Houston, 1978-79, exec. v.p., 1983-88, pres., chief exec. officer Gulf Life Ins. Co., 1988-90; pres., chief exec. officer Am. Gen. Life and Accident Ins. Co., Nashville, 1990-93, also bd. dirs.; pres. Am. Gen. Corp., Houston, 1993—; mem. adv. com. to bd. trustees, St. Joseph's Coll.; bd. dir. YMCA Greater Houston, Sam Huston Coun. Boy Scouts Am., St. Joseph Hosp. Found., Am. Coun. Life Ins. Fellow Life Mgmt. Inst. Soc. Houston (life). Republican. Roman Catholic. Office: Am Gen Corp 2929 Allen Pky Houston TX 77019-2197

TUGGLE, GLORIA HARRIS, school system administrator; b. Kerrville, Tenn., May 23, 1933; d. Isaiah and Lillian (Gary) Harris; m. Owens E. Tuggle, Nov. 18, 1955; 1 child, Kenneth Tyrone. BS, LeMoyne-Owen Coll., Memphis, 1955; MA, Memphis State U., 1965, postgrad., 1973. Cert. math. tchr., adminstr. Math. instr. spl. programs LeMoyne-Owen Coll., 1968-69, Memphis State U., 1972-74; part-time math. instr. State Tech. Inst., Memphis, 1975-76, Shelby State Coll., Memphis, 1976-79; math. tchr., guidance counselor Memphis City Schs., 1955-79, math. supr., 1979-92, dir. secondary programs, 1992-94, coord. office of accountability, 1994—; adv. bd. educator's channel Whittle Ednl. Network, 1990—; site visitor U.S. Dept. Edn., 1986-87, 88-89, 90-91, 92-93, 93-94, rev. panel, 1989-90, 92-96; vis. com. So. Assn. Colls. and Schs., 1981, 82, 88; cons. Nat. Assessment Edn. Progress, 1985-86; reviewer Math. Sci. Edn. Bd., 1987. Bd. dirs. Nat. Civil Rights Mus., Memphis, 1990—, Jessie Mahan Day Care Ctr., Memphis, 1985—, Southeastern Consortium Minorities in Engring., 1994—; chairperson Silver Star News Cmty. Adv. Bd., 1993. Named Greek of Yr. Memphis Pan Hellenic Coun., 1990, Outstanding Educator Memphis City Coun., 1987, Global Mentor for Youth Macedonia Bapt. Ch., 1990, Inspirational Role Model, 1991; recipient Disting. Role Model award Memphis Alliance Black Sch. Educators, 1995, Leadership Memphis award, 1991, Exemplary Svc. award Southeastern Consortium Minorities in Engring., 1995. Mem. ASCD, Nat. Coun. Suprs. Maths. (nomination com. 1987-89), Nat. Coun. Tchrs. Math. (co-chair Memphis meeting 1984, chair miniconf. for ednl. leaders 1990), Tenn. Math. Tchrs. Assn., Benjamin Banneker Assn., Memphis Area Coun. Tchrs. Math. (v.p. 1982-84), Memphis City Schs. Adminstrs. Assn., Phi Delta Kappa, Alpha Kappa Alpha (pres. Memphis chpt. 1990-91, Woman of Distinction 1990, Pres. of Yr. Southeastern region 1992, chairperson Southeastern Regional Conf. 1992). Democrat. Home: 4870 Ortie Dr Memphis TN 38109-6529 Office: Memphis City Schs 2597 Avery Ave Memphis TN 38112-4818

TULANON, PAITOON, surgeon; b. Ayutthaya, Thailand, 1947. MD, Siriraj Hosp. U., 1972. Diplomate Am. Bd. Surgery, Am. Bd. Colon and Rectal Surgery. Intern St. Agnes Hosp., Balt., 1974-75, resident in gen. surgery, 1975-79; resident in colon and rectal surgery Baylor U. Med. Ctr., Dallas, 1984-85; mem. staff Baylor Univ. Med. Ctr., Dallas.

TULIS, JEFFREY KENT, political scientist; b. Long Branch, N.J., Oct. 1, 1950; s. Murray A. and Lenore (Hirsch) T.; m. Sara Jean Ehrenberg, July 16, 1978; children: Elizabeth, Hanna. BA, Bates Coll., 1972; MA, Brown U., 1974; PhD, U. Chgo., 1982. Rsch. assoc. Miller Ctr., Charlottesville, Va., 1977-80; asst. prof. Princeton (N.J.) U., 1981-87; assoc. prof. U. Tex., Austin, 1988—, acting chair govt., 1992-93; vis. instr. U. Notre Dame, Ind., 1980-81; vis. assoc. prof. Harvard U., Cambridge, Mass., 1991. Author: The Rhetorical Presidency, 1987; editor: The Presidency in the Constitutional Order, 1981; co-editor Johns Hopkins Series on Constitutional Thought, 1987—; contbr. articles to profl. jours. Recipient Pres.'s Assoc.'s Tchg. Excellence award, 1996; Am. Coun. Learned Socs. fellow, 1983-84, Olin Found. fellow, 1986-87, Liberal Arts fellow Harvard Law Sch., 1986-87; Mellon preceptor Princeton U., 1985-88. Mem. Am. Polit. Sci. Assn. (chair sect. exec. politics 1990-91, history and politics pres. 1991-92), Phi Beta Kappa. Jewish. Home: 7105 Running Rope Austin TX 78731-2127 Office: U Tex Dept Govt Austin TX 78712

TULL, C. THOMAS, investment advisor; b. Dayton, Ohio, Sept. 5, 1946; s. James Theron and Emma Louise (Geppinger) T.; m. Carole Lynn Thoryk, June 20, 1970; children: Christopher James, Matthew Thomas. BS, Ohio State U., 1971; MBA, Xavier U., 1975. Chartered fin. analyst. Asst. trust investment officer Nat. City Bank, Cleve., 1973-75; dir. investments Cleve.-Cliffs Iron Co., 1975-83; v.p. Western Res. Capital Mgmt., Inc., Cleve., 1983-87, Dallas, 1987-90, 1984-87; dir. employee benefit fund investments LTV Corp., Dallas, 1987-90; pres. Tull, Doud, Marsh & Triltsch, Inc., Dallas, 1990—; mng. dir., CEO Gulfstream Global Investors, Ltd., Dallas, 1990—; vis. lectr. Cleve. State U., 1980-83. Sgt. U.S. Army, 1964-67. Mem. Assn. for Investment Mgmt. and Rsch., Dallas Assn. Investment Analysts, Fin. Execs. Inst., Sentinel Pension Inst., Dallas Metroplex Group, N.Y. Assn. for Internat. Investment, Inst. Chartered Fin. Analysts. Office: Gulfstream Global Investors 100 Crescent Ct Ste 550 Dallas TX 75201-1869

TULLIS, BILL, broadcasting company executive, sound engineer, music producer; b. Valdosta, Ga., Feb. 3, 1953; s. Vennis (Avery) T. BA, Valdosta State Coll., 1974, Ga. State U., 1976. Audio and music dir. Turner Broadcasting System, Inc., Atlanta, 1975—. Recipient Emmy award, 1980, 81, 84, 88, Clio award, 1987, 88. Mem. IEEE, Audio Engring. Soc., Nat. Assn. Broadcasters. Home: PO Box 49567 Atlanta GA 30359-1567 Office: Turner Broadcasting System 1050 Techwood Dr NW Atlanta GA 30318-5604

TULLIS, EDWARD LEWIS, retired bishop; b. Cin., Mar. 9, 1917; s. Ashar Spence and Priscilla (Daugherty) T.; m. Mary Jane Talley, Sept. 25, 1937; children: Frank Loyd, Jane Allen (Mrs. William Nelson Offutt IV). AB, Ky. Wesleyan Coll., 1939, LHD, 1975; BD, Louisville Presbyn. Theol. Sem., 1947; DD, Union Coll., Barbourville, Ky., 1954, Wofford Coll., 1976; LHD, Claflin Coll., 1976, Lambuth Coll., 1984. Ordained to ministry Methodist Ch., 1941; service in chs. Frenchburg, Ky., 1937-39, Lawrenceburg, Ky., 1939-44; asso. pastor 4th Ave. Meth. Ch., Louisville, 1944-47, Irvine, Ky., 1947-49; asso. sec. ch. extension sect. Bd. Missions, Meth. Ch., Louisville, 1949-52; pastor First Meth. Ch., Frankfort, Ky., 1952-61, Ashland, Ky., 1961-72; resident bishop United Meth. Ch., Columbia, S.C., 1972-80, Nashville area, 1980-84; ret. United Meth. Ch., 1984; instr. Bible Ky. Wesleyan Coll., 1947-48; instr. Louisville Presbyn. Theol. Sem., 1949-52; mem. Meth. Gen. Conf., 1956, 60, 64, 66, 68, 70, 72, Southeastern Jurisdictional Conf., 1952, 56, 60, 64, 68, 72, bd. mgrs. Bd. Missions, 1962-72, mem. bd. discipleship, 1972-80, v.p. Gen. Council on Fin. and Adminstrn., 1980-84; Chaplain Ky. Gen. Assembly, 1952-61; chmn. Frankfort Com. Human Rights, 1956-61, Mayor's Advisory Com. Human Relations, Ashland, 1968-72. Author: Shaping the Church from the Mind of Christ, 1984. Contbr. articles to religious jours. Sec., bd. dirs. Magee Christian Edn. Found.; trustee Emory U., 1973-80, Alaska Meth. U., 1965-70, Ky. Wesleyan Coll., Martin Coll., Lambuth Coll., McKendree Manor, Meth. Hosps., Memphis, Lake Junaluska Assembly, 1966-88; chair adv. bd. Found. for Evangelism, United Meth. Ch., 1991—. Recipient Outstanding Citizen award Frankfort VFW, 1961, Mayor's award for outstanding service. Ashland, 1971. Club: Kiwanis. Home: PO Box 754 Lake Junaluska NC 28745-0754

TULLY, CHRISTOPHER CARL, retired physician, hospital administrator; b. Charleston, W.Va., June 22, 1913; s. Christopher Columbus and Eva Lena (Lanham) T.; BS magna cum laude, Morris Harvey Coll., 1937; BS, W.Va. U., 1945; MD, Med. Coll. Va., 1947; m. Virginia Belle Tully, Apr. 9, 1937 (dec. 1963); children: Christopher Carl II, Richard R.; m. 2d, Margaret A. Plumley, Oct. 29, 1966. With Charleston Fire Dept., 1935-39, U.S. P.O., Charleston, 1939-43; intern U.S. Marine Hosp., 1947-48; gen. practice medicine, South Charleston, W.Va., 1948-79; mem. staff H. J. Thomas Meml. Hosp., South Charleston, 1948-93, pres., 1966, med. coordinator, 1979-81; med. coordinator St. Francis Hosp., Charleston, W.Va., 1981-93; ret. 1993; prof. family practice Kanawha Valley Family Practice Center, 1973-79; bd. dirs., mem. exec. com. First Nat. Bank of South Charleston. Mem. South Charleston Recreation Com.; chmn. South Charleston Park Bd.; mem. Kanawha County Bd. Edn., 1959-70, pres., 1963-64; mem. Charter Bd. South Charleston, W.Va.; pres. W.Va. div. Am. Cancer Soc., 1981-83. Served with U.S. Army, 1944-46, 47-48, 51-53, 71. Diplomate Am. Bd. Family Practice. Fellow Am. Acad. Family Physicians; mem. Am. Acad. Family Practice (pres. Kanawha chpt. 1962-63; pres. W.Va. chpt. 1969-70, chmn. bd.), W.Va. Acad. Family Practice (dir. 1960-64), AMA, W.Va., Kanawha med. socs., So. Med. Assn., Am. Soc. Contemporary Medicine and Surgery, Phi Beta Pi. Lodges: Masons, Shriners, Lions (pres. Spring Hill 1957-58, Citizen of Yr. South Charleston 1956-57). Home: 4530 Spring Hill Ave Charleston WV 25309-2213

TULLY, MARGIE GAINES, school system administrator; b. Berkeley, Calif., Oct. 5, 1960; d. John Lyle and Marlise Elizabeth (Gunther) Gaines; m. R. Scot Tully, May 30, 1992. BA, U. San Francisco, 1982; MA, U. Tex., 1987, PhD, 1989. Evaluator Austin (Tex.) Ind. Sch. Dist., 1985-87; dir. program evaluation York County Pub. Schs., Yorktown, Va., 1987-92; assessment specialist Virginia Beach (Va.) City Schs., 1992—; pvt. practice cons., Yorktown, 1992—; adj. prof. George Washington U., Hampton, 1994—. Recipient Excellence in Reporting Test Results award Am. Ednl. Rsch. Assn., Div. 4, 1989. Mem. Va. Ednl. Rsch. Assn. (pres. 1991-92), Va. Test Dirs., Assn. for Supervision and Curriculum Develop., Am. Ednl. Rsch. Assn. Home: 101 Tully Cove Tr Yorktown VA 23692 Office: Va Bch City Pub Schs 2512 George Mason Dr Virginia Beach VA 23456

TULLY, SUSAN STURGIS, adult education educator; b. Augusta, Ga., July 5, 1954; d. John Milledge and Nancy Frances (Watson) Sturgis; m. Christopher Carl Tully Jr., Apr. 1, 1978. BS in Edn., U. Ga., 1976; MEd, U. S.C., 1987, EdD, 1995. Tchr. Richmond County Schs., 1977-79, Episc. Day Sch., Augusta, 1979-81, Augusta Country Day Sch., Martinez, Ga., 1982-85; dir. edn. Walton Rehab. Hosp., Augusta, 1988-89; dir. occupl. and cmty. programs Aiken (S.C.) Tech. Coll., 1985-88; tchr., career awareness Aiken (S.C.) County Pub. Schs., 1989-90; tng. specialist Westinghouse Savannah River Co., Aiken, 1990-91; dept. chmn. devel. studies Aiken (S.C.) Tech. Coll., 1991-94; dean acad. support divsn., 1994—. Contbr. articles to profl. jours. Mem. S.C. State Employees Assn. Am. Assn. Women in Cmty. Colls., S.C. Assn. for Devel. Educators (pres.-elect 1995, pres. 1996), Nat. Staff Devel. Coun., North Augusta C. of C., Phi Delta Kappa, Alpha Delta Kappa. Home: 35 Rapids Ct North Augusta SC 29841-6015 Office: Aiken Tech Coll PO Box 696 Aiken SC 29802-0696

TUNG, SHIH-MING SAMUEL, medical physicist; b. Taipei, Aug. 18, 1954; came to U.S., 1983; s. Yao-Ching and Chen-Ping (Yen) T.; m. Hilda Tung, Oct. 16, 1983; children: Margaret, David. BS in Nuclear Engring., Nat. Tsing Hua U., Hsinchu, Taiwan, 1976, MS in Nuclear Engring., 1980; MS in Radiol. Sci., U. Colo. Health Sci. Ctr., Denver, 1985. Cert. Am. Bd. Radiology, Taiwan Nat. Bd. Health Physics; lic. med. physicist, Tex. Med. physicist Chung Gung Meml. Hosp., Taipei, 1980-81; health physicist Atomic Energy Coun., Taipei, 1981-83; physicist, radiation safety officer Bishop Clarkson Meml. Hosp., Omaha, 1986-89; med. physicist U. Tes. MD Anderson Cancer Ctr., Houston, 1989—. Contbr. articles to profl. jours. Mem. Am. Assn. Physicists in Medicine, Health Physics Soc. Baptist. Home: 12710 Water Oak Dr Missouri City TX 77489-3902 Office: U Tex MD Anderson Cancer Ctr 1515 Holcombe Blvd # 94 Houston TX 77030-4009

TUNNELL, CLIDA DIANE, air transportation specialist; b. Durham, N.C., Nov. 20, 1946; d. Kermit Wilbur and Roberta (Brantley) T. BS cum laude, Atlantic Christian Coll., 1968; pvt. pilot rating, instr. rating, Air Care, Inc., 1971, 83. Cert. tchr. Tchr. Colegio Karl C. Parrish, Barranquilla, Colombia, 1968-69, Nash County Schs., Nashville, N.C., 1969-86; ground sch. instr. Nash. Tech. Coll., Nashville, 1984-85; specialist Am. Airlines, Dallas-Ft. Worth Airport, Tex., 1987—, A300 lead developer in flight tng. program devel., 1988-89, with flight ops. procedures flight ops. tech., 1990—, F100-fleet specialist flight ops. tech., 1992—; ednl. cons., Euless, Tex., 1989—; profl. artist. State Tchrs. Scholar N.C., 1964-68, Bus. and Profl. Women Scholar, 1980-81. Mem. 99, Internat. Orgn. Women Pilots (various offices), AMR Mgmt. Club. Home: PO Box 234 Euless TX 76039-0234

TUNNELL, WILLIAM NEWTON, JR., tourism executive; b. Washington, Nov. 16, 1945; m. Janet Tunnell, Dec. 26, 1969 (div. Feb. 1975); children: Holly, Trey; m. Annette Bush, Feb. 14, 1976 (div. Apr. 1992); 1 child, Leigh. BA in History, U. of the South, 1968; postgrad., U. S.C., 1968-69. Cert. hotel adminstr., tour profl., travel industry specialist. Asst. cashier Comml. Bank, Andalusia, Ala., 1969-72; asst. v.p. Covington County Bank, Andalusia, 1972-76, First Nat. Bank of Dothan (Ala.), 1976-77; asst. gen. mgr. Ramada Inn, Dothan, 1977; gen. mgr. Holiday Inn, Ozark, Ala., 1977-79, Holidy Inn I-65, Mobile, Ala., 1979-87; hotel cons. Howard Johnson Beach Resort, Bilox, Miss., 1987; dir. sales Radisson Admiral Semmes Hotel, Mobile, 1987-88; dir. tourism and spl. events Mobile Conv. and Visitors Corp., Mobile, 1988-91; dir. mktg. and pub. rels. USS Ala. Battleship Commn., 1991—. Past pres. Lions Club, Mobile, Andulusia; past v.p., bd. dirs. Jr. Achievement of Mobile; past mem., bd. dirs. Mobile Area C. of C.; dir. Ala. Travel Coun. Mem. Am. Hotel & Motel Assn. (past bd. dirs.), Ala. Hotel & Motel Assn. (bd. dirs., past pres.), Mobile Area Hotel/Motel Assn. (life mem., past pres.), Lions (bd. dirs. Mobile chpt. 1985—). Republican. Roman Catholic. Home: 5701 Green Hill Ct Mobile AL 36609-5250 Office: Battleship USS Ala PO Box 65 2703 Battleship Pky Mobile AL 36601-0065

TURANCHIK, MICHAEL, research and development director. Dir. R&D Editek, Inc., Burlington, N.C. Office: 1238 Anthony Rd Burlington NC 27215

TURCOT, MARGUERITE HOGAN, innkeeper, medical researcher; b. White Plains, N.Y., May 19, 1934; d. Joseph William (dec.) and Marguerite Alice (dec.) Barrett) Hogan; children: Michael J., Susan A. Turcot, William R. Student, Syracuse U., 1951-54; BS in Nursing, U. Bridgeport, 1968. RN, Conn., N.C. Staff nurse Park City Hosp., Bridgeport, Conn., 1968-69, Meml. Mission Hosp., Asheville, N.C., 1969-70; instr. St. Joseph's Hosp., Asheville, 1970-71; oper. rm. nurse St. Joseph's Hosp., 1973-77, charge nurse urology-cystoscopy, 1977-85; tchr. Asheville-Buncombe Tech. Coll., Asheville, 1971-72, Buncombe County Child Devel., Asheville, 1972-73; researcher VA Med. Ctr., Asheville, 1988—; owner Reed House Bed & Breakfast, Asheville, 1985; bd. dirs. RiverLink. Charter mem. French Broad River Planning Com., Asheville, 1987—, Biltmore Village Hist. Mus.; mem. Asheville Bicentennial Commn., 1990-93. Recipient Griffin award, 1994, Friend of the River award Land of Sky Regional Coun., 1995; faculty scholar Syracuse U., 1951-54, U. Bridgeport, 1967-68, Sondley award Hist. Resources Commn. Asheville and Buncombe County, 1996. Mem. Am. Urology Assn. (presenter VA urology workshop Asheville chpt. 1981, nat. meeting allied), Am. Bd. Urologic Allied Health Profls., Nat. Trust for Hist. Preservation, Preservation Found. N.C., Blue Ridge Pkwy. Assn., Preservation Soc. Asheville and Buncombe County (bd. dirs., past pres.), Asheville Newcomers Club (founder, 1st pres.), Earthwatch, Friends of Blue Ridge Pkwy. Inc. Republican. Roman Catholic. Home: 119 Dodge St Asheville NC 28803-2731 Office: VA Med Ctr Tunnel Rd Asheville NC 28805-1233

TURJANICA, MARY ANN, clinical nurse specialist, consultant; b. Youngstown, Ohio, Oct. 30, 1960; d. Harold and Elizabeth Jane (Bartos) T. ADN, Youngstown State U., 1981, BSN, 1984; MS in Nursing, U.Va., 1985; post-MSN in Adult Nurse Practitioner, George Washington U., 1994. Cert. clin. nurse specialist, ANA; cert. adult nurse practitioner, ANA. Med.-surg. nurse St. Elizabeth's Hosp., Youngstown, 1981-84; med. intensive care nurse NIH, Bethesda, Md., 1985-88; asst. head nurse Fairfax Hosp., Falls Church, Va., 1988, clin. nurse specialist, 1988—; mem. faculty Am. Healthcare Inst., 1996—. Columnist Healthy Adults, MEDSURG Nursing, 1995—. Mem. Am. Coll. Nurse Practitioners, No. Va. Coun. Nurse Practitioners, Va. Coun. Nurse Specialists, Acad. Med./Surg. Nursing, Assn. Nurses in AIDS Care. Home: 4129 Meadow Field Ct Fairfax VA 22033-2830

TURK, DAVID SCOTT, intelligence research specialist; b. Washington, Feb. 2, 1964; s. Howard Sanford and Ann Elizabeth (Bostic) T.; m. Janet Lynn Vogel, Oct. 11, 1986; 1 child, Ryan McQuain. BBA, Longwood Coll., 1986; postgrad., George Mason U., 1991—. Acct. U.S. Marshals Svc., Arlington, Va., 1990-91; rsch. analyst historian's office U.S. Marshals Svc., Arlington, 1991-95, intelligence rsch. specialist, 1995—. Author: The Union Hole: Unionist Activity and Local Conflict in Western Virginia, 1994. Mem. Alleghany Highlands Geneal. Soc., Rose Family Assn., Phi Alpha Theta. Lutheran.

TURK, JAMES CLINTON, federal judge; b. Roanoke, Va., May 3, 1923; s. James Alexander and Geneva (Richardson) T.; m. Barbara Duncan, Aug. 21, 1954; children—Ramona Leah, James Clinton, Robert Malcolm Duncan, Mary Elizabeth, David Michael. A.B., Roanoke Coll., 1949; L.L.B., Washington and Lee U., 1952. Bar: Va. bar 1952. Assoc. Dalton & Poff, Radford, Va., 1952-53; ptnr. Dalton, Poff & Turk, Radford, 1953-72; U.S. senator from Va., 1959-72; judge U.S. Dist. Ct. (we. dist.) Va., Roanoke, 1972-73, chief judge, 1973—; dir. 1st & Mchts. Nat. Bank of Radford. Mem. Va. Senate, from 1959, minority leader.; Trustee Radford Community Hosp., 1959—. Served with AUS, 1943-46. Mem. Order of Coif, Phi Beta Kappa, Omicron Delta Kappa. Baptist (deacon). Home: 1002 Walker Dr Radford VA 24141-3018 Office: US Dist Ct 246 Franklin Rd SW # 220 Roanoke VA 24011-2204

TURK, JAMES CLINTON, JR., lawyer; b. Radford, Va., Oct. 27, 1956; s. James Clinton and Barbara (Duncan) T.; m. Allison Blanding, Oct. 16, 1993; children: Lindsey Leigh, Katherine Alexia. BA in Econs., Roanoke Coll., 1979; JD, Samford U., 1984. Bar: Va. 1984, U.S. Dist. Ct. (ea. and we. dists.) Va. 1984, U.S. Bankruptcy Ct. 1985, U.S. Ct. Appeals (4th cir.) 1985, U.S. Supreme Ct. 1988; cert. specialist in civil and criminal trial advocacy Nat. Bd. Trial Advocacy. Ptnr. Stone, Harrison, Turk & Showalter, P.C., Radford, 1985—; adj. prof. criminal justice dept. Radford U. Sec. Radford Rep. Com., 1984—; fundraising chmn. Am. Heart Assn., Radford, 1986—; bd. dirs. New River Valley Workshop, Inc., v.p., 1990-92, pres., 1992-93; bd. dirs. new River C.C. Ednl. Found.; apptd. chmn. and dir. Va. Student Assistance Authorities by Gov. George Allen, 1994—; escheator City of Radford and Pulaski County; rep. western dist. CJA Panel Attys., Va.; mem. 4th Cir. Jud. Conf. Mem. ATLA (sustaining, fellow Coll. of Advocacy), ABA, Va. Bar Assn. (civil litigation sect. coun. 1991—, criminal litigation sect. coun. 1994—), Nat. Assn. Criminal Def. Lawyers (life; death penalty com. and indigent def. com.), Va. Trial Lawyers Assn., Jaycees, Rotary. Republican. Roman Catholic. Home: 460 Quailwood Dr Blacksburg VA 24060 Office: Stone Harrison Turk & Showalter PC PO Box 2968 Radford VA 24143-2968

TURK, PAUL ALBERT, writer, editor, consultant; b. Akron, Ohio, May 26, 1942; s. Albert and Elva Margaret (Sibbald) T.; m. Jane Carol White, Aug. 15, 1970 (div. May 1973); m. Karen Susan Purdy, Oct. 28, 1989; 1 child, Katherine Antonia. AB in pol. sci., Oakland U., 1964; postgrad., Ind. U., 1968-70. City editor Courier-Tribune, Bloomington, Ind., 1968; pub. rels. rep. 150th Birthday Fund for Ind. U., Bloomington, 1969-70; staffwriter, editor The Journal Herald, Dayton, Ohio, 1970-78; comm. dir. Citizens for Tony Hall, Dayton, Ohio, 1978; corr. Am. Metal Mktg. Metalworking News, L.A., 1979-81; sr. pub. rels. rep. Goodyear Aerospace Corp., Akron, 1981-83; western editorial dir. Interavia Publs., L.A., 1984-86; dir. publs. Avmark, Inc., Arlington, Va., 1986-92; prin. Editing & Consulting Svcs., Fairfax, Va., Lenox, Mass., 1992-93, 94—; dir. media rels. USAir, 1994—; staff writer, critic Columbus Enquirer, 1967-68; staff writer The Republic, Columbus, Ind., 1964-66. Contbg. editor: Report of the National Commission to Ensure a Strong, Competitive Airline Industry, 1993. With U.S. Army, 1966-68, Army Res., 1982—. Mem. Aviation/Space Writers Assn. (pres. 1986-89), Nat. Press Club, Internat. Aviation Club, Aero Club Washington, Wings Club, Aviation Space Writers Found. (v.p. 1993—, trustee 1989—), Soc. of Aerospace Communication (bd. dirs. 1996—), N.Am. Airlines Pub. Rels. Assn. Democrat. Home: 2515 Glenlawn Pl Herndon VA 22071-2976 Office: 2345 Crystal Dr Arlington VA 22202-4801

TURK, THOMAS LIEBIG, cultural organization administrator; b. Indpls., July 4, 1936; s. Laurel Herbert and Esther Lucille (Liebig) T.; m. Judith Ann Prochnow, July 26, 1969; children: Martisha Emily, Benjamin Edward. AB, DePauw U., 1958; MA, Mich. State U., 1960; cert., Harvard U., 1973. Promotion and publicity dir. Sta. WMSB-TV Mich. State U., East Lansing, 1961, asst. editor news bur., 1962-63, fine arts assoc. producer Sta. WKAR-TV, 1963-68, fine arts producer Sta. WKAR-TV, 1969-81; acting dir. publicity DePauw U., Greencastle, Ind., 1961-62; exec. dir. Cultural Activities Ctr., Temple, Tex., 1981-91; mng. dir. Texarkana (Tex.) Regional Arts & Humanities Coun., 1991-93; exec. dir. Met. Nashville (Tenn.) Arts Commn., 1993—; pres. Met. Lansing (Mich.) Fine Arts Council, 1975-77, Mich. Assn. Community Arts Agys., East Lansing, 1979-81; Gov. apptd. mem. Mich. Council for Arts, 1979-81; chmn. Mich. Arts Forum, 1980-81. Producer, co-producer: 400 programs for local, nat. and internat. distbn. on pub. TV, 1963-81. Served with USAF, 1960. Mem. Nat. Assembly Local Arts Agys. (bd. dirs. 1979-85), Sigma Chi. Episcopalian. Lodge: Rotary. Home: 105 Harpeth Trace Ct Nashville TN 37221-3105 Office: Nashville Arts Commn 209 10th Ave S Ste 416 Nashville TN 37203-4164

TURKIA, KALEVI MATTI, engineer; b. Mikkeli, Finland, Aug. 22, 1941; came to U.S., 1959; m. Eija Raiha, Aug. 17, 1963; children: Jari K., Leena M. BS in Mktg., U. Minn., 1966, MS in Engring., 1967, postgrad., 1971. Planning engr. Rauma-Repola Oy, Lahti, Finland, 1968-70; exec. v.p. Puutalo Ltd., Helsinki, 1971-75; dir., rsch. and devel. UGI Devel. Co., Valley Forge, Pa., 1975-79; head, bldg. systems So. Solar Energy Ctr., Atlanta, 1979-81; pres., chief exec. officer Pohjola Am. Ins. Corp., Atlanta, 1990—; pres., chmn. Kaltek, Inc., Atlanta, 1981—; bd. dirs. Pohjola Am. Ins. Corp., Scandinavian-Am. Found.; com. mem. US-USSR Sci. Com. on Constrn., 1980; appointee UN Internat. Devel. Orgn., 1973. Recipient numerous scholarships. Mem. Finnish Am. C. of C. of the S.E. (pres. S.E. chpt. 1987-89), Xi Sigma Pi. Office: Kaltek Inc 2310 Peachford Rd Atlanta GA 30338-5823

TURKIN, MARSHALL WILLIAM, symphony orchestra, festival and opera administrator, arranger, composer; b. Chgo., Apr. 1, 1926; 4 children. Student, U. Kans., 1946-48; Mus. B. in Music Composition, Northwestern U., 1950, Mus. M., 1951; postgrad., Juilliard Sch. Music, Columbia U., U. Ind. Record rev. columnist, classical music commentator, gen. mgr., Honolulu Symphony and Opera Co., 1959-66; orch. festival mgr.; Ravinia Festival for Chgo. Symphony, 1966-68; founding mgr.; Blossom Festival for Cleve. Orch., 1968-70; gen. mgr. Detroit Symphony, 1970-73, exec. dir., 1973-79, mng. dir., Pitts. Symphony Orch., 1979-88; gen. dir. Hawaii Opera Theatre, Honolulu, 1988-91. Served with USN, World War II.

TURLEY, ROBERT JOE, lawyer; b. Mt. Sterling, Ky., Dec. 6, 1926; s. R. Joe and Mavis Clare (Sternberg) T.; m. Mary Lynn Sanders, Dec. 17, 1948 (div.); children: Leighton Turley Isaacs, Lynn Turley McComas, R. Joe, Mavis Lee Turley Scully. Student Berea Coll., 1944-45, St. Mary's Coll. (Calif.), 1945-46; LL.B., U. Ky., 1949. Bar: Ky. 1949, U.S. Dist. Ct. (ea. dist.) Ky. 1950, U.S. Ct. Appeals (6th cir.) 1958, U.S. Supreme Ct. 1959. Ptnr. Mooney & Turley and successor firms, Lexington, Ky., 1949-84, Turley & Moore, Lexington, 1984-89, of counsel, 1990-93; chmn. Fed. Jud. Selection Commn. Ky., 1985-89; gen counsel Shriners Hosps. for Crippled Children, 1976-77, trustee, 1981-90, emeritus trustee, 1990—. Served with USNR, 1944-46. Diplomate Nat. Bd. Trial Advocacy, 1980. Fellow Am. Coll. Trial Lawyers; mem. Ky. Bar Assn. Republican. Baptist. Clubs: Lafayette, St. Ives Jour., Champions Golf. Lodges: Masons, Shriners. Contbr. articles to legal jours. Home: 111 Woodland Ave Lexington KY 40502-6415

TURLINGTON, PATRICIA RENFREW, artist, educator; b. Washington, Sept. 14, 1939; d. Henry Wilson and Anne Ruth (Bright) Renfrew; m. William Troy Turlington III, June 3, 1963 (div. Oct. 1971); children: William

Troy IV, David Yelverton; m. William Archie Dees, Jr., June 4, 1994. Student, Meredith Coll., 1957, Washburn U., 1965-66, N.C. State UY., 1969-72. Comml. artist Adlers Inc. & McJoseph's, Raleigh, N.C., 1959-62; exec. dir. Goldsboro (N.C.) Art Ctr., 1973-78; elem. art tchr. Wayne Country Day Sch., Goldsboro, 1979-86; art prof. Wayne C.C., Goldsboro, 1986—; artist-in-residence Edward Laredo Inst. of the Humanities, Cochabamba, Bolivia, summer 1988; vis. artist Va. Western C.C., Roanoke, Va., 1986, Wake Forest U., Winston Salem, 1987, Catawba Valley C.C., Hickory, N.C., 1989, Salem Coll., Winston Salem, N.C., 1992. Works represented in permanent colections Blue Cross-Blue Shield, Durham, N.C., Duke Med. Ctr., Mint Mus., Charlotte, U. N.C., Chapel Hill, Wachovia Bank and Trust Co., Winston-Salem; corp. and pub. brick sculpture commissions Brick Assn. N.C., Greensboro, Cohn Enterprises, Lenoir, N.C., Cordova Elem. Sch., Rockingham, N.C., Wilkes C.C., Wilkesboro, N.C., Hocker Bros. Brick and Tile Co., Inc., Green Bay, Wis., Kincaid Brick Co., Tampa, Fla., Koontz Masonry, Lexington, N.C., McDonald's Restaurants, Knoxville, Tenn., Jonesville, N.C., Cary, N.C., Gastonia, N.C., Knightdale, N.C., Fayetteville, N.C, N.Y.C. Transit Authority, N.Y.C., North Dr. Elem. Sch., Goldsboro, N.C., Rowan Meml. Hosp., Salisbury, N.C. Atlantic Ctr. for the Arts fellow, New Smyrna Beach, Fla., 1986; Pntrs. of the Ams. grantee, U.S. Info. Agy., Washington, 1988. Home: 709 Park Ave Goldsboro NC 27530 Office: Turlington Brickworks PO Drawer 8 Goldsboro NC 27533

TURNBULL, TERRI DURRETT, county and non-profit organization consultant; b. Marietta, Ga., May 22, 1957; d. Thomas Richard and Margaret (Mann) Durrett; m. Ian Richards, Oct. 23, 1973 (div. Nov. 1977); m. Dan Lancaster, June 22, 1989 (div. Nov. 1990); children: Angie Louise, Shannon Leigh, Matthew D.; m. Paul Douglas Turnbull, Feb. 14, 1991. Student, Kennesaw Coll., Marietta, Ga., 1989, West Ga. Coll., Carrollton, 1989. Adv. Protection & Advocacy, Rome, Ga., 1987-89; program mgr. Cobb County Cmty. Devel., Marietta, 1989—; law clk. U.S. SBA, Atlanta, 1984-85; entrepreneur, cons. Cobb Exec. Support Svcs., Rome and Marietta, Ga., 1985—. Contbr. articles to profl. jours. Mem. publicity and fundraising com. Cobb County Habitat for Humanity, Cobb St. Ministry Homeless Shelters, Cobb County Heritage Coun.; mem. Gov.'s Policy and Adv. Com. on Weatherization, DOE/HUD Initiative Com. Recipient Certs., Gov.'s Office of Energy Resources. Office: Cobb Exec Support Svcs Ste 270 3180 Bankhead Hwy Lithia Springs GA 30057

TURNER, BILLIE LEE, botanist, educator; b. Yoakum, Tex., Feb. 22, 1925; s. James Madison and Julia Irene (Harper) T.; m. Virginia Ruth Mathis, Sept. 27, 1944 (div. Feb. 1968); children: Billie Lee, Matt Warnock; m. Pauline Henderson, Oct. 22, 1969 (div. Jan. 1975); m. Gayle Langford, Apr. 18, 1980; children (adopted)—Roy P., Robert L. B.S., Sul Ross State Coll., 1949; M.S., So. Meth. U., 1950; Ph.D., Wash. State U., 1953. Teaching asst. botany dept. Wash. State U., 1951-53; instr. botany dept. U. Tex., Austin, 1953; asst. prof. U. Tex., 1954-58, assoc. prof., 1958-61, prof., 1961—, now S.F. Blake prof. botany, chmn., 1967-75, dir. Plant Resources Ctr., 1957—; Asso. investigator ecol. study vegetation of, Africa, U. Ariz., Office Naval Research, 1956-57; vis. prof. U. Mont., summers 1971, 73, U. Mass., 1974. Author: Vegetational Changes in Africa Over a Third of a Century, 1959, Leguminosae of Texas, 1960, Biochemical Systematics, 1963, Chemotaxonomy of Leguminosae, 1972, Biology and Chemistry of Compositae, 1977, Plant Chemosystematics, 1984; Asso. editor: Southwestern Naturalist, 1959—. Served to 1st lt. USAAF, 1943-47. NSF postdoctoral fellow U. Liverpool, 1965-66. Mem. Bot. Soc. Am. (sec. 1958-59, 60-64, v.p. 1969), Tex. Acad. Sci., Southwestern Assn. Naturalists (pres. 1967, gov.), Am. Soc. Plant Taxonomists (Asa Gray award 1991), Internat. Assn. Plant Taxonomists, Soc. Study Evolution, Phi Beta Kappa, Sigma Xi. Office: U Tex Plant Resources Ctr Main Bldg 228 Austin TX 78712

TURNER, DAVID LOWERY, safety engineer; b. Atlanta, Feb. 2, 1936; s. Albert Olson Sr. and Ella May (Waldrop) T.; m. Sharon Kay Brewer, May 26, 1972 (div. 1978); children: Angela Kay, Jacqueline Kay; m. Rita M. Robertson, Aug. 25, 1993. Student, Samford U., 1958-60, U. Ala., 1960-62, U. Houston, 1977-79; BS in Safety Engring., Kennedy-Western U., 1991. Registered profl. safety engr.; lic. claims adjuster, Tex., real estate agt., Tex. Safety engr. USF&G, Birmingham, Ala., 1963-69, Parker Bros. Co. Inc., Houston, 1969-80; safety dir. MGF Oil Corp./MGF Drilling Co., Houston, 1980-84; safety mgr. Creole Prodn. Svcs. Inc., Houston, 1985-86; safety div. mgr. Mason Chamberlain Inc., Stennis Space Center, Miss., 1986-91; sys. safety engr. Raytheon Engrs. and Constructors, A Raytheon Co., Johnston Island, 1991—; cons. Fullbright and Jaworski Law Firm, Houston, 1980-81. Vol. West Meml. Vol. Fire Dept., Katy, Tex., 1979-80. With USAF, 1954-58. Mem. Am. Soc. Safety Engrs. (profl.), Nat. Safety Coun., Tex. Safety Assn., Nat. Ready Mix Concrete Assn., Internat. Assn. Drilling Contractors, NASA Safety Coun., Gulf Coast Safety Coun., MCI Exec. Safety Coun. (co-chmn. 1986-91). Republican. Baptist. Home: PO Box 098 APO AP 96558 Office: Raytheon Engrs & Constructors A Raytheon Co Johnston Island APO AP 96558

TURNER, ELIZABETH ADAMS NOBLE (BETTY TURNER), healthcare executive, former mayor; b. Yonkers, N.Y., May 18, 1931; d. James Kendrick and Orrel (Baldwin) Noble; m. Jack Rice Turner, July 11, 1953; children: Jay Kendrick, Randall Ray. BA, Vassar Coll., 1953; MA, Tex. A&I U., 1964. Ednl. cons. Noble & Noble Pub. Co., N.Y.C., 1956-67; psychometrist Corpus Christi Guidance Ctr., 1967-70; psychologist Corpus Christi State Sch., 1970-72, dir. programs, asst. supt., 1972, dir. devel. and vol. svc., 1972-76, dir. rsch. and tng., 1977-79, psychologist Tex. Mental Health and Mental Retardation, 1970-79; pres. Turner Co., 1979—; program cons. Tex. Dept. Mental Health and Mental Retardation, 1979-85; mayor pro tem. Corpus Christi, 1981-85, mayor, 1987-91; CEO, pres. Corpus Christi C. of C., 1991-94; v.p. bus. and govt. rels. ctrl. and south Tex. divsns. Columbia Healthcare Corp., 1994—. Dir. alumni Corpus Christi State U., 1976-77; coord. vols. Summer Head Start Program, Corpus Christi, 1967; chmn. spl. gifts coml United Way, Corpus Christi, 1970; mem. Corpus Christi City Coun., 1979-91; family founded Barnes and Noble, N.Y.C.; with Leadership Corpus Christi II; founder Com. of 100 and Goals for Corpus Christi; pres. USO; bd. dirs. Coastal Bends Coun. Govts., Corpus Christi Mus., Harbor Playhouse, Communities in Schs., Del Mar Coll. Found., Pres.' Coun., Food Bank, Salvation Army, Jr. League; bd. govs. Southside Community Hosp., 1989-93, Gulfway Nat. Bank, 1985-92, Bayview Hosp., 1992—, strategic planning com. Meml. Hosp., 1992, Tex. Capital Network Bd., 1992—, Humana Hosp., Rehab. Hosp. South Tex., Admiral Tex. Navy; apptd. Gov.'s Commn. for Women, 1984-85, Leadership Tex. Class I; founder Goals for Corpus Christi, Bay Area Sports Assn., Assn. Coastal Bend Mayor's Alliance; founder Mayor's Commn. on the Disabled, Mayor's Task Force on the Homeless; active Port Aransas Cmty. Ch. Recipient Love award YWCA, 1970, Y's Women and Men in Careers award, 1988, Commander's Award for Pub. Svc. U.S. Army, Scroll of Honor award Navy League, award Tex. Hwy. Dept., Road Hand award Tex. Hwy. Commn., 1989; named Corpus Christi Newsmaker of Yr., 1987. Mem. Tex. Psychol. Assn. (pres., mem. exec. bd.), Psychol. Assn. (pres., founder), Tex. Mcpl. League (bd. dir.), Corpus Christi C. of C. (pres., CEO), Jr. League Corpus Christi, Tex. Bookman's Assn., Tex. Assn. Realtors, Kappa Kappa Gamma, Corpus Christi Town Club, Corpus Christi Yacht Club, Jr. Cotillion Club. Home: 4600 Ocean Dr Apt 801 Corpus Christi TX 78412-2543

TURNER, FRED LAMAR, accountant, lawyer; b. LaGrange, Ga., Oct. 8, 1949; s. John Cletus and Dean (Norris) T.; m. Mary Katherine Daws, Sept. 27, 1969; children: Jessica, Jennifer, Judson. AA in Electronics, Troup Tech. Sch., LaGrange, 1969; BA, Columbus (Ga.) Coll., 1973; M in Taxation, Ga. State U., 1979, JD, 1986. Bar: Ga. Elec. installer N. Electric Co., Orlando, Fla., 1969-70; instr. La Grange (Ga.) Coll., 1979-81; prin., owner J.K. Boatwright & Co., PC, La Grange, 1973—; pres., bd. dirs. J.K. Boatwright & Co., La Grange. Bd. dirs. Troup County Cert. Devel. Corp., 1982—, Troup County Planning Commn.; trustee LaGrange Coll., Callaway Found. Inc., Clark Holder Clinic Ednl. Found.; treas., bd. dirs. Chattahoochee Valley Art Assn., LaGrange, 1982—; chmn. bd. LaGrange Indsl. Devel. Authority. Named Acct. Advocate of Yr. for Ga. SBA, Atlanta, 1986. Mem. AICPA (tax div.), Ga. Soc. CPAs, LaGrange C. of C. (bd. dirs., treas., pres. 1988), Troup County C. of C. (pres.), Rotary (bd. dirs., treas. LaGrange chpt. 1984—, pres.). Baptist. Home: 867 Whitaker Rd La Grange GA 30240-3768 Office: J K Boatwright Co PC 17 1/2 N Lafayette Sq Lagrange GA 30240

TURNER, GERALD, academic administrator. Chancellor U. Mississippi, University, Miss. Office: SMU Office of the President Dallas TX 75275*

TURNER, GERALD RUFUS, government contracting official; b. Charlotte, N.C., Mar. 26, 1950; s. Rufus B. and Martha (Preslar) T.; m. Virginia Pinero (div. 1981); 1 child, Cheryl; m. Emerita Hernandez, Nov. 3, 1983; children: Vivian, Valerie, Jason. BA, U. La Verne, Calif., 1975; MA, Pepperdine U., 1976; BS, U. Md., 1984; postgrad., Campbell U., Buies Creek, N.C., 1988, The Citadel, 1989—. Enlisted USN, 1970-77, commd. ensign, 1978, advanced through grades to lt., 1981; dir. aviation support div., aviation dept., material dept. U.S. Naval Supply Depot, Guam, 1979-84; supply-logistics/contracting officer USN/USNR, Atsugi, Japan, 1984-88; ret., 1990; contract specialist/contracting officer so. div. Naval Facilities Engring. Command, Charleston, S.C., 1988—; instr. bus. L.A. City Coll., Guam, 1977-79, U. Md. Far East, Guam and Japan, 1980-88, Cen. Tex. Coll., Japan, 1983-84, Limestone Coll., 1990—; instr. econs. Meth. Coll., Fayetteville, N.C., 1988. Mem. Nat. Contracts Mgmt. Assn. (cert.), Citadel MBA Assn. Baptist. Home: 5576 Betty Ct Charleston SC 29418-5405 Office: Naval Facilities Engring Command So Div Code 0232GT 2155 Eagle Dr Charleston SC 29406-4804

TURNER, GLORIA TOWNSEND BURKE, social services association executive; b. Lumberton, N.C., Nov. 16, 1938; d. John B. and Alice (Haite) Townsend; m. James Rae Burke, June 3, 1957 (dec. 1974); children: William H., Sonya Kyle; m. Robert R. Turner,June 23, 1977. Student, U. S.C., 1974; degree in nursing, York Tech. Coll./U. S.C., 1976. RN, S.C. Staff nurse, head nurse York Gen. Hosp., Rock Hill, S.C., 1976-78; head med. dept., indsl. nursing J.P. Stevens Plant, Rock Hill, 1976-78; hsop., nursing home auditor S.C. Med. Found., Columbia, 1978-79; exec. dir. Kershaw County Coun. on Aging, Camden, S.C., 1979-93; dir. med.-surg. units Conway (S.C.) Hosp., 1993—; bd. dirs. S.C. Fedn. Older Ams., 1988-95; mem. state adv. com. on Alzheimers, Columbia, 1984—; trustee Kershaw County Meml. Hosp., Camden, 1989-93. Mem. Camden C. of C., Rotary. Methodist. Home: 147 Dusty Trail Ln Surfside Beach SC 29575

TURNER, HUGH JOSEPH, JR., lawyer; b. Paterson, N.J., Oct. 5, 1945; s. Hugh Joseph and Louise (Sullivan) T.; m. Charlene Chiappetta, Feb. 11, 1983. BS, Boston U., 1967; JD, U. Miami, Coral Gables, Fla., 1975. Bar: Fla. 1975, U.S. Dist. Ct. (so. & mid. dists.) Fla. 1975, U.S. Ct. Appeals (11th cir.) 1981, U.S. Supreme Ct. 1984. Tchr. Browne & Nichols, Cambridge, Mass., 1968-72; ptnr. Smathers & Thompson, Miami, Fla., 1981-87, Kelley Drye & Warren, Miami, 1987-93, English, McCaughan & O'Bryan, Ft. Lauderdale, 1993—; chmn. Fla. Bar internat. law sect., 1988-89. Contbg. author book on internat. dispute resolution Fla. Bar, 1989; contbr. articles to profl. jours. Bd. dirs. Japan Soc. South Fla., Miami, 1989—; mem. Sea Ranch Lakes Village Coun. Mem. ABA, Def. Rsch. Inst., Internat. Bar Assn. Office: English McCaughan O'Bryan 100 NE 3rd Ave Fort Lauderdale FL 33301-1176

TURNER, JAMES R., lawyer; b. Wilmington, N.C., Sept. 4, 1934; s. Reginald and Sarah Maree (Terrell) T.; m. Carolyn Frances Simpkins, Feb. 4, 1967; children: Susannah Lynn, William Joel. AB, U. N.C., 1956; LLB, Yale U., 1962. Bar: N.C., 1963. Associate Smith, Helms, Mulliss & Moore, Greensboro, N.C., 1962-69; founder, sr. ptnr. Turner, Enochs & Lloyd, P.A., Greensboro, 1969—; senator State Legislature, N.C., 1979-80; lectr. on affordable housing Carolinas Coun., NAHRO, N.C., S.C., 1972-96. Reviewer architecture Greensboro News & Record. Warden N.W. Convocation of the Episcopal Diocese of N.C., Greensboro, 1996. Capt., USN, 1956-59, Persian Gulf. Democrat. Episcopalian. Home: 18 Fountain Manor Dr # C Greensboro NC 27405-8014 Office: Turner Enochs & Lloyd PA 100 S Elm St Greensboro NC 27402-0160

TURNER, JAMES WESLEY, minister, former church administrator; b. Hampton, Va., May 30, 1914; s. James Hugh Turner and Lizzie Emma Moger; m. Ruth Clark Brown, Sept. 28, 1940; children: James Wedford, Susan Clark. BA, Randolph-Macon Coll., 1937, DD, 1961; MDiv, Emory U., 1940. Ordained to ministry Meth. Ch., 1940. Pastor Meth. Ch., Richmond, Va., 1940-82; dir. program coun. United Meth. Ch., Richmond, 1976-82; dist. supt. United Meth. Ch., Arlington, Va., 1971-76; chmn. fin. Va. Conf. Credit Union, Inc., 1954—; pres. Chaplain Svc. Va., Richmond; mem. bd. ordained ministry, Richmond, 1989—. Vice pres. Robert E. Lee coun. Boy Scouts Am., 1978—; mem. allocation panel United Way Greater Richmond, 1987-95. Recipient Gold medal Freedom Found., 1967, Silver Beaver award Boy Scouts Am., 1980. Mem. Masons. Home and Office: 10201 Glendye Rd Richmond VA 23235-2122

TURNER, JEROME, federal judge; b. Memphis, Feb. 18, 1942; s. Cooper and Eugenia (Morrison) T.; m. Shirley Broadhead, Oct. 18, 1969 (div. July 1986); children: Alexandra Cox, Christian Annette; m. Kay Farese, Aug. 22, 1987. BA, Washington and Lee U., 1964, LLB cum laude, 1966. Bar: Tenn. 1966. Law clk. to judge U.S. Dist. Ct., Memphis, 1966-67; assoc. Canada, Russell & Turner, Memphis, 1967-73, ptnr., 1974-78; ptnr. Wildman, Harrold, Allen, Dixon & McDonnell, Memphis, 1978-87; judge U.S. Dist. Ct. (we. Dist.) Tenn., Memphis, 1988—. Author: Law Rev. Comment, Washington and Lee Law Rev., 1964, 65; editor: Law Rev., 1966. Treas. Elect Don Sundquist to Congress Com., 1981-82, Reelect Don Sundquist to Congress Com., 1983-86. Fellow Tenn. Bar Found.; mem. ABA, Memphis and Shelby County Bar Found. (bd. dirs. 1982-83, 87, 96-97), Memphis and Shelby County Bar Assn. (pres. 1988, treas. 1984, bd. dirs. 1978-79), Fed. Bar Assn., Tenn. Bar Assn., Leo Bearman Sr. Am. Inn of Ct. (pres. 1995-96, 97), Order of Coif, Omicron Delta Kappa. Roman Catholic. Office: Clifford Davis Fed Bldg 167 N Main St Ste 1111 Memphis TN 38103-1830

TURNER, JOHN FREELAND, non-profit administrator, former federal agency administrator, former state senator; b. Jackson, Wyo., Mar. 3, 1942; s. John Charles and Mary Louise (Mapes) T.; m. Mary Kay Brady, 1969; children: John Francis, Kathy Mapes, Mark Freeland. BS in Biology, U. Notre Dame, 1964; postgrad., U. Innsbruck, 1964-65, U. Utah, 1965-66; MS in Ecology, U. Mich., 1968. Rancher, outfitter Triangle X Ranch, Moose, Wyo.; chmn. bd. dirs. Bank of Jackson Hole; photo-journalist; state senator from Sublette State of Wyo., Teton County, 1974-89; mem. Wyo. Ho. of Reps. Teton County, 1970-74; pres. Wyo. Senate, 1987-89; chmn. legis., minerals bus. and econ. devel. com. Teton County, Wyo., 1987-89; dir. Fish and Wildlife Svc. Dept. Interior, Washington, 1989-93; pres. Conservation Fund, Arlington, Va., 1993—; sr. cons. Sch. Environ. and Natural Resources, U. Wyo., Laramie, 1993—; exec. adv. Hancock Timber Resource Group, 1993—; bd. dirs. Land Trust Alliance, 1994—, N.E. Utilities, Nat. Assn. Chem. Distbn. Found.; mem. Nat. Coal Coun., 1995—, Teton Sci. Sch. Bd., Nat. Wetland Forum, 1983, 87; mem. exec. com. Coun. of State Govts.; chmn. Pride in Jackson Hole Campaign, 1986; bd. dirs. Wyo. Waterfowl Trust; chmn. steering com. of UN conv. on Wetlands of Internat. Importance, 1990—; head U.S. delegation to Conv. on Internat. Trade Endangered Species. Author: The Magnificent Bald Eagle: Our National Bird, 1971. Named Citizen of Yr. County of Teton, 1984; recipient Nat. Conservation Achievement award Nat. Wildlife Fedn., 1984, Sheldon Coleman Great Outdoors award, 1990, Pres.'s Pub. Svc. award The Nature Conservatory, 1990, Stewardship award Audobon Soc., 1992, Nat. Wetland Achievement award Ducks Unlimited, 1993, Chevron/Times-Mirror Nat. Conservation Leadership award, 1995. Republican. Roman Catholic.

TURNER, JUSTIN LEROY, investor, consultant; b. Madrid, Iowa, May 26, 1915; s. John and Mabel (Smith) T.; student Northwestern U., 1934-41, N.Y.U., 1949-52; m. Roberta Gertrude Beaty, Aug. 13, 1937 (dec. Feb. 1979); m. Dorothy Y. Weaver, Feb. 14, 1985. Plant controller, div. controller, mgr. adminstrv. standards Am. Can. Co., N.Y.C., 1933-56; dir. adminstrn. Remington-Rand Univac div. Sperry Rand Co., Stamford, Conn., 1956-61; pres. CEO, dir. Foregger Co., Roslyn, N.Y., 1961; pres., CEO, chmn. exec. com. Soundscriber Corp., North Haven, Conn., 1961-64; chmn. bd. Soundscriber Sales Corp., 1961-64 indsl. mgmt. cons., 1964-66; pres., chief exec. officer, dir. Ednl. Service Programs, Inc., New Haven, 1966-73; dir. Soundscriber Corp. Japan, Ltd.; cons., gen. investor, 1973—. Chmn. troop com., scout master Boy Scouts Am., Oak Park, Ill.; chmn. publicity com. Conn. Regional Export Expansion Council. Trustee Conn. Distributive Edn. Com. Mem. Nat. Mfg. Assn., AIM, (pres.'s council), Am. Assn. Mus., Am. Assn. Zool. Parks and Aquariums, Smithsonian Mus. Assos., Yale Peabody Assos., Newcomen Soc. N.Am. Baptist (deacon). Clubs: Bayside Yacht, Lake County Executive, Douglaston, Sedgwood, Quinnipac, Darien Country, Darbonne Country, Green Valley Country Club, Kiwanis, Elks. Patentee in field. Home: 11922 Lake Louisa Rd Clermont FL 34711-9153

TURNER, LISA JOYCE, paint manufacturing company executive; b. Galveston, Tex., June 1, 1959; d. Carlton and Dorothy Lee (McPeters) Pappas Kelly; m. E.D. Turner; 1 child, Alexander Carlton. Student N. Tex. State U., 1977, Richland Coll., 1978, U. Ark.-Little Rock, 1980, IBM Continuing Edn., 1981-82. Mktg. asst. Membership Services, Irving, Tex., 1978, tech. support asst., 1980; programmer, analyst Mail Mktg. Services, Little Rock, 1980-82; bus. broker VR Bus. Brokers, Longview, Tex., 1982-85; mgr., v.p. Creative Coatings Inc., Kilgore, Tex., 1985—, also bd. dirs. Mem. Mothers Against Drunk Drivers, Longview, Tex., 1985-86, v.p. Gregg County chpt.; sec. East Tex. Area Parkinsonism Soc., 1987—. Mem. Data Processing Mgrs. Assn., Nat. Assn. Sundry Distbrs. (adv. bd.). Baptist. Avocations: skiing, traveling. Home: 3715 Ben Hogan Dr Longview TX 75605-1623 Office: Creative Coatings Inc 428 N Longview St Kilgore TX 75662-5810

TURNER, LISA PHILLIPS, human resources executive; b. Waltham, Mass., Apr. 10, 1951; d. James Sinclair and Virginia (Heathcote) T. BA in Edn. and Philosophy magna cum laude, Washington Coll., Chestertown, Md., 1974; AS in Electronics Tech., AA in Engring., Palm Beach Jr. Coll., 1982; MBA, Nova U., 1986, DSc, 1989; PhD, Kennedy Western U., 1990. Cert. sr. profl. in human resources, quality engr.; lic. USCG capt.; lic. pvt. pilot FAA. Founder, pres. Turner's Bicycle Svc., Inc., Delray Beach, Fla., 1975-80; electronics engr., quality engr. Audio Engring. and Video Arts, Boca Raton, 1980-81; tech. writing instr. Palm Beach Jr. Coll., Lake Worth, Fla., 1981-82; adminstr. tng. and devel. Mitel Inc., Boca Raton, 1982-88; mgr. communications and employee rels. Modular Computer Systems, Inc., Ft. Lauderdale, Fla., 1988-89; U.S. mktg. project mgr. Mitel, Inc., Boca Raton, Fla., 1990-91; v.p. human resources Connectronics, Inc., Ft. Lauderdale, Fla., 1991-93; mgr. human resources Sensormatic Electronics Corp., Boca Raton, Fla., 1993—. With USCG Aux. Mem. Soc. for Human Resource Mgmt., Internat. Assn. Quality Cirs., Am. Soc. Quality Control, Fla. Employment Mgmt. Assn., Am. Acad. Mgmt., Employment Assn. Fla., Am. Capts. Assn., Citizens Police Acad., Aircraft Owners and Pilot's Assn., Exptl. Aircraft Assn., Fla. Aero. Club. Home: 1358 Farifax Cir E Lantana FL 33462-7412 Office: Sensormatic Electronics Corp 6600 Congress Ave Boca Raton FL 33487-1213

TURNER, MALCOLM ELIJAH, biomathematician, educator; b. Atlanta, May 27, 1929; s. Malcolm Elijah and Margaret (Parker) T.; m. Ann Clay Bowers, Sept. 16, 1948; children: Malcolm Elijah IV, Allison Ann, Clay Shumate, Margaret Jean; m. Rachel Patricia Farmer, Feb. 1, 1968; children: Aleta van Riper, Leila Samantha, Alexis St. John, Walter McCamy. Student, Emory U., 1947-48; B.A., Duke U., 1952; M.Exptl. Stats., N.C. State U., 1955, Ph.D., 1959. Analytical statistician Communicable Disease Center, USPHS, Atlanta, 1953; rsch. assoc. U. Cin., 1955, asst. prof., 1955-58; asst. statistician N.C. State U., Raleigh, 1957-58; assoc. prof. Med. Coll. Va., Richmond, 1958-63, chmn. div. biometry, 1959-63; prof., chmn. dept. statistics and biometry Emory U., Atlanta, 1963-69; chmn. dept. biomath., prof. biostats. and biomath. U. Ala., Birmingham, 1970-82, prof. biostats. and biomath., 1982—; instr. summers Yale U., 1966, U. Calif. at Berkeley, 1971, Vanderbilt U., 1975; prof. U. Kans., 1968-69; vis. prof. Atlanta U., 1969; cons. to industry. Mem. editorial bd. So. Med. Jour., 1990—; contbr. articles to profl. jours. Fellow Ala. Acad. Sci., Am. Statis. Assn. (hon.), AAAS (hon.); mem. AAUP, AMA (affiliate), Biometrics Soc. (mng. editor Biometrics 1962-69), Soc. for Indsl. and Applied Math., Mensa, Sigma Xi, Phi Kappa Phi, Phi Delta Theta, Phi Sigma. Home: 1734 Tecumseh Trl Pelham AL 35124-1012

TURNER, MARGUERITE ROSE COWLES, library administrator; b. Port Sulphur, La., June 21, 1941; d. John Clinton and Marguerite Eileen (Slaybaugh) Cowles; B.A., U. New Orleans, 1963; M.L.S., La. State U., 1966; M.A. in History, U. So. Miss., 1970; divorced; 1 son, Jeffrey Jason. Reference librarian edn. div. U. So. Miss., 1966-70; librarian Pascagoula (Miss.) Jr. High Sch., 1970-71, Irwin County High Sch., Ocilla, Ga., 1971-72; dir. Fitzgerald (Ga.) Carnegie Library, 1974-80; adminstrv. librarian Assumption Parish Library, Napoleonville, La., 1980-83; dir. Jacob S. Mauney Meml. Library, Kings Mountain, N.C., 1983—. Author poems, short stories; writer weekly column Kings Mountain Herald, Shelby Star; contbr. articles to profl. jours. Sunday sch. tchr., First Baptist Ch., librarian, 1975—, Fitzgerald, 1978-80, Napoleonville, 1980-83. Mem. ALA, N.C. Library Assn., Broad River Libr. Assn. Democrat. Office: 100 S Piedmont Ave Kings Mountain NC 28086-3414

TURNER, MARVIN WENTZ, insurance company executive; b. Lower Marion, Pa., Oct. 17, 1959; s. Gilbert Jr. and Frances (McAlister) T.; m. Julia (Davis) Turner. BBA, Howard U., 1981; postgrad., Temple U., 1984-86; MBA, George Washington U., 1988. Registered investment advisor; cert. fund specialist. Claim advisor Prudential Ins., Fort Washington, Pa., 1982-84; ptnr. Mgmt. Enterprise, Phila., 1984-86; analyst CNA Fin. Group, Washington, 1986-88; fin. analyst Bell Atlantic, Arlington, Va., 1988-93; CFO Local Govt. Ins. Trust, Columbia, Md., 1993—; adv. bd. mem. Access Washington; ptnr. Target Group Investors, Upper Marlsboro, Md., 1990—; fin. advisor Turner Mgmt. Group, Watkins Park, Md., 1991. Ptnr. The Tucker Group, Cheverly, Md., 1990. Recipient Elizabeth B. Adams Meml. award George Washington U., 1988, minority fellowship, 1987. Mem. Nat. Black MBA Assn. (exec. bd. D.C. chpt., treas. 1988-90, v.p. 1992-94), Fin. Exec. Inst. Home: 13300 Burleigh St Upper Marlboro MD 20774 Office: Fin Assets Capital LLC 1825 Eye St NW # 400 Washington DC 20006

TURNER, MARY JANE, educational administrator; b. Colorado Springs, Colo., June 1, 1923; d. David Edward and Ina Mabel (Campbell) Nickelson; m. Harold Adair Turner, Feb. 15, 1945 (dec.); children: Mary Ann, Harold Adair III. BA in Polit. Sci., U. Colo., 1947, MPA in Pub. Adminstrn., 1968, PhD in Polit. Sci., 1978. Secondary tchr. Canon City (Colo.) Sch. Dist., 1950-53; tchr. assoc. in polit. sci. U. Colo., Denver, 1968-70, Boulder, 1970-71; rsch. asst. Social Sci. Edn. Consortium, Boulder, 1971, staff assoc., 1972-77; dir. Colo. Legal Edn. Program, Boulder, 1977-84; assoc. dir. Ctr. for Civic Edn., Calabasas, Calif., 1984-88; dir. Close Up Found., Alexandria, Va., 1988-92; sr. edn. advisor Close Up Found., Arlington, Va., 1992—. Author: Political Science in the New Social Studies, 1972; co-author: American Government: Principles and Practices, 1983, 4th edit., 1996; Civics: Citizens in Action, 1986, 2d edit., 1991, U.S. Government Resource Book, 1989; contbg. author: Internat. Ency. Dictionary of Edn. Mem. Nat. Coun. for Social Studies (chair nominations 1983-84, chair bicentennial com. 1986), Social Sci. Edn. Consortium (pres. 1986-87, bd. dirs. 1984-87), Pi Lambda Theta, Pi Sigma Alpha. Democrat. Presbyterian. Office: Close Up Found 44 Canal Center Plz Alexandria VA 22314-1592

TURNER, MARY LOUISE, computer specialist; b. Glens Falls, N.Y., June 24, 1954; d. Gilmore Eldridge and Joan (Ringrose) T. AAS, Adriondack Community Coll., Glens Falls, 1974. Computer operator Glens Falls Nat. Bank & Trust Co., 1974-89; computer specialist Ace Rent A Car, Newport News, Va., 1989—; refreshment mgr. Lake George Opera Festival, Glens Falls, summer 1974. Author: (novel) Today Begins Tomorrow, 1986; (poetry) Why Me, 1983, Auf Wiedersehen, 1988, Jealousy (poetry), 1988, You've Got To Be Kidding (poetry), 1988, What If Time Stood Still (poetry), 1989. Republican. Home: 372A Circuit Ln Newport News VA 23602-2902

TURNER, NANCY DELANE, animal nutritionist; b. Atlanta, Nov. 8, 1956; d. Pheron Oclesia and Dicie Ethel (Kent) T. Student, Emory U., 1974-75; BS, Tex. A&M U., 1978, MS, 1984, PhD, 1995. Cert. nutrition specialist. Student tech. Tex. A&M U., College Station, 1980-84, rsch. assoc., 1984-95, asst. rsch. scientist, 1996—; freelance cons., manuscript editor, College Station, 1986—; editl. asst. for Jour. of Nutrition, 1995—; ptnr. O.O.C. Cons. Contbr. chpts. to books, abstracts and articles to refereed publs. Dan F. Jones Meml. scholar Tex. A&M U., 1990; recipient vice chancellor's award in excellence for rsch. support, 1995. Mem. AAAS, Am. Soc. Animal Sci., Am. Assn. Cereal Chemists, N.Y. Acad. Scis., Soc. Exptl. Biology and Medicine, Am. Inst. Nutrition, Gamma Sigma Delta. Home: 3105 Manorwood Dr Bryan TX 77801-4204 Office: Tex A&M U Dept Animal Sci College Station TX 77843

TURNER, PEGGY ANN, graphic designer, visual artist; b. Memphis, Jan. 17, 1951; d. James Patrick and Margaret Helen (Brastock) T. BFA, U. Tenn., 1974, MFA summa cum laude, 1992. Art dir. Turner Design, Knoxville, 1972-84; designer, illustrator Creative Displays, Knoxville, 1974-75; designer alumni affairs U. Tenn., Knoxville, 1975-81; sr. art dir. Whittle Comm., Knoxville, 1982-85; creative dir. Sullivan-St. Clair Advt., Mobile, Ala., 1985-89; grad. teaching asst. dept. art U. Tenn., Knoxville, 1989-91; prof. graphic design Savannah (Ga.) Coll. Art and Design, 1991-92; asst. prof. graphic design Va. Polytechnic Inst. and State U., 1992-96, Nicholls State U., Thibodaux, La., 1996—. One-woman shows include S. Morris Gallery, Savannah, 1992, Ewing Gallery, Knoxville, 1993, 94, Armory Art Gallery, Va. Poly. Inst. and State U., 1993, Gallery 303, Ga. So. U., 1994, Littman-White Gallery, Portland, Oreg., 1996; group shows include Women's Art Works III, Rochester, N.Y. (jury prize), Nat. Expos II, Chgo., 1993, Current Works '93, Kansas City, Mo., U. West Fla., 1994, Paper Stars, San Francisco, 1994, Nat. Exposures, Winston-Salem, N.C. Recipient nat. citation Coun. for Advancement Edn., 1981, award Warren Paper Co., 1984; Fred M. Roddy scholar, 1970, Blinn scholar for fgn. study, 1991; grantee Va. Poly. Inst. and State U., 1992, 93, Women's Rsch. Inst., 1993, 95. Mem. Am. Advt. Fedn., Coll. Art Assn., Alpha Lambda Delta. Democrat. Episcopalian. Home: 301 E 7th St Thibodaux LA 70301 Office: Nicholls State U Art Dept PO 2025 Thibodaux LA 70301

TURNER, R(ALPH) CHIP, public relations and telecommunications executive, religious studies educator; b. Shreveport, La., Jan. 18, 1948; s. Ralph Wilson Sr. and Gladys Pearl (MaGouirk) T.; m. Sandra Elaine Aymond, May 23, 1970; children: Christopher, Cory. BA in Speech Edn., La. Coll., 1970; MRE, Bapt. Theol. Seminary, New Orleans, 1973. Accredited pub. rels. profl., So. Pub. Rels. Fedn. Min. of edn. and youth 1st Bapt. Ch., Farmerville, La., 1968-71, Summit, Miss., 1971-73; min. edn. and adminstrn. 1st Bapt. Ch., Slidell, La., 1973-75, Port Arthur, Tex., 1975-76; min. of edn. and bus. adminstrn. 1st Bapt. Ch., Beaumont, Tex., 1976-79; instr. religious edn. New Orleans Bapt. Theol. Seminary, New Orleans, 1979-81; dir. comm./media svcs. La. Bapt. Convention, Alexandria, 1981-95; state dir. Bapt. Telecomm. Network for Religious Edn., Alexandria, La., 1981-90, ACTS Satellite Network, Alexandria, La., 1981-95, Family Net, 1991-95; teleconferencing coord. Northwestern State U. La., Natchitoches, 1995-96; asst. dir. instnl. advancement Northwestern State U. La., Alexandria, 1996—; coord. cable TV series (NSU 22 and Channel 21); prodr. 1st PBS videoconf. originating in La., 1995, contbr. to videoconf. New Directions; mem. State of La. telecom. compatibility plan work group La. Bd. Regents, 1996—; instnl. rep. Nat. U. Teleconferencing Network, 1996—. Author: The Church Video Answerbook, 1986; editor, contbr.: A Glorious Past. . .a Promising Future--75 Years at Calvary Baptist Church; author, designer ednl. videotapes, 1981—; author (filmstrips) How to Use Audio Visuals, 1985, How to Train Sunday Workers, 1985; contbr. articles to more than 30 mags. Membership officer Bel Fed. Credit Union, Alexandria, 1984-95; mem. mayor's adv. com. City of Alexandria, 1993—; deacon Calvary Bapt. Ch., Alexandria; v.p. comm. and relationships Attakapas coun. Boy Scouts Am., 1981—, mem. nat. coms., 1980—. Recipient Nat. Youth Leadership award Religious Heritage Am., 1991, Outstanding Contbns. to Cmty. Youth award South Alexandria Rotary Club, 1993. Mem. ASCD, La. Cable TV Assn. (state bd. dirs. 1994-96), So. Pub. Rels. Fedn. (state bd. chpt. pres. 1990-94, Sr. Pub. Rels. Practitioner 1993), La. Assn. Broadcasters, Bapt. Pub. Rels. Assn., Nat. Religious Pub. Relations Coun., Am. Assn. Media Specialists, Am. Soc. Educators, Commn. Ch. and Youth Agy. Relationships (mem. editl. com. 1981—, editor nat. newsletter 1985—, nat. pres. 1988-90, 92-94). Republican. Southern Baptist. Home: 605 Windermere Blvd Alexandria LA 71303-2642 Office: Northwestern State U La Office Instnl Advancement Alexandria LA 71303

TURNER, REBECCA SUE, writer; b. Norman, Okla., Dec. 10, 1947; d. George Henry and Freda Mae (Plumb) Yoakum; m. Harry F. Turner, Jr., May 19, 1974; children: H. Fletcher III, Della Renee. BA, U. Tex., 1969; postgrad., Daytona Beach C.C., 1985-88, U. Ctrl. Fla., 1985-88. Make-up editor, writer Dallas Times Herald, 1972-74; layout artist, copywriter Sears, Roebuck and Co., Dallas, 1974-77; copywriter S.H. Heironimus Dept. Store, Roanoke, Va., 1979-80; salesperson Jensen Watson Realty Co., Port Orange, Fla., 1984-85; math. aide Chpt. 1 program Volusia County Sch. System, De Land, Fla., 1985-86; publicity asst. Daytona Beach (Fla.) Kennel Club, 1989-91; freelance writer, Port Orange, Fla., 1991—; teller Halifax Tchrs.' Credit Union, Daytona Beach, 1992-93. Author: (chapbook) Hard Core Life, 1992; contbr. articles and poems to mags. and jours. Speaker Volusia County Schs., 1992, 93. Recipient cert. of appreciation City of Port Orange, 1988, 90. Mem. Fla. Poets Assn., Chickasaw Nation. Home and Office: 5944 Broken Bow Ln Port Orange FL 32127-5999

TURNER, ROBERT CARLTON, manufacturing company executive; b. Winston-Salem, N.C., Apr. 10, 1952; s. Charlie Frank and Marjorie Ramsey (Bodenhamer) T.; m. Vickie Hope Wynne, Aug. 9, 1975; children: Lauren Hope, Robert Jr. BS, Upper Iowa U., 1979; BA, High Point Coll., 1980; Cert., U. N.C., 1987; cert. sales and mktg. mgmt., Syracuse U., 1990. V.p. C & M Co., Winston-Salem, 1974-79, sec., treas., 1979-82, pres., 1982-92; v.p. Mosley Machinery, Inc., Winston-Salem, 1992-95, Marathon Equipment Co., 1995—. Mem. Winston-Salem Better Bus. Bur. Mem. Winston-Salem C. of C., Winston-Salem BBB, Sales and Mktg. Execs. Internat., Kiwanis (pres. Carolinas Dist. Found. 1990-94, pres. 1980-81, sec.-treas. 1986-87, lt. gov. 1987-88). Democrat. Presbyterian. Office: Marathon Equipment Co 271 Flintshire Rd Winston Salem NC 27104-2737

TURNER, ROBERT FOSTER, law educator, former government official, writer; b. Atlanta, Feb. 14, 1944; s. Edwin Witcher and Martha Frances (Williams) T. AB, Ind. U., Bloomington, 1968; postgrad., Stanford U., 1972-73; JD, U. Va., 1981, SJD, 1996. Bar: Va. 1982, U.S. Supreme Ct. 1986. Rsch. assoc., pub. affairs fellow Hoover Instn. on War, Revolution and Peace, Stanford U., 1971-74; spl. asst., legis. asst. U.S. Sen. Robert P. Griffin, 1974-79; assoc. dir. Ctr. for Nat. Security Law U. Va., Charlottesville, 1981, 87—; sr. fellow, 1985-86; spl. asst. undersec. for policy Dept. Def., 1981-82; counsel Pres.'s Intelligence Oversight Bd., White House, 1982-84; prin. dep. asst. sec. for legis. and intergovtl. affairs Dept. State, 1984-85; pres. U.S. Inst. Peace, Washington, 1986-87; lectr. in law and in govt. and fgn. affairs U. Va., Charlottesville, 1988-93, assoc. prof., 1993—; Charles H. Stockton prof. internat. law Naval War Coll., 1994-95. Author: Myths of the Vietnam War: The Pentagon Papers Reconsidered, 1972, Vietnamese Communism: Its Origins and Development, 1975, The War Powers Resolution: Its Implementation in Theory and Practice, 1983, Nicaragua v. United States: A Look at the Facts, 1987, Repealing the War Powers Resolution: Restoring the Rule of Law in U.S. Foreign Policy, 1991, (with John Norton Moore) The Legal Structure of Defense Organization, 1986, International Law and the Brezhnev Doctrine, 1987, Readings on International Law, 1995, (with John Norton Moore and Frederick Tipson) National Security Law, 1990, (with John Norton Moore and Guy B. Roberts) National Security Law Documents, 1995, (with John Norton Moore) Readings on International Law, 1995; contbr. articles to profl. jours. and newspapers. Pres. Endowment of U.S. Inst. Peace, 1986-87; trustee Intercollegiate Studies Inst., 1986-92. Capt. U.S. Army, 1968-71, Vietnam. Grantee Hoover Press, 1972, Earhart Found., 1980, 1989-90, Inst. Ednl. Affairs, 1980, Carthage Found., 1980. Mem. ABA (chmn. com. on exec.-congl. rels., sec. internat. law and practice 1983-86, adv. com. on law and nat. security 1984-86, standing com. on law and nat. security 1986-92, chmn. 1989-92, editor ABA Nat. Security Law Report 1992—), Bd. Rsch. Cons., Inst. Fgn. Policy Analysis, Mensa, Am. Soc. Internat. Law, Nat. Eagle Scout Assn., Coun. on Fgn. Rels. Home: RR 18 Box 59 Charlottesville VA 22911-9819 Office: Univ Va Sch of Law Ctr for Nat Security Law Charlottesville VA 22903-1789

TURNER, ROBERT GERALD, academic administrator; b. Atlanta, Tex., Nov. 25, 1945; s. Robert B. and Oreta Lois (Porter) T.; m. Gail Oliver, Dec. 21, 1968; children: Angela Jan, Jessica Diane. AA, Lubbock Christian Coll., 1966, LLD (hon.), 1985; LLD (hon.), Pepperdine U., 1989; BS, Abilene Christian U., 1968; MA, U. Tex., 1970, PhD, 1975. Tchr. Weatherford High Sch., Tex., 1968-69; tchr. Lanier High Sch., Austin, Tex., 1969-70; instr. psychology San Antonio Coll., 1970-72; instr. Prairie View A & M U., Tex., 1973-75; asst. prof. psychology Pepperdine U., Malibu, Calif., 1975-78, assoc. prof. psychology, 1978-79, dir. testing, 1975-76, chmn. social sci. div., 1976-78, assoc. v.p. univ. affairs, 1979; assoc. prof. psychology U. Okla., Norman, 1979-84, exec. asst. to pres., 1979-81, acting provost, 1982, v.p. exec. affairs, 1981-84; chancellor U. Miss., University, 1984-95; pres. So. Meth. U., Dallas, 1995—; Pres. Southeastern Conf., 1985-87; rsch. asst. Tex. Adoption Study, 1973-75; mem. Pepperdine U., 1994-95; mem. Commn. on Telecomm., Nat. Assn. State Univs. and Land-Grant Colls., 1985-86, chmn. Commn. on Edn. for Tchg. Profession, 1990-91; mem. Pres.'s Commn., NCAA, 1989-92, chmn., 1991-92; mem. Knight Commn. on Intercollegiate Athletics, 1991-95; chmn. pres. coun. Miss. Assn. Colls., 1985-86; mem. def. adv. com. Svc. Acad. Athletic Programs, 1992—. Author: (with L. Willerman) Readings About Individual and Group Differences, 1979. Contbr. articles to profl. jours. Dir. area 2, Miss. Econ. Coun.; bd. dirs. First Miss. Corp., 1987; mem. Yocona Area coun. Boy Scouts Am. NIMH grantee, 1972; recipient Outstanding Alumni award Abilene Christian U., 1989, Communicator of Yr. award Toastmasters Club, 1987; named Miss. Amb., 1986; inducted New Boston High Sch. Athletic Hall of Fame, 1993. Mem. Young Pres. Orgn., Coun. on Competitiveness, Am. Inst. Pub. Svc. (bd. nominators 1989), Sigma Xi, Beta Alpha Psi, Phi Theta Kappa, Alpha Chi, Phi Kappa Phi. Mem. Ch. of Christ. Office: So Meth Univ Office of the Pres Dallas TX 75275

TURNER, STEVEN CORNELL, agricultural economics educator; b. Atlanta, Dec. 4, 1953; s. Arthur Cleaborn and Charlotte Elizabeth (Cornell) T.; m. Virginia Louise Bond, Aug. 27, 1988. BA, Mercer U., 1975; MS, U. Ga., 1981; PhD, Va. Tech., 1986. Asst. prof. U. Ga., Athens, 1986-92, assoc. prof., 1993—. Mem. Am. Econ. Assn., Am. Agrl. Econ. Assn., So. Agrl. Econ. Assn., Western Agrl. Econ. Assn. Mem. Ch. of Christ. Home: 234 Greystone Ter Athens GA 30606-4461 Office: U Ga Conner Hall Athens GA 30602

TURNER, TED (ROBERT EDWARD TURNER), television executive; b. Cin., Nov. 19, 1938; s. Robert Edward and Florence (Rooney) T.; m. Judy Nye (div.), m. Jane Shirley Smith, June 1965 (div. 1988); children: Beau, Rhett, Jennie; children by previous marriage: Laura Lee, Robert Edward IV; m. Jane Fonda, Dec. 21, 1991. Grad. in classics, Brown U.; DSc in Commerce (hon.), Drexel U., 1982; LLD (hon.), Samford U., 1982, Atlanta U., 1984; D Entrepreneurial Sci. (hon.), Cen. New Eng. Coll. Tech., 1983; D in Pub. Adminstrn. (hon.), Mass. Maritime Acad., 1984; D in Bus. Adminstrn. (hon.), U. Charleston, 1985. Account exec. Turner Advt. Co., Atlanta, 1961-63, pres., chief oper. officer, 1963-70; pres., chmn. bd. Turner Broadcasting System, Inc., Atlanta, 1970-96; vice chmn. Time Warner Inc. (merger Turner Broadcasting System), 1996—; bd. dirs. Atlanta Hawks; owner Atlanta Braves. Chmn. bd. Better World Soc., Washington, 1985-90; bd. dirs. Martin Luther King Ctr., Atlanta. Won America's Cup in his yacht Courageous, 1977; named Yachtsman of Yr. 4 times.Recipient Outstanding Entrepreneur of Yr. award Sales Mktg. and Mgmt. Mag., 1979, Salesman of Yr. award Sales and Mktg. Execs., 1980, Pvt. Enterprise Exemplar medal, Freedoms Found. at Valley Forge, 1980, Communicator of Yr. award Pub. Rels. Soc. Am., 1981, Communicator of Yr. award N.Y. Broadcasters, 1981, Internat. Communicator of Yr. award Sales and Mktg. Execs., 1981, Nat. News Media award VFW, 1981, Disting. Svc. in Telecommunications award Ohio U. Coll. Communication, 1982, Carr Van Anda award Ohio U. Sch. Journalism, 1982, Spl. award Edinburgh Internat. TV Festival, Scotland, 1982, Media Awareness award United Vietnam Vets. Orgn., 1983, Bd. Govs. award Atlanta chpt. NATAS, 1982, Spl. Olympics award Spl. Olympics Com., 1983, Dinner of Champions award Ga. chpt., Multiple Sclerosis Soc., 1983, Praca Spl. Merit award N.Y. Puerto Rican Assn. for Community Affairs, 1983, World Telecommunications Pioneer award, N.Y. State Broadcasters Assn., 1984, Golden Plate award Am. Acad. Achievement, 1984, Outstanding Supporter Boy Scouting award Nat. Boy Scout Coun., 1984, Silver Satellite award Am. Women in Radio and TV, Lifetime Achievement award N.Y. Internat. Film and TV Festival, 1984, Corp. Star of Yr. award Nat. Leukemia Soc., 1985, Disting. Achievement award U. Georgia, 1985, Tree of Life award Jewish Nat. Fund, 1985, Bus. Exec. of Yr. award Ga. Security Dealers Assn., 1985, Life Achievement award Popular Culture Assn., 1986, George Washington Disting. Patriot award S.R., 1986, Mo. Honor medal Sch. Journalism, U. Mo., 1987, Golden Ace award Nat. Cable TV Acad., 1987 Sol Taishoff award Nat. Press Found., 1988, Citizen Diplomat award Ctr. for Soviet-Am. Dialogue, 1988, Chmn.'s award Cable Advt. Bur., 1988, Directorate award NATAS, 1989, Paul White award Radio and TV News Dirs. Assn., 1989 Bus. Marketer of Yr. Am. Mktg. Assn., 1989, Disting. Svc. award Simon Wiesenthal Ctr., 1990, Glasnost award Vols. Am. and Soviet Life mag., 1990, numerous others; inducted into Hall of Fame, Promotion and Mktg. Assn., 1980, Dubuque (Iowa) Bus. Hall of Fame, 1983, Nat. Assn. for Sport and Phys. Edn. Hall of Fame, 1986. Mem. Nat. Cable TV Assn. (Pres.'s award 1979, 89, Ace Spl. Recognition award 1980), NAACP (life, bd. dirs. Atlanta chpt., Regional Employer of Yr. award 1976), Nat. Audubon Soc., Cousteau Soc., Bay Area Cable Club (hon.). Office: Turner Broadcasting 1 CNN Ctr PO Box 105366 Atlanta GA 30348-5366*

TURNER, THOMAS MARSHALL, telecommunications executive, consultant; b. Cumberland, Md., Aug. 17, 1951; s. James Richard and Laura Roselie (Durst) T. BS in Indsl. Tech. and Mgmt., U. Md., 1973, MA in Indsl. Tech. and Mgmt., 1980. Grad. asst U. Md., College Park, 1975-76; sales assoc., gen. mgr. Equity Trades Reality, Riverdale, Md., 1976-83; account exec. RCA Corp., Greenbelt, Md., 1983; sr. telecommunications cons. CMC, Inc., Washington, 1984-86, ORS Assoc., McLean, Va., 1986-87; owner, pres. T-1 Communications, Boca Raton, Fla., 1987—; cons. Marriott Corp., Bethesda, Md., 1990—, Group Health, Inc., N.Y.C., 1991-92, Colgate-Palmolive Co., 1993-94, State of Md., 1993, Trump Corp., 1993, Martin-Marietta, 1994, Matsushita, 1994, Montgomery Wards, 1994, Nabisco Foods, 1994, Harris Corp., 1995, Urban League, 1995, EDS, 1995—, Chem. Bank, 1996—; grad. asst. instr. Dale Carnegie Inst., 1992. Contbr. articles to profl. jours. Vol. ARC, Riverdale, Md., 1977-80; instr. Jr. Achievement Bus. Co-op, Rockville, Md., 1979-82. Recipient Highest Achievment award Dale Carnegie Inst., 1989. Mem. Am. Soc. Tng. and Devel., Telecommunications Mgrs. Assn. of Capital Area, Toastmasters, Sigma Alpha Epsilon Alumni Assn.

TURNER, WILLIAM JOSEPH, bank executive; b. Coral Gables, Fla., June 11, 1957; s. David Marshal and Emily (Wiech) T. BBA in Fin., U. Miami, 1983. Nat. bank examiner Comptr. of Currency, Miami, Fla., 1983-88; sr. v.p. Republic Bank, N.A., Miami, Fla., 1988—; mem. Bank Adminstrn. Inst., Miami, 1990—; assoc. mem. Robert Morris Assocs., 1993—. Mem. Young Reps., Miami, 1990. Appointment to Nat. Bank Examiner, Sec. Treasury, James A. Baker, 1988. Mem. Greater Miami C. of C. Republican. Episcopalian. Office: Republic Bank NA 10 N Le Jeune Rd Miami FL 33126-5431

TURNER, WILLIAM REDD, urologist, educator; b. Portsmouth, Va., June 20, 1936; s. William Redd and Mary (Rudd) T.; m. Kathleen Bouldin Stevenson; children: William Redd, Randall Williams, John Persons. BS, Davidson Coll., 1958; MD, Med. U. S.C., 1962. Diplomate Am. Bd. Urology. Resident in urology Med. U. S.C., Charleston, 1962-68, asst. prof. urology, 1970-74, assoc. prof. pediat., urology, 1978-80, prof. urology and pediat., 1980—; chief divsn. urology Charleston VA Hosp., 1970-75; dir. Ann. Ravenel Meml. lectureships dept. urology Med. U. S.C., 1971-75, acting chmn. dept. urology, 1974-75, chmn. faculty senate, 1976-77, chief divsn. pediat. urology, 1978-87, chmn. univ. grievance com., 1980-84, acting chmn. dept. urology, 1988-91, chmn. dept. urology, 1991—; assoc. med. dir. Med. U. S.C. Hosp., 1986-88; cons. urology VA, Roper Hosp., Bon Secours St. Francis Xavier Hosp., Charleston Meml. Hosp. Contbr. over 50 articles to profl. jours. Trustee Charleston Mus., 1974-75, 93—, mem. exec. com., 1975-84, v.p., 1980-85; trustee Am. Found. for Urologic Disease; ruling elder First Scots Presbyn. Ch., 1975-82, 84—, clk. of session, 1980-82; exec. com. Charleston Presbytery, 1983-84, chmn. Presbytery boundary com., 1984-86, vice chmn. exec. com., 1984, chmn. exec. com., 1985-86, exec. com. Cursillos in Christianity, 1989—, ; bd. dirs. Friends of State Mus., 1986-87; mem. Charles Webb Easter Seal Ctr. Cmty./Profl. Adv. Coun., 1989—. Capt. maj. USMC, 1968-70. Recipient Trident Vol. Physician of Yr. award, 1989. Fellow ACS, Am. Acad. Pediat.; mem. AMA (Merit award 1974), Am. Urol. Assn. (sec. 1992—, bd. dirs. 1988—, sec. S.E. sect. 1985-87, pres. sect. 1987-88), Am. Assn. Clin. Urologists, Soc. Univ. Urologists, Soc. for Pediat. Urology, S.C. Med Soc., Soc. Internat. D'Urologie, Carolina Urol. Assn., Charleston County Med. Soc., So. Soc. Pediat. Urologists, So. Soc. Urol. Surgeons, S.C. Urol. Assn., Brit. Assn. Urologic Surgeons (hon.), Alpha Omega Alpha. Office: Med Univ SC Dept Urology 171 Ashley Ave Charleston SC 29425-0001

TURNEY, JAMES EDWARD, computer scientist; b. Greensburg, Pa., May 14, 1933; s. James Edward and Mary Elizabeth (Koch) T.; m. Joan Lois Sweeney, Sept. 1, 1957 (dec. Jan. 1982); m. Audra Varnagy, Mar. 27, 1982; children: Audrey, Jennifer, Jill, Joy. BS in Indsl. Engring., Northeastern U., 1961; MS in Indsl. Mgmt., MIT, 1964; PhD in Mgmt., Calif. Coast U., 1993. Sr. cons. Peat Marwick Mitchell Co., L.A., 1965-68; gen. mgr. Technicolor, Inc., Hollywood, Calif., 1968-70; dir. Intercontinental Computing, Inc., Kansas City, Mo., 1970-72; v.p. Insight Systems, Ltd., Des Moines, 1972-76; pres. Pro Data Systems, Inc., Corpus Christi, Tex., 1976—. Bd. dirs. Luth. Ch., Wayland, Mass., 1964-66, Palos Verdes, Calif., 1967-71, Overland Pk., Kans., 1973-76, San Jose, Calif., 1991-92, Corpus Christi, Tex., 1993-95; pres. Tex. Jazz Festival Soc., 1995—. Sgt. U.S. Army, 1953-56. Mem. Am. Inst. Indsl. Engrs. (pres. 1966-67), Mensa (local sec. 1994—), Tex. Jazz Festival Soc. (pres. 1995—). Republican. Home and Office: Pro Data Systems Inc 5219 Summerset Trail Austin TX 78749-1357

TURNQUIST, DONALD KEITH, orthodontist; b. Pitts., Mar. 8, 1943; s. Arvid Gunnar and Ethel Elizabeth (Waddell) T.; m. Kathryn Druce, June 17, 1967; children: Juliana, Erik. AB, U. Pa., 1965; DMD, U. Pitts., 1972, MSD in Orthodontics, 1975. Cert. othodontist. Pvt. practice specializing in orthodontics, Winter Haven, Fla., 1975—. Bd. Elders Grace Luth. Ch., Winter Haven, 1975-85. Mem. ADA, Polk County Dent Assn., Am. Assn. Orthodontists, Fla. Assn. Orthodontists, Rotary, Omicron Kappa Upsilon. Republican. Lutheran. Home: 700 Island Way Winter Haven FL 33884-3616 Office: 1153 1st St S Winter Haven FL 33880-3907

TUROV, DANIEL, financial writer, investment executive; b. Bklyn., Jan. 15, 1947; s. Bernard and Mildred (Stevelman) T.; B.A. in Econs., CCNY, 1969; m. Rosalyn B. Kalishock, Aug. 25, 1968 (dec.); children: Joshua Nathaniel, Steven Russell. Registered investment advisor. Account exec. Walston & Co., 1969-72, Thomson McKinnon Securities, 1972-75; sr. v.p. Faulkner Dawkins & Sullivan, 1975-77, Cowen & Co., N.Y.C., 1977-80; dir. Turov Investment Group div. Moore & Schley, Cameron & Co., N.Y.C., 1980-82; v.p. Dean Witter Reynolds, Inc., 1982-83, sr. v.p., 1983-84; pres. Just Right Comm., 1992—; chmn. Philtrum Advt. Corp., 1982-84. Author: (monthly) Turov on INvestments and Hedging, 1972-80, monthly; investment column Best Buys Mag., 1982-83; editor New Innovations Pub. Corp., 1979-86, Turov on Timing, 1993—; contbr. articles to profl. jours. and newspapers. Mem. faculty N.Y. Inst. Fin., New Sch. Social Research; mem. panel The Wall St. Transcript's Option Roundtable; speaker in field. Office: Just Right Comm 154 Whippoorwill Ln Oak Ridge TN 37830-8645

TURPEN, MICHAEL CRAIG, lawyer; b. Tulsa, Nov. 10, 1949; s. Wallace Kendall and Marjorie Allyce (Kinkaid) T.; m. Susan Lynn Haugen; children: Sean Michael, Patrick Michael, Sarah Allyce. BS in History Edn., U. Tulsa, 1972, JD, 1974. Bar: Okla. 1975. Legal advisor Muskogee Police Dept., Okla., 1975-76; asst. dist. atty. City of Muskogee, 1976, dist. atty., 1977-82; atty. gen. State of Okla., 1983-87; ptnr. Riggs, Abney, Neal & Turpen, Oklahoma City, 1987—; conf. speaker; mem. Okla. Spl. Legis. Com. on Criminal Justice System, 1978-79; adj. prof. bus. law N.E. Okla. State U.-Tahlequah, 1977; adj. prof. criminal law Connors State Coll., 1977-79. Author: Police-Prosecutor Training Manual, 1975; contbr. articles to profl. jours. Mem. Gov.'s Alts. to Incarceration Com., 1980-81; bd. dirs. Call Rape, Inc., Okla. Acad. State Goods; apptd. by Pres. Clinton JFK Performing Arts Ctr. Adv. Bd.; vice chmn. Okla. Crime Commn., 1980-81; commr. Okla. State Bur. Investigation, 1978-79; bd. dirs., coach Muskogee Green Country Girls Softball Assn.; mem. Muskogee H.S. Booster Club; mem., coach Muskogee Knothole League Boys Baseball Assn.; mem. Muskogee County Human Soc., Muskogee County Women's Dem. Club; hon. mem. Okla. Hwy. Patrol, 1980; co-chmn. Clinton/Gore Okla., 1992, 96, Al Gore for Pres., 1988; chmn. State Dem. Party Okla., 1992-94; active Westminster Presbyn. Ch., Okla. City. Recipient Maurice Merrill Golden Quill award Okla. Bar Jour., 1981, Donald Santarelli award Nat. Orgn. Victim Assistance, Toronto, 1981, Mayor's commendation City of Muskogee, 1976, Mayor's commendation City of Owasso, 1975, $10,000 Cash award Found. for Improvement Justice, Inc., Achievement award Found. for Improvement Justice, Inc., 1986; named Outstanding Young Oklahoman, Okla. Jayees, 1979, Outstanding Young Lawyer, Okla. Bar Assn., 1975, Outstanding Young Man, Muskogee Jaycees, 1979, One of Ten Outstanding Nat. Leaders in field of victim rights, Nat. Orgn. for Victim Assistance, 1986, One of Men and Women Under 40 Who are Changing Nation, Esquire Mag., 1985. Mem. ABA, Okla. Bar Assn., Muskogee County Bar Assn. (past sec.), Okla. Dist. Attys. Assn. (pres. 1980-81, bd. dirs.), Tulsa U. Alumni Assn., Rotary, Tulsa U. Hurricane Club, Fraternal Order of Police. Office: Riggs Abney Neal & Turpen Ste 101 5801 Broadway Ext Oklahoma City OK 73118-7489 also: 502 W 6th St Tulsa OK 74119-1016

TURRELL, RICHARD HORTON, SR., retired banker; b. Kingston, Pa., Apr. 9, 1925; s. George Henry and Margaret (Clark) T.; m. Sally Wolfe, May 28, 1955; children: Richard H. Jr., David C., Douglas W. (dec.). Student, Cornell U., 1943; BS in Commerce, Washington and Lee U., 1949. Rep. sales Del. Lackawanna and Western Coal Co., Phila., 1949-51; asst. to pres. N.Y.C., 1951-58; broker Auchincloss Parker & Redpath, N.Y.C., 1958-61; mgr. investments Fiduciary Trust Co. Internat., N.Y.C., 1961-94, v.p., 1968-94, sr. v.p., 1968-94, sec., 1971-84; asst. sec. Blue Coal Corp., N.Y.C., 1953-58; v.p., bd. dirs. Pine Raleigh (N.C.) Corp., 1966-93. Trustee, overseer Simon's Rock of Bard Coll., Gt. Barrington, Mass., 1968-93; trustee Monmouth Coll., West Long Branch, N.J., 1980—, chmn. bd. trustees, 1989-92; chmn. Millburn-Short Hills (N.J.) Rep. Com., 1973-78; trustee Children's Specialized Hosp. Found., Mountainside, N.J., 1989-95. With Signal Corps, U.S. Army, 1943-46, PTO. Named Disting. Alumnus, Washington and Lee U., 1986. Mem. Baltusrol Golf Club (Springfield, N.J., gov. 1977), Capitol Hill Club (Washington), Turtle Creek Club (Tequesta, Fla.), Masons, Irem Temple Aaonms, Phi Beta Kappa, Phi Eta Sigma, Alpha Kappa Psi, Omicron Delta Kappa (hon.), Beta Gamma Sigma, Phi Delta Theta. Presbyterian. Home: 114 Turtle Creek Dr Tequesta FL 33469-1547

TUSA, DOMINIC FRANK, radio communications consultant; b. New Orleans, La., Apr. 28, 1953; s. Frank John and Frances (Campo) T.; div. BS in Elec. Engring., Tulane U., 1976. Assoc. engr. Allis Chalmers, Inc., New Orleans, 1976-78; comm. engr. Exxon Co., New Orleans, 1978-80; br. mgr., cons. EB Comm., Metairie, La., 1980-85; owner, founder Crescent Radio Electronics, Inc., Metairie, 1985-92; cons. Covington, La., 1992—. Recipient Outstanding Achievement award Gulf Oil, Houston, 1983, Silver Scribe, Entelec News, Houston, 1991. Home and Office: 19 Augusta Dr Covington LA 70435

TUSEO, NORBERT JOSEPH JOHN, marketing executive, consultant; b. N.Y.C., Apr. 9, 1950; s. Joseph R. and Lorraine (Babcock) T.; 1 child, Christine. AAS in Hotel and Restaurant Mgmt., N.Y. C.C., 1969, AA in Real Estate Mgmt., 1978; B degree. Lic. real estate broker, Fla.; lic. mortgage broker; lic. securities series 63, 22; cert. radon measurement technician, Fla. Mgr. Steak & Brew, N.Y.C., 1971-75; pres. Howard Beach (N.Y.) Racquet Club, 1978-80; dir. sales mktg. and tng. Vacation Interval Mktg., Ponta Gorda, Fla., 1980-83; v.p. sales mktg. and tng. Treco/Sunstate, Jacksonville, Fla., 1984-86; pres. Sunstate Mktg., Inc., St. Augustine and Jacksonville, Fla., 1986—; pres. Sunstate Radon Cons., 1986—; mortgage broker Sunstate Fin. Svcs.; real estate broker Interval Sunstate Mktg. and Sunstate Realty & Devel., Inc.; mgr. Sunstate Travel Agy.; developer Frank B. Butler Cert. 1906 Historic Bldg.; pub., founder St. John's County edit. The Real Estate Book, Jacksonville edit. The Real Estate Book. Appeared in TV commercials; pub. (periodicals) Real Estate Books; contbr. 30 articles to profl. jours. Leader Boy Scouts Am., Queens, N.Y., 1963-70, vol. campaign to elect Neil Perry sheriff St. John's County, Robert Vogal sheriff Volusia County. Recipient Capitol award Nat. Leadership Coun., 1991. Fellow World Literary Acad. (Cambridge, Eng.); mem. Am. Resort and Residential Devel. Assn. (registered resort profl., Nat. Silver award Mktg., 1991, Silver award Sales, 1991, Silver award Tng., 1991, 92, 93, Capitol award 1992), Kiwanis (pub. rels. com. 1980). Home: 4670 Aia Colony Reef Clb Saint Augustine FL 32084 Office: Sunstate Mktg 101 La Quinta Pl Saint Augustine FL 32084-4318

TUSING, JAMES C., retired association executive; b. South Bend, Ind., July 22, 1926; s. Ralph William and Gladys Clare T.; m. Rita A. Husvar, May 30, 1950; 1 child, Thomas William. Student, Ala. Polytech., 1944; diploma, Holdiday Inn U., Olive Branch Miss., 1966, AH&MA, 1976;

student, Cornell U., 1979-80, Notre Dame U., 1984. Cert. hotel adminstr. Gen. mgr., leasee Spring Mill Inn, Mitchell, Ind., 1961-66; gen. mgr. Holiday Inns (8 states), 1967-82; exec. v.p. Okla. Hotel, Motel Assn., Okla. City, 1982-93; ret. Okla. Hotel, Motel Assn., 1993. With U.S. Navy, 1943-46, PTO. Mem. Internat. Soc. Hotel Assn., Okla. City SKAL (treas. 1988—), Am. Soc. Assn. Execs. Okla. Soc. Assn. Execs., Rotary Club. Home and Office: Okla Hotel & Motel Assn 8612 S Kentucky Ave Oklahoma City OK 73159-6243

TUSSING, BERT BUD, military officer; b. Portsmouth, Va., Mar. 24, 1953; s. Jerold Anthony and Iva Denver (Milam) T.; m. Dianne Cleo Day, June 21, 1975; children: Amber Christine, Crystal Dianne. BA in English, The Citadel, 1975. Commd. 2d lt. USMC, 1975; advanced through grades to lt. col., 1002; squadron pilot 2d Marine Aircraft Wing, Jacksonville, N.C., 1977-81; platoon comdr., ops. officer Comms. Co., 2d Marine divsn., Jacksonville, 1981-82; weapons and tactics instr. 2d Marine Aircraft Wing, Jacksonville, 1982-84, squadron exec. officer, 1984-87; CH-53 br. head Marine Aviation Weapons and Tactics Squadron, Yuma, Ariz., 1985-88; Presdl. helicopter command pilot Marine Exptl. Helicopter Squadron 1, Quanitco, Va., 1989-92; exec. officer 22d Marine Expeditionary Unit, Jacksonville, 1992-94; USMC analyst, office of program appraisal Sec. of the Navy, Washington, 1994—; govt. analyst Dept. of Def. Sci. Bd., Washington, 1996. Sunday sch. tchr., 1st tenor Chamber Chorale of Fredericksburg. Fellowship MIT Ctr. for Internat. Studies, Cambridge, 1996. Mem. Marine Corps. Assn., Marine Corps. Aviation Assn., Naval Inst. Episcopalian. Office: Sec of the Navy Office of Program Appraisal The Pentagon Washington DC 20350

TUSSING, MARILEE APPLEBY, music educator; b. Decatur, Ill., Feb. 6, 1953; d. Robert William and Dorothymaie (Mallory) Appleby; m. Donald Tussing, April 17, 1976; 1 child, Torrance Ashley. B in Music Edn., Ill. State U., 1975; M in Music Edn., U. Okla., 1985. Music tchr. Shannon Elem., Shannon, Ill., 1976-80, Thompson Schs., Thompson, Ill., 1980-82; Kodaly music specialist Southgate Elem., Moore, Okla., 1982—; riding instr. Shenandoah Riding Ctr., Galena, Ill. 1977-81, freelance Norman, Okla., 1982—. Dist. Commr. Sooner Pony Club, 1985—; judge Okla. Kids Talent Search, 1993; mem. Moore Assn. Classroom Tchrs. 1982—; pres. Moore Elem. Music Orgn., 1990-91; founder Southgate Entertainer's Club. Recipient Equestrian Event Silver medal Sooner (Okla.) State Games, 1989. Mem. Midwest Kodaly Music Educators (bd. dirs. 1983-85), U.S. Pony Club (knowdown judge, 1990-93), U.S. Combined Tng. Assn. (cert. of achievement, 1985, 89, area V adult team mem. award, 1993), Nat. Edn. Assn., Okla. Edn. Assn., Am. Quarter Horse Assn. Republican. Mem. Christian Ch. (Disciples of Christ). Home: 11850 E Rock Creek Rd Norman OK 73071-8155

TUSZYNSKI, DANIEL J., JR., sales, management and marketing consultant; b. Erie, Pa., Aug. 22, 1947; s. Daniel and Dorothy (Tlyman) T. Grad., Iroquois Trade Sch., 1968; AA, L.A. City Coll., 1971; BS, Calif. State U., 1975; MBA, Gannon U., 1979; postgrad., The Cons. Inst., 1989. Cert. profl cons. Indsl. engr. Gen. Electric Co., Erie, Pa., 1965-75; sales mgr. Burroughs Corp., Culver City, Calif., 1975-76; regional sales mgr. Gen. Electric Co., Erie, 1976-81; dir. sales, mktg. Peerless Mfg. Co., Inc, Dallas, 1981-85; v.p. sales, mktg. Consumat Systems, Inc., Richmond, Va., 1985-88; v.p. mktg. Sutton Holding Co., Richmond, 1988-89; pres., chief exec. officer Tech. Mktg. Inc., Richmond, 1989—; v.p. sales and mktg. Hobart Tafa Technologies, Inc., Concord, N.H., 1990-91; pres. Music Treasures Co., Richmond, 1991—. Author: (manual) Peerless Air Inlet Systems, 1984. 1st lt. USNG, 1968-75. Mem. Am. Mktg. Assn., Am. Cons. League, Porsche Club Am. Roman Catholic. Home: 11227 Linderwood Dr Mechanicsville VA 23116-3137 Office: Music Treasures Co PO Box 9138 Richmond VA 23227-0138

TUTCHER, LARRY CLIFFORD, middle school educator; b. Topeka, Apr. 23, 1945; s. Ernest Arthur and Margaret Edna (Fawl) T. BS in Edn., Ga. So. U., 1967. Cert. tchr., Ga.; profl. songwriter. Tchr. math. McIntosh Jr. High Sch., Albany, Ga., 1967-84, Albany Mid. Sch., 1984—. Author poetry; profl. songwriter. Mem. Republican Nat. Com., Washington, 1982; sponsor Math League; eucharistic min. St. Joseph's Cath. Ch. Recipient Presdl. award Ga. Nominee for Excellence in Teaching of Math. Republican. Home: 1202 E Water St Bainbridge GA 31717-3861

TUTKO, ROBERT JOSEPH, radiology administrator, educator; b. Buffalo, Nov. 18, 1955; s. Robert Edward and Agatha (Pagliaccio) T.; m. Susan Joy Biddle, Oct. 29, 1976; children: Suzan Denise, Nicola Marie. Student, SUNY, Brockport, 1973-74; AAS, Trocaire Coll., 1982; BS, Pacific Western U., 1992, MS, PhD, 1995. Dir. X-ray svcs. Fla. Ctr. for Knee Surgery, Clearwater, 1985-86; surgery X-ray technologist St. Joseph's Hosp., Tampa, Fla., 1986-90; dir. radiology Met. Gen. Hosp., Pinellas Park, Fla., 1990-91; dir. med. imaging Univ. Gen. Hosp. and Women's Med. Ctr., Seminole, Fla., 1991-92; program dir. Sch. Radiology St. Joseph Hosp., Memphis, 1992-94; physician asst. DeSoto Family Practice, Olive Branch, Miss., 1995-96; founder, dir. continuing edn. TCB Med. Edn., Palm Harbor, Fla., 1985-91, pres., CEO, Germantown, Tenn., 1992—; tchr. Hillsborough County Schs., Tampa, 1989-92; lectr. profl. confs.; nat. radiology specialist Concorde Career Colls., Inc., Kansas City, Mo., 1994-95. Author: Limited X-Ray Course and Curriculum, 1995; contbr. articles to profl. jours. County chmn. radiology group Pinellas County Non-Profit Hosp. Venture Group, 1990-91; lectr. Pinellas County Sch. System, 1984-91. Sgt. U.S. Army, 1974-75. Recipient commendation letter Pinellas Park Police Dept., 1991. Mem. Am. Legion, Am. Educators Radiol. Scis., Am. Soc. Radiol. Technologists, Tenn. Soc. Radiol. Technologists, Fla. Soc. Radiol. Technologists, Ga. Soc. Radiol. Technologists, Colo. Soc. Radiol. Technologists, Am. Healthcare Radiology Adminstrs., KC (treas. 1989-91, Knight of Month Dec. 1989). Democrat. Roman Catholic. Home and Office: 4701 Falling Oak Cove Memphis TN 38125-4723

TUTT, GLORIA J. RUTHERFORD, insurance company executive; b. Texarkana, Ark., Sept. 1, 1945; d. William Thomas and Lois Elizabeth (Vick) Rutherford; m. F. David Tutt, Nov. 27, 1964; children: David Wayne, Danny Ray, Darryl Wilson. Student, Texarkana Jr. Coll., 1962-63. Agy. adminstr. Nat. Found. Life Ins., Oklahoma City, 1973-77; office mgr. NFC Assocs., Little Rock, 1977-78; owner, corp. sec. So. Capitol Enterprises, Baton Rouge, 1980—; exec. sec. Ins. Mgmt. & Assocs., 1989—; exec. v.p., chief oper. officer Southern Capitol Enterprises, Inc., Baton Rouge, 1990—; sec. Ins. Mgmt. Consultants, 1991—. Scoutmaster Boy Scouts Am., Baton Rouge, 1977-78; officer PTA, Bethany, Okla., 1971-74; PTF v.p. Parkview Bapt. Sch., Baton Rouge, 1989-90; corp. sponsor, bd. dirs. Baton Rouge chpt. Am. Heart Assn., 1991-92, 93. Democrat. Baptist. Office: So Capitol Enterprises 10915 Perkins Rd Baton Rouge LA 70810-3014

TUTT, NANCY JEAN, physical therapist; b. Washington, July 4; d. Lewis Jackson and Louise Monroe (Abbott) T. BS, U. Ky., 1947; MA, Columbia U., 1951, Cert. in Phys. Therapy, 1952. Staff Columbia-Presbyn. Med. Ctr., N.Y.C., 1952-54, 56-57; sr. phys. therapist St. Vincent's Hosp., N.Y.C., 1957-60; staff Hans Kraus, M.D., N.Y.C., 1955-56; pvt. practice N.Y.C., 1955-63; phys. therapist James Ewing Hosp., N.Y.C., 1962-63; sr. phys. therapist Inst. Phys Rehab., N.Y.C., 1963-66, Mt. Sinai Hosp./Elmhurst City Hosp., N.Y., 1966-68; asst. dir. phys. rehab. U. N.C. at Dix Hosp., Raleigh, 1968-70, Medictr., Raleigh, 1970-71; pres. Therapeutic Home Care Assocs., Inc., Raleigh, 1970-72, Tammy Lynn Ctr., Raleigh, 1971-72; with Rex Hosp. Wellness Ctr., Raleigh, 1991—. Vol. VA Hosp., Durham, N.C., 1980-82, Rex Hosp., Raleigh, 1983-84, Duke Inst. for Learning in Retirement, Durham, 1985—. With WAC, 1943-45. Named Ky. Col.; March of Dimes scholar, 1951-52. Mem. AAUW, DAV, Am. Soc. on Aging, Am. Phys. Therapy Assn., Rex Hosp. Wellness Ctr. Home: PO Box 51536 Durham NC 27717-1536

TUTTLE, ARTHUR NORMAN, JR., architect, university administrator; b. Balt., May 14, 1929; s. Arthur Norman and Georgia Pauline (Roberts) T.; m. Betty Gray Finney, Aug. 9, 1952 (dec. 1979); children: Arthur Norman III, George Gray; m. Barbara Jean Hassler, Apr. 15, 1983; 1 child, Katherine Elizabeth James Olsen. BS, Va. Poly. Inst. and State U., 1952; MFA, Princeton U., 1956; M in Regional Planning, U. N.C., 1962. Registered architect, N.C., Va., S.C., Okla.; cert. planner. Urban planner City of Charlestown, S.C., 1957; rsch. fellow U. N.C., Chapel Hill, 1958, dir. planning, 1959-70; architect-planner U. Health Scis. Ctr., Oklahoma City, 1970-73; univ. architect U. Okla., Norman, 1973-95, spl. asst. to v.p., 1995; cons. architect Norman, 1996—; hosp. planning cons. U. N.C., 1962-66, lectr. in planning, 1965-69; assoc. prof. health U. Okla., Oklahoma City, 1970-95, prof. architecture, 1970-95. Chmn. Town Planning Bd., Chapel Hill, 1964-69; sec. Capitol-Med. Ctr. Planning Commn., Oklahoma City, 1974-81. Fellow Assn. Univ. Architects (pres. 1990-91); mem. AIA, Am. Inst. Cert. Planners, Acad. Architecture for Health (v.p. 1970—). Presbyterian. Home and Office: 1813 Cedar Hill Rd Norman OK 73072-3161

TUTTLE, DONALD LATHAM, finance executive; b. Miami, Fla., Oct. 6, 1934; s. William Otha and Evelyn (Latham) T.; m. Margaret Joan Conkling, Dec. 29, 1956; children: Laura T. Pivateau, Angeline E. BSBA, U. Fla., 1956, MBA, 1961; PhD, U. N.C., 1965. Chartered fin. analyst. Asst. prof. U.N.C., Chapel Hill, 1965-70; prof. fin. Ind. U., Bloomington, 1970-91; v.p. Assn. Investment Mgmt. and Rsch., 1992—; vis. prof. U. Fla., Gainesville, 1969-70, INSEAD, Fontainbleu, France, 1977-78, U. Va., Charlottesville, 1982-83, Georgetown U., Washington, 1988-89; trustee Pegasus Funds, Detroit; v.p. Trust & Investment Advisers, Inc., Indpls., 1990-91. Editor: Managing Investment Portfolios, 1982, rev. edit. 1990; author: Essentials of Modern Investments, 1977, Security Analysis and Portfolio Management, 1970, rev. edit. 1975; editorial adv. bd. CFA Digest, 1973-91. Regent Coll. for Fin. Planning, Denver, 1989-91; trustee retirement system ARC, 1991—. Capt. USAF, 1956-60. Mem. Inst. Chartered Fin. Analysts (trustee 1984-87, C. Stewart Sheppard award 1990), Fin. Mgmt. Assn. (pres. 1974-75). Home: 2550 Holly Knoll Ln Charlottesville VA 22901-7572 Office: Assn Investment Mgmt Rsch PO Box 3668 Charlottesville VA 22903-0668

TUTTLE, MARCIA LEE, librarian; b. Charlotte, N.C., Apr. 11, 1937; d. Lee Foy and Lula Mae (Simpson) T. AB in Religion, Duke U., 1959; M Librarianship, Emory U., 1962; MA in Geography, U. N.C., 1974. Res. libr. Theology Libr., Emory U., Atlanta, 1959-61; cataloger Princeton (N.J.) Theol. Sem. Libr., 1962-64; asst. ref. libr. Firestone Libr., Princeton, 1964-66; head reference dept. U. Vt., Burlington, 1966-68; head Interlibr. Svc. Ctr., U. N.C. Libr., Chapel Hill, 1968-69, head serials dept., 1969—, instr. libr. sci., 1991-92; lectr. libr. sci. U. N.C., Chapel Hill, 1994—; mem. faculty coun. U. N.C. Libr., Chapel Hill, 1984-85; presenter in field to profl. confs. and meetings, profl. assns.; editor, pub. electronic Newsletter on Serials Pricing Issues. Co-editor: Advances in Serials Management, Vol. 1, 1986, Vol. 2, 1988, Vol. 3, 1990, Vol. 4, 1992 Vol. 5, 1995; mng. editor Title Varies, 1975-79; N.Am. corr. U.K. Serials Group Newsletter, 1985-87; author: Managing Serials, 1996; contbr. articles to profl. jours. Mem. ALA (chmn. serials sect. resources and tech. svcs. divsn. 1979-81, pres. 1985-86, chmn. Esther J. Piercy award jury 1982-83, orgn. and bylaws com. 1986-87, chmn. subcom. on serials pricing issues pub.-vendor-libr. rels. com. 1988-91, 1st Bowker-Ulrich's Serials Librarianship award 1985), N.Am. Serials Interest Group (exec. bd. 1985-89), Soc. for Scholarly Pubs. (edn. com. 1992—, exec. bd. 1994—). Democrat. Episcopalian. Home: 215 Flemington Rd Chapel Hill NC 27514-5637 Office: U NC Serials Dept Cb 3938 Davis Libr Chapel Hill NC 27514-8890

TUTTLE, MERLIN D., zoologist; b. Honolulu, Aug. 26, 1941; s. Horace L. and Myrna June (Colburn) T.; m. Diane Stevenson, Apr. 1975 (div. May 1980). MA, U. Kans., 1969, PhD with honors, 1974. Curator of mammals Milw. Pub. Mus., 1975-86; founder, pres. Bat Conservation Internat., Austin, Tex., 1986—; vis. scholar U. Tex., Austin, 1986-88; disting. lectr. Cornell U.; lectr. Harvard U., U. Chgo., U. Mich., Nat. Mus. Can., Am. Mus. Natural History; guest ABC's World News Tonight, Good Morning Am., NBC's Today Show, David Letterman Show; adj. assoc. prof. biology U. Wis., Milw., 1975-85. Contbr. numerous articles to profl. jours. Recipient Best Film of Festival award, Best Profl. Film award, Spl. Merit award for Advancement of Sci. Knowledge, Ann. Internat. Wildlife Film Festival, 1983, Garret S. Miller award and numerous grants. Mem. Am. Soc. Mammalogists (life), Am. Soc. Naturalists, Ecol. Soc. Am., Nat. Speleol. Soc., Soc. for Study of Evolution, U.S. Fish and Wildlife Svc. (endangered species recovery team for bats), Sigma Xi. Office: U Tex Zoology Dept Austin TX 78712*

TUTTLE, TONI BRODAX, swimming pool company executive; b. Bklyn., July 19, 1952; d. Abraham Paul and Marilyn (Monte) Brodax; m. Roy Lee, May 21, 1978; 1 child, Sean Monte. student Lesley Coll., 1972; B.A. in Journalism, U. R.I., 1974. Reporter Mexico City Daily News, 1972; freelance photographer, writer N.Y. Yankees, Comm. Group, Ft. Lauderdale, Fla., 1974-78; editl. asst. Boating Mag., N.Y.C., 1974-76; pub. rels. cons. B. Altmans Dept. Store, N.Y.C., 1975-76; dir. pub. rels. Windjammer Barefoot Cruises, Miami, Fla., 1976-78; acct. exec. Art Jacobson Advt., Miami, 1978-79; v.p. Tuttle's Pool Co., Inc., Miami, 1979—. Mem. Dramatists Guild, Inc. Jewish. Home: 6740 SW 94th St Miami FL 33156-1735

TWEEL, PHILLIP CORY, import-export company executive; b. Chattanooga, Apr. 15, 1958; s. Tanal William and Janet Marina (Corey) T. BA in Acctg., U. Tenn., 1979; MBA, Auburn U., 1985. Controller, chief fin. officer Eastern Moving Systems United Van Lines Inc., Atlanta, 1979-81, MEDIMCO, Inc., Atlanta, 1981-82, UNICORP, Ltd., Atlanta, 1985-86; chief exec. officer Mid. Ea. Devel. Investment Assn., Inc., Atlanta, 1986—; CEO Atlanta Nat. Holdings, Inc., 1993—; chief exec. officer Royal Moroccan Leather Co., Atlanta, 1990—; bd. dirs. Phoenix Trading, Atlanta; founder MEDIA Servicing, Inc., 1991—. V.p. Coll. Young Dems. Tenn., Nashville, 1978; pres. U. Tenn. Young Dems., Knoxville, 1977-78. Office: 612 Commodore Ln Knoxville TN 37922-4073

TWIFORD, H. HUNTER, III, lawyer; b. Memphis, Sept. 19, 1949; s. Horace Hunter and Elizabeth (Andrews) T.; m. Frances Dill, June 27, 1970; children—Elizabeth Smith, Horace Hunter IV. B.A., U. Miss., 1971, J.D., 1972. Bar: Miss. 1972, U.S. Dist. Ct. Miss. 1972, U.S. Ct. Appeals (5th cir.) 1972, U.S. Ct. Appeals (11th cir.) 1977, U.S. Supreme Ct. 1977. Assoc., Holcomb, Dunbar, Connell, Merkel & Tollison, Clarksdale, Miss., 1972-75, H. Hunter Twiford III, Clarksdale, 1975-77; ptnr. Garmon, Wood & Twiford, Clarksdale, 1977-78, Wood & Twiford, P.A., Clarksdale, 1978-85, Twiford & Webster, P.A., Clarksdale, 1985-90, Tollison, Austin & Twiford (Clarksdale, Oxford, Hernando, Southaven), 1990-94; Twiford Webster & Gresham, 1994—; adj. prof. Coahoma C.C., Clarksdale, 1976—; city atty. Town of Friars Point, Miss., 1981-89, Town of Jonestown, Miss., 1973-76; mcpl. judge City of Clarksdale, 1974-76; city atty. City of Clarksdale, Miss., 1985—. Author: Mississippi Annexation Law, 1992. Mem. vestry St. George's Episc. Ch., Clarksdale, 1974-76, 82-83, 87-90, sr. warden, 1984-86; mem. Coahoma County C. of C., Clarksdale, 1975—, bd. dirs. indsl. found., 1989—; mem. Gov.'s Commn. on Drug Abuse, Jackson, Miss., 1976-80; sec. Clarksdale-Coahoma County Joint Airport Bd., Clarksdale, 1981-86; dir. Indsl. Devel. Authority Coahoma County, Miss., 1988—. Mem. Assn. Trial Lawyers Am., Miss. Trial Lawyers Assn., Nat. Assn. Criminal Def. Lawyers, Nat. Inst. Mcpl. Legal Officers (chmn. pers. sect. 1989, state chmn. Miss. 1991-96),Internat. Municipal Lawyers Assn., (formerly NIMLOS), Miss. Bar Assn., Miss. Mcpl. Assn. (pres. attys. sect. 1995-96), Coahoma County Bar Assn. Lodge: Rotary (pres. 1984-85, Paul Harris fellow). Office: Twiford Webster & Gresham 144 Sunflower Ave Clarksdale MS 38614-4219

TWIGG, DAVID KEITH, public administrator, writer; b. Columbus, Ohio, Apr. 16, 1950; s. Duane C. and Roberta J. (Lee) T.; m. Rita Suarez, Dec. 29, 1989. BA, Fla. So. Coll., 1972; MS in Mgmt., Fla. Internat. U., 1973. Adv., adj. instr. Pub. Adminstr. Program Fla. Internat. U., Miami, 1973-74; program analyst Dade County Comprehensive Drug Program, Miami, 1974-78; asst. adminstr. Dade County Comprehensive Alcohol Program, Miami, 1978-81; chief, ind. monitoring office South Fla. Employment and Tng. Consortium, Miami, 1981-91, asst. dir., 1991—; mng. rep., area coord. Excel Telecom., 1996—. Editorial bd. Southern Review of Pub. Administration, 1973-75. Scoutmaster Troop 66, Miami, 1977-84. Mem. Fla. Trail Assn. (dir. 1983-87), Fla. Skyliners of Miami (pres. 1988-90, v.p. 1987-88, editor 1986-87, Hall of Fame, 1989, MacMcintire award 1987-88, Skyliner of Yr. 1986-87), Bent Tree Parcel I-C Assn. (dir., officer 1980-91). Methodist. Home: 8951 SW 60th Ter Miami FL 33173-1612

TWINING, HENRIETTA STOVER, retired English language educator; b. Pawnee, Okla., Feb. 25, 1931; d. Leonard E. and Olga (Wolf) Stover; children: Patricia T. Rioux, Donald E. BS in Edn. summa cum laude, Ctrl. State U. (now called U. Ctrl. Okla.), Edmond, Okla., 1962, M in Teaching cum laude, 1967; postgrad., Old Dominion U., 1970, Ala. A&M U., 1980-82. Cert. elem. sch. tchr., secondary sch. tchr., post secondary, Ala. Secondary tchr. Huntsville (Ala.) City Pub. Schs.; elem. and secondary tchr. Okla. City Pub. Schs., Okla.; prof. English Ala. A&M U., Huntsville, 1969-93; also chmn. textbook selection com. Ala. A&M U., Normal, Ala., 1981-93; ret., 1993; chair, co-chair sessions Conf. Coll. Composition & Comm. Internat. Orgn., 1988-93; co-chair Nat. Coun. Accreditation of Tchr. Edn., Ala. A&M U., 1988-89; chair editorial com. instl. self-study reaffirmation accreditation So. Assn. Colls. & Schs., Ala. A&M U., 1992-93. Author: Instructor's Quiz Book to accompany Prentice Hall Reader, 2d edit.; mem. editorial adv. bd. Collegiate Press, 1988-92; textbook reviewer Prentice Hall, Harcourt Brace, Collegiate Press, Allyn & Bacon, Wadsworth, et al., 1982-92. Sr. staff mem. Cmty. Action Agy. of Huntsville-Madison/Limestone Counties, Inc., 1978-92. Named Most Outststanding Female Instr., Ala. A&M U. Student Govt. Assn., 1979-80; recipient Recognitions for Cmty. Svc. Mem. NEA, MLA, Ala. Edn. Assn., Nat. Coun. Tchrs. English, Ala. Coun. Tchrs. English, Assn. Coll. English Tchrs. Ala., Ctrl. State U-U. Ctrl. Okla. Alumni Assn. (life), Alpha Chi, Kappa Delta Pi. Home: 2524 Leeshire Rd Tucker GA 30084-3026

TWITCHEL, NANCY LOU, medical/surgical and emergency room nurse; b. Overland, Mo., June 21, 1957; d. Francis Evan and Marie Louise (Carter) T. AS, No. Va. Community Coll., 1981; BSN, George Mason U., 1993. Cert. med./surg. nurse. Staff nurse Washington Hosp. Ctr., 1982-92; emergency dept. nurse Potomac Hosp., Woodbridge, Va., 1992-95; office nurse Internal Medicine Group, Reston, Va., 1996—. Vol. summer missionary Bapt. Student Union of No. Va., Bangalore, India, 1981; camp nurse Potomac Bapt. Assn. Youth Retreat at Summit Lake, Emmitsburg, Md., 1988—; vol. Ashburn (Va.) Sr. Citizens Group, 1992—; vol. nurse Tall Oaks of Reston Sr. Living Ctr., 1996—. Mem. Bapt. Nurses Fellowship, Va. Bapt. Nursing Fellowship (v.p. 1989-90, pres. 1990-94), Emergency Nurses Assn. Southern Baptist. Home: 9260 Niki Pl Apt 201 Manassas VA 20110

TWITTY, H. R., hospital official; b. Columbia, S.C., May 9, 1941; s. Archie Hazel Twitty and Sara (Murphy) Avritt; m. Marlene Faye Wingate, June 9, 1961; children: William Thomas, Michael David. BA, Tenn. Temple Coll., 1964. Cert. profl. for hosp. material mgmt. Mgr. store room Erlanger Hosp., Chattanooga, 1961-69; purchasing agt. Meml. Hosp., Chattanooga, 1969-71, dir. material, 1972—, bd. dirs. credit union, 1986-92. Chmn. bd. deacon Duncan Park Bapt. Ch., Chattanooga, 1983, 88, deacon, 1986-88, 90-92, 95-96, leadership com., 1995-96. Mem. Am. Hosp. Assn. Purchasing Mgrs. (cert. sr.), Internat. Hosp. Soc. Material Mgrs. (Disting. Profl.), Tenn. Hosp. Soc. Material Mgrs. (bd. dirs. region III 1979-82, pres. 1983-84, 89-92, Mgr. of Yr. award 1991, bd. dirs. 1994—), Chattanooga Area Purchasing Soc. (pres. 1985-87), Optimist. Home: 2017 Prater Rd Rossville GA 30741 Office: Meml Hosp 2525 Desales Ave Chattanooga TN 37404-1161

TWITTY, MYRTIS JOLENE, medical/surgical nurse, psychiatric nurse; b. Kershaw, S.C., May 21, 1938; d. Minor and Madge Myrtis (Johnson) Sullivan; m. Francis Warren Twitty, Aug. 28, 1958; children: William Joseph, Cindy Darlene, Tony Warren, Larry Wayne, Danny Calvin. ADN, U. S.C., Lancaster, 1982. RN, S.C. Med-surg. nurse Elliot White Meml. Hosp., Lancaster, 1982-84; mem. IV team Chesterfield (S.C.) Gen. Hosp., 1984-85; nurse in residence St. Francis Hosp., Greenville, S.C., 1990; mental health nurse Chestnut Hill Psychiat. Hosp., Travelers Rest, S.C., 1990-91; primary care/med.-surg. nurse St. Francis Hosp., Greenville, S.C., 1990-93; primary neuro/surg. nurse Gaston Meml. Hosp., Gastonia, N.C., 1993-94; home health nurse Total Care, Inc., Monroe, N.C., 1994-95; nurse Health South Rehab., Lancaster, S.C., 1995—; entrepreneur home bus. FranJo Enterprise. Den mother Boy Scouts Am., McAllen, Tex., 1964-66. Mem. S.C. Nurses Assn., UDC. Republican. Baptist.

TYLER, CARL WALTER, JR., physician, health research administrator; b. Washington, Aug. 22, 1933; s. Carl Walter and Elva Louise (Harlan) T.; m. Elma Hermione Matthias, June 23, 1956 (dec. Dec. 1991); children: Virginia Louise, Laureen, Jeffrey Alan, Cynthia T. Crenshaw. A.B., Oberlin Coll., 1955; M.D., Case-Western Res. U., 1959. Diplomate Am. Bd. Ob-Gyn. Rotating intern Univ. Hosps. of Cleve., 1959-60, resident in ob-gyn, 1960-64; med. officer USPHS, 1964; obstetrician-gynecologist USPHS Indian Health Service, Tahlequah, Okla., 1964-66; epidemic intelligence service officer Bur. Epidemiology, Ctrs. for Disease Control, Atlanta, 1966-67; dir. family planning evaluation div. Bur. Epidemiology, Ctrs. for Disease Control, 1967-80, asst. dir. for sci., 1980-82, acting dir. Ctr. for Health Promotion and Edn., 1982, dir. epidemiology program office, 1982-88, med. epidemiologist Office of Dir., 1988-90, asst. dir. for acad. programs, pub. health practice program office, 1990—; clin. assoc. prof. ob.-gyn. Emory U. Sch. Medicine, Atlanta; clin. asst. prof. ob-gyn Emory U. Sch. Medicine, Atlanta, 1966-80, clin. assoc. prof., 1980—, also clin. assoc. prof. preventive medicine and community health, adj. assoc. prof. sociology Coll. Arts and Scis., 1977-90; adj. assoc. prof. pub. health Sch. Pub. Health, 1990—; clin. prof. pub. health and community medicine Morehouse Sch. Medicine, Atlanta, 1990—; mem. Nat. Sleep Disorders Rsch. Commn., 1990—; mem. adv. com. on oral contrapection WHO, Geneva, 1974-77, mem. adv. com. maternal and child health, 1982-88; lectr. in field. Editor: (monograph) Venereal Infections; assoc. editor: Maxcy-Rosenau Textbook of Public Health and Preventive Medicine, 13th edit., 1992; contbr. articles to profl. jours. Chmn. Dekalb County Schs. com. on instruction programs, subcom. on health, phys. edn. and safety, (Ga.), 1967-68; active Ga. State Soccer Coaches Assn., Atlanta, 1973-79, DeKalb County YMCA. Josiah Macy Found. fellow, 1956-58; NIH grantee, 1961-64; recipient Superior Service award, 1974, Meritorious Service medal USPHS, 1984, Disting. Service medal, 1988; Carl S. Shultz Population award APHA, 1976, medal of Excellence Ctrs. for Disease Control, 1984. Fellow Am. Coll. Ob-Gyn (chmn. community health com. 1974-77), Am. Coll. Preventive Medicine, Am. Coll. Epidemiol.; mem. Am. Epidemiologic Soc., Internat. Epidemiologic Assn., Assn. Tchrs, Preventive Medicine (bd. dirs. 1988-89), Am. Pub. Health Assn. (governing council 1976-78), Assn. Planned Parenthood Profls., Population Assn. Am., Sierra Club. Office: HHS Ctrs for Disease Control Mailstop E-42 1600 E Clifton Rd NE Atlanta GA 30333*

TYLER, K. SCOTT, JR., manufacturing company executive; b. 1940. BA, U. Va., 1962, MBA, 1964. With Lane Furniture Co., Inc., Altavista, Va., 1968—, sec., 1980-83, v.p., 1983-89, pres., 1989—, CEO, 1992—. Office: Lane Co Inc E Franklin Ave Altavista VA 24517*

TYLER, MICHAEL AUGUSTUS, telecommunication industry consultant; b. Richmond, Va., Sept. 27, 1963; s. Millard Augustus and Johnetta Inez (Gilliam) T. BS, Va. Polytech. Inst., 1985; MPA, George Washington U., 1993. Customer svc. rep. Va. Fed. Savs. and Loan, Richmond, 1986-87; from customer svc. rep. to ops. analyst U.S. Sprint Telecomm., Reston, Va., 1987-89; sr. analyst Sprint Comm., Herndon, Va., 1989-92; budget analyst U.S. Dept. Commerce, 1992-94. Tutor STEP Found. Greater Washington, 1993-95. Mem. Am. Soc. Pub. Adminstrn. (bd. dirs. 1994-96), Nat. Young Profls. Forum, Capitol Telecomms. Profls. (bd. dirs. 1995—), Phi Alpha Alpha. Democrat. Baptist. Home: 14809 Edman Rd Centreville VA 20121

TYLER-DILLARD, DEBORAH MARIE, county official, consultant; b. Marin, Calif., July 2, 1952; d. Jesse L. and Dorothy M. (Stewart) Tyler. BA in Behavioral and Social Sci., U. Calif., Riverside, 1976; grad. Calif. Crime Prevention Inst.,, Calif. Poly. U., Pomona, 1977; postgrad., Tex. So. U., 1980. Community svc. counselor Riverside Police Dept., 1977-78; data processing analyst car share program Met. Transit Authority, Houston, 1979-81; adminstrv. aide Harris County Atty.'s Office, Houston, 1981—; mem. Houston grievance com. State Bar Tex., 1994—. Bd. dirs. Sickle Cell Assn. Tex. Gulf Coast, 1987—, Police Adv. Com., 1989-92; treas. Tex. Dem. Women Harris County, 1992-93; bd. dirs. Houston Area Urban League Guild, sec., 1987-90. Recipient Young Black Achiever award H.E.L.P., Inc., 1986, appreciation award Oak Village Mid. Sch., 1986, Miss Black Houston Pageant, 1987, Jack and Jill Am., Inc., 1990, Disting. Leadership award United Negro Coll. Fund, 1990, cert. of appreciation Sickle Cell Assn. Tex. Gulf Coast, 1991, Christopher Columbus award Quincentenary Tex. Jubilee Commn., 1991. Mem. Fedn. Houston Profl. Women, Nat. Coun. Negro Women, Century Club, Delta Sigma Theta (Dedicated Svc. award 1987). Roman Catholic. Office: Harris County Atty's Office 1001 Preston St Ste 634 Houston TX 77002-1816

TYNDALL, RANDY R., multimedia artist; b. DuBois, Pa., Feb. 5, 1955; s. Eugene Melvin and Dorothy Allan (Taylor) T.; m. Lynn Sexton, Mar. 24, 1976; 1 child, Samuel Cameron. BS in Comms., Ga. State U., 1978, MS in Comms., 1988. Media utilization specialist DeKalb Coll., Decatur, Ga., 1979-88, info. sys. coord., 1989-92; coord. ednl. affairs DeKalb Coll., Clarkston, Ga., 1992-95; multimedia artist Digitation, Decatur, Ga., 1995—. Cub scout den leader Boy Scouts Am., Decatur, 1989. Mem. Assn. for Edn. and Comms. Tech., Ga. Assn. for Indsl. Tech. (bd. dirs. 1994-95), S.E. Regional Media Leadership Coun. (bd. dirs. 1994-95). Home: 199 Avery St Decatur GA 30030

TYNDALL, RICHARD LAWRENCE, microbiologist, researcher; b. Mt. Joy, Pa., Mar. 29, 1933; s. William Leroy and Reba May (Ream) T.; m. Thelma Mae Sherk, June 19, 1955; children: Sharon Tyndall Headley, Michael L., Sandra Tyndall Holland. BS in Microbiology, Pa. State U., 1955, MS in Microbiology, 1959, PhD in Microbiology, 1961. Rsch. staff biology div. Oak Ridge (Tenn.) Nat. Lab., 1961-73; rsch. staff med. div. Oak Ridge Assoc. Univs., 1973-76; assoc. prof. rsch. zoology dept. U. Tenn., Knoxville, 1976-87; adj. assoc. Biology and Environ. Scis. div. Oak Ridge Nat. Lab., 1976-87; rsch. staff mem. Health and Safety Rsch. div. Oak Ridge Nat. Lab., 1988—; founder, CEO Microbial Monitoring, Clinton, Tenn., 1985—; co-founder Reprotech Inc., Knoxville, 1981; cons. in field. Contbr. numerous articles to profl. jours.; patentee in field. Mem. com. for control of Legionella, State of Wis. With U.S. Army, 1955-57. AEC postdoctoral fellow. Fellow Am. Acad. Microbiology; mem. AAAS, ASHRAE (subcom. on Legionella), Am. Soc. Microbiology, Phi Sigma, Gamma Sigma Delta (awards). Methodist. Home: 209 Woodland View Rd Clinton TN 37716

TYNES, SUSAN FOURNET, counselor, educator; b. Lafayette, La.; d. J. Briant and Patricia T. Fournet; m. L. Lee Tynes, 1984. BS, U. Southwestern La., Lafayette, 1982, MS, 1983; PhD, U. New Orleans, 1993. Lic. profl. counselor; cert. disability mgmt. specialists. Acad. advisor, counselor U. Southwestern La., Lafayette, 1984; rehab. cons. Rehab. Providers, Baton Rouge, La., 1984-85; rehab. counselor Cmty. Re-Entry Svcs., Lynn, Mass., 1986-89; grad./rsch. asst. U. New Orleans, 1989-93, vis. asst. prof., 1993-94; pvt. practice profl. counselor New Orleans, 1993—; adj. asst. prof. U. New Orleans, 1994-95, vis. asst. prof., dir. grad. gerontology program, 1995—; clin. asst. prof. Tulane U. Sch. Medicine, New Orleans, 1995-96; adj. asst. prof., 1996—. Vol. spkr. Daus. of Charity, Neighborhood Health Partnership, New Orleans, 1995. Recipient Disting. Dissertation award Phi Delta Kappa Coll. Edn., U. New Orleans, 1994. Fellow Chi Sigma Iota (chpt. pres. 1990-91, nationally elected sec. 1992-94, chpt. faculty advisor 1993-94, coord. La. state chpt. 1994-95, Outstanding Mem. 1992); mem. ACA, AAUP, Assn. Adult Devel. and Aging, La. Counseling Assn., La. Assn. Counseling Edn. and Supervision. Office: U New Orleans New Orleans LA 70148

TYNES, THEODORE ARCHIBALD, educational administrator; b. Portsmouth, Va., Sept. 24, 1932; s. Theodore Archibald and Mildred Antonette (Lee) T.; m. Bettye Clayton, June, 1955 (div. June 1970); children: Karen A. Culbert, David Lee, Tammy Alecia Simpers; m. Cassandra Washington, Nov. 17, 1989; 1 child, Jordan Alexandria. BS in Edn., W.Va. State Coll., 1954; postgrad., Calif. State U., L.A., 1959, Mt. San Antonio Coll, 1962, Chaffey Coll., 1962, Azusa Pacific Coll., 1967; MA in Ednl. Adminstrn., U. Calif., Berkeley, 1969; PhD in Adminstrn. and Mgmt., Columbia Pacific U., 1989. Tchr., athletic dir., coach Walker Grant High Sch., Fredericksburg, Va., 1958-59; dir. programs and aquatics L.A. Times Boys Club, L.A., 1959-62; tchr., dir. recreation, acting edn. supr. youth tng. sch. Calif. Youth Authority, Chino, 1962-68; tchr., dir. drug abuse program Benjamin Franklin Jr. High Sch., San Francisco, 1968-70; asst. prin. Pomona (Calif.) High Sch., 1970-72; prin. Garey High Sch., Pomona, 1972-75; adminstrv. asst. to supt. Bd. Edn., East Orange, N.J.; asst. to commr. U.S. Dept. Edn., Washington; Rockefeller fellow, supt. adminstrv. intern Rockefeller Found., N.Y.C., 1975-76; supervising state coord. sch. programs Office Essex County Supt. N.J. State Dept. Edn., East Orange, 1976-77; rsch. asst., dir. tech. assistance career info. system U. Oreg., Eugene, 1977-79; dir. ednl. placement U. Calif., Irvine, 1979; prin. edn. svcs. Woodrow Wilson Rehab. Ctr., Fisherville, Va., 1980-87; med. courier Urology Inc., Richmond, Va., 1988-90; vice prin. Ithaca (N.Y.) High Sch., 1991—; cons. Fielder and Assocs., Berkeley, 1969-80, Jefferson High Sch., Portland, Oreg., 1970, U. Calif., Berkeley, 1972, U. Calif., Riverside, 1972, Calif. Luth. Coll., 1972, Compton Unified Sch. Dist., 1973, Goleta Unified Schs., 1973, Rialto Sch. Dist., 1973, Grant Union Sch. Dist., Sacramento, Calif., 1973-75, San Mateo Sch. Dist., Tri Dist. Drug Abuse project, 1973, North Ward Cultural Ctr., Newark, N.J., 1976, Nat. Career Conf., Denver, 1978, Opportunities Indulstrialization Ctrs. Am., Phila., Bklyn., Detroit, Poughkeepsie, N.Y., 1980, Tynes & Assocs., 1988; lectr. seminar San Francisco City Coll., 1968-69. Author various curricula, monitoring procedures, grants. 1965—. City commr. Human Rels., Pomona, Calif., 1972-74; pres. San Antonio League, Calif., 1972-75. With USAF, 1954-57. Named Coach of Yr. L.A. Times Boys Club, 1959; fellow Rockefeller Found., 1975; recipient Administrv. award for Excellence Woodrow Wilson Rehab., 1987. Mem. NAACP, Am. Assn. Sch. Adminstrs., Nat. Assn. Secondary Sch. Prins., Nat Alliance Black Sch. Adminstrs., Assn. Supervision and Career Devel., Assn. Ednl. Data Systems., Assn. Calif. Sch. Adminstrs., Va. Govtl. Employees Assn., Va. Rehab. Assn., South Bay Pers. Guidance Assn., Pomona Adminstrs. Assn., Ithaca Prins. Assn., Fisherville Ruritan, Phi Delta Kappa, Omega Psi Phi (Basilius Pi Rho chpt. 1965). Democrat. Episcopalian. Home: 102 Sherwood Dr Waynesboro VA 22980-9286

TYNG, SHARON ANN, former federal agency administrator; b. Troup, Tex., Jan. 19, 1948; d. Clarence Nathan and Thelma Musselwhite; m. Frederick Regan Tyng, Nov. 8, 1985 (div. Feb. 1993); children: Melody Ann Hosek, Mark Wade Hosek. Student, Victoria Coll., 1967, 79, 85-86. Rental property mgr. Victoria, Tex., 1973-79; tchr. St. Mark's Daycare, Victoria, 1979-81; mem. staff Tex. Dept. Human Resouces, Victoria, 1981-83; audit/appointment clk. IRS, Victoria, 1984-91, taxpayer svc./office collection rep., 1991-95; ret., 1996. Contbr. poems to profl. publs. Vol. Food Bank, Victoria, 1982, VITA Program, Victoria, 1985. Roman Catholic. Home: 343 Sutton mott Rd Victoria TX 77905

TYRRELL, TAMARA JOAN, public affairs executive; b. St. Louis, Dec. 24, 1968; d. Charles Louis and Ann Wilken T. BA in Polit. Sci., Principia Coll., 1992. Press. asst. Clinton-Gore Campaign, Denver, 1992; mgr. Am. Trucking Assn., Alexandria, Va., 1993-94; mgr. pub. affairs Club Mgrs. Assn. Am., Alexandria, Va., 1994—. Co-author: Heartland Ethics, 1992. Donator Carpenter's Shelter, Alexandria, 1994-96, Prevention of Blindness Thriftshop, Alexandria, 1995-96. Recipient Cert. of Appreciation for Editl. Excellence, Unltd. Ideas for Editors, 1995. Mem. Am. Soc. Assn. Execs., Pub. Rels. Soc. Am. Office: Club Mgrs Assn Am 1733 King St Alexandria VA 22314

TYSON, ANNE ELIZABETH DODGE, theologian; b. Phila., May 10, 1959; d. Harold Stuart and Anne (Zillger) Dodge; m. John Horton Tyson, Jan. 6, 1990; 1 child, John Horton Jr. BA, U. Calif., 1981; MDiv, Gordon Conwell Theol. Sem., 1986; STM, Yale U., 1987; PhD, U. Edinburgh, 1993. Sr. rsch. assoc. World Vision, Internat., Monrovia, Calif., 1987-88; program dir. Trinity United Meth. Ch., Jacksonville, N.C., 1991-93; dir. Christian Edn. Haymount United Meth. Ch., Fayetteville, N.C., 1993—. Scholarship Leighton F.S. Ford Found., 1985. Republican. Home: PO Box 64132 Fayetteville NC 28306-0132 Office: Haymount United Meth Ch 1700 Fort Bragg Rd Fayetteville NC 28303-6800

TYSON, DONALD JOHN, food company executive; b. Olathe, Kans., Apr. 21, 1930; s. John W. and Mildred (Ernst) T.; m. Twilla Jean Womochil, Aug. 24, 1952; children: John H., Cheryl J., Carla A. Student, U. Ark. Plant mgr. Tyson Foods, Inc., Springdale, Ark., 1951-55, pres., 1955-67, chmn., chief exec. officer, 1967-95, sr. chmn., 1995—; chief exec. officer Eagle Distbg. Inc., Tyson Export Sales Inc., Poultry Growers Inc., Tyson Carolina Inc., Spring Valley Farms Inc., Lane Processing Inc., Lane Farms Inc. Lodge: Elks. Home: 2210 W Oaklawn Dr Springdale AR 72762-6900 Office: Tyson Foods Inc PO Box 2020 Springdale AR 72765-2020*

TYSON, JOSEPH BLAKE, religion educator; b. Charlotte, N.C., Aug. 30, 1928; s. Joseph B. and Lucy (Lewis) T.; m. Margaret H. Helms, June 12, 1954; 1 child, Linda S. BA, Duke U., 1950, BD, 1953; STM, Union Theol. Sem., 1955, PhD, 1959. Prof. religious studies So. Meth. U., Dallas, 1958—. Author: The New Testament and Early Christianity, 1984, The Death of Jesus in Luke-Acts, 1986, Images of Judaism in Luke-Acts, 1992; editor: Luke-Acts and the Jewish People, 1988. Mem. Soc. Bibl. Lit., Am. Acad. Religion, Cath. Bibl. Assn., Soc. for N.T. Studies. Methodist. Office: So Meth U Dept Religious Studies Dallas TX 75275-0202

TYSON, ROSENDO FELICITO, JR., urban planner; b. Araunustadt, Aruba, May 27, 1951; came to the U.S., 1952; s. Rosendo Felicito and Marie Albertine (Gumbs) T.; m. Lora Lea Trail, Aug. 14, 1976; children: Ian Scott, Brent Marshall. BA in Sociology, Wheaton Coll., 1973; MS in Higher Mil. Strategic Studies, U.S.A. Command/Gen. Staff Coll, 1984; MS in Urban Planning, U. Louisville, 1989; postgrad. diploma, Nat. Def. U., 1991. Commd. 2d lt. U.S. Army, 1973, advanced through grades to maj., 1984, ret., 1986; cons., trainer U.S. Postal Mgmt. Acad., Potomac, Md., 1986-88; cons., trainer, faculty U. Louisville, 1988—; chief planner bd. adjustment Lexington-Fayette (Ky.) Urban County Govt., 1989-94, sr. planner, 1994—; commr. Planning Commn., Vine Grove, Ky., 1987-89; mem. adv. bd. Ctrl. Ky. Regional Planning Coun., Lexington, 1995-96. Author: Tank Platoon Leader's Notebook, 1985, Cavalry Platoon Leader's Notebook, 1985; contbr. articles to profl. jours. Area facilitator dialogue group Christian Unity Task Force on Race Rels., Lexington, 1995, 96; dist. dir. Dem. Ctrl. Com. Ky., Lexington, 1995. Decorated Army Commendation medal, Medallion of Freedom, Regiment du March de Chad; named Ky. Col., 1986—. Mem. Civil Svc. (bd. dirs., v.p. 1995, pres. 1996), Govt. Adv. Bd. on Tng. Facilities and Instrn. (chair 1995). Presbyterian. Home: 2980-A Candlelight Way Lexington KY 40502-2826 Office: Lexington-Fayette Urban County Govt 200 E Main St Lexington KY 40500

TYSON-AUTRY, CARRIE EULA, legislative consultant, researcher, small business owner; b. Fayetteville, N.C., July 13, 1943; d. Henry McMillan II and Adeline Amelia (Williams) Tyson. BA in Social Studies and Lang. Edn., U. N.C., 1974, MA in Adminstrn., 1992; postgrad., U. Sterling, Scotland, 1978, Coll. Charleston, 1986-87; postgrad., doctoral candidate, Fayetteville State U., 1995—. Cert. tchr., N.C., S.C. Legislative aide, cons. N.C. Gen. Assembley, Raleigh, 1957-86; tchr. various states, 1963-88; rschr. U. N.C., Chapel Hill, 1991—; columnist Orkney, Scotland, 1992—; instr. Pope Air Force Base (CIC), Pope AFB (CTC), 1995—; mem. N.C. joint legis. com. edn., 1976-80; mem. N.C. gov. adv. com. exceptional children, 1977-78; gov. state coord. task force on reading, 1977; U.S. del. to world congr. edn., Scotland, 1978; mem. gov. conf. rural edn., Hilton Head, S.C., 1987. Author: Marlboro County Handbook, 1982-86; developer various curricula, 1977-88. Mem. adminstrv. campaign staff numerous nat. and state candidates; active St. John's Episc. Ch. With U.S. Army, 1973-77. Grantee GED, 1974-75. Mem. ASCD, Am. Heritage Assn., Scotland's Land Trust Soc., Scottish-Am. Geneol. Soc., Nat. Trust Hist. Preservation, Smithsonian Soc., Mus. Cape Fear (docent), Mensa, Phi Beta Kappa. Republican. Home: Grays Creek RR7 Box 284 Fayetteville NC 28306-9535

TYTANIC, CHRISTOPHER ALAN, lawyer; b. Oklahoma City, July 12, 1961; s. Stanley Martin and Stella Rose (Fillips) T. AA, Oscar Rose Jr. Coll., 1981; BA, U. Okla., 1983, JD, 1986. Bar: Okla. 1986. Legal intern Zuhdi & Denum, Oklahoma City, 1986; atty. Kerr-McGee Corp., Oklahoma City, 1986—. Recipient Letzeiser award U. Okla.; named Scholastic All-Am., 1982. Mem. ABA, Okla. Bar Assn., Nat. Polled Hereford Assn., Okla. Polled Hereford Assn., Phi Beta Kappa, Phi Theta Kappa, Pi Sigma Alpha, Omicron Delta Kappa, Phi Delta Phi. Home: 3245 S Westminster Rd Oklahoma City OK 73150-1312 Office: Kerr-McGee Corp 123 Robert S Kerr Ave Oklahoma City OK 73102-6425

UCHIDA, PRENTISS SUSUMU, entrepreneur, management executive; b. San Jose, Calif., Nov. 30, 1940; s. Fred Toshio and Elise Chioye (Kurasaki) U.; BA, San Jose State U., 1963; postgrad. Santa Clara U. Bus. Sch., 1965; m. Patricia Ann White, Oct. 17, 1981; children: S. Akemi, Toshio C., K. Kansai P. Programmer, Lockheed Missiles & Space Co., Sunnyvale, Calif., 1963-66, Adage Inc., Los Angeles, 1966-69; founder, pres., chmn. Vector Gen. Inc., Woodland Hills, Calif., 1969-79; pres. InnerGame Corp., Los Angeles, 1979-83; chmn. bd., chief exec. officer Secom Gen. Corp., Calabasas, Calif., 1984-86; pres. Rice Systems Co., Calabasas, Calif., 1981—; bd. dirs. Instar Informatique, Paris, 1981—; chmn. bd. dirs. Potter Electronics, Inc., Yanceyville, N.C., 1984-86, Secom Communications Co., Southfield, Mich., 1984-86, Nickel Equipment Co., Grand Rapids, Mich., 1985-86; mgmt. cons., Agoura, Calif., 1986-87; real estate developer, Palm Beach County, Fla., 1987-91, Futurestrader, Jupiter, Fla., 1989—, nat. mktg. dir. and ind. distbr. Nat. Safety Assocs., Memphis, 1990—, pres. VanderBolt Co., 1995—; Mem. adv. com. Stanford U. Exec. Inst., 1975-76; bd. dirs. United Crusade/United Way, 1977-79. Mem. Assn. Computer Machinery, Am. Mgmt. Assn., Aircraft Owners and Pilots Assn., Jupiter C. of C. Democrat. Club: Te Ken Jutsu Kai.

UDALL, JOHN NICHOLAS, JR., pediatric gastroenterologist; b. Washington, Dec. 30, 1940. BS, Brigham Young U., 1965; MD, Temple U., 1969; PhD, MIT, 1980. Diplomate Nat. Bd. Med. Examiners, Am. Bd. Pediatrics, Sub-bd. Pediatric Gastroenterology, Am. Bd. Nutrition; lic. physician Calif., Mass., Ariz., La. Rotating intern L.A. County/U. So. Calif. Med. Ctr., L.A., 1969-70, resident in pediatrics, 1972-74; postdoctoral rsch. fellow in pediatric gastroenterology Baylor Coll. Medicine, Houston, 1974-76; postdoctoral rsch. fellow pediatric pharmacology neonatology U. Ariz. Health Scis. Ctr., Tucson, 1976-77; postdoctoral rsch. fellow in clin. nutrition Children's Hosp., Harvard Med. Sch., Boston, 1977-79; instr. pediatrics, asst. prof. pediatrics Harvard Med. Sch., Boston, 1979-81, 81-86; lectr. dept. nutrition/food sci., asst. dir. clin. rsch. ctr MIT, Cambridge, Mass., 1980-85; sci. staff, dir. pediatric rsch. Shriners Burn Inst., Boston, 1981-86, 85-86; assoc. prof. pediatrics U. Ariz. Coll. Medicine, Tucson, 1986-92; prof. pediatrics La. State U., New Orleans, 1992—; chief sect. pediatric gastroenterology and nutrition New Orleans Children's Hosp., 1992—; clin. prof. pediatrics Sch. Medicine Tulane U., New Orleans, 1992—; resident physician Clin. Rsch. Ctr., MIT, 1977-80, prin. investigator, 1980-85; assoc. staff physician Mass. Rehab. Hosp., Boston, 1978-85; asst. in pediatrics Mass. Gen. Hosp., Boston, 1979-86; dir. nutrition support svc. Children's Hosp., Boston, 1983-85, assoc. in medicine/gastroenterology, 1983-86; dir. sect. pediatric gastroenterology U. Ariz. Health Scis. Ctr., Tucson, 1986-92. Contbr. numerous articles to profl. jours., chpts. to books; editorial bd. Mass. Gen. Hosp. Dietary Manual, 1982, Seminars in Pediatric Gastroenterology and Nutrition, 1990—, Healthy Kids: The Magazine for Parents, 1990—, Jour. Pediatric Gastroenterology and Nutrition, 1991—, Nutrition: The Internat. Jour. of Applied and Basic Nutrition Scis., 1993—; editorial adv. bd. Snyder Comms., Rockville, Md., 1990-92; book rev. editor Jour. Pediatric Gastroenterology and Nutrition, 1983-90. With USPHS, 1970-72. Grantee NIH, 1978-80, 81-83, 83-86, 84-89, 86-89, 1993, Shriners Hosp., 1986-89, Ariz. Disease Control Rsch. Commn., 1988-90, U. Ariz. Small Grants Project, 1988-89, Joseph and Mary Cacioppo Found., 1988-89. Fellow Am. Acad. Pediatrics; mem. Internat. Soc. Supramolecular Biology, N.Am. Soc. for Pediatric Gastroenterology, Soc. for Pediatric Rsch., Am. Burn Assn., AAAS, Am. Soc. Clin. Nutrition (nomination com. 1993), Am. Inst. Nutrition, Western Soc. Pediatric Rsch., Am. Gastroenterol. Assn., Nat. Ileitis and Colitis Found., Am. Soc. Parenteral and Enteral Nutrition, Pima County Pediatric Soc. (sec. 1988), Ariz. Pediatric Soc., Am. Pediatric Soc., Tucson Area Soc. Parenteral and Enteral Nutrition. Office: Children's Hosp Pediatric Gastroenterology 200 Henry Clay Ave New Orleans LA 70118-5720

UDASHEN, ROBERT N., lawyer; b. Amarillo, Tex., June 10, 1953; s. Leo Joe and Esther K. (Klugsberg) U.; m. Dale Lynn Sandgarten, Aug. 15, 1976. BA with high honors, U. Tex., 1974, JD, 1977. Bar: Tex. 1977, U.S. Ct. Appeals (5th cir.) 1978, U.S. Dist. Ct. (no. and so. dists.) Tex. 1978, U.S. Ct. Appeals (11th cir.) 1981, U.S. Supreme Ct. 1981, U.S. Dist. Ct. (ea. dist.) Tex. 1989, U.S. Dist. Ct. (we. dist.) Tex. 1991. Staff atty. Staff Counsel for Inmates, Huntsville, Tex., 1977-79; assoc., ptnr. Crowder, Mattox & Udashen, Dallas, 1979-85; ptnr. Udashen & Goldstucker, Dallas, 1985-87; pvt. practice, 1987-94; ptnr. Milner, Lobel, Goranson, Sorrels, Udashen & Wells, Dallas, 1995—; bd. dirs. Open, Inc., Dallas. Contbr. articles to profl. publs. Adv. bd. Coalition for Safer Dallas, 1994. Mem. State Bar Tex. (penal code com. 1992-93), Nat. Assn. Criminal Def. Lawyers, Tex. Criminal Def. Lawyers Assn., Dallas Criminal Def. Lawyers Assn. Office: Milner Lobel Goranson Sorrels Udashen & Wells 2515 Mckinney Ave # 21 Dallas TX 75201-1978

UDDIN, RIZWAN, engineering educator, researcher; b. Karachi, Sind, Pakistan, Nov. 13, 1959; came to U.S., 1982; s. Halim and Safia (Khatoon) U.; m. Naznin Iqbal, Oct. 11, 1988; children: Ammar, Nabeel. BSME, Middle East Tech. U., Ankara, Turkey, 1980; MS in Nuclear Engring., U. Ill., 1983, PhD in Nuclear Engring., 1987. Student asst. Middle East Tech. U., Ankara, 1979-82; rsch. asst. U. Ill., Urbana-Champaign, 1982-84; rsch. asst. U. Va., Charlottesville, 1984-88, rsch. asst. prof., 1988-92, asst. prof., 1992—. Reviewer Nuclear Sci. and Engring. jour., 1988—; contbr. articles to profl. jours. Recipient scholarship Regional Coop. for Devel., Ankara, 1976-80, Allan Talbott Gwathmey award U. Va., 1988. Mem. ASME, Am. Nuclear Soc. (Mark Mills award 1987). Muslim. Office: Univ Va Mech Aero Nuclear Engring Thornton Hall Charlottesville VA 22903-2442

UDDIN, WAHEED, civil engineer, educator; b. Karachi, Pakistan, Feb. 8, 1949; came to U.S., 1981; s. Hameed and Amjadi (Begum) U.; m. Rukhsana Tayyab, July 1, 1978; children: Omar W., Usman W., Asad W. BSCE, U. Karachi, 1970; MS in Geotech. Engring., Asian Inst. Tech., Bangkok, 1975; PhD in Transp. Engring., U. Tex., 1984. Registered profl. engr., Tex. Lab. engr. Airport Devel. Agy., Ltd., Pakistan, 1971-73; materials engr. Netherlands Airport cons., Jeddah, Saudi Arabia, 1975-78; asst. rsch. engr. U. Petroleum and Minerals Rsch. Inst., Dhahran, Saudi Arabia, 1978-81; rsc. engr. Austin (Tex.) Rsch. Engrs., Inc., 1984-87; pavement/materials engr. Tex. R&D Found., Riverdale, Md., 1987-89; UN pavement expert UNCHS/Dubai Municipality, Dubai, 1989-91; asst. prof. U. Miss., University, 1991—; infrastructure cons. Engring. Mgmt. Applications, Inc., Silver Spring, Md., 1992—; liaison officer for Saudi Arabia and UAE Asian Geotech. Info. Ctr., Bangkok, 1976-81; numerous conf. presentations in field. Contbr. over 60 articles to profl. jours. M Engring. scholar Govt. of U.K., 1973-75. Mem. ASCE, ASTM, Internat. Soc. Asphalt Pavements (founder), Chi Epsilon. Office: U Miss Dept Civil Engring University MS 38677

UDEN, DAVID ELLIOTT, cardiologist, educator; b. Montreal, Sept. 7, 1936; s. Reginald and Elsie Ada (Elliott) U.; children: Thomas Elliott, Linda Ann, Christopher Elliott. BSc, McGill U., 1958; MD, McGill U., Quebec, Can., 1962. Diplomate Am. Bd. Internal Medicine; cert. cardiovascular disease. Attending cardiologist Toronto Western Hosp., 1972-93, The Wellesley Hosp., Toronto, 1990-93; asst. prof. medicine U. Toronto, 1975-93; chief of cardiology Oconee Meml. Hosp., Seneca, S.C., 1993—, chief of medicine, 1994-96. Contbr. articles to sci. and profl. jours. With RCAF, 1963-66. Fellow Am. Coll. Cardiology, Am. Heart Assn. Coun. on Clin. Cardiology. Office: 103 Omni Dr # B Seneca SC 29672-9448

UDICK, ROBERT ALAN, political science and media educator; b. Bellvue, Nebr., Nov. 27, 1957; s. Earl Walter Udick and Rosemarie (Hicks) Richards. BA in History, La. State U., 1980, MA in Polit. Sci., 1983; PhD in Social Scis., Syracuse U., 1994. Rsch. asst. Inst. Govt. Rsch. La. State U., Baton Rouge, 1981-83; Blueprint editor and labor studies coord. Inst. Human Rels. Loyola U., New Orleans, 1983-87; rsch. asst., program coord. Ctr. for Study of Citizenship Syracuse (N.Y.) U., 1987-89, rsch. assoc. social sci. program Maxwell Sch. Citizenship, 1988-91; univ. senator, univ. senate hon. degrees com. Syracuse (N.Y.) U., N.Y., 1992-93; univ. senate affirmative action grievance handling com. Syracuse (N.Y.) U., 1992-93, grad. study ad hoc parking and transit com., 1992-93, grad. student rep. to bd. trustees, 1991-92; vis. prof. polit. sci. Colgate U., Hamilton, N.Y., 1994, La. State U., 1994; mgr. front office Prytania Pk. Hotel, New Orleans, 1995-96; presented papers at Assn. for Edn. in Journalism and Mass. Comm., Ga. State U., Atlanta, 1993, Nat. Social Sci. Assn., Memphis, 1991, Orlando, Fla., 1992, New Orleans, 1994, N.Y. State Polit. Sci. Assn., Buffalo, 1992. Founding editor The Pulse, 1989-91, Maxwell Progress, 1989-91; contbr. articles to profl. jours. Bd. dirs. New Orleans Progressive Alliance, 1985-87. Mem. Assn. for Edn. in Journalism and Mass Comm., Nat. Social Sci. Assn., Educators for Social Responsibilty (nat. bd. dirs. 1987-89).

UDOFF, ERIC JOEL, diagnostic radiologist; b. Balt., Oct. 8, 1948; s. Melvin Jerome and Esther (Fisher) U.; m. Ronni Ann Chapin, June 7, 1980; children: Brian Evan, Jonathan Andrew. AB, Washington U., 1969; MD, U. Rochester, 1973. Intern, resident in diagnostic radiology U. Chgo., 1973-77; instr. in cardiovasc. radiology Johns Hopkins U., Balt., 1977-79; radiologist Sinai Hosp., Balt., 1979-86, Mt. Sinai Med. Ctr., Milw., 1986-88, Sinai Hosp., Balt., 1988-90; asst. prof. radiology Johns Hopkins U. Hosp., 1990-91; radiologist North Fulton Regional Hosp., Roswell, Ga., 1991—. Mem. AMA, Am. Roentgen Ray Soc., Am. Coll. Radiology, Radiol. Soc. N.Am., Soc. Cardiovasc. and Interventional Radiology, Ga. Radiol. Soc. Office: North Fulton Regional Hosp 3000 Hosp Blvd Roswell GA 30076

UDOUJ, RONALD ERIC, army reserve officer; b. Ft. Smith, Ark., Mar. 25, 1965; s. Ronald Herman and Jane Taylor (Massey) U. BS cum laude, Ea. N.Mex. U., 1987; grad., Armor Officers Basic, Ft. Knox, Ky., 1988. Area rep. U.S. Student Exch., Hot Springs Nat. Park, Ark., 1993-95; recruiting ops. officer for Ala. and N.W. Fla., USAR, Montgomery, Ala.; found. program officer The Darby Found. Capt. U.S. Army Res., 1987-96. Mem. Orgn. Am. States Guild, Am. Legion, Wilson Ctr. Assocs., Naval Inst., Ala. World Affairs Coun., Kappa Sigma (guard 1986-87). Roman Catholic. Home: 2739 The Mdws Montgomery AL 36116-1162 Office: USARB Montgomery Bldg 1510 Gunter APS Montgomery AL 36114

UEHLEIN, E(DWARD) CARL, JR., lawyer; b. Boston, May 7, 1941; s. Edward Carl and Elizabeth (Thatcher) U.; m. Judith Taylor, June 16, 1962; children: Christine, Sara. Student, Bowdoin Coll., Brunswick, Maine, 1958-59; BA, Swarthmore Coll., 1962; LLB, Boston Coll., 1965. Bar: Mass. 1965, D.C. 1968. Atty. Nat. Labor Relations Bd., Atlanta, 1965-68; assoc. Morgan, Lewis & Bockius, Washington, 1968-71; exec. asst. to sec. U.S. Dept. Labor, Washington, 1971-73; ptnr. Morgan Lewis & Bockius, Washington, 1973—; sec.-treas. Carlou Corp., Wilmington, Del., 1969-71. Fellow Ford Found., 1961. Mem. ABA, FBA, D.C. Bar Assn., Belle Haven Country Club, Ballybunion Golf Club, Royal Dornoch Golf Club. Republican. Office: Morgan Lewis & Bockius 1800 M St NW Washington DC 20036-5802

UFEMA, JOHN WILLIAM, radiologist, educator; b. Johnstown, Pa., July 31, 1946; s. George and Loretta Cecilia (Bent) U.; m. Mary Jo Federici, June 21, 1980; 1 child, Anthony M. Oliver. Student, Johns Hopkins U., 1964-67; MD, Emory U., 1971; MBA, Nova U. Adminstrn. Studies Ctr., 1987. Cert. in Diagnostic Radiology, 1975. Intern in internal medicine Emory affiliated hosps., 1971-72, resident in diagnostic radiology, 1972-75; attending physician Ponce de Leon Infirmary, Atlanta, 1972-75; clin. assoc. Emory U., Atlanta, 1976; attending radiologist Diagnostic Clinic, Largo, Fla., 1977-80; pres., chmn. Med. Imaging Services, Port Charlotte, Fla., 1980-88; mng. gen. ptnr. Ufema Capital Equipment Leasing, Port Charlotte, 1984-89; med. dir. Palm Harbor (Fla.) Imaging, 1988-92; pres. Diagnostic Imaging, Palm Harbor, 1992-94; sr. staff radiologist Scott and White Clinic, College Station, Tex., 1994—; asst. prof. radiology Tex. A&M U. Coll. Medicine, 1994—; pres. Physician's Reference Lab. Charlotte County, 1987-88. Contbr. numerous articles to profl. jours. Mem. Soc. for Entertainment and Arts Devel., Port Charlotte, 1984-88. Maj. USAF, 1975-77. Mem. AMA (Physicians' Recognition award in Continuing Med. Edn.), Am. Coll. Radiology, Radiol. Soc. N.Am., Tex. Radiol. Soc., Tex. Med. Assn., Brazos-Robertson Counties Med. Soc., Mensa, NRA (life). Republican. Roman Catholic. Office: 1600 University Dr East College Station TX 77842

UGELOW, SEYMOUR JOSEPH, retired lawyer; b. Bklyn., Sept. 14, 1920; s. Abraham and Sarah Ugelow; m. Leah Payenson, Dec. 27, 1942; children: Albert, Seth, Robin. BA, CCNY, 1941; LLB, Columbia U., 1948. Bar: N.Y. 1949, N.J., Ga., Tenn, S.C., U.S. Dist. Cts. N.Y., Fla., Tex., N.Mex., N.J., U.S. Ct. Appeals (2d, 3d and 5th cirs.). Atty. Conrad & Smith, N.Y.C., 1949-65; pvt. practice Jamaica, Queens, N.Y., 1965-66; ptnr. Goldweber, Ugelow, Hershkowitz & Balsam, Jamaica, Queens, 1966-69; sr. atty., counsel Rein, Mound & Cotton, N.Y.C., 1969-86; counsel Mound, Cotton & Wollan, N.Y.C., 1986-89, ret., 1990. Pres., dir. Jewish Cmty. House of Laurelton-Springfield, Queens, N.Y., 1960-65, Pembridge E Condominium Assn., Lakes of Delray, 1992-94; pres. Lincoln-Congress Benevolent Soc., Bklyn., 1960-70; mem. Temple Emeth, 1992—, mem. chmn. legal com., 1993—, v.p. edn., 1994—. Staff sgt. U.S. Army, 1943-46, ETO.

Mem. Am. Arbitration Assn. (nat. panel arbitrators), N.Y. County Lawyers Assn. (com. on arbitration and conciliation), N.Y. State Bar Assn. (property and casualty com. and life ins. com., negligence and workers compensation sect.), K.P. (chancellor comdr., lower officer Abraham Lincoln Lodge, also chief dep. grand chancellor, chmn. law com., chief tribune Grand Lodge), Phi Beta Kappa. Jewish. Home: 15450 Pembridge Ave Apt 188E Delray Beach FL 33484-4175

UGWU, MARTIN CORNELIUS, pharmacist; b. Enugu, Anambra, Nigeria, Aug. 22, 1956; came to U.S., 1978; s. Nneji and Maria Uchenwa (Igwesi) U.; m. Renee Mashell Momon, June 30, 1990; children: Martin Cornelius Jr., Kyla Chikanya. AA/AS in Civil Engring. and Gen. Studies, Brevard Community Coll., 1980; BS in chemistry, Grambling State U., 1982; PharmD, Fla. A&M U., 1986. Registered clin. pharmacist Dept. Profl. Regulation, Fla. Pharmacist Rite Aid Pharmacy, Miami, Fla., 1986-87, mgr., 1989-93; clin. pharmacist Mercy Hosp., Miami, 1987-88; pharmacist Miami Heart Inst., Miami Beach, Fla., 1994—; mem. pharmacy and therapeutic com. Palmetto Gen. Hosp., Miami, 1986. Named one of Outstanding Young Men of Am., 1986. Mem. Am. Pharm. Assn., Am. Soc. Hosp. Pharmacists, Am. Soc. Parenteral and Enteral Nutrition, Fla. Pharmacy Assn., Fla. Soc. Hosp. Pharmacists. Roman Catholic. Home: 1801 NE 140 St #106 North Miami FL 33181 Office: Miami Heart Inst 4701 N Meridian Ave Miami FL 33140-2910 Mailing: PO Box 600651 North Miami Beach FL 33160

UHDE, GEORGE IRVIN, physician; b. Richmond, Ind., Mar. 20, 1912; s. Walter Richard and Anna Margaret (Hoopes) U.; m. Maurine Elizabeth Whitley, July 27, 1935; children—Saundra Uhde Seelig, Thomas Whitley, Michael, Janice. M.D., Duke U., 1936. Diplomate: Am. Bd. Otolaryngology. Intern Reading (Pa.) Hosp., 1936-37, resident in medicine, 1937-38; resident in otolaryngology Balt. Eye, Ear, Nose and Throat Hosp., 1938-40, U. Oreg. Med. Sch., Portland, 1945-47; practice medicine specializing in otolaryngology Louisville, 1948—; asst. prof. otolaryngology U. Louisville Med. Sch., 1945-62, prof. surgery (otolaryngology), head dept., 1963-92, prof. emeritus, 1992—, dir. otolaryngology services, 1963—; mem. staffs Meth., Norton's-Children's, Jewish, St. Joseph's, St. Anthony's, St. Mary and Elizabeth's hosps.; cons. Ky. Surg. Tb Hosp., Hazlewood, VA Hosp., Louisville, U. Louisville Speech and Hearing Center. Author 4 books.; Contbr. articles to profl. jours. Bd. dirs. Easter Seal Speech and Hearing Ctr. Lt. col. M.C. U.S. Army, 1940-45, ETO, Gen. Eisenhower staff, 1943-45. Recipient Disting. Service award U. Louisville, 1972. Fellow A.C.S., Am. Acad. Ophthalmology and Otolaryngology, So. Med. Soc.; mem. N.Y. Acad. Scis., Am. Coll. Allergists, Am. Acad. Facial Plastic and Reconstructive Surgery, AAAS, Assn. U. Otolaryngologists, AAUP, Assn. Mil. Surgeons U.S., Am. Laryngol., Rhinol. and Otol. Soc., Am. Audiology Soc., Soc. Clin. Ecology, Am. Soc. Otolaryngology Allergy, Centurian Otol. Research Soc. (Ky. rep.), Am. Council Otolaryngology (Ky. rep. 1968—), Hoopes Quaker Found., SAR (life), Gen. Soc. Colonial Wars (hereditary mem.), Alpha Kappa Kappa. Democrat. Methodist. Clubs: Filson, Big Spring Country, Jefferson. Home: 708 Circle Hill Rd Louisville KY 40207-3627 Office: Med Towers Louisville KY 40202

UHLER, BRUCE DEAN, medical company executive; b. Warrensburg, Mo., May 10, 1955; s. Earl Dean Jr. and Jane (Russell) U.; m. Kerstin Margareta Lihv, Aug. 24, 1984; children: Christopher, Michael. Student in Real Estate, U. Mo., 1976; BSBA in Fin., Ctrl. Mo. State U., 1977. Lic. real estate broker, Mo. Recruiter Ctrl. Mo. State U., Warrensburg, 1977-78; v.p., owner Warrensburg Broadcasters, Inc., 1979-87; adminstrv. svc. officer Tanini-Fovad Global Assocs., Abqaiq, Saudi Arabia, 1981-82; regional owner Qualitech Computer Ctrs., Orlando, Fla., 1983-85; owner Movie Gallery, Orlando, 1985-89; Cobb Theatres territory dir. Cobb Prime Time, Birmingham, Ala., 1989-91; owner Fantini Internat., Longwood, Fla., 1990-91; pres., ptnr., dir. Mediflex Systems, Inc., Longwood, 1991—; bd. dirs. Mediflex Systems Inc., Orlando. Co-developer spinal rehab. continuous passive motion, 1992. Named Outstanding Young Man, U.S. Jaycees, Mo., 1979. Mem. Scandinavian Club (editor, pub. 1991—, v.p. 1994—). Republican. Methodist. Home: 372 Goldstone Lake Mary FL 32746

UHM, DAN, process engineer; b. Seoul, Korea, Jan. 23, 1964; came to U.S. 1965; s. Do Sung Uhm and Eun Sook Park; m. Sang Hee Lee, Sept. 10, 1989. BS in Ceramic Engring., U. Wash., 1986; postgrad., Furman U., Greenville, S.C., 1989-91, Clemson (S.C.) U., 1991-92; MBA, Radford U., 1995. With CIA, Washington, 1985-87; process engr. Kyocera Corp., Vancouver, Wash., 1987-89, Kemet Electronics Corp., Fountain Inn, S.C., 1989-92, Alcatel Telecom., Roanoke, Va., 1992—; cons. Korean Capacitor Industry, 1987-92; cons. tech. contracts Tongkook Electronics, Samryoong Corp., Sangyong Corp. Author tng. manual/text: Statistical Process Control, 1988, Quality Circles, 1989. Mem. Am. Ceramic Soc., Nat. Inst. Ceramic Engrs., Internat. Soc. Hybrid Microelectronics, Am. Soc. Quality Control. Home: 1005 Chestnut Mountain Dr Vinton VA 24179-1717 Office: Alcatel Telecom 7635 Plantation Rd Roanoke VA 24019-3222

ULISS, BARBARA TURK, accountant; b. Cleve., Aug. 7, 1947; d. Louis A. and Shirley L. (Petersen) Turk.; m. Howard I. Uliss, Aug. 21, 1969; 1 child, Masen W. BA, Ohio State U., 1969; M.Acctg., Case Western Reserve U., 1985, PhD, 1991. CPA; CCP. Programmer analyst AT&T Co., Cleve., 1969-74; CPA Champa, Uliss & Soss, Cleve., 1979-85; instr. acctg. Hiram (Ohio) Coll., 1985-86; lectr. in acct. Case Western Reserve U., Cleve., 1987-90; asst. prof. sch. acctg. Fla. Internat. U., Miami, 1991—. Author: Reporting Interest Rate Swaps, 1994. Recipient Dean's Outstanding Acad. Achievement award Weatherhead Sch. Mgmt., Cleve., 1985. Mem. AICPA, Am. Women's Soc. CPAs, Ohio Soc. CPAs, Am. Acctg. Assn., Acad. Acctg. Historians, Bus. History Conf., Beta Alpha Psi, Beta Gamma Sigma. Office: Met State Coll Denver Campus Box 80 PO Box 173362 Denver CO 80217-3362

ULLESTAD, MERWIN ALLAN, tax services executive; b. Hampton, Iowa, June 29, 1949; s. Alan L. and Georgene E. (Simms) U.; m. Crystal R. (Kleppinger), Sept. 17, 1977. BS, Iowa State U., 1971. CPA, PFS, Iowa, Tenn.; lic. capt. inland waters USCG. Ptnr. Coopers and Lybrand, Des Moines, 1971-83; ptnr. in charge, tax svcs. Touche Ross and Co., Nashville, 1983-89; ptnr. in tax svcs. Deloitte & Touche, Nashville, 1989—; chmn. fin. com. Watkins Inst. Editor: Abingdon Clergy Income Tax Guide, 1989-96. Bd. dirs., mem. exec. com., treas. United Way Mid. Tenn., 1990-96, mem. allocations panel, 1983-89; bd. dirs., mem. exec. com. Am. Cancer Soc., Des Moines, 1977-83, Nashville City Ballet, 1983-85; bd. dirs. Watkins Inst., 1996—; sustaining membership capt. Mid. Tenn. Coun. Boy Scouts Am., 1985-88; mem. Econ. Devel. Com., 1988-90. Mem. AICPA (cert. Pers. Fin. Specialist), Tenn. Soc. CPAs, Iowa Soc. CPAs, Am. Mgmt. Assn., Internat. Assn. for Fin. Planning (pres., bd. dirs. Nashville chpt. 1987-90), Nashville Estate Planning Coun. (pres., dir.), Nashville Songwriters Assn. Internat. (fin. cons. to bd. dirs. 1990—), Nashville C. of C., Kiwanis (treas. Nashville 1990-91), Nashville City Club, Old Hickory Country Club, Gildas Club Nashville (bd. dirs. 1996). Office: Deloitte and Touche 424 Church St Nashville TN 37219

ULLMER, (R.) JOHN, computer company executive, retired educator; b. Chgo., Oct. 16, 1932; s. Ray Joseph and Eleanore (Domagalski) U. BA, St Mary's U., San Antonio, 1955; MA, St. Louis U., 1966, PhD, 1969. Asst. prof. St. Mary's U., San Antonio, 1968-69; prof. San Antonio Coll., 1969-90; ret., 1990; ptnr. Data Backup Svc., San Antonio, 1989—, DOEL Software Svc., San Antonio, 1990—. Author: (manual) Learning VI in Unix, 1987; designer, programmer: (software) Freshman Eng. Course, 1987, DOEL Writing Skills, 1989, DOEL Reading Skills, 1990. Recipient Chancellor's grant, Alamo Community Coll. Dist., San Antonio, 1989-90, Programming grant, San Antonio Coll., 1989-90. Mem. Assn. of Shareware Profls. Home: 3211 Thrush Bend San Antonio TX 78209-5138

ULM, LES, social services administrator; b. Jacksonville, Ill., Mar. 18, 1946; s. Marshall D. and Dorothy (Tyler) U.; m. Sharleen Mick, May 27, 1972; 1 child, Evan Rolando. BA, Ill. Wesleyan U., 1968; MDiv, Wesley Theol. Sem., Washington, 1974. Program coord. East Bay Camp, Hudson, Ill., 1968; VISTA tchr. Estate Brookman Pre-Sch., St. Thomas, V.I., 1969; dir. day camp Rock Days, Washington, 1971-72; counselor, adminstrv. asst. Second Mile House, Hyattsville, Md., 1971-78; exec. dir. W.Va. Child Care Assn., Huttonsville, 1979-87; v.p. for residential programs Burlington (W.Va.) United Meth. Family Svcs., 1987—; cons. United Meth. Disaster Response Com., Charleston, W.Va., 1987, 93,Florence Crittenton Home, Wheeling, W.Va., 1984, 91; grant reviewer HHS, Washington, 1988-90, 1995-96. Editor: Residential Services for Children and Youth in West Virginia, 1980-87. Nat. chmn. Nat. NEtwork Runaway and Youth Svcs., Washington, 1975; chmn. W.Va. Youth Coalition, Charleston, 1986; corr. sec. Ea. Regional Family Resource NEtwork, Burlington, W.Va., 1991-95. Mem. W.Va. Human Resources Assn. (bd. dirs. 1991—), Kiwanis (sec. Keyser Breakfast Club 1991—, Outstanding Sec. award 1992). Democrat. Home: RR 2 Box 229 Keyser WV 26726-9231 Office: Burlington United Meth Family Svcs PO Box 69 Burlington WV 26710-0096

ULOSEVICH, STEVEN NILS, management consultant, educator; b. Tampa, Fla., Nov. 19, 1947; s. Steven Anthony and Coragene (Paulson) U.; m. Pamela Elmeda Locke, June 27, 1970; children: Christina, Garrett. BA, U. N.C., Greensboro, 1969; MBA, Webster U., 1981; EdD, U. So. Calif., 1990. Sr. assoc. JWK Internat., Inc., Universal City, Tex., 1992-93; prin. Ulosevich & Assocs., China Grove, Tex., 1993—; sr. scientist Sys. Rsch. Labs. Inc., San Antonio, 1995—; asst. prof. Embry-Riddle Aero U., Honolulu, 1988-91, San Antonio, 1992—; prof. Troy State U. Sch. Edn., Honolulu, 1990-91, Webster U., San Antonio, 1992—, U. of the Incarnate Word, San Antonio, 1996—; with San Antonio New Schs. Devel. Found., 1991—, San Antonio 2000; bd. dirs. Universal LEarning Sys., Inc., 1993, Northside Edn. Found., 1995; bd. govs. Character Edn. Inst., 1996—. Contbr. articles to profl. jours. Mem. Am. Security Coun., Washington, 1979—, mem. nat. adv. bd., 1981—; state advisor U.S. Congl. Adv. Bd., 1981—; mem. U.S. Def. Com., 1982—. Educare scholar U. So. Calif., 1989; recipient Meritorious Svc. award for excellence in teaching Embry-Riddle Aero U., 1995. Mem. ASCD, ASTD, Survival and Flight Equipment Assn. (chpt. pres. 1986-88), Human Factors and Ergonomics Soc., Air Force Assn., Order of Daedalians, Phi Delta Kappa, Delta Epsilon.

ULRICH, ROGER STEFFEN, environmental design educator, researcher; b. Birmingham, Mich., Feb. 20, 1946; s. Victor Frederick and Eunice (Williams) U.; m. Ann-Margret Gunilla Nilsson, July 18, 1970; children: Kenneth, Michael. BA in Econs., U. Mich., 1968, MA in Geography, 1971, PhD in Geography, 1973. Asst. prof. geography U. Del, Newark, 1974-78, assoc. prof., 1979-88; prof., depts. arch. and landscape arch. Tex. A&M U., College Station, 1988—, assoc. dean for rsch. Coll. Architecture, 1988—; vis. prof. Lund (Sweden) Inst. Tech., 1977-78; vis. rschr. dept. clin. psychology Uppsala (Sweden) U., 1984-85; numerous presentations in field; mem. urban ecosystems directorate U.S. man and biosphere program, Dept. State and UNESCO, 1987-91; mem. exec. bd. Archtl. Rsch. Ctrs., Consortium, 1992—; mem. Healthcare Design Rsch. Com., 1992—; reviewer sci. and design jours. Author: Scenery and the Shopping Trip: The Roadside Environment as a Factor in Route Choice, 1974; mem. editl. bd. Man-Environ. Sys., 1978-83, Urban Ecosystems, 1995—; mem. editl. adv. bd. Landscape Rsch., 1982-96, also numerous articles. Recipient nat. award for exemplary team leadership in higher edn. Am. Assn. Univ. Adminstrs., 1990; rsch. fellow Nat. Swedish Coun. for Bldg. Rsch., 1977-78, 84-85. Mem. APA (population-environ. divsn.), Environ. Design Rsch. Assn., Landscape Rsch. Group, Assn. Am. Geographers. Office: Tex A&M U Coll Architecture College Station TX 77843-3137

ULVILA, JACOB WALTER, management consultant; b. Chgo., May 13, 1950; s. Toivo Einor and Belle Evelyn (Vanderbilt) U.; m. LouAnna Notargiacomo, Aug. 7, 1976; 1 child, Alexander Michael. BSEE, U. Ill., 1972; MBA, U. Mich., 1974; DBA, Harvard U., Boston, 1979. Decision analyst Decisions & Designs, Inc., McLean, Va., 1974-77, 79-80; vis. assoc. prof bus. adminstrn. U. Va., Colgate Darden Grad. Sch. Bus. Adminstrn., Charlottesville, Va., 1982-83; exec. v.p., also dir. Decision Sci. Consortium, Inc., Reston, Va., 1980-91; founder, prin. Decision Sci. Assocs., Inc., Manassas, Va., 1991—. Contbr. articles to profl. jours., chpts. to books. Recipient Franz Edelman award for mgmt. sci. achievemednt, Inst. Mgmt. Sci., 1987. Mem. Inst. Mgmt. Sci., Maserati Club Am., Lamborghini Owners Club, Lamborghini Club Am., Maserati Club Internat. Office: Decision Sci Assocs Inc 10980 Poplar Ford Trl Manassas VA 20109

UMAKANTHA, KAGGAL V., physiatrist; b. Bellary, India, 1943. BS, MD, MS (orthop.), Karnatak Med. Coll., Hubli, India, 1965. Diplomate Am. Bd. Phys. Medicine and Rehab. Intern Karnatak Med. Coll. Hosp., Hubli, 1965-66; resident in orthopedic surgery King George's Med. Hosp., Lucknow, India, 1967-69; resident in phys. medicine and rehab. Rehab. Inst. Chgo., 1975-78; chief, phys. medicine and rehab. VA Med. Ctr., Tuscaloosa, Ala.; clin. asst. prof. Coll. Community Health Scis. Lt. col. USAFR. Office: VA Hosp 117 Tuscaloosa AL 35404

UMBAUGH, LLOYD DAVID, computer science educator; b. South Bend, Ind., Nov. 23, 1935; s. Loyd Devon and Elfrieda Emma (Scope) U.; m. Loretta May Moore, Mar. 21, 1959; 1 child, Bruce David. BS, U.S. Mil. Acad., 1958; MS in Computer Info. Sci., Ohio State U., 1979, PhD in Computer Info. Sci., 1983. Commd. 2d lt. U.S. Army, 1958, advanced through grades to lt. col., 1975, ret., 1978; asst. prof. U. Tex., Arlington, 1983-90, sr. lectr., 1990—. Decorated Bronze Star with oak leaf cluster, Purple Heart. Mem. IEEE, Assn. for Computing Machinery, Inst. Elec. Engrs. Computer Soc., Sigma Xi. Democrat. Lutheran. Home: 1809 Mossy Oak St Arlington TX 76012-5619 Office: Univ Tex Arlington Dept CSE PO Box 19015 Arlington TX 76019

UMBAYEMAKE, LINDA, librarian; b. Cleve., Feb. 19, 1953; d. Charles Morgan and Helen Loretta (Ballard) McDonald; m. Bari S. Zaka, Dec. 17, 1972 (div. Jan. 1979); children: Manu, Kumar, Bari; m. Nola UmBayemake Joachim, Dec. 20, 1984 (div. June 1989); children: Mayi, Thurayya; m. Glenn Mitchell Hurt; 1 child, GlennChinua. AA, Cuyahoga C.C., Cleve., 1980; BA, Kent State U., 1984; MLS, Tex. Woman's U., 1989; postgrad., U. Ky. Libr. African Am. Ctr. Toledo (Ohio)-Lucas County Pub. Libr., 1989; libr. young adult, correctional and homebound Cuyahoga County Pub. Libr., Warrensville, Ohio, 1989-90; libr. supr. Western N.Mex. Correctional Facility, Grants, 1990; instr., libr. supr. Santa Fe C.C., Grants, 1990; libr. supr. Ga. Dept. Corrections, Buford, 1991; instr., head circulation Ky. State U., Frankfort, 1992-93, instr./ILL reference libr., 1993-96; pub. svcs. libr. Owensboro (Ky.) C.C., 1996. Mem. New Mem. Round Table, Shirley Olofson award com. and minority recruitment com. Parent Tchr. Orgn., Frankfort, 1995—. Mem. ALA (Black Caucus 1989—, chair new mem. orientation com., mem. pub. rels. com.). Office: Learning Resource Ctr Owensboro CC 4800 New Hartford Rd Owensboro KY 42303-1800

UMFLEET, LLOYD TRUMAN, electrical engineering technology educator; b. Grangeville, Idaho, June 2, 1944; s. Lloyd Truman Sr. and Bessie Viola (MacKay) U.; m. Ruth Ann Strickland, Oct. 26, 1968. BSEE, U. Mo., 1966; MSIM, Poly. Inst. Bklyn., 1971; M in Engring., U. Colo., 1988. Registered profl. engr., Tex. Asst. engr. Union Electric, St. Louis, 1966; elec. engr. Power Authority State of N.Y., N.Y.C., 1967-68, Consol. Edison, N.Y.C., 1968-71; ind. engring. cons. Toledo, 1971-76; chief elec. engr. Goldston Engring., Inc., Corpus Christi, Tex., 1976-80; mgr. elec. engring. Berry Engring., Inc., Corpus Christi, 1980-84; instr. elec. tech. Bee County Coll., Beeville, Tex., 1984-86; asst. prof. Del Mar Coll., Corpus Christi, 1988—; cons. engring. Ctrl. Power and Light, Corpus Christi, 1991, 92, INDTECH, Inc., Corpus Christi, 1994, 95, Schneider Engring., Boerne, Tex., 1996, Schneider Engring., Inc., 1996. Mem. IEEE (sr.), Am. Soc. Engring. Edn., Instrument Soc. Am., Rockport Sailing Club (commodore 1982). Office: Del Mar Coll 101 Baldwin Corpus Christi TX 78404

UMHOLTZ, CLYDE ALLAN, financial analyst; b. Du Quoin, Ill., Dec. 20, 1947; s. Frederick Louis and Opal Kathleen (Beard) U. BS, U. Ill., 1969; postgrad. U. Ark., 1969-70; MS, U. Miss., 1972; MBA, Memphis State U., 1983, PhD, 1986. CFA; cert. systems profl., tax practitioner; registered profl. engr.; cert. in data processing. Supr. quality control Champion Internat. Corp., Oxford, Miss., 1971-72; mgr. div. quality control Cook Industries, Memphis, 1973; engring. planner Northwest Industries and subsidiaries, Memphis, 1974-75; long range planning and analysis, W.R. Grace & Co. and subsidiaries, Memphis, 1975-78, mgr. planning and analysis Center Nuclear Studies, Memphis State U., 1979-83; data processing mgr. Shelby County Govt., 1983-87, deputy adminstr., 1987—, spl. asst. to county exec., 1989—; adj. prof. U. Tenn.-Memphis, 1985—; ptnr. Custom Data Systems Inc., Memphis, 1987—, Western Techs. Inc., Memphis, 1988—; bd. dirs. Am. Tech. Inst., Memphis, Am. Info. Cons. , Atlanta; bd. underwriters Lloyd's of London; diplomate editl. adv. bd. Brent's Peerage, London; cons. in field. Contbr. articles to profl. publs; inventor angle trisector, 1966; researcher energy considerations of Haber cycle, 1969, comprehensive bus. and fin. studies of sulfur, sulfuric acid, and phosphate industries, 1975-78, cost and materials sci. studies for nuclear industry, 1979-80, studies of distillation with vapor recompression, 1983, studies of prototyping in devel. computerized fin., systems, 1985-86, Context Analysis in System Design, 1987, The Family Partnership-An Estate Planning Model, 1994, Spectral Field Effects on Photosynthesis, 1995. Active presdl. election campaigns, 1968, 72, 80, 84, 88, 92, 96, mayoral campaign Memphis, 1975, 83, 87, 91, mayoral campaign Shelby County, 1990, 94, sheriff's campaign Shelby County, 1990, 94, Mid-South Billy Graham Crusade, 1978; mem. Southern Governors' Conf., del. 1992-93, gov. staff, State Tenn., 1993-94, mayor's adv. com., Memphis, 1991, steering com. Future Memphis, 1992, steering com. Arena Football League, Memphis, 1994; mem. Houston Oilers relocation com., 1996; mem. adv. coun. Kordes' Gardens, Hamburg, Germany. Recipient Oratorical award Optimist Club, 1963, Leadership and Human Rels. award Dale Carnegie Inst., 1977, Disting. Svc. award State of Tenn., 1991; NSF fellow, 1970-72. Fellow NAS, Australian Acad. Scis., N.Y. Acad. Scis.; mem. AAAS, Memphis Jaycees, U. Ill. Alumni Assn., U. Miss. Alumni Assn., Memphis State U. Alumni Assn., Am. Mgmt. Assn., Am. Rose Soc. (accredited life rose judge 1990), Am. Iris Soc., Am. Hemerocallis Soc., Elvis Presley Meml. Soc. (1993—), Am. Inst. Chem. Engrs., Fin. Execs. Inst., Am. Chem. Soc., Assn. MBA Execs., Data Processing Mgmt. Assn., Planning Execs. Inst., Am. Horticultural Soc., Internat. Platform Assn., Great Am. Pyramid Boosters Memphis, Mensa, Adms. Club, Oxford Club, London, Exec. Club of Memphis, Petroleum Club of Memphis, Olympic Soc. Atlanta, Order of De Molay. Baptist. Home: 3580 Hanna Dr Memphis TN 38128-3451

UNDERHILL, MARK LYNN, marine surveyor; b. Port Arthur, Tex., July 1, 1958; s. Robert Joseph and Sue Jean (Perkins) U.; m. Rebecca Raye Rhodes, Aug. 6, 1983; children: Robert Lewis, Allison Elizabeth, Michael Benjamin. BBA in Gen. Bus., Lamar U., 1985. Cert. all lines ins. adjustor, Tex. Marine surveyor, cons. Capt. R.J. Underhill & Assocs., Inc., Port Arthur, Tex., 1979-95. Author (software) Wedge Formula Calculation Program, 1982. Cub scout troop den leader Boy Scouts Am., Nederland, Tex, 1994, cubmaster, 1995. Mem. Marine Surveyors Guild, Nautical Inst. (Eng.), Propeller Club Am. Republican. Roman Catholic. Home: 2614 12th St Port Neches TX 77651 Office: Capt RJ Underhill & Assocs Inc 1335 Procter St Port Arthur TX 77640

UNDERNEHR, LAURA LEE, elementary education educator; b. Tulsa, Apr. 22, 1947; d. James Marion and Opal Lee (Bradford) Garman; m. Donnie Ray Undernehr, Aug. 12, 1971. BS, Northeastern State U., 1969, MEd, 1973; postgrad., Okla. State U., 1973-85, cert., 1988. Cert. elem. edn. and reading tchr., Okla. Tchr., team leader Tulsa Pub. Schs., 1969-88, tchr., 1988—. Treas. Tulsa Daniel Webster Alumni Found., 1991—. Mem. NEA, Okla. Edn. Assn., Tulsa Classroom Tchrs. Assn., Tulsa County Reading Coun., Civitans (v.p., pres.-elect Tulsa 1987-88, pres. 1989), Delta Zeta (pres. Tulsa chpt. 1989—). Home: 8125 S 40th West Ave Tulsa OK 74132-3042 Office: Alice Robertson Elem Sch 2720 W 48th St Tulsa OK 74107-7606

UNDERWOOD, BERNARD EDWARD, religious organization administrator; b. Bluefield, W.Va., Oct. 26, 1925; s. W. B. and Annie Theresa (Bain) U.; m. Esther Parramore, Dec. 22, 1947; children: Paul, Karen, Pam. BA, Emmanuel Coll., Franklin Springs, Ga., 1947; MA, Marshall U., 1954. Lic. to ministry Pentecostal Holiness Ch., 1942; ordained, 1944. Mem. Pentecostal Holiness Youth Soc. bd. Va. conf. Pentecostal Holiness Ch., Kingsport, Tenn., 1946-53; Christian edn. dir. Pentecostal Holiness Ch., Va. Conf., 1951-60, asst. supt., 1958-64; supt. Va. conf. Pentecostal Holiness Ch., Roanoke, 1964-69, 74-78; exec. dir. world missions Pentecostal Holiness Ch., Oklahoma City, 1969-73, 77-89, vice chmn., 1981-89, gen. supt., 1989—. Author: Gifts of the Spirit, 1967, Spiritual Gifts: Ministries and Manifestations, 1984, 16 New Testament Principles for World Evangelization, 1988; contbr. numerous articles to profl. jours. Phi Alpha Theta scholar, 1954. Mem. Nat. Assn. Evangelicals (mem. exec. com. 1989—), Pentecostal Fellowship N.Am. (pres. 1991—), Pentecostal Renewal Svcs. (chmn. 1987—), Evang. Fgn. Missions Assn. (bd. adminstrn. 1981—). Republican. Office: Pentecostal Holiness Ch PO Box 12609 Oklahoma City OK 73157-2609*

UNDERWOOD, CECIL H., company executive, past governor of West Virginia; b. Josephs Mills, W.Va., Nov. 5, 1922; s. Silas and Della (Forrester) U.; m. Hovah Hall, July 25, 1948; children: Cecilia A., Craig Hall, Sharon. AB, Salem (W.Va.) Coll., 1943; AM, W.Va. U., 1952; AM research fellow, Amelia Earhart Found., Ann Arbor, Mich., 1954-56; LLD, Marietta (Ohio) Coll., 1957, Bethany (W.Va.) Coll., 1957, W.Va. U., 1957, W.Va. Inst. Tech., 1957, W.Va. State Coll., 1961, Concord Coll., 1960; D of Humanics, Salem Coll., 1957; Dr. Pub. Adminstrn., W.Va. Wesleyan Coll., 1958; LHD (hon.), Shepherd Coll., 1964; LittD, Western New Eng. Coll., 1969. Tchr. high sch., 1943-46; mem. staff Marietta Coll., 1946-50; v.p. Salem Coll., 1950-56; gov. State of W.Va., 1957-61; v.p. Island Creek Coal Co., 1961-64; dir. civic affairs Monsanto Co., 1965-67, v.p., 1967; pres. Cecil H. Underwood Assocs., 1965-80, Franswood Corp., 1968-75, Bethany (W.Va.) Coll., 1972-75, Princess Coals, Inc., Huntington, 1978-81, Morgantown (W.Va.) Indsl. Park, Inc., 1983—, Software Valley, 1989-92, Mon View Heights of W.Va., 1993—; field underwriter N.Y. Life Ins. Co., 1976-78;, 1994; chmn. bd. Princess Coals, Inc., Huntington, 1981-83; Gov. Council of State Government, WV, 1996; sec. bd. dirs. Huntington Fed. Savs. and Loan Assn.; bd. dirs. Huntington Found. Mem. W.Va. Ho. Dels., 1944-56, minority floor leader, 1949, 51, 53, 55; Mem. exec. com. Gov.'s Conf., 1959; chmn. So. Regional Edn. Bd., 1959-60; Pres. Young Republican League of W.Va., 1946-50; parliamentarian Young Rep. Nat. Conv., Boston, 1951; del.-at-large Rep. Nat. Conv., 1960, 64, 72, 76, 80, 84, 88, temporary chmn., 1960; Chmn. bd. dirs. W.Va. Found. Ind. Colls., Appalachian Regional Hosps.; chmn. bd. dirs. W.Va. div. Am. Cancer Soc., nat. bd. dirs., chmn. nat. crusade com., 1976-77, chmn. com. on legacies and planned giving, 1979; chmn. bd. dirs. Salem Coll., 1978-89, Salem Teikyo U., 1989—; bd. dirs. Higher Edn. Loan Program of W.Va., 1980-94; chair W.Va. Coun. on Vocat. Edn., 1982—; chair W.Va. State Coll. System, 1991; regional vice chmn. Boy Scouts Am., 1961-67. With U.S. Army Enlisted Res. Corps, 1942-43. Mem. Nat. Assn. State Coun. Vocat. Edn. (pres. 1994—), Masons, Shriners, Elks, Rotary, Sigma Phi Epsilon, Pi Kappa Delta. Methodist. Home: 609 13th Ave Huntington WV 25701-3227 Office: PO Box 2685 Huntington WV 25726-2685

UNDERWOOD, GERALD TIMOTHY, business consultant; b. Nogales, Ariz., June 15, 1928; s. Timothy Irve and Ellen Christine (Rentzmann) U.; m. Marie Lois Steadman, Aug. 7, 1949; children: Lynn Gaye Underwood Gordon, Keri Ann Underwood Horrell. B in Engring., U. So. Calif., L.A., 1951. Mgr. factory sys. Deere & Co., Dubuque, Iowa, 1966-70, mgr. product engring. svcs., 1970-75; mgr. mgmt. devel. Deere & Co., Moline, Ill., 1975-77; factory mgr. Deere & Co., Monterrey, Mex., 1977-79; mgr. corp. engring. stds. Deere & Co., Moline, 1979-81, dir. engring. resource planning, 1981-84; dep. dir. internat. trade SBA, 1983; dir. metric program, dir. internat. programs E.A. divsn., U.S. Dept. Commerce, Washington, 1984-91; pres. INTRX Assocs., Trophy Club, Tex., 1991—; mgr. PC coord. Deere & Co. Europe, Mannheim, Germany, 1960-65, sys. analyst, Moline, 1958-60; sys. mgr./PC mgr. Beckman Instruments, Fullerton, Calif., 1954-58, Statham Labs., Santa Monica, Calif., 1951-54. Contbr. articles to profl. jours. Pres. Dubuque Cmty. Sch. Bd., 1974-75; steering com. YMCA of Washington, 1987; scout leader Boy Scouts Am., Fullerton, 1955. Recipient Bronze Medal award U.S. Dept. Commerce, Washington, 1989. Mem. ASTM, Soc. Automotive Engrs., Am. Soc. Agrl. Engrs., Am. Nat. Metric Coun. (pres. 1991-93, Presdl. award 1991), Am. Legion. Republican.

UNDERWOOD, HARVEY COCKRELL, real estate executive. BA, U. Mo.; LLB, Oklahoma City U. Cert. master sr. appraiser, master residential appraiser, master farm and land appraiser. Prin. H.C. Underwood Real Estate Co., Ft. Worth; mem. Greater Ft. Worth Bd. Realtors. Mem. Nat. Assn. Master Appraisers (cert.), Internat. Orgn. Real Estate Appraisers (cert.), Internat. Real Estate Inst. (sr. mem., sr. cert. valuer), Nat. Assn. Real Estate Appraisers (cert.), Nat. Assn. Rev. Appraisers (cert.), Nat. Inst. for Real Estate Cons. (cert.), Cert. Appraisal Orgn., Tex. Assn. Realtors (realtor/lawyer com.), Nat. Assn. Realtors, Realtor Farm Inst. Lodges:

Kiwanis, Shriners. Office: HC Underwood Real Estate Co 4151 Oakcrest Ln Rt 5 Box 275-G Fort Worth TX 76126

UNDERWOOD, SANDRA JANE, planning and management director; b. Highland Park, Mich., Dec. 14, 1941; d. Donald Earl and Delores Irene (Campbell) Hayes; m. Richard Allan Underwood, Nov. 17, 1962; 1 child, Eric Michael. BA in Polit. Sci. and Pub. Adminstrn., Stephens Coll. Data mgr., rsch. analyst, div. bus. and fin. Clemson (S.C.) U., 1977-81, higher edn. project adminstr., planning/budgets, 1981-84, planning and rsch. coord., planning/budgets, 1984-86, dir. mgmt. svcs., 1986-88, asst. to v.p. bus. and fin., 1988-90, dir. univ. planning, 1989-90, dir. strategic planning and quality mgmt., 1990—; cons. colls. and univs. S.C. and Calif., 1989—. Author: Economic Development in S.C.--The Research University Link, 1987; co-editor: Alternatives for Growth, 1978. W.K. Kellogg Found. co-grantee, 1994. Mem. Am. Mgmt. Assn., World Future Soc., Assn. Women Profls., Soc. Coll. and Univ. Planning, Clemson Lions (bd. dirs. 1991-92). Home: 111 Lakeview Cir Clemson SC 29631-1713 Office: Clemson U 201 Brackett Hall Clemson SC 29634-5160

UNDERWOOD, SHAWN MICHAEL, newspaper editor; b. Houston, Nov. 14, 1965; s. Cecil Wayne Underwood and Erica Bronwyn (Martin) Maratea; m. Sara Charlotte Smith, Sept. 23, 1965. Student, Hiram Coll., 1983-87. Pub. First Amendment Mag., Hiram, Ohio, 1986-88; reporter Warren (Ohio) Tribune, 1988-89; v.p. Right/Wood Enterprises, Kure Beach, N.C., 1989-93; reporter Island Gazette, Carolina Beach, N.C., 1992—, city news editor, 1993, editor, 1994, mng. editor, 1994—; freelance writer Encore mag., Wilmington, N.C., 1992—; cons. The Visitor newspaper, Garrettsville, Ohio, 1988-89. Author: Quest for the Hashish Trail, 1994. Mem. Soc. Profl. Journalists, N.C. Working Press. Office: Island Gazette 1009 N Lake Park Blvd B-4 Carolina Beach NC 28428

UNGARO, PETER CURT, hematology and oncology educator; b. Salinas, Calif., July 9, 1943; s. Ludwig Edmund and Ursula (Berliner) U.; m. Hannah Frances Hoopes, June 28, 1974; children: Cynthia Ann, Andrew Edward. Student, Oberlin Coll., 1961-64; MD, U. Miami, 1968. Diplomate Am. Bd. Internal Medicine, Med. Oncology and Hematology, Nat. Bd. Med. Examiners. Intern in medicine U. Pa. Hosp., Phila., 1968-69, med. resident, 1969-70; clin. assoc. Nat. Cancer Inst./Balt. Cancer Rsch. Ctr., 1970-72; hematology fellow U. Utah Med. Ctr., Salt Lake City, 1972-73; asst. prof. medicine divsn. hematology-oncology U. Ky. Med. Ctr., Lexington, 1973-75; chief hematology sect. VA Hosp., Lexington, 1974-75; assoc. prof. medicine medicine divsns. hematology and oncology U. N.C. Sch. Medicine and Area Health Edn. Ctr., Wilmington, 1975-84, prof. medicine divsns. hematology and oncology, 1984—. Author: Hematologic Diseases--New Directions in Therapy, 1976, 3d edit., 1984, Portuguese edit., 1978, Med. Examination Rev., Vol. 32, Hematology, 3d edit., 1985; contbr. over 37 articles and revs. to med. and profl. jours., 8 chpts. to books. Surgeon USPHS, 1970-72. Wyeth Traveling fellow, 1981. Fellow ACP; mem. Am. Soc. Hematology, Am. Soc. Clin. Oncology, Alpha Omega Alpha. Home: 109 Darley Ln Wilmington NC 28409-4503 Office: U NC Costal Area Health Edn Ctr PO Box 9025 Wilmington NC 28402

UNGARO-BENAGES, URSULA MANCUSI, federal judge; b. Miami Beach, Fla., Jan. 29, 1951; d. Ludivico Mancusi-Ungaro and Ursula Berliner; m. Michael A. Benages, Mar., 1988. Student, Smith Coll., 1968-70; BA in English Lit., U. Miami, 1973; JD, U. Fla., 1975. Bar: Fla. 1975. Assoc. Frates, Floyd, Pearson et al, Miami, 1976-78, Blackwell, Walker, Gray et al, Miami, 1978-80, Finley, Kumble, Heine et al, Miami, 1980-85, Sparber, Shevin, Shapo et al, Miami, 1985-87; cir. judge State of Fla., Miami, 1987-92; U.S. dist. judge Miami, 1992—; mem. Fla. Supreme Ct. Race & Ethnic & Racial Bias Study Commn., Fla., 1989-92, St. Thomas U. Inns of Ct., Miami, 1991-92. Bd. dirs. United Family & Children's Svcs., Miami, 1981-82; mem. City of Miami Task Force, 1991-92. Mem. ABA, Fed. Judges Assn., Fla. Assn. Women Lawyers, Dade County Bar Assn., Eugene Spellman Inns of Ct. U. Miami. Office: US Dist Ct 300 NE 1st Ave Ste 243 Miami FL 33132-2135*

UNGER, ALBERT HOWARD, allergist, immunologist; b. Chgo., June 24, 1923. MD, Northwestern U., 1947. Diplomate Am. Bd. Allergy and Immunology. Rotating intern Wesley Meml. Hosp., Chgo., 1946-47; resident in Internal Medicine Cook County Hosp., Chgo., 1947-49; with Sierra Med. Ctr., El Paso, Tex. Fellow AMA, Am. Assn. Allergy and Immunology; mem. Am. Assn. Clin. Immunology and Allergy, Am. Coll. Chest Physicians. Office: 6232 Gateway Blvd E El Paso TX 79905-2005

UNGER, GERE NATHAN, physician, lawyer; b. Monticello, N.Y., May 15, 1949; s. Jessie Aaron and Shirley (Rosenstein) U.; m. Alicen J. McGowan, July 21, 1990; children: Elijah, Breena, Ari, Sasha, Arlen. JD, Bernadean U., 1979; MD, Inst. Polytecnico, Mexico City, 1986; D Phys. Medicine, Met. U., Mexico City, 1987; postgrad., Boston U., 1993, Harvard Law Sch., 1994-95. Dipomate Am. Bd. Forensic Examiners, Am. Bd. Med. Legal Analysis in Medicine and Surgery, Am. Bd. Forensic Medicine, Am. Bd. Risk Mgmt. Med. dir. Vietnam Vets. Post-Traumatic Stress Disorder Program, 1988-90; emergency rm. physician, cons. in medicaid fraud Bronx (N.Y.)-Lebanon Hosp., 1990—; clin. legal medicine Paladin Profl. Group, P.A., Palm Beach, Fla., 1992—; mediator, arbitrator, negotiator World Intellectual Property Orgn., 1994; mem. peer rev. com. Nat. Inst. on Disability and Rehab. Rsch., Office Spl. Edn., U.S. Dept. Edn., 1993; mem. clin. ethics com. Inst. Medecine Legale et de Medecine Sociale, Strasbourg, France, 1994; mem. surg. critical care com. Am. Soc. Critical Care Medicine, 1992; N.Y. state capt. Am. Trial Lawyers Exch., 1992. Editl. rev. bd. Am. Bd. Forensic Examiners, 1993, Jour. Neurol. and Orthopaedic Medicine and Surgery, 1993. Commandant Broward County Marine Corps League, 1995—. With USMC, 1968-72. Fellow Internat. Coll. Surgeons (mem. ethics com. 1994, mem. emergency response program Ea. region 1994), Am. Acad. Neurol. and Orthopaedic Surgeons, Am. Coll. Legal Medicine, Am. Coll. Forensic Examiners; mem. ABA, ATLA, FBA (mem. health com., rep. ABA 1994, chmn. med. malpractice/tort com. and FBA liaison to AMA), Nat. Coll. Advocacy, Internat. Bar Assn., Am. Coll. Physician Execs. (chair forum on law and med. mgmt. 1995), Kennedy Inst. Ethics, Nat. Health Lawyers Assn., Am. Soc. of Laser Medicine and Surgery, Nat. Assn. of Forensic Econs. Office: 235 S County Rd Ste 9 Palm Beach FL 33480-4292

UNGER, PAUL TEMPLE, search firm executive, consultant; b. N.Y.C., June 9, 1942; s. Samuel Unger and Estelle (Temple) Unger Slater; m. Patricia Ann Coffin, Feb. 4, 1967 (div. June 1977); children: Kimberly Anne, David Temple; m. Susan Jean McCarthy, Oct. 1, 1983; 1 child, Samantha Leigh. BS, Upsala Coll., 1966; MBA, Case Western Res. U., 1969. Personnel recruiter RCA, Harrison, N.J., 1966-67; personnel mgr. Parker Hannifin Corp., Cleve., 1967-69; dir. indsl. rels. Indian Head, Inc., Dallas, Pa., 1969-72; dir. indsl. rels., gen. mgr. Macke Co., Cheverly, Md., 1972-76; pres. P.T. Unger Assocs., Washington, 1976-94; v.p. A.T. Kearney Exec. Search, 1994—; chmn. Florington Group, Inc., Washington, 1980—. Mem. Soc. Satellite Profls. (pres. Mid-Atlantic charter 1987-88), Armed Forces Communications and Electronics Assn., Old Crows, Security Affairs Support Assn. Republican. Home: 1711 Raleigh Hill Rd Vienna VA 22182

UNGER, ROBERTA MARIE, special education educator; b. Oakland, Calif., Apr. 22, 1944; d. Lowber and Roberta June (Hedrick) Randolph; m. William Mitchell Unger, Jr., June 29, 1970; 1 child by previous marriage, Diana Marie Holt; 1 child, William Mitchell III. BA in Edn., San Francisco State U., 1965; postgrad., Utah State U., 1967, 73, Frostburg (Md.) State U., 1973, 84, Lamar U., 1991; MA in Ednl. Adminstrn., W.Va. U., 1984. Cert. tchr., Calif., Utah, Md., W.Va.; cert. elem. tchr., supervising tchr. elem. edn./mentally retarded, English tchr., gifted edn., learning disabilities, behavior disorders, pre-sch. tchr., mentally retarded, W.Va. Tchr. 2d grade North Park Elem. Sch., Box Elder County, Utah, 1965-67; tchr. spl. edn. emotionally disturbed grades 5-8 Centre St. Sch., Allegany County, Md., 1967-68; tchr. 3rd grade Dennett Rd. Elem. Sch., Garrett County, Md., 1968-69; tchr. 2d & 3rd grades Grantsville Elem. Sch., Garrett County, Md., 1969-70; tchr. 1-high sch. grades spl. and regular edn. Short Gap Elem. Sch., Mineral County, W.Va., 1970-77; supervising tchr. W.Va. U., Morgantown, 1973-76; tchr. summer satellite program gifted edn. Frostburg State U., 1985; tchr. spl. edn. Frankfort H.S., Ridgeley, W.Va., 1977—, collaborative and consulting spl. edn. tchr., 1983—, mentor tchr., 1991-92, 96-97. Former vol. San Francisco Hosp.; past usher Oakland Civic Light Opera Assn.; mem. Cmty. Concert Assn., Allied Arts Coun., St. Thomas Woman's Study Group, No. Maidu Tribe Calif. Native Ams., Frostburg Cmty. Orch., 1968; dir. youth programs grades 7-12 Emmanuel Episcopal Ch., Cumberland (Md.) Sunday Sch. tchr.; coach Odyssey of the Mind, 1987—; club sponsor Ski Club, AFS, Classic Club. Grantee W.Va. Dept. Edn., 1986, 87, 89-91. Mem. NEA, W.Va. Edn. Assn., Mineral County Edn. Assn. (past bldg. rep., past dept. chair spl. edn., past county chair mentally impaired, past chair county secondary integrative collaboration com., county chair integrative collaboration spl. edn. svc. ages 6-12), Nat. Coun. for Exceptional Children (nat. conv. presenter 1989, 92, 93, 95, 97), W.Va. State Coun. for Exceptional Children (Mem. of Yr. award 1991, state conf. presenter 1984—, sec. 1990, 91, 92, v.p. 1993, pres.-elect 1994, pres. 1995-96, newsletter editor 1992—, subdivsn. mental retardation developmental disabilities organizing chair 1992-93, pres. divsn. mental retardation 1994-95, pres., chair state conv. 1993—, coun. exceptional children Nat. MRDD membership com. 1995—, coun. exceptional children Nat. DLD multicultural com., 1995—), Coun. for Exceptional Children (v.p. W.Va. divsn. learning disabilities 1988, membership chmn. 1988-89, pres. 1990, newsletter editor divsn. learning disabilities 1991—, sec. Coun. Exceptional Children Am. Indian caucus 1989—, del. nat. conv. 1990—), Am. Indian Soc. Washington, Allegany County Hist. Soc., Mineral County Hist. Soc., Mooretown Maidu Rancheria. Episcopalian. Office: Frankfort High Sch RR 3 Box 169 Ridgeley WV 26753-9510

UNGLESBY, LEWIS O., lawyer; b. New Orleans, July 6, 1949; s. Lewis Huber and Mary Jane (Holloway) U.; m. Gail Hoy, Aug. 15, 1970; children: Lewis, Lance, Blake. BS, U. Miss., 1971; JD, La. State U., 1974. Bar: La. 1974, U.S. Dist. Ct. (ea., mid. and we. dists.) La. 1974, U.S. Ct. Appeals (5th cir.) 1974, U.S. Supreme Ct. 1980; cert. criminal trial adv. Nat. Bd. Trial Advocacy. Ptnr. Unglesby & Koch; mem. judge's benchbook com. La. Supreme Ct., 1982—; spl. counsel La. State Senate, 1991—; lectr. La. Assn. Criminal Def. Lawyers, 1987-91. Editor criminal law sect. La. Trial Lawyers Brief, 1988—. Fellow Am. Bd. Criminal Lawyers; mem. ABA, La. Bar Assn. (ho. of dels. 1979-87, lectr.), Nat. Assn. Criminal Def. Lawyers, Assn. Trial Lawyers Am. (criminal law com. 1989-90), La. Trial Lawyers Assn. (chmn. criminal law sect. 1983-85, bd. govs. 1983-94, exec. com. 1991-96, lectr.). Home: 14415 Highland Rd Baton Rouge LA 70810-5312 Office: 246 Napoleon St Baton Rouge LA 70802-5937

UNTERMEYER, CHARLES GRAVES (CHASE), computer company executive; b. Long Branch, N.J., Mar. 7, 1946; s. Dewitt Edward and Marguerite Alonza (Graves) U.; m. Diana Cumming Kendrick, Oct. 6, 1990; 1 child, Ellyson Chase. AB, Harvard Coll., 1968. Polit. reporter Houston Chronicle, 1971-74; exec. asst. County Judge of Harris County, Houston, 1974-76; state rep. Tex. Ho. of Reps., Austin, 1977-81; exec. asst. V.P. U.S., Washington, 1981-83; from dep. asst. sec. to asst. sec. Navy Dept., Washington, 1983-88; asst. to the pres. White House, Washington, 1989-91; dir. Voice of Am., Washington, 1991-93; dir. pub. affairs Compaq Computer Corp., Houston, 1993—; bd. visitors U.S. Naval Acad., Annapolis, Md., 1993-96, chmn., 1995. Author: Houston Survival Handbook, 1980. Commnr. Port of Houston, 1995—; bd. dirs. Nat. Pub. Radio, 1996—. Lt. USNR, 1968-70. Inst. Politics fellow Harvard U., 1980; recipient George Washington Honor medal Freedoms Found., 1969. Mem. Asia Soc./Tex. (bd. dirs. 1993—). Republican. Episcopalian. Home: 3608 Locke Ln Houston TX 77027 Office: Compaq Computer Corp 20555 SH 249 Houston TX 77070

UNTHANK, G. WIX, federal judge; b. Tway, Ky., June 14, 1923; s. Green Ward and Estell (Howard) U.; m. Marilyn Elizabeth Ward, Feb. 28, 1953. J.D., U. Miami, Fla., 1950. Bar: Ky. 1950. Judge Harlan County, 1950-57; asst. U.S. atty., Lexington, Ky., 1966-69; commonwealth atty. Harlan, 1970-80; judge U.S. Dist. Ct. (ea. dist.) Ky., Pikeville, 1980-88; sr. judge U.S. Dist. Ct. (ea. dist.) Ky., London, 1988—. Served with AUS, 1940-45, ETO. Decorated Purple Heart, Bronze Star, Combat Inf. badge. Mem. ABA, Am. Judicature Soc., Ky. Bar Assn., Fla. Bar Assn. Democrat. Presbyterian. Office: Sr Judge's Chambers PO Box 5112 London KY 40745-5112*

UPDIKE, SAMUEL D., business executive; b. 1947. Grad., Notre Dame U., 1971. V.p. Alcoma Assn., Inc., Lake Wales, Fla., 1971—. Office: Alcoma Assn Inc 5937 State Road 60 E Lake Wales FL 33853-9279

UPTON, HOWARD B., JR., management writer, lawyer; b. Tahlequah, Okla., May 17, 1922; s. Howard B. and Marjorie (Ross) U.; m. Jean Devereaux, June 14, 1945; children—Pamela, Barbara, Martha, Brian. BA, U. Okla., 1943, LLB, 1948. Cert. assn. exec. Dir. indsl. relations Western Petroleum Refiners Assn., Tulsa, 1948-51; exec. v.p. Petroleum Equipment Inst., Tulsa, 1951-87; dir. Telex Corp., Tulsa, 1972-88; mgmt. columnist Inflight Mag. of Southwest Airlines, 1988-93; lectr. dept. engring. profl. devel. U. Wis., 1988—, U. Alaska, Fairbanks, 1991—. Frequent contbr. to Wall St. Jour. Dir. Tulsa Zoo Friends, Inc., 1993—. Mem. Am. Soc. Assn. Execs. (bd. dirs. 1964-68, Gold Circle award 1977, 82), Okla. Bar Assn., Mens Forum of Tulsa. Republican. Home: 5133 E 25th Ct Tulsa OK 74114-3749 Office: Upton Comm PO Box 4634 Tulsa OK 74159-0634

UPTON, SHARON LAKIN, university program director; b. Dubuque, Iowa, Nov. 28, 1956; d. Donald Lamar and Margaret Ann Lakin; m. Laurence R. Upton, July 22, 1986. BA in Urban Studies, Augsburg Coll., 1979. Rschr. U. Minn. Found., Mpls., 1981-85; rsch. coord. Mpls. YWCA, 1985-87; cons. Campaign Cons. Am., Mpls., 1987-91; rsch. mgr. United Way Mpls. Area, 1991-93; dir. rsch. N.C. State U., Raleigh, 1993—; tutor ESL, Mpls., 1982-84. Mem. Assn. Profl. Rschrs. in Advancement (dir. 1987-88), Carolina's Assn. Profl. Rschrs. for Advancement (dir. 1995—). Democrat. Lutheran. Office: NC State U Box 7111 Raleigh NC 27695

URAL, OKTAY, civil engineering educator. BA in Math., Trinity U., 1956; BS in Civil Engring., Tex. A&M U.; MSCE, U. Tenn., 1959; PhD in Civil Engring., N.C. State U., 1964; BSCE, 1958. Asst. prof. U. Mo., Rolla, 1967-69, assoc. prof., 1969-73, prof., 1973, founding dir. Inst. for Interdisciplinary Housing Studies; prof. Fla. Internat. U., Miami, 1973—, founding dir. constrn. div. Coll. Engring. and Applied Scis., dir. Inst. Housing and Bldg.; lectr. various univs.; chmn., dir., 30 nat. and internat. confs.; bd. dirs. Internat. Found. Earth Constrn., Internat. Coun. Bldg. Rsch. Studies and Documentation, Rotterdam, The Netherlands, 1978-80; mem. sci. adv. panel UN Disaster Relief Orgn.; pres. Turkish Housing Authorit, advisor to prime min. Turkish Republic, 1990-92. Author: Matrix Operations and Use of Computers in Structural Engineering, 1971, Finite Element Method: Basic Concepts and Applications, 1973, A Systematic Approach to Basic Utilities in Developing Countries, 1974, Construction of Lower-Cost Housing, 1980; editor-in-chief Internat. Jour. Housing Sci. and Its Applications, 1977—; editor 22 vols. of sci. congress procs.; contbr. articles to profl. jours. Grantee HUD, Washington, Com. on Banking and Currency, U.S. Ho. of Reps., NSF, Fla. Power and Light Co., Fla. Internat. U. Found., Inc., Dept. Edn., State Fla.; recipient Medail de Vermeil for Experts, Govt. France. Fellow ASCE (chmn. structures com. on electronic computation edn. com., urban planning and devel. div. housing com., control group, Harland Bartholomew award); mem. Internat. Assn. Housing Sci. (pres.), Am. Soc. Engring. Edn. (internat. com.), Sigma Xi, Tau Beta Pi, Phi Kappa Phi, Chi Epsilon. Home: 3608 Anderson Rd Coral Gables FL 33134-7053 Office: Fla Internat U Internat Inst Housing & Bldg Civil Engring Dept Miami FL 33199

URATO, BARBRA CASALE, entrepreneur; b. Newark, Oct. 10, 1941; d. Dominick Anthony and Concetta (Castrichini) Casale; m. John Joseph Urato, June 20, 1965; children: Concetta U. Graves, Gina E., Joseph D. Student, Seton Hall U., 1961-63. File clk. Martin Gelber Esquire, Newark, 1956-58; policy typist Aetna Casualty Ins., Newark, 1959-61; sec. to dean Seton Hall U., South Orange, N.J., 1961-63; paralegal sec. Judge Robert A. McKinley, Newark, 1963-65, Joseph Garrubbo, Esquire, Newark, 1965-66; office mgr. Valiant I.M.C., Hackensack, N.J., 1971-73; asst. pers. mgr. Degussa Inc., Teterboro, N.J., 1975-78; night mgr. The Ferryboat Restaurant, River Edge, N.J., 1976-78; mgr. Fratello's and Ventilini's, Hilton Head, S.C., 1978-80; day mgr. Ramada Inn Restaurant, Paramus, N.J., 1980-81; mgr. Gottlieb's Bakery, Hilton Head, 1982-83; asst. mgr. closing dept. Hilton Head Mortgage Co., 1983-84; owner, mgr. All Cleaning Svc., Hilton Head, 1984—; owner Hilton Head Investigations, 1990-93, Hilton Head Island, 1990-92; owner Aaction Investigators, 1992-94. Mem. NAFE, Profl. Women of Hilton Head, Assn. for Rsch. and Enlightenment, Rosicrucian Order. Roman Catholic. Office: PO Box 4953 Hilton Head Island SC 29938

URBAN, GARY ROSS, computer and information processing consultant; b. Corpus Christi, Tex., May 17, 1947; s. Ross O. and Nell (Hall) U.; m. Jeanette Corbitt, Dec. 14, 1968 (div. 1979); children: Kimberly, Bryan, Sheryl. Pvt. practice computer and info. processing cons. GRU Enterprises, Houston, 1972—. Recipient Achievement cert. U.S. Army, 1971. Mem. Mensa.

URBINA, MANUEL, II, legal research historian, history educator; b. Rodriguez, Nuevo Leon, Mex., Sept. 23, 1939; came to U.S., 1947; s. Manuel and Irene (Salce) de Urbina. BA, Howard Payne Coll., 1962; postgrad., Nat. Autonoma U. Mex., Mexico City, 1963-64; MA, U. Tex., 1967, PhD, 1976; postgrad., Cambridge (Eng.) U., 1982; JD, U. Houston, 1983. Prof. Latin Am. history Coll. of the Mainland, Texas City, Tex., 1967—; founder, curator Urbina Mus. History of Mex., Houston, 1990—; chmn., legal counsel Urbina Found., Houston, 1985—; chmn., CEO Urbina Pub. Co. Inc., Houston and Mexico City, 1985—. Editor, interviewer history videos, oral history interviews with participants in the Mexican Revolution. Founder Cinco de Mayo Assn., Galveston County, Tex., 1976; founder, faculty sponsor Mex. Am. Student Assn., Coll. of Mainlan, 1974—. Named Hispanic of Yr. Galveston County League of United Latin Am. Citizens, 1982; NEH grantee, 1971-72; U.S. Dept. State scholar diplomat, 1979. Mem. League of United Latin Am. Citizens, Tex. State Hist. Assn., Howard Payne U. Alumni Assn., U. Houston Law Alumni Assn., Interam. C. of C. Democrat. Baptist. Home: 889 Old Genoa Red Bluff Rd Houston TX 77034-4010 Office: Museo Urbina de Historia de Mexico 889 Old Genoa Red Bluff Rd Houston TX 77034-4010

URESTI, RONDA VEVERKA, elementary bilingual education educator; b. Newton, Iowa, May 23, 1963; d. Terry Joe and Carol Jean VeVerka; m. Eulalio Uresti, Dec. 18, 1993. BA in Elem. Edn., Ctrl. U., 1994. Instr. mentally challenged adults Progress Ind., Newton, 1989-94; bilingual tchr. San Carlos Elem. Sch., Edinburg, Tex., 1994—; mem. adv. bd. J & E Opporation, Edcouch, Tex., 1989-94; 1st grade curriculum writer, Edinburg Sch. Dist., 1995, 96, mem. assessment adv. com., 1996, mem. tech. com., 1996. Grantee Jasper Charter Am. Bus. Women's Assn., Newton, 1992, 93. Mem. Ind. Order of Odd Fellows Rebekah Lodge (sec. 1992—). Mem. Church of Christ. Home: PO Box 1454 Edcouch TX 78538-1454

URIBE, JAVIER MIGUEL, investment executive; b. Baranquilla, Colombia, Sept. 4, 1941; s. Jose and Ofelia (Diaz-Granados) U.; m. Dena Rue Whitaker, Apr. 1, 1963 (div. Sept. 1987); children: Sandra J., Joseph J., Cristina; m. Diana L. Anglada, Dec. 4, 1987. BS in Indsl. Mgmt., Purdue U., 1967. With Citibank, N.A., 1967; resident v.p. Citibank, N.A., Bogota, Colombia, 1975-76; v.p. Citibank, N.A., Port of Spain, Trinidad, 1976-78, N.Y.C., 1978-80, San Juan, P.R., 1980-85; pres. Citicorp Fin. Svcs. Corp., San Juan, P.R., 1980-85; chmn., chief exec. officer Merrill Lynch Govt. Securities, San Juan, 1985-88; pres. San Juan Capital Corp., 1988—; advisor exec. program Ind. U., Bloomington, 1978-80; chmn. Trinfinance Leasing, Port of Spain, Trinidad, 1976-78, Met. Mortgage Co., San Juan, 1989—; trustee Ashford Presbyn. Community Hosp., San Juan, 1990—. Bd. dirs. Maracaibo (Venezuela) Botanical Gardens Found., 1974-75. Mem. Securities Industry Assn. of P.R. (founder, treas. 1985-86), N.Am. Assn. (bd. dirs. Caracas, Venezuela chpt. 1973-74), Berwind Country Club, Centro Ecuestre de P.R. (pres. 1989-91), P.R. Equestrian Fedn., Ingenio Polo Club. Roman Catholic. Home: PO Box 3462 San Juan PR 00902 Office: San Juan Capital Corp Banco Popular Ste 908 San Juan PR 00901

URMY, NORMAN B., hospital administrator; b. Ft. Smith, Ark., June 26, 1944; married. BA, Williams Coll., 1966; MA, U. Chgo., 1969. Various positions Mass. Gen. Hosp., Boston, 1966-67; adminstrv. resident NYU Med. Ctr., 1968, adminstrv. asst., 1969-70, asst. adminstr., 1970-76, assoc. adminstr., 1976-79, adminstr., v.p. ops., 1979-82; exec. dir. Vanderbilt Univ. Hosp. & Clinic, Nashville, 1985—. Mem. ACHE. Office: Vanderbilt U Hosp & Clinic 1161 21st Ave S Nashville TN 37232*

URQUHART, SALLY ANN, environmental scientist, chemist; b. Omaha, June 8, 1946; d. Howard E. and Mary Josephine (Johnson) Lee; m. Henry O. Urquhart, July 31, 1968; children: Mary L. Urquhart Kelly, Andrew L. BS in Chemistry, U. Tex., Arlington, 1968; MS in Environ. Scis., U. Tex., Dallas, 1986. Registered environ. mgr.; lic. asbestos mgmt. planner, Tex.; Asbestos Hazard Emergency Response Act accredited inspector, mgmt. planner, project designer. Rsch. asst. U. Tex. Dallas, Richardson, 1980-82; high sch. sci. tchr. Allen (Tex.) Ind. Sch. Dist., 1983-87; hazardous materials specialist Dallas Area Rapid Transit, 1987-90, environ. compliance officer, 1990-94, environmental compliance coordination officer, 1994-95; pres. Comprehensive Environ. Svcs. Inc., Dallas, 1995—. Pres. Beacon Sunday Sch. Spring Valley United Meth. Ch., Dallas, 1987, adminstrv. bd. dirs., 1989, com. status and role of women, 1992. Scholar Richardson (Tex.) Br. AAUW, 1980. Mem. Am. Inst. Chemists, Am. Chem. Soc., Am. Soc. Safety Engrs., Am. Indsl. Hygiene Assn., Am. Conf. Govtl. Indsl. Hygienists (affiliate), Nat. Registry Environ. Profls., Soc. Tex. Environ. Profls. (sec.-treas. Dallas chpt. 1994, v.p. 1996), U. Tex.-Dallas Alumnae Assn. (com. 1992-94), Soc. of Environ. Mgmt. and Tech. Home: 310 Sallie Cir Richardson TX 75081-4229

URSETTA, TERRANCE THOMAS, anesthesiologist; b. Sharon, Pa., Sept. 29, 1945; s. Frank James and Helen (Thomas) U. BA, Thiel Coll., 1967; MA, Bowling Green State U., 1969; DO, Coll. Osteo. Medicine, Kansas City, Mo., 1974. Diplomate Am. Osteo. Bd. Anesthesiologists. Staff anesthesiologist Cherry Hill (N.J.) Anesthesia Assn., 1978-83, Fox Chase Anesthesia Assn., Phila., 1983-90, Sheridan Health Corp., Hollywood, Fla., 1991—; assoc. prof. Univ. N.J. Sch. Medicine and Dentistry, Camden, 1980—. Mem. AMA, Am. Osteo. Assn., Am.Soc. Anesthesiologists, Fla. State Soc. Anesthesiologists, Am. Coll. Osteo. Anesthesiologists, Broward County Med. Assn. Republican. Lutheran. Home: 10821 Santa Fe Dr Cooper City FL 33026-4956 Office: Sheridan Health Corp 4651 Sheridan St Ste 400 Hollywood FL 33021-3430

URVAL, KRISHNA RAJ, health facility administrator, educator; b. Mangalore, India, July 3, 1955; came to U.S., 1984; s. Rajgopal Rao and Bhoomi Devi (Kanemar) U.; m. Purnima K. Hebbar, May 23, 1985; children: Nikita, Nikhil. MBBS, MD, Govt. Med. Coll., Mysore City, India, 1979; DCH, U. West Indies, Kingston, Jamaica, 1985. Bd. cert. pediatrics, allergy/immunology. Resident pediatrics U. West Indies, Jamaica, 1980-85; resident pediatrics Interfaith Med. Ctr., Bklyn., 1985-88, chief resident, 1987-88; fellow immunology U. South Fla., St. Petersburg, 1988-90; assoc. Wyo. Chest and Allergy Clinic, Casper, 1990-91; med. dir. Ohio Valley Allergy Inst., Wheeling, W.Va., 1991—; clin. asst. prof. W.Va. U., Morgantown, 1991—; bd. dirs. W.Va. Am. Lung Assn., Charleston. Bd. dirs. Child Care Resource Ctr., Wheeling, 1992—; med. dir. Asthma Support Group, Wheeling, 1992—. Fellow Am. Acad. Pediatrics; mem. AMA, Am. Coll. Allergy/Immunology, Am. Acad. Allergy/Immunology. Democrat. Hindu. Office: Ohio Valley Allergy Inst 2101 Jacob St Ste 601 Wheeling WV 26003

USHER, CHARLES LINDSEY, social work educator, public policy analyst; b. Portsmouth, Va., Aug. 12, 1949; s. Henry George and Lottie Frances (Dickens) U.; m. Janan Bailey, Aug. 14, 1971; children: Lindsay Erin, Ellen Ashley. BA in Polit. Sci., Old Dominion U., 1971, M in Urban Studies, 1974; postgrad., U. Mich., 1975; PhD in Polit. Sci., Emory U., 1976. Planning and evaluation specialist Dept. Social Svcs., Portsmouth, 1972-73; asst. prof. polit. sci. Miami U. of Ohio, Oxford, 1976-78, U. N.C., Charlotte, 1978-80; policy analyst, sr. policy analyst Rsch. Triangle Inst., Rsch. Triangle Park, N.C., 1980-84, dir. Ctr. for Policy Studies, 1985-92; exec. dir. Northeastern N.C. Tomorrow, Inc., Elizabeth City, 1984-85; Wallace H. Kuralt Sr. prof. pub. welfare policy/adminstrn. U. N.C., Chapel Hill, 1993—; presenter in field. Assoc. editor Evaluation Rev., 1987-89; contbr. articles to profl. jours. Bd. dirs. Arc of Durham County, 1992—, Concern of Durham, Inc., 1989-94; mem. steering com. Children's Summit, N.C. Child Advocacy Inst., 1992-93. Grantee Dept. Labor, 1980, NIMH, 1980-81, Nat. Inst. Justice, 1980-83, Social Security Adminstrn., 1982-83, Office of Analysis and Evaluation/Food and Nutrition Svc./USDA, 1981-83, 87-91, Conn.

Gen. Assembly, 1986-87, United Way of Wake County, 1987, Office of Policy Devel. and Rsch./HUD, 1987-90, Fla. Legis., 1988, Ctr. for Study of Social Policy, 1990-93, Annie E. Casey Found., 1992—, Edna McConnel Clark Found., 1995—. Mem. ASPA, Am. Evaluation Assn., Am. Pub. Welfare Assn. Home: 4215 Swarthmore Rd Durham NC 27707-5389

USHER, TOMMY, computer software engineer, consultant; b. Fairfield, Ala., Nov. 12, 1954; s. Howard Thomas and Polly Elizabeth (Sanders) U.; m. Rebecca Aleen Hawkins, Aug. 11, 1980; 1 child, Elizabeth Marie. Student, Walker Jr. Coll., Jasper, Ala., 1973-74, Indian River Coll., Ft. Pierce, Fla., 1984-88, U. Ala., 1990-91. Owner No Frills Software, Birmingham, Ala., 1984—; Birmingham. Office: No Frills Software 2030 Highland Ave S Apt C-1 Birmingham AL 35205-3831

USRY MABRY, TINA, family nurse practitioner; b. Forest, Miss., Aug. 1, 1959; d. Travis and Nancy Jane (Lott) U. Diploma, Matty Hersee Hosp. Sch. Nsg., 1980; BS, U. So. Miss., Meridian, 1984; MS, U. So. Miss., Hattiesburg, 1986; Cert. Nurse Practitioner, Miss. U. for Women, Columbus, 1991. RN, Miss. Staff nurse Lackey Hosp., Forest, Miss.; head nurse Miss. Meth. Rehab. Ctr., Jackson; dir. nursing Lackey Hosp., Forest, Miss.; family nurse practitioner Rush Med. Group, Lake, Miss. Mem. ANA, Am. Acad. Nurse Practitioners, Miss. Nurses Assn., Sigma Theta Tau. Home: 5115 Newton-Conehatta Rd Decatur MS 39327

UTHMAN, BASIM MOHAMMAD, neurologist, epileptologist, consultant; b. Tripoli, Lebanon, Sept. 25, 1958; came to the U.S., 1984; s. Mohammad Assa'ad and Mariam Mohammad (Moukalled) U. BSc, Am. U. Beirut, 1978, MD, 1984. Diplomate Am. Bd. Psyhciatry and Neurology, Am. Bd. Clin. Neurophysiology. Intern Am. Univ. Beirut Med Ctr., Lebanon, 1983-84; resident in neurologyDept. Neurology U. Cin., 1984-87, clin. fellow in neurophysiology, epilepsy, preceptor, 1987-88; clin. rsch. fellow in epilepsy, neurophysiology and neuropharmacology U. Fla., Gainesville, 1988-90, clin. instr., 1990-91; vis. assoc. prof. dept. neurology U. Fla., 1991-92; asst. prof. dept. neurology, brain inst. U. Fla., Gainesville, 1992-96, assoc. prof. dept. neurology, brain inst., 1996—; staff neurologist VA Med. Ctr., Gainesville, 1990—, asst. chief neurology svc., 1992—, dir. status epilepticus team, 1990-95, contracting officers tech. rep., 1990-92, acting chief neurology svc., 1993, dir. clin. neurophysiology lab. EEG/EP, 1991—; chmn. med. record rev. com. VA, 1995—; staff neurologist VA Med. Ctr. Gainesville, 1990—, dir. status epilepticus team, 1990-95, asst. chief neurology svc., 1991—, contracting officers tech. rep., 1990-92, dir. clin. neurophysiology lab. EEG/EP, 1991—, acting chief neurology svc., 1993; chmn. Adminstrv. Bd. Investigation VA Med. Ctr., Gainesville, 1993; attending epideptologist Shands Hosp., 1993—; permanent mem. U. Fla. Instnl. Rev. Bd. Health Sci. Ctr., 1994—. Ad hoc referee U.S. Pharmacopeial Conv., 1988-89, Drug Evaluations, 1990, Epilepsia, 1990—, Jour. Neuroimaging, 1990—, Drugs, 1993—; contbr. articles to profl. jours., chpts. to books. Active emergency blood donation campaign, Beirut, 1982-83, worker war disaster plan, 1982-83; vol. Lebanese Red Cross, Beirut, 1982-83; organizer children's med. ednl. presentations, 1984; profl. adv. bd. Epilspsy Found. Fla., 1992-93, chmn., 1993—. A.S. Khalidi scholar Am. U. Beirut, 1978, Azeez B. Ajloini scholar, 1979, Tamari-Saab scholar, 1979, Dr. Haddad, 1980; fellow Bowman Gray Med. Sch., Winston-Salem, N.C., 1987; grantee Epilepsy Rsch. Found. Fla., 1988-90, Cyberonics, 1989—, Coop. Studies Program Coordinating Ctr., 1990-95, VA Affairs Med. Ctr. Allotment, 1991-92, Abbott Labs., 1991—, U. Fla., 1991-92, Ceiba-Geigy, 1991-94, U. Fla. Brain Inst., 1992, Parke-Davis 1993—. Mem. AMA, Am. Acad. Neurology, Am. Epilepsy Soc., Am. Sleep Disorders Assn., Am. Electroencephalographic Soc., Am. Soc. Neurophysiological Monitoring, Am. Coll. Internat. Physicians, Nat. Stroke Assn., So. Clin. Neurol. Soc., So. Electroencephalographic Soc., Fla. Med. Assn., Alachua County Med. Soc., Nat. and Internat. Spkrs. Bur. (Parke-Davis, Marion Merryl Dow, Burroughs Wellcome, Abbott Labs., Ciba-Geigy, Cyberonics 1993—). Moslem. Office: VA Med Ctr-Neurology Svc 127 1601 SW Archer Rd Gainesville FL 32608-1135

UTNIK, DAVID ALAN, newspaper editor, journalist; b. June 17, 1960; s. Valentine Peter and Jessie Lenora (Land) U.; m. Pamela Annette Clyburn, May 11, 1991. BS in Journalism, Radford U., 1983. Sports reporter Md. Ind., Waldorf, 1983-84, Potomac News, Woodbridge, Va., 1984-85; sports info. dir. Radford (Va.) U., 1985-87; feature contbr. Radford U. Mag., 1986; sports editor Culpeper (Va.) Star Exponent, 1987-94, news editor, 1994-96, sports editor, 1987-94, 96—; guest lectr. AP seminar series, 1991; freelance writer Balls and Strikes Mag., 1992, Carolina League Beat, 1993; guest features writer AP, 1993-95. Coach Culpeper Little League, 1988—, fast pitch softball team Culpeper Recreation Dept., 1988-89, NCAA Div. I Women's Softball, Radford U., 1986-87; chmn. comm. Culpeper United Meth. Ch., 1993—. Recipient 1st place award Page Design and Column Writing Worrell Pub. Co., 1989, Layout and Sports Writing award Chesapeake Pub., 1984. Mem. Md.-Del.-D.C. Press Assn. (1st pl. feature photography award 1983), Coll. Sports Info. Dirs., Radford U. Sports Info., Va. Press Assn. (1st pl. column writing award 1988, 89, feature writing award 1987, 90, 1st pl. for page design 1989, 1st pl. sports event writing 1993, 1st pl. lifestyle writing 1993, sports page design award 1994, feature writing award 1994, sports news writing award 1994, 1st pl. editorial writing 1995), Soc. Collegiate Journalists (v.p. 1982). Home: 124 W Mason St Culpeper VA 22701-3239 Office: Culpeper Star Exponent 122 W Spencer St Culpeper VA 22701-2628

UTSMAN, FAYE MILDRED, surgical patient educator; b. Tenn., Sept. 14, 1926; d. Lawrence and Trula (Howard) Sanders; m. Andrew J. Utsman, Sept. 29, 1954; children: Andrew T., Tinah, Sanya, Flara Jan. Diploma, Fort Sanders Sch. Nursing, 1951; BS, U. Tenn., 1974, MS, 1985. Licensed real estate agt. Pvt. scrub nurse Thoracic Surgeons, Knoxville, Tenn.; surg. nurse Ft. Sanders Hosp., Knoxville, St. Thomas Hosp., Nashville; surg. patient educator U. Tenn. Med. Ctr., Knoxville, Tenn. Mem. Assn. Operating Rm. Nurses, Pi Lambda Theta.

UTTERBACK, WILL HAY, JR., labor union administrator; b. Amarillo, Tex., Mar. 10, 1947; s. Will Hay and Marie (Willey) U.; m. Margaret Jane Smith, July 31, 1982. JD (hon.), Pacific Northwestern U., 1980. Pres. BillCo Enterprises, Amarillo, Tex., 1974-86, Communications Workers Am. Local 6128, Amarillo, 1988—; audiovisual cons. Franklin D. Roosevelt Libr., Hyde Park, N.Y., 1971—; cons. Smithsonian Instn., Washington, 1983; lectr. Ind. Scholar Network, Amarillo, 1982—; spl. cons. Ednl. Video Group, Greenwood, Ind., 1989—; dir. state sect. Mufon, Inc., 1991—. Contbr. articles to profl. publs.; reconstructor newsreel film, 1974—. Bd. dirs. Panhandle Tech-Prep Consortium; mem. citizens budget com. United Way. Mem. Am. Hist. Assn., Nat. Hist. Soc., Ctr. for Study of Presidency. Mem. Ch. of Christ. Home: PO Box 150 Amarillo TX 79105-0150

UWUJAREN, GILBERT PATRICK, economist, consultant, realtor; b. Oza Agbor, Bendel, Nigeria, May 6, 1945; came to U.S., 1985; s. Jacob Aghahowa and Victoria (Lasila) Uwujaren; m. Ngozi Buzugbe, Aug. 25, 1973; children: Jane, Janice, Jacob, Jo-Anne, Joseph, Jarune. BSc, U. Ibadan, Nigeria, 1971; MA, Columbia U., 1975, MPhil, 1977, PhD, 1977. Asst. lectr. U. Ife, Ibadan, 1972-73; sr. lectr. U. Ife, Ile-Ife, Nigeria, 1977-85; economist World Bank, Washington, 1985-89, cons., 1989-95; pres. Econ. Devel. Assocs., Burke, Va., 1993—; realtor Weichert Realtors, Springfield, Va., 1993-95, Fairfax Realty, Inc., Springfield, Va., 1995—. Contbr. articles to profl. jours. Recipient German Acad. award Govt. Fed. Republic Germany, Ibadan, 1970-71, Rockefeller award Rockefeller Found., Ibadan, 1971-73. Mem. Am. Econ. Assn. Office: 5801 Shana Pl Burke VA 22015-3663

UZE, IRVING, automotive executive; b. Chelsea, Mass., June 21, 1918; s. Philip and Ann (Connoers) U.; m. Rosalynn Siegel, Apr. 6, 1941 (dec. May 1985); m. Meriam Breitholz, July 17, 1990; children: Martin Andrew, Beth Ellen, Vicki Jean. Grad., N.E. Conservatory of Music, Boston, 1939. Pres. ESCO Corp., Waterloo, Iowa, 1946-83, Cen. States Distbn. Warehouse, Waterloo, 1961-83, Royal Oaks Co., Cedar Falls, Iowa, 1969-91; pres., treas., sec. BANVIR Corp., Waterloo, 1961—; pres. Banyan Pt., Inc., PGI. Solicited Iowa rep. for Richard Nixon, 1961, Ronald Reagan, 1979-80. With USN, 1943-45. Mem. Seminole Lakes Country Club, Sunnyside Country Club, Burnt Store Country Club, Shriner, Mason (32 degree). Home: 601 Shreve St Apt 52B Punta Gorda FL 33950-3346

UZSOY, PATRICIA J., nursing educator and administrator; b. Corning, Ark.; m. Namik K. Diploma, Mo. Bapt. Hosp. Sch. Nursing, St. Louis, 1960; BSN, Washington U., St. Louis, 1962; MEd, Lynchburg Coll., 1977, EdS, 1981; MS in Nursing, U. Va., 1987. RN, Va. Dir. sch. nursing Lynchburg (Va.) Gen. Hosp., dir. Mem. ANA, NLN, Va. Nurses Assn. (Nurse of Yr. dist. III 1987).

VACHHER, PREHLAD SINGH, psychiatrist; b. Rawalpindi, Punjab, Pakistan, Nov. 30, 1933; came to U.S., 1960; s. Thakar Singh and Harbans Kaur (Ghai) V.; m. Margaret Mary Begley, Oct. 9, 1963; children: Paul, Sheila, Mary Ann, Eileen, Mark. Grad., Khalsa Coll., India, 1950; MD, Panjab U., Amritsar, India, 1956. Diplomate Am. Bd. Psychiatry. Staff N.J. State Hosp., Trenton, 1965-66, Wayne County Gen. Hosp., Eloise, Mich., 1966-68; pvt. practice Livonia, Mich., 1966-75, Woodstock, Va., 1991—; pres. Vachher Psychiat. Ctr., P.C., Livonia, 1975-91; dir. community psychiatry Northville (Mich.) State Hosp., 1968-71; cons. staff Kingswood Hosp., Ferndale, Mich., 1967-72, Annapolis Hosp., Wayne, 1967-88, St. Joseph Mercy Hosp., Ann Arbor, 1970-89; westland staff Margaret Montgomery Hosp., 1988-91; bd. dirs. Oakland Rental Housing Assn., 1990-91; med. dir. mental health unit Shenandoan County Meml. Hosp., Woodstock, Va., 1991-94. Mem. Am. Psychiat. Assn., Va. Psychiat. Soc., Sikh Physicians in Mich. (bd. dirs. 1987), Canton C. of C. (pres. 1975), Sikh Bus. Profl. Coun. (pres. 1988—), Rotary (Canton and Plymouth, Mich., Woodstock), Prince William County C. of C. Office: 14573 Potomac Mills Rd Woodbridge VA 22192

VACHON, REGINALD IRENEE, engineer; b. Norfolk, Va., Jan. 29, 1937; s. Rene Albert Vachon and Regina (Galvin) Radcliffe; student U.S. Naval Acad., 1954-55; BME, Auburn U., 1958, MS, 1960; PhD, Okla. State U., 1963; LLB, Jones Law Sch., 1969; m. Mary Eleanor Grigg, Jan. 16, 1960; children: Reginald Irenee, Eleanor Marie. Engr., Hayes Internat., 1958; instr., rsch. asst. Auburn U., 1958-60, rsch. assoc., 1961, assoc., prof., 1963-78; R & D engr. E.I. DuPont, 1960; aerospace engr., technologist NASA Marshall Space Flight Center, summers, 1964, 65; pres. Vachon Nix & Assocs., 1977—, VNA Systems Inc., 1982—; chmn. bd. Optimal Systems Internat., Inc., 1969-95; COO Thacker Constrn. Co., Thacker Orgn. Inc., 1981-90; pres., CEO Compris Techs., Inc., 1991-92; chmn., Global Risk Managers, Inc., 1992—; prin. Gipco Holdings Internat., Ltd., 1994—. Admitted to Ala. bar, 1971. Served with U.S. Army, 1960-61. Registered profl. engr., Ala., Ga., Miss., La., Wis., Tex. Fellow ASME; mem. Am. Inst. Aeros. and Astronautics, Nat. Soc. Profl. Engrs., Ala. Bar Assn., Am. Bar Assn., The Phoenix Soc. of Atlanta. Roman Catholic. Club: Cosmos (Washington). Contbr. articles to profl. jours.; patentee in field. Home: 1414 Epping Forest Dr NE Atlanta GA 30319-2539 Office: PO Box 467069 Atlanta GA 30346-7069

VADIA, RAFAEL, visual artist; b. Havana, Cuba, Nov. 27, 1950; came to U.S., 1959; s. Alberto and Rosario (Rodriguez-Caceres) V. AA, Miami Dade C.C., 1971; student, Ecole des Beaux-Arts, Paris, 1972-73; BFA, Fla. Internat. U., 1976. Keynote speaker Fla. Art Edn. Assn. Conf., Naples, Fla., 1991, Miami Internat. Art Fair, Miami Beach, Fla., 1992; lectr. Broward C.C., Pembroke Pines, Fla., 1992, North-South Ctr., Coral Gables, Fla., 1995. One-man shows include Gloria Luria Gallery, Miami, 1988, Broward C.C., Hollywood, Fla., 1992, Broward County Main Libr. Gallery, Ft. Lauderdale, Fla., 1992, Cultural Resource Ctr./Metro-Dade Govt. Ctr., Miami, 1993; exhibited in group shows at Gloria Luria Gallery, Miami, 1990, Brigham Young U., Provo, Utah, 1990, Metro-Dade Cultural Ctr., Miami, 1991, The Americas Collection Gallery, Coral Gables, Fla., 1992, Orlando (Fla.) City Hall, 1992, Miami-Dade C.C., 1992, Aqueous Open 1995, Pitts. Ctr. for the Arts; also corp. collections. Recipient Cintas Found. fellowship Inst. Internat. Edn., N.Y.C., 1991-92, John Gordon Meml. award Soc. Four Arts, Palm Beach, Fla., Amerifirst award Met. Mus. and Art Ctr., Coral Gables, Judge's Recognition award Broward Art Guild, Ft. Lauderdale, Fla., 1983, Patron award Met. Mus. and Art Ctr., Coral Gables, Verna Lammi Meml. award Norton Gallery Art, West Palm Beach, Fla., Judge's merit award Grove House, Coconut Grove, Fla, Patron award WPBT Galleries, Miami. Republican. Roman Catholic. Home and Studio: 3130 Center St Coconut Grove FL 33133-4671

VAETH, AGATHA MIN-CHUN FANG, quality assurance nurse, wellness consultant, home health nurse; b. Beijing, Feb. 19, 1935; d. Yung-Cheng and Wen-Pu (Cheng) Fang; m. Randy H. Vaeth, July 20, 1971; children: David Sun, Elizabeth Cheng, Philip Cheng. Diploma, Mary View Hosp. Sch. Nursing, Portsmouth, Va., 1959; student, Okla. State U., 1969-73; BS, St. Joseph's Coll., North Windham, Maine, 1986, postgrad., 1989—; postgrad., La. State U., 1986. Staff nurse, charge nurse Stillwater (Okla.) Mcpl. Hosp., 1969-74; clin. nurse USIHH Hosp., Pawnee, Okla., 1974-75; clin. nurse, relief supr. Gillis W. Long Hansen's Disease Ctr., Carville, La., 1975-91, supervisory clin. nurse, 1991—; wellness cons.; part-time home health nurse, 1993—. Translator video cassettes on Hansens Disease; illustrator herpetology lab manuel; art exhbns. at Barton Rouge Art & Artist Guild, 1976-77. Recipient Outstanding Performance award GWLHD, PHS, DHHS, 1991, 1993, High Quality Performance award, 1978, Dedicated Svc. to Clin. Br. award, 1981, Outstanding Nurses award Baton Rouge Dist. Nurses' Assn., 1994. Fellow Internat. Biog. Assn. (life); mem. ANA, AAUW, La. Nurses Assn. (nominating com. 1990-94), Baton Rouge Nurses Assn., Am. Coll. Health Execs. Home: 1274 Marilyn Dr Baton Rouge LA 70815-4928

VAFEADES, PETER, mechanical engineering educator; b. Detroit, Dec. 26, 1957; s. George and Agnes-Athena (Kellargi) V.; m. Katherine Dakie, July 2, 1980. BS, U. Detroit, 1982; MS, Mich. State U., 1983, Mich. State U., 1984; PhD, Mich. State U., 1987. Lectr. U. Minn., Mpls., 1987-89; assoc. prof. mech. engring. Trinity U., San Antonio, Tex., 1989—. Author: (software) PDELIE: Automatic Symbolic Solution of Partial Differential Equations, 1991; contbr. articles to profl. jours. Mem. AAUP, Am. Math. Soc., Soc. Indsl. and Applied Math., Soc. Automotive Engrs. Office: Trinity U 715 Stadium Dr San Antonio TX 78212-3104

VAIDHYANATHAN, SIVA, journalist, educator; b. Buffalo, June 16, 1966; s. Vishnampet S. and Virginia Ann (Evans) V. BA, U. Tex., 1992, postgrad., 1992—. Reporter Dallas Morning News, 1988, Austin (Tex.) Am. Statesman, 1989-91, Ft. Worth (Tex.) Star-Telegram, 1992; freelance journalist, 1992—; history lectr. Concordia U., Austin, 1996—; instr. Am. studies U. Tex., 1997—. Election judge Travis County (Tex.), 1984—. Mem. MLA (exec. com. 1996), Am. Studies Assn. of Tex. (students com. 1995-97). Hindu. Office: Am Studies Dept 303 Garrison Hall U Texas Austin TX 78712

VAILLANCOURT-ROSENAU, PAULINE MARIE See ROSENAU, PAULINE VAILLANCOURT

VALA, MARTIN THORVALD, chemistry educator, researcher; b. Bklyn., Mar. 28, 1938; s. Martin Thorvald and Norun (Nilson) V.; m. Vibeke Wilken-Jensen, June 23, 1966; children: Lars, Carsten, Steffen. BA, St. Olaf Coll., Northfield, Minn., 1960; MS, U. Chgo., 1962, PhD, 1964. NSF postdoctoral fellow U. Copenhagen, 1965-66; NSF U.S.-Japan coop. sci. postdoctoral fellow Nagoya (Japan) U., 1966-67; asst. prof. chemistry U. Fla., Gainesville, 1967-72, assoc. prof., 1972-78, prof., 1978—. Contbr. more than 90 articles to phys. chemistry jours. Fellow Merck Found., 1970-71, NATO, Paris, 1973, sr. Fulbright fellow, Paris, 1974. Fellow Am. Inst. Chemists; mem. Am. Chem. Soc., Am. Phys. Soc., Interam. Photochem. Soc., Phi Beta Kappa. Democrat. Lutheran. Office: U Fla Dept Chemistry Gainesville FL 32611

VALADKA, ALEX BRUNO, neurosurgeon, educator; b. Chgo., Oct. 21, 1961; m. Patricia Croasdale; children: Patrick Ryan, Jaclyn Sorelle. BA in Biology, U. Dallas, 1983, BS in Biochemistry summa cum laude, 1983; MD, U. Chgo., 1987. Intern in surgery Med. Coll. Va., Richmond, 1987-88, resident in neurosurgery, 1988-93; med. dir. neurosurg. ICU, Meth. Hosp., Houston, 1993-95; asst. prof. Baylor Coll. Medicine, Houston, 1993—; chief neurosurgery Ben Taub Gen. Hosp., Houston, 1994—; presenter Soc. for Neurosci., 1991, 93, Soc. Critical Care Medicine, 1993. Contbr. articles to med. jours., chpts. to books. Participating spkr. THINK FIRST Program, Richmond, 1993. Mem. AAAS, AMA, Am. Assn. Neurol. Surgeons, Congress Neurol. Surgeons (presenter 1991, 92), Neurotrauma Soc. (travel fellow 1991), So. Med. Assn., Tex. Med. Assn., Harris County Med. Soc., Houston Neurol. Soc., Med. Soc. Va., Hastings Ctr., Children's Mus. Houston, Zool. Soc. Houston, Houston Mus. Natural Sci. Office: 6560 Fannin St Ste 944 Houston TX 77030

VALASQUEZ, JOSEPH LOUIS, industrial engineer; b. Balt., Apr. 15, 1955; s. Jose Louis and Edith Rosabel (Saunders) V.; m. Nicole Diane Feldser, Sept. 4, 1983; children: Alexandra Nicole, Joseph Jr. AA, Essex Coll., 1977; BS in Indsl. Engring., U. Ariz., 1982; MBA in Fin., So. Ill. U., 1985. Registered profl. engr., Fla.; cert. quality engr.; cert. quality auditor; cert. quality mgr.; pvt. pilots license. Machinist Bausch & Lomb, Balt., 1974-77; indsl. engr. IBM Corp., Tucson, 1980-81; sr. indsl. engr. Gen. Dynamics, San Diego, 1981-83; supr. engring. Avco Corp., Nashville, 1983-84; mgr. engring. Burroughs Corp., Coral Springs, Fla., 1984-85; dir. total quality mgmt. Lambda Novatronics, Inc., Pompano Beach, Fla., 1985—; pres. Woodland Properties; computer cons., Margate, Fla., 1987; founder, owner E.P.I. Cons., Pompano Beach. Mem. Am. Inst. Indsl. Engrs., Fla. Engring. Soc. Republican. Roman Catholic. Home: PO Box 9821 Coral Springs FL 33075-0821

VALDES, JUAN B., engineering educator; b. Resistencia, Chaco, Argentina, July 8, 1944; s. Oscar and Aurelia (Dentone) V.; m. Maria Aurelia Alday, Aug. 2, 1969; children: Santiago, Javier, Jimena. Cert. civil engr., Cath. U. Cordoba, Argentina, 1970; MS in Civil Engring., MIT, 1975, PhD in Water Resources, 1976. Registered profl. engr., Tex. Assoc. prof. Simon Bolivar U., Caracas, Venezuela, 1976-87; faculty rsch. assoc. Climate Sys. Rsch. Program, Coll. Geoscis., Tex. A&M U., College Station, 1988-92, prof., divsn. head environ., ocean and water resources divsn., 1993—; vis. rsch. engr. MIT, 1970-72, rsch. asst., 1974-76, rsch. assoc., 1976, vis. assoc. prof. dept. civil engring., 1982-83; prof., head grad. program in hydrology and water resources Simon Bolivar U., Caracas, 1987; vis. assoc. prof. Tex. A&M U., 1987-88, assoc. prof., 1988-93, prof., area leader environ. and water resources engring. area, 1993, assoc. dir., 1992—. Contbr. articles to profl. jours., chpts. to books. Fellow ASCE; mem. Am. Geophys. Union, Am. Water Resources Assn., Am. Meteorological Soc., Internat. Assn. Hydraulic Rsch., Internat. Assn. Hydrologic Scis., Argentinean Inst. Water Resources, Venezuelan Hydraulic Engring. Soc., Sigma Xi. Office: Tex A&M U 205 A Wisenbaker College Station TX 77843

VALDÉS, KAREN W., art gallery director, educator; b. L.A., May 25, 1945; d. Richard Victor and Eleanor M. (Tomte) V.; m. Thomas E. Schwarz, Oct. 14, 1989. BFA, U. Calif., Irvine, 1968; MFA, Fla. State U., 1974. Dir. cultural events Fla. State U., Tallahassee, 1973-75; curator exhbn. Art Mus. So. Tex., Corpus Christi, 1975-76; assoc. prof., dir. gallery Miami (Fla.)-Dade Community Coll., 1976-84; dir. Gloria Luria Gallery, Miami, 1985; curator exhbn. Mus. Art, Ft. Lauderdale, Fla., 1985-89; assoc. prof., dir. univ. galleries U. Fla., Gainesville, 1989—; panelist NEA, Ft. Lauderdale, 1978-80, Dade County Art in Pub. Places, Miami, 1980-83, GSA Commn., 1982, Arts in State Bldgs., Gainesville, 1989—. Mem. Am. Assn. Mus., Coll. Art Assn., U. Fla. Hispanic Faculty Assn. Democrat. Office: U Fla Galleries 102 Fab Gainesville FL 32611

VALDES, ROLANDO HECTOR, library director, law librarian; b. Havana, Cuba, Jan. 13, 1939; came to U.S., 1966; s. Juan Manuel Valdes-Anciano and Sylvia (Nunez) Marasco. BA, Sancti-Spiritus Coll., Las Villas, Cuba, 1961; MLS, Havana (Cuba) U., 1963, postgrad. in tchr. edn., 1963-65. Libr. asst. The Newberry Libr., Chgo., 1966-68; reference libr. Sandard and Poor's Corp., N.Y.C., 1968-72; evening supr. Hunter Coll. Libr., N.Y.C., 1970-72; med. social worker Flower and Fifth Ave. Hosps., N.Y.C., 1973-76; social worker Mt. Carmel Guild, Union City, N.J., 1976-79, Queensborough Soc. for Prevention of Cruelty to Children, 1979-82, State of Fla. Dept. Health and Rehab. Svcs., 1982-84; libr. specialist, law libr., libr. dir. Dade Correction Instn. Librs., Florida City, Fla., 1984—. Contbr. articles to profl. jours. Mem. Dade County Libr. Assn., Reforma. Home: 38277 SW 192nd Ave Lot 28 Florida City FL 33034-6606 Office: Dade Correctional Libr 19000 SW 377th St Florida City FL 33034-6407

VALDEZ, ANA MARIA BRIONES, English language educator; b. San Diego, July 26, 1948; d. Vitalio C. and Leonor (Tiblier) Briones; m. Erasmo Valdez Sr., July 2, 1966; children: Elida, Melissa, Erasmo Jr. MS in Ednl. Admin., Tex. A&M U., 1996. English lang. educator San Diego Ind. Sch. Dist., San Diego, Tex. Vice-pres. Duval County/San Diego Friends of the Libr.; mem. Dist. Site Based Decision Making Team, 1994-96. Mem. Am. Fed. Tchrs., Nat. Assn. Secondary Sch. Prins., Nat. Assn. Student Activity Advisers, Assn. of Tex. Profl. Educators. Democrat. Roman Catholic. Home: 306 E Dix Ave San Diego TX 78384 Office: San Diego Ind Sch Dist 609 Labbe Ave San Diego TX 78384

VALDEZ, MARIA DEL ROSARIO, perinatal nurse; b. San Antonio, Nov. 4, 1955; d. Guadalupe Garza and Beatrice Consuelo (Martinez) V. BS in Nursing, BA in Psychology, Incarnate Word Coll., San Antonio, 1978; MS in Nursing, U. Tex. Health Sci. Ctr., San Antonio, 1986; postgrad., Tex. Woman's U. RN, Tex. Nurse, team leader Santa Rosa Med. Ctr., San Antonio, 1979-81, Met. Gen. Hosp., San Antonio, 1981-85; childbirth educator Santa Rosa Hosp., 1985-87, obstetrics clin. educator, 1987-94; instr. nursing Incarnate Word Coll., 1989-94; part-time perinatal staff nurse several nursing agys., Houston, 1994—; staff nurse North Ctrl. Bapt. Hosp., San Antonio, 1995—; instr. in Basic Life Support/CPR, Am. Heart Assn., 1985—, Prepared Childbirth, Coun. of Childbirth Edn. Specialists, 1985, instr. neonatal resucitation, 1989, instr.; mem. adv. bd. Hispanic Nurse Practice in Medically Underprivileged Areas, Ctr. for Health Policy Devel., San Antonio, 1989-91, Tex. Works Together program United Way, San Antonio, 1990—. Mem. ANA, NAACOG, Tex. Nurses' Assn., Nat. Assn. Hispanic Nurses, Am. Soc. Psychoprophy Obstets., Internat. Childbirth Edn. Assn., Coun. Childbirth Edn. Specialists, Sigma Theta Tau. Roman Catholic. Home: 303 Cosgrove San Antonio TX 78210

VALENTINE, HERMAN EDWARD, computer company executive; b. Norfolk, Va., June 26, 1937; s. Frank and Alice Mae (Heigh) V.; m. Dorothy Jones, Nov. 27, 1958; children: Herman Edward, Bryce Thomas. BS in Bus. Adminstrn., Norfolk State Coll., 1967; postgrad., Am. U., 1968; grad. student, Coll. William and Mary. Asst. bus. mgr. grad. sch. Dept. Agr., 1967, exec. officer grad. sch., 1967-68; bus. mgr. Norfolk State Coll., 1968; chmn., pres. Systems Mgmt. Am. Corp., Norfolk, 1969—, chmn., CEO, 1995—; chmn. Century Capitol Holders, Inc. Bd. dirs. PUSH Internat. Trade Bur., Cooperating Hampton Roads Orgn. for Minorities in Engring., Operation Smile, Greater Norfolk Corp.; mem. president's coun. Old Dominion U.; mem. adv. bd. Tidewater Vets. Meml. Project; mem. adv. coun. Va. Stage Co. Named Entrepreneur of Yr. Dept. Commerce Minority Bus. Devel. Agy., 1984, one of 10 Top Minority Owned Fed. Govt. Contractors Govt. Computer News, 1988, Outstanding Business Person of Yr. Va. Black Pres.'s Roundtable Assn., 1987, Amb. City of Norfolk, Va., 1986, Citizen of Yr. William A. Hunton YMCA, 1986, Pres.'s Coun. Am. Inst. Mgmt.; recipient Cert. of Merit City of Chg., 1985, McDonald's Hampton Roads Black Achievement award United Negro Coll. Fund., 1986, Colgate Whitehead Darden award, U. Va., 1987, cert. recognition Lt. Gov. Commonwealth of Va., 1987, Class III Supplier of Yr. award Nat. Minority Supplier Devel. Coun., 1987, Regional Minority Mfr. of Yr. award Minority Bus. Devel. Agy., 1988, Patriotic Svc. award U.S. Treasury Dept., 1989, Black Diamond award Operation Push, 1989; recognized by Upscale Mag., 1993. Mem. Armed Forces Communications and Electronics Assn., Tidewater Regional Minority Purchasing Coun., Downtown Norfolk Devel. Corp., Air Traffic Control Assn., Soc. Logistics Engrs., U.S. Navy League, Hampton Roads C. of C. Office: Systems Mgmt Am Corp 5 Koger Ctr Ste 219 Norfolk VA 23502

VALENTINE, KATHRYN LOIS, mortgage company executive; b. Atlanta, Nov. 24, 1961; d. Willie James and Marjorie Ann (McGee) Jones; 1 child, Brandon Paul Valentine. Student, Katherine Gibbs Bus. Sch., N.Y.C., 1980-82. Sec. Damson Oil Co., N.Y.C., 1983-85, Internat. Paper Co., N.Y.C., 1985-87, Am. Express, N.Y.C., 1987-93; resident mgr. Mortgage Co., Atlanta, 1994—. Author: He Walks with Me. Staff mem., campaign supporter Regina Davis State Rep. 53rd Dist., 1996; vol. Hospice.

VALENTINE, RAWSON JAMES, surgeon, educator; b. Pensacola, Fla., July 15, 1954; s. Andrew Jackson and Marjorie Ann (Parks) V.; m. Tracy

Williams, Oct. 2, 1982; children: Elizabeth Atlee, John Randol. BA cum laude, Vanderbilt U., 1976; MD cum laude, Emory U., 1980. Diplomate Am. Bd. Surgery, cert. added qualifications in gen. vascular surgery. Resident in surgery U. Tex. Southwestern Med. Sch., Dallas, 1980-85, vascular fellow, 1985-86, asst. prof. surgery, 1990-93, assoc. prof. surgery, 1993—, dir. grad. med. edn., dept. surgery, 1996—; asst. prof. surgery Uniformed Svcs. U. of Health Scis., Bethesda, Md., 1986-90; head divsn. vascular surgery dept. surgery Naval Hosp., Bethesda, 1986-90; chief vascular surgery sect. VA Med. Ctr., Dallas; mem. attending staff dept. surgery Parkland Meml. Hosp., Dallas, Zale Lipshy U. Hosp., Dallas; lectr. in field. Author: (with G.G. Wind) Anatomic Exposures in Vascular Surgery, 1991; contbr. articles to profl. jours. Lt. M.C., USNR, 1980-86, lt. comdr. 1986-90, comdr., 1990-93. Traveling fellow Royal Coll. Surgeons, 1992, R&D grantee USN, 1989-90, Instl. Rsch. grantee, 1990-91, AHA grantee, 1991-93, 93-95, VA grantee, 1991-96. Fellow ACS; mem. AMA (stroke coun.), Am. Assn. Clin. Anatomists, Internat. Soc. Cardiovascular Surgery, Soc. for Vascular Surgery, So. Assn. Vascular Surgery (budget com. 1993, Pres.'s award 1994), Assn. Acad. Surgeons, Ea. Vascular Soc., Soc. University Surgeons, Chesapeake Vascular Soc., Dallas County Med. Soc., Parkland Surg. Soc. (program chmn. 1993, 94), Peripheral Vascular Surg. Soc. Episcopalian. Office: U Tex Southwestern Med Ctr Dept Surgery 5323 Harry Hines Blvd Dallas TX 75235-7200

VALERI-GOLD, MARIA, reading educator; b. Clinton, Mass., July 10, 1948; d. Frank and Lena (Turini) Valeri; m. Stephen Gold, July 9, 1983. AB, Anna Maria Coll., 1970; MA, Worcester State Coll., 1972; PhD, Fla. State U., 1982. Tchr. Chpt. 1 Worcester Pub. Schs., 1972; tchr. Clinton Pub. Schs., 1978-82, reading specialist, 1982-85; asst. prof. reading Ga. State U., Atlanta, 1978-91, assoc. prof., 1992—. Author: Hurricanes, The Alphabet Book of Feelings; author numerous poems. Mem. Nat. Coun. Tchrs. English, Internat. Reading Assn., Metro Atlanta IRA, MACDRC (v.p.; Tchr. of Yr. award). Home: 10009 Point View Dr Jonesboro GA 30236-7806

VALK, JUDY P., librarian; b. Danville, Ill., May 6, 1937; d. Elmer James and Marjorie Lois (Schwartz) Pickrell; m. Robert Delvan Carlton, Mar. 14, 1958 (div. Jan. 1962); 1 child, Jean Lynn Valk; m. James Melvin Valk, Nov. 28, 1963; children: Anne Marie, Heidi Jo, Eli James. BA in Secondary Edn., Fla. State U., 1959, MLS, 1963. Tchr. Sopchoppy (Fla.) H.S., 1959-60; dir. Clay County Pub. Libr., Green Cove Springs, Fla., 1962-63; children's libr. Sante Fe Regl. Libr., Gainesville, Fla., 1963-64; dir. City island Libr., Daytona Beach, Fla., 1964-66; cataloguer Arthur D. Little, Inc., Cambridge, Mass., 1978-86; automation and tech. svcs. coord. Pollard Meml. Libr., Lowell, Mass., 1986-93, Volusia County Pub. Libr., Daytona Beach, Fla., 1993—. Mem. ALA, Fla. Libr. Assn. Democrat. Episcopalian. Office: Volusia County Pub Libr Libr Ops Ctr 12900 Indian Lake Rd Daytona Beach FL 32124

VALLONE, RALPH, JR., lawyer; b. Phila., Apr. 15, 1947; s. Ralph and Carmen Maria (Perez) V. BA, Yale U., 1966, M. Philosophy (Carnegie fellow), 1966; LLD Harvard U., 1972. Bar: P.R., 1972, U.S. dist. ct. P.R., 1972, U.S. Sup. Ct., 1972. Ptnr. Ralph Vallone Law Firm, San Juan, P.R., 1972—; prof. comml. law Interam. U. Law Sch., P.R., 1972—; chief hearing examiner for Environ. Quality Bd. of P.R. Author: Tiene Usted un Caso de Malapractica Medica, 1985, Second Vision, 1994. Past Trustee Bronx Mus. Arts. Mem. P.R. Inst. Registry Law, Jud. Conf. of P.R. Office: 1411 Ashford Ave 2d Fl Santurce San Juan PR 00907

VALLYATHAN, VAL, pathologist and educator; b. Haripad, Kerala, India, Oct. 14, 1936; came to U.S., 1971; s. Neelakanta Pillal and Subnadra Amma; m. Usha Kumari, Nov. 7, 1965; children: Veena, Sanjay. BSc with honors, U. Baroda, India, 1957, MSc, 1959, PhD, 1963. Teaching assoc. U. Baroda, 1958-59, Govt. of India rsch. fellow, 1959-64, asst. prof., 1964-68, rsch. assoc., 1964-68; NRC postdoctoral fellow U. Guelph, Ont., Can., 1968-71; rsch. assoc. Inst. for Muscle Disease, N.Y.C., 1971-74; rsch. assoc./asst. prof. U. Vt., Burlington, 1974-79; rsch. pathologist/prof. pathology Nat. Inst. for Occupational Safety, W.Va. U., Morgantown, 1979—; panel mem. NIOSH/CAP com. asbestosis, 1981-84, com. on silicosis, 1984-88; chmn. Work Group Silica/Silicosis, Morgantown, 1989-91, Oxygen Radicals Conf., Morgantown, 1993. Editor, co-editor meeting procs. Environ. Health Perspectives, 1993, Silica/Silicosis, 1994; contbr. numerous articles to profl. jours.; patentee in field. Industry team leader Am. Heart Assn., Morgantown, 1992, 93. Recipient U.S. Patent Office award, 1993, Hon. Recognition award Nat. Inst. Occupational Safety, Atlanta, 1990, Spl. Recognition award NIOSH, 1993; fellow Univ. Grants Commn., Govt. of India, 1959-64, Nat. Rsch. Coun. Can., 1968-71. Democrat. Office: Nat Inst Occupational Safety 1095 Willowdale Rd Morgantown WV 26505-2819

VALSARAJ, KALLIAT THAZHATHUVEETIL, chemical engineering educator; b. Tellichery, Kerala, India, Oct. 2, 1957; came to U.S., 1980; s. Mundayat B. Nambiar and Kalliat T. Bhanumathy; m. Nisha Valsaraj, Dec. 24, 1990; 1 child, Viveca. MS, Indian Inst. Tech., Madras, India, 1980; PhD, Vanderbilt U., 1983. Affiliate faculty U. Ark., Fayetteville, 1983-86; sr. rsch. assoc. Hazardous Waste Rsch. Ctr. La. State U., Baton Rouge, 1986-90, asst. prof., 1990-93, assoc. prof., 1994—, dept. chem. engring.; mem. panel directions in separations NSF, 1989-90; cons. Balsam Engr. Cons., Salem, N.H., 1990-91; presenter in field. Author: Elements of Environmental Engineering: Thermodynamics and Kinetics, 1995; contbr. over 70 articles to profl. jours. Grantee Dept. of Def., 1986-89, NSF, 1989, 92-95, EPA, 1989-91, 90-92. Mem. Am. Chem. Soc., Am. Inst. Chem. Engrs., Nat. Geographic Soc., Indian Chem. Soc. Home: 1924 Hobbiton Rd Baton Rouge LA 70810-3414 Office: La State U Dept Chem Engring Baton Rouge LA 70803

VAN AKEN, JOHN HENRY, marine surveyor, engineer, consultant; b. Haarlem, Netherlands, Sept. 26, 1922; came to U.S., 1952; s. Antony and Maria Petronella (Renzen) van A.; m. Hendrika A. Bonneur, Sept. 25, 1947 (div. Feb. 1960); 1 son, Antony Laurens; m. 2d, Helen Jemison, July 17, 1962 (dec. Feb. 1978); m. 3d, Marilyn McDaniel, July 13, 1980. Marine Engr., Acad. Tech. Sci. and Arts of Design, Rotterdam, Holland, 1940. Asst. mgr. repair dept. Wilton-Feyenoord Dockyards, Schiedam, Netherlands, 1945-52; supt. machinery Ala. Dry Dock & Shipbldg. Co., Mobile, 1958-60; project mgr. Kerr-McGee Oil Industries, Oklahoma City, 1954-58, 60-63; insp. George Sharp Co., naval architects, Newport News, Va., 1960; pres. John H. van Aken Co., Inc., marine surveyors and cons., Mobile, 1963—; non-exclusive surveyor Panama Bur. Shipping, Internat. Cargo Gear Bur., Registr. Italiano Navale, Lloyd's Register of Shipping. Named hon. consul gen. Republic of South Africa; decorated comdr. Order Good Hope (South Africa). Mem. Soc. Naval Architects and Marine Engrs., Nat. Assn. Marine Surveyors, Netherlands Soc. Marine Technologists, Am. Boat and Yacht Coun. Republican. Clubs: Athelstan, Fairhope Yacht. Lodge: Mobile Rotary. Home: 188 Rolling Hill Dr Daphne AL 36526-7806 Office: John H van Aken Co Inc PO Box 1738 Daphne AL 36526-1738

VAN ALSTYNE, JUDITH STURGES, English language educator, writer; b. Columbus, Ohio, June 9, 1934; d. Rexford Leland and Wilma Irene (Styan) Van A.; m. Dan C. Duckham (div. 1964); children: Kenton Leland, Jeffrey Clarke. BA, Miami U., Oxford, Ohio, 1956; MEd, Fla. Atlantic U., 1967. Sr. prof. Broward C.C., Ft. Lauderdale, Fla., 1967-88; ret., 1988; spl. asst. for women's affairs Broward C.C., 1972-88, dir. cmty. svcs., 1973-74, dir. cultural affairs, 1974-75; spkr., cons. Malaysian Coll., 1984; ednl. travel group tour guide, 1984-88; v.p., ptnr. Downtown Travel Ctr., Ft. Lauderdale, Fla., 1993—. Author: Write It Right, 1980, Professional and Technical Writing Strategies, 3d edit., 1994; freelance writer travel articles; contbr. articles and poetry to profl. jours. Bd. dirs. Broward C.C. Found., Inc., 1973-89, Broward Friends of the Libr., 1994—, Broward Friends of Miami City Ballet, 1994—; active Sister Cities/People to People, Ft. Lauderdale, 1988—; docent Ft. Lauderdale Mus. Art, 1988—; officer Friends of Mus., Ft. Lauderdale, 1992—. Recipient award of achievement Soc. for Tech. Comm., 1986, award of distinction Fla. Soc. for Tech. Comm., 1986. Mem. English-Speaking Union (bd. dirs. 1984-89). Democrat. Episcopalian. Home: 1688 S Ocean Ln # 265 Fort Lauderdale FL 33316-3346

VAN ALSTYNE, VANCE BROWNELL, arbitration management consultant; b. Rochester, N.Y., Feb. 3, 1924; s. Guy Brownell and Jessie Cary Van A.; B.A., U. Rochester, 1948; LL.B., Blackstone Coll. Law, 1964; m. Jane Kotary, Aug. 12, 1950; children—Cary B., Stacey E. Research asst. Gilbert Assos., Inc., N.Y.C., 1950-56; corp. sec., v.p., dir. R.C. Simpson & Staff, Inc., Newark and Ridgewood, N.J., 1956-74, pres., dir. R.C. Simpson, Inc., Ridgewood, 1975—. Served to 2d lt. USAF, 1943-45. Decorated Air medal. Mem. Am. Mgmt. Assn., Indsl. Relations Research Assn., Am. Arbitration Assn., Internat. Atlantic Salmon Fedn., Swiss-Icelandic Salmon Assns., Trout Unltd. Republican. Home: 6853 N Baltusrol Ln Charlotte NC 28210-7365 Office: RC Simpson Inc 5950 Fairview Rd Ste 604 Charlotte NC 28210-3104

VAN ALSTYNE, WILLIAM WARNER, legal educator; b. Chico, Calif., Feb. 8, 1934; s. Richard Warner and Margaret (Ware) Van A.; BA, U. So. Calif., 1955; JD, Stanford U., 1958; certificate Hague Acad. Internat. Law, 1961; LLD, Wake Forest U., 1976, Coll. William and Mary, 1979. Bar: Calif. 1958. m. Carol Frances Engstrom, Sept. 18, 1955 (div. 1979); children: Marshall, Allyn, Lisa; m. Pamela Gann, Jan. 1980. Dep. atty. gen. Calif., 1958; atty. civil rights div. U.S. Dept. Justice, Washington, 1959; from asst. prof. to prof. Ohio State U. Law Sch., 1959-63; prof. Duke U. Law Sch., Durham, N.C., 1965-73, William R. Perkins prof. law, 1974—. Mem. nat. bd. dirs. ACLU, 1972-76; mem. adv. council Carnegie Found. for Advancement Teaching, 1974-76. With USAF, 1959. Mem. AAUP (nat. pres. 1974-76, gen. counsel 1988-90), AAAS. Author: Interpretations of the First Amendment, 1984, First Amendment Cases and Materials, 2nd edit., 1995, Freedom and Tenure in the Academy, 1993; contbr. articles to profl. jours. Office: Duke U Sch Law Rm 106 Durham NC 27706

VAN ARNAM, MARK STEPHEN, sales executive; b. Erie, Pa., Oct. 27, 1949; s. George Mark and Patricia Anne (Dunne) Van A.; m. Judy Ann Windham, May 25, 1979; children: Leigh, Heather, J.R. Student, Geneseo State U., 1967-68, Daytona Beach Community Coll., 1971-73. EMT, Fla. Dir. ops. Emergency Med. Svcs., Daytona Beach, Fla., 1972-81; v.p. Wheeled Coach Industries, Orlando, Fla., 1982-91; pres. and CEO Am. Emergency Vehicles, Jefferson, N.C., 1991—; bd. dirs. VDS Electronics, Daytona Beach; mem. risk adv. bd. Azstar Casualty Co., Scottsdale, Ariz., 1989-92; lectr. U. Cen. Fla., 1987, Fleet Mgmt., 1989, EMS Safety, Cleve., 1991; instr. Tex. Tech U., 1991. Mem. Indsl. Devel. Bd., Orlando, 1984-86. With USN, 1967-71, Vietnam. Mem. Nat. Ambulance Mfrs. Assn. (pres. 1987-90), Am. Ambulance Assn., Calif. Ambulance Assn., Internat. Assn. Fire Chiefs (task force), Profl. Car Soc. Methodist. Office: Am Emergency Vehicles PO Box 1059 Jefferson NC 28640-1059

VAN ARSDALE, LEE ARNOLD, career military officer; b. Akron, Ohio, Oct. 6, 1952; s. Frank William and Mary Maxine (Hipsher) Van A.; m. Marilee Jane Schalk, Dec. 30, 1977; children: Lucas Franklin, Nathan Scott, Paul Matthew. BS, U.S. Mil. Acad., 1974; MS, U. Colo., 1994. Commd. U.S. Army, 1974; platoon leader 101st Airborne Divsn., Ft. Campbell, Ky., 1974-77; detachment cmdr. 10th Spl. Forces Group, Ft. Devens, Mass., 1977-79; pres. High Country Enterprises, Inc., Colorado Springs, 1980-82; co. cmdr. 172d Light Infantry Brigade, Ft. Richardson, Alaska, 1983-85; cmdr. U.S. Spl. Ops. Command, Fort Bragg, N.C., 1985—. Leader Boy Scouts Am., Fayetteville, 1991. Decorated silver star U.S. Army, 1995, purple heart, 1995. Mem. MENSA, Elks Club. Home: 525 E Hedgelawn Way Southern Pines NC 28387

VAN ARSDALE, STEPHANIE KAY LORENZ, cardiovascular clinical specialist, nursing educator, researcher; b. Butte, Mont., June 20, 1952; d. Hubert Nelson and Pauline Anna (Tebo) Lorenz; m. Roy Burbank Van Arsdale, June 18, 1978; children: Christopher, Erica. Diploma, St. Johns McNamara, Sch. Nursing, 1975; BSN cum laude, U. Utah, 1978, MSN, 1979; EdD, U. Ark., 1993. RN, Ark.; cert. ACLS instr., Am. Heart Assn.; cert. BLS instr.-trainer, Am. Heart Assn. Staff nurse cardiovascular surg. ICU Presbyn. Hosp. Ctr., Albuquerque, 1975-76; staff nurse surg. ICU and CCU U. Utah Med. Ctr., Salt Lake City, 1976-78; clin. specialist residency LDS Hosp., Salt Lake City, 1979; asst. prof. dept. Baccalaureate Nursing Ea. Ky. U., Richmond, 1980-84; staff nurse critical care unit Pattie A. Clay Hosp., Richmond, 1981-83; med. clinician Washington Regional Med. Ctr., Fayetteville, Ark., 1985; cardiovascular clin. specialist VA Med. Ctr., Fayetteville, 1985-93; assoc. prof. U. Memphis, 1993-96; asst. prof. U. Ark. for Med. Scis., Little Rock, 1996—; CPR instr. in cmty., Fayetteville and Richmond, 1980-93; mem. adj. faculty div. nursing Northeastern State U., Tahlequah, Okla., 1986-93, U. Ark., Fayetteville, 1989-93; mem. adj. clin. faculty U. Ark. for Med. Scis. Coll. Nursing, Little Rock, 1988-93; charter mem., spkr. N.W. Ark. Critical Care Consortium, Area Health Edn. Ctr., Fayetteville, 1989-93; presenter in field. Contbr. articles to profl. jours. Coord., vol. Home Meals Delivery Program, Richmond, Ky., 1981-84; adminstrv. bd., Sunday sch. tchr., sec. adult forum Ctrl. United Meth. Ch., Fayetteville, 1986-87; troop leader Girl Scouts Am. NOARK Coun., Fayetteville, 1987-90; sound sys. operator Christ United Meth. Ch., 1993—. Recipient Nurse of Yr. award for excellence in nursing practice Dist. 9, Ark. State Nurses Assn., 1987; grantee Ctrl. U.S. Earthquake Consortium, 1993, U.S. Geologic Survey, 1994, Miss. Emergency Mgmt. Agy., 1996. Mem. ANA (v.p. Dist. 9 1985-86, pres. 1987-88, mem. image com. 1990-93, chmn. program com. 1986-87, state 2d v.p. 1988-90, clin. nurse specialist coun. 1991—), AACN (CCRN; bd. dirs., chpt. sec. program com. 1994—), Nat. League for Nursing (mem. nominating com. Ky. 1984-85), Sigma Theta Tau. Methodist. Home: 8872 Farmoor Rd Germantown TN 38139-6517 Office: U Ark for Med Scis Coll Nursing Slot 529 4301 W Markham St Little Rock AR 72205-7199

VANARSDALE, WILLIAM EUGENE, chemist, researcher; b. Marshall, Mo., Oct. 5, 1949; s. Johnson William and Betty (Hilton) VanA.; children: Rachel Kyle, Sarah Windsor, Matthew William. AB in Chemistry, U. Mo., St. Louis, 1978; PhD in Organic Chemistry, U. Mo., 1983. NSF postdoctoral fellow Ind. U., Bloomington, 1983-84; vis. asst. prof. chemistry U. Houston-Cen. Campus, 1984-85; asst. prof. chemistry U. Houston-Clear Lake, 1985-89; process chemist, product steward Rohm & Haas Tex., Inc., Deer Park, 1989—; cons. Fina Oil & Chem., Houston, 1987—, Dixie Chem. Co., Houston, 1987-89, Ethyl Corp., Houston, 1989—. Contbr. articles to profl. jours. Vol. judge Houston Regional Sci. Fair, 1986—, Pasadena (Tex.) High Sch. Sci. Fair, 1991, Clear Creek Mid. Sch. Sci. Fair, League City, Tex., 1986-88; vol. Deer Park C. of C., 1990. Monsanto Found. Rsch. fellow, 1981. Mem. AAAS, Am. Chem. Soc. Office: Rohm & Haas Tex Inc PO Box 672 Deer Park TX 77536-0672

VAN ASSENDELFT, ONNO WILLEM, hematologist; b. Brummen, The Netherlands, Aug. 23, 1932; came to U.S. 1976; s. Frederik and Anna Maria (Veenbaas) Van A.; m. Theodora Henriette Teunissen, July 15, 1960; children: Anne C.E., Frederik H.B., Albert H.P., Diederik A.A., Catharina E.E. MD, U. Groningen, 1959, PhD, 1970. Rsch. scientist, assoc. prof. Lab. Regulatory Physiology, Groningen, 1961-76; sec., dean Groningen Med. Sch., 1973-75; supervisory med. rsch. officer Ctrs. for Disease Control and Prevention, Atlanta, 1976—; cons. FDA, 1979—; bd. secretariat Internat. Coun. Standardization in Hematology, 1978—, chmn. secretariat, 1994—; bd., exec. com. Nat. Comm. Clin. Lab. Stds., Villanova, Pa., 1982-94, pres., 1990-92; chmn. U.S. delegation to ISO/TC 212 on clin. lab. testing and in vitro diagnostic test sys., 1995—. Author: Spectrophotometry of Hemoglobin Derivatives, 1970; editl. bd. ECRI Healthcare Product Comparison System, Lab. Hematology; contbr. articles to profl. jours., chpts. to books. Capt. Royal Netherlands Army, 1959-61. Recipient Sec. Group award USPHS, 1986, Bronze plaque Ministry of Health, Chile, 1983, Russel J. Eilers award Nat. Com. for Clin. Lab. Stds., Villanova, 1988, Spl. award Nat. Hemophilia Found., 1992. Mem. AAAS, Am. Soc. Hematology, Internat. Soc. Lab. Hematology, N.Y. Acad. Scis. Office: Ctrs Disease Control Prevention 1600 Clifton Rd NE Atlanta GA 30329-4018

VAN AUKEN, ROBERT DANFORTH, business administration educator, management consultant; b. Chgo., Oct. 31, 1915; s. Howard Robert and Mable (Hanlon) Van A.; student Guilford Coll., 1933-35, Gen. Motors Inst. Tech., 1936-38, U. Pitts., 1953-54; BS, U. Dayton, 1958; MA, U. Okla., 1967; m. Ruth Bowen Cutler, Nov. 24, 1939 (dec.); children: Robert Hanlon, Joseph Marshall, David Danforth, Howard Evans, Jonathan Lewis; m. Vernia Maurine Long, July 9, 1993. Commd. aviation cadet U.S. Air Force, 1938; advanced through grades to lt. col., 1961; fighter pilot, squadron comdr., ops. officer, 1939-45; asst. air attaché, Paris, 1946-49; staff officer, Pentagon 1950-53; procurement-prodn. staff officer Wright-Patterson AFB, 1954-58, Tinker AFB, 1958-60, Holloman AFB, 1960-61, ret., 1961; personnel officer U. Okla., Norman, 1962-65, mem. faculty, 1965—, asst. prof. mgmt., 1979-83, prof. emeritus bus. adminstrn., 1983—, dir. student programs and career devel. Coll. Bus. Adminstrn., 1975-79; cons. seminars mgmt. amd compensation, 1963—; adj. instr. Park Coll., 1991—; instr. Park Coll., 1991—; cattle rancher, 1970—; owner VA Farms. Mem. Oklahomans for Improvement in Nursing Care Homes; Decorated Silver Star, Purple Heart. Mem. NRA, Newcomen Soc. U.S., Oklahoma City Human Resources Assn., Acad. Mgmt., Internat. Platform Assn., Nat. Cattlemen's Beef Assn., Okla. Cattlemans Assn., Okla. Alliance Aging, Air Force Assn., Am. Legion, (life mem.), Ret. Officers Assn., Mil. Order of World Wars, (life. mem.), Order of Deadalians, 5th Air Force Meml. Found., 49th Fighter Group Assn., 31st Fighter Officers Assn., (life mem.), Disabled Am. Vets., Masons, Beta Gamma Sigma, Delta Sigma Pi. Republican. Contbr. monographs in field. Home: 420 S Highland Rd Oklahoma City OK 73110-2138 Office: U Okla 307 W Brooks St Norman OK 73069-8822

VANBEBBER, MICHAEL CRAIG, public relations executive; b. Bowie, Tex., Oct. 5, 1961; s. Ernest William and Reta Ann (Yerby) V.; m. Cheryl Lynn Harbert, Jan. 7, 1989; children: Austin Michael, Hope Mackenzie. BS in Pub. Rels., U. North Tex., 1985. Coord. pub. rels. HyperGraphics Corp., Denton, Tex., 1985-87; account exec. pub. rels. C. Pharr & Co., Dallas, 1987-89; mgr. corp. rels. UTA Robotics Inst., Ft. Worth, 1989-92; mgr. corp. comm. Lockheed Martin Vought Sys., Dallas, 1992—; mem. adv. coun. Automation and Robotics Rsch. Inst., Ft. Worth, 1989-92. Vol. Am. Diabetes Assn., Dallas, 1989-91; tchr. youth dept. First Bapt. Ch., Euless, Tex., 1993-96, tchr. adult divsn., 1996—. Named Outstanding Young Men of Am., 1989, 92. Mem. Internat. Assn. Bus. Communicators, Pub. Rels. Soc. Am., Tex. Pub. Rels. Assn. Home: 7420 Steward Ln North Richland Hills TX 76180 Office: Lockheed Martin Vought Sys 1701 W Marshall PT-42 Grand Prairie TX 75051

VAN BERKEL, GARY JOSEPH, research scientist; b. Appleton, Wis., Nov. 4, 1959; s. Raymond Lawrence and Dorthy Jane (Schermitzler) Van B. BA magna cum laude, Lawrence U., Appleton, Wis., 1982; MS in Analyt. Chemistry, Wash. State U., 1984, PhD in Analyt. Chemistry, 1987. Teaching asst. Lawrence U., 1981, student rsch. asst., 1981-82; rsch. asst. Wash. State U., Pullman, 1983-87; postdoctoral assoc. Oak Ridge (Tenn.) Nat. Lab., 1987-89, staff rsch. scientist, 1989—; lectr. and presenter in field. Contbr. numerous articles to profl. jours. Mem. Am. Chem. Soc., Am. Soc. Mass Spectrometry. Home: 116 Cayuga Ln Clinton TN 37716-6073 Office: Oak Rige Nat Lab PO Box 2008 Oak Ridge TN 37831-2008

VANBIESBROUCK, JOHN, professional hockey player; b. Detroit, Sept. 4, 1963; m. Rosalinde V. With N.Y. Rangers, 1981-93, Vancouver Canucks, 1993, Florida Panthers, 1993—; mem. NHL All-Star team, 1985-86; player NHL All-Star game, 1994. Recipient Vezina Trophy (NHL outstanding goaltender), 1985, 86, (with Ron Scott) Terry Sawchuk trophy, 1983-89, (with Marc D'Amour) F.W. Dinty Moore trophy, (with D. Bruce Affleck) Tommy Ivan trophy, 1983-84; named NHL All-Star, 1985-86, Sporting News NHL All-Star, 1985-86, 93-94. Office: Florida Panthers 100 NE 3rd Ave Fl 10 Fort Lauderdale FL 33301-1155*

VAN BULCK, HENDRIKUS EUGENIUS, accountant; b. Beek en Donk, The Netherlands, Dec. 13, 1950; came to U.S., 1972; s. Marcellus Maria and Josephina Theodora (Koelman) Van B.; m. Margaret West, Aug. 7, 1976; children: Marcel Allen, Sydney Josette. Grad., Nijenrode, The Netherlands, 1972; MBA, U. Ga., 1974, PhD in Bus. Adminstrn., 1979. CPA, S.C. Instr. U. S.C., Sumter, 1975-77; asst. prof. Clemson (S.C.) U., 1977-80; chmn. dept., assoc. prof. St. Andrew's Presbyn. Coll., Laurinburg, N.C., 1980-83; staff acct. L. Allen West, CPA, Sumter, 1983-84; ptnr. West & Van Bulck, CPAs, Sumter, 1984-88, Van Bulck & Co., Sumter, 1989—; part time instr. U. S.C., Sumter, 1983-85; cons. in field. Contbr. articles to profl. jours. Chmn. Make-a-Wish Found., Midlands, S.C., 1983-90. Recipient Mktg. award Netherlands Ctr. of Dirs., 1972. Mem. AICPA, Sumter Estate Planning Coun., S.C. Assn. CPAs, Nat. Assn. Estate Planning Couns., Physicians Viewpoint Network, Habitat for Humanity, Kiwanis (pres. Sumter chpt. 1996—), Beta Gamma Sigma. Presbyterian. Home: 234 Haynsworth PO Box 1327 Sumter SC 29151-1327 Office: Van Bulck & Co CPAs 15 Broad St Sumter SC 29150-4224

VAN BURKLEO, BILL BEN, osteopath, emergency physician; b. Tulsa, Nov. 21, 1942; s. Walter Russell and Joan Vera (Brimm) Van B.; m. Paula Mae Brinkley, Mar. 5, 1965 (div. Feb. 1974); children: Baron, Kristy and Kelly (twins). BS, U. Tulsa, 1965; DO, Okla. State U., 1981. Diplomate Nat. Bd. Osteo. Examiners. Defensive back, quarterback, punter Can. Football League, Ottawa, Calgary, 1966-73; dir. sports and spl. events Tulsa Cable TV, 1974-78; rotating intern Corpus Christi (Tex.) Osteo. Hosp., 1981-82; family physician Antlers (Okla.) Med. Clinic, 1982-90, Colbert (Okla.) Med. Clinic, 1989-90; dir. dept. emergency Valley View Regional Hosp., Ada, Okla., 1990-94; regional med. dir. Okla., N.Mex., Ariz., So. Calif. Okla. Spectrum Emergency Care, Inc., 1994—; mem. clin. faculty Coll. Osteo. Medicine, Okla. State U. Author newspaper column, several computer programs. Mem. Rep. Senatorial Inner Ctr., Washington, 1990-91 (medal of Freedom 1994); affiliate faculty Am. Heart Assn. Named to Alltime Greats of Okla., Jim Thorpe Award Com., 1975. Fellow Assn. Emergency Physicians; mem. Am. Osteo. Assn., Am. Coll. Gen. Practitioners, Okla. Osteo. Assn., S.W. Okla. Osteo. Assn. (pres. 1990-91). Home: PO Box 2740 Ada OK 74821-2740

VANCE, CHARLES RANDALL, minister; b. Huntington, W.Va., May 28, 1953; s. Tony and Rinda Gertrude (Caserta) V.; m. Patricia Ann Armstrong, Oct. 29, 1971; children: Charles Stephen, Cynthia Denise. DD (hon.), Internat. Sem., Plymouth, Fla., 1991. Lic. minister Church of God, 1990; ordained to ministry Spirit of Victory Ministries, 1993. Min. music Spirit of Victory, Barboursville, W.Va., 1983-86, asst. pastor, 1986-90, assoc. pastor, 1990-94; pastor Spirit of Victory, Barboursville, 1994—; pres. Spirit of Victory Ministries, Barboursville, 1986—. Author: Retaining What You Receive, 1994; host, exec. prodr.: Spirit of Victory Radio and Television, Barboursville, 1986—. Republican. Home: 4756 Route 10 Barboursville WV 25504-9650 Office: Spirit of Victory 5800 Us Route 60 E Barboursville WV 25504-1032

VANCE, CYNTHIA LYNN, psychology educator; b. Norwalk, Calif., Mar. 31, 1960; d. Dennis Keith and Donna Kay (Harryman) V. BS, U. Oreg., 1982; MS, U. Wis., Milw., 1987, PhD, 1991. Teaching asst. U. Wis., Milw., 1983-89; computer graphics mgr. Montgomery Media, Inc., Milw., 1987-92; asst. prof. Cardinal Stritch Coll., Milw., 1992-93, Piedmont Coll., Demorest, Ga., 1993—. Contbr. articles to profl. jours. Vol. Dunwoody (Ga.)-DeKalb Kiwanis Club, 1993—. Mem. AAUP, APA, Assn. Women in Psychology, S.E. Psychol. Assn., Am. Psychol. Soc., Am. Assn. Higher Edn. Office: Piedmont Coll PO Box 10 Demorest GA 30535-0010

VANCE, DAMA LEE, obstetrical/gynecological nurse, ultrasound sonographer; b. Beckley, W.Va., Mar. 13, 1967; d. Peter Lee, Sr. and Nancy Lee (Calfee) H. BSN, W.Va. U., 1989. RN, W.Va. Office nurse Dr. John L Hahn, Petersburg, W.Va. Mem. Sigma Theta Tau (Alpha Rho chpt.). Home: PO Box 144 Wardensville WV 26851-0144

VANCE, RALPH BROOKS, oncologist and educator; b. Jackson, Miss., Dec. 4, 1945; s. Brooks C. and Chrystine G. (Gober) V.; m. Mary Douglas Allen, June 18, 1979; children: Brooks, Barrett. BA in Biology and German, U. Miss., 1968, MD, 1972. Asst. prof. medicine U. Miss., Jackson, 1978-86, assoc. prof. medicine, 1986-93, prof. medicine, 1993—; chief of staff U. Miss. Hosp. and Clinics, Jackson, 1989-90; pres. faculty senate Univ. Med. Ctr., Jackson, 1986-87, univ. clin. assoc., pres., 1987-89. Author (with others) Development in Molecular Virology: Herpes Virus DNA, 1982; contbr. numerous articles and abstracts to profl. jours. Bd dirs. Am. Cancer Soc., Atlanta, nat. bd. dirs., exec. com.; bd. dirs. ARC, Jackson; med. adv. bd. Blue Cross/Blue Shield, Jackson, 1989-92. Named to Hall of Fame, U. Miss., 1968. Mem. Am. Assn. for Cancer Edn., Am. Fedn. for Clin. Rsch., Am. Soc. Clin. Oncology, Am. Assn. for Cancer Rsch., Miss. Acad. Scis., S.W. Oncology Group, Sigma Xi. Episcopalian. Office: Univ of Miss Sch Medicine 2500 N State St Jackson MS 39216-4500

VANCE, ROBERT DALE, philosophy educator, sculptor; b. Dayton, Ohio, Jan. 26, 1941; s. B. Bernarr and Erma Margene (Euverard) V.; m. Terry Goldman, June 4, 1942; children: Aaron Reed, Brandon Jeremy. BA with honors, Kenyon Coll., 1962; MFA, U. N.C., 1982; PhD, Duke U., 1966. Asst. lectr. U. Leeds, Eng., 1964-65; asst. prof. U. N.C., Chapel Hill, 1966—; dir. undergrad. studies U. N.C., 1968-87, 91-95, dir. honors program, 1969-87, 91-95, dir. Worth award competition, 1977-87, 91-95, dir. undergrad. logic program, 1966-68. Contbr. articles to profl. jours.; artist various sculptures. Mem. Internat. Sculpture Ctr., Am. Soc. Aesthetics, N.C. Art Soc., Tri-State Sculptors' Guild, Durham Art Guild. Home: 1419 Gray Bluff Tr Chapel Hill NC 27514 Office: Univ NC Dept Philosophy CB # 3125 Caldwell Hall Chapel Hill NC 27514

VANCE, ROBERT PATRICK, lawyer; b. Birmingham, Ala., Feb. 12, 1948; s. James Robert and Lucy Juanita (McMath) V.; m. Sarah Elizabeth Savoia, June 11, 1971; 1 son, Robert Patrick, Jr. B.A. with honors, La. State U., 1970, J.D., 1975. Bar: La. 1975, U.S. Dist. Ct. (ea. dist.) La. 1975, U.S. Dist. Ct. (mid. dist.) La. 1978, U.S. Dist. Ct. (we. dist.) La. 1979, U.S. Ct. Appeals (5th cir.) 1975, U.S. Ct. Appeals (11th cir.) 1981, U.S. Supreme Ct. 1981. Assoc. Jones, Walker, Waechter, Poitevent, Carrere & Denegre, New Orleans, 1975-80, ptnr., 1980—, exec. com. 1991-95, mng. ptnr., 1994-95. Contbr. La. Law Rev.; author, editor: Bankruptcy Rules: Parts I, II, VII, VIII and IX, 1983; Overview of the Bankruptcy Code and the Court, 1983. Co-author: Bankruptcy-Current Developments, 1983, Current Developments in Commercial Law, 1984, Basic Bankruptcy of Louisiana, 1989, Fundamentals of Bankruptcy Law & Procedure in La., 1993; contbr. articles to profl. jours. Fellow Am. Coll. Bankruptcy, Nat. Bankruptcy Conf.; mem. ABA (chair bankruptcy litigation com.), Am. Law Inst., Am. Bankruptcy Inst., Fed. Bar Assn. (mem. bankruptcy law com., polit. campaign and election law com., editorial bd. Bankruptcy Briefs), La. State Bar Assn. (pres. consumer and bankruptcy law sect., chmn. CLE com.), New Orleans Bar Assn., La. Bankers Assn. (chmn. bank counsel com. 1992-93), Pi Sigma Alpha, Phi Beta Kappa (Faculty Group award), Phi Kappa Phi. Democrat. Roman Catholic. Home: 1821 State St New Orleans LA 70118-6219 Office: Jones Walker Waechter Poitevent Carrere & Denegre 201 Saint Charles Ave New Orleans LA 70170-1000

VANCE, VINCE, entertainer/bandleader, composer; b. Oakland, Calif., Jan. 31, 1957; s. Andrew John and Melvina Annie Franichevich; m. Debora Diane Barnes Stone, 1974 (dec. Mar. 1987); children: christopher Andrew, Steven Michael. BA in English/Music, Southeastern La. U., 1969. Bandleader/entertainer Vince Vance & The Valiants, New Orleans, 1971-79, Dallas, 1980—; CEO Valiant Records, Dallas, 1980—; pres., CEO Brightstone Pub., Dallas, 1985—. Author: You Made Me Love Me, 1984, The Vince Vance Rock and Roll Reader, 1996; composer: (musical album) All I Want for Christmas Is You, 1989, Don't Touch My Hair, 1996. Team capt. Dem. Nat. Com., Washington, 1992; spokesperson Tex. Narcotics Officers Assn., Dallas, 1990-92; trustee The Vince Vance Scholarship Fund, 1995-96. Named Keyboardist of the Yr., Dallas Observer Music Awards, 1988; named to Tex. Tornado Keyboard Hall of Fame, Buddy Mag., 1983; recipient Critics Choice Best Pop Band award Boddy Music Awards, 1982. Mem. Internat. Entertainment Buyers Assn., Internat. Assn. of Fairs and Exhbns., The Spl. Event Assn. Democrat. Roman Catholic. Office: PO Box 180099 Dallas TX 75218-0099

VAN CLEAVE, KIRSTIN DEAN (KIT VAN CLEAVE), martial arts educator, writer, educator, publishing executive; b. Ft. Worth, Jan. 9, 1940; d. Henry Shibley and Lola Kathryn (Wimberly) van C. BA in Journalism, North Tex. State U., 1961; MA in English, U. Houston, 1972; DL in English, London Inst., 1973. Cert. self-defense instr. Tex. Commn. Law Enforcement Officer Standards and Edn., 1992, Nat. Women's Martial Arts Fedn., 1994. Reporter Associated Gen. Contractors News Svc., Houston, 1961-62; dir. pub. rels. Diboll Advt. Agy., Tex., 1963-64; writer Goodwin, Dannenbaum, Littman and Wingfield Advt. Agy., Houston, 1964-65; reporter Houston Tribune, 1965-68; copywriter sales promotion dept. Gulf Pub. Co., 1968-70; Houston editor, then mng. editor Metrobeat, Dallas, 1970; editor publs., dir. pub. rels., press rep. Baroid div. NL Industries, Inc., Houston, 1973-74; presdl. speechwriter Gulf Oil Co., 1974-76; CEO Inner-View Pub. Co., Houston, 1980-88; instr. self-def. Houston Area Women's Ctr., 1989-94, Harris County Sheriff's Dept., 1991-94; guest lectr. Univ. Coll., Cork, Ireland, 1994-95; chief instr. Kingwood Karate Chayon-Ryo, 1995—; past mem. faculty U. Houston, Coll. of Mainland, Texas City, Tex., St. Agnes Acad., Houston. Author: They Still Do, 1973, Folklore of Texas Cultures, 1975, (poetry) Day of Love (set into a song cycle which was nominated for Pulitzer prize in Mus. Composition), 1978, Amourette, 1979, Laurels, 1980; librettist: Four Songs (composer Thomas Pasatieri), 1980; editor Inner-View mag., Houston; columnist: Houston Home & Garden, Houston Guide, Scene mag., In Houston, Billboard; contbr. articles to mags. Regional coord. South and S.W. region, leader Houston chpt. Guardian Angels, 1986-90. Recipient Mayor's Vol. award City of Houston, 1988, Excellence in Journalism award Houston Exec. Adv. Council, 1986, 1st Place award Harris County Med. Soc., 1986, Clean Houston Pub. Service award, 1986-87, Presdl. Sports award, 1994; named one of fifty Most Interesting Houstonians, City Mag., 1985, Goodwill Amb. City of Houston, 1994. Mem. S.W. C. of C., Houston C. of C., AAUP, Music Critics Assn., Internat. Assn. Bus. Communicators, Am. Soc. Authors and Journalists, World Tae Kwon Do Fedn., Cha Yon Ryu Black Belt Assn., Nat. Women's Martial Arts Fedn., Pacific Assn. Women Martial Artists, Am.-Ireland Martial Arts Assn. (pres. 1992—). Home: PO Box 66127 Houston TX 77266-6127

VAN CLEVE, RUTH GILL, retired lawyer, government official; b. Mpls., July 28, 1925; d. Raymond S. and Ruth (Sevon) Gill; m. Harry R. Van Cleve, Jr., May 16, 1952; children: John Gill, Elizabeth Webster, David Hamilton Livingston. Student, U. Minn., 1943; A.B. magna cum laude, Mt. Holyoke Coll., 1946, LL.D., 1976; LL.B., Yale, 1950. Bar: D.C. 1950, Minn. 1950. Intern Nat. Inst. Pub. Affairs, 1946-47; atty. Dept. Interior, 1950-54, asst. solicitor, 1954-64; dir. Office Territorial Affairs, 1964-69, 1977-80, dep. asst. sec., 1980-81, acting asst. sec., 1993; atty. Solicitor's Office, 1981-93; atty. FPC, 1969-75, asst. gen. counsel, 1975-77. Author: The Office of Territorial Affairs, 1974, The Application of Federal Laws to the Territories, 1993. Recipient Fed. Woman's award, 1966, Disting. Service award Dept. Interior, 1968, Presdl. Rank award, Pres. U.S., 1989. Mem. Phi Beta Kappa. Unitarian. Home: 4400 Emory St Alexandria VA 22312-1321

VAN CURA, BARRY JACK, ballet dancer, choreographer; b. Berwyn, Ill., Nov. 13, 1948; s. John J. and Eleanor (Knize) Van C.; m. Anna Baker Miller, Aug. 18, 1979; children—Anamarie, Anthony, Victoria. B.F.A., N.C. Sch. Arts, Winston-Salem. Trainee, Rebeccah Harkness Found., 1972; dancer, soloist Chgo. Ballet and Lyric Opera, 1970-74, Milw. Ballet, 1974-75; dir., choreographer Ballet Midwest, Chgo., 1977-84; dir. Nat. Acad. of Dance, Champaign, Ill., 1979-81; dir., choreographer Chattanooga Ballet, 1984—; mem. part-time faculty U. Ill., Champaign, 1980-82; resident choreographer theatre dept., Youngstown U., Ohio, 1984-85; choreographer Allegheny Coll., Meadville, Pa. 1984-85; cons. on dance Warren Dance Ctr., Ohio, 1983-84. Choreographer; Firebird/Gemstones, 1984, Liebeslieder/Interlude, 1983, Seasons/Canon/Congregation, 1979; Tribute to the Beatles, 1980. Founder Friends of Ballet Midwest, Youngstown, 1982, Chattanooga Ballet Guild, 1984; Ohio Arts Council grantee, 1983, 84. Mem. Assn. Ohio Dance Co. (trustee 1983-85), Nat. Assn. Regional Ballet, Southeastern Regional Ballet Assn. Buddhist. Office: Chattanooga Ballet PO Box 6175 Chattanooga TN 37401-6175

VANCURA, STEPHEN JOSEPH, radiologist; b. Norton, Kans., June 26, 1951; s. Cyril William J. and Clara Mae (Ruthstrom) V.; BA in Chemistry magna cum laude, Kans. State U., 1972; MD, Kans. U., 1976; m. Lydia Acker, Dec. 10, 1976. Intern in medicine Letterman Army Med. Center, San Francisco, 1976-77, resident in radiology, 1977-80; practice medicine specializing in radiology, 1980—; chief dept. radiology Darnall Army Hosp., Ft. Hood, Tex., 1980-82; pvt. practice diagnostic radiology, 1982—; chief of staff Metroplex Hosp., 1985-86, 88-90. Served to maj. M.C., U.S. Army, 1976-82 Recipient Ollie O. Mustala award in clin. pharmacology Kans. U. Med. Center, 1974; A. Morris Ginsberg award in phys. diagnosis Kans. U. Med. Center, 1975; Resident Tchr. of Yr. award Letterman Army Med. Center, 1979; Staff Tchr. of Yr. award Darnall Army Hosp., 1982. Trembly Meml. scholar, 1972. Diplomate Am. Bd. Radiology. Mem. Am. Coll. Radiology, Radiologic Soc. N. Am., AMA, Tex. Med. Assn., Tex. Radiol. Soc., Ind. Med. Practitioners Assn. Ctrl. Tex. (pres.), Clinical Magnetic Resonance Soc., Sigma Xi, Alpha Chi Sigma, Alpha Omega Alpha. Home: 3302 Walnut Cir Harker Heights TX 76542 Office: Metroplex Hosp Dept Radiology 2201 Clear Creek Rd Killeen TX 76548-4110

VAN DAALEN, JAMES MICHAEL, thoracic surgeon; b. Grand Rapids, May 22, 1956; s. Jay Meyer and Jean Mary (Noorderwier) Van D.; m. Cheryl Ann Cook, Apr. 23, 1985; 1 child, Rachel Ann. BS, Calvin Coll., 1978; MD, U. Chgo., 1982. Diplomate Am. Bd. Thoracic Surgery, Am. Bd. Surgery. Pvt. practive Louisville, 1990—; clin. asst. prof. U. Louisville, Ky., 1990—. Presbyterian. Home: 3707 Trail Ridge Rd Louisville KY 40241-6222 Office: 201 Abraham Flexner Way Louisville KY 40202-1817

VANDEL, DIANA GEIS, management consultant; b. San Antonio, Apr. 2, 1947; d. John George and Elma Ruth (Triplett) Geis; m. Jerry Dean Vandel, Apr. 17, 1976; 1 child, Jeremy Kyle. MusB, U. Tex., 1969. Cert. tchr., Tex.; lic. nursing home adminstr., Tex. Tchr. music Zilker Elem. Pub. Sch., Austin, Tex., 1969-70, Isely Sch., Austin, 1986; asst. adminstr. Hillside Manor Nursing Home, Inc., San Antonio, 1970-76, cons. to nursing homes, 1976-78, asst. adminstr., 1978-79, cons. adminstr., 1979-91, adminstr., 1988; mgmt. cons. Promoting Excellence Consultation, Austin, 1991-95, Winning Solutions, Austin, 1995—; owner, facilitator creative music and relaxation in motion classes, workshops and retreats, San Antonio, 1982-84; fine arts facilitator Cedar Creek Elem. Sch., Austin, 1988-91; seminar leader Movement Spiritual Inner Awareness, Austin, 1986—, min., 1989—. Austin rep. Peace Theol. Sem., L.A., 1988-93; mem. exec. bd. Cedar Creek Booster Club, 1989-91. Mem. ASTD (Austin chpt.), NAFE, Inst. Individual and World Peace, Nat. Spkrs. Assn.-Heart of Tex., Austin Internat. Soc. for Performance Improvement (v.p. mem.), S.W. Facilitators' Network. Home: 916 Terrace Mountain Dr Austin TX 78746-2732 Office: Winning Solutions 916 Calithea Austin TX 78746-2732

VANDERBEEK, ANN RANDLE, elementary education educator; b. Tupelo, Miss., Feb. 6, 1947; d. Hugh Enoch and Dimple Frances (Conway) Randle; m. James V. Hemphill III, June 3, 1968 (div. 1984); children: James V. IV, Angie Randle; m. Glen Ray Vanderbeek, Aug. 9, 1986. BS, Miss. State U., 1969, MEd, 1970, EdS, 1977. Cert. tchr., Ga. Elem. tchr. Starkville (Miss.) Pub. Schs., 1969-84, Gwinnett County (Ga.) Schs., 1984-88; adj. prof. Kennesaw State U., Marietta, Ga., 1988-89, dir. tchr. resource activity ctr., 1989-91; 5th grade tchr. Anniston Elem. Sch., Lithonia, Ga., 1991-95; extension tchr. Troup County Schs., LaGrange, Ga., 1995—; mem. SACS accreditation com. Paulding County Schs., Dallas, Ga., 1994-95; mem. tchr. adv. coun. Troup County Schs., 1995—; vis. prof. LaGrange Coll., 1996. Sec.-treas. Brookwood Orch. Orgn., Snellville, Ga., 1988-89; participant Leadership Kennesaw, 1990. Mem. ASCD, Ga. Assn. Tchr. Educators (state sec. 1988-90), Profl. Assn. Ga. Educators, Phi Delta Kappa (spl. projects chair 1988), Kappa Delta Pi.

VANDERBURG, PAUL STACEY, insurance executive, consultant; b. Detroit, Apr. 13, 1941; s. Harold Stacey and Alice Bertha (Lyle) V. Cert. in plastics tech., Oakland U., 1966; AS in Bus., C.S. Mott Community Coll., 1971; Casualty Claims Law Assoc., Am. Ednl. Inst., 1986; BA in Bus. Adminstrn. and Mgmt., Columbia Pacific U., 1990; cert. in Human Resource Devel., U. South Fla., 1992; fraud claims law assoc., Am. Ednl. Inst., 1995. Lic. ins. adjuster, Mich., Fla. Ins. field claims adjuster Underwriters Adjusting Co., Pontiac, Mich., 1972-76; pres., chief exec. officer Sun Cycle, Inc., Drayton Plains, Mich., 1975-77; sr. ins. claims adjuster Kemper Ins. Group, Tampa, Fla., 1979-80; ins. field claims adjuster Auto-Owners Ins. Co., Lakeland, Fla., 1981-82; sr. recovery specialist CIGNA Corp., Tampa, 1984-85; ins. field claims adjuster Seaboard Adjustment Bur., Lakeland, 1985-87; sr. field claims ins. adjuster Hallmark Ins. Adjusters, Clearwater, Fla., 1987-88; ind. ins. claims cons., adjuster Tampa, 1988—. Staff sgt. U.S. Army, 1963-69. Mem. Am. Security Coun. (nat. adv. bd.), Fla. Sheriffs Assn., Am. Legion, Ctr. for Internat. Security Studies, Assn. of Workers' Compensation Claims Profls., Soc. of Claims Law Assocs. Republican. Home and Office: 6505 Dimarco Rd Tampa FL 33634-7311

VANDER GHEYNST, CAROL M., coordinator of planning; b. Chgo., Mar. 11, 1948; d. Raymond C. and Sophie G. (Hanczar) Cadek; m. Paul J. Vander Gheynst, July 25, 1970; children: John, Amy, Sally. BS with honors, U. Ill., 1970; MEd, Columbus Coll., 1976; PhD, Ga. State U., 1986. Dir. spl. svcs. Columbus (Ga.) Coll., 1983-87, adj. asst. prof., 1984-87, 1984-87, dir. challenge program for gifted elem. students, 1987-91; asst. prin. Muscogee County Sch. Dist., Columbus, Ga., 1987-90, prin., 1990-94, coord. of planning, 1994—. Contbr. articles to profl. jours. Bd. dirs. Springer Opera House, Columbus Youth Orch. Mem. Kappa Delta Pi, Phi Delta Kappa.

VAN DERLASKE, DENNIS PETER, electrical engineer; b. Mineola, N.Y., Jan. 15, 1948; s. Peter Joseph and Emily (Shenocka) Van D.; m. Mary Lou Hunn, Oct. 7, 1978; children: Kristin Claire, Rebecca Laraine. B of Engring., SUNY, Stony Brook, 1969; MS, George Washington U., 1975; MA, Ctrl. Mich. U., 1981. Elect. engr. comm. and electronics command U.S. Army Night Vision & Electronic Sensors Directorate, Ft. Belvoir, Va., 1969—; chmn. rsch. study group NATO, 1982-85. Patentee for thermal imaging technology. Mem. Friends of Chinn Park Regional Libr., Prince William, Va., 1991—. Mem. IEEE, Nat. Trust for Hist. Preservation, Mencken Soc. Home: 4924 Lanyard Ln Woodbridge VA 22192-5746 Office: CECOM Nigh Vision & Elect Sensors Directorate AMSEL RD-NV-HTI Fort Belvoir VA 22060

VAN DER VINK, GREGORY EVANS, geologist, educator. AB in Geology, Colgate U., 1979; MA in Geol. and Geophys. Scis., Princeton U., 1981, PhD in Geol. and Geophys. Scis., 1983. NRC postdoctoral fellow Naval Rsch. Lab., Washington, 1983-85; fellow U.S. Congress, Washington, 1985-89; dir. sci. and tech. studies U.S. Congress Office Tech. Assessment, Washington, 1988-89; dir. planning The IRIS Consortium, Arlington, Va., 1989—; vis. faculty dept. geoscis. Princeton (N.J.) U., 1991—; vis. faculty Woodrow Wilson Sch. Internat. Affairs, spring, 1992; internat. affairs fellow Coun. on Fgn. Rels., Washington, 1992-93; Pres. Clinton appointee Sci. and Policy Adv. Com., ACDA; lectr. in field. Contbr. chpts. to books, articles to profl. jours. Princeton U. fellow, 1979-83. Office: IRIS Consortium 1616 Fort Myer Dr # 1050 Arlington VA 22209-3100

VAN DERVORT, THOMAS RAYMOND, political science educator; b. Ft. Myers, Fla., Aug. 22, 1933; s. Carlton and Josephine (Wade) V.; m. Elsa Wolf, Sept. 15, 1956; children: Nadine, Shawn. BA, U. Tenn., 1959; MA, Fletcher Sch. Internat. Law, 1962; PhD, U. Tenn., 1967. Prof. polit. sci. Mid. Tenn. State U., Murfreesboro, 1963—; rsch. dir. Adv. Commn. on Intergovtl. Rels., Nashville, 1981-82. Author: Equal Justice Under the Law, 1994. With USAF, 1955-57. Fellow AAUP, So. Polit Sci. Assn., Tenn. Polit Sci. Assn. (pres. 1985-86, chair edn. com. 1988—). Democrat. Episcopalian. Home: 1407 Parklawn Dr Murfreesboro TN 37130-2154 Office: Mid Tenn State U PO Box 462 Murfreesboro TN 37133-0462

VAN DEVENTER, JON NELSON, physiatrist; b. Tulsa, 1948. MD, U. Ariz., 1984. Diplomate Am. Bd. Phys. Medicine and Rehab. Intern Baylor Coll. Medicine, Houston, 1984-85, resident in phys. medicine and rehab., 1985-87; with Harris-Meth. Hosp., Ft. Worth, 1987—. Mem. AMA, TMA, Am. Assn. Phys. Medicine and Rehab., Am. Coll. Rehab. Medicine. Office: 1325 Pennsylvania Ave Ste 290 Fort Worth TX 76104-2100*

VAN DEVENTER, MICKI JO, magazine writer, editor; b. Clay Center, Kansas, Dec. 31, 1940; d. Joe Fleming and Ida J. (Morton) Farmer; m. James Edward Goins III, Mar. 22, 1964 (div. Dec. 1966); 1 child, Kent Alan Goins; children from second marriage: Cynthia Van Deventer, Greg Van Deventer, Kevin Van Deventer. BS in English, Northeastern State U., Tahlequah, Okla., 1963; MS in Comms., Okla. State U., Stillwater, 1965; Summer fellow, Syracuse U., 1966. Tchr. English, journalism C.E. Donart H.S., Stillwater, 1965-67; lifestyle editor Stillwater News Press, Stillwater, 1967-76; investigative reporter Tulsa (Okla.) Tribune, 1976-77; lifestyle, entertainment editor Stillwater News Press, 1977-81; asst. lifestyle editor Tulsa World, 1981-82; dir. publs. ColorGraphics Corp., Tulsa, 1982-90, Nat. Cowboy Hall of Fame, Okla. City, 1990—; journalism instr. Okla. State U., Stillwater, 1967-88; adj. journalism prof. U. Cen. Okla., Edmond, 1993—; freelance mag. writer variuos publs. including Better Homes & Gardens, Traditional Home, Cowboys & Indians, Cowboys & Country, American Cowboy, others. Author: (books) Western Design, 1995; contbg. author Dictionary of the American West, 1995. Chmn. creative writers conf. Stillwater Arts & Humanities, 1980—; mem. bd. dirs. Okla. Arts Coun., Okla. City, 1984-90, Okla. Arts Inst., Okla. City, 1982-90. Nom. for Pulitzer prize for public svc. reporting Tulsa Tribune, 1977. Mem. Internat. Philanthropic and Ednl. Org. Democrat. Presbyn.

VAN DE WATER, SUSAN D., physiatrist. BA in Biology, Oberlin Coll., 1974; MD, U. Rochester, 1979; postgrad., U. Tex., San Antonio, 1982-86. Diplomate Am. Bd. Physical Medicine and Rehabilitation. Postdoctoral fellow U. Tex. Med. Br., Galveston, 1979-81; resident Rehab. Inst. Chgo., 1986-90; med. dir. Meml. Rehab. Hosp., Midland, Tex., 1990-94; psychiatrist Health South Rehab. Hosp., Midland, 1994—; chmn. phys. medicine and rehab. com. Meml. Hosp. and Med. Ctr., Midland, 1991-92, 93-94, Med. Ctr. Hosp., Odessa, Tex., 1990-92. Contbr. articles to profl. jours. Louise Barekman Meml. scholar Tex. Med. Assn., 1985, Bowen-Vogt Med. scholar, 1984, J. Belcher Trust scholar, 1983, So. Med. Assn. scholar 1982; Grad. fellow NSF, 1974-77, Rush Rhees Grad. fellow U. Rochester, 1974-77. Fellow Am. Acad. Phys. Medicine and Rehab.; mem. AMA, Assn. Acad. Physiatrists, Tex. Soc. Phys. Medicine and Rehab., Tex. Med. Assn., Midland County Med. Assn., U. Tex. San Antonio Alumni Assn., Alpha Omega Alpha, Phi Beta Kappa. Office: PO Box 4766 Midland TX 79704-4766

VAN DYK, MICHAEL ANTHONY, software designer; b. Moscow, Idaho, Sept. 14, 1950; s. Victor and Alice (LaFrance) Van D.; m. Lorna Veraldi, 1984; children: Nathan, Daniel. BS, U. Wash., 1973. Cons. Salomon Bros., Inc., 1980-82, Citicorp/Citibank, N.Y.C., 1982-85, Drexel, Burnham, Lambert, Inc., N.Y.C., 1987-88; ptnr., pres. Mintz, Pappas & Van Dyk, Inc., N.Y.C., 1982-83; adj. prof. Fordham U., N.Y.C., 1984. Designer of software including Trader Workstation, 1988, Trading System, 1985, Toddlerware, 1991. Vice chair N.Y. Assn. Computing Machinery, 1980-84. Home and Office: 20565 NE 6th Ct Miami FL 33179-2415

VAN DYKE, GENE, oil company executive; b. Normal, Ill., Nov. 5, 1926; s. Harold and Ruby (Gibson) Van D. B.S. in Geol. Engring., U. Okla., 1950; children: Karen, Scott, Janice, Mary Katherine. Geologist Kerr-McGee, Oklahoma City, 1950; chief geologist S.D. Johnson Co., Wichita Falls, Tex., 1950-51; ind. geologist and oil operator, 1951-58; ptnr. Van Dyke and Mejlaender, Houston, 1958-62; owner, pres. Van Dyke Oil Co. (name now Vanco Energy Co.), Houston, 1962—; also bd. dirs.; bd. dir. Van Dyke Netherlands, Inc. With AC, U.S. Army, 1945. Mem. Am. Petroleum Inst., Ind. Petroleum Assn. Am., Am. Assn. Petroleum Geologists. Republican. Methodist. Clubs: Houston, Houston Petroleum, Houstonian, University. Compiler index of geol. articles in South La. Home: 49 Briar Hollow Ln Houston TX 77027-9307 Office: Vanco Energy Co One Greenway Pla Houston TX 77046

VAN FLEET, SHARON KAY, psychiatric clinical nurse; b. Denver, Dec. 16, 1960. Student, Coe Coll., 1979-80; BS cum laude, U. Colo., Denver, 1984; MS in Psychiat.-Mental Health Nursing, U. Mich., 1990. Cert. psychiat.-mental health nurse. Staff nurse U. Chgo. Hosps., 1984-89; clin. nurse specialist psychiat. sect. M.D. Anderson Cancer Ctr., Houston, 1991—. Recipient Edith Galt Morgan Meml. award for outstanding grad. rsch. U. Mich., 1991; dean's fellowship, 1989-90. Mem. ANA, Tex. Nurses Assn., Houston Area Psychiat. Nurses, Internat. Soc. Psychiat. Consultation-Liaison Nurses, Oncology Nursing Soc., Alpha Omicron Pi. Home: 1800 El Paseo St Apt 1210 Houston TX 77054-3013 Office: MD Anderson Cancer Ctr Box 100 Dept Neuro-Oncology 1515 Holcombe Blvd Houston TX 77030-4009

VAN GILDER, DEREK ROBERT, lawyer, engineer; b. San Antonio, Feb. 26, 1950; s. Robert Ellis and Genevieve Delphine (Hutter) Van G.; m. Charlene Frances Madison, Jan. 21, 1984. Student, U.S. Mil. Acad., 1969-71; BS in Civil Engring., U. Tex., 1974, JD, 1981; MBA, U. Houston, 1976. Bar: Tex. 1981, U.S. Ct. Appeals (5th and 9th cirs.) 1982, Calif. 1982, U.S. Dist. Ct. (cen. dist.) Calif. 1982, U.S. Dist. Ct. (ea. and so. dists.) Tex. 1982, U.S. Dist. Ct. (we. dist.) Tex. 1983, U.S. Dist. Ct. (no. dist.) Tex. 1988, U.S. Supreme Ct. 1988, D.C. 1990, U.S. Patent/Trademark 1990. Engr. various engring cos., Houston, Longview and Austin, Tex., 1974-81; assoc. Thelen, Marrin, Johnson & Bridges, Los Angeles, 1981-82, Bean & Manning, Houston, 1982-85; pvt. practice Van Gilder & Assocs., Houston, 1985-94, Law Office of Derek R. Van Gilder, Bastrop, Tex., 1995—; instr. Houston C.C., 1981-82; life mem., committeeman Houston Livestock Show & Rodeo, 1991—. Bd. dirs. Children's Advocacy Ctr. of Bastrop City. Mem. ABA, ASCE, NSPE, Houston Bar Assn., Coll. State Bar Tex., Am. Arbitration Assn. (panel of arbitrators), Houston Med.-Legal Soc., Tex. Soc. Profl. Engrs., Rotary Club Bastrop County. Republican. Roman Catholic. Office: 916 Main St Bastrop TX 78602

VAN GROEN, THOMAS, neurobiologist; b. Amsterdam, The Netherlands, Apr. 28, 1953; came to U.S., 1986; s. Jacob Hendrik and Fenna (Klok) Van G.; m. Judith Anna-Maria Zijlstra, Apr. 11, 1980. Degree, Goois Lyceum, Bussum, The Netherlands, 1971; MS, U. Utrecht, 1975; PhD, U. Amsterdam, 1985. Instr. U. Amsterdam, 1975-78; researcher FUNGO, Amsterdam, 1981-85, U. Amsterdam, 1985; rsch. assoc. U. Ala., Birmingham, 1986-87; rsch. fellow U. Edinburgh, Scotland, 1988-89; rsch. asst. prof. U. Ala., 1989-93, asst. prof., 1994—. Mem. Royal Dutch Soc. Med. Rsch., European Neurosci. Assn., Soc. for Neurosci. Office: U Ala Sta VH302 1670 University Blvd Birmingham AL 35233-1709

VAN HORN, GAGE, III, neurologist, educator; b. Pecos, Tex., Dec. 28, 1936; s. Gage, Jr. and Louise (Briscoe) Van H.; m. Virginia Jenkins, Mar. 21, 1964; children: Margaret Louise, Michael Gage. BA in Chemistry, U. Tex., 1959; MD, Baylor Coll. Medicine, 1963. Diplomate Am. Bd. Psychiatry & Neurology. Asst. prof. sch. medicine U. Pitts., 1969-74; assoc. prof. U. Tex. Health Sci. Ctr., Houston, 1974-83, prof., 1983—. With USN, 1967-69. Fellow Am. Acad. Neurology; mem. Tex. Neurol. Soc. (pres.-elect 1996—). Office: U Tex Health Sci Ctr 6431 Fannin # 7044 Houston TX 77030

VAN HORN, RICHARD LINLEY, academic administrator; b. Chgo., Nov. 2, 1932; s. Richard Linley and Mildred Dorothy (Wright) Van H.; m. Susan Householder, May 29, 1954 (dec.); children: Susan Elizabeth, Patricia Suzanne, Lynda Sue; m. Betty Pfefferbaum, May 29, 1988. BS with highest honors, Yale U., 1954; MS, MIT, 1956; PhD, Carnegie-Mellon U., 1976; D of Bus. (hon.), Reitsumeikan U., Kyoto, Japan, 1991. Asst. dir. Army EDP Project, MIT, Cambridge, 1956-57; research staff Rand Corp., Santa Monica, Calif., 1957-60; head mgmt. systems group Rand Corp., 1960-67; dir., prof. mgmt. systems European Inst. Advanced Studies in Mgmt., Brussels, Belgium, 1971-73; asso. dean Grad. Sch. Indsl. Adminstrn., Carnegie-Mellon U., Pitts., 1967-71, dir. budget and planning, 1973-74, v.p. for bus. affairs, 1974-77, v.p. for mgmt., 1977-80, provost and prof. mgmt., 1980-83; chancellor U. Houston, 1983-86, pres., 1986-89; pres. U. Okla., 1989-94; pres. emeritus and regent's prof. Coll. of Bus. U. Okla., Norman, 1994—; Clarence E. Page prof. aviation U. Okla., Norman, 1995—. Author: (with Robert H. Gregory) Automatic Data Processing Systems, 1960, 2nd edit. 1963, (with R.H. Gregory) Business Data Processing and Programming, 1963, (with C.H. Kriebel and J.T. Heames) Management Information Systems: Progress and Perspectives, 1971; contbr. articles to profl. jours.; asso. editor: Jour. Inst. Mgmt. Scis, 1964-78. Bd. dirs. Last Frontier coun. Boy Scouts Am., Kirkpatrick Ctr., Nelson-Atkins Art Mus., Truman Libr. Inst., State Fair Okla., Okla. Futures Commn., Okla. Health Scis. Ctr. Found., Inc., Okla. Ednl. TV Authority. Mem. Inst. Mgmt. Sci. (nat. council mem. 1963-65, sec.-treas. 1964), Assn. for Computing Machinery (nat. lectr. 1969-70), Council on Govt. Relations (bd. dirs. 1981-83). Home: 701 NW 14th St Oklahoma City OK 73103-2211 Office: U Okla Coll of Bus Norman OK 73019

VAN HORN, TRENDA R., retail marketing management executive, consultant; b. Chevy Chase, Md., Apr. 1, 1949; d. Trenton M. and Angela M. (Vandoren) Richards; m. Jon H. Clayton, May 25, 1968 (div. 1971); 1 child, Kimberly Anne; m. Michael Van Horn, Sept. 1976 (div. 1980). BBA in Mktg. and Comm., U. Calif., Berkeley, 1968. With retail sales/mgmt. Dallas, N.Y.C., Mpls., 1971-82; pres., owner Van Horn Enterprises, Dallas, 1982-86; dir. retail RFD Inc. divsn. Designer Fragrances, Inc., Carrollton, Tex., 1986-87; exec. v.p., COO Designer Fragrances, Inc., Carrollton, 1987-

88; mgr. ops., mktg. Gump's, the Galleria, Dallas, 1988-91; contract cons., v.p. Bolos' Associated Cos., Inc., Carrollton, 1991-93; contract cons., 1991—. Democrat. Home and Office: 4412 Windhaven Lane Dallas TX 75287

VAN HOWE, ANNETTE EVELYN, retired real estate agent; b. Chgo., Feb. 16, 1921; d. Frank and Susan (Linstra) Van Howe; m. Edward L. Nezelek, Apr. 3, 1961. BA in History magna cum laude, Hofstra U., 1952; MA in Am. History, SUNY-Binghamton, 1966. Editorial asst. Salute Mag., N.Y.C., 1946-48; assoc. editor Med. Econs., Oradell, N.J., 1952-56; nat. mag. publicist Nat. Mental Health Assn., N.Y.C., 1956-60; exec. dir. Diabetes Assn. So. Calif., L.A., 1960-61; corp. sec., v.p., editor, pub. rels. dir. Edward L. Nezelek, Inc., Johnson City, N.Y., 1961-82; realtor, broker, Ft. Lauderdale, 1980-96, ret., 1996; mgr. condominium, Fort Lauderdale, Fla., 1982-83; dir. Sky Harbour East Condo, 1983-88; substitute tchr. high schs., Binghamton, N.Y., 1961-63. Editor newsletters Mental Health Assn., 1965-68, Unitarian-Universalist Ch. Weekly Newsletter, 1967-71. Bd. dirs. Broome County Mental Health Assn., 1961-65, Fine Arts Soc., Roberson Ctr. for Arts and Scis., 1968-70, Found. Wilson Meml. Hosp., Johnson City, 1972-81, White-Willis Theatre, 1988—, Found. SUNY, Binghamton, mem., 1991-95; mem. Fla. Women's Alliance, 1989—; v.p. Fla. Women's Polit. Caucus, 1989-92; chair Women's History Coalition, Broward County, 1986—; pres. Fla. Women's Consortium, 1989-92; trustee Broome C.C., 1973-78; v.p. Broward County Commn. on Status of Women, 1982-93; bd. dirs. Ft. Lauderdale Women's Coun. of Realtors, 1986-88, Broward Arts Guild, 1986; grad. Leadership Broward Class III, 1985, Leadership Am., 1988; trustee Unitarian-Universalist Ch. of Ft. Lauderdale, 1982-89; mem. adv. bd. Planned Parenthood, 1991-93; pres. Broward Alliance of Planned Parenthood, 1993-94; sec. Nat. Women's Conf. Com., 1994-96; bd. dirs. Nat. Women's Party, 1987-93. Named Feminist of Yr., Broward County, 1987; Women's Hall of Fame, Broward County, 1992, Feminist Heroine Nat. Am. Humanist Assn., 1996. Mem. AAUW (legis. chair Fla. divsn. 1986-87, chair women's issues 1989-94, v.p. Ft. Lauderdale br. 1993—), NAFE, Am. Med. Writers Assn., LWV (bd. dir. Broome County 1969-70), Alumni Assn. SUNY Binghamton (bd. dir. 1970-73), Fla. Bar Assn. (grievance com. 1991-94), Am. Acad. Polit. and Social Sci. Broward Women's Alliance, Broward County Voice for Choice (pres. 1995—), Am. Heritage Soc., Nature Conservancy, Nat. Hist. Soc., Symphony Soc., Pacers, Zonta, Alpha Theta Beta, Phi Alpha Theta, Phi Gamma Mu, Binghamton Garden Club, Binghamton Monday Afternoon Club, Acacia Garden Club (pres.), 110 Tower Club, Tower Forum Club (bd. dirs. 1989—), Downtown Coun., Ft. Lauderdale Woman's Club. Home: 2100 S Ocean Dr Fort Lauderdale FL 33316-3806

VANIMAN, JEAN ANN, manufacturing executive; b. Huntsville, Ala., Dec. 3, 1960; d. Jerold L. and Janis (Taylor) V. BSChemE, U. Ala., Tuscaloosa, 1984; MBA, Utah State U., 1989. Rsch. analyst dept. chem. engring. U. Ala., 1983-84; process engr. Rsch. & Devel. Lab. Morton Thiokol Corp., Brigham City, Utah, 1984-86; program mgr. Trident Strategic Programs, 1986-88; program mgr. advanced launch vehicle ops. Morton Thiokol, Inc., Brigham City, Utah, 1988-89; program mgr. space shuttle program Thiokol Corp., Huntsville, 1989-91; participant exec. Leadership Program Thiokol Corp., Brigham City, Utah, 1991-94; program mgr. Thiokol Yellow Creek Nozzle Divsn., Iuka, Miss., 1994—; dir. Thiokol Recreation Coun., 1989—. Vol. counselor Huntsville Crisis Line; vol. Utah Mus. Natural History, 1992—. Mem. NAFE, Am. Inst. Chem. Engrs., Capstone Engring. Soc. (bd. dirs.), Am. Mgmt. Assn., Soc. Women Engrs., Tau Beta Pi Alumni Assn., Chi Omega Alumni Assn. Home: 4145 S 850 E Ogden UT 84403-2973 Office: Thiokol Corp Nozzle Divsn 1 Nasa Dr Bldg 1000 Iuka MS 38852-8935

VAN KUREN, NANCY ELLEN, academic administrator; b. Endicott, N.Y., Feb. 23, 1956; d. Lawrence Russell and Minnie Pauline (Linehan) Van K. BA, Wilkes Coll., 1978; MS, Alfred U., 1980; EdD, Va. Tech., 1987. Residential coord. N.H. Coll., Manchester, 1980-81; asst. dir. residence life Mansfield (Pa.) U., 1981-84; dean students Juniata Coll., Huntington, Pa., 1987-92; v.p. N.C. Wesleyan Coll., Rocky Mount, 1993—; cons. U.S. Dept. Edn., 1994; bus. adv. bd. Ea. N.C. Bus., 1994—. Mem. Nat. Assn. Student Personnel Adminstrs., Am. Coll. Personnel Assn., Phi Kappa Phi, Wilkes U. Alumni Assn. (nat. exec. bd. 1994-96). Office: NC Wesleyan Coll 3400 N Wesleyan Blvd Rocky Mount NC 27804

VAN LANDINGHAM, LEANDER SHELTON, JR., lawyer; b. Memphis, July 15, 1925; s. Leander Shelton and Bertha (Shumaker) Van L.; m. Henrietta Adena Stapf, July 5, 1959; children: Ann Henrietta, Leander Shelton III. BS in Chemistry, U. N.C., 1948, MA in Organic Chemistry, 1949; JD, Georgetown U., 1955. Bar: D.C. 1955, Md. 1963, Va. 1976. Patent adviser Dept. Navy, Washington, 1953-55; sole practice comml. law and patent, trademark and copyright law, Washington met. area, 1955—. Served to lt. USNR, 1943-46, 51-53. Mem. Am. Chem. Soc., Sci. Assn., Fed. Bar Assn., ABA, D.C. Bar Assn., Va. Bar Assn., Md. Bar Assn., Am. Intellectual Property Law Assn., Am. Judicature Soc., Sigma Xi, Phi Alpha Delta. Home: 10726 Stanmore Dr Potomac MD 20854-1518 Office: 2001 Jefferson Davis Hwy Arlington VA 22202-3603

VANMEER, MARY ANN, publisher, writer, researcher; b. Mt. Clemens, Mich., Nov. 22; d. Leo Harold and Rose Emma (Gulden) VanM. Student Mich. State U., 1965-66, 67-68, Sorbonne U., Paris, 1968; BA in Edn., U. Fla., 1970. Pres. VanMeer Tutoring and Translating, N.Y.C., 1970-72; freelance writer, 1973-79; pres. VanMeer Publs., Inc., Clearwater, Fla., 1980-88, VanMeer Media Advt., Inc., Clearwater, 1980-88; exec. dir., founder Nat. Ctrs. for Health and Med. Info., Inc., Clearwater, 1987-88, Nat. Health and Med. Info. Ctr., Palm Beach, Fla., 1990-93; pres., CEO The Thrifty Traveler, Inc (formerly Traveling Free Publs., Inc.), 1993—. Author: Traveling with Your Dog, U.S.A., 1976, How to Set Up A Home Typing Business, 1978, Freelance Photographer's Handbook, 1979; See America Free, 1981, Free Campgrounds, U.S.A., 1982, Free Attractions, U.S.A., 1982, VanMeer's Guide to Free Attractions, U.S.A., 1984, VanMeer's Guide to Free Campgrounds, 1984, The How to Get Publicity for Your Business Handbook, 1987, Asthma: The Ultimate Treatment Guide, 1991, Allergies: The Ultimate Treatment Guide, 1992, Cancer: The Ultimate Treatment Guide, 1993, Thrifty Traveling, 1995; pub. Nat. Health and Med. Trends Mag., 1986-88, Thrifty Traveler Newsletter, 1993—, The Over-50 Thrifty Traveler Newsletter, 1996—. Pub. info. chairperson, bd. dirs. Pinellas County chpt. Am. Cancer Soc., Clearwater, 1983-84, 86-88; mem. fin. devel. com. ARC, Palm Beach County, 1990-92. Mem. Am. Booksellers Assn., PACT (Performing Arts, Concert, and Theatre), Author's Guild. Office: The Thrifty Traveler, Inc PO Box 5126 Clearwater FL 34618

VAN METER, CLIFFORD HOLLY, JR., surgeon; b. Mar. 22, 1955; s. Clifford and Patty Sue (Henry) Van M.; m. Marianne Joan Mattingly; children: Logan Jade, Clifford Chancellor, Merritt Grace. BS in Biology cum laude with honors, Tulane U., 1977, MD, 1981. Diplomate Am. Bd. Surgery, Am. Bd. Thoracic Surgery. Surg. intern U. Va. Med. Ctr., Charlottesville, 1981-82, resident in gen. surgery, 1982-85, chief resident, 1985-86; fellow dept. surgery div. cardiothoracic surgery Washington U. Med. Ctr., St. Louis, 1986-88; staff dept. surgery Ochsner Clinic, New Orleans, 1988—; mem. transplant adv. bd. Ochsner Clinic, New Orleans, 1988—; clin. asst. prof. dept. surgery Tulane U. Med. Ctr., 1993; mem. utilization review subcom. Alton Ochsner Med. Found., New Orleans, 1989—, coronary care unit com., 1989—, intensive care unit com., 1989—, cardiac transplant com., 1989—; presenter in field. Contbr. articles to profl. jours. Bd. dirs. La. Organ Procurement Assn.; rep. to thoracic organ com. United Network for Organ Sharing. Mem. AMA. Alton Ochsner Surg. Soc., New Orleans Surg. Soc., Tulane Surg. Soc., Muller Soc., So. Med. Assn., Orleans Parish Med. Soc., Southeastern Surg. Congress, Internat. Soc. Heart and Lung Transplant Assn., Assn. Am. Indian Physicians, Soc. Thoracic Surgeons, So. Thoracic Surg. Assn., Soc. Transplant Surgeons, Pi Eta Sigma, Beta BEta Beta. Republican. Episcopalian. Home: 32 Pelham Dr Metairie LA 70005-4454 Office: Ochsner Clinic Dept Surgery Thoracic Cardiovascular 1514 Jefferson Hwy New Orleans LA 70121-2429

VAN METER, KENNETH DON, telecommunications company executive; b. Clarksburg, W.Va., Mar. 4, 1947; children: Ryan, Adam. BS, W.Va. U., 1969; MBA, U. Ga., 1979. Sales mgr. Pfizer, Inc., Atlanta, 1977-80; mgr. AT&T, Atlanta, 1980-84; dir. Sprint, Atlanta, 1984-89; group v.p. Nat. Data Corp., Atlanta, 1989-91; v.p., gen. mgr. Thomas Cook, Atlanta, 1991-93; pres. Bell Atlantic Video Svcs., Arlington, Va., 1993-94; sr. v.p. Tele-TV Systems, Reston, Va., 1994—. Contbr. articles to mags. Capt., jet pilot USAF, 1971-77. Named Most Outstanding Person in Industry, Teleconferencing mag., 1986. Home: 1236 Weatherstone Ct Reston VA 20194-1350 Office: Tele-TV Systems 1880 Campus Commons Dr Reston VA 22091-1512

VANN, DIANE E. SWANSON, nursing educator; b. San Antonio, Aug. 10, 1952; d. Ralph A. and Imogene E. (Harrison) Swanson; m. James R. Vann III, May 15, 1982. BSN, U. Nebr., Omaha, 1974; MS in Nursing, U. Tenn., Knoxville, 1986. Asst. charge nurse, emergency room U. So. Ala. Med. Ctr., Mobile; instr. nursing Chattanooga State Tech. Community Coll.; asst. prof. Middle Ga. Coll., Cochran, Macon (Ga.) Coll. Capt., U.S. Army, 1972-77. W.K. Kellogg Found. fellow. Mem. ANA, Sigma Theta Tau.

VANNAHMEN, AVA MARIE, public relations executive; b. Spearville, Kans., Jan. 1, 1955. AA, Dodge City C.C., 1975; BS in Journalism, U. Kans., 1977, MPA, 1995; postgrad., U. South Fla., 1993—. Lic. vision cable community access producer; lic. Jones intercable producer. Broadcast writer, on-air talent, voice talent KEDD Radio, Dodge City, Kans., 1973-75, KLWN, Lawrence, Kans., 1975-77, KARN, Little Rock, 1978-79; copywriter, asst. film coord. Ogilvy & Mather Advt., Houston, 1977-78; asst. press sec. Gov. Bill Clinton, Ark., 1979-80; mktg. strategist, advt. writer, pub. rels. exec. HLA Advt., 1980-82; account exec. The Dick Leonard Group (now Paradigm Advt.), 1982-84; pub. info. officer, acting asst. v.p. instl. advancement St. Petersburg (Fla.) Jr. Coll., 1984-91; asst. dir. pub. and govt. rels., community rels. coord. Tampa Port Authority, 1991—. Past mem. Pinellas County Met. Planning Commn. Citizen's Adv. Coun., Tiger Bay of Hillsborough and Pinellas County. Recipient Addy awards, awards for broadcast and print media, Ark., Fla. Mem. Am. Soc. Pub. Adminstrn., Nat. Acad. Cable Producers Pub. Rels. Bd., Hospice of Pinellas County, Propeller Club, Internat. Assn. Bus. Comm., Greater Tampa C. of C. Home: 13937 Egret Ln Clearwater FL 34622-4510

VAN NESS, JAMES SAMUEL, academic administrator, historian; b. Houston, Feb. 26, 1932; s. John Bishop and Ruth (Ryan) Van N.; m. Nedra Tracy, June 18, 1955; children: Lynn, Paul. B.A., U. Md., 1954, M.A., 1962, Ph.D., 1968. Asst. prof. history U. Md., Coll. Park, 1967-74, supt. history and govt. European div., Heidelberg, Fed. Republic Germany, 1969-71, dir. summer sch., Coll. Park, 1972-74; asst. dean St. Lawrence U., Canton, N.Y., 1974-78; dean instrn. Central Wyo. Coll., Riverton, 1978-82; dean arts and scis. Temple Coll., Tex., 1982-92, dean of instrn., 1992—; bd. dirs. Temple Sister Cities Corp. Editor: (with J. Raths and J. Pancella) Studying Teaching, 1971; contbr. chpt. to book, articles to profl. jours. Bd. dirs. Inst. for Humanities at Salado, Tex., 1989-95; vice chmn. Wyo. Council for Humanities, Laramie, 1981-82; mem. exec. com. Assn. for Innovation in Higher Edn., 1977-79; bd. dirs. Central Tex. Orchestral Soc., Temple, 1984-85; chmn. Canton Village Rep. Club, 1975-78. Named Rotarian of Yr., Canton, 1978, Temple, 1992, Outstanding Tchr., U. Md. History Honorary, 1969; faculty devel. fellow U. Md., 1961-63. Mem. Inst. for Early Am. History and Culture, Orgn. Am. Historians, Nat. Assn. Instructional Adminstrs., Rotary (past pres., Temple South Rotary). Home: 4502 Cactus Trl Temple TX 76504-3243 Office: Temple Coll 2600 S 1st St Temple TX 76504-7435

VAN OEVEREN, EDWARD LANIER, lawyer, biologist, physician; b. Washington, Apr. 12, 1954; s. Donald James and Sarah Margaret (Clardy) Van O. BA with high distinction, U. Va., 1976; M.D., Med. Coll. Va., 1995; JD, U. Va., 1981; BS with distinction, George Mason U., 1983. Bar: Va. 1981, U.S. Dist. Ct. (ea. dist.) Va. 1988, U.S. Temporary Emergency Ct. Appeals 1989. Pvt. practice legal cons., Falls Church, Va., 1984-85; pvt. practice law, Falls Church, 1986-89, pvt. practice law and biology,, 1989—. Editor: Federal Special Court Litigation, 1982. Election officer Fairfax County (Va.) Electoral Bd., 1989-90, 94-96. Capt. Va. Army NG, 1996—; 1st lt. USAR, 1995-96. Mem. AMA, Va. State Bar Assn., George Mason U. Alumni Assn. (scholarship, awards, rules and policies coms. 1989-91), Alpha Chi. Home: 3304 Patrick Henry Dr Falls Church VA 22044-1514

VANOVER, BOYD RUSSELL, engineer; b. Vinita, Okla., Apr. 19, 1950; s. Bezonny Calvin and Audrey Colleen (Bump) V.; m. Glenda Sue Moore, Sept. 8, 1973; children: Michael, Carrie. AA, Northeastern Okla. A&M Coll., 1970; student, Harvard U., 1990. Owner Van Design Svc., Commerce, Okla., 1970-73; dir. engring. Newell Coach Corp., Miami, 1973—; bd. dirs. NEO Fed. Credit Union. Mem. Soc. Automotive Engrs. Home: 1519 Lincoln Blvd Miami OK 74354-3830 Office: Newell Coach Corp Hwy 69 N Miami OK 74355

VAN PATTEN, JAMES JEFFERS, education educator; b. North Rose, N.Y., Sept. 8, 1925; s. Earl F. and Dorothy (Jeffers) Van P.; married. BA, Syracuse U., 1949; ME, Tex. Western Coll., 1959; PhD, U. Tex., Austin, 1962. Asst. prof. philosophy and edn. Central Mo. State U., Warrensburg, 1962-64, assoc. prof., 1964-69; assoc. prof. vis. overseas U. Okla., Norman, 1969-71; prof. edn. U. Ark., Fayetteville, 1971—; visiting scholar, U. Mich., 1981, UCLA, 1987, U. Tex., Austin, 1987; vis. prof./scholar U. Fla., Gainesville, 1994. Served with inf., U.S. Army, 1944-45. Decorated Purple Heart. Mem. Am. Ednl. Studies Assn., Southern Future Soc., World Future Soc., Am. Philosophy Assn., Southwestern Philosophy of Edn. Soc. (pres. 1970), Am. Ednl. Rsch. Assn., Phi Delta Kappa (pres. chpt. U. Ark. 1976-77), NOLPE. Club: Kiwanis. Editor: Conflict, Permanency and Change in Education, 1976, Philosophy, Social Science and Education, 1989, College Teaching and Higher Education Leadership, 1990, Social-Cultural Foundations of Educational Policy in the U.S., 1991; Author: Academic Profiles In Higher Education, 1992, The Many Faces of the Culture of Higher Edn., 1993, (with John Pulliam) History of Education in America, 1995, The Culture of Higher Education: A Case Study Approach, 1996, What's Really Happening In Education: A Case Study Approach, 1997; contbr. articles to books, profl. jours.; founder Jour. of Thought. Home: 434 Hawthorne St Fayetteville AR 72701-1934

VAN REENEN, JANE SMITH, speech and language pathologist; b. Baton Rouge, Sept. 16, 1949; d. William Robert and Mary Jane (Laidlaw) Smith; m. Dirk Andries van Reenen, Mar. 3, 1973; children: Andrea Lee, Erika Lynn. BS in Speech Pathology, La. State U., 1971; MEd in Speech Pathology, Ga. State U., 1984. Cert. clin. competence Am. Speech-Lang.-Hearing Assn.; lic. Ga.; cert. tchr. Ga. Speech-lang. pathologist Livingston Parish Schs., La., 1971-73, Gwinnett County (Ga.) Schs., 1973-75, 94—; pvt. practice speech-lang. pathology Norcross, Ga., 1975—; speech-lang. pathologist Nova Care, Atlanta, 1979—; grad. asst. Ga. State U., Atlanta, 1983-84, substitute clin. supr., 1988-90, interim clinic coord., 1991; speech-lang. pathologist Americana Nursing Home, Decatur, 1984; chairperson Atlanta (Ga.) Orofacial Myology Study Group, 1987-89; adv. com. Comm. Disorders Program, Atlanta, 1990-94; mem. Ga. Supervision Network, 1991-94; mem. Cognitive Remediation Interest Group, Atlanta, 1993—. Mng. editor: Internat. Jour. Orofacial Myology, 1989-91; contbr. articles to profl. jours. Ruling elder Northminster Presbyn. Ch., Roswell, Ga., 1981; mem. local sch. adv. com. Pinckneyville Middle Sch., Norcross, 1987-92, co-founder sch. based drug/alchol abuse prevention program, 1988; v.p. Parent Tchr. Student Assn. Norcross High Sch., 1990-91; pres. River Valley Estates Homeowners Assn., Norcross, 1991; local sch. adv. com. Norcross High Sch., 1993—, AIDS rep. PTSA, 1993-96, drug/alcohol abuse rep., 1993-96, care team, 1993-96. Recipient Positive Parenting awards Ga. State Supt. of Schs., Atlanta, 1987-88, 88-89; named Outstanding Sch. Vol., Gwinnet County Bd. Edn., Lawrenceville, Ga., 1989-90. Mem. Am. Speech-Lang.-Hearing Assn. (congl. action contact com. 1991—), Ga. Speech-Lang.-Hearing Assn. (honors and ethics com. 1989-91), Internat. Assn. Orofacial Myology (mng. editor 1989-91). Republican. Home and Office: 3992 Gunnin Rd Norcross GA 30092-1953

VANSELOW, NEAL ARTHUR, university administrator, physician; b. Milw., Mar. 18, 1932; s. Arthur Frederick and Mildred (Hoffmann) V.; m. Mary Ellen McKenzie, June 20, 1958; children: Julie Ann, Richard Arthur. AB, U. Mich., 1954, MD, 1958, MS, 1963. Diplomate: Am. Bd. Internal Medicine, Am. Bd. Allergy and Immunology. Intern Mpls. Gen. Hosp., 1958-59; resident Univ. Hosp., Ann Arbor, Mich., 1959-63; instr. medicine U. Mich., 1963-64, asst. prof., 1964-68, assoc. prof., 1968-72, prof., chmn. dept. postgrad. medicine and health professions edn., 1972-74; dean Coll. Medicine U. Ariz., Tucson, 1974-77; chancellor med. ctr. U. Nebr., Omaha, 1977-82, v.p., 1977-82; v.p. health scis. U. Minn., 1982-89, prof. internal medicine, 1982-89; chancellor Tulane U. Med. Ctr., New Orleans, 1989-94; prof. internal medicine, adj. prof. health sys. mgmt. Tulane U., New Orleans, 1989—; chmn. Joint Bd. Osteo. and Med. Examiners Ariz., 1974-77; chmn. coun. on Grad. Med. Edn., Dept. Health and Human Svcs., 1986-91; mem. com. on educating dentists for future Inst. Medicine, NAS, 1993-95, chairperson com. on future of primary care, 1994-96, co-chairperson com. on the U.S. physician supply, 1995-96, scholar in residence, 1994-95. Bd. dirs. Devel. Authority for Tucson's Economy, 1975-77, Minn. Coalition for Health Care Costs, 1983-87, La. Health Care Authority, 1989-90, United Way Greater New Orleans Area, 1992—; mem. exec. com. United Way Midlands, 1980-82, vice chmn. 1981 campaign; bd. dirs., mem. exec. com. Health Planning Coun. Midlands, Omaha, 1978-82, v.p., 1981-82; bd. dirs. Minn. High Tech. Coun., 1983-86; mem. commn. on Health Professions Pew Charitable Trusts, 1990-92; mem. Gov.'s Pan Am. Commn., La., 1991-92; mem. mktg. mgmt. governing coun. U. Hosp. Consortium, 1993-95. Fellow ACP, Am. Acad. Allergy, Am. Coll. Physician Execs.; mem. Assn. Acad. Health Ctrs. (bd. dirs. 1983-89, chmn. bd. dirs. 1988), Soc. Med. Adminstrs., Phi Beta Kappa, Sigma Xi, Alpha Omega Alpha, Beta Theta Pi, Nu Sigma Nu. Home: 1828 Palmer Ave New Orleans LA 70118-6216 Office: Tulane U 1430 Tulane Ave New Orleans LA 70112-2699

VAN SLYKE, LEONARD DUBOSE, JR., lawyer; b. Hattiesburg, Miss., Oct. 6, 1944; s. Leonard D. and Edith Loraine (Barksdale) Van S.; m. Donna Joyce McIntyre, June 3, 1967; children: Lendy DeLane, Guy McIntyre. BS, U. So. Miss., 1966; JD, U. Miss., 1970; LLM in Taxation, Georgetown U., 1974. Bar: Miss. 1970, U.S. Ct. Claims 1974, U.S. Tax Ct. 1974. Trial atty. U.S. Dept. Justice, Washington, 1970-74; ptnr. Knight, Ballew & Van Slyke, Jackson, Miss., 1974-79, Van Slyke & Houston, Jackson, Miss., 1979-80, Thomas, Price, Alston, Jones & Davis, Jackson, Miss., 1980-92, Alston, Rutherford & Van Slyke, Jackson, Miss., 1992—; trustee Miss. Tax Inst., 1982-84. Bd. dirs. Bethlehem Ctr., Jackson, 1982-87; treas. Ellington Congl. Campaign, 1982; mem. adminstrv. bd. Galloway United Meth. Ch., Jackson, chmn. fin. com., 1991-92. Served with U.S. Army Res., 1962-70. Fellow Miss. Bar Found.; mem. Fed. Bar Assn. (pres. Miss. chpt. 1980-81), Miss. State Bar (chmn. taxation com. 1978-80), Hinds County Bar Assn. (dir. 1984-85, chmn. jud. poll com. 1980-82, pres. 1990-91), Capitol City Petroleum Club. Democrat. Methodist. Home: 106 Hillcroft Pl Jackson MS 39211-2915

VAN TASSEL-BASKA, JOYCE LENORE, education educator; b. Toledo, July 28, 1944; d. Robert Rae and Eleanor Jane (Kenyon) Sloan; m. Thomas Harold Van Tassel, May 21, 1964 (div. 1975); m. Leland Karl Baska, July 25, 1980; 1 child, Ariel Sloan. BEd cum laude, U. Toledo, 1966, MA, MEd, 1969, EdD, 1981. Tchr. Toledo Pub. Schs., 1965-72, coord. gifted programs, 1973-76; dir. Ill. gifted program Ill. State Bd. Edn., Springfield, 1976-79; dir., area svc. ctr. Matteson (Ill.) Sch. Dist., 1979-82; dir. Ctr. for Talent Devel. Northwestern U., Evanston, Ill., 1982-87; Smith prof. edn. Coll. William and Mary, Williamsburg, Va., 1987—; dir. Ctr. for Gifted Edn. Coll. William and Mary, Williamsburg, 1988—; mem. Va. Adv. Bd. on Gifted and Talented, 1988—; mem. State Ohio Adv. Bd. Gifted and Talented, 1975-76; mem. edn. coun. Nat. Bus. Consortium, 1981-84. Mem. editorial bd. Roeper Rev., 1980-82; pub. Talent Devel. Quar., 1983-87; manuscript rev. editor Jour. Edn. of Gifted, 1981—; mem. editorial adv. bd. Critical Issues in Gifted Edn. series; mem. editorial bd. Gifted Child Quar., 1984—, Jour. Advanced Devel.; column editor Understanding the Gifted Newsletter author 8 books; contbr. chpts. and over 200 articles to profl. jours. Bd. trustees Lourdes High Sch., Chgo., 1985-86. Recipient Outstanding Faculty award State Coun. Higher Edn. Va., 1993; grantee U.S. Office Edn., 1977-78, 78-79, 89—, Ill. State Bd. Edn., 1979-82, 84-91, Richardson Found., 1986, 89, Fry Found., 1987-90, Va. State Coun. Higher Edn., 1987-89, 90-91, 93-95, Bur. Indian Affairs, 1989, Hughes Found., 1989-94, Va. State Libr., 1989-90, Va. State Dept. Edn., 1990-93, 93-95, Funding Agy. U.S. Dept. Edn., 1989—, 90-93, 93-95; eminent scholar Coll. William and Mary, 1987—, Nat. Ednl. policy fellow U.S. Office Edn., 1979-80, Paul Witty fellow in gifted edn., 1979, Outstanding Rsch. Paper award Mensa, 1995. Mem. ASCD, Nat. Assn. Gifted Children (bd. dirs. 1984-90), Coun. Exceptional Children, Assn. for Gifted (pres. 1980-81), World Coun. on Gifted, Am. Ednl. Rsch. Assn., Phi Beta Kappa, Phi Delta Kappa (pres. Northwestern chpt. 1986-87). Home: 225 Richard Burbydge Williamsburg VA 23185-5115 Office: Coll William and Mary Jones Hall Williamsburg VA 23185

VANTREASE, ALICE TWIGGS, marketing executive; b. Augusta, Ga., Mar. 29, 1943; d. Samuel Warren and Harriett Alice (Wright) Twiggs; m. John Mulford Marks, July 8, 1964 (div. Oct. 1972); children: John Mulford, Sarah Elizabeth; m. James David Vantrease, May 9, 1980 (div. Mar. 1988). Student Winthrop Coll., 1961-62, Augusta Coll., 1962-64. Sales staff Chalker Publ. Co., Waynesboro, Ga., 1972-74; with Creative Displays, Inc., Tuscaloosa, Ala., 1974-78; sales mgr. GMC Bdcasting, Chattanooga, 1978-80; corporate sales, mktg. dir. Creative Displays Inc., Augusta, 1980-83; pres. Creative Mktg. Svcs., Augusta, 1983-91, Beaufort, S.C., 1991-95, Twiggs of Savannah, 1995—. Bd. dirs. Better Bus. Bur., 1987-89; pres. Good Luck Found., 1988-91. Author: The Rabbit in the Moon, 1996; editor: The Met. Spirit Newspaper, 1989-91, Beaufort Mag., 1991-92. Named to Co-op Advt. Hall of Fame, 1989. Mem. Outdoor Advt. Suppliers Assn. (v.p. 1984-87, pres. 1987-88, editor newspaper 1985-88), Nat. Speakers Assn., Am. Assn. Coop Advt. Profls., Outdoor Advt. Assn. Am. Instr. Episcopalian. Avocations: painting, writing. Home: 5203 Waters Ave Savannah GA 31404 Office: 202 W St Julian St Savannah GA 31401-2514

VANVLECK, AMY ANN, editor, communications executive; b. Memphis, Tex., Apr. 22, 1967; d. Jack Bryan and Ann (Atkinson) McNabb; m. Albert Louis VanVleck, Dec. 30, 1989; 1 child, Victoria Grace. BS, Tex. Christian U., 1990. Comms. coord. Dallas Chpt. of Tex. Soc. CPAs, 1990-95; comms. dir., mng. editor Dallas County Med. Soc., 1995—; mem. comms. com. Am. Cancer Soc., Dallas, 1996—. Mem. Internat. Assn. Bus. Communicators. Republican. Office: Dallas Med Jour Sta A PO Box 4680 Dallas TX 75208-0680

VAN VLECK, PAMELA KAY, commercial real estate broker; b. St. Cloud, Minn., Aug. 26, 1951; d. Kipp James Gillespie and Lorraine Marie (Johnson) Storck; m. Clinton Eugene Van Vleck, Jan. 29, 1985. Student, St. Cloud State U., 1969-70, Washburn U., 1971-72. Lic. pilot; lic. cmty. assn. mgr. Mgr., broker Coldwell Banker-Pioneer Realty, Jackson, Wyo., 1980-85; owner, broker Tri-Corp Realty, Ltd., Scottsdale, Ariz., 1985-87, Affiliated Properties Group, Inc., Phoenix, Las Vegas, Nev., 1987-91; mgr., broker Machan Hampshire Properties, Las Vegas, Nev., 1990-91; v.p. Affiliated Property Mgmt. Corp., 1990-92; retail properties specialist Grubb & Ellis, Tucson, 1991-92; commercial broker/realtor assoc. Cameron Real Estate Svcs., Naples, Fla., 1992—; dir. Lee County Cameron Real Estate Svcs., Inc., Ft. Myers, Fla., 1994—; bd. dirs., owner Affiliated Properties Group Inc./Affiliated Property Mgmt. Corp., Phoenix, 1985-92; bd. dirs., cons. Realty Software Svcs. Ariz., Inc., Phoenix, 1986-91, MHP Realty & Mgmt., Inc., Las Vegas, 1989-91. Developer, copywriter computer software program REMMI (Real Estate Matching, Mktg. and Inventory). Grad. Leadership Lee County, 1996. Mem. NAFE, Women in Comml. Real Estate, Nev. Devel. Authority, Women's Conv. Sales Assn., Internat. Coun. Shopping Ctrs., Resl Estate Investment Soc., Exec. Womens Golf League. Republican. Office: The Cameron Bldg 6309 Corporate Ct Fort Myers FL 33919

VAN VRANKEN, ROSE, sculptor; b. Passaic, N.J., May 15, 1919; d. Gilbert and Rose (Camwell) Van V.; m. Robert C. Hickey, June 11, 1942; children: Kathryn, Robert, Stephen, Dennis, Sarah. BA in Art with honors, Pomona Coll., 1939; studied with Laurent and Zorach, Art Students League, N.Y.C., 1939-42; postgrad., NYU, 1941-42; MA in Sculpture, U. Iowa, 1943. Works represented in collections including Temple Emanuel, Houston, M.D. Anderson Cancer Ctr., Houston, John Whitney Payson Family Collection, N.Y.C., Jewish Cmty. Ctr., Houston, St. Cyril of Alexandria Ch., Houston, Tex. Commerce Bank, Houston, Med. Ctr., Houston, Coventry Cathedral, Eng., U. Iowa Mus. Fine Arts, Iowa City, Des Moines Art Ctr.; one-woman shows include C.J. Jung Ctr., Houston, 1992, Bibl. Arts Mus., Dallas, 1992, U. Dayton, Ohio, 1992. Recipient Medal of Honor Acad. Artists Assn., 1985. Mem. Internat. Platform Assn. (Best of Show Gold medal 1990, 1st prize for sculpture 1987, 95), Nat. Assn. Women Artists (Sculpture award 1980, Medal Honor for Graphics 1952), Artists Equity, Profl. Sculptors

Guild, Salmagundi Club (4 1st prize and 3 2d prize awards), Tex. Soc. Sculptors.

VAN WIJK, MAIKE HEDWIG GISELA, reporter; b. Vinkeveen, The Netherlands, Aug. 22, 1973; came to the U.S., 1990; d. Pieter Deventer and Birgitt (Gosse) van W. BA in Journalism cum laude, U. Houston, 1996. Clk. Little Prof. Bookcenter, Kingwood, Tex., 1995; reporter The Daily Cougar, Houston, 1995, The Baytown (Tex.) Sun, 1996. Vol. newsletter coord. Forest Cove Bapt. Ch., Kingwood, 1992-94, middle sch. youth leader, 1992-94, 95-96. Scholar Press Club Houston, 1995-96. Mem. Soc. Profl. Journalists, Women in Comm., Golden Key. Home: 2115 Crystal River Dr Kingwood TX 77345

VAN WOLKENTEN, RAYMOND VINCENT, medical educator; b. L.A., May 29, 1943; s. Raymond V. and Janet (Carmichael) van W.; m. Jane M. van Wolkenten, July 19, 1966; children: Kristen, Megan. BS in Physics, U. N.C., 1965; MS in Info. and Computer Sci., Ga. Inst. Tech., 1971, PhD, 1975; MD, Med. Coll. Va., 1981. Diplomate Am. Bd. Family Practice. Asst. prof. info. systems and math. Va. Commonwealth U., Richmond, 1974-77; instr., assoc. prof. Ea. Va. Med. Sch., Norfolk, 1984—. Pres. med. staff Hillhouse Rehab. Ctr., Norfolk, 1991—. Lt. comdr. USNR, 1965-70. Mem. AAAS, Am. Med. Info. Assn., Rotary Internat. Office: Ea Va Med Sch 721 Fairfax Ave Norfolk VA 23507-2007

VARADARAJAN, POONDI RAJAN, marketing educator; b. Bangalore, Karnataka, India, Apr. 20, 1948; came to U.S., 1976; BS, Bangalore U., 1968; BE, Indian Inst. Sci., Bangalore, 1971; M in Tech., Indian Inst. Tech., Madras, India, 1973; PhD, U. Mass., 1978. Account exec. M/S Swamy Advt. Assocs., India, 1973-74; lectr. Indian Inst. Tech., Madras, 1974-76; teaching asst. U. Mass., Amherst, 1976-78; asst. prof. SUNY, Albany, 1978-81; asst.prof. Tex. A&M U., College Station, 1981-86, assoc. prof., 1986-90, prof., 1990—, coord. PhD program in mktg., 1989-94, dept. head, 1996—. Editor: Jour. Mktg., 1993-96, The Mktg. Concept: Perspectives and Viewpoints, 1983; guest editor: Jour. Bus. Rsch., 1994, (with others) Enhancing Knowledge Development in Marketing, 1993; mem. editl. rev. bd. Jour. Mktg., 1985-93, Jour. Mktg. Rsch., Jour. Bus. Rsch., Jour. Internat. Mktg.; reviewer jours.; contbr. articles to profl. jours. Recipient Nat. Merit cert. Ministry of Edn., India, 1968; Strategic Planning Inst. fellow, 1978; grantee faculty SUNY, 1980, Tex. A&M U., 1982-89, Inst. New Ventures and Tech., 1984-85, AT&T, Inc., 1986, 88, Strategic Planning Inst., 1988, Office of U.S. Small Bus. Adminstrn., 1989. Fellow Am. Mktg. Assn.; mem. Acad. Mktg. Sci. (Best Paper award 1992), Acad. Mgmt., Strategic Mgmt. Soc. Office: Tex A&M U Mktg Dept College Station TX 77843-4112

VARDI, MOSHE YA'AKOV, computer science researcher; b. Haifa, Israel, July 4, 1954; came to U.S., 1981; s. Pinchas and Zipporah (Mandel) V.; m. Pamela K. Geyer, Dec. 1986; 1 child, Aaron P. Hertzmann. BSc in Physics, Computer Sci., Bar-Ilan (Israel) U., 1974; MSc, Weizmann Inst., Rehovot, Israel, 1980; PhD, Hebrew U., Jerusalem, 1981. Teaching asst. dept. math. Bar-Ilan U., 1972-73; programmer The Weizmann Inst.Sci., Rehovot, 1978-79; rsch. asst. Inst. Math. and Computer Sci. Hewbrew U., Jerusalem, 1979-80, instr. Inst. Math. and Computer Sci., 1980-81; postdoctoral scholar dept. computer sci. Stanford U., Palo Alto, Calif., 1981-83, rsch. assoc. Ctr. for Study Lang. and Info., 1984-85; vis. scientist dept. computer sci. IBM Rsch. Lab., San Jose, Calif., 1983-84; mem. rsch. staff IBM Almaden Rsch. Ctr., San Jose, 1985-94, 2d-level mgr. dept. math and related computer sci., 1989-94; Noah Harding prof., chair computer sci. Rice U., Houston, 1994—; cons. assoc. prof. dept. computer sci. Stanford U., 1988-91, cons. prof. dept. computer sci., 1991-95; program chair 6th Assn. for Computing Machinery Symposium on Prins. Database Systems, 1987, 2d Conf. on Theoretical Aspects Reasoning About Knowledge, 1988; conf. chair 3d Conf. on Theoretical Aspects Reasoning About Knowledge, 1990, 11th ACM Symposium on Prins. Database Systems, 1992, 7th IEEE Symposium on Logic in Computer Sci., 1993, others; bd. dirs. Theoretical Aspects Reasoning About Knowledge, Inc., 1991—. Co-author: Reasoning About Knowledge, 1995; editor conf. procs. Theoretical Aspects Reasoning About Knowledge, 1988; assoc. editor Info. and Computation, 1989—, Jour. of Computer and System Scis., 1993—; contbr. articles to profl. jours. Mem. Beth Yeshurum Temple. Sharpiro fellow Bar-Ilan U., 1971-73, Weizmann postdoctoral fellow, 1981-83; recipient Fulbright award U.S.-Israel Edn. Found., 1981. Office: Rice U Dept Computer Sci PO Box 1892 Houston TX 77251-1892

VARGA, JONALYNN RUTH, real estate salesperson; b. Tonawanda, N.Y., Nov. 24, 1954; d. Peter and Dorothy Louise (Stevens) Duzy; m. Bruce A. Morehouse, Mar. 3, 1973 (div. 1975); m. George Francis Brown, Nov. 26, 1977 (div. Dec. 1984); children: Bruce Andrew Morehouse II, Christopher George Brown; m. Louis Stephen Varga, Jr., June 20, 1987 (div. Nov. 1994); m. Louis Stephen Varga, Jr. Mar. 27, 1996. Commdl. notary pub., Fla.; lic. real estate salesperson, Fla.; cert. fin. cons. On-site resident mgr. Argo Corp./Hollywood Apts., Las Vegas, 1985-86; co-owner L & L Classic Fashions, Sarasota, Fla., 1986-87; asst. mgr., leasing agt. Gill Co./The Colony Apts., Bradenton, Fla., 1988; asst. corp. sec., property mgr. A.A.D.D.R. Investments, Inc., Bradenton, Fla., 1988-90; real estate agt., fin. cons. Bay View Real Estate and Trust, Bradenton, Fla., 1990-94; real estate assoc., bus. investments specialist North Star Properties, Inc., Bradenton, Fla., 1994-95; real estate assoc. Waters Realty, Inc., Bradenton, Fla., 1996. Contbr. to World of Poetry Anthology, 1990-91, 96. Fund raising sponsor Muscular Dystrophy Assn., Sarasota, Fla., 1993. Mem. Nat. Assn. Realtors (IREM designation), Manatee County Bd. Realtors, Tri-City Apt. Assn. (sec. 1988). Republican. Christian. Home: 5726 Cortez Rd W # 285 Bradenton FL 34210-2701

VARGAS, JOE FLORES, insurance claims executive; b. Corpus Christi, Tex., Dec. 18, 1940; s. Jose Arispe and Francisca (Flores) V.; m. Anita Munoz, Feb. 16, 1963; children: Joseph Dean, Bernice Ann Vargas Burns. AA, Del Mar Jr. Coll., 1973; BS, Tex. A&M at Corpus Christi, Corpus Christi, 1979. Ct. interpreter Nueces County, Corpus Christi, 1966-70, dep. sheriff, ct. bailiff, 1970-78; ins. adjuster Greene Claims Svc., Corpus Christi, 1978; pvt. investigator Equifax, Corpus Christi, 1978-79; ins. claims rep. Crum & Forster Commercial Ins., Corpus Christi, 1979-86; owner, pres., ins. claims adjuster South Tex. Claims Svc. Inc., Corpus Christi, 1986—. Mem. Corpus Christi Claims Assn., Tex. Claims Assn., Ins. Women of Corpus Christi, Fedn. Ins. Women of Tex., Nat. Acad. Conciliators, Nat. Ctr. Dispute Settlement. Office: South Tex Claims Svc Inc PO Box 270276 Corpus Christi TX 78427-0276

VARIA, INDIRA MAHESH (INDU VARIA), psychiatry educator; b. Jamnagar, India, Sept. 26, 1942. Grad. intersci. exam. Gujarat State, D.K.V. Arts and Sci. Coll., Jamnagar, 1962; med. degree, M.P. Shah Med. Coll., Jamnagar, 1968. Diplomate Am. Bd. Psychiatry and Neurology. Intern Gujarat State Hosps., India, 1968; resident in anesthesiology Gujarat Med. Coll., Ahmedabad Civil Hosp., India, 1968-69; med. officer Min. Health Hosps., Uganda, 1970-71; family planning physician Better Family Planning Clinic and Family Planning Clinic Phila., 1973-75; resident Duke U., Durham, N.C., 1978-82, chief resident, 1982, clin. instr. divsn. psychosomatic medicine, 1982-83, clin. asst. prof. affective disorder program, 1985, acting dir. residency edn. in psychosomatic medicine, 1987, dir., consultation liaison svc. psychosomatic medicine, 1987-92, clin. asst. prof. dept. psychiatry, 1992—; rsch. coord. John Ulmsted Hosp., Butner, N.C., 1984-86; with WRAL Doctors on Call, 1991-92; examiner Am. Bd. Psychiatry and Neurology, 1994; presenter numerous seminars, confs. Author: (book chpt.) Somatic Symptoms in Depression: In Affective Disorders, 1993; contbr. articles to profl. jours. Pres. Jain Study Ctr. N.C., 1990. Named Table Tennis Champion Saurashtra Championships, India, 1967; grantee Hoffman La-Roche, Inc., 1984, Sandoz Pharm. Co., 1992, Burroughs Wellcome Co., 1993. Mem. Am. Psychiat. Assn., Am. Soc. Clin. Psycho-Pharmacology, Anxiety Disorders Assn. Am., Acad. Psychosomatic Medicine, N.C. Med. Soc., N.C. Neuropsychiat. Assn. Office: Duke Univ Med Ctr Dept Psychiatry PO Box 3889 Durham NC 27710

VARIN, ROGER ROBERT, textile executive; b. Bern, Switzerland, Feb. 15, 1925; came to U.S., 1951; s. Robert Francois and Anna (Martz) V.; m. Annemarie Louis, May 24, 1951; children: Roger R.R., Edward C.H., Viviane A.H. BBA, Mcpl. Coll., Bern, 1944; PhD in Chemistry, U. Bern, 1951. Rsch. fellow Harvard U., Cambridge, Mass., 1951-52; rsch. assoc. E.I. DuPont De Nemours, Wilmington, Del., 1952-62; dir. rsch. Riegel Textile Corp., Ware Shoals, S.C., 1962-71; founder, chief exec. officer Varinit Corp., Greenville, S.C., 1971—; founder, chief exec. officer Varinit S.A., Geneva, 1974—. Pres. Greenville Sister City Internat., 1993. Mem. Am. Chem. Soc., Fiber Soc., Soc. Advanced Materials and Process Engrng., Rotary (pres. Greenville chpt. 1979-80), Sigma Xi. Office: Varinit Corp PO Box 6602 Greenville SC 29606-6602

VARLEY, ROBERT CHRISTOPHER GOUGH, management consultant, economist; b. Perth, Scotland, Dec. 11, 1949; came to U.S., 1990; s. Rowland Michael Gough and Elizabeth Joan (Asher) V.; m. Widayati Ambarkahi Supangat, Sept. 4, 1986; children: Krishna, Harold, Lucy Maharani. BSc in Econ., London U., 1971, MSc in Econ., 1973; cert. edn., Inst. Edn., London, 1975; MPPM, Yale U., 1992. Econs. lectr. U. South Bank, London, 1973-75; researcher U.K., Fiji, 1975-77; sr. economist Hunting Tech. Svcs., Elstree, U.K., 1977-85; cons., project assoc. Harvard Inst. for Internat. Devel., Cambridge, Mass., 1985-91; cons. ADB, HIID, 1991-93; sr. pub. fin. specialist Rsch. Triangle Inst., 1993—. Author: Tourism in Fiji, 1978, (monograph) Irrigation Policy, 1989, Household Credit and Urban Water Supply and Sanitation, 1995, Masalah dan Kebijakan Irigasi, 1995; contbr. articles to profl. jours. Home: 3508 Prince William Dr Fairfax VA 22031

VARNER, BRUCE H., JR., fire department official, educator; b. Washington, June 21, 1946; s. Bruce H. Varner and Rose A. (Parrish) Lewis; m. Elaine L. Nelson (div. 1974); 1 child, Paul A.; m. Susan A. Nungesser, Oct. 7, 1989. AA in Fire Protection, Phoenix Coll., 1972; student, Ariz. State U., 1973-77. Firefighter Phoenix Fire Dept., 1967-72, fire engr., 1972-77, fire capt., 1977-83, div. chief, 1983-85, dep. chief, 1985-92; fire chief Carrollton (Tex.) Fire Dept., 1992—. Mem. Nat. Fire Protection Assn. (tech. corr. com. fire svc. protective clothing and equipment), Internat. Assn. Fire Chiefs, Dallas County Fire Chiefs, S.W. Fire Chiefs, North Tex. Fire Chiefs Assn. (pres. 1996), Internat. Soc. Fire Svc. Instrn., Hon. Order Ky. Cols., Nat. Exch. Club of Carrollton (chmn. svc. chair 1994-96), Wingspread IV Conf., 1996. Office: Carrollton Fire Dept 1945 Jackson PO Box 110535 Carrollton TX 75011

VARNER, CHILTON DAVIS, lawyer; b. Opelika, Ala., Mar. 12, 1943; s. William Cole and Frances (Thornton) Davis; m. K. Morgan Varner III, June 19, 1965; 1 child, Ashley Elizabeth. AB with distinction, Smith Coll., 1965; JD with distinction, Emory U., 1976. Assoc. King & Spalding, Atlanta, 1976-83, ptnr., 1983—; trustee Emory U., Atlanta, 1995—. Author: Appellate Handbook for Georgia Lawyers, 1995. Mem. Leadership Atlanta, 1984-85; asst. clk., elder, bd. elders Trinity Presbyn. Ch., Atlanta, 1985-88; exec. com. Ate Arts Alliance, Atlanta, 1981-85; mem. Atlanta Symphony Chorus, 1970-74. Fellow Am. Coll. Trial Lawyers; mem. ABA, Ga. Bar Assn., Atlanta Bar Assn., Bleckley Inn of Ct. (master), Order of Coif, Phi Beta Kappa. Office: King & Spalding 191 Peachtree St NE Atlanta GA 30303-1740

VARNER, JOYCE EHRHARDT, librarian; b. Quincy, Ill., Sept. 13, 1938; d. Wilbur John and Florence Elizabeth (Mast) Ehrhardt; m. Donald Giles Varner, Sept. 12, 1959; children: Amy, Janice, Christian, Matthew, Nadine. BA, Northeastern Okla. State U., 1980; MLS, U. Okla., 1984. Lab. analyst Gardner Denver Co., Quincy, 1956-60; sales rep. Morrisonville, Ill., 1963-69; libr. clk. U. Ill., Urbana, 1973-75; libr. tech. asst. Northeastern Okla. State U., Tahlequah, 1976-86; asst. reference libr. Muskogee (Okla.) Pub. Libr., 1986-90; libr. Jess Dunn Correctional Ctr., Taft, Okla., 1990—. Editor Indian Nations Audubon Nature Notes, 1977-81, 96—; contbr. articles to newspaper. Vol. Lake-Wood coun. Girl Scouts U.S.A., 1975—, bd. dirs. 1992—, pres., 1995-96; sec.-treas. Cherokee County Rural Water Dist. 7, 1987—; edn. chmn. Indian Nations chpt. Nat. Audubon Soc., 1989—. Recipient Thanks Badge, Lake-Wood coun. Girl Scouts U.S.A., 1990. Mem. ALA, AAUW, Okla. Libr. Assn. (nominating com. 1989), Okla. Acad. Sci., Okla. Ornithol. Soc. (chmn. libr. com. 1978-88, Award of Merit 1990, pres.-elect 1994, pres. 1995-96), Am. Correctional Assn., Okla. Correctional Assn., Alpha Chi, Beta Beta Beta, Phi Delta Kappa (Found. rep. 1984-86, historian 1992—). Home: RR 1 Box 1 Welling OK 74471-9701 Office: Jess Dunn Correctional Ctr Leisure Libr PO Box 316 Taft OK 74463-0316

VARNER, ROBERT EDWARD, federal judge; b. Montgomery, Ala., June 11, 1921; s. William and Georgia (Thomas) V.; children: Robert Edward, Carolyn Stuart.; m. Jane Dennis Hannah, Feb. 27, 1982. BS, Auburn U., 1946; JD, U. Ala., 1949. Bar: Ala. 1949. Atty. City of Tuskegee, 1951; asst. U.S. atty. U.S. Dist. Ct. (mid. dist.) Ala., 1954-58; pvt. practice Montgomery, 1958-71; ptnr. Jones, Murray, Stewart & Varner, 1958-71; U.S. dist. judge Montgomery, 1971—; guest lectr. bus. law Huntingdon Coll. Pres. Montgomery Rotary Charity Found.; v.p., fin. chmn. Tukabatchee Area coun. Boy Scouts Am.; mem. Macon County Bd. Edn., 1950-54. With USNR, 1942-46. Recipient Silver Beaver award Boy Scouts Am. Mem. ABA, FBA, ATLA, Montgomery Bar Assn. (pres. 1971), Macon County Bar Assn., Jud. Conf. U.S. (mem. com. on operation of jury sys.), Rotary (pres. club 1961), Phi Alpha Delta (Outstanding Alumnus award 1996), Phi Delta Theta. Republican. Methodist. Office: US Dist Ct PO Box 2046 Montgomery AL 36102-2046

VARNES, JILL TUTTON, university official, health educator; b. Rome, Ga., Sept. 15, 1947; d. Mather M. and Patti L. (Fricks) Tutton; m. G. Peter Wilson, Dec. 1966 (div. Oct. 1973); children: James G. II, Jennifer Anne; m. Paul R. Varnes, Nov. 24, 1977; 1 child, Julia Rae. AA, Lake Sumter Community Coll., Leesburg, Fla., 1967; BS in Phys. Edn., U. Fla., 1973, MA, 1974; EdD, U. So. Miss., 1978. Cert. tchr., health educator, health edn. specialist, Fla. Tchr., coach Marion County Schs., Dunnellon, Fla., 1974-76; asst. coord. comprehensive health edn. demonstration model Fla. Dept. Edn., Tallahassee, 1977-78; asst. prof. health edn. U. Fla., Gainesville, 1978-83, assoc. prof., 1983-96, dir. living well employee wellness program, 1985-89, asst. dean Coll. Health and Human Performance, 1989—, assoc. dir. Ctr. for Health Promotion, Rsch. and Devel., 1989—, prof., 1996—; presenter to numerous internat., nat., state and local orgns. on wellness, sch. health programs, profl. preparation and gerontology; cons. to numerous govt., pub. and pvt. agys. on curriculum devel., health promotion, program and pers. evaluation, and worksite wellness programs. Contbr. articles to profl. jours. Bd. dirs. Am. Lung Assn. Fla., also various coms., also mem. NE br. bd. dirs.; mem. nat. coms. Am. Lung Assn., N.Y.C. Grantee Fla. Dept. Edn., 1987-89, Nat. Cancer Inst., 1989—. Fellow Assn. for Fitness in Bus. (pres. region 3, 1988-89); mem. AAHPERD (nominating com. 1986, bd. govs., bd. dirs. so. dist., 1989-91, pres., v.p. health 1986-89, honor award 1989), Fla. Assn. for Health, Phys Edn., Recreation and Dance (v.p. health div. 1978-80, pres. 1980-83, honor award 1983), Fla. Assn. Profl. Health Educators (sec., Health Edn. award 1990), Assn. for Advancement of Health Edn. Office: U Fla Coll Health & Human Performance FLG 232 Gainesville FL 32611

VARTANIAN, ISABEL SYLVIA, dietitian; b. Duquesne, Pa.; d. Apel and Mary (Kasparian) V. BS, U. Ala., 1957; MS, Columbia U., 1962. Registered dietitian. Dietetic intern N.Y. Hosp./Cornell Med. Ctr., N.Y.C., 1957-58; therapeutic dietitian Vets. Affairs Med. Ctr., Bronx, N.Y., 1958-60, adminstrv. dietitian, 1960-62, nutrition clinic dietitian, 1962-63; rsch. and nutrition clinic dietitian Vets. Affairs Med. Ctr., Coral Gables, Fla., 1963; nutrition clinic dietitian Vets. Affairs Med. Ctr., Richmond, Va., 1963-66, chief nutritional therapy edn. and rsch. sect., 1966-83, nutrition support dietitian, 1983—. Bd. dirs. Richmond Cmty. Action Program, 1978-83; adv. com. Social Svcs., Hopewell, Va., 1991—. Recipient Outstanding awards Vets. Affairs Med. Ctr., Superior Performance awards, Outstanding award. Mem. Richmond Dietetic Assn. (chairwoman diet therapy sect. 1966-67, pres.-elect 1967-68, pres. 1968-70, chairwoman Dial-A-Dietitian 1972-74, chairwoman pub. rels. 1973-74, 78-81, chairwoman Divsn. Cmty. Dietetics 1983-85, chairwoman program planning com. 1985), Va. Dietetic Assn. (chairwoman career guidance com. 1963-65, ednl. exhibits 1967, Dial-A-Dietitian 1972-74, pub. rels. 1982-84, visibility campaign 1984, exhibit com. 1984, program planning com. 1988, divsn. cmty. dietetic 1989-91), Va. Soc. Parenteral and Enteral Nutrition (chairwoman program planning com. 1988-89, membership com. 1990), Am. Dietetic Assn. (life, membership com.), Nat. Kidney Found. (renal nutrition sect.), Am. Soc. Parenteral and Enteral Nutrition. Home: 2005 Jackson St Hopewell VA 23860-3633 Office: VA Med Ctr 1201 Broad Rock Blvd Richmond VA 23249-0001

VASSBERG, LILIANE MANGOLD, foreign language educator; b. Paris, Sept. 9, 1943; came to U.S., 1962; d. Eugene S. and Erna (Motzer) Mangold; m. David E. Vassberg, Nov. 10, 1962; children: Mark A., Alan H. BA in French, U. Tex., 1969; MA in Eng., Pan American U.; PhD in applied linguistics, U. Tex., 1989. Lecturer in French Pan Am. U., Edinburg, Tex., 1980-88; asst. prof. in French Pan Am. U., Edinburg, 1988-94, assoc. prof. in French, 1994—; dir. French program U. Tex., Pan American, 1993—; mem. faculty senate, 1994—. Author: Alsatian Acts of Identity, 1993; contbr. articles to profl. jours. Pres. Alliance Francaise, McAllen, 1983. Mem. Am. Assn. Tchrs. French, Linguistic Assn. Southwest, MLA, Am. Coun. Teaching Fgn. Langs., Nat. Assn. Ethnic Studies, Soc. French Hist. Studies, Phi Beta Kappa, Kappa Delta Pi, Phi Kappa Phi, Phi Alpha Theta. Home: 5000 N 5th St Mcallen TX 78504-2807 Office: U Tex Dept Modern Lang Edinburg TX 78539

VATANDOOST, NOSSI MALEK, art school administrator; b. Teheran, Iran, May 22, 1935; d. Abdullah Goodar and Mahtaban (Goodar) Malek; B.A., Western Ky. U., 1970; m. Ira Vatandoost, May 30, 1964; children: Debbie, Cyrus. Art tchr. Met.-Davidson County Sch. System, Nashville, 1970-71; dir., owner Nossi Coll. Art, Goodlettsville, Tenn., 1973—, dir. Tenn. Proprietary Bus. Sch. Assn., Inc., pres. Crimson Corp.; treas. Malek & Assos. Inc., 1976; dir. EXCEL Edn. Corp., 1980—; vis. lectr., cons. EXCEL Bus. Inst., 1980—. Active mem. Nat. Trust for Hist. Preservation. Mem. NAFE, Nat. Mus. Women in the Arts (charter), Nat. Assn. of Schs. of Art and Design, Hendersonville Art Council, Hendersonville Art Guild (com. chmn.). Club: Soroptimists (Upper Cumberland Valley, Tenn.). Home: 105 Country Club Dr Hendersonville TN 37075-4024 Office: 907 Two Mile Pky Goodlettsville TN 37072-2324

VATAVUK, WILLIAM MICHAEL, chemical engineer, author; b. Sharon, Pa., Jan. 30, 1947; s. William James and Amelia Agnes (Lenarcic) V.; m. Betsy Ann Chandler, Oct. 27, 1973; 1 child, William Chandler. B in Engring., Youngstown State U., Ohio, 1969. Registered profl. engr., N.C. Chem. engr. E.I. DuPont de Nemours, Richmond, Va., 1969-70; sr. chem. engr. U.S. EPA, Durham, N.C., 1970—. Author: Dawn of Peace, 1989 (Pulitzer nomination 1990), Estimating Costs of Air Pollution Control, 1990, Marketing Yourself with Technical Writing, 1992; inventor Vatavuk Air Pollution Control Cost Indexes; contbr. articles to profl. jours. Chmn. Bennett Pl. Hist. Site Adv. Com., Durham, 1992—; publicity chmn. Hist. Preservation Soc. Durham, 1989-90; bd. dirs. N.C. 4-H Devel. Fund, Raleigh, N.C., 1990-93, budget review com., 1994—; tchr., Sunday sch. CCD, 1993. Comdr. USPHS, 1970—. Mem. N.C. Farm Bur., N.C. Grange, USPHS Commd. Officers Assn. (pres. N.C. br. 1975-76, 84-85), Ret. Officers Assn., Author's Guild. Democrat. Roman Catholic. Office: US EPA Mail Drop 15 Durham NC 27711

VATT, RICHARD DOUGLAS, medical corps officer; b. Denver, Nov. 8, 1957; s. Karl Daniel and Lougine Mae (Amundsen) V.; m. Sharon Kay Weeks, Apr. 13, 1979; children: Seth Tyler, Garrett Douglas. BS, Colo. State U., 1979; DO, Chgo. Coll. Osteo. Medicine, 1987; MPH, U. Tex., 1992. Diplomate Am. Bd. Aerospace Medicine. Intern Southeastern Med. Ctr., North Miami Beach, Fla., 1987-88; commd. 2d lt. USAF, 1988, advanced through grades to maj., 1994; flight surgeon Regional Med. Ctr., Eglin AFB, 1988-91; resident in aerospace medicine Sch. Aerospace Medicine, Brooks A.F.B., 1991-94; squadron comdr., chief aeromed. svcs. 7th Med. Group, Dyess AFB, Tex., 1994—. Mem. Am. Osteo. Assn., Aerospace Med. Assn., Am. Coll. Occupational Safety and Environ. Medicine, USAF Soc. Flight Surgeons, Am. Osteo. Coll. Preventive Medicine. Office: 697 Hospital Rd Dyess AFB TX 79607

VAUGHAN, ALICE FELICIE, accountant, real estate executive, tax consultant; b. Laredo, TX, July 14, 1937; d. Wilfred John and Mayme Alice (Mitchell) Peck; m. Sam J. Vaughan, Feb. 27, 1960; children: Nicole Pam, Bonnie Kay, Kimberly Ann, Linda Marie. AS, AA, Del Mar Coll., 1981; BBA, Corpus Christi State U., 1982, MBA, 1983. Staff acct. Robin Perrone, CPA, Corpus Christi, Tex., 1985-86; owner Alice Vaughan Realty, Corpus Christi, 1982—; mgr. Country Club Estates Parks, Inc., Corpus Christi, 1986-89; tax acct. Jon Hurt, CPA, Corpus Christi, Tex., 1989—; v.p., sec., treas. Sa-Gu Corp., 1989—; bus. tchr. Incarnate Word Acad. High Sch., Corpus Christi, 1988. Aquatic instr. YMCA, Corpus Christi, 1986-88; water safety instr. ARC, Corpus Christi (20 Yr. Svc. award, 1991); vice-chmn. Corpus Christi Housing Improvement Corp./Loan Rev. Com., mem. water allocation and adv. com. Mem. Tex. Assn. Realtors, Nat. Assn. Realtors, Country Club Civic Assn. Republican. Roman Catholic. Home and Office: 6410 Coral Gables Dr Corpus Christi TX 78413-2612

VAUGHAN, CLYDE VERNELSON, program director; b. Nashville, Mar. 5, 1941; s. Clearwood Vernelson and Mamie May (Patterson) V.; m. Linda Carol Bean, Dec. 7, 1977; children: Vaudi, Gary, Christopher, Patrick, Cheryl, Pamela. AA in Mgmt., Hawaii Pacific Coll., 1984; BBA in Econs., Campbell U., 1987, MBA, 1990. Printer Palm Beach Post, West Palm Beach, Fla., 1960-64; coord. VA Campbell U., Buies Creek, N.C., 1987-90; dir. Campbell U., Pope AFB, N.C., 1990—; mem. bd. transfer com. Fayetteville (N.C.) Tech. Coll., 1993—. Vice chmn. Cumberland County Bd. Adjustments, Fayetteville, 1992—. With U.S. Army, 1964-87. Mem. VFW, Am. Vets. Fgn. Wars, Am. Legion, Am. Motorcycle Assn. Baptist. Home: 126 W Circle Ct Fayetteville NC 28301 Office: Campbell Univ Campus 384 Maynard St Ste A Pope AFB NC 28308

VAUGHAN, DENNIS J., business executive. Dir. R&D Clark-Schwebel, Inc., Anderson, S.C. Office: Clark-Schwebel Inc 2200 S Murray Ave Anderson SC 29622

VAUGHAN, EUGENE H., investment company executive; b. Brownsville, Tenn., Oct. 5, 1933; s. Eugene H. Sr. and Margaret (Musgrave) V.; m. Susan Bolinger Westbrook, May 11, 1963; children: Margaret Corbin, Richard Bolinger. BA, Vanderbilt U., 1955; MBA, Harvard U., 1961. CFA, 1967. Security analyst Putnam Mgmt. Co., Boston, 1961-64; dir., dir. rsch. Underwood, Neuhaus & Co., Inc., Houston, 1964-70; pres., chief exec. officer Vaughan, Nelson & Boston, Inc., Houston, 1970-77, Vaughan, Nelson, Scarborough & McConnell, Inc., Houston, 1970—; bd. dirs. Founders Asset Mgmt. Co., Denver, 1970—. Chair Fin. Analyst Fedn., N.Y.C., 1973-74, bd. dirs., 1969-76; pres. Houston Soc. Fin. Analysts, 1967-68; founder Internat. Coordinating Com., 1974; bd. dirs., chmn. investment com. Presbyn. Bd. Pensions (USA), Phila., 1988—; mem. investment com. Tex. State Employees Retirement System, Austin, 1988-93; trustee Vanderbilt U., Nashville, 1972—, St. John's Sch., Houston, 1980-85, Goodwill Industries, Houston, 1978—; elder First Presbyn. Ch., 1976—; founding chmn., trustee Presbyn. Sch., Houston, 1986-90. Lt. USN, 1955-58. Recipient Disting. Svc. award Fin. Analyst Fedn., 1978, Humanitarian award Am. Jewish Com., 1993, Disting. Svc. award Houston Soc. Fin. Analysts, 1993. Mem. Inst. Chartered Fin. Analysts (trustee 1986-93, chmn. 1989), Assn. for Investment Mgmt. and Rsch. (founding chmn. 1990-91, gov. 1990-93), Greater Houston Partnership (bd. dirs. 1990—, exec. com. 1993—), Houston Club (pres. 1983-84, bd. dirs. 1979-85, chair centennial celebration, 1992-94), Houston Country Club, Forum Club Houston (pres. 1991-92, chmn. 1992-93), Harvard U. Bus. Sch. Club Houston (pres. 1968-69, bd. dirs. 1966-71, 86-90), Vanderbilt Club Houston (chmn. 1984—, pres. 1966-68, Disting. Svc. award 1994), Conferie des Chevaliers du Tastevin, Belle Meade Country Club (Nashville), Argyle Club (San Antonio). Republican. Home: 3465 Inwood Dr Houston TX 77019-3129 Office: Vaughan Nelson Scarborough & McConnell 6300 Texas Commerce Towers Houston TX 77002

VAUGHAN, OTHA H., JR., aerospace engineer, research scientist; b. Anderson, S.C., July 1, 1929; s. Otha H. and Ethel (Mayfield) V.; m. Betty Frances McCoy; children: Thera Virginia, Leslie, Frances. BS in Mech. Engring, Clemson U., 1951, MS in Mech. Engring., 1959; postgrad., U. Tenn. Space Inst., Tullahoma, 1975-81, U. Ala., Huntsville, 1974-75. Registered profl. engr., Ala. Commd. 2nd lt. USAF, 1951, advanced through grades to lt. col., 1972; mem. Von Braun R&D group Army Ballistic Missile Agy. (ABMA), Redstone Arsenal, Ala., 1956-60; retired USAF, 1979; rsch. engr., charter mem. NASA Marshall Space Flight Ctr., Huntsville, Ala., 1960—. Contbr. over 60 articles to profl. jours. Charter Mem. Aviation Hall of Fame, Dayton, Ohio. Fellow AIAA (assoc.); mem. Air Force Assn. (past v.p. Huntsville chpt., life), Res. Officers Assn. (past pres. Huntsville, life), Minute Man Soc. Ala., Antique Aircraft Assn. (life), Exptl. Aircraft

Assn., Soc. Interplanetary Free Floaters (zero-gravity flights in NASA KC-135 aircraft), Masons, Shriners. Home: 10102 Westleigh Dr SE Huntsville AL 35803-1647

VAUGHAN, ROBERT E., diagnostic radiologist, army officer; b. Fontana, Calif., Aug. 18, 1964; s. Frank Jimmy and Maurita Ann (Fillman) V.; m. Tamara Reneé Ellis, Aug. 2, 1987; children: Matthew Joseph Manning, Lucas James Linton. BA in Biology, So. Coll. 7th-day Adventists, Collegedale, Tenn., 1986; MD, Loma Linda U., 1990. Diplomate Am. Bd. Radiology. Layout worker art dept. Coll. Press, Collegedale, 1983-84; tutor Tchg.-Learning Ctr. So. Coll. Seventh-day Adventist, 1984-86; commd. capt. U.S. Army, 1990; transitional intern Letterman Army Med. Ctr., San Francisco, 1990-91; resident in diagnostic radiology Madigan Army Med. Ctr., Tacoma, 1991-95; staff radiologist Martin Army Cmty. Hosp., Ft. Benning, Ga., 1995—, East Ala. Med. Ctr., Opelika, 1996—, Bapt. Med. Ctr., Montgomery, Ala., 1996—. Mem. Am. Roentgen Ray Soc., Am. Coll. Radiology, Radiol. Soc.N.Am., Alpha Omega Alpha, Beta Beta Beta. Office: Martin Army Cmty Hosp Dept Radiology 9200 Marne Rd Fort Benning GA 31905-5515

VAUGHAN, STEPHANIE RUTH, water aerobics business owner, consultant; b. Winchester, Va., Feb. 27, 1956; d. Robert Hall Sr. and Peggy (Owen) Hahn; m. Ward Pierman Vaughan, Nov. 29, 1980; children: Carol Owen, Eva Virginia, Robert Alexander. BS in Biology, Shenandoah U., 1983, MBA, 1985. Sales rep., cashier Best Products, Roanoke, Va., 1977-78; dir. Peg-Ell Sch. Modeling, Winchester, 1978-79; mgr. purchasing and metal fabrication materials Fabritek Co., Inc., Winchester, 1979-84, sec. bd. dirs., 1980—; CEO, owner Splash Internat., Winchester, 1991—, internat. mktg. dir. original cabinet; tennis instr. Camp Camelot, Wilmington, N.C., summer 1978; cons. Fabritek Co., Inc., 1993-95; membership dir. Stonebrook Swim and Racquet Club, Winchester, 1992-93, corp. fitness dir., 1993; instr. Workout in Water class Crooked Run Fitness and racquet Club, Front Royal, Va., 1992—, Winchester Parks and Recreation Dept., 1991-92; instr., designer Children's Water Fitness Classes Winchester County Club, Va., 1993, Stonebrook Country Club, 1994; keynote spkr. Women's Fiar, 1996. Author: Water Exercises for Physicians, Physical Therapists and Water Fitness Instructors, 1994 (award); contbr. articles to profl. jours.; internat. aquatic exercise and therapy presenter. Steering com. mem. Habitat for Humanity, 1995; bd. dirs. Winchester Fred County. Patentee for water fitness product. Mem. AAHPERD, NAFE, AAUW, AMA, Am. Coll. Sports Medicine, Va. Assn. Health, Phys. Recreation and Dance (conf. presenter, chair aquatic coun. 1994-95, v.p. recreation coun. 1996—), Va. Recreation and Parks Soc. (conf. presenter), U.S. Water Fitness Assn. (adv. bd., chair tech. com. 1993—, mem. nat. tech. com. 1992—, C. Carson Conrad Top Water Fitness Leader for Va. award 1993, Deep Water Running Champion 1993, BEMA Nat. Water Fitness Champion 1993, cert. pool coord., cert. instr., nat. conf. aquatic fashion show dir. 1992, 93, 94, conf. presenter, leader 1st Nat. Aquatic Summit, Washington, Team Water Aerobics aquatic champion 1994, June Andrus Entrepreneur of Yr. award 1995, Champion Deep Water Instr. 1995), United Daus. of Confederacy, Aquatic Exercise Assn. (conf. presenter, regional rep. 1994-96), U.S. Synchronized Swimming, Shenandoah U. Alumni Assn. (bd. dirs.), Aquatic Alliance Internat. (internat. mktg. dir. 1996—), Aquatic Edn. Assn. Home: 115 Old Forest Cir Winchester VA 22602

VAUGHEN, JUSTINE L., rehabilitation hospital medical professional; b. Wilmington, Del., Apr. 21, 1930; d. John Victor and Charlotte (Leicht) V.; m. Richard M. Fry, June 26, 1955; children: Martha Hilary Morrow, Amanda Tung. BS, Stetson U., 1950; MD, Temple U., 1954. Diplomate Am. Bd. Physical Medicine and Rehab. Resident physical medicine, rehab. U. Mich., Ann Arbor, 1954-59; asst. prof. physical medicine, rehab. U. Mich. Hosp., Ann Arbor, 1959-60; private practice Gainesville, Fla., 1961—; chief rehab. med. svc. VA Med. Ctr., Gainesville, Fla., 1971—; med. dir. Upreach Rehab. Hosp., Gainesville, Fla., 1986-95; co-clin. prof. U. Fla., Gainesville, 1967—; cons. Vocat. Rehab., State Fla., 1986—; adv. coun. State Divsn. Vocat. Rehab., Tallahassee, 1980-95. Pres. D.A.R.E., Gainesville, 1992-94; bd. dirs. Altrusa House, Gainesville, 1991—. Mem. AMA, Am. Acad. Phys. Medicine and Rehab., Fla. Soc. Phys. Medicine and Rehab. (pres. 1992-94), Fla. Med. Assn., Altrusa Internat., Am. Assn. Electrodiagnostic Medicine. Office: Rehab Medicine Assoc 4881 NW 8th Ave Ste 2 Gainesville FL 32605-4582

VAUGHN, JAMES ELDON, retired military officer, civic volunteer; b. Newkirk, Okla., Aug. 22, 1925; s. Melvin Bud and Vanda Leah (Shurtz) V. Bd. dirs., v.p. ways and means Lyric Theatre Guild, Oklahoma City, 1985-93; mem. com. Jewel Box Theatre, Oklahoma City, 1988-90; cons., leader State Theatre Planning Retreat, Okla., 1990, 91; adv. bd. Bank One. Del. State Rep. Conv., Tulsa, 1983; founder Carpenter Sq. Theatre Vols., 1984—; div. chair SWTA Children's Theatre, 1990-91, exec. dir., 1992—; bd. dirs., v.p. devel. Canterbury Chorale Soc., 1991-92; mem. adv. bd. Physically Ltd. Theatre, Tulsa, 1991-93. co-founder Canterbury Choral Vol., 1992. Sgt. U.S. Army, 1950-52. Recipient Community Svc. Arts award Gov. of Okla. 1986, several Vol. of Yr. awards; inducted in to Okla. Theatre Hall of Honor, 1991. Mem. S.W. Theatre Assn. (Okla. theatre rep. 1988-90, Svc. citation 1989, Disting. Svc. award 1994, Meritorious award 1994), Okla. Cmty. Theatre Assn. (bd. dirs., v.p. membership com. 1987-93), UN Assn. (bd. dirs. Okla. chpt. 1989—, pres. 1995—), SAR (chaplain 1991). Home: 2632 NW 12th St Oklahoma City OK 73107-5420

VAUGHN, JOANN WOLFE, family nurse practitioner; b. Knoxville, Tenn., Mar. 4, 1947; d. Paul Albert and Elizabeth (Umburger) Wolfe; m. Neville Dewayne VAughn, Nov. 8, 1985. Diploma, Johnston Meml. Hosp., Abingdon, Va., 1968; BSN, East Tenn. State U., Johnson City, 1981, MSN, 1996. Cert. family nurse practitioner, ACLS. Staff nurse Bristol (Tenn.) Meml. Hosp., 1968-70, Med. Coll. Va., Richmond, 1970-72; staff nurse ICU/CCU Chippenham Hosp., Richmond, 1972-73; staff nurse Bristol Regional Med. Ctr., 1973-92, asst. nurse mgr. emergency dept., 1992-96; family nurse practitioner Johnston Meml. Hosp., Abingdon, Va., 1996—. Mem. ANA, Emergency Nurses Assn. (pres. Appalachian chpt. 1983-84), Sigma Theta Tau. Republican. Lutheran. Home: PO Box 201 Bristol VA 24203-0201 Office: Family Physicians of Abingdon 227 E Main St Abingdon VA 24210

VAUGHN, JOHN CARROLL, minister, educator; b. Louisville, Sept. 22, 1948; s. Harold D. and Morel (Johnson) V.; m. Brenda Joyce Lyttle, June 17, 1968; children: Deborah, John, Rebecca, Daniel, Joseph. BA, Bob Jones U., 1977, MMin, 1991, DD, 1989. Ordained to ministry Bapt. Ch., 1978. Sr. pastor Faith Baptist Ch., Greenville, S.C., 1977—; founder/adminstr. Hidden Treasure Christian Sch., Greenville, S.C., 1980-84; founder Iglesia Bautista de la Fe, Greenville, S.C., 1981-93; founder/dir. Hidden Treasure Ministries, Greenville, 1985—; exec. bd. Associated Gospel Chs., Hopewell, Va., 1987-93; chaplain Greenville Police Dept., 1987—. Editor: (instrnl. video) Sufficient Grace, 1987; author: (textbook) Special Education: A Biblical Approach, 1991, (biography) More Precious Than Gold, 1994. Chmn. Greenville County Human Rels. Commn., 1986-89; lt. col., chaplain Greenville Composite Squadron CAP, 1985—; counselor Greenville County Crisis Response Team, 1987-91; co-chmn. Greenville County Sex Edn. Adv. Com., 1988-91; mem. exec. bd. dirs. Fundamental Bapt. Fellowship, 1988—, The Wilds, 1992—, Internat. Bapt. Missions, 1993—, Christians for Religious Freedom, 1993—. Mem. Internat. Conf. Police Chaplains, Am. Assn. Christian Schs. (exec. bd. dirs. 1992—), ACFT Owners and Pilots Assn., S.C. Law Enforcement Assn., S.C. Assn. Christian Schs. (pres. 1988—). Republican. Home: 117 Frontline Dr Taylors SC 29687-2675 Office: Faith Bapt Ch 500 W Lee Rd Taylors SC 29687-2513

VAUGHT, DARREL MANDEL, accountant; b. Oklahoma City, Sept. 8, 1943; s. Rubin A. Vaught and Lula B. (Burris) Pierce. BS, Cen. State U., Edmond, Okla., 1971. CPA, Okla. Staff auditor Authur Andersen & Co., Oklahoma City, 1971-72; auditor Office of Inspector Gen. HUD, Ft. Worth, 1972-78, area audit supr., 1978-83, asst. dist. insp. gen. for audit, 1983—. Chief of staff Civil Air Patrol, Okla., 1977-78. Served as sgt. USAF, 1965-69. Mem. AICPA, Okla. Soc. CPAs, Assn. Govt. Accts. (sec. Ft. Worth chpt. 1984-85, edn. dir. 1985-86, pres. 1988-89, regional v.p. Tex.-Okla. 1996, Acct. of Yr. 1985, Nat. Edn. award 1993, Fin. Mgr. of Yr. 1993), Cert. Fraud Examiners (assoc.). Republican.

VAUGHT, WILMA L., foundation executive, retired air force officer; b. Pontiac, Mich., Mar. 15, 1930; d. Willard L. and Margaret J. (Pierce) V. BS, U. Ill., 1952; MBA, U. Ala., 1968; postgrad., Indsl. Coll. Armed Forces, 1972-73; D Pub. Affairs (hon.), Columbia Coll., 1992. Cert. cost acct. Commd. 2d lt. USAF, 1957, advanced through grades to brig. gen., 1980; chief data services div. 306th Combat Support Group USAF, McCoy AFB, Fla., 1963-67; mgmt. analyst Office Dep. Chief of Staff, comptroller Mil. Assistance Command USAF, Saigon, Vietnam, 1968-69; chief advanced logistics systems plans and mgmt. group Air Force Logistics Command USAF, Wright-Patterson AFB, Ohio, 1969-72; chief cost factors br., chief security assistance br. USAF, Washington, 1973-75, Directorate Mgmt. Analysis, Office of Comptroller, 1973-75; dir. program and budget Office Dep. Chief of Staff, comptroller Hdqrs. Air Force Systems Command USAF, Andrews AFB, Md., 1980-82; comdr. U.S. Mil. Entrance Processing Command USAF, North Chicago, Ill., 1982-85; ret. USAF, 1985; pres. Women in Mil. Svc. Meml. Found., Arlington, Va., 1987—; pres. bd. dirs. Pentagon Fed. Credit Union, 1975-82; bd. regents Inst. Cost Analysis, 1979-83; Air Force sr. mil. rep. Def. Adv. Com. on Women in Services, 1982-85; chmn. Com. on Women in Armed Forces, NATO, Brussels, 1984-85. Bd. dirs. Air Force Retired Officer Community, 1986-90; mem. adv. bd. Jane Addams Conf.; mem. bd. trustees The Teller Found. Decorated Bronze Star medal, Def. Disting. Service medal, U.S. Air Force Disting. Service medal; recipient Ill. Achievement award U. Ill., 1983. Mem. Internat. Women's Forum. Methodist. Home: 6658 Van Winkle Dr Falls Church VA 22044-1010 Office: Women in Mil Svc Meml Found 5510 Columbia Pike Ste 302 Arlington VA 22204-3123

VAZQUEZ, GILBERT FALCON, lawyer; b. Eagle Pass, Tex., Oct. 29, 1952; s. Catalina (Falcon) Vazquez. AB in Polit. Sci., Yale U., 1975; JD, Harvard U., 1978. Bar: Tex. 1978, U.S. Dist. Ct. (we. dist.) Tex. 1980, U.S. Ct. Appeals (5th and 11th cirs.) 1981. Ptnr. Matthews & Branscomb, San Antonio, Tex., 1978-85, Akin, Gump, Strauss, Hauer & Feld, L.L.P., San Antonio, 1985—. Co-chmn. issues com. H. Cisneros Mayoral Campaign, San Antonio, 1981; bd. dirs. Bexar County-San Antonio United Way, 1982-87, 91—, San Antonio World Affairs Coun., 1993—, San Antonio Mus. Assn., 1993-95; mem. exec. com. Mayor's Target 90 Commn., San Antonio, 1985-89, vice chmn., 1987-89; chmn. City of San Antonio Charter Rev. Com., 1991-93, State of Tex. Pension Rev. Bd., 1991—, vice-chmn., 1994, chair, 1995; bd. dirs. San Antonio Zool. Soc., 1988—, mem. exec. com. Named Outstanding Young San Antonian, U.S. Jaycees, 1985, Outstanding Vol., J.C. Penny Co., 1984. Mem. ABA (internat. law sect., assoc. editor newsletter 1985-87), Nat. Assn. Bond Lawyers, Tex. Bar Assn. (governing coun. internat. law sect. 1985-88), San Antonio Bar Assn., San Antonio Young Lawyers Assn. (Outstanding Young Lawyer 1987), Hispanic Nat. Bar Assn. (regional pres. 1987-88, nat. sec. 1988-89, v.p. 1989-90), San Antonio World Trade Assn. (bd. dirs. 1987-90), Mexican C. of C. (bd. dirs. 1984-85), Greater San Antonio C. of C. (bd. dirs. 1992-95), Yale Club South Tex. (pres. 1982-85). Democrat. Roman Catholic. Office: Akin Gump Strauss Hauer & Feld LLP 300 Convent St Ste 1500 San Antonio TX 78205-3716

VEACH, ROBERT RAYMOND, JR., lawyer; b. Charleston, S.C., Nov. 28, 1950; s. Robert Raymond and Evelyn Ardell (Vegter) V.; m. Lori Sue Erickson, May 27, 1989. Student, St. Olaf Coll., 1968-70; BS in Acctg., Ariz. State U., 1972; JD, So. Meth. U., 1975. Bar: Tex. 1975, Nebr. 1975, U.S. Dist. Ct. Nebr. 1975, U.S. Dist. Ct. (no. dist.) Tex. 1975, Temporary Emergency Ct. Appeals 1975. Acctg. instr. Sch. Bus. So. Meth. U., Dallas, 1973-74; law clk. to Hon. Joe E. Estes U.S. Dist. Ct. No. Dist. Tex.-Temp. Emergency Ct. Appeals, Dallas, 1975-76; assoc. Locke Purnell Boren Laney & Neely, Dallas, 1976-80; v.p. The Lomas & Nettleton Co., Dallas, 1980-83, Rauscher Pierce Refsnes, Inc., Dallas, 1983-87; pres. RPR Mortgage Fin. Corp., Dallas, 1985-87; sr. shareholder Locke Purnell Rain Harrell, Dallas, 1987—; allied mem. N.Y. Stock Exch., 1985-87; lectr. securities and banking confs.; bd. dirs. pvt. corps. Author legal articles. Dir. North Tex. affiliate Am. Diabetes Assn., Dallas, 1978-81; mem. Gov.'s Task Force Wash. State Housing Commn., 1982-83. Mem. ABA, State Bar of Tex., Nebr. State Bar Assn., Fed. Bar Assn., Dallas Bar Assn. Republican. Methodist. Home: 4223 Brookview Dr Dallas TX 75220-3801 Office: Locke Purnell Rain Harrell 2200 Ross Ave Ste 2200 Dallas TX 75201-6766

VEAL, REX R., lawyer; b. Lafayette, Ga., May 2, 1956; s. Boyd Herman and Barbara Ann (Sharp) V.; m. Vicky Elizabeth Wilkins, Dec. 13, 1980; children: Matthew Aaron and Richard Andrew (twins). BA, U. Tenn., 1978, JD, 1980. Bar: Tenn. 1981, U.S. Dist. Ct. (ea. dist.) Tenn. 1981, U.S. Ct. Appeals (10th cir.) 1981, U.S. Ct. Appeals (6th cir.) 1984, U.S. Ct. Appeals (4th cir.) 1987, Ga. 1991, U.S. Dist. Ct. (no. dist.) Ga. 1991, U.S. Ct. Appeals (11th cir.) 1991, D.C. 1993, U.S. Dist. Ct. D.C. 1993, U.S. Ct. Appeals (D.C. and fed. cir.) 1993. Assoc. Finkelstein, Kern, Steinberg & Cunningham, Knoxville, Tenn., 1980-83; atty. FDIC, Knoxville, 1983-84, sr. atty., 1984-88; counsel liquidation FDIC, Washington, 1988-89, assoc. gen. counsel, 1989-90; spl. counsel Resolution Trust Corp., Washington, 1989-90; ptnr. Powell, Goldstein, Frazer & Murphy, Atlanta and Washington, 1990—; lectr. in field. Contbr. articles to profl. jours. Mem. ABA, Tenn. Bar Assn., Ga. Bar Assn., Atlanta Bar Assn. Home: 6201 Blackberry Hl Norcross GA 30092-1375 Office: Powell Goldstein Frazer & Murphy 191 Peachtree St NE Fl 16 Atlanta GA 30303-1741 also: Powell Goldstein Frazer & Murphy 6th Flr 1001 Pennsylvania Ave NW Washington DC 20004

VEASEY, BYRON KEITH, information systems consultant; b. Washington, Mar. 17, 1957; s. Columbus Jr. and Joan Marie (Ingram) V. BS in Indsl. and Sys. Engring., U. So. Calif., 1979; MBA, Ball State U., 1982; M Mgmt. in Info. Sys., U. Dallas, 1989. Cert. quality analyst Quality Assurance Inst., computing profl. Inst. for Certification of Computer Profls. CIM engr. Mason & Hanger, Amarillo, Tex., 1983-87; bus. sys. analyst E-Sys., Garland, Tex., 1987-89; consulting mgr. Deloitte & Touche, Dallas, 1989-93; sr. cons. CSC, Dallas, 1993—. Mem. Dallas Heart Ball, 1991-92; mem. PM League Dallas Mus. of Art, 1992-93; bd. dirs. Dallas Wind Symphony, 1992; pres. Inst. of Indsl. Engrs., Dallas, 1992-93; v.p. programs Assn. for Sys. Mgmt., Dallas, 1991-93. Capt. USAF, 1979-82. Mem. Am. Legion. Republican. Home: 12010 Ridge Knoll Dr # 10 Fairfax VA 22033 Office: AT&T Solutions 1921 Gallows Rd Ste 500 Vienna VA 22182

VEAZEY, DORIS ANNE, state agency administrator; b. Dawson Spring, Ky., Feb. 16, 1935; d. Bradley Basil and Lucy Mable (Hamby) Sisk; m. Herman Veazey Jr., Aug. 15, 1964 (dec. Sept. 1987); 1 child, Vickie Dianne Veazey Kicinski. Murray State U., 1952-54. Unemployment ins. examiner Dept. for Employment Svcs., Madisonville, Ky., 1954-73, unemployment ins. supr., 1973-85, field office mgr., 1985-96; bd. dirs., adv. bd. region II Vocat. Tech. Schs., Madisonville, 1988-92. Mem. Mayor's Work Force Devel. Com., 1993—, Ky. Indsl. Devel. Com., 1992-96; dept. dir. Adult III Sunday Sch., 1994-96, ch. choir, 1990—. Mem. Internat. Platform Assn., Internat. Assn. of Pers. in Employment Svcs., Southeastern Employment and Tng. Assn., Tenure, Order of Ky. Cols., Greater Madisonville C. of C. (dir. leadership 1988-93). Baptist. Office: Dept Employment Svcs 56 Federal St # 1226 Madisonville KY 42431-2043

VEAZEY, JOHN HOBSON, internist; b. Van Alstyne, Tex., June 27, 1901; s. James and Malta Augusta (Blassingame) V.; m. Elizabeth May Chandler, Mar. 14, 1935; children: Samuel, James. Grad., Austin Coll., 1918-22; MD, U. Tex., 1926. Intern Sherman (Tex.) Hosp., 1926-28; pvt. practice medicine, Madill, Okla., 1929-35, Ardmore, Okla., 1935—; co-founder Med. Arts Clinic, Ardmore, 1952—; pvt. practice internal medicine, Ardmore, 1957—; chief staff Meml. Hosp., So. Okla., 1958—, chmn. dept. internal medicine, 1973, chmn. pattern gift com., 1983, mem. staff Ardmore Hosp.; pres. Med. Arts Bldg. Co. Ardmore, 1952-88, Med. Arts Clinic of Ardmore, 1952-88. Co-chmn. profl. div. United Fund, 1969; trustee Presbyn. Ch. Recipient 50-Year cert. of appreciation Bd. Trustees U. Tex. Med. Br. Alumni Assn., 1976; hon. at homecoming banquets U. Tex. Med. Br., 1987, 90-92. Mem. AMA (Physician's Recognition award 1976, 79, 82, 85-88, 90—), Okla. State Med. Assn. (council 1944-56, life) Carter-Love-Marshall Med. Soc. (pres. 1955, life), Ardmore C. of C. (bd. dirs., v.p.), Am. Soc. Internal Medicine. Lodge: Masons. Home: 2 Overland Route St Ardmore OK 73401-2916 Office: 921 14th Ave NW Ardmore OK 73401-1837

VEDLIK, CSABA SANDOR, JR., political science educator; b. Aalen, Germany, May 13, 1947; came to U.S., 1950; s. Csaba Imre and Eva Alice (Biro) V. BA, Fla. Atlantic U., 1969; MA, U. Ariz., 1974. Legis. asst. U.S. Ho. Reps., Washington, 1978-82; rsch. dir. Am. Space Frontier Polit. Action Com., Falls Church, Va., 1983-84; writer, editor The White House, Washington, 1984-89; lobbyist Am. Life Lobby, Washington, 1989-90; instr. Polit. Sci. Keiser Coll. Tech., Melbourne, Fla., 1992; concierge La Bonne Vie Condominium, Palm Beach, Fla., 1993-95; writer Eternal Word TV Network, Irondale, Ala., 1995—. Author: Judicial Supremacy: The Supreme Court on Trial, 1980. Richard M. Weaver fellow, 1981. Mem. Eta Kappa Phi. Republican. Roman Catholic.

VEENHUIS, PHILIP EDWARD, psychiatrist, educator, administrator; b. Kalamazoo, Mich., Aug. 4, 1935; s. Claude Albert and Placide Mary (Steger) V.; m. Joanne Elizabeth Williams, Aug. 8, 1959; children: Mark Edward, Suzanne Marie. BA, Kalamazoo Coll., 1957; MD, U. Mich., 1961, MPH in Health Svcs. Adminstrn., 1990. Diplomate Am. Bd. Psychiatry; cert. of added qualifications in geropsychiatry; cert. in adminstrv. psychiatry. Intern James Decker Munson Hosp., Traverse City, Mich., 1961-62; resident Lafayette Clinic Wayne State U., Detroit, 1962-65; dir. psychiat. edn. Med. Coll. Wis., Milw., 1970-73, acting chmn. dept. psychiatry, 1973-75, 82-86, dir. continuing edn. dept. psychiatry, 1975-86, dir. psychiat. tng., 1984-86; chmn. dept. psychiatry Providence Hosp., Southfield, Mich., 1986-93; med. dir. divsn. mental health/devel. disabil. subs. abuse N.C. Dept. Human Resources, Raleigh, 1993—; assoc. prof. psychiatry Med. Coll. Wis., 1973-86; clin. prof. psychiatry Mich. State U., 1988-92, U. N.C., Chapel Hill, 1993—; clin. assoc. prof. Wayne State U., 1991-92. Contbr. articles to profl. jours. Served to lt. comdr. USNR, 1965-67. NIMH grantee, 1982-86. Fellow Am. Psychiat. Assn.; mem. Mich. Psychiat. Soc., North Psychiat. Assn. Office: NC Dept Human Resources Divsn Mental Health 325 N Salisbury St Raleigh NC 27603-1388

VEGA, ELI SAMUEL, nurse anesthetist; b. Guayama, P.R., Oct. 26, 1945; came to U.S., 1979; m. Maria J. Ramos, Apr. 22, 1972; children: Marieely, Samarys. Diploma in Nursing, Bella Vista Sch. Nursing, Mayaguez, P.R., 1971; cert. in Anesthesia, Damas Hosp., Ponce, P.R., 1973; posgrad., U. West Fla., 1990-92. RN. Staff nurse Bella Vista Hosp., Mayaguez, P.R., 1974-79; commd. lt. (j.g.) USN, 1979, advanced through grades to comdr., 1993; staff nurse anesthetist U.S. Naval Hosp., San Diego, 1979-81; head anesthesiology dept. U.S. Naval Hosp., Twentynine Palms, Calif., 1981-84; staff nurse anesthetist U.S. Naval Hosp., Jacksonville, Fla., 1984-87; asst. anesthesia dept. head U.S. Naval Hosp., Rota, Spain, 1987-90; staff nurse anesthetist U.S. Naval Hosp., Pensacola, Fla., 1990-94; asst. anesthesia dept. head Naval Hosp. Keflavik, Iceland, 1994-95; sr. nurse anesthetist Naval Hosp., Pensacola, Fla., 1995—, 1996—. Developer, instr. intravenous therapy program U.S. Naval Hosp., Rota, Spain, 1989. Decorated two Navy commendation medals. Mem. Am. Assn. Nurse Anesthetists, Fla. Nurse Anesthetist Assn., P.R. Nurse Anesthetist Assn. (v.p. 1976-77). Home: 3691 Monteigne Dr Pensacola FL 32504-4538

VEGA, MARIO, family practice physician; b. Encarnación, Itapua, Paraguay, Jan. 26, 1928; came to U.S., 1966; s. Manuel and Maria Clotilde (Perini) V.; m. Sady Diaz de Bedoya (dec. 1988); 1 child, Jennifer Alexandra. BS, Nat. Coll., Paraguay, 1949; MD, Nat. U. Asunción, Paraguay, 1954; postgrad., U. Miami, 1966-67. Diplomate Am. Bd. Family Practice. Resident Med. Sch. Nat. U. Asunción, 1955; Med. Sch. fellow Nat. U. Asunción, 1956; Polytech. Inst. Surgery fellow Britanic Hosp., Rosario, Argentina, 1957; pvt. practice Rosario, 1957-66; rotating intern Mt. Sinai Hosp., Miami Beach, Fla., 1967; pvt. practice Charles Town, W.Va., 1968-70; resident in anesthesiology Albert Einstein Coll. Medicine, Bronx, N.Y., 1971-72, Meml. Hosp. Cornell U., N.Y.C., 1972-73, Jackson Meml. Hosp. U. Miami, 1973; anesthesiology fellow Wilmington (Del.) Med. Ctr., 1973-74; pvt. practice Bradenton, Fla., 1975—; staff Charles Town Gen. Hosp., Ranson, W.Va., 1968-70; founder Non Invasive Vascular Lab., Tampa, Fla., 1981—. Fellow Am. Acad. Family Physicians; mem. Fla. Med. Assn., Orange County Med. Soc., Internat. Assn. Bilingual Physicians, Am. Assn. Residents and Interns, Royal Soc. Medicine (Eng., affiliate). Democrat. Adventist. Home: 1055 Beach Rd #302 Sarasota FL 34242 Office: Profl Med Ctr 503 Manatee Ave Ste E Bradenton Beach FL 34217-1992

VEIGEL, JON MICHAEL, science administrator; b. Mankato, Minn., Nov. 10, 1938; s. Walter Thomas and Thelma Geraldine (Lein) V.; m. Carol June Bradley, Aug. 10, 1962. BS, U. Washington, 1960; PhD, UCLA, 1965. Program mgr. Office of Tech. Assessment, U.S. Congress, Washington, 1974-75; div. mgr. Calif. Energy Commn., Sacramento, 1975-78; asst. dir. Solar Energy Rsch. Inst., Golden, Colo., 1978-81; pres. Alt. Energy Corp., Rsch. Triangle Park, N.C., 1981-88, Oak Ridge (Tenn.) Associated Univs., 1988-96; bd. dirs. Am. Coun. Energy Efficient Economy, Washington, Pacific Internat. Ctr. for High Tech. Rsch., Honolulu. Contbr. articles to jours. Bd. dirs. Oak Ridge Community Found., also chmn.; trustee Maryville Coll., Mendeleyev U., Moscow, Russia. 1st lt. USAF, 1965-68. Mem. AAAS (com. on sci. and engring. pub. policy). Office: SunRunner Assocs PO Box 2005 Cedar City UT 84721

VEILLE, JEAN-CLAUDE, maternal-fetal medicine physician, educator; came to U.S., 1982; m. Beatrice Buehler; children: Olivier, Xavier, Patrique. BS, McGill U., 1971; MD, U. Montpellier, France, 1977. Fellow in maternal-fetal medicine Oreg. Health Scis., Portland, 1982-84; from asst. prof. to assoc. prof. Case Western Res. U., Cleve., 1984-90; chief maternal, fetal medicine Case Western Reserve U., Cleve., 1989-90; assoc. prof., dir. maternal fetal med. fellowship program Bowman Gray Sch. Medicine, Winston-Salem, N.C., 1990-95, prof., 1995—. Contbr. articles to med. jours. Grantee NIH, 1991—. Office: Bowman Gray Sch Medicine Medical Center Blvd Winston Salem NC 27157

VELA, FILEMON B., federal judge; b. Harlingen, Tex., May 1, 1935; s. Roberto and Maria Luisa Cardenas V.; m. Blanca Sanchez, Jan. 28, 1962; children: Filemon, Rafael Eduardo, Sylvia Adriana. Student, Tex. Southmost Coll., 1954-56, U. Tex., 1956-57; JD, St. Mary's U., San Antonio, 1962. Bar: Tex. 1962. Mem. Vela & Vela, 1962-63; atty. Mexican-Am. Legal Def. Fund, 1962-75; pvt. practice law Brownsville, 1963-75; judge dist. 107, Tex. Dist. Ct., 1975-80; judge U.S. Dist. Ct. (so. dist.) Tex., Brownsville, 1980—; instr. Law Enforcement Coll. City commr., Brownsville, 1971-73. Served with U.S. Army, 1957-59. Mem. State Bar Tex. Democrat. Office: US Courthouse PO Box 1072 Brownsville TX 78520*

VENDITTI, CLELIA ROSE See PALMER, CHRISTINE

VENDITTO, JAMES JOSEPH, chemical engineer; b. Dobbs Ferry, N.Y., Nov. 13, 1951; s. Vincenzio Rocco and Maria Nichola (Cassetti) V.; m. Debora R. Bruncak; children: Vincent James, Joseph Ryan. BSChemE, U. Okla., 1973. Registered profl. engr., Tex. Engr.-in-tng., Victoria, Tex., 1973-74; field engr. Halliburton Svcs., Alice, Tex., 1974-75, dist. engr., Mission, Tex., 1975-77, regional svc. sales engr., New Orleans, 1977-80, asst. div. engr., Corpus Christi, Tex., 1980-83, supt. stimulation dept., 1983, div. engr., 1983-88, rsch. engring. advisor, 1988-93, stimulation PSL mgr., 1993-94, PSL tech. mgr., 1994-95, global sand control dir., 1995, global sand control, stimulation, conformance svcs. dir., 1995, prodn. enhancement mgr. Latin Region, 1996; cons. in field; researcher high temperature fracturing fluids, chem. stimulation S. Tex. sandstones. Devel. new API cementing temperatures and new refracturing tech. for oil and gas industry; contbr. articles to profl. jours.; patentee in field. Mem. Am. Inst. Chem. Engrs., Soc. Petroleum Engrs., AIME, Am. Petroleum Inst. Republican. Roman Catholic. Home: 4518 Keneshaw Sugar Land TX 77479 Office: Halliburton Ctr 5151 San Felipe Ste 2433 Houston TX 77056

VENKATARAMAN, TIRUNELVELI VISWANATHAN, nephrologist; b. Madras, Tamilnadu, India, June 28, 1947; came to U.S., 1972; s. Tirunelveli R. Viswanathan and Annapurni Venkatarama Aiyar; m. Pankaja Sundaram, Jan. 24, 1974; children: Anna, Anita. BS, MB, Madras Med. Coll., 1970. Diplomate Am. Bd. Internal Medicine, Am. Subspecialty Bd. Nephrology. Registrar dept. medicine Jipmer Hosp., Pondicherry, India, 1971-72; pvt. practice Oklahoma City, 1983—; intern Grasslands Hosp., Valhalla, N.Y., 1972-73; resident, renal fellow Westchester County Med. Ctr., Valhalla, 1973-77; asst. prof. medicine U. Okla. Health Scis. Ctr., Oklahoma City, 1983—; med. dir. Capitol Hill Dialysis Ctr., Oklahoma City, 1992—, St. Anthony Hosp. Dialysis Ctr., Oklahoma City, 1992—; active staff St. Anthony and Presbyterian Hosps., Oklahoma City. Pres. India Assn. Okla.,

Oklahoma City, 1986-87. Named Ky. Col. Gov. Julian Carroll, 1977. Fellow ACP; mem. AMA, Am. Assn. Physicians of Indian Origin (v.p. Okla. chpt. 1993-94, pres. 1994—). Home: 14 Oakdale Farm Rd Edmond OK 73013-8220 Office: 1110 N Classen Blvd # 200 Oklahoma City OK 73106-6840

VENUTI, RUTH LOUISE, secondary school educator, counselor; b. Spokane, Wash., July 1, 1957; d. Louis Jesse and Ruth Virginia (Mussetter) V. BA, Fla. So. Coll., 1979; MA in Counseling, Liberty U., Lynchburg, Va., 1990; specialist degree, Stetson U., 1992. Cert. elem., mid. sch. math. and secondary Spanish tchr., Fla. Elem. tchr. Polk County Sch. Bd., Auburndale, Fla., 1979, Bartow, Fla., 1979-84; jr. high sch. tchr. Volusia County Sch. Bd., Deltona, Fla., 1984-88, mid. sch. tchr., 1988—, NEAT observer, 1982, peer tchr., 1988—; tutor Fla. Sheriff's Girls' Villa, Bartow, 1979-80, Fla. United Meth. Children's Home, Enterprise, 1984; ednl. dir. Rohr House, abuse shelter, Bartow, 1980-81. Recipient Cert. of Commendation from Pres. Nixon, 1974, Apple pin Volusia County Sch. Bd., 1988. Mem. ACA, Nat. Coun. Tchrs. Math., Am. Assn. Tchrs. Spanish and Portuguese, Assn. Spiritual, Ethical & Religious Values in Counseling, Kappa Delta Pi. Mem. Assembly of God Ch. Home: 670 Montclair Ave Orange City FL 32763-4842 Office: Galaxy Mid Sch 2400 Eustace Ave Deltona FL 32725-1765

VERBLE, FRANCES HELEN, librarian; b. Memphis, Apr. 26, 1951; d. William David and Mildred Lorene (Hickman) V. AA, Cumberland U., 1971; BS, Austin Peay State U., 1973; MLS, Vanderbilt U., 1976. Bookmobile libr. Upper Cumberland Regional Libr., Cookeville, Tenn., 1973-75; govt. docs. cataloger Memphis and Shelby County Pub. Libr. and Info. Ctr., Memphis, 1977-78; cataloger U. Tenn., Memphis Health Sci. Ctr. Libr., 1978—. Mem. Med. Libr Assn. (chairperson govt. rels. com. So. chpt. 1993-95, sr. mem. Acad. Health Info. Profls.), Spl. Librs. Assn. (pres. Mid-South chpt. 1995-96), Tenn. Libr. Assn. (mem. legis. com. 1983-85), Assn. Memphis Area Health Scis. Librs. (U. Tenn. rep. 1985-90, sec. 1990). Methodist. Office: Univ Tenn Health Sci Ctr Libr 877 Madison Ave Memphis TN 38103-3408

VERDON, JANE KATHRYN, lawyer; b. Manchester, N.C., 1943. BA, Newton Coll., 1964; JD, U. San Diego, 1991. Bar: N.C. 1992. Legal intern San Diego City Atty. - Criminal Divsn., 1991; law clk. criminal def. Cheshire, Parker, Hughes and Manning, Raleigh, N.C., 1991-92; pvt. practice Raleigh, 1992—; creative dir., corp. v.p., ptnr. Internat. Creative Sys.; account exec., publicity dir., TV spokesperson H. Richard Silver, Inc.; fashion, beauty editor, spokesperson for major consumer mags., newspapers, TV; advt. and promotion in all areas of health, beauty and fashion. Assoc. fashion editor, assoc. managing editor Seventeen Mag.; fashion dir. Woman's World Mag.; contbg. editor, writer for newspapers and consumer mags.; designer newspaper, radio and TV features, brochures, scripts, promotional programs, mediation, negotiations; TV and comml. appearances. Mem. AFTRA, ABA, ATLA, N.C. Bar Assn., N.C. Trial Lawyers Assn., N.J. Foster Parents' Assn., Lawyers' Club, Phi Alpha Delta. Office: 514 Daniels St Raleigh NC 27605

VERHOVSEK, MARY ANN DANA, radio news anchor, reporter; b. Johnstown, Pa., Aug. 6, 1955; d. Rudolph Fred and Mary Teresa (Walls) V. Announcer various radio stas., 1974-76; anchor newscasts, exec. producer Sta. WCRO Radio, Johnstown, Pa., 1976-78; with Sta. WTAJ TV, Altoona, Pa., 1978-79; anchor Sta. WFBG FM & AM, Altoona, 1983-84, WJAC FM & AM, Johnstown, 1979-82, Sta. WAJE AM, Ebensburg, Pa., 1982-83; news reporter Sta. WIXV/WBMQ, Savannah, Ga., 1984-86; anchor WBBQ FM & AM, Augusta, Ga., 1986—. Media com. City of Augusta's Forth of July parade and celebration, 1991; hospitality com. chmn. Olde Town Neighborhood Assn.'s first Tour of Homes, 1991; active Celebrity Fashion Show, 1991, Leadership Augusta, Leadership Aiken, 1989—, Richmond County Sch. System, 1988—, Augusta Players, 1986-87; judge ann. Pet-a-Fair Humane Soc., 1988-92; drama club advisor Immaculate Conception Sch., 1989-91; fund raiser Med. Coll. Ga., 1987—; bd. dirs. Olde Towne Neighborhood Assn., Augusta, 1994. Mem. Soc. Profl. Journalists (sec. Agusta profl. chpt.), Ga. Assn. of Newscasters, Augusta Lions Club (pres. 1994-95), Ga. Associated Press Broadcasters Assn. (excellence spl. staff coverage 1990, excellence-best regularly scheduled newscast 1989, excellence-specialized reporting 1986), S.C. Press Broadcasters Assn. (1st pl. spot news 1990), West Augusta Rotary Club (1st pl.-pub. svc. reporting 1988). Democrat. Roman Catholic. Home: 305 Broad St Augusta GA 30901-1517 Office: WBBQ Radio 1305 Georgia Ave North Augusta SC 29841-3019

VERKLER, KAREN WOLZ, foreign language educator; b. Rockville Center, N.Y., Aug. 27, 1956; d. Frank Kurt and Jean (Mylner) W.; m. James Thomas Verkler, July 8, 1978; 1 child, Erin Kristin. BA magna cum laude, Stetson U., 1978; MEd, U. Ctrl. Fla., 1988; PhD in Instrn./Curriculum, U. Fla., 1993. Cert. tchr., Fla. Tchr. Marion County Schs., Ocala, Fla., 1979-82, Seminole County Schs., Oviedo, Fla., 1983-95; instr. U. Ctrl. Fla., Orlando, 1995—; ad. prof. Stetson U., DeLand, Fla., 1994-95, Rollins Coll., Winter Park, Fla., 1995; fgn. lang. cons. U. Fla., Gainesville, 1994, various ctrl. Fla. schs., 1994. Bilingual edn. fellow U.S. Dept. Edn., 1991. Mem. Am. Assn. Tchrs. Spanish & Portuguese, Am. Coun. Teaching Fgn. Lang., Am. Assn. Counseling & Devel., Fla. Fgn. Lang. Assn. Lutheran. Home: 1012 Big Oaks Blvd Oviedo FL 32765

VERMYLEN, DEBRA MAE SINGLETON, sales executive; b. Tulsa, May 7, 1955; d. George Monroe and Jacqueline Romaine (Redman-Williams) Singleton; m. Patrick Roger Guy Vermylen, July 21, 1984; children: Nathan Christopher, Nicholas Patrick, Alexandria Jacqueline. AA, Erie Community Coll., Williamsville, N.Y., 1976; BS, SUNY, Buffalo, 1978. Sales rep. Kraft Inc., Columbia, Md., 1979-80, key sales rep., 1980-81, account mgr., 1981-82, sales supr. for Balt., 1982-84, sales supr. for Washington, 1984, supr. mil. sales, 1984-89; unit mgr. Kraft Gen. Foods, Columbia, 1989-90, sales mgr. ops., 1990-91; sales mgr. Kraft Gen. Foods, Houston, San Antonio, Rio Grande Valley, Austin, 1991-96, Fleming, Tom Thumb & Randalls, Humble, Tex., 1996—. Coord. Children's Time Presch., Columbia, 1990; aide The Learning Tree Sch., 1993-96, Humble, Tex., 1994-95. Republican. Baptist. Home and Office: 6007 Matt Rd Humble TX 77346

VERON, J. MICHAEL, lawyer; b. Lake Charles, La., Aug. 24, 1950; s. Earl Ernest and Alverdy (Heyd) V.; m. Melinda Anne Guidry, Jan. 2, 1993; children: John Heyd, Katharine Leigh, Dylan Michael Earl. BA, Tulane U., 1972, JD, 1974; LLM, Harvard U., 1976. Bar: La., U.S. Dist. Ct. (we., ea.. and mid. dists.) La., U.S. Dist. Ct. (ea. dist.) Tex., U.S. Ct. Appeals (5th cir.), U.S. Ct. Appeals (fed. cir.), U.S. Tax Ct. Law clk. to presiding justice La. Supreme Ct., New Orleans, 1974-75; sole practice Lake Charles, 1976-78; ptnr. Scofield, Gerard, Veron, Pohorelsky & Singletary (formerly Scofield, Gerard, Veron, Hoskins & Soileau), Lake Charles, 1978—; instr. legal method and rsch. Boston U., 1975-76; lectr. environ. law McNeese State U., 1976-79; faculty Tulane Trial Adv. Inst., 1980; adj. proj. La. State U. Sch. Law, 1993—. Mem. bd. editors Tulane Law Rev., 1972-73, assoc. editor, 1973-74. Mem. athletic adv. com. Tulane U., 1983-86; pres. Krewe of Barataria, 1980-86; bd. dirs. Friends of Gov.'s Program for Gifted Children, Inc., 1985. Named to La. State U. Law Ctr. Hall of Fame, 1993. Mem. U.S. Golf Assn. (sectional affairs com.), La. Golf. Assn. (bd. dirs., pres. 1990), Order of Coif, Maritime Law Assn., Lake Charles Country Club (pres. 1986), Tulane Green Wave (pres. Lake Charles chpt. 1984), English Turn Golf & Country Club. Roman Catholic. Home: 4116 Beau Chene Dr Lake Charles LA 70605-2763 Office: Scofield Gerard Veron Singletary & Pohorelsky 1114 Ryan St Lake Charles LA 70601-5252

VERSTEGEN, DEBORAH A., education educator; b. Neenah, Wis., Oct. 27, 1946; d. Gerald C. and Margaret A. (Lamers) V. BA, Loretto Heights Coll., 1969; EdM, U. Rochester, 1972; MS, U. Wis., 1981, PhD, 1983. Adminstr. Iditarod Area Sch. Dist., McGrath, Alaska, 1976-79; rsch. asst. Wis. Ctr. for Edn. Rsch., 1981-84; dir. asst. prof. mid-mgmt. program U. Tex., Austin, 1984-86; asst. prof. U. Va., Charlottesville, 1986-91, assoc. prof., 1992—; rsch. assoc. Oxford U., Eng., 1991; adv. bd. U.S. Dept. Edn., 1989-92. Author over 100 books, reports, chpts., articles and revs., latest being The Impacts of Litigation and Legislation on Public School Finance, 1990, Spheres of Justice in Education, 1991; editor Jour. Edn. Fin., 1990-93, editor edn. policy, 1993—. Treas. LWV, 1986, mem. state board, Va., 1995—. Mem. AAUP, Am. Ednl. Fin. Assn. (bd. dirs., disting. svc. award 1989), Am. Ednl. Rsch. Assn., Univ. Coun. on Ednl. Adminstrn. (disting svc. award 1991, adv. bd. fin. ctr.), Phi Delta Kappa, Phi Kappa Phi. Home: 2030 Lambs Rd Charlottesville VA 22901-8978 Office: U Va Curry Sch Edn Ruffner Hall 405 Emmet St S Charlottesville VA 22903-2424

VERTIZ, VIRGINIA CASTLEN, educational administrator; b. Washington, Mar. 8, 1949; d. Oscar R. and Castlen (Bear) V.; children: Peter James Isenberg, Carrie Venetia Gouskos. BFA, Va. Commonwealth U., 1972; MS, Va. Polytechnic Inst./State U., 1981, cert. advanced grad. study, 1984, PhD, 1984; doctoral program, George Washington U., 1981-82. cert. tchr., adminstr., Va. Social worker model cities divsn. Dept. Pub. Welfare, Richmond, Va., 1972-75; industrial cooperative tng. coord., dept. chmn. George Marshall H.S., Fairfax, Va., 1977-79; tng. coord. Project YEELD (Youth Employment Experience Learning Demon.), Fairfax, 1980-82; cross-cultural rels. coord., cmty. liason J.E.B. Stuart H.S., Fairfax, 1982-86; assessment specialist, asst. to superintendant Arlington (Va.) Pub. Schs., 1986-87; lobbyist Am. Assn. of Sch. Adminstrs. (AASA), Arlington, 1988-90; dir., nat. curriculum Audit Ctr. Am. Assn. of Sch. Adminstrs. (AASA), 1990-96; ednl. cons., 1996—; adj. assoc. prof. Inst. for Ednl. Transformation George Mason U., Fairfax, 1994—; affiliate prof. McGill U., Montreal, Quebec, 1994; adj. rsch. prof. George Washington U., Washington, 1990; quality mgmt. cons. Quality Enhancement Sems., L.A., 1993, Behavioral Scis. Inst. Fed. Way, Wash., 1993, W. Edwards Deming: sems. and cons. practice, 1992-93. Guest editor of Project Innovations Jour. Edn., Winter, 1992; contbr. publs. and profl. papers; author various book chpts. Mem. Phi Kappa Phi Honor Soc. Home and Office: 5607 S Second St Arlington VA 22204

VESELY, PAUL T., imaging software development firm executive, consultant; b. Newburgh, N.Y., June 27, 1959; s. Frank and Anna Marie (Kusman) V. BS in Computer Sci. and Math., SUNY, Albany, 1981. Programmer Sperry Computer Systems, Lexington Park, Md., 1981-83; engring. mgr., systems designer Grumman Data Systems Corp., Holtsville, N.Y., 1983-89; asst. v.p., chief engr. PRC Inc., Reston, Va., 1989-92; v.p. engring. BIIS Corp., Herndon, Va., 1992-93; pres. Blue Mountain Data Systems Inc., Reston, Va., 1993—. Contbr. articles to profl. jours. Mem. Assn. for Info. and Image Mgmt. (founding, vertical market adv. com. 1993), Nuclear Info. Records Mgmt. Assn. Democrat. Roman Catholic. Office: Blue Mountain Data Systems 11495 Sunset Hills Rd Ste 202 Reston VA 20190

VESOLE, DAVID H., physician; b. Davenport, Iowa, Feb. 4, 1953; s. Herman and Esther (Siegel) V.; m. Karen Sherman, Aug. 7, 1976; children: Lori Michelle, Steven Michael. BS, U. Iowa, 1974; PhD, Med. U. S.C., 1978; MD, Northwestern U., 1984. Diplomate Am. Bd. Internal Medicine, Hematology, Med. Oncology. Asst. prof. U. Ark., Little Rock, 1990-95; assoc. prof. Med. Coll. Wisc., Milw., 1995—. Contbr. articles to profl. jours./books. Recipient Career Devel. award Am. Cancer Soc., 1991-94. Fellow Am. Coll. Physicians; mem. Am. Soc. Clin. Oncology, Am. Soc. Hematology, Am. Soc. Blood and Marrow Transplantation, Sigma Xi. Home: 7320 N Beach Dr Fox Point WI 53217 Office: Med Coll Wis Physicians & Clinics Bone Marrow Transplant Program 9200 W Wisconsin Ave Milwaukee WI 53226

VESSEL, ROBERT LESLIE, lawyer; b. Chgo., Mar. 21, 1942; s. Louis Frank and Margaret Ruth (Barber) V.; m. Diane White, Oct. 12, 1966; m. Lise Vessel, Dec. 19, 1992. BA, U. Ill., 1964; JD, Seton Hall U., 1973; LLM in Taxation, U. Miami, Coral Gables, Fla., 1980. Bar: N.J. 1973, Fla. 1981, U.S. Dist. Ct. (so. and mid. dists.) Fla. 1981, U.S. Ct. Appeals (11th cir.) 1981; bd. cert. civil trial, Fla. Assoc. Bennett & Bennett P.A., East Orange, N.J., 1973-76; ptnr. Kantor & Vessel, P.A., Wayne, N.J., 1976-81; assoc. Haddad Josephs & Jack, P.A., Coral Gables, Fla., 1981-85; ptnr. Mitchell Alley Rywant & Vessel, Tampa, 1985-89, Moffitt & Vessel, P.A., Tampa, 1989-94, Vessel & Morales, P.A., Tampa, 1994—. With USNR, 1964-66. Mem. Assn. Trial Lawyers Am., Nat. Inst. Trial Advocacy, Acad. Fla. Trial Lawyers, Hillsboro County Bar Assn. Office: Vessel & Morales PA 5401 W Kennedy Blvd Tampa FL 33609-2428

VEST, FRANK HARRIS, JR., bishop; b. Salem, Va., Jan. 5, 1936; s. Frank Harris and Viola Gray (Woodson) V.; m. Ann Jarvis, June 14, 1961; children: Nina Woodson, Frank Harris III, Robert Alexander. BA, Roanoke Coll., 1959; MDiv, Va. Theol. Sem., 1962, DD, 1985; DD (hon.), U. of South, 1987; LHD (hon.), St. Paul's Coll., 1991. Ordained to ministry Episcopal Ch. as deacon, 1962, as priest 1963. Curate St. John's Episcopal Ch., Roanoke, Va., 1962-64; rector Grace Episcopal Ch., Radford, Va., 1964-68; rector Christ Episcopal Ch., Roanoke, 1968-73, Charlotte, N.C., 1973-85; suffragan bishop Diocese of N.C., Raleigh, 1985-89; bishop coadjutor Diocese of So. Va., Norfolk, 1989-91, bishop, 1991—. Chmn. exec. com. Thompsons Children's Home, Charlotte, 1976-79; pres. Crisis Assistance Ministry, Charlotte, 1983-85; trustee Va. Theol. Sem., Alexandria, 1968-73, 91—, U. of South, Sewanee, Tenn., 1985-89, Episc. Radio TV Found., Atlanta, 19786-82; chair Dispatch of Bus., House of Bishops, 1988—. Democrat. Office: Diocese of So Va 600 Talbot Hall Rd Norfolk VA 23505-4361*

VEST, JAMES MURRAY, foreign language and literature educator; b. Roanoke, Va., Mar. 27, 1947; s. Eddie Lewis and Irene (Cannaday) V.; m. Nancy Foltz, June 6, 1970; 1 child, Cecelia. BA, Davidson (N.C.) Coll., 1969; MA, Duke U., 1971, PhD, 1973. From asst. to assoc. prof. Rhodes Coll., Memphis, 1973-91, prof., 1991—; adminstr. Rhodes in Paris Program, France, 1978-87; organizer faculty teaching seminars, 1988—. Author: The French Face of Ophelia, 1989, The Poetic Works of Maurice de Guérin, 1991; contbr. articles to profl. jours. Chmn. Urban Outreach Commn., Memphis, 1978-81; leader youth groups, 1983—. Capt. U.S. Army Res., 1973—. Recipient campus svc. award Sears-Roebuck, 1990, Outstanding Teaching award Clarence Day Found., Memphis, 1984, Am. Assn. Higher Edn., 1988; Woodrow Wilson fellow, 1971, NDEA Title IV fellow, 1969. Mem. MLA, So. Atlantic Modern Lang. Assn., Am. Assn. of Tchrs. of French. Office: 2000 N Pkwy Rhodes C Memphis TN 38112

VEST, STEVEN LEE, gastroenterologist, hepatologist, internist; b. Mpls., July 30, 1948; s. Lee Herbert and Marian Mize (Rains) V.; m. Gayle Maureen Southworth, Nov. 27, 1971; 1 child, Matthew Steven. BA, U. Minn., 1970, MD, 1974. Diplomate Am. Bd. Intenal Medicine, Am. Bd Gastroenterology. Intern internal medicine Milw. County Hosp., 1974-75; resident internal medicine So. Ill. U., Springfield, 1975-77; fellow in gastroenterology and hepatology Duke U. Med. Ctr., Durham, N.C., 1978-80; gastroenterology-hepatology and internal medicine cons. Lonesome Pine Hosp., Big Stone Gap, Va., 1980—; gastroenterology and internal medicine cons. St. Mary's Hosp., Norton, 1983, Norton Community Hosp., Norton, Va., 1985—; chmn. med. care evaluation, Lonesome Pine Hosp., Big Stone Gap, 1984-88; chief of medicine Norton Community Hosp., 1991-93, bd. dirs., 1993—. Fellow ACP, Am. Coll. Gastroenterology; mem. Am. Gastroent. Assn., Am. Soc. Internal Medicine, Va. Med. Soc. (state del. 1992), Wise County Med. Soc. (treas. 1984-86, pres. 1992-93), Am. Assn. Christian Counselors. Methodist. Home: Powell Valley 1800-B Egan Rd Big Stone Gap VA 24219 Office: NCH Med Arts Bldg #2 Med Arts Bldg # 2 98 15th St NW Ste 202 Norton VA 24273

VESTAL, JUDITH CARSON, occupational therapist; b. Memphis, Dec. 22, 1939; d. Carl Thomas and Emma Winifred (Stewart) Carson; m. Tommy Vestal, June 22, 1974. BS in Elem. Edn., U. Tenn., 1961; BS in Occupl. Therapy, Washington U., St. Louis, 1964; MA in Guidance and Counseling, La. Tech. U., 1978; postgrad., Tex. Woman's U., 1993. Cert. occupl. therapist, La. Occupl. therapist Sewall Rehab. Ctr., Denver, 1964-67, Whittingham Hosp., London, 1967-70, The London Hosp., 1970-74, N.W. La. Rehab., Shreveport, 1975-77, Caddo Bossier Assn. for Retarded Children, Shreveport, 1977-81; occupl. therapist La. State U. Med. Ctr., Shreveport, 1981-87, asst. prof. occupl. therapy, 1986-92, assoc. prof. clin. occupl. therapy, 1992—. Editorial bd. Am. Jour. Occupl. Therapy, 1984-87; contbr. articles to profl. jours. Bd. dirs. Children's Learning Ctr., Shreveport, 1980-89; mem. Spl. Edn. Adv. Coun., Shreveport, 1985-91; mem., sec. vestry Ch. of Epiphany, Shrevnport, 1992—. Mem. Am. Occupl. Therapy Assn. (sec. com. on state assn. pres. 1989-92, Svc. award 1992), La. Occupl. Therapy Assn. (v.p. 1983-86, pres. 1986-90, Pres.'s award 1991, Award of Merit 1994), Soc. for Rsch. in Child Devel., Neurodevelopmental Treatment Assn., Internat. Soc. for Alternative and Augmentative Comm., Phi Kappa Phi. Anglican Ch. Home: 176 Preston Shreveport LA 71105-3306 Office: Louisiana State University Medical Center Sch Allied Health Prof 1501 Kings Hwy Shreveport LA 71130-3932

VESTER, PAULA JEAN, artist in textiles, educator; b. Vallejo, Calif., Feb. 23, 1951; d. Harvey Louis and Margaret Marie (Cole) Waldroup; m. David Lee Vester, Mar. 8, 1973; children: Jeremy Lee, Aaron Earl. BS in Psychology, Olivet Coll., 1978. Fiber instr. CAllanwalde Arts Ctr., Atlanta, 1990—. Author, publisher: (book) Beginning Spinning, 1994, 95, 96; also article. Mem. Handweavers Guild of Am., Peachtree Handspinners Guild (life, pres. 1987-88, newsletter editor 1991-96), Chatthoochee Handweavers Guild, S.E. Fiber Forum (co-chair 1995).

VIA, JOHN ALBERT, priest; b. Gorman, Tex., Oct. 13, 1937; s. Albert Hoyt and Hallie Mae Fleming; m. Marcia Lilian Mains, 1960 (div. 1973); m. Susan Claire Pillans, Aug. 20, 1974 (div. Dec. 1987); children: Laura Elizabeth, Rebecca Robinson; m. Alison Standifer Hardwick, Sept. 9, 1989. BA, Baylor U., 1959; MA, Miss. State U., 1961; PhD, U. Ill., 1968. Asst. prof. U. Ky., Lexington, 1967-74; assoc. prof., chmn. English dept. Mercer U., Atlanta, 1974-90; assoc. rector Holy Trinity Parish, Decatur, Ga., 1982-86; co-dir. The Field Sch., Washington, 1988-89; vicar Ch. of the Redeemer, Greensboro, Ga., 1990—, Ch. of the Mediator, Washington, Ga., 1990—; dean N.E. Ga. convocation Diocese of Atlanta, 1993—; chmn. commn. on ministry in higher edn. Diocese of Atlanta. Contbr. articles to profl. jours. Sgt. USAR, 1963-69. Episcopalian. Home: 310 E Liberty St Washington GA 30673-1761 Office: Ch of the Mediator PO Box 716 Washington GA 30673-0716

VIAMONTE, MANUEL, surgeon; b. Havana, Cuba, Feb. 3, 1958; came to U.S., 1959; s. Manuel Jr. and Maria Eugenia (Rosado) V.; m. Olga del Carmen Gonzalez, APr. 14, 1966; children: Manuel Aurelio, Michael Alexander. BS, U. Miami, 1986; MD, U. Fla., 1986. Diplomate Am. Bd. Surgery, Am. Bd. Colon and Rectal Surgery, Nat. Bd. Med. Examiners; cert. controlled substances, advance trauma life support. Intern, resident in gen. surgery U. Miami, Jackson Meml. Hosp., Fla., 1986-91; fellow in colon and rectal surgery St. Luke's/Roosevelt Hosp. Ctr., Columbia Coll. Physicians and Surgeons, N.Y.C., 1991-92; clin. asst. prof. surgery sch. medicine U. Miami, 1992—; presenter in field. Contbr. articles to profl. jours. Fellow ACS (assoc.); mem. AMA, Am. Soc. Colon and Rectal Surgeons, Fla. Med. Assn., Med. Soc. of State of N.Y., Dade County Med. Assn., N.Y. County Med. Soc. Republican. Roman Catholic. Office: 9195 Sunset Dr Ste 230 Miami FL 33173-3488

VIAMONTES, RALPH, agricultural services executive; b. 1949. With Ziegler Corp., Vero Beach, Fla., 1969-87, Vista Packing Co., Fort Pierce, Fla., 1987—; now pres. Vista Packing Co. Office: Vista Packing Co 3487 S Us Highway 1 Fort Pierce FL 34982-6697*

VIAULT, BIRDSALL SCRYMSER, history educator; b. Mineola, N.Y., Sept. 20, 1932; s. Joseph Choate and Helen Lee (Scrymser) V.; m. Sarah Reed Underhill, May 9, 1970. BS, Adelphi U., 1955, MA, 1956; MA, Duke U., 1957, PhD, 1963. Instr. history Adelphi U., Garden City, N.Y., 1959-63, asst. prof. history, 1963-68; assoc. prof. history Winthrop U., Rock Hill, S.C., 1968-72, prof. history, 1972—, chmn. dept. history, 1979-89; vis. assoc. prof. Duke U., Durham, N.C., 1970. Author: World History in the 20th Century, 1969, American History Since 1865, 1989, rev. edit., 1993, Western Civilization Since 1600, 1990, Modern European History, 1990, English History, 1992; author weekly column, 1979-87; contbr. articles and revs. to profl. jours. Mem. Nassau County (N.Y.) Dem. Com., 1961-68, S.C. Commn. for Archives and History, 1979-89, S.C. Bd. Rev. for Nat. Register of Hist. Places, 1988—; del. S.C. State Dem. Conv., 1972, 74, 94, 96; leader ann. tours to Europe, 1977—. Ford Found. Coop. Program for Humanities Postdoctoral fellow U. N.C., Duke U., 1969-70. Mem. So. Hist. Assn., Am. Cath. Hist. Assn., Soc. Historians of Am. Fgn. Rels., S.C. Hist. Assn., Kiwanis Club Rock Hill, Phi Kappa Phi, Phi Alpha Theta, Zeta Beta Tau. Roman Catholic. Home: 2186 Wentworth Dr Rock Hill SC 29732-1242 Office: Winthrop U Dept History Rock Hill SC 29733

VICK, FRANCES BRANNEN, publishing executive; b. Trinity, Tex., Aug. 14, 1935; d. Carl Andrew and Bess (courtney) B.; m. Ross William Vick Jr., June 23, 1956; children: Karen Lynn, Ross William III, Patrick Brannen. BA, U. Tex., 1958; MA, Stephen F. Austin State U., 1968. Teaching fellow Stephen F. Austin State U., Nacogdoches, Tex., 1966-68, lectr., 1968-69; lectr. Angelina Coll., Lufkin, Tex., 1969-71, Baylor U., Waco, Tex., 1974-75, 77-78; vice prin. Vanguard Sch., Waco, 1975-77; pres. E-Heart Press, Inc., Dallas, 1979—; co-dir. UNT Press U. North Tex., Denton, 1987-89, dir., 1989—. Publisher 120 books; editor 40 books. Leadership coun. Ann Richards Com., Austin, 1990-94; amb. Inst. Texan Cultures; mem. Tex. Commn. on Arts, Lit., 1991. Mem. AAUW, Book Pubs. Tex. (v.p. 1990-96, pres. 1996), Tex. Folklore Soc. (councillor 1991-93), Tex. Humanities Resource Ctr. (bd. dirs. 1990-91), Conf. Coll. Tchrs. English, Western Lit. Assn., Western Writers Am., Philos. Soc. Tex., Pen Ctr. U.S.A. West, Tex. State Hist. Assn. (life), East Tex. Hist. Assn. (life), Western Writers Am., Western Lit. Assn., Soc. Scholarly Pub., Women in Scholarly Pub., Rocky Mountain Book Pubs. Assn., Leadership Tex., Leadership Am., Tex. Humanities Alliance, UNT League Profl. Women. Democrat. Episcopalian. Home: 3700 Mockingbird Ln Dallas TX 75205-2125 Office: U North Tex PO Box 13856 Denton TX 76203-6856

VICK, JOHN, engineering executive; b. Feb. 12, 1933. B in Elec. Engring., Tex. A&M U., M in Elec. Engring. Mem. aerophysics group rsch. and engring. Gen. Dynamics, Ft. Worth, 1959-61, from sr. aerosystems engr. to project aerosystems engr. F-111 radar group, 1961-67, group engr. F-111 aerosystems project office, 1967-68, asst. project engr., 1968-73, aerosystems group engr. electronic fabrication ctr., 1973-75, chief, 1975-77, mgr., 1977-80, dir. support requirements and systems dept., 1980-88, divsn. v.p. mil. electronics, 1988-91, divsn. v.p. rsch. and engring., 1991—; v.p. rsch. and engring. Lockheed Ft. Worth Co. Office: Lockheed Corp PO Box 748 Lockheed Blvd Fort Worth TX 76101*

VICK, MARIE, retired health science educator; b. Saltillo, Tex., Jan. 22, 1922; d. Alphy Edgar and Mollie (Cowser) Pitts; m. Joe Edward Vick, Apr. 5, 1942; children: Mona Marie, Rex Edward. BS, Tex. Woman's U., Denton, 1942, MA, 1949. Tchr. Coahoma (Tex.) High Sch., 1942-43, Santa Rita Elem. Sch., San Angelo, Tex., 1943-45, Crozier Tech. High Sch., Dallas, 1946-47, Monroe Jr. High Sch., Omaha, 1947-48; instr. Tex. Woman's U., Denton, 1948-50; tchr. San Angelo (Tex.) Jr. High Sch., 1957-58, San Angelo (Tex.) Sr. High Sch., 1957-58, Harlingen Bonham Elem. Sch., 1958-59, Harlingen (Tex.) High Sch., 1959-62; prof. health sci. Coll. Edn. U. Houston, 1962-80. Author: A Collection of Dances for Children, 1970; Health Science in the Elementary School, 1979; contbr. articles to profl. jours.; artist in oil, watercolor and acrylic. Mem. exec. bd. Health Care Task Force of Walker County. Recipient Cert. of Achievement, Tex. Commn. Intercollegiate Athletics for Women, 1972, Research Service award Tex. Cancer Control Program, 1978-79, Plaudit award Nat. Dance Assn., 1982, Disting. Service award Pan Am. U., 1983, Service citation Am. Cancer Soc., Cert. of Appreciation, Tex. div. Am. Cancer Soc., 1980; Favorite Prof. honoree Cap and Gown Mortar Bd., U. Houston, 1974. Mem. AAHPERD (dance editor 1971-74), NEA, AARP (chmn. legis. com. Huntsville chpt. 1988-90, bd. dirs., liaison person Walker County commrs. 1989-90, chmn. cmty. svc. project Walker County Unpaved Rd. Survey, 1989, mem. exec. bd. 1992—), Am. Sch. Health Assn., So. Assn. Health, Phys. Edn. Coll. Women (sec. dance sect. 1970-73), Tex. State Tchrs. Assn. (sect. chmn. 1964-65), Tex. Assn Health, Phys. Edn. and Recreation (chmn. dance sect. 1968-69), Tex. Assn. Coll. Tchrs., Nat. Ret. Tchrs. Assn. (legis. chmn. 1988-89), Tex. Assn. Ret. Tchrs., Property Owners Assn. (organizer, 1st pres.), U. Houston Assn. Ret. Profs., Tex. Women's U. Nat. Alumnae Assn. (life), Tex. Women's Pioneer Club, U. Houston 20 Yr. Club. Democrat. Methodist. Home: RR 15 Box 345 Huntsville TX 77340-0980

VICK, MARSHA COOK, writer, African American studies educator; b. Charlotte, N.C.; d. Conley and Elizabeth (Voltz) Cook; m. Paul Allen Vick, Apr. 6, 1968; children: Paul Allen Jr., Brian Conley. BA, U. N.C., 1963, MEd, 1965; MA, Duke U., 1985; PhD, U. N.C., 1996; MA, Duke U., 1985. Spanish translator transl. svc. Duke U., Durham, N.C., 1974-76, speech writer for v.p., 1976-77, speech writer for pres., 1977-85; rsch. and editorial asst. U.S. Senate, Durham, 1986-92; lectr. Afro-Am. studies U. N.C., Chapel Hill, 1990—; writer Durham, 1996—. Contbr. essays to various publs. Mem. MLA, Coll. Lang. Assn., Sigma Delta Pi, Alpha Chi Omega. Home: 2502 Auburn St Durham NC 27706 Office: U NC Office African and Afro Am Studies Curriculum 401 Alumni Hall CB # 3395 Chapel Hill NC 27955

VICK, MARY POSTELL, biology educator; b. Palatka, Fla., July 5; d. Allen Presley and M. Alfreda (Miller) Postell; m. Norman D. Vick, Dec. 16, 1972; children: Dwight, Kimberly. BA, Hampton Inst., 1972; MA, Hampton U., 1987. Tchr. Norfolk (Va.) State U., 1987-89, Tidewater C.C., Virginia Beach, Va., 1989-90, Hampton (Va.) U., 1990-96, Isle of Wight (Va.) County Sch., 1996—. Author: Student Study Guide for Biology, 1996. Mem. AAUP, Delta Sigma Theta. AME. Home: 50 Azalea Dr Hampton VA 23669 Office: Isle of Wight County Schs PO Box 78 Isle of Wight VA 23397-0078

VICKERS, GEORGE LEWIS, computer consultant; b. South Charleston, W.Va., Sept. 22, 1954; s. Arthur Archibold and Elizabeth Mae (Coleman) V. BA, Alderson-Broaddus Coll., 1976; MDiv, Ea. Baptist Theol. Seminary, 1979; MA in Comm., Wheaton Coll., 1984-85; postgrad. in Comm., U. Ky., 1990-92. Pastor West Union (W.Va.) Bapt. Ch., 1979-82; disability examiner I disability determination sect. W.Va. Dept. Vocat. Rehab., Charleston, 1982-83; freelance marketer Wheaton, Ill., 1985-86; dir. mktg. SGACAW Tech., Charleston, W.Va., 1986-88; systems cons. Todays Computer Bus. Ctr., Charleston, 1988-89; mgr. microcomputers RMI Ltd., Charleston, 1988-89; instr., teaching asst. dept. comm. U. Ky., 1990-91; system cons. Lexington Computer Store, 1990—; acct. exec. Max Web, 1995, 96. Mem. IEEE Computer Soc. (multimedia sect.), Assn. Computing Machinery (multimedia sect.). Republican. Mem. Christian/Missionary Alliance Ch. Office: Lexington Computer 2909 Richmond Rd Lexington KY 40509-1715

VICKERY, GLENN WHEELER, lawyer; b. Houston, Nov. 27, 1938; s. Barney Burren and Bonnie Beatrice (Wheeler) V.; m. Lucille Burks, June 20, 1992; children: Ronda, Teresa, Kay, Jessica. BS in Econs. U. Houston, 1963, JD, South Tex. Coll. Law 1966. Bar: Tex. 1966; cert. personal injury trial law. Pvt. practice, Houston, 1966—, Baytown, Tex., 1966—; justice of peace 1968-70. Mem. Tex. Ho. of Reps. 1966-68; active various civic assns. Mem. ABA, State Bar Tex., Houston Bar Assn., Trial Lawyers Am., Tex. Trial Lawyers Assn. (bd. dirs.), Goose Creek Country Club. Office: Citizens Bank Tower 6th Fl 1300 Rollingbrook Dr Baytown TX 77521

VICKERY, ROBERT BRUCE, oil industry executive, consultant; b. Shreveport, La., Aug. 25, 1938; s. Wilbur Claude and Clara Louise (Powell) V.; m. Margaret Lynn Gray, April 6, 1961; children: Joy Lynn, Andrew Gray, William Charles. Degree in Petroleum Engring., Colo. Sch. Mines, 1962; degree in Arctic Engring., U. Alaska, 1974. Petroleum engr. Pan Am. Petroleum Corp., Worland, Wyo., 1962-64; v.p. ops. Vickery Drilling Co., Inc., Evansville, Ind., 1964-73; mgr. drilling BP Alaska, Inc., Sohio-BP, Sohio Petroleum Corp., Anchorage, 1973-80; chmn. Artic Alaska Drilling Co., Inc., Anchorage, 1980-85; pres. Walker Energy Ptnrs., Houston, 1986-87; pres. Refuge Exploration, Inc., Houston, Tex., 1988—, Owensboro, Ky., 1988—. Author: World Oil, 1982. Pres. Boys Club of Alaska, 1978-80; trustee Boys Clubs Am., 1980-87; Alaska fin. chmn. Re-election of Pres. Reagan Com., 1984. Recipient Alaska Engr. of the Year award SPE of AIME, 1982. Mem. Soc. Petroleum Engrs., Ky. Oil and Gas Assn. (dir.). Office: Refuge Exploration Co Inc 730 Carlton Dr Owensboro KY 42303-7719

VICKS, JOANN, biology educator; b. Starkville, Miss., Nov. 3, 1938; d. Adolphus and Ella (Perkins) V. BS, Tougaloo Coll., 1961; MA, Ind. U., 1967; edn. specialist, Miss. State U., 1976, D in edn., 1979. Ordained minister. Sci. tchr. Moor High Sch., Crawford, Miss., 1961-63, John Hay High Sch., Cleve., 1963-69; prof. biology Mary Holmes Coll., West Point, Miss., 1970—; instr. Miss. State U. for Women, Columbus, Miss., summer 1993; dir. CASET, West Point, 1989-91, NSF Instrumentation, West Point, 1989-91. Contbr. articles to profl. jours. Recipient Faculty Fellowship award Nat Sci. Found., 1965, 76. Mem. AAAS, Am. Biology Tchrs. Assn., Phi Delta Kappa. Home: PO Box 604 Starkville MS 39759-0604 Office: Mary Holmes Coll PO Box 1257 West Point MS 39773-1257

VICTOR, JAMES STUART, III, political consultant; b. Frankfort, Ky., June 6, 1961; s. James Stuart Jr. and Agnes (Rowan) V. BA in History, U. Ky., 1984, BA in Polit. Sci., 1984. Dir. vol., dep. dir. coalitions Bush/Quayle Victory 88 Campaign, Lexington, Ky., 1988; pers. polit. affairs asst. to dir. vol. Bicentennial Presdl. Inaugural Commn., Washington, 1988-89; staff asst. to spl. asst. to dep. sec. Dept. of Interior, Washington, 1989-90; staff asst. to spl. advisor to dep. undersec. Ctr. for Choice, U.S. Dept. Edn., Washington, 1990-93; mem. Bush-Quayle Ky. Reps., Internat. Big Men of Achievement, 1993—; asst. to mgr. local theaters Chevy Chase, Md. and Brighton Park; asst. to coalition dir. NOVA for George Allen, asst. to dep. campaign mgr. Tom Davis-11th dist., del. coord. Jim Miller for Sen. Campaign, Va.; Young Rep. chmn. Franklin County, Ky., 1996; mem. rules com. Franklin County 6th Dist. Rep. Party, 1996. Vol. Reagan/Bush campaign, Lexington, 1980-84, Policy Innovation Polit. Action Com., Washington, 1989, Pres.' Dinner, Washington, 1989, 90, 91, Nat. Victory Celebration, Washington, 1991; asst. vol., asst. to art dir. Nat. Bush/Quayle Com. Primary, 1992, Ky. asst. for George Allen for Gov. of Va., asst. vol. for Jim Miler for Senate from Va.; mem. Ky. Soc. Schedule C. Bush-Quayle, Ky. Reps. Mem. Nat. Geog. Soc. Home: 5021 Seminary Rd Apt 1425 Alexandria VA 22311-1941

VIDERMAN, LINDA JEAN, paralegal, corporate executive; b. Follansbee, W.Va., Dec. 4, 1957; d. Charles Richard and Louise Edith (LeBoeuf) Roberts; m. David Gerald Viderman Jr., Mar. 15, 1974; children: Jessica Renae, April Mae, Melinda Dawn. AS, W.Va. No. Community Coll., 1983; Cert. income tax prep., H&R Block, Steubenville, Ohio, 1986. Cert. surg. tech.; cert. fin. counselor; lic. ins. agt. Food prep. pers. Bonanza Steak House, Weirton, W.Va., 1981-83; ward clk., food svcs. Weirton Med. Ctr., 1982-84; sec., treas. Mountaineer Security Systems, Inc., Wheeling, W.Va., 1983-86; owner, operator The Button Booth, Colliers, W.Va., 1985—; paralegal, adminstr. Atty. Dominic J. Potts, Steubenville, Ohio, 1987-92; gen. ptnr., executrix Panhandle Homes, Wellsburg, W.Va., 1988-96; sec./treas., executrix Panhandle Homes, Inc., 1996—; ins. agt. Milico, Mass. Indemnity, 1991-92, L&L Ins. Svcs., 1992-94; paralegal Atty. Fred Risovich II, Weirton, 1991-93; sec. The Hon. Fred Risovich II, Wheeling, 1993; paralegal atty. Christopher J. Paull, Wellsburg, W.Va., 1993—; owner Wellsburg Office Supply, 1993-94; notary pub., 1991—. Contbr. articles numerous jours.; author numerous poems. Chmn. safety com. Colliers (W.Va.) Primary PTA, 1985-87; mem., sec. LaLeche League, Steubenville, Ohio, 1978-80; vol. counselor W.Va. U. Fin. Counseling Svc., 1990—; IRS vol. Vol. Income Tax Assistance Program, 1991—. Mem. W.Va. Writers Assn., Legal Assts. of W.Va., Inc., Am. Affiliate of Nat. Assn. Legal Assts., W.Va. Trial Lawyers Assn., Wellsburg Art Assn., Phi Theta Kappa. Jehovah's Witness. Home: 137R St Johns Rd Colliers WV 26035 Office: Panhandle Homes Inc RR 2 Box 27A Wellsburg WV 26070-9500

VIEWEG, CHRISTIAN SEITZ, airline pilot; b. South Bend, Ind., Oct. 14, 1951; s. Robert Seitz and Vera Nancy (Crank) V.; m. Kathryn Lynne Romig, Oct. 6, 1984. BS in History, USAF Acad., 1974; MA in History with distinction, George Mason U., 1995; postgrad., U. Md. Airline pilot U.S. Air, Washington, 1980—. Mem., officer Middleburg (Va.) Lions Club, 1987—; vol. fireman Middleburg Vol. Fire Dept., 1992—. Capt. USAF, 1974-80.

VIEWEG, WALTER VICTOR RUDOLPH, psychiatrist, educator; b. East Orange, N.J., May 15, 1934; s. Walter Victor R. and Anne Elizabeth (Reinken) V.; m. Nina McIntyre Burks; children: Ann Vieweg Allam, Eric, Catherine Vieweg Jones, Sara; m. Elizabeth Blackburn Lowe, Feb. 13, 1982; stepchildren: Dabney Elizabeth Hammer, David Garrett Hammer. Student, Pomona Coll., 1952-53; BS, U.S. Naval Acad., 1957; MD, George Washington U., 1965. Diplomate Am. Bd. Psychiatry and Neurology with qualifications in geriatric psychiatry, subspecialty of cardiovascular Disease, Am. Bd. Internal Medicine, Nat. Bd. Med. Examiners; lic. physician, Va. Rotating intern U.S. Naval Hosp., San Diego, 1965-66; internal medicine resident U.S. Naval Hosp., Oakland, Calif., 1966-69; cardiovascular disease fellow U.S. Naval Hosp., Bethesda, Md., 1970-72; tng. officer, staff dept. internal medicine U.S. Naval Hosp., Oakland, 1969-70; dir. catheterization lab. U.S. Naval Hosp., San Diego, 1972-77, head cardiology br., 1977-81; psychiat. resident U. Va., Charlottesville, 1981-84; dir. rsch. dept. behavioral medicine and psychiatry U. Va. Sch. Medicine, Charlottesville, 1984-91; dir. geriatric psychiatry dept. psychiatry Med. Coll. Va., Richmond, 1991—, prof. psychiatry, prof. internal medicine, 1991—; sci. dir. Western State Hosp., Staunton, Va., 1983-91; assoc. prof. behavioral medicine and psychiatry U. Va. Sch. Medicine, Charlottesville, 1984-88, assoc. prof. internal medicine, 1985-89, prof., 1989-91, prof. behavioral medicine and psychiatry, 1988-91; clin. instr. medicine U. Calif. Sch. Medicine, San Diego, 1974-75, asst. clin. prof., 1975-77, assoc. clin. prof., 1977-81; clin. assoc. prof. medicine Uniformed Svcs., U. Health Scis., Bethesda, 1979-81; condr. presentations sci. meetings. Mem. editorial bd. Catheterization and Cardiovascular Diagnosis, 1981-83; contbr. articles to profl. jours., chpts. to books. Capt., M.C. USN, 1953-81. Fellow ACP, Am. Coll. Cardiology (coll. gov. Navy 1980-81), Am. Psychiat. Assn.; mem. AMA, Am. Geriatrics Soc., Assn. Medicine and Psychiatry, Am. Assn. Geriatric Psychiatry. Home: 9296 Rappahannock Trail Ashland VA 23005 Office: Med Coll Va Dept Psychiatry Box 980710 MCV Richmond VA 23298-0710

VIJAYARAGHAVAN, VASU, systems consultant; b. Madras, Tn, India, Apr. 8, 1962; came to U.S., 1987; s. Rangachari and Mythili V.; m. Sudha Thiruvengadam, Oct. 27, 1992. BSEE, Bangalore U., 1983; P.G.D. Mgmt., I.I.M. Bangalore, 1987; MBA, U. Iowa, 1988; MS in Computer Engring., U. Tex., 1991. Project engr. Siemens, Madras, 1984-85; tech. mktg. exec. Intersoft, Inc., Portland, Oreg., 1989-90; systems analyst Super Collider, Dallas, 1991-92; mgr. Andersen Cons., Houston, 1992—. Vol. United Way, Houston, 1993-94. Grantee in rsch. U. Iowa, 1987, U. Tex., 1990, in tchg. U. Iowa, 1988. Mem. IEEE, Assn. for Computing Machinery. Office: Andersen Consulting 711 Louisiana Houston TX 77002

VIJVERBERG, WIM PETRUS MARIA, economics educator; b. The Hague, The Netherlands, Sept. 30, 1955; came to U.S., 1977; s. Wilhelmus P.M. and Apollonia E. (Barendse) V.; m. Chu-Ping Chen, May 26, 1981; children: Michelle, Andrea, William. BA, Erasmus U. of Rotterdam, The Netherlands, 1975; MA, U. Pitts., 1979, PhD, 1981. Postdoctoral fellow Yale U., New Haven, 1981-84; vis. asst. prof. econs. U. Hawaii at Manoa, Honolulu, 1984-85; asst. prof. Ill. State U., Normal, 1985-86; asst. prof. econs. and polit. economy U. Tex. at Dallas, Richardson, 1986-91, assoc. prof., 1991—; cons. The World Bank, Washington, 1985-91, 94-96. Contbr. articles to profl. jours., 1980—. Deacon, Calvary Chapel Assembly of God, Richardson, 1991—. Andrew Mellon Found. predoctoral fellow, Pitts., 1979-81. Mem. Am. Econ. Assn., Econometric Soc. Office: Univ Tex Dallas Sch Social Sci 2601 N Floyd Rd Richardson TX 75080-1407

VILARDEBO, ANGIE MARIE, management consultant, parochial school educator; b. Tampa, Fla., July 15, 1938; d. Vincent and Antonina (Fazio) Noto; m. Charles Kenneth Vilardebo, June 26, 1960; children: Charles, Kenneth, Michele, Melanie. BA, Notre Dame Md., 1960; postgrad., Rollins Coll., 1980. Cert. tchr., Fla. Tchr. Sea Park Elem. Sch., Satellite Beach, Fla., 1960-61; office mgr. Computer Systems Enterprises, Satellite Beach, 1973-76; artist Satellite Beach, 1976-79; employment counselor Career Cons., Melbourne, Fla., 1979-80; tchr. Our Lady of Lourdes Parochial Sch., Melbourne, 1980-89; pres. Consol. Ventures, Inc., Satellite Beach, 1989—, Versatile Suppliers, Inc., Satellite Beach, 1989—; prin. search com. Diocese of Orlando, Fla., 1989-90. Patentee personal grading machine. V.p. Jaycees, Satellite Beach, 1976-77, pres., 1977-78. Recipient 1st Place Art award Fla. Fedn. Woman's Clubs, 1978, 2nd Place Art award, 1979, Honorable Mention, 1980. Mem. Satellite Beach Woman's Club, Paper Chaser's Investment Club, Brevard Arts Ctr. & Mus., Space Coast Art League (social chmn. 1987—). Roman Catholic. Home: 606 Barcelona Ct Melbourne FL 32937

VILASI, VINCENT JOHN, anesthesiologist; b. Valhalla, N.Y., Mar. 13, 1961; s. Joseph Anthony and Joan Patricia (Grieco) V. BA, U. Pa., 1982; MD, Duke U., 1986. Diplomate Am. Bd. Internal Medicine, Am. Bd. Anesthesiology. Instr. U. Tchg. Hosp., Lusaka, Zambia, 1992; assoc. Fair Oaks Anesthesia Assocs., Fairfax, Va., 1992—. Mem. AMA, Am. Soc. of Anesthesiologists, Va. Soc. of Anesthesiologists. Office: Fair Oaks Anesthesia Assocs 3600 Joseph Siewick Rd Fairfax VA 22033

VILCHES-O'BOURKE, OCTAVIO AUGUSTO, accounting company executive; b. Havana, Cuba, Aug. 15, 1923; came to U.S., 1962, naturalized, 1967; s. Bartolome and Isabel Susana (O'Bourke) Vilches; CPA, U. Havana, 1949, JD, 1951, PhD in Econ. Scis., 1953; m. Alba Del Valle Junco, July 24, 1954; 1 son, Octavio Roberto. Owner, Octavio Vilches & Assos., Havana, 1949-61; comptr. United R.R. of Cuba, 1950-53; cons. econ. affairs Cuban Dept. Labor, Havana, 1953; auditor Cuban Dept. Treasury, 1952-59; pres. Roble Furniture, Inc., San Juan, P.R., 1963-65, owner, Hato Rey, P.R., 1963—; pres. Mero Constrn. Corp., San Juan, 1973. Mem. Circulo Cubano P.R., Colegio Contadores Publicos en el Exilio, Colegio Abogados en el Exilio, Cuban Nat. Bar Assn.; Nat. Soc. Pub. Accts. Republican. Roman Catholic. Club: American (Miami, Fla.). Home: Golden Gate 146 Turquesa St Caparra Heights PR 00920 Office: Condominio El Centro II Ste 1402 Hato Rey PR 00920

VILE, JOHN RALPH, political science educator; b. Wilmington, Del., Apr. 29, 1951; s. Ralph and Joanna Virginia (Griffith) V.; m. Linda Kay Christensen, June 27, 1976; children—Virginia, Rebekah. B.A. in Govt., Coll. William and Mary, 1973; Ph.D. in Govt., U. Va., 1977. Asst. prof. McNeese State U., Lake Charles, La., 1977-81, assoc. prof. polit. sci., 1981-86, prof. 1986—; head dept. soc. sci., 1981—; prof., chair polit. sci. Mid. Tenn. State U., 1989—. Author 6 books; contbr. articles to profl. jours. NEH fellow, summers 1979, 82, 85. Mem. Am. Polit. Sci. Assn., So. Polit. Sci. Assn., Southwestern Polit. Sci. Assn., Tenn. Polit. Sci. Assn. (v.p. 1993, pres.-elect 1994, pres. 1995-96), Phi Beta Kappa, Omicron Kappa, Lychns Hon. Soc. Baptist. Office: Middle Tennessess St U Dept Polit Sci Murfreesboro TN 37132

VILELLA, FRANCISCO JOSÉ, wildlife research biologist; b. Arecibo, P.R., Sept. 25, 1955; s. Juan José and Olga Maria (Janeiro) V.; m. Ana B. Arnizaut, Sept. 24, 1988; 1 child, Isabela Beatriz. BS, U. P.R., Mayaguez, 1978; MA, Hofstra U., 1983; PhD, La. State U., 1989. NSF rsch. fellow Water Resources Rsch. Inst., U. P.R., Mayaguez, 1978-79; teaching asst. biology dept. Hofstra U., Hempstead, N.Y., 1981-83; rsch. asst. Wild Fish Dept. La. State U., Baton Rouge, 1984-89; fish and wildlife biologist USFWS-Caribbean Field Office, Boqueron, P.R., 1989-90, FWS-P.R. Parrot Field Office, Luquillo, P.R., 1990-94; asst. unit leader Miss. Coop. F&W Rsch. Unit Miss. State U., Mississippi State, 1994—; v.p. La. State U. chpt. of The Wildlife Soc., 1984-85. Contbr. articles to profl. jours. Recipient Outstanding Performance award U.S. Fish & Wildlife Svc., 1992-94. Mem. Soc. Caribbean Ornithology (bd. governors 1993-94), Am. Ornithologists Union, Soc. Conservation Biology, Am. Mus. Natural History. Democrat. Roman Catholic. Home: 1101 Robin Dr Starkville MS 39759-9108 Office: Mississippi State U Dept of Wildlife & Fishery PO Drawer BX Mississippi State MS 00762

VILETTO, CHRISTINA ANN, elementary education educator; b. Alexandria, Va., Nov. 24, 1971; d. John Jr. and Bev Viletto. Bachelor's degree, James Madison U., MEd. Cert. elem. edn. NK-3, reading. Grad. asst. James Madison U., Harrisonburg, Va.; tchr. elem. edn. Mantua Elem., Fairfax, Va. Recipient Award of Appreciation, Fed. Govt., 1990, 92, Award of Accomodation, 1990, 92; Elsie Wiggly Meml. scholar James Madison U., 1992, Godwin scholar, 1992. Mem. Internat. Reading Assn., Phi Delta Kappa, Kappa Delta Pi. Roman Catholic.

VILLA, EDMOND ROLAND, corporate executive; b. Westfield, N.J., Sept. 22, 1929; s. Guy Sr. and Settemia (Ceremele) V.; m. Virginia Ann Chadwick, Oct. 14, 1950; children: Edmond Jr., Vicki Villa, J. Scott Sr. Grad. high sch., Westfield. Asst. sec. Guy Villa & Sons Inc., Westfield and Clark, N.J., 1947-75; v.p. Guy Villa & Sons Inc., Stuart, Fla., 1975-77; pres. Villa Bros. Inc., Stuart, 1977-87; v.p. Villa Enterprises Ltd., Cookeville, Tenn., 1979—; pres. Villa Bros. Equipment Co., Cookeville, 1987—. Mem. code enforcement bd. Town of Sewalls Point, Fla., 1980-86. Home: 24 S Sewalls Point Rd Stuart FL 34996-6728 Summer Home: 1963 Mackie Rd Cookeville TN 38506-7065 Office: Villa Bros Equipment Co Inc 1427 Interstate Dr Cookeville TN 38501-4122

VILLALOBOS, HECTOR, insurance agent; b. San Jose, Costa Rica, May 28, 1949; s. Hector and Josefina (Rodriguez) de Villalobos; m. Ana Herran, July 15, 1970 (div. 1983); children: Leonel, Danilo; m. Guiselle Umana, Feb. 14, 1984; children: Elaine, Hector J. BBA, 1982. Informatics gen. mgr. Lacsa, Costa Rica, 1968-84; informatics cons. Micro Compulacion, Costa Rica, 1984-85; gen. mgr. Auto-Lac de Costa Rica, 1985-86; insurance broker Serfimex S.A., 1986—; cons. C.R. Internat. Enterprises, Miami, 1980-84. Author: Introduction to Informatics, 1978. V.p. Union Solidarista Costarric, San Jose, Costa Rica, 1987-84. Office: Seofinex S.A. # 2d1 175 Fountainbleu 88th Ave Miami FL 33172

VILLALÓN, SILVIA DURÁN, real estate executive; b. La Havana, Cuba, Apr. 7, 1941; d. Mario Andrés and Ondina (Paredes) Durán; m. Jose R. Garrigó, Apr. 5, 1959 (div. Oct. 1983); children: Jose R., Silvia M., Jorge I.; m. Andrés Villalón, Aug. 17, 1984. BS, Instituto Del Vedado, La Havana, 1958; AA, Miami Dade Community Coll., 1984. Pres. Silvia Garrigo Interiors, Key Biscayne, Fla., 1974-92, Garrigo, Duran & Assocs., Realtors, Key Biscayne, 1976-87; v.p. The Royal Poinciana Group, Inc., Cape Coral, Fla., 1984-89; pres. Sailfish Co., Realtors, Cape Coral, 1986-87, Poinciana Realty of Cape Coral, Inc., Cape Coral, 1987-89, The Tile Wholesaler, Inc., Key Biscayne, Fla., 1987—; pvt. practice mortgage broker Key Biscayne, 1986, pvt. practice realtor, 1976—; sr. sales cons., internat. sales coord. The Gables, Coral Gables, Fla.; interior designer Burdines Interior Designs, Miami, 1991—; v.p. Ferré Villalón Designs, Miami, 1991—. Home: 600 Grapetree Dr Apt 3cs Miami FL 33149-2704

VILLARREAL, CARLOS CASTANEDA, engineering executive; b. Brownsville, Tex., Nov. 9, 1924; s. Jesus Jose and Elisa L. (Castaneda) V.; m. Doris Ann Akers, Sept. 10, 1948; children: Timothy Hill, David Akers. BA, U.S. Naval Acad., 1948; MS, U.S. Navy Postgrad. Sch., 1950; LLD (hon.), St. Mary's U., 1972. Registered profl. engr. Commd. ensign U.S. Navy, 1948, advanced through grades to lt., 1956; comdg. officer U.S.S. Rhea, 1951, U.S.S. Osprey, 1952; comdr. Mine Div. 31, 1953; resigned, 1956; mgr. marine and indsl. operation Gen. Electric Co., 1956-66; v.p. mktg. and adminstrn. Marquardt Corp., 1966-69; head Urban Mass Transit Adminstrn., Dept. Transp., Washington, 1969-73; commr. Postal Rate Commn., 1973-79, vice chmn., 1975-79; v.p. Washington ops. Wilbur Smith and Assocs., 1979-84, sr. v.p., 1984-86, exec. v.p., 1987—, also bd. dirs.; lectr. in field; mem. industry sector adv. com. Dept. Commerce; mem. sect. 13 adv. com. Dept. Transp., 1983-86. Contbr. to profl. jours. Mem. devel. com. Wolftrap Farm Park for the Performing Arts, 1973-78; mem. council St. Elizabeth Ch., 1982-86, chmn. fin. com.; mem. bd. edn. St. Elizabeth Sch.; bd. dirs. Assoc. Catholic Charities, 1983-86; mem. fin. com. Cath. Charities, U.S.A. Decorated knight Sovereign Mil. Hospitaller Order St. John of Jerusalem of Rhodes and Malta, 1981, Knight Equestrian Order of the Holy Sepulchre of Jerusalem; recipient award outstanding achievement Dept. Transp. Fellow ASCE, Am. Cons. Engrs. Coun. (vice chmn. internat. com.); mem. IEEE, NSPE (pres. D.C. soc. 1986-87, bd. dirs. 1988-91), Am. Pub. Transit Assn., Soc. Naval Architects and Marine Engrs., Soc. Am. Mil. Engrs., Am. Rds. and Transp. Builders Assn. (chmn. pub. transp. adv. coun.), Transp. Rsch. Bd., Washington Soc. Engrs., Internat. Bridge, Tunnel and Turnpike Assn., Inst. Traffic Engrs., Intelligent Transp. Soc. Am. (chmn. fin. com., bd. dirs.), Univ. Club, Army-Navy Club. Republican. Roman Catholic. Office: Wilbur Smith Assocs 2921 Telestar Ct Falls Church VA 22042-1205

VILLARREAL, JESUS MORÓN, newswriter, publisher, poet, artist; b. Key West, Fla., Dec. 7, 1952; s. Gonzalo and Clariza (Villarreal) M.; m. Maria Marroquin Guerra (div.); children: Nancy, Ruby, Xochitl Linda; m. Maria de Jesus Hernandez; 1 child, Mario de Jesus. Course in black and white photography, Martinez Studios, Coahuila, Mexico, 1967; course in photo retouching, coloring, restoration, lighting techniques, Jesus Trejo Labs., Monterrey, Mexico, 1969; course in chromegacolor processor, color print finishing and negative processing, Wabash Photo Labs., Chgo., 1973; cert., Photo Lab. Tech., 1988; course in videography and cinematography, Martinez Photography Studios, Houston, 1989. Journalist, photographer El Sol Newspaper, Houston, 1978-90; v.p. La Prensa News, Houston, 1978-79, El Torniquete, Monterrey, Mex., 1980; journalist, photographer Mas Noticias, Houston, 1981; subdirector Diario de Houston, 1982; art critic Critica Magazine, Houston, 1983-85; pub., editor Gaceta de Texas News, Houston, 1992—; lectr. U. Houston, 1978; artist Machtilli Gallery, 1978-93; photographer Gaceta de Tex. News, 1993-94; writer Machtilli Publs., 1992; historian Universidad Autonoma de Nuevo Leon, Monterey, Mex., 1992. Solo exhbns. include Mayors of Zuazua Photo Exhbn. Mus. Casa de Cultura, Imagenes C.R.O.C. Fedn. Gallery, 1981; group exhbns. at Art and Photography Festival Buckingham Found., 1975, Bilingual Bicultural Ctr. R. Salazar Gallery, 1976, S.S.C.C. Phot Contest South Side Camera Ctr., 1978, S.W. Chgo. Arts Ctr., Houston, 1978, The Glassell Sch. Art, Mus. Fine Arts, Houston, 1982, Fala Mems. Exbhn. Fala Midtown Art Gallery, 1983, Ceestem Gallery, Mexico City, 1983, O'Kane Gallery, Houston, 1983, Leopoldo Carpinteyro Gallery, Mex., 1986; permanent exhbn. Hacienda San Pedro, Zuazua, Mex.; author: (book) How to Write Poems, Como Declamar y Escribir Poesia, 1992, Manual de Pintura Nahuatl, 1995, Gutierrez and Magee Tex-Mex Heroes, 1995. union rep. Cesar Chavez United Farmworkers, 1968-69. Recipient 3d Place in Painting award Mus. Sci. and Industry, 1975, 1st Place in Photography award South Side Camera, 1980, Painting award Mus. Casa de Cultura, 1981, 4th Pl. in Painting award Vitro Art Mus., 1980, Editors Choice award Nat. Libr. of Poetry, 1994. Mem. Houston Arts Coun., Seventh Flower Artists, Bar of Artists and Critics Assn., Croc Syndicate of Photographers, Internat. Soc. Poets (life mem.). Democrat. Office: Gaceta de Tex Pub Co PO Box 87236 Houston TX 77287-7236

VILLECCO, JUDY DIANA, substance abuse, mental health counselor, director; b. Knoxville, Tenn., Jan. 19, 1948; d. William Arthur and Louise (Reagan) Chamberlain; m. Tucker, June 10, 1965 (div. 1974); children: Linda Louise (Tucker) Smith, Constance Christine; m. Roger Anthony Villecco, May 3, 1979. BA in Psychology, U. West Fla., 1988, MA in Psychology, 1992. Lic. mental health counselor, Fla.; cert. addiction profl., Fla.; internat. cert. alcohol and drug counselor. Counselor Gulf Coast Hosp., Ft. Walton Beach, Fla., 1986-87; peer counselor U. West Fla., Ft. Walton Beach, 1987-89; family and prevention counselor Okaloosa Guidance Clinic, Ft. Walton Beach, 1988-89; family svc. dir. Anon Anew of Tampa (Fla.), Inc., 1989-91; dir. Renew Counseling Ctr., Ft. Walton Beach, 1990-92; substance abuse dept. dir. Avalon Ctr., Milton, Fla., 1992-93; adult coord. Partial & Rivendell, Ft. Walton Beach, 1994-95; pvt. practice Emerald Coast Psychiat. Care, P.A., Fort Walton Beach, 1994-95, Associated Psychotherapists, Ft. Walton Beach, 1995—; internat. substance abuse counselor, dir. and presenter in field. Author: Co-dependency Treatment Manual, 1992; creator Effective Treatment for Codependants, 1992. Named Outstanding Mental Health Profl. of Yr. Mental Health Assn., 1994. Mem. Internat. Assn. for Offender Counselors, Fla. Alcohol, Drug, Substance Abuse Assn. (bd. dirs., regional rep., Regional Profl. of Yr. 1992-93, 95—), Am. Counseling Assn. (alt. rep.), Internat. Assn. for Marriage and Family Counseling, Phi Theta Kappa, Alpha Phi Sigma. Office: 348 Miracle Strip Pkwy SW Fort Walton Beach FL 32548-5264

VILLEGOUREIX-RITAUD, PATRICK, diplomat; b. Bordeaux, France, July 23, 1948; came to U.S., 1971; s. Edmond and Simone (Mendoza) Villegoureix-R.; m. Phyllis Sheila Flashner, Jan. 7, 1971; children: Katia, Andrew, Marc. French Baccalaureat, Bordeaux, France; postgrad., Bordeaux; cert. proficiency in Acctg., Ohio State U., cert. proficiency in bus. mgmt. Exec. dir. U.S. C. of C., Morocco, 1975-77; dir. U.S. Exhibits U.S. Dept. Commerce, Morocco, Algeria, 1977-80; attache U.S. Dept. State Fgn. Svc., Poland, Mexico, Niger, Haiti, 1980—. Producer monthly bulletin for U.S. C. of C. in Morocco. Recipient City of Bordeaux medal, Meritorious Honor award U.S. State Dept. Office: US State Dept IO/OICA 2201 C St NW Washington DC 20520-2418

VILLELLA, EDWARD JOSEPH, ballet dancer, educator, choreographer, artistic director; b. L.I., N.Y., Oct. 1, 1936; s. Joseph and Mildred (DeGiovanni) V.; m. Janet Greschler (div. Nov. 1980); 1 child, Roddy; m. Linda Carbonetta, Apr. 1981; children: Christa Francesca, Lauren. BS in Marine Transp., N.Y. State Maritime Coll., 1957; LHD (hon.), Boston Conservatory, 1985; hon. degree, Skidmore Coll., Fordham U., Nazareth Coll., Siena Coll., Union Coll., Schenectady, N.Y., 1991; DHL (hon.), St. Thomas U., Miami, Fla., 1994. Mem. N.Y.C. Ballet, 1957, soloist, 1958-60, prin. soloist, 1960-83; artistic dir. Ballet Okla., Oklahoma City, 1983-86; founding artistic dir. Miami (Fla.) City Ballet, 1985—; vis. artist U.S. Mil. Acad., West Point, 1981-82; vis. prof. dance U. Iowa, 1981; resident Heritage chair arts and cultural criticism George Mason U.; lectr. in field. Performed dances in Symphony C, Scotch Symphony, Western Symphony, Donizetti Variations, Swan Lake, La Source, The Nutcracker, Agon, Stars and Stripes, The Prodigal Son; premiered in Balanchine works including The Figure in the Carpet, 1960, Electronics, 1961, A Midsummer Night's Dream, 1962, Bugaku, 1963, Tarantella, 1964, Harlequinade, 1965, The Brahms-Schoenberg Quartet, 1966, Jewels, 1967, Symphony in Three Movements, 1972, Schéhérazade, 1975; choreography includes Narkissas, 1966, Shostakovitch Ballet Suite, 1972, Shenandoah, 1972, Gayane Pas de Deux, 1972, Salute to Cole, 1973, Sea Chanties, 1974, Prelude, Riffs and Fugues, 1980; TV appearances include The Ed Sullivan Show, Bell Telephone Hour, Mike Douglas Show, (TV spl.) Harlequin, 1975 (Emmy award), summer theaters, festivals, U.S. and abroad, 1957—; co-author: (autobiography) Prodigal Son, 1991. Mem. Nat. Coun. of Arts, 1968-74; chmn. Commn. for Cultural Affairs City N.Y., 1978; bd. visitors N.C. Sch. for the Arts; mem. dance adv. panel Nat. Endowment for Arts; trustee Wolf Trap Found. for the Arts. Recipient Dance Mag. award, 1964, Lions of the Performing Arts award N.Y. Pub. Libr., 1987, Capezio Dance award, 1989, Gold medal Nat. Soc. Arts and Letters, 1990, William G. Anderson merit award AAHPERD, 1991; named Miamian of Yr., UNICO Nat., 1993.

VILLENA-ALVAREZ, JUANITA I., language educator, consultant; b. Baguio, Philippines, Aug. 27, 1965; arrived in France, 1987, Spain, 1986; came to U.S., 1988; d. Juan J. V. and Milagros M. Ibarra; m. Beda E. Alvarez, Jr., June 27, 1992; 1 child, Natalie Noelle. BA magna cum laude, U. Philippines, Quezon City, 1986; Magistère French Civilization, U. Paris, 1988; MA in French Lit., U. Cin., 1989, PhD in French Lit., 1994. Instr. French, Spanish U. Philippines, Quezon, 1986; grad. tchg. asst. U. Cin., 1988-93; instr. French Miami U., Oxford, Ohio, 1993; asst. prof. U. S.C., Beaufort, 1994—; lang. cons. Software Clearing House, Cin., 1989-90; material devel. Judith Muyskens, Cin., 1988-90. Author: The Allegory of Literary Representation, 1997; contbr. article to profl. jour. Charles Phelps Taft fellow, 1993-94; recipient Rotary Amb. Goodwill Rotary Internat., 1987-88. Mem. MLA, Am. Assn. French Tchrs., S.C. Assn. Fgn. Lang. Tchrs., Alliance Française (Cin., lang. cons. 1993), French Circle (Beaufort, lang. coord. 1994—), Phi Kappa Phi. Home: 2 Quail Loop Beaufort SC 29902 Office: U SC 801 Carteret St Beaufort SC 29902

VILLOCH, KELLY CARNEY, art director; b. Kyoto, Japan, July 22, 1950; d. William Riley and stepdaughter Hazel Fowler Carney; m. Joe D. Villoch, Aug. 9, 1969; children: Jonathan Christopher, Jennifer. A in Fine Arts, Dade C.C., Miami, Fla., 1971; student, Metro Fine Arts, 1973-74, Fla. Internat. U., 1985-88. Design asst. Lanvin, Miami, 1971—, Fieldcrest, Miami, 1974-77; art dir. Advercolor, Miami, 1977-78; art dir. copywriter ABC, Miami, 1978-89; writer Armed Forces Radio & TV Network; multimedia dir. ADVITEC, 1989-91; art dir. writer Miami Write, 1979—; owner Beach Point Prodns., 1992—; lectr. Miami Dade C.C., cons. Studio Masters, North Miami, 1979-89. Prin. works include mixed media, 1974 (Best of Show 1974), pen and ink drawing, 1988 (Best Poster 1988); writer, dir., editor, prodr. (video film): Bif, 1988, Drink + Drive = Die, 1994; writer, dir., prodr. (pub. svc. announcement) Reading is the Real Adventure, 1990; film editor Talent Times Mag.; author: Winds of Freedom, 1994; art dir., exec. com. Miami Hispanic Media Conf., 1992, 93, 94; editor-in-chief, film editor: In Grove Miami Mag., 1994-96; webmaster, web content provider, website design cons., writer, graphic artist Guru Comms., 1996; editor-in-chief In Grove Miami Mag., 1994-96; web content provider WEBCOM; webmaster Guru Comm., 1996; web site designer, multimedia dir. State of Fla. grantee LimeLite Studios, Inc., 1990, William Douglas Pawley Found. grantee, Frances Wolfson scholar, Cultural Consortium grantee, 1993. Mem. Am. Film Inst., Phi Beta Kappa.

VIMONT, RICHARD ELGIN, lawyer; b. Lexington, Ky., Aug. 3, 1936; s. Richard Thompson and Christine Frazee (Anderson) V.; m. Louise Marie Salyer, Sept. 10, 1960; children: Richard Thompson II, Margaret Anderson; m. 2d, Martha Jane Murray, Nov. 13, 1982. BS, U. Ky., 1958, JD, 1960. Bar: Ky. 1960, U.S. Dist. Ct. (ea. dist.) Ky. 1960, U.S. Dist. Ct. (we. dist.) Ky. 1964, U.S. Ct. Appeals (6th cir.) 1964, U.S. Supreme Ct. 1966. Assoc. Brown, Sledd and McCann, 1960-64; ptnr. Core, Vimont and Combs, 1964-68, Breckinridge, Vimont and Amato, 1968-70, Anggelis, Vimont and Bunch, 1970-78, Vimont and Wills PLLC, Lexington, Ky., 1978—; city commr., Lexington, 1971-72; Lexington Mounted Police Bd., asst. commonwealth atty., 1973-75; vis. prof. Transylvania U., 1978-80, Midway Coll., 1992; bd. dirs. Ky. World Trade Ctr., 1990—, Equitania Ins. Co.; mng. dir. Equitania Ins. Co., 1990-93, pres., CEO, 1993—; gen. counsel Pavenstedt Pauli (U.S.A.), Inc., 1990-92. Bd. dirs. Lexington Ballet Co., 1989-90. U. Ky. fellow. Mem. ABA, Am. Acad. Trial Attys., Ky. Bar Assn., Ky. Acad. Trial Attys., Fayette County Bar Assn., Lexington C. of C., Thoroughbred Club of Am., Lexington Polo Club, Lexington, Lafayette Club, Spindletop Hall Club (bd. dirs. 1978-81, 86-90), Rotary (sec. Lexington endowment). Democrat. Mem. Disciple of Christ Ch. Office: 155 E Main St Fl 3 Lexington KY 40507-1300

VINCENT, BRUCE HAVIRD, investment banker, oil and gas company executive; b. Laramie, Wyo., Nov. 7, 1947; s. Dale Leon and Mildred Sara (Havird) V.; m. Pamela Jean Benson, Dec. 20, 1968 (div. May 1986); children: Jennifer Jean, Bryce Havird; m. Julia Rae Dilly, Nov. 16, 1991. BBA, Duke U., 1969; MBA in Fin., U. Houston, 1976. Asst. v.p. First City Nat. Bank, Houston, 1975-77, v.p., group mgr. energy dept., 1977-80; exec. v.p., chief operating officer, bd. dirs. Peninsula Resources Corp., Corpus Christi, Tex., 1980-82; ptnr. investment banking Johnson & Vincent, Houston, 1982-85; pres., chief exec. officer Tangent Oil and Gas, Inc., Houston, 1985-86, also bd. dirs.; exec. v.p., chief operating officer, chief fin. officer Energy Assets Internat. Corp., Houston, 1986-88, also bd. dirs.; pres. Vincent & Co., 1988—; sr. v.p. funds mgmt. Swift Energy Co., 1990—; co-chmn. Houston Energy Fin. Group. Bd. dirs. Big Bros./Big Sisters Greater Houston. Lt. USN, 1969-73. Mem. Ind. Petroleum Assn. Am. (chmn. internat. com., bd. govs., regional bd. trustees, bd. dirs. advisors oil and gas investment symposium, chmn. London E&P investment sumposium), Tex. Mid-Continent Oil and Gas Assn., Tex. Ind. Prodrs. and Royalty Owners Assn., N.Am. Prospect Expo (bd. dirs.), Internat. Assn. Fin. Planning, Investment Program Assn. (chmn. bd. trustees). Republican. Episcopalian.

VINCENT, CARL G., JR., real estate portfolio manager; b. Milford, Del., June 30, 1964; s. Carl G. Sr. and Phylis F. (Cash) V.; m. Rhonda L. Ross, May 26, 1990. BS, Oral Roberts U., 1985, MBA, 1988; JD, U. Tulsa, 1991. Bar: Okla. 1991. Real estate market analyst 1st Am. Realty, Tulsa, 1985-87; real estate fin. analyst Boston Mgmt. Co., Tulsa, 1987-91; real estate tax cons. Burke & Nickel, Tulsa, 1991-94; dir. Tulsa ops. Ruffin Properties, Tulsa, 1994—; bus. advisor Alzheimers Found., Tulsa, 1991—. Mem. Phi Delta Phi, Phi Alpha Phi. Office: Ruffin Properties 7130 S Lewis Ste 200 Tulsa OK 74136

VINCENT, MERLE ALLEN, learning center administrator, educator; b. Jet, Okla., Apr. 13, 1936; s. Herman and Dorothy (Dillon) V.; 1 child, Whitney. BS, Northwestern Okla. State U., 1959; MLS, Emporia State U., 1965, postgrad., 1967-74. Tchr. Madison (Kans.) Pub. Schs., 1959-62, Junction City (Kans.) Pub. Schs., 1962-63, Atchison (Kans.) Pub. Schs., 1963-65; head libr. Bonner Springer (Kans.) Jr. H.S., 1965-67, Cowley County C.C., Arkansas City, Kans., 1967-74; dir. learning resources ctr. North Ark. Cmty. Tech. Coll., Harrison, 1975—, libr. cons., 1974—. Mem. NEA, ALA, Ark. Libr. Assn. (chmn. libr. roundtable 1995-96), Lions. Republican. Methodist. Home: PO Box 1755 Harrison AR 72602 Office: North Ark Cmty Tech Coll Pioneer Ridge Harrison AR 72601

VINCENT, THOMAS ESTES, engineering executive; b. Potsdam, N.Y., Oct. 7, 1951; s. Gardiner Estes and Arlene Frances (Steele) V.; m. Joanne LaJuett, Feb. 14, 1976; Children: Tracy Jo, Thomas Jr. AAS, Jefferson C.C., 1971; BSME, Rochester Inst. Tech., 1974. Project engr. Black-Clawson Co., Fulton, N.Y., 1974-75; design engr. Hall Ski-Lift Company, Watertown, N.Y., 1975-78; sr. project engr. Leroi divsn. Dresser Industries, Sidney, Ohio, 1978-80; project mgr. rotary recip compressor divsn. Ingersoll-Rand Co., Davidson, N.C., 1980—. Patentee in field. Pres. Brownes Ferry Homeowners Assn., 1992—, v.p., 1990-91. Mem. ASME, NSPE. Republican. Home: 7213 Brassy Creek Ln Charlotte NC 28269-1292 Office: Ingersoll-Rand Co Rotary-Recip Compressor Divsn PO Box 1600 800A Beaty St Davidson NC 28036

VINECOUR, ONEIDA AGNES, nurse; b. Port Arthur, Tex., Oct. 15, 1917; d. Ernest Eugene and Gertrude Mary (Wooldridge) Thorn; m. Seymour Vinecour, Jan. 14, 1943 (dec. 1976); children: Seymour Jacob, Rebecca Leah. Diploma, St. Mary's Hosp. Sch. Nursing, Port Arthur, 1939; postgrad., cert. Surg. Tech., Anesthesia, Cook County Hosp., 1939-40; postgrad. U. Chgo., 1939-40, Tex. Coll. Mines, 1943, U. Tex. Health Ctr. R.N., cert. occupational audiometric technician, occupl. spirometric technician. Operating room supr., instr. Schumpert Meml. Hosp., Shreveport, La., 1940-41; anesthetist St. Joseph Hosp., Albuquerque, 1941-42; operating room supr., instr. Lynn City Hosp. (Mass.), 1946-48; staff anesthetist St. Mary's Hosp., Port Arthur, Tex., 1951-53, in service dir., 1971-73; staff nurse Tyler County Hosp., Woodville, Tex., 1964-65; dept. head, supr. Park Pl. Hosp., Port Arthur, 1965-71; operating room supr. Mid-County Hosp., Nederland, Tex., 1973-81; staff nurse Baptist Meml. Hosp., Beaumont, Tex., 1973-81; part time staff Health Care Svcs., Port Arthur, 1983—; indsl. nurse Synpol Inc., 1984-86; staff nurse Texaco Chem. Plant, Port Arthur, 1986-92, Olsten Health Care Svcs., 1992—. Served as officer U.S. Army Nurse Corps, 1942-46. Mem. Am. Nurses Assn., Mass. Nurses Assn., Tex. State Nurses Assn., Assn. Occupational Health Nurses. Republican. Methodist. Home: 2502 Glenwood Dr Port Arthur TX 77642-2639

VINEL, CATHERINE DAVIS, elementary education educator; b. Auburn, Ala., Oct. 23, 1940; d. Charles Shepard and Mary Greenfield (Merritt) Davis; m. Antoine Jean Bernard, May 20, 1938; children: Jean, Marie, Caroline, Antoinette, Juliette. BA, U. S.C., 1962, MA, 1993, PhD, 1994; MAT, Smith Coll., 1963. Cert. tchr. Spanish, French, English and Latin, Mass., S.C. Instr. Queens Coll., Charlotte, N.C., 1964-65; tchr. Protestant Sch. Grater Montreal, Can., 1965-66, Halco Mining Sch., Kamsar, Guinea, 1974-80, Thomas Heyword, Ridgeland, S.C., 1980-85, Hilton Head (S.C.) High, 1985-91; instr. U. S.C., Columbia, 1994-96; tchr. Dent Middle Sch., Columbia, 1995—. Author: Narrators as Characters in Cervantes's Novelas Ejemplares, 1995. Mem. MLA, Am. Assn. Tchrs. French, Am. Classical League, Cervantes Soc. Home: 602 Graymont Ave Columbia SC 29205 Office: 2719 Decker Blvd Columbia SC 29206

VINES, ANGELA, molecular biologist; b. LaFayette, Ala., Jan. 11, 1959; d. Julius S. and LeMerle (Brooks) V. BS in Biology magna cum laude, Tuskegee U., 1980; AS in Mortuary Sci., Gupton Jones Coll., 1983; MS in Biology, Clark Atlanta U., 1987, PhD in Molecular Biology, 1993. Rsch. asst. dept. immunology Morehouse Sch. Medicine, Atlanta, 1983; biology lab. tchr. Clark Atlanta U., 1989-91, Spelman Coll., Atlanta, 1986; rsch. assoc. Ctrs. for Disease Control, Atlanta, 1987-88; doctoral rschr. Ctrs. for Disease Control, 1988-93; postdoctoral rsch. assoc. dept. virology molecular biology St. Jude Children's Rsch. Hosp., Memphis, 1993—. Contbr. articles to profl. jours. Patricia Harris fellow, 1983, 88-91; recipient 1st place award Sigma Xi, 1980. Mem. Am. Soc. Microbiology, Am. Soc. Virology, Alpha Kappa Mu, Beta Kappa Chi. Office: St Jude Children's Hosp 332 N Lauderdale St Memphis TN 38105-2729

VINES, CHARLES JERRY, minister; b. Carroll County, Ga., Sept. 22, 1937; s. Charles Clarence and Ruby Johnson V.; m. Janet Denney, Dec. 17, 1960; children: Joy Vines Williams, Jim, Jodi, Jon. BA, Mercer U., 1959; BD, New Orleans Bapt. Sem., 1966; ThD, Luther Rice Sem., Jacksonville, Fla., 1974; DD (hon.), Criswell Coll., 1991, Liberty U., 1991. Pastor West Rome Bapt. Ch., Rome, Ga., 1968-74, 79-81, Dauphin Way Bapt. Ch., Moblie, Ala., 1974-79, 1st Bapt. ch., Jacksonville, Fla., 1981—. Author: Practical Guide to Sermon Preparation, An Effective Guide to Sermon Delivery, Great Events in the Life of Christ, I Shall Return - Jesus, Family Fellowship, Great Interviews of Jesus, God Speaks Today, Exploring the Epistles of John, Exploring Daniel, Exploring Mark, Wanted: Soul Winners, Wanted: Church Growers, Basic Sermons on the Ten Commandments. Pres. So. Bapt. Conv., 1988-89. Office: First Bapt Ch 124 W Ashley St Jacksonville FL 32202-3104*

VINES, MARY CHASE AUSTIN, nursing educator; b. Kingsport, Tenn., July 26, 1947; d. Harold Lee and Helen Virginia (Glass) Austin; m. Frank Davis Vines, Feb. 8, 1974; children: Donna Leigh, Mark Andrew, Scott Davis. BS in Nursing, U. Tenn., 1969; MS in Nursing, Miss. U. for Women, Columbus, 1980. Cert. family nurse practitioner. Staff nurse, head nurse Bapt. Meml. Hosp., Memphis, 1970-74; staff nurse U. Tex. Med. Units, Galveston, 1974-75, St. Francis Hosp., Memphis, 1975-76; instr. med.-surg. nursing Northwest Miss. Community Coll., Sentobia, Miss., 1978-84; assoc. prof. med.-surg. nursing Shelby State Community Coll., Memphis, 1984—. Mem. Miss. State Nurses Assn. (past pres., v.p. dist. 28), Nat. League Nursing. Home: 41 Penny Cv Senatobia MS 38668-9649

VINING, F(RANCIS) STUART, architect, consultant; b. Sanford, Fla., Oct. 11, 1934; s. J. Martyn Rufus and Hazel Leota Elizabeth (Greer) V. Cert. sr. divsn., Norton Sch. Fine Art, West Palm Beach, Fla., 1949; cert. archtl. drafting, Orange County Vocat. Tech., Orlando, Fla., 1957; BSCE, L.A. U., North Hollywood, Calif., 1970; BSArch (degree equivalency), Fla. State Bd. Architecture, Tallahassee, 1978. Registered architect, Fla. Draftsman, designer Broleman & Rapp, Orlando, Fla., 1957-60; indsl. labs. cons. Lockwood Greene, A-E, Spartanburg, S.C., 1967, archtl. design cons., 1977; archtl. design cons. Hayes, Saey, Mattern & Mattern, A-E, Roanoke, Va., 1969; structural precast cons. Xerox Corp., Webster, N.Y., 1969; structural, indsl. ventilation designer GE Capacitor Divsn., Irmo, Columbia, S.C., 1973; archtl. engrng. designer Rogers, Lovelock & Fritz, A-E, Winter Park, Fla., 1974; cons. Proctor & Gamble, Cin., 1978; clean rm. labs. and indsl. interiors cons. IBM Gen. Techs. Divsn., Essex Junction, Vt., 1979; H.V.A.C. and indsl. interiors cons. Gen. Dynamics, Electric Boat Divsn., Groton, Conn., 1980; architect, indsl. cons. Am. Tech. Svcs. Group, Inc., Tucker, Ga., 1988-89; pres., CEO F. S. Vining and Co., Inc., Orlando, Fla., 1965—; student, computer-aided design Mid-Fla. Tech. Inst., Orlando, 1991—. Staff employment and transp. specialist Orange County Sheriff, Work Release Program, Orlando, 1991; adminstrv. staff, program asst. Mid-Fla. Tech. Inst., Orlando, 1992-94; adminstrv. staff fin. aid Orlando (Fla.) Tech., 1994—. Seaman USNR, 1951-55. Mem. AIA, Am. Concrete Inst., Am. Inst. Steel Constrn., Am. Mgmt. Assn., Constrn. Specifications Inst., Nat. Fire Protection Assn. Democrat. Roman Catholic. Office: F S Vining and Co Inc PO Box 530006 Orlando FL 32853-0006

VINING, ROBERT LUKE, JR., federal judge; b. Chatsworth, Ga., Mar. 30, 1931; m. Martha Sue Cates; 1 child, Laura Orr. BA, JD, U. Ga., 1959. With Mitchell & Mitchell, 1958-60; ptnr. McCamy, Miner & Vining, Dalton, 1960-69; solicitor gen. Conasauga Judicial Cir., 1963-68; judge Whitfield County Superior Ct., Dalton, 1969-79; judge U.S. Dist. Ct. (no. dist.) Ga., 1979-95, chief judge, 1995—. Served to staff sgt. USAF, 1951-59. Office: US Dist Ct PO Box 6226 600 E 1st St Rm 345 Rome GA 30162*

VINING, WILLIAM MACON, JR., industrial hygienist; b. Jacksonville, Tex., Dec. 19, 1947; s. William M. and Eddie B. Vining; m. Tonya Jo Kallsen, July 27, 1985; children: William Macon III, Theodore John Peter. BA, Tex. Christian U., 1970; MS, U. Tex., Dallas, 1978. Diplomate Am. Acad. Indsl. Hygiene; cert. comprehensive practice of indsl. hygiene and indoor environ. quality. Safety and health coord. Globe Union, Inc. (Johnson Controls), Garland, Tex., 1973-77; corp. sr. indsl. hygienist Tex. Industries, Inc., Dallas, 1977-81, Dresser Industries, Inc., Dallas, 1981-85; pres. Occupational-Environ. Control, Inc., Dallas, 1985—. Author: (design guide) Ventilation System Design Guide, 1980. Judge Dallas Regional Sci. Fair, 1985—, Ft. Worth (Tex.) Regional Sci. Fair, 1985—, Highland Park (Tex.) Ind. Sch. Dist. Sci. Fair, 1985—. Mem. ASHRAE, EPA-S.W. Indoor Air Network, Am. Indsl. Hygiene Assn. (pres. North Tex. chpt. 1983), Am. Soc. Safety Engrs. (profl.), Tex. Indsl. Hygiene Coun. (co-founder, treas. 1993—). Office: Occupat-Environ Control Inc 12959 Jupiter Rd Ste 175 Dallas TX 75238-3200

VINROOT, RICHARD ALLEN, lawyer, mayor; b. Charlotte, N.C., Apr. 14, 1941; s. Gustav Edgar and Vera Frances (Pickett) V.; m. Judith Lee Allen, Dec. 29, 1964; children: Richard A., Laura Tabor, Kathryn Pickett. BS in BA, U. N.C., 1963, JD, 1966. Bar: N.C. 1966, U.S. Dist. Ct. (ea. mid. and we. dists.) N.C. 1969, U.S. Ct. Appeals (4th cir.) 1969. Ptnr. Robinson, Bradshaw & Hinson, P.A., Charlotte, 1969—; mayor City of Charlotte, N.C., 1991-95. Mem. Charlotte City Coun., 1983-91. Mem. ABA, N.C. Bar Assn., Mecklenburg County Bar Assn. (sec. 1976). Republican. Presbyterian.

VINSANT, GEORGE O'NEAL, surgery educator; b. Lafollette, Tenn., July 19, 1951; s. George Finley and Cleo Alta (O'Neal) V.; m. Ortrun E. Bonsiepe, Mar. 5, 1991; 1 child, Oliver O'Neal. BS, Lincoln Meml. U., 1974; MD, U. Tenn., Memphis, 1983. Intern U. Tenn. Med. Ctr., Knoxville, 1983-84, resident, 1984-87, chief resident surgery, 1987-88; trauma fellow, instr. surgery U. Fla. Health Sci. Ctr., Jacksonville, 1988-89, asst. prof. surgery, 1989-96, med. dir. trauma ICU, 1989-93, chmn. nutrition com., 1990—, med. dir. Trauma One Flight Program, 1992-93. Contbr. articles to profl. jours. Mem. AMA, Am. Trauma Soc., Ea. Assn. Surgery Trauma (assoc.), Southeastern Surg. Congress (gold medal paper 1985), Fla. Med. Assn., Duval Med. Soc. Home: 5259 Alloaks Ct Jacksonville FL 32258-2299 Office: U Fla Health Sci Ctr 653 W 8th St Jacksonville FL 32209-6511

VINSON, C. ROGER, federal judge; b. Cadiz, Ky., Feb. 19, 1940; m. Ellen Watson; children: Matt, Todd, Cate, Patrick, Joey. BS, U.S. Naval Acad., 1962; JD, Vanderbilt U., 1971. Commd. ensign USN, 1962, advanced through grades to lt., 1963, naval aviator, until 1968, resigned, 1968; assoc. to ptnr. Beggs & Lane, Pensacola, Fla., 1971-83; judge U.S. Dist. Ct. (no. dist.) Fla., Pensacola, 1983—; mem. Jud. Conf. Adv. Com. on Civil Rules, 1993—; mem. 11th Cir. Pattern Instrn. Com. Office: US Courthouse 100 N Palafox St Pensacola FL 32501-4858*

VINSON, LEILA TERRY WALKER, retired gerontological social worker; b. Lynchburg, Va., July 28, 1928; d. William Terry and Ada Allen (Moore) Walker; m. Hughes Nelson Vinson, Aug. 11, 1951; children: Hughes Nelson, William Terry. Student, Agnes Scott Coll., 1946-48; BA, U. Ala., Tuscaloosa, 1950; postgrad., U. Ala., Birmingham, 1980-81, U. Va., 1950-51. Cert. gerontol. social worker, Ala. Tchr. English and Latin Marion County Bd. Edn., Hamilton, Ala., 1952-59; social worker I Marion County Dept. Pensions and Security, 1963-72, gerontol. social worker II, 1972-85; ret., 1985. Bd. dirs. Marion County Dept. Human Resources, 1985—; speaker on gen. subjects. Recipient Ala. Woman Committed to Excellence award Tuscaloosa coun. Girl Scouts U.S., 1987; named Mrs. Marion County, PTA, Gwin, Ala., 1969, Woman of Yr. Town of Hamilton, 1980, New Retiree of Yr. Ala. Ret. State Employees Assn., 1988, Woman of Yr. BPW, 1985; Gessener Harrison fellow U. Va., 1950-51. Mem. AAUW, DAR (flag chmn. Bedford chpt. 1988-90), UDC, Bus. and Profl. Women's Club (dist. dir. 1984-86, Outstanding Dir. award 1986), Ala. Fedn. Women's Club. Home: PO Box 1112 Hamilton AL 35570-1112 also: Military Rd Hamilton AL 35570

VINSON, MARK ALAN, English language and literature educator; b. Murray, Ky., July 14, 1958; s. C.D. Jr. and Betty Sue (Outland) V.; m. Lisa Carole Fennell, July 16, 1994. Student, Murray State U., 1976-79; BA, BSE, Memphis State U., 1981, MA, 1983; Specialist of Arts in English, U. Miss., 1987. Ordained to ministry Bapt. Ch. as deacon, 1989. Teaching asst. Memphis (Tenn.) State U., 1982-83; instr. English Memphis State U., 1987-90; teaching asst. U. Miss., Oxford, 1984; instr. English N.W. Miss. Jr. Coll., Oxford, 1984-87, Shelby State C.C., Memphis, 1989, State Tech. Inst., Memphis, 1989; asst. prof. English Union U., Memphis, 1990-95, Crichton Coll., Memphis, 1995—. Named one of Outstanding Young Men of Am., 1988, 92. Mem. Am. Cut Glass Assn. (life), Conf. on Christianity and Lit., Sigma Tau Delta (charter mem., program chmn. 1981-83), Modern Lang. Assn. Republican. Southern Baptist. Home: 191 Perkins Extd Memphis TN 38117 Office: Crichton Coll 6655 Winchester Rd Memphis TN 38115-4335

VINSON, MORTY (CONRAD), oil company executive, rancher; b. Mertzon, Tex., Dec. 12, 1921; s. Albert Frank and May Victoria (Miller) V.; m. Anna Louise Rowan, Sept. 25, 1947; children: Bryan, Wayne, Wade, David. BS in Geology, U. Tex., 1951. Registered petroleum geologist. Subsurface geologist Magnolia Petroleum Co., Oklahoma City, 1951-55; area geologist Magnolia Petroleum Co., Midland, Tex., 1955-59, dist. geologist, 1959-60; dist. geologist Mobil Oil Corp., Midland, 1960-62, div. geologist, 1962-66; v.p. Sams Oil Corp., Midland, 1966-68; gen. mgr. N.Am. Royalties Inc., Midland, 1968-70; pres. Tejas Energy Exploartiaon Inc., Midland, 1970-72, Vinson Exploration Inc., Midland, 1972—; pres. Vinson Oper. Co., Midland, 1991—, Concho Creek Corp., Midland, 1992—; finder Brown-Bassett Gas Field, 1959, Frances Hill, Companero Gas Field, 1971; joint finder Coynosa, Rojo Cabollos Gas Field, 1960-61. Supporter ARC, Salvation Army, 1955—, Republican Party, 1975—, Stewarts of the Range, 1992—. Sgt. USMC, 1942-46. Mem. Am. Assn. Petroleum Geologists, Nat. Cattlemen's Assn., West Tex. Geol. Soc. (hon. life; pres. 1964-65), Permian Basin Petroleum Assn., Soc. Ind. Petroleum Earth Scientists, S.W. Tex. Cattlemen's Assn. Republican. Home: 1505 Douglas Ave Midland TX 79701-4055 Office: Vinson Exploration Inc 507 N Marienfeld St Ste 201 Midland TX 79701-4355

VINTON, WILLIAM BRIAN, mental health nurse, educator; b. Oakland, Calif., Nov. 20, 1947; s. Luke Vinton and Rena T. (Conley) Davies; m. Nancy K. Vinton, Feb. 6, 1971; children: Brenda Reneé William Brian Jr., Ryan James. BA in LAS, U. Ill., Chgo., 1975, MS in Nursing, 1985; AS in Nursing, Triton Coll., River Grove, Ill., 1979. Cert. clin. specialist in adult psychiatry and mental health nursing. Counseling supr., staff nurse River Edge Hosp., Forest Park, Ill., 1975-79; staff nurse St. Anne's Hosp., Chgo., 1979-80; staff nurse Hines (Ill.) VA Med.Ctr., 1980-81, clin. nurse adminstr., coord. drug detox and treatment, 1981-85; clin. nurse adminstr. psychiatry Hines (Ill.) VA Med. Ctr., 1986-88; nurse counselor, case mgr. substance abuse treatment program Lake City (Fla.) VA Med. Ctr.; mem. Nat. League Nursing accreditation com. dept. nursing Lake City C.C., 1993-94, instr. ADN program, 1992-94. Sec. com. for parent edn. Cook County (Ill.) Sch. Bd., 1984. With U.S. Army, 1968-70, Vietnam. Recipient Scholar award Fed. Women's Program, Chgo., 1985, Spl. Contbn. award Dept. Vets. Affairs, Lake City, 1994. Mem. ANA. Constitutionalist. Home: RR 10 Box 624 Lake City FL 32025-9148 Office: Lake City VA Med Ctr 108 S Marion St Unit 8 Lake City FL 32025-4343

VINZÉ, AJAY S., information systems educator; b. New Delhi, India, July 24, 1959; came to U.S., 1980; s. Shreekrishna N. and Kalindi (Chitale) V.; m. Amita Kohli, Dec. 31, 1983; children: Anika A., Arjun A. B in Commerce with honors, U. Delhi, India, 1980; MBA, U. Conn., 1982; PhD in Bus. Adminstrn., U. Ariz., 1988. Tech. staff SyCip, Gorres, Velayo & Co., Manila, Philippines, 1982-83; MIS mgr. Indo-Phil Textile Mills, Bulacan, Philippines, 1983-84; rsch. asst. prof. MIS dept. U. Ariz., 1984-86, rsch. assoc. MIS dept., 1986-88; asst. prof. MIS dept. bus. analysis and rsch. Tex. A & M Univ., College Station, 1992-96, assoc. prof., 1994—; computer cons. U. Ariz. Found., Tucson, 1985-87; cons. MIS St. Luke's Episc. Hosp., Houston, 1991; faculty advisor Epsilon Delta Pi, 1992—; presenter in field. Assoc. editor: Internat. Jour. Human Computer Studies, 1992—; guest editor: Expert Sys. with Applications, 1994; reviewer for various jours. including Internat. Jour. Man-Machine Studies, 1990, 91, ORSA Jour. Computing, 1991, Internat. Jour. Expert Systems with Applications, 1992, IEEE Transactions on Sys., Man and Cybernetics, 1992, IEEE Computer, 1992, Mgmt. Sci., 1992; contbr. articles to profl. jours. Recipient Best Paper awards Hawaii Internat. Conf. on Sys. Scis., Kauai, Hawaii, 1988, 93, Tucson Mayors award City of Tucson, 1985, Rsch. grant IBM, Endicott, N.Y., 1988, Tex. Instruments, Dallas, 1991. Mem. IEEE Computer Soc., Assn. Computing Machinery, Inst. Mgmt. Sci., Am. Assn. for Artificial Intelligence. Hindu. Office: Tex A & M Univ CBA/GSB BANA College Station TX 77843-4217

VIOLETTE, PETER RAYMOND, logistician; b. Houlton, Maine, Mar. 23, 1952; s. Joseph I. and Margret Ann (Melville) V.; m. Elizabeth Ann Paradis, Feb. 26, 1972; children: Stacey Lee, Joseph Peter. Cert., No. Maine VoTech, 1972; AAS, Nat. U., Vista, Calif., 1988. Commd. USMC, 1982, advanced through grades to capt., 1986, co. maintenance officer, 1980-86, battalion maintenance officer, 1986-88, maintenance officer, 1988-93; svc. mgr. Pep Boys, Fredericksburg, Va., 1993-95; owner The Packaging Store, Fredericksburg, Va., 1994—, logistic analyst, 1995—. Decorated Meritorious Svc. medal. Mem. Marine Corps Assn., Marine Corps Mustang Assn. Home: 25 Little Creek Ln Fredericksburg VA 22405-3643

VIRTANEN, PERTTU HANNES, urban planner, consultant; b. Dallas, May 22, 1935; s. Perttu Hannes and Sophie Louise (Hiegert) V.; m. Carol Elizabeth Headrick, Sept. 28, 1963 (div. Sept. 1977); children: Meri Elizabeth, Elsa Kaarina Virtanen Jordan, Anna Kristiina; m. Gerrene Marie Izzo, Jan. 18, 1978. BA, Rice U., 1957, BS in Architecture, 1959; MArch, U. Manitoba, Can., 1962. Cert. planner. Planning dir. City of Irving, Tex., 1962-63; community planner State of N.C., Raleigh, 1963-65; planning dir., asst. planning dir. Guilford County, Greensboro, N.C., 1965-73; v.p., planning mgr. Clarke-Frates Corp., Dallas, 1973-79; devel. mgr. U.S. Lend Lease, Inc., Dallas, 1979-82; dir. planning Cook Cons., Inc., Dallas, 1982-87, William H. Gordon Assocs., Inc., Reston, Va., 1987-89; ind. cons. and contract svcs. Dallas, 1989-93; contract planning svcs. City of Mesquite, Tex., 1993—; mem. steering com. County Soil Conservation Dist., USDA, Greensboro, 1972. Contbr. articles to profl. jours. Mem. City of Dallas Hist. Landmark Com., 1978; bd. dirs. Rockwall (Tex.) C. of C., 1978; mem. indsl. devel. com. Greensboro C. of C., 1972. With U.S. Army Corps of Engrs., 1959-61. Recipient Grad. assistantship U. Manitoba, 1961. Mem. Am. Inst. Cert. Planners (Tex. chpt. North Ctrl. Tex. sect. dir. 1978). Home: 1505 Glastonbury Dr Plano TX 75075

VISCELLI, THERESE RAUTH, materials management consultant; b. Bitburg, Fed. Republic Germany, Nov. 18, 1955; d. David William and Joyce (Kelly) Rauth; m. Eugene R. Viscelli, Feb. 4, 1978; children: Christopher, Kathryn, Matthew. BS, Ga. Inst. Tech., 1977; postgrad., So. Tech. Inst., 1977-78, Ga. State U., 1982-83. Mktg. engr. Hughes Aircraft Corp., Carlsbad, Calif., 1978-79; indsl. engr. Kearfott-Singer, San Marcos, Calif., 1979-80; product analyst Control Data Corp., Atlanta, 1981-84; dir. R&D Am. Software, Inc., Atlanta, 1984-92; acct. mgr. The Coca-Cola Co., 1992-93; dir. info. sys. Mizuno, USA, Norcross, Ga., 1993—. Mem. Am. Prodn. and Inventory Control Soc. (program chmn. 1982-83, v.p. 1983-84). Republican. Roman Catholic.

VISH, DONALD H., lawyer; b. Ft. Benning, Ga., Jan. 18, 1945; s. D.H. Jr. and Dorris (Parrish) V.; m. Catherine Hamilton, Aug. 20, 1966 (div. 1986); children: Donald Hamilton, Daphne Mershon Sullivan; m. Margaret A. Handmaker, July 16, 1991. BA in English, Bellarmine Coll., 1968; JD cum laude, U. Louisville, 1971. Bar: Ky. 1971, Fla. 1972, U.S. Ct. Appeals (6th cir.) 1974. Sec., gen. counsel Gen. Energy Corp., Lexington, Ky., 1978-83; ptnr. firm Wyatt, Tarrant & Combs, Lexington, 1980-88, Frost & Jacobs, Lexington, 1988-89, Brown & Heyburn, 1991—; apptd. assoc. solicitor U.S. Dept. Interior, 1989-91; assoc. prof. Coll. of Law, U. Ky., Lexington, part-time 1977-80, adj. assoc. prof. mineral law, 1979-85. Contbr. to legal ency. American Law of Mining, 2d edit., 1984; co-editor, contbr. Coal Law and Regulation, 1983, Ky. Election Law, 1995. Trustee Sayre Sch., Lexington, 1980-88, chmn. bd., 1986-88; coun. Blue Grass Boy Scouts Am., Lexington, 1988—; apptd. gov. Ky. Registry of Election Fin., 1991-93. Fellow Am. Bar Found.; mem. ABA (chmn. coal com., nat. resources sec. 1987), Am. Law Inst., Ea. Mineral Law Found. (trustee 1979—, exec. com. 1979-82, chmn. coal subcom. 1984-85), Am. Judicature Soc., Fla. Bar Assn., Ky. Bar Assn. (ethics com. 1983-85) Home: 6306 Shadow Wood Dr Prospect KY 40059-9626 Office: Brown Todd & Heyburn 2700 Lexington Fin Ctr Lexington KY 40507 also: B200 Providian Ctr Louisville KY 40202

VISSCHER, PIETER BERNARD, physicist, educator; b. Mpls., Dec. 11, 1945; s. Maurice B. and Janet Gertrude (Pieters) V.; m. Helga Bjarney Björnson, June 17, 1972; children: Kristina Maria, Paul Jon. BA, Harvard U., 1967; MA, U. Calif., Berkeley, 1968, PhD, 1971. Rsch. assoc. U. Ill., Urbana, 1971-73; rsch. physicist U. Calif., San Diego, 1973-75; asst. prof. physics U. Oreg., Eugene, 1975-78; from asst. prof. to assoc. prof. physics U. Ala., Tuscaloosa, 1978-84, prof. physics, 1984—; cons. Los Alamos (N.Mex.) Nat Lab., 1985-86, Sci. and Engring. Rsch. Coun. fellow U. Surrey, Britain, 1992-93. Author: Fields and Electrodynamics, 1988, simulation software for electrodynamics, 1991; contbr. articles to profl. jours. Recipient grants Cottrell Rsch. Corp., 1979, NSF, 1979, 81, 92, 94, Dept. Energy, 1994. Mem. AAUP (chpt. v.p. 1983, 84), Am. Phys. Soc. Democrat. Home: 4301 Kendlewood Ln Northport AL 35476-1625 Office: U Ala Dept Physics Tuscaloosa AL 35487-0324

VISSICCHIO, ANDREW JOHN, JR., linen service company executive; b. N.Y.C., Dec. 21, 1941; s. Andrew John and Anne (Renna) V.; m. Patricia Ann Hunken, Jan. 18, 1964; children: Andrew John III, Douglas David. BS in Bus., L.I. U., 1963; postgrad., A.T. Roth Grad. Sch., Brookville, N.Y., 1963-64. Gen. mgr. Allied Coat & Apron Inc., Bklyn., 1963-72; ops. officer N.Y. Ocean Sci. Lab., Montauk, N.Y., 1972-76; gen. mgr. Am. Svc. Corp., Miami, Fla., 1976-79, dist. mgr., 1979-83, v.p. ops., 1983-87; gen. mgr. Nat. Linen Svc., West Palm Beach, Fla., 1987-88; dist. mgr. Nat. Linen Svc., Atlanta, 1988-90, v.p., gen. mgr. linen supply divsn., 1990-94, regional v.p., 1994-96; v.p. Internat. Trading South Fla., Inc., Palm Beach Gardens, Fla., 1996—. Pianist in recital at Carnegie Hall, 1956, 57. Pres. Little Flower Parish Assn., Montauk, N.Y., 1970; mem. Montauk Hosp. Assn., 1970; v.p. Frost Pond Civic Assn., Glen Head, N.Y., 1971-72. Recipient Dedicated Svc. award Montauk Fire Dept., 1976. Mem. Textile Rental Svc. Assn. (mem. strategic mgmt. com. 1984-86), Phi Sigma Kappa. Republican. Roman Catholic. Home: 2350 NW 38th St Boca Raton FL 33431-5439 Office: Nat Linen Svc 1420 Peachtree St NE Atlanta GA 30309-3002

VITAL, RAFAEL, JR., auditor; b. Lodi, Calif., Nov. 11, 1952; s. Rafael and Maria E. Vital; m. Gloria Santana, Aug. 1, 1974 (div. May 1987); children: Patricia, Priscella. BBA in Acctg., U. Tex., 1976. Auditor Tex. Alcoholic Beverage Commn., San Antonio, 1976-95; auditor Tex. Lottery Commn., San Antonio, 1995—; umpire U.S. Tennis Assn. Treas. Alamo City Tennis Officials, 1993. Recipient Cert. of Honor for Excellence in Scholarship Laredo Ind. Sch. Dist., 1983. Mem. U.S. Profl. Tennis Registry (tchg. profl.). Democrat. Roman Catholic. Home: # 3908 7600 Blanco Rd San Antonio TX 78216-4108 Office: Tex Lottery Commn 105 SW Military Dr San Antonio TX 78221

VITELLO, ROBERT BLAIR, sales executive; b. Jamestown, N.Y., Apr. 2, 1958; s. Joseph Louis and Barbara Anne (Gifford) V.; m. Susan Margaret Kosch, May 28, 1983; children: Amanda Leigh, Ryan Blair. BSChemE, N.J. Inst. Tech., 1979; MBA in Fin., Mktg., Rutgers U., 1987. Inside sales rep. indsl. products mktg. Dresser Industries, Florham Park, N.J., 1979-80, outside sales rep. indsl. products mktg., 1980-87; sr. sales rep. roots ops. Dresser Industries, Riverdale, N.J., 1987-90; regional mgr. roots ops. Dresser Industries, Atlanta, 1990—; cons. Hoffman La Roche, Clifton, N.J., 1987. Sr. comdr. Royal Ranger youth program Full Gospel Ch., Livingston, N.J., 1983-88; supt. Sunday sch. Calvary Temple A/G, Wayne, N.J., 1988-90; leader young married group Calvery Assemblies of God, Dunwoody, Ga., 1990—. Mem. TAPPI, Atlanta Lawn Tennis Assn., Tau Lambda Chi (pres. 1974-75). Republican. Home: 110 St Ignaius Close Alpharetta GA 30202-6149 Office: Dresser Industries Roots Ops 5672 Peachtree Pky # J Norcross GA 30092-2847

VITIELLO, ERIC CHARLES, SR. (RIC VITIELLO), roofing consultant; b. Evansville, Ind., Mar. 23, 1946; s. Joseph Frances and Rose Marie (Gehlhausen) V.; m. A. Ann Betts, July 8, 1966 (div. 1973); m. Helen Patricia Sprecher, July 26, 1974; children: Eric C. Jr., Helen Brook. Grad. high sch., Louisville. Territory salesman Overhead Door Co., Louisville, 1978-81; sales estimator Wayco Engring., Louisville, 1981-83, Newcor Constrn. Co., Louisville, 1983-84; sales cons. Frederick Roofing Corp., Louisville, 1984-87; mktg. dir. Commonwealth Roofing Corp., Louisville, 1987-89; pres. Benchmark Svcs. Inc., Louisville, 1989—; arbitrator Nat. Panel Consumer Arbitrators, Better Bus. Bur., Louisville, 1988—; mem. nat. adv. bd. Duro-Last Inc., Saginaw, Mich., 1990-94. Author: (computer software) The Benchmark Estimator, 1989. Mem. spkrs. bur. Habitat for Humanity, Louisville, 1989—; bd. dirs. Louisville BBB, 1982—. With USNR. Named Speaker of Yr., Colo. Jaycees, 1969, Hon. Capt. of Belle of Louisville, 1981; named to Hon. Order of Ky. Cols., State of Ky., 1977. Mem. Nat. Spkrs. Assn., Ky. Spkrs. Assn., Greater Louisville Roofing Contractors Assn. (pres. 1987-88), Jaycees (pres. Okolona chpt. 1977-78, Ky. Jaycee Thorobred # 97 1978), Rotary, Woodhaven Country Club. Republican. Roman Catholic. Office: Benchmark Svcs Inc 2902 N Melrose St Louisville KY 40299-1621

VITT, LOIS A., non-profit organization director, finance sociologist; b. Rochester, N.Y., Dec. 14, 1936; d. Noel Pius and Delabeth (Loughlin) Omlor; m. Donald J. Vitt, July 1, 1954 (div. 1962); children: John, Michael, Virginia, Lois, Ellen, Patricia; m. Joel H. Bernstein, Dec. 24, 1980 (div. 1985); m. Noel A. Schweig, May 17, 1987. BPS in Business, Pace U., 1980, MBA, 1980; MA in Sociology, The Am. U., 1991, PhD in Sociology, 1993. Mortgage officer Associated Mortgage Cos., Washington, 1961-66; v.p. Dominion Mortgage Co., Reston, Va., 1966; dir. office housing devel. and dep. chief land disposition D.C. Redevelopment Land Agy., Washington, 1967-69; cons. Vitt Assocs., 1969-71; dir., pres., CEO Eastdil Housing Svcs., Inc., N.Y., Washington, L.A., 1971-74; pres. RAMA, Inc., Washington, 1975-82; gen. securities prin. Lowry Fin. Svcs. Corp., Washington, 1981-90; pres., CEO The Home Ptnrs. Cos., 1979-89; dir. Inst. for Socio-Fin. Studies, Washington, 1991—; adj. faculty The Am. U., 1988—. Co-editor: The Encyclopedia of Financial Gerontology, 1996; contbr. articles to profl. jours. Recipient Significant Achievement award D.C. Redevelopment Land Agy., 1967, Achievement citation Nat. Inst. Architects, 1971; Technical Asst. grant Arrow Inc., 1968, U.S. Small Bus. Adminstrn., 1969, Rsch. Support grant U.S. Dept. Commerce, Econ. Devel. Adminstrn., 1980, Tech. Assist. grant, 1981, Rsch. Support grant Inst. Socio-Fin. Studies, 1992. Mem. Am. Polit. Sci. Assn., Gerontol. Soc. Am., Am. Sociol. Assn., Nat. Assn. Realtors, Internat. Soc. Assn., Internat. Assn. Fin. Planners, Fin. Mgmt. Assn., Soc. Advancement Socio-Econs. Office: Inst Socio Fin Studies 4 W Federal St PO Box 1824 Middleburg VA 22117

VITTUM, KENNETH FRANKLIN, city manager; b. Wolfeboro, N.H., Aug. 4, 1952; s. Kenneth Franklin Vittum Sr. and Frances Viola (Lord) Bailey; m. Janet Eileen Hook, June 1, 1974; children: Jonathan Kenneth, Adam Thomas. BS in Social Sci., Plymouth State U., 1974; M in City Mgmt., E. Tenn. State, 1983. Tchr. Isle of Wight (Va.) Acad., 1974-75; welfare specialist Va. Dept. for Visually Handicapped, Bristol, 1975-83; city mgr. City of Norris, Tenn., 1983-88; town mgr. Town of Pearisburg, Va., 1988—. Pres., bd. dirs. Pearisburg C. of C., 1988-92; bd. dirs. Giles Homeless Shelter, Pearisburg, 1990—. Mem. Internat. City Mgmt. Assn., Am. Pub. Works Assn., Am. Assn. Pub. Adminstrn., Am. Soc. Pub. Adminstrn. (treas. S.W. Va. chpt. 1991-94), Va. Local Govt. Mgmt. Assn. Home: 501 Mcguire Ln Pearisburg VA 24134-1835 Office: Town of Pearisburg 112 Tazewell St Pearisburg VA 24134-1646

VITULLI, WILLIAM FRANCIS, psychology educator; b. Bklyn., July 17, 1936; s. William S. and Sadie Rosaria (Stallone) V.; m. Betty Jean Sheubrooks, June 15, 1961; children: Paige Vitulli Baggett, Quinn Anthony, Sherik Denise. BA, U. Miami, 1961, MS, 1963, PhD, 1966. Lic. psychologist, Ala. Grad. asst. U. Miami, Coral Gables, Fla., 1961-65; asst. prof. psychology U. South Ala., Mobile, 1965-69, assoc. prof., 1969-75, prof., 1975—; v.p. Ala. Bd. Examiners in Psychology, Montgomery, 1982-84; rsch. cons. Drug Edn. Coun., Mobile, 1988-94. Mem. editorial bd. Jour. Sport Behavior, 1978—; contbr. articles to profl. jours. Mem. adv. bd. Contact Mobile, 1987-92. Named Prof. of Quar., Alpha Lambda Delta, Faculty Mem. of Yr., 1993-94; recipient Outstanding Prof. award Alumni Assn., 1994. Mem. APA, Southeastern Psychol. Assn., Ala. Psychol. Assn. (pres. 1975), Italian-Am. Cultural Soc. South Ala. (chair hist.-cultural com. 1982), Sigma Xi, Psi Chi (faculty adviser U. South Ala. chpt. 1972-80). Roman Catholic. Home: 2025 Maryknoll Ct Mobile AL 36695-3829 Office: U South Ala 307 University Blvd N Mobile AL 36688-3053

VIVEKANANDA, FRANKLIN CHINNA, economics educator; b. Ramnagram, India, Nov. 7, 1943; came to U.S., 1987; m. Jeevalatha, Aug. 25,1975. MA, U. Gothenburg, 1971; PhD, Uppsala U., 1979. Tchr. Uppsala U., Sweden, 1973-79; rsch. faculty Inst. Alternative Devel. Rsch., Oslo, Norway, 1979-83; rsch. assoc., cons. Internat. Devel. Agys., Bangladesh, 1982-84; cons. to devel. agy. Martin Peace Inst. U. Idaho, Moscow, 1988-89; tchr. dept. fin. and econs. Southwest Tex. State U., San Marcos, 1990-91; tchr. dept. econs. St. Mary's U., San Antonio, 1991-93; tchr. Palo Alto Coll., San Antonio, 1994-96; educator Our Lady of the Lake U., San Antonio, 1996—; editl. bd. Nigerian Jour. Pub. Adminstrn., Internat. Jour. Devel. Issues; editor-in-chief Scandinavian Jour. Devel. Alternatives, Ahimsa; mem. adv. bd. Ryan Found.; rsch. assoc. Immigration Inst. Dept. Labour and Employment, Sweden, 1981. Author: Unemployment in Karnataka, South India, 1979, Bangladesh Economy Some Selected Issues, 1985, Development Alternatives, 1986, Economic Development of Cameroon, 1989, Bilateral and Multinational Economic Cooperation in West Africa, 1990, Asia--The 21st Critical Century, 1991New Hopes but Old Seeds: The Political Economy of Capital Accumulation, State, National Development, Agrarian Transformation, and the Nigerian Peasantry, 1992, Beyond the Illusion of Primary Health Care in an African Society: The Political Economy of Health Care and Crisis in Nigeria: with a Discourse on Kenya, Tanzania, Brazil and Cuba, Tiger Torture Under One-Party Rule: Exploring Africa's Human Rights Abuses in Kenya, with a Discourse on Rwanda, Somalia and Malawi; also 15 books on social sci., 11 collections of poems. Mem. United Christian Congregation Stockholm. Mem. Am. Econ. Assn., Internat. Studies Assn., African Studies Assn., Asian Studies Assn., Internat. Polit. Sci. Assn., Internat. Peace Rsch. Assn., Internat. Soc. Intercomm. New Ideas, Swedish Peace Found. Home: 6358 Mustang Point Dr San Antonio TX 78240-2687

VIVELO, FRANK ROBERT, college administrator, anthropologist; b. Bklyn., Dec. 27, 1943; s. Frank Robert and Gloria Judith (Figliuolo) V.; m. Jacqueline Jean Jones, June 19, 1965; 1 child, Alexandra Jones. BA summa cum laude, U. Tenn., Knoxville, 1970; MPhil, MA, Rutgers, 1972, PhD, 1974. Instr. anthropology Rutgers U., New Brunswick, N.J., 1972-73; vis. lectr. anthropology U. Pa., Phila., 1974; from asst. prof. to assoc. prof. U. Mo., Rolla, 1974-78; sr. rsch. assoc. Manpower Demonstration Rsch. Group, N.Y.C., 1978-80; chair social sci. div. Harrisburg (Pa.) Area C.C., 1980-89, dean Sch. Arts and Sci., 1989-92; v.p., dean acad. affairs Columbia (Mo.) Coll., 1992-94; pres. Wharton County Jr. Coll., Wharton, Tex., 1994—. Author: The Herero of Western Botswana, 1977, Cultural Anthropology Handbook, 1978, Cultural Anthropology, 1994, (novels) Michael Deal, 1984, Adventure in Suicide, 1995; co-editor: We Wait in the Darkness: American Indian Prose and Poetry, 1974; contbr.: Ency. of World Cultures; contbr. articles to profl. jours. Served with USAF, 1961-65. Fellow Am. Anthrop. Assn.; mem. Phi Beta Kappa, Phi Kappa Phi. Office: Wharton County Jr Coll 911 Boling Hwy Wharton TX 77488

VIVELO, JACQUELINE JEAN, author, English language educator; b. Lumberton, Miss., Jan. 23, 1943; d. Jack and Virginia Olivia (Bond) Jones; m. Frank Robert Vivelo, June 19, 1965; 1 child, Alexandra J. BA, U. Tenn., Knoxville, 1965, MA, 1970. Caseworker N.Y.C. Dept. Welfare, 1965-66; instr. reading Knoxville Coll., 1968-70; instr. English Middlesex County Coll., Edison, N.J., 1970-72, U. Mo., Rolla, 1975-77, Middlesex County Coll., Edison, 1978-80; instr. English Lebanon Valley Coll., Annville, Pa., 1981-87, asst. prof. English, 1987-91. Author: Super Sleuth, 1985 (Best Book award), Beagle in Trouble, 1986, A Trick of the Light, 1987, Super Sleuth and the Bare Bones, 1988, Writing Fiction: A Handbook for Creative Writing, 1993, Reading to Matthew, 1993 (Best Book award), Mr. Scatter's Magic Spell, 1993, Chills Run Down My Spine, 1994, Have You Lost Your Kangaroo?, 1995; editor: College Education Achievement Project's Handbook for College Reading Teachers, 1969; co-editor: American Indian Prose and Poetry, 1974: contbr. articles/short stories to various publs. Recipient Best Book award Am. Child Study Assn., 1985, Young Book Trust, U.K., 1994, Pa. Coun. of the Arts Fellowship award for Lit., 1992; NIMH grantee, 1969-70. Mem. Children's Lit. Coun. Pa. (v.p. 1991), Soc. Children's Book Writers, Sigma Tau Delta (sponsor Omicron Omicron chpt. 1988-90), Pi Lambda Theta. Home: 1309 Half Moon Dr Wharton TX 77488-9439

VO-DINH, TUAN, physical chemist, researcher; b. Nhatrang, Vietnam, Apr. 11, 1948; came to U.S., 1975; s. Kinh and Dinh Thi (Dang) Vo-D.; m. Kim-Chi Le-Thi. BS in Physics, Ecole Polytechnique Federale, Lausanne, Switzerland, 1971; PhD in Phys. Chemistry, Eth-Swiss Fed. Inst. Tech., Zurich, 1975. Rsch. assoc. dept. chemistry divsn. analytical chemistry U. Fla., Gainesville, 1975-76; staff rsch. scientist monitoring devel. group divsn. health and safety rsch. Oak Ridge (Tenn.) Nat.Lab., 1977-84, group leader advanced monitoring devel. group, 1984—; corp. fellow Oak Ridge (Tenn.) Nat. Lab., 1994—; organizer, chmn. monitoring imstrumentation for occupational health rsch. program Office Health and Environ. Rsch., U.S. Dept. Energy, 1984; mem. exec. com. Internat. Com. on Polycyclic Aromatic Compounds, 1984-91; mem. symposium on laser spectroscopy SPIE, L.A., 1988; mem. program com. IVth Internat. Symposium on Quantitative Luminescence Spectrometry, Ghent, Belgium, 1991, Internat. Symposium on Polycyclic Aromatic Compounds, Tan-Tara, Mo., 1993; chmn. Symposium on Optical Fiberoptics Sensors, Pitts., 1991, Conf. on Methods and Techs. for Environ. and Process Monitoring, L.A., 1992, Internat. Conf. on Monitoring Toxic Chems. and Biomarkers, Berlin, 1992; hon. chmn. Symposium on Analytical Scis., Deauville, France, 1993; bd. dirs. Biochem Tech., Inc.; U.S. del. NATO Indsl. Adv. Bd.; cons. Affymax, Arco, Ely Lilly, Environ. Systems Corp., Rockwell, Rohm and Haas; presenter and lectr. in field. Author: Room Temperature Phosphorimetry for Chemical Analysis, 1984; editor: Chemical Analysis of Polycyclic Aromatic Compounds, 1989, Environmental and Process Control Technologies, 1992, (with D. Eastwood) Laser-Based Approaches in Luminescence Spectroscopy, 1990, (with K. Cammon) Monitoring Toxic Chemicals and Biomarkers, 1993; topical editor Polycyclic Aromatic Compounds; assoc. editor Analusis; mem. editorial bd. Applied Spectroscopy, Talanta, Spectrochemia Revs.; contbr. over 200 papers to sci. jours., 10 chpts. to books. Recipient Technol. Advance award RD-100, 1981, 87, 92, 94, 96, Tech. Transfer Excellence award Fed. Lab. Consortium, 1986, Gold medal Soc. for Applied Spectroscopy, Medal Languedoc-Rousillon award, 1989, Thomas Jefferson Silver Cup award Martin Marietta Corp., 1992, Inventor Internat. Hall of Fame award Inventors Club Am., 1992, Advanced Tech. award, 1993; grantee U.S. Dept. Energy, U.S. EPA, Dept. Army, Am. Petroleum Inst., NIH, NSF. Fellow Am. Inst. Chemists; mem. ASTM (chmn. fiberoptics subcom. E13.09, co-chmn. symposium on spectroscopy and fiberoptics), Internat. Union Pure and Applied Chemistry (chmn. commn. V-4), Internat. Soc. on Polycyclic Aromatic Compounds (co-founding pres. 1991-93), Internat. Symposium on Polyaromatic Hydrocarbons (program com. 1987—). Office: Oak Ridge Nat Lab PO Box 2008 Oak Ridge TN 37831-6101

VODYANOY, VITALY JACOB, biophysicist, educator; b. Kiev, Ukraine, USSR, June 2, 1941; came to U.S., 1979; s. Jacob and Vera (Reznik) V.; m. Galina Rubin, Apr. 22, 1967; 1 child, Valerie. MS in Physics, Moscow Physical Engring. Inst., 1964; PhD in Biophysics, Agrophysical Rsch. Inst., Leningrad, USSR, 1973. Asst. prof. Inst. of Semiconductors, Leningrad, USSR, 1965-72; assoc. prof. A.F. Ioffe Physicotech. U., Leningrad, 1972-78; sr. rsch. scientist NYU, 1979-82; rsch. assoc. U. Calif., Irvine, 1982-89; assoc. prof. Auburn (Ala.) U., 1989-93, prof., 1993—; ad hoc reviewer NSF, Washington, 1985—; dir. Biosensor Lab. of Inst. for Biol. Detection Sys. Author: (with others) Membrane Biophysics, 1971, Physics of Solid State and Neutron Scattering, 1974, Receptors Events and Transduction Mechanisms in Taste and Olfaction, 1989, Molecular Electronics: Biosensors and Biocomputers, 1989, Central Nervous System Neurotransmitters and Neuromodulators, 1994; contbr. more than 60 articles to profl. jours.; inventor device for film deposition. Recipient grants NSF-U. Calif., 1982-85, 85-88, U.S. Army Rsch. Office, 1985-88, U. Calif., 1986-88, 88-92, U. Calif., FAA, 1993—, Auburn U. Mem. AAAS, Am. Phys. Soc., Biophys. Soc., Fedn. Am. Socs. for Exptl. Biology, Phi Beta Delta. Republican. Jewish. Home: 541 Summertrees Dr Auburn AL 36830-6766 Office: Auburn U Coll of Vet Medicine 212 Greene Hall Auburn AL 36830-6121

VOELKEL, JANE CLAUDETTE, elementary education educator, home economist; b. Lexington, Ky., Jan. 30, 1937; d. George Edward Ross and Esther (Brigman) Hayes; m. Eugene Voelkel, Dec. 31, 1957; children: Claudette Ann, Robert Scott, Janet Elizabeth. BS, Tex. Woman's U., 1958, postgrad., 1966-67; MEd, Tarleton State U., Stephenville, Tex., 1981. Profl. home economist; cert. elem. tchr., kindergarten learning lang. disabilities, Tex. Tchr. Mineral Wells (Tex.) Ind. Sch. Dist., 1965-66, Holly Hill (Fla.) Sch., Volusia County, 1967, Lawson (Okla.) Ind. Sch. Dist., 1978-79, Three Way Common Sch. Dist., Hico, Tex., 1979-81, Bryan (Tex.) Ind. Sch. Dist., 1981—; mem. curr. coun. Bryan Ind. Sch. Dist., 1986-87, mem. supts. forum, 1988-90, chmn. forum, 1990-91, bldg. rep. book selection in lang. arts, 1988-89, in sci., 1990-91, grade level chmn., 1994-95. Deacon 1st Presbyn. Ch., Bryan, 1988-91; vol. Hospice, Bryan and College Station, 1990-93, v.p., 1989-92; vol. LOVES (Loving Outreach and Visitation to Elderly and Shut=Ins), 1985-95. Mem. Tex. Woman's U. Nat. Alumnae Assn. (life, v.p. 1989-92), Tex. Woman's U. Brazos Valley Alumnae Assn. (pres. 1986—), Assn. Tex. Profl. Educators, Internat. Reading Assn., Tex. State Reading Assn., Sam Houston Area Reading Coun. Republican. Home: 4 Ravens Perch St Bryan TX 77808-9719

VOGAN, DAVID NICHOLAS, architect; b. Norfolk, Va., Dec. 17, 1951; s. Charles Edward and Frieda (Op't Holt) V. BA, Coll. of William & Mary, 1974; BArch, U. Minn., 1979. Lic. architect, Va. Architect Jennings Archtl. Firm, Williamsburg, Va., 1981-85, RWK & B Architects, Tabb, Va., 1985-87; lectr. Hampton (Va.) U., 1987-89, Langley AFB, Hampton, 1989—; cons. in field. Mem. rev. bd. City of Williamsburg Architecture; mem. Bruton Parish Choir, Williamsburg, 1982—; cellist Puccini Festival Orch., Lucca, Italy, 1984. Mem. AIA (Va. Soc.), Nat. Trust for Hist. Preservation, Assn. of Collegiate Schs. of Architecture. Home: 415 Burbank St Williamsburg VA 23185-3628 Office: ICES/CECH Langley Afb Hampton VA 23665

VOGE-BLACK, VICTORIA MAE, retired military officer, physician; b. Mpls., June 27, 1943; d. Donald Oscar and Veryl Shirley (Harms) Voge; m. Gerald R. Black, Jan. 10, 1976; children: Robert, John, Catherine, Kimberly. BA, U. Minn., 1964; MD, Nat. Autonomous U. Mexico, Mexico City, 1971; MPH, Johns Hopkins U., 1977, Med. Coll. Wis., 1990. Cert. in aerospace medicine, occupational medicine. Commd. USN, 1971, advanced through grades to commdr., 1980; intern Naval Hosp., Phila., 1971-72; student flight surgeon Naval Aerospace Medicine Inst., Pensacola, Fla., 1972-73; resident, aerospace medicine Naval Aerospace Medicine Inst., Pensacola, 1975-78; head acceleration physiology br. Naval Air Devel. Ctr., Warminster, Pa., 1973-76; head aeromedical div. Naval Safety Ctr., Norfolk, Va., 1978-81; head aviation medicine Naval Air Station, Agana, Guam, 1981-83; flight surgeon U.S. Air Force Sch. of Aerospace Medicine, San Antonio, Tex., 1983-84; head aviation medicine, occupational medicine Corpus Christi (Tex.) Naval Hosp., 1984-88; chief flight surgeon Naval Air Devel. Ctr., Warminster, Pa., 1988-91; flight surgeon, biomed. specialist Armstrong Lab., San Antonio, 1991—; cons. acceleration, Franklin Inst., Phila., 1975-76. Contbr. articles to prof. jours. Bd. dirs. ARC, Corpus Christi, Tex., 1984-85. Fellow Aerospace Med. Assn. (Wiley Post award 1981), Internat. Acad. Aviation and Space Medicine, Am. Coll. Preventive Medicine, Aerospace Human Factors Assn., Am. Coll. Occupl. and Environ. Medicine; mem. AMA, Aircraft Owners and Pilots Assn. LDS Church. Home: RR 3 Box 73 Gonzales TX 78629-9403 Office: Detar Hosp Victoria TX

VOGEL, HOWARD H., lawyer; b. Paris, Tenn., Sept. 4, 1949; s. Herman Lentz and Caroline Powell (Carothers) V.; m. Kathryn Lynn Massey, Sept. 14, 1974; children: Caroline Carothers, Patrick Alexander, Anna Kathryn. BA, Vanderbilt U., 1971; JD, U. Tenn., 1974. Assoc. atty. O'Neil, Parker & Williamson, Knoxville, Tenn., 1976-77; ptnr. O'Neil, Parker & Williamson, 1977—. Pres. Dogwood Arts festival Inc., Knoxville, 1990-92. Fellow Tenn. Bar Found., Am. Bar Found.; mem. ABA (bd. govs. 1985-88, chmn. standing com. on meetings and travel 1990-92, chair 1993-94), Tenn. Young Lawyers Conf. (pres. 1980-81), Knoxville Bar Assn. (pres.-elect 1990-92, pres. 1993), Tenn. Bar Assn. (v.p. 1993-94, pres.-elect 1994—). Office: PO Box 217 Knoxville TN 37901-0217 also: O'Neil, Parker & Williamson 416 Cumberland Ave Knoxville TN 37902-2301*

VOGEL, WERNER PAUL, retired machine company executive; b. Louisville, June 15, 1923; s. Werner George and Emma (Bartman) V.; B. Mech. Engring., U. Louisville, 1950; m. Helen Louise Knapp, Oct. 2, 1954. With Henry Vogt Machine Co., Louisville, 1942-86, asst. plant supt., 1957-60, plant supt., 1961-73, v.p., 1974-86. Trustee, City of Strathmoor Village, Ky., 1959-61; clk. City of Glenview Manor, Ky., 1967-73, trustee, 1974-75, treas. 1986-89; bd. dirs. Louisville Protestant Altenheim, 1979-90, pres., 1985-90, ret.; mem. adv. coun. Lindsey Wilson Coll., 1988—. Served with USAAF, 1944-46. Mem. ASME, Tau Beta Pi, Sigma Tau. Republican. Methodist. Home: 29 Glenwood Rd Louisville KY 40222-6168

VOGT, C. O., geophysical research company executive. Pres. Geophys. Rsch. Corp., Tulsa. Office: Geophys Rsch Corp 6540 E Apache St Tulsa OK 74115

VOINCHE, WOODY MARK, commercial property entrepreneur; b. Alexandria, La., Aug. 14, 1952; s. M. A. an dGeraldine (Lemoine) V. BS, La. Coll., Pineville, 1974; MS, La. Tech. U., 1976; student health scis., U. Okla., 1979. Self employed comml. property Marksville, La., 1980—. Contbr. over 100 artilces to local papers. Home and Office: 1107 N Main St Marksville LA 71351-2123

VOLENTINE, RICHARD J., JR., lawyer; b. Tampa, Fla., Apr. 2, 1955; s. Richard J. Sr. and Mary Francis (Shaw) V.; m. Susan Ruth Zimmerman, May 16, 1981; children: Rachel Elizabeth, Scott Thomas, Melissa Mary. BS, Spring Hill Coll., 1977; JD, U. Ala., 1980. Bar: Ala. 1980, Mo. 1982, Fla. 1984. Staff atty. Ala. Jud. Coll., Tuscaloosa, 1980-81; staff counsel Citicorp Person-to-Person, Inc., St. Louis, 1982; regional counsel Citicorp Person-to-Person Corp., Tampa, 1982-84; asst. gen. counsel Citicorp Savs. Fla., Miami, 1984-85; assoc. counsel Nationwide Capital Corp., Atlanta, 1985-86; regional atty. FDIC, Atlanta, 1986-88; counsel, v.p. Altus Bank, Mobile, Ala., 1988-90; v.p., assoc. gen. counsel Chase Home Mortgage Corp., Tampa, Fla., 1990-91; sr. v.p., real estate lending counsel Prudential Bank & Trust Co., Atlanta, 1991—. Mem. ABA, Am. Corp. Counsel Assn., Ala. Jud. Coll. Faculty Assn. (hon.). Republican. Roman Catholic. Home: 2688 Tritt Springs Dr Marietta GA 30062-5268 Office: Prudential Bank & Trust Co One Ravinia Dr Ste 1000 Atlanta GA 30346

VOLKMAN, ALVIN, pathologist, researcher, educator; b. Bklyn., June 10, 1926; s. Henry Phillip and Sarah Lucille (Silverstein) V.; m. Winifred Joan Grinnell, June 12, 1947 (div. Aug. 1967); children: Karl Frederick, Nicholas James, Rebecca Jane Evans, Margaret Rose Werrell, Deborah Ann Falls; m. Carol Ann Fishel, Jan. 26, 1973 (dec. Sept. 1992); 1 child, Natalie Fishel; 1 stepchild Jeffrey C. Moore. BS, Union Coll., 1947; MD, U. Buffalo, 1951; D.Philosophy, U. Oxford (Eng.), 1963. Diplomate Nat. Bd. Med. Examiners, Am. Bd. Pathology. Intern, Mt. Sinai Hosp., Cleve., 1951-52; research fellow dept. anatomy Western Res. U. Sch. Medicine, 1952-54; resident, then sr. resident, then asst. in pathology Peter Bent Brigham Hosp., Boston, 1956-60; asst. prof. pathology Columbia U. Coll. Physicians and Surgeons, 1960-66; asst. mem., then assoc. mem. Trudeau Inst., Saranac Lake, N.Y., 1966-67; prof. dept. pathology East Carolina U. Sch. Medicine, Greenville, N.C., 1977—, acting chmn. dept. pathology, 1989-90, assoc. dean for rsch. and grad. studies, 1989-95, prof. emeritus, 1995—; mem. NIH study sect. immunological scis., 1975-79, chmn., 1977-79. Served to lt. USNR, 1954-56. Am. Cancer Soc. scholar, 1961-63; Arth and Rheumat Found. fellow 1952-54. Mem. AAAS, Am. Soc. Investigative Pathology, Am. Assn. Immunologists, Am. Soc. Hematology, Reticuloendothelial Soc., Am. Soc. Microbiologists, N.Y. Acad. Scis., Soc. Leukocyte Biology (hon. life). Contbr. articles to sci. jours. Office: East Carolina U Sch Medicine Brody Bldg Greenville NC 27858

VOLLMANN, JOHN JACOB, JR., cosmetic packaging executive; b. Elizabeth, N.J., Apr. 10, 1938; s. John Jacob and Marie Louise (Sirois) V.; m. Marian Ethel Snetsinger, May 29, 1976; children: Andrea Leah, John Jacob III. BA, Queen's U., Kingston, Ont., 1973, BA with honors, 1976; postgrad., Rutgers U., 1977; PhD, Walden U., Naples, Fla., 1991. Cert. hypnotherapist; criminal justice instr., Fla. V.p. No. Trading Co., Inc., Madawaska, Maine, 1976—, also chmn., bd. dirs., 1996—; instr. Sch. of Justice and Safety Adminstrn., Miami-Dade Community Coll., 1978—; bd. dirs. Edward Sagarin Inst. for Study of Deviance and Social Issues. Contbr. articles to profl. jours. Vice chmn. Police & Fire Pension Bd., Dania, Fla., 1984; chmn. Unsafe Structures Bd., Dania, 1984; code Enforcement Bd., Dania, 1984; adv. dep. Broward County Sheriff, Ft. Lauderdale, Fla., 1986-92; maj. Fla. Sheriff's Adv. Coun., 1992—. Recipient Richard A. McGhee award Am. Justice Inst., 1992. Mem. NRA, Am. Correctional Assn., Am. Soc. Criminology (life), Acad. Criminal Justice Scis. (life), Am. Jail Assn., Am. Probation and Parole Assn., Northeastern Criminal Justice Assn. (life), Fla. Criminal Justice Educators (pres. 1984-88), So. Assn. Criminal Justice (bd. dirs. 1981-90), Internat. Assn. for Study Organized Crime, N.Am. Assn. Wardens and Supts., Optimists (lt. gov. South Fla. dist. 1993-96, lt. gov. New Eng. 1995-97), Internat. Assn. Chiefs of Police. Home: 411 SE 3rd Pl Dania FL 33004-4703 Office: No Trading Co Inc 190-202 E Main St Madawaska ME 04756-1510

VOLLMER, RICHARD WADE, federal judge; b. St. Louis, Mar. 7, 1926; s. Richard W. and Beatrice (Burke) V.; m. Marilyn S. Stikes, Sept. 17, 1949. Student, Springhill Coll., 1946-49; LLB, U. Ala., 1953. Bar: Ala. 1953, U.S. Dist. Ct. (so. dist.) Ala. 1956, U.S. Ct. Appeals (5th cir.) 1963, U.S. Ct. Appeals (11th cir.) 1983. Judge U.S. Dist. Ct. (so. dist.) Ala., 1990—. Mem. Mobile Bar Assn. (pres. 1990), Rotary (Paul Harris fellow 1988). Roman Catholic.

VOLP, ROBERT FRANCIS, chemistry educator; b. Elkhorn, Wis., Oct. 20, 1952; married, Aug. 13, 1977; 4 children. BS, U. Wis., Stevens Point, 1975; MS, U. Wis., Madison, 1977, PhD, 1979. Asst. prof. Priv. Rsch. Inst./N.Mex. State U., Alamogordo, 1982-83; asst. prof. chemistry Murray (Ky.) State U., 1983-89, assoc. prof. chemistry, 1989—. Office: Murray State U Dept Chemistry PO Box 9 Murray KY 42071-0009

VOLPE, ANGELO ANTHONY, university administrator, chemistry educator; b. N.Y.C., Nov. 8, 1938; s. Bernard Charles and Serafina (Martorana) V.; m. Jennette Murray, May 15, 1965. B.S., Bklyn. Coll., 1959; M.S., U. Md., 1962, Ph.D., 1966; M.Engring. (hons.), Stevens Inst. Tech., 1975. Rsch. chemist USN Ordnance Lab., Silver Spring, Md., 1961-66; asst. prof. to prof. chemistry Stevens Inst. Tech., Hoboken, N.J., 1966-77; chmn. dept. chemistry East Carolina U., Greenville, N.C., 1977-80, dean. coll. arts and scis., 1980-83, vice chancelor for acad. affairs, 1983-87; pres. Tenn. Tech. U., 1987—; adj. prof. textile chem. N.C. State U., Raleigh, 1978-82; guest lect. Plastics Inst. Am., Hoboken, 1967-82. Contbr. articles to profl. jours. Recipient Ednl. Svc. award Plastics Inst. Am., 1973; named Freygang Outstanding Tchr., Stevens Inst. Tech., 1975. Mem. Am. Chem. Soc., Tenn. Acad. of Scis., Sigma Xi, Phi Kappa Phi. Democrat. Roman Catholic. Avocations: golf; reading. Home: Tenn Tech U Walton House Box 5007 Cookeville TN 38505 Office: Tenn Tech U Office of Pres Cookeville TN 38505

VOLZ, MARLIN MILTON, law educator; b. Cecil, Wis., Sept. 3, 1917; s. Edward A. and Mae C. (Winter) V.; m. Esther R. Krug, Aug. 23, 1941; children: Marlin M., Karen D., Thomas A. BA, U. Wis., 1938, JD, 1940, SJD, 1945; LLD (hon.), San Juan (P.R.) Law Sch., 1957. Bar: Wis. 1940, Mo. 1951, Ky. 1958. Asst. prof. law sch. faculty U. Wis., 1946-50; prof., dean sch. law U. Kansas City (now U. Mo. in Kansas City), 1950-58; dean sch. law U. Louisville, 1958-65, prof. sch. law, 1965-87, ret., 1987; county judge pro tem, probate judge Jefferson County, Ky., 1970-74; chmn. Ky. Pub. Svc. Commn., Frankfort, 1981-82; mem. panel labor arbitrators Fed. Mediation and Conciliation Svc., Am. Arbitration Assn.; reporter on legal draftsmanship Am. Law Inst.; adviser San Juan (P.R.) Sch. Law; mem. Nat. Coun. Legal Clinics, Chgo., 1960-67; mem. Louisville Labor Mgmt. Com. Co-author: Drafting Partnership Agreements, 7th edit., 1984, 86, Wisconsin Practice Methods, 1949, Missouri Practice Methods, 1953, Iowa Practice Methods, 1954, Kansas Practice Methods, 1957; co-author, gen. editor rev. edit. West's Federal practice Manual; co-author, gen. editor Kentucky Legal Forms, vol. 3 and 4, 1965, co-author, vol. 5 and 6, gen. editor revision, 1985; co-author, gen. editor Caldwell's Kentucky Form Book; editor: Cases and Materials, Civil Procedure, 1975, 83; co-editor Elkouri and Elkouri, How Arbitration Works, 5th edit. Chmn. Ky. Com. Correctonal Rsch., Frankfort, 1962-65, Louisville Human Rels. Commn., 1962-65; candidate for mayor, Louisville, 1965. Sgt. U.S. Army, 1943-46. Recipient Teaching and Major Svc. awards. Mem. ABA (co-chair arbitration com. 1986-89), Fed. Bar Assn., Ky. Bar Assn., Wis. Bar Assn., Am. Judicature Soc. (bd. dir. 1976-80), Nat. Orgn. Legal Problems Edn. (nat. pres. 1963), Nat. Acad. Arbitrators (com. chmn. 1987-88, bd. govs. 1989-92), Rotary. Democrat. Methodist. Home: 1819 Woodfill Way Louisville KY 40205-2433 Office: U Louisville Sch Law Louisville KY 40292

VON ARX, DOLPH WILLIAM, food products executive; b. St. Louis, Aug. 30, 1934; s. Adolph William and Margaret Louise (Linderer) von A.; m. Sharon Joy Landolt, Dec. 21, 1957; children: Vanessa von Arx Gilvarg, Eric S., Valerie L. BSBA, Washington U., St. Louis, 1961; LHD, St. Augustine Coll., 1988. Account exec. Compton Advt., N.Y.C., 1961-64; v.p. mktg. Ralston Purina Co., St. Louis, 1964-69; exec. v.p. mktg. Gillette Personal Care Div., Chgo., 1969-72; exec. v.p. gen. mgmt. group T.J. Lipton Inc., Englewood Cliffs, N.J., 1973-87; pres., chief exec. officer R.J. Reynold Tobacco Co., Winston-Salem, N.C., 1987-88; chmn., chief exec. officer Planters LifeSavers Co., Winston-Salem, 1988-91; bd. dirs. Carolina Medicorp, Winston-Salem, Cree Rsch. Inc., Durham, N.C., Ruby Tuesday Inc., BMC Fund Inc.; chmn. Morrison's F.C. Atlanta, 1992-96, Morrison Fresh Cooking, 1996—. Bd. visitors U. N.C., 1988-92; chmn. bd. trustees Wake Forest U. Grad. Sch. Mgmt., 1988—; pres. bd. trustees N.C. Dance Theater, Winston-Salem, 1989-90; bd. dirs. Forsyth Meml. Hosp., 1988-92, Naples Conservancy, Naples Philharmonic Ctr. for Arts, Wheeling Thunderbirds Hockey, Inc., Reynolds Mus. Am. Art, Naples Cmty. Hosp., chmn., 1994—, bd. dirs. health care sys., chmn., 1995—. Mem. Belle Haven Club (Greenwich) (bd. dirs. 1983-87), Naples Yacht Club, Univ. Club (N.Y.C.), Linville Ridge Country Club (Linville, N.C.), Collier Res. Club (Naples, Fla.). Home: Pent House 1 4351 Gulf Shore Blvd N PH1 Naples FL 34103

VON BRAUN, PETER CARL MOORE STEWART, company executive; b. Greenwich, Conn., June 24, 1940; s. Carl Conrad and Martha Irwin (Moore) von B.; m. Elisabeth Esser, July 1, 1967 (div. Dec. 1980); m. Denene Jensen, Sept. 26, 1987; children: Christina Stewart, Alexander Stewart. BA with high honors, Yale U., 1964; PhD summa cum laude, U. Cologne, 1966. Assoc. McKinsey & Co., Inc., N.Y.C., 1966-72, prin., 1972-77; chief internat. program devel. Order of St. John, London, 1977-80; exec. dir. Sight Programme, London and Sultanate of Oman, 1977-84; chmn., CEO Am. Microtrace Corp., Virginia Beach, Va., 1987-95, RusPetrol (USA), LLC, Greenwich, Conn., 1989—; chmn., CEO CLEW, LLC, Austin, Tex., 1995—. Author: Die Verteidigung Indiens, 1968, How to Save An Eye, 1981; contbr. articles to profl. jours.; producer (film) How to Save a Life, 1977. Chmn. Battle Harbour Found., Greenwich, 1972—; vestryman Trinity Parish, N.Y.C., 1977-84; chmn. Anglican Svc. Tng. & Relief Orgn., London, 1986—; bd. dirs. Presiding Bishop's Fund, N.Y.C., 1977-81; mem. Internat. Adv. Bd. Yale U., 1989—. Served with USN, 1956-58, U.S. Army, 1958-64. Decorated knight of grace and knight of justice Order of St. John, companion with star Order of Merit (Cyprus); Fulbright scholar, 1964-66. Republican. Episcopalian. Clubs: Cavalry, Guards Polo (London); N.Y. Yacht (N.Y.C.), Yale Club, Indian Harbor Yacht (Greenwich, Conn.), Battle Harbour Yacht (Newfoundland, Can.), Commodore. Home: 36 Zaccheus Meades Ln Greenwich CT 06831 Office: Clew LLC 12010 Hwy 290 W Austin TX 78736

VON BUEDINGEN, RICHARD PAUL, urologist; b. Rochester, N.Y., Sept. 14, 1938; s. Wilmer Edward and Clara Elma von B.; BS, U. Wis., 1960, MA in Philosophy, 1961, MD, 1965; m. Bari Luwe Solesky, Nov. 26, 1966 (dec. 1992); children: Kirsten Karla, Christian Karl. Commd. ensign U.S. Navy, 1964, advanced through grades to capt., 1975, intern, U.S. Naval Hosp., St. Albans, N.Y., 1965-66, resident in internal medicine, in plastic and thoracic surgery, in urology affiliate programs Naval Regional Med. Ctr., Oakland, Calif., and U.S. Hosp., Oakland, U. Calif. San Francisco, Stanford U., 1969-73, fellow in pediatric urology, 1973, scientist astronaut trainee Naval Aerospace Med. Inst., Pensacola, Fla., 1966-67, group flight surgeon Marine Corp Air Sta., Beaufort, S.C., 1967-69, chief urology Naval Regional Med. Ctr., Long Beach, Calif., 1973-75, asst. clin. prof. urology, U. Calif., Irvine, 1973-75, resigned, 1975; pvt. practice urology, Aiken, S.C., 1975-80; bd. trustees, chief of surgery HCA Aiken Regional Med. Ctrs., 1985-91. Fellow Internat. Coll. Surgeons, ACS; mem. AMA, Am. Urol. Assn., S.C. Med. Assn. (com. on continuing edn. 1981-83), S.C. Urol. Assn., So. Med. Assn., Soc. Govt. Urologists, Aiken County Med. Soc., Am. Cancer Soc. (chmn. com. profl. edn. in S.C. 1980-82, nat. award for contbns. to profl. edn. 1982), Am. Diabetes Assn. (state bd. dirs., med. edn. com.), Am. Fertility Soc., Am. Lithotripsy Soc. Club: Edisto River Hounds (Master of Foxhounds). Contbr. articles to profl. publs. Home: 1500 Huntsman Dr Aiken SC 29803-5236 Office: 210 University Pky Ste 2300 Aiken SC 29801-6808

VONDRACEK, BETTY SUE, interior designer, remodeling contractor, real estate agent; b. Tulsa, Aug. 27, 1938; d. John Carson and Susan Elizabeth (Nall) Bumgarner; m. Rudy J. Vondracek, Feb. 4, 1961 (dec. Sept. 1990); children: Richard, John (dec.), Vikki. BFA, U. Kans., 1960. Lic. interior designer; lic. real estate agt. Comml. artist Hall & Floyd Advt., Tulsa, 1960-62; freelance artist El Dorado, Ark., 1962-67, Chgo., 1967-69; interior designer Jeanette Interiors, Dallas, 1974-76; owner, designer, contractor Bee Vee Studio, Dallas, 1976—; real estate agt. Mahoney Realty Svcs., Dallas, 1992—; mem. grievance com. Greater Dallas Bd. Realtors, 1992—; mem. Dallas Supts. Adv. Com. Designer Scottish Rite Hosp. Parade of Homes, 1984, March of Dimes Holiday Tour of Homes, 1985-86, Christmas at DeGolyer, 1988-90, Dallas Symphony Showhouse, 1985, 87, 89, 92. Elected ofcl. Dallas Ind. Sch. Dist., 1986-92; pres. West-Lake Rep. Women, Dallas, 1975-77, 92-94; chmn. bd. dirs. Am. Heart Assn., Dallas, 1990-91, Tex. chpt. bd. dirs., 1990—, chmn. bd. Tex. affiliate, 1996—, chmn. capital campaign, chmn. pub. affairs; mem. edn. com. Women's Coun. Dallas County. Recipient Dwight D. Eisenhower award Am. Heart Assn., 1993, Douglas S. Perry Vol. of Yr., Am. Heart Assn., 1990, Key Communicator award Tex. Sch. Pub. Rels., 1984, Disting. Svc. award Nat. Com. for Citizens in Edn., 1984. Mem. Am. Soc. Interior Designers. Roman Catholic. Office: Bee Vee Studio 6215 Chesley Ln Dallas TX 75214-2118

VON ENDE, FREDERICK (TED), English language educator, university director; b. Pitts., June 12, 1942; s. Richard C. and Generva (Brady) von E.; m. Catharyn Lee Seago, Aug. 15, 1964; children: Sara Catharyn von Ende Orr, Gretchen Anne. BA, McMurry Coll., 1964; MA, Tex. Christian U., 1966, PhD, 1972. Asst. prof. English Pan Am. Coll., Edinburg, Tex., 1968-72; assoc. prof. Pan Am. U., Edinburg, 1972-79, head dept. English, 1975-77, coord. policy planning, 1977-81, prof., 1979—, chairperson dept. English, 1986; dir. Inst. Rsch. and Planning U. Tex.-Pan Am., Edinburg, 1991—; planning cons. various ednl. instns., South Tex., 1991—. Author: Essential Articles: George Herbert, 1979; contbr. articles and poems to profl. publs. Planning cons. McAllen (Tex.) Internat. Mus., 1994. Mem. Soc. Coll. and Univ. Planners, Assn. Instnl. Rsch., Tex. Assn. Coll. Tchrs. (life). Home: 717 N 9th McAllen TX 78501 Office: Univ Tex-Pan Am 1201 W University Dr Edinburg TX 78539

VON ESCHEN, ROBERT LEROY, electrical engineer, consultant; b. Glasgow, Mont., Oct. 3, 1936; s. Leroy and Lillian Victoria (Eliason) Von E.; m. Carolyn Kay Frampton, Dec. 14, 1965; children: Eric Leroy, Marc Alfred. BSEE, Mont. State U., 1961; postgrad., U. Liberia, Lakeland C.C., Glendale C.C. Registered profl. engr., Pa. Hydro constrn. engr. U.S. Army Corps of Engrs., Mont. and S.D., 1961-62; hdqrs. chief engr. Eagle Constrn. Co., Colo., 1962; resident transp./distbn. elec. engr. Stanley Cons., Inc., West Africa, 1962-63; hydro cons., startup engr. Stanley Cons., Inc., Manila, West Africa, 1965-66; with Stanley Cons., 1962-68, Gilbert Assoc./United Energy Svc., 1968-92; PBAP sect. engr., maintenance pplanning engr., CAS sec. mgr. Gilbert Assocs., Inc., Tex., 1992—; cons. engr. fossil power plant, Ky., Colo., Mo., Korea; site project mgr., Ariz., Aruba; nuclear constrn. startup engr., Pa., Ala., Ohio; safety sys. functional inspector, Calif., Wis., OE; PBAP project mgr., Tex.; tech. cons. World Bank, Liberia; engring. cons. USN, Manila, 1967; founding dr. Madison Comptr. Soc., Ohio, 1983-85; v.p., dr. Boy Scouts Am., 1981-84. Founder, dir. Madison (Ohio) Computer Soc., 1983-85; v.p., bd. dirs. N.E. coun. Boy Scouts Am., Painesville, 1983-85. Recipient Silver Beaver award Boy Scouts Am., 19 other awards. Mem. IEEE, NRA, NPSE, Nat. Assn. Ret. Persons, Soc. Am. Mil. Engrs., Am. Def. Preparedness Soc., Profl. Engring. Soc. Ohio, Profl. Engring. Soc. Tex., Masons (life), Shriners. Home: 3445 Gladstone Ln Amarillo TX 79121-1525 Office: Mason & Hanger-Silas Mason Co Inc PO Box 30020 Amarillo TX 79177-0001

VON HAGGE, ROBERT, design company executive. Pres. von Hagge Design Assocs. Address: 17823 Theiss Mail Rte Rd Spring TX 77379-6110

VON HILSHEIMER, GEORGE EDWIN, III, neuropsychologist; b. West Palm Beach, Fla., Aug. 15, 1934; s. George E. Jr. and Dorothy Sue (Bridges) Von H.; m. Catherine Jean Munson, Dec. 27, 1968 (div. Oct. 1987); children: Dana Germaine, George E. IV, Alexandra; m. Jonnie Mae Warner, June 29, 1991. BA, U. Miami, 1955; PhD, Saybrook Inst., 1977. Diplomate Acad. Psychosomatic Medicine, Am. Bd. Behavioral Medicine, Am. Acad. Pain Mgmt., Am. Bd. Cert. Managed Care Providers, Am. Acad. Psychol. Treating Addiction, Nat. Register Neurofeedback. Sr. minister Humanitas, N.Y.C., 1959-64; cons. Pres. Kennedy's Commn. Nat. Vol. Svc., Juv. Del., Migration Labor, 1963-64; headmaster Summerlane Sch., North Branch, N.Y., 1964-69; supt. Green Valley Sch., Orange City, Fla., 1969-74; neuropsychologist Growth Insts., Twyman's Mill, Va., 1974-79, Growth Inst., DeLand, Fla., 1980-82; assoc. health profl. Maitland, 1982—; cons. Sci. Adv. Bd. EPA, Washington, 1974-84; chmn. Certification Bd., Internat. Coll. Environ. Medicine, 1991-94; mem. Bd. Assn. Diagnostic Efficiency and Brief Therapy, dir. curriculum, 1993-94. Author: How to Live With Your Special Child, 1970, Understanding Problems of Children, 1975, Allergy, Toxins and the LD Child, 1977, Psychobiology of Delinquents, 1978, Depression Is Not a Disease, 1989, Brief Therapy, 1993, Brief Therapy: Antecedent Scientific Principles, 1994; editor Human Learning, Washington. Mem. spl. bd. Fla. Symphony Orch., 1992-93. With U.S. Army, 1957-59. Fellow Royal Soc. Health (life), Internat. Coll. Applied Nutrition, Acad. Psychosomatic Medicine; mem. Toastmasters, Phi Kappa Phi, Omicron Delta Kappa, Alpha Sigma Phi. Mem. Ch. of Brethren. Home: 160 W Trotters Dr Maitland FL 32751-5736 Office: AAT 175 Lookout Pl # 1 Maitland FL 32751-4494

VON KAP-HERR, CHRISTOPHER GERHART, cytogeneticist; b. Laufen, Germany, July 18, 1950; came to U.S., 1987; s. Gerhart and Gerhardine (Fahrencamp) von K.-H.; m. Elizabeth J. Ampleford, May 17, 1980. BSc, Loyola Coll., Montreal, Que., Can., 1971; MSc, McGill U., Montreal, 1976; postgrad., York U., Toronto, 1978-80. Cert. Nat. Cert. Agy. for Med. Lab. Pers. Rsch. asst. in human genetics Roswell Park Meml. Inst., Buffalo, 1976-78; rsch. technologist in cytogenetics Toronto (Ont., Can.) Gen. Hosp., 1981-83, cytogenetics technologist, 1984-87; rsch. technologist in immunopathology Queen Elizabeth Hosp., Toronto, 1983-84; cytogenetics technologist Cytogenetics Lab., U. Va. Hosp., Charlottesville, 1987-90; rsch. asst. Cytogenetics Lab., U. Va. Hosp., 1990-96; sr. technologist dept. Ob/Gyn U. S.C., Columbia, 1996—. Contbr. articles to sci. jours., chpt. to book. Del. to Va. Fedn. Dog Clubs and Breeders, Charlottesville, 1993-95. Mem. Assn. Cytogenetics Technologists, Can. Soc. Lab. Technologists, Charlottesville Kennel Club (bd. dirs. 1991-93). Episcopalian. Home: 8100 Bayfield Rd Apt 8-I Columbia SC 29223-5650 Office: Dept Ob Gyn 2 Richard Medical Park Ste 208 Columbia SC 29203

VON MERING, OTTO OSWALD, anthropology educator; b. Berlin, Germany, Oct. 21, 1922; came to Switzerland, 1933, to U.S., 1939, naturalized, 1954; s. Otto O. and Henriette (Troeger) von M.; m. Shirley Ruth Brook, Sept. 11, 1954; children: Gretchen, Karin, Gregory. Grad., Belmont Hill Sch., 1940; BA in History, Williams Coll., 1944; PhD in Social Anthropology, Harvard U., 1956. Instr. Belmont Hill Sch., Belmont, Mass., 1945-47, Boston U., 1947-48, Cambridge Jr. Coll., 1948-49; rsch. asst. lab. social rels. Harvard U., 1950-51, Boston Psychopathic Hosp., 1951-53; Russell Sage Found. fellow N.Y.C., 1953-55; asst. prof. social anthropology U. Pitts. Coll. Medicine, 1955-60, assoc. prof., 1960-65, prof. social anthropology, 1965-71; prof. child devel. and child care U. Pitts. Coll. Allied Health Professions, 1969-71; prof. anthropology and family medicine U. Fla., 1971-76, prof. anthropology in ob-gyn, 1979-84, prof. anthropology and gerontology, 1986—, joint prof. dept. medicine, coll. medicine, 1994—; lectr. Sigmund Freud Inst., Frankfurt, Germany, 1962-64, Pitts. Psychoanalytical Inst., 1960--71, Interuniv. Forum, 1967-71; tech. adviser Maurice Falk Med. Fund; Fulbright vis. lectr., 1962-63; Richard-Merton guest prof. Heidelberg U., Germany, 1962-63; vis. prof. Dartmouth, 1970-71; vis. lectr. continuing edn. Med. Coll. of Pa., 1990-92, vis. lectr. U. Sheffield, Eng., Fall, 1995, U. Liverpool, 1995; bd. dirs. Tech. Assistance Resource Assocs., U. Fla., 1979-84; supr. grad. study program Ctr. Gerontologic Studies, U. Fla., 1983-85, assoc. dir. 1985-86, dir. 1986-95; mem. coordinating com. Geriatric Edn. Ctr., Coll. of Medicine, U. Fla.; mem. nat. tech. expert panel on long-term care Health Care Financing Adminstrn., Washington; chair, mem. adv. bd. Internat. Exchange Ctr. on Gerontology State U. System of Fla., 1987-92; adv. bd. Second Season Broadcasting Network, Palm Beach, Fla., 1989-92, Fla. Policy Exch. Ctr. on Aging, State U. System Fla., 1991-95, Assoc. Health Industries of Fla., Inc., Nat. Shared Housing Resource Ctr., Balt.; cons. mental hosps. Author: Remotivating the Mental Patient, 1957, A Grammar of Human Values, 1961, (with Mitscherlich and Brocher) Der Kranke in der Modernen Gesellschaft, 1967, (with Kasdan) Anthropology in the Behavioral and Health Sciences, 1970, (with R. Binstock and L. Cluff) The Future of Long Term Care, 1996; also articles; commentary editor: Human Organization, 1974-76; corr. editor Jour. Geriatric Psychiatry; mem. editl. bd. Med. Anthropology, 1976-84, Ednl. Gerontology, 1990—, Australasian Leisure for Pleasure Jour., 1995—. Mem. nat. adv. bd. Nat. Shared Housing Resource Ctr., 1994-95; pres. Dedicated Alt. Resources for the Elderly, 1996—. Recipient Fulbright-Hayes Travel award, 1962-63; grantee Wenner-Gren Found., N.Y., 1962-63, Am. Philos. Soc., 1962-63, Maurice Falk Med. Fund, 1970-71, US-DHHS, 1979-83, Walter Reed Army Inst. Rsch., 1987-91. US-ADA/Fla. Dept. of Elder Affairs, 1993-94; spl. fellow NIMH, 1971-72. Fellow AAAS, Am. Anthrop. Assn. (mem. James Mooney award com. 1978-81, vis. lectr. 1961,-62, 71-74, 91-92), Am. Gerontol. Soc., Royal Soc. Health, Acad. Psychosomatic Medicine, Am. Ethnological Soc., Soc. Applied Anthropology, Royal Anthrop. Inst.; mem. Assn. Am. Med. Colls., Assn. Anthrop. Gerontol. (pres.-elect 1991-92, pres. 1992-93), Am. Fedn. Clin. Research, Am. Public Health Assn., Canadian Assn. Gerontology, British Soc. Gerontology, Med. Group Mgmt. Assn., World Fedn. Mental Health, Internat. Assn. Social Psychiatry (regional counselor), Internat. Hosp. Fedn., Help Age Internat. (London). Home: 818 NW 21st St Gainesville FL 32603-1027 Office: U Fla Dept Anthropology 1350 Turlington Hall Gainesville FL 32611

VON OHAIN, HANS JOACHIM P., aerospace scientist; b. Dessau, Germany, Dec. 14, 1911; came to U.S., 1947; s. Wolf and Katherine L. (Nagel) von O.; m. Hanny Lemke, Nov. 26, 1949; children: Stephen, Christopher, Catherine, Stephanie. PhD in physics and aerodyn., U. Goettingen, Fed. Republic of Germany, 1935; DSc (hon.), U. W.Va., 1982. Head jet proplusion devel. div. Heinkel Aircraft Corp., Rostock, Fed. Republic of Germany, 1935-45; cons. U.S. Navy, Stuttgart, Fed. Republic of Germany, 1945-46; chief scientist USAF, Dayton, Ohio, 1947-79, with Aerospace Research Lab., 1963-75, with Propulsion Lab., 1975-79; now aerospace research cons. U. Dayton Research Inst. Multiple patents in field; contbr. article to profl. jours. Recipient R. Tom Sawyer award ASME, 1990, Godfrey L. Cabot award Aero Club New Eng., 1993. Fellow AIAA (hon., Goddard prize 1966, Daniel Guggenheim Medal award 1991); mem. NAE (Charles Stark Draper prize 1991). Club: Wings (N.Y.C.). Home and office: 3305 Nan Pablo Dr Melbourne FL 32934-8392

VON RECUM, ANDREAS F., bioengineer; b. Dillingen, Bavaria, Germany, July 5, 1939; came to U.S., 1971; s. Bogdan Freiherr and Ilse Freifrau (von Rosenberg) von R.; m. Grudrun F. Bredenbröker-Hardt, Oct. 2, 1965; children: Derik F., Vera F., Uta F., Horst F., Thomas F., Elsa F. BS, U. Giessen, 1965; DVM, Free U. Berlin, 1968, PhD, 1969; PhD in Vet. Surgery, Colo. State U., 1974. Practitioner farm animal medicine and surgery Meitingen, Germany, 1968-69; clin. staff small animal clinic Free U. Berlin (Germany), Coll. Vet. Medicine, 1969-72; rsch. asst. surg. lab. Colo. State U., Coll. Vet. Medicine, Ft. Collins, 1972-74; dir. surg. rsch. lab. Sinai Hosp. Detroit, 1975-77; prof. dept. bioengring. Clemson (S.C.) U., 1978-93, head dept. bioengring., 1982-93; chmn. bioengring. alliance S.C. Coll. Engring., Clemson U., 1984-88; scientific staff Shriners Hosp., Greenville, S.C., 1989-95; prof. Hunter endowed chair bioengring. Clemson U. Coll. Engring., 1993—; adj. assoc. prof. comparative surgery Wayne State U. Sch. Medicine, Dept. Comparative Medicine, 1975-77; adj. prof. surgery U. S.C. Sch. Medicine, 1984—, Med. U. S.C., 1987—; adj. prof. biomaterials Coll. Dentistry U. Nijmegen, 1993—; cons. in field. Editor Jour. Investigative Surg.; patentee in field. Recipient Fulbright Scientist award, 1990-91, Alexander von Humboldt Sr. Scientist award, 1990-91; nat. and internat. fellow Biomaterials Sci. and Engring., 1996. Mem. AVMA, Am. Soc. Lab. Animal Practitioners (governing body), Coll. Vet. Medicine (elected), Blue Ridge Vet. Med. Assn. (pres. 1984), Soc. Biomaterials (asst. editor 1986—, editl. bd. 1983, program chmn. 1990, sec.-treas. 1990-92, pres. 1993-94), Internat. Soc. Artificial Internal Organs, Am. Soc. Artificial Organs, Am. Heart Assn., Acad. Surg. Rsch. (founder 1982, pres. 1982-83, newsletter editor 1982-85), Biomed. Engring. Soc., Am. Soc. Engring. Edn., Assn. Advancement Med. Instrumentation. Presbyterian. Office: Clemson Univ Dept of Bioengineering Clemson SC 29631

VON ROSENBERG, GARY MARCUS, JR., parochial school educator; b. Baumholder, Federal Republic of Germany, Feb. 22, 1956; s. Gary Marcus and Maria Gwendolyn (Pickett) Von R. BA, Cleve. State U., 1979; BS, U. Tex., 1991. Jr. high sch. sci. tchr. St. Andrew's Sch., Ft. Worth, 1982-86; math. tchr., coach, moderator Monsignor Nolan High Sch., Ft. Worth, 1986—. Creator jr. high Sci. Fair program. Capt. U.S. Army field artillery, 1979-82. Recipient Sci. Fair Tchr. award Ft. Worth Regional Sci. Fair, 1985, runner-up, 1984. Mem. ASCD, Nat. Coun. Tchrs. Math., The Math. Assn. Am., The Nat. Sci. Tchrs. Assn. Home: 1525 Lincolnshire Way Fort Worth TX 76134-5583

VON TAAFFE-ROSSMANN, COSIMA T., physician, writer, inventor; b. Kuklov, Slovakia, Czechoslovakia, Nov. 21, 1944; came to U.S., 1988; d. Theophil and Marianna Hajossy; m. Charles Boris Rossmann, Oct. 19, 1979; children: Nathalie Nissa Cora, Nadine Nicole. MD, Purkyne U., Brno, Czechoslovakia, 1967. Intern Valtice (Czechoslovakia) Gen. Hosp., 1967-68, resident ob-gyn, 1968-69; med. researcher Kidney Disease Inst., Albany, N.Y., 1970-71; resident internal medicine Valtice Gen. Hosp., 1972-73; gen. practice Nat. Health System, Czechoslovakia, 1973-74; pvt. practice West Germany, 1974-80; med. officer Baragwanath Hosp., Johannesburg, South Africa, 1984-85, Edendale Hosp., Pietermaritzburg, South Africa, 1985-86; pvt. practice Huntingburg, Ind., 1988-90, Valdosta, Ga., 1990—; med. researcher, 1966—. Contbr. articles on medicine to profl. jours.; inventor, patentee in field. Office: 2301 N Ashley St Valdosta GA 31602-2620

VONTUR, RUTH POTH, elementary school educator; b. Beeville, Tex., Sept. 10, 1944; d. Robert Bennal and Ruth (Matejek) Poth; m. Robert F. Vontur, Aug. 8, 1964; children: Catherine Anne, Craig Robert, Cynthia Anne. BS in Edn., Southwest Tex. State U., 1966. Cert. health and phys. edn. tchr., biology tchr. Tex. Teachng asst. Blessed Sacrament Confraternity Christian Doctrine, Poth, Tex., 1958-64; phys. edn. tchr. Judson Ind. Sch. Dist., Converse, Tex., 1966-68; substitute tchr. St. Monica's Confraternity Christian Doctrine, Converse, 1971—; substitute tchr. Judson Ind. Sch. Dist., Converse, 1972-75, 80, phys. edn. tchr., 1966-68, 81—; county adv. bd. Am. Heart Assn., San Antonio, Tex., 1985-88, jump rope for heart coord., 1984—, heart ptnr., 1992—. Pres. St. Monica's Coun. Cath. Women, Converse, 1975; sponsor Young Astronauts, 1993—, Hall Patrol, 1990-93, 96—, Flag Patrol, 1996—. Mem. NEA, AAHPERD, Alamo Area Tex. Assn. Health, Phys. Edn., Recreation and Dance, Tex. Assn. Health, Phys. Edn., Recreation and Dance, Judson Tchrs. Assn. (exec. dir. 1993-95), Tex. State Tchrs. Assn., Judson Athletic Booster Club. Roman Catholic. Home: 105 Norris Dr W Converse TX 78109-1905 Office: Judson Ind Sch Dist Converse Elem Sch 102 School St Converse TX 78109-1320

VOORHEES, RICHARD LESLEY, chief federal judge; b. Syracuse, N.Y., June 5, 1941; s. Henry Austin and Catherine Adeline (Fait) V.; m. Barbara Holway Humphries, 1968; children: Martha Northrop, Steven Coerte. BA, Davidson Coll., 1963; JD, U. N.C., Chapel Hill, 1968. Bar: N.C. 1968, U.S. Dist. Ct. (we. dist.) N.C. 1969, U.S. Tax Ct. 1969, U.S. Ct. Appeals (4th cir.) 1978, U.S. Dist. Ct. (mid. dist.) N.C. 1981. Mem., ptnr. Garland, Alala, Bradley & Gray, Gastonia, N.C., 1968-80; pvt. practice Gastonia, N.C., 1980-88; judge U.S. Dist. Ct., Charlotte, N.C., 1988—, chief judge, 1991—. Mem. N.C. State Rep. Exec. Com., Gaston County Rep. Com., chmn., 1979-83, U.S. Jud. Conf. Com., 1993—, case mgmt. and ct. adminstrn. com., 4th Cir. Ct. Appeals Jud. Coun., 1992-93; chmn. Gaston County Bd. Elections, Gastonia, 1985-86; alt. del. Rep. Nat. Conv., Kansas City, Kans., 1976. 1st lt. U.S. Army, 1963-65. Mem. N.C. Bar Assn., Fed. Judges Assn., Dist. Judges Assn. Office: US Dist Ct WDNC 195 CR Jonas Fed Bldg 401 W Trade St Charlotte NC 28202*

VOORNEVELD, RICHARD BURKE, education educator, college official; b. L.I., N.Y., Nov. 16, 1949; s. Albert Henery and Margaret Rita (Burke) V.; m. Susan Monroe Straus, Aug. 3, 1974; children: Edward Corrie, Margaret Brice. BA in Elem. Edn., St. Leo (Fla.) Coll., 1972; MA in Edn. for Gifted, U. So. Fla., 1973; PhD in Spl. Edn., U. Fla., 1982. Cert. elem. tchr., gifted and talented edn., behaivor disorders, adminstrv. supr., Fla. Tchr. gifted child edn. Alachua County Sch. Bd., Gainesville, Fla., 1973-79, chmn. gifted edn. program, 1974-78, coord. community leadership program (gifted), 1079-81; clinic liaison multidisciplinary and tng. program Shands Teaching Hosp., Gainesville, 1981-83; asst. prof. edn. Coll. of Charleston, S.C., 1981—, dir. spl. edn., 1987-88, dir. student devel., 1988-90; dean of students, 1990—; dean of students, dir. Ctr. for Student Wellness, 1994—; participant, presenter numerous nat. and internat. workshops, 1972—. Contbr. articles to profl. jours., editor 2 books. Bd. dirs. PUSH, Charlotte, N.C., 1989. Recipient merit award Alachua County Tchrs. of Gifted, 1976; grantee S.C. Commn. on Higher Edn., 1985-86. Mem. Nat. Assn. Student Pers. Adminstrsn., Coun. for Exceptional Children, Am. Coll. Health Assocs., Assn. Frat. Advisors, S.C. Inter-Frat. Coun., St. Leo Coll. Alumni Assn. (treas. bd. dirs. 1989), Pi Kappa Phi, Kappa Delta Pi. Roman Catholic. Home: 38 Brisbane Dr Charleston SC 29407-3419 Office: Coll of Charleston Office Student Affairs Charleston SC 29424

VORDERMARK, JONATHAN SAWYER, retired military officer, pediatric urologist; b. Albuquerque, Dec. 25, 1948; s. Jonathan Sawyer and Jeffie V.; m. Alyson Howard, Dec. 23, 1972 (div. 1996); children: Jonathan, Matthew. BA with honors, Va. Mil. Inst., 1970; MD, Med. Coll. Va., 1974. Commd. 2d lt. U.S. Army, 1970, advanced through grades to col., 1989; ret., 1990; intern Brooke Army Med. Ctr., San Antonio, 1974-75; resident Madigan Army Med. Ctr., Tacoma, Wash., 1975-79; chief urology Darnall Army Community Hosp., Ft. Hood, Tex., 1979-82; fellow in plastic and reconstructive urology Middlesex Hosp. and Inst. Urology, London, 1982-84; chief pediatric urology Fitzsimmons Army Med. Ctr., Denver, 1984-85; surgeon 2d Armored Div., Ft. Hood, 1985-86; chief pediatric urology Letterman Army Med. Ctr., San Francisco, 1986-90, chmn. dept. clin. rsch., 1987-88; prof., dir. divsn. urology Tex. Tech. U., Lubbock, 1990-96; chief pediatric urology Tex. Tech. U., 1990—. Contbr. articles to profl. jours. Fellow ACS, Am. Acad. Pediat.; mem. Am. Urol. Assn., Brit. Assn. Urol. Surgeons, Soc. Pediatric Urologists, Am. Coll. Physician Execs., Internat. Continence Soc., Naut. Rsch. Guild, Urodynamics Soc., Soc. Fetal Urology (pres., Best Dr. Am. South Ctrl. region). Republican. Episcopalian. Home: 4601 94th St Lubbock TX 79424-5015 Office: Med Office Plaza 3502 9th St Ste 260 Lubbock TX 79415-3368

VOROUS, MARGARET ESTELLE, primary and secondary school educator; b. Charles Town, W.Va., Feb. 14, 1947; d. Benjamin Welton and Helen Virginia (Owens) Vorous. AA in Pre-Edn. (Laureate Scholar), Potomac State Coll., W.Va. U., 1967; BS in Elem. Edn., James Madison U., 1970, MS in Edn., 1975, postgrad., spring 1978, fall 1979, summer 1979, 81; postgrad. U. Va., summers 1977, 78, fall 1978, 89, 91, James Madison U., fall 1981-82, summer 1979, 81-82; MEd in Media Svcs., East Tenn. State U., 1988, 89. Cert. library sci., cert. adminstrn./supervisory. Tchr. 3d-4th grade Highview Sch., Frederick County, Va., 1968-69, 3d grade Kernstown Elem. Sch., Frederick County, 1970-71, E. Wilson Morrison Elem. Sch., Front Royal, Va., 1971-72, Stonewall Elem. Sch., Frederick County, 1972-78; tchr. 4th grade South Jefferson Elem. Sch., Jefferson County (W.Va.) Schs., 1978-79, Emergency Sch. Aid Act reading tchr./reading specialist, 1980-82, reading tchr./specialist Page Jackson Solar Elem. Sch., 1983-87; adult basic edn. tchr. Dowell J. Howard Vocat. Ctr., Winchester, Va., 1984-87, G.E.D. tchr., coordinator, 1985-87; libr., media specialist Powell Valley Middle Sch., 1988-91; ABE/GED/ESL tchr. for JOBS program Berkeley County Schs., 1992-94; libr., media specialist Northwestern Elem., 1994-95, first grade tchr., 1995—; tchr. 4th grade Ranson (W.Va.) Elem. Sch., 1979; reading tutor; reading tutor, trainer Laubach Literacy Internat., 1989; art rep. Creative Arts Festival at Kernstown, 1971, Stonewall elem. schs., 1973-77; mem. cultural task force Frederick County Sch., 1974-75, music task force, 1973-74, textbook adoption com. for reading, writing, 1976-77. Founder, editor: The Reading Gazette, The Reading Tribune, Emergency Sch. Aid Act Reading Program, South Jefferson Elem. Sch., 1980-81, Shepherdstown Elem. Sch., 1981-82; creator numerous reading games, activities. Vol. fundraiser Am. Cancer Soc., Frederick County, Va., 1981; vol. blood donor Am. Red Cross, 1978—; mem. Frederick County Polit. Action Com., Jefferson County Polit. Action Com.; del. 103-109th Ann. Diocesan Convs., Episc. Ch., registrar of vestry Grace Episc. Ch., Middleway, W.Va., 1980-87, lic. lay reader, 1980-90, lic. chalice bearer, 1983-90; lic. lay reader, lay eucharistic min. St. Paul's Episc. Ch.-on-the-Hill, Winchester, Va., 1996—; committeeperson Lebanon Dems., 1988-89; commd. mem. Order of Jerusalem, 1985—; VEMA leadership participant, 1989-91, 95; facilitator VEMA Conf., 1994; participant Seven Habits program Covey Leadership Ctr., 1993; Recipient various awards, including being named Miss Alpine Princess, award for Excellence in Adult Basic Edn. Dept. Edn., Charleston, W.Va., 1994, RIF Site Coord. for Honorable mention, 1995, Asst Coord. Pritt for Gov. Campaign (DEM), 1995-96, RIF Nat. Poster contest Storyteller for Chpt. I workshop and Ctrl. Elementary, 1994-96, Sigma Phi Omega, 1967. Mem. Internat. Reading Assn., NEA, Va. Reading Assn., Shenandoah Valley Reading Council, Assn. Supervision and Curriculum Devel., W.Va. Edn. Assn., NEA. Jefferson County Edn. Assn. (faculty rep.), Fauquier County Edn. Assn., Va. Edn. Assn., W.Va. Adult Edn. Assn., Va. Ednl. Media Assn., South Jefferson PTA, Potomac State Coll. Alumni Assn., James Madison U. Alumni Assn., Frederick County Dem. Women, Kappa Delta Pi, Phi Delta Kappa, Phi Kappa Phi.

VORWERK, E. CHARLSIE, artist; b. Tennga, Ga., Jan. 28, 1934; d. James A. and Hester L. (Davis) Pritchett; m. Norman T. Vorwerk, Feb. 9, 1956; children: Karl, Lauren, Michael. AB, Ga. Coll. for Women, Milledgeville, 1955. Billboard design artist Vanesco Poster, Chattanooga, 1955; cartographic draftsman TVA, Chattanooga, 1955; fashion illustrator Loveman's, Chattanooga, 1956; freelance comml. artist Chattannoga, Charleston, S.C., 1957—; pvt. art instr. for children and adults, Chattannoga, Charleston, 1066—; art instr. continuing edn. Charleston So. U., 1979-82; exhbn. chmn. Charleston Artist Guild, Summerville Artist Guild; chair Flowertown Festival, Summerville, S.C., 1972—; co-coord. Picolo-Spoleto Outdoor Art Exhibit, City of Charleston, 1983—, others. Illustrator: (jokes) Tales and Taradidles, (elem. book) St. Paul's Epitahs, others. Mem. Bd. Archtl. Rev., Summerville, 1976—; mem. women's bd. St. Paul's Ch., Summerville, 1968-84; active Boy Scouts Am., Girl Scouts U.S.; vol. Mental Health Clinic. Recipient art show ribbons. Mem. Charleston Artist Guild, Summerville Artist Guild. Episcopalian. Home and Office: 315 W Carolina Ave Summerville SC 29483

VOSS, TERENCE J., human factors scientist, educator; b. Cin., June 29, 1942; s. Harold A. and Marguerite (Canavan) V.; m. Charmaine E. Wilson, Sept. 3, 1983. BA, SUNY, Geneseo, 1965; MA, Fla. Atlantic U., 1972; postgrad., U. Mont., 1973-78. Cert. profl. ergonomist. Dept. dir., sr. staff scientist Essex Corp., Alexandria, VA., 1980-88; sr. human factors scientist Advanced Resources Devel. Corp., Columbia, Md., 1988-90; lead human factors scientist, fellow engr. Westinghouse Savannah River Co., Aiken, S.C., 1990—; cons. in field; mem. adj. faculty psychology dept. DePaul U., Chgo., 1990; human factors cons. U.S. Dept. Energy, 1990—. Contbr. articles to profl. jours. Named Citizen Amb., People to People Internat., 1985. Mem. Am. Psychol. Soc., Am. Nuclear Soc., Human Factors Soc., Sci. Rsch. Soc. N.Am., Sigma Xi. Home: 19 Shrewsbury Ln Aiken SC 29803-6299 Office: Westinghouse Savannah River Co River Co/Bldg 719-8A Aiken SC 29808

VOTAW, DONALD GENE, quality assurance professional. BS in Bus., Eastern Ky. U., Richmond, 1972. Assembly line leader Square D Mfg. Co., Lexington, Ky., 1966-67, dept. mgr., 1970-75; sr. supr. Michelin Tire Corp., Greenville, S.C., 1975-78; quality control mgr. Michelin Tire Corp., Spartanburg, S.C., 1978-81; quality assurance mgr. Uniroyal Tire Corp., Opelika, Ala., 1981-84, sect. mgr., 1984-85, statis. process control mgr., 1985-88; mgr. quality assurance and prodn., plant mgr. Dunlop Tire Corp., Buffalo, 1988-91; quality assurance dir. Am. Tokyo Rope, Danville, Ky., 1991—. Served with U.S. Army, 1967-70. Office: ATR Wire & Cable Co Inc Us 127 Byp Danville KY 40422

VOUGHT, BARBARA BALTZ, secondary school educator; b. Pocahontas, Ark., July 9, 1936; d. George Henry and Margaret Frances (Dust) Baltz; m. Carl David Vought, June 5, 1962; children: Vivian Eugenia, Stewart Lee, Stephanie Vought Ortel. BS, Siena Coll., 1958; student, St. Louis U., 1960-61, La. State U., 1962-63, U. Ala., 1972-74. Cert. secondary tchr., Ala. Rsch. asst. Kennedy VAMTG Hosp., Memphis, 1958-60; tchr. Corning (Ark.) High Sch., 1961-62; grad. asst. La. State U., Baton Rouge, La., 1962-63; instr. U. Ala., Huntsville, 1965-76; tchr. Lee High Sch., Huntsville, 1976; tchr. sci. Randolph Sch., Huntsville, 1976-83, chmn. sci., 1983—; grad. fellow St. Louis U., 1960-61; bd. dirs. Ala. State Sci. Fair, Decatur. Cocontbr. articles to profl. jours. Recipient Excellence in Sci. Teaching award U.S. Army Sci. and Humanities, 1984; named Sci. Tchr. of Yr., Calhoun Found., 1985, 87, Outstanding Faculty Mem., Randolph Sch., 1993. Mem. Botanical Garden Soc., Hist. Huntsville Found., Women's Guild Mus. Art (team capt. art bldg. fund campaign 1993), Heritage Club, Delta Kappa Gamma. Roman Catholic. Office: Randolph Sch 1005 Drake Ave SE Huntsville AL 35802-1036

VOYTKO, MARY LOU, neuroscientist; b. Cleve., May 22, 1957; d. Thomas Lee and Rita Ann (Pekarcik) V.; m. Joseph R. Tobin, Sept. 21, 1985. BS, Baldwin-Wallace Coll., 1979; PhD, SUNY, Syracuse, 1985. Postdoctoral fellow SUNY, Syracuse, 1985-87; from postdoctoral fellow to instr. Johns Hopkins Sch. Medicine, Balt., 1987-93; asst. prof. Bowman Gray Sch. Medicine, Winston-Salem, N.C., 1993—. Mem. Internat. Primatologic Soc., Internat. Brain Rsch. Orgn., Found. Biomed. Rsch., Soc. for Neurosci. (councilor Western N.C. chpt. 1994—). Office: Bowman Gray Sch Medicine Dept Comparative Medicine Med Ctr Blvd Winston Salem NC 27157-1040

VREELAND, RUSSELL GLENN, accountant, consultant; b. Princeton, N.J., Apr. 27, 1960; s. Glenn Earl and Barbara Ann (Jungels) V.; m. Traci Ann Harbold, Dec. 17, 1988; children: Hans Russell, Anna Patricia. BSBA, Bloomsburg (Pa.) U., 1982. CPA, Pa., Md. Sr. acct. Louis H. Linowitz & Co., Trenton, N.J., 1982-85; tax supr. Horty & Horty, P.A., Wilmington, Del., 1985-87; tax mgr. Stewart Waddell & Co. P.A., Columbia, Md., 1988-92; assoc. in charge of tax Hillman & Glorioso, P.L.L.C., Vienna, Va., 1993—; pvt. practice acct., 1994—; speaker in field. Author: Foreign Sales Corporations - A Primer, 1992, Exporting-Are You Ready?, 1993; contbr. articles to profl. jours. Chmn. fin. com. Woodland Village Condominium Assn., 1989-90. Mem. AICPAs (tax. div.), Nat. Assn. Cert. Valuation Analysts, Md. Assn. CPAs (fed. taxation com. 1990-91), D.C. Inst. CPAs. Republican. Lutheran. Office: Hillman & Glorioso PLLC 1950 Old Gallows Rd Ste 700 Vienna VA 22182

VROOM, STEVEN MICHAEL, director university gallery; b. Dearborn, Mich., Feb. 26, 1961; s. Edmond Montcrief Montbatten-Bain and Gisela Mathilda (Ansbach) Vroom. BPh, Cornell Coll., Mt. Vernon, Iowa, 1986, B in Spl. Studies, 1986; MA, U. Iowa, 1989. Gallery technician Armstrong Gallery, Mt. Vernon, Iowa, 1981-85; mgr. Lazy T Motor Lodge, Estes Park, Colo., 1983-87; asst to th curator Office of Visual Materials, Iowa City, Iowa, 1987-88; tchg. asst. U. Iowa, Iowa City, 1988-89; vis. asst. prof. St. Ambrose U., Davenport, Iowa, 1989; dir. exhibits Iowa City, Johnson County Arts, 1991-93; instr. U. Iowa, Iowa City, 1990-93; vis. assoc. prof. Knox Coll., Galesburg, Ill., 1993; dir. Univ. Gallery, Sewanee, Tenn., 1993—; chmn. Strike for the Arts Com., Iowa City, 1990. Author: (book) Form and Meaning: The Taj Mahal, 1989; (art catalogs), 6 Americans, 1993, The Romantic Vision of J.A. Oertel, 1995, New Sculpture: Geoff Bowie, 1996. Bd. dirs. Iowa City Childrens Theatre, 1989-91, Iowa City Arts Ctr., 1991-93. Recipient Shaw scholarship Cornell Coll., Mt. Vernon, Iowa, 1982-86, Grad. Coll. scholarship U. Iowa, Iowa City, 1990. Mem. Coll. Art Assn., Am. Assn. Mus., Tenn. Assn. Mus. (recording sec. Nashville, 1996, Hon. Mention 1994, Award of Excellence, 1996), Am. Fedn. of Art, Am. Coll. and Univ. Galleries, People for the Am. Way. Democrat.

VUŠKOVIĆ, LEPOSAVA, physicist, educator; b. Lešnica, Yugoslavia, Apr. 23, 1941; d. Djordje and Kristina (Obućina) Jovanović; m. Marko Vušković, Feb. 2, 1964 (div. Oct. 1982); children: Kristina, Ivo; m. Svetozar Popović, July 18, 1987; 1 stepchild, Ljubica Popović. Diploma in Phys. Chemistry, U. Belgrade, Yugoslavia, 1963, MS in Physics, 1968, PhD in Physics, 1972. Rsch. fellow Inst. Physics U. Belgrade, 1964-73, from rsch. scientist to head Atomic Physics Lab., 1973-78, dir. atomic laser and high energy physics div., 1981-85; assoc. prof. U. of Arts, Belgrade, 1973-85; assoc. rsch. prof. dept. physics NYU, N.Y.C., 1985-93; assoc. prof. dept. physics Old Dominion U., Norfolk, Va., 1993—; mem. gen. com. Internat. Conf. on Physics of Electronic and Atomic Collisions, 1977-81, 95—, mem. organizing com. VIII Conf., 1973, mem. organizing com. VII Symposium on Physics of Ionized Gases, Dubrovnik, Yugoslavia, 1976, 82. Author: (textbook) The Physics of Cinematography, 1985, (with others) Metrology of Gaseous Pollutants, 1981, Investigation of Electron-Atom Laser Interactions, 1982. Mem. Am. Phys. Soc. (mem. divsn. atomic, molecular and optical physics, publ. com. 1994—), Optical Soc. Am., European Phys. Soc., Sigma Xi (Tidewater, Va. chpt.). Office: Old Dominion U Physics Dept Norfolk VA 23529

VYAS, VIJAY CHANDRAKANT, nephrologist; b. Vaso, Gujarat, India, Dec. 28, 1944; came to U.S., 1972; s. Chandrakant B. and Saroj C. (Bhatt) V.; m. Darshana V. Vin, June 6, 1972; children: Shilpa, Shweta. MB, BS, M.S. U., Baroda, India, 1966; MD, Baroda Med. Coll., 1970. Diplomate Am. Bd. Internal Medicine, Am. Bd. Nephrology. Resident internal medicine Cook County Hosp., Chgo., 1972-75, resident nephrology, 1975-77; chief med. staff Andalusia (Ala.) Hosp., 1983-84; med. dir. Diaylsis Clinic Andalusia, pvt. practice. Bd. trustees Andalusia Hosp., 1985-90, 94—. Mem. AMA, Am. Assn. Physicians from India (sec.), Covington County Med. Soc. (pres. 1987), Ala. State Med. Soc., Baroda Med. Soc., Rotary. Home: 114 Fosdick St Andalusia AL 36420-4110 Office: Vyas & Vyas PO Box 1065 Andalusia AL 36420-1065

WAAGE, MERVIN BERNARD, lawyer; b. Spirit Lake, Iowa, May 12, 1944; s. Bernard and Pearl Peterson W.; m. Eileen Barbara Waage, Feb. 17. 1947; children: Love Lee, Mark Warren. BA, Northwestern Coll., Roseville, Minn., 1966; MDiv, Southwestern Sem., 1969; JD, So. Methodist U., 1974. Bar: Tex. 1974, U.S. Dist Ct (no. dist.) Tex. 1974, U.S. Dist. Ct. (ea. dist.) Tex. 1976, U.S. Supreme Ct. 1977, U.S. Tax Ct. 1978, U.S. Ct. Claims, 1978, U.S. Dist. Ct. (we. dist) Tex. 1988, U.S. Ct. Appeals (5th cir.) 1989. Asst. dist. atty. Denton County (Tex.) Atty.'s Office, 1974-76; pvt. practice law Denton, Tex., 1977—; bankrupcy trustee, 1980-87. Mem. Tex. Bar Assn., Tex. State Bar (bankruptcy com.), Tex. Bd. Legal Specialization (cert. in consumer bankruptcy 1986, cert. in bus. bankruptcy 1988). Republican. Baptist. Home: 107 Lexington Ln Denton TX 76205-5473 Office: Waage & Waage LLP 8350 S Stemmons St Denton TX 76205-2424

WABLER, ROBERT CHARLES, II, retail and distribution executive; b. Dayton, Ohio, Dec. 14, 1948; s. Robert Charles Sr. and Eileen Marie (Langen) W.; m. Linda Adele Rayburn; 1 child, Robert Charles III. BS in Acctg. cum laude, U. Dayton, 1971; MS in Acctg. magna cum laude, U. Ga., 1976. Sr. auditor Touche Ross and Co., Dayton, 1971-73; internal auditor So. Company Services, Atlanta, 1974-75; acctg. mgr. Rich's div. Federated Dept. Stores, Atlanta, 1976-77; dir. auditing Munford, Inc., Atlanta, 1977-81, v.p., controller, 1982-83, v.p. fin. analyses, 1983-86; v.p. adminstrn. World Bazaar div. Munford, Inc., Atlanta, 1981-82, sr. v.p. fin., 1986-89; sr. v.p. fin. and administrn., sec. The Athlete's Foot Group, Inc., Atlanta, 1989-93; exec. v.p., CFO, treas. Just for Feet Inc., Birmingham, Ala., 1993—. Author: The Minimum Expenses Needed Technique, 1985. Mem. AICPA, Ga. Soc. CPAs, Inst. Internal Auditors, Assn. Systems Mgmt., EDP Auditor Assn. (bd. dirs. 1978-79). Home: 1541 Fairway View Dr Hoover AL 35244-1316 Office: Just For Feet Inc 153 Cahaba Valley Pkwy N Pelham AL 35124

WACHSMANN, SHELLEY A.Z., archaeology educator; b. Regina, Sask., Can., Nov. 9, 1950; came to U.S., 1990; s. Haskel Armin and Friedel (Zeisler) W.; m. Pearl Atzmona, Feb. 26, 1974 (div.). BA, Hebrew U., 1974, MA, 1984, PhD, 1990. Inspector underwater antiquities Israel Antiquities Authority, 1976-89; Meadows vis. asst. prof. Bibl. Archaeology Tex. A&M U., College Station, 1990-93, Meadows asst. prof. Bibl. Archaeology, 1993—; advisor Time-Life, Inc., 1987; lectr. numerous instns. including Anglo-Israel Archaeol. Soc., London, Ashmolean Mus., Oxford, Bible Lands Mus., Jerusalem, Bibl. Arts Ctr., Dallas, Cambridge (Eng.) U., Carnegie Mus., Pitts., City Mus., London, Cobb Inst. Archaeology, Miss. State U., Coun. for the Advancement of Sci. Writing, New Horizons in Sci. Briefing, Chgo., Drew U., Harvard U. Semitic Mus., Inst. Archaeology, Oxford, London U., Manchester Nautical Mus., Princeton U., St. Andrews U., Scotland; participant numerous confs. Author: Aegeans in the Theban Tombs, 1987, The Excavations of an Ancient Boat from the Sea of Galilee, 1990, Seagoing Ships and Seamanship in the Bronze Age Levant, The Sea of Galilee Boat: An Extraordinary 2000 Year Old Discovery, 1995; author: (with others) The Sea Remembers, 1987, Commerce in Palestine Throughout the Ages: Studies, 1990, Conway's History of the Ship: The Age of the Galley; mem. editl. bd. Studies in Nautical Archaeology; contbr. articles to profl. jours. Served with Israeli Mil., 1969-70, to sgt. maj. Res., 1973-90. Decorated Yom Kippur War ribbon, Lebanese War ribbon. Fellow Nat. Explorers Club; mem. Am. Schs. Oriental Rsch., Archaeol. Int. Am., Bibl. Archaeology Soc., Soc. for Nautical Rsch., Nautical Archaeology Soc., Israel Exploration Soc., Inst. Nautical Archaeology, Hellenic Inst. Marine Archaeology (corr.). Office: Tex A&M U Nautical Archaeology Program College Station TX 77843

WACHSMUTH, ROBERT WILLIAM, lawyer; b. Crowell, Tex., Jan. 20, 1942; s. Frederick W. and Dorothy (McKown) W.; children: Wendi Leigh, Ashley Beth, Matthew McKown; m. Cynthia Faught Malone, June 29, 1994. BA, U. Tex., 1965, JD, 1966, grad. bus. sch., 1976. Bar: Tex. 1966, U.S. Dist. Ct. (we. dist.) Tex. 1970, U.S. Ct. Appeals (5th cir., 11 cir.) 1975, U.S. Supreme Ct. 1979, U.S. Dist. Ct. (so. dist.) Tex. 1987. Assoc. Foster, Lewis, Langley, Gardner and Banack, San Antonio, 1969-73; of counsel H.B. Zachry Co., San Antonio, 1973-79; ptnr. Johnson, Johnston, Bowlin, Wachsmuth and Vives, San Antonio, 1973-79, Kelfer, Coatney & Wachsmuth, San Antonio, 1979-81, Kelfer, Coatney, Wachsmuth & Saunders, San Antonio, 1981-83, Brock & Kelfer, P.C., San Antonio, 1983-88, Coatney & Wachsmuth, P.C., San Antonio, 1989-92, Gendry, Sprague & Wachsmuth, P.C., San Antonio, 1992-94, The Kleberg Law Firm, P.C., San Antonio, 1994—; panel arbitrators Fed. Ct. Annexed Program, San Antonio, 1987—, Bexar County Arbitration Program, San Antonio, 1988; instr. San Antonio Jr. Coll., 1972-74; bd. cert./civil trial law Tex. Bd. Legal Specialization, 1981—; mem. faculty constrn. mgmt. and contrn. exec. program Tex. A&M U. Contbr. articles to profl. jours. Bd. dirs. Halfway House San Antonio. Capt., mil. judge USMCR, 1966-69, Vietnam. Mem. ABA, Tex. State Bar Assn. (bd. dirs., treas., sec., vice chmn. constrn. law sect. 1989-92, chmn. 1992-93), Am. Arbitration Assn. (panel of arbitrators, panel of mediatros), San Antonio Bar Assn. (chmn. alternative dispute resolution com.), Fed. Bar Assn., Am. Subcontractors Assn. (gen. counsel San Antonio chpt. 1984-92), Assn. Gen. Contractors (gen. counsel San Antonio chpt. 1995—), Plaza Club (social com.), Masons, Scottish Rite, Shriners, Optimists (pres. 1977-78). Republican. Episcopalian. Office: The Klebery Law Firm PC 112 E Pecan Ste 2200 San Antonio TX 78205

WACKENHUT, RICHARD RUSSELL, security company executive; b. Balt., Nov. 11, 1947; s. George Russell and Ruth Johann (Bell) W.; m. Mariane Hutson Ball, Mar. 13, 1971; children: Jennifer Anne, Lisa Renee, Ashley Elizabeth, Lauren Hutson. BA in Polit. Sci., The Citadel Mil. Coll., 1969; grad. bus. sch. advanced mgmt. program, Harvard U., 1987. With Wackenhut Corp., Coral Gables and Palm Beach Gardens, Fla. and Columbia, S.C., 1973—; v.p. ops. Wackenhut Corp., Coral Gables, 1981-82, sr. v.p. domestic ops., 1982-83, sr. v.p. ops., 1983-86, pres., chief operating officer, 1986—, also bd. dirs. various subs.; bd. dirs. Assoc. Industries of Fla. Mem. Internat. Assn. Chiefs Police, Internat. Security Mgmt. Assn., Am. Soc. Indsl. Security. Republican. Christian Scientist. Office: Wackenhut Corp 4200 Wackenhut Dr Ste 100 Palm Bch Gdns FL 33410-4243

WADDELL, PHILLIP DEAN, lawyer; b. Covington, Ky., Nov. 14, 1948; s. Ewell Edward and Sarah Isobel (Dean) W.; m. Jill Annette Tolson, Aug. 23, 1975; children: Nathan Ewell, James Seth. BA, Centre Coll. Ky., 1971; JD, No. Ky. U., 1982. Bar: Ky. 1982, Ohio 1983, Tenn. 1986. V.p., mgr. escrow Eagle Savings Assn., Cin., 1973-83; v.p. Union Planters Nat. Bank, Memphis, 1983-84; sr. v.p., liason First Nat. Bank & Trust Co., Oklahoma City, 1984-86; sr. v.p., sec., gen. counsel First Mortgage Strategies Group, Inc., Memphis, 1986-92; atty. pvt. practice, Memphis, 1992—. Mem. ABA, Am. Judicature Soc., Ky. Bar Assn., Tenn. Bar Assn. Republican. Presbyterian. Lodge: Kiwanis. Home: 2095 Allenby Rd Memphis TN 38139-4343 Office: 1789 Kirby Pkwy Ste 2 Memphis TN 38138-3657

WADDELL, R. EUGENE, minister; b. Wayne County, N.C., Feb. 7, 1932; s. Robert Lee and Rena (Holland) W.; m. Elva Leah Nichols, July 22, 1954 (dec. Apr. 1962); children: Rhonda Waddell Sagraves, Robert, Paul, Marcia Waddell Thompson; m. Genevieve Johnson, July 4, 1963; children: Michael, John. BA, Free Will Bapt. Bible Coll., Nashville, 1954; MA, Columbia (S.C.) Bibl. Sem., 1966. Ordained to ministry Free Will Bapt. Ch., 1952. Pastor Bay Branch Free Will Bapt. Ch., Timmonsville, S.C., 1954-56, 1st Free Will Bapt. Ch., Portsmouth, Va., 1956-60, Garner (N.C.) Free Will Bapt. Ch., 1960-64, Cofer's Chapel Free Will Bapt. Ch., Nashville, 1964-81; assoc. dir. Free Will Bapt. Fgn. Missions Dept., Nashville, 1981-86, gen. dir.,

1986—; bd. dirs. Free Will Bapt. Fgn. Missions, Nashville, 1959-78, bd. sec., 1971-78; founder, editor Free Will Bapt. Witness, Garner, 1962-63. Office: Free Will Bapt Fgn Missions 5233 Mount View Rd Antioch TN 37013-2306*

WADDELL, WILLIAM ROBERT, lawyer; b. Ft. Thomas, Ky., Nov. 24, 1940; s. Ewell Edward and Sara Isabel (Dean) W.; m. Linda Kay Waddle, Aug. 25, 1962; children: Robert William, Keith Edward, Alex Watson. AB, Williams Coll., 1962; JD, U. Va., 1965. Bar: Va. 1965, U.S. Dist. Ct. (ea. dist.) Va. 1966, U.S. Ct. Appeals (4th cir.) 1966, U.S. Suprme Ct. 1966, N.C. 1991. Assoc. McGuire, Woods, Battle & Boothe, Richmond, Va., 1965-69, ptnr., 1969—; lectr. Sch. Law, U. Va.; bd. dirs. Steward Sch. Found., Richmond, The George Found., Hickory, N.C., Daughtie's Foods, Inc., Road Atlanta, Ltd., Alex Lee, Inc. Contbr. articles to profl. jours. Pres. Bon Air Community Assn., Richmond, 1979-80; bd. dirs., sec. Va. Advanced Tech. Assn., Richmond, 1986—; chmn. The Steward Sch., 1985-88, Jr. Achievement of Richmond, Inc., 1989-90. Mem. ABA (comml. code com., sales subcom. 1982—, chmn. telecomms. com. 1986-90, 94-96, vice-chmn. com. on laws of commerce in cyberspace 1996—, dispute resolution com. 1990—), Va. Bar Assn., Richmond Bar Assn. (chmn. econs. of law practice com. 1978-79), Norfolk/Portsmouth Bar Assn., George Mason U. Century Club (founder), Willow Oaks Country Club, Bull & Bear Club, Order of Coif. Office: McGuire Woods Battle Boothe 1 James Ctr 901 E Cary St Richmond VA 23219

WADDLE, CHRIS, editor; b. Ft. Worth, Oct. 30, 1944; s. James Addison and Doris Bell (Cunningham) W.; m. Sherrell Hardin, Dec. 26, 1965; children: Hardin, Virginia. BA, Birmingham-So. Coll., 1965; MS, Columbia U., 1971. Copy editor Birmingham (Ala.) Post-Herald, 1965-66, edn. reporter, 1968-70; reporter The Courier-Jour., Louisville, 1971-73, Washington corr., 1973-74, features editor, 1974-76, city editor, 1976-78; Sunday mag. editor Kansas City (Mo.) Times, 1978-79, mng. editor, 1979-82; mng. editor, editorial page editor The Anniston (Ala.) Star, 1982—, chief editorial writer, 1982—; chair New Coun. Ala., 1985; speaker social and civic orgns. Commentator Ala. Pub. TV, Montgomery, 1984—. Mem. Leadership Ala., Montgomery,1992—; cmty. advisor Jr. League, Anniston, 1995—; mem., founder 100 Citizens of Anniston, 1994—; pres. Com. of Unified Leadership, Anniston, 1982—. With U.S. Army, 1966-68. Pulliam fellow Soc. Profl. Journalists, 1988; Exch. fellow Internat. Pub. Inst., Japan, 1984, German Acad. Fellowship, 1983. Mem. Commentary Page Editors Ala. (founding mem.), Nat. Conf. Editorial Page Editors, So. Ctr. for Internat. Studies (assoc.), Ala. AP Assn. Episcopalian. Office: Anniston Star PO Box 189 Anniston AL 36202

WADE, JAMES BRADLEY, writer; b. Garden Grove, Calif., Feb. 14, 1964; s. Robert Dale and Ruth Elizabeth (Ameen) W. BA in English, Conn. Coll., 1988. Writer Galesburg (Ill.) Post, 1981-82; corr. aide James Merrill, Stonington, Conn., 1986-88; tutor Conn. Coll., New London, 1987-88; sect. mgr. Oxford Books, Atlanta, Ga., 1989-93, Oxford Too Books, Atlanta, 1993-94; writing tutor DeKalb Coll., Decatur, Ga., 1995—; rater Regent's Test, Atlanta, 1996. Vol. Clinton '92 Campaign, Atlanta, 1992. Democrat. Roman Catholic. Home: 229 Valley Brook Crossing Decatur GA 30033

WADE, JAMES P., JR., government official, industry executive; b. Richmond Heights, Mo., Dec. 26, 1930. BS, U.S. Mil. Acad., 1953; MS, U. Va., 1959; PhD in Physics, 1961. Mem. staff NATO Def. Coll., Paris, 1955-57; mem. physics staff Lawrence Radiation Lab., 1961-65; ops. directorate USCINCEUR, Paris, 1966-67; mem. staff Def. Advanced Research Agy., 1968-69, Office of Strategic and Space Systems, Def. Research & Engring., 1970-72; dir. Office of Sec. of Def. Salt Support Group, 1972-74, 1974-77; asst. for analysis Office of Under Sec. of Def. for Research and Engring., 1977-78; chmn. Mil. Liaison Com. to Dept. Energy, 1978-80; asst. to Sec. Def. for Atomic Energy, 1978-81; prin. dep. undersec. for Research and Engring. Dept. Def., 1981-85; asst. sec. of def. for devel. and support Dept. Def., Washington, 1984-85, acting under-sec. of def. for research and engring., 1984-85; asst. sec. of def. Acquisition and Logistics, 1985-86; chmn. of bd., CEO Def. Group Inc., 1987—. Recipient Dept. Def. medal for disting. Pub. Svc. with Silver Palm. Home: 11417 Hook Rd Reston VA 22090-4420 Office: Def Group Inc 307 Annandale Rd Falls Church VA 20190-2400

WADE, JULIA HOWARD, interior designer; b. Alexandria, La., Dec. 2, 1928; d. Samuel Eugene and Louis D'Or (Moore) Howard; B.A., Baylor U., 1948; student La. Coll., 1946; m. Nelsyn Ernest Brooks Wade, June 29, 1948; children: Sylvia Laureen, Lisa Frances, William Alan, David Eugene. Organizer, dir. Children's Theatre, San Augustine, Tex., 1948-52; tchr. English San Augustine High Sch., 1948; ptnr., decorator, advt. mgr., buyer Nelsyns Furniture Store, San Augustine, 1958—; lectr. in field. Hist. chmn. 8-County Deep East Tex. Devel. Assn., 1975; bd. dirs. San Augustine Public Library, 1980-82, pres., 1984-85; bd. devel. E. Tex. Bapt. Coll., 1978-82; chmn. San Augustine County Hist. Commn., 1993-96, WWII Commemorative Com. Celebrations San Augustine County. Named Outstanding Small Retailer, S.W. Home Furnishings Assn., 1979; recipient Pres.'s award, C. of C., 1973, Rotary award, 1980, Outstanding Dealer, Kirsch, 1985, George Washington medal of Honor Freedoms Found. Valley Forge, 1988. Mem. C. of C. (v.p. 1972-77, co-recipient Outstanding Citizens award 1987), v.p. Regent, 1996-97, S.W. Home Furnishings Assn. (cert.), Nat. Assn. Retail Dealers of Am., NAFE, Tex. Old Missions and Forts Restoration Assn., Nat. Trust Hist. Preservation, Baylor U. Alumni Assn., Tex. Forestry Assn., DAR (chmn. Constn. com. 1980—, writer, dir. U.S. Constn. 200th Anniversary drama 1987), (pres. 1975-77, sec. 1993-96), San Augustine County Hist. Soc., Am. Soc. Interior Designers, (ASID), Window Coverings Assn. Am. (charter 1986-87). Republican. Baptist. Clubs: Heritage (pres. 1963), Bible (pres. 1953, 57). Lodge: Gideons (v.p. and program chmn. aux. 1986-96). Home: 412 Baxter St San Augustine TX 75972-2608 Office: 128 E Columbia St San Augustine TX 75972-1902

WADE, MALCOLM SMITH, chemist, chemical engineer; b. Owensville, Ind., June 3, 1923; s. Frank Eliot and Margaret (Smith) W.; m. Mary Lou Gurley, May 17, 1958; 1 child, Marvin Lee. AB in Chemistry, Ind. U., 1949, BS in Edn., 1950, AB in Social Sci., 1950; postgrad., U. Kans., 1960. Project chemist Gulf Oil Corp. AG Div., Pittsburg, Kans., 1959-66; start-up advising engr. Kuwait Chem. Fertilizer Co., Pittsburg, 1966; chief chemist, fin. mgr. Chinhae Chemn. Co., Chinhae, Korea, 1966-69; sr. project chemist Gulf Oil Corp., Shuiba, Kuwait, 1969-70; start-up chief chemist and engr. PIC, Gulf Oil Corp., Shuiba, 1970-72; tech. dept. mgr. Fertilizer Co. of Saudi Arabia, Dammam, 1973-76; LNG storage and sect. head ops. R.M. Huffington, Bontang, Indonesia, 1976-78; advisor, trainer P.T. Arun (Mobil Oil assignment), Lhukseu, Indonesia, 1978-83, engr. for LNG expansion, 1983-84, spl. project engr., 1984-86. Deacon Grace Presbyn. Ch., Jackson, Tenn. Home: Apt 91-L Carolane Dr Jackson TN 38301

WADE, MARGARET GASTON, real estate property manager, educator; b. Shreveport, La., Feb. 26, 1948; d. Leroy Evans and Helena (DeWitt) Gaston; m. William Burgess Wade, May 24, 1969; children: Helena Elizabeth, Catherine Frances. BA, Stephen F. Austin State U., 1969; EdD, Tex. Tech U., 1995, Texas Tech. U., 1995. Cert. tchr., Tex. Tchr. Redland (Tex.) Sch. Dist., 1969-70, Lubbock (Tex.) Ind. Sch. Dist., 1971-73, San Antonio Coll., 1974-75, Midland (Tex.) Coll., 1975-78; owner, mgr. real estate investments BHM Enterprises, Midland, 1977—; tchr. Odessa Coll., Midland Coll., 1989-90, Midland Coll., 1989—; tchr. Hillander Sch., Midland, 1980-81. Troop leader Girl Scouts U.S., Midland, 1983-89; bd. dirs. Planned Parenthood, Midland, 1980-83; chmn. teen ct. Midland Jr. League, 1985-87, bd. dirs., 1987-88. Mem. Chi Omega Alumnus Assn. (pres. Midland chpt. 1978-79). Republican. Methodist. Club: Midland Lawyer's Wives (corr. sec. 1986-87). Home and Office: 705 Doral Ct Midland TX 79705-1926

WADE, RONALD E., state municipal administrator; b. Gilmer, Tex., Sept. 15, 1950; s. Ellis Whitfield and Rosedyne (Langford) W.; m. Catherine Sue Rachel, Feb. 16, 1985. AA, Kilgore Coll., 1971; BBA, U. Tex., 1973. Office mgr. Lt. Gov. Tex., Austin, 1971-73; press liaison Pres. Richard M. Nixon, Washington, 1973-74; office mgr. Gen. Pub. Rels., Palm Springs, Calif., 1975-77; owner, operator Wade Mart Stores, Lone Star, Tex., 1978-84; social svc. supervisor Tex. Dept. Human Svcs., Carthage, 1985—; pres. liaison V.p. George Bush, Washington, 1984; vice chmn., chmn. Pres.'s Youth Adv. Coun. Selective Svc., Washington, 1970-74; mem. Pres. Bush's Inaugural Com., Washington, 1988-89. Author: A Pioneer Southern Family Life, 1967, The Langford Legacy, 1986. Pres. Upshur County Young Reps., Gilmer, Tex, 1968-71, Kilgore (Tex.) Coll. Young Reps., 1970-71; del. Rep. Nat. Convention, New Orleans, 1988, state convs., Tex., 1974-94. Mem. Am. Political Item Collectors. Methodist. Home: 2100 Lafayette Dr Longview TX 75601

WADE, SUZANNE, computer software company consultant; b. Chgo., Dec. 29, 1938; d. Edward Peter and Dorothy Rose Traxel; m. Robert Gerald Wade (div. Feb. 1980); children: Peter John, Robert Gerald Jr., Suzette Marie, Francesca Louise Felde, Elizabeth Rose Quigley. AA, Orange Coast Coll., 1980; BA, Calif. State U., Fullerton, 1985. Analyst data info. Motorola, Mesa, Ariz., 1972-75; planner prodn. Ford Aerospace, Newport Beach, Calif., 1975-79; supr. prodn. control Shiley, Inc., Irvine, Calif., 1979-81; mgr. bus. systems Hughes Aircraft Co., Fullerton, 1981-85; systems adminstr. Long Beach, Calif., 1985-89; cons. IBM, Gaithersburg, Md., 1989-94; computer assoc. project mgr. U.S. Mint Project, 1994-95; cons. Oracle Corp., 1996—; lectr. to clubs, classes Calif. State U., Fullerton, 1984-85; speaker in field. Author: (manual) Data Services, 1985; columnist, 1984-85. Mem. NAFE, Am. Prodn. and Inventory Control Soc. (editor Digest 1990-91), L.A. Aerospace and Def. Spl. Interest Group (editor Digest 1987-90), Toastmasters (treas. Long Beach 1986). Episcopalian. Home: 7630 Coddle Harbor Ln Potomac MD 20854-3202 Office: Oracle Corp 196 Van Buren St Herndon VA 20170

WADE, THOMAS EDWARD, health and social services executive; b. Kansas City, Mo., Apr. 15, 1950; s. Wilford DeBerry and Anne Marie (Mallen) W.; m. Eleanor Regina Signs, Sept. 18, 1972; children: Rebecca Signs Wade, Katherine Signs Wade. BA, U. Ga., 1974, MPA, 1976. Caseworker Fulton County Dept. Family and Children Svcs., Atlanta, 1976-77; planning dir. Community Action for Improvement, Inc., LaGrange, Ga., 1977-80; planner Ga. Dept. Human Resources, Atlanta, 1980-83, dep. dir. adminstrv. svcs., 1983-89; dir. adminstrv. svcs. Ga. Dept. Human Resources, Pub. Health, Atlanta, 1989-92; asst. commr. Ga. Dept. Human Resources, Atlanta, 1992—. Contbr. articles to profl. jours. Vol. Grady Hosp., Atlanta, 1988—. Mem. ASPA, Ga. Soc. for Pub. Adminstrn., Ga. Pub. Health Assn. Democrat. Office: Ga Dept Human Resources 47 Trinity Ave SW Atlanta GA 30334-9006

WADE, THOMAS EDWARD, electrical engineering educator, university research administrator; b. Jacksonville, Fla., Sept. 14, 1943; s. Wilton Fred and Alice Lucyle (Hedge) W.; m. Ann Elizabeth Chitty, Aug. 6, 1966; children: Amy Renee, Nathan Thomas, Laura Ann. BSEE, U. Fla.-Gainesville, 1966, MSEE, 1968, PhD, 1974. Cert. Rsch. Adminstr., 1992—. Interim asst. prof. U. Fla.-Gainesville, 1974-76; prof. elec. engring. Miss. State U., Starkville, 1976-85, state-wide dir. microelectronics rsch. lab., Miss., 1978-85, assoc. dean., prof. electrical engring. U. South Fla., Tampa, 1985—, dir. Engring. Indsl. Experiment Sta., 1986-93, exec. dir. Ctrs. for Engring. Devel. and Rsch., 1985-90, mem. presdl. faculty adv. com. for rsch. and tech. devel., 1986-88, mem. fed. demonstration project com. for contracts and grants, 1986-88; mem. adv. bd. USF Exec. Fellows Program, 1987-91; chmn. evaluation task force applied rsch. grants program High Tech. and Industry Coun. State of Fla., 1988-90, vice chmn. microelectronics and materials subcom. 1987-93, mem. telecom. subcom., 1988-89, chmn. legis. report com. FHTIC, 1989-90; vice chmn. subcom. on microelectronics and materials Enterprise Fla. Innovation Partnership, 1993-94; mem. Tampa Bay Internat. Super Task Force, 1986-92, vice chmn. edn. com. 1988; dir. Fla. Ctr. for Microelectronics Design and Test, 1986-88; bd. dirs. NASA Ctr. Comml. Devel. of Space Comm. Ctr., Fla., 1990-93; rev. panel govt.-univ.-industry rsch. round table for fed. demonstration project, NAS, 1988; solid state circuit specialist Applied Micro-Circuits Corp., San Diego, 1981-82; sr. scientist NASA Marshall Space Flight Ctr., Huntsville, Ala., 1983; scientist Trilogy Semiconductor Corp., Santa Clara, Calif., 1984; organizer, chmn. Very Large Scale Integrated/Ultra Large Scale Integrated Multilevel Interconnection Conf., Seminar and Exhbn., editor proceedings, 1991—; organizer, gen. chmn. Dielectrics for Ultra Large Scale Integrated Multilevel Interconnection Conf., 1995—, Chem.-Mech.-Polish Planarization for Ultra Large Scale Integrated Multilevel Interconnection Conf., 1996—; cons. in field. Author: Polyimides for Very Large Scale Integrated Applications, 1984, (U.S. Army handbook) Modern Very Large Scale Integrated Circuit Fabrication Processess, 1984, Photosensitive Polyimides for Very Large Scale Integrated Applications, 1986, Very Large Scale Multilevel Interconnection Tutorial, 1987—, Very Large Scale Multilevel Interconnection Tutorial, 1987—; contbr. to encys.; contbr. 120 articles to profl. jours. Treas. Tampa Palms Civic Assn., 1994-95; vol., United Fund, Miss. State U., 1983-85. Recipient Outstanding Engring. Teaching award Coll. Engring. U. Fla., 1976, Cert. of Recognition NASA (5 times), 1981-88, Outstanding Rsch. award Sigma Xi, 1984, Outstanding Contbn. to Sci. and Tech. award Fla. Gov., 1989, 90. Mem. AAAS, NSPE, IEEE (sr. mem., guest editor periodical 1982, gen. chmn. Internat. Very Large Scale Integrated Multilevel Interconnection Conf. annually 1984-90, editor conf. proceedings 1984-90, chmn. acad. affairs com. CHMT Soc. 1984-86, gen. chmn. univ./govt./industry microelectronics symposium, 1981, tech. program commn., 1991, bd. dirs. workshop on tungsten and other refractory metals 1987-90), Am. Soc. Engring. Edn. (gen. chmn. engring. research counc. ann. meeting 1987, chmn. engring. rsch. coun. adminstrv. com. 1987-90, chmn. coun., 1990-92, session chmn. ann. meeting 1990, 92, bd. dirs. 1990-92, mem. Nominations Com. 1992-94, mem. Long Range Planning Com. 1992-95, recipient ASEE Centennial Cert. 1992, 2d Century Cert. 1993), World Future Soc., Internat. Soc. Hybrid Microelectronics, Assn. U.S. Army (bd. dirs. Suncoast chpt. 1991-93), Soc. Photo Optical Instrumentation Engring., Univ. Faculty Senate Assn. of Miss. (organizer 1985), Am. Vacuum Soc., Am. Phys. Soc., Am. Electronics Assn., Am. Inst. Physics, Nat. Coun. Univ. Rsch. Adminstrn., Soc. Rsch. Adminstrs. (external rels. com. for SRA 1988-91), Fla. Engring. Soc. (v.p. edn. com. 1987-92, pres. 1989-90, bd. dirs. 1989-90, Fla. engring. found. trustee 1989-90, ann. meeting steering com. 1989-90, Outstanding Svc. to the Profession award 1992), Soc. Am. Mil. Engring., Order of Engrs., 1991, Sigma Xi (v.p. 1985), Tau Beta Pi (Fla. Alpha chpt. pres. 1969, 71, nat. outstanding chpt. award 1969, 71, faculty advisor Miss. Alpha chpt. 1977-85, faculty advisor Fla. Gamma chpt. 1986—, recipient outstanding hon. soc. advisor award, 1994), Eta Kappa Nu (pres. 1968), Sigma Tau, Omicron Delta Kappa, Soc. Am. Inventors, Fla. Blue Key (v.p. 1972, sec, 1971), Epsilon Lambda Chi (founder 1970, pres. 1971). Club: Downtown Tampa Rotary (Paul Harris Fellow 1987, perfect attendance award 1986—, chmn. com. on environ. issues 1990), Rotary Club New Tampa (organizer, charter mem., pres. 1995-96, v.p. 1996—). Active First Bapt. Ch., Temple Terrace, Fla., vice-chmn. bd. deacons 1989-90, chmn. bd. deacons, 1990-91, 93-94, chmn. pastor search com. 1990-91, vice chmn. long range plannning com., 1989-91, vice chmn. pastor search com., 1994-95, dir. adult coed III Sunday sch. dept. 1993-94; ch. coun. 1994-95. Avocations: collecting antique furniture, carpentry, restoring antique sports cars, basketball. Home: 5316 Witham Ct E Tampa FL 33647-1026

WADENBERG, MARIE-LOUISE GERTRUD, psychopharmacologist, researcher; b. Stockholm, Nov. 11, 1944; d. Sten Helge and Maj Gertrud (Vilgon) Borgendahl; m. Anders Einar Wadenberg, Aug. 4, 1973 (div. Dec. 1988); children: Andreas, Sofia, Mattias. Pianist diploma, Borgarskolan, Stockholm, 1971; BA, U. Stockholm, 1984, PhD, 1994. Piano playing instr. Stockholm, 1968-86; asst. rschr. Astra Pharms., Södertälje, Sweden, 1989-90; postdoctoral fellow, prin. investigator Scott & White Clinic, Temple, Tex., 1994—. Contbr. articles to profl. jours. and sci. meeting abstracts. Grantee Swedish Med. Rsch. Coun., Stockholm, 1994, Swedish Rsch. Coun. in Humanities and Social Scis., Stockholm, 1995, 96, Swedish Inst., Stockholm, 1994, 95. Mem. AAAS, Soc. Neurosci., Internat. Brain Rsch. Orgn., European Neurosci. Assn., Serotoni Club, J.B. Johnston Club. Office: Scott and White Clinic Dept Psychiatry 2401 S 31st St Temple TX 76508

WAESCHE, R(ICHARD) H(ENLEY) WOODWARD, combustion research scientist; b. Balt., Dec. 20, 1930; s. J(oseph) Edward and Margaret Steuart (Woodward) W.; m. Lucy Spotswood White, June 29, 1957; children: Charles Russell, Ann Spotswood. BA, Williams Coll., 1952; postgrad. U. Ala., 1956-58; MA, Princeton U., 1962, PhD, 1965. Rsch. scientist Rohm & Haas Redstone div., Huntsville, Ala., 1954-59; rsch. asst. Princeton U., 1961-64; sr. rsch. scientist Rohm & Haas, Huntsville, 1964-66; sr. rsch. engr. United Tech. Rsch. Ctr., East Hartford, Conn., 1966-81; prin. sci. Atlantic Rsch. Corp., Gainesville, Va., 1981-93; sr. sci. Sci. Applications Internat. Corp., 1993—; cons. Goodyear Corp., 1959-60, Princeton U., 1965, NRC, 1985-86, NASA, 1987—, Def. Adv. Rsch. Project Agy., 1988—, Directed Techs, 1989—, Atlantic Rsch. Corp., 1992—, Battelle Meml. Inst., 1992—, Calif. Inst. Tech., 1995—. Assoc. editor Jour. Spacecraft and Rockets, 1975-80, editor-in-chief, 1980-86, Jour. Propulsion and Power, 1986—; contbr. numerous articles to profl. jours.; mem. exec. bd. Dictionary of Modern Science and Technology; mem. exec. adv. bd. Encyclopedia of Physical Science and Technology. Chmn. Fine Arts Commn., Glastonbury, Conn., 1975-77. Served to cpl. U.S. Army, 1952-54. Recipient JANNAF Recognition award, 1988; Guggenheim fellow, 1959-61. Fellow AIAA (chmn. propellants and combustion tech. com. 1975-77, propulsion tech. group coord. 1979-81, tech. activities com. 1979—, publs. com. 1980—, inst. devel. com. 1988—, fin. com. 1988—, dir. propulsion & energy 1992-95, bd. dirs. 1992-95, Best Paper in Solid Rockets 1989); mem. Am. Phys. Soc., Combustion Inst., Am. Def. Preparedness Assn., Internat. Pyrotechnics Soc., Sigma Xi. Episcopalian. Home: 4319 Banbury Dr Gainesville VA 20155 Office: Sci Applications Internat Corp 1710 Goodridge Dr Mc Lean VA 22102-3701

WAGAR, CHARLES KIGHTLY "KIT", journalist, educator; b. Castro Valley, Calif., Aug. 25, 1958; s. James Harwood and Billie Ruth (Lamb) W.; m. Linda Jean Saper, Jan. 25, 1981; 1 child, Clayton Eugene. BA in Econs., Journalism, San Francisco State U., 1980. Regional reporter The Idaho Statesman, Boise, 1980-82; polit. reporter The Evansville (Ind.) Courier, 1982-85; spl. projects reporter Lexington (Ky.) Herald-Leader, 1985—; instr. investigative reporting U. Ky., Lexington, 1995—; instr. pub. affairs reporting Ea. Ky. U., Richmond, 1988-94; spkr. Ky. Broadcasters Assn. Conf., 1991; reporting cons. Long Beach (Calif.) Press-Telegram, 1995. Advisor No. Calif. Scholarship Found., Oakland, 1981—. Recipient Best Comprehensive Spot News Coverage award Soc. Profl. Journalists, 1981, Best Comprehensive Spot News Coverage award Idaho Press Club, 1981, Best News Story, Inda. AP Mng. Editors, 1983, Best Investigative Story, Ky. Press Assn., 1987, 94, Best Spot News Story, Ky. Press Assn., 1988, Benjamin Fine award for Edn. Reporting, 1990, Pub. Svc. Journalism award Soc. Profl. Journalists, 1990, Investigative Reports and Editors award, 1990, Selden Ring award for investigative reporting, 1990, Best Extended Coverage, Ky. Press Assn., 1991, Best Bus. Story, Ky. Press Assn., 1994, finalist in investigative reporting AP Sports Editors Nat. Contest, 1994, Pub. Svc. Journalism award Soc. Profl. Journalists, 1995. Mem. Investigative Reporters and Editors (spkr. nat. conf. 1990, 91, 95). Home: 227 Irvine Rd Lexington KY 40502 Office: Lexington Herald Leader 100 Midland Ave Lexington KY 40508-1943

WAGENER, JAMES WILBUR, social science educator; b. Edgewood, Tex., Mar. 18, 1930; s. James W. and Ima (Crump) W.; m. Ruth Elaine Hoffman, May 31, 1952; children: LuAnn Wagener Powers, Laurie Kay Wagener Ulman. BA, So. Methodist U., 1951, BD, 1954; MA, U. Tex., Austin, 1967, PhD (Ellis fellow 1967-68), 1968. Instr. edn. U. Tex., Austin, 1967-68, asst. prof., 1970-74; asst. prof. U. Tenn., Knoxville, 1968-70; asst. to chancellor acad. affairs U. Tex. System, 1974; assoc. prof. U. Tex., San Antonio, 1974-78, acting pres., 1978, pres., 1978-89, prof. div. edn. Coll. Social and Behavioral Scis., 1978—; asst. to pres., then exec. asst. to pres. U. Tex. Health Sci. Center, San Antonio, 1974-78, acting dean Dental Sch., 1976-78. Author articles, book revs. in field. Bd. govs. Southwest Found. Research and Edn., San Antonio, 1978-89; bd. dirs., trustee Southwest Research Inst., 1978-89. Office: Dept Social Behavioral Scis U Tex at San Antonio San Antonio TX 78249-0654

WAGER, MICHAEL, company executive. Pres. Robert H. Wager Co. Address: Forum 52 Industrial Park 570 Montroyal Rd Rural Hall NC 27045

WAGES, VIRGINIA ANNE SOBOL, pediatrics nurse; b. Memphis, June 20, 1962; d. John Andrew and Jean Duffy (Gordon) Sobol; m. David Paul Wages, June 2, 1986; children: Ashley Anne, Julie Nichole, David Paul, Sarah Catherine. Student, Memphis State U., 1980-82; BSN, U. Tenn., 1985. RN, Tenn.; cert. pediatric nurse. Grad. nurse intern LeBonheur Children's Med. Ctr., Memphis, 1985, med.-surg. pediatric nurse, 1988-95, quality assurance coun., 1988-95, recruitment retention com., 1990-92, chair unit clin. practice coun., 1992; neurol./seizure monitoring nurse Le Bonheur Children's Med. Ctr., Memphis, 1995—. Mem. Memphis Maternal Welfare League, 1992—, Memphis Mus. Sys., 1987—, Memphis Zool. soc., 1987—, Children's Mus., 1995—, Dixon Gallery and Gardens, 1995—, Lactation Edn. and Promotion, Memphis, 1992, St. Luke's Meth. Ch., United Meth. Women's Group, Meth. Hosp. Women's Aux., 1996—; fundraising chairperson Christ the King Lutheran Sch., 1996-97. Named one of Top 100 Nurses in Memphis, Celebrate Nursing, 1991. Mem. Alpha Lambda Delta, Phi Eta Sigma, Gamma Beta Phi, Alpha Delta Phi (Gamma Eta chpt.). Methodist. Home: 4558 E Dearing Rd Memphis TN 38117-6509 Office: LeBonheur Childrens Med Ctr 848 Adams Ave Memphis TN 38103-2816

WAGGONER, JAMES VIRGIL, chemicals company executive; b. Judsonia, Ark., Oct. 29, 1927; s. Loren Dye and Vera (Meacham) W.; m. M.E. June Howell; children: Liz Waggoner Quisenberry, Jay. BS in Chemistry and Math., Ouachita Bapt. U., 1948, DSc (hon.), 1990; MS in Organic Chemistry and Math., U. Tex., 1950. Successively rsch. chemist, sales asst., asst. sales mgr., sales mgr. Monsanto, Texas City, Tex., 1950-57; dir. sales Monsanto, Springfield, Mass., 1957-59; product adminstr. Monsanto, St. Louis, 1959-61, dir. sales, 1961-63, dir. mktg., 1963-67, bus. dir., 1967-68, gen. mgr. petrochems. div., 1972-76, gen. mgr. cycle-safe div., 1976, corp. v.p., mng. dir. Plastics & Resins Co., 1977, group v.p., 1978-80; pres. petrochem. and plastics unit El Paso Co., Odessa, Tex., 1980-83; cons. to petrochem. industry Houston, 1984-85; pres., chief exec. officer Sterling Chems., Inc., Houston, 1986—; mem. adv. bd. 1st Comml. Bank, N.A., Little Rock; bd. dirs. Kirby Corp., Houston, Mail-Well Holdings, Inc., Englewood, Colo. Chmn. adv. coun. Coll. Natural Scis., U. Tex., Austin; mem. devel. coun. Ouachita Bapt. U.; bd. dirs. Tex. Rsch. League; bd. dirs., chmn. Good Samaritan Found., 1993-94; supporter, patron Star of Hope Mission; corp. leader, contbr. United Way, Texas City, LaMarque Area, Houston; mem. chmn.'s adv. bd. Rep. Nat. Conv. Mem. Nat. Petroleum Refiners Assn. (v.p., bd. dirs., exec. com.), Tex. Assn. Taxpayers (bd. dirs.). Home: 11 Shadder Way Houston TX 77019-1415 Office: Sterling Chems. Inc. 1200 Smith St Ste 1900 Houston TX 77002-4312*

WAGNER, CHARLENE BROOK, middle school educator, consultant; b. L.A.; d. Edward J. and Eva (Anderson) Brook; m. Gordon Boswell Jr. (div.); children: Gordon, Brook, John. BS, Tex. Christian U., 1952; MEd, Sam Houston U., 1973; postgrad., U. Tex., Austin, 1975, Tex. A&M U., 1977. Sci. educator Spring Branch Ind. Sch. Dist., Houston, 1970—; cons. Scott Foresman Pub. Co., 1982-83; owner Sci. Instrnl. Sys. Co., 1988—; rep. World Class Network; ind. travel agt. Mem. Houston Opera Guild, Houston Symphony League, 1992, Mus. Fine Arts, Mus. of Art of Am. West, Houston, 1989, Women's Christian Home, Houston, 1991; social chmn. Encore, 1988; mem. Magic Circle Rep. Women's Club. Mem. NEA, NAFE, AAUW, Tex. State Tchrs. Assn., Spring Branch Edn. Assn., Internat. Platform Assn., Wellington Soc. for Arts (Houston chpt.), Shepherd Soc., Watercolor Arts Soc., Art League Houston, Clan Anderson Soc., Heather and Thistle Soc., Houston Highland Games Assn. Episcopalian. Home: B54 2670 Marilee Ln Houston TX 77057-4264 Office: Spring Oaks Mid Sch 2150 Shadowdale Dr Houston TX 77043-2608

WAGNER, DOUGLAS ALAN, secondary school educator; b. Washington, June 20, 1957; s. Robert Earl and Bernice (Bittner) W.; m. Linda Sue Tinsley, July 18, 1981; 1 child, John Robert. BS in Indsl. Mgmt., Ga. Inst. Tech., 1980; student, N.C. State U., 1975-76; MEd in Math., Ga. State U., 1987, EdS, 1991, PhD in Math. Edn., 1994. Cert. spl. edn. tchr., Ga. Mfrs. rep. Hitachi Corp., Atlanta, 1981; tchr. math., football coach Gwinnett Bd. Edn., Lawrenceville, Ga., 1981-84, 85—, chmn. math. dept., 1995—; prodn. supr. Campbell Soup Co., Maxton, N.C., 1984-85; asst. varsity football coach Parkview H.S., Lilburn, Ga., 1981-90, head jr. varsity football coach, 1983-88; grad. rsch. asst. Atlanta Math. Project/NSF, 1990-94; steering com. Coll. Mgmt., Ga. Inst. Tech., Atlanta, 1983-84. Author curriculum materials. Tchr. ch. sch. St. Andrews Presbyn. Ch., Tucker, Ga., 1977-80, ordained elder, 1979—; pres. Westminister Presbyn. Ch. Choir, Snellville, Ga., 1989-90, elem. sch. coord., 1995-96. Mem. NEA, Ga. Assn. Educators, Nat. Coun. Tchrs. Math., Ga. Coun. Tchrs. Math., So. Assn. Colls. and Schs. (steering com. Parkview High Sch. 1988-89). Republican. Home: 1995 Pinella Dr Grayson GA 30221-1705 Office: Parkview High Sch 998 Cole Rd SW Lilburn GA 30247-5422

WAGNER, FRED JOHN, JR., petroleum geologist; b. Phila., Feb. 7, 1929; s. Fred John and Dorothy V. (Burrows) W.; m. Carolyn Lipe, June 4, 1955; children: Fred John III, Kristin L. BS in Geology, Franklin and Marshall Coll., 1951; MA in Geology, Washington U., St. Louis, 1954; postgrad. Tulsa U., 1969-71. Rsch. geologist Standard Oil Co. of N.J. including Carter Oil Co., Tulsa, Jersey Prodn. Rsch. Co., Tulsa, Esso Standard Libya, Tripoli, 1953-68; petroleum systems engr. IBM, Tulsa, 1968-69; staff geologist, profl. specialist, planning geologist Skelly Oil Co. (merged with Getty Oil Co.), Tulsa, 1969-79, ops. rsch. coord. Getty Oil Co., Tulsa, supr. geologic rsch., Houston, 1979-81; mgr. exploration/exploitation, Williams Exploration Co., Tulsa, 1981-82; lead geologist offshore ops., mgr. exploration computing systems, Getty Oil Co., Houston, 1982-84, regional exploration geologist, 1984-85; exploration systems adviser; instr. continuing edn. Tulsa U., 1981, 82, 90; v.p. info. svcs. Petrocons. SA, Geneva, 1986-88, pres. North Am. ops., 1988-89; instr. geol. computer applications Oil and Gas Cons. Internat., Tulsa, 1986-93. Editor Geobyte, Am. Assn. Petroleum Geologists, Tulsa, 1985-93. Served with U.S. Army, 1955-57. Mem. Am. Assn. Petroleum Geologists (AAPG-Am. Petroleum Inst. joint com. for statis. integrity of discovery data 1981-88, mem. com. on U.S. drilling stats., AAPG com. on drilling and producing expenditures, adv. coun. petroleum data system, cert. petroleum geologist, chmn. com. on stats. of drilling 1973-75, cert. of merit 1975, 93), Am. Inst. Profl. Geologists (cert. geologist), Soc. Petroleum Engrs. of AIME, Tulsa Geol. Soc., Houston Geol. Soc. Home: 4454 S Columbia Ave Tulsa OK 74105-5221

WAGNER, JAMES PEYTON, lawyer; b. McKinney, Tex., July 22, 1939; s. Otto James and Jane Peyton (Adams) W.; m. Patricia Anne Squires, June 16, 1962; children: Jarrod Shannon, Anne Paige, Leslie Lauren, James Russell. BA, Tex. Tech. U., Lubbock, 1961; LLB, So. Meth. U., 1964. Bar: Tex. 1964, U.S. Dist. Ct. (no. dist.) Tex. 1965, U.S. Ct. Appeals (3rd and 5th cirs.) 1996, U.S. Supreme Ct. 1996. Atty. United American Ins. Co., Dallas, 1969-70, Employer's Ins. of Wausau, Dallas, 1970-73, Crumley Murphy and Shrull, Ft. Worth, 1973-77, Fillmore & Camp, Ft. Worth, 1977-78, Penner, Jones, Keith & Wagner, Ft. Worth, 1978-80, Law Offices James P. Wagner, Ft. Worth, Dallas, 1964-69, 80-85; prin. Keith and Wagner, P.C., Ft. Worth, 1985-89; assoc. Brockermeyer & Assocs., Ft. Worth, 1989-90; ptnr. Fielding, Barrett & Taylor, Ft. Worth, 1990—. Author, contbr. course book: State Bar of Texas Personal Injury and Workers Compensation Practice Skills, 1987, 89. Mem. ATLA, State Bar Tex., Tarrant County Bar Assn., Coll. of State Bar Tex. Baha'i World Faith. Home: 4240 Sudith Ln Midlothian TX 76065-6332 Office: Fielding Barrett & Taylor 3400 Bank One Tower 500 Throckmorton St Fort Worth TX 76102-3708

WAGNER, JOHN PHILIP, safety engineering educator, science researcher; b. Trenton, N.J., Feb. 29, 1940; s. Joseph and Anna Wagner; m. Carol Anne Hammond, June 14, 1969; children: John Joseph (Jay), Timothy Andrew. BS in Chemistry, St. Joseph's U., 1961; MSChemE, Johns Hopkins U., 1964, PhDChemE, 1966. Registered profl. engr., Tex. Rsch. asst. chemistry Johns Hopkins U., Balt., 1961-62, rsch. fellow chem. engring., 1962-66; assoc. chemist Applied Physics Lab. Johns Hopkins U., Silver Spring, Md., summer 1962, sr. engr. Applied Physics, 1966-72; sr. rsch. scientist Factor Mut. Rsch. Corp., Norwood, Mass., 1972-73; rsch. supr. Gillette Rsch. Inst., 1973-78; staff engr., sr. staff engr. EXXON Rsch. and Engring. Co., 1978-83; assoc. prof. indsl. engring. Tex. A&M U., 1985-89, assoc. prof. nuclear engring., 1989—; assoc. dir. and rsch. engr. Food Protein Rsch. Devel. Ctr. Tex. Engring. Expt. Station., 1983-90; assoc. dir., rsch. engr. Engring. Bioscis. Rsch. Ctr Tex. A&M U., College Station, 1990—; cons. O'Melveny & Myers, L.A., 1987-88, Lawrence Livermore Nat. Lab., Exxon Co.-USA, Englehard Industries, Gillette Rsch. Inst., Liberty Mut., Champion Internat, John Deere. Mem. editl. adv. bd. Jour. Polymer-Plastics Tech. and Engring., 1987—, Indsl. Crops and Products, 1991-95; co-guest editor Jour. Bioresources Tech., 1991; contbr. chpts. to books, articles to profl. jours.; patentee in field. Grantee USDA/DOD, 1984-93. Mem. Am. Oil Chemists Soc. (environ. com. 1985-86), Assn. for the Advancement of Indsl. Crops, Am. Chem. Soc., Am. Inst. Chem. Engrs., Am. Soc. Engring. Edn., Cath. Alumni Club Balt. (pres. 1968), Sigma Xi, Phi Lambda Upsilon. Office: Tex A&M U Dept Nuclear Engring College Station TX 77843

WAGNER, LYNN EDWARD, lawyer; b. Mt. Holly, N.J., Feb. 10, 1941; s. Edward John and Alma Elizabeth (Mason) W.; m. Maureen Elizabeth Bach, May 25, 1973; children: Daniel Preston, Matthew Evan. BS, Drexel U., 1965; JD, Duke U., 1968. Bar: Mass. 1968, U.S. Dist. Ct. Mass. 1968, Fla. 1972, U.S. Dist. Ct. (mid. dist.) Fla. 1972, U.S. Ct. Appeals (5th cir.) 1972, U.S. Supreme Ct. 1972, Pa. 1975, U.S. Dist. Ct. (we. dist.) Pa. 1975, U.S. Ct. Appeals (4th cir.) 1977, U.S. Ct Appeals (11th cir.) 1978, U.S. Ct. Appeals (D.C. cir.) 1980, U.S. Ct. Appeals (3d cir.) 1985, U.S. Dist. Ct. (so. dist.) Fla. 1991, U.S. Dist. Ct. (no. dist.) Fla. 1992; cert. cir. ct. mediator, Fla. Assoc. Foley, Hoag & Elliot, Boston, 1968-70; asst. prof. law U. Fla., Gainesville, 1971-73; sr. trial atty. U.S. EEOC, Washington, 1973-74; assoc. Pitts, Eubanks, Ross & Rumberger, Orlando, Fla., 1974-75; ptnr. Berkman, Ruslander, Pohl, Lieber & Engel, Pitts., 1975-84, Kirkpatrick & Lockhart, Pitts., 1985-86, Rumberger, Kirk, Caldwell, Cabaniss, Burke & Wechsler, Orlando, 1986-91, Cabaniss, Burke & Wagner, Orlando, 1991-94, Baker & Hostetler, Orlando, 1995—. With USAR, 1960-61. Scholarship recipient Sch. Law, Duke U., Durham, N.C., 1965-68. Mem. ABA (litigation sect., employment law sect., forum on constrn. industry, dispute resolution section), Mass. Bar Assn., Pa. Bar Assn. (labor sect.), Fla. Bar Assn. (labor sect., fed. ct. practice sect., dispute resolution sect.), Am. Arbitration Assn. (mem. S.E. regional employment panel, constrn. panel, securities and comml. arbitration panel), Nat. Assn. Securities Dealers (mem. regulation arbitration and mediation panels for securities and employment cases), Fla. Acad. Profl. Mediators, Soc. Profls. in Dispute Resolution. Home: 198 Promenade Circle Heathrow FL 32746 Office: Baker & Hostetler 2300 SunBank Ctr 200 S Orange Ave Orlando FL 32801-3410

WAGNER, MICHAEL GRAFTON, investor, corporation executive, resources advisor, business consultant; b. Greenville, Ohio, May 31, 1935; BA, Vanderbilt U., 1957; With Henny Penny Corp., Eaton, Ohio, 1957-76, sales, 1957-60, dir. advt., 1960-63, dir. mktg., 1963-68, pres., chief exec. officer, 1968-76, also of Henny Penny, Ltd., Toronto, Ont., Can.; pvt. investor, 1976—; pres. Schaefer Corp., Madison, Ala., 1979-81; cons., pvt. investor Rair Systems Inc., Nashville, 1985-87; nat. accounts mgr. spl. products and projects Vulcan Hart Corp. Div. Premark Corp., 1987-89, Wagner Investments, 1989—. Area chmn. Vanderbilt U. Endowment Fund, Nashville, 1961-66, 70-74; fin. chmn. Tenn. Republican Com., 1977-78. Mem. Nat. Commadore Club, Alpha Tau Omega. Episcopalian (sec., treas., warden 1969-71). Home: PO Box 50338 Nashville TN 37205-0338

WAGNER, ROBERT DAVID, JR., banker; b. Bklyn., Jan. 17, 1942; s. Robert D. and Grace (Panitz) W.; m. Patricia M. Nicholson, Dec. 19, 1964; children: Lisa M., Christopher R., Kimberly A. A.B. in History, Holy Cross Coll., 1963; M.B.A., NYU, 1971. Asst. treas. Bankers Trust Co., N.Y.C., 1966-69, asst. v.p., 1969-71, v.p., 1971-78; v.p. First City Nat. Bank, Houston, 1978-80, sr. v.p., 1980-81, exec. v.p., 1981-86; dir. Bear Stearns & Co., N.Y.C. and Dallas, 1986-89; mng. dir. Bankers Trust Securities, Houston, 1989—. Served to capt. USMC, 1963-66. Mem. Ind. Petroleum Assn. Am., Internat. Assn. Drilling Contrators, Nat. Ocean Industries Assn.

WAGNER, ROBERT WAYNE, real estate executive; b. Lake Wales, Fla., Aug. 25, 1956; s. Robert G. and Bessie M. (Safford) W. Grad., Polk Community Coll., 1977. Lic. real estate profl. Tennis profl. U.S. Tennis Assn., Miami, Fla., 1975; troubleshooter Athletic Attic, Inc. Hdqrs., Gainesville, Fla., 1976-82; ops. mgr. Armel, Inc., Ft. Lauderdale, Fla., 1983-85; gen. mgr., mktg. dir. Cons. Realty Co., Clearwater, Fla., 1986-87; investment cons. Sudler Marling, Inc., Tampa, Chgo., 1987-89; gen. mgr., mktg. dir. Wilkow Real Estate Cos./Metro Mall, Ft. Myers, Fla., 1989-94; v.p. Trammell Crow Co., Ft. Myers, Fla., 1994—. Co-author: Athletic Attic, Inc. Corporate Manual, 1979; author: Bayonet Point Mall Tenant Handbook, 1986, Pompano Outlet Mall Tenant Handbook, 1987; asst. producer video tng. films Athletic Attic, Inc., 1980. Mem. Fla./Korea Econ. Com., 1988—. Recipient Meritorious Service award U. Fla., Gainesville, 1981, Disting. Service award Santa Fe Community Coll., Gainesville, 1981. Mem. S.E. U.S.-Japan Assn., Japan-Am. Soc. Fla., Real Estate Investment Soc., Internat. Coun. Shopping Ctrs., Fla. Coun. Shopping Ctrs., U.S. Tennis Assn. Republican. Office: Metro Mall Office 2855 Colonial Blvd Ste 100 Fort Myers FL 33912-1040

WAGNER, ROY, anthropology educator, researcher; b. Cleve., Oct. 2, 1938; s. Richard Robert and Florence Helen (Mueller) W.; m. Brenda Sue Geilhausen, June 14, 1968 (div. Dec. 1994); children: Erika Susan, Jonathan Richard. AB, Harvard U., 1961; AM, U. Chgo., 1962, PhD, 1966. Asst. prof. anthropology So. Ill. U., Carbondale, 1966-68; assoc. prof. Northwestern U., Evanston, Ill., 1969-74; prof. U. Va., Charlottesville, 1974—, chmn. dept., 1974-79; mem. cultural anthropology panel NSF, Washington, 1981-82. Author: Habu, 1972, The Invention of Culture, 1975, Lethal Speech, 1978, Symbols That Stand for Themselves, 1986. Social Sci. Research Council faculty research grantee, 1968; NSF postdoctoral research grantee, 1979. Fellow Am. Anthropol. Assn. Home: 726 Cargil Ln Charlottesville VA 22902-4302 Office: U Va Dept Anthropology University Station Charlottesville VA 22906

WAGNER, SAMUEL, V, secondary school English language educator; b. West Chester, Pa., Dec. 28, 1965; s. Samuel and Mary Ann (Baker) W.; m. Allison Lee Lewis, May 25, 1991; 1 child, Samuel Jackson. BS in English Lit., Haverford Coll., 1988; MEd, U. New Orleans, 1995. Intern in English, asst. coach Westtown (Pa.) Sch., spring 1989; tchr. upper sch. English Metairie (La.) Pk. Country Day Sch., 1989—; asst. varsity soccer coach Metairie Pk. Country Day Sch., 1989-94; advisor to student senate Metairie Country Day Sch., 1990-95, chairperson/headmaster adv. com., 1994—, coll. counselor, 1995—; presenter ann. conf. Ind. Sch. Assn. of the South, New Orleans, 1992, 96. Mem. NASAA, NASSP, So. Assn. for Coll. Admissions Counseling, Nat. Assn. of Coll. Admissions Officers, Nat. Coun. Tchrs. of English, La. Coun. Tchrs. of English, Alpha Theta Epsilon, Phi Delta Kappa, Kappa Delta Pi. Republican. Mem. Soc. of Friends. Home: 416 Severn Ave Metairie LA 70001-5145 Office: Metairie Pk Country Day Sch 300 Park Rd Metairie LA 70005-4142

WAGNER, STEPHEN DEAN, editor; b. Oklahoma City, Jan. 25, 1962; s. Jerry Dean and Joyce Marie (Smith) W.; m. Denise Renee Tobey, Jan. 26, 1985. As in wildlife mgmt. entomology, E. Okla. State Coll., 1982; BA in photojournalism, Okla. State U., 1984. Newspaper sportswriter Donrey Media Group, Barlesville, Okla., 1985-86, Fort Smith, Ark., 1986-87; magazine writer Outdoor Okla., Oklahoma City, 1987-91; mng. editor Outdoor Okla., 1991-93, editor, 1993—. Contbr. articles to profl. jours. Recipient Okla. Media award Okla. Bowhunting Coun., Director's award Okla. Dept. of Wildlife Conservation, 1996. Mem. Assn. for Conservation Information, Outdoor Writers Assn. of Am. Office: Outdoor Oklahoma 1801 N Lincoln Oklahoma City OK 73105

WAGNER, WILLIAM BRADLEY, lawyer; b. Memphis, Dec. 30, 1949; s. William G. and Wilmeth (Norman) W. BS in Econs., U. Fla., 1971; JD, U. Va., 1974. Bar: U.S. Ct. Appeals (5th and 11th cirs.) 1981, Tex. 1989, U.S. Dist. Ct. (ea., fed. and so. dists.) Tex. 1989, U.S. Tax Ct. Ptnr. Fulbright & Jaworski, Austin, Tex., 1974—. Contbg. author: (handbook) Natural Gas Regulation. Home: 1600 Westlake Dr Austin TX 78746-3740 Office: Fulbright & Jaworski 600 Congress Ave Ste 2400 Austin TX 78701-3248*

WAGNER, WILLIAM ROBERT, lawyer; b. Ann Arbor, Mich., Dec. 30, 1959; s. Robert Lewis and Effie Roberta (Elftmann) W.; m. Marilyn Kay Jarvey, Mar. 24, 1986; children: Nicole, Luke. BA magna cum laude, Western Mich. U., 1982; postgrad., St. Louis U., 1986. Bar: Mo. 1986, U.S. Ct. Appeals (6th, 8th and D.C. cirs.) 1986. Officer 37th Jud. Cir. Mich., Battle Creek, 1982-83; legal counsel U.S. Senate, Washington, 1986; chief appellate litigation, asst. U.S. atty. Washington, 1987-89, 91—; chief counsel Mich. Senate Judiciary Com.; adj. prof. Mich. State U., 1989-91. Editor-in-chief St. Louis U. Law Rev.; co-author: Federal Practice Manual, 1993; contbr. articles to legal jours. Pres. Gethsemane Luth. Ch., Evang. Luth. Ch. Am. Thomas J. White scholar; St. Louis U. law fellow, Danforth fellow. Mem. ABA (vice chair victim rights com.), St. Louis Bar Assn., Am. Judicature Soc., Western Mich. U. Alumni Assn. Office: Dept Justice 104 N Main St Fl 4 Gainesville FL 32601-3347

WAHL, WILLIAM BRYAN, marketing professional, real estate officer; b. Aurora, Colo., Dec. 17, 1963; s. Harold Edward Wahl and Dianne (Fowler) Armstrong. BBA in Mgmt., St. Edward's U., 1987; MBA in Gen. Bus., Kent Coll., 1991. Asst. store mgr. Handy Dan, Austin, Tex., 1981-88; real estate broker Powell/Armstrong Realty, Austin, 1985—, S&W Realty, Austin, 1988—; nat. mktg. dir. Am. Home Products, Austin, 1988—; pres. Wahl Success Systems, Austin, 1989—; bd. dirs. Pahl Enterprises, Austin, 1988—. Named Outstanding Citizen, Berkeley Davis, Inc., Berkeley, Calif., 1988. Mem. Austin Assn. Life Underwriters, Austin Bd. Realtors, Tex. Assn. Realtors, Nat. Assn. Realtors, Nat. Assn. Life Underwiters, Mktg. and Distributive Edn. Roman Catholic. Home: 1206 Greenlawn Blvd Round Rock TX 78664-6918

WAHLBERG, KATHERINE ELEANOR, anthropologist; b. Ft. Myers, Fla., Jan. 10, 1955; d. Wesley Merriet and Lucy Keeling (Sisson) Higgins; m. Andrew Richard Wahlberg, June 1, 1974; children: Kurt Alexander, Megan Nicole. BA in Anthropology cum laude, NYU, 1983; postgrad., Fla. Atlantic U., 1993—. Archaeology lab. asst. Soil Systems, Inc., N.Y.C., 1981-82; tching. asst. Fla. Atlantic U., Boca Raton, 1991-92, contract work, dept. ethnic affairs, 1994. Recipient Founders Day award, NYU, 1983. Mem. Film Soc. S.W. Fla. (pres. 1990-92), Phi Beta Kappa, Lambda Alpha, Phi Kappa Phi. Home: 6548 Hartland St Fort Myers FL 33912

WAHLBRINK, JAMES ROY, construction executive; b. St. Charles, Mo., Mar. 15, 1941; s. Roy J. and Jennie Mae (Davidson) W.; m. Jeslyn Rader Wahlbrink, Apr. 6, 1968; children: Kara, Steven. BS in Real Estate, U. Mo., 1968. Sales ITT Terryphone, St. Louis, 1963-64; dealer sales Shell Oil Co., St. Louis, Springfield, 1964-67; mktg. mgr. Bank of St. Louis, 1968-69; property mgr. Crow Development Corp., Lake St. Louis, 1969-70; owner Wahlbrink's Gifts, St. Charles, Mo., 1970-84; dir. divns. Home Builders Assn., St. Louis, 1976-80; exec. dir. Home Builders Assn. Memphis, 1980-85; Contractors Assn. Sarasota, Fla., 1985-91; exec. officer Homebuilders Assn. Raleigh-Wake County, 1991—; dir. Exec. Officer Coun. NAHB, Washington, 1983, 84, 93, 94, 95, 96; pres. Exec. Officer Coun. NCHBA, Raleigh, N.C., 1996; mem. Neighborhood Resources Com., Raleigh, N.C., 1995-96, Affordable Housing Task Force, Raleigh, N.C., 1995. Mem. Kiwanis Clubs, St. Charles, Memphis, Raleigh, Sarasota, 1981—. Recipient Assoc. Exec. Achievement awards Exec. Officer Coun. NAHB, 1981-96; named Exec. Officer of Yr., 1993, Outstanding American, 1996, Exec. Officer Coun. NAHB. Mem. Am. Soc. Assn. Execs. Republican. Home: 8609 Davishire Dr Raleigh NC 27615 Office: Home Builders Assn Raleigh-Wake Co 6510 Chapel Hill Rd Raleigh NC 27607

WAHLS, HARVEY EDWARD, civil engineering educator; b. Evanston, Ill., Aug. 8, 1931; s. Albert C. and Lydia E. (Kutz) W.; m. Margaret B. Waggoner, Sept. 3, 1960; children: Richard A., Nancy K. BSCE, Northwestern U., Evanston, Ill., 1954, MS, 1955, PhD, 1961. Registered profl. engr., N.C. Instr. civil engring. Worcester (Mass.) Poly. Inst., 1955-57, asst. prof., 1957-60; instr. Northwestern U., 1957-59; asst. prof. N.C. State U., Raleigh, 1960-63, assoc. prof., 1963-69, prof. civil engring., 1969—, assoc. dept. head, 1983—; cons. in field. Fellow ASCE (chair geotech. divsn. 1982-83); mem. ASTM, Am. Soc. Engring. Edn., Internat. Soc. Soil Mechanics and Found. Engring., U.S. Nat. Soc. for Soil Mechanics and Found. Engring. (sec. 1985—). Office: NC State U Box 7908 Civil Engring Dept Raleigh NC 27695

WAHLSTROM, PAUL BURR, television producer; b. N.Y.C., Sept. 16, 1947; s. Frederick Dagget and Dorothy Borst (Rickard) W.; m. Kathryn Gabel, June 9, 1990; 1 child, Paul Jr.; 1 stepchild, Candice Wynn. Student, U. of Americas, Mexico City, 1968; BSBA, U. Denver, 1969. Exec. producer Irving (Tex.) Cmty. TV Network, 1981—; prodn. mgr. Channel 10, Danbury, Conn., 1979-81; mem. adv. com. North Lake Coll., Irving. Recipient Cable Ace award Nat. Acad. Cable Programming, 1983, 86-96, award Nat. Fedn. Local Cable Programmers, 1985-91, profl. video award JVC Corp., 1988, award Nat. League Cities, 1986-96, C.P. Snow award DeVry Inst., 1995. Mem. Dallas Comm. Coun., Press Club of Dallas (Katie award 1992, 93, 96). Office: Irving Community TV 233 S Rogers Rd Irving TX 75060-2608

WAID, STEPHAN HAMILTON, publishing executive; b. Richmond, Va., Oct. 6, 1948; s. Lewis Carroll and Helen Lois (McCann) W.; m. Margaret Rose Bouldin, Oct. 3, 1970; children: Ann Celeste, Stephan Andrew. BA, Old Dominion Univ., 1970. Sports writer Martinsville (Va.) Bulletin, 1970-71, Roanoke (Va.) Times, 1971-81; exec. editor Griggs Publ. Co., Concord, N.C., 1981-93; pub. Street & Smith's Sports Group, Charlotte, N.C., 1993—; cons. Am. City Bus. Jours., Charlotte, 1993—, Diamond Sports Group, Charlotte, 1995—. Editor: Circle of Triumph, 1990; editor, writer (newspaper) Winston Cup Scene, 1981—. With USMCR, 1970-76. Mem. Nat. Motorsports Press Assn. (pres. 1988—, awards), Nat. Driver of Yr. Panel (dir.). Home: 1400 Chadmore Ln Concord NC 28027 Office: Street & Smiths Sports Group 128 S Tryon St # 2275 Charlotte NC 28202

WAINBERG, SALOMON, accountant; b. Zelechow, Poland, Apr. 15, 1936. Acct. degree, Acad. Comml. Minerva, San Jose, Costa Rica, 1958; BBA, U. Miami, Fla., 1963; postgrad., Fla. Internat. U. CPA. Acct. Wiener, Stern and Hantman, Miami, 1960-65; ptnr. Goldstein Schechter Price Lucas Horwitz & Co., Miami, 1965—; adj. prof. Miami-Dade C.C., Fla. Internat. U. Bd. dirs. Metro Bank Dade County, Temple Zion, Temple Samuel, Greater Miami Chamber Orch., Greater Miami Jewish Fedn., Univ. Miami Citizens. Mem. AICPA, Nat. Assn. Accts., Fla. Inst. CPA (pres. Dade chpt., at large mem. bd. govs.), Colegio de Contabilidad Privados San Jose, Costa Rica, Bankers Club. Home: 8270 SW 86th Ter Miami FL 33143-6940 Office: Goldstein Schechter Price Lucas Horwitz & Co 2121 Ponce De Leon Blvd Coral Gables FL 33134-5224

WAIT, GEORGE WILLIAM, sales executive; b. Balt., Oct. 23, 1958; s. Frank H. Jr. and Betty (Cartwright) W.; m. Susan Erwin, Oct. 16, 1982; children: J. Stokes, Hannah S., C. Sam. BSBA, Western Carolina U., 1982. From sales rep. to regional sales asst. Gen. Mills Inc., Kinston, N.C., 1982-85; dist. sales mgr. Gen. Mills Inc., Charlotte, N.C., 1985-87; product sales mgr. Gen. Mills Inc., Mpls., 1987-89; mgr. promotions and merchandising Gen. Mills Inc., Raleigh, N.C., 1989-90, regional merchandising mgr., 1990—, regional tri healthway dir., 1992—, mgr. bus. devel., 1993—; corp. ops. mgr. Gen. Mills Inc., Cary, N.C., 1995—. Author: The Job Plan, 1991. Pres. A.V. Baucom Elem. Sch. PTO, Apex, N.C., 1991-93, chmn. Wake County Fun Festival; head coach '84 Explorers Soccer Team, 1990—; mem. YMCA Indian Guides, 1991—; mem. YMCA Youth Com., 1995—; mem. adv. com. Wake County Sch. Bd., 1996—. Mem. Grocery Mfrs. Retail Assn., KC (3d degree, outside guard 1982-83, inside guard 1983-84), Lambda Chi Alpha. Republican. Roman Catholic. Office: Gen Mills Inc PO Box 4349 Cary NC 27519

WAITE, JOY ELIZABETH, interior decorator; b. Boynton Beach, Fla., Aug. 29, 1964; d. John Henry and June (Thompson) W. AS in Interior Design, Art Inst. Ft. Lauderdale, 1984. Interior designer J.J. Chalk, West Palm Beach, Fla., 1984-88; supr. foreman Waite Painting Corp., Lake Worth, Fla., 1988-91; pres./owner J.E. Waite Corp., Lake Worth, Fla., 1991—. Mem. Am. Soc. Interior Designers (allied practioner), The Associated General Contractors of Am. (assoc.). Office: J E Waite Corp 3010A Broward Ave Lake Worth FL 33463-2006

WAITE, LEMUEL WARREN, library director; b. Ashland, Ky., July 13, 1955; s. Lemuel Crenshaw and Polly Jane (Davidson) W. BS, U. Ky., 1980, MLS, 1988. Bookkeeper Ky. Geol. Survey, Lexington, 1981-84; libr. asst. Ky. Christian Coll., Grayson, 1986-88, libr., 1988-89, dir. libr., 1989—; minister Blue Bank Christian Ch., Flemingsburg, Ky., 1988—, Moore's Ferry Christian Ch., Salt Lick, Ky., 1986-88. Author various poems and essays. Mem. ALA, APA, ACD, Speech Comm. Assn., Am. Theol. Libr. Assn., Disciples of Christ Hist. Soc., Ind. Hist. Soc., Beta Phi Mu. Democrat. Home: 501 Snodgrass Ln Grayson KY 41143-2102 Office: Ky Christian Coll Libr 100 Academic Pkwy Grayson KY 41143-2205

WAITES, WILLIAM ERNEST, advertising executive; b. Detroit, Dec. 14, 1934; s. William Ernest and Jean (Bryant) W.; m. Susanne Pinkett, Jan. 5, 1957; children: Bryant Andrew, Randel Schumann. BA, Mich. State U., 1956. Sr. v.p., creative dir. Young & Rubicam, Detroit, 1973-77; mng. dir. Young & Rubicam, Adelaide, Australia, 1977-79; sr. v.p., dir. creative svcs. Young & Rubicam, Chgo., 1979-81; vice chmn., chief creative officer Stone & Adler, Chgo., 1981-83; sr. v.p., group creative dir. Ogilvy & Mather, Chgo., 1983-89; pres. Huryup & Waites Creative Cons., Ft. Myers, Fla., 1989-94; chmn. The Spiro Group, Inc., Double W. Ltd., Taos, N.Mex., The Waites Group. Served to capt. USAF, 1957-60. Mem. Advt. Fedn. S.W. Fla. (bd. dirs.), Fla. Direct Mktg. Assn., Lambda Chi Alpha. Office: 6296 Corporate Ct Ste B202 Fort Myers FL 33919-3536

WAJIMI, TAKESHI, hematologist, medical oncologist, researcher; b. Ogi, Japan, Jan. 10, 1931; came to U.S., 1969; s. Kiichi and Hatsue (Nitta) W.; m. Yoshie Francis Furukawa, Jan. 9, 1964; children: Yutaka, Hiroshi, Makoto, Hikaru. BS in Pharmacy, Kanazawa (Japan) Pharm. Coll., 1952; MD, U. Kanazawa, 1960; PhD, Yamaguchi U., Ube, Japan, 1966. Rsch. fellow in pharm. sci. Kanazawa U., 1952-54; instr. medicine Yamaguchi U. Sch. Medicine, 1966-69; staff hematology/oncology Wilford Hall Med. Ctr., Lackland AFB, Tex., 1976-84; asst. prof. Uniformed Svcs. U. Health Sci., Bethesda, Md., 1980-84; clin. asst. prof. U. Tex. Health Sci. Ctr., San Antonio, 1977-84; staff physician Olin E. Teague Vets. Ctr., Temple, Tex., 1984—; asst. prof. Tex. A&M U. Sch. Medicine, Temple, 1984-87, assoc. prof., 1987-91, prof. internal medicine, 1991—; vis. rsch. assoc. Atomic Bomb Casualty Commn., Hiroshima, Japan, 1967-69; mem. S.W. Oncology Group, San Antonio, 1977—. Lt. col. USAF, 1976-82. Decorated Air Force Commendation medal, Meritorious Svc. medal. Mem. ACP, Am. Soc. Hematology, Internat. Soc. Hematology, Internat. Soc. Thrombosis and Haemostasis, Internat. Soc. Fibrinolysis, Soc. Air Force Physicians, Assn. Mil. Surgeons U.S. Episcopalian. Home: 3332 Red Cliff Cir Temple TX 76502 Office: Olin E Teague Vets Ctr 1901 S 1st St Temple TX 76504

WAJSMAN, ZEV, urologist educator; b. Lublin, Poland, Apr. 8, 1937; came to U.S., 1973; s. Moses and Frania (Kestenbaum) W.; m. Alina Szemet, Mar. 8, 1957; children: Renata, Ilan, Dan. MD, Hebrew U., Hadassah, Jerusalem, 1963. Cert. Israeli Bd. Urology, 1976, Can. Bd. Urology, 1979; lic. MD, N.Y., Nebr., Fla. Intern, resident Cen. Emek Hosp., Afula, Israel, 1963-65; resident gen. surgery Cen. Emek Hosp., Afula, 1969-70, sr. resident dept. urology, 1971-73; rsch. assoc. surgery/urology SUNY, Buffalo, 1973-76, asst. prof. surgery/urology, 1977-80, rsch. assoc. prof. surgery/urology, 1980-83; assoc. prof. surgery/urology U. Fla., Gainesville, 1983-84, David A. Cofrin prof. urologic oncology, 1984—; cancer rsch. urologist Roswell Park Meml. Inst., Buffalo, 1974-75, 76-80, clin. fellow 1973-75, sr. attending physician, 1979-80, assoc. chief dept. Urologic Oncology, 1980-83; clin. cons. Nat. Prostatic Cancer Project, 1976-80; prin. investigator Nat. Bladder Cancer Collaborative Group A., 1980-83; chief Urology Svc. VA Hosp., Gainesville, 1983-89; chief Urologic Oncology, U. Fla., Gainesville, 1983—. Mem. editorial bd.: Jour. Surg. Oncology, 1993; contbr. articles to profl. jours. Recipient Letter of Award Internat. Cancer Rsch. Tech. Transfer Programme, 1980. Fellow ACS, Royal Coll. Surgeons Can.; mem. Am. Urologic Assn. (Southeastern sect.), Am. Soc. Clin. Oncologists, Internat. Soc. Urology, Soc. Surg. Oncology, Soc. Urologic Oncology, Soc. Univ. Urologists, Fla. Med. Assn., Fla. Urol. Soc.

WAKE, ERIC L., history educator; b. Louisville, Oct. 18, 1943; s. Arthur and Tunnie Wake; m. Elizabeth Sue Doan, Apr. 5, 1969; children: Kimberly, Jennifer. BA, Cumberland Coll., 1965; MA, Tex. Christian U., 1967, PhD, 1973. Asst. prof. history Cumberland Coll., Williamsburg, Ky., 1967-71, assoc. prof., 1973-85, prof., chmn. dept. history and polit. sci., 1985—. Contbr. articles to profl. jours. Chmn. nominating com. Main Street Bapt. Ch., Williamsburg, 1982-83; mem. president's coun. Williamsburg City Sch., 1983, pres. PTA, 1984-85. Named Honored Prof. by faculty Cumberland Coll., 1980, Honored Male prof. by students, 1988; recipient Outstanding Teaching award U. Ky., 1990; Univ. fellow Tex. Christian U., 1972-73. Mem. Am. Hist. Assn., Ky. Assn. Tchrs. History (exec. com. 1991—, pres.-elect 1995-96), Phi Alpha Theta (advisor chpt. 1985—, editor the Upsilonian 1989—). Home: 522 Elm St Williamsburg KY 40769-1313 Office: Cumberland Coll 7657 College Station Dr Williamsburg KY 40769-1387

WAKEFIELD, STEPHEN ALAN, lawyer; b. Olney, Ill., Oct. 18, 1940; s. George William and Blanche Lucille (Sheesley) W.; children from previous marriage: Melissa Cox, Tracy Lenz, Stephen Alan Jr.; m. Patricia Ann

McGuire, Nov. 29, 1980; 1 child, Mark. LLB, U. Tex., Austin, 1965. Bar: Tex. 1965. Assoc. Baker & Botts, Houston, 1965-70, ptnr., 1974-84, sr. ptnr., chmn. energy dept., 1986-89; atty. Federal Power Commn., Washington, 1970-72; dep. asst. sec. energy programs Dept. Interior, Washington, 1972-73, asst. sec. energy and minerals, 1973-74; asst. adminstr. Fed. Energy Office, Washington, 1973-74; vice chmn., gen. counsel United Energy Resources, Inc., Houston, 1985-86; pres. United Gas Pipe Line Co., Houston, 1985-86; exec. v.p. MidCon Corp., 1985-86; gen. coun. Dept. Energy, Washington, 1989-91; ptnr. Akin, Gump, Strauss, Hauer & Feld, L.L.P., 1991—. Bd. dirs. Houston Advanced Rsch. Ctr.; bd. visitors M.D. Anderson Cancer Ctr. Mem. ABA, Tex. Bar Assn., Fed. Energy Bar Assn. Clubs: River Oaks Country, Coronado (Houston). Home: 16 West Ln Houston TX 77019-1008 Office: Akin Gump Strauss Et Al 711 Louisiana St Ste 1900 Houston TX 77002-2720

WAKEHAM, RONALD T., protective services official. AAS, Tidewater C.C., 1977; BS in Govtl. Adminstrn., Christopher Newport U., 1980; M in Pub. Adminstrn., Old Dominion U., 1985. Investigator, firefighter Dept. Fire and Paramed. Svcs., Norfolk, Va., 1972-80, in-svc. training, lt., 1981-82, coord. lt. Tidewater Regional Fire Acad., 1982-83, lt. media prodn., 1983, lt. rescue squad, 1984-85, lt. prevention/edn. bureau, 1985-87, commdr., acting battalion chief, 1987-91, dir., 1991—; dir. fire sci. program Tidewater C.C., 1980-83; adj. faculty, instr. fire adminstrn. program Hampton U., 1986-90; cons. Tech. Adv. Svc. for Attys., 1985—. Office: Dept Fire & Paramedical Services 540 E City Hall Ave Norfolk VA 23510-2305*

WALCOTT, CHARLES ELIOT, political science educator; b. Pasadena, Calif., Apr. 19, 1943; s. Stuart and Mary (Eliot) W.; m. Anne Stillman, June 8, 1963 (div. Feb. 1990); children: Stuart S., Donald A.; m. Karen Marie Hult, June 16, 1990. AB, Occidental Coll., 1964; MA, U. Calif., Santa Barbara, 1965, PhD, 1971. Teaching asst. U. Calif., Santa Barbara, 1967-68; asst. prof. U. Minn., Mpls., 1968-78, assoc. prof., 1978-89; assoc. prof. Va. Tech. Inst., Blacksburg, 1989—; adj. prof. Hamline U., St. Paul, 1983-89. Author: Simple Simulations, 1976; co-author: Governing Public Organizations, 1990, Governing the White House, 1995; editor: Simple Simulations II, 1980; assoc. editor Tchg. Polit. Sci., 1970-78; contbr. articles to profl. jours. Mem. Ramsey County Local Govt. Study Commn., St. Paul, 1973-74; treas. Linwood Booster Club, St. Paul, 1979-80; dir. St. Peter (Minn.) Soccer Assn., 1983-85. Recipient Morse Alumni award U. Minn., 1988. Mem. Am. Polit. Sci. Assn. (exec. com. undergrad. edn. sect. 1995—), Midwest Polit. Sci. Assn. Episcopalian. Home: 2507 Manchester St Blacksburg VA 24060-8225 Office: Va Tech Inst Dept Polit Sci Blacksburg VA 24061

WALCOTT, DEXTER WINN, allergist; b. Greenville, Miss., Dec. 20, 1954; s. Charles DeWitt and Ruth LaFon (Stillions) W.; m. Virginia Shackelford, Sept. 20, 1980; children: Arrington, Winn. Grad. cum laude, U. Miss., 1977; postgrad., U. Miss. Sch. Medicine, 1978-82. Diplomate Am. Bd. Pediatrics, Am. Bd. Allergy and Immunology; lic. physician, Miss. Intern U. Miss. Med. Ctr., Jackson, 1982-83, resident in pediatrics, 1983-85; pvt. practice Oxford, Pa., 1985-91; with Miss. Asthma and Allergy Clinic, Jackson, 1993—; pres. house staff U. Med. Ctr., 1984-85, U. Med. Ctr. del. to Miss. State Med. Soc., 1985; ethics com. mem. North Miss. Retardation Ctr.; rev. physician Miss. Found. for Med. Care; participant vis. clinician program LeBonheur Children's Hosp.; mem. staff Miss. Bapt. Med. Ctr., Meth. Med. Ctr., River Oaks Hosp., St. Dominic's Med. Ctr., U. Med. Ctr. dept. pediatrics divsn. allergy/immunology; spkr. in field. Allergy/Immunology fellow La. State U. Med. Ctr., 1991-93. Fellow Am. Bd. Allergy and Immunology; mem. AMA, Am. Coll. Allergy/Immunology, Am. Acad. Allergy and Immunology, Am. Acad. Pediatrics, Miss. State Med. Assn., Miss. State Acad. Pediatrics, Ctrl. Miss. Med. Soc. (exec. com. mem. 1994—), Ctrl. Miss. Pediatric Soc. (pres. 1996), Alpha Epsilon Delta, Order of Omega, Eta Sigma Phi, Beta Beta Beta, Sigma Alpha Epsilon (pres. 1976-77). Office: Miss Asthma & Allergy Clin 940 N State St Jackson MS 39202-2646

WALD, MARLENA MALMSTEDT, librarian; b. Elkhorn, Wis., Feb. 7, 1950; d. Philip John and Evelyn Jean (Romeril) Malmstedt; m. Michael Leonard Wald, June 10, 1972. BA in Psychology, George Washington U., 1980; MLS, U. Md., 1986; MPH, Emory U., 1996. Program asst. NSF, Washington, 1980; reference asst. Johns Hopkins U., Balt., 1981-86; sci. reference libr. U. Ga., Athens, 1986-90, coord. collection devel., 1990-93; mem. mgmt. intern coun. on libr. resources reference dept. U. Ga. Sci. Libr., Athens, 1988-89; rsch. assoc. Ctr. for Injury Control Rollins Sch. Pub. Health, Emory U., Atlanta, 1996—; video reviewer ABC-Clio publs., 1989-93; lectr. internet applications and resources for health scis. issues. V.p. Clarke County Dem. Women, 1988-89. Mem. ALA (mem. com. 1986-88), APHA, Nat. Rural Health Assn., Spl. Librs. Assn., Phi Kappa Phi, Phi Mu. Democrat. Lutheran. Home: 257 Morton Ave Athens GA 30605-1407

WALD, MICHAEL LEONARD, economist; b. Balt., Jan. 5, 1951; s. Leonard Marvin and Frances (Kosinski) W.; m. Marlena Malmstedt, June 10, 1972. BA, Am. U., 1972. Mgr. Woodward and Lothrop Dept. Store, Washington, 1972-75, Hecht Co., Washington, 1975-76; store mgr. W.J. Sloane & Co., Washington, 1976-77; economist U.S. Bur. of Labor Stats., Balt., 1977-85, Washington, 1985-86; economist U.S. Bur. of Labor Stats., Atlanta, 1986—, S.E. regional economist, 1996—; lectr. on fed. compensation issues; peer reviewer ACA Jour. Editl. bd. HR Atlanta, 1993-95; contbr. articles on compensation issues to profl. publs.; reviewer Monthly Labor Rev., 1992—; peer reviewer ACA Jour., 1995—. Bd. dirs. Athens (Ga.) Habitat for Humanity, 1990-93; venue mktg. liaison mgr. 1996 Centennial Olympic Games. Mem. Am. Compensation Assn. (cert. compensation profl.), Atlanta Compensation Assn. (v.p. 1992, 93, 94, pres. 1996), Am. Sociol. Assn. (co-chair software vendor fair 1996), Alpha Tau Omega. Home: 257 Morton Ave Athens GA 30605-1407 Office: US Bur Labor Stats 1371 Peachtree St NE Atlanta GA 30367-3102

WALDEN, RUTH, communications educator, writer; b. Milw., Oct. 17, 1948; d. Peter A. and Rose T. (Ruszkiewicz) Flegel; m. Dennis V. Walden, Nov. 27, 1971; children: Matthew D., Rebecca R. BA, U. Wis., 1970, MA, 1978, PhD, 1981. Reporter Wis. State Jour., Madison, 1969-74; asst. dir. judicial edn. Wis. Supreme Ct., Madison, 1980; asst. prof. U. Utah, Salt Lake City, 1981-85, U. N.C., Chapel Hill, 1985-88; assoc. prof. U. N.C., 1988-95, prof. journalism and mass communication, 1995—. Author: Mass Communication Law in North Carolina, 1993; contbr. articles to profl. jours. Mem. Assn. for Edn. in Journalism and Mass Communication (head of law divsn. 1991-92, 1st pl. paper Bicentennial of the 1st Amendment 1991), N.C. News Media Adminstrn. of Justice Coun. Home: 4425 Highgate Dr Durham NC 27713 Office: CB #3365 Sch Journalism & Mass Comm U NC-CH Chapel Hill NC 27599

WALDER, DEBBY JEAN, program director, quality manager, nursing service administrator, nurse, educator; b. Watertown, S.D., Nov. 25, 1947; d. James Russell and Gladys Elizabeth (Owen) W. BS in Nursing with honors, S.D. State U., 1970; MS in Nursing, U. Minn., 1977. Staff nurse VA Med. Ctr., Mpls., 1970-71, instr., 1971-75, coordinator, 1976-77, trainee-assoc. chief nursing service for edn., 1977; assoc. chief nursing service for edn. VA Med. Ctr., Wilmington, Del., 1977-80, Richmond, Va., 1980-83; chief nursing service VA Med. Ctr., Huntington, W.Va., 1983-85, VA Med. Ctr., Cin., 1985-87; quality mgmt. coord. VA Hosp., Madison, Wis., 1987-91; clin. program mgr., dir. risk mgmt. VA Ctrl. Office, Washington, 1991-93, dir. risk mgmt., 1993—; adj. faculty Med. Coll. Va., Richmond, 1980-82; basic cardiac life support inst.-trainer Am. Heart Assn., Richmond, 1980-83; clin. prof. Marshall U. Sch. Nursing, Huntington, 1983—. Mem. task force Richmond Area chpt. Am. Heart Assn. Recipient Outstanding Cardiopulmonary Resuscitation Instr. award Richmond Area chpt. Am. Heart Assn., 1982, Achievement award VA Med. Ctr., Richmond, 1983, recognition award for excellence in mgmt. VA Med. Ctr., Huntington, 1983, Spl. Contbn. award, 1992-95, Unsung Heroes award, 1994; Bush Found. fellow, 1975-76. Mem. Nat. Assn. Quality Assurance Profls., Phi Kappa Phi, Sigma Theta Tau (Phi chpt. scholar 1969-70), Nat. Assn. Quality Assurance Profls., Pi Lambda Theta. Roman Catholic. Office: VA Cen Office Office Quality Mgmt 810 Vermont Ave NW Washington DC 20420-0001

WALDMAN, ALAN I. (ALAWANA), songwriter, composer, lyricist, computer programmer; b. Elkins Park, Pa., Jan. 20, 1955; s. Harry and Anna Waldman. Student, U. Okla., 1973-76, U. Oreg., 1978, 79; BS in Econs., U. Wis., 1979; MS in Stats., U. Iowa, 1985. Performing songwriter, composer, lyricist Deerfield Beach, Fla., 1986—; ind. computer programmer; cons. Internet and World Wide Web. Author: Poetic Universe Collection, How to Form Your Own Publishing Entity and Operating it Thereafter; lyricist, composer (song collections) Hit The Market, Down to Home, Sphere of Influence, Next Galaxy, Quality Rainbow, Predicaments of Life, Great Guidelines for Living, Collection of Alawana, Vol. I, 1993, The Artist Dimension Song Collection, Vols. II, III, Artsist Dimension Collection. Charter mem. Rep. Presdl. Task Force, Washington, 1984—. Mem. U. Iowa Alumni Assn. Republican. Home: PO Box 4581 Deerfield Beach FL 33442-4581

WALDO, CATHERINE RUTH, private school educator; b. Erie, Pa., Nov. 5, 1946; d. James Allen and Ruth Catherine (Rubner) Babcock; m. James Robert Waldo, June, 1968; children; Robert, Ruth Ann. BA in History magna cum laude, Duke U., 1968. Cert. tchr., Okla. Tchr. Shawnee (Okla.) Pub. Schs., 1968-70; tchr., team leader Norman (Okla.) Pub. Schs., 1971-73; tchr., social studies chmn. Westminster Sch., Oklahoma City, Okla., 1990—. Mem. edn. commn. Westminster Presbyn. Ch., Oklahoma City, 1980-93, deacon, 1981-84, coord. early childhood programs, 1988-90, elder, 1990-93; mem. coun. Ward 2 City of Nichols Hills, Okla., 1989-93; bd. dirs. Assn. Ctrl. Okla. Govts., Oklahoma City, 1989-93; vol., planning com. World Neighbors. Recipient Colonial Williamsburg Summer Inst., Okla. Found. for Excellence, 1994. Mem. Nat. Coun. Tchrs. English, Nat. Coun. for Social Studies, Okla. Coun. for Social Studies, Okla. Coun. Tchrs. English. Presbyterian. Home: 1100 Tedford Way Oklahoma City OK 73116-6007 Office: Westminster Sch 612 NW 44th St Oklahoma City OK 73118-6627

WALDON, GRACE ROBERTA, insurance agent; b. Surry County, N.C., July 8, 1941; d. Brady Warren and Kathleen (Riggs) Felts; m. Jesse James Waldon Jr., May 17, 1958; children: James, Forrest. BS in Econs., U. N.C., 1981, postgrad., 1983-84. Registered rep. NML Investment Svcs., Inc. Real estate agt. Rob Ramby Real Estate, Abilene, Tex., 1982-84; asst. to v.p. Life Ins. Svcs., Charlotte, N.C., 1984-85; v.p. James R. Worrell Gen. Agy., N.W. Mut. Life,, Charlotte, 1985—; investment officer Robert W. Baird & Co. Inc. Officer Symphony Guild, Abilene, 1972, Internat. Mgmt. Coun., Charlotte, 1989; chmn. faculty wives La. Tech. Inst., Ruston, 1966. Named Outstanding Mem. St. Paul's Meth. Ch., 1973. Mem. CLU, Chartered Fin. Cons., Charlotte Sales and Mktg. Execs. Republican. Office: NW Mut Life 1900 Rexford Rd Ste 120 Charlotte NC 28211-3481

WALDREP, ALVIS KENT, JR., non-profit foundation administrator; b. Austin, Tex., Mar. 2, 1954; s. Alvis Kent and Denise Carol (Wolfe) W.; m. Lynn Burgland, Dec. 6, 1980; children: Trey, Charles. BBA, Tex. Christian U. and Kennedy Western U., 1992. Exec. Nat. Paralysis Found., Dallas, 1985—; chmn. Turbo Resins Internat., Dallas, 1991—, Dallas Rehab. Inst., 1981-93; bd. dirs. Tex. Rehab. Commn., Austin, 1989—. Member Job Accomodations Network, Washington, 1986-89, Internat. Alliance on Disability, Washington, 1986—; chmn. Tex. Gov.'s Com. for Disabled Persons, Austin, 1987-90; founder Am. Paralysis Assn., 1979—. Recipient Spirit of Tex. award ABC-TV Affiliate, 1984, Spl. award Tex. Sports Hall of Fame, 1975; named one of Ten Outstanding Young Ams., U.S. Jaycees, 1985. Mem. Nat. Soc. Fund Raising Execs. (bd. dirs. 1983-84), Nat. Coun. on Disability (vice chair 1983-94), Nat. Rehab. Assn., Neurotrauma Soc., Tex. Jaycees. Republican. Methodist. Home: 1501 Anglebluff Ln Plano TX 75093-4826 Office: Nat Paralysis Found 16415 Addison Rd Ste 550 Dallas TX 75248

WALDREP, LEIGH BARNHARDT, primary school educator; b. Charlotte, N.C., June 5, 1959; d. Charles Franklin Barnhardt and Anne Marie (Calhoun) Smith; m. Ronald Carson Waldrep, May 23, 1986. Student, St. Mary's Coll., Raleigh, N.C., 1979; AA, Ctrl. Piedmont C.C., Charlotte, 1987; BA, U. N.C., Charlotte, 1991; MA, Queens Coll., 1996. Cert. elem. tchr., N.C. Tchr., asst. dir., dir. La Petite Acad., Charlotte, 1988-92; asst. mgr. Talbots Kids, Charlotte, 1992-93; substitute tchr. Charlotte Mecklenburg Schs., 1993—; dir. Barnhardt Bros. Co., 1991-92, asst. sec., 1992—. Home: 2317 Laburnum Ave Charlotte NC 28205

WALDRON, RONALD JAMES, protective services official; b. Dover, N.J., Sept. 3, 1939; s. Chauncey and Evelyn May (White) W.; m. Jean M. Jacober; children: Diana, Jennifer, Michelle. BA in Criminology, Indiana U. Pa., 1970; MA in Criminal Justice, CUNY, 1972; MPA, Harvard U., 1989; PhD in Criminal Justice, Sam Houston State U., 1973. State trooper N.J. State Police, 1963-67; teaching fellow Sam Houston State U., 1971-73; chief rsch. br. Tex. Dept. Corrections, 1973-76; correctional programs officer U.S. Bur. Prisons, Washington, 1976-78, chief office of program devel., 1978-83, dep. ast. dir. adminstrv. div., 1983-88, dep. asst. dir. program rev. div., 1988-89, sr. dep. asst. dir. health svcs. div., 1989—. Contbr. article to profl. jours. Active Woodson High Sch. Boosters, Neighborhood Watch, Providence Ch. Served with USAF, 1957-61. Recipient Letter of Commendation from Pres. Ronald Reagan, 1988, awards from Fed. Prison System, 1980, 87, 91; Sam Houston State U. fellow in criminal justice; U.S. Office Edn. fellow in criminal justice, others. Mem. Am. Soc. for Pub. Adminstrn. (nat. officer 1987, nat. program com. 1991-93, exec. com. sect. criminal justice adminstrn. 1985-87, 91-93), Am. Correctional Assn., Acad. Criminal Justice Scis., Pi Gamma Mu, Alpha Kappa Delta, Gamma Theta Upsilon. Office: 320 1st St NW Washington DC 20534-0002

WALDROP, BEVERLY ELIZABETH, volunteer administrator; b. San Francisco, Dec. 17, 1940; d. Ray Emory and Maria Josfeua (Nenzel) Preffer; m. John William Waldrop, Nov. 18, 1960; children: Sandra Louise Waldrop Gross, Tamara Jean Waldrop Cornelison, Pamela Ann Waldrop Clever, John Daniel, Wayne Houston, Sharon Marie. Grad. high sch., Phoenix. Cert. vol. adminstr. Comml. artist Phoenix, Milpilās, Calif., 1960-75; instr. visual aids Milpilās, 1972; exec. dir. CASA of Jackson County, Scottsboro, Ala., 1980—; bd. dirs. CASA, Scottsboro; dir. religious edn. St. Elizabeth Ch., 1971. Bd. dirs. Jackson County Christmans Charities, 1986—, sec., 1987—; pres. Jackson County Community Resource Devel. Com., 1988, chmn. emergency preparedness com., 1989; pres. Jackson County Interagy. Coun., 1985, bd. dirs., 1981—; active Ala. Assembly Volunteerism, 1985-87, Give Five, 1989, Jackson County Voting Asessability Project; mem. liturgy com. St. Jude Cath. Ch. Mem. Ala. Leaders in Vol. Efforts (pres. elect/pres. 1991-94), Jackson County Coun. Aging (bd. dirs. 1980-94, long term care com. 1981—, chmn. 1982), Jackson County Health Coun. (sec. 1982-90), Jackson County Community Resource Devel. (chmn. 1990), Jackson County C. of C. Office: CASA of Jackson County 215 S Scott St Scottsboro AL 35768-1930

WALDROP, ENID JOHNSON, nurse; b. Waco, Tex., Mar. 22, 1945; d. Elbert Medley and Agnes Lorraine (Fulbright) Johnson; m. George William Waldrop, Aug. 6, 1964; children: Suzanne Elaine, Charlotte Michelle, Christy Lynn. BS in Nursing, U. Mary Hardin-Baylor, Belton, Tex., 1980. RN, Tex.; cert. women's health care nurse practitioner, RNC, NCC. Staff nurse Hillcrest Bapt. Med. Ctr., Waco, 1980-81, Waco-McLennan County Pub. Health Dist., Waco, 1981-93; women's health care nurse practitioner Scott and White Clinic, Temple, Tex., 1993—. Mem. AWHONN, Tex. Nurse Practitioners, Am. Acad. Nurse Practitioners. Republican. Methodist.

WALDROP, LINDA M., medical administrator; b. Jefferson County, Ala., Oct. 24, 1942; d. Luther Grady Jr. and Anna Katherine (Gray) McGill; m. Bennie Lee Waldrop Jr., Mar. 14, 1961; children: Tracy L., Terry L. AS, Jefferson State Jr. Coll., 1971; BSN, Samford U., 1985; MA, U. Ala., Birmingham, 1989. Head nurse open heart ICU Bapt. Med. Ctr.-Montclair, Birmingham, 1976-82, head nurse telemetry unit, 1985-87, head nurse med. unit, 1983-85, head nurse oncology unit, 1987-90, edn. coord.; internal auditor Bapt. Med. Ctr.-Montclair, 1991; dir. med.-surg. telemetry nursing Shelby Med. Ctr. (now Shelby Bapt. Med. Ctr.), Alabaster, Ala., 1991-96, dir. gastroenterol. svcs., 1993-95, nursing internal auditor, 1993—, dir. women's svcs., 1994-95, dir. edn., 1996—. Mem. ANA (cert. nursing adminstrn.), AACN, Oncology Nursing Soc., Nat. Mgmt. Assn., Ala. Orgn. Nurse Execs., Birmingham Regional Orgn. Nurse Execs.

WALDROP, MARY LOUISE, nursing educator; b. Spartanburg, S.C., Feb. 7, 1947; d. Clarence Daniel and Esther Lorena Waldrop. BSN, U. S.C., 1975; MSN, Med. Coll. Ga., 1978; ABD, U. Ga., 1984. Lic. perinatal nurse, ob-gyn. nurse practitioner; cert. advance practice, Ga. Bd. Nursing, pediat. advanced life support. Staff nurse labor and delivery Greenville (S.C) Hosp. Sys., 1968-70; head nurse CCU/ICU St. Francis Comty. Hosp., Greenville, 1970-73; team coord. adolescent psychology Marshall I. Pickens Psych./Mental Health, Greenville, 1973-74; DON, patient care coord. Piedmont Health Care Corp., Greenville, 1975-76; teaching assoc. ADN program U. S.C., Spartanburg, 1976-77; instr. maternal child nursing Clemson (S.C.) U., 1978-84; asst. prof. Med. Coll. Ga., Augusta, 1985-86; nurse practitioner prem. prev. project Med. Coll. Ga./Ga. Human Resource, Augusta, 1986-87; joint appt. asst. prof., clinician Incarnate World Coll./Santa Rosa Med. Ctr., San Antonio, 1987-88; mem. faculty obstets. Bapt. Hosp. Sch. Nursing, San Antonio, 1988-90; mem. faculty pediatrics St. Phillips Coll., San Antonio, 1990-91; asst. dir. nursing, program dir. Howard Coll., Del Rio, Tex., 1992-93; asst. prof. Valdosta (Ga.) State U., 1992—; coord. 3d Ann. Women's Health Seminar, 1985; prodr. workshop continuing edn. dept. Clemson U., Greenville; adv. bd. Head Start, Valdosta, 1994; adv. com. Nursing Ctr., Valdosta State U., 1994. Co-author: (videotape) Complemental Nursing Care, 1975; group author: (newspaper column) Pregnancy & Nutritive During Holidays, 1984. Vol. Greenville chpt. ARC, 1981—. Recipient Nat. Disting. Svc. award Libr. of Congress, 1988; univ. rsch. grantee, 1984. Mem. ANA (item writer cert. exam 1987), AAUP, S.C. Nurses Assn. (mem. coun. on edn. 1982-84), S.C. Perinatal Assn. (program com. 1928-84), Ga. Nurses Assn. (1st v.p. 1993—, exec. com. 1995—), Tex. Nurses Assn. (program com. 1991-92). Home: 113 Runnymeade Ln Spartanburg SC 29301-2621 Office: Valdosta State U Coll of Nursing Brookwood Hall Valdosta GA 31601

WALDROP, WILLIAM RHEUBEN, chemical engineer; b. Demopolis, Ala., July 1, 1939; s. William Clyde and Christine (Andrews) W.; m. Marjorie Kirk, July 1, 1961; children: Amy Susanne, Joan Kathleen. BS in Aero. Engring., Auburn U., 1961; MS in Fluid Mechanics, U. Ala., Huntsville, 1968; Engr. Exptl. Fluid Dynamics, von Karman Inst. Fluid Dynamic, Belgium, 1969; PhD in Chem. Engring., La. State U., 1972. Registered profl. engr., Tenn. Engr. Northrop Space Lab., Huntsville, 1965-68, Lockheed Missile & Space Co., Huntsville, 1969-70; rsch. assoc. Coastal Studies Inst., La. State U., Baton Rouge, 1970-74; civil engr. TVA, Knoxville, 1974-80, mgr. projects, 1980-94; pres. Quantum Engring. Corp., Loudon, Tenn., 1994—. Contbr. articles to profl. jours. 1st lt. USAF, 1961-65. NATO fellow. Mem. ASCE, Nat. Mgmt. Assn., Am. Geophys. Union, Internat. Assn. Hydraulic Rsch., Sigma Xi. Episcopalian. Home and Office: Quantum Engring Corp Tellico Village 112 Tigitsi Ln Loudon TN 37774-2509

WALENTA, RONALD JAMES, risk management consultant; b. Austin, Dec. 27, 1948; m. Janie Osborn, May 26, 1980. BBA in Ins., U. Tex., 1976. Cert. ins. counselor, Soc. Cert. Ins. Counselors. Risk mgr. DFW Internat. Airport, Dallas, 1988-90, Chili's Restaurants, Dallas, 1990, Trailway's Transit, Dallas, 1990-92, Chief Auto Parts, Dallas, 1992-94; pres., owner EEI Support Svcs., Inc., Dallas, 1992—; guest spkr. Coun. Edn. Mgmt., Dallas, 1990—; cons. Lloyds of London, 1993—; dir. Transcon Mgrs. Ltd., Reno, 1994—. Vice chair Dallas Police Review Bd., 1991-95. maj. Tex. N.G., 1985-93. Mem. Fair Park Trust Fund Bd., Masons, Scottish Rite, Shriners. Republican. Office: EEI Support Svcs Inc PO Box 8107 Dallas TX 75205

WALIGORA, JAMES, financial services consultant; b. Harvey, Ill., Sept. 30, 1954; s. John Joseph and Lucille Patricia (Gargala) W.; m. Cheryl L. Stewart. AA, Thornton Community Coll., 1976; BS in Acctg. and Fin., U. Ala., Birmingham, 1978. CPA, Ala. Sr. acct. Ernst & Whinney, Birmingham, Ala., 1978-81; dir. internal auditing Motion Industries Inc., Birmingham, 1981-82; registered rep. DeRand Investment Corp., Arlington, Va., 1983-85; pvt. practice acctg., Birmingham, 1982—; pres. Equity Ptnrs. Inc., Birmingham, 1986-87, James Waligora Assocs., Birmingham, 1987—; pres. Metro Acctg. Svc. Inc., 1995—. Mem. Birmingham Mus. Art, 1985, Big. Bros. Birmingham, 1979-86; pres. Greater Birmingham Arts Alliance, 1985, Greater Birmingham Habitat for Humanity, 1992; advisor Jr. Achievement Project Bus., Birmingham, 1989. Mem. Am. Inst. CPA's, Ala. Soc. CPA's, Internat. Assn. Fin. Planning (treas. Ala. chpt. 1986). Lodge: Civitan Internat. (charter mem. local club 1983, pres. 1986, award 1987). Home: 1131 11th Pl S Birmingham AL 35205-5206 Office: 167 Oxmoor Blvd Birmingham AL 35209-5955

WALKER, ALICE DAVIS, retired audio-visual specialist educator; b. Takoma Pk., Md., Sept. 18, 1931; d. Bryan and Helen (Bilsborough) Davis; m. Richard David Walker, June 6, 1953; children: Patricia Walker Jordan, Jean, Sharyl Elise. BA in English, U. Md., 1953; MS in Adult Edn., Va. Poly. Inst. and State U., 1974, Cert. Adv. Grad. Studies, 1981. Workshop coord. Purdue U., Lafayette, Ind., 1953-55; editor Va. Poly. Inst. and State U., Blacksburg, 1976-86, learning resources specialist, 1986-88, audio visual edn. specialist, 1988-96, ret., 1996. Co-author: Lift Your Voices, 1974; editor: Visual Literacy: Enhancing Human Potential, 1984; contbr. articles to profl. jours. Treas., bd. dirs. Mental Health Assn., Blacksburg, 1970-80; sec. County Coun. PTA, Montgomery County, Va., 1972; leader, trainer Girl Scouts U.S., Blacksburg, 1975. Mem. Internat. Visual Literacy Assn. (exec. treas. 1987-95, bd. dirs. 1976-95, Presdl. award 1987, John Debes award 1994), Assn. Ednl. Comms. and Tech. (chairperson awards com. 1992-94, scholarship and leadership award 1979), Higher Edn. Media Assn. (treas. 1986-88), S.E. Regional Media Leadership Coun., Va. Ednl. Media Assn. (leadership chairperson 1988). Presbyterian.

WALKER, ANNETTE, counseling administrator; b. Birmingham, Ala., Sept. 20, 1953; d. Jesse and Luegene (Wright) W. BS in Edn., Huntingdon Coll., 1976; MS in Adminstrn. and Supervision, Troy State U., 1977, 78, MS in Sch. Counseling, 1990, AA in Sch. Adminstrn., 1992; diploma, World Travel Sch., 1990; diploma in Cosmetology, John Patterson Coll., 1992; MEd in higher Edn. Adminstrn., Auburn (Ala.) U., 1995. Cert. tchr., adminstr., Ala.; lic. cosmetologist, Ala. Tchr. Montgomery (Ala.) Pub. Sch. System, 1976-89, sch. counselor, 1989—; gymnastics tchr. Cleveland Ave. YMCA, 1971-76; girls coach Montgomery Parks and Recreation, 1973-76; summer sch. sci. tchr. grades 7-9, 1977-88; chmn. dept. sci. Bellingrath Sch., 1987-90, courtesy com., 1987-88, sch. discipline com., 1977-84; recreation asst. Gunter AFB, Ala., 1981-83; calligraphy tchr. Gunter Youth Ctr., 1982; program dir. Maxwell AFB, Ala., 1983-89, vol. tchr. Internat. Officer Sch., 1985—, Ala. Goodwill Amb., 1985—, day camp dir., 1987, calligraphy tchr., 1988; trainer internat. law for sec. students, Ala., 1995—; leader of workshops in field; evening computer tchr. high sch. diploma program, 1995—; sales rep. Ala. World Travel, 1990—; behavior aid Brantwood Children's Home, 1996—; computer tchr. h.s. diploma program Montgomery County Sch., 1995—; behavior aide Brantwood Children's Home, 1995—; hotel auditor, 1995—. Mem. CAP; tchr. Sunday sch. Beulah Bapt. Ch., Montgomery; vol. zoo activities Tech. Scholarship Program for Ala. Tchrs. Computer Courses, Montgomery, Ala.; bd. dirs. Cleveland Ave. YMCA, 1976-80; sponsor Bell-Howe chpt. Young Astronauts, 1986-90, Pate Howe chpt. Young Astronauts, 1991-92; judge Montgomery County Children Festival Elem. Sci. Fair, 1988-90; bd. dirs. Troy State U. Drug Free Schs., 1992—; chmn. Maxwell AFB Red Cross-Youth, 1986-88; goodwill amb. sponsor to various families (award 1989, 95); State of Ala. rep. P.A.T.C.H.-Internat. Law Inst., 1995. Recipient Outstanding High Sch. Sci./Math. Tchr. award Sigma Xi, 1989, Most Outstanding Youth Coun. Leader award Maxwell AFB Youth Ctr., 1987, Outstanding Ala. Goodwill Amb. award, 1989, 95; named Tchr. of the Week, WCOV-TV, 1992, Ala. Tchr. in Space Program, summer 1989, Local Coord. Young Astronaut Program, 1988. Mem. NEA, Internat. Platform Assn., Nat. Sci. Tchrs. Assn., Ala. Sch. Counselors, Montgomery Sch. Counselors Assn., Montgomery County Ednl. Assn., Space Camp Amb., Huntingdon Alumni Assn. (sec.-treas.), Ala. Goodwill Amb., Montgomery Capital City Club, Young Astronauts, Ea. Star, Zeta Phi Beta, Chi Delta Phi, Kappa Pi. Home: 2501 Westwood Dr Montgomery AL 36108-4448 Office: Bellingrath Sch 3488 S Court St Montgomery AL 36105-1608

WALKER, ARTHUR LONZO, religious organization administrator; b. Birmingham, Ala., Apr. 10, 1926; s. Arthur Lonzo and Nannie Agnes (Bynum) W.; m. Gladys Evelyn Walker, Aug. 4, 1949; children: Marcia Lea Hamby, Gregory Arthur. BA, Samford U., 1949; MDiv, So. Bapt. Theol. Sem., 1952; ThD, New Orleans Bapt. Theol. Sem., 1956; LHD (hon.), Campbell U., 1984; HHD (hon.), Houston Bapt. U., 1985. Prof. theology Samford U., Birmingham, 1956-76, v.p. student affairs, 1965-68, v.p. adminstrv. affairs, 1968-73; v.p. student affairs So. Bapt. Theol. Sem., Louisville, 1976-78; exec. dir. edn. commn. So. Bapt. Conv., Nashville, 1978—; sec.-treas. So. Bapt. Commn. Am. Bapt. Theol. Sem., Nashville, 1978—; mem. adv. bd. Ctr. for Constl. Studies, Macon, Ga., 1978-90; mem. nat. adv. coun. J.M. Dawson Inst. of Ch. State Studies, Waco, Tex., 1990—. Author: By Their Fruits, 1982; editor: Educating For Christian Missions, 1981, Directory of Southern Baptist Colleges, 1986; (jour.) The Southern Baptist Educator, 1978—. Pres. Birmingham Council of Christian Edn., 1970-71. Served as sgt. U.S. Army, 1944-46, PTO. Mem. Nat. Assn. Ind. Colls. and Univs. (bd. dirs. 1987-91). Office: Assn So Baptist Colls 901 Commerce St Ste 750 Nashville TN 37203-3629*

WALKER, BRIGITTE MARIA, translator, linguistic consultant; b. Stolp, Germany, Sept. 20, 1934; came to U.S., 1957; d. Joseph Karl and Ursula Maria Margot Ehrler; m. John V. Kelley (div.); 1 child, John V. Jr.; m. Edward D. Walker, July 3, 1977. Grad., Erlangen Translator's Sch., Germany, 1956; grad. fgn. corres., Berlitz Sch., Germany, 1956. Bilingual sec., translator Spencer Patent Law Office, Washington, 1959-62; office mgr., translator I. William Millen, Millen and White, Patent Law, Washington, 1962-67; prin. Tech. Translating Bur., Washington, 1967-68, St. Petersburg Beach, Fla., 1968—; cons. for patent law offices, Washington, 1962—; ofcl. expert for ct. Paul M. Craig, Patent Atty., Rockford, Ill., 1981; cons. to sci. editor Merriam-Webster, Inc., Springfield, Mass., 1987—. Author: German-English/English-German Last-Resort Dictionary for Technical Translators, 1991, (poetry) The Other Side of the Mirror, 1992 (Poetry award Nat. League Am. Pen Women 1994); co-translator: The Many Faces of Research, 1980; holder of trademark in field. Evaluator fgn. textbooks Pinellas County Sch. Bd., St. Petersburg, 1987, German judge, 1988. Recipient Recoginition award Pinellas County Sch. Bd., 1988, Meritorious Pub. Svc. award City of St. Petersburg Beach, 1987, Poetry award Nat. League Am. Pen Women, 1994, Essay award, 1996. Mem. Mensa. Democrat. Lutheran. Home and Office: 7150 Sunset Way Apt 1007 Saint Petersburg FL 33706-3650

WALKER, CAROL ELLEN BURTON, elementary school educator; b. Owensboro, Ky., July 23, 1934; d. Merle Wilson and Helen Mildred (Thomas) Burton; m. William Marvin Walker, June 28, 1958; children: Sara Helen, David William. BA, Ky. Wesleyan Coll., 1956; postgrad., Ind. U., 1957, U. Louisville, 1972. Cert. elem. music tchr. Tchr. Owensboro Pub. Schs., 1956-58; tchr. Jefferson County Pub. Schs., Louisville, 1958-63, 71-91; master exec. state dir. Oxyfresh, USA, Inc., 1991; curriculum writer, music textbook selection com., music workshop leader Jefferson County Pub. Schs., Louisville; supr. for student tchrs. Bellarmine Coll., U. Ky., Murray State U., U. Louisville, 1971-91. Named Elem. Music Tchr. of Yr., Ky. Music Educators, 1988. Mem. NEA, Ky. Edn. Assn., Jefferson County Edn. Assn., Nat. Fedn. Music Clubs (nat. bd. dirs. 1991—), Ky. Fedn. Music Clubs (pres. 1987-91), Music Educators Nat. Conf., Ky. Music Educators Assn. (pres. Dist. 12 1986-88), MacDowell Music Club (pres. 1969-71), Thoroughbred Ladies Aux. (treas. 1980-93, Woman of Yr. 1987), Delta Kappa Gamma. Republican. Methodist. Home: 4029 Brookfield Ave Louisville KY 40207-2003

WALKER, CAROLYN SMITH, college services administrator, counselor; b. Atlanta, May 9, 1946; d. George Taft and Lonnie Bell (Bates) Smith; 1 child from previous marriage, Gary Sherard Walker II. BA in Psychology, Clark Coll., Atlanta, 1970; MS in Counseling & Guidance, U. Nebr., Omaha, 1975. Lic. profl. counselor, Ga. Adult basic edn. instr. Atlanta Pub. Schs., 1970-71, adult basic edn. site coord., 1971; adult basic edn. instr. Omaha-Nebr. Tech. C.C., Omaha, 1971-74, dir. adult basic edn., 1974; guidance counselor Omaha Pub. Schs., 1974-76; recruitment counselor Minority Women Employment Program, Atlanta, 1976-77; career planning and employment preparation instr. Discovery Learning Inc., Job Tng. and Pntrship Act, Atlanta, 1985-86; dir. counseling and testing svcs. Atlanta Met. Coll., 1977—; test supr. Ednl. Testing Svc., Princeton, N.J., 1980—, Psychology Corp., San Antonio, 1991—, Law Sch. Admissions Test, Newtown, Pa., 1991—; cons. Commn. on Colls., So. Assn. Colls. and Schs., Atlanta, 1978—; jr. c.c. rep. Placement & Coop. Edn., Atlanta, 1987-90. Editor newsletters The Brief, 1984, 85, Guided Studies News, 1974; contbg. author: (manual) AJC Self-Study, 1981; author: (manual) Policies and Procedures for Coordinated Counseling, 1981, 2d edit., 1991, Women's Coalition for Habitat for Humanity in Atlanta, 1993-95. Pres. Atlanta Barristers Wives Inc., 1984, 85; mem. steering com. Atlanta Mayor's Masked Ball, 1987; mem. memberships sales com. Atlanta Arts Festival, 1986, Neighborhood Arts Ctr., 1986; state host Dem. Nat. Conv., Atlanta, 1988; mem. Heritage Valley Cmty. Neighborhood Assn., 1982—. Recipient Outstanding Svc. award Nat. Orientation Dirs. Assn., 1985, 86, Literacy Action, Inc., 1978, Atlanta Met. Coll., 1987, others. Mem. Ga. Coll. Personnel Assn., Ga. Mental Health Counselors Assn., Nat. Coun. Student Devel., Univ. System Counseling Dirs., 100 Women Internat. Inc. (charter mem.), Am. Assn. Community and Jr. Colls., The Links Inc., Ga. Assn. Women Deans, Counselors and Adminstrs., Ga. Coll. Conselors Assn. Democrat. Methodist. Home: 3511 Toll House Ln SW Atlanta GA 30331-2330 Office: Atlanta Metro Coll 1630 Stewart Ave SW Atlanta GA 30310-4448

WALKER, CECIL L., broadcast executive. Office: Gannett Co Inc 1100 Wilson Blvd Arlington VA 22239*

WALKER, CHARLES B., chemicals company executive; b. 1939. Attended, Univ. of Richmond, Richmond, VA, 1961. With Southern States Co-Op, Inc., 1961-64, Albemarle Paper Mfg. Co., 1965-68; pres. Spotless Stores, Richmond, Va., 1969-74; with State Comp. State of Va., 1974-81, sec. adminstrn. and fin., 1978; v.p. Ethyl Corp., Richmond, 1981—; now CFO, vice chmn., tng. dir. Ethyl Corp, Richmond. Office: Ethyl Corp 330 S 4th St Richmond VA 23219-4304*

WALKER, CLARENCE WESLEY, lawyer; b. Durham, N.C., July 19, 1931; s. Ernie Franklin and Mollie Elizabeth (Cole) W.; m. Ann-Heath Harris, June 5, 1954; children: Clare Ann, Wesley Gregg. A.B., Duke U., 1953, LL.B., 1955. Bar: N.C. 1955. Assoc. Mudge Stern Baldwin & Todd, 1955-59; ptnr. Kennedy, Covington, Loddell & Hickman, Charlotte, N.C., 1959—; bd. dirs. Lawyers Mut. Liability Ins. Co., Legal Services Corp. N.C., Oakwood Home Corp. Glendale Hosiery Co.; lectr. N.C. Bar Found. Continuing Legal Edn. Insts., N.C. Jud. Planning Com., 1978-79; pres. Pvt. Adjudication Found. Chmn. bd. mgrs. Charlotte Meml. Hosp. and Med. Ctr., 1981-87; trustee N.C. Ctrl. U., 1979-83; vice-chmn. Charlotte-Mecklenburg Hosp. Authority; adv. bd. Ctrl. Piedmont Paralegal Sch.; pres. Charlotte-Mecklenburg Hosp. Found.; trustee Charlotte Country Day Sch., 1977-81; state chmn. Nat. Found. March of Dimes, 1968-70; chmn. Charlotte Park and Recreation Commn., 1970-73; bd. dirs. Charlotte Symphony, 1965-71, Bethlehem Ctr., 1975-77, N.C. Recreators Found., 1973-75; adv. bd. Charlotte Children's Theatre, 1972; bd. dirs. Charlotte C. of C., 1970-72; bd. visitors Duke U. Law Sch.; dir., gen. campaign chmn. United Way Ctrl. Carolinas, 1985. Fellow Am. Bar Found.; mem. N.C. Bar Assn. (pres. 1978-79, gov. 1971-75), ABA (state del. 1980-89, assembly del.) 26th Jud. Dist. Bar Assn., Mecklenburg Bar Found. (trustee), Am. Law Inst., Order of Coif, Phi Eta Sigma, Phi Beta Kappa. Democrat. Methodist. Home: 1047 Ardsley Rd Charlotte NC 28207-1815 Office: Kennedy Covington Lobdell & Hickman NationsBank Ctr 100 N Tryon St Ste 4200 Charlotte NC 28202-4000

WALKER, DANA EUGENE, evangelist; b. Ancourage, Ala., Nov. 3, 1956; s. Robert Dale and Kathryn Jean (Ruhl) W.; m. Dorcas Annette, June 11, 1976; children: Dawn Annette, Dwight Eugene. Grad., Penn View Bible Coll., 1978. V.p. youth ministry Bible Meth. Connection of Tenn., Jamestown, 1981-83, home missions chmn., 1993-96, evangelist, 1991—; owner Christian Stuff, Jamestown, 1994—. Author: Full and Complete Salvation, 1984, Remarks on Romans, 1991, Holiness Truths from the Hebrew Tabernacle, 1995; author, compiler (religious periodical) Holiness Messenger, 1986-96. Home and Office: Christian Stuff 154 N Wildwood Ln Jamestown TN 38556

WALKER, DANIEL JOSHUA, JR., lawyer; b. Gibson, N.C., Nov. 27, 1915; s. Daniel Joshua and Annie (Hurdle) W.; m. Sarah Elizabeth Nicholson, June 14, 1941. A.B., U. N.C., 1936, J.D., 1948. Bar: N.C. 1948, U.S. Dist. Ct. (mid. dist.) N.C. 1956, U.S. Ct. Appeals (4th cir.) 1956. Clk. of Superior Ct. of Alamance County, Graham, N.C., 1948-53; ptnr. firm Long, Ridge, Harris & Walker, Graham, 1953-67; county atty. Alamance County, 1964-77, county mgr., 1971-76; sr. mem. firm Walker Harris & Pierce, Graham, 1967-71; ptnr. firm. Allen & Walker and predecessor, Burlington, N.C., 1977-91; pvt. practice, Graham, 1991—; of counsel Floyd, Allen & Jacobs, Greensboro and Burlington, 1991—. Mem. Human Rels. Coun. of Alamance County, 1963-71, chmn., 1970; mem. N.C. Environ. Mgmt. Commn., 1972-77; pres. Alamance County Young Democratic Club, 1950; chmn. Alamance County Dem. Exec. Com., 1956-58; mem. N.C. Dem. Exec. Com., 1958-66; trustee Tech. Inst. of Alamance, 1964-71, Presbyn. Found., Presbyn. Ch. of U.S., 1969-73; moderator Orange Presbytery, 1980, mem. council, 1972-74; bd. dirs. Alamance County United Fund, Cherokee council Boy Scouts Am., Burlington Community YMCA.; mem. adv. bd. Salvation Army, 1980—, chmn., 1990-91. Served to capt. AUS, 1942-46, ETO. Decorated Bronze Star. Mem. Alamance County C. of C. (pres. 1981), ABA, N.C. Bar Assn., Alamance County Bar Assn. (pres. 1977-78), N.C. Assn. County Attys. (pres. 1972, named County Att. of Yr. 1971), 15th Jud. Dist. Bar Assn. (pres. 1967-68), Phi Alpha Delta. Lodge: Burlington Kiwanis (pres. 1957, named Alamance County Citizen of Yr. 1969). Home: 215 Long Ave Graham NC 27253-2315 Office: PO Box 772 Graham NC 27253-0772

WALKER, DONALD WILLIAM, home health care nurse, critical care nurse; b. Ft. Smith, Ark., June 27, 1964; s. Donald Edward Walker and Nancy Coradelia (Simpson) Pigg; m. Barbara J. Jester, May 3, 1986 (div. May 1990); 1 child, Christopher Michael Shane; m. Deborah Jo Hiner, July 26, 1991. LPN, Ark. Valley Vocat.-Tech. Inst., 1988; ADN, Westark Community Coll., 1994. LPN, Ark., Okla.; RN, Ark., Okla. LPN ICU nurse St. Edwards Mercy Med. Ctr., Ft. Smith, 1988-90; home health field nurse Med. Home Health Inc., Sallisaw, Okla., 1990-92; home health aid liaison Med. Home Health Inc., Spiro, Okla., 1992-94; field nurse Med. Home Health Inc., Sallisaw, Okla., 1994-95; home health aide supr. Med. Home Health, Inc., Poteau, Okla., 1995—. Cub scout leader Boy Scouts Am. With USAF, 1982-85. Recipient Achievement medal USAF, 1982-83; Ark. Valley Vocat.-Tech. Inst. scholar, 1987. Democrat.

WALKER, DOROTHY KEISTER, minister; b. Lock Haven, Pa., Sept. 24, 1920; d. Charles Lester and Eva Derr (Schuyler) K.; m. Dean E. Walker, May 28, 1962 (dec. 1988). BS in Elem. Edn., Lock Haven U., 1942; BD in Ch. History, MS in Religious Edn., Butler U., 1949; DD (hon.), Milligan Coll., 1962. Ordained to ministry Ch. of Christ, 1949. Asst. min. Fleming Garden Christian Ch., Indpls., 1946-49; with Jones-Keister Evang. Team, nat., 1949-59; dir., lectr. Mission to Women, nat., 1959—; elder Hopwood Christian Ch., Milligan Coll., Tenn., 1985—; co-founder Emmanuel Sch. of Religion, Johnson City, Tenn.; asst. bd. mem. N.Am. Christian Conv., 1985-87; trustee Appalachian Christian Village, Johnson City, 1986—, European Evang. Soc., Tubingen, Germany, 1989—. Contbr. articles to religious jours. Mem. Phi Kappa, Theta Phi, Kappa Delta Pi. Home and Office: PO Box 449 Milligan College TN 37682-0449

WALKER, EDWIN STUART, III, retired missionary organization executive; b. Cumberland, Va., Sept. 12, 1928; s. Edwin Stuart Jr. and Thea Boyd (Womack) W.; m. Mary Lee Fry, Sept. 11, 1953; children: Stuart, Mary Anne, David, Thomas, Sara. BA, Columbia (S.C.) Bible Coll., 1951; postgrad., Wheaton (Ill.) Coll., 1951, 53, U. Haiti, Port-au-Prince, 1972, Columbia Bibl. Sem., 1982. Ordained to ministry Fellowship Ind. Evang. Chs., 1951. Pastor Grace Presbyn. Ch., Lexington, Va., 1952-56; tchr. Inst. Biblique Lumière, Cayes, Haiti, 1957-64; chief exec. officer Radio Lumière, Port-au-Prince, 1965-79; min. missions Worldteam, Norfolk, Va., 1980-84; pres., chief exec. officer, bd. dirs. Worldteam USA, Miami, Fla., 1985-92; pres. Alumni Assn. Columbia Internat. U., 1995—; chmn. Communications Commn., Concile des Eglise Evangelique, Haiti, 1965-79; bd. dirs. Worldteam Internation, Inc., Atlanta, 1985-92, Worldteam Assocs., Inc., Morton, Ill., 1985-92. Author: (booklets) La Trinite, 1960, Church/Mission Partnership, 1982, Philosophy of Resource Development, 1991; contbr. article to ency. Mem. cen. com. Haitian Red Cross, Port-au-prince, 1974-79; mem. curriculum com. Haiti Dept. Agr., 1970-75; pres. Pedodontic Found., Port-au-Prince, 1972-75; cons. on radio edn. Haiti Presdl. Cabinet, 1978-79. Recipient Disting. Lectureship in Communications award Wheaton Coll. Grad. Sch., 1976. Mem. Christian Mgmt. Assn. Office: World Team USA 1431 Stuckert Rd Warrington PA 18976

WALKER, EVELYN, retired educational television executive; b. Birmingham, Ala.; d. Preston Lucas and Mattie (Williams) W.; AB, Huntingdon Coll., 1927; student Cornell U., 1927-28; MA, U. Ala., 1963; LHD, Huntingdon Coll., 1974. Speech instr. Phillips High Sch., Birmingham, 1930-34; head speech dept. Ramsay High Sch., Birmingham, 1934-52; chmn. radio and TV, Birmingham Pub. Schs., 1944-75, head instructional TV programming svcs., 1969-75; mem. summer faculty extension div. U. Va., 1965, 66, 67; former regional cons. ednl. TV broadcasting; Miss Ann, broadcaster children's daily radio program, Birmingham, 1946-57; prodr. Our Am. Heritage radio series, 1944-54; TV staff prodr. programs shown daily Ala. Pub. TV Network, 1954-75; past cons. Gov.'s Ednl. TV Legis. Study Com., 1953; nat. del. Asian-Am. Women Broadcasters Conf., 1966; former regional cons. Ednl. TV Broadcasting. Mem. emerita Nat. Def. Adv. Com. on Women in Svcs.; past TV-radio co-chmn. Gov.'s Adv. Bd. Safety Com.; past chmn. creative TV-radio writing competition Festival of Arts; past audio-visual chmn. Ala. Congress, also past mem. Birmingham coun. PTA; media chmn. Gov.'s Commn. on Yr. of the Child; bd. dirs. Women's Army Corps Mus., Fort MiClellen, 1960-93. Recipient Alumnae Achievement award Huntingdon Coll., 1958; Tops in Our Town award Birmingham News, 1957; Air Force Recruiting plaque, 1961; Spl. Bowl award for promoting arts through Ednl. TV. Birmingham Festival of Arts, 1962; citation 4th Army Corps., 1962; cert. of appreciation Ala. Multiple Sclerosis Soc., 1962; Freedoms Found. at Valley Forge Educator's medal award, 1963; Top TV award ARC, 1964; Ala. Woman of Achievement award, 1964; Bronze plaque Ala. Dist. Exch. Clubs, 1969; cert. of appreciation Birmingham Bd. Edn., 1975; Obelisk award Children's Theatre, 1976; 20-Yr. Svc. award Ala. Ednl. TV Commn.; key to city of Birmingham, 1966; named Woman of Yr., Birmingham, 1965; named Ala. Woman of Yr., Progressive Farmer mag., 1966; hon. col. Ala. Militia. Mem. Am. Assn. Ret. Persons, Ala. Assn. Ret. Tchrs., Huntingdon Coll. Alumnae Assn. (former internat. pres.), Former Am. Women in Radio and TV, Arlington Hist. Assn. (dir., pres. 1981-83), Magna Charta Dames (past state sec.-treas.), DAR (former pub. rels. com. Ala., TV chmn., state program chmn. 1979-85, state chmn. Seimes Microfilm com. 1985-88, state chmn. Motion Picture, Radio TV com. 1988-94, tricom. chmn. 1988-94), Colonial Dames 17th Century, U.S. Daus. 1812 (past state TV chmn.), Daus. Am. Colonists (past 2d v.p. local chpt., past state TV and radio chmn.), Ams. Royal Descent, Royal Order Garter, Plantagenets Soc. Am., Salvation Army Women's Aux., Symphony Aux., Humane Soc. Aux., Eagle Forum, Nat. League Am. Pen Women, Womens's Com. 100 for Birmingham (bd. dirs.), Royal Order Crown, Women in Communications (past local pres., nat. headliner 1965), Internat. Platform Assn., Birmingham-Jefferson Hist. Soc., Delta Delta Delta (mem. Golden Circle), Ladies Golf Assn., Birmingham Country Club, The Club. Methodist. Home: Mountain Brook 744 Euclid Ave Birmingham AL 35213-2538

WALKER, F. K., executive. Chmn. Broward County Host. Commn., Ft. Lauderdale, Fla. Office: Broward County Hist Commn 100 S New River Dr E Fort Lauderdale FL 33301-2929

WALKER, FRANCIS ROACH, rehabilitation counselor; b. Dallas, Mar. 1, 1944; s. Anan Orville and Vonda Mae (Roach) W.; m. Sherry Lynn Robins (div. Dec. 1977); children: John, Christian, Lorri; m. Karen Sue Newhouse, Aug. 2, 1980. BGS in Psychology, Chaminade U. of Honolulu, 1980; MA in Psychology, U. No. Colo., 1982. Cert. tchr., Hawaii; cert. rehab. counselor. Br. mgr. Internat. Savs. & Loan, Honolulu, 1982-83; ops. mgr. C.M. Assocs., Inc., Kaneohe, Hawaii, 1983-84; instr. adult div. St. Louis High Sch., Honolulu, 1984-87; owner Commonwealth Distbrs., Norfolk, Va., 1987-88; dir. edn. Gulf Coast Marine Inst., Inc., Sarasota, Fla., 1989-91; vocat. evaluator vets. svcs. Goodwill Industries-Suncoast, Inc., St. Petersburg, Fla., 1991—; adj. prof. City Colls. of Chgo., 1984-87, Ctrl. Tex. Coll., 1988-89. Capt. USMC, 1962-82. Mem. Am. Legion Nat. Sojourners (chpt. pres.), Marine Corps. League, Marine Corps Mustang Assn., Fla. Mustangs (co-founder, pres.), Shriners. Republican. Home: 340 Colony Point Rd S Saint Petersburg FL 33705-6227 Office: Goodwill Industries Suncoast Inc 10596 Gandy Blvd N Saint Petersburg FL 33702-1422

WALKER, FRANK ALEXANDER, pediatrician, educator; b. San Francisco, Dec. 5, 1934; s. Lawrence Howe and Jane Johanna (Koskiniemi) W.; m. Rosina Neidich, June 20, 1958; children, Katharina Ray, Julia Beran, Francesca Knutson. Student, U. Calif., Berkeley, 1952-55; MD, McGill U., 1959. Diplomate Am. Bd. Pediat. Intern So. Pacific, San Francisco, 1959-60; resident and fellow Children's Meml. Hosp., Chgo., 1960-63; fellow U. Wis., Madison, 1963-66; instr. clin. pediat. U. Ore., Portland, 1966-67; asst. prof. pediat. Med. Coll. Wis., Milw., 1967-74; pvt. practice Milw., 1974-83; sr. pediatrician KKESH, Riyadh, Saudi Arabia, 1983-85; cons. pediatrician Hamad Gen. Hosp., Doha, Qatar, 1985-87; pediatrician Health Am.-Maxicare-Humana, Louisville, 1987—; assoc. clin. prof. Marquette U. Dental Sch., Milw., 1968-80; clin. assoc. U. Ky., 1993—; clin. asst. prof. pediat. U. Louisville, 1995—. Wyeth Labs. fellow, 1961-63. Fellow Am. Acad. Pediat.; mem. Am. Coll. Physicians. Republican. Lutheran. Office: 2650 W Broadway Louisville KY 40211-1333

WALKER, GARY CHITWOOD, author; b. Wytheville, Va., May 24, 1946; s. Carl David and Mary (Cassell) W.; m. Sue Adams, June 11, 1968; children: Christopher, Kevin. BS, Va. Poly. Inst. and State U., 1968. Truck driver Dodson Specialties, Roanoke, Va., 1978-79; sales rep. Palco, Roanoke, 1979; field underwriter Life and Casualty, Roanoke, 1979-81; founder, mgr. Mobile Communications Systems, Wytheville, 1981-83; sales rep. Life of Va., Roanoke, 1983-85; author A&W Enterprise, Roanoke, 1985—; chmn. Civil War Roundtable, Roanoke, 1987-88; writer, cons., actor Wythe County Bicentennial, Wytheville, 1989-90; cons. Roanoke County Dept. Pks. and Recreation, 1991-92. Author: Footprints, 1983, The War in Southwest Virginia, 1961-65, 1985, Hunter's Fiery Raid through Virginia Valleys, 1989, Civil War Tales, Civil War Tales Vol. II, Ode to Wythe County, 1990. Mem. Roanoke spl. events com. Recipient Cert. Commendation, Fair View Centennial, 1990, Cert. Appreciation, Nat. Pk. Svc., 1990, Redbud Festival, 1990, Wolf Hills Archeol. Chpt., 1990. Mem. Sons of Confederate Vets. (commdr. 1988-90), Roanoke Valley Hist. Soc., Confederate Meml. Soc., Assn. for the Preservation of Civil War, Wythe County Hist. Soc., Saltville Historic Found. (cons. re-enactment 1989). Mem. Christian Ch. (Disciples of Christ). Office: A&W Enterprise PO Box 8133 Roanoke VA 24014-0133

WALKER, GARY LINN, materials and logistics executive, consultant; b. Cin., Apr. 26, 1947; s. Ward Walkie and Cora Lee (Reynolds) W.; m. Mary Lee Robertson, Aug. 30, 1969; 1 child, Charlotte Anne. BA, Samford U., 1969. Cert. fellow in prodn. and inventory mgmt. Prodn. planner, prodn. foreman, indsl. engr., Cin., 1969-74; mfg. mgr. Xomox Inc., 1974-77; materials mgr. Textron Inc.-Sprague Meter Divsn., 1977-80; dir. materials and mgmt. info. Fairchild Inc., Beckley, W.Va., 1980-83; materials mgr., corp. mgr. distbn. and logistics Pelikan Inc./Dennison Mfg. Co., Franklin, Tenn., 1983-94; internat. mgr. mfg. and logistics Pelikan Inc./Dennison Mfg. Co., Franklin, 1983-94; application cons. The Everest Group, Nashville, 1994—; cons. Nukote/Pelikan, Derry, Pa., 1995—, Pelikan Europa, Egg, Switzerland, 1989-94. V.p. Young Dems., Samford U., 1967-69. With U.S. Army, 1970-71. Home: 200 Green Valley Blvd Franklin TN 37064-5271 Office: Nukote/Pelikan 1 Imaging Ln Derry PA 15627

WALKEP, GEORGE KONTZ, law educator; b. Tuscaloosa, Ala., July 8, 1938; s. Joseph Henry and Catherine Louise (Indorf) W.; m. Phyllis Ann Sherman, July 30, 1966; children: Charles Edward, Mary Neel. BA, U. Ala., 1959; LLB, Vanderbilt U., 1966; AM, Duke U., 1968; LLM, U. Va., 1972; postgrad. (Sterling fellow), Law Sch. Yale U., 1975-76. Bar: Va. 1967, N.C. 1976. Law clk. U.S. Dist. Ct., Richmond, Va., 1966-67; assoc. Hunton, Williams, Gay, Powell & Gibson, Richmond, 1967-70; pvt. practice Charlottesville, Va., 1970-71; asst. prof. Law Sch. Wake Forest U., Winston-Salem, N.C., 1972-73, assoc. prof. Law Sch., 1974-77, prof. Law Sch., 1977—; mem. bd. advisors Divinity Sch. Wake Forest U., 1991-94; Charles H. Stockton prof. internat. law U.S. Naval War Coll., 1992-93; vis. prof. Marshall-Wythe Sch. Law, Coll. William and Mary, Williamsburg, Va., 1979-80, U. Ala. Law Sch., 1985; cons. Naval War Coll., 1976—, Nat. Def. Exec. Res., 1991—, Naval War Coll., Operational Law Adv. Bd., 1993—. Author: International Law for the Naval Commander, 1985; contbr. articles to profl. jours. With USN, 1959-62, capt. USNR, ret. Woodrow Wilson fellow, 1962-63; recipient Joseph Branch Alumni Svc. award, Wake Forest, 1988; named Hon. Atty. Gen. N.C., 1986. Mem. ABA, Va. Bar Assn., N.C. Bar Assn. (chair internat. law & practice sect. 1995-96), Am. Soc. Internat. Law (exec. coun. 1988-91), Internat. Law Assn., Am. Judicature Soc., Am. Law Inst., Maritime Law Assn., Order of Barristers, Piedmont Club, Phi Beta Kappa, Sigma Alpha Epsilon, Phi Delta Phi. Democrat. Episcopalian. Home: 3321 Pennington Ln Winston Salem NC 27106-5439 Office: Wake Forest U Sch Law PO Box 7206 # U Winston Salem NC 27109

WALKER, GLORIA LEE, service company executive; b. Oklahoma City, Dec. 31, 1942; d. Russell Holland and Ethel Wanita (Kierig) Walker; m. Thomas William Rupprath, June 3, 1966 (dec. Feb. 1995); children: Robert, John. BA in Sociology, U. S.C., 1965; MS in Elem. Edn., U. Nebr., 1971; EdD in Adminstrn., Fla. Atlantic U., 1986. Ops. rsch. analyst U.S. Bur. Mines, Washington, 1988-90; employee devel. specialist IRS, Dallas, 1991-92; pres. AMERITRAIN, Dallas/Lubbock, Tex., 1992—. Author: Training a Diversified Workforce, 1993, Developing Training Materials, 1995, Instructing Diversified Employees 1995: Seminars in Training, 1995.

WALKER, HARRIETTE KATHERINE, religious administrator; b. Cad, Ga., Jan. 7, 1929; d. James Wilden and Eugie Arleen (Harton) Pack; m. William Daniel Walker, June 4, 1960. AA, Tenn. Wesleyan Coll., 1948; BA, U. Tenn., Chattanooga, 1953. Edn. dir. 1st United Meth. Ch., Copperhill, Tenn., 1953-55, Morristown, Tenn., 1955-57, Alcoa, Tenn., 1957-59; field exec. Citrus Coun. Girl Scouts, Inc., Orlando, Fla., 1968-85; program dir. United Meth. Ch., Satellite Beach, Fla., 1985-87; del. Fla. Ann. Conf., Lakeland, 1978-96, Meth. World Conf., Nairobi, 1986, Singapore, 1991, Rio de Janeiro, 1996; mem. Meth. World Coun., 1991, 96; mem. exec. bd. Haitian Refugee Ministry, Ft. Pierce, Fla., 1988-96; United Meth. rep. Fla. Coun. Chs., Orlando, 1990—; mem. lay-clergy adv. coun. Bethune-Cookman Coll., 1994-96. Mem. Girl Scouts USA; mem. Daus. of the Nile, Shilah Temple No. 151, 1993, bd. lay ministry, 1993, Melbourne lay dist. leader, 1993, mem. Fla. conf. commn. on archives and history, 1992. Recipient Conf. Laity Christian Svc. award United Meth. Ch. Fla. Conf., 1988, Thanks Badge Citrus Coun. Girl Scouts U.S., 1988. Mem. AAUW, Nat. Assn. United Meth. Scouters Ministry, Missile, Space and Range Pioneers, Inc. (life), Fla. So. Coll. Pres. Coun., Pi Beta Phi. Home: 145 Allan Ln Melbourne FL 32951

WALKER, HARRY WEBSTER, II, food products executive; b. Bridgeport, Conn., Feb. 28, 1921; s. Webster Upson and Edith May (Camp) W.; m. Alethea Kunhardt, June 17, 1950; children: Antoinette Hamner, Alethea K. Overholser, H. Webster III, Gilford B. BA, Yale U., 1944; LHD (hon.), Piedmont Coll., Demorest, Ga., 1989. Sale mgr. St. Regis, Chgo., 1946-60; gen. mgr. Bates do Brasil, Sao Paulo, 1961-64; exec. v.p. and gen. mgr. Clint Davis Co., Ft. Pierce, Fla., 1965-67; pres., chief exec. officer Sunsweet Fruit, Inc., Vero Beach, Fla., 1968—, also bd. dirs.; bd. dirs. Carpenter Tech. Corp., Reading, Pa., The Walker Group, Inc., Southport, Conn. Contbr. articles on yachting to various mags., 1960—. Bd. dirs. Vero Beach YMCA, Blue Ridge Assemblies, Inc., Black Mountain, N.C.; chmn. Camp-Younts Found., 1989—; vice chmn. Ruth Camp Campbell Found.; sec. Elms. Found.; chmn. Olympic com. Internat. Star Class Yacht Racing Assn.; deacon United Congl. Ch.; active devel. bd. Yale U.; mem. Nat. Boating Safety Adv. Coun. Lt. USNR, 1944-46, PTO. Mem. U.S. Yacht Racing Union, Assn. Yale U. Alumni, Rotary. Republican. Office: Sunsweet Fruit Inc PO Drawer T Vero Beach FL 32961

WALKER, JACKSON VENUS, systems analyst, consultant; b. Port Angeles, Wash., Jan. 2, 1957; s. James Venus and Betty Jean (Kilgore) W.; m. Shawn Marshall, June 13, 1981 (div. Oct. 1982). BSEE, Tenn. Technol. U., 1981. Engr. Ga. Power Co., Augusta and Columbus, 1977-84; mfg. engr. Phillips Consumer Electronics, Knoxville, Tenn., 1984; tech. engr. Dynage Controls, Hartford, Conn., 1985; tech. sales rep. CBM Computer Sys., Oak Ridge, Tenn., 1986; programmer/analyst Scitek, Inc., Oak Ridge, 1987-90; project control engr. EBASCO, Inc., Watts Bar/Spring City, Tenn., 1990; mem. tech. staff Micah Sys., Inc., Knoxville, 1990-92; pres., owner Softwalk Cons. Group, Knoxville, 1993—. Author: (computer manuals) Operation of PC Modeling Software, 1987, Fortran Modeling Software, 1987. Student organizer Bob Clement campaign, Cookeville, Tenn., 1979. Democrat. Office: Softwalk Cons Group 7509 Kingston Pike Ste 267 Knoxville TN 37919-5625

WALKER, JAMES E., academic administrator, educator; b. Phenix City, Ala.; s. Curtis and Mamie (Milner) W.; m. Gwendolyn Pompey, Dec. 22, 1968; children: Jamell E., Jabrina E. BS, Ala. State U., 1963; MA, Atlanta U., 1967; EdD, Pa. State U., 1972; LhD, Mt. St. Mary's Coll., 1991. Chmn., tchr. Parks Jr. High Sch., Atlanta, 1967-69; instr. Western Mich. U., Kalamazoo, 1971; asst. prof. spl. edn. So. Ill. U., Edwardsville, 1972-74; exec. asst. to supt. Bryce Hosp., Tuscaloosa, Ala., 1975-77; chmn. spl. edn. Ill. State U., Normal, 1977-80; dean edn. Calif. State U., Hayward, 1980-87; v.p. provost U. No. Colo., Greeley, 1987-91; pres. Mid. Tenn. State U., Murfreesboro, 1991—; adj. prof. U. Ala., Tuscaloosa, 1975-77; presenter in field. Author: Behavior Management: A Practical Approach for Educators, 1987, 5th edit., 1992. Commr. Boy Scouts Am., Nashville, 1992—; mem. Black Health Care Task Force, Nashville, 1992—. USDE/BEH fellow Pa. State U., 1969-72, State of Ga. Dept. Edn. fellow, 1966-67; recipient Outstanding Alumni award Ala. State U., 1986, Coll. Edn. Alumni award Pa. State U., 1988. Mem. AAUW, Am. Assn. Higher Edn., Rotary. Democrat. Roman Catholic. Office: Mid Tenn State U Office of Pres 110 Cope Adminstrn Bldg Murfreesboro TN 37132*

WALKER, JAMES ROBERT, software products developer; b. Union, S.C., Oct. 21, 1951; s. James Robert and Virginia Carolyn (Farmer) W. BS in Computer Sci., U. S.C., 1973. Programmer trainee Spartan Mills, Spartansburg, S.C., 1973-74; sr. programmer Cone Mills, Greensboro, N.C., 1974-77, Luth. Gen. Hosp., Park Ridge, Ill., 1977, Equifax, Atlanta, 1985-92; programmer analyst Bus. Data, Chgo., 1977-79, Hargray Telephone Co., Hilton Head, S.C., 1993-96; system software specialist Digital Systems, Columbia, S.C., 1979-80; tech. specialist Draper Corp., Greensboro, 1980-85; with Trilogy Cons., Inc., Research Triangle Park, N.C., 1996—. Recipient 5th place award Anderson Running Club, 1982. Mem. Audubon Soc., Sierra Club (chair stream watch 1983-85). Home: 4600 University Dr Apt 1721 Durham NC 27707-6123 Office: PPD Pharmaco 1400 Perimeter Park Ave Morrisville NC 27560-5519

WALKER, JERALD CARTER, university administrator, minister; b. Bixby, Okla., May 22, 1938; s. Joseph Carter and Trula Tosh (Jackson) W.; m. Virginia Canfield, Apr. 14, 1963; children: Elisabeth Katherine, Anne Carter. BA in Sociology, Oklahoma City U., 1960; BD, U. Chgo., 1964; D of Religion, Sch. Theology at Claremont, 1966; LHD (hon.), Shiller U., 1994. Ordained to ministry Meth. Ch., 1964. Dir., campus minister Campus Christian Assn., Chgo., 1961-64; minister of outreach Temple Meth. Ch., San Francisco, 1965-66; chaplain, asst. prof. religion Nebr. Wesleyan U., Lincoln, 1966-69; pres. John J. Pershing Coll., Beatrice, Nebr., 1969-70; v.p. univ. rels., assoc. prof. Southwestern U., Georgetown, Tex., 1970-74; pres. Baker U., Baldwin, Kans., 1974-79, Oklahoma City U., 1979—; ednl. adv. to bd. dirs. Tianjin U. Commerce, People's Republic of China; participant Okla. Ann. Conf. of United Meth. Ch. Co-author: The State of Sequoyah: An Impressionistic View of Eastern Oklahoma, 1985; contbr. chpt. book, articles to profl. jours. Bd. dirs., past chmn. Okla. Ind. Coll. Found. Recipient Alumni Recognition award Nebr. 4H Club, 1970, Okla. 4H Club, Disting. Alumnis award Oklahoma City U., 1974, Outstanding Citizen award Dist. 575 Rotary Internat., 1990, Award for Excellence Asia Soc. Okla., 1990, Humanitarian award for Okla/Ark. region NCCJ, 1992, Nat. Police Adminstrn. award for promotion or peace and order Rep. of China, 1992, Francis Asbury award for fostering United Meth. Ministries in Higher Edn., 1994, Excellent Leader award Mgmt. Devel. Inst. Singapore, 1996, Benjamin Franklin award Downtown Olka. City Sertoma Club, 1992, Excellent Leader award Mgmt. Devel. Inst. of Singapore, 1996. Mem. Nat. Assn. Schs. and Colls. of United Meth. Ch. (past pres.), Nat. Assn. Colls. and Univs. (bd. dirs.). Office: Oklahoma City U 2501 N Blackwelder Ave Oklahoma City OK 73106-1493

WALKER, JEWETT LYNIUS, clergyman, church official; b. Beaumont, Tex., Apr. 7, 1930; s. Elijah Harvey and Ella Jane (Wilson) W.; BA, Calif. Western U., 1957; MA, Kingdom Bible Inst., 1960; B.R.E., St. Stephens Coll., 1966, D.D., 1968; LLD, Union Bapt. Sem., 1971; grad. Nat. Planned Giving Inst., 1981, St. Paul Sch. Theology, 1979, Philanthropy Tax Inst., 1982; D.D., Clinton Jr. Coll., 1992; m. Dorothy Mae Croom, Apr. 11, 1965; children: Cassandra Lynn, Jewett L., Kevin, Michael, Ella, Betty Renne, Kent, Elijah H. Ordained to ministry A.M.E. Zion Ch., 1957; pastor Shiloh A.M.E. Zion Ch., Monrovia, Calif., 1961-64, Martin Temple A.M.E. Zion Ch., L.A., 1964-65, 1st A.M.E. Zion Ch., Compton, Calif., 1965-66, Met. A.M.E. Zion Ch., L.A., 1966-73, Logan Temple A.M.E. Zion Ch., San Diego, 1973-74, Rock Hill A.M.E. Zion Ch., Indian Trail, N.C., 1974-79, Bennettsville A.M.E. Zion Ch., Norwood, N.C., 1979-86, Price Meml. A.M.E. Zion Ch., Concord, N.C., 1986-89, Mt. Zion A.M.E. Zion Ch., Hickory Grove, S.C., 1989-91, New Hope A.M.E. Zion Ch., Lancaster, S.C., 1992, Mt. Zion A.M.E. Zion Ch., Lancaster, S.C., 1993—; sec.-treas. dept. home missions, brotherhood pensions and relief A.M.E. Zion Ch., Charlotte, N.C., 1974-94; mem. exec. bd. Prophetic Justice Unit Com. Nat. Coun. Chs., co-chairperson pers. com.; mem. World Meth. Coun., del. 14th World Conf. Chmn. Minority Affairs Adv. Com., Mecklenburg County; trustee Clinton Coll., dir. planned giving, 1992; trustee Rock Hill, Lomax-Hannon Coll., Greenville, Ala., Union Bapt. Theol. Sem., Birmingham, Ala.; bd. mgrs. McCrorey br. YMCA; pres. Am. Ch. Fin. Service Corp., Carolina Home Health Service Inc., Methodist Life Ins. Soc. Inc., bd. trustees State N.C. Coll. Found., Inc., 1987, del. Presbyn. Partners in Ecumenism Nat. Council Chs. Christ, 1986, pres., 1988—; pres. The House of Irma Funeral Home, Concord; del. Presbyn. Ch. U.S. Gen. Assembly, 1985; mem. citizens parole accountability com. Mecklenburg County, Charlotte, N.C., 1993; mem planned giving adv. bd. Livingston Coll., Salisbury, N.C.; pres. Jewett L. Walker & Assocs.; chmn. minority affairs adv. com. Mecklenburg County. Fellow Nat. Assn. Ch. Bus. Adminstrs., Ch. Bus. Adminstrn., Presbyn. Ch. Bus. Adminstrn. Assn., com. mem. Charlotte Meckienburg Citizen Parole Accountability Com., 1994; mem. NAACP (life), Nat. Soc. Fund Raising Execs., Am. Bible Soc. (state dir. vols., N.C. and S.C. dir. vol.), Nat. Spkr.'s Bur., Christian Ministries Mgmt. Assn., Am. Soc. Assn. Execs., Shriners, Masons (33 deg.), Prince Hall Club. Republican. Author: Is There a Man in the House, 1975, Lets Get Serious about Missions, 1991, The Denominational Dollar, 1992; also articles. Home: 910 Bridlepath Ln Charlotte NC 28211-2022 Office: 4501 Walker Rd Charlotte NC 28211-2047

WALKER, JOHN SAMUEL, retired pediatrician; b. Brevard, N.C., June 25, 1921; s. Hugh Raven and Mary Jane (King) W.; m. Jean Lane Davis, June 9, 1945 (div. Mar. 1986); children: Virginia Davis, Hugh Raven, Samuel Vivian, Joseph Andrew, Jean Lane; m. Chieko Akahori, May 31, 1986; 1 child, Mary Jane Haruko Walker. BS, Wake Forest U., 1943; MD, Jefferson Med. Coll., 1946. Diplomate Am. Bd. Pediatrics. Resident in pediatrics Crawford W. Long Meml. Hosp., Atlanta, 1950-51, Children's Hosp., Cin., 1951-52; pvt. practice pediatrics Children's Med. Group, Atlanta, 1952-61; mgr. clin. rsch. Upjohn Co., Kalamazoo, Mich., 1961-67; v.p. med. affairs Riker Labs., Northridge, Calif., 1967-69; dir., sr. dir. clin. rsch. Merck Rsch. Labs., West Point, Pa., 1969-77, sr. dir. regulatory affairs, 1977-92; ret., 1992. Lt. (j.g.) Med. Corps USN, 1946-49. Fellow Am. Acad. Pediatrics, Am. soc. for Clin. Pharmacology and Therapeutics, Royal Soc. Medicine; mem. AMA. Republican. Episcopalian. Home: 4190 Sulgrave Ct Winston Salem NC 27104

WALKER, JOSEPH HILLARY, JR., lawyer, banker; b. Birmingham, Ala., Apr. 7, 1919; s. Joseph Hillary Sr. and Nora D. (Arnold) W.; m. Ann Tucker, Dec. 31, 1944; children: Joseph Hillary III, Harriet E., Mildred Katherin, Bonnie Jo. AB, U. Ala., 1941, JD, 1947. Bar: Ala. 1947, Tenn. 1947, U.S. Dist. Ct. (we. dist.) Tenn. 1947, U.S. Ct. Mil. Appeals 1956, U.S. Supreme Ct. 1956. Sole practice, Ripley, Tenn., 1947-76; sr. mem. Walker & Walker, Ripley, 1976—; mem. Tenn. Ho. of Reps., 1949-51, Tenn. Senate, 1951-53; chmn. bd. Farmers Union Bank, Ripley, 1964-86; dir. Lauderdale Devel. Corp., Ripley. Pres. Tenn. Constl. Conv., 1959, mem. 1965; chmn. Lauderdale County Bd. of Edn., 1964-67; trustee Lauderdale County Hosp., 1962-89; deacon Bapt. Ch., 1954—, treas., 1962—; trustee Union U., 1970—. Mem. Sigma Nu. Lodge: Rotary. Home: 233 Lackey Ln Ripley TN 38063-1619 Office: Walker & Walker PO Box 287 Ripley TN 38063-0287

WALKER, MARK LESLIE, financial executive; b. Enid, Okla., Feb. 18, 1962; s. Bobby Gene and Daphenee Viola Walker; m. Becky Ruth Birdwell; 1 child, Ryan Patrick. BA, BBA, Tex. Christian U., 1985. Cert. investment mgmt. analyst. Acct. exec. Johnston Lemon & Co., Washington, 1988-89, Dean Witter, Ft. Worth, 1989-91; asst. v.p., sales mgr. Merrill Lynch, Ft. Worth, 1991-96; 1st v.p. Smith Barney, Dallas, 1996—;, 1996—. Bd. dirs. Ft. Worth Ballet Concerto, 1990-93, Fellowship Christian Athletes, 1991-96; bd. dirs., chair devel. Easter Seals North Tex., 1993-96, Bobby Bragan Youth Found., 1993-96. Capt. U.S. Army, 1986-88, Korea. Republican. Roman Catholic. Home: 3501 Bellaire Park Ct Fort Worth TX 76109-2640 Office: Smith Barney 200 Cresent Ct Ste 1200 Dallas TX 75201-7837

WALKER, MARY ERLINE, critical care nurse; b. Newport, R.I., June 4, 1951; d. Edgar Hergor and Doris Elizabeth (Allen) Sherman; m. Michael Robert Walker, Dec. 22, 1970; 1 child, Michael Robert II. AS in Nursing, Lake City (Fla.) Community Coll., 1971; AA, Santa Fe Community Coll., Gainesville, Fla., 1974; BS in Profl. Arts, St. Joseph's Coll., North Windham, Maine, 1980; BSN, Regent's Coll., Albany, N.Y., 1996. RN; cert. critical care nurse, med./surg. nurse. Staff nurse Cape Fear Valley Hosp., Fayetteville, N.C., 1971-72, surg. staff nurse, 1975-76; staff nurse Alachua Gen. Hosp., Gainesville, 1972-74; staff nurse male medicine Womack Army Community Hosp., Ft. Bragg, N.C., 1976-81, staff nurse, 1986-87, inservice coordinator, 1987; staff nurse Reynolds Army Community Hosp., Ft. Sill, Okla., 1981-83, evening supr., 1983-84; staff nurse cardiology Lettermen Army Med. Ctr., San Francisco, 1984-85, clin. nurse specialist recovery room, 1985-86, charge nurse cardiac rehab., 1985; staff nurse, insvc. coord. Bayne Jones Army Hosp., Ft. Polk, La., 1988-90; staff nurse MICU Brooke Army Med. Ctr., Fort Sam Houston, Tex., 1990—. Pres. Bay Bandits Volksmarch, San Francisco, 1985-86; cub scout den leader Boy Scouts Am., 1993—. Mem. Am. Assn. Critical Care Nurses (North Cen. Fla. chpt. pres. 1974), Am. Nurses Assn., Am. Heart Assn., Nat. League Nursing, Phi Theta Kappa. Republican. Methodist. Home: 9719 Fortune Ridge Dr Converse TX 78109-2752 Office: Brooke Army Med Ctr San Antonio TX 78234

WALKER, MATTHEW, III, biomedical engineer; b. Newark, Nov. 10, 1964; s. Matthew Walker Jr. and Ramona Muldrow; m. Kellye Williams, Mar. 13, 1993. BSE in Biomed. Engrng. with honors, U. Tenn., 1987, MS in Biomed. Engrng., 1991; postgrad., Vanderbilt U., 1991-95, Tulane U., 1995—. Biomed. engr. in tng., rsch. fellow in space medicine NASA, Lyndon B. Space Ctr., Houston, 1982-86; grad. teaching asst. Vanderbilt U. Grad. Sch., Nashville, 1991-92; instr. U. Tenn., Knoxville, 1990; rsch. fellow in surgery Cornell Med. Ctr.-Meml. Sloan Kettering Cancer Ctr., N.Y.C., 1992—. Big bro. Ch. of Christ, Knoxville, Tenn., 1985-87, Evangelism Sunday sch. tchr., Nashville, 1990—; advisor, tutor Black Cultural Ctr., 1987-91; leader, mentor YMCA, Nashville, 1993-94. Recipient NASA Biomed. Engrng. rsch. award 1982, Coop. Engrng. Outstanding Achievement award, 1987, Delta Sigma Theta Outstanding Grad. Student award, 1990; U Tenn. Engrng. Acad. scholar, 1982, James King Acad. scholar, 1985; Vanderbilt U. fellow and acad. rsch. award, 1990, Patricia Harris Nat. Acad. Grad. fellow, 1989-91, Tulane Chancellor's fellow, Grad. Med. Acad. fellow, Exptl. Biology NIDOR Travel fellow. Mem. Biomed. Engrng. Soc. (pres. 1982-87), Minority Engrng. Scholars (advisor), Master's Music City Swim Club, Nashville Sportsman Club, Am. Physiol. Soc., Student Nat. Med. Assn., Mortar Bd., Alpha Epsilon Delta (pres. 1986-87).

WALKER, NANCY ANN, American studies educator, English language educator; b. Shreveport, La., Sept. 5, 1942; d. Kirkby Alexander and Phyllis (Pettegrew) W.; m. John Thomas Hand, Nov. 23, 1965 (div. Aug. 1974); m. Burton Michael Augst, Jan. 24, 1976. BA, La. State U., 1964; MA, Tulane U., 1966; PhD, Kent State U., 1971. Instr. Kent State U., East Liverpool, Ohio, 1966-68; teaching fellow Kent (Ohio) State U., 1968-71; faculty mem. Stephens Coll., Columbia, Mo., 1971-89, exec. asst. to pres., 1984-85; dir. women's studies, assoc. prof. English Vanderbilt U., Nashville, 1989-96, prof. English, 1992—; bd. dirs. James M. Wood Inst. for Study of Women's Edn., Columbia, 1981-87. Author: The Tradition of Women's Humor in America, 1984, A Very Serious Thing: Women's Humor and American Culture, 1988, Feminist Alternatives: Irony and Fantasy in the Contemporary Novel by Women, 1990, Fanny Fern, 1992, The Disobedient Writer: Women and Narrative Tradition, 1995; editor: Humor in America: The View from Open Places, 1985, Redressing the Balance: American Women's Humor from the Colonies to the 1980's, 1988, Communication: The Autobiography of Rachel Maddux, 1991, Kate Chopin's The Awakening, 1992, The Way Things Are: The Stories of Rachel Maddux, 1992; mem. editl. bd. American Studies, Tulsa Studies in Women's Lit., Studies in American Humor, LIT: Literature, Interpretation Theory, Legacy; chair editl. com. Vanderbilt U. Press, 1995-96; contbg. editor: Santa Barbara Rev. Woodrow Wilson fellow, 1964, NEH fellow. Mem. MLA (exec. coun. 1992-95), South Atlantic MLA, Am. Studies Assn., Am. Humor Studies Assn.

WALKER, PATRICIA D., critical care nurse; b. Glenwood Springs, Colo., Aug. 30, 1948; d. O. Dale and Lucy D. (MacKenzie) St. John; m. Dennis A. Walker; children: Stephanie Ann, Steven Charles. ADN, Indian Hills Community Coll., Ottumwa, Iowa, 1986. Cert. emergency nurse; cert. ACLS, ENPC, TNCC. Emergency rm. nurse Naples (Fla.) Community Hosp., 1986-92, 94—; nurse chemical dependency treatment program New Beginnings, Ft. Collins, Colo., 1992-94. Home: 169 Fairway Cir Naples FL 33942-1115

WALKER, PAUL DEAN, manufacturing executive; b. Donelson, Tenn., May 9, 1937; s. Alvin McKinley and Selma Pauline (Fendley) W.; m. Joyce Ellen Garrett, Sept. 13, 1959; children: Jeffrey Alvin, Connie Joyce. BSBA, Belmont U., 1959. From trainee and mfg. mgr. to v.p. Jamison Bedding, Inc., Nashville, Franklin, Tenn., 1959-72; pres. LaCrosse (Kans.) Furniture Co., 1972-75; gen. mgr. Consol. Packaging Corp., Pulaski, Tenn., 1975-84; pres. and CEO Valley Packaging Corp., Pulaski, 1984—, also bd. dirs. Treas., bd. dirs. Cmty. Coun. for Developmentally Delayed, Pulaski, 1976-82; bd. dirs. Giles County Econ. Devel. Commn.; vice-chmn., bd. dirs. Colonial Bank Tenn., Columbia-Hillside Hosp.; trustee Belmont U. Mem. Rotary (pres. local chpt. 1980-81, Paul Harris fellow 1983). Baptist. Office: Valley Packaging Corp 275 Industrial Blvd Pulaski TN 38478-5221

WALKER, PEGGY JEAN, social work agency administrator; b. Carbondale, Ill., Aug. 9, 1940; d. George William and Lola Almeda (Black) Robinson; children: Edith Nell and Keith Alan. BA, So. Ill. U., 1962, PhD, 1986; MSW, Washington U., St. Louis, 1967. Lic. clin. social worker. Caseworker, casework supr. Ill. Dept. Pub. Aid, 1964-71; child welfare adminstr. Ill. Dept. Children and Family Svc., 1971-75; mem. faculty social work program So. Ill. U., 1975-79; exec. dir. Western divsn. Children's Home Soc. of Fla., Pensacola, 1979—; appointed to Fla. State Coord. Coun. for Early Childhood Devel., 1994—; adj. adv. bd. dept. social work U. West Fla., 1982—; appt. by Fla. Dept. Edn. to task force Edn. for Children of the Homeless, 1989—, Dept. of Health and Rehab. Svcs. Dist. Task Force on Family Preservation and Support Svcs., 1985—, chmn. 1988, 89; dept. juvenile justice coun., 1994, chmn., 1996. Bd. dirs. United Way Escambia County, Fla., 1992—, co-chair chief judge task force for children, 1994—; mem. Leadership Fla., 1988—; mem. Escambia County Juvenile Justice Coun., 1994, chmn., 1996. Home: 613 Silverthorn Rd Gulf Breeze FL 32561-4625 Office: PO Box 19136 Pensacola FL 32523-9136

WALKER, R. TRACY, personnel director; b. North Wilkesboro, N.C., July 27, 1937; m. Nena Watkins; children: Randy, Kirk. Student, Wilkes C.C., Wake Forest U. With CMI Industries Inc., Elkin, N.C., 1967—, plant human resource mgr. Commr. Wilkes County, mem. region "D" exec. bd., regional econ. devel. coun., indsl. park com., chmn. regional transp. com., mem. regional adv. com. to WNCREDC, liaison between Wilkes County Bd. Edn. and Wilkes County Commrs.; past chmn. region"D" coun. govts. Wilkes County, northwestern housing authority, past mem. bd. edn., 1972-76, airport authority; past vice-chmn., chmn. Wilkes County Commrs.; past bd. dirs. Blue Ridge Water Assn.; pres. Northwestern Devel. Assn.; trustee Health Ins. N.C. Assn. County Commrs.; mem. N.C. Regional Econ. Devel. Commn.; apptd. mem. N.C. Adv. Coun. Vocat. and Technical Edn., 1972-76, N.C. Dept. Correction, 1984-92. Rep. candidate for N.C. Commr. of Labor, 1996. With USAF, 1955-59. Recipient Leadership award Western N.C., 1996. Office: CMI Industries Inc PO Box 620 Elkin NC 28621

WALKER, RETIA SCOTT, dean, researcher, educator, consultant; b. Hatchechubbee, Ala., June 21, 1940; d. Samuel David and Julia Lee (Gary) Scott; m. James H. Walker, Dec. 23, 1967 (div. June 1, 1986); 1 child, JaRee S. BS, Tuskegee U., 1963; MS, Hunter Coll., 1968, Pace U., 1978; PhD, Iowa State U., 1982. Cert. tchr., edn. adminstr., N.Y., sch. supt. N.Y., Iowa. Sch. lunch mgr. N.Y.C. Schs., 1963-65, tchr., 1965-71, edn. adminstr., 1971-80; rsch. asst. Iowa State U., Ames, 1980-82, instr. Coll. Edn., 1982; asst. prof. Tex. Woman's U., Denton, 1982-83; chair dept. human ecology U. Md. Ea. Shore, Princess Anne, 1983-94; dean Coll. Human Environ. Sci. U. Ky., Lexington, 1994—; cons. pub. schs. dists. Ft. Worth, Detroit, Mpls., 1981-83, aging agys., Salisbury, Md., 1990-94; mem. adv. bd. Somerset County Sch. Dist., Princess Anne, Md., 1988-90. Contbr. chpt. to book, articles to profl. jours.; host (radio program) The Retirement Years, 1987-92. Mem. adv. bd. One-Parent Housing Bd., Lexington, Ky., 1994—, Lower Shore Area Agy. on Aging, Salisbury, Md., 1991-94; mem. civil. svc. com. Lexington-Fay Urban County Govt., Lexington, 1996; mem. Somerset County Com. on Aging, Princess Anne, Md., 1990; v.p. Greenwood Middle Sch. PTA, Princess Anne, 1986. Postdoct. fellow U. Md., Balt., College Park, 1985-87; named Disting. Lectr. Ala. A&M U., Huntsville, Ala., 1993. Mem. Am. Assn. Family and Cons. Sci. (chair higher edn. unit 1995—), Assn. Geronotology and Human Devel (pres., v.p. 1990-92, Rsch. award 1988), Pub. Policy Coun. (vice chair 1988-82, Svc. award 1988, 95), Assn. Adminstrs. Human Sci. (sec. 1992-94), Kappa Omicron Nu. Office: U Ky 102 Erikson Hall Lexington KY 40506-0050

WALKER, RICHARD, JR., nephrologist, internist; b. Dayton, Ohio, Sept. 1, 1948; m. Madeleine Ann Walker. BS cum laude, Ohio State U., 1970, MD, 1973. Diplomate Nat. Bd. Med. Examiners, internal medicine, nephrology, critical care medicine Am. Bd. Internal Medicine. Intern medicine U. Tex. Southwestern, Dallas, 1973-74, resident internal medicine, 1974-76, fellow nephrology, 1976-78; staff nephrologist and internist Bay Med. Ctr., Panama City, Fla., 1978—, HCA Gulf Coast Hosp., Panama City, 1978—; med. dir. Panama City Artificial Kidney Ctr., 1978—; assoc. med. dir. North Fla. Artificial Kidney Ctr., 1993—. Mem. AMA, ACP, Soc. Critical Care Medicine, Fla. Physicians Assn., The Bays Med. Soc., Fla. Med. Assn., Am. Soc. Nephrology, Internat. Soc. Nephrology, Fla. Soc. Nephrology, Renal Physicians Assn., Am. Soc. Internal Medicine, Fla. Soc. Internal Medicine, Nat. Kidney Found., Alpha Omega Alpha. Home: 320 Bunkers Cove Rd Panama City FL 32401-3912 Office: Nephrology Assocs PA 504 N Macarthur Ave Panama City FL 32401-3636

WALKER, RICHARD BRIAN, chemistry educator; b. Quincy, Mass., May 14, 1948; s. George Edgar and Eva Mary (Taylor) W. BS in Biochemistry, U. So. Calif., 1970; PhD in Pharm. Chemistry, U. Calif., San Francisco, 1975. Rsch. assoc. Oreg. State U., Corvallis, 1975-76, U. Wash., Seattle, 1976-78; lectr. U.S. Internat. U., San Diego, 1978-81, Hamdard Sch. Pharmacy, New Delhi, India, 1981-82; rsch. scientist Biophysica Found., San Diego, 1982-83; assoc. prof. chemistry U. Ozarks, Clarksville, Ark., 1983-84; asst. to assoc. prof. chemistry U. Ark., Pine Bluff, 1984-96, prof. chemistry, 1996—; prin. investigator minority biomed. rsch. support program NIH, Bethesda, Md., 1986—; project dir. Ark. Systemic Sci. Initiative. Contbr. articles to profl. jours. Coord. home Bible fellowship The Way Internat., Pine Bluff, 1984—; judge Ctrl. Ark. Sci. Fair, Little Rock, 1986—. NIH rsch. grantee, 1986, 89, 93. Mem. Am. Chem. Soc., Ark. Acad. Scis., Coun. on Undergrad. Rsch., Sigma Xi. Office: U Ark Dept Chemistry 1200 University Dr Pine Bluff AR 71601-2799

WALKER, ROBERT BERNARD, sports executive; b. Asheboro, N.C., May 5, 1963; s. Douglas and Mary Louise (Yow) W.; m. Jacqueline Sue Purdie, June 1, 1991. BS in Phys. Edn., cert. tchr., Liberty U., 1985; MS in Sports Mgmt., U.S. Sports Acad., 1989. Athletic dir., head coach varsity basketball Wise (Va.) County Christian Sch., 1985-88, head coach varsity soccer, 1985-87, head coach varsity baseball, 1988; athletic dir., soccer coord., varsity basketball asst. Charlotte (N.C.) Christian Sch., 1988-94; pres. Unlimited Success Sports Mgmt. Inc., 1994—, U.S. Sports Mgmt. Inc., Charlotte; golf tournament organizer Unlimited Success Spkrs. Bur. for Profl. Athletes Sport Mgmt., Charlotte; spkr. and basketball camps; asst. coach, score Summer Nat. USA Team in Russia, 1993. Author: Athletic Manual Advantage. Mem. N.C. Ind. Sch. Athletic Assn. (bd. dirs. 1993-94, asst. coach 1992 state basketball champions), Charlotte Ind. Athletic Assn. (pres. 1993-94). Republican. Baptist. Office: PO Box 13291 Charlotte NC 28270-0079

WALKER, SAMMIE LEE, retired elementary education educator; b. Elkhart, Tex., July 10, 1927; d. Samuel and Mary (Pigford) Nathaniel; m. R.L. Walker, Oct. 12, 1952 (dec. 1994); children: Winfred, Frederick, Mary, Pearlene, Gladys, Robert, Ethel. BS, Tex. Coll., 1951; MEd, Tex. So. U., 1979. Cert. tchr., home econs. educator, elem. educator. Seamstress Madonna Guild Factory, Houston, 1958-60; presch. tchr. Project Head Start, Houston, 1961-64; tchr. Houston Ind. Schs., 1964-86; tchr. Harris County Youth Authority, Clear Lake, Tex., 1985; costume maker CETA program Houston Ind. Sch. Dist., 1984. Tchr. Trinity Garden Ch. of Christ, 1956—; phys. fitness coord. Kashmere Garden Sr. Citizen Club, Houston, 1986-92; home care provider Tex. Home Health Care, Houston, 1988-93. Recipient Friendship award Houston Christian Inst., 1993. Mem. NEA. Home: 7911 Shotwell St Houston TX 77016-6548

WALKER, SARAH FRANCES, marketing, public relations consultant; b. Midland, Tex., Mar. 2, 1953; d. Walter Thomas and Virginia Elizabeth (Thomas) Ross; m. Bill J. Rogers, Aug. 7, 1975 (div. Mar. 1982); 1 child, Amber Elizabeth; m. O.W. Pete Wiggins, Apr. 23, 1982 (div. Jan. 1987); 1 child, Joshua Ross; m. William Raymond Kremer, Nov. 11, 1988 (div. Nov. 1992); m. Dale A. Walker, May 1993. BS in Mktg., Fashio Mdse., Tex. Christian U., 1975. Owner Sarah Rogers & Assocs., Houston, 1975-81; art dir. Heritage Publishing, North Little Rock, Ark., 1982-84, Ark. Bus., Little Rock, 1984-85; owner, pres. Sarah Wiggins & Assocs. Inc., Little Rock, 1985-91; creative dir. Ark. Bus., Little Rock, 1989-91; owner, pres. Kremer Communications Inc., Little Rock, 1991-94; pres. Marketing by Design Ltd., Little Rock, 1994—; mktg. dir. Ballet Ark., Little Rock, 1991-92, dir. exec. bd., 1989-94; advt. dir. The Quapaw Chronicle, Little Rock, 1991-92. Pres. Greater Little Rock Heart Guild, 1990-92; aux. mem. Ctrl. Ark. Radiology Therapy Inst., Little Rock, 1990-95. Mem. Ark. Women Execs. Roman Catholic. Office: Marketing by Design Ltd PO Box 21208 Little Rock AR 72221-1208

WALKER, STANLEY MAURICE, nuclear physicist; b. Uvalde, Tex., Aug. 23, 1952; s. Sam A. and Eleanor G. (Shaw) W.; m. N. Eileen Smith, July 4, 1975; children: Julie L. and Cyndi M. AS Engrng., San Antonio Coll., 1972; BS in Applied Physics, U. of Tex., San Antonio, 1982. Cert. ASNT Level III in ultrasonic, liquid penetrant, and magnetic particle exam. methods. NDE technician S.W. Rsch. Inst., San Antonio, 1974-82, rsch. scientist, 1982-83; sr. engr. J.A. Jones Applied Rsch. Co., Charlotte, N.C., 1983-89; mgr. J.A. Jones Applied Rsch. Co., Charlotte, 1989-95, program mgr., 1995—; instr. Saint Philip's Coll., San Antonio, 1982. Co-author: Stress Corrosion Cracking, 1992; contbr. articles to profl. jours. Mem. ASME, Am. Soc. of Metals. Home: 10211 Meadow Hollow Dr Charlotte NC 28227 Office: EPRI NDE Ctr 1300 Harris Blvd Charlotte NC 28262

WALKER, VICTOR LOUIS, computer company executive; b. Bessemer, Ala., Dec. 10, 1958; s. William Louis and Barbara (Smitherman) W.; m. Natalie F. Reaves, Apr. 18, 1980; children: Greg, Kevin, Barry. AA, Bessemer State Tech. U., 1979. Registered EMT. Programmer Mason Corp., Birmingham, Ala., 1977-80, McGrief Siebels, Birmingham, 1980-81; programmer/analyst Atrax R&D, Tuscaloosa, Ala., 1981-84; systems analyst McDonnell Douglas Corp., Birmingham, 1984-85; systems cons. Tel-Data Systems, Birmingham, 1985-89; pres. ViComp, Inc., Birmingham, 1989—. Author: (software) Nutritional Information System, 1994. Asst. chief McAdory Fire & Rescue #3, McCalla, Ala., 1994, vol. firefighter, 1987, EMT, 1993, bd. dirs., 1992—. Named Firefighter of Yr. McAdory Fire & Rescue #3, 1993, 94. Republican. Baptist. Home: 2163 Rock Mountain Lake Dr Mc Calla AL 35111

WALKER, WALTER GRAY, JR., small business owner, program statistician; b. Newport News, Va., June 6, 1931; s. Walter Gray and Verna Elizabeth (Haughton) W.; divorced; children: James Gray, Thomas Shelton, Martha Anne Crute. AB, William and Mary Coll., 1956; AAS magna cum laude, No. Va. Community, 1983; D of Noetic Scis. (hon.), Fergle U., 1987. Broadcast engr. Sta. WGH, Hampton, Va., 1957-58; instr. Chesterfield Sch. Bd., Va., 1958-63; asst. coord. Va. Mental Health Study Commn., Richmond, Va., 1964; asst. dir. Community Action Agency, Hampton, Va., 1965; statistician U.S. Govt., Washington, 1966-78; pres. Diversified Svcs. Co., Arlington, Va., 1980—; automotive tech. instr. No. Va. Community

Coll., Alexandria, Va., 1983; radio electronics officer Vulcan Carriers, Inc., N.Y.C., 1991; real estate broker Va. Real Estate Commn., Richmond, Va., 1962; bd. dir. Chesterfield Hosp. Corp., Va., 1963-64. Author: Public Housing Review, 1973, Automotive Technical Document Study of Northern Virginia Community College, 1983. Treas. 1st Congregational Ch., Washington, 1972; del. Arlington (Va.) Dem. Party, 1992; active mem. Common Cause, Washington, 1968—; Am. for Dem. Action, Washington, 1993—; active The Unitarian Universalist Ch. of Arlington, Va. With USNR, 1949-53, Korea, 1950-52. Mem. Am. Radio Assn., World Federalist Assn., Vets. for Peace, UN Assn. of the Nat. Capitol Area, Chesterfield Jaycees (external affairs rep. 1962-63, Arlington Radio Club (treas. 1988-89), Oxford Club. Democrat. Home: 900 N Livingston St Arlington VA 22205-1423 Office: Diversified Svcs Co PO Box 5315 Arlington VA 22205-0415

WALKER, WALTER WAYNE, retail management executive; b. Rosiclare, Ill., Dec. 27, 1938; s. Walter Perkins W. and Rachel (Denton) Scott; m. Marilyn Janice Ashford, Feb. 13, 1960; children: Kimberly Kay, Mark Wayne. BS, So. Ill. U., 1960. Mgr. office and credit Firestone Tire & Rubber Co., Kokomo, Ind., 1960-61; coord. mdse. Interstate Dept. Stores, N.Y.C. and Evansville, Ind., 1961-74; pres., chief exec. officer S.W. Anderson Co., Inc., Owensboro, Ky., 1974-89; retail/bus. cons., 1989—. Pacesetter chmn., bd. dirs. United Way Owensboro, 1978-82; pres., bd. dirs. Downtown Owensboro, Inc., 1979—. Named to Alumni Hall Fame Coll. Bus. Adminstrn. So. Ill. U., 1988. Mem. Nat. Retail Mchts. Assn., Ky. C. of C., Owensboro C. of C., Nat. Fedn. Ind. Bus., Ky. Retail Fedn. (bd. dirs. 1985-89), Downtown Bus. and Profl. Assn. (past pres., bd. dirs.), Masons, Shriners, Lions. Republican. Presbyterian. Home: 3249 Santana Ln Plano TX 75023-3602

WALKER, WANDA GAIL, special education educator; b. Montgomery, Ala., June 7, 1946; d. Carter Warren Gamaliel and Ruth Jones (Carter) Walker. BS in Elem. Edn., Campbell U., 1968; MA in Christian Edn., Scarritt Coll., 1970; cert. in tchg. of learning disabled, Pembroke U., 1994. Cert. tchr. class A, N.C. Dir. Christian edn. United Meth. Ch., Roxboro, N.C., 1970-76; diaconal min. United Meth. Ch., Hamlet, N.C., 1976-77, Rockingham, N.C., 1977-85; head teller Montgomery Savs. and Loan, Rockingham, 1985-87; loan officer-credit R.W. Goodman Co., Rockingham, 1987-89; tchr. spl. edn. Richmond County Schs., Hamlet, 1989—; active Richmond County Reading Coun., Hamlet, 1989—. Bd. dirs. Sandhill Manor Group Home, Hamlet, 1977—; mem. Woman's Club Hamlet, 1989-94, treas., 1989-91, 1st v.p., 1992-94. Eisenhower grantee U. N.C., 1994; recipient Mission award United Meth. Women, N.C. Conf., 1990; named Best Working Mem., Women's Club Hamlet, 1991. Democrat. Home: 344 Raleigh St Hamlet NC 28345-2750 Office: Richmond County Schs Hamlet Ave Hamlet NC 28345

WALKER, WENDY K., marketing executive; b. Elizabeth, N.J., Nov. 11, 1961; d. William Henry Jr. and Catherine Lillian (Fulton) Knight; m. George Russell Walker Jr., Oct. 25, 1986; 1 child, Faith Corinne. Student, U. Warwick, Eng., 1981-82; BA, Duke U., 1983. Cert. ins. counselor, assoc. in risk mgmt.; CPCU. Mktg. exec. Aon Risk Svc., Inc. of the Carolinas, 1994—; tchr. internship program Howard U., N.Y.C., 1986; bus. advisor internship program Inroads, Inc. Mem. NAFE, CPCU Soc., PIA, Am. Biog. Inst. (mem. rsch. bd. advisors), Soc. Cert. Ins. Counselors, Young Profls. Coun. Democrat. Episcopalian. Home: 4146 Rosalie St Winston Salem NC 27104

WALKER, WILLIAM ALFRED, colon and rectal surgeon; b. Lubbock, Tex., Apr. 28, 1952; s. Alfred Leonard and Louise Dolly (Burgess) W.; m. Lynn Carol Bancroft, May 28, 1977; children: Richard B., Carol B. BA in Chemistry and Psychology, U. N.C., 1974, MD, 1978. Diplomate Am. Bd. Surgery, Am. Bd. Colon and Rectal Surgery. Intern, then resident U. Mich., Ann Arbor, 1978-84; fellow in colon and rectal surgery U. Minn., Mpls., 1984-85; colon and rectal surgeon Charlotte (N.C.) Colon and Rectal Surgery Assocs., P.A., 1985—; co-dir. colorectal cancer divsn. Presbyn. Cancer Ctr., 1992—; mem. staff Mercy Hosp., Charlotte, Presbyn. Hosp., Charlotte; cancer liaison physician Am. Cancer Soc. Commn. on Cancer, 1994—; asst. consulting prof. surgery Duke U., 1995—. Contbr. articles to profl. jours. Coach little league baseball South Park Youth Assn., 1989—; den leader pack 79 Cub Scouts, 1991. F.A. Coller Travelling fellow U. Mich., 1984. Fellow ACS, Am. Soc. Colon and Rectal Surgeons; mem. AMA, Am. Lung Assn. (bd. dirs. Mecklenburg County 1991-92), Am. Cancer Soc. (bd. dirs. Mecklenburg County 1991—), F.A. Coller Surg. Soc., N.C. State Med. Soc., Mecklenburg County Med. Soc. Office: Charlotte Colon and Rectal Surgery Assoc 2015 Randolph Rd Ste 201 Charlotte NC 28207-1200

WALKER, WILLIAM OLIVER, JR., religion educator, dean; b. Sweetwater, Tex., Dec. 6, 1930; s. William Oliver and Frances Baker (White) W.; m. Mary Scott Daugherty, Dec. 22, 1955 (div. Dec. 1978); children: William Scott, Mary Evan, Michael Neal. BA, Austin Coll., 1953; MDiv, Austin Presbyterian Sem., 1957; MA, U. Tex., 1958; PhD, Duke U., 1962. Instr. religion Austin Coll., Sherman, Tex., 1954-55, Duke U., 1960-62; from asst. to prof. religion Trinity U., San Antonio, 1962—, chair dept., 1980-88, acting dean div. Humanities and Arts, 1988-89, dean, 1989—. Contbr. articles and book reviews to profl. jours. Editor: The Relationships, 1978, The Harper Collins Bible Pronunciation Guide, 1994; assoc. editor Harper's Bible Dictionary, 1985. Mem. Studiorum Novi Testamenti Soc., Soc. Bibl. Lit. (regional sec.-treas. 1980-86), Am. Acad. Religion (regional pres. 1966-67), Soc. Sci. Study Religion, Cath. Bibl. Assn. Am., Coll. Theology Soc. Democrat. Presbyterian. Avocations: tennis, traveling, photography. Home: 315 Cloverleaf Ave San Antonio TX 78209-3822 Office: Trinity U Office Dean Humanities & Arts 715 Stadium Dr San Antonio TX 78212-7200

WALKER, WOODROW WILSON, lawyer, cattle and timber farmer; b. Greenville, Mich., Feb. 19, 1919; s. Craig Walker and Mildred Chase; m. Janet K. Keiter, Oct. 7, 1950; children: Jonathan Woodrow, William Craig, Elaine Virginia. BA, U. Mich., 1943; LLB, Cath. U., 1950. Bar: D.C. 1950, U.S. Supreme Ct. 1958, Va. 1959. Atty. Am. law div. legis. reference Library of Congress, Washington, 1951-60; sole practice Arlington, Va., 1960—; counsel Calvary Found., Arlington, 1970-85, first pres., 1972; judge moot ct. George Mason Law Sch., 1986; owner-operator Walker Farm Front Royal, Va., 1972—. Co-author rsch. publs. for U.S. Govt. V.p. Jefferson Civic Assn., Arlington, 1955-61; pres. Nellie Custis PTA, Arlington, 1960-61; sec. Arlington County Bd. Equalization Real Estate Assessment, 1962, chmn. 1963; com. chmn. Arlington Troop 108 Boy Scouts Am., 1964-69; mem. Arlington County Pub. Utilities Commn., 1964-66, vice chmn., 1965-66; pres. Betschler Class Adult Sunday Sch., Calvary United Meth. Ch., Arlington, 1965. Served with U.S. Army, 1943-45, PTO. Mem. ABA, Arlington County Bar Assn., Va. Farm Bur., Va. Cattleman's Assn. Methodist. Democrat. Home: 2822 Ft Scott Dr Arlington VA 22202-2307 Office: 2055 15th St N Ste 2203 Arlington VA 22201-2613

WALKOWIAK, VINCENT STEVEN, lawyer, educator; b. Chgo., Apr. 22, 1946; s. Vincent Albert and Elizabeth (Modla) W.; m. Linda Kae Schweigert, Aug., 1968; children—Jenifer, Steven. B.A., U. Ill., 1968, J.D., 1971. Bar: Ill. 1971, Tex. 1981, U.S. Ct. Appeals (8th cir.) 1971, U.S. Ct. Appeals (5th cir.) 1982, U.S. Dist. Ct. (ea., we., so. and no. dists. Tex.) 1982. Assoc., Dorsey, Marquart, Windhorst, West & Halladay, Mpls., 1971-74; ptnr. Fulbright & Jaworski, Houston, 1982—; prof. Fla. State U., Tallahassee, 1974-76, So. Meth. U., Dallas, 1976-84. Editor: Uniform Product Liability Act, 1980; Trial of a Product Liability Case, vol. 1, 1981, vol. 2, 1982; Preparation and Presentation of Product Liability, 1983. Office: Fulbright & Jaworski 2200 Ross Ave Ste 2800 Dallas TX 75201-6773

WALKUP, CHARLOTTE LLOYD, lawyer; b. N.Y.C., Apr. 28, 1910; d. Charles Henry and Helene Louise (Wheeler) Tuttle; m. David D. Lloyd, Oct. 19, 1940 (dec. Dec. 1962); children—Andrew M. Lloyd, Louisa Lloyd Hurley; m. Homer Allen Walkup, Feb. 4, 1967. AB, Vassar Coll., 1931; LLB, Columbia U., 1934. Bar: N.Y. 1935, U.S. Supreme Ct. 1939, U.S. Dist. Ct. D.C. 1953, Va. 1954. Asst. solicitor Dept. Interior, Washington, 1934-45; asst. gen. counsel UNRRA, Washington and London, 1945-48; assoc. and cons. firms, Washington, 1953, 55, 60; atty., spl. asst. Office Treasury, Washington, 1961-65; asst. gen. counsel Dept. Treasury, Washington, 1965-73; cons. Rogers & Wells, Washington, 1975-86. Editor, Columbia Law Rev., 1933, 34. Pres. Alexandria Community Welfare Coun., 1950-52; bd dirs. Alexandria Coun. Human Rels., 1958-60, New Hope Found., 1977. Recipient Meritorious Svc. award Dept. Treasury, 1970, Exceptional Svc. award, 1973, Career Svc. award Nat. Civil Svc. League, 1973; named Hon. fellow Harry S. Truman Libr. Inst. Mem. Columbia U. Alumni Assn., Phi Beta Kappa. Democrat. Episcopalian. Home: 2501 Ridge Road Dr Alexandria VA 22302-2830

WALL, ARTHUR EDWARD PATRICK, editor; b. Jamestown, N.Y., Mar. 12, 1925; s. George Herbert and Doris (Olmstead) W.; student pub. schs., LLD (hon.) Rosary Coll., 1979; m. Marcella Joan Petrine, Nov. 5, 1954; children: John Wright, Marie Ann, David Arthur Edward. Copy editor Worcester (Mass.) Telegram, 1958; Sunday editor Hawaii Island Corr., Honolulu Star-Bull., 1958-60; editor Hilo (Hawaii) Tribune-Herald, 1960-63; Sunday editor Honolulu Advertiser, 1963-65, mng. editor, 1971-72; mng. editor Cath. Rev., 1965-66, editor, 1966-71; editor-in-chief Nat. Cath. News Service, Washington, 1972-76; editor, gen. mgr. The New World (name changed to Chgo. Catholic 1977), Chgo., 1976-86, pres., 1979-86; pres. New World Pub. Co., 1977-86; comm. officer Diocese of Cen. Fla., Orlando, 1988—; editor Cen. Fla. Episcopalian, Orlando, 1989—; dir. Noll Printing Co., Inc., Huntington, Ind. Dir. bur. info. Archdiocese Balt., 1965-66; mem. fin. com. Archdiocese Chgo., 1979-82; mem. council Internat. Cath. Union of Press, Geneva, 1972-84, v.p., 1974-77. Chmn., Gov.'s Com. Ednl. TV, Honolulu, 1964-65; regent Chaminade Coll., Honolulu, 1959-65, chmn., 1963-65; trustee St. Mary's Sem. and Univ., Balt., 1975-76; bd. dirs. Cath. Journalism Scholarship Fund, 1976-84, Our Sunday Visitor, Inc., Huntington, Ind., 1977-87, dir. emeritus, 1987—; mem. spiritual renewal and devel. com. 41st Internat. Eucharistic Congress, Phila., 1975-76; bd. dirs. Bible Reading Fellowship, 1996—. Named Young Man of Year, Hilo, Hawaii, 1960, Fla. Writer of Yr., 1988; recipient St. Francis de Sales award Cath. Press Assn., 1977; Father of Year, Honolulu C. of C., 1964; Spl. award U.S. Cath. Conf., 1980. Mem. Internat. Fedn. Cath. Press Agys. (pres. 1974-77), Internat. Fedn. Cath. Journalists (pres. 1977-80, v.p. 1981-83), Chgo. Acad. Sci., Cath. Press Assn. U.S. and Can. (bd. dirs. 1978-86), Bible Reading Fellowship (bd. dirs. 1996—), Fla. Cath. Exec. Bd., Sigma Delta Chi (past chpt. pres.), Internat. Order St. Luke the Physician (religious pub. rels. coun.). Episcopalian. Clubs: Nat. Press (Washington); Overseas Press (N.Y.C.). Author: The Big Wave, 1960, The Spirit of Cardinal Bernardin, 1983, If I Were Pope, 1989; contbr. articles to periodicals including The Orlando Sentinel, The Living Ch.; editor: Origins and Catholic Trends, 1972-76. Office: Diocese Cen Fla 1017 E Robinson St Orlando FL 32801-2023

WALL, BETTY JANE, real estate consultant; b. Wichita Falls, Tex., Mar. 23, 1936; d. Albert Willis and Winnie Belle (Goodloe) Beard; m. Richard Lee Wall, Feb. 21, 1959; 1 child, Cynthia Lynn. BS, Vocat.Home Econs. Edn, U. Okla., 1958; MEd, Midwestern U., 1959. Lic. real estate salesperson, Tex. Tchr. San Diego County Schs., 1959-60, Long Beach (Calif.) City Schs., 1960-61, Norman (Okla.) Kindergarten Assn., 1961-65; real estate salesperson WestMark Realtors, Lubbock, Tex., 1983-85; now ind. real estate salesperson Lubbock; coll. adviser Nat. Panhellenic Conf., Tex., 1979-91; judge talent and beauty pageants, Tex. N.Mex., Okla., 1984—. Treas. Lubbock Symphony Guild, 1985-87, v.p. ways and means com., 1987-88, chmn. ball, 1990, pres. elect, 1993-94, pres., 1994-95; bd. dirs. Tex. Assn. of Symphony Orchs., 1994-95, Ballet Lubbock, 1996—; pres., bd. dirs. Miss Lubbock Pageant, 1992—. Recipient Tex. Tech. U. Outstanding Greek Alumni award, 1994. Mem. Tex. Real Estate Assn., Jr. League Lubbock (treas. 1976-78, sustaining advisor fin. com. 1979-83, hdqrs. commn. advisor 1989-94), West Tex. Mus. Assn. (chmn. planetarium com., 1996, bd. dirs., women's coun., trustee 1997—), Nat. Platform Assn., Women's C. of C., Lubbock Women's Club (bd. dirs. 1996—), Tex. Tech. U. Faculty Women's Club (v.p. & pres. 1967-69, Lubbock chpt. Achievement Rewards for Coll. Sci. bd. 1995—), Alpha Chi Omega (nat. coun., nat. panhellenic del. 1978-83, 88-90, nat. v.p. membership 1985-88, nat. v.p. collegians 1990-92, co-chmn. Performance Lubbock '96 1996). Republican. Methodist. Home and Office: 3610 63rd Dr Lubbock TX 79413-5308

WALL, DIANE EVE, political science educator; b. Detroit, Nov. 17, 1944; d. Albert George and Jean Carol (Young) Bradley. BA in History and Edn., Mich. State U., 1966, MA in History, 1969, MA in Polit. Sci., 1979, PhD in Polit. Sci., 1983. Cert. permanent secondary tchr., Mich. Secondary tchr. Corunna (Mich.) Pub. Schs., 1966-67, N.W. Pub. Schs., Rives Junction, Mich., 1967-73; lectr. Tidewater Community Coll., Chesapeake, Va., 1974-77; instr. Lansing (Mich.) Community Coll., 1981-83; prof. dept. polit. sci. Miss. State U., 1983—, undergrad. coord., 1993—; instr. Wayne State U., Detroit, fall 1980, Ctrl. Mich. U., Mt. Pleasant, spring 1982; pre-law advisor Miss. State U., 1990-93, chair, 1993—. Contbr. articles, revs. to profl. jours., chpt. to book. Evaluator Citizen's Task Force, Chesapeake, Va., 1977; panelist flag burning program Ednl. TV, Mississippi State, 1990. Recipient Paideia award Miss. State U. Coll. Arts and Scis., 1988, Miss. State U. Outstanding Woman Teaching Faculty award Pres.'s Commn. on Status of Women, 1994, Acad. Advising award Miss. State U., 1994, Outstanding Advisor award Nat. Acad. Advising Assn., 1995; Grad. Office fellow Mich. State U., 1980; Miss. State U. rsch. grantee, 1984. Mem. ASPA (exec. bd. Sect. for Women 1987-90, Miss. chpt. pres. 1992-93), LWV (Chesapeake charter pres. 1976-77), Miss. Polit. Sci. Assn. (exec. dir. 1991-93), Miss. State U. Soc. Scholars (pres. 1992-93), Miss. State U. Faculty Women's Assn. (v.p. 1985-86, pres. 1986-88, scholar 1987-89), Phi Kappa Phi (v.p. 1985-86, pres. 1986-88), Pi Sigma Alpha (Ann. Chpt. Activities award 1991). Democrat. Methodist. Office: Miss State U PO Drawer PC Mississippi State MS 39762

WALL, EDWARD MILLARD, environmental consulting executive; b. Newburyport, Mass., Dec. 17, 1929; s. Millard Edward and Edith Noyes (Carter) W.; m. Jean Titus, Jan. 27, 1951 (dec. 1989); children: Karen, Kenneth, Kathryn; m. Gertrude Knott, Nov. 18, 1992. BSME, Tufts U., 1951; MBA, Xavier U., 1962. Cert. hazardous materials mgr. Tech. service engr. Goodyear Tire, Akron, Ohio, 1951-53; mgr. engine test facilities Gen. Electric, Cin., 1956-62; mgr. mfg. Williams Mfg., Portsmouth, Ohio, 1962-74; sr. project mgr. N-Ren Corp., Cin., 1975-78; v.p. mfg. Nelson Electric, Tulsa, 1979-88; v.p. Techrad Environ. Svcs., Oklahoma City, 1988-92, pres., 1992—. Mem. Vo-Tech Edn. Adv. Com., Tulsa, 1982-88. Lt.(j.g.) USNR, 1953-56. Mem. ASME, NSPE, Am. Prodn. and Inventory Control Soc. (cert.), Am. Mgmt. Assn. Republican. Presbyterian. Lodges: Rotary, Masons. Home: 4100 NE 143rd St Edmond OK 73013-7205 Office: Techrad Environ Svcs Inc 4619 N Santa Fe Ave Oklahoma City OK 73118-7905

WALL, JACQUELINE REMONDET, industrial and clinical psychologist, rehabilitation counselor; b. Paris, Dec. 25, 1958; came to U.S., 1959; d. Jack Whitney and Hazel Aline (Riley) Hargett; m. Mel Dennis Remondet, Aug. 5, 1977 (div. Mar. 1984); m. David Gordon Wall, Jan. 27, 1990; 1 child, Jeanette Renee. BA, Southeastern La. U., 1978; MA, U. Tulsa, 1982, PhD, 1989; postgrad. in clin. psychology, Ill. Inst. Tech., 1995. Lic. profl. counselor, Okla. (ret.); limited lic. psychologist, Mich. Program coord. Hillcrest Med. Ctr., Tulsa, 1982-88; coord. psychol. svcs. Rebound Inc.-Cane Creek Hosp., Martin, Tex., 1989-90; psychologist Sea Pines Rehab. Hosp., Melbourne, Fla., 1990; indsl. psychology intern Morris & Assocs., Jackson, Miss., 1990-91; ind. cons. indsl. psychology, 1991-92; clinic coord. Ill. Inst. Tech., Chgo., 1992-94, postdoctoral fellow clin. respecialization program, 1992-94; intern psychology dept. U. Miss. Med. Ctr., Jackson, 1994-95; postdoctoral fellow Rehab. Inst. Mich., Detroit, 1995—; instr. Tulsa Jr. Coll., 1989; rsch. asst. U. Tulsa, 1981-82, 84-86, La. State U., Baton Rouge, 1980, Med. Sch., Tulane U., New Orleans, 1979-80; part-time instr. Wayne State U., 1991, IIT, 1994; presenter in field. Contbr. book chpts. and articles to profl. jours. Recipient rsch. grant U. Tulsa, 1982. Mem. APA, Soc. for Indsl.-Orgnl. Psychology, Southeastern La. U. Thirteen Club, Sigma Xi, Psi Chi, Phi Kappa Phi, Phi Lambda Pi. Office: Rehab Inst Mich Dept Psych-Neuropsychology 261 Mack Ave Detroit MI 48201

WALL, JIM, metals company executive; b. 1945. Positions with various cos. including NSW's Hunter Valley, Mt. Newman Mining Co., Aztec, Australia; chmn. Savage Zinc, Inc., Sydney, Australia. Office: Savage Zinc Inc 1800 Zinc Plant Rd Clarksville TN 37040

WALL, KENNETH E., JR., lawyer; b. Beaumont, Tex., Apr. 6, 1944; s. Kenneth E. and W. Geraldine (Peoples) W.; m. Marjorie Lee Hughes, Dec. 21, 1968; children—Barbara, Elizabeth, Kenneth. Grad. Lamar U., 1966, U. Tex.-Austin, 1969. Bar: Tex. 1969, U.S. Supreme Ct. 1979. Asst. city atty., Beaumont, 1969-73, city atty., 1973-84; with firm Olson & Olson, Houston, 1984—; dir. Tex. Mcpl. League Ins. Trust, 1979-84, vice chmn., 1983-84; counsel S.E. Tex. Regional Planning Commn., 1974, 76. Active Boy Scouts Am., Girl Scouts U.S.A. Mem. Nat. Inst. Mcpl. Law Officers (chmn. com. on local govt. pers. 1979-81, 82-84), State Bar Tex., Tex. City Attys. Assn. (pres. 1982-83), Jefferson County Bar Assn. (dir. 1975-77), Houston Bar Assn., Phi Delta Phi. Methodist. Office: 333 Clay St Houston TX 77002-4000

WALL, MARION PRYOR, judge; b. Chattanooga, Jan. 7, 1954; s. Junius F. and Tilda C. (Caldwell) W.; m. Jeanne Kuertz, Mar. 1, 1980 (div. Apr. 1987); 1 child, Laura; m. Donna Dorian, July 4, 1992. JD, Vanderbilt U., 1980. Bar: Tenn. 1980. Clk. to fed. judge Hon. Kent Sandidge U.S. Dist. Ct., Nashville, 1980-82; atty. Nashville, 1982-88; adminstrv. judge State of Tenn., Nashville, 1988—; instr. S.E. Paralegal Inst., Nashville, 1991-93. Office: Secretary of State James K Polk Building Ste 1700 Nashville TN 37243

WALL, P.Q. (LUCIUS JOHN), financial analyst, money manager; b. Sioux Falls, S.D., July 22, 1931; s. Lucius John and Theresa (Finnell) W.; m. Phyllis Alper, 1954 (div. 1966); children: Brian, Fred, Jeff, Jack, William; m. Lola Marie Bagby, 1966 (div. 1979); children: Patrick S., Lucius J. III; m. Ellen Claire Toppel, Jan. 3, 1980; children: Charles M., James H. Diploma in English, NYU, 1956. Registered money mgr. Registered rep. Bosworth Sullivan, Denver, 1972-74, Dean Witter Reynolds, Denver, 1974-79, Rauscher Pierce, Denver, 1979-83, Hamilton Bohner & Van Vleck, Inc., Denver, 1984-85; chief tech. analyst Boettcher & Co., Denver, 1983-84; dir. sales J.W. Gant & Assoc., Englewood, Colo., 1984; ptnr. Griffin & Co., Denver, 1985-89; owner Wall & Griffin, Denver, 1989—, P.Q. Wall Forecast, Denver, 1989—. Author: Magic is Real, 1987; contbr. numerous articles to profl. jours. Featured in articles Barron's, Sun News, Times-Picayune, Seattle Daily Journal, others; TV appearances include Good Morning America. Mem. Market Technicians Assn. (speaker), Technician Soc., Found. for Study of Cycles. Republican. Office: Wall & Griffin PO Box 15558 New Orleans LA 70175-5558

WALL, ROBERT THOMPSON, secondary school educator; b. Luray, Va., May 31, 1943; s. Robert Alexander and Mary Ann (Coffman) W.; m. Sarah S. Wall, Aug. 19, 1967; children: Melissa Coffman, Jennifer Grey. BA, Va. Poly. Inst. and State U., 1966; MA, Radford (Va.) U., 1971; postgrad., U. Fla., 1978. Tchr. instrumental and choral music Halifax County Schs., Halifax, Va.; tchr. instrumental music Montgomery County Schs., Christiansburg, Va.; chmn. fine arts dept. Christiansburg Middle Sch., 1991—; judge, clinician for marching and concert bands; curriculum and instrn. clin. affiliate Va. Poly. Inst. and State U., Blacksburg, Radford (Va.) U.; clinician, guest condr. for mid-Atlantic band camps Ferrum Coll., Va.; guest condr. all-dist. bands in Va., N.C., S.C. Composer: Published Windsor Portrait, 1990, Adagio for horn and piano, 1982, Nocturne for flute and piano, 1987, Royal Brigade, 1988, Prelude and tarantelle, 1991, An American Tattoo, 1994; compositions commd. by Va. State Symphony Orch., Charlotte (N.C.) Mecklenburg County Schs., Rural Retreat (Va.) H.S.; music performed at Va. Music Educators Conf., 1990, 95, Midwest Band Conv., Chgo., 1990, Finland Radio, 1993, Great Britain, 1993, 94, France, 1995. Recipient Young composers award Va. Music Clubs, 1960, Va. Govs. Sch. Presdl. citation, 1990, 92, Teaching award Halifax County Schs., 1972. Mem. ASCAP, Music Educators Nat. Conf., Nat. Band Assn., Va. Music Educators Assn. (exec. bd.), Va. Band and Orch. Dirs. Assn. (instrumental chmn. dist. VI), Modern Music Masters (life, past adv. coun., exec. bd.), Phi Beta Mu, Phi Delta Kappa. Home: 2810 Mt Vernon Ln Blacksburg VA 24060-8121

WALL, ROBERT THORP, JR., internist, hematologist, oncologist; b. Manchester, N.H., Dec. 23, 1946; s. Robert Thorp and Anne (Hedderman) W.; m. Susan T. Wall, June 7, 1969; children: Spencer Seabury, Elizabeth Dodd. BA in Biology, Williams Coll., 1968; MD, Med. Coll. S.C., 1972. Diplomate Am. Bd. Internal Medicine, Nat. Bd. Med. Examiners, Am. Bd. Hematology, Am. Bd. Med. Oncology; lic. physician, S.C. Intern, then asst. resident dept. medicine Med. Sch. U. Tex., Houston, 1972-74; sr. fellow in hematology, dept. medicine Sch. Medicine U. Washington, Seattle, 1974-76, instr. dept. medicine, 1976-78; asst. prof. dept. medicine Sch. Medicine Stanford (Calif.) U., 1978-82; mem. staff Roper Hosp., 1982—, Bon Secours St. Francis Xavier Hosp., Charleston, S.C.; with Charleston Hematology-Oncology, 1982—; invited spkr. Gordon Conf. on Hemostasis, 1980, Kroc Conf. on Diabetes and Atherosclerosis, 1980. Contbr. chpt. to: Basic Clinical Pharmacology, 1982, Diabetic Retinopathy, 1983; contbr. many articles to profl. publs. Recipient Nat. Rsch. Svc. award, 1975-76, Young Investigator's Rsch. award Nat. Heart, Lung, and Blood Inst., 1977-80. Fellow ACP; mem. AAAS, Am. Soc. Hematology (session chmn. nat. meeting 1981), Am. Fedn. for Clin. Rsch. (sect. counsellor 1981-83, abstract reviewer, session chmn. Western sect. 1982), Am. Soc. Clin. Oncology, Am. Heart Assn. (mem. coun. on thrombosis, mem. grant rev. study sect. Calif. affiliate 1981-82), So. Assn. for Oncology, S.C. Med. Assn., Med. Soc. S.C., Charleston County Med. Soc., Alpha Omega Alpha. Office: Charleston Hematology-Oncology 125 Doughty St Charleston SC 29403-5740

WALLACE, ALICEANNE, civic worker; b. Chgo., Sept. 28, 1925; d. Alexander and Mary (Zurek) Zalac; m. Henry Clay Wallace, Jr., Apr. 10, 1948; children: Laura Lillian Wallace Bergin, Christine Claire Wallace Stockwell. Student, St. Teresa Coll., Winona, Minn., 1944-45, DePaul U., 1946-48, North Tex. State U., 1971, 72. City sec. City of Southlake, Tex., 1969-77; pres. AZW, Inc., real estate sales, Roanoke, Tex., 1977-84. Mem. Trinity Valley Mental Health-Mental Retardation, Ft. Worth, 1971-72; chmn. ways and means Tex. Silver-Haired Legis., Austin, 1986-90, parliamentarian, 1991-94; treas. TSHL Found., 1990-92, pres., 1992-96; sec., bd. dirs. Sr. Citizens Activities, Inc., Temple, Tex., 1989-90; sec. CTCOG Area Agy. on Aging, Citizens Adv. Comm. Bd., Belton, Tex., 1991; bd. dirs. Tex. Dept. on Aging, Austin, 1991—; congl. sr. intern U.S. Ho. of Reps., Washington, 1991; pres. Tri-County Tex. Dem. Women, 1990-94; congl. del. White House Conf. on Aging, 1995; elected State Dem. Exec. Com. Senatorial Dist. #24, 1994—. Mem. Am. Assn. Ret. Persons (legis. chmn. Temple chpt. 1990-94, regional coord. VOTE 1991-96, assoc. state coord. 1996—), Tex. Fedn. Women's Clubs (state legis. chmn. 1990-92, resolutions chmn. 1992-94, parliamentarian Capitol dist. 1990-92), North Ctrl. Tex. Secy. Assn. (pres. 19760, City Fedn. Women's Clubs (corr. sec. 1991-92, records custodian 1991—), Triangle Forum (pres. 1992-94), Daus. Republic Tex. (assoc.), Internat. Inst. Mcpl. Clks. (state cert.), Epsilon Eta Phi. Home: RR 2 Box 2585 Belton TX 76513-9611

WALLACE, BETTY JEAN, elementary school educator, lay minister; b. Denison, Tex., Dec. 5, 1927; d. Claude Herman and Pearl Victoria (Freels) Moore; m. Billy Dean McKneely, Sept. 2, 1950 (div. Nov. 1964); children: Rebecca Lynn, Paul King, David Freels, John Walker, Philip Andrew McKneely. Student, Tulane U., 1947; BA, Baylor U., 1949; postgrad., U. Houston, 1949-50, 74, 81, Rocky Mountain Bible Inst., 1959, U. Colo., 1969-70, U. No. Colo., 1965, 68, 72, U. St. Thomas, 1992, Autonomous U. Guadalajara, summer 1993; MEd, Houston Bapt. U., 1985. Cert. life profl. elem., high sch., life profl. reading specialist, secondary field ESL tchr., Tex. Tchr. Galena Park (Tex.) Ind. Sch. Dist., 1949-50, 52-53, 72—, Corpus Christi (Tex.) Independent Sch. Dist., 1950-51, Denver Pub. Schs., 1953-54, 63-72. Author: The Holy Spirit Today, 1989, Our God of Infinite Variety, 1991, God Speaks in a Variety of Ways, 1991. Sunday sch. tchr. So. Bapt. Conv. chs., Tex., 1946-50, Denver, 1952-56; tchr. kindergarten Emmanuel Bapt. Ch., Denver, 1956-59, 60-63; missionary, Queretaro, Mex., 1977, 78; mem. Rep. Senatorial Inner Circle, Washington, 1989-91, Round Table for Ronald Reagan, Washington, 1989-90; helper Feed the Poor, Houston, 1983-85; active Suicide Prevention, Houston, 1973-76, Literacy, Houston, 1978-81; rep. NEA, Denver, 1966-72; mem. Retirement Com., Denver, 1970-72; bd. advisors Oliver North, 1994. Recipient Rep. Senatorial medal of freedom, 1994; grantee NSF, 1969-70. Mem. Tex. Classroom Tchrs. Assn. (officer rep., pres. Galena Park chpt. 1988-91), Delta Alpha Pi (pres. Waco chpt. 1948-49), Alpha Epsilon Delta. Republican. Home: 14831 Anoka Dr Channelview TX 77530-3201 Office: North Shore Elem Sch 14310 Duncannon Dr Houston TX 77015-2514

WALLACE, CAROLYN MARIE, administrative assistant; b. Fayetteville, N.C., Mar. 31, 1961; d. William and Patricia Lee (Ladley) Waterson; m. Loston R. Wallace, Apr. 13, 1996. BA in Edn., U. N.C., 1982. Tchr.'s asst. St. Thomas More Sch., Chapel Hill, N.C., 1983-84; transfer coord. pers.

dept. U. N.C., Chapel Hill, 1984-85, adminstrv. sec. IV, Morehead Planetarium, 1985-88, level V, 1988-94; adminstrv. asst. Niagara Conservation Corp., 1995-96; word processor PACE, Inc., 1996—. Contbr. articles to profl. jours. Mem. Phi Eta Sigma, Kappa Delta Pi.

WALLACE, DONALD JOHN, III, rancher, former pest control company executive; b. Houston, May 17, 1941; s. D.J. Jr. and Doris Jill (Gano) W.; m. Patricia Anne McShane, Sept. 3, 1964 (div. 1984); children: Donald John IV, Megan; m. Nena Jo Isenhower, June 1, 1985 (div. 1989); 1 child, Andrew. BBA in Mktg., Texas A&M U., 1963. Regional sales dir. Orkin Exterminating Co., Inc., Dallas, 1977-79, br. mgr., 1979-80, dist. mgr., 1980-83, comml. region mgr., 1983-85, regional sales dir., 1985-86; owner Omega Telex, Dallas, 1986-88; rancher Valley View, Tex., 1988—. Mem. Tex. Structural Pest Control Bd., Austin, 1983-84. Mem. Nat. Pest Control Assn., Tex. Pest Control Assn., Dallas Pest Control Assn. Republican. Roman Catholic. Home: 1400 Trails End Valley View TX 76272-9530

WALLACE, DUNCAN SARON, psychiatrist, educator; b. N.Y.C., Nov. 15, 1937; s. Bruce Cameron Sr. and Carolyn (Jones) W.; m. Bernadene Lewis, June 12, 1961; children: Rochelle, Julia, Jennifer, Matthew. Student, U. Denver; BS, U. Wis., 1959; MD, U. Colo., 1962. Diplomate Am. Bd. Psychiatry and Neurology-Psychiatry, Am. Bd. Psychiatry and Neurology-Child Psychiatry. Intern U. Pitts. Hosps., 1962-63; resident U. Colo. Sch. Medicine, 1963, Colo. Psychiat. Hosp., 1965-67; fellow in child psychiatry Children's Hosp. D.C., 1968-70; from instr. to assoc. prof. George Washington U., Washington, 1968-71; staff psychiatrist Children's Treatment Ctr. Colo. State Hosp., 1967-68; staff psychiatrist area B Mental Health Ctr., Washington, 1970-71; asst. prof. Howard U., Washington, 1970-71; ptnr. Psychiat. Assocs. of Tidewater, Inc., 1971-88, Beach Psychiat. Svcs., Inc., 1988-91; assoc. prof. Ea. Va. Med. Sch., Norfolk, 1971-93; med dir. adolescent svcs. Tidewater Psychiat. Inst., Virginia Beach, 1974-76; chmn. dept. psychiatry Humana Bayside Hosp., Virginia Beach, 1983-84, Virginia Beach Gen. Hosp., 1983-84; med. dir. adult svcs. Virginia Beach Psychiatry Ctr., 1989-94. Contbr. book chpt.: Dimensions for Growing Up, 1983, (bull.) Virginia Child Protection Soc., 1983. Active Virginia Beach Sch. Bd., 1978-84. Lt. USN, 1963-65. Recipient Exemplary Psychiatrist award Nat. Alliance for Mentally Ill, 1993. Fellow Am. Acad. Psychiat. Assn., Am. Psychiat. Assn.; mem. Psychiat. Soc. Va. (pres. 1991-92), Virginia Beach Med. Soc. (chmn. ethics com. 1982, pres. 1987). Congregational. Office: 837 First Colonial Rd Ste C Virginia Beach VA 23451-6125

WALLACE, GARY, bank executive; b. 1936. With Commonwealth Credit Union, Inc., 1976—, now pres. Office: Commonwealth Credit Union Inc 417 High St Frankfort KY 40601-2112*

WALLACE, GEORGE CORLEY, former governor; b. Clio, Ala., Aug. 25, 1919; s. George C. and Mozell (Smith) W.; m. Lurleen Burns, May 23, 1943 (dec.); children: Bobbie Jo, Peggy Sue, George Corley, Janie Lee; m. Cornelia Ellis Snively, Jan. 1971 (div. Jan. 1978); m. Lisa Taylor, Sept. 1981 (div. Jan. 1987). LLB, U. Ala., 1942. Bar: Ala. 1942. Asst. atty. gen. State of Ala., 1946-47, mem. Barbour County Legis., 1947-53, judge 3d jud. dist., 1953-58, gov., 1963-66, 71-79, 83-87; sole practice Clayton, Ala., 1958-62; dir. rehab. resources U. Ala., Birmingham, 1979-83; chair pub. adminstrn. Troy State U., Montgomery, Ala., 1987-95; pres. Ala. Bd. Edn. Sponsor, Wallace Act for state trade schs., 1947. Candidate for pres. Am. Ind. Party, 1968, Dem. primary, 1972, 76; bd. dirs. Ala. Tb Assn.; past Sunday sch. tchr. and supt. Meth. Ch. Served with USAAF, 1942-45, PTO. Mem. Am. Legion, VFW, DAV. Lodges: Masons, Shriners, Moose, Elks, Modern Woodman of World, Order Eastern Star, Civitan Internat. Home: 3140 Fitzgerald Rd Montgomery AL 36106-2633 Office: The Wallace Found PO Box 667 Montgomery AL 36101

WALLACE, JAMES JOSEPH, banking executive; b. Louisville, Oct. 21, 1939; s. James Joseph and Florence Eva (Morgan) W.; m. Marietta Chambers, Aug. 12, 1967; children: James, Christine, Margaret. AB, Spring Hill Coll., Mobile, Ala., 1961; MBA, Ga. State U., 1967. Reporter Atlanta Constn., 1961-62; comml. banking rep. Trust Co. of Ga., Atlanta, 1965-68; communications assoc. Coca-Cola U.S.A., Atlanta, 1968-70; mgr. pub. relations and advt. The Southern Co., Atlanta, 1970-78; dir. communications Mid. South Utilities, New Orleans, 1978-82; gen. mgr. Ogilvy & Mather Pub. Relations, Atlanta, 1982-83; v.p. communications Fulton Fed. Savs. Bank, Atlanta, 1983-91; dir. mktg. and corp. comms. Fed. Home Loan Bank of Atlanta, 1991—. Lt. USN, 1962-65. Mem. BBB (bd. dirs. 1986-90), Pub. Rels. Soc. Am. (bd. dirs. Ga. chpt. 1984—, pres. 1985, S.E. dist. chmn. 1996, Coll. of Fellows 1996—). Roman Catholic. Home: 3120 Bolero Dr Atlanta GA 30341-5758 Office: Fed Home Loan Bank Atlanta 1475 Peachtree St NE Atlanta GA 30309-3003

WALLACE, JAMES OLDHAM, librarian; b. San Antonio, Sept. 22, 1917; s. James Vance and Violet Edyth (Oldham) W.; m. Lillie Ruth Franklin, July 23, 1968; children: Carolyn Denning, Edith Frances Peterson, Thelma Ruth Pittman. AA, San Antonio Coll., 1936; BA, St. Mary's U., 1938, MA, 1940; BLS, Our Lady of the Lake U., 1950. Tchr. Natalia (Tex.) Ind. Sch. Dist., 1940-41; tchr. L.A. Heights Ind. Sch. Dist., San Antonio, 1941-42; clk. USAAF, Kelly AFB, Tex., 1942-43; payroll chief, certifying officer USAAF, Randolph AFB, Tex., 1943-49; tchr., libr. Lanier High Sch., San Antonio, 1949-50; asst. libr. San Antonio Coll., 1950-51, libr., prof., dir. learning resources, 1951-85, dir. emeritus, 1985—; libr. dir. Hispanic Bapt. Theol. Sem., San Antonio, 1986-94; pres. Friends of San Antonio Pub. Libr., 1986-88; cons. U.S. Office Edn., Washington, 1967-68. Contbr. articles to profl. jours. Trustee Bapt. Meml. Hosp., San Antonio, 1965-67, Mexican Bapt. Bible Inst., San Antonio, 1975-83; pres. adv. com. Hispanic Bapt. Theol. Sem., 1983-90. Named Libr. of Yr. Tex. Libr. Assn., 1968; recipient Disting. Svc. citation Assn. Coll. and Rsch. Librs., 1989, Disting. Svc. award Tex. Libr. Assn., 1991, Outstanding Svc. award, Assn. Coll. and Rsch. Librs., 1991. Mem. ALA (life), Tex. Libr. Assn. (life, pres. 1983-84), Bexar Libr. Assn. (life, pres. 1951-52). Home: PO Box 13041 San Antonio TX 78213-0041

WALLACE, JANE HOUSE, geologist; b. Ft. Worth, Aug. 12, 1926; d. Fred Leroy and Helen Gould (Kixmiller) Wallace; A.B., Smith Coll., 1947, M.A., 1949; postgrad. Bryn Mawr Coll., 1949-52. Geologist, U.S. Geol. Survey, 1952—, chief Pub. Inquiries Offices, Washington, 1964-72, spl. asst. to dir., 1974—, dep. bur. ethics counselor, 1975—, Washington liaison Office of Dir., 1978—. Recipient Meritorious Service award Dept. Interior, 1971, Disting. Svc. award, 1976, Sec.'s Commendation, 1988, Smith Coll. medal, 1992. Fellow Geol. Socs. Am., Washington (treas. 1963-67); mem. Sigma Xi (asso.). Home: 3003 Van Ness St NW Washington DC 20008-4701 Office: Interior Bldg 19th and C Sts NW Washington DC 20240 also: US Geol Survey 103 National Ctr Reston VA 22092

WALLACE, JEFFREY LEIGH, surgeon; b. Pitts., Apr. 4, 1951; s. Walter R. and Mary E. Wallace; m. Patricia Waters, June 16, 1977; children: Forrest, Marcus. BS, U. Tenn., 1973; MD, U. Tenn., Memphis, 1976. Diplomate Am Bd. Gen. Surgery. Resident in surgery Charity Hosp., New Orleans, 1977-81; staff Athens (Tenn.) Community Hosp., 1984—. Fellow ACS. Episcopalian. Office: 719 Cook Dr Athens TN 37303-3495

WALLACE, CARL JERRY, zoo director; m. Molly Wallace; children: Beth, Carrie, Laura. Student Zoology, Chemistry, U. Cin.; student Mortuary Sci, Chemistry, Xavier U., Cin. Staff mem. Cin. Zoo, 1970-80; team leader Toledo Zoo, 1980-92; dir. Birmingham (Ala.) Zoo, 1992—; collector insects in C.Am. for 1st zoo insectarium in N.Am., Cin. Zoo; condr. travels to Africa; condr. classes at Cin. univs., until 1980; condr. travels to Kenya, Tanzania, India, Nepal, Peru, and China fo Toledo Zoo; negotiator with China for visit of giant pandas to Toledo, summer 1988; established programs to study pandas in wild and protection of their habitat. Office: Birmingham Zoo 2630 Cahaba Rd Birmingham AL 35223-1106

WALLACE, JERRY MCLAIN, academic administrator; b. Rockingham, N.C., Apr. 20, 1935; s. William M. and Lillie (Edwards) W.; m. Betty Blanchard, Apr. 15, 1956; children: Betty Lynne Johnson, McLain, Kelly. BA, East Carolina U., 1956; M in Divinity, Southeastern Sem., Wake Forest, N.C., 1959, ThM, 1960; MS, N.C. State U., 1969, EdD, 1971. Pastor Elizabethtown (N.C.) Bapt. Ch., 1960-75; chmn. dept. religion and philosophy Campbell U., Buies Creek, N.C., 1975-81, v.p. acad. affairs, 1981—. Mem. Am. Acad. Religion. Democrat. Baptist. Home: PO Box 246 Buies Creek NC 27506-0246 Office: Campbell U Office of the Provost PO Box 578 Buies Creek NC 27506-0578*

WALLACE, JOHN ROBERT, county administrator; b. Princeton, Ind., Mar. 24, 1939; s. Robert Floyd and Marjorie Eloise (Steele) W.; m. Karen Sue Katilius, June 18, 1967 (div. Mar. 1985). BS in Engring. with honors, USCG Acad., 1961; BS in Civil Engring. with honors, U. Ill., 1967. Commd. ensign USCG, 1961, advanced through grades to capt., 1982; facilities engr. Coast Guard Res. Tng. Ctr., Yorktown, Va., 1975-77; chief engr. Coast Guard Activities Europe, Am. Embassy, London, 1977-80; mem. planning/plans evaluation staff USCG Chief of Staff, Washington, 1980-82; dep. chief civil engring. USCG Office Engring., Washington, 1982-83; chief, dep. chief office USCG Office Rsch. and Devel., Washington, 1983-86; commanding officer, sr. engr. USCG Facilities Design and Constrn. Ctr., Norfolk, Va., 1986-89; asst. county adminstr. planning and community devel. Pittsylvania County, Chatham, Va.; county adminstr. County of Amelia, Va., 1992—. Recipient Man of Yr. award Optimists, 1982, Spl. award Kennedy Found., 1984, Haskel Small USO Vol. awards, Washington, 1985, 86. Fellow Soc. Am. Mil. Engrs.; mem. VFW, NRA (life), Am. Def. Preparedness Assn., U.S. Lighthouse Soc., Naval Airship Assn., Royal Nat. Lifeboat Instn. Eng., Scottish Soc. Tidewater, St. Andrews Soc. Tidewater, Clan Wallace Soc., Scottish-Am. Mil. Soc., Am. Legion, Retired Officers Assn., Am. Planning Assn., Va. Citizen's Planning Assn., Va. Econ. Developers Assn., Va. Assn. County Ofcls., Coast Guard Combat Vets. Assn., Va.-Carolina Scottish Soc., Lions. Office: County of Amelia PO Box A Amelia Court House VA 23002-0066

WALLACE, LINDA JO, elementary education educator; b. Lubbock, Tex., Jan. 7, 1950; d. Edward Burt and Ella Beatrice (Tapp) Green; m. David Paul Wallace, Aug. 7, 1971; children: David Paul II, Matthew Edward, Sharon Lynn. Student, Tex. Tech., 1968-69; BS, Abilene Christian Univ., 1972. Tchr. Cleburne (Tex.) ISD, 1972-75; phys. edn. tchr. Waco (Tex.) Christian Sch., 1987; presch. tchr. Beltway Bapt. Ch., Abilene, 1989-90; tchr. Wylie Intermediate, Abilene, 1990—; Supt. adv. bd. Wylie Ind. Sch. Dist., Abilene, 1991-94. Tchr. bible classes Ch. of Christ, Cleburne, Midland, Waco, Abilene, 1972-95. Mem. Big Coungry Coun. Tchrs. Eng. (sec. 1993-94), Big Country Reading Coun., Internat. Reading Assn. Home: 526 Country Pl Rd Abilene TX 79606 Office: Wylie Intermediate Sch 7650 Hardwick Rd Abilene TX 79606

WALLACE, MARK ALLEN, hospital executive; b. Oklahoma City, Apr. 24, 1953; s. William Howell and Mollie Marie (Godsy) W.; children: Emily, Benjamin. BS, Okla. Bapt. U., 1975; MS, Washington U., St. Louis, 1978. Adminstrv. asst. Bapt. Med. Ctr., Oklahoma City, 1975-77; administrv. resident Meth. Hosp., Houston, 1977-78; asst. v.p. Tex. Meth. Hosp., Houston, 1978-80, v.p., 1980-83, sr. v.p., 1983-89; exec. dir., chief exec. officer Tex. Children's Hosp., Houston, 1989—; adj. instr. Washington U., 1984—; adj. asst. prof. Tex. Womans U., Houston, 1983—; bd. dirs., chmn. fin. com., treas. Greater Houston Hosp. Svc. Corp., 1986-90. Contbr. articles to profl. jours. Chmn. campaign drives United Way, Houston, 1984, 86; class chmn. alumni vision for excellence and growth for future campaigns Okla. Bapt. U., 1982; bd. dirs. Tex. Gulf Coast chpt. March of Dimes Birth Defects Found., 1985-91. Recipient Emerging Leaders in Health Care award Healthcare Forum Mag. and Korn/Ferry Internat., 1987, Robert S. Hudgens Meml. award, 1992. Fellow Am. Coll. Healthcare Execs. (com. on membership, subcom. on recruitment 1990—, Young Healthcare Exec. of Yr.), mem. Am. Heart Assn. (med. adv. com. 1990-91), Healthcare Forum (pres. emerging leaders alumni group 1988-91), Am. Hosp. Assn., Tex. Hosp. Assn. (bd. dirs., bd. dirs. polit. action com. 1988—), Greater Houston Hosp. Coun. (bd. dirs. 1991—), Houston Area Health Care Coalition, Childrens Hosp. Assn. Tex. (pres. 1992—), Tex. Gulf Coast Arthritis Found. (bd. dirs. 1990-91). Republican. Baptist. Office: Tex Children's Hosp PO Box 300630 Houston TX 77230-0630*

WALLACE, MARK HARRIS, minister; b. Albany, Ga., Sept. 14, 1955; s. Lawrence Theodore and Grace (Justice) W.; m. Kelly Sue Noe, Mar. 3, 1979; children: Justin, Andrew, Brittany Hope, Marcie Faith. BS in Psychology, Ga. State U., 1978; MS in Clin. Psychology, Augusta Coll., 1985; M of Ministry, Internat. Bible Inst., Plymouth, Fla., 1983, D of Ministry, 1985. Ordained to ministry Faith Christian Fellowship Internat., 1988 ; lic. to ministry Ch. of God, 1989. Assoc. pastor Riverdale (Ga.) Ch. of God, 1977-82; youth pastor Maranatha Fellowship, Augusta, 1982-84; sr. pastor, founder New Hope Christian Ctr., Augusta, 1984-89; resident pastor New Hope Ch. of God, Augusta, 1989-90, world missions pastor, 1990-91; elder, co-pastor Living Word Christian Ctr., Augusta, 1991-92; CEO, founder EagleFire Graphics Design & Pub., Inc., Marietta, Ga., 1991—; comml. real estate prin. agt. Comml. Assets Group, Inc., Atlanta, 1995—; co-elder minister Oneln Spirit Ministries, Augusta, 1986-92; praise team musician and singer A Great Love Ministries, Toccoa, Ga., 1987-93; pres., founder Wallace Ministries Internat. Augusta, 1989—; minister Internat. Conv. Faith Ministries, Tulsa, 1988-91; motivational conf. speaker, U.S., S.Am., Ctrl. Am., Caribbean Islands, Europe, Sweden, 1984—; highend computer operator, computer graphic designer, computer illustrator, computer typesetter, 1994—. Author 10 books including: The Servant's Heart, The Christian's Call to War, Grace: God's Greatest Gift; songwriter gospel music; contbr. articles to profl. jours. Co-founder, co-dir. Augusta Thanksgiving Dinner of Love Outreach, 1986—, Augusta Christmas Food/Toy Baskets Outreach, 1986-92. Mem. Nat. Assn. Desktop Publs., Ga. State U. Alumni Assn., Augusta Coll. Alumni Assn., Golden Key, Psi Chi.

WALLACE, MILTON DENARD, school system administrator; b. Tyler, Tex., July 7, 1957; s. John Milton and Thelma Louise (Jackson) W.; m. Gwendolyn Ann Wheeler, Apr. 8, 1989. BS, E. Tex. State U., 1978, MEd, 1979. Tchr. Commerce (Tex.) Mid. Sch., 1978-84, asst. prin., 1983-84; prin. Union Hill H.S., Gilmer, Tex., 1984-87; asst. prin. Denton (Tex.) H.S., 1987-90, prin., 1990—; camp dir. Tex. Assn. Student Coun., Austin, 1984-90. Mem. Nat. Assn. Secondary Prins., Tex. Assn. Secondary Prins. Democrat. Baptist.

WALLACE, MINOR GORDON, JR., architect, landscape architect, mayor; b. Texarkana, Tex., Oct. 30, 1936; s. Minor Gordon and Dessie (Bledsoe) W.; children: Rayma, Minor Gordon III. BA, U. Ark., 1961, BArch., 1961. Project architect Bruce R. Anderson, Architect, Little Rock, 1964-67; univ. architect U. Ark., Fayetteville, 1968—; prin. Minor G. Wallace, Jr., Architect, 1969—, Wallace & Estes, Architects, Fayetteville, 1978-80; dir. facilities planning and constrn. U. Ark. System, Fayetteville, 1968-81, dir. facilities planning, 1981-84, asst. v.p. facilities planning, 1984—; cons. edn. planning, architecture. Alderman, City of Prairie Grove, (Ark.), 1981-83, mayor, 1983-86; chmn. bd. dirs. Northwest Ark. Arts and Crafts Guild, 1977-79; bd. dirs. Northwest Ark. Cultural Center, 1978—, acting pres., 1981-84, pres., 1984—; pres. D & W Devel. Co., Inc., 1985—; ptnr. Country Inn Restaurants and Antiques, 1985—. Campus landscaping Pine Bluff and Fayetteville campuses U. Ark., 1977-78, indoor tennis ctr., Fayetteville campus, 1979-80, also botany greenhouse and sports arena, Ch. for Fayetteville Christian Fellowship, 1987. Mem. AIA, Am. Soc. Landscape Architects, Council Ednl. Planners, Soc. Coll. and Univ. Planning, Nat. Trust Hist. Preservation, Assn. Univ. Architects, Am. Planning Assn. Democrat. Unitarian. Office: Univ Tower Bldg Ste 601 1123 S University Ave Little Rock AR 72204-1609

WALLACE, NATHANIEL OWEN, English language educator; b. Charleston, S.C., July 26, 1948; s. James Irvin Sr. and Bella Goldin W.; m. Janet Lynn Kozachek, May 26, 1979. AB in French, Classics, Coll. Charleston, 1969; MA in Comparative Lit., Rutgers U., 1975, PhD in Comparative Lit., 1979. Instr. Rutgers U., New Brunswick, N.J., 1974-77, Rider Coll., 1978-80; lectr. Brit. and Am. lit. Hebei U., Baoding, China, 1981-82, Jilin U., Changchun, China, 1982-83; lectr. English and comparative lit. Beijing (China) Normal U., 1983-85; lectr. English Univ. Coll.-European Divsn. U. Md., 1985-87; asst. prof. English Del. Valley Coll., 1988-91, S.C. State U., Orangeburg, 1991—; grad. student rep. bd. trustees, Rutgers U., 1975-76; mem. faculty coun. Del. Valley Coll., 1990-91; rsch. com. S.C. State U., 1991-93; chmn. Internat. Programs comm., 1994-96; vis. lectr. U. Konstanz, Germany, 1994-95; papers presented at various confs. Contbr. articles to profl. jours. NEH fellow, 1994-95; Walter C. Russell grad. scholar Rutgers U.; NEH summer programs, 1980, 87, 89, 90. Mem. MLA, Am. Comparative Lit. Assn., So. Comparative Lit. Assn., Renaissance Soc. Am., South Atlantic MLA, Am. Assn. Chinese Studies. Democrat. Jewish. Office: SC State U Dept English Orangeburg SC 29117

WALLACE, RICHARD LEA, marketing professional; b. Bloomington, Ind., Mar. 19, 1958; s. Richard Lee and Lucee Ann (Williams) W.; m. Priscilla Burcham, Aug. 13, 1983. BA, N.C. State U., 1983. Account exec. Glesby-Marks Leasing, Houston, 1984; distrbn. mgr. Va. Paper Co., Raleigh, N.C., 1985-87; account exec. Glover Printing, Raleigh, 1987-89, Meredith Webb Printing, Burlington, N.C., 1989-93, Hutchinson-Allgood Printing, Raleigh, 1993—. Bd. dirs. Watts-Hosp. N.A., Durham, N.C., 1993—; pres.-elect, pres. Inter Neighborhood Coun., Durham, 1993-95. Named Salesperson of Yr. Sales and Mktg. Execs., 1995. Mem. Triangle Prodn. Assn. (bd. dirs. 1995—), Carolina's Direct Mktg. Assn. Democrat. Episcopalian. Home: 801 Snowcrest Trail Durham NC 27707 Office: Cary Printing Co 920 Morrisville Pkwy Morrisville NC 27560

WALLACE, ROANNE, hosiery company executive; b. Greenwood, Miss., Dec. 18, 1949; d. Robert Carter and Lois Anne (Vick) W. BM, U. Tenn., 1971; MA, U. N.C., 1976; MBA, Wake Forest U., 1982. Exec. dir. Am. Bd. Clin. Chemistry, Winston-Salem, N.C., 1977-78; administrv. officer Winston-Salem/Forsyth County Office Emergency Mgmt., 1978-79, sr. asst. dir., 1979-82; with Sara Lee Hosiery, Winston-Salem, 1982—, mktg. dir., 1988—; product mgr. L'eggs Products, Inc., Winston-Salem, 1986-88. Mem. adv. coun. Winston-Salem/Forsyth County Office Emergency Mgmt.; bd. dirs. Piedmont Opera Theatre, Inc. Miss U. Tenn., 1970. Home: 803 Devon Ct Winston Salem NC 27104-1263 Office: L'Eggs Products Inc PO Box 2495 Winston Salem NC 27102-2495

WALLACE, ROBERT BARNES, JR., lawyer; b. Corpus Christi, Tex., Mar. 6, 1951; s. Robert Barnes and Beverley (Bird) W.; m. Louella Caldwell, July 27, 1974; children: Emily, Lorraine. BBA, So. Meth. U., 1973, JD, 1976. Bar: Tex. 1976, U.S. Dist. Ct. (so. dist.) Tex. 1976, U.S. Tax Ct. 1978. Ptnr. Wallace, Wallace & Wheeler, L.L.P., Corpus Christi, 1976—; bd. dirs. H.&K. Constrn. Co. Bd. dirs. 100 Club Corpus Christi, Comty. Blood Bank, past pres., exec. com.; pres., trustee Coastal Bend Bays Found.; adv. com. mem. Trans-Tes Water Program; Coastal Mgmt. Program mgmt. com. mem. Gen. Land Office; adv. com. mem. Tex. Water Commn., Corpus Christi Nat. Estuary Program; Kennedy Causeway com. mem. TexDOT/MPO; com. for littering locations mem. USCG. Mem. ABA (estate and gift tax com. 1978—), State Bar Tex. (real estate, probate and trust sect. 1976—, taxation sect. 1983—), Nueces County Estate Planning Coun., Corpus Christi Bar Assn. Office: 1800 American Bank Plz Corpus Christi TX 78475

WALLACE, ROBERT W., sociologist, educator; b. Borger, Tex., Nov. 1, 1956; s. Richard W. and F. Roberta (Smith) W.; m. Rosemary Kovach, Dec. 18, 1980. M in Gerontol. Studies, Miami U., 1980; MA, Columbia U., 1985, M in Philosophy, 1987, PhD, 1989. Social svc. worker John Knox Retirement Village, Lubbock, 1977-79; rsch./teaching asst. dept. sociology Scripps Found. Gerontology Ctr. Miami U., Oxford, Ohio, 1979-80; rsch. analyst Margaret Blenkner Rsch. Ctr. Benjamin Rose Inst., Cleve., 1981-84; Paul F. Lazarsfeld fellow Columbia U., N.Y.C., 1984-88, lectr. in sociology, 1987-88; asst. prof., chairperson sociology McMurry U., Abilene, Tex., 1990-93, assoc. prof., chairperson, 1993—; adj. lectr. Hunter Coll. CUNY, Kingsborough C. C., N.Y.C., 1989-90. Contbr. articles to profl. jours. Mem. Southwestern Social Sci. Assn., Soc. for Study of Social Problems, Ea. Sociol. Soc., Am. Sociol. Assn., Alpha Kappa Delta. Home: 1118 Sayles Blvd Abilene TX 79605-4205 Office: McMurry U Dept Sociology Abilene TX 79697

WALLACE, STEVEN CHARLES, judge; b. Lubbock, Tex., Jan. 19, 1953; s. Charles Andrew Wallace and Alice Hillene (McMillin) Stone; m. Kathleen Louise Merrill, Apr. 3, 1976; children: Christine Merrill, Zachary Charles, Steven Kyle. BA, Tex. Tech U., 1975, JD, 1979. Bar: Tex. 1979, U.S. Dist. Ct. (no. dist.) Tex. 1980, U.S. Ct. Appeals (5th cir.) 1981. Asst. county atty. Parker County, Weatherford, Tex., 1979-80; asst. dist. atty. Tarrant County, Ft. Worth, 1980-83; pvt. practice Ft. Worth, 1983-90; judge Tarrant County Ct. at Law # 2, Ft. Worth, 1991—; chmn. prosecution and adjudication subcom. Tarrant 2000 Task Force, 1987—. Recipient Am. Jurisprudence award Bancroft Whitney Co., 1979. Fellow Coll. State Bar of Tex.; mem. Am. Judges Assn., State Bar Tex., Tarrant County Bar Assn., Ridotto Club, Ridgelea Country Club, Phi Alpha Delta, Phi Alpha Theta. Office: County Ct at Law # 2 100 W Weatherford St Fort Worth TX 76196-0234

WALLACE, WILLIAM EDWARD, research physicist; b. Charleston, W.Va., Sept. 25, 1942; s. William Edward and Zoe Wallace; m. Elisabeth Ann Hornsby-Fehl, July 1, 1970; children: Sarah Hart, David Bransford. BS in Physics, W.Va. U., 1963, MS in Physics, 1967, PhD, 1969. Postdoctoral associateship NRC U.S. Bur. of Mines, Morgantown, W.Va., 1969-70, rsch. physicist, 1970-76; asst. ctr. dir. U.S. Dept. of Energy, Morgantown, W.Va., 1976-80; rsch. physicist div. respiratory disease studies, div. health effects lab. Nat. Inst. for Occupational Safety and Health, Morgantown, W.Va., 1980—; adj. prof. dept. chem. engring. W.Va. U., Morgantown, 1982—, Coll. Mineral and Energy Resources, W.Va. U., Morgantown, 1990-95; grad. faculty Coll. Engring., W.Va. U., Morgantown, 1988—; com. synthetic fuels facilities safety NRC, LaJolla and Washington, 1981-82; working group WHO, Internat. Agy. for Rsch. on Cancer, Lyon, France, 1983; chmn. radiation safety com. Appalachian Lab. for Occupl. Safety and Health, Nat. Inst. Occupl. Safety and Health, 1983—; postdoctoral rsch. adv. associateship program NRC, 1991—. Editor: Silica and Silica-Induced Lung Diseases, 1995; referee Jour. Magnetic Resonance, 1972, ACS Jour. Environ. Sci. and Tech., 1974, Jour. Toxicology and Environ. Health, 1990, 93, Annals Occupl. Hygiene, 1991; patentee in field; contbr. articles to profl. jours. Chmn. admissions and allocations United Way Monongalia and Preston Counties, W.Va., 1992, chmn. donor rels. com., 1993-95, chmn. vol. action com., 1996—. Recipient Shepard Sci. award nominee U.S. Ctr. for Disease Control, 1988, 93, Leadership award United Way, 1993. Office: Nat Inst Occupational Safety & Health 944 Chestnut Ridge Rd Morgantown WV 26505-2819

WALLACE, WILLIAM RAY, fabricated steel manufacturing company executive; b. Shreveport, La., Mar. 25, 1923; s. Jason Mohoney and Mattie Evelyn (Adair) W.; m. Minyone Milligan Rose, Oct. 5, 1966; children: Jayne Cecile Rose McDearman, Susan Rose O'Brien, H. Robert Rose; children by previous marriage: Patrick Scott, Michael B., Timothy R., Shelly W. Taetz. BS in Engring., La. Tech., 1944. Field engr. Austin Bridge Co., Dallas, 1944-45; core analyst Core Labs., Bakersfield, Calif., 1945-46; chief engr., then sec.-treas., exec. v.p. Trinity Industries, Inc., Dallas, 1946-58, pres., CEO, 1958—, also bd. dirs.; bd. dirs. Lomas Fin. Corp., Trinity Industries, ENSERCH Corp. Trustee Dallas Meth. Hosps. Found. Methodist. Office: Trinity Industries Inc 2525 N Stemmons Fwy Dallas TX 75207-2401*

WALLCRAFT, MARY JANE LOUISE, religious organization executive, songwriter, author; b. Deloraine, Man., Can., Nov. 2, 1933; d. Norman Zephaniah and Mary Jane (McKinney) Sexton; m. James Orval Wallcraft, Oct. 13, 1956; children: Angela Mae, Ronald Clarke. Assoc. in piano, Royal Conservatory Toronto, Brandon, Man., 1952; AA, Victor Valley Coll., 1973. Tchr. piano Souris, Man., 1963-67; church organist St. George's Anglican, Brandon, 1960-63, St. Lukes Anglican, Souris, Man., 1963-67, Victorville (Calif.) United Meth. Ch., 1970-74; tchr. piano Hines House of Music, Victorville, 1969-72; ch. sec. Fredericksburg (Va.) United Meth. Ch., 1977-79; med. transcriptionist Mary Washington Hosp., Fredericksburg, 1985-87, Shady Grove Adventist, Rockville, Md., 1987-89; founder, pres. Make Me a Blessing Ministries, Inc., Zellwood, Fla., 1992—. Author: Make Me a Blessing, 1991, Sing Your Way to Victory, "Reflections", 1994, A Modern Day Psalter, Shadows, Symbols, and Strategies, 1994; songwriter (albums) Make Me a Blessing, 1992, Grandkid's Praise, 1993, Grandma Jane's Unity Rap, 1993, A Word of Encouragement From Make Me A Blessing, Music from the Psalms, Vol. 1, 1995, vols. 2 and 3, 1996; recorded music tapes of Psalms, book of scripture songs Sing to the Lord a New Song...Every Day of the Year, 1996; completion of 5-yr. investigation of Benny Hinn; recommenced ministry to Care Homes, 1996. Choir accompanist, alt. pianist New Hope Presbyn. Ch., Eustis, Fla., 1995—; weekly ministry to Care Homes, 1994, 96. Republican. Home and Office: 4162 Greenbluff Ct Zellwood FL 32798-9005

WALLENSTEIN, PETER, historian, educator; b. East Orange, N.J., May 22, 1944; s. Crandall R. and R. Carol (Van Duyne) W.; m. Sookhan Ho. AB, Columbia U., 1966; PhD, Johns Hopkins U., 1973. Asst. prof. history Sarah Lawrence Coll., Bronxville, N.Y., 1970-75, U. Toronto, Ont., Can., 1975-77; assoc. prof. history Va. Poly. Inst. and State U., 1983—. Author: From Slave South to New South, 1987; contbr. articles to profl. jours. and mags. Fellow Am. Hist. Assn., 1983, 91, Va. Found. for Humanities, 1989, 92, Va. Hist. Soc., 1990, 91. Mem. So. Hist. Assn. (life), Orgn. Am. Historians (life). Office: Va Poly Inst and State U Dept History Blacksburg VA 24061-0117

WALLER, DAVID VINCENT, sociology educator; b. Miami, Fla., Apr. 15, 1961; s. Gladys Theodore W.; m. Dorothy June Church, July 27, 1996; children: Ian David Murray, Tres Church Tinsley, Marianna Sylvia Fusich-Waller. BA, U. Fla., 1985; MA, U. Calif., Riverside, 1989, PhD, 1993. Asst. prof. sociology U. Tex., Arlington, 1993—. Editor: (textbook) Analyzing Social Problems, 1996; contbr. articles to profl. publs., chpt. to books. Mem. Am. Sociol. Assn., Southwestern Sociol. Assn., Pacific Sociol. Assn. Office: U Tex Dept Sociology/Anthropology Box 19599 Arlington TX 76010

WALLER, GARY WILTON, administration educator, minister; b. Ft. Worth, July 16, 1948; s. Robert Preston and Lillian Lee (Taylor) W.; m. Cindy Ann Dollar, Jan. 3, 1975; children: Stephanie, RyAnn. BS in Phys. Edn., Baylor U., 1970; MRE, Southwestern Bapt. Theol. Sem., Ft. Worth, 1972, PhD, 1979; PhD, U. North Tex., 1992. Ordained to ministry, Bapt. Ch., 1979. Min. music and youth North Cleburne Bapt. Ch., Cleburne, Tex., 1970-72; min. edn. Trinity Bapt. Ch., Ft. Worth, 1972-74, Gambrell Street Bapt. Ch., Ft. Worth, 1978-82; min. edn. and evangelism North Ft. Worth Bapt. Ch., 1974-78, 1st Bapt. Ch., Waco, Tex., 1982-84; prof. adminstrn. Southwestern Bapt. Theol. Sem., 1984—; em. Com. To Nominate Coordinating Bds., Dallas, 1983-84; trustee Latham Springs Encampment, Aquilla, Tex., 1971-72, 76-78. Trustee Castleberry Ind. Sch. Dist., Ft. Worth, 1977-79; pres. bd. Aerials Gymnastics, Arlington, Tex., 1991-94. Fellow Scarborough Inst.; mem. So. Bapt. Religious Educators (v.p. 1995), Tarrant Bapt. Religious Educators (pres. 1981), Bapt. Religious Educators S.W., Am. Mgmt. Assn., Castleberry Alumni Assn. (treas. 1978-80, Outstanding Ex award 1978), Woodhaven Country Club. Office: Southwestern Bapt Theol Sem PO Box 22487 Fort Worth TX 76122

WALLER, JOHN HENRY, author, international consultant; b. Paw Paw, Mich., May 8, 1923; s. George and Marguerite (Rowland) W.; m. Barbara Steuart Hans, Sept. 2, 1947; children—Stephanie Robinson, Gregory, Maria. B.A., U. Mich., 1946. Vice consul U.S. Fgn. Service, Iran, 1947-53, 2d sec., Khartoum, Sudan, 1960-62, spl. asst. to ambassador, New Delhi, 1955-57, 68-71; polit. analyst State Dept., Washington, 1962-68; insp. gen. CIA, Washington, 1976-80; free-lance author, Washington, 1968—. Author: (pen name John Rowland) Hostile Co-existence, History of Sino-Indian Relations, 1988, Gordon of Khartoum: The Saga of a Victorian Hero; (pen name John MacGregor) Tibet, A Chronicle of Exploration, 1970, Beyond The Khyber Pass, 1990, The Unseen War in Europe, 1996; contbg. editor Mil. History Mag., Leesburg, Va., 1985—; contbr. articles to popular history to profl. jours. Recipient Career Service award Nat. Civil Service League, 1979, 80, Disting. Intelligence medal CIA, 1980. Mem. Washington Inst. Fgn. Affairs, Middle East Inst. Club: Cosmos (Washington).

WALLER, JOHN HENRY, judge; b. Mullins, S.C., Oct. 31, 1937; s. John Henry and Elnita (Rabon) W.; m. Jane McLaurin Cooper, Nov. 16, 19633 (div.); children: John Henry III, Melissa McLaurin; m. Debra Ann Meares, May 9, 1981; children: Ryan Meares, Rand Ellis. AB in Psychology, Wofford Coll., 1959; LLB, U. S.C., 1963. Mem. S.C. Ho. of Reps., 1967-77, S.C. Senate, 1977-80; judge S.C. Cir. Ct., 1980-94, S.C. Supreme Ct., 1994—; mem. S.C. Cir. Ct. Adv. Com., 1981-94, chmn., 1991-94; mem. S.C. Jud. Std. Com., 1991-94, chmn., 1992-94. Capt. U.S. Army, 1959-60. Mem. Millins Rotary Club (1st pres.), Masons. Office: SC Supreme Ct Courthouse Main St Marion SC 29571

WALLER, JOHN LOUIS, anesthesiology educator; b. Loma Linda, Calif., Dec. 1, 1944; s. Louis Clinton and Sue (Bruce) W.; m. Jo Lynn Marie Haas, Aug. 4, 1968; children: Kristina, Karla, David. BA, So. Coll., Collegedale, Tenn., 1967; MD, Loma Linda U., 1971. Diplomate Am. Bd. Anesthesiology. Intern Hartford (Conn.) Hosp., 1971-72; resident in anesthesiology Harvard U. Med. Sch.-Mass. Gen. Hosp., Boston, 1972-74, fellow, 1974-75; asst. prof. anesthesiology Emory U. Sch. Medicine, Atlanta, 1977-80, assoc. prof., 1980-86, prof., chmn. dept., 1986—; svc. chief anesthesiology Emory Univ. Hosp., Atlanta, 1986-94, med. dir., 1993-95; assoc. v.p. info. svcs. Woodruff Health Scis. Ctr., 1995—; chief info. officer Emory U. System Healthcare, Atlanta, 1995—; cons. Arrow Internat., Inc., Reading, Pa., 1988—; bd. dirs. Clifton Casualty Co., Colo.; mem. adv. com. on anesthetic and life support drugs FDA, Washington, 1986-92; numerous vis. professorships and lectures. Contbr. articles to med. jours. Maj. M.C., USAF, 1975-77. Recipient cert. of appreciation Office Sec. Def., 1983. Fellow Am. Coll. Anesthesiologists, Am. Coll. Chest Physicians; mem. AMA, Am. Soc. Anesthesiologists, Soc. Cardiovascular Anesthesiologists (pres. 1991-93), Internat. Anesthesia Rsch. Soc. (trustee 1984—, sec. 1993—), Assn. Univ. Anesthetists, Soc. Acad. Anesthesia Chairmen (councillor 1989—), Assn. Cardiac Anesthesiologists. Office: Emory U Hosp Dept Anes 1364 Clifton Rd NE Atlanta GA 30322-1059

WALLER, MICHAEL LAWRENCE, headmaster; b. Duluth, Minn., Dec. 29, 1955; s. Lawrence Edward and Suzanne Edith (Klein) W.; m. Maria-Elena Curiel Alcocer, Feb. 8, 1991; children: Michael Ignacio, Monica Maria. BA in Social Scis., U. Calif., Irvine, 1979; MA in Edn., U. San Francisco, 1989. Tchr. Trinity Pawling (N.Y.) Sch., 1979-82, St. Matthew's Parish Sch., Pacific Palisades, Calif., 1982-85; asst. headmaster Cathedral Sch. for Boys, San Francisco, 1985-89, The Chandler Sch., Pasadena, Calif., 1990-94; headmaster St. Clement's Episcopal Parish Sch., El Paso, 1994—. Mem. exec. bd. Am. Heart Assn. of El Paso, 1996—. Mem. Southwestern Assn. of Episcopal Schs. (bd. dirs. 1994—), Ind. Sch. Assn. of the S.W. (com. mem.). Home: 542 Rosinante Rd El Paso TX 79922 Office: St Clement's Episcopal Parish Sch 605 E Yandell Dr El Paso TX 79902

WALLER, WILLIAM KENNETH, health physicist; b. Yazoo City, Miss., May 28, 1954; s. William Thomas and ruth Inez (Gary) W.; m. Gail Paige Knott, Aug. 11, 1979; children: Enid Michelle, William Charles. AA, Holmes C.C., Goodman, Miss., 1974; BS, Delta State U., Cleveland, Miss., 1976; Cert., Oak Ridge Assoc. U., 1977. Chief radioactive materials sect. Divsn. Radiol. Health, Miss. State Bd. Health, Jackson, 1976-80; from project mgr. to dir. waste mgmt. US Ecology, Inc., Louisville, 1980-90; sr. scientist Battelle Pacific NW Lab., Richland, Wash., 1990-91; tech. dir. environ. restoration and radiation svcs. Law Engring. and Environ. Svcs., Inc., Kennesaw, Ga., 1991—. Co-author: Guidance Manual of REviewing RCRA and CERCLA Documentation, 1989, Comparative Review of U.S. DOE CERCLA Federal Facility Agreements, 1989; contbr. articles to profl. jours. Chmn. ops. stewards Summit Bapt. Ch., Kennesaw, 1994, 95; chmn. pers. stewards Towne View Bapt. Ch., Kennesaw, 1992. Mem. Am. Nuclear Soc., Am. Mgmt. Assn., Health Physics Soc., Internat. Soc. for Decontaimination/Decommissioning Profls. Home: 1073 Boston Rdg Woodstock GA 30189 Office: Law Engring Environ Svcs 114 Townpark Dr Kennesaw GA 30144-5561

WALLER, WILMA RUTH, retired secondary school educator and librarian; b. Jacksonville, Tex., Nov. 15, 1921; d. William Wesley and Myrtle (Nesbitt) W. BA with honors, Tex. Woman's U., 1954, MA with honors, 1963, MLS with honors, 1976. Tchr. English Dell (Ark.) High Sch., 1953-54, Jefferson (Tex.) Ind. Schs., 1954-56, Tyler (Tex.) Ind. Schs., 1956-68; librarian Wise County Schs., Decatur, Tex., 1969-71, Thomas K. Gorman High Sch., Tyler, 1971-74, Sweetwater (Tex.) Ind. Sch. Dist., 1974-86; ret.; lectr., book reviewer for various clubs. Active in past as vol. for ARC, U. Tex. Health Ctr. Ford Found. fellow, 1959; recipient Delta Kappa Gamma Achievement award, 1992. Mem. AAUW (past chmn. book, critique, drama and contemporary interests groups), UDC, Smith County Ret. Sch. Pers., Bible Study Group, Delta Kappa Gamma. Republican. Baptist. Home: 1117 N Azalea Dr Tyler TX 75701-5206

WALLIN, EVE LINDA, engineering executive; b. Vineland, N.J., Oct. 5, 1948; d. David Irving and Helen Judith (Cotler) Kaplan; m. LeRoy Alvin Wallin, June 17, 1982. BS, West Liberty State Coll., 1970; MS, W.Va. U., 1973. Mathematician Naval Surface Weapons Ctr., White Oak, Md., 1979-83; sr. engr. HRB Singer, Inc., Lanham, Md., 1983-85; sr. analyst BTG, Inc., Vienna, Va., 1985-87; tech. staff GTE Govt. Sys., Rockville, Md., 1988-94; sr. staff mem. BDM Enterprise Integration, McLean, Va., 1994—. Home: 1909 Olivine Silver Spring MD 20904

WALLIN, LELAND DEAN, artist, educator; b. Sioux Falls, S.D., Oct. 14, 1942; s. Clarence Forrest and Leona Mae (McInnis) W.; m. Meredith Maria Hawkins, Mar. 26, 1977; 1 child, Jessica Hawkins. Student, Columbus Coll. Art and Design, 1961-62; BFA in Painting, Kansas City (Mo.) Art Inst., 1965; MFA in Painting, U. Cin. and Cin. Art Acad., 1967. Prof., coord. drawing St. Cloud (Minn.) State U., 1967-86; prof. Queens Coll., CUNY, Flushing, 1983-84; prof., coord. MFA painting Marywood Coll., Scranton, Pa., 1985-90; assoc. prof. painting and drawing East Carolina U., Greenville, N.C., 1993—; lectr. Carnegie-Mellon U., Pitts., 1988; juror Belin Arts Grant Com., Waverly, Pa., 1989; curator Philip Pearlstein Retrospective Exhibit, Scranton, 1988; vis. prof. painting East Carolina U., Greenville, N.C., 1992-93; judge/juror No. Nat. Art Competition, 1993. One man shows include Mpls. Coll. Art and Design, 1978, Harold Reed Gallery, 1983, Gallery Henoch, N.Y.C., 1991, others; group shows at The Bklyn. Mus., 1979, Greenville County Mus. of Art, 1983, The Mus. of Modern Art, 1993, Huntsville Mus. Art, 1994, Sacramento Fine Arts Ctr. Internat., 1995, Salon Internat., 1994, San Bernardino County Mus. Internat., Calif., 1995; represented in permanent collections N.Y.C. Gallery, Gallery Henoch, 1986—; contbr. articles to profl. jours. Named Outstanding Tchr., East Carolina U., 1994, 95; recipient numerous rsch. awards East Carolina U., 1992—. Mem. Coll. Art Assn. Am., Pa. Soc. Watercolor Painters. Home and Studio: 218 York Rd Greenville NC 27858

WALLINGER, M(ELVIN) BRUCE, lawyer; b. Richmond, Va., Dec. 27, 1945; s. Melvin W. and Ellen Scott (Barnard) W.; m. Rosemary Moore Hynes, Aug. 8, 1970; children: Mary Moore, Ann Harrison, Carrie. BA, U. Va., 1968, JD, 1972. Bar: Va. 1972, U.S. Dist. Ct. (ea. dist.) Va. 1986, (we. dist.) Va. 1972, U.S. Ct. Appeals (4th cir.) 1976, U.S. Supreme Ct. 1978; cert. comml. mediator Am. Arbitration Assn. Assoc. Wharton, Aldhizer & Weaver, Harrisonburg, Va., 1972-76, ptnr., 1976—. Bd. dirs. Shrine Mont, Inc., Orkney Springs, Va.; trustee Stuart Hall Sch., Staunton, Va. 1st lt. Army N.G., 1968-74. Fellow Am. Coll. Trial Lawyers; mem. ABA, Va. Bar Assn. (exec. com. 1996—), Harrisonburg Bar Assn. (pres. 1984), Va. State Bar (pres. young lawyers conf. 1981-82, chmn. 6th dist. disciplinary com. 1988-89), Va. Assn. Def. Attys. (pres. 1989-90), Def. Rsch. and Trial Lawyers Assn. Republican. Episcopalian. Office: Wharton Aldhizer & Weaver 100 S Mason St Harrisonburg VA 22801-4022

WALLINGFORD, JOHN RUFUS, lawyer; b. Artesia, N.Y., Apr. 6, 1940; s. Joseph Keevil and Ellen (Williams) W.; m. Katharine Tapers, July 22, 1966; children: Halley Martha, John Beckett. BA, U. of the South, 1962; LLB, So. Meth. U., 1965. Bar: Tex. 1965. Sr. ptnr. Fulbright & Jaworski, Houston, 1967-93; sr. v.p., gen. counsel Browning Ferris Industries, Houston, 1994—. Bd. dirs. St. Luke's Episcopal Hosp., Houston, 1986—, The Children's Mus., Houston, 1994—. Fellow Am. Coll. Trial Lawyers; mem. Internat. Soc. of Barristers, Am. Bd. Trial Advocates. Office: Browning Ferris Industries 757 N Eldridge Pky Houston TX 77079-4435*

WALLIS, BEN ALTON, JR., lawyer; b. Llano County, Tex., Apr. 27, 1936; s. Ben A. and Jessie Ella (Longbotham) W.; children from previous marriage: Ben A. III, M. Jessica.; m. Joan Mery, 1987. BBA, U. Tex. 1961, JD, 1966; postgrad. Law Sch. So. Meth. U., 1971. Bar: Tex. 1966, U.S. Dist. Ct. (no. dist.) Tex. 1971, U.S. Ct. Appeals D.C. 1974, U.S. Dist. Ct. D.C. 1975, U.S. Dist. Ct. (we. dist.) Tex. 1975, U.S. Dist. Ct. (no. dist.) Calif. 1983, U.S. Ct. Appeals (5th cir.) 1975, U.S. Ct. Appeals (8th cir.) 1980, U.S. Ct. Appeals (11th cir.) 1981, U.S. Dist. Ct. (ea. dist.) Wis. 1983. U.S. Supreme Ct. 1974. Pvt. practice, Llano, Tex., 1966-67, Dallas, 1971-73; investigator, prosecutor State Securities Bd. Tex., 1967-71; v.p. of devel. Club Corp. Am., Dallas, 1973; assoc. counsel impeachment task force U.S. Ho. of Reps. Com. on Judiciary, Washington, 1974; prin. Law Offices of Ben A. Wallis, Jr., San Antonio, Tex., 1974—. Chmn. Nat. Land Use Conf., 1979-81; mem. Gov.'s Areawide Planning Adv. Com., 1975-78; pres. Inst. Human Rights Rsch., 1979-82. Mem. ABA, State Bar Tex. (chmn. Agr. Tax Commn.), D.C. Bar Assn., San Antonio Bar Assn., Fed. Bar Assn., Assn. Trial Lawyers Am., Delta Theta Phi, Delta Sigma Pi. Republican. Baptist. Office: GPM South Tower 800 NW Loop 410 Ste 350 San Antonio TX 78216-5619

WALLIS, CARLTON LAMAR, librarian; b. Blue Springs, Miss., Oct. 15, 1915; s. William Ralph and Tellie (Jones) W.; m. Mary Elizabeth Cooper, Feb. 22, 1944; 1 child, Carlton Lamar. B.A. with spl. distinction, Miss. Coll., 1936; M.A., Tulane U., 1946; B.L.S., U. Chgo., 1947; L.H.D., Rhodes Coll., Memphis, 1980. English tchr., coach Miss. Pub. Schs., 1936-41; teaching fellow Miss. Coll. and Tulane U., 1941-42; chief librarian Rosenberg Library, Galveston, Tex., 1947-55; city librarian Richmond, Va., 1955-58; dir. Memphis Pub. Library, 1958-80, ret., 1980. Author: Libraries in the Golden Triangle, 1966; contbr. articles to library jours. Trustee Belhaven Coll., 1978-82, Nat. Ornamental Metal Mus., 1989—. Served as chief warrant officer AUS, 1942-46. Decorated Bronze Star. Mem. ALA (chmn. library mgmt. sect. 1969-71), Pub. Library Assn. (dir. 1973-77), Tex. Library Assn. (pres. 1952-53), Va. Library Assn., Southwestern Library Assn. (exec. bd. 1950-55), Southeastern Library Assn. (chmn. pub. library sect. 1960-62), Tenn. Library Assn. (pres. 1969-70, Distinguished Service award 1979). Presbyterian (elder). Club: Egyptian (pres. 1973-74). Home: 365 Kenilworth Pl Memphis TN 38112-5405

WALLIS, JOHN JAMES (JIMMY WALLIS), entertainer, ventriloquist, comedy writer, video production executive; b. Searcy, Ark., Mar. 21, 1939; s. Prentiss Bascom and Maxine (James) W.; children: Lori Diana Wallis Waterman, Shauna Kathleen. Grad., Okla. U., 1960. advisor Am. Acad. for Entertainment at U.S. Vets. Hosps., N.Y.C., 1988—. Nat. TV debut Art Linkletter's Hollywood Talent Scouts, 1966; entertained troops in S.E. Asia, 1967-70; performed with Ann Murray, Lou Rawls, Lola Falana, Ben Vereen, Al Hirt, Debbie Reynolds, Rip Taylor, Suzanne Somers, others; performed in numerous clubs including Tropicana, Las Vegas, The Sahara, Las Vegas, The Flamingo, Las Vegas, Chauteau Champlain, Montreal, The Cave, Vancouver, The Paradise Island Casino, The Bahamas, The Superstar Theater, Atlantic City, Riviera, Las Vegas, Harrah's, Reno, The Reno Hilton, Las Vegas Hilton, Flamingo Hilton; featured in Royal Caribbean Cruise Lines, Premier's Disney Theme Cruises, Norwegian Cruise Lines, Holland Am. and Celebrity Cruise Lines, Night of the Stars, Las Vegas. Named Okla.'s Top Comedian, Okla. Ho. of Reps.; recipient Am. Legion medal. Mem. Internat. Platform Assn., Nat. Park and Conservation Assn., Planetary Soc., Nat. Space Soc., Smithsonian Assocs., NRA. Presbyterian. Office: PO Box 276100 Boca Raton FL 33427-6100

WALLIS, OLNEY GRAY, lawyer, educator; b. Llano, Tex., July 27, 1940; s. Ben Alton and Jessie Ella (Longbotham) W.; m. Linda Lee Johnson, June 29, 1963; children—Anne, Brett. B.A., U. Tex., 1962, J.D., 1965. Bar: Tex. 1965, U.S. Dist. Ct. (so. dist.) Tex. 1966, U.S. Ct. Mil. Appeals 1968, U.S. Supreme Ct. 1970, U.S. Dist. Ct. (we. dist.) Tex. 1976, U.S. Ct. Appeals (5th cir.) 1977, U.S. Tax Ct. 1980, U.S. Ct. Appeals (10th cir.) 1981, U.S. Ct. Appeals (11th cir.) 1983, U.S. Dist. Ct. (no. dist.) Tex. 1985, U.S. Dist. Ct. (ea. and we. dists.) Ark. 1985, U.S. Ct. Appeals (8th cir.) 1985. Assoc., Brown & Cecil, Houston, 1965-66; asst. U.S. atty. Dept. Justice, Houston, 1971-74; mem. Jefferson, Wallis & Sherman, Houston, 1975-81; mem. Wallis & Pruitt, Houston, 1981-87, Wallis and Short, 1987—; instr. U. Md., Keflauik, Iceland, 1968-69; mem. faculty continuing legal edn. U. Houston, 1981-84. Served to capt. USAF, 1966-70. Decorated Air Force Commendation medal, 1970; recipient Disting. Service award U.S. Dept. Justice, 1973. Mem. Assn. Trial Lawyers Am., Am Judicature Soc., Tex. Trial Lawyers Assn., Houston Trial Lawyers Assn., Houston Bar Assn., Houston Bar Found., Phi Delta Phi, Phi Kappa Tau. Democrat. Episcopalian. Office: Wallis & Short 4300 Scotland St Houston TX 77007-7328

WALLIS, ROBERT JOE, pharmacist, retail executive; b. Lawton, Okla., Dec. 26, 1938; s. John L. and Bertha Leora (Blake) W.; m. Rubena Ann Hennessee, June 1, 1958; children: Jeffrey Allen, Joseph Robert, Justin Matthew. BS in Pharmacy, Okla. U., 1962. Pharmacist, mgr. Hyde Drug, Oklahoma City, 1962-77, v.p., mgr., 1977-82, pres., 1982—; mem. McKesson Drug Co. Small Chain Adv. Bd., San Francisco, 1986-87. Bd. mgmt. YMCA, 1989—. Mem. Oklahoma City Profl. Businessmen's Assn. (pres. 1962, 72), Nat. Assn. chain Drug Stores (sml. chain com. 1991—). Republican. Methodist. Office: Hyde Drug Inc 5108 N Shartel Ave Oklahoma City OK 73118-6025

WALLS, CARL EDWARD, JR., communications company official; b. Magnolia, Ark., Sept. 9, 1948; s. Carl E. and Melba Rene (Garrard) W.; m. Doris Duhart, Aug. 1, 1970; children: Carl Edward, Forrest Allen. Student San Antonio Coll., 1966-68. Div. mgr. Sears Roebuck & Co., San Antonio, 1967-73, area sales mgr., 1973-78; service cons. Southwestern Bell, 1978-79, account exec., 1979-82; account exec., industry cons. AT&T Info. Systems, 1983-88, account mgr., 1988-89; gen. mgr. Tex. State Govt., 1989—. Mem. citizens advisory com. Tex. Senate, 1975-81; legis. aide Tex. Ho. of Reps., 1981-85; commr. Alamo Area council Boy Scouts Am., 1970-79, Capitol Area council, 1980—, nat. jamboree staff, 1973, 77, 81, 85, 89, 93; mem. Republican Nat. Com., 1980—, Rep. Presdl. Task Force, 1980—, Rep. Senatorial Club, 1981—. Recipient Patriotic Service award U.S. Treasury Dept., 1975-76; Scouters Key and Commrs. award Boy Scout Am., Dist. Merit award Boy Scouts Am., 1978. Mem. Scouting Collectors Assn. (pres. South Central region 1979-80, v.p. region 1980-81, sec. 1983-86), U. Ark. Alumni Assn. (life), Am. Legion. Baptist. Home: 11712 D K Ranch Rd Austin TX 78759-3770 Office: 1624 Headway Ct Austin TX 78754

WALLS, CARMAGE LEE, JR., newspaper executive, consultant; b. Cleveland, Tenn., May 4, 1962; s. Carmage Lee Walls Sr. and Sarah (Smith) Bailey; m. Jeanne Marie Waller, June 4, 1989; children: Courtney Marie, Kathryn Jessica. BA in Journalism and English, U. Ala., Birmingham, 1988. Writer Birmingham News, 1987; exec. v.p. Cleveland Newspapers Inc., Birmingham, 1987—. Republican. Methodist.

WALLS, JAY DAVID, hematologist, oncologist; b. Chattanooga, Jan. 31, 1959; s. J.D. and Carol Sue (Norrell) W.; m. Kimberly Jo Alley, Nov. 24, 1990; 1 step child LIndsey Jo Howes, 1 child, Alley Elizabeth Walls. BS in Molecular Biology, Vanderbilt U., 1981; MD, U. Tenn, Memphis, 1986. Diplomate Am. Bd. Internal Medicine, Am. Bd. Hematology, Oncology. Intern and resident Beth Israel Hosp. Harvard Med. Sch., Boston, 1986-89; fellow in hematology, oncology Vanderbilt U. Med. Ctr., Nashville, 1989-92; physician Muhlenberg Hematology, Oncology Assocs., Charlotte, N.C., 1992-94, Hematology, Oncology Assocs., Greenville, S.C., 1994—. Mem. S.C. Med. Soc., Alpha Omega Alpha. Office: Hematology Oncology Assocs LLC PO Box 9108 Greenville SC 29604

WALLSTROM, RANDI RUTH, rheumatologist, educator; b. Hamadan, Iran, Nov. 2, 1956; d. Ira Clarke and Doris Elaine (Rylander) W.; m. Howard Takiff, May 18, 1991. BS, Stanford U., 1978; MD, Loma Linda U., 1984. Internal medicine resident UCLA-San Fernando Valley Program, Sepulveda, Calif., 1984-87, Kennamer fellow, 1987-88, fellow rheumatology, 1988-90; physician Scripps Clinic Med. Group, La Jolla, Calif., 1991-93; asst. prof. rheumatology Tulane U., New Orleans, 1993—; med. adv. com. Arthritis Found. San Fernando Valley, Calif., 1989-90. Recipient Janet M. Glasgow award Am. Med. Woman's Assn., 1984. Mem. ACP, Alpha Omega Alpha. Office: Tulane U Med Ctr 1430 Tulane Ave New Orleans LA 70112-2699

WALNE, SARAH WEST, writer, educator; b. Clarksdale, Miss., Oct. 2, 1957; d. Felix Karr and Mary Ann (Cooper) West; m. James Austin Walne, Jr., Aug. 2, 1980; children: James Austin III, Charles Hunt. BA in Edn., U. Miss., 1978, MEd, 1981. Cert. tchr., kindergarten-grade 8. Tchr. Small World Kindergarten, Oxford, Miss., 1979-80, Clarksdale (Miss.) Bapt. Sch., 1980-83, Grace-St. Luke's Episcopal, Memphis, 1983-85; pvt. practice as tutor Memphis, 1986—, freelance writer, 1992—; speaker in field. Author: (book, tape and guidebook) Memphis Mazes, 1992 (named Ofcl. Children's Book of Memphis 1993), (book) Holiday Gifts, 1993; writer Memphis Parent, 1993—; asst. editor Vol. Voices, 1994-95, editor, 1995-96. Active Memphis Zool. Soc., 1986—, Jr. League Memphis, Inc., 1989—, mem. membership coun., 1994-95, mem. comm. coun., bd. dirs., 1995-96; active Children's Mus. Memphis, 1991-93; vol. Memphis Literacy Coun., 1990-91, bd. dirs., 1995—; vol. Memphis 2000 Edn. Task Force, 1991-92. Named Community Vol. of Yr., Jr. League of Memphis, Inc., 1990-91. Mem. Soc. Children's Bookwriters and Illustrators. Episcopalian. Office: 1947 Linden Ave Memphis TN 38104-4036

WALRAVEN, JOSEPH WILLIAM (BILL WALRAVEN), writer, publisher; b. Dallas, July 1, 1925; s. Orange Daniel Sr. and Valerie (Garrison) W.; m. Marjorie Kathryn Yeager, May 28, 1950; children: Valerie Ruth, Wilson Frederick, Joseph William Jr. BA, Tex. A&I U., 1950; postgrad. sch. profl. writing, U. Okla., 1950-51. Copy editor San Antonio Light, 1951-52; reporter Corpus Christi (Tex.) Caller-Times, 1952-68, daily columnist, 1968-89; pub. Sandcrab Press, Corpus Christi, 1983—, Javelina Press, Corpus Christi, 1989—; freelance writer Corpus Christi, 1989—. Author, pub.; Real Texans Don't Drink Scotch in Their Dr Pepper, 1983; author: Corpus Christi, History of a Texas Seaport, 1983, Walraven's World or Star Boarder (and other) Wars, 1985, El Rincon, A History of Corpus Christi Beach, 1990, (with Marjorie Kathryn Walraven) The Magnificent Barbarians, Little-Told Tales of The Texas Revolution, 1993, All I Know Is What's On TV, 1995. V.p. South Tex. Hist. Soc., 1978; active Tex. State Hist. Assn. With USN, 1943-45, PTO. Recipient 1st pl. gen. interest column Harte-Hanks Newspapers, 1979, 2nd prize, 1987; recipient 2nd pl. news story Tex. AP, 1954, 1st pl. features, 1958; recipient 2nd prize series Animal Def. League Tex., 1987; award recipient Corpus Christi Police Officers Assn., 1967, ARC, 1970, Tex. Hist. Commn. and Tex. Hist. Found., 1980, 81, Corpus Christi Landmark Commn., 1987, Nueces County Hist. Commn., 1989; named Civic Salesman of Yr., Sales and Mktg. Execs. Corpus Christi, 1984. Mem. Nat. Soc. Newspaper Columnists, Corpus Christi Press Club (v.p. 1964, pres. 1965, many awards). Democrat. Methodist. Home: 4609 Wilma Dr Corpus Christi TX 78412-2357 Office: Sandcrab Press PO Box 1479 Corpus Christi TX 78403-1479

WALSER, SANDRA TERESA JOHNSON, rehabilitation nurse, preceptor; b. Lexington, N.C., Dec. 9, 1951; d. Thomas Victory and Mary (Ingle) Johnson; m. Ellis Kent Walser, Nov. 14, 1970; children: Andrea Elise, Joshua Kent, Jonathan Patrick. ADN, Forsyth Tech. Community Coll., Winston-Salem, N.C., 1989. RN, N.C. Nurse physical neuro brain injury rehab. unit Forsyth Meml. Hosp., Winston-Salem, 1989—; mem. career ladder devel. level II Forsyth Meml. Hosp., 1989—. Mem. Assn. Rehab. Nurses (cert. rehab. RN). Home: 559 Baileys Chapel Rd Advance NC 27006-7142

WALSH, AL E., protective services official. Chief of police Lexington, Ky. Office: Police Dept Fayette County 150 E Main St Lexington KY 40507-1318

WALSH, CHERYL L., women's health nurse; b. East St. Louis, Ill., June 30, 1956; d. John T. and Bernetta M. (Hoef) McPherson; m. Michael F. Walsh, May 4, 1979; children: Brendan, Erin. BSN, So. Ill. U., Edwardsville, 1978. RN, Ill.; cert. PALS instr.; cert. pediatric nurse. Staff nurse hemodialysis Clovis (N.Mex.) High Plains Hosp., acting head nurse; charge nurse pediatrics St. Mary's Hosp., Decatur, Ill.

WALSH, F. HOWARD, oil producer, rancher; b. Waco, Tex., Feb. 7, 1913; s. P. Frank and Maude (Gage) W.; m. Mary D. Fleming, Mar. 13, 1937; children: Richard F., F. Howard, D'Ann E. Walsh Bonnell, Maudi Walsh Roe, William Lloyd. BBA, Tex. Christian U., 1933, LLD (hon.), 1979. Self employed oil producer, rancher, 1942—; pres. Walsh & Watts, Inc. Mem. Tex. Jud. Qualifications Commn., 1970-74; pres. Walsh Found.; v.p. Fleming Found.; hon. trustee Tex. Christian U.; guarantor Ft. Worth Arts Council (also hon. bd. mem.), Schola Cantorum, Ft. Worth Ballet, Tex. Boys' Choir, Ft. Worth Theatre, Ft. Worth Opera; bd. dirs. Southwestern Expdn. and Fat Stock Show, Ft. Worth. Named Valuable Alumnus, Tex. Chriatisn U., 1967, Patron of Arts in Ft. Worth, 1970, 91, Edna Gladney Internat. Grandparents, 1972, PAtron of Yr. Live Theater League Tarrant County, 1996; recipient spl. recognition for support Univ. Ranch Tng. Program,

Royal Purple (with wife) Tex. Christian U., 1979, Disting. Svc. award So. Bapt. Radio and TV Commn., 1972, tng. Commn., 1976, Brotherhood citation NCCJ, 1978, Friends of Tex. Boys' Choir, 1981, donor Walsh Med. Bldg., Southwestern Bapt. Theol. Sem., land and bldgs. to Tex. Boys Choir, 1971, Wurlitzer Organ of Cana Manana, 1972, appreciation award an citation Southwestern Bapt. Theol. Sem., 1981, B.H. Carroll Founders Southwestern Bapt. Theol. Sem., 1982, (with wife) St. Citizen award, 1985, Silver Spur award, 1990, Horizon award Fine Arts Dept. Tex. Christian U., 1995, Disting. Philanthropist award, 1995; Tarrant County Jr. Coll. Libr. dedicated in his honor, 1978, ballet season dedicated in his honor by Ft. Worth Ballet Assn., 1978-79, TCU Athletic Complex dedicated in his honor, 1994, benefactor ann. prodn. Littlest Wiseman, Christmas Gift to City of Ft. Worth. Mem. Tex.-Mid-Continent Oil and Gas Assn., West Central Tex. Oil and Gas Assn., North Tex. Oil and Gas Assn., Ind. Petroleum Assn., Tex. Ind. Producers and Royalty Owners, Am.-Internat. Charolais Assn., Tex. Christian U. Ex-Letterman's Assn. Baptist bd. sr. deacons. Clubs: Garden of Gods; Colorado Springs Country (Colorado Springs); Steeplechase, Fort Worth, Ridglea, Frog, Colonial Country, Shady Oaks Country, Century II, Petroleum, City, River Crest Country. Home: 2425 Stadium Dr Fort Worth TX 76109-1055 Office: Walsh & Watts Inc 1007 InterFirst Ft Worth Bldg Fort Worth TX 76102 also: 1801 Culebra Colorado Springs CO 80907

WALSH, JAMES ANTHONY (TONY WALSH), theater and film educator; b. Bklyn., Aug. 21, 1947; s. Henry Michael and Clara (Nappi) W. BA in Theater, Hofstra U., 1968; MA in Theater, Adelphi U., 1976. Tchr., dir. theater N.C. Sch. of Arts, Winston-Salem, 1976-81; artistic dir. Cross and Sword/State Play of Fla., St. Augustine, 1982-91; dean Fla. Sch. of Arts, Palatka, 1982-91; dir. Inst. of Entertainment Technologies Valencia C.C., Orlando, Fla., 1992-93, dir. Ctr. Profl. Devel., 1993—; producing dir. TV and video prodn. Valencia Coll., Orlando, 1996—; freelance theater dir., acting coach, N.Y.C., 1973-76; cons. Network of Performing and Visual Arts Schs., Washington, 1980—, Inst. Outdoor Drama, Chapel Hill, N.C., 1989—, Univ. Film and Video Assn., Sarasota, Fla., 1992, Internat. Film Workshops, Rockport, Maine, 1992, Dir. Guild Am. Educators Workshop, L.A., 1993, Dir.'s Workshop, 1996, Acad. TV Arts and Scis. Educators Seminar, L.A., 1995. Writer PBS documentary World of Family, NCCJ, 1995; exptl. theater playwright; lyricist (off-Broadway mus.) Sugar Hill, 1990. bd. dirs. Enzian Film Theatre. NEH grantee, 1978; recipient playwriting fellowships Atlantic Ctr. for Arts, 1983, Fla. Divsn. Cultural Affairs, 1983; named Winner Fla. Playwrite Competition, 1994. Mem. Assn. Theater in Higher Edn., Fla. Motion Picture and TV Assn. (bd. dirs., v.p.), Ctrl. Fla. Film Commn. (bd. dirs.), Fla. Inst. for Film Edn. (bd. dirs.) Actors Equity Assn., Dramatists Guild N.Y.C., Players Club (N.Y.C.). Home: 100 Detmar Dr Winter Park FL 32789-3901 Office: Valencia CC PO Box 3028 Orlando FL 32802-3028

WALSH, KENNETH ALBERT, chemist; b. Yankton, S.D., May 23, 1922; s. Albert Lawrence and Edna (Slear) W.; m. Dorothy Jeanne Thompson, Dec. 22, 1944; children: Jeanne K., Kenneth Albert, David Bruce, Rhonda Jean, Leslie Gay. BA, Yankton Coll., 1942; PhD, Iowa State U., 1950. Asst. prof. chemistry Iowa State U., Ames, 1950-51; staff mem. Los Alamos Sci. Lab., 1951-57; supr. Internat. Minerals & Chem. Corp., Mulberry, Fla., 1957-60; mgr. Brush Beryllium Co., Elmore, Ohio, 1960-72; assoc. dir. tech. Brush Wellman Inc., Elmore, 1972-86; cons., patentee in field. Democratic precinct chmn., Los Alamos, 1956, Fremont, Ohio, 1980. Mem. AIME, Am. Chem. Soc. (sect. treas. 1956), ASM Internat., Toastmasters Internat., Theta Xi, Phi Lambda Upsilon. Methodist. Home: 2106 Kensington Dr Tyler TX 75703-2232

WALSH, LYNN RENEE, library director; b. Flint, Mich., Oct. 31, 1946; d. Samuel J. and E. Lucile (Moore) Seirmarco; m. William P. Walsh, July 8, 1972 (div. Sept. 1992); children: Sarah, Virginia, Louisa. MusB, Mich. State U., 1969; MLS, Western Mich. U., Kalamazoo, 1970. Audiovisual libr. Triton C.C., River Grove, Ill., 1970-72; tchr. Libr. and Music Cotter (Ark.) Pub. Schs., 1974-76; tchr. Promise Land Acad., Mountain Home, Ark., 1978-81; tech. svcs. libr. St. Lucie County Libr., Ft. Pierce, Fla., 1981-83; libr. dir. Sebastian (Fla.) River Libr. Assn., 1983-86, Indian River County BCC, Vero Beach, Fla., 1986—. Mem. Exchange Club, Sebastian, Fla., 1986-90. Mem. ALA, Fla. Libr. Assn. Mem. Ch. of God. Office: N Indian River County Library 1001 State Road 512 Sebastian FL 32958-4861

WALSH, MARIE LECLERC, nurse; b. Providence, Sept. 11, 1928; d. Walter Normand and Anna Mary (Ryan) Leclerc; m. John Breffni Walsh, June 18, 1955; children: George Breffni, John Leclerc, Darina Louise. Grad., Waterbury Hosp. Sch. Nursing, Conn., 1951; BS, Columbia U., 1954, MA, 1955. Team leader Hartford (Conn.) Hosp., 1951-53; pvt. duty nurse St. Luke's Hosp., N.Y.C., 1953-57; sch. nurse tchr. Agnes Russel Ctr., Tchrs. Coll. Columbia U., N.Y.C., 1955-56; clin. nursing instr. St. Luke's Hosp., N.Y.C., 1957-58; chmn. disaster nursing ARC Fairfax County, Va., 1975; course coord. occupational health nursing U. Va. Sch. Continuing Edn., Falls Church, 1975-77; mem. disaster steering com. No. Va. C.C., Annandale, 1976; adj. faculty U. Va. Sch. Continuing Edn., Falls Church, 1981; disaster svcs. nurse ARC, Wichita, Kans., 1985-90; disaster svcs. nurse Seattle-King County chpt. ARC, Seattle, 1990-96; rsch. and statis. analyst U. Va. Sch. Continuing Edn. Nursing, Falls Church, 1975; rsch. libr. Olive Garvey Ctr. for Improvement Human Functioning, Inc., Wichita, 1985. Sec. Dem. party, Cresskill, N.J., 1964-66; county committeewoman, Bergen County, N.J., 1965-66; pres., v.p., Internat. Staff Wives, NATO, Brussels, Belgium, 1978-80; election officer, supr. Election Bd., Wichita, 1987, 88. Mem. AAAS, AAUW, N.Y. Acad. Sci., Pi Lambda Theta, Sigma Theta Tau. Home: 8800 Prestwould Pl Mc Lean VA 22102

WALSH, MARY D. FLEMING, civic worker; b. Whitewright, Tex., Oct. 29, 1913; d. William Fleming and Anna Maud (Lewis) Fleming; B.A., So. Meth. U., 1934; LL.D. (hon.), Tex. Christian U., 1979; m. F. Howard Walsh, Mar. 13, 1937; children: Richard, Howard, D'Ann Walsh Bonnell, Maudi Walsh Roe, William Lloyd. Pres. Fleming Found.; v.p. Walsh Found.; partner Walsh Co.; charter mem. Lloyd Shaw Found., Colorado Springs; mem. Big Bros. Tarrant County; guarantor Fort Worth Arts Council, Scholar Cantorum, Fort Worth Opera, Fort Worth Ballet, Fort Worth Theater, Tex. Boys Choir; hon. mem. bd. dirs. Van Cliburn Internat. Piano Competition; co-founder Am. Field Service in Ft. Worth; mem. Tex. Commn. for Arts and Humanities, 1968-72, mem. adv. council, 1972-84; bd. dirs. Wm. Edrington Scott Theatre, 1977-83, Colorado Springs Day Nursery, Colorado Springs Symphony, Ft. Worth Symphony, 1974-81; hon. chmn. Opera Ball, 1975, Opera Guild Internat. Conf., 1976; co-presenter (with husband) through Walsh Found., Tex. Boys Choir and Dorothy Shaw Bell Choir ann. presentation of The Littlest Wiseman to City of Ft. Worth; granted with husband land and bldgs. to Tex. Boys Choir for permanent home, 1971, Walsh-Wurlitzer organ to Casa Manana, 1972. Sem. Recipient numerous awards, including Altrusa Civic award as 1st Lady of Ft. Worth, 1968; (with husband) Disting. Service award So. Bapt. Radio and Television Commn., 1972; Opera award Girl Scouts, 1977-79; award Streams and Valleys, 1976-80; named (with husband) Patron of Arts in Ft. Worth, 1970, 91, Edna Gladney Internat. Grandparents of 1972, (with husband) Sr. Citizens of Yr, 1985; Mary D. and Howard Walsh Meml. Organ dedicated by Bapt. Radio and TV Commn., 1967, tng. ctr. named for the Walshes, 1976; Mary D. and Howard Walsh Med. Bldg., Southwestern Bapt. Theol. Sem.; library at Tarrant County Jr. Coll. N.W. Campus dedicated to her and husband, 1978; Brotherhood citation Tarrant County chpt. NCCJ, 1978; Spl. Recognition award Ft. Worth Ballet Assn.; Royal Purple award Tex. Christian U., 1979; Friends of Tex. Boys Choir award, 1981; appreciation award Southwestern Bapt. Theol. Sem., 1981, B. H. Carroll Founders award, 1982, (with husband) Patrons of the Arts award, 1991; Outstanding Women of Fort Worth award City of Fort Worth, 1994, numerous other award for civic activities. Mem. Ft. Worth Boys Club, Ft. Worth Children's Hosp., Jewel Charity Ball, Ft. Worth Pan Hellenic (pres. 1940), Opera Guild, Fine Arts Found. Guild of Tex. Christian U., Girl's Service League (hon. life, hon. chmn. Fine Arts Guild Spring Ballet, 1985), AAUW, Goodwill Industries Aux., Child Study Center, Tarrant County Aux. of Edna Gladney Home, YWCA (life), Ft. Worth Art Assn., Ft. Worth Ballet Assn., Tex. Boys Choir Aux., Friends of Tex. Boys Choir, Round Table, Colorado Springs Fine Art Center, Am. Automobile Assn., Nat. Assn. Cowbelles, Ft. Worth Arts Council (hon. bd. mem.), Am. Guild Organists (hon., Ft. Worth chpt.), Rae Reimers Bible Study Class (pres. 1968), Tex. League Composers (hon. life), Children's Hosp. Woman's Bd. (hon. 1991), Chi Omega (pres. 1935-36, hon. chmn. 1986), others. Baptist. Clubs: The Woman's (Club Fidelite), Colorado Springs Country, Garden of Gods, Colonial Country, Ridglea Country, Shady Oaks Country, Chi Omega Mothers, Chi Omega Carousel, TCU Woman's. Home: 2425 Stadium Dr Fort Worth TX 76109-1055 also: 1801 Culebra Ave Colorado Springs CO 80907-7328

WALSH, MILTON O'NEAL, lawyer; b. Memphis, Tenn., June 17, 1941; s. J. Milton and Rebie (Willis) W.; m. Janet Parker; children: Susan, Neal. BS, La. State U., 1964, JD, 1971. Bar: La. 1971. Salesman Met. Ins. Co., Baton Rouge, 1963-65; claims adjustor Safeco Ins. Co., Baton Rouge, 1965-68; law clk. Franklin, Moore, Beychok & Cooper, Baton Rouge, 1968-71, assoc., 1971-73; ptnr. Franklin, Moore, Cooper & Walsh, Baton Rouge, 1973-74, Franklin, Moore & Walsh, Baton Rouge, 1974-90; prin. O'Neal Walsh and Assocs., Baton Rouge, 1990—; chmn. rules com. Baton Rouge City Ct., 1975-76, liaison com. 19th Jud. Dist. Ct., 1977; instr. in bus. law La. State U., 1974. Mem. ABA (mem. products liability com. 1978-79), Baton Rouge Bar Assn., La. Bar Assn., La. Assn. Def. Counsel (bd. dirs. 1982-84), Internat. Assn. Def. Counsel (mem. casualty ins. com. 1980-81, mem. faculty 14th ann. counsel trial acad. 1986), Def. Rsch. Inst. (state chmn. 1980-82, regional v.p. 1983-86, bd. dirs. 1986-89, mem. arbitration com., Scroll of Merit award 1981, 82), Assn. Def. Trial Attys. (state chmn. 1984—, S.W. mem. chmn. 1985-95, v.p./pres.-elect 1995-96, pres. 1996—, mem. exec. coun. 1990-93), Sherwood Forest Country Club (bd. dirs. 1977-79, pres. 1979), Phi Delta Phi. Office: O'Neal Walsh & Assocs 501 Louisiana Ave Baton Rouge LA 70802-5921

WALSH, ROBERT RAYMOND, librarian, consultant; b. Chgo., Aug. 14, 1943; s. Robert A. and Jane (Wright) W. BA in Archtl. Scis. cum laude, Harvard U., 1965; MA, U. Chgo., 1990. Libr. asst. Art Libr., U. Chgo., 1965-67; adminstrv. asst. Harvard U. Libr., Cambridge, Mass., 1967-71, asst. univ. libr. for bldg. planning, 1971-76; asst. v.p. The New Eng. Deposit Libr., Boston, 1972-76; asst. to chief libr. Queens Coll., CUNY, 1981-85; libr. bldgs. cons. Va. State Libr. and Archives, Richmond, 1988-92; libr. bldgs. and networking cons. Libr. of Va., Richmond, 1992—; vis. lectr. Grad. Sch. Libr. Sci., U. Ill., summer 1970; libr. planning cons., 1970—; vis. critic Grad. Sch. Arch., Yale U., New Haven, 1981, Harvard U. Grad. Sch. Design, 1975, 77, 80; vis. lectr. Sch. Libr. Svc., Memphis State U., 1974, Grad. Sch. Libr. Sci., U. Ill., 1970; cons. over 200 acad., pub. and govt. librs. Editor The Harvard Librarian and HUL Notes, 1971-74; contbr. articles to profl. jours. Nat. Merit scholar, 1961-65, Harvard Coll. scholar, 1964-65; U. Chgo. Grad. Libr. Sch. fellow, 1965-67. Mem. ALA, Assn. Coll. and Rsch. Librs., Libr. Adminstrn. and Mgmt. Assn. (circulation svcs. com., ins. for librs. com., univ. libr. bldgs. com.), New Eng. Assn. Coll. and Rsch. Librs., Greater N.Y. Assn. Coll. and Rsch. Librs. Office: Libr of Va 808 E Broad St Richmond VA 23219-1905

WALSH, SARAH FEENEY, elementary education educator; b. Somerset, Pa., Jan. 13, 1961; d. William Joseph and Catherine O'Bryn (Feeney) W. BS, Duquesne U., 1983, MS in Edn., 1985; postgrad., Tex. Women's U., 1987. Cert. reading specialist/elem. edn. Resident asst. Duquesne U., Pitts., 1981-82, grad. asst., 1984-85; tchr. St. Canice Sch., Pitts., 1982-83, William Brown Miller, Dallas, 1985-86, J.P. Starks Elem. Sch., Dallas, 1986-89, W.W. Bushman Elem. Sch., Dallas, 1989—, Preston Hollow Sch., Dallas, 1994—. Tchr. Sunday sch. Holy Trinity Parish, Dallas, 1987-93, mem. Edn. Coun., mem. Singles Group, 1987—; mem. St. Thomas Aquinas Coun./Edn.; mem. 500 Inc., Dallas Mus. Art. Mem. Tchrs. Applying Whole Lang., Internat. Reading Assn. (mem. Dallas coun., membership chair 1992-94, historian 1994—, recording sec. 1995-96), Kappa Delta Epsilon (pres. 1983). Roman Catholic. Home: 6630 Vanderbilt Ave Dallas TX 75214

WALSH, THOMAS JAMES, JR., lawyer; b. Memphis, Oct. 22, 1947; s. Thomas James and Lois Rhine (Gibson) w.; m. Jean Clay McKee, May 31, 1969; children: Courtney Michelle, Meredith McKee. BA, Yale Coll., 1969; JD, U. Va., 1975. Bar: Tenn. 1975, U.S. Dist. Ct. (we. dist.) Tenn. 1976, U.S. Ct. Appeals (5th cir.) 1982, U.S. Ct. Appeals (6th cir.) 1985, U.S. Ct. Appeals (11th cir.) 1986, U.S. Supreme Ct. 1986, U.S. Ct. Appeals (10th cir.) 1991, U.S. Ct. Appeals (8th cir.) 1992. Assoc. Canada, Russell & Turner, Memphis, 1975-78; assoc. Wildman, Harrold, Allen, Dixon & McDonnell, Memphis, 1978-80, ptnr., 1981-89; ptnr. McDonnell, Boyd, Smith & Solmson, Memphis, 1989-90, McDonnell Boyd, Memphis, 1990-94; atty. Wolff Ardis, P.C., Memphis, 1995—; hearing officer Bd. of Profl. Responsibility Supreme Ct. Tenn., 1988-95. Chmn. bd. dirs. Multiple Sclerosis Soc. mid-south chpt., Memphis, 1978, World Affairs Coun. Memphis, 1985—; vol. atty. pro bono panel for sr. citizens, Memphis, 1982—; v.p. Bapt. Peace Fellowship of N.Am., Memphis, 1984-89; coun. chmn. Prescott Meml. Bapt. Ch., Memphis, 1993-95. Mem. Class award Leadership Memphis, 1985, Community Class award Unitarian Universalist Fellowship, Memphis, 1989. Mem. ABA, Tenn. Bar Assn., Memphis Bar Assn. Democrat. Office: 6055 Primacy Pky Ste 360 Memphis TN 38119-5724

WALSH, WILLIAM ARTHUR, JR., lawyer; b. Washington, Mar. 17, 1949; children: Jesse Creighton, Patrick McKay. BS in Econs. and Fin., U. Md., 1972; JD, U. Richmond, 1977. Bar: Va. Ptnr. Hunton & Williams, Richmond, Va.; mem. adv. bd. for law rev. U. Richmond. Bd. trustees Va. Commonwealth U. Real Estate Found. Mem. ABA, Va. Bar Assn. (chmn. real estate legal opinions com.), Richmond Bar Assn., Ctrl. Richmond Assn. (mem. bd. dirs.), Omicron Delta Kappa. Home: 4705 Leonard Pky Richmond VA 23226-1337 Office: Hunton & Williams Riverfront Pla East Tower 951 E Byrd St Richmond VA 23219-4040*

WALSH, WILLIAM B., JR., foundation administrator; b. Washington, Aug. 8, 1945; s. William B. and Helen R. (Runvold) W.; children: William III, Deirdre Murphy. BA, Trinity Coll., 1968; M in Pub. Health, U. Mich., 1973; student, U. Pa., 1990; Diploma (hon.), Presidium Supreme Soviet, 1992. Adminstr. U.S. programs Project HOPE, Millwood, Va., 1968-71, dir. personnel, 1971-72, health planner Colombia, 1973-75, dir. Middle East, Africa, 1975-80, v.p. strategic planning, dir. foundation planning, 1981-82, v.p. opers., 1984-91, pres., COO, 1991-92, pres., CEO, 1992—; presdl. exch. exec. President's Exec. Exch. Com., Washington, 1983; also bd. dirs., 1992—; mem. European Adv. Bd., London, 1990—, Project HOPE Swiss Fondation, Geneva, 1991—, Hong Kong Adv. Bd., 1993—, Project HOPE Deutschland, 1994—, Project HOPE U.K., 1994—, Asia Adv. Bd., 1995—; developer health care, ednl. schs. program, Southwest U.S.A., 1969—. Author: (health planning manual) Estructora Para el Desarrollo de un Plan Para la Prestacion de Servicio, 1974; contbr. articles to profl. jours. Mem. Internat. Action Commn. for St. Petersburg, 1994, Prince Charles Bus. Roundtable, Eng., 1994. Recipient Disting. Svc. award MacAlaster Coll. Internat., 1970, U.S. Border Coll. Consortium, 1987, Republic of Armenia, 1990, Recognition award Chinese Am. Cooperation in Health Scis., U. Ala., 1988. Mem. Am. Assn. Sovereign Mil. Order of Malta (knight), Rotary Club (Disting. Svc. award 1982). Office: Project HOPE 7500 Old Georgetown Rd #600 Bethesda MD 20814-6133

WALSH, WILLIAM JOHN, educational administrator; b. Natrona Heights, Pa., Mar. 29, 1941; s. William Henry and Helen Constance W.; BA in Sociology, Duquesne U., 1969; MEd in Ednl. Adminstrn., Pa. State U., 1971; JD, LaSalle U., 1993; m. Carol Jean Miller, Sept. 3, 1966; children: Keirsten, Shannon. Classification analyst Pa. State U., University Park, 1969-73; asst. pers. dir. W.Va. U., Morgantown, 1973-78; exec. asst. to pres., 1977; dir. pers. adminstrn., dir. purchasing audit W.Va. Bd. of Regents, Charleston, 1978-86; dir. salary adminstrn. and benefits Pa. State U., 1986-92; dir. employee benefits and retirement U. Miami, 1992-96; exec. dir. employee benefits U. Miami, Fla., 1996—; cons. in field. Served with USMC, 1962-66; Vietnam. Mem. Coll. and Univ. Personnel Assn., South Fla. Health Coalition, Coral Gables C. of C., Med. Found. Svcs., Inc. Republican. Roman Catholic. Home: 2126 Harbor Way Fort Lauderdale FL 33326-2345

WALSH HANSEL, JEANETTA LYNN, home infusion nurse; b. Providence, June 14, 1947; d. Herman David and Carmela Rosemary (Coletta) Harris; m. R.J. Walsh, Dec. 16, 1967 (div. 1983); children: Robert A., Shawn M.; m. Robert Raymond Hansel, Mar. 21, 1991. AA, R.I. Jr. Coll., 1968; BSN, U. Tex., Arlington, 1981. RN, Tex., RNC; cert. chemotherapy nurse. Staff nurse Osteo. Med. Ctr., Ft. Worth, 1981-82; charge nurse Duncan Meml. Hosp., Ft. Worth, 1983; supr. Northwest Hosp., Ft. Worth, 1983-85; staff nurse St. Joseph Hosp., Ft. Worth, 1985-86; relief charge nurse All Saint's Hosp., Ft. Worth, 1986-87; staff nurse, asst. supr., staff devel. John Peter Smith Hosp., Ft. Worth, 1987-93; home infusion therapy nurse AACU Care Infusion, Burleson, Tex., 1993—; peripherally inserted ctrl. catheter line specialist John Peter Smith Hosp., Ft. Worth, 1992; mem. test devel. com. for gen. practice ANCC, 1995-98. Mem. ANA, NAACOG, INS, Tex. Nurse's Assn., Am. Paint Horse Assn., Pinto Horse Assn. Roman Catholic. Home and Office: 4501 Cross Timber Rd Burleson TX 76028-6723

WALSH-MCGEHEE, MARTHA BOSSE, conservationist; d. Leon and Lenore (Carter) Bosse; m. Leo S. Walsh, Sept. 30, 1972 (div. Oct. 1982); m. Donald B. McGehee, Aug. 6, 1992. Student, U. Mo., 1966, Baker U., 1966-67, Marymount-Manhattan, 1980-82. Flight attendant TWA, N.Y.C., 1967-78; pres. Island Conservation Effort, 1988—; chmn. bd. dirs. The Tortoise Preserve; trustee Rare Ctr. for Tropical Bird Conservation, Phila., 1987-91; rsch. assoc. N.C. Mus. Natural Sci. Ptnr. in conservation World Wildlife Fund, Washington, 1986—; assoc. World Resources Inst., Washington, 1987—; mem. St. Croix Environ. Assn., 1987—; mem. Saba Conservation Found. Nature Conservancy. Mem. Caribbean Conservation Assn., St. Lucia Naturalists Soc., Cedam Internat., Soc. Caribbean Ornithology (exec. coun. mem.), Friends of Abaco Parrot, Assn. Parrot Conservation Tropical Audubon, Ctr. for Marine Conservation, Fla. Wildlife Fedn. Republican. Home: 90 Edgewater Dr Apt 901 Coral Gables FL 33133-6918 also: Windwardside, Saba Netherlands Antilles

WALTER, DONALD ELLSWORTH, federal judge; b. Jennings, La., Mar. 15, 1936; s. Robert R. and Ada (Lafleur) D'Aquin; m. Charlotte Sevier Donald, Jan. 5, 1942; children: Laura Ney, Robert Ellsworth, Susannah Brooks. BA, La. State U., 1961, JD, 1964. Bar: La. 1964, U.S. Supreme Ct. 1969. Assoc. Cavanaugh, Brame, Holt & Woodley, 1964-66, Holt & Woodley, Lake Charles, La., 1966-69; U.S. atty. U.S. Dept. Justice, Shreveport, La., 1969-77; lawyer Hargrove, Guyton, Ramey & Barlow, Shreveport, La., 1977-85; judge U.S. Dist. Ct. (west. dist.) La., Monroe, 1985-92, Shreveport, La., 1993—. Served with AUS, 1957-58. Office: US Dist Ct 300 Fannin St Rm 4200 Shreveport LA 71101-3121*

WALTER, GARY STEVEN, hotel manager; b. Rochester, N.Y., Nov. 18, 1949; s. Richard Stanley and Leona (Caswell) W. BA in English and History, U. Rochester, 1972; BS in Hotel Mgmt., U. Houston, 1976; postgrad., Rice U., 1985—. Asst. mgr. Americana Hotels, Rochester and N.Y.C., 1972-75, Marriott Hotels, Houston, Denver, Chgo., 1975-79, Shamrock Hilton Hotel, Houston, 1979-80; front office mgr. Adam's Mark Hotel, Houston, 1980-82, Remington on Post Oak Pk., Houston, 1982-84; rooms div. mgr. Hotel Intercontinental, Houston, 1984-88; mgr. Med. Ctr. Hilton, Houston, 1989, Ft. Worth Hilton, 1990-91, DFW Hilton Exec. Conf. Ctr., Dallas, 1992-93, Melrose Hotel, Dallas, 1994—. Mem. Houston Symphony Chorale, 1974-76. Mem. Houston Hotel Assn., Hilton Coll. Alumni Assn. of U. Houston (v.p. 1980-82, pres. 1988-90, coll. dean selection com. 1983, editor news monthly 1986-87), U. Rochester Alumni Assn. (mem. alumni admissions com. 1974—), Houston Grand Opera Soc., Wortham Theatre Found., Phi Kappa Phi. Republican. Methodist. Home: 1118 Millview Dr Apt 406 Arlington TX 76012-2345 Office: Melrose Hotel 3015 Oak Lawn Ave Dallas TX 75219-4134

WALTER, JAMES W., diversified manufacturing executive; b. Lewes, Del., 1922; m. Monica Saraw, 1946 (wid. 1982); children: James W., Robert; m. Constance Spoto, 1983. Ptnr. Walter Constrn. Co., 1948-55; chmn. bd., dir. Walter Industries Inc. (formerly Jim Walter Corp.), Tampa, Fla. , 1955—; bd. dirs. Gen. Telephone & Electronics Co., Contel Cellular, Inc., Anchor Glass Container Corp. With USN, 1942-46. *

WALTERS, BILL, state senator, lawyer; b. Paris, Ark., Apr. 17, 1943; s. Peter Louis and Elizabeth Cecelia (Wilhelm) W.; m. Joyce Leslie Garrett Moore, Jan. 9, 1964 (div. 1970); children: Jamie, Sherry Ann; m. Shirley Ann Dixon, Aug. 20, 1971; 1 child, Sandra. BS, U. Ark., 1966, JD, 1971. Bar: Ark. 1971, U.S. Dist. Ct. Ark. 1971. Asst. prosecuting atty. 12th Jud. Dist. Ark., Ft. Smith, 1971-74; pvt. practice Greenwood, Ark., 1975—; mem. Ark. Senate, Little Rock, 1982—; bd. dirs. 1st Ark. Title Co., Pine Bluff; bd. dirs., sec.-treas. Mineral Owners Collective Assn. Inc., Greenwood; v.p., bd. dirs. Sebastian County Abstract & Title Ins. Co., Greenwood; mem. Ark. Real Estate Commn., Ark. Abstract and Title Commn. Committeeman Rep. Ctrl. Com. Ark., Ft. Smith, 1980; search pilot CAP, Ft. Smith. Decorated Silver Medal of Valor; recipient Cert. of Honor Justice for Crime's Victims, 1983. Mem. Ark. Bar Assn., South Sebastian County Bar Assn. (pres. 1991-94), Profl. Landmen's Assn. Roman Catholic. Home: PO Box 280 Greenwood AR 72936-0280 Office: 44 Town Square St Greenwood AR 72936-4019

WALTERS, CYNTHIA VOIGT, internal medicine physician; b. Knoxville, Tenn., Apr. 10, 1958; d. William Carl and Evelyn (Kidd) Voigt; m. Gordon W. Walters, Aug. 12, 1980. BS cum laude, Auburn U., 1980; MD, U. South Ala., 1987. Diplomate Am. Bd. Internal Medicine. Anesthesiology residency U. Ala., Birmingham, 1988-89; internal medicine residency Carraway Meth. Medical Ctr., Birmingham, Ala., 1989-91; internal medicine physician Lloyd Noland Hosp., Fairfield, Ala., 1991—. Instr. Advanced Trauma Life Support. Mem. ACP, Jefferson County Med. Soc., Med. Assn. State of Ala., Soc. Critical Care Medicne, Alpha Omega Alpha. Office: Lloyd Noland Hosp 701 Lloyd Noland Pky Fairfield AL 35064-2660

WALTERS, GEORGE JOHN, oral and maxillofacial surgeon; b. Balt., June 16, 1956; s. George John Sr. and Henrietta Jean (Parker) W.; m. Melanie Ann Goodreau, June 23, 1989. BS, Loyola Coll., 1978; DDS, U. Md., 1983; postgrad., John Hopkins, 1991, U. Pa., 1992, U. Pa., 1993. Cert. argon laser. Rsch. asst. dept. otolaryngology The Johns Hopkins Sch. Medicine, Balt., 1978-79; ind. learning ctr. technician Balt. Coll. Dental Surgery, Dental Sch., U. Md., 1980-81; audio-visual technician U. Md. Law Sch., Balt., 1981-82, res. material circulation asst., 1982-83; resident gen. practice residency York (Pa.) Hosp., 1983-84; resident dept. anesthesia The Med. Coll. of Pa. and Hosp., Phila., 1984-85; resident dept. dentistry div. oral and maxillofacial surgery U. Md. Med. System, Balt., 1985-89, chief adminstrv. resident dept. dentistry, 1988-89; assoc. in oral and maxillofacial surgery Miller Oral Surgery and Pa. Jaw Treatment Ctr., Harrisburg, Pa., 1989-91; ptrn. Oral and Maxillofacial Surgery, Panama City, Fla., 1991-95; individual practice oral and maxillofacial surgery Panama City, Fla., 1995—; explorer advisor for health career explorer post Balt. Coll. Dental Surgery, Dental Sch., U. Md., 1981, dental rsch. student com., 1982, vol. for recruitment of minority students, 1983; testifier Sen. House Com. on Medicaid Funding, State House, Annapolis, Md., 1987-88; lectr. Gulf Coast C.C., 1991—. Copntbr. to profl. jours. Health vol. overseas Nepal Mission for Cleft Lip and Palate, 1989; vol. Guatemala Med. Mission Cleft Lip and Palate, 1994; bd. dirs. Am. Cancer Soc., 1996. John Hopkins fellow 1989. Mem. ADA, Am. Assn. Oral and Maxillofacial Surgery, Mid. Atlantic Soc. Oral and Maxillofacial Surgery, Bay County Dental Soc., Fla. Dental Soc., N.W. Dental Soc. Fla., Fla. Soc. Oral and Maxillofacial Surgery, Gorgas Odontological Soc., Rotary, Bay County Civil War Roundtable, Gamma Pi Delta. Roman Catholic. Home: PO Box 27473 1702 Wahoo Cir Panama City FL 32411-7230 Office: 2202 State Ave Ste 200 Panama City FL 32405-4539

WALTERS, GREGORY NORMAN, college administrator; b. Johnson City, Tenn., Mar. 2, 1964; s. Norman Keith and Wanda Juanita (Cooter) W. BS in Mass Comm., East Tenn. State U., 1987, postgrad., 1988-89. Asst. dir. pub. rels. Milligan (Tenn.) Coll., 1987; asst. to dir. pub. info. N.E. State Tech. C.C., Blountville, Tenn., 1989—; advisor N.W. State Student Ambs., 1991—; chair N.E. State Cultural Activities Com., 1993-94, N.E. State Student Activities Com., 1994-95. Author: (poem) American Collegiate Poets, 1986, American Poetry Anthology, 1987; editor: The Buccaneer, 1985, East Tennessean, 1986, The Star, 1990—. Recipient Outstanding Adminstr. award N.E. State Tech. C.C., 1993. Mem. Nat. Coun. Mktg. and Pub. Rels., N.E. Coun. Adminstrv. Awareness (v.p. 1994-95, pres. 1995-96), Student Alumni Assn./Student Found. Network, Phi Kappa Phi. Methodist. Office: NE State Tech CC PO Box 246 Blountville TN 37617-0246

WALTERS, JERRY WILLARD, retired federal agency administrator; b. Paducah, Ky., Aug. 26, 1936; s. Rex Willard and Dorothy Maureen (Smith) W.; m. Rita Ann Middledorf, Oct. 10, 1960; children: Rex Robert, Wade Alan, Stacy Lee. BA, U. Md., 1959. Fingerprint specialist FBI, Washington, 1955-57; commd. ensign USN, 1960; served as intelligence officer U.S. Naval Security Group, Alaska, and the Philippines, 1960-70; intelligence analyst Nat. Security Agy., Washington, 1966-69; human intelligence case officer U.S. Naval Intelligence, Japan, 1973-77; intelligence ops. officer Bur. Alcohol, Tobacco & Firearms, Washington, 1978-82; mgr. customs intelligence officer U.S. Customs Svc., Washington, 1982-93. Mem. Internat. Assn. Law Enforcement Intelligence Analysts (charter, bd. dirs. 1980-90, pres. 1986-89). Republican. Home: Bull Run Mountain 2254 Mountain Rd Haymarket VA 20169-1549

WALTERS, LORI J., medieval literature and language educator; b. Bklyn., Oct. 14, 1947; d. William Joseph and Jean (Spizuoco) W.; m. Alexandre Georges Djokic, Sept. 13, 1972 (div. Apr., 1985). BA, Douglass Coll., 1969; MA in Teaching, U. Chgo., 1971; postgrad., Northwestern U., 1972-75; MA in French, Princeton U., 1982, PhD in Romance Langs. and Lit., 1986. Instr. Northwestern U., Summer 1974, 75; asst. to dean of students U. Chgo., 1976-78, asst. dir. admissions, 1978-80; lectr. Princeton (N.J.) U., 1985-87; assoc. prof. Fla. State U., Tallahassee, 1987-96, prof., 1996—; nat., internat. conf. speaker. Author, editor: Lancelot and Guinevere: A Casebook, 1996; author poetry; translator: De la sorisete des estopes, The Resistence of Reference, Philosophy, Linguistics and the Literary Text (Ora Avni), 1990; co-editor: The Manuscripts of Chrétien de Troyes, 2 vols., 1993; mem. editorial bd. Studies in Iconography, Vol. 15; contbr. book revs., articles to profl. jours. NEH fellow, 1993-94, Donald and Mary Hyde fellow, 1982-84, fellow Northwestern U., teaching assistantships, 1972-75; grantee Coun. on Faculty Rsch. Support, 1991, 95, NEH, 1988-89, Fla. State U., summer 1988, 89, 90; France scholar U. Poitiers, summer 1982, Princeton U. assistantships, 1980-82, 84-85, Fulbright-French govt. teaching assistantship, 1969-70. Mem. MLA (exec. com. 1994-98), Internat. Arthurian Soc., Internat. Courtly Lit. Soc. (sec. SAMLA br. 1989), Medieval Acad. Am. Home: 3306 Lemoyne Ct Tallahassee FL 32312-2071

WALTERS, NORMAN EDWARD, hospital administrator; b. Williamsburg, Ky., Nov. 21, 1941; s. Winford and Dorothy Florence (Clifford) W.; m. Elizabeth Lou Custer, Sept. 7, 1963; children: Pamela Denise, Scot Edward. BS, Southeastern U., 1969; MS, St. Joseph's U., Windham, Maine, 1991. Br. mgr. GEICO, Chevy Chase, Md., 1965-68; asst. dept. head, internal audit mgr., dir. of fin. Commonwealth of Va., Alexandria and Richmond, 1968-77; asst. contr. Cumberland County Hosp. System, Fayetteville, N.C., 1978-81; contr., asst. adminstr. Hosp. Mgmt. Assoc., Williamson, W.Va., 1981; asst. adminstr. Advanced Health System, Inc., Marlow and Elk City, Okla., 1981-87; asst. adminstr., CFO Taylor County Hosp., Campbellsville, Ky., 1987—; v.p. Pikeville (Ky.) Meth. Hosp., 1991—; govt. cons. healthcare com. Health Care Fin. Mgmt. Assn., Campbellsville, 1991. Contbr. articles to profl. jours. Member Christian Profl. Bus. Men, Alexandria, 1970-80, Lions, Marlow and Elk City, 1981, 83Gov. Jim Hunt's Health Care Task Force, Raleigh, N.C., 1980; ; treas. Rotary, Campbellsville, 1987. Capt. USAF, 1959-65. Decorated Hon. Order of Ky. Cols. Mem. Am. Mgmt. Assn. (chmn. 1968-75, 88-89), Health Care Fin. Mgmt. Assn. (nat. matrix 1978—, health care task force com. Charleston, W.Va. chpt. 1981-82, program chmn. N.C. chpt. 1980-81, health care reform task force Ky. chpt. 1991-92, mem. adv. com. health care task force nat. com., Leffer Plaque 1981), Health Law Mgmt. Assn. (assoc. chmn. Ky. chpt. 1988-89, Leffer Plaque 1989, 90). Democrat. Baptist. Home: 224 College St Apt 2A Pikeville KY 41501-1771

WALTERS, PHILIP RAYMOND, foundation executive; b. Frankfort, Ind., Jan. 26, 1938; s. Raymond and Ruth Edna (Grimes) W.; m. Sharon Pearl Wilfong, May 31, 1958 (div. Nov. 1992); children: Raymond (dec.), Robert, Sharon Ruth; m. Candace Gina Oden, Jan. 29, 1994. BSBA, Olivet Nazarene Coll., 1959; JD, Ind. U., Indpls., 1969; postgrad., NYU, 1969-70. Bar: Ind. 1969, U.S. Dist. Ct. (so. dist.) Ind. 1969. Co-corp. counsel Ind. Farm Bur. Ins., Indpls., 1975-79; dir. gift and estate planning Orlando (Fla.) Regional Healthcare Found., 1991-96; regional dir. planned giving Arthritis Found., Longwood, Fla., 1996—; dep. atty. gen. State of Ind., Indpls.; planned giving officer Wheaton (Ill.) Coll.; campaign dir. Ketchum, Inc., Pitts.,; dir. planned giving Presbyn. Sch. Christian Edn., Richmond, Va.; presenter in field. Contbr. articles to profl. jours. Mem. Wekiva Presbyn. Ch., Longwood. Mem. Nat. Soc. Fundraising Execs, Ind. State Bar Assn., Ctrl. Fla. Estate Planning Coun. Republican. Home: 897 Cutler Rd Longwood FL 32779-3525

WALTERS, REBECCA RUSSELL YARBOROUGH, medical technologist; b. Lancaster, S.C., Mar. 9, 1951; d. William Peurifoy and Anna Beth (Cheatham) Yarborough; m. Thomas Edward Walters, Oct. 15, 1983; 1 child, Katherine Rebecca. BA, Winthrop Coll., 1972; postgrad. in med. tech., Bapt. Med. Ctr., Columbia, S.C., 1974; MA, Cen. Mich. U., 1978. Diplomate in Lab. Mgmt. ASCP. Teaching asst. in biology Winthrop Coll., Rock Hill, S.C., 1972-73; microbiology technologist Bapt. Med. Ctr., 1974-76, night shift supr., 1976-77, asst. adminstrv. dir., 1977—, tchr. Sch. Med. Tech., 1974—; article reviewer Med. Lab. Observer; mem. Nat. Cert. Agy. for Med. Lab. Personnel. Hycel, Inc. scholar, 1976, 77. Mem. Am. Soc. for Med. Tech. (scholar 1977), S.C. Soc. Med. Tech. (pres. 1979-80, scholar 1976), Am. Soc. Clin. Pathologists (assoc.), Clin. Lab. Mgmt. Assn., Beta Beta Beta, Alpha Mu Tau (scholar 1977). Republican. Presbyterian. Home: 155 Shawn Rd Chapin SC 29036-9215 Office: Bapt Med Ctr Taylor At Marion Columbia SC 29220

WALTERS, ROBERT ANCIL, II, protective services coordinator; b. Washington, Sept. 21, 1945; s. Robert Ancil and Etha Jane (McKinley) W.; m. Sandra Faye Roy, June 30, 1969; children: Anthony Wayne, Byron Edward. Student, Western Ky. U., 1964-65, Internat. Acad., 1965-66, U. Md., 1969-70. Cert. fire tng instr., Ky., emergency med. technician, Ky., profl. emergency mgr., Md. Computer operator U.S. Naval Weapons Lab., Dahlgren, Va., 1969-70; instr. computer programming Brentwood Acad., Lexington, Ky., 1970-71; data control supr. Dept. Child Welfare, State of Ky., Frankfort, 1971-74; military personnel supr. Ky. Army Nat. Guard, Frankfort, 1974-77; area coord. Ky. Disaster and Emergency Svcs., Somerset, Ky., 1977—. Chmn. bd. dirs. Somerset-Pulaski County Rescue Squad, Ky., 1982-86, active mem., 1978-89; bd. dirs. Nancy Fire Dept., 1986-87, active mem., 1979-95; bd. dirs., disaster chmn. Lake Cumberland (Ky.) chpt. ARC, 1982-86, instr. CPR and first aid, 1979-88; mem. prospect listing and evaluation com. Ptnrs. in Progress, Somerset C.C., 1994. Sgt. U.S. Army, 1968-69, Vietnam. Recipient Ky. Commendation medal, 1975, 77, 79, Ky. Merit citation, 1976, 80, 892, Ky. Humanitarian citation, 1974, 77, Ky. Achievement medal, 1978, 82, 93. Mem. Ky. Disaster and Emergency Svcs Assn., Ky. Emergency Mgmt. Assn., Nat. Emergency Mgrs. Assn., Order of Kentucky Colonels, Somerset Colonel, Adair County General. Democrat. Baptist. Home: 1063 Prather Dr Nancy KY 42544-8722

WALTERS, ROBERT P., manufacturing executive; b. 1957. Grad., U. N.C., 1979. With Broyhill Furniture INdustries, Lenoir, N.C., 1979-80, Riverside Furniture Co., Ft. Smith, Ark., 1980-82, Trendline Furniture Co., Hickory, N.C., 1982-84, Bernardt Furniture Co., Lenoir, 1984-90; with Thomasville Upholstery Inc., Statesville, N.C., 1990—, pres. Office: Thomasville Upholstery Inc 820 Cochran St Statesville NC 28677-5657*

WALTERS, ROLAND A, III, ophthalmologist; b. Oklahoma City, Apr. 18, 1943; s. Roland A. Jr. and Marie V. (Rogers) W.; m. Kelsey Price, June 24, 1964; children: Michele, Allison. Student, Stanford U., 1964; MD, U. Okla., 1968. Emergency physician St. Anthony Hosp., Oklahoma City, 1969-70; resident U. Okla. Health Scis. Ctr., Oklahoma City, 1970-73; ophthalmologist pvt. practice, Oklahoma City, 1973—. Pres. Lyric Theatre Okla., Oklahoma City, 1992, bd. dirs. Capt. USAFR, 1969-74. Fellow Am. Acad. Ophthalmology (councillor 1986-89); mem. Am. Soc. cataract and Refractive Surgery, Okla. State Med. Soc. (bd. trustees 1995-96), Okla. State Soc. Eye Surgeons and Physicians (pres. 1982), Okla. County Med. Soc. (pres. 1993), Vis. Nurses Assn. (pres. 1996). Republican. Episcopalian. Home: 1607 Guilford Ln Oklahoma City OK 73120 Office: 5701 N Portland #101 Oklahoma City OK 73112

WALTERS, SUE FOX, business executive, accountant; b. Louisville, June 9, 1941; d. Thomas Burke and Reva (Crick) Fox; m. Hugh Alexander Walters; children: Thomas Wade, Susan Alexandra Walters Ebling. Student, N.C. State U., Ky. Wesleyan Coll. Acct., paralegal for fin. instns. and firms; ct. adminstr. 45th Jud. Cir. Ct. Ky.; v.p., treas. Alexander and Assocs., CATV cons. firm, Greenville, Ky.; corp. adminstr. pub. corp., Bellevue, Wash.; acctg. specialist Japanese/Am. automotive mfg. co., Bowling Green, Ky.; land developer. Pres., Jr. Woman's Club Greenville, 1964-65, Woman's Club Greenville, 1976-78; vice gov. 2nd dist. Ky. Fedn. Women's Clubs, 1980. Avocations: historical restoration, design, antiques, dogs, flying. Home: 151 N Main St Greenville KY 42345-1503

WALTERS, SYLVIA ANNETTE, public relations and communications executive. BS, U. N.C., Greensboro, 1973; MS, Cornell U., 1978. Lectr. Cornell U., Ithaca, N.Y., 1976-78; dir. Domestic Sugar Industry Info. Ctr., Washington, 1981; dir. comms. Nat. Agrl. Chems. Assn., Washington, 1982-85; pres. Sylvia Walters & Assocs., Pierre, S.D., 1985-91; dir. corp. comms. U.S. Sugar Corp., Clewiston, Fla., 1991-93; prin. Walters Comms., Welcome, N.C., 1993—; specialist in mktg., pub. rels. and media rels. Home: PO Box 509 Welcome NC 27374-0509

WALTERS, WILFRED NELSON, JR., resource management company executive, engineering and economics educator; b. Tarentum, Pa., Mar. 31, 1942; s. Wilfred Nelson and Rebecca I. (Hamilton) W.; m. Mary Ellen Espinosa; children: Quentin Scott, Amy Beth, Kristin Jill. Student, USAF Air War Coll., 1967; BS in Engring. Mgmt., Clayton U., 1979; LLD, Toccoa Falls Coll., 1986; MA in Edn., Internat. Sem., 1993, PhD, 1994. Constrn. mgr. Walters and Haas, Inc., 1960-65; mgr. fin. and projects Walters and Walters, Ltd., 1965-67; rep. mem. of Congress and staff cons. Select Com. on Small Bus., 1968-70; project mgr., v.p. Del E. Webb of Colo., 1971-72; sr. project engr., asst. to v.p. project mgmt. Alyeska Pipeline Svc. Co., 1973-77; dir. contracts, mgr. ops. and govt. rels. Williams Bros. Engring. Co., 1977-79; pres. Walters Consol. Group Ltd., 1979—; chmn. Blackwater Whitehall Sebring & Humphries, 1994; prof. engring. econs. Okla. Res. U., 1988—. Author: Organization of Ideas - The Key to Good Writing, 1962, New Communities A Challenge for Today, 1971, Union Organization Do's and Don'ts, 1975, New Concepts for a More Effective Organization, Principals of Management, 1975, Corporate Acquisitions Procedures, 1978, Spiritual Concepts for Troubled People, 1979, Development of a Management Organization, 1981, The Intimacy of Real Living, 1984, Project Delivery Systems, 1990, The Search, 1991, Self Evaluation Guide Rating, 1992, Real Life Principles, 1993; contbr. articles to profl. jours. Bd. dirs. Victory Christian Ctr., Ron Kite Ministries, Assoc. in Mgmt.; trustee Sharing and Caring Found., Fla., Good Shepard Found., Haiti; past dir. Partnership Ministries, N.Y.C.; chmn. Nahum Jonah Ministries; co-chmn. Heart Found., 1966. Recipient Westinghouse Design award of Excellence, Presdl. Sports award, award Freedoms Found.; named one of Top 500 Design Firms, Engring. New Record. Mem. NSPE, Okla. Soc. Profl. Engrs., Am. Soc. Mil. Engrs. (past v.p.), United Contractors Assn. Western Pa. (past pres.), Rocky Mountain Developers Assn. (past bd. dirs.). Home: 3712 E 107th At Myrtlewood Tulsa OK 74137

WALTERS, WILLIAM LEE, accountant; b. New Orleans, Feb. 26, 1946; s. Elton E. and Helen (England) W.; m. Wanda Lovorn, Aug. 24, 1968; 1 child, Jack. BS in Acctg., Miss. State U., 1969. CPA, Miss. Acct. Ellis & Hirsberg, CPA's, Clarksdale, Miss., 1969-75; prin. W.L. Walters, CPA's, Clarksdale, 1975—. Founding dir. Found. for N.Am. Wild Sheep, Cody, Wyo., 1978-82; com. man U.S. Golf Assn., Far Hills, N.J., 1986—; panel mem. Golf Digest 100 Greatest Courses, 1985—; bd. dirs. Lula-Rich Ednl. Found., Clarksdale, 1995—. Mem. AICPA, Miss. Soc. CPAs, Clarksdale Country Club (pres. 1980, 85), Bulldog Club (bd. dirs. 1986—), Old Waverly Golf Club. Methodist. Home and Office: PO Box 896 Clarksdale MS 38614-0896

WALTHER, RICHARD ERNEST, psychology educator, library administrator; b. Des Moines, Nov. 12, 1921; s. Rudolph Herman and Ruth Viola (Leekley) W.; m. Viola Eugenia Godwin, May 4, 1951; children: Mark Edward, Diane Elaine. Student, U. Ill., 1941-42; BA, Tex. Christian U., 1949-50, MA, 1950-52; EdD, North Tex. State U., Denton, 1954-62. Cert. Lifetime Teaching Credentials, Tex. Supt. Dallas Juvenile Home, 1951-61; v.p. rsch and devel. U.S. Industries, Ednl., N.Y.C., 1961-69; pres. Walther & Assoc., Silver Springs, Md., 1969-72; dir. of libr. Ambassador U., Pasadena, Calif., 1972-90; dir., instl. rsch. Ambassador U., Big Sandy, Tex., 1990-92, assoc. dir. Coll. Libr., prof. psychology, 1992-96; prof. emeritus, 1996—; v.p. rsch. Humane Soc. of the U.S., Washington, 1968-70; tng. cons. Bell Telephone Labs., Piscataway, N.J., 1968-72. Author: Handling Behavior Problems, 1959. Mem. APA, Am. Ednl. Rsch. Assn. Home: PO Box 211332 Bedford TX 76095 Office: Ambassador University PO Box 111 Big Sandy TX 75755-0111

WALTMAN, LYNNE MARIE, medical illustrator; b. Lake Forest, Ill., July 4, 1952; d. John Dieffenbach and Marie Elizabeth (Dahl) Kleis; m. William DeWitt Waltman III, July 24, 1976; children: Katherine Marie, William DeWitt IV. BA, Va. Poly. Inst. and State U., 1974; MA in Biomed. Communications, U. Tex., Dallas, 1976; MBA, Okla. U., 1984. Cert. med. illustrator. Med. illustrator Maine Med. Ctr., Portland, 1976; freelance med. illustrator Dallas, 1976-78; sr. med. illustrator Tex. Coll. Osteo. Medicine, Ft. Worth, 1978-79; sr. med. illustrator support services, health edn. ARAMCO, Dhahran, Saudi Arabia, 1980-84; owner Med. Graphics, Ft. Worth, 1984—. Illustrator: Clinical Surgery, 1987, Pathological Basis of Disease, 1989, Saunders Basic Pathology, 5th edit., 1991; assoc. editor Jour. Biocommunication, 1985-88; producer of graphics 60 Second Housecall broadcast, 1987—. Sustaining mem. Jr. League; bd. dirs. Easter Seal Soc. Tarrant County, 1988-93; chair St. Cecelia's Guild, 1990—; mem. vestry All Saint's Episcopal Ch., 1994-97, jr. warden, 1996. Mem. Assn. Med. Illustrators, Ft. Worth Boat Club, Demonstrative Evidence Specialists Assn. Republican. Episcopalian.

WALTON, CAROLE LORRAINE, clinical social worker; b. Harrison, Ark., Oct. 20, 1949; d. Leo Woodrow Walton and Arlette Alegra (Cohen) Armstrong. BA, Lambuth Coll., Jackson, Tenn., 1971; MA, U. Chgo., 1974. Diplomate Clin. Social Work, Acad. Cert. Social Workers; bd. cert. diplomate; lic. clin. social worker. Social worker Community Mental Health, Flint, Mich., 1971-72; clin. social worker Community Mental Health, Westchester, Ill., 1974-76; dir. self-travel program Chgo. Assn. Retarded Citizens, 1973; coord. family svcs. Inner Harbors Psych. Hosp., Douglasville, Ga., 1976-83; sr. mental health clinician Northside Mental Health Ctr., Atlanta, 1983—. Mem. NASW, Ga. Soc. for Clin. Work (pres. 1981-82, pres. 1993-95). Office: Northside Mental Health Ctr 5825 Glenridge Dr NE Bldg 4 Atlanta GA 30328-5387

WALTON, CHESTER LEE, JR., management consultant; b. Annapolis, Md., Oct. 10, 1926; s. Chester Lee and Mildred Dolores (Farnen) W.; m. Doris Lange, Nov. 3, 1981; children by previous marriage: Bret Lee, Candace Susan Walton Poole, Gregory Tod; stepchildren: Charles Edward Lange III, Eric Stephen Lange. Maintenance engr. Pam Am. Petroleum and Transport Co., Texas City, Tex., 1948-51; rsch. engr. Babcock & Wilcox Co., Alliance, Ohio, 1953-54; sales engr. Bunting Brass & Bronze Co., Indpls., 1954-55; cons. McKinsey & Co., Inc., Chgo., London, 1955-60; prin. McKinsey & Co., Inc., London, N.Y.C., 1960-63, dir., mgr., Chgo., 1963-67, mng. dir., 1967-73, dir. Dallas, mgr. Tex. offices, 1973-84; ret., 1988; bd. dirs. Wingate Ptnrs. Mem. adv. bd. Dallas Symphony Assn., 1979-90; dir. Dallas Symphony Found., 1982-90; chmn. adv. coun. U. Tex., Dallas, 1976—, mem. centennial commn., 1982—, devel. bd., 1988—, chancellors coun. U. Tex. System, 1978—; trustee U. Dallas, 1992—; bd. dirs. The Family Place, 1988—; bd. vis. McDonald Obs., 1985—. With USNR, 1944-46; 1st lt. USAF, 1951-53. Recipient Nelle C. Johnston award U. Tex., Dallas, 1979. Republican. Lutheran. Office: 2200 Ross Ave Ste 5200 Dallas TX 75201-2794

WALTON, CONRAD GORDON, SR., architect; b. Houston, June 18, 1928; s. John Edward and Evelyn Lucille (Gordon) W.; BS (Walsh scholar), Rice U., 1951; postgrad. U. Houston, 1955; m. Rilda Ellen Akin, Dec. 10, 1954; children: Conrad Gordon, Jr., Evelyn Coleman, Roberta Agnes. Registered architect, Tex. Chief supt. Welton Becket & Assos., Houston, 1961-63; partner Alexander, Walton & Hatteberg, Houston, 1963-68; owner Conrad G. Walton, Houston, 1968-73, D.C.W. Architects, 1973; Realtor, 1982—; co-developer subdiv. Holiday Oaks, Lake Somerville, Tex., 1972—; registered fallout shelter analyst Def. Dept., 1966—. Pres. Woodrow Wilson Elem. PTO, Houston, 1969-70, Houston Great Books Council, 1976-77, Binglewood Civic Club, 1985-87; chmn. Troop 345, Roberts Sch., Boy Scouts Am., 1960-71; Republican precinct chmn., 1964-71; trustee Fair Haven United Meth. Ch., 1976-77. Served with AUS, 1952-54, Korea. Mem. AIA (treas. 1968), Tex. Soc. Architects, Optimist (pres. Greenway Pla. ch. 1990-91). Architect Blinn Coll. Gym renovation, 1993. Methodist. Home: 9014 Springview Ln Houston TX 77080-1755 Office: 2425 Fountain View Dr Ste 225 Houston TX 77057-4811

WALTON, DEWITT TALMAGE, JR., dentist; b. Macon, Ga., May 25, 1937; s. DeWitt T. Sr. and Jimmie (Braswell) W.; m. Joan Robinson, June 11, 1960; children: Jimmie Walton Paschall, Gwen N., Gayle N., Joy A. BS, Howard U., 1960, DDS, 1961. Pvt. practice Macon, 1963—; Chmn. dental adv. com. Ga. Dept. Med. Assistance; dental svcs. adv. com. Dept. Physical Health, Ga. Dept. Human Resources. Fin. chmn. Boy Scouts Am., Piedmont/Creek Dist., 1978-80, exec. bd., 1978-82, v.p. exec. com., 1983-84; apptd. Bibb County Bd. Edn., 1969-73; vice chmn. Macon-Bibb County Transit Authority, 1981-87; dir. exec. com. Devel. Corp. Mid. Ga., 1984-91; sec.-treas. Urban Devel. Authority, Macon-Bibb County, 1984-87; trustee Macon Heritage Found., 1983-87; bd. dirs. Ctrl. Ga. Speech and Hearing Ctr., 1984-87, Boys' Club Macon, Inc., 1986, 87, 88, The Grand Opera House, 1988, 89, 90, Booker T. Washington Ctr., 1993, Pub. Edn. Found., 1995—, Douglass Theater, 1995—; mem. oversight com. Minority Bus. Assistance Program, 1984-91; active Bibb County Commn. on Excellence in Edn., 1984; trustee United Way Macon-Bibb County, 1985, 86, 87; deacon, elder, treas. Washington Ave. Presbyn. Ch.; active Downtown Coun., Coalition for Polit. Awareness, So. Poverty Law Ctr., NAACP; mem. "Cmty. Hero"-torchbearer Olympic Torch Relay for 1996 Olympic games, Atlanta. With U.S. Army, 1961-63. Recipient Cert. of Appreciation State Bar of Ga., Citizenship award Bibb County Voter's Registration League, Inc., 1977, Community Svc. award NAACP, 1982, Community Svc. award Alpha Kappa Alpha Sorority, 1982, Meritorious Svc. award United Negro Co. Fund, 1983, Comml. Bldg. of Yr. award Macon Heritage Found., 1983, Faithful Svc. award Bibb County Dept. Family and Children's Svcs., 1983-90, citation Macon-Bibb County Beautification Clean Community Comm., 1983-84, Cert. appreciation Macon-Bibb County Econ. Opportunity Coun., 1984, Outstanding Svc. award So. Poverty Law Ctr., 1984, Proclamation Mayor George Israel Svc. on Macon-Bibb County Transit Authority, 1984, Outstanding Alumni award Coll. Dentistry Howard U., 1985, award for Outstanding Svc. Macon-Bibb County Urban Devel. Authority, 1987, award for Outstanding Svc. Macon-Bibb County Transit Authority, 1987, cert. Appreciation Close-Up Found., 1988, cert. Appreciation Ga. Dental Edn. Found., 1988, Community Svc. award United Way Macon-Bibb County, 1988, cert. Disting. Svc. Devel. Corp. Middle Ga., 1990, Continuous Corp. Support award Entrepreneurship and Black Youth Program U. Ga., 1990, cert. Recognition Outstanding Svc. So. Poverty Law Ctr., 1990, cert. Appreciation Keep Macon-Bibb Beautiful Commn. and Cherry Blossom Festival, 1990, James E. Carter award Ga. Dental Soc., 1993; named Olympic Torchbearer, 1996. Fellow Acad. Gen. Dentistry (Membership award 1983-85), Acad. Dentistry Internat., Am. Coll. Dentists, Ga. Dental Assn. (hon.), Internat. Coll. Dentists, Pierre Fauchard Acad.; mem. AAAS, ADA (alt. del. Ga. 1986-91), Am. Analgesic Soc., Am. Endodontic Soc., Am. Fund Dental Health, Am. Sch. Health Assn., Am. Soc. Dentistry for Children, Nat. Dental Assn., Nat. Rehab. Assn., Ga. Dental Soc. (pres., 1978, Citizenhip award 1979-80, Humanitarian award 1981-82, James E. Carter Jr. award 1993), North Ga. Dental Soc. (pres. 1978-79), Cen. Dist. Dental Soc. (peer rev. com., legis. com., alt. del. to Ga. Dental Assn. 1982, 83, 84, del. 1984, 85, 86, 87), Bibb County Dental Soc. (charter), Acad. Continuing Edn., Fed. Dentaire Internat. (life), Pres'. Club Howard U. (life), Am. Running and Fitness Assn. (life), Greater Macon C. of C. (bd. dirs. 1995—), Macon Tracks, Sigma Pi Phi, Omega Psi Phi (life). Presbyterian. Home: 2988 Malibu Dr Macon GA 31211-2609 Office: DeWitt T Walton Jr DDS 591 Cotton Ave Macon GA 31201-7504

WALTON, EDMUND LEWIS, JR., lawyer; b. Salisbury, Md., Sept. 4, 1936; s. Edmund Lewis and Iris Tull (White) W.; m. Barbara Post, Sept. 18, 1965; children: Southy E., Kristen P. BA, Coll. William and Mary, 1961, JD (Godwin scholar), 1963; postgrad. U. Md. 1957-59. Bar: Va. 1963, U.S. Dist. Ct. (ea. dist.) Va. 1964, U.S. Supreme Ct. 1971, U.S. Dist. Ct. (we. dist.) Va. 1972, U.S. Ct. Appeals (4th cir.) 1980, Grad. asst. Coll. William and Mary 1961-62; assoc. Simmonds, Coleburn, Towner & Carman, Arlington and Fairfax, Va., 1963-68, ptnr. 1968-74; ptnr. Putbrese and Walton, McLean, Va., 1975; mem. Edmund L. Walton, Jr., P.C., McLean, 1976-82, Walton and Adams, P.C., McLean, 1983—; judge pro tem Fairfax County Cir. Ct. 1977—, commr. in chancery, 1990—; legis. com. Va. State Bar 1974-76, 10th dist. com. 1975-78, bus. law sect. exec. com. 1983-88, sec. 1984-85, vice chmn. 1985-86, chmn. 1986-87. Bd. dirs. Home Run Acres Civic Assn. 1968-70, v.p. 1969-70; bd. dirs. McLean Citizens Assns. 1976-79, 1st v.p. 1977-78; bd. dirs., pres. Rocky Run Citizens Assn. 1973-74; bd. dirs. Langley Sch., Inc. 1975-77, treas. 1976-77; mem. Fairfax County Rep. Com. 1966-82, chmn. 1970-72; del. Rep. Nat. Conv. 1972; mem. Va. Rep. Cen. Com. 1974-77, exec. com. 1976-77; chmn. Providence Dist. Rep. Com. 1968-70; mem. 10th Congl. Dist. Rep. Com. 1970-77, vice chmn. 1974-76, chmn. 1976-77; mem. 8th Congl. Dist. Rep. Com. 1967-70; v.p. Arlington County Young Reps. 1965-66; counsel Arlington County Rep. Com. 1965-66; bd. dirs. McLean Planning Com. 1975-79, chmn. 1976-77; bd. dirs. McLean Office Square Condominium Assn. 1979-83, pres. 1979-82; chmn. Tysons Corner Citizens Task Force 1977-78; mem. Fairfax County Council on Arts; bd. dirs. Fairfax YMCA 1974-75; bd. dirs. Friends of Turkey Run Farm 1981—, counsel, 1981—, mem. exec. com. 1981-83. With U.S. Army 1956-59. Editor William and Mary Law Sch. Rev., 1961-63. Named McLean (Va.) Bus. Citizen of Yr., 1996. Fellow Am. Bar Found., Va. Law Found. (dir. 1991—, mem. com. on continuing legal edn. 1990-91, chmn. 1992-93); mem. ABA, Am. Law Inst., Va. Bar Assn. (spl. com. to study rules of ethics 1981-84, membership com. 1981-84, exec. com. 1982-88, chmn. 1984-85, pres. elect 1985-86, pres., 1986-87), Va. Continuing Legal Edn. Bd. (chmn. 1995—), Arlington County Bar Assn., Fairfax County Bar Assn. (cts. com. 1975-77, dir. 1976-77), McLean Bar Assn. (dir. 1978-79, 80-83, sec. 1978-79, pres. 1980-82), Va. Trial Lawyers Assn., Am. Judicature Soc., William and Mary Law Sch. Assn. (dir. 1970-76), Fairfax County C. of C. (dir. ex officio 1981-83), McLean C. of C. (bd. dirs. 1995-96), McLean Bus. and Profl. Assn. (dir. 1976-85, 89-90, pres. 1981-83), Washington Golf and Country Club, Melrose Club, Lowes Island Club, Phi Alpha Delta. Episcopalian. Home: 914 Peacock Station Rd Mc Lean VA 22102-1021 Office: 6862 Elm St Ste 400 PO Drawer EE Mc Lean VA 22101

WALTON, G. CLIFFORD, family practice physician; b. Richmond, Va., Jan. 5, 1968; s. Eugene Marion and Mary Ann (McNabb) W. BS summa cum laude, Hampden-Sydney Coll., 1990; MD, Med. Coll. Va., 1994. Intern Med. Coll. Va., Richmond, 1994-95; resident Blackstone (Va.) Family Practice, 1995—; physician Patient First, Richmond, 1996—; med. examiner Va. Dept. Health, Richmond, 1996—; housestaff coun. Med. Coll. Va., 1995—. Sci. fair judge Southside Va. H.S., Farmville, 1988—. Mem. AMA, Am. Acad. Family Physicians, Med. Soc. Va., Phi Beta Kappa, Omicron Delta Kappa, Sigma Xi. Baptist. Home: 1618 Cedar Ln Powhatan VA 23139 Office: Blackstone Family Practice 820 S Main St Blackstone VA 23824

WALTON, HARRY A., JR., retired dairy manager; b. Covington, Va., Sept. 24, 1918; s. Harry A. and Madeline Lillian (Gaylor) W.; m. Virginia Robinson, May 4, 1942; children: Harriet Ann, Jeannie Marie, Bonita Carol, Mary Allyn, Dawn Elizabeth. Student, U. Va., 1937, Columbia U., 1939; BS, Lynchburg (Va.) Coll., 1939. Analytical chemist Indsl. Rayon Corp., Covington, Va., 1940-42; mgr. White Oak Dairy, Covington, 1945-80. Author: (catalogs) Exhibits at Lynchburg Coll., Coll. of William and Mary, Trinity Coll., Norfolk Mus., 1968-93; compiler selective index documents of Allegheny County, 1822-90. Chmn., mem. 5th Planning Dist., Roanoke, Va., 1960—, Alleghany Bd. of Suprs., Alleghany County, Val, 1962-86, Alleghany Sch. Bd., 1948-62; founder, pres., mem. Alleghany Assn. Retarded Citizens, 1948-96; fellow Pierpont Morgan Libr., N.Y.C., 1968-86; charter mem. Boiling Spring Ruritan, 1950—. With USAF, 1942-45, ETO. Mem. Holstein-Friesian Assn., U. Va. Bibliographic Soc. Home: White Oak Dairy Drawer 790 Covington VA 24426

WALTON, JOHN WAYNE, lawyer; b. Kingsport, Tenn., May 3, 1947; s. Willard J. and Katherine H. (Syrad) W.; m. Anna Marie Laws, Oct. 24, 1969; children: Natasha Lee, John Adam. BS, East Tenn. State U., 1970; JD, Memphis State U., 1975. Bar: Tenn. 1976, U.S. Dist. Ct. (ea. dist.) Tenn. 1977. Assoc. Dan M. Laws, Jr., Elizabethton, Tenn., 1976-80; ptnr. Laws & Walton P.C., Elizabethton, 1980—. City atty. City of Elizabethton, 1982—. Served to capt. U.S. Army, 1970-72. Mem. ABA., Tenn. Bar Assn.,

Carter County Bar Assn. (pres. 1978), Tenn. Mcpl. Attys. Assn. Baptist. Lodge: Rotary (bd. dirs. Elizabethton club 1978).

WALTON, RODNEY EARL, lawyer; b. Corvallis, Oreg., Apr. 28, 1947; s. Ray Daniel Jr. and Carolyn Jane (Smith) W. BA, Coll. of Wooster, 1969; JD, Cornell U., 1976. Bar: Fla. 1976, U.S. Dist. Ct. (so. dist.) Fla. 1976, U.S. Dist. Ct. (mid. dist.) Fla. 1977, U.S. Supreme Ct. 1980, U.S. Ct. Appeals (11th cir.) 1981. Assoc. to jr. ptnr. Smathers & Thompson, Miami, Fla., 1976-87; ptnr. Kelley, Drye and Warren, Miami, 1987-93; atty. Heinrich Gordon Hargrove Weihe & James, P.A., Ft. Lauderdale, 1994—. Sec. bd. dirs. Kings Creek Condominium Assn., Miami, 1984-89, treas., 1984, pres., 1990-91. 1st lt. U.S. Army, 1969-73, Vietnam. Decorated Bronze Star. Mem. ABA, Fla. Bar, Broward County Bar Assn., Maritime Law Assn. Republican. Methodist. Home: 2331 NW 33rd St Apt 301 Fort Lauderdale FL 33309-6444 Office: Heinrich Gordon PA 500 E Broward Blvd Ste 1000 Fort Lauderdale FL 33394-3002

WALTON, RONALD ELWOOD, retired school superintendent; b. Elkhart, Ind., Mar. 5, 1932; s. Marvin Glenn and Faye (Beisel) W.; m. Bernita Jo Yunker, June 3, 1956; 1 child, Ronald Yunker. BS, Manchester Coll., 1953; MS, Ind. U., 1958, EdD, 1962. Vocal and instrumental music and speech tchr. Berne (Ind.)-French Twp. Schs., 1953-56; instrumental music tchr. John Adams High Sch., South Bend, Ind., 1956-58; supervising prin. Galveston (Ind.) Sch., 1958-60; adminstrv. asst. MSD of Pery Twp., Indpls., 1962-63; supt. of Schs. Southeastern Sch. Corp., Cass County, Ind., 1963-64, Jeffersonville (Ind.) City Schs., 1964-66, Monroe County Com. Schs., Bloomington, Ind., 1966-84, Fayette County Pub. Schs., Lexington, Ky., 1984-94; ret., 1994; bd. dirs. Ky. Coun. of Econ. Edn., Louisville, Bluegrass Chpt. Goodwill Industries, Jr. Achievement Bluegrass Inc., Friends of Music-Univ. Ky. Contbr. articles to profl. jours. Recipient Sch. Adminstr. award Kennedy Ctr./Alliance for Arts, 1988, Sch. Adminstr. Yr. award Ky. Assn. of Ednl. Office Pers., 1989, Top 100 Exec. Educators award The Exec. Educator, 1987, 93, Roundtable Educator award George Peabody coll. 1987, Ky. Assn. Sch. Supt. of Yr. award, 1990-91, Nat. Art Edn. Assn. Disting. Svc. award, 1990-91. Mem. Am. Assn. Sch. Adminstrs. (adv. coun. 1986-89, chmn. and suburban supt. planning com. 1986-89), Nat. Acad. Sch. Exec. (bd. dirs. 1989-92), Mid-Am. Assn. Sch. Supt., Network U. Com. Sch. Dist., Ky. Assn. Sch. Adminstrs. (conf. planning com. 1989-90), Ky. Assn. Sch. Supts. (bd. dirs. 1984-94, sec. treas. 1989-90, pres. 1990-91), Ky. Ednl. Leadership Inst. (bd. dirs. 1985-94), Ky. Congress of PTA (Supt. of Yr. award 1988), Cen. Ky. Assn. Sch. Supt., Nat. Assn. Ednl. Office Pers. (Adminstr. of Yr. 1990), Greater Lexington C. of C., Lexington Rotary. Republican. Methodist.

WALTON, SUZANNE MARIE CHAPMAN, clinical pharmacist, educator; b. Plattsburgh, N.Y., July 31, 1965; d. Robert Frank and Mary Louise (Gamble) Chapman; married. BS in Pharmacy, Albany Coll. Pharmacy, 1988; PharmD, Med. Coll. Va., 1991. Lic. pharmacist, N.Y., R.I., Ohio, W.Va.; cert. pharmacotherapy specialist. Pharmacy intern Champlain Valley Physicians' Hosp., Plattsburgh, 1986, 87; pharmacy extern Fay's Drugs, Plattsburgh, 1988, Health Scis. Ctr. SUNY, Syracuse, 1988; Am. Soc. Hosp. Pharmacists resident in hosp. pharmacy R.I. Hosp., Providence, 1989; staff pharmacist VA Med. Ctr., Richmond, Va., 1989-91; Am. Soc. Hosp. Pharmacists resident in oncology splty. U. Cin. Hosp., 1992; oncology clin. pharmacist specialist Charleston (W.Va.) Area Med. Ctr., 1992—; preceptor for baccalaureate pharmacy students, tchr. oncology case conf. Med. Coll. Va., 1991; adj. instr. clin. pharmacy U. Cin., 1991-92; clin. asst. prof. Coll. Pharmacy W.Va. U., 1992—; chmn. oncology collaborative practice group Charleston Area Med. Ctr., 1994, mem. cancer com., 1992—; presenter Gt. Lakes Pharmacy Resident Conf., Chgo., 1992, many ednl. instns. and med. facility orgn. confs., mtgs. and seminars, 1989—. Participant Do the Charleston Health Fair, 3d Ann. Children's Classic Golf Tournament, Charleston Area Med. Ctr. Cancer Ctr., 1993, Am. Cancer Soc.'s Relay for Life, 1994; active Speakers Bur., Kanawha Hospice Care. Recipient George B. Ceresia award Am. Chem. Soc., 1987, Roche Pharmacy Comm. award, 1988, Ohio Soc. Hosp. Pharmacists/Upjohn Clin. Pharmacy Rsch. award, 1993. Mem. Am. Soc. Hosp. Pharmacists (oncology preceptor accredited residency in pharmacy practice 1993—, mem. ad hoc com. on off label uses oncology splty. practice group 1992), Am. Soc. Clin. Oncology, Am. Coll. Clin. Pharmacy, W.Va. Soc Hosp. Pharmacists (mem. manpower and edn. com. 1992—), Rho Chi. Office: Charleston Area Med Ctr Dept Pharmacy & Drug Info 3200 Maccorkle Ave SE Charleston WV 25304-1200

WALTON, WILLARD FRED, principal; b. Dec. 8, 1942; s. Willard Jennings and Katherine (Syard) W.; m. Anita Urceal Buck, Aug. 1, 1970; children: Jason Frederick, Lindsay Michelle. AA, Lees-McRae Jr. Coll., 1966; BS, East Tenn. State U., 1968, MS, 1986. Tchr., coach Wise (Va.) County Sch. System, 1968-69; tchr., coach Kingsport (Tenn.) City Schs., 1969-85, prin., 1985—; pres. Mum. Employees Credit Union, Kingsport, 1989—; dir. N.E. Tenn. Prep Tech Bd., Grey, Tenn., 1996. Mem. Lions Club, Moose. Baptist. Home: 1024 Starling Dr Kingsport TN 37660 Office: Kingsport City Schs 1800 Legion Dr Kingsport TN 37664-2658

WALTON, WILLIAM ROBERT, academic administrator; b. Macon, Ga., Aug. 28, 1949; s. Swift Jessie and LouVenia Mattie (Helms) W.; m. Cynthia Bonell Pollock, Dec. 14, 1969; children: David Anthony, Kelly Melissa. Student, Marsh-Draughon Bus. Coll., 1968; BBA, Ga. State U., 1972, M Pub. Adminstrn., 1977. Acct. K.L. Kemp, Atlanta, 1968-72, Berman Mills & Co., Atlanta, 1972; internal auditor U. Ga. System, Atlanta, 1972-74, asst. dir. budgets, 1974-78; dir. bus. and fin. Ft. Valley (Ga.) State Coll., 1978-82; v.p. bus. affairs Roanoke Coll., Salem, Va., 1982-92; adminstr. Joseph W. Jones Ecol. Rsch. Ctr., Newton, Ga., 1992—; treas. bd. trustees Roanoke Coll, Salem, 1983-92; trustee June Cheelsman Unitrust, Salem, 1984-92, Lois C. Fisher Unitrust, Salem, 1984-92, Harold W. Harris Unitrust, Salem, 1983-92, James W. Sieg Annuity Trust, Salem, 1984-92, T.B. & R.E. Meador Annuity Trust, Salem, 1985-92, Pendleton Hogan Unitrust, Salem, 1989-92, Francis T. West Annuity Trust, Salem, 1988-92. Pres. West Salem PTA, 1985-87; bd. dirs. Am. Lung Assn. Va., 1991-93; bd. dirs., treas. Albany Area Primary Health Care, 1993—; commr. Albany-Dougherty County County. Commn., 1993—; vestryman St. Patrick's Episcopal Ch. Mem. Nat. Assn. Coll. and Univ. Bus. Officers, Nat. Coun. Rsch. Adminstrs., Luth. Coll. Bus. Officers, Coll. and Univ. Pers. Assn., Assn. Phys. Plant Adminstrs., Salem-Roanoke County C. of C., Rotary Internat. (bd. dirs. Salem 1985-89, pres. 1987-88), South Ga. C. of C. (bd. dirs.), Albany C. of C., Rotary. Home: 2718 Somerset Dr Albany GA 31707-9127 Office: Joseph W Jones Ecol Rsch Ce Newton GA 31770

WALTRIP, BURROUGHS ALLEN, dance band leader, retired navy officer; b. Seguin, Tex., May 27, 1928; s. Burroughs Allen and Jessie Anna Belle (Johnson) W.; m. Joyce Renneberg, Aug. 30, 1975 (dec. June 1989); children: Cynthia Kay, Jeffrey Lee, Bambi Lynn, Carla Christine, Keely Ann, Lisa Evelyn, Burroughs Allen III m. Mary Frances Graham, Feb. 13, 1990. BJ, U. Tex., 1977. Instrumentalist USN Unit Bands, 1945-53; biologist's asst. Tex. Game & Fish Commn., Mathis, 1953-54; comml. diver Gulf Coast Divers Co., Corpus Christi, Tex., 1953; yard clk. T&NO RR, Austin, Tex., 1954-56; instrumentalist USN Unit Bands, 1956-60, band leader, 1960-65, band officer, 1966-72; exec. officer Navy Sch. Music, Little Creek, Va., 1972-74; comm. coord. Grumman Am., Savannah, Ga., 1977-80; leader own band B.A. Waltrip Big Band, Buffalo Gap, Tex., 1990—. Contbr. articles to publs. Instrumentalist, arranger Abilene (Tex.) Community Band, 1982—. Lt. USN, 1945-74, PTO, ATO, MTO. Mem. Tex. Music Educators Assn., Internat. Trumpet Guild, Tex. Bandmasters Assn., Dallas-Ft. Worth Profl. Musicians Assn., Ret. Officers Assn., VFW (life), Silver Wings (life), Mensa, Kappa Tau Alpha. Home and office: B A Waltrip Big Band PO Box 370 Buffalo Gap TX 79508-0370

WALTRIP, ROBERT L., environmentalist; b. Austin, TX, 1931. BBA in Mgmt., U. Houston, 1954. With Heights Funeral Home, 1954-62; founder, chmn. bd. dirs., chief exec. officer Service Corp. Internat., Houston, 1962—; founder, chmn. bd. dirs. Waltrip Enterprises Inc., Houston, 1982—; with Tanknology Corp. Internat., Houston, 1988—, Tanknology Environ. Inc., Houston, 1989—. Office: Service Corp International 1929 Allen Pky Houston TX 77019-2507 Office: Tanknology Environ Inc 5225 Hollister St Houston TX 77040-6205*

WALZER, PHILIP SAMUEL, journalist; b. N.Y.C., May 14, 1960; s. Alexander and Belle Esther (Rosner) W.; m. Mary Ann Green, Oct. 18, 1987; children: Jacob, Benjamin. BA, Princeton U., 1981. Copy editor, book editor, Sunday book columnist Buffalo (N.Y.) Courier-Express, 1981-82; copy editor Am. Banker/Bond Buyer, N.Y.C., 1983-84, Phila. Inquirer, 1984-88; education writer Virginian-Pilot, Norfolk, Va., 1988—; panelist, spkr. in field. Mem. Congregation Beth El, Norfolk, Va., 1989—. Fellowship in Higher Edn. Knight Ctr. Specialized Journalism U. Md., 1993; recipient Award for Excellence in Coverage of Higher Edn. AAUP, 1995, Third Place Enterprise Reporting award Nat. Assn. Blacck Journalists, 1996, Second Place News Series award Va. Press Assn., 1995. Mem. Edn. Writers Assn. (panelist, spkr.), Investigative Reporters and Editors. Jewish. Office: Virginian-Pilot 4565 Virginia Beach Blvd Virginia Beach VA 23462

WAMP, ZACH P., congressman; b. Ft. Benning, Ga., Oct. 28, 1957; m. Kim Wamp; 2 children. Student, U. N.C., U. Tenn. Chmn. Hamilton County Rep. Party, 1987; regional dir. Tenn. Rep. Party, 1989; v.p. Charter Real Estate Corp., 1989-92; real estate broker Fletcher Bright Co., 1992-94; mem. 104th Congress from 3d Tenn. dist., 1995—. Office: US House Reps 423 Cannon House Office Bldg Washington DC 20515-4203

WAMPLER, ANDREW TODD, English language educator; b. Bristol, Tenn., Apr. 4, 1973; s. Donald Edward and Sharon Anne (Baines) W.; m. Jennifer Leigh Douglas, June 3, 1995. BA summa cum laude with honors, Presbyn. Coll., Clinton, S.C., 1995; postgrad., U. Tenn., 1995—. Lab. asst. Presbyn. Coll., 1993-95; grad. tchg. asst. English dept. U. Tenn., Knoxville, 1995-96, grad. tchg. assoc., 1996—. Poetry pub. in New river Free Press Lit. Supplement. Coord. Laurens County Soup Kitchen, Laurens, S.C., 1993-95. John C. Hodges fellow U. Tenn., 1995-96. Mem. MLA, South Atlantic MLA, Sigma Delta Tau, Omicron Delta Kappa. Presbyterian. Home: Apt T-11 3700 Sutherland Ave Knoxville TN 37919 Office: U Tenn Dept English Knoxville TN 37996

WANENMACHER, KATHLEEN MURPHY, executive producer; b. Danville, Ky., Apr. 3, 1944; d. Dudley C. Sr. and Gladys (Royce) Murphy; married; children from previous marriage: Robert C. King II, Lydia Marie King. BA, U. Tulsa, 1966; MS, Okla. State U., 1989. Chief exec. officer Data Share, Oklahoma City, 1982-83; exec. adminstr. Whole World Family Pub., Tulsa, 1983-84; supr. media ctr. Coll. of Edn. Okla. State U., Stillwater, 1986-92; exec. producer Wanenmacher Prodns., Inc., Tulsa, 1991—; mgmt. cons. cablecast of Homecoming Parade, Stillwater, 1988; curriculum design cons. Applied Bus. Telecomm., San Ramon, Calif., 1990. Writer, producer, dir. (video) Tough Love, 1986, (radio documentary) What Future the Past, 1987; producer, co-dir. (radio dramas) A Turkey's Tale, 1988, The Most Valuable Gifts, 1989; author: (manual) Cablecasting the Homecoming Parade at Okla. State U., 1989, (children's book) The Bedtime Book of the Lion and the Little Lark, 1996. Mem. Women in Comm., Internat. TV Assn. Republican. Episcopalian. Office: Wanenmacher Prodns Inc 5110 S Yale #414 Tulsa OK 74135

WANG, FRANK YU-HENG, publishing executive, mathematician, consultant; b. Boston, Sept. 6, 1964; s. Leon Ru-Liang and Joyce Chieh-Chun (Tien) W.; m. Judy Yu-Hsin Tsao, May 30, 1992. AB, Princeton U., 1986; PhD, MIT, 1991. V.p. Saxon Pubs., Norman, Okla., 1991-92; exec. v.p. Saxon Pubs., Norman, 1992-93, pres., 1994—; guest lectr. numerous schs., 1992—. Co-author: (textbook) Calculus, 1988. Grad. fellow NSF, 1986. Mem. Am. Math. Soc. Office: Saxon Publishers 1320 W Lindsey St Norman OK 73069-4319

WANG, JIE, computer science educator; b. Guangzhou, China, Aug. 28, 1961; s. Yeu-Yun and Lian-Fang (Hu) W.; m. Helen Hong Zhao, Dec. 26, 1986; 1 child, Jesse. BS, Zhongshan U., Guangzhou, 1982, ME, 1984; PhD, Boston U., 1990. Asst. prof. Wilkes U., Wikles-Barre, Pa., 1990-93, U. N.C., Greensboro, 1993—. Contbr. articles to profl. confs.; referee jours. Boston U. Presdl. fellow 1989-90; grantee NSF, 1991—. Mem. IEEE Computer Soc., Assn. Computing Machinery (spl. internest group on algorithsm and computation theory 1988—), European Assn. Theoretical Computer Sci. Office: U NC Dept Math Scis Greensboro NC 27412

WANG, JINGSONG, immunologist; b. Xiyang, Jiangsu, China, Apr. 29, 1964; came to U.S., 1991; . Kai-Cheng and Xiu-Hua (Yu) W. MD, Xuzhou Med. Coll., Jiangsu, 1986; MMS, Bethune U. Med. Scis., Changchun, Jilin, China, 1989. Intern Xuzhou Med. Coll. Hosp., 1985; resident Zuzhou Med. Coll. Hosp.; grad. student trainee dept. microbiology and immunology Bethune U. Med. Scis., 1986-88; rsch. fellow dept. biochemistry and molecular biology Peking Union Med. Coll. and Chinese Acad. Med. Sci.; instr. dept. pharmacology NYU Med. Ctr., N.Y.C., 1990-91; postdoctoral rsch. assoc. U. N.C., Chapel Hill, 1991—. Contbr. articles to profl. jours. Recipient Achievement award Ministry Pub. Health, Beijing, China, 1991; postdoctoral fellow Arthritis Found., Atlanta, 1993. Office: U NC CB7280 3330 Thurston Chapel Hill NC 27599

WANG, LIANG-GUO, research scientist; b. Foochow, People's Republic of China, Apr. 23, 1945; parents Chi-hsi Wang and Yunqing Chen; m. Shu-fen Zhang, Sept. 27, 1977; children: Zhijing, Zhijian. BS in Physics, Peking U., Beijing, 1969; MS in Physics, Ohio State U., 1983, PhD in Physics, 1986. Tech. mgr. and electronics engr. various cos., People's Republic of China, 1971-78; rsch. asst. Inst. of Academia Sinica, Beijing, 1978-80, U. Ky., Lexington, 1981, Ohio State U., Columbus, 1981-86, U. Va., Charlottesville, 1987-89; rsch. scientist Coll. of William and Mary, Williamsburg, Va., 1989—; cons. NASA Langley Rsch. Ctr., Hampton, Va., 1989—. Contbr. articles to profl. jours. Recipient Pub. Svc. medal NASA, 1992. Mem. Am. Phys. Soc., Am. Geophys. Union, Optical Soc. Am., Internat. Soc. for Optical Enging, Photonics Soc. of Chinese-Ams. Home: 4 Poulas Ct Hampton VA 23669-1863 Office: NASA Langley Rsch Ctr M S #472 Hampton VA 23665 Office: NASA Langley Rsch Ctr M S #472 Hampton VA 23665

WANG, PAUL WEILY, materials science and physics educator; b. Kao-Hsiung, Taiwan, Republic of China, Nov. 4, 1951; came to U.S., 1979; s. Yao Wen Wang and Yue Hua Lo; m. Diana Chung-Chung Chow, June 9, 1979; children: Agnes J., Carol H., Alfred Z. PhD, SUNY, Albany, 1986. Rsch. asst. prof. Vanderbilt U., Nashville, 1986-90; asst. prof. U. Tex., El Paso, 1990-96, assoc. prof., 1996—; hon. prof. Dalian Inst. Light Industry, 1995—; cons. EOTec Inc., 1987-88, Midtex Comm. Instruments Inc., 1996—. Contbr. articles to Jour. Applied Physics, Nuclear Instru. and Math., Springer Series in Surface Scis., Applied Surface Sci., Applied Optics, Jour. of Am. Ceramic Soc., Jour. Materials Sci., Jour. Luminescence, Jour. Non-cyrs. Solids, Lasers, Thin Solid Films. Fellow Inst. for Study of Defects in Solids; mem. Am. Ceramic Soc., Am. Phys. Soc., Materials Rsch. Soc., Am. Vacuum Soc. Home: 6890 Orizaba Ave El Paso TX 79912-2324 Office: U Tex Dept Physics and Materials Rsch El Paso TX 79968

WANG, PETER ZHENMING, physicist; b. Quanzhou, Fujian, People's Republic of China, Nov. 30, 1940; came to U.S., 1983; s. Guohua and Shunhua (Chen) W.; m. Grace Ruhui Xu, Mar. 14, 1967; children: Yili, Yile. MS, Qinghua U., Peking, People's Republic of China, 1964; postgrad., U. Tex., Dallas, 1983-84. Sr. engr. Particle Accelerator Inst., Shanghai, 1964-83; electronic engr. Benchmark Media Systems, Inc., Syracuse, N.Y., 1984-87; project engr. McGaw Inc., Carrollton, Tex., 1988—; physicist High Energy Physics Inst., Peking, 1978-79. Co-author: (book) Vacuum World, 1984. Tchr. Bible study, Plano, Tex., 1990. Baptist. Home: 1510 Chesterfield Dr Carrollton TX 75007-2847 Office: McGaw Inc 1601 Wallace St Carrollton TX 75006-6652

WANG, TONG, mechanical engineer, senior research scientist; b. Shanghai, China, July 17, 1937; came to U.S., 1982; s. Zao Xiang and Fanyian (Chen) W.; m. Yueying Qi, 1967; 1 child, Lifeng. BS, Beijing U., 1962; PhD, Rice U., 1985. Rsch. engr. Beijing Rsch. Inst., 1962-82; rsch. assoc. Rice U., Houston, 1982-85, sr. rsch. assoc., 1985-87, sr. rsch. scientist, 1987—. Recipient O. Hugo Schuck award Am. Automatic Control Coun., 1988. Fellow AIAA (assoc.). Office: Rice U Dept Mech Engring 6100 Main St Houston TX 77005-1827

WANG, YANG, science researcher; b. Yangzhou, Jiangsu, China, Dec. 5, 1961; came to U.S., 1986; s. Yun Ye and Yaotong Wang; m. Rose Sihong, May 1, 1988; 1 child, Albert Miao. BS, U. Sci. and Tech. China, Hefei, 1982; ME, Chinese Acad. Scis., Beijing, 1985; PhD, Fla. Atlantic U., 1993. Rsch. asst. Inst. Electronics Chinese Acad. Scis., 1985-86; teaching asst. Fla. Atlantic U., Boca Raton, 1986-89, rsch. asst., 1989-93; postdoctoral rschr. Oak Ridge (Tenn.) Nat. Lab., 1993—. Contbr. articles to profl. jours. Newell fellow, 1989, 90. Mem. Am. Phys. Soc., Am. Soc. Materials, Orgn. Chinese Am., East Tenn. Chinese Assn. (pres. 1993—).

WANGBERG, LOUIS M., academic administrator. B in Geography, U. N.D., 1963, M in Geography, 1964, D in Sch. Adminstrn. and Mgmt., 1970. Tchr., asst. prin. Granite Falls (Minn.) H.S., 1964-66; prin. Cosmos (Minn.) H.S., 1966-68; grad. tchg. asst. U. N.D., Grand Forks, 1968-69; adminstrv. asst. to supt. Grand Forks Pub. Schs., 1969-70; asst. supt. Worthington (Minn.) Pub. Schs., 1970-72; supt. Bemidji (Minn.) Pub. Schs., 1972-79; lt. gov. State of Minn., 1979-83; v.p., gen. mgr. Jostens Corp., Mpls., 1983-85; chmn., pres., CEO Bus., Industry Tng. Sys., Jacksonville, Fla., 1985—, Flagler Career Insts., Jacksonville, St. Augustine, Ft. Lauderdale and Miami, 1985—; speaker, cons. We, Inc., Waynesville, N.C., 1985—; adj. prof. Bemidji State U., 1974-81; vice chair Nat. Conf. Lt. Govs., 1981, 82, human resources com., 1979-83; mem. accrediting commn. Career Schs. and Colls. of Tech.; mem. com. Allied Health Edn. and Accreditation, AMA; cons. Jr. Achievement. Pres. Mt. Valley Estates Assn.; past bd. dirs. Fla. Speakers Assn.; founder Sigma Nu Epsilon Kappa Ednl. Found. Bd.; bd. trustees So. Ohio Coll., 1983-85, Watterson Coll., 1983-85; mem. Minn. Youth in Govt. Bd., 1979-85, Minn. Bus. Found. Excellence in Edn., 1981-86, Minn. State Retirement Bd., 1979-83, Duke U. Forum on the Presidency, 1981, Citizens League; chair Capitol Area Archtl. and Planning Bd., 1979-83, vice chair exec. coun., 1979-83; advisor/spokesperson Lions Internat. Hearing Ctr. Recipient Wall St. Jour. fellowship, Honor award Epsilon Kappa chpt., Sigma Nu, Terrance Quirke award Sigma Nu, Outstanding Vol. Leadership Congl. award U.S. Congress, Excellence award Ventures for Excellence, Disting. Svc. award Vocat. Tech. Divsn., Minn. Dept. Edn., Disting. Svc. award In Plant Printing Mgmt. Assn.; named hon. chair Minn. D Day, 1981, Multiple Sclerosis Read-a-Thon, 1981, hon. Am. farmer Nat. Future Farmers Am., hon. citizen Medford, Minn., hon. Turkey King, Worthington, Minn. Mem. Minn. Assn. Sch. Adminstrs. (emeritus), Career Coll. Assn. (bd. dirs.), Fla. Assn. Postsecondary Schs. and Colls., Parent Tchr. Student Assn. (hon. lifetime), Norman County Hist. Soc. (hon. lifetime), Minn. State Hist. Soc., Norwegian Am. Hist. Soc., Shriners (past master), Masons (past grand orator), Grand Lodge Minn., Rotary Internat., Elks, Sons of Norway, Phi Delta Kappa, Kappa Delta Pi. Home: 125 Mount Valley Rd Waynesville NC 28786-8637

WANI, MANSUKHLAL CHHAGANLAL, chemist; b. Nandurbar, Maharastra, India, Feb. 20, 1925; came to U.S., 1958, naturalized, 1977; s. Chhagnalal Kikabhai and Maniben Chhanganlal (Shah) W.; m. Ramila Mansukhlal Dalal, Dec. 4, 1954; 1 child, Bankim M. BS with honors, St. Xavier's Coll., Bombay U., 1947, MS, 1950; PhD, Ind. U., 1962. Lectr. chemistry Bhavan's Coll., Bombay, 1951-58; rsch. asst. Ind. U., Bloomington, 1958-61; rsch. assoc. U. Wis., Madison, 1961-62; prin. scientist Rsch. Triangle Inst., Rsch. Triangle Park, N.C., 1962—. Inventor anticancer drugs. Recipient B.F. Cain Meml. award Am. Assn. Cancer Rsch., 1994, City of Medicine award Durham, N.C., 1994, Award of Recognition Nat. Cancer Inst., 1996. Mem. AAAS, Am. Chem. Soc., Am. Soc. Pharmacognosy, N.Y. Acad. Scis., India Assn. 9pres. 1970-72), Hindu Soc. (dir. 1976-81), Assn. Indians in Am., Indo-Am. Forum, Sigma Xi, Phi Lambda Upsilon. Democrat. Home: 2801 Legion Ave Durham NC 27707-1921 Office: Rsch Triangle Inst 3040 W Cornwallis Rd Research Triangle Park NC 27709-2194

WANTLING, BRIAN DOUGLAS, county official, data processor; b. Columbus, Ohio, Apr. 16, 1942; s. George Kenneth Dale and Leola Mary (Ross) W.; m. Bonnie Darlene Wiener, Aug. 9, 1963; children: Wendy Denise, Brian Keith, Melissa Lynn. BS in Econs., U. Tenn., 1964. Systems analyst UNIVAC Corp., Richmond, Va., 1965-66; systems and programming mgr. Med. Data Svcs., Richmond, 1966-68; sr. systems analyst Sperry UNIVAC Corp., Richmond, 1968-72, systems analyst mgr., 1972-77; dir. data processing Henrico County, Richmond, 1977—; mem. local govt. adv. com. Va. Coun. on Info. Mgmt., Richmond, 1993—. Pres. Shipwatch Villas Homeowners Assn., Sneads Ferry, N.C., 1987—; treas. Queenspark Civic Assn., Midlothian, Va., 1989. Recipient numerous awards Nat. Assn. Counties, 1987-96, Innovation in Info. Mgmt. award City and Tech New-spaper, 1991. Fellow Unisys Info. and Tech. Exch.; mem. Va. Local Govt. Info. Tech. Execs. Republican. Home: 2501 Castle Hill Rd Midlothian VA 23113-1145

WAPLES, DAVID LLOYD, athletic director; b. Columbus, Ohio, Nov. 14, 1941; s. Melvin D. and Bonnie (Rankin) W.; m. Mary J. King, Dec. 8. 1990; 1 child, Jennifer. BA, West Liberty State Coll., 1963; MEd, Temple U, 1964; EdD, W.Va. U., 1972. Grad. asst. Temple U., Phila., 1963-64; coach/instr. U. N.Mex., Albuquerque, 1964-66, Pleasant View High Sch., Grove City, Ohio, 1966-67, West Liberty (W.Va.) State Coll., 1967-69, W.Va. U., Morgantown, 1969-71; instr. Jacksonville (Ala.) State U., 1971-72; coach/instr. Valdosta (Ga.) State Univ., 1972-83; commr. Gulf Star Conf., Lake Charles, La., 1984-87; athletic dir. Kennesaw State U., Marietta, Ga., 1987—. Recipient W.Va. Baseball Coach-of-the-Yr. award W.Va. Sports Writers, 1969, Region Cross Country Coach-of-the-Yr. award NCAA Div. II Cross Country Coaches Assn., 1976, 77, 78. Office: Kennesaw State Coll PO Box 444 Marietta GA 30061-0444

WARBURTON, RALPH JOSEPH, architect, engineer, planner, educator; b. Kansas City, Mo., Sept. 5, 1935; s. Ralph Gray and Emma Frieda (Niemann) W.; m. Carol Ruth Hychka, June 14, 1958; children: John Geoffrey, Joy Frances W. Tracey. B.Arch., MIT, 1958; M.Arch., Yale U., 1959, M.C.P., 1960. Registered architect, Colo., Conn., Fla., Ill., La., Md., N.J., N.Y., Va., D.C.; registered profl. engr., Conn., Fla., N.J., N.Y.; registered cmty. planner, Mich., N.J.; licensed interior designer, Fla. With various archtl. planning and engring. firms Kansas City, Mo., 1952-55, Boston, 1956-58, N.Y.C., 1959-62, Chgo., 1962-64; chief planning Skidmore, Owings & Merrill, Chgo., 1964-66; spl. asst. for urban design HUD, Washington, 1966-72, cons., 1972-77; prof. architecture, archtl. engring. and planning U. Miami, Coral Gables, Fla., 1972—, chmn. dept. architecture, archtl. engring. and planning, 1972-75, assoc. dean engring. and environ. design, 1973-74; dir. grad. urban and regional planning program, 1973-75, 81,, 87-93; advisor govt. Iran, 1970; advisor govt. France, 1973, govt. Ecuador, 1974, govt. Saudi Arabia, 1985; cons. in field, 1972—, lectr., critic design juror in field, 1965—; mem./chmn. Coral Gables Bd. Archs., 1980-82. Assoc. author: Man-Made America: Chaos or Control, 1963; editor: New Concepts in Urban Transportation, 1968, Housing Systems Proposals for Operation Breakthrough, 1970, Focus on Furniture, 1971, National Community Art Competition, 1971, Defining Critical Environmental Areas, 1974; contbg. editor: Progressive Architecture, 1974-84; editl. adv. bd.: Jour. Am. Planning Assn., 1983-88, Planning for Higher Edn., 1986-94, Urban Design and Preservation Quar., 1987-94; contbr. over 100 articles to profl. jours.; mem. adv. panel Industrialization Forum Quar., 1969-79, archtl. portfolio jury Am. Sch. and Univ., 1993. Mem. Met. Housing and Planning Coun., Chgo., 1965-67; mem. exec. com. Yale U. Arts Assn., 1965-70; pres. Yale U. Planning Alumni Assn., 1983—; mem. ednl. adv. com. Fla. Bd. Architecture, 1975; mem. grievance com. The Fla. Bar, 1996—. Recipient W.E. Parsons medal Yale U., 1960; recipient Spl. Achievement award HUD, 1972, commendation Fla. Bd. Architecture, 1974, Fla. Trust Historic Preservation award, 1983, Group Achievement award NASA, 1976; Skidmore, Owings & Merrill traveling fellow MIT, 1958; vis. fellow Inst. Architecture and Urban Studies, N.Y.C., 1972-74; NSF grantee, 1980-82. Fellow AIA (nat. housing com. 1968-72, nat. regional devel. and natural resources com. 1974-75, nat. sys. devel. com. 1972-73, nat. urban design com. 1968-73, bd. dirs. Fla. S. chpt. 1974-75), ASCE, Fla. Engring. Soc., Nat. Acad. Forensic Engrs.; mem. NSPE, Am. Inst. Cert. Planners (exec. com. dept. environ. planning 1973-74), Am. Soc. Engring. Edn. (chmn. archtl. engring. divsn. 1975-76), Nat. Sculpture Soc. (allied profl.), Nat. Trust Hist. Preservation (principles and guidelines com. 1967), Am. Soc. Landscape Architects (hon., chmn. design awards jury 1971, 72), Am. Planning Assn. (Fla. chpt. award excellence 1983), Am. Soc. Interior Designers (hon.), Urban Land Inst., Fla. Bar (grievance com. 1996—), Omicron Delta Kappa, Sigma Xi, Tau Beta Pi. Home: 6910 Veronese St Coral Gables FL 33146-3846 Office: 420 S Dixie Hwy Coral Gables FL 33146-2222 also: U Miami Sch Architecture Coral Gables FL 33124-5010

WARD, ALICE FAYE, elementary education educator; b. Swartz, La.. BS, Grambling (La.) U., 1973; postgrad., N.E. U., 1976-79. Tchr. Robinson Elem. Sch., Monroe, 1971-73, Poinciana Elem. Sch., Boynton Beach, Fla., 1973-76, Melaleuca Elem. Sch., West Palm Beach, Fla.; tchr., dir. after sch. program Melaleuca Elem. Sch., West Palm Beach. Dir. Just Say No Club, 1994-95, K-Kid Club, 1994-95, After Sch. Program, 1994. Named Tchr. of Week Palm Beach Post Newspaper, 1994. Mem. NEA, CTA. Democrat. Baptist. Office: Melaleuca Elem Sch 5759 W Gun Club Rd West Palm Beach FL 33415-2505

WARD, BETHEA, artist, small business owner; b. Montgomery, Ala., July 6, 1924; d. Charles E. and Lucy (Walter) W. BFA, Syracuse U., 1946; postgrad., Trinity U., San Antonio, 1965, 66, 68, San Antonio Art Inst., 1967, Houston Mus. Fine Arts Sch., 1973-75. Interior designer Davison-Paxon, Atlanta, 1946-47; assoc. prof. interior design U. Tex., Austin, 1947-51; interior designer Heminways-Bundrick, Shreveport, La., 1951-55; draftsman, supr. Ark. Fuel subs. Cities Service Co., Shreveport, 1955-60, Cities Svc. Co. Midland, San Antonio, 1961-82; visual artist, owner Tex. Notables Studio-Gallerie, Houston, 1983—. Juried shows include (watercolor paintings) Midland (Tex.) Art Fest. (2d place award, 1962), 35th Ann. Local Artist Exhbn., San Antonio (Wofford award 1965), Wichita, Kas. Centennial Nat. Exhbn. (inclusion award 1970), Cen. Tex. Hist. on Canvas Exhbn. (1st place award TFAA 1972), Laguna Gloria, Austin; group exhibits include U. Houston, 1986; contbr. ink drawing to Southwestern Hist. Quarterly, 1977; commns. include drawing for Moody Found. of Galveston; one person shows include Star of the Republic Mus., Houston Pub. Libr., Harris County Heritage Soc., San Antonio Pub. Libr. Recipient Award of Distinction Juried Art Fair, Houston Internat. Festival, 1987, numerous awards for watercolor paintings. Mem. Hoover Watercolor Soc. (founding mem. 1952), Watercolor Art Soc. Houston (chmn bd. social chmn., sec., co-founder), Art League Houston, Cultural Arts Council Houston, Coppini Acad. Fine Arts (life), Tex. Arts Alliance, Tex. Commn. on the Arts, Southwestern Watercolor Soc. (founding mem., pub. chmn.), Tex. State Hist. Assn., Tex. Hist. Found., Cultural Arts Council of Houston. Presbyterian. Home and Studio: Tex Notables Studio-Gallerie 9614 Val Verde St Houston TX 77063-3702

WARD, CALVIN H., academic director, environmental science educator, federal agency administrator; b. Strawberry, Ark., Mar. 1, 1933; married; 3 children. BS in Biology, N.Mex. State U., 1955; MS in Plant Pathology-Genetics, Cornell U., 1958, PhD in Plant Pathology-Physiology, 1960; MPH in Environ. Health, U. Tex., 1978. Rsch. scientist Sch. Aerospace Medicine USAF, San Antonio, 1960-63, physiologist, dir. bioregenerative life support systems rsch. Sch. Aerospace Medicine, 1963-66; assoc. prof. dept. chem. engrng. Rice U., Houston, 1966-68, assoc. prof. environ. sci. and engring. program, 1968-70, prof., 1970-88, chair dept. environ. sci. and engring., 1970-92, prof. environ. sci./engring., ecology, evolutionary biology, 1970—; Foyt Family chair engrng. Rice U., 1993—; dir. Energy and Environ. Systems Inst., Rice U., Houston, 1992—; vis. prof. environ. health U. Tex. Sch. Pub. Health, 1973-74; editor-in-chief intl. jnl. Environmental Toxicology and Chemistry, 1980—; dir. Nat. Ctr. Ground Water Rsch., Rice U., U.S. EPA Exploratory Rsch. Ctr. of Excellence, 1981—; dir. Superfund Univ. Tng. Inst., Rice U., U.S. EPA Office Solid Wastes and Emergency Response, 1989—; co-dir. Hazardous Substances Rsch. Ctr.-South and S.W., La. State U., Rice U., Ga. Tech., U.S. EPA Superfund Rsch. Ctr., 1991—; dir. Advanced Applied Tech. Demonstration Facility, U.S. Dept. Def., 1993—; mem. profl. sci. adv. coms.; cons. Mem. editorial bd. Houston Engr., 1979-83; assoc. editor SIM News, 1979-90; editor-in-chief Environ. Toxicology and Chemistry, 1981—; sr. editor Jour. Indsl. Microbiology, 1985-91, Internat. Adv. Bd. Enzyme and Microbial Tech., 1994—, Devels. in Indsl. Microbiology, 1985-91; co-editor 10 books; contbr. more than 200 articles to peer-reviewed jours., chpts. to books, provs. of confs., symposia, others. Mem. SW Ctr. Urban Rsch., 1969-82, treas., 1974-75, chmn., bd. dirs., 1977-79. Roger Boles scholar 1951; Shell Found. grad. fellow 1957-59; Regents grad. fellow 1957-59; recipient Bausch and Lomb award in Sci., 1951, Achievement award Nat. Aeronautics and Space Adminstrn., 1981, Controlled Ecol. Life Support Systems award, 1993; named Corr. in Gravitational Physiology, Internat. Union Physiol. Scis., 1985. Fellow Soc. Indsl. Microbiology (sec. 1979-82, bd. dirs. 1982-85, pres. 1983-84, Charles Porter award 1986), Am. Acad. Microbiology; mem. AAAS, Am. Soc. Microbiology, Am. Inst. Biol. Scis. (gov. bd. mem.-at-large 1977-82, exec. com. 1982-86, pres. 1984-85), Am. Soc. Plant Physiologists, Am. Phytopathological Soc., Internat. Water Resources Assn. (v.p. U.S. nat. com. 1977—), Soc. Environ. Toxicology and Chemistry (founder, bd. dirs. 1979-82, Disting. Svc. award 1990), Assn. Ground Water Scientists and Engrs., Assn. Environ. Engring. Profs. Office: Rice U Energy & Environ Sys Inst 6100 S Main MS-316 Houston TX 77005

WARD, DANIEL BERTRAM, botanist, educator; b. Crawfordsville, Ind., Mar. 20, 1928; s. Forrest Archibald and Ursula (Caster) W.; m. Suzanne Siegfried, July 28, 1956 (dec. 1990); children: Forrest Siegfried, Gordon Caster, Sylvia Jane, Douglas Harris. AB, Wabash Coll., 1950; MS, Cornell U., 1952, PhD, 1959. Asst. prof. U. Fla., Gainesville, 1958-67, assoc. prof., 1967-75, prof. botany, 1975—. Mem. Am. Soc. Plant Taxonomists, Internat. Assn. Plant Taxonomy, Fla. Acad. Scis. (pres. 1981-82), So. Appalachian Bot. Club. Home: 733 SW 27th St Gainesville FL 32607 Office: Univ of Florida Dept of Botany Gainesville FL 32611

WARD, EDITH BURNETTE, business educator; b. Wakulla, Fla., Sept. 3, 1930; d. Andrew Joshua and Delia Leanna (Green) Hargrett. BS, Fla. Agrl. and Mech. U., 1951; MEd, Am. U., 1964; EdD, Va. Poly. Inst. and State U., 1992. Cert. of advanced grad. studies. Sec. Fla. Agrl. and Mech. U., Tallahassee, 1951-52; sec., adminstrv. asst. Fed. Govt., Washington, 1952-64; tchr. D.C. Pub. Schs., 1964-90; acad. advisor Va. Poly. Inst. and State U., Blacksburg, 1990-92; asst. prof. St. Augustine's Coll., Raleigh, N.C., 1992—, acting chair divsn. bus., 1995-96. Chairperson fin. com. Tabernacle Bapt. Ch., Washington, 1982-90; treas. PTA, Washington, 1975-87; tchr. Mayor's Summer Youth Program, Washington, 1980-89; advisor Future Bus. Leaders of Am., Washington, 1975-90; vol. Dem. Party, Prince George's County, Md., 1988, NAACP, Washington, 1958-64; vol. tutor Sargeant Meml. Presbyn. Ch., Washington, 1963; sec. Hyde Park Cmty. Families, 1993—. Mem. Am. Vocat. Assn., Washington Tchrs. Union, Fla. Agrl. and Mech. U. Alumni Assn. (D.C. chpt. sec. 1970-85), Phi Eta Sigma, Delta Pi Epsilon, Phi Delta Kappa, Omicron Tau Theta, Sigma Gamma Rho. Democrat. Home: 1316 Oakwood Ave Apt C Raleigh NC 27610 Office: Saint Augustine's College 1315 Oakwood Ave Raleigh NC 27610

WARD, HARRY PFEFFER, physician, university chancellor; b. Pueblo, Colo., June 6, 1933; s. Lester L. and Alysmai (Pfeffer) W.; m. Betty Jo Stewart, Aug. 20, 1955; children—Stewart, Leslie, Elizabeth, Mary Alice, Amy. A.B., Princeton U., 1955; M.D., U. Colo., 1959; M.S., U. Minn., 1963. Intern Bellevue Hosp., N.Y.C., 1959; resident Mayo Clinic, Rochester, Minn., 1960-63; practice medicine specializing in hematology; chief medicine Denver VA hosp., 1968-72; dean, asso. v.p. U. Colo. Sch. Medicine, 1972-78, prof. medicine, 1972; chancellor U. Ark. Med. Sci., Little Rock, 1979—; clin. investigator VA, 1964-67. Chmn. Assn. Acad. Health Ctr., 1993-94. Mem. ACP, AMA, Am. Fedn. Clin. Research, Central Soc. Clin. Investigation, Am. Soc. Hematology, Internat. Soc. Hematology, Western Soc. Clin. Research. Home: 369 Valley Club Cir Little Rock AR 72212-2900 Office: U Ark Med Scis 4301 W Markham St Little Rock AR 72205-7101

WARD, HIRAM HAMILTON, federal judge; b. Thomasville, N.C., Apr. 29, 1923; s. O.L. and Margaret A. W.; m. Evelyn M. McDaniel, June 1, 1947; children: William McDaniel, James Randolph. Student, Wake Forest Coll., 1945-47; J.D., Wake Forest U., 1950, LLD (hon.), 1996. Bar: N.C. bar 1950. Practiced law Denton, N.C., 1950-51; staff atty. Nat. Prodn. Authority, Washington, 1951-52; partner firm DeLapp, Ward & Hedrick, Lexington, N.C., 1952-72; U.S. dist. judge Mid. Dist. N.C., 1972—, chief judge, 1982-88, sr. judge, 1988—; mem. com. on Codes of Conduct of Jud. Conf., U.S., 1990-95; mem. Fourth Cir. Jud. Coun., 1984-87. Contbr. legal opinions to Fed. Supplement, F.2d & F.R.D., 1972—. Bd. visitors Wake Forest U. Sch. Law, 1973—; Mem. N.C. Bd. Elections, 1964-72; trustee Wingate Coll., 1969-72. Served with USAAF, 1940-45. Decorated Air medal, Purple Heart; recipient Liberty Bell award N.C. Bar Assn., 1994. Mem. ABA, N.C. Bar Assn., Am. Judicature Soc., N.C. State Bar, Masons, Lions, Phi Alpha Delta (hon. life). Republican. Baptist. Home: 188 Forest Park Dr Denton NC 27239 Office: US Courthouse 246 Fed Bldg 251 N Main St Winston Salem NC 27101-3914

WARD, HORACE TALIAFERRO, federal judge; b. LaGrange, Ga., July 29, 1927; m. Ruth LeFlore (dec.); 1 son (dec.). AB, Morehouse Coll., 1949; MA, Atlanta U., 1950; JD, Northwestern U., 1959. Bar: Ga. 1960. Instr. polit. sci. Ark. A.M. and N. Coll., 1950-51, Ala. State Coll., 1951-53, 55-56; claims authorizer U.S. Social Security Adminstrn., 1959-60; assoc. firm Hollowell Ward Moore & Alexander (and successors), Atlanta, 1960-69; individual practice law Atlanta, 1971-74; judge Civil Ct. of Fulton County, 1974-77, Fulton Superior Ct., 1977-79; U.S. Dist. Ct. judge No. Dist. Ga., Atlanta, 1979—; lectr. bus. and sch. law Atlanta U., 1965-70; dep. city atty., Atlanta, 1969-70, asst. county atty., Fulton County, 1971-74. Former Trustee Friendship Baptist Ch., Atlanta; mem. Ga. adv. com. U.S. Civil Rights Commn., 1963-65; assisting lawyer NAACP Legal Def. and Edn. Fund, Inc., 1960-70; mem. Jud. Selection Commn., Atlanta, 1972-74, Charter Commn., 1971-72; mem. Ga. Senate, 1964-74, jud. com., rules com., county and urban affairs com.; mem. State Democratic Exec. com., 1966-74; former bd. dirs. Atlanta Legal Aid Soc.; bd. dirs. Atlanta Urban League, Fed. Defender Program, No. Dist. Ga.; trustee Met. Atlanta Commn. on Crime and Delinquency, Atlanta U., Fledgling Found. Mem. Am. Bar Assn., Nat. Bar Assn. (chmn. jud. council 1978-79), State Bar Ga., Atlanta Bar Assn., Gate City Bar Assn. (pres. 1972-74), Atlanta Lawyers Club, Phi Beta Kappa, Alpha Phi Alpha, Phi Alpha Delta, Sigma Pi Phi. Office: US Dist Court 2388 US Courthouse 75 Spring St SW Atlanta GA 30303-3309

WARD, JACQUELINE ANN BEAS, nurse, healthcare administrator; b. Somerset, Pa., Oct. 23, 1945; d. Donald C. and Thelma R. (Wable) Beas; divorced; children: Charles L. Jr., Shawn M. BS in Nursing, U. Pitts., 1966; MA in Counseling and Guidance, W.Va. Coll. Grad. Studies, 1976; MBA, Columbus Coll., 1983. Cert. in advanced nursing adminstrn. Staff nurse W.Va. U. Hosp., Morgantown, 1966-67; staff nurse, head nurse Meml. Hosp. Charleston, W.Va., 1967-69; staff nurse Santa Rosa Hosp., San Antonio, 1969; staff nurse, supr. Bexar County Hosp., San Antonio, 1970; charge, staff nurse Rocky Mountain Osteo. Hosp., Denver, 1971; staff nurse Charleston Area Med. Ctr., 1971-74, asst. dir. nursing, 1974-82; dir. nursing H.D. Cobb Meml. Hosp., Phenix City, Ala.; clin. instr. Chattahoochie Valley C.C., Phenix City, 1982-84; v.p. nursing Venice (Fla.) Hosp., 1984-90, v.p. ops., 1990-94, exec. dir., v.p. Life Counseling Ctr., Osprey, Fla., 1994-95, dir. skilled unit and spl. projects Bon Secours/Venice Hosp., 1995—; support svcs. cons. Bon Secours Healthcare, Fla., 1996—. Mem. Am. Coll. Healthcare Exec., Fla. Hosp. Assn., Nat. League Nursing, Articulation Coun. Sarasota and Manatee Counties, Am. Orgn. of Nurse Execs. (pres. region II south Fla. 1985-86, 90-94), Fla. Orgn. Nurse Execs., Fla. Commn. on Nursing. Office: Bon Secours-Venice Hosp 540 The Rialto Venice FL 34285-2900

WARD, JAMES EVERETT, library director; b. Dardanelle, Ark., Apr. 10, 1934; s. Norman E. and Nellie Ina (Ross) W.; m. Betty Jo Wells, Dec. 20, 1964; children: Bradlee Milton, David Everett. BA, Hendrix Coll., 1954; MEd, U. Ark., 1956, EdD, 1962; MLS, George Peabody Coll., 1968. Tchr. Carlisle (Ark.) High Sch., 1955-57, Rogers (Ark.) High Sch., 1959-60; chair dept. health, phys. edn. & recreation Cen. Meth. Coll., Fayette, Mo., 1961-63; prof. health & phys. edn. David Lipscomb U., Nashville, 1963-66, dir. library, 1966—. Contbr. articles to profl. jours. With U.S. Army, 1957-59. Recipient Honor award Tenn. Libr. Assn., 1983, James E. Ward Libr. Instrn. award Tenn. Libr. Assn., 1984, So. Dist. Honor award AAHPERD, 1996. Mem. NEA, ALA, AAHPERD, Assn. Coll. Rsch. Librs. (mem. clearinghouse com. bibliog. instrn. sects. 1986-88, mem. nominating com. 1978, mem. chpt. coun. for Tenn. 1978-80), S.E. Libr. Assn. (hon., mem. libr. instrn. roundtable nominating com. 1985-86, pres. 1990-92, parliamentarian 1987-88, 94-96, treas. 1987-88, chair nominating com. 1994-96), Tenn. Libr. Assn. (pres. 1973-74, bd. dirs. 1976-77, 78-80, 83-86, 93—, chairperson bylaws and procedures com. 1985-90, 93—, mem. spl. projects com. 1979-80, chmn. 1981-82, mem. fin. com. 1977-80, 85-86), Mid-State Libr. Assn. (chmn. exec. coun. 1971-73), Tenn. Assn. Health, Phys. Edn., Recreation and Dance (exec. dir. 1974-95, Honor award 1996), Tenn. Edn. Assn., Nashville Libr. Club (pres. 1972-73, mem. exec. com. 1973-74). Home: 3710 Rosemont Ave Nashville TN 37215-3040

WARD, JANET LYNN, magazine editor, sports wire reporter; b. Albany, Ga., Feb. 20, 1955; d. Andrew Johnson and Dorothy Iris (Pipera) W.; m. William Thomas Hankins III, Apr. 25, 1981 (div. Feb. 1990); m. Jack Wilkinson, May 22, 1993. AB in Journalism, U. Ga., 1977; JD, Woodrow Wilson Coll. Law, 1984. Sports editor Marietta (Ga.) Daily Jour., 1977-79, North Fulton extra-Atlanta Jour. Constitution, 1979-80; asst. editor In town extra-Atlanta Jour. Constitution, 1980-84; lawyer Atlanta, 1984-89; editor Am. City & County Mag., Atlanta, 1989—. Democrat. Roman Catholic. Home: 372 Oakdale Rd NE Atlanta GA 30307-2070 Office: Am City & County Ste 1200 6151 Powers Ferry Rd NW Atlanta GA 30339-2943

WARD, JEANNE LAWTON, family counselor, consultant; b. Bklyn., Mar. 23, 1945; d. James Joseph and Grace Frances (Brennan) Lawton; m. Robert L. Bucher, June 11, 1966 (div. Aug. 1977); children: Barbara Anne, Laura Jeanne; m. Charles F. Ward Jr., Aug. 19, 1983. BA in Edn., St. Catherine's Coll., St. Paul, 1966; MA in Counseling and Psychology, Coll. St. Thomas, St. Paul, 1970. Elem. tchr. Cooper Elem. Sch., 1966-69; spl. edn. resource tchr. Susie Tolbert 6th Grade Ctr., Jacksonville, Fla., 1976-78, sch. counselor, Arlington Heights Elem. Sch., Jacksonville, Fla., 1978-83; instr. Fla. C. C., Jacksonville, 1978-88; pvt. practice family counseling, Jacksonville, 1984-88; dir. tng. staff devel. City of Jacksonville, Fla., 1987-88; adj. prof. U. North Fla., 1990-92; dir. legis. affairs Mayors Office Jacksonville, Fla., 1992—. cons. mktg. tng. design and devel. Am. Transtech, Jacksonville, 1985-87; cons. child care Community Coll. Jacksonville, 1990-92; founder, dir. Divorce Ministry Diocese of St. Augustine, Jacksonville, 1979-83; Fla. del. White House Conf. on Families, 1980; regular panelist Sta. WJXT, Jacksonville, 1982—, editorial writer, 1990-92. Author curriculum. Bd. dirs., chmn. pers. com. Child Guidance Clinic, Jacksonville, 1977—; bd. dirs. Girls Club of Jacksonville, 1981-83; chairperson Mayors Commn. on Status of Women, Jacksonville, 1985-87; bd. dir. tng. and staff devel. City of Jacksonville, 1986-87; chmn. task force Corp. Child Care, 1985—, founding dir., 1985—; cons. Fla. Community Coll., 1988—; bd. dirs. YWCA, Jacksonville Symphony, Hope Haven, Family Care Connections, Inc., Nutcracker Ballet; chmn. bd. dirs. Child Guidance Ctr.; mem. Literacy Coalition, Coalition for a Drug Free Jacksonville, Leadership Jacksonville. Recipient Eve award Fla. Times Union, 1990, Woman of Achievement award Bus. and Profl. Women. Mem. AAUW, NAFE, ASTD, Nat. Coun. of Family Rels., Phi Delta Kappa, N.E. Fla. Soc. Parents of Visually Impaired Children Club (program chmn. 1985—). Democrat. Roman Cathlic. Home: 3523 Park St Jacksonville FL 32205-7726 Office: Office of the Mayor 220 E Bay St Jacksonville FL 32202-3429

WARD, JO ALICE, computer consultant, educator; b. Ft. Worth, Aug. 14, 1939; d. Boyd Wheeler and Frances Elizabeth (Wheeler) Patton; m. John Oliver Ward, Mar. 19, 1960 (div. Feb. 1976); children: Russell Scott, Pamela Joan Ward Watson. BA in Math., North Tex. State U., 1961, MA in Math., 1965, postgrad., 1969-72. Instr. math. North Tex. State U., Denton, 1965-67, grad. asst., 1968-72; instr. math. Tarrant County Jr. Coll., Ft. Worth, 1967-68; math. tchr. Aldine Ind. Schs., Houston, 1973-76; math. instr. U. Houston Downtown, 1974-80; sys. analyst Conoco Inc, Houston, 1981-93; computer cons. Quality First Computer Svcs., Houston, 1994—. Vol. facilitator for family violence program Houston Area Women's Ctr., 1993-94; adminstrv. vol. Citizens for Animal Protection, 1993—; vol. Bering Cmty. Svc. Found., 1995—. Recipient Outstanding Adminstrv. Vol. award Citizens for Animal Protection, 1995. Home: 11943 Briar Forest Dr Houston TX 77077-4132

WARD, JOE HENRY, JR., lawyer; b. Childress, Tex., Apr. 18, 1930; s. Joe Henry and Helen Ida (Chastain) W.; m. Carlotta Agnes Abreu, Feb. 7, 1959; children—James, Robert, William, John. BS in Acctg., Tex. Christian U., 1952; JD, So. Meth. U., 1964. Bar: Tex. 1964, Va. 1972, D.C. 1972; CPA, Tex. Mgr. Alexander Grant & Co., CPA's., Dallas, 1956-64; atty. U.S. Treasury, 1965-68; tax counsel U.S. Senate Fin. Com., 1968-72; sole practice, Washington, 1972-83; asst. gen. counsel, tax mgr. Epic Holdings, Ltd. and Crysopt Corp., 1983-87; pvt. practice, Washington and Va., 1987—. Lt. USNR, 1952-56. Mem. ABA, AICPA, Am. Assn. Atty.-CPA's, Univ. Club. Home: 2639 Mann Ct Falls Church VA 22046-2721 Office: Murphy & Hearn PC 202 G St NE Washington DC 20002

WARD, JOSEPH MARSHALL, SR., retired art educator; b. Phoenix, Ariz., Feb. 11, 1922; s. Elde Hulet and Ethel (Thornton) W.; m. Vivian Paula Moore, Sept. 2, 1950; children: Joseph Marshall Jr., McDaniel Moore. BA, U. Ky., 1946; cert. in illustration, Phila. Coll. Art, 1949; MA in Art Edn., East Tenn. State U., 1965. Artist Bapt. Sunday Sch. Bd., Nashville, 1949-53, artist-illustrator, 1953-59; instr. applied art Va. Intermont Coll., Bristol, 1959-68; assoc. prof. art, chmn. dept. art Bapt. Coll. Charleston (now named Charleston So. U.), S.C., 1968-87, ret.; advisor to yearbook Va. Intermont Coll., Bristol, 1953-58; judge art exhibits, Nashville, Bristol and Charleston. Exhibited in group shows at Nashville Watkins Inst., 1950, Smithsonian Inst., 1940, Art Dirs. Club; commd. oil painting North Charleston City Coun. Chambers, 1996. Mem. publicity com. Colony North Civic Club, North Charleston, 1968—. With U.S. Army, 1941-43. Recipient Coastal Carolina Fair Merit award 1984, 86, 93. Mem. Charleston Artist Guild (bd. dirs. 1975-77, v.p. 1976, chmn. scholarship com. 1983-85). Baptist. Home and Office: 8019 Nantuckett Ave Charleston SC 29420

WARD, KENNY, food products executive; b. 1945. BS in Agr., U. Ky., 1967; postgrad., Auburn U., 1967-69. Salesperson Allied Mills, Inc., Memphis, 1970-74; pres. Farmer's Gin & Peanut Co., Inc., Clinton, Ky., 1974—, sec., treas., 1975—; ptnr. Ward Farm, Bardwell, Ky., 1982—, sec.-treas., 1984—. Office: Farmers Gin & Peanut Co Inc Depot Extd Clinton KY 42031

WARD, KEVAN EULIS, video specialist; b. Bremen, Ga., May 6, 1969; s. Jim Collier and Kanea Sue (Sprewell) W. ABJ in Telecom. summa cum laude, U. Ga., 1991. Radio station corr. WPPI-FM, Carrollton, Ga., 1984-86; film reviewer The Bowdon (Ga.) Bulletin, 1987; various positions from editor to sr. reporter The Red & Black, Athens, Ga., 1987-1990; production asst. Creative Video, Atlanta, 1990; disc jockey WUOG-FM, Athens, 1988-1991; sr. news stringer WUGA-FM, Athens, 1989-1991; video specialist Prestige Cablevision, Catersville, Ga., 1993—; chief exec./artistic dir. Videodrome Prodns., Bremen, Ga., 1993—. Writer/dir. (film) Love Is ..., 1990; photographer (book) Faking It, 1991. Recipient Best Review award Ga. Coll. Press Assn., 1988, Outstanding Public Svc. Through Broadcasting award WSB Radio, 1991; Cox fellow Cox Ctr. for Internat. Telecom., Europe, 1991-92; Scripps-Howard Found. scholar, Governor's scholar, William I. Ray and Barrett scholar U. Ga., Alumni scholar, UAW of Am. scholar. Mem. Soc. of Profl. Journalists, Zodiac, Phi Eta Sigma, Gamma Beta Phi, Kappa Tau Alpha Honor Socs. Home: 130 Barnes Mill Rd Carrollton GA 30117 Office: Prestige Cablevision PO Box 190 Cartersville GA 30120

WARD, LLEWELLYN O(RCUTT), III, oil company executive; b. Oklahoma City, July 24, 1930; s. Llewellyn Orcutt II and Addie (Reisdorph) W.; m. Myra Beth Gungoll, Oct. 29, 1955: children: Casidy Ann, William Carlton. Student, Okla. Mil. Acad. Jr. Coll., 1948-50; BS, Okla. U., 1953; postgrad. Harvard U., 1986. Registered profl. engr., Okla. Dist. engr. Delhi-Taylor Oil Corp., Tulsa, 1955-56; ptnr. Ward-Gungoll Oil Investments, Enid, Okla., 1956—; owner L.O. Ward Oil Ops., Enid, 1963—; mem. Okla. Gov.'s Adv. Coun. on Energy; rep. to Interstate Oil Compact Commn.; bd. dirs. Community Bank and Trust Co. Enid. Chmn. Indsl. Devel. Commn., Enid, 1968—; active YMCA; mem. bd. visitors Coll. Engring., U. Okla.; mem. adv. coun. Sch. Bus., trustee Phillips U., Enid, Univ. Bd., Pepperdine, Calif.; Okla. chmn. U.S. Olympic Com., 1986—; chmn. bd. Okla. Polit. Action Com., 1974—, Bass Hosp.; Rep. chmn. Garfield County, 1967-69; Rep. nat. committeeman from Okla.; bd. dirs. Enid Indsl. Devel. Found. Served with C.E., U.S. Army, 1953-55. Mem. Ind. Petroleum Assn. Am. (chmn. 1996—), Okla. Ind. Petroleum Assn. (pres., bd. dirs.), Nat. Petroleum Council, Enid C. of C. (v.p., then pres.), Alpha Tau Omega. Methodist. Clubs: Toastmasters (pres. Enid chpt. 1966), Am. Bus. (pres. 1964). Lodges: Masons, Shriners, Rotary (pres. Enid 1990-91). Home: 900 Brookside Dr Enid OK 73703-6941 Office: 502 S Fillmore St Enid OK 73703-5703

WARD, LYNDA SUE SCOVILLE, special education educator, writer; b. Pampa, Tex., Jan. 5, 1945; d. Kenneth E. and Opal Myrle (Turner) Scoville; m. Bruce C. Ward, Oct. 1, 1976; children: J. Wade Bainum, Jennifer L. Bainum. BS in Edn., Emporia (Kans.) State U., 1967; MS in Edn., U. Kans., 1973; postgrad., Wichita (Kans.) State U. Cert. learning disabled, educable mentally handicapped, psychology, composition and lit., Kans., Tex. Tchr. educable mentally handicapped and learning disabled Shawnee Mission (Kans.) Pub. Schs., 1967-69; tchr. headstart program Hutchinson Pub. Schs., 1968; tchr. educable mentally handicapped Chanute High Sch., Iola, Kans., 1974-76; tchr. learning and behavior disabled Sedgwick County Area Spl. Edn. Svcs. Coop., Goddard, Kans., 1979-80; tchr. learning disabled coun. spl. edn. program Butler County Sch. Bd., El Dorado, Kans., 1986-87; tchr. learning disabled Wichita Pub. Schs., 1987-89; writer and researcher, Andover, Kans., 1989-91; legal adminstrv. asst., 1992-94; tchr. learning and behavior disabled So. Tex. Ind. Sch. Dist., Mercedes, 1995-96. Author: A Scoville Branch in America: A Genealogy and Story (1660-1990). Grantee U. Kans. Mem. AAUW, ASCD, DAR (Eunice Sterling chpt. registrar), Coun. for Exceptional Children, Psi Chi.

WARD, MICHAEL DELAVAN, congressman, former state legislator; b. Jan. 7, 1951; s. Jasper Dudley III and Lucretia (Baldwin) W.; m. Christina Heavrin, July 18, 1975; children: Jasper Dudley IV, Kevin Michael. BS, U. Louisville, 1975. Salesperson Matthew Bender & Co., Louisville, 1979-83; owner Campaign Svcs., Polit. Cons., Louisville, 1983—; campaign mgr. Ron Mazzoli for Congress, Louisville, 1984; salesman Sta. WAVG, Louisville, 1984-85; spl. asst. Jefferson County, Louisville, 1985-88; state rep. Ky. Gen. Assembly, Frankfort, 1988-93; mem. 3rd congl. dist. U.S. Ho Reps., 1994—. State chair Common Cause/Ky. Louisville, 1975-77, 79-80; treas. Jefferson County Dem. Com., Louisville, 1984-91; bd. dirs. Ohio Valley March of Dimes, 1987-88. Mem. Kentuckiana Hemophilia Soc. (bd. dirs. 1987—), Action League for Physically Handicapped Adults (bd. dirs. 1987—). Home: 1905 Deer Park Ave Louisville KY 40205-1201 Office: 1032 Longworth Washington DC 20015*

WARD, MICHAEL DENNIS, chamber of commerce executive; b. July 31, 1958; s. Robinson Jester and Barbara (Byrne) W.; m. Cathryne Hunt, Apr. 7, 1990; 1 child, Cathryne Hanly. BS in Bus. Adminstrn., U. Ala., 1983; postgrad., Colo. U., 1992-95. Legis. asst. Med. Assn. State of Ala., Montgomery, 1983-84; asst. dir. govtl. affairs Med. Assn. State of Ala., Huntsville, 1984-87, dir. legis. affairs, 1987; mgr. pub. affairs Jim Walter Cos./Walter Industries, Birmingham, 1987-88; dir. pub. affairs Jim Walter Cos./Walter Industries, Huntsville, 1989-91; v.p. govtl. affairs C. of C. Huntsville/Madison County, 1991—. Bd. dirs. Ala. Cultural and Heritage Found., 1989-91, Ala. Voters Against Lawsuits, 1996—, Ala. Tax Reform Coalition, 1996—; mem. bus. adv. coun. Lt. Gov., 1996—; founding mem., exec. com. Huntsville Heritage Found., 1993; bd. dirs. Green Mountain Civic League, 1991-93; dir. advanced sales Panoply of the Arts, Huntsville, 1992. Recipient scholarship U. Ala., 1976-78, Degree of Distinction, Nat. Forensics League. Mem. Bus. Coun. Ala., C. of C. Execs. Ala., Am. C. of C. Execs. (adv. coun., govt. coun. 1994—, govt. rels. coun. 1991—, vice chmn. communications 1996). Office: Chamber of Commerce HSV/MAD Co PO Box 408 Huntsville AL 35804-0408

WARD, PHILLIP WAYNE, electrical engineer; b. Warren, Ark., June 10, 1935; s. Jake M. and Violet M. (Skees) W.; m. Nancy Ward, Jan. 27, 1958; children: Christopher T., Stephen M., Ivy Ward O'Malley, Andrew L. BSEE, U. Tex., El Paso, 1958; MSEE, So. Meth. U., 1965; postgrad., MIT, 1967-69. Registered profl. engr., Tex. Design engr. Tex. Instruments, Inc., Dallas, 1960-70; sr. mem. tech. staff Tex. Instruments, Inc., Plano, 1970-91; mem. tech. staff MIT Instrumentation Lab, Cambridge, 1967-70; pres. Navward GPS Cons., Dallas, 1991—; propr. Word Works, Dallas, 1981—. Patentee in field; contbr. articles to profl. jours. Asst. scoutmaster Boy Scouts Am., Dallas, 1970-84, scoutmaster, 1974; spl. minister of eucharist St. Patrick Ch., Dallas, 1978—. Served to lt. (j.g.) U.S. Coast and Geodetic Survey, 1958-60. Recipient Golden Pelican award Boy Scouts Am., 1982; O.J. Gramly Meml. scholar, U. Tex., El Paso, 1954; named to PhD Research Asst. Program, Tex. Instruments, Inc., 1968. Mem. IEEE (sr.), Inst. Navigation (exec. v.p. ctrl. region 1990-91, exec. v.p. 1991-92, pres.

1992-93, chair ION Satellite Divsn. 1994-96, Col. Thomas L. Thurlow Navigation award 1989), Sigma Alpha Epsilon. Republican. Roman Catholic. Home: 9629 Cove Meadow Dr Dallas TX 75238 Office: Navward GPS Cons PO Box 38451 Dallas TX 75238-0451

WARD, ROBERT CARL, library director, consultant; b. Louisville, May 6, 1953; s. Andrew Lee and Vera May (Klumb) W.; m. Patricia Ann Vedder, May 20, 1975 (div. Oct. 1992). BA in Polit. Sci., Bellarmine Coll., 1971; MLS, U. Ky., 1976; MPA, Drake U., 1983; postgrad., Va. Polytechnic Inst., 1993. Br. coord. Jefferson-Madison Regional Libr., Charlottesville, Va., 1977-80; libr. adminstr. Cen. Iowa Regional Libr., Des Moines, 1980-86; libr. dir. Rockingham County Pub. Libr., Eden, N.C., 1987-90, Horry County Pub. Libr., Myrtle Beach and Conway, S.C., 1990-93; instr. libr. adminstrn. Des Moines C.C., 1981-85, instr. libr. collection devel., 1981-85, instr. libr. pers. mgmt., 1982-84, instr. libr. automation, 1982-85; instr. libr. adminstrn. U. N.C., Greensboro; lectr pub. interest groups Drake U., 1986. Contbr. articles to profl. jours. Named to Hon. Order of Ky. Cols.; recipient numerous grants. Mem. ALA, ASPA, Am. Soc. Info. Sci., Pub. Libr. Assn. (legis. com. 1989-92, mtkg. com. 1991—, tech. com. 1990—, systems com. 1982-86), S.C. Libr. Assn. (legis. com. 1990-93), Assn. S.C. Libr. Adminstrs. (legis. com. 1990-93, exec. com. 1992), Libr. Adminstrn. and Mgmt. Assn. (membership com. 1989-91, risk mgmt. com. 1988-90, program com. 1988-90, fund raising com. 1988-90), N.C. Libr. Assn., Pi Alpha Alpha, Beta Phi Mu. Democrat. Roman Catholic. Office: Ward Mgmt Svcs 404 Clay St Ste B Blacksburg VA 24860

WARD, SHARON DEE, secondary school educator; b. Tulsa, Okla., Sept. 15, 1958; d. Earl Edmond and Wilma Rose (Hurst) Walker; m. Ricky Lee Yates, Dec. 24, 1977 (div. Apr. 1986); children: Pamela, Lisa; m. William Eugene Ward, Apr. 8, 1988; children: Christian, William. AA, Rogers State Coll., 1987; BS cum laude, U. of the Ozarks, 1989; tchr. cert., Coll. of the Ozarks, 1992. Cert. tchr. Ark. Bus. mgr. Dr. Phillips D.D.S., Owasso, Okla., 1982-85, Dr. Franklin D.D.S., Owasso, 1986; office asst. U. Ozarks, Clarksville, Ark., 1987-89; bus. mgr. M&R Container, Berryville, Ark., 1990; office bus. mgr. Carroll County News, Berryville, 1990; v.p. of fin. The Cookie Bouquet, Inc., Dallas, 1991; vocat. bus. educator Eureka Springs (Ark.) H.S., 1992—; mem. Eureka Springs Day Care, 1994-95; sponsor, leader First Eureka Springs Jr. Bank, Eureka Springs, 1993—; cons. Ark. Vocat. Bd., Little Rock, 1994—. Mem. Girl Scouts Am., cookie coun. Mem. Ark. Vocat. Assn., Bus. Edn. Assn., Ark. Edn. Assn. (sec. 1995—), Am. Vocat. Assn., Future Bus. Leaders of Am. Democrat. Methodist. Home: 304 Spring St Eureka Springs AR 72632

WARD, THOMAS A(UGUSTINE), III, federal immigration officer; b. Evergreen Park, Ill., Apr. 18, 1948; s. Thomas Augustine Jr. and Elizabeth Mary (Bruzan) W.; m. Maureen H. Germain, Sept. 20, 1969 (div. June 1974); 1 child, George Earl; m. Marie Stanford, May 29, 1979. BA, DePaul U., 1971; student, Border Patrol Acad., Port Isabel, Tex., 1973, Civil Svc. Commn., Chgo., 1978, Fed. Law Enforcement Tng. Ctr., 1979. Clk. U.S. Postal Svc., Chgo., 1971-73; border patrol agt. U.S. Immigration and Naturalization Svc., Chula Vista, Calif., 1973-76; immigrant inspector U.S. Immigration and Naturalization Svc., Chgo., 1976-78, supervisory inspector, 1978-85; asst. officer in charge U.S. Immigration and Naturalization Svc., Milw., 1985-87, Jacksonville, Fla., 1987—; instr. U.S. Immigration and Naturalization Svc., Chgo., 1977-88; computer programmer U.S. Immigration and Naturalization Svc., Jacksonville, 1989—. Author computer applications and programs for immigrant processing. Recipient 7 medals for pistol shooting Fla. Sunshire State Games, 1988. Mem. NRA (expert class 1988—), Gateway Rifle and Pistol Club.

WARD, WILLIAM E., mayor. Mayor City of Chesapeake, Chesapeake, VA., 1990—. Office: Office of Mayor PO Box 15225 Chesapeake VA 23328

WARE, CARL, bottling company executive; b. Newnan, Ga., Sept. 30, 1943; s. U.B. and Lois (Wimberly) W.; m. Mary Clark, Jan. 1 1966; 1 son, Timothy Alexander. B.A., Clark Coll., 1965; M.P.A., U. Pitts., 1968; postgrad., Carnegie Mellon U., 1965-66. Dir. Atlanta Housing Authority, 1970-73; pres. city council City of Atlanta, 1974-79; v.p. The Coca-Cola Co., Atlanta, 1974-86, sr. v.p., 1986—; dir. Ga. Power Co. Mem. adv. council U.S. Civil Rights Commn., 1983; bd. dirs. Nat. Council Black Agencies, 1983—, United Way of Met. Atlanta, 1983—; trustee Clark Coll. Mem. Gammon Theol. Sem. (trustee), Ga. State U. Found. (trustee), Sigma Pi Phi. Democrat. Methodist. Office: The Coca-Cola Co PO Drawer 1734 Atlanta GA 30301-1734*

WARE, JAMES T., electric company executive; b. Hattiesburg, Miss., June 11, 1926; s. Joseph L. and Effie M. (Sullivan) W.; m. Vera M. Shepard, Aug. 10, 1946; children: Charles L., James Larry. BSBA, U. So. Miss., 1949, postgrad., 1967-68; postgrad., U. Mich., 1980. Bd. commrs. East Forrest (Miss.) Utility Dist., 1960-67; supt. Standard Oil Gen. Sta. Miss. Power Co., Pascagoula, Miss., 1967-69; mgr. plant Jack Watson Miss. Power Co., Gulfport, Miss., 1969-74; indsl. rels. mgr. Combustion Engrs./Nat. Tank Co., Gulfport, 1974-76; mgr. Vermillion Power Sta. Ill. Power Co., Danville, 1976-78; dir. power prodn. Ill. Power Co., Decatur, 1978-82; v.p. Cajun Electric Power Coop, Baton Rouge, La., 1982-89; mgmt. cons. in China and U.S., Hattiesburg, Miss., 1989—; spkr. in field. With USN, 1944-46. Mem. Rotary. Baptist. Home and Office: 2602 Sierra Cir Hattiesburg MS 39402-2541

WARE, JOHN DAVID, valve and hydrant company executive; b. Beaumont, Tex., Feb. 2, 1947; s. Clarence David Ware and Lois Pearl (Coffey) Hardy; m. Dorothy Ann Jones, Mar. 27, 1986. Cert. in mgmt., James Madison U. Announcer Stas. KAYC and KAYD-FM, Beaumont, 1966-71; Stas. KAYC and KAYD-FM, 1971-77; asst. supr. Am. Valve & Hydrant, Beaumont. Mem. Am. Soc. for Quality Control (chmn. SE Tex. 1989-90), Nat. Mgmt. Assn., Inst. Cert. Profl. Mgrs. (cert. mgr.). Baptist. Home: 385 Needles St Vidor TX 77662-6513 Office: Am Valve & Hydrant 3350 Hollywood St Beaumont TX 77701-3820

WARE, LEIGH ANN CARTER, neonatal critical care nurse; b. Hobbs, N.Mex., Nov. 15, 1953; d. Amos Lee Jr. and Nettie Maxine (Harris) Carter; m. Ernest Ray Ware, Dec. 21, 1974; children: Carol Michelle, Tamara Leigh, Carter Ray. BSN, Tex. Woman's U., 1976; MS in Nursing, Fla. State U., 1991. Cert. Brazelton neonatal assessment. Newborn nursery staff nurse St. Paul's Hosp., Dallas; neonatal ICU staff nurse Sacred Heart Hosp., Pensacola, Fla., devel. case mgr., parent support coord.; instr. Pensacola Jr. Coll. Nursing. Mem. Nat. Assn. Neonatal Nurses, Parent Care, Inc. (bd. dirs.), Assn. for Care of Children's Health, Sigma Theta Tau.

WARE, STEWART ALEXANDER, biologist, educator; b. Stringer, Miss., Aug. 20, 1942; s. Rufus Alexander and Selena Artimatha (Grantham) W.; m. Donna Marie Eggers, Sept. 7, 1968. BS, Millsaps Coll., 1964; PhD, Vanderbilt U., 1968. Asst. prof. biology Coll. William and Mary, Williamsburg, Va., 1967-72, assoc. prof., 1972-82, chair biology, 1976-82, prof., 1982—. Editor: Jeffersonia, 1970-73, Va. Jour. Sci., 1979-84, Bull. Torrey Botan. Club, 1993—; contbr. articles to profl. jours. and chpts. to books. Fellow Va. Acad. Sci.; mem. Botan. Soc. Am., Ecol. Soc. Am., Torrey Botan. Club, So. Appalachian Botan. Soc., Assn. S.E. Biologists (Teaching award 1987). Democrat. Methodist. Home: 14 Buford Rd Williamsburg VA 23188-1505 Office: Coll William & Mary Dept Biology Williamsburg VA 23187

WARE, THOMAS EARLE, building consultant; b. Cleve., Apr. 13, 1931; s. Orval Bertele and Dorothy Lillian (Brammar) W.; m. Ann Sanborn Gilkey, Dec. 21, 1955 (div. Dec. 1960); 1 child, Thomas Earle Jr.; m. Gillian May Arnold, June 8, 1968 (div. Dec. 1983); 1 child, Elizabeth; m. Mary Erin Chandler, Apr. 19, 1994. BArch, Cornell U., 1955. Assoc. ptnr. Kelly and Kress and Assocs., Architects and Planners, Cleve., 1955-59; project architect J. Gordon Lorimer, F.A.I.A., N.Y.C., 1959; gen. mgr., ptnr. Project Design, Inc., Cleve., 1960-64; project architect, mgr. Cleve. dist. and hdqrs. The Austin Co., 1961-68; project architect, mgr., asst. and acting chief bldg. systems sect., bldg. rsch. divsn. Inst. Applied Tech., Nat. Bur. Standards U.S. Dept. Commerce, Washington, 1968-71; sr. program specialist, Office of the Sec., Office of Asst. Sec. for Sci. and Tech., Office of Dep. Asst. Sec. for Environ. Affairs U.S. Dept. Commerce, 1971-72; with Bldg. Cons., Reston, Va., 1972-73; v.p., dir. Bldg. Tech., Inc., Silver Spring, Md., 1973—, TCSB, Inc., Silver Spring, Md., Tehran and Shiraz, Iran, 1974-82; instr. continuing engring. edn. program, Sch. Engring. and Applied Sci., George Washington U., 1969-71; lectr. dept. architecture The Cath. U. Am., 1969-71; lectr., discussion leader U. Wis.-Ext., 1980-83; presenter in field. Contbr. articles to profl. jours. Named Architect of Yr., D.C. Coun. Engring. and Archtl. Socs., 1971; recipient Sci. and Tech. fellowship U.S. Dept. Commerce, 1971. Mem. Nat. Inst. Bldg. Scis., Soc. Am. Mil. Engrs., Constrn. Specifications Inst. Home: 11478 Links Dr Reston VA 22190-4814 Office: Bldg Tech Inc 1109 Spring St Silver Spring MD 20910-4002

WARE, WILLIAM BRETTEL, education educator; b. Glen Ridge, N.J., June 17, 1942; s. Howard Brettel and Helen Burd (Dickson) W.; m. Andrea Lou Gartley, June 24, 1967 (div. May 1989); children: Emily Dickson, Matthew Brettel, Erin Johanna Ware; m. Barbara Ann McClave Reynolds, Dec. 26, 1991; stepchildren: Dianne Catherine, Kristin Elise. AB, Dartmouth Coll., 1964; MA in Tchg., Northwestern U., 1965, PhD, 1968. Classroom tchr. Chgo. Pub. Schs., 1964-65; asst. prof. U. Fla., Gainesville, 1968-73, assoc. prof., 1973-76, prof., 1976-78; prof. U. N.C., Chapel Hill, 1978—. Contbr. chpts. to books and articles to profl. jours. Mgr. youth soccer team Ctrl. Carolina Youth Soccer Assn., Chapel Hill, 1980-86. Recipient J. Minor Gwynn professorship Sch. Edn., U. N.C., 1994-95. Mem. Am. Ednl. Rsch. Assn., Nat. Coun. on Measurement in Edn., N.C. Assn. for Rsch. in Edn. (bd. dirs. 1991—, pres. 1996-97), Psychometric Soc., Am. Evaluation Assn. Home: 110 Princeton Rd Chapel Hill NC 27516-3222 Office: Sch Edn U N C CB #3500 Chapel Hill NC 27599-3500

WAREHAM, JAMES LYMAN, steel company executive; b. Clinton, Iowa, Oct. 8, 1939; s. Lyman Hugh and Ulainee Maria (Pitts) W.; m. Patricia Josephine Wrubel, June 18, 1966; children: Lisa Jo, Tara Lynn. BSEE, U. Notre Dame, 1961. Various mgmt. positions U.S. Steel-Gary Works, Ind., 1961-69, div. mgr., 1976-79; various mgmt. positions U.S. Steel-Tex. Works, Baytown, 1969-72; various mgmt. positions U.S. Steel-South Works, Chgo., 1972-76, gen. plant mgr., 1979-84; v.p. engring. U.S. Steel, Pitts., 1984-86; pres., CEO Bliss Salem, Inc., Ohio, 1986-89; pres., COO Wheeling-Pitts. Steel Corp., W.Va., 1989-92, chmn., pres., CEO, 1992—; pres., bd. dirs. Wheeling-Pitts. Corp.; bd. dirs. Bliss-Salem Inc., Wesbanco, Am. Iron and Steel Inst. Area coord. Thompson for Gov., Homewood, Ill., 1978; div. chmn. United Way, Gary, Ind., 1976; gen. chmn., United Way Wheeling, W.Va., 1990; bd. dirs. United Way of Upper Ohio Valley, Wheeling Jesuit Coll., 1989—, Wheeling Hosp., 1990—. Named Small Businessman of Yr. Salem C. of C., 1988, Entrepreneur of Yr. Ernst & Young, Pitts., 1989. Mem. Assn. Iron & Steel Engrs., Inst. Mining & Metall. Engrs., Ohio Steel Industry Adv. Commn., W.Va. Mfg. Assn., Wheeling C. of C. Home: 234 Greenwood Dr Canonsburg PA 15317-5211 Office: 1134 Market St Wheeling WV 26003-2906*

WARFEL, JOSEPH ROSSER, local government official, retired military officer; b. Fayetteville, N.C., July 26, 1944; s. Joseph M. and Jane (Rosser) W.; m. Jo Thomas, Jan. 11, 1969; children: Paul, Jill, Scott. BA in Econs., U. N.C., 1966; postgrad., U. Okla., 1974, Cath. U., Washington, 1981. Lic. comml. pilot. Commd. 2d lt. USAF, 1996, advanced through grades to lt. col., 1982, pilot, 1966-73; logistics planner HQ Strategic Air Command, Omaha, Nebr., 1973-75; acad. and flying instr. USAF Instrument Flight Ctr., San Antonio, Tex., 1975-77; air ops. staff officer The Pentagon, Washington, 1978-82; regional rep. southern region USAF, Atlanta, 1982-89; budget and revenur mgr. Fulton County Pub. Works, Atlanta, 1990-92; mgr. capital inprovements Fulton County, Atlanta, 1993—; chmn. U.S. delegation NATO Air Traffic Com., Brussels, Belgium, 1978-82; U.S. del. Air Standardization Com., Ottawa, Can., 1980, Wellington, New Zealand, 1982. Author: Handbook for Instrument Instructor Pilots, 1978; contbr. articles to profl. jours. Decorated Bronze Star, Air medal, Meritorious Svc. medal, Commendation medal; named to Outstanding Young Men of Am., 1979. Fellow Nat. Order Scabbard and Blade, Alpha Phi Omega; mem. Air Force Assn., Ret. Officers Assn. (life), Order of Daedalians, Sigma Phi Epsilon (chaplain), Lake Colony Assn. (treas. 1986-89), Northside Soccer Assn. (asst. coach 1974-77). Home: 1222 Colony Dr Marietta GA 30068

WARGETZ, GEORGIA LYNN RANCE, accountant; b. Oklahoma City, Feb. 7, 1959; d. William and Ruth Virginia (Kemp) Rance; m. David John Wargetz, Jan. 2, 1981. BBA in Acctg., Baylor U., 1981. CPA, Tex. Revenue agt. asst. IRS, Dallas, 1980-81; tax acct. Computer Lang. Rsch., Inc. (Fast-Tax), Carrollton, Tex., 1982-83, sr. tax acct., 1983-84, tax acctg. supr., 1984-87, mgr. sales adminstrn., 1987-94, mgr. product support and system assurance testing, 1994-96, nat. accounts exec., 1996—; pvt. practice acctg., Grapevine, Tex., 1983—. Mem. Nat. Arbor Day Found., Nebraska City, Nebr., 1984—, Wilderness Soc., Washington, 1985—; charter mem. Lone Star Composting Corps, master composter, 1993—. Recipient Star Performer Intensity award CLR-FAST-TAX, 1988, v.p. award, 1989. Mem. Am. Inst. CPA's, Tex. State Bd. Pub. Accountancy (Dallas chpt.), Baylor U. Alumni Assn., Tex. Enrolled Agts. Soc. (Metroplex chpt.). Republican. Baptist. Home: 1107 Silverlake Dr Grapevine TX 76051-3391 Office: Computer Lang Rsch Inc 2395 Midway Rd Carrollton TX 75006-2521

WARING, MARY LOUISE, social work administrator; b. Pitts., Feb. 15, 1928; d. Harold R. and Edith (McCallum) W. AB, Duke U., 1949; MSS, Smith Coll., 1951; PhD, Brandeis U., 1974. Lic. clin. social worker, Tenn. Sr. supervising social worker Judge Baker Guidance Ctr., Boston, 1955-65; dir. social svc. Cambridge (Mass.) Mental Health Ctr., 1965-70; assoc. prof. Sch. Social Work Fla. State U., Tallahassee, 1974-77; prof. Fordham U., N.Y.C., 1977-82; cons. Dept. Human Svc., N.J., 1983-84; cons., sr. staff mem. Family Counseling Svc. Bergen County, Hackensack, N.J., 1984-86; dir. Step One Employee Assistance Program Fortwood Ctr., Inc., Chattanooga, 1986—; mem. ethics com. Chattanooga Rehab. Hosp., 1995. Contbr. articles to profl. jours. Mem. Citizen Amb. Program Human Resource Mgmt. Delegation to Russia, 1993; active Nat. Trust for Hist. Preservation, Nature Conservancy, Hunter Mus. Am. Art, Chattanooga Symphony and Opera Assn., Friends of Hamilton County Bicentennial Libr. Recipient Career Tchr. award Nat. Inst. Alchohol and Alchohol Abuse, 1972-74; traineeship NIMH, 1949-51. Mem. NASW (charter), Acad. Cert. Social Workers, Nat. Mus. Women in Arts (charter), Smithsonian Assocs., Cmty. Svcs. Club Greater Chattanooga (pres. 1995, 96, v.p. 1994, 97). Office: Fortwood Ctr Inc 1028 E 3rd St Chattanooga TN 37403-2107

WARKENTIEN, PAUL DAVID, electronics technology educator; b. Enid, Okla., Jan. 10, 1947; s. Jacob M. and Frances A. (Rice) W. B of Comml. Sci., Enid Bus. Coll., 1967; AAS, Okla. State U., 1989, BS, 1991. Cert. Accountable chief examiner. Programmer indsl. engring., pers. asst. George E. Failing Co., Enid, 1968-89; electronics tech. instr. O.T. Autry Tech. Ctr., Enid, 1992—; accountable chief examiner Nat. Radio Examiners, Dallas, 1994—, amateur radio examiner, 1991—. Mem. Tau Alpha Pi, Psi Eta Sigma. Home: 1910 W Rupe Ave Enid OK 73703

WARLICK, KARLA JAN, school counselor; b. Levelland, Tex., Aug. 6, 1949; d. Milton Jr. and Mary Tom (Bradford) Tankersley; m. Philip Owen Warlick, Aug. 24, 1968 (div. Oct. 1994); children: Allyson Wynn, Philip Owen II. BS, Tex. Women's U., 1970; MA, U. Tex., Odessa, 1991. Tchr. Richardson (Tex.) Ind. Sch. Dist., 1970-72; agt. Irene Smith Realtors, Austin, 1977-79; broker Bohannan Realtors, Midland, Tex., 1979-80; broker in pvt. practice Midland, 1980-92; tchr. Hillander Sch., Midland, 1980-81; assessment coord. Midland Coll., Midland, 1988-90; therapist, substance abuse supr. Dept. Family Svcs., Midland, 1990-91; counselor Midland Ind. Sch. Dist., Midland, 1991—; counselor in pvt. practice Midland, 1992—; counselor Grapevine-Colleyville (Tex.) Ind. Sch. Dist., 1995—; mem. gifted and talented com. Midland Ind. Sch. Dist., 1992—. Active Midland Symphony Guild; bd. dirs. Am. Heart Assn., Midland, 1982-85. Mem. Am. Counseling Assn., Tex. Counseling Assn., Permian Basin Counseling Assn. (mem. legis. com. 1992—), Zeta Tau Alpha. Methodist. Home: 365 Parkway Blvd Coppell TX 75019

WARNER, CECIL RANDOLPH, JR., lawyer; b. Ft. Smith, Ark., Jan. 13, 1929; s. Cecil Randolph and Reba (Cheeves) W.; m. Susan Curry, Dec. 10, 1955 (dec. 1982); children: Susan Rutledge, Rebecca Jane, Cecil Randolph III, Matthew Holmes Preston, Katherine Mary; m. Barbara Ragsdale, May 26, 1983. B.A. magna cum laude, U. Ark., 1950; LL.B. magna cum laude, Harvard U., 1953, Sheldon fellow, 1953-54. Bar: Ark. 1953. Ptnr. Warner & Smith and predecessor firm, 1954-89; pres., CEO, Fairfield Communities Inc., Little Rock, 1973-81; chmn., CEO Fairfield Communities Inc., 1981-85, chmn., pres., CEO, 1985-91; chmn., pres., CEO Environ. Systems Co., Little Rock, 1991-93; cons., 1993-95; chmn. bd. Wortz Co., Poteau, Okla., 1993—; instr. U. Ark. Sch. Law, 1954, 56; vice chmn. Ark. Constl. Revision Study Commn., 1967; v.p. 7th Ark. Constl. Conv., 1969-70. Scoutmaster troop 23 Boy Scouts Am., Fort Smith, 1955-58; commr. Ark. State Police Commn., 1970; bd. dirs. St. Vincent Infirmary Found., Ctrs. for Youth and Family. Fellow Am. Bar Found., Ark. Bar Found.; mem. ABA, Ark. Bar Assn. (past chmn. exec. com., past chmn. young lawyers sect.), Pulaski County Bar Assn., Am. Law Inst., Fifty for the Future, Phi Beta Kappa, Phi Eta Sigma, Omicron Delta Kappa, Sigma Alpha Epsilon. Methodist. Office: PO Box 7462 Little Rock AR 72217-7462 also: One Treetop Ln Little Rock AR 72201

WARNER, DAVID COOK, public affairs educator; b. Boston, Apr. 22, 1940; s. Roger Lewis and Dorothy Flora (Cook) W.; m. Phyllis Gail Erman, July 9, 1967; children—Ann Fitch, Michael Beers. B.A., Princeton U., 1963; M.P.A., Syracuse U., 1965, Ph.D. in Econs., 1969. Research assoc. Ctr. Urban Studies, Wayne State U., Detroit, 1969, asst. prof. econs., 1969-71; dep. dir. program analysis and budget N.Y.C. Health and Hosp. Corp., 1971-72; postdoctoral fellow, Yale U., New Haven, 1972-73, lectr., 1973-75; assoc. prof. L.B.J. Sch. Pub. Affairs, U. Tex., Austin, 1975-81, prof. pub. affairs, 1981—; vis. prof. pub. health, 1983—. Bd. dirs. Brackenridge Hosp., Austin, 1976-83; mem. Tex. Diabetes Coun., 1983-88, chmn., 1985-88; mem. adv. bd. Found. for Mental Health, 1990-93. Mem. U.S.-Mex. Border Health Assn. (chmn. rsch., edn., tng. com. 1982-84), Am. Pub. Health Assn., Tex. Philosophical Soc. Democrat. Congregationalist. Author: Health of Mexican Americans in South Texas, 1979; Developing Programs to Prevent and Control Diabetes, 1982, Maternal and Child Health on the U.S.-Mexico Border, 1987, Health Care Across the Border, 1993; editor: Toward New Human Rights, 1977, Public Affairs Comment, 1978—; mem. editorial bd. Jour. Health, Politics, Policy and Law, 1975-93; contbr. numerous articles to profl. publs. Home: 5701 Trailridge Dr Austin TX 78731-4226 Office: U Tex LBJ Sch Pub Affairs Austin TX 78712

WARNER, DOUGLAS WAYNE, education educator; b. San Angelo, Tex., Oct. 30, 1942; m. Shirley Mae Caskey, Jan. 25, 1964; children: Ben, David, Tamara. BBA, Abilene (Tex.) Christian U., 1965, MS, 1967; EdD, Nova U., 1975, PhD, 1989; postgrad., Ambert U., 1982—. V.p. Abilene Christian Univ., dean of men, prof. of bus.; founding pres. Amber U., Garland, Tex., 1971—. Author: The Parable of Aman, 1980, Ethics for Decision Making, 1984. Recipient Outstanding Svc. award U.S. Postal Svc., 1986. Mem. IEEE, Kappa Delta Pi. Office: Amber U Office of President 1700 Eastgate Dr Garland TX 75041-5510*

WARNER, ELIZABETH JANE SCOTT, exceptional education educator; b. Memphis, June 19, 1953; d. William Edward and Augusta Grace (Cushman) Scott; m. Russell Curtis Warner II, June 25, 1977; 1 child, Brittany Elizabeth. BS in Edn., U. Louisville, 1975, MEd, 1977. Cert. educable mentally handicapped, emotionally handicapped, elem. edn., early childhood, adminstr., supervision, Fla. Tchr. Jefferson County Sch. Bd., Louisville, 1975-77, Lee County Sch. Bd., Ft. Myers, Fla., 1977—; chmn. dept. Ft. Myers Mid. Acad., Lee Sch. Bd., 1980—, pres. prin. adv. coun., 1988-90. Mem. Coun. for Exceptional Children, Phi Delta Kappa. Republican. Roman Catholic. Home: 2302 SE 11th Ave Cape Coral FL 33990-4644 Office: Ft Myers Mid Acad 3050 Central Ave Fort Myers FL 33901-7305

WARNER, HEIDI C., clinical research nurse; b. Thomasville, N.C., Nov. 7, 1962. BSN, N.C. U., Charlotte, 1985. RN, N.C.; cert. in audiometry. Clin. rsch. assoc. tng. The Blethen Group, Research Triangle Park, N.C.; clin. rsch. nurse Monitor-BRI, Inc., Arlington, Va. Walter C. Teagle Found. nursing scholar, Exxon Co. USA. Mem. Nat. Assn. Female Execs., Phi Eta Sigma. Democrat. Methodist.

WARNER, JAMES BARRY, school system administrator; b. Jasper, Tex., Oct. 18, 1941; s. James M. and Lessie L. (Dickerson) W.; m. Linda G. Solly, June 30, 1962; 1 child, Lisa G. BA in English, Lamar U., 1964, MA in History, 1971, mid-mgmt. cert., 1981; superintendency cert., Tex. A&M U., 1985, EdD in Ednl. Adminstrn., 1987. Tchr. Goose Creek Ind. Sch. Dist., Baytown, Tex., 1964-65, Beaumont (Tex.) Ind. Sch. Dist., 1965-67; tchr. Port Neches (Tex.) Ind. Sch. Dist., 1967-77, dir. student activities, 1977-80, asst. prin., 1980-85, prin. Port Neches-Groves H.S., 1985-88, asst. supt. schs., 1988—; lectr. Lamar U., Beaumont,1990—; cons., Jasper, 1996—. Mem. Rotary, Kiwanis (bd. dirs. 1996—). Democrat. Mem. Ch. of Christ. Home: Rt 1 Box 554-B Jasper TX 75951

WARNER, JOHN WILLIAM, senator; b. Washington, DC, Feb. 18, 1927; s. John William and Martha Stuart (Budd) W.; children: Mary Conover, Virginia Stuart, John William IV. BS Engring., Washington and Lee U., 1949; LL.B., U. Va., 1953. Law clk. to U.S. judge, 1953-54, spl. asst. to U.S. atty., 1956-57; asst. U.S. atty. Dept. Justice, 1957-60; ptnr. Hogan & Hartson, 1960-68; owner, operator Cattle Farm, 1961—; undersec. of navy, 1969-72, sec. of navy, 1972-74; adminstr. Am. Revolution Bicentennial Adminstrn., 1974-76; U.S. senator from Va., 1979—. Served with USNR, 1944-46; to capt. USMCR, 1949-52. Mem. Bar Assn. D.C. Republican. Episcopalian. Club: Metropolitan. Office: Office of Senate 225 Russell Senate Bldg Washington DC 20510-4601*

WARNER, RICHARD ALLEN, small business owner; b. Washington, Feb. 18, 1936; s. Harold Ellsworth Warner and Cynthia Adeline (Brooker) Crocker; m. Druwanda Joan Woolam, June 14, 1958 (div. June 21, 1995); children: Devin Bertwill, Daree Woolam. Waiter/cashier Hot Shoppes, Silver Springs, Md., 1953; apprentice brick mason K&S Brickmasons, Takoma Park, Md., 1954; tractor operator U.S. Dept. Agr., Beltsville, Md., 1954; life underwriter Volunteer State Life Ins. Co., Pensacola, Fla., 1960-62; salesman, divsn. mgr. Sears, Roebuck & Co., Pensacola, 1965-67; mgmt. analyst Civil Svc., Pensacola, 1967-84; profl. driver Poole Truck Line, Pensacola, 1984-86, Puritan-Bennett Corp., Pensacola, 1986-95; owner/operator True-blue Truckin, Orlando, Fla., 1995—; Contbr. letters in various mags., newspapers. Capt. USMC, 1957-65. Mem. NRA (life), Consumers (Reports) Union. Libertarian. Baptist. Office: 4630 S Kirkman Rd # 333 Orlando FL 32811-2873

WARNKEN, BYRON, food products executive; b. 1950. Student, Tex. A&M U.; grad., U. Tex., Austin. Pres. Wilco Peanut Co., Pleasanton, Tex., 1971—. Office: Wilco Peanut Co 2 Mi N US Hwy 281 Pleasanton TX 78064

WARNOCK, CURTLON LEE, lawyer; b. Mpls., Nov. 30, 1954; s. Lowell Wayne and Peggy Joan (Teague) W.; children: Curtlon Lee II, Joshua Douthit, Vanessa Ann, Melissa Kay; m. Jamie Beth Hood, Aug. 24, 1991. Student, Baylor U., 1973-77, JD, 1979. Bar: Tex. 1979, U.S. Dist. Ct. (so. dist.) Tex. 1981, U.S. Supreme Ct. 1986. Assoc. Culpepper & Conway, Houston, 1979-81; atty. Pogo Producing Co., Houston, 1981-86; sr. atty. Burlington Resources Inc, Houston, 1986—. Editor newspaper First Amendment, 1978. Mem. Com. for Pub. Info. Radio Show, Waco, Tex., 1978; bd. dirs., cons. Acad. Devel. Svc., Inc., Houston, 1979-91; counselor Baylor U. Law Sch., Waco, 1980; bd. dirs. Hugh O'Brien Youth Found., Houston, 1982-83. Nat. Merit scholar, Baylor U., 1973. Mem. ABA, Houston Bar Assn., Tex. Bar Assn., Houston Young Lawyers, Houston Jaycees (bd. dirs., legal counsel 1979-82). Republican. Baptist. Home: 17902 Saint Helen Ct Spring TX 77379-6151 Office: Burlington Resources Inc 5051 Westheimer Rd Ste 1400 Houston TX 77056-5604

WARNOCK, DAVID GENE, nephrologist; b. Parker, Ariz., Mar. 5, 1945. MD, U. Calif., San Francisco, 1970. Diplomate Am. Bd. Internal Medicine, Am. Bd. Nephrology. Intern U. Calif., San Francisco, 1970-71, resident, 1971-73; fellow nephrology NIH, Bethesda, Md., 1973-75; prof. medicine and pharmacology U. Calif., San Francisco, 1983; prof. U. Ala., Birmingham, 1988—; chief nephrology sect. VA Med. Ctr., Birmingham, 1983-88; prof., dir. divsn. nephrology U. Ala., Birmingham, 1988—, prof. medicine & physiology, 1988—. Mem. AAAS, Am. Physiol. Soc., Am. Soc. Clin. Investigation, Am. Soc. Nephrology. Office: U Ala Nephrology Rsch & Tng Ctr UAB Sta Birmingham AL 35294*

WARREN, DANIEL CHURCHMAN, health facility administrator; b. Washington, Sept. 23, 1939; s. Walter Thomas and Laura Katherine W.; m. C. Frederica Lescure, June 5, 1958; 1 child, Christopher C. BS, Roanoke Coll., 1960; MD, Med. Coll. Va., 1964; MPH, U. N.C., 1971; MMAS, U.S. Army Command & Gen. Coll., 1974. Diplomate Nat. Bd. Med. Examiners, Am. Bd. Preventive Medicine; lic. physician, Val. Intern Georgetown U. Hosp., 1964-65; resident in surgery Med. Coll. Va., 1967-68, William Beaumont Gen. Hosp., 1968-69; resident in preventive medicine Walter Reed Army Inst. Rsch., 1971-73; commd. 2d lt. U.S. Army, 1965, advanced through grades to col., 1986; asst. med. dir. HealthAm. Va., 1986; pvt. practice travel, 1987-89; dir. Peninsula Health Dist., Newport News, Va., 1990—; clin. asst. prof. family and cmty. medicine Ea. Va. Med. Sch., Norfolk; cons. Riverside Regional Med Ctr., Newport News, Williamsburg (Va.) Cmty. Hosp. Active Gloucester County Rep. Com., 1987—, chmn. 1992-95, Gloucester County Redistricting Adv. Com., 1991; hon. chmn. Combined Va. Campaign United Way the Va. Peninsula, 1992. Fellow Am. Coll. Preventive Medicine, Royal Soc. Medicine; mem. Am. Coll. Physician Execs., Med. Soc. Va., Mid-Tidewater Med. Soc., Ret. Officers Assn. (pers. affairs com.), Cremona Fiddlers, Kiwanis. Republican. Anglican. Office: Peninsula Health Dist 416 J Clyde Morris Blvd Newport News VA 23601-1927

WARREN, DEAN STUART, artist; b. Mpls., June 30, 1949; s. Jefferson Trowbridge and Dorothy Ann (Edin) W.; m. Betty Sharon Poe, Aug. 14, 1971; children: Jeremy, Adam. BFA, Fla. Atlantic U., 1973; MA, Northwestern State U., 1975; MFA, Stephen F. Austin State U., 1980. Instr. art Cisco (Tex.) Jr. Coll., 1976-78; staff craftsworker Walt E. Disney Show Prodn. Walt Disney World, Lake Buena Vista, Fla., 1981-83, staff craftsworker staff shop, 1983, property craftsworker, 1983-87, artist preparator animation dept., 1987—; lead prodn. artist Marvac, Inc., Seminole County, Fla., 1983; founder Dean S. Warren Studio, 1991—; cons. Mt. Dora (Fla.) Ctr. for Arts Children's Edn. Program. Author: Runemaster, 1991; project artist Youth Art Symposium, U. Ctrl. Fla., 1993, Children's Art program, Atlantic Ctr. for arts, 1993, 95, Children's Art Program Mount Dora Ctr. for Arts, 1995; one-man shows include Ormond Beach (Fla.) Meml. Art Gallery and Gardens, 1987, U. Ctrl. Fla. Art Gallery, Orlando, 1991, Harris House Atlantic Ctr. for Arts, New Smyrna Beach, Fla., 1993; exhibited in group shows at U. Miami (Fla.) Sculpture Invitational, 1982, Valencia C.C. Fine Arts Gallery, Orlando, 1989, Polk C.C. Fine Arts Gallery, Winter Haven, Fla., 1990, U. Ga., Athens, 1990, U. Tampa (Fla.) Scarfone Gallery, 1991, World Cup Soccer, Valencia C.C., 1994, Mt. Dora Ctr. of Arts, 1996, others. Recipient Artist in the Schs. grant Tex. Commn. on the Arts, 1980, awards U. Ga. Bot. Gardens, Athens, 1980, Valencia C.C., East Campus, Orlando, 1983, Arts on The Park, Lakeland, Fla., 1995. Home: 8069 Wellsmere Cir Orlando FL 32835-5361

WARREN, DOUGLAS EDGAR, accountant; b. Loudon, Tenn., Nov. 10, 1955; s. Chester Lee and Mary Sue (Burris) W.; m. Letha Ann Cardin, Dec. 7, 1974; children: Erica M., Brenton D. AA in Bus. Adminstrn., Hiwassee Coll., 1975; BS in Acctg., Tenn. Wesleyan U., 1977. CPA, Tenn., Ga. Staff acct. C.L. Warren Co., Madisonville, Tenn., 1975-77; staff acct., ptnr. Warren & Warren, Madisonville, 1977-82; prin. Douglas E. Warren, CPA, Madisonville, 1982-85; pres. Warren & Bales CPA, P.C., Sweetwater, Tenn., 1985-87; mgr. G.R. Rush & Co. CPA, P.C., Sweetwater, 1987-88; mng. ptnr. Warren & Tallent CPA, Sweetwater, 1988—; bd. dirs., vice chair Sweetwater Hosp. Assn.; mem. Tenn. Bd. Accountancy, 1994—. Contbr. to acctg. publs. Past capt. Monroe County Rescue Squad; bd. dirs. Monroe County United Way, Sweetwater, 1986—, Tenn. Fire and Emergency Svcs. Inst., Inc.; mem. Presbytery of East Tenn., 1992; trustee Bachman Meml. Hosme; mem. Sweetwater Indsl. Adv. Bd. Mem. AICPA, Tenn. Soc. CPAs (CPE com.), Tenn. Assn. Pub. Accts. (pres. 1984-85, Outstanding Pub. Acct. award 1984-85), Ga. Soc. CPAs, Ind. Bus. Appraisers, Tenn. Assn. Rescue Squads (treas. 1985—), Monroe County Health Access Coun., Monroe County C. of C. (chmn. 1989), Sweetwater Kiwanis Club (pres. 1991), Masons. Presbyterian. Home: 285 Old Athens Rd Madisonville TN 37354-6166 Office: Warren & Tallent CPA 606 Main St S Ste C Sweetwater TN 37874-2731

WARREN, EMILY P., retired secondary school educator; b. Dayton, Ky., Oct. 6, 1928; d. Morris C. and Kathleen (B.) Parker; m. Richard E. Warren (dec.); children: Richard Warren Jr., George Michael. BS in Home Econs., U. Ky., 1950; MS in Edn., Barry U., 1968; postgrad., Fla. State U. Cert. tchr., Fla. Tchr. home econs. Vevay, Ind., 1950-52, Ludlow, Ky., 1952-53, Cin., 1953-54; part-time adult home econs. tchr. Sch. Practical Nursing Mt. Sinai Hosp., Miami Beach, Fla., 1955-57; elem. tchr. Dade County, Fla., 1957-59, tchr. home econs., 1960-66; coord. vocat. home econs. Dade County Pub. Schs., 1966-91; group leader home econs. tchrs., Russia, 1993, China, 1994, Russia/Hungary, 1995; cons. in field. Named Fla. Tchr. of Yr., 1965. Mem. Am. Assn. Family and Consumer Scis., Am. Vocat. Assn., Dade County Adminstrs. Assn., Dade County Home and Family Edn. Assn., Fla. Adult Edn. Assn., Fla. Assn. for Supervision and Curriculum Devel., Fla. Assn. Family and Consumer Scis., Nat. Assn. Local Suprs. Home Econs. Econs. Assn. (pres.), Internat. Furnishings and Design Assn. (Fla. chpt. v.p. and sec.), Ret. Educators Assn. (pres. Dade County 1994-98, Delta Kappa Gamma. Home: 165 NE 162nd St Miami FL 33162-4226

WARREN, JERRY LEE, academic administrator, conductor; b. Montgomery, Ala., Jan. 12, 1935; s. H.L. and Lula B. (Dowdy) W.; m. Dorothy Glen Floyd, Aug. 17, 1955; children: Dorothy Lee, Laura Ellen, John Floyd. B.M., Samford U., 1955; M.C.M., Sch. Ch. Music, So. Bapt. Theol. Sem., 1959, D.M.A., 1967. Minister music First Bapt. Ch., Cartersville, Ga., 1956-57, Auburn, Ala., 1959-63; asst. prof. music Shorter Coll., Rome, Ga., 1966-69; chmn. dept. music Belmont U., Nashville, 1969-83, dean Sch. Music, 1983-91, acting v.p. acad. affairs, 1991-92, provost, 1992—; choral performer Broadman Singers Rec. Group, Nashville, 1972-80; clinician sch. and ch. choral groups. Tenor soloist 1st Presbyn. Ch., Nashville, 1970-75, 77-79. Mem. Am. Choral Dirs. Assn. (state pres. 1979-81, editor so. div. newsletter 1987-93, editorial bd. Choral Jour. 1987-94, program chair nat. conv. 1989, so. divsn. conv. 1994), Music Educators Nat. Conf., Tenn. Music Educators Assn. (state bd. 1976-88), Mid. Tenn. Vocal Assn. (coll. rep. 1976-88), Coll. Music Soc., Nat. Assn. Tchrs. Singing (local pres. 1974-76), Pi Kappa Lambda. Republican. Baptist. Avocations: golf, reading. Home: 5325 Overton Rd Nashville TN 37220-1924 Office: Belmont U 1900 Belmont Blvd Nashville TN 37212-3758

WARREN, JOHN HERTZ, III, lawyer; b. Charleston, S.C., June 6, 1946; s. John Hertz Jr. and Louise (Hammett) W.; m. Helen Smith, Oct. 7, 1968; children: Louise Capers, Caroline Gregorie, John Alexander. BS in English, Coll. Charleston, 1967; JD, U. S.C., 1972. Bar: S.C. 1972, U.S. Dist. Ct. S.C. 1973, U.S. Ct. Appeals (4th cir.) 1973. Assoc. Brockinton & Brockinton, Charleston, 1972-73; assoc., then ptnr. Sinkler, Gibbs & Simons, Charleston, 1973-85; ptnr. Hutcheson & Warren, Charleston, 1986-92, Warren & Sinkler, Charleston, 1993—. Pres. Charleston Symphony Orch., 1984-85; trustee Hist. Charleston Found., 1987—, pres., 1994—; trustee Coll. of Charleston Found., 1987—, pres., 1995—; bd. dirs. Med. Soc. Health Sys., Inc., 1993—. Mem. ABA, S.C. Bar Assn., Charleston County Bar Assn., Ocean Cruising Club (London), Carolina Yacht Club. Episcopalian. Home: 6350 Oak Grove Plantation Rd Wadmalaw Island SC 29487 Office: 171 Church St Ste 340 Charleston SC 29401-3140

WARREN, KAREN COHEN, librarian; b. Albuquerque, Mar. 19, 1944; d. Edward I. and Corinne Marie (Hall) C.; m. William Francis Warren, May 1, 1938; children: Lisa Marie, Leslie Gail. BA, U. N.Mex., 1966; MLS, U. Tex., 1972. Br. libr. Twin Oaks and Manchaca Rd. Br. Libraries, Austin, 1972-74; libr. assoc. Austin Travis County Collection, 1974-80; reader svcs. libr. Austin History Ctr., 1981—. Mem. Soc. of Southwest Archivists, Austin Heritage Alliance. Office: Austin History Ctr PO Box 2287 Austin TX 78768

WARREN, LARRY ESTEL, internist; b. Clinton, N.C., Apr. 24, 1944; s. Estel M. and Sallie (Sutton) W. BS, N.C. State U., 1966; PhD, U. N.C., 1971, MD, 1974. Diplomate Am. Bd. Internal Medicine. Intern U. Tenn. Hosp., 1974-75; resident in internal medicine New Hanover Hosp., Wilmington, N.C., 1975-77; clinic physician Wake Med. Ctr., Raleigh, 1978-89; pvt. practice, Raleigh, 1990—. Contbr. articles to chemistry jours. Mem. Wake County Med. Soc. Democrat. Baptist. Home: 503 Sunnybrook Rd Raleigh NC 27610-2850

WARREN, LLOYD VAN, software engineer, conceptual designer; b. Little Rock, Ark., May 24, 1956; s. David Sutton Warren and Doris Ann Brannon; m. Lynn Marie Mittelstadt, Jan. 7, 1978; children: Nicholas, Naomi, Bethany. BS in Aerospace Engring., U. Ill., 1981, MS in Aerospace Engring., 1983; MS in Computer Sci., U. Utah, 1985. Systems engr. Jet Propulsion Lab., Pasadena, Calif., 1985; automotive engr. Modular Motors, Pasadena, 1990; software engr. Jet Propulsion Lab., Pasadena, 1991, parachute engr., 1992; conceptual designer Warren Design Vision, Pasadena, 1993, Little Rock, Ark., 1994; cons. U.S. Army CERL, Champaign, Ill., 1981; cons. MCA Universal Inc., Universal City, Calif., 1986, Eyes on Earth, Santa Monica, Calif., 1990, Evans & Sutherland, Salt Lake City, 1991; Rigging Innovations, Romoland, Calif., 1993. Designer Vertical Windtunnel Project, 1981, Bendix Competition: Space Escape Simulation, 1981, CERL Geographic Information System, 1983, "Sound into Graphics" Animation Project, 1984, USAF Simulation87 SDI Project, 1987, USAF Transportation C2 System, 1989, Encyclopedia of Software Components, 1990, Geo Storm Hybrid Electric Car, 1991, AweThenTick Electric Car, 1991, Mars Pathfinder Parachute System, 1993, StratoBike Racing Bicycle, 1993, Micr-Plane Experimental Aircraft, 1994, Designer's CALCbook Software, 1994; dir. "Sky Church" Skydiving Film, 1980; tech. dir. GeoSphere Project, 1989; collaborator Foxbat Indy 500 Racing Telemetry Display, 1989; engr. EOS Spacecraft AIRS Data Processing, 1991. Recipient Hypercube Group Achievement award NASA, 1989. Mem. AIAA, USPA, SKA.

WARREN, MICHAEL DAVID, journalist; b. Pasadena, Calif., June 27, 1968; s. Terry Douglas and Colleen (Moore) W.; m. LuAnne Girard, Mar. 18, 1990. BA in Journalism, Calif. State U., L.A., 1992; postgrad., Ref. Theol. Sem., Orlando, Fla., 1996—. Assoc. editor Youth '86 to Youth '92 Mag., Pasadena, 1986-92, contbg. editor, 1993-96; free-lance journalist Ocala, Fla., 1993—. Contbr. articles to profl. jours.; corr. N.Y. Times Regional Newspapers, 1993-96; columnist Plain Truth Mag., 1996—. Recipient Nat. Collegiate Journalism award USAA, 1988. Mem. Soc. Profl. Journalists, Golden Key, Phi Kappa Phi. Home: 5037 SE 33rd Ter Ocala FL 34480

WARREN, PATSY RUTH, elementary school educator; b. Bryan, Tex., June 19, 1950; d. Arnold Jacob Zgabay and Loretta Joyce (Merchant) Leatherman; m. James Wiatt, Jan. 8, 1972; children: Anna Marie, Mark Pearce. BS in Elem. Edn., U. North Tex., 1972, M of Elem. Supervision, 1977. Cert. elem. tchr. and supervision, Tex. Elem. tchr. Lewisville (Tex.) Ind. Sch. Dist., 1972-77, Eagle Mountain/Saginaw (Tex.) Ind. Sch. Dist., 1983-84, Bridgeport (Tex.) Ind. Sch. Dist., 1985-87, Quitman (Tex.) Ind. Sch. Dist., 1987—; cons. learning styles Quitman Ind. Sch. Dist., 1995—; lectr. in field. Lectr. Weight Watchers, Arlington/Dallas area, 1973-74; mem. Pilot Club, Quitman, 1988-90. Mem. ASCD (site base edn. com. chmn. 1994—), Tex. Classroom Assn., Quitman Classroom Tchrs. Assn. (v.p., treas., rep.), Tex. Coun. of Tchrs. of Math. Southern Baptist. Home: PO Box 697 Quitman TX 75783 Office: Quitman Ind Sch Dist 902 E Goode Quitman TX 75783

WARREN, RICHARD ERNEST, advertising executive; b. Managua, Nicaragua, Jan. 27, 1942; came to U.S., 1948; s. Ernest R. and Marina E. (Echeverria) W.; m. Betty Lou Murray (dec. Apr. 1980); 1 child, Deborah Marie; m. Cynthia Ann Welch, Sept. 13, 1975; 1 child, James Lymon Kendrick III. Degree in bus. adminstrn., Loyola U., New Orleans, 1968, B in Comml. Sci., 1971. Sales office mgr. Avoncraft div. Avondale Shipyards, Inc., New Orleans, 1964-68; exec. dir. Info. Council Ams., New Orleans, 1968-73; account supr. Ladas Advt. Agy., New Orleans, 1973-76; pres., gen. mgr. Warren Advt. Agy., New Orleans, 1976-77; regional account exec. Mace Advt., Inc., New Orleans, 1977-79; nat. account supr. J. Walter Thompson USA, Chgo., 1979-83; v.p., dir. advt. Snapper Power Equipment, McDonough, Ga., 1983-89; pres., gen. mgr. Henco Advt., Inc., McDonough, 1983-89; owner Confectionately Yours, Inc., Atlanta, 1985—; pres. Dick Warren Advt. Agy., Marietta, Ga., 1989—; owner Dick Warren Worldwide Travel, 1992—; cons. Fuqua Industries, Inc., Atlanta, 1984-89; nat. adv. bd. Internat. Care Exploration Soc., 1989, Merehurst Press, Ltd., London, 1989; cons. Nicholas Lodge Brand Products; chmn. adv. com. WFOM-AM; nat. spkr. on effective advt. to travel industry; nat. advisor Holland Am. Cruise Lines, 1996—; bd. dirs. Consortium of N.Y. Editor: (newspapers) Singles Critique, 1972-79, Metairie/Fat City News, 1974-75; producer: Jerry Lewis Muscular Dystrophy Telethon, New Orleans, 1970-73, (TV shows) Spirit '76, New Orleans, 1976, Sportsmen's Paradise, New Orleans, 1976. Served with USAF, 1960-64. Chmn. bus. and fin. com. World Outreach Missionary Ch., 1992—; bd. dirs. Internat. N.T. Ch.; sec. Cobb County Rep. Party; adv. bd. The Consortium. Mem. Am. Film Inst., Joseph's Investment Group, Internat. Confectioner Exploration Soc. (mem. adv. bd. nat. cake decorating and candy supply shops), Young Men's Bus. Club (chmn. 1970), Cruise Line Internat. Assn., Assn. Retail Travel Agts. Republican.

WARREN, SANDRA KAY, writer; b. Grand Rapids, Mich., Oct. 17, 1944; d. Marinus Dieleman and Adrianne Jeanne (Mol) Dieleman-Sjoerdsma; m. Roger Dennis Warren, Sept. 10, 1966; children: Kerri Sue, Leslie Ann, Michelle Lynn. A in Home Econs. Edn., Grand Rapids Jr. Coll., 1964; BS in Home Econs. Edn., Mich. State U., 1966; postgrad., Merrill Palmer Inst., 1967. Writer Trillum Press Royal Fireworks, Unionville, N.Y., 1986—, Mind Play/Methods & Solutions, Tucson, 1988—, Pieces of Learning, Beavercreek, Ohio, 1992-95, Kane Press, N.Y.C., 1994; editor Creative Leaning Conss., Beavercreek, 1992-93, cons., writer, mem. sales dept., 1992-95; sales rep. Synergetics, East Windsor Hill, Conn., 1992—; owner, writer Arlie Enterprises, Strongsville, Ohio, 1992—. Author: Being Gifted: Because You're Special From the Rest, 1987, If I Were a Road, 1987, If I Were a Table, 1987, The Great Bridge Lowering, 187, (book, audio tape, puppet) Arlie the Alligator, 1992, (booklet) Kwanzaa, 1994; author Pieces Ednl. Newsletter, 1993, Nat. State Leadership Tng. Bull., 1978; author, prodr.: (video study kit) Being Gifted: The Gift, 1990; editor Nat. Assn. Gifted Children Parent-Cmty. Newsletter, 1996—. Named Hon. Life mem. Strongsville PTA, 1991. Mem. Mid-Am. Pubs. Assn., Nat. Assn. Gifted Children, Pubs. Mktg. Assn., North East Ohio Pubs. Group (bd. dirs. 1992—), Strongsville Assn., Gifted/Talented Children (founder, past pres., bd. dirs. 1977—), Strongsville C. of C., Ohio assn. Gifted Children (Civic Leadership award 1983), Soc. Children's Book Writers and Illustrators, Great Lakes Booksellers Assn., No. Ohio Pubs. Assn. (v.p. 1995-96), Ohio Libr. Assn., World Coun. Gifted and Talented Children. Office: Arlie Enterprises PO Box 360933 Cleveland OH 44136

WARREN, STEPHEN THEODORE, human geneticist, educator; b. Grosse Point, Mich., Nov. 30, 1953; s. Theodore Stephen and Frances (Fedo) W.; m. Karen Lee Pierce, Aug. 27, 1978; 1 child, Thomas. BS, Mich. State U., 1976, PhD, 1981. Diplomate Am. Bd. Med. Genetics. Grad. asst. Mich. State Univ., East Lansing, 1976-81; rsch. assoc. Univ. Ill., Chgo., 1981-83, instr., 1983-85; asst. prof. Emory U. Sch. of Medicine, Atlanta, 1985-91, assoc. prof., 1991-93, W.P. Timmie prof. human genetics, 1993—; assoc. investigator Howard Hughes Med. Inst., 1991—; vis. scientist European Molecular Biol. Lab., Heidelberg, Germany, 1984.; cons. Ctrs. for Disease Control, Atlanta, 1988-89, NIH, Bethesda, Md., 1989—; collaborator Ctr. D'Etude du Polymorphysme Humain, Paris, 1989—. Mem. editorial bd. Human Molecular Genetics, Am. Jour. Human Genetics, Cytogenetics, Cell Genetics, Mammalian Genome, others; contbr. chpts. to books and more than 60 articles to profl. jorus. Recipient Sigma Xi prize Mich. State Sigma Xi, East Lansing, 1981, NIH fellowship NIH, Bethesda, 1982, Basil O'Connor award March of Dimes, N.Y.C., 1986, Albert E. Levy award Emory Univ., Atlanta, 1987. Mem. Am. Soc. Human Genetics (nominating com. 1991, awards con. 1992—), Am. Soc. Biochemistry and Molecular Biology, Am. Soc. Microbiology, Genetics Soc. Am. Home: 2305 Kimbrough Ct Atlanta GA 30350-5635 Office: Emory Univ Sch Medicine 4035 Rollins Rsch Ctr 1510 Clifton Rd NE Atlanta GA 30329-4218*

WARREN, W. K., JR., oil industry executive; b. 1911. Vice chmn. The William K. Warren Found., Tulsa; also with Warren Am. Oil Co., Tulsa, 1938—, now pres. and chmn. bd. Office: The William K Warren Found PO Box 470372 Tulsa OK 74147-0372*

WARREN, WILLIAM FRAMPTON, JR., religion educator; b. Shelbyville, Tenn., Nov. 16, 1954; s. William Frampton Sr. and Miriam (O'Quinn) W.; m. Katie Cutrer, Dec. 22, 1979; children: William Frampton III, Benjamin Isaac. AA, Okaloosa Walton Jr. Coll., 1974; BS, Miss. Coll., 1976; MDiv, New Orleans Bapt. Theol. Sem., 1979, ThD, 1983. Asst. pastor Istrouma Bapt. Ch., Baton Rouge, 1978-80; pastor Plank Road Bapt. Ch., Slaughter, La., 1980-83; missionary prof. Seminario Teologico Bautista Internat., Cali, Colombia, 1983-89; prof. New Orleans Bapt. Theol. Sem., 1990—; coord., advisor, missionary Buenaventura, Colombia, 1985-89, coord. hunger relief program, 1987-89; coordinating com. pres. grad. program Sem. Teologica Bautista, Cali, 1988-89; mem. exec. com. Colombian Bapt. Mission Bogota, Colombia, 1988-89. Editor: La Teologia De La Liberacion: Una Respuesta Evangelica, 1990; contbr. articles to profl. jours. Mem. Am. Acad. Religion, Soc. Bibl. Lit., Coll. Theology Soc. Democrat. Office: New Orleans Bapt Theol Sem 3939 Gentilly Blvd # 60 New Orleans LA 70126-4858

WARSHAK, RICHARD ADES, clinical and research psychologist, author; b. N.Y.C., Dec. 18, 1949; s. Henry L. and Raye (Ades) W.; m. Sandra Lee Brock, June 22, 1979. BS, Cornell U., 1971; postgrad., CUNY, 1972-74; PhD, U. Tex., 1978. Lic. clin. psychologist, Tex.; cert. health svc. provider, Tex. Staff psychologist Children's Psychiat. Unit Terrell (Tex.) State Hosp., 1976-79; clin. psychologist Dallas Child Guidance Clinic, 1978-81; rsch. scientist U. Tex., Dallas, 1981-83, asst. prof., 1983-85; dir. Tex. Custody Rsch. Project, Dallas, 1977—; clin. instr. dept. psychiatry U. Tex. S.W. Med. Ctr., Dallas, 1980-84, clin. asst. prof. dept. psychiatry, 1984-87, clin. assoc. prof. dept. psychiatry, 1987-93, clin. prof. dept. psychiatry, 1993—; pvt. practice Dallas, 1980—; lectr. U. Tex., Dallas, 1978-81; psychol. cons. McKinney (Tex.) Ind. Sch. Dist., 1976-81; editorial reviewer Jour. Family Psychology, 1992; cons. reviewer Child Devel., 1984—; bd. dirs. Brain-Behavior Ctr., Dallas, 1986—; mem. Scientists' Inst. Pub. Info., 1986—. Author: The Custody Revolution: The Father Factor and the Motherhood Mystique, 1992, (clin. instrument) Warshak Inventory for Child and Adolescent Assessment, 1988, rev. edit., 1995, (audio tape) Custody Consultation with Divorcing Families: How to Avoid Therapeutic Pitfalls, 1983; contbr. chpts. to books, numerous articles to profl. jours., mags. and newspapers. Recipient N.Y. State Bd. Regents scholarship, 1966-70, U. Tex. Health Sci. Ctr. fellowship, 1974-77, Invitation to White House, Pres. Clinton's Dep. Domestic Policy Advisor, Washington, 1993; NIMH rsch. grantee, 1981. Mem. APA, Soc. Rsch. in Child Devel., Tex. Assn. Mediators (profl. mem.), Dallas Soc. Psychoanalytic Psychology (founding mem., adv. coun., editor-in-chief newsletter 1984-91, pres. 1991-92). Office: Clinical Psychology Assocs 16970 Dallas Pky Ste 202 Dallas TX 75248-1928

WARSHAW, DONALD, police chief. Chief Miami Police Dept. Office: Police Dept PO Box 330708 Miami FL 33233-0708*

WARSHAW, IRA GREG, family physician; b. Jan. 17, 1950; m. Jane Warshaw; children: Hayley, Lauren, Emily. BA, Washington U., 1972; MD, Rutgers U., 1979. Resident in family practice Meml. Hosp. R.I., Pawtucket, 1979-82; emergency rm. physician Charlton Meml. Hosp., Fall River, Mass., 1981-83; with Family Doctors Group Ltd., East Providence, R.I., 1982-93, Good Samaritan Primary Care, Palm Beach Gardens, Fla., 1993; physician group coord. Butler Hosp., Providence, 1980-82; clin. asst. prof. Brown U., Providence; clin. mem. Meml. Hosp. R.I., Pawtucket, Woman and Infants Hosp., Providence, Miriam Hosp., Providence, R.I. Hosp., Providence; active Govt. Rite Track Commn., 1992-93; mem. Health Com. on Primary Care, 1992-93. Mem. AMA, Am. Acad. Family Physicians (R.I. chpt. bd. dirs. 1986-93, alt. del. 1987-93, v.p. 1987-89, pres.-elect 1989-91, pres. 1991-93, Fla. chpt. bd. dirs., govt. affairs com. 1993). Home: 2611 Embassy Dr West Palm Beach FL 33401-1016 Office: 3401 Pga Blvd Ste 240 Palm Beach Gardens FL 33410

WARSICK-RINZIVILLO, MARY KATRINA, counselor, educator; b. Tampa, Fla., Aug. 3, 1956; d. Frank McDonough and Mary Margaret (Laxton) W.; m. Ronald Carl Rinzivillo, Nov. 18, 1990. BA in English Edn., U. South Fla., 1979, MA in Counselor Edn., 1984. Lic., cert. mental health counselor, Fla.; nat. cert. counselor; cert. English and mass comm. tchr., Fla. Tchr. Mango (Fla.) Bapt. Sch., 1979-80; tchr. English Eisenhower Jr. High Sch., Gibsonton, Fla., 1980-84; counselor, chair guidance svcs. Dowdell Jr. High Sch., Tampa, 1984-85; counselor Lake Weir Mid. Sch., Summerfield, 1985-87; counselor West Hernando Mid. Sch., Spring Hill, 1987—, counselor, chair guidance svcs., 1989—; pvt. practice Cen. Fla. Counseling Ctr., 1992; contract therapist Cath. Charities, 1992—. Co-facilitator Parent Support Group, Hernando County, Fla., 1988-89, Parents Anonymous, 1990-92. Named Counselor of Yr., Hernando County Mid. Sch., 1987, 88, 91-92. Mem. Hernando County Assn. Counseling and Devel. (pres. 1989-90), Phi Kappa Phi, Phi Delta Kappa. Presbyterian. Office: Hernando County Schs 14325 Ken Austin Pky Brooksville FL 34613-4907

WARTELLA, ELLEN ANN, communications educator, consultant; b. Kingston, Pa., Oct. 16, 1949; d. Nicholas and Margaret (Lipko) W.; m. D. Charles Whitney, Aug. 1, 1976; children: David Charles, Stephen Wright. BA, U. Pitts., 1971; MA, U. Minn., 1974, PhD, 1977. Asst. prof. Ohio State U., Columbus, 1976-79; rsch. asst. prof. communications U. Ill., Champaign, 1979-83, rsch. assoc. prof., 1983-89, rsch. prof., 1989-93; dean Coll. Comm., Walter Cronkite Regents Chair in Comm. U. Tex., Austin, 1993—; vis. prof. U. Calif., Santa Barbara, 1992-93; cons. Children's TV Workshop, N.Y.C., 1988-89, FTC, Washington, 1978, 1991-92, FCC, Washington, 1979. Co-author: How Children Learn to Buy, 1977; editor: Mass Communications Review Yearbook, 1982-83, Rethinking Communication, vols. I and II, 1989. Mem. bd. advisors Am. Children's TV Festival, Chgo., 1988; bd. trustees Children's TV Workshop, 1996—; bd. dirs. Headliners Found., Austin, Sta. KLRU-TV (ex officio), Austin. Recipient Krieghbaum award Assn. for Edn. in Journalism and Mass Communication, 1984; Univ. scholar U. Ill., 1989-93; Gannett Ctr. for Media Studies fellow, 1985-86. Fellow Internat. Comm. Assn. (pres. 1992-93), Broadcast Edn. Assn. (bd. dirs. 1990-94), Speech Comm. Assn., Soc. for Rsch. in Child Devel.

WARWICK, JOHN BENJAMIN, marketing professional; b. Washington, Sept. 28, 1948; s. John B. and Helen (Wagner) W.; m. Cynthia A. Christie, Aug. 16, 1986. BA, St. Bernard Coll., 1970; postgrad., Frostburg State U., 1980. Account exec. AT&T, Washington, 1972-77, market mgr., 1978-81; dist. mgr. edn. AT&T, Cin., 1981-83; v.p. mktg. and sales Lockheed Data Plan, Los Gatos, Calif., 1983-86; pres., cons. Investment Mgmt. Assn., Hillsboro, N.J., 1986-88; dir. mktg., edn. and sales tng. Harris Corp., Melbourne, Fla., 1988-89; pres. Investment Mgmt. Assocs., Inc., Melbourne, 1989—; cons. various corps., Cin., 1981-84; lectr. in field. Author: Successful Telemarketing Skills, 1983, Global Communications in the 90's, 1991, How to Get the Most Bang for Your Marketing Buck, 1992, Wireless Telecommunications, Domestic and Global, 1993, PCS Industry Sales, 1995, Business Negotiations Skills, 1995, Selling Against the Competition, 1996. Mem. Am. Mktg. Assn., Nat. Soc. Sales Tng. Execs., Am. Soc. Tng. and Devel., Dir. Mktg. Assn. Republican.

WASHBURN, CARYL ANNE, occupational therapist; b. Los Cruces, N.Mex., May 3, 1943; d. Peyton Randolph Walmsley and Eleanor (Kellar) Walmsley Davis; m. Arlon Craig Washburn, Dec. 19, 1981. BS, Tex. Woman's U., 1983, MA, 1991. Registered occupational therapist. Flight attendant Am. Flyers Airline, Ardmore, Okla., 1969; libr. asst. Douglas County Libr., Roseburg, Oreg., 1970-71; clk. Forrest Industries, Roseburg, Oreg., 1971-73; adminstrv. asst. pers. Alaska Hosp., Anchorage, 1974-77; psychiat. occupational therapist Harris-H.E.B. Hosp., Bedford, Tex., 1983-84; self-contractor Multiple Home Health Agys., Dallas, 1984-87; prin. Caryls Clinic Occupational Therapy, Denton, Tex., 1987—; co-owner, operator Applied Therapeutic Scis., South Lake, Tex., 1994—; mentor O.T. students; condr. seminars for reversal of carpal tunnel syndrome without surgery (Washburn Technique). Contbr. articles to profl. jours. Vol. horseback therapy for handicapped Freedom Ride, 1983. Mem. Am. Occupational Therapy Assn., Am. Soc. Hand Therapists, Tex. Occupational Therapy Assn. (Clin. Excellence award 1995), South Lake C. of C., Phi Theta Kappa.

WASHBURN, JOHN ROSSER, entrepreneur; b. Hopewell, Va., July 24, 1943; s. Winthrop Doane and Mary Virginia (Overstreet) W.; m. Rebecca M. Wells, Sept., 1991; 1 child, Amanda Ashley Washburn; stepchildren: Eric Joseph Harrison, Leo M. Cicone, Suzann R. Weldon. Student Louisburg Jr.

Coll., 1963, Va. Commonwealth U., 1963-64, U. Richmond Extension, 1967-69, Williams Coll., 1985, Stanford U., 1986-87. Asst. mgr. Liberty Loan Corp., Richmond, Va., 1965-67; loan interviewer Cen. Fidelity Bank, Richmond, 1967-69; regional credit/sales supr. Moores Bldg. Supplies, Inc., Roanoke, Va., 1969-74; corp. credit mgr. Owens & Minor, Inc., Richmond, 1974-88; fin., investment cons. JA-GO Enterprises, Richmond, 1982—; instr., lectr. investment, fin., credit mgmt. Washburn Enterprises, Richmond, 1970—; sec.-treas. Multi-Enterprises, Inc., 1988—; ind. agent N.Y. Life Ins. Co., 1994—; dir., v.p. Forbes Clin. Rsch. Group, Inc., 1995—. Active Nat. Rep. Congl. Com., 1980—, YMCA, 1979—, Am. Mus. Nat. History, 1982—, U.S. Def. Com., 1981—; mem. Credit Rsch. Found. Mem. Internat. Platform Assn., Nat. Assn. Credit Mgmt. (Appreciation cert for outstanding svc. 1980-81, pres. Cen. Va. sect. 1979-80, chmn. legis. com. 1977-79, dir. 1983—), Am. Mgmt. Assn., Nat. Wildlife Fedn., Va. Assn. Life Underwriters, Congressional Club, Hopewell Yacht Club. Episcopalian. Office: Multi-Enterprises Inc 40 Seyler Dr Petersburg VA 23805-9244

WASHBURN, RONALD GLENN, infectious disease physician; b. Lake Forest, Ill., July 14, 1954; s. William Henry and Dorothy (Kohlhepp) W.; m. Deborah Edwards, May 16, 1981. AB magna cum laude, Brown U., 1976; MD, Duke U., 1979. Diplomate Am. Bd. Internal Medicine, subspecialty infectious diseases. Med. intern Duke U., Durham, N.C., 1980-81, med. resident, 1981-83; med. staff fellow NIH, Bethesda, Md., 1983-87; asst. prof. medicine Wake Forest U. Med. Ctr., Winston-Salem, N.C., 1987-91, assoc. prof., 1991—. Ad hoc reviewer VA Merit Review Bd., Infection and Immunity Jour., Infectious Diseases, Clin. Infectious Disease, 1987—. Recipient Scholarship Mallinckrodt Found., St. Louis, 1989, Rsch. Career Devel. award NIH, Bethesda, 1991. Fellow ACP, Infectious Diseases Soc. Am.; mem. Am. Fedn. Clin. Rsch. (nat. coun. 1993—), Am. Soc. Microbiology, Internat. Soc. Human and Animal Mycology, Alpha Omega Alpha. Home: 673 Peoples Creek Rd Advance NC 27006-7442 Office: Wake Forest U Med Ctr Med Ctr Blvd Winston Salem NC 27157

WASHINGTON, AARON ANTHONY, biologist; b. Clarksdale, Miss., Nov. 7, 1954; s. Aron and Minnie Mae (Woods) W.; m. Josie Mae Burrell, Aug. 18, 1978 (div. Sept. 28, 1988); children: Aaron Anthony III, Nadaria, Dwylette. BS, Tougaloo Coll., 1981; postgrad., Jackson State U., 1995. Psychiat. tech. Miss. Mental Hosp., Whitfield, 1981, VA Med. Ctr., Jackson, 1981-83; sr. store mgr. Church's Fried Chicken, Metairie, La., 1983-85; clk. Schwegmann's, Metairie, La., 1985-87; inspector USDA, Morton, Miss., 1987—. Coach Spl. Olympics, Forest, Miss., 1990; vol. GED tchr., Forest, 1994—. Servedin U.S. Army, 1976-79. Mem. Kappa Alpha Psi. Democrat. Baptist. Home: PO Box 641 Forest MS 39064

WASHINGTON, ALBERT, health facility administrator; b. Bostic, N.C., May 10, 1952; s. Sam and Katherine (Toms) W.; m. Phileria Ann Evans, Sept. 3, 1983; children: Reonda, Reginald. BA in Social Studies, Livingstone Coll., 1974; MS in Spl. Edn., MS in Ednl. Media, N.C. A&T State U., 1978, cert. prin., 1990. Cert. spl. edn. tchr., N.C. Tchr. Emotionally Handicapped students Broughton Hosp., Morganton, N.C., 1975-89; ednl. adminstr. III, prin. dir. Enola Learning Ctr Broughton Hosp., Morganton, 1989—; mem. adv. bd. dirs. Burke County Lit. Coun. Chmn. Mountain View Recreation Ctr. Adv. Bd., Morganton, 1988—. Mem. NEA, Nat. Assn. Secondary Sch. Prins., Nat. Assn. Black Social Workers, State Employees Assn. N.C., N.C. Coun. for Exceptional Children, N.C. Hosp. Tchrs. Assn., Alpha Phi Alpha. Baptist. Home: 322 Morehead Street Ext Morganton NC 28655-3054 Office: Broughton Hosp Enola Learning Ctr Morganton NC 28655

WASHINGTON, ALICE HESTER, human services professional; b. Durham, N.C., Oct. 28, 1960; d. Melvin and Martha Elizabeth Hester; m. Melvin Preston Washington, Aug. 13, 1988; 1 child, Melvin Preston Washington II. BS in Home Econs., N.C. Agrl. and Tech. State U., 1983. Dietetic technician N.C. divsn. mental health Mental Retardation and Substance Abuse Svcs., Butner, 1984-85; dietary supr. Svcs. Systems, Marriott Corp., Boca Raton, Fla., 1985; dietetic technician HBA Mgmt. Corp., Ft. Lauderdale, Fla., 1986-87; registered dietetic technician Boca Raton (Fla.) Community Hosp., 1987-89; pub. assistance specialist II Fla. Dept. of Health and Rehab. Svcs., Lauderhill, 1989-91, human svcs. counselor III, 1993—; case worker Fla. Fin. Assistance Specialists, Inc., Ft. Lauderdale, 1991-93. Mem. Mount Bethel Bapt. Ch. Social Svc. Ministry, Ft. Lauderdale, 1993, young women for Christ ministry, 1993; pres. Saint Luke Primitive Bapt. Ch. Young Matrons Aux., Hollywood, Fla., 1989. Mem. Am. Dietetic Assn., Broward County Dietetic Assn. Baptist. Office: Fla Dept Health and Rehab 3800 Inverrary Blvd Ste 203 Fort Lauderdale FL 33319-4313

WASHINGTON, GERALD, manufacturing executive; b. 1939. With Futorian Mfg. Co., New Albany, Miss., 1960-69, De Ville Furniture Co., Pontotoc, Miss., 1969-74, Astro Lounger Co., Okolona, Miss., 1974-76; with Washington Furniture Mfg. Co., Houlka, Miss., 1977—, now chmn. bd. Office: Washington Furniture Mfg Co 6496 Redlane Rd Houlka MS 38850*

WASHINGTON, JAMES EARL, healthcare administrator; b. Grenada, Miss., July 3, 1959; s. Edmond Sr. and Beulah Mae (Ross) W.; m. Ester Stephnie Hope, May 12, 1984; children: Franchesca, Ashli, Amanda. BS in Edn., Jackson (Miss.) State U., 1983, MS in Edn., 1985. Cert. Nat. Coun. for Therapeutic Recreation; ordained to ministry Baptist Ch. Recreation supr. Miss. State Hosp., Whitfield, 1983-88; sr. therapist in therapeutic recreation Rehab. Inst. New Orleans, 1987-88; dir. therapeutic recreation Touro Rehab. Ctr., New Orleans, 1988—; assoc. min. Second New Guide Bapt. Ch., Metairie, La., 1993—; mem. adv. bd. So. U., Baton Rouge, 1994—, Grambling (La.) State U., 1992—; presenter, speaker in field. Bd. dirs. Second New Guide Bapt. Ch., 1989—, United Cerebral Palsy of Greater New Orlans, 1993-95. With ROTC, U.S. Army, 1979-80. Named to Outstanding Young Men of Am., 1985, 94. Mem. Nat. Therapeutic Recreation Assn. (rep.), La. Therapeutic Recreation Assn. (bd. dirs. 1991—, Mem. of Yr. 1994), Am. Therapeutic Recreation Assn. (chair), Nat. Recreation and Parks Assn., Alpha Phi Alpha (1st v.p. 1983). Home: 4128 South Dr Jefferson LA 70121 Office: Touro Rehab Ctr 1401 Foucher St New Orleans LA 70115

WASHINGTON, JAMES MACKNIGHT, former chemical engineer; b. Hackensack, N.J., Dec. 1, 1938; s. Everett Gladstone and Josephine Alice (MacKnight) W.; m. Anne LeBaron Allen, Aug. 18, 1956 (dec. Sept. 1987); children: Jean LeBaron Hall, James MacKnight Jr., John Allen, David Emory; m. Laura Elizabeth Jenison, Feb. 14, 1988 (div. Dec. 1993); 1 child, George Trowbridge. BSChemE, Clemson U., 1961; MSChemE, Va. Polytech. Inst., 1964, PhD, 1969. Assoc. prof. U. New Brunswick, Fredericton, Can., 1965-66; rsch. engr. DuPont, Martinsville, Va., 1966-68; scientist Allied Chem. Corp., Petersburg, Va., 1968-72; rsch. engr. Philip Morris Rsch. Ctr., Richmond, Va., 1972-79, assoc. sr. engr., 1979-93; ret., 1993. With U.S. Army, 1956-59. Mem. AIChE, Sigma Xi. Episcopalian. Home: 2400 Stuts Ln Richmond VA 23236-1638

WASHINGTON, MICHAEL O'NEAL, musician; b. Dania, Fla., Apr. 6, 1951; s. Alfonsa and Sarah W.; m. Evelyn Cooper, Mar. 2, 1993; children: Rodney Dobronozynco, Michael O'Neal Washington, Jr. AS, Miami U., 1972; postgrad., Fla. U., 1984-85. Foreman Southern Bell, Ft. Lauderdale, Fla., 1969-70; musician Raw Soul Express, Miami, Fla., 1972-79; musician, composer Hollywood, Fla., 1979—; judo instr. Model City Sports, Miami, 1972-74; photographer West Hollywood, Fla. Author: The Boy and the Common House Fly, ESP The Unexplained Now Explained, (poem and song) Its Lonely, 1993; composer, musician Its For Real, 1993. Home: 4001 SW 20th St Apt 1 Hollywood FL 33023-3417

WASHINGTON, WALTER, retired academic administrator; b. Hazlehurst, Miss., July 13, 1923; s. Kemp and Mable (Comous) W.; m. Carolyn Carter, July 31, 1949. BA, Tougaloo Coll., 1948, LLD (hon.), 1972; MS, Ind. U., 1952, LLD (hon.), 1983; Edn. Specialist, Peabody Coll., 1958; postgrad., Yale, 1953; EdD, U. So. Miss., 1969; postgrad., Harvard U., 1989; DSc (hon.), Purdue U., 1993. Tchr. Holtzclaw High Sch., Crystal Springs, Miss., 1948-49; asst. prin., tchr. Parrish High Sch., Hazlehurst, 1949-52; prin. Utica Jr. Coll. High Sch., Miss., 1951-54; dean Utica Jr. Coll., 1954-55, pres., 1957-69; prin. Sumner Hill High Sch., Clinton, Miss., 1955-57; pres. Alcorn (Miss.) State U., 1969-94, pres. emeritus, 1994—; past ptnr. Klinger Industries, Ltd.; bd. dirs. Blue Cross and Blue Shield Miss. Pres. Nat. Pan-Hellenic Council, 1964-67, Nat. Alumni Council of United Negro Coll. Fund, 1959-60; past. mem. adv. council Miss. Vocational Edn. Program, Miss. Regional Med. Programs; mem. Miss. Econ. Council; mem. S.E. regional exec. com. Boy Scouts Am.; mem. exec. com. Andrew Jackson council; past mem. adv. council Miss. 4-H Clubs; bd. dirs. Miss. Mental Health Assn., Miss. Easter Seal Soc.; past bd. dirs. Miss. Heart Assn. Recipient Presdl. citation for outstanding leadership to Univ./Industry Cluster, 1980-81, Disting. Alumni award Vanderbilt-Peabody, 1991, George Washington Carver Lifetime Achievement award Tuskegee Inst., 1993; named to U. So. Miss. Alumni Hall of Fame, 1987; Walter Washington Bldgs. named in his honor U. So. Miss., 1993, Alcorn State U., 1994. Mem. NEA, ASCD, Am. Assn. Sch. Adminstrs. (So. Regional Edn. bd.), Nat. Assn. State Univs. and Land Grant Colls., So. Assn. Colls. Secondary Schs. (past bd. dirs., past chmn. secondary commn., past chmn. commn. on colls., past trustee), Miss. Educators Assn. (pres. 1964-65), Miss. Tchrs. Assn., Nat. Soc. for Study of Higher Edn., Tougaloo Nat. Alumni Assn. (pres. 1960), George Peabody Coll. Alumni Assn. (past v.p. exec. com., Disting. Alumni of Yr. 1991), John Dewey Soc., Delta Kappa Pi, Phi Delta Kappa, Alpha Kappa Mu, Alpha Phi Alpha (gen. pres. 1974-76).

WASKA, ROBERT E., SR., retired diplomat, consultant; b. St. Cloud, Minn., Apr. 8, 1925; s. Charles D. and Mildred (Jablonski) W.; m. Frances R. Waska, Oct. 9, 1954; 1 child, Robert E. Jr. BA in Econs., Carleton Coll., 1950; MEd, U. Houston, 1951; MBA, Harvard U., 1971, grad. Advanced Mgmt. Program. Exec. trainee Air Reduction Magnolia Co., Houston, 1950-51; joined Fgn. Svc., U.S. Dept. State, Washington, 1951; assigned to Greece, Pakistan, Italy, Jamaica, Romania, Nigeria, Taiwan, Lebanon, 1951-80, 80-84; sr. Fgn. Svc. insp., 1980-84; sr. examiner DOS Dept. of State; ret., 1986; sr. examiner, security cons. U.S. Dept. State, Washington, cons., 1986-96. Vol. St. James Ch., Falls Church, Va. 2d lt. U.S. Army, 1943-46. Recipient Meritorious Honor award U.S. Dept. State, 1968, 73, 80. Mem. cath. War Vets. USA (comdr. 1988—). Home: 7601 Dominion Dr Falls Church VA 22043-2557

WASKA, RONALD JEROME, lawyer; b. Helena, Mont., Aug. 18, 1942; s. Charles Daniel and Mildred (Jablonski) W.; m. Elizabeth Ann Helten, Dec. 3, 1973; children: Amber Ann, Autumn Ann. BA, U. Tex., 1964; JD in Law, U. Houston, 1969. Bar: Tex. 1969, U.S. Supreme Ct. 1975, U.S. Dist. Ct. (no., so., we., and ea. dists.) Tex., U.S. Tax Ct., U.S. Ct. Appeals (5th, 8th and 11th cirs.). Asst. U.S. atty. Civil and Criminal Div., chief Criminal Div. So. Dist. of Tex., Houston, 1970-75; pvt. practice law Houston, 1976—. Recipient Outstanding Performance Rating Dept. of Justice, Washington, 1970-75, AV Rating Martindale-Hubbell, 1974. Mem. ABA, Houston Fed. Bar, Tex. Trial Lawyers Assn., Assn. Trial Lawyers Am., Fed. Bar Assn. (Outstanding svc. 1974, Younger Fed. Lawyer award 1974), Assn. of Criminal Attys., Tex. Assn. of Criminal Attys., Harris County Assn. Criminal Attys., Phi Alpha Delta, Pi Kappa Alpha. Republican. Roman Catholic. Office: 952 Echo Ln Ste 180 Houston TX 77024-2757

WASMER, CHARLOTTE CARLTON, secondary school educator; b. Pensacola, Fla., Jan. 5, 1967; d. Peter Rudolph and Gene (Brown) W. BA, Coll. of Charleston, S.C., 1989; MA in Tchg., Johns Hopkins U., 1994. Internat. banker Nationsbank, Atlanta, 1989-92; tchr. Balt. City Schs., 1993-94; Caribbean product mgr. Vacation Express Inc., Atlanta, 1994-96; tchr. DeKalb County Schs., Atlanta, 1996—. Vol. Hands on Atlanta, 1990—; mem. Jr. League of Altanta, 1989—. Mem. ASCD, Nat. Coun. for the Social Studies, Ga. Coun. Econ. Edn., Ga. High Sch. Coaches Assn. Democrat. Episcopalian. Home: 1146 Saint Augustine Pl Atlanta GA 30306

WASSELL, STEPHEN ROBERT, mathematics educator, researcher; b. Santa Monica, Calif., Jan. 17, 1963; s. Desmond Anthony and Catherine Ann (Stephens) W. BS in Architecture, U. Va., Charlottesville, 1984, PhD in Math., 1990. Programmer, analyst UNISYS, McLean, Va., 1984-85, graphics artist, 1986; tutor, Summer Transition Program U. Va., Charlottesville, 1987-88, teaching asst., 1986-90; asst. prof. math. Sweet Briar (Va.) Coll., 1990-96, assoc. prof. math., 1996—, dept. chair, 1996—; prof. of record Ctr. for the Liberal Arts, U. Va., 1991; vis. asst. prof. math., Charlottesville, Va., 1992; doctoral cons., Charlottesville, 1989-90; tutor, Charlottesville, 1987-90. Author: (with L.E. Thomas) Schrödinger Operators, 1992; contbr. chpt. to book. Awarded grad. assistantship U. Va., 1986-90; Gordon T. Whyburn fellow, 1985-86. Mem. AAUP (Sweet Briar chpt. sec./treas. 1993—), Am. Math. Soc., Math. Assn. Am., Am. Solar Energy Soc., Sigma Nu (Beta chpt. treas. 1985-86). Home: RR 1 Box 196 North Garden VA 22959-9602 Office: Sweet Briar Coll Dept Math Scis Sweet Briar VA 24595

WASSENICH, LINDA PILCHER, health policy analyst, fund raiser; b. Washington, Aug. 27, 1943; d. Mason Johnson and Vera Bell (Stephenson) Pilcher; m. Mark Wassenich, May 14, 1965; children: Paul Mason, David Mark. BA magna cum laude, Tex. Christian U., 1965; MSW, U. N.C., 1970. Licensed advanced practitioner, cert. social worker, Tex. Counselor family ct. Dallas County Juvenile Dept., Dallas, 1970-73, 75-76; dir. govt. rels. Vis. Nurse Assn., Dallas, 1980-84, exec. officer of hospice, 1984-85; exec. dir. Incest Recovery Assn., Dallas, 1985-86; assoc. exec. dir. Lone Star Coun. Camp Fire, Dallas, 1986-89; exec. v.p. Vis. Nurse Assn. Found., Dallas, 1989-91; dir. policy & resource devel. Vis. Nurse Assn. Tex., Dallas, 1992—. Contbr. articles to profl. publs. Bd. dirs. Women's Coun. Dallas County, 1986-95, pres., 1992-93; chmn. Dallas County Welfare Adv. Bd., 1991-95; bd. dirs. United Way of Met. Dallas, 1992-94, Youth Impact Ctrs., Dallas, 1993-94; mem. adv. bd. Maternal Health and Family Planning Dallas, 1990-94; mem. Leadership Dallas, 1988-89. Recipient AAUW, Dallas, Laurel award, 1995. Mem. NASW (Tex. bd. dirs., nominating chmn. 1990-92, co-chmn. Dallas unit 1981-82, Social Worker of Yr. award 1988), LWV (bd. dirs. Dallas 1974-80, 95—, pres. 1995—), Acad. Cert. Social Workers, Nat. Soc. Fundraising Execs. (cert., bd. dirs. Dallas chpt. 1994—, v.p. governance 1995-96). Home: 6948 Kenwhite Dr Dallas TX 75231-5640 Office: 1440 W Mockingbird Ln Dallas TX 75247-4929

WASSERMAN, FRED, III, internist; b. Phila., May 17, 1955; m. Susan Valesky; 1 child, Sara Elisabeth. MBA, U. South Fla., 1990; MD, U. Miami, 1981. Diplomate Am. Bd. Internal Medicine. Resident in gen. surgery U. Miami (Fla.) Affiliated Hosps., 1981-82; resident in internal medicine Baylor Coll. Medicine Affiliated Hosps., Houston, 1982-85; chief med. officer, clin. of jurisdiction Dept. Vets. Affairs Bay Pines (Fla.) VA Med. Ctr., 1991—. Mem. ACP, Am. Coll. Physician Execs. Office: Dept Vets Affairs Bay Pines VAMC Bay Pines FL 33744

WASSERMAN, KAREN BOLING, clinical psychologist, nursing consultant; b. Olney, Ill., July 29, 1944; d. Kenneth G. and Betty Jean (Varner) Boling; m. James M. Wasserman, Apr. 14, 1965; children: Nicole C., Michael B. RN, Barnes Hosp. Sch. Nursing, St. Louis, 1965; BA, Antioch Coll., 1977; Dr. of Psychology, Wright State U., 1986. Lic. psychologist, Miss., Ohio, Ind.; RN, Miss., Mo., Ohio. Staff nurse various med. facilities, 1965-76; instr. practical nurse program Ind. Vocat. Tech. Coll., Richmond, 1976-77; staff, float nurse Good Samaritan Hosp., Dayton, Ohio, 1977-78; pub. health nurse coord. Bur. Alcoholism Svcs., Dayton, 1978-79; alcoholism counselor IV Bur. Alcoholism Svcs., Dayton, Ohio, 1979-82; practicum student Wright State U. Sch. Profl. Psychology, Dayton, 1983-85; psychology intern Balt. VAMC Consortium, 1985-86; clin. psychologist Dayton VAMC, 1987-89; dir. clin. svcs., pvt. mental health Fairhaven Clinic, P.A., Biloxi, Miss., 1989—; clin. psychologist Gulf Oaks Hosp., Biloxi, 1989—; Sand Hill Hosp., Gulfport, Miss., 1993—; psychiatric nursing cons. Mercy Hosp., Omaha, Council Bluffs, Iowa, 1987; instr. William Carey Coll. on the Coast, 1993; owner/proprietor Angel Garden Books, Biloxi, 1996—. Chmn. cmty. svcs. Altrusa Internat., Biloxi, 1990-94, treas., 1993-94; mem. Evangelism com. First United Meth. Ch., Gulfport, Miss., 1991-93, coun. on ministries, 1994-95; Friend of the Rainbow Warrior, Greenpeace, 1986-93. Recipient Alumnae award in Acads., Barnes Hosp. Sch. Nursing, 1965, Career Woman of Yr. award, Lighthouse of Biloxi chpt., Bus. and Profl. Women, 1994. Fellow Am. Acad. Psychologists Treating Addiction; mem. APA, Ohio Psychol. Assn., Miss. Psychol. Assn. (continuing edn. com. 1990-95, chair 1994-95). Office: Fairhaven Clinic PA Pvt Mental Health 2635 Pass Rd Biloxi MS 39531-2729 also: Angel Garden Books 2635A Pass Rd Biloxi MS 39531

WASSERMAN, RICHARD LAWRENCE, pediatrician, educator; b. Bklyn., Oct. 28, 1948; s. Isidore and Gladys W.; m. Tina D. Wasserman; children: Jonathan A., Leslie R. BS in Chemistry, Hobart Coll., 1970; PhD, CUNY, 1975; MD, U. Tex. Southwest, Dallas, 1977. Diplomate Am. Bd. Pediatrics, Am. Bd. Allergy and Immunology. Resident in pediatrics Children's Hosp. Phila., 1977-79, fellow in immunology, 1979-80; rsch. assoc. in immunology Rockefeller U., N.Y.C., 1980-82; asst. prof. pediatrics and microbiology U. Tex. S.W. Med. Ctr., Dallas, 1982-88, asst. clin. prof. pediatrics, 1988—; asst. chief pediatrics Baylor U. Med. Ctr., Dallas, 1989; adj. attending physician Mt. Sinai Hosp., N.Y.C., 1981-82; cons. Am. Assn. Blood Banks, Arlington, Va., 1983-95; med. dir. pediatric allergy and immunology Columbia Hosp. at Med. City, Dallas, 1994—. Mem. Am. Assn. Immunologists, Clin. Immunology Soc., Am. Assn. Allergy Asthma and Immunology, So. Soc. for Pediatric Rsch. (coun. 1986-87, Founder's award 1988), Phi Beta Kappa Zeta. Home: 7153 Lavendale Ave Dallas TX 75230-3650

WASSERMAN, SUSAN VALESKY, accountant; b. St. Petersburg, Fla., June 5, 1956; d. Charles B. Valesky and Jeanne I. (Schulz) Morgan; m. Fred Wasserman III, May 19, 1990; 1 child, Sara Elisabeth. BS in Merchandising, Fla. State U., 1978; BA in Acctg., U. South Fla., 1983; ChFC, Am. Coll., 1991. CPA, Fla.; ChFC, Fla. Mgmt. trainee Burdines Dept. Stores, Miami, Fla., 1978-79; store mgr. Levi Straus Inc., San Francisco, 1979; pvt. practice St. Petersburg, Fla., 1980—; internet practice, 1996—. Paintings shown at Longboat Key (Fla.) Art Ctr. Watercolor 10 Art Show, 1993, Fla. Suncoast Watercolor Soc. Aqueous Show, Sarasota, 1994; quoted in The Tax Advisor (nat. syndicated column); developer 1st worldwide Internet discussion group on fin. planning. Mem. AICPA (personal fin. specialist), Am. Soc. CLUs and ChFCs (bd. dirs.), Fla. Inst. CPAs. Office: PO Box 406 Terra Ceia FL 34250-0406

WASSON, ELIZABETH ANNE, newspaper editor; b. Springfield, Mo., Oct. 13, 1951; d. Harry O. and Mary S. (Kennedy) Howard; m. Calvin E. Wasson, Aug. 8, 1970; children: Sarah Elizabeth, John Calvin. BA, Ark. State U., 1974, MA, 1977. Lic. social worker, Ark. Tchg. asst. Ark. State U., Jonesboro, 1975; rschr., planner Office of Youth Svcs., Jonesboro, 1977; program adminstr. East Ark. Area Agy. on Aging, Jonesboro, 1977-87; exec. dir. Ark. Assn. of Area Agys. on Aging, Little Rock, 1987-90, Ark. Aging Found., Little Rock, 1990—; editor, pub. Aging Ark. newspaper, 1990—; bd. dirs., v.p. Nonprofit Resources, Inc., Little Rock. Justice of the Peace, Craighead County Quorum Ct., Jonesboro, 1974-76; v.p. Craighead County Young Dems., Jonesboro, 1974-75; Greene County del. Dem. State Nominating Conv., Little Rock, 1980, 84; elected Ark.'s del. Ctr. for the Study of the Presidency, N.Y., 1975, 77. Mem. DAR, LWV (bd. dirs.), Phi Kappa Phi. Democrat. Presbyterian. Home: 66 Lakeshore Dr Little Rock AR 72204 Office: Ark Aging Found 706 S Pulaski St Little Rock AR 72201

WASSON, JOHN MARVIN, English language educator; b. Thayer, Mo., Feb. 23, 1928; s. David Ratliff and Florence Myrtle (MacDonald) W.; m. Janis Ahola Ho, June 15, 1969 (div. Oct. 1982); children: Jo Marie Galt, David Carlisle, Adam Jon, Matthew Frederick; m. Barbara Lee Dallas Palmer, July 31, 1982. BA, Cen. Meth. Coll., Fayette, Mo., 1950; MA, U. Mo., 1953; PhD, Stanford U., 1959. Tchg. asst. U. Mo., Columbia, 1952-53, Stanford (Calif.) U., 1953-57; prof. of English Wash. State U., Pullman, 1957-92; adj. prof. Mary Washington Coll., Fredericksburg, Va., 1995—. Author: (book) Subject and Structure, 8 edits., 1963-83; editor: Malone Society Collections IX, 1980, Records of Early English Drama: Devonshire, 1986. Actor in 54 plays various locations. Sgt. paratroops, 1946-48, Japan, 1950-51, Korea. Grantee Nat. Endowment for Humanities, 1978, 85, 91. Mem. MLA, Internat. Shakespeare Assn., Shakespeare Assn. of Am., Malone Soc. Democrat. Home: 120 Woodland Rd Fredericksburg VA 22401

WATANABE, ALBERT TOHRU, classical studies educator; b. Honolulu, May 7, 1956; s. Reizo and Hanako (Yamachika) W. BA in Liberal Arts, St. Mary's Coll., 1978; MA in Classics, U. Calif., Santa Barbara, 1982; PhD in Classics, U. Ill., 1988. Instr. Monmouth (Ill.) Coll., 1987-88; adj. prof. U. South Fla., Tampa, 1988-89; vis. asst. prof. U. Calif., Irvine, 1989-91; instr. Univ. Memphis, 1991—; Bernice L. Fox Classics lectr., Monmouth, Ill., 1995. Mem. Am. Philol. Assn., Phi Kappa Phi. Office: Univ Memphis Dept Fgn Lang & Lit Memphis TN 38152

WATANABE, WADE OSAMU, marine biologist; b. Honolulu, Sept. 19, 1951; s. Charles Shujiro and Clara Mieko (Hasegawa) W.; m. Colleen Aiko Sasaki, June 26, 1976; children: Skye, Laine, Landon. BS in Zoology, Oreg. State U., 1973; MS in Zoology, U. Hawaii, 1975, PhD in Zoology, 1982. Lab. technician Fish Physiology Lab., Oceanic Inst., Hawaii, 1976-77, rsch. asst., 1977-81; marine biologist Internat. Ctr. for Living Aquatic Resources Mgmt., Manila, Philippines, 1982-84; chief scientist Caribbean Marine Rsch. Ctr., Vero Beach, Fla., 1986-95, Sea Change Found., Vero Beach, Fla., 1996—; adj. grad. faculty mem. Dept. Biol. Scis., Fla. Inst. Tech., 1991—; cons. in field; lectr. in field; grant reviewer NSF, Nat. Coastal Resources Rsch. and Devel. Inst., Univ. Hawaii Sea Grant Coll. Program, Nat. Marine Fisheries Svc. Co-editor: Aquaculture of the Milkfish, 1986; reviewer Aquaculture Jour., Jour. World Aquaculture Soc., Aquaculture Engring., Can. Jour. Zoology, Jour. Fish Biology, Aquatic Living Resources, Jour. Applied Aquaculture, Asian Fisheries Soc., Gulf and Caribbean Fisheries Inst., Jour. Aquaculture in the Tropics; contbr. articles to profl. jours. Grad. rsch. assistantship Hawaii Inst. Marine Biology, 1975; Jessie Smith Noyes Found. pre-doctoral fellow, 1977-81, Rockfeller Found. postdoctoral rsch. fellow, 1982-84; grantee Caribbean Marine Rsch. Ctr., 1987-91, 92, Oceanic Inst. Hawaii, 1993, 94, George F. Baker Trust, 1993, 94, 95, Marine Scis. and Tech. Ctr./U. Conn., 1995, 96. Mem. Am. Tilapia Assn. (bd. dirs. 1991-92), Fla. Foodfish, Gamefish and Aquatic Bait Farmers Assn. (bd. dirs. 1992), Internat. Ctr. for Living Aquatic Resources Mgmt. (affiliate scientist 1984-88), World Aquaculture Soc., Asian Fisheries Soc., Caribbean Aquaculture Assn. (bd. dirs. 1993-96), Fla. Aquaculture Assn., Network of Tropical Aquaculture Scientists. Home: 5846 62nd Ln Vero Beach FL 32967-5263 Office: Sea Change Found 4731 N Hwy AIA Ste 222 Vero Beach FL 32963

WATCHORN, THOMAS M., bank executive; b. 1949. Former cons. McGladrey & Pullen, CPA; with Citizens Savings Bank, Inc., Newton, N.C., 1987—, now pres., CEO. Office: Citizens Savings Bank Inc 22 S Main Ave Newton NC 28658-3319*

WATERHOUSE, MONA ELISABETH, artist; b. Grangesberg, Dalarna, Sweden, June 9, 1942; came to U.S., 1966; d. Rolf Folke and Gunborg Sofia (Skog) Johansson; m. John Fredric Waterhouse, Aug. 17, 1961; 1 child, Andrew John. Student, Coventry (Eng.) Coll. Art, 1961-63; BFA summa cum laude, U. Mass., 1975, MAT, 1978. Cert. art instr., Mass., Wis. Tchr. art Covington (Va.) High Sch., 1968-70; art and critic tchr. Clarke Sch. for Deaf, Northampton, Mass., 1976-78; tchr. art John F. Kennedy Jr. High Sch., Florence, Mass., 1978, Westfield (Mass.) State Coll., 1979; instr. art U. Mass., Amherst, 1978-81; tchr. art Hadley (Mass.) Elem. Schs., 1979-81; asst. adminstr. Appleton (Wis.) Gallery Arts, 1981-84; instr. art St. Thomas More Sch., Appleton, 1983-89; free-lance artist Peachtree City, Ga., 1989—; art cons. Dignity of Man Found., San Francisco, 1975-81; art judge various art events; artist-in-residence Ga. Coun. for the Arts, 1991—, Fulton County Sch. Arts Program, 1991—. One-person shows include Bergstrom-Mahler Mus., Neenah, Wis., 1996; exhbns. include Heter Gallery, U. Mass., Amherst, 1980, Hampshire Coll., Amherst, 1981, U. Wis., Oshkosh, 1984, Edna Carlsten Gallery U. Wis., Stevens Point, 1985, U. Wis., Menasha, 1985, Marquette Haggerty Mus., Milw., 1986, Dard Hunter Mus., Appleton, Wis., 1986, 87, The Arts Ctr., Iowa City, 1986, Neville Pub. Mus., Green Bay, Wis., 1986, 87, Milw. Inst. Art and Design, 1986, GEF Bldg., Madison, Wis., 1987, Edgewood Orchard Galleries, Fish Creek, Wis., 1987, No. Mich. U., Marquette, 1987, Fine Arts Gallery Ind. U., Bloomington, 1988, Wis. Women in the Arts, 1988-89 (travelling exhibit), Mindscape Gallery, Evanston, Ill., 1988, Milw. Art Mus., 1989, West Bend Gallery of Fine Arts, Wis., 1989, TAPPI's Internat. Paper Art Festival, Atlanta, 1990, Columbia Coll., Mo., 1991, Perspectives Gallery, Mpls., 1991, Arts Ctr., Athen, Ohio, 1991, Arts Ctr., Cartersville, Ga., 1992, Forum Gallery, Jamestown, N.Y., 1992, Hastings Seed Bldg., Atlanta, 1993, Univ. Milw. Art Gallery, 1993, Westbrook Gallery, Atlanta, 1993, Kvarnen, Sundborn, Sweden, 1995; publs. include Chgo. Art Rev., 1989, Fiber Arts Design Book 4, 1991, Book 5,

1995. Active Amnesty Interant., Save the Children. Individual Artist grantee Ga. Coun. for Arts and Fulton County Arts Coun., 1994, Hartsfield Internat. Airport Olympic Centennial Youth Art Project grantee, Atlanta, 1996. Mem. Nat. Art Edn. Assn., Internat. Assn. Paper Artists, Friends Dard Hunter Paper Mus. Democrat. Home and Office: 102 Delbank Pt Peachtree City GA 30269-1184

WATERS, CURTIS JEFFERSON, retired minister, evangelist; b. Spartanburg, S.C., Apr. 8, 1929; s. Leroy Belton and Lillian Isola (Tucker) W.; m. Nancy Carol Taylor, Oct. 25, 1947; children: Curtis Michael, Ronald Stephen, Gloria Lynn. BA, North Greenville Coll., Tigerville, S.C., 1953; BD, Luther Rice Sem., Jacksonville, Fla., 1973; DD (hon.), North Fla. Bapt. Theol. Sem., 1988, ThD, 1991. Ordained to ministry So. Bapt. Conv., 1950; lic. real estate broker, N.C. Pastor Gap Creek Bapt. Ch., Marietta, S.C., 1950-51, Fairmont (S.C.) Bapt. Ch., 1951-55, Francis Bapt. Ch., Palatka, Fla., 1955-60, Double Springs Bapt. Ch., Greer, S.C., 1960-63, Churchwell Avenue Bapt. Ch., Knoxville, Tenn., 1963-71, Tuxedo (N.C.) 1st Bapt. Ch., 1971-75, City View 1st Bapt. Ch., Greenville, S.C., 1975-93; retired, 1993; chmn. bd. dirs. Champions for Christ Found. City View 1st Bapt. Ch., Greenville, S.C., 1987-93; ret., 1993, evangelist, 1993—; dir. E.J. Daniels Crusade, Palatka, Fla.; evangelist 9 states and Jamaica; sem. commencement speaker North Fla. Bapt. Theol. Sem., 1989-90, 90-91; speaker Bible confs. Bd. dirs. Jacksonville (Fla.) Bapt. Theol. Sem. Republican. Home: 148 Pilot Rd Greenville SC 29609-6348

WATERS, CYNTHIA WINFREY, media advertising specialist; b. Atlanta, Feb. 25, 1951; d. Tommie Lee Winfrey; m. Leroy Hollaway Jr., June 7, 1970 (div. 1981); children: Marechalnelle, Geoffrey; m. Leamond Howard Waters, Sept. 1, 1985. Cert. in acctg., Atlanta Area Tech. Inst., 1982; cert. in human relations, Chattahoochee Tech. Inst., 1988. Customer svc. rep. Atlanta Gaslight Co., 1975-83; asst. mktg. mgr. Vorwerk, U.S.A., Atlanta, 1983-86; fgn. sec. coord. Focal Point Inc., Atlanta, 1986-91, safety facilitator, 1988-91; pub. svc. dir. Sta. WYZE Radio, Atlanta, 1991—, media advt. specialist, 1996—; TV host A New Look in Gospel, Atlanta, 1991—; sec. Emory U., Atlanta, 1993-94; owner operator Water Print Media Creations, 1995—. Mem. Atlanta Prevention Connection, Edwin Hawkins Arts & Music Seminar Choir Metro Atlanta chpt.,Gateway Baptist Church youth job training pgm., cons. Home: 2968 Chipmunk Trl Marietta GA 30067 Office: PO Box 813056 Smyrna GA 30081-8056

WATERS, DOUGLAS STUART, JR., engineering company consultant, civil engineer; b. Phila., Nov. 21, 1946; s. Douglas Stuart Waters and Betty Jean Elizabeth (Hamilton) Underwood; m. Edna Josephine Medina, Aug. 30, 1969; children: Patricia Renee Williamson, Natalie Waters, Jennifer Michelle Waters. BS in Civil Engring., U. Del., 1972; postgrad., U. Houston, 1974-77; M in Mgmt. cum laude, Webster U., 1987. Registered profl. engr., Tex., Ala., Tenn. Civil engr. U.S. Army Corps of Engrs., Phila., 1972-73, Galveston, Tex., 1973-77, Mobile, Ala., 1977-82; project engr. U.S. Army 21th Support Command, Kaiserslavtern, Germany, 1982-83; dep. dir. engring. and housing U.S. Army 29th Area Support, Kaiserslavtern, 1983-85; project engr. Air Logistics Ctr., USAF, San Antonio, 1985-87; chief ops. divsn., dir. engring. and housing Walter Reed Army Med. Ctr., Washington, 1987-89; dep. dir. engring. and housing U.S. Army 7th Corps, Stuttgart, Germany, 1989-91; dir. installation svcs. Def. Logistics Agy., Memphis, 1991-94; regional mgr. Allen & Hoshall, Inc., Irving, Tex., 1994-96; cons. U.S. Postal Svc. in energy Pickering Environ. Svcs., Memphis, 1996—. Dir. U.S. Jaycees, League City, Tex., 1975; bd. mem. Montgomery Village Bd., Gaithersburg, Md., 1989; treas. Parent, Tchr., Student Assn., Stuttgart, 1990. Sgt. USAF, 1966-70. Mem. ASCE (chpt. sec. Mobile, Ala., 1981), Am. Pub. Works Assn., Soc. Am. Mil. Engrs., Nat. Soc. of Environ. Cons. Presbyterian. Home: 8418 King William St Cordova TN 38018

WATERS, H. FRANKLIN, federal judge; b. Hackett, Ark., July 20, 1932; s. William A. and Wilma W.; m. Janie C. Waters, May 31, 1958; children—Carolyn Denise, Melanie Jane, Melissa Ann. B.S., U. Ark., 1955; LL.B., St. Louis U., 1964. Engr., atty. Ralston-Purina Co., St. Louis, 1958-66; ptnr. Crouch, Blair, Cypert & Waters, 1967-81; judge U.S. Dist. Ct. (we. dist.) Ark., from 1981, now chief judge. Former bd. dirs. Springdale Schs.; former bd. govs. Washington Regional Med. Ctr. Mem. ABA, Ark. Bar Assn., Springdale C. of C. (past bd. dirs.). Office: US Dist Ct PO Box 1908 Fayetteville AR 72702-1908*

WATERS, JOHN W., minister, educator; b. Atlanta, Feb. 5, 1936; s. Henry and Mary Annie (Randall) W. Cert., U. Geneva, Switzerland, 1962; BA, Fisk U., 1957; STB, Boston U., 1967, PhD, 1970. Ordained to ministry Bapt. Ch., 1967. Min. religious edn. Ebenezer Bapt. Ch., Boston, 1965-67, assoc. min., 1967-69; min. Myrtle Bapt. Ch., West Newton, Mass., 1969, Greater Solid Rock Bapt. Ch., Atlanta, 1981—; prof. Interdenominational Theol. Ctr. , Atlanta, 1976-86, trustee, 1980-83; bd. dirs. Habitat for Humanities, Atlanta, 1984-90; chmn. South Atlanta Joint Urban Ministries, 1983-93. Contbr. articles to profl. jours. Mem. Va. Highlands Neighborhood Assn., Atlanta, 1977-87, Butler St. YMCA, 1980-86, South Atlanta Civic League, 1983, others; treas. Prison Ministries with Women, Inc.; v.p. South Met. Ministries Fellowahip, Atlanta, 1990-94. Fund for Theol. Edn. fellow, 1965-67, Nat. Fellowship Fund fellow, 1968-70, Rockefeller doctoral fellow, 1969. Mem. AAUP (chpt. pres. 1971-72), Am. Acad. Religion, Soc. Bibl. Lit., Blacks in Bibl. Studies, New Era Missionary Bapt. Conf. Ga., So. Bapt. Conv. Democrat. Home: 1516 Niskey Lake Trl SW Atlanta GA 30331-6318 Office: The Greater Solid Rock Bapt Ch 6280 Camp Rd Riverdale GA 30296-2803

WATERS, MARY BASKIN, state agency administrator, educator; b. Sumter, S.C., Aug. 31, 1945; d. Norwood Fleming and Nan Richardson (Rickenbaker) Baskin; m. Samuel C. Waters, Sept. 14, 1968. Cert. d'Etude, Sorbonne U., Vichy, France, 1966; BA, U. S.C., 1985, MA in Tchg., 1987; Grad. Cert. in Women's Studies, S.C. Exec. Inst., 1993. Instr. art Newberry (S.C.) Coll., 1987-92; instr. women's studies U. S.C., Columbia, 1988—; instr. art U. S.C., Lancaster, 1990-92; dir. S.C. Commn. on Women, A Divsn. of Gov.'s Office, Columbia, 1992—; budget and control bd. mem., 1993—; vis. lectr. U. S.C., Columbia, 1988; art cons., broker Carolina Editions Gallery, Columbia, 1990; instr. art Midlands Tech. Coll., Columbia, 1991; exec. bd. Advs. for Women on Bds. and Commns., Columbia; adv. bd. Pathways for Women at Richland Meml. Hosp., Columbia; mem. Leadership Inst., Columbia (S.C.) Coll.; lectr. in field. Contbr. articles to profl. jours. Mem. S.C. Dept. Edn. Visual and Performing Arts Transition Com., Columbia, 1991; adv. com. Women in State Work Force Symposium, 1993; adv. com. Women in State Work Force Symposium, 1993; adv. bd. S.C. Women in Higher Edn. Adminstrn., 1994; S.C Del. leader U.S. Southeastern Regional Conf. Beijing World Conf., 1995, commn. USIA Grant Commn. Exchange Program Women and Civic Participation, 1996—; adv. bd. The Leadership Inst. Columbia Coll. Mem. Nat. Art Edn. Assn., Nat. Coun. for Rsch. on Women, Southeastern Women's Studies Assn., Nat. Assn. Commns. on Women (S.C. delegation leader U.S. Southeastern Regional Conf. on Women, UN Preparatory Meeting for Beijing World Conf. 1995, commr. USIA, Grant Cmmn. Exch. Program, Women and Civic Participation 1996, adv. bd. A Leadership Jour.: Women in Leadership-Sharing the Vision, The Leadership Inst., Columbia Coll.), Richland County Legal Aux. (pres. 1982-83), Brennen Elem. Sch. PTO (pres. 1980-81), Golden Key Honor Soc., Gamma Beta Phi, Kappa Phi Kappa. Office: Office of Gov SC Commn on Women 2221 Devine St Ste 408 Columbia SC 29205-2418

WATERS, MICHAEL VINCENT, music and Spanish language educator; b. N.Y.C., Mar. 24, 1959; s. Michael F.X. and Margaret (O'Carroll) W.; m. Mary Kay Bauer, July 1, 1989. MusB, Cath. U. Am., Washington, 1981; diploma, Bklyn. Conservatory Music, 1988; diploma in Spanish, U. Complutense Madrid, 1991. Cert. music tchr., N.Y., N.C., cert. elem. Spanish tchr., N.C. Tchr. St. Catherine of Genoa Sch., Bklyn., 1982-88; music dir. Highlands's (N.C.) United Meth. Ch., 1988-89; tchr. Macon County Pub. Schs., Franklin, N.C., 1989—; instr., dir. classical guitar studies Western Carolina U., Cullowhee, N.C., 1989—; adjudicator N.C. State Teaching Fellowships, Raleigh, N.C., 1994, 95, 96. Author: Irish Pipe Music, 1987, The Kirking of the Pipers, 1994; arranger: Songs of Yellow Mountain, 1992; piper Clann Eireann Piper's Band, Bklyn., 1976-88; pipe maj. Highlands Pipes and Drums, 1988—; performer All Ireland Music Competitions, Listowel, Kerry, Ireland, 1987, Vail Internat. Celtic Music Festival, 1995; rec. artist (CD) Scottish and Irish Music ffrom Highlands, N.C., 1995. Recipient King Juan Carlos fellowship Ortega y Gasset Found., Madrid, 1991, Teaching fellowship N.C. Ctr. for Advancement of Teaching, 1993. Mem. ASCD, Am. Coun. Teaching Fgn. Langs., Am. Assn. Tchrs. of Spanish, Ea. U.S. Pipe Band Assn., Scottish Tartan's Soc., Classical Guitar Soc. Western Carolinas. Democrat. Roman Catholic. Home: 795 Pressley Creek Rd Cullowhee NC 28723-9546 Office: Western Carolina Univ Dept Music Cullowhee NC 28723

WATERS, ROLLIE ODELL, consulting company executive; b. Charleston, S.C., Oct. 14, 1942; s. Rollie Robert and Mary Olivia (Brown) W.; divorced; children: Wendie Kay, Lauren Olivia. A.A., Spartanburg Coll., 1968; BS, U. S.C., 1969; MBA, Pepperdine U., 1980; cert. mgmt. cons. Supr. comms. and spl. activities Owens-Corning Fiberglas, Aiken, S.C., 1970-71, asst. pers. dir., Fairburn, Ga., 1971-72; pers. dir. Meisel Photochrome Corp., Atlanta, 1972-73, dir. corp. pers., Dallas, 1973-76, asst. v.p., dir. human resources, after 1976; co-founder, sr. ptnr. chief exec. officer Waters, Trego & Davis, Dallas, 1976-88; owner The Waters Cons. Group, 1988—; publicity dir., program dir. 35th and 36th North Tex. Pers. Confs.; guest lectr. Lorch Found., London, Calif. Inst. Tech., U. Md., Am. Mgmt. Assn. So. Meth. U.; spkr. in field. Author: (tng. sys.) The Manager, CASS-Computer Software for Computation, PAMS-Computor Software for Performance Appraisal; contbr. articles to profl. jours. With USAF, 1962-66. Mem. Internat. Personnel Mgmt. Assn., Inst. Mgmt. Cons. (cert., bd. dirs. Texoma chpt.), Soc. Human Resource Mgmt. (nat. compensation and benefits com.), Internat. Pers. Mgmt. Assn., Dallas Pers. Assn. (v.p. membership 1977-78), Am. Compensation Assn., Am. Soc. for Tng. and Devel., Inst. Mgmt. Cons. (cert., bd. dirs.), Mensa, Psi Chi, Phi Theta Kappa, Omicron Delta Kappa, Beta Phi Gamma. Home: 6211 W NW Hwy Ste G203 Dallas TX 75225 Office: Ste B104 2695 Villa Creek Dr Dallas TX 75234

WATERS, RUDOLPH EARL, university administrator; b. Brookhaven, Miss., May 21, 1932; s. Leonard Douglas and Annie Mae (Thadison) W.; m. Kathleen Graham; children Rudolph E. Jr., Veronica. BSC, DePaul U., 1954; EdM, Boston U., 1958; PhD, Kans. State U., 1977. Registrar Utica (Miss.) Jr. Coll., 1954-55, dean of instrn., 1955-57; dean of students Alcorn State U., Lorman, Miss., 1957-58; dean of instrn. Alcorn State U., Lorman, 1958-70, coord. of title III programs, 1967-75, v.p., 1970-93, exec. v.p., 1993—, interim pres., 1994-95; mem. adv. com. So. Growth Policies Bd., 1995—. Alumni fellow Kans. State U., 1988. Mem.ASCD, Am. Assn. for Higher Edn., Nat. Soc. for the Study of Edn., Am. Assn. of Univ. Adminstrs., Phi Delta Kappa (chpt. pres. 1992), Delta Mu Delta. Home: Rte 2 Box 29C Lorman MS 39096 Office: Alcorn State U 1000 Asu Dr # 359 Lorman MS 39096-9400

WATERS, WALTER KENNETH, JR., theatre educator; b. Kansas City, Mo., Apr. 27, 1927; s. Walter Kenneth and Margaret Elizabeth (Piper) W.; m. Irene Ruth Holtzinger, Aug. 25, 1956; children: Wendy Kay Waters McNeill, Brian David. AB, Park Coll., 1950; MA, Stanford U., 1951, PhD, 1964. Instr. speech and drama Doane Coll., Crete, Nebr., 1952-53; asst. dir., bus. mgr. Hillcrest divsn. Kans. State Hosp., Topeka, 1954; instr. speech and drama Dillard U., New Orleans, 1954-57; asst. prof. theatre arts Portland (Oreg.) State Coll., 1960-63; stage dir., designer New Savoy Opera Co., Portland, 1962-65; chmn. speech and drama, dir. cultural affairs Monticello Coll., Alton, Ill., 1962-65; assoc. prof. theatre Stephen F. Austin State U., Nacogdoches, Tex., 1965-70, prof. theatre, 1970—. Author: Understanding Theatre, 1995; contbr. articles to profl. jours. and Encyclopedia USA. With USN, 1945-46. Recipient award for contbn. to arts Portland Arts Coun., 1960. Mem. Am. Theatre Assn. (ethics com. 1965-68), Tex. Ednl. Theatre Assn. (pres., v.p., chmn. comm. com., Founders award 1980, Lifetime Achievement award 1994), Assn. for Theatre in Higher Edn., Nat. Assn. Schs. of Theatre (treas. 1979-88), Lions (bd. dirs.). Presbyterian. Home: 307 Brookshire Dr Nacogdoches TX 75961 Office: Stephen F Austin State U Box 9090 SFA Sta Nacogdoches TX 75962

WATERS, WRIGHT, sports association executive; b. Montgomery, Ala., June 22, 1949; m. Sara Anderson; 1 child, Ashley. BS in Phys. Edn., Livingston U., 1974, masters degree in secondary edn., 1975. Head trainer, student asst. football coach Livingston U., 1972-74; tchr., football coach Vincent (Ala.) H.S., 1976; asst. trainer, equipment mgr. U. So. Miss., 1975, adminstrv. asst., acad. dir., 1976-79; asst. athletic dir. U. Fla., 1979-83; assoc. athletic dir. U. Southwestern La., 1983-84; assoc. athletic dir., interim athletic dir. Tulane U., 1984-88; asst. commr. So. Conf., 1989-91, commr., 1991—; chmn. football issues com. NCAA 1-AA. Mem. Nat. Assn. Coll. Dirs. Athletics (exec. com.), Collegiate Commrs.' Assn. (exec. v.p.). Office: Southern Conf 1 W Pack Sq Ste 1508 Asheville NC 28801-3402*

WATKINS, CATHY COLLINS, corporate purchasing agent; b. Memphis, Sept. 20, 1952; d. Amos Verlyn and Ruby Etoile (Mayo) Collins; m. Lewis McGill Watkins Jr., May 21, 1988. AA, Clarke Coll., 1972; BMus, William Carey Coll., 1974. Sales assoc., mgr. inventory and receiving Waldoff's Inc., Hattiesburg, Miss., 1974-80; buyer Forrest Gen. Hosp., Hattiesburg, 1980-81; asst. mgr. Ward's Fast Food of Laurel (Miss.), Inc., 1981-82; buyer, sole purchasing agent Eagle Distbrs., Hattiesburg, 1982-85; inventory coord., purchasing agent Miss. Music, Inc., Hattiesburg, 1985—. Photographer campus yearbook Carey Crusader, 1974; editor: (newsletter) Mississippi Bandmaster, 1988—. Mem. Nat. Assn. Music Merchants. Baptist. Home: 105 Elaine Cir Hattiesburg MS 39402-3305 Office: Miss Music Inc PO Box 1705 222 S Main Hattiesburg MS 39401

WATKINS, HAYS THOMAS, retired railroad executive; b. Fern Creek, Ky., Jan. 26, 1926; s. Hays Thomas Sr. and Minnie Catherine (Whiteley) W.; m. Betty Jean Wright, Apr. 15, 1950; 1 son, Hays Thomas III. BS in Acctg., Western Ky. U., 1947; MBA, Northwestern U., 1948; LLD (hon.), Baldwin Wallace Coll., 1975, Alderson Broaddus Coll., 1980, Coll. of William and Mary, 1982, Va. Union U., 1987. CPA, Ill., Ohio. With C. & O. Ry. Cleve., 1949-80, v.p. fin., 1964-67, v.p. adminstrv. group, 1967-71, pres., chief exec. officer, 1971-73, chmn. bd., chief exec. officer, 1973-80; with B. & O. R.R., 1964-80, v.p. finance, 1964-71, pres., chief exec. officer, 1971-73, vice chmn. bd., chief exec. officer, 1973-80; chmn., chief exec. officer Chessie System, Inc., 1973-80; pres. and co-chief exec. officer CSX Corp. (merger of Chessie System, Inc. and Seaboard Coast Line Industries, Inc.), Richmond, Va., 1980-82, chmn. bd., chief exec. officer, 1982-89, chmn. bd., 1989-91; chmn. emeritus, 1991—. Vice rector bd. visitors Coll. William and mary, 1984-87, rector, 1987-93. With AUS, 1945-47. Named Man of Yr., Modern R.R. mag., 1984; recipient Excellence in Mgmt. award Industry Week mag., 1982. Mem. Nat. Assn. Accts., Am. Inst. C.P.A.'s. Clubs: Commonwealth (Richmond, Va.); Country of Va. (Richmond). Home: 22 Lower Tuckahoe Rd W Richmond VA 23233-6108 Office: CSX Corp PO Box 85629 Richmond VA 23285-5629

WATKINS, LEWIS BOONE, artist; b. Beckely, W.Va., July 24, 1945; s. Fred Boone and Margaret Theodoris (Laurie) W.; m. Marinda Ann Hogan, Aug. 18, 1979; children: Mary Sheridan, Marinda Laurie. B.S., W.Va. State Coll., 1978; postgrad. U. South Fla., 1979-82. Artist in residence Boxwood Gallery, Brooksville, Fla., 1978-79; instr. of gifted, Hernando County, Fla., 1979-81; artist in residence Casa Serena Gallery, Brooksville, 1981—; vis. artist W. Va. State Coll., Samford U., St. Leo Coll., U. Tampa (Fla.); works include numerous lithograph print edits., sculpture represented in permanent collections Fla. State Mus., U. Fla., Gainesville, Vatican Mus., Vatican City, Italy, W.Va. Fine Arts and Cultural Ctr., Charleston, Nat. Fine Arts Mus., Santiago, Chile, Nat. Art Gallery, Chile, St. Petersburg Fine Art Mus., Nat. Baseball Hall of Fame and Mus., Cooperstown, N.Y., Boston Sport Mus., San Diego Sport Mus., also numerous pvt. collections; sculptures include Hernando Heritage Sculpture, 1981, Crosses of Life, 1982, Youth of Today, 1983; Am. Farmer Meml. Sculpture, Bonner, Kans., 1986. Bd. advisors Hernando County YMCA (Fla.); pres. Boxwood Art Guild, 1978; treas. Hernando County Young Republicans, 1981. Recipient various awards including Amb. Artistic Achievement award State of W.Va., 1981, Amb. of Art award, 1989; Outstanding Achievement award State of Fla., 1982; proclamation declaring Lewis Watkins Day, Hernando County, Fla., 1981; cert. of Recognition in Art, State of Ga., 1983, award for sculpture, Tampa, Fla., 1984, Pub. Service award City of Atlanta, 1984. Mem. Hernando Heritage Mus. Assn. (bd. dirs.), Hernando County C. of C.

WATKINS, NANCY HOBGOOD, sales executive; b. Oxford, N.C., Mar. 7, 1949; d. Ruben Northington and Julia Clyde (Hobgood) W. AA, Vardell Hall Jr. Coll., Red Springs, N.C., 1967-68; BS in Edn., Atlantic Christian Coll., 1971. Tchr. Granville County Schs., 1972-74; with Combined Ins. Co., 1974-76; dist. mgr. Investors Heritage Life Ins. Co., 1976-80; mfrs. rep. Jerry Elsher Co., N.Y.C., 1982-85, Down South, Atlanta, 1985-90; nat. sales mgr. Chang Seng, Inc., Charlotte, N.C., 1990-93; mfrs. rep. Good Ship, Atlanta, 1993—. Mem. Young Reps., Charlotte, 1985-91. Episcopalian.

WATKINS, SAMUEL RAYBURN, association executive; b. Benton, Ky., Apr. 21, 1923; s. Gipp and Keron (Wyatt) W.; student Tufts U., 1942-43; BS in History, Econs. and Journalism, Murray State U., 1944; MS in Mass Communications, History and Econs., U. Ill., 1951; m. Evelyn W. Ellis, Mar. 6, 1954; children: Julia Ellis, Samuel R.; m. Nancy Spann Kelley, Jan. 30, 1993. Night editor S.I. (N.Y.) Advance, 1946-48; instr. journalism U. Ill., 1948-49; editor, pub. Tribune-Democrat, Benton, 1948-54; adminstrv. sec. Louisville Area C. of C., 1950-55; pres. Assoc. Industries of Ky., Louisville, 1955-85; pres. Ky. Safety Coun. 1980—. Pres. Nat. Labor-Mgmt. Found., 1970—; mem. Pres.' Com. on Employment of Physically Handicapped, 1968-72; mem. Ky. Labor Mgmt. Adv. Coun., 1979-89; vice chmn. Ky. Employer Com. Support Guard and Res., 1979-88, chmn., 1985-88. Served to lt. USNR, 1942-46. Recipient Disting. Alumnus award Murray State U., 1977. Mem. Am. Soc. Assn. Execs. (past pres., chartered assn. exec.), Govt. Rsch. Assn., Kappa Delta Pi, Tau Kappa Alpha, Sigma Delta Chi. Clubs: Louisville Pendennis, Louisville Boat. Author: Management Success Patterns, 1965, How to Be A Good Supervisor, 1969, Management Strategy in Labor Relations, 1970. Home: 2704 Poplar Hill Ct Louisville KY 40207-1171 Office: 2303 Greene Way Louisville KY 40220-4009

WATKINS, STEPHEN LEE, music educator; b. New Orleans, June 8, 1957; s. Charlie Wesley and Octavia Julia (Toussaint) W.; m. Janice Marie Smothers, Mar. 14, 1981; children: Stefnee Leetasha, Janell Marie. B in Music Edn., Loyola U., 1980; MA, Xavier U., 1990. Vocal music tchr. Orleans Pub. Schs., New Orleans, 1981—; CEO Unity Home Health, Inc., New Orleans, 1992—, v.p., sec., 1991—. Mem. ASCD, United Tchrs. New Orleans, Phi Delta Kappa, Alpha Theta Epsilon. Home: 12920 Chanelle Ct New Orleans LA 70128-2512

WATKINS, TED ROSS, social work educator; b. Terrell, Tex., Dec. 2, 1938; s. Daniel Webster and Iva Lucy (Lowrie) W.; m. Betty Diane Dobbs, May 30, 1959; children: Evan Scott, Brett Dobbs, James David. BA in Psychology, U. North Tex., 1961; MSW, La. State U., 1963; D of Social Work, U. Pa., 1976. Staff social worker Mercer County Mental Health Ctr., Sharon, Pa., 1963-65; chief social worker, assoc. exec. Talbot Hall Treatment Ctr., Jonestown, Pa., 1965-70; chief social worker Harrisburg (Pa.) Mental Health Ctr., 1970-71; asst. prof. social work U. Tex., Arlington, 1971-76; dir. counseling svcs. Family Svcs., Inc., Ft. Worth, 1976-79; assoc. prof. social work U. Tex., 1979-85, dir. criminal justice, 1985-87, chair dept. sociology, 1987-91, assoc. prof., grad. advisor social work, 1991—; cons. in field. Author: (with James Callicutt) Mental Health Policy and Practice Today. Tex. del. to Pres.'s Commn. in Mental Health, Austin, 1978. Recipient Golladay Teaching award Coll. Liberal Arts, Arlington, 1990; named Outstanding Profl. Human Svcs., 1972. Mem. NASW (state bd. dirs. 1976-78, 80-82, unit chair, vol. lobbyist 1982), Acad. Cert. Social Workers (lic. master social worker, advanced clin. practitioner). Democrat. Methodist. Office: U Tex Box 19129 UTA Arlington TX 76019

WATKINS, WESLEY LEE, accountant; b. Norfolk, Va., Dec. 4, 1953; s. Morrell and Mary Elizabeth (Washington) W. BS, Norfolk State U., 1977. Inventory acct. specialist Norfolk State U. Bookstore (Va.), 1977-79; acct., auditor DMTS, HEW, 1979-80; acct. McClure Lundberry Assocs., 1980-81; contractual acct. Acad. Contemporary Problems, Washington, 1982; fin. cons. Watkins & Watkins, Washington, 1982-86, U.S. Tax Svc., Suffolk, Va., 1987; tax cons., acct. H&R Block, Norfolk, 1988—; tax cons. Watkins & Watkins Fin. Cons., Norfolk, Va., 1987—; cons. Watkins & Watkins Auto Shop, Norfolk, 1983-84. Bd. dirs. Jerusalem Baptist Ch. Credit Union, 1976—. Named Young Adult of Yr. Jerusalem Bapt. Ch., Norfolk, 1978, 91. Mem. NAACP, Nat. Assn. Accts., Nat. Assn. Black Accts., Phi Beta Lambda. Democrat. Home: 2209 Marshall Ave Norfolk VA 23504-2610

WATKISS, REGINA (REGINA MONKS), secondary school educator; b. Worcester, Mass., Apr. 21, 1952; d. Albin and Victoria (Babicz) Linga; m. G. Philip Watkiss. BA, Assumption Coll., 1974; MA, Western Md. Coll., 1980; postgrad., U. Ala.; MS, Western Md. Coll., 1992. Cert. sci. tchr., Ga., Colo. Sci. tchr. Randolph Sch., Huntsville, Ala.; sci. coord. Divine Redeemer Sch., Colorado Springs, Colo.; sci. curriculum cons. U.S. Space Found., Colorado Springs; head dept. sci. Heritage Sch., Newnan, Ga.; workshop presenter, curriculum author in field. Recipient Dreyfus Master Tchr. award in chemistry, 1986, Colo. Sci. Tchr. of Yr. award, Seismic Sleuths award State of Ga.; Woodrow Wilson fellow, 1986; State of Ala. grantee. Mem. Nat. Sci. Tchrs. Assn., Ala. Sci. Tchrs. Assn., Am. Chem. Soc. (Operation Chemistry award).

WATNE, ALVIN L., surgeon, educator; b. Shabbona, Ill., Jan. 13, 1927; m. Diana Folio, Dec. 3, 1966; children: Carrie, Matthew, Andrew, Valerie. B.S., U. Ill.-Chgo. Coll. Medicine, 1950, M.D., 1952, M.S., 1956. Diplomate: Am. Bd. Surgery. Intern Indpls. Gen. Hosp., 1952-53; resident U. Ill. Research and Edn. Hosps., Chgo., 1954-58; assoc. cancer surgeon Cancer Research, Roswell Park, Buffalo, N.Y., 1958, assoc. chief cancer research, 1959; assoc. prof. surgery W.Va. U., 1962-67, prof., 1967-72, acting chmn. dept. surgery, 1973-75, prof., chmn. dept. surgery, 1975-86; prof., chmn. dept. surgery U. Ill., Peoria, 1986-91; dir. Cancer Ctr. of Ga., 1991-94; assoc. dir. dept. surgery GBMC, 1994—; cons. surgery VA, Clarksburg, W.Va., 1963—. Author: Gardner's Syndrome, 1977, (2d edit.), 1979, Melanoma of Head and Neck, 1981, Polyposis Coli, 1982. Pres. W. Va. div. Am. Cancer Soc., 1967-68, 80—, v.p., 1981. Recipient Hektoen Gold medal AMA, 1958; recipient Hektoen Silver medal AMA, 1960. Mem. ACS (pres. W.Va. chpt. 1972-73, chmn. local com. 1978—, gov. 1985—), Southeastern Surg. Congress (councilor 1980—), Soc. Surg. Oncology (exec. council 1980), Soc. Head and Neck Surgeons (pres. 1982), Am. Cancer Soc. (dir.-at-large 1985—).

WATSON, ADA, secondary education educator; b. Memphis, Oct. 21, 1951; d. Leroy and Helen Marie (Sparks) Preyer; m. William Elton Watson, June 2, 1973; children: William Elton Jr., Moneka Nésha. BS in Edn., Memphis State U., 1974, care-guidance of children endorsement, 1976; MS in Human Resource Devel., U. Tenn., 1995. Parenting educator Sea Isle Adult Vocat.-Tech. Ctr., Memphis, 1975-76; tchr. child care Sheffield Vocat.-Tech. Ctr., Memphis, 1976-88; tchr. home econs. and teen parenting edn. Booker T. Washington H.S., Memphis, 1989—. Author teen parenting videos; co-author child care curriculum. Mem. adv. bd. Golden Leaf Day Care Ctr., Memphis, 1979-81; chmn. March of Dimes, Sheffield Vocat.-Tech. Ctr., 1985-86; craft coord. Vacation Bible Sch., Greater Imani Bapt. Ch., Memphis, 1991; Sunday sch. tchr. St. Matthew Bapt. Ch., Millington, Tenn., 1992—, dir. Vacation Bible Sch., 1992-95. Recipient svc. award Future Homemakers Am., 1986-89. Mem. NEA, Am. Vocat. Assn., Tenn. Edn. Assn., Memphis Edn. Assn. (faculty rep. 1978-86, bargaining com. 1981, ins. chmn. 1983, svc. awards 1981, 83), Nat. Assn. Vocat. Home Econs. Tchrs. (local arrangements com., membership com., svc. award 1993), Tenn. Vocat. Assn. (v.p. home econs., svc. award 1994), Tenn. Assn. Vocat. Home Econs. Tchrs. (bd. dirs., v.p., pres.-elect, pres. 1995, svc. award 1985, 90, 91, 92-94), Assn. Supvsn. and Curriculum Devel. Democrat. Home: 2614 Monette Ave Memphis TN 38127-6835 Office: Booker T Washington HS 715 S Lauderdale St Memphis TN 38126-3910

WATSON, ARTHUR DENNIS, government official; b. Brownsville, Pa., May 11, 1950; s. Arthur Francis Puglia and Margaret Teresa Mastile; stepson of John Leslie Watson; m. Kathleen Frances Zaccardo, July 16, 1983; 1 child, Fiona Kathleen. BSBA, U. Richmond, 1972; MS in Bus.-Govt. Rels. Am. U., 1977, MA in Lit., 1979; PhD in English Lang. and Lit. Cath. U., 1987. Statisical asst. U.S. Postal Svc. Hdqrs., Washington, 1972-73, economist assoc., 1973-74, staff economist, 1974-77, mktg. analyst, 1977; rate analyst U.S. Postal Rate Commn., Washington, 1977-79, dir. pub. affairs, 1979-82; spokesman, pub. affairs officer ICC, Washington, 1982-89, dep. dir. pub. affairs, 1989-93, assoc. dir. congl. and pub. affairs, 1993-95, assoc. dir. congressional and pub. affairs surface transp. bd., U.S. DOT, 1996—; pres. Arthur D. Watson and Co., Clifton, Va., 1983—. Washington corr. Linn's Stamp News, Sidney, Ohio, 1983-84; pub. rels. columnist

Arundel Communications, Reston, Va., 1991-92; contbr. articles to profl. jours.; reader Washington Ear, WETA-FM radio side channel, 1977. With USCG, 1972-78. Recipient Meritorious Svc. medal, Pub. Svc. award ICC, 1989. Mem. Nat. Assn. Govt. Communicators, E. Claiborne Robins Sch. Bus. Alumni Assn., Assn. Transp. Law, Logistics and Policy, USS Natoma Bay Assn., Pub. Rels. Soc. Am. Roman Catholic. Avocations: classical music, reading, writing, model building, travel. Home: 6521 Rockland Dr Clifton VA 20124-2415 Office: ICC Surface Transp Bd Rm 4136 1201 Constitution Ave NW Washington DC 20423-0001

WATSON, BARRY LEE, real estate and mortgage broker, investor, contractor, builder, developer; b. Morris, Minn., June 10, 1963; s. Richard Jay and Lila Richa (Goll) W. Student, Havti U., 1981-82. Metalergist Reinheart & Assoc., Pasadena, Tex., 1982-83; realtor ISI Inc., Winter Park, Fla., 1983—; owner First Am. Capital Corp., Orlando, 1984—; bd. dirs. Farmbank Real Estate, Inc., Orlando; v.p. Oak Harbour Assn., Altamonte Springs, Fla., 1985-86, pres., 1986—; pres. Watson Fin. Corp., Orlando, 1986—, U.S. Devel. Corp., Orlando, 1986—, Southeastern Capital of Orlando, Inc., 1986—, The Watson Group Inc. Bus. Mgmt.,1991—. Author: Watson Winning and Wealth, 1985, 86. Advisor Cen. Fla. Young Reps., Orlando, 1984-89, bd. dirs., 1987, 88, 89. Mem. Orlando C. of C. Lutheran. Office: 1st Am Capital/The Watson Group 832 Irma Ave Orlando FL 32803-3807

WATSON, BEVERLY ANN, nurse; b. Springfield, Mass., Aug. 31, 1948; d. Paul Michael and Ann Theresa (Wheeler) Urekew; m. Kenneth A. Watson Jr., Dec. 17, 1977. Diploma in Nursing, Framingham Union Hosp., 1970. RN; cert. nursing supr., Ga. Staff nurse Hartford (Conn.) Hosp.; charge nurse Ridgeview Nursing Home, Springfield, Vespers Nursing Home, Wilkesboro, N.C.; asst. dir. nurses North Macon Health Care, Macon, Ga.; medical supr. Hospitality Care Ctr., Macon, Ga. Mem. ANA, Ga. Nurses Assn. Address: PO Box 13144 Macon GA 31208-3144

WATSON, BOB, professional baseball executive. Gen. mgr. Houston Astros. Office: Houston Astros PO Box 288 Houston TX 77001-0288*

WATSON, C. L. (CHUCK WATSON), gas industry executive; b. 1950. Grad., Okla. State U., 1972. With Conoco, Inc., Houston, 1972-85; pres, CEO Natural Gas Clearinghouse, Houston, 1985—. Office: Natural Gas Clearinghouse 13430 Northwest Fwy Houston TX 77040-6000*

WATSON, DAVID L(EE), nuclear energy training specialist, educator; b. Clarksburg, W.Va., Feb. 22, 1946; s. James R. and Gladys B. (Sedars) Howard; m. Donna M. Blair, June 23, 1973; children: Keri, Matthew. B.S., W.Va. Wesleyan U., 1968; MEd, Fla. Atlantic U., 1976. Cert. tchr., adminstr./supr., Fla.; pvt. pilot; lic. water/wastewater plant operator. Tchr., coach Martin County Schs., Stuart, Fla., 1969-72, 74-80; nuclear cons. various locations, 1980-83; health physics instr. Fla. Power Corp., Crystal River, 1983-86, nuclear support supr., 1986, nuclear tng. supr., 1986-94, nuclear tng. acad. supr., 1994—; nuclear security mgr. Fla. Power Corp., 1996—. Mem. Citrus County Sch. Bd., Inverness, Fla., 1984—, chmn. bd., 1989-90, 93-94, vice chmn., 1991-92, creator, adminstr. Yellow Sch. Bus. award, 1991—, also coord. environ. conservation Blueprint 2000 program, coord. Earth Days event; coach Youth Soccer, Little League, Youth Basketball, 1983-91; bd. dirs. North Suncoast Rep. Club, 1988—. Maj. USAR. Mem. Am. Nuclear Soc., Fla. Sch. Bds. Assn., Citrus County C. of C., Am. Assn. Pilots, Res. Officers Assn., Sugarmill Woods Tennis Assn. (com. chmn.), U.S. Lawn Tennis Assn., Chi Phi. Methodist.

WATSON, DENISE SANDER, medical products sales executive; b. Bellville, Tex., July 19, 1960; d. Charles Morris and Corinne Olive (Bakke) S. Assoc., S.W. Tex. State U., 1981, BS in Allied Health Mgmt., 1982. Cardiodiagnostician Katy Community Hosp., Katy, Tex., 1982-84; staff cardiodiagnostician Sharpstown Gen. Hosp., Houston, 1984-85; cardiodiagnostician, noninvasive lab. supr. W. Houston Med. Ctr., Houston, 1985-86; with Pro-Tech Med. Assocs., Houston, 1985-86; clinical applications specialist Hewlett-Packard Co., Houston, 1986-87; field application specialist Acuson, Houston, 1987-92; dist. medical product sales rep. Acuson, St. Louis, 1992—. Named Field Application Specialist of Yr., Western Cardiology Region, 1990. Fellow Am. Registry Diagnostic Med. Sonographers, Am. Soc. Diagnostics Med. Sonographers, Am. Soc. Echocardiography, Soc. Vascular Tech.; mem. Ctrl. West End Assn., Bluebonnet Soc. Bellville, Alpha Delta Pi. Republican. Episcopalian. Office: Acuson 1899 Powers Ferry Rd Ste 100 Atlanta GA 30339-5653

WATSON, DIANE B., librarian; b. Bklyn., Aug. 25, 1946; d. Stanley and Jean (Juncewicz) Haberek; m. Jerry Walker Rutledge, Jan. 20, 1966 (div.); children: Quentin, Jason; m. Robert Ray Reedy, July 20, 1995. BS, U. Okla., 1968; MLS, Vanderbilt U., 1973. Tchr. English Bowling Green (Ky.) City Schs., 1970-71; tchg. asst. We. Ky. U., Bowling Green, 1971-72, acquisitions libr., sci. cataloger, 1973-86; libr. asst. Vanderbilt U., Nashville, 1972-73; head libr. Bowling Green Jr. Coll., 1986-87; pub. svc. libr. Tex. A&M U., Galveston, Tex., 1988—; chmn. acad. requirements and regulations com., acad. coun. We. Ky. U., Bowling Green, 1980-84; mem. faculty exchange team We. Ky. U., 1981-82; ednl. cons. Naval Air Sta., Pensacola, Fla., 1984. Contbr. articles to profl. jours., encyclopedia, poems to Ky. Poetry Rev. Mem;. Women's Propeller Club, Galveston, Tex. 1994—; coord. local Save Our Ships Campaign, Washington, 1994—. Mem. S.E. Affiliate of Internat. Marine Sci. Librs., Pelican Club, Beta Pi Mu. Home: 7310 Seawall Blvd Apt 1207 Galveston TX 77551 Office: Tex A&M Univ Libr PO 1675 Galveston TX 77553

WATSON, DONALD CHARLES, cardiothoracic surgeon, educator; b. Fairfield, Ohio, Mar. 15, 1945; s. Donald Charles and Pricilla H. Watson; m. Susan Robertson Prince, June 23, 1973; children: Kea Huntington, Katherine Anne, Kirsten Prince. BA in Applied Sci. Lehigh U., 1968, BS in Mech. Engring., 1968; MS in Mech. Engring., Stanford U., 1969; MD, Duke U., 1972. Diplomate Am. Bd. Thoracic Surgery, Am. Bd. Surgery. Intern in surgery Stanford U. Med. Ctr., Calif., 1972-73, resident in cardiovascular surgery, 1973-74, resident in surgery, 1976-78, chief resident in heart transplant, 1978-79, chief resident in cardiovascular and gen. surgery, 1978-80; clin. assoc. surgery br. Nat. Heart and Lung Inst., 1974-76, acting sr. surgeon, 1976; assoc. cardiovascular surgeon dept. child health and devel. George Washington U., Washington, 1980-84, asst. prof. surgery, asst. prof. child health and devel., 1980-84, attending cardiovascular surgeon dept. child health and devel., 1984-89; assoc. prof. surgery, 1984-89; assoc. prof. pediatrics U. Tenn.-Memphis, 1984-90, prof. surgery, 1989—, prof. pediatrics, 1990—, chmn. cardiothoracic surgery, 1984—; mem. staff Le Bonheur children's Med. Ctr., Memphis, chmn. cardiothoracic surgery, 1984—; mem. staff William F. Bowld Med. Ctr., Memphis, Regional Med. ctr. at Memphis, Baptist Meml. Med. Ctr., Memphis; cons. in field; instr. advanced trauma life support; profl. cons., program reviewer HHS. Contbr. chpts., numerous articles, revs. to profl. publs. Bd. dirs. Internat. Children's Heart Found., Child Health Alliance of the Mid-South. Served to lt. comdr. USPHS, 1974-76. Smith Kline & French fellow Lehigh U., 1967; NSF fellow Lehigh U., 1968; univ. interdepartmental scholar and univ. scholar Lehigh U., 1968. Fellow Am. Coll. Cardiology, Am. Coll. Chest Physicians (forum cardiovascular surgery, council critical care), Southeastern Surg. Congress, Am. Acad. Pediatrics (surgery sect.), ACS; mem. Assn. Surg. Edn., Am. Assn. Thoracic Surgery, Soc. Thoracic Surgeons, So. Thoracic Surg. Assn., Am. Thoracic Soc., Assn. Acad. Surgery, Internat. Soc. Heart Transplantation, Am. Fedn. Clin. Research, Found. Advanced Edn. in Scis., Andrew G. Morrow Soc., Norman E. Shumway Soc. (multiple bd. dirs.). Council on Cardiovascular Surgery of Am. Heart Assn., Soc. Internat. di Chirig, AAAS, N.Y. Acad. Sci., AMA, NIH Alumni Assn., Stanford U. Med. Alumni Assn., Duke U. Med. Alumni Assn., Duke U. Alumni Assn., Stanford U. Alumni Assn., Lehigh U. Alumni Assn., Smithsonian Assocs., Sierra Club, U. Tenn. Pres.'s Club, LeBonheur Pres.'s Club, U.S. Yacht Racing Assn., Pilots Internat. Assn., Nat. Assn. Flight Instrs., Aircraft Owners and Pilots Assn., Order Ky. Cols., Phi Beta Kappa, Tau Beta Pi, Pi Tau Sigma, Phi Gamma Delta. Republican. Presbyterian. Club: Crescent. Avocations: sailing, racquet sports, flying, computers. Office: The Heart Ctr 777 Washington Ave Ste 215 Memphis TN 38105-4567

WATSON, ELIZABETH MARION, protective services official; b. Phila., Aug. 25, 1949; d John Julian and Elizabeth Gertrude (Judge) Herrmann; m. Robert LLoyd Watson, June 18, 1976; children: Susan, Mark, David. BA in Psychology with honors, Tex. Tech. U., 1971. With Houston Police Dept., 1972-92, detective homicide, burglary and theft, 1976-81, lt. records div. northeast patrol div., 1981-84, capt. inspections div., auto theft div., 1984-87, dep. chief west patrol bur., 1987-90, police chief, 1990-92; with Austin, Tex. Police Dept., 1992—, police chief, 1992—; mem. adv. bd. S.W. Law Enforcement Inst., Richardson,Tex., 1990—. Mem. editorial bd. Am. Jour. Police, 1991—. mem. Internat. Assn. Chiefs of Police (mem. major cities chiefs, mem. civil rights com.), Police Exec. Rsch. Form, Tex. Police Chiefs Assn. Roman Catholic. Office: Police Department 715 E 8th St Austin TX 78701-3397

WATSON, EVELYN EGNER, radiation scientist; b. Corbin, Ky., Dec. 15, 1928; d. Edgar Mattison and Bertha Mae (Mayfield) Egner; m. Earl Greene Watson, Nov. 10, 1953; children: Nancy Eileen, Philip Allen. AA, Cumberland Coll., 1946; student, Lincoln Meml. U., 1947-48; BA, U. Ky., 1949; postgrad., U. Tenn., 1968. Math. and sci. tchr. Lynch (Ky.) High Sch., 1949-50; office mgr. Whitley County Sch. System, Williamsburg, Ky., 1950-53; sr. lab. tech. Radiation Internal Dose Ctr. Oak Ridge (Tenn.) Assoc. Univs., 1961-71, scientist, 1971-79, program mgr., 1979-89, program dir., 1989-94; lectr. in field; cons. USFDA, Rockville, Md., 1983-88. Assoc. editor Jour. Nuclear Medicine, 1981-86; editor newsletter Soc. Nuclear Medicine S.E. chpt., 1988—; co-author: MIRD Primer, 1988; contbr. articles to profl., chpts. to books. Bd. dirs. Youth Haven, Oak Ridge, Tenn., 1970-74, Clinch River Home Health, Clinton, Tenn., 1988-94. Recipient Excellence in Tech. Transfer award Fed. Lab. Consortium, 1985, Lifetime Scientific Achievement award Assn. Women in Sci., 1993. Mem. Soc. Nuclear Medicine (med. internal radiation dose com. 1980—, chmn. 1994—), Health Physics Soc. (Disting. Svc. award 1981, treas. 1976-77), European Assn. Nuclear Medicine, Nat. Coun. on Radiation Protection and Measurements (sci. com. 1986—), Sigma Xi. Mem. Ch. of Christ. Home: 104 New Bedford Ln Oak Ridge TN 37830-8289 Office: Oak Ridge Assoc Univs PO Box 117 Oak Ridge TN 37831-0117

WATSON, FORREST ALBERT, lawyer, bank executive; b. Atlanta, May 7, 1951; s. Forrest Albert and Virginia Doris (Ritch) W.; m. Marlys Wise, Oct. 16, 1982; children: Annaliese Marie Elizabeth, Forrest Albert Watson III. AB, Emory U., 1973; JD, U. Ga., 1975; postgrad., Mercer U., 1979-80. Bar: Ga. 1975, U.S. Dist. Ct. (mid. dist.) Ga. 1976, U.S. Tax Ct. 1976, U.S. Ct. Appeals (5th cir.) 1977, U.S. Supreme Ct. 1980; cert. data processor; CFP. Assoc. Banks, Smith & Lambdin, Barnesville, Ga., 1976-78; ptnr. Watson & Lindsey, Barnesville, 1978-82; v.p., gen. counsel United Bank Corp., Barnesville, 1981-91, chief ops. officer, 1990—, exec. v.p., gen. counsel, 1991—, mem., bd. dirs., exec. v.p., 1991; pres. United Bank Mortgage; exec. v.p., sr. trust officer United Bank, Griffin, Ga., 1995—; pres. United Bank Mortgage, 1993-95; gen. counsel Lamar State Bank, Barnesville, 1976-84; judge Small Claims Ct., Lamar County, Ga., 1976, City Ct. of Milner, Ga., 1977; lectr. IBM, 1984-85; atty. City of Meansville, Ga., 1976, City of Milner, 1977; bd. dirs. United Bank Corp. Assoc. editor Ga. Jour. Internat. Law, 1975. Gen. counsel Lamar County Devel. Authority, Barnesville, 1977; bd. dirs. Legaline Inc., Atlanta, 1983-85. Mem. ABA, Ga. Bar Assn., Cir. Ct. Bar Assn., Griffin Cir. Bar Assn., Ga. Rural Health Assn. (trustee 1981-82), S.E. Bank Card Assn. (operating com. 1986-91), Assn. Cert. Fin. Planners, Assn. Inst. Cert. Computer Profls., Internat. Assn. Fin. Planners. Methodist. Home: PO Box 347 Zebulon GA 30295-0347 Office: United Bank Corp PO Box 144 595 South Hill St Griffin GA 30224

WATSON, FRANKIE RHODES, homemaker; b. Auburn, Ala., Aug. 6, 1947; d. Theodore Milton and Frances Epting (Fulmer) Rhodes; m. Emory Olin Watson, Jr., June 8, 1969; children: Frances Patricia, Bryan David, Grace Elizabeth. BS, Coker Coll., 1969. Pre-sch. tchr. United Meth. Ch., Conway, S.C., 1976-79; swimming instr. Conway and Irmo, S.C., Ala., 1976-96; dir. instrnl. staff Cold Stream Country Club, Irmo, S.C., 1980-83. Author: (Bible study book/course) Just Between Us Women, 1993, Handling Emotions Biblically, 1991. Founder Pastor's Wives Fellowship, Palmetto Presbytery, S.C., 1988-89, Southeast Ala., 1992, Ladie's Comm. Bible Ministry, Greenville, Ala., 1993-96; pres. Southeast Ala. Ladies Ministry, 1996-98; vol tchr. West Columbia Evangel. Ch., West Cola, S.C., 1980-85, St. Andrews Presbyn. Ch., Irmo, 1988-90. Mem. Sasanqua Garden Club (award judge 1993-96). Republican. Presbyterian.

WATSON, GARY L., newspaper executive; Pres. newspaper divsn. Cin. Enquirer. Office: Gannett Co Inc 1100 Wilson Blvd Arlington VA 22234

WATSON, GEORGE WILLIAM, lawyer, legal consultant; b. Eaton Rapids, Mich., Mar. 1, 1926; s. George W. and Agnes R. (Nissen) W.; m. Ruth Carpenter Murphy, Oct. 1, 1949; children: G. William, Linda, Daniel, Thomas, Rose Mary. AB, U. Mich., 1947, JD, 1950. Bar: Mich. 1951, U.S. Dist. Ct. (ea. and we. dists.) Mich. 1951, U.S. Ct. Military Appeals, 1991. Pvt. practice law Charlotte, Mich., 1951-53; dir. Kalamazoo Legal Aid Bur., 1953-54; asst. pros. atty. Kalamazoo County, 1955-56; gen. atty. Office Civil and Def. Mobilization, Battle Creek, Mich., 1956-62, Def. Civil Preparedness Agy., Washington, 1962-80; assoc. gen. counsel Fed. Emergency Mgmt. Agy., Washington, 1980=88, gen. counsel, 1988-91; cons. on adminstrn. law and govtl. affairs pvt. practice, Alexandria, Va., 1991—. Pres. Mt. Vernon/Lee Enterprises, Alexandria, Va., 1988-94; commordor Nat. Yacht Club, Washington, 1981. With USN, 1944-46, PTO. Mem. State Bar of Mich. Episcopalian. Home and Office: 2108 Huntington Ave Alexandria VA 22303-1534

WATSON, JACK CROZIER, retired state supreme court justice; b. Jonesville, La., Sept. 17, 1928; s. Jesse Crozier and Gladys Lucille (Talbot) W.; m. Henrietta Sue Carter, Dec. 26, 1958; children: Carter Crozier (dec.), Wells Talbot. BA, U. Southwestern La., 1949; JD, La. State U., 1956; completed with honor, Appellate Judges Seminar, N.Y. U., 1974, Sr. Appellate Judges Seminar, 1980. Bar: La. 1956. Atty. King, Anderson & Swift, Lake Charles, La., 1956-58; prosecutor City of Lake Charles, 1960; asst. dist. atty. Calcasieu Parish, La., 1961-64; ptnr. Watson & Watson, Lake Charles, 1961-64; judge 14th Jud. Dist., La., 1964-72; judge ad hoc Ct. Appeals, 1st Circuit, Baton Rouge, 1972-73; judge Ct. Appeals, 3rd Circuit, Lake Charles, 1973-79; assoc. justice La. Supreme Ct., New Orleans, 1979-96, ret., 1996; faculty advisor Nat. Coll. State Judiciary, Reno, 1970, 73; adj. prof. law summer sch. program in Greece, Tulane U., 1988-97; del. NEH Seminar, 1976; La. del to Internat. Conf. Appellate Magistrates, The Philippines, 1977; mem. La. Jud. Coun., 1986-92. 1st lt. USAF, 1950-54. Mem. ABA, La. Bar Assn., S.W. La. Bar Assn. (pres. 1973), Law Inst. State of La., La. Coun. Juvenile Ct. Judges (pres. 1969-70), Am. Judicature Soc., S.W. La. Camellia Soc. (pres. 1973-74), Am. Legion (post comdr. 1963), Lake Charles Yacht Club (commodore 1974), Blue Key, Sigma Alpha Epsilon, Phi Delta Phi, Pi Kappa Delta. Democrat. Baptist.

WATSON, JACK H., JR., lawyer; b. El Paso, Tex., Oct. 24, 1938; children: Melissa Woodward, Lincoln Hearn. BA, Vanderbilt U., 1960; LLB, Harvard U., 1966. Bar: Ga. 1965, D.C. 1978. Assoc. King & Spalding, Atlanta, 1966-71; partner King & Spalding, 1972-77; asst. to Pres. for intergovtl. affairs and sec. to cabinet Washington, 1977-80; chief of staff White House, 1980-81; ptnr. Long, Aldridge & Norman, Atlanta, 1981—; mem. vis. com. Harvard Law Sch., 1987-93; permanent chmn. Ga. Joint Commn. on Alt. Dispute Resolution, 1990-93, chmn. Ga. Commn. on Dispute Resolution, 1993—. Counsel Met. Atlanta Commn. Crime and Juvenile Delinquency, 1966-67; trustee Milton S. Eisenhower Found., 1994—; pres. Met. Atlanta Mental Health Assn., 1971-72; chmn. Gov.'s Study Commn. Alcohol, 1971-72, Ga. Alcoholism Adv. Council, 1972; chmn. bd. Ga. Dept. Human Resources, 1972-77; candidate gov. of Ga., 1982; mem. nat. adv. com. Ctr. for Study of Presidency, 1983; mem. Franklin D. Roosevelt Library Bd., 1986—; chmn. 20th Century Fund Task Force on the U.S. Vice Presidency, 1987-88; active Franklin and Eleanor Roosevelt Instnl. Bd., 1990—. Served as officer USMC. Named One of Atlanta's Five Outstanding Young Men Jaycees, 1970. Mem. ABA (standing com. on dispute resolution 1991-93, coun. mem. sect. dispute resolution 1993—, chmn. ABA task force on N.Am. Free Trade Agreement 1993), State Bar Ga., Atlanta Bar Assn., Atlanta Lawyers Club, Phi Beta Kappa, Phi Eta Sigma, Omicron Delta Kappa. Office: Long Aldridge & Norman 701 Pennsylvania Ave NW Ste 600 Washington DC 20004-2608

WATSON, JAMES RAY, JR., education educator; b. Anniston, Ala., Dec. 6, 1935; s. James Ray and Mary Garrity (Profumo) W.; m. Shirley Jean Lesesne, 1960 (div. 1972); children: Laura Catherine, Gregory Andrew, Jennifer Ann; m. Louise Edmonds, 1973. BS in Animal Sci., Auburn U., 1957, MS in Agronomy, 1960; PhD in Botany, Iowa State U., 1963. Rsch. asst. dept. agronomy Auburn (Ala.) U., 1958-60; rsch. asst. dept. botany Iowa State U., Ames, 1960-61, teaching asst. dept. botany, 1961-63; asst. prof. dept. botany Miss. State U., Mississipi State, 1963-68, assoc. prof. dept. botany, 1968-77, head dept. botany, 1975-78, prof. dept. botany, 1977-78, prof. dept. biol. sci., 1978—; participant Smithsonians Summer Inst. Systematics, Washington, 1968; vis. scholar U. Mich., Ann Arbor, 1964-65. Contbr. articles to profl. jours. Mem. The Nature Conservancy. With U.S. Army, 1957-58. NSF postdoctoral fellow U. Mich., 1963-64; Nat. Natural Landmarks Miss. grantee, 1973-74. Mem. Natural Areas Assn., Bot. Soc. Am. (paleobot. sect.), Miss. Native Plant Soc., Sigma Xi, Xi Sigma Pi. Republican. Roman Catholic. Home: 217 Seville Pl Starkville MS 39759-2133 Office: Miss State U Dept Biol Sci PO Drawer GY Mississippi State MS 39762

WATSON, JAMES STANLEY, secondary education educator; b. Glen Ridge, N.J., Feb. 2, 1948; s. James G. and Bernice T. (Frail) W. BS in Natural Sci. Edn., U. Tenn., 1971; MA in Environ. Edn., Glassboro State Coll., 1978; postgrad., U. Tenn., 1984, 89, Coll. Atlantic, U. Maine, 1986. Cert. secondary sci. curriculum, Tenn. Tchr. geology, chemistry, biology and applied sci., asst. coach wrestling Red Bank High Sch., Chattanooga, 1972-76; tchr. earth sci. 8th grade Red Bank Jr. High Sch., Chattanooga, 1976-78; tchr. gen. sci. and ecology, coach wrestling Ooltewah High Sch., Chattanooga, 1978-81; tchr. biology, earth sci., chemistry, gen. sci., geology and physical sci., coach boys and girls soccer, asst. coach wrestling Red Bank High Sch., 1981-92; tchr. honors biology, asst. coach boys and girls soccer Soddy-Daisy High Sch., Chattanooga, 1992—; textbook reviewer for scis. Tenn. Dept. Edn., 1996—, Praxis reviewer for earch sci., 1996; writer, tchr. new geology course Red Bank High Sch., 1973, new ecology course Ooltewah High Sch., 1979; writer energy conservation plan Hamilton County Sch. Dist., 1978, gen. sci. curriculum guide, 1979; planner, contributing writer tchr. workshop field activity design and procedures Chattanooga Nature Ctr., Keystone (Colo.) Sci. Sch., 1985, tchr. workshop volcanoes Mt. St. Helens Nat. Monument, Washington, 1986, tchr. workshop marine mammals in Gulf of Maine, 1989; writer solar energy sect. Tenn. Valley Authority Energy Source Book for Tchrs., 1985; participant Tenn. Valley Authority Water Quality Monitoring Network, 1986; presenter environ. edn. conf. N.Am. Assn., Eugene, Oreg., 1986; mem. task force on earth sci. curriculum Tenn. Dept. Edn., 1988; mem. adoption com. sci. textbooks Hamilton County Sch. Dist., 1990; textbook reader, evaluator geology, gen. sci. and phys. sci. Tenn. Dept. Edn., 1990; asst. to instr. dept. geoscis. U. Tenn., 1990, 91; presenter workshops Ctr. Excellence for Sci. and Math. Edn. Tenn. Dept. Edn., 1991. sponsor winner Chattanooga Sci. Fair, 1973, runner-up, 1974; mem. dual team championships wrestling rules com. Tenn. Secondary Sch. Athletic Assn., 1987, speaker bureau Tenn. River Aquarium, 1990, 91, ednl. adv. com. Spangler Farm Environ. Edn. Ctr., 1991, adv. coun. Chattanooga YMCA Earth Sci. Corps, 1992; horticulture vol. Tenn. River Aquarium, 1992. Grantee Lyndhurst Found., 1982, 84, 86, Pub. Edn. Found., 1990, 94, Pub. Edn. Found., 1994, GeoTrek, 1996; recipient Soccer Coach of Yr. award News Free Press, 1985, 89, Mini-grant Chattanooga Jr. League, 1985, 87. Mem. NEA, Am. Littoral Soc., Nat. Assn. Geology Tchrs. (Outstanding Earth Sci. Tchr. award 1992), Nat. Marine Edn. Assn., Ga. Assn. Marine Edn., Tenn. Edn. Assn., Hamilton County Edn. Assn. (Outstanding Svc. award 1980, trustee Hamilton County Sch. Dist. Sick Leave Bank 1982—), Tenn. Conservation League, Chattanooga Nature Ctr., Internat. Oceanographic Found., Nature Conservancy, Tenn. Earth Sci. Tchrs. Assn. (pres. 1995-97). Baptist. Office: Soddy-Daisy High Sch 618 Sequoyah Access Rd Soddy Daisy TN 37379-4049

WATSON, JEAN VAUGHN, critical care nurse, ambulatory surgery nurse; b. Commerce, Ga., July 31, 1954; d. Butler Dock and Lula May (Long) Vaughn; m. John Robert Watson, Sept. 5, 1989. Lic. practical nurse diploma, Oconee Vocat. Ctr., Seneca, S.C., 1973; ADN, Greenville (S.C.) Tech. Coll., 1979; cert. cardiovascular nursing specialist, Meth. Hosp., Houston, 1981. RN, S.C.; cert. CCRN; cert. ACLS, BCLS instr. Staff nurse neurol. ICU, Greenville Meml. Hosp.; staff nurse CCU, Oconee Meml. Hosp., Seneca; head nurse CCU, Cannon Meml. Hosp., Pickens, S.C., outpatient coord., employee health nurse, insvc. edn. coord. Mem. AACCN (cert.). Home: 372 Blazer Trl Walhalla SC 29691-4400

WATSON, JERRY CARROLL, advertising executive; b. Greenville, Ala., Aug. 22, 1943; s. William J. and Georgia Katherine (Mixon) W.; m. Judith Zeigler Brooks, Sept. 16, 1988; 2 child, Theodore William, Hunter Brooks. BS, U. Ala., Tuscaloosa, 1967; MS, U. Va., 1995. Staff writer Phillips, Eindhoven, The Netherlands, 1967-68; mgr. mktg. Fuller & Dees Mktg., Montgomery, Ala., 1968-70; v.p. Univ. Programs, Washington, 1970-73; pres. Coll. & Univ. Press, Washington, 1973-80; ptnr. Direct Response Consulting Svcs., McLean, Va., 1981-96; bd. dirs. Foxhall Corp., The Art Co. Founding mem. Am. Inst. Cancer Rsch. Mem. Direct Mktg. Assn., Non-Profit Mailer Fedn., Promotional Mktg. Assn., Nature Conservancy, Sierra Club, Falls Church (Va.) C. of C. (bd. dirs.). Home: 850 Dolley Madison Blvd Mc Lean VA 22101-1821 Office: Direct Response Cons Svcs 6849 Old Dominion Dr Ste 300 Mc Lean VA 22101-3705

WATSON, JIM ALBERT, lawyer; b. Rotan, Tex., Feb. 1, 1939; s. Morris Gilbert and Mae (Montgomery) W.; m. Paula Gayle Hickman, June 3, 1962; children: Michael Montgomery, Jennifer Ruth. BA, U. Tex., 1962, JD, 1964. Bar: Tex. 1964. Ptnr. Johnson & Gibbs, Dallas, 1975-95, also bd. dirs.; ptnr. Vinson & Elkins L.L.P., Dallas, 1995—; adj. prof. law U. Tex., 1987—; adj. prof. legal history So. Meth. U., 1989—. Mem. exec. council The Tex. State Hist. Assn., 1992—. Home: 7235 Lakewood Blvd Dallas TX 75214-3511

WATSON, JOHN ALLEN, lawyer; b. Ft. Worth, Sept. 18, 1946; s. John and Mary (Barlow) W.; m. Patricia L. Clardy, Oct. 24, 1946; 1 child, Virginia E. B.A., Rice U., 1968; J.D., U. Tex., Austin, 1971. Bar: Tex. 1971. Assoc. Fulbright & Jaworski, Houston, 1971-78, ptnr., 1978—. Mem. ABA. Office: Fulbright & Jaworski LLP 1301 Mckinney St Ste 5100 Houston TX 77010*

WATSON, KAY, school system administrator, retired; b. Rotan, Tex., Feb. 5, 1942; d. C.M. and Marie (Reeder) W. BA, Baylor U., 1964; MA, Colo. State Coll., 1968; MEd, Sul Ross State U., Alpine, Tex., 1982; EdD, Tex. Tech. U., 1988. Tchr. grade 6 Dallas Ind. Sch. Dist., Dallas, 1964-67, counselor J.L. Long Jr. H.S., 1968-70, tchr. grade 7, 1970-72; tchr. grade 5 Weatherford (Tex.) Ind. Sch. Dist., 1972-73; spl. edn. counselor Parker County Coop., Weatherford, 1973-74; spl. edn. counselor Monahans (Tex.)-Wickett-Pyote Ind. Sch. Dist., 1974-78, dir. spl. edn., 1978-85; supr. pre-sch. ctr. Ector County Ind. Sch. Dist., Odessa, Tex., 1985-86, prin. elem. Magnet Sch. at Travis, 1986-89, prin. LBJ Elem. Sch., 1989-90, assoc. dir. elem. edn., 1990-92, assoc. exec. dir., clusters I and II, 1992; asst. supt. Calhoun County Ind. Sch. Dist., Port Lavaca, Tex., 1992-96; vis. asst. prof. U. Tex. of the Permian Basin, Odessa, 1996—; vis. asst. prof. U. Tex., Odessa, 1996—. Bd. dirs. Am. Cancer Soc., Odessa, 1991-92; mem. Odessa Symphony Guild, 1990-92, Port Lavaca Crisis Hotline Vol.; bd. dirs. United Way of Calhoun County, 1996. Mem. ASCD, Tex. Elem. Prins. and Suprs. Assn., Tex. Assn. Secondary Sch. Adminstrs., Tex. Assn. Sch. Adminstrs., Tex. Assn. Profl. Educators, Pilot Club Internat. (dir. 1991-92, 93-96), Rotary Club Internat. (dir. 1995-96), Delta Kappa Gamma Soc. Internat. Baptist. Home: 1204 S Eric Monahans TX 79756 Office: Univ of the Permain Basin #307 Sch Edn 4901 E University Blvd Odessa TX 79762-0001

WATSON, KERR FRANCIS, management educator; b. Winston-Salem, Jan. 31, 1944; s. Kerr Francis and Mary Lee (Nalley) W.; m. Atalie Carol Marvin, July 31, 1965 (div. 1973); 1 child, David William; m. Carolyn Kay Rambo, July 23, 1974; children: Rebecca Marie, Benjamin Lee. BS in Chemistry, Math., Greensboro (N.C.) Coll., 1967; MBA in Mgmt., East Tenn. State U., 1977; PhD in Bus. Adminstrn., U. Tenn., 1990. Chemist Tenn. Eastman Co., Kingsport, 1967-71; chemist/mgr. Holliston Mills, Kingsport, 1971-74; chemist Great Lakes Rsch. Corp., Elizabethton, Tenn., 1974-77; economist First Tenn.-Va. Devel. Dist., Johnson City, Tenn., 1977-81; mgr. Johnson City Chem. Co., 1981-82; rsch. and devel. mgr. Strahan

Ink Co., Kingsport, Tenn., 1982-83; rsch. and teaching asst. U. Tenn., Knoxville, 1983-85; asst. prof. Western Carolina U., Cullowhee, 1986-88; assoc. prof. mgmt. Tusculum Coll., Greenville, Tenn., 1988-89; assoc. prof. mgmt. Va. Intermont Coll., Bristol, 1989—, faculty sec., 1991-92; mem. adj. faculty East Tenn. State U., 1983-90, Tusculum Coll., 1984; cons. in field. Contbr. articles to profl. jours. Chmn. long-range planning, head usher Cherokee Meth. Ch., Johnson City, 1989-91; mem. long-range planning com. Va. Intermont Coll., 1991—, mem. orgnl. mgmt. steering com., 1989-92. Recipient Chemistry Achievement award, Greensboro Coll., 1967, Rsch. award, N.C. Acad. Sci., 1965. Mem. Acad. Mgmt., So. Mgmt. Assn., N.Am. Case Rsch. Assn., Am. Mgmt. Assn., Assn. Coll. Bus. Schs. and Programs (program chmn. 1992, sec.-treas. 1993 region II), Greenwood Ruritan (past pres., zone gov.), Beta Gamma Sigma. Methodist. Home: 1621 Mill Springs Rd Jonesborough TN 37659-6221 Office: Va Intermont Coll Moore St Bristol VA 24201-4309

WATSON, LAURA HUMPHREYS, structural engineer; b. Chamblee, Ga., June 11, 1954; d. Warren Patrick Humphreys and Jane Brice (Caldwell) Cruse; m. Ronnie Lee Watson, Feb. 22, 1975. Student, U. Ga., 1972-75; BSCE with highest honors, Clemson U., 1978. Registered profl. engr., S.C. Assoc. engr. II Fluor Daniel, Greenville, S.C., 1978-80; assoc. engr. III Fluor Daniel, Greenville, 1980-82, engr. I, 1982-85, engr. II, 1985-92, engr. III, 1992-94; cons. Watson and Watson, Martin, Ga., 1994—. Recipient Nat. Merit scholar, Nat. Merit Found., 1972; Walter Lowry award, Clemson U., 1977, 78. Mem. ASCE, Toccoa Bird Club (Toccoa, Ga.), Phi Kappa Phi, Tau Beta Phi, Chi Epsilon. Home: RR 1 Box 499W Martin GA 30557-9652 Office: Watson and Watson Watson Rd Martin GA 30557

WATSON, MARILYN KAYE, elementary education educator; b. Liberty, Ky., Nov. 30, 1950; d. Lewis Joshua and Lois Sue (Ross) W. BA, Ea. Ky. U., 1974, postgrad., 1977, 81. Tchr. Casey County Bd. of Edn., Liberty, 1977—. Mem. NEA, Ky. Edn. Assn., Order of Eastern Star (sec. Casey chpt. 1979-85, grand Esther 1981-82, worthy matron 1989-90). Republican. Methodist.

WATSON, MERLYN FOHRELL, retired public school media specialist; b. St. Louis, Dec. 3, 1934; d. Eugene E. and Ora Meta (Teschmacher) Fohrell; m. Marvin Albert Watson, June 7, 1953 (dec. June 12, 1985); children: Jeffrey, Patrick, Merrall Keith. BS, Henderson State U., 1960, MS, 1980. Libr. clk. Hempstead/Nevada Pub. Libr., Hope, Ark., 1960-70; libr. Prescott (Ark.) Mid. Sch., 1970-76; office mgr. Ark. Pine Lumber Co., Inc., Prescott, 1977-85; media specialist Little Rock Sch. Dist., 1987-95. Mem. ALA, NEA, Ark. Edn. Assn., Ark. Libr. Assn. Methodist.

WATSON, ROBERT FRANCIS, lawyer; b. Houston, Jan. 9, 1936; s. Louis Leon and Lora Elizabeth (Hodges) W.; m. Marietta Kiser, Nov. 24, 1961; children: Julia, Melissa, Rebecca. BA, Vanderbilt U., 1957; JD, U. Denver, 1959. Bar: Colo. 1959, U.S. Dist. Ct. (no. dist.) Tex. 1967, U.S. Supreme Ct. 1968, Tex. 1973, U.S. Ct. Appeals (5th cir.) 1973, U.S. Dist. Ct. (so. dist.) Tex. 1980, U.S. Ct. Appeals (11th cir.) 1981. Law clk. U.S. Dist. Ct. Colo., 1960-61; trial atty. SEC, Denver, 1961-67, asst. regional adminstr., Ft. Worth, 1967-72, regional adminstr., 1972-75; ptnr. Law, Snakard & Gambill, P.C., Ft. Worth, 1975—; counsel City of Ft. Worth Police Investigation Commn., 1975; spl. counsel Office Atty. Gen. State Ariz., 1977-78. Mem. Ft. Worth Crime Commn., 1987-93; pres. bd. trustees Trinity Valley Sch., Ft. Worth; adv. dir., pres. Lena Pope Home for Dependent and Neglected Children, Ft. Worth. Honoree 27th Ann. Rocky Mountain State-Fed.-Provincial Securities Conf. Mem. ABA, State Bar Tex., Tarrant County Bar Assn., Colo. Bar Assn. (life fellow), Tex. Bar Found., Tex. Bus. Law Found. (bd. dirs. 1988-93), Am. Counsel Assn., Fed. Bar Assn., Am. Judicature Soc., Coll. of the State Bar Tex., Phi Delta Phi. Republican. Presbyterian. Clubs: Ft. Worth, Shady Oaks Country (Ft. Worth). Contbr. articles to profl. jours. Office: Law Snakard & Gambill PC 500 Throckmorton St Ste 3200 Fort Worth TX 76102-3819

WATSON, ROBERT JAMES, lawyer; b. Oceanside, N.Y., Mar. 30, 1955; s. Ralph Joseph and Mildred Adeline (Knapp) W.; m. Ann M. Goade, May 27, 1988; children: Emily Allyn, Caroline Elisabeth. BA, Biscayne Coll., 1976; JD, U. Fla., 1979. Bar: Fla. 1979, U.S. Dist. Ct. (so. dist.) Fla. 1980, U.S. Dist. Ct. (no. dist.) Fla. 1981, U.S. Dist. Ct. (mid. dist.) Fla. 1982, U.S. Ct. Appeals (11th cir.) 1982. Asst. pub. defender Law Offices of Elton Schwarz, Ft. Pierce, Fla., 1979-81; ptnr. Wilkinson & Watson P.A., Stuart, Fla., 1981-86; pvt. practice Stuart, 1986-90; ptnr. Frierson & Watson, Stuart, 1990—. Mem. Fla. Bar Assn., Nat. Assn. Criminal Def. Lawyers, Acad. Fla. Trial Lawyers, Martin Assn. Criminal Def. Lawyers, Fla. Assn. Criminal Def. Lawyers. Democrat. Roman Catholic. Home: 9 Emarita Way Stuart FL 34996-6704 Office: Frierson & Watson 3601 SE Ocean Blvd Ste 004 Stuart FL 34996-6737

WATSON, ROBERTA CASPER, lawyer; b. Boise, Idaho, July 11, 1949; d. John Blaine and Joyce Lucile (Mercer) C.; m. Robert George Watson, July 22, 1972; 1 child, Rebecca Joyce. BA cum laude, U. Idaho, 1971; JD, Harvard U., 1974. Bar: Mass. 1974, U.S. Dist. Ct. Mass. 1975, U.S. Supreme Ct. 1979, U.S. Ct. Appeals (1st cir.) 1979, U.S. Tax Ct. 1979, Fla. 1985, U.S. Dist. Ct. (mid. dist.) Fla. 1985, U.S. Dist. Ct. (so. dist.) Fla. 1987. Assoc. Peabody & Brown, Boston, 1974-78, Mintz, Levin, Cohn, Ferris, Glovsky & Popeo, Boston, 1978-84; sr. dir. Wolper Ross & Co., Miami, 1983-85; assoc. Trenam, Kemker, Scharf, Barkin, Frye, O'Neill & Mullis, P.A., Tampa, Fla., 1985-87, ptnr., 1988—. Contbr. articles to profl. jours.; co-author: A Physician's Guide to Professional Corporations. Pres. Performing Arts Ctr. Greater Framingham, Mass., 1983; bd. dirs. Northside Commmunity Mental Health Ctr.; trustee Unitarian Universalist Found., Clearwater, Fla. Named bd. mem. of yr. Fla. Cmty. Mental Health, 1994. Mem. ABA (chair employee benefit com. sect. taxation 1995-96), Fla. West Coast Employee Benefits Coun. (bd. dirs.), Harvard Club (bd. dirs. West Coast Fla. chpt.), Ivy League Club Tampa Bay (bd. dirs.), Tampa Club, Order Ea. Star. Democrat. Home: 124 Adalia Ave Tampa FL 33606-3304 Office: Trenam Kemker et al Ste 2700 2700 Barnett Pla Tampa FL 33602

WATSON, ROGER ELTON, state agency administrator; b. Goldsboro, N.C., Jan. 5, 1944; s. Robert Elton and Maggie (McCabe) W.; m. Barbara S. Baus, June 30, 1973; children: Michelle E., Stephanie Ann. BS, N.C. State U., 1968. Collection mgr. Planters Bank, Hopkinsville, Ky., 1976-80; pres., owner Watson Enterprises, Hopkinsville, 1980-85; cabinet for human resources Commonwealth of Ky., Hopkinsville, 1985—. Vice-pres. Hopkinsville Girsl Softball, 1979. Capt. AUS Spl. Forces, 1968-76, Vietnam. Decorated Disting. Svc. Cross, 2 Silver Stars, 2 Bronze Stars, Purple Heart. Mem. Lions Club (pres. 1978). Republican. Presbyterian. Home: 313 Mark Dr PO Box 1237 Hopkinsville KY 42241-7237

WATSON, RONALD, painter, art educator; b. Grand Island, Nebr., Oct. 9, 1941; m. Diana Shaffer. BFA in Edn., U. Nebr., 1964, MFA in Painting, 1967; postgrad., U. Colo., 1977, Picasso Mus., Barcelona, Spain, 1989, Columbia U., 1991. Instr. No. Mich. U., Marquette, 1967-68; asst. prof. Aquinas Coll., Grand Rapids, Mich., 1970-77, assoc. prof., 1977-79, prof., 1979-82, chmn. art dept., 1971-81; prof. art Tex. Christian U., Ft. Worth, 1982—, chmn. and gallery dir. dept. art and art history, 1982-89, dir. grad. studies Coll. Fine Arts and Comm., 1991-94, chmn., dir. gallery Coll. Fine Arts and Comm., 1994—; mem. selection panel Art in Pub. Places program Nat. Endowment for Arts, 1975-79, project dir. for grant, 1974, mem. artists' svcs. panel, 1975; founder, dir. Urban Inst. for Contemporary Arts, Grand Rapids, 1977-82; cons. in field; vis. artist Cranbrook Acad. Art, Bloomfield Hills, Mich., 1982, Calvin Coll., Grand Rapids, 1982, Miami-Dade C.C., Fla., 1981, Ferris State Coll., Big Rapids, Mich., 1979, Ohio State U., Columbus, 1978, Lehman Coll., Bronx, N.Y., 1973. One man shows at Lehman Coll., 1973, Ohio State U., 1978, Ferris State Coll., 1979, Miami-Dade C.C., 1981, Dobrick Gallery, Chgo., 1982, Brown-Lupton Gallery, Tex. Christian U., 1982, Wichita Falls (Tex.) Art Assn., 1983, San Antonio Art Inst., 1987, William Campbell Contemporary Art, Ft. Worth, 1988, Tex. Christian U., 1991, Broadway Bapt. Ch., Ft. Worth, 1992; performance works exhibited at Tex. Christian U., 1991, Modern Art Mus. of Ft. Worth, 1993; contbr. articles to profl. pubis. Artist fellow Nat. Endowment for Arts, 1975; recipient Key to City of Grand Rapids, 1973. Mem. Nat. Coun. Art Adminstrs. (chmn. 1987). Home: 6416 Greenway Rd Fort Worth TX 76116-4426 Office: Tex Christian U Dept Art and Art History Box 30793 Fort Worth TX 76129

WATSON, S. MICHELE, home health nurse; b. Selma, Ala., Apr. 21, 1965; d. Kenneth and Linda (Bishop) Wilds; m. H. Alan Watson, May 30, 1987. AAS, Cleveland State Community Coll, Tenn., 1987, AS, 1985. RN, Tenn. Emergency room staff nurse Cleveland Community Hosp.; staff nurse ICU Meml. Hosp., Chattanooga; team leader Bradley Meml. Home Health, Cleveland. Home: 146 Hicks Rd NE Cleveland TN 37312-5853

WATSON, STANLEY ELLIS, clergyman, financial company executive; b. New Orleans, July 25, 1957; s. Joseph and Dorothy (Jones) W.. EdB, Jarvis Christian Coll., Hawkins, Tex., 1977; MRE, Tex. Christian U., Ft. Worth, 1979; spl. edn., So. U. A&M, Baton Rouge, 1986; grad., U.S. Acad. Pvt. Investigation, 1991; DD (hon.), Charter Ecumenical Ministries, 1994. Cert. tchr.; registered notary Mich. Asst. min. Jarvis Christian Coll., Hawkins, Tex., 1974-77; tchr. pub. sch., Daingerfield, Tex., 1977-78; asst. min. Park Manor Christian Ch., Chgo., 1980-81; asst. mgr. K Mart, Shreveport, La., 1981-82; min. United Christian Ch., Jackson, Miss., 1982-83; tchr. pub. sch., Napoleonville, La., 1986-87, Zachary, La., 1987-88; min. Vermont Christian Ch., Flint, Mich., 1988-90; sr. pastor Mich., 1990—; owner Waton Diversified Fin. Co., 1989—. Mem. NAACP, NEA. Christian Women's fellow, 1975-77, St. Louis Bd. Edn. fellow, 1977-79, Tex. Christian U. Brite Div. Sch. scholar, 1977; Jarvis Christian Coll. cert. of Honor, Merit, 1974-77; named Rev. Stanley Watson Day City of Flint, Mich., 1989. Mem. Nat. Assn. Investigative Specialists, Am. Inst. Profl. Bookeepers, Am. Fin. Coord. Assn. (fin. coord.), Christian Counselors Assn., Nat. Assn Investigative Specialist, Nat. Assn Federated Tax Preparers, Am. Soc. Notaries, Aircraft Owners and Pilots Assn. Coun. for Exceptional Children, Forgotten Man Ministries, Jarvis Christian Coll. Alumni Assn. (v.p.), NAACP, Urban League of Flint, Urban Coalition of Greater Flint, Flint C. of C., Internat. Reading Assn., NEA, Phi Beta Sigma, Kappa Delta Pi. Dem. Office: Watson's Detective Agy PO Box 1664 Donaldsonville LA 70346-1664

WATSON, WILLIAM DOWNING, JR., economist, educator; b. Durango, Colo., Aug. 9, 1938; s. William Downing and Carrie Elizabeth (Bailey) Blanchard; m. Dolores Marie Boisclair, Sept. 7, 1968; children: Kelli, Adam, Seth. BA in Math., No. Colo. U., 1964; MA in Econs., Syracuse U., 1965; PhD in Econs., U. Minn., 1970. Asst. prof. Wash. State U., Pullman, 1971-72; economist EPA-Washington, 1972-73; sr. fellow Resources for the Future, Washington, 1973-78; adj. prof. Va. Poly. Inst. and State U., Falls Ch., 1981—; economist U.S. Geol. Survey, Reston, Va., 1978—; staff economist dirs. office U.S. Geol. Survey, Reston, 1984-88; sr. economist Ministry of Fin. and Nat. Economy Kingdom of Saudi Arabia, 1989-91; economist Office of Energy and Marine Geology U.S. Geol. Survey, Reston, 1991-95; assoc. prof. Ga. Inst. Tech., Atlanta, 1995—. Author: To Choose a Future, 1980; contbr. articles to profl. jours. Served with U.S. Army, 1956-59. Earhart fellow, U. Minn., 1967; Resources for the Future Dissertation fellow, Washington, 1969. Mem. Am. Econs. Assn., Internat. Assn. Energy Economists, Assn. Environ. and Resource Economists. Avocations: tennis; hiking; skiing. Home: 659 Peachtree St #1004 Atlanta GA 30308

WATT, CHARLES, research scientist. Grad., Clemson U., George Washington U. With Bendix Corp., 1959, Bell Sys.; dir. def. test and evaluation Office Sec. Def.; lab. dir., mem. faculty Ga. Inst. Tech.; chmn., CEO Sci. Rsch. Corp., Atlanta; lectr. univs., profls. socs., and C. of C. meetings on tech. trends and their impact on soc.; mem. faculty Clemson U., mem. elec. envring. dept. adv. bd., mem. pres.'s adv. coun.; bd. dirs. Tech-Sym Corp. Recipient Def. Meritorious Disting. Svc. award, Commendation for Spl. Svc. to U.S. Congress on Telecom., George Washington U. Alumni Achievement award, Gazelle award Atlanta Bus. Chronicle, 1995. Mem. IEEE (sr.), Internat. Test and Evaluation Assn. (bd. dirs.), Atlanta C. of C. Chmn.'s Club, Tau Beta Pi, Sigma Xi. Office: Sci Rsch Corp Ste 400 2300 Windy Ridge Pky Atlanta GA 30339

WATT, (ARTHUR) DWIGHT, JR., computer programming and microcomputer specialist; b. Washington, Jan. 25, 1955; s. Arthur Dwight and Myrtle Lorraine (Putnam) W.; m. Shari Elizabeth Gambrell, July 30, 1988. BA, Winthrop U., 1977, MBA, 1979; EdD, U. Ga., 1989. Cert. computer profl. Inst. Cert. Computer Profls.; cert. instr. cmty. first aid and safety, ARC; cert. Home Fire Arms Safety. Data processing instr. York Tech. Coll., Rock Hill, S.C., 1977-78; computer ctr. asst. Winthrop U., Rock Hill, 1976-79; data processing instr. Brunswick (Ga.) Coll., 1979-80; system operator, asst. programmer Sea Island (Ga.) Co., The Cloister, 1981; pvt. practice data processing cons. Swainsboro, Ga., 1981—; computer programming/microcomputer specialist instr. Swainsboro Tech. Inst., 1981-96; sr. programmer/analyst Policy Mgmt. Sys. Corp., Columbia, S.C., 1996—; cons., speaker in field; chmn. exec. bd. computer curricula Ga. Dept. Tech. and Adult Edn., 1990-92, mem. exec. bd. computer curricula, 1994-96; chmn. East Ctrl. Ga. Consortium for Computer Occupations, 1990-93, 94-96. Author: District Revenue Potential and Teachers Salaries in Georgia, 1989; co-author: District Property Wealth and Teachers Salaries in Georgia, 1990, Factors Influencing Teachers Salaries: An Examination of Alternative Models, 1991, Local Wealth and Teachers Salaries in Pennsylvania, 1992, School District Wealth and Teachers' Salaries in South Carolina, 1993, Structural COBOL for Technical Students, 1996. Chmn. Emanuel County chpt. ARC, Swainsboro, 1989-90, 92-93, bd. dirs., 1989—; pres. United Meth. Men. Swainsboro, 1984-86; trustee Greater Swainsboro Tech. Inst. Found., Inc., 1995-96. Recipient Nat. Tech. Tchr. of Yr. finalist award Am. Tech. Edn. Assn., 1994; named Olypmpic Cmty. Hero Torchbearer, 1996. Mem. Ga. Bus. Edn. Assn. (dir. dist. 1 1986, 96, dist. sec.-treas. 1993-95, dist. 1 dir.-elect 1995-96, Dist. 1 Postsecondary Tchr. of Yr. 1985, state postsecondary tchr. of yr. 1995), Ga. Vocat. Assn., Data Processing Mgmt. Assn., Swainsboro Jaycees (Outstanding Young Citizen 1985, treas. 1984-89, pres. 1987-88, pres. S.E. Ga. Jaycee Fair 1995, treas. S.E. Ga. Jaycee Fair 1995), Ga. Jaycees (v.p. area C. mem. 1988-89, chaplain 1989-90, dir. region 6 1990-91, chmn. state shooting edn. 1991-92), U.S. Jr. C. of C. (nat. rep. shooting edn. program 1992-95, Shooting Edn. State Program Mgr. of Yr. 1992), Swainsboro Kiwanis. Methodist. Home: 8100 Bayfield Rd Apt 24-E Columbia SC 29223 Office: Policy Mgmt Sys Corp PO Box 10 Columbia SC 29223

WATT, JOSEPH MICHAEL, state supreme court justice; b. Austin, Tex., Mar. 8, 1947. BA in History, Tex. Tech U., 1969; JD, U. Tex., 1972. Bar: Tex., Okla. Pvt. practice, Altus, Okla., 1972-85; judge Dist. Trial Ct., 1985-91; gen. counsel to gov. State of Okla., Oklahoma City, 1991-92; justice Okla Supreme Ct., Oklahoma City, 1992—. Office: Okla State Supreme Ct State Capitol Rm 240 Oklahoma City OK 73105

WATT, MELVIN L., congressman, lawyer; b. Mecklenburg County, N.C., Oct. 26, 1945; m. Eulada Paysour; children: Brian, Jason. BS in Bus. Adminstrn., U. N.C., 1967; JD, Yale U., 1970. Atty. Ferguson, Stein, Watt, Wallis, Adkins, & Grensham, 1971—; U.S. senator from N.C. 95th Congress, 1985-86; co-owner East Towne Manor, 1989—; mem. 103rd-104th Congress from 12th N.C. dist., Washington, D.C., 1993—; pres. Mecklenburg County Bar. Active Ctrl. Piedmont C.C. Found., Legal Aid of Southern Piedmont, N.C. NB Community Devel. Corp., Auditorium-Coliseum-Civic Ctr. Authority, United Way, Mint Mus., Family Housing Svcs., Pub. Edn. Forum, Dilworth Community Devel. Assn., Cities in Schs., Housing Authority Scholarship Bd., Morehead Scholarship Selection Com.; bd. visitors Johnson C. Smith Univ. Mem. N.C. Assn. Black Lawyers, N.C. Acad. Trial Lawyers, Charlotte C. of C. (sports action coun.), West Charlotte Bus. Incubator, Inroads Inc., Phi Beta Kappa. Democrat. Presbyterian. Office: US Ho of Reps 1230 Longworth Ho Office Bldg Washington DC 20515-3312*

WATT, WILLIAM STEWART, physical chemist; b. Perth, Scotland, Feb. 25, 1937. BSc, U. St. Andrews, Scotland, 1959; PhD in Phys. Chemistry, U. Leeds, 1962. Fellow Cornell U., 1962-64; rsch. chemist Cornell Aeronautics Lab., Buffalo, 1964-71; head chem. laser sect. Naval Rsch. Lab., 1971-73, dep. head laser physics br., 1973-76, head laser physics br. optical sci. divsn., 1976-79; gen. mgr. wash ops. W. J. Schafer Assoc., Arlington, Va., 1979-80, v.p. program devel., 1980-90, sr. v.p., dir. programs, 1991-94; CEO Lawrence Assocs., Inc., Arlington, 1994-95; pres. WSW Consulting Inc., McLean, Va., 1996—. Recipient J. B. Cohen Rsch. prize, 1962. Mem. IEEE (assoc. editor Jour. Quantum Electronics), Am. Phys. Soc., Combustion Inst., Sigma Xi. Office: WSW Consulting Inc PO Box 121 Mc Lean VA 22101

WATTERSON, GENE LEE, clergyman; b. Decatur, Ala., Dec. 10, 1929; s. Aulton Douglas and Eva Rose (Couch) W.; m. Yvonne Caudle, Aug. 7, 1954; children: Pamela Yvonne Watterson Runyans, Gene L. Jr., Lisa Dawn. Student, Samford U., 1948-51; BA, Jones U., 1952; MA, Coll. William and Mary, 1956; MDiv, Southeastern Bapt. Theol. Sem., 1960; DD (hon.), Gardner-Webb Coll., 1974. Ordained to ministry So. Bapt. Conv., 1952; cert. clin. counselor, Va., Fla., N.C. Pastor Woodlawn Bapt. Ch., Colonial Heights, Va., 1953-60, 1st Bapt. Ch., Crestview, Fla., 1960-67; sr. min. Murray Hill Bapt. Ch., Jacksonville, Fla., 1967-69, 1st Bapt. Ch., Shelby, N.C., 1969—; mem. exec. com. N.C. Bapt. State Conv., Carey, 1969-74, pres. coun. on Christian higher edn., 1971-74, 1st v.p., 1988-89, pres., 1990-91; officer exec. com. So. Bapt. Conv., Nashville, 1975-83. Author: (with others) Evangelism Today, 1966; also articles. Chmn. Commn. on Housing and Urban Devel., Shelby, 1969-74; mem. Commn. on Human Rels., Shelby, 1969-74; bd. dirs. Coun. on Abuse Prevention, Shelby, 1978-82; mem. N.C. Legislature Study Commn. on Youth Suicide, Raleigh, 1987-89; mem. Commn. on the Family, 1990-95. With USN, 1945-48, ETO, Asia. Recipient citation for excellence in Christian ministry Gardner-Webb Coll., 1972, citation for outstanding svc. So. Bapt. Conv., 1983. Mem. Friends of Missions, Religious Liberty Coun. Home: 617 Peach St Shelby NC 28150-5544 Office: 1st Bapt Ch 120 N Lafayette St Shelby NC 28150-4456

WATTS, ANTHONY LEE, bank executive; b. Griffin, Ga., Jan. 24, 1947; s. Edgar Lee and Eula Mae (Benton) W.; m. Barbara Malinda Harp, Oct. 11, 1969; children: Natalie Paige, Barbara Leigh, Melanie Marie. AA, Gordon Mil. Coll., 1967; ABJ, U. Ga., 1969. Conventional loan rep. Fed. Nat. Mortgage Assn., Atlanta, from 1971, asst. regional appraiser, quality control and property mgr., until 1976; v.p., dir. ins. svcs. Ticor Mortgage Ins. Co., Atlanta, 1976-82, v.p., regional sales and exec. v.p. Ticor Indemnity Co., 1982-85; sr. v.p., regional mgr. Ticor Mortgage Ins. Co., Atlanta, 1984, sr. v.p. Ea. div. mgr., 1984-85; pres. Mt. Vernon Fed. Savs. Bank, Dunwoody, Ga., 1985-95; pres. Mt. Vernon Fin. Corp., 1993-95; pres. Banc Mortgage Fin. Corp., 1996—; lectr. trade assns. With U.S. Army, 1969-71. Decorated Bronze Star; Paul Harris fellow, 1987. Mem. Ga. Mortgage Bankers Assn., Rotary. Office: 2408 Mount Vernon Rd Atlanta GA 30338-3004

WATTS, AUBREY VERNON, JR., city manager; b. Norfolk, Va., Mar. 12, 1941; s. Aubrey V. Sr. and Mildred (Mullins) W.; m. Emily Wingate, Aug. 24, 1963; children: Barbara Lynn, Aubrey Vernon III. BS in Bus. Adminstrn., Va. Poly. Inst., 1963; Cert. in Pub. Adminstrn., U. Va., 1973. Dep. City Treas. City of Virginia Beach, 1963-67, asst. dir. fin., 1967-71, dir. personnel, 1971-74, dir. pub. utility, 1974-84, dep. city mgr., 1984-87, city mgr., 1987-91; city mgr. City of Greenville (S.C.), 1991—; mem. state water commn., Va., 1988-91, state com. jails and prisons, Va., 1989-91. Recipient Fuller award Am. Water Works Assn., Award of Merit Am. Legion, 1989, Technology Leadership, Pub. Tech. Inc., 1990. Mem. Internat. City Mgrs. Assn. (30 Yr. Svc. award 1990), S.C. City County Mgrs. Assn., Rotary. Methodist. Office: City of Greenville 206 S Main St Greenville SC 29601

WATTS, BEVERLY L., civil rights executive; b. Nashville, Feb. 4, 1948; d. Willliam E. and Evelyn L. (Bender) Lindsley; 1 child, Lauren. BS, Tenn. State U., 1969; MS, So. Ill. U., 1973. Mgr., exec. sec. State of Ill. Minority and Female Bus. Enterprise Program, Chgo.; equal opportunity specialist U.S. Dept. of Health, Edn., and Welfare, Chgo.; reginal dir., civil rights/equal employment opportunity USDA, Chgo. Grad. Leadership Louisville, 1994, Leadership Ky., 1995, Duke U. Strategic Leadership for State Execs.; mem. long term planning commn. Ky. Health Policy Bd.; mem. Ohio Valley March of Dimes; mem. equal opportunity com. Ky. Coun. on Higher Edn., Louisville Met. Housing Coalition. Recipient Chgo. Forum Gavel award, BEEP Gold Seal award. Mem. Nat. Urban Affairs Coun., Ky. Women's Leadership Network, Chgo. Forum, Affirmative Action Assn., Chgo. Urban Affairs Coun. (pres.), Coalition 100 Black Women. Office: Ky Commn on Human Rights 322 W Broadway Fl 7 Louisville KY 40202-2106

WATTS, CHRISTOPHER LEE, physical education educator; b. Alexandria, Va., Dec. 8, 1955; s. James Carlos and Carole Joyce (Blake) W.; m. Virginia Lynne Dodd, Jan. 5, 1980; children: Katti Lynne, Rebecca Summer, Krista Brooke, Alexandria. BS, Mars Hill Coll., 1980; MEd, West Ga. Coll., 1989. Tchr. elem. phys. edn. Mt. Carmel Elem., Douglasville, Ga., 1980—; football coach Lithia Springs (Ga.) H.S., 1986-91, coach girls tennis, 1986-92; football coach Douglas County H.S., Douglasville, 1993—; mem. strategic planning com. Douglas County Bd. Edn., Douglasville, 1993—. Coord. Jump Rope for Heart, Am. Heart Assn., Douglas County, 1983—; sch. coord. D.A.R.E. Fun Run, Drug Awareness Resistance Orgn., Douglas County, 1994—. Mem. NEA, AAHPERD, Assn. for Sport and Phys. Edn., Ga. Assn. Educators, Ga. Assn. Health, Phys. Edn., Recreation and Dance, Ga. H.S. Assn. Republican. Baptist. Home: 9153 Saddlebrook Way Douglasville GA 30135 Office: Douglas County Bd Edn Mount Carmel Elem 2356 Fairburn Rd Douglasville GA 30135

WATTS, CLAUDIUS ELMER, III, retired air force officer; b. Bennettsville, S.C., Sept. 22, 1936; s. Claudius Elmer and Blanche Robey (Wannamaker) W.; m. Patricia Jane Sims, July 23, 1960; children: Claudius Elmer IV, Patricia Watts Heck. A.B. in Polit. Sci., The Citadel, 1958; postgrad. (Fulbright scholar), London Sch. Econs. and Polit. Sci., 1958-59; M.B.A., Stanford U., 1967. Commd. officer USAF, 1958, advanced through grades to lt. gen., 1986; comdr. 438th Mil. Airlift Group USAF, McGuire AFB, N.J., 1978-80; comdr. 63d Mil. Airlift Wing USAF, Norton AFB, Calif., 1980-82; asst. dep. chief staff plans Mil. Airlift Command USAF, Scott AFB, Ill., 1982-83, dep. chief staff plans Mil. Airlift Command, 1982-84; dir. budget Hdqrs. U.S. Air Force, Washington, 1984-85; sr. mil. asst. to dep. sec. def. U.S. Dept. Def., Washington, 1985-86; compt. USAF, Washington, 1986-89; pres. The Citadel, Charleston, S.C., 1989-96; ret.; former mem. adv. coun. grad. sch. bus. Stanford U.; former mem. bd. visitors Air U.; mem. NCAA Coun., rep. on acad. requirements, chmn. peer rev. teams for cert. Bd. trustees Palmetto Partnership; chmn. Marion Sq. Commn.; bd. dirs., mem. fin. com. Air Force Aid Soc. Decorated Def. Disting. Svc. medal, USAF Disting. Svc. medal, Legion of Merit with oak leaf cluster, DFC with two oak leaf clusters, Air Medal with 10 oak leaf clusters, Gallantry Cross with Palm (Vietnam), Vietnamese Svc. Cross with 2 svc. stars. Mem. Air Force Assn. (audit com. nat. hdqrs.), Am. Soc. Mil. Comptrollers, Mil. Order World Wars, Air Force Sgts. Assn., Airlift Assn., VFW, Royal Order of St. Stanislas, Order of Daedalians, Soc. of the Cincinnati (hon.), Assn. Mil. Colls. and Schs. of U.S. (exec. com.), Aerospace Edn. Found. (trustee), Air Force Aid Soc. (bd. dirs., mem. finance com.), Rotary. Methodist. Office: Mil Coll of SC MSC # 150 The Citadel Charleston SC 29409

WATTS, ELIZABETH ANNE, journalism educator; b. Denver, Aug. 6, 1948; d. Leslie V. and Barbara M. (Kleber) W. BA, Adams State Coll., 1970; Ednl. Specialist, U. No. Colo., 1976; PhD, Ohio U., 1992. Corr. United Am. Life Ins. Co., Denver, 1970-71; tchr. Peetz (Colo.) H.S., 1971-73, Trona (Calif.) H.S., 1973-74; clk. Pike Safe Co., Denver, 1976-77; reporter Sidney (Nebr.) Telegraph, 1977-78, McCook (Nebr.) Gazette, 1978-80; prof. journalism Kearney (Nebr.) State Coll., 1981-90, St. Bonaventure (N.Y.) U., 1990-92, Tex. Tech U., Lubbock, 1992—. Mem. Soc. Profl. Journalists, Assn. for Edn. in Journalism and Mass Comm., Tex. Profl. Communicators (asst. treas. 1995-96), N.Y. Press Women (treas. 1991-92), Nebr. Press Women (treas. 1982-84), Nat. Fedn. of Press Women. Lutheran. Office: Tex Tech U Sch Mass Comm Lubbock TX 79409

WATTS, GERALD DALE, software engineer, researcher; b. Norman, Okla., July 7, 1959; s. Gerald Dale Sr. and Berle Janet (Orr) W.; m. Loretta Olline Meurer, July 2, 1988 (div.); 1 child, Michael A. Grad., Moore Norman Vocat. Tech., 1978, postgrad., 1978—. System operator Cablistic Rsch., Norman, 1987—. Author: (software) Cipher version 1.0, 1992, version 2.0, 1993, version 3.0, 4.0, 1994, Generator version 1.0, 1992, version 2.0, 1993, version 3.0, 4.0, 1994. Home: 110 W Haddock St Norman OK 73069-8720

WATTS, HELENA ROSELLE, military analyst; b. East Lynne, Mo., May 29, 1921; d. Elmer Wayne and Nellie Irene (Barrington) Long; m. Henry Millard Watts, June 14, 1940; children: Helena Roselle Watts Scott, Patricia Marie Watts Foble. B.A., Johns Hopkins U., 1952, postgrad., 1952-53. Assoc. engr., Westinghouse Corp., Balt., 1965-67; sr. analyst Merck, Sharp & Dohme, Westpoint, Pa., 1967-69; sr. engr. Bendix Radio div. Bendix Corp., Balt., 1970-72; sr. scientist Sci. Applications Internat. Corp., McLean, Va., 1975-84; mem. tech. staff The MITRE Corp., McLean, 1985-94, ret., 1994;

adj. prof. Def. Intelligence Coll., Washington, 1984-85. Contbr. articles to tech. jours. Mem. IEEE, AAAS, AIAA, Nat. Mil. Intelligence Assn., U.S. Naval Inst., Navy League of U.S., Air Force Assn., Assn. Former Intelligence Officers, Assn. Old Crows, Mensa, N.Y. Acad. Sci. Republican. Roman Catholic. Avocations: photography, gardening, reading. Home: 4302 Roberts Ave Annandale VA 22003-3508

WATTS, J. C., JR., congressman; b. Eufaula, Okla., Nov. 8, 1957; m. Frankie Watts; 5 children. BA in Journalism, U. Okla., 1981. Profl. football player Ottawa and Toronto Teams Can. Football League, 1981-86; youth min. Sunnylane So. Bapt. Ch., Del City, 1987-94; mem. Okla. Corp. Commn., 1990-94, chmn., 1993-94; mem. 104th Congress from 4th Okla. dist., 1995—; mem. Nat. Drinking Water Adv. Coun.; mem. electricity com. Nat. Assn. Regulatory Utility Commrs. Republican. Office: US House Reps 1713 Longworth Washington DC 20515-3604

WATTS, JUDITH-ANN WHITE, academic administrator; b. Moline, Ill., Nov. 11, 1955; d. Harry Cameron and Jennie Elizabeth (Brockevelt) White. BSEd, Ill. State U., 1976; MSEd, Western Ill. U., 1987; postgrad., George Mason U., 1992-96, U. So. Calif., 1996—. English tchr. United Twp. High Sch., East Moline, Ill., 1976-77, English tchr., curriculum designer/asst. theatre dir., 1978-84; county coord. Simon for Senate Campaign, Rock Island, Ill., 1984; legis. asst. U.S. Sen. Paul Simon, Washington, 1985-89; program devel. specialist NEA, Washington, 1989-90; dir. constituent rels. Nat. Coun. Accreditation Tchr. Edn., Washington, 1990-92; exec. assoc. policy devel. Nat. Bd. Profl. Teaching Standards, Washington, 1992-93; spl. asst. to pres. Va. State U., Petersburg, 1993-96; exec. asst. ofc. of the dean U. So. Calif. Sch. of Edn., L.A., 1996—; v.p. bd. dirs. Rappahannock Mediation Ctr., Fredericksburg, Va., mediator, 1989—, trainer, 1991—. Mem. Fredericksburg Singers, 1990—, Fredericksburg Community Chorus, 1990—; precinct capt. Spotsylvania County (Va.) Dem. Com., 1989—; campaign worker various polit. campaigns, Va., Ill., 1972—; exec. com. of vestry St. George's Ch., Fredericksburg, mem. ch. choir, 1990—. Mem. NEA, ASCD, AERA, Am. Assn. Sch. Adminstrs., Nat. Assn. Sec. Sch. Prins., Ill. Edn. Assn. (regional vice chair 1982-84, regional pub. rels. chair 1982-84), Va. Edn. Assn., Va. Meditation Network. Episcopalian. Home: 120 21st St Huntington Beach CA 92648-3918 Office: USC Sch of Edn Office of Dean WPH 1100 Los Angeles CA 90089-0031

WATTS, MARIE ELIZABETH (MITZI WATTS), mining and heavy construction executive, art consultant; b. Dallas, Feb. 17, 1936; d. Milan and Marie Elizabeth Martha (Eichinger) Furtula; student St. Mary's Coll., Notre Dame, Ind., 1954-55; student art Dallas Mus. Fine Art, Ark. Art Center, So. Meth. U., Honolulu Art Center; cert. interior designer Tex. Archtl. Bd.; m. Cleal Thomas Watts, Jr., July 28, 1956; children—Cleal Thomas, III, John Milan, Elizabeth, Lawrence Budd. A founder, 1962, since chief exec. officer H.F. Constrn. Co., Inc., Dallas; a founder, 1970, since chief exec. officer HFCO, Inc., Dallas; a founding partner Cleal T. Watts, research, design, mfg. and purchasing internat. sales and services, Dallas, 1962—; co-founder and chief exec. officer SOD Unltd., Inc., Dallas, 1986—; profl. artist, 1979—; founder, dir., owner Mitzi Watts, art cons. firm, 1982—. One-woman exhbn. Tokyo, 1988-89, Georgetown Gallery, Atlanta, 1980, Lynn Kottler Gallery, N.Y.C.; represented in permanent collection Chanel NYC, Andy Granatelli-STP Mus. Pres. Ark. Art Ctr., 1965; co-founder San Marcos Art League, 1962; metal mobile of three kings and annunciation statues St. Mary's Coll., Notre Dame Dist. dir. Tex. Republican Party, 1963; mem. bd. Ursuline Acad. Sch., 1978-80, women's exec. bd. Dallas Bapt. U., 1986—; mem. mother's club, 1976-80; bd. dirs. So. Meth. U., 1984-86, also bd. dirs. Parents Council; chair Christ the King Sch. Endowment Fund, 1994-96, St. Bernard's Sch. Bd., 1996. Recipient Linz scholar award, 1950-54; named Vol. of Yr. So. Meth. U., 1986; recipient Golden Plate award Dallas Bapt. U., 1985. Mem. Assn. Gen. Contractors Am., Am. Mining Congress, Internat. Platform Assn., Tex. Fine Artists Assn. Dallas So. Mem. Assn. (exec. bd.). Office: PO Box 181867 Dallas TX 75218

WATTS, NELSON BARNETT, endocrinologist, medical educator; b. San Antonio, Nov. 11, 1944; s. Walter Moore and Adelene (Barnett) W.; m. Bettie Griffin, June 9, 1966; children: Parker Neely, Alison Barnett. BS, U. N.C., 1966, MD, 1969. Cert. Am. Bd. Internal Medicine (subspecialty endocrinology and metabolism). Intern in medicine Eugene Talmadge Meml. Hosp., Augusta, Ga., 1969-70; fellow in endocrinology N.C. Meml. Hosp., Chapel Hill, 1970-71; resident in medicine Charlotte (N.C.) Meml. Hosp., 1971-72; pvt. practice endocrinology and diabetes W.N.C. Internal Medicine Cons., Asheville, N.C., 1972-83; attending physician Meml. Mission Hosp. and St. Joseph's Hosp., Asheville, 1972-83, Emory U. Hosp., Grady Meml. Hosp., Atlanta, 1983—; endocrinologist The Emory Clinic, Inc., Atlanta, 1983-85, endocrinologist, ptnr., 1985—, lab. dir., 1987—, assoc. subsect. head endocrinology sect. internal medicine, 1989—, co-dir. Bone Densitometry Svc., 1990—; clin. asst. prof. medicine U. N.C. Sch. Medicine, 1976-81, clin. assoc. prof., 1981-83; pres. Buncombe County (N.C.) Med. Soc., 1980; sr. assoc. medicine Emory U. Sch. Medicine, Atlanta, 1983-84, asst. prof., 1984-88, assoc. prof., 1988-96, prof., 1996—; mem. subcom. on urinalysis Nat. Com. for Clin. Lab. Stds., 1989—, subcom. on hemoglobinopathies, 1990—; grant reviewer Nat. Osteoporosis Found., NIH (NIDDK), 1993; ad-hoc reviewer for various jorus.; presenter in field; others. Author: Disorders of Glucose Metabolism, 1987; author: (with others) Practical Endocrine Diagnosis, 1978, 3d edit., 1982, Diagnostico Endocrinologico Practico, 1983, Emory University Hospital Diabetes Manual, 1985, Practical Endorcinology, 4th edit., 1989, Medicine for the Practicing Physician, 3d edit., 1992, Comprehensive Management of Menopause, 1993, others; editor: The Emory Clinic Dialogue, 1988—; mem. editorial bd. Diabetes Care, 1992—; contbr. chpts. to books and articles to jours. Mem. Asheville (N.C.) Community Theater, 1972-83, bd. dirs., 1980-83, v.p., 1982-83; mem. annual ball com. Ga. Coun. Internat. Visitors, 1986-88, active, 1986—; mem. nightflight night fantasy host com. Callanwolde Found., 1987—; active Asheville (N.C.) Art Mus., 1972-83, Rhododendron Royal Brigade of Guards, Asheville, 1972-83, Biltmore Forest Country Club, Asheville, 1972—, First Presbyn. Ch., Asheville, 1972-83, ruling elder, 1983, Western N.C. Nature Ctr., Asheville, 1976-83, City-County Blue Ribbon Com. for the Arts, Asheville, 1982-83, United Arts Fund Dr., Asheville, 1982-83, High Mus. Art, 1983—, Friends of Zoo Atlanta, 1986—; others. Recipient cert. appreciation Mountain Area Health Edn. Ctr., Family Practice Residents, 1980, Spl. award for Significant Contbns. to the Health Profls. of Western N.C., 1983. Fellow ACP; mem. AMA, Am. Assn. Clin. Chemistry, Am. Assn. Clin. Endocrinologists, Am. Diabetes Assn. (pres. Ga. affiliate 1991-92, numerous others), Am. Fedn. for Clin. Rsch., Am. Soc. for Bone and Mineral Rsch., Am. Soc. Clin. Pathologists (coun. on continuing edn. commr.'s medal 1989, pres.'s award 1990, others), The Endocrine Soc., Internat. Soc. for Calcium Related Hormones, Med. Assn. Atlanta, Med. Assn. Ga., Soc. for Clin. Densitometry, N.Am. Menopause Soc. Home: 625 Greystone Park NE Atlanta GA 30324-5284 Office: The Emory Clinic Inc 1365 Clifton Rd NE Atlanta GA 30322

WATTS, ROBERT GLENN, retired pharmaceutical company executive; b. Norton, Va., Apr. 28, 1933; s. Clifford Amburgey and Stella Lee (Cornette) W.; m. Doris Juanita Slaughter, Aug. 29, 1953 (dec. 1980); children: Cynthia L. Watts Waller, Robert Glenn, Kelly L.; m. Sara Lowry Childrey, Aug. 20, 1982; stepchildren: J. Eric Alexander, Matthew R. Alexander. B.A., U. Richmond, 1959. Dir. ops. A.H. Robins Co., Inc., Richmond, Va., 1967-71, asst. v.p., 1971-73, v.p., 1973-75, sr. v.p., 1975-79, exec. v.p., 1979-92; ret., 1992; bd. dirs. Little Oil Co., Richmond, Fidelity Fed. Savs. Bank, Richmond. Bd. dirs. United Way, Richmond, 1982—; Pvt. Industry Council, Richmond, 1983—; sec. YMCA, Richmond, 1984—. Served with USN, 1952-56. Mem. Met. Richmond C. of C. (chmn. 1985-86), Bull and Bear Club, Hermitage Country. Episcopalian. Home: 2409 Islandview Dr Richmond VA 23233-2525

WATTS, SARA CASEY, marriage and family therapist; b. Magnolia, Ark., June 9, 1948; d. William Alexander and Leslie Frances (Gunn) Casey; m. John Phillip Watts, Nov. 22, 1968 (div. Apr. 1993); children: Damion, Jonathan. Student, Centenary Coll. of La., 1966-69; BA in Psychology cum laude, Tex. Woman's U., 1975, MA in Psychology, 1977. Lic. profl. counselor, marriage and family therapist. Therapist Tex. Mental Health/Mental Retardation, Gainesville, 1977-78, Richland Coll., Dallas, 1978-80; pvt. practice Dallas, 1980—. Columnist Family Living mag. Legis. activist, State of Tex., 1989. Mem. ACA, Am. Mental Health Counselors Assn., Am. Assn. for Marriage and Family Therapy, Tex. Mental Health Counselors Assn. (pres. 1990-91), Tex. Counseling Assn., Tex. Assn. for Marriage and Family Therapy, Dallas Assn. for Marriage and Family Therapy. Office: 12830 Hillcrest Rd Ste 111 Dallas TX 75230-1425

WATTS, THOMAS DALE, social work educator; b. Hattiesburg, Miss., Sept. 19, 1941; s. Thomas Dale and Martina Catherine (Landwehr) W.; m. Ilene Mary Peters, Nov. 28, 1970; children: Rebecca A., Jeanine L. BA, Wichita State U., 1963; MSW, Ariz. State U., 1970; DSW, Tulane U., 1976. Prof. Sch. Social Work U. Tex., Arlington, 1974—; bd. dirs. Am. Indian Ctr., Euless, Tex., Arlington Pub. Libr.; precint chair Precinct 2181, Arlington, 1978—. Author: The Societal Learning Approach..., 1981; co-author: Pathways for Minor into the Health Professions, 1989, Transcultural Perspectives in the Human Services..., 1983, Preschoolers and Substance Abuse..., 1993; editor: Social Thought on Alcoholism, 1986; co-editor: Black Alcoholism..., 1983, Prevention of Black Alcoholism..., 1985, Black Alcohol Abuse and Alcoholism: An Annotated Bibliography, 1986, Native American Youth & Alcohol: An Annotated Bibliography, 1989, Alcoholism in Minority Populations, 1989, Alcohol Problems of Minority Youth in America, 1989, The World of Social Welfare..., 1990, Hispanic Substance Abuse, 1993, International Handbook on Social Work Education, 1995. Mem. Coun. on Social Work Edn., Internat. Assn. Schs. Social Work. Home: 1108 Briarwood Blvd Arlington TX 76013-1509 Office: U Tex at Arlington PO Box 19129 Arlington TX 76019-0129

WATTS, WENDY HAZEL, wine consultant; b. York, Pa., Oct. 9, 1952; d. Alphonso Irving and Daphne Jean (Gainsford) Watts; m. Frederic Joseph Bonnie, (div. 1986); m. Kenneth Scott Herron, Feb. 14, 1987 (div. Jan. 1992). BS, U. Cin., 1975. Store mgr. The Grapevine, Inc., Birmingham, Ala., 1978-81; sales rep. Supreme Beverage Co., Birmingham, 1981-84, Internat. Wines Co., Birmingham, 1984-90; nat. sales exec. Kermit Lynch Wine Mcht., Berkeley, Calif., 1990-91; on-premise mgr., fine wine mgr. Premier Beverage Co., Birmingham, 1991-94; key accounts mgr. Ala. Crown Distbg. Co., Birmingham, 1994-95; dir. of wine Western Supermarkets, 1995—, Western Mountain Brook, Ala., 1995—; instr. ednl. wine tasting classes, 1996—; spkr., instr. various groups, Birmingham; co-chmn. Sonoma Wine Tour of Birmingham, 1987-88, chmn., 1989-90; chmn. Wine Tour of France, Birmingham, 1988-89; mem. exec. com. Taste of the Nation, 1992—. Wine columnist Black and White, 1992—; wine radio show host, 1992—. Co-chmn. Multiple Sclerosis Wine Auction, 1992—, mem. exec. com., 1990—. Mem. Wine Educator's Soc., Tuesday Tasting Group. Democrat. Mem. United Ch. Christ.

WATTS, WILLIAM DAVID, corporate executive, business owner; b. Birmingham, Dec. 2, 1938; s. Edgar Reid and Ruth (Appling) W.; m. Lynda Louise Moseley, Aug. 1964 (div. Aug. 2, 1974); children: William David, Jr., Mark Chadwick; m. Lynn Saccone, June 28. 1975; children: Trudy, Paul William. BS in Indsl. Arts, Auburn U., 1963; student, Dale Carnegie, Birmingham, Ala., 1969, Ed Winner, Hagerstown, Md., 1971-72. Field erector engr. Pangborn Corp., Hagerstown, Md., 1963-64; sales svc. engr. Pangborn Corp., Hagerstown, 1964-68, dist. sales engr., 1968-71, acct. exec., 1971-76; owner, pres. Watts Equipment & Supply Co., Atlanta, 1976-89, Blastec, Inc., Alpharetta, Ga., 1989—. Holder 14 U.S. blast machine patents. Ticket chmn. Am. Foundry Soc., Birmingham, 1964-66, arrangements chmn., 1966-68, dir., 1968-69, treas., 1969-72. With USAR, 1957-63. Mem. Atlanta Athletic, Lake Arrowhead Yacht & Country, Masonic Lodge. Office: Blastec Inc 4965 Hwy 9 N Alpharetta GA 30201-2922

WATTS, WILLIAM PARK, naval officer; b. Huntsville, Ala., Mar. 25, 1916; s. Clarence Lee and Inez Elizabeth (Looney) W.; m. Eleanor Ruth Roth, July 2, 1949; children: Deborah Clark Watts, Lauren McCrary Watts Buchner. BS, U.S. Naval Acad., 1938; grad. Naval War Coll., 1949; MBA, NYU, 1961; PhD in Bus. Adminstrn., U. Ala., 1977. Commd. ensign U.S. Navy, 1938, advanced through grades to capt., 1962, duty assignments include commdg. officer of naval supply depot, various Navy, joint, NATO staffs and in combatant ships; adminstrv. mgr. Rsch. Inst., U. Ala., Huntsville, 1963-70, mem. faculty, 1970-77, asst. prof. 1970-74, acting chmn. dept. bus. adminstrn., 1974-75; mgmt. cons. Mgmt. Sci. Applications Assocs., Huntsville, 1979-82. Pres., 1st v.p., sec., mem. exec. com. Huntsville-Madison County Council for Internat. Visitors, 1978-93; bd. trustees Huntsville Symphony Orch. Assn., 1983-93, sec., mem. exec. com., 1988-90; vestryman Episcopal Ch. of the Nativity, Huntsville, 1982-84; founding pres. Randolph Sch. Athletics and Activities Assn., Huntsville, 1966-67; mem. Huntsville-Madison County Library Devel. Council, 1985; mem. Huntsville Community Chorus, 1980-86, bd. dirs., 1981-82, mem. Huntsville Pilgrimmage Assn, 1987-93; chmn. storm water mgmt. bd. City of Huntsville, 1991-92. Decorated Asiatic-Pacific Campaign medal with three stars, WWII Victory medal, Occupation service medal, Am. Campaign, Navy Commendation medal, 1946, Nat. Defense Service medal, 1954; Paul Harris fellow. Mem. Carl Jung Soc. of Tenn. Valley, Inc. (founder and founding chmn., pres., 1993, bd. dirs. 1993—), Huntsville Rotary Club. Republican. Episcopalian. Avocations: music, photography, gardening, reading, family history. Home: 2300 Big Cove Rd SE Huntsville AL 35801-1350

WAUFLE, ALAN DUANE, museum director, consultant; b. Hornell, N.Y., Feb. 11, 1951; s. Robert Karl and Heather (Gunn) W.; m. Catherine Lynn Chandler, Aug. 11, 1973; children—Erik Alan, Mark Chandler. A.B., Coll. William and Mary, 1973; M.A., Duke U., 1976. Dir., Gaston County Mus., Dallas, N.C., 1976—; cons. Gaston Hist. Properties Commn., Gastonia, N.C., 1983—. Author: Guide to North Carolina Galleries, 1982. Bd. dirs. Gastonia Little Theater, 1977-79; v.p. Gaston County Art Guild, Gastonia, 1980-82. Mem. N.C. Mus. Council (bd. dirs. 1978-83), Am. Assn. of Mus., Nat. Trust, Am. Assn. of State and Local History. Democrat. Methodist. Lodge: Rotary (Gastonia). Avocations: collecting cut glass; cooking; gardening. Home: 3308 Sherwood Cir Gastonia NC 28056-6636 Office: Gaston County Mus 131 Main St PO Box 429 Dallas NC 28034-2019

WAUGAMAN, PAUL GRAY, management consultant; b. Pitts., Dec. 4, 1939; s. Charles Miller and Jane Elizabeth (Walton) W.; m. Dorothy Owen Murray, June 3, 1961; children: Barbara Lynne, Donald Paul. BA in Polit. Sci., Am. U., Washington, 1961, MA in Public Policy, 1966; MPA, Ind. U., 1970. Various adminstrv. positions NIH, Bethesda, Md., 1961-77, exec. officer, 1975-84; innovation devel. officer Office of Gov., Raleigh, N.C., 1984; assoc. dean rsch. adminstrn. Bowman Gray Sch. Medicine, Winston-Salem, N.C., 1985-91; dir. tech. adminstrn. N.C. State U., Raleigh, 1991-92; dir. spl. mgmt. project Duke U. Med. Ctr., Durham, N.C., 1992; cons. U. P.R., San Juan, 1989-92, Bell Seltzer Park & Givson, P.A., Charlotte, N.C., 1992—, German Cancer Rsch. Ctr., 1993—, So. Tech. Coun., 1994—. Author: (with others) Strategies and Practices for Technological Innovation, 1986, Biomedical Research: Collaboration and Conflict of Interest, 1992; contbr. a rticles to profl. jours. Bd. dirs. Area Health Systems Agy., Durham, 1979-84. Capt. USAFR, 1962-73. Mem. Soc. Rsch. Adminstrs. (pres. So. sect. 1977—, Hartford-Nicholson award 1989), Assn. U. Tech. Mgrs. (chair com. 1985-92), Licensing Execs. Soc. Presbyterian. Office: Signa Tech Inc 1045 Bullard Ct Raleigh NC 27615-6801

WAWEE, ROBERT WILLIAM, priest; b. Grand Rapids, Mich., Nov. 19, 1953; s. Gustave and Donna Mae (Grit) W.; m. Donna Ann Nicholas, May 11, 1979; children: Jonathan Paul, Christopher Robert Gustave. BA, U. Mary Hardin Baylor, Belton, Tex., 1980; MA, U. Dallas, 1995. Ordained to ministry Bapt. Ch., 1976; ordained deacon Episcopal Ch., 1990, priest, 1994. Enlisted U.S. Army, 1971, active, 1971-76, reenlisted, 1983, resigned, 1986; min. area Bapt. ch.; adminstr. Loaves and Fishes Metroplex Foodbank, Ft. Worth, 1989-90, Tarrant Area Community of Chs., Ft. Worth, 1990-91; program adminstr. Episcopal Diocese of Ft. Worth, 1992-93; deacon-in-charge St. Paul's Episc. Mission, Olney, Tex., 1992-93; vicar St. Patrick's Episc. Ch., Bowie, Tex., 1995—; coord. relief funds Episcopal Diocese of Ft. Worth, 1991—, also comm. officer; priest-in-charge St. Patrick's Episcopal ch., Bowie, Tex., 1995—; evangelism cons. Episc. Diocese Ft. Worth, 1984-85, coord. relief funds, 1991—, comm. officer; instr. humanities Tex. Wesleyan U., 1996—. Author: A New Social Consciousness, 1989; editor: Resource Book on Evangelism, 1984; editor Ft. Worth ForWard, publ. of Episc. Diocese of Ft. Worth, 1992—; contbr. articles and book revs. to profl. publs. and newspapers. Active Tarrant County Homeless Coalition, Ft. Worth, 1991. With Tex. Army N.G. Res. Mem. Acad. Polit. Sci., Cath. Clerical Union. Republican. Home: 1206 Trenton Ln Euless TX 76040-6365 Office: Tex Western U 1201 Wesleyan Dr Fort Worth TX 76102

WAX, GEORGE LOUIS, lawyer; b. New Orleans, Dec. 6, 1928; s. John Edward and Theresa (Schaff) W.; LL.B., Loyola U. of South, 1952, B.C.S., 1960; m. Patricia Ann Delaney, Feb. 20, 1965; children: Louis Jude, Joann Olga, Therese Marie. Admitted to La. bar, 1952, practiced in New Orleans, 1954—. Served with USNR, 1952-54. Mem. La., New Orleans bar assns., Am. Legion. Roman Catholic. Kiwanian. Clubs: New Orleans Athletic, Suburban Gun and Rod, Southern Yacht. Home: 6001 Charlotte Dr New Orleans LA 70122-2731 Office: Nat Bank Commerce New Orleans LA 70112

WAY, WILSON SPENCER, retired osteopathic physician and surgeon; b. Guatemala City, Guatemala, Feb. 24, 1910; s. Wilson Spencer and Lydia Caroline (Walker) W.; m. Louise Edrington, May 20, 1938 (div. May 1953); children: Flora Ann Way Arnold, Wilson Edrington; m. Olga Cheves, May 25, 1953 (dec. 1990); m. Annie Mae Hardesty, 1991. DO, Kirksville Coll. Osteo. Medicine, 1941; PhD, Donsbach U., 1979; D. Christian Lit. (hon.), Freedom U., 1984. Gen. practice osteo. medicine, Orlando, Fla., 1941; staff Orlando Gen. Hosp., 1941-72; cert. instr. Dale Carnegie, Orlando, 1957-63. Author: Total Life, 1978; Miracle of Enzymes, 1979. Bd. dirs. Sta. WTGL-TV, Cocoa-Orlando, 1980—; deacon Assembly of God Ch. Fellow Internat. Coll. of Applied Nutrition; mem. Am. Osteo. Assn., Fla. Osteo. Med. Assn., Fla. Acad. Osteopathy, Nat. Acad. Osteopathy, Internat. Acad. of Preventive Medicine. Democrat. Lodge: Toastmasters Internat. (pres. Orlando, Fla. 1966-67). Avocation: fishing.

WAYBRIGHT, JEFFREY SCOTT, county clerk; b. Ripley, W.Va., Oct. 22, 1960; s. Conard Coleman and Carolyn Sue (Boggess) W.; m. Edwina Jane Angus, Nov. 7, 1980; children: Jeffrey Coleman, Cara Linn. Student, Marshall U., 1978-79. Dir. purchasing Broughton Foods Co., Charleston, W.Va., 1983-88; account mgr. Dot Foods Co., New Castle, Del., 1988-89; sales agt. State Farm Ins. Co., Ripley, W.Va., 1989-91; county clk. Jackson County Commn., Ripley, 1992—. Bd. edn. Jackson County Schs., Ripley, 1988-92; deacon Ripley Tabernacle Ch., 1989—; v.p. Ripley Youth Basketball League, 1995. Mem. Jackson County Optimist Club. Republican. Baptist. Home: 311 Edgewood Circle Ripley WV 25271 Office: Jackson County Clk PO Box 800 Ripley WV 25271

WAYLAND, RUSSELL GIBSON, JR., retired geology consultant, government official; b. Treadwell, Alaska, Jan. 23, 1913; s. Russell Gibson and Fanchon (Borie) W.; m. Mary Mildred Brown, 1943 (div. 1964); children: Nancy, Paul R.; m. Virginia Bradford Phillis, Dec. 24, 1965. B.S., U. Wash., 1934; A.M., Harvard, 1937; M.S., U. Minn., 1935, Ph.D., 1939. Engr., geologist Homestake Mining Co., Lead, S.D., summers 1930-39; with U.S. Geol. Survey, 1939-42, 1952-80, chief conservation div., 1966-78; research phys. scientist Office of Dir., 1978-80; energy minerals cons., 1980—; Washington rep. Am. Inst. Profl. Geologists, 1982-88; commr. VA Oil and Gas Conservation Bd., 1982-90; with Army-Navy Munitions Bd., 1942-45, Office Mil. Govt. and Allied High Commn., Germany, 1945-52; instr. geology U. Minn., 1937-39. Author sci. bulls. in field. Served to lt. col. AUS, 1942-46. Decorated Army Commendation medal; recipient Distinguished Service award Dept. Interior. Mem. AIME, Mineral Soc. Am., Geol. Soc. Am., Am. Inst. Profl. Geologists, Soc. Econ. Geologists, Assn. Engring. Geologists, Cosmos Club, Sigma Xi, Tau Beta Pi, Phi Gamma Delta, Sigma Gamma Epsilon, Gamma Alpha, Phi Mu Alpha Sinfonia. Episcopalian. Home and Office: 4660 35th St N Arlington VA 22207-4462

WAYNE, BILL TOM, secondary school educator, coach; b. Evansville, Ind., Oct. 31, 1946; s. George William and Agnes Ledbetter W.; m. Donna Marie Agnew, Aug. 24, 1968; 1 child, Erin Marie. BS, Murray (Ky.) State U., 1971; MS, Western Ky. U., 1978. Tchr., coach Henderson County (Ky.) Sr. High Sch., 1971—; scout Kansas City Royals, 1985—. Deacon 1st Christian Ch. Named Coach of Yr. Ky. High Sch. Big 8 Conf., 1979, 1982, 1984, 87; named to Hon. Order Ky. Cols. Mem. NEA, Ky. Edn. Assn., Ky. High Sch. Athletic Assn., Am. Baseball Coaches Assn., Ky. Baseball Coaches Assn. (pres. 1989-91), U.S. Baseball Fedn., Nat. Hot Rod Assn., Waterfowl U.S.A, Ducks Unltd., Elks. Democrat. Home: 847 Lamont Ln Henderson KY 42420-2472 Office: Henderson County Sr High Sch 2424 Zion Rd Henderson KY 42420-4713

WEAKLEY, CLARE GEORGE, JR., insurance executive, theologian, entrepreneur; b. Dallas, Apr. 14, 1928; s. Clare George and Louise (Cunningham) W.; children: Clare George III, Carol J., Charles E.; m. Jean C. Burrow, July 20, 1962. BBA, So. Meth. U., 1948, ThM, 1967. Ordained minister Christian Community, 1967. With Employers Ins., Dallas, 1948-52; owner Weakley & Co., Dallas, 1952—; founder, pres. Am. Svc. Found., Inc., 1967—, Small Bus. Assn., Inc., 1988—; vis. prof. western bus. theory and Christian ethics Internat. Mgmt. Inst. (formerly Leningrad Internat. Mgmt. Inst.), St. Petersburg, Russia, 1990—. Author, editor: The Wesley Library Series for Today's Reader, The Nature of the Kingdom, The Nature of Spiritual Growth, The Nature of Revival, The Nature of Salvation, The Nature of Christian Life. Mem. Dallas County Grand Jury, 1959. Republican. Home: 7106 Gateridge Dr Dallas TX 75240-8028 Office: Weakley & Co PO Box 516065 Dallas TX 75251-6065

WEATHERALL, WILLIAM BAILEY, human resources administrator; b. Port Arthur, Tex., July 2, 1949; s. Lee Thomason and Joyce (Bailey) W.; m. Marguerite Ciccosanti, Dec. 18, 1971; children: Jennifer, Benjamin, Kathryn. BS in Psychology, Lamar State Coll. of Tech., Beaumont, Tex., 1971. Employee rels. asst. Texaco, Port Arthur, Tex., 1972-74, coord. employee rels., 1974-76; asst. supr. employee rels. Texaco, Lawrenceville, Ill., 1976-78; mgr. indsl. rels. Kerr-McGee, Corpus Christi, Tex., 1978-80; mgr. employee rels. Mitchell Energy and Devel., Houston, 1980-86; coord. St. Lukes Episc. Hosp., Houston, 1986-89; dir. Human Resources Internat. Drilling Fluids, Houston, 1989-90; mgr. Human Resources Foster Valve Corp., Houston, 1990-93; dir. human resources GSE Lining Tech., Inc., Houston, 1993-95, Eco Resources, Inc., Sugar Land, Tex., 1996—. Elder The Woodlands (Tex.) Cmty. Presbyn. Ch., 1987—. Mem. Soc. for Human Resource Mgmt., Inst. for Internat. Human Resources, Human Resource Systems Profls. Presbyterian. Home: 12 Sand Piper Pl The Woodlands TX 77381-3117 Office: Eco Resources Inc 12550 Emily Ct Sugar Land TX 77478

WEATHERBY, MICHAEL F., security technology executive; b. Royal Oak, Mich., Jan. 30, 1950; s. Philip Grandin and Jean Clair (Walsh) W.; 1 child, Shadow Smith. BSBA, Shaw U., 1993; AA, Vance Granville C.C., 1993. Pres. Eagle Builders, New Haven, 1973-78, Renovation Assocs., New Haven, 1978-83, Bi-Coastal Builders, Woodbridge, Conn., 1983-89, MFW Assocs., Butner, N.C., 1989-96; v.p. Cashcard Internat., San Cristobel, Venezuela, 1996—. Copywriter Soc. for Ethical Restraint, 1996. Mem. Toastmasters Internat. (v.p. edn. 1994-96, pres., 1993-94). Episcopalian. Home: 5059 Commonwealth Dr Sarasota FL 34242 Office: Cashcard Internat, 5 Torr E Piso, San Cristobel Venezuela

WEATHERFORD, CATHERINE J., state insurance commissioner; b. Miami, Okla., Jan. 26, 1955; d. Joseph E. and Norma J. (Hankins) Mountford; m. Stephen R. Weatherford, July 24; children: Holly Catherine, Allyson Taylor, Chelsey Elizabeth. BA in Polit. Sci., U. Ctrl. Okla., 1991. Exec. sec. Okla. Ins. Dept., Oklahoma City, 1976-79, life accident & health policy analyst, 1980-83, adminstrv. asst., 1983-85, asst. commr., 1985-90; exec. asst. to Gov. State of Okla., Oklahoma City, 1990-91, state ins. commr., 1991-95; chmn. Okla. Real Estate Appraise Bd., Oklahoma City, 1991—, State Bd. Property and Casualty Rates, Oklahoma City, 1991—; state dir. Okla. Motor Vehicle Assigned Risk Plan, Oklahoma City, 1991—; active Oklahoma Police Pension & Retirement Bd., Oklahoma City, 1991—, Okla. Firefighters Pension & Retirement Bd., Oklahoma City, 1991—, Okla. Linked Deposit Rev. Bd., Oklahoma City, 1991, Oklahoma State and Edn. Employees Group Ins. Bd., Oklahoma City, 1991, Interagency Coordinating Coun. on Early Childhood Intervention, Oklahoma City, 1992—, Okla. Health Care Study Commn., Oklahoma City, 1992—; bd. trustees Okla. Pub. Employees Retirement Sys., Oklahoma City, 1991—. chmn. Okla. Real Estate Appraisal Bd., 1991—, State Bd. for Property and Casualty Rates; state dir. Okla. Motor Vehicle Assigned Risk Plan, 1991—; mem. Okla. Police Pension & Retirement Bd., 1991—, Okla. Firefighters Pension & Retirement Bd., Okla. Linked Deposit Review Bd., Okla. State and Edn. Employees Group Ins. Bd.; mem. bd. trustees Okla. Pub. Employees Retirement System; mem. Inter Agy. Coord. Coun. on Early Childhood Intervention, 1992—, Okla. Health Care Study Commn. Named Outstanding Young Oklahoman, Jaycees, 1994. Mem. Nat. Assn. Ins. Commrs. (zone chair 1993, treas. edn. and rsch. found. 1993). Democrat. So. Baptist. *

WEATHERFORD, DAVID C., insurance training manager; b. Great Lake, Ill., Dec. 16, 1953; s. Charles A. and Ann E. W.; m. Diane L., Aug. 17, 1984; children: Kimberly Anne, Tyler David, Hannah Michelle. BA, Nat. Louis U., 1990. Cert. life underwriter tng. course fellow. Owner Weatherford & Assocs., Tampa, Fla., 1974-81; dist. mgr. Mut. Savs. Life, Marianna, Fla., 1981—; life underwriter tng. course moderator, 1991, 92. Mem. Optimist Club, 1991-93. Recipient Sales Excellence award Mut. Savs. Life, 1981-93; named Life Underwriter Tng. Course fellow, 1986. Mem. Panhandle Assn. Life Underwriters (sec.-treas. 1990-91, v.p. 1991-92, pres. 1993-94, nat. committeeman 1993—), Fla. Assn. Life Underwriters (region 2 v.p. 1995), Tampa Assn. Life Underwriters. Office: Mut Savs Life PO Box 2222 Decatur AL 35609-2222

WEATHERFORD, GREGORY OSINA, journalist; b. Seoul, Korea, June 30, 1965; s. William Osina and Judith Ann (Rahorn) W.; m. Anne Shannon Roberts, Dec. 19, 1992. BS in Mass. Comm., Va. Commonwealth U., 1995. Reporter The Hopewell (Va.) News, 1994, Richmond (Va.) Times-Dispatch, 1994; editor The Goochland (Va.) Gazette, 1995; editl. asst. The AP, Richmond, 1995; asst. editor Style Weekly Mag., Richmond, 1995—. Musician: (45 rpm record) Rain on Me, Spike the Dog, Clubland Records, 1996, (compact disc) Post Modern Tradition, BS&M Alcove Records, 1992, Richmond Music Cooperative, RMC Records, 1993. Recipient Outstanding Grad. award Va. Commonwealth U. and Soc. Profl. Journalists, 1995. Mem. Va. Press Assn. (Best in Show award 1995, 1st place for in-depth reporting 1995, 1st place continuing story 1994), Soc. Profl. Journalists. Office: Style Weekly Publications 1118 W Main St Richmond VA 23220

WEATHERFORD, KEITH ANDERSON, information system specialist; b. Memphis, Feb. 9, 1957; s. Kenneth Malone and Flor Mai (Anderson) W.; m. Judy Ann Murphy, Aug. 30, 1985 (dec. Jan. 1986); m. Sheryl Ann Gregory, Feb. 29, 1988; children: Andrea Mai, Gregory Arthur. BS, U. Tenn. Martin, 1979; MS, Tex. Christian U., 1981. Specialist employee rels. Whittaker Saudi Arabia Ltd., Riyadh, 1981-83; analyst sr. compensation Memphis City Govt., 1983-87; analyst sr. compensation Internat. Paper, Memphis, 1987-90, specialist info. sys., 1990-96; analyst sr. compensation Fed. Express, Memphis, 1996—. Republican. Methodist. Home: 8013 CD Smith Rd Germantown TN 38138 Office: Fed Express 3128 Director's Row Memphis TN 38131

WEATHERFORD, ROY CARTER, philosophy educator, academic unionist; b. Middlebrook, Ark., May 30, 1943; s. Frank Carter and Opal Wynona (Luter) W.; m. Doris Linda Barge, Feb. 8, 1966; 1 child, Margaret Marie (Meg). BA, Ark. Tech. Coll., 1964; MA, Harvard U., 1970, PhD, 1972. Prof. philosophy U. South Fla., Tampa, 1972—. Author: Philosophical Foundations of Probability Theory, 1982, Implications of Determinism, 1991, World Peace and the Human Family, 1992. Mem. Dem. Exec. Com., Tampa, 1976—, ctrl. com. Fla. Dem. Party, 1993—; v.p. Ctrl. Labor Coun., Tampa, 1976-82. Danforth Found. fellow, 1964-72; recipient Bechtel Prize in Philosophy, Harvard U., 1970. Mem. NEA (bd. dirs. 1988-91), AAUP, Harvard Club of the West Coast of Fla. (bd. dirs. 1985—), United Faculty of Fla. (pres. 1983-87), Fla. AFL-CIO (lobbyist 1979-81), Fla. Exec. Coun. Democrat. Home: 5425 County Road 579 Seffner FL 33584-7305 Office: Univ South Fla Dept Philosophy CPR 259 Tampa FL 33620

WEATHERFORD-BATMAN, MARY VIRGINIA, rehabilitation counselor, educator; b. St. Louis, Mar. 28; d. John Ely and Virginia Louise (Cox) Weatherford; m. Aug. 28, 1965 (div. Jan. 1976); 1 child, Christopher James Batman. Cert. med. technologist, Jackson Meml. Hosp., Miami, Fla., 1966; BS, Barry U., 1984, MBA, 1986, EdS, 1992; postgrad., Union Inst. Cert. rehab. counselor; cert. case mgr. Crossmatch technologist John Elliott Blood Bank, Miami, 1966-68; nurse D. E. Fortner MD, P.A. Gutlohn MD, Miami, 1969-75; allergy technologist Dadeland Allergy, Ear, Nose and Throat Assocs., Miami, 1975-78; tech. mgr. Morris Beck MD, Miami, 1978-86; sales rep. Glaxo, Inc., Research Triangle Park, N.C., 1987-88; med. ctr. specialist Wyeth Ayerst, Phila., 1988-90; hosp. rep. Allen & Hanburys, Div. Glaxo, Inc., Research Triangle Park, 1990; sales cons. Profl. Detailing Network, Princeton, N.J., 1991—; adj. prof. Union Inst., Miami, 1993—; chief psychology intern Miami Heart Inst., 1994-95; rehab. counselor Nat. Health and Rehab. Cons., Inc., Miami, 1991-94; therapist Ctrs. for Psychol. Growth, 1994; chief psychology intern Miami Heart Inst., 1994-95. Vocat. devel. vol. Jackson Meml. Hosp., U. Miami, 1991—; vol. Crippled Children's Soc., Miami, 1968-69, South Miami Hosp., 1959-63. Recipient award DAR, 1962; Tng. scholar NIH, 1962, Lucille Funk Keely Trust scholar, 1991, 92. Mem. ACA, APA, Assn. for Adult Devel. and Aging, Am. Rehab. Counseling Assn., Fla. Counseling Assn., Fla. Assn. for Adult Devel. and Aging (pres.), Fla. Soc. Med. Technologists, Barry U. Counseling Assn., Toastmasters Internat. Inc., Miami Parrot Club, Country Club of Coral Gables, Delta Epsilon Sigma. Methodist. Office: PO Box 141217 Coral Gables FL 33114-1217

WEATHERS, LAWRENCE MARTIN, agricultural executive; b. Bowman, S.C., Mar. 26, 1924; s. George Whetsell and Gladys (Shuler) W.; m. Frances Fitzhugh Landrum, June 18, 1948; children: Landrum, Virginia, Martin, Hugh. Student, The Citadel, 1941-42. Pres. Weathers Farms, Inc., Bowman, 1969—; mem exec. com. Dairy div. U.S. Farm Bur., Columbia, S.C., 1968—; bd. dirs. Fed. Land Bank Assn. Orangeburg. sec., treas. Sunday Sch. Bowman So. Meth. Ch., 1951-84, steward; councilman city of Bowman, 1958-64; mem. Orangeburg (S.C.) County Bd. Edn., 1965-75; commr. Orangeburg County Devel. Commn., 1980—. Served as sgt. U.S. Army, 1942-46, ETO. Named Man of Yr. Co-op, 1968; recipient Dairy Leadership award Clemson U., 1988; named to Dairy Hall of Fame, Clemson U., 1990. Mem. Am. Dairy Assn. (bd. dirs. S.C. chpt. 1968-72, pres. 1972-73), S.C. Council Milk Producers (bd. dirs. 1958—), Palmetto Milk Producers of Carolinas (bd. dirs. 1982—). Home: PO Box 615 Bowman SC 29018-0615 Office: Weathers Farms Inc PO Box 126 Bowman SC 29018-0126

WEATHERS, MELBA ROSE, hospital administrator; b. Ladonia, Tex., Mar. 31, 1940; d. E. Carl and Rosa Lee (Evans) W. BSN, Holy Family Coll., 1974; BS, Tex. Woman's U., 1989. Staff/charge nurse maternal and child health St. Paul Med. Ctr., Dallas, 1974-87; rev. coord. Tex. Med. Found., Austin, 1989-95; utilization review mgmt. coord. Marshall (Tex.) Meml. Hosp., 1995—. Mem. Am. Health Info. Mgmt. Assn., VFW Ladies Aux. Roman Catholic. Home: 100 Stonecreek Dr #210 Marshall TX 75670-4580

WEATHERS, WILLIAM TRAVIS, pediatrician, educator; b. Batesburg, S.C., Oct. 20, 1940; s. Samuel H. and Frances E. (Bull) W.; m. Nancy Ann Walker, Oct. 7, 1967; children: Paul T., Mark A., Steven D. Student, Coll. of Charleston, S.C., 1958-60, U. S.C., 1960-61; MD, Med. U. S.C., 1965. Intern Greenville (S.C.) Hosp. Sys., 1965-66; resident in pediatrics U. Okla. Med. Ctr., Oklahoma City, 1966-68; pediatrician Charlotte (N.C.) Pediat. Clinic, 1970-73; rsch. investigator Mead Johnson Co., Evansville, Ind., 1973-74; dir. pediats. St. Mary's Hosp., Evansville, 1974-77; dir. ambulatory pediats. Greenville (S.C.) Hosp. Sys., 1977-91; dir. pediats. Shriner's Hosp. for Crippled Children, Greenville, 1991—; cons. JAARS, br. of Wycliffe Translators, Waxhaw, N.C., 1970-73. Author: Principles of Parenting, 1994. Elder, Presbyn. Ch., Greenville, 1979—; adv. com. Ref. Theol. Sem., Charlotte, 1992-94; vol. Greenville Free Clinic, 1995—. Capt. USAF, 1968-70. Fellow Am. Acad. Pediats.; mem. S.C. Acad. Pediats. (chmn. com. on disabilities 1985-89), S.C. Med. Assn., Christian Med. and Dental Soc. Republican. Presbyterian. Home: 107 Highbourne Dr Greenville SC 29615 Office: 890 W Faris Rd Greenville SC 29605

WEATHERSBY, CECIL JERRY, accounting and finance manager; b. Birmingham, Ala., Oct. 28, 1952; s. E.W. and Dorothy M. (Zuiderhoek) W.; m. Julia Diane Harris, Feb. 26, 1976; children: Matthew, Blake, Nathan. BBA, St. Bernard Coll., 1975; MS in Adminstrv. Sci., U. Ala., Huntsville, 1988. Asst. plant acct. Cullman (Ala.) Electric Coop., 1977-82, contr., 1982-88, mgr. acctg. and fin., 1988-95; chief fin. officer Hired Hand Inc., 1995—. Acct. City of Cullman, 1977; bd. dirs. Cullman Regional Med. Ctr., 1994—. Recipient Founders award Cullman Family Recreation Complex, 1990. Mem. Nat. Assn. Accts., North Ala. Power Accts. Assn. (chmn. 1986-87), Tenn. Valley Pub. Power Assn. (pres. acctg. sect. 1989), Kiwanis (bd. dirs. 1994—). Presbyterian. Office: Hired Hand Inc PO Box 99 Bremen AL 35033

WEATHERSBY, JAMES ROY, lawyer; b. Pine Bluff, Ark., Aug. 28, 1935; s. Willard Alton and Francis (McCormick) W.; children: Jim, Brad; m. Lydia Huber, Jan. 20, 1990. BScE, U. Tenn., 1958; JD, Vanderbilt U., 1964. Bar: Ala. 1965, Tenn. 1965, Ga. 1971, U.S. Dist. Ct. (no. dist.) Ala. 1966, U.S. Dist. Ct. (no. dist.) Ga. 1971, U.S. Dist. Ct. (middle dist.) Ga. 1985, U.S. Dist. Ct. (so. dist.) Ga. 1990. Labor counsel Rust Engring. Co., Pitts., Birmingham, Ala., 1964-70; ptnr. Wilson & Wilson, Atlanta, 1971-76; ptnr., head labor sect. Powell Goldstein Fraser & Murphy, Atlanta, 1976-90; mng. ptnr. Ogletree Deakins Nash Smoak & Stewart, Atlanta, 1991-95, Littlen, Mendelson, Fastiff, Tashy & Mathiason, Atlanta, 1996—; dep. atty. gen. State of Ga., Atlanta, 1974—; gen. counsel Gen. Assocs. Ga. Associated Builders & Contractors, Atlanta, 1976—; bd. dirs. Kamtech Inc., Glen Falls, N.Y. Mem. ABA, Lawyers Club Atlanta, Ga. Bar Assn., Atlanta Bar Assn. Home: 510 Valley Rd Atlanta GA 30305 Office: Littler Mendelson Fastiff Tichy & Mathiason 1100 Peachtree St Ste 2000 Atlanta GA 30309

WEATHERSTON, GEORGE DOUGLAS, JR., food service executive; b. San Antonio, Apr. 5, 1952; s. George Douglas and Ann (Waide) W. BA in Latin Am. Studies, U. Tex., 1981. Market analyst Warlick & Assocs., Inc., Houston, 1981-83; petroleum landman Discorbis Oil Co., San Antonio, 1983-84; market planning mgr. Smith Internat., Inc., Houston, 1984-86; mgr. sales and mktg. Petroconsultants, Houston, 1986-87; pres. Miramar Internat. Corp., San Antonio, 1987-94; mgr. Pecan Street Market Group LLC, 1994—; cons. Analytix Group, Houston, 1987-94. With USN, 1970-74. Episcopalian. Home: 152 E Pecan St Apt 1004 San Antonio TX 78205-1518 Office: Pecan St Market 152 E Pecan St # 102 San Antonio TX 78205-1522

WEAVER, CARRIE ETTA, sales executive; b. Brenham, Tex., Oct. 5, 1935; d. Arthur and Matilda Marietha (Atkinson) Correthers; m. Frank Jay Weaver, July 13, 1956; children: Deborah Lene Weaver Nash, Dianna Lynn Weaver Baronville. AS, Seminole Community Coll., 1978. With Emerson Electric Co., Sanford, Fla., 1976-88; buyer Emerson Electric Co., 1978-86, sr. buyer, 1986-88; beauty cons. Mary Kay Cosmetics, Inc., Winter Springs, Fla., 1982-89, sales dir., 1989—. Chmn. Winter Springs Bd. Adjustment, 1975-80; chmn. adminstrv. com. St. Augustine Cath. Ch., Casselberry, Fla., 1987-89; chmn. pers. policy, bd. dirs. Seminole Cmty. Vol. Program, Sanford, 1988-93, Seminole County Ret. Srs. Vol. Program. Democrat.

WEAVER, CHARLES H., internist, oncologist; b. Nov. 17, 1961. BS, U. Puget Sound, 1983; MD, U. Wash., 1988. Diplomate Am. Bd. Internal Medicine, Am. Bd. Oncology; lic. physician Pa., Wash., Tenn. Fellow NIH, Bethesda, Md., 1986; intern U. Pa. Hosp., Phila., 1988-89; resident in internal medicine U. Pa., Phila., 1989-91; fellow in oncology-bone-marrow transplantation Fred Hutchinson Cancer Rsch. Ctr., Seattle, 1991-94; acting instr. dept. internal medicine U. Wash., Seattle, 1991-94; sci. dir. Response Oncology, Inc., Memphis, 1994-96, chief med. officer, 1996—. Bd. trustees Patrons of Northwest Civic, Cultural and Charitable Orgns., 1993—. Author: (book) High Dose Chemotherapy and Stem Cell Transplantation, 1996; co-author: (with others) Technical and Biological Components of Marrow Transplantation, 1995; contbr. articles and abstracts to profl. jours. Mem. Am. Coll. Physicians (assoc.), Am. Soc. Clin. Oncology, Am. Soc. for Blood and Marrow Transplantation, Am. Soc. Hematology, Internat. Soc. Hematotherapy and Graft Engring., Internat. Soc. for Exptl. Hematology. Home: 1775 Moriah Woods Blvd Memphis TN 38117

WEAVER, DAVID CHRISTOPHER, lawyer; b. Tuscaloosa, Ala., Jan. 21, 1960; s. Billy Don and Gail (Williams) W.; m. Connie Mitchell, July 28, 1984. BS in Mktg., U. Ala., 1982; JD, Samford U., 1985. Staff atty. FERC, Washington, 1985-87; govt. affairs rep. SONAT Inc., Birmingham, Ala., 1988-92, legis. counsel, 1992—. Bd. dirs. Ala. Civil Justice Reform com., Montgomery, 1994—, Fla. Energy Pipeline Assn., Tallahassee, 1990—; mem. Ala. Oil & Gas Study com., Montgomery, 1992-94. Republican. Office: SONAT Inc PO Box 2563 Birmingham AL 35202

WEAVER, EDGAR SHELDON, mayor; b. Schenectady, N.Y., June 22, 1925; s. Caius Edgar and Grace Marion (Patterson) W.; m. Jeanne Ann Bisgrove, Sept. 13, 1950; children: Christine A., Jo Ann M., Nancy L. BSCE, U. Okla., 1951; postgrad., Harvard U., 1967. Registered profl. engr. Various Gen. Electric Realty Corp., 1951-67; pres., dir. Gen. Electric Realty Corp., Schenectady, N.Y., 1968-80; v.p. J.A. Jones Constrn. Co., Charlotte, N.C., 1980-84; mem. city coun. City of Tega Cay, S.C., 1986-90, mayor, 1990-94; bd. dirs. York County (S.C.) Natural Gas Authority. With U.S. Army, 1943-46, ETO. Mem. Lions Internat. (bd. dirs. 1985-86, 96-97).

WEAVER, ESTHER RUTH, medical and surgical, geriatrics and oncology nurse; b. Kansas City, Mo., Mar. 20, 1951; d. Fred Bicknell and Mary Elizabeth (Williams) Crigler; 1 child, Scott Lee McPhee; m. Charles Edward Weaver, June 10, 1995; stepchildren: Alan Bower, Ward. ADN, Eastern N.Mex. U., Roswell, 1989. Cert. chemotherapy nurse. Staff nurse med. floor St. Mary's Hosp., Roswell, Eastern N.Mex. Med. Ctr., Roswell; night nurse Sunset Villa Care Ctr., Roswell; nurse supr. Turtle Creek Health Care Ctr., Jacksonville, Fla.; oncology staff nurse, active with dept. corrections unit Meml. Med. Ctr., Jacksonville. Mem. Merrill Rd. Bapt. Ch.; dir. children's ch. Merrill Rd. Cmty. Ch. Nursing Found. scholar. Mem. N.Mex. Nurses Assn. (publicity chmn. Dist. 5), Oncology Nurses Soc., Phi Theta Kappa (v.p.).

WEAVER, JAMES PAUL, minister; b. Rocky Mount, N.C., Dec. 6, 1933; s. William David and Betty (Langley) W.; m. Mary Helen Pridgen, Oct. 20, 1956; children: Paula, Jamie, Kim. Student, So. Bapt. Sem. Extension Dept., 1960-69. Ordained to ministry So. Bapt. Conv., 1962. Pastor Aenon Bapt. Ch., Elm City, N.C., 1962-64, Elm Grove and Wakelon Bapt. Chs., Colerain, N.C., 1964-69, Cedar Branch Bapt. Ch., Jamesville, N.C., 1969—. Mem. South Roanoke Bapt. Assn. (chm. fin. com., pres. pastors, vice moderator 1979-80, moderator and exec. chmn. 1981-82). Home: 2051 NC Hwy 171 Jamesville NC 27846-9801 Office: 2407 NC Hwy 171 Jamesville NC 27846

WEAVER, JEANNE MOORE, retired history educator; b. Elba, Ala., July 9, 1927; d. Joseph Jackson and Mamie (Rushing) Moore; divorced; children: Claudia Smalley, Paul, Phoebe Stern, Noccalula M. Moon, Mary Croninger, Julia Weaver Bernstein. AA, Freed-Hardeman Coll., 1946; BA, George Peabody Coll., 1948; MA, Mid. Tenn. State U., 1962; PhD, Auburn U., 1988. Instr. Freed-Hardeman Coll., Henderson, Tenn., 1948-49, Jefferson State C.C., Birmingham, Ala., 1965-94; emeritus, 1994; chmn. faculty senate Jefferson State C.C., 1991-93; writer, lectr., reviewer in field. Mem. Ala. chpt. ACLU, 1985—, Common Cause, Washington, 1985—; vol. programs for homeless, including Bread and Roses Shelter, Birmingham, 1989, Firehouse Shelter, 1991-92, YWCA Kids Korner, 1996—; vol. Amnesty Internat., Birmingham, 1980—, Planned Parenthood, 1985—, Dem. Fundraising, Birmingham, 1980—. Mem. AAUW, So. Assn. Women Historians, So. Hist. Assn., Ala. Assn. Historians (exec. bd. 1989-91), Phi Alpha Theta. Unitarian. Home: 2409 5th St NW Birmingham AL 35215-2321

WEAVER, JO NELL, elementary school educator; b. Dallas, Apr. 22, 1941; d. Robert Glen and Lottie (Harris) Bryant; m. L. Ben Weaver, Sr., June 20, 1963 (div. Mar. 1968); children: Carolyn Cantrell, L. Ben Weaver, Jr. BA, So. Meth. U., Dallas, 1968; MEd, U. North Tex., 1974. Cert. elem. tchr., elem. supr. Tchr. Richardson (Tex.) Ind. Sch. Dist., 1968—. Curriculum writer Delta Edn., Inc., 1984-85; critic reader Silver Burdett & Ginn, 1989. Mem. Sch. Dist. edn. coun., Richardson, Ind., 1994-95; area communication coun. R.I.S.D., 1995-96. Recipient Tex. Congress of Parents and Tchrs. scholarship/grant Tex. PTA, 1974, Ross Perot award for Excellence in Tchg., 1978; named one of Outstanding Elem. Tchrs. of Am., 1975. Mem. Richardson Edn. Assn., North Tex. Reading Assn., Assn. Tex. Profl. Educators, ASCD, TEx. State Tchrs.' Assn., Alpha Delta Kappa. Republican. Baptist. Home: 4505 Hanover Dr Garland TX 75042-5131 Office: Richardson Ind Sch Dist 2100 Copper Ridge Dr Richardson TX 75080-2312

WEAVER, JOHN LAWSON, III, vocational education educator; b. Nashville, June 23, 1938; s. John Lawson Jr. and Alice Marie (Patterson) W.; m. Alice Fay Everett Benson, June 6, 1981; 1 stepchild, Edwin Welburn III. BA, Vanderbilt U., 1961; MA, Middle Tenn. State U., 1969. Tchr. Hickman Elem. Sch.-Davidson County Schs., Nashville, 1961-66; secondary sch. drafting tchr. Two Rivers High/Metro-Nashville, 1966-72, McGavock Comprehensive High/Metro-Nashville, 1972-81; gymnastics coach Two Rivers & McGavock, Nashville, 1966-80; secondary sch. drafting tchr. Hillwood H.S., Nashville, 1981-83; secondary sch. drafting tchr. Whites Creek H.S., Nashville, 1983-85, program asst. vocat./tech. edn., 1985—; pres. Stargold Design divsn. of Stargold Publs., Nashville, 1980—; cons. Nashville Ford Glass Plant, 1984—. Asst. rabban Al Menah Shrine Temple, Nashville, 1996, high priest and prophet, 1995, oriental guide 1994. Mem. Hendersonville Masons, McWhirtersville Masons, Scottish Rite Bodies, Order of DeMolay (advisor), Royal Order of Jesters. Office: Stargold Publs Inc PO Box 78124 Nashville TN 37202-8124

WEAVER, LYNN EDWARD, academic administrator, consultant, editor; b. St. Louis, Jan. 12, 1930; s. Lienous E. and Estelle F. (Laspe) W.; m. JoAnn D., 1951 (div. 1981); children: Terry Sollenberger, Gwen, Bart, Stephen, Wes; m. Anita G. Gomez, Oct. 27, 1983. BSEE, U. Mo., 1951; MSEE, So. Meth. U., 1955; PhD, Purdue U., 1958. Devel. engr. McDonnell Aircraft, St. Louis, 1952-53; aerophysics engr. Convair Corp., Ft. Worth, 1953-55; instr. elec. engring. Purdue U., Lafayette, Ind., 1955-58; assoc. prof., then prof., dept. head U. Ariz., Tucson, 1959-69; assoc. dean coll. engring. U. Okla., Norman, 1969-70; exec. asst. to pres. Argonne Univs., Chgo., 1970-72; dir. sch. nuclear engring. and health physics Ga. Inst. Tech., 1972-82; dean engring., disting. prof. Auburn (Ala.) U., 1982-87; pres. Fla. Inst. Tech., Melbourne, 1987—; cons. Ga. Power; bd. dirs. Oak Ridge Associated Univs., 1984-87, DBA Systems, Inc., Melbourne, Fla.; chmn. pub. affairs coun. Am. Assn. Engring. Soc., Washington, 1984-87; bd. advisors Ctr. for Sci., Tech. & Media, Washington. Author: (textbook) Reactor Dynamics & Control, State Space Techniques, 1968; exec. editor Annals of Nuclear Energy; contbr. numerous articles to tech. jours. U.S. rep. World Fedn., Engring. Orgn. Energy Com., 1981-86. Served to lt. USAF, 1951-53. Recipient Mo. Honors award for disting. svc. in engring., 1996. Fellow Am. Nuclear Soc.; mem. IEEE (sr.), Am. Soc. Engring. Edn., Sigma Xi. Republican. Roman Catholic. Club: Eau Gallie Yacht. Office: Fla Inst Tech 150 W University Blvd Melbourne FL 32901-6982

WEAVER, MARGUERITE MCKINNIE, plantation owner; b. Jackson, Tenn., June 7, 1925; d. Franklin Allen and Mary Alice (Caradine) McKinnie; children: Elizabeth Lynn, Thomas Jackson III, Franklin A. McKinnie. Student, U. Colo., 1943-45, Am. Acad. Dramatic Arts, 1945-46, S. Meisner's Profl. Classes, 1949, Oxford U., 1990, 91. Actress, 1946-52; mem. staff Mus. Modern Art, N.Y.C., 1949-50; woman's editor radio sta. WTJS-AM-FM, Jackson, Tenn., 1952-55; editor, radio/TV Jackson Sun Newspaper, 1952-55; columnist Bolivar (Tenn.) Bulletin-Times, 1986—; chmn. Ho. of Reps. of Old Line Dist., Hardeman County, Tenn., 1985-91, 94—. Founder Paris-Henry County (Tenn.) Arts Coun., 1965; pres. Assn. Preservation of Tenn. Antiquities, Hardeman County chpt., 1991-95; charter mem. adv. bd. Tenn. Arts Commn., Nashville, 1967-74, Tenn. Performing Arts Ctr., Nashville, 1972—; chmn. Tenn. Libr. Assn., Nashville, 1973-74; regional chmn. Opera Memphis, 1979-91; mem. nat. coun. Met. Opera, N.Y.C., 1980-92, Tenn. Bicentennial Com., Hardeman County, 1993—. Mem. DAR, Nat. Soc. Colonial Dames Am. (treas. Memphis chpt. 1996—), Am. Women i Radio and TV, Jackson Golf and Country, English Speaking Union (London chpt.), Summit (Memphis), Dilettantes (Memphis). Methodist.

WEAVER, MARSHALL GUERINGER, lawyer; b. New Orleans, Mar. 8, 1954; s. Walter Albert and Virginia (Dove) W. BA, Washington and Lee U., 1977; JD, Tulane U., 1980. Bar: La. 1980. Law clk. to judge 24th Jud. Dist. Ct., Jefferson, La., 1980-81; assoc. Donovan & Lawler, Metairie, La., 1981-86; assoc. Henican, James & Cleveland, Metairie, 1986-88, ptnr., 1988—; mem. New Orleans Pro Bono Project, 1988—. Mem. student editorial bd. Maritime Lawyer, 1979-80. Mem. France-Amerique La., Inc. New Orleans, 1985—, Preservation Resource Ctr., New Orleans, 1987—. Mem. ABA, La. Bar Assn., New Orleans Bar Assn., Def. Rsch. Inst., La. Mayflower Soc., New Orleans Mus. Art, So. Yacht Club. Republican. Episcopalian. Home: 1217 Amelia St New Orleans LA 70115-2529 Office: Henican James & Cleveland 111 Veterans Memorial Blvd Metairie LA 70005-3028

WEAVER, VIRGINIA DOVE, museum executive; b. Westerly, R.I.; d. Ronald Cross and Elva Gertrude (Burdick) Dove; m. Water Albert Weaver, Jr. (div. Apr. 1982); children—Marshall Gueringer, Claudia Cross, Leila Jane. B.A., Tulane U., 1973; M.A., 1977. Dir. vols.Hermann Grima Hist. House, New Orleans, 1976-77; adminstrv. analyst City Chief Adminstrv. Office, New Orleans, 1977-83; dir. pub. rels. New Orleans Mus. Art, 1983-95, Vincent Mann Art Gallery, New Orleans, 1996—; chmn. publicity 15th Triennial Vol. Commns. Art Mus. Internat. Conf., New Orleans, 1994. Coeditor: Letters From Young Audiences, 1971; contbr. articles to profl. jours. Bd. dirs. New Orleans chpt. Young Audiences, Inc., 1968-77; co-chmn. New Orleans Symphony Book Fair, 1973-74; mem. city coun. investigative panel SPCA, New Orleans, 1981-82; nat. pub. rels. chmn. Nat. Soc. Daus. of Founders and Patriots Am., 1985-88, publicity chmn. Spirit of 76 chpt. DAR, 1988-90. Nat. Coun. Jewish Women grantee, 1977. Episcopalian. Bd. dirs. Symphony Womens Com., 1982-86; mem. steering com. Mayors Arts Task Force, New Orleans, 1978-79. Clubs: Orleans (fine arts com., current events com., hist. com. 1990-92, chair lecture com. 1996, chmn. Discovery Tours 1996—); Le Petit Salon (chmn. publicity for 150th anniversary 1988, co-chmn. programs 1989, 90-96, chmn. summer programs 1994), France-Amérique de la Louisiane, Inc. (bd. dirs. 1992-96, 1st v.p. 1996—), Vol. Commits. of Art Mus. (host. com. internat. triennial conf. 1994). Avocation: piano. Home: 7478 Hurst St New Orleans LA 70118-3641 Office: New Orleans Mus Art PO Box 19123 New Orleans LA 70179-0123

WEBB, BERNICE LARSON, writer, consultant, press owner, publisher; b. Ludell, Kans.; d. Carl Godfred and Ida Genevieve (Tongish) Larson; m. Ralph Raymond Schear, Aug. 9, 1942 (div. July 1956, dec. Aug., 1981); children: William Carl Schear, Rebecca Rae Schear Gentry; m. Robert MacHardy Webb, July 14, 1961 (dec. June 1983). BA, U. Kans., 1956, MA, 1957, PhD, 1961; postgrad., U. Aberdeen, Scotland, 1959-60. Cert. counseler Nat. Multiple Sclerosis Soc., peer counselor for cancer, ARC. Asst. instr. English U. Kans., Lawrence, 1958-59, 60-61; asst. prof. U. Southwestern La., Lafayette, 1961-67, assoc. prof., 1967-80, prof., 1980-87; owner, publisher Spider Press, 1991—; vis. assoc. prof. S.S. Universe Campus/World Campus Afloat, 1972; coord. Poetry in the Schs., Lafayette Parish, La., 1974; dir. grad. seminars NDEA Inst. Intellectual and Cultural History, Lafayette, summer 1966; poetry cons. Acadiana Arts Coun., 1976-87, Lafayette Parish Schs., 1976-87; bd. dirs. Deep South Writers Conf., 1978-87; acting dir. English reading-writing lab. U. Southwestern La., summers 1977, 78, 79, writing cons., 1987—; founder, coord. Webb's Writers, 1974—. Author: The Basketball Man, 1973, transl. to Japanese, 1981, new edit., 1994, Beware of Ostriches, 1978, Poetry on the Stage, 1979, Lady Doctor on a Homestead, 1987, Two Peach Baskets, 1991 (with J. Allan) Born to Be a Loser, 1993, Spider Web, 1993, Mating Dance, 1996; contbr. poetry and articles to various publs.; book reviewer Jour. Am. Culture, Jour. Popular Culture, 1980-87; actress Little Theater, La., 1969-83, off-off Broadway, 1980. Vol. Mayor's Commn. on the Needs of Women, City of Lafayette, 1976-86; vol. La. Talent Bank of Women, 1978-86; judge of writing contests for schs., clubs, profl. socs., La. and U.S., 1961—; newsletter editor Bayou coun. Girl Scouts of Am., 1964-66; guest editor The New Laurel Rev., 1976. Mem. AAUW (bd. dirs. br. 1967-71, state editor 1967-71, grantee 1978-80, faculty rsch. grant U. Southwestern La. 1980-81, 85-86), Soc. for Values in Higher Edn. (Svc. award 1995), South Cen. Coll. English Assn. (pres. 1986-87), S.W. Br. Poetry (pres. 1988—), La. State Poetry Soc. (Disting. Lifetime mem., pres. 1978-79, 81-82, editor 1970-90), South Cen. MLA, Coll. English Assn. (life mem.), Am. Folklore Soc., Conf. on Christianity and Lit., Nat. Fedn. State Poetry Socs., Inc. (Queen of Poetry 1993), Phi Beta Kappa (regional pres. 1976-77, 83-84). Democrat. Roman Catholic. Home: 159 Whittington Dr Lafayette LA 70503-2741

WEBB, BILLIE JEAN, retired middle school educator; b. London, Ky., Aug. 4, 1952; d. Marris and Grace (Allen) Baker; m. Billy Lynn Webb, July 19, 1980. BS, Cumberland Coll., 1974; 5th yr. degree (hon.), Ea. Ky. U., 1978. Cert. elem. tchr., Ky. Tchr. Clay County Sch. System, Manchester, Ky., 1974-90; tchr. South Laurel Jr. High Sch., Laurel County Bd. Edn., London, 1990-91, disability ret., 1991. Recipient Outstanding Svc. award Ward, Cundiff and Aaron Meml., 1987. Mem. NEA. Home: 682 Reed Rd London KY 40741-8662

WEBB, BRIAN LOCKWOOD, lawyer; b. Phila., Apr. 12, 1949; children: Brant, Natalie. BA, U. N.Mex., 1971; JD, So. Meth. U., 1975. Bar: Tex. 1975, U.S. Dist. Ct. (no. dist.) Tex. 1981. Assoc. Brewer & Price Inc., Irving, Tex., 1975-76; sole practice Irving, 1976-86; ptnr. Webb & Kinser, P.C., Dallas, 1985-95, Nelson & Nelson, N.Y.C., 1995—, McCurley, Webb & Kinser, Limited Liability Partnership, Dallas, 1992-93, McCurley, Webb, Kinser, McCurley & Nelson, LLP, Dallas, 1993—; lectr. in field. Author seminars/course books. Mem. exec. com. Com. for a Qualified Judiciary, Dallas, 1983—. Fellow Am. Acad. Matrimonial Lawyers (chmn. Tex. chpt. 1991-93, sec.-treas. 1988-89, bd. govs. 1993—), Internat. Acad. Matrimonial Lawyers, Tex. Bar Found., Dallas Bar Found.; mem. State Bar Tex. (family law coun. 1981—, chmn. 1994—), Dallas Bar Assn. (pres. family law sect. 1986, judiciary com. 1987—, ethics com. 1993—), Irving Bar Assn. (pres. 1978-79), Tex. Acad. Family Law Specialists (pres. 1993). Office: McCurley Webb Kinser McCurley & Nelson LLP 4242 Renaissance Tower 1201 Elm St Dallas TX 75270

WEBB, DENNIS WAYNE, protective services official; b. Washington, Sept. 7, 1955; s. Clarence Edward and Henrietta Agnes (Rison) W.; m. Linda Faye Morgan, May 31, 1991; children: Shaun Dennis, Brian Patrick. BA, Bold Christian U., 1987. Dep. sheriff Price William County Sheriff Dept., Manassas, Va., 1977-79, supr., 1979-82; lt., asst. shift comdr. Prince William-Manassas Regional Adult Detention Ctr., 1982-83, lt., tng./staff devel. and security liaison, 1983-87, capt./ dir. tng., staff devel. and recruitment, 1987-89, dir. adminstrn., 1989—; cons., trainer Eppanhannock Regional acad., Fredericksburg, Va., 1985—; corrections sci. curriculum advisor No. Va. C.C., Arlington, 1983—; chmn. tng. subcom. Coun. Govts. Corrections Chiefs, 1990-91; chmn. spl. ops. and tactics workgroup, 1994; owner, pres. Commonwealth Tng. Cons. Contbr. articles to profl. jours. Bd. dirs. Prince William-Manassas Acad., 1987-89; mem. Manassas Dem. Com., 1989; chmn. spl. edn. adv. com. Manassas City Schs., 1991; instr. ARC, Manassas, 1984—. Recipient Cert. of Appreciation, ARC, 1991, 92, 93. Mem. Am. Criminal Justice Assn., Am. Jail Assn., Police Marksman Assn., Fraternal ORder Police (charter, treas. 1984-87, guard 1988, chaplain 1989, dir. 1994—), Nat. Tactical Officers Assn., Spl. Equipment and Tactics Assn., Internat. Assn. Chiefs of Police, Internat. Assn. Law Enforcement Firearms Instrs. Office: Adult Detention Ctr 9320 Lee Ave Manassas VA 22110-5517

WEBB, EDSEL PHILIP, retired textile engineer; b. Birmingham, Ala., May 18, 1928; s. Evan Hall and Mary Lee (Hough) W.; m. Mary Ann Pritchett, 1954; children: Phyllis Ann, Rebecca Hough Webb Campbell, Jeffery, Richard. BS in Textiles, Ga. Inst. Tech., 1954, MS in Indsl. Mgmt., 1955. Textile mfr. Callaway Mills, Manchester and LaGrange, Ga., 1954-59; devel. engr. Firestone Tire and Rubber Co., Akron, Ohio, 1959-62, tire and process engr. radial tires, 1962-65, mgr. internat. radial tire engring., 1965-68; sales engr., mgr. water mgmt. Firestone Coated Fabrics Co., Magnolia, Ark., 1968-70, product sales mgr. fuel cells and allied products worldwide, 1970-75, developer of rubber-coated fuel tank for GM Corvette, 1973-75, sales mgr. coated fabrics northern divsn. and internat., 1975-79, sales mgr. Ea. U.S., Can. and all exports, 1979-80, staff prodn., processing, testing and R & D engr., 1980-83; staff prodn., processing, testing and R & D engr. Am. Fuel Cell and Coated Fabric Co., Magnolia, 1983-92, ret., 1992; exec. v.p. TFR Financial Svcs., Magnolia, 1990-93; participant internat. conf. for radial tire devel. and engring. Firestone Tire & Rubber Co., London, Rome, Madrid, and Hamburg, Germany, 1965; served on team with reps. of Belgium, Sweden, Italy, Eng. and Germany for NATO, 1974. Asst. scoutmaster Troop 54 Boy Scouts Am., Anchorage, 1947-50; asst. scoutmaster and scoutmaster Troop and Post 24, Manchester, Ga., 1955-56, explorer advisor, 1956-58, explorer, scout commr., 1957-59, instl. rep., 1957-58; asst. scoutmaster, mem. troop com. Troop 50, Akron, Ohio, 1960-70; asst. scoutmaster Troop 49, Magnolia, Ark., 1971-73, scoutmaster, 1973-76, dist. chmn., dist. vice chmn., 1973-76, mem. coun. exec. bd., 1974—, dist. commr., 1976-79, 90-92, fin. chmn., 1977-78; numerous other positions Boy Scouts Am.; chmn. mfg. com. Am.'s Pub. Works Assn. 85th Congress FWPA, 1968-69; deacon Presbyn. Ch., Ohio and Ga., supt. Sunday Sch., Ohio and Ga., asst. supt. Sunday Sch., Ark.; pres. Men of Ch., Ohio, Ark. and Ga.; pres. Couples Club, Ohio; elder, trustee 1st Presbyn. Ch., Magnolia; tchr. Sunday Sch.; Stephen's min. Peachtree Presbyn. Ch., Atlanta, 1995—; mem. various chs. orgnl. coms.; mem. Vols. in Probation, Vols.-in-Drug-Abuse Edn. Program, Ohio and Ark.; mem. adv. bd. Magnolia Adult Drug Edn. Program; mem. DeSoto Area Coun. Exec. Bd., 1971-93; exec. bd. Atlanta Area coun., 1993—, v.p. camping com., 1993-95; asst. leader Boy Scouts Am. Atlanta group to 1st Russian Boy Scouts Am. Jamboree, Russia, 1994—; mem. internat. com. as ptnr. to World Scouting Program, Boy Scouts Am., Atlanta, 1990—, mem. Japanese com. Atlanta area coun., 1997. Staff sgt. USAF, 1946-49, USAFR, 1949-52. Recipient Wood Badge award Boy Scouts Am., 1972, Scouter Trainer award and cert. Boy Scouts Am., 1977, Scouter Key Tng. Recognition award Boy Scouts Am., 1978, Silver Beaver award, 1978, cub scout cub master and dist. cub commr., 1978-90, Man of Achievement award, 1979, 17th edit., 1996, Vigil Honor Order of Arrow award, 1980, Dist. Merit award, 1993; recognized for 50 years in scouting as a vol., 1996—, Com. Nat. Jamboree Boy Scouts Am.; recipient Good Neighbor award City of Magnolia, 1993. Mem. Am. Assn. Textile Chemists and Colorists, Nat. Fire Protection Assn., So. Overseers Assn., Soc. Automotive Engrs. (mem. and cons. G9 and AE5 com.), Kiwanis, Jaycees, Rotary, Masons, Toastmasters Internat. (pres. club 151, dist. commr.), Scottish Rite, Akron Rubber Group, Sigma Nu, Alpha Phi Omega (pres., commr. of scouting). Home: 1631 Willow Way Woodstock GA 30188-4649

WEBB, ERMA LEE, nurse educator; b. Hitchcock, Okla., Mar. 16, 1933; d. Edward B. and Annabelle G. (Schnell) Haffner; m. James M. Webb, Apr. 4, 1959; children: Scott, Sandee, Steve. BSN, Union Coll., 1957; MSN, Loma Linda (Calif.) U., 1976. Charge and staff nurse pediatrics and surg. units Porter Meml. Hosp., Denver, 1960-68; dir. LPN program Hialeah (Fla.) Hosp., 1969-72; asst. prof. Loma Linda U., 1972-76; assoc. prof. So. Coll. 7th Day Adventists, Orlando, Fla., 1976—, coord. BS program Fla. campuses, 1976—. Mem. Fla. Nurse's Assn., Fla. League Nursing, So. Regional Edn. Bd., Sigma Theta Tau. Home: 3233 Holiday Ave Apopka FL 32703-6635

WEBB, GLORIA O., mayor; b. Omaha, Apr. 4, 1931; m. Thomas H. Webb; children: Wendy, Tom IV, Patricia, Bob. BS in Social Work, U. Nebr.; postgrad. in Guidance Counseling, Old Dominion U. Former stewardess United Airlines; former recreation dir. Omaha Urban League; probation officer Douglas County Juvenile & Domestic Relations Ct., Omaha, until 1988; mayor City of Portsmouth (Va.), 1988—. Bd. dirs. Nat. Women's Polit. Caucus, Friends of Women's Studies Old Dominion U., Salvation Army, ARC; mem. community and econ. devel. Va. Mcpl. League; mem. Portsmouth Partnership Council, Auxs. of Medicine, Faculty Wives Eastern Va. Med. Sch., Portsmouth City Council, Colonial Coast Girl Scouts Council Adv. Bd., Established Concerned Parents for Quality Edn. Churchland Elem. Sch., Family Life Com. Tidewater Planning Council, COMPLAN Task Force; mem. steering com. med. symposium Second Ann. Citizens Trust Disting. Prof. Lectures; sec. Portsmouth Service League; v.p. Churchland Parks & Recreation Forum; elected to bd. dirs. Women in Local Govt. Nat. League of Cities; participant C. of C. Leadership Devel. Inst.; chmn. C. of C. Leadership Com.; chmn. hon. membership sect. PTA Council; campaign co-chmn. Spl. Gifts to Women United Way; former mem. Portsmouth Sch. Bd., 1972-80, chmn., 1978-80; former mem. Mental Health Assn.; vol. worker Girl Scouts, Portsmouth Girl's Club, Kirk Cone Ctr., Wesley Community Ctr. Kindergarten, Friends of Juvenile Ct., Drug Referral/Crisis Ctr., Churchland Elem. Sch. Recipient Portsmouth Woman of Yr. award Portsmouth Jaycettes for Outstanding Service to Community, 1981. Home: 201 Park Rd Portsmouth VA 23707-1211 Office: City of Portsmouth 801 Crawford St Fl 6 Portsmouth VA 23704-3822*

WEBB, JAMES CALVIN, minister; b. Washington, Ga., Dec. 16, 1947; s. Mack Clifton and Thelma (Walker) W.; m. Lynda Sue Gravely, Mar. 18, 1967; children: Wendell Lewis, Christopher Andrew. BA, Mercer U., Atlanta, 1977; MDiv, Southwestern Bapt. Theol. Sem., Ft. Worth, Tex., 1980, DMin, 1987. Ordained to ministry So. Bapt. Conv., 1980. Pastor Abbott (Tex.) Bapt. Ch., 1978-81, Bethesda Bapt. Ch., Burleson, Tex., 1981-84, White Oak Bapt. Ch., Lilburn, Ga., 1985—. Contbr. articles to profl. jours. With Army N.G. 1967-73. Home: 3083 Fireside Dr Snellville GA 30278-6523 Office: White Oak Bapt Ch 1352 Martin Nash Rd SW Lilburn GA 30247-1939

WEBB, JAMES DAVID, editor, publisher; b. Louisville, Miss., Aug. 17, 1936; s. James David Sr. and Frances Virginia (Watson) W.; m. Mary Lou Jones, Mar. 17, 1962; children: Marsha Lee, Mary Heather. BA, U. So. Miss., 1962. Writer Sea Coast Echo, Bay St. Louis, Miss., 1959-60, Bristol (Va.) Herald Courier, 1960; editor/pub. Franklin Advocate, Meadville, Miss., 1962—, Wilk-Amite Record, Gloster, Miss., 1963—. Author/writer (newspaper column) Southwest Scene, 1962—. Pub. rels. counsel Gov. Paul Johnson Jr., Jackson, Miss., 1963; past chmn. Franklin County Dem. Exec. Com.; mem. Bude, Miss. to Bude, Cornwall Cities Exch. Group, 1992; pres. Franklin Promtions, 1992—. Recipient Merit award Gov. William A. Waller, 1976, Miss. Cmty. Leadership award, 1996; named Col. and aide de camp Gov. Paul Johnson Jr., 1964-68. Mem. Franklin County C. of C. (bd. dirs. 1988-91), Bude Miss. Pub. Rels. Com., Franklin County Forestry Assn., Franklin County Fair Assn. (sec.). Baptist. Office: Franklin Advocate 111 Main St Meadville MS 39653

WEBB, JAMES DAVID, assistant principal; b. Bentonville, Ark., Nov. 4, 1947; s. Wilson C. and Letta L. (Cooper) W.; m. Jane Lynn Demanzuk, Sept. 28, 1990; children: Allison E. Scott, Michael A. Scott. BA, Coll. of the Ozarks, Clarksville, Ark., 1970; MPA, U. Ark., 1980, BSin Edn., 1984, EdS, 1994. Adminstrv. asst. to mayor City of Wynne, Ark., 1975-76; dir. ops. City of Bentonville, Ark., 1976-78; bus. office mgr. Bates Meml. Hosp., Bentonville, Ark., 1978-80; social studies tchr. Decatur Pub. Schs., Ark., 1984-86; career orientation tchr. Rogers Pub. Schs., Ark., 1986-96; asst. prin. Fayetteville Pub. Schs., Ark., 1996—; regional and state scorekeeper Odyssey of the Mind, 1989-96; chair 5 yr. planning com. Oakdale Jr. H.S., Rogers, 1994-96. Author: (book review) Book Review of Small Rural Schools, 1996; presenter in field. Mem., elder, Sunday sch. tchr. Presbyn. Ch., Rogers, Ark. Named Tchr. of Yr. Technology and Learning Mag., 1992. Mem. ASCD, Nat. Mid. Sch. Assn., Ark. Assn. Ednl. Adminstrs., Ark. Assn. Mid. Level Edn., Phi Delta Kappa. Democrat. Office: Ramay Jr HS 401 S Sang Ave Fayetteville AR 72701

WEBB, JAMES ROBERT, strategic management consultant; b. Houston, May 20, 1954; s. Marion Strode and Theresa Ann (Hailstones) W.; m. Karen Aldyth Hutson, May 26, 1984; children: James Robert Jr., Courtney Aldyth. BS in Engring. and Applied Sci., U.S. Mil. Acad., 1976; MBA, U. Dallas, 1984; MSME, Pacific Western U., 1985; Exec. Program in Corp. Strategy, MIT, 1994; Cert. of Holmesian Studies, 1994. Cert. mgmt. cons. Commd. 2d lt. U.S. Army, 1976, advanced through grades to capt., 1980; with spl. forces U.S. Army, Ft. Bragg, N.C., 1976-81; resigned U.S. Army, 1981; engring. mgr. Tex. Instruments, Inc., Dallas, 1981-84; project mgr. Lockwood Greene, Inc., Dallas, 1984-85; mgr. Price Waterhouse & Co., Dallas, 1985-88; sr. mgr. Deloitte & Touche, Dallas, 1988-92; dir. corp. strategic planning Stevens Graphic Corp., Ft. Worth, 1992-94; mng. cons. strategic mgmt. Electronic Data Sys., Plano, Tex., 1994-96; with AT&T Solutions, Irving, Tex., 1996—; bd. dirs. Franco-Midland Hardware Co.; bd. dirs., treas. Tex. Judo, Inc.; instr. Am. Mgmt. Assn., N.Y.C., 1985-90; spkr. in field. Mem. Rep. Presdl. Task Force, Washington, 1990; bd. dirs. Brookhaven Bus. Assn., Dallas, 1989-91; mem. fin. com. nat. governing body for judo U.S. Olympic Com.; ordained elder Presbyn. Ch. Recipient Korean Master Parachutist badge Rep. of Korea Army, 1989, Presdl. medal of Merit, 1990. Mem. Inst. Mgmt. Cons. (chpt. pres.), U.S. Tennis Assn., U.S. Judo, U.S. Judo Assn. (treas., bd. dirs.), U.S. Judo Fedn., Planning Forum, Spl. Forces Assn., Brookhaven Country Club, Sigma Iota Epsilon. Recipient Presdl. medal of merit, 1990. Home: 3811 Wooded Creek Dr Dallas TX 75244-4751 Office: AT&T Solutions East Tower 5429 LBJ Freeway Ste 500 Dallas TX 75240

WEBB, JOHN, state supreme court justice; b. Rocky Mount, N.C., Sept. 18, 1926; s. William Devin and Ella (Johnson) W.; m. Martha Carolyn Harris, Sept. 13, 1958; children: Caroline Webb Smart, William Devin. Student, U. N.C., 1946-49; LLB, Columbia U., 1952. Judge Superior Ct., Wilson, N.C., 1971-77, N.C. Ct. Appeals, Raleigh, 1977-86; justice Supreme Ct. N.C., Raleigh, 1986—. Served with USN, 1944-46. Mem. N.C. Bar Assn. Democrat. Baptist. Home: 808 Trinity Dr W Wilson NC 27893-2131 Office: NC Supreme Ct PO Box 1841 Raleigh NC 27602-1841

WEBB, JOHN WEBER, JR., minister; b. Memphis, Oct. 18, 1962; s. John Weber and Virginia (Thompson) W.; m. Trudy Marie DenHartog, July 18, 1992; 1 child, Zachary John. BA, Memphis State U., U. Memphis, 1986; MDiv, Ref. Theol. Sem., Jackson, Miss., 1989. Summer intern Commnity Presbyn. Ch., Live Oak, Fla., 1987, First Presbyn. Ch., West Point, Miss., 1988; dir. youth ministries Fifth St. Presbyn. Ch., Tyler, Tex., 1989-92; tchr. Good Shepherd Sch., Tyler, TX, 1992-93, 96—; dir. after-sch. program, 1994-96, devel. dir., 1996—; adminstr. The Castle (Youth Outreach Ctr.), 1993-94; dir. jr. ministry Grace Cmty. Ch., Tyler, TX, 1994—; worship team Grace Cmty. Ch., 1993-94; dir. ops. Boys & Girls Club Smith County, Tyler, Tex., 1995—; pres. Tyler Area Youth Ministries Network, 1990-92; dir. Robert E. Lee chpt. Soldiers for Jesus, Tyler, 1990-92; bd. dirs. Tyler Area Youth Ctr., 1990—. Author/contbr. PCA Bull., 1990. Republican. Home: 1600 Rice Rd Apt 1514 Tyler TX 75703-3309 Office: Boys & Girls Club Smith County 325 S Broadway Ave Tyler TX 75702-7337

WEBB, LAMAR THAXTER, architect; b. Hapeville, Ga., Sept. 13, 1928; s. Eugene Garnette and Sara Ethel (Moore) W.; m. Bettye Jayne Jackson, Dec. 6, 1957; children: Mark Maynard, Robin Lynn. BBA in Fin., U. Ga., 1950; BS, Ga. Inst. Tech., 1959, BArch, 1960. Registered architect, Ga., Fla. Intern architect Abreu and Robeson, Inc., Brunswick, Ga., 1960-66; architect, pres. Webb & Baldwin, Inc., St. Simons Island, Ga., 1966-72; pres., owner Lamar Webb, Architect, Inc., St. Simons Island, 1966—. lst lt. USAF, 1953-55. Mem. AIA (State bd. dirs. 1985—, v.p. Golden Isles chpt. 1988-89, pres. 1989-90), Am. Soc. Interior Designers, Am. Soc. Landscape Architects (assoc.), Audubon Soc., Nat. Hort. Soc., Humane Soc. (local bd. dirs. 1985-87), Smithsonian Assocs., Coastal Alliance for Arts, Nat. Trust for Hist. Preservation, Ga. Trust for Hist. Preservation, Coastal Ga. Hist. Assn., Met. Mus. Art, Golden Isles Gourmet Club (bd. dirs.) Chien de Rotessieurs, G.I. Chap. Home: Marsh Oaks Saint Simons GA 31522 Office: 13 Retreat Pl Saint Simons GA 31522-2401

WEBB, LYNNE MCGOVERN, communication educator, consultant; b. Shamokin, Pa., Mar. 20, 1951; d. Charles Ralph and Ethel Elizabeth (Harris) McGovern; m. Ronald E. Webb, Sept. 28, 1978 (div. June 1981); m. Robert Blakely Moberly, Apr. 6, 1984; children: Laura Ellen, Richard Edward, Reed JeeMinSeo. BS, Pa. State U., 1972; MS, U. Oreg., 1975, PhD, 1980. Field rep. East Central Ill. Area Agy. on Aging, Campaign, Ill., 1972-74; grad. teaching asst. U. Oreg., Eugene, 1974-78; instr. Berea Coll., Berea, Ky., 1978-80; asst. prof. U. Fla., Gainesville, 1980-86, assoc. prof., 1986-90; vis. assoc. prof. U. Hawaii, Honolulu, 1990-91; assoc. prof. U. Memphis, 1991—; cons. Fla. Farm Bur., Gainesville, 1981, Clay County Electric Coop., Keystone Heights, Fla., 1987, Retirement Rsch. Found., Chgo., 1988. Mem. Fla. Speech Comm. Assn. (v.p. 1986-87), So. States Comm. Assn. (chair applied comm. divsn. 1989-90, chair gender studies divsn. 1992-93, chair membership 1993, v.p. 1994, pres. 1995), Speech Comm. Assn. (chair com. on comm. and aging 1982-83, legis. coun. 1989-92, 93-96, chair applied comm. sect. 1994-95, chair resolutions com. 1996). Democrat. Methodist. Office: Univ Memphis 143 Theatre and Comm Arts Memphis TN 38152

WEBB, MARTY FOX, principal; b. Des Moines, July 15, 1942; d. Joseph John and Jean (Way) Fox; m. Andrew H. Rudolph, Aug. 17, 1963 (div. Jan. 1988); children: Kristen Ann, Kevin Andrew; m. Eugene J. Webb, Nov. 23, 1991. BS, U. Mich., 1964; MEd, Houston Bapt. U., 1982; EdD, U. San Francisco, 1993. Cert. adminstr., Tex., elem. and spl. edn. educator, Mich., Tex. Tchr. spl. edn. Hawthorn Ctr., Northville, Mich., 1964-70; tchr. Bellaire (Tex.) Sch. for Children, 1977-80; dir., owner Ednl. Consulting, Houston, 1979-80; prin. Corpus Christi Sch., Houston, 1980—; cons. Hawthorn Ctr., Northville, 1970-72, Bellaire Sch. for Young Children, 1974-78; instr. Excellence in Edn. Seminars, Galveston, Houston, 1985—; speaker in field. Recipient Elem. Sch. Recognition award U.S. Dept. Edn., 1989-90, Blue Ribbon Sch. award, 1990, Outstanding Doctoral Student award, 1994. Mem. ASCD, Nat. Cath. Edn. Assn., Child Abuse Prevention Network, U. Mich. Alumni. Home: 3531 Sun Valley Dr Houston TX 77025-4148 Office: Corpus Christi Sch 4005 Cheena Dr Houston TX 77025-4701

WEBB, RANDY, business executive; b. 1956. Grad., Bethany Coll. With Landmark Land Co., Oklahoma City, Okla., 1979-87, contr., 1988-91; v.p. Premier Parks Inc., Oklahoma City, Okla., 1991—. Office: Premier Parks Inc 11501 NE Expressway St Oklahoma City OK 73131

WEBB, RICHMOND JEWEL, professional football player; b. Dallas, Jan. 11, 1967. BA in Indsl. Distbn., Texas A&M. Offensive tackle Miami Dolphins, 1990—. Named NFL Rookie of Yr., Sporting News, 1990, Sporting News All-Pro Team, 1992. *

WEBB, ROGER STUART, forestry educator; b. Richmond, Va., Apr. 22, 1950; s. Robert Morris Hewes and Mary Ellen (Todd) W.; m. Patricia Margaret Gardner, Dec. 24, 1981; children: Michael, Austin, Lauren, Chandler, Jordan. AB, Coll. William and Mary, 1972; MF, Duke U., 1976; PhD, Va. Poly. Inst and State U., 1980. Asst. prof. forest pathology U. Fla., Gainesville, 1980-86, assoc. prof., 1986—; cons. agroforestry AID, Port-au-Prince, Haiti, 1985—; tech. advisor forestry Taiwan Forest Rsch. Inst., Taipei; tech. coord. agroforestry program Khartoum, Sudan. Author: Introduction to Forestry, 1987. Recipient Meritorious Service award Nat. Forestry Inst., Guatemala City, Guatemala, 1984, Recognition award Min. Agriculture, Japan, 1988. Mem. Am. Phytopath. Soc. (mem. forest pathology commn.), Soc. Am. Foresters, Internat. Soc. Tropical Foresters, Fla. Christmas Tree Assn. (sec. 1981-89), Fla. Mushroom Growers Assn. (sec. 1989—). Republican. Methodist. Home: RR 1 Box 281-38 Micanopy FL 32667-9727 Office: U Fla Dept Forestry 208 Newins Ziegler Hall Gainesville FL 32611-2091

WEBB, ROSS ALLAN, historian, educator; b. Westchester, N.S., Can., July 22, 1923; came to U.S. 1929; s. William Oswald and Permilla Madge (Purdy) W.; m. Ruth evangeline Keil, June 19, 1954; children: Eric Seth, Alan George. BA with honors in history, Acadia U., Wolfville, N.S., 1949; MA in History, U. Pitts., 1951, PhD in History, 1956. Lectr. U. Pitts., 1950-56; asst./assoc. prof., dir. undergrad. studies in history U. Ky., Lexington, 1956-67; prof., chair dept. history Winthrop Coll., Rock Hill, S.C., 1967-68, prof. history, dean faculty, v.p. acad. affairs, 1968-75, prof. history, 1975-89, univ. historian, prof. emeritus, 1989—; cons. in field; vis. prof. summer sch. Wesleyan U., 1966, Acadia U., 1951-64. Author: A Book of Remembrance, 1956, The Alaskan Boundary Dispute, 1779-1903, 1951, Benjamin Helm Bristow Border State Politician, 1969, Kentucky in the Reconstruction Era, 1978; contbr. articles to profl. jours., chpts. in books; contbr. to: Ency. of Southern History, 1979, Kentucky Governors, 1985, The Kentucky Ency., 1992; book reviewer scholarly jours. including The Am. Hist. Rev., Civil War History, The Register of the Kentucky Hist. Assn., Western Pennsylvania Hist. Mag. Mem. S.C. Commn. of Archives and History, 1967-69, York Tech. Edn. Commn., 1968-77; bd. trustees Diocese of Upper S.C.; priest Episcopal Ch. Am. Philos. Soc. grantee, 1977, S.C. Com. on Humanities grantee, 1984; recipient Algernon Sydney Sullivan award, Winthrop Coll., 1981. Mem. Am. Assn. Ret. Persons (S.C. state legis. com. chmn. 1991-93, mem. nat. legis. coun. 1996—), So. Conf. Brit. Studies, So. Hist. Assn. (European sect.), Ky. Hist. Soc., Kiwanis (pres. 1980-81), Phi Beta Kappa, Omicron Delta Kappa, Phi Kappa Phi, Phi Alpha Theta. Home: 2534 Shiland Dr Rock Hill SC 29732-1543 Office: Winthrop Univ Dept History Rock Hill SC 29733

WEBB, SCHUYLER CLEVELAND, naval officer; b. Springfield, Mass., June 28, 1951; s. Cleveland and Bettye Laconia (Wright) W. BA, Morehouse Coll., Atlanta, 1974; MS, U. Mass., 1978; MBA, Nat. U., San Diego, 1986; PhD, U.S. Internat. U., San Diego, 1994. Ednl. coordinator/counselor Springfield Ctr. for Alcoholic Treatment and Edn., Springfield, Mass., 1975-76; asst. trainer Western Mass. Minority Recruitment and Tng., Springfield, 1976-77; research asst. Inst. for Study of Ednl. Policy, Washington, 1978; counseling psychologist Concerned Parents for Ednl. Excellence, Columbia, Md., 1979-80; asst. project ldr. Lawrence Johnson & Assocs., Inc., Washington, 1978-81; commd. USN, 1981, advanced through grades to lt.; research psychologist Naval Health Research Ctr., San Diego, 1983-86; instr./research psychologist Diving & Salvage Sch., Panama Beach, Fla., 1986-87; rsch. psychologist, adminstrv./equal opportunity officer Naval Biodynamics Lab., New Orleans, 1987-91; rsch. intern Def. Equal Opportunity Mgmt. Inst., Patrick AFB, 1991; dep. dir., rsch. psychologist Naval Bur. Pers., Washington, 1994—; tech. cons. Navy Inspector Gen. Office, Washington, 1994—; mktg. cons. Primam./T. Frank and Assocs., New Orleans, 1989-91, Virginia Jackson and Assocs. Inc., Washington, 1979-81; editorial cons. Howard U. Ctr. for Sickle Cell Disease, Washington, 1979-81; cons. Higher Horizons Day Care ctr. Inc., Crossroads, Va., 1980-81; prorgram cons. Project Impact-Tutorial Program, Springfield, Mass., 1974. Contbr. articles to profl. jours. and community newspaper. Mem. Second Harvest Food Bank, New Orleans, 1987-91; chmn. Combined Fed. Campaign, San Diego, 1984; bd. dirs. Project 2000, Inc. Mem. APA, Nat. Naval Officers Assn. (v.p. 1987-89), Nat. Opinion Assn., Assn. Black Psychologists (chpt. rec. sec. 1995—), Soc. Indsl. and Organizational Psychology, Human Factors Soc., Morehouse Coll. Alumni Assn., Assn. for Study of Classical African Civilizations, Alpha Phi Alpha, Psi Chi. Democrat. Office: Bur of Naval Pers Pers 6EB FOB #2 Washington DC 20370

WEBB, THOMAS GEORGE, aircraft manufacturing engineer; b. N.Y.C., Oct. 5, 1944; s. Charles George and Mary-Louise (Hollaman) W.; m. Laurie Jean Dallmer. BS, N.Y. Inst. Tech., 1979; MA, Calif. State U., 1994. Prodn. control mgr. Bischoff Chem. Co. Inc., Hicksville, N.Y., 1968-71; fin. analyst Dun & Bradstreet, Rockville Centre, N.Y., 1971-74; instr. Human Resources Ctr., Albertson, N.Y., 1975-76; indsl. engr. Alarm Device Mfg. Co. Inc., Syosset, N.Y., 1977-80; sr. indsl. engr. Fairchild Republic Co. Inc., Farmingdale, N.Y., 1980-82; mfg. engr. Grumman Aerospace, Bethpage, N.Y., 1983-85; engring. cons. Brunswick Nuclear Project, Southport, N.C., 1985-86; pres. T&L Mgmt. Co. Inc., Holden Beach, N.C., 1987—; owner Tom Webb's Seminars; cons. Deknatel Inc., Floral Park, N.Y., 1977-78, U.S. Dept. Energy, Savannah River Site, Aiken, S.C., 1993; sr. indsl. engr. Grumman Electronics Systems, 1987; indsl. engring. cons. Wilson Concepts of Fla., 1987; engring. cons. McDonnell Douglas Astronautics Co., Huntington Beach, Calif., 1988-89, FL Aerospace, Greenwood, S.C., 1989, Douglas Aircraft Co., Long Beach, Calif., 1990. Served with U.S. Army, 1966-68, Vietnam. Mem. AIAA, Inst. Indsl. Engrs. (sr.), Wilmington Engrs. Club. Episcopalian. Home: 151 Marlin Dr Supply NC 28462-1803

WEBB, THOMAS RICHARD, environmental services administrator; b. Whitesburg, Ky., Jan. 4, 1960; s. James Edward and Allie (Evanoff) W.; m. Lynnell Benton, Apr. 4, 1992. BS in Geology, U. Ky., 1983. Cert. profl. geologist, Ky., Ind., Tenn. Geologist Skelly & Loy Engrs., Lexington, 1983-87, McCoy & McCoy Consultants, Lexington, 1988-90; project mgr. Groundwater Tech., Lexington, 1990-93; environ. svcs. program mgr. Lex-Fayette Urban County Govt., Lexington, 1993—; liaison Local Emergency Planning Com., Lexington, 1993—, Tech. Adv. Commn., Lexington, 1993—. Chief warrant officer 3 USAR, 1988-95. Mem. Am. Inst. Profl. Geologists, Inst. Hazardous Materials Mgmt., Army Aviation Assn. Am. Office: Divsn Environ and Emergency Mgmt 121 N Martin Luther King Lexington KY 40507

WEBB, W. ROGER, university president; b. Bristow, Okla., Apr. 28, 1941; s. E.A. and Grace (Dameron) W.; m. Gwen Moulton, Sept. 7, 1963; children—Roger Brett, Brandon R. B.A., Okla. State U., 1963; J.D., U. Okla., 1967. Bar: Okla. Asst. to sec. U.S. Senate, Washington, 1965; commr. Okla. Dept. Pub. Safety, 1974-78; now pres. Northeastern State U., Tahlequah, Okla. Pres. Okla. Acad. for State Goals, 1989, Leadership Okla., 1987-88; chmn. N.E. Okla. Pub. Facilities Authority, 1978—, Tahlequah Main St. U.S.A. Program, 1987-89; mem. Blue Ribbon Task Force on Corruption in County Govt., 1982; nat. bd. dirs. Explorer Scouts Am., 1977-78; chair Okla.

Homecoming, 1990; bd. dirs. Okla. Found. for Humanities. Ford Found. legis. intern, 1963. Mem. Okla. Bar Assn., Okla. State C. of C., Tulsa Area C. of C. (bd. dirs.), Lambda Chi Alpha. Baptist. Office: Northeastern State U Office of President Tahlequah OK 74464*

WEBBER, RICHARD LYLE, dental radiology educator; b. Akron, Ohio, Nov. 2, 1935; s. George Alfred and Alice Caroline (Yaw) W.; m. Katherine Stanlay Eggert, Aug. 30, 1991; children: Robert Lawrence, Lauren Michele. AB in Physics, Albion Coll., 1958; DDS, U. Mich., 1963; PhD in Physiol. Optics, U. Calif., Berkeley, 1971. Cert. Am. Bd. Maxillofacial Radiology. Staff dentist materials and tech. br., div. dental health USPHS, San Francisco, 1964-72; staff dentist NIDR, NIH, Bethesda, Md., 1972-73, chief clin. investigatios br., 1973-80, chief diagnostic systems br., 1980-88; prof., chmn. dept. diagnostic scis. U. Ala. Sch. Dentistry, Birmingham, 1988-90; prof. depts. dentistry and radiology Bowman Gray Sch. Medicine, Wake Forest U., Winston-Salem, N.C., 1990—. Contbr. articles to Jour. ADA, Sci., Internat. Jour. Tech. Assessment in Health Care, Advances in Dental Rsch. Mem. Soc. Photo-Optical Instrumentation Engrs., Diagnostic Systems Group (pres. 1989-90), Internat. Assn. for Dental Rsch., Omicron Kappa Upsilon, Sigma Xi, Kappa Mu Epsilon. Home: 1240 Chester Rd Winston Salem NC 27104-1355 Office: Wake Forest U Bowman Gray Sch Med Dept Dentistry Medical Center Blvd Winston Salem NC 27157

WEBBER, WENDY ELIZABETH, association management company executive; b. Chestnut Hill, Pa., Jan. 10, 1963; d. William Wallace and Constance Mae (Russell) W.; m. Andrew Taylor Scheid, Aug. 3, 1991; 1 child, Taylor William. BA in Sociology, Lafayette Coll., 1984. Dir. pub. rels., telethon prodr. March of Dimes, Phila., 1984-87; exec. dir. Outdoor Power Equipment Distbn. Assn., Phila., 1987-91, N.Am. Hort. Supply Assn., Phila., 1987-91; owner, mgr. Mahi Mgmt., Charlotte, N.C., 1991—. Office: Mahi Mgmt 235 N Brackenbury Ln Charlotte NC 28270

WEBER, ALBAN, association executive, lawyer; b. Chgo., Jan. 29, 1915; s. Joseph A. and Anna (von Plachecki) W.; m. Margaret Kenny, Dec. 29, 1951; children: Alban III, Peggy Ann, Gloria, Brian. AB, Harvard U., 1935, JD, 1937, MA, Northwestern U., 1962; LLM, John Marshall Law Sch., 1967. Bar: Ill. 1938, Mich. 1985, U.S. Supreme Ct., 1946. Ptnr. Weber & Weber, 1937-41; gen. counsel Fgn. Liquidation Commn., State Dept., 1946; trust officer Lake Shore Nat. Bank, Chgo., 1952-55; univ. counsel Northwestern U., Evanston, Ill., 1955-70; pres. Fedn. Ind. Ill. Colls. and Univs., Evanston, 1971-85; of counsel Schuyler, Roche & Zwirner, Evanston, 1984-94; pres. Benjamin Franklin Fund, Inc., 1965-75, Northwestern U. Press, Inc., 1961-70; chmn. State Assn. Execs. Coun., 1981. Pres. Northeast Ill. Coun. Boy Scouts Am., 1970-71, dist. chmn. Gulfstream Coun., 1994—; alderman City of Chgo., 1947-51. Comdr. USNR, 1941-45, rear adm., 1969-75. Recipient Silver Beaver award Boy Scouts Am., Meritorious Svc. award Loyola U., 1978, Edn. for Freedom award Roosevelt U., 1984. Mem. Nat. Assn. Coll. and Univ. Attys. (pres. 1962), Harvard Law Soc. Ill. (pres. 1984), Navy League (pres. Evanston coun. 1967-70, Univ. Risk Mgmt. Assn. (pres. 1965), Naval Order of U.S. (nat. comdr. 1970-72), Law Club, Econs. Club, Harvard Club, Execs. Club, Chicago Yacht Club, White Lake Golf Club, White Lake Yacht Club, Kiwanis (lt. gov., pres. Port St. Lucie club), St. Lucie River Power Squadron (comdr.), Anchor Line Yacht Club (commodore). Home: 1555 SE Sunshine Ave Port Saint Lucie FL 34952-6011

WEBER, DEAN LEE, athletic trainer; b. Washington, Sept. 4, 1945; s. Raymond Louis and Gladys Louise (Beckner) W.; m. Antoinette Francis Le Grand, Nov. 25, 1990. BA, Bridgewater Coll., 1967. Tchr. Rockingham County Schs., Harrisonburg, Va., 1967-68; athletic trainer U. N.C., Chapel Hill, 1968-72; dir. sports medicine, athletic tng. U. Ark., Fayetteville, 1973—; athletic trainer Nat. Sports Festival-USOC, 1978, 82, 83, Japan Bowl All-Star Game, Tokyo, 1978-83, U.S. Olympic Team-USOC, L.A., 1984; cons. Nike, Inc., Beaverton, Oreg., 1980—, Bike Athletic Co., Knoxville, Tenn., 1982-83, Rawlings Sporting Goods, St. Louis, 1990, Reebok, 1993—. Contbr. articles to profl. jours. Mem. Nat. Athletic Trainers Assn. (cert.), Am. Orthopaedic Soc. Sports Medicine, S.W. Athletic Trainers Assn. (Hall of Fame 1993), Ark. Athletic Trainers Assn. (pres. 1987-89). Home: 10185 Thunder Rd Fayetteville AR 72701-3747 Office: U Ark Broyles Ctr Fayetteville AR 72702

WEBER, FREDRIC ALAN, lawyer; b. Paterson, N.J., July 31, 1948; s. Frederick Edward and Alida (Hessels) W.; m. Mary Elizabeth Cook, June 18, 1983. BA in History, Rice U., 1970; JD, Yale U., 1976. Bar: Tex. 1976, U.S. Dist. Ct. (so. dist.) Tex. Assoc. Fulbright & Jaworski, Houston, 1976-80, participating assoc., 1980-83, ptnr., 1983—. Dir. Houston Symphony Soc., 1993—. Recipient Benjamin Scharps prize Yale Law Sch., 1976, Ambrose Gherini prize Yale Law Sch., 1976. Mem. ABA, Am. Coll. Bond Counsel, Nat. Assn. Bond Lawyers (bd. dirs. 1988-89, treas. 1989-90, pres.-elect 1991, pres. 1991-92), Houston Bar Assn. Office: Fulbright & Jaworski LLP 1301 Mckinney St Ste 5100 Houston TX 77010

WEBER, KATIE, special education educator; b. Delhi, La., Dec. 6, 1933; d. Sullivan and Teresa McClain Aytch; m. Hilliard Weber Jr., June 16, 1956; children: Barrett Renwick, Sandra Anita, Dawna Lynn, Thaddeus Marc. BA, So. U., 1957; MEd, Tex. So. U., 1982. Cert. elem. and spl. edn. tchr., La., Tex. Elem. tchr. Port Arthur (Tex.) Ind. Sch. Dist., 1957-73, elem. spl. edn. tchr., 1974-85, secondary spl. edn. tchr., 1985—; part-time prin. Port Arthur Ind. Sch. Dist., 1976-83, interim prin., 1983-85; mem. Tex. assessment acad. skills test Tex. Edn. Agy., Austin, 1988-90, scorer master tchr. test, 1990; also curriculum writer. Candidate for city coun. City of Port Arthur, Tex., 1974; active Rock Island Bapt. Ch., Port Arthur, 1975—, Buchanan Cir., 1980—, Port Child Svc. League, Port Arthur, 1989—, Life PTA-Tex. PTA, 1985, Clean Cmty. Commn., Port Arthur, 1990—. Named One of Top 20 Tchrs. in Tex., Leadership Edn., 1984-85, Bus. Assoc. of Yr. plaque Energy City chpt. Am. Women Bus. Assn., 1984. Mem. Assn. Tex. Profl. Educators (Leadership cert. 1989), Zeta Phi Beta. Democrat. Home: 741 E 10th St Port Arthur TX 77640

WEBER, MARY LINDA, preschool educator; b. Hermon, N.Y., May 21, 1947; d. Stanley Albert and Shirley Lucille (Holland) Morrill; m. John Weber, July 23, 1966 (div. Nov. 1980); children: James, Mark. AAS, Agrl. and Tech. Coll., Canton, N.Y., 1971; BA, SUNY, Potsdam, 1973; MA, U. South Fla., 1981. Cert. pre-sch., elem. and reading K-12 tchr., N.Y., Fla.;. Tchr. elem. Hermon-DeKalb Ctrl. Sch., DeKalb Junction, N.Y., 1974-76, Westside Elem. Sch., Spring Hill, Fla., 1976-77; tchr. kindergarten Spring Hill Elem. Sch., 1977-89; tchr. pre-kindergarten Deltona Elem. Sch., Spring Hill, 1989—. Author mini-grant Home-Sch. Partnerships, 1990, Multi-Cultural Ctr., 1992, Family Info. Ctr., 1993, Parent Partners in Literacy, 1996. Mem. NEA (Young Children sect.), Assn. Childhood Edn. Internat., Internat. Reading Assn., So. Early Childhood Assn., Fla. Reading Assn., Hernando County Reading Coun. Home: 4132 Redwing Dr Spring Hill FL 34606-2425 Office: Deltona Elem Sch 2055 Deltona Blvd Spring Hill FL 34606-3216

WEBER, MICHAEL HOWARD, senior nuclear control operator; b. Provo, Utah, Sept. 9, 1960; s. Allen Howard and Bonnie Jilene (Hoggan) W.; m. Laura Jean Smith, May 19, 1990. AAS in Nuclear Tech., Aiken Tech. Coll., 1983; BS in Nuclear Sci., U. Md., 1995. Lic. sr. reactor operator. Aux. operator Carolina Power & Light Co., New Hill, N.C., 1983-88, control operator, 1988-92, sr. control operator, 1992-96, control rm. supr., 1996—. Recipient scholarship Aiken County Homebuilders Assn., 1982. Mem. Am. Nuclear Soc. Republican. Lutheran. Home: 3008 Brozak Dr Fuquay Varina NC 27526-8466 Office: Carolina Power & Light Co PO Box 165 New Hill NC 27562-0165

WEBER, MICHAEL JAMES, conductor; b. Grand Forks, ND, Jan. 28, 1957; s. James Warren and Donna Jean (Christiansen) W. BS in Edn., U. N.D., 1980; MusM, Calif. State U., 1986; MusD, U. Ariz., 1990. Music tchr. Hillsboro (N.D.) Pub. Schs., 1980-84, Grand Forks (N.D.) Pub. Schs., 1990-92; choral conductor The Victoria (Tex.) Coll., 1992—; organist, choir master Trinity Episcopal Ch., Victoria, Tex., 1994—; conductor Victoria (Tex.) Master Chorale, 1995—. Arranger (choral music): I Wonder As I Wander, 1996. Mem. adv. bd. Hopkins Fine Arts Sch., Victoria, Tex., 1994—. Mem. Am. Choral Dirs. Assn., Victoria (Tex.) Symphony Soc. (bd. dirs. 1993—), Victoria Fine Arts Assn. (bd. dirs. 1992—), Music Educators Nat. Conf., Tex. Music Educators Nat. Conf., Tex. ACDA. Office: The Victoria Coll 2200 E Red River Victoria TX 77901

WEBER, PATRICIA, speaker, human resources training executive; b. Glen Cove, N.Y., Mar. 19, 1949; d. Michael R. and Agnes P. (Abbondondolo) Pasucci; m. Boyd Martin Weber, June 28, 1970; 1 child, Christopher Lee. BS in Edn., SUNY, Plattsburgh, 1971; MS in Bus., Troy (Ala.) State U., 1976. European registrar Troy State U., Adana, Turkey, 1974-76; ter. mgr. Burroughs Corp., Newport News, Va., 1976-78; area sales mgr. CCH Computax (PSCI), Norfolk, Va., 1978-81; dept. mgr. Tandy Corp., Norfolk, 1981; sales mgr. Reams Computer Corp., Newport News, 1981-83; saleswoman ComputerLand in Hampton & Norfolk, Norfolk, 1983-85, store mgr., 1985-88, dir. sales and mktg., 1988-90; pres. Profl. Strategies, Inc., Newport News, 1990—. Mem. Chesapeake Bay Found., Md., 1989—. Recipient Tribute to Women in Industry and Bus., YWCA, Hampton, Va., 1985. mem. ASTD, Nat. Assn. Women Bus. Owners (founding pres. Tidewater chpt. 1991), Va. Peninsula C. of C. (Small Bus. Women Adv. 1992), Kiwanis. Office: Profl Strategies Inc 732 Thimble Shoals Blvd Newport News VA 23606-4258

WEBER, ROBERT CHARLES, adapted physical education educator, academic administrator; b. West Union, Iowa, Oct. 11, 1948; s. Victor Duane and Elaine I. (Johnson) W.; m. Debra Elaine Nay, Aug. 12, 1972 (div.); childrenL Heidi, Mindy Rae; m. Nancy Jo Johnson, Aug. 9, 1986; 1 child, Ryan Anthony. BS in Phys. Edn. and Health, Bemidji (Minn.) State U., 1971; MS in Phys. Edn., Ea. Ill. U., 1973; EdD in Spl. Phys. Edn. and Adminstrn., U. Utah, 1985. Dir. recreation and adult edn., coach Cass Lake (Minn.) Pub. Schs., 1971-72; tchr. elem. phys. edn., asst. coach basketball Charleston (Ill.) Pub. Schs., 1972-73; grad. asst. Ea. Ill. U., Charleston, 1972-73, asst. prof., 1987-89; instr., coach, dir. intramural sports Iowa Wesleyan Coll., Mt. Pleasant, 1973-75; tchr. driver edn., head football and track coach Virden (Ill.) High Sch., 1975-78; asst. prof. health and phys. edn., coach Dakota State Coll, Madison, S.D., 1978-80; counselor N.W. Juvenile Tng. Ctr. Bemidji State U., 1980, adj. prof. edn., 1985-86; supr. spl. phys. edn. Lubbock (Tex.) State Sch., 1981-83; asst. prof., coord. adapted phys. edn. program Tex. Tech U., Lubbock, 1989—; lectr. U. N.C., Wilmington, 1983-84, So. Ill. U., Carbondale, 1986-87; part-time instr. U. Utah, Salt Lake City, 1981; counselor therapeutic recreation Camp Kostopulos, Salt Lake City, 1981, Salt Lake City EBD and TMR Group, 1981; cons., lectr. in field. Developer audio-visual aids. Vol. Spl. Olympics, 1987—, mem. adv. bd. Region 17, 1989—; v.p. Lubbock Ind. Sch. Dist. Swimming and Diving Booster Club, 1991-91; v.p. Lubbock High Sch. Gymnastic Booster Club, 1991-92, v.p. Swimming and Diving Booster Club, 1991-92, active other booster clubs; cons. Lubbock Office Planning for Cruise for Disabled Program, 1990-91; co-captain His Step Stewardship Drive St. Luke's Meth. Ch., 1990; advisor South Plains Wheelchair Spokers, 1989—. Grantee numerous founds. and orgns.; recipient 15 Yr. Svc. award Spl. Plympics Internat., 1990, Spl. Svc. award Ill. High Sch. Athletic Assn., 1989, Internat. Man of Yr., 1994-95, citation of Meritorious Achievement in Edn. and Habilatation, 1994; named one of Outstanding Young Men. Am. Jaycees, 1990, Hon. Coach Tex. Tech. U. Football Team, 1990, Honored Guest Can. Spl. Olympics for Summer Games, Vancouver, 1990. Mem. AAHPERD (presenter various confs.), Nat. Assn. Sports and Phys. Edn., Adapted Phys. Edn. Acad., Nat. Consrotium Phys. Edn. and Recreation Handicapped, Internat. Fedn. Adapted Phys. Activities, Leisure Spl. Populations, Therapeutic Coun., Tex. Alliance Health, Phys. Edn., Recreation and Dance (rep. region 17 1989—). Home: 5223 71st St Lubbock TX 79424-2015 Office: Tex Tech U PO Box 4070 Lubbock TX 79409-0005

WEBER, STEVEN JOHNSON, emergency flight nurse; b. Frankfort, Ky., May 11, 1962; s. Robert Lee and Alice (Dews) W. Diploma, Appalachian Sch. Practical Nursing, 1982; ADN, Ky. State U., Frankfort, 1988. RN, Ky., N.C.; cert. flight RN, CEN; cert. BCLS, ACLS, ACLS instr., PALS, BTLS, TNCC ENPC instr. Staff nurse med./surg. unit King's Daus. Meml. Hosp., Frankfort, 1982-88; staff nurse pediatric ICU U. of Ky. Med. Ctr., Lexington, 1988-89; charge nurse emergency dept. U. Ky. Albert B. Chandler Med. Ctr., Lexington, 1989-92; flight nurse Careflight Air Med. St. Joseph Hosp., Lexington, 1992-94, chief flight nurse, 1994-96; flight nurse Life Flight, Duke U. Med. Ctr., Durham, N.C., 1996—. Mem. AACN, Emergency Nurses Assn., Nat. Flight Nurses Assn. Home: 5110 Copper Ridge Dr #6-101 Durham NC 27707

WEBER, WILLIAM P., electronics company executive; b. 1940; married. BS, Lamar U., 1962; MS, So. Meth. U., 1966. With Tex. Instruments, Inc., Dallas, 1962—, mgr. assembly and test equipment group, 1965-70, mfr. mgr. electro-optics div. equipment group, 1970-71, mgr. ops. digital systems, 1971-75, asst. v.p., mgr. missile div. equipment group, 1975-79, 1979-80, mgr. Lewisville site, 1979-80, v.p., mgr. electro optics div., 1980-81, mgr. Forest Ln. site, 1980-81, v.p., mgr. equipment group, 1981-82, v.p. and pres. defense systems and electronics group, 1982-84, exec. v.p., mgr. corp. devel., 1984-87, exec. v.p., pres. semiconductor group, 1987—, also bd. dirs. Office: Tex Instruments Inc PO Box 655474 13500 N Central Expy Dallas TX 75265*

WEBERPAL, MICHAEL ANDREW, lawyer; b. Sycamore, Ill., Sept. 16, 1951; s. Michael Andrew Sr. and Mary Elizabeth (Egan) W.; m. Michelle Vinet, Aug. 20, 1971. BA in Econs., U. Wis., Milw., 1975; JD, U. Wis., Madison, 1978; LLM, So. Meth. U., 1992. Bar: Wis. 1978, Tex. 1980, U.S. Dist. Ct. (we. dist.) Wis. Assoc. LaRowe & Gerlach, Reedsburg, Wis., 1978-79; tax specialist Laventhol & Horwath, Dallas, 1980-81; sr. atty. Otis Engring. Corp. (subsidiary of Halliburton Co.), Dallas and London, 1983-88; sr. tax counsel Halliburton Co., Dallas, 1988-92, sr. atty., asst. sec., 1992-93; v.p., gen. counsel, sec. Highlands Ins. Co., Houston, 1993—. Mem. ABA, State Bar Tex., State Bar Wis., Houston Bar Assn. Republican. Roman Catholic. Home: 61 Ambleside Crescent Dr Sugar Land TX 77479-2528 Office: Highlands Ins Co 10370 Richmond Houston TX 77042-4123

WEBSTER, DAVID STEVEN, education educator; b. Bklyn., Aug. 3, 1940; m. Sandrel Adelaide Jones-Isom, Dec. 22, 1984. BA in English, Brandeis U., 1964; MA in English, U. Chgo., 1965; postgrad. in English, U. Calif., Berkeley, 1965-70; PhD in Higher Edn., UCLA, 1981. Manuscript editor pvt. practice, L.A., 1970-76; rsch. analyst Higher Edn. Rsch. Inst. (prof. Alexander W. Astin), L.A., 1976, 78-79; reader asst. English dept. W. L.A. Coll., 1976-81; asst. prof. edn. U. Pa., Phila., 1981-88; asst. prof. ednl. adminstrn. and higher edn. Okla. State U., Stillwater, 1988-90, assoc. prof. ednl. adminstrn. and higher edn., 1990—; cons. Presdl. Com. on Acad. Quality, Rutgers U., New Brunswick, N.J., 1982, Peirce Jr. Coll. Liberal Arts Program, Pa., 1982; reviewer Change, 1986, Econs. of Edn. Rev. 1988, Edn. Librs., Ednl. Rscher. 1982, Focus on Learning, 1984-85, Johns Hopkins Univ. Press, 1991, Jossey-Bass Pubs., 1987, Jour. of Higher Edn., 1984—, NSF, 1985, Rsch. in Higher Edn., 1991—, Rev. of Higher Edn., 1984—, Student Svcs. Program, U.S. Dept. Edn., 1993, Transaction Books, 1989—; organizer, speaker in field. Author: Academic Quality Rankings of American Colleges and Universities, 1986; Editor: Foundations of Higher Edn. Series, 18 books; assoc. editor: Foundations of American Higher Education, 1991; co-editor PEN, 1987-88, editor, 1988-89; editor U. Pa. Grad. Sch. of Edn. Newsletter, 1981-82; co-editor: Faculty and Faculty Issues in Colleges and Universities, 1996; contbg. writer Coll. Digest, 1985-86; contbr. numerous articles to profl. jours., chpts. to books;. Nominated for AAUP Annual Higher Edn. Writers award, 1985, History of Edn. Soc. award, 1984; grantee: UCLA Grad. Divsn. Rsch. Conf. travel grant 1979, Computer Bibliography Search grant, 1980, Travel Rsch. grant, 1980, Acad. Senate Com. on Rsch. grant 1980, Chancellor's Fund grant, 1981, U. Pa. Rsch. Found. grant, 1984, 85; recipient NYU Inst. Fine Arts scholarshp, 1964-65, U. Chgo. Humanities scholarship, 1965, English Dept. scholarship 1965-66, UCLA's Chancellor's fellowship 1977-81. Mem. Am. Assn. for Higher Edn., Am. Ednl. Rsch. Assn. (chmn. E.F. Lindquist award com. 1991-92, mem. at large exec. com. divsn. J 1986-88, mem. outstanding book award com. 1990-91, nominee Outstanding Book award 1986, Rsch. award in higher edn. 1987), Assn. for Study of Higher Edn. (program com. 1987, nominating com. 1988, 90-91, membership com. 1989-91, nominee Outstanding Dissertation award 1980-81), Nat. Book Critics Circle, Soc. for History Authorship, Reading and Pub. Home: 121 W Hartman St Stillwater OK 74075-3608 Office: Okla State U Stillwater OK 74078-0146

WEBSTER, JAMES KELSEY, IV, legal assistant; b. Batavia, N.Y., Apr. 13, 1966; s. James Kelsey III and Carol Joan (Mast) W. BA in History, SUNY at Buffalo, 1989, BA in Polit. Sci., 1989. Staff intern Congressman Bill Paxon, Williamsville, N.Y., 1989; records clk. Keller & Heckman, Law Offices, Washington, 1990, legal asst. in telecomms., 1990—; grad. student internat. rels. The Am. U., Washington, 1993—. Mem. World Future Soc., World Affairs Coun. Washington. Democrat. Methodist. Home: Apt 528N 1600 S Eads St Arlington VA 22202-2918 Office: Keller and Heckman Law Offices 1001 G St NW #500 West Washington DC 20001

WEBSTER, MURRAY ALEXANDER, JR., sociologist, educator; b. Manila, Philippines, Dec. 10, 1941; s. M.A. and Patricia (Morse) W.; A.B., Stanford U., 1963, M.A., 1966, Ph.D., 1968. Asst. prof. social relations Johns Hopkins U., Balt., 1968-74, assoc. prof., 1974-76; prof. sociology, adj. prof. psychology U. S.C., Columbia, 1976-86; vis. prof. sociology Stanford U., 1981-82, 85, 88-89; sr. lectr. San Jose State U., 1987-89; sociology program dir. NSF, 1989-91; prof. sociology U. N.C., Charlotte, 1993—; NIH fellow, 1966-68; grantee NSF, Nat. Inst. Edn. Mem. AAAS, Am. Sociol. Assn., So. Sociol. Soc., Am. Psychol. Assn., Am. Psychol. Soc., N.Y. Acad. Scis. Presbyterian. Author: (with Barbara Sobieszek) Sources of Self-Evaluation, 1974; Actions and Actors, 1975, (with Martha Foschi) Status Generalization: New Theory and Research, 1988; mem. editorial bd. Am. Jour. Sociology, 1976-79, Social Psychology Quar., 1977-80, 84-87, 93—, Social Sci. Research, 1975—. Office: Univ NC Dept Sociology Charlotte NC 28223

WEBSTER, PETER DAVID, judge; b. Framingham, Mass., Feb. 12, 1949; s. Waldo John and Helen Anne (Borovek) W.; m. Michele Page Hernandez, Jan. 13, 1989; 1 stepchild, Alana Perryman. BS, Georgetown U., 1971; JD, Duke U., 1974; LLM, U. Va., 1995. Bar: Fla. 1974, U.S. Dist. Ct. (mid. dist.) Fla. 1975, U.S. Ct. Appeals (5th cir.) 1975, U.S. Dist. Ct. (so. dist.) Fla. 1977, U.S. Dist. Ct. (no. dist.) Fla. 1978, U.S. Supreme Ct. 1978, U.S. Ct. Appeals (11th cir.) 1981. Law clk. U.S. Dist. Judge, Jacksonville, Fla., 1974-75; assoc. Bedell, Bedell, Dittmar, Smith & Zehmer, Jacksonville, 1975-78; ptnr. Bedell, Bedell, Dittmar & Zehmer, Jacksonville, 1978-85; cir. judge State Fla., Jacksonville, 1986-91; judge Dist. Ct. of Appeal, First Dist., State of Fla., Tallahassee, 1991—; master of bench Chester Bedell Am. Inn of Ct., 1988-91, Tallahassee Am. Inn of Ct., 1992—; mem. com. on standard jury instrns. in civil cases, com. on trial ct. info. sys.; com. on confidentiality of records of jud. br. Fla. Supreme Ct. Contbg. author: Sanctions: Rule 11 and Other Powers, 1986, Florida Criminal Rules and Practice Manual, 1990. Bd. dirs. Jacksonville Area Legal Aid, Inc., 1978-82, River Region Human Svcs., Inc., Jacksonville, 1986-88; mem. adv. bd. P.A.C.E. Ctr. for Girls, Inc., Jacksonville, 1986-91; com. mem. Shawnee dist. North Fla. coun. Boy Scouts Am., 1974-78; mem. delinquency task force Mayor's Commn. on Children and Youth, City of Jacksonville, 1988-91; officer, mem. exec. bd. Suwanee River Area coun. Boy Scouts, 1991—. Mem. Fla. Conf. Appellate Judges, Jacksonville Bar Assn., Tallahassee Bar Assn., Phi Beta Kappa, Phi Alpha Theta, Phi Eta Sigma. Office: 1st Dist Ct Appeal 301 Martin Luther King Blvd Tallahassee FL 32399-1850

WEBSTER, RAYMOND EARL, psychology educator, psychotherapist; b. Providence, Dec. 3, 1948; s. Earl Harold and Madeline (D'Antuono) W.; m. Angela Grenier, Jan. 31, 1984; children: Matthew Raymond, Patrick Gregory, Timothy Andrew. BA, R.I. Coll., 1971, MA, 1973; MS, Purdue U., 1976; PhD, U. Conn., 1978. Diplomate Am. Bd. Forensic Examiners; lic. psychologist, N.C. Dir. pupil svcs. and spl. edn. Northeastern Area Regional Edn. Svcs., Wauregan, Conn., 1978-79; dir. alternative vocat. sch. Capital Region Edn. Coun., West Hartford, Conn., 1979-83; prof. psychology, dir. sch. psychology program East Carolina U., Greenville, N.C., 1983—; rsch. assoc. ednl. psychology U. Conn., Storrs, 1976-78; cons. Bolton (Conn.) Pub. Schs., 1976-78, Columbia (Conn.) Pub. Schs., 1976-78, N.C. Dept. Instrn., Raleigh, 1983—; speaker at profl. meetings. Guest reviewer Jour. Applied Behavior Analysis, 1975, Clin. Psychology Pub. Co., 1992, Psychol. Reports, 1993—, Perceptual and Motor Skills, 1993—; mem. editl. bd. Psychology in Schs., 1987—; contbr. numerous articles to profl. jours., chpts. to books. Trustee N.C. Ctr. for Advancement of Teaching, Cullowhee, 1990-93. Sgt. U.S. Army Spl. Forces N.G., 1969-75. Recipient spl. distinction award Conn. Assn. Sch. Psychologists, 1983. Mem. APA, Am. Coll. Forensic Examiners (cert. Forensic Examiner), Nat. Assn. Sch. Psychologists (cert., alt. del. 1985-86, spl. distinction in profl. devel. 1982, 83), Nat. Acad. Neuropsychology, Sigma Xi. Methodist. Home: 200 Williams St Greenville NC 27858-8712 Office: East Carolina U Rawl Bldg Greenville NC 27834-4353

WECHSLER, ARNOLD, osteopathic obstetrician, gynecologist; b. N.Y.C., June 10, 1923; s. David and Eva (Kirsch) W.; m. Marlene Esta Jurnovoy, Sept. 11, 1955 (div. Sept. 1986); children: Diane, Paul, Stewart. Grad., Rutgers U.; DO, Phila. Coll. Osteo. Medicine, 1952. Diplomate Am. Bd. Osteo. Obstetricians and Gynecologists; lic. physician, Pa., N.Y., Fla. Intern Hosps. of Phila. Coll. Osteo. Medicine, 1952-53, resident in obstetrics/gynecology and gen. surgery, 1953-56; lectr. in obstetrics and gynecology Nursing Sch. Phila. Coll. Osteo. Medicine; founder, mem. staff Tri County Hosp., Delaware County, Pa., from 1960, chief staff, 1960-62, chief dept. obstetrics and gynecology surgery, 1960-77, dir. med. edn., 1968-71; attending and cons. in obstetrics and gynecol. surgery Met. Hosp., Phila., 1956-60, 71-75; chief dept. obstetrics and gynecology Humana Hosp.-South Broward, Hollywood, Fla., 1980-84; cons. and attending in gynecol. surgery Drs. Hosp. of Hollywood, 1982-86; insp. for intern and resident tng. programs Bur. Hosps. of Am. Osteo. Assn., 1965-66; founder, med. dir. Women's Med. Svcs., 1973-77, Nutrients Inc., Phila., 1977-79, Supplements Inc., Phila., 1979-80, Alternative Lifestyle Ctr., Fla., 1983-86; founder, dir. A.W. Profl. Consultants, Inc.; cons. Practice Mgmt. Group, Med Temps Plus, Plantation, Fla.; provider ambulatory gyn. surgery for multiple gyn ctrs. in Dade, Broward and Palm Beach Counties, Fla. Author: Dr. Wechsler's New You Diet, 1978. Staff Sgt. Signal Corps, USAF, 1942-46, PTO, Japan. Fellow Am. Coll. Osteo. Obstetricians and Gynecologists, Internat. Coll. Applied Nutrition; mem. Am. Osteo. Assn., Pa. Osteo. Med. Assn., Philadelphia County Osteo. Soc., Fla. Osteo. Med. Assn., Broward County Osteo. Med. Assn., Am. Soc. Bariatric Physicians, Assn. Maternal and Child Welfare, Internat. Acad. Preventive Medicine, Inst. Food Technologists, Coun. for Responsible Nutrition, Internat. Coll. Gynecologic Laparoscopists, Assn. Reproductive Health Profls.

WECKERLY, WILLIAM CLARENCE, minister; b. Butler, Pa., Apr. 9, 1937; s. Albert K. Sr. and Helen Marjorie (Kepple) W.; m. Sheila Faye Saxman, May 26, 1962; children: William S., Eric S., Erin B., Brian T. BS in Edn., Indiana U. of Pa., 1959; MDiv, Pitts. Sem., 1967; D. Ministry, Christian Theol. Sem., 1987. Ordained to ministry Presbyn. Ch. (U.S.A.), 1967; cert. secondary tchr., Pa. Assoc. pastor 1st Presbyn. Ch., Batavia, N.Y., 1967-72; pastor Eastminster Presbyn. Ch., Cin., 1972-76, 1st Presbyn. Ch., Monticello, Ind., 1976-90, Graham (N.C.) Presbyn. Ch., 1990—; commr. Presbytery of Salem, Clemmons, N.C., 1990—. Author: Conflict in the Church: A Case Study, 1987. Chaplain Graham Police Dept., 1990; bd. dirs. Habitat for Humanity. Recipient Civic Svc. award Batavia City Coun., 1972, Brotherhood award NCCJ, 1976. Mem. Graham Ministerial Alliance (pres. 1991), Alban Inst., Alamance Ministerial Assn., Rotary, United Comml. Travelers. Home: 1045 Camelot Ln Graham NC 27253-9539 Office: Graham Presbyn Ch 216 W Harden St Graham NC 27253-2828

WEDINGER, ROBERT SCOTT, research chemist, business manager; b. Fairbanks, Alaska, Dec. 19, 1957; s. Robert Howard and Beatrice Ann (Hrbacek) W.; m. Barbara Jean Bergmann, Aug. 4, 1979; children: Kathryn Lyann, Robert Michael. BS in Chemistry and Biology with honors, Wagner Coll., 1979; PhD in Chemistry, SUNY, Stony Brook, 1984. Post-doctoral fellow Harvard U., Cambridge, Mass., 1984-85; rsch. chemist FMC Agrl. Chem. Group, Princeton, N.J., 1986-87; group leader FMC Lithium Divsn., Gastonia, N.C., 1987-88; mgr. organic rsch. FMC Lithium Divsn., Gastonia, 1989-90, mgr. preservation systems, 1988-92, assoc. dir. devel., 1992-93, bus. mgr. synthesis, 1993—. Contbr. articles to profl. jours; patentee chemicals and processes for mass deacidification and strengthening of paper in bound books. Scoutmaster Troop #4 Boy Scouts of Am., Staten Island, N.Y., 1976-79. Recipient Outstanding Chem. Tchg. award SUNY, Stony Brook, 1980, 83, Pres.' award for tchg. excellence, 1984, Exec. of Yr. award Spindelette chpt. Profl. Secs. Internat., 1991. Mem. AAAS, Am. Chem Soc., Organic Chem. Div. and Med. Chem. Div. of Am. Chem. Soc., Order of

Arrow (VIGIL honor), Sigma Xi. Office: FMC Lithium Div 449 Cox Rd Gastonia NC 28054-0615

WEDOW, DAVID WALTER, marketing analyst; b. LaPorte, Ind., July 12, 1953; s. Lyle Thomas and Rosemary Katherine (Stone) W. BA in Criminology, Ind. U., 1978. Field data analyst Nat. Hwy. Traffic Safety Adminstrn., Bloomington and Columbus, Ind., 1978-80; office mgr., then outside sales Quality Mill Supply Co., Columbus and Indpls., 1980-82; territorial sales rep. McCulloch Corp., Indpls., 1982-83; dist. sales rep. McCulloch Corp., Detroit, 1983-85; nat. account mgr. McCulloch Corp., Jacksonville, Fla., 1985-86; nat. account sales mgr. Bush Internat., Inc., Jacksonville, 1986-87; sales and mktg. analyst The Mktg. Connection, Jacksonville, 1987-88; regional sales mgr. Western Hemisphere Sales, Inc., Clearweater, Fla., 1988-89; nat. account mgr. S.E. S.E. McCulloch Corp., Ponte Vedra Beach, Fla., 1989—; regional mgr. Shop-Vac/McCulloch Corp., Williamsport, Pa., 1991-95; nat. account sales mgr. McCulloch Corp., Tucson, 1996—. Active Young Reps.; vol. Spl. Olympics, Detroit, 1984, 85; basketball coach YMCA Youth, Jacksonville, Fla., 1986-87. Mem. Ind. U. Alumni Assn., Nat. Rifle Assn. (instr. 1978-85), Nat. Hardware Mfrs. Assn., Nat. Assn. Gen. Mcht. Reps. Republican. Methodist. Club: Jacksonville Execs. Home: 63 Jackson Ave Ponte Vedra Beach FL 32082-2808 Office: McCulloch Corp 6085 S Mcculloch Dr Tucson AZ 85706-9411

WEDZICHA, WALTER, foreign language educator; b. Jezor, Poland, June 5, 1920; came to U.S., 1946; s. Wladyslaw and Maria (Kruczek) W.; m. Sabina Purzynska, Nov. 28, 1945; children: John M., Christine S. AB, U. Miami, 1965; MA, U. Pitts., 1966. Attaché Consulate Gen. of Poland, N.Y.C., 1946-49; acct. Miami, 1950-65; asst. prof. German and Russian Clarkson U., Potsdam, N.Y., 1967-86, prof. emeritus, 1986—. Author: Song of the City, 1957, From Love of God and All Creation, 1992. Fellow NDEA, U. Pitts., 1965-66; grantee NEH, Ohio State U., 1977, NEH, U. Ill., 1978. Mem. MLA. Democrat. Home: 2311 SE Bowie St Port Saint Lucie FL 34952-7317

WEECH, WILLIAM ALLEN, foreign service officer; b. Balt., Sept. 8, 1959; s. C. Sewell and Ann (McCord) W.; m. Jane Elizabeth Moller, Jan. 2, 1988; 1 child, Alexander. BA, Ohio State U., 1983; MA, Sch. for Internat. Tng., Brattleboro, Vt., 1987. Peace corps vol. U.S. Peace Corps, Costa Rica, 1983-85; rsch. assoc. No. Ill. U., DeKalb, 1987; fgn. svc. officer U.S. Dept. of State, Belgrade, Yugoslavia, 1988-90, Guadalajara, Mex., 1990-91, Tirana, Albania, 1991-92, Washington, 1992—. Mem. ASTD, Nat. Orgn. Devel. Network. Home: 607 Truman Circle SW Vienna VA 22180 Office: Fgn Svc Inst 4000 Arlington Blvd Arlington VA 22180

WEED, KERI ANITA, psychology educator; b. Vallejo, Calif., Feb. 1, 1956; d. Harold Vernon and Juanita Kimbal (Knox) W.; m. Douglas Barnes Slifer, July 24, 1986. BA in Psychology, Northwest Nazarene Coll., 1976; MA in Devel. Psychology, U. Notre Dame, 1982, PhD in Devel. Psychology, 1984. Rsch. assoc. SUNY, Binghamton, 1984-86; asst. prof. U. S.C., Aiken, 1986-91, assoc. prof., 1991-94, prof., 1994—; chair, bd. dirs. Mental Health Assn. S.C., 1993-94; pres., bd. dirs. Mental Health Assn. Aiken County, 1990-91; mem. children's planning coun. S.C. Dept. Mental Health, Columbia, 1993—. Dir. Mothers as Mentors, Aiken, 1991-95. Mem. Am. Psychol. Soc. (charter), Am. Ednl. Rsch. Assn., Am. Assn. Mental Retardation (mem.-at-large 1994, chair S.C. chpt. 1996—), Soc. Rsch. Child Devel. Office: U SC 171 University Pky Aiken SC 29801-6309

WEED, ROGER OREN, rehabilitation educator and counselor; b. Bend, Oreg., Feb. 2, 1944; s. Chester Elbert and Ruth Marie (Urie) W.; m. Paula J. Keller; children: Nicholette, Andrew. BS in Sociology, U. Oreg., 1967, MS in Rehab. Counseling, 1969; PhD in Rehab. Counseling, U. Ga., 1986. Cert. rehab. counselor; cert. disability mgmt. specialist; lic. profl. counselor. Vocat. rehab. counselor State of Alaska, Anchorage, 1969-71; instr. U. Alaska, Anchorage, 1970-76; counselor Langdon Psychiat. Clinic, Anchorage, 1971-74; from asst. dir. to exec. dir. Hope Cottages, Anchorage, 1974-79; owner Profl. Resources Group, Anchorage, 1978-80; mng. ptnr. Collins, Weed & Assocs., 1980-84; assoc. dir. Ctr. for Rehab. Tech. Ga. Tech. U., Atlanta, 1986-87; catastrophic injury rehab. Weed & Assocs., Atlanta, 1984—; assoc. prof. Ga. State U., Atlanta, 1987—; adj. faculty Ga. Inst. Tech. Co-author: Vocational Expert Handbook, 1986, Transferable Work Skills, 1988, Life Care Planning: Spinal Cord Injured, 1989, 94, Life Care Planning: Head Injured, 1994, Life Care Planning for the Amputee, 1992, Rehab Consultant Handbook, 1994; mem. editl. bd. Jour. of Pvt. Sector Rehab., Athens, Ga., 1986—; mem. Disting. Editl. Bd. Vanguard Series in Rehab., Athens, 1988—; contbr. articles to profl. publs. Recipient Gov.'s award Gov.'s Com. on Employment, Alaska, 1982, Goldpan Svc. award Gov.'s Com. on Employment, Alaska, 1978, Profl. Svcs. award Am. Rehab. Counselors Assn., 1993. Fellow Nat. Rehab. Assn. (chair legis. com., bd. dirs. met. Atlanta chpt. 1988—, pres. Pacific region 1983-85, pres.'s award Pacific region 1986), Nat. Assn. Rehab. Profls. in Pvt. Sector (chair resh. and tng. com. 1988-93, pres. 1994-95, Educator of the Yr. award 1991), Nat. Brain Injury Assn., Pvt. Rehab. Suppliers Ga., Rehab. Engring. Soc. N.Am., Anchorage Amateur Radio Club. Republican. Methodist. Office: 9th Fl College of Education Ga State U Dept Counseling Atlanta GA 30303

WEEDMAN, KENNETH RUSSELL, artist, art educator; b. Little Rock, Sept. 26, 1939; s. Charles Kenneth and Elna Alice (Lumpkin) W.; m. Elizabeth Sue Wheeler, Apr. 3, 1963; children: Russell Scott, Elizabeth, Melissa. BA, U. Tulsa, 1964, MA, 1968. Artist Philbrook Art Ctr., Tulsa, 1963-64, Sul Ross State Coll., Alpine, Tex., 1965-66; dir. Pine Bluff (Ark.) Art Ctr., 1966-67; prof. art, chmn. dept. Cumberland Coll., Williamsburg, Ky., 1968—; vis. artist Nicholls State U., Thibodaux, La., 1970-71; dealer Gallery BAI, N.Y.C. One-person shows include Bienville Gallery, 1971, Gallery BAI, N.Y.C., 1996; art editor Nimrod, 1964-65; editor Sculpture Quar., 1974-75. With U.S. N.G., 1957-65. Recipient purchase award Ark. Arts Ctr., 1963, Baldwin-Wallace Coll., 1973, Mus. Arte Contemporanea, Brazil, 1986, exhibit hon. Brown-Forman Corp., 1987; grantee Mellon Devel. Found., 1988. Mem. Coll. Art Assn. Home: 191 Florence Ave Williamsburg KY 40769-2718 Office: Cumberland Coll Box 7523 College Station Dr Williamsburg KY 40769

WEEKS, ALBERT LOREN, author, educator, journalist; b. Highland Park, Mich., Mar. 28, 1923; s. Albert Loren and Vera Grace (Jarvis) W. Student, U. Mich., 1942-43; MA, U. Chgo., 1949; PhD, Columbia U., 1965; cert., Russian Inst., 1960. Reporter Chgo. City News Bur., 1946; polit. analyst U.S. Dept. State, 1950-53, Free Europe Com., Inc., 1953-56; editorial asst. Newsweek mag., 1957-58; Russian tech. glossary compiler McGraw-Hill Book Co., 1960-61; prof. continuing edn. NYU, 1959-89; lectr. U.S. diplomatic history and soviet govt. Columbia U., 1951-52; mem. adv. coun. Nat. Strategy Info. Ctr., 1979-89; instr. Ringling Sch. Art and Design, 1991—; pub. spkr. S.W. Fla. Host: A Week's View of Red Press, Sta. WNBC, 1965-68; series Myths That Rule America, NBC-TV, 1979-82; author: Reading American History, 1963, The First Bolshevik: A Political Biography of Peter Tkachev, 1968, The Other Side of Coexistence: An Analysis of Russian Foreign Policy, 1970, Richard Hofstadter's The American Political Tradition and the Age of Reform, 1973, Andrei Sakharov and the Soviet Dissidents, 1975, The Troubled Detente, 1976, Solzhenitsyn's One Day in the Life of Ivan Denisovich, 1976, Myths That Rule America, 1980, War and Peace: Soviet Russia Speaks, 1983; editor/compiler Brassey's Soviet and Communist Quotations, 1987, The Soviet Nomenklatura, 1987-1991; internat. affairs editor Def. Sci. mag., 1982-85; columnist Def. Report, 1982-90; nat. sec., editor N.Y.C. Tribune, 1982-90; contbr. articles N.Y. Times, New Republic, New Leader, Annals, Russian, Slavic revs., Christian Sci. Monitor, Problems of Communism, Survey, Mil. Intelligence, Strategic Rev., World War II mag., Air Univ. Rev., L.A. Times, Washington Times, Orbis, Global Affairs, Panorama, Sarasota Herald-Tribune, Bradenton Herald, Defense and Diplomacy, Am. Intelligence Jour., USA Today, Rossiiskiye Vesti. Home: 4884 Kestral Park Cir Sarasota FL 34231-3369

WEEKS, CHARLES, JR., real estate executive, retired publishing company executive; b. Palo Alto, Calif., Apr. 25, 1919; s. Charles and Mary Alice (Johnson) W.; m. Patricia Anne Blair, Apr. 7, 1949; children: Patricia Alice, Charles Blair, Clayton Brian, Phyllis Anne. Student, U. Fla., 1936-38. Prin. Fla. Airmotive, Inc., Lantana, 1946-50; v.p., dir. Perry Publs., Inc., West Palm Beach, Fla., 1950-69; bd. dirs. Perry Oceanographics, Inc., Riveria Beach, Fla., 1969-84; dir. mgmt. bd. Flagler Nat Bank, West Palm Beach, 1992. Mem. Planning and Zoning Bd., Lantana, 1962-65; assoc. trustee John. F. Kennedy Hosp., Atlantis, Fla., 1985. Served as pilot USAF, 1943-46, ETO. Decorated Air medal; recipient Pilot Safety award Nat. Bus. Aircraft Assn., 1970, 74, 78. Mem. Quiet Birdman, Handersonville (N.C.) Country Club, Sailfish of Fla. (Palm Beach) Club. Episcopalian. Democrat. Home: PO Box 3411 Lantana FL 33465-3411 Office: Palermo-Long Realty Inc 204 E Ocean Ave Lantana FL 33465

WEEKS, EDWARD FRANCIS (TED), art appraiser, art critic, lecturer; b. Boston, Apr. 11, 1935; s. Edward Augustus and Frederica (Watriss) W.; m. Janis Hardin, June 21, 1964; 1 child, Edward Augustus Jr. BS, Columbia U., 1962; cert. in German lang., Goethe Inst. für Auslanders, Bavaria, Germany, 1962; cert. in Art Adminstrn., Harvard U., 1974; MA in Art History, NYU, 1970. Gen. and sr. curator permanent collections and exhbns. Birmingham (Ala.) Mus. of Art, 1970-84; gen. consulting curator Birmingham Mus. Art Found., 1984-85; asst. to owner Sheila Atchinson Gallery, Birmingham, 1984-86; cons. and agt. for private and corp. collectors pvt. practice, Montgomery, Ala., 1987-89; prin. Weeks Fine Arts, Art Cons. Internat., Jacksonville, Fla., 1989—; cons. The Downtown Club Collection, 1973, Birmingham Eye Found. Hosp., 1973; guide art tours Montgomery, Washington, S.E., N.Y.C., 1972—; adjunct tchr. history and appreciation of art, Auburn U., Montgomery, 1988-89. Contbr. articles to art and antiques publs.; developed numerous exhbns. and provided catalogs and brochures; art critic, 1990—; contbg. writer Folio Weekly, Jacksonville. Mem. com. on pub. murals Greater Birmingham Arts Alliance, 1977-87, Mayor's Commn. on Pub. Art, Birmingham, 1977-84, Arts Adv. Com., Birmingham-Jefferson Civic Ctr. With U.S. Army Airborne, 1957-59. Mem. Friends Am. Art (co-founder, sec. 1981, bd. dirs.), Nat. Inst. Arts and Letters, Alumni Assn. Inst. Fine Arts. Home and Office: 1786 Challen Ave Apt 1 Jacksonville FL 32205-8528

WEEKS, GWENDOLEN BRANNON, nurse, educator; b. Durham, N.C., Aug. 23, 1943; d. Gus Travers and Valerie Dunster (Baker) B.; m. John Luther Weeks, May 28, 1983; step-children: Cynthia Weeks Kelly, John Luther Weeks Jr. BS in nursing, U. N.C., 1967; MS, Med. Coll. Va., 1971. Maternity staff nurse N.C. Meml. Hosp., Chapel Hill, 1967-68; obstetrics instr. Watts Hosp. Sch. Nursing, Durham, N.C., 1968-69; maternity instr. U. N.C., Greensboro, N.C., 1971-72; clin. specialist Petersburg (Va.) Gen. Hosp., 1972-77; assoc. prof. J. Sargeant Reynolds Community Coll., Richmond, Va., 1977—; clin. assoc., staff nurse St. Mary's Hosp., Richmond, 1969-83. Bd. dirs. Jr. League of Richmond, 1969—; hospitality bd. dirs. Hist. Richmond Coun., 1987-93. Mem. Nat. AWOHN (cert. inpatient obstetric nursing 1987—), Nurses Assn. Am. Coll. Ob-Gyn. (Richmond sect. chmn. 1972-74), Nat. Soc. for Colonial Dames, George Mason Meml. Soc., Sigma Theta Tau (sec. 1974-77). Home: 3803 Timber Ridge Rd Midlothian VA 23112-4539 Office: J S Reynolds Community Coll 8th Jackson St Richmond VA 23232

WEEKS, KENT MCCUSKEY, lawyer; b. Cleve., Nov. 21, 1937; s. John Henry and Helen (McCuskey) W.; m. Karen Weeks, July 27, 1962; children: Kevin, Barton, Kristen. BA, Coll. of Wooster, 1955-59; MA, U. New Zealand, 1960; LLB, Duke U., 1961-64; PhD, Case Western Res. U., 1969. Bar: Ohio 1964, Iowa 1972, Tenn. 1976. Priv. practice Schlesinger, Galvin, Cleve., 1964-67; asst. prof. Coll. of Wooster (Ohio), 1967-72; dean, prof. U. Dubuque (Iowa), 1972-75; assoc. dir. United Methodist Higher Edn., Nashville, 1975-77; priv. practice Weeks & Anderson, Nashville, 1977—; prof. edn. George Peabody Coll., Vanderbilt U., Nashville, 1983—. Author: Adam Clayton Power & Supreme Court, 1971, Ombudsmen Around the World, 1973, Complying with Federal Law, 1995, Faculty Evaluation and the Law, 1995. Dir. Iowa Humanities Adv. Coun., 1973-75; adv. bd. Finley Hosp. Nursing, Dubuque, 1973-75; chmn., mem. bd. Pub. Edn. Davidson City, Nashville, 1980—; mem. Nashville, Pub. TV Coun., 1980—; mem. exec. com. Coun. of the Gt. City Schs., 1994—. Nat. Defense Edn. Act fellow Office Edn. 1966-67; U.S. Office of Edn. fellow Dept. Edn., Washington, 1970-71; recipient Human Rights award Human Rights Commn., Nashville, 1984. Mem. Tenn. Bar Assn., Nashville Bar Assn., Iowa Bar Assn., Am. Polit. Sci. Assn. Home: 6025 Sherwood Dr Nashville TN 37215 Office: Weeks Turner Anderson and Russell 2021 Richard Jones Rd Ste 350 Nashville TN 37215-2860

WEEKS, MARIE COOK, health and physical education educator; b. High Point, N.C., Jan. 21, 1949; d. Paul Hue Cook and Beulah Edna (Smith) Townsend; m. Lewis Tirey Weeks, June 5, 1970; children: Gina, Corby. BS in Edn., Western Carolina U., 1971. Tchr. grades 6,7,8, math. science, health, physical edn. Ramseur (N.C.) Elem. Sch., 1971-91; tchr. grades 6,7,8, health and physical edn. Archdale-Trinity Middle Sch., Trinity, N.C., 1991—; coach girls softball and volleyball Randolph County Schs., Asheboro, N.C., 1971—; mentor tchr. Randolph County Schs., Asheboro, 1989—; student tchr. supr. Archdale Trinity Middle Sch. 1993—, head of health and phys. edn. dept., 1993—. Coach girls' softball Hillsville (N.C.) Civitan's Youth Softball League, 1984—. Named Ramseur Sch. Tchr. of Yr., Ramseur Faculty, 1983, 89, Outstanding Young Educator Asheboro/Randolph County, Asheboro Jaycees, 1989. Mem. NEA, N.C. AAHPERD, Nat. Fedn. Coaches, N.C. Assn. Educators. Baptist. Home: 3725 Lynn Oaks Dr Trinity NC 27370-9445 Office: Archdale-Trinity Mid Sch 5105 Archdale Rd Trinity NC 27370

WEEKS, MARTA JOAN, priest; b. Buenos Aires, May 24, 1930; came to U.S., 1932; d. Frederick Albert and Anne (Newman) Sutton; m. Lewis Austin Weeks, Aug. 17, 1951; children: Kermit Austin, Leslie Anne. BA in Polit. Sci., Stanford U., 1951; MDiv, Episcopal Theol. Sem. S.W., 1991. Ordained priest Episcopal Ch., 1992. Legal libr., sec. Mene Grande Oil Co., Caracas, Venezuela, 1948; English tchr. Centro-Venezolano Americano, Caracas, 1948; sec. Household Fin. Corp., Salt Lake City, 1951; legal sec. McKelvey & McKelvey Attys., Durango, Colo., 1952; sec., dir. Weeks Air Mus., Miami, Fla., 1985—; chaplain Jackson Meml. Hosp., 1992-93; priest-at-large Episcopal Diocese of S.E. Fla., until 1996; interim asst. St. James Episcopal Ch., Salt Lake City, 1994-95. Trustee Beloit (Wis.) Coll., 1980-82, U. Miami, 1983-88, 95—, Bishop Gray Inns, Lake Worth and Davenport, Fla., 1992—. Mem. Am. Soc. Order St. John of Jerusalem. Address: 7350 SW 162nd St Miami FL 33157-3820

WEEMS, FRANCES ELIZABETH, lawyer, county official; b. Lutherville, Md., Mar. 3, 1945; d. Charles Louis and Mary-Elizabeth Kathleen (Bentley) W. BA, U. Ala., 1977; JD, Miles Law Sch., 1989. With Jefferson County Commn., Birmingham, Ala., 1976—, community devel. specialist; bd. dirs. Indsl. Devel. Bd., Birmingham, 1990—. Composer and lyricist: Message to His Deciples, 1978; photographer: Lest We Forget, 1980 (award 1980). Sponsor, trainer Spl. Olympics, Birmingham, 1979—; bd. dirs. Kiwanis Internat., Bessemer, Ala., 1990. Recipient Meritorious Svc. award United Negro Coll. Fund, Inc., 1990; named Minority Advocate of Yr. U.S. Dept. Commerce, 1991, Minority Enterprise Devel. award, 1992, 93. Mem. Nat. Assn. County Community and Econ. Devel., Assn. Pub. Adminstrs., Delta Theta Phi. Roman Catholic. Office: Jefferson County Commn 805 22nd St N Birmingham AL 35203-2303

WEEMS, JOHN EDWARD, writer; b. Grand Prairie, Tex., Nov. 2, 1924; s. J. Eddie and Anna Lee (Scott) W.; m. Jane Ellen Homeyer, Sept. 11, 1946; children: Donald (dec.), Carol, Mary, Barbara, Janet. BJ, U. Tex., 1948, M.Journalism, 1949; MA in Libr. Sci., Fla. State U., 1954. Tel. editor Temple (Tex.) Daily Telegram, 1950; instr. Calif. State Poly. Coll., San Dimas, 1950-51; night news editor San Angelo (Tex.) Standard-Times, 1951; copy editor Dallas Morning News, 1952-53; asst. prof., head cataloger main library Baylor U., 1954-57; asst. prof. U. Ala., also asst. mgr. Ala. Press Assn., 1957-58; asst. to dir. U. Tex. Press, 1958-68; prof. English, Baylor U., 1968-71, lectr. creative writing, fall 1979; reference librarian McLennan Community Coll., Waco, Tex., 1969-70; freelance writer, 1971—. With USNR, 1943-46, 51-52; lt. Res. (ret.). Am. Philos. Soc. grantee, 1964. Fellow Tex. State Hist. Assn., Tex. Inst. Letters; mem. PEN, Nat. Book Critics Circle, Authors Guild, Western Writers Am., Sigma Delta Chi, Beta Phi Mu. Author: A Weekend in September, 1957; The Fate of the Maine, 1958; Race for the Pole, 1960; Peary: The Explorer and the Man, 1967; Men Without Countries, 1969; Dream of Empire (Amon G. Carter award), 1971; To Conquer a Peace: The War Between the United States and Mexico (Richard Fleming award), 1974; Death Song, 1976; The Tornado, 1977; (with John Biggers and Carroll Simms) Black Art in Houston, 1978; "If You Don't Like the Weather," 1986; editor: A Texas Christmas: A Miscellany of Art, Poetry, Fiction, Vol. I, 1983, Vol. II, 1986; (San Antonio Conservation Soc. Spl. award), The Story of Texas, 1986, Austin (Texas): 1839-1989, 1989 (Tex. Inst. Letters Barbara McCombs Lon Tinkle award lifetime Writing achievement 1989). Address: 2012 Collins St Waco TX 76710-2626

WEGER, WILLIAM JOHN, public relations executive; b. Washington, Nov. 11, 1960; s. Adolph John and Janet Virginia (Warren) W. BS in Journalism, U. Md., 1985; MA in Pub. Comm., Am. U., 1995. Reporter Daily Banner, Cambridge, Md., 1984-85; writer, media rels. asst. ARC Nat. Hdqs., Washington, 1985-87; publs. editor, writer Aspen Pubs., Inc., Rockville, Md., 1987-89; dir. comm. Hardwood, Plywood and Veneer Assn., Reston, Va., 1989-91; dir. pub. affairs Am. Trucking Assns., Inc., Alexandria, Va., 1992-94; mgr. media rels. for Mass. Transit Adminstrn. Md. Dept. Transp., Balt., 1994—; stringer AP, Easton, Md., 1984, Times Jour. Newspapers, Springfield, Va., 1985-87. Fundraiser, vol. Muscular Dystrophy Assn., Fairfax, Va., 1985—. Recipient 1st place best newspaper award for ARC news Soc. Nat. Assn. Publs., 1986, dedicated svc. award MADD, 1994. Mem. Pub. Rels. Soc. Am., Am. Soc. Assn. Execs. Home: 3304 Pendleton Dr Silver Spring MD 20902-2427 Office: Mass Transit Adminstrn Md Dept Transp Baltimore MD 21203

WEGMANN, MARY KATHERINE, art director; b. New Orleans, Sept. 18, 1948; d. Joseph A. and Catherine (Lyons) W. BA in English lit., Spring Hill Coll., Mobile, Ala., 1970; MA in English Lit., U. New Orleans, 1972. Asst. mgr., actor, dir. La Mise En Scene Theatre, New Orleans, 1970-72; loan processor First Homestead Savs. and Loan, New Orleans, 1972-74; home improvement contractor Superior Distbrs., New Orleans, 1974-75; adminstr. Freeman-Anacker, Inc., New Orleans, 1975-77; assoc. dir. Contemporary Arts Ctr., New Orleans, 1978-91, acting dir., 1986-88, 88-89; owner MK Arts Co., New Orleans, 1991—; cons. Junebug Prodn., New Orleans, 1985-93, Alternate Roots, Atlanta, 1986, 92, Cultural Arts Coun. Houston, 1988-89, Seven Stages Performing Arts Ctr., Atlanta, 1989, 91, Nat. Endowment Arts, Washington, 1983-93, Assn. Performing Arts Presenters, 1994, Arts Coun. New Orleans, 1991, 92, La. Philharm. Orch., New Orleans, 1992, Melanie Beene and Assocs., 1991-93, La. Divsn. Arts, 1992—, Arts Coun. New Orleans, 1991—; mem. various panels, juries and adv. coms., 1980—. Bd. dirs. Dog & Pony Theatre Co., New Orleans, 1993—; bd. dirs., treas. Junebug Prodns., 1985—. Office: MK Arts Co PO Box 71914 New Orleans LA 70172-1914

WEGNER, JUDITH WELCH, law educator, dean; b. Hartford, Conn., Feb. 14, 1950; d. John Raymond and Ruth (Thulen) Welch; m. Warren W. Wegner, Oct. 13, 1972. BA with honors, U. Wis., 1972; JD, UCLA, 1976. Bar: Calif. 1976, D.C. 1977, N.C. 1988, U.S. Supreme Ct. 1980, U.S. Ct. Appeals. Law clk. to Judge Warren Ferguson, U.S. Dist. Ct. for So. Dist. Calif., L.A., 1976-77; atty. Office Legal Counsel and Land & Natural Resources Divsn. U.S. Dept. Justice, Washington, 1977-79; spl. asst. to sec. U.S. Dept. Edn., Washington, 1979-80; vis. assoc. prof. U. Iowa Coll. Law, Iowa City, 1981; asst. prof. U. N.C. Sch. Law, Chapel Hill, 1981-84, assoc. prof., 1984-88, prof., 1988—, assoc. dean, 1986-88, dean, 1989—; spkr. in field. Chief comment editor UCLA Law Rev., 1975-76; contbr. articles to legal publs. Mem. ABA (chmn. planning com. African Law Sch. Initiative 1994, co-chmn. planning com. 1994 mid-yr. deans meeting sect. on legal edn. and admission to bar), AAUP, N.C. Assn. Women Attys. (Gweneth Davis award 1989), N.C. State Bar Assn., Assn. Am. Law Schs. (mem. exec. com. sect. on law & edn. 1985-88, mem. exec. com. sect. on local govt. law 1989-92, mem. accreditation com. 1986-88, chmn. 1989-91, program chmn. 1992 ann. meeting, program chmn. 1994 ann. meeting, mem. exec. com. 1992-94, pres. 1995), Soc. Am. Law Tchrs., Nat. League Cities (coun.-mentor program 1989-91), Women's Internat. Forum, Order of Coif (nat. exec. com. 1989-91), Phi Beta Kappa. Democrat. Office: U NC Sch Law Van Hecke-Wettach Hall Campus Box 3380 Chapel Hill NC 27599-3380

WEHNER, HENRY OTTO, III, pharmacist, consultant; b. Birmingham, Ala., Mar. 3, 1942; s. Henry O. Jr. and Carolyn (Kirkland) W.; m. Sammye Ruth Murphy, June 8, 1974 (div. July 1989). AA, Daytona Beach Community Coll., 1967; BS in Biology, North Ga. Coll., Dahlonega, 1971; BS in Pharmacy, U. Ga., 1978. Registered pharmacist, Fla., Ga.; cert. sci. tchr. grades 7-12, Ga. Tchr. biology Irwin County High Sch., Ocilla, Ga., 1971-75; extern Eckerd Drugs, Athens, Ga., 1977; intern/extern St. Mary's Hosp., Athens, 1977; pharmacy intern Button Gwinnett Hosp., Lawrenceville, Ga., 1978; co-owner, mgr. Hiawassee (Ga.) Pharmacy, 1978-79; staff pharmacist Dyal's Pharmacy, Daytona Beach, Fla., 1979, Little Drug Co., New Smyrna Beach, Fla., 1979-80; staff pharmacist, mgr. Super X Drugs, New Smyrna Beach, 1980-81; staff pharmacist Fish Meml. Hosp., New Smyrna Beach, 1981-92, Halifax Med. Ctr., Daytona Beach, Fla., 1992—. With USAF, 1961-65. Mem. Am. Pharm. Assn., Fla. Soc. Hosp. Pharmacists, Volusia County Pharm. Assn., Ea. Shores Soc. Hosp. Pharmacists (charter, pres. 1995-96), Eastern Shores Fla. Soc. Hosp. Pharmacists, Phi Lambda Sigma, Phi Theta Kappa. Methodist. Office: Halifax Med Ctr PO Box 1350 303 N Clyde Morris Blvd Daytona Beach FL 32114-2709

WEHRS, ROGER E., physician; b. Seward, Nebr., Mar. 26, 1925; s. Edward and Maurine Matilda (Miller) W.; m. Mary Ann Pettee, June 18, 1950; children: Donald, Suzanne. BS, U. Nebr., Lincoln, 1949; MD, U. Nebr., Omaha, 1952. Diplomate Am. Bd. Otolaryngology; lic. physician, Okla., Kans., Calif. Intern Alameda County Hosp., Oakland, Calif., 1952; resident in otolaryngology U. Kans. Med. Ctr., Kansas City, 1952-55; physician, specializing in diseases and surgery of the ear Tulsa, 1958—; assoc. clin. prof. otology Tulsa br. U. Okla. Coll. Medicine; instr. in field. Contbr. articles to profl. jours., chpts. to books. Served to 1st lt. M.C., U.S. Army, 1953-55. Fellow Am. Acad. Ophthalmology and Otolaryngology, Am. Laryngol., Rhinol. and Otol. Soc.; mem. AMA, Am. Otological Soc., Okla. State Med. Soc., Tulsa County Med. Soc., Oosclerosis Study Club (sec.-reas. 1986-87, pres. 1989-90), Triological Soc. (v.p. Middle sec.). Office: Otology Assocs Inc 6465 S Yale Ave Tulsa OK 74136-7822

WEI, CHENG-I, toxicologist, microbiologist; b. Taiwan, July 22, 1948; came to U.S., 1974; s. Chin-Shoei and Chin-ing (Tseng) W.; m. Wen-pei Chien, Dec. 26, 1973; children: Alfreda, Kane. BS, Tunghai (Taiwan) U., 1970; MS, Nat. Taiwan U., Taipei, 1972; PhD, U. Calif., Davis, 1979. Asst. prof. dept. food sci. and human nutrition U. Fla., Gainesville, 1981-85, assoc. prof. dept. food sci. and human nutrition, 1985-89, prof. dept. food sci. and human nutrition, 1989—. Contbr. rsch. articles to profl. jours. Mem. Inst. Food Technologists, Am. Soc. Microbiology, Am. Inst. Fishery Rsch. Biologists. Office: Univ of Fla Dept Food Sci Nutri Gainesville FL 32611

WEI, JOHN PIN, surgery educator; b. Hsinchu, Taiwan, Oct. 20, 1958; U. S. citizen; m. Sharon Chiang, June 21, 1986; children: Jeremy, Emily. BA summa cum laude, Boston U., 1982, MD, 1982. Diplomate Am. Bd. Surgery; lic. physician, Ga. Intern Boston U. Med. Ctr., 1982-83, resident in gen. surgery, 1983-87; fellow in immunotherapy Nat. Cancer Inst., Bethesda, Md., 1987-88, fellow in surg. oncology, 1988-90; asst. prof. surg. oncology, dept. surgery Med. Coll. Ga., Augusta, 1990-94; assoc. prof. surg. oncology dept. surgery Med. Coll. Ga., Augusta, 1994—, chief sect. of surg. oncology, 1996—. Contbr. numerous articles to profl. jours. Fellow ACS; mem. AMA, AAAS, SHNS, AAES, IAES, ISS, Soc. Surg. Oncologists, Am. Soc. Clin. Oncologists, Assn. for Acad. Surgery, Soc. for Study of Breast Diseases, Southeastern Surg. Congress, Clin. Immunology Soc., Mass. Med. Soc., Med. Assn. Ga., Richmond County Med. Soc., So. Med. Assn., So. Assn. for Oncology, Moretz Surg. Soc. Home: 3673 Cypress Point Dr Martinez GA 30907-9020 Office: Med Coll Ga BIW 442 Dept Surgery Augusta GA 30912

WEI, MING, epidemiology researcher; b. Nanning, China, May 5, 1958; came to U.S., 1989; s. Shi-Phan Wei and Wan-Yan Liu; m. Kun Wang, July 14, 1987; children: Murlin K., Glyn K. MD, Guang Xi Med. Coll., Nanning, China, 1983, MS, 1986; MPH, U. S.C., 1992. Physician Guang Med. Coll. Hosp., Nanning, China, 1986-89; med. assoc. Iwate Med. U., Marioca, Japan, 1989; path. assoc. U. Pitts., 1989-91; rsch. asst. prof. U. S.C., Columbia, 1993-94; fellow U. Tex. Health Sci. Ctr., San Antonio, 1994—. Contbr. articles to profl. jours. Mem. AAAS, Am. Diabetes Assn., Soc. Epidemiol. Rsch., Chinese Med. Assn. Home: 2626 Babcock San Antonio TX 78229 Office: U Tex Health Sci Ctr Dept Medicine/Clin Epidem 7703 Floyd Curl Dr San Antonio TX 78284

WEIBLEN, MICHAEL DON, electrical engineer; b. Castroville, Tex., Dec. 23, 1948; s. Arthur Fritz and Adeline Helen Weiblen; m. Judith Ann Toudre, Dec. 26, 1970; children: Amanda Lee, Natalie Kate, Lorin Michael. BSEE, Tex. A&I U., 1972. Jr. engr. City Pub. Svc., San Antonio, Tex., 1972-77; sr. engr. Alexander Engring., San Antonio, 1977-80; chief engr. Medina Elec. Coop., Hondo, Tex., 1980-87, mgr. engring., 1987-94; so. regional sales mgr. ILEX Sys., Inc., 1994; sr. applications engr. Cannon Techs., Inc., 1994—. Mem. IEEE, Tex. Soc. Profl. Engrs., Elec. Reliability Coun. Tex., Tex. Elec. Coop. Engrs. Assn. (pres. 1991-93). Roman Catholic. Home and Office: 175 Cr 373 Rio Medina TX 78066-2529

WEIDEMEYER, CARLETON LLOYD, lawyer; b. Hebbville, Md., June 12, 1933. BA in Polit. Sci., U. Md., 1958; JD, Stetson U., 1961. Bar: Fla. 1961, D.C. 1971, U.S. Dist. Ct. (mid. dist.) Fla. 1963, U.S. Ct. Appeals (5th cir.) 1967, U.S. Ct. Appeals (D.C. cir.) 1976, U.S. Supreme Ct. 1966, U.S. Ct. Appeals (11th cir.) 1982. Research asst. Fla. 2d Dist Ct. Appeals, 1961-65; ptnr. Kalle and Weidemeyer, St. Petersburg, Fla., 1965-68; asst. pub. defender 6th Jud. Cir., Fla., 1966-69, 81-83; ptnr. Wightman, Weidemeyer, Jones, Turnbull and Cobb, Clearwater, Fla., 1968-82; pres. Carleton L. Weidemeyer, P.A. Law Office, 1982—; guest lectr., Stetson U., 1978-80; lectr. estate planning seminars; bd. dirs. 1st Nat. Bank and Trust Co., 1974-78, Fla. Bank of Commerce, 1973-77. Author: (handbook) Arbitration of Entertainment Claims, Baltimore County's Second District, The Emerging Thirties, 1990, Area History, Baltimore County, 1990; editor: Ad Lib mag., 1978-81; contbr. numerous articles to profl. jours. & geneal. pubs.; performer This Is Your Navy Radio Show, Memphis, 1951-52; leader Polka Dots, The Jazz Notes, 1976—; mem. St. Paul Ch. Orch., Fla. Hist. Soc., 1973—, Md. Hist. Soc., 1990—; performer Clearwater Jazz Holiday, 1980, 81, co-chmn., 1981. Bd. advisors Musicians Ins. Trust; trustee Francis G. Prasse Meml. Scholarship Trust, 1984—. Served with USN, 1951-54. Mem. SAR, Musicians Assn. Clearwater (pres. 1976-81), Fla.-Ga. Conf. Musicians (sec., treas. 1974-76), NRA, ABA (sr. bar sect.), Fed. Bar Assn., Fla. State Hist. Soc., Md. Hist. Soc., Greater St. Petersburg Musicians Assn., Clearwater Fla. Bar Assn. (probate divsn.), Am. Fedn. Musicians (internat. law com.; pres. so. conf. musicians 1979-80), Clearwater Genealogy Soc., Pinellas Genealogical Soc. (lectr. on genealogical rsch.), Md. Geneal. Soc., Pa. Geneal. Soc., Pinellas (Fla.) Geneal. Soc. (lectr. 1995—), Balt. County Geneal. Soc., Lancaster (Pa.) Mennonite Hist. Soc., Navy Hurricane Hunters, Sons Union Vets. Civil War, Md. Hist. Soc., Catonsville (Md.) Hist. Soc., Am. Legion, German Am. Geneal. Assn. D.A.V. Fleet Res., Masons, Egypt Temple Shrine, Scottish Rite, Moose, Sertoma (bd. dirs. Clearwater chpt. 1984-86, v.p. 1989-92), Phi Delta Phi, Sigma Pi, Kappa Kappa Psi. Home: 2261 Belleair Rd Clearwater FL 34624-2761 Office: 501 S Fort Harrison Ave Clearwater FL 34616

WEIGAND, DENNIS ALLEN, dermatologist, educator; b. Alva, Okla., Mar. 17, 1939; s. Carl and Helen J. (Wesner) W.; m. Janet DeAnn White, July 7, 1961; children—Christopher, Rebecca. B.S., Northwestern Okla. State Coll., 1960; M.D., U. Okla., 1963. Diplomate Am. Bd. Dermatology, Am. Bd. Dermatopathology. Intern, St. Francis Hosp., Wichita, Kans., 1963-64; resident in dermatology U. Okla. Health Sci. Ctr., Oklahoma City, 1964-67; asst. prof. dermatology U. Okla., Oklahoma City, 1970-74, assoc. prof. dermatology, 1974-78, adj. prof. pathology, 1977—, prof. dermatology, 1978—, vice-head dept. dermatology; chief dermatology service VA Med. Ctr., Oklahoma City, 1978—. Served to maj. U.S. Army, 1968-70. Decorated Army Commendation medal. Fellow Am. Acad. Dermatology, Am. Soc. Dermatopathology; mem. Am. Dermatological Assn., AMA, Alpha Omega Alpha. Episcopalian. Contbr. articles to books and profl. jours. Home: 141 Barbara Dr Edmond OK 73013-4437 Office: 619 NE 13th St Oklahoma City OK 73104-5001

WEIGEL, PAUL HENRY, biochemistry educator, researcher, consultant; b. N.Y.C., Aug. 11, 1946; s. Helmut and Jeanne (Wakeman) W.; m. Nancy Shulman, June 15, 1968 (div. Dec. 1987); 1 child, Dana J.; m. Janet Oka, May 17, 1992. BA in Chemistry, Cornell U., 1968; MS in Biochemistry, Johns Hopkins U., Balt., 1969, PhD in Biochemistry, 1975. NIH postdoctoral fellow Johns Hopkins U., Balt., 1975-78; asst. prof. U. Tex. Med. Br., Galveston, Tex., 1978-82, assoc. prof., 1982-87; prof. biochemistry and cell biology U. Tex. Med. Br., Galveston, 1987-94, vice chmn. dept. human biol. chemistry and genetics, 1990-93, acting chmn. dept. human biology, chemistry and genetics, 1992-93; prof., chmn. dept. biochemistry and molecular biology U. Okla. Health Scis. Ctr., Okalahoma City, 1994—; mem. NIH Pathobiochemistry Study Sect., Washington, 1985-87; cons. Teltech, Mpls., 1985—. Contbr. articles to profl. jours.; patentee in field. Treas. Bayou Chateau Neighborhood Assn., Dickinson, Tex., 1981-83, v.p., 1983-84, pres., 1984-86. With U.S. Army, 1969-71. Grantee NIH, 1979—, Office Naval Rsch., 1983-87, Tex. Biotech., 1989-94; recipient Disting. Tchr. award U. Tex. Med. Br., 1989, Disting. Rsch. award, 1989. Mem. Am. Chem. Soc., Am. Soc. Cell Biology, Am. Soc. Biochemistry and Molecular Biology. Democrat. Lutheran. Home: 817 Hollowdale Edmond OK 73003-3022 Office: U Okla Health Scis Ctr Dept Biochem & Mol Biology BMSB Rm 860 Oklahoma City OK 73190

WEIL, JESSE LEO, physicist, educator; b. Ann Arbor, Mich., Dec. 9, 1931; s. Herbert Louis and Pearl Esther (Arnovits) W.; m. Esther Kirkland, Jan. 23, 1960 (div. 1984); children: Janna G., Alexandra A. BS, Calif. Inst. Tech., 1952; PhD, Columbia U., 1959. Rsch. assoc. Rice U., Houston, 1959-60, 61-63, Hamburg (Germany) U., 1960-61; asst. prof. U. Ky., Lexington, 1963-65, assoc. prof., 1965-73, prof. physics, 1973—; rsch. assoc. Rutherford Lab., Eng., 1971-72. Contbr. articles to profl. jours. NSF grantee, 1965—. Mem. AAUP (chpt. pres. 1975-76, 1996—), Am. Phys. Soc., Sigma Xi. Office: Univ of Kentucky Dept Physics/Astronomy Lexington KY 40506

WEILAND, STEPHEN CASS, lawyer; b. San Antonio, Apr. 29, 1948; s. Frank H. and Eileen (Pitman) W.; m. Jessica Buhler; children: Bradley, Cartwright, Kathryn. AB, Coll. William and Mary, Williamsburg, Va., 1970; JD, U. Tex., 1973. Bar: Tex. 1973, D.C. 1974. Trial atty. U.S. Dept. Justice, Washington, 1973-80; asst. dir. Commodity Futures Trading Commn., Washington, 1980-81; chief counsel U.S. Senate Permanent Subcom. on Investigations, Washington, 1981-85; of counsel Matthews & Branscomb, Corpus Christi, Tex., 1985-86; litigation ptnr. Jackson & Walker, Dallas, 1986—. Mem. ABA (mem. white collar crime com., criminal justice sect.). Republican. Office: Jackson & Walker 901 Main St Ste 6000 Dallas TX 75202-3748*

WEILER, HAROLD EDWARD, municipal executive, military officer; b. Medford, Wis., Feb. 9, 1934; s. Nicholas Theodore and Elsa Elizabeth (Bartelt) W.; m. Dolores Elizabeth Easton, June 15, 1963; children: Drew, Deborah, Richard. BS, U. Alaska, 1955; MS, Shippensburg (Pa.) U., 1975. Commd.2d lt. U.S. Army, 1955, advanced through grades to col., 1977, advisor to N.G., 1975-77; comdr. Support Ctr., Frankfurt, Germany, 1977-79; ret. U.S. Army, 1979; asst. city mgr. City of Harken Heights, Tex., 1979-84, city mgr., 1984-92; city mgr. City of Bridgeport, W.Va., 1994—; advisor Area Emergency Med. Svc. Dirs., Killeen, Tex., 1990-92. Dir. Sch. Improvement Coun., Bridgeport, 1994-96. Decorated Legion of Merit (3), Bronze Star (3). Mem. Internat. City Mgrs. Assn., W.Va. City Mgrs. Assn., VFW, Am. Legion, Kiwanis Internat. (dir. 1979-92). Office: City of Bridgeport 156 Thompson Dr Bridgeport WV 26330

WEILER, JAMES G., computer scientist; b. Fargo, N.D., Apr. 11, 1954; s. F.S. and Lorraine M. W. Grad., DeVry Inst., 1978. Data ctr. support technician Burroughs Santa Barbara Plant, Calif., 1978-79; lead data ctr. technician Burroughs Santa Barbara Plant, 1979-81, Burroughs Rancho Bernardo Plant, Calif., 1981-83; programmer, editor, product mgr. Softdisk Pub., Shreveport, La., 1983-92; editl. dir. Softdisk Pub., Shreveport, 1992, editor, product mgr., 1992-94, online sales, 1994—. Editor The Naked Word, 1995—. Office: Softdisk Pub 606 Common St Shreveport LA 71101

WEIMAR, ROBERT HENRY, counselor, clinical hypnotherapist; b. Chgo., July 4, 1946. BA in Psychology, U. Ill., 1968; MS in Community Mental Health, No. Ill. U., 1971. Cert. med. hypnotherapist, cert. clin. mental health counselor. Cons., edn. coord. No. Community Mental Health Ctr., Ashland, Wis., 1978-79; pvt. practice counselor and cons. Ashland, 1981-88; alcohol prevention coord. Bad River Chippewa Tribe, Odanah, Wis., 1982-88; prodr. freelance radio programs Ashland, Wis., 1984-90, Lynchburg, Va., 1984-90; mental health counselor Ctrl. Health (Bridges), Lynchburg, 1988-90, mental health cons. 1990—; coord. Va. Divsn. Drug Abuse Control, Richmond, 1972-74; planner N.Y. State Drug Abuse Control Commn., N.Y.C., 1974-75. Contbr. numerous articles to profl. jours. Recipient Outstanding Svc. award Nat. Indian Bd. on Alcohol and Drug Abuse, 1987. Office: Hypnosis For Health 3313 Old Forest Rd Lynchburg VA 24501

WEIMER, MICHAEL JOHN, researcher, writer, editor; b. Washington, Feb. 19, 1945; s. Clifford E. Sr. and LaRue (McFadden) W. BA, Yale U., 1967, M.Phil., 1969, PhD, 1973. Vis. asst. prof. U. Oreg., Eugene, 1973-74; asst. prof. C.W. Post Coll./L.I. U., Old Brookville, N.Y., 1977-80; adj. asst. prof. Nassau County C.C., Garden City, N.Y., 1980-81, Hofstra U., Hempstead, N.Y., 1981-82; vis. assoc. prof. Keimung U., Taegu, Republic of Korea, 1982-88; vis. prof. Keimung U., 1988-90; rsch. asst. NYU, N.Y.C., 1981-82; lectr. English Lang. and Lit. Assn. Korea, 1984; instr. Yale Transitional Yr. Program, New Haven, 1970-71; reader Folger Shakespeare Libr., Washington, 1993. Contbr. articles to profl. jours. Vista vol. Action/Vista, Cheyenne, Wyoming, 1971-72. Woodrow Wilson Nat. fellow Woodrow Wilson Found., Princeton, N.J., 1967. Mem. Phi Beta Kappa. Home: PO Box 1844 Alexandria VA 22314-1844

WEIMER, PETER DWIGHT, mediator, lawyer, corporate executive; b. Grand Rapids, Mich., Oct. 14, 1938; s. Glen E. and Clarabel (Kauffman) W.; children: Melanie, Kim; m. Judith Anne Minor. BA, Bridgewater Coll., 1962; JD, Howard U., 1969. Assoc. counsel Loporto & Weimer Ltd., Manassas, Va., 1970-75; chief counsel Weimer & Cheatle Ltd., Manassas, 1975-79, Peter D. Weimer, P.C., Manassas, 1979-82; pres., mediator Mediation Ltd., Manassas, 1981—; pres. Citation Properties, Inc., Manassas, 1971-93; pres. Preferred Rsch. of No. Va., Inc., 1985-89, Pro Rsch. Inc., 1989-93, Pro Mgmt., Inc., 1990—; cons. Continental Title & Escrow, Inc., 1992—, Pegusas Title & Escrow, Inc., 1994-95, Pro, Inc., 1995—. Address: PO Box 1616 Manassas VA 20108-1616

WEINACHT, JOHN WILLIAM, lawyer; b. Orange, Tex., Nov. 13, 1963; s. Charles and Mary Ann W.; m. Luz Marina Lara, Aug. 21, 1985; children: Lara, Jake, Claire. BA, U. Tex., 1987; JD, Baylor U., 1989. Bar: Tex. 1989, N. Mex. 1994, U.S. Dist. Ct. (all dists.) Tex. 1993, U.S. Dist. Ct. N. Mex. 1994, U.S. Ct. Appeals (5th cir.) 1993, U.S. Ct. Appeals (10th cir.) 1995, U.S. Ct. Internat. Trade 1995; U.S. Supreme Ct. 1995. Atty. pvt. practice, Pecos, Tex., 1989—; county atty. Reeves County, Pecos, Tex., 1993—. Mem. ABA, Tex. Trial Lawyers Assn., Reeves County Bar Assn., Trans-Pecos Bar Assn. Democrat. Office: 420 S Cypress Pecos TX 79772

WEINBERG, BELLA REBECCA, art gallery director, writer; b. N.Y.C., Aug. 30, 1912; d. Alexis and Maria (Okin) Kudisch; m. William Weinberg (dec.). Student, Bklyn. Coll., 1930-34, N.Y. U. City Coll. Workshop Md. Sch. Art-Design, Silver Spring, Md., 1940—; tutor U. Md., College Park, Md., 1980-85; writer on small museums in Washington Voice of Am.; docent Nat. Gallery of Art, Hirshhorn Mus., 1960—; dir., gallery owner Chevy Chase Galerie, Bethesda, Md., 1963-69; art dir. W.J. Sloane Fine Arts Gallery, Washington, 1969-71; instr. Tonalities in Fabrics, Sarasota, 1991; tutor in reading and art Gulf Gate Elem. Sch., 1996. One-person shows include Cosmos Club, Washington, 1975, Berry Coll., Rome, Ga., 1992; exhibited in Art in Embassy showings U.S. State Dept. abroad, 1969-80, Grand Piano Art Gallery, West Venice; permanent exhbns. at Sarasota Opera House, Gulf Gate Libr.; exhibited in circus show Robarts ARena, 1995; designer note cares for Sarasota Opera House. mem., dir. JCC Greater Washington Fine Arts Gallery, Rockville, Md., 1971-77; vol., tutor Pineview Sch., Sarasota, Fla., 1986-89, bd. dirs. Pub. Libr., Sarasota, 1986-89, bd. mem. Art Orgn., Sarasota, 1989-93. Recipient Achievement award, 1969, Arvida award, 1986, Painting award Renewal, Venice, Fla., 1991, Jazz award Batik, 1994. Mem. Sarasota Arts Ctr (exhbn. mem.), Women's Caucus for Arts. Democrat. Jewish. Home: 6553 Gulf Gate Pl Apt 256 Sarasota FL 34231-5849

WEINBERG, FLORENCE MAY, modern language and literature educator; b. Alamogordo, N.Mex., Dec. 3, 1933; d. Steven Horace and Olive Gladys (Edgington) Byham; m. Kurt Weinberg, May 8, 1955 (dec. Feb. 1996). PhD, U. Rochester, 1968. Instr. modern langs. St. John Fisher Coll., Rochester, N.Y., 1967, asst. prof. modern langs., 1967-71, assoc. prof. modern langs., 1971-75, prof. modern langs., 1975-89, dept. chmn. modern langs., 1972-79, dir. internat. studies, 1983-86; prof. French and Spanish Trinity U., San Antonio, Tex., 1989—, chair modern langs. and lits., 1989-95. Author: The Wine and the Will, 1972, Gargantua in a Convex Mirror, 1986, The Cave, 1986. Recipient grant-in-aid Am. Coun. Learned Socs., 1974-75, sr. fellowship NEH, 1979-80, grant NEH, 1983, Rsch. grant Ludwig Vogelstein Found., 1986. Mem. MLA, N.E. MLA (sec. French 16th century sect. 1978, chmn. 1979), South Ctrl. MLA, Am. Assn. Tchrs. French, Renaissance Soc. Am. Democrat. Home: 331 Royal Oaks Dr San Antonio TX 78209-1623 Office: Trinity Univ 715 Stadium Dr San Antonio TX 78212-3104

WEINBERG, JOSEPH ARNOLD, pediatrician, educator; b. Newark, N.J., Sept. 30, 1947; married; 2 children. BA, Johns Hopkins U., 1969; MD, Harvard U., 1973. Diplomate Am. Bd. Pediats., Am. Bd. Emergency Medicine; cert. ACLS instr., Advanced Pediat. Life Support, Pediat. Advanced Life Support. Intern then resident in pediats. Harbor Gen. Hosp., Torrance, Calif., 1973-76; pvt. practice Twin Falls Idaho, 1978-80, Willimantic, Conn., 1980-81; mem. med. staff East Tenn. Children's Hosp., Knoxville, 1981-85, assoc. dir. pediatric ICU, 1984-85; dir. emergency svcs., mem. med. staff Le Bonheur Children's Med. Ctr., Memphis, 1985—; mem. med. staff Twin Falls Clinic and Hosp., 1978-80, Magic Valley Meml. Hosp., Twin Falls, 1978-79, Windham Cmty. Meml. Hosp., Willimantic, Conn., 1979-80; affiliate faculty, asst. prof. pediatrics U. Tenn., Memphis, 1985-90, affiliate faculty, assoc. prof., 1990—, dir. pediatric emergency medicine fellowship, 1987-92; mem. Harvard Schs. Com., Memphis, 1986—, chmn., 1987-89, 91-92; cons. State of Tenn., 1990—; lectr. in field. Mem. editorial bd. Pediatric Emergency Trends, 1987—; reviewer jours.; contbr. articles to profl. jours. and abstracts. Mem. Knox County Ambulance Commn., Knoxville, 1982-85; mem. med. adv. com. Knox County Indigent Care Program, 1982-85; mem. med. rev. and disaster coms. MidSouth EMS Coun., 1985—, chmn. quality assurance com., 1992—; mem. emergency med. adv. com. Shelby County, Tenn., 1987—; mem. Tenn. Pediat. Trauma Ctr. Task Force, 1987-88; mem. med. adv. bd. So. Poison Ctr., 1990—; chairperson subcom. pediat. emergency care Tenn. Licensing Bd. for Health Care Facilities, 1993—; mem. EMS Bd. State Tenn.; mem. sub-bd. pediat. emergency medicine Am. Bd. Pediatrics. Fellow Am. Acad. Pediats. (com. pediat. emergency medicine 1988-96, chmn. 1992-96), Am. Coll. Emergency Physicians; mem. AMA, ASTM, Am. Trauma Soc., Am. Heart Assn. (com. 1985-95), MidSouth Pediats. Soc., Tenn. Pediat. Soc., Tenn. Med. Assn. (com. 1983—), Tenn. Trauma Soc. (bd. dirs. 1990—), Memphis-Shelby County Med. Soc. (EMS com. 1987—, chmn. 1992—), Soc. Critical Care Medicine, Soc. Pediat. Emergency Medicine, Soc. Acad. Emergency Medicine.

WEINBERG, LOUISE, law educator, author; b. N.Y.C.; m. Steven Weinberg; 1 child, Elizabeth. AB summa cum laude, Cornell U.; JD, Harvard U., 1969, LLM, 1974. Bar: Mass. Sr. law clk. Hon. Chas. E. Wyzanski, Jr., Boston, 1971-72; assoc. in law Bingham, Dana & Gould, Boston, 1969-72; teaching fellow Harvard Law Sch., Boston, 1972-74; lectr. law Brandeis U., Waltham, Mass., 1974; assoc. prof. law Suffolk U., Boston, 1974-76, prof., 1977-80; vis. assoc. prof. law Stanford U., Palo Alto, Calif., 1976-77; vis. prof. law U. Tex., Austin, 1979; prof. law Sch. Law, U. Tex., Austin, 1980-84, Thompson prof., 1984-90, Andrews and Kurth prof. law, 1990-92; Fulbright and Jaworski regents rsch. prof. U. Tex., Austin, 1991-92, Angus G. Wynne, Sr. prof. civil jurisprudence, 1992—, Fondren chair faculty excellence, 1995-96, Eugene R. Smith Centennial rsch. prof. law, 1993; vis. scholar Hebrew U., Jerusalem, 1989; Forum fellow World Econ. Forum, Davos, Switzerland, 1995—; lectr. in field. Author: Federal Courts: Judicial Federalsim and Judicial Power, 1994, and ann. supplements; co-author: Conflict of Laws, 1990; contbr. chpts. to books, articles to profl. jours. Bd. dirs. Ballet Austin, 1986-88, Austin Coun. on Fgn. Affairs, 1985—. Recipient Disting. Educator award Tex. Exes Assn., 1996. Mem. Am. Law Inst. (consultative com. complex litigation 1989-93, consosultative com. enterprise liability 1990—, adv. com. fed. judicial code revision project 1996—), The Philos. Soc. Tex., Assn. Am. Law Schs. (chmn. com. on conflict laws 1991-93, exec. coun. 1989-90), Maritime Law Assn., Scribes, Phi Beta Kappa, Phi Kappa Phi. Office: U Tex Sch Law 727 E 26th St Austin TX 78705-3224

WEINBERG, MARCY, psychologist; b. Detroit; m. Michael Eugene Weinberg, June 1, 1966. BA, Northeastern Ill. U., 1977; MA, Northwestern U., 1978; PhD, Nova Univ., 1989. Lic. psychologist. Psychology intern Broward Gen. Med. Ctr., Ft. Lauderdale, Fla., 1984-85; psychology resident U. Miami Sch. Medicine, 1989-90; psychologist Marcy Weinberg, Hollywood, Fla., 1991—; adj. prof. dept. psychiatry U. Miami, 1991-92; diagnostician Cen. Agy. for Jewish Edn., Miami, 1981-87; invited lectr., guest WLRN-TV, Miami, 1987, 90, Hollywood Meml. Hosp. Contbg. author: Pediatric Nephrology, 1991; author computer prog., 1985. Fundraiser Transplant Found. of South Fla., Miami, 1989—; invited speaker Dialysis/Organ Transplant Support Groups, Miami, Boca Raton, 1990. Recipient Svc. award Stratford Ctr. Sch., Highland Park, Ill., 1977. Fellow Am. Orthopsychiat. Assn.; mem. APA, Fla. Psychol. Assn. Office: 3990 Sheridan St Ste 204 Hollywood FL 33021-3656

WEINBERG, ROGER DAVID, communications executive; b. Balt., Feb. 10, 1954; s. James Henry Weinberg and Anne (Horowitz) Meyers; m. Nancy Rosenthal, July 23, 1977 (div. 1984); m. Jacquelyn Scully, Apr. 5, 1986. BA cum laude, U. Pa., 1976; grad., Broadcast Acad. Richmond, 1979. Copywriter Heilig-Meyers Co., Richmond, Va., 1976-82; dir. video tng. Heilig-Meyers Co., Richmond, 1982-88, asst. v.p. corp. communications, 1988—. Producer numerous videotapes, including Sir Moses Ezekiel, 1988, History of Beth Ahabah Congregation, 1989. Vol. reader Va. Voice for Print Handicapped, Richmond, 1980—. Mem. Internat. TV Assn. (sec. 1989-90), chmn. membership com, 1989-90 Richmond chpt.), Sigma Chi (steward 1973-74); charter mem. (inductee) Va. Voice Vol. Hall of Fame. Democrat. Jewish. Home: 7616 Cornwall Rd Richmond VA 23229-6718 Office: Heilig-Meyers Co 2235 Staples Mill Rd Richmond VA 23230-2942

WEINBERG, STEVEN, physics educator; b. N.Y.C., NY, May 3, 1933; s. Fred and Eva (Israel) W.; m. Louise Goldwasser, July 6, 1954; 1 child, Elizabeth. BA, Cornell U., 1954; postgrad., Copenhagen Inst. Theoretical Physics, 1954-55; PhD, Princeton U., 1957; AM (hon.), Harvard U., 1973; ScD (hon.), Knox Coll., 1978, U. Chgo., 1978, U. Rochester, 1979, Yale U., 1979, CUNY, 1980, Clark U., 1982, Dartmouth Coll., 1984, Columbia U., 1990, U. Salamanca, 1992, U. Padua, 1992; U. Barcelona, 1996, U. Barcelona, 1996; PhD (hon.), Weizmann Inst., 1985; DLitt (hon.), Washington Coll., 1985. Rsch. assoc., instr. Columbia U., 1957-59; rsch. physicist Lawrence Radiation Lab., Berkeley, Calif., 1959-60; mem. faculty U. Calif., Berkeley, 1960-69, prof. physics, 1964-69; vis. prof. MIT, 1967-69, prof. physics, 1969-73; Higgins prof. physics Harvard U., 1973-83; sr. scientist Smithsonian Astrophys. Lab., 1973-83; Josey prof. sci. U. Tex., Austin, 1982—; sr. cons. Smithsonian Astrophys. Obs., 1983—; cons. Inst. Def. Analyses, Washington, 1960-73, ACDA, 1973; Sloan fellow, 1961-65; chair in physics Coll. de France, 1971; mem. Pres.'s Com. on Nat. Medal of Sci., 1979-82, Coun. of Scholars, Libr. of Congress, 1983-85; sr. adv. La Jolla Inst.; mem. Com. on Internat. Security and Arms Control, NRC, 1981, Bd. on Physics & Astronomy, 1989-90; dir. Jerusalem Winter Sch. Theoretical Physics, 1983-94; mem. adv. coun. Tex. Superconducting Supercollider High Energy Rsch. Facility, 1987; Loeb lectr. in physics Harvard U., 1966-67, Morris Loeb vis. prof. physics, 1983—; Richtmeyer lectr., 1974; Scott lectr. Cavendish Lab., 1975; Silliman lectr. Yale U., 1977; Lauritsen Meml. lectr. Calif. Inst. Tech., 1979; Bethe lectr. Cornell U., 1979; de Shalit lectr. Weizman Inst., 1979; Cherwell-Simon lectr. Oxford U., 1983; Bampton lectr. Columbia U., 1983; Einstein lectr. Israel Acad. Arts and Scis., 1984; Hilldale lectr. U. Wis., 1985; Clark lectr. U. Tex., Dallas, 1986; Dirac lectr. U. Cambridge, 1986; Klein lectr. U. Stockholm, 1989; Brittin lectr. U. Colo., 1994; Sackler lectr. U. Copenhagen, 1994; Gibbs lectr. Am. Math. Soc., 1996; Sloan fellow, 1961-65; mem. Supercollider Sci. Policy Com., 1989-93. Author: Gravitation and Cosmology: Principles and Application of the General Theory of Relativity, 1972, The First Three Minutes: A Modern View of the Origin of the Universe, 1977, The Discovery of Subatomic Particles, 1982; co-author (with R. Feynman) Elementary Particles and the Laws of Physics, 1987, Dreams of a Final Theory, 1992, The Quantum Theory of Fields - Vol. I: Foundations, 1995, Modern Applications, Vol. II, 1996; rsch. and publs. on elementary particles, quantum field theory, cosmology; co-editor Cambridge U. Press, monographs on math. physics; mem. adv. bd. Issues in Sci. and Tech., 1984-87; mem. sci. book com. Sloan Found., 1985-91; mem. editl. bd. Jour. Math. Physics, 1986-88; mem. bd. editors Daedalus, 1990—; mem. bd. assoc. editors Nuclear Physics B. Bd. advisors Santa Barbara Inst. Theoretical Physics, 1983-86; bd. overseers SSC Accelerator, 1984-86; bd. dirs. Headliners Found., 1993—. Recipient J. Robert Oppenheimer meml. prize, 1973, Dannie Heineman prize in math. physics, 1977, Am. Inst. Physics-U.S. Steel Found. sci. writing award, 1977, Nobel prize in physics, 1979, Elliott Cresson medal Franklin Inst., 1979, Madison medal Princeton U., 1991, Nat. Medal of Sci. NSF, 1991. Mem. Am. Acad. Arts and Scis. (past councilor), Am. Phys. Soc. (past councilor at large, panel on faculty positions com. on status of women in physics), NAS (supercollider site evaluation com. 1987-88), Einstein Archivess (adv. bd. 1988—), Internat. Astron. Union, Coun. Fgn. Rels., Am. Philos. Soc., Royal Soc. London (fgn. mem.), Am. Mediaeval Acad., History of Sci. Soc., Philos. Soc. Tex. (pres. 1994), Tex. Inst. of Letters, Phi Beta Kappa. Clubs: Saturday (Boston); Headliners, Tuesday (Austin); Cambridge Sci. Soc.

WEINBERGER, GWEN LEE SCHALLER, academic administrator; b. Phila., July 20, 1931; d. Max A. and Minnie A. (Apparies) Schaller; m. Morton L. Weinberger, July 3, 1952; children: Marc Bennett, Barrett Neil, Cynthia R. Schulman. BA in Edn., Temple U., 1952; MA in Edn., Fla. Internat. U., 1982. Classroom tchr. various sch. systems, Phila., 1953-55; ednl. statistician Sch. Medicine U. Miami, Fla., 1955-58; classroom tchr. Miami, 1962-64; ednl. adminstr. Fla. Internat. U., Miami, 1983—; mem. adminstrv. and profl. senate Fla. Internat. U., chairperson, 1994-95; mem. Greater Miami Jewish Fedn. Planning and Budget, 1970—. Pres. Women's Am. ORT, Miami, 1975; mem. Ctr. Agy. for Jewish Edn., Miami, 1970—, pres., 1979-81; mem. Miami Jewish Fedn., 1968—, pres. women's divsn., 1982; bd. dirs. Hillel Founds. of Fla., 1989-95; Jewish Chaplaincy Svc., Miami, 1990—; charter mem. Nat. Holocaust Mus., Washington. Mem. Nat. Univ. Continuing Edn. Assn., Nat. Coun. Jewish Women (life). Office: Fla Internat U North Miami Campus North Miami Beach FL 33181

WEINBERGER, MALVIN, pediatric surgeon; b. Phila., Sept. 1, 1937; s. Emanuel Milton and Molly Weinberger; m. Irene H. Segall, July 5, 1959; children: Audrey, Benjamin, Jeremy. AB, U. Pa., 1958; MD, Temple U., 1962. Intern Phila. Gen. Hosp., 1962-63; resident in gen. surgery Temple U. Health Scis. Ctr., Phila., 1965-69; resident in pediatric surgery Columbus Ohio Children's Hosp./Ohio State U., 1969-71; instr. surgery Ohio State U., Columbus, 1969-71; asst. prof. surgery/pediats. U. Miami, Fla., 1971-73; attending surgeon Miami Children's Hosp., 1973-85, sr. attending surgeon, 1985—, dir. trauma, 1992—; clin. assoc. prof. surgery U. Miami, 1992—. Mem. Dade County Trauma Adv. Coun., Miami, 1989—. Lt. Med. Corps USN, 1963-65. HEW, USPHS Sr. Clin. traineeship, 1969-70. Fellow ACS (Dade County councillor 1990-96), Am. Acad. Pediats.; mem. Fla. Assn. Pediat. Surgeons (pres. 1984-86). Republican. Jewish. Office: 3200 SW 60th Ct Miami FL 33155-4000

WEINBRENNER, GEORGE RYAN, aeronautical engineer; b. Detroit, June 10, 1917; s. George Penbrook and Helen Mercedes (Ryan) W.; BS, M.I.T., 1940, MS, 1941; AMP, Harvard U., 1966; ScD (hon.), Mapua Inst. Tech., Manila, 1994; m. Billie Marjorie Elwood, May 2, 1955. Commd. 2d lt. USAAF, 1939, advanced through grades to col., 1949; def. attaché Am. embassy, Prague, Czechoslavakia, 1958-61; dep. chief staff intelligence Air Force Systems Command, Washington, 1962-68; comdr. fgn. tech. div. U.S. Air Force, Wright-Patterson AFB, Ohio, 1968-74; comdr. Brooks AFB, Tex., 1974-75; ret., 1975; exec. v.p. B.C. Wills & Co., Inc., Reno, Nev., 1975-84; lectr. Sch. Aerospace Medicine Brooks AFB, Tex., 1975-84; chmn. bd. Hispaño-Technica S.A. Inc., San Antonio, 1977—; adv. dir. Plaza Nat. Bank, San Antonio; cons. Def. Dept., 1981, Dept. Air Force, 1975-84. Decorated D.S.M., Legion of Merit, Bronze Star, Air medal, Purple Heart; Ordre National du Merite, Medaille de la Resistance, Croix de Guerre (France). Fellow AIAA (asso.); mem. World Affairs Council, Air Force Assn. (exec. sec. Tex. 1976-94), Assn. Former Intelligence Officers (nat. dir.), Air Force Hist. Found. (dir.), U.S. Strategic Inst., Nat. Mil. Intelligence Assn., Tex. Aerospace & Nat. Def. Tech. Devel. Coun., Am. Astronautical Soc., Aerospace Ednl. Found. (trustee), Disabled Am. Vets. (life), Mil. Order World Wars, Am. Legion, Assn. Old Crows, Kappa Sigma. Roman Catholic. Clubs: Army-Navy (Washington). Home: 7400 Crestway Dr Apt 903 San Antonio TX 78239-3094 Office: PO Box 8121 San Antonio TX 78208-8121

WEINER, DEBRA KAYE, physician, educator; b. St. Louis, July 28, 1956; d. Harry Leo and Mary (Katz) W. BA, Washington U., St. Louis, 1978; MD, U. Mo., 1983. Diplomate Am. Bd. Internal Medicine. Intern Jewish Hosp. St. Louis, 1983-84, resident in internal medicine, 1984-86, fellow in geratrics, 1986-87; fellow in rheumatology Duke U. Med. Ctr., Durham, N.C., 1987-89, rsch. fellow in geriatrics, 1989-90, assoc. in medicine, 1990-92, asst. prof. medicine, 1992—; dir. geriatrics outpatient clinic Durham Veterans Affairs Med. Ctr., 1992—. Contbr. articles and abstracts to profl. jours. Ctr. for Study of Aging and Human Devel. fellow, 1991; grantee A.W. Mellon, 1989-90. Mem. ACP, Am. Geriatrics Soc., Gerontol. Soc. Am., Phi Beta Kappa, Alpha Lambda Delta. Home: 107 Boulder Ln Chapel Hill NC 27514-2000 Office: Duke U Med Ctr PO Box 3003 Durham NC 27715-3003

WEINER, JEFFREY STUART, lawyer; b. N.Y.C., Nov. 14, 1948; s. Mac and Lee W.; m. Duchess Weiner; children: Charlee, Max, Jake. Student, U. Miami, Coral Gables, Fla., 1966-70; JD, Ill. Inst. Tech., 1974. Bar: Fla. 1974, Ill. 1974, U.S. Dist. Ct. (so. dist.) Fla. 1974, U.S. Ct. Appeals (5th cir.) 1978, U.S. Tax Ct. 1981, U.S. Supreme Ct. 1981, U.S. Ct. Appeals (4th and 11th cirs.) 1981, U.S. Dist. Ct. (cen. dist.) Ill. 1982, U.S. Ct. Appeals (6th and 9th cirs.) 1984, U.S. Ct. Appeals (2d cir.) 1986, U.S. Ct. Appeals (7th cir.) 1990. Apptd. spl. pub. defender Dade County, Miami, Fla., 1974—; ptnr. Weiner, Robbins, Tunkey & Ross, P.A., Miami, 1976-92; hon. prof. law S.E. Fla. Inst. Criminal Justice, Miami, 1976—; mem. faculty, bd. regents Nat. Criminal Def. Coll. Mercer U., Macon, Ga., 1985—; hearing examiner Met. Dade County, Miami, 1982—; del. U.S. 11th Jud. Conf., Panama City, Fla, 1988, New Orleans, 1989; witness U.S. Sentencing Guidelines Com., 1991. Author: Inside Drug Law, 1985, Taking the Lid Off the Government's Silent Partner, 1990; contbr. articles to profl. jours. Recipient Fla. Bar Media award for Excellence for Jeff Weiner Radio Program, 1988; named to Iron Arrow Hon. Fellow Am. Bd. Criminal Lawyers; mem. ABA, Am. Arbitration Assn. (panel arbitrators), Am. Inns of Ct. (barrister), Nat. Bd. Trial Advocacy (cert. criminal trial advocate), Nat. Assn. Criminal Def. Lawyers (pres. 1991-92, chair Dept. of Justice dialogue com. 1993—, Robert C. Henney Meml. award 1985), Assn. Trial Lawyers Am., Jud. Conf. of U.S. (witness com. to rev. the criminal justice act 1989), Acad. Fla. Trial Attys. (past chmn. criminal law sect.), Fla. Criminal Def. Lawyers (pres. 1981-82), Dade County Bar Assn. (past chmn. criminal law sect.). Home and Office: Two Datran Ctr Ste 1910 9130 S Dadeland Blvd Miami FL 33156-7858

WEINER, LAWRENCE, lawyer; b. Phila., Aug. 20, 1942; s. Robert A. and Goldie Weiner; m. Jane M. Coulthard, Feb. 28, 1976; 1 child, Kimberly. BS in Econs., U. Pa., 1964, JD, 1967. Bar: Pa. 1967, U.S. Dist. Ct. (ea. dist.) Pa. 1967, Fla. 1970, U.S. Dist. Ct. (so. dist.) Fla. 1976, U.S. Ct. Appeals (5th cir.) 1976, U.S. Tax Ct. 1984. Assoc., ptnr. Blank, Rome, Klaus & Comisky, Phila., 1967-71, 1975-77; ptnr. Weiner & Weisenfeld, P.A., Miami Beach, Fla., 1971-73, Pettigrew & Bailey, Miami, Fla., 1973-75; pres. Lawrence Weiner, P.A., Miami, 1977-83; ptnr. Spieler, Weiner & Spieler, P.A., Miami, 1983-89, Weiner & Cummings, P.A., Miami, 1989-94, Weiner, Cummings & Vittoria, Miami, 1994—; lectr. Wharton Sch. U. Pa., Phila., 1968-70; instr. bus. law and acctg. Community Coll. Phila., 1967-70; lectr. estate planning various non-lawyer groups, Miami, 1972—. Mem. ABA (pension, profit sharing trust coms. 1976-77), Fla. Bar (liaison non-lawyers groups 1980-87), Pa. Bar Assn., Phila. Bar Assn., Dade County Bar Assn. (chmn. ins. com. 1977-78, probate law com. 1992—). Democrat. Jewish. Office: Weiner Cummings & Vittoria 1428 Brickell Ave Ste 400 Miami FL 33131-3436

WEINER, MYRON FREDERICK, psychiatrist, educator, clinical investigator; b. Atlantic City, June 4, 1934; s. Jack and Eva (Friedman) W.; m. Jeanette Harmon; children: Daniel, Gary, Darrel, Holli. MD, Tulane U., 1957. Diplomate Am. Bd. Psychiatry, qualifications in geriatric psychiatry. Intern Parkland Hosp., Dallas, 1957-58, resident, 1960-63; fellow in geriatrics and adult devel. Mt. Sinai Med. Ctr., N.Y.C., 1984-85; clin. instr. to assoc. prof. U. Tex. Southwestern Med. Ctr., Dallas, 1963-77, prof. psychiatry, 1980—; head geriatric psychiatry U. Tex Southwestern Med. Ctr., Dallas, 1985—; asst. prof. neurology U. Tex. Southwestern Med. Ctr., Dallas, 1989, head clin. core Alzheimer Disease Ctr., 1988—, vice-chair clin. affairs psychiatry, 1993—. Author: Techniques of Group Psychotherapy, 1984, Practical Psychotherapy, 1986; editor: The Dementias: Diagnosis and Management, 1991, 2d edit., 1996; co-author: The Psychotherapeist Patient Privilege, 1987. Mem. Tex. Alzheimer's Coun., 1991—. Capt. USAF, 1958-60. Mem. AMA, Am. Psychiatric Assn., Am. Assn. Geriatric Psychiatry, Tex. Soc. Psychiatry Physicians (pres. 1985-86). Office: U Tex Southwestern Med Ctr 5323 Harry Hines Blvd Dallas TX 75235-7200

WEINER, RICHARD DAVID, psychiatrist, researcher; b. N.Y.C., Nov. 25, 1945. BS, MIT, 1967; M of Systems Engring., U. Pa., 1969; MD, PhD, Duke U., 1973. Diplomate Am. Bd. Psychiatry and Neurology. Assoc. prof. psychiatry Duke U. Med. Ctr., Durham, N.C., 1984—, dir. electroconvulsive therapy program, 1991—; chief, psychiatry svc. VA Med. Ctr., Durham, N.C., 1993—. Recipient Merit award NIMH, 1988. Mem. Am. Psychiat. Assn. (chmn. electroconvulsive therapy task force 1987—). Office: Duke U Med Ctr PO Box 3309 Durham NC 27710-3309

WEINER, ROBERT HAROLD, clinical psychologist; b. Dallas, Aug. 3, 1951; s. Abe Arnold and Lillian Weiner; m. Doris Kephart, Mar. 20, 1994. BA, Northwestern U., 1973; PhD, Tex. Tech U., 1983. Lic. psychologist, health svc. provider, Tex. Staff psychologist Tex. Back Inst., Plano, 1984-86, dir. psychol. svcs., 1986-87; pvt. practice Plano, 1987—. Intern Human Rights Rsch. Coun., Crownpoint, N.Mex., 1974. Recipient Am. Jurisprudence award U. Tex. Sch. Law, 1974. Mem. APA, Tex. Psychol. Assn., Collin County Psychol. Assn., North Tex. Soc. Clin. Hypnosis, Assn. Applied Psychophysiology and Biofeedback, Physicians for a Nat. Health Program, Biofeedback Cert. Inst. Am.-EEG Biofeedback. Office: 2801 Regal Rd Ste 107 Plano TX 75075-6315

WEINGER, STEVEN MURRAY, lawyer; b. Chgo., Feb. 7, 1954; s. Paul and Joan (Taxay) W.; children: Blake, Paige, Haley. BA, Hampshire Coll., 1975; JD, U. Chgo., 1978. Bar: Fla. 1979, Ill. 1979, U.S. Dist. Ct. (so. dist.) Fla. 1979, U.S. Ct. Appeals (5th cir.) 1980, U.S. Ct. Appeals (11th cir.) 1981, U.S. Supreme Ct. 1982, U.S. Dist. Ct. (mid. dist.) Fla. 1989. Mem. faculty U. Miami Sch. Law, Coral Gables, Fla., 1978-79; ptnr. Kurzban, Kurzban & Weinger, P.A., Miami, Fla., 1979—. Bd. dirs. Sunrise Cmty. for Mentally Retarded, Miami, United Cerebral Palsy Tallahassee, Inc., Palmer-Trinity Sch., Miami. Recipient Chmn.'s award Sunrise Community for Mentally Retarded, 1987, Bd. Dirs. of the Yr., 1989. Mem. ABA, Assn. Trial Lawyers Am., Fla. Assn. Trial Lawyers. Office: Kurzban Kurzban & Weinger 2650 SW 27th Ave Fl 2D Miami FL 33133-3003

WEINHAGEN, SUSAN POUCH, emergency care nurse; b. Dallas, Jan. 17, 1954; d. Arnold Cornwall and Barbara Anne (Noakes) Pouch; m. Charles Winthrop Weinhagen, Apr. 23, 1977 (div. May 1985); children: Francine Melanie, Kurt Woodbury; m. Giles Milton Ellis, Apr. 14, 1989. Diploma in nursing, Jackson Meml. Hosp. Sch., 1977. RN, N.C., Wis.; cert. ACLS, basic trauma life support, mobil intensive care nurse, pediatric advanced life support. Nurse pvt. med. office, Ellensburg, Wash., 1977; staff nurse orthopedics floor St. Joseph Hosp., Madison, Wis., 1977-80; staff nurse emergency St. Joseph Hosp., Madison, 1980-83, Haywood County Hosp., Waynesville, N.C., 1983; staff nurse emergency care ctr. Meml. Mission Hosp., Asheville, N.C., 1983-86, charge nurse emergency care ctr., 1986-89, mgr. emergency care ctr., 1989-95; charge nurse, Emergency Care Ctr., 1995—; mem. nursing practice coun. Meml. Mission Hosp., Asheville, 1992-94, mem. nursing adminstrv. coun., 1994-95, charge nurse emergency care ctr., 1995—. Mem. Emergency Nurses Assn. Home: 8 Simpson Hollow Rd Asheville NC 28803-9003 Office: Meml Mission Hosp 509 Biltmore Ave Asheville NC 28801-4601

WEINHAUER, WILLIAM GILLETTE, retired bishop; b. N.Y.C., Dec. 3, 1924; s. Nicholas Alfred and Florence Anastacia (Davis) W.; m. Jean Roberta Shanks, Mar. 20, 1948; children: Roberta Lynn, Cynthia Anne, Doris Jean. BS, Trinity Coll., Hartford, Conn., 1948; MDiv, Gen. Theol. Sem., 1951, STM, 1956, ThD, 1970. Ordained to ministry Episcopal Ch., 1951. Pastor Episcopal parishes Diocese N.Y., 1951-56; prof. N.T. St. Andrews Theol. Sem., Manila, Philippines, 1956-60; asst. prof. N.T. Gen. Theol. Sem., 1961-71; rector Christ Ch., Poughkeepsie, N.Y., 1971-73; bishop Episcopal Diocese of Western N.C., Black Mountain, 1973-90, ret., 1990; vis. prof. religion Western Carolina U., Cullowhee, N.C., 1991-96; adj. faculty Seabury-Western Theol. Sem., Evanston, Ill., 19991-94. Served with USN, 1943-46. Mem. Soc. Bibl. Lit.

WEINRIB, DAVID A., infectious disease physician, consultant; b. Cin., Oct. 29, 1963; s. Mark Michael and Louisa (Herzfeld) W.; m. Elizabeth T. Wahls, Aug. 31, 1991; 1 child, Benjamin Wahls. AB in History, Brown U., 1985; MD, U. Ala., Birmingham, 1989. Chief med. resident Beth Israel Hosp., Boston, 1994-95; faculty physician Carolinas Med. Ctr., Charlotte, N.C., 1995—; asst. clin. prof. U. N.C., chapel Hill, 1996—. Mem. N.C. Med. Soc., Infectious Disease Soc. Am. Office: Carolinas Medical Center Dept Internal Medicine PO Box 32861 Charlotte NC 28232-2861

WEINSTEIN, ART TED, marketing professional, educator; b. Bklyn., Aug. 18, 1955; s. Jesse and Sylvia W.; m. Sandra Lee Press, Apr. 19, 1977. BA in Mktg., U. South Fla., 1976; MBA in Mktg., Fla. Internat. U., 1982, PhD, 1991. Asst. store mgr. F.W. Woolworth Co., Atlanta, 1976-78; sr. mktg. rsch. rep. A.C. Nielsen Co., Northbrook, Ill., 1978-82; regional mgr., mktg. analyst Small Bus. Devel. Ctr. Fla. Internat. U., Miami, 1982-89, adj. instr., instr. mktg. and environ., 1986-91; adj. instr. Entrepreneurial Inst. U. Miami, Coral Gables, 1986-89; ptnr.. dir. mktg. ops. Pro-Mark Svcs., Cooper City, Fla., 1987-90; asst. prof. mktg. and internat. bus. Hofstra U., Hempstead, N.Y., 1991-93; assoc. prof. mktg. Nova Southeastern U., Ft. Lauderdale, Fla., 1993—. Author: Market Segmentation: Using Demographics, Psychographics and Other Niche Marketing Techniques to Predict Customer Behavior, 1987, rev. edit., 1994 (alt. monthly selection Macmillan Exec. Book Club, 1987); contbr. articles to profl. jours. Mem. Am. Mktg. Assn., Acad. Mktg. Sci., Internat. Acad. Bus. Disciplines. Office: Nova Southeastern U Sch Bus & Entrepreneurship 3100 SW 9th Ave Fort Lauderdale FL 33315-3025

WEINSTEIN, DAVID, lawyer, educator; b. Phila., Feb. 6, 1926; s. Harry and Bertha (Berman) W.; m. Florine S. Dutkin, May 18, 1952; children: Lee M., Norman J., Debra E. BS in Edn., U. Pa., 1949, MS, 1953, postgrad., 1953-55; JD, Temple U., 1959. Bar: Pa. 1960, U.S. Dist. Ct. (ea. dist.) Pa. 1960, U.S. Ct. Appeals (3d cir.) 1961; cert. tchr., ednl. adminstr., Pa. Tchr. Phila. Sch. Dist., 1952-60; legal adviser Phila. Dept. Revenue, 1960-62; pvt. practice, Phila., 1962-89; ptnr. Weinstein, Goss, Katenstein, Schleifer & Eisenberg, Phila., 1989—; prof. Coll. of Boca Raton, Fla., 1989—, Lynn U., Boca Raton, 1989—; bd. dirs. various corps., Phila. Mem. Temple U. Law Rev., 1958-59. Mem. Boynton Beach (Fla.) Edn. Adv. Com., 1993, 96. Served with USAAC, 1944-45, to 1st lt. U.S. Army, 1950-52. Mem. Fed. Bar Assn. (fed. jud. com. Phila. 1988-89), Phila. Bar Assn. (edn. com. 1982-84), Masons, Phi Delta Kappa, Kappa Phi Kappa. Home: 11 Southport Ln Apt B Boynton Beach FL 33436-6418 Office: 1634 Spruce St Philadelphia PA 19103-6719

WEINSTEIN, EUGENE, pharmacist; b. N.Y.C., Oct. 29, 1929; s. Samuel Weinstein and Ethel (Horowitz) Bernstein; m. Thelma Saphir, May 10, 1954 (div. June 1992); children: Daniel, Wendy, Michael, Richard, Dana. BS in Pharmacy, Rutgers U., 1952. Registered pharmacist Fla., N.J., Calif.; registered cons. pharmacist Fla. Pres. Wards Pharmacy Inc., Butler, N.J., 1958-67, Bloomingdale, N.J., 1967-70; pharmacist, asst. mgr. SuperX Drugs, Miami Beach, Fla., 1971-72; mgr. SuperX Drugs, Hallandale, Fla., 1972-75, Lauderhill, Fla., 1975-79, Margate, Fla., 1979-80; owner, operator, pharmacist Coral Springs (Fla.) Pharmacy, 1980-85; pharmacist, asst. mgr. Gray Drugs, Margate, Fla., 1985; pharmacist Rite Aid Drugs, Margate, 1986; pharmacy supr. Rite Aid Drugs, Miami, Fla., 1987; pharmicist mgr. Rite Aid Drugs, Naranga, Fla., 1988—. V.p. Pompton Lakes (N.J.) Bd. Edn., 1967, mem., 1964-68; apptd. mem. Passaic County (N.J.) Bd. Edn; active Drug Abuse Speakers Bureau, Morris County, N.J. Pvt. U.S. Army, 1953-55. Mem. Fla. Pharmacists Assn., Broward County Pharmacists Assn. (dir.), Dade County Pharmacists Assn., Rotary Club (pres. 1984-85). Democrat. Jewish. Home: 10620 SW 74th Ave Miami FL 33156-4144 Office: Eckerd Pharmacy 27365 S Dixie Hwy Homestead FL 33032-8210

WEINTRAUB, ABNER EDWARD, information services executive; b. Miami, Fla., Aug. 30, 1954; s. William Albert Weintraub and Miriam (Mayers) Lemberg; m. Kimbal Reisig, Aug. 31, 1979; 1 child, Sarah Lee. BS, U. N.C., 1983. Prin. rschr. DynaSearch Group, Orlando, Fla., 1983-86, dir. rsch., 1986-94; mgr. consumer markets rsch. Sprint/United Telephone of Fla., Altamonte Springs, Fla., 1995—. Originator databases, 1985-86; patentee in field. Mem. Soc. for Investigation of Unexplained (assoc. investigator 1982—). Democrat. Office: Sprint/United Telephone of Fla MC 5302 PO Box 5000 Altamonte Springs FL 32717-0002

WEIR, JULIA MARIE, psychic readings company executive; b. St. Louis, Nov. 14, 1950; d. Charles Daniel and Elliott (Chambers) Smith; m. Sanford David Weir, Dec. 22, 1976; 1 child, David Daniel. Student, Syracuse U., 1968. With Sears, Roebuck and Co., Syracuse, N.Y., 1968-72; credit corresp. Allis-Chalmers Credit Corp., Syracuse, 1974-75; dir. systems Mutual of N.Y., Syracuse, 1975-87; systems mgr. Claims Adminstrn. Corp., Rockville, Md., 1988-92; pres. Jordan's Journey, Centreville, 1992—; cons. Banner Life, Rockville, 1988. Author: Numerology Profile, 1993, Excursion of Life, 1993, Planes of Expression, 1993, Name Profile, 1993, Your Name's Aura, 1995, Natal Horoscope, 1995, Karmic Challenges, 1995, What's Your Tarot Card?, 1995, Money Tree, 1996. Fellow Life Mgmt. Inst.; mem. Health Ins. Assn. Am. Democrat. Episcopalian. Office: Jordan's Journey 15314 Jordans Journey Dr Centreville VA 22020-3904

WEIR, RICHARD DALE, elementary education educator; b. Diamond Springs, Calif., Oct. 2, 1940; s. Martin Gaines and Phyllis Lorene (Sargent) W.; m. Carol Jean Baker, Dec. 25, 1976; children:, David Richard, Barbara Anne, Susan Michelle, Roger Allen. BS in Elem. Edn., Oklahoma City U., 1976, MEd, 1988; BS in Mgmt. Info. Sys., Coleman Coll., LaMesa, Calif., 1987. Cert. tchr. K-8, Okla. Joined USCG, 1961, advanced through grades to chief warrant officer, 1976; adminstrv. officer USCG, Washington, 1976-82; ret. USCG, 1982; platform instr. IBM Corp., Oklahoma City, 1985-86; mid. sch. tchr. Archdiocese Oklahoma City, 1987-88; adj. prof. Oklahoma City U., 1988-91; elem. tchr. Oklahoma City Pub. Schs., 1988—; cons. in tng. math.-sci. tchrs.; trainer for Activities Integrating Math./Scis. Nat. Leadership Network. Recipient Presdl. award for excellence in sci. and math. teaching NSF, Washington, 1993, Okla. Outstanding Tchr. award Math. Assn. Am., Washington, 1996. Mem. ASCD, Nat. Sci. Tchrs. Assn., Nat. Coun. Tchrs. Math., Coun. Presdl. Awardees Math., Okla. Coun. Tchrs. Math. (advisor Metro Oklahoma City), Soc. Elem. Presdl. Awardees. Republican. Methodist. Home: 9109 NW 99th Pl Yukon OK 73099-8313 Office: PO Box 720226 Oklahoma City OK 73172-0226

WEIRICK, WILLIAM NEWTON, economics educator, university administrator; b. Long Beach, Calif., June 16, 1952; s. Richard Carver and Jane Margaret (Rumble) W.; m. Ellen Ann Johnson, Oct. 29, 1975; children: Lauren, Carlin. BA, Pomona Coll., 1974; PhD, U. Wyo., 1984. Fin. mgr. So. Calif. Coop. Community, Los Angeles, 1975-79; rsch. asst. U. Wyo., Laramie, 1980-84; asst. prof. econs. N.E. La. Univ., Monroe, 1983-89, assoc. prof. econs., 1990-91, assoc. dir. Ctr. for Bus. and Econs. Rsch., 1989-91, acting v.p. bus. affairs, N.E. La. U., 1991-92; v.p. bus. affairs, N.E. La. U., 1992—; research aide EPA, 1981-84; faculty advisor Delta Sigma Pi N.E. La. Univ., 1986-90; assoc. prof. econs., 1990—. Bd. dirs. N.E. La. Arts Coun., 1990-91, Northeast Campus Ministries, 1992-94; v.p. Twin City Arts Found., 1993, pres., 1994—, bd. dirs., 1989—; contract adminstr., La. Real Estate Commn., 1989-91; mem. CDBG rev. com. City of Monroe, 1989-91; ex-oficio bd. mem. Monroe Downtown Devel. Authority, 1989-92; bd. mem. Grace Episcopal Sch., 1990-93. Contbr. articles to profl. jours. Interim period rsch. grantee N.E. La. Univ., 1984-86, La. Real Estate Bd. grantee N.E. La. Univ., 1985, La. Arts Coun. grantee, 1987; Bugas fellow U. Wyo., 1982-84; Outstanding Rsch. Award nominee Coll. Bus. Adminstrn., N.E. La. U., 1986. Mem. Am. Econ. Assn., Acad. La. Economists (parliamentarian 1985, program chmn. 1986, v.p. 1987, pres. 1988). Avocations: auto restoration, gardening. Home: 2313 Jasmine St Monroe LA 71201-4125 Office: VP Bus Affairs 700 University Ave Monroe LA 71209-9000

WEIS, ARTHUR JOHN, naval officer; b. Bay Shore, N.Y., Oct. 30, 1953; s. Arthur Herbert and Evelyn Frances (Smith) W. BS, U.S. Merchant Marine Acad., 1975. Commd. USNR, 1975—, advanced through grades to comdr.; lic. master mariner USCG, 1980; ship's officer Brotherhood of Marine Officers, Bklyn., 1975-77; ship's officer Am. Maritime Officers, Dania, Fla., 1977-82, ship master, 1982—;, 1977—; marine cons. COSCOL Marine, Houston, 1983—, Marine Safety Internat., Laguardia, N.Y., 1982-85; info. rep. U.S. Merchant Marine acad., King's Point, 1975. Mem. Am. Coun. Master Mariners, U.S. Merchant Marine Acad. Alumni Assn. SC (v.p. 1990), First City Club of Savannah (charter mem.), Club at Point o' Woods. Episcopalian. Home: 12 Spanish Moss Rd Hilton Head Island SC 29928

WEIS, LAURA VISSER, lawyer; b. Mich., June 6, 1961; d. Roger Leonard and Genevieve (Gore) V.; m. Barton Dale Weis, Jan. 12, 1991. BA cum laude, U. Va., 1983, JD, 1986. Bar: Calif. 1987, D.C. 1988, Va. 1991. Assoc. Shaw, Pittman, Potts & Trowbridge, Washington, 1986-90, Christian, Barton, Epps, Brent & Chappell, Richmond, Va., 1990—. Co-author: (with others) National Institute on Construction Law & Practice, 1987, Law and Business, 1988. Del. Nat. Rep. Inst. for Internat. Affairs, Czechoslovakia, 1990. Mem. ABA, Va. State Bar, Calif. Bar Assn., D.C. Bar Assn., Richmond Bar Assn. (exec. com., sec. real estate sect.), Philanthropy By Design (bd. dirs. 1992-95), Comml. Real Estate Women of Richmond, Va., French-Am. C. of C. (bd. dirs., asst. sec. 1988-90). Office: Christian Barton Epps Brent & Chappell 909 E Main St Fl 12 Richmond VA 23219-3002

WEISFELD, SHELDON, lawyer; b. McAllen, Tex., Feb. 20, 1946; s. Morris and Pauline (Horwitz) W.; m. Eve F. Weisfeld, Jan. 23, 1994; BBA, U. Tex., 1967; postgrad. Nat. U.Mex., Mexico City, 1969; JD, U. Houston, 1970. Bar: Tex. 1971, U.S. Dist. Ct. (so. dist.) Tex. 1978, U.S. Ct. Appeals (5th cir.) 1978, U.S. Ct. Appeals (11th cir.) 1981, U.S. Supreme Ct. 1982. Pvt. practice, Austin, Tex., 1973-77, pvt. practice law, Brownsville, Tex., 1980—; asst. fed. pub. defender U.S. Dist. Ct. (so. dist.) Tex., Brownsville, 1977-80; dir., sec.-treas. Flying Nurses Inc. Mem. Nat. Assn. Criminal Def. Lawyers, Tex. Criminal Def. Lawyers (dir.), ABA, Fed. Bar Assn., State Bar Tex., Cameron County (Tex.) Bar Assn., Hidalgo County (Tex.) Bar Assn. Democrat. Club: B'nai B'rith, Rotary (Brownsville). Office: 602 E Saint Charles St Brownsville TX 78520-5218 also: 55 Waugh Dr Ste 900 Houston TX 77007

WEISHAMPEL, JOHN FREDERICK, environmental scientist; b. Reading, Pa., Aug. 24, 1963; m. Teresa M. Riedel, 1988; 1 child, Anthony Christopher. BS in Biology magna cum laude, Duke U., 1985; MS in Environ. Scis., U. Va., 1990, PhD in Ecology, 1993. Undergrad. rsch. asst. dept. botany Duke U., Durham, N.C., 1984-85; asst. dir. Reading Emergency Shelter, Reading Urban Ministry, 1985-86; tchr. high sch. biology and phys. sci. Reading Sch. Dist., 1986-87; rsch./tchg. asst. dept. environ. scis. U. Va., Charlottesville, 1987-93; NRC rsch. assoc. Goddard Space Flight Ctr. biospheric scis. br. NASA, Greenbelt, Md., 1993-95; asst. prof. dept. biology U. Cen. Fla., Orlando, 1995—; new investigator Mission to Plant Earth; NASA planetary biology intern Marine Biol. Lab., Woods Hole, Mass., 1990; grad. student fellow in global change rsch. NASA, 1990-93; presenter sci. confs. and symposia, 1989—; co-organizer environ. scis. rsch. forum U. Va., 1991. Co-contbr. chpt. to: Natural Sinks of CO2, 1992; contbr. articles to profl. jours. and conf. procs. Luden's scholar, 1981-85. Mem. Ecol. Soc. Am., Internat. Assn. Landscape Ecology, Phi Eta Sigma. Office: U Cen Fla Dept Biology PO Box 2368 Orlando FL 32816

WEISHUHN, CAROLYN ANN, elementary education educator; b. El Campo, Tex., Mar. 7, 1962; d. Lawrence Clarence and Lillian Marie (Wendel) Pavlu; m. James Clarence Weishuhn, Dec. 30, 1989; children: Nicole Leigh, James Christopher. AA, Wharton County Jr. Coll., 1982; BA in Tchg., Sam Houston State U., 1984. Cert. tchr. elem. edn., math. Tchr. Sheridan (Tex.) Elem., 1984-92, Sacred Heart Sch., LaGrange, Tex., 1992—; number sense sponsor U. Ill. Democrat. Roman Catholic. Office: Sacred Heart Sch 545 E Pearl La Grange TX 78945

WEISINGER, CHARLES, produce executive, consultant; b. N.Y.C., Mar. 31, 1942; s. Charles and Sheila Weisinger; m. Sheryl Ann Lipman; children: Michele Lynn, Lisa Beth, Max Jaime. BA, U. Miami, Fla., 1964. V.p. sales Six L's Packing, Immokalee, Fla., 1964-91; pres. Paragon Produce, Immokalee, 1987—; pres., CEO Weis Buy Svcs., Ft. Meyers, Fla., 1992—, Coastline Inc. Builders, Beaufort, S.C., 1992—. Mem. founding com. Ctr. for Produce Quality, Alexandria, Va., 1988; initiated travelling exhibit for produce State of Fla., Tallahassee, 1985; bd. dirs. Jewish Fedn. Lee County; chmn. Israel Independence Day. Mem. United Fruit and Vegetable Assn. (chmn. tomato div. 1983-87, bd. dirs. 1987—, exec. com. 1989-90, vice chmn. nat. conv., mem. dist. com., mem. search com. for new pres. 1989, sci. and tech. liaison, membership awards 1986-89), Fla. Fruit and Vegetable Assn. (mktg. div. 1990-91), S.W. Fla. Sportsmen's Assn., Eagles. Republican. Jewish.

WEISINGER, RONALD JAY, economic development consultant, real estate developer; b. Youngstown, Ohio, Feb. 13, 1946; s. David S. and Sterna (Woolf) W.; married; children: Morgan, Megan. BS, Carroll Coll., 1968; MBA, U. Palm Beach, 1970. Dir. cash dept. Nat. United Jewish Appeal, 1975-77; exec. dir. Jewish Fedn. Pinellas County, Inc., Fla., 1978-80; prin. VIP Mortgage Trust Co., VIP Mgmt. and Realty, Inc., West Palm Beach, 1984-91; developer, builder affordable housing, 1991—; econ. devel. in Eastern Europe, former countries of Soviet Union and Mid. East. Jewish.

WEISMAN, R(OBERT) BRUCE, physical chemist, educator; b. Balt., Nov. 23, 1950; s. Samuel and Eva (Abramson) W.; m. Kathleen Mary Beckingham, July 25, 1986; 1 child, Caroline Mary. BA, Johns Hopkins U., 1971; PhD, U. Chgo., 1977. Postdoctoral fellow U. Pa., Phila., 1977-79; asst. prof. Rice U., Houston, 1979-84, assoc. prof., 1984-93, prof., 1993—. Mem. editl. bd. Rev. Sci. Instruments, 1991-93; contbr. more than 40 articles to profl. and sci. jours. Grad. fellow Fannie and John Hertz Found., 1973-76, NSF, 1971-73; postdoctoral fellow NSF, 1977-78; rsch. fellow Alfred P. Sloan Found., 1985-89. Mem. AAAS, Am. Chem. Soc., Am. Phys. Soc., Sigma Xi. Office: Rice U Dept Chemistry Houston TX 77005

WEISMULLER, CONNIE LYNN GARDNER, ambulatory care nurse; b. Huntington, W.Va., Dec. 3, 1950; d. William Lacy and Inez Florene (Farley) Gardner; m. Jerome A. Jacobson, May 12, 1971 (div. Sept. 1980); 1 child, Scott M.; m. John Weismuller Jr., Sept. 17, 1988; 1 child, Kenneth. Diploma, Grady Meml. Hosp. Sch. Nursing, 1971; student, Fayetteville State U., 1972-73, Harris County C.C., 1983-85, Houston C.C., 1985, Graceland Coll., 1995. Cert. commun. health nurse, ANA. Staff nurse vascular surgery Grady Meml. Hosp., Atlanta, 1971-72; staff nurse ICCU/CCU Fayetteville (N.C.) VA Med. Ctr., 1972-74; staff nurse ICU/CCU Houston VA Med. Ctr., 1975-78, charge nurse emergency rm., 1978-81, relief nurse clinics, 1981-85, charge nurse med. clinic, 1985-91; staff nurse Lufkin (Tex.) VA Outpatient Clinic, 1991—; facilitator HIV Support Group, Houston, 1988-89; conf. presenter Topeka VA Med. Ctr., 1989, Ohio Rsch. Conf., Columbus, 1989; instr. self breast exam. Am. Cancer Soc.; Women Vet.'s coord., 1995—. Author numerous patient teaching plans. Mem. Nurse Orgn. Vet. Affairs, Washington, 1989—; com. mem. Boy Scouts Am., Houston, 1986-90, cub scout master, Spring,, Tex., 1985-86; historian for Angelina Christian Sch.; active Pavcat Tchrs. Fellowship, 1995-96. Mem. NAFE, Am. Assn. Ambulatory Nurse Admnistrs., Nurse Orgn. Vets. Affairs. Democrat. Methodist. Home: 2804 Fuller Springs Dr Lufkin TX 75901-6746 Office: Lufkin VA Outpatient Clinic 1301 W Frank Ave Lufkin TX 75904-3305

WEISS, GARY M., neurologist; b. Denver, Feb. 23, 1954; s. Joseph H. and Ruth (Huttner) W.; children from previous marriage: Nicole, Joshua; m. Priscilla (Cathleen) Brown, Aug. 23, 1991; children: Michael, Robert. BS in Medicine, Northwestern U., 1976, MD, 1978. Cert. Am. Bd. Psychiatry Neurology, 1984, Am. Bd. Electrodiagnostic Medicine, 1989. Intern Mayo Clinic, 1978-79, residency, 1979-82; chief exec. officer, Internat. Recovery Ctr., Cannes, France, Sebastian, Fla., 1990—, Bowling Green, Fla., 1988—; mem. exec. com., Sea Pines Rehab., Melbourne, Fla., 1988—, Humana Hosp., Sebastian; rsch. assn., Mayo Clinic; med. cons. Next Step Recovery Inst., Palm Bay, Fla., 1994—. Contbr. articles to profl. jours. Chmn. Weiss Found., Melbourne, 1989, co-chmn. Substance Abuse Com. Congressman Bacchus, Orlando, Fla., 1990. Mem. AMA, ANA, Am. Acad. Neurology,

Am. Bd. Electrodiagnostic Medicine, Am. Electroenephelographic Assn., Fla Med. Assn., Indian River Med. Soc., Sigma Xi. Democrat. Roman Catholic. Office: 1051 Port Malabar Blvd NE Ste 6 Melbourne FL 32905-5153

WEISS, JUDITH MIRIAM, psychologist; b. Chgo., June 29, 1939; d. Louis and Annette (Frazin) Schmerling; m. Jon Howard Kaas, May 19, 1963 (div. Dec. 1984); children: Lisa Karen, Jon Michael; m. Stephen Fred Weiss, Dec. 22, 1988. AB in Liberal Arts, Northwestern U., 1961; PhD, Duke U., 1969. Lic. clin. psychologist, Tenn. Postdoctoral fellow U. Wis. Hosp., Madison, 1969-71; neuropsychologist Mental Health Assocs., Madison, 1971-72; asst. prof. George Peabody Coll., Nashville, 1972-77, Vanderbilt U., Nashville, 1972-77; neuropsychologist Comprehensive Clin. Svcs., Nashville, 1977—; advocate, cons. Tenn. Protection and Advocacy, Inc., Nashville, 1976—. Mem. CABLE, Nashville. Mem. APA, Tenn. Psychol. Assn., Internat. Neuropsychol. Assn., Nat. Acad. Neuropsychology, U.s.-China Peoples Friendship Assn., Tenn. Head Injury Assn., B.R.A.I.N., Tenn. Assn. for the Talented and Gifted, Tenn. Assn. Audiologists and Speech-Lang. Pathologists, Nashville Area Psychol. Assn., Coun. for Learning Disabilities, Assn. for Children with Learning Disabilities. Jewish. Home: 893 Stirrup Dr Nashville TN 37221-1918 Office: Comprehensive Clin Svcs 102 Woodmont Blvd Ste 215 Nashville TN 37205-2287

WEISS, LARRY DAVID, medical educator; b. Pitts., Aug. 8, 1953. BA in Biology, Northwestern U., 1975; MD, Hahnemann Med. Coll., Phila., 1979; postgrad., Loyola U., New Orleans, 1993—. Diplomate Am. Bd. Emergency Medicine, Am. Bd. Hyperbaric Medicine; lic. physician, Pa., La. Rotating intern Mercy Hosp. of Pitts., 1979-80; emergency medicine resident Charity Hosp. of La., New Orleans, 1980-82; active staff dept. emergency medicine Western Pa. Hosp., 1982-84; chmn. dept. emergency medicine Mercy Hosp. of Pitts., 1984-87; active staff dept. emergency medicine Children's Hosp. of Pitts., 1987-90; staff, asst. med. dir. dept. hyperbaric & emergency medicine Presbyn.-Univ. Hosp., 1987-90; active staff emergency medicine Charity Hosp. La., New Orleans, 1990—, Meadowcrest Hosp., 1990-93; asst. dir. hyperbaric medicine Jo Ellen Smith Med. Ctr., New Orleans, 1990-94; co-dir. emergency svcs. Charity Hosp., New Orleans, 1994—; clin. instr. medicine U. Pitts., 1983-87, asst. prof., 1987-90; clin. asst. prof. medicine La. State U., New Orleans, 1990-93, clin. assoc. prof. medicine, 1993—, co-dir. hyperbaric medicine fellowship, 1992—, asst. dir. emergency medicine residency, 1991-94; vis. prof. U. Pitts., 1991; lectr. in field; instr. advanced cardiac life support Am. Heart Assn., 1980—, affiliate faculty Pa. chpt., 1982-90, La. chpt., 1992—. Contbr. numerous articles to profl. jours., chpts. to books; editor Triage newsletter of Nat. Bd. Diving and Hyperbaric Med. Tech., 1992—; co-editor Monitor newsletter of Ctr. for Emergency Medicine of Western Pa., 1989-90. Vol. United Jewish Fedn. of Greater Pitts., 1983-90; mem. Big Bros. and Sisters of Greater Pitts., 1987-90, Am. Jewish Com., 1988—, Am. Acad. Assn. for Peace in Middle East, 1988-90; bd. dirs. Congregation Beth Israel, New Orleans, 1992—; mem. Nat. Jewish Dem. Coalition, 1992—. Recipient Tchr. of the Yr. award La. State U. Emergency Medicine Residency Program, 1992-93; named Hon. Asst. Coroner, Orleans Parish, 1981-82; grantee Ocean Advanced rsch. Found., Pitts. Emergency Medicine Found., 1988, 92. Fellow Am. Coll. Emergency Physicians (bd. dirs. La. chpt. 1992—, sec. sect. hyperbaric medicine 1991-93, Pa. chpt. edn. com. 1989-90, Continuing Edn. award 1984, 87, 90, 93, 96); mem. AMA (Physicians Recognition award 1987, 87, 90, 93), Undersea and Hyperbaric Med. Soc., Soc. for Acad. Emergency Medicine, Orleans Parish Med Soc. (young physicians task force 1992—), La. Med. Soc., Am. Coll. Hyperbaric Medicine, Nat. Assn. EMS Physicians (charter mem.), Beta Beta Beta. Office: Charity Hosp Dept Emerg Med 1532 Tulane Ave Ste 1311 New Orleans LA 70140

WEISS, PATRICIA FINNERTY, educational consultant; b. Providence, R.I., Sept. 11, 1947; d. John and Stella P. Finnerty; m. James R. Weiss, 1971. BA, Boston Coll., 1969; MEd, U. N.C., 1974, PhD, 1978. Rschr., prin. investigator Frank Porter Graham Child Devel. Ctr., Chapel Hill, N.C., 1983-88; acting dir. U. N.C. Nat. Ctr. for The Paideia Program, Chapel Hill, N.C., 1988-91; pres. The Paideia Group Inc., Chapel Hill, N.C., 1991—, P.F. Weiss & Assocs., Chapel Hill, N.C., 1991—. Author: The History of Gifted Education, 1979, Paideia Teaching, co-author: (videotape series) Paideia Teaching. Grantee Smith Reynolds, Dupont Found., Exxon Found., NSF. Mem. ASCD, Coun. Exceptional Children. Office: The Paideia Group Inc PO Box 3423 Chapel Hill NC 27514-3423

WEISS, RANDALL A., television producer, supermarket executive; b. Gary, Ind., Sept. 3, 1952; s. Arthur and Sylvia (Mednick) W.; m. Adrienne J. Weiss, Feb. 5, 1973; children: Benjamin, Caleb, Joshua, James, Abigail, Emma. AA, Coll. DuPage, 1977; BA, Dallas Bapt. U., 1993; MA in Religious Studies, Greenwich U., 1994; diploma of practical theology, Christ for the Nations Inst., 1993; PhD, Greenwich U., 1995; MS in Jewish Studies, Spertus Inst. Jewish Studies, 1996; DMin, Faraston Theol. Sem., 1996. Gen. mgr. We Care Food Stores, Inc., Knox, Ind., 1975-84; pres., CEO We Care Food Stores, Inc. subs. Five Star Foods, Knox, Ind., 1984—; asst. prof. on adj. faculty ICI U.; dean Jewish studies dept. Faraston Theol. Sem. Author: Jewish Sects of the New Testament Era, Does Jacob's Trouble Wear a Cross?: Christianity: A Jewish Religion, In Search of the Lost Jewish Atonement; writer, artist: (TV show) Crosstalk, 1994, 95, 96; production mgr. Excellence in Christian Broadcasting; songwriter/pub. Internat. dir. Lesea Global Feed the Hungry, South Bend, Ind., 1988—. Mem. Full Gospel Bus. Men's Fellowship Internat. (life, banquet spkr.), Soc. for Pentecostal Studies, Evang. Theol. Soc. Office: Five Star Foods 1209 S Heaton St Knox IN 46534-2311

WEISS, RHETT LOUIS, lawyer; b. Kyushu, Japan, May 22, 1961; came to U.S., 1961; s. Armand Berl and Judith (Bernstein) W.; m. Kristen Sue Krieger, Oct. 11, 1987; children: Aaron Bradford, Alexander Donald. BS in Mgmt. cum laude, Tulane U., 1983; JD, Coll. William and Mary, 1986; exec. internat. bus. cert., Georgetown U., 1996. Bar: Va. 1986, D.C. 1993, N.Y. 1995, U.S. Ct. Appeals (4th cir.) 1986, U.S. Tax Ct. 1987, U.S. Dist. Ct. (we. dist.) Va. 1989, U.S. Bankruptcy Ct. (we. dist.) Va. 1989, U.S. Dist. Ct. (ea. dist.) Va. 1989, U.S. Bankruptcy Ct. (ea. dist.) Va. 1996. Vice pres., chief ops. officer First Fed. Savs. Bank Shenandoah Valley, Front Royal, Va., 1990-92; sr. assoc. Weil, Gotshal & Manges, Washington, 1992—; former prin., dir. Adamson, Crump, Sharp & Weiss, P.C., Front Royal; bd. dirs. Pentathlon Corp., Winchester, Va., Assns. Internat. Inc., McLean, Va., Weiss Pub. Co., Inc., Richmond, Va.; asst. town atty., counsel to Front Royal Planning Commn., 1987-90. Author: Portfolio Transactions: The Anatomy of a Deal, 1994, The Basics of Successful Negotiating, 1994, The Negotiating Process: Optimizing Give and Take, 1995, 96. Bd. dirs. Blue Ridge Arts Coun., Inc., 1987-92, v.p., 1989-90, pres., 1990-91; bd. dirs. Front Royal Little Theatre, Inc., 1988-89, Front Royal Warren County Unit Am. Heart Assn., 1991-92, Lord Fairfax C.C. Ednl. Found., 1991-94, Build-A-Future Found., 1994—; Shenrapawa dist. chmn. Shenandoah area coun. Boy Scouts Am., 1988-89, coun. treas., 1991-92, coun. bd. dirs., 1987-94; adv. com. Small Bus. Assistance Ctr., Lord Fairfax C.C.; mem. Seaton Elem. Sch. devel. team D.C. Pub. Schs. Ptnrs. In Edn. Program, 1994—. Recipient Nat. Quality Dist. award Boy Scouts Am., 1988, 89, Statuette award, 1992. Mem. ABA (loan practices subcom., loan practices and lender liability com., partnerships joint ventures and other investment vehicles com.), D.C. Bar (vice chmn. comml. trans. com. 1994-96, vice chmn. real property trans. com. 1996—, real estate, housing and land use sect.), Va. Bar Assn. (fellow John Marshall Soc.), Valley Estate Planning Coun. (bd. govs. 1989-92, pres. 1992), Front Royal-Warren County C. of C. (small bus. com. 1990-91), Univ. Club Washington (resident), Country Club Fairfax (Va.), Delta Tau Delta (sec. 1980-81), Beta Gamma Sigma, Beta Alpha Psi. Home: 7419 Kincheloe Rd Clifton VA 20124-1831 Office: Weil Gotshal & Manges 1615 L St NW Ste 700 Washington DC 20036-5610

WEISS, SALLY ANN, nursing educator; b. Wilkes-Barre, Pa., May 5, 1950; d. Bernard S. and Eleanor F. (Friedman) Barton; m. R. Joel Weiss, June 11, 1972; children: Stefan Craig, Alyssa Danielle. BSN, Am. U., 1972; MSN, U. Miami, 1986. RN, Fla. Clin. nurse ICU Wilkes-Barre Gen. Hosp., 1972; pub. health nurse team leader Luzerne County Vis. Nurse Assn., Wilkes-Barre, 1972-73; pub. health nurse II, coord. Pa. State Health Dept., Wilkes-Barre, 1973-74; clin. instr. community health nursing, BSN program Coll. Misericordia, Dallas, Pa., 1974; recovery rm. charge nurse Ambulatory Surg. Facility, Hollywood, Fla., 1978-85; assoc. prof. med.-surg. nursing, ADN program Broward C.C., Ft. Lauderdale, 1981—; clin. nurse specialist Neurol. Cons., P.A., Hollywood, 1994—; nursing coord. project Headstart, Broward County Health Dept., Ft. Lauderdale, 1979-81; nursing cons. spl. projects Hollywood Meml. Hosp., 1987-90, developer standards of care and practice; mem. adj. faculty, instr. state bd. rev. course Med. Coll. Pa., Phila., 1990—; presenter in field. Mem. Art and Cultural Ctr., Hollywood, 1993—, Friends of Broward Ctr. Performing Arts, Ft. Lauderdale, 1994—. Mem. AACN, Am. Assn. Neuroscience Nurses, Sigma Theta Tau. Office: Broward Community Coll 7200 Pines Blvd Hollywood FL 33024-7225

WEISS, SHIRLEY F., urban and regional planner, economist, educator; b. N.Y.C., Feb. 26, 1921; d. Max and Vera (Hendel) Friedlander; m. Charles M. Weiss, June 7, 1942. BA, Rutgers U., 1942; postgrad., Johns Hopkins U., 1949-50; M in Regional Planning, U. N.C., 1958; PhD, Duke U., 1973. Assoc. research dir. Ctr. for Urban and Regional Studies U. N.C., Chapel Hill, 1957-91, lectr. in planning, 1958-62, assoc. prof., 1962-73, prof., 1973-91, prof. emeritus, 1991—; joint creator-sponsor Charles and Shirley Weiss Urban Livability Program, U. N.C., Chapel Hill, 1992—; research assoc. Inst. for Research in Social Sci., U. N.C., 1957-73; research prof. U. N.C., Chapel Hill, 1973-91, acting dir. women's studies program Coll. Arts and Scis., 1985, faculty marshal, 1988-91; mem. tech. com. Water Resources Rsch. Inst., 1976-79; mem. adv. com. on housing for 1980 census Dept. Commerce, 1976-81; cons. Urban Inst., Washington, 1977-80; mem. rev. panel Exptl. Housing Allowance Program, HUD, 1977-80; mem. adv. bd. on built environ. Nat. Acad. Scis.-NRC, 1981-83, mem. program coordinating com. fed. constrn. coun. of adv. bd. on built environ., 1982-83; mem. Planning Accreditation Bd., Site Visitation Pool, Am. Inst. Cert. Planners and Assn. Collegiate Schs. Planning, 1985—; mem. discipline screening com. Fulbright Scholar awards in Architecture and City Planning, Coun. for Internat. Exchange of Scholars, 1985-88. Author: The Central Business District in Transition: Methodological Approaches to CBD Analysis and Forecasting Future Space Requirements, 1957, New Town Development in the United States: Experiment in Private Entrepreneurship, 1973; co-author: A Probabilistic Model for Residential Growth, 1964, Residential Developer Decisions: A Focused View of the Urban Growth Process, 1966, New Communities U.S.A., 1976; co-author, co-editor: New Community Development: Planning Process, Implementation and Emerging Social Concerns, vols. 1, 2, 1971, City Centers in Transition, 1976, New Communities Research Series, 1976-77; mem. editl. bd.: Jour. Am. Inst. Planners, 1963-68, Rev. of Regional Studies, 1969-74, 82-92, Internat. Regional Sci. Rev., 1975-81. Trustee Friends of Libr., U. N.C., Chapel Hill, 1988-94, Santa Fe Chamber Music Festival, adv. coun., 1990-91, trustee, 1991—; bd. dirs. Triangle Opera Theatre, 1986-89, 91—. Recipient Cornelia Phillips Spencer Bell award in recognition of contbns. to life and success of U. N.C. at Chapel Hill, 1996, Disting. Alumni award in recognition of outstanding contbns. in field of city and regional planning Alumni Assn. Dept. City and Regional Planning, U. N.C. at Chapel Hill, 1996, Mary Turner Lane award Assn. Women Faculty, 1994; Adelaide M. Zagoren fellow Douglass Coll., Rutgers U., 1994. Fellow Urban Land Inst. (sr., exec. group, community devel. coun. 1978—); mem. Am. Inst. Planners (sec., treas. southeast chpt. 1957-59, v.p. 1960-61), Am. Inst. Cert. Planners, Am. Planning Assn., Am. Econ. Assn., So. Regional Sci. Assn. (pres. 1977-78), Regional Sci. Assn. (councillor 1971-74, v.p. 1976-77), Nat. Assn. Housing and Redevelopment Ofcls., Interamerican Planning Soc., Internat. Fedn. Housing and Planning, Town and Country Planning Assn., Internat. Urban Devel. Assn., Econ. History Assn., Am. Real Estate and Urban Econs. Assn. (regional membership chmn. 1976-82, 84-85, dir. 1977-80), AAUP (chpt. pres. 1976-77, pres. N.C. Conf. 1978-79, mem. nat. council 1983-86, William S. Tacey award Assembly of State Confs.), Douglass Soc., Order of Valkyries, Phi Beta Kappa. Home: 155 N Hamilton Rd Chapel Hill NC 27514-5628

WEISS, STEVEN GARY, physician; b. Gary, Ind., June 28, 1949; s. Morris Eugene and Edith (Wolinsky) W.; m. Irene Cohn, May 14, 1977; children: Leah Rose, Julia Inger, Mara Emily, Max martin. BA, Ind. U., 1971, MD, 1974. Intern Highland Gen. Hosp., Oakland, Calif., 1974; resident Mt. Zion Hosp. and Med. Ctr., San Francisco, 1977; fellow U. Chgo., 1982; Assoc. prof. U. South Fla. Coll. Medicine, Tampa, 1984—; physician pvt. practice, Clearwater, Fla., 1984—; chief of med. staff Mease Hosps., Dunedin, Fla., 1991-92. Trustee Mease Health Care, 1991-94. Fellow Am. Acad. Allergy/Immunology, Am. Coll. Allergy. Office: 3251 McMullen Booth Rd Safety Harbor FL 34695

WEISSKOPF, BERNARD, pediatrician, child behavior, development and genetics specialist, educator; b. Berlin, Dec. 11, 1929; came to U.S., 1939, naturalized, 1944; s. Benjamin and Bertha (Loew) W.; m. Penelope Allderdice, Dec. 26, 1965; children: Matthew David, Stephen Daniel. BA, Syracuse U., 1951; MD, U. Leiden, Netherlands, 1958. Diplomate Am. Bd. Med. Mgmt. Intern Meadowbrook Hosp., East Meadow, N.Y., 1958-59; resident Meadowbrook Hosp., 1959-60, Johns Hopkins Hosp., Balt., 1962-64; fellow child psychiatry Johns Hopkins U. Sch. Medicine, Balt., 1962-64; asst. prof. pediatrics U. Ill. Coll. Medicine, Chgo., 1964-66; faculty U. Louisville, 1966—, prof. pediatrics, 1970—; also assoc. in psychiatry, pathology and Ob-gyn, dir. Child Evaluation Ctr., Louisville, 1966—; chmn. Gov.'s Adv. Com. Early Childhood, Gov.'s Council on Early Childhood, Ky., 1986-88. Contbr. articles to profl. jours. Trustee Jewish Hosp., Louisville, 1974-77. Served to capt. USAF, 1960-62. Fellow Am. Acad. Pediatrics, Am. Assn. Mental Deficiency; mem. Am. Soc. Human Genetics, So. Soc. Pediatric Rsch., Am. Soc. Law and Medicine, Am. Coll. Physician Execs. Home: 6409 Deep Creek Dr Prospect KY 40059-9422 Office: Child Evaluation Ctr 571 S Floyd St Louisville KY 40202-3818

WEISTROFFER, HEINZ ROLAND, information systems professional, educator; b. Herne, Germany, Jan. 24, 1950; came to the U.S., 1983; s. Rudolf Peter and Ursula (Krause) W.; m. Linda Massey Duke, June 8, 1974; children: George, Richard Peter, Charles. MA, Duke U., 1973; DSc, Free U. Berlin, 1976. Lectr., sr. lectr. Natal U., Durban, 1977-79; chief rsch. officer CSIR, Pretoria, South Africa, 1980-83; asst. prof. Va. Commonwealth U., Richmond, 1983-91, assoc. prof., 1991—; mem. mgmt. info. systems commn. Cath. Diocese of Richmond, 1995—. Contbr. articles to profl. jours. Mem. Assn. Info. Systems Profls. (v.p. publs. 1996—, v.p. meeting participation 1995, v.p. edn. 1994), INFORMS, Decision Scis. Inst., Internat. Soc. for Multiple Criteria Decision Making, others. Office: Va Commonwealth U Sch of Business Richmond VA 23284

WEISZ, PETER R., lawyer; b. Providence, Dec. 18, 1953; s. Paul B. and Lillian R. (Brown) W.; m. Pauline R. Cameron, June 3, 1973; children: Leah D., Samuel A., William J. BA in Econs. and Polit. Sci., Boston U., 1975; JD cum laude, U. Mich., 1978. Bar: Ga. 1979, Ga. Ct. Appeals 1979, U.S. Ct. Appeals (5th cir.) 1979, 81, U.S. Ct. Appeals (11th cir.) 1981, U.S. Dist. Ct. (no. dist.) Ga. 1979, U.S. Ct. Claims 1979, U.S. Supreme Ct. 1989. Ptnr. Stokes, Shapiro, Fussell & Genberg, Atlanta, 1984-85, Robinson & Weisz, Decatur, Ga., 1985-89, Weisz & Assocs., Atlanta, 1989-91; bd. dirs. HSP, Inc., Detroit, Harry S. Peterson Co., Inc., Detroit, Harry S. Peterson Co. of Can., Detroit, Harry S. Peterson Co. of Ga., Atlanta. Mem. ABA, Atlanta Bar Assn., Am. Trial Lawyers Assn., Forum Com. Constrn. Industry, Arbitrators' Panel Am., Am. Arbitration Assn. Home: 5325 Brooke Farm Dr Atlanta GA 30338-3150

WEITZ, JEANNE STEWART, artist, educator; b. Warren, Ohio, Apr. 30, 1920; d. William McKinley and Ruth (Stewart) Kohlmorgan; m. Loyal Wilbur Weitz, Aug. 1, 1940 (dec. 1986); children: Gail, Judith, John, Marc. BS in Art and English, Youngstown U., 1944; MEd in Art, U. Tex., El Paso, 1964; postgrad., Tex. Tech U., 1976. Indsl. engr. Republic Iron & Steel, Youngstown, Ohio, 1942-43; art tchr. pub. schs., Bessemer, Pa., 1943-44; art tchr. El Paso (Tex.) Independent Sch. Dist., 1944-50, 54-78, art. cons., 1978-87; art tchr. Hermosa Beach (Calif.) Independent Sch. Dist., 1950-53, El Paso Mus. Art, 1960-65; lectr. in art U. Tex., El Paso, 1963-66; instr. El Paso Community Coll., 1970-78; free-lance artist, lectr. El Paso, 1987—; supr. student tchr. U. Tex., El Paso, 1989-91. Represented in group exhibitions at Sun CarnivalExhbn., 1961, El Paso Mus. Art, 1962; author highsch. curriculum guide; exhibited at LVAA Shows, 1990 (5 First Places), Westside Art Guild, 1992, LVAA, 1992 (1st in Watercolor). Coordinator art edn. El Paso Civic Planning Coun., 1985-86; chmn. art edn., art resources dept. City of El Paso, 1982-83. Recipient Purchase award El Paso Art Assn. Spring Show, 1995. Mem. Tex. Art Edn. Assn. (conf. planner, local orgn. 1981, Hon. Mention award 1972), Nat. Soc. Arts and Letters (sec. El Paso chpt. 1988—), El Paso Mus. Art Guild, Lower Valley Art Assn. (Hon. Mention award 1988), Nat. Art Edn. Assn. (sec. 1988—, two 1st Place award LVAA shows 1989). Republican. Presbyterian. Home and Studio: 890 Forrest Hills Dr El Paso TX 79932-3017

WEITZNER, STANLEY WALLACE, physician, medical educator; b. N.Y.C., Feb. 12, 1929; s. HArry and Esther (Friedlander) W.; m. Nina Silver, Jan. 9, 1955; children: Howard, Gregg, Mitchell, Bradley. BA, NYU, 1949, MD, 1953. Diplomate Am. Bd. Anesthesiology. From asst. prof. to prof. SUNY, Bklyn., 1959-77; prof. anesthesiology Duke U. Med. Ctr., Durham, N.C., 1977—; cons. anesthesiology med. devices Bur. Med. Devices, FDA, Washington, 1973-76; mem. U.S. Tech. Adv. Group to Internat. Electrotech. Commn., 1981—; del. to Internat. Standards Orgn. Tech. Com. T21, 1969—. Contbr. articles to profl. jours. Capt. U.S. Army, 1957-59. Grantee NIH, 1960-65. Mem. ASTM (chmn. 1993-97). Home: 104 Hampshire Pl Chapel Hill NC 27516-8748 Office: Duke U Med Ctr PO Box 3094 Durham NC 27715-3094

WEKEZER, JERZY WLADYSLAW, civil engineering educator; b. Czestochowa, Poland, June 27, 1946; came to U.S., 1982; s. Kazimierz and Janina (Rosikon) W.; m. Mariola Nowak, July 15, 1969 (div. July 1980); 1 child, Michal; m. Henryka Debska, Dec. 27, 1983; 1 child, Joanna Amy. BSCE, Gdansk Tech. U., Poland, 1969, PhD in Applied Mechanics, 1974. Registered profl. engr., Alaska, Fla. Lectr., asst. prof. Gdansk Tech. U., Poland, 1969-81; rsch. assoc. Inst. Fluid-Flow Machinery, Gdansk, 1973-74; lectr. U. Basrah, Iraq; vis. asst. prof. U. So. Calif., L.A., 1983-85; assoc. prof. U. Alaska, Anchorage, 1985-87, prof., 1987—, head, civil engring. dept., 1990-94; dept. chmn. civil engring. Fla. Agrl. and Mech. U./Fla. State U. Coll. Engring., Tallahassee, 1994—; cons. Autogenesis, Anchorage, 1990, Fed. Hwy. Adminstrn., 1991-96, ARCO Alaska, Inc., 1992-93. Co-author two books, monographs; reviewed jour. articles. Mem. ASCE. Office: Fla A&M U/Fla State U Coll Engring Civil Engring 2525 Pottsdamer St Tallahassee FL 32310-6046

WELBORN, ANNIE B., primary school educator; b. Cameron, Tex., May 22, 1952; d. Frank Emil and Angellee Mathilda (Posival) Lesikar; m. Gibson VanCleave Vodrey, Nov. 7, 1972 (div. 1979); m. William Steven Welborn, Oct. 2, 1982. BSc in edn., U. Mary Hardin Baylor, 1977; MEd, Ga. So. U., 1991. Cert. tchr., Ga. Tchr. Copperas Cove (Tex.) ISD, 1978-81, Bryan County Schs., Richmond Hills, Ga., 1981-82; tchr., coach Vernon Parish Sch. Sys., Leesville, La., 1982-85; tchr. Killeen (Tex.) ISD, 1985-87, Liberty County Schs., Hinesville, Ga., 1987—; chairperson Liberty County Sci. Fair com., Hinesville, 1991—, So. Assn. of Colls. and Schs. sch. com., Hinesville, 1995-96; mem. Principals Organizational Team, Hinesville. Adv. bd. Am. Lung Assn., Hinesville, 1994-95; bd. dirs. Ft. Stewart Women's Bowling Assn., 1994-95. Recipient Outstanding Sci. Tchr. State Ga., Atlanta, 1993. Mem. Nat. Sci. Tchrs. Assn., Nat. Earth Sci. Tchrs. Assn., Profl. Assn. of Ga. Educators, Ga. Sci. Tchrs. Assn. (ednl. cons. Tchrs. Tng. Tchrs. 1994-96), Alpha Delta Kappa (treas.). Lutheran. Home: 111 Saint Andrews St Hinesville GA 31313 Office: Lewis Frasier Mid Sch Hinesville GA 31313

WELBORN, DAVID MORRIS, political science educator; b. Sept. 18, 1934; s. Claud Alson and Olga Nell (Morris) W.; m. Aline T. Bergeron, May 9, 1959; 1 child, Amélie. BA, U. Tex., 1956, PhD, 1962. Rsch. assoc. Ind. U., Bloomington, 1959-61; asst. prof. Tex. Tech. U., Lubbock, 1962-64; from asst. to assoc. prof. No. Ill. U., DeKalb, 1964-68; assoc. prof. U. Kans., Lawrence, 1968-73; prof. polit. sci. U. Tenn., Knoxville, 1973—; cons. Adminstrv. Conf. of U.S., Washington, 1973-75, 82-84. Author: Governance of Federal Regulatory Agencies, 1977, Regulation in the White House, 1993; co-author: Intergovernmental Relations in the American Administrative State, 1989. Recipient Rsch. award Johnson Adminstrv. History Project, 1979-85, Baker Oral History Project, 1991—; Congl. fellow Am. Polit. Sci. Assn., 1961-62, Pub. Policy fellow Am. Soc. Pub. Adminstrn., 1967-68. Home: 5213 Sunset Rd Knoxville TN 37914-4351 Office: Univ Tenn Dept Polit Sci Mcclung Towers Knoxville TN 37996

WELBORN, JAMES TODD, physician; b. Lexington, N.C., Oct. 7, 1923; s. William Fowle and Bessie Lee (Todd) W.; m. Lillian Marie Summers, Feb. 27, 1926; children: James Todd, Jr., Olivia Leigh, David Summers. BS in Chemistry & Biology, Davidson Coll., 1944; Cert. in Medicine, U. N.C., 1946; Med. Degree, U. Md., 1948. Lic. physician, N.C. Intern Charlotte (N.C.) Meml. Hosp., 1948-49; resident physician Vols. Am. Hosp., Balt., 1948; med. ofcr./capt. Tokyo U.S. Army Hosp., 1956-58; staff physician Lexington (N.C.) Meml. Hosp., 1949-94; coroner and med. examiner Davidson County, 1968-72; contractual physician N.C. Dept. of Corrections; chief of staff Lexington Hosp., 1966-68; trustee Lexington Hosp., 1966-68. Elder First Presbyn. Ch., Lexington, 1972—. Maj. U.S. Army, 1956-58, Japan. Mem. So. Med. Assn. (life), U. Md. Med. Alumni Assn. (life), Lexington Hosp. Med. Staff (hon.), Davidson County Med. Soc. (pres. 1964). Home: 504 Weaver Dr Lexington NC 27292

WELCH, EDWIN HUGH, academic administrator; b. Balt., Apr. 11, 1944; s. Lester Kenneth and Catherine (Dodrer); m. Janet Gail Boggess, Nov. 22, 1977. BA, Western Md. Coll., 1965; STB, Boston U. Sch. Theology, 1968; postgrad., London Sch. Econs. and Polit. Sci., 1968-69; PhD, Boston U., 1971. Assoc. prof., chmn. W.Va. Wesleyan Coll., Buckhannon, 1971-75; assoc. prof., chmn. Lebanon Valley Coll., Annville, Pa., 1975-79, dir. weekend coll., 1979-80; dean Lakeland Coll., Sheboygan, Wis., 1980-81; provost Wartburg Coll., Waverly, Iowa, 1981-89; pres. U. Charleston, W.Va., 1989—; chmn. Iowa Deans Confs., Des Moines, 1984-89; title III evaluator Iowa Wesleyan Coll., Mt. Pleasant, 1983-85. Contbr. articles to edn. jours. Bd. dirs. Bus. and Indsl. Devel. Corp., One Valley Bank, Charleston Area Med. Ctr.; v.p. Nat. Inst. Chem. Studies; creator, dir. Community Leadership Devel. Program, Waverly, 1986-88; bd. dirs., pres. Lebanon (Pa.) Family Planning Assn., 1976-81. Named Tchr. of Yr., W.Va. Wesleyan Coll., 1974. Mem. Nat. Assn. Ind. Colls. and Univs., Balt. Conf. United Meth. Ch. (ordained), Appalachian Coll. Assn., Coun. Ind. Colls., Rotary Internat. (bd. dirs. Charleston). Democrat. Methodist. Office: U Charleston Office of Pres Charleston WV 25304-1099*

WELCH, JEANIE MAXINE, librarian; b. L.A., Jan. 22, 1946; d. Howard Carlton and Roberta Jean (Dunsmuir) W. BA, U. Denver, 1967, MA, 1968; M of Internat. Mgmt., Am. Grad. Sch. Internat. Mgmt., 1981. Asst. libr. Am. Grad. Sch. Internat. Mgmt., Glendale, Ariz., 1968-83; reference libr. Lamar U., Beaumont, Tex., 1983-85, head reference, 1985-87; reference unit head U. N.C., Charlotte, 1988—. Author: The Spice Trade, 1994; contbr. articles to profl. jours. Chpt. pres. NOW, Beaumont, 1985-87, state sec., Tex., 1986; exec. bd. Ariz. State Libr. Assn., 1976-80. Rsch. grantee Tex. Libr. Assn., 1986; named Dun & Bradstreet Info. Svcs. Online Champion of Yr., 1996. Mem. ALA, N.C. Libr. Assn. Democrat. Methodist. Office: U NC Atkins Libr Charlotte NC 28223

WELCH, JOE LLOYD, marketing educator; b. Texarkana, Tex., Dec. 30, 1948; s. Morris Eugene and Billie Jo (Boyd) W.; m. Lydia Cowan, May 9, 1975; children: Erin, Christina. BBA, Tex. Christian U., 1970; MBA, U. North Tex., 1972, PhD, 1975. Regional v.p. Sales Corp. Am., Memphis, 1970-71; asst. prof. U. North Fla., Jacksonville, 1975-76, U. Dallas, Irving, 1976-80; nat. sales mgr. Standard Meat Co., Ft. Worth, 1980-81; v.p. Savitz Rsch. Ctr., Dallas, 1981-83; assoc. prof. U. North Tex., Denton, 1983-88, prof., 1988—; pres. Syndics Rsch. Corp., Dallas, 1983—. Author: Marketing Law, 1980, Sales Force Management, 1983; contbr. articles to profl. jours. Named one of Outstanding Young Men of Am., U.S. Jaycees, 1978. Mem. Am. Mktg. Assn. Home: 4566 Mill Run Rd Dallas TX 75244-6431 Office: U North Tex Coll Bus Adminstrn Denton TX 76203

WELCH, KATHY JANE, information technology executive; b. San Antonio, Aug. 5, 1952; d. John Dee and Pauline Ann (Overstreet) W.; m. John Thomas Unger, Jan. 8, 1977. BAS in Computer Sci., So. Meth. U., 1974; MBA in Fin., U. Houston, 1978. Programmer, analyst Tex. Instruments, Houston, 1974-76, project leader, 1976-78, br. mgr., 1978-81; mgr. systems and programming Global Marine, Houston, 1981-84, mgr. office automation, 1984-85, mgr. user systems, 1985-88, dir. MIS, Advanced Tech. div. Browning-Ferris Industries, Houston, 1988-89, dir. Telecom. and Computer Svcs., 1989-93; v.p. info. tech. Talent Tree Svcs., Inc., Houston, 1993-96; info. tech. cons. Tech. Ptnrs., Inc., Houston, 1996—. Mem. Mensa, Beta

Gamma Sigma. Office: Talent Tree Svcs Inc 9703 Richmond Ave Houston TX 77042-4620

WELCH, MADELEINE LAURETTA, medical/surgical and occupational health nurse; d. Roger M. and Aldea (Fortier) LeComte; m. Raymond F. Welch Jr. Diploma, St. Anne's Hosp., 1965; postgrad., SMTI, 1967. RN, Mass., Fla., N.J., R.I. Relief occupational health nurse Gen. Mills, Pawtucket, R.I., 1983; occupational health nurse Providence Jour. Co., 1980-84, Davol div. Bard, Cranston, R.I.; staff nurse St. Cloud (Fla.) Hosp.; instr. CPR ARC, 1981-84. Eucharistic min., 1990, Bereavement Ministry St. Thomas Aquinas, 1992—. Recipient Svc. to Youth award Cub Scouts, 1980; grantee State of Fla., 1988.

WELCH, ROBERT BALLINGER, investment planner; b. Baton Rouge, Nov. 16, 1936; s. Jasper Arthur and Oramay (Ballinger) W.; m. Janice I. Perrine; children: Robert B. Jr., Mary Inger, Carlton Arthur; m. Judith Dorene Brace, Apr. 17, 1971. BA in Comm. and Mktg., U. Ill., 1961. Lic. investment broker and planner. Advt. account mgr., TV writer, dir. sales Nat. Advt. Agy. & TV Broadcasting, Baton Rouge, Dallas, Houston, until 1972; gen. ptnr. real estate devel. Nat. Firms, New Orleans, 1972-80, investment broker, 1980—; mem. adv. bd. Computer Mentors. Co-prodr.: (TV documentary) No Bells at Carville, 1959 (Emmy award). Mem. student life adv. bd. Tulane U. Mem. Carl G. Jung Soc. (treas., bd. dirs.), Sigma Chi (regional officer). Home and Office: 106 Westchester Pl New Orleans LA 70131

WELCH, ROBYN PERLMAN, pediatric critical care nurse; b. N.Y., Feb. 10, 1963; d. Jared Charles and Joan Phyllis (Kastin) Perlman; m. Martin Edward Welch, Apr. 22, 1989; children: Jacquelyn Hope, Alison Paige. BSN, U. Fla., 1986, MSN, 1994. Cert. pediatric ALS. Home health nurse Home Choice, Orlando, Fla., 1986-87; charge nurse Orlando Regional Med. Ctr., 1986-87; nurse clinician Home Nutritional Support, Tampa/Gainesville, Fla., 1989; staff nurse pediatric ICU Shands Teaching Hosp., Gainesville, 1987-94; pediatric emergency rm. nursing care coord. St. Mary's Hosp., West Palm Beach, Fla., 1994-95; pediatric educator West Boca Med. Ctr., Boca Raton, Fla., 1995—. Mem. Emergency Nurses Assn., Fla. Nurses Assn., Sigma Theta Tau.

WELDON, DAVID JOSEPH, JR., congressman, physician; b. Amityville, N.Y., Aug. 31, 1953; s. David Joseph and Anna (Mallardi) W.; m. Nancy Sourbeck, Nov. 26, 1956; 1 child, Kathryn. BS, SUNY, Stony Brook, 1978; MD, SUNY, Buffalo, 1981. Elder Zion Christian Fellowship, Palm Bay, Fla., 1991—; mem. 104th Congress from 15th Fla. dist., Washington, DC, 1995—; pvt. practice, Melbourne, Fla., 1987—; pres. Space Coast Family Forum, Melbourne, 1988-91. Maj. USAR, 1981—. Mem. AMA, Am. Coll. Physicians, Fla. Med. Assn. Home: 1602 Willard Rd NW Melbourne FL 32907-6320 Office: US House of Reps 216 Cannon Bldg Washington DC 20515-1015*

WELGE, JACK HERMAN, JR., lawyer; b. Austin, Tex., Sept. 12, 1951; s. Jack Herman and Regina Victoria (Hunger) W.; m. Frances Ava Roddy Avent, Dec. 23, 1977; children: Kirsten Frances Page Welge, Kathleen Ava Regina Welge. BA, U. Tex., 1974; JD, St. Mary's U., 1977. Bar: Tex. 1977, U.S. Dist. Ct. (ea. dist.) Tex. 1979, U.S. Dist. Ct. (no. dist.) Tex. 1982, U.S. Ct. Appeals (5th cir.) 1983, U.S. Supreme Ct., 1984; cert. family law Tex. Bd. Legal Specialization. Asst. dist. atty. Gregg County Criminal Dist. Atty., Longview, Tex., 1978-79; assoc. Law Office of G. Brockett Irwin, Longview, 1979-81; judge Mcpl. Ct. of Record, Longview, 1979-81; ptnr. Adams & Sheppard, Longview, 1981-83; pvt. practice, 1983—; of counsel East Tex. Assn. for Abused Families, Longview, 1985-90. Bd. dirs. Longview Mus. and Arts Ctr., 1991-94, East Tex. Coun. on Alcoholism and Drug Abuse, Longview, 1981-83, Longview Comty. Theater, 1979-82, East Tex. Assn. for Abused Families, Longview, 1983-85, Salvation Army, 1994—; vestry Trinity Episcopal Ch., Longview, 1993-96. Mem. State Bar of Tex. (pro bono coll., contested custody case panel, protective case panel, Gregg County lawyers pro bono project, Outstanding Contbn. award 1990, Disting. Svc. award 1993, 95, Outstandiing Pro Bono Atty. 1994), Rotary (pres. Longview club 1987-88, Paul Harris fellow 1982), Gregg County Bar Assn. (pres. 1983), Gregg County Family Law Coun., Tex. Acad. Family Law Specialists, East Tex. Knife and Fork Club (pres. 1983-84), Mason, Delta Theta Phi (dean 1977). Office: 211 E Tyler St Longview TX 75601-7209

WELGE, WILLIAM D., archivist; b. San Antonio, Apr. 29, 1953; s. Frederick C. and Iva L. (Greenawalt) W. BA in Journalism, U. Okla., 1976; MA and History summa cum laude, Ctrl. State U., Edmond, Okla., 1988. Cert. archivist Acad. Cert. Archivists. Customer svc. rep. J.C. Penney Co., Oklahoma City, 1973-84; microfilm technician Okla. Hist. Soc., Oklahoma City, 1977-82, asst. archivist, 1990-81, archivist, records mgmt. specialist I, 1981-90, dir. archives and manuscripts div., 1990—; presenter in field to profl., geneal. and patriotic socs.; judge State History Day, 1981—. Recipient cert. of merit Rochester Inst. Tech., 1980, Vol. Action Ctr. Oklahoma City, 1987, ednl. support award Oklahoma City Pub. Schs., 1984. Mem. Soc. S.W. Archivists, Okla. State Hist. Soc. (life), Oklahoma County Hist. Soc. (life, treas., v.p., pres. 1983-87), Presbyn. Hist. Soc. S.W. (chmn. 1990—), U.S. Grant High Sch. Alumni Assn. (historian 1991—), Phi Alpha Theta. Republican. Presbyterian. Office: Okla Hist Soc 2100 N Lincoln Blvd Oklahoma City OK 73105-4915

WELLBERG, EDWARD LOUIS, JR., insurance company executive; b. Eagle Pass, Tex., June 5, 1945; s. Edward L. Wellberg and Nell L. (Kownslar) Walker; children: Elizabeth, Ashley, Jennifer; m. Yvonne Hill, Feb. 4, 1989. Student, St. Mary's U., San Antonio, 1978. CLU, Life Underwriters Tng. Coun. Fellow. Sales agt. Washington Nat. Ins. Co., San Antonio, 1969-82; ptnr. Mazur Bennett Wellberg Assocs., San Antonio, 1982-91; mktg. exec. Wellberg Assocs., San Antonio, 1991—; bd. dirs. Tex. State Ins. Bd. Adv. Coun., Austin, 1988-94. Contbr. articles to trade publs. Mem. Am. Soc. CLU's, Tex. Assn. Life Underwriters (bd. dirs. 1983-86, 92-93, pres. 1996), Tex. Life Underwriters Polit. Action Com. (vice chmn. 1981-83, 88-90, chmn. 1990-92), San Antonio Assn. Life Underwriters (pres. 1982). Home: 1707 Ashley Cir San Antonio TX 78232-4710 Office: Wellberg Assocs 12500 San Pedro Ave Ste 650 San Antonio TX 78216-2858

WELLER, LAURIE JUNE, artist, educator; b. Warsaw, N.Y., May 18, 1953; d. Charles M. and Mary (Loysen) W.; m. Gary B. Washmon, Sept. 5, 1980; children: Katelin, Jesse. BFA, U. Ill., 1976; MFA, Tyler Sch. of Art, Phila., 1980. Instr. Laguna Gloria Art Mus. Sch., Austin, Tex., 1980-83; lectr. S.W. Tex. State U., San Marcos, 1981-83; v.p. Austin Contemporary Visual Arts Assn., 1984-85; lectr. Tex. Woman's U., Denton, 1988-90, adj. asst. prof., 1990—. One woman shows include Hadler/Rodriguez Gallery, Houston, 1981, 85, U. Gallery Southwest Tex. State U., San Marcos, Tex., 1983, Air Gallery, Austin, 1984, Amarillo Art Ctr., Tex., 1984, Objects Gallery, San Antonio, Tex., 1984, East & West Galleries Tex. Women's U., Denton, Tex., 1987, Gardiner Art Gallery Okla. State U., Stillwater, 1987, Patrick Gallery, Austin, 1989, Mountain View Coll., Tex., 1993, William Campbell Contemporary Art, Ft. Worth, 1993, Tex. Woman's U., Denton, 1994, Lakeside Gallery Richland Coll., Dallas, 1995, Harry Nohr Gallery U. Wis., Platteville, 1996; exhibited in two person shows at Illini Union Gallery U. Ill., Urbana, 1984, Patrick Gallery, Austin, Tex., 1986, Tarrant County Jr. Coll., Ft. Worth, Tex., 1990, Parkland Coll. Art Gallery, Champaign, Ill., 1990, Brookhaven Coll., Dallas, 1993, Irving Art Ctr., Irving, Tex., 1993, N. Lake Coll., Dallas, 1994; exhibited in group shows at Butler Inst. Am. Arts, Youngstown, Ohio, 1976 , Springfield (Mo.) Art Mus., 1979, Laguna Gloria Art Mus., Austin, 1982, San Antonio Mus. Art, Tex., 1985, Abilene Art Mus, Texas, 1988, William Campbell Contemporary Art, Ft. Worth, Tex., 1989, Matrix Gallery, Austin Tex., 1990, Charles P. Goddard Ctr. Visual Arts, Ardmore, Ohio, 1991, Laguna Gloria Art Mus., Austin, 1991, Longview Mus. Arts Ctr. Longview, Tex., 1992, Brookhaven Coll., Dallas, 1994, Meadows Gallery, Denton, 1994, Coll. of the Mainland, Texas City, Tex., 1995, Maurice Sternberg Gallery, Chgo., 1996; represented in permanent collections Pepsi-Cola South, Texas Instruments, Radisson Hotels, 3M Corp., Amoco Oil Co., Prudential Ins. Co., Steak & Ale Corp., Tambrands. Fellow Va. Ctr. for Creative Arts, Sweet Briar, 1982, 84. Home: RR 2 Box 637-m Denton TX 76208-9303 Office: Tex Woman's U PO Box 425469 Denton TX 76204-0995

WELLER, RICHARD IRWIN, physics educator; b. Newark, Mar. 3, 1921; married, 1989; 2 children. BEE, CCNY, 1944; BS, Union Coll., 1948; MS, Fordham U., 1950, PhD in Physics, 1953. Elec. engr. N.Am. Phillips Co., Mt. Vernon, N.Y., 1944, 45-46, Guy F. Atkinson Co., Alaska, 1944-45, Crow, Lewis & Wick, N.Y.C., 1947, Edward E. Ashley, N.Y.C., 1948, Allied Processes Co., N.Y.C., 1950, V.L. Falotico & Assocs., N.Y.C., 1950-51; electrical engr. Singmaster & Breyer, 1951; instr. physics Bklyn. Coll., 1952-53; asst. prof. SUNY Maritime Coll., N.Y.C., 1953-54; med. physicist Brookhaven Nat. Lab., Upton, N.Y., 1954-57; prof., chmn. dept. physics Franklin and Marshall Coll., Lancaster, Pa., 1957-70; prof. physics, dean. Sch. Sci. and Math. Edinboro (Pa.) State Coll., 1970-81; instr. Manhattan Coll., 1949-50, Fordham U., N.Y.C., 1950-52, Newark Coll. Engring., 1952-53, Broward C.C., Ft. Lauderdale, Fla., 1981-83, Brevard C.C., Cocoa, Fla., 1983-84, Fla. Inst. Tech., Melbourne, 1984-85; cons. Brookhaven Nat. Lab., Fairchild Camera & Instrument Corp., Nuclear Sci. & Engring. Corp.; mem. nat. resch. coun. subcom. Nat. Acad. Sci. Mem. AAAS, IEEE, Am. Soc. Engrng. Educators, Am. Physics Soc., Am. Assn. Physics Tchrs., Health Physics Soc., Sigma Xi.

WELLFORD, HARRY WALKER, federal judge; b. Memphis, Aug. 6, 1924; s. Harry Alexander and Roberta Thompson (Prothro) W.; m. Katherine E. Potts, Dec. 8, 1951; children: Harry Walker, James B. Buckner P., Katherine T., Allison R. Student, U. N.C., 1943-44; BA, Washington and Lee U., 1947; postgrad. in law, U. Mich., 1947-48; LLD, Vanderbilt U., 1950. Bar: Tenn. 1950. Atty. McCloy, Myar & Wellford, Memphis, 1950-60, McCloy, Wellford & Clark, Memphis, 1960-70; judge U.S. Dist. Ct., Memphis, 1970-82; judge U.S. Ct. Appeals (6th cir.), Cin. and Memphis, 1982-92, sr. judge, 1992—; mem. pres.' adv. coun. Rhodes Coll. Chair Senator Howard Baker campaigns, 1964-66; chair Tenn. Hist. Commn., Tenn. Constnl. Bicentennial Commn., 1987-88; mem. charter drafting com. City of Memphis, 1967, Tenn. Am. Revolution Bicentennial Commn., 1976, com. on Adminstrn. Fed. Magistrates Sys., Jud. Conf. Subcom. Adminstrn. of Criminal Law Probation; clk. session, commr. Gen. Assembly; elder Presbyn. Ch.; moderator Memphis Presbytery, 1994. Recipient Sam A. Myar award for svc. to profession and community Memphis State Law U., 1963. Mem. Phi Beta Kappa, Omega Delta Kappa. Home: 91 N Perkins Rd Memphis TN 38117-2425 Office: US Ct Appeals 1176 Federal Bldg 167 N Main St Memphis TN 38103-1816

WELLINGTON, MARIE ANNETTE, French language educator; b. Chgo., Dec. 4, 1953; d. John Adam and Marie Adele (Zeilstra) W. BA in French and Spanish, Wellesley Coll., 1976; AM in Romance Langs., Harvard U., 1977, PhD in Romance Langs., 1981. Teaching fellow in French Harvard U., Cambridge, Mass., 1977-81; asst. prof. French Mich. State U., East Lansing, 1981-83, Loyola U., Chgo., 1986-87, U. Notre Dame, South Bend, Ind., 1987-91; asst. prof. French Mary Washington Coll., Fredericksburg, Va., 1991-94, assoc. prof., 1994—; teaching fellow in French Harvard U., 1977-81; rsch. fellow Inst. Scholarship, U. Notre Dame, summer 1988. Contbr. articles and books revs. to profl. jours. Vol. Historic Fredericksburg Found., 1991—. Named Best Teaching fellow, 1980, 81; Durant scholar, 1976. Mem. MLA, Am. Assn. Tchrs. French, Am. Soc. Eighteenth-Century Studies, N.Am. Assn. for Study Jean-Jacques Rousseau, South Ctrl. MLA, South Atlantic MLA, Midwestern Am. Soc. Eighteenth-Century Studies, N.E. Am. Soc. Eighteenth Century Studies, Southeastern Am. Soc. Eighteenth-Century Studies. Office: Mary Washington Coll Dept Modern Fgn Langs Fredericksburg VA 22401

WELLMAN, GERALD EDWIN, JR., safety and fire inspector; b. Steubenville, Ohio, Feb. 27, 1948; s. Gerald Edwin Sr. and Rose Marie (Bonacci) W.; 1 child, Jerad Anthony. AS Data Processing, West Liberty State Coll., 1974, BSBA, 1974; MS in Safety Mgmt., W.Va. U., 1991, cert. of advanced study, 1995. With production, mechanical Wheeling and Pitts. Steel Corp., Beech Bottom, W.Va., 1966-76; with production, mechanical, safety Wheeling and Pitts. Steel Corp., Steubenville, Ohio, 1976—, also safety and fire insp., safety coord.:, 1993, 95; mem. wellness com. Wheeling and Pitts. Steel Plant; safety coord. Wheeling and Pitts. Steel Corp. Hazardous Material Team; safety chmn., trustee local 1190 United Steel Workers Am.; mem. Am. Iron and Steel Inst. R.R. Com. Contbr. articles to profl. jours. With U.S. Army, 1967-69, Vietnam. Mem. Am. Iron and Steel Inst. (railroad com.), West Liberty State Coll. Alumni Club, West Liberty State Coll Hilltops Club, W.Va. U. Alumni Club, Mountaineer Athletic Club, Dapper Dan Club Upper Ohio Valley, Brooke High Sch. Boosters Club, W.Va. Sheriffs Assn., Follansbee Blue Waves Boosters Club, Nat. Fire Protection Assn., Nat. Safety Coun., W.Va. Safety Coun., Western Pa. Safety Coun., U.S. Steel Workers Am., Eagles Club, Am. Soc. Safety Engrs. (nominating com. 1989—), Alpha Kappa Psi. Home: 311 Hillcrest Dr Wellsburg WV 26070-1943

WELLON, ROBERT G., lawyer; b. Port Jervis, N.Y., Apr. 18, 1948; s. Frank Lewis and Alice (Stephens) W.; m. Jan Montgomery, Aug. 12, 1972; children: Robert F., Alice Wynn. AB, Emory U., 1970; JD, Stetson Coll. Law, 1974. Assoc. Turner, Turner & Turner, Atlanta, 1974-78; ptnr. Ridley, Wellon, Schwieger & Brazier, Atlanta, 1978-86; of counsel Wilson, Strickland & Benson, Atlanta, 1987—; adj. prof. Atlanta Law Sch., 1981-94; adj. prof. law Emory U. Sch. of Law, 1995—. Gov.'s task force chmn. Atlanta 2000, 1978; exec. com., treas., 2d v.p. Atlanta Easter Seals Soc., 1983-88; rep. Neighborhood Planning Unit, 1981-83; adminstrv. bd. Northside United Meth. Ch.; bd. dirs. Atlanta Found. for Psychoanalysis, Inc. Served with USAR, 1970-76. Recipient Judge Joe Morris award Stetson Coll. Law, St. Petersburg, 1974, Charles E. Watkins svc. award 1995). Mem. Fla. Bar, State Bar. Ga. (professionalism com. 1994—), Atlanta Bar Assn. (bd. dirs. 1978-88, pres. 1986-87, bd. trustees CLE), Lawyers Club Atlanta, Old War Horse Lawyers Club. Methodist. Office: 1100 One Midtown Pla 1360 Peachtree St NE Atlanta GA 30309-3214

WELLS, ANNE SHARP, historian, researcher; b. Jackson, Miss., Mar. 25, 1952; d. Elden C. and Jean (Robinson) W. BA in History, Miss. State U., 1974, MA in History, 1975; MLS, U. Ala., Tuscaloosa, 1981. Cert. archival adminstr. Rsch. asst. Douglas MacArthur Biog. Project Miss. State U., Mississippi State, 1974-85, manuscript libr., assoc. prof., 1975-88; adminstrv. faculty Va. Mil. Inst., Lexington, 1988—; cons. Evans Meml. Libr., Aberdeen, Miss., 1985. Co-author: From Pearl Harbor to V-J Day: The American Armed Forces in World War II, 1995, A Time for Giants: Politics of the American High Command in World War II, 1987, Refighting the Last War: Command and Crisis in Korea, 1950-53, 1992; contbr. articles to profl. jours. Mem. Am. Hist. Assn., Soc. Mil. History, Soc. Am. Archivists, Soc. Miss. Archivists (pres. 1982-83), WWII Studies Assn. (formerly Am. Com. on History of 2d World War, editor 1990-93), Soc. for Historians of Am. Fgn. Rels., Phi Kappa Phi (pres. Va. Mil. Inst. chpt. 1992-93). Office: Va Mil Inst Dept History And Polit Lexington VA 24450

WELLS, BENJAMIN GLADNEY, lawyer; b. St. Louis, Nov. 13, 1943; s. Benjamin Harris and Katherine Emma (Gladney) W.; m. Nancy Kathryn Harpster, June 7, 1967; children: Barbara Gladney, Benjamin Harpster. BA magna cum laude, Amherst (Mass.) Coll., 1965; JD cum laude, Harvard U., 1968. Bar: Ill. 1968, Tex. 1973, U.S. Tax Ct. 1973, U.S. Ct. Claims 1975, U.S. Ct. Appeals (5th cir.) 1981, U.S. Dist. Ct. (so. dist.) Tex. 1985, U.S. Dist. Ct. (we. dist.) Tex. 1993. Assoc. Kirkland & Ellis, Chgo., 1968-69; assoc. to ptnr. Baker & Botts, L.L.P., Houston, 1973—; mem. Harvard Legal Aid Bur., 1966-68. Contbr. articles to profl. jours. Mem. devel. com. St. John's Sch., Houston, 1987—, chmn. planned giving com., 1987—; active Harvard Legal Aid Bureau, 1966-68. Capt. U.S. Army, 1969-72. Fellow Am. Coll. Tax Counsel; mem. Houston Tax Roundtable (pres. 1994-95), The Forest Club, The Houston Club, Phi Beta Kappa. Presbyterian. Office: Baker & Botts LLP One Shell Plaza 910 Louisiana St Houston TX 77002-4995

WELLS, BETTY CALHOUN, elementary education educator; b. Haywood County, N.C., Feb. 28, 1938; d. Fred Herbert and Agnes Lee Calhoun; m. Keller Wells, June 15, 1956; children: Cynthia Lee Register, Jeffrey Lane Wells. BS in Elem. Edn., Bob Jones U., Greenville, S.C., 1961; MRE, Bethany Theol. Sem., Dothan, Ala., 1989; postgrad., U. S.C. Cert. elem. tchr. N.C., S.C., Fla. First grade tchr. Greenville County Sch. Dist., S.C., 1961-71; first grade tchr. Providence Christian Sch., Riverview, Fla., 1971-80, pre-sch. dir., 1980-91, elem. supr., 1991—. Leader Girl Scouts of Am., Greenville, 1961-65; appointee Child Care Facilities Adv. Bd., 1996; mem. various Bapt. Ch. orgns. Recipient awards for profl. and ch. activities. Mem. Fla. Assn. of Christian Schs. Home: 210 Mary Ellen Ave Seffner FL 33584 Office: Providence Christian Sch 5416 Providence Rd Riverview FL 33569

WELLS, CHARLES TALLEY, judge. Bar: Fla. 1965, U.S. Dist Ct. (middle dist. of Fla.), U.S. Ct. Appeals,(5th cir.) now (11th cir.) 1966, U.S. Supreme Ct., 1969, U.S. Dist. Ct., U.S. Dist. Ct. (So. dist), Fla., 1976, U.S. Ct. of Claims, 1990. Trial atty. U.S. dept justice Washington, 1969; pvt. practice maguire, Voohris and Wells, PA, Orlando, Fla., 1965-68, 1970-75, Wells, Gattis, Hollowes & Carpenter, PA, Orlando, Fla., 1976-94; justice Fla. Supreme Ct., Tallahassee. Methodist. Office: Fla Supreme Ct Supreme Ct Bldg 500 S Duval St Tallahassee FL 32399-6556

WELLS, CLAUDIA MAE ELLIS, nutritionist, educator; b. Reform, Ala., Apr. 25, 1911; d. Leven Handy and Mary (Sibley) Ellis; m. John Walter Wells, Sept. 10, 1935; 1 child, John Walter. BS in Home Econs., U. Ala., 1931, MS, 1933. Registered dietitian. Dietitian U. Ala., 1931-33; tchr. home econs., sci. Ala. high schs., 1942-50; sci. tchr. Marietta (Ga.) High Sch., 1950-53, head sci. dept., 1953-56; instr. biology U. Ga. Ctr., Marietta, 1953-56; asst. prof. nutrition and food sci. U. Ky., 1956-76; organizer Ga. Sci. Fairs, 1954-56, Lafayette (Ky.) High Sch. Band Club, Ctrl. Ky. Youth Orch. Assn., 1956-58; presenter papers in field. Author: History of Aiken Garden Club, 1990, Laborers Together, 1995; contbr. articles to profl. jours. Active ARC, YWCA, PTA, Ala., Ga., Ky.; sponsor Bapt. Student Union U. Ky., 1964; assoc. Young People's Dir., mem. Bapt. Tng. Union, Cmty. Missions divsn. Woman's Missionary Union, chmn., 1963-64, Elkhorn (Ky.) Assn.; tchr. ladies' Sunday Sch. class Aiken (S.C.) 1st Bapt. Ch., 1976—, pres. ch. tng. group, 1978, 80, chm. nominating com., 1978-79; pres. Aiken Garden Club, 1978-80; active Aiken Garden Coun., 1978-80, parliamentarian, 1979-84; vol. Multiple Sclerosis Soc., 1980; pres. Sunshine Club, 1988-90, mem. sr. adult choir, 1990—; active Nat. Arbor Day Found., 1995—. Named Honorable Order of Ky. Col., 1976; honoree 50th Anniversary of Coll. Home Econs., U. Ala., 1981; named to Faculty Hall of Fame, U. Ky. Mem. NEA, Am. Ednl. Assn., Ga. Edn. Assn., Biology Tchrs. Am., Inst. Technologists, Inst. Food Technologists (historian Bluegrass sect. 1965-71), Am. Home Econs. Assn., Ky. Home Econs. Assn., Am. Dietetic Assn., Ky. Dietetic Assn. (pub. rels. chmn. 1968-71, co-editor bull. 1971-75), Bluegrass Dietetic Assn. (v.p. 1963-64, pres. 1964-65), Sigma Xi. Home: 174 Wise Hollow Rd Aiken SC 29803-9613

WELLS, COLIN MICHAEL, Roman history educator, archaeologist; b. West Bridgford, Eng., Nov. 15, 1933; s. Alfred Henry and Ada (Nicholls) W.; m. Catherine P. Wells, July 23, 1960; children: Christopher William Llewellyn, Dominic Richard Alexander. BA, Oriel Coll., Oxford, Eng., 1958, MA, 1959, DPhil, 1965. Classical VIth form master Beaumont Coll., Old Windsor, Eng., 1958-59; lectr., asst. prof. U. Ottawa, Ont., 1964-66, assoc. prof., 1966, chmn. classical studies, 1967-72, prof., 1971—, vice-dean of arts, 1974-77; T. Frank Murchison dist. prof. classical studies Trinity U., San Antonio, 1987—, chmn. dept., 1987—; vis. prof. U. Calif., Berkeley, 1978; adj. prof. Carleton U., Ottawa, Ont., 1985-88; prof. invité U. Scis. Humaines, Strasbourg, France, 1990 spring; vis. lectr. Inst. of Archaeology, Oxford, 1973-74; dir. Can. excavations at Carthage, Tunisia, 1977-86; dir. Trinity U. excavations at Carthage, 1990—; vis. fellow Brasenose Coll., Oxford, 1973-74. Author: The German Policy of Augustus, 1972, The Roman Empire, 1984, 2nd edit., 1995 (translated to German, Italian, Spanish); editor: L'Afrique romaine: les Conférences Vanier 1980, 1982. 2d lt. British Army, 1954-56. Doctoral fellowship Can. Coun., 1962-64; rsch., travel grants Can. Coun., Social Scis. and Humanities Rsch. Coun. of Can., U. Ottawa, Trinity U. Fellow Soc. of Antiquaries of London; mem. Am. Philol. Assn., Archaeol. Inst. of Am. Office: Trinity U 715 Stadium Dr San Antonio TX 78212-7200

WELLS, DAMON, JR., investment company executive; b. Houston, May 20, 1937; s. Damon and Margaret Corinne (Howze) W.; BA magna cum laude, Yale U., 1958; BA, Oxford U., 1964, MA, 1968; PhD, Rice U., 1968. Owner, CEO Damon Wells Interests, Houston, 1958—, pres.,Damon Wells Found., 1993—. Bd. dirs. Child Guidance Ctr. of Houston, 1970-73; trustee Christ Ch. Cathedral Endowment Fund, 1970-73, 84-88, chmn., 1987-88, Kinkaid Sch., 1972-86, Kinkaid Sch. Endowment Fund, 1981-86; hon. friend of Somerville Coll., Oxford U., 1988—; mem. Sr. Common Room, Pembroke Coll., Oxford U., 1972—; trustee Camp Allen retreat of Episc. Diocese of Tex., 1976-78; founding bd. dirs. Brit. Inst. U.S., 1979-80; mem. pres.'s coun. Tex. A&M U., 1983-89. Named Hon. Comdr. Most Excellent Order of Brit. Empire by Her Majesty Queen Elizabeth II, 1991, Outstanding Alumnus Yr. by Kinkaid Sch., 1994. Fellow Jonathan Edwards Coll. (assoc.), Yale U., 1982—; hon. fellow Pembroke Coll., Oxford U., 1984—. Mem. English-Speaking Union (nat. dir. 1970-72, v.p. Houston br. 1966-73), Coun. Fgn. Rels., Phi Beta Kappa, Pi Sigma Alpha. Episcopalian. Clubs: Houston Country, Houston, Yale (N.Y.C.), United Oxford and Cambridge U. (London); Cosmos (Washington), Buck's (London), Coronado (Houston), Little Ship Club (London) . Author: Stephen Douglas: The Last Years, 1857-1861, 1971 (Tex. Writer's Roundup prize 1971), paperback edit., 1990. Home: 5555 Del Monte Dr Houston TX 77056-4116 Office: 2001 Kirby Dr Ste 806 Houston TX 77019-6033

WELLS, DONALD EUGENE, hospital administrator; b. Phoenix, May 10, 1940; married. BHA, Ga. State U., 1970, MHA, 1972. Adminstrv. resident Emory Univ. Hosp., Atlanta, 1971-72, asst. adminstr., 1972-77, assoc. adminstr., 1977-78, dep. exec. dir., 1978-81, adminstrv. dir., 1981-91, exec. dir., 1991—. Mem. Ga. Hosp. Assn. (del., mem. coms.). Office: Emory U Hosp 1364 Clifton Rd NE Atlanta GA 30322-1059*

WELLS, JERRY WAYNE, police official; b. Hodgenville, Ky., Dec. 17, 1950; s. Lawrence and Margaret Evelyn (Locke) W. BA in History, Western Ky. U., 1973; postgrad., So. Police Inst., Louisville, 1987; MS in Criminal Justice Adminstrn., Ea. Ky. U., 1990; grad., Ky. Dept. Criminal Justice Tng., 1993. Cert. police officer, police mgmt. instr., Ky. Audio visual technician, police dispatcher Western Ky. U., Bowling Green, 1972-74, police officer, detective and sgt., 1975-76; police officer City of Bowling Green, 1976-83, police sgt., 1983-87, police capt., 1987-94, sector comdr., capt., 1994—; part-time tchr. police related topics; also legal mgmt. rschr. Mem., grad. Leadership Bowling Green, 1989. Mem. Fraternal Order Police (treas. 1981-84, svc. award 1979, 81), Internat. Assn. Chiefs of Police, Western Ky. U. Alumni Assn., So. Police Inst. Alumni Assn., Ea. Ky. U. Alumni Assn., Leadership Bowling Green Alumni Assn., Coll. Law Enforcement Alumni Assn. Republican. Baptist. Home: PO Box 684 Bowling Green KY 42102-0684 Office: Bowling Green Police Dept PO Box 1287 Bowling Green KY 42102-1287

WELLS, JOHN CALHOUN, physics educator; b. Tampa, Fla., May 12, 1941; s. John Calhoun and Ethel Bernice (Hitchcock) W.; m. Marilee Winifred Mays, Dec. 21, 1963; children: Sarah Kathleen, John Bryan. BS, Fla. State U., 1961; PhD, Johns Hopkins U., 1968. Postdoctoral researcher U.S. Naval Ordnance Lab., Silver Spring, Md., 1968-70; asst. prof. Tenn. Tech. U., Cookeville, 1970-75, assoc. prof., 1975-80, prof. physics, 1980—; adj. rsch. scientist nuclear physics Oak Ridge (Tenn.) Nat. Lab., 1976—. Mem. Am. Phys. Soc., Am. Assn. Physics Tchrs., AAUP, Tenn. Acad. Scis., Sigma Xi. Office: Tenn Tech U Dept Physics Cookeville TN 38505

WELLS, JOHN GAULDEN, technology education educator; b. Guatanamo Bay, Cuba, Sept. 9, 1954; s. Peter Frailey II and Helen Erwin (Reed) W.; m. Deborah Lee Colvett, June 5, 1993; 1 child, Alexander John. BS in Indsl. Arts Edn., Fla. State U., 1978, BS in Biol. Sci., 1979; MS in Tech. Edn., Va. Poly Inst. & State U., 1990, PhD in Technology Edn., 1992. Sci. and reading instr. dyslexic and hyperkinetic students Woodland Hall Acad., Tallahassee, 1979-80; secondary biology and tech. edn. instr. Antilles Consol. Sch. System, Ceiba, Puerto Rico, 1980-89; biotechnology instr. Va. Govs. Sch. Tech./Va. Poly. & State U., Blacksburg, 1991-92; grad. rsch. assoc. Va. Poly. Inst. & State U., Blacksburg, 1989-92; asst. prof. dept. tech. edn. Coll. Human Resources and Edn./W.Va. U., Morgantown, 1992—; tech. edn. resource ctr. com. mem. W.Va. U., 1994, diversity task force com. mem., 1993, PDS assessment study com. mem., 1993, profl. devel. schs. comm. subcom. mem. Benedum project, 1992, assoc. mem. grad. faculty, 1992; cons. Biotechnology, 1992, James Madison U., 1992, Delmar Publ., 1992; nat. selection panel for Mcauliffe fellowship recipients Challenger Ctr. for Space

Sci. Edn., 1991, cons., 1992, steering com. for devel. aerospace teaching package, 1989, mem. steering com. Nat. Faculty Conf.,1990, design team for Mars simulation instrnl. model, 1992; participant confs. in field; presenter in field. Contbr. articles to profl. jours. Named NASA Space Amb. and Educator, 1987—. Mem. NASA Tchr. in Space, Challenger Ctr. for Space Sci. Edn., Internat. Tech. Edn. Assn., Coun. on Tech. Tchr. Edn., Va. Tech. Edn. Assn., Epsilon Pi Tau, Phi Delta Kappa. Office: WVa Univ PO Box 6122 706 Allen Hall Morgantown WV 26506

WELLS, JON BARRETT, engineer; b. Sewickley, Pa., Oct. 21, 1937; s. Calvin and Martha Barrett (Byrnes) W.; m. Nancy Lou LaFrance, Nov. 18, 1967; children: James Jonathan, Tiffany Lynn. BSEE, Calif. Poly U., 1961. Various positions Bell & Howell Co. Datatape Div., Pasadena, Calif., 1961-73; chief engr. Bell & Howell Co. Datatape Div., 1973-75; engring. mgr. Bell & Howell Co. Datatape Div., Baldwin Park, Calif., 1975-87; remittance projects mgr. Lundy Fin. Systems, Rancho Cucamonga, Calif., 1987-92; engring. mgr. Recognition Internat. (formerly Lundy Fin. Systems), Irving, Tex., 1992-96; project mgr. BancTec (formerly Recognition Internat.), Irving, 1996—; pres. Datatape Fed. Credit Union, Pasadena, 1978-93; v.p. Recognition Tech. Users Assn., Boston, 1987—; sec. Am. Nat. Standard Inst. X9B6, Washington, 1989-92. Patentee in field; contbr. articles to publs. Sec., founder Pasadena Neighborhood Housing Svcs., Pasadena, 1976-80. Mem. IEEE, Pasadena IBM Personal Computer Users Group, U.S. Power Squadrons, Aircraft Owners and Pilots Assn., Internat. Underwater Explorers Soc. Republican. Home: 32921 Arrowhead Dr Trabuco Canyon CA 92679 Office: BancTec Inc 2701 E Grauwyler Rd Irving TX 75061-3414

WELLS, PALMER DONALD, performing arts executive; b. Keokee, Va., Jan. 31, 1937; s. Lon S. Wells and Ada Mae (Russell) Craft. BA in Journalism, U. Ky., 1960. Founder, mng. dir. Theatre in the Square, Marietta, Ga., 1982—; v.p. IBM Drama Club, White Plains, N.Y., 1976. Appeared in The Three Penny Opera, 1963; director plays The Glass Menagerie, 1965, Dark of the Moon, 1966, The Little Foxes, 1983, Tobacco Road, 1985, Mary Shelly's Frankenstein, 1988; director musicals The 1940's Radio Hour, 1987. Founder Lonesome Pine Players, Cumberland, Ky., 1960; mem. Cobb Landmarks Soc., Marietta, 1990. With U.S. Army, 1961-63. Democrat. Home: 43 Mcdonald St Marietta GA 30064-3217 Office: Theatre in the Square 11 Whitlock Ave Marietta GA 30064-2321

WELLS, ROBERT HARTLEY, chemistry professional; b. Springfield, Mass., Mar. 23, 1926; s. Cecil and Anna (Coates) W.; m. Mary G. Frinzi, May 30 1952 (wid. May 1969); children: Michael J., Brian H., Donald L.; m. Alice G. Asplund, June 20, 1970. BS in Chemistry, U. Maine, 1948, MS in Chemistry, 1950. Instr. in chemistry Lafayette Coll., Easton, Pa., 1950-51; rsch. chemist Celanese Corp., Summit, N.J., 1952-56, S.D. Warren, Westbrook, Maine, 1956-58; epoxy rsch. engr. CIBA Corp., Toms River, N.J., 1958-66; sect. head Foundry Products Borden Cem., Bainbridge, N.Y., 1966-70; sr. rsch. engr. Amoco Chem., Naperville, Ill., 1970-73; product mgr. epoxies Wilmington (Del.) Chem., 1973-76; product mgr. epoxy resins AZS Corp., Lakeland, Fla., 1976-83; cons. chemist Lakeland, 1983—. Patentee in field; contbr. articles to profl. jours.; photographer exhibits in field. Mem. Toms River Sch. Bd., 1962-66, Garden State Symphony, Toms River, 1963-66; pres. Toms River Jaycees, 1962; photographer SPCA, Lakeland, 1993—. Sgt. U.S. Army, 1944-46. Mem. AAAS, Am. Chem. Soc., Photographic Soc. (mem. chmn. 1993-95, Merit Svc. award 1994), Am. Contract Bridge League, Bartow Camera Club (pres. 1988-91), Sigma Xi, Kappa Phi Kappa. Republican. Methodist.

WELLS, ROBERT LOUIS, priest; b. Alexandria, La., Mar. 18, 1939; s. Charles Alexander Jr. and Elouise (Hinton) W.; m. Michal Ann McCubbin, Mar. 12, 1966 (div. Oct. 1982); children: Steve, David (dec.), Melissa; m. Carol Hunter, Apr. 3, 1983; 1 child, Matthew. BA, La. State U., 1961; MDiv, Golden Gate Bapt. Theol. Sem., 1965. Pastor Second Bapt. Ch., Lubbock, Tex., 1966-78; exec. dir. CONTACT Lubbock, Inc., 1979-91; religion tchr. All Saints Episcopal Sch., Lubbock, 1988-91, dir. counseling, 1988-91; pvt. practice pastoral counselor Lubbock, 1982-91; asst. rector St. Paul's Episcopal Ch., Waco, Tex., 1991-95; chaplain Canterbury Assn. at Baylor U., Waco, Tex., 1991-95; exec. dir. The William Temple Found., Galveston, Tex., 1995—; vicar Univ. Ch. of St. Luke the Physician, 1995—; mem., chmn. bd. dirs. CONTACT USA, Inc., Harrisburg, Pa., 1971-82; mem., treas. secretariat Life Line Internat., Harrisburg, 1979-87; bd. dirs. Nat. Assn. Contact Dirs., Harrisburg, 1984-85. Editor (NASCOD jour.) Chiasma, 1984. Mem., chmn. Community Planning Coun., Lubbock, 1976-79; bd. dirs. United Way of Lubbock, Inc., 1977-78; mem. City-County Child Welfare Bd., Lubbock, 1968-71, South Plains Info. and Referral Bd., Lubbock, 1981, Nat. Assn. Eagle Scouts, Boy Scouts Am., 1979—. Parish Minister's fellow The Fund for Theol. Edn., Inc., 1975-76; named Citizen of Yr. Lubbock unit Tex. chpt. Nat. Assn. Social Workers, 1980. Mem. Am. Assn. Pastoral Counselors, Assn. for Psychol. Type, Masons, Rotary, Lambda Chi Alpha. Democrat. Episcopalian. Home: 103 Water St Galveston TX 77550-3209 Office: The William Temple Found 427 Market Galveston TX 77550

WELLS, RONA LEE, consumer products company executive; b. Beaumont, Tex., Aug. 23, 1950; d. Ray Peveto and Frances (Manning) Reed; m. Harry Hankins Wells, Mar. 22, 1975. BS in Systems Engring, So. Meth. U., 1972. Registered profl. engr., Tex. With initial mgmt. devel. program Southwestern Bell Corp., Houston, 1972-73, engr. and inventory coord., 1973-74, sr. engr. supr., 1974-75, engring. project supr., 1975-77, dist. supr. maj. project, 1977-79, dist. supr. materials, 1979; mgr. field svcs. CNA Fin. Corp., Chgo., 1979-80, mgr., asst. to v.p., 1980, area mgr. support svcs., 1980-82, area mgr. acctg. svcs., 1982; dir. bldg. and office mgmt. Kimberly-Clark Corp., Neenah, Wis., 1982-85; ops. specialist Kimberly-Clark Corp., New Milford, Conn., 1985-86, acting supt., 1985, project leader, 1985-88, ops. mgr., 1988-89; mill mgr. Kimberly-Clark Corp., Neenah, 1990-92, Kimberly Clark Corp., Hendersonville, N.C., 1992-95; v.p. Roswell, Ga., 1995—. Mem. Nat. Def. Exec. Res., Washington, 1979—, Hendersonville C. of C.; bd. dirs. Faulkner County United Way, 1989-90, Henderson County United Way, 1992-95. Named one of Outstanding Young Women of Am., 1978. Mem. NSPE, NAFE, Inst. Indsl. Engrs. (sr.), Soc. Women Engrs., C. of C. (treas. com. 100), Sigma Tau. Office: Kimberly Clark Corp 1400 Holcomb Bridge Rd Roswell GA 30076

WELLS, STEVEN CHARLES, media company executive; b. Roanoke, Va., Jan. 13, 1954; s. B.T. and Barbara (Bailey) W. BA in Phys. Edn., Degrees in Gen. Studies and Bus. Mgmt. Owner, dir. United Network, Virginia Beach, Va., 1979—. Contbr. articles to profl. jours. Mem. Am. Mgmt. Assn., Soc. Applied Learning & Tech., Nat. Inst. Bus. Mgmt., Internat. Ski Writers Assn. Office: United Media PO Box 62044 Virginia Beach VA 23466-2044

WELMAKER, FORREST NOLAN, lawyer; b. McKinney, Tex., Aug. 13, 1925; s. Felix E. and Forrest Love (Baker) W.; div.; children: Forrest Nolan Jr., Mary Elizabeth Welmaker Young, Byron Skillin. BBA, U. Tex., 1950, LLD, 1953. Bar: Tex. 1953, U.S. Dist. Ct. (so. and we. dists.) Tex. 1956, U.S. Ct. Appeals (5th cir.) 1956, U.S. Tax Ct. 1959, U.S. Supreme Ct. 1956. Pvt. practice San Antonio, 1953—. Past bd. dirs., officer United Fund San Antonio, San Antonio chpt. ARC, Children Welfare Bur. San Antonio, San Antonio YMCA. Capt. USNR, 1945-46, PTO, 1950-52, Korea. Fellow Tex. Bar Found., San Antonio Bar Found.; mem. San Antonio Bar Assn. (past bd. dirs., v.p., pres.), Tex. Assn. Def. Counsel, San Antonio Res. Officer Assn., Tex. Bar Assn. (past bd. dirs.), San Antonio Pla. Club, San Antonio German Club. Episcopalian. Home: 114 W Brandon Dr San Antonio TX 78209-6404

WELSH, ALFRED JOHN, lawyer, consultant; b. Louisville, May 10, 1947; s. Elvin Alfred and Carol (Kleymeyer) W.; m. Lee Mitchell, Aug. 1, 1970; children: Charles Kleymeyer, Kathryn Thomas. BA, Centre Coll., 1969; JD, U. Ky., 1972; LLM in Internat. Law cum laude, U. Brussels, 1973. Bar: Ky. 1972, U.S. Dist. Ct. (we. and ea. dists.) Ky. 1972, U.S. Ct. Appeals (6th cir.) 1972. Atty. Ky. Atty. Gen. Office, Frankfort, 1973-74; legis. counsel to congressman Ho. of Reps., Washington, 1974-77; mng. ptnr. Nicolas Welsh Brooks & Hayward, Louisville, 1977—, Boone Welsh Brooks and Hayward Internat. Law; hon. counsel of Belgium, 1983—; econ. devel. advisor Kingdom of Belgium; mem. Ky. Econ. Adv. Coun.; pres. Transcontinental Trading Cons., Ltd.; participant in North African Mideast Econ. Summit Conf., Morocco, 1994. Bd. dirs. Greater Louisville Swim Found., 1983-94, exec. com., 1994—, Louisville com. Coun. Fgn. Rels., 1983—, Jefferson County Alcohol and Drug Abuse Found., Louisville, 1986—. Decorated knight Order of the Crown (Belgium). Mem. ABA (internat. law sect., commn. on impairment), Ky. Bar Assn. (bd. dirs. 1981-82, pres. young lawyers divsn. 1981-82), Am. Judicature Soc., Louisville C. of C. Democrat. Presbyterian. Office: Barristers Hall 1009 S 4th St Louisville KY 40203-3207

WELSH, JAMES JOHN, computer consultant; b. Huntington, N.Y., Nov. 4, 1966; s. Brian James and Alice Theresa (Weiler) W.; m. Diane Romano, July 9, 1988; children: Matthew James, Daniel Joseph, Jake Alexander. AS, Champlain Coll., 1990. Programmer Whalstrom & Co., Inc., Stamford, Conn., 1990-91; cons. software WELCON, Port Chester, N.Y., 1991-92; dir. mktg. Dancik-On-Disk Internat., Ltd., Raleigh, N.C., 1993—; pres. Weller Enterprises, Inc., Raleigh, 1995—. Republican. Lutheran. Home: 8900 Leader Ln Raleigh NC 27615 Office: Weller Enterprises Inc PO Box 98996 Raleigh NC 27624

WELSH, JUDITH SCHENCK, communications educator; b. Patchogue, L.I., N.Y., Feb. 5, 1939; d. Frank W. and Muriel (Whitman) Schenck; B.Ed., U. Miami (Fla.), 1961, M.A. in English, 1968; m. Robert C. Welsh, Sept. 16, 1961; children: Derek Francis, Christopher Lord. Co-organizer Cataract Surg. Congress med. meetings, 1963-76; grad. asst. instr. Dale Carnegie Courses Internat., 1967; adminstr. Office Admissions, Bauder Fashion Coll., Miami, 1976-77, instr. communications, 1977—, also pub. coll. monthly paper; freelance writer regional and nat. publs.; guest speaker Optifair Internat., N.Y.C., 1980, Fla. Freelance Writers Assn. ann. conf., Ft. Lauderdale, 1991; guest speaker, mem. seminar faculty Optifair West, Anaheim, Calif., 1980, Optifair Midwest, St. Louis, 1980, Face to Face, Kansas City, Mo., 1981. Mem. NAFE, Fla. Freelance Writers Assn., Nat. Writers Club (award), Delta Gamma. Congregationalist. Clubs: Coral Reef Yacht, Riviera Country, Royal Palm Tennis. Co-editor: The New Report on Cataract Surgery, 1969, Second Report on Cataract Surgery, 1974; editor: Surgidev's Cataract Surgery N.O.W., 1982—; contbr. Miami Today, 1985—, Ft. Lauderdale Sun/Sentinel, 1986—, Prime Times, Club Life, Gainesville Sun, The Oklahoman, South Fla. mag, Miami Herald. Home and Office: 1600 Onaway Dr Miami FL 33133-2516

WELSH, LEONARD WOODROW, JR., computer programmer; b. Oklahoma City, Nov. 1, 1943; s. Leonard W. and Martha Maria (Zvonek) Welsh; m. Sharon Anne Norton, Sept. 20, 1980; children: Jennifer Lynne, John Thomas. BS in Math., U. Okla., 1968; MS in Indsl. and Sys. Engring., U. Fla., 1976; MS in Computer Sci., U. Tex., Dallas, 1992. Computer programmer Rockwell Internat., Cedar Rapids, Iowa, 1976-80; mem. tech. staff Tex. Instruments, Dallas, 1980—. Capt. USAF, 1968-75. Mem. IEEE, Assn. for Computing Machinery, KC. Republican. Roman Catholic. Home: 1428 Debon Dr Plano TX 75075 Office: Tex Instruments Inc PO Box 655303 MS 3657 Dallas TX 75265-5303

WELSH, MICHAEL L., business executive; b. Clayton, Ga., June 14, 1959; s. John F. and Mary Ann (Casimes) W.; m. Susie Googe, June 5, 1982; children: Sarah Alex, Daniel. BBA magna cum laude, U. Ga., 1981, MACC, 1986. Consolidation acct. Tex. Instruments, Dallas, 1981-82, fin. analyst, 1982-84; v.p. cons. MISA, Atlanta, 1986-87; consolidation analyst Coca-Cola Enterprise, Atlanta, 1987-88; mid-Atlantic supr., mgr. Coca-Cola Bottling Co., Columbia, Md., 1988-90; div. mgr. Coca-Cola Enterprises-North, Columbia, 1990-91; ops. controller Cott Beverages USA, Columbus, Ga., 1993-95; v.p. adminstrn. Thompson Hardwoods, Inc., Hazlehurst, Ga., 1995—; acctg. and system implementation cons., Dallas and Athens, Ga., 1982-86. Youth leader Ascension Ch., Dallas, 1982-83, St. Michael's Ch., Stone Mountain, Ga., 1986-88, St. John's Episc. Ch., Ellicott City, Md., 1988-91; pres., co-founder Youth Soccer Assn., 1996. Mem. Internat. Platform Assn., U. Ga. Alumni Soc. (pres. Dallas chpt. 1983-84), Blue Key, Golden Key, Phi Kappa Phi, Beta Gamma Sigma, Phi Eta Sigma, Beta Alpha Psi, Phi Kappa Psi. Baptist. Home: PO Box 1067 Hazlehurst GA 31539 Office: Thompson Hardwoods Inc PO Box 646 Hazlehurst GA 31539

WELSH, RONALD DEAN, veterinary microbiologist; b. Garnett, Kans., Nov. 18, 1946; s. Olin and Marjorie (Steele) Welsh; m. Patricia J. Paine, May 31, 1948; children: Michelle L., Jacquelyn E., Lindsey M., Austin W. BS, Kans. State U., 1968, MS, 1970, DVM, 1978; postgrad., U. Minn., 1972-73. Diplomate Am. Coll. Vet. Microbiologists, Am. Coll. Vet. Preventive Medicine. Rsch. technician Theracon Rsch., Inc., Topeka, 1967; grad. teaching asst. Kansas State U. Coll. Vet. Medicine, Manhattan, 1968-70; clin. microbiology technician dept. clin. microbiology Mayo Clinic, Mayo Found., Rochester, Minn., 1970-72, grad rsch. fellow microbiology, 1972-74; pvt. practice St. Charles Vet. Clinic, 1974; teaching asst. dept. infectious diseases Kans. State U., 1974-77; intern Acad. Acres Vet. Hosp., Colorado Springs, Colo., 1977-78; veterinarian Jessamine Vet. Clinic, Nicholasville, Ky., 1978-80; vet. microbiologist Tex. Vet. Med. Diagnostic Lab. Tex. A&M U., Amarillo, 1980-88; vet. microbiologist Okla. Animal Disease Diagnostic Lab. Okla. State U., Stillwater, 1988—; prof. dept. vet. medicine and surgery Coll. Vet. Medicine, 1988—; mem. honors and awards com. Coll. Vet. Medicine, Okla. State U., 1991-95. Contbr. articles to profl. jours. Capt. U.S. Army, 1970-78. Mem. Am. Vet. Med. Assn., Am. Soc. Microbiology, Okla. Vet. Med. Assn., Am. Assn. Vet. Lab. Diagnosticians (com. on devel. of stds. for vet. antimicrobial susceptibility testing 1986—), U.S. Animal Health Assn. (com. on salmonella 1984—, biologics com. 1989), Am. Coll. Vet. Microbiologists (bd. govs. 1989-92), Southwestern Assn. Clin. Microbiology, Gamma Sigma Delta, Phi Zeta. Office: Okla Animal Disease Diagnostic Lab Okla State U Stillwater OK 74078

WELSH, SACHIKO ANN, Japanese language educator, librarian; b. Tokyo, Feb. 10, 1931; came to U.S., 1957; d. Makizo and Tama (Takino) Kasama; m. Kenneth A. Welsh, Apr. 26, 1956 (div. 1988); children: Kay Dianne, June Joanne, Kim Susanne Welsh Hajaistron. B Gen. Studies cum laude, U. Miami, Coral Gables, Fla., 1978; MLS, Fla. State U., 1981. Cert. tchr., sch. libr., Fla. Sec. CBS-TV, NBC-TV and UPI, Tokyo, 1950-53; adminstrv. asst. USIA, Tokyo, 1953-56; computer edn. tchr. Dade County Pub. Schs., Miami, 1981-85, Japanese language tchr., 1985—, media specialist, 1979-92; freelance translator, Miami, 1977—. Prodr., host: (multi-media Japanese Lang. Inst. program) Ichiban, 1992-94; contbr. articles to profl. jours. Fulbright scholar U.S. Dept. Edn., Japan, 1986. Mem. AAUW, Assn. of Tchrs. of Japanese, Fulbright Alumni Assn. Democrat. Home: 11844 Hickorynut Dr Tampa FL 33625-5688

WELSH, TIMOTHY JOHN, human resources specialist; b. Salt Lake City, Dec. 18, 1962; s. John Francis and Mary Imelda (Sullivan) W. BS, U. Utah, 1985; MBA, U. N. Fla., 1991. Safety dir. Atlantic Marine, Inc., Jacksonville, Fla., 1991-92; safety, environ. mgr. Atlantic Marine, Inc., Jacksonville, 1992-94, human resources mgr., 1994—. Lt. U.S. Navy, 1985-90. Environ. Protection Bd. award City of Jacksonville, 1996. Mem. N.E. Fla. Assn. Environ. Profls. (pres. 1994-95), Shipbuilder's Coun. of Am., (chmn. environ. com.), First Coast Mfrs. Assn., (bd. dirs.), Soc. Naval Architects and Marine Engrs., U.S. Naval Inst. Republican. Roman Catholic. Office: Atlantic Marine Inc 8500 Heckscher Dr Jacksonville FL 32226-2434

WELSH, WILMER HAYDEN, music educator, composer, organist; b. Cin., July 17, 1932; s. Wilmer Wesley Welsh and Dorothy Mary (Exon) Hamilton; m. Constance Teri DeBear, June 30, 1957 (div. 1982); children: Benjamin Hayden, Stephen Andrew. B.S., Johns Hopkins U., 1953; artist diploma Peabody Conservatory Music, 1953, B.Music, 1954, M.Music, 1955. Asst. prof. music Winthrop Coll., Rock Hill, S.C., 1959-63; assoc. prof. music Davidson Coll., N.C., 1963-72, prof. music, 1972-91, chmn. dept. music 1981-87, composer in residence, 1987-91; prof. emeritus, 1992—; organ recitalist specializing in Am. music from Colonial period to present; subject doctoral dissertation, 1985. Composer symphonies, concertos, operas, music for ch. festivals; performances throughout world. Contbr. articles to profl. jours. Grantee Ford Found., 1959, Nat. Endowment Arts, 1969, N.C. Arts Council, 1985; recipient Thomas Jefferson award McConnell Found., 1976. Mem. AAUP. Republican. Episcopalian. Avocations: writing; antiques; gardening; swimming, Ile Ere collection African art. Home: 103 Tradd St Charleston SC 29401-2422

WELTZHEIMER, MARIE KASH, artist; b. Akron, Ohio, May 5, 1960; d. John Eugene and Florence Marie (McConnell) Kash; m. Ronald George Weltzheimer, Apr. 28, 1984; 1 child, Jordan James. BA in Comml. Art, U. Ctrl. Okla., 1982, postgrad., 1987. Layout artist Scrivner, Inc., Oklahoma City, 1982-83; graphic media artist Okla. Water Resources Bd., Oklahoma City, 1984-88; visual artist Oklahoma City, 1986—. One-woman shows include Okla. Heritage Ctr. Oklahoma City, 1995, Kirkpatrick Gallery for Okla. Artists, Oklahoma City, 1995, Charles B. Goddard Art Ctr., Ardmore, Okla., 1993, Flips Wine Bar & Trattoria, Oklahoma City, 1989, Plains Indians and Pioneers Mus., Woodward, Okla., 1989; two women shows include M.A. Doran Gallery, Tulsa, 1991, Okla. State Capitol, Oklahoma City, 1993; exhibited in group shows at Telluride (Colo.) Pastel Invitational, 1995, Longview (Tex.) Art Mus., 1996, ArtsPlace, Oklahoma City, 1990, 92, Charles B. Goddard Art Ctr., 1991, Pastel Soc. the S.W., 1988, 89, 91-95, Pastel Soc. Am., N.Y.C., 1991, 93, Okla. Painting Biennial II, Okla. City, 1993, Artisan 9 Gallery, 1989, Festival the Arts, Okla. City, 1992, 93, 96, Midwest Pastel Soc., St. Charles, Ill., 1992; represented in permanent collections Coca-Cola, Moscow, Laureate Psychiat. Clinic and Hosp., Am. Bank and Trust, Lawyers Title Oklahoma City, Inc., Charles B. Goddard Art Ctr. Sunday sch. tchr. 8th grade N.W. Bapt. Ch., Oklahoma City, 1993-95. Recipient Best of Show awards Charles B. Goddard Art Ctr., 1989, 91, 93, Judges award, 1994, Okla. Art Workshops, Tulsa, 1994, Pastel Soc. Okla., 1989, 1st pl. pastel Okla. Art Guild, 1992, 3d pl. pastel, 1991, 2d pl. pastel, 1989-90, 2d pl. pastel Art in the Park, 1990, 1st pl. pastel, 1988-89. Mem. Pastel Soc. Am. (Steven Leitner award 1991), Pastel Soc. S.W. (First award of excellence 1991, S.W. Gallery award 1992). Republican. Southern Baptist. Home and Office: 2724 NW 45th St Oklahoma City OK 73112-8220

WEMMERS, FREDERICK RICHARD, JR., advertising executive; b. Miami, Fla., Oct. 19, 1939; s. Frederick Richard and Ethel (Durham) W.; m. Jayanne Haines, Jan. 11, 1969; children: Susan Allison, Jason Douglas. AB in Journalism, U. Ga., 1961; postgrad., Wharton Bus. Sch., 1970. Account exec. Fox Advt., High Point, N.C., 1966-68, Cargill, Wilson & Acree Advt., Richmond, Va., Charlotte, N.C., 1968-70; v.p. J. Walter Thompson, N.Y.C., Chgo., Washington, Atlanta, 1970-78; owner Wemmers Comm., Atlanta, 1978—. Speaker various orgns., 1965—. Mem. adminstrv. bd. Sandy Springs United Meth. Ch.; mem. New Zealand Olympic Com., 1995-96. 1st lt. U.S. Army, 1962-64. Named Outstanding Young Ad Man, Greensboro Ad Club, 1969, Outstanding Jaycee, Ark. Jaycees, 1966. Mem. Pub. Rels. Soc. Am., Am. Mktg. Assn., S.E. Software Assn. (bd. dirs. 1993—), U.S. Polo Assn., Atlanta Advt. Club (bd. dirs. 1991-93), Atlanta Polo Club (pres. 1990-92), Atlanta Ad Club (pres. 1994-95). Republican. Home: 4955 Olde Towne Way Marietta GA 30068 Office: Wemmers Communications Inc 6100 Lake Forest Dr Ste 330 Atlanta GA 30338

WEMPLE-KINDER, SUZANNE FONAY, history educator; b. Veszprém, Hungary, Aug. 1, 1927; came to U.S., 1949; d. Ernest Fonay and Magda (Mihalyfy) Széchényi; m. George Barr Wemple, June 17, 1956 (dec. Apr. 1988); children: Peter, Stephen, Carolyn; m. Gordon T. Kinder, May 26, 1990. Student, English Sisters, Budapest, Hungary, 1945; BA, U. Calif., Berkeley, 1953; MLS, Columbia U., 1955, PhD, 1967. Reference asst. Columbia U. Libr., N.Y.C., 1955-58, Stern Coll., N.Y.C., 1963-64, Tchr.'s Coll., N.Y.C., 1964-66; prof. Columbia U., Barnard Coll., N.Y.C., 1966-92, prof. emerita, 1992—. Author: Atto of Vercelli, Church, State and Society in the Tenth Century, 1979, Women in Frankish Society, Marriage and the Cloister, 1981 (Berkshire Book prize 1982); co-editor: Women in Medieval Society, 1983; contbr. essay to A History of Women Vol. II: Silences of the Middle Ages, 1992; contbr. articles to profl. jours., essays to books. Grantee Spivak-Summer Barnard Coll., 1970, 81, NEH, 1974-75, 81-86, Fulbright Found., 1982. Home: 1285 Gulf Shore Blvd N Naples FL 34102

WEN, HELEN HWA JUNG, occupational health nurse; b. Tainan, Taiwan, Feb. 9, 1935; came to U.S., 1967; d. Yong-Shing and Jung-Yong (Lee) Wu; m. Michael M. Wen, Sept. 4, 1956; children: Tony, Ted. Diploma nursing, St. Anthony Hosp. Med. Ctr., Rockford, Ill., 1979; B Health Profession, S.W. Tex. State U., 1988; MA in Human Svcs., St. Edward's U., Austin, Tex., 1992. Cert. occupational health nurse, cert. for Andiometry, cert. for Pulmonary FUnction Test, 1990, cert. Emergency Care Asst., 1995. Tchr. Chung Chang Grade Sch., Tainan, 1953-67; med. asst. Beloit (Wis.) Clinic, 1973-76; nursing asst. Carlye Nursing Home, Beloit, 1977; staff nurse, team leader, surg. and med. Beloit Meml. Hosp., 1979-80; occasional charge nurse Seton Med. Ctr., Austin, 1980-94; occupational health nurse, sr. nurse, CPR instr. Motorola Inc., Austin, 1986—. Instr. CPR Seton Good Health, Austin, 1992—. Mem. Austin Assn. Occupational Health Nurses.

WENDEL, CHARLES ALLEN, lawyer; b. Lockport, N.Y., Aug. 13, 1942; s. Harold Henry and Doris Lillian (Gardner) W.; m. Helen W. Roberts, June 23, 1973; children: William Charles, Jonathan David. BChem. Engring., Rensselaer Poly. Inst., 1964; JD, Am. U., 1968. Bar: N.Y. 1969, Va. 1971, D.C. 1980, U.S. Supreme Ct., U.S. Ct. Appeals (fed. and 4th cirs.), U.S. Dist. Ct. (ea. and we. dists.) Va. Patent examiner U.S. Patent and Trademark Office, Washington, 1964-66; patent trainee Union Carbide Corp, Washington, 1966-68, patent atty., N.Y.C., 1968-70; assoc., then ptnr. Stevens, Davis, Miller & Mosher, Arlington, Va., 1970-83; ptnr. firm Wegner & Bretschneider, Washington, 1983-85, assoc. solicitor U.S. Patent and Trademark Office, 1985-88; assoc. Lyon & Lyon, Washington, 1988-90; founding ptnr. Parkhurst, Wendel & Rossi, Alexandria, Va., 1990-95. Contbr. articles to profl. jours. Mem. Va. State Bar (patent trademark copyright sect., chmn. 1977-78), Am. Intellectual Patent Law Assn., Patent Lawyers Club Washington (pres. 1982-83), Delta Theta Phi. Republican. Office: Parkhurst Wendel & Burr LLP 1421 Prince St Ste 210 Alexandria VA 22314-2805

WENDEL, PAMELA LOIS, auditor, banker; b. St. Albans, N.Y., Aug. 18, 1960; d. Henry H.H. and Lois H. (Paul) Plehn; m. William A. Wendel, June 28, 1980. Diploma, Am. Bankers Assn. Nat. Compliance Sch., Norman, Okla., 1983; diploma in audit mgmt., Sch. for Bank Adminstrn., Madison, Wis., 1989; AA in Bus. Adminstrn., Miami-Dade Community Coll., Fla., 1991. Cert. bank compliance officer. Compliance officer Creditbank, Miami, Fla., 1983-86, internal auditor, 1983-87; internal auditor Megabank, Miami, 1987-95; asst. v.p., bus. devel. mgr. Bank Atlantic, Miami, 1995—. Mem. Fin. Women Internat. (pres. 1990-91, formerly Nat. Assn. Bank Women), Bank Adminstrn. Inst. (bd. dirs. S. Fla. chpt. 1989, dir. 1989-91, v.p. 1991—, pres. 1992, Chuck Myers scholar 1987), S. Dade Bankers Assn. (chmn. 1985-87), S. Fla. Compliance Assn., NAFE, Inst. Internal Auditors (bd. govs., chmn. Speakers Bur. 1989-90). Office: Bank Atlantic 13751 SW 152nd St Miami FL 33177-1106

WENDELIN, MARIAN, computer systems analyst; b. Lansing, Mich., July 14, 1946; d. Ralph and Helen (Prosser) Bowersox; m. Jerry Wendelin, June 8, 1968; 1 child, Holly. BA in English, Stanford U., 1968; MEd, Staford U., 1969. Programmer So. Pacific Transp. Co., San Francisco, 1969-71, Computer Scis. Corp., San Diego, Calif., 1972-73; programmer/analyst City and County of Denver, 1976-79; analyst distributed systems support Manville Corp., Denver, 1979-82; sr. analyst data adminstrn. Manville Corp., Danver, 1982-83, project leader data adminstrn., 1983-86; programmer/analyst Associated Credit Svcs., Houston, 1987-88; sr. programmer/analyst Variable Annuity Life (subs. Am. Gen. Corp.), Houston, 1988-93, cons. sys. analyst, 1993-94, application mgr., 1994—. Unitarian. Home: 12867 Kingsbridge Ln Houston TX 77077-2232 Office: Variable Annuity Life Ins 2929 Allen Pky # A4 55 Houston TX 77019-2197

WENDELL, EARL W., entertainment company executive; b. 1928. Grad., Wooster Coll., 1950. Officer Opryland USA Inc. and affiliates and predecessors, Nashville, 1950—, pres., 1983—, pres., CEO Gaylord Entertainment Co., 1991—. Office: Opryland USA Inc 2802 Opryland Dr Nashville TN 37214-1200

WENDTLAND, MONA BOHLMANN, dietitian, consultant; b. Schulenburg, Tex., Mar. 30, 1930; d. Willy Frank and Leona A. (Bruns) Bohlmann; m. Charles William Ewing, Mar. 8, 1953 (div. Sept. 1975); children: Charles William Jr., Deborah Susan Ewing Richmond; m. William Wolters Wendtland, Jan. 12, 1991. BS in Home Econs., U. Tex., 1952, postgrad., 1952-57. Registered dietitian, Tex. Dietitian sch. lunch program Port Arthur (Tex.) Ind. Sch. Dist., 1952-53; elem. tchr. Portsmouth (Va.) Sch. Dist., 1953-54; dietitian, mgr. lunch room E.M. Scarbrough Dept. Store, Austin, Tex., 1955-57; asst. chief adminstrv. dietitian John Sealy HOsp., Galveston, Tex., 1957-59; chief therapeutic dietitian USPHS Hosp., Galveston, 1959-60, asst. chief dietitian, 1960-62; cons. dietitian Sinton (Tex.)

Nursing Home, 1963-65; dietary cons. Deaton Hosp., Galena Park, Tex., 1966-68; dir. food svcs. Nat. Health Enterprises, Houston, 1975-76; dietary cons. to nursing homes and retirement ctrs. Drug Abuse Ctr., Houston, 1976—. Del. Internat. Congress Arts & Comm., 1993. Mem. Am. Dietetic Assn. (registered), Tex. Dietetic Assn., South Tex. Dietetic Assn. (chmn. cons. interest group 1978-79), U. Tex. Home Econs. Assn., Dietitians in Bus. and Industry (nat. rep. to mgmt. practices group 1980-83, treas. Houston chpt. 1980-81, pres. 1981-82, advisor 1983-84), Tex. Gerontol Nutritionists (sec. 1994-95), Tex. Cons. Dietitians in Healthcare Facilities, Tex. Nutrition Coun., Dietary Mgrs. Assn. (advisor Houston dist. 1979-92). Republican. Methodist. Home and Office: 5463 Jason St Houston TX 77096-1238

WENG, CHUAN, mechanical engineer; b. Guang Zhou, China, July 13, 1963; came to U.S., 1986; B of Engring., Changsha (China) Ry. U., 1983; MSME, Ohio U., 1990. Registered profl. engr., N.C. Asst. engr. Guang Zhou Railway Adminstrn., Guang Zhou, 1983-86; rsch. asst. Ohio U./ Forma Sci., Athens, Ohio, 1988-90; project engr. Revco/Lindberg, Asheville, N.C., 1990—. Patentee in field. Mem. NSPE, N.C. Soc. Profl. Engrs. Home: 3 Dorman Dr Weaverville NC 28787

WENGER, DOROTHY MAE, retired dietitian; b. Rozel, Kans., Jan. 20, 1917; d. John Edward and Irene Margaret (McElroy) Franz; m. Edward Lawrence Wenger (dec.); 1 child, Edward Lawrence III; m. Jacob Eric Iverson, 1995. Student, Iowa State Tchrs. Coll., Cedar Falls, 1937-39; BS, Lindenwood Coll. for Women, St. Charles, Mo., 1940; postgrad., U. W.Va., 1941, Columbia U., 1945, 47. Registered dietitian. Dietetic intern Mayo Clinic, Rochester, Minn., 1941, Western Pa. Hosp., Pitts., 1941-42; head dietitian, dir. dept. St. Luke's Hosp., Bluefield, W.Va., 1942-44, Monongalia Gen. Hosp., Morgantown, W.Va., 1944-49, Elyria (Ohio) Meml. Hosp., 1949-57; chief dietitian Lakewood Hosp., Cleve., 1957-58; dir. dietary dept. Beach Hosp., Ft. Lauderdale, Fla., 1959-61, North Broward Med. Ctr., Pompano Beach, Fla., 1961-75; chief dietitian North Broward Med. Ctr., Pompano Beach, 1975-89; ret., 1989; supr. clin. practicum program for student from various schs. including Atlantic Vocat. Sch., Broward Community Coll., Fla. Internat. Coll.; community nutrition lectr. North Broward County Hosp. Dist., 1985-89. Developer dietetic course programs for various levels. Guidance vol. children and adults with dyslexia, 1965—; lector Episc. Ch., 1988—; mem. Bible Study Fellowship Internat., 1990—, St. mary's Guild, 1993—; pres. Order of Daus. of the King, 1995—. Mem. Am. Dietetic Assn., Tri-county Clin. Mgrs., W.Va. Dietetic Assn. (state pres. 1942-44), Greater Miami Dietetic Assn. (adv. com. for dietetic tech. 1974-80), Cons. Dietitians for Long Term Facilities (Fla. state dietetic rep. 1978-79), Fla. Dietetic Assn. (chmn. dist. edn. com. 1975-77), Nat. Honor Soc. (Norfolk, Nebr.), Quota Club (Morgantown), Triangle Club (St. Charles).

WENGROVITZ, JUDITH, artist, educator; b. Bklyn., Jan. 3, 1931; d. Harry and Hilda (Seigal) Kanarick; m. Seymour Wengrovitz, Feb. 23, 1952; children: Michael, Phillip, David. BA in Art Edn., Hunter Coll., 1952. Layout artist, copywriter Woodward & Lothrop, Washington, 1952-55; artist Va., 1955—; art dir., instr. Judy Wengrovitz Sch. Art, Springfield, Va., 1962—. One-artist shows include Art League-Torpedo Factory, Alexandria, 1981, 88, 97, George Mason U., Arlington, Va., 1984, Design Studios Gallery, McLean, Va., 1984, Gallery West, Alexandria, 1986, City Gallery, Washington, 1989, US Too Studio, Fairfax, Va., 1990, Twentieth Century Gallery, Williamsburg, Va., 1991, NIH, Bethesda, Md., 1994; group exhbns. include Capricorn Gallery, 1995, 96, Art League-Torpedo Factory, Alexandria, 1986-96, Fairfax County Coun. Arts, 1987-95, Springfield Art Guild, 1987-96, Nat. League Pen Women (award 1987), Miniature Soc. Internat. Exhibit (2nd pl. landscape award 1991), others; permanent collections includeAllen Corp., Alexandria, Edward Bennett Williams, Wash., McGuire, Woods, Battle & Boothe, Mitre Corp., Falls Church, Va., Texaco, Harrison, N.Y., NIH Clin. Ctr. Galleries, others. Recipient Gilham award Art League-Torpedo Factory, Alexandria, Va., 1986, 92, Miniature Internat. Exhibit 2nd Pl. Landscape award Miniature Soc., Washington, 1991-95. Mem. Southern Watercolor Soc., Washington Watercolor Assn. (Juror's Choice award 1992), Potomac Valley Watercolor Assn. (pres. 1978), Va. Watercolor Soc. (pres. 1987-88, Best in Show award 1986), Art Guild Springfield and Vienna (Va.), Nat. League Am. Pen Women (pres. 1974-76).

WENNER, MICHAEL ALFRED, retired diplomat, writer; b. Macclesfield, Eng., Mar. 17, 1921; came to U.S., 1977; s. Alfred Emil and Simone Marguerite (Roussel) W.; m. Gunilla Ståhle, Mar. 16, 1950 (div. Oct. 1978); children: Miles, Charles Andrew, Christopher, Martin; m. Holly Adrianne (Raven) Johnson, Apr. 27, 1990. BA, Oxford (Eng.) U., 1947, MA, 1952. 3d sec. Brit. Embassy, Stockholm, 1948-51; 2d sec. Brit. Embassy, Washington, 1951-53; 1st sec. Brit. Embassy, Tel Aviv, 1956-59; head of chancery Brit. Embassy, La Paz, Bolivia, 1959-61, Vienna, Austria, 1961-63; mem. Am. Dept. Fgn. Office, London, 1953-55; inspector diplomatic establishments worldwide, 1964-67; Brit. Amb. to El Salvador San Salvador, 1967-70; Latin Am. Rep.-Designate Thomas De La Rue Ltd., 1971-72; dep. head energy dept. Rio Tinto Zinc, London, 1974-75; v.p. Micron Corp., Houston, 1977-81; comml. and econ. advisor Consulate Gen. of Switzerland, Houston, 1984-91; pres. Wenner Comm., Houston, 1992—. Author: (autobiography) So It Was, 1993, (children's stories) Telephone Tales, 1995; translation: (hist. account) Captured by Brigands, 1994. Capt. Brit. Army, 1940-45. Recipient Cert. of Appreciation Mayor of Houston, 1991. Mem. Sunrise Toastmasters, Houston Choral Soc., Houston Consular Corps (hon. life), Oxford Union (life). Roman Catholic. Home and Office: Wenner Comm 7917 Westwood Dr Houston TX 77055

WENRICH, JOHN WILLIAM, college president; b. York, Pa., June 8, 1937; s. Ralph Chester and Helen Louise (McCollam) W.; m. Linda Larsen, June 23, 1961 (dec. Sept. 1966); 1 child, Thomas Allen; m. Martha Gail Lofberg, Sept. 1, 1967; 1 child, Margaret Ann. A.B., Princeton U., 1959; M.A., U. Mich., 1961, Ph.D., 1968. Fgn. service officer Dept. State, Washington, 1962-65; rep. Internat. Devel. Found., N.Y.C., 1965-66; project dir. U. Mich., Ann Arbor, 1966-69; asst. to pres. Coll. San Mateo, Calif., 1969-71; v.p. Ferris State U., Big Rapids, Mich., 1971-75, pres., 1984-88; pres. Canada Coll., Redwood City, Calif., 1975-79, Santa Ana Coll., Calif., 1979-84; chancellor San Diego Community Coll. Dist., 1988-90, Dallas County Community Coll., 1990—. Co-author: Leadership in Administration of Technical and Vocational Education, 1974, Administration of Vocational Education. Recipient Meritorious Service medal Dept. State, 1966; Hinsdale scholar Sch. Edn. U. Mich., 1968. Home: 1520 Wyndmere Dr De Soto TX 75115-7808 Office: 701 Elm St Dallas TX 75202-3250

WENTWORTH, MALINDA ANN NACHMAN, former small business owner, real estate broker; b. Greenville, S.C.; d. Mordecai and Frances (Brown) Nachman; m. William A. Wentworth, June 22, 1964; children: William Allen Jr., Linda Ann. BBA, U. Miami, 1960. Registered rep. brokerage, real estate broker. Personnel Mgrs. Asst. Jordan March, Miami, 1960-61; stock broker Barron & Co., Inc., Greenville, 1961-64; real estate agt. Par Realty, Inc., Conyers, Ga., 1969-72; real estate broker Par Realty, Inc., Conyers, 1972-83; owner/ops. Rockdale Cablevision, Conyers, 1979-83; real estate broker Coldwell Banker, Conyers, 1983-85; owner, operator Wentworth's Gym & Fitness Ctr., Conyers, 1981-90; real estate broker First Realty, Conyers, 1981-89; ptnr. and dir. Santa Barbara (Calif.) Cellular Systems, Inc., 1986-89; v.p. Santa Barbara Cellular Systems, Inc., Atlanta, 1986-87; investor Cocoa Beach, Fla., 1990—. Producer and dir.: local sport events on cable to sta., 1979, 80, 81, 87. Founding dir., past pres. Porterdale PTO, 1972-79; mem. Nat. Cable TV Assn., 1979-83, pres. Unity Ch. of Rockdale, Conyers, 1984-85, dir., 1984-89. Named Lt. Col.--Aide-De-Camp, Gov. Staff, state of Ga., Gov. George Busbee, 1979, Appreciation Plaque award, Rockdale County High Sch. Football, 1987. Mem. Nat. Health & Strength Assn., Rockdale County Bd. of Realtors, Cellular Telephone Industry Assn., Rockdale County C. of C.

WENZEL, JOAN ELLEN, artist; b. N.Y.C., July 23, 1944; d. Irwin S. and Pearl (Silverman) Rever; m. Allen Jay Wenzel, June 12, 1966 (div. June 1987); 1 child, Kimberly Anne; m. Robert Harold Messing, July 23, 1987 (dec.). Student, Syracuse U., 1962-64; BS in Painting, NYU, 1966, MA in Painting, 1976; postgrad., Harvard U., 1967. One-woman shows include Esperante Sculpture Ctr., 1996, Lighthouse Sch. and Gallery, Tequesta, Fla., 1996, Helander Gallery, Palm Beach, Fla., 1985, 89, 95, Adamar Fine Art, Miami, 1993, Gallery Contemporena, Jacksonville, Fla., 1993, Alexander Brest Mus., Jacksonville, 1993, Albertson Peterson Gallery, Winter Park, Fla., 1992, Amerifest, Miami, 1991, Gallery Yves Arman, N.Y.C., 1982, Palm Beach County Court House, West Palm Beach, Fla., 1991, One Brickall Square, Miami, 1992, Lighthouse Gallery, Tequesta, Fla., 1995-96, Esperante Ctr., West Palm Beach, 1996; exhbns. include Aldrich Mus., Ridgefield, Conn., 1977, Queens Mus., N.Y.C., 1981. Democrat. Jewish. Home: 2275 Ibis Isle Rd W Palm Beach FL 33480-5307

WERLE, ROBERT GEARY, academic administrator; b. Washington, Mar. 28, 1944; s. Francis Bernard and Evelyn Mae (Case) W. BA, Christian Bros. Coll., 1970; MEd, U. Toronto, Ont., Can., 1976. Cert. Ednl. Adminstr. Tchr. La Salle H.S., Cin., 1970-73; tchr., adminstr. Roncalli H.S., Omaha, 1973-77; asst. prin. O'Hara H.S., Kansas City, Mo., 1977-79; dir. Stritch Retreat Ctr., Memphis, 1979-82; vocation dir. La Salle Inst., St. Louis, 1982-84; admissions counselor Christian Bros. U., Memphis, 1984-85, dir. campus ministry, 1985-86, dir. campus activities, 1986-91, assoc. dir. Stritch Conf. Ctr., 1991-94; archivist Christian Bros. U., C.B. Midwest Dist.; curator of art Christian Bros. U. Mem. Soc. Am. Archivists, Religious Archives Assn., De La Salle Regional Archivist Assn. (founder, chair USA-Toronto region), Pi Kappa Phi (adv. 1986-89, 94-96, Founder's Svc. award 1989, Alumni award 1995), Memphis in May Archives Com. (Founders award 1994). Democrat. Roman Catholic. Office: Christian Bros Univ O Donnell Archives 2455 Avery Ave Memphis TN 38112-4824

WERLEIN, EWING, JR., federal judge, lawyer; b. Houston, Sept. 14, 1936; s. Ewing and Ruth (Storey) W.; m. Kay McGibbon Werlein, June 29, 1963; children: Ewing Kenneth, Emily Kay. BA, So. Meth. U., 1958; LLB, U. Tex., 1961. Bar: Tex. 1961, U.S. Dist. Ct. (so. dist.) Tex. 1965, U.S. Dist. Ct. (ea. dist.) Tex. 1990, U.S. Ct. Appeals (5th cir.) 1970, U.S. Ct. Appeals (10th cir.) 1980, U.S. Claims Ct. 1985, U.S. Tax Ct. 1985, U.S. Supreme Ct. 1983. Ptnr. Vinson & Elkins, Houston, 1964-92; dist. judge U.S. Dist. Ct. (so. dist.) Tex., 1992—. Trustee So. Meth. U., Dallas, 1976-92, Asbury Theol. Sem., Wilmore, Ky., 1989—; mem. gen. bd. pub. United Meth. Ch., Nashville, 1974-84, chmn., 1980-84, chancellor Tex. ann. conf., 1977—; mem. exec. com. World Meth. Counh., 1981—, treas., 1991-93. Capt. USAF, 1961-64. Fellow Am. Coll. Trial Lawyers, 1984, Internat. Soc. Barristers, 1987; recipient Disting. Alumni award SMU Alumni Assn., 1994. Fellow Am. Bar Found., Tex. Bar Found., Houston Bar Found.; mem. State Bar Tex. (dir. 1990-93), Nat. Conf. Bar Pres., Houston Bar Assn. (pres. 1988-89), Houston C. of C. (life), SAR, Order of Coif, Ramada Club (Houston), Houston Club, Phi Beta Kappa. Office: US Dist Ct Tex US Courthouse 515 Rusk St Ste 9136 Houston TX 77002-2605

WERNER, DAVID FRANCIS, forensic serologist; b. Port Jervis, N.Y., Aug. 23, 1950; s. David John and Rosemary Ann (Witt) W.; m. Paula Cline Werner, May 22, 1976; children: Stephanie, David. AA, Orange County C.C., 1970; BS, SUNY, Albany, 1972. Med. technologist St. Francis Hosp., Port Jervis, 1974-78; enlisted U.S. Army, 1978, advanced through grades to chief warrant officer 4, 1995; mil. policeman 205th MP Co., Ft. Leavenworth, Kans., 1978-80; forensic serologist U.S. Army Criminal Investigation Lab.-CONUS, Ft. Gordon, Ga., 1980-81, U.S. Army Criminal Investigation Lab.-CONUS, Ft. Gillem, Ga., 1984—, U.S. Army Criminal Investigation Lab.-PACIFIC, Camp Zama, Japan, 1981-84; expert witness in field. Mem. Forensic Sci. Soc., Soc. of Forensic Hemogenetics, Internat. Soc. of Bloodstain Pattern Analysts. Home: 175 Glenloch Pky Stockbridge GA 30281-5915 Office: USACIL-CONUS Fort Gillem Forest Park GA 30050

WERNER, ELIZABETH HELEN, librarian, Spanish language educator; b. Palo Alto, Calif., June 21, 1944; d. Fielding and Lucy Elizabeth (Hart) McDearmon; m. Michael Andrew Werner, Aug. 21, 1976. BA, Mills Coll., 1966; MA, Ind. U., 1968; MLS, U. Md., 1973. Instr. Spanish, Western Md. Coll., Westminster, 1968-72; libr., assoc. prof. Clearwater (Fla.) Christian Coll., 1975—; sec. Sunline Libr. users group Tampa Bay Libr. Consortium, Tampa, Fla., 1993-94. Contbr. book revs. to profl. jours. Com. mem. Upper Pinellas County Post Office Customers' Adv. Coun., Clearwater, 1992—. Mem. Fla. Libr. Assn., Assn. Christian Librs., Fla. Assn. Christian Librs. (pres. 1991-94, sec. 1987-90, 95-96), Friends of the Clearwater Libr., Am. Assn. Tchrs. Spanish and Portuguese. Office: Clearwater Christian Coll 3400 Gulf To Bay Blvd Clearwater FL 34619-4514

WERNER, STUART LLOYD, computer services company executive; b. N.Y.C., June 2, 1932; s. Leroy Louis and Frances Werner; m. Davideen Price, Jan. 6, 1990; children by previous marriage: Joan Leslie, Susan Lyn, Richard Wayne. BArch, Rensselaer Poly. Inst., 1954. Ptnr. in charge architecture Werner-Dyer & Assos., Washington, 1959-68; v.p. Rentex Corp., Phila., 1968-70; pres. Werner & Assos., Inc., Washington, 1970-81; v.p. spl. projects ARA Svcs., Inc.; v.p. ARA, 1981-83; chmn. STN, Inc., Falls Church, Va., 1982-83; pres. Werner & Monk, Inc., 1983-87; pres. STN, Inc., 1981—; mem. indsl. engring. terminology U.S. Stds. Inst. Bd. dirs. Watergate South, Washington Opera Soc., Friends of the Corcoran Gallery, Washington. With AUS, 1955-57. Mem. AIA, Am. Inst. Indsl. Engrs., Marinette Yacht Club, Masons,Tau Beta Pi. Republican. Contbr. articles to tech. jours. Home: 700 New Hampshire Ave NW Washington DC 20037-2406 Office: STN Inc 5113 Leesburg Pike Falls Church VA 22041-3204

WERNER, THOMAS LEE, hospital administrator; b. Hazen, N.D., Dec. 8, 1945; married. BA, Union Coll., 1967; MA, U. Nebr., 1969. Asst. dir. pers. Portland (Oreg.) Adventist Med. Ctr., 1971-72; v.p. Verticare Ambulatory Care Program, Portland, 1972-73; adminstr. Tillamook (Oreg.) CountyGen. Hosp., 1973-77, Walla Walla (Wash.)Gen. Hosp., 1977-81; exec. v.p. Fla. Hosp. Med. Ctr., Orlando, 1981-85, pres., 1985—. Office: Fla Hosp Med Ctr 601 E Rollins St Orlando FL 32803-1248*

WERRIES, E. DEAN, food distribution company executive; b. Tescott, Kans., May 8, 1929; s. John William and Sophie E. Werries; m. Marjean Sparling, May 18, 1962. B.S., U. Kans., 1952. With Fleming Foods Co., Topeka, 1955-89, exec. v.p., 1973-76; exec. v.p. Eastern ops. Fleming Foods Co., Phila., 1976-78; pres. Fleming Foods Co., Oklahoma City, 1978-81; pres., chief operating officer Fleming Cos., Inc., Oklahoma City, 1981-88, also dir.; pres., chief exec. officer Fleming Cos., Inc., 1988-89, chmn., CEO, 1989-93; chmn. bd. Sonic Corp., 1995—. Sec. of Commerce State of Okla., 1995. With U.S. Army, 1952-54, Korea. Mem. Nat. Am. Wholesale Grocers Assn. (bd. dirs. 1979-93), Food Mktg. Inst. (bd. dirs. 1984—, chmn. 1989-91), Ind. Grocers Alliance (bd. dirs. 1984-94). Republican. Presbyterian. Office: Fleming Cos Inc PO Box 26647 6301 Waterford Blvd Oklahoma City OK 73126-0647

WERT, MARY COX, health facility administrator; b. Chattanooga, Dec. 29, 1935; d. Joseph Cecil and Frances Evelyn (Payne) Soc.; m. Harry Emerson Wert, May 9, 1959; children: Kimberley Dawn, Joanna Reed, Stephen Emerson. Diploma, Baroness Erlanger Sch. Nursing, 1956; BSN, U. Phoenix, 1984. Staff nurse emergency room Fla. Hosp., Orlando; admissions coord. Americana Healthcare, Winter Park, Fla.; dir. utilization mgmt. Hawthorne (Calif.) Meml. Hosp., 1979-83; dir. utilization/diagnosis related groups Robert F. Kennedy Med. Ctr., Hawthorne, 1983-89; quality assurance reviewer Cen. Fla. Rehab. Specialists, Maitland, Fla., 1995-96.

WERTH, SUSAN, lawyer; b. N.Y.C., Nov. 29, 1948. BA, Barnard Coll., 1970; JD, Columbia U., 1973. Bar: Fla. 1973, U.S. Dist. Ct. (so. dist.) Fla. 1974, U.S. Dist. Ct. (mid. dist.) Fla. 1975, U.S. Dist. Ct. (no. dist.) Fla. 1976, U.S. Ct. Appeals (5th cir.) 1974, U.S. Ct. Appeals (11th cir.) 1978, U.S. Supreme Ct. 1978, U.S. Ct. Appeals (11th cir.) 1981. Ptnr. Weil, Gotshal & Manges, Miami, Fla., 1989-96; sr. v.p. of law Vistana Development, Miami, Fla.; adj. prof. law Sch. Law U. Miami, 1976-77. Mem. Fla. Bar Found. (bd. dirs. 1986-88, sec.-treas. 1988-90, pres.-elect 1991-92, pres. 1992-93), Fla. Bar. Office: Weil Gotshal & Manges 701 Brickell Ave Ste 2100 Miami FL 33131-2861*

WERTHEIM, MICHAEL STANLEY, oncologist; b. N.Y.C., Mar. 1, 1952; s. Julius and Herta (Levy) W.; m. Susan Wertheim (div.); children: Mariell, Jonathan. BS cum laude, SUNY, Stony Brook, 1974; MD, SUNY, Bklyn., 1980. Diplomate Am. Bd. Internal Medicine, Med. Oncology, Nat. Bd. Med. Examiners. Intern, resident Downstate Kings County Hosp., Bklyn., 1980-81, resident, 1981-83; clin. fellow med. oncology Meml. Sloan Kettering Cancer Ctr., N.Y.C., 1983-85; hematologist, oncologist Assocs. Treasure Coast, Port St. Lucie, Fla., 1985—; med. dir. Hospice of Treasure Coast, Ft. Pierce Fla., 1985-93, HCA Med. Ctr. Port St. Lucie, 1993, chief of staff, 1995. Contbr. articles to profl. jours. Fellow Cornell U. Med. Coll., 1983-85. Mem. ACP, Am. Soc. Clin. Oncology, Fla. Med. Assn., Fla. Soc. Oncology, Flying Physicians Assn. Office: Hematology/Oncology Assocs Treasure Coast PA 1801 SE Hillmoor Dr Ste B-101 Port Saint Lucie FL 34952-7545

WESCOTT, LYLE DUMOND, JR., chemistry educator; b. Hackensack, N.J., Jan. 27, 1937; s. Lyle DuMond Sr. and Tula (Williams) W.; m. Paula Ruth Moore, June 9, 1959 (div. 1980); children: Douglas Allen, Paul Stuart; m. Sheena Joyce Clymer, Sept. 27, 1985 (div. 1996). BS, Ga. Tech., 1959; PhD, Pa. State U., 1963. Research fellow Pa. State U., University Park, 1963-64; research chemist Esso Research and Engring., Baytown, Tex., 1964-68; prof. chemistry Christian Bros. U., Memphis, 1968—; cons. Accrabond, Inc., Olive Branch, Miss., 1976—, Am. Telephone and Telegraph Bell Labs., Murray Hill, N.J., 1981-85. Author: Polymer Additives, 1984; contbr. articles to profl. jours.; patentee in field. Served with USNR, 1954-62. Mem. Am. Chem. Soc. (chair 1985-86), Royal Soc. Chemistry. Office: Christian Bros U 650 E Parkway S Memphis TN 38104-5519

WESELIN, MARY LOU, interior designer; b. Salem, Ohio, Nov. 15, 1946; d. Andrew Herbert and Wilma Gertrude (Bauman) Herbert Berry; m. Robert Pross, May 29, 1966 (div. 1978); m. Dietmar Weselin, Apr. 27, 1979; 1 child, Adrian. Cert., N.Y. Sch. Interior Design, N.Y.C., 1968. Self-employed interior designer Jamaica Estates, N.Y., 1968-78; prin. Mary Lou Weselin, Interior Design, Fredericksburg, Va., 1981—. Designer mag. cover Better Homes & Gardens, Decorating, 1986; mag. articles Decorating, 1986-87, Window & Wall Ideas, 1989; books: In Fredericksburg, 1984, Expression of Style, 1990. Co-chair fundraising Rappahannock Hospice-In-Motion, Fredericksburg, 1987, chairperson benefit, 1990; co-chair benefit auction Mary Washington Hosp., Fredericksburg, 1989; bd. dirs. Mary Washington Hosp. Found., 1989-92, Fredericksburg Festival of Arts, 1996—; mem. gift shop com. Kenmore Mus., Fredericksburg, 1990-91. Lutheran. Home and Office: 1206 Prince Edward St Fredericksburg VA 22401-3732

WESLEY, JAMES WYATT, JR., communications company executive; b. Atlanta, Sept. 5, 1933; s. James Wyatt Wesley and Nellie (Johnson) Poston; m. Mary Phillips, Mar. 20, 1954; children: James Alan, David Wyatt. BS in Indsl. Mgmt., Ga. Inst. Tech., 1955; MBA, U. Miami, 1974. Announcer, sales mgr. Sta. WSB, Atlanta, 1955-62; local sales mgr. Sta. WSB, Altanta, 1962-65; v.p., gen. mgr. Stas. WIOD/WAIA Radio, Miami, Fla., 1965-73, Stas. KFI/KOST Radio, L.A., 1973-81; exec. v.p. radio Cox Broadcasting Corp., Atlanta, 1981-84; pres., chief exec. officer DKM Broadcasting Corp., Atlanta, 1984-88; chmn., chief exec. officer Summit Communications Group, Inc., Atlanta, 1988—; bd. dirs. Radio Advt. Bur., 1982-83. Mem. Nat. Assn. Broadcasters (bd. dirs. 1973—), Fla. Assn. Broadcasters (pres. 1972—), So. Calif. Broadcasters Assn. (chmn. bd. dirs. 1979—), Greater Miami Radio Broadcasters (pres. 1969—). Office: Summit Comm Group Ste 1150 115 Perimeter Center Pl NE Atlanta GA 30346-1282*

WESLEY, STEPHEN BURTON, training professional; b. Louisville, July 13, 1949; s. Leon and Montie C. (Burton) W.; m. Kun Wanna Jarusin, May 22, 1972; 1 child, Thomas Jayson. AA, Somerset (Ky.) Coll., 1969; student, Community Coll. of Air Force, Maxwell, AFB, 1970-77; AA, Watterson Coll., 1977 student, U. Louisville, 1978-80. Cert. energy mgr., lighting efficiency profl. Electronics tech. Kegco, Somerset, 1973-74; instrument tech. Ky. Air Nat. Guard, Louisville, 1974-78; application engr. Johnson Controls, Inc., Louisville, 1978-81, sales engr., 1981-88, energy svcs. mgr., 1988-96; regional tng. dir. Excel Telecom., 1995—; adv. bd. Ivy Tech Vocat. Sch., Jeffersonville, Ind., 1988-90. Inventor pitot tube removal tool. Lay dir. Walk to Emmaus, Elizabethtown, Ky., 1989. Sgt. USAF, 1969-73. Mem. Assn. Energy Engrs. Baptist. Home and Office: 8652 Navarre Pkwy #146 Navarre FL 32566

WESLEY, STEPHEN HARRISON, pharmaceutical company executive; b. Knoxville, Tenn., Aug. 13, 1961; s. Robert Louis and Doris Ruth (Rogers) W.; m. Kittie Conner, May 28, 1988; children: Robert Allen, Kellie Elizabeth. BA in Econs., U. Tenn., 1984. Sales rep. Newark Electronics, Knoxville, Tenn., 1984-85; sales engr. Carolina Controls Co., Knoxville, 1986-88; profl. rep. Winthrop Pharmaceuticals, Knoxville, 1988-90; med. ctr. specialist Winthrop Pharmaceuticals, Nashville, 1990—; wound care market specialist Convatec divsn. Bristol-Myers Squibb, Knoxville, 1995—, ConvaTec divsn. Bristol-Myers-Squibb, Knoxville, 1995—; exec. v.p., bd. dirs. Maverick Med. Corp., Knoxville, 1996—. Recipient Mayor's Merit award City of Knoxville, 1974, Silver Pen Editl. award The Nashville Banner, 1993. Home and Office: 2804 Pebblestone Ln Knoxville TN 37938-3934

WESSLING, GREGORY JAY, retail executive; b. Chgo., Dec. 11, 1951; s. Robert J. and Doris (Tosch) W.; m. Mary Anne Richmond, Nov. 16, 1974; children: Douglas A., James R., Robert E. BBA, U. N.C., 1974; postgrad., Wake Forest U. Sch. Bus., 1974-76, MBA, 1987. Store mgr. Lowe's Co., Inc., Winston-Salem, N.C., 1973-76; mktg. mgr. Lowe's Co., Inc., North Wilkesboro, N.C., 1976—, dir. merchandising, 1978-80, v.p. merchandising, 1980-96, sr. v.p., gen. merchandise mgr., 1996—; bd. dirs. DJR Corp., Winston-Salem; mem. alumni coun., bd. visitors Babcock Grad. Sch. Mgmt., Wake Forest U. Mem. Home Ctr. Leadership Council. Republican. Methodist. Office: Lowes Cos Inc PO Box 1111 North Wilkesboro NC 28659-1111

WEST, BENJAMIN B., advertising executive; b. 1951. BA, Washington and Lee U. With West Advt. & Mktg., Tampa, Fla., 1973—, now pres., CEO. Office: West & Company Marketing & Adver 401 E Jackson St Ste 3600 Tampa FL 33602-5232*

WEST, CAROL CATHERINE, law educator; b. Phila., May 23, 1944; d. Scott G. and Helen (Young) West. BA, Miss. U. for Women, 1966; MLS, U. So. Miss., 1984; JD, U. Miss., 1970. Pub. svcs. law libr., U. Va., Charlottesville, 1966-67; catalog law libr. U. Miss., Oxford, 1967-70; legis. reference libr. Miss. Legislature, Jackson, 1970-75; law libr. Miss. Coll., Jackson, 1975-94, prof. law, 1975—; del. White House conf. Libr. and Info. Svcs., 1991; cons. to Parliament of Armenia, 1995; mem. bd. commr. Miss. Libr. Comm., 1993—. Mem. ABA, Miss. Bar, Hinds County Bar (bd. dirs. 1994-96), Miss. Women Lawyers Assn. (bd. dirs. 1991-93), Miss. Libr. Assn., ALA. Methodist. Office: Miss Coll Law Sch 151 E Griffith St Jackson MS 39201-1302

WEST, DELOURIS JEANNE, project management company executive; b. Durham, N.C., July 13, 1943; d. James Hayward and Daisy Lilly (Penwell) O'Neal; m. Larry Alexander West, Aug. 10, 1961; children: Gregory Alexander, Dedrea Lynne, Brandon James. Grad. high sch., Mebane, N.C. Inventory control clk. Avon Products, Inc., Atlanta, 1962-67; dir., tchr. United Meth. Kindergarten, Woodstock, Ga., 1972-77; owner, mgr. Gift Emporium, Roswell, Ga., 1977-79; exec. dir. North Fulton C. of C., Roswell, 1979-88; pres. Project Ptnrs., Inc., Roswell, 1988—; founder, dir. Environ. Edn. Ctr., Alpharetta, Ga., 1991; founder, adminstr. Project Ripple Water Quality Program, 1991, Green Sch. Program, 1990; mem. Fulton County Soil and Water Conservation Dist. Bd.; adv. bd. Alpharetta Greenways System, Ga. DNR/EPD Stream Watch. Author: The Acorn, 1972; editor Nova News, 1966, The Acorn, 1972, News and View, 1980-88, Clean and Green Report, 1990—; newspaper columnist Rainbows and Butterflies, 1973. Active numerous civic orgns., including mem. Fulton County Devel. Bd., Fulton County Metro Pvt. Industry Coun., Chattahoochee River Corridor Adv. Coun.; bd. dirs. YMCA, North Fulton Regional Hosp., 1983-86, Chattahoochee Theater, 1990-91; chmn. vocat. com. Milton H.S., Alpharetta, Ga., 1987; trustee Chattahoochee Nature Ctr., 1988-92; chmn., founder North Fulton Ednl. Consortium, 1987-90; candidate County Commn., 1986, Ga. Ho. of Reps., 1989; exec. dir. Alpharetta Clean & Beautiful Commn., 1990—. Recipient Outstanding Layman award Roswell Jaycees, 1982, Supt.'s award Fulton County Bd. Edn. 1983, Perserverance award Am. Med. Internat., 1982, Appreciation award Adopt-A-Sch., 1986, svc. Appreciation award North Fulton Regional Hosp., 1987, Community Builder award Masons Lodge 739, 1987, Keys to Cities of Roswell and Alpharetta, 1990, Appreciation award Dept. Natural Resources, 1994; named One of Atlanta's 100, Sta. WRMM, 1985, One of Ten Most Powerful People in North Fulton County, Atlanta Jour. and Constn., 1986. Mem. Am. Water Works Assn., Groundwater Found. (charter mem.), Nat. Coun. for Urban Econ. Devel.,

Ga. C. of C. Execs. Assn., Ga. Indsl. Developers Assn., Roswell Hist. Soc., Alpharetta Hist. Soc., Ga. Clean and Beautivul Exec. Dirs. Assn., Nat. Arbor Day Found., Civitans (co-founder, charter v.p. Roswell 1982-83, Pres.'s award 1983). Methodist. Office: EEC 131 Roswell St Ste A-1 Alpharetta GA 30201-1900

WEST, GLENN EDWARD, business organization executive; b. Kansas City, Mo., Nov. 19, 1944; s. Ernest and Helen Cecil (Johnson) W.; m. Vicki Lynn Knox, May 22, 1970; children: Keele Kay, Kollen Chandler, Ashley Knox. BS in Acctg. and Mktg. cum laude, Northwest Mo. State U., 1966; student U. Colo. Inst. Orgn. Mgmt., 1974; student Notre Dame U. Acad. Orgn. Mgmt., 1977. Auditor Arthur Young & Co., Kansas City, Mo., 1966-68; sales mgr. Procter & Gamble, Kansas City, Mo., 1968-69; mgr. pub. relations St. Joseph Area C. of C., Mo., 1969-71, mgr. econ. devel., 1971-74; exec. v.p. Lawrence C. of C., Kans., 1974-81, Greater Macon C. of C., Ga., from 1981; now pres. Austin C. of C.; mem. bd. dirs. Tex. Assn. Bus. and C. of C., 1995, U.S. C. of C., 1995. Contbr. articles to profl. jours. Chmn. chpt. ARC, Macon, 1984; pres. Quality of Life Found. Austin, Greater Austin Sports Found.; cen. campaign chair Capital Area United Way, 1995. Recipient Leadership award Kiwanis Club, St. Joseph, Mo., 1974. Served with USNG, 1967-73. Mem. Kans Assn. Commerce and Industry (bd. dirs. 1977-79, leadership award 1981), Kans. C. of C. Execs. (bd. dirs. 1977-80, pres. 1979), Ga. C. of C. Execs. (bd. dirs. 1982—), Am. C. of C. Execs. (bd. dirs. 1979-81, 83-84, vice chmn. 1989—, chmn.-elect 1990, chmn. 1991, cert. chamber exec. 1980), C. of C. of U.S. (adv. com. 1981-89, bd. dir. 1995), Rotary, Barton Creek Country Club. Republican. Methodist. Office: Greater Austin C of C PO Box 1967 111 Congress Ave Plz Austin TX 78767-1967

WEST, JADE CHRISTINE, legislative staff; b. Cleve., Oct. 8, 1950; d. Roy Leo and Arleen Vivien (Trimmer) W.; m. Raymond J. LaJeunesse, Jr., Aug. 16, 1975. Student, Duke U., 1969-71. Rsch. dir. Nat. Right to Work Legal Def. Found., Springfield, Va., 1972-76; realtor George Mason Green Co., Arlington, Va., 1976-82; staff dir. U.S. Senate Steering Com., Washington, 1982-86; staff dir. Rep. Policy com. U.S. Senate, Washington, 1996—. Candidate Va. Gen. Assembly, 1975; delegate Rep. Nat. Conv., 1976, 1980. Republican. Office: US Senate Rep Policy Com 347 Russell Senate Bldg Washington DC 20510

WEST, JAMES ODELL, JR., finance executive; b. Newport News, Va., Mar. 1, 1960; s. James Odell and Margaret Alice (Schweida) W.; m. Elizabeth Ann Healy, May 21, 1983; children: James Odell III, William Charles. BA in History, Coll. of William and Mary, 1983, MBA, 1990. Analyst govt. contract adminstrn. Newport News Shipbuilding, 1984-90, supr., govt. audit liaison, 1990-93; dir. capital budgeting Tenneco, Inc., Houston, 1993—. Capt. USAR, 1984-93. Mem. Am. Mgmt. Assn., Beta Sigma. Republican. Home: 74 Rumplecreek Pl The Woodlands TX 77381 Office: Tenneco Inc PO Box 4100 The Woodlands TX 77387-4100

WEST, JANET L., German language educator; b. Nashville, Aug. 15, 1969; d. David J. and Nancy E. (Hagewood)) W. BA, Centre Coll., Danville, Ky., 1991; postgrad., U. N.C., 1991—. Tchg. asst. U. N.C., Chapel Hill, 1992—, asst. to dir. tchg. program dept. German, 1994-96, coord. tchg. tng. program, 1994-96, grad. tchg. cons. Ctr. for Tchg. and Learning, 1996—. Grantee German Acad. Exec. Svc., summer 1991. Mem. MLA, Am. Assn. Tchrs. German, Am. Comparative Lit. Assn., South Atlantic MLA (sec. spl. session 1995-96, presenter 1995). Home: 101 Hwy 54 Bypass Apt H-6 Carrboro NC 27510 Office: U NC Dept Germanic Langs 438 Dey Hall CB 3160 Chapel Hill NC 27599-3160

WEST, JOHN CHARLES, financial consultant; b. Fayetteville, Ark., Oct. 14, 1950; s. Charles Richard and Eileen Patricia West; m. Joan Gail Quinters, Oct. 18, 1980; children: Benjan Paul, Mark Aaron. BA, U. New Orleans, 1977; JD, Loyola U., New Orleans, 1982. Bar: La. 1983. Supr. Cigna Corp., Los Colinas, Tex., 1985-91; pres. West's Fin. Svcs., Arlington, Tex., 1996—; lawyer Jminos Simon, Lafayette, La., 1991. Sgt. U.S. Army, 1969-71, Vietnam. Office: One Galleria Tower 5805 Fox Hunt Dr Arlington TX 76017

WEST, LEE ROY, federal judge; b. Clayton, Okla., Nov. 26, 1929; s. Calvin and Nicie (Hill) W.; m. MaryAnn Ellis, Aug. 29, 1952; children: Kimberly Ellis, Jennifer Lee. B.A., U. Okla., 1952, J.D., 1956; LL.M. (Ford Found. fellow), Harvard U., 1963. Bar: Okla. 1956. Individual practice law Ada, Okla., 1956-61, 63-65; faculty U. Okla. Coll. Law, 1961-62; Ford Found. fellow in law teaching Harvard U., Cambridge, Mass., 1962-63; judge 22d Jud. Dist. Okla., Ada, 1965-73; mem. CAB, Washington, 1973-78; acting chmn. CAB, 1977; practice law Tulsa, 1978-79; spl. justice Okla. Supreme Ct., 1965; judge U.S. Dist Ct. (we. dist.) Okla., 1979-94; sr. judge U.S. Dist. Ct. (we. dist.), Okla., 1994—. Editor: Okla. Law Rev. Served to capt. USMC, 1952-54. Mem. U. Okla. Alumni Assn. (dir.), Phi Delta Phi (pres. 1956), Phi Eta Sigma, Order of Coif. Home: 6500 E Danforth Rd Edmond OK 73034-7601 Office: US Dist Ct 3001 US Courthouse 200 NW 4th St Oklahoma City OK 73102-3003

WEST, MACDONALD, real estate executive; b. Bournemouth, Eng., July 15, 1943; came to U.S., 1968; s. Joseph Stanley and Maisie Siswick (Hollom) W.; m. Charlotte Denise Duvall, Nov. 1, 1980. Diploma London U. Coll. Estate Mgmt., 1968; MBA, Columbia U., 1970. Trainee surveyor Navy Works Dept., Admiralty, London, 1960-64; sr. assoc. Robinson & Roods, London, 1965-68; dir. cost control Nat. Liberty Corp., Valley Forge, Pa., 1970-71; v.p., dir. Philipsborn Cos., Coral Gables, Fla., 1972-76, Allen Morris Co., Miami, Fla., 1976-89 ; sr. v.p., COO Allen Morris Constrn. Co., 1978-89, also sr. v.p. asset mgmt. div.; pres. Miami Lakes (Fla.) Devel., Inc., 1989-91; exec. v.p. The Graham Cos., Miami Lakes, 1989-91; pres., CEO The Macdonald West Co., Coral Gables, 1991—. Deacon Univ. Bapt. Ch., Coral Gables, 1977—. Fellow Royal Instn. Chartered Surveyors; mem. Counselors of Real Estate (pres. 1995), Urban Land Inst., Nat. Assn. Indsl. and Office Parks, Indsl. Assn. Dade County, Realtor Assn. Miami, Bldg. Industry Assn. South Fla. (pres. 1996), Nat. Assn. Home Builders, Miami City Club, Ocean Reef Club, Rotary (Miami club). Republican. Home: 5325 Orduna Dr Coral Gables FL 33146-2640 Office: 1390 S Dixie Hwy Ste 2217 Coral Gables FL 33146-2945

WEST, MARSHA, elementary school educator; b. DeQueen, Ark., Sept. 1, 1950; d. Marshall T. and Mildred L. (Davis) Gore; m. Larry T. West, May 19, 1972; 1 child, Zachary. BS in Edn., So. State Coll., Magnolia, Ark., 1971; MEd, U. Ark., 1975; postgrad., Henderson State Coll., Arkadelphia, Ark., Purdue U.; specialist's degree, U. Ga., 1991. Cert. elem. and spl. edn. tchr., Tex., elem. tchr., early childhood, mid. sch. tchr., media specialist, Ga. Spl. edn. resource tchr. Gatesville (Tex.) Ind. Sch. Dist.; tchr. early childhood spl. edn. Bryan (Tex.) Ind. Sch. Dist.; elem. tchr. Tippecanoe Sch. Corp., Lafayette, Ind.; elem. tchr. Clarke County Sch. Dist., Athens, Ga., media specialist. Mem. ALA, NEA, Am. Assn. Sch. Librs., Internat. Reading Assn., Ga. Assn. Educators, Ga. Assn. Instrnl. Tech., Ga. Libr. Media Assn. (dist. V chair), N.E. Ga. Reading Coun., Clarke County Assn. Educators, Kappa Delta Pi.

WEST, MARY ELIZABETH, psychiatric management professional; b. Spartanburg, S.C., Aug. 27, 1939; d. Thomas Benjamin and Virginia Milster (Smith) Anderson; m. William Duane West, Sept. 13, 1960; children: William Kevin, Walter Duane, Litia Allyn West Harrison, Thomas Anderson. Diploma in nursing, Ga. Bapt. Hosp., 1960; BS in Nursing Leadership, Tift Coll., 1966; MS in Counseling, U. Scranton, 1972; EdD, Nova U., 1979. RNC, Tenn.; cert. profl. counselor, Tenn., nurse adminstr. advanced. Staff nurse pub. health Fulton County Health Dept., Atlanta, 1960-61; instr. in nursing Macon (Ga.) Hosp. Sch. Nursing, 1965-66, Western Piedmont C.C., 1973-74; dir. nursing Tyler Meml. Hosp., Tunkhannock, Pa., 1967-70; assoc. dir. nursing Nesbitt Meml. Hosp., Kingston, Pa., 1971; assoc. adminstr. Home Health Svcs. Luzerne County, Wilkes-Barre, Pa., 1972; cons. nursing Hosp. Affiliates Internat., Nashville, 1974-76, v.p. nursing, 1976-78, v.p. quality assurance, 1978-80; v.p. nursing cons. svc. Advanced Mgmt. Sys., Nashville, 1981; sr. v.p. planning Hosp. Affiliates Devel. Corp., Nashville, 1982-83; v.p. ops. Winter Haven (Fla.) Hosp., 1986-90; pres. Hope Psychiat. Mgmt., Inc., Winter Haven, 1994—. Contbg. author: Political Action Handbook for Nurses, 1985 (Am. Jour. Nursing Book of Yr. 1986); co-author, editor manual Hosp. Affiliates International, 1978; contbr. articles to mags., chpt. to book. V.p. part time svcs. Winter Haven Hosp., 1987-90; insvc. tng. dir. Rotary Internat., Winter Haven, 1989-91; v.p. Winter Haven C. of C., 1988-90; pres. Polk County Nurse Exec. Orgn., Lakeland, Fla., 1989-90; bd. dirs. Women's Resource Ctr., Inc., Winter Haven, 1989-91; bd. dirs., founder Mothers Alone, Haines City, Fla., 1991—; nat. chair Sunhealth Nursing Coun., Charlotte, N.C., 1990; founder, bd. chmn. Hope Christian Counseling Inc., 1994; state bd. dirs., dir. profl. edn. Bapt. Nursing Fellowship, 1995—. Mem. ANA, Fla. Nursing Assn., Am. Orgn. Nurse Execs., Inner Wheel (v.p., treas., bd. dirs. 1992—), Theta Chi Omega. Republican. Baptist. Home: 3208 Lake Breeze Dr Haines City FL 33844 Office: HOPE Psychiat Mgmt Ste 5013 5665 Cypress Gardens Blvd Winter Haven FL 33884-2273

WEST, PHILIP WILLIAM, chemistry educator; b. Crookston, Minn., Apr. 12, 1913; s. William Leonard and Anne (Thompson) W.; m. Tenney Constance Johnson, July 5, 1935 (dec. Feb. 1964); children: Dorothy West/Farwell, Linda West Gueho (dec.), Patty West Elstrott; m. Foymae S. Kelso, July 1, 1964. B.S., U. N.D., 1935, M.S., 1936, D.Sc. (hon.), 1958; Ph.D., State U. Iowa, 1939; postgrad., Rio de Janeiro, 1946. Chemist N.D. Geol. Survey, 1935-36; research asst. san. chemistry U. Iowa, 1936-37; asst. chemist Iowa Dept. Health, 1937-40; research microchemist Econ. Lab., Inc., St. Paul, 1940; faculty La. State U., 1940-80, prof. chemistry, 1951-80, Boyd prof., 1953-80, emeritus, 1980—, chmn. ann. symposium modern methods of analytical chemistry, 1948-65, dir. Inst. for Environmental Scis., 1967-80; co-founder, chmn. bd. West-Paine Labs. Inc., Baton Rouge, 1980-93; O. M. Smith lectr. Okla. State U., 1955; vis. prof. U. Colo., 1963, Rand Afrikaans U., 1980; adj. prof. EPA, 1969-80; founder Ken-Tech. Labs., Inc., Baton Rouge, 1954, chmn. bd., 1965-74; co-founder West-Paine Labs., Inc., Baton Rouge, 1978, pres., 1978-93, chmn. bd., lab dir., 1990; mem. 1st working party sci. com. on problems of environment, 1971-74; pres. analytical sect. Internat. Union Pure and Applied Chemistry, 1965-69, mem. sect. indsl. hygiene and toxicology, 1971-73, mem. air quality sect., 1973-75; mem. tech. adv. com. La. Air Pollution Control Com., 1979—; mem. Gov.'s Task Force Environ. Health, 1983-85; mem. sci. adv. bd. EPA, 1983-84; cons. WHO; tech. expert Nat. Bur. Standards Nat. Vol. Lab. Accreditation Program, 1988—; chmn. bd., CEO West & Assoc., Inc., 1992—; mem. adv. com. Coll. Basic Sci. La. State U. Author: Chemical Calculations, 1948, (with Vick) Qualitative Analysis and Analytical Chemical Separations, 2d edit., 1959, (with Bustin) Experience Approach to Experimental Chemistry, 1975; editor: (with Hamilton) Science of the Total Environment, 1973-78, (with Macdonald) Analytica Chimica Acta, 1959-78, Reagents and Reaction for Qualitative Inorganic Analysis; co-editor: Analytical Chemistry, 1963; asst. editor: Mikrochemica Acta, 1952-78, Michrochem. Jour, 1957-75; adv. bd.: Analytical Chemistry, 1959-60; publ. bd.: Jour. Chem. Edn, 1954-57; contbr. articles to profl. jours. Recipient Honor Scroll award La. sect. Am. Inst. Chemistry, 1972. Fellow AAAS; mem. Am. Chem. Soc. (Southwest award 1954, Charles E. Coates award 1967, Analytical Chemistry award 1974, award for Creative Advances in Environ. Sci. and Tech.), La. Acad. Sci., Air Pollution Control Assn., Am. Indsl. Hygiene Assn., Austrian Microchem. Soc. (hon.), Soc. of Analysts Eng. (hon.), Internat. Union Pure and Applied Chemistry (pres. commn. I, pres. analytical div.), Japan Soc. for Analytical Chemistry (hon.), La. Cancer and Health Found., Sigma Xi, Phi Lambda Upsilon, Phi Kappa Phi, Alpha Epsilon Delta, Alpha Chi Sigma, Tau Kappa Epsilon. Office: West-Paine Labs Inc 7979 G S R I Rd Baton Rouge LA 70820-7402

WEST, RAYMOND L., nurse; b. Newport News, Va., July 28, 1968; s. Raymond and Louise (Gray) W. AAS cum laude, Thomas Nelson Community Coll., Hampton, Va., 1990; BS cum laude, Med. Coll. Va., 1992. Qualified in Pediat. Advanced Life Support, 1995; cert. pediat. nurse. Staff nurse Williamsburg Commun. Hosp., 1992-93, Children's Hosp. of the Kings Daus., 1993—; mem. Coordinating Coun. Progressive Care Unit, 1995; mem. Progressive Care Unit Logistic Com., 1995; mem. adv. bd. Thomas Nelson C.C. Sch. of Nursing, 1994—. Mem. Sentara Hampton Gen. Hosp. Aux., 1984—, Am. Heart Assn., 1988-89. With USAF, 1987. Mem. AACN, Nat. Legue for Nursing, Va. Nurses Assn. (treas. dist. 10 1994-96), Va. Commonwealth U.-Med. Coll. Va. Alumni Assn., Thomas Nelson C.C. Alumni Assn., Soc. of Pediatric Nurses, Am. Pediat. Surg. Nurses Assn.

WEST, ROGER SEIKER, III, finance executive; b. Exmore, Va., Mar. 23, 1949; s. Roger Seiker Jr. and Midred (Shockley) W.; m. Terry Haynie, Aug. 15, 1981. Student, Gulf Coast Coll., Panama City, Fla., 1968-69. Pres. Peninsula Home Improvement, Exmore, 1970-80; chmn., chief exec. officer BSI Holdings Inc., Norfolk, Va., 1980—; also bd. dirs. Brokers Securities, Inc., Norfolk, Va.; chmn. AutoBanc Inc., Norfolk, 1991—; dir. AutoBanc Corp.; Amb. City of Norfolk; vol. worker for homeless. Named Man of Yr., SBA, 1976. Mem. Regional Investment Brokers Syndicate (bd. dirs. regional), Va. Traders Assn. Republican. Methodist. Lodge: Moose. Office: AutoBanc Inc 5 Koger Ctr Ste 105 Norfolk VA 23502-4107

WEST, RUTH TINSLEY, lawyer; b. Scranton, Pa., Mar. 4, 1945; d. Joseph Woodford and Martha McLendon (Ross) W.; children: Bowman Staples Garrett, III, McLendon West Garrett. BA in Polit. Sci., Duke U., 1966; JD, Mercer U., 1974. Bar: Ga. Ptnr. King & Spalding, Atlanta, 1980—. Editor-in-chief Mercer Law Rev. Me. bd. visitors Walter F. George Sch. Law Mercer U., 1979-80, sec. bd. visitors, 1980-81, chmn. bd. visitors, 1981-82; bd. dirs. Met. Atlanta YMCA, 1988-90, Nexus Contemporary Art Ctr., 1983-93, New Visions Gallery, 1987-89, Ga. Justice Project, 1989—, Pro-Choice, 1990-92, Mercer Univ. Press, 1991—, Atlanta Women's Fund, 1993—, High Mus. Art, 1995—; participant Leadership Ga., 1981; participant Leadership Atlanta, 1986-87, mem. exec. com., 1991-92; mem. Commerce Club, 1987—; trustee Ga. Ctr. for Children, 1994—, Arts Festival Atlanta, 1996—; mem. Ctrl. Ala. Hospitality Childcare, Inc., 1995—; mem. Regional Leadership Inst. Mem. ABA (tax-exempt fin. sect. taxation com. 1978—), State Bar Ga., Atlanta Bar Assn. (dir. 1985-86, chmn. minority clerkship program 1985-87, adv. bd. 1989—), Bond Attys. Workshop (chmn. 1978-79, steering com. 1977-78, 85-86, instr. 1979-89), Nat. Assn. Bond Lawyers (dir. 1977-80, treas. 1978-80, instr. fundamentals mcpl. bonds 1980, chmn. legis. seminar 1987), Lawyers Club Atlanta (treas. 1983-85, sec. 1986-87, exec. com. 1983-89), Ga. Bar Found. (trustee 1993—), Mercer U. Alumni Assn. (sec. 1982-83, v.p. 1983-84, pres. 1985-86), Phi Alpha Delta. Democrat. Episcopalian. Home: 245 Peachtree Cir NE Atlanta GA 30309-3206 Office: King & Spalding 191 Peachtree St Atlanta GA 30303*

WEST, THOMAS LOWELL, JR., insurance company executive; b. Cedar Bluff, Va., June 7, 1937; s. Thomas Lowell and Kathleen (Bowling) W.; m. Katharine Thompson, Feb. 13, 1960; children: Thomas Lowell III, John Gardner, Katharine Covington. BS in Indsl. Engring., U. Tenn., 1959. CLU, 1967; chartered fin. cons., 1987. Asst. supr. Aetna Life Ins. Co., Memphis, 1960-62, supr., 1962-67, asst. gen. agt., 1967-69; gen. agt. Aetna Life Ins. Co., Jackson, Miss., 1969-80; regional v.p. Aetna Life & Casualty, Hartford, Conn., 1980-85; v.p. Aetna Life Ins. and Annuity Co., Hartford, 1985-88, sr. v.p. exec. com. and investment com., 1988-94, also bd. dirs.; v.p. Aetna Fin. Services, Hartford, 1986-87; pres., bd. dirs. Structured Benefits, Inc., Hartford, 1985-94, Systemized Benefits Adminstrn., Inc., SBFI, 1988; pres., dir. exec. com., mgmt. com., investment com. The Variable Annuity Life Ins. Co., 1994—; exec. v.p., dir. Am. Gen. Series Portfolio Co.; mem. bd. dirs. Houston Symphony. Named to Hall of Fame, Jackson Assn. Life Underwriters, 1977. Mem. Am. Soc. CLU's and CHFC, Am. Soc. Pension Actuaries (assoc.), Assn. for Advanced Life Underwriters (assoc.), Nat. Assn. Life Underwriters, Internat. Assn. Fin. Planners, Nat. Assn. Variable Annuities (bd. dirs.). Republican. Presbyterian. Home: 2120 Brentwood Dr Houston TX 77019-3512 Office: The Variable Annuity Life Ins Co 2929 Allen Pky Houston TX 77019-2197

WEST, WALLACE MARION, cultural organization administrator; b. N.Y.C., Aug. 30, 1921; s. Florian and Mary (Wziatek) Wesolowski. BSBA, L.I. U., 1966; cert. mus. mgmt., Columbia U. Estimating engr. Sperry Rand Corp., Lake Success, N.Y., 1957-65; sys. analyst Grumman Aerospace, Bethpage, N.Y., 1965-71; exec. dir. Queens Coun. on Arts, Jamaica, N.Y., 1971-76, Hall of Sci. of City of N.Y., Flushing, 1976-79; pres. Am. Inst. Polish Culture, Pinellas Park, Fla., 1982—; cons. arts mgmt. N.Y. State Coun. on Arts, 1968-71. Author: Handbook for Directors of Non-Profit Corporations, 1974; editor: Sharing Our Heritage, 1996; contbr. articles to profl. jours. Recipient Order of Merit Republic of Poland, 1992; named Notable Am. of Bicentennial Era Am. Biog. Inst., 1976. Mem. Am. Inst. Polish Culture (pres., Polonian of Yr. 1985), Am. Coun. Polish Culture (bd. dirs., Founders award 1992, editor 1985—), Polish Am. Soc., Polish Inst. Arts/Scis. in Am., Polish Am. Pulaski Assn., Kosciuszko Found. Republican. Roman Catholic. Home: 6507 107th Ter N Pinellas Park FL 33782 Office: Am Inst Polish Culture 9190 49th St Pinellas Park FL 33782-5228

WEST, WILLIAM ROBERT, history educator; b. Woodbury, N.J., Feb. 4, 1947; s. William Robert Sr. and Genevieve Jane (Cooper) West; m. Rhonda Gaye Foster, Apr. 4, 1981; children: Shaun Cooper Foster West, Ryan William Foster West. BA, Ky. Wesleyan Coll., 1970; MA, Western Ky. U., 1973; postgrad., U. Louisville, U. Shanghai, U. Denver, U. Wash., others. Ky. secondary cert. life. Tchr. Daviess County Pub. Schs., Owensboro, 1971-86; assoc. prof. history U. Ky., Owensboro (Ky.) C.C., 1984—; Ky. C.C. faculty senate coun. rep. univ. studies; U. Ky. C.C.S. coun. mem., 1994—; parent rep. local sch. based coun. Mem. Leadership Owensboro Class of 1988; exec. dir. Owensboro Sister Cities Program, 1990—; mem. state mgmt. team Ky. Sister Cities, 1991—. Recipient cert. of merit Ky. Ednl. TV-Ashland Oil Found., 1982; rsch. scholar Lyndhurst Found., 1984, scholar Japan Endowment at U. Wash., 1983, N.E. Asia Coun. of Assn. for Asian Studies, 1983; travel grantee U.S.-Japan Found., 1983. Mem. Am. Assn. Individual Investors, Nat. Geographic Soc., Daviess County Hist. Soc., So. Regional Honors Count., Nat. Trust Historic Preservation, Hon. Order Ky. Cols., Nat. Collegiate Honors Coun., C.C. Humanities Assn., U.S.-China Peoples Friendships Assn., Nat. Assn. Humanities in Edn., UN Assn. U.S.A., N.Am. Congress on Latin Am., Ky. C.C. Humanities Assn., The So. Hist. Assn. (European history sect.), others. Democrat. Unitarian Universalist. Home: 5829 Jack Hinton Rd Philpot KY 42366-9641 Office: Univ Ky Owensboro C C 4800 New Hartford Rd Owensboro KY 42303-1800

WESTBROOK, JAY LAWRENCE, law educator; b. Morristown, N.J., Dec. 11, 1943; s. Joel W. and Elaine Frances (Summers) W.; m. Pauline June Travis, Feb. 15, 1969; 1 child, Joel Mastin. BA in Polit. Sci./Philosophy, U. Tex., 1965, JD, 1968. Bar: Tex. 1968, D.C. 1969, U.S. Ct. Appeals (D.C. cir.) 1969, U.S. Supreme Ct. 1976, U.S. Ct. Appeals (4th cir.) 1978, U.S. Ct. Appeals (2d cir.) 1979. Assoc. Surrey & Morse (name now Jones, Day, Reavis, Pogue), Washington, 1969-74; ptnr. Surrey & Morse (name now Jones, Day, Reavis, Pogue, Surrey & Morse), Washington, 1974-80; mem. law faculty U. Tex., Austin, 1980—, Benno C. Schmidt Chair Bus. Law, 1991—; vis. prof. U. London, 1990, Harvard Law Sch., 1991-92; advisor Tex. Internat. Law Jour., 1985-91; reporter Am. Law Inst. Transnat. Insolvency Project, 1994—; co-leader U.S. delegation to UN Commn. on Internat. Trade Law Working Group on Model Law Internation Insolvency, 1995—. Co-author: As We Forgive Our Debtors: Bankruptcy and Consumer Credit in America, 1989 (Silver Gavel award ABA 1989), The Law of Debtors and Creditors: Text, Cases and Problems, 3d edit., 1996, Teacher's Manual, The Law of Debtors and Creditors, 3d edit., 1996; contbr. articles to profl. jours. Grantee U. Tex. Law Sch. Found., 1982, U. Rsch. Inst., 1982-83, NSF, 1983-86, Policy Rsch. Inst., Lyndon Johnson Sch. Pub. Affairs, 1984, Tex. Bar Found., 1985, Nat. Inst. Child Health and Human Devel., 1986, Nat. Conf. Bankruptcy Judges, 1991, 93. Mem. ABA (bus. bankruptcy com., internat. bankruptcy subcom., internat. sect., Meyer rsch. grant 1986), Am. Law Inst., Am. Coll. Bankruptcy, Nat. Bankruptcy Conf., State Bar Tex. (governing coun. internat. sect. 1987-89), Internat. Bar Assn., Internat. Bankruptcy Com. (com. J), Internat. Acad. Comml. and Consumer Law, Order of Coif. Office: U Tex Sch Law 727 E 26th St Austin TX 78705-3224

WESTBROOK, SUSAN ELIZABETH, horticulturist; b. Canton, Ohio, Sept. 27, 1939; d. Walter Simon and Rosella Hunt Tolley; m. Edward D. Westbrook, July 2, 1966 (div. 1980); 1 child, Tyler Hunt. Student, Smithdeal-Massey, Richmond, Va., 1958-59; student in Spanish, U. Honduras, 1960; student biology/geology, Mary Washington Coll., 1960, 72, 73; student hort., Prince Georges Community Coll., 1987-88. Farm owner Spotsylvania, Va., 1972-83; office mgr. Tolley Investments, Inc., Fredericksburg, Va., 1980-83; real estate agt. Cooper Realty, Fredericksburg, Va., 1981-83; salesperson Meadows Farms Nursery, Chantilly, Va., 1986-93; student Geology Dept. Mary Washington Coll., Fredericksburg, Va., 1993—; master gardener Va. Poly. Inst., 1993. Author booklets: Japanese Maples, 1990, Fruit Trees, 1989; author radio format: Gardening in Virginia, 1960; co-author computer program: Plantscape, 1990. Sec. Rep. Party, Spotsylvania, 1972-83, Elko County, Nev., 1968; judge Bd. Elections, Spotsylvania, 1980-83, cand. bd. suprs., 1979. Named Master Gardener Va. Poly. Inst., Blacksburg, Va., 1993. Mem. Nat. Wildlife Fedn., Md. Nurserymen's Assn., Friends of the Nat. Arboretum. Home: 6110 S Virginia Ln PO Box 8 Dahlgren VA 22448

WESTBROOK, WALTER WINFIELD, minister; b. Chattanooga, Sept. 15, 1955; s. Robert Stanley and Ruth Louise (Fisher) W.; m. Betty Blevins, June 3, 1978; 1 child, Cassandra Noel. BA, Emory (Va.) and Henry Coll., 1977; MDiv, Drew U., 1980; postgrad., Asbury Theol. Sem., 1991-96, Ruah, 1993-95. Ordained to ministry United Meth. Ch., 1980. Min. Dahlgren (Va.) United Meth. Ch., 1980-87, Highland Springs (Va.) United Meth. Ch., 1987-95, Bethany United Meth. Ch., Reedville, Va., 1995—; dir. health and welfare ministries Ashland dist. United Meth. Ch., Va., 1989-90, dir. spiritual formation, 1990-92, chmn. spiritual formation com., 1993—; mem. bd. comm. Va. Conf. United Meth. Ch., 1990, mem. bd. discipleship, chmn. divsn. spiritual formation, 1995—; creator, facilitator Monday Morning Meditation Group, Ashland Dist. Clergy; trainer for clergy, laity and mixed groups in 8 districts. Author: Two Sermons in Verse, 1994, Two More Sermons in Verse, 1994; creator, host, producer weekly radio program Tell Me Why, 1987-93; religion columnist The King George Jour., weekly newspaper, 1986-87; contbr. adult Sunday sch. lessons to Va. Adv., 1990; contbr. to Lenten Devotional Books, 1993-96. Bd. dirs. The Haven, battered women shelter, Fredericksburg, Va., 1983-86, The Bethlehem Ctr., Richmond, Va., 1989-90, Richmond Hill, Christian Retreat Ctr., Richmond, 1990-95; coordinating coun. Interfaith Svcs. Henrico County, Richmond, 1987-89; active Habitat for Humanity, 1986-90, Bread for World, 1986-90; vol. reader for Virginia Voice, 1989-90. Co-recipient Couple of Yr. award Rappahannock Big Bros.-Big Sisters, 1985. Mem. Disciplined Order of Christ, Fellowship Merry Christians, Internat. Jugglers Assn., Renovaré, United Meth. Vols. in Mission (mission trip to Haiti 1977, to Charleston, S.C. 1989). Address: PO Box 77 Reedville VA 22539

WESTBY, TIMOTHY SCOTT, lawyer; b. Fargo, N.D., Apr. 16, 1957; s. Joseph Arlo and Dorothy Mae (Nye) W.; m. Holli Leigh Huber, Mar. 17, 1987; 1 child, Katherine Elizabeth. SBChemE, MIT, 1979; PhDChemE, U. Tex., 1984; JD, U. Houston, 1994. Bar: U.S. Dist. Ct. (so. dist.) Tex. Researcher Energy Lab., MIT, Cambridge, 1976-79; rsch. asst. U. Tex., Austin, 1979-84, teaching asst., 1981-83; assoc. rsch. engr. Shell Devel. Co., Houston, 1984-87, rsch. engr., 1987-91, sr. rsch. engr., 1991-94; assoc. Conley, Rose & Tayon, P.C., 1994—; mem. adv. com. Ohio Combustion Rsch., Columbus, 1985-90, Pa. Coal Rsch. Coop., University Station, 1986-89. Contbr. articles to profl. jours.; patentee method for in situ coal drilling, patentee coal blends having improved ash viscosity. Campaigner United Way, Houston, 1989-91. Scholar MIT, 1975-79; fellow U.S. dept. Energy, 1979-82, Getty Oil Co., 1983-84. Mem. ABA, State Bar of Tex., Houston Bar Assn., Houston Intellectual Property Law Assn., ASTM (com. D-5 1989-94), ASME (advisor rsch. com. on corrosion and deposits from flue gases 1988—), Phi Delta Phi. Office: Conley Rose & Tayon PC Ste 1850 600 Travis Houston TX 77002-2912

WESTERFIELD, FRANCIS CLARK, quality assurance professional; b. Owensboro, Ky., June 2, 1950; s. William Allen and Mary Catherine (Clark) W.; m. Frances Elaine Hall, June 2, 1973; 1 child, James. BSEE, U. Cen. Fla., 1981, MS in Engring. Adminstrn., 1987. Registered profl. engr., cert. quality engr., cert. quality mgr. Sr. prin. quality engr. NCR Corp., Lake Mary, Fla., 1974-92; v.p. quality assurance ETI-FETCO, Sanford, Fla., 1992—. Mem. IEEE, Am. Soc. Quality Control (treas. 1991-95, chmn. 1995-96). Home: 365 Westwind Ct Lake Mary FL 32746-6003 Office: ETI-FETCO 421 Cornwall Rd Sanford FL 32773-5871

WESTERMAN, ALBERT BARRY, marine surveyor; b. Phila., July 8, 1941; s. William Edward and Alice Beverly (Martin) W.; m. Madeline Rose Lauginger, July 23, 1943 (div. July 1974); children: Debra Lee Westerman Bordelon, Allan Keith; m. Lynn Marie Nesser, May 31, 1947; children: David William, Dawn Marie. Student, U. Md., Augsburg, Germany, 1961,

Bucks County Tech., 1966, Tulane U., 1970-71, La. State U., 1987. Journeyman machinist Honeywell Corp., Tampa, Fla., 1967-68; resident surveyor Owensby & Kritikos, Inc., Gretna, La., 1968-70; field constrn. supr. Ocean Drilling & Exploration Co., New Orleans, 1970-73; gen. mgr. Weldit Engrng. Ltd., Scunthorpe, Eng., 1973; v.p. Ocean-Oil Internat. Engrng. Corp., New Orleans, 1973-74; pres. Internat. Cons. & Brokers, Inc., Metairie, La., 1974-76; v.p. Am. Gulf Shipping, Inc., Metairie, 1982-88; pres., dir. Nat. Radiometric Agy., Inc., Metairie, 1987—; pres. Albert B. Westerman & Co., Inc., Metairie, 1973—. Author, editor: Procedure and Operations Manual, 1987. With U.S. Army, 1960-61. Mem. NRA, Nat. Assn. Marine Surveyors, Soc. of Naval Arch. and Marine Engrs., Am. Boat & Yacht Coun., Propeller Club. Lutheran. Home: 2800 Sells St Metairie LA 70003-3543 Office: Nat Radiometric Agy PO Box 7784 Metairie LA 70010-7784

WESTERMAN, HARRIET HEAPS, nurse, certified case manager; b. Houston, Nov. 16, 1947; d. Neal Barton and Billye Katherine (Cookenboo) Heaps; m. Eric Lane Westerman, Apr. 29, 1967; children: Tracey Lynn Westerman-Peterson, Meredith Lane. Student, Tex. Christian U., 1965-66, U. Tex., 1966-68; diploma in nursing, Hermann Hosp., 1971; BSN, U. Tulsa, 1990. Cert. case mgr. Staff nurse post-neurosurgery The Meth. Hosp., Houston, 1971; charge nurse/staff nurse Neurosurgery Intensive Care/Intermediate Care Ben Taub Gen. Hosp., Houston, 1971-72; clinic float nurse Kelsey-Seybold Clinic, Houston, 1972-73; office mgr./nurse Tulsa Infectious Disease Clinic, Tulsa, 1977-84; cons. Fiber-Seal of Tulsa, 1986-87; sales assoc. McGraw/Breckinridge Realtors, 1984-87, Rodger Erker Realtors, Tulsa, 1987-90; staff nurse/charge nurse ARC, 1990-91; supr. ARC, Tulsa, 1991-92; rehab. cons. Okla. Rehab. Cons., Tulsa, 1992-93; clin. RN Laureate Psychiat. Clinic and Hosp., Tulsa, 1993; managed care coord. Pacificare, Tulsa, 1993-94; DON Vis. Nurses Assn., Tulsa, 1994; disaster nurse ARC, Tulsa, 1983-86. Bd. dirs. Tulsans Against Property Tax Discrimination, 1983-87, PTAG, Tulsa, 1980-83, YMCA Camp Takatoka, Tulsa, 1984-86, Shanti, Tulsa, 1991-92, HIV Resource Consortium, 1991-92; mem. polit. action com. Tulsa Med. Wives Aux., 1977-84; chmn. arts and crafts for ann. Holland Hall Book and Art Fair, 1978, 79; vol. Parents Anonymous, Tulsa, 1980-81, Tulsa Vols. for Philharm., 1977-78, 84-85, 90-91; mem. Hillcrest Svc. Assn., Tulsa, 1980-84; asst. leader Girl Scouts U.S.A., Houston, 1974-76, Tulsa Camp Fire Girls, 1979-82; candidate for county commr., Tulsa, 1986; chmn. Tulsa Dist. 18; initiator, officer Homeowners Assn., 1986-89, 95; vol. Day Ctr. for Homeless, 1995, Family Mental Health, 1995—; vol. comm. svc. coun. AIDS Partnership Grant Com., 1995—. Women of the Moose scholar, 1970-71. Mem. AAUW, ANA, LWV, Embroiders Guild Am. (mem. com. 1978, Nat. Conv. in Tulsa), Okla. Nurses Assn., Individual Case Mgmt. Assn., Case Mgmt. Soc. of Am., Sigma Theta Tau, Pi Beta Phi (bd. dirs. 1973-74, 77-79).

WESTFALL, BERNARD G., university hospital executive; b. Lockney, W.Va., July 12, 1941; s. Edward C. and Wilma (Dotson) W.; m. Marion Williams, July 26, 1969; 1 child, Gregory. BS, W. Va. U., 1963, MBA, 1972. Tchr. sci. Monongalia County Schs., Morgantown, W.Va., 1963-65; assoc. dir. purchasing W. Va. U., Morgantown, 1965-73; hosp. computer mgr. W. Va. U. Hosp., Morgantown, 1973-74, assoc. adminstr. fin. and systems, 1974-82; interim adminstr. W.Va. U. Hosp., Morgantown, 1982-83, sr. assoc. adminstr., 1983-84, exec. v.p., adminstr., 1984-87, pres., 1987—; bd. dirs. One Valley Bank; guest lectr. W. Va. U., 1984—. Author: Central Breakout at West Virginia University, 1970. Trustee W.Va. Hosp. Assn. Mem. Am. Coll. Hosp. Adminstrs., Hosp. Fin. Mgmt. Assn. Lodge: Rotary. Home: RR 9 Box 69A Morgantown WV 26505-9809*

WESTGATE, JAMES WILLIAM, geologist; b. Washington, July 17, 1952; s. John Edward and Elizabeth Theresa (Dickhaut) W.; married; children: Erin, Jeffrey. BS in geology, Coll. William & Mary, 1975; MS in geology, U. Nebr., 1978; MS in biology, Southwest Mo. State U., 1983; PhD in geology, U. Tex., 1988. Asst. instr. and rsch. asst. dept. geology U. Nebr., Lincoln, 1975-78; lab. supr. dept. geosciences Southwest Mo. State U., Springfield, 1978-83; paleontology cons. Tex. Historical Commn. and Prewitt & Assocs., Inc., Austin, Tex., 1986-88; rsch. scientist asst Tex. Meml. Mus. U. Tex., Austin, 1986-88; sci. lectr. sci. dept. European div. U. Md., Heidelberg, Germany, 1988-89; asst. prof. geology dept. Lamar U., Beaumont, Tex., 1988-94, assoc. prof. geology, 1994—; rsch. assoc. Tex. Meml. Mus., U. Tex., Austin, 1991—; asst. sci. instr. Arlington County Va. Pub. Schs., 1969-71. Contbr. articles to profl. jours. Recipient numerous grants for rsch. in field. Mem. Paleontological Soc., Soc. Vertebrate Paleontology, Gulf Estuarine Rsch. Soc., Tex. Acad. Sci., Lamar Univ. Club, Sigma Xi (pres. 1992-93, 94-95, v.p. 1991-92, sec./treas. 1990-91), Phi Kappa Phi, Sigma Gamma Epsilon. Office: Lamar U Geology Dept PO Box 10031 Beaumont TX 77710-0031

WESTHEIMER, JEROME MAX, SR., petroleum executive, geologist; b. Marietta, Okla., Feb. 14, 1910; s. Simon and Rose (Munzesheimer) W.; m. Ellen Louise Woods, Feb. 22, 1936; children: Beverly, Jerome M., Jr., Valerie. B.A., Stanford U., 1933. Chief geologist Simpson-Fell Oil Co., Ardmore, Okla., 1936-40, Samedan Oil Corp., Ardmore, 1940-51; cons. geologist, Ardmore, 1951—. Primary trustee C.B. Goddard Ctr. for the Visual and Performing Arts, Ardmore, 1974—; trustee Mid-Am. Arts Alliance, Kansas City, Mo., 1978—, Okla. Art. Ctr., Oklahoma City, 1967—, chmn., 1987—; dir. Okla. Summer Arts Inst., Okla. City, 1977—, pres. 1983, Valbel West Corp., 1986—. Contbr. articles to profl. jours. Mem. Am. Assn. of Petroleum Geologists, Am. Inst. of Profl. Geologists, Soc. of Econ. Paleontologists, Soc. of Ind. Exploration Scientists, Sigma Xi. Avocation: art collectors.

WESTLAKE, JAMES ROGER, retired federal program manager; b. Kansas City, Mo., Feb. 11, 1928; s. Roger A. and Helen (Treadway) W.; m. Joyce Rosemary Covey, May 14, 1946; children: Joyce Ann Westlake Morgan, Beverly Jeanne Westlake Simpson, James R. Jr., Richard Christopher. Student, Mo. U., 1944-45; BBA, Ga. State U., 1958, MBA, 1960; MPA, U. Ga., 1974. Sales Wohl Shoe Co., Kansas City, 1946-47; sales mgr. Bankers Life & Casualty Co., Kansas City, 1947-49; from ptnr. to pres. So. Agys., Inc., Atlanta, 1949-71; dep. adminstr. EPA, Atlanta, 1971-76; dep. sec. rep. U.S. Dept. of Commerce, Atlanta, 1976-81; from specialist to program mgr. Econ. Devel. Adminstrn., Atlanta, 1981-95; chief econ. adj. divsn. NOV, 1989-95; chmn. bd. Atlanta Sch. Bib. Studies, Decatur, Ga., 1975—. Author: The Republicans Are Coming, 1968; columnist Decatur-DeKalb News, 1965-71; contbr. articles to profl. jours. State legis. (Ga.) representing DeKalb County, 1965-71; chmn. 4th dist. Ga. Rep. Com., Decatur, 1966-68; mem. adv. bd. Nat. Independence Day Parade and Festival Com., 1990-92; ruling elder Trinity Presbyn. Ch. With USN, 1945-46. Mem. SAR (pres. gen. 1989-90, Minuteman award 1989), Soc. CPCUs (pres. Ga. chpt. 1961), Soc. CLUs, Am. Coll. Chartered Fin. Cons., Nat. Soc. Washington Family Descendants (pres. gen. 1988-90), Nat. Congress Patriotic Orgns. (pres. 1991-92), Barons of Magna Carta, Nat. Gavel Soc. and Old Guard of Atlanta, Sons Am. Colonists, Order Founders and Patriots, Honey Creek Golf and Country Club, Omicron Delta Kappa, Phi Kappa Phi, Sigma Chi, Delta Sigma Pi, Beta Gamma Sigma. Home: 2221 Shady Ln Covington GA 30209-8719

WESTMAN, STEVEN RONALD, rabbi; b. Chgo., Sept. 16, 1945; s. Kurt S. and Hilda (Schmoller) W.; m. Sherri, Nov. 30, 1980; children: Rachel Dara, Emily Nicole, Molly Sarah Levin. BA, U. Ill., 1967; B of Hebrew Letters, Hebrew Union Coll., 1969, MA in Hebrew Letters, 1972. Ordained rabbi, 1972. Asst. rabbi Congregation Rodeph Shalom, Phila., 1972-75; rabbi Temple Israel, Stroudsburg, Pa., 1975-83, Temple Beth Torah, Wellington, Fla., 1993-95, Temple Beth El Israel, Ft. Pierce, Fla., 1996—; mem. Commn. for Jewish Edn., West Palm Beach, Fla., 1990-94; bd. dirs. Jewish Cmty. Day Sch., West Palm Beach, 1988-91, Jewish Cmty. Ctr., 1987-89; pres. Palm BEach County Bd. Rabbis, 1989-92. Bd. dirs. Palms West Hosp., Loxahatchee, Fla., 1986-91, Pocono Hosp., East Stroudsburg, Pa., 1979-83; found. bd. dirs. Hospice of Monroe County, East Stroudsburg, 1978-83; bd. dirs. Palm Beach Liturgical Culture Soc., West Palm Beach, 1986—. Recipient Tower of David award State of Israel Bonds, 1988, Leadership award Jewish Fedn. of Palm Beach County, 1985. Mem. Cen. Conf. of Am. Rabbis, Rotary. Home: 13587 Jonquil Pl West Palm Beach FL 33414-8557 Office: Temple Beth El Israel PO Box 12128 Fort Pierce FL 34979

WESTMORELAND, THOMAS DELBERT, JR., chemist; b. near Vivian, La., June 2, 1940; s. Thomas Delbert and Marguerite Beatrice (Moore) W.; BS, N. Tex. State U., 1963, MS, 1965; PhD, La. State U., 1971, postdoctoral fellow, 1971-72; m. Martha Verne Beard, Jan. 1, 1966; children: Anne Laura, Kyle Thomas. Chemistry tchr., rsch. dir. Lewisville (Tex.) H.S., 1964; summer devel. program student Tex. Instruments, Inc., Dallas, 1966; sr. exptl./analytical engr. Power Systems div. United Technologies, South Windsor, Conn., 1972-76; sr. research chemist Pennzoil Co., Shreveport, La., 1976-82, rsch. assoc., 1983-93, sr. environ. engr. Pennzoil Products Co. Tech. Ctr., The Woodlands, Tex., 1993—; chem. cons. Recipient E.I. du Pont tching. award La. State U., 1968-69. Mem. Am. Chem. Soc. (treas. 1978-79, chmn. 1979-80), Assn. Rsch. and Enlightenment, Soc. Automotive Engrs., Sigma Xi (sec.), Phi Eta Sigma (pres. 1959-60), Alpha Chi Sigma, Kappa Mu Epsilon. Clubs: Jaycees (state dir. Conn. 1976, gov.'s civic leadership award Conn. 1975-76, C. William Brownfield Meml. award 1976), Masons (Scottish Rite, 32d degree). Contbr. sci. articles to profl. jours; patentee in field. Home: 143 Melmont Ln Conroe TX 77302-1022 Office: PO Box 7569 The Woodlands TX 77387-7569

WESTON, AUGUSTENE, women's health nurse, perinatal grief counselor; b. Markedtree, Ark., Aug. 4, 1949; d. Willie and Dorothy (Pitts) Parker; m. Joe B. Weston, May 8, 1976; children: Douglas, Dykeshia, Dana. LPN, Memphis Area Vocat., 1970; diploma, St. Joseph Hosp. Sch. Nursing, Memphis, 1975; BSN, Memphis State U., 1988; MSN, Ark. State U., 1994. RN, Tenn., Del., Tex.; cert. grief counseling; cert. clin. nurse specialist in adult health, Ark. Staff nurse SICU Regional Med. Ctr. at Memphis, head nurse gynecology, nurse mgr. gynecol. oncology, nurse mgr. maternal-child; juvenile probation officer; adminstrv. supr. Regional Med. Ctr. at Memphis; instr. maternal child USAR. Maj. USAR, 1979—. Named Family of Yr. for Tenn., 1986; recipient Excellence in Mgmt. award, 1989, Shelby County Top 100 Nurses award, 1991. Mem. Tenn. Nurses Assn. (com. on continuing edn.), Res. Officers Assn. (life). Home: 5126 Queen Elizabeth Fwy Memphis TN 38116-8543

WESTON, WILLIAM JOSEPH (BEAU WESTON), sociologist, educator; b. Norristown, Pa., Apr. 13, 1960; s. William John and Jean Sherry Weston; m. Susan Kristina Perkins, May 29, 1982; children: Margaret Blum, Eleanor Hudson, Samuel Josiah. BA, Swarthmore Coll., 1982; MA in Religion, Yale U., 1986, PhD in Sociology, 1988. Rsch. assoc. U.S. Dept. Edn., Washington, 1987-90; asst. prof. Centre Coll., Danville, Ky., 1990—. Editor: Education and the American Family, 1989; author: (chpt. in book) Religious Seminaries in America, 1989. Ruling elder Presbyn. Ch., Danville, Ky., 1993—; mem. speakers bur. Ky. Humanities Coun., 1993—. Lilly scholar Louisville Sem., 1989. Mem. Am. Sociol. Assn. (sect. officer 1992-93), Assn. Sociology of Religion, Anthropologists and Sociologists of Ky. (pres. 1994-95), So. Sociol. Soc., Religious Rsch. Assn. Democrat. Office: Centre Coll 600 W Walnut St Danville KY 40422-1309

WESTPHAL, DOUGLAS HERBERT, engineering company executive; b. Houston, Feb. 21, 1940; s. Herbert Hugo and Olga Clara (Brune) W.; m. Blanche Elizabeth Berkley; children: Barbara A., Christi A. BS in Mech. Engring., U. Houston, 1964. Ops. technician Sinclair Refining Co., Houston, 1964-67; asst. buyer Sinclair Oil Corp., N.Y.C., 1967-69; buyer BP Oil Corp., Atlanta, 1969-70; procurement engr. Standard Oil Co., Cleve., 1970-73; sr. buyer Alyeska Pipeline Svc. Co., Anchorage, 1973-76, Fluor Engrs. and Constructors, Inc., Houston, 1976-80; mgr. purchasing and stores Coastal Refining and Mktg., Inc., Corpus Christi, Tex., 1980-89; mgr. project procurement Fluor Daniel, Inc., Houston, 1989-93; mgr. procurement MES Engrng., Houston, 1993-94; mgr. project procurement Fluor Daniel, Inc., Sugar Land, Tex., 1994—. Mem. Corpus Christi Kennel Club, 1982-90, show chmn., 1989; life mem. Houston Livestock Show and Rodeo; mem. ch. coun. Trinity Luth. Ch., Frelsburg, Tex., fin. sec., 1992, pres., 1993-94. Mem. ASME, NSPE, Gulf Coast Purchasing Mgmt. Assn. (pres. 1986-87, bd. dirs. 1987-90), Houston Farm and Ranch Club (life), Kappa Kappa Psi (hon. band fraternity). Democrat. Lutheran. Home: RR 2 Box 49 New Ulm TX 78950-9515 Office: Fluor Daniel Inc One Fluor Daniel Dr Sugar Land TX 77478

WESTPHAL, ROGER ALLEN, electrical engineer; b. Waterloo, Iowa, Feb. 17, 1946; s. Clifford Henry and Pauline Vere (Kleinow) W.; foster children: Rajathi, Ponnammal. BSEE, U. Fla., 1981, MS, 1990. Registered profl. engr., Fla. Instrumentation technician Gen. Dynamics, Ft. Worth, 1966-68, Gen. Dynamics/Convair, Edwards AFB, Calif., 1968-71; electronics technician Lockheed Calif. Co., Burbank, Calif., 1973-74, field svc. rep., 1974-78; engring. technician engring. scis. dept. U. Fla., Gainesville, 1980-84, instr. elec. engring. dept., 1984-86, 90; engr. elec. utility Gainesville Regional Utilities, 1987—. Mem. Friends of Classic 89, Gainesville, Friends of Five, Gainesville; supporting mem. Smithsonian, Washington. With USN, 1968-71. Mem. IEEE, Am. Solar Energy Soc., Internat. Solar Energy Soc., Phi Kappa Phi, Eta Kappa Nu, Tau Beta Phi. Republican. Methodist. Home: PO Box 846 Gainesville FL 32602-0846 Office: Gainesville Regl Utilities # A 136 PO Box 147117 Gainesville FL 32614-7117

WESTROPE, MARTHA RANDOLPH, psychologist, consultant; b. Gaffney, S.C., May 19, 1922; d. Gordon Robert and Hannah (Brown) W.; 1 adopted child, Ashley Randolph. BS, Winthrop Coll., 1942; MA, U. N.C., 1944; PhD, State U. of Iowa, Iowa City, 1952. Lic. psychologist, S.C. Pvt. practice Greenville, S.C., 1960—, part-time pvt. practice, 1987—; part-time staff mem. Spartanburg (S.C.) Mental Health Clinic, 1971-73, Greenville Mental Health Ctr., 1974-85, Patrick B. Harris Psychiat. Hosp., Anderson, S.C., 1985-87; med. cons. S.C. Vocat. Rehab. Dept., Greenville, 1987-91, part-time med. cons., 1993—; cons. S.C. Parole Bd. for Psychol. Evaluation, S.C. Dept. Corrections, 1983-87. Mem. Am. Psychol. Assn., Southeastern Psychol. Assn., S.C. Psychol. Assn., Am. Assn. for Advancement of Psychology, Greenville County Mental Health Assn., Am. Group Psychotherapy Assn., Coun. for the Nat. Register of Health Svc. Providers in Psychology. Democrat. Presbyterian. Home: 11 Darien Way Greenville SC 29615-3236 Office: 506 Pettigru St Greenville SC 29601-3117

WETHERBEE, JAMES MILTON, librarian; b. Poughkeepsie, N.Y., June 13, 1959; s. Clifton Ward and Carol Alice (Pike) W.; m. C. Renee Abercrombie, Jan. 31, 1981; children: J. Milton, Cynthia R., Jonathan E., Charles A. BA in Philosophy of Religion, Taylor U., 1981; MA in Philosophy of Religion, Trinity Evang. Div. Sch., 1987; MDiv, Louisville Presbyn. Sem., 1987; MS in Libr. Sci., U. Ky., 1988. Reference/serials libr. Wingate (N.C.) Coll. (now Wingate U.), 1988-89; reference/system libr. Wingate (N.C.) Coll., 1990—. Mem. ALA, Soc. Christian Philosophers, N.C. Libr. Assn., Evang. Theol. Soc. Office: Ethel K Smith Libr 110 Church St Wingate NC 28174

WETHERELL, VIRGINIA BACON, state legislator, state agency administrator, engineering company executive; b. Anniston, Ala., May 15, 1947; d. William Dennis and Mary (Perkins) Bacon; children: Virginia Blakely, Page Perkins. BA, Auburn U., 1968; MS, Jacksonville State U., 1971. Tchr. Biology and Physiology Anniston High Sch., 1968-72; planner East Ala. Regional Planning & Devel. Com., Anniston, 1974-82; exec. dir. City-County Drug Abuse Commn., Pensacola, Fla., 1976-82; dir., officer Coastal Transp., Pensacola, 1980-86; mem. Fla. Ho. of Reps., 1982-88; dir., officer Ammons, Bass, Bass & Boys, Pensacola, 1985-86, Gulf Coast Mortgage & Investments, Pensacola, 1985-86; mktg. adminstr. Baskerville-Donovan Engrs., Pensacola, 1986-91; exec. dir. Fla. Dept. Natural Resources, 1991-93; secy. Fla. Dept. Environ. Protection, 1993—; mem. exec. com. Gulf Coast Econs. Club, Pensacola, 1985—, Homeporting Commn., Pensacola, 1985—; chmn. internat. trade and econ. devel. Fla. Ho. of Reps., 1986-88; active Commn. Sustainable South Fla. Environ. Coun. States; bd. dirs. Bapt. Health Care Found., Pensacola. Bd. dirs. Fla. Council on Asian Affairs, 1985—, Fla. Com. on Future, 1987-88; mem. exec. com. Fla. Dem. Party, 1985—. Named Profl. Leader of Yr. Pensacola C. of C. and Pensacola News Jour., 1981, Fla.'s Outstanding Young Woman Fla. Jaycees, 1982, Woman of Yr. Pensacola Breakfast of Champions, 1983. Mem. Nat. Conf. State Legislatures, Council of State Govt., Fla. Chpt. of Dem. Leadership. Episcopalian. Clubs: Leadership Pensacola (founding mem., pres. 1981), Pensacola Heritage Found. (pres. 1980-82). Home: 3770 Bobbin Mills Rd Tallahassee FL 32312-1202*

WETHINGTON, CHARLES T., JR., academic administrator. AB, Ea. Ky. U., 1956; postgrad., Syracuse U., 1958-59; MA, U. Ky., 1962, PhD, 1965. Instr. ednl. psychology U. Ky., Lexington, 1965-66; dir. Maysville (Ky.) C.C., 1967-71; asst. v.p. c.c. system U. Ky., Lexington, 1971-81, v.p. c.c. system, 1981-82, chancellor c.c. system, 1982-88, chancellor c.c. system and univ. rels., 1988-89, interim pres., 1989-90, pres., 1990—; chmn. legis. com. State Dirs. Community and Jr. Colls., 1983-85, chmn. nat. coun., 1985-86; mem. commn. on colls. So. Assn. Schs. and Colls., 1978-84, vice chmn. exec. coun., 1984, trustee, 1986-89; mem. So. Regional Edn. Bd., 1988—, mem. exec. com., 1989-93, vice chmn., 1991-93. Bd. dirs. Bluegrass State Skills Corp., 1984-91, vice-chmn. bd. dirs., 1986-87; bd. visitors Community Coll. of Air Force, 1986-90; mem. Ky. Ednl. TV Adv. Com., 1984—; mem. jud. nominating commn. 22nd Jud. Dist., Fayette County, Ky., 1988-91; mem. Ky. Coal Authority, 1990—, So. Growth Policies Bd., 1990—; served with sec. svc. USAF, 1957-61. Home: Maxwell Pl 471 Rose St Lexington KY 40508 Office: U Ky 104 Administration Bldg Lexington KY 40506*

WETSCH, JOHN ROBERT, information systems specialist; b. Dickinson, N.D., Aug. 27, 1959; s. Joseph John and Florence Mae (Edwards) W.; m. Laura Jean Johnson, Aug. 29, 1981; children: Julie Elizabeth, Katherine Anne, John Michael. BS, U. State of N.Y.-Regents Coll., Albany, 1984; MA, Antioch U., 1989; PhD, Nova S.E. U., 1994. Radiation physics instr. Grand Forks (N.D.) Clinic, 1983-85; sr. programmer PRC, Inc., Cavalier Air Force Sta., N.D., 1987-91, PARCS project-SAFEGUARD sys.; pres. Dakota Sci. Inc., Langdon, N.D., 1988-95; instr. U. N.D.-Lake Region, Devils Lake, 1988-91; systems adminstr. U.S. Courts Nat. Fine Ctr., Raleigh, N.C., 1991-94; bus. project leader Raleigh (N.C.) Info. Sys. Svc. Ctr., 1994—; cons. on Wave Obs./N.D. Proposal, Gov.'s Office, Bismarck, 1991; founder, developer Dakota Sci., Inc., Langdon, 1988-95; instr. divsn. continuing edn. Wake Tech. C.C., 1993—. Author: (with others) COMPUTE!'s 2nd Book of Amiga, 1988; contbr. articles to COMPUTE! Jour. of Progressive Computing, 1987, other profl. jours. Mem. coll. scholarship selection com. Cavalier Air Force Sta., N.D., 1990; program coord. Lake Region Outreach, U. N.D., Cavalier Air Force Sta., 1988-91; mem. Bd. Alumni Trustees, SUNY-Regents Coll., Albany, 1995—, v.p., 1996—; pres. Zeta Rho chpt. Pi Kappa Alpha, Grand Forks, 1981. SMITS scholar N.D. Acad. Sci., 1990; Larimore-Mathews scholar U. N.D., Grand Forks, 1978, N.D. Acad. Sci. scholar, 1978; recipient Westinghouse Sci. Talent Search award, 1978. Mem. AAAS, IEEE, IEEE Computer Soc., N.Y. Acad. Scis., Regents Coll. Degrees (grad. resource network), Assn. for Computing Machinery, Dakota Astron. Soc. (co-founder, pres. 1987-91). Republican. Roman Catholic. Home: 5009 Rampart St Raleigh NC 27609-5100 Office: RAISSC 4200 Wake Forest Rd Raleigh NC 27668-9000

WETZEL, ALBERT JOHN, university executive, systems engineer, former air force officer, consultant; b. New Orleans, Dec. 29, 1917; s. Albert John and Emelie (Willoz) W.; B.Engring., Tulane U., 1939, M.S., Johns Hopkins U., 1950; postgrad. UCLA, George Washington U., 1952, Armed Forces Staff Coll., 1955; grad. Command and Gen. Staff Coll., Advanced Flying Sch. (Jet); m. Helen Elizabeth Zurad, Sept. 7, 1946; children—Albert John, Elizabeth Ann, Joan Clark, Edward Russell. Commd. 2d lt. C.E., U.S. Army, 1941, advanced through grades to col. USAF, 1956; exptl. test pilot, 1943-45; fighter pilot, 1945-47; tech. staff officer Armed Forces Spl. Weapons Project, Washington, exec. asst. to dir. of guided missiles, office of Sec. of Def., 1950-55; service in Europe, Asia, Middle East; wing comdr. SAC, 1955-57; dir. Titan ICBM and Gemini Space Program, 1957-62; exec. dir. USAF Council, 1962-63; dir. strategic programs, def., research and engring. Office Sec. of Def., 1963-65, ret., 1965; dir. research and sponsored programs, then dir. univ. devel. Tulane U., 1965-76, v.p. alumni and univ. affairs, 1976-80, sr. adviser to pres., 1980-81, asst. to pres., 1981-94, adj. prof. mgmt. and engring. mgmt., 1965-94, v.p.- emeritus, 1994—; mem. rocket and space panel Pres.'s Sci. Adv. Com., 1965-71; bd. dirs. Gulf South Research Inst., Inst. Def. Analysis, Washington; del. Nat. Conf. Advancement Research. Bd. dirs. Walter Clark Teagle Found. (N.Y.C.), also exec. com., Crippled Children's Hosp., New Orleans, La. Council Music and Performing Arts, Council. Devel. French in La.; trustee Delgado Jr. Coll.; pres. bd. dirs. New Orleans Catholic Found.; bd. dirs. Girl Scouts U.S.A.; exec. com. local Boy Scouts Am.; commr. La. Ednl. TV Authority. Decorated Legion of Merit, Command Pilot, Armed Forces and Air Force Commendation Medal. Registered profl. engr., Ohio. Paul Harris fellow. Fellow AIAA; mem. AAAS (sci. mem.), Greater New Orleans Area C. of C. (v.p.), Oak Ridge Assn. Univs., Paul Tulane Soc., Air Force Assn., Eagle Scout Assn., Navy League U.S., Sigma Xi Kappa Sigma, Tau Beta Pi, Omicron Delta Kappa. Clubs: Internat. House, Bienville, Plimsoll (New Orleans); Univ. (N.Y.C.); Army-Navy (Washington). Lodges: Knights of Malta, Rotary, Order of St. Louis, Order Holy Sepulchre of Jerusalem (Knight Comdr. with star), Papal Order-Pro Ecclesia et Pontifice. Contbr. articles on aeros., strategic mil. weapons and strategy, instl. devel., planned gift programs and univ. advancement to profl. jours. Home: 7 Richmond Pl New Orleans LA 70115-5019 Office: Tulane U Mgmt & Engring Mgmt Dept New Orleans LA 70118

WETZEL, ROBERT GEORGE, botany educator; b. Ann Arbor, Mich., Aug. 16, 1936; s. Wilhelm and Eugenia (Wagner) W.; m. Carol Ann Andree, Aug. 9, 1959; children: Paul Robert, Pamela Jeanette, Timothy Mark, Kristina Marie. BS, U. Mich., 1958, MS, 1959; PhD, U. Calif. at Davis, 1962; PhD (hon.), U. Uppsala, Sweden, 1984. Research assoc. Ind. U., Bloomington, 1962-65; asst. prof. botany Mich. State U., Hickory Corners, 1965-68; assoc. prof. Mich. State U., 1968-71, prof., 1971-86; prof. U. Mich., Ann Arbor, 1986-90; Bishop prof. biology U. Ala., Tuscaloosa, 1990—; cons. Internat. Biol. Program, London, 1967-75; chmn. Internat. Seagrass Commn., 1974-75; founding mem. Internat. Lake Environment Com., 1986—. Author: Limnology, 1975, 2d rev. edit., 1983, Limnological Analyses, 1979, 2d rev. edit., 1990, To Quench Our Thirst: Present and Future Freshwater Resources of the United States, 1983, Freshwater Ecosystems: Revitalizing Educational Programs in Limnology, 1996; editor: Periphyton of Freshwater Ecosystems, 1983, Wetlands and Ecotones, 1993, Recent Studies on Ecology and Management of Wetlands, 1994, Wetland Ecology, 1995, Lake Okeechobee: A Synthesis, 1995, Limnology of Developing Countries, vol. 1 1995; contbr. numerous articles on ecology and freshwater biology sys. to profl. jours.; mem. editl. bd. Aquatic Botany, 1975—, Jour. Tropical Freshwater Ecology, 1987—, Internat. Jour. Salt Lake Resources, 1991—, Biogeochemistry, 1993—, Lakes and Reservoirs, 1995—; N.Am. editor Archiv f. Hydrobiologie, 1989—. Served with USNR, 1954-62. Recipient First T. Erlander Nat. professorship Swedish Nat. Research Council and U. Uppsala, 1982-83, award of Distinction U. Calif. at Davis, 1989; AEC grantee, 1965-75; NSF grantee, 1962—; ERDA grantee, 1975-77; Dept. Energy grantee, 1978—. Fellow AAAS; mem. Royal Danish Acaad. Scis. (elected fgn. mem. 1986), Am. Acad. Arts and Scis. (elected 1993), Am. Inst. Biol. Scis., Am. Soc. Limnology and Oceanography (edtl. bd. 1971-74, v.p. 1979-80, pres. 1980-81, G.E. Hutchinson medal 1992), Aquatic Plant Mgmt. Soc., Ecol. Soc. Am., Internat. Assn. Ecology, Freshwater Biol. Assn. U.K., Internat. Assn. Theoretical and Applied Limnology (gen. sec. treas. 1968—, Baldi Meml. award 1989, Naumann-Thienemann medal 1992), Internat. Phycological Soc., Mich. Acad. Scis., N.Am. Benthological Soc., Phycological Soc. Am., Internat. Assn. Great Lakes Rsch., Internat. Consortium Salt Lake Rsch. (edtl. bd. 1991—), Japanese Soc. Limnology, Mich. Bot. Soc., Internat. Assn. Aquatic Vascular Plant Biologists (founder, pres. 1979—), Water Assn. Finland (edtl bd 1990—), Asociacion Argentina de Limnologia (hon.), Brazilian Soc. Limnology, Finnish Limnological Soc. (edtl. bd. 1989—), Internat. Lake Environ. Comm. Found. (exec. bd. 1986—), Netherlands Soc. Aquatic Ecology, Soc. Wetland Scientists, Sigma Xi, Phi Sigma. Home: 16 Dunbrook Tuscaloosa AL 35406-1962 Office: U Ala Dept Biol Scis Tuscaloosa AL 35487-0206

WEXLER, JEFFREY F., education educator, Montessori training administrator; b. Casper, Wyo., Apr. 3, 1941; s. Daniel Louis and Florence (Jamison) W.; m. Jennifer Forest, May 9, 1966; children: Paul, Jared, Denise, Flora, Danielle. BEd, U. So. Calif., 1964, M in Early Childhood Edn., 1965. Cert. elem. sch. tchr. and early childhood edn. Teller Casper Fed. Savs., 1961-63, loan officer, 1963-65; teacher to asst. dir. Early Childhood Tng. Ctr., 1964-78; asst. dir. Montessori Tng. Inst., Charlotte, N.C., 1978-89; dir., CEO Little Flower Montessori Sch., Charlotte, N.C., 1989—; Vis. instr. Montessori Sch., Ayden, N.C., Summers 1990—, Montessori instr., Alexander Mills, N.C., 1992—; bd. dirs. Little Flower Montessori Sch. Mem. Elem. Tchrs. Assn., Montessori Tchrs. Soc., (pres. Charlotte chpt. 1988-91, 95—), Edn. Found.

WEYRAUCH, WALTER OTTO, law educator; b. Lindau, Germany, Aug. 27, 1919; came to U.S., 1952; s. Hans Ernst Winand and Meta Margarete

(Lönholdt) W.; m. Jill Carolyn White, Mar. 17, 1973; children from previous marriages—Kurt Roman, Corinne Harriet Irene, Bettina Elaine (dec.). Student, U. Freiburg, 1937, U. Frankfurt Main, Germany, 1940-43; Dr. iur, U. Frankfurt Main, Germany, 1951; LL.B., Georgetown U., 1955; LL.M., Harvard, 1956; J.S.D., Yale, 1962. Referendar Frankfurt, Germany, 1943-48; atty. German cts. U.S. Ct. Appeals, Allied High Commn., Frankfurt, 1949-52; expert on trade regulations, visit in U.S. under auspices Dept. State, 1950; Harvard U. Dumbarton Oaks Library and Collection, Washington, 1953-55; asst. in instrn. Law Sch., Yale, 1956-57; assoc. prof. law U. Fla., Gainesville, 1957-60, prof., 1960-89, Clarence J. TeSelle prof. law, 1989-94, Stephen C. O'Connell chair, 1994—; hon. prof. law Johann Wolfgang Goethe U., Frankfurt Main, 1980—; vis. cons. U. Calif. at Berkeley, Space Scis. Lab., 1965-66; vis. prof. law Rutgers U., 1968; vis. prof. polit. sci. U. Calif. at Berkeley, 1968-69; vis. prof. law U. Frankfurt, 1975; cons. Commn. of Experts on Problems of Succession of the Hague Conf. on Pvt. Internat. Law, U.S. Dept. State, 1968-71; Rockefeller Found. fellow, Europe, 1958-59. Author: The Personality of Lawyers, 1964, Zum Gesellschaftsbild des Juristen, 1970, Hierarchie der Ausbildungsstätten, Rechtsstudium und Recht in den Vereinigten Staaten, 1976, Gestapo V-Leute: Tatsachen und Theorie des Geheimdienstes, 1989, 2d edit., 1992; co-author: (with Sanford N. Katz) American Family Law in Transition, 1983, (with Katz and Frances E. Olsen) Cases and Materials on Family Law: Legal Concepts and Changing Human Relationships, 1994; contbr. to: Clinical Law Training-Interviewing and Counseling, 1972, Law, Justice, and the Individual in Society-Psychological and Legal Issues, 1977, Marriage and Cohabitation in Contemporary Societies: Areas of Legal, Social and Ethical Change-An International and Interdisciplinary Study, 1980, Dutch trans., 1981, Group Dynamic Law: Exposition and Practice, 1988. Mem. Am. Acad. Fgn. Law, Law and Soc. Assn., Internat. Soc. on Family Law, Assn. Am. Law Schs. (chmn. com. studies beyond 1st degree in law 1965-67), Order of Coif. Home: 2713 SW 5th Pl Gainesville FL 32607-3113 Office: U Fla Coll Law Gainesville FL 32611

WHALEN, PAUL LEWELLIN, lawyer; b. Lexington, Ky.; s. Elza Boz and Barbara Jean (Lewellin) W.; m. Teena Gail Tanner, Jan. 26, 1985; children: Ashley, Lars, Lucy. BA, U. Ky.; JD, Northern Ky. U.; cert., Bonn U., Fed. Republic Germany, 1981; student, U.S. Army J.A.G. Sch., 1988. Bar: W.Va. 1984, U.S. Ct. Appeals (6th cir.) 1984, Ky. 1985, U.S. Ct. Appeals (4th cir.) 1985, Ohio 1993. Assoc. Geary Walker, Parkersburg, W.Va., 1984-85; prin. Paul L. Whalen, Ft. Thomas, Ky., 1985—; atty. Dept. of Air Force, Office of Chief Trial Atty. Contract Law Ctr., Wright Patterson AFB, 1988—; prosecutor Ky. Dept. Edn. Profl. Stds. Bd., 1995—. State sec. Ky. Young Dems., 1981-82; mem. Campbell County Foster Care Rev. Bd., Newport, Ky., 1986, Leadership No. Ky.; bd. dirs. Ky. Coun. Child Abuse, Inc. Com. for Kids; mem. Ft. Thomas Bd. Edn., 1987—, chmn., 1990-94; dir. Ky. Sch. Bd. Assn., 1993—. Recipient Commendation No. Ky. Legal Aid, 1986-96. Mem. No. Ky. Bar Assn., Optimist Club, Kiwanis Club, Phi Alpha Delta. Democrat. Methodist. Home: 113 Ridgeway Ave Fort Thomas KY 41075-1333 Office: PO Box 22 Fort Thomas KY 41075

WHALEY, CHARLES E., state agency administrator; b. Bloomington, Ind., Aug. 12, 1948; s. Lawrence Ellsworth and Mary Beth (Bennett) W. BS, Ind. U., 1973, MS, 1975, EdS, 1977; postgrad. U. Houston; postgrad., U. South Fla. Tchr. Ctr. for World Studies, Grand Rapids, Mich.; tchr. social studies Leon County Schs., Tallahassee; instr. social studies Devel. Rsch. Sch. Fla. State U., Tallahassee; dir. Fla. Gov.'s Summer Coll.; program coord. instrnl. strategies br. Ky. Dept. Edn., Frankfort. Author: Future Images: Futures Studies for Grades 4-12, 1986, The Futures Primer for Classroom Teachers, 1987, Enhancing Thinking & Creativity with Futures Studies, 1991, also other books, chpts. and articles. Named Ky. Col., 1985; recipient Disting. Svc. award, Ky., 1987, 94; grantee NDEA, ESEA, also others. Office: Ky Dept Edn Instrnl Strategies Branch Frankfort KY 40601

WHAPLES, ROBERT MACDONALD, economic history educator; b. Augsburg, Fed. Republic Germany, Mar. 23, 1961; came to U.S., 1963; s. Gene C. and Marlene (Dreher) W.; m. Regina T. Tatarewicz, June 16, 1984; children: Thomas, Antonina, Rebecca, Rose, Charles. BA in Econs. and History, U. Md., 1983; PhD in Econs., U. Pa., Phila., 1990. Asst. editor Jour. Econ. History, Phila., 1985-88; asst. prof. history U. Wis., Milw., 1988-91; asst. prof. econs. Wake Forest U., Winston-Salem, 1991-96, assoc. prof., 1996—; assoc. dir. EH.Net. Author: (with Dianne Betts) Historical Perspectives on American Economy, 1994; contbr. articles to profl. publs. Recipient Allen Nevins prize for outstanding dissertation in Am. econ. history, 1990. Mem. Am. Econ. Assn. (assoc. dir. 1996—), Econ. History Assn., Social Sci. History Assn., Cliometric Soc. Office: Wake Forest U Dept Econs Winston Salem NC 27109

WHATLEY, JACQUELINE BELTRAM, lawyer; b. West Orange, N.J., Sept. 26, 1944; d. Quirino and Eliane (Gruet) Beltram; m. John W. Whatley, June 25, 1966. BA, U. Tampa, 1966; JD, Stetson U., 1969. Bar: Fla. 1969, Alaska 1971. Cert. real estate law specialist. Assoc. Gibbons, Tucker, McEwen Smith & Cofer, Tampa, Fla., 1969-71; pvt. practice, Anchorage, 1971-73; ptnr. Gibbons, Tucker, Miller, Whatley & Stein, P.A., Tampa, 1973-81, pres., 1981—. Bd. dirs. Travelers Aid Soc., 1982-94; trustee Humana Women's Hosp., Tampa 1987-93, Keystone United Meth. Ch., 1986-89. Mem. ABA, Fla. Bar Assn. (real estate cert. com. 1993-95), Alaska Bar Assn., Tenn. Walking Horse Breeders and Exhibitors Assn. (v.p. 1984-87, dir. for Fla. 1981-87, 1990-93, adv. com. Tenn. Walking Horse Nat. Celebration 1994—), Fla. Walking and Racking Horse Assn. (bd. dirs. 1988-89, pres. 1980-82), Athena Club (Tampa). Republican. Methodist. Home: PO Box 17595 Tampa FL 33682-7595 Office: 101 E Kennedy Blvd Ste 1000 Tampa FL 33602-5146

WHAYNE, THOMAS FRENCH, JR., cardiologist; b. Ft. Leavenworth, Kans., Aug. 25, 1937; s. Thomas French and Mary Lutenia (Porter) W.; m. Eugenia McDonald Ingram, June 22, 1963; children: Thomas French III, James Givens, Katherine Ingram. AB in Chemistry, U. Pa., 1959, MD, 1963; PhD in Biochemistry, U. Calif., San Francisco, 1970. Intern in medicine The N.Y. Hosp., 1963-64, resident in medicine, 1964-66; fellow in cardiovascular disease Cardiovascular Rsch. Inst., San Francisco, 1966-69, U. Toronto, Ontario, Can., 1969-70; asst. prof. medicine Ohio State U., Columbus, 1970-72; assoc. prof. medicine U. Okla., Oklahoma City, 1972-77; clin. prof. medicine U. Ky., Lexington, 1977—; assoc. med. Okla. Med. Rsch. Found., 1972-77; staff cardiologist Lexington Clinic, 1977—. Named man of yr, Okla. Heart Assn., 1975-76. Fellow Am. Coll. Cardiology, Am. Coll. Physicians, Am. Heart Assn., Coll. Physicians of Phila. Presbyn. Office: Lexington Clinic 1221 S Broadway St Lexington KY 40504-2701

WHEALTON, JOHN H., physicist, educator; b. Bklyn., Apr. 27, 1943; s. Daniel J. and Isabelle K. (Baines) W.; m. Katharine M. Owens, Aug. 1, 1972; children: Karl, Linda, Thomas. BS, U. Mass., 1966; MS, U. Del., 1968, PhD, 1971. Rsch. assoc. Brown U., Providence, 1971-73, U. Colo., Boulder, 1973-75; staff scientist Oak Ridge (Tenn) Nat. Lab., 1975—; bd. editors Rev. Sci. Instruments. Contbr. over 280 articles to profl. jours.; patentee in field. Mem. Bd. Edn., Oak Ridge, 1990. Fellow Am. Phys. Soc.; mem. Nat. Sci. Tchrs. Assn., Am. Assn. Physics Tchrs., Math. Soc. Am., Nat. Sch. Bd. Assn., Nat. Coun. Tchrs. Math., Tenn. Inventors Soc., The Inventors Forum Martin Marietta Energy Systems Inc., Tenn. Sch. Bd. Assn. Home: 185 Outer Dr Oak Ridge TN 37830-5364 Office: Oak Ridge Nat Lab Fusion Energy Div Engring Tech Divsn Oak Ridge TN 37831-8088

WHEAT, EDWARD MCKINLEY, political science educator, researcher; b. Kansas City, June 18, 1943; s. Edward McKinley and Ruth Beckwith (Parry) W.; m. Stella Ilene Hubbard, Aug. 9, 1969; 1 child, Walter Whitman. BA in Polit. Sci., U. Mo., 1968, MA in Polit. Sci., 1971; PhD in Polit. Sci., U. Calif., Santa Barbara, 1975. Lectr. U. Calif., Santa Barbara, 1973-75; asst. prof. Salem (W.Va.) Coll., 1975-77; prof. polit. sci. U. So. Miss., Hattiesburg, 1977—; dir. Am. studies U. So. Miss., Hattiesburg, 1983—, dir. grad. studies in polit. sci., 1988-89. Contbr. articles to profl. jours. With U.S. Army, 1962-65, Korea. Mem. Am. Polit. Sci. Assn., So. Polit. Sci. Assn., Western Polit. Sci. Assn., Am. Studies Assn., Miss. Polit. Sci. Assn., Mid Am. American Studies Assn. Home: 110 W Ray Dr Hattiesburg MS 39402-1041 Office: Univ Sothern Mississippi Hattiesburg MS 39406-5108

WHEAT, JOHN NIXON, lawyer; b. Liberty, Tex., Dec. 15, 1952; s. Thomas Allen and Dora (Arrendell) W. BA, Tulane U., 1975; JD, St. Mary's U., San Antonio, 1977. Bar: Tex. 1978, U.S. Dist. Ct. (ea. dist.) Tex. 1978, U.S. Ct. Appeals (5th cir.) 1979. Law clk. U.S. Dist. Ct. Ea. Dist. Tex., Beaumont, 1978-79; pvt. practice The Wheat Firm, Liberty, Tex., 1979—. Active various polit., ednl. orgns. Mem. ABA, Tex. Bar Assn., Liberty-Chambers County Bar Assn., Houston Bar Assn., Tower Club of Beaumont, Magnolia Ridge County Club, Knights of Neches, Delta Theta Phi. Republican. Episcopalian. Office: The Wheat Firm 714 Main St PO Box 10050 Liberty TX 77575

WHEAT, MYRON WILLIAM, JR., cardiothoracic surgeon; b. Sapulpa, Okla., Mar. 24, 1924; s. Myron William and Mary Lee (Hudiburg) W.; m. Erlene Adele Plank, June 12, 1949 (div. June 1970); children: Penelope Louise, Myron William III, Pamela Lynn, Douglas Plank; m. Carol Ann Karmgard, June 18, 1970 (div. Apr. 1996); 1 child, Christopher West. AB, Washington U., St. Louis, 1949; MD cum laude, Washington U., 1951. Diplomate Am. Bd. Surgery, Am. Bd. Thoracic Surgery. Instr., clin. fellow Washington U., St. Louis, 1956-58; asst. prof. surgery U. Fla., Gainesville, 1958-65, prof. surgery, 1965-72; dir. profl. svcs., chief clin. physician U. Fla. Shands Teaching Hosp., Gainesville, 1968-72; prof. surgery, dir. thoracic and cardiothoracic surgery U. Louisville Sch. Medicine, 1972-75; clin. prof. surgery U. Louisville Sch. of Medicine, 1975—; cardiothoracic surgeon Cardiac Surg. Assocs., P.A., St. Petersburg, Fla., 1975-91; cons., thoracic surgery Bay Pine VA Hosp., St. Petersburg, Fla., 1994—; clin. prof. surgery U. So. Fla. Sch. Medicine, Tampa, 1995—; cardiothoracic surgeon Cardiac Surg. Assocs., P.A., Clearwater, Fla., 1991—; clin. prof. surger U. South Fla., 1995—; cons. Bay Pines VA Hosp., St. Petersburg, Fla., 1991—. Author (with others) 14 books; contbr. over 100 articles to profl. jours.; developed drug therapy for acute dissecting aneurysms of the aorta. 1st lt. USAF, 1943-46, ETO. Named First Howard W. Lillenthal Meml. lectr. Mt. Sinai Hosp., 1963; recipient DFC Air medal, Presdl. Citation. Fellow Am. Coll. Cardiology (chmn. bd. govs. 1968-69), Am. Coll. Surgeons (gov.); mem. Am. Surg. Assn., Am. Assn. for Thoracic Surgery, So. Surg. Assn., So. Thoracic Surg. Assn., Soc. Thoracic Surgeons, Soc. Thoracic Surgeons Great Britain and Ireland, Alpha Omega Alpha. Republican. Home and Office: 1772 Long Bow Ln Clearwater FL 34624-6402

WHEATLEY, JOSEPH KEVIN, physician, urologist; b. N.Y.C., Jan. 5, 1946; s. Patrick Owen and Catherine (Malloy) W.; m. Anne Johanna Foody, Aug. 22, 1970; children: Joseph, Thomas. BSChemE, Manhattan Coll., 1967; MSChemE, U. Del., 1969; MD, N.J. U. of Medicine, 1974. Diplomate Am. Bd. Urology. Rsch. engr. NASA, Houston, 1965, 66, Exxon, Florham Park, N.J., 1968-69; urology resident Emory Univ., Atlanta, 1975-79, assoc. prof. urology, 1979—; clin. urology practice Urology Assocs., Atlanta, 1986—; chief of urology Kennestone Hosp., Marietta, Ga., 1990-93; medicare care cons. Ga. Found. med. Care, Atlanta, 1982—; tchr. Atlanta VA Med. Ctr., Atlanta, 1979—; mem. hosp. exec. com. Kennestone Hosp., Marietta, 1990-93. Contbr. chpts. to books and articles to profl. jours. Active various Rep. actitives, 1992—. Named Top Drs. in Atlanta Atlanta Mag., 1995-96. Fellow ACS; mem. AMA, Urol. Assn., Urodynamics Soc., Am. Fertility Soc., Soc. of Reproductive Surgeons, Lithotripsy Soc. Roman Catholic. Home: 692 N Saint Mary's Ln Marietta GA 30064 Office: Urology Assocs 833 Campbell Hill Rd #300 Marietta GA 30060

WHEDON, GEORGE DONALD, medical administrator, researcher; b. Geneva, N.Y., July 4, 1915; s. George Dunton and Elizabeth (Crockett) W.; m. Margaret Brunssen, May 12, 1942 (div. Sept. 1982); children: Karen Anne, David Marshall. AB, Hobart Coll., 1936, ScD (hon.), 1967; MD, U. Rochester, 1941, ScD (hon.), 1978. Diplomate Am. Bd. Internal Medicine, Am. Bd. Nutrition. Intern in medicine Mary Imogene Bassett Hosp., Cooperstown, N.Y., 1941-42; asst. in medicine U. Rochester Sch. Medicine; also asst. resident physician medicine Strong Meml. Hosp., Rochester, 1942-44; instr. medicine Cornell U. Med. Coll., 1944-50, asst. prof. medicine, 1950-52; chief metabolic diseases br. Nat. Inst. Arthritis, Diabetes, Digestive and Kidney Diseases, NIH, Bethesda, Md., 1952-65, asst. dir., 1956-62, dir., 1962-81, sr. sci. adv., 1981-82; sr. assoc., dir. conf. program Kroc Found., Santa Ynez, Calif., 1982-84; adj. prof. medicine (endocrinology) UCLA Sch. Medicine, 1982-84; dir. med. rsch. programs Shriners Hosps. for Crippled Children, Tampa, 1984-91; mem. subcom. on calcium, com. dietary allowances Food and Nutrition Bd., NRC, 1959-64; cons. to office manned space flight NASA, 1963-78, chmn. Am. Inst. Biol. Scis. med. program adv. panel to, 1971-75, chmn. NASA life scis. com., 1974-78, mem. space program adv. coun., NASA, 1974-78; cons. on endocrinology and metabolism adv. com. Bur. Drugs, FDA, 1977-82; mem. subcommn. on gravitational biology Com. on Space Rsch., Internat. Union Physiol. Scis., 1979-85; mem. rsch. adv. bd. Shriners Hosps., 1981-84; mem. subcom. spacecraft maximum allowable concentrations, com. toxicology, bd. on environ. studies and toxicology Commn. on Life Scis. NRC, 1989—; cons. in medicine Wadsworth Gen. Hosp. VA Ctr., L.A., 1982-84; mem. U.S. Del. of U.S.-Japan Coop. Med. Sci. Program, 1984-93; mem. Internat. Soc. Gravitational Physiol., 1991—. Mem. editorial bd. Jour. Clin. Endocrinology and Metabolism, 1960-67; adv. editor Calcified Tissue Rsch., 1967-76; contbr. articles to profl. publs. Mem. med. alumni coun. Sch. Medicine, mem. trustees' coun. U. Rochester, 1971-76, vice chmn. trustees' coun., 1973-74, chmn., 1974-75; trustee Dermatology Found., 1978-82; bd. dirs. Osteogenesis Imperfecta Found., 1991—, med. adv. coun., 1993-96. Recipient Superior Svc. award USPHS, 1967, Alumni citation U. Rochester, 1971, Alumni citation Hobart Coll., 1986, Exceptional Sci. Achievement medal NASA, 1974, NASA award of Merit, 1996. Fellow Royal Soc. Medicine; mem. AAAS, Am. Fedn. Clin. Rsch. Assn., Am. Physicians, Aerospace Med. Assn. (Arnold D. Tuttle Meml. award 1978), Internat. Bone and Mineral Soc., Internat. Soc. Gravitational Physiology, Md. Acad. Scis. (sci. coun. 1964-70, 81-82), Endocrine Soc. (Robert H. Williams Disting. Leadership award in endocrinology 1982, Ayerst award 1974), Am. Physiol. Soc., Am. Inst. Nutrition, Am. Acad. Orthopaedic Surgeons (hon.), Am. Soc. Bone and Mineral Rsch., Orthopaedic Rsch. Soc., Am. Soc. Gravitational/Space Biology (Founders award 1994), Theta Delta Chi. Episcopalian. Home: 880 Mandalay Ave Apt 1002S Clearwater FL 34630

WHEEDLETON, KATHARINE MARIE, elementary school educator; b. Tucson, Ariz., Nov. 15, 1968; d. Ronald Kent and Mary Carol (Crane) B.; m. Christopher Carroll Wheedleton, June 27, 1992. BA in Edn., Va. Tech. U., 1990. Cert. elem. sch. tchr., Va. Tchr. Loudoun County (Va.) Pub. Schs., 1990—. Mem. Reston (Va.) Homeowner Assn. (treas., sec. 1994-96). Office: Sanders Corner Elem Sch 43100 Ashburn Farm Pkwy Ashburn VA 22011

WHEELAN, R(ICHELIEU) E(DWARD), lawyer; b. N.Y.C., July 10, 1945; s. Richard Fairfax and Margaret (Murray) W. BS, Springfield (Mass.) Coll., 1967; MS, Iona Coll., 1977; JD, Pace U., 1981. Bar: N.Y. 1982, Minn. 1983, Colo. 1989, Tex. 1990, U.S. Dist. Ct. (no dist.) Calif. 1982, (so. dist.) Tex. 1991, U.S. Internat. Trade 1982, U.S. Ct. Appeals (2d cir.) 1982, (9th cir.) 1983, (5th cir.) 1993, U.S. Supreme Ct. 1994; bd. cert. criminal law, trial advocacy. Lt. of detectives White Plains (N.Y.) Police Dept., 1969-81; area counsel IBM, Armonk, N.Y., 1981-89; gen. counsel Kroll Assocs. (Asia), Hong Kong, 1989-91; pvt. practice, Houston, 1991—. Mem. ABA (mem. sentencing guidelines com.), Nat. Assn. Criminal Def. Lawyers (life mem., mem. death penalty com.), Houston Bar Assn., Coll. of State Bar Tex., Pro Bono Coll. State Bar Tex., Tex. Assn. Criminal Def. Lawyers, Harris County Criminal Def. Lawyers Assn. (treas. 1993). Office: 602 Sawyer St Ste 480 Houston TX 77007-7510

WHEELER, ALBERT LEE, III, real estate appraiser, consultant, lawyer; b. Oklahoma City, Sept. 28, 1954; s. Albert Lee Jr. and Mercedes Elizabeth (Ball) W. BS in Mus. Edn., Central State U., Edmond, Okla., 1979; Oklahoma City U., Okla. City U., 1983, JD with honors, 1990. Real estate appraiser Market Data Research Inc., Oklahoma City, 1977-78; real estate mgr. Kerr McGee Corp., Oklahoma City, 1978-79; prin. Al Wheeler Appraisal Co., Oklahoma City, 1980—; pvt. practice law Oklahoma City, 1990—; assoc. attorney Gary B. Homsey & Assocs., Oklahoma City, 1996—. Editor Oklahoma City U. Law Rev., 1989-90; contbr. articles to profl. jours. Mem. Employee Relocation Coun., Washington, 1986-94. Mem. ABA, Am. Inst. Real Estate Appraisers, Nat. Assn. Realtors, Nat. Assn. Criminal Def. Lawyers, Merit Scholars Assn., Phi Delta Phi. Republican. Methodist. Office: Al Wheeler Appraisal Co 9517 N Regal Ln Oklahoma City OK 73162-7223 also: 8208 Crestline Ct Oklahoma City OK 73132-1321

WHEELER, ALVINA P., education educator; b. Boston, July 30, 1944; d. William John and Sarah Alvina Pheeny; m. Jeremy duQuesnay Adams, Dec. 21, 1975; 1 stepchild, Constance. AB, Stonehill Coll., 1966; MA, Brown U., 1967, PhD, 1971. Asst. prof. Columbia U., N.y.C., 1970-75; assoc. prof. So. Meth. U., Dallas, 1975—, dir. medieval studies program, 1978—; bd. dirs. Teams, Inc., Kalamazoo; lectr. in field. Editor: Arthuriana jour., 1994—; editor: (books) Fresh Verdicts on Joan of Arc, 1996, Feminea Medievalia, 1994, Medieval Mothering, 1996, The Block Book, 1996, Becoming Male in the Middle Ages, 1997; contbr. articles to profl. jours. Grantee in field; NDEA fellow Brown U., 1968-70; recipient Coun. for Rsch. in Humanities fellowship Columbia U., 1971, 74, Chamberlain fellowship, 1974-75, Coun. for Humanities fellowship So. Meth. U., 1976, numerous others. Mem. Internat. Courtly Lit. Soc., Fifteenth Century Studies, The Medieval Acad. of Am., MLA, New Chaucer Soc., Soc. Internat. Arthurienne, Phi Beta Kappa. Home: 3425 University Blvd Dallas TX 75205 Office: Medieval Studies Program So Meth Univ Dallas TX 75275-0432

WHEELER, CATHY JO, government official; b. Birmingham, Ala., Feb. 14, 1954; d. Charles Edwin and Hazel Josephine (Hollis) W.; m. David Arthur Tate. BA, U. Montevallo, 1975; postgrad., U. Ala., 1982-84. With Social Security Adminstrn., Birmingham, 1975—, mgmt. analyst, 1991—, sr. employment devel. specialist, 1983-85, mgr. tech. tng. dept., 1985-91, mgmt. analyst, 1991—; v.p. Fed. Women's Program, Birmingham, 1984-85; treas., charter mem. Federally Employed Women, Birmingham, 1984-88. Alumni bd. dirs. U. Montevallo, Ala., 1991-94, v.p. fin., 1994—. Mem. ASTD (treas. 1987-88, pres. elect 1989, pres. 1990, asst. regional dir. 1991-92), Soc. Govt. Meeting Planners (chartered, v.p. 1989-90, sec. 1990-91), Ala. Designer-Craftsmen, Riverchase Women's Club, Jaycees (v.p. mgmt. devel. Hoover, Ala. chpt. 1988-89), Chi Omega Alumni Assn. (treas. 1991, advisor 1991—). Home: 4001 Fairchase Ln Birmingham AL 35244 Office: Social Security Adminstrn 2001 12th Ave N Birmingham AL 35234-2717

WHEELER, CLARENCE JOSEPH, JR., physician; b. Dallas, Sept. 25, 1917; s. Clarence Joseph Sr. and Sadie Alice (McKinney) W.; m. Alice Mary Freels, Dec. 6, 1942; deceased; m. Patsy Lester Butler, Sept. 2, 1995; children: Stephen Freels, C.J. III, Robert McKinney, Thomas Michael, David Ritchey. BS in Math., So. Meth. U., 1941, BA in Psychology, 1946; MD, John Hopkins U., 1950. Diplomate Am. Bd. Surgery; cert. provider ACLS and advanced trauma life support, Am. Heart Assn. Intern John Hopkins Hosp., Balti., 1950-51; resident in surgery Barnes Hosp., St. Louis, 1951-54; fellow thoraic surgery U. Wis. Hosp., Madison, 1954-56, instr. surgery, 1955-56; attending surgeon Welborne Clinic Baptist Hosp., Evansville, Ind., 1956-57; mem. consulting staff Tex. Children's Hosp., 1957-70; courtesy and consulting staffs Pasadena Hosp., Spring Br. Hosp., others, Houston, 1957-70; mem. active staff Hermann Hosp., Houston, 1957-70, St. Luke's Hosp., Houston, 1957-70, Meth. Hosp., Houston, 1957-70, St. Joseph's Hosp., Houston, 1957-70, Meml. Hosp., Houston, 1957-70, Ben Taub Gen. City/County Hosp., Houston, 1957-70, Diagnostic Hosp., &, 1957-70; attending surgeon Lindley Hosp., Duncan, Okla., 1970-71; sr. attending, chief surgery Gordon Hosp., Lewisburg, Tenn., 1971-73; chief thoracic surgery Lewisburg Community Hosp., 1973-75; mem. active med. staff, med. dir. Carver Family Health Clinic, 1975-82; dir. emergency dept. Meth. Med. Ctr. Ill., Peoria, 1975-82; mem. staff Contract Emergency Med. Care, Houston and Dallas, 1982-88; med. dir. substance abuse unit Terrell (Tex.) State Hosp., 1988-90; med. dir. Schick-Shadel Hosp., Dallas-Ft. Worth, 1991—; med. dir., chief of staff Schick-Shadel Hosp., Ft. Worth, 1991-93; med. dir. Skillman Med. Ctr., Dallas, 1993-95, Centers for Preventative Medicine, Dallas, 1996—; instr. surgery U. Wis. Med. Sch., 1955-56; clin. instr. Baylor Coll. Medicine, Houston, 1959-70; lectr. U. Tex. Postgrad. Sch., Houston, 1957-70; clin. asst. prof. U. Ill. Sch. Medicine, Peoria, 1977-82; sr. med. advisor Thue Tien Province, So. Vietnam, 1968-69; chief of surgery Bien Vien Hué So. Vietnam, 1968-69. Treas. Samuel Clark Red Sch. PTA, Houston, 1959-61; bd. dirs. Salvation Army Boys Club, Houston; mem. Am. Mus. of Nat. History, Met. Mus. Art, Smithsonian Inst., Dallas Symphony Assn., Dallas Opera Soc., Dallas Theatre Ctr., Theatre Three Assn. Capt. USMCR, 1942-45, PTO. Decorated DFC with three stars, Air medal with four stars, Pacific Combat Theatre Ribbon with three stars, Purple Heart, Vietnamese Medal of Health (1st class), Vietnamese Medal Social Welfare, Navy Commendation medal, Presdl. Unit citation medal, Meritorious Bronze Star. Fellow ACS, Am. Coll. Angiology, Am. Coll. Chest Physicians, Royal Soc. Medicine, Internat. Coll. Surgeons, Am. Coll. Gastroenterology, Southea. Surg. Congress, Southwestern Surg. Congress, Internat. Assn. Proctologists; mem. AAAS, AMA, Am. Thoracic Soc., Nat. Tb Assn., Am. Assn. History of Medicine, Am. Soc. Contemporary Medicine and Surgery, Am. Soc. Addiction Medicine (cert.), Am. Heart Assn., Am. Cancer Soc., Am. Soc. Abdominal Surgeons, Marine Corps Officer's Assn., Naval Res. Officer's Assn., Nat. Geog. Soc., Mil. Order of the World Wars, Navy League, Indsl. Med. Assn., So. Med. Assn., Tex. Med. Assn., Tex. Thoracic Soc., Tex. Heart Assn., Tex. Anti-Tb Assn., Postgrad. Med. Assembly So. Tex., St. Louis Med. Soc., Dallas County Med. Soc., Marshall County Med. Soc. (pres.), Harris County Med. Soc., Houston Heart Assn., Houston Gastroent. Soc., Houston Surg. Soc., Greater Dallas Res. Officers Assn., Sierra Club, Rotary, Kappa Sigma, Phi Eta Sigma, Kappa Mu Epsilon, Psi Chi. Episcopalian. Address: 7111 Chipperton Dr Dallas TX 75225-1708

WHEELER, DAVID WAYNE, accountant; b. Charlottesville, Va., June 1, 1952; s. Daniel Gordon and Marion Elaine (Booth) W. BS in Acctg., Va. Poly. Inst. and State U., 1975. CPA, Va. Staff acct. Robert M. Musselman, Charlottesville, Va., 1971-76; pvt. practice acctg. Charlottesville, Va., 1976-77; sec., treas. Wheeler & Hancher Ltd., Charlottesville, Va., 1977-79; pres. David W. Wheeler Ltd., Charlottesville, Va., 1980—. Contbr. articles to profl. jours. Treas., bd. dirs. East Rivanna Vol. Fire Dept., Albemarle County, Va., 1983-91; bd. dirs. Literacy Vols. of Am., Charlottesville, Albemarle, 1988-90. Mem. AICPA (taxation div.), Va. Soc. CPAs (bd. dirs. 1992-93, chpt. sec. 1990-91, v.p. 1991-92, pres. 1992-93). Baptist. Home: 1112 Beaverdam Rd Keswick VA 22947 Office: The Massie-Smith House 211 4th St NE Charlottesville VA 22902-5205

WHEELER, ED, natural gas company executive; b. N.Y.C., Jan. 22, 1938; s. Edward George and Eleanor (Stehle) W.; m. Marcia Jane Largen, Aug. 24, 1963; 1 child, Brian Edward. Student, Tex. A&M U., 1956-57; BA in History/Polit. Sci., U. Tulsa, 1971, MA in History, 1994; grad., U.S. Army War Coll., 1983. Creative writer Whitney Advt. Agy., Tulsa, 1960-61; dir. promotion KVOO Radio, Tulsa, 1961-63; with Okla. Natural Gas Co., Tulsa, 1964—, gen. mgr. corp. comm., 1986—. Author radio scripts 1300 prodns., 1964-73. Past pres. 45th Infantry Divsn. Assn., 1981, West Point Parent's Assn., Tulsa, 1986-90. Brig. gen. U.S. Army, 1956-91. Decorated DSM, DSC, Meritorious Svc. medal, Legion of Merit; recipient George Washington honor medals Freedoms Found., Valley Forge, Pa. Mem. NRA, APR, Am. Legion (post 1 1971—), Pub. Rels. Soc. Am. (Coll. Fellows, pres. Tulsa chpt. 1989), Mil. Order World Wars (charter chpt. pres.), U.S. Army War Coll. Alumni Assn., Phi Kappa Phi, Phi Alpha Theta, Pi Kappa Alpha. Republican. Presbyterian. Home: 5122 S Madison Ave Tulsa OK 74105-5622 Office: Okla Natural Gas Co PO Box 871 Tulsa OK 74102-0871

WHEELER, EDWARD NORWOOD, chemical consultant; b. Yancey, Tex., Oct. 11, 1927; s. Wilber Basel and Clara Clementine (Stafford) W.; m. Luella Jean Brossette, Nov. 21, 1950; children: Gordon A., Sterling R., Darrell S., Charlotte, Murray H. BS, Tex. A&I U., 1947, BSChemE, 1949; MA, U. Tex., 1951, PhD, 1953. Rsch. chemist Celanese Chem. Co., Corpus Christi, 1953-55, group leader, 1955-62, section mgr., 1962-67, dir. rsch., 1967-72, dir. devel., 1972-74; planning dir. Celanese Chem. Co., N.Y.C., 1974-75, dir. rsch. devel. planning, 1975-76, v.p. rsch. devel. planning, 1976-79; v.p. rsch. & devel. Celanese Chem. Co., Dallas, 1979-83; cons. and expert witness White and Case, Hong Kong and N.Y.C., 1986-91; mem. adv. coun. U. Tex. Natural Sci. Found. Contbr. articles to profl. jours., patentee 14 inventions. Treas. Dallas Bethlehem Ctr., 1985-89; hon. life mem., mem. adv. coun. U. Tex. Coll. Natural Sci. Found.; bd. trustees Tex. A&M U.-Kingsville Found., 1994—; pres. North Tex. Conf. Coun. on Fin. and Adminstrn., United Meth. Ch., 1992-96. Recipient Disting. Alumnus award Tex. A&I U., Kingsville, 1981. Mem. Am. Chem. Soc., Indsl. Rsch. Inst., Synthetic Organic Chem. Mfrs. Assn. (bd. govs. 1977-81), Littlefield Soc. U.

Tex. Methodist. Home and Office: 9238 Moss Haven Dr Dallas TX 75231-1412

WHEELER, ELLEN JAYNE, music educator; b. Durant, Okla., Aug. 12, 1936; d. Harold Wayne and Edith Lucinda (Records) Maris; m. Donald Keith Miller, May 28, 1961 (div.); 1 child, Donald Wayne; m. Joseph Clyde Wheeler, June 2, 1969. BMus, U. Tex., El Paso, 1958; MA in Tchg., Okla. City U., 1967; D of Musical Arts, U. Okla., 1987. Youth dir. Trinity Meth. Ch., El Paso, Tex., 1958; music tchr. El Paso Pub. Schs., 1959, Ysleta (Tex.) Pub. Schs., 1959-60, Okeene (Okla.) Pub. Schs., 1963-64, Kingfisher (Okla.) Pub. Schs., 1964-66; ch. choir dir. First Meth. Ch., Kingfisher, 1965-67; prof. voice Oklahoma City U., 1966-69, 86—; ch. choir dir. St. Matthews Meth. Ch., Midwest City, Okla., 1967-68, Christ Meth. Ch., Oklahoma City, 1968-69. Editor: Cherokee Outlet Cowboy, 1995. Precinct chmn. Rep. Party, Oklahoma City, 1968; pres. PTA, Oklahoma City, 1979-80; fine arts adv. bd. Oklahoma City Pub. Schs., 1974-76; docent in pub. schs. Women's Com. for the Symphony, Oklahoma City, 1978-80. Fellowship Rotary Club of West Tex., 1960. Mem. DAR (vice-regent 1978-80), AAUP, Magna Charta Dames (v.p. 1983), Okla. Music Tchrs. Assn. (dist. pres. 1988-92, historian 1994—), Col. Dames of XVII Century (pres. 1975-77), PEO Sisterhood (treas. 1972-76, chaplin), Zeta Tau Alpha (panhellenic rep. 1974-76), Sigma Alpha Iota (v.p. 1994—). Disciples of Christ. Home: 2324 Northwest 45th St Oklahoma City OK 73112 Office: Oklahoma City Univ 25th & Blackwelder Oklahoma City OK 73106

WHEELER, EVERETT LYNN, historian, editor; b. New Albany, Ind., July 22, 1950; s. Newland Everett and Esther (Smith) W. AB cum laude, Ind. U., 1972; postgrad., SUNY, Buffalo, 1972-73; PhD, Duke U., 1977; postgrad., Am. Sch. Classical Studies, Athens, Greece, 1975-76. Scholar in residence dept. classical studies Duke U., Durham, N.C., 1986—, asst. editor Greek, Roman and Byzantine Studies, 1991—; vis. prof. U. Mo., Columbia, 1979-81; vis. lectr. U. Louisville, Ky., 1983, 86. Translator: (Hans Delbruck) History of the Art of War Within the Framework of Political History II, History of the Art of War Within the Framework of Political History III, History of the Art of War Within the Framework of Political History IV, Polyaenus, Stratagems of War, 1994; author: Stratagem and the Vocabulary of Military Trickery, 1988; co-author: Hoplites: The Classical Greek Battle Experience, 1991, Terrorism Research and Public Policy, 1991, The Roman Army in the East, 1996; contbr. articles to profl. jours. Alexander Von Humboldt Found. fellow, Bonn, Germany, 1981-83, Harry Frank Guggenheim Found. fellow, N.Y., 1986-87. Mem. Soc. for Mil. History (Moncado prize 1994), Am. Philol. Assn., Am. Hist. Assn., Ernst Kirsten Assn. for Hist. Geography Alten Welt, Soc. for the Study Caucasia, Assn. for Preservation of Civil War Sites, Phi Beta Kappa. Office: Duke Univ Dept Classical Studies PO Box 90103 Durham NC 27708-0103

WHEELER, GENEVIEVE STUTES, library administrator, educator; b. Duson, La., Dec. 13, 1937; d. Noah and Natalie (Falcon) Stutes; m. Richard Anthony Musemeche, Feb. 3, 1956 (div. 1975); children—Sabrina Marie Musemeche Beckham, Susan Ann Lowrie; m. 2d, Berle Steele Wheeler, July 1, 1978. B.A., U. Southwest La., Lafayette, 1959; M.S. in Library Sci., La. State U., Baton Rouge, 1970. Cert. tchr. Tchr. Iberia Schs., New Iberia, La., 1959-60; sch. librarian Lafayette Parish Sch., 1960-69; tchr., librarian La. State Sch. Deaf, Baton Rouge, 1970-71; librarian East Baton Rouge System, 1971-78; library adminstr. St. Bernard Community Coll., Chalmette, La., 1978—, cons., 1978-92; dir. libr. sci. Nunez Community Coll., Chalmette, 1992—; cons. library La. State Dept. Edn., Baton Rouge, 1975-76. Author tchr. guides, 1975, 77. Co-organizer, co-sponsor Project LesEnfants, 1975. Mem. Am. Library Assn., Am. Assn. Jr. and Community Colls., La. Assn. Sch. Librarians (pres. 1982-83), ALA, La. Assn. Sch. Execs., La. Library Assn., Gov.'s Conf. Libraries, Delta Kappa Gamma (v.p. Baton Rouge 1975-76), Phi Kappa Phi. Home: 913 Cross Gates Blvd Slidell LA 70461 Office: Nunez CC 3700 La Fontaine St Chalmette LA 70043-1249

WHEELER, HAROLD AUSTIN, SR., lawyer, former educational administrator; b. Montverde, Fla., Oct. 5, 1925; s. Bureon Kylus and Susan Ella (Bible) W.; m. Myrtle Edna Suggs, Sept. 30, 1949; children—Brenda Lynn, Harold Austin, Stephen Wayne, Donna Kay. B.S.B.A., U. Fla., 1950; M.Ed., Fla. Atlantic U., 1970; J.D., U. Miami (Fla.), 1973, LL.M., 1977. C.P.A., Fla.; bar: Fla. 1973. Auditor to supr. auditor Fla. State Auditing Dept., 1950-62; asst. supt. fin. and acctg. Palm Beach County, Fla. Pub. Schs., 1962-65; dir. fin., treas. Fla. Pub. Schs., Dade County, 1966-81; ptnr. Wheeler & Segarra, Miami, 1982—. Mem. Fla. Inst. C.P.A.s, Am. Inst. C.P.A.s, Fla. Bar Assn., Dade County Bar Assn., Assn. Sch. Bus. Ofcls. of U.S. and Can. Democrat. Baptist. Lodge: Kiwanis. Home: 6695 SW 112th St Miami FL 33156-4856 Office: 5825 Sunset Dr Ste 300 Miami FL 33143-5222

WHEELER, IRVING, association executive. Pvt. practice law, 1960—; claims ct. judge Polk County, Fla., 1962-72; pres. Wheeler Farms, Inc., 1972—; pres., bd. dirs. Haines City Citrus Growers Assn., Winter Haven, Fla. Mem. ABA, Fla. Bar Assn. Office: Haines Cy Citrus Growers Assn PO Box 2796 Winter Haven FL 33882

WHEELER, JEANETTE NORRIS, entomologist; b. Newton, Iowa, May 21, 1918; d. David Ottis and Esther (Miles) Norris; widowed; 1 child, Ralph Allen. BA, U. N.D., 1939, MS, 1956, PhD, 1962. Tchr. Casselton (N.D.) High Sch., 1939-40; instr. U. N.D., Grand Forks, 1944-49, asst. prof., 1963-65, rsch. assoc., 1965-67; rsch. assoc. Desert Rsch. Inst., U. Nev., Reno, 1967-80, Fla. Collection of Arthropods, 1985—, Los Angeles County Natural History Mus., 1979—; rsch. assoc. Natural History Mus. L.A. County, Fla. Collection Arthropods. Co-author: The Ants of North Dakota, 1963, The Amphibians and Reptiles of North Dakota, 1966, Ants of Deep Canyon, Colorado, Desert, California, 1973, Ant Larvae: Review and Synthesis, 1976, The Ants of Nevada, 1986; contbr. over 100 articles to profl. jours. Recipient Sioux award U. N.D. Alumni Assn., 1989. Home: 3338 NE 58th Ave Silver Springs FL 34488-1867

WHEELER, LAWRENCE J., art museum administrator. BA cum laude in History and French, Pfeiffer Coll., 1965; MA in European History, U. Ga., 1969, PhD in European History, 1972; cert., Fed. Execs. Inst., Charlottesville, Va., 1977, U. N.C., 1982. Asst. prof. European history Pfeiffer Coll., Misenheimer, N.C., 1970-74; dep. sec. N.C. Dept. Cultural Resources, Raleigh, 1977-85; asst. dir. mus. and dir. devel. Cleve. Mus. Art, 1985-94; staff liaison for bldg. and staffing N.C. Mus. Art, Raleigh, 1977-83, dir., 1994—; cons. on fundraising and pub. rels. N.C. Mus. History, Raleigh; coord. 400th anniversary celebration Sir Walter Raleight's voyages festival, 1984. Bd. dirs. Am. Arts Alliance, 1991-92. Mem. Am. Assn. Mus. (chmn. dvel. and membership profl. com. 1990-92, sr. reviewer mus. assessment program 1992—), Inst. Mus. Svcs. (reviewer 1988—), Art Mus. Devel. Assn. (pres. 1987-88). Office: NC Mus Art 2110 Blue Ridge Rd Raleigh NC 27607-6494

WHEELER, STEVE DEREAL, neurologist; b. Chgo., Sept. 15, 1951; s. Clarence and Tommie L. (Andrews) W.; m. Debra B. Buckingham; children: Winter N., Ryan S., Gabrielle S. Student, Mich. State U., 1970-73; MD, Dartmouth Coll., 1976. Diplomate Am. Bd. Psychiatry and Neurology, Nat. Bd. Med. Examiners; lic. Mich., Ohio, Fla. Intern Thomas Jefferson U., Phila., 1976-77; emergency physician River Dist. Hosp. Emergency Cons., Inc., St. Clair, Mich., 1977-78; fellow Dartmouth Med. Sch., 1978; resident U. Miami, Fla., 1978-81; fellow Washington U., St. Louis, 1981-82; instr. in neurology Med. Coll. Pa., Phila., 1982-83; electroencephalograph reader, attending neurologist VA Med. Ctr., Phila., 1982-83; asst. neurologist, attending neurologist Muscle Clinic U. Hosps. Cleve., 1983-86; electromyographer Rainbow Babies and Children's Hosp., U. Hosps. Cleve., 1983-86; chief neuromuscular diseases divsn., asst. prof. neurology Case Western Res. U., Cleve., 1983-86, co-dir. muscle disease ctr. and lab., 1985-86; clin. assoc. prof. of neurology U. Miami, 1987-89; pvt. practice Miami, 1987—; lectr. Myasthenia Gravis Found., Vermillion, Ohio, 1984, Student Nat. Med. Assn., Cleve., 1983-86; vol. assoc. prof. U. Miami Sch., 1992—, vis. lectr., 1983—; neurology cons. Low Back Pain Team U. Hosps. Cleve., 1984-86; mem. quality assurance com. Coral Reef Hosp., Miami, 1987-88; cons. dir. planning Bapt. Headache Clinic Bapt. Hosp., Miami, 1993—; mem. adminstrv. com. Deering Hosp. Pain Mgmt. Ctr., Miami, 1993-94; mem. sleep diagnostic ctr. com. Bapt. Hosp., 1990-92, 94—, advisor to headache support group, 1995—; lectr. in field. Author (chpt.) Intensive Care For Neurological Trauma and Disease, 1982; contbr. articles to profl. jours. Named Internat. Man Yr., 1991-92; recipient Celebration Excellence Black Achiever award Family Christian Assn. Am., 1992. Fellow Royal Soc. Medicine, Am. Acad. Neurology; mem. Am. Acad. Clin. Neurophysiology, Am. Soc. Internal Medicine, Am. Assn. Study of Headache, Am. Coll. Physicians, Nat. Headache Found., Nat. Chronic Pain Outreach Program, Nat. Stroke Assn., Internat. Headache Soc., Fla. Med. Assn., Fla. Soc. Neurology, Fla. Soc. Internal Medicine, N.Y. Acad. Scis., Muscular Disease Soc. Northeastern Ohio (bd. trustees 1984-86), Dade County Med. Assn., So. Pain Soc., Internat. Assn. Study of Pain, Dartmouth Club Greater Miami, Am. Coun. for Headache Edn. Office: 8950 N Kendall Dr Ste 501 Miami FL 33176-2132

WHEELER, SUSIE WEEMS, retired educator; b. Cassville, Ga., Feb. 24, 1917; d. Percy Weems and Cora (Smith) Weems-Canty; m. Dan W. Wheeler Sr., June 7, 1941; 1 child, Dan Jr. BS, Fort Valley (Ga.) State U., 1945; MEd, Atlanta U., 1947, EdD, 1978; postgrad., U. Ky., 1959-60; EdS, U. Ga., 1977. Tchr. Bartow County Schs., Cartersville (Ga.) City Schs., 1938-44, Jeanes supr., 1946-58; supr., curriculum dir. Paulding Sch. Sys.-Stephens Sch., Calhoun City, 1958-64; summer sch. tchr. Atlanta U., 1961-63; curriculum dir. Bartow County Schs., 1963-79; pres., co-owner Wheeler-Morris Svc. Ctr., 1990—; mem. Ga. Commn. on Student Fin., 1985-95. Coord. Noble Hill-Wheeler Meml. Ctr. Project, 1983—. Recipient Oscar W. Canty Cmty. Svc. award, 1991, Woman in History award Fedn. Bus. and Profl. Women, 1994-95. Mem. AAUW (v.p. membership 1989-91, Ga. Achievement award 1993), Ga. Assn. Curriculum and Supervision (pres.-elect 1973-74, pres. 1974-75, Johnnye V. Cox award 1975), Delta Sigma Theta (pres. Rome alumnae chpt. 1978-80, mem. nat. bd. 1984, planning com. 1988—, Dynamic Delta award 1967, 78), Ga. Jeanes Assn. (pres. 1968-70). Home: 105 Fite St Cartersville GA 30120-3410

WHEELER, TOWNSEND, III, academic administrator; b. Bridgeport, Conn., Oct. 21, 1942; m. Carolyn Bardwell, July 5, 1980; children: Bethany, Carrie, Jennie. BS, Union Coll., Schnectady, 1966; postgrad., Syracuse U., 1969-73. Tchr. Marcellus (N.Y.) Schs., 1968-86; owner S&W Builders, Inc., Louisville, 1986-89; prin., dir. devel. Alliance Christian Acad., Louisville, 1989-96. Cpl. USMC, 1966-68. Mem. Internat. Fellowship Christian Sch. Adminstrs., Beuchel Bus. Assn. (sec. 1994, v.p. 1995), Rotary Club of Buechel (v.p. 1996).

WHEELER, VIRGINIA ANN, secondary school educator; b. Atlanta, May 16, 1954; d. Vincent D. and Carrie L. (Huiet) W. B Music Edn., Shorter Coll., Rome, Ga., 1976; MusM, Ga. State U., Atlanta. Music tchr. Floyd Middle Sch., Mableton, Ga., 1976-85; choral dir. South Cobb High Sch., Austell, Ga., 1985—. Pianist Powder Springs (Ga.) 1st United Meth. Ch. Recipient Heritage Music Festival award, 1989, Fla. Music Fantasy award, Orlando, 1990, Manhattan Skyline Choral Festival, 1991. Mem. Nat. Music Educators Assn., Am. Choral Dirs. Assn., Ga. Music Educators Assn. Office: South Cobb H S 1920 Clay Rd Austell GA 30001-2299

WHEELER, WILLIAM BRYAN, III, systems company executive; b. Kissimmee, Fla., June 21, 1940; s. William Bryan and Olive Mae (Criner) W.; m. Mary Sue Lewis, Dec. 29, 1961 (div. Jan. 1987); children: Alicia Nanette, Bryan; m. Vickie Lynn Von Tempske, Mar. 20, 1988. Student U. Fla., 1958-59, U. Md., 1967-68; B.L.A., U. Ga., 1975; Ph.D., Bangor Inst., 1978. Meteorol. supr. Pan Am. World Airways, 1962-63; asst. engr. Fla. Road Dept., Orlando, 1963-64; tech. supr. Xerox Corp., 1964-65; sr. field engr. Fed. Electric Corp., Rome, 1965-66; systems engr. Bendix Corp., 1966-70; devel. dir. East Coast Stainless Steel, Lanham, Md., 1970-71; regional planner Middle Flint Planning and Devel. Commn., Ellaville, Ga., 1975-78; planning dir. Northeast Ga. Area Planning and Devel. Commn., Athens, 1978-81; dist. mgr. CASA Data Systems, Athens, 1981-82; v.p. Select Systems, Inc., Atlanta, 1982-86; network mgr. Universal Data, Atlanta, 1987-88; pres. Camelot Data, 1988-91; regional sales mgr. W.H. Assocs., 1991—. V.p. Sumter County Bicentennial Beautification Com., 1976-77. Author: (Pseudonym Rhuddlwm Gawr) The Quest--The Discovery of the Cauldron of Immortality, 1976, The Way Part II of The Quest, 1984, Celtic Crystal Magick, vols. 1 and 2, 1988, The Word, The Story of Welsh Witchcraft. Served with USMC, 1958-61. Mem. Am. Soc. Landscape Architects, Am. Soc. Med. Computing and Electronics, Am. Planning Assocs. Democrat.

WHEELER, WILLIAM EARL, general surgeon; b. Fort Benning, Ga., Feb. 23, 1952; s. Thomas Harvey and Martha (Donaldson) W.; m. Rebecca Sue Shafer, May 6, 1984; children: Thomas Andrew, William Matthew. AA, East Ctrl. C.C., 1972; BS, Millsaps Coll., 1974; MD, U. Miss., 1977. Diplomate Am. Bd. Surgery. From asst. prof. to assoc. prof. Marshall Univ., Huntington, W.Va., 1983-91; staff surgeon Upstate Carolina Med. Ctr., Gaffney, S.C., 1991—; staff surgeon VA Med. Ctr., Huntington, 1983-91; chief surgical svc., 1985-91; staff and burn surgeon, Cabell Huntington Hosp, 1983-91; staff surgeon St. Mary's Hosp., Huntington, 1983-91; chief surg. sect. Upstate Carolina Med. Ctr., 1994-95; staff surgeon Mary Black Meml. Hosp., Spartanburg, S.C., 1992—; asst. clin. prof. surgery Med. Coll. S.C., Charleston, 1994—. Camp physician, committeeman Boy Scouts Am., Huntington, 1986-91; water safety instr. ARC, Decatur, Miss., 1971-80; elder Limestone Presbyn. Ch., Gaffney, 1994-96, fin. com., 1993-96. Recipient Eagle Scout award, Boy Scouts Am., 1967. Fellow Am. Coll. Surgeons; mem. AMA, Am. Burn Assn., S.C. Med. Assn., So. Med. Assn., Kiwanis. Home: 118 Greenbriar Dr Gaffney SC 29341 Office: 117 E Montgomery St Gaffney SC 29340

WHEELING, ROBERT FRANKLIN, computer consultant; b. Springboro, Pa., Sept. 10, 1923; s. Alfred Abraham and Louwaive Letty (Hollabaugh) W.; m. Luella Mae Race, June 2, 1951; 1 child, Eric Wayne. BSEE, Pa. State Coll., 1944; MS in Math., U. Rochester, 1949; postgrad., Brown U., 1947-51. Project engr. Eastman Kodak Co., Rochester, N.Y., 1944-47; mathematician Mobil Research and Devel. Corp., Paulsboro, N.J., 1952-70; mgr. computer technology Mobil Oil Corp., N.Y.C., 1971-72; engrng. cons. Mobil Research and Devel. Corp., Princeton, N.J., 1973-84; pvt. practice computer cons. Naples, Fla., 1985—. Contbr. chpt. to book Optimizers, 1964; contbr. articles to profl. jours.; patentee in field. Mem. Mathematical Assn. of Am., Assn. for Computing Machinery (lectr. 1963). Home and Office: 2718 Shoreview Dr Naples FL 34112-5840

WHEELOCK, ELIZABETH SHIVERS, trade association executive, small business owner; b. Marion, Ala., Nov. 29, 1932; d. William Lewitt and Willie Mae (Perkins) Shivers; m. Hugh Franklin Wheelock, Aug. 23, 1955; children: Hugh Franklin Jr., Elizabeth McLaurin, Lewitt Shivers. Student, Judson Coll., Marion, 1951-53, Wallace Community Coll., Dothan, 1973-74, 80. Credit mgr. Ted's Jewelers, Dothan, 1975-79; with mktg. and spl. projects depts. City Nat. Bank, Dothan, 1979-81, new account adminstr., 1980-81; founder, sec. Art Gallery, City Nat. Bank Art Gallery, Dothan, 1980-83; exec. officer Home Builders Assn. Dothan and Wiregrass Area, 1981—; cons., tchr., designer Needle Arts, Dothan, 1970—; owner, mgr. Elizabeth's Needle, Dothan, 1973; ptnr. Magnolia Springs Antiques, Foley. Editor newsletteers Perri-Winkle, 1950-51, Tapeline, 1981—; designer, pattern maker needle work, 1970—. Mem. Vivian B. Adams Sch. Parents Orgn., Ozark, Ala., 1973—, Wiregrass Art Mus., 1989—, Shakespeare Theatre Found., Montgomery, Ala.; bd. dirs. March of Dimes, Dothan, 1987-89. Recipient award March of Dimes, 1989, Pres. award Home Builders Assn. Dothan, 1994; nominee Small Bus. Prson of Yr. Dothan-Houston C. of C., 1994. Mem. DAR, Nat. Trust for Hist. Preservation, Internat. Platform Soc., Zonta Internat. Episcopalian. Home: 1405 W Newton St Dothan AL 36303-3924 Office: Home Builders Assn Dothan and Wiregrass Area 2207B Denton Rd Dothan AL 36303-2219

WHEELOCK, MOIRA MYRL BREWER, real estate broker, educator, church musician; b. Kirkland, Tex.; d. William Cassius and Marjorie (Lindsey) Brewer; m. Robert Denton Wheelock, June 5, 1938 (dec. July 1993); children: John Robert, Mary Ann Wheelock Reynolds. BA, Tex. Tech U., 1938; MA, W. Tex. State U., 1951. Cert. tchr.; lic. real estate broker. Tchr. various schs., Tex., 1936-40, 51-78; owner, broker Wheelock Real Estate, Canyon, Tex., 1979—. Contbr. artices to local newspaper. Active Friends to Save Our Courthouse, Canyon, 1984-86; musician First Bapt. Ch.; pianist Canyon Sr. Citizens. Mem. NEA (life), Tex. State Tchrs. Assn. (life), Tex. Classroom Tchrs. Assn. Ilife), Tex. Ret. Tchrs. Assn. (life), Canyon Ret. Tchrs. Assn., Tex. Assn. Realtors, Nat. Assn. Realtors, Sue Hite Federated Club (past pres.), Order Eastern Star (organist), Dalta Kappa Gamma (past pres. Eta Phi chpt.). Democrat. Home and Office: PO Box 122 Canyon TX 79015-0122

WHELAN, KAREN MAE LEPPO, manufacturing executive; b. Lancaster, Pa., Mar. 20, 1947; children: Katherine, John. BA, U. Pitts., 1967; MS in Bus., Va. Commonwealth U., 1977. Sr. acct. Arthur Young, Richmond, Va., 1977-80; various positions, advanced to v.p. fin. reporting James River Corp., Richmond, 1980-92; v.p., treas. Universal Corp., Richmond, 1993—. Mem. AICPA (Elijah Watts Sells award 1976), Nat. Investor Rels. Inst., Fin. Execs. Inst., Va. Soc. CPAs (cert. CPA, gold medal award 1976). Office: Universal Corp PO Box 25099 Richmond VA 23260

WHICHARD, WILLIS PADGETT, state supreme court justice; b. Durham, N.C., May 24, 1940; s. Willis Guilford and Beulah (Padgett) W.; m. Leona Irene Paschal, June 4, 1961; children: Jennifer Diane, Ida Gilbert. AB, U. N.C., 1962, JD, 1965; LLM, U. Va., 1984, SJD, 1994. Bar: N.C. 1965 Law clk. N.C. Supreme Ct., Raleigh, 1965-66; ptnr. Powe, Porter, Alphin & Whichard, Durham, 1966-80; assoc. judge N.C. Ct. Appeals, Raleigh, 1980-86; assoc. justice N.C. Supreme Ct., Raleigh, 1986—; instr. grad. sch. bus. adminstrn. Duke U., 1978; vis. lectr. U. N.C. Sch. Law, 1986—. Contbr. articles to profl. jours. Rep. N.C. Ho. of Reps., Raleigh, 1970-74; senator N.C. Senate, 1974-80, chair numerous coms. and commns.; N.C. legis. rsch. commn., 1971-73, 75-77, land policy coun., 1975-79; bd. dirs. Sr. Citizens Coordinating Coun., 1972-74; chair local crusade Am. Cancer Soc., 1977, state crusade chair, 1980, chair pub. issues com., 1980-84; pres., bd. chmn. Downtown Durham Devel. Corp., 1980-84; bd. dirs. Durham County chpt. ARC, 1971-79; Durham county campaign dir. March of Dimes, 1968, 69, chmn., 1969-74, bd. dirs. Triangle chpt., 1974-79; bd. advisors Duke Hosp., 1982-85, U. N.C. Sch. Pub. Health, 1985—, U. N.C. Sch. Social Work, 1989—; bd. visitors N.C. Ctrl. U. Sch. Law, 1987—; mem. law sch. dean search com. U. N.C., 1978-79, 88-89, self-study com., 1985-86; pres. N.C. Inst. Justice, 1984-94; bd. dirs. N.C. Ctr. Crime and Punishment, 1984-94. Staff sgt. N.C. Army NG, 1966-72. Recipient Disting. Service award Durham Jaycees, 1971, Outstanding Legis. award N.C. Acad. Trial Lawyers, 1975, Outstanding Youth Service award N.C. Juvenile Correctional Assn., 1975, Citizen of Yr., Eno Valley Civitan Club, Durham, 1982, Faith Active in Pub. Life award N.C. Council of Churches, 1983, Outstanding Appellate Judge award N.C. Acad. Trial Lawyers, 1983, inducted Durham High Sch. Hall of Fame, 1987. Mem. ABA, N.C. Bar Assn. (v.p. 1983-84), Durham County Bar Assn., U. N.C. Law Alumni Assn. (pres. 1978-79, bd. dirs. 1979-82), Nat. Guard Assn. (judge advocate 1972-73, legis. com. 1974-76), Order of Golden Fleece, Order of Grail, Order of Old Well, Amphoterothen Soc., Order of Coif, Phi Alpha Theta, Phi Kappa Alpha. Democrat. Baptist. Clubs: Durham-Chapel Hill Torch (pres. 1984-85), Watauga (Raleigh, pres. 1994—). Home: 5608 Woodberry Rd Durham NC 27707-5335 Office: NC Supreme Ct 2 E Morgan St Raleigh NC 27601-1445

WHICKER, CHRISTINE SPAINHOUR, municipal official; b. Winston-Salem, N.C., Apr. 3, 1947; d. William Henry and Evelyn Abigail (Long) Spainhour; m. Randall Grey Whicker, July 1, 1966; 1 child, Vanessa Whicker Flynt. BS in Bus. Adminstrn. and Econs., High Point (N.C.) U., 1993. Office mgr. King (N.C.) Dist. Water System, 1976-89; fin. dir. City of King, 1989—. Mem. Inst. Mgmt. Accts., Govt. Fin. Officers Assn., N.C. Govt. Investment Officers Assn. Democrat. Methodist. Office: City of King 229 S Main St King NC 27021-1132

WHIDDON, FREDERICK PALMER, university president; b. Newville, Ala., Mar. 2, 1930; s. Samuel Wilson and Mary (Palmer) W.; m. June Marie Ledyard, June 14, 1952; children: Charles Wilson, John Tracy, Karen Marie and Keith Frederick (twins). AB, Birmingham So. Coll., 1952; BD cum laude, Emory U., 1955, PhD in Philosophy, 1963, LittD (hon.), 1991. Asst. prof. philosophy, dean of students Athens (Ala.) Coll., 1957-59; dir. Mobile Ctr. U. Ala., 1960-63; pres. U. South Ala., Mobile, 1963—; mem. presdl. adv. com. Fed. Home Loan Bank, Atlanta. Contbr. articles to profl. jours. Chmn. Marine Environ Scis. Consortium. Named Outstanding Adminstr. in Ala., Am. Assn. Univ. Adminstrs., 1981. Mem. Am. Assn. Univ. Adminstrs., Fhi Kappa Phi. Lodge: Kiwanis (Mobile). Office: U South Alabama Pres Office Mobile AL 36688*

WHIDDON, THOMAS GAYLE, retired marketing executive; b. Chappell Hill, Tex., Aug. 1, 1916; s. Thomas Eugene an Melissa (Smith) W.; m. Virginia Cotten, Apr. 2, 1941. Engrng./bus. adminstrn./mktg. student, U. Houston, 1935-41. Contract svc. mgr. shell and aircraft landing gear divsn. Hughes Tool Co., Houston, 1943-45, adv. dept., 1946-47; export office mgr. Hughes Tool Co., N.Y.C., 1947-48; field sales rep. Hughes Tool Co., various counties, Tex., 1948-51; spl. sales rep. east Tex. to Fla. Hughes Tool Co., Shreveport, La., 1951-55; no. regional and Can. spl. rep. Hughes Tool Co., Tulsa, Okla., 1955-58; first sales coord. Hughes Tool Co., Tex., N.Mex., Colo., Ariz., 1958-59; regional mgr. Hughes Tool Co., Dallas, 1959-61; v.p. nat. exec. sales rep. Hughes Tool Co., Houston, 1961-81; founder/cons. Gayle Whiddon Co., Houston, 1981—; Petroleum Adminstr. of Def. Korean War, Washington, 1951-52; cons. Hughes Tool Co., Houston, 1981-83; asst. to chmn. bd. Wilson Supply and Wilson Industries, 1983-85. Mem. Am. Petroleum Inst., Petroleum equipment Supplies Assn., Soc. Petroleum Engring., Internat. Assn. Drilling Contractor, Nat. Oil Equipment Mfrs. and Dels. Soc., (v.p. Dallas/Ft. Worth chpt.) NOMA DS, Houston Petroleum Club, Braeburn Country Club (Houston). Office: Gayle Whiddon Co 12326 Mossycup Dr Houston TX 77024-4907

WHIGHAM, MARK ANTHONY, computer scientist; b. Mobile, Ala., Jan. 14, 1959; s. Tommie Lee Sr. and Callie Mae (Molette) W. BS in Computer Sci., Ala. A&M U., 1983, MS in Computer Sci., 1990; postgrad., Ala. A&M Univ., 1995—. Computer programmer U.S. Army Corps of Engrs., Huntsville, Ala., 1985-88; programmer analyst, coord. acad. computing Ala. A&M U., Normal, Ala., 1988-89; programmer analyst II, DEC systems coord., instr. part-time computer sci. dept. Ala. A&M U., 1989-91; systems engr. Advanced Bus. Cons. Inc.-La. div. Dow Chem. Co., 1991-93; owner Whigham's Computer Cons., 1990—; sys. engr. DOW Chem. Co.-USA La. Divsn., Plaquemine, La., 1991-93; instr. computer info. system Calhoun C.C., Decatur, Ala., 1993—; network specialist/cons. Ala. A&M U., Normal, 1994—; computer info. sys. instr. Calhoun C.C., Decatur, Ala., 1994—; instr. computer sci. dept. Ala. A&M U., 1989-91; network specialist, cons. Ala. A&M U., Normal, 1994—. Active Huntsville Interdenominational Ministerial Fellowship, Huntsville, 1984. Mem. Nat. Assn. Sys. Programmers, Ala. Coun. for Computer Edn., Assn. for Computing Machinery, Huntsville Jaycees, Nat. Soc. Black Engrs., So. Poetry Assn., Nat. Arts Soc., Internat. Black Writers and Artists Assn., Optimists, Sigma Tau Epsilon, Alpha Phi Omega. Baptist. Home: 1507 C Barrington Rd Huntsville AL 35816 Office: Calhoun CC Bus Divsn PO Box 2216 Decatur AL 35609-2216

WHIGHAM, THOMAS LYLE, historian, educator; b. San Diego, Feb. 2, 1955; s. Frank Frederick and Laura Frances (Davis) W.; m. Marta Carolina Fernandez, Oct. 10, 1987; children: Paul Alexander, Nicholas Isaac. BA, U. Calif., Santa Cruz, 1977; AM, Stanford U., 1979, PhD, 1986. Assoc. prof. U. Ga., Athens, 1986—; vis. lectr. San Francisco State U., 1985, U. Calif., Riverside, 1985-86, Calif. Poly., Pomona, 1985-86, Calif. State U., San Bernardino, 1986. Author: The Politics of River Trade, 1991, La Yerba Mate del Paraguay, 1991; editor: Economía y sociedad en la intendencia del Paraguay, 1990. Recipient Fulbright grant, 1989, 92, Sarah Moss grant U. Ga., 1988, grant Am. Philos. Soc., 1992. Mem. Com. Latin Am. History, Latin Am. Studies Assn., Centro Paraguayo de Estudios Paraguayos, Southeastern Coun. Latin Am. Studies. Democrat. Office: Univ Ga Dept History Leconte Hall Athens GA 30602

WHINERY, MICHAEL ALBERT, physician; b. Watsford, Eng., June 30, 1951; s. Leo Howard and Doris Eileene W. and Alma Piper; m. Tatjiana Dunnebier, 1976 (dec. Jan. 1981); m. Judy Renee Wright, Apr. 30, 1982; children: Rhiannon Daire Eileene, Terron Rae Lee. BS, Okla. U., 1976; D of Osteopathy, Okla. State U., 1980. Bd. cert. physician in gen. practice. Intern Hillcrest Health Ctr., Oklahoma City, Okla., 1980-81; with McLoud Clinic, McLoud, Okla.; house physician McLoud Nursing Ctr., 1988—; med. examiner Pottawatomie County Health, McLoud, 1983—. Author: Poetic Voices of America, 1991. Mem. Presdl. Order Merit Nat. Repub. Senatorial Com., Washington, 1991, Presdl. Task Force, 1983—, Senatorial Commn. Repub. Senatorial Inner Circle, Washington, 1991; mem. U.S. Congrl. Adv. Bd., 1993. With USMC, Vietnam. Recipient Acknowledgement of Outstanding Contbn. in Clin. Rsch. award SANDOZ Labs., 1992, Rep. Presdl. Legion of Merit, 1994. Mem. Am. Legion, C. of C., Jr. C. of C., U.S. Senatorial Club (preferred mem.), U.S. Congressional Act Bd. (state advisor 1990-91). Baptist. Office: McLoud Clinic PO Box 520 107 S Main Mc Loud OK 74851

WHISENAND, JAMES DUDLEY, lawyer; b. Iowa City, Aug. 14, 1947; s. J.D. and Barbara Pauline (Huxford) W. BA in Mktg. cum laude, U. No. Iowa, 1970; MBA, Fla. State U., 1973, JD cum laude, 1973. Bar: Fla. 1973, U.S. Dist. Ct. (no., mid. and so. dists.) Fla. 1974, U.S. Tax Ct. 1974, U.S. Ct. Appeals (11th cir.) 1975, U.S. Supreme Ct. 1976. Law clk. U.S. Dept. Justice, Fla., 1972, Office of Fla. Atty. Gen., 1971-73; asst. atty. gen. Tax Div., 1973-74; head adminstr. law div., 1974-75; cabinet counsel Atty. Gen. Office, Fla., 1975; dep. atty. gen. Fla., 1975-78; ptnr. Sage, Gray, Todd & Sims, N.Y.C., Miami, 1979-81; of counsel Paul & Thomson, Miami, 1981-82; founding ptnr. Hornsby & Whisenand, Miami, 1982-90, Whisenand & Assocs., P.A., Miami, 1990-91; ptnr. Patton Boggs & Blow, Washington and Miami, 1991-93; founding ptnr. Whisenand & Turner, P.A., Miami, Fla., 1993—; pres. Americas Conf. Corp., 1994—. Publ.: The Cuba Report, 1992—; contbr. articles to profl. jours. Bd. advisors New World Sch. Arts, Miami, 1988; bd. dirs. Fla. State U. Sch. Law Alumni Assn., 1988-89; bd. trustees U. No. Iowa Found., 1993—; mem. bd. advisors Ctrl. European (Euromoney). Mem. Fla. Bar Assn., D.C. Bar Assn., Inter-Am. Bar Assn., Internat. Bar Assn., Greater Miami C. of C., European Forum. Office: Whisenand & Turner PA 501 Brickell Key Dr Ste 200 Miami FL 33131-2608

WHISENANT, B(ERT) R(OY), JR., insurance company executive; b. Brownsville, Tex., Oct. 10, 1950; s. Bert R. and Jimmie Lee (Tallon) W.; m. Margaret Elizabeth Bugge, Aug. 21, 1970; children: Michelle, Bert III, Bryan, Monette. BBA in Ins., S.W. Tex. State U., 1972. Ptnr. Bert Whisenant Ins., McAllen, Tex., 1972—; pres. JJ & BW, Inc. Investment Co., McAllen, 1987—; bd. dirs. Ind. Agy., Inc., Harlingen, Tex., 1977—. Contbr. articles to Tex. Insuror, 1984. Recipient Blue Ribbon Honors award Aetna Life and Casualty, Co., 1974, Charter Pacesetter award West Coast Life Ins. Co., 1982. Mem. Ind. Ins. Agts. Am. (bd. dirs. 1984—), Ind. Ins. Agts. Tex. (com. person 1986—), Ind. Ins. Agts. McAllen (pres. 1985-86), Associated Risk Mgrs. of Tex., Upper Valley Life Underwriters (sec.-treas. 1978), Jaycees (bd. dirs., chaplain 1974). Republican. Lodges: Optimists (pres. McAllen club 1986), Rotary. Office: 816 E Hackberry Ave Mcallen TX 78501-5739

WHITACRE, EDWARD E., JR., telecommunications executive; b. Ennis, Tex., Nov. 4, 1941. BS in Indsl. Engring., Tex. Tech U., 1964. With Southwestern Bell Telephone Co., 1963-85; various positions in ops. depts. Tex., Ark., Kans.; pres. Kans. div. Topeka, 1984-85; group pres. Southwestern Bell Corp., 1985-86; v.p. revenues and pub. affairs, vice-chmn., chief fin. officer Southwestern Bell Corp., St. Louis, 1986-88, pres., chief oper. officer, 1988-89, chmn., chief exec. officer, 1990—, also bd. dirs.; bd. dirs. Anheuser-Busch Cos., Inc., May Dept. Stores Co., Emerson Electric Co., Burlington No., Inc. Bd. regents Tex. Tech. U. and Health Scis., Lubbock; mem. exec. bd. nat. coun. and so. region Boy Scouts Am. Presbyterian. Office: SBC Communications Inc PO Box 2933 175 E Houston St 6th Fl San Antonio TX 78205*

WHITAKER, BRUCE EZELL, college president; b. Cleveland County, N.C., June 27, 1921; m. Esther Adams, Aug. 22, 1947; children: Barry Eugene, Garry Bruce. BA, Wake Forest U., 1944; BD, So. Bapt. Theol. Sem., 1947, ThM, 1948, PhD, 1950; postgrad., George Peabody Coll., 1952; DL, Wake Forest U., 1987. Ordained to ministry Bapt. Ch., 1945; pastor Smithfield, Ky., 1945-49; instr. sociology and philosophy Ind. U., 1947-50; prof. religion Cumberland U., Lebanon, Tenn., 1950-51, Belmont Coll., Nashville, 1951-52; prof. sociology, asst. to pres. Shorter Coll., Rome, Ga., 1952-53; asso. pastor, minister edn. Atlanta, 1953-54; state sec., student dept. Bapt. State Conv., N.C., 1954-57; pres. Chowan Coll., Murfreesboro, N.C., 1957-89, pres. emeritus, 1989—; mem. adv. com. to Nd. Higher Edn., 1962-66; to N.C. Commn. Higher Edn. Facilities, 1964—; pres. N.C. Conf. Social Svc., 1965-67, Assn. Governing Bds., 1973-82, Assn. So. Baptist Colls. and Schs., 1967-68, Assn. Eastern N.C. Colls., 1968-69; bd. dirs. Regional Edn. Lab. for Carolinas and Va. Pres. bd. trustees N.C. Found. Church-Related Colls., 1970-74; bd. dirs., v.p. Nat. Coun. Ind. Jr. Colls., 1974-75, pres., 1975-76; mem. adv. coun. presidents Assn. Governing Bds., from 1973; mem. N.C. Bd. Mental Health, from 1966; bd. dirs. Am. Assn. Cmty. and Jr. Colls., 1976-82; pres. N.C. Assn. Colls. and Univs., 1977-78; chmn. N.C. Commn. Mental Health/Mental Retardation Sers., 1978-81; mem. N.C. Commn. on Mental Health, Developmental Disabilities, and Alcohol and Drug Svcs., 1995—. V.p. Bapt. State Conv. N.C., 1989-91. Named Tarheel of Week Raleigh News and Observer, 1962, Boss of Year N.C. Jaycees, 1972; tribute paid in Congl. Record, 1962, 89; Whitaker Libr. at Chowan Coll. named for him; Whitaker Sch. at Butner, N.C. named for him; selected one of nation's 18 most effective coll. pres. in 1985, funded study Exxon Found.; featured in We the People of North Carolina, 1989. Mem. N.C. Lit. and Hist. Assn. (pres. 1970-71), Am. Acad. Polit. and Social Scis., NEA, Am. Assn. Community and Jr. Colls. (dir. 1976-82, Leadership Recognition award 1989), Nat. Assn. Ind. Colls. and Univs (dir. 1977-78, 81-85), Am. Assn. Higher Edn., Am. Coun. Edn. (bd. dirs. 1985-89), Internat. Platform Assn., Omicron Delta Kappa. Clubs: Capital City (Raleigh, N.C.), Capitol Club (Raleigh); Rotary (chmn. dist. student exchange com. 1969-72, Paul Harris fellow); Optimist; Beechwood Country (Ahoskie, N.C.); Harbor (Norfolk, Va.). Office: PO Drawer 40 Murfreesboro NC 27855-0040

WHITAKER, C. BRUCE, postal worker; b. Asheville, N.C., Oct. 28, 1953; s. Clyde Maskel and Elizabeth (Ingle) W. BA, U. N.C., 1974. Machine operator Beacon Mfg. Co., Swannanoa, N.C., 1974-76; coord. Eaton-Cutler Hammer, Arden, N.C., 1976-81; customer svc. rep. U.S. Postal Svc., Asheville, 1981—; bd. dirs. Cane Creek Cemetery, Fairview, N.C. Author: The Whitaker Family NC, 1989; contbr. articles to profl. jours. Registrar Buncombe County Bd. Election, Swannanoa, 1977-85; election supervisor Swannanoa Fire Dept., 1980-83; libr. vol. Old Buncombe County Genealog. Soc., Asheville, 1981-89; dept. sec. First Bapt. Ch., Swannanoa, 1974-80, 86—. Recipient Family History Book award N.C. Soc. of Historians, 1989, Foster Sondley award Old Buncombe County Genealog. Soc., 1989. Mem. Cane Creek Cemetery Assn. (treas. 1985—). Republican. Southern Baptist. Home: 661 Old Fort Rd Fairview NC 28730 Office: US Postal Svc 1302 Patton Ave Asheville NC 28816

WHITAKER, EVANS PARKER, academic administrator; b. Shelby, N.C., Nov. 4, 1960; s. Howard Vernon and Helen Louise (Parker) W. BSBA, Gardner-Webb U., 1983; MEd in Instn. Mgmt., Vanderbilt U., 1986, postgrad., 1991—. Dir. found. and corp. rels. Gardner-Webb U., Boiling Springs, N.C., 1983-86; exec. asst. to pres. Gardner-Webb Coll., Boiling Springs, N.C., 1986-88, assoc. v.p., 1990-92; v.p. devel. Wingate (N.C.) U., 1992-96; dir. endowment and trust devel. N.C. Bapt. Found., Cary, 1988-90; dir. development Belmont U., Nashville, 1996—; bd. dirs. Bapt. Employee Credit Union, Cary. President Boiling Springs Rotary, 1988; mem. Shelby (N.C.) Rotary, 1991. Vanderbilt U. scholar, 1985; recipient Resolution of Appreciation, Gardner-Webb U., 1987, 88. Mem. Coun. for Advancement and Support of Edn. Home: 420-1004 Elmington Ave Nashville TN 37205 Office: Belmont Univ 1900 Belmont Blvd Nashville TN 37212-3758

WHITAKER, FREDERICK STAMEY, pilot; b. Galax, Va., Apr. 8, 1960; s. Baxter Dale and Phyllis Ann (Johnson) W.; m. Janet Faye Redwine, May 5, 1955; 1 child, Allison Claire. AAS in Aviation, Cen. Tex. Coll., 1988. Lic. comml. pilot-helicopter and fixed wing FAA. Chief warrant officer 3, pilot U.S. Army, 1982-93; pilot Columbia Helicopters, Portland, Oreg., 1994; owner, operator P.C. House Calls, Fayetteville, N.C., 1995—; cons. Advanced Internet Tech., Fayetteville, 1996—. Founder Neighbors, Fayetteville, 1993. Republican. Home: 313 N Churchill Dr Fayetteville NC 28303

WHITAKER, HALFORD SNYDER, physician; b. Oliver Springs, Tenn., July 27, 1934; s. Lorenzo Robert and Virginia Belle (Snyder) W. BS, U. S.C., 1954; MD, U. Tenn., 1956. Cert. Am. Bd. Pediatrics, Am. Bd. Emergency Medicine, Am. Bd. Family Practice (Geriatrics). Intern Regional Med. Ctr., Memphis, 1956-57; resident pediatrics U. Tenn., U. Ky., Emory U., 1960-62; fellow pediatric neurology Harvard U., 1964; asst. resident internal medicine New Eng. Deaconess Hosp., 1965; tchr. Med. Coll. Ga., 1966-68, U. Tenn., Knoxville, 1968-69, 73-74; dir. Eval. Ctr. Eastern Tenn., 1969-70; physician emergency medicine Babies Hosp., Wrightsville Beach, N.C., 1970-71, Morristown, Tenn., 1971-77, various orgns., Fla., S.C., N.C., Ga., Tenn., 1977-92; med. dir. Sandhills Med. Found., McBee, S.C., 1992—. Contbr. articles to profl. jours. With USPHS, 1958-60. Fellow Am. Acad. Pediatrics, Am. Coll. Emergency Physicians (charter mem.), Acad. Family Practice; mem. So. Med. Assn. Office: Sandhills Med Found Hwy One Mc Bee SC 29101-0366

WHITAKER, RUTH REED, retired newspaper editor; b. Blytheville, Ark., Dec. 13, 1936; d. Lawrence Neill and Ruth Shipton (Weidemeyer) Reed; m. Thomas Jefferson Whitaker, dec. 29, 1961; children: Steven Bryan, Alicia Morrow. BA, Hendrix Coll., 1958. Copywriter, weather person KTVE TV, El Dorado, Ark., 1958-59; nat. bridal cons. Treasure House, El Dorado, 1959; bridal cons. Pfeifers of Ark., Little Rock, 1959-60; dir. of continuity S. M. Brooks Advt. Agy., Little Rock, 1960-61; layout artist C. V. Mosby Co., St. Louis, 1961-62; editor, owner Razorback Am. Newspaper, Ft. Smith, Ark., 1979-81; ret., 1981. Host Crawford Conversations TV show; contbr. author indsl. catalog, 1979 (Addy award). State sec. Rep. Party of Ark., 1992-94; mem. Ben Geren Regional Park Commn., Sebastian County, Ark., 1984-89, pres., 1990; past pres. Jr. Civic League; mem. Ft. Smith Orchid Com.; mem. com. of 21 United Way; publicity chmn. Sebastian County Rep. Com., 1983-84; state press officer Reagan-Bush Campaign, 1984; exec. dir. Ark. Dole for Pres., 1995-96; pres. Women's Aux. Sebastian County Med. Soc., 1974; mem. Razorback Scholarship Fund; class agt. alumni fund Hendrix Coll., 1990, 91, 92; mem. Sparks Woman's Bd.; 1st vice chmn. 3d Dist. Rep. Party; state committeewoman Rep. Party Ark. Recipient Disting. Vol. Leadership award Nat. Found. March of Dimes, 1973, Appreciation award Ft. Smith Advt. Fedn., 1977, 78, Hon. Parents of Yr. award U. Ark., 1984, Recognition award United Cerebral Palsy, 1980. Mem. AAUW, Alden Soc. Am. (life), Ft. Smith C. of C., Ark. Nature Conservancy, Am. Legion Aux., Frontier Rschrs. Soc. (pres. 1995-96), Daus. Union Vets. Presbyterian. Home: PO Box 349 Cedarville AR 72932-0178

WHITAKER, SHIRLEY ANN, telecommunications company marketing executive; b. Asmara, Eritea, Ethiopia, Oct. 13, 1955; (parents Am. citizens); d. Calvin Randall and Ruth (Ganeles) Peck; m. John Marshall Whitaker, June 16, 1973; l child, Kathryn Ann. AA, Tacoma Community Coll., 1974; BA, Wash. State U., 1977, MBA, 1978. Planning adminstr. for econ. rsch. GTE NW, Everett, Wash., 1978-80; specialist in demand analysis western region GTE Svc. Corp., Los Gatos, Calif., 1980-81; fin. analyst GTE Svc. Corp., Stamford, Conn., 1981-83, staff specialist demand analysis and forecasting, 1983-84; group mgr. for rate devel. Nat. Exch. Carrier Assn., Whippany, N.J., 1984-87; mgr. pricing strategy and migration GTE Calif., Thousand Oaks, 1987-88; mgr. market forecasting GTE Telephone Ops. Hdqrs., Irving, Tex., 1989-90, dir. revenue analysis, 1990-92, dir. market rsch., 1992-93, dir. process re-engring., 1993-94; dir. network and resource mgmt., 1994—. Mem. Am. Mktg. Assn. (membership com. 1984), Beta Gamma Sigma, Phi Kappa Phi.

WHITAKER, VON BEST, nursing educator; b. New Bern, N.C.; d. Cleveland W. and Lillie (Bryant) Best; m. Roy Whitaker Jr., Aug. 9, 1981; 1 child, Roy Whitaker III. BS, Columbia Union Coll., 1972; MS, U. Md., 1974; MA, U. N.C., 1980, PhD, 1983. Lectr. U. N.C., Chapel Hill, 1981-82; asst. prof. U. Mo., Columbia, Mo., 1982-85; asst. prof. grad. sch. Boston Coll., Newton, Mass., 1985-86; asst. prof. U. Tex. Health Sci. Ctr., San Antonio, 1986-94; assoc. prof. Ga. So. U., Statesboro, 1994—; mem. cataract guideline panel Agy. for Health Care Policy Rsch., 1990-93; rsch. coord. glaucoma svc. Georgia Eye Inst., Savannah. Contbr. articles to profl. jours., chpts. to textbooks; presenter in field. Vol. to prevent blindness. Bush fellowship, 1979-81; recipient Cert. of Appreciation, Prevent Blindness South Tex., 1988, 89. Mem. ANA (cert. community health nurse), APHA, Am. Soc. Ophthalmic Nursing (chair rsch. com.), Assn. Black Faculty in Higher Edn., Nat. Black Nurses Assn., Sigma Theta Tau. Home: 1 Chelmsford Ln Savannah GA 31411

WHITAKER, WILMA NEUMAN, mathematics instructor; b. Chgo., Aug. 18, 1937; d. August P. and Wilma M. (Kaiser) Neuman; m. G.D. Whitaker, Mar. 28, 1970; children: Brett Allan Karlsen, Karen J. Whitaker Laflin, Mark D. Whitaker, David R. Whitaker. BA in Math., DePauw U., 1959; MEd in Math., Francis Marion Coll., 1988. Cert. secondary tchr., Ill., Mich., S.C.; cert. realtor Mich. High sch. math tchr. Dist. 209, Hillside, Ill., 1959-61, Dist. 214, Mt. Prospect, Ill., 1961-65; apprentice pharmacist Karlsen Pharmacy, Mt. Prospect, 1961-67; realtor Durbin Co., Clarkston, Mich., 1977-81; substitute tchr. Clarkston (Mich.) Community Schs., 1979-80; math instr. Florence (S.C.)-Darlington Tech. Coll., 1981-85, math dept. head, 1985-87, dean arts and scis., 1987-95, instr. math., 1995—. Stephen min. St. Lukes Luth. Ch., Florence, 1991—, coun., 1989-92, tchr., 1981—; founder, organizer Spring Cmty. Walk Along Rotary Beauty Trail, Florence, 1988, 89, 91. Named Faculty Mem. of Yr., Florence-Darlington Tech. Coll., 1987, Adminstr. of Yr., 1992, Exec. of Yr., Florence chpt. Profl. Secs. Internat., 1993. Mem. ASTD, AAUW, Am. Assn. Women in C.C.s, Am. Assn. C.C.s, S.C. Assn. Devel. Educators, S.C. Assn. Math. Tchrs. Two-Yr. Colls., S.C. Tech. Edn. Assn., S.C. Women in Higher Edn., Optimist Club of Florence (v.p. 1991-92, pres. 1992-93), Optimist Internat. (lt. gov. Zone 6 S.C. 1993-94, 95-96, gov.-elect S.C. dist. 1994-95, gov. 1995-96), Theta Sigma Phi, Delta Zeta. Office: Florence-Darlington Tech Coll PO Box 100548 Florence SC 29501-0548

WHITBY, RODNEY SCOTT, internist, pediatrician; b. Dyersburg, Tenn., Apr. 3, 1965; s. Willie D. Whitby and Betty Ann (White) Williams; m. Karen Remae, Oct. 29, 1994. BS, Memphis State U., 1987; MD, U. Tenn., Memphis, 1991. Diplomate Am. Bd. Internal Medicine, Am. Bd. Pediatrics. Resident in internal medicine and pediatrics U. Tenn., 1991-95, chief resident in internal medicine, 1995-96; pvt. practice, Paris, Tenn., 1996—; emergency physician Henry County Med. Ctr., Paris, 1994-96; med. cons. Boystown Youth Villages, Memphis, 1996-96. Contbr. articles to profl. jours. Fellow Am. Acad. Pediatrics; mem. ACP. Office: East Wood Clinic 1323 E Wood St Paris TN 38242

WHITCOMB, CARL ERVIN, horticulturist, researcher; b. Independence, Kans., Oct. 26, 1939; s. Albion Carlyle and Marie V. (Burck) W.; m. LaJean C. Carpenter, June 2, 1963; children: Andrew Carl, Benjamin Dwight. BS, Kans. State U., Manhattan, 1964; MS, Iowa State U., 1966, PhD, 1969. Asst. prof. horticulture U. Fla., Gainesville, 1967-72; prof. horticulture Okla. State U., Stillwater, 1972-85; pres. Lacebark Inc, Stillwater, 1985—; cons. Sierra Chem. Co., Milpitas, Calif., 1987-90. Author: Know It and Grow It, 1975, rev., 1978, 80, 85, 95, Plant Production in Containers, 1984, rev., 1990, Establishment and Maintenance of Landscape Plants, 1989, Production of Landscape Plants, 1991. Recipient Chadwick award Am. Assn. Nurserymen, 1983, Wight award So. Nurserymens Assn., 1986. Fellow Internat. Plant Propagators Soc.; mem. Am. Soc. Hort. Sci., Am. Soc. Agronomy, Weed Sci. Soc. Am. Office: Lacebark Inc PO Box 2383 Stillwater OK 74076

WHITE, ALBERT CORNELIUS, entomologist, researcher; b. Clearwater, Fla., July 17, 1927; s. Jack F. and Mary C. White; m. Frances L. White; children: Albert C. Jr., J. Patrick, Stephen M.; stepchildren: Gary A. Young, Kenneth E. Young. BS, Clemson U., 1951; MS, U. Wis., 1953. With rsch. dept. Chevron Chem. Co., Goldsboro, N.C., 1953-56, Columbia, S.C., 1956-59, McAllen, Tex., 1959-62, Orlando, Fla., 1962-67, Fresno, Calif., 1967-69, San Jose, Costa Rica, 1969-73; rsch. mgr. Chevron Chem. Co., Tokyo, 1973-76; entomologist Fla. Arthropod Rsch. Lab., Panama City, 1976-78; cons. Orlando, 1978—. With USMC. Mem. Entomol. Soc. Am., Fla. Entomol. Soc. (pres. 1983), Fla. Mosquito Control Assn., Fla. State Hort. Soc., Internat. Soc. Citriculture, Mex. Entomol. Soc. Home: 817 Fairbanks Ave Orlando FL 32804-2044

WHITE, ALICE VIRGINIA, volunteer health corps administrator; b. Wichita, Kans., June 30, 1946; d. Harry Houston White and Margaret V. (Milligan) Gabbert. BA in Russian (hons.) and Spanish, U. Kans., 1967; PhD in Journalism, U. Tex., 1991. Tchr. Russian and Spanish Ingalls Sch. Dist., Kansas City, Mo., 1967-72; instr. Dodge City (Kans.) C.C., 1972-73, 84; tchr. Arrowhead West, Inc., 1984-85; asst. dir. Ctr. for Bus. & Industry Dodge City (Kans.) Community Coll., 1984-85, dir. community rels. and resource devel., 1985-87; co-founder, treas. Breitenbach Farms, Inc., Dodge City, 1970-79, pres., 1979-85; asst. to dean for devel. Coll. Comm., U. Tex., Austin, 1990-93, asst. instr. journalism, 1988-90, lectr. pub. rels., 1992; asst. immunization strategic coord. Tex. Dept. Health, Austin, 1993-95, coord. spl. health initiatives, 1995-96; dir. Tex. Vol. Health Corps, 1996—; media judge Headliners Found., Austin, 1989, Tex. Hosp. Assn., 1990, 91; dir. job placement Kans. Elks Tng. Ctr. for Handicapped, 1984-85; mgr. dental office, 1973-83; bd. dirs. Dispute Resolution Ctr., 1992-93. Treas. Ford County Hist. Soc., 1972-77, Ofcl. Bicentennial Com. Ford County, 1975-77; active Leadership Kans., 1986, Leadership Austin, 1990-91; co-founder Leadership Dodge, 1987; founder Walk-a-Dog project Williamson County SPCA, Austin State Sch., 1991; media judge Tex. PTA, 1992, Tex. Med. Assn., 1993; mem. chancellors coun. U. Tex. Sys.; mem. endowment com. United Way Capital Area. Recipient Most Creative Vol. Project award Tex. Mental Health and Mental Retardation, 1992, Athena winner Women's C. of C., 1987, Kans. PRIDE honoree, 1988; U. Tex. fellow, 1987-89; named of one of 100 Best-Managed Farms in U.S., Farm Futures Mgr., 1983. Mem. AAUW (pres. Kans. 1979-81, gift honoree 1973, 81, 91), Nat. Assn. Individual Investors (life), Pub. Rels. Soc. Am. (mentor, profl. advisor U. Tex.), Tex. Pub. Rels. Soc. (bd. dirs. 1993), Women in Comm. (liaison to student chpt. 1989-91), Tex. Exes Alumni Assn. (life), U. Kans. Alumni Assn. (nat. bd. dirs. 1977-82), Austin C. of C., U. Tex. Pres.' Assocs., U. Kans. Chancellor's Club, Austin-Travis County Humane Soc. (life), Waterloo Benevolent Soc. of United Way Capital Area, Phi Beta Kappa, Phi Kappa Phi. Home: 5914 Upvalley Run Austin TX 78731-3669 Office: Tex Dept Health Comms & Spl Health Initiatives 1100 W 49th St Austin TX 78756-3101

WHITE, ANN WELLS, community activist; b. Kansas City, Mo., Mar. 16, 1927; d. William Gates and Annie Loretta (Morton) Wells; m. Norman E. White, Oct. 2, 1949 (div. Dec. 1977); children: Thomas Wells, Norman Lee. BJ, U. Mo., 1948. Asst. to pres. Cities in Schs., 1978-79. Lobbyist Common Cause, Atlanta, 1972-73; vol. Jimmy Carter's Peanut Brigade, 1976, Carter/Mondale campaign, 1980; bd. dirs., vice chair Atlanta Area Svcs. for the Blind, 1973-81; Gov.'s Commn. on the Status of Women, Atlanta, 1974-76; office mgr. Carter/Mondale Transition Office, Atlanta, 1976; chair evaluation com. United Way Met. Atlanta, 1980-90; bd. dirs. Mems. Guild, The High Mus. of Art, Atlanta, 1982-83, Hillside Hosp., Atlanta, 1989-94, Ga. Forum, Atlanta, 1988-91; bd. dirs. Planned Parenthood of Atlanta area, 1975-89, pres., 1978-81; bd. dirs. Planned Parenthood Fedn. Am., N.Y.C., 1980-86, chair ann. meeting, New Orleans, 1986; legis. chair, lobbyist Ga. Women's Polit. Caucus, 1984-90; convenor, founding chair Georgians for Choice, 1989. Democrat. Presbyterian. Home: Colony House 1237 145 Fifteenth St Atlanta GA 30309

WHITE, ANNETTE JONES, early childhood education administrator; b. Albany, Ga., Aug. 29, 1939; d. Paul Lawrence and Delores Christine (Berry) Jones; m. Frank Irvin White, Nov. 13, 1964; children: Melanie Francine, Sharmian Lynell. BA, Spelman Coll., 1964; MEd, Va. State U., 1980. Tchr. Flint Ave Child Devel. Ctr., Albany, 1966-67; tchr., supr. Flintside Child Devel. Ctr., Albany, 1967-68; tchr., dir. Albany Ga. Community Sch., 1968-69; tchr. Martin Luther King Community Ctr., Atlanta, 1975-77, The Appleton Sch., Atlanta, 1977-78; sec., proofreader The Atlanta Daily World, 1978-80; tchr. kindergarten Spelman Coll., Atlanta, 1981-88, dir. nursery and kindergarten, lectr. in edn., 1988—; cons., presenter child devel. assoc. program Morris Brown Coll., Atlanta, 1991; presenter ann. child care conf. Waycross (Ga.) Coll., 1993. Contbr. articles to profl. jours. Mem. Peace Action, Washington, 1990—, Children's Def. Action Coun., Washington, 1990—; mem. Native Am. Rights Fund, Am. Indian Rights Coun. Mem. AAUW, ASCD, Acad. Am. Poets, Assn. Childhood Edn. Internat., Nat. Asn. Edn. Young Children, Nat. Black Child Devel. Inst., Ga. Assn. Young Children (cons., presenter 1992), Nat. Coun. Negro Women, Atlanta Assn. Edn. Young Children, Sierra Club. Office: Spelman Coll Nursery-Kinder 350 Spelman Ln SW # 89 Atlanta GA 30314-4346

WHITE, BETTY MAYNARD, retired social worker; b. N.Y.C., May 22, 1922; d. William and Madge (Hooks) Maynard; B.A., Hunter Coll., 1964; M.S.W., Columbia U., 1969; m. Charles E. White, Sept. 8, 1941; 1 child, Charles B. Case worker Bur. Child Welfare, Jamaica, N.Y., 1964-69; supr. foster care Spl. Services for Children, Jamaica, 1969-73, case supr. application sec., family services, group services, 1973-83, supr. III, borough coordinator for Manhattan and Bronx, Office Home Care Services, Div. Med. Rev., 1983-84, dir. div. Med. Rev., 1984; pvt. practice, 1986-90. Mem. Nat. Assn. Social Workers, Acad. Cert. Social Workers, Hunter Coll. Alumni Assn. Democrat. Roman Catholic. Home: 3720 Dorrington Dr Las Vegas NV 89129

WHITE, BRIAN DOUGLAS, public relations executive; b. Lafayette, Tenn., Oct. 2, 1956; s. J. Robert and Hazel Christine (Deckard) W.; m. Rita Fay Breeding, June 6, 1977; children: Briann Douglas, Westly Ryan, Alexander Demps. BS in English and Journalism, Tenn. Tech. U., 1979. Accredited bus. communicator. Staff writer The Dispatch, Cookeville, Tenn., 1976-77; asst. dir. info. svcs. Tenn. Farm Bur. Fedn., Columbia, Tenn., 1979-81; mktg. communications coord. Fla. Power Corp., St. Petersburg, 1981-85, pub. info. specialist, 1985-86; pub. affairs mgr. GTE Telephone Ops.-Ga., Dalton, 1986-88; pub. affairs dir. GTE Telephone Ops.-S.E., Durham, N.C., 1988-91; mgr. pub. affairs planning GTE Telephone Ops., Irving, Tex., 1991-93, dir. employee comms., 1993—. Bd. dirs. Jr. Achievement, Dalton, Ga., 1987; active pub. rels. com. Bus. Coun. Ga., Atlanta, 1988; bd. dirs. Durham Coalition on Chem. Dependency, Durham, 1990-91; troop leader Oconeechee Coun. Boy Scouts Am., Durham, 1990-91; active mktg. com. United Way of Greater Durham, 1990-91. Named Jaycee of Month, Jaycees, St. Petersburg, 1983, Outstanding Young Man of Yr., 1984; recipient Mktg. Communications award of Distinction, Fla. Pub. Rels. Assn., Tampa, Fla., 1985. Mem. Internat. Assn. Bus. Communicators (chpt. bd. 1982-86, chpt. pres. 1986, dist. bd. 1986-89, accrediation bd. 1988-91, exec. bd. 1991—; chpt. svc. award Tampa, 1984, profl. devel. award 1986). Office: GTE Telephone Ops HQE04N13 600 Hidden Rdg Irving TX 75038-3809

WHITE, BRUCE DAVID, law and ethics educator; b. Elizabethton, Tenn., Jan. 10, 1951; s. Darold S. and Anna Ruth (Lewis) W.; m. Sarah Jo Pugh, Dec. 28, 1974; children: Sarah Elizabeth, Meredith Ruth, Rebecca Mae. B.S. in Pharmacy, U. Tenn., 1974, J.D., 1976; D.O., N. Tex. State U. Tex. Coll. Osteo. Medicine, 1985. Bar: Tenn. 1977, U.S. Dist. Ct. (we. dist.) Tenn. 1979; diplomate Am. Bd. Pediatrics. Asst. prof. U. Tenn. Health Scis. Ctr., Memphis, 1977-81, assoc. prof., 1981; lectr. U. Miss., Oxford, 1980-81; asst. prof. North Tex. State U. Tex. Coll. Osteo. Medicine, Fort Worth, 1981-85; ptnr. Swafford & White, Memphis, 1979-81; resident pediatrics U. Louisville, 1985-88; asst. prof. pediatrics Meharry Med. Coll., 1988-93; asst. prof., asst. dir. Ctr. Clin. Rsch. Ethics Vanderbilt U. Med. Ctr., 1988-94; fellow clin. med. ethics U. Chgo., 1989-91; dir. Clin. Ethics Ctr. St. Thomas Hosp., Nashville, 1993—. Author: (with H. Wetherbee) Cases and Materials on Pharmacy Law, 1980; (with W.B. Swafford) Tennessee Pharmacy Law Handbook, 1980, Mississippi Pharmacy Law Handbook, 1981. Fellow Am. Soc. Pharmacy Law, Am. Coll. Legal Medicine. Lodge: Masons. Office: Clin Ethics Ctr St Thomas Hosp 4220 Harding Rd Nashville TN 37205-2005

WHITE, BRUCE EMERSON, JR., restaurant chain executive; b. Winston-Salem, N.C., Feb. 26, 1961; s. Bruce Emerson and Earline Syble (Nelson) W.; m. Wendy Melynn Potter; children: Monica Joy, Nicole Melynn, Bryson Elliott. With Arby's, Inc., Ft. Lauderdale, Fla., 1977-92; field rep. Arby's, Inc., Miami, Fla., 1984-87, ops. devel. mgr., 1987-91, franchise dist. mgr., 1992; dist. mgr. Trefz & Trefz, Inc., Augusta, Ga., 1992—; owner White Market Enterprises, Uniform & Career Apparel, 1993—. Bd. dirs. resource com. Big Bros./Big Sisters Charlotte, N.C., 1995—. Republican. Mem. Ch. of Christ. Home: 1813 Stoney Fork Rd York SC 29745-8527

WHITE, CARL EDWARD, JR., pharmaceutical adminstrator; b. Huntington, W.Va., Apr. 4, 1955; s. Carl Edward Sr. and Peggy Joan (Church) W.; m. Denise Karen McDaniel, May 26, 1979; children: Daniel Aaron, David Kenton, Caitlin Ruth. BS, Purdue U., 1977; MBA, Ga. State U., 1996. Profl. sales rep. Ciba-Geigy Pharms., Huntington, 1977-85, dist. sales mgr., 1985-93; area bus. dir Ciba-Geigy Pharms., Atlanta, 1993-94; dist. bus. mgr. , Huntington, 1994—. Bd. dirs. Coventry Homeowners' Assn., Peachtree City, Ga., 1991, Park Brooke Homeowners' Assn., Alpharetta, Ga., 1996; chmn. deacons First Bapt. Ch., Peachtree City, 1992. Republican. So. Bapt. Home: 3905 Brookline Dr Alpharetta GA 30202

WHITE, (EDWIN) CHAPPELL, retired music educator; b. Atlanta, Sept. 16, 1920; s. Goodrich Cook and Helen Dean (Chappell) W.; m. Barbara Tyler, Aug. 22, 1959; children: Patricia Dean, Tyler Goodrich, Victoria Helen. BA, Emory U., 1940; MusB, Westminster Choir Coll., 1947; MFA, Princeton (N.J.) U., 1950, PhD, 1957. Instr. Agnes Scott Coll., Decatur, Ga., 1950-52; from asst. prof. to assoc. prof. Emory U., Atlanta, 1953-73; prof. music history Kans. State U., Manhattan, 1974-91; ret., 1991; vis. prof. U. Ga., Athens, 1970-71, Ind. U., Bloomington, 1972-73; violist Atlanta Symphony Orch., 1950-56; music critic Atlanta Jour., 1958-70. Author: Life & Works, Wagner, 1967, Catalog, Works of Viotti, 1985, From Vivaldi to Viotti: A History of the Early Classical Violin Concerto, 1992. Staff sgt. USAF, 1942-45, ETO. Rsch. grantee NEH, 1982; Brown Found. fellow U. of South, 1993. Mem. Am. Musicol. Soc. (chmn. South Cen. chpt.), Coll. Music Soc. (pres. 1979-80), Phi Kappa Phi, Pi Kappa Lambda. Democrat. Office: Kans State U Music Dept McCain Auditorium Manhattan KS 66506

WHITE, CHARLES EDWIN, real estate management company executive; b. Alexandria, La., Dec. 5, 1952; s. Charles Harvey White and Nita (Cooper) Mitchell; m. Robin Ellen Lewis, Dec. 4, 1976; children: Daniel P., C. Matthew. BS in Bldg. Tech., Auburn U., 1976; AS in Computer Programming, Data Processing Inst., Tampa, Fla., 1983. Chief field engr. BE&K, Inc., Birmingham, Ala., 1974-78; project mgr. Venture Constn. Co. Inc., Tampa, 1978-79; v.p. West Coast Comml. Contractors Inc., Port Richey, Fla., 1979-80; gen. mgr. C. White Constrn. Co., Inc., Tampa, 1980-82; project mgr. Puckett & Assocs., Tampa, 1982-84, Kroh Bros. Devel. Corp., Tampa, 1984-87; sr. project mgr. Western Devel. Corp., Cin., 1987-89; dir. ops., constrn. and property mgmt. Paran Mgmt. Co., Cleve., 1989-92; dir. ops. Rockwood Ltd., Atlanta, 1992—. Mem. Am. Inst. Constrn., Phi Kappa Psi. Republican. Methodist.

WHITE, DALE TIMOTHY (TIM WHITE), television journalist; b. Mt. Pleasant, Mich., May 12, 1949; s. Dale Glenn and Norma Jean (Lessender) W.; m. Basha Banczyk, Sept. 12, 1991 (div. Sept. 17, 1993); 1 child, Elizabeth Natalia. BA in Film and TV, Mich. State U., 1971; MA in Polit. Sci., U. So. Calif., 1975; PhD in Comm., U. Md., 1994. Exec. prodr. film and TV svc. U.S. State Dept./U.S. Info. Agy., Worldwide, 1975-80; pres. T White Comms., Arlington, Va., 1985—; chmn. Lives and Legacies Films, McLean, Va., 1994—; pres. First Person Films Inc., McLean, 1994—. Moderator PBS-TV TechnoPolitics, 1991-95; host Fox Morning News, 1990-92, FOX-TV Sightings, 1991-95, Network Cable, 1996—; host for CBS News, Turner Broadcasting, WorldNet. Bd. dirs. WAVE Inc., 1990—, Coun. on Internat. Non-Theatrical Events, 1995—. With USAF, 1971-75; col. USAFR, 1976—. Recipient CINE Golden Eagle awards, 1976-80, Emmy awards, 1991, 92. Mem. NATAS, AFTRA, Screen Actors Guild, Army Navy Country Club, Air Force Assn., Am. Legion, Reserve Officers Assn., Potomac Club, Cosmos Club, Nat. Press. Club. Congregationalist. Home: 1200 N Nash St Arlington VA 22209-3616

WHITE, DAVID ALAN, municipal official; b. Buffalo, July 13, 1947; s. William Thornton and Lois Magdeline (Mislin) W.; m. Sally Steward, Jan. 9, 1976; 1 child, Lindsay Elizabeth. Student, Clarkson Coll Tech, 1965-66; BA in English, SUNY, Buffalo, 1970; student, U. Ark., 1970, 71, 72; diploma, Revenue Sources Mgmt. Sch., 1983. Mgr. city pool Dept. Parks and Recreation, Fayetteville, Ark., 1973, asst. dir., 1973-75; asst. dir. Fayetteville Youth Ctr. and Boys Club, 1973-75; dir. Dept. of Parks and Recreation, Siloam Springs, Ark., 1976-79; exec. dir. Meadville (Pa.) Area Recreation Authority, 1979-86; dir. City of Palm Bay (Fla.) Parks and Recreation, 1986-96; mgr. City of Palm Bay Spl. Projects and Grants, 1996—; adv. Fla. Recreational Trails Coun., State Dept. of Environ. Protection. Contbr. articles to newspapers. Vol. Spl. Olympics, St. Jude Hosp., Pub. Schs.; bd. mem Brevard County Libr.; steering com. BCC Inst. of Govt. Mem. Nat. Recreation and Park Assn. (cert. leisure profl.), Fla. Recreation and Park Assn., Mid-Atlantic Ice Ring Mgrs. Assn. (founder), League of Am. Wheelmen, All-Am. Soap Box Derby (city dir.), Palm Bay Kiwanis. Home: 134 Copenhaver Ave NE Palm Bay FL 32907-3153 Office: City Hall 120 Malabar Rd SE Palm Bay FL 32907

WHITE, DAVID ALAN, JR., manufacturing company executive; b. Chgo., Feb. 18, 1942; s. David Alan and Janet (Fate) W.; m. Catherine Elizabeth Harman, June 12, 1971; children: Christopher Alan, John Michael. BS, U.S. Mil. Acad., 1964; MBA, U. Pa., 1971. Planning analyst Cooper Industries, Houston, 1971-74; exec. asst. The Cooper Group, Raleigh, 1974-76; v.p. fin. and planning Cooper Energy Svcs. Group, Mt. Vernon, Ohio, 1976-80; v.p., gen. mgr. Cooper Power Tools, Columbia, S.C., 1980-88; v.p. corp. planning and devel. Cooper Industries, 1988-96, sr. v.p. strategic planning, 1996—; dir. Wyman-Gordon Co. Capt. U.S. Army, 1964-69. Decorated Army Commendation medal. Republican. Episcopalian. Office: Cooper Industries Inc PO Box 4446 Houston TX 77210-4446

WHITE, DONALD FRANCIS, financial planner, insurance agent; b. Everett, Mass., Oct. 28, 1955; s. Donald Francis Sr. and Joan Frances (Cannatelli) W.; m. Grace Restrepo, May 10, 1975. MS in Fin. Svcs., Am. Coll., 1994. CLU, ChFC. Agt. N.Y. Life, Hollywood, Fla., 1976-79; sales mgr. Pacific Mutual Life, Coral Springs, Fla., 1979-82; owner Treasure Coast Fin. Svcs. former Donald F. White & Assocs., Ft. Lauderdale and Stuart, Fla., 1982—; speaker in field. Author: Legacy Leadership, Legacy Planning; broadcaster radio program Your Money From God's Perspective, 1993—. Bd. dirs. Martin County Estate Planning Coun., Stuart, 1988-95, pres., 1993-94; mem. Treasure Coast Planned Giving Coun., speaker liaison, 1993-94; bd. dirs., founder Treasure Coast Cmty. Ch., 1992—; active Leadership Martin County, 1995, bd., 1996. Named Agt. of Yr., Gen. Agt. and Mgrs. Assn. of the Palm Beaches, 1990. Mem. Am. Soc. CLU and ChFC, Am. Messianic Mission (bd. dirs. 1986-94), Nat. Assn. Life Underwriters (legis. liaison 1993-96, nat committeeman 1995—), Treasure Coast Assn. Life Underwriters (founder, bd. dirs. 1992—, nat. committeeman 1995—), Stuart/Martin County C. of C. (stategovt. affairs committeeman 1993-94, grad. leadership Martin County 1995-96), Assn. for Advanced Life Underwriting (polit. involvement committeeman 1994-96), Million Dollar Round Table (life, qualifying mem. 1986—, mem. productivity com. 1994—). Republican. Office: Treasure Coast Fin Svcs Inc Ste 300 901 SE Monterey Commons Blvd Stuart FL 34996-3339

WHITE, EDITH ROBERTA SHOEMAKE, elementary school educator; b. Hattiesburg, Miss., Feb. 24, 1948; d. Robert Ellis and Helen C.M. (Hinton) Shoemake; m. Robert Q. White, May 31, 1971. Student, Perkinston (Miss.) Jr. Coll., 1968; BS, U. So. Miss., 1970, MA, 1985. Cert. elem. tchr., Miss. Tchr. Ouachita Parish Schs., Monroe, La., Meridian (Miss.) City Schs., Lauderale County Schs., Meridian, Perry County Schs., New Augusta, Miss.; mid. sch. tchr. Hancock County Schs., Bay St. Louis, Miss., Pass Christian (Miss.) Pub. Schs. Dist. Mem. NEA, Miss. Assn. Educators. Methodist. Home: 124 Clower Ave Long Beach MS 39560-3302

WHITE, EDWARD ALFRED, lawyer; b. Elizabeth, N.J., Nov. 23, 1934. BS in Indsl. Engring., U. Mich., 1957, JD, 1963. Bar: Fla. 1963, U.S. Ct. Appeals (5th cir.) 1971, U.S. Supreme Ct. 1976, U.S. Ct. Appeals (11th cir.) 1981. Assoc. Jennings, Watts, Clarke & Hamilton, Jacksonville, Fla., 1963-66, ptnr., 1966-69; ptnr. Wayman & White, Jacksonville, 1969-72; pvt. practice, Jacksonville, 1972—; mem. aviation law com. Fla. Bar, 1972-94, chmn., 1979-81, bd. govs., 1984-88, admiralty com., 1984—, chmn., 1990-91, chmn. pub. relations com., 1986-88, exec. coun. trial lawyers sect., 1986-91. Fellow Am. Bar Found.; mem. ABA (vice chmn. admiralty law com. 1995—), Fla. Bar Assn. (bd. cert. civil trial lawyer, bd. cert. admiralty lawyer), Jacksonville Bar Assn. (chmn. legal ethics com. 1975-76, bd. govs. 1976-78, pres. 1979-80), Assn. Trial Lawyers Am. (sustaining mem. 1984—), Acad. Fla. Trial Lawyers (diplomate), Fla. Coun. Bar Assn. Pres.'s, Lawyer-Pilots Bar Assn., Am. Judicature Soc., Maritime Law Assn. (proctor in admiralty), Southeastern Admiralty Law Inst. (bd. dirs. 1982-84, chmn./pres. 1994). Home: 1959 Largo Rd Jacksonville FL 32207-3926 Office: 610 Blackstone Bldg Jacksonville FL 32202

WHITE, EDWARD GIBSON, II, lawyer; b. Lexington, Ky., Nov. 7, 1954; s. Russell Edwin White and Betty Lee White-Estabrook; m. Cynthia Ann Reisz, Mar. 10, 1979; children: Edward Gibson III, William Elliot, John Alexander, Albert Grahm. BA, U. Tenn., Chattanooga, 1980; JD, U. Tenn., Knoxville, 1983. Bar: Tenn. 1983, U.S. Dist. Ct. (ea. dist.) Tenn. 1984, U.S. Ct. Appeals (6th cir.) 1985. Assoc. Hodges, Doughty & Carson, Knoxville, 1983-87, ptnr., 1988—. Pledge vol. Knoxville Mus. Art, 1986—; vol. Winfield Dunn Gubernatorial Campaign, Tenn., 1985-86. Mem. ABA (litigation sect. 1985—), Tenn. Bar Assn. (interprofl. code com. 1989—, med./legal com. 1991—), Knoxville Bar Assn. (treas. 1995-96, continuing legal edn. com. 1985-86, 88-91, chmn. 1992-94, mem. naturalization com. 1985-87, bd. govs. 1993-94, pres. elect 1996, pres. 1997, Pres.'s award 1992), Tenn. Def. Lawyers Assn., Knox Bar Assn. (pres.-elect 1995-96), Def. Rsch. Inst. (med./legal com. 1985—), U. Tenn. Pres.'s Club, U. Tenn. Faculty Club, Cherokee Country Club. Republican. Episcopalian. Office: Hodges Doughty & Carson 617 Main St # 869 Knoxville TN 37902-2602

WHITE, EUGENE VADEN, pharmacist; b. Cape Charles, Va., Aug. 13, 1924; s. Paul Randolph and Louise (Townsend) W.; m. Laura Juanita LaFontaine, Aug. 28, 1948; children: Lynda Sue, Patricia Louise. BS in Pharmacy, Med. Coll. Va., 1950; PharM (hon.), Phila. Coll. Pharmacy and Sci., 1966. Pharmacist McKim & Huffman Drug Store, Luray, Va., 1950, Miller's Drug Store, Winchester, Va., 1950-53; pharmacist, ptnr. Shiner's Drug Store, Front Royal, Va., 1953-56; pharmacist, owner Eugene V. White, Pharmacist, P.C., Berryville, Va., 1956—; Sturmer lectr. Phila. Coll. Pharmacy and Sci., 1979; Lubin vis. prof. U. Tenn. Sch. Pharmacy, Memphis, 1974; mem. bd. visitors Sch. Pharmacy, U. Pitts., 1969. Author: The Office-Based Family Pharmacist, 1978; created first office practice in community pharmacy, 1960, developed patient medication profile record, 1960. 2d lt. USAAC, 1943-45. Recipient Nat. Leadership award Phi Lambda Sigma, 1979, Outstanding Pharmacy Alumnus award Med. Coll. Va. Sch. Pharmacy Alumni Assn., 1989; Eugene V. White scholarship named in his honor Shenandoah U. Sch. Pharmacy, 1996. Fellow Am. Coll. Apothecaries (J. Leon Lascoff award 1973); mem. Am. Pharm Assn. (Daniel B. Smith award 1965, Remington Honor medal 1978), Va. Pharm. Assn. (Pharmacist of Yr. award 1966, Outstanding Pharmacist award 1992). Methodist. Office: 1 W Main St Berryville VA 22611-1340

WHITE, FRANK WILLIAM, editor; b. Cleveland, Tenn., Dec. 25, 1953; s. William Virgil White and Elsie L. (Dorrow) Rymer; m. Natalie Andrews, May 24, 1975; 1 child, Andrew William. BS, Mid. Tenn. State U., 1977; MA, Ind. U., 1979. Assoc. prof. Mid. Tenn. State U., Murfreesboro, 1978-80; reporter, news editor Leaf-Chronicle, Clarksville, Tenn., 1980-84; feature reporter Bapt. Sun. Sch. Bd., Nashville, 1984-90, mag. editor, 1991-92; print officer U.S. Army, Saudi Arabia and Iraq, 1991; mng. editor Broadman & Holman Pubs., Nashville, 1992-94, prodn. mgr., 1994—. Contbr. articles to profl. jours. Deacon First Bapt. Ch., Clarksville, 1984—, Sunday sch. tchr., 1983—; bd. dirs., pres. Clarksville Nat. Little League, 1996-97; officer Tenn. Army NG, Nashville, 1979-91. With U.S. Army, 1972-75, USAR, 1991—. Decorated Meritorious Svc. medal, Army Commendation medal, Liberation of Kuwait medal, S.W. Asia Svc. medal. Mem. Soc. Profl. Journalists, Religious Pub. Rels. Coun. (pres. Nashville chpt. 1987), Bapt. Pub. Rels. Assn., Windows Prepub. Assn., Res. Officers Assn. Home: 3065 Clydesdale Dr Clarksville TN 37043-5491 Office: Broadman & Holman Pubs 127 9th Ave N Nashville TN 37203-3601

WHITE, GEORGE EDWARD, legal educator, lawyer; b. Northampton, Mass., Mar. 19, 1941; s. George LeRoy and Frances Dorothy (McCafferty) W.; m. Susan Valre Davis, Dec. 31, 1966; children: Alexandra V., Elisabeth McC. BA, Amherst Coll., 1963; MA, Yale U., 1964, PhD, 1967; J.D., Harvard U., 1970. Bar: D.C. 1970, Va. 1975, U.S. Supreme Ct. 1973. Vis. scholar Am. Bar Found., 1970-71; law clk. to Chief Justice Warren, U.S. Supreme Ct., 1971-72; asst. prof. law U. Va., 1972-74, assoc. prof., 1974-77, prof., 1977-86, John B. Minor prof. law and history, 1987-92, Disting. Univ. prof., John B. Minor prof. law and history, 1992—; vis. prof. Marshall-Wythe Law Sch. spring 1988, N.Y. Law Sch., fall 1988. Mem. Am. Acad. Arts and Scis., Am. Law Inst., Am. Soc. Legal History (bd. dirs. 1978-81), Soc. Am. Historians. Author books, including The American Judicial Tradition, 1976, 2d edit., 1988, Tort Law in America: An Intellectual History (Gavel award ABA 1981), 1980, Earl Warren: A Public Life (Gavel award ABA 1983), 1982, The Marshall Court and Cultural Change, 1988, 2d edit. 1991 (James Willard Hurst prize 1990), Justice Oliver Wendell Holmes: Law and the Inner Self, 1993 (Gavel award ABA 1994, Scribes award 1994, Littleton-Griswold prize 1994, Triennial Order of the Coif award 1996), Intervention and Detachment: Essays in Legal History and Jurisprudence, 1994; Oxford, U. Press, Creating the National Pastime: Baseball Transforms Itself, 1903-1953, 1996—,editor Studies in Legal History, 1980-86, Delegate in Law, 1986-96—. Office: U Va Law Sch Charlottesville VA 22903-1789

WHITE, HENRY ALLEN, journalism educator; b. Harlan, Ky., Jan. 19, 1953; s. Henry Allen and Berniece (Jones) W. BS, Murray State U., 1976, MS, 1985; PhD, U. Tenn., 1989. Sports editor Paris (Tenn.) Post-Intelligencer, 1981-84, reporter, 1984-85; Bickel rsch. scholar coll. communications U. Tenn., 1985-86, grad. teaching assoc. sch. journalism, 1986-88; asst. prof. A.Q. Miller Sch. Journalism Kans. State U., 1988-90; asst. prof. dept. communication Duquesne U., 1990-91; assoc. prof., grad. coord. dept. journalism and radio-TV Murray State U., 1991—; text reviewer Holt, Rinehart and Winston, 1989, 90. Contbr. articles to profl. jours. and newspapers. With USN, 1976-81. Named Ky. Col. Gov. of Ky., 1990; recipients awards Tenn. Press Assn., 1982-85. Mem. Assn. for Edn. in Journalism and Mass Communications, Soc. Collegiate Journalists, Midwest Assn. for Pub. Opinion Rsch., Kappa Tau Alpha. Office: Murray State U Dept Journalism Radio TV 1 Murray St Murray KY 42071-3300

WHITE, HERBERT LAVERNE, meterologist, federal agency administrator; b. Waverly, N.Y., Oct. 28, 1950; s. Howard Chauncey and Edith Baylis (Soper) W.; m. Gayle Maureen Shannon, Dec. 28, 1975. BS in Meteorology, Pa. State U., 1972; postgrad., Marine Forecasting Naval, Postgrad. Sch., 1980. Meteorologist-student trainee Nat. Weather Svc., Charleston, S.C., 1970-71; meteorologist intern Nat. Weather Svc., Pitts., 1972-76, meteorologist, 1976-77; forecaster Nat. Weather Svc., Raleigh, N.C., 1977-80, evaluations officer, computer mgr., 1980-94; warning coordination meteorologist Nat. Weather Svc., Binghamton, N.Y., 1994-96; pub. safety meteorologist Nat. Weather Svc., Silver Spring, Md., 1996—. Asst. scoutmaster Boy Scouts Am., 1969-72, neighborhood commr. 1973-74. Recipient Gold Medal award U.S. Dept. Commerce, 1993; Modernization award Nat. Oceanic and Atmospheric Adminstrn., 1995. Mem. Am. Meteorol. Soc. (vice chmn. cen. N.C. chpt. 1993-94, newsletter editor Pitts. chpt. 1976-77), Nat. Weather Assn. (charter), Nat. Weather Svc. Employees Orgn. (sec. ea. region 1987-88, chmn. 1988-91, dir. legis. and pub. affairs 1991-94, mem. nat. negotiating com. 1988-94), Pa. State U. Alumni Assn. (life). Methodist. Office: National Weather Svc Headqtrs OM11 SSMC 2 #14394 1325 East-West Hwy Silver Spring MD 20910

WHITE, IRENE, insurance complex case manager; b. Taumuning, Guam, Jan. 3, 1961; d. Antonio Gill and Irma Magdalena (Idrogo) Gill; m. William Paul Franck, Aug. 4, 1979 (div. July 1984); m. Richard Nelson White, May 12, 1989 (div. Dec. 1993). Cert. ins. adjuster, Tex. Ins. adjuster Gen. Accident Group, San Antonio, 1983-85, Crum & Forster Ins., San Antonio, 1985-89, Aetna Life & Casualty, San Antonio, 1979-83; adjuster, analyst, cons., complex case mgr. Aetna Life & Casualty, Dallas, 1989-96; complex case mgr. Travelers/Aetna Property Casualty Corp., Dallas, 1996—. Big sister Big Bros. and Sisters, San Antonio, 1987-89; vol. counselor March of Dimes, San Antonio, 1988-89. Republican. Roman Catholic. Office: Travelers/Aetna Property 2350 Lakeside Blvd Richardson TX 75082-4311

WHITE, JAMES CLAIBORNE, manufacturing engineer executive; b. Xenia, Ohio, May 6, 1962; s. John Delano and Janice Claire (Ingram) W.; m. Janna Unger, Aug. 24, 1985; children: Dakota James, Tristan Garrett, Colton Laramy. BS in Mech. Engring., Tenn. Tech. U., Cookeville, 1987; MS in Indsl. Engring., Purdue U., 1993. Registered profl. engr., Ky., Tenn. Quality assurance analsyt Johnson Controls, Inc., Greenfield, Ohio, 1987-88; mech. engr. Big Rivers Electric Corp., Henderson, Ky., 1988-95; sr. mfg. engr. Calsonic N.Am.-Tenn. Ops., Shelbyville, 1995-96, mfg. engring. supr., 1996—. Pres. Collegiate Bowling League, Cookeville, Tenn., 1984-85, U. Christian Student Ctr., Cookeville, 1984-85; fin. dir. local non-profit orgn., Evansville, Ind., 1993-95. Mem. ASME (assoc.), NSPE (engr. amb. 1989—, mathcounts co-chair 1989). Republican. Mem. Ch. of Christ. Office: Calsonic NAM-Tenn Ops One Calsonic Way PO Box 350 Shelbyville TN 37160

WHITE, JAMES M., III, lawyer; b. 1938. BA, Washington & Lee U., 1960; BCL, Coll. William & Mary, 1966. V.p., gen. counsel Universal Corp., Richmond, Va., 1973-90, sec., gen. counsel, 1990—; mem. joint commn. to study revision Va. Stock Corp. Act Va. State Bar/Va. Bar Assn., 1986. Mem. Va. State Bar (bd. govs. bus. law sect. 1983-86), Richmond Bar Assn. (chmn. corp. counsel sect. 1975). Office: Universal Corp Hamilton St at Broad PO Box 25099 Richmond VA 23260-5099*

WHITE, JAMES PATRICK, creative writing educator, writer; b. Wichita Falls, Tex., Sept. 28, 1940; s. Joe B. White and Minnie Orlene (Mann) Ware; m. Janice Lou Turner, Sept. 12, 1960; 1 child, Christopher Jules. BA with honors, U. Tex., 1961; MA in History, Vanderbilt U., 1963; MA in Creative Writing, Brown U., 1973. From asst. prof. to assoc. prof. U. Tex., Permian Basin, 1973-77; vis. univ. prof. U. Tex., Dallas, 1977-78; instr. novel writing UCLA, 1979; dir. Master's profl. writing U. So. Calif., L.A., 1979-82; dir. creative writing U. South Ala., Mobile, 1982—. Author: Birdsong, 1977, 78, 85, 95, (novellas) The Persian Oven and California Exit, 1987, Clara's Call, 1992; co-editor: Where Joy Resides: A Christopher Isherwwod Reader, 1989. Fulbright grantee, India, 1991; Guggenheim fellow, 1988-89; Dean's lectr. Coll. Arts & Scis., U. South Ala., 1990. Mem. Am. Lit. Translators Assn. (mem. internat. adv. bd. 1996), Tex. Assn. Creative Writing Tchrs. (founder, pres. 1974-78), Gulf Coast Assn. Creative Writing Tchrs. (founder, past pres. 1992-94), Associated Writing Programs (mem. nat. editl. bd. 1976-77), Ala. Writers Forum (bd. dirs. exec. com. 1994-97). Office: U South Ala Creative Writing/English Dp HumB 240 Mobile AL 36688

WHITE, JAMES ROBERT, minister; b. Crescent, Okla., Aug. 31, 1936; s. James Franklin and Nellie Verona (Moffitt) W.; m. Willa June Mason, June 3, 1960; children: Jeri Lynn, James Robert Jr. BA, Okla. Bapt. U., 1959; MDiv, Southwestern Bapt. Theol. Sem., Ft. Worth, 1963. Ordained to ministry So. Bapt. Conv., 1960. Pastor Beaty Bapt. Ch., Pauls Valley, Okla., 1961-62; pastor 1st Bapt. Ch., Stratford, Okla., 1962-65, Ft. Cobb, Okla., 1965-67, Stroud, Okla., 1968-70; dir. students and missions and Bapt. Student Union, Kay Assn., Tonkawa, Okla., 1966-68; assoc. pastor Trinity Bapt. Ch., Oklahoma City, 1970-73; pastor Capitol Hill Bapt. Ch., Oklahoma City, 1973—; chmn., initiator Southside Crusade, Oklahoma City, 1975-79; trustee Okla. Bapt. U., Shawnee, 1978-81; mem. exec. bd. Capitol Bapt. Assn., 1973—, Union Bapt. Assn., 1989—. Contbg. author: Christian Life Bible, 1985. Pres. Olde Capitol Hill Coun., Oklahoma City, 1985-89; bd. dirs. Andrews Square Steering Com., Oklahoma City, 1980-91; mem. Oklahoma City Mayor's Adv. Com., 1987. Recipient svc. award Salvation Army, 1986-90. Mem. Lions (pres. Capitol Hill club 1993-94). Office: Capitol Hill Bapt Ch 304 SW 134th St Oklahoma City OK 73170

WHITE, JEFF V., information services company executive; b. Mobjack, Va., Jan. 8, 1925; s. Leonard S. and Gracie F. (Drisgill) W.; m. Rosalyn White, Dec. 25, 1946; children: Robert, Lynne. With Equifax, Inc., Atlanta, 1942—; from asst. v.p. to pres. Credit Bur. Inc. affiliate Equifax, Inc., Atlanta, 1962-74; v.p. Equifax, Inc., Atlanta, 1976-77, group v.p., 1977-79, exec. v.p., 1979-81, pres., 1981-87, CEO, 1983-89, vice chmn., 1987-88, chmn., CEO, 1988-89, chmn., 1988, now chmn. exec. com., also bd. dirs.; bd. dirs. affiliated cos. 1st Nat. Bank Atlanta, 1st Atlanta Corp., Cen. Atlanta Progress; mem. adv. council Coll. Bus. Adminstrn. Ga. State U., IN-ROADS/Atlanta. Bd. dirs. adv. coun. Ga. State U. Coll. Bus. Asminstrn.; mem. adv. council United Way of Metro Atlanta; bd. visitors Emory U.; bd. trustees Fernbank Sci. Ctr.; mem. The Conf. Bd., 1988. Served to lt. U.S. Army, 1943-46. Mem. Can. Am. Soc. Southeast U.S. Office: Equifax Inc 1600 Peachtree St NE Atlanta GA 30309-2403*

WHITE, JEFFERY HOWELL, lawyer; b. Tyler, Tex., Aug. 4, 1959; s. Bluford D. and Tempie R. (Tunnell) W.; m. Michael Anne Mackley, May 21, 1989; children: Kristin, Alex. BS in History, So. Ark. U., 1983; JD, Oklahoma City U., 1986. Bar: Tex. 1987. Assoc. Dean White, Canton, Tex., 1986-90; asst. dist. atty. Van Zandt Co., Canton, 1991-94; ptnr. Elliott Elliott & White, Canton, 1994—. Mem. Van Zandt County Bar Assn., Tex. Criminal Def. Lawyers Assn. Democrat. United Methodist. Home: PO Box 102 Canton TX 75103-0102 Office: Elliott Elliott & White 166 N Buffalo St Canton TX 75103-1338

WHITE, JOE E., JR., lawyer; b. Roswell, N.Mex., Oct. 27, 1962. BA in Polit. Sci., Ctrl. State U., 1985; JD, U. Okla., 1988. Bar: Okla. Assoc. Hughes, White, Adams & Grant, Oklahoma City, Okla., 1985-93, ptnr., 1993-94; ptnr. White & Adams, Oklahoma City, Okla., 1995—; barrister Am. Inns of Ct, Oklahoma City, 1994—. Trustee Okla. Student Loan Authority, Oklahoma City, 1992-96; vice chmn. bd. dirs. U. Ctrl. Okla. Found., Edmond, 1992—. Democrat. Baptist. Office: White & Adams 25th Fl 204 N Robinson City Pl Bldg Oklahoma City OK 73102

WHITE, JOHN AUSTIN, JR., engineering educator, dean, consultant; b. Portland, Ark., Dec. 5, 1939; s. John Austin and Ella Mae (McDermott) W.; m. Mary Elizabeth Quarles, Apr. 13, 1963; children: Kimberly Elizabeth White Brakmann, John Austin III. BS in Indsl. Engring., U. Ark., 1962; MS in Indsl. Engring., Va. Poly. Inst., 1966; PhD, Ohio State U., 1969; PhD (hon.), Cath. U. of Leuven, Belgium, 1985, George Washington U., 1991. Registered profl. engr., Va. Indsl. engr. Tenn. Eastman Co., Kingsport, 1961-63, Ethyl Corp., Baton Rouge, 1965; instr. Va. Poly. Inst. and State U., Blacksburg, 1963-66, asst. prof., 1970-72, assoc. prof., 1972-75; teaching assoc. Ohio State U., Columbus, 1966-70; assoc. prof. Ga. Inst. Tech., Atlanta, 1975-77, prof., 1977-84, Regents' prof., 1984—, Gwaltney prof., 1988—, dean engring., 1991—; asst. dir. engring. NSF, 1988-91; founder, chmn. SysteCon Inc., Duluth, Ga., 1977-84; exec. cons. Coopers & Lybrand, N.Y.C., 1984-93; mem. mfg. studies bd. NRC, Washington, 1986-88; bd. dirs. CAPS Logistics, Russell Corp., Eastman Chem. Co., Motorola Corp.; pres. Nat. Consortium for Grad. Degrees for Minorities in Engring. and Sci., Inc., 1993-95; bd. dirs. Southeastern Consortium for Minorities in Engring., 1992—; apptd. U.S. del. to the Internat. Steering Com. of the Intelligent Mfg. System, 1995-97; mem. Nat. Sci. Bd., 1994—. Co-author: Facility Layout and Location: An Analytical Approach, 1974 (Book of Yr. award Inst. Indsl. Engrs. 1974), 2d edit., 1991, Analysis of Queueing Systems, 1975, Principles of Engineering Economic Analysis, 3d edit., 1989, Capital Investment Decision Analysis for Management and Engineering, 1980, 2d edit., 1996, Facilities Planning, 1984 (Book of Yr. award Inst. Indsl. Engrs. 1984), 2d edit., 1996; editor: Production Handbook, 1987; co-editor: Progress in Materials Handling and Logistics, Vol. 1, 1989; also numerous articles to profl. jours., chpts. to books and handbooks in field, conf. procs. Recipient Outstanding Tchr. award Ga. Inst. Tech., 1982, Disting. Alumnus award Ohio State U. Coll. Engring., 1984, Disting. Indsl. Engring. alumnus award Va. Polytech. Inst. and State U., 1993, Reed-Apple award Material Handling Edn. Found., 1985, Disting. Svc. award NSF, 1991, Rodney D. Chipp Meml. award Soc. Women Engrs., 1994. Fellow Am. Inst. Indsl. Engrs. (pres. 1983-84, facilities planning and design award 1980, outstanding indsl. engr. award region III 1974, region IV 1984, Albert G. Holzman disting. educator award 1988, outstanding pub. award 1988, David F. Baker disting. rsch. award 1990, Frank and Lillian Gilbreth award 1994), Am. Assn. Engring. Socs. (bd. govs., chmn. 1986, Kenneth Andrew Roe award 1989); mem. Nat. Acad. Engring., Ark. Acad. Indsl. Engring., Am. Soc. Engring. Edn. (Donald E. Marlowe award 1994), Coun. Logistics Mgmt. Internat. Material Mgmt. Soc. (material mgr. of yr. 1989), Soc. Mfg. Engrs. (mfg. educator award 1990), Nat. Soc. Profl. Engrs. Inst. for Ops. Rsch. and the Mgmt. Scis. (hon.), Golden Key, Sigma Xi, Alpha Pi Mu, Omicron Delta Kappa, Phi Kappa Phi, Tau Beta Pi, Omega Rho. Baptist. Office: Ga Inst Tech Coll Engring Office of Dean Atlanta GA 30332

WHITE, JUNE MILLER, mathematics educator, education consultant; b. E. Bernstadt, Ky., June 13, 1938; d. James Fulton and Ida Mae (Hansel) Miller; m. Richard Allen White, Aug. 27, 1960; children: Jennifer Lynn, Richard Allen Jr. BS with high honors, Denison U., 1960; MA, U. Rochester, 1969; PhD, Bryn Mawr Coll., 1980. Engirng. asst. AT&T, Kansas City, Mo., 1960-61; math. tchr. William Chrisman High Sch., Independence Pub. Schs., Independence, Mo., 1961-62, Brighton High Sch., Brighton, N.Y., 1962-69, Conestoga High Sch., Tredyffrin-Easttown Pub. Schs., Berwyn, Pa., 1970-72; chair math. dept. Hill Top Prep. Sch., Rosemont, Pa., 1972-76; curriculum coord. Hill Top Prep. Sch., 1976-81; math. instr. St. Petersburg Jr. Coll., Clearwater, Fla., 1982-84; dir. math. program St. Petersburg Jr. Coll., Clearwater, 1984—; presenter at various confs. Author: A Collection of Mathematics Applications for College

Students, 1989; editor SPECTRUM, 1983-95; contbr. articles to profl. jours. Elder Northwood Presbyn. Ch., Clearwater, 1986-90; chmn. blood drive ARC, King of Prussia, Pa., 1973-74; chmn. citizens adv. com. Upper Merion Pub. Schs., King of Prussia, 1975-76. Mem. Am. Math. Assn. of Two Yr. Colls., Math. Assn. Am. (v.p. Fla. and Caribbean sect. 1988-91, sec. 1994—), Nat. Coun. Tchrs. Math., Fla. Assn. Cmty. Colls., Rsch. Coun. for Diagnostic and Prescriptive Math., Pinellas County Assn. for Children and Adults with Learning Disabilities (bd. dirs. 1987-88), Phi Beta Kappa. Home: 4951 Bacopa Ln S #103 Saint Petersburg FL 33715 Office: St Petersburg Jr Coll Drew St Clearwater FL 34621

WHITE, KEVIN LEE, officer of marines; b. Munich, Jan. 11, 1960; s. William and JoNeil (Mathis) W.; m. Melinda Lee Shaw, Mar. 8, 1986; 1 child Justin Lee. BS in Mech. Engring., U.S. Naval Acad., 1985; postgrad., The Basic Sch., Quantico, Va., 1985-86, Landing Force Tng. Command, Norfolk, Va., 1986; MS in Mgmt. with distinction, Naval Post Grad. Sch., 1994. Enlisted USN, 1978; commd. 2d lt. USMC, 1985; advanced through grades to maj., 1995; with marine expeditionary unit USN, Camp Lejeune, N.C., 1986-88; with 2d Radio Bn., 2d SRIG USN, Camp Lejeune, 1989-90; co. comdr. Hdqs Svc. Co., 1st Med. Bn., 1st Force Svc. Support Group USN, Camp Pendleton, Calif., 1990-91, with Hdqs. Svc. Bn., 1991-92, staff sec., 1992-93; asst. program mgr. logistics MARCORSYSCOM, Quantico, 1995—. Decorated Combat Action Ribbon. Mem. Internat. Soc. Logistics (cert. profl. logistician), Marine Corps Assn. Republican. Methodist. Office: MARDORSYSCOM C411C 2033 Barnett Ave Ste 315 Quantico VA 22134-5010

WHITE, MARY LOU, fundraiser, writer, educator; b. Davenport, Iowa, Feb. 17, 1939; d. Edward Joseph and Madeleine (Levart) Briglia; m. Morton Bartho White, Dec. 6, 1965 (dec. Jan. 1973). Cert. d'etudes francaises, U. Grenoble, France, 1959; BA, Gettysburg Coll., 1960; postgrad., Sorbonne, Paris, 1961; MA, Middlebury Coll., 1962; MS, U. Bridgeport, 1972. Writer CIA, N.Y.C., 1962-64; tchr. French Miss Porter's Sch., Farmington, Conn., 1964-66; fundraiser N.Y. Philharm., N.Y.C., 1966-72; tchr. French Fairfield (Conn.) Country Day Sch., 1973-77, Greens Farms (Conn.) Acad., 1977-79; spl. events coord. N.Y. Philharm., N.Y.C., 1979-80; econ. devel. Broward C.C., Ft. Lauderdale, Fla., 1989-91; programming grants writer Broward Ctr. for the Performing Arts, Ft. Lauderdale, 1992—. Vol. Polit. Party, Ft. Lauderdale, 1990-93. Mem. Hereditary Register of U.S. Home: 888 Intracoastal Dr Fort Lauderdale FL 33304-3638

WHITE, MARY LOUISE, management consultant; b. N.Y.C., Aug. 8, 1933; d. Henry Fred and Martha (Meyer) Behrmann; m. Roger Stevenson White, July 15, 1953; children: Stevenson Rogers, William Henry. BBA, Hofstra Coll., 1954. Instr. Dept. Army, Poitiers, France, 1954-55; bus. office rep. N.Y. Telephone Co., Hempstead, N.Y., 1955-56; sec. admissions Duke U. Med. Sch., Durham, N.C., 1955-56; substitute tchr. St. Paul's Episcopal Sch., Clearwater, Fla., 1968-74; tutor Clearwater, 1974-77; adminstrv. asst. Arthur Rutenberg Homes, Clearwater, 1977-80, Castro Homes, Juno Beach, Fla., 1980-81; purchaser Jack Eckerd Vision Group divsn. Jack Eckerd Corp., Clearwater, 1982-92, supr., 1992-94; pres. Lou White Cons., Clearwater, 1994—; mgmt. cons. Clearwater, 1983-96. Pres. South Ward Sch. PTA, Clearwater, 1966. Mem. AAUW, NAFE. Republican. Methodist. Home: 1565 Alexander Rd Clearwater FL 34616-1907

WHITE, MARY RUTH WATHEN, social services administrator; b. Athens, Tex., Dec. 27, 1927; d. Benedict Hudson and Sara Elizabeth (Evans) W.; m. Robert M. White, Nov. 10, 1946; children: Martha Elizabeth, Robert Miles, Jr., William Benedict, Mary Ruth, Jesse Wathen, Margaret Fay, Maureen Adele, Thomas Evan. BA, Stephen F. Austin State U., Nacogdoches, Tex., 1948. Chmn. Regional Drug Abuse Com., San Antonio, 1975-81, Met. Youth Coun., San Antonio, 1976-78; state chmn. Citizens United for Rehab. Errants, San Antonio, 1978-91; sec. Bexar County Detention Ministries, San Antonio, 1979-88; chmn. Bexar County (Tex.) Jail Commn., 1980-82; chmn. com. on role of family in reducing recidivism Tex. Dept. Criminal Justice, Austin, 1985—; chmn. Met. Cmty. Corrections Com., San Antonio, 1986-90; bd. dirs. Tex. Coalition for Juvenile Justice, 1975-93, Target 90 Youth Coordinating Coun., San Antonio, 1986-89; local chmn. vol. adv. bd. Tex. Youth Commn., 1986-87. Pres. San Antonio City Coun. PTA, 1976-78, Rep. Bus. Women Bexar County, San Antonio, 1984-86, North Urban Deanery, San Antonio Alliance Mental Illness, 1995-96, also legis. chmn.; bd. dirs. CURE, 1978-92; legis. chmn. Archdiocese of San Antonio Coun. Cath. Women; mem. allocation com. United Way, San Antonio, 1986-91. Named Today's Woman, San Antonio Light newspaper, 1985, Outstanding Rep. Woman, Rep. Bus. Women Bexar County, 1987; honoree Rep. Women Stars over Tex., 1992. Mem. Am. Corrections Assn., Assn. Criminal Justice Planners, LWV (pres. San Antonio chpt. 1984-86), Conservation Soc., Fedn. Women (bd. dirs. 1984-90), DAR (regent), Colonial Dames (pres.), Cath. Daus. Am. (profl. registered parliamentarian, past regent Ct. of St. Anthony), Tex. Cath. Daus. Am. (state legis. chair), San Antonio Alliance for Mentally Ill (pres. 1996-97). Home: 701 E Sunshine Dr San Antonio TX 78228-2516 Office: 5372 Fredericksburg Rd Ste 114 San Antonio TX 78229-3559

WHITE, MELVIN JEFFREY, ophthalmologist, environmental medicine physician; b. Sept. 3, 1927; s. William and Rose (Jacob) W.; (div.); 1 child, Sharon (dec.); m. D. Olga Llano Kuehl, Feb. 25, 1996. AB in Psychology, U. Louisville, 1948, MD, 1953; MA in Anthropology, U. Chgo., 1949; postgrad., U. Pa., 1958. Diplomate Am. Bd. Ophthalmology, Am. Bd. Environ. Medicine. Intern Fitzsimmons Army Hosp., Denver, 1953-54; flight surgeon Carswell AFB, Ft. Worth, 1954-55; resident U. Pa., Phila., 1955-58; ophthalmologist, flight surgeon MacDill AFB, Tampa, Fla., 1958-62; pvt. practice ophthalmologist Tampa, 1962—, pvt. practice environ. medicine physician, 1985—; asst. prof. ophthalmology U. South Fla. Med. Sch., Tampa, 1970—. Col. USAF (ret.), 1953-87; cpl. USMC, 1945-46, CBI. Fellow Am. Acad. Environ. Medicine; mem. Royal Order Jesters (dir. Ct 89 1990), Mystic Shrine, Scottish Rite, Masons. Republican. Baptist. Home: 50 Albermarle Ave Tampa FL 33606 Office: White Eye Clinic-EnviroMed Clinic 3715 W Azeele St Tampa FL 33609-2807

WHITE, MICHAEL JAMES, managed care/case management consultant; b. Malone, N.Y., May 19, 1950; s. Lyle J. and Patricia M. (Finnegan) W. AAS in Nursing, SUNY, Canton, 1973; BSN, Case Western Reserve U., 1978. Cert. case mgr. Adminstrv. supr. The Inst. for Rehab. & Rsch., Houston, 1978-81; regional dir. NSI Svcs., Inc., Houston, 1981-85; dir. home care Tulane U. Med. Ctr., New Orleans, 1985-88; supr. case mgmt. Sanus/N.Y. Life Health Plan, Houston, 1988-91; lectr. 3d party reimbursement and medicare Sch. of Nursing U. Tex. Health Sci. Ctr.; dir. splty. svcs. Vis. Nurse Assn., Houston; mng. ptnr. Sills, White and Assocs., managed care cons., Houston; dir. resource case mgmt., asst. v.p. Columbia Healthcare Corp. Mid-Am. Group Columbia Bayshore MC, 1996—; dir. splty. svcs. Vis. Nurse Assn. Chmn. nurses campaign United Way, Houston; adv. bd. ARC, Houston. Mem. ANA (rep. nat. ho. of dels.), Tex. Nurses Assn. (numerous local offices including pres., bd. dirs., state level rep. ho. of dels., coms.), Assn. Rehab. Nurses (local and state bd. dirs., state sec.-treas.), Case Mgmt. Soc. Am. (pres. local chpt., sec.-treas. state chpt.), Sigma Theta Tau. Home: 401 Stratford St Houston TX 77006-3019 Office: Columbia Bayshore Med Ctr 4000 Spencer Hwy Pasadena TX 77504

WHITE, MICHAEL LEE, lawyer; b. Dilley, Tex., Mar. 27, 1953; s. Deryl and Ruby Alice (Gillis) W. BA, Tex. A&M U., 1975; JD, U. Houston, 1978. Bar: Tex. 1979. Briefing atty. 14th Ct. Appeals, Houston, 1979; contracts analyst Texaco Inc., Houston, 1979-80, legis. coord., 1980-82; mgr. state govt. rels. Pennzoil Co., Houston, 1982-85, mgr. employee comms., pub. affairs liaison, 1985-87, mgr. media comms., 1987-88; dir. govt. affairs Met. Transit Authority Harris County, Houston, 1988-90; v.p. C. of C. divsn. Greater Houston Partnership, 1990-94; legis. cons. Austin, Tex., 1994—. Fellow Houston Bar Found.; mem. ABA, State Bar Tex., Houston Bar Assn., Tex. Lyceum Assn. (bd. dirs., exec. com. 1984-89), Travis County Bar Assn. Office: PO Box 1667 Austin TX 78767-1667

WHITE, NANCY G., journalism educator; b. N.Y.C., Oct. 21, 1923; d. John C. and Mamie (Comparetto) Giunta; m. Paul Michael White, June 16, 1946; children: Paul Michael Jr., Nancy Melissa. BA, U. Tampa, 1944; MEd, U. Fla., 1954; Advanced Masters Degree, Fla. State U., 1956. Tchr. journalism, dir. student publs. Hillsborough High Sch., Tampa, Fla., 1952-55; tchr. journalism, newspaper advisor Chamberlain High Sch., Tampa, Fla., 1956-68; tchr. journalism, head English dept., newspaper advisor Plant High Sch., Tampa, Fla., 1968-69; prof. journalism, dir. student publs. Hillsborough C.C., Tampa, Fla., 1969—; chair profl. devel. Coll. Media Advisors, Inc., 1993-95, chair awards com., 1990-93, pub. rels. chair, 1988-90; mem. U. West Fla. Adv. Coun., Pensacola, 1984—; mem. State Dept. Edn. Common Course Numbering System Com., 1974—. Contbr. articles to profl. jours.; reporter Tallahassee Dem., 1955-57. Newsletter editor Ybor City Mus. Soc., Tampa, 1990-95; pres., newsletter editor Suncoast Aux. U.S. Submarine Vets. WWII, Tampa, 1986-92; mem., newsletter editor Tampa Women's Club, 1973—. Recipient Columbia U. Gold Key, Columbia Scholastic Press Assn., 1971, Disting. Svc. award Kappa Tau Alpha, 1984, Gold medallion Fla. Scholastic Press Assn., 1989, Disting. Newspaper Adviser award Coll. Media Advisers, 1983, also Disting. Mag. Adviser award, 1988; named to Acad. Hall of Fame, Fla. C.C. Activities Assn., 1995, Hall of Fame, Fla. C.C. Press Assn., 1991. Mem. Nat. C.C. Journalism Assn. (pres. 1992-94), Fla. C.C. Press Assn. (pres. 1971-73, Hall of Fame), Pan Am. Univ. Women (pres.-elect 1996), Fla. Scholastic Press Assn. (pres. 1954-57), Alpha Delta Kappa (pres. 1976-78), Phi Kappa Phi, Kappa Delta Pi, Sigma Delta Chi, Alpha Psi Omega. Democrat. Methodist. Home: 5105 Homer St W Tampa FL 33629 Office: Hillsborough C C 2001 N 14th St Tampa FL 33605-3662

WHITE, NICHOLAS J., retail company executive; b. Sacramento, 1945. Grad., Mo. So. State Coll. Exec. v.p. Wal-Mart Supercenter div. Wal-Mart Stores Inc. Home: 81 Champions Blvd Rogers AR 72758 Office: Wal-Mart Stores Inc 702 SW 8th St Bentonville AR 72712-6209

WHITE, NORMAN LEE, marketing professional; b. Kansas City, Mo., May 10, 1955; s. Norman E. and Ann Louise (Wells) W.; m. Laura Lynn Orman, Aug. 11, 1984; 1 child, Michael Wells White. BA magna cum laude, Dartmouth Coll., 1977; MBA, U. Chgo., 1979. Mktg. rep. IBM, Atlanta, 1979-85, regional mktg. staff, 1985, area mktg. staff, 1986, adminstrv. asst. to area v.p. and gen. mgr., 1989; mktg. mgr. IBM, Orlando, Fla., 1986-88; br. mgr. IBM, Winston Salem, N.C., 1989-91; mgr. retail enterprise mktg. IBM, Raleigh, N.C., 1991-93; bus. exec. sales force automation IBM, Washington, 1993—; ptnr. KPMG Peat Marwick Strategic Svcs. Consulting. Bd. dirs. Sawtooth Ctr. for Creative Design, Winston Salem, 1990; sect. chmn. Winston Salem United Way, 1990, div. chmn., 1991; co-com. chmn. PGA Golf Tournament, Atlanta, 1981; supr. U.S. Open Golf Tournament, Atlanta, 1976. Mem. Atlanta Athletic Club. Office: 303 Peachtree St NE Ste 2000 Atlanta GA 30308-3252

WHITE, OLIVIA A., clinical therapist; b. Metairie, La., June 10, 1951; d. John Arthur and Betty (Van Cleave) W. AA, So. U., New Orlean, postgrad. Cert. addictions counselor I, Nat. and La.; cert. substance abuse counselor and trainers reciprocity in 40 states and Can. Detox counselor, psychiat. technician adolescent unit dePaul Hosp., New Orleans; clin. aftercare counselor Coliseum Hosp., New Orleans; clin. sr. counselor Eastlake Hosp., New Orleans, program dir.; pvt. practice clin. therapist Metairie, La., 1991—. Mem. Coun. on Alcoholism and Drug Abuse, New Orleans, 1986, New Orleans AIDS Task Force, 1990. Mem. La. Bd. Substance Abuse Counselors, La. Assn. Counselors and Trainers, Nat. Assn. Substance Abuse and Drug Abuse Counselors, Suprs. Orgn. of Counselors. Roman Catholic. Home and Office: 2209 Edenborn Ave Apt 20 Metairie LA 70001-1807

WHITE, RAYE MITCHELL, educational administrator; b. Gilmer, Tex., Jan. 21, 1944; d. R.E. and Addie Belle (Collum) Mullican; children: Victoria, William Brett. BS, East Tex. State U., 1966, MS, 1973; EdD, U. Ga., 1984. Cert. tchr., supr., Tex. Tchr. Arabian Oil Co., Ras Tanura, Saudi Arabia, 1978-84; cons. Region VII Edn. Svc. Ctr., Kilgore, Tex., 1985; curriculum dir. Gilmer Ind. Sch. Dist., 1985-87, 92-96; tchr., coord. at-risk mentoring program L.V. Stockard Middle Sch., Dallas, 1987-89; curriculum dir. Chapel Hill Ind. Sch. Dist., Tyler, Tex., 1989-92; part-time prof. U. Tex., Tyler, 1991-93. Mem. editorial bd. The Reading Tchr., 1987-90. Mem. ASCD, Internat. Reading Assn., Nat. Coun. Tchrs. English, Phi Delta Kappa, Kappa Delta Pi, Delta Kappa Gamma. Home: Rt 7 Box 5 Gilmer TX 75644-1747 Office: Gilmer Ind Sch Dist 1447 Hwy 248-D Branson MO 65616-0040

WHITE, ROBERT BROWN, medical educator; b. Ennis, Tex., Jan. 5, 1921; s. Robert Brown and Willia Elizabeth (Latimer) W.; m. Jimmie Estelle Sims, Oct. 18, 1942; children: Robert B., Canelia White Layton, Margaret White Gilbert. BS, Tex. A & M Coll., 1941; MD, U. Tex., 1944; cert., Western New Eng. Psych. Inst., 1959. Intern Phila. (Pa.) Gen. Hosp., 1944-45; psychiat. residency John Sealy Hosp., Galveston, Tex., 1945-46, 48-49; psychiatry fellow Austen Riggs Ctr., Stockbridge, Mass., 1949-51; staff psychiatrist Austen Riggs Ctr., Stockbridge, 1951-62; assoc. prof. U. Tex. Med. Br., Galveston, 1962-67, prof., 1967—, Marie Gale prof. of psychiatry, 1981-93; prof. emeritus, 1993—; tng. analyst New Orleans (La.) Psychoanalytic Inst., 1966-76; tng. analyst Houston-Galveston Psychoanalytic Inst., 1974-94; analyst emeritus, 1994—. Author: Elements of Psychopathology, 1975; contbr. chpts. to books and articles to profl. jours. Capt. U.S. Army, 1946-48. Recipient David Rapaport prize Western New Eng. Psychoanalytic Inst., New Haven, 1959; Ohio State award Ohio State Univ., 1976. Fellow Am. Psychiat. Assn., Am. Coll. Psychiatrists, Am. Coll. Psychoanalysts (bd. regents 1988-91); mem. Alpha Omega Alpha. Democrat. Home: 1013 Harbor View Dr Galveston TX 77550-3109 Office: Univ Tex Med Br Galveston TX 77550

WHITE, ROBERT BRUCE, keyboard instruments company acoustical consultant; b. Casper, Wyo., Aug. 16, 1937; s. Steel Bruce and Julia Doris (Mace) W.; m. Nancy Inez Christian, Sept. 3, 1961; children: Jane Marie, Richard Bruce. BS, Okla. State U., 1959. Field engr. GE, Charlotte, N.C., 1961-63; physics, electronics specialist Derring-Milliken Rsch., Spartanburg, S.C., 1963-66; engring. mgr. Consultants, Inc., Woodruff, S.C., 1966-67; div. mgr. Case Bros., Spartanburg, 1967—; acoustical cons. for religious bldgs.; tchr. Spartanburg Tech. Coll.,1965-66. Contbg. author cookbooks. With USAF, 1959-61. Mem. Inst. Radio Engring., Am. Soc. Engring. Technicians, Am. Guild Organ Technicians, Elks, Masons. Republican. Methodist. Home: 225 Singing Woods Ln Spartanburg SC 29301-2622 Office: Case Bros 906 S Pine St Spartanburg SC 29302-3311

WHITE, ROBERT FREDERICK, landscape architect; b. Pitts., June 18, 1912; s. Edward John and Sarah Ann (Romaine) W.; m. Florence Hilda Kusian, Aug. 21, 1937; children: Hans Willi, Ross (by adoption). BS in Landscape Architecture, Pa. State U., College Park, 1934; MA in Landscape Architecture, U. Mich., 1951. Park staff City of Pitts., 1934-35, 2 parks mgr., 1934-37, mem. planning dept., 1937-43, 45; assoc. Office of Ruth Z. London, Houston, 1946-47; asst. prof. Coll. of Architecture Tex. A&M U., College Station, 1947-58, prof., head landscape architecture dept., 1962-75, prof. emeritus Coll. of Architecture, 1975—; prin. Robert F. White Assoc., Houston, 1958-62; cons. LB Johnson Home Site Restoration, Stone Wall, Tex., 1965. Judge hwy. dept. contest award LB Johnson, Ranch, Tex., 1970, nat. contest ASLA Mag., Washington, 1978; mem. Action Group, Houston, 1960-61, Planning Com., College Station, 1967-68. With USAF, 1943-45. Recipient Citation award Ho. of Reps./State of Tex., 1975. Fellow Am. Soc. Landscape Architecture (S.W. chpt. emeritus); mem. Alpha Gamma Rho, Tau Sigma Delta.

WHITE, ROBERT MILES FORD, life insurance company executive; b. Lufkin, Tex., June 9, 1928; s. Sullivan Miles and Faye Clark (Scurlock) F.; m. Mary Ruth Wathen, Nov. 10, 1946; children: Martha, Robert, Benedict, Mary, Jesse, Margaret, Maureen, Thomas. BA, Stephen F. Austin State U., 1948; BBA, St. Mary's U., San Antonio, 1955; MS in Fin. Services, Am. Coll., Bryn Mawr, Pa., 1981, MS in Mgmt., 1986. CLU. Tchr. Douglas (Tex.) Pub. Schs., 1946-47, Houston Pub. Schs., 1948-51; office mgr. Heat Control Insulation Co., San Antonio, 1951-53; acct. S.W. Acceptance Co., San Antonio, 1953-55; sec.-treas. Howell Corp., San Antonio, 1955-64; agt. New Eng. Mut. Life Ins. Co., San Antonio, 1964-71; br. mgr. Occidental Life Ins. Co. of Calif., San Antonio, 1971-84; gen. agt. Transam. Occidental Life Ins. Co., 1984—. Regional planner Estate Planning for the Disabled; mem. citizens liaison com. San Antonio Ind. Sch. Dist., 1972-78, EEO Coun., 1974-80; Mem. San Antonio Estate Planners Coun., S.W. Pension Conf., Nat., Tex., San Antonio assns. life underwriters, Am. Soc. CLU's., Internat. Assn. Fin. Planners, Gen. Agts. and Mgrs. Assn., Am. Risk and Ins. Assn., Internat. Platform Assn., Tex. Hist. Soc., East Tex. Hist. Soc., San Antonio, S.E. Tex. Geneal. Soc., S.E. Tex. Hist. Soc., Sons of Republic of Tex., SAR, Kappa Pi Sigma. Republican. Roman Catholic. Home: 701 E Sunshine Dr San Antonio TX 78228-2516 Office: Ste 114 5372 Fredericksburg Rd San Antonio TX 78229-3559

WHITE, RONALD LEON, financial management consultant; b. West York, Pa., July 14, 1930; s. Clarence William and Grace Elizabeth (Gingerich) W.; m. Estheranne Wieder, June 16, 1951; children: Bradford William, Clifford Allen, Erick David. BS in Econs, U. Pa., 1952, MBA, 1957. Cost analysis supr. Air Products & Chem. Corp., Allentown, Pa., 1957-60; cost control mgr. Mack Trucks, Inc., Allentown, 1960-64; mgmt. cons. Peat, Marwick, Mitchell & Co., Phila., 1964-66; mgr. profit planning Monroe, The Calculator Co. (div. Litton Industries), Orange, N.J., 1966-67, controller, 1967-68; v.p. fin. Bus. Systems Group of Litton Industries, Beverly Hills, Calif., 1968-70; pres. Royal Typewriter Co. div., Hartford, Conn., 1970-73; exec. v.p., chief operating officer, treas. Tenna Corp., Cleve., 1973-75, pres., dir., 1975-77; v.p. fin. Arby's, Inc., Youngstown, Ohio, 1978-79; exec. v.p., dir. Roxbury Am., Inc., 1979-81; v.p. fin., treas. Royal Crown Cos., Inc., Atlanta and Miami Beach, Fla., 1981-86, TDS Healthcare Systems Corp., Atlanta, 1987-88; v.p. Corp. Fin. Assocs., Atlanta, 1988-90; prin. The Janelle Co., Atlanta, 1991—; instr. acctg. Wharton Sch. U. Pa., 1952-53, instr. industry, 1953-54. Served to lt. USNR, 1954-57. Mem. Am. Mgmt. Assn., Nat. Assn. Accountants, Nat. Assn. Corp. Dirs., Fin. Execs. Inst., Acacia. Mem. United Ch. Christ (deacon). Lodges: Masons, Rotary. Home: 2362 Kingsgate Ct Atlanta GA 30338-5931 Office: The Janelle Co 2362 Kingsgate Ct Atlanta GA 30338-5931

WHITE, SHARON ELIZABETH, lawyer; b. Galveston, Tex., July 5, 1955; d. Edward and Clara Adelia (Haden) W. BA, Baylor U., 1977; JD, So. Meth. U., 1981. Bar: Tex. 1981, U.S. Dist. Ct. (no. dist.) Tex. 1983, U.S. Ct. Appeals (5th cir.) 1985. Assoc. Underwood, Wilson, Berry, Stein & Johnson, Amarillo, Tex., 1981-86, ptnr., 1987-89, shareholder, 1990—. Asst. editor-in-chief Southwestern Law Rev., Dallas, 1980-81. Bd. dirs., sec. council Amarillo Girl Scout U.S., 1983-85, 3d v.p., 1985, 1st v.p. 1985-88, pres., 1988-90; bd. dirs. Amarillo Little Theatre, 1984-91, treas., 1985-89; grants chmn. Don Harrington Discovery Ctr., 1984-86, future planning and devel. chmn., 1986-87; active Amarillo Symphony Guild (bd. dirs. 1994-95), Amarillo Art Alliance (bd. dirs. 1993—), Panhandle Plains Hist. Soc.; mem. Jr. League Amarillo, 1987—, bd. dirs., 1993-94; chair Amarillo Race for the Cure Devel. Coun. of Don & Sybil Harrington Cancer Ctr., 1995—. Fellow Tex. Bar Found.; mem. ABA, Amarillo Bar Assn. (sec.-treas. 1989-90, bd. dirs. 1994-96), Phi Delta Phi, Delta Delta Delta. Republican. Presbyterian. Office: Underwood Wilson PO Box 9158 Amarillo TX 79105-9158

WHITE, SHARON LARUE, social worker, therapist; b. Jefferson County, Tex., Oct. 3, 1950; d. Jack Dayton Sr. and Jessie Larue (Daniels) W. BSN cum laude, Tex. Christian U., 1976; BFA with honors, U. Tex., 1987, MS in Social Work with highest honors, 1988. RN Palo Pinto Gen. Hosp., Mineral Wells, Tex., 1976-77; RN, asst. head nurse All Saint's Hosp., Ft. Worth, 1977-78, charge nurse, 1979, supr. in-svc. edn., 1979-80, acting dir. nurses, 1980; team leader surg. fl. Harris Hosp., Ft. Worth, 1981-82, edn. coord., 1980-81; acting charge nurse cardiac fl. Med. Pla., Ft. Worth, 1982; psychiat. social worker intensive treatment unit Wyo. State Hosp., 1989-90; clin. therapist Pioneer Counseling Svcs., 1990—. Co-facilitatior Rape Crisis Ctr., Ft. Worth, 1985-87. Episcopalian.

WHITE, SHARON LEE, critical care nurse; b. Bluefield, W.Va., Oct. 5, 1960; d. Walter Stuart III and Adele (Osborne) Hamlin; m. Gary White, June 24, 1978; 1 child, Stephen Stuart. AS, John Tyler Community Coll., 1988, student, 1989—; postgrad., Broward Community Coll., Ft. Lauderdale, Fla., 1985. RN. Ophthalmic technician Dr. Stanley D. Swinton, Ft. Lauderdale; opthalmologic technician Va. Eye Inst., Richmond; staff nurse evening shift Southside Regional Med. Ctr., Petersburg, VA. Mem. Phi Theta Kappa.

WHITE, SUSIE MAE, school psychologist; b. Madison, Fla., Mar. 5, 1914; d. John Anderson and Lucy (Crawford) Williams; m. Daniel Elijah White, Oct. 20, 1958 (dec. Sept. 29, 1968). BS, Fla. Meml. Coll., St. Augustine, 1948; MEd, U. Md., 1953; postgrad., Mich. State U., 1955, Santa Fe Community Coll., 1988; Cert. Child Care Supervision, W.T. Loften Edn. Ctr., Gainesville, Fla., 1994. Elem. tchr. Grove Park (Fla.) Elem. Sch., 1943; tchr. Douglas High Sch., High Springs, Fla., 1944-55; sch. psychologist Alachua County Sch. Bd., Gainesville, Fla., 1956-69; coord. social svcs. Alachua County Sch. Bd., Gainesville, 1970; owner, dir. Mother Dear's Child Care Ctr., Gainesville, 1988—. Del. Bapt. World Alliance, Bapt. Conv. Fla., Tokyo, 1970; state dir. leadership Fla. Bapt. Gen. Conv., 1971-85. Recipient Cert. of Appreciation Fla. State Dept. Edn., Tallahassee, 1971, Appreciation for Disting. Svc. award Fla. Gen. Bapt. Conv., Miami, 1979, Hall of Fame award Martin Luther King Jr. Hall of Fame, 1994; The Susie Mae White scholarship fund established Mt. Sinai Congress Christian Edn., 1995. Mem. Nat. Ret. Tchrs. Assn., Alachua County Tchrs. Assn., Fla. Meml. Coll. Nat. Alumni Assn., AAUW, Heroines of Jerico, Masons. Democrat. Office: Child Care Ctr 811 NW 4th Pl Gainesville FL 32601-5049

WHITE, TERRY EDWARD, physician; b. Springfield, Mo., May 30, 1954; s. Roy Edward and Eselean (Moffis) W.; m. Susan Marie Peters, Aug. 16, 1981. BA, Drury Coll., 1976; MD, U. Mo., 1980. Diplomate Am. Bd. Physical Medicine and Rehab. Staff physician Lakeshore Hosp., Birmingham, Ala., 1983-86; clin. instr. U. Ala., Birmingham, 1984-86; staff physician Thomas Rehab., Asheville, N.C., 1986—, chief staff, 1987-88, 91-92, 94—, vice chief staff, 1992-94; alternate Medicare State Carrier adv. com., Greensboro, N.C., 1993; bd. dirs. Nationwide Post Polio Support Group, Dallas, N.C., 1992-94; vice chmn. Western N.C. Health Care Provider Coun., 1995-96, chmn., 1996-97; mem. editl. adv. com. Stroke Rehabilitation. Author: A Patient's and Physician Guide to Late Effects of Polio, 1995; mem. editl. staff Stroke Rehabilitation-Patient Education Guide. Named Rehab. Physician Yr., N.C. Med. Soc., 1993. Fellow Am. Acad. Phys. Medicine and Rehab.; mem. N.C. Soc. Phys. Medicine and Rehab. (v.p. 1989-91, pres. 1991-93). Republican. Mem. Christian Ch. Office: Thomas Rehab Hosp 68 Sweeten Creek Rd Asheville NC 28803-2318

WHITE, THOMAS PATRICK, county official, small business owner; b. Red Bank, N.J., Mar. 17, 1945; s. Edwin Hardy and Alice G. (Olah) W.; m. Jeanette Haydee Gonzalez, Oct. 22, 1966; children: Kimberley Ann, Tiffany Lynne. AS in Criminal Justice, Indian River C.C., Ft. Pierce, Fla., 1977; student, Northeastern U., 1964-65, Rutgers U., 1969, U. Fla., 1984. Cert. law enforcement officer, N.J., Fla.; cert. evaluator, Fla. State ranger N.J. Bur. Forests and Parks, Trenton, 1966-70; pres., owner Whiteford Enterprises Inc. T/A Colonial Automotive Svc. Ctr., Eatontown, N.J., 1970-75; dep. sheriff, criminal investigator, instr. firearms Indian River County Sheriff's Dept., Vero Beach, Fla., 1975-90; dir. investigations Indian River County Property Appraiser's Office, Vero Beach, 1990—; owner TeeJays' Awards, Vero Beach, 1978—. Dir. Rep. Club Indian River County, Vero Beach, 1994-95; treas. Men's Rep. Club, Vero Beach, 1995; former v.p. and pres. Fla. Police Combat League; former mem. Econ. Crime Coun. With USCG, 1962-66. Named Man of Yr., March of Dimes, 1987, Entrepreneur of Yr., Vero Beach Jaycees, 1992. Mem. Internat. Assn. Assessing Officers, Fraternal Order Police (state trustee 1978-85, state asst. dir. 1987-88, state dist. dir. 1989-90, pres. 1985-87, lodge v.p. 1993-94, Mem. of Yr. award 1982, 84, 88), Ducks Unltd. (1990—), 100 Club Indian River County, Elks, Kiwanis (v.p. Vero Beach 1991-92, pres. 1992-93, lt. gov. 1994-95, Kiwanian of Yr. award 1992). Roman Catholic. Home: 1556 30th Ave Vero Beach FL 32960-3288 Office: Indian River County Property Appraiser's Office 1840 25th St Vero Beach FL 32960-3384

WHITE, TOM WILLINGHAM, wholesale beer/beverage distributor executive; b. McAllen, Tex., Feb. 16, 1943; s. Louis Thomas and Leota Faye (Grimm) W.; m. Lauryn G. Longwell, Mar. 8, 1968; children: Brad Edward, Parker Thomas, Landon Allen. BBA, U. Tex., 1965. Acct. Haskins & Sells, CPA's, Houston, 1965-67, Paul Veale, CPA, McAllen, Tex., 1967-68; pvt. practice acctg., Corpus Christi, Tex., 1969-79; pres. Tower Beverage Group, LLC, Dallas; chmn., CEO Tower Beverages of Colo., Inc., Denver, 1986—, Tower Beverages of E. Tex., Inc., CEO Tower Beverages of the Front Range, Inc., 1995—, Tower Beverages of W. Tex., Inc., El Paso, 1996—. Mem. chancellor's coun. U. Tex. Sys.; mem. bd. trustees St. Marks Sch. Tex. Mem.

Wholesale Beer Distbrs. Tex., Nat. Beer Wholesalers Assn., U. Tex. Ex-Students Assn., Corpus Christi Yacht Club, Crescent Club, Brookhollow Golf Club. Home: 5026 Middlegate Rd Dallas TX 75229-5456 Office: 300 Crescent Ct Ste 1640 Dallas TX 75201-1890

WHITE, WARREN TRAVIS, educational consultant firm executive; b. Thrift, Tex., Apr. 28, 1926; s. Warren Travis and Leika (Clark) W.; m. Genevieve Greer; children: Warren Travis, Grady Spruce, Robert Coulter, Carroll Greer; m. Elizabeth Jean Dinkmeyer, June 12, 1964; children: Naomi Kimberly, Stacey Michèle. BA, U. Tex., 1949, MA, 1955; EdD, Vanderbilt U., 1967. Cert. pub. sch. teaching and adminstrn., Tex. Tchr. Ft. Worth (Tex.) Ind. Sch. Dist., 1952-56, adminstr., 1971-89; prin. Midland (Tex.) Sch. Dist., 1956-61, Riverview Gardens Sch. Dist., St. Louis, 1963-64; adminstr. Richmond (Va.) Pub. Schs., 1964-68; supt. Caesar Rodney Sch. Dist., Camden, Del., 1968-71; v.p. White and White, Ft. Worth, 1989—; cons. Office of Indian Edn., Region VI; adj. prof. U. Va., 1964-68, U. Del., 1968-71. Contbr. articles to profl. jours. Mem. ushers com. Univ. Christian Ch.; mem. steering com. Ft. Worth Mayor's Adv. Com. on Energy Conservation; trustee Masonic Temple Assn., Ft. Worth Masonic Libr. and Mus., Ft. Worth Scottish Rite Found., Inc.; bd. dirs. Knights Templar Edn. Found. With U.S. Army, 1944-46, ATO. Mem. NRA, Tex. Assn. Sch. Adminstrs. (chmn. Tex. Pub. Schs. Week com.), Masons (chmn. pub. edn. com. Grand Lodge of Tex., past master Ft. Worth lodge 148, past high priest Ft. Worth chpt. 58, past master Ft. Worth coun. 42), Order of DeMolay (dist. gov., Legion of Honor), Knights Templar (past comdr. Worth Commandery 19), Shriners. Home: 4109 Wedgworth Rd S Fort Worth TX 76133-3614 Office: White and White PO Box 330936 Fort Worth TX 76163-0936

WHITE, WILLIAM CLINTON, pathologist; b. Scottsville, Va., Nov. 22, 1911; s. Llewellyn Gordon and Caroline Rebecca (Rawlings) W.; m. Frances Evelyn Daniel, July 2, 1938; children: William Clinton, Elizabeth White Martin. BS, Va. Mil. Inst., 1933; MD, U. Va., 1937. Diplomate Am. Bd. Pathology. Intern, Walter Reed Gen. Hosp., Washington, 1937-39; resident in pathology U. Colo. Med. Ctr., Denver, 1949-53, assoc. prof., 1949-65; med. dir. Los Alamos Hosp., 1946-49; cons. U. Calif. Sci. Labs., Los Alamos, 1949-59; chmn. dept. pathology Denver Gen. Hosp., 1953-65; dir. med. edn. and rsch. Pensacola Found. for Med. Edn. and Research (Fla.), 1965-78; bd. dirs., 1976—; cons. med. edn., emeritus dir. med. edn. Pensacola Edn. Program (Fla.); co-founder, dir. Rocky Mountain Natural Gas Co.; dir. Midwest Nat. Gas Co. Bd. govs. Fellowship Concerned Churchmen, 1982-85, pres., 1983-85. Mem. Selective Service Bd., N.Mex., 1946-49; mem. adv. bd. on cancer to Gov. of Colo., 1960-65; mem. Community Hosp. Council, Fla. Bd. Regents, 1971-74; mem. vestry, chmn. fin. com., sr. warden Christ Ch.; active Salvation Army, Boy Scouts Am. Served to col., M.C., U.S. Army, 1938-46. Recipient cert. of appreciation SSS, 1951; citation of merit Bd. Health and Hosps., Denver, 1963. Mem. AMA, Am. Soc. Clin. Pathologists (counselor), Colo. Soc. Pathology (pres.), Internat. Acad. Pathology (hon. life), Colo. State Med. Soc., Denver Med. Soc., Escambia County Med. Soc. (hon. life), Los Alamos County Med. Soc. (pres.), Andalusia Country Club, Pensacola Country CLub, Rotary Internat., St. Andrew's Soc. (trustee 1981—), Masons, Shriners, K.T. Contbr. articles to profl. jours. Home and Office: 615 Bayshore Dr Apt 101 Pensacola FL 32507-3500

WHITE, WILLIAM DUDLEY, safety engineer; b. Birmingham, Mich., June 11, 1958; s. Paul Richard and Annetta Carole (Manhart) W.; m. Tamara Jean Wishon, Mar. 13, 1992; 1 child, Stacy Michelle; 1 stepchild, Royce Edward Vorel. BS cum laude, U. Ctrl. Okla., 1994. Chief maintenance engr. First Union Mgmt., Oklahoma City, 1984-89; safety rep., chmn. safety and suggestion coms. E-Systems, Inc., Greenville, Tex., 1994—; creator curriculum for various safety programs, 1994, 96. Pack master Boy Scouts Am., Edmond, Okla., 1991-92; CPR instr., std. first aid instr. ARC, Hunt County, Tex., 1993—. Mem. Am. Soc. Safety Engrs., Alpha Chi. Roman Catholic. Home: 2507 Hillcrest St Greenville TX 75402-8050 Office: E-Systems PO Box 6056 CBN072 Greenville TX 75403

WHITED, STEPHEN REX, English literature and language educator; b. Knoxville, Tenn., Mar. 6, 1955; s. Victor R. and Peggy J. (Rice) W.; m. Jo Moira Miller, Apr. 22, 1958; children: Samuel Stephen, Walker Lewis. BA, Ga. State U., 1981, MA, 1984; PhD, U. Ky., 1992. Teaching fellow U. Ky., 1985-90; asst. prof. Lakeland Coll., Sheboygan, Wis., 1990-93; asst. prof. Piedmont Coll., Demorest, Ga., 1993—, asst. to pres., 1995—. Editor jour. Limestone, 1986-89; poetry editor Habersham Rev., 1993—; contbr. articles to profl. jours. Pres. Task Force on Race Rels., 1992-93, Task Force on Enrollment, 1994. Dissertation Yr. fellow U. Ky., 1989-90; U. Ky. travel grantee, 1990; Lakeland Coll. grantee, 1992. Mem. Am. Assn. Higher Edn., South Atlantic MLA, So. Humanities Coun. Home: 419 Yonah St Cornelia GA 30531 Office: Piedmont Coll English Dept PO Box 10 Demorest GA 30535

WHITEFIELD, CAROLYN LEE, lawyer; b. Texarkana, Ark., Mar. 1, 1946; d. William Parker, Sr. and Julia Arabella (Rayburn) Whitefield; BS, So. State Coll., 1970; JD, U. Ark., 1973; m. Jerry Allen McDowell, Sept. 21, 1974. Bar: Ark. 1973, Tex. 1974; pvt. practice, Texarkana, Ark., 1973—. Mem. Ark. Bar Assn., Tex. Bar Assn. Republican. Baptist. Home: RR 4 Box 360-b Texarkana AR 71854 Office: 1600 Arkansas Blvd Ste 104 Texarkana AR 71854

WHITEHEAD, BARBARA ANN, secondary school educator; b. Shreveport, La., Apr. 25, 1941; d. Clifton John and Leona Elizabeth (Lemoine) W. BA, McNeese State U., 1963, MEd, 1967; postgrad., Centenary Coll., 1982-83, La. Tech. U., 1983. Cert. secondary edn. tchr., La. Tchr. Calcasieu Parish Sch. System, Lake Charles, La., 1963-68, Caddo Parish Sch. System, Shreveport, 1968—; chair social studies dept. C.E. Byrd Math./Sci. Magnet High Sch., Shreveport, 1987—. Author: Teaching the Historical Origins of Nursery Rhymes and Folk Tales, 1982. Named La. Tchr. of Yr. DAR, 1983. Mem. NEA, La. Assn. Educators, Caddo Assn. Educators, Sigma Tau Delta. Roman Catholic. Office: CE Byrd Math Sci Magnet High Sch 3201 Line Ave Shreveport LA 71104-4241

WHITEHEAD, CHRISTOPHER CLEO, industrial engineer, researcher; b. Fort Carson, Colo., Dec. 9, 1954; s. Robert Joseph and Iris Ellen (Thomason) W.; m. Susie Manuelita Gallegos, Dec. 29, 1972; children: Christopher Michael, Charles Alexander, Stephanie Michell, Steven Andrew, Sean Michael. BSEE, U. Tex., 1978; MS in Ops. Rsch., Naval Postgrad. Sch., Monterey, Calif., 1986. Cert. naval aviator; lic. real estate agent, Ga. Enlisted USMC, 1972; commd. 2d lt. USN, 1978; advanced through grades to lt. comdr., 1988; aviation radar technician U.S. Marine Corps., Denver, 1972-75; naval aviator Patrol Squadron Fifty, Moffett Field, Calif., 1980-84, pilot-in-command, mission comdr., 1982-84; staff comm. officer Carrier Group Seven, San Diego, 1986-89; asst. prof. math. scis. USAF Acad., Colo., 1989-92, ret., 1992; exec. dir. Computers With A Smile, Pueblo, Colo., 1992-93; indsl. engr. Dept. Army, Ft. Benning, Ga., 1993—; aviation safety officer Patrol Squadron Fifty, 1982-84; sci. analyst math dept. USAF Acad., 1989-92, sci. rschr. UN AIDS model, 1989-91, Coast Guard drug interdiction program, 1990; dir. computer resources, 1990-92; lectr. U. So. Colo., Pueblo, 1992; adj. prof. computer sci. Troy State U., 1993—, Chattahoochee Valley C.C., 1993—. Contbr. articles to profl. jours. Mem. Ops. Rsch. Soc. Am., Am. Soc. Quality Control, Planetary Soc., Pi Mu Epsilon. Home: 6925 Sandstone Ct Columbus GA 31907-5725 Office: US Army Inf Ctr Directorate of Logistics Fort Benning GA 31905

WHITEHEAD, DAVID LYNN, school counselor; b. Crockett, Tex., Mar. 24, 1950; s. Clifton Baine and Corene (Stowe) W.; m. Joyce Stalmach, June 23, 1973; children: Christopher, Kimberly, Allison. BA with honor, Sam Houston State U., Huntsville, Tex., 1972, MA, 1975. Cert. tchr., speech pathologist, learning disabilities, mental retardation, ednl. diagnostician, counseling, Tex. Speech pathologist Texas City Ind. Sch. Dist., 1972-73; speech pathologist Brenham (Tex.) Ind. Sch. Dist., 1973-75, ednl. diagnostician, 1975-86; ednl. diagnostician Austin County Edn. Coop., Sealy, Tex., 1986-88; sch. counselor Sealy (Tex.) Ind. Sch. Dist., 1988-92; counselor Alton Elem. Sch., Brenham, Tex., 1992—; ednl. cons., Austin County, Tex., 1987-88; reviewer spl. edn. program College Station (Tex.) Ind. Sch. Dist., 1983; feature artist Gov.'s Mansion, State of Tex., Austin, 1985. Pres. Whitehead Cemetery Assn., Grapeland, Tex., 1986-90. Mem. AACD, Tex. Assn. for Counseling and Devel., Ft. Bend County Counseling Assn., Region VI Educational Diagnosticians (pres. Bluebonnet chpt. 1977-78), Nat. Egg Art Guild (SW regional bd. dirs. 1986), Tex. Guild Egg Shell Artists (state pres. 1984-85). Mem. Brethren Ch. Home: RR 1 Box 74 New Ulm TX 78950-9729

WHITEHEAD, JOHN WAYNE, law educator, organization administrator, author; b. Pulaski, Tenn., July 14, 1946; s. John M. and Alatha (Wiser) W.; m. Virginia Carolyn Nichols, Aug. 26, 1967; children: Jayson Reau, Jonathan Mathew, Elisabeth Anne, Joel Christofer, Joshua Benjamen. BA, U. Ark., 1969, JD, 1974. Bar: Ark. 1974, U.S. Dist. Ct. (ea. and we. dists.) Ark. 1974, U.S. Supreme Ct. 1977, U.S. Ct. Appeals (9th cir.) 1980, Va. 1981, U.S. Ct. Appeals (7th cir.) 1981, U.S. Ct Appeals (4th and 5th cirs.). Spl. counsel Christian Legal Soc., Oak Park, Ill., 1977-78; assoc. Gibbs & Craze, Cleve., 1978-79; sole practice law Manassas, Va., 1979-82; pres. The Rutherford Inst., Charlottesville, Va., 1982—, also bd. dirs.; frequent lectr. colls., law schs.; past adj. prof. O.W. Coburn Sch. Law. Author: The Separation Illusion, 1977, Schools on Fire, 1980, The New Tyranny, 1982, The Second American Revolution, 1982, The Stealing of America, 1983, The Freedom of Religious Expression in Public High Schools, 1983, The End of Man, 1986, An American Dream, 1987, The Rights of Religious Persons in Public Education, 1991, Home Education: Rights and Reasons, 1993, Religious Apartheid, 1994, several others; contbr. numerous articles to profl. jours.; contbr. numerous chpts. to books. Served to 1st lt. U.S. Army, 1969-71. Named Christian Leader of Yr. Christian World Affairs Conf., Washington, 1986; recipient Bus. and Profl. award Religious Heritage Am., 1990, Hungarian Freedom medal, Budapest, 1991. Mem. ABA, Ark. Bar Assn., Va. Bar Assn. Office: The Rutherford Inst PO Box 7482 Charlottesville VA 22906-7482

WHITEHEAD, LUCY GRACE, health facility administrator; b. Jacksonville, Fla., Jan. 12, 1935; d. William Alexander and Hester Grace (Gray) Fisackerly; m. John Vernon Whitehead, Sept. 4, 1957; children: Marilyn Ruth, John Vernon Jr., James Andrew. BA, Fla. So. Coll., 1956; M of Christian Edn., Emory U., 1957; BSN, U. North Fla., 1990. RN, Fla. Staff nurse Venice (Fla.) Hosp., 1977, Med. Personnel Pool, Largo, Fla., 1978; charge nurse/nurse educator Gadsden Nursing Home, Quincy, Fla., 1979-85; primary nurse Meml. Regional Rehab. Hosp., Jacksonville, Fla., 1990-92; staff nurse, nurse mgr. Nassau Gen. Hosp., Fernandina Beach, Fla., 1992-94; clin. coord. Integrated Health Svcs., Ft. Pierce, Fla., 1994, dir. nursing, 1994-95. Mem. ANA, Fla. Nurses Assn., Order Ea. Star (worthy matron), Sigma Theta Tau. Methodist. Home: 1083 Tallavana Trail Havana FL 32333

WHITEHEAD, MARTHA, state official. Treas. State of Tex., Austin. Office: State Treasury Bldg PO Box 12608 Capitol Station Austin TX 78711-2608

WHITEHEAD, ZELMA KAY, special education educator; b. Tupelo, Miss., Sept. 20, 1946; d. Henry Neal and Zelma Lee (Rye) W. BS in Spl. Edn., Miss. State Coll. for Women, Columbus, 1968; MEd in Spl. Edn., Miss. State U., Starkville, 1971, Edn. Specialist, 1975; postgrad., U. Miss., Oxford, 1978, 85, Miss. Coll., 1990-92. Cert. tchr. spl. edn., elem. edn., adult basic edn., spl. subject supervision, ednl. adminstrn., elem. principal, secondary principal, elem. supr. Tchr. spl. edn. Nettleton (Miss.) Elem. Sch., 1968-71; site monitor Appalachian Edn. Satellite Program Itawamba Jr. Coll., Tupelo, Miss., 1977-79; instr. spl. edn. Spl. Vocat. Edn. Ctr. Itawamba Jr. Coll., Tupelo, 1971-85, supr. Spl. Vocat. Edn. Ctr., 1984-85, instr. adult basic edn., 1979-85; tchr. spl. prevocat. edn. Shannon (Miss.) High Sch., 1985; edn. specialist Miss. State Dept. Edn., Jackson, 1986, edn. specialist sr., 1986-90; acad. tchr. III Miss. State Hosp., Whitfield, 1990-93, coord. patient edn. and skill tng., 1993—. Mem. Coun. Exceptional Children, Miss. Orgn. Spl. Edn. Suprs. Methodist. Home: 560 Boardwalk Blvd Ridgeland MS 39157-4125 Office: Miss State Hosp Whitfield MS 39193

WHITE-HURST, JOHN MARSHALL, lawyer; b. Washington, May 30, 1942; s. Bernard Marshall and Viola (Hailman) W.-H.; m. Elizabeth Kibler, Oct. 17, 1964 (dec. 1981); 1 child, Elizabeth Marshall; m. Barbara Ann Paliwoda, July 7, 1984. BA, U. Richmond, 1964, JD, 1972. Bar: Va. 1972. Pvt. practice Chase City, Va., 1973-94; asst. commonwealth's atty. Mecklenburg County, Boydton, Va., 1975-89, commonwealth's atty., 1989—; bd. dirs. Va. Legal Aid Soc., Inc., Lynchburg, 1985-92. Bd. dirs. Southside Regional Juvenile Group Home, South Boston, Va., 1980-85, Cmty. Diversion Program, Farmville, Va., 1988-95. Capt. U.S. Army, 1964-68. Mem. Nat. Dist. Atty. Assn., Va. Bar Assn., Va. Trial Lawyers Assn., Mecklenburg County Bar Assn. (pres. 1980-81, 91-92), Local Govt. Attys. Va. (bd. dirs. 1974-77), Chase City Lions (pres. 1976), Am. Legion, Mason, Moose. Baptist. Office: Commonwealth Atty Office MacKlenburg County PO Box 7 350 Washington St Boydton VA 23917

WHITELEY, HAROLD LEE, director; b. Graham, Tex., Aug. 5, 1948; s. Arthur Wiley and Cecilia Elizabeth (Boisclair) W.; m. Linda Sue Day, Dec. 27, 1969; children: Michael Kevin, Jason Lee, Christopher Brian, Kristen Michelle. BS, N. Tex. State U., 1970, MS, 1972; PhD, U. North Tex., 1995. Tchr. math., coach Newcastle (Tex.) Ind. Sch. Dist., 1970-71; tchr. biolog, head football, basketball, track & field coach Munday (Tex.) Ind. Sch. Dist., 1971-73; asst. prin., athletic dir., head coach, tchr. Argyle (Tex.) Rural H.S., 1973-77; mgr. southeast mktg. Turbo Refrigerating Co., Denton, Tex., 1977-82; pres., owner ICE Sys. Internat. Inc., Marietta, Ga., 1982-85, Whiteley & Assocs., Lewisville, Tex., 1983-92; transp. rep. Spl. Programs for Assisting the Needy, Inc., Lewisville, 1992—; pres., owner So. Developers, Inc., Marietta, 1980-84; aerial crop photo technician Agrl. Stabilization and Conservation Svc. Denton, 1991—; bd. dirs Ultra Techs., Inc., Wichita Falls, Tex., 1987-90. Inventor (game boards) Bass Classic, 1986, Golf Classic, 1986; developer Amateur Sports Network Nat. Golf Assn., 1991; contbr. articles on HIV issues in athletics to profl. jours. Grantee Bertha Found., 1991. Mem. Nat. Athletic Trainers Assn., Nat. Assn. Acad. Advisors for Athletes, Am. Assn. Wellnes Edn. Counseling and Rsch., Nat. Assn. Coll. Dirs. of Athetics, Am. Medieval Athletic Assn., Golden Key Soc. Baptist. Home and Office: 531 W Main St Lewisville TX 75057

WHITELEY, JAMES MORRIS, retired aerospace engineer; b. Bangs, Tex., Jan. 27, 1927; s. Charles David and Ruby May (Snead) W.; m. Oleta Wright Basham, Nov. 6, 1993. BS, Daniel Baker Coll., 1951; postgrad., U. Va., 1951-52, So. Meth. U., 1954-57. Rsch. scientist Nat. Adv. Com. for Aeronautics, Hampton, Va., 1951-52; engring. specialist Gen. Dynamics, Ft. Worth, 1952-91; ret., 1991. With USN, 1945-46, PTO. Assoc. fellow AIAA; mem. AARP, The Air Force Assn., Am. Legion. Home: PO Box 297 Bangs TX 76823-0297

WHITEMAN, STEPHANIE ANN, neonatal nurse; b. New Kensington, Pa., May 15, 1967; d. Oran Jr. and Cecilia (Skultety) L. BSN, U. Pitts., 1989. RN, N.J.; cert. BLS, N.J., Va.; cert. neonatal resuscitation Am. Heart Assn. Neonatal ICU nurse Overlook Hosp., Summit, N.J., 1989-90, Med. Coll. of Va. Hosp., Richmond, Va., 1991-95; pediat. mgr. clin. practice Olsten Kimberly Quality Care, 1995—. Benz scholar, Foodland scholar. Mem. Nat. Assn. for Neonatal Nurses. Home: 4603 Patterson Ave Richmond VA 23226-1341

WHITENER, LAWRENCE BRUCE, political consultant, consumer advocate, educator; b. Alexandria, Va., Mar. 5, 1952; s. Ralph Verly and Alice Lee (Beard) W.; m. Deborah Susan Koons, Dec. 7, 1985; 2 foster children. BA in History and Polit. Sci., Va. Commonwealth U., 1975; diploma, Nat. Inst. Real Estate, 1986; AA in Sci., No. Va. C.C., Annandale, 1987, student, 1995—. Tchr. Fairfax (Va.) County Pub. Schs., 1975—; wholesaler Consignment Auto, Falls Church, Va., 1975-77; coach Groveton High Sch. Wrestling Team, Alexandria, 1975-77; senate aide Va. Gen. Assembly, Richmond, 1978; pres. Whitener Cons., Springfield, Va., 1977-86, Real Estate Fin. Svcs., Springfield, 1986-90; U.S. Postal Svc., 1989—; pres. Amicus Curiae & Co., Springfield, 1992—; coach wrestling team Langley H.S., McLean, 1991-93, J.E.B. Stuart H.S., Falls Church, 1993-95; panelist Am. Arbitration Assn., Washington; automotive and banking specialist, 1994—. Author poetry, 1975, 76, 94, screenplays Sorrow, 1993, Saro, 1996; photographer landscapes; subject of article in The Postal Record, 1996. Mem. Athletic Coun., Fairfax County, 1975-84; appointee Housing Assistance Adv. Com., Fairfax County, 1990; commr. Indsl. Devel. Authority, Fairfax County, 1985-93; candidate Fairfax County Bd. Suprs., Springfield Dist., 1991, Fairfax County Sch. Bd., 1995; chmn. vol. rev. com. Fairfax County Access Cable Ch. 10, 1994—; chmn. W.T. Woodson High Sch.'s Class of '70 25th Reunion, 1995; umpire Am. Softball Assn., 1996—. Recipient Cert. of Appreciation, Fairfax County Bd. of Suprs., 1990, Cert. of Appreciation, Nat. Ctr. for Missing and Exploited Children, 1990. Mem. Am. Arbitration Assn. (panel 1994—), Mortgage Bankers Assn. (legis. com. 1985-90, edn. com. 1986-89), No. Va. Bd. Realtors (pub. rels. com. 1985-90, Cert. of Appreciation, Am. Home Week 1986, 90). Office: Amicus Curiae & Co PO Box 611 Springfield VA 22150-0611

WHITESIDE, ANN BIRDSONG, university public relations director; b. Gallatin, Tenn., Dec. 3, 1955; d. Jack Johnson and Dethel (Key) Birdsong; m. Lee Frank Whiteside, Oct. 10, 1975; children: Erica Evette, Kelli Danielle. Student, Stephens Coll., 1989; BA cum laude, Trevecca Nazarene Coll., 1992; grad. Leadership Inst., Mid. Tenn. State U., 1994; MS cum laude, U. Tenn., 1996. Keypunch operator Gallatin Aluminum Products, 1971-76; keypunch operator, computer operator, supr. Space Age Computer Sys., Madison, Tenn., 1976-79; PBX operator, receptionist Vol. State C.C., Gallatin, 1979-80, sec. humanities, 1982, exec. aide, 1982-83, asst. to dir., 1983-86, dir. community rels., 1986—; speaker Vol. State C.C. Speakers Bur., Gallatin, 1986—; instr. student journalism workshop Fisk U., Nashville, 1991. Editor publs. com. Tenn. Higher Edn. Commn., 1990-91. Mem. Tenn. Homecoming 86 Campaign Com., Sumner County, 1986; mem. Gov.'s 3 Star Com., Gallatin, 1988, Tenn. 2000 Steering Com.; Leadership Sumner, Gallatin, 1990-91, coord., 1991-92; sec. bd. dirs. Gallatin Day Care Ctr., 1986-94; mem. exec. bd. United Way, 1995—; active Sumner County Families 1st Coun. Recipient Leadership Support award, Challenge '92 award Returning Women Orgn., Vol. State C.C., 1988, 90, 91. Mem. Nat. Coun. Mktg. and Pub. Rels. (bd. dirs.-at-large 1988-92, treas.), Am. Assn. Women in Cmty. and Jr. Colls., Tenn Higher Edn. Commn. (mem. publ. com.), Tenn. Coll. Pub. Rels., Gallatin C. of C. (mem. exec. bd. 1993—, pres.-elect 1996—), Tenn. Alumni Rels. Coun., Gamma Beta Phi. Democrat. Mem. African Methodist Episcopal Ch. Home: 103 Canterbury Close Gallatin TN 37066-4546 Office: Vol State CC Nashville Pike Gallatin TN 37066

WHITESIDE, DAVID POWERS, JR., lawyer; b. Tupelo, Miss., Jan. 1, 1950; s. David Powers and Delores Dean (Gerkin) W. m. Roseanna McCoy, June 2, 1972; children: David III, Lauren. BA, Samford U., 1972; cert. Exeter Coll., Oxford U., England, 1974; JD, Duke U., 1975; LLM, U. Ala.-Tuscaloosa, 1980. Bar: Ala. 1975, U.S. Dist. Ct. (no. dist.) Ala. 1975, U.S. Ct. Appeals (5th cir.) 1975, U.S. Ct. Appeals (11th cir.) 1981, U.S. Supreme Ct. 1978. Assoc. Johnston, Barton, Proctor et al., Birmingham, Ala., 1975-81, ptnr., 1981—; gen. counsel, Personnel Bd. Jefferson County, Birmingham, 1981-86; legal counsel Jefferson County Citizens Supervisory Commn., Birmingham, 1982-85; lectr. Ala. Jud. Coll., 1985. First. v.p. Birmingham Music Club, 1979-81; mem. Com. for a Better Ala., Birmingham, 1981-82. Recipient Mark Donahue Meml. award Ala. Sports Car Club, 1981-82; winner Palm Beach Hist. Races, 1984, Bahama Vintage Grand Prix, 1987, 89, Grand Bahama Grand Prix, 1990, Lola Cars Cup, Jefferson 500, 1992, Dunlop Cup, 1992; named SVRA Driver of Yr., 1989, Rolex Endurance Champion, 1993, 94. Mem. U.S. Ct. of Appeals Fifth Cir. Jud. Conf. (Host com. 1977, del. 1978), U.S. Ct. Appeals 11th Cir. Jud. Conf. (del. 1982, 86), U.S. Ct. Appeals 5th and 11th Cirs. Jud. Conf. (del. 1989), Newcomen Soc. N.Am., Omicron Delta Kappa. Episcopalian. Club: Mountain Brook. Lodge: Rotary. Home: 2840 Overton Rd Birmingham AL 35223-2734 Office: Johnston Barton Proctor Swedlaw & Naff 2900 Am-South/Harbert Plz Birmingham AL 35203

WHITESIDE, EDWIN, allergist, immunologist; b. Bentonville, Ark., May 3, 1932; s. Thomas C. and Grayce Broyles (Pickens) W.; m. Carole Dowdy, Dec. 22, 1954; children: Scott, Kirk, Susan, Tom, David. Student, USAF Pilot Tng., 1953-55; BS, U. Ark., 1957, MD, 1961. Diplomate Am. Bd. Allergy and Immunology. Commd. USAF, 1953, advanced through grades to col.; intern Lackland AFB (Tex.) Hosp., 1961-62, allergy and immunology tng., 1962-65; chief Aero. Medicine and Allergy Clinic, Dyess AFB, Tex., 1965; comdr. 188th TAC Clinic, Ft. Smith, Ark.; asst. prof. clin. allergy and immunology Sch. Medicine, U. Ark, Little Rock; pres. Northwest Ark. Allergy Clinic, P.A., Ft. Smith, 1965—; mem. staff Washington Regional Med. Ctr., Fayetteville, Ark., 1994, courtesy cons., 1965-85, St. Mary's Hosp., Rogers, Ark., 1994. Deacon Univ. Bapt. Ch., Fayetteville, Ark. Fellow Am. Assn. Cert. Allergists, Am. Coll. Allergy and Immunology; mem. AMA, Am. Acad. Allergy/Immunology, Southwest Allergy Forum, Sebastian County Med. Soc., Allen Cazort State Allergy Soc. Office: NW Ark Allergy Clinic PA 3416 Old Greenwood Rd Fort Smith AR 72903-5462

WHITESIDE, JERRY EUGENE, human resources administrator, consultant; b. Aragon, Ga., May 3, 1937; s. William E. and Mary E. Whiteside; m. Sylvia Lee, Aug. 31, 1958; children: Lee J., Lynn. BS in Poultry Sci., Agrl. Econs., U. Ga., 1959, MBA in Mgmt., 1974, DEd in Bus. Edn., 1985. Commd. 2d lt. U.S. Army, 1959, advanced through grades to col., 1982; various managerial positions, 1959-72; sec. of gen. staff U.S. Army Tng. Ctr., Ft. Jackson, S.C., 1967-69; systems mgr. U.S. Army Computer Systems Command, Ft. Belvoir, Va., 1974-76; bn. comdr. 1st Basic Tng. Brigade, Ft. Jackson, 1976-77, brigade exec. officer, 1977-79; dir. installation systems U.S. Army Computer Systems Command, Ft. Lee, Va., 1980-82; personnel and staff devel. specialist Coop. Ext. Svc. U. Ga., Athens, 1982-89, personnel and staff devel. dir. Coop. Ext. Svc., 1989—, sr. pub. svc. assoc., 1996; speaker numerous workshops and confs., 1983—. Bd. dirs. Beech Haven Bapt. Ch., coord. deaf ministry, pers. com.; merit badge counsellor, former scoutmaster Boy Scouts Am.; state pres. Ga. 4-H Club, 1953-54, del. Nat. Camp, Washington, 1955, counsellor Rock Eagle Ctr., 1955, 56, 57, Cherokee chief, 1956, 57; Danforth fellow, del. Camp Minnewaca, Mich., 1957. Decorated Legion of Merit, Bronze Star with V (3 awards), Air medal (2 medals), Republic of Vietnam Gallantry Cross with gold palm; recipient Refrigerated Transport Co. scholarship, U. Ga., Freshman Merit scholarship, Charles Pfizer Co. scholarship, Polk County Home Demonstration Clubs scholarship, 1955-59. Mem. Am. Mgmt. Assn., Am. Assn. Adult and Continuing Edn., Nat. Assn. Ext. 4-H Agts.(meritorious Svc. award, 1988, Achievement in Svc. award, 1989), Ga. Agri-Bus. Coun., Ga. Adult Edn. Assn., Ga. Master 4-H Club (pres. 1989-91), Rock Eagle Counsellor's Assn., Assn. U.S. Army, Ga. Registry Interpreters for Deaf, Eterna Club, Toastmasters Internat., Epsilon Sigma Phi, Alpha Zeta, Agrl. Honor Soc., Blue Key Fraternity, Sigma Iota Epsilon, Phi Kappa Phi, Gamma Sigma Delta. Southern Baptist. Home: 390 Milledge Ter Athens GA 30606-4940 Office: Univ Ga Lumpkin House Athens GA 30602

WHITESIDES, JOHN LINDSEY, JR., aerospace engineering educator, researcher; b. San Antonio, Feb. 27, 1943; s. John Lindsey and Florene Lyndelle (Wheelis) W.; m. Sheila LaVerne Beadle, May 30, 1964 (div. 1975); children: Lisa Diane, John Gregory; m. Andrea Martina Chavez Lewis, Mar. 26, 1994. BS in Aerospace Engring., U. Tex., 1965, PhD, 1968. Asst. prof. George Washington U., Hampton, Va., 1968-74, assoc. prof., 1974-80, prof., 1980—; assoc. dir. Joint Inst. for Advancement of Flight Scis., Hampton, 1986—. Contbr. articles to profl. jours. Mem. Simga Series Lectures, Hampton, 1990—. Recipient disting. pub. svc. medal NASA, 1993, Malina medal Internat. Astronautical Fedn., 1995. Mem. AIAA (assoc. fellow, dir. 1987-93, nat. faculty advisor 1989), Am. Soc. Engring. Edn., Soc. Engring. Sci. (organizing com. 1975, 76, 77), Tau Beta Pi, Phi Eta Sigma, Sigma Gamma Tau. Home: 218 Cheadle Loop Rd Seaford VA 23696 Office: George Washington U-JIAFS Ms 269 Nasa Lrc Hampton VA 23665

WHITESIDES, THOMAS EDWARD, JR., orthopaedic surgeon; b. Gastonia, N.C., Nov. 4 1929; s. Thomas Edward and Ferne (Bell) W.; m. Peggy Sue Patrick, Jan. 28, 1967; children: William Taylor, Lisa Elizabeth, Edward Patrick, John Thomas. BS, Emory U., 1952, MD, 1955. Diplomate Am. Bd. Orthopaedic Surgeons (dir. 1980-90, trustee 1991—). Resident in orthopaedics Barnes Hosp.-Washington U., St. Louis, 1957-60; asst. prof. surgery Emory U., 1962-66, assoc. prof. surgery, 1966-70, prof. orthopaedic surgery, 1970—, chmn. dept. orthopaedics, 1974-81; instr. orthopaedics Washington U., St. Louis, 1957-60; Alan DeForrest Smith lectr. Columbia U., N.Y.C., 1974; McCarroll lectr. Washington U., St. Louis, 1978, Stein Meml. lectr., 1982; Phesant Meml. lectr. U. So. Calif.; vis. prof. Washington U., Harvard U., Iowa U., U. Pa., others. Author, editor: Evarts Surgery of Musculoskeletal System, 1984, Spine Section, 1984; contbr. numerous articles to profl. jours. Capt. orthopedist MC, USAF, 1960-62. Recipient Kappa Delta rsch. award, Am. Acad. Orthopaedic Surgeons/Orthopaedic Rsch. Soc., 1980. Mem. Am. Acad. Orthopaedic Surgeons; mem. Am. Orthopaedic

Assn., Alpha Omega Alpha. Republican. Presbyterian. Home: 958 Calvert Ln NE Atlanta GA 30319-1202 Office: Emory Clinic Spine Ctr 1265 N Decatur Rd Decatur GA 30033

WHITE-SIMS, SUSANNE TROPEZ, pediatrician, educator; b. New Orleans, Apr. 13, 1949; d. Maxwell Sterling and Ethel (Ross) Tropez; m. James Carnell White, Apr. 10, 1971 (div. 1992); children: Lisa, Janifer, James Carnell; m. Michael Milroy Sims, Feb. 18, 1995. BS, Bennett Coll., 1971; MD, U. N.C., 1975, M.P.H., 1982. Diplomate Am. Bd. Pediatrics. Resident in pediatrics N.C. Meml. Hosp., Chapel Hill, 1975-76, 77-79; pediatrician Darnell Army Hosp., Ft. Hood, Tex., 1976-77; acting dir. pediatric day clinic Wake County Med. Ctr., Raleigh, N.C., 1979-82, dir. pediatric day clinic, 1982-88, dir. teens with tots clinic, 1980-88; asst. prof. pediatrics U. N.C., Chapel Hill, 1982-88, assoc. prof. pediatrics La. State U., New Orleans, 1988—; dir. div. pediatric emergency rm., 1988-89; chief div. ambulatory care, 1989-92, clin. dir. maternal and child health units, 1992, chief divsn. community pediatrics and adolescent medicine, 1992—; pediatrician Shelly Child Devel. Ctr., Raleigh, 1981-88, child med. examiner program, Raleigh, 1979-88; chairperson sch. health com. local chpt. AAP, 1993; adminstrv. bd. chair Cornerstone U.M.C., 1993—, chairperson edn. com., 1991-92; mem. Nat. Com. Sch. Health, 1993—. Contbr. articles to profl. jours. Mem. United Meth. Women. Mem. Walnut Terr. Child Devel. Ctr., Raleigh, 1981-83, chmn., 1982-83; chmn. pastor of parish com. Longview Ch., Raleigh, 1982-84, 87-88, chmn. membership care com.; chmn. edn. com. Cornerstone UMC, 1989-90. Fellow preventive medicine, 1979-82, Faculty Devel. fellow U. N.C. Sch. Medicine, 1985-87. Fellow Am. Acad. Pediatrics (mem. sch. health com.); mem. N.C. Pediatric Soc. (com. child abuse and neglect, adolescent pregnancy), La Pediatric Soc., Ambulatory Pediatric Assn., Adolescent Pregnancy Coalition United Way, Bennett Coll. Alumnae Assn. Democrat.

WHITFIELD, DAVID, company executive. Exec. dir. SGM Internat./ U.S.A. Address: PO Box 195575 Winter Springs FL 32719-5575

WHITFIELD, EDWARD (WAYNE WHITFIELD), congressman; b. Hopkinsville, Ky., May 25, 1943; m. Constance Harriman; 1 child, Kate. BS in Bus., U. Ky., 1965, JD, 1969. Mem. Ky. Ho. of Reps., 1973-74; pvt. practice law, 1973-79; govt. affairs counsel Seaboard Sys. R.R. subs. CSX Corp., 1979-82, counsel to pres., 1982-85; v.p. state rels. CSX Corp., 1986-88, v.p. fed. r.r. affairs, 1988-91; legal counsel to chmn. Interstate Commerce Commn., 1991-93; mem. 104th Congress from 1st Ky. dist., 1995—. 1st lt. USAR. Republican. Office: US Ho of Reps 1541 Longworth HOB Washington DC 20515

WHITFIELD, GRAHAM FRANK, orthopedic surgeon; b. Cheam, Surrey, Eng., Feb. 8, 1942; came to U.S., 1969, naturalized, 1975; s. Reginald Frank and Marjorie Joyce (Bennett) W. BSc, King's Coll., U. London, 1963, PhD, Queen Mary Coll., U. London, 1969; MD, N.Y. Med. Coll., 1976. Rsch. scientist Unilever Rsch. Lab., Eng., 1963-66; postdoctoral fellow dept. chemistry Temple U., 1969-71, instr., 1971-72, asst. prof., 1972-73; resident in surgery N.Y. Med. Coll. Affiliated Hosps., N.Y.C., 1976-78, resident in orthopedics, 1978-79, sr. resident in orthopedic surgery, 1979-80, chief resident, 1980-81; attending orthopedic surgeon Good Samaritan Hosp., West Palm Beach, Fla., 1981-87, JFK Med. Ctr., Lake Worth, Fla., 1981—, Palms Wellington Surgical Ctr., West Palm Beach, Fla., 1994-96, Wellington Regional Med. Ctr., 1996—; instr. health professions divsn. Nova Southeastern U., North Miami, Fla., 1994-95, clin. asst. prof. dept. surgery, Coll. Osteo. Medicine, Ft. Lauderdale, Fla., 1995—. Recipient N.Y. Med. Coll. Surg. Soc. award, 1976. Fellow Internat. Coll. Surgeons; mem. AMA, Fla. Med. Assn., Palm Beach County Med. Soc., Royal Inst. Chemistry (Eng.), So. Orthopedic Assn., Fla. Orthopedic Soc., Sigma Xi. Clubs: Brit. Schs. and Univs., Soc. Sons of St. George (N.Y.C.); Explorers' Club (N.Y.C.). Lodges: Rotary, Sovereign Order Knights of St. John. Author: (with Joseph Cohn and Louis Del Guercio) Critical Care Readings, 1981; editorial bd., contbg. editor Hosp. Physician, 1978-82; cons. editor Physician Asst. and Health Practitioner, 1979-82; orthopedic cons. Conv. Reporter, 1980-82; assoc. editor in chief Critical Care Monitor, 1980-82; edit. bd. Complications in Orthopedics, 1986—; practice panel cons. in orthopedic surgery Complications in Surgery, 1982—. Office: 2150 S Congress Ave West Palm Beach FL 33406-7604

WHITFIELD, JONATHAN MARTIN, pediatrician; b. Edinburgh, Scotland, Sept. 26, 1946; s. Robert Percy and Miriam (Rosenberg) W.; m. Clare Anne Larabie; children: Mark, Andrew, Nicola. MB BChir cum laude, Glasgow (Scotland) U., 1970. Fellow in neonatology U. Toronto, Ont., Can., 1977-78; fellow in neonatology U. Colo., 1976-77, from asst. prof. to assoc. prof. pediats., 1978-91; dir. neonatology and pediat. critical care Baylor U. Med. Ctr., Dallas, 1991—. Comdr. M.C. USN, 1986—. Fellow Am. Coll. Chest Physicians, Am. Acad. Pediats., Royal Coll. Physicians Can. Office: Baylor U Med Ctr 3500 Gaston Ave Dallas TX 75246-2045

WHITFORD-STARK, JAMES LESLIE, geologist, educator; b. London, Sept. 28, 1948; s. Thomas Arthur and Ruby Anne (Frost) W.; m. Judith Ann Perolle, Aug. 6, 1979 (div. Aug. 1981); m. Seta Zaven Choubaralian, Dec. 16, 1983; 1 child, Amy Sylvia; 1 stepchild, Edward. BA in Geology/Geography, U. Keele, U.K., 1971; MSc in Environ. Scis., U. Lancaster, U.K., 1976; PhD in Geology, Brown U., 1980. Geologist Inst. of Geol. Scis., London, 1969-70; rsch. asst. Lancaster U., 1971-76; teaching asst. Brown U., Providence, 1976-77, rsch. asst., 1977-80; vis. asst. prof. U. Mo., Columbia, 1980-82; asst. prof. Sul Ross State U., Alpine, Tex., 1982-87, assoc. prof., chmn. dept. geology/chemistry, 1987-92, prof., 1993—; mem. bd. scientists Chihuahua Desert Rsch. Inst., Alpine, 1991—; rep. Tex. Space Grant Consortium, Austin, 1993—. Author: A Survey of Cenozoic Volcanism on Mainland Asia, 1987; contbr. numerous articles and abstracts to profl. jours. Grantee NASA, 1982-86, NSF, 1988-90, 89-91, 94. Fellow Geol. Soc. London, Geol. Soc. Am.; mem. Am. Geophys. Union, Planetary Soc., NRA (life), N.Am. Hunting Club (life), Alpine Noon Lions (pres. 1992), Big Bend Sportsman Club (sec. 1993—). Home: 1305 N 6th St Alpine TX 79830 Office: Sul Ross State Univ C-139 Dept Geology/Chemistry Alpine TX 79832

WHITING, HENRY H., state supreme court justice. LLB, Univ. Va., 1949. Former judge 26th Jud. Cir. of Va.; sr. justice Va. Supreme Ct., Richmond, 1987—. Office: Va Supreme Ct Judicial Ctr 5 N Kent St Winchester VA 22601-5037*

WHITING, MARTHA COUNTEE, retired secondary education educator; b. Marshall, Tex., Mar. 24, 1912; s; d. Thomas and Nannie Selena (Yates) Countee; m. Samuel Whiting, June 8, 1937; children: Jacqueline Bostic, Sammie Ellis, Nan Broussard, Tommye Casey, Martha Goddard. BA in Sci., Bishop Coll., 1934; M of Secondary Edn., Tex. So. U., 1959; postgrad., U. Colo., 1963. Tchr., sci., math. Houston Ind. Sch. Dist., 1942-73; researcher, local history Houston, 1973—; lectr. in field. Mem. exec. com. Houston YWCA, 1976; advisor Preservation 4th Ward, Houston, 1991—; trustee Antioch Missionary Bapt. Ch., Houston, 1977; instrumental in getting the Antioch Missionary Bapt. Ch. in Christ Inc. on the Nat. Register of Hist. Places, 1976; presented Queen Elizabeth II with miniature history of Antioch Missionary Bapt. Ch. in Christ, 1991; author nomination form for Tex. hist. marker Antioch Missionary Bapt. Ch. in Christ, 1994; presenter to Harris County Heritage Soc. of Jack Yates House, the only house built by a former slave to be maintain ed by a U.S. city, and chmn. Pathfinder presentation of achievements of 64 Negro pioneers in Harris County, 1966-1986. Named Woman Courage, Houston Radcliffe Club, 1985, Black Womens Hall Fame Mus. Africal Am. Life, Dallas, 1986; recipient Friend of the Soc. award Harris County Heritage Soc., 1994. Mem. Tex. Ret. Tchrs. Assn., Houston Mus. Fine Arts, Harris County Heritage Soc. (exec. com. 1984), Bluebonnet Garden Club (pres. 1968), Jack & Jill Am. (pres. Houston chpt. 1955-57), Smithsonian, Nationwide Trust for Historic Preservation. Home: 3446 Southmore Blvd Houston TX 77004-6349

WHITLEY, JOHN QUENTION, JR., orthodontal educator, researcher; b. Burkesville, Ky., Jan. 24, 1955; s. John Quention Sr. and Pauline (Reid) W.; m. Daun Shearin Whitley, Aug. 9, 1980; children: Nicole Dominique, Zachary Cannon. BS, Middle Tenn. State U., Murfreesboro, 1977; postgrad., U. N.C., 1977-78. Rsch. technician U. N.C., Chapel Hill, 1979—, lab. instr. orthodontics, 1988—, lab. instr. biomed. engring., 1989—; cons. Enron Chem. Corp., Rolling Meadows, Ill., 1987, Ormco Corp., Unitek/3M, 1992. Contbr. numerous articles to profl. jours.; patentee in field. Mem. Am. Chem. Soc., Biomaterials Soc., Am. Assn. Dental Rsch., N.Am. Thermal Analyis Soc. Democrat. Baptist. Home: 9101 Greenbriar Sta Chapel Hill NC 27516-9747 Office: U NC CB#7455 Rm 318 DRC Chapel Hill NC 27599

WHITLOCK, DARRELL DEAN, manufacturing company executive; b. Mercedes, Tex., Dec. 24, 1941; s. William Edgar and Luella Anna (Bruggeman) W.; m. Carol Ann Stoneberger, July 6, 1968; children: Troy Dean, Heather LeAnn. BA, Tex. A&I U., 1965. Area supr. Burger King Corp., Miami, Fla., 1970-71; area mgr. The Krystal Co., Jacksonville, Fla., 1971-82; dir. ops. So. Food Svcs., Chattanooga, 1982-83; regional dir. ops. Po Folks Inc., Nashville, 1983-84, dir. mgmt. devel. and tng., 1984-85; regional v.p. Banditree, Inc., Jupiter, Fla., 1985-86; pres. Favorite Foods, Inc., Round Rock, Tex., 1986-89; exec. dir. Nat. Assn. Restaurant Mgrs., Austin, 1987-88; v.p. The Pegasus Group, Austin, 1988-90; pres. Discover Products, Inc., Round Rock, 1989—. Inventor Fling-a-Ring yard game. Chmn. adv. bd. Fla. Jr. Colls., Jacksonville, 1980-81; asst. scoutmaster Boy Scouts Am., 1980-81, Jacksonville, 1980-82; brotherhood mem. Order of Arrow Boy Scouts, Jacksonville, 1980-82. Served as capt. U.S. Army, 1965-69, Vietnam. Mem. Am. Legion. Republican. Office: Discover Products Inc 800 Brandi Ln Round Rock TX 78681-4103

WHITLOCK, JAMES ALAN, pediatrics educator; b. Kingsport, Tenn., July 19, 1958; s. James M. and Ethel E. (Hawk) Wh.; m. Deborah A. Wrenn, Apr. 26, 1986; 1 child, Christopher. BS, Southwestern U., Memphis, 1980; MD, Vanderbilt U., 1984. Diplomate Am. Bd. Pediatrics, Nat. Bd. Med. Examiners. Intern Vanderbilt U. Med. Ctr., Nashville, 1984-85, resident, 1985-87, fellow, 1987-90, asst. prof., 1990—. Mem. AMA, Am. Assn. for Cancer Rsch., Am. Soc. Hematology, Am. Soc. Pediatric Hematology-Oncology, Phi Beta Kappa. Office: Vanderbilt U Med Ctr 517 MRB II 220 Pierce Ave Nashville TN 37232

WHITLOW, JAMES ADAMS, lawyer; b. Mayfield, Ky., Jan. 29, 1968; s. Charles William and June (Hawkens) W. BA, Transylvania U., 1990; JD, Harvard U., 1993. Bar: N.C. 1994. Assoc. Parker Poe Adams & Bernstein, L.L.P., Charlotte, N.C., 1993-95, Akin, Gump, Strauss, Hauer & Feld, L.L.P., Dallas, 1995—. Office: Akin Gump Strauss Hauer & Feld LLP 1700 Pacific Ave Ste 4100 Dallas TX 75201

WHITMAN, HOMER WILLIAM, JR., investment counseling company executive; b. Sarasota, Fla., Jan. 8, 1932; s. Homer William and Phoebe (Corr) W.; m. Anne Virginia Sarran, May 8, 1954; children: Burke William, Michael Wayne. BA in Econs. optime merens, U. South, 1953; grad., U.S. Naval Officer Candidate Sch., 1953; postgrad., Emory U., 1969. Served to group v.p. 1st Nat. Bank Atlanta, 1956-72; pres., dir. Palmer 1st Nat. Bank & Trust Co., Sarasota, 1973-74, Hamilton Bank & Trust Co., Atlanta, 1974-76; v.p. Lionel D. Edie & Co., Atlanta, 1976-78, Mfrs. Hanover Trust Co., Atlanta, 1978-85; sr. v.p. Montag & Caldwell, Inc., Atlanta, 1985—. Dir. Asolo State Theatre. Trustee Selby Found., 1973-74, West Paces Ferry Hosp., Ringling Sch. Art, St. Stephens's Sch.; bd. vis. Emory U.; mem. Leadership Atlanta. Lt. j.g. USNR, 1953-56. Named Hon. French Consul, Atlanta, Atlanta's Outstanding Young Man of Yr., 1963. Mem. Govt. Fin. Officer's Assn., Gla. Govt. Fin. Officers Assn., Ga. Govt. Fin. Officers Assn., Assn. Investment Mgmt. Sales Execs., Atlanta Soc. Fin. Analysts, Healthcare Fin. Mgmt. Assn., Fla. Pub. Pension Trustees Assn., Assn. Pvt. Pension and Welfare Plans (regional chmn.), Am. Cancer Soc. (dir. Atlanta city unit), Newcomen Soc., 300 Club, Atlanta C. of C. (life mem.), Piedmont Driving Club, Peachtree Golf Club, Commerce Club, Buckhead Club (bd. govs.), Union League Club (N.Y.), Breakfast Club, Sarasota U. Club (bd. dirs.), Rotary. Episcopalian. Home: 77 E Andrews Dr NW Apt 353 Atlanta GA 30305-1344 Office: Montag & Caldwell Inc 1100 Atlanta Fin Ctr 3343 Peachtree Rd NE Atlanta GA 30326-1022

WHITMER, WILLIAM EWARD, retired accountant; b. Ft. Wayne, Ind., May 6, 1933; s. Frank Edward and Helen (Eward) W.; m. Signa Charity Dukes, Apr. 11, 1958 (div. 1972); children: Charles Edward, Michael Lee; m. Judith Rehm, Feb. 11, 1984. BA in Econs., Denison U., 1954. CPA, Calif. Staff auditor Arthur Young & Co., San Francisco, 1957-61, audit mgr., 1961-66, audit principal, 1966, cons. prin., 1967, dir. mgmt. cons., 1968-71; office mng. ptnr. Arthur Young & Co., Sacramento, 1971-75; regional dir., mgmt. cons. Arthur Young & Co., Atlanta, 1975-81, regional dir., office mgr., ptnr. mgmt. cons., 1981-89; assoc. mng. dir. Ernst & Young, Atlanta, 1989-92; ret., 1992. Bd. dirs. Acalanes Union High Sch. Dist., LaFayette, Calif., 1965-71, pres. bd. 1969-70. Served with USAF, 1954-57. Mem. AICPA, Ga. Soc. CPA's, Atlanta Country Club, Sea Pines Country Club, Long Court Club. Republican. Presbyterian. Office: 45 Oyster Landing Lane Hilton Head Island SC 29928

WHITMIRE, BRYANT ANDREW, JR., lawyer; b. Birmingham, Ala., Oct. 5, 1946; s. Bryant A. and Sue (Pryor) W.; m. Virginia Neighbors, June 21, 1975; children: Courtney, Elizabeth. BA, U. Richmond, 1969; JD, U. Ala., 1972. Bar: Ala. 1972. Assoc. Whitmire, Morton & Coleman, Birmingham, 1972-78, ptnr., 1978-82; ptnr. Whitmire, Coleman, Whitmire, Birmingham, 1982-86; pvt. practice Birmingham, 1986—. Mem. Child Code Com., Tuscaloosa, Ala., 1986-90, Child Support Guidelines, Montgomery, Ala., 1988-89; founder Keeping Us Together, Birmingham, 1986. Lt. Col. USAR, 1972—. Mem. Am. Acad. Adoption Attys., Birmingham Bar (exec. com. 1986-88, treas.), Pub. Rels. for State Bar (chmn. 1990—), Ala. Legal Svcs. (bd. dirs. 1989—), Ala. Family Law Sect. (bd. dirs. 1993—, pres. 1995-96). Home: 2941 Pine Haven Dr Birmingham AL 35223-1251 Office: 215 21st St N Ste 501 Birmingham AL 35203-3710

WHITMIRE, JOHN LEE, daycare provider; b. Brevard, N.C., June 17, 1924; s. John Leander and Betty Burr (Owen) W.; m. Eva Lee Wilson, Aug. 13, 1950; 1 child, Bonita Dawn. Student, Brevard Coll., 1948-49; BS in Acctg., U. Balt., 1960. Asst. tchr. agr. pub. schs., Brevard, 1946-48; office mgr. Peninsula Poultry Co., Balt., 1955-59; auditor accounts receivable Ea. Products Corp., Balt., 1959-62; chief acct. Texize Corp., Mauldin, S.C., 1962-63; contr. Atlas Vending Co., Greenville, S.C., 1966-69; owner, dir. Twinkle Kiddie Kollege & Day Care, Greenville, 1969—; lobbyist state day care regulation, Columbia, S.C., 1977-81; mem. Adv. Com. on Regulation Child Day Care Facilities, Columbia, 1982-83; field counselor Day Care Child Trend, N.C., S.C., Ga., Ala., Miss., Tenn., Ark. Recipient 100% Dist. Leader Dog award Leader Dogs for the Blind, 1992, 100% Dist. Gov.'s award 1992. Mem. long range planning com. Grove Sch., East Gantt Sch., Greenville; precinct committeeman Greenville Dem. Com., 1970—. Sgt. AUS, 1944-46, ETO; with U.S. Army, 1950-52, Korea. Decorated Purple Heart. Recipient Model Sector Coord. award Campaign Sight First, 1993, Key Leader award, 1993, Leadership award, 1995. Mem. ASCD, Lions (1st v.p. Pleasantburg, L.C. 1985-86, pres. 1987-88, zone chmn. dist. 32-A 1988-89, region chmn. 1989-90, lt. gov. 1990-91, dist. gov. 1991-92, extension chmn., bd. dirs. S.C. Lions Sight Conservation Assn., contbr. Internat. Lions Mag., 1992, Palmetto Lion, 1993-94, Lion of Yr. award 1985, cert. of appreciation from internat. pres. 1989, 91, S.C. Eye Bank Vol. of Yr. award 1992). Baptist. Home: 13 Pecan Dr Greenville SC 29605-3729

WHITMORE, WILLIAM HARVEY, retired physician, securities dealer; b. Portsmouth, Va., Sept. 14, 1926; s. William Harvey and Harriet Weiss (Angeny) W.; m. Katharine Lamar Kimberly, Dec., 1951; children: William H. III, Brent C., Katherine K., Margaret M., John K., Harriet L. BS in Chemistry, Va. Mil. Inst., 1948; MD, U. Va., 1952. Diplomate Am. Bd. Family Practice. Intern Johnston-Willis Hosp., Richmond, Va., 1952-53; resident in internal medicine Norfolk (Va.) Gen. Hosp., 1953-54; Pvt. practice Norfolk, 1954-89, securities dealer, 1985—. With USN, 1944-45. Mem. Norfolk Yacht and Country Club. Episcopalian. Home and Office: 2068 Hunters Trl Norfolk VA 23518-4921

WHITNEY, EDWIN JOSEPH, airlines executive; b. Oklahoma City, June 24, 1931; s. Earl Wayne and Mary Elizabeth (Phillips) W.; m. Shirley Ann Curry, 1958 (div. 1976); m. Kathleen Lou Donaldson, May 30, 1981; children: Sheri Laraine Whitney Dewitt, Eric Wayne. BBA, U. Okla., 1953; LLB, Tulsa U., 1960. Flight mgr. United Airlines, Denver, 1966-91; mng. ptnr. Menor Whitney Co., Tulsa, 1962—. Lt. col. USAF, 1953-56, 61-62, Oklahoma Air Nation Guard, 1957-75, ret. Republican. Presbyterian. Home: 7351 Shady Hollow San Antonio TX 78255 Office: Menor Whitney Co PO Box 472146 Tulsa OK 74147-2146

WHITNEY, ENOCH JONATHAN, lawyer; b. Jacksonville, Fla., Oct. 7, 1945; s. Enoch Johnson and Iris Ida (Sperber) W.; m. Diane Marie Dupuy, Aug. 29, 1968; children: Elizabeth, William, Edward. BA, Fla. State U., 1967, JD, 1970; grad., FBI Nat. Law Inst., 1989. Bar: Fla. 1970, U.S. Dist. Ct. (no. dist.) Fla. 1970 U.S. Dist. Ct. (mid. dist.) Fla. 1982, U.S. Dist. Ct. (so. dist.) Fla. 1989, U.S. Ct. Appeals (5th cir.) 1971, U.S. Ct. Appeals (11th cir.) 1981, U.S. Supreme Ct. 1974. Rsch. asst. Fla. 1st Dist. Ct. Appeals, Tallahassee, 1971; asst. atty. gen. Fla. Dept. Legal Affairs, Tallahassee, 1971-74; asst. gen. counsel Fla. Dept. Hwy. Safety & Motor Vehicles, Tallahassee, 1974-79, gen. counsel, 1979-82, 86—; gen. counsel Fla. Parole and Probation Commn., Tallahassee, 1982-85; instr. Fla. Hwy. Patrol Tng. Acad., Tallahassee, 1977-82, 86—. Named Able Toastmaster, Toastmasters Internat., 1977. Mem. ABA, Tallahassee Bar Assn., Fla. Govt. Bar Assn. (pres. 1977-78), Fla. Bar (bd. govs. 1989—, charter mem. govt. law sect. 1991, bd. cert. appellate lawyer 1994), Fla. Coun. Bar Assn. Pres. (life), Fla. State U. Alumni Assn., Fla. Supreme Ct. Hist. Soc., Supreme Ct. U.S. Hist. Soc., Atty. Gen.'s Hist. Soc. Fla., Fla. Sheriff's Assn., Govs. Club, Capital Tiger Bay Club, Kiwanis (pres. Tallahassee 1984-85, lt. gov. Fla. dist. 1986-87). Democrat. Roman Catholic. Home: 5001 Vernon Rd Tallahassee FL 32311-4534 Office: Fla Dept Hwy Safety & Motor Vehicles 2900 Apalachee Pky Tallahassee FL 32399-6552

WHITNEY, GLAYDE DENNIS, psychologist, educator, geneticist; b. Sidney, Mont., Apr. 25, 1939; s. Russell Taylor and Althea May (Zuber) W.; m. Yvonne Marie Miels, June 20, 1965 (div. 1990); children: Scott, Timothy. BA cum laude, U. Minn., 1961, PhD, 1966. Postdoctoral fellow Inst. Behavior Genetics U. (Boulder) Colo., 1969-70; asst. prof. psychology Fla. State U., Tallahassee, 1970-73, assoc. prof., 1973-78, prof., 1978—; cons. NIH and NSF, Washington, 1976—; adv. group mem. Colo. Alcohol Rsch. Ctr., Boulder, 1986—. Assoc. editor Jour. Behavior Genetics, 1981-84; contbr. over 100 articles to profl. jours. Capt. USAF, 1966-69. Recipient Claude Pepper award Nat. Inst. Deafness and Comm. Disorders, 1990, Mannheimer award for career contbns. to chem. senses, 1994; grantee NIH and NSF, 1970—; fellow NIMH, 1963. Mem. AAAS, Nat. Assn. Scholars, Assn. Chemoreception Scis., Behavior Genetics Assn. (treas. 1978-81, pres. 1994), NRA, Phi Beta Kappa. Republican. Roman Catholic. Office: Fla State U Psychology Dept Tallahassee FL 32306-1051

WHITNEY, J. LEE, home health care administrator; b. Sacramento, Calif., May 11, 1933; d. J. Pierotte and Laura Mae (Parke) Hill; children: M. Thomas Swift III, James E. Swift, Lisa Swift O'Steen. AA, L.A. Valley Coll., 1973; postgrad., Graceland Coll., 1988-89, Barry U., 1990-91. RN, Fla.; cert. advanced cardiac life support. Staff nurse Riverside Hosp., Sherman Oaks, Calif.; home care cons. Home Care Plus, Vero Beach, Fla.; charge nurse med.-surg. and uro-pediatrics unit Indian River Meml. Hosp., Vero Beach, 1988-91, imaging scis. nurse, 1991-93; nurse liaison R.N. Home Health Care, Ft. Pierce, Fla., 1993-95; cmty. coord. Housecall Home Healthcare, Ft. Pierce, 1995—; owner Green Dolphin Interiors, Inc., 1993—; instr. Webster Coll., 1991; past mem. Internat. Urol. Soc., Intravenous Therapy Nurse Soc. Mem. Rep. Exec. Com. Indian River County. Home: 536 Holly Rd Vero Beach FL 32963-1461

WHITNEY, THOMAS PORTER, writer, translator; b. Toledo, Jan. 26, 1917; s. Herbert Porter and Louise (Metzger) W.; m. Marguerite Carusone, Sept. 21, 1974; children by previous marriages: John Herbert, Louise Whitney Christofferson, Julia Forrestel. Grad., Phillips Exeter Acad., 1934; AB summa cum laude, Amherst Coll., 1937; MA, Columbia U., 1940. Instr. social scis. Bennett Coll., 1940-41; social sci. analyst OSS, Washington, 1941-44; attache, chief econ. sect. U.S. Embassy, Moscow, USSR, 1944-47; staff corr. AP of Am., Moscow, USSR, 1947-53; bur. chief, 1953; fgn. news analyst AP of Am., N.Y.C., 1953-59; propr. Whitney Book Shops Conn., 1975—; pres. Book Call, New Canaan, Conn., 1982—. Author: Has Russia Changed, 1960, Russia in My Life, 1962; editor: The Communist Blueprint for the Future, 1962, Khrushchev Speaks, 1963; editor, translator: The New Writing in Russia, 1964, In a Certain Kingdom, Twelve Russian Fairy Tales, 1972, The Young Russians, A Collection of Stories About Them, 1972; translator: One Day in the Life of Ivan Denisovich, 1963, Scarlet Sails, 1967, Prince Ivan, The Firebird and the Gray Wolf, 1968, The First Circle, 1968, Vasilisa the Beautiful, 1970, Forever Flowing, 1972, The Nobel Lecture on Literature, 1972, The Foundation Pit, 1973, The Gulag Archipelago, Vol. I, 1973, Vol. II, 1975, Children of the Street, 1979, Memoirs of General Peter Grigorenko, 1982, The Month Brothers, 1982, Dangerous Thoughts, 1990, No Return, 1990; contbr. articles to popular mags. including Wall Street Jour., N.Y. Times. Trustee Julia A. Whitney Found., Washington, Conn., Saratoga Performing Arts Ctr., 1989—. Mem. Overseas Press Club Am. (pres. 1958-59), ASCAP, PEN Am. Ctr., Thoroughbred Owners and Breeders Assn., Nat. Mus. Racing, Yaddo Corp. (corp. mem.), Phi Beta Kappa, Alpha Delta Phi. Clubs: The Brook (N.Y.); Century Assn., Thoroughbred of Am., Saratoga Reading Rooms. Office: 901 Georgia St Key West FL 33040-7217

WHITSELL, SUNNY SUZANNE, assistant principal; b. McKinney, Tex., Feb. 20, 1953; d. James Hershell Harris and Nancy Sue (Sonntag) Morphis; m. John Wayne Whitsell, Nov. 25, 1971; 1 child, Jeffrey. BA, U. Mo., Kansas City, 1975; MA, U. Tex., 1991. Cert. tchr., endl. supervision, edni. adminstrn. Tchr. Little Elm (Tex.) Ind. Sch. Dist., 1976-79, Lewisville (Tex.) Ind. Sch. Dist., 1981-83; tchr. Midland (Tex.) Ind. Sch. Dist., 1983-91, appraiser, 1991-93, staff devel. intern, 1993-94, asst. prin., 1994—; presenter in field. Mem. Tex. Assn. of Secondary Sch. Prins., Phi Delta Kappa (found. rep.).

WHITT, JOHN, company executive; b. Athens, Ala., Feb. 11, 1946; s. Ervin L. and Mary V. (Guthrie) W.; m. Diana D. Hassenforder, May 27, 1965 (div. Dec. 1980); children: John A., Sean A. BA in Bus., U. Ala., 1967. Prodn. clk. Sherman & Reilly, Inc., Chattanooga, 1967-70, asst. prodn. mgr., 1970-72, sales office mgr., 1972-75, regional sales mgr., 1975-78, asst. v.p. ops., 1978-86, v.p. ops., 1986—. Recipient Human Rels. award Dale Carnegie Course, Chattanooga, 1973; named Impromptu Champion speaker Dale Carnegie Course, Chattanooga, 1973-74. Mem. Adminstrv. Mgmt. Soc., C. of C. (Chattanooga). Office: Sherman & Reilly Inc PO Box 11267 Chattanooga TN 37401-2267

WHITT, MARCUS CALVIN, public relations and marketing executive; b. Paintsville, Ky., Feb. 5, 1960; s. Calvin Leo and Dora Sue (Spears) W.; m. Jennifer Marie McGuire, Jan. 4, 1986; children: Emily Marie, Elizabeth Anne. BA, Eastern Ky. U., 1982, MA, 1985. Intern, dir. student rels. dept. music Eastern Ky. U., Richmond, 1982-85; assoc. for ch. rels. Cumberland Coll., Williamsburg, Ky., 1985-87; dir. communications Conv. & Visitors Bur., Louisville, 1987; staff corr. The Western Recorder, Louisville, 1987—; dir. pub. rels. Georgetown (Ky.) Coll., 1988-92; dir. pub. rels. and mktg. Campbellsville (Ky.) U., 1992-95, asst. to pres., 1995—; bd. dirs. Coun. for Advancement and Support of Edn., Ky., 1990-96, pres.-elect, 1992, pres., 1993, 94, program co-chair, 1989-91, chair III pub. and promotion, 1994; mem. program com. Bapt. Pub. Rels. Assn., Louisville, 1987; lectr. higher edn. instrl. advancement. Contbr. articles to profl. jours. Bd. dirs. Taylor County Tourism Commn., 1995—. Recipient Gold award for Instnl. Rels., Mktg. Higher Edn., 1991, Silver medal Coun. for Advancement and Support of Edn., 1991, award of excellence, 1992, 94, 95, Spl. Merit award, 1991, 94, 95, Grand award, 1991, 94, Silver medal, 1991, 92, Gold medal Image Improvement Mktg. Higher Edn., 1991, Gold award Outdoor Transit Billboard, Admissions Advt. awards, 1990, 91, Merit award in TV advt. Mem. Campbellsville/Taylor County C. of C. (bd. dirs. 1995—, pres.-elect 1996-97), Leadership Scott County (publicity 1990-92), Scott County Adult Lit., Scott County Cmty. Showcase (publicity chair 1989-92), Ky. Bapt. Communicators Forum (co-founder 1991), Mil. Order of the Stars and Bars (Ky. comdr. 1987). Republican. Baptist. Home: 109 E Yorkshire Place Campbellsville KY 42718 Office: Campbellsville U Office Pub Rels and Mktg Campbellsville KY 42718-2799

WHITT, MARY F., reading specialist, educator; b. Montgomery, Ala.; d. Clarence and Georgia W. BS, Ala. State U., 1958; MEd, U. Ariz., 1971; EdD, U. Ala., 1980; postgrad., various colls. ongoing. Camp counselor N.Y.C. Mission Soc., Port Jervis, summer 1956; recreation counselor Dayton

(Ohio) Parks and Recreation Dept., summer 1963; adminstrv. asst. Wiley Coll./NDEA Inst., Marshall, Tex., summer 1965; tchr. Montgomery (Ala.) County Schs., 1958-62; coordinator sci. and math. Dayton (Ohio) pub. schs., 1962-67; reading and spl. edn. tchr. Vacaville (Calif.) Unified Sch. Dist., 1967-70; coord. reading Dallas Pub. Schs., 1971-72; prof. reading Ala. State U., Montgomery, 1972—. Contbr. articles to profl. jurs. U.S. Office Edn. fellow, 1970, 76, 77, NSF fellow, 1961, 62, 64, 66. Mem. Internat. Reading Assn., Capstone Coll. of Edn. Soc., AAUW, Phi Delta Kappa, Kappa Delta Pi. Home: 717 Genetta Ct Montgomery AL 36104-5701

WHITT, RICHARD ERNEST, reporter; b. Greenup County, Ky., Dec. 15, 1944; s. Walter Charles and Irene (Hayes) W.; children: Hayes Chadwick, Emily. Student, Ashland (Ky.) Community Coll., 1966-68; B.A. in Journalism, U. Ky., 1970. Reporter Middlesboro (Ky.) Daily News, 1970-71; asst. state editor Waterloo (Iowa) Courier, 1971-72; city editor Kingsport (Tenn.) Times, 1972-76; No. Ky. bur. chief Courier-Jour., Louisville, 1977; Frankfort bur. chief Courier-Jour., 1977-80, spl. projects reporter, 1980-89; investigative reporter Atlanta Jour. & Constn., 1989—. Served with USN, 1962-66. Decorated Air medal; recipient Pulitzer prize for coverage of Beverly Hills Supper Club fire, 1978; named Outstanding Ky. Journalist, 1978; recipient John Hancock award for excellence, 1983; named to U. Ky. Journalism Hall of Fame, 1995. Democrat. Office: Atlanta Jour & Constn 72 Marietta St NW Atlanta GA 30303-2804

WHITTAKER, CHRISTOPHER JAMES, army officer; b. Phila., Mar. 12, 1968; s. James Miller and Carol Jeane (Oberle) W.; m. Katherine Ann Welte, June 28, 1992; children: Allison Marie, Brock James. BA in History, Va. Mil. Inst., 1990. Commd. 2d lt. U.S. Army, 1990, advanced through grades to capt., 1994; armor platoon leader CCO 5/77 AR 8th Infantry Divsn., Mannheim, Germany, 1990-91; asst. BDE S4 HHC 3d BDE 1st Armor Divsn., Mannheim, 1991-92; maint. platoon leader B Co 202d FSB 1st Armor Divsn., Mannheim, 1992; maint. officer HHC 125th FSB 1st Armor Divsn., Mannheim, 1992-93; shop officer B Co. 125th FSB 1st Armor Divsn., Mannheim, 1993-94; bn. adjutant HHC 296th FSB 2ID, Ft. Lewis, Wash., 1994-95; brigade maint. officer HHC 35th Signal BDE (ABN), Ft. Bragg, N.C., 1996—. Mem. Assn. U.S. Army, Ordnance Corps Assn., Armor Officers Assn., Kappa Alpha Order. Republican. Home: 22 Volturo St Fort Bragg NC 28307

WHITTAKER, MARY FRANCES, educational and industrial company official; b. Portsmouth, Va., Jan. 27, 1926; d. Milton Ernest and Esther (Morgan) Claud; m. Edmund H. Whittaker, June 21, 1947; 1 child, Richard W. BS, Coll. of William and Mary, 1958; MEd, U. Fla., 1966. Tchr., curriculum asst. Duval County Sch. Bd., Jacksonville, Fla., 1958-67; elem. prin. Duval County Sch. Bd., Jacksonville, 1967-70, 76-79, elem. supr., 1970-71, elem. area dir., 1971-76, coordinator planning and constrn., 1979-80, dir. pupil acctg., 1980-85, founding prin. Sch. of Arts, 1985-86, facilities planner, 1986-88, project mgr., 1988-90; asst. prof., coord. of interns Edward Waters Coll., Jacksonville, Fla., 1990-92; v.p. Ednl. & Indsl. Inc., Jacksonville Beach, Fla., 1988—; asst. prof. Edward Waters Coll., Jacksonville, Fla., 1993—, dir. of interns, 1994—. Mem. Nat. Assn. Tchrs. of Singing, Nat. League Am. Pen Women (sec. 1980-82).

WHITTEMORE, LINDA GENEVIEVE, clinical psychologist; b. Ft. Bragg, N.C., Nov. 1, 1948; d. James and Nancy (Caudill) White; children: Trevor Johnson, Dylan Lane. BA in Anthropology, East Carolina U., 1972, MA in Clin. Psychology, 1980. Rehab. svcs. coord. Social Center, Fairfax, Va., 1978-79; site coord. Mental Health Assn. of N. Va., Annandale, 1979-80; program asst. Alliance to Save Energy, Washington, 1981-82; ednl. psychology officer APA, Washington, 1984-88; exec. mktg. dir. I.D.N., Provo, Utah, 1989-93; supr. 24th Dist. Ct. Svcs. Unit, Lynchburg, Va., 1994-96; psychologist Ctrl. Va. Tng. Ctr., Lynchburg, 1996—; prof. Benjamin Franklin U., Washington, 1986-87. Editor: Activities Handbook for the Teaching of Psychology, Vol. 2, 1987, Vol. 3, 1990. Mem. Noetic Soc., Assn. of Employee Assistance Counselors, Toastmasters Internat. Home: Villa Mozart 517 Washington St Lynchburg VA 24504

WHITTEMORE, RONALD P., hospital administrator, retired army officer, nursing educator; b. Saco, Maine, Aug. 10, 1946; s. Ronald B. and Pauline L. (Larson) W.; m. Judy D. McDonald, Feb. 17, 1967; 1 child, Leicia Michelle. BGS, U. S.C., 1974, MEd, 1977; BSN, Med. Coll. Ga., 1975. Enlisted U.S. Army, 1968, advanced through ranks to maj., 1985, ret., 1991; adult/oncology nurse practitioner Martin Army Community Hosp.; asst. head nurse SICU, infection control practitioner Moncrief Army Community Hosp.; infection control practitioner U.S. Army Hosp., Seoul, Korea; chief nurse 2d Combat Support Hosp., Ft. Benning, Ga.; community health nurse Brooke Army Med. Ctr., Ft. Sam Houston, Tex.; comty. health nurse Giessen (Fed. Republic Germany) Mil. Comty.; clin. instr. Eisenhower Army Med. Ctr., Ft. Gordon, Ga.; chief nursing adminstrn. E/N Frankfurt (Germany) Army Med. Ctr.; adminstr., dir. quality improvement Gracewood (Ga.) State Sch. and Hosp., 1995—; instr. Augusta (Ga.) Tech. Inst.; nurse epidemiologist Med. Coll. Ga., Augusta. Mem. ANA, Ga. ANA (3d Dist. honoree, pres. 1983-85), Am. Holistic Nurses Assn., Nat. Asns. Health Care Quality Profls., Sigma Theta Tau. Home: 801 Bon Air Dr Augusta GA 30907 Office: Gracewood State Sch & Hosp Gracewood GA 30812

WHITTEN, BESSIE EMRICK, editor; b. Opelika, Ala., Aug. 9, 1945; d. Veri Roy and Eleanor (Craig) Emrick; m. David Owen Whitten, Sept. 1, 1987. Student, Auburn U., 1963-66. Editl. asst. U. Fla. Law Rev. U. Fla. Law Sch., 1974-76; copy editor Jour. Mgmt. Auburn (Ala.) U., 1978-79, supr. manuscript preparation ctr., copy editor Coll. Bus., 1978-92, co-editor Bus. Libr. Rev., 1993—. Editor: A History of Economics and Business at Auburn University, 1992; co-editor: (with David O. Whitten) Manufacturing: A Historiographical and Bibliographical Guide, Vol. 1, Handbook of American Business History, 1990, Eli Whitney's Cotton Gin, 1793-1993, 1994; asst. editor: Wall St. Rev. Books, 1983-88, Bus. Libr. Rev., 1988—; editor, exec. dir. The Cotton Gin Symposium, Auburn, 1993; copy editor (with others): The Entrepreneur, 1982, The Essentials of Money and Banking, 1982; others. Mem. Am. Econ. Assn., Bus. History Conf., Econ. and Bus. Hist. Soc., Econ. History Assn.

WHITTEN, C. G., lawyer; b. Abilene, Tex., Apr. 1, 1925; s. C.G. and Eugenia (St. Clair) W.; m. Alene Henley, Nov. 25, 1945; children: Julie, Jennifer, Blake; m. Carol Owen, Apr. 22, 1977. BS, U. Tex.-Austin, 1943, JD, 1949. Bar: Tex. 1949, U.S. Dist. Ct. (no. dist.) Tex. 1950, U.S. Supreme Ct. 1955. Assoc. Grisham & King, Abilene, Tex., 1949-52; ptnr. Jameson & Whitten, 1952-54, Jameson, Whitten, Harrell & Wilcox, 1954-58, Whitten, Harrell, Erwin & Jameson, 1958-68, Whitten, Sprain, Wagner, Price & Edwards, 1968-79, Whitten, Haag, Cobb & Hacker, 1979-82; sr. ptnr. Whitten, Haag, Hacker, Hagin & Cutbirth, 1983-87; pres. Whitten, Hacker, Hagin, Anderson & Rucker, P.C., 1987-92, Whitten & Young, 1992—; gen. counsel Pittencrieff Comms., Inc., 1992—, sr. v.p., dir., 1994—; pres. Abilene Improvement Corp., 1994—; mem. adv. coun. U. of Tex. Press, 1995—. Mem. Abilene Ind. Sch. Dist., 1959-67, pres., 1972-76. Office: PO Box 6088 Abilene TX 79608-6088

WHITTEN, DAVID OWEN, economics educator; b. Beaver Falls, Pa., Nov. 30, 1940; s. Paul Harry and Bula (Owens) Ehrenbergh. BS, Coll. Charleston, 1962; MA, U. S.C., 1963; PhD, Tulane U., 1970. Instr. econs. and fin. U. New Orleans, 1965-68; asst. prof. econs. Auburn U., Ala., 1968-74, assoc. prof., 1974-82, prof., 1982—; cons. U.S. Army C.E., New Orleans, summers 1964, 65. Author: Andrew Durnford: A Black Sugar Planter in the Antebellum South, 1981, 95 (La. honor award 1982), Emergence of Giant Enterprise, 1983, A History of Economics and Business at Auburn University, 1992; editor: (with Bessie E. Whitten) Manufacturing: A Historiographical and Bibliographical Guide Vol. 1 Handbook of American Business History, 1990, Two-Hundred Years of Eli Whitney's Cotton Gin, 1994, Andrew Durnford: A Black Sugar Planter in the American South, 1995; editor, Wall St. Rev. of Books, 1981-89, Bus. Libr. Rev., 1990—; contbr. articles to profl. jours. Served with USMCR, 1957-63. Tulane Edn. Found. fellow, 1964, 65. Mem. Am. Econ. Assn. Agrl. History Soc., Soc. for History Early Am. Rep., Econ. History Assn., So. Econs. Assn., Bus. History Conf., Econ. and Bus. Hist. Soc. (v.p. 1988-91, pres. 1991-92), Rexford G. Tugwell Internat. Inst. for Great Depression Era Studies (v.p., treas., dir. 1992—). Home: 1309 Gatewood Dr Apt 909 Auburn AL 36830-2839 Office: Auburn U Dept Econs Bus Bldg 209 Auburn AL 36849

WHITTINGTON, FLOYD LEON, economist, business consultant, retired oil company executive, foreign service officer; b. Fairfield, Iowa, May 27, 1909; s. Thomas Clyde and Ora E. (Trail) W.; m. Winifred Carol McDonald, July 31, 1933; children: Susan Whittington West, Thomas Lee. A.B., Parsons Coll., 1931; M.A., U. Iowa, 1936; student, U. Minn., 1940, Northwestern U., 1941-42. Econs., speech instr. Fairfield High Sch., 1931-36, Superior (Wis.) High Sch., 1936-40; supr. tchr. tng. Superior State Tchrs. Coll., 1936-40; econs., finance instr. Carroll Coll., Waukesha, Wis., 1940-42; price exec. OPA, Wis. and Iowa, 1942-46; indsl. relations mgr. Armstrong Tire & Rubber Co., Des Moines, 1946-48; dir. price and distbn. div. SCAP, Tokyo, Japan, 1948-51; Far East economist ODM, Washington, 1951-52; asst. adviser to sec. on Japanese financial and econ. problems Dept. State, Washington, 1952-53; chief Far Eastern sect. Internat. Finance div.; bd. govs. FRS, Washington, 1953-56; officer charge econ. affairs Office S.E. Asian Affairs, Dept. State, 1956-57, dep. dir., 1957-58; became counselor of embassy Am. embassy, Bangkok, 1958; counselor, polit. officer Am. embassy, Djakarta, Indonesia, 1962-65; counselor of embassy for econ. affairs Seoul, Korea, 1965-66; v.p. Pacific Gulf Oil, Ltd., Seoul, 1966—; exec. v.p. S.E. Asia Gulf Co., Bangkok, 1967-72, Gulf Oil Co. Siam, Ltd., Bangkok, 1967-72; v.p. Gulf Oil Co.-South Asia, Singapore, 1970-72; now Asian bus. cons. Recipient Meritorious Civilian Service citation Dept. Army, 1950. Mem. Am. Econ. Assn., Am. Acad. Polit. Sci., World Affairs Council Seattle (pres.), Seattle Com. Fgn. Relations, Pi Kappa Delta, Theta Alpha Phi. Presbyterian. Clubs: Royal Bangkok (Thailand); Sports; Lakes (Sun City, Ariz.). Lodges: Masons; Shriners; Rotary. Home: 1 Towers Park Ln Apt 515 San Antonio TX 78209-6421

WHITTINGTON, FREDERICK BROWN, JR., business administration educator; b. Sept. 22, 1934; m. Marjorie Ann Babington; children: Frederick Brown III, Marjorie Ellen, Lisa Anne. SB, MIT, 1958; MBA, Tulane U., 1965; PhD, La. State U., 1969. Staff economist Miss. Rsch. Commn., Jackson, 1961-64; sr. assoc. econ. rsch. Gulf South Rsch. Inst., Baton Rouge, 1966-69; asst. prof. bus. adminstrn. Emory U., Atlanta, 1969-73, assoc. prof., 1973-79, prof. bus. adminstr., 1979—, dir. customer bus. devel. track, 1991—; bd. dirs. Gwinnett Industries, Inc.; mem. forecasting panel Fed. Res. Bank Atlanta; vis. prof. Johannes Kepler U., Linz, Austria, 1983, 84, 89, 95, 96; guest lectr. Austrian Univs., Linz, Vienna, Innsbruck and Klagenfurt; presenter workshops; cons. in field. Contbr. articles and reports to profl. jours. Mktg. plan, mgmt. audit State of Miss., Park Commn.; past chmn., bd. deacons Decatur Presbyn. Ch.; mem. adv. bd. DeKalb/Rockdale Svc. Ctr., ARC. Capt. USNR, ret. Sears, Roebuck Found. fellow, 1965-66. Mem. Am. Mktg. Assn., Nat. Assn. Purchasing Mgmt., So. Mktg. Assn., Coun. for Logistics Mgmt., Warehousing Edn. and Rsch. Coun., Omicron Delta Kappa, Beta Gamma Sigma, Delta Tau Delta. Office: Goizueta Bus Sch Emory Univ Atlanta GA 30322

WHITTINGTON, ROBERT WALLACE, business executive; b. Birmingham, Ala., Sept. 25, 1939; s. Dorsey and Frances (Kohn) W. BS, Auburn U., 1959; BA, U. Miami, 1961; MS, Cornell U., 1963. Cert. landscape architect. Pres. Balt. Travel Ctr., 1965-69, CTC, Inc., Chgo., 1969-75, Prestige Vacations, Inc., Chgo., 1970-75, Hort. Svcs., Inc., Sarasota, Fla., 1975-89, Exotics, S.A., San Jose, Costa Rica, 1985—, Internat. Travel Ctr., Miami, Fla., 1985—. Author: Bibliography of American Fishing Books, 1979. Recipient Key to the City, City Coun. of Miami, 1981, Govt. of Mexico City, 1982. Mem. Fedn. Fly Fishermen, Am. Hort. Soc. Office: Exotics SA PO Box 025216 Miami FL 33102-5216

WHITTLE, MELISSA SUE, kindergarten educator; b. Nashville, May 18, 1972; d. William Thomas and Sandra Oleta (Jarvis) W. BS, Freed-Hardeman U., 1994. Kindergarten tchr. Friendship Christian Sch., Lebanon, Tenn., 1994—. Mem. Ch. of Christ. Office: Friendship Christian Sch Coles Ferry Pike Lebanon TN 37087

WHITTON-HENLEY, LYNDA JEAN, librarian; b. Shreveport, La., Sept. 18, 1942; d. Lynford and Rowena Laurence (Belgard) Feazel; m. John Evan Whitton Jr., June 22, 1963 (div. Mar. 1990); children: Suzette F., Patricia L., Brian E., Charle L.; m. Thomas Eugene Henley, Dec. 12, 1992. BA in Sociology, Corpus Chrsiti State U., 1991, MS in Counseling, 1992; MLS, U. Tex., 1995. Crew leader U.S. Census Bur., Ft. Worth, 1980; ind. market researcher, coord. Arbitron, Ft. Worth, 1980-87; field interviewer U.S. Census Bur., Corpus Christi, Tex., 1983-87; youth counselor City of Corpus Christi, 1987; career counselor Corpus Christi Pub. Libr., 1987-94, bus. libr. II, 1994—. Mem. ALA, ASTD, Pub. Libr. Assn., Tex. Libr. Assn. (vol. coord. 1994). Baptist. Office: Corpus Christi Pub Libr 805 Comanche St Corpus Christi TX 78401-2715

WHYDE, JANET MARCIEL, literature educator, editor; b. Arkansas City, Kans., Feb. 24, 1963; d. Jack Stephen W. and Carmen Marciel (Bennett) Cline; m. Keith William Hendrix, June 5, 1985 (div. May 15, 1991); 1 child, Jakob William. BA, Tex. A & M U., 1985; MA, N.C. State U., 1991; PhD, La. State U., 1995. Copy editor Oxford U. Press, Cary, N.C., 1989-92, AMS Press, N.Y.C., 1992-96; mng. editor Henry James Rev., Baton Rouge, 1992-94; instr. La. State U., Baton Rouge, 1995-96; tchr. UMS-Wright Prep. Sch., Mobile, Ala., 1996—. Compiler: (journal) Poe Studies, 1989-93; contbr. articles to profl. jours. Vol. Habitat for Humanity, Baton Rouge, 1993-96, Urban Art and Culture Collective, Baton Rouge, 1994-96; reader E. Baton Rouge Pub. Schs., 1993. Mem. Am. Studies Assn., MLA, South Ctrl. Modern Lang. Assn. Democrat. Presbyterian. Office: UMS-Wright Prep Sch 65 N Mobile St Mobile AL 36607

WHYTE, BRUCE MACGREGOR, health service executive director; b. Brisbane, Australia, June 29, 1947; came to U.S., 1989; s. Henry Malcolm and Marguerite Mary (Lamont) W.; m. Hanya L. Baran, Aug. 26, 1972; children: Jeremy MacGregor, Timothy Bruce. MB, BS, U. Sydney, Australia, 1972. Med. resident, registrar Royal Hobart (Australia) Hosp., 1972-74; pvt. practice Hobart, 1975-76, Canberra, Australia, 1976-85; dir. Fed. AIDS Coord. Unit, Sydney, 1986-87; sr. scientist, med. adminstr. spl. unit AIDS, epidemiology and clin. rsch. Nat. Health and Med. Rsch. Coun., 1987-89; vis. scientist Ctrs. for Disease Control, Atlanta, 1989-90; med. epidemiologist pub. health Dept. Human Resources, Atlanta, 1991-93; exec. dir. Ga. Mountains Health Svcs., Morganton, Ga., 1994—; cons. in field. Contbr. articles to profl. jours. Australian Fed. Govt. fellow, 1989. Office: Ga Mountains Health Svcs PO Box 540 Morganton GA 30560-0540

WHYTE, JOHN JOSEPH, internist; b. Phila., Apr. 14, 1966; s. John and Anna Marie (Alberti) W. BA, U. Pa., 1984-88; MD, Hahnemann U., 1993; MPH, Harvard U., 1993. Diplomate Nat. Bd. Med. Examiners. Med. resident Duke U. Med. Ctr., Durham, N.C., 1993-96; attending physician Stanford, Palo Alto VA Hosp., Palo Alto, Calif., 1996—; chmn. Nat. Consortium Resident Physician Orgns., Washington, 1995-96,. Author: (editorials) in newspapers and med. jours. Mem. AMA (chmn. resident physician sect. 1996-97), Am. Coll. Physicians, Am. Soc. Internal Medicine. Roman Catholic. Home: 801 Church St # 1219 Mountain View CA 94041

WIATT, CAROL STULTZ, elementary education educator; b. Roanoke, Va., July 9, 1946; d. Hubert Grant and Irene Ella (Barbour) Stultz; m. Alexander Lloyd Wiatt, June 14, 1969; children: Alexander Todd II, Christopher Campbell. BS in Elem. Edn., Radford U., 1968; cert., Coll. of William and Mary, 1991. Cert. elem. and mid. sch. prin., geography and elem. grades tchr. Tchr. 4th grade Roanoke Pub. Schs. Sys., 1968-70; tchr. 6th grade Richmond (Va.) Pub. Schs. Sys., 1970-73; tchr. 5th and 6th grades Newport News (Va.) Pub. Schs. Sys., 1974-91, staff devel. specialist, 1991-93, tchr. 5th grade, 1993—; adj. faculty, master tchr. Hampton (Va.) U., 1988—; adj. faculty Christopher Newport U., Newport News, 1988-93, prof., 1993-94; computer specialist Newport News Pub. Schs. Sys., 1987-91; prin. Hidenwood Elem. Sch., summer 1994. Author: DESIGNS, 1986; contbr. articles to profl. jours. and newspapers. Active Friends of Mariners' Mus., Newport News, 1987—; chmn. cultural arts com. Newport News Coun. PTA, 1980-83, 1st v.p., 1981-83, treas., 1983-85; mem. hospitality com. Hidenwood Sch. PTA, 1985-86, chmn. membership com., 1986-88; bd. dirs. Hidenwood Recreational Assn., Newport News, 1988-92. Recipient Hon. Mention, Tchr. of Yr. awards The Consortium for Interactive Instrn., 1987, 90; fellow Old Dominion U. Coll. Edn. Mem. ASCD, NEA, ICCE, AAUW, Va. Assn. Curriculum and Devel., Va. Edn. Assn., Va. Edn. Math. Assn., Va. Tech. Edn. Assn., Va. Geography Soc., Newport News Edn. Assn., Peninsula Coun. Math. of Va. (v.p. 1987-88), Newport News Reading Coun, Kappa Delta Pi. Republican. Baptist. Home: 24 S Madison Ln Newport News VA 23606-2855 Office: McIntosh Elem Sch 185 Richneck Rd Newport News VA 23608

WICH, DONALD ANTHONY, JR., lawyer; b. Detroit, Apr. 13, 1947; s. Donald Anthony and Margaret Louise (Blatz) W. BA with honors, Notre Dame U., Ind., 1969, JD, 1972. Bar: Fla. 1972, U.S. Dist. Ct. (so. dist.) Fla. 1972; U.S. Ct. Appeals (5th and 11th cirs.) 1982, U.S. Supreme Ct. 1976; cert. civil trial lawyer 1983. Assoc. VISTA, Miami, Fla., 1972-74; atty. Legal Svcs., Miami, 1973-75; adj. prof. law U. Miami, Fla., 1974-75; ptnr. Wich, Wich & Wich, P.A., Ft. Lauderdale, Fla.; pres., dir. Legal Aid of Broward, Ft. Lauderdale, 1976-82. Mem. ABA, ATLA, Am. Arbitration Assn., North Broward Bar Assn. (pres. 1983-84), Acad. Fla. Trial Lawyers Assn. (sustaining mem.), Broward County Trial Lawyers Assn. (pres. 1988-89, sustaining mem.), Broward Bar Assn. (chmn. legis. com. 1984-85, exec. com. 1986-92, 94—, chmn. bench-bar com. 1993-94, chmn. clerk-bar com. 1993—, pres.-elect 1996—), Tex. Trial Lawyers Assn., N.Y. Trial Lawyers Assn., Pompano Beach C. of C. (pres. 1989-90, dir. 1984-87, 92—, govtl. affairs chmn. 1983-84, art show chmn. 1984-85, seafood festival chmn. 1986-90), Notre Dame Frederick Sorin Soc., Rotary (bd. dirs. 1987-91), Woodhouse (bd. dirs. 1990-91). Office: Wich Wich & Wich PA 2400 E Commercial Blvd Fort Lauderdale FL 33308-4030

WICK, GARY ALLEN, police officer; b. Steubenville, Ohio, Mar. 13, 1942; s. Gordon Edward and Virginia Agnes (Core) W.; m. Rebecca Ann Boyles, Aug. 13, 1965; 1 child, Angela Ann. Student, Ohio Valley Coll., 1960, 61, U. Va., 1978; BA, Marshall U., 1983, MS, 1987. With W.Va. State Police, 1971-94; detachment comdr. W.Va. State Police, Glasgow, 1982-83, Big Chimney, 1983-88; insp. internal affairs W.Va. State Police, South Charleston, 1988-94, acad. instr., 1978-94; with chem. div. Pitts. Plate Glass Co., Natruim, W.Va., 1965-71; with FBI, Clarksburg, W.Va., 1994—. Named Law Officer of Yr. for W.Va., Am. Legion-40 and 8 Soc., 1985. Mem. Am. Soc. Safety Engrs. (cons. 1989), FBI Acad. Assocs. (pres. W.Va. chpt. 1987-88), Nat. Troopers Coalition, W.Va. Troopers Assn., W.Va. Safety Coun., Fraternal Order Police (guard 1989), W.Va. Chiefs of Police Assn., Nat. Internal Affairs Investigators Assn. (pres. 1994). Republican. Home: PO Box 100 Rivesville WV 26588 Office: FBI/CJIS Clarksburg WV 26306

WICKER, DENNIS A., state official; b. Sanford, N.C., 1952; s. J. Shelton and Clarice (Burns) W.; m. Alisa O'Quinn; children: Quinn Edward, Jackson Dennis, Harrison Lee. BA in Econs. with honors, U. N.C., 1974; JD, Wake Forest U., 1978. Atty. Love & Wicker, 1978-92; mem. N.C. Ho. of Reps., 1981-92; lt. gov. State of N.C., 1993—; chmn. law enorcement com., 1983, house com. cts. and adminstrn. justice, 1985, house jud. com., 1987; chmn. N.C. Small Bus. Coun., 1993—, N.C. State C.C. Bd., 1993—, N.C. State Health Purchasing Alliance Bd., 1993—, Gov.'s Task Force on Driving While Impaired, 1994—, N.C. Local Govt. Partnership Coun.; mem. N.C. Capitol Planning Com., 1993—, N.C. Coun. of State, 1993, N.C. Commn. on Bus. Laws and The Economy. Chmn. N.C. Local Govt. Partnership Coun.; chmn. Gov.'s Task Force on Driving While Impaired. Named Legis. of Yr., Children's Learning Disability Assn. N.C.; recipient Jane Alexander Pub. Svc. award MADD, 1993, Pres.'s award N.C. Assn. Educators, Legis. Leadership award Nat. Commn. Against Drunk Driving, 1994; listed among 10 most effective legis. N.C. Ctr. Pub. Policy Rsch. Mem. Phi Beta Kappa. Democrat. Methodist. Office: Office of Lt Gov State Capitol Raleigh NC 27603-8006

WICKER, JAMES ROBERT, minister; b. Corpus Christi, Tex., Sept. 30, 1954; s. David Elzy III and Carolyn (Reed) W.; m. Dana Abernathy, Dec. 22, 1978; children Jessica Helen, Matthew Robert, Stephen Paul. BA in Oral Communications, Baylor U., 1977; MDiv., Southwestern Bapt. Theol. Sem., 1980, PhD in N.T., 1985. Lic. to ministry So. Bapt. Conv., 1973, ordained, 1981. Sunday Sch. cons. Mo. Bapt. Conv., Jefferson City, 1978; asst. dir. Youth Evangelism Schs. Evangelism div. Bapt. Gen. Conv. Tex., Dallas, 1979-81, dir., 1982-85; pastor 1st Bapt. Ch., Lavon, Tex., 1981-84; teaching fellow Southwestern Bapt. Theol. Sem., Ft. Worth, 1982-83; pastor 1st Bapt. Ch., Farmersville, Tex., 1984-91, 1st Bapt. ch., Frisco, Tex., 1991—; magician, 1974—; moderator Collin Bapt. Assn., 1989-91, evangelism com., 1982-85, Dallas Bapt. U. com., 1985-87, prayer com., 1986-89, exec. com., 1988-91, fin. com., 1992-94, ch. growth com., 1993-95, D.O.M. search com., 1994, mission com. 1995—; adj. prof. Old and N.T., Dallas Bapt. U., 1988—; missions advance team Bapt. Gen. Conv. Tex., 1989-90. Mem. Comm. Network, Farmersville Ind. Sch. Dist., 1989-91; mem. Farmersville Alliance, 1984-91, pres., 1985, 87; mem. cmty. rels. com. Collin County United Way, 1993-94, chmn., 1994; mem. bd. YMCA, Frisco, 1992-94; mem. Marketplace Ministries Bd., 1993—. Recipient awards talent shows, tng. award for religious leadership Order Ea. Star, Lavon, 1983. Mem. World Clown Assn., Unicycling Soc. Am., Farmersville C. of C. (bd. dirs. 1985-87, v.p. 1986, pres. 1987), Tex. Assn. Magicians (awards in comedy magic 1977, 79), Internat. Brotherhood Magicians, Fellowship Christian Magicians, Farmersville Rotary (pres.-elect 1986-87, pres. 1987-88), Kappa Omega Tau. Home: 5100 Ashland Belle Ln Frisco TX 75035 Office: 1st Bapt Ch PO Box 1170 Frisco TX 75034-1170

WICKER, MARIE PEACHEE, civic worker; b. Detroit, July 9, 1925; d. Charles Andrew and Bessie Louise (Sullivan) Peachee; m. Warren Jake Wicker, July 31, 1948; children: Beth Wicker Walters, Jane Fields Wicker-Miurin, Thomas Alton. BA, Westhampton Coll., 1946; MA, U. N.C., 1950. Test technician N.C. Merit System Coun., Durham, 1950-51; classification analyst N.C. Personnel Dept., Raleigh, 1951-52; engring. placement dir. N.C. State U., Raleigh, 1952-57. Author: You Can Make It Yourself, 1988, First Women of Orange County, N.C., 1994, 2d edit., 1995, A History of the Chapel Hill Woman's Club, 1910-1995, 1995. Chmn. Chapel Hill Recreation Commn., 1961-62; legis. chmn. N.C. Congress Parents and Tchrs., 1972-73; mem. Chapel Hill-Carrboro Bd. Edn., 1973-75, Historic Hillsborough (N.C.) Commn., 1987-93. Recipient Dist. Conservation award N.C. Wildlife Resources Commn., 1987. Mem. N.C. Fedn. Women's Clubs (dist. pres. 1984-86, dist. chmn. conservation dept. 1992-94, state chmn. conservation dept. 1992-94, sec.-treas. past dist. pres. club 1992-94, Sallie Southall Cotten scholarship com. 1994—), N.C. Coun. Women's Orgns. (bd. dirs. 1990, 1st v.p. 1992-93), Chapel Hill Women's Club (pres. 1985-87, 1st v.p. 1996-98), Orange County Commn. for Women. Democrat. Home: 1024 Highland Woods Rd Chapel Hill NC 27514-4410

WICKER, ROGER F., congressman; b. Pontotoc, Miss., July 5, 1951; m. Gayle Wicker; children: Margaret, Caroline, McDaniel. BA in Polit. Sci. and Journalism, U. Miss., 1973; JD, Ole Miss Law Sch., 1975. Judge advocate USAF, 1975-79; mem. staff rules com. Staff of U.S. Rep. Trent Lott, 1980-82; pvt. practice, 1982—; mem. Miss. State Senate, 1988-94, 104th Congress from 1st Miss. dist., 1995—. Republican. Office: US House Reps 206 Cannon Washington DC 20515

WICKER, THOMAS CAREY, JR., judge; b. New Orleans, Aug. 1, 1923; s. Thomas Carey and Mary (Taylor) W.; children: Thomas Carey III, Catherine Anne; m. Jane Anne Trepanier, Dec. 29, 1995. BBA, Tulane U., 1944, LLB, 1949, JD, 1969. Bar: La. 1949. Law clk. La. Supreme Ct., New Orleans, 1949-50; asst. U.S. Atty., 1950-53; practiced in New Orleans, 1953-72; mem. firm Simon, Wicker & Wiedemann, 1953-67; partner firm Wicker, Wiedemann & Fransen, 1967-72; dist. judge Jefferson Parish (La.), 1972-85, judge, Court of Appeals 5th cir., 1985—, mem. faculty Nat. Jud. Coll., 1979-93, Tulane U. Sch. Law, 1978-83. Past bd. visitors Tulane U.; bd. dirs. La. Jud. Coll.; past pres. Sugar Bowl. Author: (with others) Judicial Ethics, 1982, (with others) Modern Judicial Ethics, 1992; editor Tulane Law Review, 1949. Lt. (j.g.), USNR, 1944-46. Mem. ABA (jud. div. council), La. (chmn. jr. bar sect. 1958-59, gov. 1958, mem. ho. of dels. 1960-72), Jefferson Parish, bar assns., Tulane U. Alumni Assn. (past pres.), Am. Judicature Soc., La. Dist. Judges Assn. (past pres.), Order of Coif, Beta Gamma Sigma, Pi Kappa Alpha. Republican. Episcopalian. Clubs: Rotary (pres. 1971-72), Metairie (La.) Country. Avocations: golf, photography, military history, duplicate bridge. Home: 500 Rue St Ann #127 Metairie LA 70005 Office: La Ct Appeal 5th Cir Gretna Courthouse Fl 4 Gretna LA 70053

WICKHAM, CHRISTOPHER JOHN, foreign language educator; b. Reading, Berkshire, Eng., May 26, 1950; came to the U.S., 1976; m. Sherry A. Whitmore. BA with honors, U. Reading, Eng., 1972; MPhil, U. Reading, 1974; PhD, U. Wis., 1982. Lectr. U. Regensburg, Germany, 1974-76; asst.

prof. Allegheny Coll., Meadville, Pa., 1982-85, U. Ill., Chgo., 1985-91, U. Tex., San Antonio, 1991—; faculty mem. Middlebury (Vt.) Coll. German Sch., 1986, 91, 93. Author: Diendorf Kr Nabburg, 1987; co-editor: Was in den alten Buechern steht, 1991, Framing the Past, 1992. Recipient fellowships German Acad. Exchange Svc., 1972-73, King Edward VII British-German Found., 1973-74, Wis. Alumni Rsch. Found., 1976-77, Travel grant German Acad. Exch. Svc., 1990, 95. Mem. Am. Assn. Tchrs. German, Soc. for Lit. and Sci., N.E. Modern Langs. Assn., German Studies Assn., MLA. Office: Univ Tex Divsn Fgn Langs 6900 N Loop 1604 San Antonio TX 78249-0644

WICKHAM, M(ARVIN) GARY, optometry educator; b. Ft. Morgan, Colo., Dec. 23, 1942; s. Marvin Gilbert W. and Dorothy Mae (Frazell) West; m. Irene Mary Wilhelm, Mar. 20, 1965. BS, Colo. State U., 1964, MS, 1967; PhD, Wash. State U., 1972. Rsch. physiologist VA, Gainesville, Fla., 1971-74; asst. prof. U. Fla., Gainesville, 1972-74; rsch. physiologist VA, San Diego, 1974-79; asst. rsch. biologist morphology of the eye U. Calif., San Diego, 1974-79; assoc. prof. histology, ocular anatomy and physiology Northeastern State U., Tahlequah, Okla., 1979-85, prof. histology, gen. biology, 1986-88; prof. optometry, histology, human genetics and immunology Northeastern State U., Tahlequah, Okla., ., 1988—; prof. ocular anatomy and physiology and gen. biology Northeastern State U., Tahlequah, Okla.; ad hoc reviewer vision scis. study sects. divsn. rsch. grants NIH, 1990—. Contbr. articles to profl. jours. Recipient Glaucoma Studies grant VA, 1975, Core Em Facility grant, 1977-79, Focal Argon Laser Lesions grant, 1979; Morphology of Mammal Eyes grant NIH, 1980, Computer-Based Image Analysis grantee Nat. Eye Inst., 1990. Mem. AAAS, Soc. Integrative Comparative Biology, Am. Inst. Biol. Scis., Assn. for Rsch. in Vision and Ophthalmology. Office: Northeastern State U Coll Optometry Tahlequah OK 74464

WICKLIFFE, JERRY L., lawyer; b. Dallas, Jan. 12, 1941; s. John A. and Ola (Kirk) W.; m. Lynda Hart, Aug. 26, 1961; children: Lisa Schmalhausen, Jeffrey, Mark. BBA, U. Tex., 1963, JD, 1965. Bar: Tex. 1965. Assoc. Fulbright & Jaworski, Houston, 1965-73, ptnr., 1973—. Office: Fulbright & Jaworski 1301 Mckinney St Fl 51 Houston TX 77010

WICKS, HARRY OLIVER, III, mechanical engineer; b. Wyandotte, Mich., Jan. 2, 1931; s. Harry O. Jr. and Dorothy Ellsworth (Worthman) W.; m. Sharon Lee Kirsch, July 10, 1989; stepchildren: Kenneth M. Burrows, Michael F. Cilano, Jill M. Cilano. Student, Rensselaer Poly. Inst., Troy, N.Y., 1948-51; BS, SUNY, Buffalo, 1967. Cert. tchr., N.Y., N.Mex. Design engr. Ford Motor Co., Buffalo, 1963-70; chief engr. Acme Hwy. Products Co., Buffalo, 1970-72; pres. Harwick Design, Inc., Hamburg, N.Y., 1975-90; mgr. engring. Curtiss-Wright Corp., Buffalo, 1978-79; chief engr. Railmaster System, Inc., Hamburg, 1983-87; bd. dirs. ReilRunner Syss., Inc., Griffin, Ga.; cons. RoadRailer, Chicago Heights, Ill., 1987-90, RailRunner Systems, Inc., Griffin, Ga., 1993—. Patentee in field of intermodal transp. Mem. dist. com. Erie County (N.Y.) Dem. Com., 1963-83. Served with U.S. Army, 1952-54. Mem. Hamburg C. of C., El Paso C. of C., Masons (32 degree), Shriners. Presbyterian. Home: # 38 Sutton Place 350 Thunderbird Dr El Paso TX 79912-3841

WICKSTROM, JON ALAN, telecommunications executive, consultant; b. San Antonio, Apr. 17, 1949; s. Stanley Alan and Louise (MacMillan) W.; m. Mary Carmen Sparkman, Jan. 25, 1969 (div. Jan. 1978); children: Dana Marie, Jon Alan Jr.; m. Jane Bielbey Slawson, June 19, 1988. BS, Tex. Tech. U., 1975. Ptnr. Hensley & Assocs., Albuquerque, 1976-78; dealer svcs. mgr. Gulf States Toyota, Houston, 1978-80; comms. mgr. Hughes Tool Co., Houston, 1980-85; network svcs. mgr. Tenneco Oil Co., Houston, 1986-89; comms. mgr. Clarke Am., San Antonio, 1989-94; I/T planner USAA, San Antonio, 1994-96; IS audit mgr. E & Y, San Antonio, 1996—; prin. Comm. Tech. Cons., Houston, 1980-89; cons. Comms. Consulting Group, Inc., San Antonio, 1989-96, Ernst & Young, San Antonio, 1996—. Author: (reference) 1976 Population Estimates for Bernalillo County, New Mex., 1976. Rep. precinct chmn. Bexar County, Tex., 1992-94; cons. Houston Symphony Orch., 1988. Mem. Alamo Area Telecomms. Assn. (bd. dirs 1990-94, pres., 1992-93), S.W. Comms. Assn. (bd. dirs. 1981-85, pres. 1982-84), Tex. Telecomms. Conf. (bd. dirs. 1982-84, chmn. 1983). Office: USAA 9800 Fredericksburg Rd San Antonio TX 78288-0001

WIDENER, HIRAM EMORY, JR., federal judge; b. Abingdon, Va., Apr. 30, 1923; s. Hiram Emory and Nita Douglas (Peck) W.; children: Molly Berentd, Hiram Emory III. Student, Va. Poly. Inst., 1940-41; B.S., U.S. Naval Acad., 1944; LL.B., Washington and Lee U., 1953, LL.D., 1977. Bar: Va. 1951. Pvt. practice law Bristol, Va., 1953-69; judge U.S. Dist. Ct. Western Dist. Va., Abingdon, 1969-71; chief judge U.S. Dist. Ct. Western Dist. Va., 1971-72; judge U.S. Ct. Appeals 4th Circuit, Abingdon, 1972—; U.S. commr. Western Dist. Va., 1963-66; mem. Va. Election Laws Study Commn., 1968-69. Chmn. Rep. party 9th Dist. Va., 1966-69; mem. Va. Rep. State Ctrl. Com., 1966-69, state exec. com., 1966-69. Served to lt. (j.g.) USN, 1944-49; to lt. USNR, 1951-52. Decorated Bronze Star with combat V. Mem. Am. Law Inst., Va. Bar Assn., Va. State Bar, Phi Alpha Delta. Republican. Presbyterian. Home and Office: 180 Main St Rm 123 Abingdon VA 24210-0868

WIDMAN, LAWRENCE EDWARD, cardiology and computer science educator; b. Phila., Sept. 15, 1950. BS in Physics and Life Scis., MIT, 1973; PhD, Columbia U., 1980, MD, 1981. Diplomate Am. Bd. Internal Medicine, Am. Bd. Cardiovascular Diseases, Am. Bd. Clin. Cardiac Electrophysiology. Med. intern Johns Hopkins U. Hosp., Balt., 1981-82; resident in pathology Mass. Gen. Hosp., Boston, 1982-83; resident in medicine Case Western Res U., Cleve., 1983-85, fellow in cardiology, 1985-87; asst. prof. cardiology U. Tex. Health Sci. Ctr., San Antonio, 1987-90; asst. prof. computer sci. U. Tex. Health Sci. Ctr., Austin, 1989-90; asst. prof. cardiology U. N.Mex. Sch. Medicine, Albuquerque, 1990-92; asst. prof. cardiology U. Okla. Health Scis. Ctr., 1992-96, assoc. prof. cardiology, 1996; assoc. prof. cardiology U. Tex. Health Sci. Ctr., San Antonio, 1996—; cons. Arthur D. Little, Inc., Boston, 1982-85, NIH, Bethesda, Md., 1987—; adj. asst. prof. biomed. engring. La. Tech. U., Ruston, 1991—; referee Jour. Am. Coll. Cardiology, Circulation, Circulation Rsch., ACM Transactions on Modeling & Computer Simulation, IEEE Expert, Med. Decision Making, others. Author: Artificial Intelligence, Simulation, and Modeling, 1989; contbr. articles to sci. jours. Ednl. counsellor MIT, Cambridge, 1987-92. Rsch. grantee Am. Heart Assn., 1987-90, VA, 1988-92, NIH, 1992—. Office: Divsn Cardiology U Tex Health Sci Ctr 7703 Floyd Curl Dr San Antonio TX 78284

WIDMER, CHARLES GLENN, dentist, researcher; b. Daytona Beach, Fla., Jan. 8, 1955; s. Ernest Clyde and Martha Elizabeth (Hunter) W.; m. Alyson Lynn Byrd, Jul. 11, 1981; children: Kathryn Michelle, Elizabeth Ann. BS, Emory Univ., 1977, DDS, 1981; MS, SUNY, 1983. Asst. prof. Sch. Dentistry Emory Univ., Atlanta, 1983-91; assoc. prof. Coll. Dentistry Univ. Fla., Gainesville, 1991—, acting assoc. dean for rsch., 1996—; reviewer NIH, Washington, 1988-89, 93-94, NIH Reviewer's Res., 1995-99. Contbr. articles to profl. jours. Contbr. Atlanta Zoo, 1985-91. NIH grantee for utilization of Trigeminal Evoked Potentials in dentistry, 1986-92, for orgn. and function of human masseter muscles, 1991—, for methods for conducting temporomandibular joint imaging using MRI, 1988-89, Rsch. Career Devel. award, 1991-96. Mem. ADA, Internat. Assn. Dental Rsch. (sec., treas., v.p., then pres., councilor neurosci. group 1989-95), Assn. Univ. Temporomandibular Disorders and Orofacial Pain Programs (sec., treas., v.p., then pres. 1990-95), Soc. Neurosci., Internat. Brain Rsch. Orgn., N.Y. Acad. Scis. Office: Univ Fla Dept Oral and Maxillofacial Surgery PO Box 100416 Gainesville FL 32610-0416

WIDNER, NELLE OUSLEY, retired elementary education educator; b. Loyston, Tenn., May 20, 1924; d. Jacob Milas and Myrtle (Longmire) Ousley; m. John DeLozier Widner; children: Stephen John, Beth Widner Jackson, David Earl. BA, Maryville (Tenn.) Coll., 1946; postgrad., U. Tenn. Cert. profl. educator. 1st grade tchr. Alcoa (Tenn.) City Schs., 1946-50, 74-87, tchr. remedial reading, 1966-74. Mem. AAUW, Alpha Delta Kappa (publicity chmn. 1982-84, chaplain 1984-86, sec. 1994-96), Order Ea. Star (worthy matron local chpt. 1941), Chilhowee Club, Epsilon Sigma Omicron (chmn. 1991-92), Passion Play Guild. Democrat. Methodist. Home: 1629 Peppertree Dr Alcoa TN 37701-1514

WIEBER, PATRICIA MCNALLY, medical/surgical nurse, orthopaedics nurse; b. Albany, N.Y., Oct. 4, 1952; d. Stephen A. and Catherine E. (Dyer) McNally; children: Stephen, James. Diploma, Physician's Hosp. Med. Ctr., Plattsburg, N.Y., 1973; student, St. Joseph's Coll., Windham, Maine, 1986. Cert. nursing adminstr., orthopaedic nurse cert. Staff nurse Albany Meml. Hosp., 1972; staff nurse West Volusia Meml. Hosp., Deland, Fla., 1975, asst. head nurse, 1981; head nurse, mgr. Meml. Hosp. West Volusia, Deland, Fla., 1982—. Mem. Nat. Assn. Orthopaedic Nursing, Fla. Orgn. Nurse Execs.

WIECZOREK, ROBERT CLAYTON, financial consultant; b. San Antonio, Dec. 26, 1959; s. Leonard William Wieczorek and Mary Alice (Cullifer) Paddock; m. Ashley Lamarr; 1 child, Madison Elizabeth Alice. BS in Psychology, Valdosta State Univ., 1982. Lic. pastor, 1978. Pastor So. Ga. Conf. United Meth. Ch., 1978-82; sales rep. JA Kirven Co., Columbus, Ga., 1982-83; rep. Pre-Paid Legal Svcs., Inc., Ada, Okla., 1983-89, sr. v.p. mktg., 1989-91; interim pastor Antioch Primative Bapt. Ch., Louvale, Ga., 1991-93; fin. cons. New Eng. Fin. Group, Atlanta, 1991—. Vol. Contact of Columbus, Ga., 1993-94. Mem. Nat. Assn. Life Underwriters, Sigma Pi, Pi Gamma Mu. Republican. Home: Hwy 27 South PO Box 100 Louvale GA 31814 Office: New Eng Fin Group 3001 Hamilton Rd Columbus GA 31904-8209

WIEDENKELLER, BARRY ARNOLD, bookseller, art director; b. St. Louis, May 3, 1936; s. Lester and Margaret Ann Wiedenkeller. BFA, Washington U., 1966. Sr. designer Ginn & Co., Boston, 1967-72; art dir. Allyn & Bacon, Boston, 1974-82; pres. Printer's Devil, Ltd., Decatur, Ga., 1982-94; registered rep. The Equitable, 1994-95. Mem. Antiquarian Booksellers' Assn. Am. (bd. govs. 1986-88, treas. 1989), Andiquarian Booksellers London, Provincial Book Fairs Assn. Democrat. Home: 290 Heaton Park Dr Decatur GA 30030-1029

WIEDER, BRUCE TERRILL, lawyer, electrical engineer; b. Cleve., Dec. 9, 1955; s. Ira J. and Judith M. (Marx) W. BSEE, Cornell U., 1978; MBA, U. Tex., 1980, JD with honors, 1988. Bar: Tex. 1988, U.S. Dist. Ct. (we. dist.) Tex. 1989, U.S. Patent and Trademark Office 1989, U.S. Ct. Appeals (fed. cir.) 1990, D.C. 1991, U.S. Dist. Ct. (no. dist.) Tex. 1995. Engr. Motorola, Inc., Austin, Tex., 1979-85; assoc. Arnold, White & Durkee, Austin, 1988-90; law clk. U.S. Ct. Appeals (Fed. cir.), Washington, 1990-91; assoc. Burns, Doane, Swecker & Mathis, Alexandria, Va., 1991—. Mem. IEEE, ABA, Am. Intellectual Property Law Assn., Alpha Phi Omega (life), Beta Gamma Sigma (life). Office: Burns Doane Swecker & Mathis 699 Prince St Alexandria VA 22314-3187

WIEDMAN, TIMOTHY GERARD, management educator; b. Detroit, Nov. 3, 1951; s. Charles Albert and Doris Gertude (Kreager) W.; m. Lisa Kyle Mattimore, Mar. 24, 1987. BA, Oakland U., 1976; MS, Ctrl. Mich. U., 1978; cert. profl. fin. planning, Old Dominion U., 1995. Gen. mgr. Burger Chef Sys., Inc., Detroit, 1969-75; area mgr. Fotomat Corp., Cleve., Columbus, Ohio, 1978-85; instr. bus. mgmt. Ctrl. Ohio Tech. Coll., Newark, 1986-88, Ohio U., Lancaster, 1988-92; asst. prof. Thomas Nelson C. C., Hampton, Va., 1992-95; assoc. prof. Thomas Nelson C.C., Hampton, Va., 1995—; workshop leader Va. Peninsula Total Quality Inst., Hampton, 1994—; quality trainer Quality Union of Bus., Industry and Cmty. Program, Lancaster, 1991-92; invited spkr. Svc. Corps. Ret. Execs., Newark, 1988, USCGR Tng. Ctr., Yorktown, Va., 1994, USMCR, Hampton, 1994, So. Assn. Coll. and Univ. Bus. Officers, Memphis, 1996. Contbg. author: Great Ideas for Teaching Marketing, 1992, Great Ideas for Teaching Introduction to Business, 1994; contbr. articles to profl. jours.; author: (newsletter) The Quality Management Forum, 1993. Judge regional competition Future Bus. Leaders Am., Hampton, 1993—; judge team excellence competition Ohio Mfrs. Assn., Lancaster, 1991; county rep. UNICEF, Fairfield County, Ohio, 1988-91. Mem. Am. Soc. for Quality Control (invited speaker 1993), Soc. for Indsl. and Orgnl. Psychology, Nat. Assn. Profl. Fin. Planners, Va. Quality Network. Office: Thomas Nelson CC 99 Thomas Nelson Dr Hampton VA 23670-1433

WIEGEL, JUERGEN KURT WILHELM, education educator; b. Berlin-Spandau, Germany, Apr. 2, 1941; arrived in U.S., 1982; m. Heide Wiegel, Apr. 7, 1966; children: Markus, Michaela. MS in Chemistry, U. Gottingen, Germany, 1969, PhD in Microbiology, 1973, DSc, 1982. Horticulturist Gärtnerei Ev. Johannesstift, Berlin-Spandau, 1960-61; rsch. assoc. dept. biochemistry U. Ga., Athens, 1977-79, assoc. prof., 1985-90, mem. Ctr. for Biol. Resource Recovery, 1982—, mem. Inst. of Ecology, 1983—, prof. dept. microbiology, 1990—; vis. assoc. prof. U. Ga., 1982-85, adj. prof. dept. biochemistry, 1989—; mem. internat. subcom. for Taxonomy of Methanogens and Acidothermophiles; chmn. internat. subcom. for Taxonomy of Clostridia and related organisms; presenter papers at seminars in field. Mem. editl. bd. Jour. Environ. Sci. and Health, 1990—, Jour. for Indsl. Microbiology, 1991—, Applied Environ. Microbiology; mng. editor Extremophiles; contbr. articles to profl. jours., chpts. to books; patentee in field. Fulbright travel grantee Kristjanson, Reikjavik, Iceland, 1992; bacterial species names in honor of his work on thermophiles; numerous grants in field including Ga. Environ. Tech. Consortium, 1993, USN Rsch., 1991-94, U.S. EPA, 1985-87, 88, DOE, 19846, U.S. Dept. Transp., 1983-86, Rsch. Found. of Ga., 1984-87, others. Home: 165 Torrey Pine Pl Athens GA 30605-3350 Office: U Ga Dept Microbiology Athens GA 30602-2605

WIELAND, PAUL OTTO, environmental control systems engineer; b. Louisville, Apr. 9, 1954; s. Otto George and Flora Carolyn (Wolf) W. BS in Botany, U. Louisville, 1982, BS in Applied Sci., 1985, M. in Engring., 1987. Lic. profl. engr., Ala., Va.; cert. environ. insp. Paper carrier Courier-Jour., Louisville, 1976-77; youth program dir. UNICORN, Louisville, 1978; recreation worker Met. Parks Dept., Louisville, 1978-80; retail sales clk. Lose Bros. Lawn and Garden, Louisville, 1980-82; trainee engr. Sealand Svc., Inc., Elizabeth, N.J., 1982; engr. NASA Marshall Space Flight Ctr., Huntsville, Ala., 1983—. Author: Designing for Human Presence in Space: An Introduction to Environmental Control and Life Support Systems, 1994, Living Together in Space: The Design and Operation of the Life Support Systems on the International Space Station, 1996; contbr. articles to profl. jours. Vol. advocate R.A.P.E. Relief Ctr., Louisville, 1977-80; vol. tutor Adult Basic Edn. Program, Huntsville, 1988-89; vol. projectionist Film Co-op., Huntsville, 1990-91; vol. tech. advisor Am. Lung Assn. Health House '96, Huntsville. Mem. ASME, ASHRAE, AIAA (chmn. student chpt. 1984-85), NSPE (mathcounts vol. 1990-91), Environ. Assessment Assn., Inst. for Advanced Studies in Life Support (treas. 1990-92). Home: 4219 Hawthorne Ave SW Huntsville AL 35805-3423 Office: NASA/MSFC/ED62 Marshall Space Flight Ctr Huntsville AL 35812

WIELAND, ROBERT GRAHAM, journalist, media relations consultant; b. Havana, Cuba, Dec. 7, 1949; parents Am. citizens; s. Robert Earl and Mara (Kipling) W.; m. Kristina Moody Van Cleave, Apr. 20, 1974; children: Beth, Wendy, Anne, Bob. BA in Comm., Beloit Coll., 1971. News dir. Sta. KLEF, Houston, 1971-73; dir. A.P. Tex. Sound, Austin, 1973-76; exec. asst. rsch. mktg. dept. Gordon McLendon, Dallas, 1980-81; broadcast supr. A.P., Dallas, 1976-80, newsman, 1981-96. Mem. Writers Guild Am./East. Office: Ste 300 4851 Lyndon B Johnson Fwy Dallas TX 75244-6017

WIELAND, WERNER, biology educator; b. Backnang, Wuttenburg, Germany, May 29, 1950; came to U.S., 1954; s. Ernst and Emilie (Datphaus) W.; m. Linda Marie Donnelly, May 17, 1986; children: Elyce Marie, Joseph Charles. BS in Biology, Va. Commonwealth U., 1973, MS, 1976; PhD in Zoology/Fisheries Biology, Auburn U., 1983. Faculty rsch. asst. dept. biology Va. Commonwealth U., Richmond, 1972-76, adj. faculty, 1976; biol. technician Ala. Coop. Fisheries Rsch. Unit U.S. Dept. Interior, Fish and Wildlife Svc., Auburn, 1977-78; prof. ecology, vertebrate zoology Mary Washington Coll., Fredericksburg, Va., 1983—; allied health advisor Mary Washington Coll., Fredericksburg, 1985-89; mem. various coms. Mary Washington Coll., including faculty governance com., 1994, self-study com. on student devel. svcs., 1991-93, com. on tenure, 1991-93, strategic planning com., 1992-94; tech. cons. Sharply Labs., Inc., Fredericksburg, 1973, J.R. Reed & Assocs., Inc., Newport News, Va., 1976-77, Law Engring. Testing, Inc., Atlanta, 1979, Olin Chem. Group, Charleston, Tenn., 1983, Dames and More, Inc., Atlanta, 1987, others. Reviewer Va. Jour. Sci., 1984, 86, 87, 93, 94; contbr. chpts. to books, articles to profl. jours. Mem. Am. Fisheries Soc. (so. divsn., Va. chpt. chair resolutions com. 1991-94, pres. 1996), Am. Soc. Ichthyologists and Herpetologists (southeastern divsn.), Assn. Southeastern Biologists, Assn. Systematic Collections, Soc. Systematic Biologists, Southeastern Fishes Coun. (sec., treas. 1987-91), Va. Acad. Scis. (chair biol. sect. 1987-88, 88-89, vice chair, bd. sec. 1986-87, sec. 1985-86), Va. Assn. for Biology Edn. (pres. 1993-94), Va. Herpetological Soc., Va. Natural Soc., Va. Mus. Natural History, others. Office: Mary Washington Coll Dept Biol Scis Fredericksburg VA 22401-5358

WIELAND, WILLIAM DEAN, health care consulting executive; b. Peoria, Ill., Feb. 15, 1948; s. George William and Virginia Lee (Delicath) W.; m. Joyce Lumia; 1 child, William Michael. BBA, Bradley U., 1971. Asst. adminstr. Galesburg (Ill.) Cottage Hosp., 1973-74; v.p. Anton & Damian, Iowa City, 1975-76; mgr. Clifton, Gunderson & Co., Peoria, 1977-80; v.p. OHMS Health Mgmt. Services, Columbus, 1980-84; dir., cons. VHA Cons. Services, Tampa, Fla., 1984-88; divsn. mgr. VHA, Inc., Tampa, Fla., 1988-95; sr. cons. mgr. Cost Sys. Group, Inc., Tampa, Fla., 1995—; small bus. cons. Glifton, Gunderson & Co., 1977-80; cons. OHMS Health Mgmt. Svcs., Columbus, 1980-84. Mem. Healthcare Info. and Mgmt. Systems Soc., Healthcare Fin. Mgmt. Assn., Soc. Hosp. Planning and Mktg., Inst. Indsl. Engrs., American Bus. Club (Peoria) (bd. dirs. 1978-80). Office: 4830 W Kennedy Blvd Ste 950 Tampa FL 33609-2574

WIEMKEN, DEBORAH LYNN, elementary education educator; b. S.I., N.Y., Sept. 15, 1971; d. Paul Albert and Carole Anne (Wakefield) W. B of Elem. Edn., Fla. So. Coll., 1993; MS of Reading and Lang. Arts, Cen. Conn. State U., 1994. Fitness instr. Lifestyle Fitness Ctr., Lakeland, Fla., 1992-93; grad. asst. Cen. Conn. State U., New Britain, 1993-94; tchr. 5th grade Mango Elem., Tampa, Fla., 1994—; mem. reading/lang. arts com., mem. multicultural edn. com. Mango Elem., Tampa. U.S. Achievement Acad. All-Am. scholar, 1993. Mem. Internat. Reading Assn., Phi Delta Kappa (scholar 1994), Kappa Delta Pi (v.p. 1993-94). Republican. Roman Catholic. Home: Apt 3702 2225 131st Ave E Tampa FL 33612

WIENANDT, CHRISTOPHER, newspaper desk chief; b. Iowa City, Aug. 2, 1951; s. Elwyn Arthur and Lois Patricia (Trachsel) W.; m. Beverly Bundy, June 27, 1987; 1 child, James Joseph Bundy. BA, Baylor U., 1973; MA in German Lit., U. Iowa, 1976; M of Internat. Journalism, Baylor U., 1978; PhD in English, U. North Tex., 1995. Copy editor Abilene (Tex.) Reporter News, 1978-79, entertainment editor, 1979; copy editor, universal desk chief Dallas Morning News, 1980-83; asst. city editor, copy desk chief European Stars and Stripes, Darmstadt, Germany, 1983-86; universal desk chief Dallas Morning News, 1986—. Contbr. books sect. Dallas Morning News. Mem. Phi Kappa Phi. Office: Dallas Morning News Universal Desk Box 655237 Dallas TX 75265

WIENER, JACQUES LOEB, JR., federal judge; b. Shreveport, La., Oct. 2, 1934; s. Jacques L. and Betty (Eichenbaum) W.; children: Patricia Wiener Shifke, Jacques L. III, Betty Ellen Wiener Spomer, Donald B. BA, Tulane U., 1956, JD, 1961. Bar: La. 1961, U.S. Dist. Ct. (we. dist.) La. 1961. Ptnr. Wiener, Weiss, Madison & Howell, A.P.C., Shreveport, 1961-90; judge U.S. Ct. Appeals (5th cir.), Shreveport, 1990—; mem. coun. La. State Law Inst., 1965—; master of the bench Am. Inn of Ct., 1990—. Pres. United Way N.W. La., 1975, Shreveport Jewish Fedn., 1969-70. Fellow Am. Coll. Trust & Estates Counsel, Am. Bar Found., La. Bar Found.; mem. ABA, La. State Bar Assn., Shreveport Bar Assn. (pres. 1982), Am. Law Inst., Internat. Acad. Trust & Estate Law (academician). Office: US Ct Appeals 5th Cir US Ct House 300 Fannin St Ste 5101 Shreveport LA 71101-3070

WIENER, KATHLEEN MARIE, elementary education educator; b. Covington, Ky., July 2, 1964; d. Louis Clarence and Rose Alma (Crowe) Blackburn; m. David Michael Wiener Sr., June 1, 1985; children: David Michael II, Elizabeth Anne, Anna Marie. BA in Elem. Edn., Thomas More Coll., 1985; MA in Elem. Edn., No. Ky. U., 1989, postgrad. Cert. resource tchr., Ky. Tchr. kindergarten Little Red Sch. House, Erlanger, Ky., 1985-87; tchr. Diocese of Covington, 1987-91; tchr., resource tchr. Boone County Schs., Union, Ky., 1991—; cons., resource tchr. Ky. Tchr. Intern Program, 1990—; conf. workshop presenter Ohio Cath. Educators Assn., 1989; extended sch. svcs. tutor, 1993—; tutor Maplewood Children's Home, 1993-94, report card rev. com., 1991, 95; chmn. Parents As reading Ptnrs. Program, 1995, 96; guest lectr. early childhood No. Ky. U.; dept. chairperson Boone County Schs., Union, 1996, ednl. specifications steering com. new elem., 1996. Sec. St. Anthony Bd. Edn., Taylor Mill, Ky., 1982-85; vol. Spl. Olympics, 1993, 94, 95. Mem. Nat. Educators Assn., Nat. Cath. Educators Assn., Ky. Assn. Children Under six (conf. presenter), Ky. Educators Assn., Boone County Educators Assn., No. Assn. Children Under Six (conf. workshop presenter, v.p. 1990-94, conf. chmn. 1992, 93). Home: 617 S Arlington Rd Covington KY 41011-2806 Office: New Haven Elem Sch 10854 Us Highway 42 Union KY 41091-9596

WIENKER, CURTIS WAKEFIELD, physical anthropologist, educator; b. Seattle, Feb. 3, 1945; s. Curtis Howard and Ruth (Daniels) W.; m. Cherie Kolbeck, Sept. 19, 1966 (div. 1987); 1 child, Heather. MA, U. Ariz., 1972, PhD, 1975. From instr. to prof. anthropology U. South Fla., Tampa, 1972—, assoc. dean coll. social and behavioral scis., 1988-90, assoc. dean Coll. Arts and Scis., 1990-93. Contbr. articles to sci. jours. Mem. Friends of Mus. of Sci. and Industry, Tampa,1 973—; trustee Nat. Kidney Found. Fla., Tampa, 1985-88. Chautauqua fellow NSF, 1974-75; grantee NSF, 1977-78, Fla. Regional Med. Program, 1975-76. Fellow Human Biology Assn., Soc. Applied Anthropology, Am. Acad. Forensic Scis.; mem. Am. Assn. Phys. Anthropologists, Sigma Xi. Office: Univ South Fla Dept Anthropology Tampa FL 33620-8100

WIERICH, JOCHEN, American studies educator; b. Neuss, Germany, Feb. 6, 1961; came to U.S., 1990; s. Hans and Anneliese (Rheidt) W. MA, U. Frankfurt, Germany, 1990; postgrad., Coll. William and Mary, 1993—. Rschr. Terra Mus. Am. Art, Chgo., 1990-92, Muscarelle Mus. Art, Williamsburg, Va., 1992-93; instr. Coll. William & Mary, Williamsburg, 1993—. Co-author: Winslow Homer in Gloucester, 1990, Lasting Impressions, 1992. Home: 1109 N Rochester St Arlington VA 22205

WIERSMA, KAREN GUTHRIE, learning disabilities educator; b. Jasper, Ala., June 21, 1952; d. William Leo and Gwen (Ellis) Guthrie; m. Gary Stuart Wiersma. BS, U. Ala., Birmingham, 1974, MA, 1976, postgrad., 1986-89. Hostess Walt Disney World, Lake Buena Vista, Fla., 1972-73; tchr., coach Birmingham Bd. Edn., 1975-79; tchr., coach Walker County Bd. Edn., Jasper, 1979-84, learning disabilities tchr., 1984—; textbook reviewer State Textbook Rev. Com., Birmingham, summer 1984, Eagle Forum, Montgomery, Ala., 1983-86; coach Girls Basketball Team, Farmstead Sch., 1994-95. Sec. Parrish (Ala.) PTA, 1979-81; counselor Right to Life Orgn., Birmingham, 1985-86; vol. Beacon House, Jasper, 1980-82. Author: Adapting the Kumon Math. Program for Children with Special Needs, 1990. Mem. NEA, Nat. Assn. Univ. Women, Nat. Poetry Soc., Ala. Edn. Assn. (Walker County rep. 1978-80), Ala. State Poetry Soc., Walker County Edn. Assn. Home: 1502 Laurin St Jasper AL 35501-3038 Office: Farmstead Sch RR 1 Box 478 Sumiton AL 35148-9747

WIESE, TERRY EUGENE, consulting executive, financial services, telecommunications and utilities sales and marketing executive; b. East St. Louis, Ill., Apr. 2, 1948; s. Herman and Opal F. (Terry) W.; m. Janet T. Kimmel, Apr. 1988; 1 child, Travis B.; stepchildren: Meghan R. Kimmel, Kristen M. Kimmel. BS in Engring., U.S. Mil. Acad., 1973; MBA in Mktg. and Fin., Wash. U., 1981. Commd. 2d lt. U.S. Army, 1973, advanced through grades to capt., resigned, 1978; sales rep. McDonnell Douglas Automation Co., St. Louis, 1978-80; br./dist. mgr. United Computing Systems, St. Louis, 1980-81; dir. affiliate sales Uninet, Inc., Kansas City, Mo., 1981-82, dir. hdqrs. sales, 1982-83, dir. central area sales, Lenexa, Kans., 1983-84, dir. nat. accounts/central area sales, 1984, dir. field engring. and ops., 1984; dir. nat. accounts MCI Telecom., Washington, 1984-86; v.p. mktg. Instnl. Comm. Co., McLean, Va., 1986-87; v.p. market devel. No. Telecom Co., Richardson, Tex., 1987-88, v.p. networks mktg., 1988-89, v.p., gen. mgr. cellular systems, 1989; exec. v.p. Sonitrol Corp., Alexandria, 1989—; pres. Results Cons., Inc., 1990—; owner, regional v.p. Primerica Fin. Svcs., 1990—; v.p. Philip Crosby Assocs./Proudfoot PLC, 1992—, regional pres. Proudfoot USA; prin. A.T. Kearney/EDS, 1995—; telecom. cons. United Way, 1982—. Author: ARTEPS for Nuclear Units, 1977; Lance Nuclear Missile ARTEP, 1978; Honest John Rocket ARTEP, 1978; ARTEP for Division/Brigade Elements, 1978; contbr. articles to various periodicals.

Pres. Aid Assn. for Lutherans, Collinsville, Ill., 1978-80; chmn. stewardship/budget com. Good Shepard Luth. Ch., Collinsville, 1979-81; chmn. United Way campaign, 1982-84; elder Messiah Luth. Ch., Richardson, Tex. Mem. Am. Assn. Cost Engrs., Regional Commerce and Growth Assn., Assn. of Grads. U.S. Mil. Acad., West Point Soc. North Tex., Fellowship Christian Athletes. Republican. Home: 3305 Terry Dr Plano TX 75023-1128

WIESEHUEGEL, RICHARD ERWIN, science, engineering and mathematics educator; b. Columbus, Ohio, Dec. 18, 1935; s. Erwin George and Katherine Veach (Hale) W.; m. Katherine Lillian Dickson, Nov. 18, 1979 (div. Apr. 1990); m. Kay Stilz, July 14, 1990; children: William Vinson, Susan Hale, Robert Erwin. BS in Indsl. Engring., U. Tenn., 1957, MS in Indsl. Engring., 1967; PhD in Higher Edn. Adminstrn., George Peabody Coll. for Tchrs, 1978. Registered profl. engr., Tenn. Indsl. analyst Bethlehem Steel Co., Williamsport, Pa., 1957-63; sr. indsl. engr. Huyck Formex, Greenville, Tenn., 1963-68, mgr. quality assurance, 1968-70, mgr. mfg. svcs., 1970-73; coord. pub. svcs. and rsch. U. Tenn., Nashville, 1973-78; divsn. chmn. State Tech. Inst. at Knoxville, 1978-80; program dir. Oak Ridge (Tenn.) Assoc. Univs., 1980—; mem. adv. bd. Roane State C.C., Oak Ridge, 1990-95. Contbr. to Measuring Learning in Continuing Education for Engineers and Scientists, 1984. Chpt. pres. Am. Inst. Indsl. Engrs., Kingsport, Tenn., 1972; charter mem. Tenn. Alliance for Continuing Higher Edn., 1979; elder, deacon various Presbyn. chs., 1959—; vol. fireman Andersonville (Tenn.) Fire Dept., 1984. Mem. Am. Soc. for Engring. Edn., Am. Forest Found., Tenn. Forestry Assn. Office: Oak Ridge Assoc Univs PO Box 117 Oak Ridge TN 37831-0117

WIEST, JOHN ANDREW, dentist; b. Cheverly, Md., Apr. 13, 1946; s. Louis Madox and Martha Elizabeth (Wilson) W.; m. Billie Ann O'Hern, Aug. 1968 (div. June 1981); children: Laurie Carrolin, Courtney Elizabeth; m. Dawn Michelle McCain, Oct. 13, 1984. Student, Bridgewater Coll., 1964-65; BSc, U. Md., 1965-68, postgrad., 1968-69, DDS summa cum laude, 1975. Lic. dentist, Fla. Med. technician USPH Hosp., Balt., 1972-75, Balt. County Hosp., 1973-75; assoc. dentist Richard R. Powell DDS, Tampa, Fla., 1975-79; ptnr. Richard R. Powell DDS, Tampa, 1979-88; pvt. practice Tampa, 1988—; cons. DentAll of Fla., Tampa, 1978-79. With U.S. Army, 1969-71, Vietnam. Mem. ADA, Acad. Gen. Dentistry, Fla. Dental Assn., West Coast Dental Assn., Hillsborough County Dental Assn., Psi Omega, Dental Frat. Alumno Assn., U. Md. Dental Sch. Alumni Assn., Elks, Tampa Handball Group (recruitment/devel. chmn.). Office: 315 W Busch Blvd Tampa FL 33612-7829

WIETOR, MICHAEL GEORGE, real estate executive, commodity trading advisor, export purchasing agent; b. Chgo., Oct. 26, 1937; s. Henry George and Marion (Englehardt) W.; m. Patricia Heimbrodt; children: Tracey Michael, Kristen Marie; m. Marti Agudo. Student, Lake Forest Coll., 1967-69; cert. real estate brokerage mgr., Realtors Nat. Mktg. Inst., 1985. Engrs. aide State of Ill., Elgin, 1960-64; prodn. mgr. Ardmore Products, Inc., Northbrook, Ill., 1964-68; mgr. purchasing and sales Fullerton Metals, Inc., Northbrook, 1968-69; mgr. ops. Fullerton Metals, Hialeah, Fla., 1970; pres. Wietor Realty, Inc., Hollywood, Fla., 1971-81, Century 21 AAA Realty, Inc., Ft. Lauderdale, Fla., 1981-88, Tahoe Trading Co., Ft. Lauderdale, 1985—, Country Squire, Inc. Realtors, 1988—; instr. Hollywood Area Bd. Realtors, 1978-85, bd. dirs., 1979, 82, 85, 88, 90, 91, v.p., 1980, chmn. com., 1980-91, treas., 1983, 89, pres., 1984, 92. Pres. Grant Twp. Dem. Orgn., Fox Lake, Ill., 1962-66, Chain-O-Lakes Parks Assn., Fox Lake, 1968, Everglades Artists Guild, Hollywood, Fla., 1976-77, 80-81; v.p. Hollywood Art Guild, 1975. Served with USAF, 1955-59. Named to honor society Hollywood Area Bd. Realtors, 1984-87, Life Mem. of Honor Soc., 1988, CRB Ambassador Realtors Mktg. Inst., 1985; named Realtor of Yr. Hollywood Area Bd. Realtors, 1987. Mem. Nat. Assn. Realtors (MLS com. 1984-86), Fla. Assn. Realtors (bd. dirs. 1983-86), Nat. Futures Assn., Lions (v.p. Pembroke Pines Fla., 1983-84). Office: Country Squire Inc Realtors 4801 S University Dr Fort Lauderdale FL 33328-3839

WIGGINS, NANCY BOWEN, real estate broker, market research consultant; b. Richmond, Va., Oct. 9, 1948; d. William Roy and Mary Virginia (Colson) Bowen; m. Samuel Spence Saunders, Aug. 16, 1969 (div. 1977); m. Edwin Lindsey Wiggins, Jr., Apr. 16, 1983; children: Neal Bowen, Mark Edwin. AA, St. Mary's Coll., Raleigh, N.C., 1968; postgrad., Trinity U., 1968-69; BA, U.S. Internat. U., San Diego, 1970; MA, U. Tex., Arlington, 1975; postgrad., Tulane U., 1976-77. Bank teller Bank of Am., San Diego, 1971-72; lectr. U. Tex., Arlington, 1974-76; instr. Johnson C. Smith U., Charlotte, N.C., 1977-78; human svcs. planner Centralina Coun. of Govt., Charlotte, 1978-80; mktg. rsch. analyst First Union Nat. Bank, Charlotte, 1980-81; mktg. rep. Burroughs Corp., Charlotte, 1981-83; ptnr., mktg. researcher George Selden & Assocs., Charlotte, 1983-84; pres., broker Bowen Wiggins Co., Charlotte, 1984-92; pres. WRB, Inc. (merger Bowen Wiggins Co. and W. Roy Bowen Co., Inc.), Charlotte, 1992-96; mgr., prin. Nancy Wiggins, LLC, Charlotte, 1996—; instr. U. N.C., Charlotte, 1984-85, 87-90, Winthrop U., Rock Hill, S.C., 1985-86, 91-92; bd. dirs. Roy Bowen, Inc., Frogmore, S.C., v.p., sec., 1990. Contbr. articles to profl. jours. Vice chmn. United Cerebral Palsy Coun., Charlotte, 1984; chmn. bd. dirs. Carriage House Condominium Assn., Charlotte, 1980-82; mem. Charlotte Mayor's Budget Adv. Com., 1980-81, Charlotte-Mecklenburg Planning Commn., 1994—, mem. planning com., 1994-95, zoning com., 1995-96; pres. Mecklenburg Dem. Women's Club, 1990; mem. state exec. com. N.C. Dem. Party, 1991-95; mem. Charlotte Women's Polit. Caucus, Mecklenburg County Solid Waste Adv. Bd., 1991-92, chmn. recycling com., 1991-94, reappointed 1995-96. Mem. Com. of 100 Women for Johnson C. Smith Univ., Charlotte Region Comml. Bd. Realtors, N.C. Assn. Appraisers (bd. dirs., pres. 1989-90), Internat. Coun. Shopping Ctrs., Multimillion Dollar Club, Tournament Players Club Piper Glen, Good Friends, Pi Sigma Alpha. Democrat. Episcopalian. Home: 6919 Seton House Ln Charlotte NC 28277 Office: Nancy Wiggins LLC 501 N Church St Ste 30 Charlotte NC 28202

WIGGINS, NORMAN ADRIAN, university administrator, legal educator; b. Burlington, N.C., Feb. 6, 1924; s. Walter James and Margaret Ann (Chason) W.; m. Mildred Alice Harmon. AA, Campbell Coll., 1948; BA, Wake Forest Coll., 1950, LLB, 1952; LLM, Columbia U., 1956, JSD, 1964; Exec. Program, U. N.C., 1968-69; LLD, Gardner-Webb Coll., 1972. Deacon Wake Forest Baptist Ch., Winston-Salem, N.C., 1963-66, Buies Creek (N.C.) Bapt. Ch., 1973—; deacon, tchr. Sunday sch., 1952—, lay preacher, 1953—; pres. N.C. Found. of Ch.-Related Coll., 1969-70, Campbell U., Buies Creek, 1967—; prof. law Campbell U., 1976—. Author: Wills and Administration of Estates in North Carolina, 1964—, (with Gilbert T. Stephenson) Estates and Trusts, 1973; Editor: N.C. Will Manual, 1958—, Trust Functions and Services, 1978; Contbr. articles to legal jours. Chmn. Gov.'s Task Force Com. on Adjudication of the Com. on Law and Order, 1969-71; mem. Com. on Drafting Interstate Succession Act for N.C., 1957-59; mem. Com. for Revision of the Laws Relating to the Adminstrn. of Descs.' Estates, 1959-67, chmn., 1964-67; trustee Sunday Sch. Bd., So. Bapt. Conv., 1975—, chmn. bd. trustees, 1978—, nominations com., 1988—; pres. Bapt. State Conv. N.C., 1983-85; bd. dirs. N.C. Citizens for Bus. and Industry, 1982—. Recipient Outstanding Civilian Svc. award Dept. Army, 1985; Campbell Law Sch. renamed in his honor the Norman Adrian Wiggins Sch. of Law, 1989; recognized for outstanding svc. to high edn. and legal edn. Newcomen Soc. U.S., 1993; Comdr.'s award for Pub. Svc., 1995, Internat. Freedom of Mobility award, 1995. Mem. ABA, Nat. Assn. Coll. and Univ. Attys. (pres. 1972-73, Disting. Svc. award 1991), Am. Assn. Presidents Ind. Colls. and Univs. (pres. 1981-83), N.C. Assn. Colls. and Univs. (exec. com. 1980—, pres. 1984-85), N.C. Assn. Ind. Colls. and Univs. (pres. 1970-72, exec. com. 1980-81), N.C. Bar Assn., Harnett County Bar Assn., Nat. Fellowship Baptist Men (pres. 1987-90), Jay Waugh Evang. Assn. (dir./pres. 1970-72), Dunn Area C. of C., Wake Forest Alumni Assn., Rotary (hon. mem. Dunn club), Phi Alpha Delta, Phi Kappa Phi, Omicron Delta Kappa. Office: Campbell U PO Box 127 Buies Creek NC 27506-0127

WIGGINS, ROBERT ALLAN, physician; b. Glen Ridge, N.J., Oct. 27, 1949; s. Asa Garfield and Juanita (Caballero) W.; m. Gillian Kay Springstun, Feb. 2, 1982 (div.); Nancy Allison North, Dec. 24, 1984. BA in English magna cum laude, Rutgers U., 1972, MD, 1976. Diplomate Am. Bd. Internal Medicine; cert. ACLS, advanced trauma life support provider, instr. Intern dept. family practice Baylor Coll. Medicine Affiliated Hosps., Houston, 1976-77, resident dept. internal medicine, 1978-79; emergency physician Dept. Pub. Health, Houston, 1979-80, acting bur. chief Bur. Emergency Med. Svcs., 1980; emergency physician Meml. City Gen. Hosp., Houston, 1980-81, Brackenridge Hosp., Austin, 1981-84; internist dept. mental health and mental retardation E. Austin Clinic-Methadone Maintenance Program, 1982-83; emergency physician S. Austin Cmty. Hosp., 1983-84, St. Davids Cmty. Hosp., Austin, 1984-94; pvt. practice ambulatory medicine Bozeman, Mont., 1994-95; emergency physician Meml. Med. Ctr., Corpus Christi, Tex., 1995—; med. dir. emergency dept. Meml. Med. Ctr., Corpus Christi, 1996—; clin. instr. Ctrl. Tex. Med. Found. residency programs dept. internal medicine Brackenridge Hosp., Austin, 1984; med. cons. Pharmacodynamics Rsch. Corp., Austin, 1986; cons. Tex. Med. Liability Trust, Austin, 1991—; lectr. Wellness Program St. Davids Cmty. Hosp., Austin, 1990—. Contbr. (with others) article to Jour. Molecular Biology. Mem. AMA, Tex. Med. Assn., Nueces County Med. Soc. Roman Catholic. Home: 4350 Ocean Dr Corpus Christi TX 78412-2569

WIGGS, ROBERT HOWARD, advertising agency executive; b. Brunswick, Ga., Sept. 8, 1947; s. George Robert and Jean (Harrison) W.; m. Carole Lynette Hernandez (div. 1984); children: Johnny R., Christopher H., Scott B.; m. Linda Bagley, May 10, 1985; 1 child, Kimber Lauren. Student, U. Fla., 1980; student, U. Colo., Boulder, 1985; BS, Fla. So. Coll., 1986. Master advt. specialist. Lab. technician Internat. Minerals Co., Bartow, Fla., 1967-73; v.p. lending, mktg. Flagship/SunBank, Mulberry, Winter Haven, Fla., 1974-85; pres. Bagley Advt., Lakeland, Fla., 1985—. Exec. producer (TV program) Inside Lakeland. Commr. Lakeland City; bd. dirs. Retired Sr. Vol. Program, Lakeland, Vols. in Svc. to the Elderly, Lakeland, 1985-89, Polk Sr. Games, Polk County Community Rels. Coun.; adv. bd. dirs. PRIDE Polk County (drug edn.), 1988—; co-founder Lakeland Coun. Alcohol and Drug Abuse, Lakeland Coun. on the Aging; adv. com. Polk County Pub. Schs. Substance Abuse Program; founder Lakeland Community Rels. Coun.; mem. adv. bd. Boys & Girls Clubs of Lakeland; active Met. Planning Orgn. Recipient Golden Addy award Polk Advt. Fedn., 1988. Mem. Leadership Lakeland Alumni (past pres., bd. dirs), Fla. Pub. Rels. Assn., Sales and Mktg. Execs. (bd. dirs. 1988), Grad. Leadership Ctrl. Fla., Citizen's Police Acad., Lakeland C. of C. (past bd. dirs., v.p., local and county legis. task force), Pres.'s Roundtable Club (Sports-A-Rama chmn.), Rotary (bd. dirs.), Kiwanis (past pres. Mulberry chpt.). Republican. Methodist. Home: 4602 Highlands Place Dr Lakeland FL 33813-2120

WIGGS, SHIRLEY JOANN, secondary school educator; b. Johnston County, N.C., Nov. 6, 1940; d. William H. and Sallie P. (Barden) W.; BA, Atlantic Christian Coll., 1963; postgrad. Duke U., 1966, East Carolina U., 1979-80; grad. Newspaper Inst. Am. Tchr. public schs. South Hill, Va., 1963-64; tchr. lang. arts and social studies Glendale Chapel High Sch., Kenly, N.C., 1964-65, Benson (N.C.) High Sch., 1965—; tchr. advanced placement English, lang. arts, journalism South Johnston High Sch., Four Oaks, N.C., 1969-96, ret., 1996; chairperson lang. arts dept., 1971-86, coordinating adminstr. curriculum, 1974-76, student adv., 1978-80, coach Acad. Super Bowl, 1982-87; evaluator profl. books Allyn and Bacon, Inc., 1974, 79; yearbook judge Columbia Scholastic Press Assn., 1986-92, yearbook advisor, 1980-94. Sunday sch. tchr. 1st Bapt. Ch., Smithfield, N.C., 1964-66, asso. supt. young people's dept., 1964-67; scholarship chairperson 1st Bapt. Ch., 1987-91, ch. libr., 1992—; chmn. Keep Johnston County Beautiful, 1979-81. Named Woman of Yr., Atlantic Christian Coll., 1962; recipient Keep Johnston County Beautiful Appreciation award, 1980, Internat. Cheerleading Found. award, 1972, Acad. Booster Club award, 1986. Mem. NEA, Nat. Council Tchrs. English, Assn. Supervision and Curriculum Devel., N.C. English Tchrs. Assn. (dir. dist. 12, 1980-85), Johnston County Assn. of Educators, N.C. Assn. Educators (past pres. Johnston County chpt.). Home: 102 E Sanders St Smithfield NC 27577-4211 Office: South Johnston High Sch RR 3 Four Oaks NC 27524-9803

WIGINTON, JAY SPENCER, sales executive; b. Lubbock, Tex., Sept. 21, 1941; s. Clarence Elbert and Faye (George) W.; BS, Tex. Tech. U., 1963, MS, 1968; m. Billye Kay Freitag, Nov. 28, 1968 (div. Feb. 1993); children: Lauren, Lindsay; m. Laverne Shook, June 18, 1993. Sales rep. West Tex. ter. Syntex Labs., Lubbock, 1968-70, regional sales rep., 1970-72, Far East regional mgr., Des Moines, 1972-73, dir. mktg., 1973-74; regional sales mgr. Zoecon Corp., Dallas, 1974-76, nat. accounts mgr. Custom div., 1976-78; gen. mgr. V.A. Snell & Co. div. Gt. Plains Chem. Co., San Antonio, 1978-83, Southwest regional mgr., 1983-84, dir. field devel., 1984-85; dist. mgr. Agri-Sales Assocs., Inc., 1985-87; sales mgr. western region Allflex U.S.A., Inc., 1987-91; gen mgr Pro. Vet. S., 1991-93; dist. sales mgr. Rhone Merieux, Inc., 1993—. Served with AUS, 1964-66; Vietnam. Mem. Tex. Grain and Feed Assn., Tex. Cattle Feeders Assn., Tex. Chem. Assn., Kappa Sigma. Mem. Christian Ch. (Disciples of Christ). Office: 2611 Fm 1960 Rd W Ste F-122 Houston TX 77068-3733

WIGLEY-MORRISON, KAREN, accountant, travel consultant, paralegal, administrative assistant; b. Dallas, July 14, 1950; d. Willard Robert Jr. and Jerry (McDonald) Wigley; m. Jon Edwin Morrison, Jan. 20, 1982. Student, Dallas Bapt. Coll., 1968-69; BA, U. Okla., 1971; diploma, Exec. Secretarial Sch., Dallas, 1971. Profl. model Kim Dawson Model Agy., Dallas, 1962-72; legal sec. Gardere & Wynne, Dallas, 1972-76; paralegal, sec. Geary, Brice Law Firm, Dallas, 1983-84; v.p., sec.-treas. Astraea Co., Dallas, 1984-90; paralegal, sec. Geary, Bryce Law Firm, Dallas, 1983-84; paralegal Gardere & Wynne, Dallas, 1972-76; corp. sec. X Part, Inc., Dallas, 1987-90; pvt. cons. Dallas, 1990—, acct., 1992—. Vol. I Have a Dream Found., Dallas, 1988—, exec. vol. coun., 1990—; vol. Texans' War on Drugs, Austin. Mem. NAFE, Am. Bus. Women's Assn., North Dallas Network Career Women, Dallas Summer Musicals Guild, Dallas Symphony Assn., Arboretum and Botanical Gardens, Phi Beta Lambda. Republican. Episcopalian.

WIIG, KARL MARTIN, knowledge management expert and consultant; b. Karasjok, Norway, Feb. 8, 1934; came to U.S., 1957; s. Alf Kristian and Margarethe (Sylann) W.; Elisabeth Hemmersam Nielsen, June 10, 1958; children: Charlotte Elisabeth, Erik Daniel. BS, Case Inst. Tech., 1959, MS, 1964. Researcher Chr. Michelsen Inst., Bergen, Norway, 1960-64; systems engr. GE, Cleve., 1964-66; mgr. systems engring. Dundee (Mich.) Cement Co., 1966-70; chmn. of the bd. Abacus Alpha, Inc., Newton, Mass., 1980-81; mgr. systems and policy analysis Arthur D. Little, Inc., Cambridge, Mass., 1970-80, dir. artificial intelligence, 1981-87; ptnr. Coopers & Lybrand, Dallas, 1987-89; mng. ptnr. The Wiig Group, Arlington, Tex., 1989-95; chmn. bd., CEO Knowledge Rsch. Inst., Inc., Arlington, Tex., 1995—; presenter in field; co-founder Internat. Knowledge Mgmt. Network. Author: The Economics of Offshore Oil and Gas Supplies, 1977, Expert Systems: A Manager's Guide, 1990, Knowledge Management Foundations: Thinking About Thinking - How People and Organizations Create, Represent and Use Knowledge, 1993, Knowledge Management: The Central Management Focus for Intelligent-Acting Organizations, 1994, Knowledge Management Methods: Practical Approaches to Manage Knowledge, 1995; (publs.) Managing Knowledge: Executive Perspectives, 1989, Knowledge-Based Systems and Issues of Integration, 1988, Management of Knowledge: A New Opportunity, 1988; contbr. articles to Mgmt. Rev., Asset-Based Fin. Jour., The Bankers Mag., Computer, Annales de AICA. With Norwegian Army, 1953-54. Home and Office: 5211 Vicksburg Dr Arlington TX 76017

WIITA, PAUL JOSEPH, astrophysicist; b. Bronx, N.Y., Feb. 18, 1953; s. Paul Elias and Martha Jenny (Knippenberg) W.; m. Brinda Umberkoman, May 31, 1978; children: Arun, Neil. BS in Physics, Cooper Union Coll., 1972; PhD in Physics, Princeton U., 1976. Rsch. assoc. U. Chgo., 1976-79; asst. prof. U. Pa., Phila., 1979-86; asst. prof. Ga. State U., Atlanta, 1986-89, assoc. prof., 1989-93, prof., 1993—; vis. prof. Indian Inst. Astrophysics, Bangalore, India, 1989, 94—, Tata Inst. of Fundamental Rsch., Pune, India, 1990-92, 94—. Editor: (books) Active Galactic Nuclei, 1988, Variability of Active Galactic Nuclei, 1991; contbr. numerous articles to profl. jours. Predoctoral fellow NSF, Princeton, 1972-75, NATO postdoctoral fellow Cambridge U., NSF, 1977-78; grantee NSF, 1982-85, 87-95, NASA, 1995—. Fellow Royal Astron. Soc.; mem. Am. Astron. Soc., Am. Physical Soc., Internat. Astron. Union. Democrat. Home: 4387 Dunmore Rd Marietta GA 30068-4222 Office: Ga State U Dept Physics & Astronomy Atlanta GA 30303-3083

WIKE, ANDREW, data processing executive; b. Warrington, Cheshire, Eng., Nov. 19, 1952; came to U.S., 1984; s. Raymond Harry and Edna (Bottomley) W.; m. Jennifer Lynne Hooley, Aug. 2, 1975 (div. 1987); m. Pamela Ann Wolfson, Nov. 21, 1987. BSc with hons., The Polytech., Wolverhampton, G.B., 1975; student, U. Kent, Canterbury, 1970-71. Programmer/analyst Logica B.V., Rotterdam, The Netherlands, 1975-78; cons. Logica B.V., 1978-79, sr. cons., 1979-81, prin. cons., 1981-83, bus. mgr., 1983-84; gen. mgr. Logica Energy Sys., Houston, 1984-87; dir. tech. svcs. Stoner Assocs., Inc., Houston, 1988-91, dir. bus. devel., 1991—; cons. in field. Contbr. articles to profl. jours. Mem. Instrument Soc. Am., Am. Gas Assn. (mem. automation and telecommunications com.). Office: Stoner Assocs Inc # 900 5177 Richmond Ave Houston TX 77056-6736

WIKE, D. ELAINE, business executive; b. Ridgecrest, Calif., Sept. 26, 1954; d. Robert G. and Jimmie Mae (Sallee) Field; student U. Houston, 1975-77; m. Mike Wike, Oct. 14, 1978; children: Mike II, Angelina Elaine, William V., Danielle Elizabeth, Edward Lawrence, Windy Gale. Legal sec. Morgan, Lewis & Bockius, Washington, 1977-78; legal asst. Alfred C. Schlosser & Co., Houston, 1972-77, 78-81, Jerry Sadler, atty., Houston, 1982-83; founder, owner DEW Profl. & Bus. Svcs., Houston, 1979—; office mgr. Law Offices Mike Wike, Houston, 1983—. Treas., Wilhelm Schole Parents Orgn., 1981-82; mem. Free, Inc.; vol. campaign worker, (Ron Paul for Congress and Reagan for Pres.), 1975, 76. Recipient 3d place Nassau Bay Tex. Christmas Boat Lane Parade First Ann. Photography Contest, 1990. Mem. Young Ams. for Freedom, Nat. Notary Assn., Nat. Assn. Female Execs., Am. Soc. Notaries, Nat. Paralegal Assn. Republican. Libertarian. Mem. Christian Ch. Office: 2421 S Wayside Dr Houston TX 77023-5318

WIKLE, THOMAS ADAMS, geography educator, researcher; b. Pasadena, Calif., Jan. 26, 1962; s. John William and Ellen Cecil (Betts) W.; m. Michelle Ann Hist, Oct. 7, 1989; children: Paige Kathryn, Garrett Adams. BA, U. Calif., Santa Barbara, 1983; MA, Calif. State U., Fullerton, 1985; PhD, So. Ill. U., 1989. Staff cartographer, dept. geography Calif. State U., Fullerton, 1983-85; rsch. asst. dept. geography So. Ill. U., Carbondale, 1982-89; asst. prof. dept. geography Okla. State U., Stillwater, 1989-93, assoc. prof., 1993—, head dept. geography, 1994—. Contbr. articles to profl. jours. Recipient Regents Disting. Teaching award, 1996; Nat. Geog. Soc. grantee, 1993, NSF grantee, 1991, 94. Mem. Okla. Acad. Scis. (sect. chair 1990-91), Assn. Am. Geographers, Southeastern Conf. on Linguistics, Soc. for Photogrammetric Engring. and Remote Sensing (cert. mapping scientist), Nat. Coun. Geographic Edn. (media editor), Gamma Theta Upsilon (S.W. regional coord. 1994—), Phi Kappa Phi. Democrat. Home: 12 N Canyon Rim Dr Stillwater OK 74075-6901 Office: Okla State U Dept Geography Stillwater OK 74078

WILBANKS, DANIEL PINCKNEY, dentist, director; b. Tallassee, Ala., Oct. 18, 1937; s. William Calvin and Effie Lee (Lett) W.; m. Alice Thompson Ogletree, June 12, 1960 (dec. Aug. 1970); children: Daniel Pinckney Jr., Bruce Ogletree, John Todd; m. Nancy Jane Stovall, Dec. 27, 1971; children: Mark Stovall, James Mattison. BS, U. Ala., 1960, DMD, 1966. Prin. Wilbanks Family Practice, Tallassee, 1966—; bd. dirs. Bank of Tallassee; chmn. bd. Sylacauga (Ala.) Health Care Ctr. Inc., 1983—. President City of Tallassee Bd. of Edn., 1975-90; vice chmn. Blount Ednl. & Charitable Found., Tallassee, 1980—. 1st lt. U.S. Army, 1959-61. Recipient Resolution of Commendation, City of Tallassee Coun., 1990. Mem. ADA, Ala. Dental Assn. (Silver cert. 1991), 2d Dist. Dental Assn. (pres. Ala. chpt. 1979-80), Ala. Nursing Home Assn., Ind. Bankers Assn., Montgomery Country Club, Lions (various offices Tallassee chpt. 1975-80). Home: PO Box 706 Tallassee AL 36078-0706 Office: 1 S Dubois Ave Tallassee AL 36078-1419

WILBANKS, DARREL JAY, automation applications executive; b. Dover, N.J., May 12, 1944; s. Carey J. and Laura (Hill) W.; married; children: Denise, Cale. Student Newark Coll. Engring., 1962-65. Mech. engr. Haggar Slacks, Dallas, 1966-78, prodn. mgr., 1979-81, tng. dept. mgr., 1982-83; human resource devel. mgr. Fox Photo, San Antonio, 1983—; tng. cons. Phlash Prodns., San Antonio, 1984-86; automation applications mgr. Mitsubishi Electric Sales, Inc., Irving, Tex., 1986—; photog. cons. La Quinta Motels, San Antonio, 1984—. Patentee mech. devices. Mem. Internat. TV Assn. (v.p. San Antonio chpt. 1985, pres. 1986), Am. Soc. Tng. and Devel. Avocations: raquetball, travel, photography. Office: Mitsubishi Electric Sales Inc 9000 W Royal Ln Irving TX 75063-2418

WILBANKS, JOHN FLANDERS, town administrator; b. Eastman, Ga., June 21, 1938; s. Hollis Woodrow and Florence E. (Flanders) W.; m. Patricia Anne Jamison, June 11, 1961; children: Shannon, Shelly, John Flanders. BS in History and Polit. Sci., Coll. of Charleston, S.C., 1960; postgrad., U. S.C., 1979. Ins. investigator Retail Credit Co. (now Equifax), Charleston, 1960-68; ins. agt. Integon Corp., Charleston, 1968-72; city mgr. City of Folly Beach, S.C., 1972-76; county adminstr. Dorchester County, St. George, S.C., 1976-79; town adm nstr. Town of Summerville, S.C., 1979—; cons. in field. Served with U.S. Army, 1961-64. Mem. S.C. City Mgmt. Assn. (pres. 1985-86), S.C. Mcpl. Assn. (bd. dirs. 1986-89), Internat. City Mgmt. Assn., Elks, Kiwanis (pres. Summerville 1986), Toastmasters (pres. 1991, Disting. Toastmaster). Lutheran. Home: 116 Spring St Summerville SC 29485-4826 Office: Town of Summerville 104 Civic Ctr Summerville SC 29483-6000

WILBORN, RANDY CHARLES, banker; b. Tuskegee, Apr. 3, 1966; s. Daniel Webster and Evia Mae (Giles) W. BS in Acctg., Tuskegee U., 1990; postgrad., Birmingham So. Coll., 1994—. Product coord. Compass Bank; market rsch. analyst Compass Bank, Birmingham, Ala., 1990-94; banker Central Bank of the South, Birmingham, Ala., 1994—. Mem. Vulcan Kiwanis, Birmingham, 1991-94, Birmingham Jaycees, 1993-94. Recipient Baub Pres. award. Mem. Am. Mktg. Assn., Am. Inst. Banking, Birmingham Assn. Urban Bankers, Omega Psi Phi. Baptist. Home: 301-11 Beacon Crest Ln Birmingham AL 35209 Office: Compass Bank 15 20th St S Birmingham AL 35233-2034

WILBORN, WOODY STEPHEN, lawyer; b. Cin., Apr. 20, 1947; s. R. Walter and Viola (Eades) W.; 1 child, Christopher B. BA, Eastern Ky. U., 1969; JD, U. Ky., 1973. Bar: Ky. 1973, U.S. Dist. Ct. (ea. dist.) Ky. 1976, U.S. Supreme Ct. 1978, U.S. Dist. Ct. (we. dist.) Ky. 1982. Sole practice Shelbyville, Ky., 1973-94; exec. dir. Ky. Petroleum Coun., 1994—; gen. coun. ho. leadership Ky. Gen. Assembly, Frankfort, 1985-93; co-host People's Bus. Ky. Ednl. TV, 1984-85; chmn. Ky. Ins. and Liability Task Force, 1986-87; spl. justice Ky. Supreme Ct., 1990; mem. Uniform Law Commrs., 1989—. State rep. 58th legis. dist. Ky. Gen. Assembly, 1978-81. Served with U.S. Army, 1970-71. Mem. ABA, Ky. Bar Assn. (pres. young lawyers sect.). Democrat. Baptist. Home: 306 Tower Dr Shelbyville KY 40065-8914 Office: 403 State National Bank Bld 305 Ann St Frankfort KY 40601-2847

WILBUR, MARK, environmental executive. V.p. engring. Kemron Environ. Svcs., Inc., McLean, Va. Office: Kemron Environ Svcs Inc Ste 1100 7926 Jones Branch Dr Mc Lean VA 22102

WILBUR, ROBERT LYNCH, botanist, educator; b. Annapolis, Md., July 4, 1925; s. Ralph Sydney and Elizabeth Ellen (Lynch) W.; m. Jeanne Marie Doucette; children: Martha, Ralph, Ellen, Mark, Margaret, Lenore. BS, Duke U., 1946, MA, 1947; PhD, U. Mich., 1952. Asst. prof. botany U. Ga., Athens, 1952-53, N.C. State U., Raleigh, 1953-57; asst. prof. botany Duke U., Durham, N.C., 1957-63, assoc. prof., 1963-69, prof. dept. botany, systematic botanist, 1970—. Roman Catholic. Home: 2613 Stuart Dr Durham NC 27707-2835 Office: Duke U Dept Of Botany Durham NC 27707

WILCOX, BARBARA MONTGOMERY, accountant; b. Corpus Christi, Tex., Dec. 23, 1939; d. Archie James and Jewel (Williams) Montgomery; m. William L. Wilcox, Nov. 7, 1958 (div. June 1966); 1 child, Lawrence Montgomery. Office mgr., acct. Cattleland Oil Co., Corpus Christi, 1966-68; acct. Sanford E. McCormick, Houston, 1968-69; sr. acct. Penn Cen.(formerly Bus. Funds Inc. and Marathon Mfg. Co.), Houston, 1969-74; treas., acct. Frame It Inc., Houston, 1974-76; owner Wilcox Fin. Reporting, Houston, 1976—; owner The Office Gallery, Houston, 1981-96, Pocketwatch, Houston, 1985—; sec. to trustees Pauline Sterne Wolff Meml. Found., Houston, 1977-85; treas. Ouisie's Inc., Houston, 1993-95. Author: Accounting Procedure Manual for Frame Shop Franchises, 1975. Vol. Mus. Fine Arts, 1988—, Tex. Agrl. Ext. Svc. Master Gardener Program, 1986. Mem. Beta Sigma Phi (Outstanding Woman 1964, 65). Republican. Home and Office: 8626 Oakford Dr Houston TX 77024-4604

WILCOX, BENSON REID, cardiothoracic surgeon, educator; b. Charlotte, N.C., May 26, 1932; s. James Simpson and Louisa (Reid) W.; m. Lucinda Holderness, July 25, 1959; children: Adelaide, Alexandra, Melissa, Reid. BA, U. N.C., 1953, MD, 1957. Diplomate Am. Bd. Surgery, Am. Bd. Thoracic Surgery (chmn. 1991-93). Resident Barnes Hosp., St. Louis, 1958-59, N.C. Meml. Hosp., Chapel Hill, 1959-60, 62-64; clin. assoc. Nat. Heart Inst., Bethesda, Md., 1960-62; instr. U. N.C., Chapel Hill, 1963-65, asst. prof., 1965-68, assoc. prof., 1968-71, chief divsn. of cardiothoracic surgery, 1969—, prof., 1971—; cons. NIH Grant Com., Bethesda, 1986-89. Contbr. articles to profl. jours.; author (with others): Atlas of the Heart, 1988, Surgical Anatomy of the Heart, 1992. Pres. Atlantic Coast Conf., Greensboro, N.C., 1980-81; dir. Am. Bd. Thoracic Surgery, 1983-93, chmn., 1991-93. Markle scholar John and Mary Markle Found., 1967; recipient Hadassah Myrtle Wreath award, 1979. Mem. Am. Assn. Thoracic Surgery, Am. Surg. Assn., Soc. Thoracic Surgeons (treas. 1980-86, pres. 1994-95), Soc. Univ. Surgeons, So. Surg. Assn., Thoracic Surgery Dirs. Assn. (pres. 1985-87), Womack Soc. (pres. 1991-93). Democrat. Presbyterian. Office: U NC Med Sch Div Cardiothoracic Surgery 108 Burnett-Womack CB-7065 Chapel Hill NC 27599-7065

WILCOX, CHARLES JULIAN, geneticist, educator; b. Harrisburg, Pa., Mar. 28, 1930; s. Charles John and Gertrude May (Hill) W.; m. Eileen Louise Armstrong, Aug. 27, 1955; children: Marsha Lou, Douglas Edward. BS, U. Vt., 1950; MS, Rutgers U., 1955, PhD, 1959. Registered profl. animal scientist. Dairy farm owner, operator Charlotte, Vt., 1955-56; prof. U. Fla., Gainesville, 1959-95; prof. emeritus, 1995—; cons. in internat. animal agrl. Gt. Britain, France, Sudan, Can., Mex., El Salvador, Ecuador, Brazil, Bolivia, Peru, Colombia, Venezuela, Dominican Republic, Saudi Arabia, Sweden, Norway, 1965—. Author: (with others) Animal Agriculture, 1973, 2d edit., 1980, Improvement of Milk Production in Tropics, 1990; editor: Large Dairy Herd Management, 1978, 93. 1st Lt. U.S. Army, 1951-53, Korea. Decorated Combat Infantryman badge; 3 Korean campaigns. Recipient Disting. Svc. award Fla. Purebred Dairy Assn., 1986, Jr. Faculty award Gamma Sigma Delta, 1968, Sr. Faculty award, 1984, Internat. award for Disting. Svc. to Agr., 1987, Sr. Rsch. Scientist award Sigma Xi, 1994. Mem. Am. Dairy Sci. Assn., Am. Soc. Animal Sci., Brazilian Soc. Genetics (editorial bd. 1979—), Am. Registry Profls. Animal Sci. (examining bd. 1987—), Fla. Holstein Assn. (pres. 1979), Fla. Guernsey Cattle Club (pres. 1974-76), Fla. Jersey Cattle Club (bd. dirs.). Republican. Office: Univ Fla Dairy and Poultry Sci Dept Gainesville FL 32611-0920

WILCOX, DIANE POU, guidance counselor; b. Dallas, July 10, 1947; d. Robert Louis Jr. and Phyllis E. (Carter) Pou; m. Donald E. Wilcox, May 25, 1968; children: Dana Erin, Deren Pou. BFA, So. Meth. U., 1969, MEd, 1972. Tchr. Dallas Ind. Sch. Dist., 1969-72, counselor, 1973, 87-90; guidance counselor, event coord. Highland Park High Sch. Highland Park Ind. Sch. Dist., Dallas, 1990—; sec. bd. dirs. FOCAS, 1980; bd. dirs. Trinity River Mission, 1990-91. Former Duchess, chmn. Fiesta de Las Seis Banderas, Dallas, 1994, asst. Duchess chmn., 1995, gown display, 1996; mem. Dallas Symphony Orch. League, Jr. League Dallas; Symphony Assembly assoc., com. chmn. Jr. Symphony Ball. Recipient Eisenhower award North Tex. West Point Soc., 1992. Mem. ACA, Tex. Counseling Assn., Tex. Assn. Coll. Admissions Counselors (presenter, membership chmn. 1995—, Coll. Band CSS assembly del.), Nat. Assn. Coll. Admissions Counselors, Kappa Alpha Theta Alumni. Republican. Methodist. Office: Highland Park High Sch 4220 Emerson Ave Dallas TX 75205-4620

WILCOX, JAMES ALLEN, psychiatrist; b. Davenport, Iowa, July 1, 1956. BS cum laude, U. Iowa, 1978, MS, 1987; DO, Coll. Osteo. Medicine, Des Moines, 1981; PhD in Biology, U. San Jose, 1995. Diplomate Am. Bd. Psychiatry and Neurology. Intern, resident in psychiatry U. Iowa. Hosps. and Clinics, Iowa City, 1981-85; clin. instr. U. Iowa Med. Sch., 1985-88; asst. prof. U. Iowa, 1989; assoc. prof., dir. rsch. Tex. Tech U., El Paso, 1989—; adj. prof. U. Tex., El Paso, 1990—; med. dir. MECCA, Iowa City, 1983—. Contbr. articles to profl. publs. Recipient Cert. of Recognition Thomason Hosp., 1990. Mem. AAAS, AMA, Am. Psychiat. Assn., Soc. Biol. Psychiatry, Behavioral Neurology Soc. Office: Tex Tech U Dept Psychiatry 4800 Alberta Ave El Paso TX 79905-2709

WILCOX, NANCY DIANE, nurse, administrator; b. Griffin, Ga., Oct. 28, 1951; d. Robert Wayne Birdwell and Eula F. (Maddox) Tatum; m. David Reed Wilcox, May 29, 1970; children: David Jr., Melanie, Bradley, Amy. AS, Panola Coll., 1971; lic. vocat. nurse, Kilgore Coll., 1990, ASN, 1993; BSN magna cum laude, U. Tex., Tyler, 1994. RN, Tex. Hemodialysis nurse Good Shepherd Hosp., Longview, Tex., 1990-91, critical care and telemetry nurse, 1993-94; staff nurse Roy H. Laird Hosp., Kilgore, 1991-93; case mgr. TLC Home Health Agy., Longview, 1994-95; owner, operator LifeCare Home Nursing, Inc., Kilgore, Longview, 1995—. Mem. ANA, Tex. Nurses Assn., Home Care Nurses Assn., Phi Theta Kappa, Alpha Chi, Sigma Theta Tau. Home: 1705 Oakwood Dr Kilgore TX 75662-8803

WILCOX, ROBERT HOWARD, mechanical engineer; b. Lockport, N.Y., Aug. 21, 1930; s. Robert Herrick and Ruth Beatrice (Cullingford) W.; m. Doris Marie Gillis, June 19, 1955; children: Susan, Janet, Robert A., Heather R. BSME, Stevens Tech., 1952; MS in Nuclear Engring., MIT, 1958. Mech. engr. Babcock & Wilcox Co., N.Y.C., 1952-57, U.S. Atomic Energy Commn., Germantown, Md., 1957-63; asst. to exec. sec. U.S. Atomic Energy Commn., Washington, 1963-67; sci. rep. U.S. AEC, Rio de Janeiro/Brussels, 1967-73; sci. and tech. counselor U.S. Dept. State, Buenos Aires/Mexico City, Argentina, Mexico, 1973-81; project mgr. Stone & Webster Engr. Corp., Boston, 1981-87; cons. Falmouth, Mass., 1987-89; program mgr. Westinghouse Savannah R. Co., Aiken, S.C., 1989-96. Mem. Am. Nuclear Soc. (sect. dir. 1986-87, 94—, emeritus). Republican. Roman Catholic.

WILCOX, WILLIAM EDWARD, physician; b. Lexington, Va., Aug. 6, 1946; s. William Stilwell and Lois Jane W.; m. Shirley Fay Crowson, May 29, 1980; children: Patrick, Sarah. AB, U. N.C., 1968, MD, 1977. Gen. practice internal medicine Alabaster, Ala., 1980-86; prin. Health Am.-MCE, Birmingham, Ala., 1986-89; physician Simon Williamson Clinic, Birmingham, Ala., 1990-92, Ea. Med. Specialists, Birmingham, 1992—. Served with U.S. Army, 1969-71. Home: 4448 Briar Glen Dr Birmingham AL 35243-1743 Office: Ea Med Specialists 48 Medical Park Dr E Ste 354 Birmingham AL 35235-3411

WILCOXEN, JOAN HEEREN, fitness company executive; b. Flushing, N.Y., May 30, 1948; d. Paul Arnold and Helena Catherina (Laskowski) Heeren; m. Eddie Dean Wilcoxen, Dec. 31, 1981. BA, Long Island U., 1971; grad., Radford U. Karate Coll., 1994. Cert. referee AAU. Real estate broker Heeren Agy., Riverhead, N.Y., 1970-72; 2d v.p. Levitt House, Inc., Medford, N.Y., 1972-78; radio broadcaster Sta. KWHW Radio, Altus, Okla., 1979-84; exec. dir. Ironworks Family Gym and Heartland Health Club, Altus, Okla., 1984-94, Wilcoxen's Acad. of the Martial Arts, Altus, Okla., 1994—; lectr. martial arts; lectr. Shortgrass Arts and Humanities Coun., Altus, 1988—. Vol. United Way of Jackson County, Altus, 1989—, project co-chair, 1994; fundraiser Muscular Dystrophy Assn., Wichita Falls, Tex., 1987—; mem. Shortgrass Arts and Humanities Coun., 1988-93, Nat. Bd. Realtors, 1978-79; state coord., co-chair Sooner State Games Karate, Oklahoma City, 1989-93; bd. dirs. Am. Heart Assn. 1993-95; mem. Altus 2000 edn. task force. Named for civic leadership Okla. State U. Coop. Extension Svc., Altus, 1988, S.W. Bell Tel. Co., Altus, 1989, Rotary Club and March of Dimes, Altus, 1989, Jackson County Free Fair, Altus, 1988, 89; Okla. State AAU karate champion, 1990, black belt, Nat. AAU women's karate (sparring) champion, 1995. Mem. AAUW (v.p. Altus chpt. 1990, pres. 1992-93), Altus C. of C. (amb. 1989-90), Am. Bus. Women's Assn., Biz Tips Women's Assn. (v.p. 1989-90, pres. 1991-92), Am. Heart Assn. (bd. dirs. Altus chpt. 1994, pres. Jackson County divsn. 1996), Altus C. of C., Air Force Assn. Cmty. Ptnrs., Am. Ind. Karate Instrs. Assn. (instr. Christiansburg, Va. chpt. 1986—). Home: 1100 N Main St Altus OK 73521-3122 Office: Wilcoxen's Acad Martial Art Altus Plz Shopping Ctr 1100 N Main St # C5B Altus OK 73521-3122

WILCZYNSKI, WALTER, psychology educator, neuroscience researcher; b. Trenton, N.J., Sept. 18, 1952; s. Alexander Walter and Eugenia Mary (DiGuiseppi) W. BS in Psychology/BA in Biology, LeHigh U., 1974; PhD in Neurosci., U. Mich., 1978. Postdoctoral fellow Cornell U., Ithaca, N.Y., 1979-83; asst. prof. U. Tex., Austin, 1983-89, assoc. prof., 1989-95, prof., 1995—. Mem. editorial bd. Brain Behavior and Evolution, 1986—; editor: The Evolution of the Amphibian Auditory System, 1988; contbr. articles to profl. jours. and chpts. to 4 books. Grantee NIMH, 1989-93, 95—, NSF, 1984, 86, 91, Smithsonian Instn., 1987, 90, 95. Mem. Soc. for Neurosci., Am. Soc. Zoologists, Internat. Soc. for Neuroethology, Am. Soc. for Advancement Sci. Office: U Tex Dept Psychology Austin TX 78712

WILDENTHAL, C(LAUD) KERN, physician, educator; b. San Marcos, Tex., July 1, 1941; s. Bryan and Doris (Kellam) W.; m. Margaret Dehlinger, Oct. 15, 1964; children—Pamela, Catharine. B.A., Sul Ross Coll., 1960; M.D., U. Tex. Southwestern Med. Ctr., Dallas, 1964; Ph.D., U. Cambridge, Eng., 1970. Intern Bellevue Hosp., N.Y.C., 1964-65; resident in medicine, fellow cardiology Parkland Hosp., Dallas, 1965-67; research fellow Nat. Heart Inst., Bethesda, Md., 1967-68; vis. research fellow Strangeways Research Lab., Cambridge, 1968-70; asst. prof. to prof. internal medicine and physiology U. Tex. Southwestern Med. Ctr., Dallas, 1970-76, prof., dean grad. sch., 1976-80, prof., dean Southwestern Med. Sch., 1980-86, prof., pres., 1986—; hon. fellow Hughes Hall, U. Cambridge, 1994—; bd. dirs. Westcott Comm. Inc. Author: Regulation of Cardiac Metabolism, 1976, Degradative Processes in Heart and Skeletal Muscle, 1980; contbr. articles to profl. jours. Bd. dirs. Dallas Symphony, Dallas Opera, Dallas Mus. Art, S.W. Mus. Sci. and Tech., Dallas Citizen's Coun., Am. Friends Cambridge U. Recipient rsch. career devel. award NIH, 1972; spl. rsch. fellow USPHS, 1968-70; Guggenheim fellow, 1975-76. Mem. AMA, Am. Soc. Clin. Investigation, Am. Coll. Cardiology, Royal Soc. Medicine Gt. Britain, Am. Physiol. Soc., Internat. Soc. Heart Rsch. (past pres. Am. sect.), Am. Fedn. Clin. Rsch., Assn. Am. Med Colls., Assn. Am. Physicians, Am. Heart Assn. (past chmn. sci. policy com.), Assn. Acad. Health Ctrs. (past chmn. sci. policy com.). Home: 4001 Hanover Ave Dallas TX 75225-7010 Office: U Tex Southwestern Med Ctr 5323 Harry Hines Blvd Dallas TX 75235-7200

WILDER, CECIL CREIGHTON, educational association administrator; b. Andalusia, Ala., Aug. 17, 1944; s. Cecil O. and Syble Grace (Posey) W.; m. Elizabeth Ann Romine, June 11, 1966; children: Elizabeth Grace, Deborah Ann. BS, Auburn U., 1966, MEd, 1972; postgrad., Northwestern U., 1991, West Ga. Coll., 1993-95. Tchr. Elmoe County Bd. Edn., Wetumpka, Ala., 1966-67, Muscogee County Sch. Dist., Columbus, Ga., 1967-77, Clayton County Bd. Edn., Jonesboro, Ga., 1977-96; exec. sec.-treas. Ga. Music Educators Assn., Jonesboro, 1996—; adj. asst. prof. Auburn (Ala.) U., 1973-77; music dir. Miss Ga. Pageant, Columbus, 1969-84. Fellow Northwestern U., summer 1991. Mem. Am. Soc. Assn. Execs., Ga. Music Educators Assn. (pres. 1985-87), Phi Beta Mu. Methodist. Home: PO Box 702 Jonesboro GA 30317 Office: Ga Music Educators Assn 145-B N Main St Jonesboro GA 30236

WILDER, JAMES SAMPSON, III, lawyer, judge; b. Knoxville, Tenn., Mar. 15, 1949; s. James Sampson and Florence Louise (Summers) W. BS, Lambuth Coll., Jackson, Tenn., 1971; JD, Memphis State U., 1974. Bar: Tenn. 1974, U.S. Dist. Ct. (we. dist.) Tenn. 1975, U.S. Supreme Ct. 1981, U.S. Ct. Appeals (6th cir.) 1982. Assoc. Lt. Gov. John S. Wilder, Somerville, Tenn., 1974-75, ptnr., 1975-76; ptnr. Wilder, Wilder & Johnson, Somerville, 1976-83; pvt. practice James S. Wilder III, Somerville, 1983-95; gen. sessions judge Fayette County, Somerville, Tenn., 1985-90; assoc. Petkoff and Lancaster, Memphis, 1995—. Scoutmaster troop 95 Boy Scouts Am., Somerville, 1975-77, com. person, 1977—. Paul Harris fellow Rotary, Somerville, 1977. Mem. ABA, Assn. Trial Lawyers Am., Tenn. Bar Assn., Tenn. Trial Lawyers Assn. (dir. 1983-86), Fayette County C. of C. (dir. 1979—), Somerville Rotary (dir. 1976—, charter pres. 1976-78). Methodist. Home: PO Box 187 Somerville TN 38068-0187 Office: Washington Courtyard 305 Washington Ave Memphis TN 38103-1911

WILDER, JOHN SHELTON, state official, state legislator; b. Fayette City, Tenn., June 3, 1921; s. John Chamblee and Martha (Shelton) W.; m. Marcelle Morton, Dec. 31, 1941; children: John Shelton, David Morton. Student, U. Tenn.; LL.B., Memphis Law U., 1957. Bar: Tenn. 1957. Engaged in farming Longtown, Tenn., 1943—; supr. mgmt. Longtown Supply Co.; judge Fayette County Ct.; mem. Tenn. Senate, 1959—; lt. gov. Tenn., 1971—; past pres. Nat. Assn. Soil Conservation Dists., Tenn. Soil Conservation Assn., Tenn. Agrl. Council; exec. com. So. Legis. Conf., Conf. Lt. Govs.; dir. Oakland Deposit Bank, Tenn., Somerville Bank and Trust Co., Tenn. Served with U.S. Army, 1942-43. Mem. Tenn. Cotton Ginners Assn. (past pres.), Delta Theta Phi. Democrat. Methodist. Club: Shriners. Office: Legislative Plz Ste 1 Nashville TN 37243-0026*

WILDER, ROBERT ALLEN, finance and leasing company executive, leasing broker, investment consultant; b. Memphis, Feb. 13, 1944; s. Donald Byrd and Marion S. (Brown) W.; m. Betty Michael, Apr. 23, 1977; 1 child, Elizabeth Michael. BS, Memphis State U. Sch. Engring., 1967, MS, 1973. Regional sales mgr. Hertz Corp. Truck div., Atlanta, 1974-77; regional dir. Itel Corp., Atlanta, 1978, 79, 90, 91, 92; pres. Interstate Systems, Inc., Atlanta, 1979-81; dir. corp. lease programs, 1981-83, dir PBX sales, 1983-87, dir., gen. mgr. distbr. sales, 1988-90, No. Telecom Fin. Corp., Atlanta and Nashville, 1981-90; cons.; sr. v.p. First Tenn. Equipment Fin. Corp., Nashville, 1990-91; investment cons. Am. Wealth Mgmt., Inc., Atlanta, 1992—. With U.S. Army, 1967-72. Mem. Am. Assn. Equipment Lessors (speaker 1988 conf.), Memphis State U. Alumni. Ga. (pres. 1986-88). Methodist. Home: 955 River Overlook Ct Atlanta GA 30328 Office: 3525 Piedmont Rd Bldg 7 Atlanta GA 30305

WILDSCHUETZ, HARVEY FREDERICK, electric industry executive; b. Independence, Mo., Sept. 3, 1943; s. George Frederick and Dorothy Mae (Knapheide) W.; m. Sharon Kay Eigenmann; children: Holly Dawn, Michael Dean. BSEE, U. Mo., Rolla, 1966. Registered profl. engr., Ill., Mo., N.Mex.; real estate broker, N.Mex. Elec. engr. power div. Burns & McDonnell Engring. Co., Kansas City, Mo., 1966-69; supt. elec. engring. City Water Light & Power, Springfield, Ill., 1969-76; asst. v.p. Plains Electric G&T Corp., Albuquerque, 1976-89; dir. Light and Power Dept., Highland, Ill., 1989-91; mgr. engring. and ops. Ill. Mcpl. Electric Agy., Springfield, 1991-93; utilities dir. City of Lake Worth, Fla., 1993—. Coach Little League. Mem. IEEE, NSPE, N.Mex. Soc. Profl. Engrs., Optimist, Exch. Club. Home: 1739 Kelso Ave Lake Worth FL 33460 Office: City of Lake Worth 1900 2nd Ave N Lake Worth FL 33461-4204

WILDUN, REGINA DUNCAN, songwriter, writer, singer; b. Memphis, Oct. 7, 1960; d. Roy and Delight Carmen (Pratt) Duncan; m. Ronnie Wildun Williams, July 15, 1989; 1 child, Ashlin Blake. MusB, Lambuth U., 1982. Courier Fed. Express Corp., Nashville, 1983-96, key account sales rep. for sanctuary distbn., 1996—. Home and Office: Songwriter Cir Music 604 Songwriter Cir Nashville TN 37220

WILEMAN, GEORGE ROBERT, lawyer; b. Ironton, Ohio, June 1, 1938; s. George Merchant and Marguerite (McCormack) W.; m. Patricia M. Wileman; children: John Chandler, Julie Jo. AB, Duke U., 1960; JD, Georgetown U., 1963. Bar: Ohio 1968, Tex. 1977, U.S. Supreme Ct. 1993. Pvt. practice Dallas, 1977—. Mem. Coll. State Bar of Tex. Republican. Home: 5313 Paladium Dr Dallas TX 75240 Office: 5220 Spring Valley # 520 Dallas TX 75240

WILES, BETTY JANE, accountant; b. Scott County, Ark., Dec. 21, 1940; d. Edd and Nellie Margaret (Richey) Staggs; m. Ralph A. Wiles, July 18, 1959; children: Ralph A. Jr., Penny Margaret. BBA magna cum laude, Henderson State Coll., 1983. CPA, Ark. Sec. Royalty Holding Co., Oklahoma City, 1959-65, Rector & Eubanks, Mena, Ark., 1966-69; paralegal Shaw & Shaw Attys., Mena, Ark., 1969-83; pvt. practice acctg. Mena, Ark., 1984—. Cons. adv. bd. Mena H.S., 1985-86; cons. adv. bd. St. John Libr., Rich Mountain C.C., 1987-90, mem. svc. adv. com., 1988-90; mem. bd. trustees Mena Hosp. Com., 1991-97. Mem. AAUW (pres. Mena br. 1993-95), Ark. Soc. CPAs (emergency assistance com., govt. acct. and auditing com. 1993-95), Ouachita Chpt. CPAs (v.p. 1996-97), Mena Lioness, Quachita Writer's Guild. Baptist. Club: Mena Lioness. Home: PO Box 522 Mena AR 71953-0522 Office: 513 Mena St Mena AR 71953-3337

WILES, JERRI FULP, microcomputer educator, accountant, consultant; b. Winston-Salem, N.C., Mar. 19, 1951; d. Lemuel McArthur and Beulah Mae (Poarch) Fulp; m. Bruce R. Rudd, July 3, 1971 (div. 1982); m. Toby N. Wiles, Jan. 13, 1996. AAS in Acctg., Forsyth Tech. C.C., Winston-Salem, 1978; BS in Bus. and Econs., High Point U., 1987; MBA, Appalachian State U., Boone, N.C., 1990, postgrad., 1996—. Capital budgeting specialist The Hanes Corp., Winston-Salem, 1978-80; acctg. supr. The Fortis Corp., King, N.C., 1980-84; acctg. mgr. L'Erin Cosmetics, Winston-Salem, 1984-85; contr. Avtex Properties, Inc., Winston-Salem, 1985-86; mgr. Coble Dairy Coop., Lexington, N.C., 1986-87; instr. microcomputing Forsyth Tech. C.C., 1987—; pres. MBA & Assocs., Inc., Walnut Cove, N.C., 1992—; trainer Bowman Gray Sch. Medicine, Wake Forest U., Winston-Salem, 1993; reviewer microcomputer textbooks. Advisor Jr. Achievement, Winston-Salem; judge N.C. Future Bus. Leaders of Am., Winston-Salem, 1992. Mem. Am. Assn. Women in C.C.s (pres.), Multimedia Users Group (DCC N.C. 1991-93), Nat. Bus. Edn. Assn., N.C. Assn. for Women in Edn. Republican. Moravian. Home: RR 2 Box 202 Walnut Cove NC 27052-9608 Office: Forsyth Tech CC 2100 Silas Creek Pky Winston Salem NC 27103-5150

WILEY, ALBERT LEE, JR., physician, engineer, educator; b. Forest City, N.C., June 9, 1936; s. Albert Lee and Mary Louise (Davis) W.; m. Janet Lee Pratt, June 18, 1960; children: Allison Lee, Susan Caroline, Mary Catherine, Heather Elizabeth. B in Nuclear Engring., N.C. State U., 1958, postgrad., 1958-59; MD, U. Rochester, N.Y., 1963; PhD, U. Wis., 1972. Diplomate Am. Bd. Nuclear Medicine, Am. Bd. Radiology, Am. Bd. Med. Physics. Nuclear engr. Lockheed Corp., Marietta, Ga., 1958; intern in surgery-medicine U. Va. Med. Sch., Charlottesville, 1963-64; resident in radiation therapy Sanford U., Palo Alto, Calif., 1964-65; resident and NCI postdoctoral fellow U. Wis. Hosp., Madison, 1965-68; med. dir. USN Radiol. Def. Lab., San Francisco, 1968-69; staff physician Balboa Hosp., USN, San Diego, 1969-70; asst. prof. radiotherapy M.D. Anderson Hosp. U. Tex., Houston, 1972-73; assoc. dir., clin. dir. radiation oncology U. Wis., Madison, prof. radiology, human oncology, med. physics, 1970-88; prof., chmn. radiation oncology, dir. cancer ctr. East Carolina U. Med. Sch., Greenville, N.C., 1988-93; cons. U.S. NRC, 1981-82, Nat. Cancer Inst., U.S. Dept. VA, 1990-93; advisor, cons. numerous univs. and govt. agys.; mem. Wis. Radioactive Waste Bd., Wis. Gov.'s Coun. on Biotech., Gov.'s Com. on UN. Author more than 140 articles and abstracts on med. physics, environ. health, nuclear medicine, biology and cancer treatment. Rep. candidate for U.S. Congress for 2d Wis. dist., 1982, 84; rep. primary candidate for gov., State of Wis., 1986; mem. Greenville Drug Task Force; bd. dirs. Greenville Salvation Army. Lt. comdr. USNR, ret. Oak Ridge Inst. Nuclear Studies fellow N.C. State U., 1958-59. Fellow Am. Coll. Radiology, Am. Coll. Preventive Medicine, N.C. Inst. Polit. Leadership; mem. IEEE, AMA, AAUP, Am. Assn. Physicists in Medicine, Am. Soc. Therapeutic Radiation Oncologists, Am. Assn. Physics Tchrs., Am. Bd. Sci. in Nuclear Medicine (sec.-treas.), Am. Acad. Health Physics, Am. Cancer Soc. (N.C. bd. dirs.), C. of C., VFW, Vietnam Vets. Am., Am. Legion, Masons, Rotary, Sigma Xi, Tau Beta Pi. Home: Salter Path Rd Box 588 Indian Beach NC 28575 Office: Watson Clinic Radiation Medicine PO Box 95000 Lakeland FL 33805-5000

WILEY, ELIZABETH GREENE WILLIAMS, secondary education educator; b. Daytona Beach, Fla., Dec. 31, 1948; d. William Alfred Greene and Katherine Caufman (Thatcher) G.; m. Steve T. Williams, June 6, 1970 (dec. 1977); m. Larry Eugene Wiley, Aug. 9, 1985; 1 child, Emily Faith. BS, East Tex. State U., 1972, MS, 1974. Cert. art tchr., Tex., mentally retarded, Tex. Tchr. art Commerce (Tex.) Ind. Sch. Dist.; instr. art Dalton (Ga.) Jr. Coll.; tchr. art Granbury (Tex.) Ind. Sch. Dist., Alvord (Tex.) Ind. Sch. Dist.; visual art tchr. Mineral Wells (Tex.) High Sch. Recipient Nat. Humanities Coun. award. Mem. Internat. Coun. Learning Disabilities, Nat. Art Edn. Assn., Am. Fedn. Tchrs., Tex. Fedn. Tchrs., Tex. Classroom Tchrs. Assn.

WILEY, JEROLD WAYNE, environmental services executive, retired air force officer; b. Urbana, Ill., Jan. 7, 1944; s. Jesse Scott and Eula Eileen (Deffenbaugh) W.; BS, So. Ill. U., 1967; MS, U. N.D., 1973; m. Gloria J. Uselton, May 6, 1982; children: Jackson Scott, Justin Wayne. Commd. 2d lt. U.S. Air Force, 1968, advanced through grades to maj., 1982; Minuteman II launch officer 321 Strategic Missile Wing, Grand Forks AFB, N.D., 1969-73; Minuteman II initial qualification instr. 4315 Combat Crew Tng. Squadron, Vandenberg AFB, Calif., 1973-76; asst. prof. aerospace studies Coll. St. Thomas, St. Paul, 1976-79; dir. tng. and devel. 325 Fighter Weapons Wing, Ops. Tng. Devel. Team, Tyndall AFB, Fla., 1979-83; chief internat. tng. Joint U.S. Mil. Mission for Aid to Turkey, Ankara, 1983-85; comdr. 3743 Basic Mil. Tng. Squadron, Lackland AFB, Tex., 1985-87; chief acads. br. Hdqrs. Basic Mil Tng. Sch., Lackland AFB, 1987-88, retired, 1988; asst. dir. environ. svcs. North Miss. Med. Ctr., Tupelo, 1989-90, asst. dir. environ. svcs.; dir. environ. svcs. Bapt. Hosp. Miami, 1990-91; dir. housekeeping Great Oaks Nursing Home, Roswell, Ga., 1992-93; dir. environ. svcs. St. Francis Hosp., Columbus, Ga., 1993-94; asst. dir. environ svcs. Baptist Med. Ctr., Montgomery, Ala., U. Va. Med. Ctr., Charlottesville, Va., 1995—. Decorated Meritorious Svc. medal with 1 oak leaf cluster, Combat Readiness medal, Air Force Commendation medal with 2 oak leaf clusters, Humanitarian Svc. medal, Defense Meritorious Svc. medal. Mem. Am. Soc. Tng. and Devel., Am. Mgmt. Assns., Am. Assn. Community and Jr. Colls., Nat. Community Edn. Assn., Soc. Am. Foresters, Air Force Assn. (life), USTA (cert. umpire), Am. Soc. Healthcare Environ. Svcs., So. Ill. U. Alumni Assn. (life), Ret. Officers Assn. (life), Exch. Club. Republican. Contbr. articles to Tng. mag. Home: 1307 Carter Ln Charlottesville VA 22901-3103

WILEY, JOHN EDWIN, cytogeneticist; b. Roanoke, Va., Mar. 2, 1951; s. James Edwin and Marie Rita (Cassell) W. BA, U. N.C., Greensboro, 1973, MA, 1976; PhD, N.C. State U., 1981. Diplomate Am. Bd. Med. Genetics-Clin. Cytogenetics. Biomed. researcher St. Paul's Coll., Lawrenceville, Va., 1981-82; postdoctoral trainee U. Wis., Madison, 1982-84; mem. faculty East Carolina U. Sch. Medicine, Greenville, N.C., 1984—. Contbr. articles to profl. jours. Biomed. rsch. support grantee United Way, Greenville, 1986-87, USPHS, Washington,1987-90. Mem. AAAS, Am. Soc. Human Genetics, Am. Soc. Zoologists, Am. Soc. Ichthyologists and Herpetologists. Democrat. Home: 1461 Hunters Ln Greenville NC 27834-8829 Office: East Carolina U Sch Medicine Moye Blvd Greenville NC 27858-4300

WILEY, KENNETH LEMOYNE, physician; b. San Antonio, Jan. 10, 1947; s. Elmer Lee and Dolores (Shields) W.; m. Linda Nixon, June 29, 1974; children: Kenneth Jr., Brian. BS, Trinity U., 1968; MS, Okla. State U., 1970; MD, Meharry, Nashville, 1977. Resident in internal medicine George W. Hubbard Hosp., Nashville, 1977-80; with USPHS, Lebanon, Tenn., 1980; pvt. practice medicine Lebanon, 1980-93; pvt. practice in internal medicine MD Care, Inc., New Orleans, 1993—. Capt. U.S. Army, 1969-73, Vietnam. Mem. Sigma Pi Sigma, Soc. of the Sigma Xi, Alpha Omega Alpha, Alpha Phi Alpha. Home: 6150 Eastover Dr New Orleans LA 70128-3614 Office: 3840 Saint Bernard Ave New Orleans LA 70122-1146

WILEY, MILLICENT YODER, retired secondary school educator, realtor; b. Mercedes, Tex., June 7, 1923; d. Frank and Grace Mae (Setter) Yoder; m. William Gregory Wiley, Mar. 25, 1946; children: Sandra Kay Wiley, Patti Gayle Wiley Diamond. BS, Tex. State Coll. Women, 1949; postgrad. U. Houston, 1950-53. Choral dir., music tchr. schs. in Tex. and La., 1945-60; tchr. Kingsville (Tex.) Ind. Sch. Dist., 1960-80, trustee 1981-87; choral dir. H.M. King High Sch., 1964-80, ret., 1980; area admissions adv., adminstr. Pacific Am. Inst., 1976-80; state dir. South Tex. for Am. Internat. Edn. and Tng., 1980-83; Tex. rep. Internat. Travel Study, Inc., 1983-90; adminstr. Travel Selections, 1990-96; pianist Kingsville Rotary Club, 1966—, Tex. State Fedn. of Women's Club, 1994-96, Dist. Fedn. of Women's Club, 1994-96. Bd. dirs. Kingsville chpt. Am. Heart Assn., Community Concerts Assn., Helen Kleberg Community Ctr., 1994—, Kingsville Action Com.; adjudicator Tex. Choral Contests; mem. Tex. All-State Alumni Bd., 1995; active Mayor's City Com., Mayor's Future Com., Rep. Task Force. Recipient various certs. appreciation. Mem. NEA, Am. Sch. Bd. Assn. (trustee 1980-87), Am. Choral Dirs. Assn., Music Educators Nat. Conf., Tex. Assn. Sch. Bds. (trustee 1980-87), Tex. Music Educators Assn. (dir. 1973-74), Tex. Choral Dirs. Assn. (state clinic condr. 1977), Tex. State Tchrs. Assn., Tex. Music Adjudicators Assn., Kingsville Bd. Realtors (bd. dirs. 1994-95), Tex. Assn. Realtors, Multiple Listing Service Kingsville, Nat. Bd. Realtors, Fgn. Study League (adv., adminstr. 1971-76), Music Club of Kingsville (pres. 1982-84, 3rd v.p. 1987-91), Nat. Ret. Tchrs. Assn., Kingsville Ret. Tchrs. Assn. (sec. 1986-88, 2nd v.p. 1988-89, 1st v.p. 1989-91), Tri-City Ret. Tchrs. (sec.), Kingsville C. of C., 36th Divsn. Assn. (2d v.p. nat. ladies aux. 1988-89, 1st v.p. nat. ladies aux. 1989-90, pres. 1990-91), Women's Club Kingsville, (chmn. As You Like It dept. 1988-90, 1st vice chmn. 1992-94),

General Women's Club of Kingsville (parliamentarian 1992-94, pres. 1994—), Exxon Annuitant Club (bd. dirs. 1992-94), Rotary (pianist 1966—, 1st Woman mem. 1987—, past social chmn., program chmn., membership chmn. 1993-94, chmn. membership devel. com. 1994—), Kiwanis (pianist Kingsville club 1985—), Exxon Bridge Club, Monday Night Bridge Club, Kingsville Country Club. Methodist. Home: 229 Helen Marie Dr Kingsville TX 78363-7305

WILEY, MYRA, mental health nurse; b. Lexington, Ala., Jan. 20, 1938; d. Joseph Aaron and Annie Lura (Putnam) Haraway; m. Robert Harold Wiley, Sept. 17, 1960; children: Sonya, Robert, Marie. BSN, U. Ala., Huntsville, 1989. RN, Ala.; cert. in chem. dependency. Nursing asst., night-weekend coord. Upjohn Health Care, Huntsville, 1983-87; nursing asst. North Ala. Rehab. Hosp., Huntsville, 1987-89; staff nurse Humana Hosp., Huntsville, 1989-91; staff nurse counselor Bradford-Parkside, Madison, Ala., 1991-95; relief charge nurse for behavioral health Columbia Med. Ctr. of Huntsville (formerly Crestwood Hosp.), Huntsville, Ala., 1995—. Mem. ANA, Nat. Nurses Soc. on Addictions, Ala. State Nurses Assn., Madison County Nurses Assn, Nat. Consortium Chem. Dependency Nurses, Inc. Baptist.

WILEY, RONALD ROSS, librarian; b. Flushing, N.Y., July 19, 1936; s. Harold Foster and Alice (Ross) W. BA, U. Pitts., 1959, MLS, 1963. Libr. Bklyn. Pub. Libr., 1963-65, W.Va. State Coll., Institute, 1966—. Disaster svc. vol. ARC, Charleston, W.Va., 1988—; vol. Jay Rockefeller for Gov., 1972, Charleston. Democrat. Home: 283 Roxalana Hills Dr Dunbar WV 25064-1919 Office: WVa State Coll Institute WV 25112

WILHELM, MARY EVELYN, writer; b. Stamford, Tex., Jan. 7, 1947; d. Charlie and Cecilia Jane (Reznik) Vasek; m. Vernon Wilhelm, Aug. 16, 1969; children: Lisa, Theresa, David, Daniel, Michael. Student, Draughon's Bus. Coll. Author: (cook book) Welcome to Happy, Texas, The Town Without a Frown, 1994. Treas. St. Ann's Cath. Ch., Canyon, Tex., 1990-91. Named Outstanding Conservation Homemaker award Palo Duro Soil and Water Conservation Dist., 1987. Roman Catholic. Home: PO Box 104 Happy TX 79042

WILHELM, WILBERT EDWARD, industrial and systems engineering educator; b. Pitts., Oct. 24, 1942; married; 2 children. BSME, W. Va. U., 1964; MS in Indsl. Engring., Va. Poly. Inst. and State U., 1970; PhD in Indsl. Engring. and Ops. Research, 1972. Registered profl. engr., Ohio. Facilities engr. lamp glass dept. Gen. Electric Co., Logan, Ohio, 1965, quality control engr. and subcontract adminstr., ordinance dept., Pittsfield, Mass., 1966; quality control foreman, Salem, Va., 1966-67, mfg. analyst, 196769, specialist mfg. adminstrn., instr. Va. Poly. Inst., Blacksburg, 1969-72; from asst. to assoc. prof. dept. indsl. and systems engring. Ohio State U., Columbus, 1972-78; prof. dept. indsl. engring. Tex. A&M U., 1989—; cons. Columbus Coated Fabrics, United Airlines, Dorcey Cycle, Gen. Elec. Co., Cen. Ohio Transit Authority, Ohio State Internat., Ohio Dept. Transp., Def. Constrn. Supply Ctr., Tex. Instruments; dir. Flexible Mfg. Lab. Contbr. numerous articles to profl. jours. Recipient Ralph Boyer award Ohio State U. Coll. Engring., 1984, research award, 1985; Tex. Engring. Experiment Sta. Sr. Rsch. fellow, 1991, 92, 93, NSF fellow, NASA fellow. Fellow IIE (dir. OR divsn. 1988-89, Spl. Citation award 1993, David F. Baker Disting. Rsch. award 1996); mem. Am. Inst. Indsl. Engrs. (sr., pres. local chpt. 1979-80, bd. dirs. 1980-81, program chmn. 1982-83, chpt. devel. adviser 1983-84, Region Community Affairs award 1980, Chpt. Devel. award 1980), Soc. Mfg. Engrs. (sr., editl. bd. Jour. Mfg. Syss. 1989—), Ops. Research Soc. Am. (chair, tech. sect. on mfg. mgmt. 1991-93), Phi Kappa Phi (editor in chief IIE Transactions, 1993-96), Alpha Pi Mu. Home: 2912 Colton Pl College Station TX 77845-7720 Office: Tex A & M U Industrial Engr 237M Zachry Engring Ctr College Station TX 77843

WILHELMI, MARY CHARLOTTE, education educator, college official; b. Williamsburg, Iowa, Oct. 2, 1928; d. Charles E. and Loretto (Judge) Harris; m. Sylvester Lee Wilhelmi, May 26, 1951; children: Theresa Ann, Sylvia Marie, Thomas Lee, Kathryn Lyn, Nancy Louise. BS, Iowa State U., 1950; MA in Edn., Va. Poly. Inst. and State U., 1973, cert. advanced grad. studies, 1978. Edn. coord. Nova Ctr. U. Va., Falls Church, 1969-73; asst. adminstr. Consortium for Continuing Higher Edn. George Mason U., Fairfax, Va., 1973-78; adminstr., asst. prof. George Mason U., Fairfax, 1978-83; dir. coll. rels. and devel., assoc. prof. No. Va. C.C., Annandale, 1983—; bd. dirs. No. Va. C.C. Ednl. Found., Inc., Annandale, 1984—; v.p. mktg. Fairfax (Va.) Symphony, 1995—; chmn. Health Systems Agy. No. Va., Fairfax; mem. George Mason U. Inst. for Ednl. Transformation. Edtl. bd. Va. Forum, 1990-93; contbr. articles to profl. jours. Bd. dirs. Fairfax County chpt. ARC, 1981-86, Va. Inst. Polit. Leadership, 1996—, Fairfax Com. of 100, 1986-88, 90—, Hospice No. Va., 1983-88, No. Va. Mental Health Inst., Fairfax County, 1978-81, Fairfax Profl. Women's Network, 1981, Arts Coun. Fairfax County, 1989—; vice chmn. Va. Commonwealth U. Ctr. on Aging, Richmond, 1978—; mem. supt.'s adv. coun. Fairfax County Pub. Schs., 1974-86, No. Va. Press Club, 1978—; pres. Fairfax Ext. Leadership Coun., 1995; mem. Leadership Fairfax Class of 1992. Named Woman of Distinction, Soroptimists, Fairfax, 1988, Bus. Woman of Yr., Falls Church Bus. and Profl. Women's Group, 1993; fellow Va. Inst. Polit. Leadership, 1995. Mem. State Coun. Higher Edn. Va. (pub. affairs adv. com. 1985—), Greater Washington Bd. Trade, Fairfax County C. of C. (legis. affairs com. 1984—) Va. Women Lobbyists, 1991—, No. Va. Bus. Roundtable, Internat. Platform Assn., Phi Delta Kappa (10-Yr. Continuous Svc. award 1991), Kappa Delta Alumni No. Va., Psi Chi, Phi Kappa Phi. Roman Catholic. Home: 4902 Ravensworth Rd Annandale VA 22003-5552 Office: No Va CC 4001 Wakefield Chapel Rd Annandale VA 22003-3744

WILHELMI, WILLIAM MERLE, artist; b. Garwin, Iowa, Feb. 4, 1939; s. Ray and Dorothy Clarine (Cronhardt) W. BA, San Diego State U., 1960; MFA, UCLA, 1969. Studio potter Dos Patos Gallery, Corpus Christi, Tex., 1969-75, Kaffie Gallery, Corpus Christi, Tex., 1976-83, Carancahua Gallery, Corpus Christi, Tex., 1983-86, Wilhelmi/Holland Gallery, Corpus Christi, Tex., 1986—; workshop leader various univs. and confs. Exhibited in group shows at Art Mus. South Tex., 1973, Nat. Conf. Edn. for Ceramic Arts Conf., Ann Arbor, Mich., 1980, Am. Crafts Mus., N.Y.C., 1980, Renwick Gallery, Washington, 1980, Asher/Faure Gallery, L.A., 1982, Libr. Congress, Washington, 1983, Cayman Gallery, N.Y.C., 1983, Emily Edwards Gallery, San Antonio, 1989, S.W. Tex. State U., San Marcos, 1993, Art Mus. of South Tex., 1996, numerous others; represented in permanent collections Long Beach (Calif.) Mus. Art, Everson Art Mus., Syracuse, N.Y., Tweed Mus. Art, Duluth, Minn., Renwick Gallery Smithsonian Instn., Washington, Cooper-Hewitt Mus., N.Y.C., Gene Autry Mus. Western Art, L.A.; numerous public collections; works published in (books) Decorative Art in Modern Interiors, 1970, 71, 77, 78, Claywork: Form and Idea in Ceramic Design, 1975, Ceramics, 1978, Teapots, 1980, American Porcelain: New Expressions in an Ancient Art, 1981, Ceramics of the 20th Century, 1982, American Cowboy, 1983, The New York Art Review, 1989, Southwest Art Review, 1990, American Ceramics, 1990, The Book of Cups, 1990, Art Today, 1996, numerous others, numerous periodicals. Lt. USNR, 1962-65. Recipient Cert. of Merit, Am. Ceramic Soc., L.A., 1968, 2d Place prize Expo Art in All Media, Del Mar, Calif., 1968, Purchase prize 25th Ceramic Nat., Syracuse, N.Y., 1968, Cert. of Merit, Calif. Crafts VI, Sacramento, 1969, 2 Purchase awards Ceramics '69, San Mateo, Calif., 1969, Honorable Mention award Corpus Christi Art Found. Exhbn., 1971, Honorable Mention award 15th Tex. Crafts Exhbn., Dallas, 1971, 1st Place award Corpus Christi Art Found. Exhbn., 1972, Honorable Mention award 16th Tex. Crafts Exhbn., 1974, Winedale, 1981, Tex. Arts award for Creativity, Tex. Arts Alliance and Tex. Commn. on Arts, Austin, 1981, The Corpus Christi Arts Coun. award for Creativity, 1991, Dir.'s award Creativity and Community Svc., Arts Coun. Corpus Christi, 1992. Mem. Art Mus. South Tex. (bd. trustees). Home: 1129 Ocean Dr Corpus Christi TX 78404-2331 Office: Wilhelmi Studio 300 S Chaparral St Corpus Christi TX 78401-2806

WILHOIT, GENE, state agency administrator. Edn. dir. Ark. Dept. Edn., Little Rock. Office: Ark Dept Edn Capitol Mall Bldg 4 Little Rock AR 72201*

WILHOIT, HENRY RUPERT, JR., federal judge; b. Grayson, Ky., Feb. 11, 1935; s. H. Rupert and Kathryn (Reynolds) W.; m. Jane Horton, Apr. 7, 1956; children: Mary Jane, H. Rupert, William. LLB, U. Ky., 1960. Ptnr. Wilhoit & Wilhoit, 1960-81; city atty. City of Grayson, Ky., 1962-66; county atty. Carter County, Ky., 1966-70; judge U.S. Dist. Ct. (ea. dist.) Ky., 1981—. Recipient Disting. Service award U. Ky. Alumni Assn., 1980. Mem. ABA, Ky. Bar Assn. Office: US Dist Ct 320 Fed Bldg 1405 Greenup Ave Ashland KY 41101-7542*

WILHOITE, LAURA J., occupational health nurse; b. Dublin, Ga., May 22, 1959; d. Donald R. and Sally J. (Kingman) Jarvis; m. Arnold M. Wilhoite, Dec. 19, 1981; children: Wesley, Donna Jean. BS, Ga. So. Coll., 1981, MEd, 1982; AS, Manatee Community Coll., Bradenton, Fla., 1987. Cert. occupational hearing conservationist, 1st aid instr., occupational health nurse. Staff nurse, neonatal and newborn Bulloch Meml. Hosp., Statesboro, Ga., 1987-89; occupational health nurse King Finishing Co., Dover, Ga., 1989-95, Torrington Co., Sylvania, Ga., 1995—. Mem. Am. Assn. Occupational Health Nurses, Ga. Assn. Occupational Health Nurses (corr. sec. 1995—), Coastal Ga. Assn. Occupational Health Nurses (pres. 1992—). Home: 216 N Edgewood Dr Statesboro GA 30458-5522

WILKE, CHET, real estate executive; b. Chgo., Dec. 10, 1942; m. Beverly J. Galuska, July 31, 1981; children: Lisa Michelle, Rebecca Ann, Christa Leann. BA in Comm., Columbia Coll., L.A., 1970. Cert. real estate mktg. cons. Sta. mgr., dir. TV news, personality Armed Forces Radio & TV, 1965-69; acct. exec. Sta. KALI, L.A., 1970-72; sr. acct. exec. HR/Stone Radio Reps., L.A., 1972-75; gen. sales mgr. Sta. KYXY-FM, San Diego, 1975-77; pres., founder Wilke Enterprises Inc., San Diego and Houston, 1977-81; gen. sales mgr. Sta. KEYH, Houston, 1982; gen. sales mgr., acting mgr. Sta. KYST, Houston, 1982-85; mgr., mktg./creative dir. Advt. Concepts Inc., Houston, 1985-88; exec. v.p. First Hanover Real Estate/Mortgage, Houston and Sugar Land, Tex., 1988-89; pres., real estate broker Ameristar Group Corp., Plano, Tex., 1989—; CEO PRO, Profl. Realty Office Network, Inc., Plano, Tex., 1995—. With USAF, 1964-69. Mem. Nat. Assn. Realtors, Tex. Assn. Realtors, Greater Dallas Assn. Realtors, Collin County Assn. Realtors, Lions. Republican. Methodist. Home: 2312 Cardinal Dr Plano TX 75023-1470 Office: PRO Network 3033 W Parker Rd #106 Plano TX 75023

WILKE, RICHARD B., bishop. Bishop Little Rock Conf. United Meth. Ch. Office: United Meth Ch 715 Center St Ste 202 Little Rock AR 72201-4317*

WILKENS, LEONARD RANDOLPH, JR. (LENNY WILKENS), professional basketball coach; b. Bklyn., Oct. 28, 1937; s. Leonard Randolph Sr. and Henrietta (Cross) W.; m. Marilyn J. Reed, July 28, 1962; children: Leesha Marie, Leonard Randolph III, Jamée McGregor. BS in Econs., Providence Coll., 1960, HHD (hon.), 1980. Counselor Jewish Employment Vocat. Services, 1962-63; salesman packaging div. Monsanto Co., 1966; profl. basketball player St. Louis Hawks, 1960-68; player-coach Seattle SuperSonics, 1969-72, head coach, 1977-85, gen. mgr., 1985-86; profl. basketball player Cleve. Cavaliers, 1972-74, player NBA All-Star Game, 1973, head coach, 1986-93; player-coach Portland (Oreg.) Trail Blazers, 1974-76; head coach Atlanta Hawks, 1993—; coach 4 NBA All-Star Teams including Ea. Conf. team All-Star game, Mpls., 1994, World Champion basketball team, 1979, IBM NBA Coach of the Year, 1994; winningest coach of all time, 1995, coach 1996 Olympic Basketball Team, asst. coach 1992 Olympic Basketball. Author: The Lenny Wilkens Story, 1974. Bd. regents Gonzaga U., Spokane; bd. dirs. Seattle Ctr., Big Bros. Seattle, Bellevue (Wash.) Boys Club, Seattle Opportunities Industrialization Ctr., Seattle U.; co-chmn. UN Internat. Yr. of Child program, 1979; organizer Lenny Wilkens Celebrity Golf Tournament for Spl. Olympics. 2d lt. U.S. Army, 1961-62. Recipient Whitney Young Jr. award N.Y. Urban League, 1979, Disting. Citizens award Boy Scouts Am., 1980; named MVP in NBA All-Star Game, 1971, Man of Yr., Boys High Alumni chpt. L.A., 1979, Sportsman of Yr., Seattle chpt. City of Hope, 1979, Congl. Black Caucus Coach of Yr., 1979, CBA Coach of Yr., 1979, Coach of Yr., Black Pubs. Assn., 1979, NBA Coach of Yr., 1994; named to NIT-NIKE Hall of Fame, 1988; named to 9 NBA All-Star Teams, elected to Naismith Memorial Basketball Hall of Fame, 1988. *

WILKERSON, JAMES NEILL, lawyer; b. Tyler, Tex., Dec. 17, 1939; s. Hubert Cecil and Vida (Alexander) W.; m. Cal Cantrell; children: Cody, Ike. A.A., Tyler Jr. Coll., 1960; B.B.A., U. Tex., 1966, JD, 1968. Bar: Tex. 1968, U.S. Dist. Ct. (we. dist.) Tex. 1974, U.S. Supreme Ct. 1973. Sole practice, Georgetown, Tex., 1977—; instr. Cen. Tex. Coll., Copperaas Cove, Tex., 1973-74; asst prof. law U.S. Mil. Acad., West Point, N.Y., 1971-73; pres. W.I.N. Ranch, Inc., 1995—; pres. C&N Bus. Developers, 1992—. Pres. Beautify Georgetown Assn., 1977-80, 81-82; pres. U. Tex. Young Reps., 1964-65; co-chmn. Bush for Pres., 1988, Reagan-Bush campaign, 1980; mem. Williamson County Rep. Com., 1977-81; chmn. Hist. Preservation Com., 1979-85; trustee 1st Unied Meth. Ch., 1994—, chmn. bd. trustees, 1996. Col., USAR, 1968—, trial judge JAGC, 1975-91; appellate judge Army Ct. Mil. Rev., 1991-93. Decorated Legion of Merit, Bronze Star, Air medal. Mem. Williamson County Bar Assn., Tex. State Bar Coll., Sertoma (v.p. 1981-83, 87, sec. 1988-89, pres. 1992-93), Lions (pres. 1982-83), Vietnam War Vets. Office: PO Box 1090 Georgetown TX 78627-1090

WILKERSON, MATHA ANN, oil company executive; b. Mill Creek, Okla., Sept. 1, 1937; d. Frank and Lottie Evelyn (Cordell) Stie; m. Ronald Gene Wilkerson, Dec. 22, 1956; 1 child, Mitchell Linn. BS in Edn., East Cen. U., 1966. Elem. sch. tchr. Moore (Okla.) Pub. Schs., 1966-74; office mgr. S. S. Sanbar, M.D., Oklahoma City, 1974-78; ops. mgr., acct. John A. Taylor Oil Co., Oklahoma City, 1978-84; office mgr., controller Lance Ruffel Oil & Gas Corp., Oklahoma City, 1984—. Mem. Coun. of Petroleum Accounts Soc. (com. mem. 1979—). Baptist. Office: Lance Ruffel Oil & Gas 100 Park Ave Ste 500 Oklahoma City OK 73102-8006

WILKERSON, RITA LYNN, special education educator, consultant; b. Crescent, Okla., Apr. 22. BA, Cen. State U., Edmond, Okla., 1963; MEd, Cen. State U., 1969; postgrad., U. Okla., 1975, Kans. State U. Elem. tchr. music Hillsdale (Okla.) Pub. Sch., 1963-64; jr. high sch. music and spl. edn. Okarche (Okla.) Pub. Sch., 1965-71; cons. Title III Project, Woodward, Okla., 1971-72; dir. Regional Edn. Svc. Ctr., Guymon, Okla., 1972-81; dir., psychologist Project W.O.R.K., Guymon, 1981-90; tchr. behavioral disorders Unified Sch. Dist. 480, Liberal, Kans., 1990—; sch. psychologist Hardesty (Okla.) Schs., 1994; cons. Optima (Okla.) Pub. Schs., 1990, Felt (Okla.) Pub. Schs., 1990, Texhoma (Okla.) Schs., 1994, Balko (Okla.) Pub. Schs., 1996; spl. edn. cons. Optima Pub. Schs., 1992—, Goodwell (Okla.) Pub. Schs., 1992—; diagnostician Tyrone, Okla. Pub. Schs., 1992-95; home svcs. provider Dept. Human Svcs., Guymon, 1990; active Kans. Dept. Social and Rehab. Svcs., 1993—; adj. tchr. Seward County C.C., 1994—. Grantee Cen. State U., 1968-69, Oklahoma City Dept. Edn., 1988-89. Mem. ASCD, NAFE, NEA (liberal Kans. chpt.), AAUW, Coun. Exceptional Children, Okla. Assn. Retarded Citizens, Okla. Assn. for Children with Learning Disabilities, Phi Delta Kappa. Republican. Home: 616 N Crumley St Guymon OK 73942-4341 Office: Unified Sch Dist 480 7th And Western Liberal KS 67901

WILKERSON, WILLIAM HOLTON, banker; b. Greenville, N.C., Feb. 16, 1947; s. Edwin Cisco and Agnes Holton (Gaskins) W.; m. Ellen Logan Tomskey, Oct. 27, 1973; 1 child, William Holton Jr. AB in Econs., U. N.C., 1970. Asst. v.p. First Union Nat. Bank, Greensboro, N.C., 1972-77; v.p. Peoples Bank & Trust Co., Rocky Mount, N.C., 1977-79; sr. v.p. Hibernia Nat. Bank, New Orleans, 1979-86; exec. v.p. Peoples Bank and Trust Co., 1987-89, pres., 1989-90; group exec officer, bd. dirs. Centura Banks, Inc., 1990—; chmn., Centura Ins. Svcs., Inc., 1995—, Centura Securities, Inc., 1995—, Carolinas Gateway Partnership, Inc., 1995—. Mem. Robert Morris Assoc., Rocky Mount C. of C. (bd. dirs. 1989—, vice chmn. 1992-94, chmn.-elect 1994, chmn. 1995), Benvenue Country Club, Kiwanis, Omicron Delta Epsilon, Chi Beta Phi, Phi Sigma Pi. Republican. Home: 336 Iron Horse Rd Rocky Mount NC 27804-2118

WILKES, ADELINE WOOD, library science educator; b. Dalton, Ga.; d. John Henry and Ruth Rebecca (Hassler) Wood; m. Judson Stanley Wilkes, Jr., June 8, 1948; children: Mary Adeline, Judson Stanley, Wendy Ann, Kevin Wood. AB in English cum laude, Wesleyan Coll., Macon, Ga., 1947; MS in Libr. Sci., Fla. State U., 1968, AMD in Libr. Sci., 1977, PhD in Libr. Sci., 1983. Owner/mgr. Discount Sporting Goods House, Thomasville, Ga., 1970-72; instr. Fla. State U., Tallahassee, 1969-70, assoc. libr., 1972-80, univ. libr., 1980-88, adj. faculty mem., 1982-88, dir. libr. sci. libr., 1969-70, 72-86; libr. Study Ctr. Libr. Fla. State U., Florence, Italy, 1986; head spl. collections Fla. State U., Tallahassee, 1986-88; asst. prof. libr. sci. Tex. Woman's U., Denton, 1988-91, assoc. prof., 1991—; lectr. in field; evaluator U.S. Dept. Edn., Office Ednl. Rsch. and Improvement, Libr. Programs, Fgn. Lang. Materials Acquisition Program, Title V of the Libr. Svcs. and Constrn. Act, 1991. Contbr. articles to profl. jours. Mem. Friends of Fla. State U. Libr., 1985-88, bd. dirs., 1985-86, adv. com., 1987-88, other coms. Recipient Faculty Devel. award Tex. Woman's U., 1990; HEA Title IIB fellow, 1990, 92, 93. Mem. ALA (Libr. Rsch. Round Table), Assn. for Libr. and Info. Sci. Edn. (faculty liaison Sch. Libr. and Info. Studies, Tex. Woman's U. 1992—, faculty devel. com. 1989-92, 92-94, Spl. Award for Rsch. 1984), Sch. Libr. and Info. Studies Alumni Assn. (bd. dirs. 1972-85, exec. sec.-treas. 1972-85), Assn. for Libr. Svc. to Children (nat. planning for spl. collections com. 1983-87), Tex. Libr. Assn. (councilor Automation and Tech. Round Table 1991-94), Beta Phi Mu (exec. bd./faculty liaison 1992— Lambda chpt.). Home: 1812 Westminster St Apt 7 Denton TX 76205-7833 Office: Texas Woman's Univ Sch Libr and Info Studies Denton TX 76204

WILKES, CLEM CABELL, JR., stockbroker; b. Johnson City, Tenn., Apr. 5, 1953; s. Clem Cabell Sr. and Dorothy Jane (Miller) W.; m. Tonya Jean McCall, July 20, 1974; children: Elizabeth Layne, Clem Cabell III. BS, East Tenn. State U., 1975; postgrad., Med. Coll. Pa., 1978, Owen Sch. Mgmt., Nashville, 1984. Salesman Beecham Labs., Bristol, Tenn., 1975-78, Smith Kline & French Labs., Phila., 1978-81; stockbroker J.C. Bradford & Co., Johnson City, 1981-85; stockbroker, ptnr. Robert Thomas Securities, Inc., Johnson City, 1985—. Vestry mem. St. John's Epis. Ch., 1986-89, treas., 1986—, sr. warden, 1989; mem. com. Am. Cancer Soc., Johnson City, 1986-87, 2d v.p., 1989—. Melvin Jones fellow Johnson City Ties for Blind Found., 1989. Mem. Johnson City C. of C. (membership chmn. 1987), Robert Thomas Securities Pres. Club, Lions (v.p. Johnson City 1986-88, pres. 1989-90 Lion of Yr. award 1985, Lion of Decade award 1992), Kappa Alpha. Office: Robert Thomas Securities Inc 901 N Roan St Johnson City TN 37601-4604

WILKINS, (GEORGE) BARRATT, librarian; b. Atlanta, Nov. 6, 1943; s. George Barratt and Mabel Blanche (Brooks) W. B.A., Emory U., 1965; M.A., Ga. State U., 1968, U. Wis., 1969. Reference libr. S.C. State Libr., Columbia, 1969-71; instl. libr. cons. Mo. State Libr., Jefferson City, 1971-73; asst. state libr. State Libr. Fla., Tallahassee, 1973-77; state libr. State Libr. Fla., 1977—; dir. div. Libr. and Info. Svcs. State of Fla., Tallahassee, 1986—, acting asst. sec. state, 1987; abstractor Hist. Abstracts, 1967-71; dir. survey project Nat. Ctr. Edn. Statistics, 1976-77; del. The White House Conf. on Libr. and Info Svcs., 1991; mem. planning com. Fla. Gov.'s Conf. on Libraries and Info. Svcs.; bd. dirs. Southeastern Libr. Network, Inc., 1979-82, treas., 1980-81, vice chmn., 1981-82; mem. adv. coun. U.S. Pub. Printer, 1983-86, Southeastern/Atlantic Regional Med. Libr. Svcs. 1986-89; mem. planning com., Fla. Automated Edn. Commn., 1989-94; bd. dirs. Fla. Distance Learning Network, Inc., First Am. Found., Inc.; cons. in field. Contbr. articles to profl. jours. Mem. adv. com. statewide jail project Mo. Assn. Social Welfare, 1971-73, bd. dirs. central div., 1971-73; mem. State Univ. System Interinstl. Library Com., 1977—; bd. dirs. Fla. Ctr. Libr. Automation, 1984—, Fla. Ctr. for the Book, 1984—, Fla. Coll. Ctr. for Libr. Automation, 1990—. Recipient Exceptional Achievement award Assn. Specialized and Coop. Libr. Agys., 1991, Outstanding Pub. Svc. award Gov. of Fla., 1991; U. Wis. fellow, 1969. Mem. ALA (coun. 1981-85, legis. com. 1982-86, com. cn orgn. 1988-90, planning com., 1993-95, standards, 1996—), Assn. State Libr. Agys. (pres. 1976-77), Assn. Hosp. Instl. Librs. (bd. dirs. 1973-74), Am. Correctional Assn. (instn. libr. com.), Southeastern Libr. Assn. (pres. 1982-84), Chief Officers of State Libr. Agys. (bd. dirs. 1980-82, pres. 1990-92, chair legis. com. 1992-96), Beta Phi Mu, Phi Alpha Theta. Democrat. Episcopalian. Office: Dept State Divsn Libr Svcs RA Gray Bldg Tallahassee FL 32399-0250

WILKINS, FLO, elementary education educator; b. Jamaica, N.Y., July 12, 1946; d. Raymond and Jeanette (Brown) Fardy; m. Robert Wilkins, Dec. 21, 1969; children: Nancy, Julie, Emily, Mary Grace. AA, Nassau Community Coll., Garden City, N.Y., 1966; BA, SUNY, New Paltz, 1969. Cert. elem. tchr., W.Va., instr. for Lions Quest and Jr. Great Books. Tchr. Sachem Bd. Edn., Holbrook, N.Y., Doddridge County Bd. Edn., West Union, W.Va., Wayne County Bd. Edn., Philippi, W.Va., Barbour County Bd. Edn., Philippi, W.Va. Active community orgns.; remedial reading tutor. Mem. NEA, W.Va. Edn. Assn., Delta Kappa Gamma. Home: RR 3 Box 278 A-5 Philippi WV 26416-9803

WILKINS, JERRY L., lawyer, clergyman; b. Big Spring, Tex., June 1, 1936; s. Claude F. and Grace L. (Jones) W.; children by previous marriage: Gregory, Tammy, Scott, Brett; m. Valerie Ann Nuanez, Aug. 1, 1986. BA, Baylor U., 1958, LLB, 1960. Bar: Tex. 1960, U.S. Dist. Ct. (no. dist.) Tex. 1960, U.S. Ct. Appeals (5th cir.); ordained to ministry, 1977. Pvt. practice, Dallas, 1960—; capt. Air Am., Vietnam, 1967-68, Joint Church Aid, Biafra, 1969-70, TransInternat. Airlines, Oakland, Calif., 1977-79; gen. counsel First Tex. Petroleum, Dallas, 1982; owner Wooltex, Inc., Dallas, 1983—; owner, dir., legal counsel Intermountain Gas Inc., Dallas, 1983-84; legal counsel, dir. USA First (co-founder USA First Panama); co-founder Nederlandse Fin. Panama; founder, dir. Comanche Peak Reclamation Inc.; bd. dirs. Engineered Roof Cons., Continental Tex. Corp., Arlington, Landlord Rsch. Inc., Acklin Pain Rsch. Inst., Inc., Irving, Tex., Silver Leaf Metals Internat. Inc., Silver Leaf Mining Inc., Tex. Recycling Industries, Inc., Minerals Exploration Inc., Land Techs. Inc., Environ. Techs. Inc., Environ. Contractors Inc., Environ. Enterprises Inc., Desert Resources Inc.; founder, chmn. bd. dirs. Tex. Reclamation Industries, Inc.; founder Oxford Securities Funding Inc., Manchester Securieties Funding Inc., Cambridge Securities Funding Inc.; bd. dirs., v.p for legal affairs, underwriter Lloyds U.S. Inc.; bd. dirs., co-founder R.O.A.S., Inc., Maritime Internat., Inc., Maritime Oil Recovery, Inc., Moriah Oil Recovery Barges, Inc., Megas Homes Internat., Urex Internat., Landlord Rsch. Co., Inc.; mem. legal counsel, bd. dirs. U.S. Fiduciary Co. Inc., U.S. Fiduciary Trust Co. Inc.; bd. dirs., legal counsel Lloyds U.S. Corp., Lloyds Link Inc., Lloyds Am. Inc., Image Security Co., Inc., Manchester Funding, Inc.; founder Kenai Cold Storage Inc., Kenai Pure Water Co., Arctic Pure Water Co., Arctic Cold Storage Inc., Shiloh Inc., Receivers, Inc., Internat. Equity Founding, Inc., C3 Plus Inc., UBO Sonoma Fin., UBO Caribbean Funding, Capstone Corp., Prowler Fouler Inc., Pacific Atlantic Funding Inc., Atlantic Funding, Inc.; bd. dirs., CEO Celex Nev., Inc.; bd. dirs. Minerals Exploration, Inc., Land Tech., Inc., Environ. Techs., Inc., Environ. Enterprises, Inc., Desert Gold Resources, Inc., Environ. Contractors, Inc.; co-founder USA First; cons. in field. Author: Gods Prosperity, 1980; So You Think You Have Prayed, 1980, Gods Hand in my Life, America, The Land of Sheep for Slaughter, I.R.S., America's Gestapo; Editor numerous books; contbr. articles to profl. jours. Bd. dirs., pres. Beasley For Children Found. Inc., Dallas, 1978—; mem. Rep. Presdl. Task Force, Washington, 1984—, Rep. Senatorial Inner Circle; bd. dirs., pilot Wings for Christians, Dallas, 1976—, Wings for Christ, Waco, Tex., 1976—. Recipient Cert. of Appreciation Parachute Club of Am., 1966; cert. of record holder for high altitude sky diving State of Tex., 1966, 67; Cert. of Achievement, Tex. State Guard, 1968. Mem. ABA, Nat. Lawyers Assn., Plaintiff Trial Lawyers Assn., Internat. Platform Assn., Tex. Trial Attys. Assn., Assn. Trial Lawyers Am., Quiet Birdmen, Tex. Outdoor Writers Assn., NRA, Tex. Rifle Assn., Parachute Assn. Am., P51 Mustang Pilots Assn., Phi Alpha Delta, U.S. Parachute Club (Monterey, Calif.). Avocations: shooting, hunting, fishing, flying, sports. Achievements: atty. (2 Tex. landmark cases) securing custody of female child for stepfather against natural parents (set the precedent which is now the standard visitation regarding children in divorce cases in Tex.), securing outside jail work program for convicted man, others. Office: PO Box 59462 Dallas TX 75229-1462

WILKINS, LUCIEN SANDERS, gastroenterologist; b. Sanford, N.C., Mar. 30, 1942; s. Alexander Betts and Olive Elizabeth (Pittman) W.; m. Freda Barry Hartness, July 16, 1966; children: Lucien Sanders Jr., Elise Perryman. BA, Duke U., 1963; MD, Med. Coll. Va., 1967. Diplomate Am. Bd. Internal Medicine. Intern Medical Coll. Va., Richmond, 1967-68, resident in internal medicine, 1970-72, gastroenterology fellow, 1972-73; clin. gastroenterologist Wilmington (N.C.) Health Assoc., 1973—; vis. physician Hopital St. Croix, Leogane, Haiti, 1979-84; founder Divsn. Gastrointestinal Endoscopy Hopital St. Croix, Leogane, 1984, 1st Endoscopic Ambulatory Surgery Facility in State of N.C., 1990; chmn. dept. medicine New Hanover Regional Med. Ctr., Wilmington, N.C., 1990-92; asst. prof. clin. medicine U.

N.C., Chapel Hill, 1974—; bd. dirs. Br. Banking and Trust, Wilmington, 1991—; physican adv. Nat. Found. Ileitis and Colitis, 1976-78. Author: Progeny, 1994. Bd. dirs. Cape Fear Coun. for the Arts, Wilmington, 1976-77, New Hanover Regional Med. Ctr. Found., Wilmington, 1993-95, exec. com., 1994-95, Com. of 100, Wilmington, 1992-95. Lt. comdr. M.C., USN, 1968-70. A. D. Williams rsch. fellow, 1965, Paul Harris fellow Rotary, 1986; winner GTP-L Al Holbert Meml. Race, Sebring, Fla., 1995. Mem. ACP, New Hanover-Pender County Med. Soc. (pres. 1980), Cape Fear Country Club, Surf Club, Hist. Stock Car Racing Group, Figure Eight Island Yacht Club (charter), Wrightsville Beach Ocean Racing Assn. (commodore). Presbyterian. Home: 2215 Lynnwood Dr Wilmington NC 28403-8026 Office: Wilmington Health Assoc 1202 Medical Ctr Dr Wilmington NC 28401-7307

WILKINS, PAUL COLE, psychiatrist; b. Buffalo, Aug. 21, 1947; s. John Paul and Grace Estelle (Sammons) W.; Wenche Larsson, June 1, 1968; 1 child, Jon Cole. BA in Psychology magna cum laude, Yale U., 1969; MD, U. Va., 1973. Diplomate Am. Bd. Psychiatry and Neurology., Am. Bd. Geriat. Psychiatry. Resident in psychiatry U. Va. Hosp., Charlottesville, 1973-76; clin. instr. in psychiatry U. Va. Med. Ctr., Charlottesville, 1976-78; pvt. practice, 1978—; clin. asst. prof. U. Va. Med. Ctr., Charlottesville, 1987—; med. dir. Region 10 Community Mental Health Svc., Charlottesville, 1976-79, staff psychiatrist, 1979-80, cons. psychiatrist, 1981-86; med. dir. Charter Hosp. Charlottesville, 1986-88; dir. Piedmont Psychiat. Profls., Charlottesville, 1985—; mem. cons. staff Martha Jefferson Hosp., Charlottesville, 1979-82, assoc. staff, 1982-84, active staff, 1984—. Contbr. articles to profl. jours. Bd. dirs. Mental Health Assn. Charlottesville-Albemarle, 1988-91, chmn. pub. edn. com., 1988-90, chmn. nominating com., 1990-91; bd. dirs. Coalition for Mentally Disabled, 1986-91. Fellow Am. Psychiat. Assn.; mem. Psychiat. Soc. Va. (mem. ins. com. 1986—, chmn. 1988-90, co-chmn. 1990-91), Albemarle County Med. Soc., Med. Soc. Va., AMA, Va. Psychoanalytic Soc., Alpha Omega Alpha. Office: Piedmont Psychiat Profls 1139 E High St Ste 103 Charlottesville VA 22902-4854

WILKINS, ROBERT PEARCE, lawyer; b. Jesup, Ga., Sept. 10, 1933; s. Ransom Little and Sarah (Pearce) W.; m. Rose Truesdale, Jan. 7, 1956; children: Robert Pearce, Chisolm Wallace (dec.), Sarah Ruth Weiss, Rose Anne Brooks. B.A., U. S.C., 1953, J.D., 1954; LL.M., Georgetown U., 1957. Bar: S.C. 1954; cert. mediator and arbitrator, S.C. Atty. Office Gen. Counsel, Sec. Army, Washington, 1956; trust officer First Nat. Bank S.C., Columbia, 1957-60; practice law Columbia, 1960-64; ptnr. McLain, Sherrill & Wilkins, Columbia, 1964-68, McKay, Sherrill, Walker, Townsend & Wilkins, Columbia, 1969-75; sole practice law Columbia and Lexington, S.C., 1975-88; of counsel Nelson, Mullins, Riley & Scarborough, Lexington, 1988—; pres. Sandlapper Press, Inc., 1967-72, pub. Sandlapper Mag. S.C., 1968-72; editor Sandlapper Mag. S.C., 1968-69, 89—; editor, pub. S.C. History Illustrated, 1970; pres. R.P.W. Pub. Corp.; mem., chmn. S.C. Splty. Adv. Bd. Estate Planning and Probate, 1982-85; lectr. in law U. S.C., 1971-78. Author: Draftin Wills and Trust Agreements in South Carolina, 1971, Drafting Wills and Trust Agreements in Michigan, 1978, Wills and Trust System (Arkansas), 1978, Drafting Wills and Trust Agreements: A Systems Approach, 1995, 3d edit., 1995, software edit.; (with others) Word Processing for a Law Office, 1979, also articles; editor: The Lawyer's Microcomputer, 1982-85, The Lawyer's PC, 1983—, What a Lawyer Needs to Know to Buy and Use a Computer, 1984, The Perfect Lawyer, 1990—, The Lawyers' Word, 1991, Shepard's Elder Care/Law Newsletter, 1991-95. Del., Spl. Liaison Tax Com. Southeastern Region, 1967-70; exec. com. Richland County Rep. Com., 1960-64; sec.-treas. Richland County Rep. Club, 1960; bd. dirs. Ctrl. Tb-RD Assn.; trustee Sch. Dist. 1, Lexington County, S.C., 1971-78, sec., 1972-75, chmn., 1975-78; mem. S.C. Commn. on Higher Edn., 1978-80, S.C. Commn. on Lawyer Competence, 1980-82; bd. dirs. Crime Stoppers of the Midlands, 1983-85, RPW Learning Ctr., 1987-94, Mt. Hope Cemetary, 1991—, also v.p., 1992—; v.p. 11th cir. Alumni Coun. U. S.C., 1993-95, mem. awards com., 1995—; mem. commn. Riverbanks Zoo, 1986—, sec., 1991-95, chmn., 1995—. With AUS, 1954-55. Fellow Am. Bar Found., Am. Coll. Trust and Estate Counsel (publs. com. 1984-87, bd. regents 1986-87, mem. tech. com. 1989—), Am. Coll. Tax Counsel, Coll. Law Practice Mgmt. (charter, trustee), S.C. Bar (tax coordinating com. 1968-70, chmn. legal econs. com. 1973-75, ho. of dels. 1978-80, editor S.C. Lawyer 1989-91, mem. alternative dispute resolution sect. 1993—), S.C. Bar Found. (life, bd. dirs. 1984-88, v.p. 1986-87, pres. 1987-88); mem. ABA (ho. of dels. 1986-87, chmn. valuation subcom., estate and gift tax com., taxation sect. 1967-73, vice chmn. svc. and assistance to law student div. com. gen. practice sect. 1971-72, vice chmn. corp. counsel com. gen. practice sect. 1972-74, editor econs. of law practice sect. legal econs. 1974-78, sec. 1977-78, vice chmn. 1978-79, chmn. 1980-81, mem. standing com. assn. comm. 1981-84, real property, probate and trust law, mem. publs. com. 1985-89, editor Probate and Property, 1986-89), Richland County Bar Assn. (chmn. probate sect. 1973-74, unauthorized practice of law com. 1976), Lexington County Bar (chmn. mediation com. 1994—), Columbia Jaycees (sec.-treas. 1958-59), Columbia Estate Planning Coun. (pres. 1964-65), Am. Y-Flyer Yacht Racing Assn. (area v.p. 1971, internat. dir. 1972-73), Omicron Delta Kappa, Sigma Chi. Clubs: Columbia Sailing (dir. 1968-71), Columbia Tip Off (dir. 1968-73), Columbia (pres. 1971-72). Home: PO Box 729 Lexington SC 29071-0729 Office: 334 Old Chapin Rd Lexington SC 29072-8801*

WILKINS, WILLIAM WALTER, JR., federal judge; b. Anderson, S.C., Mar. 29, 1942; s. William Walter and Evelyn Louise (Horton) W.; m. Carolyn Louise Adams, Aug. 15, 1964; children: Lauren, Lyn, Walt. B.A., Davidson Coll., 1964; J.D., U. S.C., 1967. Bar: S.C., 1967, U.S. Dist. Ct. S.C. 1967, U.S. Ct. Appeals (4th cir.) 1969, U.S. Supreme Ct. 1970. Law clk. to judge U.S. Ct. Appeals 4th Cir., 1969; legal asst. to U.S. Senator Strom Thurmond, 1970; ptnr. Wilkins & Wilkins, Greenville, S.C., 1971-75; solicitor 13th Jud. Cir., 1974-81; judge U.S. Dist. Ct., Greenville, 1981-86, U.S. Ct. Appeals (4th cir.), 1986—; lectr. Greenville Tech. Coll.; chmn. U.S. Sentencing Commn., 1985-94. Editor-in-chief S.C. Law Rev., 1967; contbr. articles to legal jours. Served with U.S. Army, 1967-69. Named Outstanding Grad. of Yr. U. S.C. Sch. Law, 1967. Mem. S.C. Bar Assn., Wig and Robe. Republican. Baptist. Office: US Cir Ct 4th Ct PO Box 10857 Greenville SC 29603-0857

WILKINSON, CAROL LYNN, mycologist; b. Raleigh, N.C., July 29, 1953; d. James Spencer and Eva Elizabeth (Hitchner) W. BA, SUNY, Albany, 1976, A.Bus., 1986. Pub., editor N.C. Rev. Press, 1976. Mem. AAAS, APHA, DAR, Intertel, Mensa, Girls Scouts U.S. (life). Presbyterian.

WILKINSON, DAVID ANDY, writer; b. Slaton, Tex., June 26, 1948; s. James Richard Wilkinson and Betty Jane (Dickson) Baker; m. Mary Ann Louise Alley, Aug. 17, 1968; children: Ian Stuart, Emily Louise. BA in Sociology, Tex. Tech. U., 1972. Police officer Police Dept., Lubbock, Tex., 1967-73; supv., mgr. Dept. of Pub. Safety, Lakewood, Colo., 1973-79; v.p. Wilkinson Brokerage, Lubbock, 1979-82; fin. planner Lubbock, 1982-88; fin. officer Operator Svc. Co., Lubbock, 1988-91; writer, performer Lubbock, 1991—. Author, performer (album) Texas When Texas Was Free, 1990, Deep in the Heart, 1992, Charlie Goodnight, 1994; author: (play) Charlie Goodnight's Last Night, 1995. Named New Folk songwriter Kerrville Folk Festival, 1985, Western Heritage Wrangler Nat. Cowboy Hall of Fame, 1994. Fellow Ctr. for Great Plains Studies; mem. Western Writers of Am., Western Folklife Ctr., Tex. Tech. Ex-Students Assn., Nashville Assn. of Songwriters Internat., West-Tex. Hist. Soc. Democrat. Methodist. Home: 5205 92nd St Lubbock TX 79424

WILKINSON, EDWARD STARSMEARE, JR., federal agency executive; b. Norfolk, Va., Aug. 17, 1948; s. Edward Starsmeare and Marguarite Pricilla (Adams) W. BS, Sam Houston State U., 1973, MA, 1974; MS, Nat. Def. U., Washington, 1995. Spl. agt./investigator Office of Sec. of Def., Washington, 1975-89; adminstrv./security officer Office of Sec. of Army/Dept. of Def., Washington, 1989-91; exec./sr. officer CIA, Washington, 1991—. Capt. U.S. Army, 1968-71, Tex. Army N.G., 1971-75. Mem. Criminal Justice Rsch. Soc. (assoc.), Indsl. Coll. of Armed Forces Assn., Mil. Order of Purple Heart, Phi Theta Kappa, Lambda Alpha Epsilon. Republican. Baptist. Home: 2472 Ridgehampton Ct Reston VA 20191

WILKINSON, G. THOMAS, gas and oil industry executive; b. 1937. BSE, St. Louis U., 1959. With AMOCO, ARCO, Seagull Energy S&P; pres. Ashland Exploration, Inc., 1990—; v.p. Ashland Oil, Inc., 1990-91, sr. v.p., 1992—. Office: Ashland Exploration Inc 14701 Saint Marys Ln Ste 700 Houston TX 77079-2905

WILKINSON, GREGG STUART, epidemiologist; b. Alexandria, La., July 25, 1942; s. Stanley Stuart and Erna G. (Adleff) W.; m. Jacqueline Neil Roemer, Nov. 12, 1966; children: Julie Caroline, Garret Stuart, Glen Jeffrey, Scott Graham. BA, SUNY, Buffalo, 1969, MA, 1971, PhD, 1973. Assoc. cancer rch. scientist Roswell Park Meml. Inst., Buffalo, 1974-78; sr. epidemiologist EPA, Research Triangle Park, N.C., 1978-80; epidemiology group leader Los Alamos (N.Mex.) Nat. Lab., 1980-87; assoc. epidemologist Epidemiology Resources Inc., Chestnut Hill, Mass., 1987-89; assoc. prof. med. br. U. Tex., Galveston, 1989-90, chief div. of epidemiology and biostats., 1990—, prof., 1993—; cons. U. Tex. Sch. Health Scis., Houston, 1980-82, NSF, Washington, 1985-88, KACST, Saudi Arabia, 1988-90, N.Mex. Dept. of Health, 1991—, Colo. Dept. Health, 1992—, UCLA Sch. Pub. Health, 1993—, Simultec Ltd., 1995—; pres., treas. HealthEffects Press, Inc., New Orleans, 1992—; pres. Wilkinson Rsch., Inc., Santa Fe, Tex., 1993—; mem. neural tube defects sci. adv. bd. Tex. Dept. Health, 1992-95; mem. Tex. Radiation Adv. Bd., 1992—. Author: An Evaluation of a Cancer Information Telephone Facility; Candial, Praeger Scientific, 1985; editor: The Nuclear Energy Industry, Occupational Medicine: State of The Art Reviews, 1991; contbr. articles to profl. jours. Del. Buffalo Council of Chs., 1977, 78. Nat. Cancer Inst. grantee, 1975-78, NIOSH, 1985-86, 94—, John Sealy Found., 1990-93, One Borde Found., 1992-94. Mem. AAAS, APHA, Soc. Epidemiologic Rsch., N.Y. Acad. Scis., Phi Kappa Psi (chpt. chaplain 1961-62). United Methodist. Home: 2335 Avenue L Santa Fe TX 77510-9031

WILKINSON, HARRY EDWARD, management educator and consultant; b. Richmond Heights, Mo., June 30, 1930; s. Harry Edward and Virginia Flo (Shelton) W.; m. Sara Beth Kikendall, Aug. 30, 1958; children: Linda Beth, Cheryl Susan. BA in Physics, Princeton U., 1952; MBA, Washington U., St. Louis, 1957; D Bus. Adminstrn., Harvard U., 1960. Lic. psychologist, Mass. Staff engr. Southwestern Bell Tel. Co., St. Louis, 1954-57; traffic engr. New Eng. Tel. & Telegraph Co., Boston, 1957-60; sr. mgmt. cons. Harbridge House Inc., Boston, 1961-65; dean bus. adminstrn., dir. Mgmt. Inst., Northeastern U., Boston, 1965-67; pres., chmn. bd. Univ. Affiliates Inc., North Port, Fla., 1967—; vis. prof. mgmt. Rice U., Houston, 1990-94, dir. office of exec. devel., 1994—; cons. to various industries and govt., 1961—. Author: Influencing People in Organizations, 1993; contbr. articles to mgmt. jours. Lt. (j.g.) USN, 1952-54, Korea. Mem. APA, Acad. Mgmt., N.Am. Case Rsch. Assn., S.W. Case Rsch. Assn., Harvard Bus. Sch. Assn. Office: Jones Grad Sch Rice U 6100 Main St Houston TX 77005-1892

WILKINSON, JAMES HARVIE, III, federal judge; b. N.Y.C., Sept. 29, 1944; s. James Harvie and Letitia (Nelson) W.; m. Lossie Grist Noell, June 30, 1973; children: James Nelson, Porter Noell. B.A., Yale U., 1963-67; J.D., U. Va., 1972. Bar: Va. 1972. Law clk. to U.S. Supreme Ct. Justice Lewis F. Powell, Jr., Washington, 1972-73; asst. prof. law U. Va., 1973-75, assoc. prof., 1975-78; editor Norfolk (Va.) Virginian-Pilot, 1978-81; prof. law U. Va., 1981-82, 83-84; dep. asst. atty. gen. Civil Rights div. Dept. Justice, 1982-83; judge U.S. Ct. Appeals (4th cir.), 1984—, chief judge, 1996—. Author: Harry Byrd and the Changing Face of Virginia Politics, 1968, Serving Justice: A Supreme Court Clerk's View, 1974, From Brown to Bakke: The Supreme Court and School Integration, 1979. Bd. visitors U. Va., 1970-73; Republican candidate for Congress from 3d Dist. Va., 1970. Served with U.S. Army, 1968-69. Mem. Va. State Bar, Va. Bar Assn., Am. Law Inst. Episcopalian. Home: 1713 Yorktown Dr Charlottesville VA 22901-3035 Office: US Ct Appeals 255 W Main St Rm 230 Charlottesville VA 22901-5058

WILKINSON, REBECCA ELAINE, human resources systems analyst; b. Dallas, Nov. 11, 1960; d. John Cephas and Mary Magdeline (Rhea) Bishop; m. Billy Don Wilkinson, July 31, 1982; children: Eric Tyler, Kristen Rhea. BEd, U. Dallas, 1982, MBA, 1995. Human resources/payroll systems analyst IBM, Irving, Tex., 1982-85; equal opportunity coord. IBM, Irving, 1985-90; human resources data analyst IBM, Roanoke, Tex., 1990-94; systems analyst specialist Westinghouse Security Systems, Irving, 1994—; team leader finance & adminstrv. sys. Westinghouse Security Sys., 1996—. Mem. NOW, Greenpeace, Sigma Iota Epsilon. Democrat. Episcopalian.

WILKLOW, CHARLES MANFRED, air transportation executive, pilot; b. Tacoma, Dec. 25, 1960; s. Charles Francis and Sonoe (Yutani) W.; m. Veronica Lynn Gantt, June 4, 1988; children: Charles Alexander, Rachel Erin. AS, Cen. Tex. Coll., 1988; BS in Aviation Mgmt., Pacific Western U., 1992. Cert. airline transport pilot. Infantryman U.S. Army, Ft. Bragg, N.C., 1979-82; aviator 2d infantry div. U.S. Army, Camp Casey, Korea, 1983-84; aviator 82d airborne div. U.S. Army, Ft. Bragg, 1984-87; aviator U.S. Army Nat. Guard, Raleigh, N.C., 1987—; pilot Ram Air Freight, Raleigh, 1987-88, Mid-Atlantic Freight, Greensboro, N.C., 1988, Metro Airlines, Dallas-Ft. Worth, 1988-93; pres. Airways Internat., Inc., Miami Springs, Fla., 1993-95; chief pilot Biscayne Helicopters, Inc., Miami, Fla., 1995—; instr./FAA check airman Airways Internat., Inc., 1993, Civil Air Patrol, Beckely, W.Va., 1992. Recipient humanitarian svc. medal U.S. Army, 1981, Army achievement medal, 1984, Army commendation medal, 1984, nat. def. svc. medal, 1992. Mem. Nat. Guard Assn. of U.S., N.C. Nat. Guard Assn. Republican. Methodist. Home: 205 Fox View Pl Cary NC 27511-7264 Office: Biscayne Helicopters Inc PO Box 163639 12760 SW 137th Ave Miami FL 33186

WILKS, LARRY DEAN, lawyer; b. Columbia, S.C., Jan. 8, 1955; s. Ray Dean and Jean (Garrett) W.; m. Jan Elizabeth McIllwain, May 2,1981; children: John Ray, Adam Garrett. BS, U. Tenn., 1977, JD, 1980. Bar: Tenn. 1981, U.S. Dist. Ct. (mid. dist.) Tenn. 1981, U.S. Supreme Ct. 1986, U.S. Ct. Appeals (6th cir.) 1993, U.S. Dist. Ct. (we. dist.) Tenn. 1996. Assoc. Mayo & Norris, Nashville, 1981-82; sole practice Springfield, Tenn., 1982-84; ptnr. Walton, Jones & Wilks, 1984, Jones & Wilks, 1984-89. Chmn. Dem. Orgn. Robertson County Tenn., 1986-93. Fellow Tenn. Bar Found.; mem. ABA, ATLA, Tenn. Bar Assn. (assoc. gen. counsel 1991-94, gen. counsel 1994—, bd. profl. responsibility 1993—, bd. govs. 1991—, young lawyers divsn. lifetime fellow), Tenn. Assn. Criminal Def. Lawyers, Tenn. Trial Lawyers Assn., Robertson County Bar Assn. (pres. 1993-96), Nat. Assn. Criminal Def. Laywers, Tenn. Young Lawyers Conf. (bd. dirs. 1987, editor quar. newsletter 1987-88, Mid. Tenn. v.p. 1988-89, v.p. 1989-90, pres.-elect 1990-91, pres. 1991-92). Methodist. Office: 509 W Court Sq Springfield TN 37172-2413

WILKS, WILLIAM LEE, educator, dean; b. Ft. Wayne, Ind., Nov. 12, 1931; s. Lee and Mildred (Roberts) W.; children: Sara P., Margaret E., Amy P., David E., Ariel J. BA, Yale U., 1952; JD, U. Mich., 1955; LLM, George Washington U., 1973; LLD, Dickinson Sch. Law, 1988. Bar: Ind. 1955, Mich. 1955. With Hunt, Suedhoff & Wilks, Ft. Wayne, 1957-70; asst. prof. Dickinson Sch. Law, Carlisle, Pa., 1970-73, assoc. prof., 1973-74, prof., asst. dean, 1974-77, prof., dean, 1977-89; pres., dean South Tex. Coll. Law., Houston, 1989-95; cons. Juvenile Ct. Judges Commn., 1971-75; reporter Commonwealth Ct. of Pa., 1973-89; adv. Motor Vehicle Code Revision, 1973-74; lectr. Pa. Law Enforcement Acad., 1971-88, Pa. Bar Inst., 1970-88. Contbr. articles to legal jours. Bd. dirs. Cumberland-Perry Assn. Retarded Citizens, 1973-76, Legal Svcs., Inc., 1973-77; mem. bd. advisors Cumberland County Children's Svcs., 1975-78; pres. United Way Carlisle, 1986. With U.S. Army, 1955-57. Fellow Am. Bar Found.; mem. ABA, ATLA, Def. Rsch. Inst., Ind. Bar Assn., Pa. Bar Assn., Houston Bar Assn. Home: 10734 Old Coach Ln Houston TX 77024-3124 Office: S Tex Coll Law 1303 San Jacinto St Houston TX 77002-7013*

WILLANS, RICHARD JAMES, religious organization executive, human resources management consultant; b. Detroit, July 24, 1943; s. James Cyril and Georgie Agnes (Ray) W.; m. Jean Stone, Mar. 28, 1966; 1 child, Suzanne Jeanne. Student, Dartmouth Coll., 1960-63; BS in Orgnl. Behavior, U. San Francisco, 1984; DD (hon.), Am. Coll. Seminarians, Santa Cruz, Calif., 1996. Assoc. editor Trinity Mag., Van Nuys, Calif., 1963-66; co-founder, pres., chmn. Soc. of Stephen, Altadena, Calif., 1967—; missionary pastor Soc. of Stephen, Hong Kong, 1968-81; tchr. Hong Kong Christian Coll., Caineway English Coll., Hong Kong, 1968-71; ops. mgr. RCM Svcs., Hong Kong, 1972-74; dir. exec. selection Peat, Marwick, Mitchell & Co., Hong Kong, 1974-81; pers. dir. Gen. Bank, L.A., 1982-83; dir. human resources Calif. Commerce Bank, L.A., 1984-88; mgr. human resources info. ctr. Union Bank of Calif., Monterey Pk., 1988-96; lectr. in field. Co-editor: (collection of personal stories) Charisma in Hong Kong, 1970, (song book) Spiritual Songs, 1970, (book series) The People Who Walked in Darkness, Vol. I, 1977, Vol. II, 1992, (book) The Acts of the Green Apples, 1995. Monument in his honor for drug addict rehab. work Kowloon Walled City Pk., Hong Kong, 1996. Republican. Office: Soc of Stephen PO Box 6225 Altadena CA 91003-6225

WILLARD, ANN ELAM, retired special education educator; b. Luling, Tex., Mar. 23, 1932; d. George Henry and Leah (Wright) Elam; widowed; children: Sharon Darlene Denison, Rita Ann Bush, Sindy Rene Burroughs. BS, Sul Ross U., 1952; MS, U. Ala., 1971, EdS, 1975. Tchr., third grade Fort Stockton (Tex.) Pub. Schs., 1953-54; tchr., elem. music San Angelo (Tex.) Pub. Schs., 1954-55; tchr., spl. EMR class Caddo Pub. Schs., Shreveport, La., 1966-67; tchr., fourth grade Albamarl County Schs., Charlottesville, Va., 1967-69; tchr. spl. EMR class Tuscaloosa County Schs., Brookwood, Ala., 1969-70, Cresmont Elem. Sch., Northport, Ala., 1970-82; tchr. TMR/OHI Class Tuscaloosa County Schs., Northport, Ala., 1982-89; tchr. EMR class Matthews Elem. Sch., Northport, Ala., 1989-1996; ret., 1996; tchr. adult edn. Tuscaloosa County Schs., 1974-80. Active Internat. Parents Without Ptnrs., 1980. Named Elem. Tchr. of Yr., Tuscaloosa County Schs., 1978-79, Single Parent of Yr., Parents Without Ptnrs., Tuscaloosa, 1978. Mem. AAUW (newsletter editor 1978-80), Coun. Exceptional Children (award 1981, sec. 1981, past pres. mentally retarded), Tuscaloosa County Tchrs. Assn., Toastmasters (Toastmaster of Yr. 1986, gov. of dist. #48 1995), Delta Kappa Gamma (sec. 1990-91, pres. 1992-94), Kappa Delta Pi. Baptist. Home: 1737 Ridgemont Dr Tuscaloosa AL 35404-4892

WILLARD, RALPH LAWRENCE, surgery educator, physician, former college president; b. Manchester, Iowa, Apr. 6, 1922; s. Hosea B. and Ruth A. (Hazelrigg) W.; m. Margaret Dyer Dennis, Sept. 26, 1969; children: Laurie, Jane, Ann, H. Thomas. Student, Cornell Coll., 1940-42, Coe Coll., 1945; D.O., Kirksville Coll. Osteo. Medicine, 1949; EdD (hon.), U. North Tex., 1985; ScD (hon.), W.Va. Sch. Osteo. Medicine, 1993. Intern Kirksville Osteo. Hosp., 1949-50, resident in surgery, 1954-57; chmn. dept. surgery Davenport Osteo. Hosp., 1957-68; dean, prof. surgery Kirksville Coll. Osteo. Medicine, 1969-73; asso. dean acad. affairs, prof. surgery Mich. State U. Coll. Osteo. Medicine, 1974-75; dean Tex. Coll. Osteopathic Medicine, 1975-76, pres., 1981-85, prof. surgery, 1985-87; v.p. med. affairs North Tex. State U., Denton, 1976-81; assoc. dean W.Va. Sch. Osteo. Medicine, Lewisburg, 1988-91; mem. Nat. Adv. Council Edn. for Health Professions, 1971-73, Iowa Gov.'s Council Hosps. and Health Related Facilities, 1965-68; chmn. council deans Am. Assn. Colls. Osteo. Medicine, 1970-73, pres., 1979-80. Served with USAAF, 1942-45; Served with USAF, 1952-53; col. USAFR, ret. Decorated D.F.C., Air medal with 4 oak leaf clusters, Meritorious Svc. medal, Legion of Merit; recipient Robert A. Kistner Educator award Am. Assn. Colls. Osteo. Medicine, 1989. Fellow Am. Coll. Physician Execs., Am. Coll. Osteo. Surgeons; mem. Am. Osteo. Assn. (Disting. Svc. cert. 1992), Tex. Osteo. Assn., W.Va. Soc. Osteo. Medicine, Am. Acad. Osteopathy, Acad. Osteo. Dirs. Med. Edn., Aerospace Med. Assn., Flying Physicians Assn., Quiet Birdmen, Davis-Monthan Officers Club, Masons, Shriners, Lewisburg Rotary (Paul Harris fellow), Internat. Comanche Soc., Order of Daedalians. Democrat. Episcopalian. Home: PO Box 749 Lewisburg WV 24901-0749 Office: WVa Sch Osteo Medicine 400 N Lee St Lewisburg WV 24901-1128

WILLCOTT, EARLINE FAY, social worker; b. San Juan, Tex., Aug. 26, 1936; d. William Earl and Autie (Phillips) Hinkle; m. Mark Robert Willcott III, June 4, 1955; children: Julie Willcott Bell, June Elinor, Mark Robert III, Ashley. BA in Eng., U. Houston, 1972, MSW, 1982. Lic. master social work, Tex.; advanced clin. pracititioner; accredited cert. social worker. Regulatory affairs officer NMR Imaging, Inc., Houston, 1983-89; coord. of social work Alive Hospice, Inc., Nashville, 1990-94; coord. of social svcs. Hospice Galveston County, Tex. City, Tex., 1995—; sec. Mid. Cumberland Coun. of Health Care Social Workers, 1990-94; mem. selection com. Nat. Hospice Orgn., Arlington, 1993; facilitator White House Conf. on Aging, Houston, 1995. Mem. editl. adv. bd. The Hospice Jour. Adv. bd. Tenn CARE: Population at Risk, Nashville, Tenn., 1993-94. Named Notable Women of Tex. State of Tex., 1984. Mem. NASW. Presbyterian. Office: Hospice of Galveston County 1708 Auburn Texas City TX 77591

WILLE, LOIS JEAN, retired newspaper editor; b. Chgo., Sept. 19, 1931; d. Walter and Adele S. (Taege) Kroeber; m. Wayne M. Wille, June 6, 1954. B.S., Northwestern U., 1953, M.S., 1954; Litt.D. (hon.), Columbia Coll., Chgo., 1980, Northwestern U., 1990, Rosary Coll., 1990. Reporter Chgo. Daily News, 1958-74, nat. corr., 1975-76, assoc. editor charge editorial page, 1977; assoc. editor charge editorial and opinion pages Chgo. Sun-Times, 1978-83; assoc. editor editorial page Chgo. Tribune, 1984-87, editor editorial page, 1987-91, ret., 1991. Author: Forever Open, Clear and Free: the Historic Struggle for Chicago's Lakefront, 1972. Recipient Pulitzer prize for public svc., 1963, Pulitzer prize for editorial writing, 1989, William Allen White Found. award for excellence in editorial writing, 1978, numerous awards Chgo. Newspaper Guild, numerous awards Chgo. Headline Club, numerous awards Nat. Assn. Edn. Writers, numerous awards Ill. AP, numerous awards Ill. UPI. Home: 120 Charmont Dr Radford VA 24141-4205

WILLEMS, CONSTANCE CHARLES, lawyer; b. Zuilen, Utrecht, Netherlands, Oct. 31, 1942; came to U.S., 1967, naturalized, 1977; d. Anton Henri and Maria (Van der Meys) Charles; m. Cornelis Franciscus Willems, May 25, 1965; 1 son, Maurice. B.A. in Sociology magna cum laude, U. New Orleans, 1974; J.D. with honors, Tulane U., 1977. Bar: La. 1977, U.S. Dist. Ct. (ea. dist.) La. 1977, U.S. Ct. Appeals (5th cir.) 1977, U.S. Supreme Ct. 1983. Assoc. McGlinchey, Stafford, Mintz, Cellini, and Lang, New Orleans, 1977-81, ptnr., 1982—; instr. law office mgmt. Loyola U. Sch. Law, 1986-90; instr. European law Tulane U. Sch. Law, New Orleans, 1994, 96. Mem. Task Force on Municipalization; hon. consul for The Netherlands, 1989—; bd. dirs. United Way Agy. REls. Com., 1987-91, Coun. Internat. Visitors, 1992-94, Com. of 21, 1994—, New Orleans Opera Assn., 1995—; sec./treas. Consular Corps; bd. visitors Coll. Liberal Arts U. New Orleans, 1995—. Recipient Disting. Alumni award U. New Orleans, 1989. Mem. ABA, La. Assn. Women Attys. (pres. 1983-85, 86-87), La. State Bar Assn. (mem. ho. of dels. 1984-85, chair internat. law sect. 1994—). Office: McGlinchey Stafford Lang 643 Magazine St New Orleans LA 70130-3405

WILLER, EDWARD HERMAN, real estate broker; b. Concord, N.C., June 12, 1941; s. Emil Francis and Mary (McKinley) W.; m. Cornelia Campbell, Nov. 30, 1963; children: Laura Campbell, Edward Groves. AB, Davidson Coll., 1963. V.p., sales mgr. Bacon & Co., Realtors, Raleigh, N.C., 1971-84; pres. residential div. York Properties, Inc., Raleigh, 1984—; treas. N.C. Real Estate Ednl. Found., Greensboro, 1984, pres., 1988; bd. dirs. Rex Hosp. Found., Raleigh, 1988-89, Relo, The Internat. Referral Network, Inc., Chgo., dir., 1988—, treas., 1992. Author: Real Estate Exam Ready Book, 1984; contbr. articles to profl. jours. Bd. dirs. Ea. N.C. Multiple Sclerosis Soc., Raleigh, 1982-85; campaign chair United Way of Wake County, 1996, bd. dirs., 1995—, mem. exec. com., 1996—. 1st lt. U.S. Army, 1963-66, Vietnam. Named Realtor of the Year, 1984. Mem. Nat. Assn. Realtors (cert.), N.C. Assn. Realtors (bd. dirs. 1978-82), N.C. Real Estate Ednl. Found. (pres.), Raleigh Bd. Realtors (pres. 1979), Greater Raleigh C. of C. (bd. dirs. 1991-94), Quite Birdmen Club. Democrat. Presbyterian. Home: 1512 Saint Mary's St Raleigh NC 27608-2217 Office: York Properties Inc 801 Oberlin Rd Raleigh NC 27605-1170

WILLETT, A. L. THOMPSON, public relations executive, consultant; b. Bardstown, Ky., Jan. 27, 1909; s. Aloysius Lambert and Mary Catherine (Thompson) W.; BA, Xavier U., Cin., 1931; m. Mary Virginia Sheehan, Jan. 14, 1942; children: Mary Tabitha (Mrs. Frank J. Fisher, Jr.), James (dec.), Martha Harriet (Mrs. Even Kulsveen), John David, Susan Virginia (Mrs. Thomas C. Dawson), Richard Francis, Alice Jane. Editor Loveland (Ohio) Herald, 1931-32; comptroller Ky. Hwy. Dept., 1932-33; asst. supt. Bernheim Distilling Co., Louisville, 1933-36; pres. Willett Distilling Co., Bardstown, Ky., 1936-82, also dir.; pres. Thompson Willett, pub. rels., Bardstown, 1982—; officer Willett Distributing, Inc., Wines Importer, 1982—; internat. rep. Pub. Translation of Lemarié Life of Bishop Flaget. Chmn. Bardstown-Nelson County Hist. Commn., 1938-53; Ky. advisor Nat. Trust for Historic Preservation, Washington, 1943-40. Bd. dirs. Xavier U., 1960-63; bd. dirs.

Bellarmine Coll., 1964—; dir. Ida Lee Willis Meml. Found., Frankfort, Ky., 1982—. Recipient Disting. Cath. Alumnus award Archdiocese of Louisville, 1994. Mem. Ky. Distillers Assn. (pres. 1960), Newcomen Soc. N.Am., Distilled Spirits Coun. U.S. (dir. 1940-82). Club: Old Kentucky Home Country (Bardstown), Xavier U. 1931 Soc. Lodge: K.C. Contbr. articles to various publs. Home: Beechwold E Stephen Foster Bardstown KY 40004 Office: Box PO Box 91 Bardstown KY 40004-0091

WILLETT, ALBERT JAMES, JR., family historian; b. Hampton, Va., June 13, 1944; s. Albert James and Mamie Rose (Gilbert) W.; m. Diane Lynn Myers, May 8, 1963; children: Albert James III, Karen Diane. AA, Christopher Newport Coll., 1972, BSBA, 1976. Cert. comml. pilot, FAA. Enlisted warrant officer candidate U.S. Army, 1968; helicopter pilot, 1969-73; editor, pub. Willett House Quarterly, Middlesex County, Va., 1985-89; chief warrant officer, master aviator Ft. Bragg, N.C., 1991-96; cons., rschr. Logistics Civil Augmentation Program, Alexandria, Va., 1996—. Author: Willett Families of North America, 1985, Poquoson Watermen, 1989; co-author: Martin Family of Poquoson, Va., 1994. With USAR, 1984-90; with Va. N.G., 1974-76; ret., 1996. Mem. Vietman Helicopter Pilots Assn., Poquoson Historical Soc., Assn. One-Name Studies, Alpha Kappa Psi. Baptist. Home: PO Box 7 Topping VA 23169-0007

WILLETT, HOLLY GENEVA, librarian, educator; b. Brunswick, Maine, Apr. 15, 1948; d. Hollis Eugene and Gene Edith (Stratton) W. BA magna cum laude, San Francisco State Coll., 1971; MLS, U. Calif., Berkeley, 1972; MA, Simmons Coll., Boston, 1980; PhD, U. N.C., 1986; postgrad., U. North Tex., Denton, 1993-94. Cert. tchr. Spanish, Tex., learning resources endosement, Tex. Libr. I, II Alameda County Free Libr., Fremont, Calif., 1972-78; coord. children's svcs. New Bedford (Mass.) Free Pub. Libr., 1980-81; asst. prof. U. Wis., Madison, 1985-92; asst. vis. prof. Tex. Woman's U., Denton, 1992-93, adj. asst. prof., 1993, 96; libr. media specialist Dallas Pub. Schs., 1993—; planner, spkr. Children's Svcs. Inst., U. Wis.-Madison, 1989, 91. Editl. cons. Highsmith Press, Ft. Atkinson, Wis., 1992-93; author: Public Library Youth Services, 1995; author environ. rating scale for children's svcs., 1989— (Hannigan award 1991); contbr. articles to profl. jours. Treas. Denton (Tex.) Intercultural Assn., 1995—; bd. mem. Denton Unitarian Universalist Fellowship, 1994-96. Fellow Bush Inst. for Child & Family Policy, Chapel Hill, 1983-85, Margaret Kelp fellow U. N.C., Chapel Hill, 1981-83. Mem. ALA, Am. Folklore Soc., Assn. Libr. and Info. Sci. Edn. (Hannigan award 1991), Calif. Libr. Assn., Children's Lit. Assn., Nat. Storytelling Assn., six other nat. orgns. Democrat. Office: Arcadia Park Sch 911 N Morocco Ave Dallas TX 75211

WILLIAMS, ALBERT THEOPHILUS WADI, consulting engineer, educational guidance executive; b. Leopoldville, Zaire, Africa, Apr. 14, 1922; came to U.S., 1968; s. Vidal Athanasius and Joanna Dorcas (Jarret) W.; m. Arimah Adeline King, Nov. 12, 1949 (div. Feb. 1981); children: Wadiike, Warimah, Wamahdri, Arimah; m. Barbara Booker, Mar. 7, 1993. BS in Engring., Leeds (U.K.) U., 1946; diploma, Huddersfield (U.K.) Coll., 1948. Registered profl. engr., N.J., Pa., Md., Va., Ga., Tenn., Wis., Mo.; registered structural engr., Ill. Sr. engr. David Geiger & Horst Berger, N.Y.C., 1968-69; v.p. structures Gerard Engring., Jersey City, 1969-74; chief engring. David Volkert & Assocs., Bethesda, Md., 1974-76; assoc. and chief engr. Williams & Sheladia, Inc., Mt. Rainier, Md., 1976-77; v.p. Washington office Fleming Corp., 1977-80; v.p. engring. Urban Svcs. Inc., Richmond, Va., 1980-83; dir. phys. plant Commonwealth of Va. Longwood Coll., Farmville, 1983-88; owner Wadi Williams Enterprises, Farmville, 1988—; cons. United Design Engrs., Washington, 1988; structural engring. cons. Capitol Engrs. P.C., Washington. Spkr. world energy confs., 1985, spkr. TVA energy conf., 1988. Asst. coach jr. H.S. soccer County of Henrico, Va., 1982-83; active Heart of Va. Festival, Farmville, 1985; treas. Race St. Bapt. Ch., 1990—; apptd. to bd. dirs. Farmville Habitat for Humanity, 1994—. Mem. NSPE (rep. 1979-80), D.C. Soc. Profl. Engrs. (pres. 1979-80). Baptist. Home: PO Box 283 Farmville VA 23901-0283

WILLIAMS, ALFRED BLYTHE, business communication educator; b. Oakland City, Ind., Sept. 17, 1940; s. Ross Merl and Jesse Adell (Helsley) W. B.S. cum laude, Oakland City Coll., 1963; M.S., Ind. U., 1964; Ph.D., Ga. State U., 1974. Cert. tchr. bus. edn. and English, Ind. Tchr. Arlington High Sch., Indpls., 1964-65, Oakland City Coll., Ind., 1965-69; editor Southwestern Pub. Co., Cin., 1969-72, cons., 1981-93; adj. prof. Ga. State U., Atlanta, 1972-74; prof. bus. communications U. Southwestern La., Lafayette, 1975—, chmn. dept., 1986-96; cons. John Wiley Pub. Co., N.Y., 1988-89, Irwin Pub., 1989. Author study guides. Editor Information Systems Bus. Communication Jour., 1983, 93. Patron Lafayette Community Concerts, 1984—; contbr. La. and Nat. Rep. parties, Baton Rouge, Washington, 1983—. Mem. AAUP, Assn. Bus. Communicators (bd. dirs. 1986-90, Francis W. Weeks Merit award 1984), La. Assn. Higher Edn., Sierra Club, Kiwanis, Phi Delta Kappa, Phi Kappa Phi, Delta Pi Epsilon. Methodist.

WILLIAMS, AMANDA KYLE, writer; b. Norfolk, Va., Aug. 17, 1957; d. Fred Kyle and Violet Elizabeth (Mizzle) W. V.p. mfg. Sovereign Carpet Mills, Dalton, Ga., 1976-86; writer, 1990—. Author: Club Twelve, 1990, The Providence File, 1991 (nominated Lambda Lit. award 1992), A Singular Spy, 1992, The Spy in Question, 1993; contbr. short stories to various anthologies; freelance writer articles, op-ed material and advt. copy. Office: 3082 Brook Dr Decatur GA 30033-3910

WILLIAMS, ANDREW D., secondary school educator. BS in History, St. John's U., 1960, MS, 1972; EdS, Stetson U., 1984. Cert. tchr. secondary social studies and English, N.Y., N.J.; cert. prin., supr., N.J.; cert. tchr. secondary social studies and English, adminstr., supr., cert. ofcl. observer performance learning measurement system, Fla. Social studies tchr. N.Y.C. Bd. Edn., Bklyn., 1960-64, North Babylon Sr. High Sch., Babylon, N.Y., 1964-66, Glen Cove (N.Y.) High Sch., 1970-71; social studies and English tchr. Island Trees Pub. Schs., Levittown, N.Y., 1971-73; lang. arts and History tchr. Glen Ridge (N.J.) Pub. Schs., 1973-76; humanities and English tchr. Volusia County Pub. Schs., Fla., 1977-80; history and sociology tchr. Berkely Inst., Bklyn., 1980-81; lang. arts and Am. history tchr. Seminole County Pub. Schs., Fla., 1981—, social studies dept. chmn., 1993—; part-time instr. Daytona Beach (Fla.) C.C., 1978—. Recipient Outstanding Social Studies Tchr. of Yr. award Fla. Coun. Social Studies, 1985, 94, Outstanding Tchr. Am. History 1985, 94, Outstanding H.S. Social Studies Tchr. award, 1994; named Outstanding Am. History Tchr. of Yr., DAR, 1985. Mem. Phi Delta Kappa. Home: 151A Cascade St Deltona FL 32725-8007 Office: Seminole High Sch 2701 Ridgewood Ave Sanford FL 32773-4916

WILLIAMS, ANNE, English studies educator; b. Stephenville, Tex., Mar. 23, 1947; d. Charles Bunyan and Gary (Palmer) Williams; m. John D. Boyd, May 30, 1978. BA, Baylor U., 1969; MA, Cornell U., 1971, PhD, 1973. Asst. prof. Cornell Coll., Mt. Vernon, Iowa, 1973-76; asst. prof. U. Ga., Athens, 1976-83, assoc. prof., 1983-91; prof. U. Ga., Athens, Mass., 1994—; assoc. prof. Holy Cross Coll., Worcester, Mass., 1991-92. Author: Prophetic Strain: The Greater Lyric in the 18th Century, 1984, Art of Darkness: A Poetics of Gothic, 1995. Fellow NEH, 1977-78, Am. Coun. Learned Socs., 1985, Rockefeller Found., 1990. Mem. MLA, N.Am. Soc. for Study of Romanticism, Am. Soc. for Eighteenth-Century Studies. Office: U Ga Dept English Athens GA 30602

WILLIAMS, BARBARA ELAINE, design production company executive; b. Bartlesville, Okla., Aug. 12, 1952; d. B. Joe and Roy Marie (Smith) W.; m. Charles M. Ellertson, Apr. 20, 1985. B.A. cum laude, Duke U., 1974. Asst. to bus. mgr. Duke U. Press, Durham, N.C., 1974-75, prodn. asst., 1975-78, assoc. prodn. mgr., 1979-82, jours. mgr., 1982-84; prodn., design mgr. Menasha Ridge Press, 1984-88; owner B. Williams & Assocs. Design and Prodn. Studio, 1988—; instr. Carolina Pub. Inst, Chapel Hill, N.C., 1994-96; panelist Career Counseling Conf., Durham, 1983, 84, Conf. Editors Learned Jours., Modern Lang. Assn., 1985. Photographer Latent Image 3, 1976, Latent Image 4, 1978, Latent Image 5, 1980, N.C. Mus. Art Ann. Show, 1978, 79. Chair comm. com. St. Paul's Luth. Ch., 1992-94. Mem. Assn. Am. Univ. Presses (jours. com. 1983-85, Design award 1988), Women in Scholarly Pub. Democrat. Home: 1412 Pennsylvania Ave Durham NC 27705-3544

WILLIAMS, BETTIE WHITE, special education educator; b. Miami Beach, Fla., Jan. 19, 1957; d. Mosey and Bettie Jean (Littleton) W. BS, Troy State U., 1979, MS in Spl. Edn., 1989; cert. psychometry, U. South Ala., 1991. Cert. elem. tchr., elem., secondary spl. edn. tchr., sch. psychometrist, Ala. Elem. tchr. Cen. Bapt. Sch., Moblie, Ala., 1979-80; elem. tchr. educable mentally retarded Baldwin County Bd. Edn., Bay Minette, Ala., 1980-89, tchr. emotionally disturbed, learning disabled, 1989—; cheerleader advisor Loxley (Ala.) Jr. High Sch., 1982-87; chair screening com. psychiat. evaluation Loxley Elem. Sch., 1985-89; co-presenter South Ala. Regional Insvc. Ctr. program, 1992. Mem. Nat. Assn. Sch. Psychometrists, Coun. for Children with Learning Disabilities, Am. Bus. Women's Assn., Coun. Exceptional Children (sec.-treas. 1988-89, co-presenter conf. 1992), Ala. Assn. Sch. Psychometrists, Troy State U. Alumni Assn., Kappa Delta Alumni Assn., Baldwin County Assn. Profl. Educators, Phi Delta Kappa. Republican. Episcopalian. Office: Daphne Mid Sch Baldwin County Bd Edn 1 Jubilee Cir Daphne AL 36526-6109

WILLIAMS, BETTY OUTHIER, lawyer; b. Woodward, Okla., Sept. 11, 1947; d. Robert E. and Ethel M. (Castiller) Outhier; children: Amanda J., Emily Rebecca. BA, Oklahoma City U., 1969; JD, Vanderbilt U., 1972. Bar: Okla. 1972, U.S. Dist. Ct. (no. dist.) Okla. 1972, U.S. Dist. Ct. (ea. dist.) Okla. 1973, (U.S. Ct. Appeals (10th cir.) 1973, U.S. Supreme Ct. 1980, U.S. Dist. Ct. (we. dist.) Okla. 1988. Atty. Reginal Heber Smith Community Lawyer Fellowship, Tulsa, 1972-73; asst. U.S. atty. Robinson, Gage & Williams, Muskogee, Okla., 1973-81; U.S. atty. U.S. Dept. Justice, Muskogee, Okla., 1981-82; ptnr. Robinson, Locke, Gage, Fite & Williams, Muskogee, 1982-96, Robinson, Gage, Fite & Williams, Muskogee, 1996—; chairperson local rules com. U.S. Bankruptcy Ct. Ea. Dist., Okla., 1994, U.S. Dist. Ct. Ea. Dist. Okla., 1995. Mem. bd. editors Okla. Law Enforcement Ops. Bull., 1993-94. Pres. Bus. and Profl. Women, Muskogee, 1975-77, 83; pres., bd. dirs. YWCA, Muskogee, 1975-82; bd. dirs. Green County Mental Health, Muskogee, 1986-88; trustee Frontier Heritage Found., 1990—; bd. dirs. WISH, 1990—; chmn. bd. commrs. Muskogee Housing Authority. Named one of Outstanding Young Career Women Bus. and Profl. Womens, 1974. Fellow Okla. Bar Found. (trustee 1989—, v.p. 1994, pres. elect. 1995, pres. 1996); mem. ABA, Okla. Bar Assn., Muskogee County Bar Assn. (pres. 1984-85), Soroptimists (pres. 1986-88), Gamma Phi Beta. Republican. Methodist. Home: 4326 Oklahoma St Muskogee OK 74401-2351 Office: Robinson Gage Fite PO Box 87 Muskogee OK 74402-0087

WILLIAMS, CAROLYN ANTONIDES, university dean; b. Louisville, Oct. 27, 1939; d. John Dwight and Dorothy Ida Marie (Hoffman) Antonides; m. Frank Canon Williams, Dec. 26, 1961. BS with honors in Nursing, Tex. Woman's U., 1961; MS in Pub. Health Nursing Edn., U. N.C., 1965, PhD in Epidemiology, 1969. Asst. prof. nursing Emory U., Atlanta, 1968, assoc. prof., 1969, prof., dir. grad. programs and rsch., 1969-71; assoc. prof. nursing, asst. prof. epidemiology U. N.C., Chapel Hill, 1971-81, assoc. prof. nursing, rsch. assoc. Health Svcs. Rsch. Ctr., from 1971, assoc. prof. epidemiology, 1981-84; dean Coll. Nursing, U. Ky., Lexington, 1984—; mem. Pres.'s Commn. Study of Ethical Problems in Medicine and Biomed. and Behavioral Rsch., 1980-82; chair rsch. adv. com. Am. Nurses Found., 1979-81; mem. planning com. study of nursing and nursing edn. Inst. Medicine of NAS, 1980; cons. WHO in S.Am. Mem. editorial bd. Family and Community Health, 1977-90, Advances in Nursing Sci., 1979-88, Internat. Jour. Nursing Studies, 1981—; also articles, chpts. to books. USPHS fellow U. N.C., 1969. Fellow APHA (publs. bd., Young Practitioner award 1973), Am. Acad. Nursing (pres. 1983-85); mem. ANA (chair commn. nursing rsch. 1980-82), Coun. Nurse Researchers, Soc. Epidemiol. Rsch., Delta Omega, Sigma Theta Tau (bd. dirs.). Democrat. Baptist. Office: U Ky Coll Nursing 500 S Limestone St Lexington KY 40508-3217*

WILLIAMS, CAROLYN RUTH ARMSTRONG, university official; b. Birmingham, Ala., Feb. 17, 1944; d. Lonnie and Lois Adel America (Merriweather) Armstrong; m. James Alvin Williams Jr., Mar. 16, 1968. BS, Tenn. State U., 1966; cert., Hawaii U., 1970; MA, Northwestern U., 1972; MA, PhD, Cornell U., 1978; postgrad., Exeter U., Eng., 1985, MIT, 1990, 93, Chinese U. of Hong Kong, 1992. Postdoctoral fellow Harvard U., 1982-83; spl. project asst. U.S. Senator Paul Tsongas, Boston, 1983; asst. vice chancellor N.C. Cen. U., Durham, 1983-87; asst. dean for minorities and women engring. programs Vanderbilt U. Sch. Engring., Nashville, 1987—; assoc. dir. Cornell U. Career Ctr., Ithaca, N.Y., 1976-82, edn.cons. Youth Data, Ithaca, 1981—, LeMoyne Coll. Higher Edn. Preparation Program, 1977-83; cons. U.S. Dept. Edn. Rev. Bd.; judge Goodrich Collegiate Inventor Program; bd. dirs. Sta. WBGH TV, Boston; participant Nat. Scis. Resources Ctr. Conf. on pre-coll. edn. for scientists and engrs. Calif. Inst. Tech., 1992. Contbr. articles to profl. jours. Bd. dirs. So. Policies Ednl. Bd., 1983-87, Clean Commn. System of Durham Bd., 1982-87. Recipient Woman of Achievement and Recognition award YWCA, 1984-87, Affirmative Action award Vanderbilt U., 1989, 90. Mem. Nat. Assn. Women Deans and Adminstrv. Counselors (exec. bd. 1981—), Cornell Women Studies Program (exec. bd. 1981—), Nat. Soc. Black Engrs. (adv. bd., pres. region III 1990—, Black Engr. Leadership award 1988, Charles E. Tunstall award 1990, 91), Assn. Women in Sci. (exec. bd. 1990—, nat. sec. 1992—), Soc. Women Engrs. (tech. coord. 1988—, coord. tech. paper competition, chair adv. bd. 1990—), Nat. Assn. Minority Engring. Program Adminstrs. (sec., pres.-elect, chair region B 1990—, exec. bd., bd. dirs., nat. editor newsletter 1990—), Rotary, Phi Delta Kappa, Delta Sigma Theta, Omicron Delta (Vanderbilt chpt.), Phi Lambda Theta. Home: 305 Summit Ridge Cir Nashville TN 37215-3806 also: 36 Morningside Dr Cortland NY 13045-1423 Office: Vanderbilt U Sch Engring PO Box 6006 Nashville TN 37235

WILLIAMS, CATHLENE ANN, association executive, researcher; b. Waterloo, Iowa, Apr. 17, 1945; d. Harold Stanley and Martha Elizabeth (Loonan) Nation; m. Jan Adrian DeYoung, June 10, 1967 (div. Feb. 20, 1976); 1 child: Laura Elizabeth; m. Clyde Roydon Williams, Jan. 3, 1977. BS, Iowa State U., 1967; MA, U. N. Iowa, 1971; PhD, George Washington U., 1995. Tchr. Oak Park (Ill.) Pub. Schs., 1967-69, Cedar Falls (Iowa) Pub. Schs., 1969-75; adminstrv. asst. Sys. Rsch. Inc./Ednl. Methods, Washington, 1975-77; adminstrv. asst. to exec. dir. Nat. Assn. State Bds. Edn., Alexandria, Va., 1985-86, project specialist, 1978-80, project dir., 1980-82, dir., 1985-86; communications mgr. Nat. Soc. Fund Raising Execs., Alexandria, Va., 1987-89, dir. external affairs, 1989-91, dir. libr. and rsch. svcs., 1991-94, dir. edn. and rsch. programs, 1994—. Author: (with others) Manual on State Policies Related to Adolescent Parenthood, 1980, A Guide to Employment and Training Programs for Adolescent Parents, 1981; editor: The Journal, 1987-92, Nat. Soc. Fund Raising Execs. News, 1987-91, The State Bd. Connection, 1981-86. Vestry Ch. of the Resurrection Episcopal Ch. (register 1988, jr. warden 1989, 93, assoc. sr. warden 1990, lay ordination com. 1990, cmty. concerns com. 1993—, stewardship com.). Mem. Am. Soc. Assn. Execs., PRSA, Internat. Soc. for 3d Sector Rsch., AAUW (newsletter editor 1986-87, treas. 1986-87, v.p. mem. 1984-85, pres. Alexandria br. 1988-89), Assn. Rsch. on Nonprofit Orgns. and Voluntary Action, Phi Gamma Delta, Phi Upsilon Omicron, Omicron Nu. Office: Nat Soc Fund Raising Execs 1101 King St Ste 700 Alexandria VA 22314-2944

WILLIAMS, CHARLOTTE EVELYN FORRESTER, civic worker; b. Kansas City, Mo., Aug. 7, 1905; d. John Dougal and Georgia (Lowerre) Forrester; student Kans. U., 1924-25; m. Walker Alonzo Williams, Sept. 25, 1926; children: Walker Forrester, John Haviland. Trustee, Detroit Grand Opera Assn., 1960-87, dir., 1955-60; chmn. Grinnell Opera Scholarship, 1958-66; founder, dir., chmn. adv. bd. Cranbrook Music Guild, Inc., 1952-59, life mem.; bd. dirs. Detroit Opera Theater, 1959-61, Severo Ballet, 1959-61; Detroit dist. chmn. Met. Opera Regional Auditions, 1958-66; Fla. Atlantic U. Found.; past pres. Friends of Caldwell Playhouse, Boca Raton. Mem. Debbie-Rand Meml. Svc. League (life), DAR, English-Speaking Union, Vol. League Fla. Atlantic U., PEO, Order Eastern Star. Home: 2679 S Ocean Blvd Apt 5C Boca Raton FL 33432-8353

WILLIAMS, CHERYL, service company executive; b. Neosho, Mo., July 7, 1957; d. Allen and Travestine Williams. BS in Math., East Tex. State U., 1978, postgrad., 1978-79; postgrad., Rose State Coll., 1980-81, Sheppard Tech. Tng. Ctr., 1980-81; MS in Math., U. Tex., 1997. Computer scientist Tinker AFB, Oklahoma City, 1980-81, Defense Comm. Agy., Washington, 1986; tchr. Parent Child Inc., San Antonio, 1989; asst. sec. Antioch Bapt. Ch., San Antonio, 1989-92; substitute tchr. San Antonio Ind. Sch. Dist., 1990-93; instrnl. asst. Northside Ind. Sch. Dist., San Antonio, 1995-96, asst. tchr., 1994-95; rep. West Telemarketing, 1996—; asst. mgr. Fashion Place, San Antonio, 1994-95. Counselor YMCA, San Antonio, 1989-91; active Girl Scouts U.S., 1964-86; mem. choir, asst. sec. area ch., 1972, tutor, 1970—, tchr. Sunday Sch., 1973-86, asst. sec. Sunday Sch., 1973-86, 88—, asst. ch. sec., 1988-91; mem. Dorcas Circle, Lupus Found. Am., Biomed. Rsch. U. Tex., 1995—; mem. Epilepsy Found. Am., Tex. Head Injury Assn., Nat. Head Injury Assn., Smithsonian Instn. Mem. NEA, Tex. Edn. Assn., Mu Alpha Theta.

WILLIAMS, CLYNN WORTHINGTON, social studies educator; b. Hammond, Ind., May 23, 1933; d. Clinton L. and Olive V. (Peck) Worthington; m. Harry J. Altemus, Nov. 1957 (div. 1974); 1 child, Clinton L. Altemus. AA, Stephens Coll., Columbia, Mo., 1953; BS in Math., Rollins Coll., Winter Park, Fla., 1974; MEd, 1979. Cert. Math., Social Studies, Bus. Edn., Adminstrn./Supv. Tchr. Math. Osceola H.S., Kissimmee, Fla., 1975-87; tchr. Computers Parkway Middle Sch., 1987-89; tchr. Social Studies, Math, Computers, Bus. Edn. Osceola H.S., 1989—; adjunct prof. Valencia Cmty. Coll., Orlando, Fla., 1980-90; instr. Computer Tutor Tng. Ctr., St. Cloud, Fla., 1992-94. Author, exhibitor: (3 projects) ASCD Nat. Symposium, 1994; co-presenter Fla. Ednl. Computer Conf., 1985; contbr. articles to profl. jours. Recipient Disney Teacherrific (3 projects) Walt Disney World, Orlando, Fla., 1990, 92, 93, Best Vocat. Practices award Fla. DOE, Tallahassee, Fla., 1993. Mem. FTP/NEA, Phi Delta Kappa. Home: PO Box 420937 Kissimmee FL 34742 Office: Osceola HS 420 S Thacker Ave Kissimmee FL 34741-5963

WILLIAMS, CURT ALAN, mechanical engineer; b. Dallas, Nov. 4, 1953; s. Arthur Berri and Betty Lou (Calvert) W.; m. Cynthia Ann Corliss, Sept. 25, 1976; children: Christopher Aaron, Craig Allen. BSME, U. Tex., 1976. Registered prof. engr., Tex. Engring. coop. Vought Aeros., Dallas, 1973-75; tech. svc. engr. nordel EPDM process E.I. duPont de Nemours and Co., Beaumont, Tex., 1976-79; tech. svc. engr. dacron yarn rsch. E.I. duPont de Nemours and Co., Old Hickory, Tenn., 1979-81; project engr. supr. photo systems div. E.I. duPont de Nemours and Co., Rochester, N.Y., 1981-84; product engring. supr. connector systems E.I. duPont de Nemours and Co., Camp Hill, Pa., 1984-85, tech. svcs. supr. connector systems, 1985-86; gold recovery engr. E.I. duPont de Nemours and Co., Emigsville, Pa., 1986; rsch. assoc. Electronics Tech. Ctr. E.I. duPont de Nemours and Co., Research Triangle Park, N.C., 1986-88, facilities and safety cons., 1988-91; rsch. assoc. duPont Beaumont Works E.I. duPont de Nemours and Co., Inc., Beamont, Tex., 1991-95, tech. assoc. duPont Beaumont Works, 1993-96; tech. assoc. duPont Dow Elastomers, L.C.C., Beamont, 1996—. Co-patentee method for eluting absorbed golf from carbon. Mem. ASME, Am. Soc. Safety Engrs. Home: 2090 Savannah Trce Beaumont TX 77706-2552

WILLIAMS, DAVID HOWARD, lawyer; b. Las Vegas, Nev., Sept. 21, 1945; s. Howard Cummins and Alice Emma (Taufenbach) W.; m. Kathleen Graham, Sept. 2, 1967; children: David Howard Jr., Jonathan Graham. BA in History cum laude, Denison U., 1967; MA in Polit. Sci., Columbia U., 1969; JD cum laude, Ohio State U., 1973. Bar: Ohio 1973, Ga. 1980. Assoc. Vorys, Sater, Seymour & Pease, Columbus, Ohio, 1973-79; from assoc. to ptnr. Powell, Goldstein, Frazer & Murphy, Atlanta; ptnr. Hunton & Williams, Atlanta; adj. prof. U. Ga. Sch. Law, 1994—; lectr. workshop ann. conv. Ohio League of Savs. Assns., others. Former mem. profl. adv. bd. Ohio Assn. for Children with Learning Disabilities; bd. dirs. Northside Youth Orgn., Atlanta, 1985—; active Peachtree Presbyn. Ch., Atlanta, 1982—. Served to 1st lt. Ohio NG, 1969-75. Mem. ABA (exec. compensation com. corp. sect., taxation and employee benefits sects.), Ga. Bar Assn. (taxation sect.), Atlanta Bar Assn., So. Pension Conf., Midwest Pension Conf. (cen. Ohio chpt. organizer, former vice chmn.). Republican. Office: Hunton & Williams NationsBank Plz 600 Peachtree St NE Atlanta GA 30308*

WILLIAMS, DAVID LOREN, employment interviewer; b. Peoria, Ill., Jan. 9, 1970; s. Donald Kay and Virginia Lynn (Kiser) W. AAS, Ill. Ctrl. Coll., East Peoria, 1990; BA, Eastern Ill. U., Charleston, 1992. Employment interviewer Employment Security Commn. N.C., Raleigh, 1994—. Named to Outstanding Young Men of Am., 1992. Mem. Am. Polit. Sci. Assn., Internat. Assn. Profls. in Employment Security (local office chair 1995—), Am. Birding Assn., NRA, Sigma Iota Lambda. Republican. Mem. Disciples of Christ Ch. Home: 2013 Valley Ct Clayton NC 27520

WILLIAMS, DOLORES LOUISE, retired telecommunications executive; b. Rockford, Ill., Apr. 20, 1937; d. Arthur F. and Erma Lee (Johnson) Warner; divorced; 1 child, Leona Marie Williams. BE, Ottawa (Kans.) U., 1959. Cert. tchr., Kans., Tenn. Tchr., acting prin. Navajo Indian Reservation, N.Mex. and Ariz., 1959-62; svc. rep. Ill. Bell., Rockford, 1962-64; sr. svc. rep. Mich. Bell, Jackson, 1964-67, South Cen. Bell, Memphis, 1967-70; unit supr. bus. office South Central Bell, Memphis, 1974-81; asst. sales mgr. AT&T and South Cen. Bell, Nashville and Memphis, 1981-90; asst. staff mgr. Bellsouth tng. staff State of Tenn., 1991; asst. dir. HWPC Child Care Tng. Program, Memphis, 1970-71; dir. Shelby County Headstart, Memphis, 1971-73. Recipient Outstanding Svc. award Warren Headstart Ctr., Memphis, 1973, Bell System Eagle award, 1981, Ops. Mgrs.' Coun. Excellence award, 1986, 87, 88, 89, 90, Disting. Leadership award Outstanding Svc. in Communications Industry, 1989, White House Communication Cert. of Appreciation, 1988, 89. Home: 500 Michele Dr Antioch TN 37013-4109

WILLIAMS, EDA DUNSTAN, civic worker; m. Ichabod Thomas Williams, June 25, 1930 (dec. Aug. 1987); children: Thomas, Samuel Dunstan, Resolvert Waldron. AB, Vassar Coll., 1929; postgrad., Columbia U., 1957-58. Past chmn., bd. dirs. Far Rockaway (N.Y.) Mother's Health Ctr., Planned Parenthood Greater N.Y., N.Y.C., Peninsula Child Guidance Ctr., Woodmere, N.Y.; past bd. dirs. Family Svcs. Five Towns, Cedarhurst, N.Y.; past mem. conservation com. Garden Club Am.; bd. dirs., officer Garden Club Lawrence (N.Y.), Clermont Hist. Site, Tivoli, N.Y.; former vol. Bok Tower Gardens, Lake Wales, Fla. Mem. Nat. Soc. Colonial Dames in N.Y. (past v.p., chmn. hist. activities), Pen and Brush Club (pub. poet). Democrat. Home: Mountain Lk Lake Wales FL 33859-0832

WILLIAMS, EDDIE KYENE, martial arts team executive; b. Wineheim, Germany, June 9, 1951; adopted s. Stanely C. and Edna E. (Bowen) Williams; m. Debbie VanDyke, June 5, 1971 (div. Aug. 1974); m. Beverly Denise Wall, June 27, 1975; children: Jason Aaron, Derek Lee. Student, U. Louisville, 1976-78, Bowling Green State Transp., 1991. Cert. Internat. Labor Bd., martial arts instr., cert. body guard. Instr. Cowan's Kawanza Karate, Louisville, 1966-71; head instr. Three Rivers Martial Arts, Louisville, 1971-74, Street Justice, Louisville, 1974-76, Wonderlust Internat., Louisville, 1982-84, Sho Chi Ku Bai Martial Arts Acad., Louisville, 1976-84, Budokan Martial Arts Fedn., Lexington, Ky., 1984-85, Shadowing Martial Arts Acad., Lexington, 1985-86; owner, oper. Warriorz USA World Karate Team, Lexington, 1985, Powen House Gym, Lexington, 1986—; coach at nats. U.S. Kaekwondo Union, Portland, Oreg., 1992. Contbr. articles to newspapers. Head coach Ky. AAU Jr. Karate Team, Elizabeth, N.J., 1983, cert. chmn. exec. bd., 1981-83, tournment dir., 1983; exec. mem. Ky. Soc. Marital Arts, Clarksville, Ind., 1975; mem. AAU Taekwodo Olympic Team, L.A.; instr., olympic coach Jr. Yung Song; head instr. Royal Bhutanese Army Thundarr, 1987. Recipient 1st Pl. Fighting Pro Kickboxing World Belt Champion, 1986, letters of recommendation from Pres.'s Carter, Reagan, Bush and Clinton; unducted Internat. Karate Hall of Fame, 1988; ranked 4th in World Kickboxing Kata, 1988, 3d in World full contact USKA, 1991, world champion full contact, 1993. Mem. World Karate Assn. (registered fighter), Profl. Karate Commn. (registered fighter), World Kickboxing Coun. (registered fighter), U.S Karate Fedn. (1st place award State Competition 1987), Internat. Martial Arts Assn. (competitor, 1st Place award 1985). Home: 119B Lynnwood Dr Nichalsville KY 40356 Office: Pwoen House Gym 3460 Richmond Rd Lexington KY 40509-1801

WILLIAMS, EDWARD EARL, JR., entrepreneur, educator; b. Houston, Aug. 21, 1945; s. Edward Earl and Doris Jewel (Jones) W.; m. Susan M. Warren, June 28, 1983; children: Laura Michelle, David Brian. BS, U. Pa., 1966; PhD, U. Tex., 1968. Asst. prof. econs. Rutgers U., New Brunswick, N.J., 1968-70; assoc. prof. fin. McGill U., Montreal, Que., Can., 1970-73; v.p., economist Service Corp. Internat., Houston, 1973-77; prof. adminstrv. sci. Rice U., Houston, 1978-82, Henry Gardiner Symonds prof., 1982—, prof. stats., 1995—; chmn. bd. Edward E. Williams & Co., Houston, 1976-92; chmn. bd., pres. Tex. Capital Investment Co., 1979-95; chmn. bd. First Tex. Venture Capital Corp., 1983-92; mng. dir. First Tex. Venture Capital,

LLC, 1992—; dir. Video Rental of Pa. Inc., Svc. Corp. Internat, EQUUS II, Inc.; adv. dir. Frost Nat. Bank. Benjamin Franklin scholar, Jesse Jones scholar, U. Pa., 1966, Tex. Savs. and Loan League fellow, NDEA fellow, U. Tex., 1968. Mem. Am. Statis. Assn., Coll. Innovation Mgmt. and Entrepreneurship, Fin. Mgmt. Assn., Beta Gamma Sigma, Alpha Kappa Psi. Author: Prospects for the Savings and Loan Industry, 1968, An Integrated Analysis for Managerial Finance, 1970, Investment Analysis, 1974, Business Planning for the Entrepreneur, 1983, The Economics of Production and Productivity: A Modeling Approach, 1996; contbr. articles to profl. jours. Home: 7602 Wilton Park Dr Spring TX 77379-4672 Office: Rice U Jesse H Jones Grad Sch Adminstrn Houston TX 77251

WILLIAMS, EDWARD F(OSTER), III, environmental engineer; b. N.Y.C., Jan. 3, 1935; s. E. Foster Jr. and Ida Frances (Richards) W.; m. Sue Carol Osenbaugh, June 5, 1960; children: Cecile Elizabeth, Alexander Harmon. BS in Engring., Auburn U., 1956; MA in History, U. Memphis, 1974. Registered profl. engr., Tenn. Engr. Buckeye Cellulose Corp. (subs. of Procter & Gamble), Memphis, 1957, process safety engr., 1960; resident constrn. engr. Buckeye Cellulose Corp. (subs. of Procter & Gamble), Perry, Fla., 1960-61; staff engr. Buckeye Cellulose Corp. (subs. of Procter & Gamble), Memphis, 1961-70; chief engr., v.p. Enviro-trol, Inc., Memphis, 1970-73; v.p., then pres. Ramcon Environ. Corp., Memphis, 1973-80; pres. E.F. Williams & Assocs., Inc., Memphis, 1980—, EFW Comml. Ventures Inc., 1990—; bd. dirs. Mobile Process Tech. Inc., Memphis; v.p. Environ. Testing and Cons., Inc., Memphis, 1985-94; environ. coord. Shelby County, Tenn., 1995-96. Author: Fustest with the Mostest, 1968, Early Memphis and Its River Rivals, 1969; editor Environ. Control News for So. Industry, 1971—. State rep. Tenn. Gen. Assembly, 1970-78; mem. Shelby County Bd. Commrs., Memphis, 1978-94, chmn., 1987-88, 90-92; mem. Shelby County Records Commn., 1978—, chmn., 1993—; historian Shelby County, 1994—; environ. coord. Shelby County Mayor's staff, 1995-96; trustee Bolton Coll., 1982—, chmn., 1987-88, 90-92; del. Rep. Nat. Conv., 1988, 92, 96, Rep. state exec. com., 1994—; state chmn. Nat. Conf. Rep. County Ofcls., 1993-96; vice-chmn. Memphis-Shelby local Emergency Planning Com., 1986—; bd. dirs. Better Bus. Bur., Memphis, 1995—. Capt. USAF, 1957-60. Named Tenn. Water Conservationist of Yr., Tenn. Conservation League, 1973, Tenn. Legis. Conservationist of Yr., Nat. Wildlife Fedn., 1974, Memphis Outstanding Engr., Memphis Joint Engrs. Coun., 1980; recipient Shelby County Environ. Improvement award, 1983, Tenn. Lifetime Environ. Stewardship award Tenn. Dept. Environ. and Conservation, 1995. Mem. NSPE, ASME, Am. Acad. Environ. Engrs. (diplomate), Water Environ. Fedn., Am. Indsl. Hygiene Assn. (chpt. pres.), Am. Soc. Safety Engrs. (outstanding achievement award 1995-96), Air and Waste Mgmt. Assn., Engrs. Club Memphis (bd. dirs. 1979-80), Rotary, C. of C. (environ. coun. chmn. 1988—), Tenn. Hist. Soc. (v.p. 1972), Tenn. Hist. Commn. (vice chmn. 1987—), West Tenn. Hist. Soc. (pres. 1983-85), Am. Hist. Assn., Memphis-Shelby County Tenn. Bicentennial Commn. (chmn. 1994-96). Republican. Presbyterian. Home: 148 Perkins Ext Memphis TN 38117-3127 Office: EF Williams & Assocs 751 E Brookhaven Cir Memphis TN 38117-4501 also: PO Box 241813 Memphis TN 38124-1813

WILLIAMS, EDWIN NEEL, newspaper editor; b. Rives, Mo., Jan. 14, 1942; s. Carl Edwin and Vina Marie (Edmonston) W.; m. Marylyn Lentine, 1973; 1 child, Jonathan Lentine. BA in History, U. Miss., 1965. Reporter Clarksdale (Miss) Press-Register, 1965; reporter, editor Delta Dem.-Times, Greenville, Miss., 1967-72; Nieman fellow Harvard U., Cambridge, Mass., 1972-73; writer, researcher Ford Found., N.Y.C., 1973; editorial writer Charlotte (N.C.) Observer, 1973-76, editor of editorial pages, 1976-80, 87—. Chmn. KinderMourn, Charlotte, 1988, N.C. Harvest, 1993-94; bd. dirs. N.C. Ctr. for Pub. Policy Rsch., Raleigh, 1992-95. With U.S. Army, 1965-67. Baptist. Home: 916 Mount Vernon Ave Charlotte NC 28203-4845 Office: Charlotte Observer PO Box 30308 Charlotte NC 28230-0308

WILLIAMS, EMILY ALLEN, English language educator; b. Nottoway, Va., Aug. 14, 1955; d. Joseph Robert and Cornelia (Scott) Allen; m. Kenneth Jerome Williams, Feb. 29, 1992. BA, St. Paul's Coll., 1977; MA, Va. Commonwealth U., 1979; DAH, Clark Atlanta U., 1996. Instr. adult edn. Med. Coll. Va./Va. Commonwealth U., Richmond, 1977-79; instr. English Richmond Bus. Coll., 1979-80; regional grants coord. Va. Com. for Arts, Richmond, 1980-85; grants program coord. Ga. Coun. for Arts, Atlanta, 1986-87; grants dir. City of Atlanta Bur. Cultural Affairs, 1987-91; prof. English Clark Atlanta U., 1991-92, Morehouse Coll., Atlanta, 1992—, Spelman Coll., 1995—; adj. instr. English Reynolds C.C., Richmond, 1983-85; site reviewer NEA, Washington, 1990-91; panelist Nat. Black Arts Festival, Atlanta, 1991, Ga. Coun. Arts, Atlanta, 1987-90; cons. Fulton County Arts Coun., Atlanta, 1991-92, African Am. Philharmonic Orch., Atlanta, 1991-92. Contbr. numerous articles to profl. publs. Advisor student newspaper Morehouse Coll., 1992-93, grant com. chmn. English dept., 1992-93; speaker arts sem. Va. Commonwealth U., Richmond, 1982; cons. The APEX Mus., Atlanta, 1992-93. E. Bradlee Watson scholar, St. Paul's Coll., 1976. Mem. Popular Culture Assn., Coll. Lang. Assn., Delta Sigma Theta, Alpha Kappa Mu. Home: 6196 Spring Lake Walk Lithonia GA 30038-3467 Office: Morehouse Coll 830 Westview Dr SW Atlanta GA 30314-3773

WILLIAMS, EMMA CRAWFORD, business owner; b. Dillon, S.C., Aug. 16, 1945; d. Moses and Sallie Lee (McInnis) Crawford; m. Johnny Lee Williams, Nov. 25, 1967; 1 child, GiGi T. A in Bus. Adminstrn., Durham (N.C.) Bus. Coll., 1964; A in Acctg., Strayer Coll., Washington, 1969. From sec. to office mgr. Ferris & Co., Washington, 1965-68; exec. asst. mgr. Manpower Assistance Program, Washington, 1968-71; adminstrv. asst./office mgr. Appalachian Regional Com., Washington, 1971-81; adminstrv. sec. Home Owners Warranty Ins., Washington, 1981-82; office mgr. Hilton Internat. Hotels, Washington, 1986-89; pres., CEO, owner AHA Enterprises, Inc. (Added Hands Agy.), Ft. Washington, Md., 1989—; mem. Fairfax County Commerce Dept.; motivational spkr. D.C. Treatment Facility; guest spkr. Julia Jackson's Other Office on Bus. and Fins., Va., 1996. Block capt. Ft. Washington Citizen Assn., 1975—; active Laura House Assn., Tex., 1992—; vol. office asst. nat. presdl. campaign, Washington, 1976. Mem. Am. Woman's Econ. Devel., Nat. Notary Assn., Dillionite, Inc. Democrat. Home: 9108 Overlook Trail Washington MD 20744 Office: AHA Enterprises Inc Added Hands Agy 1800 Diagonal Rd Ste 600 Alexandria VA 22314

WILLIAMS, ETHEL LAVERNA (ETHEL LAVERNA WILLIAMS STEED), painter; b. Brownsville, Tex., Jan. 3, 1920; d. John Francis and Clara Alice (Moore) Contantine; m. Alvis Williams, Mar. 23, 1940 (dec. July 1974); children: Glenda, Deanna, Gaylen, Wade; m. William Sherman Steed, Feb. 25, 1985. Self-taught artist Art Assn. Corpus Christi (Tex.), 1969-84. Pub., collector: (folk songs book) Lamplighting Time, 1976. Precinct worker Democratic Party, Corpus Christi, 1988. Mem. Art Community Ctr. (Corpus Christi), Nat. Mus. Women in the Arts, Thomas Gilcrease Mus. (Tulsa), The Nature Conservancy. Democrat. Nazarene. Home: 1125 Stratton Dr Corpus Christi TX 78412-3570

WILLIAMS, FRANKLIN CADMUS, JR., bibliographer; b. Palestine, Tex., July 30, 1941; s. Franklin Cadmus and Cathryn Lucille (Pessoney) W. BA, Baylor U., 1963; MA, Stephen F. Austin State U., 1965; PhD, U. Wis., 1975. Cert. in secondary edn. English and History. Teaching fellow Stephen F. Austin State U., Nacogdoches, Tex., 1964-65, U. Wis., Madison, 1965-68; instr. English Austin Peay State U., Clarksville, Tenn., 1970-71; adj. asst. prof. East Tex. State U., Commerce, 1975; asst. prof. English Jarvis Christian Coll., Hawkins, Tex., 1976-78, 79-81; ind. scholar Palestine, Tex., 1981—; owner, bibliographer Goldsmith Archive, Palestine, 1981—; cons. Diocese of Galveston-Houston, 1977-84, Tex. State Hist. Assn., Austin, 1988; speaker, editor Jarvis Christian Coll., Hawkins, Tex., 1976-78, 79-81; nat. teaching fellow Office Edn., Washington, 1976-77; del. to Baylor U., U. Wis. System, Madison, 1981. Contbr. articles to profl. jours. Mem. Modern Lang. Assn., Tex. State Hist. Assn., Tex. Cath. Hist. Soc., Baylor Alumni Assn. (life), Wis. Alumni Assn. (life), Sigma Tau Delta. Office: PO Box 96 Palestine TX 75802-0096

WILLIAMS, GAYLEN EUGENE, accountant; b. Marlow, Okla., June 24, 1940; s. Gaylen Lafayette and Myrtle Francis (Sage) W.; m. Janice Ladean Moore, July 19, 1958; children: Mark, Gayla, Leland, Charm. Assoc. degree, Cameron Coll., Lawton, Okla., 1960. With Whiteway Grocery, Marlow, 1950-60; store mgr. Pratt Foods, Marlow, 1960-67; sales mgr. Jewel Co., Chgo., 1967-76; pvt. practice acct. Midwest City, Okla., 1976—.

WILLIAMS, GLEN MORGAN, federal judge; b. Jonesville, Va., Feb. 17, 1920; s. Hughy May and Hattie Mae W.; m. Jane Slemp, Nov. 17, 1962; children: Susan, Judy, Rebecca, Melinda. A.B. magna cum laude, Milligan Coll., 1940; J.D., U. Va., 1948. Bar: Va. 1947. Pvt. practice law Jonesville, 1948-76; judge U.S. Dist. Ct. (we. dist.) Va., 1976-88, sr. judge, 1988—; commonwealth's atty. Lee County, Va., 1948-51; mem. Va. Senate, 1953-55. Mem. editorial bd.: Va. Law Rev, 1946-47. Mem. Lee County Sch. Bd., 1972-76; trustee, elder First Christian Ch., Pennington Gap, Va. Lt. USN, 1942-46, MTO. Recipient Citation of Merit Va. Def. Lawyers Assn., Outstanding Alumnus award Milligan Coll., 1980. Mem. ABA, Va. State Bar (citation of merit), Va. Bar Assn. (citation of merit), Fed. Bar Assn., Va. Trial Lawyers Assn. (Meritorious Svc. award 1986, Disting. Svc. award), Am. Legion, 40 and 8. Clubs: Lions, Masons, Shriners. Office: US Dist Ct Fed Bldg PO Box 339 Abingdon VA 24212

WILLIAMS, GRETCHEN MINYARD, food store executive; b. Dallas, Dec. 18, 1956; d. Marvin Tipton and Clarine (Cooper) Minyard; m. Joseph Larry Williams, June 10, 1978. BBA, Tex. Christian U., 1978. Dir. employee rels. Minyard Food Stores, Inc., Coppell, Tex., 1978-80, v.p. employee rels., 1980-83, v.p. corp. rel., 1983-85, vice chmn. of bd. dirs., 1985-88, co-chmn. bd. dirs., 1988—; bd. dirs. Cullen/Frost Bank, N.A., Dallas. Adv. bd. mktg. edn. Dallas Ind. Sch. Dist., Dallas, 1981—; campaign mem. Old City Park, Dallas, 1988, Tex. Christian U. Fund Drive, Ft. Worth, 1987-88; adv. bd. Dallas Bapt. U., 1985—. Mem. Dallas/Ft. Worth Retail Grocers Assn. (chmn. bd. 1988—, avt. com.), AGAPE Social Svcs. Inc. (bd. dirs. 1987—), Baylor Health Care System (bd. dirs. 1989—), Zeta Tau Alpha (pres 1986-87). Office: Minyard Food Stores Inc 777 Freeport Pky Coppell TX 75019-4411*

WILLIAMS, HARRY GEORGE, minister; b. Kokomo, Ind., Aug. 9, 1925; s. Thomas Ralph and Marguerite Ann (Bergman) W.; m. Mary Virginia Carroll, Aug. 25, 1952 (dec. 1972); children: Barbara, Thomas, Kathleen, Mary Beth, Harry, Timothy; m. Trudy Anne Sly, June 17, 1980. BFA in Broadcast Edn., Cin. Coll. Music, 1949; MDiv, Gen. Theol. Sem., N.Y.C., 1978. Ordained priest Episcopal Ch., 1979. Tchg. asst., reading Gen. Theol. Seminary, 1976-77; canon residentiary St. Peter's Cathedral, St. Petersburg, Fla., 1978-80; rector/vicar St. Luke's Ch./Our Savior Ch., Lincolnton, N.C., 1980-83; founding rector St. Anne of Grace Ch., Seminole, Fla., 1983-92; ret., 1992; mem. Diocesan Coun. St. Luke's Ch., Lincolnton, 1981-83, St. Anne of Grace Ch., Seminole, 1986-89; founding dir. Mission 4 Consortium of Small Chs., 1981-83; dean Shelby Deanery, 1982-83; founding legis. del. Episc. Synod of Am., Ft. Worth, 1989—. With USN, 1943-45. Mem. Soc. Holy Cross, Evang. and Cath. Mission, Nat. Orgn. Episcs. for Life. Republican. Home: 8021 Bayhaven Dr Largo FL 34646-3320

WILLIAMS, HENRY RUDOLPH, retired railroad executive; b. Wilmington, N.C., Oct. 23, 1919; s. Henry R. and Virginia L. (Hewlett) W.; m. Elsie Virginia Gray, Apr. 25, 1942; children: Cheryl A., Deborah L. BCS, Benjamin Farnklin U., 1949; MBA, George Washington U., 1952. With Hamilton Nat. Bank, Washington, 1937-42, IRS, 1945-52, ICC, Washington, 1952-67, Office of Sec., U.S. Dept. Transp., Washington, 1967-69, U.S. Fed. R.R. Adminstrn., Washington, 1969-74; sr. fin. analyst U.S. Ry. Assn., Washington, 1974-75; asst. to v.p.-fin. Mo.-Kans.-Tex. R.R. Co., Denison, Tex., 1975, ret. 1988, successively asst. v.p.-fin., asst. v.p. and comptroller; dir. Okla.-Kans.-Tex. R.R. Co. With U.S. Army, 1942-45, 61-62. Recipient Achievement award U.S. Dept. Transp., Sec.'s award meritorious achievement. Mem. R.R. Ins. Mgmt. Assn., Assn. Am. R.Rs, Denison C. of C., Denison Rod and Gun Country Club. Republican. Baptist. Home: 2600 Brookhaven Cir Denison TX 75020-4003

WILLIAMS, HUGH ALEXANDER, JR., retired mechanical engineer, consultant; b. Spencer, N.C., Aug. 18, 1926; s. Hugh Alexander and Mattie Blanche (Megginson) W.; BS in Mech. Engring., N.C. State U., 1948, MS in Diesel Engring. (Norfolk So. R.R. fellow), 1950; postgrad. Ill. Benedictine Coll. Inst. Mgmt., 1980; m. Ruth Ann Gray, Feb. 21, 1950; children: David Gray, Martha Blanche Williams Heidengren. Jr. engr.-field service engr. Baldwin-Lima Hamilton Corp., Hamilton, Ohio, 1950-52, project engr., 1953-55; project engr. Electro-Motive div. Gen. Motors Corp., La Grange, Ill., 1955-58, sr. project engr., 1958-63, supr. product devel. engine design sect., 1963-86, staff engr., advanced mech. tech., 1986-87. Trustee Downers Grove (Ill.) San. Dist., 1965-92, pres., 1974-91, v.p., 1991-92; pres. Ill. Assn. San. Dists., 1976-77, bd. dirs., 1977-89; mem. statewide policy adv. com. Ill. EPA, 1977-79; mem. DuPage County Intergovtl. Task Force Com., 1988-92; elder Presbyn. Ch. Served with USAAC, 1945. Registered profl. engr., Ill. Recipient Trustee Svc. award Ill. Assn. San. Dists., 1986, Citizens award Downers Grove Evening chpt. Kiwanis, 1991. Fellow ASME (chmn. honors and awards com. 1993—, Diesel and Gas Engine Power Div. Speaker awards 1968, 84, Div. citation 1977, Internal Combustion Engine award 1987, exec. com. Internal Combustion Engine div. 1981-87, 88-92, chmn. 1985-86, sec. 1988-92); mem. Soc. Automotive Engrs. (life), ASME (chmn. Soichiro Honda medal com. 1987-92), Ill. Assn. Wastewater Agys. (Outstanding Mem. award 1990, hon. mem. 1992), Raleigh Host Lions Club (pres. 1996—), Masons (32 degree), Sigma Pi. Republican. Editor: So. Engr., 1947-48; contbr. articles to profl. jours. Patentee in field. Home: 2108 Weybridge Dr Raleigh NC 27615-5562

WILLIAMS, JAMES BRYAN, banker; b. Sewanee, Tenn., Mar. 21, 1933; s. Eugene G. and Ellen (Bryan) W.; m. Betty G. Williams, July 11, 1980; children: Ellen, Elizabeth, Bryan. AB, Emory U., 1955. Chmn., CEO SunTrust Banks, Inc., Atlanta, 1991—; bd. dirs. The Coca-Cola Co., Atlanta, Genuine Parts Co., Atlanta, Rollins, Inc., Ga.-Pacific Corp., Atlanta, RPC, Inc., Atlanta, Sonat Inc., Birmingham, Ala. Trustee Emory U.; chmn. bd. trustees Robert W. Woodruff Health Scis. Ctr. Lt. USAF, 1955-57. Mem. Bankers Roundtable. Presbyterian. Clubs: Piedmont Driving (Atlanta), Capital City (Atlanta), Commerce (Atlanta), Peachtree Golf (Atlanta), Augusta Country. Office: SunTrust Banks Inc 25 Park Pl NE Atlanta GA 30303*

WILLIAMS, JAMES HOWARD, sociologist, research agency executive; b. Wheat, Tenn., Dec. 19, 1920; s. William Wess and Sallie (Shelton) W.; AB, Carson-Newman Coll., 1942; MA, George Peabody Coll., 1947; PhD, Vanderbilt U., 1956; m. Mary Helen Mewshaw, Aug. 31, 1946; children: James Howard, Edward Robert, Nancy Jean. Instr. dept. sociology U. S.C., 1950-55; asst. dir. Nat. Inst. Mental Health Project, Vanderbilt U., 1956-58; asst. prof. social welfare and sociology Fla. State U., 1958-61; rsch. dir. Fla. Bur. Alcoholic Rehab., Avon Park, 1961-75; rsch. assoc. Fla. Aging and Adult Svcs., 1975-76; planner, evaluator Fla. Alcoholic Rehab. Program, Tallahassee, 1976—. Social sci. cons. City of Columbia (S.C.) Planning Comm., 1950-55. Lt. USNR, 1942-46. Mem. N.Am. Assn. Alcohol Programs, So. Sociol. Soc., Soc. Study Social Problems, Am. Sociol. Assn., Nat. Rehab. Assn., Population Assn. Am., Fla. Acad. Sci. Kiwanian (pres. Avon Park club 1970-71, 74-75). Contbr. articles to profl. jours. Home: 1537 Woodgate Way Tallahassee FL 32312-3228 Office: 1323 Winewood Blvd Tallahassee FL 32399-6571

WILLIAMS, JAMES KELLEY, diversified resources company executive; b. Bentonia, Miss., Mar. 29, 1934; s. James C. and Katheryn (Kelley) W.; m. Jean Pittman, June 16, 1956; children: James Kelley Jr., George P., Clifford C. B.S. in Chem. Engring, Ga. Inst. Tech., 1956; M.B.A., Harvard U., 1962. Asst. to pres. Tyrone Hydraulics, Corinth, Miss., 1962-67; mgr. corp. planning and devel. First Miss. Corp., Jackson, 1967-69, v.p., 1969-71, pres., CEO, 1971-88, chmn., pres., CEO, 1988—, also chmn. exec. com., bd. dirs.; chmn. B.C. Rogers Poultry, Inc., Morton, Miss., 1981—; mem. adv. coun. Degussa Corp.; dir. Deposit Guaranty Corp., Deposit Guaranty Nat. Bank. Dirs. Miss. Econ. Coun., Com. for Econ. Devel., Washington; deacon Northminster Bapt. Ch.; trustee Miss. Found. Ind. Colls., Nature Conservancy; chmn. Inst. Tech. Devel. for Miss. With USAR, 1957-60. Mem. Fertilizer Inst., Chief Execs. Orgn., Mfg. Chemists Assn., Agribus Promotion Coun., World Bus. Coun., Hundred of Jackson. Clubs: Jackson Country, River Hills, Hundred of Jackson. Office: First Miss Corp PO Box 1249 700 North St Jackson MS 39215-1249 also: BC Rogers Poultry Inc 121 Old Hwy 80 E Morton MS 39117*

WILLIAMS, JAMES KENDRICK, bishop. Ed., St. Mary's Coll., St. Mary's, Ky., St. Maur's Sch. Theology, South Union, Ky. Ordained priest Roman Catholic Ch., 1963; ordained titular bishop Catula and aux. bishop of Covington, 1984; ordained first bishop of Lexington, Ky., installed 1988. Office: Bishop of Lexington PO Box 12350 1310 Leestown Rd Lexington KY 40582-2350*

WILLIAMS, JAMES LAWRENCE, pharmaceutical executive; b. Phila., Apr. 3, 1950; s. Edward J. Max and Margery Jean (Wiseman) Williams; m. Patricia Ann Rice, June 24, 1972; children: James Jr., John, Thomas. BA, West Chester (Pa.) U., 1972; postgrad., Temple U., 1972. Regional dir., mgr. pub. affairs Pharm. Mfrs. Assn., Washington, 1978-91; dir. state govt. affairs Glaxo Wellcome Inc., Rsch. Triangle Pk., N.C., 1991-95. Author (civic presentations) Value of Medicines, 1991; corporate civic action c ampaign, brochures. State rep. Rep. candidate Pa., 1976; polit. cons. Pa., 1976-78, coach youth sports leagues, N.C., Pa., 1986-95; dir. Tex. Civil Justice League, Austin, 1983-93, AMA Steering Com. on Prescription Drug Abuse, Washington, 1981-89. Mem. Am. Polit. Sci. Assn. Home: 8414 Inverness Way Chapel Hill NC 27516 Office: Glaxo Wellcome Inc 5 Moore Dr Research Triangle Park NC 27709

WILLIAMS, JAMES ORRIN, university administrator, educator; b. New Orleans, Jan. 8, 1937; married, 1956; 3 children. BS, Auburn U., 1960, MEd, 1963, EdD, 1967; postgrad., Tchrs. Coll., Columbia U., summer 1964. Tchr. social sci., coach Columbus High Sch. Ga., 1960-61; tchr., coach Eufaula High Sch. Ala., 1961-63; prin. Troy Jr. High Sch., 1963-65; grad. asst. Sch. Edn. Auburn U., 1965-66, interim dir. field service, 1966-67; asst. prof. edn. adminstrn. U. Fla., 1967-68; asst. prof. Columbus Coll., 1968-69; assoc. prof., chmn. div. Auburn U., Montgomery, 1969-73, vice chancellor acad. affairs, 1973-80, chancellor, 1980—. Contbr. articles to profl. jours. Phi Delta Kappa grantee, 1967. Mem. Am. Assn. State Colls. and Univs., Am. Assn. Coll. Tchr. Edn., Assn. Tchr. Edn., So. Regional Council Edn. Adminstrn., Phi Delta Kappa (v.p. 1965), Phi Kappa Phi. Office: Auburn U-Montgomery Office of Chancellor 7300 University Dr Montgomery AL 36117-3531*

WILLIAMS, JAN KORET, secondary school educator; b. Carmi, Ill., Oct. 17, 1953; d. Ted J. and Ruth Ann (Ward) Smith; m. S. Eric Williams, Nov. 25, 1971; children: Ryan Eric, Worth Smith. BA, Ea. Ill. U., 1974, MA, 1975. Tchr. Ea. Ill. U., Charleston, 1976-77; tchr. English Williams Middle Sch., Rockwall, Tex., 1984-90, Summit Middle Sch., Edmond, Okla., 1990-91, Edmond Meml. High Sch., 1991, Rockwall (Tex.) High Sch., 1992—. Author: In Shape for Learning: Interdisciplinary Curriculum Enhancements. Named Tchr. of Yr. Rockwall Ind. Sch. Dist., 1990; finalist Apple Computer Thanks to Tchr. award, Tex., 1990. Mem. Nat. Coun. Tchrs. English, Nat. Fedn. Tchrs., Rockwell Fedn. Tchrs. Republican. Baptist. Home: 1606 N Hills Dr Rockwall TX 75087-3241 Office: Rockwall High Sch 901 Yellow Jacket Ln Rockwall TX 75087-4839

WILLIAMS, JEANNE MARIE, editor, writer; b. Palo Alto, Calif., Nov. 26, 1965; d. Michael David and Joan (Stephens) Kelly; m. Douglas Lee Williams, June 15, 1991. BA, Coll. William and Mary, 1989; postgrad., George Washington U., 1993. Analyst Legis-Slate, Inc., Washington, 1987-90, supr., 1988-90; editor Local, State Funding Report Govt. Info. Svcs., Arlington, Va., 1990—, exec. editor, 1991—; judge Newsletter Publishers Assn. Competition, Washington, 1995. Contbr. editor periodicals, guides. Vol. Friends United for Need, Washington, 1994, Steven Greenwood Found. Heritage Walk, Alexandria, Va., 1994. Democrat. Roman Catholic. Home: 3346 Wheatwheel Ln Annandale VA 22003 Office: Govt Info Svcs 4301 N Fairfax Dr #875 Arlington VA 22203

WILLIAMS, JEFFREY JAMES, English language educator; b. Bay Shore, N.Y., Dec. 14, 1958; s. Sidney Harvey and Muriel Antoinette (Overton) W.; 1 child, Virginia Ann. BA, SUNY, Stony Brook, 1984, PhD, 1990. Asst. prof. East Carolina U., Greenville, N.C., 1990-96, assoc. prof., 1996—. Author: Narrative, The Question of Theory, and the English Novel, 1996; editor: PC Wars: Politics and Theory in the Academy, 1995; editor, pub. The Minn. Rev.: A Jour. Committed Writing, 1992—; co-editor: The Norton Anthology of Literary Theory and Criticism; adv. editor Symploke, 1993, Works and Days, 1994—, Journal X, 1995—. Fellow Sch. Criticism and Theory Dartmouth Coll., 1992, 89; fellow, grantee NEH, 1995. Mem. MLA (del. from South 1995—), AAUP, South Atlantic MLA, Tchrs. for Dem. Culture, Radical Caucus, Marxist Lit. Group (coord. So. region 1994—). Socialist. Office: East Carolina U Dept English Greenville NC 27858

WILLIAMS, JEFFREY LEE, credit union association executive; b. Ft. Worth, Oct. 30, 1958; s. Gary Lee and Barbara Ann (Womack) W.; m. Holly Holcomb, Dec. 2, 1978; children: Candice Gabrielle, Crysti Leigh. BS in Econs., Tex. A&M U., 1982. Owner, chief exec. officer Williams Maintenance Svcs., College Station, Tex., 1978-81; assoc. analyst Continental Pipeline Co., Inc., Lake Charles, La., 1982-83; adminstrv. coordinator Conoco, Inc., Atlanta, 1984-86; contr., asst. treas. Ga. Credit Union Affiliates, Atlanta, 1987-95, v.p., 1987—; owner, CEO Coop. Underwriters, Inc., Snellville, Ga., 1994—; asst. treas. Ga. Credit Union League and Affiliate, Atlanta, 1986-95, Ga. Ctrl. Credit Union, Atlanta, 1986-95, Credit Union Svc. Corp., Atlanta, 1987-95; pres., CEO South Atlanta C.A.R., 1990-94, 1990-94; v.p. Credit Union Coop. Automotive Resources, Inc., 1990-95. Author, editor: Introduction to Oil Pipeline Industry, 1984; contbr. author: Disaster Recovery: A Special Report, Credit Union Directors, 1989. Outreach leader 1st Bapt. Ch., Lake Charles, 1983, Sunday sch. tchr., Snellville, Ga., 1987; legis. chmn., bd. dirs. Hunters Pond Homeowners Assn., R.L. Norton Sch. PTA; mem. Citizens Lobby for Kids, 1989-91; state rep. Dist. 83, GOP Welfare Reform Task Force, GOP House Policy Com., 1995—; legis. vice chmn. Nat. Conf. State Legislatures Legis. Effectiveness Com. Mem. Am. Credit Union League Execs., Ga. Ind. Automobile Dealers Assn. Republican. Baptist. Home: 2815 Hunters Pond Ln Snellville GA 30278-6903 Office: Coop Underwriters Inc PO Box 954 Snellville GA 30278-0454

WILLIAMS, JESSIE WILLMON, church worker, retired librarian; b. Boynton, Okla., Feb. 23, 1907; d. Thomas Woodard and Eliza Jane (Adams) Willmon; m. Austin Guest, Aug. 13, 1932 (div. 1945); m. Thomas Washington Williams, Dec. 12, 1946 (dec.). BA, East Tex. State U., 1930, MA, 1944. cert. English and Spanish tchr., Tex. Libr. Gladewater (Tex.) Pub. Libr., 1935-46; med. libr. VA Hosp., North Little Rock, Ark., 1946-58; base libr. Little Rock AFB, 1958-68; ret., 1968; lay worker 1st Bapt. Ch., Pecan Gap, Tex., 1988—. Mem. Delta Kappa Gamma, Phi Beta Kappa. Democrat. Mem. So. Bapt. Conv. Home: PO Box 43 Pecan Gap TX 75469-0043

WILLIAMS, JOCELYN JONES, reading educator; b. Greenville, N.C., Sept. 24, 1948; d. William Edward and Elinor Suejette (Albritton) Jones; m. Robert Alexander Simpkins Jr., Sept. 7, 1969 (div. May 1972); m. Oscar James Williams Jr., July 12, 1985 (div. Mar. 1989). BS, Bennett Coll., 1970; MEd, N.C. Cen. U., 1988; MS, N.C. Agrl. & Tech. State U., 1992. Kindergarten/1st grade tchr. Greenville City Schs., 1970-74; elem./reading tchr. Orange County Schs., Hillsborough, N.C., 1974—; mem. N.C. Reading Recovery Adv. Bd., 1994—, Reading Recovery Coun. N.Am., 1994—. Mem. NEA, ASCD, Internat. Reading Assn., Nat. Assn. Edn. Young Children, N.C. Assn. Educators, Phi Delta Kappa, Alpha Kappa Alpha, Progressive Sertoma Club. Democrat. Baptist. Home: 47 Celtic Dr Durham NC 27703-2894

WILLIAMS, JOHN CLIFFORD (JACK WILLIAMS), journalist; b. Jacksonville, Fla., June 12, 1936; s. Clifford Lester and Rhoda Jane (Schenck) W.; m. Shirley Aichel, Oct. 11, 1963 (div. Dec. 1984); 1 child, Kurt John; m. Darlene Shields, Feb. 28, 1987. BS in History and Govt., Jacksonville U., 1962; postgrad., SUNY, Brockport, 1976-82. Lic. pvt. pilot FAA. Reporter Jacksonville Jour., 1962-63, The Times Union, Rochester, N.Y., 1964-70; dir. news svcs. SUNY, 1970-76; copy editor, weekly columnist on weather The Democrat and Chronicle, Rochester, 1976-82; editor weather page USA Today, Arlington, Va., 1982—; dep. editor/weather USA Today Online, 1995—. Author: USA Today Weather Book, 1992 (Louis J. Buttan author's award Am. Meteorol. Soc. 1994), The USA Today Weather Almanac, 1994. Sgt. USMC, 1955-59. Mem. Am. Meteorol. Soc., Aircraft Owners and Pilots Assn., Exptl. Aircraft Assn., Am. Geophys. Union. Home: 6022 Hardwick Pl Falls Church VA 22041-2413 Office: USA Today 1000 Wilson Blvd Arlington VA 22209-3901

WILLIAMS, JOHN TOLLIVER, media executive; b. San Angelo, Tex., Nov. 4, 1944; s. Tom L. and Virginia W. (Potter) W.; BBA, Baylor U., 1967; MBA, U. Pa., 1969; m. Carol Anne Tennison, June 1, 1968; children: Christina, Tolliver. Supr. Ernst & Whinney, San Antonio, Tex., 1971-75; treas. Harte-Hanks Communication, Inc., San Antonio, 1975-79; gen. mgr. San Angelo Standard-Times, 1979-80; pres., pub. Bryan-College Station (Tex.) Eagle, 1980-86; pub. Plano (Tex.) Star Courier, 1986-91; pres., chief oper. officer Garden State Newspapers, Houston, 1991-92; pres., chief exec. officer Gray Communications Systems, Inc., 1992—; v.p. Harte-Hanks Communications, Inc., pres., 1986-91, Harte-Hanks Community Newspapers, Inc., 1986-91; founder Tex. Poll.; pres. Albany State Coll. Found. With U.S. Army, 1969-71. CPA, Tex. Mem. AICPA, Ga. C. of C. (bd. dirs.). Office: PO Box 48 Albany GA 31702-0048

WILLIAMS, JOHN TRENT, public policy company executive; b. Memphis, July 23, 1952; s. William H. and Betty (Schneider) W.; m. Melinda Angel, Dec. 29, 1974 (div. 1980); 1 child, Courtney; m. Lise Morreale, Feb. 4, 1983; children: Corinne, Adele, Peter. BBA magna cum laude, Memphis State U., 1974; MS, La. State U., 1976. Rsch. analyst, div. rsch. La. State U., Baton Rouge, 1975-76, instr. microecons., 1976; rate analyst La. Pub. Svc. Commn., Baton Rouge, 1976-77; project leader, assoc. dpet. mgr. Gulf South Rsch. Inst., Baton Rouge, 1977-79, program mgr. econ. div., 1979-83, rsch. div. dir., 1984-85, v.p., 1985-88; undersec. La. Dept. Commerce, Baton Rouge, 1983-84; v.p. La. Partnership for Tech. and Innovation, Baton Rouge, 1988-92, exec. v.p., 1993-94; prin. Regional Tech. Strategies, Inc., Chapel Hill, N.C., 1994—; dir. USNet, Chapel Hill, N.C., 1994—; bd. dirs. AUG Inc., New Orleans, Life Monitor Sys., Inc., New Orleans, CCF, Inc., Baton Rouge, La.; mem. Operation Bootstrap, La. Power & Light, New Orleans, 1988-90; cons. So. Tech. Coun., Research Triangle Park, N.C., 1991—, co-chmn., 1988-89; founding mem. Modernization Forum, Metrovision Task Force, New Orleans, 1992, mayor's strategic planning com. Econ. Devel., New Orleans, 1992; faculty mem. So. Tech. Coun. Regional Acad. Indsl. Modernization, 1992. Author: (with Shapira Rosenfeld) Smart Firms in Small Towns, 1992; also speeches; contbr. articles to profl. jours. Mem. Leadership La., Baton Rouge, 1991. Mem. Phi Kappa Phi, Gamma Sigma, Omicron Delta Epsilon. Home: 108 Ivy Brook Ln Chapel Hill NC 27516-8083 Office: RTS Inc PO Box 9005 Chapel Hill NC 27515-9005

WILLIAMS, JOHN YOUNG, merchant banker; b. Cordele, Ga., Apr. 13, 1943; s. George Wilmer and Minnie Converse (Roberts) W.; m. Julian Perdue Boykin; m. Joyce, Isabel. BS in Indsl. Engring., Ga. Inst. Tech., 1965; MBA in Fin., Harvard U., 1969. CFA, Ga. Assoc. Kuhn, Loeb & Co., N.Y.C., 1969-71; asst. v.p. Stone & Webster Securities Corp., N.Y.C., 1971-74, Chem. Bank, N.Y.C., 1974-75; mng. dir. Dean Witter Reynolds, Inc., Atlanta, 1975-84; sr. v.p., ltd. ptnr. Bear Stearns & Co., Atlanta, 1984-85; mng. dir. Robinson Humphrey Co., Atlanta, 1985-87; mng. dir., co-founder Grubb & Williams, Ltd., Atlanta, 1987—, Equity South Ptnrs., 1995—; bd. dirs. Tech Data Corp., Clearwater, Fla., Law Cos. Group, Inc., Atlanta, Frisco Furniture Co., High Point, N.C., co-chmn. 1st lt. U.S. Army, 1965-67, Korea. Fellow Soc. Internat. Bus. Fellows (sec. 1988-89); mem. Assn. for Investment Mgmt. and Rsch. (CFA), Assn. for Corp. Growth (pres. 1983-84), Harvard Bus. Sch. Club (pres. 1982-83), Phi Delta Theta (alumni pres. 1980-81). Episcopalian. Home: 750 Arden Close NW Atlanta GA 30327-1275 Office: Equity South Advisors, LLC 3399 Peachtree Rd NE Ste 1790 Atlanta GA 30326-1151

WILLIAMS, JOSEPH HILL, retired diversified industry executive; b. Tulsa, June 2, 1933; s. David Rogerson and Martha Reynolds (Hill) W.; children: Joseph Hill Jr., Peter B., James C.; m. Terese T. Ross, May 7, 1977; stepchildren: Margot Ross, Jennifer Ross. Diploma, St. Paul's Sch., 1952; B.A., Yale U., 1956, M.A. (hon.), 1977; postgrad., Sch. Pipeline Tech. U. Tex., 1960. Field employee div. domestic constrn. The Williams Cos., Inc., Tulsa, 1958-60; project coord. div. engring. The Williams Cos. Inc., Tulsa, 1960-61; project supt. Iran, 1961-62, asst. resident mgr., 1962-64; project mgr., 1964-65, resident mgr., 1965-67; exec. v.p. Tulsa, 1968—, pres., chief operating officer, 1971-78; chmn., chief exec. officer The Williams Cos., Inc., Tulsa, 1979-93; chmn. bd. The Williams Cos., Inc., 1994; now chmn. & CEO The Williams Co., Inc., Tulsa, O.K.; dir. The Williams Co., Inc., Tulsa, 1995—. Former fellow, trustee Yale Corp. Served with AUS, 1956-58. Mem. (hon.) Am. Petroleum Inst. (hon. bd. dirs.), Met. Tulsa C. of C. (past chmn.), Okla. State C. of C. and Industry (past. chmn.), Bus. Coun., Nature Conservancy (past chmn. bd. govs.). Episcopalian. Clubs: Springdale Hall (Camden, S.C.); Augusta (Ga.); Grandfather Golf and Country (Linville, N.C.); Old Baldy Club, (Saratoga, Wyo). Office: Williams Cos Inc 1 Williams Ctr PO Box 2400 Tulsa OK 74102-2400

WILLIAMS, JUDITH L., library administrator; b. Jacksonville, Fla., Sept. 3, 1948; d. Herman D. and Lucille T. (Jaskowiak) W. BA, Fla. State U., 1970, MLS, 1971. From librarian to sr. librarian to asst. dir. to dir. Jacksonville Pub. Libraries, 1971—. Active Jacksonville Community Council. Mem. ALA, Fla. Library Assn., Southeastern Library Assn., League of Women Voters, Jacksonville C. of C. Office: Jacksonville Pub Librs 122 N Ocean St Jacksonville FL 32202-3314*

WILLIAMS, JUDY ANN, biological scientist; b. Ft. Lauderdale, Fla., Dec. 30, 1947; d. Lowell LaVerne Bair and Betty Lynn (Chancey) Prominski; m. James Franklin Williams, June 14, 1965 (div. Feb. 1979); children: Joanna, David, Douglas; m. Jerry Lee Williams, Mar. 1, 1982. BS in Biology, U. Ala., Huntsville, 1982; MS in Biology, U. North Tex., 1984; PhD in Molecular Biology, Tex. Woman's U., 1988. Adj. faculty Collin County C.C., McKinney, Tex., 1988-89, El Centro Coll., Dallas, 1989-90; postdoctoral rsch. assoc. U. North Tex., Denton, 1989-90, Tex. Woman's U., Denton, 1990-91; asst. prof. dept. biol. scis. Southeastern Okla. State U., Durant, 1991—. Contbr. articles to profl. jours. Bd. dirs. Denton County Mental Health-Mental Retardation, Denton, 1990-91. Grantee Nat. Inst. Gen. Med. Scis., 1991, 92, 95, Southea. Okla. State U., 1991, 93, Okla. Ctr. for Advancement Sci. and Tech., 1992. Mem. AAAS, Soc. Neurosci., Okla. Acad. Scis., Sigma Xi. Home: 208 Rollingwood Hills Dr Durant OK 74701 Office: Southeastern Okla State U Fifth and University Durant OK 74701

WILLIAMS, JULIA REBECCA KEYS, secondary school educator; b. Bristol, Va., July 13, 1922; d. Walter King and Eleanor Fell (Fickle) K.; m. Charles Edwin, Feb. 19, 1944; children: James Edwin, Eleanor Lynn. BA, Queens Coll., Charlotte, 1943; MA, Appalachian State U., Boone, N.C., 1969; EdS, Nova U., 1989. Fla. Tchr. Cert. in Bible, History, English. Tchr. Watauga County Sch. Bd., Blowing Rock, N.C., 1943-44; bank teller, mgr. The Northwestern Bank, Boone, Blowing Rock, N.C., 1944-51; owner, mgr. Yonahlossee Motel, Blowing Rock, N.C., 1952-65; tchr. Sarasota County Sch. Bd., Fla., 1965-89; English Dept. Chmn. McIntosh Jr. High Sarasota Fla. 1976-82; English Curriculum Coordinator McIntosh Middle Sch. 1982-87. Author Poems 1986 (Golden Poet award), Interdisciplinary Units for Middle Sch., Ch. History Bee Ridge Presbyn. Ch. (elder 1981). Elder Bee Ridge Presbyn. Ch., 1990-92. Mem. Sarasota English and Reading Coun. (pres. 1974-75), Nat. and Fla. Coun. of English Tchrs., Presbyn. Womens Club (Life Mem. award), Delta Kappa Gamma Soc. (pres. Beta Upsilon chpt. 1990-92), Alpha Delta Kappa (pres. 1972-74). Democrat. Presbyterian. Home: 4509 Beacon Dr Sarasota FL 34232-5215

WILLIAMS, JUSTIN, retired government official; b. Greenbrier, Ark., Mar. 2, 1906; s. Isom G. and Susan Elizabeth (Clements) Williams; m. Ellawitt Brewer, Aug. 13, 1927; children: Justin Jr., Nicholas B. AB, U. Cen. Ark., 1926; MA, U. Iowa, 1928, PhD, 1933. Instr. U. Cen. Ark., Conway, 1926-27; prof. history U. Wis., River Falls, 1928-42, chmn. dept., 1932-42; div. chief govt. sect. Gen. Hdqrs., SCAP, Tokyo, 1946-52; div. chief ICA (now AID), Washington, 1953-59, ICA, Am. Embassy, Paris, 1960-62; asst. to pres. U. Md., College Park, 1962-67; fgn. affairs cons. U.S. Army Inst. Land Combat, Washington, 1967-71; ret., 1971; TV commentator in documentaries on Japan occupation, Cineworld, BBC, NHK, 1987-91. Author: Japan's Political Revolution under MacArthur, 1979 (Japanese edit. 1989); also articles. Capt. USAAF, 1942-46. Recipient Outstanding Performance commendation Dept. Army, 1952, 53, Disting. Alumnus award U. Cen. Ark., 1991. Mem. Japanese Govt. Order of the Sacred Treasure, 1992. Home: 690 Bird Bay Dr W Venice FL 34292-4030

WILLIAMS, KAREN JOHNSON, federal judge; b. Orangeburg, S.C., Aug. 4, 1951; d. James G. Johnson and Marcia (Reynolds) Johnson Dantzler; m. Charles H. Williams, Dec. 27, 1968; children: Marian, Ashley, Charlie, David. BA, Columbia Coll., 1972; postgrad., U. S.C., 1973, JD cum laude, 1980. Bar: S.C. 1980, U.S. Dist. Ct. S.C. 1980, U.S. Ct. Appeals (4th cir.) 1981. Tchr. Irmo (S.C.) Mid. Sch., 1972-74, O-W High Sch., Orangeburg, 1974-76; assoc. Charles H. Williams P.A., Orangeburg, 1980-92; circuit judge U.S. Ct. Appeals (4th cir.), 1992—; mem. exec. bd. grievance commn. S.C. Supreme Ct., Columbia, 1983-92. Mem. child devel. bd. First Bapt. Ch., Orangeburg; bd. dirs. Orangeburg County Mental Retardation Bd., 1986-94, Orangeburg-Calhoun Hosp. Found.; bd. visitors Columbia Coll., 1988-92; dir. Reg. Med. Ctr. Hosp. Found., 1988-92; mem. adv. bd. Orangeburg-Calhoun Tech. Coll., 1987-92. Mem. ABA, Am. Judicature Soc., Fed. Judges Assn., S.C. Bar Assn., Orangeburg County Bar Assn. (co-chair Law Day 1981), S.C. Trial Lawyers Assn., Bus. and profl. Women Assn., Rotary, Order of Wig and Robe, Order of Coif. Home: 2503 Five Chop Rd Orangeburg SC 29115 Office: 1021 Middleton St Orangeburg SC 29115

WILLIAMS, KAREN OLIVIA, nurse manager, maternal/child health nurse; b. Alexandria, La., Nov. 23, 1959; d. Edward and Calian (Jacobs) W.; 1 child, Edward DeSean Marquis Williams. AS, La. State U., Alexandria, 1980; BS with honors, Northwestern State U., 1991. RN, La.; cert. ACLS, BLS, neonatal resusciation provider, PALS, TNCCP; cert. nurse oper. rm. Nurse ob.-gyn. Huey P. Long Med. Ctr., Pineville, La., 1980-83, nurse labor and delivery, 1983-87, charge nurse oper. rm., 1987-91, emergency rm. supr., 1992-94; maternal child health mgr., 1994—; nurse ARC, 1991. Mem. ANA, Assn. Women's Health Obstet. and Neonatal Nurses, La. Assn. Nurse Practitioners, La. Nurse Polit. Action Com., Emergency Nurse Assn., Assn. Oper. Rm. Nurses (cert., bd. dirs. 1991-92), La. State Nurses Assn. (polit. action com.), Alexandria Dist. Nurses Assn. (bd. dirs. 1992-93, pres. 1993-95), Sigma Theta Tau. Republican. Roman Catholic. Home: 107 Navaho Pl Pineville LA 71360-5931 Office: Huey P Long Med Ctr Hospital Blvd Pineville LA 71360

WILLIAMS, KARMEN PETERSEN, secondary school educator; b. Kansas City, Mo., Sept. 19, 1942; d. Hans Jorgen and Rosella Petersen; m. James Emmett Williams, Aug. 28, 1965; children: Jan Elizabeth Williams Parks, James Jorgen. BA in English, Okla. Bapt. U., 1964; MS in Edn., Ouachita Bapt. U., 1983. Cert. secondary tchr., reading specialist, K-12, Ark. Instr. English/reading Fern Creek H.S., Louisville, 1966-69; dir. kindergarten 1st Bapt. Ch., Texarkana, Ark., 1970-73; staff devel. specialist Divsn. Children & Family Svc., Pine Bluff, Ark., 1974-85; instr. English, speech, drama White Hall (Ark.) High Sch., 1985—, chairperson English dept., 1989—. Vol. Casa Women's Shelter, Pine Bluff, 1992—. Mem. MLA, Nat. Fedn. Interscholastic Speech & Debate Assn., Nat. Coun. Tchrs. English. Southern Baptist. Home: 517 E 7th St Little Rock AR 72202

WILLIAMS, KATHRYN SANDERS, elementary education administrator; b. Lexington, Ky., May 18, 1961; d. Gerald Louis and Donna Lee (Freeman) Sanders; m. R. Duane Williams, Jr., May 21, 1983; children: Bryan, Brad. BS in Elem. Edn., U. Louisville, 1983, M in Elem. Curriculum, 1990, rank I in ednl. adminstrn., 1995. Tchr. elem. sch. Indpls. Pub. Schs., 1984-85; tchr. mid. sch. Jefferson County Pub. Schs., Louisville, 1985-96; asst. prin. Mt. Washington (Ky.) Elem. Sch., 1996—. Vol. Talent Ctr. grantee, Louisville, 1990. Mem. ASCD, Ky. Assn. for Supervision and Curriculum Devel., Ky. Assn. Sch. Adminstrs., Ky. Edn. Assn., Nat. Assn. for Yr.-Round Edn., Ky. Assn. of Elem. Sch. Prins., Bullitt County Assn. of Sch. Adminstrs. Democrat. Roman Catholic. Home: 4319 Saratoga Hill Rd Jeffersontown KY 40299-8306 Office: Mt Washington Elem Sch 9234 Highway 44 E Mount Washington KY 40047-7309

WILLIAMS, KENNETH HOWARD, historical editor; b. Birmingham, Ala., Apr. 16, 1964; s. Elbert Taylor and Janelle (Mitchell) W.; m. Melinda Ann Tyler, Mar. 27, 1993. BA, Auburn U., 1985; MA, U. Ky., 1988. Rschr. The Papers of Henry Clay, U. Ky., Lexington, 1989-90, asst. editor, 1990-91; asst. editor The Papers of Jefferson Davis, Rice U., Houston, 1991-95, assoc. editor, 1995—. Editor: The Papers of Henry Clay, Vol. 10, 1991, supplement, 1992, The Papers of Jefferson Davis, Vol. 8, 1995, Vol. 9, 1997; rec. album One Accord, 1995. Mem. So. Hist. Assn., Assn. for Documentary Editing. Baptist. Office: Papers of Jefferson Davis Rice U MS 43 6100 Main St Houston TX 77005-1827

WILLIAMS, (ROBERT) KENT, artist; b. New Bern, N.C., Jan. 12, 1962; s. Robert Floyd and Janice Fay (May) W.; m. Sherilyn Van Valkenbugh, Dec. 7, 1985; 1 child, Kerig Sun. BFA, Pratt Inst., 1984. vis. instr. Pratt Inst., N.Y., 1987-89; lectr. Pratt Inst., 1987; lectr. and workshop No. Ariz. U., Flagstaff, 1989, Cleve. Inst. Art, Ohio, 1992. One-person shows include Gallery Americas, Carrboro, N.C., 1995; exhibited in group shows including Jack Meier Gallery, Houston, 1987, No. Ariz. U. Art Mus. and Galleries, 1989, 91, Soc. Illustrators, N.Y.C., 1984-94, Bess Cutler Gallery, N.Y.C., 1993, San Jose State U., Calif., 1993, Four Color Images Gallery, N.Y.C., 1993-94; represented in permanent collections No. Ariz. U. Art Mus. and Galleries; represented in pvt. collections U.S., Eng., France, Germany, Japan; artist (with Dematteis) Blood: a tale, 1987, 88, 89, (with Muth, Walter and Louise Simonson) Meltdown, 1989, 90, Kent Williams: Drawings and Monotypes, 1991, (with Wagner, Rieber) Tell Me, Dark, 1992; illustrator for numerous publs. nationally and internationally including Playboy, Omni and Penguin Books. Recipient Silver Medal award Soc. Illustrators, 1985, 96, The Yellow Kid and Torre Gunigi award, Italy, 1990, Best in Show Joseph Morgan Henninger award Illustration West 32, 1993. Home: 102 Sidney Grn Chapel Hill NC 27516-9038

WILLIAMS, KRISTINA (MICHELLE SPURRIER), executive secretary; b. Hagerstown, Md., Oct. 10, 1965; d.; d. Michael Keenan and Patricia Salome (Summers) Spurrier; m. George Scott Williams, Aug. 4, 1990; 1 child, Aston Tyler. AA, Prince George's C.C., Largo, Md., 1985. Cert. profl. sec. Sec. Price Waterhouse, Washington, 1986-89; adminstrv. asst. Encore Mktg. Internat., Lanham, Md., 1989-90, exec. sec., 1991-92; adminstrv. asst. to city mgr. City of Beaufort, S.C., 1990-91; exec. sec. Beaufort County Parks and Leisure Svcs., Beaufort, 1992-95. Mem. Officers' Wives Club, Beaufort, 1990-95, Key Vols., USMC, Beaufort, 1992-95. Mem. Acad. Profl. Sec., Profl. Secs. Internat. (at-large). Home: 306 Jodeco Station Cir Stockbridge GA 30281

WILLIAMS, LA RONNIA VERNON DOBSON, retired educator, news correspondent, educational consultant; b. Kansas City, Mo., July 28, 1934; d. Arthur Burkes and Mary (Briscoe) Vernon; adopted parents: William Augustus and Gladys (Martin) Dobson; m. Elmo Green Jr., July 1956 (div. June 1970); children: Ruth Annette Sims, Patricia Griffin, Gladys Faye Haile, Elmo Green III; m. Franklin Don Williams, Mar. 24, 1973. BA, Spelman Coll., 1955; MA, Atlanta U., 1960; postgrad., U. Md., Annapolis, 1974-76; MA, Valdosta State Coll., 1980. Tchr. Telfair County Bd. Edn., Lumber City, Ga., 1955-65; tch. spl. edn. Telfair County Bd. Edn., McRae, Ga., 1965-70, Atlanta City Schs. Bd. Edn., 1970-73; tchr. learning disabilities, dept. head Anne Arundel County Bd. Edn., Ft. Meade, Md., 1973-77; tchr. learning disabilities, secondary math, English Valdosta (Ga.) City Schs. Bd. Edn., 1977-90; tchr. math. Valwood Pvt. Sch., Valdosta, 1991—; co-owner, dir. Valdosta Reading Clinic., Valdosta, Lowndes, Ga., 1986-88; workshop dir., presenter Valdosta City Schs. and Valdosta State Coll., 1985—; dept. head Valdosta Jr. High Sch., 1978-81. Weekly columnist, corr. Valdosta Daily Times, 1989—. Vol. instr. Camp Relitso Cmty. Learning Ctr., Valdosta, 1979—; bd. dirs., treas., charter mem. Adoption Svcs.-Children with Spl. Needs South Ga., 1988—; choir pres., clk., Bible sch. dir. St. James Missionary Bapt. Ch., Valdosta, 1981—; coord., com. mem. Census Edn. Project, 1990; chmn. Martin L. King Commemoration, 1990—; mem. Valdosta/Lowndes County Theater Guild, 1988—; bd. dirs. 1991—, v.p. 2000 Partnership; bd. dirs. Conv. and Visitors Bur., 1995; clk. election polls, 1990—; mem. Lowndes/Valdosta PAC, others; mem. Olympic Flag Celebration Com. for 1996 Olympic Games, Atlanta, 1992—. Recipient Congl. Citation/Civic Svc., U.S. Ga. Congressman, 1983, Proclamation Mayor of Valdosta, 1983, citations for Outstanding Svc. Vols. Pub. Schs., 1981-89, Intellectual Freedom award Ga. Libr. Media Assn., 1991; named Tchr. of Yr., Telfair County Tchrs. and Edn. Assn., 1971, to Ga. Tchr. Hall of Fame in State Capitol, Ga. Assn. Educators, 1987, Educator of Yr., Black Hist. Action Soc., 1989, Woman of Achievement S.E. dist. Bus. and Profl. Women, 1990, Mother of Yr., Community Bapt. Ch., 1976, Progressive Citizen of Yr., Citizens in Action, 1983, Citizen Amb. USSR People to People Internat., 1990-91, Valdosta Woman of Yr. Valdosta Jr. Women's Club, 1991. Mem. NEA, AAUW (br. v.p. 1987-89, br. pres. 1989—, state divsn. chairperson-elections 1988-89, chairperson state divsn. internat. rels., regional leadership trainer 1988—, nat. diversity trainer 1989—, Ga. Program v.p., 1992-94, Ga. pres.-elect 1994-96, Ga. pres. 1996), Assn. Bus. and Profl. Women, Ga. Libr. Media Assn., Social Issues Resources Series, Telfair County Tchrs. Assn. (sec., v.p., pres. 1955-72), Valdosta Assn. of Educators (v.p., pres., chairperson 1982-86), Ga. Assn. Educators (chairperson women's concerns 1988-90, lobbyist and moderator fo r legis. forums 1979—), South Ga. Coun. Exceptional Children (sec.-treas. 1983, v.p., pres. 1989-90), Ga. Coun. Exceptional Children (named direct svc. tchr. of yr. 1987), Internat. Reading Assn., Valdosta-Lowndes Black Action Com. (Educator of Yr. 1990), Valdosta/Lowndes County Mental Health Assn. (bd. dirs.), Delta Sigma Theta Sorority, Inc. (alumnae, Disting. Soror of Yr. 1990). Democrat. Home: 505 New Hudson St Valdosta GA 31601-6144

WILLIAMS, LARRY BILL, academic administrator; b. Cushing, Okla., June 9, 1945; s. Louis Albert and Morene Ruth (Cox) W.; m. Pam Bryan, May 1, 1993; children: Natalie Michelle, Nicole Diane, Louis Bradley, Sharla Dianne Bryan, Vanessa Joy Bryan. BS, Cen. State U., Edmond, Okla., 1967, MBA, 1972; PhD, U. Okla., 1985. Office mgr. Okla. State U., Stillwater, 1967-69; asst. comptroller Cen. State U., Edmond, 1969-71, dir. affirmative action, 1971-72, assoc. dir. univ. personnel services, 1971-72, dir. affirmative action, 1972-80, dir. univ. personnel services, 1972-80, asst. v.p. adminstrn., 1980-84, v.p. adminstrn., 1984-87; interim pres. Southeastern Okla. State U., Durant, 1987, pres., 1987—; managerial cons. various municipalities; mktg. cons. State of Okla.; arbitrator Met. Fraternal Order of Police; bd. dirs. Okla. Small Bus. Devel. Ctr., 1987—, Okla. Acad. State Goals, 1992—, southeast region chmn. 1995. Bd. dirs. Bryan County Econ. Devel. Corp., 1989—, Bryan County United Way, 1988-94; mem. adv. bd. Med. Ctr. Southeastern Okla., 1987-92; bd. dirs. Bryan County Ret. Sr. Vol. Program, 1990-92, Leadership Okla. Class IV, 1991, mem. adv. bd., 1991-95; mem. exec. bd. Boy Scouts Am., 1991; com. mem. Okla. Ctr. for Advancement Sci. and Tech. Long Range Planning Task Force, Most Eminent Scholars and Rsch. Equipment, 1990-91; mem. higher edn. alumni coun. Okla. State Regent for Higher Edn. Tuition Com., budget com., outreach com., quality initiative com., capital com., chmn. legis. affairs com., 1995; mem. adv. coun. Ea. Okla. Schs., 1987—; trustee Southeastern Found., 1990—; past pres. Kickingbird Golf Course Mgmt., Edmond; bd. dirs. Edmond C. of C., 1984; mem. Okla. State Regents for Higher Edn. Coun. of Pres., 1987—, chair, 1994; Chocktaw Nation of Okla. JTPA Adv. Coun., 1987—; mem. Okla. Regional Pres.' Coun., 1987—, chair, 1994; vice chmn. Diamond Jubilee Commn., Edmond; mem. found. bd. trustees Ctrl. State U., Edmond; mem. adv. com. Durant Airport. With USNG, 1962-70. Named One of Outstanding Young Men of Am., Edmond Jaycees, 1971, 74, 79; recipient Presdl. Leadership award Nat. U.S. Jaycee Pres., 1971, Presdl. Leadership, Achievement and Honor awards Nat. Jaycees, 1972, Nat. Presdl. award of Honor Nat. Coll. and Univ. Pers. Assn., 1973, Disting. Svc. award City of Edmond, 1974, Dwight F. Whelan Meml. award for Outstanding Leadership, Edmond, 1972; named to Cushing Alumni Hall of Fame, 1988, recipient Nat. Order Omega (charter hon. mem), 1991. Mem. Okla. Assn. Coll. and Univ. Pers. Adminstrs. (founder, bd. dirs., chmn.), Nat. Coll. and Univ. Pers. Assn., Nat. Coll. and Univ. Bus. Officers Assn., Okla. Assn. Affirmative Action (co-founder, pres., bd. dirs.), Okla. City Pers. Assn. , Am. Assn. State Colls. and Univs., Okla. Assn. Coll. and Univ. Bus. Officers (bd. dirs., pres.), Acad. Cert. Adminstrv. Mgrs., Okla. Small Bus. Devel. Ctr. (bd. dirs. 1987—), Industry Ednl. Coun. McCurtain County, Okla. Acad. for State Goals (bd. dirs. 1992—, vice chair S.E. region 1995), Okla. Advocates for Arts and Humanities (steering com. 1995), Durant C. of C. (past pres., bd. dirs.), Okla. State C. of C. (bd. dirs. 1991—), Blue Key, Rotary. Democrat. Presbyterian. Lodge: Rotary (sec. Edmond club 1986-87). Office: Southeastern Okla State U Office of Pres Durant OK 74701*

WILLIAMS, LAWRENCE CARROLL, data processing executive; b. Benton, Ark., June 11, 1934; s. Henry Pascal and Maurine (Slaughter) W.; m. Mary Lee Carter, June 3, 1954. BEd, U. Miami, 1960; MA, U. Denver, 1966. Electronic technician Boeing Airplane Co., Seattle/Wichita, 1954-59, Convair div. Gen. Dynamics, Ft. Worth, Tex., 1960-61; tchr. history Dade County (Fla.) Pub. Schs., Miami, 1961-67, Jefferson (Colo.) High Sch., 1967-68; prof. history and econs. Arapahoe Community Coll., Littleton, Colo., 1968-89; owner C&M Data Svcs., Tallahassee, Fla., 1990—. With USAF, 1951-54. Coe Found. fellow, 1962. Mem. Tallahassee C. of C. Methodist. Home and Office: C&M Data Svcs 6516 War Admiral Trl Tallahassee FL 32308-1753

WILLIAMS, LENA HARDING, English language educator; b. Portsmouth, Va., June 12, 1947; d. Arthur McKinley and Mildred (Smith) Harding; m. Leroy Stephen Williams, July 8, 1966; children: Michael LaMar, Darryl LaVon Stephen LaSean. AB in English Edn. and Speech, Norfolk State U., 1969; postgrad., U. Va., 1972-73, Norfolk State U., 1987, Old Dominion U., 1973-88; MS in Ednl. Adminstrn., Old Dominion U., 1993. Cert. 7-12 English and speech tchr., mid. sch. and h.s. prin., collegiate profl., Va. English tchr. S.H. Clarke Sch. Portsmouth Schs., 1969-70, English tchr., W.E. Waters Sch., 1970-71, English tchr., Churchland Mid. Sch., 1971-74, English dept. chmn., 1974-86, 88—; fieldtester Va. Standards of Learning Lang. Arts; tchr./trainer Portsmouth Schs., 1986-88, lead mentor tchr., 1990—; presenter SAT prep. workshop, New-Tchr. Insvc., Writing Across the Curriculum, Reading to Learn, Technology in the Classroom. Active Hodges Manor Civic League, Portsmouth, 1985—, PTA; dir. Christian edn., summer camp youth adv., coord. vol. tutorial svc., mem. sr. choir, usher, coord. youth activities, mem. ch. coun., bd. dir. kindegarten, Edna Hyke Corbett Achievement award found.; coord. Multiple Sclerosis Read-a-Thon, Back to Sch. Seminar; community campaign vol. Mother's March, Am. Cancer Soc., Muscular Dystrophy, Am. Heart Assn.; co-sponsor Cavalier Manor Deep Doubles Tennis Tounament. Named State Tchr. of Yr., State Bd. Edn., Richmond, Va., 1992, Outstanding Young Educator, Portsmouth Jaycees, 1978; recipient 25 svc. and honor awards from local orgns. Fellow Hampton Rds Inst. for Advanced Study of Teaching; mem. ASCD, NEA, NAACP, Va. Edn. Assn., Nat. State Tchrs. of Yr. Assn., Va. State Secondary Reading Assn., Va. Congress English Teachers, Va. Assn. Tchrs. of English, Portsmouth Edn. Assn., Portsmouth Reading Coun.,Tidewater Assn. Tchrs. English, Hampton Roads Inst. for the Advanced Study of Teaching, Delta Sigma Theta. Democrat. Home: 801 Nottingham Rd Portsmouth VA 23701-2118 Office: Churchland Mid Sch 4051 River Shore Rd Portsmouth VA 23703-2001

WILLIAMS, LOIS ANN, secondary and elementary education educator; b. Yonkers, N.Y., Sept. 12, 1956; m. James Michael Williams; Mar. 30, 1986. BA in Elem. Edn., SUNY, Plattsburgh, 1978; MEd in Curriculum, U. Va., 1981, EdS in Math Edn., 1991, EdD in Curriculum, 1997—. Tchr. Albemarle County Schs., Charlottesville, Va., 1980-93; math specialist K-12 Albemarle County Schs., 1993—. Jesse Ball DuPont fellow U. Va., 1991; Fulbright scholar, Scotland, 1982. Mem. Jefferson Coun. Tchrs. of Math. (pres. 1992). Office: Albemarle County Schs 401 McIntire Rd Charlottesville VA 22901

WILLIAMS, LUTHER STEWARD, science foundation administrator; b. Sawyerville, Ala., Aug. 19, 1940; s. Roosevelt and Mattie B. (Wallace) W.; m. Constance Marie Marion, Aug. 23, 1963; children: Mark Steward, Monique Marie. BA magna cum laude, Miles Coll., 1961; MS, Atlanta U., 1963; PhD, Purdue U., 1968, DSc (hon.), 1987; DSc (hon.), U. Louisville, 1992. NSF lab. asst. Spelman Coll., 1961-62; NSF lab. asst. Atlanta U., 1962-63, instr. biology, faculty rsch. grantee, 1963-64, asst. prof. biology, 1969-70, prof. biology, 1984-87, pres., 1984-87; grad. tchg. asst. Purdue U., West Lafayette, Ind., 1964-65, grad. rsch. asst., 1965-66, asst. prof. biology, 1970-73, assoc. prof., 1973-79, prof., 1979-80, NIH Career Devel. awardee, 1971-75, asst. provost, 1976-80; dean Grad. Sch., prof. biology Washington U., St. Louis, 1980-83; v.p. acad. affairs, dean Grad. Sch. U. Colo., Boulder, 1983-84; Am. Cancer Soc. postdoctoral fellow SUNY-Stony Brook, 1968-69; assoc. prof. biology MIT, 1973-74; spl. asst. to dir. Nat. Inst. Gen. Med. Scis., NIH, Bethesda, Md., 1987-88; dep. dir. Nat. Inst. Gen. Med. Scis. NIH, Bethesda, 1988-89; sr. sci. advisor to dir. NSF, Washington, 1989-90, asst. dir. for edn. and human resources, 1990—; chmn. rev. com. MARC Program, Nat. Inst. Gen. Med. Scis., NIH, 1972-76; grant reviewer NIH, 1971-73, 76, NSF 1973, 76-80, Med. Research Council of N.Z., 1976; mem. life scis. sreening com. recombinant DNA adv. com. HEW, 1979-81; mem. nat. adv. gen. med. sci. council NIH, 1980-85; mem. adv. com. Office Tech. Assessment, Washington, 1984-87; chmn. fellowship adv. com. NRC Ford

Found., 1984-85; mem.-at-large Grad. Record Exam. Bd., 1981-85, chmn. minority grad. edn. com., 1983-85; mem. health, safety and environ. affairs. com. Nat. Labs., U. Calif., 1981-87; mem. adv. panel Office Tech. Assessment, U.S. Congress, 1985-86; mem. fed. task force on women, minorities and the handicapped in sci. and tech., 1987-91; mem. adv. panel to dir. sci. and tech. ctrs. devel. NSF, 1987-88; mem. nat. adv. com. White House Initiative on Historically Black Colls. and Univs. on Sci. and Tech., 1986-89; numerous other adv. bds. and coms. Contbr. sci. articles to profl. jours. Vice chmn. bd. advisors Atlanta Neighborhood Justice Ctr., 1984-87; bd. dirs. Met. Atlanta United Way, 1986-87, Butler St. YMCA, Atlanta, 1985-87; trustee Atlanta Zool. Assn., 1985-87, Miles Coll., 1984-87, Atlanta U., 1984-87, 90-96; mem. nominating com. Dana Found. NIH predoctoral fellow Purdue U., 1966-68. Fellow AAAS, Am. Acad. Microbiology; mem. Am. Soc. Microbiology, Am. Chem. Soc., Am. Soc. Biol. Chemists (mem. ednl. affairs com. 1979-82, com. on equal opportunities for minorities 1972-84), AAAS, N.Y. Acad. Scis. Home: 11608 Split Rail Ct Rockville MD 20852-4423 Office: NSF Education & Human Resources 4201 Wilson Blvd Arlington VA 22230-1803

WILLIAMS, LYLE KEITH, federal agency administrator; b. Glencoe, Okla., Feb. 11, 1915; s. Frank Lee and Ana (McGuire) W.; m. Jean Emma Batchelor, Sept. 28, 1941; children: Dan Batchelor, David Neal. Grad. high sch., Newkirk, Okla. Various positions U.S. Civil Service (War Dept.), 1946-75; numerous com. assignments; ret. Regional Commr. FSS Gen. Svcs. Adminstrn. Author: Matthew Williams of Wethersfield, Conn., The Batchelor Family, The Lane-Robertson Families, Joseph Jackson Genealogy, The Stovall Family and Related Lines, 2 vols., The Batchelor-Williams Families and Related Lines. V.p. Tarrant Co., Tex. United Way, Ft. Worth, 1973. Methodist. Home: 5000 Rock River Dr Fort Worth TX 76103-1226

WILLIAMS, M. JANE, marketing and sales executive; b. Salem, Ohio, Aug. 17, 1955; d. Robert Angus and Mary Elizabeth (Riddle) W.; 1 child, Landon Matthew Betsworth; m. Wyman A. Rousseau. BSBA, Youngstown State U., 1984. Lic. real estate broker, N.C. Corp. acct. Westminster Co., Greensboro, N.C., 1984-86; market analyst Zaremba Coms. N.C., Inc., 1986; sales mgr. Stonehaven Zaremba, Winston-Salem, N.C., 1987; sales and mktg. mgr. Laurel Brook at Adams Farm and Windsor Park R&D Homes, Inc., Greensboro, 1987-88, Westminster Co., Greensboro, 1988-90; dir. mktg. East West Ptnrs. Mgmt. Co., Chapel Hill, N.C., 1990-94; divsn. mktg. mgr. Centex Crosland Homes, Charlotte, N.C., 1996—. Mem. NAFE (dir. Charlotte chpt.), Profl. Women's Consortium (bd. dirs., pres. elect 1987, pres. 1988-89), Nat. Assn. Homebuilders (chmn. sales and mktg. coun. 1989), North Charlotte Profl. Women (founder). Unitarian Universalist. Home: 9241 Heritage Woods Pl Charlotte NC 28269-0300

WILLIAMS, MARC H., electroencephalography technologist; b. L.A., Mar. 31, 1952; s. Edward S. and Florence R. (Fisher) W.; m. Rebecca L. May, May 29, 1976 (div. 1980); 1 child, James S.; m. Corinne A. Woolley, June 17, 1989; 1 child, Matthew J. B in Vocat. Edn., Calif. State U., Long Beach, 1992. Reg. EEG technologist, 1976. Hosp. corpsman USN, 1969-77; dept. mgr. Mansfield (Ohio) Gen. Hosp., 1977-78; rsch. technologist UCLA-NPI, L.A., 1978-83; EEG technologist Long Beach Meml. Med. Ctr., 1983-88, dept. mgr., 1988-93; mgr. clin. neurophysiology svcs. Med. Univ. of S.C., Charleston, 1994—; cons. Electroneuronisgnostics, 1988—; exec. com. Am. Soc. of ELectro-Neurodiagnostic Technologists, 1983—. adj. instr. Orange Coast Coll., 1984. With USN, 1969-77, tech. sgt. ANG, 1980-89. Mem. Am. Soc. of Electro-Neurodiagnostic Technologists (bd. trustees 1983-85, v. p. 1987-89, 1991-93), am. EEG Soc., Western Soc. EEG Technologists (nominating chair, 1972-76, 1985-92), S.C. END Soc. (pres 1995-97), So. EEG Soc. (mem. 1994, pres-elect 1996). Democrat. Home: 1239 Center Lake Dr Mount Pleasant SC 29464-7419 Office: Med Univ S C Clin Neurophysiology Svcs 171 Ashley Ave Charleston SC 29425-0001

WILLIAMS, MARCUS DOYLE, judge; b. Nashville, Oct. 24, 1952; s. John Freelander and Pansy (Doyle) W.; m. Carmen Myrie, May 21, 1983; children: Aaron Doyle, Adam Myrie. BA with honors, Fisk U., 1973; JD, Cath. U. of Am., 1977. Bar: Va. 1977, D.C. 1978. Asst. commonwealth's atty. County of Fairfax, Fairfax, Va., 1978-80; asst. county atty. County of Fairfax, Faifax, Va., 1980-87; dist. ct. judge 19th Jud. Dist., Va., 1987-90; judge 19th Jud. Cir., Va., 1990—; lectr. bus. legal studies George Mason U., Fairfax, 1980—; instr. pvt. investigators North Va. Community Coll., Fairfax, 1979; mem. Fairfax Criminal Justice Adv. Bd., 1980-86; faculty advisor Nat. Jud. Coll., 1991, faculty, 1992—; Am. participant lectr. for USIA, 1990; lectr. George Mason U. Law Sch., 1987. Book reviewer for ABA Jour., 1981-84; contbr. articles to legal jours. Recipient Cert. Appreciation for Outstanding Svc. Burke-Fairfax Jack & Jill; Thomas J. Watson Found. fellow, 1977. Mem. ABA (chair subcom. Victims of Crimes), Fairfax Bar Assn. (CLE com., vice chmn. 1986-87), Am. Bus. Law Assn., Am. Judges Assn., Phi Alpha Delta, Beta Kappa Chi, Omega Psi Phi. Methodist. Office: Cir Ct 4110 Chain Bridge Rd Fairfax VA 22030-4009

WILLIAMS, MARGARET LU WERTHA HIETT, nurse; b. Midland, Tex., Aug. 30, 1938; d. Cotter Craven and Mollie Jo (Tarter) Hiett; m. James Troy Lary, Nov. 16, 1960 (div. Jan. 1963); 1 child, James Cotter; m. Tuck Williams, Aug. 11, 1985. BS, Tex. Woman's U., 1960; MA, Tchrs. Coll., N.Y.C., 1964, EdM, 1974, doctoral studies, 1981; postgrad., U. Tex., 1991-92, U. Wis.; cert. completion, U. Wis., Scotland. Cert. clin. nurse specialist, advanced practice nurse; cert. psychiat./mental health nurse, nursing continuing edn. and staff devel. Nurse Midland Meml. Hosp., 1960-63; instr. Odessa (Tex.) Coll., 1963-67; dir. ADNP Laredo (Tex.) Jr. Coll., 1967-70; asst. prof. Pan Am. U., Edinburgh, Tex., 1970-72; rsch. asst. Tchrs. Coll., 1973-74; nursing practitioner St. Luke's Hosp., N.Y.C., 1975-79; sgt. Burns Security, Midland, 1979-81; with Area Builders, Odessa, 1981-83; field supr. We Care Home Health Agy., Midland, 1983-87; clin. educator, supr. Glenwood, A Psychiat. Hosp., Midland, 1987-92; dir. nursing Charter Healthcare Systems, Corpus Christi, Tex., 1992-93; RN III Brown Sch., San Marcos, Tex., 1993—; owner MTW Nursing Consultation, Lockhart, Tex., 1996—, Margaret Hiett Williams RN, CNS, Lockhart, Tex., 1996—; co-owner, operator MTW Med. Legal Cons.; adj. prof. Pace U., 1974-75, S.W. Tex. State U., 1995. Mem. Gov. Richards' Exec. Leadership Coun., 1991-95, re-election steering com., 1994. Recipient Isabelle Hampton-Robb award Nat. League for Nursing, 1976, Achievement award Community Leaders of Am., 1989, Ladies 1st of Midland, 1974. Mem. NAFE, ANA, Tex. Nurses Assn. (pres. dist. 21 1962-65, dist. 32 1970-72), Am. Psychiat. Nurses Assn., Parkland Meml. Hosp. Nurses Alumnae Assn., Tex. Women's U. Alumnae Assn., Midland H.S. Alumni, Bus. and Profl. Women's Club, Mensa, Lockhart Breakfast Lions Club. Democrat. Office: PO Box 324 Lockhart TX 78644

WILLIAMS, MARILYN, health care organization executive; b. Ashland, Ky., July 28, 1950; d. Charley Thurman and Wilma Margaret (Burke) W. BS, Queens Coll., 1971; MS, U. Ala., Birmingham, 1977. Diplomate Am. Coll. Healthcare Execs. Asst. biochemist So. Research Inst., Birmingham, 1972-75; asst. exec. dir. Jefferson County Med. Soc., Birmingham, 1977-78; dir. project rev. Birmingham Regional Health Systems Agy., 1978-80; v.p. planning and regulation Miss. Hosp. Assn., Jackson, 1980-82; v.p. planning, regulation and data Miss. Hosp. Assn., 1982-85; coord. for corp. planning Commn. on Profl. and Hosp. Activities, Ann Arbor, Mich., 1986-89, chief oper. officer, 1990-91; dir. ops. Vis. Nurse Assn., Birmingham, Ala., 1991-93; pres. Future Health Concepts, Birmingham, 1994—; wellness and prevention specialist Choice Behavioral Health Partnership, Birmingham, 1996—; wellness and prevention specialist Choice Behavioral Health Partnership. Contbr. articles to profl. jours. Mem. allocations com. United Way, Jackson, 1985; bd. dirs. Modern Dance Collective, Jackson, 1985; commr. for Housing Authority for Birmingham Dist.; chairperson Magic City Harvest, 1993-94; bd. dirs. A Baby's Place, 1994-95, Positive Maturity, 1994. Richards Co. scholar, 1970; named an Outstanding Young Women of Am., 1974, Woman of Yr. Jackson Bus. and Profl. Women's Club, 1984; recipient Commendation award VA, 1977. Mem. Am. Hosp. Assn., Soc. Hosp. Planning and Mktg., U. Ala. Alumni Assn. Grad. Program in Hosp. and Health Adminstrn., Birmingham Area C. of C. (chair health svcs. com. 1996). Democrat. Home: 1508-G 33rd St S Birmingham AL 35205-2142 Office: Future Health Concepts PO Box 130716 Birmingham AL 35213-0716

WILLIAMS, MARK ANTHONY, minister; b. Morristown, Tenn., Jan. 5, 1957; s. Robert Burl Williams and Betty Lois (Pinkston) W.; m. Deborah Ann Walker, Dec. 27, 1980; children: Brett Anthony, Kasey Ann. BS, Carson Newman Coll., 1979; MDiv, Southwestern Bapt. Theol. Sem., 1983; postgrad., Luther Rice Sem., 1991—. Ordained to ministry So. Bapt. Conv., 1982. Pastor Happy Hills Bapt. Ch., Alvarado, Tex., 1982-85, Blue Springs Bapt. Ch., Rutledge, Tenn., 1985-88, New Hopewell Bapt. Ch., Knoxville, Tenn., 1988-96, Rock Hill Bapt. Ch., Inman, S.C., 1996—. Office: Rock Hill Baptist Church 511 Edwards Rd Inman SC 29349

WILLIAMS, MARK LEON, medical educator, researcher; b. Portsmouth, Va., July 25, 1953; s. Marvin L. and Kathleen J. (Clements) W. BGS, U. Iowa, 1976, PhD, 1983; MA, U. Nebr.-Lincoln, 1979. Asst. prof. U. St. Thomas, Houston, 1983-87; v.p. rsch. Affiliated Systems Corp., Houston, 1987-94; v.p. for behavioral rsch. NOVA Rsch. Co., Bethesda, Md., 1994—; adj. assoc. prof. U. Miami Sch. Medicine, Miami, Fla., 1994—, U. Tex. Sch. Pub. Health, Houston, 1996—; bd. dirs. HIV adv. bd. Dept. Health, Houston, 1992-94; mem. adv. bd. Good Neighbor Health Clinic, Houston, 1992-94; peer reviewer Am. Jour. Pub. Health, N.Y.C., 1994—. Contbr. book chpts., articles to profl. jours. Recipient Nat. Inst. Drug Abuse grant, 1986, 92, 95. Mem. APHA, Soc. for Prevention Rsch. Office: NOVA Rsch Co 4600 East West Hwy Bethesda MD 20814-3415

WILLIAMS, MARK MASON, engineering educator, consultant; b. Paris, Tenn., Aug. 2, 1960; s. Bobby Mason and Martha Faye (Throgmorton) W.; m. Kerri Linn Reed, July 2, 1982; 1 child, Laura Elizabeth. BS in Engring. Tech., Memphis State U., 1982, MS in Tech. Edn., 1984. Asst. prof. dept. engring. technology U. Memphis, 1984—; cons. indsl. controls, Productive Syss., Inc., Memphis, 1987-94, other cos. Memphis area, 1994—. Mem. Am. Soc. Engring. Edn. (newsletter editor, vice chmn. engring. technology divsn. S.E. sect. 1988-91), Soc. Mfg. Engrs. Office: U Memphis Dept Engring Central Ave Memphis TN 38152

WILLIAMS, MARSHA RHEA, computer scientist, educator, researcher, consultant; b. Memphis, Aug. 4, 1948; d. James Edward and Velma Lee (Jenkins) W.; BS, Beloit Coll., 1969; MS in Physics, U. Mich., 1971; MS in Systems and Info. Sci., Vanderbilt U., 1976, PhD in Computer Sci., 1982. Cert. data processing (CDP). Engring. coop. student Lockheed Missiles & Space Co., Sunnyvale, Calif., 1967-68; asst. transmission engr. Ind. Bell Telephone Co., Indpls., 1971-72; systems analyst, instr. physics Memphis State U., 1972-74; computer-assisted instrn. project programmer Fisk U., 1974-76; mem. tech. staff Hughes Rsch. Labs., Malibu, Calif., 1976-78; assoc. systems engr. IBM, Nashville, 1978-80; rsch. and teaching asst. Vanderbilt U., Nashville, 1980-82, spl. asst. to dean Grad. Sch., spring 1981, minority engr. advisor, 1975-76; cons. computer-assisted instrn. project Meharry Med. Coll., Nashville, summer 1982; assoc. prof. computer sci. Tenn. State U., Nashville, 1982-83, 84-90, full, tenured prof., 1990—, univ. marshal, 1992—; assoc. prof. U. Miss., Oxford, 1983-84, faculty senator; assoc. program dir. Applications of Advanced Techs. Sci. and Engring. Edn., NSF, 1987-88, apptd. USRA Sci. and Engring. Edn. Coun., Advanced Design Program, 1992-94; cons. on minority scientists and engrs. Univ. Space Rsch. Assn., Washington, 1988; vis. scientist CSNET-Minority Instn. Networking Project Bolt, Beranek & Newman, Cambridge, Mass., 1989; mem. tech. staff Bell Communications Rsch., Red Bank, N.J., 1990; presenter papers profl. meetings. Editor-in-chief newspaper Pilgrim Emanuel Bapt. Ch., 1975-76; adv. Chi Rho Youth Fellowship, Temple Bapt. Ch., 1975-81, adv. com. Golden Outreach Sr. Citizens Fellowship, 1979-80, 86-87, 89-93, Women's Day speaker, 1979, 81, Ebenezer Missionary Bapt. Ch., 1993; adviser Nat. Soc. Black Engring. Students, 1983-84; founder, coord. Tenn. State U. Assn. for Excellence in Computer Sci., Math. and Physics (AE-COMP), 1986-87, coord. Tech. Opportunites Fair, 1986, 87; dir. Tenn. State U. Minorities in Sci., Engring. & Tech. Rsch. Project-MISET, 1989—; child sponsor World Vision, 1981—; mem., newsletter staff Lake Providence Missionary Bapt. Ch. Recipient Disting. Instr. award 1984, Disting. Svc. citation Beloit Coll. Alumni Assn., 1994; grantee Digital Equipment Corp., 1989-92; faculty rsch. grantee Tenn. State U., 1993, 94. Mem. NAACP (nat. judge ACT-SO sci. olympics 1992), Assn. Computing Machinery, Data Processing Mgmt. Assn. (edn. chmn., bd. dirs. 1986), Tenn. Acad. Sci., Phi Kappa Phi. Achievements include founding Assn. for Excellence in Computer Sci., Math., and Physics, research in database, network and human-computer interfacing for broadening minority participation in science, engineering and technology, research on a general theory of completeness. Home: PO Box 270093 Nashville TN 37227-0093 Office: Tenn State U Dept Computer Sci PO Box 136 Nashville TN 37203-3401

WILLIAMS, MARVIN, management consultant; b. St. Petersburg, Fla., May 23, 1944; s. Early and Valeria Lee (Wilcox) W.; m. Margaret Davis, May 12, 1944 (div. June 1974); m. Rena Joseph, Dec. 23, 1949; children: Tracey Yvette, Courtney Berrien J., Yolan Yasmin J. BS in Comml. Industries, Tuskegee U., 1967. Assemblyman E-A Indsl. Corp., Atlanta, 1970-72; system engr. devel. Electronic Data Systems Corp., Atlanta, 1972-74; shop mgr. H. Salt Fish and Chips, Atlanta, 1974-75; data preparation mgr. Electronic Data Systems Ga., 1975-76; claims processing mgr. Title XIX pharm. program Electronic Data Systems N.C., 1976-77, provider svc. mgr. Title XIX Medicaid program, 1977-78, adminstrn. dir. Title XIX Medicaid program, 1978-79; systems engr., indsl. engr. Electronic Data Systems Corp., Dallas, 1979-83; indsl. engring. mgr., cons. Electronic Data Systems Corp., Plano, 1983-96; v.p., gen. mgr. WESTCORP, 1996—. With U.S. Army, 1967-70, Vietnam. Decorated Bronze Star. Democrat. Baptist. Home: 602 Bush Dr Allen TX 75002-1546

WILLIAMS, MARY ELEANOR NICOLE, writer; b. Atlanta, May 14, 1938; d. Edward King Merrell and Bernice I. (Pitts) Smith; m. Charlie Lloyd Williams, July 25, 1993; children: Mary Palmer, Susan Gober, Traci Cox. Student, Fla. Jr. Coll., 1974. Lic. real estate broker, Fla. Editor, writer, former owner Southwestern Advt. and Pub., Carrollton, Ga., 1991-94; freelance writer children's stories, 1992—. Author, editor: West Georgia Area Guide, 1991-93. Mem. Carroll County C. of C. Home: 103 Ferndale Rd Carrollton GA 30117-4312

WILLIAMS, MARY ELMORE, English language and history educator, educational administrator; b. San Angelo, Tex., Sept. 19, 1931; d. Taylor and Florrine (Gee) Elmore; m. Mark B. Williams, Sept. 6, 1951; children: John Mark, Mary Jean. AA, San Angelo Coll., 1950; BS, Tex. Christian U., 1951; MS, Corpus Christi State U., 1983; postgrad. U. Chgo., 1954, Princeton U., 1961, Mansfield Coll., Oxford U., 1966. Tchr. 1st grade First Methodist Ch., Dallas, 1951-52; tchr. 8th grade Pleasant Grove Jr. High, Dallas, 1952-54; tchr. Bible Ray High Sch., Corpus Christi, 1957, tchr. history Hamlin Jr. High Sch., 1958; tchr. 6th grade St. Christopher's Episcopal Sch., Lubbock, Tex., 1968; tchr. English and history Hamlin Jr. High, Corpus Christi, 1974—, asst. prin., 1989—; coord. Adopt-a-School Program, 1983—; organizer of Vet.'s Day Patriotic Rally; cons. KEDT-TV Tex. History series The Lone Star, Corpus Christi, 1984-85; cons. textbook com. Corpus Christi Ind. Sch. Dist., 1983, 86, mem. curriculum writing team, 1985-86, chmn. supt.'s adv. com., 1991-92, chmn. Quincentennial Edn. Com., 1991-92. Mem. Animal Control Bd.; campaign coord. Ruth Gill for Mayor, Corpus Christi, 1979; del. Gov.'s Commn. for Women, San Antonio, 1985, Tex. Sch. Assembly Gov. Ann Richards, 1991; participant Leadership Corpus Christi XIX, 1990-91; mem. Corpus Christi Coun. for Women; chmn. Tchr. Task Force on Edn. for state rep. Ted Roberts, 1986-88, chmn. tchr. com. Better Sch. Program, 1987, chmn. tchr. Task Force Excellence Edn. for State Rep. Todd Hunter, 1988— . Named Outstanding Tchr. Am. History-Tex., DAR, 1986; recipient Robert A. Taft accolade for Excellence in Tchng. Govt. and Politics, 1986, Women in Careers Edn. award YWCA, 1991; named Tchr. of Yr. Corpus Christi Ind. Sch. Dist., 1990-91. Mem. AACD, Corpus Christi Council Social Studies (v.p. 1981-83, supt.'s adv. com. 1991—, co-chmn. children's com. A Kid's Place 1991—), Tex. Nat. Coun. Social Studies (conv. chmn. 1988, chmn. nominating com. 1990-91), Corpus Christi C. of C. (events chmn. 1983), PTA (life), YWCA (v.p., chmn. bldg. com. 1983-88), AAUW (v.p. 1983-85, pres. 1986-88), Phi Delta Kappa, Delta Kappa Gamma, Kappa Delta Pi. Avocations: tennis, reading. Home: 601 Barracuda Pl Corpus Christi TX 78411-2112 Office: Hamlin Mid Sch 3900 Hamlin Dr Corpus Christi TX 78411-2237

WILLIAMS, MARY LEE, elementary school educator; b. Hearne, Tex., Feb. 24, 1950; d. William Penn and Joanna (Wiley) Robinson; m. James Curtis Williams, July 22, 1972; children: Uhura Michelle, James Curtis II, Charles Istan. BS, Bishop Coll., Dallas, 1972; MS, Stephen F. Austin State U., 1979. Tchr. Rosemont Sch., Dallas, 1973-75; tchr. Blackshear Sch., Hearne, Tex., 1977-93, asst. prin., 1993-94, tchr., TAAS coord. alternative acad. edn., 1994—, summer sch. program adminstr./tchr., 1996. Mem. NAACP, NEA, Tex. tchrs. Assn., Robertson County Tchrs. Assn. (pres. 1988-92), Order Ea. Star (worthy matron), Chums Club (pres. 1994—), Phi Delta Kappa. Democrat. Baptist. Home: Box 715 700 W Gregg Calvert TX 77837-0715 Office: Blackshear Elementary School 1401 W Blackshear Ave Hearne TX 77859

WILLIAMS, MARY MARGARET LAHIFF, park ranger; b. Buffalo, Apr. 1, 1943; d. John Vincent and Mildred B. (Kelly) Lahiff; m. John R. Williams Jr., Nov. 30, 1968; children: Meghan, John Robert III. BA, Daemen Coll., 1964; MA in History, U. Conn., 1965. Park technician Nat. Park Svc., Ft. Davis, Tex., 1969-83, park ranger, historian, 1983—. Editor: Army Wife's Cookbook, 1972; contbr. articles to mags. Mem. restoration com. Jeff Davis County Courthouse; active Preservation Ft. Davis, 1994. Mem. Ft. Davis Hist. Soc. (life), Friends of Ft. Davis Nat. Hist. Site (life), Western History Assn., West Tex. Hist. Assn., S.W. Parks and Monuments Assn. (life, Spl. Achievement award 1986). Roman Catholic. Office: Ft Davis Nat Hist Site Nat Park Svc PO Box 1456 Fort Davis TX 79734-1456

WILLIAMS, MICHAEL BURL, librarian; b. Kansas City, Mo., Apr. 13, 1949; s. Burl and Ethel Doris (Brown) W.; m. Sandra Kay McSpadden, May 3, 1969 (div. June 1980); children: Lori Kathryn Williams Gastineau, Nathan Blair. Student, Okla. Bapt. U., 1967-69; BA, U. Okla., 1981; MA, U. Tulsa, 1988. Enlisted USN, 1969, resigned, 1978, ret., 1991; data processing technician USNR, 1979-91; libr. Tulsa City-County Libr. Sys., 1981—; chmn. in-svc. tng. com. Tulsa City-County Libr., 1994-96, pres. staff assn., 1996-97. Mem. Govt. Day, Tulsa County Govt., 1988; mem. fund distbn. Tulsa Area United Way, 1991—. Mem. ALA, Pub. Libr. Assn., Phi Alpha Theta, Sigma Delta Phi. Republican. Episcopalian. Home: 1722 S Carson Ave # 2700 Tulsa OK 74119-4642 Office: Tulsa City-County Libr Sys 6737 S 85 E Ave Tulsa OK 74135

WILLIAMS, MICHAEL E., social services administrator; b. Bryson City, N.C., Sept. 10, 1953; s. Frank E. and Virginia L. (Conley) W. BA in History and Polit. Sci., U. N.C., Greensboro, 1976, Masters Pub. Affairs, 1979. Asst. dir. planning and allocations United Way of Grtr. Greensboro, 1980-82, campaign dir., 1982-87; past participant in leadership dev. prog. Ctr. for Creative Leadership, 1986; pres. United Way Aiken (S.C.) County, 1987-92, United Way of the Coastal Empire, Savannah, Ga., 1992—; Instr. for United Way of America Nat. Acad. for Voluntarism, 1987—; Sec. 1997 SE Regl. Conf. United Way of America; Pres Ga State Profl. Assn. of United Way, 1995-96; NAV instr. Small City Workshops, United Way of Am., 1987—, nat. profl. adv. coun. on comty. problem solving, 1990-91; operation spotlight mentor United Way S.E. Ga., 1990-92; chmn. United Way S.C. Exec. Coun., Columbia, 1990. Active Ctr. for Creative Leadership, Greensboro, 1986, Leadership Aiken County, 1988, First City Club, mem. Youth Futures Authority Chatham County, 1992—, Savannah Crime Control Collaborative; mem. adv. bd. Jr. League Savannah, 1994-96, Rotary Club of Savannah. Mem. Am. Soc. for Pub. Adminstrn. (treas. 1981, v.p. 1982, pres. 1983). Office: United Way of Coastal Empire 428 Bull St Savannah GA 31401-4963

WILLIAMS, MILLER, poet, translator; b. Hoxie, Ark., Apr. 8, 1930; s. Ernest Burdette and Ann Jeanette (Miller) W.; m. Lucille Day, Dec. 29, 1951 (div.); m. Rebecca Jordan Hall, Apr. 11, 1969; children: Lucinda, Robert, Karyn. BS, Ark. State Coll., 1951; MS, U. Ark., 1952; postgrad., La. State U., 1951, U. Miss., 1957; HHD (hon.), Lander Coll., 1983; DHL, Hendrix Coll., 1995. Instr. in English La. State U., 1962-63, asst. prof., 1964-66; vis. prof. U. Chile, Santiago, 1963-64; assoc. prof. Loyola U., New Orleans, 1966-70; Fulbright prof. Nat. U. Mex., Mexico City, 1970; co-dir. grad. program in creative writing U. Ark., 1970-84, assoc. prof., 1971-73, prof. English and fgn. langs., dir. program in transl., 1973-87, univ. prof., 1987—, dir. poetry-in-the prisons programs div. continuing edn., 1974-79, chmn. program in comparative lit., 1978-80; dir. U. Ark. Press, 1980—, Bank of Elkins, Ark. 1988—; fellow Am. Acad. in Rome, 1976—, mem. adv. coun. Sch. Classical Studies, 1985-91; first U.S. del. Pan Am. Conf. Univ. Artists and Writers, Concepcion, Chile, 1964; invited del. Internat. Assembly Univ. Press Dirs., Guadalajara, Mex., 1991; mem. poetry staff Bread Loaf Writers Conf., 1967-72; founder, exec. dir. Ark. Poetry Cir., 1975; participant Assn. Am. Univ. Presses Soviet Mission, 1989. Author: (poems) A Circle of Stone, 1964, Recital, 1965, So Long At the Fair, 1968, The Only World There Is, 1971; (criticism) The Achievement of John Ciardi, 1968, The Poetry of John Crowe Ransom, 1971; (with John Ciardi) (criticism) How Does a Poem Mean?, 1974; (poems) Halfway From Hoxie: New & Selected Poems, 1973, Why God Permits Evil, 1977, Distractions, 1981, The Boys on Their Bony Mules, 1983; translator: (poems) Poems & Antipoems (Nicanor Parra), 1967, Emergency Poems (Nicanor Parra), 1972, Sonnets of Giuseppe Belli, 1981; editor: (poems) 19 Poetas de Hoy en Los Estados Unidos, 1966, (with John William Corrington) Southern Writing in the Sixties: Poetry, 1967, Southern Writing in the Sixties: Fiction, 1966, Chile: An Anthology of New Writing, 1968, Contemporary Poetry in America, 1972, (with James A. McPherson) Railroad: Trains and Train People in American Culture, 1976, A Roman Collection: An Anthology of Writing about Rome and Italy, 1980, Ozark, Ozark: A Hillside Reader, 1981, (criticism) Patterns of Poetry, 1986, (poetry) Imperfect Love, 1986, Living on the Surface: New and Selected Poems, 1989, Adjusting to the Light, 1992, Points of Departure, 1995; poetry editor La. State U. Press, 1966-68; contbr. articles to profl. publs. Mem. ACLU. Recipient Henry Bellaman Poetry award, 1957, award in poetry Arts Fund, 1973, Prix de Rome, Am. Acad. Arts and Letters, 1976, Nat. Poets prize, 1990, Charity Randall citation Internat. Poetry Forum, 1993, John William Corrington award for excellence in lit., Centenary Coll., Shreveport, La., 1994, Acad. Lit. award AAAL, 1995; named Bread Loaf fellow in poetry, 1963. Mem. MLA, PEN, AAUP, South Ctrl. MLA, Am. Lit. Translators Assn. (v.p. 1978-79, pres. 1979-81), Authors' Guild, Soc. Benemerito dell'Assn. Centro Romanesco Trilussa (Rome). Home: 1111 Valley View Dr Fayetteville AR 72701-1603 Office: U Ark Press 201 Ozark Ave Fayetteville AR 72701-4041

WILLIAMS, MORGAN LEWIS, pharmacist; b. Summerville, S.C., Feb. 28, 1948; s. Carroll S. and Venie Aline (Pound) W. BS in Pharmacy, U. S.C., 1971; Dipl., Niles Bryant Sch., Sacramento, 1982, Am. Sch. Piano Tuning, Morgan Hill, Calif., 1979. Lic. pharmacist, S.C., N.C.; registered tuner technician. Pharmacist VA Hosp., Columbia, S.C., 1972-75, Med. Ctr. Pharmacy, Florence, S.C., 1975-78, Revco Drugs, Cheraw, S.C., 1978—; organist Mt. Hebron United Meth. Ch., W. Columbia, S.C., 1967-76, Latta (S.C.) United Meth. Ch., 1977-81, Swansea (S.C.) United Meth. Ch., 1983-86, St. David's Episcopal Ch., Cheraw, 1989—; piano technician, Florence, Columbia, Cheraw, 1978—; inst. piano tech. Cheraw, 1991. Asst. editor Lodge Newsletter, Trestle Board, 1985-89. Mem. Piano Technicians Guild (former newsletter editor local chpt., sec./treas.), Am. Guild Orangists, S.C. Pharm. Assn. (pres. 1981-82), Optimist Club, Masons (master 1989, musician 1990—), Am. Pharm. Assn., Order of the Ea. Star, Past Royal Patron of the Order of the Amaranth. Republican. Episcopalian. Office: Revco Drugs 932 Chesterfield Hwy Cheraw SC 29520-7008

WILLIAMS, NELSON GARRETT, lawyer, mediator, arbitrator; b. Detroit, Feb. 16, 1926; s. Nelson Wallace and Sylvia Marie (Bowen) W.; m. Marian Pearl Stemme, May 29, 1948 (dec. 1972); children: Elizabeth, Margaret, Roberta. BA, Bowling Green State U., 1947; MA, U. Mich., 1950; MEd, U. South Fla., 1980; JD with honors, Fla. State U., 1987. Bar: Fla. 1987. Editor Huron County Tribune, Bad Axe, Mich., 1947-48; asst. prof. Keuka Coll., Keuka Park, N.Y., 1954-57, Ball State Tchrs. Coll., Muncie, Ind., 1957-63; lectr. Ind. U., Bloomington, 1963-65; assoc. prof. Dana Coll., Blair, Nebr., 1965-69, Sch. of Ozarks, Point Lookout, Mo., 1969-72; exec. dir Am. Cancer Soc., Gainesville, Fla., 1972-74; tchr. Sumter Correctional Inst., Bushnell, Fla., 1974-88; staff atty. Withlacoochee Area Legal Svcs., Floral County, Fla., 1987-89, ret., 1989. Author: Labor Journalism, 1963; contbr. articles to popular jours. Grad. fellow U. Fla., 1951-54, Fla. Bar Found. pub. svc. fellow, 1984-87; econs. fellow Case Inst. Tech., 1954, U. Wis., 1958. Mem. Fla. Bar Assn., AAUP (chpt. pres. 1968-69), AFSCME (local v.p., del. 1978-84), Assn. for Union Democracy, Soc. Profl. Journalists, Train Collectors Assn., Am. Flyer Collectors Club, Toy Train Operating Soc.,

Lionel Collectors Club Am., Sigma Delta Chi, Phi Alpha Theta, Pi Sigma Alpha, Pi Gamma Mu, Phi Kappa Phi. Democrat. Home: 7589 S Grovewood Loop Floral City FL 34436-2915

WILLIAMS, PAIGE ASHLEY, reporter, writer; b. Oxford, Miss., Nov. 29, 1966; d. Billy Wayne and Joann (Ashley) W. BA in Journalism, U. Miss., 1988. Reporter, news dir. The Daily Mississippian, Ole Miss, 1984-87; reporting intern Tupelo (Miss.) Daily Jour., 1986, The Clarion-Ledger, Jackson, Miss., 1987; reporter The Oxford Eagle, 1987-88; reporting intern The Washington Post, 1988; reporter The Charlotte (N.C.) Observer, 1988—; part-time instr. journalism U. N.C., Charlotte, 1995. Contbr. articles to mags. Nieman fellow Harvard U., 1996—; recipient Casey medal for meritorious journalism, 1st place awards N.C. Press Assn., Investigative and Enterprise Reporting award N.C. Press Assn., Walter Spearman award for feature writing. Mem. Investigative Reporters and Editors. So. Bapt.

WILLIAMS, PATRICE DALE, linguist, educator; b. Fairfield, Ala., Dec. 20, 1952; d. Silas and Bertha Mae (Allen) W. BS in Music, U. Ala., 1974, BA in English, 1975; MA in Secondary Reading, U. Ala., Birmingham, 1978; PhD in Linguistics, U. Fla., 1991. Reading tchr. Chattanooga Pub. Schs., 1978-80; instr. Ala. State U., Montgomery, 1980-93; asst. prof. English Troy State U., Montgomery, Ala., 1993—; cons. Ala. State Pers. Dept., 1994—, Montgomery City and County Pers., 1994—, Auburn U. in Montgomery, 1994—; approved reader SAT writing (ETS), 1994; evaluator Head Start, Birmingham, 1976; field rep. Ala. Edn. Study Commn., Montgomery, 1977; acting dir. writing lab. Ala. State U., Montgomery, 1981-82. Ch. musician, music dir., 1968—. Mem. MLA, Am. Dialect Soc., Phi Delta Kappa. Democrat. Baptist.

WILLIAMS, PAUL E., agricultural company executive; b. 1927. Pres. Budd Leaf Tobacco, Quincy, Fla., 1949—; ptnr. Quincy Liquors, 1976—; v.p. Gadsden Tomato Co., Quincy, 1983—. Office: Gadsden Tomato Co 218 Graves St Quincy FL 32351-2100

WILLIAMS, PAUL LELAND, transportation executive; b. Mpls., Aug. 22, 1938; s. Paul Oliver and Marian Louise (Crail) W.; m. Diana Doherty, June 29, 1974. BS, Syracuse U., 1966; MA, Ctrl. Mich. U., 1973; cert., Indsl. Coll. of Armed Forces, 1987. Commd. 2d lt. USAF, 1966, advanced through grades to col., 1986, various postions, 1956-73; quality assurance mgr. B-1 Program Office, Wright-Patterson AFB, Ohio, 1974-77; contract inspector Inspector Gen., Wright-Patterson AFB, 1978-80; F-15 spl. projects F15 System Program Office, Wright-Patterson AFB, 1980-83; F-15 program mgr. Warner Robins Air Logistics Ctr., Robins AFB, Ga., 1983-85; dir. logistics Joint U.S.-Korea Adv. Group, Taegu, Korea, 1985-86; dir. contracts USAF, Marietta, 1987-91; ret. USAF, 1991; logistics mgr. Lockheed, Marietta, Ga., 1992—. Author: Is the Department of Defense organized to Manage Security, 1987, Managing Quality Assurance in the System Acquisition Process, 1978. Named Disting. Toastmaster Toastmaster Internat., 1974, 76. Fellow Nat. Contract Mgmt. Assn. (chpt. pres. 1992-93, cert. profl. contracts mgr.); mem. Soc. of Logistics Engrs. (sr. mem., chpt. chmn. 1993-94, cert. profl. logistician), Air Force Assn., Lockheed Ga. Mgmt. Assn. (bd. dirs. 1993-95, pres. 1996—). Republican. Baptist. Home: 607 Trailwood Ln Marietta GA 30064-4630 Office: Lockheed Aeronautical System Co 86 S Cobb Dr Marietta GA 30063-0970

WILLIAMS, PAUL WHITCOMB, lawyer; b. Rochester, N.Y., July 12, 1903; s. Henry B. and Lillian Gray (White) W.; m. Minerva Fedyn Sawdon, Aug. 10, 1956. AB magna cum laude, Harvard U., 1925, LLB, 1929; student, Emmanuel Coll., Cambridge (Eng.) U., 1925-26; LLD, New Bedford Inst. Tech., 1958, Southeastern Mass. U., No. Dartmouth, 1975; LHD, Bard Coll., 1975. Bar: N.Y. 1931. Assoc. Cravath, de Gersdorf, Swaine & Wood, 1929-31; assoc. Cahill, Gordon & Reindel, N.Y.C., 1933-39, ptnr., 1939-42, 45-54, 58-77; asst. atty. U.S. Dist. Ct. (so. dist.) N.Y., 1931-33, atty., 1955-58; spl. counsel to Ins. Dept. State N.Y., 1951-52; spl. asst. atty. gen. in charge investigations State of N.Y., Saratoga and Columbia counties, 1952-54; justice Supreme Ct. State of N.Y., 1954; bd. dirs. Sterling Bancorp, Sterling Nat. Bank & Trust Co., N.Y.; chmn. minimum wage bd. Confectionery Industry, N.Y., 1947. Pres. Manhattan council Boy Scouts Am., 1952-56, mem. exec. bd. of Greater N.Y. councils, 1956—, pres., 1962-65, chmn. bd., 1965-67, hon. chmn. bd., 1967-77; chmn. bd. N.Y.C. div. Am. Cancer Soc., 1965-74, chmn. exec. com. nat. orgn., 1975-77, vice chmn. bd., 1977-79; chmn. exec. com. Am. Cancer Soc. Palm Beach Benefit, 1985—; chmn. bd. trustees Bard Coll., 1964-74, life trustee, 1974—; mem. bd. advisors St. Mary's Hosp., Palm Beach, 1985—; N.Y.C. Republican candidate for Congress, 8th N.Y. Dist., 1946. Served as lt. comdr. USNR, 1942-45. Decorated officer Order of Merit (France). Mem. Assn. Bar City N.Y. (chmn. sect. on trials and appeals 1949-51, 58-59, v.p. 1958-59), Harvard Law Sch. Assn. N.Y. (v.p. 1958-59), Pilgrims of U.S., Soc. Colonial Wars (Fla. gov. 1985—), Roundtable Palm Beach (pres. 1986—), N.Y. County Lawyers Assn., Am. Law Inst., Am. Judicature Soc., Inst. Jud. Adminstrn., Am. Bar Found., Am. Coll. Trial Lawyers, ABA, Fed. Bar Assn. (pres. Empire chpt. 1956-58), N.Y. State Bar Assn., Southwestern Legal Found., VFW, S.R. (pres. 1962-64), Mil. Order World Wars, Am. Legion, English Speaking Union, Soc. of the Four Arts, Phi Beta Kappa. Episcopalian. Clubs: Brook, N.Y. Young Rep. (pres. 1936), Harvard U., Univ. (N.Y.C.); Southampton, Shinnecock Hills Golf (Southampton, L.I.); L.I. (pres. 1974-77) (Eastport); Quantuck Beach (L.I.); Anglers (N.Y.); Everglades, Seminole Golf, Bath and Tennis, Old Guard Golfers (Palm Beach, Fla.). Lodge: Masons. Home: 12445 Plantation Ln North Palm Beach FL 33408

WILLIAMS, PAULINE ELIZABETH, special education educator; b. Spanish Town, Jamaica, Nov. 11, 1949; came to U.S., 1972; d. Limwell and Julia Ann (Thomas) Cranston; m. Boswell Frank Williams, May 18, 1975; children: Boswell Frank Jr., Latesha, Conrad. Student, Church Tchrs. Coll., Mandeville, Jamaica, 1969; BS in Edn., Northeastern U., 1975; MA in Pre-Sch. Handicapped, Chgo. State U., 1983; postgrad., U. Fla., 1990. Cert. English for speaker of other lang. tchr., Fla. Tchr. McAuley's Primary Sch., Jamaica, 1970-72; tchr. spl. edn. Chgo. Bd. Edn., 1975-85; varying exceptional tchr. College Park Elem. Sch., Ocala, Fla., 1985-86, Wyomina Park Elem. Sch., Ocala, 1986-87, Fessenden Elem. Sch., Ocala, 1987—. Dir. Vacation Bible Sch., Silver Springs Shores 7th-day Adventist Ch., Ocala, 1986-94. Tchr. mini-grantee Marion County Pub. Schs. Found., 1990-91. Mem. NEA, Marion Edn. Assn. (bldg. rep.), Fla. Teaching Profession. Office: Fessenden Elem Sch 4200 NW 90th St Ocala FL 34482-1542

WILLIAMS, PAULINE M., psychiatric-mental and community health nurse; b. Mt. Pleasant, Mich., Feb. 26, 1942; d. George Francis and Eva May (Cotter) Campbell; m. Clyde H. Williams, Apr. 16, 1966; 1 child Lynette M. Williams Disberry. Diploma, St. Mary's Hosp. Sch. Nursing, Saginaw, Mich., 1963; student, Cen. Mich. U. RN, Ind., Mich., Fla., N.C. Pub. health nurse Saginaw County Health Dept., Saginaw, 1972-80; staff nurse Mercy Wood Psych. Hosp., Ann Arbor, Mich., 1980-81; psych. staff nurse Meth. Hosp., Indpls., Ind., 1981-83; head nurse Meml. Hosp., South Bend, Ind., 1983-88; nursing supr. Ball Meml. Hosp., Muncie, Ind., 1988-90, Valley Inst. Psychiatry for Children and Adolescents, Owensboro, Ky., 1990-91; staff nurse Psychiat. Ctr., Tallahassee Meml. Hosp., 1991-92; staff nurse psychiatry Duke Med. Ctr. Duke U., Durham, N.C., 1992—. Speaker on pub. health. Mem. ANA (cert. psychiat.-mental health nurse), Am. Psychiat. Nurses Assn. Home: 142 Cow Pasture Ln Semora NC 27343-9611

WILLIAMS, PERCY DON, lawyer; b. Dallas, Sept. 19, 1922; s. Percy Don and Frances (Worrill) W.; m. Helen Lucille Brunsdale, Aug. 4, 1954; children—Anne Lucy, Margaret Frances, Elizabeth Helen. B.A. with honors, So. Methodist U., 1942, M.A., 1943; LL.B. magna cum laude, Harvard U., 1946. Bar: Tex. 1951. Instr. So. Meth. U. Law Sch., 1946-47; asst. prof., then assoc. prof. U. Tex. Law Sch., Austin, 1947-49; lectr. U. Va. Law Sch., 1951; law clk. to Justice Tom C. Clark U.S. Supreme Ct., 1949-51; pvt. practice Houston, 1952—; master dist. ct. Harris County, Tex., 1980-95. Contbr. articles to legal jours. Decorated Order of Sacred Treasure Gold Rays, Rosette, Japan. Fellow Tex. Bar Found.; mem. ABA, State Bar Tex. (col.), Fed. Bar Assn., Houston Bar Assn., Am. Law Inst., Am. Judicature Soc., Order of Coif, Phi Beta Kappa, Phi Eta Sigma, Pi Sigma Alpha, Tau Kappa Alpha, Kappa Sigma. Clubs: Houston, Houstonian. Home: 31 Briar Hollow Ln Houston TX 77027-9301 Office: 5685 1st Interst Bank Plz Houston TX 77002

WILLIAMS, PETER JOHN, world bank officer; b. Bristol, England, Oct. 23, 1939; came to the U.S., 1968; s. Gilbert John and Evelyn Mary (Lee) W.; m. Jette Seier-Poulsen, Sept. 29, 1962; children: Rolf Peter Jeffrey, Kristina Suzanne, Jennifer Louise. Student, Univ. Coll., London, 1958-61. Mgmt. trainee Pickfords Removals & Travel Ltd., Bristol, 1963-64; shipping mgr. Michael Gerson Ltd., London, 1964-68; mgr. internat. divsn. Security Storage Co., Washington, 1968-75; dir. Victory Van Internat., Alexandria, Va., 1976-83; from shipping officer to sect. chief shipping and materials mgr. World Bank, Washington, 1983—. Pres. Arthur S. Flemming Awards Commn., Washington, 1992—, Children's Theater of Arlington, Va., 1979-80. Mem. Jaycees (life, v.p. Downtown chpt. 1973-74, Jaycee of Yr. 1975). Episcopalian. Home: 2646 Jackson Dr Falls Church VA 22043

WILLIAMS, PHILLIP WAYNE, state official, former army officer, consultant; b. Birmingham, Ala., Nov. 1, 1939; s. Louie Alfred and A. Banks (Osborn) W.; (divorced); children: Phillip Wayne, Christopher N., Charles, Marion, William; m. Ramsey Waddell, Mar. 19, 1988. BS in Math. and Physics, Florence State Coll. (Ala.), 1961; M in Adminstrv. Sci., U. Ala.-Huntsville, 1977; D. Pub. Adminstrn., Nova U., 1978. Dep. sheriff, Lauderdale County, Florence, 1960-61; commd. 2d lt. U.S. Army, 1961, advanced through grades to lt. col., 1977; served as comdr., staff officer, platoon co., bn., project mgr. laser designators Redstone Arsenal, Ala., 1973-74, ret., 1982; chmn., pres. COMTEL-South, Inc., Huntsville, Ala., 1982-85, Joint Capital Securities, Inc., Joint Capital Svcs., cons. def. industry, 1983-95; dir. fin. State of Ala., 1995-96. Bd. dirs. Better Bus. Bur. No. Ala., 1985. Decorated Legion of Merit, Bronze Star with V and 5 oak leaf clusters, Air Medal with V and no. 7, Army Commendation medal with V and 3 oak leaf clusters; Vietnam Gallantry Cross with Silver Star, Vietnam Gallantry Cross with Palm, Vietnam Tech. Svc. Medal 1st Class, Vietnam Honor Medal 1st Class, Vietnam Civic Action Medal. Mem. U.S. Armor Assn., Assn. U.S. Army, Blackhorse Assn., Am. Def. Preparedness Assn. (dir. 1982-84, regional v.p. 1985—), Am. Soc. Pub. Adminstrn. (pres. 1982-84), Rotary Club (pres. 1993-94, dist. gov. group rep. 1994-95). Office: 105-N State Capitol 600 Dexter Ave Montgomery AL 36104-3734

WILLIAMS, REBECCA WALLS, non-profit organization executive; b. Dallas, Apr. 3, 1954; d. Henry Leon McBee and Sarah Elizabeth (Scudder) Tindle; m. Larry D. Walls, May 4, 1974 (div. 1982); children: Robert Glen Walls, Zachary James Walls; m. Keith D. Williams, Sept. 15, 1990. AA, Richland Coll., 1980; BSW, Tex. Woman's U., 1984; postgrad., U. Tex., Arlington, 1984-86. Cert. fundraising exec. Project mgr. South Dallas Comty. Ctr., Dallas, 1970-72; graphic artist Blanks Engraving Co., Dallas, 1973-77, Rabbit Reprodns., Dallas, 1977; dir. social svcs. Family Planning and Treatment Ctrs., Dallas, 1978-81; dir. Soma Health Sys., Dallas, 1981-84, Richardson (Tex.) YWCA, 1984-87; dir. program planning and analysis YWCA of Met. Dallas, 1988-89; asst. regional dir. S.W. regional office CARE, Internat. Relief and Devel., Dallas, 1989-94; regional dir. south ctrl. U.S. Soc. of St. Andrew, Dallas, 1994-95; exec. dir. Stress Rsch. Fedn., 1995-96; dir. Dallas Nature Ctr., 1996—. Bd. dirs. YWCA of Met. Dallas; chair Richardson Outreach Project, Vol. Ctr. of Dallas, 1986; chair com. on adminstrn. Garland (Tex.) YWCA, 1990-91; bd. dirs. young profl. league Dallas World Salute; mem. fin. adv. com. Circle Ten Explorer Scouts divsn. Boy Scouts Am. Recipient Speaker's Bur. award United Way of Met. Dallas, 1984-89, Spl. Svc. award Assn. of Retarded Citizens, 1986, 10 Yrs. of Vol. Svc. award Dallas Ind. Sch. Dist., 1989, Gov.'s Humanitarian award for outstanding vol. svc. State of Tex., 1991. Mem. NASW (internat. task force), Nat. Soc. Fundraising Execs., Network Masters, The Women's Ctr. Dallas, Fedn. of Women's Clubs, Assn. of Dirs. of Vols. (advisor to bd. of dirs.).

WILLIAMS, REGINALD ANTHONY, educator, author, artist, actor; b. Daytona Beach, Fla., Sept. 13, 1960; m. Jewelle Denise Doris, July 16, 1994. BS in African-Am. Studies, English, Ohio U., 1984; MFA in Creative Writing, Bowling Green (Ohio) State U., 1988. Instr. English Sinclair C.C., Dayton, Ohio, 1989-92; counselor Ohio State U., Columbus, 1993-94; instr. English Bethune-Cookman Coll., Daytona Beach, 1994—; owner/pres. RAW Prodns., Daytona Beach, 1992—. Author: (collection of poetry and short stories) Manhood, 1994, (play) The Wife and the Bachelor, 1993, (film) Zoom, 1996. Office: RAW Productions PO Box 1421 Daytona Beach FL 32115

WILLIAMS, RICHARD KENNON, ophthalmologist; b. Richmond, Va., Dec. 8, 1923; s. Carter Nelson Jr. and Hattie Maclin (Lifsey) W.; m. Ann Hughes Preston, Nov. 12, 1948 (div. June 1968); children: Elizabeth Kennon, Anna Strudwick, Richard Kennon Jr.; m. Yvonne Kay Hynes, May 1, 1993. BS, U. Richmond, 1943; MD, Med. Coll. Va., 1946. Diplomate Am. Bd. Ophthamology. Physician staff Stuart Circle Hosp., Richmond, 1950-93, Richmond EENT Hosp., 1950-93; asst. prof. ophthalmologist clin. M.C.V., Richmond, 1950-65; physician staff St. Marys Hosp., Richmond, 1987-93, Henrico Drs. Hosp., Richmond, 1987-93, Rappahanock Gen. Hosp., Kilmarnock, Va., 1993—. Lt. (j.g.) USN, 1947-50. Fellow ACS. Home: PO Box 1210 White Stone VA 22578-1210 Office: Lancaster Office Park 650 S Main St Kilmarnock VA 22482-1936

WILLIAMS, RICHARD LEROY, federal judge; b. Morrisville, Va., Apr. 6, 1923; s. Wilcie Edward and Minnie Mae (Brinkley) W.; m. Eugenia Kellogg, Sept. 11, 1948; children: Nancy Williams Davies, R. Gregory, Walter L., Gwendolyn Mason. LLB, U. Va., 1951. Bar: Va. 1951. Ptnr. McGuire, Woods & Battle and predecessor firms, 1951-72; judge Cir. Ct. City of Richmond, 1972-76; ptnr. McGuire, Woods & Battle, 1976-80; dist. judge U.S. Dist. Ct., Richmond, Va., 1980—, sr. judge, 1992—. Served to 2d lt., USAAF, 1940-45. Fellow Am. Coll. Trial Lawyers; mem. Va. State Bar, Va. Bar Assn., Richmond Bar Assn. Office: US Dist Ct/Lewis F Powell Ste 307 1000 E Main St Richmond VA 23219-3525

WILLIAMS, ROBERT C., company executive. Chmn. James River Corp. Address: 120 Tredegar St Richmond VA*

WILLIAMS, ROBERT CARLTON, electrical engineer; b. Copperhill, Tenn., July 14, 1948; s. Robert Carlton and Ruth Vivian (Becker) W.; m. Evelyn Snyder; 1 child, Sean Phillip. BS in Mech. Engring., U. Tenn., 1971. Designer NASA, Huntsville, Ala., 1968-69, Tenn. Chem. Co., Copperhill, 1969-70; draftsman TVA, Knoxville, 1970-71, design engr., 1971-76, tech. supr., 1976-81, sr. elec. engr., 1981-84, prin. mech. engr., 1984-86, prin. nuclear engr., 1984-86; lead elec. engr. TVA, Chattanooga, 1986-87; asst. chief electrical engr. TVA, Knoxville, 1987-89; instrumentation and controls engring. mgr. TVA, Knoxville, Tenn., 1989-90, chief elec. engr., 1990-91, chief I&C engr., 1991-94, chief elec. engr., 1994—. Mem. IEEE, Nat. Mgmt. Assn., Instrument Soc. Am. Republican. Baptist. Home: 815 Divot Ct Soddy Daisy TN 37379-4519 Office: 1102 Market St Chattanooga TN 37402-2861

WILLIAMS, ROBERT CHADWELL, history educator; b. Boston, Oct. 14, 1938; s. Charles Reagan and Dorothy (Chadwell) W.; m. Ann Bennett Kingman, Aug. 27, 1960; children: Peter, Margaret, Katharine. B.A., Wesleyan U., 1960; A.M., Harvard U., 1962, Ph.D., 1966. Asst. prof. history Williams Coll., Williamstown, Mass., 1965-70; prof. history Washington U., St. Louis, 1970-86; dean of faculty Davidson Coll., N.C., 1986—; pres. Central Slavic Conf., 1971-72; v.p. History Assocs. Inc., Gaithersburg, Md., 1980—; sr. research assoc. St. Antony's Coll., Oxford, 1985. Author: Culture in Exile, 1972, Artists in Revolution, 1976, Russian Art and American Money, 1980 (Pulitzer nominee), The Other Bolsheviks, 1986, Klaus Fuchs, Atom Spy, 1987; co-author: Crisis Contained, 1982; mem. editorial bd.: Slavic Rev., 1979-82. Fellow Kennan Inst., 1976-77; fellow Am. Council Learned Socs., 1973-74, W. Wilson Found., 1960-61. Mem. Am. Assn. for Advancement of Slavic Studies, Phi Beta Kappa, Sigma Xi. Presbyterian. Office: Davidson Coll Office VP Acad Affairs Davidson NC 28036

WILLIAMS, ROBERT HENRY, oil company executive; b. El Paso, Jan. 12, 1946; s. William Frederick and Mary (Page) W.; m. Joanne Marie Mudd, Oct. 22, 1967; children: Lara, Michael, Suzanne, Jennifer. BS in Physics, U. Tex., El Paso, 1968; PhD in Physics, U. Tex., Austin, 1973; MS in Physics, Va. Poly. Inst., 1971. Dir. Gulf Oil R&D, Houston, 1978-81; tech. mgr. Gulf Oil Internat., Houston, 1981-83; exploration mgr. Gulf Oil Co., Houston, 1983-85; mgr. geophys. rsch. Tenneco Oil Co., Houston, 1985-87, mgr., chief geophysicist, 1987-88; founder, mng. dir. Dover Energy, Houston, 1988—; exec. v.p. Tatham Offshore Inc, Houston, 1989-95, also bd. dirs.; chmn., CEO Dover Tech. Inc., Houston, 1989—; cons. Tenneco Inc., Houston, 1989—; DeepTech Internat., 1992-95; Ukraine Acad. Sci., 1993; bd. dirs., exec. v.p. DeepTech Inc., 1991-95; founder, pres. Westway tech. Assocs., 1986—; co-founder, chmn. CEO Castaway Graphite Rods, Inc., 1990—; owner, CEO Team Tex. Inc., 1993—; Bulldog Lures, Inc., 1994—; founder, CEO Houston Books Inc., 1994—; founder, CEO, chmn. Dover Energy Exploration, 1995—; pres. Westway Interests, 1995—; bd. dirs. Tatham Offshore. Contbr. articles to profl. jours. Mem. coun. Boy Scouts Am., Houston, 1989—; patron Mus. Fine Arts, Houston, 1990-96, Houston Zool. Soc., 1990-96; leader Girl Scouts U.S., Houston, 1989—. Mem. Soc. Exploration Geophysics, Am. Assn. Petroleum Geologists, Am. Geophys. Union. Republican. Office: Dover Tech 11767 Katy Frwy Ste 1000 Houston TX 77079

WILLIAMS, ROBERT JOSEPH, energy journalist; b. Eschwege, Germany, Feb. 17, 1951; s. Lewis Bert and Erika Maria (Russenberg) W.; m. Aletha Jane Yoder Williams, June 4, 1988; children: Heidi, Wesley. BA in Journalism, U. Tulsa, 1973. Bookstore mgr. B. Dalton, Tulsa, Oklahoma City, 1973-77; freelance writer pvt. practice, Tulsa, 1977-80; dist. editor Oil and Gas Jour., Tulsa, 1980-81, west coast editor, 1981-86, sr. staff writer, 1987-91, assoc. mng. editor, 1991—; contbg. editor: Internat. Petroleum Encyclopedia, Tulsa, 1985—, World Book Encyclopedia, Chgo., 1990—, Asian Oil & Gas Projects rev.; consulting map editor Pennwell Pub., Tulsa, 1993—; editor: Oil & Gas Jour. Revista Latinoamericana; OGJ online contbg. editor. Author: U.S. Petroleum Strategies in the Decade of the Environment, 1991, Institutional Investor, 1990-93, (play) Lost in Lotusland, 1992. Chmn. Tulsa Film Soc., 1974-75; tutor, organizer Adopt-A-School, Tulsa, 1991-93; newsletter copy editor Swan Lake Neighborhood Assn., Tulsa, 1990—; speaker Energy and Environmental Issues, 1991—; vol. St. Peter and Paul Sch., Tulsa, 1993—. Recipient Scripps-Howard scholarship Tulsa, 1971; named Pres.'s Club Univ. Tulsa, 1972-73, Outstanding Journalist Sigma Delta Chi, Tulsa, 1973. Mem. Petroleum Club, Assn. Petroleum Writers, Sigma Delta Chi. Roman Catholic. Home: 1724 S Quaker Ave Tulsa OK 74120-7018 Office: Oil and Gas Journal 1421 S Sheridan Rd Tulsa OK 74112-6619

WILLIAMS, ROBERT LARRY, environmental toxicologist; b. Jacksonville, Fla., July 25, 1950; s. James Clifford and Mable (Johnson) W. BS in Biology, Edward Waters Coll., Jacksonville, 1980; MS in Toxicology, Fla. A&M U., 1987, PhD in Toxicology, 1991. Environ. toxicologist Agy. for Toxic Substances and Disease Registry, Atlanta, 1991-93, 94—; region 5 rep. Agy. for Toxic Substances and Disease Registry, Chgo., 1993-94. Contbr. articles to profl. jours. With U.S. Army, 1974. Recipient McKnight Fellowship award Fla. Endowment Fund, 1985. Mem. Soc. of Neurosci. (pres. 1996), Commd. Officers Assn. (pres.-elect 1993), Nat. Geog. Soc. Islam. Home: 1521 Tunbridge Wells Cres Lithonia GA 30058 Office: 1600 Clifton Rd NE Atlanta GA 30333

WILLIAMS, ROBERT LEEDWARD, academic administrator, dean; b. Flora, Miss., Feb. 17, 1947; s. Albert and Paralee (Henry) W.; m. Virginia Williams, Dec. 10, 1966; children: Zealyne, Marchelle, Keisha. BA, Jackson (Miss.) State U., 1970; MBA, Atlanta U., 1981, EdD, 1985; postdoctoral, U. Ala., 1987-88, Harvard U., 1989, MIT, UCLA, 1990. Bus. mgr. Saints Coll., Lexington, Miss., 1974-76; purchasing mgr. Pineywoods (Miss.) Sch., 1976-77; asst. prof. bus. Jarvis Christian Coll., Hawkins, Tex., 1977-78; chief acct. Atlanta Ga., 1979-81; asst. prof. bus. Tuskegee (Ala.) U., 1981-88; dir. bus. adminstr. Fisk U., Nashville, 1988-91; now assoc. v.p. for acad. affairs, dean Sch. Bus. Alcorn State U., Lorman, Miss.; cons. Cons. and Developers of Bus. Enterprises, Atlanta, 1979—; assoc. v.p. acad. affairs, dean sch. bus. Alcorn State U., Lorman, Miss. Author: Organizational Management, 1986, Instructional Case Guide, 1986; editor The Rsch. Jour., 1988, Organizational Behavior and Institutional Effectiveness in Higher Edn.; contbr. articles to profl. jours. Pres. One-Way Boys' Mission, Jackson, Miss., 1976—. Nat. Dean scholar Ednl. Com. Inc., 1983-84. Mem. Researchers Assn. (pres. 1985—), Case Rsch. Assn., Nat. Bus. League, Acad. Mgmt., Alpha Kappa Psi, Delta Mu Delta, Alpha Phi Alpha. Home: 108 Los Pueblos Ct Clinton MS 39056-5914 Office: Alcorn State Univ PO Box 569 Lorman MS 39096-0569

WILLIAMS, ROBERT MICHAEL, insurance executive; b. Balt., Mar. 1, 1949; s. Robert E. and Miriam W. Williams; BBA, North Tex. State U., 1971; m. Dianne Starr, Apr. 14, 1973. Constrn. acct. Redman Devel. Co., Dallas, 1971-72; with J.C. Penney Co., Dallas, 1972-74, 76—, area audit mgr. adminstrn. and tng., 1978-80, audit project mgr., 1981-82; supervising sr. auditor J.C. Penney Life Ins. Co., 1982-83, v.p. ops. sales div., 1983-86, v.p. adminstrv. svcs., 1987-90, v.p. customer svc., 1990-94, v.p. telemktg., 1994—; systems and fin. auditor Sanger Harris-Fed. Dept. Stores, Dallas, 1974-76. Chmn. bd. Plano Balloon Festival, Inc., 1992-94; chmn. career edn. adv. bd. Plano Ind. Sch. Dist., 1992-93; bd. dirs. United Way Collin County, 1993, Vol. Ctr. Collin County, 1995—; active Jr. Achievement Bus. Tchrs. Home: 909 Sunningdale Cir Garland TX 75044-4117 Office: JC Penney Life Ins Co 2700 W Plano Pky Plano TX 75075-8205

WILLIAMS, ROBERT WESTON, music educator; b. Newberry, S.C., Dec. 30, 1964; s. George Henry Jr. and Susanna (Weston) W. BA, Stillman Coll., 1987; MusM, U. S.C., 1988, D in Musical Arts, 1996. Instr. music Benedict Coll., Columbia, S.C., 1988-90; asst. prof. music Barber-Scotia Coll., Concord, N.C., 1990-94; lectr. Fayetteville (N.C.) State U., 1994—; condr. Robeson Civic Chorale, Lumberton, N.C., 1995—; bd. dirs. N.C. Symphony Orch., Fayetteville, 1995—. Mem., soloist Simon Temple AMEZ Ch., Fayetteville, 1995. Recipient Citation City of Camden, N.J., 1992, Fort Bragg (N.C.) EEOC, 1995. Mem. AAUP, Soc. for Ethnomusicology, Alpha Phi Alpha. Methodist. Home: 846-10 King Arthur Dr Fayetteville NC 28314 Office: Fayetteville State U 1200 Murchison Rd Fayetteville NC 28301

WILLIAMS, ROGER COURTLAND, lawyer; b. Atlanta, June 11, 1944; s. Ralph Roger and Beatrice (Hill) W.; m. Jo Ann Davenport, June 9, 1968; children: Melissa, Kimberly, Courtland. BS, U. Ala., 1966, JD, 1969. Bar: Ala. 1969, U.S. Dist. Ct. (no. and mid. dists.) Ala. 1969, U.S. Supreme Ct. 1972. V.p. Williams, Williams & Williams, P.C., Tuscaloosa, Ala., 1969-90; pres., 1990—. Mem. bd. trustees Tuscaloosa Acad., 1987—, pres., 1990-94; bd. dirs. Children's Hands On Mus., Tuscaloosa, 1986—. 1st lt. U.S. Army, 1969-71. Mem. ABA, Ala. Bar Assn., Assn. Trial Lawyers Am., Nat. Acad. Arbitrators, Am. Arbitration Assn., Jaycees (nat. assoc. legal counsel 1979-80, state pres. 1978-79, pres. Ala. Found. 1980-81, Internat. Senator), Toastmasters (pres. 1975), Kiwanis (bd. dirs. 1974, 90, v.p. 1995-96), Indian Hills Country Club (bd. dirs. 1996). Methodist. Office: Williams Williams & Williams PC PO Box 2690 Tuscaloosa AL 35403-2690

WILLIAMS, ROGER FRANCIS, state agency administrator; b. Marlinton, W.Va., July 5, 1948; s. Edgar Moffett and Frances Willard (Miller) W. BA magna cum laude, U. Pa., 1976. Civil servant State of W.Va., Charleston, 1984—. Author of poems. Home: 3547 Teays Valley Rd Hurricane WV 25526-9054

WILLIAMS, RUTH ELIZABETH (BETTY WILLIAMS), retired secondary school educator; b. Newport News, Va., July 31, 1938; d. Lloyd Haynes and Erma Ruth (Goodrich) W. BA, Mary Washington Coll., 1960; cert. d'etudes, Converse Coll., 1961, U. Oreg., 1962. Cert. tchr., Va. French tchr. York High Sch., York County Pub. Schs., Yorktown, Va., 1960-65; French resource tchr. Newport News Pub. Schs., 1966-74, tchr. French and photography, 1974-81, tchr. French, Spanish, German and Latin, 1981-91, ret., 1991; pres. Cresset Publs., Williamsburg, Va., 1977—; lectr. Sch. Edn., Coll. Williamand Mary, Williamsburg, 1962-65; French tchr., coord. fgn. langs. York County Pub. Schs., 1962-65; workshop leader dept. pub. instrn. State of Del., Dover, 1965; cons. Health de Rochemont Co., Boston, 1962-71. Driver Meals on Wheels, Williamsburg, 1989-90; contbr. Va. Spl. Olympics, Richmond, 1987—; charter mem. Capitol Soc. Colonial Williamsburg Found., Inc., 1994; mem. Colonial Williamsburg Assembly, Colonial Williamsburg Found., Inc.; mem. Altar Guild, Bruton Parish Ch., Williamsburg, 1960—. Grantee Nat. Def. Edn. Act, 1961, 1962. Mem. AAAU, Fgn. Lang. Assn. Va., AARP (ret. tchrs. divsn.), Heritage Soc., Mary Washington Coll. Alumni Assn., Va. Hist. Soc., Am. Assn. Tchrs. French, Mortar Bd., Women in the Arts, Alpha Phi Sigma, Phi Sigma Iota. Episcopalian. Home and Office: 471 Catesby Ln Williamsburg VA 23185-4732

WILLIAMS, SALLY BROADRICK, infection control nurse and consultant; b. Dalton, Ga., Dec. 25, 1943; d. Columbus N. and Anne M. (McHan) Broadrick; m. Joe P. Williams, Aug. 30, 1969; children: Michael J., Andrew B. Diploma in Nursing, Grady Meml. Hosp., Atlanta, 1969; BS in Health Arts, Coll. of St. Francis, Joliet, Ill., 1981. Cert. in infection control. Emergency dept. nurse Hamilton Med. Ctr., Dalton, 1963-69; patient care coord. Wesley Woods Health Ctr., Atlanta, 1969-70; critical care nurse DeKalb Gen. Hosp., Decatur, Ga., 1970-71, emergency dept. nurse, 1971-73, infection control and employee health nurse, 1973-75; infection control dir. DeKalb Med. Ctr., Decatur, 1973-94; infection control/employee health dir. R.T. Jones Hosp.(formerly Promina R.T. Jones Hosp.), Canton, 1994—; tng. cons. CDC, Atlanta, 1984-89; bloodborne pathogen cons. Merck, 1992, 93. Author: Infection Control for Emergency Medical Technicians, 1990, Infection Control for Pre-Hospital Care Givers, 1989, Infection Control for Pre-Hospital Care Givers and Emergency Departments, 1994. Observer/reporter Cherokee LWV, Cherokee County, Ga., 1993-94; vol. Am. Cancer Soc.; fin. chairperson Cherokee County Relay for Life; mem. adv. com. Boy Scouts Am. Med. Explorer Post #23, Canton, Ga. Mem. Ga. Infection Control Network (pres. 1981-84, 90, 95, dist. 3 liaison 1981-84, 90, dist. 1 liaison 1995-96, Infection Control Practitioner of Yr. award 1984, 89, Outstanding Contbr. award 1985, 87, 91), Assn. Practitioners in Infection Control (pres. 1978, Outstanding Practitioner award 1990), Assn. for Profls. in Infection Control and Epidemiology (nominating chmn. 1993, pres.-elect 1995, pres. Greater Atlanta chpt. 1996), Internat. Assn. for AIDS Educators, Southeastern Assn. Microbiologists. Democrat. Methodist. Home: 1454 White Columns Blvd Canton GA 30115 Office: RT Jones Hosp 201 Hospital Dr Canton GA 30114

WILLIAMS, SANDRA WHEELER, commercial pilot; b. Glenns Falls, N.Y., Apr. 2, 1957; d. John Wheeler and Phyllis Yoder (Reihl) W.; m. Allen James Gencarelle, Sept. 18, 1980. BA, U. So. Fla., 1981. Mgr. prodn. Skydiving mag., DeLand, Fla., 1982-86; pres. AVOT Industries Inc., Orange City, Fla., 1987—; internationally rated skydiving judge Federale Aeronautique Internationale, Paris, 1982—; pres. Misty Blues All-Woman Skydiving Team, Inc., Orange City, 1987—; participated in world record for 1st coed 100-way free-fall formation and current world record 200 way, 1986, fixed wing pilot ratings; pvt. multi instrument, comml., multi. CFI, CFII, MEI and ATP (air transport pilot); organized five women's world record skydiving events between 1984-95, 60 way 1986, 79 way 1989, 104 way, 1995. Mem. MENSA. Home and Office: 549 Daley St Orange City FL 32763-4901

WILLIAMS, STEVEN DALE, political science educator; b. Huntington, Ind., July 25, 1944; s. Lester Dale and Marjorie Adele (McMullen) W.; m. Elaine Bowden Tomlin, Sept. 12, 1970; 1 child, Laura Nicole. BA in Polit. Sci., Ind. U., 1966; PhD in Am. Polit. Process, U. Ky., 1972. Asst. prof. polit. sci. Tenn. Tech. U., Cookeville, 1970-85, assoc. prof., 1985-90, prof., 1990—. Contbr. articles to profl. jours. Mem. So. Polit. Sci. Assn., Southeastern Polit. Sci. Assn., Tenn. Polit. Sci. Assn. (pres. 1993-94). Republican. Methodist. Home: 2390 Cane Creek Rd Cookeville TN 38506-6407 Office: Tenn Tech U N Dixie Ave Cookeville TN 38505

WILLIAMS, SUE DARDEN, library director; b. Miami, Fla., Aug. 13, 1943; d. Archie Yelverton and Bobbie (Jones) Eagles; m. Richard Williams, Sept. 30, 1989. B.A., Barton Coll., Wilson, N.C., 1965; M.L.S., U. Tex., Austin, 1970. Cert. librarian, N.C., Va. Instr. Chowan Coll., Murfreesboro, N.C., 1966-68; libr.'s asst. Albemarle Regional Libr., Winston, N.C., 1968-69; br. libr. Multnomah County Pub. Libr., Portland, Oreg., 1971-72; asst. dir. Stanly County Pub. Libr., Albemarle, N.C., 1973-76; dir. Stanly County Pub. Libr., 1976-80; asst. dir. Norfolk (Va.) Pub. Libr., 1980-83; dir., 1983-94, Rockingham County Pub. Libr., Eden, N.C., 1996—. Mem. ALA (orientation com. 1990-92, chair 1991), Libr. Adminstrv. and Mgmt. Assn. (pub. rels. sec. 1985-87), Southeastern Libr. Assn. (staff devel. com. 1986-88, Rothrock award com. 1984-86, sec. pub. libr. sect. 1982-84), Va. Libr. Assn. (SELA rep. 1993-96, coun. 1984, 88-91, 93-96, ad hoc conf. guidelines com. 1985-86, chmn. conf. program 1984, awards and recognition com. 1983), Pub. Libr. Assn. (bd. dirs.-at-large Met. area 1986-89), Va. State Libr. (coop edn. com. 88-89). Home: 817A Carter St Eden NC 27288-5923 Office: Rockingham County Pub Libr 527 Boone Rd Eden NC 27288

WILLIAMS, SUZANNE, pediatric cardiovascular nursing educator; b. Murray, Ky., Sept. 23, 1961; d. Clifton Eugene and Mary Helen (Lee) W. Diploma, Bapt. Meml. Hosp. Sch. Nursing, 1982; BSN, U. Ky., 1985; MSN, Vanderbilt U., 1989; postgrad., U. N.C., 1996—. Staff nurse pediatric ICU U. Ky. Hosp., Lexington, 1982-86, divisional charge nurse pediatrics, 1988-89, pediatric clin. nurse specialist/case mgr., 1989-90; staff nurse pediatric ICU Vanderbilt U. Hosp., Nashville, 1986-87; pediatric cardiovascular case mgr. Med. U. of S.C., Charleston, 1990-94, clin. nurse V/nurse educator, 1994-96. Mem. AACN, ANA, Assn. for the Care of Children's Health (program planning com. 1990-92), Soc. Pediatric Cardiovascular Nurses, Sigma Theta Tau. Home: 412 Tinkerbell Rd Chapel Hill NC 27514

WILLIAMS, SYLVESTER EMANUAL, III, elementary school educator, consultant; b. Chgo., Feb. 4, 1937; s. Sylvester Emanual and Carita (Brown) W.; children: Sylvia, Sylvester, Sydnee, Steven. BS, No. Ill. U., 1958; MA, Chgo. State U., 1968; PhD, U. S.C., 1992. Cert. tchr., S.C., N.C., Ill. From asst. to supt. Washington D.C. Pub. Schs., 1968-69; tchr. Chgo. Pub. Schs., 1958-68; program officer Dept. Edn., Washington, 1971-86; prof. Lander U., Greenwood, S.C., 1986-89, U. S.C., Akin, 1990-91; tchr., coach Charlotte (N.C.) Mecklenburg Pub. Schs., 1992—; bd. dirs. John de Home Sch., McCormick, S.C., 1986—. Mem. Phi Delta Kappa. Republican. Baptist. Home: 205 Briggs Ave Greenwood SC 29649-1603

WILLIAMS, THOMAS ARTHUR, biomedical computing consultant, psychiatrist; b. Racine, Wis., May 11, 1936; s. Robert Klinkert and Marion Anne (Wisneski) W.; m. Rexanne Louise Smith, Aug. 8, 1988; children: Jennifer, Thomas, Ted, Susan, Hailey. BA, Harvard Coll., 1958; MD, Columbia U., 1963; postgrad., NIH, 1967-68. Diplomate Nat. Bd. Med. Examiners, Am. Bd. Psychiatry and Neurology. Intern in surgery Presbyn. Hosp., N.Y.C., 1963-64; resident in psychiatry N.Y. State Psychiat. Inst., N.Y.C., 1964-67; chief depression sect. NIMH, Bethesda, Rockville, Md., 1967-71; asst. prof. U. Pitts., 1969-70; assoc. prof. U. Utah, Salt Lake City, 1971-77; prof., chmn. dept. psychiatry Eastern Va. Med. Sch., Norfolk, Va., 1977-78; clin. dir. Sheppard & Enoch Pratt Hosp., Towson, Md., 1978-80; prof. U. South Fla., Tampa, 1980-83; practitioner psychiat. medicine, med. dir. St. Augustine (Fla.) Psychiat. Ctr., 1983-89, 89-90; prin. Williams & Assocs., Tampa, 1990—. Chief editor: Psychobiology of Depression, 1972, Mental Health in the 21st Century, 1979; contbr. numerous articles to profl. jours. and chpts. to books. Mem. Gov.'s Adv. Com. on Mental Health, Salt Lake City, 1971-77, Gov.'s Adv. Com. on Penal Code, Richmond, Va., 1978, Dist. Mental Health Bd., Tampa, 1980-83; mem. U.S. Govt. Mission on Psychiatry to USSR, 1974; sponsor, coach Forest Hills Little League Baseball, Tampa, 1980-83. Sr. surgeon USPHS, 1958-67. Recipient Predoctoral fellowship NIMH, 1960-61, Alumni Rsch. award N.Y. State Psychiat. Inst., 1964, Rush Bronze Medal award Am. Psychiat. Assn., 1973, Rsch. grants VA, 1971-77. Mem. AMA, Fla. Med. Assn., Hillsborough County Med. Assn., Columbia U. Alumni Club (dir. 1995—), Harvard Club of the West Coast of Fla. Home: 831 S Delaware Ave Tampa FL 33606 Office: Williams & Assocs 831 S Delaware Ave Tampa FL 33606-2914

WILLIAMS, THOMAS ARTHUR, lawyer; b. Wilmington, N.C., Sept. 26, 1943; s. Louis C. and Mary Alice (Elmore) W.; m. Karen Barbara Hoster, Feb. 2, 1978; children—Morgan, Duncan; stepchildren: Quentin, Marady. B.S. In Journalism, Okla. State U., 1966; J.D.S., U. Okla., 1972. Bar: Okla. 1972, U.S. Dist. Ct. (we. dist.) Okla. 1972, U.S. Dist. Ct. (ea. and no. dists.) Okla. 1973, U.S. Ct. Appeals (10th cir.) 1973. Assoc. Jones, Atkinson, Williams, Bane & Klingenberg, Oklahoma City, 1972-73, Jones, Williams, Bane, Ray & Klingenberg, Oklahoma City, 1973-74; owner Bane & Williams, Oklahoma City, 1974-76; ptnr. Kratz, Thomas, Williams & Patton, Oklahoma City, 1978-79; ptnr. Drummond, Patton, Williams & Tullius, Oklahoma City, 1979-81; ptnr. Williams, Patton, Patton & Hyde, Oklahoma City, 1981-83; prof. corrections law Rose State Coll., 1976-78; judge Temporary Ct. Appeals 124, Okla., 1982. Mem. Okla. Bar Assn. (exec. bd. family law sect. 1987-89, membership chmn. 1987-89), Oklahoma County Bar Assn., Okla. Criminal Def. Lawyers Assn., ABA, Phi Delta Phi.

WILLIAMS, THOMAS E., pharmaceuticals executive; b. 1944. With Grabette H.S., 1968-71, Dunn Hall Pharms., Grabette, 1971-81; pres. T.E. Williams Pharms., Guthrie, Okla., 1992—. Office: TE Williams Pharms 2005 Ruhl Dr Guthrie OK 73044

WILLIAMS, THOMAS EUGENE, pharmaceutical consultant; b. Texarkana, Ark., May 13, 1936; s. Thomas Earle and Frankie Jo (Garner) W.; m. Peggy Jane O'Neill, May 31, 1958; children: Thomas Eugene, Elizabeth Anne, James David. BA, Yale U., 1958; MD, U. Tex. Southwestern Med. Sch., 1962. Diplomate Am. Bd. Pediatrics, Am. Bd. Pediatric Hematology and Oncology. Rotating intern Hermann Hosp., Houston, 1962-63; pediatric resident Children's Med. Ctr., Dallas, 1963-65; fellow pediatric hematology U. Va. Sch. Medicine, Charlottesville, 1967-68; rsch. assoc. Cancer Rsch. Lab., U. Va., Charlottesville, 1968-69; asst. prof. pediatrics and pathology U. Tex. Health Sci. Ctr. at San Antonio, 1969-72, assoc. prof. pediatrics, asst. prof. pathology, 1972-73, assoc. prof. pediatrics and pathology, 1973-79, assoc. prof. pediatrics, 1985-94; med. dir. Santa Rosa Children's Hosp. Cancer Rsch. and Treatment Ctr., 1974-79, South Tex. Comprehensive Hemophilia Ctr., 1977-79, dir. pediatric bone marrow transplantation program, 1986-93; dir. new drug devel. Orphan Med., Inc., 1994-96; sr. clin. rsch. scientist Burroughs Wellcome Co., 1979-85; clin. assoc. prof. pediatrics U. N.C. Sch. Medicine, 1979-85; clin. fellow bone marrow transplantation program Johns Hopkins U. Sch. Medicine, Balt., 1985. Contbr. articles to med. jours. Served to lt. comdr. USN, 1965-67. Am. Cancer Soc. advanced clin. fellow, 1968-69, 70-72; Am. Soc. Pharmacology and Exptl. Therapeutics travel awardee, 1968. Mem. Am. Soc. Clin. Oncology, Am. Soc. Hematology, Am. Assn. for Cancer Rsch. Episcopalian. Office: 11303 Vance Jackson Rd G6 San Antonio TX 78230-1850

WILLIAMS, THOMAS RHYS, anthropologist, educator; b. Martins Ferry, Ohio, June 13, 1928; s. Harold K. and Dorothy (Lehew) W.; m. Margaret Martin, July 12, 1952; children: Rhys M., Ian T., Tom R. B.A., Miami U., Oxford, Ohio, 1951; M.A., U. Ariz., 1956; Ph.D., Syracuse U., 1956. Asst. prof., asso. prof. anthropology Calif. State U., Sacramento, 1956-65; vis. asso. prof. anthropology U. Calif. Berkeley, 1962; vis. prof. anthropology Stanford U., 1976; prof. anthropology Ohio State U., Columbus, 1965-78; chmn. dept Ohio State U., 1967-71, mem. grad. council, 1969-72, mem. univ. athletic council, 1968-74, chmn. univ. athletic council, 1973-74, exec. com. Coll. Social and Behavior Scis., 1967-71; dean Grad. Sch. George Mason U., Fairfax, Va., 1978-81, prof. anthropology, 1981—; dir. Ctr. for Rsch. and Advanced Studies George Mason U., 1978-81, fed. liaison officer, 1978-81, chmn. faculty adv. bd. grad. degree program in conflict resolution, 1980-86. Author: The Dusun: A North Borneo Society, 1965, Field Methods in the Study of Culture, 1967, A Borneo Childhood: Enculturation in Dusun Society, 1969, Introduction to Socialization: Human Culture Transmitted, 1972, Socialization, 1983; editor, contbg. author: Psychological Anthropology, 1975, Socialization and Communication in Primary Groups, 1975, Cultural Anthropology, 1990; contbr. articles to profl. jours. Mem. United Democrats for Humphrey, 1968, Citizens for Humphrey, 1968. Served with USN, 1946-48. Research grantee NSF, 1958, 62, Am. Council Learned Socs.-Social Sci. Research Council, 1959, 63; Ford Found. S.E. Asia, 1974, 76; recipient Disting. Faculty award Calif. State U., Sacramento, 1961, George Mason U., 1983; Disting. Teaching awards Ohio State U., 1968, 76. Fellow Am. Anthrop. Assn., Royal Anthrop. Inst. Gt. Britain; assoc. mem. Current Anthropology; mem. AAAS, Sigma Xi. Office: George Mason U Robinson Hall B-315 4400 University Dr Fairfax VA 22030-4443

WILLIAMS, THRESIA WAYNE MATTHEWS, occupational health nurse; b. Moultrie, Ga., Oct. 20, 1945; d. James Wayne and Ola (Cone) Matthews; m. William Ensey Williams, Dec. 31, 1966; children: Darren Ensey, April Thresia Williams McIntosh. ADN, Abraham Baldwin Coll., Tifton, Ga., 1966. Nat. cert. occupational health nurse-specialist, Ga. Supr. Floyd Med. Ctr., Rome, Ga., 1967-71, 74-75; instr. Coosa Valley Vocat. H.S., Rome, 1972-73; med. dept. supr. Riegel Textile Corp., Trion, Ga., 1975-78, CBS Records, Carrollton, Ga., 1980-83, Carriage Industries, Inc., Calhoun, Ga., 1984-94, Galey & Lord, Inc., Shannon, Ga., 1994-96; COHN specialist, 1996—; specialist and spokesperson disaster health svcs. ARC, Rome, 1993—, chair disaster health svcs. cluster com., 1993—, mem. disaster action team, 1993—, vol. local, state and nat. disasters, 1991—, instr. HIV-AIDS, CPR/first aid, blood borne pathogens, freedom from smoking, 1996. Mem. Nat. Assn. Occupational Health Nurses, Am. Lung Assn. (Freedom from Smoking instr. 1996), Ga. Assn. Occupational Health Nurses (scholarship com. 1991—, chair com. 1994—, dir. 1995, proctor Atlanta 1994), N.W. Ga. Assn. Occupational Health Nurses (v.p. 1990-94, Ga. rep. 1993, 95, newsletter editor 1991-94), Jane Delano Soc. Methodist. Home: PO Box 86 208 Floyd Springs Rd Armuchee GA 30105 Office: Galey & Lord Inc PO Box 972 401 Burlington Dr Shannon GA 30172

WILLIAMS, TIM, administrator wild life sanctuary. Mgr. Clyde E. Buckley Wildlife Sanctuary, Frankfort, Ky. Office: Clyde F Buckley Sanctuary 1305 Germany Rd Frankfort KY 40601-8257

WILLIAMS, TOM, recreational facility executive; b. 1947. Degree, Calif. State U. Various leading mgmt. roles MCA Recreation Svcs. Group, Hollywood, Calif., 1970-87; with Universal City Fla. Ptnr., Orlando, 1987—, pres., 1990. Office: Universal City Fl Ptnr 1000 Universal Studios Plz Orlando FL 32819-7601*

WILLIAMS, TRUDY ANNE, English language educator, college administrator; b. Winnipeg, Man., Can., Mar. 4, 1946; d. Herbert Francis and Melita French (Russell) Sly; m. Harry G. Williams, June 17, 1980; 1 child, David Langdon Jr. BA, U. Southwestern La., 1969, MA, 1970. Teaching asst. U. Southwestern La., Lafayette, 1968-72; instr. Gaston Coll., Dallas, N.C., 1980-83; asst. prof. English, St. Petersburg (Fla.) Jr. Coll., 1983—, also acting program dir., comm., program dir. acad. svcs.; program dir. acad. svcs. St. Petersburg (Fla.) Jr. Coll., Tarpon Springs Campus; adj. prof., cons. St. James Sch. Theology, Tarpon Springs, Fla., 1992—. Founding mem. Episcopal Synod of Am.; dir. Christian edn. St. Anne of Grace Episcopal Ch., Seminole, Fla. Mem. MLA, Nat. Coun. Tchrs. English, Southeastern Conf. on English in 2-Yr. Colls., Fla. Assn. Community Colls., Fla. Devel. Edn. Assn., Fla. Coll. English Assn., Pinellas County Tchrs. of English, South Atlantic Modern Lang. Assn., Fla. Coun. Instructional Affairs. Home: 8021 Bayhaven Dr Largo FL 34646-3320

WILLIAMS, WILLIAM BRYANT, JR., publisher; b. Paris, Tenn., Aug. 20, 1934; s. William Bryant Sr. and Julia Margaret (Sensing) W.; m. Anne Chatten Corbett, June 21, 1956; children: Cynthia B. Williams Barnett, Michael B., Julia L. Williams Ray, Joan C. Williams Stevens. BA, Murray State U., 1956. Reporter Memphis Press-Scimitar, 1956-57, Tullahoma (Tenn.) News, 1957-60; from reporter, to news editor, to assoc. pub. Paris Post-Intelligencer, 1960-78, editor, pub., 1978-91, pub., 1992—. Pres. Leadership Henry County, Paris, 1986-87, Henry County Literacy Coun., Paris, 1988-90, Support Tenn. Adult Readers Inc., Hendersonville, 1993-94, Land Between the Lakes Assn., Golden Pond, Ky., 1993-94; trustee Tenn. Press Found., 1992—; exec. dir. Paris-Henry County Heritage Ctr., 1995—. 2d lt. U.S. Army, 1957. Named Man of Yr., C. of C., Paris, 1980; recipient Sequoyah Literacy award Tenn. Hist. Commn., 1992. Mem. Tenn. Press Assn. (pres. 1980-81), Mid-Am. Press Inst. (founding dir. 1968-81), Tenn. AP Mng. Editors Assn. (pres. 1981), UPI Tenn. Assn. Newspapers (pres. 1973), Optimist Club Paris (pres. 1966-67, Optimist of Yr. 1989), Tenn. Press Svc. (bd. dirs. 1993—). Presbyterian. Home: 323 Highwood Circle Paris TN 38242 Office: Paris Post-Intelligencer 208 E Wood St Paris TN 38242-4139

WILLIAMS, WILLIAM HENRY, II, publisher; b. Birmingham, Ala., Oct. 21, 1931; s. Calvin Thomas and Lillian Elizabeth (Levey) W.; m. Lewis Mozelle Hensley, Feb. 28, 1959; 1 child, William Henry III. Student, Baylor U., 1952-55. Printer Waco (Tex.) Tribune-Herald, 1950-59; internat. rep. Internat. Typog. Union, Colorado Springs, Colo., 1960-68; editor, gen. mgr. Colorado Springs Free Press, 1969-70; dir. labor relations The Morning Telegraph, N.Y.C., 1970-72; gen. mgr. Daily Racing Form, Hightstown, N.J., 1972-89, nat. gen. mgr. for U.S. and Can., 1990-91, pub., 1991-92; ret., 1992; pub. Kerrville (Tex.) Mountain Sun, 1993-96; mem. adv. council journalsim dept. Baylor U., Waco, 1970-72. Chmn. CentraState Med. Ctr., Freehold, N.J., 1982-83, CentraState Health Affiliates, Freehold, 1987-94; vice chmn. Ctr. for Aging, Inc., Freehold, 1985-90; dep. mayor Freehold Twp. Com., 1987, mayor, 1989-90, 93, committeeman, 1985-94; chmn. Freehold Mayor's Task Force on Substance Abuse, 1987-91; mem. Upper Guadalupe River Authority, 1995—, Kerr Econ. Devel. Found. Named an Hon. Trustee Freehold Area Hosp., 1985—. Mem. Am. Newspaper Pubs. Assn., Newspaper Pers. Rels. Assn., Tex. Press Assn. (bd. dirs. 1995-96), NCCJ (Brotherhood award 1986), Exch. Club (Hightstown; carter pres.), Masons (32 deg.), Shriners, Optimists (charter mem. Freehold chpt.). Republican. Lutheran. Club: Exchange (Hightstown) (charter pres.). Lodges: Masons (32 degree), Shriners, Optimists (charter mem. Freehold chpt.). Home and Office: 172 Saint Andrews Loop Kerrville TX 78028-6441

WILLIAMS, WILLIE JOHN, II, marketing consultant; b. Mobile, Ala., Mar. 3, 1960; s. Willie John and Augustine (Dacus) W. BS in Mktg. and Mgmt., Ala. State U., 1984. Account exec. Thomas May & Assocs., Montgomery, Ala., 1984-85, v.p. mktg., 1986-88; dir. mktg. Imex Comm., Atlanta, 1985-86; v.p. mktg. Tempo Advt. & Mktg., Mobile, 1988-91; mktg. cons., Mobile, 1991—; v.p. mktg. Thomas May & Assocs., Montgomery, Ala., 1994—; mem. bd. Ala. Dept. Human Resources, Montgomery, 1991—, sec. bd., 1992-95. Founder Baldwin County Reverend M.L. King Celebration Com., 1989; v.p. Young Rep. Club Baldwin County, 1993-94, sec., 1991, pres., 1994-95; mem. Baldwin County Rep. Exec. Com., 1991—; mem. State of Ala Voter Registration Adv. Bd. Recipient award of merit City of Daphne, Ala., 1990, 91; named to Mobile PressRegister Top 60 young leaders for the next century. Mem. Masons, Alpha Phi Omega (v.p., pres.). Baptist. Home: PO Box 434 Point Clear AL 36564-0434 Office: 11370 Confederate Rest Rd Point Clear AL 36564

WILLIAMS, WINTON HUGH, civil engineer; b. Tampa, Fla., Feb. 14, 1920; s. Herbert DeMain and Alice (Grant) W.; m. Elizabeth Walser Seelye, Dec. 18, 1949; children: Jan, Dick, Bill, Ann. Grad. Adj Gens. Sch., Gainesville, Fla., 1943; student U. Tampa, 1948; grad. Transp. Sch., Ft. Eustis, Va., 1949; BCE, U. Fla., 1959; grad. Command and Gen. Staff Coll., Ft. Levenworth, Kans., 1964, Engrs. Sch., Ft. Belvoir, 1965, Indsl. Coll. Armed Forces, Washington, 1966, Logistics Mgmt. Center, Ft. Lee, Va., 1972. Registered profl. engr., Fla., N.C. Constrn. engr. air fields C.E., U.S. Army, McCoy AFB, Fla., 1959-61, Homestead AFB, Miami, Fla., 1961-62; civil engr. C.E., Jacksonville (Fla.) Dist. Office, 1962-64, chief master planning and layout sect., mil. br., engring. div., 1964-70; chief master planning and real estate div. Hdqrs. U.S. Army So. Command, Ft. Amador, C.Z., 1970-75, spl. asst. planning and mil. constrn. programming Marine Corps Air Bases Eastern Area, Marine Corps Air Sta., Cherry Point, N.C., 1975-82; cons. engr., Morehead City, N.C., 1982—. Mem. Morehead City Planning Bd., 1982-94; mem. Carteret County N.C. Health Bd., 1990—, chmn. 1995—; active Boy Scouts, C.Z.; mem. nat. council U. Tampa. Served with AUS, World War II, ETO, Korean War; col. Res. Decorated Breast Order of Yun Hi (Republic of China); presdl. citation, Meritorious Service medal (Republic of Korea); eagle scout with gold palm. Fellow ASCE (life); mem. NSPE (life), Res. Officers Assn. (life, v.p. C.Am. and S.Am.), Profl. Engrs. N.C., Am. Soc. Photogrammetry, Prestressed Concrete Inst. (profl.), Soc. Am. Mil. Engrs. (life, engr.), Nat. Eagle Scout Assn., Nat. Rifle Assn. Am., Am. Legion (life), Order Arrow, Theta Chi. Presbyterian. Home and Office: 4322 Coral Point Dr Morehead City NC 28557-2745

WILLIAMS, WRIGHT, psychologist, educator; b. Houston, May 10, 1949; s. Marvin Wright and Mary Katherine (Lacey) W.; m. Brenda Eileen Wobig, Apr. 6, 1985 (dec. Nov. 1993); 1 child, Christopher Wright. BA, U. Tex., 1971; MS, Fla. State U., 1976, PhD, 1978. Lic. psychologist, Tex.; cert. group psychotherapist; health service provider in psychology. Clin. psychologist VA Med. Ctr., Houston, 1979—; pvt. practice, Houston, 1980—; asst. prof. Baylor U. Coll. of Medicine, Houston, 1980—; adj. clin. asst. prof. U. Houston, 1982—. Contbr. articles to profl. jours. USPHS/NIMH fellow Fla. State U., 1973-76; recipient Cert. of Recognition, DAV, 1980. Mem. APA (cert. of recognition 1981), Am. Group Psychotherapy Assn., Tex. Psychol. Assn., Houston Psychol. Assn. (exec. com. 1984-93, 95-96, sec.-treas. 1986-87), Houston Group Psychotherapy Soc. (exec. com. 1995-96). Presbyterian. Home: 4126 Falkirk Ln Houston TX 77025-2909 Office: VA Med Ctr Psychology Svc 2002 Holcombe Blvd Houston TX 77030-4211

WILLIAMS-DALY, ANGELIA EVETTE, marketing executive, small business owner; b. Chattanooga, Apr. 17, 1960; d. Tedi (Chester) W. BS in Nursing, U. Tenn., Chattanooga, 1988. Mktg. dir. Echols Furniture Co., Chattanooga, 1979-91; owner Daly Enterprises, Baton Rouge, La., 1991—. Bd. dirs. La. Make-A-Wish Found. 1991-94; mem. Chattanooga Rep. Com. Mem. Chattanooga Apt. Assn. (bd. dirs. 1988-90), Chattanooga Hotel-Motel Assn. (bd. dirs. 1988-90), Chattanooga Jaycees (bd. dirs. 1985-86, v.p. 1986-88, pres. 1989-90, chmn. bd. dirs. 1990-91, Dir. of Yr. award 1986, Exec. of Yr. award 1988, Pres. of Yr. award 1990). Roman Catholic. Office: 1225 Carrollton Ave Baton Rouge LA 70806-7302

WILLIAMS-MADDOX, JANICE HELEN, nurse; b. Boston; d. Arthur Hamilton Wade and Edith Josephine (Weekes) Williams; B.S. in Nursing, Boston U., 1957; M.A., Atlanta U. Sch. Edn., 1971; M.Community Health, Emory U., 1976; m. Larry Maddox, May 21, 1977 (dec.). Staff nurse Beth Israel Hosp., Boston, 1957-58, N.Y. Hosp.-Cornell U. Med. Center, N.Y.C., 1958-59; ward supr. Jewish Meml. Hosp., Boston, 1959-61; staff and pvt. duty nurse Mass. Gen. Hosp., Boston, 1961-63; public health nurse Boston Health Dept., 1963-64; intravenous nurse Hughes Spalding Hosp., Atlanta, 1964-66; public health nurse Fulton County (Ga.) Health Dept., 1966-69; sr. tchr. Atlanta Southside Comprehensive Health Center, 1970-73, acting dir. edn., 1973-74, assoc. dir. clin. nursing, 1974-76; asso. dir. mental health planning project So. Region Edn. Bd., Atlanta, 1976-78; nursing cons. Dept. Health and Human Services, Atlanta, 1978-81; head nurse VA Med. Center, Atlanta, 1982-85; br. mgr. Am. Home Health Care of Ga., Inc., Jonesboro, 1985-86; mem. staff Med. Emergency Clinic-Grady Meml. Hosp., 1986-91; project dir. Morehouse Sch. Medicine Initiative, N.K. Kellogg Found., 1991-95; evening coordinator, instr. for innovative practical nursing program for health para-profl. Atlanta Area Tech Sch., 1971-81; mem. admissions com. M. Pub. Health program Emory U. Sch. Medicine, 1979—. Mem. coms., including Women's Day com. Central United Meth. Ch., Atlanta. Recipient spl. recognition Am. Cancer Soc., 1975. Mem. Sigma Theta Tau (Epsilon chpt.).

WILLIAMSON, BARBARA JO, community health nurse, educator; b. Hopkins County, Tex., July 13, 1931; d. Wallace G. and Ellie (Williams) Swindell; m. Billy W. Williamson, Nov. 5, 1952; children: Joellyn Brickhouse, Jan Boyett. Diploma, Dallas Meth. Hosp., 1951; BS, East Tex. State U., 1981. Cert. in vision and hearing, scoliosis screening, CPR instr. Dir. Sch. Vocat. Nursing Titus County Meml. Hosp., Mt. Pleasant, Tex.; dir. nursing and edn. Winnsboro (Tex.) Hosp. Inc.; sch. nurse Winnsboro Ind. Sch. Dist., Mesquite (Tex.) Ind. Sch. Dist.; ret., 1996. Mem. Tex. Assn. Sch. Nurses, Tex. Sch. Health Assn., Dallas Area Sch. Health Assn. (nomination com.). Home: 2233 Aloha Dr Mesquite TX 75150-3728

WILLIAMSON, CHRISTINE WILDER, preschool specialist, educational consultant, small business owner; b. Sylvester, Ga., Jan. 1, 1929; d. Thomas Herman and Irene (Beverly) Wilder; m. James Bryant Williamson, Aug. 10, 1947; children: James Robert, Joseph Nathan, Janet Marie. BS, Tift Coll., Forsyth, Ga., 1972; MEd, Mercer U., 1973; D Ministry, Luther Rice Sem., Jacksonville, Fla., 1983. Tchr. Houston County Bd. Edn., Warner Robins, Ga., 1947-50, Kathleen Pape Kindergarten, Macon, Ga., 1963-66, Vineville Bapt. Kindergarten, Macon, 1966-71; elem. dir. Vineville Bapt. Ch., 1971-80; presch. specialist, cons. Ga. Bapt. and So. Bapt. Conv., 1970—; instr. Macon Tech. Inst., 1980-85; owner, founder Splendid Difference Ent., 1990—. Author: I Can Do It Myself, 1983, Creative Art Activities for Children, 1991. Fund raiser Ga. Cancer Assn., Macon, 1970-88; dir. Mission Friends, Macon Bapt. Women's Missionary Union, 1989—; dir. Royal Ambassadors. Mem. Nat. Assn. Edn. Young Children, So. Assn. Children under Six, Ga. Assn. Young Children, Ga. Presch. Assn. (pres. 1984-86, chaplain 1990—), Bibb County Presch. Assn. (pres. 1975-77, chaplain, treas. 1988—), MADD. Democrat. Home and Office: 577 Old Lundy Rd Macon GA 31210-4305

WILLIAMSON, HENRY GASTON, JR., banker; b. Whiteville, N.C., Aug. 18, 1947; s. Henry Gaston and Elizabeth Lee (Brittain) W.; m. Nancy Thomas Williamson, Aug. 30, 1969; children: Leigh, Clay. BSBA, East Carolina U., 1969, MBA, 1972; grad. bus. adminstrn., U. N.C., 1979. Mgr.

bus. loans Branch Banking & Trust Co., Fayetteville, N.C., 1973-77; v.p., regional loan adminstr. Branch Banking & Trust Co., Wilson, N.C., 1977-80; v.p., city exec. Branch Banking & Trust Co., Tarboro, N.C., 1980; exec. v.p., mgr. ops./human resources div. Branch Banking & Trust Co., Wilson, N.C., 1981-83, sr. exec. v.p., adminstrv. group mgr., 1983-89, pres., 1989—, COO, 1991—; bd. dirs. BB&T Fin. Corp., BB&T; bd. dirs. BB&T Ctr. for Leadership Devel. Author: American Antiques: A Case Study, 1973 (First Place award Robert Morris Assocs.). Bd. dirs. Wilson County chpt. ARC, 1984—, East Carolina U. 1985—, N.C. Med. Soc. Found., Inc., 1991; mem. exec. com., bd. dirs. East Carolina coun. Boy Scouts Am., 1985—; bd. dirs. Wilson Heart Fund Assn., 1983-87, pres., 1985-86. East Carolina faculty scholar, 1969; recipient Outstanding Alumni award East Carolina U., 1988. Mem. Omicron Delta Epsilon, Beta Gamma Sigma. Club: Wilson Country. Lodge: Kiwanis (pres. Wilson club 1984-85). Home: 1210 Cambridge Rd NW Wilson NC 27896-1458 Office: BB&T Fin Corp PO Box 1250 Winston Salem NC 27102*

WILLIAMSON, HUGH JACKSON, statistician; b. Dallas, Jan. 12, 1943; s. Hugh and Edna (Mays) W.; m. Sheri Lynn Wooten, Jan. 19, 1980; 1 child, Laura Elizabeth. B.A. in Math. with honors, U. Tex., 1965, M.A. in Math., 1967, Ph.D. in Mech. Engring., 1975. Engr., scientist Tracor, Inc. and subs. Austin, Tex., 1967-73; research engr., scientist assoc. U. Tex.-Austin, 1973-77; sr. scientist Radian Internat. LLC , Austin, 1977-85, sr. staff scientist, 1986-91, prin. scientist, 1992—. Contbr. articles, reports to profl. publs. Mem. Am. Statis. Assn., Sigma Xi, Phi Kappa Phi. Baptist. Avocations: reading, gourmet cooking, music appreciation, golf. Home: 2401 Indian Trl Austin TX 78703-2337 Office: Radian Internat LLC PO Box 201088 Austin TX 78720-1088

WILLIAMSON, JOHN THOMAS, SR., minerals company executive; b. Atlanta, Oct. 1, 1925; s. Walter Berry and Clare (Mathews) W.; m. Ava Gene Shealy, June 11, 1949; children: John Thomas, Ava Clare, Robin E., Leila Ann. Diploma, N. Ga. Coll., 1942-43; BS in Indsl. Engring., Ga. Inst. Tech., 1949. Registered profl. engr. and land surveyor, Ga. Chief engr. Thiele Kaolin Co., Sandersville, Ga., 1949-57; assoc. W.C. Davis and Assocs., Atlanta and Tallahassee, 1957-60; chief engr. So. Clays, Inc., Gordon, Ga., 1960-63; asst. gen. mgr. Freeport Kaolin Co., N.Y.C., 1972-77, v.p., gen. mgr., 1977-78, pres., 1978-85; cons., gen. mgr. Gordon ops. Engelhard Corp., N.J., 1985-86; pres. IMPEX Corp., Milledgeville, Brunswick, Ga., 1987—; bd. dirs. Freeport Export Corp., Freeport Overseas Sales Co., 1978-83. Patentee on processing kaolins; contbr. articles to profl. jours. Mem. adv. bd. Ga. Coll., 1979-82, found. bd., 1983—, vice chmn. found. bd., 1988-89, chmn., 1989-90; mem. nat. adv. bd. Ga. Tech. Inst., 1979-85, emeritus; adv. bd. sch. mgmt. U. Ga., 1979-80; mem. Ga. Mil. Coll. Found. Bd., 1993—, exec. com., 1995. With USNR, 1943-46. Recipient Robert Earll McConnell award AIME, 1996. Mem. TAPPI, China Clay Producers, Ga. State Mining Assn., Ga. Soc. Profl. Engrs., Ga. Bus. and Industry Assn. (bd. dirs. 1978-83), Bus. Coun. Ga. (bd. dirs. 1983-88), Ga. Soc. Mining Metallurgy and Exploration, Inc., Ga. C. of C., Jaycees, Lions (pres. 1957), Alpha Tau Omega. Baptist (deacon). Home: 1810 Tanglewood Rd Milledgeville GA 31061-2461 Office: IMPEX Corp PO Box 1028 Milledgeville GA 31061-1028 also: IMPEX Corp 157 Darien Hwy Brunswick GA 31525-2423

WILLIAMSON, JON CREIGHTON, federal agency administrator; b. Washington, July 29, 1943; s. Henry Creighton and Mary Evelyn (Brunton) W.; m. Carol Elizabeth Cheney Kelly, June 5, 1965 (div. Dec. 1983); children: Robert Creighton, Richard Carroll, Jon Christopher; m. Laura Jean Waters, Jan. 3, 1986; 1 child, Whitney Lynn. BS, U. Md., 1965; MSM, Houston Bapt. U., 1983. Group mgr. IRS, Houston, 1971-86, br. chief, 1986-96, chief spl. procedures, 1996—; Chmn. bd. dirs. US Employees Credit Union, Houston. Co-author: Pro Greek, 1980. Staff sgt. U.S. Army, 1966-69, Vietnam. Decorated Bronze Star; recipient Roy F. Bergengren Premier award Tex. Credit Union League, 1993. Mem. Masons, Shriners, Chinar Grotto, Lambda Chi Alpha (nat. sports editor 1970—, Disting. Svc. award 1986). Republican. Methodist. Home: 13010 Queensbury Houston TX 77079 Office: IRS 1919 Smith Houston TX 77002

WILLIAMSON, NORMA BETH, adult education educator; b. Hamilton, Tex., Nov. 2, 1939; d. Joseph Lawrence and Gladys (Wilkins) Drake; m. Stuart Williamson, Mar. 14, 1981. BA, Baylor U., 1962; MA, Tex. A&I U., 1969; postgrad., Tex. Tech. U., 1976-80, CIDOC, Cuernavaca, Mex., 1973, 75. Instr. English, Tex. Southmost Coll., Brownsville; lectr., Spanish; coll. prep. tchr. Tex. Dept. Corrections, 1995—; lectr. Spanish Sam Houston State U. Music chmn. Huntsville Unitarian Universalist Ch.; pres. S.W. Dist. Unitarian Universalist Assn., 1982-86. Mem. AAUW (pres. Huntsville br. 1995-96). Home: RR 1 Box 349 Bedias TX 77831-9625

WILLIAMSON, PAUL RICHARD, medical educator, surgeon; b. Asheville, N.C., Aug. 11, 1956; s. William Cooper and Joyce Lee (Sluder) W. BS in Biology, Wake Forest U., 1978, MD, 1982. Asst. clin. prof. surgery U. Ill., Urbana, 1988-89, U. Fla., Gainesville, 1989—; clin. prof. surgery Orlando (Fla.) Regional Med. Ctr., 1989—, co-dir. colon-rectal fellowship program, 1990—, chief of surgery Sand Lake Divsn., 1991—. Contbr. articles to profl. jours. Fellow ACS, Am. Soc. Colon and Rectal Surgery, So. Med. Assn. (pres., mem. rectal sect. 1994), Phi Beta Kappa. Baptist. Office: Colon Rectal Clinic 110 W Underwood St Orlando FL 32806-1112

WILLIAMSON, RICHARD JOSEPH, English language educator; b. Houston, Apr. 11, 1962; s. Robert Michael and Martha Jo (Bourland) W.; m. Leigh Montgomery Range, Dec. 26, 1992; 1 child: Ethan Merritt. BA in English, French, journalism, Sam Houston State U., 1988, MA in English, 1992; PhD in English, U. of North Tex., 1996. Tutor and tchg. asst. Sam Houston State U., Huntsville, Tex., 1990-92; tutor and tchg. asst. U. North Tex., Denton, Tex., 1992-96, fellow dept. English, 1992-96; asst. prof. English Muskingum Coll., New Concord, Ohio, 1996—. Contbr. poems to jours., including North Tex. Rev., 1994, Outstanding North Tex. Poets. Don Reid scholar in Journalism, Sam Houston State U., 1985, Eugene Edge grad. scholar, Eng., 1992. Mem. MLA, South Ctrl. MLA, Nathaniel Hawthorne Soc., Nat. Women's Studies Assn., Conf. of Coll. Tchrs. of English, Pi Delta Phi. Democrat. Office: Muskingum Coll English Dept New Concord OH 43762

WILLIAMSON, SAMUEL RUTHVEN, JR., historian, university administrator; b. Bogalusa, La., Nov. 10, 1935; s. Samuel Ruthven and Frances Mitchell (Page) W.; m. Joan Chaffe Andress, Dec. 30, 1961; children: George Samuel, Treeby Andress, Thaddeus Miller. BA, Tulane U., 1958; AM, Harvard U., 1960, PhD, 1966, grad. advanced mgmt. program, 1986; hon. degrees, Furman U. Va. Theol. Sem. Asst. prof. U.S. Mil. Acad., 1963-66; instr. history Harvard U., 1966-68, asst. prof., 1968-72, Allston Burr sr. tutor, 1968-72, asst. to dean of Harvard Coll., 1969-70; rsch. assoc. Inst. Politics, faculty asso. Ctr. for Internat. Affairs, 1971-72; mem. faculty J.F. Kennedy Sch. Govt., 1971-72; assoc. prof. history U. N.C., Chapel Hill, 1972-74; prof. U. N.C., 1974-88, dean Coll. Arts and Scis., 1977-85, provost univ., 1984-88; pres., vice chancellor The U. of the South, Sewanee, Tenn., 1988—; cons. Historian's Office, Office of Sec. Def., 1974-76; vis. fellow Churchill Coll., 1976-77; mem. vis. com. Harvard Coll., 1986-92; dir. Research Triangle Inst., 1984-88; trustee N.C. Sch. Sci. and Math., 1985-88, Day Found., 1990-93; mem. bd. visitors Air U., 1994—. Author: The Politics of Grand Strategy: Britain and France Prepare for War, 1904-1914, 1969, 2d edit., 1990; co-author: The Origins of U.S. Nuclear Strategy, 1945-53, 1993; editor: The Origins of a Tragedy: July 1914, 1981; co-editor: Essays on World War I: Origins and Prisoners of War, 1983, Austria-Hungary and the Origins of the First World War, 1991; Am. editor: War and Soc. Newsletter, 1973-88. Mem. cen. com. Morehead Found., 1978-93; vice chmn. bd. visitors Air U., 1996—. Capt. U.S. Army, 1963-66. Fulbright scholar U. Edinburgh, 1958-59; Woodrow Wilson fellow, 1958-63; Danforth fellow, 1958-63; Nat. Endowment Humanities fellow, 1976-77; Ford Found. grantee, 1976; fellow Nat. Humanities Ctr., 1983; recipient George Louis Beer prize for best book on internat. history Am. Hist. Assn., 1970. Mem. Am. Hist. Assn., Internat. Inst. Strategic Studies, Nat. Assn. Ind. Colls. and Univs. (chairperson bd. dirs. 1994-95). Democrat. Episcopalian. Home: PO Box 837 Sewanee TN 37375-0837 Office: U of the South Office of Pres Sewanee TN 37375-4013

WILLIAMSON, WALKER KENDRICK, insurance executive; b. Ft. Worth, Tex., May 14, 1924; s. Mertz Kendrick and Bertie Hearn (Carson) W.; m. Nancy Jane Wilson, May 1, 1948 (dec. 1969); children: Blake Kendrick, Jane Elise; m. Laura Mary McKee, Jan. 29, 1972. BS in Econs., Tex. A & M U., 1947. Mgr., ptnr. Williamson Ins. Agy., Okla. City, Okla., 1947-55; spl. agt. No. British Ins. Group, OKla. City, 1955-58; mgr. No. British Ins. Group, Dallas, 1958-60; asst. mgr. Comml. Union, Dallas, 1960-61; spl. agt. Hartford Ins. Group, Okla. City, 1961-62; sr. spl. agt. Hartford Ins. Group, Dallas, 1962-72, asst. agy. mgr., 1972-76, mktg. mgr., 1976-82, mktg. adminstr., 1982-90. Hon. dep. commr. Okla. Ins. Commn., Oklahoma City, 1956; active Dallas Mus. Art, 1989—, Dallas Hist. Soc., 1989—, Dallas County Heritage Soc., 1989—, Highland Park Community League, Dallas, 1989—, Dallas Symphony Assn., 1989—. Capt. U.S. Army, 1943-46. Decorated Asiatic-Pacific Campaign medal with battle star, Am. Campaign medal, Army of Occupation medal with Japan clasp, World War II Victory medal. Mem. North Tex. Fieldmen's Assn. (pres. 1965-66), Okla. Fire Underwriters Assn. (pres. 1965-66), Okla. Fire Underwriters Assn. (pub. rels. dir. 1956-58), Dallas Country club (bd. govs. 1988-91, 93-96, chmn. ins. com. 1988-91, 94-96, ins. com. mem. 1981-82, 88-95, ho. com. mem. 1979-80, 84-85, 86-87, 91-95, interview com. mem. 1993-95), Masons (master). Republican. Presbyterian. Home: 4205 Arcady Ave Dallas TX 75205-3701

WILLIAMSON, WILLIAM ALLEN, optometrist; b. Dossville, Miss., July 29, 1933; s. Donald Wodsworth and Ruth Beatrice (Doss) W.; m. Martha Pearl Taylor, Mar. 28, 1959; children: Lamar Arthur, William Allen, Donna Taylor. AA, Northwest Jr. Coll., Senatobia, Miss., 1952; OD, So. Coll. Optometry, Memphis, 1956. Pvt. practice optometry Greenville, Miss., 1959—; chmn. Adv. Com. to Medicaid, Miss., 1972-75. Mem. Miss. Blind & Deaf Bd. Trustees, 1974-76; charter mem. Optomist Club, Greenville, Miss., 1964; pres. Wash. County Assn. Retarded Citizens, Greenville, 1981-83, S.O.S. Retarded Workshop, Inc., Greenville, 1985-87, Christian Mission Concerns of Miss., Greenville, 1987-89. 1st lt. U.S. Army, 1956-59. Mem. Am. Optometric Assn. (legis. keyman 1971-72), Miss. Optometric Assn. (legis. chmn. 1973-74), Masons (32 degree), Shriners, Elks. Presbyterian. Office: Eye Clinic of Optometry 239 S Washington Ave Greenville MS 38701-4234

WILLIFORD, CLIFFORD FREDERICK, system engineer, retired air force officer; b. Norfolk, Va., July 12, 1950; s. Clifford and Frances Josephia (Rest) W.; m. Lorraine Ann Prytulak, July 18, 1970; children: Clifford Frederick Jr., Brandon Peter. BSEE, Va. Poly. Inst. and State U., 1976; MSEE, Air Force Inst. Tech., 1985. Cert. mgr., Inst. Cert. Profl. Mgrs., 1995. Enlisted USAF, 1970, commd. 2d lt., 1976, advanced through grades to maj., 1987; undergrad. pilot tng. Air Tng. Command, Williams AFB, Ariz., 1976-77; aircraft comdr. 492d and 493d Tactical Fighter Squadron, RAF Lakenheath, Eng., 1978-81; flight examiner standardization and evaluation 27th Tactical Fighter Wing, Cannon AFB, N.Mex., 1981-84; lead electronic warfare engr. Aeronautical System Div., Air Force Systems Command, Wright-Patterson AFB, Ohio, 1986-89; aircraft comdr. 493d Tactical Fighter Squadron, RAF Lakenheath, Eng., 1989-91, also squadron sect. comdr., ops. dir. resources, 1989; flight comdr., asst. ops. officer 493rd Tactical Fighter Squadron, Taif, Saudi Arabia, 1990; air force hdqrs. planning officer, combat pilot 48th Tactical Fighter Wing, Riyadh, Taif, 1991; ret. USAF, Marietta, Ga., 1991; tech. mgr. Lockheed Aero. Sys. Co., Marietta, Ga., 1991—; adj. asst. prof. Wright State U., Dayton, Ohio, 1986. Asst. scoutmaster Boy Scouts Am., Bellbrook, Ohio, 1986-88. Mem. Order Daedalians, VFW, Etta Kappa Nu.

WILLIFORD, JAMES RICHARD, university administrator; b. Tampa, Fla., Nov. 4, 1925; s. James Richard and Ella Lee (Burts) W.; m. Laurie Nill, Dec. 18, 1948; children: James R., Jerald J. BS, Ga. Inst. Tech., 1950; postgrad., USN Postgrad. Sch., 1957; MS, George Washington U., 1971. Commd ensign USN, 1949-77, advanced through grades to capt., 1971, ret., 1977; advisor to Iran Stanwick Internat., Kharg Island, 1977-79; resident dir. Fla. Inst. Tech., Orlando, 1983-91; dir. Orlando (Fla.) Met. Ctr. Webster U., 1991—. Adv. bd. to select mgr. City of Maitland, Fla., 1995-96; v.p. Maitland civic Ctr., 1995-96. Mem. Rotary (pres. 1995—). Office: Webster Univ 151 S Wymore Rd Altamonte Springs FL 32714-4224

WILLIFORD, MABON LESLIE, II (BEAU WILLIFORD), boxing promoter; b. Fayetteville, N.C., Apr. 18, 1950; s. Mabon Leslie I and Thelma Alice (Starling) W.; m. Teri Anne Logue, Nov. 27, 1983; children: Mabon Leslie III, Wesley Logue I, Christian Thomas I, Alexander Robert I. BA in Bus. Adminstrn., Coll. of New Rochelle, 1978; diploma in sports mgmt., Riley Coll., 1991. Cert. in bus. law Real Estate Inst. Salesman Jim Breswitz Realty, Fayetteville, 1970-75; profl. boxer Al Braverman Sports, Ltd., N.Y.C., 1975-78; gen. mgr. Arrow Electric Line, Inc., Lafayette, La., 1978-82, also bd. dirs.; pres. Beau Williford's Knockout, Ltd., Lafayette, 1982—; chief exec. officer Spl. Events Ltd., 1991—, bd. dirs.; bd. dirs. Arrow Environ. Controls, Inc., Lafayette; bd. dirs., founder Ragin' Cajun Amateur Boxing Club, Lafayette, 1988—; chief exec. officer williford, Otts and Sims Prodns.; ptnr. B-W Boxing, ptnr. Freeman, Guidry & Williford; chief exec. officer Beau Williford Sports Promotions, London; ptnr. King of the Hill Sports and Edn., Ltd. Bd. dirs., founder Fayetteville Athletic Club, 1971; bd. dirs. Downtown Sporting Club, Ltd. Named Ky. Col., La. Col. and Duke of Hazard. Mem. World Boxing Coun., World Boxing Assn., Universal Boxing Assn. (bd. dirs. 1987—, Man of Yr. 1991), Internat. Boxing Fedn., N.Am. Boxing Fedn., U.S. Boxing Assn., World Boxing Fedn. (Man of Yr. 1994), Internat. Boxing Coun., Acadian Hill Country Club, Kiwanis, Royal Legion. Republican. Episcopalian. Office: 305 Arnould Blvd Lafayette LA 70506-6217

WILLIFORD, ROBERT MARION, civil engineer; b. Murhpysboro, Ill., Nov. 4, 1937; s. Paul Marion and Helen Margaret (Heilig) W.; m. Jewell Eleanor Winkler, Aug. 15, 1959; children: Robert Marion II, Andrew Blaine, Sally Ann. BS, U. Ill., 1960; postgrad., U. Calif., Berkeley, 1971. Registered profl. engr., Calif., Ill., Minn., W.Va., S.C., N.C. Field engr. Bechtel Corp., San Francisco, 1962-66; supt. Bechtel Corp., Weirton, W.Va., 1966-68, Bechtel Pacific Corp., Irian Jaya, Indonesia, 1969-71; tech. mgr. Bechtel Pacific Corp., Queensland, Australia, 1972-73; gen. supt. Bechtel Corp., Virginia, Minn., 1974-77, Bechtel Power Corp., Phoenix, 1977-78; project mgr. BE & K Inc., Birmingham, Ala., 1979-85; pres. CRS Sirrine Svcs. & Power, Greenville, S.C., 1986-88; project dir. Gaylord Container Corp., Antioch, Calif., 1989; mgr. projects BE & K Constrn., Birmingham, Ala., 1990-94; constrn. mgr. Bechtel Am. Inc., Brisbane, Queensland, Australia, 1994-95, Bechtel Corp., Gaithersburg, Md., 1995—. Lt. U.S. Army Corps of Engrs., 1960-62. Fellow ASCE; mem. Am. Soc. Mil. Engrs., Am. Soc. Profl. Engrs., Tech. Assn. Pulp & Paper Inst., Constrn. Industry Inst. (mem. tech. com. 1983-85, bd. advisors alternate 1985-87, mem. membership com. 1986-87). Presbyterian. Home: 1674 Winfield Dr Birmingham AL 35242 Office: Bechtel Corp 9801 Washingtonian Blvd Gaithersburg MD 20878-5356

WILLINGHAM, DENNIS RAY, secondary education educator; b. Jasper, Ala., July 6, 1969; s. Clarence Wayne and Martha Marie (Patton) W. AA, Wallace State U., Hanceville, Ala., 1989; BS in Social Scis., Edn., U. Ala. Birmingham, 1991, MA in Social Scis., Edn., 1995. Part time disk jockey WARF-WEFN Radio, Jasper, Ala., 1985-91; tchr., coach Walker County Bd. Edn., Jasper, 1992—; designated asst. prin. Sumiton (Ala.) Sch. 1993, Martin Sch., Goodsprings, Ala., 1996; Student Govt. Assn. Sponsor Martin Sch., Goodsprings, 1994-96; mem. Effective Schs. Program, Martin Sch., 1995. Mem. NEA, Ala. Edn. Assn., Nat. Assn. Student Activity Advisors, Nat. Assn. Secondary Sch. Prins. Democrat. Baptist.

WILLINGHAM, EMAGENE EMANUEL, social worker; b. Bainbridge, Ga., June 1, 1937; d. Frank Wooten and Louie (Coburn) Emanuel; children: Tracy Coburn, Robert Wesley, Jeffrey Reeves. BA in Psychology and Sociology, Jacksonville U., 1959; MSW, U. N.C., 1984; postgrad., Duke U. Diplomate in clin. social work; cert. CEAP. Personnel asst. Jacksonville (Fla.) Paper Co., 1959-60; social worker Dept. Social Svc., Raleigh, N.C., 1984-86, Wake County Alcohol Treatment Ctr., Raleigh, N.C., 1986-88; counselor Duke U., Durham, N.C., 1988—; psychotherapist pvt. practice, Chapel Hill, N.C., 1989—. Mem. NASW, Nat. Fedn. Soc. Clin. Social Work (com. on psychoanalysis), N.C. Soc. Clin. Social Work, N.C. Psychol. Assn. Office: 727 Eastowne Dr Ste 300A Chapel Hill NC 27514-2214

WILLINGHAM, MARY MAXINE, fashion retailer; b. Childress, Tex., Sept. 12, 1928; d. Charles Bryan and Mary (Bohannon) McCollum; m. Welborn Kiefer Willingham, Aug. 14, 1950; children: Sharon, Douglas, Sheila. BA, Tex. Tech U., 1949. Interviewer Univ. Placement Svc., Tex. Tech U., Lubbock, 1964-69; owner, mgr., buyer Maxine's Accent, Lubbock, 1969—; speaker in field. Leader Campfire Girls, Lubbock, 1964-65; sec. Community Theatre, Lubbock, 1962-64. Named Outstanding Mcht., Fashion Retailor mag., 1971, Outstanding Retailer; recipient Golden Sun award Dallas Market, May 1985. Mem. Lubbock Symphony Guild, Ranch and Heritage Ctr. Club: Faculty Women's. Office: 16 Briercroft Shopping Ctr Lubbock TX 79412-3022

WILLINGHAM, OZELLA M., medical/surgical and cardiac nurse; b. Hot Springs, Ark., Sept. 24, 1965; d. George E. and Ora Mae (Adams) W. ADN, Garland County Community Coll., Hot Springs, 1986. RN, Ark.; cert. in ACLS, cardiovascular nursing. Charge nurse diabetic-cardiac unit St. Joseph Regional Health Ctr., Hot Springs, 1986—. Named Sweetheart Nurse of Yr., Am. Assn. Ret. Persons, 1988.

WILLIS, C. PAUL, minister; b. Harkers Island, N.C., Dec. 14, 1932; s. Cleveland Paul and Bertha Gray (Lewis) W.; m. Mary Jane Roberts, June 1, 1951; children: Deborah, Tamalie, Dennis. BA, Campbell U., 1966; Clin. Pastoral Edn. degree, Bowman Gray Sch. Medicine, Winston Salem, N.C., 1969; MDiv, Southeastern Bapt. Sem., Wake Forest, N.C., 1970; DMin, Oral Roberts U., 1989. Pastor Northside Bapt. Ch., Greensboro, N.C., 1970-73; pres. Christian Word Ministries, Greensboro, 1973-82; sr. pastor Cathedral of His Glory, Greensboro, 1982—; pres. Ministerio de Su Gloria, Antigua, Guatemala, 1990—. Author: Bells and Pomegranates, 1991, Born to Triumph, 1992, Christ of the Apocalypse, 1993; (booklets) Abiding Power, 1976, Visions of the Victory, 1976, Signs That Make You Wonder, 1993, When the Spirit Comes, Whoosh, 1994. Mem. Charismatic Bible Ministries. Republican. Office: Cathedral of His Glory 4501 Lake Jeanette Rd Greensboro NC 27455-2807

WILLIS, CLAYTON, broadcaster, corporation executive, former government official, educator, arts consultant, photojournalist, lecturer; b. Washington, Aug. 11, 1933; s. William H. and Elizabeth Carl (Keferstein) W. Student, The Sorbonne, Paris, 1953-54; BA, George Washington U., 1957; student, U. Oslo, 1953; grad., N.Y. Inst. Fin., 1966, Assn. Commodities Exch. Firms Inc., 1966. Spl. assignment Am. Embassy, London, 1957; writer NBC Network radio show Tex and Jinx, 1958; spl. corr. NBC News, La Paz, Bolivia, 1959; spl. Washington corr. Fin. News TV Network (now CNBC), N.Y.C., 1988; contbr., corr. Saudi Arabian TV, Newsweek mag., Philips News Svc. The Hope (Ark.) Star, Christian Sci. Monitor, L.A. Times-Mirror Syndicate, The Palm Beach (Fla.) Post, The Greenwich (Conn.) Time, The Bar Harbor (Maine) Times, Info-Explo Mining Jour., Rouyn-Noranda, Que., Can., Fin. News TV Network, New York, The Mainichi, Tokyo, The China Post, Taipei, Taiwan, Chattanooga Times, The Nashville Tennesseean, the Daily Nation of Kenya, The Khartoum Echo, Sudan, The Washington Daily News, Washington Post, Cape Argus of Capetown, South Africa, Bangkok Post, Irish Times, Dublin; reporter, movie, art critic Albuquerque Tribune, 1959-61; asst. editor Newsweek Mag., N.Y.C., 1961-62; TV broadcaster-writer UPI Newsfilm, N.Y.C., 1962; White House, Washington corr., chief bur., anchor World Radio News, Houston; White House, Washington corr. WAVA Radio Sta., Washington, 1963-65; editorial writer, corr. Hearst Newspapers, N.Y.C., 1965; press officer UN, N.Y.C., 1965-66; spl. assignment Am. Embassy, Reykjavik, Iceland, 1967; editorial writer, critic, reporter N.Y. Amsterdam News, N.Y.C., 1967-68; cons. Ford Found., N.Y.C., 1968-69; dir. pub. affairs U.S. EEOC, Washington, 1969-70; cons. OEO, Washington, 1970, Pres.'s Nat. Coun. on Indian Opportunity, Washington, 1970-71, Community Rels. Svc., U.S. Dept. Justice, Washington, 1970-73, Cabinet Com. on Opportunities for Spanish-Speaking People, 1971-72, Fed. Energy Adminstrn., Washington, 1973-74; dir. pub. affairs Office Petroleum Allocation U.S. Dept. Interior, 1973-74; dir. Congl. rels., dir. pub. affairs Pres.'s Nat. Commn. on Fire Prevention and Control, 1971-73; pub., editor, owner Four Corners Chieftain, Ignacio and Durango, Colo., 1972-73; lectr. Sch. of Bus., U. D.C., Washington, 1973-74; owner, White House corr., photojournalist Willis News Svc., Washington, 1974—; pub. affairs dir. Inaugural Vets. Com., 1976-77; White House corr., photojournalist Washington Life mag., 1993—; anchor Channel 33, Arlington, Va., 1991—; adviser to Fernando E.C. de Baca, spl. asst. to the Pres., White House, 1974-76; lectr. nat., internat. affairs, Haiti, art, communications, strategic and precious metals, diamond, nickel, copper, and cobalt mining, energy; corr.-broadcaster Sta. KTEN-TV, Ada, Okla., 1985; mem. staff presdl. transition office U.S. Pres. Bush, 1988-89, 90; anchor, pres. 30 minutes with Clayton Willis, 2000 Today With Clayton Willis; pres., anchor, exec. producer TV show 30 Minutes with Clayton Willis, PBS, 1990; dir. L. Clayton Willis Art Collection, Washington; anchor, corr. Channel 33 Arlington, Va., 1991—; pres., White House corr., congressional corr., photojournalist, Evening News Broadcasting Co., Collector Watch TV Show Ltd. with Clayton Willis, Alexandria, 1991—, 30 Mins. with Clayton Willis, and Willis News Service; prodr., anchor documentary programs Saudi Arabian TV, 1992—; exec. prodr., anchor Glimpses of the World documentaries, 1993; White House corr., photojournalist Hope (Ark.) Star, 1994—. Contbg. author: Capital Fare; contbr. articles to Daily Mail, London, London Sunday Express, Umtali Post, Zimbabwe, Gwelo (Zimbabwe) Times, To the Point news mag., Johannesburg, The Citizen, Johannesburg, Hartford Courant, Sacramento Union, Chattanooga Times, UPI Radio Networks, Washington Post, The Hope (Ark.) Star, Phillips News Svc., also other mags. and newspapers. Broadcaster with Bush/Quayle Nat. Campaign Hdqrs., Washington, 1988; adviser Presdl. Transition Office of Pres. George Bush, 1988-89; loaned Haitian paintings for spl. exhbn. to Haitian Embassy, Washington, 1991, Milw. Art Mus., 1992. Recipient Outstanding Svc. award Harlem Prep. Sch., Johannes Gutenberg medal, 1984, Letters of Cert. Appreciation Pres. of U.S., 1989. Mem. Blue Ridge Summit, Penna. Club: Overseas Press of Am.; Monterey Country Club, Blue Ridge Summit, Pa. Home and Office: Evening News Broadcasting Co PO Box 25615 Washington DC 20007*

WILLIS, DONNA ROSE, oil company executive; b. Fairfax, Okla., Mar. 29, 1931; d. Willard Lewis and Ruby (DeNoya) Oller; m. J.E. McAlpine, Oct. 14, 1950 (div. 1968); children: Louis, Jennifer, Jacqueline, Jaime, Jonna. Student, Stephens Coll., 1948-50, Okla. State U., 1951-52. Okla. landman Tulsa, 1952-55, ind. prodr., 1955-65; oil promotions Oklahoma City, 1975-78; ind. oil operator Willis Exploration Co., Oklahoma City, 1978-87; oil/gas cons.; owner, mgr. Horse Breeder's Farm; discoverer unknown geol. sandstone, Okla., 1979. Mem. Am. Paint Horse Assn. (2 world champions), Nat. Reining Horse Assn. (Internat. Reining Cup Winner 1992). Roman Catholic. Office: Willis Exploration Co PO Box 851052 Yukon OK 73085-1052

WILLIS, DWAYNE DAVID, information systems consultant; b. Ashland, Ky., Apr. 4, 1964; s. Ronald Ray and Mae (Hensley) W.; m. Nanette Marie Felty, Aug. 6, 1988; children: Emily Adrienne, Ian Krystoffer Scott. BBA, Morehead State U., 1992, MA, 1995. Steelworker Armco Steel Co., L.P., Ashland, 1987-92; account mgr. Van Dyke, Inc., Ashland, 1993-94; contr. Coleman Constrn., Inc., Portsmouth, Ohio, 1994-96; pvt. practice MIS cons. Darkstar Cons., Flatwoods, Ky., 1996—; bd. dirs. T.T.&K., Inc., Portsmouth, Ohio. Chmn. Greenup County (Ky.) Young Reps., 1991. Named to Outstanding Young Men of Am., 1989; named Century III Leader, Century III Leadership Found., 1982. Mem. Computer Users Group of Ashland (pres. 1992), Order of Ky. Cols., Kappa Delta Pi. Methodist. Home: 912 Mary Sue Dr Flatwoods KY 41139 Office: Darkstar Cons 912 Mary Sue Dr Flatwoods KY 41139-1332

WILLIS, ELEANOR LAWSON, university official; b. Nashville, Sept. 15, 1936; d. Harry Alfred Jr. and Helen Russell (Howse) Lawson; m. Alvis Rux Rochelle, Aug. 25, 1956 (div. Mar. 1961); m. William Reese Willis Jr., Mar. 7, 1964 (div. June 1994) children: Alfred Russell Willis, William Reese III, Brent Lawson. BA cum laude, Vanderbilt U., 1957. Host children's syndicated TV show Sta. WSIX-TV, Nashville, 1961-64; tchr. head start program Metro Pub. Sch., Nashville, 1965-67; co-investigator cognitive edn. curriculum project Peabody Coll., Nashville, 1979-81; dir., founder Heads Up Child Devel. Ctr., Inc., Nashville, 1973-87; dir. Tenn. Vols. for Gore for Pres. Campaign, Nashville, 1987-88; dir. devel. Vanderbilt Inst. Pub. Policy Studies, Vanderbilt U., Nashville, 1988—; mem. task force on child abuse Dept. Human Svcs., Nashville, 1976; mem. mental health ctr. adv. bd.

Vanderbilt U., 1978-80, bd. dirs. Vanderbilt Child Devel. Ctr.; mem. instrumental enrichment adv. bd. Peabody/Vanderbilt U., 1981-82. Author: (with others) I Really Like Myself, 1973, I Wonder Where I Came From, 1973. Pres. Nashville Bar Aux., 1967-68, Nashville Symphony Guild, 1984-85, W.O. Smith Nashville Community Music Sch., 1987-89; founder, bd. mem. Rochelle Ctr., Nashville, 1968-96; vice chmn. Century III Com., Nashville, 1978-80; chmn. so. region Am. Symphony Orch. League Vol. Coun., Washington, 1984-86, Homecoming 1986 Steering Com., Nashville, 1985-86; mem. Cheekwood Fine Arts Ctr., Nahville City Ballet, Nashville Symphony Assn., Dem. Women of Davidson County; appointed Metro Arts Commn., 1992; exec. dir. Friends of Warner Park, 1994. Recipient Leadership Nashville award, 1982; Seven Leading Ladies award Nashville Mag., 1984; Eleanor Willis Day proclaimed by City of Nashville, 1987. Mem. Exchange Club of Nashville, Tenn. Conservation League, Vanderbilt Alumni Assn. Presbyterian. Office: 50 Vaughn Rd Nashville TN 37221-3706

WILLIS, ISAAC, dermatologist, educator; b. Albany, Ga., July 13, 1940; s. R.L. and Susie M. (Miller) W.; m. Alliene Horne, June 12, 1965; children: Isaac Horne, Alliric Isaac. BS, Morehouse Coll., 1961, DSc (hon.), 1989; MD, Howard U., 1965. Diplomate Am. Bd. Dermatology. Intern Phila. Gen. Hosp., 1965-66; fellow Howard U., Washington, 1966-67; resident, fellow U. Pa., Phila., 1967-69, assoc. in dermatology, 1969-70; instr. dept. dermatology U. Calif., San Francisco, 1970-72; asst. prof. Johns Hopkins U. and Johns Hopkins Hosp., Balt., 1972-73, Emory U., Atlanta, 1973-77, assoc. prof., 1977-82; prof. Morehouse Sch. Medicine, Atlanta, 1982—, chief dermatology, 1991—; dep. commdr. of 3297th USA Hosp. (1000B), 1990—; attending staff Phila. Gen. Hosp., 1969-70, Moffit Hosp., U. Calif., 1970-72, Johns Hopkins Hosp., Balt. City Hosp., Good Samaritan Hosp., 1972-74, Crawford W. Long Meml. Hosp., Atlanta, 1974—, West Paces Ferry Hosp., 1974—, others; mem. grants rev. panel EPA, 1986—; mem. gen. medicine group IA study sect. NIH, 1985—, mem. nat. adv. bd. Arthritis and Musculoskeletal and Skin Diseases, 1991—; chmn. instl. rev. bd., mem. pharmacy and therapeutic com.; mem. nat. adv. coun. U. Pa. Sch. Medicine, 1995—, charter mem. nat. alumni coun., 1995—; bd. mem. Comml. Bank Gwinnett; West Paces Med. Ctr.; mem. gov.'s commn. on effectiveness and economy in govt. State of Ga. Human Resources Task Force, 1991—; charter mem. Nat. Alumni Adv. Coun. U. Pa. Med. Ctr., 1995—; mem. com. adv. bd. sch. pub. health Emory U., 1994—; cons. in field. Bd. dirs. Heritage Bank, Comml. Bank of Ga., chmn. audit rev. com., 1988-96; chmn. State of Ga. Dermatology Found., 1995; bd. dirs. Lupus Specialists, Inc., 1996—, InterVu, Inc., 1995—. Served to col. USAR, 1983-95. EPA grantee, 1985—. Author: Textbook of Dermatology, 1971—; Contbr. articles to profl. jours. Chmn. bd. med. dirs. Lupus Erythematrosus Found., Atlanta, 1975-83; bd. dirs. Jacquelyn McClure Lupus Erythematrosus Clinic, 1982—; bd. med. dirs. Skin Cancer Found., 1980—; trustee Friendship Bapt. Ch., Atlanta, 1980-82 . Nat. Cancer Inst. grantee, 1974-77, 78—; EPA grantee, 1980—. Fellow Am. Acad. Dermatolgy, Am. Dermtol. Assn.; mem. AAAS, Soc. Investigative Dermatology, Am. Fedn. Clin. Research, Am. Soc. Photobiology, Am. Med. Assn., Nat. Med. Assn., Internat. Soc. Tropical Dermatology, Pan Am. Med. Assn., Phi Beta Kappa, Omicron Delta Kappa. Clubs: Frontiers Internat., Sportsman Internat. Subspecialties: dermatology; cancer research (medicine). Home: 1141 Regency Rd NW Atlanta GA 30327-2719 Office: NW Med Ctr 3280 Howell Mill Rd NW Ste 342 Atlanta GA 30327-4109

WILLIS, JERRY WELDON, computer systems educator, writer; b. Tuscumbia, Ala., Jan. 27, 1943; s. Elbert Carter and Lavice Mae (McAlpin) W.; m. Dee Anna Smith, Mar. 28, 1987; 1 child, Amy Elizabeth. BA, Union U., 1966; MA, PhD, U. Ala., 1970. Asst. prof. U. Guelph (Ont., Can.), 1972-74, U. Western Ont., London, 1974-76, U. B.C., Vancouver, 1976-78; prof. edn. Tex. Tech U., Lubbock, 1978-87; dean Edn. and Home Econs. Miss. U. for Women, 1987-88; prof., program coord. Instrnl. Tech.-Ednl. Computing, E. Carolina U. Sch. of Edn., 1988-91; prof., dir. ctr. for info. tech. and tchr. edn. Coll. of Edn. U. Houston, 1991—; pres. Willis Pub. Group; adv. Pres's. Panel on Technology in Edn., 1995. Author: Peanut Butter and Jelly Guide to Computers, 1978 (Outstanding Computer Book, Am. Library Jour.); Nailing Jelly to a Tree, 1981; Computers for Everybody, 1981 (Outstanding Computer Book, Am. Library Jour.); Computers for People, 1982; Computers, Teaching and Learning, 1983; The Essential Commodore 128 User's Guide, 1986; The Essential Atari ST User's Guide, 1986; Super Calc 3: Learning, Mastering, and Using, 1986; Using Super Calc 4, 1987; Desktop Publishing with your IBM PC and Compatible, 1987; Educational Computing: An Introduction, 1986, 96; Computer Simulations: A Guide to Educational Applications, 1986, Teaching with Artificial Reality, 1990, Works Tutorial and Applicatons, 1990, Computers, Reading and Language Arts, 1996; assoc. editor: Computers in the Schools; contbg. editor Educational Technology; also 34 other books and transls. in 9 langs.; contbr. chpt. to book. Mem. Internat. Soc. for Tech. in Edn., Assn. for Computing Machinery, Assn. for Tchr. Educators, Soc. for Info. Tech. and Tchr. Edn. (founder, pres. 1991-95, jour. co-editor 1991—, Outstanding Contbns. award 1996). Home: 1007 N Sunset Dr Pearland TX 77581-6766 Office: U Houston Coll Of Edn Houston TX 77204

WILLIS, KEVIN ALVIN, professional basketball player; b. L.A., Sept. 6, 1962. Student, Jackson C.C., Mich., Mich. State U. Basketball player Atlanta Hawks, 1984-94; with MiamiHeat, 1994—. Named NBA All-Star, 1992. Office: Miami Heat The Miami Arena Miami FL 33136*

WILLIS, MARILYN, medical librarian; b. Magnolia, Ark., Mar. 10, 1933; d. Louie Mansfield and Mary Eleanor (Casey) W. MusB, La. State U., 1955, MLS, 1966. Acquisitions, serials libr. La. State U., Shreveport, 1967-69; serials libr. La. State U. Med. Sch., Shreveport, 1969-75; med. libr. Schumpert Med. Ctr., Shreveport, 1976-94. Mem. Med. Libr. Assn. (cert., s. ctrl. region). Home: 7800 Youree Dr Apt 101 Shreveport LA 71105-5543

WILLIS, PAUL ALLEN, librarian; b. Floyd County, Ind., Oct. 1, 1941; s. Clarence Charles and Dorothy Jane (Harritt) W.; m. Barbara Marcum, June 15, 1963; children: Mark, Sally. A.B., U. Ky., 1963, J.D., 1969; M.L.S., U. Md., 1966. Cataloger, Library of Congress, Washington, 1963; head descriptive cataloging br. Sci. and Tech. Info. Facility NASA, College Park, Md., 1963-66; law librarian, prof. law U. Ky., Lexington, 1966-73; dir. libraries U. Ky., 1973—, acting dean Coll. Library Sci., 1975-76, 88; exec. sec. Ky. Jud. Retirement and Removal Commn., 1977-81; mem. adv. com. Center for Jud. Conduct Orgns., Am. Judicature Soc., Chgo., 1979-81; bd. dirs. Southeastern Library Network, Atlanta, 1980-83, 96—; mem. exec. com. Ky. Hist. Soc., 1984-88; mem. Ky. Adv. Coun. on Libraries, 1985—, adv. com. Online Computer Library Ctr., 1986-90; cons. S.E. Consortium for Internat. Devel., U. Sriwijaya, Palembang, Sumatera, Indonesia, 1987-88. Sr. fellow UCLA, summer 1982. Mem. Assn. Southeastern Research Libraries (chair 1986-88). Home: 2055 Bridgeport Dr Lexington KY 40502-2615 Office: U Ky Libr Office of Dir Lexington KY 40506

WILLIS, RALPH HOUSTON, mathematics educator; b. McMinnville, Tenn., Dec. 26, 1942; s. Carl Houston and Carrie Lee (Hill) W.; m. Gayle Catherine Celestin, June 29, 1973 (div. Apr. 1985); m. Velma Inez Church, Aug. 10, 1985; stepchild, Bobbie Lynn White. BS in Math., Mid. Tenn. State U., 1964, MA in Math., 1966. Cert. secondary edn. Instr. math. dept. Western Carolina U., Cullowhee, N.C., 1968-73, asst. prof. math. dept., 1973-83, assoc. prof. math. dept., 1983—. Editor: (newsletters) Abelian Grapevine-Secondary Math, 1970-88, The Child of Mathematics-Elementary-Middle Grade Math., 1972-78; mem. editl. bd. The Centroid, 1995—; contbr. articles to profl. jours. Dir., coord. Western Carolina U. High Sch. Math. Contest, Cullowhee, 1970—; solicitor-coord. Math. Contest Scholarship Program, Cullowhee, 1971-82; initiator-coord. Math. Dept.'s Vis. Speaker Program, Western Carolina U., Cullowhee, 1974-77; faculty sponsor N.C. Coun. Tchrs. Math. Student Affiliate, Cullowhee, 1988—. 1st lt. U.S. Army, 1966-68. Recipient Paul A. Reid Disting. Svc. award Western Carolina U., 1991, hon. mention N.C. Gov.'s Award for Excellence, 1991, Innovator award N.C. Coun. Tchrs. in Math., 1994. Mem. Nat. Coun. Tchrs. Math. (Innovator award 1994), N.C. Coun. Tchrs. Math. (historian 1993—, Innovator award 1994. editl. bd. Centroid 1995—), Phi Kappa Phi, Kappa Mu Epsilon. Office: Western Carolina U Math Dept Stillwell Bldg Cullowhee NC 28723

WILLIS, RONI MAY LEWIS, library administrator; b. Springfield, Mass., Dec. 27, 1954; d. Ralph Mansfield and Ruth Harriet (Williamson) Lewis; m. Arnold Thomas Willis, Aug. 7, 1976; 1 child, Dana Rene. BS in Edn., Winthrop Coll., 1976, MEd, 1979; M of Librarianship, U. S.C., 1982. Cert. pub. libr., Ga. Media specialist Chesterfield County S.C. Schs., Pogeland, 1976-79, Lancaster County S.C. Schs., 1979-81; young adult and audiovisual libr. West Ga. Reg. Libr., Carrollton, 1983-84; asst. dir. West Ga. Reg. Libr., 1984—; chair-elect, chair North Ga. Associated Librs., 1988-90. Mem. Carroll County Cmty. Theatre; treas. Carroll County Heart unit Am. Heart Assn., 1994—, sec., 1992-94. Mem. ALA, Ga. Libr. Assn. (chair pub. rels. com. 1988-90), Pub. Libr. Assn., Carroll County C. of C., Pilot Club of Carrollton (pres. 1986-87). Republican. Baptist. Office: West Ga Reg Libr Carrollton GA 30117

WILLIS, RUSSELL EARL, consultant; b. Tallahassee, Dec. 21, 1966; s. John Gibson and Patricia Sue (Kaiser) W. AA, Tallahassee C.C., 1987; BSME, Fla. A&M U.-Fla. State U., 1992. Computer cons. Fla. State U. Acad. Computing and Network Svcs., Tallahassee, 1989-95; computer sys. specialist Bur. Hist. Preservation, Dept. State, Tallahassee, 1995. Mem. ASME, AIAA, Assn. for Computing Machinery, Nat. Space Soc., Planetary Soc., Libr. of Congress Assocs. (charter), Distributive Edn. Clubs U.S. (cert. of appreciation 1992, 93), Phi Theta Kappa.

WILLIS, THOMAS DELENA, health insurance company executive; b. Barstow, Calif., May 26, 1955; s. William Thomas and Delena (Curtis) W.; m. Olena Ann Seaton, Jan. 1, 1977 (div. Mar. 1981); 1 child, Amber LaShelle. Student, South Plains Coll., Levelland, Tex., 1973-74, 76, Mid. Tenn. State U., 1975-76. Computer technician NCR, Lubbock, Tex., 1976-77; loan officer Southwestern Investment Co., Lubbock, 1977-78; agt., sales mgr. Am. Nat. Ins. Co., Lubbock, 1978-81; owner, mgr. Willis Ins., Lubbock, 1981-86; regional sales mgr. Time Ins. Co., Dallas, 1986-90; pres., CEO Gt. S.W. Brokerage, Dallas, 1990—; instr. Life Underwriters Tng. Coun., Dallas, 1991—. Fouding mem. Heritage Bapt. Ch., Lubbock, 1984, Am. Men's Bus. Club, Lubbock, 1984-85; mem. president's cabinet Nat. Farm Life, 1985; vol. United Way, ARC, Dallas and Milw., 1986—. With USMC, 1973-75. Mem. Nat. Assn. Health Underwriters (chmn. health ins. tng. coun. 1988-90), Nat. Assn. Life Underwriters (chmn. membership com. 1989-90, industry awards 1990-91). Republican. Office: 15400 Knoll Trail Dr Ste 204 Dallas TX 75248-3465

WILLMANN, DONNIE GLENN, safety executive; b. Waco, Tex., Aug. 25, 1955; s. Robert and Marie Louise (Schraeder) W.; m. Susan Lynn Martin, June 14, 1975. Student, Tarleton State U., 1973-75; BS in Indsl. Tech., Tex. A & M U., 1978. Cert. safety profl. Mfg. ops. devel. trainee Sii Drilco, Houston, 1978-80, loss control rep., 1980-81; safety mgr. Weatherford/Lamb U.S. Inc., Houston, 1981-83; corp. safety mgr. Weatherford Internat., Houston, 1983-86; loss control specialist CNA Ins., Houston, 1986-88; sr. safety adminstr. Enron Ops. Corp., Houston, 1988—. Mem. Am. Soc. Safety Engrs. (membership chmn. 1989-90, treas. 1990-91, v.p. membership 1991-92, program chmn. 1992-94, pres.-elect. 1994-95, pres. 1995-96, named Gulf Coast chpt. Safety Profl. of Yr. 1994-95, asst. v.p. region III 1995-96), Nat. Safety Mgmt. Soc. Lutheran. Home: 19911 Sweetgum Forest Dr Humble TX 77346-2119 Office: Enron Ops Corp 1400 Smith St Houston TX 77002

WILLMARTH, ROGER A., budget director; b. Concord, Calif., Apr. 30, 1943; s. Gardiner B. and Ruth M. (Lundquist) W.; m. Gay Willmarth, Nov. 25, 1967 (div. Jan. 1990); children: James Scott, Melissa Gay. BA, San Jose State U., 1966; BS, U. No. Colo., 1971. Bus. mgr. Sidney (Nebr.) Pub. Schs., 1976-81; dean of adminstrv. svcs. Labette C.C., Parson, Kans., 1981-87; budget dir. El Paso (Tex.) C.C., 1988—; bd. dirs. Better Bus. Bur., El Paso, 1989—. Home: 4401 Marcus Uribe Dr El Paso TX 79934-3724 Office: EPCC PO Box 20500 El Paso TX 79998

WILLNER, EUGENE BURTON, food and liquor company executive; b. Chgo., July 27, 1934; s. Fred and Mae (Goodhartz) W.; B.A., Northwestern U., 1956; m. Karen Nell Kaye, Feb. 22, 1962; children—Tracy Fran, Kelly Kaye. Pres., World Wide Fisheries Inc., Chgo., 1956-60; merchandiser Edison Bros. Stores Inc., St. Louis, 1960-66; v.p. Mo. Supreme Life Ins. Co., St. Louis, 1966-67; exec. v.p. Exec. Agys., Inc., St. Louis, 1966-67; pres. Bluff Creek Industries, Inc., Ocean Springs, Miss., 1967-69, Purse String Stores, Inc., Miami, Fla., 1968-69, World Wide Fisheries, Inc., Miami, Fla., 1969-73, Universal Fisheries, Inc., Miami, 1974—, Renwill Seafoods, Inc., 1979—; chmn. bd. Astral Liquors, Inc., Foxy Laidy Lounges, Prime Universal Seafood Corp., Miami, also Key West, Fla., Caracas, Venezuela, San Juan del Sur, Nicaragua, Quito, Ecuador; pres., chmn. bd. Common Markets, Inc., Miami, London and Moscow, 1980—; dir. Mo. Supreme Life Ins. Co., Lite Am. Corp. Clubs: Deering Bay Country, Turnberry, Grove Isle, Fisher Island, Palm Beach Country. Office: 29000 S Dixie Hwy Homestead FL 33033-2302 Address: PO Box 570337 Miami FL 33297-0337

WILLNER, LARRY ELLIOTT, telecommunications company executive, consultant; b. New Haven, May 16, 1932; s. Abraham Louis and Ann (Kaye) W.; m. Inga Katz, Oct. 28, 1956; children: Allan, Susan. BS in Engring., U.S. Mil. Acad., 1954; MBA in Fin., Stanford U., 1964; diploma with distinction, Nat. Def. U., 1975. Commd. 2d lt. U.S. Army, 1954, advanced through grades to Col., ret., 1980; dir. Govt. Systems Div. Western Union Corp., McLean, Va., 1981, sr. dir., 1981-82, div. dir., 1983-84, div. v.p., 1984-85, v.p., gen. mgr., 1985-86; sr. v.p. Govt. Networks Div. Contel Corp., McLean, 1986-87; group v.p. Info. Systems and Networks Inc., Bethesda, Md., 1988-89; exec. v.p. INTACT Inc., Chantilly, Va., 1989—; chmn. bd. dirs. Western Union Hawaii, Honolulu, 1985-86; cons. Identity Rsch. Inc., McLean, 1981-92, U.S. Sprint Corp., Herndon, Va., 1989—, Ops. Rsch., Arlington, Va., 1981, GTE Corp., McLean, 1990-91, Computer Scis. Corp., Falls Church, Va., 1991-96, ARINC, Inc., 1991-92, Boeing Computer Svcs., 1992-94, Harris Corp., 1992, Grumman Corp., 1992, GSI/Infonet, 1993-95, Boeing Info. Svcs., 1994-95, AT&&T, 1994—, Andrulis Rsch. Corp., 1993-94, SRC Corp., 1994, DC Net, Inc., 1993-95, UNITEl Communication Corp., 1993-96, A.T. Kearney Corp., 1995-96. Contbr. articles on telecommunications, fgn. policy, weapons systems acquisition, etc. to profl. jours. Decorated Legion of Merit, Bronze Star, Disting. Svc. medal; Disting. Rsch. fellow Nat. Def. U., 1975; named Hon. Prof. systems acquisitions Def. Systems Mgmt. Coll., 1974. Mem. IEEE, Armed Forces Communications-Electronics Assn. (internat. bd. 1986-90), Nat. Def. Exec. Res., Fed. Communications Commn. Nat. Industry Adv. Com., Stanford Grad. Sch. Bus. Alumni Assn. (chpt. bd. dirs. 1980-83), Masons, Scottish Rite. Republican. Jewish. Home: 4160 Elizabeth Ln Annandale VA 22003-3648 Office: INTACT Inc 14500 Avion Pky Chantilly VA 22021-1108

WILLS, DONALD, bank executive; b. 1936. With Broward Schs. Credit Union, 1955—, now pres. Office: Broward Schools Credit Union 1879 N State Road 7 Fort Lauderdale FL 33313-5007*

WILLSON, ROBERT (WILLIAM), glass sculpture and watercolor artist; b. Mertzon, Tex., May 28, 1912; s. James Thomas and Birdie Alice (Blanks) W.; m. Virginia Lambert, Aug. 12, 1941 (div. 1977); 1 child, Mark Joseph; m. Margaret Pace, May 30, 1981. BA, U. Tex., 1934; MFA, U. Bellas Artes, Mex., 1941. Pub. sch. tchr. various small Tex. towns, 1936-40; chmn. art dept. Tex. Wesleyan Coll., Ft. Worth, 1940-48; owner Nob Hill Tourist Resort, Winslow, Ark., 1948-52; prof. art U. Miami, 1952-77, ret., 1977; represented by Sol Del Rio Gallery, San Antonio, Galleria d'Arte Moderna Ravagnan, Venice, Italy, Lyons-Matrix Gallery, Austin, Tex., Sandra Ainsley Gallery, Toronto, Stein Gallery, Portland, Maine, Painted Horse Gallery, Aspen, Colo., Parchman-Stremmel Gallery, San Antonio; tchr. U. Mex., 1935; dir. Nob Hill Art Gallery, Ark. Ozarks, 1948-52; dir. Tex. Wesleyan Coll. Art Gallery, 1940-48; cons.-dir. Peoria Art Mus., Ill., 1969. One-man shows include U. Tex., Austin, 1980, McNay Art Mus., San Antonio, 1982, Art Inst. of the Permian Basin, Odessa, Tex. 1985, 96, Tulane U., New Orleans, 1986, San Antonio Mus. Art, 1986, San Angelo (Tex.) Mus. of Art, 1989, Lyons-Matrix Gallery, Austin, 1989, 92, 95, Mus. of Modern Art, Venice, Italy, 1984, Galleria d'Arte Sant'Apollonia, 1989, Galleria d'Arte Moderna, San Marco, Venice, 1984-89, Martin Mus. of Art, Baylor U., Waco, Tex., 1991-92, N.Mex. Mus. of Fine Art, Santa Fe, 1993, Bee County Coll., Beeville, Tex., 1996; exhibited in group shows at Internat. Glass Art 982 Show, Venice, Italy, 1994; juried shows include San Francisco Mus. Art, 1971, Mus. Modern Art, Mexico City, Adria Gallery, N.Y.C., Harmon Gallery, Naples, Fla., Lowe Art Mus., Fucina degli Angeli Internat. Glass Scuplture Exhbns., Venice, 1966-88, La Biennale di Venizia, 1972; selected to 1st Biennial of Glass, Venezia Aperto Vetro, 1996; permanent collections include Museo Correr, Venice, Victoria and Albert Mus., London, Nat. Italian Glass Mus., Murano, Italy, Auckland Nat. Art Mus., New Zealand, U. Tex., Austin, Corning Mus. Glass, N.Y., Witte Art Mus., San Antonio, San Antonio Mus. Art, Phila. Mus. Art, Little Rock Ctr., Ark., Ft. Lauderdale (Fla.) Art Mus., Peoria Art Mus., Lowe Art Mus., Miami, Fla., Columbus (Ga.) Art Mus., Duke U. Art Mus., N.C., Oxford (Eng.)-Wilson-Willson Glass Collection, New Orleans Mus. Art, New Mex. Mus. Fine Art, Santa Fe, others; contbr. articles to profl. jours. Capt. USMCR, 1942-45. Tex. Regents scholarship U. Tex., 1930-34, Farmer Internat. fellowship to Mex., 1935; Nat. study grant Corning Mus. of Glass, 1956, rsch. grant U. Miami, 1964, 66, Feldman Found., 1976, Internat. rsch. grant U.S. Office of Edn., 1966-68, Coll. grants Shell Co. Found., 1971, 73. Mem. AAUP, Coun. of Ozark Artists and Craftsmen (founder), Fla. Craftsmen, Coll. Art Assn., Am. Assn. Mus., Fla. Sculptors, Tex. Sculptors, Tex. Watercolor Soc., others. Home: 207 Terrell Rd San Antonio TX 78209-5915

WILMER, HARRY ARON, psychiatrist; b. New Orleans, Mar. 5, 1917; s. Harry Aron and Leona (Schlenker) W.; m. Jane Harris, Oct. 31, 1944; children: Harry, John, Thomas, James, Mary. BS, U. Minn., 1938, MB, 1940, MS, 1940, MD, 1941, PhD, 1944. Intern, Gorgas Hosp., Ancon, C.Z., 1940-41; resident in neurology and psychiatry Mayo Clinic, Rochester, Minn., 1945-49, cons. in psychiatry, 1957-58; physician Palo Alto (Calif.) Clinic, 1949-51; pvt. practice medicine, Palo Alto, 1951-55, 1958-64; prof. psychiatry U. Calif. Med. Sch., San Francisco, 1964-69; sr. psychiatrist Scott & White Clinic, Temple, Tex., 1969-74; prof. psychiatry U. Tex. Health Sci. Ctr., San Antonio, 1974-87; mem. staff Audie Murphy VA Hosp., San Antonio, part-time 1974-82; founder, dir. Internat. Film Festivals on Culture and Psychiatry, U. Tex. Health Sci. Center, 1972-80; founder, pres., dir. Inst. Humanities, Salado, Tex., 1980—; practice medicine, specializing in psychiatry, Salado, Tex., 1982—. Served to capt. M.C., USNR, 1955-57. Guggenheim fellow, Zurich, 1969-70; NRC fellow, Johns Hopkins Hosp., 1944-45. Fellow Am. Psychiat. Assn. (life, emeritus), Am. Coll. Psychiatrists, Am. Acad. Psychoanalysis; mem. AAAS, Internat. Assn. Analytical Psychology, Author: Huber the Tuber, 1942, Corky the Killer, 1945, This is Your World, 1952, Social Psychiatry in Action, 1958, First Book for the Mind, 1963, Vietnam in Remission, 1985, Practical Jung, 1987, Closeness: A Dictionary of Ideas, Vol. I, 1989, Father Mother, 1989; (film) People Need People, 1961, Facing Evil, 1988, Evil, 1989, Creativity, 1990, Creativity Paradoxes and Relflections, 1991, Closeness: Personal and Professional Relations, 1992, Understandable Jung, 1994. Home: 506 S Ridge Rd Mill Creek PO Box 528 Salado TX 76571

WILMER, MARY CHARLES, artist; b. Atlanta, Aug. 25, 1930; d. William Knox and Harriott Creighton (Thomas) Fitzpatrick; student Wellesley Coll., 1948-50; AB, Agnes-Scott Coll., 1970; BFA, Coll. of Art, 1974; m. John Grant Wilmer, Dec. 28, 1950; children: John Grant, Knox Randolph, Charles Inman, Mary Catherine; m. Olin Grigsby Shivers, May 18, 1982. One-woman shows: Image South Gallery, 1974, Aronson Gallery, 1977, 79, Heath Gallery, 1982, Coach House Gallery, 1983, 89; exhibited in group show: Colony Sq., 1975; portrait painter, 1974—. Bd. dirs. Hillside Cottages, 1963-65, Atlanta Child Svcs., 1965-68, Atlanta Coll. Art, 1965-85, Atlanta Puppetry Arts, 1982-87; co-chmn. Ga. Commn. Nat. Mus. of Women in the Arts, 1985-87. Mem. Piedmont Driving Club, Jr. League, Piedmont Garden Club. Episcopalian. Address: 1 Vernon Rd NW Atlanta GA 30305-2964

WILMORE, FAYE C., elementary and secondary education educator; b. nr. Smith County, Tex., Mar. 6, 1938; d. Alfred C. and Melba E. (Ray) McClanahan; m. H. Eugene Wilmore, June 5, 1959; children: Jack Carter, Barry Eugene. BS in Biology, Middle Tenn. State U., 1959; MA, U. No. Colo., 1976. Tchr. various sch. sys., Tenn., 1959-72, Ind., 1959-72; prodr., narrator, tchr. Sta. WDCN-TV, Nashville, 1972-77; tchr. Dodson Elem. Sch., Hermitage, Tenn., 1978-86; coord. Apple Classrooms of Tomorrow (ACOT), Met. Nashville Pub. Sch. Sys., 1986-89, coord. ACOT tchr. devel., 1989—. Author guides and workbooks, 1972-77; creator tchr. devel. model, 1989-92; contbr. articles to profl. jours. Mem. NSF steering com., 1992—; mem. Tenn. Info. Infrastructure Task Force, Nashville, 1994-95; mem. Nashville's Am. 2000 steering com., 1992. Selected Tenn. rep. U.S. Sec. of Edn. Tech. Conf., Washington, 1994-95; NSF grantee, 1992-96. Mem. NEA, Delta Kappa Gamma (pres. 1988-90). Baptist. Office: ACOT TDC Dodson Elem 4401 Chandler Rd Hermitage TN 37076-4304

WILNER, MORTON HARRISON, retired lawyer; b. Balt., May 28, 1908; s. Joseph A. and Ida (Berkow) W.; m. Zelda Dunkelman, Nov. 3, 1940; children: James D., Thomas B., Lawrence J., Theodora. B.S. in Econs, U. Pa., 1930; J.D., Georgetown U., 1934. Bar: D.C. 1933. Gen. counsel emeritus Armed Forces Benefit Assn.; vice chmn. AFBA Indsl. Bank; bd. dirs. Armed Forces Benefit Svcs., Inc.; mem. emeritus Giant Food, Inc. Past pres. Jewish Community Center of Greater Washington.; Emeritus life trustee U. Pa.; past pres. Nat. Child Research Center; bd. govs. St. Albans Sch., 1968-72. Served to maj. USAAF; dep. dir. aircraft div. WPB 1942-45. Decorated Legion of Merit; recipient Ourisman Meml. award for civic achievement, 1970; Ben Franklin award U. Pa., 1973; alumni award of merit, 1975; Friar of Yr. award U. Pa., 1976; Wharton Sch. Club Joseph Wharton award, 1980. Mem. Fed. Bar Assn., ABA (ho. dels. 1971-73), D.C. Bar Assn., Internat. Bar Assn., Fed. Communications Bar Assn. (pres. 1969-70). Clubs: Army and Navy, Woodmont Country. Home: 2701 Chesapeake St NW Washington DC 20008-1042 Office: AFBA 909 N Washington St Alexandria VA 22314-1555

WILSON, ALBERT JOHN ENDSLEY, III, social gerontologist, administrator, consultant; b. Pitts., Oct. 9, 1934; s. Robert Endsley and Dorothy Mae (Parry) W.; m. Nancy Jean Hooton, Sept. 29, 1955 (div. Mar. 1963); children: Linda Jean, Albert John Endsley IV, Patrick Lee; m. Nera Bernice Kennedy, Nov. 24, 1965. AA in Liberal Arts, St. Petersburg Jr. Coll., 1954; BS in Mgmt., Fla. State U., 1956; MRC, U. Fla., Gainesville, 1958, PhD in Sociology, 1966. Research sociologist Fla. Dept. Health, St. Petersburg, 1961-66; dir. Inst. on Aging, U. So. Fla., Tampa, 1967-74; dep. dir. geriatric ctr. VA, Bay Pines, Fla., 1974-76, cons., Bay Pines and Waco, Tex., 1972-74, 76-77, 79-82; dir. grad. study gerontology Baylor U., Waco, 1978-81; dir., prof. Beard Gerontology Ctr., Lynchburg Coll., Va., 1983-94, prof. emeritus, 1994—; vis. prof. Calif. State U.-Chico, 1976-77; adj. prof. rural sociology Pa. State U., 1978-79; cons. in field; del. White House Conf. on Aging, Washington, 1971; expert witness U.S. Senate Com. on Aging, Washington, 1973; bd. dirs. Adult Care of Central Va., Lynchburg, 1984-87, Alzheimers Disease Support, Lynchburg, 1984-89; mem. geriatric prescription team Cen. Va. Cmty. Svcs. Bd., 1986-94; vice chmn. Va. Gov.'s Adv. Bd. on Aging, 1990-94; bd. dirs. Va. Coalition for the Aging, sec. 1987-88; chmn. adv. coun. Cen. Va. Area Agy. on Aging, 1986-92. Author: Social Services for Older Persons, 1984, revised edit. 1988; also chpt., articles; editor: Total Health and Aging, 1976, Ethical Considerations in Long Term Care, 1977, Centenarians: The New Generation, 1990. V.p. bd. Presbyn. Social Ministries, St. Petersburg, 1972-76, Interfaith Coalition on Aging, Pinellas County, Fla., 1974-76; mem. adv. com. Va. Baptist Hosp. Day Ctr., Lynchburg, 1984-94. Recipient Disting. Faculty Scholar award Lynchburg Coll., 1987, Mildred M. Seltzer Disting. Svc. award Assn. for Gerontology in Higher Edn., 1995; grantee Adminstrn. on Aging, HEW, 1969-72, 71-74, Health Services and Mental Health Adminstrn., USPHS, 1972-73, Calif. Dept. on Aging, 1976-77, Bedford Meml. Found., 1986-87, LWV, 1990-92. Mem. Gerontol. Soc. Am., Nat. Council on Aging, Am. Pub. Health Assn., So. Sociol. Soc., Va. Assn. on Aging (pres. 1985-86, Outstanding Svc. award 1986, Outstanding Educator of Yr. award 1993), So. Gerontol. Soc. (bd. dirs. 1988-90, Pres.'s award 1990). Democrat. Methodist. Avocations: antique and special interest autos, hiking, exploring, traveling. Home: 2024B Nature's Bend Dr Fernandina Beach FL 32034

WILSON, ALMA, state supreme court justice; b. Pauls Valley, Okla.; d. William R. and Anna L. (Schuppert) Bell; m. William A. Wilson, May 30, 1948 (dec. Mar. 1994); 1 child, Lee Anne. AB, U. Okla., 1939, JD, 1941, LLD (hon.), 1992. Bar: Okla. 1941. Sole practice Muskogee, Okla., 1941-43; sole practice Oklahoma City, 1943-47, Pauls Valley, 1948-69; judge Pauls Valley Mcpl. Ct., 1967-68; apptd. spl. judge Dist. Ct. 21, Norman, Okla., 1969-75, dist. judge, 1975-79; justice Okla. Supreme Ct., Oklahoma City, 1982—, now chief justice. Mem. alumni bd. dirs. U. Okla.; mem. Assistance League; trustee Okla. Meml. Union. Recipient Guy Brown award, 1974, Woman of Yr. award Norman Bus. and Profl. Women, 1975, Okla. Women's

Hall of Fame award, 1983, Pioneer Woman award, 1985, Disting. Svc. Citation U. Okla., 1985. Mem. AAUW, Garvin County Bar Assn. (past pres.), Okla. Bar Assn. (co-chmn. law and citizenship edn. com.), Okla. Trial Lawyers Assn. (Appellate Judge of Yr. 1986, 89), Altrusa, Am. Legion Aux. Office: Okla Supreme Ct State Capitol Rm 245 Oklahoma City OK 73105*

WILSON, ALPHUS DAN, plant pathologist, researcher; b. Ft. Worth, Tex., Sept. 27, 1958; s. Alphus James and Essie Morris (Nugent) W.; m. Lisa Beth Forse, July 11, 1992; 1 child, Jon Colter. BS in Bioenviron. Sci., Tex. A&M U., 1981, MS in Plant Pathology, 1983; PhD in Plant Pathology, Wash. State U., 1988. Grad. rsch. asst. Tex. A&M U., College Station, 1981-83, Wash. State U., Pullman, 1984-88; postdoctoral plant pathologist USDA-Agrl. Rsch. Svc., Pullman, 1989-90, rsch. plant pathologist, 1990-91; rsch. plant pathologist USDA-Forest Svc., Stoneville, Miss., 1991—; tech. cons. Tex. Oak Wilt Suppression Adv. Bd., Austin, 1992—, Tex. Forest Svc. Strategic Plan Team, Austin, 1994—. Author: (chpt.) Systematics, Ecology, and Evolution of Endophytic fungi in Grasses and Woody Plants, 1996; contbr. articles to profl. jours. Project judge Delta Regional Sci. Fair, Greenville, Miss., 1992; sci. demonstrator Delta Schs. Sci. Awareness Day, Stoneville, 1993. Recipient fellowship Chevron Chem. Corp., 1981-83, Rsch. fellowship Wash. State U., 1984-88. Mem. AAAS, N.Y. Acad. Scis., Am. Phytopathological Soc., Mycol. Soc. Am., Soc. Am. Foresters, Alpha Zeta. Republican. Methodist. Home: 2202 Highway 1 N Greenville MS 38703-9471 Office: USDA Forest Svc So Hardwoods Lab PO box 227 Stoneville MS 38776

WILSON, AMY LOUISE, public relations executive; b. Ferriday, La., Nov. 10, 1958; d. Perry Andrew and Mary Agnes (Weed) W. BA, U. Ark., 1980, MA in English, 1983. Teaching asst. dept. English U. Ark., Fayetteville, 1980-83; gen. assignment reporter, columnist Northwest Ark. Times, Fayetteville, 1984-85; writer, lifestyle reporter, editor Sunday Lifestyle Ark. Democrat, Little Rock, 1985-89; health reporter, feature writer, war-desk copy editor, Home and Books editor Ark. Gazette, Little Rock, 1989-91; freelance writer, pub. rels. and comm. Amy L. Wilson Comm., Little Rock, 1991-92; coord. comm./edn. Ark. Environ. Fedn., Inc., Little Rock, 1992—. Recipient First Place News Article awards Ark. Press Women, 1987, 89, Second and Third Place awards, 1990, First Place Comm. award, 1992, contest awards, 1993. Mem. Pub. Rels. Soc. Am., Nat. Fedn. Press Women (Nat. 1st Place Editing award 1989), Words Lit. Soc. Office: Ark Environ Fedn 1400 W Markham St Little Rock AR 72201-1840

WILSON, ANGELA SABURN, nursing educator; b. Norfolk, Va., May 24, 1961; d. Richard Ruben and Rose Faye (Mobley) Saburn; m. Robert Walker Wilson, Mar. 4, 1989. Diploma, Norfolk Gen. Hosp. Sch. Nsg., 1987; BSN, Old Dominion U., 1989, MSN, 1993. RN, Va.; cert. pediatric nurse. Staff nurse Children's Hosp. of King's Daus., Norfolk, 1987-90, staff devel. coord., 1990-94, nurse educator, 1994-95; nursing instr. DePaul Hosp., Norfolk, 1995-96, Christopher Newport U., 1996—. Mem. Va. Nurses Assn., Golden Key Honor Soc., Sigma Theta Tau (pres. Epsilon Chi chpt.), Alpha Chi, Phi Kappa Phi. Home: 214 Faulk Rd Norfolk VA 23502-5328

WILSON, ANNA MARIE S., magazine editor, publisher; b. Pampa, Tex., Dec. 2, 1917; d. William Alonzo and Elsie Hildegard (Voelkel) Stigler; widowed, Mar. 1993; chidlren: Lonnie W. Wilson Jr., Carole Ann Boyd. BA, U. Tex., 1936, MA, 1937. Office mgr., newsletter editor A & M Advt., Dallas, 1943-50; real estate broker Ann Wilson Real Estate, Dallas, 1952—; editor, pub. Pug Talk Mag., Dallas, 1986—. Editor Pet News, Dallas Times Herald, 1985-91. Chief ct. clk. County of Dallas, 1953-85. Mem. Dog Writers Assn. Am., Bluebonnet Pug Dog Club, Tex. Kennel Club, Inc. (corr. sec. 1988-90, breed club liaison 1990—), Phi Beta Kappa, Sigma Delta Pi, Pi Lambda Theta. Democrat. Home and Office: 223 W Louisiana Ave Dallas TX 75224-2224

WILSON, ARTHUR JESS, psychologist; b. Yonkers, N.Y., Oct. 25, 1910; s. Samuel Louis and Anna (Gilbert) W.; BS, NYU, 1935, MA, 1949, PhD, 1961; LLB, St. Lawrence U., 1940; JD, Bklyn. Law Sch., 1967; m. Lillian Moss, Sept. 16, 1941; children—Warren David, Anton Francis. Tchr., Yonkers Pub. Schs., 1935-40; dir. adult edn. Yonkers, 1940-42; supr. vocat. rehab. N.Y. State Dept. Edn., 1942-44; personnel exec. Abraham & Straus, Bklyn., 1946-47; rehab. field sec. N.Y. Tb and Health Assn., 1947-48; dir. rehab. Westchester County Med. Center, Valhalla, N.Y., 1948-67; dir. Manhattan Narcotic Rehab. Center, N.Y. State Drug Abuse Control Commn., 1967-68; clin. psychologist VA Hosp., Montrose, N.Y., 1968-73; pvt. practice clin. psychology, Yonkers, 1973—; cons. N.Y. State Dept. Edn., HEW; spl. lectr. Sch. Pub. Health and Adminstrv. Medicine, Columbia U. and Grad. Sch., N.Y. U.; instr. Westchester Community Coll., Valhalla, N.Y.; selected participant Clin. Study Tour of China, 1980. With USN, 1944-46. Recipient Founders Day award NYU, 1961. Mem. APA, Internat. Mark Twain Soc. (hon.), N.Y. Acad. Scis., N.Y. State Psychol. Assn., Kappa Delta Pi, Phi Delta Kappa, Epsilon Pi Tau. Author: The Emotional Life of the Ill and Injured, 1950; A Guide to the Genius of Cardozo, 1939; The Wilson Teaching Inventory, 1941; also articles. Honored as Westchester Author, Westchester County Hist. Soc., 1957. Home and Office: 4121 NW 88th Ave Apt 204 Coral Springs FL 33065-1820 also: 487 Park Ave Yonkers NY 10703-2121

WILSON, BARBARA DAVENPORT, writer, editor; b. Atlanta, Jan. 24, 1961; d. Robert Tedford and Madie Lou (Rudolph) Davenport; m. Edward Pierce Jr., Mar. 26, 1983 (div. Apr. 3, 1989); m. Kevin Scott Wilson, Aug. 3, 1991; 1 child, Elizabeth Kate Wilson. AA, Gulf Coast C.C., Panama City, Fla., 1992; BS, Florida State U., 1993. Pub. rels. Huff Comms., Atlanta, 1988-89; camera operator, floor dir., promotions asst., copywriter WMBB-TV, Panama City, Fla., 1989-91; writer intern News Herald, Panama City, Fla., 1991; pub. rels. coord. Nat. Multiple Sclerosis Soc., Dublin-Macon, Ga., 1994-95; staff writer, education editor Courier Herald, Dublin, Ga., 1995—. Prodr. promotional video Peters Campaign, 1990. Mem. bd. BC Drug Free, Panama City, Fla., 1990-91; with publicity Habitat for Humanity, AHA, Dublin Ga., 1996; vol. Dem. Nat. Convention, Atlanta, 1988. Recipient Sch. Bell Media award Ga. Assn. Educators, 1996. Mem. Soc. Profl. Jours. Democrat. Episcopalian. Office: Courier Herald Drawer B 655 Dublin GA 31021

WILSON, BARNETT RONALD, sales specialist, writer; b. Clarkesville, Ga., June 27, 1929; s. Elbert Barnett and Ora Irene (Carson) W.; m. Sarah Ann Parsons, Oct. 27, 1979. BBA, Ga. State Coll., 1959. Salesman Davidson Enamel Products, Lima, Ohio, 1961-67, Luster-Life, Inc., Scranton, Pa., 1967-73; pres. Glamor-Ron, Inc., Pocono Summit, Pa., 1973-80; salesman Davis & Wingard Assocs., Charlotte, N.C., 1980-86; pres. R.W. Bldg. Products, Charlotte, N.C., 1986-90; salesman/svc. man Fenestra Corp., Harrisburg, N.C., 1990-92, Mr. Doorman, Inc., Charlotte, 1992—. Contbr. hist. essays. With USNR, 1951, Korea. Mem. Am. Legion. Republican. Avocations: golf, reading, writing, travel, historical research. Home: 6536 Dwight Ware Blvd Charlotte NC 28227

WILSON, BENJAMIN FRANKLIN, JR., education educator; b. Shreveport, La., Aug. 13, 1933; s. Benjamin Franklin Wilson and Charlotte (Cornman) Dudley; m. Verna Chorine Walker, May 21, 1953; children: Carolyn Coleith, Cynthia Denise, Ben Edward. BS, U. Houston, 1956, MEd, 1964; PhD, Nat. Christian U., 1974; DEd, Baylor U., 1977. Cert. tchr., adminstr., counselor, vocat. counselor, Tex.; lic. profl. counselor, Tex. Tchr., counselor Houston Ind. Sch. Dist., 1957-65; dir. guidance and counseling Gary Job Corps, San Marcos, Tex., 1965-73; disability examiner Tex. Vocat. Rehab. Commn., Austin, 1973-74; asst. prof. edn. Southwest Tex. State U., San Marcos, 1974-79; counselor Hays Consolidated Ind. Sch. Dist., Buda, Tex., 1979-81; asst. supt., elem. prin., jr. h.s. prin. Pearsall (Tex.) Ind. Sch. Dist., 1981-89; prof. edn. Sul Ross State U, Rio Grande Coll., Rio Grande College Uvalde, Tex., 1989—. Contbr. articles to profl. jours. Mem. Prairie Lea (Tex.) Ind. Sch. Dist. Sch. Bd., 1967-74. 2d lt. USMCR, 1956. Mem. ACA, Am. Assn. Sch. Adminstrs., AF&AM Prairie Lea Lodge #114, Gonzales Commandery # 30, OES Wimberley Chpt. # 1130, Phi Delta Kappa (treas. 1976). Home: HCR 34 Box 1016 Uvalde TX 78801 Office: Sul Ross State U Rio Grande Coll 400 Sul Ross Dr Uvalde TX 78801

WILSON, BLAKE SHAW, electrical engineer, researcher; b. Orlando, Fla., Mar. 7, 1948; s. Joseph Richard Hoyle and Jacqueline Lucy (Jones) W.; m. Doris Jane Rouse, Jan. 6, 1974; children: Nadia Jacqueline, Blair Elizabeth. BSEE, Duke U., 1974. Rsch. engr. Rsch. Triangle Inst., Research Triangle Park, N.C., 1974-78, sr. rsch. engr., 1978-83, sr. rsch. scientist, 1979-83, head neurosci. program, 1983-94, dir. Ctr. for Auditory Prosthesis Rsch., 1994—; guest scientist Coleman Meml. Lab., U. Calif., San Francisco, 1983-86; adj. asst. prof. otolaryngology Duke U. Med. Ctr., 1984-94, assoc. prof., 1994—; oversight com. cochlear implants Kresge Hearing Rsch. Inst., U. Mich., 1987—, U. Iowa, 1994—; sci. adv. coun. House Ear Inst., L.A., 1990; gen. chair Conf. Implantable Auditory Prostheses, Pacific Grove, Calif., 1991; spl. panel hearing aids NIDCD, 1992, ad hoc adv. com. hearing aid R & D, 1993—; guest of honor Internat. Workshop on Cochlear Implants, Vienna, 1996; reviewer grant applications NIH, NSF, VA and Med. Rsch. Coun., Can.; cons. cochlear implants NIH; mem. faculty various continuing edn. courses; prin. investigator numerous projects; presenter numerous confs., symposia. Reviewer chpts. for books, papers and jours.; contbr. numerous articles to profl. jours. Recipient Discover award for tech. innovation, 1996. Home: 2410 Wrightwood Ave Durham NC 27705-5802 Office: Rsch Triangle Inst PO Box 12194 Durham NC 27709-2194

WILSON, BRUCE KEITH, men's health nurse; b. Alton, Ill., Aug. 18, 1946; s. Lewis Philip and Ruth Caroline Wilson; m. Karen Loughrey, Aug. 14, 1977; children: Sarah Ann, Andrew James. BSN, U. Tex., San Antonio, 1975, MSN, 1977; PhD, North Tex. State U., Denton, 1987. Cert. in nursing informatics. Coord. Pan Am. U., Edinburg, Tex., 1982-83; house supr. HCA Rio Grande Regional Hosp., McAllen, Tex., 1986-87; program dir. Tex. Southmost Coll., Brownsville, 1983-86; mem. faculty U. Tex.-Pan Am., Edinburg, 1986—. Author: Logical Nursing Math., 1987. With U.S. Army, 1966-68. Mem. ANA, Nat. League for Nursing, Am. Assembly for Men in Nursing, Tex. League for Nursing (bd. dirs. 1993—). Home: 1702 Ivy Ln Edinburg TX 78539-5367 Office: U Tex-Pan Am Dept Nursing Edinburg TX 78539

WILSON, C. DANIEL, JR., library director; b. Middletown, Conn., Nov. 8, 1941; s. Clyde D. and Dorothy M. (Neal) W.; m. M. April Jackson, Apr. 1986; children: Christine, Cindy, Clyde, Ben. BA, Elmhurst Coll., 1967; MA, Rosary Coll., 1968; MPA, U. New Orleans, 1995. Trainee Chgo. Pub. Libr., 1967-68; instr. U. Ill., 1968-70; asst. dir. Perrot Meml. Libr., Greenwich, Conn., 1970-76; dir. Wilton Pub. Libr., Wilton, Conn., 1976-79; assoc. dir. Birmingham Pub. Libr., Birmingham, Ala., 1979-83; dir. Davenport Pub. Libr., Davenport, Iowa, 1983-85, New Orleans Pub. Libr., 1985—. With USMC, 1962-65. Mem. Am. Libr. Assn., La. Libr. Assn., Am. Soc. Pub. Adminstrs., Pi Gamma Mu, Rotary. Episcopalian. Office: New Orleans Pub Libr Simon Heinsheim & Fisk Libe 219 Loyola Ave New Orleans LA 70112-2007

WILSON, CARL WELDON, JR., construction company executive, civil engineer; b. Norfolk, Va., Sept. 4, 1933; s. Carl Weldon and Janie Marie (Ludford) W.; m. Jean Roberts, Feb. 13, 1960; children: Lisa Ann, Carl Weldon III. BCE, Tex. A&M U., 1954. Registered profl. engr., Tex. Engr. Magnolia Petroleum Co., Morgan City, La., 1954-55, Brown & Root, Houston, 1957-60; project mgr. Claude Everett Constrn. Co., Houston, 1960-62; pres. Falcon Constrn. Co., Houston, 1962-63; pres., owner Wilson Engring. and Constrn. Co., Houston, 1963-68; v.p. Divcon, Inc., Houston, 1968-71, Wilson Industries, Inc., Houston, 1971-81; pres., prin. owner BS&B Engring. Co., Inc., Houston, 1981-86; chmn., majority shareholder Task Internat., Inc., Houston, 1986—. Served to 1st lt. U.S. Army, 1955-57. Republican. Episcopalian. Home: 750 Bison Dr Houston TX 77079-4401 Office: Task Internat Inc PO Box 218327 Houston TX 77218-8327

WILSON, CAROLYN TAYLOR, librarian; b. Cookeville, Tenn., June 10, 1936; d. Herman Wilson and Flo (Donaldson) Taylor; m. Larry Kittrell Wilson, June 14, 1957 (dec.); children: Jennifer Wilson Rust, Elissa Anne Wilson. BA, David Lipscomb Coll., 1957; MLS, George Peabody Coll., 1976. Tchr. English Fulton County Sch. System, Atlanta, 1957-59; serials cataloger Vanderbilt U. Libr., Nashville, 1974-77; asst. libr. United Meth. Pub. House, Nashville, 1978-80; collection devel. libr. David Lipscomb U., Nashville, 1980—; cons. and rschr. in field; project dir. Tenn.'s Lit. Legacy for Tenn. Humanities Coun., 1994—, ALA grant, Frontier in Am. Culture, 1996-98. Rsch. asst. Handbook of Tennessee Labor History, 1987-89. Adv. bd. So. Festival of Books, Nashville, 1988-90, 90—, vol. coord., 1989, 90—; project dir. Women's Words (summer grant program) for Tenn. Humanities Coun., Tenn.'s Literary Legacy (summer grant program), 1994-96, Growing Up Southern (summer grant), 1996—, ALA grant The Frontier in Am. Culture, 1996—. Recipient Nat. Honor Soc. award Phi Alpha Theta, 1956, Internat. Honor Soc. award Beta Phi Mu, 1980, Frances Neel Cheney award Tenn. Libr. Assn., 1992; nominee Athena award, 1992; Growing Up Southern summer grantee, 1996—. Mem. ALA, Tenn. Hist. Soc., Tenn. Libr. Assn. (Frances Neel Cheney award 1992), Southeastern Libr. Assn. (chmn. outstanding S.E. author award com. 1991-92, chmn. So. Books competition 1992-94), Women's Nat. Book Assn. (pres., v.p., treas., awards chmn. 1980—), Tenn. Writers Alliance (bd. dirs. 1995—). Democrat. Office: David Lipscomb U Univ Libr # 317 Nashville TN 37204

WILSON, CHARLES EDWARD, medical records administrator; b. Columbus, Miss., July 13, 1943; s. James Hugh Wilson and Wenonah Elizabeth Marsh Coble; m. Maria Corazon Junio, Nov. 30, 1968 (div. Apr. 1983); children: James Edward, Charles Edward Jr.; m. Susan Salazar Sabino, Oct. 26, 1983. BS, Okla. State U., 1966; MS, Nova U., 1980. Dir. med. records Meml. Med. Ctr., Springfield, Ill., 1972-76, Holy Cross Hosp., Ft. Lauderdale, Fla., 1976-91, Fawcett Meml. Hosp., Port Charlotte, Fla., 1991-94; dir. Wellington Regional Med. Ctr., West Palm Beach, Fla., 1994—; dir., sci. cons. Darn Communications Group and Darn Computer Corp., Boca Raton, Fla., 1981—. Author: Bar Code Applications in Hospitals, 1986. Mem. Broward County Zool. Pk. Commn., Ft. Lauderdale, Fla., 1978. Capt. USAF, 1966-70, Vietnam. Decorated Air Force Commendation medal USAF, 1968, Bronze Star medal USAF, 1970. Mem. AAAS, Am. Med. Record Assn. (registered record adminstr.), Fla. Med. Record Assn., Broward County Med. Record Assn., Cen. Ill. Med. Records Assn. (pres. 1972-74), Am. Legion, VFW. Democrat. Roman Catholic. Home: 8856 NW 76th Pl Fort Lauderdale FL 33321-2436 Office: Wellington Regional Med Ctr 10101 Forest Hill Blvd West Palm Beach FL 33414-6103

WILSON, CHARLES H(ARRISON), retired air force officer, financial planner, human resource development professional; b. Chgo., Sept. 6, 1941; s. Charles E. and Lorraine F. (Parker) W.; m. Mona Dickerson, July 2, 1988; children: Audrey M., Angela M., Andrew M., Aaron M. BS, So. Ill. U., 1964; BA, U. Md., 1976; MA, Webster U., 1979. Commd. 2d lt. USAF, 1964, advanced through grades to lt. col., 1981; pers. dir. air force logistics command USAF, Wright-Patterson AFB, Ohio, 1980-83; dir. DEF logistics agy. USAF, Washington, 1983-86; ret. USAF, 1984; exec. dir. exec. leadership program Dept. Def. (Pentagon), Washington, 1976—; adj. prof. Park Coll., St. Louis, 1977-80; mcpl. cons. City of Dayton, Ohio, 1980. Patentee microwave oven carousel. Bd. dirs. Credit Union, No. Va. Hotline. Fellow D.C. Life Under Writers Tng. Coun.; mem. Classification and Compensation Soc., Am. Soc. Tng. and Devel., Internat. Pers. Mgmt. Assn. (human rights commn.), Omega Psi Phi, Toastmasters. Democrat. Methodist. Home: 6101 Edsall Rd Apt 703 Alexandria VA 22304-4104

WILSON, CHARLES THOMAS, technology company executive, corporate restructuring consultant; b. Memphis, Feb. 8, 1941; s. Charles Lewis and Mary Frances (Parks) W.; m. Alice Elaine Ford, June 20, 1964; children: Elaine, Mary Jane. BS in Commerce, U. Ky., 1963. Dir. corp. acctg. Celanese Corp., N.Y.C., 1977-78; owner, cons. Strategic Planning Services, Charlotte, N.C., 1974-81; controller Fiber Industries, Inc., Charlotte, 1974-76, dir. planning, 1979-81; dir. L & H Techs., Inc., 1980—; dir. bus. devel. Celanese Fibers, Charlotte, 1981-82, v.p., gen. mgr. Hoechst Celanese Separations Products div., 1983-87; v.p. Textile Corp. of Am., 1987-88. Trustee Wingate (N.C.) Coll., 1986, chmn. 1989, 94, 97, vice chmn., 1993, 96; deacon, tchr. Candlewyck Bapt. Ch., Charlotte, 1986. Recipient Wall St. Jour. award, 1963. Mem. Inst. Mgmt. Accts., Beta Gamma Sigma. Baptist.

WILSON, DENISE WATTS, secondary school educator; b. Bklyn., Aug. 20, 1954; d. James and Hattie (Jowers) Watts; m. Jimmy Lee Wilson, July 30, 1983; 1 child, Gregory Alexander. BA, CUNY, 1976; MA in Christian Edn., So. Bapt. Sem., Louisville, 1978, MDiv, RE, 1982. Dir. edn. and youth Bethany Bapt. Ch., Bklyn., 1978-80; substitute tchr. Jefferson County Bd. Edn., Louisville, 1980-83; min. edn. and youth South Park Bapt. Ch., Houston, 1983-84, Greenspoint Bapt. Ch., Houston, 1986-88; tchr. Barrick Elem. Sch., Houston Ind. Sch. Dist., 1985-88; tchr. history Wells Mid. Sch., Spring Ind. Sch. Dist., Houston, 1988-93; asst. pastor and minister of edn. St. Stephen Bapt. Ch., Louisville, 1993-95; tchr. U.S. history Bruce Middle Sch. Jefferson County Schs., 1995-96; tchr. computer tech. Bruce Mid. Sch. Jefferson County Schs., Louisville, 1996—; proprietor Gifts from Home, Louisville, 1995—; youth dir. Zion Bapt. Ch., Louisville, 1982-83. Author: Devotions for Christian Staff, 1982. Benjamin Mays fellow Fund for Theol. Edn., 1981. Mem. N.G. Assn. U.S.A., N.G. Assn. Tex. (life). Democrat.

WILSON, DEREK KYLE, journalist; b. Pittsburg, Kans., Feb. 13, 1973; s. Charles Curtis and Carol Sue (Maples) W. AA in Journalism, Tulsa Jr. Coll., 1993; BA in Journalism, U. Okla., 1996. Newsroom intern KTUL TV, Tulsa, 1992; entertainment reporter intern Okla. Daily Newspaper, Norman, 1994-95, entertainment writer, 1995-96. Mem. Student Assn. Concert Series Com., 1995-96. Mem. Soc. Profl. Journalists (sec. 1995-96). Home: 716 W South Park Blvd Broken Arrow OK 74011

WILSON, DEWEY ERROL, sales and marketing executive; b. Mobile, Ala., Sept. 24, 1950; s. Guy Montieth and Gladys Jessie (Padgett) W.; m. Melody Ann Cappiali, June 15, 1974; children: Farrah, Lance, Gia. BS, U. So. Miss., 1973; postgrad., Jackson Sch. Law, 1973-74. With real estate sales Century 21 Real Estate, Mobile, 1975-76; owner Wilson Audio Svcs., Mobile, 1976-77; sales and gen. mgr. Chin Industries, Mobile, 1978-82; pres., co-owner Express Clean Inc., Mobile, 1983-86; v.p. sales and mktg. Initial U.S.A., Atlanta, 1987-92; regional v.p. Nat. Uniform Svc./Divsn. of N.S.I., 1992-97; v.p. mktg. WOM USA, Louisville, Ky., 1997—; bd. dirs. Initial Holding Inc., a BET Co., Atlanta. Mem. Kex Nat. Assn. (chmn. sales mktg. com. 1989-91), Kappa Sigma. Episcopal. Home: 7203 Summerwood Ln Alpharetta GA 30202 Office: WOM USA 1409 W Hill St Louisville KY 40210

WILSON, DONNA OWEN, author, artist; b. Wolf Mountain, N.C., Nov. 2, 1938; d. Wiley Isiah and Ella Canzada (Galloway) Owen; m. Fred Enous Ansley, Aug. 19, 1955 (div. July 1975); children: Steven Eugene, Galen Owen, Nancy Elisabeth, Robbie Scott; m. James Lester Wilson Jr., Aug. 26, 1975. Author: (poems and short stories) Memories & Dreams, 1991, (nonfiction) Footsteps From the Past, 1996; exhibited in art shows in Atlanta, Tenn., N.C., N.Y. and Calif. Mem. Talking Book Ctr., Augusta, Ga. Democrat. Baptist. Home: 949 Earle St NW Thomson GA 30824

WILSON, DOUGLAS DOWNES, lawyer; b. Astoria, N.Y., Jan. 20, 1947; s. Douglas and Mildred P. (Payne) W.; children: Douglas S., Debra J. AB, Grove City Coll., 1968; JD, Am. U., 1970; LLM, George Washington U., 1974. Bar: Md. 1971, D.C. 1971, U.S. Ct. Appeals (D.C. cir.) 1972, U.S. Ct. Mil. Appeals 1972, U.S. Supreme Ct. 1975, Va. 1978, U.S. Ct. Claims, U.S. Ct. Appeals (4th cir.), U.S. Dist. Ct. (we. dist.) Va. 1978, U.S. Dist. Ct. (ea. dist.) Va. 1979, U.S. Dist. Ct. (ea. dist.) Ky. 1981. Staff judge advocate Air Force Office Sci. Rsch., Arlington, Va., 1971-74; trial atty. Office Chief Trial Atty., Dept. Air Force, Wright Patterson AFB, Ohio, 1974-77; assoc. Martin, Hopkins & Lemon, P.C., Roanoke, Va., 1977-78; ptnr. Gardner, Moss & Brown, Washington and Roanoke, 1978-83; ptnr. Parvin Wilson & Barnett, P.C., 1984-96; mem. Wilson & Assocs., PC, 1996—; guest lectr. Old Dominion U., Norfolk, U. Wis., Madison, Alaska Pacific U., Anchorage, Va. Tech., Blacksburg. Deacon, First Presbyn. Ch., Roanoke, 1979-82, elder, 1989-92; mem. Roanoke Valley Estate Planning Coun., 1979-82; dir. Legal Aid Soc., Roanoke Valley, 1982-84; chmn. long range planning commn. Roanoke City Sch. Bd., 1986-93. Capt. USAF, 1971-77. Decorated Air Force Commendation medal with oak leaf cluster. Mem. ABA (pub. contract law sect.), Md. Bar Assn., D.C. Bar Assn., Fed. Bar Assn., Va. Bar Assn. (bd. govs., constrn. law sect. 1989-92), Nat. Assn. Bond Lawyers, Am. Road and Trans. Builders Assn., Va. Road and Trans. Builders Assn. (dir. 1993-96), Tenn. Road Builders Assn., Elks (exalted ruler 1973-74), Forest Ridge Civic Assn. (dir. 1974-77). Home: 1410 West Dr SW Roanoke VA 24015 Office: 2592 Broadway Ave SW Roanoke VA 24014

WILSON, DOUGLAS EMORY, editor, retired army officer; b. Washington, Nov. 1, 1910; s. Emory Moyers and Mabel Lawton (Lamborn) W.; m. Margaret Packwood, Dec. 26, 1943 (div. Jan. 1958); 1 child, Peter Lamborn. AB summa cum laude, Dartmouth Coll., 1931; AM, Harvard U., 1933. English instr. George Washington U., Washington, 1934-38, Rice U., Houston, 1940-41; enlisted U.S. Army, 1941, rose through ranks to maj., 1946, recalled, 1951; lt. col., battalion cmmdr. USAR, Anniston, Ala., 1958-65; tutor in English Harvard U., Cambridge, Mass., 1946-48; asst. prof. English Rutgers U., New Brunswick, N.J., 1948-51; adminstrv. officer U.S. Army Civil Svc., Ft. McClellan, Ala., 1956-73; textual editor Works of R.W. Emerson, 1975—; mem. editl. bd. Collected Works of R.W. Emerson, Harvard U. Press, 1976—, gen. editor, 1996—. Pres. Friends of the Pub. Libr., Anniston, Ala., 1981-96; bd. dirs. United Way of Calhoun County, Ala., 1974-77. Mem. MLA (inspector com. on scholarly edits.), Ralph Waldo Emerson Soc. (newsletter editor), Retired Officer Assn. (newsletter editor N.E. Ala.), Soc. for Textual Scholarship, Assn. for Document Editing. Home: 1404 Christine Ave Anniston AL 36207

WILSON, EDWARD COX, minister; b. Danville, Va., Sept. 30, 1938; s. James Thomas and Sallie Estelle (Cox) W.; m. Nancy Alva Hudson, Aug. 9, 1960; children: Michael Edward, Suzanne Adams. AB magna cum laude, Elon Coll., 1960; MDiv, Union Sem., 1965. Ordained to ministry Presbyn. Ch. (U.S.A.), 1965. Pastor Meadowbrook Presbyn. Ch., Greenville, N.C., 1965-67, Indian Trail (N.C.) Presbyn. Ch., 1971-86, Locust (N.C.) Presbyn. Ch., 1987-92; assoc. pastor Selwyn Ave Presbyn. Ch., Charlotte, N.C., 1968-71; pastor Williams Meml. Presbyn. Ch., Charlotte, 1992—; commr. Gen. Assembly, Presbyn. Ch. (U.S.A.), 1973, 79, 86; mem. com. on ministry, nomination com., mem. coun. Presbytery, also moderator, 1976-77. Author: Broken--But Not Beyond Repair, 1992, Play Ball! Reflections on Coaching Young Folk, 1994; contbr. articles, sermons and prayers to religious jours. Union Theol. Sem. fellow, 1965. Mem. Alban Inst. Democrat. Home: 8618 Appaloosa Way Ln Charlotte NC 28216-8732 Office: 4700 Beatties Ford Rd Charlotte NC 28216-2845

WILSON, ERIC LEWIS, medical technician; b. Jackson, Miss., Oct. 2, 1964; s. Aaron Wilson and Deloristeen (Bates) Omali; 1 child, DaWaine Alexander Carter. Cert. in acctg., Linds C.C., Jackson, Miss., 1988; CNA, Miss. State Hosp., Whitfield, 1991. Polit. activist AFL-CIO of Miss., Jackson, 1988-90; ctrl. svc. technician II Univ. Med. Ctr., Jackson, Miss., 1993-96; assoc. Hinds Assocs. Legal Svcs., (parliamentarian), 1984-87. Poet: A Friend and Mother, 1989, Literary Guild. Activist in labor issues, Jackson, Miss., 1988-90. Democrat. Roman Catholic. Home: PO Box 31911 Jackson MS 39286

WILSON, FRANK LYNDALL, surgeon; b. Oct. 29, 1926; children: Frank L. III, Patricia W. Major; m. Kristina F. Wilson, June 29, 1984. BS, Emory U., 1948, MD, 1952. Diplomate Am. Bd. Surgery, 1960. Surg. intern Univ. Hosps. Cleve., 1952-53; asst. surg. resident Grady Meml. Hosp., Atlanta, 1953, 55-58, chief surg. resident, 1958-59, now mem. surg. staff; pvt. practice surgery, Atlanta, 1959—; chmn. dept. surgery Piedmont Hosp., Atlanta, 1984-91 , also trustee, mem. surg. staff; clin. asst. prof. surgery Emory U. Sch. Medicine; mem. staff Crawford W. Long Meml. Hosp. Trustee Lovett Sch., 1971-79, Piedmont Hosp., 1984-91; chmn. med. div. United Way Atlanta, 1978. Served with USN, 1944-46, 53-55. Fellow ACS (pres. Ga. chpt. 1976-77); mem. Med. Assn. Atlanta (dir. 1977-82, pres. 1980, chmn. med. adv. com. selective service, peer rev. com.), Atlanta Med. Heritage Inc. (pres. 1980-83), Med. Assn. Ga. (vice councilor 1966-68, del.), Ga. Surg. Soc. (pres. 1990-91), So. Med. Assn., AMA, Atlanta Clin. Soc. Rocky Mountain Traumatological Soc. Presbyterian. Club: Piedmont Driving, Highlands Country (N.C.). Office: 95 Collier Rd NW Ste 6015 Atlanta GA 30309-1607

WILSON, GINGER, elementary education educator; b. Waurika, Okla., May 3, 1948; d. Obed and Ethel (Fulton) Bennett; m. Roy Wilson, Jr., July 1, 1978; 1 child, Melea. BS, U. Sci. and Arts Okla., 1969; MEd, Southeastern State U., Durant, Okla., 1973. Cert. elem. tchr., spl. endorsement in lang. arts and social studies, Okla. Elem. tchr. Ninnekah (Okla.) Pub. Schs., 1969—; chmn. Ninnekah Writing Festival. Mem. NEA, Okla. Edn. Assn., Okla. Reading Coun., Grady County Reading Coun., Ninnekah Classrom Tchrs. Assn. (past pres.). Office: Ninnekah Elem Sch PO Box 275 Ninnekah OK 73067-0275

WILSON, GINNY CHARLOTTE, guidance counselor; b. Luverne, Ala., Jan. 26, 1951; d. Charlie M. and Florelle (Buck) W. BS in Elem. Edn., Troy State U., 1972; MEd in Counseling, Auburn U., Montgomery, Ala., 1976; postgrad., Auburn U., 1980; PhD, Walden U., 1994. Lic. psychometrist, Ala. Tchr. Crenshaw County Bd. Edn., Highland Home, Ala., 1972-90, guidance counselor, 1990—; student counselor Fairview Med. Ctr., Montgomery, 1978, Auburn U., Montgomery, 1979; vol. counselor Dist. Atty.'s Pre-Trial Diversion Program, Montgomery, 1979-80, Cadet Ctr., Montgomery, 1980. Chmn. Leukemia Soc., Crenshaw County, 1982; active Drug Edn. Com., Crenshaw County, 1993-94, Adult Edn. Adv. Com., Crenshaw County, 1993-94, Chpt. 1 Adv. Com., Crenshaw County, 1993-94. Parenting program grantee Ala. Power Co., 1993; named one of Outstanding Young Women Am., 1980. Mem. NEA, Ala. Edn. Assn., Crenshaw County Edn. Assn. (sec., faculty rep.), Ala. Counseling Assn., Sch. Counseling Assn., Alpha Delta Kappa (pres., sec. Nu chpt.). Democrat. Home: Rt 1 Box 259 Highland Home AL 36041-9121 Office: Highland Home Sch Rt 1 Box 199A Highland Home AL 36041

WILSON, GREGORY GLENN, funeral home official; b. Fincastle, Va., Apr. 29, 1960; s. Marvin Glenn and Mildred Ruth (Williams) W. AAS in Bus. Mgmt. summa cum laude, New River C.C., Dublin, Va., 1981. Debt collection rep. Credit Bur. Svc., Christiansburg, Va., 1990-92; funeral svc. worker Maberry Funeral Home Inc., Floyd, Va., 1977-90, 92—. AuthorP Planting Your First Ginseng Garden, 1995. Mem. Moose (prelate Floyd 1988-89, jr. gov. 1989-91, gov. 1991-92, past gov. 1992—). Baptist. Home: PO Box 642 State Rt 720 Floyd VA 24091

WILSON, GUILFORD JAMES, JR., oil company executive; b. Pitts., Feb. 11, 1932; s. Guilford J. and Gladys J. (Caldwell) W.; m. Jan S. Conroy, June 1, 1991; children from previous marriage: Michael Lee, Elizabeth Marie, Bradley James. BS in Geology, Tex. A&M U., 1954, MS, 1957; postgrad., Harvard U., 1981. Cert. petroleum geologist. V.p., gen. mgr. U.S. exploration and prodn. Union Tex. Petroleum, Houston, 1981-85; pres. Wacker Oil Inc., Houston, 1985-90; exec. v.p., gen. mgr. Scana Petroleum Resources, Houston, 1991-95; pres. Amicus Energy Inc., Houston, 1995—. Bd. dirs. Greater Houston USO, past pres., 1990-92. 1st lt. U.S. Army, major gen. USAR, 1954-91. Mem. Am. Assn. Petroleum Geologists, Soc. Profl. Well Log Analysts, Sr. Army Res. Comdrs. Assn. (past pres. 1987-89, Hall of Honor 1995). Home: 1711 Cedar Creek Ct Houston TX 77077 Office: Amicus Energy Inc 921 Main Ste 1420 Houston TX 77002

WILSON, HARRISON B., college president; b. Amstead, N.Y., Apr. 21, 1928; m. Lucy Wilson; children—Benjamin, Harrison, John, Richard, Jennifer, Marquarite. B.S., Ky. State U.; M.S., D.H.S., Ind. U. Head basketball coach Jackson State Coll., 1951-60, chmn. dept. health and phys. edn., 1960-67; dir. coop. edn. Tenn. State U.; exec. asst., pres. Fisk U.; pres. Norfolk State Univ. (Va.), 1975—; dir. Va. Nat. Bank. Mem. Va. State Adv. Council on Vocat. Edn.; bd. dirs. Health, Welfare, Recreation Planning Council; mem. lay adv. bd. DePaul Hosp. Mem. Alpha Kappa Mu. Office: Norfolk State U Office of President 2401 Corprew Ave Norfolk VA 23504-3907*

WILSON, JAMES CHARLES, JR., lawyer; b. Birmingham, Ala., Sept. 13, 1947; s. James C. and Angelina (Serio) W.; m. Ann Bullock, Mar. 1, 1975; children: Brent Trammell, Lucy Bullock. BA, Tulane U., 1969, JD, 1972; MBA, Samford U., 1995. Ptnr. Bradley, Arant, Rose & White, Birmingham, 1972-90, Lange, Simpson, Robinson & Somerville, Birmingham, 1990-93, Sirote & Permutt, P.C., Birmingham, 1993-96; v.p. and gen. counsel Shop-A-Snak Food Mart, Inc., Birmingham, 1996-; adj. prof. internat. bus. transactions and internat. law U. Ala., Tuscaloosa, 1983-85, 89-, internat. bus. transactions Cumberland Sch. Law, 1990-95. Author: Alabama Business Corporation Law, 1980; co-author: Corporate Law for the Healthcare Provider: Organization, Operation, Merger and Bankruptcy, 1993, Alabama Business Corporation Law Guide, 1995. Mem. adv. bd. Jr. League of Birmingham, 1984; bd. dirs. Ala. chpt. Am. Liver Found., 1993—, sec., 1994-95; bd. trustees The Altamont Sch. With U.S. Army, 1972-76. Mem. ABA (sect. internat. law, tax and corp., banking and bus. law), Internat. Bar Assn., Nat. Health Lawyers Assn., Am. Hosp. Atty's. Assn., Ala. Bar Assn., Birmingham Bar Assn. (chmn. pub. rels. com. 1990), Birmingham Golf Assn. (pres., v.p., treas. 1982-84). Lodge: Rotary (pres. Birmingham-Sunrise club 1986-87). Office: Shop-A-Snak Food Mart Inc 833 Green Springs Hwy Birmingham AL 35209-4917

WILSON, JAMES LEE, retired geology educator, consultant; b. Waxahachie, Tex., Dec. 1, 1920; s. James Burney and Hallie Christine (Hawkins) W.; m. Della I. Moore, May 8, 1944; children: James Lee Jr., Burney Grant, Dale Ross (dec.). Student, Rice U., 1938-40; BA, U. Tex., 1942, MA, 1944; PhD, Yale U., 1949. Geologist Carter Oil Co., Tulsa, 1943-44; asst. and assoc. prof. U. Tex., Austin, 1949-52; rsch. geologist Shell Devel. Co., Houston, 1952-66; prof. Rice U., Houston, 1966-79, U. Mich., Ann Arbor, 1979-86; geol. cons. New Braunfels, Tex., 1986—; cons. Erico Corp., London, 1985-88, Masera Corp., Tulsa, 1988—, Coyote Geol. Svcs., Boulder, Col., 1990—; adj. prof. Rice U., 1986—. Author: Carbonate Facies in Geologic History, 1975; contbr. articles to tech. jours. With C.E., U.S. Army, 1944-46, Italy. Grantee NSF. Mem. Am. Assn. Petroleum Geologists (hon., Disting. Educator award), Internat. Sedimentological Soc., Soc. Econ. Paleontology and Minerology (pres. 1972-73, field trip guide books 1989), Paleontological Soc., West Tex. Geol. Soc., South Tex. Geol. Soc., Can. Soc. Petroleum Geologists. Home and Office: 1316 Patio Dr New Braunfels TX 78130-8505

WILSON, JAMES REED, industrial engineering educator; b. Waco, Tex., July 11, 1948; s. James Reed and Maydelle (Connor) W.; m. Mary Elizabeth Thibeaux, Aug. 21, 1971; children: Kate Elizabeth, Anna Christine. BA, Rice U., 1970; MS, Purdue U., 1977, PhD, 1979. Rsch. analyst Houston Lighting & Power Co., 1970-72; asst. prof. U. Tex., Austin, 1979-84; assoc. prof. Purdue U., West Lafayette, Ind., 1985-91; prof. indsl. engring. N.C. State U., Raleigh, 1991—; cons. NASA, Houston, 1980-82, Ind. U. Med. Sch., Indpls., 1985-89, Pritsker Corp., Indpls., 1995—; pres. Coll. on Simulation, Inst. of Mgmt. Scis., Providence, 1988-90, dept. editor Mgmt. Sci., 1988-92, program chair winter simulation conf., 1992. Contbr. more than 50 articles to profl. jours. Lt. U.S. Army, 1972-75. Recipient Stochastic Modeling and Simulation award NSF, 1988, Outstanding Simulation Publ. award Inst. Mgmt. Scis. Coll. on Simulation, 1985, Disting. Svc. award Inst. for Ops. Rsch. and the Mgmt. Scis. Coll. on Simulation, 1995, Excellence in Tchg. award, United Techs. Rsch. Ctr., 1996; named to N.C. State U. Acad. Outstanding Tchrs., 1996. Mem. Inst. Indsl. Engrs. (assoc. editor 1989, grad. rsch. award 1978), Phi Beta Kappa, Sigma Xi, Tau Beta Pi, Omega Rho. Home: 107 Buckden Pl Cary NC 27511-9003 Office: NC State U Dept Indsl Engring Box 7906 Raleigh NC 27695

WILSON, JANE C. LUCK, author, housecleaning specialist; b. Magnolia, Ark., Sept. 29, 1967; d. James Richard Luck and Devona Elaine (Meeks) Amis; m. James Randall Wilson, Jan. 3, 1986; children: James William, Madeline Nicole. Assoc. in Adminstrv. Svcs., So. Ark. U., 1987. Shipping clk. Atlantic Rsch. Corp., Camden, Ark., 1987-90; writer, pub. spkr. Ozark Pub. Co., Prairie Grove, Ark., 1992—; housekeeper Camden, Ark., 1995—. Author: Rufus' Big Day, 1994, Charlie's Great Escape, 1995. Vol. Nat. Ct. Appointed Spl. Adv. Assn., Camden, 1996; children's tchr. Cullendale 1st Bapt. Ch., Camden, 1993—. Mem. Soc. Children's Book Writers and Illustrators, Laubach Lit. Action. Democrat. Home: 2784 Mimosa St Camden AR 71701

WILSON, JEAN MARIE HALEY, civic worker; b. Dallas, Oct. 16, 1921; d. William Eldred and Helen Marie (Littlepage) Haley; BA, So. Meth. U., 1943; m. Edward Lewis Wilson, Jr., Mar. 19, 1943; children: Edward Lewis III, William Haley, Sarah. Bd. dirs. Dallas Symphony Orch. League, 1963-89, sec., 1964-68, 1st v.p., 1968-72, vice-chmn. spl. projects, 1977-78, rec. sec., 1984-85, 7th v.p., 1985-86, trustee, 1976-88, showhouse chmn., 1987, corresponding sec., 1987-88; v.p. activities, bd. dirs. Allegro Dallas, Inc., 1986-90; precinct chmn. Democratic Party, 1952-62; mem. Dallas County Dem. Exec. Com., 1952-62; bd. dirs. TACA (Com. for Fund Raising of the Arts), 1975-88; mem. Southwestern hospitality bd. Met. Opera; charter mem., bd. dirs., North Tex. Herb Club, 1974-78; mem. Grand Heritage Ball Com. of Old City Park, exec. com. 1992-94 exec. com. Les Femme du Monde-fundraising arm Dallas Coun. on World Affairs, 1992-95. Mem. Nat. Trust Hist. Preservation, Dallas Mus. Art/League, Decorative Arts Guild N. Tex., Herb Soc. Am. (life), Am. Hort. Soc., Pewter Collectors Club Am., Royal Hort. Soc., Le Circle Francaise of Dallas (hon. chmn. 1985-94), Herb Soc. of Old City Park, Kappa Alpha Theta. Methodist. Home: 3501 Lexington Ave Dallas TX 75205-3914 Office: 2909 Maple Ave Dallas TX 75201-1443

WILSON, JEANETTE OUREN, office manager; b. Hanska, Minn., Mar. 14, 1921; d. Marvin Gehart and Ingeborg Amanda (Blien) Ouren.; m. Edward Clark Wilson, May 14, 1949; children: Patricia, Edward Jr., Marsha. BA, U. Minn., 1943; postgrad., Northwestern U., 1943. Jr. acct. Price Waterhouse, Chgo., 1943-45; acct. ARC, Manila and Seoul, 1945-47; sec. J.P. Stevens, Inc., Greensboro, N.C., 1947-50; adminstrv. asst. Am. Friends Serv. Comm., High Point, N.C., 1967-80; office mgr. Friends Assn. for Higher Edn., Greensboro, 1985—; tchr. adult basic edn. classes, 1966-67; editl. bd. The Southern Friend, Greensboro, 1992—; founding bd. New Garden Friends Schl., Greensboro, 1973, High Point Friends Kindergarten, 1965. Author historic articles in The Southern Friend, Greensboro, 1995. Social worker Head Start Program, High Point, 1965. Mem. High Point Jr. League. Democrat. Mem Soc. of Friends.

WILSON, JEANNE IRENE, language educator; b. Quincy, Fla., Apr. 4, 1947; d. Arthur Rueben and Carolyn Rose (Wedeles) Fixel; m. John Winn, 1970 (div.); children: Sherry, Irene. AA, Chipola Jr. Coll., Maryanne, Fla., 1967; BS in Social Welfare, Fla. State U., 1970; MEd, U. North Fla., 1985; ESOL endorsement, U. Fla., 1991. Tchr. Chpt. I Putnam County Schs., Palatka, Fla., 1971-75; tchr. Putnam County Schs., Interlachen, Fla., 1975-89; tchr. ESOL Putnam County Schs., Interlachen, 1989—. Contbr. poems to profl. jours. Mem. Am. Fedn. Tchrs., ESOL Leadership Orgn. Office: Price Mid Sch RR 1 Box 15 Interlachen FL 32148-9704

WILSON, JEANNETTE SOLOMON, retired elementary education educator; b. Columbus, Ga., Sept. 5, 1915; d. John C. and Mary L. (Parham) Solomon (adoptive parents, aunt and uncle); m. Harvie L. Wilson, Aug. 9, 1952; 1 child, Katrina M. Deese Turner. BS, Ft. Valley (Ga.) Coll., 1947; MS, Tuskegee (Ala.) Inst., 1951; postgrad., Syracuse U., 1961, U. Alaska, 1967. cert. elem. tchr. Elem. tchr. Muscogee County Sch. Dist., Columbus, 1939-53, 1954-60, 1969-71, home/hosp. tchr., 1971-75; elem. tchr. Am. Dependent Schs., Heilbronn, Fed. Republic Germany, 1953-54; ret., 1975; cons. in field. Active Girls Scouts Columbus chpt. Named one of Women of Achievement Girl Scouts, Inc., 1989; recipient Outstanding Svc. award Am. Cancer Soc., 1983-84. Mem. AAUW, The Links Club (one of the founders Columbus, Ga. chpt. 1964), Urban League, Nat. Coun. Negro Women, Tuskegee Alumni Assn., Mr. and Mrs. Club (sec. 1960-64), Matrons Club (Gracious Lady of Ga. 1988), Alpha Kappa Alpha.

WILSON, JEFFERY BRAD, career officer; b. Lansing, Mich., July 18, 1968; s. James Windsor and Bonnie Carolyn (Head) W. BS in Aerospace Engring., U.S. Naval Acad., 1990. Commd. 2nd lt. USMC, 1991, advanced through ranks to capt., 1994; platoon comdr. B Co., 1st BN 6th Marines 2nd Mar. Div., Camp LeJeune, N.C., 1991-93, Recon Co., HQBN, 3rd Mar. Div., Okinawa, Japan, 1993-94; asst. ops. ofcr., G-3 3rd Marine Divsn., Okinawa, 1995; reconnaissance equipment project ofcr., ground weapons systems Marine Corps Systems Command, Quantico, Va., 1995—. Mem. Divers Alert Network, Quantico Ofcr.'s Club, U.S. Naval Acad. Alumni Assn., Army Navy Club, U.S. Rugby Football Union. Home: 605 Stonewall Ln Fredericksburg VA 22407 Office: Marcorsyscom 2033 Barnett Ave Ste 315 Quantico VA 22134

WILSON, JIM V., school system administrator; b. Muskogee, Okla., Aug. 21, 1937; s. Frank Clay and Cassie Emma (Sturm) W.; m. Neva Darlene Clark, Oct. 6, 1954; children: Pamela, Jim Jr., Guyla, Wendy, Sherri. BA in Edn., Northeastern State Coll., 1963; Diploma Metal Fabrication, Purdue U., 1970; MS in Edn., Okla. State U., 1971. Machine shop instr. Central H.S., Muskegee, Okla., 1954-64, welding instr., 1964-68; welder Boeing Aircraft, Wichita, Kans., 1954-64; adv. for contract team Kingdom of Thailand Okla. State U., Stillwater, 1968-70; asst. state coord. spl. schs. divsn. State Dept. Vocat.-Tech. Edn., %, 1970-74; supr. press divsn. Holley Carburetor, Sallisaw, 1974-75; asst. supt. Indian Meridian Vocat.-Tech. Sch., Stillwater, 1975-84; asst. supt. Francis Tuttle Vocat.-Tech. Ctr., Okla. City, 1984—, rep. Okla. Team for apprenticeship Denmark and Germany, 1993. Mem. Save Tinker AFB initiative, Okla. City, 1993-94. Mem. Am. Vocat. Assn. (pres. adult divsn. 1977-78, past officer), Nat. Sch. Bds. Assn., Nat. Coalition Advanced Tech. Ctrs. (past officer, mem. exec. com., mem. exec. coun. 1991-94), Okla. Coun. Vocat. Adminstrs. (pres. 1984-85), Soc. Mfg. Engrs., Okla. State U. Alumni Assn., Okla. Vocat. Assn. (pres. adult divsn. 1979-80, Silver Key award 1992, Francis Tuttle Award of Excellence 1994). Democrat. Baptist. Office: Francis Tuttle 12777 N Rockwell Oklahoma City OK 73142

WILSON, JOHN, protective services official. Police chief Montgomery, Ala. Office: Office of Police Chief PO Box 159 Montgomery AL 36192

WILSON, JOHN FRANK, neonatal nurse; b. Millen, Ga., May 30, 1950; s. Lamar F. and Jem (Rogers) W. BSN, Valdosta State Coll., 1977. PRNN neonatal transport nurse Med. Coll. of Ga., Augusta, 1980-90, ECMO clinician, 1987—, staff nurse NICU, 1980-90, neonatal specialist in-house edn., ECMO transport supr., 1990—; lectr. Med. Coll. of Ga., 1990—; NRP regional instr. Am. Acad. Pediatrics, Elk Grove Village, Ill., 1990—. Mem. AWHONN, Nat. Assn. Neonatal Nurses. Home: 1117 Brookwood Dr Augusta GA 30909-2305 Office: Med Coll of Ga 15th St Augusta GA 30912-3740

WILSON, LARRY JOSEPH, federal agency administrator; b. St. Charles, Mo., Mar. 21, 1948; s. Clyde Marvin and Maxine Mary (Schwendeman) W.; 1 child, Heather Renee. BA in English, U. Mo.-St. Louis, 1969; postgrad. U. Mo., 1969-70, Am. U., 1977. Tech. writer, U.S. Army Missile Command, Huntsville, Ala., 1970-71, U.S. Army Munitions Command, Dover, N.J., 1971-72; chief writer, editor Atmospheric Scis. Lab., White Sands, N.Mex., 1972-75; assoc. editor Def. Mgmt. Jour., Alexandria, Va., 1975-78, editor, 1978-82, 82-86; chief pub. affairs officer U.S. Army Depot Systems Command, Chambersburg, Pa., 1982; dir. pub. affairs, Defense Logistics Agy., Alexandria, Va., 1986-94; rsch. assoc. Inst. for the Study of Diplomacy Georgetown U., 1994-95; legis. fellow Brookings Instn. U.S. Senator Charles S. Robb, 1996; sr. internet policy advisor Def. Logistics Agy., Ft. Belvoir, Va., 1996—; lectr. in field. Contbr. articles to profl. jours. Bd. dirs. Boys' Club Am., Las Cruces, N.Mex., 1974, Brayhill Crest Citizens Assn. Avocations: bicycling, gardening, bass musician. Home: 7413 Beverly Manor Dr Annandale VA 22003-2512 Office: Russell Senate Office Bldg Rm 154 Washington DC 20510

WILSON, LAWRENCE ALEXANDER, construction company executive; b. Nashville, 1935. Grad., Vanderbilt U., 1957. With H.C. Beck Co., Inc., Dallas, 1959-80, pres., COO, 1976-80; chmn., CEO Beck Co., Inc., Dallas, 1980—; pres., CEO HCB Contractors, Dallas, 1980—. Office: HCB Contractors 1700 Pacific Ave Ste 3800 Dallas TX 75201*

WILSON, LELAND EARL, petroleum engineering consultant; b. Ft. Recovery, Ohio, Oct. 28, 1925; s. John Huffman and Matilda Caroline (Sunderhaus) W.; m. Marian Ruthetta Trygstad, Nov. 27, 1948; children: Kathleen Ann, Linda Kay, Mary Lee, John Russell. BS in Petroleum Engring., Tulsa U., 1950. Registered profl. engr., Alaska, Tex. Drilling engr. Atlantic Refining Co., Tex., Ark., and La., 1950-56; drilling supr. Atlantic Refining Co., La., Tex., 1956-65; drilling supt. Atlantic Richfield, Anchorage, 1965-67, prodn. and drilling supt., 1967-72; ops. mgr. ARCO Oil Prodn. Co., London, 1972-75; resident mgr. ARCO Greenland, Copenhagen, 1975-78; pres. ARCO Indonesia, Inc., Jakarta, 1978-82; v.p. ARCO China, Hong Kong, 1982-85; petroleum cons. Lindale, Tex., 1985—; bd. dirs. Houma Oil Treaters, Inc., DPM Non-Destructive Testing, Odessa, Tex. Author family history Dear John, 1989; contbr. articles to profl. jours.; inventor in field. Aviation cadet AAF, 1943-45. Mem. NSPE, Tex. Soc. Profl. Engrs., Tyler Petroleum Club, Soc. Petroleum Engrs., Petroleum Club (pres. Anchorage 1971-72), Indonesian Petroleum Assn. (pres. 1981-82). Republican. Roman Catholic. Home: PO Box 893 428 Lonestar Ln Lindale TX 75771 Office: PO Box 893 2715 S Main Lindale TX 75771

WILSON, LEONARD RICHARD, geologist, consultant; b. Superior, Wis., July 23, 1906; s. Ernest and Sarah Jane (Cooke) W.; m. Marian Alice DeWilde, Sept. 1, 1930; children: Richard Graham, Marcia Graham. PhB, U. Wis.-Madison, 1930, PhM, 1932, PhD, 1935. Research assoc. Wis. Geol. and Nat. Hist. Survey, Trout Lake, Wis., 1932-36; instr. to prof. geology Coe Coll., Cedar Rapids, Iowa, 1934-46; head dept. geology and mineralogy U. Mass., Amherst, 1946-56; leader Greenland Ice Cap Am. Geog. Soc., N.Y.C., 1953; prof. geology NYU, N.Y.C., 1956-57; prof. to George L. Cross research prof. geology and geophysics U. Okla., Norman, 1957-77, prof. emeritus, 1977—; geologist Okla. Geol. Survey, Norman, 1957-77, ret. 1977—; cons. in field; research assoc., mem. edn. bd. Mus. Nat. Hist., N.Y.C., 1956-77; curator paleobotany-micropaleontology Okla. Mus. Natural Hist., Norman, 1968—. Contbr. articles to profl. jours. Editor proceedings Iowa Acad. Sci., 1936-46. Melhaup fellow Ohio State U., 1939-40; NSF grantee, 1959-65. Fellow AAAS, Geol. Soc. Am., Palynological Soc. India Coll. of Fellows (Erdtman Internat. medal 1973); mem. Am. Assn. Petroleum Geologists, Am. Assn. Stratigraphic Palynologists (hon.), Nat. Assn. Geology Tchrs. (hon. life), Explorer's Club (life), Audubon Soc. (pres. Norman br. 1982-83), Sigma Xi (pres. Okla. chpt. 1965-66), Phi Beta Kappa (pres. Okla. Alpha chpt. 1978-79). Current work: Stratigraphic research in Paleozoic palynology as it relates to hydrocarbon maturation and associated strata. Subspecialties: Geology; Chronobiology.

WILSON, LEVON EDWARD, law educator, lawyer; b. Charlotte, N.C., Apr. 2, 1954; s. James A. and Thomasina Wilson. BSBA, Western Carolina U., 1976; JD, N.C. Ctrl. U., 1979. Bar: N.C. 1981, U.S. Dist. Ct. (mid. dist.) N.C. 1981, U.S. Tax Ct. 1981, U.S. Ct. Appeals (4th cir.) 1982, U.S. Supreme Ct.; lic. real estate broker, N.C.; cert. mediator. Pvt. practice Greensboro, N.C., 1981-85; asst. county atty. Guilford County, Greensboro, 1985-88; asst. prof. N.C. Agrl. & Tech. State U., Greensboro, 1988-91; asst. prof. Western Carolina U., Cullowhee, N.C., now assoc. prof., head dept. bus. adminstrn., law and mktg., $D; pres. Trade Brokers Cons.; legal counsel, bd. dirs. Rhodes Assocs., Inc., Greensboro, 1982—; legal counsel Guilford County Sheriff's Dept., Greensboro, 1985-88. Contbr. articles to profl. jours. Bd. dirs. Post Advocacy Detention Program; active mem. Prison Litigation Study Task Force, Adminstrn. Justice Study Com. Recipient Svc. award Blacks in Mgmt., 1980, Excellence in Tchg. award Jay I. Kneedler Found. of Western Carolina U., 1994-95; Student in Free Enterprise fellow. Mem. ABA, N.C. Bar Asns., Acad. Legal Studies in Bus., Southeastern Acad. Legal Studies in Bus. (editor-in-chief Jour. of Legal Studies in Bus.), N.C. Assn. Police Attys., N.C. Real Estate Eudcators Assn., So. Acad. Legal Studies in Bus., Phi Delta Phi. Democrat. Methodist. Home: PO Box 620 Cullowhee NC 28723-0620 Office: Western Carolina U Coll of Bus Cullowhee NC 28723

WILSON, LINDA ANN, renal dialysis nurse; b. Johnson City, Tenn., Feb. 22, 1947; d. Andrew Jackson and Dorothy (Pate) Robertson; m. William Eugene Wilson, Feb. 17, 1968. Student, U. Tenn., 1969. Cert. nephrology nurse. Nurse Johnson City (Tenn.) Med. Ctr., 1969-73, head nurse renal dialysis, 1973—. Vol. nurse Red Cross. Mem. NAFE, Internat. Platform Assn., Am. Nephrology Nurses Assn., Assn. Nurses Endorsing Transplantation.

WILSON, LINDA EDMISTON, secondary school science educator; b. Youngtown, Ohio, Dec. 18, 1941; d. Ernest Lyle and Florence Jeannette (Hoover) Edmiston; m. Jon Rhodes Wilson, Aug. 16, 1942; children: Scott Lyle, Jon Todd, Michelle Lynn. AB in Secondary Edn., Asbury Coll., 1963; MA in Elem. Edn., Nova Southeastern U., 1979. Tchr. health and phys. edn. Millersport, Ohio, 1964-66; tchr. Newark, Ohio, 1966-67; tchr. 2d grade Univ. Sch., Davie, Fla., 1978-80; tchr. sci. Driftwood Middle Sch., Hollywood, Fla., 1980-85; tchr. sci. and KLAS Hollywood Hills H.S., Hollywood, 1985—; coord. Silver Knights for Hollywood Hills, Miami Herald Newspaper, Ft. Lauderdale, Fla., 1991; coord at risk 10-12 grades Hollywood Hills H.S., 1985—. Illustrator: (Child's Book), The Loveable Lookalike, 1981; author, illustrator: Frankly Fortish, 1996. Named Christa McAuliffe Tchr. of Yr., Broward County Fla Engring. Soc., Ft. Lauderdale, Fla., 1989, Hills Silver Knight Tchr. of Yr., Hollywood, Fla., 1990; recipient Sunshine Medallion recognition, Sunshine State Sch. Pub. Rels. Assn., 1993. Methodist. Home: 4951 SW 29th Way Fort Lauderdale FL 33312 Office: Hollywood Hills HS 5400 Stirling Rd Hollywood FL 33021-1602

WILSON, LISA RENÉE, special education educator; b. Alexandria, La., Mar. 14, 1959; d. Arthur Alexander Jr. and Shirley Jean (Dillon) W. BS in Dance Edn., U. N.C., Greensboro, 1980; MEd, Lynchburg Coll., 1995. Tchr. learning disabilities Concord (Va.) Elem. Sch., 1994-95, Ben Franklin Mid. Sch., Rocky Mount, Va., 1995—. Mem. NEA, CEC, Coun. for Children with Behavioral Disorders, Coun. Learning Disabilities, Va. Edn. Assn. Home: Rt 1 Box 425B Glade Hill VA 24092

WILSON, LLOYD KENTON, neuropsychologist, consultant; b. San Antonio, May 9, 1948; s. Buel Woodrow and Joyce Etoy (Moore) W.; m. Teresa Cavallo, Feb. 15, 1980; 1 child, Karla Kristen. Student, San Antonio Coll., 1970-73; BA in Psychology and Fine Arts, U. Tex., Odessa, 1975, MA in Behavioral Sci., 1977; PhD in Rehab. Psychology, U. Ariz., 1984; cert. life care planning, U. Fla., 1995. Lic. psychologist, Tex.; cert. rehab. counselor. Mgr. sheltered workshop Permian Basin Mental Health/Mental Retardation Ctr., Midland, Tex., 1975-76; supr. vocat. evaluation and tng. Bexar County Mental Health/Mental Retardation Ctr., San Antonio, 1976-78; supr. vocat. exploration Goodwill Industries Santa Clara County, San Jose, Calif., 1978-80; psychol. asst., teaching asst. dept. rehab Coll. Edn. U. Ariz., Tucson, 1980-82, psychology intern Rehab. Ctr., 1983; psychology intern Rehab. Svcs. No. Calif., Pleasant Hill, 1983-84; staff psychologist Warm Springs Rehab. Hosp., Gonzales, Tex., 1984-85; neuropsychologist, assoc. dir. Community Re-entry Svcs. Mich. New Medico Assocs., Battle Creek, 1985-87; assoc. dir. South Valley Ranch Neurobehavioral Program Learning Svcs. Corp., Gilroy, Calif., 1987-88; dir. psychology and social svcs. Warm Springs Rehab. Hosp., San Antonio, 1988-91; system neuropsychologist Warm Springs Rehab. System, Gonzales, Corpus Christi, Tex., 1991-93; pvt. practice psychology, life care planning cons. San Antonio, 1993—; mem. med. staff Horizon Splty. Hosp. and Vencor Hosp., San Antonio; oral exam. panelist Tex. State Bd. Examiners. of Psychologists, 1994—; consultative exam. panelist Tex. Rehab. Commn., 1992—; registered profl. Tex. Commn. Law Enforcement Officer Stds. and Edn., 1991—; clin. asst. prof. dept. psychiatry Health Sci. Ctr. U. Tex., San Antonio, 1989-93; peer reviewer office spl. edn. and rehab. svcs. Nat. Inst. on Disability and Rehab. Rsch. U.S. Dept. Edn., 1993—; presenter in field. Author: A History of Ector County Cattle Brands, 1974. With U.S. Army, 1968-69. Mem. APA, Nat. Head Injury Assn., Tex. Head Injury Assn. (bd. dirs., treas. bd. 1994-95, Outstanding Leadership award 1990, bd. dirs. Alamo chpt. 1991, Profl. of Yr. award 1992), Alliance Tex. Head Injury Rehab. Facilities (chmn. 1991, chmn. ann. conf. 1990-91, co-chmn. 10th ann. S.W. Head Injury Symposium 1992, Outstanding Svc. award 1991). Democrat. Office: 14603 Green Oaks Woods San Antonio TX 78249-1435

WILSON, LUCINDA GLADE REES, elementary school educator; b. Beckley, W.Va., Mar. 26, 1956; d. James Ernest and Geneva Mae (Martin) Rees; m. Paul Edward Wilson, July 15, 1979; 1 child, James Paul. BSED, Concord Coll., 1977; MA in Speech Comm., W.Va. U., 1979; MA in Gifted Edn., W.Va. Grad. Coll., 1993. Tchr. elem. schs. Raleigh County, Beckley, 1977—; adv. bd. Youth Mus., 1994-96; supr. W.Va. Grad. Coll., Institute, 1996. Judge Raleigh County Soc. State Sci. Fair, Beckley, 1987—; den leader Boy Scouts, Beckley, 1990-94; citizen mem. W.Va. Humanities Coun., 1994—; presenter Raleigh County Tchrs. Acad., Beckley, 1996. Recipient MWI grant for author Marc Harshman, W.Va. Humanities Coun., 1990, Media Tchr. of Yr. award WSWP-Pub. TV, 1991. Mem. W.Va. Edn. Assn., Raleigh County & W.Va. Reading Coun., W.Va. English Lang. Arts Coun. (state dir. literacy mags. 1995-96). Home: Box 256 Stanaford WV 25927 Office: Stanaford Elem Box 19 Stanaford WV 25927

WILSON, LUCY LYNN WILLMARTH, postal service administrator; b. Russellville, Ala., May 18, 1953; d. Richard Bert and Alice Josephine (Gantt) Willmarth; m. Donald Wayne Wilson, Dec. 21, 1974; children: Beau Evan and Heath Edward (twins). BS in Home Econs., U. Ala., 1975; BS Ed. Sec. Biology/Psychology, Athens (Ala.) State Coll., 1996. Dietetic technician Athens (Ala.) Limestone Hosp., 1975-76, Med. Ctr. Hosp., Huntsville, Ala., 1976-78; kitchen supr. Lurleen B. Wallace Ctr., Decatur,

Ala., 1979; food svc. dir. Limestone Nursing Hosp., Athens, 1980; city carrier U.S. Postal Svc., Huntsville, 1986; city carrier U.S. Postal Svc., Athens, 1986-88, distbn. clk., 1988—; officer in charge U.S. Postal Svc., Lester, Ala., 1992-93. Mem. Cowart Elem. Sch. PTA, Athens, 1985-91; clinic vol. Cowart Elem. Sch., 1985; team mother Dixie Youth Baseball, Athens, 1991; mem. Athens H.S. Athletic Boosters Club, 1994—. Recipient Good Citizenship award Civitan Club, Russellville, 1971. Mem. Nat. Assn. Postmasters of U.S. (assoc.), Ala. Sci. Tchrs. Assn., U. Ala. nat. Alumni Assn, MADD (Ala. chpt.), The Studebaker Drivers Club, Psi Chi. Home: 209 Cascade Dr Athens AL 35611-2215 Office: US Postal Svc 1110 W Market St Athens AL 35611-2466

WILSON, MARGARET EILEEN, retired physical education educator; b. Kansas City, Mo., Aug. 4, 1925; d. Edward Leslie and Bertha Mae (Coe) W. BS in Edn., U. Ark., 1944, MS, 1949; PhD, U. Iowa, 1960. Cert. secondary tchr., Ark. Recreation dir. Pine Bluff (Ark.) Arsenal, 1944-45; instr. Ctrl. High Sch., Muskogee, Okla., 1945-48; grad. asst. U. Ark., Fayetteville, 1948-49; instr. Fayetteville High Sch., 1949-52; from instr. to asst. prof. Ark. Poly. Coll., Russellville, 1952-57, assoc. prof., 1959-65; grad. asst. U. Iowa, Iowa City, 1957-59; prof. Tex. Tech. U., Lubbock, 1965-90, dept. chair health, phys. edn. and recreation for women, 1967-76, prof. emerita, 1990—; mem. Tex. Tech. Faculty Senate, 1978-90, pres., 1978-79, 85-86. Active Lubbock County Dem. Ctrl. Com., 1993, 94, 96. Recipient AMOCO Found. Disting. Tchg. award, 1978, Disting. Faculty award in Tex. Tech. Moms and Dads Assn., 1987. Mem. AAHPERD (life), Tex. Assn. for Health, Phy. Edn., Recreation and Dance (Honor award 1979, David K. Bruce award 1992), Tex. Tech. Faculty Legal Action Assn. (pres. 1990-96), Lubbock Ret. Tchrs. Assn. (cmty. svc. chair 1994-96, co-treas. 1996—), Double T Connection (chair membership 1991-94), Delta Gamma (house corp. treas. 1982-91, Cable award 1978), Delta Kappa Gamma (chpt. pres. 1972-74, Chpt. Achievement award 1976, state corr. sec. 1979-81, state conv. chair 1979-80, state nominations com. 1985-87, state pers. com. 1987-89, State Achievement award 1987, state necrology com. 1993-95, state fin. com. 1995—). Presbyterian. Home: 5411 46th St Lubbock TX 79414-1513 Office: Tex Tech U Womens Gymnasium Lubbock TX 79409

WILSON, MARGARET GIBBONS, social sciences educator; b. Chgo., Nov. 14, 1943; d. Joseph and Florence (Greenberg) Gibbons; m. David Louis Wilson, July 8, 1967; 1 child, Mariah Elizabeth Gibbons Wilson. BA, U. Chgo., 1965, MAT, 1969; MA, U. So. Calif., 1972, PhD, 1978. Instr. dept. social studies Cen. YMCA C.C., Chgo., 1968-69; asst. prof. Coll. of Technology Fla. Internat. U., Miami, 1980-87, dir. rsch. Ctr. for Labor Rsch. & Studies, 1980-91, acting chairperson dept. indsl. systems, 1981-82, acting assoc. dean Coll. of Technology, 1982-83, dir. acad. programs and assoc. dir. Ctr. Labor Rsch. Studies, 1991—. Author: American Women in Transition: The Urban Influence 1876-1920, 1979, Floridans at Work: Yesterday and Today, 1989; editor Florida Labor History Symposium Procs., 1991. Mem. adv. bd. Louis Wolfson II Media History Ctr., Miami, 1986-92, PTSA Carver Mid. Sch., Miami, 1992-95, PTSA Coral Gables H.S., 1995—, Citizens for Open and Safe Streets, 1994—; mem., chmn. rsch. com. Women's Fund of Dade County, Miami, 1993—. Grantee Fla. Humanities Coun., 1984-85, 86, others. Mem. Univ. and Coll. Labor Edn. Assn. (editor Labor Studies Forum 1987—, editl. bd. Labor Studies Jour., 1987—, chmn. 1996—), Orgn. Am. Historians, Am. Hist. Assn. Democrat. Office: Fla Internat Univ Ctr for Labor Rsch & Studies Miami FL 33199

WILSON, MARLENE ANN, neuroscientist, educator; b. Cleve., June 22, 1956; d. Robert Wayne and Ann Lillian (Stuksa) W. BS in Biology, Chemistry, Muskingum Coll., 1978; student, U. Ill., PhD, 1985. Tchr., rsch. asst. U. Ill., Champaign, 1980-85; postdoctoral fellow Yale U. Sch. Medicine, New Haven, Conn., 1985-88; asst. prof. pharmacology U. S.C. Sch. Medicine, Columbia, 1988-94; assoc. prof. pharmacology U. SC. Sch. Medicine, Columbia, 1994—. Contbr. numerous articles to profl. jours. Recipient First award Nat. Inst. Drug Abuse, 1989-94, Small Instrument. award Alcohol, Drug Abuse and Mental Health Adminstrn., 1992, Stephan Mironescu award U. S.C. Sch. Medicine, 1989; Rsch. and Productive Scholarship award U. S.C.; Biomedical Rsch. Support grant U. S.C. Sch. Medicine, 1989. mem. Am. Soc. for Pharmacology & Exptl. Therapeutics, S.C. Chpt. for Neuroscience, Internat. Soc. for Psychoneuroendocrinology, Soc. for Neuroscience. Office: U SC Sch Medicine Bldg 1 Dept Pharmacology Columbia SC 29208

WILSON, MARY ELIZABETH, geriatrics nurse; b. Cin., Jan. 22, 1931; d. William S. and Mary E. (Arundel) Ferguson; m. Robert E. Wilson, Dec. 1, 1984; children: Maribeth, Deborah, Michael. Diploma, Christ Hosp. Sch. Nursing, Cin., 1952; BSN, U. Cin., 1955; postgrad., Xavier U. Instr. Christ Hosp. Sch. Nursing, 1952-56, 73-77; staff devel. coord. Deaconess Hosp., Cin., 1966-72; adminstrv. asst. health svcs. Twin Towers Retirement Home, Cin., 1977-84; staff devel. Good Samaritan Village Health Care Ctr., Kissimmee, Fla., 1985-87, DON, 1987-96; quality assurance/infection control coord., 1996—; health educator for Comty. Coord. Child Care; former mem. adv coun. LPN program and health occupations Tech. Edn. Ctr., Osceola, Fla.; employee health nurse Good Samaritan Village Health Care Ctr., Kissimmee, 1996—. Mem. Nat. League Nursing, Nat. Assn. Dirs. Nursing Adminstrn./Long Term Care, Fla. Assn. Dirs. Nursing Adminstrn./Long-Term Care (past regional coord., past com. chmn., past sec.), Assn. Practitioners in Infection Control (past sec.), Fla. Bd. Nursing (past mem. ad hoc com.).

WILSON, MELVIN NATHANIEL, psychology educator; b. St. Louis, Sept. 27, 1948; s. William F. Wilson and Mary Helen (Warder) Thompson; m. Eunice Clark, June 9, 1969 (div. June 1976); 1 child, Jibri-Akil; m. Angela Maria Davis, July 20, 1980. BA, Millikin U., 1970; MA, U. Ill., 1973, PhD, 1977. Asst. prof. U. Houston, 1976-78; vis. asst. prof. U. Ill., Champaign, 1978-79; asst. prof. U. Va., Charlottesville, 1979-86, assoc. prof., 1986—. Author: African American Family Life: Its Structural and Ecological Aspects, 1995; assoc. editor Am. Jour. Cmty. Psychology. Minority Rsch. scholar NSF, 1983-85; fellow Rockefeller Found., 1987, Social Sci. Rsch. Coun., 1991; USPHS grantee, 1970-72. Fellow APA, Am. Psychol. Soc.; mem. Soc. Rsch. on Child Devel., Nat. Coun. Family Rels., Assn. Black Psychologists (life). Office: U Va Psychology Dept Gilmer Hall Charlottesville VA 22903-2477

WILSON, NOLLIE ANDREW, Boy Scouts of America administrator; b. Big Spring, Tex., June 7, 1938; s. Silas Andrew and Vina Lee (Lloyd) W.; m. Wilma Ruth Williamson, Nov. 10, 1960; children: Valarie Ann Wilson Sullivan, Noel Andrew, Amanda Ruth. BA Biology, Tex. Lutheran Coll., 1972. From tng. specialist to dir. USAF Scouting Liaison, Dobbins AFB, Ga., 1956-82; sr. dist. exec. Bay Area Boy Scouts Am., Galveston, Tex., 1982—; adv. bd. criminal justice dept. Alvin (Tex.) C.C. Decorated commendation medal USAF, 1972; recipient Mayor's Commendation Big Spring City, 1976. Mem. Toastmasters, Rotary. Baptist. Home: 1402 Bellaire Blvd Alvin TX 77511 Office: Bay Area Coun 3020 53d St Galveston TX 77522

WILSON, PAUL EDDY, philosophy educator; b. Lebanon, Ind., Feb. 18, 1955; s. Paul Henry and Clara Marie (Essex) W.; m. Teresa Gail Marion, Aug. 5, 1977 (wid. Oct. 1989). BS, Johnson Bible Coll., Knoxville, Tenn., 1977; MDiv, Emmanuel Sch. Religion, Johnson City, Tenn., 1984; PhD in Philosophy, U. Tenn., 1989. Grad. teaching asst. U. Tenn., Knoxville, 1987-88, 88-89; asst. prof. philosophy U. of the South, Sewanee, Tenn., 1989-91, Shaw U., High Point, N.C., 1991—; adj. faculty Shaw Div. Sch., 1993, 95; lectr./presenter in field. Contbr. articles/essays to profl. jours. Min. 1st Ch. of Christ, Montoursville, Pa., 1977-88, Weber City Christian Ch., Gate City, Va., 1973-84; deacon Woodland Christian Ch., Knoxville, 1987-89; Sunday sch. tchr. 1st Ch. of Christ, High Point, N.C., 1993—, elder, 1996—. Grantee NEH, 1990, 94, Howard and Edna Hong Kierkegaard Libr., St. Olaf Coll., Northfield, Minn., 1992. Mem. Am. Acad. Religion, The Soc. Bibl. Lit., Am. Assn. Philosophy Tchrs., Am. Philos. Assn., N.Am. Soc. Social Philosophy, Kierkegaard Soc., Soc. Christian Philosophers, Soc. Advancement of Am. Philosophy, Soc. Philosophy Religion, Theta Phi. Mem. Disciples of Christ Ch. Home: 320 Summit Rd High Point NC 27265 Office: Shaw Univ Cape Ctr 329 N Main St High Point NC 27260-5044

WILSON, PAUL LOWELL, lawyer, investor; b. Rockingham County, Va., May 12, 1951; s. James Joseph and Edna Vivian (Halterman) W.; m. Thea Elaine Hermit, June 21, 1975; children: Meredith Elaine, Taylor Halterman. AB, W.Va. U., 1973; JD, Coll. of William and Mary, 1976. Bar: W.Va. 1976, U.S. Dist. Ct. (so. dist.) W.Va. 1976, Va. 1979, U.S. Dist. Ct. (ea. dist.) Va. 1991. Assoc. Brown & Peyton, Charleston, W.Va., 1976-78; title atty. Lawyers Title Ins. Corp., Williamsburg, Va., 1978-80; assoc. S.J. Baker, Williamsburg, 1981-83; counsel edn. com. W.Va. Legislature, Charleston, 1977-78; gen counsel A J & L Corp., Williamsburg, 1983-85, v.p., gen. counsel, Williamsburg, 1985-91; bd. dirs. First Va. Bank-Commonwealth, Grafton, 1983-90, 503 Cert. Devel. Co., Richmond, Sta. WHRO-TV. Mem. York County Sch. Bd. 1986-94, chmn., 1992-94; pres. Nat. Housing Corp., 1986-93, The Preservation Group, Inc., 1991—. Mem. W.Va. State Bar, EconoLodges Am. Franchisee Assn. (sec., treas. 1986-90), Kiwanis, Sigma Phi Epsilon. Methodist. Home: PO Box 1593 Williamsburg VA 23187 Office: Ste 215 402 W Duke of Gloucester St Williamsburg VA 23185

WILSON, RHYS THADDEUS, lawyer; b. Albany, Ga., May 9, 1955; s. Joseph Farr Jr. and Betty Ann (Wilkins) W.; m. Carolyn Reid Saffold, June 2, 1984. AB, Duke U., 1976; JD, U. Ga., 1979; LLM, Emory U., 1985. Bar: Ga. 1979. Pvt. practice law Atlanta, 1979-89; sr. v.p., gen. counsel Monarch Capital Group, Inc., Atlanta, 1989-92, Jackson & Coker, Inc., Atlanta, 1992-93; pres. Jackson & Coker Locum Tenens, Inc., Atlanta, 1993-95; ptnr. Robins, Kaplan, Miller & Ciresi, Atlanta, 1995—; spkr. continuing legal edn. seminars; mem. The Exec. Com. (TEC). Contbr. articles to profl. jours. Mem. ABA, Ga. Bar Assn. (chmn. internat. law sect. 1987-88, exec. com. corp. and banking law sect. 1987-89, editorial bd. Ga. State Bar Jour. 1986-89), Atlanta Bar Assn. (editor newsletter 1984-86, Outstanding Svc. award 1986), Assn. for Corp. Growth, Atlanta Alliance Network, The Exec. Com., Atlanta Venture Forum, Capital City Club. Episcopalian.

WILSON, RICHARD LEE, political science educator; b. Worthington, Minn., Dec. 20, 1944; s. G. Roy and Dorothy Eileen (Johnson) W.; m. Carolyn Ann Dirks, Aug. 24, 1968 (div.); 1 child, Kevin Richard. BA, U. Chgo., 1966, postgrad., 1966-67; PhD, Johns Hopkins U., 1971; postgrad., Columbia U., 1988, Stanford U., 1992. Congl. aide 4th Congl. Dist. Md., 1971; asst. prof. polit. sci. U. Tenn., Chattanooga, 1971-76, assoc. prof., 1976-87, prof., 1988—; registrar-at-large Hamilton County Election Commn., 1977-84; lectr. Robert A. Taft Inst. Govt., U. Tenn., Nashville, 1978, 79, 81; supr. state legis. and met. internship program U. Chattanooga, 1972-86; vis. prof. Govt. Fgn. Affairs Coll., Beijing, 1986-87; Fulbright prof. govt. Beijing U., 1988-89, Samford U., Birmingham, Ala., 1991-93. Author: Tennessee Politics, 1976, American Government, 1993; co-editor: Ready Reference: Censorship, 1996; contbr. chpts. to books. Chmn. Hamilton County Health Planning Adv. Council, 1975-79; bd. dirs. Ga.-Tenn. Regional Health Commn., 1978-82; active Tenn. State Health Coordinating Council, 1977-81; exec. com. State Health Coordinating Council, 1979-81. Named Outstanding Educator of Yr., Signal Mountain (Tenn.) Jaycees, 1973, Outstanding Prof. of Yr., SGA, 1985-86; recipient Polit. Edn. award NAACP, 1980, Excellent Prof. award Fgn. Affairs Coll., Beijing, 1987, UTC Exceptional Merit award, 1990, 94; NEH grantee, 1988, 92. Mem. So. Polit. Sci. Assn., Midwest Polit. Sci. Assn., Am. Polit. Sci. Assn. (nat. rsch. grant 1995), Nat. Soc. Internships and Exptl. Edn., SAR, China People's Friendship Assn., Aircraft Owners and Pilots Assn. Methodist. Office: Univ of Tenn Dept Political Sci Holt 232F Chattanooga TN 37403

WILSON, ROBERT GODFREY, radiologist; b. Montgomery, Ala., Mar. 18, 1937; s. Robert Woodridge and Lucille (Godfrey) W.; B.A., Huntingdon Coll., 1957; M.D., Med. Coll. Ala., 1961; m. Dorothy June Waters, Aug. 31, 1957; children—Amy Lucille, Robert Darwin, Robert Woodridge II, Lucy Elizabeth. Intern, Letterman Gen. Hosp., San Francisco, 1961-62; resident in radiology U. Okla. Med. Center, Oklahoma City, 1965-68, clin. instr. in radiology, 1968—; practice medicine specializing in diagnostic and therapeutic radiology, nuclear medicine, Shawnee, Okla., 1968—; mem. med. staff Shawnee Med. Center, Mission Hill Meml. Hosp., Shawnee, 1968—. Served to capt. M.C., USAF, 1960-65. Diplomate Nat. Bd. Med. Examiners, Am. Bd. Radiology, Am. Bd. Nuclear Medicine. Mem. AMA, Okla., Pottawatomie County med. socs., Okla., Greater Oklahoma City radiol. socs., Am. Coll. Radiology, Soc. Nuclear Medicine, Radiol. Soc. N.Am. Methodist. Home: 26 Sequoyah Blvd Shawnee OK 74801-5570 Office: 1110 N Harrison St Shawnee OK 74801

WILSON, ROBERT HINES, urban policy educator; b. Norman, Okla., Oct. 13, 1949; s. William and Claire (Hines) W.; m. Rita Santos, Aug. 12, 1977; 1 child, David. BS in Indsl. Engring., Okla. State U., 1971, MS in Indsl. Engring., 1972; MA of Regional Sci., M of City and Regional Planning, U. Pa., 1974, PhD in City and Regional Planning, 1979. Rsch. fellow Ctr. for Ecol. Rsch. in Planning, Phila., 1975; vis. prof. Fed. U. Pernambuco (Brazil) Recife, 1975-79; from asst. prof. to assoc. prof. Lyndon B. Johnson Sch. Pub Affairs U. Tex., Austin, 1979-90, asst. dean Lyndon B. Johnson Sch. Pub. Affairs, 1980-83, prof. Lyndon B. Johnson Sch. Pub. Affairs, 1990—; coord. PhD program Lyndon B. Johnson Sch. Pub. Affairs Lyndon B. Johnson Sch. Pub. Affairs, Austin, 1991-94; Mike Hogg prof. Lyndon B. Johnson Sch. Pub. Affairs U. Tex., Austin, 1993—, dir. urban issues program, 1995—; cons. rsch. project Superintendencia de Desesvolvimento do Nordeste, Recife, Brazil, 1975-76, Autarquin Metropolitana de Fortaleza, Fortaleza, Brazil, 1976, Banco do Nordeste do Brasil, Fortaleza, 1977; cons. Legal Aid Tex., Austin, 1980, Orgn. Am. States, Recife, 1987, Tex. Hist. Commn., 1988, UN Devel. Program, 1990, Tex. Govt. Today, Am. Legal Pub., 1991-92; mem. tech. com. Tex. Rural Econ. Devel. Commn., 1990; mem. panel fiscal neutrality measures Legis. Edn. Bd., State of Tex., 1990-91. Author: States and the Economy: Policymaking and Decentralization, 1993, (with Jurgen Schmandt) Promoting High Technology: Initiatives and Policies for State Government, 1987, Telecommunications and Economic Development: The New State Role, 1989, Growth Policy in the Age of High Technology: The Role of Religions and States, 1990, (with others) The New Urban Infrastructure: Cities and Telecommunications, 1990, The Political Economy of Brazil: Public Policies in an Era of Transition, 1990, Telecommunications and Rural Development: A Study of Private and Public Sector Innovation, 1991, (with Beryl Radin) New Governance for Rural America, 1996; contbr. articles to profl. jours., chpts. to books. Mellon fellow U. Pa., 1974, fellow Banco do Nordeste do Brazil, Bertha and Aaron Horwitz fellow, 1979, Elspeth Rostow Centennial fellow U. Tex., 1986-89; Fulbright lectr. Fed. U. Minas Gerais, Belo Horizonte, Brazil, 1982. Mem. Nat. Assn. Schs. of Pub. Affairs and Adminstrn. (com. on PhD programs 1991-94), Assn. for Pub. Policy Analysis and Mgmt. (policy coun. 1991-95). Office: U Tex LBJ Sch Pub Affairs PO Drawer Y Univ Sta Austin TX 78713-7450

WILSON, RONALD JAMES, geologist; b. San Antonio, Dec. 24, 1948; s. James Robert and Robbie Lee (Bell) W.; m. Beverly Ann Engelhorn, June 23, 1970 (div. May 1980); children: Jennifer, Jason; m. June Guynette Nolin, Aug. 5, 1983; 1 child, Heather. BA, Rice U., 1971. Sr. logging engr. Schlumberger, Houston, 1971-75; sr. petrophysicist Delta Drilling Co., Tyler, Tex., 1975-78; sr. log analyst Dresser Industries, Houston, 1978-81; mgr., geology and petrophysics Intercomp, Houston, 1981-83; cons. geologist C G & A, Ft. Worth, 1983-90; exec. v.p. Alpha Bio Internat., Ltd., Dallas, 1990-91; pres. Integrated Energy Solutions, Ft. Worth, 1991-94, Lahd Energy, Inc., Granbury, Tex., 1994—; bd. dirs. Tex. Energy Resources, Arlington, 1994—. Author: Practical Log Analysis, 1981, Quick-Look Techniques, 1981; contbr. articles to jour. Prodn. Log Analyst, Log Analyst. Mem. nat. edn. bd. Luth. Ch. Am., Denver, 1975; deacon Richland Hills Ch. of Christ, Ft. Worth, 1991; edn. com. Action United Meth. Ch., Acton, Tex., 1994-95; trustee The White Lake Sch., 1995—. Mem. Am. Assn. Petroleum Geologists (cert.), Soc. Profl. Well Log Analysts (pres. 1987-88), Soc. Petroleum Engrs. (bd. edn. 1976—), Divsn. Environ. Geoscientists (charter). Republican. Methodist. Home: 301 Willow Ridge Rd Fort Worth TX 76103 Office: Lahd Energy Inc 307 W 7th St Ste 1717 Fort Worth TX 76102

WILSON, SAMUEL GRAYSON, federal judge; b. 1949. BS, U. Richmond, 1971; JD cum laude, Wake Forest U., 1974. Asst. commonwealth atty. City of Roanoke, Va., 1974-76; asst. U.S. atty. Western Dist. Va., 1976; U.S. magistrate U.S. Dist. Ct. for Western Dist. Va., 1976-81; mem. Woods, Rogers & Hazlegrove, Roanoke, 1981-90; dist. judge U.S. Dist. Ct. for Western Dist. Va., Abingdon, Va., 1990—. Mem. staff Wake Forest Law Rev., 1973-74. Mem. law bd. visitors Wake Forest U. Mem. Va. State Bar, Fed. Bar Assn., Va. Bar Assn., Roanoke Bar Assn., Supreme Ct. Hist. Soc. Methodist. Office: US Dist Ct PO Box 749 180 W Main St Abingdon VA 24210-0749*

WILSON, SAMUEL V., academic adminstrator. Pres. Hampden-Sydney (Va.) Coll. Office: Hampden-Sydney Coll Office of Pres PO Box 128 Hampden Sydney VA 23943-0128

WILSON, SHERRY DENISE, speech and language pathologist; b. Rutherford, N.C., Jan. 10, 1963; d. Morris William and Betty Jean (Hudgins) Wilson. AA, Isothermal Community Coll., 1981; BS, Cen. Mo. State U., 1985, MS, 1988. Lic. speech-lang. pathologist, N.C. Speech pathologist DePaul Hosp. Home Health, Cheyenne, Wyo., 1987, 89; coord. handicap svcs., staff speech-lang. pathologist Laramie County Head Start, Cheyenne, 1987-89; speech pathologist, supr., coord., dir. inclusive pre-sch. Ednl. Svcs. Unit # 13, Scottsbluff, 1989-95, project dir. The Early Intervention Demonstration Project, 1991-95; dir. rehab. svc. Brentwood Hills Nursing Ctr. (Beverly Enterprises), Asheville, N.C., 1995—; planning region chair Interagy. coord. Coun. Presch. Spl. Edn., Scottsbluff, Nebr., 1989-93, mem. 1993-95; mem. health adv. bd. Head Start, Gering, Nebr., 1989-91; cons. trainer in field. Founding mem. S.E. Wyo. AIDS Project, Cheyenne, 1989; Odyssey of the Mind coach Gering Jr. H.S., 1989-93; project dir., mem. exec. bd. Cmty. Devel. Coalition, 1994. Named Outstanding Speech Pathologist of Yr., Sigma Alpha Eta, 1985, Two Thousand Notable Am. Women, 1992, 96. Mem. NEA, Am. Speech-Lang.-Hearing Assn. (cert. clin. competence 1989—, Cert. Excellence 1993), Nebr. State Edn. Assn., Coun. for Exceptional Children (early childhood divsn.). Office: Brentwood Hills Nursing Ctr Asheville NC 28804

WILSON, SHERYL A., pharmacist; b. Nashville, Apr. 6, 1957; d. Robert Lewis and Norma Anne (Cox) W. BS in Biology, David Lipscomb U., 1979; BS in Pharmacy, Auburn U., 1985. Lic. pharmacist, Tenn. Student extern/intern East Alabama Med. Ctr., Opelika, Ala., 1982-86; staff pharmacist Metro Nashville Gen. Hosp., 1987-95, PharmaThera, Inc., Nashville, 1995—. Flutist Nashville Community Concert Band, 1973—; preschool tchr. Donelson Ch. of Christ, 1988—. Mem. Am. Pharm. Assn., Am. Soc. Health Sys. Pharmacists, Am. Soc. Parenteral and Enteral Nutrition, Tenn. Soc. Hosp. Pharmacists, Nashville Area Pharmacists Assn. Democrat. Home: 1439 Mcgavock Pike Nashville TN 37216-3231 Office: PharmaThera Inc 1410 Donelson Pike Ste B-3 Nashville TN 37217-2933

WILSON, STANLEY PORTER, retired agricultural association executive; b. Andalusia, Ala., Sept. 4, 1931; s. Porter and Alice (Johnson) W.; m. Barbara Dee Duggan, June 20, 1953; children: Michael Stanley, Daniel Robert. BS, Auburn U., 1954, MS, 1958; PhD, Okla. State U., 1961. Postdoctoral researcher NAS-NRC, West Lafayette, Ind., 1961-63; coord. NC regional poultry breeding lab. USDA-ARS, West Lafayette, 1963-65, nat. investigation leader poultry genetics, 1965-67, dir. pioneering rsch. lab., 1967-72, rsch. leader, 1972-75; assoc. dir. Ala. Agrl. Exptl. Sta. Auburn (Ala.) U., 1975-80, v.p. agr., home econs., vet. medicine, 1980-84; cons. Auburn, 1985-86; owner, operator farm Andalusia, 1986-90; exec. v.p. Coun. Agrl. Sci. and Tech., Ames, Iowa, 1990-92; Past mem. Ala. State Bd. Agr., Ala. Rural Devel. Coun., Ala. Food and Agr. Coun., Ala. Resource and Devel. coun., Ala. Farm-City Com., Tri-States Blue Ribbon Com. on Agr. Contbr. numerous articles to profl. jours. With U.S. Army, 1954-56. Mem. Genetics Soc. Am., Am. Genetic Assn. (mem. coun.), AAAS, Am. Soc. Animal Sci., So. Assn. Agrl. Scientists, Sigma Xi, Gamma Sigma Delta.

WILSON, STEVE, museum director. Office: Mus Gt Plains PO Box 68 Lawton OK 73502-0068

WILSON, TERENCE SCOTT, osteopath; b. Lakewood, Ohio, Oct. 8, 1951; s. Walter Raymond W. and Elizabeth M. (Haller) W.; m. Grace Lucille Gettins; 1 child, Ruth Elizabeth. BS in Systems Engring., U.S. Naval Acad., 1973; DO, Kirksville Coll. Osteo. Medicine, 1981. Diplomate Nat. Bd. Med. Examiners, Am. Bd. Osteo., Am. Coll. Osteo. Family Physicians. Commd. ensign USN, 1973, advanced through grades to lt. comdr., 1982; intern NAS, Jacksonville, Fla., 1981-82; emergency rm. staff physician Naval Regional Med. Ctr., Jacksonville, Fla., 1982; dir. Family Practice Clinic Naval Air Sta., Cecil Field, Fla., 1983; dir. emergency dept. Naval Hosp., Orlando, Fla., 1983-86; pvt. practice Am. Osteo. Assn., Orlando, Fla., 1986—; med. dir. emergency svcs., Orange County, Fla., 1985—; co-med dir. Inst. Emergency Med. Svcs., Orlando, 1985—; med. dir. critical care edn., Orange County, 1989—, Greater Orlando Aviation Authority, 1986—. Recipient Adm. W.P. Blandy award U.S. Naval Acad., 1973, Charles C. Hall award Orange County Emergency Med. Svc., 1993, Fellow award Am. Coll. Osteo. Family Physicians Mem. Am. Coll. Osteo. Family Practitioners (trustee, pres. 1994-95); mem. Am. Osteo. Assn., Fla. Soc. Am. Coll. Osteo. Family Practitioners (pres. 1994-95, Fa ily Physician of Yr. award, 1990), Ctrl. Fla. Multiple Sclerosis Soc. (med. dir. 1983—, creative works editor 1985—, Unsung Hero award), Sigma Sigma Phi, Psi Sigma Alpha. Republican. Methodist. Home: 1640 Wind Harbor Rd Orlando FL 32809-6844 Office: Good Shepherd Med Clinic 8009 S Orange Ave Orlando FL 32809-6711

WILSON, THOMAS LEON, physicist; b. Alpine, Tex., May 21, 1942; s. Homer Marvin and Ogarita Maude (Bailey) W.; m. Joyce Ann Krevosky, May 7, 1978; children: Kenneth Edward Byron, Bailey Elizabeth Victoria. BA, Rice U., 1964, BS, 1965, MA, 1974, PhD, 1976. With NASA, Houston, 1965—, astronaut instr., 1965-74, high-energy theoretical physicist, 1969—. Author of two books on cosmic dust and astrophysics; contbr. articles in field to profl. jours. Recipient Hugo Gernsback award IEEE, 1964; NASA fellow, 1969-76. Mem. AAAS, Am. Phys. Soc., N.Y. Acad. Scis., Am. Assn. Physicists in Medicine. Research on grand unified field theory, relativistic quantum field theory, quantum chromodynamics, quantum probability theory, supergravity, quantum cosmology, astrophysics, deep inelastic scattering, neutrino astronomy, authority on neutrino tomography, discoverer classical uncertainty principle; subspecialty: relativity and gravitation. Patentee in field; contributor to design of NASA's proposed lunar base; originator olive branch as symbol of man's 1st landing on moon (on Susan B. Anthony and Eisenhower dollars); and manual Saturn takeover for Apollo moon program. Home: 206 Woodcombe Dr Houston TX 77062-2538 Office: NASA Johnson Space Ctr Houston TX 77058

WILSON, THOMAS WOODROW, III, research scientist, consultant; b. Greensboro, N.C., Mar. 29, 1956; s. Thomas Woodrow Jr. and Ruth Hanes (Friddle) W.; m. Rhonda Gayle Beeson, May 16, 1980. BS in Textile Chemistry with honors, N.C. State U., 1978, MS in Textile Chemistry, 1981, PhD in Fiber and Polymer Sci., 1986. Registered patent agent. Polymer scientist Rsch. Triangle Inst., Research Triangle Park, N.C., 1989-91; rsch. scientist Family Health Internat., Research Triangle Park, N.C., 1991-93, sr. rsch. scientist, 1993-94; assoc. dir., 1994—; cons. IPAS, Carrboro, N.C., 1991—. Patentee medical device; contbr. numerous articles to profl. jours. Grantee USDA, NASA, NIH/Nat. Inst. Dental Rsch., 1986. Mem. AAAS, Am. Chem. Soc. (polymeric materials sci. and engring. divsn., polymer divsn., rubber divsn., N.C. polymer group, N.C. sect.), ASTM, Sigma Xi. Office: Mayer Labs 645 Kennedy St Oakland CA 94606

WILSON, VICTORIA JANE SIMPSON, farmer, former nurse; b. Floresville, Tex., Nov. 30, 1952; d. Joseph Eugene and Eva Gertrude (Ferguson) Simpson; m. Richard Royce Wilson, May 15, 1976; children: Sarah Beth, Nathan Lawrence. BSN, U. Cen. Ark., 1977; MS in Nursing, Northwestern State U., 1981. Charge nurse surg. St. Vincent Infirmary, Little Rock; staff nurse ICU La. State U. Med. Ctr., Shreveport, La.; patient edn. coord. White River Med. Ctr., Batesville, Ark.; co-owner, chief exec. officer Health Plus, Stuttgart, Ark.; co-owner, mgr. Wilson & Son Fish Farm. Mem. Catfish Farmers Am. (bd. dirs.), Catfish Farmers Ark., Sigma Theta Tau. Home: 51 Wilson Ln Humphrey AR 72073-0310

WILSON, WILLIAM GLENN, JR., graphic designer; b. McKeesport, Pa., Mar. 16, 1955; s. William Glenn Sr. and Anna Elizabeth (Johnson) W.; m. Marie Estelle Spillias, July 13, 1983 (div. June 1986); m. Beth Lynn Lewis, July 9, 1988. Student, Art Inst., 1977-78. Pressman, mgr. Prince Printing, Clairton, Pa., 1968-76; pressman, layout artist Multiscope, Inc., Pitts., 1976-77, mgr., 1977-79; editor, pub., dir. Questar Mag., Pitts., 1978-81; artist, designer Dick Z Assocs., Pitts., 1979-81; designer, pub., adminstr. Imagine, Inc., Pitts., 1982-83; graphic designer St. (Fla.) Petersburg Times, 1983-90; owner Wilson-Lewis-Wilson Design, Palm Harbor, Fla., 1990—; comm. cons. ABR Info. Svcs., 1993—. Assoc. prodr. 7th Ann. Sci. Fiction Film Awards, Hollywood, Calif., 1980; prodr. corp. video Mus. African-Am. Art, Tampa, Fla., 1991; editor, ghostwriter Grande Illusions, 1983; editor, pub.

comic book mag. The Collector, 1966-74, sci. fiction mag. Questar, 1978-81; Fla. corres. Starlog Mag. Contbr. Popular Culture Collection Hillman Libr., U. Pitts., 1990; cons. Mus. African-Am. Art, Tampa, 1991—; designer, cons., contbr. Tampa Bay History Ctr., 1993—. Recipient Hon. Mention Printing Industry Assn. Western Pa., 1979, 80, Lifetime Achievement award Acad. Sci. Fiction, 1980, Mag. Cover of Yr., Mktg. Bestsellers, N.Y.C., 1980, Pub. Svc. award Distilled Spirits Coun., 1981, Nat. Agri-Mktg. Assn. award as designer of award winning curriculum materials for Am. Egg Bd., 1993, Graphic Arts Excellence award for outstanding achievement in design, Consolidated Papers, Inc., 1996.

WILSON, WILLIAM H., history educator; b. St. Joseph, Mo., Nov. 3, 1935; m. Katharine Lehr, June 18, 1960; children: Katharine, Margaret. Student, St. Joseph Jr. Coll., 1953-54; BJ, U. Mo., 1957, MA, 1958, PhD, 1962. Asst. prof. U. S.D., 1962-63; asst. prof. U. Alaska, Fairbanks, 1963-66, assoc. prof., 1966-67; assoc. prof. U. North Tex., Denton, 1968-75, prof. history, 1975-90, Regents' prof. history, 1990—; lectr. in field. Author: The City Beautiful Movement in Kansas City, 1964, 2d edit. 1991, Coming of Age: Urban America, 1915-1945, 1974, Railroad in the Clouds: The Alaska Railroad in the Age of Steam, 1914-1945, 1977, The City Beautiful Movement, 1989, co-author: Carl F. Gould: A Life in Architecture and the Arts, 1995; contbr. numerous articles to profl. jours., chpts. to books; book reviewer Agrl. History, Alaska History, Am. Hist. Rev., Am. West, Colo. Mag., The Historian, Jour. of Am. History, Jour. of the West, Locus, Pacific Historian, Rev. in Am. History, others. Recipient Lewis Mumford prize Soc. for Am. City and Regional Planning History, 1989, Outstanding Book of the Yr. in category of arch. and urban planning Assn. Am. Pubs., 1989; grantee Community Studies, Inc., 1960-62, Harry S. Truman Libr. Inst., summer 1964, Am. Philos. Soc., summer 1966, Am. Assn. State and Local History, summer 1966, U. N. Tex., 1969-74, 77, 78-79, 81-83, 88-92, U. North Tex., spring 1985; NEH fellow, 1968. Mem. Orgn. Am. Historians (membership com. 1964-67), Internat. Planning History Soc. (exec. com. 1979-84, 90—), Soc. for Am. City and Regional Planning History (trustee 1990—, chmn. John W. Reps prize com. 1993, pres. 1995-97), Tex. State Hist. Assn. (H. Bailey Carroll award com. 1990-92, chmn. Kate Broocks Bates award com. 1991-92). Home: 716 W Mulberry St #24 Denton TX 76201-5992 Office: Univ of North Texas Dept History PO Box 13735 Denton TX 76203-6735

WILSON, WILLIAM J., English language educator; b. Oxford, Ind., Sept. 18, 1932; s. William Woodward Wilson and Esta Ella (Burton) Dilley; m. Edith Lucille McElhaney, June 1, 1955 (dec. Mar. 1969); children: Susan Wilson Sarver, Maura A., Kyle A. BS summa cum laude, Ill. State U., 1959; MA, Peabody-Vanderbilt U., Nashville, 1968; EdD, Nova U., Ft. Lauderdale, Fla., 1983. Tchr. Manteno (Ill.) High Sch., 1959-60; teaching asst. U. Ill., Urbana, 1960-61; tchr. Wheaton (Ill.) Central High Sch., 1961-67; editor Laidlaw Pubs., Chgo., 1968-69; asst. prof. Ball State U., Muncie, Ind., 1969-70; assoc. prof. English Palm Beach C.C., Lake Worth, Fla., 1970—; test reader Ednl. Testing Svc., Princeton, N.J., 1965-96; pres. Am. Lang. Rsch. Found., Lake Worth, 1976-96. Editor: New Approaches to Language and Composition, 1969; author children's mus. Winter Comes to Florida, 1974, children's mus. play A Cruise on the S.S. Eternal, 1975, Arnold's Answering Apparatus, 1976. Bd. dirs. Village Green Condominiums, Palm Springs, 1985-86. With USN, 1951-55. No. Ill. U. fellow in linguistics, DeKalb, 1965-66, humanities fellow Peabody-Vanderbilt U., Nashville, 1967. Mem. VFW, NEA, Am. Legion, Nat. Assn. Tchrs. English., Kappa Delta Pi, Sigma Tau Delta. Democrat. Episcopalian. Home: 2100 Springdale Blvd Apt 216Y Lake Worth FL 33461-6385 Office: Palm Beach C C 4200 Congress Ave Lake Worth FL 33461-4705

WILSON, WILLIAM R., JR., judge; b. 1939. Student, U. Ark., 1957-58; BA, Hendrix Coll., 1962; JD, Vanderbilt U., 1965. Atty. Autrey & Goodson, Texarkana, Ark., 1965-66, Wright, Lindsey & Jennings, Little Rock, 1969-72, Wilson & Hodge, Little Rock, 1972-74; prin. William R. Wilson Jr., P.A., Little Rock, 1974-80, Wilson & Engstrom, Little Rock, 1980-83, Wilson, Engstrom & Vowell, Little Rock, 1984, Wilson, Engstrom, Corum & Dudley, Little Rock, 1984-93; judge U.S. Dist. Ct. (ea. dist.) Ark., Little Rock, 1993—; chair Ark. Supreme Ct. Com. on Model Criminal Jury Instrns., 1978—; active Ark. Supreme Ct. Com. on Civil Practice, 1982—. Lt. USN, 1966-69. Named Disting. Alumnus, Hendrix Coll., 1993, Outstanding Lawyer, Pulaski County Bar Assn., 1993. Mem. ABA, ATLA, Am. Bd. Trial Advocates (Nat. Civil Justice award 1992), Am. Coll. Trial Lawyers, Internat. Acad. Trial Lawyers, Internat. Soc. Barristers, Ark. Bar Assn. (Outstanding Lawyer 1991), S.W. Ark. Bar Assn., Ark. Trial Lawyers Assn. (pres. 1982, Outstanding Trial Lawyer 1988-89). Office: US Dist Ct Ark 600 W Capitol Ave Rm 149 Little Rock AR 72201-3329*

WILSON, WILLIAM ROBERTS, JR. (BOB WILSON), lawyer, apparel executive; b. Rosedale, Miss., July 6, 1941; s. William Roberts Wilson Sr. and Mary Elizabeth (Boatner) W.; m. Elizabeth Ann Smith; children: William Roberts Wilson III, Elizabeth Ann, Augusta Elliott. Student, Vanderbilt U., Tenn., 1964; JD, U. Miss., 1969. Pvt. practice Jackson, Miss.; chmn. bd., prin. owner Dunn's Supply Co. Inc., Sporting Goods Catalog Co. Chmn. founder The Charitable Food Bank Sportsman Against Hunger; active mem. Rep. Nat. Com. Team 100, Newcomen Soc. of U.S., Am. Intertrade Group, Presdl. Round Table, Rep. Senatorial Inner Circle. Mem. NRA (life mem.), Ala. State Bar Assn., Miss. Bar Assn., Miss. Trial Lawyers Assn. (life mem.), Assn. Trial Lawyers of Am. (sustaining mem.), Ark. Trial Lawyers Assn., Ala. Trial Lawyers Assn., Pa. Trial Lawyers Assn., La. Trial Lawyers Assn., Roscoe Pound Found. (fellow), Miss. State Bar Assn. (former commr.), Nat. Col. Advocacy, United Conservation Alliance (founding and interim bd. mem.), Congressional Sportsmen Found. (bd. dirs.), Congressional Sportsmen's Caucus Found. (treas.), Quail Unlimited (life mem., life sponsor), Miss. Wildlife Fedn. (life mem.), Ducks Unlimited (sponsoring mem.), Waterfowl, U.S.A., Delta Wildlife Found. (sponsoring founder), British Assn. for Shooting and Conservation (life mem.), Safari Club Internat. (v.p. regional, bd. dirs.), Catfish Point Hunting Club (gen. ptnr.), Donaldson Point Hunting Club (landowning mem.), Bell Place Duck Hunting Club, Athelstan Club, Singing River Yacht Club, Country Club of Jackson Miss., Delta Kappa Epsilon, Delta Theta Phi. Office: 4465 I 55 N Ste 201 Jackson MS 39206-6124

WILSON-WEBB, NANCY LOU, adult educational administrator; b. Maypearl, Tex., Jan. 20, 1932; d. Madison Grady and Mary Nancy Pearson (Haney) Wilson; m. John Crawford Webb, July 29, 1972. BS magna cum laude, Abilene (Tex.) Christian U., 1953; MEd with high honors, Tex. Christian U., 1985. Cert. tchr., adult edn. dir., Tex. Tchr. elem. grades Ft. Worth Ind. Sch. Dist., 1953-67, tchr., 1970-73; dir. adult edn. consortium for 38 sch. dists. Tex. Edn. Agy., 1973—; pres. Nat. Commn. on Adult Basic Edn., 1994-95; pres. Tex. Adult Edn. Adminstrn., 1994; apptd. mem. Tex. State Literacy Coun., 1987—, Tex. State Sch. Bd. Commn., 1994-95; exec. bd. Tex. Coun. Co-op Dirs., 1989—. Cons. to textbook: On Your Mark?, 1994. Pres. Jr. Womans Club, Ft. Worth, 1969, Fine Arts Guild, Tex. Christian U., Ft. Worth, 1970-72, Ft. Worth Womens Civic Club Coun., 1970; active Exec. Libr. Bd., Ft. Worth, 1990—; apptd. bd. dirs. Literacy Plus in North Tex., 1988, Greater Ft. Worth Literacy Coun.; commr. Ed-16 Task Forces Tex. Edn. Agy., 1985-92; literacy bd. dirs. Friends of Libr., 1967—, Opera Guild Ft. Worth, 1965—, Johnson County (Tex.) Corrs. Bd. Recipient Bevy award Jr. Womans Club, 1968, Proclamation Commrs. Ct. Outstanding 40 Yr. Literacy Svc. to Tarrant County, 1994, Tarrant County Woman of Yr. award, 1995, Outstanding Leadership award Ft. Worth ISD Sch. Bd., 1995; named one of Most Outstanding Educators in U.S. Nat. Assn. Adult Edn., 1983, Most Outstanding Woman Edn., City of Ft. Worth, 1991, others; named to Tex. Hall of Fame for Women, 1991; scholar Germany, 1983. Mem. NEA, DAR (Nat. Most Outstanding Literacy award 1992, Leadership Literacy award 1985-87, 89, 94), AAUW, Am. Assn. Adult and Continuing Edn. (v.p. 1987-89, chair 1993 internat. conv. 1992) Tex. Assn. Adult and Continuing Edn. (pres. 1985-86, Most Outstanding Adult Adminstr. in Tex. 1984), Tex. Coun. Adult Edn. Dirs. (pres.), Coun. World Affairs (bd. dirs. 1980-92), Am. Bus. Womens Assn., Ft. Worth C. of C., Lecture Found., Internat. Reading Assn. (Literacy Challenge award 1991), Ft. Worth Adminstrv. Assn., Zonta, Ft. Worth Garden Club, Womans Club Ft. Worth, Petroleum Club, Carousel Dance Assn., Optimist Club (Ft. Worth), Met. Dinner and Dance Club, Ridglea County Club, Crescent Club, Phi Beta Kappa, Alpha Delta Kappa (Nat. Literacy award), Phi Delta Kappa. Democrat. Mem. Church of Christ. Home: 3716 Fox Hollow St Fort Worth TX 76109-2616 Office: 100 N University Dr Fort Worth TX 76107-1360

WIMBERLEY, RONALD C., sociology educator, researcher; b. Mobile, Ala., Nov. 7, 1942. B.A., La. Coll., 1963; M.S., Fla. State U., 1967; Ph.D., U. Tenn., 1972. Instr. to prof. N.C. State U., Raleigh, 1971—, prof., head dept. sociology, anthropology and social work, 1981-85; William Neal Reynolds prof., 1996—; social scientist sci. and edn. adminstrn. USDA, 1979; economist Joint Econ. Com., U.S. Senate and Ho. of Reps., 1985-86; chmn. census adv. com. for agrl. stats. U.S. Dept. Commerce, 1984. Editor: Rural Studies Series, Rural Sociological Society, 1988-92. Recipient USDA award 1994; named Disting. Alumnus, La. Coll., 1996. Mem. Am. Sociol. Assn., So. Sociol. Soc., Rural Sociol. Soc. (pres. 1992-93), So. Assn. Agrl. Scientists (pres. sociology sect. 1983-84), Assn. Russian Sociolocists, Russian Rural Sociol. Assn. Contbr. articles to profl. jours.; also books. Office: NC State U Dept Sociology and Anthropology Raleigh NC 27695-8107

WIMBERLY, EVELYN LOUISE RUSSELL, nursing coordinator; b. Tallutah, La., Feb. 7, 1941; d. Luther Franklin and Marion Gertrude (Martin) Russell; m. William Lary Wimberly, Mar. 29, 1963; children: Collin, Holly, Allison. BSN, Northwestern State U., 1963; MSN, Northwestern State U. La., 1994. Head nurse Hanna Hosp., Coushatta, La.; dir. nurses Sr. Citizen Ctrs., Coushatta; evening supr. Riverside Med. Ctr., Bossier City, La.; house supr. La. State U. Hosp., Shreveport, coord. nursing quality improvement and policy and procedure. Mem. ANA, La. Nurses Assn., Sigma Theta Tau (Beta Chi chpt.). Home: PO Box 145 Hall Summit LA 71034-0145

WIMPEE, MARY ELIZABETH, elementary school educator; b. Karnes City, Tex., Nov. 23, 1952; d. Bernarr Floyd and Mary Jane (Putnam) Plummer; m. William Eugene Wimpee, June 7, 1975; 1 child, Matthew David. BS in Elem. Edn., Baylor U., 1974. Cert. elem. tchr., Tex. Resource tchr. 1st and 2d grades Kenedy (Tex.) Ind. Sch. Dist., 1975-76; kindergarten tutor Stride Learning Ctr., F.E. Warren AFB, Wyo., 1976-78, infant stimulation therapy asst., 1978-80; kindergarten tchr. Stockdale (Tex.) Ind. Sch. Dist., 1980-81; kindergarten tchr. Edgewood Ind. Sch. Dist., San Antonio, 1981-83, 1st grade tchr., 1983-85, 2d grade tchr., reading lang., gifted and talented tchr., 1989-93, instrnl. specialist, gifted and talented tchr., 1993-94; 3d grade tchr. Winston Elem., San Antonio, 1994—; 3rd grade tutor Wake County, Cary, N.C., 1985-86, 3rd grade tchr., 1986-89. Co-author: Curriculum Writing for Kindergarten and Second Grade Gifted and Talented, 1991. Mem. Edgewood Classrm. Tchrs. Assn. (rep. 1990—). Baptist. Home: 9658 Chelmsford San Antonio TX 78239-2308 Office: Winston Elem 2500 S General Mcmullen Dr San Antonio TX 78226-1657

WINCENTSEN, EDWARD LEE, artist; b. Jersey City, N.J., Aug. 1, 1947; m. Jacquie Sturia, Jan. 2, 1971; children: James, Daniel, Sarah. Student, Oral Roberts U., 1986. Aircraft assembler Lockheed, Burbank, Calif., 1976-78; in-house artist, art dir. Phoenix and Tulsa, 1980-88; pvt. practice artist, writer, publisher Tulsa, Okla., 1988—; spkr. in fields; pres. New Thought Jour. Press, 1995—. With USN, 1964-65. Office: PO Box 700754 Tulsa OK 74170

WINCHESTER, JACQUELINE CANTON, county government official; b. Jacksonville, Fla., Feb. 7, 1930; d. Arthur Norman and Eleanor (Lummus) Canton; children: James Jr., Jon C., Sterling R., Melissa P. BA, U. Fla., 1961. Cert. tchr., Fla. Tchr. Palm Beach County Sch. System, Belle Glade, Fla., 1966-68; supr. elections Palm Beach County, West Palm Beach, Fla., 1973—. Bd. dirs. Forum Club Palm Beaches, 1975—, Fla. Women's Alliance, Tampa, 1985—; bd. dirs. Palm Beach Regional Vis. Nurse Assn. Mem. Am. Soc. Pub. Adminstrs. (pres. 1995-96), Fla. State Assn. Suprs. of Elections, Internat. Assn. Clks. and Recorders, Soroptimist (pres. West Palm Beach chpt. 1979-81), LWV (voter svc. chair 1973). Democrat. Episcopalian. Office: Palm Beach County Rm 105 301 N Olive Ave West Palm Beach FL 33401-4705

WINCHESTER, JESSE GREGORY, real estate lending company executive; b. Charlotte, N.C., Mar. 2, 1957; s. Dewey Reece and Ruby Lee (Aldridge) W.; m. Jan Partain, May 14, 1983; children: Dustin, Mary-Elsye, Caleb, Sarah-Anne, Asa. BSBA, U. N.C., 1979; founds. diploma, Am. Inst. Banking, 1979. Asst. v.p. 1st Nat. Bank Atlanta, 1979-83; exec. v.p. Lomas Mgmt. Inc., Dallas, 1983-96; v.p. Hatfield Philips, Inc., Atlanta, 1996—; mem. Dallas Real Estate Coun. Campaign vol. United Way, Atlanta, 1982-83; participant Opportunity Dallas, 1985, Habitat for Humanity, People Helping People; treas. Coppell (Tex.) Rep. Club, 1986; Awana leader; leader Cub Scouts; Eagle Scout (God and Country award). Named Hon. Citizen Charlotte, N.C. Mem. Internat. Coun. Shopping Ctrs., Texans United for Life, U. N.C. Alumni Assn., Beta Gamma Sigma, Alpha Phi Omega. Baptist. Home: Five Oaks Ranch 921 FM 407 E Argyle TX 76226 Office: Hatfield Philips Inc 245 Peachtree Center Ave Atlanta GA 30303

WINCHESTER, JOHN WIDMER, oceanography educator; b. Chgo., Oct. 8, 1929; s. Harold Johnson and L. Darlene (Eastes) W.; m. Ellen Marie Stegenga, Feb. 1, 1958; 1 child, Kathleen Jo Sullivan. AB, U. Chgo., 1950, MS in Chemistry, 1952; PhD in Chemistry, MIT, 1955. From asst. to assoc. prof. geochemistry MIT, Cambridge, 1956-66; from assoc. prof. to prof. oceanography U. Mich., Ann Arbor, 1967-70; prof. oceanography Fla. State U., Tallahassee, 1970—; dept. oceanography chmn. Fla. State U, Tallahassee, 1970-76; acting dir. atmospheric chemistry div. Nat. Ctr. for Atmospheric Rsch., Boulder, Colo., 1988-89; asst. dir. Great Lakes rsch. div. U. Mich., Ann Arbor, 1968-70; chmn. atmospheric sci. rev. panel U. Alaska, Fairbanks, 1990-93; panel mem. study global change scis. in China, com. mem. on scholarly comm. with China, NAS, 1991-92; mem. adv. com. Southeastern Regional Ctr. Nat Inst. Global Environ. Change U.S. Dept. Energy, 1993—; convenor, program leader Internat. Global Atmospheric Chemistry IGAC Program; speaker in field. Contbr. more than 100 articles to profl. jours. Fulbright grantee, The Netherlands, 1955-56, Taiwan, 1962-63, Argentina, 1966, Yugoslavia, 1971; Rsch. scholar U.S. Nat. Acad. Sci., 1980; recipient Editors Choice award for excellence in refereeing for global biogeochemical cycles Am. Geophys. Union, Washington, 1988. Mem. Am. Geophys. Union (edn. and human resources com. 1990-92), Sigma Xi (Fla. State U. chpt. pres. 1993—, treas. 1982-83, MIT chpt. sec. 1961-63), Phi Beta Kappa. Home: 2405 Delgado Dr Tallahassee FL 32304-1303 Office: Fla State Univ Dept Oceanography Tallahassee FL 32306

WINCHESTER, SAM ALLEN, computer systems specialist; b. Claiborne County, Miss., Feb. 15, 1948; s. Sam and Ruthie (Smith) W.; m. Ella Mae Donaldson, Apr. 12, 1968; children: Samuel Keith, Kylie Ellis. BS in Math., Alcorn State U., 1973; MS in Urban System Engring., Howard U., 1975; MS in Computer Sci., U. So. Miss., 1978, Miss. State U., 1979. Heavy equipment operator Wrights Bros., Ashland, Miss., 1964-66; maintenance supr. Alcorn State U., Lorman, Miss., 1969-73; agt. Ind. Life Ins., Brookhaven, Miss., 1973; instr. math., asst. prin. Amite County Tng. Sch., Gloster, Miss., 1973-74; tech. staff mem. Mitre Corp., McLean, Va., 1974-76; mathematician U.S. Army C.E., Vicksburg, Miss., 1976-77; computer systems programmer Naval Oceanographic Office, Stennis Space Ctr., Miss., 1977—; EEO counselor Dept. of Navy, Bay St. Louis, Mo., 1978-92; chairperson Project One to One, Bay St. Louis, 1991—; tchr., counselor ch. sch. project, Lorman, Miss., 1987-94. Guest columnist Fayette Chronicle, 1991-94; contbr. articles to profl. jours. Treas. Assn. Culture Awareness, Stennis Space Ctr., 1978—; pres. Blacks in Govt., Stennis Space Ctr., 1992—; v.p. Gulf Coast EEO Forum, Gulfport, Miss., 1985-94; asst. coord. ARC, 1978-94; 2d lt. Bennit Johnson Consistory, 1989-94. 1st sgt. U.S. Army, 1966-69. Decorated Bronze Star medal; recipient Spl. Svc. awards ARC, 1979, EEO Com., 1982-93. Mem. Masons (worshipful master 1969-94, Man of Yr. 1988). Democrat. Baptist. Home: RR 2 Box 113 Lorman MS 39096-9708 Office: Naval Oceanographic Office 1002 Balch Blvd Bay Saint Louis MS 39522-5050

WINDERS, SUZAN EILEEN, preventive medicine educator; b. Seattle, Feb. 19, 1961; d. Robert Clarence and Bernice Wanda (King) W. BA in Psychology and Biology cum laude, Seattle Pacific U., 1983; PhD in Med. Psychology, Uniformed Svcs. U. Health Sci., 1990. Rsch. assst. dept. med. psychology Uniformed Svcs. U. of Health Scis., 1983-88; practicum in neuropsychology Walter Reed Army Med. Ctr., 1984; practicum in behavioral medicine Bethesda Naval Hosp., 1985; practicum in behavioral dentistry Bethesda Naval Hosp. Dental Clinic, 1985-86; asst. prof. dept. psychology Memphis State U., 1988-93, counseling practicum Psychol. Svc. Ctr., 1989-93; inpatient psychology practicum Parkwood Psychiat. Hosp., 1992-93; intern in clin. psychology U. Ala., Birmingham, 1993-95, asst. prof. Sch. Medicine divsn. preventive medicine, 1993—; dir. weight gain and smoking relapse study Nat. Heart, Lung, and Blood Inst./NIH, 1988-92, dir. pharmacologic intervention for postcessation weight gain project, 1992-93; presenter in field. Reviewer: Jour. Applied Social Psychology, Behavior Therapy, Annals Behavioral Medicine, Am. Jour. Medicine, others; cons. editor: Health Psychology, 1990-92; contbr. articles to profl. jours. grad. student fellow Uniformed Svcs. U. of Health Scis., 1983-88. Mem. APA, Soc. Behavioral Medicine, Internat. Behavioral Neurosci. Soc., N.Am. Assn. for Study of Obesity, Soc. Ingestive Behavior, Alpha Kappa Sigma. Office: U Ala 1717 11th Ave S Birmingham AL 35205-4731

WINDHAM, CUYLER LARUE, police official; b. Lamar, S.C., Nov. 29, 1936; s. Raymond Baxter and Zeloise (Parnell) W.; m. Mary Frances Dowling, Aug, 24, 1955; children: Cuyler LaRue Jr., David Baxter. Student, Ben Franklin U., 1956. With fingerprint divsn. FBI, Washington, 1955-57; night security clk. Charlotte (N.C.) divsn. FBI, 1957-62; condr. investigations resident agy. FBI, Fayetteville, N.C., 1962-67; spl. agt. N.C. State Bur. Investigation, Fayetteville & Kannapolis, 1967-72; supr. inter-agy. narcotics squad N.C. State Bur. Investigation, Fayetteville, 1968-72; asst. supr. Fayetteville divsn. N.C. State Bur. Investigation, 1972-73, asst. dir., 1974-85; sr. asst. dir. N.C. State Bur. Investigation, Fayetteville, 1985-94; ret., 1994; maj., chief of detectives Cumberland County Sheriff's Office, Fayetteville, 1994-95; chief dep. Cumberland County Sheriff's Office, Fayetteville, N.C., 1995—; speaker on law enforcement, violent crimes and narcotics problems, N.C. and southeastern U.S.; chmn. drug subcom. Law Enforcement Coord. Com., Ea. Dist. N.C. Pres. Christian Peace Officers Assn., Cumberland County chpt., Fayetteville, 1991-92; deacon Southview Bapt. Ch., Hope Mills, N.C. Named Outstanding Young Law Enforcement Officer Cumberland County, Cape Fear Jaycees, 1970-71; recipient 1st place award for outstanding young law enforcement officer N.C., N.C. Jaycees, 1971. Mem. Law Enforcement Officers Assn. (com. mem. statewide violent crimes task force, violent crimes com.), Law Enforcement Officers Alumni Assn. (pres. nat. tng. inst. drug enforcement adminstrn. 1977), Gamecock Club. Democrat. Baptist. Home: 112 Bledsoe St Hope Mills NC 28348-9701

WINDHAM, JOHN FRANKLIN, lawyer; b. Fayette, Ala., Jan. 21, 1948; s. Grover B. Windham Jr. and Nancy Katherine (McAdams) Haynie; m. Patricia Strain, Dec. 31, 1969; 1 child, John Franklin. BA, U. West Fla., 1970; JD, U. N.C., 1975. Bar: Fla. 1975, U.S. Dist. Ct. (no. dist.) Fla. 1976, U.S. Ct. Appeals (11th cir.) 1983, U.S. Supreme Ct. 1984. Acctg. supr. Monsanto Co., Research Triangle Park, N.C., 1970-72; law clk. to U.S. Atty Pensacola, Fla., 1974; assoc. Beggs & Lane, Pensacola, 1975-79, ptnr., 1979—; adj. asst. prof. bus. law Troy State U., Pensacola, 1983—. Mem. exec. com. Fla. divsn. Am. Cancer Soc., 1982-93, 95-96, chmn. legis. and planned giving, 1986-88, chmn. inc. devel., 1989-91, chmn. ad hoc adv. com., 1991—, legal advisor, 1992—, bd. dirs., 1993—, mem. scholarship com., 1995—, mem. Winn Dixie adv. com., 1996—, chmn. dist. VII steering com., 1995—; chmn. bd. Escambia Christian Sch., Pensacola, 1976-86; deacon Ch. of Christ; mem. adv. bd. Interim Healthcare, 1993—, Panhandle Rehab. Injury Mgmt. and Evaluation, 1993—; mem. founding bd. East Hill Christian Ch., 1995—; bd. govs. Pensacola chpt. Order Granaderos e Dames de Galvez, 1990-96, bd. govs. 1995-96; mem. U. West Fla. Found., 1983-85. Mem. Fla. Bar Assn. (comml. litigation com.), Fla. Def. Lawyers Assn., Fla. Workers Compensation Inst., Southeastern Admiralty Law Inst. (bd. dirs. 1986-89), U. West Fla. Nat. Alumni Assn. (bd. dirs.), Kiwanis (pres. Pensacola 1978-79, 88-89). Republican. Office: Beggs & Lane PO Box 12950 Pensacola FL 32576-2950

WINDHAM, NANCY QUINTERO, obstetrician, gynecologist; b. Maracaibo, Venezuela, May 18, 1961; came to U.S., 1976; d. George Albert and Jean Louise (Gimbert) Quintero; 1 child, Kathleen Jean. BS, Tulane U., 1982, MD, 1986. Intern Baylor Coll. Medicine, Houston, 1986-87, resident in ob-gyn., 1987-90; pvt. practice ob-gyn. Florence and Darlington, S.C., 1990-91, La Grange, Ga., 1992, Florence, 1993—. Fellow Am. Coll. Obstetricians and Gynecologists (bd. cert.); mem. AMA, S.C. Med. Soc. Office: 901 E Cheves St Ste 300 Florence SC 29506

WINDHAM, SUSAN KAY HARPER, early childhood educator; b. Lincoln, Nebr., Jan. 26, 1959; d. Eugene Findley and Dorothy May (Gertsch) Harper; m. Steven Earl Windham, Oct. 27, 1990. AA, LBW Jr. Coll., 1979; BSEd, Auburn U., 1981; MEd, Auburn U., Montgomery, 1995. Cert. early childhood tchr., Ala. Tchr. 4th grade Cass Elem. Bd. Edn. Bartow County, Cartersville, Ga., 1982-84, tchr. 5th, 6th grade, 1984-85; tchr. kindergarten Beatrice (Ala.) Elem. Sch. Bd. Edn. Monroe County, 1985-86; tchr. kindergarten Excel (Ala.) High Sch. Bd. Edn. Monroe County, 1986-87, tchr. 2d grade, 1987-88; tchr. kindergarten Floyd Sch. Bd. Edn. Montgomery (Ala.), 1988-89, tchr. 2d grade basic social studies, 1989-90; tchr. 2d grade Red Level (Ala.) Sch. Bd. Edn. Covington County, 1990-91, tchr. 2nd and 3rd grades, 1991-92, tchr. 3rd grade, 1992-93; tchr. 2d grade RedLevel Sch., 1995—. Home: HC 35 Box 196 Evergreen AL 36401-9350 Office: Covington County Bd Edn PO Box 460 Andalusia AL 36420-0460

WINDHAM, THOMAS, protective services official. Police chief Ft. Worth. Office: Police Department Office of the Police Chief 350 W Belknap St Fort Worth TX 76102-2004

WINDLE, PAMELA EVELYN, surgical nurse; b. Dumaguete City, Negros, The Philippines, Aug. 3; came to U.S., 1975; d. Lorenzo Sr. and Mary (Kho) Yang; m. David A. Windle, Jan. 12, 1980; children: Cynthia Ann, Michael Adam. BSN, Silliman U., Dumaguete City, 1973; MS in Nursing Adminstrn., Tex. Womans U., 1991. Cert. nursing adminstrn., post anesthesia nurse, ambulatory peri-anesthesia nurse. Staff nurse, charge nurse to asst. head nurse med.-surg. ICU Med. Ctr. Hosp., Tyler, Tex., 1975-81; staff nurse, unit tchr., nurse mgr. cardiovascular recovery room to nurse mgr. post-anesthesia care unit St. Luke's Episcopal Hosp., Houston, 1981-91; nurse mgr. day/ambulatory surgery, post-anesthesia care unit St. Luke's Med. Towers, Houston, 1991—. Mem. AACN (chair edn. com. 1994-95), Am. Post Anethesia Nurses (mem. rsch. com. edn., provider com. 1994-95), Tex. Assn. Post Anesthesia Nurses (state sec. 1994-95, mem. membership com. 1994-95, mem. govtl. affairs com. 1994-95, pres. 1996-97, chair bylaws and Outstanding Dist. award com. 1995-96), Tenn. Nurses Assn. (chair dist. 9 nominating com. 1995-96, bd. dirs. 1996—), Houston Orgn. Nurse Execs., Philippine Assn. Met. Houston (v.p. 1986, bd. dirs. 1994—), Sigma Theta Tau (TNA Dist. 9 award 1992). Roman Catholic. Home: 5421 Valerie St Bellaire TX 77401-4708 Office: St Lukes Episcopal Hosp PO Box 20269 Houston TX 77225-0269

WINDSOR, JAMES THOMAS, JR., printing company executive, newspaper publisher; b. Blakely, Ga., July 30, 1924; s. James Thomas and Mary Alice (Blitch) W. Student, Emory Jr. Coll., Valdosta, Ga., 1941-42, Cardiff (Wales) U., 1945-46; BA, Emory U., 1947. Insp./scientist U.S. Argl. Rsch. Adminstrn., San Augustine, Tex., 1948; pres. J.T. Windsor & Co., McRae, Ga., 1949-65; v.p. McRae Industries, Inc., 1963-64; pers. dir. Sunbeam Corp., McRae, 1965-71; editor, pub. The Laurens County News, 1973-74; editor, publisher The Soperton (Ga.) News, 1971—, The Wheeler County Eagle, Alamo, Ga., 1975—, The Montgomery Monitor, Mt. Vernon, Ga., 1987—; pres. The Mulberry Bush, Inc., Soperton, 1985-89, Suburban Printing Corp., Higgston, Ga., 1972—. Editor: Blueprint for Progress, 1963 (Washington Model award), also cookbooks and hist. books; area newspaper columnist, 1971—. Mayor City of McRae, 1962-70; adminstr. Telfair County, McRae, 1965; pres. Telfair Redevel. Corp., 1963-64; former coun. bd. dirs. Boy Scouts Am., Macon, Ga.; bd. dirs. Million Pines Festival, Soperton, 1973-87, Ga. Mcpl. Assn., Atlanta, 1963-66; dir. Eastman (Ga.) Planning and Devel. Commn., 1965-70; supt. sch. McRae Meth. Ch., 1951-71; active Eagle Scouts Am. With AUS, 1943-46, ETO. Recipient 20 yrs. perfect attendance award McRae Meth. Ch. Sch. Mem. Ga. Press Assn. (numerous awards 1972—), Nat. Newspaper Assn., Montgomery County C. of C., Soperton-Treutlen C. of C., Telfair County C. of C. (pres.), Wheeler county C. of C., Jaycees (editor jour. 1959, 1st place Jour. in Nation award, Rebel Corps col. 1991—, One of 5 Ga. Outstanding Young Men award 1961), VFW, Am. Legion (post comdr. 1957-58), Treutlen County Sportsman Club, McRae Rotary Club (pres.), Toastmasters, Lions (pres. Soperton 1975-76, 15 yrs. perfect attendance award). Home: 308 3rd St # 537 Soperton GA 30457 Office: Suburban Printing Corp RR 1 Ailey GA 30410-9801

WINEMAN, CLARENCE EDWARD, aerospace engineer; b. Latrobe, Pa., July 31, 1961; s. George Shoupe and Violet Ruth (Simmons) W.; m. Caroline Ann Linatoc, Mar. 23, 1985. B in Aerospace Engring., Ga. Inst. Tech., 1983. Student clk. Ga. Inst. Tech., Atlanta, 1981-83; engr. Aero Systems Div., Dayton, Ohio, 1983-85, Lockheed Ga., Marietta, 1985-88; configuration svcs. and integrated logistic support mgr. Intermarine USA, Savannah, Ga., 1988-90; engr. specialist Lockheed Missiles and Space Co., Iuka, Miss., 1990-93; engr. supr. Lockheed Aeronaut. Sys. Co., Marietta, Ga., 1993—. Mem. AIAA, Am. Soc. Quality Engrs. (cert. reliability engr.), Nat. Mgmt. Assn., Airlift Assn., Soc. Safety Engrs. Republican. Roman Catholic. Office: 86 S Cobb Dr D/62-13 Z/0307 Marietta GA 30063-1000

WINFREY, WALTER J., police chief; married; 1 child. BA, U. Memphis, 1981; grad., FBI Acad., 1989. Patrol officer Memphis Police Dept., 1968-73, with internal affairs bur., 1973-83, 90-91, lt., supr. uniform patrol, 1983-90, from capt. to inspector, 1990-91, comdr. East precinct uniform patrol, 1991-92, dep. chief uniform patrol divsn., 1992-94, with investigative svcs., 1994, dir. police svcs., 1994—. Mem. N.O.B.L.E. Office: 201 Poplar Ave Ste 12-01 Memphis TN 38103-1947

WING, LILLY KELLY RAYNOR, health services administrator; b. Florence, S.C., Oct. 1, 1953; d. Harold and Adlyne (Gaddy) Kelly; m. Terry Michael Wing, Apr. 29, 1989; children: Kelly Ann, Stuart James. ADN, Florence Darlington Tech, Florence, S.C., 1985; BS in Nursing, Med. U. S.C., 1987; MSN, U. S.C., 1992. RN, S.C.; lic. nat. long term care adminstr.; N.C.; lic. long term care adminstr. Staff nurse McLeod Regional Med. Ctr., Florence, S.C., 1985-88; neuro rehab. nurse mgr. HealthSouth Rehab. Ctr., Florence, 1988; dir. nursing HealthSouth Rehab Ctr., Columbia, S.C., 1988-89; program dir. orthopedic, rehab. Bruce Hosp. System, Florence, S.C., 1989-91; adminstr., mem. adv. bd. Inpatient Rehab. Svcs. of Carolinas Hosp. Svcs., Florence, S.C., 1992-95; exec. dir. Transitional Health Svcs. of Cary, N.C., 1995-96; corp. sub. mgr. WelCare Internat., Atlanta, 1995—; adj. prof. Limestone Coll., Gaffney, S.C., 1993; mem. S.C. TB Task Force, 1994, TB stds. in long term care subcom., 1994, edn. with state TB plan subcom., 1994. Mem. N.C. Peer Rev. Team for N.C. Health Care Facilities Assn., ANA (cert. nursing adminstr., past pres. local chpt. 1991-93, sec., bd. dirs. 1994), AACN, S.C. Nurses Assn., Assn. Rehab. Nurses, Pee Dee Nurses Assn., S.C. Assn. Rehab. Faculties (sec., bd. dirs. 1992—), S.C. Health Care Assn., S.C. Hosp. Assn. (long term care coun. 1994).

WING, LINDA KING, English language educator; b. Bay City, Tex., Sept. 19, 1947; d. William George and Verna Marie (Matthes) King; m. Wayne Leslie Chilcote, Nov. 24, 1967 (div. July 1978); m. Frank M. Wing Jr., Jan. 13, 1979 (div. Jan. 1995); 1 child, Deborah Lin Chilcote Crawford. BS in English Edn., U. Tenn., 1971; MEd, East Tenn. State U., 1982. Cert. tchr., Tenn. 5th grade tchr. Lynn Garden Elem. Sch., Kingsport, Tenn., 1972-75; 4th grade tchr. Brookside Elem. Sch., Kingsport, Tenn., 1975-87; tchr. English Sullivan South High Sch., Kingsport, Tenn., 1987—; pres., co-founder Teach Peace, Kingsport, Tenn., 1990—; participant Fulbright Tchr. Exch. to Bulgaria, U.S. Info. Agy., Washington, 1993-94. Participant, facilitator Sister City Project, Kingsport, Bristol, Johnson City, Tenn., 1990—. Mem. NEA, Tenn. Edn. Assn., Sullivan County Edn. Assn., Beta Sigma Phi. Home: 2028 Pendragon Rd Kingsport TN 37660-3467 Office: Sullivan South High Sch 1236 Moreland Dr Kingsport TN 37664-5222

WINGARD, JOHN REID, medical educator; b. Charleston, S.C., Jan. 30, 1947; m. Frances Diane Phillips, 1974; children: Emily, Sally, Benjamin. BA in English, Yale U., 1969; MD, The Johns Hopkins U., 1973. Diplomate Am. Bd. Internal Medicine, subspecialty of Med. Oncology. Intern City of Memphis Hosp./U. Tenn. Ctr. for Health Scis., 1973-74, resident, 1974-76; chief resident V.A. Hosp., Memphis, 1976-77; instr. in medicine U. Tenn. Ctr. for Health Scis., Memphis, 1976-77; fellow in oncology and internal medicine The Johns Hopkins U. Sch. Medicine, Balt., 1977-79, various to asst. prof. oncology, 1977-87, assoc. prof. oncology, 1987-91, assoc. prof. medicine, 1990-91; prof. medicine Emory U. Sch. Medicine, Atlanta, 1991-96, prof. Winship Cancer Ctr., 1992-96; dir. bone marrow transplant program, prof. medicine U. Fla., Gainesville, 1996—; dir. bone marrow transplant program Emory U. Sch. Medicine, 1991-96; dir. Bone Marrow Transplant Outpatient Clinic, Johns Hopkins Oncology Ctr., 1984-91; cons. Office of Disability Programs, Social Security Adminstrn., Balt., 1981-91; mem. study group Nat. Inst. Allergy and Infectious Diseases, 1988—; mem. adv. com. Internat. Bone Marrow Transplant Registry, 1989-91, 95—. Contbr. articles to profl. jours.; contbr. to abstracts and books in field; mem. editl. bd. Biology of Blood and Marrow Transplantation. Mem. AAAS, AMA, Am. Soc. Microbiology, Am. Soc. Clin. Oncology, Am. Soc. Hematology, Internat. Soc. Exptl. Hematology, Multinat. Assn. Supportive Care in Cancer, Am. Soc. Blood and Marrow Transplantation. Office: U Fla Coll Medicine PO Box 100277 Gainesville FL 32610-0277

WINGATE, DAVID ARTHUR, aircraft mechanic; b. Coventiion, Ky., Nov. 21, 1948; s. Dalton Tim Wingate and Gladys Louise (Clifford) Saenz; m. Socorro Maria Martinez, Jan. 12, 1970; children: John David, Veronica Lynn. Grad. high sch., Pensacola, Fla., 1964. Aircraft mechanic Dee Howard Co., San Antonio, 1972-75, Lear Sieglar Co., Oklahoma City, 1975-78, Mitsubishi, San Angelo, Tex., 1978-84; aircraft CADD LOFT engring. McDonnell Douglas, Calif., 1987; aircraft mechanic McDonnell Douglas, St. Louis, 1990, Chrysler Tech. Airborn, Waco, Tex., 1990-93. Author: The Highway to Texas the Untold Story, 1966, 2d edit., 1996. Home: 4714 Florida St Waco TX 76705

WINGATE, HENRY TRAVILLION, federal judge; b. Jackson, Miss., Jan. 6, 1947; s. J.T. and Eloise (Anderson) W.; m. Turner Arnita Ward, Aug. 10, 1974. BA, Grinnell Coll., 1969; JD, Yale U., 1973; LLD (hon.), Grinnell Coll., 1986. Bar: Miss. 1973, U.S. Dist. Ct. (so. dist.) Miss. 1973, U.S. Ct. Appeals (5th cir.) 1973, U.S. Mil. Ct. 1973. Law clk. New Haven (Conn.) Legal Assistance, 1971-72, Community Legal Aid, Jackson, 1972-73; spl. asst. atty. gen. State of Miss., Jackson, 1976-80; asst. dist. atty. (7th cir.), Jackson, 1980-84; asst. U.S. atty. U.S. Dist. Ct. (so. dist.), Jackson, 1984-85; judge U.S. Dist. Ct. (so. dist.) Miss., Jackson, 1985—; lectr. Miss. Prosecutors Coll., 1980-84, Law Enforcement Tng. Acad., Pearl, Miss., 1980-84, Miss. Jud. Coll., 1980-84, Nat. Coll. Dist. Attys., 1984-85; adj. prof. law Golden Gate U., Norfolk, Va, 1975-76, Tidewater Community Coll., 1976, Miss. Coll. Sch. Law, 1978-84. Former mem. adv. bd. Jackson Parks and Recreation Dept.; former mem. bd. dirs. SCAN Am. of Miss., Inc., Jackson Arts Alliance, Drug Rsch. and Edn. Assn. in Miss., Inc., United Way Jackson; mem. exec. com. Yale U. Law sch., 1989—; chmn. bd. dirs. YMCA, 1978-80. Racquetball State Singles Champion Jr. Vets. Div., 1981, State Singles Champion Srs. Div., 1982, Outstanding Legal Service award NAACP (Jackson br. and Miss. br.), 1982, Civil Liberties award Elks, 1983, Community Service award Women for Progress Orgn., 1984. Mem. ABA (co-chmn. sect. litigation liaison with judiciary 1989-91), Miss. Bar Assn., Hinds County Bar Assn., Fed. Bar Assn., Yale Club Miss. Home: 6018 Huntview Dr Jackson MS 39206-2130 Office: James O Eastland Courthouse 245 E Capitol St Ste 109 Jackson MS 39201-2409*

WINGO, CHARLES SPURGEON, medical and physiology educator; b. Oct. 5, 1949. BS in Phys. Chemistry, Stanford U., 1971; MD, La. State U., 1975. Diplomate Am. Bd. Internal Medicine; lic. physician, La., Tex., Fla. Intern Hermann Hosp. U. Tex., Houston, 1975-76, resident Med. Sch., 1976-78; fellow in clin. nephrology Parkland Meml. Hosp., 1978-79; fellow Nat. Kidney Found. U. Tex., Dallas, 1979-81; asst. prof. medicine U. Fla., Gainesville, 1981-85, asst. prof. medicine and physiology, 1985-86, assoc. prof. medicine and physiology, 1986-92, prof. medicine and physiology, 1992—, mem. grad. faculty, 1987—; Cons., lectr. and presenter in field. Contbr. numerous articles and abstracts to publs. Recipient Career Devel. award, 1985-87. Mem. ACP, AAAS, Am. Phys. Soc., Am. Fedn. Clin. Rsch., Am. Soc. Nephrology, Am.Soc. Clin. Investigation, Internat. Soc. Nephrology, So. Soc. Clin. Investigation (pres.), N.Y. Acad. Scis. Office: U Fla Divsn Nephrology PO Box 100224 Gainesville FL 32610-0224

WINHAM, GEORGE KEETH, retired mental health nurse; b. Plain Dealing, La., Nov. 25, 1934; s. Henderson and Lula Mae (Kelly) W.; m. Patricia Annie Weise, Nov. 7, 1959; children: Adrian Keeth, George Kevin, Karla Ann. ADN, La. State U., 1974; BS in Health Care, Carolina Christian U., 1986. Cert. chem. dependency nurse specialist; RN, La. Staff nurse preceptor ward 10 VAMC, Shreveport, La., 1992-96, staff nurse ward 10, 1976-88, 96; ret. Overton Brooks VA Med. Ctr., Shreveport, 1996; guest speaker in field. With USAFR, 1982-95. Mem. Drug and Alcohol Nurses Assn., Am. Soc. Pain Mgmt. Nurses, Nat. Fedn. Federal Employees (local treas. 1956, nurse of yr. 1989), Air Force Sgts. Assn., Nat. Consortium Chem. Dependency Nurses, Consol. Assn. Nurses in Substance Abuse, Masons. Baptist. Home: 106 Lancashire Dr Bossier City LA 71111-2023

WINKLER, ALLEN WARREN, lawyer; b. Chgo., Dec. 11, 1954; s. Maurice A. and Florence (Klein) W.; m. Bett C. Gibson, Nov. 1, 1986. BS, No. Ill. U., 1977; JD, Tulane U., 1981. Bar: La. 1982, Ill. 1982, U.S. Dist. Ct. (ea. dist.) La. 1982, U.S. Dist. Ct. (mid. dist.) La. 1987. Atty. La. Legal Clinic, New Orleans, 1982-84; pvt. practice law New Orleans, 1984-85; staff atty. Oak Tree Savs. Bank, S.S.B., New Orleans, 1985-87, sr. atty., asst. v.p., 1987-90; staff atty. Resolution Trust Corp., Baton Rouge, 1991-92; sr. atty. Resolution Trust Corp., Atlanta, 1992-95; sr. corp. counsel Fleet Fin., Inc., Atlanta, 1996—; pres. Legal Eagle Inc., Atlanta, 1996—; mem. faculty Franklin Coll. Ct. Reporting, Metairie, La., 1981-88; cons., guest lectr. paralegal studies Tulane U., New Orleans, 1982-90; guest lectr. U. New Orleans, 1988-90. Vol. Hawkins for Judge campaign, New Orleans. Mem. La. Bar Assn., Ill. Bar Assn. Home: 1322 Colony Dr Marietta GA 30068 Office: Fleet Fin Inc Ste 300 6 Executive Pk Dr NE Atlanta GA 30329

WINKLER, H. DONALD, public relations executive; b. Cobden, Ill., Nov. 25, 1932; s. Hugh Stelle and Vesta Marguerite (Schimpf) W.; m. Edna Azile Thomson, Dec. 21, 1956; children: Donald Thomson, James Randolph. AB, McKendree Coll., Lebanon, Ill., 1954; MS, Ohio U., 1956. Exec. adminstr. Nat. Conf. of Meth. Youth, Nashville, 1955-57; acting dir. comms. N.D. State U., 1957-59; dir. of info. svcs. Randolph-Macon Woman's Coll., Lynchburg, Va., 1959-66; dir. of pub. rels. George Washington U., 1966-72; dir. of pub. affairs Calif. State U., Fresno, 1972-78; exec. adminstr. for pub. affairs East-West Ctr., Honolulu, 1978-82; assoc. v.p. Longwood Coll., Farmville, Va., 1982-95; pres. JMB Pub. Rels., Hilton Head Island, S.C., 1995—; critic and panelist Nat. Newspaper Publishing Workshop, Coun. for Advancement and Support of Edn., 1970, dir. Dist. Pub. Rels. Workshop, 1971, judge Nat. Publications Competition, 1968, 72, mem. bd. of advisors certification program, 1977-80, mem. nat. com. on institutional rels., 1977-79, cons. and evaluator for pub. rels. programs, 1987-93. Editor Concern, 1955-57, Contact, 1973-78 (7 nat. awards), East-West Perspectives, 1979 (4 nat. awards), Va. Writing, 1986— (12 nat. awards); contbr. articles to profl. jours . Cons. San Diego State U., Innisfree Village, Va., Tri-County Sheltered Workshop, Va., Indsl. Devel. Commn., Va., Rapid Transit Sys., Va. Recipient Gold Georgi award Writer's Found. of Am., 1993, numerous others; inducted into Va. Commc. Hall Of Fame, 1995. Mem. Nat. Press Club, Soc. Profl. Journalists, Pub. Rels. Soc. of Am., Ednl. Press Assn. of Am., Coun. for Advancement and Support of Edn. (Grand award 1991, Award of exellence 1991, 1992). Methodist. Home: 10 Brassie Ct Hilton Head Island SC 29928

WINKLER, LORRAINE TOBY, psychotherapist, social worker; b. Bronx, N.Y., Oct. 27, 1942; d. Abraham and Sarah (Piperno) W.; m. Eugene Tuch, May 31, 1964 (div. Oct. 1981); children: Sherry, Deborah, David Tuch; m. William J. Lyman, Aug. 26, 1987. BSN, Fairleigh Dickinson U., Rutherford, N.J.; MSW, Rutgers U. RN, N.Y., N.J.; lic. clin. social worker, BCD, Fla., N.Y.; diplomate Nat. Assn. Social Workers, Am. Bd. Examiners. Family therapist spl. unit Div. Youth and Family Svc., 1979-80; clin. specialist Muhlenberg Hosp., Plainfield, N.J., 1980-83; pvt. practice N.J., 1980—; clin. dir., therapist Women's Haven, Paterson, N.J., 1985-86; psychiat. clinician Rahway (N.J.) Hosp., 1985-87; psychotherapist Middlesex Family Svc. Agy., Highland Park, N.J., 1987-89, Ctr. Marriage and Family Counseling, Matawan, N.J., 1987-89; pvt. practice Orlando, Fla., 1980—; mem. Drug Task Force, Somerset, Madison, N.J., 1981, 87-88. Mem. Women's Resource Ctr., Orlando, 1989, 90. Mem. NASW, Acad. Cert. Social Workers, Fla. Soc. Clin. Social Workers (diplomate), Women's Resource Ctr., Orlando C. of C., Rutgers Alumni Assn. Office: Colonial Office Ctr 1310 W Colonial Dr Ste H 12 Orlando FL 32804-7139

WINKLER, STEVEN ROBERT, hospital administrator; b. Chattanooga, Tenn., Dec. 4, 1953; s. David Wilfred and Margaret (Tepper) W.; m. Monica Sue Nijoka, July 11, 1987; children: Megan Leigh, Sara Elizabeth. BA, Vanderbilt U., 1976; M in Health Adminstrn., Duke U., 1978. Asst. adminstr. Tepper Hosp. and Clinic, Chattanooga, 1978-79, adminstr., 1979-80; assoc. exec. dir. Humana Hosp.-Brandon (Fla.), 1981-83, Humana Hosp.-Bennett, 1983-84; v.p. ops. Baton Rouge Gen. Med. Ctr., 1984-86, v.p. mktg., 1986-88; v.p. risk mgmt. Gen. Health Systems, Baton Rouge, 1988—. V.p. Beth Shalom Synagogue, 1990-93, pres., 1993-95; active Am. Diabetes Assn. (Baton Rouge, state chpts.), Arthritis Found., United Way of Baton Rouge, 1989. Fellow Am. Soc. Healthcare Risk Mgmt. (pres. midsouth region 1990); mem. Am. Coll. Healthcare Execs. (diplomat), Am. Hosp. Assn., Jewish Fedn. Greater Baton Rouge (v.p. 1990, pres. 1992-93), Tipmasters (pres., Tipmaster of Yr. 1989). Office: Gen Health Systems 5757 Corporate Blvd Ste 200 Baton Rouge LA 70808-2571

WINKLES, DEWEY FRANK, lawyer; b. Thomaston, Ga., Apr. 3, 1946; s. Dewey Monroe and Cora Marie (Whittaker) W.; children: Alexandra, Judson, Allyson. BA, U. So. Fla., 1969; JD, U. Fla., 1972. Bar: Fla. 1972, U.S. Supreme Ct. 1972, U.S. Ct. Appeals (11th and 5th cirs.) 1972, U.S. Dist. Ct. (mid. and no. dists.) Fla. 1972. Law clk. to presiding justice U.S. Dist. Ct. (mid. dist.) Fla., Tampa, 1972-73, asst. U.S. atty., 1973-75; assoc. Shackleford, Farrior, Stallings & Evans, Tampa, 1975-77; ptnr. Winkles & Trombley, Tampa, 1977-94; of counsel Anderson & Orcutt, P.A., 1993—. Master Am. Inns. Ct.; mem. ATLA, Nat. Assn. Criminal Def. Lawyers, Fed. Bar Assn. (pres.), Fed. Grievance Com., Fla. Trial Lawyers Assn. Office: 401 E Jackson St Ste 2440 Tampa FL 33602-5232

WINN, HERSCHEL CLYDE, retail electronics company executive; b. Hill County, Tex., Dec. 14, 1931; s. Herschel C. and Alta Fay; m. Dorothy Carolyn Martin, June 24, 1961; children—Celia Carol, Macey Sheryl. B.A., U. Tex., Austin, 1958, LL.B., 1960. Bar: Tex. bar 1960. Atty. Tex. Hwy. Dept., 1960-61; trial atty. Internat. Service Ins. Co., 1961-63; judge Johnson County, Tex., 1963-68; with Tandy Corp., 1968—, v.p., 1976-79, sec., 1975—, sr. v.p., 1979—; bd. dirs. Ft. Worth Crime Control and Prevention Dist. Bd. dirs. Better Bus. Bur. Tarrant County, 1971-87; dir. Van Cliburn Piano Competition, 1984—; bd. dirs. Downtown Ft. Worth, Inc., 1985—, Youth Orch. Greater Ft. Worth, 1984-87, Family Svc. Inc., 1984-89; bd. dirs., exec. com. Ft. Worth Conv. and Visitors Bur., 1986-94. With AUS, 1953-55. Mem. ABA, State Bar Tex., Tarrant County Bar Assn. (pres. corp. counsel sect. 1980-81), Fort Worth C. of C. Methodist. Office: Tandy Corp 1900 One Tandy Fort Worth TX 76102

WINN, WALTER GARNETT, JR., marketing strategist, advertising executive; b. Wilmington, N.C., Dec. 1, 1941; s. Walter Garnett and Pamela Weber (Bradham) W.; m. Linda Ann Irvin, July 1, 1964; children: Walter Welborn, Katie Hillary. BFA, U. Ga., 1966, MS with honors, 1968. Account exec. Sudler & Hennessey Advt., N.Y.C., 1968-69, Dean Burdick & Assocs. Inc., N.Y.C., 1969-70; v.p., creative dir. Buntin & Assocs. Inc., Nashville, 1970-72; pres. Smith & Winn Advt. Inc., Jacksonville, Fla., 1972-77; mktg. mgr. Standard Telephone Co., Cornelia, Ga., 1977-79; mktg., sales mgr. Commonwealth Telephone Co., Dallas, Pa., 1979-83; advt. dir. CTE Corp., Wilkes Barre, Pa., 1983-84; dir. mktg. North State Telephone Inc., High Point, N.C., 1984—. Creator, designer bus. strategy game Merchants and Movers, 1990. Bd. dirs., chair com. High Point Area Arts Coun., 1989-96; bd. dirs. Back Mountain Arts Guild, Dallas, 1980, Misericordia Coll. Arts Endowment, 1982-84. Named Advt. Person of Yr. Am. Advt. Fedn., Northeastern Pa., 1983. Mem. N.C. Tel. Assn. (chmn. mktg. 1989-91, 95-96), Civitan (pres. High Point 1994-95). Republican. Home: 381 Hunters Pointe Lexington NC 27295-9634 Office: North State Telephone Co 111 Hayden Pl High Point NC 27260-4913

WINN, WILLIAM MOYERS, JR., accountant; b. White Plains, Ga., June 18, 1928; s. William Moyers and Martha Louise (Burton) W.; m. Lillian Anne Etheridge, Mar. 12, 1949; children: William Moyers III, Carlton Muller. BBA, U. Ga., 1955, MBA, 1956. CPA, Ga. Jr. acct. Price Waterhouse & Co., L.A., 1956-58; bus. mgr. Newton County Hosp., Covington, Ga., 1958-59; staff acct. Walker Meadows Garret & Laney, CPAs, Macon, Ga., 1959-63; owner W.M. Winn, Jr., CPA, Covington, 1963—. With USN, 1946-53. Mem. AICPAs, Ga. Soc. CPAs, Rotary. Republican. Home: 2154 Monticello St SW Covington GA 30209-3754 Office: 1118 Conyers St SW Covington GA 30209-3725

WINNER, MARIAN CAROL, library director, educator; b. Toledo, Ohio, June 29, 1929; d. Howard Eldridge and Carrie Katherine (Schulte) Smith; m. Robert William Winner, Sept. 4, 1951 (div. Apr. 1987); children: Karen Lynn Winner Blackburn, Kevin Robert. BA, Otterbein Coll., Westerville, Ohio, 1951, BS in Botany cum laude, 1951; MS in Libr. Sci., U. Ky., 1977. Head sci. libr., asst. prof. Miami U. Librs., Oxford, Ohio, 1978-90; libr. dir. No. Ky. U., Highland Heights, 1990—; mem. dean's coun. No. Ky. U.; faculty Miami U., Ind. U. Coll. Libr. and Info. Sci., 1982-91, U. Ky., 1992; lectr. in field. Contbr. articles to profl. jours. Mem. Ky. State Adv. Com. for Librs., 1990-96; chair State-Assisted Acad. Libr. Coun. of Ky., 1994—, Ky. Info. Resources Discussion Group, 1995—; chair user svcs. com. Ky. Libr. Network, 1991-92, pres. bd., 1994-95; mem. exec. bd., sec.-treas. Greater Cin. Libr. Consortium, 1992-93; mem. adv. com. on univ. records State Archives and Records Com., 1992—; chair Ohio Coun. on Libr. and Info. Sources, 1983-85; mem. automated ref. coun. Ohionet, 1987-88; mem. adv. coun. OhioPi, 1985-86. Title II grantee, 1989, 93. ALA, AAUP, AAUW, Assn. Coll. and Rsch. Librs. (presdl. cand. forum chair 1993, Libr. adminstrv. Mgmt. Assn. (exec. bd. libr. orgn. and mgmt. sect. 1987-89, proram bd. 1982-86), Spl. Libr. Assn. (Cin. chpt. pres. 1985-86, chair budget com. 1988-89, Acad. Libr. of the Yr. 1986), Ohio Acad. Sci. (v.p. info. and libr. scis. sec. 1986-87, membership chair 1987-88), Ohio Libr. Assn. (sec. 1983-84), Am. Soc. Info. Sci., Beta Phi Mu, Phi Sigma Iota, Sigma Zeta. Home: 410 Keeneland Dr Fort Thomas KY 41075-4071 Office: No Ky Univ Nunn Dr Newport KY 41099

WINNEY, DAVID LEE, career officer; b. St. Louis, Sept. 21, 1952; s. Wilbur Wallace and Virginia Lee (LaRue) W.; m. Mary Kathryn McGahey, Mar. 7, 1981; 1 child, Allison Kathleen. BS in Bus. Adminstrn., U. Mo., 1975; MS in Human Resources Mgmt., Houston Bapt. U., 1987; postgrad. seminars, Harvard U., 1993. Commd. 2d lt. USAF, 1975, advanced through grades to major; pers. officer USAF, Columbus AFB, 1976-80; with 726 Tactical Control Squadron USAF, Homestead AFB, Fla., 1980-81; air weapons, tactical air controller USAF, 1981-83; sr. dir., instr. air weapons controller USAF, various locations, 1983-84; dir. ops. 6130th tactical control flight, 621 tactical control squadron USAF, Osan Air Base, Korea, 1984-85; chief CBPO USAF, Reese AFB, Tex., 1985-88; inspector ATC/IG team pers., chief mission support and pers. inspection br. USAF, numerous locations, 1988-90; chief pers. divsn. Hdqs. Recruiting Svc. USAF, Randolph AFB, 1990-92, advisor quality integration, sr. advisor Recruiting Svc., 1992—. Contbr. articles to profl. jours. Coord., team leader Habitat for Humanity, San Antonio, 1989-94; vol. San Antonio Met. Ministry Homeless Shelter, 1992-94; elder Holy Trinity Presbyn. Ch., 1993-96, Frist Bapt. Ch., Universal City; mentor Candlewood Elem. Sch., San Antonio, 1994. Mem. Am. Soc. Quality Contrs. (cert. quality auditor 1995), Univ. Alumni Assn., Nat. Eagle Scout Assn. Home: 92 Main Cir Randolph AFB TX 78148-5477 Office: USAF Hdqs Air Force Recruitment Svcs 550 D St W Ste 1 Randolph AFB TX 78150-4526

WINOKER, DIANA LEE, financial consultant, educator; b. Martinsville, Va., Feb. 20, 1953; d. Joseph A. and Julia (Mittle) W. BS in Psychology, Tulane U., 1974 MBA, U. Tampa, 1979. Registered securities rep. N.Y. Stock Exch., all regional exchs.; lic. securities rep. 25 states, gen. securities prin., rep. for life ins. and variable annuities, health and disability ins., commodity broker. Community svc. officer Tampa (Fla.) Bay Area Rapid Transit Authority, 1974-76; mgr. pub. rels. Profl. Broadcast Prodns., Inc., Tampa, 1976; account exec. Merrill Lynch, Pierce, Fenner and Smith, Tampa, 1976-79, Dean Witter Reynolds, Inc., Tampa, 1979-82; regional account mgr. ISFA Corp. (INVEST), Tampa, 1982-83; coord. cons. svcs. and qualified plan Smith Barney, Tampa, 1983—, v.p.; instr. continuing edn. program U. South Fla., Tampa, 1980—. Condr. fin. seminars for community groups; trustee, past co-chmn. Tampa Gen. Employees Pension Fund, 1985—; bd. dirs. Suncoast coun. Girl Scouts U.S.A., 1988-90; past pres. Hillsborough Community Mental Health Ctr.; mem. steering com., founding mem. Tampa Leadership Coun., 1979—; mem. allocations com. United Way Greater Tampa, Inc., 1988-90; bd. dirs. Boys and Girls Club, Tampa, 1989—. Mem. Tampa C. of C., Network Exec. Women, Tampa Club. Home: 3614 W Tacon St Tampa FL 33629-6942 Office: Smith Barney 101 E Kennedy Blvd Ste 3400 Tampa FL 33602-5151

WINOKUR, HARVEY JAY, rabbi; b. Bklyn., Aug. 16, 1950; s. Douglas Louis and Miriam (Weinberg) W. BA in Sociology, SUNY, Buffalo, 1971; MA, Hebrew Union Coll., 1974. Ordained rabbi, 1976. Rabbi The Temple, Atlanta, 1976-79, Temple Sinai, Atlanta, 1979-80, Balt. Hebrew Congregation, 1980-82, Temple Kehillat Chaim, Roswell, Ga., 1982—. Co-author: Lehava, 1979. Co-chmn. Ann. City-Wide Appeal To Address Homelessness; trustee N.W. Ga. coun. Girl Scouts U.S.A., 1983-86; officer Nat. Coalition Against Death Penalty, N.Y.C., 1982-86; mem. Atlanta-Fulton County Commn. on Children and Youth, Leadership Atlanta Class of 1992; bd. dirs. United Way Met. Atlanta, 1992—. Mem. Ctrl. Conf. Am. Rabbis (social action commn. 1987-89), N.Am. Bd. World Union for Progressive Judaism, Atlanta Rabbinical Assn. (pres. 1988-90), Am. Jewish Com. (bd. dirs. Atlanta chpt. 1991—), Interfaith Coalition Atlanta (co-chmn. 1994-96), Atlanta Jewish Bedn. (bd. dirs. 1988-91), Atlanta Black-Jewish Coalition (steering com.). Office: Temple Kehillat Chaim 45 Woodstock St Roswell GA 30075-3559

WINOKUR, MARK, secondary education educator; b. New Orleans, Aug. 22, 1955; s. Harry and Anne (Buccheri) W.; m. Katherine Eggert, July 23, 1989. BA, Brandeis U., 1977; MA, U. Calif., 1981, Phd, 1987. Asst. prof. Dickinson Coll., Carlisle, Pa., 1988-90, Kans. State U., Manhattan, 1990-92, Rhodes Coll., Memphis, 1992-96; assoc. prof. Rhodes Coll., 1996—; chair film studies Rhodes Coll., 1993—. Author: American Laughter: Immigrants, Ethnicity, and 1930's Hollywood Film Comedy, 1996.

WINSHIP, PETER, law educator; b. Pensacola, Fla., Jan. 5, 1944; s. Stephen and Frances Norinne (Hayford) W.; m. Marion Christina Nelson, June 18, 1966; children: Verity Elizabeth, Adam Edward. BA, Harvard U., 1965, LLB, 1968; LLM, London Sch. of Econs., 1973; postdoctoral, Yale U., 1973-74. Bar: Tex. 1975, U.S. Dist. Ct. (no. dist.) Tex. 1981, U.S. Ct. Appeals (5th and 11th cirs.) 1981. Legal advisor Ethiopian Ministry of Commerce, Addis Ababa, 1968-70; lectr. Haile Selassie I U., Addis Ababa, 1970-72; prof. law So. Meth. U., Dallas, 1974-90, James Cleo Thompson Sr. Trustee prof., 1990—; vis. prof. U. Calif., Berkeley, 1979-80, UCLA Sch. Law, 1986, Coll. William & Mary, 1990, U. Pa., 1992. Co-author: Texas Litigation Guide, Vols. 7-10, 1979, Commercial Transactions, 1985; editor: Background Documents of the Ethiopian Commercial Code, 1974. Mem. Am. Law Inst., Internat. Inst. for Unification Pvt. Law (corr. 1983—), UN Commn. on Internat. Trade Law (nat. corr. 1990). Home: 3448 Amherst St Dallas TX 75225 Office: So Meth U Sch Law Dallas TX 75275-0116

WINSLOW, ANNE BRANAN, artist; b. Waynesboro, Ga., July 28, 1920; d. Walter Augustus and Rubie (Griffin) Branan; m. James Addison Winslow Jr., May 8, 1943; children: Lu Anne, Jan Renee. BS in Fine Art, Queens Coll., Charlotte, N.C., 1941; postgrad., U. South Fla., 1974-75. One-woman shows include Dunedin (Fla.) Art Ctr., 1980, Tampa (Fla.) Originals Gallery, 1982, Pub. Libr., St. Petersburg, Fla., 1982, Lee Scarfone Gallery, 1983, 84, Studio 1212, Clearwater, Fla., 1983, 87, 90, Gallery 600, Largo, Fla., 1986, Gallery of State Capitol, Tallahassee, 1987, Berghoff Gallery, Clearwater, 1988, 92, Anderson-Marsh Gallery, St. Petersburg, 1989, 92, Loveland (Colo.) Mus., 1990, Gallery at City Hall of Tampa, 1990, Lawrence Charles Gallery, Tampa, 1993, Gallery Contemporanea, Jacksonville, Fla., 1994; painting, oil painting, Fla. Series II, Images II, 1980, Amagedon, 1974, Eastern Series III, 1984, original handpulled serigraphs, 1991, 92. Mem. Studio 1212, Fla. Artist Group, Mus. Women in Arts, Fla. Printmakers Soc., Generator Gallery (founding). Republican. Home and Studio: 5224 W Neptune Way Tampa FL 33609-3639

WINSTEAD, ELISABETH WEAVER, poet, writer, English language educator; b. Nashville, July 31, 1926; d. Charles Preston and Carrie Lawrence (Hadley) Weaver; m. George Alvis Winstead, July 18, 1945. BA, Vanderbilt U., 1946; MA, Peabody Coll. Vanderbilt U., 1947; postgrad., Vanderbilt U., 1980-83, Trevecca Nazarene, 1975-79. Cert. tchr. of lang. arts, bus. edn., social sci., English, Tenn., Va., Ind., Idaho, Ariz. Head bus. edn. dept. La Crosse (Ind.) High Sch., 1947-48, Franklin (Tenn.) High Sch., 1952-54, Belmont Coll., Nashville, 1954-56; with English dept. Boise (Idaho) High Sch., 1948-49; critical analyst Dept. Commerce, Washington, 1949-50; with bus. edn. dept. Averitt Coll., Danville, Va., 1950-52; elem. and high sch. tchr. Met. Nashville Schs., 1956-85; cons. Model Tchr. Program, Nashville Met. Sch., 1958-68, mem. faculty adv. coun., 1970-79, mem. profl. devel. coun., 1980-84. Author: Social Studies Curriculum Guide, 1970, Metro Beautiful Programs, 1976, Metro PTA School History, 1980; contbr. poetry to anthologies and popular mags. Chmn. TB Seal Drive, Franklin, 1956-60, March of Dimes Fund Drive, Nashville, 1982-84, Red Cross Blood Drive, Nashville, 1984-86; capt. Heart Fund Drive, Nashville, 1979-81. Recipient Tchr. Appreciation awrd Sta. WKDA, 1970, Galaxy of Stars award Nashville Met. Schs., 1982, Ednl. Appreciation award City of Nashville, 1983, Commendation for pub. svc. Tenn. Legislature, 1994; named to Honorable Order of Ky. Cols., 1988. Mem. NEA, Am. Childhood Edn. Internat., Tenn. Hist. Soc., Wisdom Soc., Kappa Delta Pi, Pi Omega Pi, Pi Gamma Mu. Baptist. Home: 3819 Gallatin Rd Nashville TN 37216-2609

WINSTEAD, GEORGE ALVIS, law librarian, biochemist, educator, consultant; b. Owensboro, Ky., Jan. 14, 1916; s. Robert Lee and Mary Oma (Dempsey) W.; m. Elisabeth Donelson Weaver, July 18, 1943. BS, We. Ky. U., 1938; MA, George Peabody Coll., 1940, MLS, 1957, MEd, 1958. Head chemistry and biology dept. Belmont Coll., Nashville, 1952-56; head chemistry dept. George Peabody Coll., Vanderbilt U., Nashville, 1956-58; assoc. law librarian Vanderbilt U., Nashville, 1958-76; dir. Tenn. State Supreme Ct. Law Libraries, Nashville, 1976—; law cons. Tenn. Youth Legis., Nashville, 1976—; cons. civic clubs, local colls., 1976—, Tenn. State Govt. Depts. Archives, Nashville, 1976—. Author: Tenn. State Law Library Progress Reports, 1975, Supreme Court Library Personnel Guide, 1981, Designing Future Law Libraries' Growth and Expansion, 1982, Problem Identification and Solutions in Law Libraries, Tenn. Supreme Courts, 1985. Mem. Col. Tenn. Gov.'s staff, Nashville, 1978. With USAAF, 1943-46. Named to Gov.'s Staff of Ky. Cols., Lexington, 1988. Fellow Am. Inst. Chemists, SAR. Baptist. Home: 3819 Gallatin Rd Nashville TN 37216-2609 Office: Tenn Supreme Ct Libr Nashville TN 37219

WINSTEAD, JOY, journalist, consultant; b. Washington, May 31, 1934; d. Purnell Judson and Mellie Richardson (Winstead) W.; m. David Boyd Propert, Jul. 28, 1956 (div. June 1980); children: Kathleen Joy, David Bruce. BA in pol. sci., U. Richmond, 1955. Reporter Richmond (Va.) Times-Dispatch, 1955-56; staff writer, pub. rels. U. Pa., Phila., 1956-58; dir. publicity Children's Hosp., Washington, 1958-59; staff writer Richmond News Leader, 1972-77; features editor Columbia (S.C.) Record, 1977-81; asst. editor lifestyles Richmond Times-Dispatch, 1981-83, fashion editor, 1983-92; coord. pub. rels. Sci. Mus. Va., Richmond, 1992-93; dir. communications Medical Soc. Va., Richmond, 1993-96; guest lectr. U. Richmond. Va. Commonwealth U., U. S.C.; book reviewer Richmond Times-Dispatch. Contbg. author: Richmond Reader; contbg. editor: A Gem of a Coll. History of Westhampton Coll.; author (introduction): University of Richmond, A Portrait. Co-chmn. alumni weekend U. Richmond, 1968, chmn. alumnae fund, 1989, chmn. lectr. series, 1992-94, mem. 75th Anniversary Com. Recipient 1st pl. award for spl. articles Nat. Fedn. Press Women, 1975, Va. Press Women, 1975, 95, Va. Press Assn., 1978. Mem. Soc. Profl. Journalists (bd. dirs. 1975), Va. Press Women (hospitality chmn. 1993), Soc. Profl. Journalists Found. (bd. dirs. 1987-91), Va. Assn. Med. Soc. Execs. (assoc.), Am. Assn. Med. Soc. Execs., Richmond Pub. Rels. Assn., Fashion Editors and Reporters Assn. (bd. dirs. 1985-91, nominating com. chmn. 1991). Presbyterian. Home: 122 Holly Rd Williamsburg VA 23185

WINSTEAD, PHILIP CONNOR, education educator, university administrator; b. Mullins, S.C., Dec. 10, 1935; s. Philip Connor and Hilda Rae (Renfrew) W.; m. Hazel Jenon Wehunt; children: Amoret Beth, Hilda Marie, Mary Connor. AB, Davidson Coll., 1957; MA, Appalachian State, 1964; EdD, Duke U., 1966. Tchr., coach McClenaghan High Sch., Florence, S.C., 1957-62, asst. prin., 1962-64; faculty, adminstr. Rollins Coll., Winter Park, Fla., 1966-68; adminstr. Nat. Lab. for Higher Edn., Durham, N.C., 1968-72; dir. institutional planning and rsch., prof. edn. Furman U., Greenville, S.C., 1972—; cons. in field, 1972—. Elder 1st Presbyn. Ch., Greenville, 1985; pres. Greenville Sister Cities Internat., 1992. Mem. Assn. for Institutional Rsch., Am. Assn. for Higher Edn., Am. Ednl. Rsch. Assn., S.C. Assn. for Institutional Rsch. Home: 107 Old Mill Rd Taylors SC 29687-4943 Office: Furman U Poinsett Hwy Greenville SC 29613

WINSTON, DAVID CHARLES, pathologist; b. St. Louis, Sept. 25, 1963; s. Donald Francis and Maxine Marie (Kertz) W.; m. Cynthia Lucille McDougal, June 17, 1989; 1 child, Zachary Lewis. BS, St. Louis U., 1985; PhD, Med. U. S.C., 1991, MD, 1993. Resident in pathology U. Va. Health Scis. Ctr., Charlottesville, 1993-97; fellow in forensic pathology Office of Med. Investigator U. N.Mex. Sch. Medicine, Albuquerque, 1997-98. Contbr. articles to profl. jours. Mem. AMA, Royal Microscopic Soc., Coll. Am. Pathologists, Am. Soc. Clin. Pathologists, Va. Soc. Pathologists, Va. Med. Soc., U.S. and Can. Acad. Pathology. Home: Rt 1 Box 604A Scottsville VA 24590 Office: U Va Health Scis Ctr Dept Pathology Box 214 Charlottesville VA 22908

WINTER, CALVIN ARNOLD, JR., agricultural and horitcultural resource specialist; b. Selma, Ala., Mar. 25, 1955; s. Calvin Arnold Winter and Mary Catherine (Morgan) Reiges; m. Martha Elaine Poss, Apr. 14, 1979; children: Douglas Ryan, Benjamin Logan. Student, Abraham Baldwin Agrl. Coll., 1974-76; BS in Agrl. Econs., U. Ga., 1983. Asst. herdsman animal sci. dept. Beef Cattle Ctr., U. Ga., Athens, 1977-78, herdsman, 1978-81, unit mgr. beef cattle ctr., 1981-82; beef cattle rsch. asst. So. Piedmont Expt. Sta., USDA, Watkinsville, Ga., 1981-83; county extension Agt. Bleckley County U. Ga., Cochran, 1983-87, Brooks County, 1987, county extension dir. Brooks County, 1987-90; county extension agent Brooks County U. Ga. Coop. Extension Svc., Quitman, 1990-93; agrl. & hort. resource specialist, cons. The Home Depot, Tallahassee, Fla., 1993—. Bd. dirs. Brooks County Heart Unit, 1989; royal amb. counselor Dawson St. Bapt. Ch.; youth sports coach YMCA, 1992—. Named Vol. of Yr., Bleckley County unit Am. Heart Assn., 1986, 87, Brooks County unit, 1988. Mem. Ga. Assn. County Agrl. Agts. (chmn. S.W. scholarship com.), Nat. Assn. 4-H Agts., Ga. Assn. 4-H Agts. (New 4-H Agt. of Yr. award 1987), Ga. Cattleman's Assn., Fla. Angus Cattle Assn. (pres. 1994—), Brooks County Cattleman's Assn., Brooks County Farm Bur. (advisor 1989), Quitman-Brooks C. of C. (bd. dirs. 1988-89, chmn. agribus com. 1988-89), Rotary (vocat. com. Quitman-Brooks 1989—), Lions (bd. dirs. Quitman 1991), Epsilon Sigma Phi (Outstanding Young Men in Am. award 1987, Young Profl. of Yr. award 1988). Office: Winters Property Evaluation 340 Plantation Ln Thomasville GA 31757-1228

WINTER, JOAN ELIZABETH, psychotherapist; b. Aiken, S.C., Feb. 24, 1947; d. John S. and Mary Elizabeth (Caldwell) Winter. BS, Ariz. State U., 1970; MSW, Va. Commonwealth U., 1977; EdS, Coll. William and Mary, 1989, EdD, 1993. Lic. clin. social worker, AMFT bd. approved supr., clin. group worker. Va. Counselor Child Psychiatry Hosp., Phoenix, 1969-70, Ariz. Job Coll., Casa Grande, 1970-71; dir. Halfway House, Richmond, Va., 1971-73; state supr. resdl. treatment, Richmond, 1973-75; psycotherapist Med. Coll. Va., Richmond, 1975-76, Va. Commonwealth U., 1976-77; adj. prof., exec. dir. Family Rsch. Project, William and Mary Coll., Richmond, Va., 1979—; dir. Family Inst. Va., Richmond, 1980—; examiner, approved supr. Bd. Behavioral Scis., Commonwealth of Va., 1982—; mem. adj. faculty dept. psychology Coll. William & Mary, Med. Coll. Va.; mem. Avanta Network, Exec. Coun. and Faculty, Nat. Inst. of Drug Abuse, Rsch. Adv. Com. Author: The Phenomenon of Incest, 1977, The Use of Self in Therapy: The Person and Practice of the Therapist, 1987, Family Life of Psychotherapists, 1987 Enhancing the Marital Relationship: Virginia Satir's Parts Party, 1990, Enhancing the Marital Relationship: Virginia Satir's Parts Party, 1991, Family Therapy Research Outcomes: Bowen, Haley and Satir; editor Jour. Couple Therapy; contbr. articles to profl. jours. Diplomate Nat. Assn. Social Workers; mem. Am. Soc. Cert. Social Workers, Am. Family Therapy Assn., Am. Assn. Marriage and Family Therapy (approved supr.), Avanta Network Faculty. Address: 2910 Monument Ave Richmond VA 23221-1404

WINTER, LARRY EUGENE, accountant; b. Williamsport, Pa., Jan. 17, 1950; s. Robert Schrader and Betty Irene (Foresman) W.; m. Constance Dianne Snyder, June 2, 1973; children: John, Matthew, Noël, James. A in Bus. Adminstrn., Palm Beach Jr. Coll., 1969; BSBA, U. Fla., 1971; cert. bus., U. Pa., 1977. CPA, Fla., Ga.; accredited fin. planning specialist. Audit supr. Touche Ross & Co., Atlanta, 1971-74; chief. fin. officer Hawthorne Industries, Dalton, Ga., 1974-79; pvt. practice acctg. Dalton, 1979-89; mng. ptnr. Winter & Harris, CPAs, Dalton, 1990—; mem. White House Conf. Small Bus., Atlanta, 1979; instr. West Ga. Coll., Carollton, 1985, Ea. European Bus. Coll., Budapest, Hungary, 1995; acct. in residence Ga. Coll., Milledgeville, Ga., 1989; cons. Christian Businessman, Chattanooga, 1986—. Author: The American Free Enterprise System and the Ethics that Make it Work, 1991. Trustee Dalton Jr. Coll. Found.; chair Whitfield County/Dalton Day Care Ctrs., 1987-92; elder Fellowship Bible Ch., 1985—; mem. adv. coun. Ga. State Bd. Workers Compensation, 1991—; mem. fee arbitration panel State Bar Ga., 1987—. Mem. AICCPA, Ga. Soc. CPAs (pres. 1983-84), Fla. Inst. CPAs (recipient), Ga. Sheriff's Assn. (Disting. Humanitarian award), Dalton-Whitfield C. of C. (Leadership 1990-91, treas. 1992-94), Walden Club, Kiwanis (life, pres. 1978-79, lt. gov. 1981-84). Office: PO Box 2644 Dalton GA 30722-2644

WINTER, MARK LEE, physician; b. Joplin, Mo., Oct. 7, 1950; s. Elza Jr. and Malbryn Lea (Everhard) W.; m. Debbie Wright, Apr. 11, 1987; children: Jason, Tarra, Allison. BA in Biology cum laude, Drury Coll., 1972; MD cum laude, U. Mo., 1976. Resident in otolaryngology U. Tex. Med. Br., 1981; clin. asst. prof. dept. otolaryngology U. Tex. Med. Br., Galveston, 1981—; pvt. practice, 1982—; clin. instr. dept. surgery Tex. Tech U. Health Scis. Ctr., Lubbock, 1984—, clin. asst. prof. dept. med. and surg. neurology, 1987—; adj. prof. Dept. Speech and Hearing Scis. Tex. Tech. U. Helath Scis. Ctr., Lubbock, 1989—. Fellow Am. Acad. Otolaryngology (mem. nat. internat. stds. com. head and neck surg. 1992-94), Am. Acad. Neurotology Soc.; mem. Pan-Am Allergy Soc., Am. Acad. Facial Plastic and Reconstructive Surgery, Lubbock C. of C. (mem. health and medicine com. 1993), Phi Eta Sigma, Phi Mu Alpha. Republican. Office: 4002 21st St Lubbock TX 79410-1102

WINTER, MARSHA TERRY, French language educator; b. N.Y.C., Apr. 1, 1947. Student, Am. Acad. Dramatic Arts, 1962-63; AAS in Secretarial Sci., Queens Coll./CUNY, 1968, BA in French Lit., 1974, MA in French Lit., 1978; MPhil. in French Lit., Grad. Ctr./CUNY, 1981, PhD in French Lit., 1985. Cert. French tchr., N.Y. Asst. de langue américaine C.E.S. Nationalisé Mixte St.-Fuscien, C.E.S. Mixte, Amiens, France, 1974-75; tchr. French and English Cordozo High Sch., Bayside, N.Y., 1978; vis. asst. prof. French Fla. Atlantic U., Boca Raton, 1993; adj. asst. prof. of French St. John's U., 1985; instr. conversational French program in pvt. enterprise, N.Y.C., 1986-93; instr. Gregg Steno Ballard Sch./YWCA; instr. sec. sci. Citibanc. Contbr. articles to The Writer, The N.Y. Times, profl. jours. and lit. mags. Participant Dark Shadows Festival, Newark; actress Colonial Ch. Players, Bayside, N.Y., 1985-86. Recipient teachng assistantship French Govt., Amiens, 1974-75; Univ. fellow CUNY, 1980-81; French Govt. grantee, Montpellier, 1981-82. Mem. MLA, Am. Assn. Tchrs. French, PhD Assn. Grad. Ctr. CUNY, CUNY Queens Coll. Alumni Assn.

WINTER, WILLIAM ERNEST, physician, educator; b. San Francisco, June 10, 1952. BS, U. Santa Clara, 1974; MD, Loyola U., 1977. Diplomate Am. Bd. Pediatrics, Am. Bd. Pediatric Endocrinology, Am. Bd. Clin. Chemistry; diplomate in chem. pathology Am. Bd. Pathology. Intern, resident in pediatrics U. Ky.-Albert B. Chandler Med. ctr., Lexington, Ky., 1977-80, chief resident in pediatrics, 1980-81; clin. fellow in pediatric endocrinology and diabetes U. Fla. Coll. Medicine, Gainesville, 1981-82, rsch. fellow in pediatric and endocrinology and diabetes, 1982-84, assoc. prof., 1990-96, prof., 1996—; med. dir. clin. chemistry Shands Hosp., Gainesville, 1992—. Office: U Fla Pathology Dept PO Box 100275 Gainesville FL 32610-0275

WINTERS, BARBARA K., geriatrics services professional, poet; b. Brooklyn, N.Y., Nov. 3, 1934; d. Jacob and Jeanie (Salomon) Klein; m. Oct. 24, 1953 (div. July 16, 1977); children: Keith, Dean. Student, Lafayette H.S., Brooklyn, N.Y., 1952; Grad. Nurse Aide, Hempstead, N.Y., 1975. Data terminal operator Fed. Divsn. County Ct. House, Ft. Lauderdale, Fla., 1978-81; mkt. rsch. star interviewer Natalie Weitzman, Ft. Lauderdale, Fla., 1981-84; activity dir. Aviva Manor/Beverly Manor Cmty., Ft. Lauderdale, Fla., 1984-88; office mgr. constrn. firm, Ft. Lauderdale, Fla., 1988-89; cons. Mary Kay, Ft. Lauderdale, Fla., 1981-84; mental health adv. liaison Broward County Mental Health, Ft. Lauderdale. Contbr. poetry to mags., newspapers, anthology. Recording sec. Dem. Party, Ft. Lauderdale, Fla., 1981-84. Recipient Award for Svc. Planning, HRS Dist. 10, 1993, Dual Diagnosis in Elderly, 1994. Mem. Broward County (Fla.) Art Guild (Blue Ribbon Winner 1991). Home: 4141 NW 26th St Lauderhill FL 33313

WINTERS, SHARON ANN, librarian, library educator; b. West Palm Beach, Fla., Mar. 4, 1955; d. Edward William and Ethel Virginia (Held) W.; m. Kendall Martin Reid, May 7, 1988. BA in History, Wake Forest U., 1977; MLS, U. N.C., Greensboro, 1985; MPA, George Washington U., 1992. Tech. svcs. libr. Morgantown (W.Va.) Pub. Libr., 1985-86; systems libr. Hampton (Va.) Pub. Libr., 1986-91, support svcs. mgr., 1991—; mem., chair budget subcom. City of Hampton (Va.) Employee Coun., 1992—; lectr. Sch. Libr. and Info. Sci., Cath. U. Am., Washington, 1993—. Bd. mem., pres. Greenspring Food Coop., Winston-Salem, 1982-84; reading tutor Hampton (Va.) Literacy Coun., 1989-93. Recipient Excellence in Info. award Dynix, Inc., Provo, Utah, 1992. Mem. ALA, Pub. Libr. Assn., Customers of Dynix, Inc. (sec. 1988-90, newsletter editor 1990-92, chair local arrangements ann. conf. 1993-94, v.p. and pres.-elect 1994-95, pres. 1995-96). Office: Hampton Pub Libr 4207 Victoria Blvd Hampton VA 23669-4243

WINTERS, STEPHEN SAMUEL, geology educator; b. N.Y.C., June 29, 1920; m. Doris Hattie Rosenblum, Jan. 31, 1943; children: Philip David, Martha Karen. BA, Rutgers U., 1942; MA, Columbia U., 1948, PhD, 1955. Instr. Newark Colls. of Rutgers U., 1948-49; from asst. prof. to prof. geology Fla. State U., 1949-89, dean basic studies, 1964-84, dir.-dean honors program, 1967-85, prof. emeritus, 1989—. Author: Supai Formation (Permian) of Eastern Arizona, Memoir 89, Geological Soc. of Am., 1963. 1st. lt. USAF, 1943-46, PTO. Fellow Geol. Soc. Am.; mem. Am. Assn. Petroleum Geologists, Nat. Assn. Geology Tchrs., Sigma Xi, Phi Beta Kappa. Home: 1919 Alban Ave Tallahassee FL 32301

WINTERSHEIMER, DONALD CARL, state supreme court justice; b. Covington, Ky., Apr. 21, 1932; s. Carl E. and Marie A. (Kohl) W.; m. Alice T. Rabe, June 24, 1961; children: Mark D., Lisa Ann, Craig P., Amy T., Blaise Q. BA, Thomas More Coll., 1953; MA, Xavier U., 1956; JD, U. Cin., 1959. Bar: Ky. 1960, Ohio 1960. Pvt. practice Covington, Ky., 1960—; city solicitor City of Covington, 1962-76; judge Ky. Ct. Appeals, Frankfort, 1976-83; justice Ky. Supreme Ct., Frankfort, 1983—, chmn. criminal rules com., 1988-94, chmn. continuing jud. edn. com., 1983—, chmn. rules com., 1994—; del. Foster Parent Rev. Bd., 1985—; mem. adv. bd. Sta. WNKU-FM, 1984-94, Am. Soc. Writers on Legal Subjects. Trustee Sta. WNKU-FM. Recipient Cmty. Svc. award Thomas More Coll., 1968; recipient Disting. Alumnus award Thomas More Coll., 1982; named Disting. Jurist Chase Coll. Law, 1983, Outstanding Jurist Phi Alpha Delta Law Frat., 1990. Mem. ABA, Am. Judicature Soc., Ky. Bar Assn., Ohio Bar Assn., Cin. Bar Assn., Inst. Jud. Adminstrn. Democrat. Roman Catholic. Home: 224 Adams Ave Covington KY 41014-1712 Office: Ky Supreme Ct Capitol Building Rm 201 Frankfort KY 40601

WINTON, JAMES C., lawyer; b. Ft. Worth, Oct. 8, 1952. AB cum laude, U. So. Calif., 1974; JD magna cum laude, Southwestern U., 1977. Bar: Calif. 1977, U.S. Ct. Military Appeals 1979, D.C. 1980, U.S. Dist. Ct. (no. dist.) Calif. 1980, U.S. Dist. Ct. (ctrl. dist.) Calif. 1981, U.S. Dist. Ct. (so. dist.) Calif. 1983, U.S. Ct. Appeals (9th cir.) 1985, Tex. 1988, U.S. Dist. Ct. (so. dist.) Tex. 1989, U.S. Ct. Appeals (5th cir.) 1991, U.S. Dist. Ct. (no. dist.) Tex. 1992. Ptnr. Baker & Hostetler, Houston. Mem. ABA, State Bar Calif., D.C. Bar, State Bar Tex., Maritime Law Assn. U.S., Houston Bar Assn. Office: Baker & Hostetler 1000 Louisiana St Ste 2000 Houston TX 77002-5009*

WINTON, ROBERT EMMETT, psychiatrist; b. Annapolis, Md., Apr. 25, 1946; s. Lowell Sheridan and Cornelia Love (Rolston) W.; m. Pamela Boyd Jackson, Dec. 23, 1969; children: Tyler, Brett, Scott. BA, U. N.C., 1968; MD, Vanderbilt U. Med. Sch., 1972. Intern U. Mich., 1972-73; resident in psychiatry Duke U., 1975-78, fellow, 1978-79; epidemiologist Ctrs. for Disease Control, Atlanta, 1973-75; psychiat. cons. Fed. Correctional Inst., Butner, N.C., 1978-80; pvt. practice psychiatry Durham, N.C., 1980—; med. dir. N.C. Preferred Providers, Inc., 1995—; med. dir. N.C. Preferred Providers, 1995—; instr. Duke U. Sch. Nursing, 1980-82; asst. dir. psychiat. svc. Durham Regional Hosp., 1985-91, dir. psychiatry and chem. dependency svc., 1991—; v.p. Piedmont Care, Inc., Durham, 1991-94, pres. 1994—. Served to 2d lt. USPHS, 1973-75. Mem. AMA, AM. Psychiat. Assn. (Nancy Roeske award 1994) , N.C. Med. Soc., N.C. Neuropsychiat. Assn. Democrat. Home: 134 Pinecrest Rd Durham NC 27705-5813 Office: Durham Regional Hosp 3643 N Roxboro Rd Durham NC 27704-2702

WINTZ, CARY DECORDOVA, history educator; b. Houston, Feb. 12, 1943; m. Celia Janet Boritz, Aug. 9, 1974; 1 child, Jason Michael. BA in History, Rice U., 1965; MA In History, Kans. State U., 1968, PhD in History, 1974. Instr. history Tex. So. U., Houston, 1971-74; asst./assoc. prof. history Tex. So. U., 1974—, prof. history, dir. acad. computing, 1988-94, asst. dir. faculty instrn. and support, 1987-88; chair dept. History, geography and econs. Tex. So. U., Houston, 1995—; lectr. USIA, The Philippines, 1985, India, 1990; cons. in field; presenter computer workshops in Egypt, 1993, 94; adv. placement reader Ednl. Testing Svc., Trenton, N.J., 1987—; grant evaluator NEH, Washington, 1984, 85, 86, 89, 90, 91, 94. Author: Black Culture and the Harlem Renaissance, 1988, Reconstruction in Texas, 1983, Texas Politics in the Gilded Age, 1983; editor: African-American Political Thought, 1980-1930: Washington, DuBois, Garvey, and Randolph, 1966, The Harlem Renaissance, 1920-1940, 7 vols., 1966; co-editor: Black Dixie: Essays on Afro-Texan History and Culture in Houston, 1992; contbr. articles to profl. jours. Bd. dirs., pres. Houston Ctr. for Humanities, 1982-83; commr. Houston Archeol. and Hist. Commn., City of Houston, 1993. Recipient Disting. Svc. award Tex. So. U., 1988; grantee NEH, 1983, 88, 92, 96, faculty rsch. grantee Tex. So. U., 1985. Mem. Southwestern Hist. Assn. (pres. 1986-87), Am. Hist. Assn., Orgn. Am. Historians, Western Hist. Assn., So. Hist. Assn., Southwestern Social Sci. Assn. (gen. program chair, mem. exec. coun., v.p., 1994-95, pres. 1996—). Home: 2001 Holcombe Blvd Apt 602 Houston TX 77030-4214 Office: Texas Southern U 3100 Cleburne St Houston TX 77004-4501

WINZELER, TED J., geologist; b. Columbus, Ohio, Dec. 24, 1948; s. Edwin Clarence and Charlotte Mae (Whiteley) W.; m. Linda Meyer, Sept. 30, 1972; children: Alissa Meyer, Elena Marie. BS in Geology, Wittenberg U., 1970; MS in Geology, Bowling Green State U., 1974. Geologist Amoco Prodn. Co., Houston, 1974-80, divsn. geologist, 1980-84, regional geologist, 1984-88, mgr. resource devel., 1991—; mgr. exploration Amoco Egypt Co., Cairo, 1988-90; dep. exploration mgr. GUPCO, Cairo, 1988-90, divsn. exploration mgr., 1990-91, resource mgr. South Permian Basin, 1991-93; v.p. Amoco Bolivia, 1993—. Vol. worker Women's Christian Home Aux., Houston, 1984. Mem. Am. Assn. Petroleum Geologists (cert.), Soc. Exploration Paleontologists and Mineralogists, Houston Geol. Soc., Meyerland Club, Westlake Club, Sigma Gamma Epsilon. Methodist. Avocations: golf, tennis. Office: Amoco Prodn Co 501 Westlake Park Blvd PO Box 3092 Houston TX 77253

WINZER, P.J., lawyer; b. Shreveport, La., June 7, 1947; d. C.W. Winzer and Pearlene Hall Winzer Tobin. BA in Polit. Sci., So. U., Baton Rouge, 1968; JD, UCLA, 1971. Bar: Bar: Calif. 1972, U.S. Supreme Ct. 1986. Staff atty. Office of Gen. Counsel, U.S. HEW, Washington, 1971-80; asst. spl. counsel U.S. Office of Spl. Counsel Merit Systems Protection Bd., Dallas, 1980-82; regional dir. U.S. Merit Systems Protection Bd., Falls Church, Va., 1982—. Mem. Fed. Bar Assn., Calif. Bar Assn., Fed. Cir. Bar Assn., Delta Sigma Theta. Office: US Merit System Protection 5203 Leesburg Pike Ste 1109 Falls Church VA 22041-3401

WIORKOWSKI, GABRIELLE KAY, senior data base consultant; b. Tulsa, Nov. 10, 1943; d. Marshall Frank and Iva Ann (Johnson) Patterson; m. John J. Wiorkowski, June 4, 1966; 1 child, Fleur. BA summa cum laude, St. Mary's U., 1971; MS, U. Tex., Dallas, 1979. Adminstrv. asst. Stritch Sch. Medicine, Loyola U., Chgo., 1963-67; sr. programmer Corn Products Co., Chgo., 1967-68; mgr. data communications Jewel Co., Chgo., 1971-74; ind. data processing cons., Dallas, 1975—; lectr. U. Tex., Dallas, 1980—; mgr. data base mgmt. systems Sun Co. Inc., Dallas, 1981-83; DBA systems supr. Tex. Instruments, Inc., Dallas, 1983-85; sr. DB2 cons., founder Gabrielle & Assocs. (subs. Codd & Date Internat.), Dallas, 1985—; pres. DB2 Forum, 1988—. Mem. Richardson Assn. Gifted and Talented (treas. 1979-80), Assn. Computing Machinery, Nat. Computer Conf. (publs. chmn., steering com. 1977), Delta Epsilon Sigma, Pi Gamma Mu. Republican. Baptist. Author: DB2: Design Development Guide, 1990, 3d edit., 1992; author chpt. in book; contbr. articles to profl. jours. Home and office: 9922 Lincolnshire Ct Rockwall TX 75087-4509

WIORKOWSKI, JOHN JAMES, mathematics educator; b. Chgo., Sept. 30, 1943; s. John Stanley and Harriet Elizabeth (Bedra) W.; BS, U. Chgo., 1965, MS, 1966, PhD, 1972; m. Gabrielle K. Hollis, June 4, 1966; 1 child, Fleurette Anne. Research asso. U. Chgo., 1972; asst. prof. Pa. State U., University Park, 1973-74; assoc. prof. U. Tex. at Dallas, Richardson, 1975, assoc. prof. and program head Math Scis. Program, 1979-81, prof., 1981—, asst. to v.p. acad. affairs, 1980-85, asst. v.p. acad. affairs, 1985-91, assoc. v.p. acad. affairs, 1991-94, assoc. provost, 1994—, head math. scis. program, 1996—; cons. to Fed. Energy Adminstrn., 1975, Tex. Instruments, 1977, Frito-Lay Inc., 1977-78, Republic Nat. Bank, 1979; mem. panel studying 55 mile per hour speed limit Nat. Acad. Sci. Served to capt. U.S. Army, 1968-71. Decorated Army Commendation medal. NSF grantee, 1975—. Am. Council Edn. fellow, 1981-82. Mem. Am. Statis. Assn. (chpt. pres. 1974, v.p. 1977, chpt. pres. 1978), AAAS, Inst. Math. Stats., Biometric Soc., Sigma Xi. Unitarian. Contbr. articles to profl. jours. Home: 9922 Lincolnshire Ct Rockwall TX 75087-4509 Office: U Tex at Dallas PO Box 830688 Richardson TX 75083-0688

WIRE, TEDDY KERMIT, psychotherapist; b. Protem, Mo., Feb. 8, 1936; d. Flora (Thornton) Brown; m. Paul W. Wire, May 30, 1953; children: Brenda, Eddie, Patty, Paula. BA, So. Nazarene U., Bethany, Okla., 1971; MEd, U. Ctrl. Okla., 1988. Lic. profl. counselor; cert. alcohol drug counselor, cert. criminal justice specialist; nat. cert. gerontological counselor. Secondary tchr. Yukon (Okla.) Pub. Schs., 1973-78; asst. mgr. Bethany Rite-Way Printing, 1978-88; psychotherapist Cmty. Counseling Ctr., Oklahoma City, 1989-95, dir. aging svcs., 1995—; adj. prof. psychology So. Nazarene U., 1990-92. Mem. ACA, APA, Am. Soc. on Aging, Phi Delta Lambda. Republican. Mem. Ch. of Nazarene. Home: 3913 Riverside Dr Bethany OK 73008

WIRTSCHAFTER, IRENE NEROVE, tax consultant; b. Elgin, Ill., Aug. 5; d. David A. and Ethel G. Nerove; B.C.S., Columbus U., 1942; cert. tax profl.; enrolled agt. IRS; m. Burton Wirtschafter, June 2, 1945 (dec. 1966). Commd. ensign Supply Corps, USN, 1944, advanced through ranks to capt., 1975; comdg. officer Res. Supply Unit, 1974-75; ret., 1976; agt. office internat. ops. IRS, 1967-75, internat. banking specialist, now pvt. practice tax cons., Cocoa Beach, Fla.; sr. intern program U.S. Senate, 1981; mem. Sec. of Navy's Adv. Com. Ret. Personnel, 1984-86, VA Adv. Com. for Women Vets., 1987-90. Past troop leader Girl Scouts U.S.A.; cons. Jr. Achievement, 1989—; lt. col. and mission pilot CAP, 21 air races; comml. instrument pilot; founder Sr. Action Com. Brevard County, 1981; chmn. College Park Airport Johnny Horizon Day, 1975; Navy liason officer Commd.'s Retiree Coun. Patrick AFB, 1985-89; elected dir. Fla. Space Coast Philharmonic, 1985—, treas. 1986-92; mem. bd. dirs., adv. mgr. Cocoa Beach Citizens League, 1990-92; co-chmn. Internat. Women's Yr. Take Off Dinner, Washington, 1976; mem. Nat. Com. Internat. Forest of Friendship, Atchison, Kans., 1976—; 1st v.p. Friends of Cocoa Beach Libr., 1988-90, pres., 1990-92, bd. dirs., 1993—, apptd. to Cocoa Beach Libr. Bd., 1996; mem. Cocoa Beach Bus. Improvement Coun., Fla.; elected senator Silver Haired Legislature, Fla., 1985—; advisor Women's Air & Space Mus., 1993—; vol., founding mem. Brevard Zoo; chmn. Cocoa Beach Code Enforcement Bd., 1989—; sr. adv. com. Cape Canaveral Hosp., co-chmn. 1994. Named hon. citizen of Winnipeg (Can.), 1966, Atchison, 1989 and New Orleans, 1988; Ky. col., La. col. Mem. AAUW, Naval Res. Assn. (nat. treas. 1975-77, nat. adv. com. 1985—, Nat. award of Merit 1992), Ninety Nines (past chpt. and sect. officer; 99 Achievement awards), Naval Order U.S. (treas. nat. capitol commandry), Assn. Naval Aviation (nat. trustee 1988—), Banana River Squadron (founder, comptr. 1984—), Assn. Enrolled Agts., Cocoa Beach Area C. of C., Internat. Platform Assn., Silver Wings (bd. dirs. 1990—, nat. sec. 1986, Woman of the Year 1985), WAVES Nat. (bd. dirs. chpt. 75 1989—), Tailhook Assn., Patrick Women's Golf Assn. (treas. 1996—), Daybreak Rotary Club. First female Supply Corps officer to be assigned sea duty, 1956. Avocations: aviation, golf, music. Home: 1825 Minutemen Cswy Apt 301 Cocoa Beach FL 32931-2033

WIRTZ, MICHAEL H., interior designer; b. Cin., Mar. 23, 1951; s. Leonard F. Wirtz and Dolores L. Schmidt. BS, U. Cin., 1972. Owner, mgr. Michael Wirtz Designer Inc., Boca Raton, Fla.; mem. adv. bd. Contract mag., N.Y.C., 1981, Design Ctr. Ams., Ft. Lauderdale, Fla., 1981-92, Interior and Sources mag., Chgo., 1989, Bauder Coll., Ft. Lauderdale, 1993—; trustee Fed. Interior Design Found., chmn., 1991-95; trustee Found. for Interior Design Edn. Rsch., 1983-91, chmn., 1989; mem. State Fla. Bd. Architecture and Interior Design, 1994—. Mem. adv. bd. Interior Resources Mag., 1984—. Trustee, chmn. bd. Fed. Interior Designers Found., 1991—. Fellow Inst. Bus. Designers (v.p. 1979-81, disting. merit award 1986; trustee Found., treas. 1985-87, pres. 1990-92); mem. Coun. Fed. Interior Designers (hon.), Internat. Soc. Designers (hon.), Interior Design Educators Coun. (hon.), Internat. Interior Design Assn. (life), Boca Raton Hist. Soc. Home: 56 NW 3rd Ct Boca Raton FL 33432-3734 Office: 34E Palmetto Park Rd Boca Raton FL 33432-3734

WISCH, DAVID JOHN, structural engineer; b. Jefferson City, Mo., Dec. 6, 1953; s. Theodore A. and Josephine (Lauf) W.; m. Leslie Babin, Oct. 24, 1981; 1 child, Christine. BSCE, U. Mo., Rolla, 1975, MSCE, 1977. Registered profl. engr., La., Calif. Civil engr. Texaco-Ctrl. Offshore Engring., New Orleans, 1977-81, advanced civil engr., 1981-86, sr. project engr., 1986-92; specialist Texaco-Ctrl. Offshore Engring., Bellaire, Tex., 1992—; chmn. fixed systems subcom. Am. Petroleum Inst., Dallas, 1991-93, mem. adv. bd. offshore standardization com., 1991-94, chmn., 1993-94, mem. exec. com. on standardization, 1994—, chmn. offshore and subsea com., 1994—, head U.S. Delegation Internat. Orgn. Stds. Tech. Com. 1967/Subcom 7, 1993—, mem. Tech. Com. 67/Subcom. 7/AG1, 1993—, convener Tech. Com. 67/Subcom 7/WG3-Fixed Steel Structures, 1993—; mem. structure subcom. Oil Soc. Internat. Exploration and Prodn. Forum, London, 1993-93. Author numerous papers/presentations, 1984—. Mem. ASCE (program. subcom. for Offshore Tech. Conf. 1993—), Sigma Xi, Phi Kappa Phi, Tau Beta Pi, Chi Epsilon (chpt. pres. 1975-76). Office: Texaco Ctrl Offshore Engring 4800 Fournace Pl Bellaire TX 77401-2324

WISDOM, JOHN MINOR, federal judge; b. New Orleans, May 17, 1905; s. Mortimer Norton and Adelaide (Labatt) W.; m. Bonnie Stewart Mathews, Oct. 24, 1931; children: John Minor (dec.), Kathleen Mathews, Penelope Stewart Wisdom Tose. AB, Washington and Lee U., 1925; LLB, Tulane U., 1929, LLD (hon.), 1976; LLD (hon.), Oberlin Coll., 1963, San Diego U., 1979, Haverford Coll., 1982, Middlebury Coll., 1987, Harvard U., 1987, So. Meth. U., 1994. Bar: La. 1929. Mem. Wisdom, Stone, Pigman & Benjamin, New Orleans, 1929-57; judge U.S. Ct. Appeals (5th cir.), 1957—, now sr. judge; mem. Multi-Dist. Litigation Panel, 1968-78, chmn., 1975-78; mem. Spl. Ct. Regional Reorgn. of R.R.s, 1975-86, presiding judge, 1986—; adj. prof. law Tulane U., 1938-57; faculty IJA Appellate Judges Seminar, 1961-70; vis. coms. law schs. U. Chgo., Harvard U., U. Miami, U. San Diego. Mem. Pres.'s Com. on Govt. Contracts, 1953-57; past pres. New Orleans Council Social Agys.; Republican nat. committeeman for La., 1952-57; trustee Washington and Lee U., 1953—. Served from capt. to lt. col. USAAF, 1942-46. Decorated Legion of Merit, Army Commendation medal; recipient 1st Disting. Jurist award La. Bar Found., 1986, St. Thomas More Medallion, Loyola U. of L.A., 1987, Devitt Disting. Svc. to Justice award, 1989, Tulane Disting. Alumnus award, 1989, Alfred E. Clay award Children's Bur., 1992, Strength in Aging award (with Mrs. Wisdom) LSU Geriatric Ctr., 1992, LPB Living Legends award, 1993, Trumpet award Turner Broadcasting, 1994. Mem. ABA (chmn. appellate judges conf. 1966-67, 1st recipient John Minor Wisdom pub. svc. and profl. award sect. litigation 1990, Am. Inns of Ct. Lewis F. Powell Jr. award 1991, Fellows award young lawyers div. 1991, Pres.'s medal of Freedom 1993, medal 1996), Am. Acad. Arts and Scis., La. Bar Assn., New Orleans Bar Assn., La. Bar Found., Am. Law Inst. (coun. mem. 1961), La. Law Inst., Am. Judicature Soc., Order of Coif, Delta Kappa Epsilon, Phi Alpha Delta (Tom C. Clark Equal Justice under Law award 1982), Omicron Delta Kappa. Episcopalian. Clubs: Boston (New Orleans), Louisiana (New Orleans); Metropolitan (Washington). Office: John Minor Wisdom 200 John Minor Wisdom Bldg 600 Camp St New Orleans LA 70130-3425

WISE, LAWRENCE GEORGE, human resources executive; b. St. Petersburg, Fla., June 20, 1946; s. Lawrence George and Janet Mary (Butler) W.; m. Bonita Mary Stockler, June 21, 1967; children: Stephanie Mary, Lawrence George III. BA in Bus., U. South Fla., 1967. Cert. bus. tchr., Fla.; lic. in real estate sales, Fla. Underwriting specialist State Farm Ins. Cos., Winter Haven, Fla., 1967-87, credit union pres., 1987-88, credit union treas. and human resources supr., 1988—; bd. dirs. Citrus Community Fed. Credit Union, 1990. Mem. Citrus County Gifted Orgn., Fla.; coord. projects Citrus County Aquatic Control Bd., Lecanto; bd. dirs. Lake Buckeye Condominium Assn., Winter Haven, Fla., 1978-80; mem. adv. bd. Citrus High Sch., 1987-90. Mem. Lambda Chi Alpha Alumni Assn. (treas. 1966). Republican. Methodist. Club: Inverness Golf and Country (Fla.). Home: 8133 S Clarkwise Pt Floral City FL 34436-3422

WISE, MIGUEL DAVID, lawyer; b. Mercedes, Tex., Feb. 11, 1960; s. Miguel and Barbara Cecilia (Barbosa) W.; m. Erin Adrienne Duffy, Aug. 4, 1984; children: Miguel David III, Mark Riborg, Zachary August. BA magna cum laude, St. Mary's U., San Antonio, 1981, JD, 1984. Bar: Tex. 1984, U.S. Dist. Ct. (so. dist.) Tex. 1986, U.S. Ct. Appeals (5th cir.) 1986, U.S. Dist. Ct. (no. and we. dists.) Tex. 1988, U.S. Supreme Ct. 1988, U.S. Dist. Ct. (ea. dist.) Tex. 1990, U.S. Ct. Appeals (D.C. cir.) 1993. Law clk. Office Atty. Gen. Tex., San Antonio, 1983-84; assoc. Richard S. Talbert, Weslaco, Tex., 1985-86, Allison, Chavez & Sweetman, Brownsville, Tex, 1986-89; ptnr. Dunn & Wise, P.C., Harlingen, Tex., 1990-92, Sweetman & Wise, LLP, Harlingen, 1992—. Contbr. articles to profl. jours. Dist. chmn. Llano Grande dist. Boy Scouts Am., 1985-90, bd. dirs. Rio Grande coun., post advisor, 1989-90; mem. state com. presdl. campaign Al Gore Jr., 1988; del. Tex. Dem. Conv., 1988, Cameron County Dem. Conv., 1988; adv. bd. mem. Adam Walsh Found., 1992—; voting del. Tech Prep of the Rio Grande Valley, Inc., 1994—. Recipient Big Pine Tree III award City of Donna, 1985, Dist. award of merit Boy Scouts Am.; Airborne qualified U.S. Army, 1993. Mem. ABA, Mexican-Am. Bar Assn., Hispanic Nat. Bar Assn., Tex. Bar Assn., State Bar of Tex. (chair editl. subcom. standing com. on legal assts. 1993—, vice chair standing com. on legal assts. 1994—), D.C. Bar Assn., Hidalgo County Bar Assn., Cameron County Bar Assn. (com. 1987—, dir. 1992—), Assn. Trial Lawyers Am. (com. 1987—), Tex. Trial Lawyers Assn., Coll. State Bar Tex., Supreme Ct. Hist. Soc., Jaycees, Rotary, Lambda Chi Alpha, Delta Epsilon Sigma, Delta Theta Phi. Roman Catholic. Home: PO Box 812 711 S Georgia St Weslaco TX 78596 Office: Sweetman & Wise LLP 1221 Morgan Blvd Harlingen TX 78550-5154

WISE, ROBERT ELLSWORTH, JR. (BOB ELLSWORTH), congressman; b. Washington, D.C., Jan. 6, 1948; m. Sandra Casber, 1984. BA, Duke U., 1970; JD, Tulane U., 1975. Bar: W.Va., 1975. Sole practice Charleston, W.Va., 1975-80; atty., legis. council for judiciary com. W.Va. Ho. of Dels., 1977-78; mem. W.Va. Senate, 1980-82, 97th-103rd Congresses from 2nd W.Va. dist., Washington, D.C., 1982—; whip at large Congress from W.Va., 1986—. Dir. West Virginians for Fair and Equitable Assessment of Taxes, Inc. Mem. ABA, W.Va. State Bar Assn. Democrat. Office: US Ho of Reps Office Bldg 2367 Rayburn House Washington DC 20515-4802*

WISE, SUSAN TAMSBERG, management and communications consultant, speaker; b. Memphis, Nov. 16, 1945; d. Joseph Lane and Mable Rosa (Koth) Tamsberg; m. Roy Thomas Wise, June 29, 1968; children: Kristin Rebecca, Mary Catherine. BA in Math., Columbia (S.C.) Coll., 1967; M in Edn., Ga. State U., Atlanta, 1986. Tchr. high sch. math. various pub. schs., N.C., S.C., and Ga., 1967-73; instr. Cen. Piedmont Community Coll., Charlotte, N.C., 1979; devel. dir. Classique, Inc., Kannapolis, N.C., 1979-81; asst. v.p. First Nat. Bank of Atlanta, 1981-87; Ga. dir. The Exec. Speaker, Inc., Atlanta, 1987-90; pres. TrimTime, Inc., Atlanta, 1988—, Wise Consulting Inc., Atlanta, 1990—; speaker Girl Scouts USA, Jr. League, numerous med. assns., Atlanta and S.E. area, 1985—. Tng. cons. Jr. League of Atlanta, 1988-89; bd. dirs. Incarnation Luth. Ch., Atlanta, 1984; mem. ch. coun., bd. dirs, Luth. Ch. of the Redeemer. Mem. ASTD (v.p., bd. dirs., Leadership award 1987), Kappa Delta Pi. Republican.

WISE, WILLIAM ALLAN, oil company executive, lawyer; b. Davenport, Iowa, July 10, 1945; s. A. Walter and Mary Virginia (Kuhl) W.; m. Marie Figge, Sept. 27, 1969; children—Vivian Marie, Genevieve Marie, Mary Elizabeth. B.A., Vanderbilt U.; J.D., U. Colo. Bar: Colo. 1970. Prin. counsel El Paso Natural Gas, Tex., 1970-80, sr. v.p. mktg., 1985-87, exec. v.p. mktg., 1987-89; pres., chief oper. officer El Paso Natural Gas, 1989-90, pres., chief exec. officer, 1990-93, chmn, pres. & CEO, 1994-96; asst. gen. counsel in Houston The El Paso Co., 1980-82, v.p., gen. counsel, 1983, sr. v.p., gen. counsel and sec., 1983-85; chmn., pres. & CEO El Paso Natural Gas Co. dba El Paso Energy Corp., 1996—; also bd. dirs. El Paso Energy Corp.; bd. dirs. Tex. Commerce Bank, El Paso, Tex. Commerce Bancshres, Inc., Houston, Interstate Natural Gas Assn. Am., Washington: mem. N.Y. Merc. Exch., Tri-Regional Com. Contbr. articles to profl. jours. Bd. dirs. Battle Mountain Gold Co., U. Colo. Found., Boulder, Gas Industry Stds., Natural Gas Coun., Tex. Gov.'s Bus. Coun.; mem. bus. adv. coun. and devel. bd. U. Tex., El Paso; bd. visitors M.D. Anderson Cancer Ctr. Mem. Nat. Petroleum Coun. (bd. dirs.), Colo. Bar Assn., El Paso Country Club, George Town Club (Washington), River Oaks Country Club (Houston), Old Baldy Club (Saratoga, Wyo.). Republican. Roman Catholic. Home: 5605 Westside Dr El Paso TX 79932-2921 Office: El Paso Energy Corp. 100 N Stanton One Paul Kayser Cen El Paso TX 79901

WISEBURN, LAWRENCE PRITCHARD, social worker, psychotherapist; b. Englewood, N.J., Oct. 15, 1947; s. Frank Pritchard and Dorothea Claire (Perry) W. BS, USAF Acad., 1969; MSW, U. S.C., 1990. Lic. baccalaureate social worker; credentialed master counselor, credentialed clin. counselor; nat. cert. addiction counselor. Commd. 2nd lt. USAF, 1969, advanced through grades to capt., discharged, 1981; asst. sales mgr., broadcaster Eagle River (Wis.) Broadcasting, 1981-83; asst. sales mgr., sales mgr. Radio Shack Computer Ctr., Columbia, S.C., 1983-84; sales mgr., gen. mgr. Computer Mart, Venice, Fla., 1984-86; residential dir. to sr. counselor, to community svcs. dir. Aiken (S.C.) Ctr. for Alcohol and Other Drug Svcs., 1986-89; pvt. practice Florence, S.C., 1995—; clin. social worker, coord. assessment and utilization rev. Bruce Hall, Florence, S.C., 1989—; mem. faculty S.C. Sch. Alcohol and Drug Studies, 1991—, Bruce Hall Inst. Family Wellness, 1990—; adj. prof. U. S.C., 1992—; presenter in field. Recipient Vocat. Rehab. Profl. and Personal Achievement award S.C. Vocat. Rehab., Aiken, 1987. Mem. NASW, Nat. Assn. Alcohol and Drug Abuse Counselors. Home: 3731 Southborough Rd 3B Florence SC 29501-8860 Office: Bruce Hall 601 Gregg Ave Florence SC 29501-4316 also: The Counseling Ctr 227 S Bargain St Florence SC 29501

WISECUP, BARBARA JEAN, medical/surgical nurse; b. Missouri Valley, Iowa, Apr. 7, 1933; d. Charles Arthur and Agnes Viola (Tollefson) W. Diploma, Meth. Hosp. Sch. Nursing, Sioux City, Iowa, 1955; postgrad., Morningside Coll., Sioux City, Sacred Heart Dominion Coll., Houston, Houston Community Coll. RN, Tex., Iowa; cert. CNOR. Staff nurse surg. floor U. Minn. Hosps., Mpls., 1955-57; staff nurse operating rooms Hermann Hosp., Houston, 1957-63, nurse mgr. operating room staff devel., 1963—. Mem. Assn. Operating Room Nurses. Home: 12037 Bob White Dr Houston TX 77035-3928 Office: Hermann Hosp 6411 Fannin St Houston TX 77030-1501

WISEHART, MARY RUTH, academic administrator; b. Myrtle, Mo., Nov. 2, 1932; d. William Henry and Ora (Harbison) W. BA, Free Will Baptist Bible Coll., 1955; BA, George Peabody Coll. Tchrs., 1959, MA, 1960, PhD, 1976. Tchr. Free Will Bapt. Bible Coll., Nashville, 1956-60, chmn. English dept., 1961-85; exec. sec.-treas. Free Will Bapt. Women Nat. Active for Christ, 1985—. Author: Sparks Into Flame, 1985; contbr. poetry to jours. Mem. Nat. Coun. Tchrs. English, Christian Mgmt. Assn., Religious Conf. Mgmt. Assn., Scribbler's Club. Avocations: photography, music, drama. Office: Women Nat Active for Christ Free Will Bapt PO Box 5002 Antioch TN 37011-5002

WISEHEART, MALCOLM BOYD, JR., lawyer; b. Miami, Fla., Sept. 18, 1942; s. Malcolm B. and Dorothy E. (Allen) W.; m. Michele I. Romanens, Dec. 11, 1976. BA, Yale U., 1965; MA in English Jurisprudence, Cambridge U., 1973; JD with honors, U. Fla., 1970. Bar: Fla. 1970, Eng. and Wales 1970, Jamaica 1970, Trinidad and Tobago 1971, D.C. 1980. Assoc. Helliwell, Melrose & DeWolf, Miami, 1970-72; sr. ptnr. Malcolm B. Wiseheart, Jr., P.A., Miami, 1973-86; sr. ptnr., Wiseheart & Joyce, P.A., Miami, 1986-88; sec., gen. counsel Wiseheart Found.; spl. master Dade County Property Appraisal Adjustment Bd., 1977-90; pres. Fla. Law Inst., 1980-91; trustee, mem. exec. com. Players State Theater, 1982-84; bd. dirs. Sta. WLRN Pub. Radio, 1982, Coun. Internat. Visitors; trustee Ransom Everglades Sch., 1995-96. Named Most Outstanding, U. Fla. Law Rev. Alumnus, 1981. Mem. Fla Bar (chmn. grievance com. 1978-81), Dade County Bar Assn. (dir. 1971-74, 86-89, treas. 1974-75, sec. 1975-77), Order of Coif, Yale Club (Miami pres. 1976-77), United Oxford and Cambridge Univs. Club (London). Office: Wiseheart Bldg 2840 SW 3rd Ave Miami FL 33129-2317

WISEMAN, DENNIS GENE, university dean; b. Anderson, Ind., Sept. 25, 1947; s. Harold Leslie and Lillian Loetta (Woods) W.; m. Susan Jean Reidenbach, June 10, 1971; children: Matthew Benjamin, Andrew Joseph. BA, U. Indpls., 1969; MA, U. Ill., 1970, PhD, 1974; postgrad., Ind. U., 1970-71. Tchr. Indpls. Pub. Schs., 1970-71; rsch. asst. U. Ill., Urbana, 1971-74, clinician, supr., 1972-74, coord. Office for Profl. Svc., 1973-74; dir., tchr. Champaign (Ill.) pub. schs., 1972-73; asst. prof. U. S.C. Coastal Carolina Coll., Conway, 1974-77, assoc. prof., 1977-84, prof., 1984—, dean Sch. Edn., 1982-93; dean Sch. Edn. and Grad. Studies, Coastal Carolina U., 1993—; field disseminator Social Sci. Edn. Consortium, Boulder, Colo., 1979-81; reviewer Ethnic Heritage Studies Program, U.S. Office Edn., Washington, 1980-81; cons. S.C. State Dept. Edn., Columbia, 1986—; dir. Oxford program U. S.C. Coastal Carolina Coll., summer, 1990; evaluator So. Assn. Colls. and Schs., Atlanta, 1991; folio reviewer for Nat. Coun. for Social Studies, Nat. Coun. for Accreditation of Tchr. Edn., 1994—. Co-author: Effective Teaching, 1st edit., 1984, 2d edit. 1991, Wondering about Thinking, 1988; contbr. articles to jours. in field. Mem. Horry County Human Rels. Coun., Conway, 1990-93; mem. curriculum frameworks rev. panel S.C. Dept. Edn., 1993—. Named Tchr. of Yr., U. S.C. Coastal Carolina Coll., 1980; S.C. Com. for the Humanities grantee, 1984, S.C. Com. on Higher Edn. grantee, 1985, 86; Japan Study Program scholar U.S. Office Edn., 1980. Mem. S.C. Assn. Colls. for Tchr. Edn. (pres. elect 1989, pres. 1989-91), Coun. Edn. Deans (pres. 1986-90), Nat. Coun. for the Social Studies, Am. Assn. Colls. for Tchr. Edn. (instl. rep. 1980—), Assn. Tchr. Educators, Phi Delta Kappa (pres. Coastal Carolina chpt. 1984-85). Methodist. Office: Coastal Carolina U Dean Sch Edn & Grad Studies PO Box 1954 Conway SC 29526-1954

WISEMAN, J(AMES) PATRICK, lawyer; b. L.A., Dec. 22, 1948; s. James Patrick and Helen (Donohue) W.; m. Bonnie Ruth McFarland, Feb. 12, 1976 (div. 1990); children: James III, Clare McFarland. BBA, Tex. A&M U., 1970; JD, U. Houston, 1973. Bar: Tex. 1974, U.S. Dist. Ct. (so. dist.) Tex. 1975, U.S. Ct. Appeals (5th cir.) 1978, U.S. Ct. Appeals (11th cir.), 1981, U.S. Dist. Ct. (we. dist.) Tex. 1985, U.S. Ct. Appeals (2nd cir.) 1986, U.S. Dist. Ct. (ea. dist.) Tex. 1986, U.S. Ct. Appeals (4th cir.) 1995. Lawyer VISTA, Houston, 1974-75, Houston ACLU, 1975-77; assoc. Pape & Mallett, Houston, 1977-79; ptnr. Nelson & Mallett, P.C., Houston, 1975-84; chief of state and city affairs Tex. Atty. Gen., Austin, 1984-87; ptnr. Richards, Wiseman & Durst, Austin, 1987-92, Wiseman, Durst, Tuddenhom & Owen, P.C., Austin, 1992—; adj. prof. U. Houston Sch. Law, 1982-84. Recipient Schwab award Tex. Human Rights Found., 1990, Advocacy award Bar Assn. for Human Rights, 1993, Tex. Law Fellowships award for excellence in pub. interest U. Tex. Sch. Law, 1994. Mem. Tex. Bar Assn. (pres. individual rights sect. 1981-82), ACLU (state bd. dirs. 1982-84, 91-92, 95—). Home: 2113 Highgrove Ter Austin TX 78703-4521 Office: Wiseman Durst et al 1004 West Ave Austin TX 78701-2019

WISEMAN, ROSE FRESCHMAN, public relations executive; b. LaGrande, Oreg., Dec. 17, 1956; d. Paul and Lucille (Allen) Freschman. BS in Journalism and Pub. Rels., U. Tenn., 1980. Pres. Campus Communicators, Knoxville, Tenn., 1978-79; dir. pub. rels. Knox County chpt. ARC, Knoxville, 1979; info. specialist, pub. rels. coord. divsn. engring. design TVA, Knoxville, 1979-82; dir. pub. rels. Bellarmine Coll., Louisville, 1982-83; freelance pub. rels. practitioner Louisville and Atlanta, 1983-86; pub. rels. account exec. Sawyer Riley Compton, Inc., Atlanta, 1989-91; v.p. pub. rels. Basinger & Assocs., Inc., Atlanta, 1991-93; prin., pres. The Pub. Rels. Group, Inc., Atlanta, 1993—. Mem. Pub. Rels. Soc. Am. (chairperson 40th anniversary com. 1992, internat. rels. com. 1991, coll. rels. com. 1990). Roman Catholic. Office: The Pub Rels Group Inc 1026 Sanfords Walk Tucker GA 30084-1429

WISEMAN, THOMAS ANDERTON, JR., federal judge; b. Tullahoma, Tenn., Nov. 3, 1930; s. Thomas Anderton and Vera Seleta (Poe) W.; m. Emily Barbara Matlack, Mar. 30, 1957; children: Thomas Anderton III, Mary Alice, Sarah Emily. B.A., Vanderbilt U., 1952, LL.B., 1954; LLM, U. Va., 1990. Bar: Tenn. Pvt. practice Tullahoma, 1956-63; ptnr. Haynes, Wiseman & Hull, Tullahoma and Winchester, Tenn., 1963-71; treas. State of Tenn., 1971-74; ptnr. Chambers & Wiseman, 1974-78; judge U.S. Dist. Ct. (mid. dist.) Tenn., Nashville, 1978—, chief judge, 1984-91, sr. chief judge, 1995—; mem. Tenn. Ho. of Reps., 1964-68; adj. prof. law Vanderbilt U. Sch. Law. Asso. editor: Vanderbilt Law Rev, 1953-54. Democratic candidate for gov., Tenn., 1974; Chmn. Tenn. Heart Fund, 1973, Middle Tenn. Heart Fund, 1972. Served with U.S. Army, 1954-56. Fellow Tenn. Bar Found.; mem. Masons (33 deg.), Shriners, Amateur Chefs Soc. Presbyterian. Office: US Dist Ct 736 US Courthouse 801 Broadway Nashville TN 37203-3816

WISENBAKER, JAMES MICHAEL, archaeologist, writer; b. Rome, Ga., Sept. 1, 1947; s. Vance Byrd and Mary Ellen (Copeland) W. AA with honors, Tallahassee C.C., 1968; BS cum laude, Fla. State U., 1970, MA, 1972. Grad. teaching asst. Fla. State U., Tallahassee, 1971-72; underwater archaeologist State of Fla., Florida Keys, 1973; instr. scuba diving Carter's Sporting Goods, Tallahassee, Fla., 1974-75; land surveying technician John R. Van Norman & Assocs., Tallahassee, 1976-77; archaeologist Nat. Park Svc., Natchez Trace Parkway, 1978, U.S. Forest Svc., Tallahassee, 1979-80; archaeol. cons. Fla., 1981-84; archaeologist, preservation planner Fla. Divsn. Hist. Resources, Tallahassee, 1984—; mem. adv. coun. Karst Waters Inst., 1992—. Author: (with I.R. Daniel) Harney Flats: A Florida Paleo-Indian Site, 1987; contbr. articles and photographs to profl. jours. Mem. Nat. Audubon Soc., Nat. Speleol. Soc. (cave diving sect.), The Nature Conservancy, Phi Beta Kappa, Phi Theta Kappa. Democrat. Mem. Ch. of Christ. Home: 2013 Longview Dr Tallahassee FL 32303-7323 Office: Fla Dept State Divsn Hist Resources 500 S Bronough St Tallahassee FL 32399-6504

WISHART, LEONARD PLUMER, III, army officer; b. Newark, Sept. 24, 1934; s. Leonard Plumer and Mabel Dorothea (Womsley) W.; m. Sandra Frances De Vito, Apr. 12, 1958; children: Leonard Plumer IV, Scott Brian. Student, Va. Mil. Inst., 1952-53; BS in Engring., U.S. Mil. Acad., 1957; MS in Nuclear Physics, U. Va., 1966. Commd. 2d lt. U.S. Army, 1957, advanced through grades to lt. gen., 1988; served in Germany and Vietnam; tactical officer U.S. Mil. Acad., West Point, N.Y., 1971-73; sr. mil. asst. to Sec. of Army, 1975-76; comdr. 1st Brigade, 24th Inf. Div., Ft. Stewart, Ga., 1977-78; chief of staff 24th Inf. Div., 1979, VII Corps in Germany, 1979-81; asst. div. comdr. 1st Armored Div., 1981-83; dep. comdr. CACDA, Ft. Leavenworth, Kans., 1983-86; comdr. 1st Inf. Div., Ft. Riley, Kans., 1986-88, Combined Arms Command, Ft. Leavenworth, Kans., 1988-91; dep. comdr. TRADOC, Ft. Leavenworth, Kans., 1988-91, ret., 1991; assoc. Burdeshaw Assocs. Ltd., Bethesda, Md., 1991-92; apptd. 1st dir. non-legis. and fin. svcs. U.S. Ho. of Reps., Washington, 1992-94, resigned, 1994; assoc. Burdeshaw Assocs., Ltd., Bethesda, Md., 1994—; program mgr. INNOLOG, McLean, Va., 1996—. Active in cmty. activities. Decorated Disting. Service Medal (2), Legion of Merit (2), D.F.C., Bronze Star medal (2), Army Commendation medal, Air medals. Mem. Assn. U.S. Army, Assn. Grads. U.S. Mil. Acad., Alumni Assn. U. Va., VFW, Soc. of the First Divsn. Methodist. Office: Burdeshaw Assocs Ltd 4701 Sangamore Rd Bethesda MD 20816-2508

WISHERT, JO ANN CHAPPELL, elementary and secondary education educator; b. Carroll County, Va., July 10, 1951; d. Joseph Lenox and Helen Alata (Wagoner) Chappell; m. Clarence Hinnant Wishert, Jr., June 10, 1987; 1 child, Kelly Marie. BA, Oral Roberts U., 1974; MS, Radford U., 1977; Degree in Advanced Postgrad Studies, Va. Poly. Inst. and State U., 1981; postgrad., U. S.C., Spartanburg, 1990. Cert. elem. music supr., Va., elem. and secondary music tchr., S.C., music tchr., ednl. specialist, N.C. Head start tchr. Rooftop of Va., Galax, 1975; elem. music tchr. Carroll County Pub. Schs., Hillsville, 1975-78; grad. asst., supr., course advisor Coll. Edn., Va. Poly. Inst. and State U., Blacksburg, 1975-81, pregrad. interviewer placement svcs., 1981-83; music dir. Heritage Acad., Charlotte, N.C., 1984-85, fine arts specialist, 1985-86; choral dir. Chester County Schs., Chester, S.C., 1986—; fine arts chairperson Chester H.S., 1995-96, chmn.; guest condr. workshop Patrick County Schs., Stuart, Va., 1980; liaison for Chester County Schs. to S.C. Gov.'s Sch. for Arts, 1990-91. Soloist PTL TV Network, Charlotte, 1984-85. Guest spkr. on battered women and marital abuse to chs and workshops; entertainer; co-dir. Chester City Schs. Choral Festival; active Arts Coun. Chester County, 1988—, S.C. Arts Alliance and Arts Advocacy; mem. steering com. Chester H.S., 1995-96, fine arts chmn. 1995—. Named Tchr. of the Yr., Chester Sr. H.S., 1989, Chester County Schs., 1991, Educator of Yr., Chester County C. of C., 1992, Tchr. of the Week, The Herald, 1995. Mem. ASCD, AAUW (mem. bylaws com. Chester br. 1987—, sec. 1988-89, fine arts chmn. 1995—), Music Educators Nat. Conf., S.C. Music Educators Assn. (del. pub. rels. network Chester County Schs. 1991), S.C. Edn. Assn., Am. Ednl. Rsch. Assn., Am. Assn. Choral Dirs., Chester County Edn. Assn., Nat. Assn. Secondary Music Edn. (team evaluator divsn. tchr. edn. cert. 1989, 91—), State So. Assn. Schs. and Colls. (mem. evaluation team, mem. steering com.), All U.S.A. Chorus Student Group (alumni), Tri-M Music Honor Soc. (sponsor), 4-H Club (life), Phi Delta Kappa. Republican. Baptist. Home: 1122 Virginia Dare Dr Rock Hill SC 29730-9669

WISLER, DARLA LEE, pastor; b. Balt., May 14, 1940; d. Hugh Charles Douglas and Angela Rita (Poffel) Mayer; m. Norman Marvin Wisler, Dec. 26, 1960; children: David Paul, Diane Lynn. A in Biblical Studies, Christian Internat. U., 1982, BTh, 1984, MDiv, 1990, D in Ministry, 1993. Asst. pastor Anderson (S.C.) Christian Assembly, 1978-80; founder, sr. pastor Living Water Ch., Anderson, 1981—; chaplain Anderson County Sheriff's Dept., 1996; mid-week devotion min. Anderson Health Care Ctr., 1980—, pres. adv. bd. 1988—; dean Living Water Bible Coll., Anderson, 1982ú; prin. Living Water Christian Sch., Anderson, 1983-88; regular co-host Dove Broadcasting TV-16, Greenville, S.C., 1984—; coord. Christian Internat. Network of Chs. Mid-East Region, 1994-96. Author: Basic Christian Teaching Made Plain and Clear, 1994, Advanced Christian Teaching Made Plain and Clear, 1995. Pres. clergy staff exec. com. Anderson Area Med. Ctr., 1993-94; sec. Anderson County Sheriff's Dept. Chaplaincy, Anderson, 1996. Republican. Office: Living Water Ch PO Box 1823 Anderson SC 29622

WISLER, GARY CLIFTON, writer, educator; b. Oklahoma City; s. Charles Clifton and Frances Joan (Higgins) W. BFA, So. Meth. U., 1972, MA, 1974; postgrad.. U. Tex., Dallas, 1991, U. North Tex., 1993—. Cert. tchr. secondary edn., journalism, English, history, Tex. Tchr. Denton (Tex.) H.S. Denton Ind. Sch. Dist., 1972-73; tchr. Jackson Mid. Sch. Garland (Tex.) Ind. Sch. Dist., 1974-84; tchr. Boman Mid. Sch. Plano (Tex.) Ind. Sch. Dist., 1986-87; writer, lectr., 1985, 87—. Author: (novels) My Brother, the Wind, 1979, paperback edit., 1987, German transl., 1988, Swedish transl., 1988, A Cry of Angry Thunder, 1980, paperback edit., 1986, Winter of the Wolf, 1981, Danish transl., 1982, The Trident Brand, 1982, paperback edit., 1986, Sunrise, 1982, The Chicken Must Have Died Laughing, 1983, Thunder on the Tennessee, 1983 (Spur award 1984, Best Western Juvenile Book award 1983), A Special Gift, 1983, Buffalo Moon, 1984, The Raid, 1985, West of the Cimarron, 1985, The Antrian Messenger, 1986 (Children's Book of Yr. 1986, Children's Choice award 1987), Starr's Showdown, 1986, Spirit Warrior, 1986, High Plains Rider, 1986, Antelope Springs, 1986, paperback edit., 1987, Texas Brazos, 1987, Purgatory, 1987, Thompson's Mountain, 1987, Texas Brazos: Fortune Bend, 1987, Comanche Crossing, 1987, Abrego Canyon, 1987, The Wolf's Tooth, 1987 (Notable Children's Book 1987, Children's Book of Yr. 1988), Texas Brazos: Palo Pinto, 1987, Illinois

Prescott, 1987, This New Land, 1987, Comanche Summer, 1987, The Return of Caulfield Blake, 1987, paperback edit., 1989, Texas Brazos: Cddo Creek, 1988, The Wayward Trail, 1988, Avery's Law, 1988, Ross's Gap, 1988, South Pass Ambush, 1988, The Seer, 1989, Sweetwater Flats, 1989, Prescott's Trail, 1989, Lakota, 1989, paperback edit., 1990, Esmerelda, 1989, Among the Eagles, 1989 (Spur award 1990), Prescott's Law, 1990, Sam Delamer, 1990, Boswell's Luck, 1990, Piper's Ferry: A Novel of the Texas Revolution, 1990, Clear Fork, 1990, Prescott's Challenge, 1990, The Mind Trap, 1990, Pinto Lowery, 1991, North of Esperanza, 1991, Red Cap, 1991 (Notable Children's Book award 1991, Best Book for Young Adults 1991, Children's Book of Yr. award 1991), The Medicine Trail, 1991, Blood Mesa, 1991, Stone Wolf's Vision, 1991, Baron of the Brazos, 1992, The Buffalo Shield, 1992, Dreaming Wolf, 1992, The Wetherbys, 1993, Jericho's Journey, 1993, The Shawnee Trail, 1993, Warrior's Road, 1994, Mr. Lincoln's Drummer, 1995, Weeping Moon, 1995, Caleb's Choice, 1996; author (as Will McLennan) The Ramseys, 1989, Ramsey's Luck, 1989, Matt Ramsey, 1989; author (with others) The Western Writers Handbook, 1987; contbr. short stories to Boys' Life. Scoutmaster Boy Scouts Am., Dallas, asst. scoutmaster, assoc. advisor Order of Arrow; Webelos leader, Plano. Recipient Dist. Award of Merit, Boy Scouts Am., 1984, Scouter's Key award Boy Scouts Am., 1984, Silver Beaver award Boy Scouts Am., 1985, Founder's award Boy Scouts Am., 1990. Mem. Soc. Profl. Journalists, Western Writers Am., Authors Guild. Methodist. Home: 1812 Savage Dr Plano TX 75023-1835

WISSINGER, ROBERT ALAN, biomedical software engineer; b. Painesville, Ohio, Sept. 16, 1950; s. Robert Ralph and Opal (Hacker) W.; m. Barbara Ellen Paul, June 7, 1974; children: John Robert, Lisa Ann. BS in Pharmacy, U. Cin., 1974; MS in Biomed. Computer Sci., Ohio State U., 1978. Registered pharmacist, Calif., Ohio. Pharmacist, asst. mgr. Gray Drug Stores, Columbus, Ohio, 1975; pharmacist Riverside Meth. Hosp., Columbus, 1976; programmer analyst Ohio State U., Columbus, 1976-77; systems coordinator M.D. Anderson Hosp. and Tumor Inst., Houston, 1977-80; dir. pharmacy systems U. Calif. Med. Ctr., San Diego, 1980-86; engring. mgr. Emtek Health Care Systems, Tempe, Ariz., 1986-92; mgr. info. sys. strategy Wal-Mart, Bentonville, Ark., 1992-95; software devel. mgr. VIPS, Inc., Towson, Md., 1995—; cons. Meml. Sloan Kettering Cancer Ctr. Pharmacy, N.Y.C., 1985-86, VA Med. Ctr. Pharmacy, San Diego, 1984-86. Contbr. articles to profl. jours. Mem. Am. Soc. Hosp. Pharmacists (chmn. working group on computer systems 1980-81), ASTM (com. mem. 1982-86), Electron Computing Health Oriented Assn., Rho Chi. Republican. Home: 13410 Blythenia Rd Phoenix MD 21131 Office: VIPS Inc One West Pennsylvania Ave Towson MD 21204

WIST, ABUND OTTOKAR, biomedical engineer, radiation physicist, educator; b. Vienna, Austria, May 23, 1926; s. Engelbert Johannes and Augusta Barbara (Ungewitter) W.; m. Suzanne Gregson Smiley, Nov. 30, 1963; children: John Joseph, Abund Charles. BS in Engring., Tech U. Graz, 1947; MEd, U. Vienna, 1950, PhD in Theoretical Physics, 1951. Research and devel. engr. Hornyphon AG, Vienna, 1952-54, Siemens & Halske AG, Munich, Germany, 1954-58; dir. research and devel. Brinkman Instruments Co., Westbury, N.Y., 1958-64; sr. scientist Fisher Sci. Inc., Pitts., 1964-69; mem. faculty U. Pitts., 1970-73; asst. prof. computer sci. Va. Commonwealth U., 1973-76, asst. prof. biophysics, 1976-82, asst. prof. physiology and biophysics, 1982-84, asst. prof. radiology, 1984-92, adj. prof. radiology, 1992—; founder, gen. chmn. Symposium Computer Applications in Med. Care, Washington, 1977-79, chmn. Biomedical Optics Conf., Clin. Application of Modern Imaging Tech. I and II, L.A., 1993, 94; session chmn., lectr. European Radiology Conf., Vienna, 1993, Advanced Laser Dentistry Conf., St. Petersburg, Russia, 1994; session chmn., lectr. Biomedical Optics Europe Conf., Lille, France, 1994; invited speaker, session chmn., co-chmn. poster session Internat. Conf. Light and Biol. Systems, Wroclaw, Poland, 1995; lectr. and session chmn. BIOS Europe 95 Conf., Barcelona, Spain, 1995; lectr. 5th European Congresson Dental and Maxillofacial Radiology, Cologne, Germany, 1995; pres. Inntech, Inc., 1985—. Author: Electronic Design of Microprocessor Based Instrumentation and Control Systems, 1986; contbr. numerous articles and chpts. to profl. jours. and books; patentee in electronic and lab. instrumentation (10). NASA/Am. Soc. Engring. Edn. faculty fellow, summer 1975; U.S. biomed. engring. del. People's Republic China, 1987, 93, Russia, 1993; lectr. in field; bd. regents Liberty U., Lynchburg, Va., 1991—. Mem. AAAS, IEEE (sr., sec. cen. Va., vice chmn. Richmond sect.), ASTM, SPIE (editor proceedings, 1993, 94), Am. Chem. Soc., N.Y. Acad. Scis., Am. Coll. Radiology (assoc.), Richmond Computer Club (founder, pres. 1977-79), Biomed. Engring. Soc., Am. Assn. Physics in Medicine, Sigma Xi. Roman Catholic. Home: 9304 Farmington Dr Richmond VA 23229-5336 Office: Med Coll Va/VCA 1101 E Marshall St Richmond VA 23298-0072

WITCHER, ANN ELIZABETH, education educator; b. S.I., N.Y., Jan. 8, 1949; d. Lloyd Smith and Pauline Kundagunda (Kangiesser) Rolufs; m. J. Wayne Witcher, July 8, 1977; children: Julie McKay, Lisa Ann. BS in Edn., U. Kans., 1972; MEd, U. Ark., 1978, EdD, 1993; EdS, U. Ctrl. Ark., 1990. Cert. mid. sch. English, social studies tchr., spl. edn. tchr., curriculum specialist, elem. prin., spl. edn. supr., elem. tchr. 1-6, moderate/profound handicapped tchr. K-12. Early childhood specialist Carrollton (Tex.)-Farmers Br. Ind. Sch. Dist., 1973-74; spl. edn. tchr. Birdville Ind. Sch. Dist., Ft. Worth, 1974-75; dir., head tchr. Carroll County Learning Ctr., Berryville, Ark., 1975-80, dir., interprogram coord., 1980-86; instr., student tchr. supr. U. Ctrl. Ark., Conway, 1986-93, asst. prof. tchr. edn., 1993—; cons. Topeka Sch. Dist., 1991-92; mem. ednl. concerns adv. com. Ark. Gov.'s Conf. on Handicapped Individuals, Little Rock, 1976-77. Author: The Degree of Progressivism Among Arkansas Public School Superintendents, 1996; co-author: School Size, Phi Delta Kappa Hot Topics vol., 1996; contbr. articles to profl. publs., chpt. to book; presentations to profl. audiences. V.p. Ark. Assn. for Hearing Impaired Children, Little Rock, 1991-93. Recipient Outstanding Svc. to Developmentally Disabled award Ark. chpt. Am. Assn. for Mental Deficiency, 1980. Mem. Soc. Philosophy and History of Edn., So. Future Soc. (conf. coord. 1994, 95), Phi Delta Kappa (local sec. 1994-95), Kappa Delta Pi. Office: U Ctrl Ark UCA Box 4917 Conway AR 72035

WITCHER, ROBERT CAMPBELL, bishop; b. New Orleans, Oct. 5, 1926; s. Charles Swanson and Lily Sebastian (Campbell) W.; m. Elisabeth Alice Cole, June 4, 1957; 2 children. BA, Tulane U., 1949; MDiv, Seabury-Western Theol. Sem., 1952, DD, 1974; MA, La. State U., 1960, PhD, 1968; DCL (hon.), Nashotah House, 1989. Ordained priest Episc. Ch., 1953; consecrated bishop, 1975. Priest-in-charge St. Andrew Ch., Linton, La. and St. Patrick Ch., Zachary, La., 1953-56; priest-in-charge St. Augustine Ch., Baton Rouge, La., 1953-54; rector St. Augustine Ch., 1954-61; canon pastor Christ Ch. Cathedral, New Orleans, 1961-62; rector St. James Ch., Baton Rouge, 1962-75; coadjutor bishop L.I., 1975-77; bishop, 1977-91; prof. ch. history Mercer Sch. Theology, 1975-91; interim bishop of Armed Forces, 1989-90; bishop in residence Baton Rouge, New Orleans, 1991-92; pres. Mercer Scholarship Fund; trustee Ch. Pension Fund, 1991-92; pres. bd. trustees estate belonging to Diocese of L.I., 1975-91; pres. Anglican Soc. N.Am., 1980-83; chmn. pastoral com. House of Bishops, 1980-90, Com. to Revise Title III, 1980-90; chmn. Com. on Developing Guidelines for Theol. Edn.; cons. Episc. Health Fund L.I. Author: The Episcopal Church in Louisiana, 1801-1861. Trustee U. of South, 1963-69, Seabury-Western Theol. Sem., 1963-82, Gen. Theol. Sem., 1979-88, Ch. Pension Fund, 1985-91, Bch. Reins. Corp.; pres. Episc. Health Svcs.; bd. dirs. Nat. Coun. Alcoholism, L.I. Coun. Alcoholism, Alcohol and Drug Abuse Coun., Baton Rouge, St. Mary's Hosp. for Children, Baton Rouge Green, La. Urban Forestry Coun., United Way; bd. dirs., trustee St. James Place; active NCCJ (Baton Rouge chpt.). Capt. USNR, ret. Mem. N.Y. State Coun. Chs., L.I. Coun. Chs. (com. social justice), Am. Legion, Mil. Order of World Wars. Address: 1934 Steele Blvd Baton Rouge LA 70808-1673

WITENGIER, MARY JOAN MACGILVRAY, retired special education educator, physical therapist; b. Worcester, Mass., Mar. 26, 1915; d. George H. and Johanna V. (Crowley) MacGilvray; m. Andrew Alfred Witengier, May 7, 1943 (dec. 1981); children: Mariann, George, Jan, Vincent. BS, Boston U., 1938; MEd, U. Fla., 1966; postgrad., U. Cen. Fla., 1983. Cert. ednl. adminstr., Fla.; lic. phys. therapist. Phys. therapist Gillette State Hosp. for Crippled Children, St. Paul, 1938-40, U. Md. Hosp., Balt., 1940, Harry Anna Home for Crippled Children, Umatilla, Fla., 1940-43, 48-49, Orlando (Fla.) Gen. Hosp., 1943-44, Forrest Park Sch. for Disabled, Orlando, 1950-68; coord. exceptional edn. Sch. Bd. Seminole County, Sanford, Fla., 1968-82; phys. therapist Woodland Elem. Sch., Orlando, 1983, Magnolia Spl. Edn. Sch., Orlando, 1983-85, Lake Silver Elem. Sch., Orlando, 1985-87; with Orlando Hosp. South, 1991-92; with pediatric home health Olsten Health Care, 1993-95; grant writer for Magruder Environ. Playground for physically handicapped children, 1966; pvt. practice phys. therapy, 1989-91; tchr. spl. edn. U. Ctrl. Fla., Orlando, 1982-83; cons. U. Fla., Gainesville, 1983; judge Seminole Program English as 2d Lang., 1989, 91, 92. Guardian ad litem Voice of Abused Child in Ct., Seminole County, 1989—; bd. dirs. dist. 7 adv. coun. Dept. Human Svcs., Seminole County, 1980-82. Recipient numerous svc. awards. Mem. Coun. for Exceptional Children (treas. Fla. chpt. 1984—, divsn. career devel., surogate parent for Seminole and Orange County Exceptional Edn.), Toastmasters. Roman Catholic. Home: 3513 Mayflower Ln Apopka FL 32703-6039

WITHERELL, PETER CHARLES, regulatory entomologist; b. Athol, Mass., Sept. 23, 1943; s. Charles Emerson and Ruth Eva (Dodge) W.; m. Beatriz Alicia Plaza Gonzales, Nov. 9, 1981; children: Tina, Philamer, Melissa. BS, U. Mass., 1965; MS, U. Calif., Davis, 1970, PhD, 1973. Asst. area supr. Aedes aegypti mosquito eradication program USPHS, Fla., 1965-68; grad. rsch. asst. entomology U. Calif., Davis, 1969-72, postdoctoral rsch. entomologist, 1973-74; asst. dir. rsch. Dadant & Sons, Inc., Hamilton, Ill., 1975-76; grain insp. USDA, Balt., 1977-78; plant protection and quarantine officer USDA, Laredo, Tex., 1978-81; sta. supr. Miami Methods Devel. Sta., USDA, 1981-85; asst. dir. Methods Devel. Ctr., Hoboken, N.J., 1985-95; quarantine treatment specialist Oxford (N.C.) Plant Protection Ctr., USDA, Oxford, N.C., 1995—; insp., tester agrl. quarantine treatment facilities. Contbr. articles to profl. jours. and tech. manuals. Mem. Entomol. Soc. Am., Orgn. Profl. Employees Dept. Agriculture, Sigma Xi. Home: 1714 Cole Mill Rd Durham NC 27712-9999 Office: USDA Oxford Plant Prot Ctr APHIS, PPQ 901 Hillsboro St Oxford NC 27565

WITHEROW, JIMMIE DAVID, secondary school educator; b. Dalton, Ga., Nov. 13, 1961; s. Jimmie W. and Jimmie Lou (Nixon) W. BA in English, Emory U., 1983; MEd in Secondary Edn., Ga. State U., 1989. Cert. English tchr., Ga. Tchr. SE Whitfield High Sch., Whitfield County Bd. Edn., Dalton, 1983-92, Murray County High Sch., Chatsworth, Ga., 1992—. Contbr. article to profl. jour. Mem. NEA, Nat. Coun. Tchrs. English, Ga. Edn. Assn., Ga. Coun. Tchrs. English, Kappa Delta Pi. Home: PO Box 891 Chatsworth GA 30705-0891

WITHEROW, WILLIAM KENNETH, physicist; b. Patuxent, Md., Jan. 12, 1954; s. William W. and Gail E. (Woodle) W.; m. Kathryn C. Price, June 25, 1977; children: Wendy L., William J. BS, U. Tenn., 1977; MS, U. Ala., Huntsville, 1981. Physicist NASA/Marshall Space Flight Ctr., Huntsville, 1973—; mem. SPIE Working Group on Holography. Named Inventor of Yr., NASA, 1990. Mem. Internat. Soc. Optical Engring., Optical Soc. Am., Huntsville Electro-Optical Soc. Office: NASA/MSFC ES76 SSL Bldg 4481 Huntsville AL 35812

WITHERS, DONALD CHRIS, university administrator; b. Binghamton, N.Y., May 1; m. Susan S. Fox; children: Christopher Todd, Wendy Bovaird, Timothy Tait. BA in Econs., Alfred U., 1963, MS in Edn., 1970. With mktg. divsn. Arco, Lake Placid, N.Y., 1963-66; dir. alumni programs Alfred U., 1966-70; dir. ann. giving, assoc. dir. devel., dir. corp. rels. U. Richmond, 1970-73, campaign dir., 1973-79, campaign dir. U. Cornerstones for the Future, 1982-86, assoc. v.p., 1980—; cons. in field. Contbr. articles to profl. jours. Mem. Com. for South Richmond Young Life, 1989-95; bd. dirs. Needles Eye Ministries, Inc., 1992-96; SME chair Boy Scouts Am., 1986; com. chair Cub Scouts of Am., 1983-86; sec. Richmond Met. Aquatic League, 1983-84; pres. Bon Air Community Assn., 1979, trustee 1988—, long range planning com., 1990; bus. area chmn. United Givers Fund, 1976; pres. Crestwood Farms Resident's Assn., 1974-76; v.p. Richmond Wine Soc., 1974-75; vice chmn. Alfred Station Community Chest, 1969. Mem. Am. Alumni Coun., Am. Coll. Pub. Rels. Assn., The Fund Raising Inst., Nat. Soc. of Fund Raising Execs., Va. Assn. of Fund Raising Execs. (pres. 1987-88), Kennedy Sinclair Course of Planned Giving, Coun. for Advancement and Support of Edn. (chair ann. assembly, trustee mgmt. 1985-87, chair profl. area trustee, 1986-87, fin. com. nat. bd. 1983-87, chair career devel, mem. svcs. com. 1985-86, dist. III bd. dirs. 1983-85, chair dist. III 1983-85, others), Omicron Delta Kappa. Office: U Richmond Office Devel Richmond VA 23173

WITHERSPOON, WALTER PENNINGTON, JR., orthodontist, philanthropist; b. Columbia, S.C., Sept. 3, 1938; s. Walter P. and Florence Evelyn (Jones) W.; m. Joyce Ann Smith, Sept. 6, 1970; 1 child, Annie Melissa. BS, U. S.C., 1960; DDS, U. N.C., 1964, MSO, 1969. Bd. qualified Am. Bd. Orthodontics. Pvt. practice in orthodontics, Columbia, 1969—; med. staff Bapt. Med. Ctr., Columbia, 1970—, Lexington County Hosp., West Columbia, 1974—. Hóst Nite Line, Dove Broadcasting Co. Adv. bd. 1st Palmetto Bank and Trust, West Columbia, 1982; mem. adv. bd. First Citizens Bank; candidate S.C. Ho. Reps., 1994; del. S.C. Rep. Com., 1989-96; mem. platform com. S.C. Rep. Party Conv., poll com., 1992; del. Rep. Nat. Conv., Houston, 1992; Rep. nat. committeeman, 1996—; bd. dirs. Southeastern Coll. Assemblies of God, Lakeland, Fla., 1984, Brookland Plantation Home for Boys, Orangeburg, S.C.; pres. Friends of Irmo Libr.; bd. dirs. Irmo-St. Andrew's Coalition of Neighborhood Home Owners' Assns.; chmn. Lexington County Rep. Party; commr. Richland/Lexington Counties Commn. for Tech. Edn., S.C. Commn. on Alcohol and Drug Abuse; bd. dirs. Centerplace for Homeless; active Campbell for Gov., Presdl. Visit-Ticket Com.; amb. Irmo C. of C. Lt. USN, 1964-66. Recipient Century Mem. award Boy Scouts Am., 1984. Mem. ADA, Greater Columbia Dental Assn. (pres. 1975-76), U. N.C. Dental Alumni Assn. (bd. dirs.), S.C. Dental Assn. (ho. of dels. 1971-73, 1991-96, legis. com. 1993), S.C. Orthodontic Assn., Cntrl. Dist. Rep., Am. Assn. Orthodontists, Sertoma (pres. 1975-76), Am. Legion., So. Assn. Orthodontists, Cen. Dist. Dental Soc., Alston Wilkes Soc. (bd. dirs.). Home: 250 Lancer Dr Columbia SC 29212-1216 Office: 205 Med Cir W Columbia SC 29169

WITHERSPOON, W(ILLIAM) TOM, engineering consultant; b. Dallas, Feb. 1, 1949; s. Vernon H. and Mary Witherspoon; m. Sandra Stein, July 10, 1970; children: Mary Jac, Stephen. BSCE, So. Meth. U., 1971; MS in Mgmt. and Adminstrv. Sci., U. Tex., Dallas, 1979. Registered profl. engr., Tex. Field engr. Robert E. McKee Constrn., 1972-73; supt. Batson Cook County, 1973-77; project mgr. Rucker Constrn. Co., 1977-81; v.p. Wynn Oil Co., 1981-85; pres. Sandco Petroleum Corp., 1985; pres. S & W Found. Contractors, Richardson, Tex., 1986—, pres., soil dr., 1992—; speaker in field. Contbr. articles to profl. jours.; patentee in field. Deacon Ch. of Christ. Recipient Gold medal Masters Pan Am. Championship; named 5-time Tex. State Weightlifting Champion. Mem. ASCE, Am. Soc. Petroleum Engrs., Am. Soc. Petroleum Geologists, Tex. Found. Repair Soc. (v.p.), North Tex. Weightlifting Assn. (pres.), Internat. Assn. Found. Drillers (bd. dirs.). Office: 1030 E Belt Line Rd Richardson TX 75081-3703

WITHEY, PAUL ANDREW, physics educator; b. Calgary, Alta., Can., Apr. 23, 1966; came to U.S., 1988; s. Alfred John and Jeanette May (Mackenzie) W.; m. Jennifer Lynn Way, May 23, 1992. BSc in Physics and Astrophysics, U. Calgary, 1988; PhD in Physics, Tex. Christian U., 1993. Obs. colleague Calgary Centennial Planetarium, 1985; rsch. assoc. U. Calgary, 1986; constrn. worker Landmark Truss, Cochrane, Alta., 1987; Green doctoral fellow Tex. Christian U., Ft. Worth, 1988-89, grad. teaching asst., 1989-93, Barnett fellow, Welch postdoctoral fellow, 1993; asst. prof. physics W.Va. Wesleyan Coll., Buckhannon, 1993—. Contbr. articles to profl. jours. Mem. Am. Phys. Soc., Sigma Xi. Office: WVa Wesleyan Coll PO Box 67 Buckhannon WV 26201-0067

WITHROW, DOLLY MAE, English language educator; b. Charleston, W.Va., Sept. 14, 1931; d. Don Paul Wood and Esther Marie (Frame) Cassinet; m. Howard W. Withrow, July 18, 1955; children: Jeffrey Paul, Risa Lynn. BA in English, W.Va. State Coll., 1976; MA in English, Marshall U., 1979. Grad. asst. instr. Marshall U.; prof. dept. English W.Va. State Coll., 1979-94; pres. Writing Svcs., Inc.; speaker, workshop leader in field. Author: From the Grove to the Stars, 1991. Mem. W.Va. Coun. Coll. English Tchrs., W.Va. Writers (charter). Home: 94 Willow Way Kenna WV 25248

WITHROW, LUCILLE MONNOT, nursing home administrator; b. Alliance, Ohio, July 28, 1923; d. Charles Edward Monnot and Freda Aldine (Guy) Monnot Cameron; m. Alvin Robert Withrow, June 6, 1945 (dec. 1984); children: Cindi Withrow Johnson, Nancy Withrow Townley, Sharon Withrow Hodgkins, Wendel Alvin. AA in Health Adminstrn., Eastfield Coll., 1976. Lic. nursing home adminstr., Tex.; cert. nursing home ombudsman. Held various clerical positions Dallas, 1950-72; office mgr., asst. adminstr. Christian Care Ctr. Nursing Home, Mesquite, Tex., 1972-76; head adminstr. Christian Care Ctr. Nursing Home and Retirement Complex, Mesquite, 1976-91; nursing home ombudsman Tex. Dept. Aging and Tex. Dept. Health, Dallas, 1991-93; legal asst. Law Offices of Wendel A. Withrow, Carrollton, Tex., 1993—; mem. con. on geriatric curriculum devel. Eastfield Coll., Mesquite, 1979, 87; mem. ombudsman adv. com. Sr. Citizens Greater Dallas; nursing home cons.; notary pub., 1995—. Vol. Dallas Arboretum and Bot. Soc., Dallas Summer Musicals Guild; mem. Ombudsman adv. com. Sr. Citizens of Greater Dallas, Health Svcs. Speakers Bur.; charter mem. Stage Show Prodns. Recipient Volunteerism awards Tex. Atty. Gen., 1987, Tex. Gov., 1992. Mem. Tex. Assn. Homes for Aging, Am. Assn. Homes for Aging, Health Svcs. Speakers Bur., White Rock Kiwanis. Republican. Mem. Ch. of Christ. Home: 11344 Lippitt Ave Dallas TX 75218-1922 Office: Law Office of W A Withrow 1120 Metrocrest Dr Ste 200 Carrollton TX 75006-5787

WITORSCH, RAPHAEL JAY, physiologist, educator; b. N.Y.C., Dec. 12, 1941; s. Benjamin and Sarah (Etkin) W.; m. Barbara Diane Margolis, Dec. 26, 1964; children: Benjamin A., Marc L. AB, NYU, 1963; MS, Yale U., 1965, PhD, 1968. Postdoctoral fellow U. Va., Charlottesville, 1968-70; asst. prof., assoc. prof. physiology Med. Coll. Va., Richmond, 1970-88, prof. physiology, 1988—; cons. Richmond, 1984—. Co-author: Review of Endocrinology and Reproduction, 1988; editor: Reproductive Toxicology, 2d edit., 1995; mem. editorial bd. The Prostate, Toxic Substances Mechanisms Jour. Grantee Nat. Cancer Inst., 1975-85, SOVRAN Trust, 1989-91, Pfeiffer Found., 1991-92, Nations Bank, 1996-97. Mem. AAAS, Am. Physiol. Soc., Endocrine Soc., Soc. Exptl. Biology and Medicine, Soc. of Toxicology. Office: Va Commonwealth U Med Coll Va Box 980551 Richmond VA 23298-0551

WITT, JUDITH ANNE, elementary education educator; b. Danville, Ill., Mar. 8, 1949; d. Dale Norman and Ruby Lou (Stonecipher) Shideler; m. Robert Witt, Feb. 24, 1970; children: Eric, Sean, Ryan. BA, U. Ariz., 1971; MA, U.S. Internat. U., San Diego, 1990; EdS, Point Loma Nazarene Coll., 1993. Tchr. Ovid-Elsie (Mich.) Schs., 1971-73; tchr., coord. gifted and talented edn. Poway (Calif.) Unified Sch. Dist., 1987-91; tchr., dist. gifted and talented coord. Ramona (Calif.) Unified Sch. Dist., 1991-95; dist. GATE coord. Castro Valley (Calif.) Unified Sch. Dist., 1995—; presenter local sch. and dist. insvc. days, state and nat. confs.; Calif. mentor tchr. learning styles. Active community orgns. Mem. ASCD, Calif. Assn. for Gifted (regional bd. rep.), Phi Delta Kappa (newsletter editor, exec. bd.).

WITT, WALTER FRANCIS, JR., lawyer; b. Richmond, Va., Feb. 18, 1933; s. Walter Francis and Evelyn Virginia (Riggleman) W.; m. Rosemary Winter, Sept. 5, 1964; children: Leslie Anne, Walter Francis III. BS, U. Richmond, 1954, JD, 1966. Bar: Va. 1966, D.C. 1974. Assoc. Hunton and Williams, Richmond, 1966-74, ptnr., 1974—. Contbr. articles to profl. jours. 1st lt. U.S. Army, 1955-57. Mem. ABA (chmn. real property com. sect. gen. practice 1995—, dep. chair urban, state and local govt. com. 1995—, sect. gen. practice), Va. Bar Assn., Richmond Bar Assn., D.C. Bar Assn., Phi Beta Kappa, Phi Delta Phi. Home: 8901 Tresco Rd Richmond VA 23229-7725 Office: Hunton & Williams Riverfront Plaza East Twr 951 E Byrd St Richmond VA 23219-4040

WITTE, MICHAEL MYRON, molecular biologist, educator; b. Richmond, Ind., Dec. 10, 1960; s. Richard Henry and Rita Catherine (Wessel) W. BS, Purdue U., 1983; PhD, U. Ky., 1990. Postdoctoral rsch. asst. dept. pathology U. Tenn., Memphis, 1990-91, instr. pathology dept. pathology, 1991-94, asst. prof. dept. pathology, 1994—; cons. Shelby County Med. Examiners Office, Memphis, 1993—. Contbr. articles to profl. jours. Vol. Memphis in May, 1995—. Mem. AAAS, Am. Soc. Biochemistry and Molecular Biology. Democrat. Roman Catholic. Office: Univ Tenn Dept Pathology 800 Madison Ave Memphis TN 38103-3400

WITTENSTEIN, MICHAEL DAVID, management consultant; b. Orlando, Fla., Dec. 29, 1958; s. Sheldon and Patsy Ruth (Printz) W. BA with honors, U. Fla., 1980; M in Internat. Mgmt., Am. Grad. Sch. Internat. Mgmt., Glendale, Ariz., 1985. Market analyst Cushman & Wakefield, Atlanta, 1986-87; info. syss. cons. Wittenstein & Assocs., Atlanta, 1987-90; CEO/co-pres./dir. mktg. strategies Galileo Inc., Atlanta, Ga., 1991—; CEO SupportWare, software pubs., 1991-92; cons. Apple Computer, Inc., The Nutrasweet Co., Xerox; speaker on implication of photo CD in digital imaging; speaker kiosks in mktg. and advt., media/options in N.Y.C., Ga. Tech., others; developer interactive media software AT&T, Apple, IBM, Turner Broadcasting, Bell South, Dept. Edn., DCA, others. Author: Managing Change: A Guide to Automation, (software) Business Presentation on PC, 1989, Help Service for PC, 1990, What Can Multimedia Do for Your Company?, Principles of Knowledge Navigation; developer: (interactive products) Talking Business Card, Laptop Sales System; contbr. articles to profl. jours. Cons. ARC, The Ga. Shakespeare Festival, Atlanta, 1990—, Jewish Family Svcs., Atlanta, 1988—, Chabad of Cobb. Mem. Internat. Interactive Comm. Assn., Bus. and Tech. Alliance, Southeastern Software Assn., Am. Mktg. Assn., Phi Beta Kappa, Omicron Delta Kappa. Office: Galileo Inc Ste 200 6055 Barfield Rd Atlanta GA 30328

WITTY, JOHN BARBER, health care executive; b. Vicksburg, Miss., Mar. 26, 1946; s. Neomah Wilks and Jennie (Barber) W.; m. Susan Deemer, June 26, 1976; children: Justin Michael, Adam David. BA, Miss. State U., 1968; MEd, U. Md., 1972, EdD, 1989. Cert. prin. regular edn. and spl. edn., curriculum coord. spl. edn., tch. spl. edn. K-12, Md. Tchr. Anne Arundel County Pub. Schs., Annapolis, Md., 1972-77; specialist in community affairs Anne Arundel County Pub. Schs., Annapolis, 1977-78, sch. based adminstr., 1978-79, county based adminstr., 1979-87; dir. svcs. devel. Am. Internat. Health Rehab. Svcs., Annapolis, 1987-88, dir. tng. & devel., 1988-89, dir. cost containment svcs., 1989-90, v.p. svcs., 1990-91; chief oper. officer AIIA/Comp Care, Daytona Beach, Fla., 1991-94; pres. Med. Advantage, Orlando, Fla., 1994—; bd. dirs. Anne Arundel County Sheltered Workshop, Glen Burnie, Md., 1987-89. Pres. Rolling Knolls Community Assn., Annapolis, 1980s, Gen.'s Hwy. Coun., Annapolis, 1980s; chmn. Anne Arundel County Stormwater Mgmt. Commn., 1984-85; mem. human rights com. Providence Ctr., 1984-85; pres. Oceantime Condominium Assn., Ocean City, Md., 1984-89, Huntington Community Assn., 1990—. With USN, 1969-72. Recipient Jaycee of Month award, 1975, C. William Brownfield award Annapolis Md. Jaycees, 1975, Jaycee Award of Svc., 1976, Md. State Jaycee award, 1975, 77, Jaycee of Month, 1977, Harold Reece award, 1977. Mem. Rotary, Annapolis Jaycees (v.p., bd. dirs.), Phi Delta Kappa, Kappa Delta Pi, Phi Mu Alpha Sinfonia. Republican. Presbyterian. Home: 2345 Westminster Ter Oviedo FL 32765-7554 Office: Med Advantage 3452 Lake Lynda Dr Ste 250 Orlando FL 32817-1481

WITTY, ROBERT WILKES, insurance services company executive; b. Vicksburg, Miss., Apr. 20, 1941; s. N.W. and Jennie (Barber) W.; m. Sally Van Tilborg, Jan 26, 1964; children: Deborah, Theresa, Robin. BBA, U. Miss., 1964; LLB, LaSalle U., 1968; postgrad., Ga. State U., 1981. With Crawford & Co., 1964-85; adjuster Lima, Ohio, 1964-66, Findlay, Ohio, 1966-68; sr. adjuster N.Y.C., 1969-72; supr. br. New Orleans, 1972-76; asst. field supr. home address Atlanta, 1976-78, asst. v.p., 1978-80, v.p., 1980-81; regional v.p., regional ops. mgr. Northeast region, Montvale, N.J., 1981-85; pres., COO Am. Internat. Adjustment Co. (subs. A.I.G.), 1985-90; pres., CEO Am. Internat. Health & Rehab. C. (subs. AIAC), 1986-90, also bd. dirs.; pres., CEO Gates McDonald & Co. (subs. Nationwide Ins. Group), Columbus, Ohio, 1991-93; exec. v.p. strategic devel. The Thomas Howell Group (Americas) Inc., 1994-95, divsn. pres. risk mgmt. svcs., 1995-96, also bd. dirs., exec. bd. mem., 1995; S.E. region v.p. GAB Robins, Atlanta, 1995—; bd. dirs. Am. Internat. Adjustment Co., Am. Internat. recoveries, Inc.; bd. trustees Kessler Rehab. Inst., 1989-90; v.p. Lindsey & Newsom Claims Mgmt., Inc., 1990, N.Am. Health & Rehab. Svcs., 1990. Recipient Outstanding Contbn. award East Orange City Council, 1987, Support award East Orange Womens Club, 1987. Mem. Atlanta Claims Assn., Profl. Ins. Agts. of N.Y., Profl. Inst. Agts. of Northeast, Loss Exec. Coun., Risk Ins. Mgmt. Soc., Inc., Atlanta Athletic Club. Presbyterian. Home: 4735 Cambridge Trace Dunwoody GA 30338-5252 Office: 4360 Chamblee Dunwoody Rd Atlanta GA 30341

WITZEL, BARBARA BINION, elementary education educator; b. Lawrence County, Ohio, June 5, 1940; d. Lee and Mary B. (Bradley) Binion; m. Leland G. Witzel, June 23, 1963; 1 child, Katrinna Lee. BS, Rio Grande (Ohio) Coll., 1966; postgrad., U. N.C., Charlotte, U. N.C., Charlotte, 1987-90. Cert. elem. tchr. Tchr. kindergarten Alliance (Ohio) Pub. Schs., 1960-74; elem. tchr. Charlotte-Mecklenburg Pub. Schs., 1976—; rep. Sch. Improvement and Accountability Act, 1990-92. Grantee NEH Inst., 1987-90; career level II mentor for beginning tchrs., 1991-92. Mem. NEA (rep., student tchr. supr. 1993), Ohio Edn. Assn. (life), N.C. Assn. Educators, Charlotte-Mecklenburg Assn. Educators (bd. dirs.). Home: 6034 Brookhaven Rd Charlotte NC 28210-3814 Office: Windsor Park Sch 3900 Sudbury Rd Charlotte NC 28205-4543

WIZNER, LINDA JEAN, communications executive; b. Cleve., Jan. 29, 1956; d. Norman John and Marjory Berniece (Malle) W. BA cum laude, Hiram (Ohio) Coll., 1978. Graphic artist Charlotte Shopping Guide, Punta Gorda, Fla., 1977-81; prodn. mgr. Sunbelt Newspapers, Ocala, Fla., 1981; product designer Sunbelt Newspapers, Naples, Fla., 1981-84; staff writer Sunbelt Newspapers, Bonita Springs, Fla., 1984-85; mng. editor Gulf Coast Weeklies, Ft. Myers, Fla., 1985-88, exec. editor, 1989; contract tech. writer GTE, No. Telecom, Tampa, Fla., Raleigh, N.C., 1990; contract media/cons. liaison Advantis, Tampa, 1991-94, mgr. media and cons. rels., 1994—. Mem., founder North Ft. Myers Ad Hoc Com., 1986-89; mem. pub. rels. com. S.W. Fla. coun. Boy Scouts Am., Ft. Myers, 1987-89, active Caloosa Dist. coun., Cape Coral, 1987-89; bd. dirs., sec. New Life Dwelling Pl., 1991-95; bd. dirs. Child Abuse Coun., Inc. Recipient Community Awareness award Kid Save, Ft. Myers, 1989, Community Svc. award Rotary, Bonita Springs, 1984, Fifth Fla., 1988. Mem. Pub. Rels. Soc. Am. (Tampa chpt. ambassador com. 1993). Democrat. Office: Advantis Martin Luther King Jr Blvd 3101 W Dr Tampa FL 33607

WLEZIEN, CHRISTOPHER BRIAN, political science educator; b. Oak Lawn, Ill., Apr. 25, 1961; s. Norbert Mathew and Marcia Joan (Nowak) W.; m. Cristina Maria Adams, Oct. 23, 1993. BA, St. Xavier Coll., Chgo., 1984; PhD, U. Iowa, 1989. Rsch. fellow U. Iowa, Iowa City, 1984-88, dir. polit. studies Iowa Social Sci. Inst., 1988-89; asst. prof. polit. sci. U. Houston, 1989-95, assoc. prof., 1995—. Mem. editorial bd. Social Sci. Quar., 1994—; contbr. articles to profl. jours. Polit. commentator, 1988—. Dirksen Congl. Ctr. grantee, 1988-89, 89-90; NSF grantee, 1993-94, 94-95. Mem. Am. Polit. Sci. Assn., Internat. Polit. Sci. Assn., S.W. Polit. Sci. Assn. (Best Paper award 1994), So. Polit. Sci. Assn., Midwest Polit. Sci. Assn., Western Polit. Sci. Assn. Office: U Houston Dept Polit Sci Houston TX 77204-3474

WNEK, JANUSZ, artificial intelligence research scientist; b. Stary Sacz, Poland, July 15, 1960; came to U.S., 1988; s. Marian and maria (Obrzud) W.; m. Agnieszka Magdalena Gawin, Apr. 26, 1991; children: Patricia marianna, Paul Christopher, Matthew John. MS in Computer Sci., Jagiellonian U., Cracow, Poland, 1983; PhD in Info. Tech., George Mason U., 1993. Software engr. Cracow Factory of Measurement Devices (KFAP), 1983-88; consulting engr. dept. radioastronomy and cosmic physics Jagiellonian U., 1983-88; chief designer Elcomp Microcomputer Software Ltd., 1987-88; system mgr. Ctr. for Artificial Intelligence, George Mason U., Fairfax, Va., 1989-92, grad. rsch. asst., 1989-93, NSF postdoctoral rsch. assoc., asst. dir. for rsch. mgmt., 1993-95; co-chair Internat. Workshop on Intelligent Adaptive Systems IAS-95, 3d Internat. Workshop on Multistrategy learning, 1996, others. Contbr. articles to profl. jours. Recipient Spl. award KFAP, Poland, 1987, 88; travel grant Internat. Joint Conf. on Artificial Intelligence, Australia, 1991, Kosciuszko Found., Australia, 1991, Scotland and Austria, 1992, Office of Naval Rsch., Scotland, 1992; postdoctoral rsch. award NSF, 1993—. Mem. Am. Assn. for Artificial Intelligence, Assn. for Computing Machinery. Home: 20 Amarillo Ct Germantown MD 20874-6100 Office: George Mason Univ 4400 University Dr Fairfax VA 22030-4443

WNUK, WADE JOSEPH, manufacturing and service company executive; b. St. Louis, Sept. 2, 1944; s. Edward Joseph and Helen Evelyn (Millick) W.; m. Judith Kay Yohe, May 3, 1969; children: Russell Nicholas, Wade Gregory. BS in Math. magna cum laude, St. Louis U., 1966; MS in Engring. Sci., Calif. Inst. Tech., 1966-67; MBA, Harvard U., 1974. Govt. research analyst, Washington, 1967-69; planner FMC Corp., Chgo., 1974-75, mgr. bus. devel. petroleum equipment div., Houston, 1975-77, group planning mgr., petroleum equipment group, 1977-78, ops. mgr. FMC Petroleum Equipment S.E. Asia, 1978-80, subsea mgr. FMC Wellhead Equipment div., Houston, 1980-81; dir. corp. devel. Marathon Mfg. Corp., Houston, 1981-82, v.p. corp. devel., 1982-84; exec. v.p. Marathon Power Tech., Houston, 1984-86; v.p., regional gen. mgr. TDW, Inc., Tulsa, 1986-90, sr. v.p., Tulsa and Singapore, 1990-94; pres. Norriseal, Houston, 1995—. Served with U.S. Army, 1969-72. Mem. Internat. Bus. Club (past v.p.), Am. Mgmt. Assn., Assn. for Corp. Growth, The Planning Forum, St. Louis U. Alumni Assn., Calif. Inst. Tech. Alumni Assn., Harvard Alumni Assns., Harvard Club (Houston). Office: Norriseal PO Box 40525 Houston TX 77240-0525

WOBBLETON, JUDY KAREN, artist, educator; b. Williamston, N.C., Aug. 31, 1947; d. Lloyd Thomas and Lillian Edith (Hudson) Letchworth; m. Albert Virgil Wobbleton Jr., Apr. 7, 1968; children: Olivia Elizabeth, Virgil Alan. Clk. Beaufort County Hosp., Washington, N.C., 1965-68; ins. supr. Mercy Hosp., Sacramento, 1968-72; adminstrv. asst. hosp. svcs. Fairbanks (Alaska) Meml. Hosp., 1972-75; basketry artist Williamston, 1983—; instr. basketry N.C. Basketmakers, 1984-94, Wayne C.C., Goldsboro, N.C., 1986-91, Wayne County Arts Coun., Goldsboro, 1990-91; co-founder N.C. Basketmakers, 1984. Contbg. artist: The Basket Book, 1988, Basketmaker's Baskets, 1990, Craft Works in The Home, 1990. Troop leader Girl Scouts U.S., Goldsboro, 1983-88, svc. unit mgr., 1987-91; active Roanoke Arts & Crafts Guild, 1991-96. Recipient 2d Pl. award Wilson Arts Coun., 1987, 3d Pl. award Martin County Arts Coun., 1992. Mem. N.C. Basketmakers Assn. (hon., co-founder 1984, bd. dirs. 1984-94, membership chmn. 1984-87, pres. 1990-94, conv. rev. com. 1994-96), Goldweavers Basketry Guild (hon.). Home and Office: Baskets By Judy 1325 Oakview Rd Williamston NC 27892

WOEHLER, THOMAS RICHARD, allergist, immunologist; b. Evansville, Ind., Feb. 20, 1939. MD, Ind. U. Sch. Medicine, 1964. Diplomate Am. Bd. Allergy and Immunology, Am. Bd. Immunology. Intern Ind. U. Med. Ctr., 1964-65, resident in immunology, 1965-66, 69-70; fellow in allergy and clin. immunology VA Hosp., U. Pitts., 1970-71; staff mem. Meml. City Med. Ctr. Hosp., Houston; clin. instr. medicine Baylor Coll.; pvt. practice. Mem. AMA, Am. Acad. Allergy and Immunology, Am. Coll. Allergy and Immunology, Am. Thoracic Soc. Office: 909 Frostwood Dr Ste 135 Houston TX 77024-2301*

WOHLFORD, JAMES GREGORY, pharmacist; b. Virginia, Minn., Nov. 4, 1956; s. James Hoover and Jeanne Katherine (Imgrund) W. AA, Indian River C.C., Ft. Pierce, Fla., 1977; BS in Pharmacy, U. Fla., 1981; MBA, Fla. Inst. Tech., 1987; PhD in Pharmacy, Southeastern U. Health Sci., 1994. Registered pharmacist, Fla., Ala. Rsch. asst. U. Fla., Gainesville, 1979-81; pharmacist Lawnwood Med. Ctr., Ft. Pierce, 1981—. Mem. Fla. Soc. Hosp. Pharmacists, Am. Soc. Hosp. Pharmacists. Roman Catholic. Home: 4250 N A 1 A Apt 904 Fort Pierce FL 34949-8340 Office: Lawnwood Regional Med Ctr PO Box 188 Fort Pierce FL 34954-0188

WOJCIECHOWSKI, FRANK ANDREW, urologist; b. Nanticoke, Pa., Mar. 16, 1939; s. Andrew and Anna (Jaskowiak) W.; m. Dolores Zaziarski, July 20, 1963 (div. 1985); children: Christopher, Lisa Marie. BA with honors, Rutgers U., 1971; DO, Coll. Osteo. Medicine & Surg., Des Moines, 1975. Diplomate Am. Bd. Urology, Am. Osteo. Bd. Urol. Surgery; lic. physician, Pa., Ga., Ala. Intern Meml. Osteopathic Hosp., York, Pa., 1975-76; commd. capt. USAF, 1976—, advanced through grades to lt. col., 1988—; chief of flight medicine Andersen AFB, Guam; resident in urology Wilford Hall Med. Ctr., Lackland AFB, Tex., 1980-85; chief urology svc. 71st Tac Hosp., Homestead, Fla., 1985-88, Wiesbaden Regional Med. Ctr., Germany, 1988-91, Wright Patterson Med. Ctr., Dayton, Ohio, 1991-92; ret. USAF, 1992; urologist Clark-Holder Clinic, LaGrange, Ga., 1992—; cons. in field. Decorated Nat. Def. medal, Air Force Meritorious Service medal. Mem. Am. Coll. Osteopathic Surgeons, Soc. of Air Force Clin. Surgeons, Soc. of Govt. Svc. Urologists, Assn. of Mil. Osteopathic Surgeons, Am. Osteopathic Assn., Am. Urology Assn. Roman Catholic.

WOJCIK, CASS, decorative supply company executive, former city official; b. Rochester, N.Y., Dec. 3, 1920; s. Emil M. and Casimira C. (Krawiecz) W.; student Lawrence Inst. Tech., 1941-43, Yale U., 1943-44, U.S. Sch. for European Personnel, Czechoslovakia, 1945; m. Lilliam Leocadia Lendzion, Sept. 25, 1948; 1 child, Robert Cass. Owner, Nat. Florists Supply Co., Detroit, 1948-88, Nat. Decorative, Detroit, 1950-89; co-owner Creation Ctr., Detroit, 1955-60; cons.-contractor hort.-bot. design auto show displays, TV prodrs., designers and decorators. Mem. Regional Planning and Evaluation Coun., 1969-75; city-wide mem. Detroit Bd. Edn., 1970-75; commr. Detroit Public Schs. Employees Retirement Commn., until 1975; mem. Area Occupl. Ednl. Commn., Ednl. Task Force; chmn., grand marshal Ann. Gen. Pulaski Day Parade, Detroit, 1970, 71; mem. Friends of Belle Isle; mem. Nat. Arboretum Adv. Coun., U.S. Dept. Agr., 1982-83; mem. pastoral coun. Archidiocese of Detroit, 1983-86, 88-92; v.p. rsch. Barna Coll., Ft. Lauderdale, Fla., 1989-94; vice chmn. 13th Congl. Dist. Rep. Party Mich., 1987-91; elected to 1988 electoral coll. With U.S. Army, 1944-46. Decorated Bronze Star; recipient citation Polish-Am. Congress, 1971, Art in Park 3d prize City of Oakland Park, Fla. Mem. S.E. Mich. Coun. Govts., Mich., Nat. sch. bd. assns., Big Cities Sch. Bd. Com., Nat. Coun. Great Cities Schs., Mcpl. Fin. Officers Assn. U.S., Nat. Coun. Tchr. Retirement, Ctrl. Citizens Com. Detroit, Internat. Platform Assn., Mich. Heritage Coun., Nat. Geog. Soc., Polish Century Club. Home: 1729 SW 14th Ct Fort Lauderdale FL 33312-4109

WOLD, DONALD CLARENCE, physicist; b. Fargo, N.D., Sept. 24, 1933; s. Clarence Leonard and Emma Mae (Saunders) W.; m. Shelley Anne Thurman, June 11, 1956; children—Sara, Steven, Sheila. B.A. in Physics, U. Wis., 1955, M.A. in Physics, 1957; Ph.D. in Physics, Ind. U., 1968. Lectr. physics and head physics dept. Forman Christian Coll., Lahore, Pakistan, 1958-63; asst. research physicist UCLA, 1968-69; prof., chmn. dept. physics and astronomy U. Ark., Little Rock, 1969-89, prof. physics, 1974—; adj. prof. U. Ark. Med. Scis., 1985—; faculty rsch. assoc. NASA/JOVE, 1982-95; editor: (with G. Yodh and W. Kropp) Arkansas Gamma Ray and Neutrino Workshop, 1990; project dir. for preparation of energy conservation plan State of Ark., 1976-77. Recipient Donaghey Urban Mission award, 1979; Ark. Research Award Am. Assn. Mental Deficiency, 1980; Region V research award, 1980; HEW research fellow, 1978. Mem. Acoustical Soc. Am., Acoustics, Speech and Signal Processing Soc. (IEEE), Am. Assn. Physics Tchrs., Am. Phys. Soc., Assn. for Computing Machinery, Internat. Soc. Phonetic Scis., Am. Speech, Lang. and Hearing Assn., Phi Kappa Phi, Sigma Xi, Sigma Pi Sigma. Home: 38 Pine Manor Dr Little Rock AR 72207-5137 Office: U Ark 2801 S University Ave Little Rock AR 72204-1099

WOLDT, GERALD D. (JAY WOLDT), nurse anesthetist; b. Chippewa Falls, Wis., May 30, 1943; s. D.C. and Blanche A. (Patrie) W.; children: Michael B., Eve A. Diploma in Nursing, St. Mary's Sch. Nursing, Wausau, Wis., 1965; diploma, Tripler Army Sch. Anesthesia, Honolulu, 1970; BSN, Med. Coll. Ga., 1977; MSN, Oreg. Health Sci. U., 1980. Cert. RN Anesthetist. Staff nurse operating rm. Fitzsimons Hosp., Denver, 1966-67; commd. U.S. Army, 1966, advanced through grades to lt. col., 1981; staff anesthetist 93d Evac Hosp., Vietnam, 1970-71, 27th Surg. Hosp., Vietnam, 1971; clin. instr., staff anesthetist Madigan Army Hosp., Tacoma, Wash., 1971-72; staff anesthetist Munson Army Hosp., Leavenworth, Kans., 1972-76; chief anesthetist Dwight D. Eisenhower Hosp., Augusta, Ga., 1976-78, 2d Gen. Hosp., Landstuhl, Germany, 1980-83; nurse anesthesia cons. 7th MEDCOM, Germany, 1980-83; chief anesthetist, clin. instr. DeWitt Army Hosp., Ft. Belvoir, Va., 1983-87; staff anesthetist Potomac Hosp., Woodbridge, Va., 1986-91; dir. nurse anesthesia Mary Washington Hosp., Fredericksburg, Va., 1991-95; dir. nurse anesthesia Fredericksburg (Va.) Ambulatory Surgery Ctr., 1996—; co-facilitator death and dying seminars, 1980-83; lectr. in field. Mem. Am. Assn. Nurse Anesthetists, Sigma Theta Tau. Roman Catholic. Home: One Charleston Ct Stafford VA 22554

WOLF, ANNE WILSON, advocate; b. Aiken, S.C., Nov. 25, 1960; d. Samuel and Evelyn (Goss) W. BA in Psychology, Emory Univ., 1983. Instr. Aiken Tech. Coll., Langley, S.C., 1983-84; office mgr. Aiken County Emergency Svcs., 1984-86; coord. domestic violence program Coalition Assist Abused Persons, Aiken, 1986-88; coord. victim assistance Aiken County Sheriff's Dept., 1988-93; vol. coord. Abused Women's Aid in Crisis, Anchorage, Alaska, 1994; claims investigator Divsn. Victim Assistance Gov.'s Office, Columbia, S.C., 1994—; organizer Conf. on Domestic Violence, Aiken, 1986; co-chair S.C. Coalition Against Domestic Violence and Sexual Assault, 1988. spkr. in field. Vice-chair, bd. dirs. Aiken County Commn. for the Handicapped, 1987-93; mem. bd. trustees Adas Yeshurun Synagogue, Aiken, 1991-92; vol. Cumbee Ctr. Assist Abused Persons, Aiken, 1995—. Jewish. Office: Gov Office Divsn Victim Assistance 1205 Pendleton St Rm 401 Columbia SC 29201

WOLF, BARRY, genetics, pediatric educator; b. Chgo., June 19, 1947; s. Bert D. and Toby E. (Urkoff) W.; m. Gail Harriet Ross, Oct. 2, 1971; children: Michael Loren, Bryan Phillip. BS, U. Ill., 1969; MD, U. Ill. Coll. Medicine, 1974; PhD, U. Ill., 1974. Diplomate Am. Bd. Pediatrics, Med. and Biochem. Genetics. Intern, resident in pediatrics Childrens Meml. Hosp., Northwestern U., Chgo., 1974-76; fellow Yale U. Sch. Medicine, New Haven, Conn., 1976-78; prof. human genetics Med. Coll. Va., Richmond, 1978—, vice chair for rsch. dept. pediatrics, 1996—. Author over 140 jour. articles and book chpts. dealing with inherited disorders of metabolism and biochem. genetics, specifically disorders of biotin metabolism. Recipient E. Mead Johnson award for pediatric rsch. Am. Acad. Pediatrics, 1988, Borden award in nutrition Am. Inst. Nutrition, 1987, Outstanding Scientist of Va. award Va. Sci. Mus., 1986, Ounce of Prevention award Action for Prevention of Va., 1985. Mem. Am. Soc. Clin. Investigation, Soc. Pediatric Rsch., Soc. for Inherited Metabolic Diseases (bd. dirs.), Am. Soc. Clin. Nutrition, Am. Inst. Nutrition, Soc. for the Study of Inborn Errors of Metabolism, Am. Soc. Human Genetics. Office: Med Coll Va Dept Human Genetics PO Box 980033 Richmond VA 23298

WOLF, FRANK R., congressman, lawyer; b. Philadelphia, Pa., Jan. 30, 1939; m. Carolyn Stover; children: Frank, Virginia, Anne, Brenda, Rebecca. B.A., Pa. State U., 1961; LL.B., Georgetown U., 1965. Bar: Va., D.C. Legis. asst. former Congressman Edward G. Biester, Jr., 1968-71; asst. to Sec. of Interior Rogers B. Morton, 1971-74; dep. asst. sec. for Congl. and Legis. Affairs, Dept. Interior, 1974-75; mem. 97th-104th Congresses from 10th Va. dist., Washington, 1981—; mem. appropriations com., chmn. transp. subcom., mem. TPS and fgn. affairs subcom. Served with USAR. Republican. Presbyterian. Office: US Ho of Reps 241 Cannon Hse Office Bldg Washington DC 20515-4610

WOLF, JAMES STUART, surgeon, administrator; b. Chgo., Mar. 1, 1935; s. Carl Walter and Margaret Vera (Goddard) W.; m. Marjorie Ann Voytilla, July 26, 1958; children: James Stuart, Jr., Anne Elizabeth. AB, Grinnell Coll., 1957; MD, U. Ill., Chgo., 1961. Diplomate Am. Bd. Surgery. Resident in surgery Med. Coll. Va., Richmond, 1967, prof. surgery, 1968-76; chief of surgery McGuire VA Hosp., Richmond, 1968-76; prof. surgery Northwestern U., Chgo., 1976-94, assoc. dean med. edn., 1990-94, emeritus prof. surgery, 1994—; chmn. divsn. transplantation Northwestern U., 1976-91; pres. United Network for Organ Sharing, 1990-91, dir. med. affairs, 1994—; chmn. Regional Bank of Ill., Chgo., 1988-89; vice chmn. Ill. Network for End Stage Renal Disease, Chgo., 1984-88. Bd. dirs. Nat. Kidney Found., Chgo., 1984-91, Chgo. Episcopal Charities, Chgo., 1990-94. Recipient Gift of Life award Nat. Kidney Found., 1992. Fellow Am. Coll. Surgeons; mem. Ctrl. Surg. Soc., Soc. Univ. Surgeons, Am. Soc. Transplant Surgeons, Transplantation Soc., Focus Club Richmond. Republican. Home: 9800 Kingsbridge Rd Richmond VA 23233 Office: United Network forOrgan Sharing 1100 Boulders Pkwy Ste 500 Richmond VA 23225

WOLF, JEFFREY STEPHEN, physician; b. Hartford, Conn., July 30, 1946; s. Abraham and Norma Wolf; m. Nina Loving Lockridge; children: Sarah Loving, Lawren Hiley. BS, McGill U., 1968; MD, Med. Coll. Va., 1972, MS, 1973. Diplomate Am. Bd. Colon and Rectal Surgery, . Intern, in surgery Mt. Sinai Hosp., N.Y.C., 1972-73, resident, 1973-75; resident N.Y. Med. Coll.-Met. Hosp., N.Y.C., 1975-77; chief resident surgery Met. Hosp., 1977-78; fellow colon-rectal surgery Greater Balt. Med. Center, 1978-79; colon-rectal surgeon, Portsmouth, Va., 1979—. Fellow ACS, Am. Soc. Colon and Rectal Surgery; mem. AMA, Portsmouth Acad. Medicine, Med. Soc. Va., Am. Soc. Colon and Rectal Surgeons, So. Med. Assn., Chesapeake Colon-Rectal Soc.. Office: 3235 Academy Ave Ste 200 Portsmouth VA 23703-3200

WOLF, JOHN HOWELL, retired publisher; b. Narberth, Pa., Mar. 19, 1918; s. W. Dale and Ruth Coryell (Howell) W.; m. Jane Belmeur, May 18, 1946 (div. Dec. 16, 1969); children: John B., Wendy J.; m. Emily West Asbury, Dec. 21, 1969. Student, DePauw U., Greencastle, Ind., 1935-39, Xavier U., Cin., 1940-41. Pub. Cin. Suburban Newspapers, Inc., 1946-73; pres., pub. Cin. Suburban Newspapers, Inc./Clermont Newspapers, Inc., 1973-82; chmn. Nat. Better Newspaper Contests, Washington, 1957-58; adv. bd. U.S. Suburban Press, Inc., Chgo., 1970-75. Dir. Suburban Press Found., Chgo., 1972; del. 5th UNESCO Conf., 1956; chmn. Police Media Adv. Com., Cin., 1968; chmn. small media com. United Appeal, Cin., 1965; mem. com. of mgmt. YMCA, Norwood, Ohio, 1947—; pres. Y Men's Club, Norwood, 1952, Carlisle (Ky.) Nicholas County Indsl. Authority, 1984-89, chmn., 1988-89. Maj. U.S. Army, 1942-46. Recipient Silver medal Advertisers Club, Cin., 1973. Mem. Soc. Profl. Journalists, Suburban Newspapers of Am. (pres. 1973, sect. pres. 1968), Nat. Newspaper Assn. (dir. 1978-83, exec. com. 1980-83, fin. com. 1980-83, Outstanding Dir. 1980), Accredited Home Newspapers of Am. (dir. 1972), Norwood Club (pres. 1950), Masons. Presbyterian. Home: 244 Azalea Ct Carlisle KY 40311-9053

WOLF, LINDA JOYCE, legal assistant; b. Johnson City, N.Y., July 5, 1955; d. Robert Gregory and Margaret Elaine (Dixon) W. BA in Polit. Sci., Baylor U., 1978. Cert. legal asst. News editor Waco (Tex.) Tribune Herald, 1975-76; prodn. asst. Sports Comm., Waco, 1976-78; legal asst. Richards, Medlock & Andrews, Dallas, 1980-85, cert. legal asst., 1985—. Pres. Dallas County Rep. Women's Caucus, 1980; dist. dir. Tex. Fedn. Rep. Women, 1982-85; regional chmn. Dallas County Rep. Com., 1985-87, precinct chmn., 1983-89, 92—; bd. dirs. Friends So. Meth. U. Libr., 1992—, v.p., 1996—; bd. dirs. EQUEST Therapeutic Horseback Riding Program, 1992—; bd. dirs. Lone Star 2000, 1993—. Mem. ABA (assoc.), Tex. Bar Assn. (legal asst. div., charter), Nat. Assn. Legal Assts., Soc. Profl. Journalists, Jr. League Richardson (bd. dirs. 1989-90), Dallas Coun. Rep. Women's Club (legis dir. 1982-83), Dallas Profl. Rep. Women (bd. dirs. 1992-93), Pub. Affairs Luncheon Club (bd. dirs. 1991—). Roman Catholic. Home: PO Box 50562 Dallas TX 75250-0562 Office: Sidley & Austin 1201 Elm St Ste 4500 Dallas TX 75270-2136

WOLF, MICHAEL ELLIS, clinical psychologist; b. Hutchinson, Kans., Oct. 27, 1950; s. Harold E. and Geraldine F. (Spencer) W.; m. Anne Dullea, July 15, 1978; children: Chris, Brian, Allison. AA, Hutchinson Community Coll., 1970; BA, U. Kans., 1972; MA, Wichita State U., 1976; PhD, Ohio U., 1980. Lic. clin. psychologist, Tex. Psychologist Kaiser Permanente, Dallas, 1980-82; clin. psychologist Dallas Rehab. Inst., 1984-87; clin. psychologist in pvt. practice Dallas, 1982—; cons. inpatient and outpatient chem. dependency and psychiatric treatment programs, Dallas, 1984—. Contbr. articles to profl. jours. Mem., chmn. pre-sch. adv. bd., 1986-88. Franklin Cramm scholar, 1968; Summer Fgn. Lang. Inst. scholar, 1971. Mem. Am. Psychol. Assn., Tex. Psychol. Assn., Dallas Psychol. Assn., Phi Beta Kappa, Phi Theta Kappa. Office: 13800 Montfort Dr Ste 200 Dallas TX 75240-4347

WOLF, SARA HEVIA, art librarian; b. Havana, Cuba, Jan. 15, 1936; came to U.S., 1961; d. Policarpo and Manuela (Ruiz) Hevia; m. Luis A. Wolf, Sept. 23, 1960; 1 child, Sara Caroline. B in Bus., Havana Bus. U., 1956. Libr. asst. N.C. State U., Raleigh, 1963-65; cataloguer Ctrl. Piedmont C.C., Charlotte, N.C., 1970-71; libr. Mint Mus. Art, Charlotte, N.C., 1972—. Bd. dirs. YMCA, Charlotte, 1985-87; co-chair All Nations Festival, Inc., Charlotte, 1977-78; pres. Cath. Hispanic Ctr., Charlotte, 1981-82, editor Spanish Newsletter, 1972-75, chair Internat. Cultural Festival, 1973-76; steering com. Latin-Am. Week, Charlotte, 1993. Mem. Art Librs. Soc., N.Am. (mem. George Wittenborn Meml. Book Awards com. 1992, chair nominating com. S.E. chpt. 1987, chair Mary Ellen Lo Presti Publ. Awards com. S.E. chpt. 1989, v.p., pres.-elect S.E. chpt. 1990, pres. S.E. chpt. 1991), Metrolina Libr. Assn. (exec. bd. 1988), L.Am. Women's Assn. (pres. 1994-96), L.Am. Coalition. Office: Mint Mus of Art 2730 Randolph Rd Charlotte NC 28207-2012

WOLFARD, LORRIE ELAINE, English language educator; b. Agana, Guam, Mar. 23, 1960; d. Wayne Esmond and Edith Evelyn (Brown) Nickerson; m. Rodney Bishop Wolfard, Jr., June 15, 1985; children: Nickolas Todd, William Henry. BA in English, Austin Coll., 1981, MA in Elem. Edn., 1982; MA in English, Hardin-Simmons U., 1988; postgrad. in English, U. N.C., 1938—. Cert. tchr., Tex. Tchr. Glad Tidings Inst., Sherman, Tex., 1982-85; grad. asst. Hardin-Simmons U., Abilene, Tex., 1985-88; tchg. asst. U. N.C., Chapel Hill, 1988-89, 92-96; instr. composition McMurry Coll., Abilene, Tex., 1988, 89. Recipient Jewel Davis Scarborough Grad. scholarship AAUW, Sherman, 1987, Earl Hartsell award for excellence in tchg. U. N.C., 1996. Mem. MLA. Baptist.

WOLFE, BARDIE CLINTON, JR., law librarian, educator; b. Kingsport, Tenn., Oct. 21, 1942; s. Bardie Clinton and Joy (Gillenwater) W.; J.D., U. Ky., 1967, M.S.L.S., 1972. Bar: Ky. 1967. Circulation librarian, dir. reader services U. Tex., 1968-71; acquisition librarian, asst. prof. U. Va., 1971-73; law librarian, asst. prof. Cleve. State U., 1973-76, librarian, assoc. prof., 1976-77; librarian, assoc. prof. law U. Tenn., Knoxville, 1977-80; librarian, prof. law Pace U., White Plains, N.Y., 1980-84; librarian, prof. law St. Thomas U., Miami, Fla., 1984—. accreditation insp. ABA, Assn. Am. Law Schs.; cons. Queens Coll. Sch. Law, 1981-82. Mem. ABA, Ky. Bar Assn., Am. Judicature Soc., Am. Assn. Law Libraries, Assn. Am. Law Schs., Nat. Micrographics Assn. Office: St Thomas U Law Libr 16400 NW 32d Ave Miami FL 33054

WOLFE, GEORGE CROPPER, private school educator, artist, author; b. New Orleans Sept. 6, 1933; s. Howard Edward and Amaryllis (Brannen) W.; m. Catherine Vasterling, June 2, 1955; children: David, Michael, Philip. BA in Fine Art, La. State U., 1956; MEd, U. New Orleans, 1972, MS in Urban Planning, 1975; postgrad., Tex. Tech U., Junction, 1986-93. Cert. tchr. art, social studies La. Elem. tchr. Live Oak Manor Sch., Waggaman, La., 1962-65; tchr. art Isidore Newman Sch., New Orleans, 1965—. Author: 3-D Wizardry (also video), Papier Maché Plaster and Foam, 1995; contbr. articles to profl. jours. Served with USCG, 1956-58. Recipient Telly award for How-to video 3D Wizardry, 1966. Mem. Nat. Art Edn. Assn. (La. Art Educator of Yr. 1990), La. Art Edn. Assn. (pres. 1978-79), Kappa Delta Pi, Phi Delta Kappa (v.p., Rsch. award 1996). Home: 342 Jefferson St Natchitoches LA 71457

WOLFE, JOHN THOMAS, JR., university president; b. Jackson, Miss., Feb. 22, 1942; s. John Thomas Sr. and Jeanette (Wallace) W.; children: Wyatt Bardouille, John Thomas Dantzler, David Andrew Dantzler. BEd, Chgo. Tchrs. Coll., 1964; MS, Purdue U., 1972, PhD, 1976. Tchr. English Englewood High Sch., Chgo., 1965-67; linguistics prof. Cuttington Coll., Liberia, West Africa, 1967-69; pres. Wolfe & Assocs., 1970-93; asst. mgr. residence hall Purdue U., West Lafayette, Ind., 1971-75, employee relations mgr., 1975-77; asst. prof. English Fayetteville (N.C.) State U., 1977-82, assoc. prof., 1982-85, coordinator area English and dramatic arts, 1978-83, head div. humaities and fine arts, 1979-84; acad. dean. Ft. Bragg U. Ctr., 1983-85; provost, v.p. for acad. affairs Bowie (Md.) State Coll., 1985-90; pres. Ky. State U., Frankfort, 1990-91; exec. dir. Nat. Rainbow Coalition, 1992-93; pres. Savannah (Ga.) State Coll., 1993—; lectr. Krannert Sch. Mgmt., 1976; mem. N.C. Humanities Commn., 1981-85. Contbr. articles in field. Active N.C. Humanities Com., Greensboro, 1979-83, Arts Coun. Fayetteville, Cumberland, N.C., 1979-85, Minority Bus. Resource Inst. Bd., Landover, Md., 1986—; bd. dirs. Entrepreneurial Devel. Program, Landover, 1986—, Savannah Econ. Devel. Auth., 1994, Savannah Area C. of C., 1994, Savannah Regional Small Bus. Capital Fund, 1994; del. White House Conf. on Librs., 1991; Ga. state rep. Am. Assn. State Colls. and Univs., 1993—. NEH grantee, 1979; Am. Council on Edn. fellow, 1982-83; recipient award Fayetteville Human Relations Commn., 1981. Mem. Nat. Coun. Tchrs. English (pres. Black Caucus 1981-88), Conf. Coll. Composition and Communication (chmn. resolutions com. 1982—), Am. Coun. Edn. (commn. leadership devel. 1995), Kappa Delta Pi, Omega Psi Phi, Alpha Kappa Mu (hon.). Roman Catholic. Home: 247 Lyman Hall Rd Savannah GA 31410-

1048 Office: Savannah State Coll Office of the Pres PO Box 20444 Savannah GA 31404

WOLFE, MARGARET ANN REED, medical scientist; b. New Orleans, Dec. 10, 1949; d. Fred William and Gertrude Mae (Detman) R.; m. Charles Christopher Wolfe, Oct. 11, 1990. BS in Zoology, La. State U., 1971; MS in Biology, Tulane U., 1983. Office mgr. Family Health Found., New Orleans, 1972-74; lab. technician Tulane U., New Orleans, 1974-78, 1979-82, rsch. specialist clin. immunology, 1982-90, rsch. asst. clin. immunology, 1990-91, rsch. asst. histocompatibility, 1991-93, assoc. scientist histocompatibility, 1993-95, DNA Lab. supr., 1995—; lectr. and presenter in field. Contbr. numerous articles and abstracts to profl. jours. Mem. Am. Soc. for Histocompatibility and Immunogenetics. Home: 6647 Avenue B New Orleans LA 70124-2124 Office: Tulane U Med Ctr Dept Medicine 1700 Perdido St New Orleans LA 70112-1210

WOLFE, MICHAEL DAVID, management educator; b. Houston, Feb. 16, 1950; s. Alfred Sigmund and Raquel Wolfe; m. Hannan McMonagle, 1991; children: Gregory Benjamin McMonagle Wolfe, Daniel John McMonagle Wolfe. BA in Math., U. Tex., 1972; student, Cambridge (Eng.) U., 1974; PhD in Math., U. Tex., 1978, PhD in Mgmt. Sci. and Info. Systems, Econs. and Fin., 1988. Staff mem. BDM Corp., Albuquerque, 1978-80, MRC Corp., Albuquerque, 1980-83; part-time staff mem. Rockwell Internat., Albuquerque, 1983-88; part-time lectr. U. Tex., Austin, 1983-88, asst. instr., 1973-77; asst. prof. W.Va. U., Morgantown, 1989—. Contbr. articles to profl. jours. Home: PO Box 712 Morgantown WV 26507-0712 Office: W Va Univ Dept of Mgmt Morgantown WV 26506

WOLFE, MICHAEL PATRICK, metal products executive; b. Fort Monroe, Va., Oct. 15, 1948; s. Ralph Leslie and Dorothy Mae W.; m. Deborah Sue Clegg, Mar. 23, 1968; children: Michael Patrick II, Tracy Lynn. Student, West Liberty State U., 1967-72, Murray State U., 1990-93. Order supr. Fostoria Glass Co., Moundsville, W.Va., 1966-72; gen. foreman Ohio Ferro Alloys, Powhattan, Ohio, 1972-77; asst. prodn. supt. Foote Mineral, New Haven, W.Va., 1977-85; prodn. supt. SKW Alloys, Inc., Calvert City, Ky., 1985-88; prodn. coord. Am. Alloys, Inc., New Haven, W.Va., 1988-89; dir. ops. SKW Metals & Alloys, Inc., Calvert City, 1989-93, Am. Alloys, Inc., New Haven, W. Va., 1993—. Pres. Wahama High Boosters Club, Mason, W.Va., 1983, New Haven Little League, 1982, New Haven Biddy League/Basketball, 1980-82. Mem. Elks. Democrat. Methodist. Home: RR 2 Box 341B Belpre OH 45714-9756 Office: Am Alloys SKW Alloys PO Box 218 New Haven WV 25265

WOLFE, MILDRED NUNGESTER, artist; b. Celina, Ohio, Aug. 23, 1912; d. Roy Clifford and Augusta Wilhelmina (Hoenie) Nungester; widowed; children: Karl Michael, Elizabeth Hoenie. AB, U. Monte Vallo, 1932; MA, Colo. Coll., 1944. Tchr. Decatur (Ala.) City Schs., 1933-42; tchr. art and art history Millsaps Coll., Jackson, Miss., 1960-70; artist Wolfe Fine Art Studio, Jackson, 1945—. Artist 4 lithographs of So. scene, 1940s, lithographs displayed in Montgomery Mus. of Art, 1940, Libr. of Congress, London, Warsaw, Coventry, 1944; oil portrait of Eudora Welty, Nat. Portrait Gallery, Washington, 1989; represented in permanent collections at Miss. Mus. of Art, 1995, Huntsville Mus. of Art, 1996, Ga. Mus. of Art, 1996. Recipient 1st prize oil painting, Ala. Art League, Montgomery, 1935, 1st prize watercolor Miss. Art League, Jackson, 1949, award of merit, Grumbacher Internat., Lakeland, Fla., 1952, Visual Arts award Miss. Inst. of Arts and Letters, Jackson, 1989. Mem. Miss. Mus. of Art, Miss. Watercolor Soc. Home: 4308 Old Canton Rd Jackson MS 39211 Office: Wolfe Fine Art Studio 4308 Old Canton Rd Jackson MS 39211-5920

WOLFE, NANCY BEALS, public relations executive, educator; b. Fargo, N.D., May 20, 1933; d. Albert Percy and Vina Beatrice (Rugg) Beals; m. Donald H. Wolfe, Aug. 9,1962; 1 child, Alison Lee. BS in Speech, U. Vt., 1954; MS in Theatre, So. Ill. U., 1960; MBA, Wake Forest U., 1980. State polit. reporter Burlington (Vt.) Free Press, 1960-62; mng. editor Montpelier (Vt.) Monitor, 1963; pub. rels. dir. Montpelier Sch. Sys., 1963-65; local govt. reporter Twin City Sentinel, Winston-Salem, N.C., 1969; pub. rels. dir. City of Winston-Salem, 1969-81; cons. Cities in Comm., 1976-81; pres. The Wolfe Group, Inc., Winston-Salem, 1981—; tchr. Eng. and speech, drama coach Shelburne (Vt.) H.S., 1954-56, Montpelier H.S., 1956-59; chmn. dept. Eng. Olathe (Colo.) H.S., 1962-63; instr. dept. speech and drama Ithaca (N.Y.) Coll., 1965-68; lectr., course coord. mgmt. issues in pub. rels. Babcock Grad. Sch. Mgmt. Wake Forest U., 1973-74; vis. assoc. prof. pub. rels. U. Tenn., Knoxville, 1987-88, mem. adv. bd. pub. rels. program, 1977-85; lectr. dept. comm. Appalachian State U., Boone, 1988-94; A.J. Fletcher Prof. Comm. Elon (N.C.) Coll., 1994—; evaluator pub. rels. courses 10 colls., univs., 1989; speaker in field. Co-author: PR Management: The Business of Public Relations, 1989; contbr. articles, abstracts to profl. jours. Chmn. pub. rels. Winston-Salem/Forsyth County Bicentennial Commn., 1973-77, mem. steering com., 1973-77; dir. The Little Theatre, Inc., 1972-75; chmn. long-range planning com. United Way Forsyth County, 1973-76, bd. dirs., 1973-76, v.p., 1973-76, sec., 1973-76, chmn. pub. rels. com., 1971-72; pres. Pub. Rels. Roundtable, Winston-Salem, 1974-75; dir. Forsyth County Rescue Squad, 1984-85; mem. nat. resources devel. com. Nat. ARC, 1986-89; dir. Salvation Army Ctrl. Command, 1974-89, chmn. devel. com., 1987-89, chmn. long range planning com., 1980-89, mem. bldg. com., 1987-89, mem. exec. com., 1985-89, mem. capital campaign steering com., 1986-87; coun. mem. rep. ctrl. command Salvation Army Girls' Club, 1978-87, pres., 1983; vice chmn. NW N.C. Red Cross chpt., 1982-87, dir., 1982-87, mem. exec. com., 1982-87, chmn. emergency svcs., 1986-87; bd. dirs. YWCA, 1980-84, mem. fin. com., 1980-84, sec., 1984, bd. dirs. clean cmty. com., 1980-83, mem. exec. com., 1980-83; chmn. pub. rels. adv. com. Winston-Salem Arts Coun., 1972-74, chmn. pub. rels. workshop, 1979; mem. budget com., 1982; founding mem. Winston-Salem Friendship Force, 1980-81, mem. exec. com., 1980-81; mem. exec. com. 3d Century Priorities Com. Cmty. Interracial Action, 1980-82. Named Outstanding Faculty Advisor by Pub. Rels. Student Soc. Am., 1992. Fellow Pub. Rels. Soc. Am. (edn. sect. chair-elect 1994, chair 1995, newsletter editor 1992-93, sec.-treas. 1992, SE dist. dir. 1992, membership com. 1993, internat. com. 1993, ednl. affairs com. 1987-90, others, past mem. numerous coms., Tar Heel chpt. pres. 1994, assembly del. 1992-94, co-chair profl. devel. com. 1993, co-chair regional conf. sponsored by chpt. 1992, founding mem. Tar Heel chpt. 1982—, vol. chpt. 1987-88, N.C. chpt. pres. 1977, Presdl. citations 1980, 81, 86, 91, 95, accredited); mem. Greater Winston-Salem C. of C. (small bus. coun. 1981-87, mgmt. devel. com. 1984-87, exec. dialogue program 1982-87, chmn. 1983). Home and Office: 3955 Windsor Place Dr Winston Salem NC 27106

WOLFE, SUSAN MARIE, program evaluation consultant; b. Flint, Mich., Sept. 13, 1957; d. Walter Vincent and Frances Lucille (Smorch) Laskowski; m. David A. Wolfe, May 21, 1983; children: Jason Mercier, Kristopher Mercier. BS, U. Mich., Flint, 1985; MA, Mich. State U., 1988; postgrad., U. Tex., Dallas, 1994—. Rsch. coord. Hurley Med. Ctr., Flint, Mich., 1984-87; teaching asst. Mich. State U., East Lansing, 1986-87; assoc. rschr. Indsl. Tech. Inst., Ann Arbor, Mich., 1987-89; evaluation cons. McKinney, Tex., 1989—; asst. dir. rsch. Dallas County Cmty. Coll. Dist., 1989-92; instr. part-time El Centro & Richland Colls., Dallas, 1991; project dir., instr. SUNY, Buffalo, 1991-92; project dir. Wayne State U., Detroit, 1992-93; dir. rsch. Dallas Child Guidance Clinic, 1993-94; rsch./tchg. asst. U. Tex., Dallas, 1995—; prin. investigator Comparative Study of Runaway/Throwaway and Housed Adolescents, Detroit, 1993-94; presenter in field. Co-author: (book chpt.) Processes of Technological Innovation, 1990; co-editor: (spl. issue on homelessness) Community Psychologist, 1993. Den leader Boy Scouts Am., Flint, 1985-86; bd. dirs. Samaritan Inn Shelter, McKinney, 1994—. Named one of Outstanding Young Women of Am., 1987; co-grantee State of Mich., 1989, grantee State of Tex., 1991. Mem. APA (student affiliate), Soc. for Psychol. Study of Social Issues, Soc. for Cmty. Rsch. and Action (Midwest student rep. 1986-88), Am. Pub. Health Assn., Am. Psychol. Soc. (student affiliate), Soc. for Rsch. on Child Devel., Soc. for Rsch. on Adolescents, Internat. Network on Personal Relationships.

WOLFE, TOWNSEND DURANT, III, art museum director, curator; b. Hartsville, S.C., Aug. 15, 1935; m. Jane Rightor Lee; 1 child, Zibilla Lee; children (by previous marriage): Juliette Elizabeth, Mary Bryan, Townsend Durant. BFA, Atlanta Art Inst., 1958; MFA, Cranbrook Acad. Art, 1959; postgrad, Harvard Inst. Arts Adminstrn., 1970. Instr. Atlanta Art Assn., 1956-59, Memphis Acad. Art, 1959-64, Scarsdale Studio Workshop and Seamen Inst., N.Y.C., 1964-65; dir. Ford Found. Fund for Advancement of Edn. Wooster Community Art Ctr., Danbury, Conn., 1965-68; lectr. art U. Ark., Little Rock, 1969—; dir., chief curator The Ark. Arts Ctr., Little Rock, 1968—; sec. Ark. Arts Ctr. Found., 1973—; pres. Ark. Consortium Arts, 1976-80; pres. Ark. Arts in Edn. Adv. Coun., 1977-79; bd. dirs. Mid-Am. Arts Alliance, 1982-89; mem. adv. bd. Ark. Artists Registry, 1986—, Ark. Repertory Theatre, 1976-84; reviewer Inst. Mus. Svcs., 1984-87, examiner mus. assessment program, 1985-87; overview panel Nat. Endowment for Arts, 1986-88, rev. panel utilization of mus. resources, 1986, grant rev. panel conservation and collection maintenance, 1987; curator 20th Century Am. Sculpture Exhbn., First Ladies' Garden, The White House, 1995. One-man shows include Madison Gallery, N.Y.C., 1961, U. Miss., 1963, Southwestern U., Memphis, 1964, Ark. State U., Jonesboro, 1964, 70; group shows include Ball State Tchrs. Coll., Muncie, Ind., 1959, 63,65, 67, Ann. New Eng. Exhbn., 1966-67, Wadsworth Atheneum, Hartford, Conn., 1967, Audubon Artists, N.Y.C., 1968; represented in permanent collections Ark. State U., Union Planters Nat. Bank, Memphis, Mint Mus. Art, Charlotte, N.C., East Tenn. State U., others; author: Trustee Handbook, 1978, Appraiser Handbook, 1979, Selections from the Permanent Collection of the Arkansas Arts Center Foundation catalogue, 1983, Twentieth Century American Drawings from the Arkansas Arts Center Foundation Collection, 1984, American Drawings, 1986, National Drawings Invitational, 1986, 87, 88, 91, 92, 93, 94, National Objects Invitational, 1987, 88, 89, 91, National Crafts Invitational, 1987, Picasso: The Classical Years 1917-1925, 1987, Carroll Cloar Arkansas Collections, 1987, Revalations Drawing/America catalogue, 1988, The Face, 1988, 90, American Abstract Drawings, 1989, The Figure, 1990, Will Barnet Drawings: 1930-90, 1991, Silverpoint Etc., 1992, Edward Faiers Retrospective, 1994, exhbn. catalogue Memphis Coll. Art. Presdl. appt. Nat. Mus. Svcs. Bd., 1995. Recipient 20 awards for painting, 1958-68, Winthrop Rockefeller Meml. award, 1973, James R. Short award Southeastern Mus. Conf., 1981, Individual Achievement award Ark. Mus. Assn., 1984, Ark. Art Edn. Advocacy award, 1985, Promethean award for excellence in the arts March of Dimes, 1986, Chevalier dans l'ordre des Arts et Lettres, 1988. Mem. Assn. Art Mus. Dirs., Assn. Am. Museums (membership com. 1982-88, accreditation com., sr. examiner 1972—). Democrat. Episcopalian. Office: The Ark Arts Ctr MacArthur Park 9th and Commerce Little Rock AR 72202

WOLFE, TRACEY DIANNE, distributing company executive; b. Dallas, June 13, 1951; d. George F. Wolfe and Helen Ruth Cline Lemons; children: Bronson Alan, Travis Aaron. BS in Edn. and Social Sci., East Tex. State U., Commerce, 1973, MS in Elem. Edn., 1976. Asst. to dir. student devel. East Tex. State U., 1973-74; corp. sec., v.p. Wolfe Distbg. Co., beer distbrs., Terrell, Tex., 1974-90, pres., 1990—. Mem., bd. dirs., exec. com. East Tex. State U. Found.; panel mem. grievance com. State Bar Tex.; bd. dirs. Friends Terrell Libr.; bd. dirs., vol. CASA Rockwall County. Mem. Terrell C. of C. (bd. dirs. 1991-94), East Tex. State U. Alumni Assn. (bd. dirs.), Rotary, Kappa Delta (alumnae v.p. 1978-79, alumnae treas. 1979-81, province pres. 1980-82). Republican. Methodist. Home: 3316 Lakeside Dr Rockwall TX 75087-5323 Office: 100 Metro Dr Terrell TX 75160

WOLFENDEN, RICHARD VANCE, biochemistry educator; b. Oxford, Eng., May 17, 1935; s. John Hulton and Josephine (Vance) W.; m. Anita Gaunitz, May 25, 1965; children: Peter, John. BA, Princeton U., 1956, Exeter Coll., Oxford U., Eng., 1958; MA, Exeter Coll., Oxford U., Eng., 1958; PhD, Rockefeller Inst., 1964. Asst. prof. chemistry Princeton U., N.J., 1964-70; assoc. prof. biochemistry U. N.C., Chapel Hill, 1970-73, prof. biochemistry, 1973-83, alumni disting. prof., 1983—; vis. fellow Exeter Coll., Oxford, 1969; vis. prof. U. Montpellier, France, 1976; mem. molecular biology panel NSF, Washington, 1973-76; mem. bio-organic and natural products study sect. NIH, Washington, 1981-86; cons. Burroughs-Wellcome Co., Research Triangle Park, N.C., 1989—. Mem. editorial bd. Bioorganic Chemistry, 1983—, Biomed. Chem. Letters, 1993—. Fellow AAAS; mem. Am. Chem. Soc., Am. Soc. Biol. Chemists. Democrat. Home: 1307 Mason Farm Rd Chapel Hill NC 27514-4609 Office: U North Carolina Dept Biochemistry Chapel Hill NC 27514

WOLFF, DAVID STEPHEN, investments and real estate development executive; b. Phila., Sept. 18, 1940; s. Leo and Carolyn (Hirsch) W.; m. Mary Edna Crawford, Dec. 28, 1972; children: Carolyn Crawford, Elizabeth Brooke. BA, Amherst Coll., 1962; MBA, Harvard U., 1964. V.p. Brookhollow Corp., Dallas, 1965-70; ptnr. Wolff, Morgan & Co., Houston, 1970-85; chmn.bd., pres. Wolff Cos., Houston, 1985—; chmn. bd. Dominion Jaguar-Volvo, 1989—. Chmn. bd. Houston Parks Bd., 1988-90; bd. dirs. Houston Econ. Devel. Coun., 1985-87, Houston C. of C., 1984-85, Harris Galveston Coastal Subsidence Dist., 1976-78; v.p. Houston Grand Opera, 1978-84; trustee Amherst Coll., 1991—. Mem. The Urban Land Inst., Coronado Club, Nantucket Yacht Club. Office: Wolff Cos 20 Briar Hollow Ln Houston TX 77027-2802

WOLFF, DEE IVONA, artist; b. Springfield, Minn., June 25, 1948; d. Herbert Edmond and Ivona Francis (Steffel) Ricke; m. Leonard Joe Wolff, Aug. 24, 1968. BA, U. Houston, 1971; cert. of art, Glassell Sch., Mus. Fine Arts, Houston, 1976; student, C.G. Jung Ctr., Houston, 1973-85, Oomoto Sch. Traditional Art, Japan, 1984. Fellow MacDowell Colony, Peterborough, N.H., 1987. One-man shows include Galveston (Tex.) Art Ctr., 1977, 90, Covo de Iongh Gallery, Houston, 1977, Watson de Nagy Gallery, Houston, 1978, Watson Gallery, Houston, 1981, 85, Tex. A&M U. Gallery, College Station, 1986, Marvin Seline Gallery, Austin, 1986, 88, Stephen F. Austin U. Gallery, Nacogdoches, Tex., 1987, Diverseworks Artspace, Houston, 1989, 90, Mus. S.E. Tex., Beaumont, 1990, C.G. Jung Ctr., 1990, D'Art, Dallas, 1990; numerous group exhbns. including Art League Houston, 1976, 96, U. Ill., 1977, Moody Gallery, Houston, 1978, Newport Harbor Art Mus., Calif., 1978, Bklyn. Mus., 1979, Witte Meml. Mus., San Antonio, 1979, So. Meth. U., Dallas, 1980, San Antonio Art Inst. Gallery, 1981, Stavanger Kunstforening, Norway, 1982, Waco (Tex.) Art Ctr., 1982, Salzburger Kunstverein, Austria, 1983-84, Houston Art League, 1983, 87, 96, Dallas Pub. Libr., 1983, Mus. Fine Arts, Houston, 1985, Midtown Arts Ctr., Houston, 1985, Galveston Art Ctr., 1986, 92, 93, 96, Aspen (Colo.) Art Mus., 1987, Judy Youens Gallery, Houston, 1987, 91, Mpls. Coll. Art & Design, 1988, Nat. Mus. Women in the Arts, Washington, 1988, Art Mus. SE Tex., Beaumont, 1989, 96, Longview (Tex.) Mus. and Art Ctr., 1989, Lynn Goode Gallery, Houston, 1990, 91, 96, Art Mus. South Tex., Corpus Christi, 1991, 96, Fine Arts Ctr., Lubbock, 1991, 96, Dallas Mus. Fine Arts, 1991, Tex. Fine Arts Assn., 1991, Karen Lanning Gallery, Houston, 1992, Women & Their Work Gallery, Austin, 1992, 96, Hooks-Epstein Gallery, Houston, 1993, 94, U. Tex. Med. Sch., 1993, Diverseworks Artspace, Houston, 1993, C.G. Jung Ctr., Houston, 1995, Houston Lawndale Art Ctr., 1996, Yekaterinburg, St. Petersburg, Russia, Tomsk, Rostovondon, Nizhnily-Novgorod, Russia, 1996, Slover McCutcheon Gallery, Houston; represented in permanent collections Aamoco Corp., Denver, Internat. Materials Mgmt. Engrs., Houston, Wilson Industries, Houston, Marriott Hotels, Jacksonville, Fla., Park Hotel, Charlotte, N.C., Oomoto, Kameoka City, Kyoto, Japan, Enron Corp., Houston, Mus. SE Tex., Art Mus. South Tex., Corpus Christi, Mus. Fine Arts, Houston; commd. St. Philip Presbyn. Ch., Houston, 23 stained glass windows St. Theresea of Lisieux, Sugarland, Tex., Corpus Christi Pub. Libr.; visual design stage sets Kabbalah; subject radio and TV interviews. Bd. dirs. Diverseworks Artspace, Houston, 1989-91, mem. artists adv. bd., 1990-91. Interdisciplinary Arts grantee Nat. Endowment Arts, 1988, Visual Arts Fellowship grantee, 1989; N.Y. State Coun. on Arts grantee, 1989; recipient Spirit of Am. Woman award Houston Performing Arts Soc. and J.C. Penney, 1989. Studio: 421 Arlington St Houston TX 77007-2617

WOLFF, NELSON W., mayor; b. San Antonio, Oct. 27, 1940; m. Tracy Wolff; 6 children. BBA, St. Mary's U., JD. Pres. Wolff Inc.; former chmn. bd. Sun Harvest Farms, now bd. dirs.; mayor City of San Antonio, 1991—. Mem. State Ho. Reps. and Tex. Senate, 1970-74, past mem. edn. com., past vice-chmn. senate fin. com; city councilman San Antonio City Coun., 1987-91; ofcl. observer elections, El Salvador and Nicaragua, 1984; bd. dirs. Alamo Area Boy Scouts; trustee St. Mary's U.; mem. exec. com., co-founder World Affairs Coun., former chmn. Recipient Outstanding Grad. award Phi Delta Phi at St. Mary's U., 1986, Golden Rule award, 1985; named Outstanding Young Man of Yr. San Antonio Jaycees, 1972. Office: Office of Mayor PO Box 839966 100 Military Pla San Antonio TX 78283-3966*

WOLFGANG, JAMES STEPHEN, history educator, minister; b. Indpls., Dec. 8, 1948; s. James Harold and Alma Jean (Cowgill) W.; m. Bette Ashworth, June 5, 1969; children: Lesley Dawn, Lindsay Brooke. BA, Ind. Wesleyan U., 1970; MA, Butler U., 1975; MDiv, So. Bapt. Theol. Sem., 1978; MA, Vanderbilt U., 1990. Ordained min., Ch. of Christ, 1969. Minister Expwy. Ch. of Christ, Louisville, 1975-79, Danville (Ky.) Ch. of Christ, 1979-96; instr. history U. Ky., Lexington, 1994—; vis. prof. Internat. Christian U., Vienna, Austria, 1990; vis. instr. Redlands Coll. Brisbane, Australia, 1993; instr. history Lexington C.C., 1993-95. Mem. editl. adv. bd. Louisville Courier-Jour., 1994-95; news reader Sta. WUKY-FM, 1994—; contbr. articles to profl. jours. Pres. PTA Danville Ind. Schs., 1983, 86, 91. Recipient Grosswirth-Salny award Mensa Ednl. Rsch. Found., 1990, Lester London award, 1991. Mem. Am. Hist. Assn., Am. Soc. Ch. History, Orgn. Am. Historians, So. Hist. Assn., Mensa (Bluegrass chpt., bd. govs. 1990-94), Hospice (Heritage chpt., bd. dirs. 1993—, v.p. 1994—). Home: 803 Sunset Dr Danville KY 40422-1156 Office: U Ky 1743 Patterson Tower Lexington KY 40506-0027

WOLF-SCHEIN, ENID GORDON, special education researcher, educator, consultant; b. Phila., June 9, 1935; d. Samuel G. and Berdie Gordon; m. Jerome D. Schein, Apr. 18, 1982; children: Marcus Wolf, Laurence Wolf. BS in Elem. Edn. and Speech Pathology, Temple U., 1956, EdM in Speech Pathology, 1958; EdD in Spl. Edn., Boston U., 1968. Speech correctionist Phila. Sch. System, 1957-58; speech pathologist pvt. practice, Phila., 1958-60, Children with Spl. Problems, Prince Georges County, Md., 1961-62; speech-lang. therapist Children's Hosp. D.C., Washington, 1963, U. Pa., Dept. Child Psychiatry, Unit Autistic Children, Phila., 1963-65; sr. clinician Boston U. Psychoednl. Clinic, 1966-67; adminstr. spl. edn. Pub. Schs. D.C., Washington, 1968-80; asst. prof. spl. edn. program NYU, 1980-81; rsch. scientist, psycholinguist N.Y. State Inst. Basic Rsch. Devel. Disabilities, Staten Island, 1981-89; adj. prof. U. Alberta, Edmonton, Can., 1989—; assoc. in psychiatry, rsch. cons. U. Pa. Sch. Medicine, Phila., 1965-70; vis. prof. Columbia U., N.Y.C., 1983-85; cons. Edn. Response Ctr., Edmonton, 1989—. Author: Behavior Rating Instrument for Autistic and Other Atypical Children, Structured Methods in Language Instruction, Pupil Attribute Study System, Wolf Inventory of Psycholinguistic Progress; contbr. articles to profl. jours. Recipient Innovative Project award Pres. Com. Supplementary Ctr. and Svcs., 1971, commendation Coun. Exceptional Children. Mem. Am. Speech, Lang. and Hearing Assn. (cert. 1967). Home: 1703 Andros Isle Apt J2 Coconut Creek FL 33066-2848

WOLFSON, AARON HOWARD, radiation oncologist, educator; b. Nashville, May 13, 1955; s. Sorrell Louis and Jacqueline Adele (Falis) W.; m. Adrienne Sue Mates, Dec. 16, 1979; children: Alexis Ellyn, Andrew Lane. BA, U. Fla., 1978, MD, 1982. Diplomate Am. Bd. Radiology. Intern internal medicine Jackson Meml. Hosp., Miami, Fla., 1982-83; staff physician Pub. Health Svc., Miami, 1983-85; pvt. practice Palm Beach Gardens, Fla., 1985-86; resident in radiation oncology Med. Coll. Va., Richmond, 1986-89; instr. radiation oncology U. Miami Sch. Medicine, 1989-91, asst. prof., 1991—. Contbr. articles to profl. jours. Bd. dirs. Children's Home Soc., Ft. Lauderdale, Fla., 1993—, Temple Beth Israel, Sunrise, Fla., 1994—; mem. spkrs. bur. U. Miami, 1993—; vol. spkr. Broward County Schs., 1990—. Sylvester Cancer Ctr. grantee, 1992. Mem. Gynecologic Oncology Group, Radiation Therapy Oncology Group, Am. Soc. Therapeutic Radiology and Oncology, Temple Beth Israel Men's Club (v.p. 1993—). Jewish. Office: Univ of Miami 1475 NW 12th Ave # D-31 Miami FL 33136-1002

WOLFSON, LAWRENCE AARON, hospital administrator; b. Chgo., July 11, 1941; s. Norman William and Doris D. (Brownstein) W.; m. Cheryl Jean Vogel, Feb. 6, 1987; children: Marc David, Sara Elizabeth, Aaron Michael, Ryan Anthony, Ashley Michelle. BA in Biology, Ind. U., South Bend, 1973, MBA, 1980. Sales rep. Gen. Med. Corp., South Bend, 1973-75, Hoechst-Roussel Pharmaceuticals, Somerville, N.J., 1975-79; purchasing agt. Simon Bros., Inc., South Bend, 1979-81; purchasing mgr. Ingalls Meml. Hosp., Harvey, Ill., 1981-83; dir. purchasing Community Hosp., Munster, Ind., 1983-86; corp. purchasing mgr. Columbus-Cuneo-Cabrini Med. Ctr., Chgo., 1986-88; materials mgmt. cons. South Western Med. Ctr., Chgo., 1988-91; asst. dir. materials mgmt. Michael Reese Hosp. and Med. Ctr., Chgo., 1989-91; dir. material mgmt. Regional Med. Ctr. at Memphis, 1991—; mem. editorial bd. Hosp. Material Mgmt. Quarterly, Aspens Pubs. Cubmaster Cub Scouts, South Bend, 1976-78, Cub Scouts, Cordova, 1995—. With USN, 1961-71. Mem. Am. Soc. Hosp. Materials Mgmt., Healthcare Materials Mgmt. Soc. (regional rep. 1984, cert. profl. in health care material mgmt., Material Mgr. of Yr. 1995), Nat. Assn. Purchasing Mgmt., Am. Soc. Clin. Pathologists (affiliate), Am. Legion, B'nai Brith (pres. 1980-81). Jewish.

WOLINSKY, IRA, nutritionist; b. N.Y.C., Mar. 30, 1938; s. Abraham and Rachel (Stupsky) W.; m. Mary Ann C. Leonard, Jan. 9, 1965; children: Daniella, David. BS, CCNY, 1960; MS, Kans. U., 1965, PhD, 1968. Lectr. Hebrew U., Jerusalem, 1968-74; assoc. prof. Pa. State U., University Park, 1974-79; prof. U. Houston, 1979—. Editor of books and series on nutrition sci., sports nutrition, nutrition methods; contbr. articles to profl. jours. Office: U Houston Dept Human Devel Houston TX 77204-6861

WOLINSKY, JERRY SAUL, neurology educator; b. Balt., Nov. 26, 1943; s. Morris and Anne Melinda (Smith) W.; m. Gerlind Stähler, Jan. 20, 1969; children: Anja Kerstin, Jean-Paul. BS in Biology, Ill. Inst. Tech., 1965; MD, U. Ill., Chgo., 1969. Diplomate Nat. Bd. Med. Examiners, Am. Bd. Psychiatry and Neurology. Instr. neurology U. Calif., San Francisco, 1973-75; rsch. assoc. neurology VA Hosp., San Francisco, 1975-78; asst. prof. neurology U. Calif., San Francisco, 1975-78; assoc. prof. neurology and immunology Johns Hopkins U., Balt., 1978-83; prof. neurology U. Tex., Houston, 1983—; program dir. Multiple Sclerosis Update Series, Houston. Author book chpts.; mem. editorial bd. Annals of Neurology, 1980-87, Neuro Virology and Multiple Sclerosis, 1994—; assoc. editor Sci. Am. Medicine, 1995—; mem. editorial adv. bd. Critical Revs. in Clin. Neurobiology, 1983-88; ad hoc reviewer numerous jours.; contbr. over 150 articles to profl. jours. Comdr. USAR, 1970-77. Recipient David M. Oklon scholarship, 1968-69, Basil O'Connor Starter Rsch. grant Nat. Found. March of Dimes, 1975-78, NIH Rsch. Career Devel. award, 1979-83; rsch. grantee NIH, Nat. Multiple Sclerosis Soc., Clayton Found. for Rsch. Fellow Am. Acad. Neurology, AAAS; mem. Am. Soc. Microbiology, Am. Neurol. Assn., Tex. Med. Assn., Am. Soc. Clin. Investigation, Am. Soc. Virology, Tex. Neurol. Soc., Harris County Med. Soc. Home: 3311 Rice Blvd Houston TX 77005-2933 Office: Univ Tex 6431 Fannin St Ste 7 044 Houston TX 77030-1501

WOLK, ROBERT GEORGE, museum administrator, biologist; b. N.Y.C., Mar. 10, 1931; s. Sol and Mary (Baker) W.; m. Wilhelmina Joan Klein, Mar. 4, 1956; children—Stephanie Elizabeth, David Paul, Jennifer Sally, Nancy Baker, Jonathan Gardner. B.S., CCNY, 1952; M.S., Cornell U., 1954, Ph.D., 1959. Asst. prof. biology St. Lawrence U., Canton, N.Y., 1957-63; assoc. prof. vertebrate morphology and behavior Adelphi U., Garden City, N.Y., 1963-67; curator life sci. Tackapausha Mus. and Preserve, Nassau County Mus., Seaford, N.Y., 1967-78; exec. dir. Nature Sci. Ctr., Winston-Salem, N.C., 1978-82; lectr. in biology Greensboro Coll. (N.C.), 1982-83; dir. edn. N.C. State Mus. Natural Scis., Raleigh, 1983-91, dir. programs, 1991-94, dir. policy and spl. programs, 1994—. Biology dept. scholar CCNY, 1952; NSF grantee, 1956, 64; Mae P. Smith Fund grantee, Am. Mus. Natural History, 1954, 55. Mem. Am. Assn. Mus., N.C. Mus. Council (v.p. 1986-88, pres. 1988-90, Profl. Svc. award 1991) Am. Ornithologists' Union, Linnaean Soc. N.Y. (editor 1970-75), Brit. Ornithologists' Union, Wilson Ornithol. Soc. (Fuertes grantee 1955), Sigma Xi (pres. Adelphi U. 1966-67). Contbr. articles to profl. jours. Office: PO Box 29555 Raleigh NC 27626-0555

WOLKING, FRED LOUIS, retired health physicist; b. Orlando, Fla., Apr. 21, 1939; s. Howard August and Harriett Loretta (Harvey) W.; m. Patricia Belle Tusing, June 10, 1961; 4 children. Enlisted, then warrant officer USN, 1959-71, commd. lt. (j.g.), 1971, advanced through grades to lt. comdr., 1979, ret., 1983; supr. radiol. monitoring and surveillance Cin. Gas and Electric, 1983-84; supr. plant radiotion protection Ill. Power, Clinton, 1984-88; sr. staff health physicist Va. Power, Richmond, 1988-94; corp. health physicist Palo Verde Nuclear Generating Sta. Ariz. Pub. Svc., Phoenix, 1995. Dist. dir. lay spkg. Richmond dist. Va. Conf. United Meth. Ch., 1991—.

Mem. Health Physics Soc. (exec. coun. Va. chpt. 1996), Am. Nuclear Soc. Home: 10231 Lakent Ln Richmond VA 23236-1901

WOLKOW, ALAN EDWARD, chiropractic physician; b. Bklyn., Nov. 9, 1946; s. Benjamin and Leanora (Pliner) W.; m. Terri Lynn Blumenfeld, May 29, 1977; children: Jana, Darren, Michael. AA, CUNY, 1966; BSME, N.Y. Inst. Tech., 1969; postgrad. mech. engring., U. Conn., 1970-71, engr.-in-tng., 1976; DChiropractic cum laude, Life Coll., Marietta, Ga., 1983. Nat. bd. qualified chiropractic orthopedist; cert. CPR; lic. real estate salesman, Ga. Mech. engr. Pratt & Whitney Aircraft Co., East Hartford, Conn., 1969-72, Combustion Engring., Windsor, Conn., 1972-74, Ebasco Svcs., Norcross, Ga., 1974-77, Simons Eastern Co., Decatur, Ga., 1977-79, Austin Co., Atlanta, 1979-80; pvt. practice Wolkow Chiropractic Clinic PC, Duluth, Ga., 1984—; injury prevention cons. Swift Atlanta, Suwanee, Ga., 1987-94. Area coord. Nat. Assn. for Seatbelt Safety,Duluth, 1984—; mem. spkr.'s bur. Ga. Safety Belt Coalition, Atlanta, 1985—, Arthritis Found. Ga., Atlanta, 1987—; asst. advisor B'nai B'rith Youth Orgn., Atlanta, 1978-93. Recipient Cornerstone award PMA, Inc., 1985, Comdr. award, 1986, Chancellor award, 1987; recognition award Found. for Advancement Chiropractic Edn., 1988. Mem. ASME, Am. Chiropractic Assn., Ga. Chiropractic Assn., Nat. Back Found., Am. Coll. Chiropractic Orthopedists, Coun. on Diagnostic Imaging, Parker Chiropractic Resource Found., Kiwanis. Democrat. Jewish. Home: 3754 Loveland Ter Atlanta GA 30341-1742 Office: 1625 Pleasant Hill Rd Ste 170 Duluth GA 30136-5863

WOLNITZEK, STEPHEN DALE, lawyer; b. Covington, Ky., Mar. 13, 1949; s. Frederick William Jr. and Mary Ruth (Meiners) W.; m. Katherine Anita Bishop, Dec. 15, 1972; children: Marcus Stephen, Justin Bishop. BA cum laude, U. Notre Dame, 1970; JD, U. Cin., 1974. Bar: Ky. 1975, U.S. Dist. Ct. (ea. dist.) Ky. 1976, U.S. Supreme Ct. 1978, U.S. Dist. ct. (we. dist.) Ky. 1981, U.S. Ct. Appeals (6th cir.) 1991. Dep. sheriff Kenton County, Covington, 1971-75; assoc. Taliaferro & Smith, Covington, 1975-80; ptnr. Taliaferro, Smith, Mann, Wolnitzek & Schachter, Covington, 1980-86; officer Smith, Wolnitzek, Schachter & Rowekamp P.S.C., Covington, 1986-96, Wolnitzek, Rowekamp, Bender & Bonar, P.S.C., Covington, 1996—; bd. dirs. Ky. Legal Svcs. Plan Inc.; adj. prof. Chase Coll. Law, No. Ky. U., 1996—; mem. Ky. Jud. Retirement and Removal Com., 1995—, chair, 1996—. Mem. exec. com. Kenton County Boys-Girls Club, 1981—, sec., 1995, v.p., 1996; mem. exec. com. Ky. Law Enforcement Coun., Frankfort, 1984-93, vice chmn., 1991-93, chair cert. com., 1986-93; mem. City Coun., Ft. Wright, Ky., 1984-85, mem. Bd. Adjustment, 1986—, vice chair, 1995—; pres. No. Ky. Comty. Ctr., Covington, 1985-86; bd. dirs. Kenton Housing Inc., 1986—, sec., 1991-93, v.p., 1993-95, pres., 1995—; trustee No. Ky. Youth Leadership Found., 1994—, exec. com. bd. dirs., 1994—, pres., 1996—. Recipient Roy Taylor award No. Ky. Legal Aid Soc., 1985; named Vol. of Yr., Community Chest United Appeal, Cin., 1986. Fellow Am. Bar Found., Ky. Bar Found. (charter life; bd. dirs. 1989-94, 95—); mem. Ky. Bar Assn. (bd. govs. 1984—, chmn. ho. of dels. 1986, v.p. 1992-93, pres. 1994-95), Coun. Sch. Bd. Attys. (bd. dirs. 1981-87), Notre Dame Club Cin., Elks, Fraternal Order Police. Democrat. Roman Catholic. Home: 1836 Beacon Hl Covington KY 41011-3684 Office: Wolnitzek Rowekamp Bender & Bonar PSC 502 Greenup St # 352 Covington KY 41011-2522

WOLTERING, MARGARET MAE, secondary school educational consultant; b. Trenton, Ohio, July 24, 1913; d. David Lindy and Nellie Stevenson; m. Elmer Charles Woltering, Apr. 9, 1938 (dec. Oct. 1994); 1 child, Eugene Anthony. Student, Mercy Sch. Nursing, Hamilton, Ohio, 1931-34; BS, Miami U., 1962, MEd, 1968, postgrad., 1975. RN, Ohio; cert. tchr., curriculum supr., Ohio. Pub. health nurse Ohio State Dept. Health, Butler County, 1936-49; supr. Swedish Hosp., Seattle, 1944-45; various h.s. teaching positions Cin., 1968-78; ednl. cons. Ohio, 1981-94; cons., Ohio, 1981—; ednl. cons. specializing in curriculum devel., 1980—; book reviewer Friends of Libr., 1991-93. Author: The National Library of Poetry Anthology, 1996, spelling book, 1981; contbr. poetry to anthology. Chmn. Hosp. Svc. for Children, Hamilton, 1981-85; lectr. Sr. Citizens Ctr., 1992-93; chmn. vol. tutorial program Hamilton High Sch., 1989-93, Audabon Tutorial Program, 1994-96. Mem. AAUW, Toastmasters. Democrat. Roman Catholic.

WOMACK, A. BARTON, business educator; b. Cheyenne, Wyo., Feb. 25, 1950; s. Travis Twyman and Beryl W.; m. Linda Jean Hart, May 24, 1980; children: Meghan, Sarah. MBA, U. Wyoming, Laramie, 1989; BS in Fin. with honors, U. Wyoming, 1986. Br. sch. dir., course leader Nat. Outdoor Leadership Sch., Lander, Wyo., 1970-87; asst. prof. Manatee C.C., Bradenton, Fla., 1989—. Bd. dirs. Tampa Bay Area Coun. of Nat. Assn. Investment Clubs, Tampa, Bradenton, Sarasota, Venice, Fla., 1992—. Mem. Phi Kappa Phi, Beta Gamma Sigma, Beta Alpha Psi. Office: Manatee C C 5840 26th St W Bradenton FL 34207-3522

WOMACK, SAMUEL EDWARD, computer company executive; b. Covington, Ga., Nov. 16, 1942; s. Oscar Ellis and Mary Lylian (Smith) W.; m. Margaret Fay O'Berry, Dec. 15, 1969 (div. 1978); 1 child, Benjamin Jay; m. Patsy McCamey, June 30, 1979 (div. 1995); stepchildren: Greg Carson, Scott Carson. AA in Bus. and Data Processing, DeKalb Coll.; grad. exec. devel. program, George Mason U. Computer specialist, sys. analyst, programmer U.S. Govt., Dept. Army, Atlanta, 1969-80; supr., computer specialist, sys. analyst U.S. Govt., Dept. Army, Alexandria, Va., 1980-82; dir. Army Regional Data Ctr. U.S. Govt., Dept. Army, Norcross, Ga., 1982-88; pres. Ind. Computer Cons., Inc., Covington, 1988—. With U.S. Army, 1960-65, Vietnam and Germany. Mem. Elks, Masons. Roman Catholic.

WOMBLE, DONALD RAY, public health director; b. Fayetteville, N.C., Feb. 9, 1950; s. James Earl and Doris Magaleen (Johnson) W.; children: James Ray, Donald Chadwick; m. Lynne Smith, June 22, 1995. BA, Meth. Coll., 1972; MPH, U. N.C., 1989. Registered sanitarian, N.C. Sanitarian I Harnett County Health Dept., Lillington, N.C., 1972-75, sanitarian II, 1975-77, sanitarian III, 1977-83, sanitarian coord., 1983-87, sanitarian supr., 1987-93; pub. health dir. Montgomery County Health Dept., Troy, N.C., 1993, Hoke County Health Dept., Raeford, N.C., 1994—; dir. Four County Cmty. Action, Hoke County Partnership for Children and Families; sec. Child Fatality Task Force. Mem. APHA, Nat. Assn. County and City Health Ofcls., N.C. Pub. Health Assn. (Ea. Dist.), N.C. Local Health Dirs. Assn. Home: 906 E Prospect Ave Raeford NC 28376

WOMBLES, ROBERT HUSTON, chemist, petroleum company executive; b. Covington, Ky., Dec. 3, 1951. BS Summa Cum Laude, Georgetown (Ky.) Coll., 1973; MS in Organic Chemistry, Vanderbilt U., 1975. Chemist Ashland (Ky.) Oil, Inc., R&D dept., 1975-78, rsch. chemist, 1978-80, sr. rsch. chemist, 1980-81, group leader heavy hydrocarbon rsch., 1981-84, mgr. heavy hydrocarbons group, 1984-86, mgr. analytical sect., 1986-92, dir. R&D, 1992—. Contbr. articles to profl. jours.; patentee: holds five U.S. patents on asphalt roofing compositions, asphalt oxidation catalyst, prodn. process for producing high grade asphalt, and for mfr. carbon fibers and feedstock therof. Recipient Honor scholarship Georgetown Coll., 1969-73, Univ. scholarship Vanderbilt U., 1973-75. Mem. ASTM (com. D-8 on roofing waterproofing and bituminous materials), AAAS, Am. Chem. Soc. (petroleum divsn.), N.Y. Acad. Scis., Ky. Acad. Scis. Home: 4662 Canterbury Ct Ashland KY 41102 Office: Ashland Petroleum R&D PO Box 391 Ashland KY 41114

WOMER, NORMAN KEITH, economist, educator; b. Meadville, Pa., Jan. 2, 1945; s. Parley Paul and Margaret L. (Miner) W.; m. Rita Kay Landis, Apr. 23, 1966; children: Jonathan, Peter, Mark. BA in Econs., Miami U., 1966; PhD, Pa. State U., 1970. Rsch. asst. Pa. Transp. and Traffic Safety Ctr. Pa. State U., 1968; asst. prof. dept. ops. rsch. and adminstrv. scis. Naval Postgrad. Sch., 1969-73; assoc. prof. dept. systems mgmt. sch. engring. Air Force Inst. Tech., 1973-79; prof. dept. mgmt. Clemson U., 1984-86, prof. dept. econ., 1979-84; prof., chair dept. econs. and fin. U. Miss., 1986—; vis. prof. U. Torino, Italy, 1992, China Textile U., Shanghai, 1985-86. Assoc. editor: Ops. Rsch., Topics in Ops. Rsch.; editor-at-large: Interfaces; coauthor: The Economics of Made-to-Order Production: Theory with Applications Related to the Airframe Industry, 1986; contbr. articles to profl. jours. and chpts. to books. Treas. Aley Meth. Ch., Beavercreek, Ohio; chair bldg. com. Univ. Luth. Ch., Clemson, S.C., coun. pres.; treas. Morrison Elem. PTO; Sunday sch. tchr. Oxford U. Meth. Ch., chair stewardship com.; troop com. chair Boy Scouts Am.; joint master Oxford U. Hash House Harriers; bd. dirs. U. Miss. Wesley Found. Navy scholar, 1962-66; NDEA fellow, 1966-69. Mem. Ops. Rsch. Soc. Am. (chmn. geographic sects. com. 1983-86, co-chmn. symposium on ops. rsch. in cost analysis 1983, vice chmn. mil. applications sect. 1986-87, chmn. 1988-89), Soc. of Cost Estimating and Analysis (founding dir., chmn. publs. com. 1985-92, ea. regional v.p. 1985-87), Am. Statis. Assn. (pres. Dayton chpt. 1975-76, mem. coun. 1976), Mil. Ops. Rsch. Soc. (bd. dirs. 1979-84, mem. edn. com. 1975—, David Rist Prize com. 1977-79), Am. Econs. Assn., Econometric Soc., others. Home: 105 Ole Miss Dr Oxford MS 38655-2614 Office: U Miss Dept Econs and Fin University MS 38677

WON, DEANNA CERISE, physicist; b. San Francisco, Mar. 27, 1966; d. Ronald Chin and Marian (Louie) W. BS in Physics, U.S. Air Force Acad., 1988. Commd. 2nd lt. USAF, 1988, advanced through grades to capt., 1992, capt., 1992—; physicist USAF, Dayton, Ohio, 1988-92; chief counter-proliferation tech. team USAF, Melbourne, Fla., 1992-95; mem. edn. with industry program Eastman Kodak Co., Rochester, N.Y., 1995-96; mil. asst. to AFMC chief scientist USAF, Dayton, Ohio, 1996—. Office: USAF Wright Field Dayton OH 45433

WON, IHN-JAE, geophysicist; b. Yokohama, Japan, Nov. 28, 1943; came to U.S., 1969; s. Y.K. and S.B. W.; m. Susan Mary Thome, Aug. 21, 1971; children: Eugene, Lianne, Henry. BS, Seoul Nat. U., 1967; MS, Columbia U., 1971, PhD, 1973. Registered profl. geologist, N.C. Lt. Korean Army, 1967-69; seismic data interpreter Western Geophys. Co., Houston, 1970; grad. rsch. and teaching asst. Columbia U., N.Y.C., 1969-73; rsch. assoc. Lamont-Doherty Geol. Observatory and Henry Krumb Sch. Mines, N.Y.C., 1973-76; vis. scientist Earthquake Rsch. Inst., Tokyo, Japan, 1981; geophysicist Naval Ocean Rsch. & Devel. Activity Nat. Sci. Lab., Bay St. Louis, Miss., 1984-85; asst. prof. geophysics Dept. Marine, Earth & Atmospheric Sci., N.C. State U., Raleigh, 1976-79, assoc. prof. geophysics, 1979-86, prof. geophysics, 1986-89; pres. Geophex, Ltd., Raleigh, 1983—; cons. in field. Contbr. articles to Jour. Geophys. Rsch., Geophysics, Mining Engring. Jour., Geophys. Rsch. Letter, Marine Geotechnology, IEEE Jour. Ocean Engring. Grantee NSF, NASA and others. Mem. AAAS, Am. Geophys. Union, Soc. Exploration Geophysicists, Carolina Geol. Soc., Internat. Assn. Engring. Geologists, Soc. Mining Engrs. Office: Geophex Ltd 605 Mercury St Raleigh NC 27603-2343

WONG, ANTONIO HAM, family physician; b. San Pedro Sula, Honduras, Oct. 7, 1960; came to U.S., 1973; s. Hui Chung and Maria (Wong) H.; m. Heidi Wong, Apr. 7, 1990; children: Lawrence, Catherine, Kristen, Keith. BS, U. Miami, Fla., 1984, MD, 1990. Chief resident dept. family medicine Jackson Meml. Hosp., Miami, 1992-93; med. dir. PCA-Century Med. Ctr., Miami, 1993-95; CEO, founder Caduceus Med. Inst., Pembroke Pines, Fla., 1995—. Mem. AMA, Am. Acad. Family Physicians, Am. Soc. Bariatric Physicians, Fla. Med. Assn., Dade County Med. Assn. Home: 6523 Champlain Ter Davie FL 33331

WONG, BENEDICT DING CHUNG, investor; b. Hong Kong, Aug. 1, 1955; came to U.S., 1974; s. Ting and Wai Yuen (Lee) W. BSCE, U. Hawaii, 1978, MSCE, 1980; PhD in Environ./Civil Engring., U. Ill., 1985. Rsch. asst./systems analyst U. Hawaii, Honolulu, 1975-78; grad. rsch. asst. U. Hawaii, 1978-80, U. Ill., Urbana, 1980-85; postdoctoral rsch. assoc. U. Ill., 1985-86; engr. Sub-Land, Inc., El Paso, Tex., 1986-87; sr. software engr. AccuGraph/Holguin Corp., El Paso, 1987-88; prin./owner Caliber, El Paso/Denton, 1988; asst. prof. U. North Tex., Denton, 1990-95, coord. mech. design engring. tech., 1993-95, supr. engring. tech. network, mgr. CAD lab., 1991-94; cons. in field; reviewer papers Internat. Computer Symposium, 1992. Mem. IEEE Computer Soc., Assn. Computing Machinery, Am. Geophys. Union, Inst. Indsl. Engrs., Ops. Rsch. Soc. Am., Inst. Mgmt. Scis. (seeion chmn. nat. meetings 1992-94), Inst. for Ops. Rsch. and Mgmt. Scis., Chi Epsilon. Home: PO Box 2987 Denton TX 76202-2987

WONG, CHEUK-YIN, physicist; b. Kwangtung, China, Apr. 28, 1941; came to U.S., 1959; s. Hong-Yu and Sau-King (Li) W.; m. Jeanne Pei-Hwa Yang, Feb. 12, 1966; children: Janet, Albert, Lisa. AB, Princeton U., 1961, PhD, 1966. Rsch. physicist Oak Ridge (Tenn.) Nat. Lab., 1966-68, 70-82, 83-86, sr. physicist, 1986—; rsch. fellow Niels Bohr Inst., Copenhagen, Denmark, 1968-69; vis. scientist MIT, Cambridge, 1982-83; vis. prof. Inst. Nuclear Study, Tokyo, 1988. Contbr. articles to sci. jours. Bd. dirs. E. Tenn. chpt. Orgn. Chinese Ams., Knoxville, 1984-88, pres., 1992. Recipient Publ. award Martin Marietta Energy Systems Inc., 1986. Fellow Am. Phys. Soc.; mem. Princeton Alumni Assn. (chmn. alumni schs. com. East Tenn. 1981-92), Energy Capital Toastmasters Club (adminstrv. v.p. 1991-92), Overseas Chinese Physicists Assn. (life, regional coord. 1992). Home: 1043 W Outer Dr Oak Ridge TN 37830-8634 Office: Oak Ridge Nat Lab PO Box 2008 Oak Ridge TN 37831-2008

WONG, ELAINE DANG, foundation executive; b. Canton, China, June 3, 1936 (parents Am. citizens); d. Robert G. and Fung Heong (Woo) Dang; A.A. (Rotary scholar), Coalinga Coll., 1956; B.S. (AAUW scholar, Grad. Resident scholar), U. Calif., Berkeley, 1958, teaching credential, 1959; m. Philip Wong, Nov. 8, 1959; children—Elizabeth, Russell, Roger, Edith, Valerie. Tchr. acctg. San Mateo (Calif.) High Sch., 1959-60; acct., 1960-75; substitute tchr. Richmond County Schs., Augusta, Ga., 1975-77; comptroller Central Savannah River Area, United Way, Augusta, 1977-82; asst. controller Hammermill Hardwoods div. Hammermill Paper Co., Augusta, 1982-84; controller SFN Communications of Augusta, Inc. (WJBF-TV), 1984-85; acct. Med. Coll. Ga. Found., Inc., 1986-88, Nat. Sci Ctr. Found., Inc., 1988-89; cons. small bus.; pvt. tutor acctg. Mem. adv. bd. Richmond County Bd. Edn., 1985-87; bd. dirs. Cen. Savannah River chpt. Girl Scouts US, 1986-92. Panel judge Jr. Achievement Treas. award, 1980, 81; treas. Chinese Lang. Sch., 1973-75, Merry Neighborhood Sch., 1974-75. Recipient Achievement award Bank of Am., 1954. Mem. Nat. Assn. Accts. (dir. 1978-85, treas. 1982-84), Chinese Assn. Republican. Presbyterian.

WONG, SYLVIA LAW, preschool education educator; b. Canton, China, July 21, 1950; came to U.S., 1970; d. Ying and Chung Shau (Ho) Law; m. Patrick K.L. Wong, Sept. 8, 1972; 1 child, Jean. BBS, Western Ill. U., 1974. Mgr. China Garden Restaurant, Euless, Tex., 1974-81; dir. Little Scholars, Grapevine, Tex., 1981—. Mem. Nat. Assn. Edn. Young Children, Tex. Licensed Child Care Assn., So. Assn. on Children Under Six, Tex. Assn. Edn. Young Children. Home: 3212 High Meadow Dr Grapevine TX 76051-4284 Office: Little Scholars 303 W Nash St Grapevine TX 76051-5512

WONG-LIANG, EIRENE MING, psychologist; b. Nassau, Bahamas, Nov. 20, 1961; came to U.S., 1969; d. Menyu and Lim Ming (Chow) Wong; m. Danqing Liang. BA, Trinity U., San Antonio, 1984; PhD, Calif. Sch. Profl. Psychology, 1992. Crisis counselor United Way Crisis Hotline, San Antonio, 1983; lab. asst. Trinity U., 1983; counselor Bayer County Women's Ctr., San Antonio, 1984, Turning Point Juvenile Diversion Project, Garden Grove, Calif., 1985-86; psychol. trainee Wolters Elem. Sch., Fresno, 1987, San Luis Obispo (Calif.) Youth Day Treatment, 1987-88, Calif. Sch. Profl. Psychology Svc. Ctr., Fresno, 1988-89; staff psychologist 314th Med. Ctr., Little Rock, Ark., 1989-93; pvt. practice, clin. psychologist Houston, 1993—. Mem. APA, Am. Soc. Clin. Hypnosis, Nat. Register Health Svc. Providers in Psychology, Tex. Psychol. Assn., Houston Psychol. Assn., Houston Assn. Clin. Hypnosis (charter, exec.), Internat. Soc. Clin. Hypnosis. Office: 10101 Southwest Fwy Ste 445 Houston TX 77074-1112

WOO, WALTER, computer systems consultant; b. San Antonio, May 12, 1948; s. Foon Foo and Man Yin (Wong) W.; m. Margaret Leong, Aug. 26, 1973; children: Ryan David, Ellery. BA, St. Mary's U., San Antonio, 1971; postgrad., U Houston, 1983. Spl. projects chemist Atlantic Richfield Chem., Channelview, Tex., 1977; programmer/analyst First City Svcs., Houston, 1978-80; systems analyst Aminoil USA, Houston, 1980-81; sr. systems analyst Occidental Petroleum Co., Houston, 1981-82; systems analyst Houston Export Crating Co., 1982-83; systems specialist (mgr.) Ford Aerospace and Comm., Houston, 1983-85; project mgr. Raytheon Corp., Houston, 1985-87; systems cons. Ciber Inc., Houston, 1987-89, Computer Horizons Corp., Houston, 1989-92; ind. cons. Innovative Tech. Info. Systems, Houston, 1992—; adj. instr. Houston C.C. Vol. United Way. With Tex. Air N.G. Dow Chem. Co. acad. scholar, 1977. Mem. Data Processing Mgmt. Assn., Golden Key. Republican. Baptist. Home and Office: 2115 Gentryside Dr Houston TX 77077-3601

WOOD, ALASTAIR JAMES JOHNSTON, physician, educator; b. Oct. 13, 1946; m. Margaret Hicks; children: Alastair, Iain. MB, BChir, St. Andrew's U., Dundee, Scotland, 1970. Lectr. Dundee U., 1975-76; rsch. fellow, clin. pharmacologist Vanderbilt U., Nashville, 1976-78; asst. prof. Vanderbilt U., 1978-82, assoc. prof., 1982-85, attending physician, 1978—, prof. medicine, pharmacology, 1985—; drug therapy editor New Eng. Jour. Medicine, 1992—; editl. bd. Clin. Pharmacology and Therapeutics, Biopharmaceutics and Drug Disposition. Author: (textbook) Drugs and Anesthesia, 1994; contbr. articles to profl. jours. Mem. adv. com. FDA, 1992-96. Recipient Sir James McKenie award, Dr. R.D. Campbell Meml. prize, William McCunn Traveling fellowship, Merck Sharp & Dome Internat. fellowship. Fellow Royal Coll. Physicians. Office: Vanderbilt U Dept Clin Pharmacology 546 MRBI Pierce & 23rd Nashville TN 37232

WOOD, ANDY, business executive. CEO Burnham Svc. Corp., Atlanta. Office: Burnham Svc Corp Ste 310 100 Hartville Center Pky Atlanta GA 30354

WOOD, BOB GAINES, JR., finance educator; b. Jonesboro, Ark., May 23, 1957; s. Bobby Gaines and Mary Lou (Cole) W.; m. Terri Ann Freeland, May 26, 1984; children: Jill, Brian, Laura. BS, Ark. State U., 1978, MBA, 1990; PhD, La. State U., 1994. Profl. sales rep. Abbott Labs., Memphis, 1979-82; broker Dean Witter Reynolds, Memphis, 1982-86; mgr. Delta Farms, Inc., Jonesboro, Ark., 1986-89; asst. prof. fin. Ark. State U., State University, 1993-94, Tenn. Tech. U., Cookeville, 1994—. Bd. Regents fellow La. State U., Baton Rouge, 1992-94. Mem. Am. Fin. Assn., Fin. Mgmt. Assn., Multinat. Fin. Soc., Ea. Fin. Assn., So. Fin. Assn. Home: 859 Oaklawn Ct Cookeville TN 38501 Office: Tenn Tech U Box 5152 Cookeville TN 38505

WOOD, CHARLES DOUGLAS, surgeon educator; b. Amherst, N.S., Can., 1937. MD, McGill U., 1970. Diplomate Am. Bd. Surgery, Am. Bd. Colon and Rectal Surgery. Intern Royal Victoria Hosp., Montreal, Can., 1970-71, resident in gen. surgery, 1971-75; resident in colon and rectal surgery U. Minn., Mpls., 1975-76; staff mem. Muskogee VA Hosp., Okla.; prof. U. Okla. Mem. Assn. for Academic Surgery, Am. Coll. Surgeons, Am. Soc. Colon and Rectal Surgeons, Royal Coll. Surgeons in Can. Office: VA Med Ctr 112 Honor Heights Rd Muskogee OK 74401*

WOOD, CHARLES MONROE, theology educator; b. Salida, Colo., Nov. 22, 1944; s. Roy Milton and Ruth (Avery) W.; m. Jean Ann Fesler, Sept. 4, 1966; 1 child, Leslie Anne. BA, U. Denver, 1966; ThM, Boston U., 1969; M. Philosophy, Yale U., 1971, PhD, 1972. Ordained to ministry United Meth. Ch. as deacon, 1967, as elder, 1973. Pastor Rocky Mountain Conf., United Meth. Ch., 1972-76; asst. prof. theology Perkins Sch. Theology, So. Meth. U., Dallas, 1976-82, assoc. prof. theology, 1982-88, prof. theology, 1988—, assoc. dean for acad. affairs, 1990-93; Lehman prof. Christian doctrine So. Meth. U., Dallas, 1992—; mem. Rocky Mountain Conf., United Meth. Ch. Author: Theory and Religious Understanding, 1975, Formation of Christian Understanding, 1981, 2d edit., 1993, Vision and Discernment, 1985, An Invitation to Theological Study, 1994; contbr. articles to profl. jours. Mem. Am. Acad. Religion, Am. Theol. Soc., AAUP, Phi Beta Kappa, Omicron Delta Kappa. Office: So Meth U Perkins Sch of Theology Dallas TX 75275-0133

WOOD, CHARLES W., financial services company executive; b. McAlester, Okla., Nov. 6, 1946; s. Edgar Scott and Jessie Doyle (Ray) W.; m. Maxie Rae Moss, July 3, 1975 (div. July 1988); 1 child, Whitney Rae. AA, Eastern Okla. State Coll., 1966; BS, Okla. State U., 1968. Regional planner Kiamichi Econ. Dist., Wilburton, Okla., 1969-73; state planner Okla. Crime Commn., Oklahoma City 1973-75, dir. planning, 1975-80, dir., 1980-81; adminstr., mgmt. cons., logistics trainer Okla. Crime Victims Bd., Oklahoma City, 1981-89; registered rep. Waddell and Reed, Inc., Edmond, Okla., 1989-91, dist. mgr., mgmt. trainer, 1991—; mgmt. cons. Author/editor/pub. Victims' Voice newsletter, 1985-91. Recipient Liberty Bell award Okla. Bar Assn., 1985. Mem. Nat. Assn. Victims Compensation (treas. 1983-87, v.p. 1987-89), Jaycees (charter pres. 1970-73), Rotary (treas. 1983-85). Democrat. Ch. of Christ. Office: Waddell and Reed Inc 508 W 15th St Edmond OK 73013

WOOD, CLINTON WAYNE, middle school educator; b. Birmingham, Ala., Nov. 13, 1954; s. Clinton Mason and Dorothy Ann (Pullen) W. BA, U. Mobile, 1978. Cert. secondary edn. tchr., Ala. Tchr., coach Westminster Christian Sch., Gadsden, Ala., 1978-79, Simmons Mid. Sch., Hoover, Ala., 1979—. Author, editor: The Marble Valley Boys, 1986; contbr. articles to profl. jours. Named one of Outstanding Young Men of Am., 1985. Mem. Nat. Edn. Assn., Ala. Edn. Assn., Coaches Assn. (state and nat.), SAR, SCV. Baptist. Home: 3400 Treeline Ct Apt 604 Hoover AL 35216-5714 Office: Simmons Mid Sch 1575 Patton Chapel Rd Birmingham AL 35226-2257

WOOD, DEBORAH CHRISTINE, critical care nurse, educator; b. Houston, Oct. 20, 1948; d. John Bud and Bettye (Miller) Lawson; m. Billy Ray Wood, May 24, 1977; children: Amy, Mike, John, Daniel. ADN, Trinity Valley Jr. Coll., 1987; BSN, U. Tex., Arlington, 1990; MSN, U. Tex., Tyler, 1994. RN, Tex.; cert. advanced practice nurse, clin. nurse specialist in pediats. Telemetry/stepdown unit staff, charge nurse Mother Frances Hosp., Tyler, 1987-88, staff nurse cardiovasc. ICU, 1987-88, charge nurse cardiovasc. ICU, 1988—; critical care instr. Tyler Jr. Coll., 1992-93, instr. AD nursing program, 1993—. Mem. AACN, Am. Heart Assn. (cardiovascular nursing coun., critical care coun.), Sigma Theta Tau. Roman Catholic.

WOOD, DOLORES FUNAI, horticultural lecturer, writer; b. Richmond, Va., Oct. 5, 1931; d. Hamlet Virginius and Viola Elizabeth Constance (Mason) Funai; m. William Tiqnor Wood, July 11, 1955; c: Deborah Elaine, William Morison III. AB in Edn., U. N.C., 1953. Educator of English Tuckahoe Junior High School, Richmond, Va., 1958-61; educator of history The Stony Point School, Richmond, Va., 1962-64; educator on herbs Virginia Commonwealth U., Richmond, Va., 1984-86, Virginia Cooperative Extension Services, Richmond, Va., 1982-87; master gardener Va. Coop. Extension Scv., Richmond, 1981—; landscape design critic. Author: Tips and Tidbits, 1981; contbr. articles to profl. jours. Developer garden for handicapped J. Sargeant Reynolds C.C., 1982, developer new herb bed Marymont Park, 1982; originator Herbs Galore Festival Marymont Park, 1985; advisor Maymont Park, Richmond, 1985—. Recipient Distinguished Work award, Virginia Federation of Garden Clubs, Richmond, 1984-88. Mem. Old Dominion Herb Soc.(pres. 1980-81), Herb Society of Am.(regional chmn. 1982-83), Thomas Jefferson Garden Club, The Women's Club, The Tuckahoe Women's Club, The Country Club of Virginia, All Saints Episcopal Church.

WOOD, EDWIN THOMAS, journalist; b. Nashville, Oct. 9, 1963; s. Stephen Fletcher and Nancy Ann Wood; m. Nicki Pendleton, Oct. 21, 1989. Student, U. Leeds, Eng., 1984-85; BA, Vanderbilt U., 1986. Writer, journalist self employed, Nashville, 1984—; editor mag. Bank Director, Franklin, Tenn., 1990-93; bus./investigative reporter The Tennessean, Nashville, 1993-95; guest lectr. bus. and investigative journalism Bucharest (Romania) U., 1997. Author: Karski: How One Man Tried to Stop the Holocaust, 1994; contbg. writer Nashville Life, 1995-96, Nashville Scene, 1989-93; contbr. articles to Wall St. Jour., N.Y. Times, Oxford Am., Spy, Columbia Journalism Rev., others. Recipient Geyer award for journalism Vanderbilt U., 1986; Holocaust rsch. grantee CUNY, 1996. Democrat. Home and Office: 3801 Woodmont Ln Nashville TN 37215

WOOD, EMILY CHURCHILL, gifted and talented education educator; b. Summit, N.J., Apr. 11, 1925; d. Arthur Burdett and Ruth Vail (Pierson) Churchill; m. Philip Warren Wood, June 22, 1946; children: Martha, Arthur, Warren, Benjamin. BA, Smith Coll., 1946; MA in Teaching, Manhattanville Coll., 1971; postgrad., U. Tulsa, 1974-79, Langston U., 1990-92. Cert. tchr. social studies, learning disabilities, elem. edn., econs., Am. history, world history. Tchr. Miss Fines Sch., Princeton, N.J., 1946-47, Hallen Ctr. for Edn., Portchester, N.Y., 1973-74, Town and Country Sch., Tulsa, Okla., 1974-79, Tulsa Pub Schs., 1979—, Tulsa Jr. Coll., 1990-92, 94; adv. bd. Great Expectations Educators, Tulsa, 1985—; leader colloquia bill of rights Arts and Humanities Coun., Tulsa, 1989; mem. literacy task force Tulsa 2000 Edn. Com., 1990-92; chmn. internat. student exch. Eisenhower Internat. Sch., Tulsa, 1992-94. Author: (with others) Visual Arts in China,

1988, Applauding Our Constitution, 1989, The Bill of Rights: Who Guarantees What, 1993; contbr. articles to profl. jours. Dir. Smith Coll. Alumnae, Northampton, Mass., 1956-59; leader, founder Am. Field Svc., Tulsa, 1982-84; pres., v.p. Booker T. Washington H.S. PTA, Tulsa, 1985; campaign mgr. auditors race Dem. Party, Tulsa, 1988, 92, 94; bd. dirs., nominations chair Sister Cities Internat., Tulsa, 1992—. Named Tulsa Tchr. of Yr. Tulsa Classroom Tchrs. Assn., 1988, Nat. Elem. Tchr. of Yr., Nat. Bar Aux., 1992; recipient Elem. Medal of Excellence, Okla. Found. for Excellence, 1990, Valley Forge Tchrs. medal Freedoms Found., 1992, Paragon award Tulsa Commn. on Status of Women, 1996. Mem. Nat. Coun. Social Studies (religion program com. 1984—), DAR, Okla. Edn. Assn., Okla. Coun. Social Studies (pres. 1995, tchr. of yr. 1984), Okla. Bar Assn. (law related com. 1988—, tchr. of yr. 1990), Okla. Coun. Econ. Edn. (state and nat. awards 1981, 89, 92), Kent Place Alumnae Assn. (disting. alumna award 1992). Home: 3622 S Yorktown Pl Tulsa OK 74105-3452

WOOD, EMMA S., nursing administrator; b. Lancaster County, Pa., June 20, 1945; d. Moses H. and Elizabeth M. (Shirk) Zimmerman; m. George Wood, Feb. 4, 1977 (dec. July 1989); 1 child, George William Jr. ADN, Edison C.C., 1979; BSN, U. South Fla., 1987, MSN, 1989. RN, Fla.; cert. psychiat. and mental health nurse, cert. profl. in health care quality, clin. specialist in psychiat. mental health. Agy. adminstr., home health nurse VNA of Desoto County, Arcadia, Fla., 1979-81; utilization rev. coord. G. Pierce Wood Meml. Hosp., 1981-85, RN specialist, 1985-89, sr. nurse supr., mgr., 1989-95, nurse educator, 1995—. Mem. ANA, Fla. Nurses Assn., Nat. Assn. for Health Care Quality, Fla. Assn. for Health Care Quality, Am. Psychiat. Nurses Assn., NLN, Sigma Theta Tau. Home: 2808 Caribbean Dr Punta Gorda FL 33982-4302

WOOD, GERALD DAVID, religious organization administrator; b. Narrows, Va., Oct. 16, 1947; s. Curtis Edmond and Myrtle Isabella (Jernigan) W.; m. Sandra Fay Harris, Aug. 24, 1968; children: Angela Dawn, Anthony David, Jonathan David, Beth Lynette. Student, Kjesaters, Vingaker, Sweden, 1966-67, Washington and Lee U., 1967-68, U. Va., 1968-69, Emmanuel Coll., 1973-81, Oxford U., 1994—; BREd, Maranatha Inst Christian Mins., 1994. Ordained to ministry Internat. Pentecostal Holiness Ch., 1968. Pastor Charlottesville (Va.) Pentecostal Holiness Ch., 1968-72, St. Paul Pentecostal Holiness Ch., Max Meadows, Va., 1972-82; sec.-treas. Va. Conf. Sunday Sch. Bd., Dublin, 1974-80; treas. Va. Conf. Christian Edn. Bd., 1980-86; pastor New Covenant Pentecostal Holiness Ch., Princeton, W.Va., 1982-86; dir. Christian edn. Appalachian Conf. Pentecostal Holiness Ch., Dublin, 1986-94; mem. Appalachian Conf. Bd., 1994; sr. pastor 1st Pentecostal Holiness Ch., Greenville, N.C., 1994—; mem. gen. Christian edn. bd. Internat. Pentecostal Holiness Ch., 1987-91, 93, mem. gen. bd. publs., 1993—; dir. radio ministry Wythe County Ministerial Assn., Wytheville, Va., 1978-80; pres. W.Va. Camp Meeting Assn., Princeton, 1982-84; bd. dirs. Church Ministries United, Greenville, N.C., 1994—. Bd. dirs. Mountaineer Food Bank, Gassaway, W.Va., 1986; bd. dirs. Marantha Inst., Dublin, 1986—, treas., 1989-92, registrar, 1992-94; pres. Dublin Elem. Sch. PTA, 1988-90, Pulaski County Advs. for Talented and Gifted, 1989-92, sec. New River Dist. PTA, 1990-92; chmn. bd. dirs., Ch. Ministries United, Greenville, N.C., 1996—. Mem. Coun. for Exceptional Children, Internat. Platform Assn., Am. Inst. Profl. Bookkeepers, Pentecostal Fellowship N.Am. (v.p. Princeton chpt. 1982-83). Republican. Office: 1st Pentecostal Holiness Ch Brinkley Rd and Plaza Dr Greenville NC 27858

WOOD, GREGORY BURTON, JR., brokerage house executive; b. Mpls., Apr. 1, 1943; s. Gregory Burton and Ramona Edith (Jackson) W.; m. Linda A. Payn, July 8, 1967 (div. 1984); children: Kelly L., G. Scott; m. Judith A. Clubb, Dec. 15, 1984; 1 child, Jennifer L. Student, Oreg. State U., 1962-66; grad., Securities Industry Inst., 1990. Sales rep. Itek Corp., Seattle, 1966-69; account exec. Shearson Hammill & Co., Seattle, 1969-78, forest products commodities analyst, 1973-78; fin. advisor, forest products commodities analyst Prudential Securities, Inc., Bellevue, Wash., 1978-82; br. mgr., 1st v.p. Prudential Securities, Inc., Ft. Worth, 1982-95; dir. regional tng. Prudential Securities, Inc., Dallas, 1995-97; exec. dir. One Prudential, Phoenix, 1997—; active Chgo. Mercantile Exchange, 1976-82. Contbr. articles to profl. jours. Past mem. bd. dirs. Ft. Worth Boys and Girls Club. Mem. Rolls-Royce Owners Club, Classic Car Club Am. Republican. Home: 4304 Briarhaven Rd Fort Worth TX 76109-4602 Office: One Prudential Ste 125 1707 E Highland Ave Phoenix AZ 85016

WOOD, IVAN, JR., lawyer; b. Corpus Christi, Tex., Oct. 1, 1947. AA, Del Mar Jr. Coll., 1967; BBA, U. Tex., 1969, JD, 1972. Bar: Tex. 1972, U.S. Ct. Military Appeals, 1974, U.S. Supreme Ct. 1991. Ptnr. Baker & Hostetler, Houston. Lt. JAGC, USN, 1972-76. Mem. ABA, State Bar Tex., Am. Acad. Hosp. Attys., Nat. Health Lawyers Assn., Beta Alpha Psi, Phi Delta Phi. Office: Baker & Hostetler 1000 Louisiana St Ste 2000 Houston TX 77002-5009*

WOOD, J. BARCLAY, technical writer, forensic firearms consultant; b. Bowling Green, Ky., June 14, 1934; s. James William and Stella Elisabeth (Stieff) W.; m. Marijo Flaherty, Jan. 1954 (dec. Oct. 1981); children: Lark Lynne, Heather Lea, Ethan Allen, Nathan Hughes; m. Judith DeGroote, June 4, 1983; 1 adopted child, Michael Paul. Grad. high sch., Henderson, Ky. Founder, owner, mgr., cons. Firearms Svc., Henderson, 1948—; gunsmithing editor Guns of Ammo mag., L.A., 1974-82, Shooting Times mag., Peoria, Ill., 1982—; Am. editor Internationales Waffen mag., Zurich, Switzerland, 1986—; instr. firearms courses Henderson C.C., 1977; condr. firearms seminar Baldini Rsch. Assocs., Virginia Beach, Va., 1990—. Author 14 books; columnist, 1972—; contbr. over 800 articles to mags., including Shooting Times, Combat Handguns, Guns mag., Am. Handgunner, Internationles Waffen, 1962—. Mem. NRA (life), Am. Pistolsmiths Guild (assoc.).. Libertarian. Home and Office: 2d St Box 72 Corydon KY 42406

WOOD, JAMES ALBERT, foreign language educator; b. Enterprise, Oreg., Nov. 9, 1949; s. Ralph Albert and Charlotte Lavona (Johnson) Wood; m. Maritza Wood, Apr. 14, 1977; 1 child, Jamie Maritza. BS in Health and Phys. Edn., David Lipscomb U., Nashville, 1975; BA in Spanish, So. Oreg. State Coll., 1979, MA in Health and Phys. Edn., 1979; EdD, Tex. A&M U., Kingsville, 1986; postgrad., U. Tenn., 1981-82. Cert. health and phys. edn. tchr., K-12, Spanish-ESL tchr., mid-mgmt. supr., supt., elem., bilingual all level ESL, Tex. Tchr. Spanish and ESL Galena Park Ind. Sch. Dist., Houston, 1986-88; tchr. ESL and reading Rice Consol. Ind. Sch. Dist., Altair, Tex., 1988-89; ESL tchr. K-5 Royalwood Elem.Sch., Houston, 1989-90; vol. Peace Corps, El Salvador, 1976-77; sr. program devel. specialist bilingual programs U. Okla., Norman, 1990-92; asst. prof. bilingual edn. Sul Ross State U. Rio Grande Coll., Uvalde, Tex., 1992—; adj. prof. Tex. So. U., Houston, U. Houston, Clear Lake, Tex., 1988-90. Sgt. U.S. Army, 1970-73. Dean's grantee Tex. A&M U.-Kingsville. Mem. ASCD, TESOL, Nat. Assn. Bilingual Edn., Tex. Assn. Bilingual Edn., Tex. Tchr. Educators Assn., Non-Commd. Officers Assn. (life), Am. Legion, VFW (life). Home: PO Box 1415 Uvalde TX 78802-1415

WOOD, JAMES E., JR., religion educator, author; b. Portsmouth, Va., July 29, 1922; s. James E. and Elsie Elizabeth (Bryant) W.; m. Alma Leacy McKenzie, Aug. 12, 1943; 1 son, James Edward III. BA, Carson-Newman Coll., 1943; MA, Columbia U., 1949; BD, So. Bapt. Theol. Sem., 1947, ThM, 1948; PhD, So. Baptist Theol. Sem., 1957; postgrad., U. Tenn., 1943-44; cert. in Chinese, Yale U., 1949-50; Japanese diploma, Naganuma Sch. Japanese Studies, Tokyo, 1950-51, Oxford U., Eng., 1983; LLD, Seinan Gakuin U., Japan, 1983; LLD (hon.), Capitol U., 1996. Ordained to ministry So. Bapt. Ch., 1942. Pastor So. Bapt. chs., Tenn. and Ky., 1942-48; Bapt. missionary to Japan, 1950-55; prof. religion and lit. Seinan Gakuin U., Japan, 1951-55; prof. history of religions Baylor U., Waco, Tex., 1955-73, dir. honors program, 1959-64; dir. J.M. Dawson Inst. Ch.-State Studies Baylor U., 1980-95, chmn. interdeptl. grad. degree program in ch.-state studies, 1962-73, 80-95, Simon and Ethel Bunn Disting. prof. ch.-state studies, 1980—, chmn. faculty-student Far Eastern exchange program, 1970-72; exec. dir. Bapt. Joint Com. on Public Affairs, Washington, 1972-80; mem. ctrl. panel Bapt. World Alliance Commn. on Religious Liberty and Human Rights, 1965-75, Commn. on Freedom, Justice and Peace, 1976-80; chmn. Bapt. Com. on Bicentennial, 1973-76; mem. So. Bapt. Inter-Agy. Coun., 1972-80, vice chmn., 1975-76, sec. 1976-77; vis. prof. So. Bapt. Theol. Sem., 1974, N.Am. Bapt. Theol. Sem., Sioux Falls, S.D., 1974, 79, Okla. Bapt. U., Shawnee, 1977, Naval Coll. of Chaplains, Providence, 1988—, others; vis. lectr. Ashland (Ohio) Theol. Sem., 1971; Vernon Richardson lectr. U. Bapt. Ch., Balt., 1975, Ea. Bapt. Theol. Sem., Phila., 1975; lectr. First World Congress on Religious Liberty, Amsterdam, 1977, 2d Congress, Rome, 1984, U. Faculty of Law, Warsaw, Poland, 1984, Brigham Young U., 1986, 95, U. Tirana, Albania, 1992, U. Malta, 1994, Austin Coll., 1995, numerous others; chair Internat. Consultation on Relig. Rights and Ethnic Identity, Budapest, 1992; co-chair Internat. Conf. Religious Freedom, Moscow, 1993; mem. internat. adv. bd. World Report on Freedom Conscious Human Rights Ctr., U. Sussex, U.K.; co-chair consultation on Freedom of Conscience and Belief, Moscow, 1993; chair Internat. Consultation Religious Liberty and Social Peace, Malta, 1994; Carver-Barnes lectr. Southeastern Bapt. Theol. Sem., 1981; Asian Found. lectr. Seinan Gakuin U., Japan, 1983; ecumenical consultation on edn. Nat. Coun. Chs., 1974; various other com. coun. positions. Author: A History of American Literature: An Anthology, 1952, (co-author) Church and State in Scripture, History and Constitutional Law, 1958, The Problem of Nationalism, 1969, Nationhood and the Kingdom, 1977, Secular Humanism and the Public Schools, 1986, Reflections on Church and State, 1995; (edited by Derek H. Davis) The Separation of Church and State Defended: Selected Writings of James E. Wood, Jr., 1995, Church-State Relations in the Modern World, 1996; editor: Markham Press Fund, Baylor U. Press, 1970-72; founding editor: Jour. Ch. and State, 1959-73, 80-93, mem. editl. coun., 1973-80; mem. editl. bd. Religion and Public Edn., Religious Freedom Reporter; editor; contbr. numerous profl. pubs. including Religion and Politics, Church and State, others; area editor, contbr. Ency. So. Bapts., 1982; contbr. Changing Trends in Education, 1992, Law, Religion and Human Rights in GLobal Perspective, 1995, Dialogue of Democracy: An American Politics Reader, 1996; contbr. over 300 articles to profl. jours. Sponsor Ams. for Public Schs., 1963-68; bd. dirs. Waco (Tex.) Planned Parenthood, 1966-72, pres., 1971-72; sponsor Christians Concerned for Israel, 1968—, Tex. Conf. Chs. Consultation on Religion and Public Edn., 1971, Nat. Christian Leadership Conf. for Israel, 1978—; pres. Waco area ACLU, bd. dirs. Tex. unit, 1968-72; pres. Nat. Council Religion and Public Edn., 1979-83, exec. com., 1975—, bd. dirs., 1972—; chmn. exec. com. Council Washington Reps. on UN, 1977-80, mem. council exec. com., 1973-80; exec. com. Nat. Coalition on Public Edn. and Religious Liberty, 1973—; mem. religious liberty com. Nat. Council Chs. U.S.A., 1972—, also mem. com. internat. concerns on human rights; Am. rep. Chs. Montreux Colloquium on Helsinki Final Act, 1977; v.p. Waco Conf. Christians and Jews, 1983-86, Internat. Acad. for Freedom of Religion and Belief, 1985-90, pres., 1990—; mem. internat. adv. bd. World Report on Freedom of Conscience, Human Rights Ctr., U. Sussex, Eng.; trustee Internat. Devel. Conf., 1974-80; nat. coun. Am.-Israel Friendship League, 1977—; founder, chmn. Waco Human Rights Week, 1981—; mem. ch. rels. com., U.S. Holocaust Meml. Coun., 1990—. Recipient Disting. Alumnus award Carson-Newman Coll., 1974, Religious Liberty award Alliance for Preservation of Religious Liberty, 1980, Henrietta Szold award Tex. region Hadassah, 1981, Human Rights award Waco Conf. Christians and Jews, 1986, Cir. of Achievement award Baylor U. Mortar Bd., 1991, Religious Freedom Lifetime award Ams. United Ctrl. Tex., 1993, W.R. White Meritorious Svc. award, 1996; hon. Tex. col., 1969. Mem. Am. Soc. Ch. History, Am. Acad. Religion, Am. Soc. Internat. Law, Am. Soc. Sci. Study of Religion, N. Am. Soc. Ecumenists, NCCJ (ad. com. on ch. state and taxation 1979-85), ACLU, Phi Eta Sigma, Pi Kappa Delta, Alpha Psi Omega. Democrat. Home: 3306 Lake Heights Dr Waco TX 76708-1543 Office: Baylor U PO Box 97308 Waco TX 76798-7308

WOOD, JAMES JERRY, lawyer; b. Rockford, Ala., Aug. 13, 1940; s. James Ronald and Ada Love Wood; m. Earline Luckie, Aug. 9, 1959; children: James Jerry, William Gregory, Diana Lynn. A.B. Samford U. 1964, J.D. 1969. Bar: Ala. 1969, U.S. Supreme Ct. 1976. Dir. legal affairs Med. Assn. State of Ala., 1969-70; asst. atty. gen. State of Ala., 1970-72; asst. U.S. atty. Middle Dist. Ala., 1972-76; ptnr. Segrest, Pilgrim & Wood, 1976-77; sole practice, 1977-78; pres. Wood & Parnell, P.A., Montgomery, Ala., 1979-89; sole practice, 1990—; gen. counsel Ala. Builders Self-Insurance Fund, Home Builders of Ala., Ala. Retail Assn. Workers Compensation Fund, Automobile Dealers Assn. of Ala. Workers Compensation Fund. chmn. character and fitness com. Ala. State Bar, 1981-84, 86-89, chair task force on quality of life, 1990-92, chair task force on mem. svcs., 1994-96. Served to capt. USAR, 1974-79. Mem. ABA (environ. litigation com., Ho. of dels. 1990—), Am. Nat. Inns of Ct., Fed. Bar Assn. (pres. Montgomery chpt. 1974-75), Ala. Bar Assn., Montgomery Bar Assn., Ala. Def. Lawyers Assn., Def. Rsch. Inst. Republican. Baptist. Lodge: Montgomery Capital Rotary (pres. 1986-87). Office: PO Box 4189 Montgomery AL 36103-4189

WOOD, JOHN THURSTON, cartographer, jazz musician; b. Chgo., Apr. 29, 1928; s. Clarence Leo and Hilda Bernice (Miller) W.; m. Erma Louise Vogt, July 3, 1957; children: John Thurston Jr., Holly Lynn, Joseph Miller II. BS, Iowa State U., 1952; postgrad., Ohio State U., 1962-64, Indsl. Coll. Armed Forces, Washington, 1974, Fed. Exec. Inst., Charlottesville, Va., 1985. Commd. 2d lt. USAF, 1952, advanced through grades to lt. col., 1968; combat airlift pilot 535th Troop Carrier Squadron, Vung Tau, Vietnam, 1966-67; comdr. USAF Operational Evaluation Detachment, Topeka, 1967-70; aerial and ground survey officer Def. Intelligence Agy., Washington (D.C.), Def. Mapping Agy., Washington (D.C.), Va., 1972-76; ret., 1976; chief user svcs. Nat. Cartographic Info. Ctr. U.S. Geol. Survey, Reston, 1976-83, dep. chief, 1983-85, chief, 1985-89, 1985-89; chief Earth Sci. Info. Office U. S. Geol. Survey, Reston, 1989-95. Tuba player Buck Creek Jazz Band, 1977—. Decorated Air medal with four oak leaf clusters. Mem. Masons, Shriners. Home: 4007 Terrace Dr Annandale VA 22003-1856

WOOD, LARRY WAYNE, human resources executive, city manager; b. Shelby, N.C., June 2, 1950; s. Richard Rufus and Marjorie Coleen (Wright) W.; m. Cynthia Kaye Alexander, May 26, 1973; children: Larry Brandon, Lane Alexander. BS in Psychology, Gardner Webb U., 1972; postgrad., Cleve. C.C., 1973, Ctrl. Piedmont C.C., 1974, U. Mich., 1980, U. S.C., 1988, City U. Lic. real estate agt., gen. contractor, N.C. Dir. personnel Carolina Throwing Co., Inc., Kings Mountain, N.C., 1973-75, Spectrum Fibers, Inc., Kings Mountain, 1975-78; personnel mgr. Foote Mineral Co., Kings Mountain, 1978-85; dir. human resources City of Gastonia, 1986-91; exec. dir. human resources and pub. safety, asst. city mgr. N050postgrad., 1991-94, exec. dir. pub. svcs., 1994—; corp. officer Alexander, Inc., Kings Mountain, 1980—; ptnr. Alexander-Wood, Kings Mountain, 1980—. Active Kings Mountain United Fund, Blue Ridge Safety Coun., Kings Mountain Rescue Squad, N.C. Local Govt. Employees Credit Union Adv. Coun., Leadership Gaston, Crimestoppers, N.C. Employment Security Commn. Employers Adv. Coun., Kings Mountain Energy Commn., Gaston United Way Campaign Cabinet; mem. ad hoc com. Gaston/Cleve. Regional Airport; deacon 1st Bapt. Ch., Kings Mountain. Mem. Soc. Human Resources Mgmt., Orgn. Mcpl. Pers. Officers, Internat. Pers. Mgmt. Assn., Kings Mountain Pers. Assn., C. of C., Gardner Webb Coll. Alumni Assn., Gaston County Pers. Assn., Rotary, others. Home: 100 Gold Dust Ct Kings Mountain NC 28086-7755 Office: City of Gastonia South St City Hall Gastonia NC 28053

WOOD, LINDA SHERRILL, secondary education educator; b. Birmingham, Ala., Aug. 16, 1947; d. Virgil Alton and Anna Ruth (Boston) W. BS, Auburn U., 1969, MEd, 1973. Tchr. math. Elberta (Ala.) Jr. High Sch., 1970-85, Foley (Ala.) High Sch., 1985—. Mem. NEA, Ala. Edn. Assn., Nat. Coun. Tchrs. Math., Ala. Coun. Tchrs. Math., Baldwin County Edn. Assn. Office: Foley High Sch 1 Pride Pl Foley AL 36535-1100

WOOD, LOREN EDWIN, aerospace engineer, consultant; b. Taunton, Mass., Dec. 25, 1927; s. Elmer Roe and Alice Eleanor (Philbrick) W.; m. Ann H. Hamilton, Aug. 6, 1952; children: Joan, Alice, Scott, Carol. BA magna cum laude, Brown U., 1949; AM in Math. Analysis and Applied Math., Cornell U., 1950. Teaching fellow Cornell U., Ithaca, N.Y., 1949-50; mgr. Minuteman silo devel. instrumentation TRW Inc., Redondo beach, Calif., 1958-60; mgr. Apollo engring. and ops. support projects TRW Inc., Houston, 1966-72, mgr. shuttle computer systems and software integration, 1973-74, mgr. shuttle payload flight control studies, 1975-77, mgr. advanced programs and program devel., 1978-87; mgr. space program integration Aerospace Corp., El Segundo, Calif., 1961, mgr. Gemini launch vehicle and target vehicle flight testing, 1962-66; mgr. Apollo mission model devel. and calculations White House Com. to Select Lunar Landing Mission Model, Washington, 1961; engr. mgr. instrumentation projects, space shuttle program Rockwell Internat., Houston, 1988-94, engr. mgr. space sta. command and data sys., 1994—; speaker to tech. socs., radio, TV, civic clubs. Author numerous tech. papers and reports. Organizer, adminstr. youth football and baseball leagues, Friendswood, Tex., 1967-69; mem. city Charter Commn., Friendswood, 1970-71, Friendswood City Coun., 1977-83; founding trustee Houston Grad. Sch. Theology, 1983—, Biblical Resources, Inc., 1989—. Capt. USAF, 1954-56. Named Citizen of Yr., Friendswood C. of C., 1983; recipient Disting. Svc. award U.S. Jaycees, 1983. Fellow AIAA (assoc., chmn. Outstanding Spl. Events 1971-73, chmn. Outstanding sect. 1975-76); mem. Instrumentation Soc. Am. (sr.), Phi Beta Kappa, Sigma Xi. Home: 905 Cowards Creek Dr Friendswood TX 77546-4407

WOOD, MARTHA SWAIN, mayor; b. Sept. 14, 1943; m. Frank B. Wood, June 1965; children: Helen Maria, Wesley Swain, Daniel Hardison. BA, Wake Forest U., 1965. Tchr. English and French city high schs., Henderson, N.C., 1965-66; buyer, v.p., sec., treas. Swain's, Inc., Fayetteville, N.C., 1972-83; mgr. Swain Investments, Fayetteville, 1984—; alderman City of Winston-Salem, N.C., 1981-89, mayor, 1989—. Named Woman of Yr., Winston-Salem Chronicle, 1987. Mem. Greater Winston-Salem C. of C., Kiwanis. Baptist. Office: Office of Mayor PO Box 2511 101 N Main St Winston Salem NC 27102-2511*

WOOD, PAULA DAVIDSON, lawyer; b. Oklahoma City, Dec. 20, 1952; d. Paul James and Anna Mae (Ferrero) Davidson; m. Andrew E. Wood; children: Michael Paul, John Roland. BS, Okla. State U., 1976; JD, Oklahoma City U., 1982. Bar: Okla. 1983, U.S. Dist. Ct. (we. dist.) Okla. 1983, U.S. Supreme Ct. 1995; cert. pub. mgr. Pvt. practice Oklahoma City, 1984-85; ptnr. Davidson & Wood, Oklahoma City, 1985-87; child support enforcement counsel Okla. Dept. Human Svcs., Oklahoma City, 1987-92, child support adminstr. (IV-D dir.), 1992—; adj. instr. Tech. Inst. Okla. State U., Oklahoma City, 1985. Articles editor Oklahoma City U. Law Rev., 1982. Mem. Okla. Bar Assn. (sec. family law sect. 1987, Golden Gavel award 1987), Nat. Child Support Enforcement Assn. (bd. dirs. 1995, sec. 1997), Okla. Child Support Enforcement Assn., S.W. Regional Child Assn. State Child Support Enforcement Adminstrs. (pres. 1996), Western Interstate Child Support Enforcement Coun. (sec. 1995). Republican. Roman Catholic. Home: 3020 Shadybrook Midwest City OK 73110 Office: PO Box 15096 Del City OK 73155-5096

WOOD, RICHARD ELGIN, JR., family physician; b. Gainesville, Tex., Aug. 6, 1947; s. Richard Elgin and Celena Lucile (Manning) W.; m. Gina Murphy Wood, Dec. 21, 1968 (div. Jan. 1982); 1 child, Kimberly Nicole; m. June Reynolds, Apr. 9, 1983; 1 child, Anne Reynolds Wood. BS, U. Ala., Tuscaloosa, 1969; MD, Tulane U., 1973. Diplomate Am. Bd. Family Physicians. Intern in internal medicine Letterman Army Med. Ctr., Presidio of San Francisco, 1973-74; resident in family practice Martin Army Hosp., Ft. Benning, Ga., 1974-76; pvt. practice Columbus, Ga., 1979-92; founding ptnr. Columbus Clinic P.C., 1992—. Bd. dirs. Columbus Alliance for Battered Women, 1983-84; vestryman St. Thomas Episcopal Ch., Columbus, 1983-86. Fellow Am. Acad. Family Physicians, Muscogee County Med. Soc., Kiwanis Club of Columbus (bd. dirs. 1983-86, chmn. fair com. 1987), Scabbard & Blade, Alpha Epsilon Delta, Phi Mu Epsilon, Gamma Sigma Epsilon. Office: The Columbus Clinic 610 19th St Columbus GA 31901-1528

WOOD, ROBERT CHARLES, financial consultant; b. Chgo., Apr. 8, 1956; s. Roy Edward and Mildred Lucille (Jones) W.; m. Jennifer Jo Briggs, Oct. 1984; children: Jacqueline Jones, Reagan Keith. BA in History, BBA in Real Estate, So. Meth. U., 1979, JD, 1982. Bar: Tex. 1983. Appraiser McClellan-Massey, Dallas, 1977-79; researcher, acquisitions officer Amstar Fin. Corp., Dallas, 1979-80; prin. Robert Wood Cons., Dallas, 1981—; cons. Plan Mktg. Cos., 1983-84; pvt. practice law, Dallas, 1983-84; gen. counsel Diversified Benefits, Inc., Dallas, 1984-86; nat. accts. mgr. L. omas & Nettleton Real Estate Group, Dallas, 1987-88; sr. pension cons., prin. Eppler, Guerin &Turner, 1988-93; chmn. adv. coun. on devel. Medisend, 1991; nat. consulting coord. fin. advisors coun., v.p. Callan Assocs., San Francisco, 1994-95; atty. at law, 1995—. Author: Electionomics: How the Money Managers View the Election, 1992, After the Congress Vote: How the Managers See Things Now, 1993; mem. So. Meth. U. Law Rev., 1981-82; contbr. articles to profl. pubs. Bd. dirs. Am. Cancer Soc., Dallas unit, 1982-87, mem. spl. events com., 1986-87, crusade com., 1987-88, corp. devel. bd. chmn. 1989—. Mem. Tex. Bar Assn., Phila. Bar Assn., Phi Gamma Delta.

WOOD, SHELTON EUGENE, college educator, consultant, minister; b. Douglas, Ga., May 20, 1938; s. Shelton and Mae Lillie (Pheil) W.; m. Edna Louise Wood, Aug. 25, 1958; children: Shelton John, Deirdre Louise. AA, St. Johns U., 1958; BA, U. Nebr., 1959; MEd, Coll. William and Mary, 1971; PhD, Sussex U., 1973; EdD, Nova U., 1975; MA, Central Mich. U., 1977, MA U. Okla., 1980. Area mgr. Marshall Fields Corp., Fla., 1957-58; transp. supr. Greyhound Corp., Jacksonville, Fla., 1959-62; commd. lt. U.S. Army, 1963, advanced through grades to lt. col., 1977; with Redstone Readiness Group, 1977-80; chief studies and analysis div. Korean Inst. for Def. Analysis, 1981-83; faculty St. Johns River C.C., 1984-90. Active Boy Scouts Am., 1977-90; lay leader United Meth. Ch., Falls Church, Va., 1977-79, St. James United Meth. Ch., 1986-90. Decorated Bronze Star with 2 oak leaf clusters, Air Medal with 3 oak leaf clusters, Purple Heart with 2 oak leaf clusters; Sussex Coll. fellow, 1969-70. Mem. NEA, Putnam County C. of C. (pres. 1990-91), Am. Soc. Trainers and Developers (pres. S.E. chpt. 1974-75), Am. Def. Preparedness Assn., Phi Kappa Delta, Phi Delta Kappa. Clubs: Masons, Shriners, Kiwanis (pres. 1989-90). Author: Strategic Planning for Churches, 1995; 127 articles and reports in field of mil. tng., edn. and mgmt. Address: PO Box 820 San Mateo FL 32187

WOOD, THOMAS WILLARD, health care industry executive; b. Logan, Utah, Jan. 21, 1939; s. Elmer Raymond and Leola (Pitkin) W.; m. Blanche Loila Dowdle, Sept. 11, 1959 (div.); children: Dianna Wood Raleigh, Jeffery Thomas (dec.); m. Charlene Taulbee, Oct. 5, 1974; children: Douglas Winston Remington, Angela Christine Douglas, Thomas Willard II, Michael Joseph, Matthew David. BA, Utah State U., 1962; MS, Cen. Mich. U., 1975; postgrad., Indsl. Coll. Armed Forces, 1975, Armed Forces Staff Coll., 1976. Commd. 2d lt. USAF, 1962, advanced through grades to col., 1983; chief protocol Hdqrs. Air Force Logistics Command, Wright-Patterson AFB, Ohio, 1972-75; chief spl. project div. Hdqrs. 21st Air Force, McGuire AFB, N.J., 1977-78; chief inquiries br. Office Legis. Liaison, The Pentagon, Washington, 1978-82; dep. dir. Directorate Competition Advocacy Ogden Air Logistics Ctr., Hill AFB, Utah, 1982-85; air attache U.S. Def. Attache Office, Am. Embassy, Wellington, New Zealand, 1985-88; chief protocol, dep. dir. pub. and govtl. affairs Hdqrs. U.S. Comdr.-in-Chief Pacific, Camp Smith, Hawaii, 1988-89; ret., 1989; adminstrv. asst. to v.p. mktg. Hawaii Med. Svc. Assn., Honolulu, 1989-91; sr. account exec. client rels. Baxter Internat. Inc., San Antonio, 1991-92; sr. account exec. prescription svc. divsn. Caremark, Inc., San Antonio, 1992-95; with corp. accts. prescription svc. divsn. Caremark Inc., San Antonio, 1996—; dean New Zealand Mil. Attache Corps, 1986-88. Elder LDS Ch., also ch. organist, pianist, tchr. Decorated DFC, Air medal with nine oak leaf clusters; Gallantry Cross with palm (Vietnam); named hon. Royal New Zealand Air Force Navigator, 1988. Republican. Home: 1351 Grey Oak Dr San Antonio TX 78213-1602 Office: Caremark Inc 7054 Alamo Downs Pky San Antonio TX 78238-4509

WOOD, VIVIAN POATES, mezzo soprano, educator, author; b. Washington, Aug. 19, 1923; d. Harold Poates and Mildred Georgette (Patterson) W.; studies with Walter Anderson, Antioch Coll., 1953-55, Denise Restout, Saint-Leu-La-Fôret, France and Lakeville, Conn., 1960-62, 64-70, Paul A. Pisk, 1968-71, Paul Ulanowsky, N.Y.C., 1958-68, Elemer Nagy, 1965-68, Vyautas Marijosius, 1967-68; MusB Hartt Coll. Music, 1968; postgrad. (fellow) Yale U., 1968; MusM (fellow), Washington U., St. Louis, 1971, PhD (fellow), 1973. Debut in recital series Internat. Jeunesse Musicals Arts Festival, 1953, solo fellowship Boston Symphony Orch., Berkshire Music Ctr., Tanglewood, 1964, St. Louis Symphony Orch., 1969, Washington Orch., 1949, Bach Cantata Series Berkshire Chamber Orch., 1964, Yale Symphony Orch., 1968; appearances in U.S. and European recitals, oratorios, operas, radio and TV, 1953-68; appeared as soloist in Internat. Harpsichord Festival, Westminster Choir Coll., Princeton, N.J., 1973; appeared as soloist in meml. concert, Landowska Ctr., Lakeville, 1969; prof. voice U. So. Miss., Hattiesburg, 1971—, asst. dean Coll. Fine Arts, 1974-76, acting dean, 1976-77; guest prof. Hochschule für Musik, Munich, 1978-79; prof. Italian Internat. Studies Program, Rome, 1986; Miss. coord. Alliance for Arts Edn., Kennedy

Ctr. Performing Arts, 1974—; mem. Miss. Gov.'s Adv. Panel for Gifted and Talented Children, 1974—; mem. 1st Miss. Gov.'s Conf. on the Arts, 1974—; bd. dirs. Miss. Opera Assn. Author: Polenc's Songs: An Analysis of Style, 1971. Recipient Young Am. Artists Concert award N.Y.C., 1955; Wanda Landowska fellow, 1968-72. Mem. Miss. Music Tchrs. Assn., Nat. Assn. Tchrs. of Singing, Music Tchrs. Nat. Assn., Am. Musicology Soc., Golden Key, Mu Phi Epsilon, Delta Kappa Gamma, Tau Beta Kappa (hon.), Pi Kappa Lambda. Democrat. Episcopalian. Avocation: sailing. Office: U So Miss Sch Music South Pt # 8264 Hattiesburg MS 39406-9539

WOOD, YVONNE MCMURRAY, nursing educator; b. Fulton County, Ind., July 23, 1931; d. Wesley Earl and Dortha (Bunn) McMurray; m. Bob C. Wood, Dec. 27, 1954; children: Teresa Wood Goble, Kevin. Diploma, Meth. Hosp. Sch. Nursing, 1955; BA, Indpls. U., 1955; MS in Nursing, Ind. U., Indpls., 1972; MS in Adult Edn., Ind. U., Bloomington, 1982. Instr. ARC, Dayton, Ohio, 1956-57; staff nurse Health and Hosp. Corp., Indpls., 1967-70; asst. prof. community health and psychiat. nursing Ind. U., Indpls., 1967-70; instr. med. terminology No. N.Mex. Community Coll., Espanola, 1982-83; instr. McCurdy Practical Nurse Sch., Espanola, 1979-82; staff nurse Mimbres Meml. Hosp., Deming, N.Mex., 1983-85, Pima County Health Dept., Tucson, 1985; day charge nurse intermediate care Presbyn. Village, Little Rock, 1986; sch. nurse McCurdy Schs., Espanola, 1989; instr. hospice program No. N.Mex. Community Coll., 1989-90; night supr. Marion County Nursing Home and Rehab. Ctr., Indpls., 1965-66; vis. asst. prof. Coll. Nursing U. N.Mex., Albuquerque, 1979-81; staff nurse Home Health Svcs. Englewood (Fla.), 1986-87; instr. Edison Community Coll., Ft. Myers, Port Charlotte, Fla., 1988. Vol. cons. for establishment of family crisis ctr. in no. N.Mex., Rio Arriba County, 1991-92, others, 1993-96; neighborhood vol. Mem. APHA, Sigma Theta Tau. Home: 229 Caddy Rd Placida FL 33947-2223

WOODARD, WALLACE WILLIAM, III, quality advocate; b. Balt., May 25, 1950; s. Wallace William and Helen Cecelia (Berger) W.; m. Patricia Ann Dunphy, Dec. 31, 1976; children: Wallace William IV, Cassaundra Ann, Lauren Ashley. BS in Indsl. Engring., Georgia Tech., 1972; MS in Mgmt., Rensselaer Poly., 1977. Sr. quality control engr. Martin Marietta Aerospace, Orlando, Fla., 1972-75; nuclear quality assurance engr. NE Utilities, Hartford, Conn., 1975-78; prin. quality engr. Fla. Power and Light, Juno Beach, Fla., 1978—; nuclear energy adv. West Palm Beach, 1990. Speaker Pvt. Industry Council, West Palm Beach, Fla., 1986; coach Palm Beach Gardens Youth Athletics, 1983-86, YMCA, Palm Beach Gardens, 1984-85; exec. advisor Jr. Achievement, Miami, Fla., 1981; asst. scoutmaster Boy Scouts Am., 1989-95; bd. dirs. Homeowners, 1992-96. Mem. Am. Soc. Quality Control (cert. quality engr., reliability engr. 1987, chmn. 1986-87, sec. mgmt. 1987-88, ISO 9000 lead assessor 1995—), Am. Inst. Indsl. Engrs., Am. Nuclear Soc., Sigma Phi Epsilon. Roman Catholic. Club: Toastmasters Internat. (treas. 1984-85). Home: 12774 S Normandy Way West Palm Beach FL 33410-1422 Office: Fla Power and Light 700 Universe Blvd North Palm Beach FL 33408-2657

WOODBURN, MARY STUART, education educator; b. Franklin, Va., June 5, 1941; d. Stuart Holland and Mary Hazel (Bryant) Jenkins; m. Robert James Woodburn, June 4, 1967; children: Robert James II, Tammy Lee Woodburn West, Robert Stuart. BS, Madison Coll., Harrisonburg, Va., 1962; MEd, U. Va., 1966, EdD, 1979. Elem. tchr. Portsmouth (Va.) City Schs., 1962-63, Lexington (Va.) Pub. Schs., 1963-64, Colonial Heights (Va.) Pub Schs., 1964-66; prof. edn. Longwood Coll., Farmwood, Va., 1966—, developer literacy and acad. retention programs, 1987-89; ednl. cons. to over 500 sch. dists., 1966—; mem. adj. faculty U. Va., Charlottesville, 1971-78; testing supr. Ednl. Testing Svc., Trenton, N.J., 1967—; vis. prof. Dalhousie U., Halifax, N.S., Can., summers 1969-71, Jyvaskyla U., Finland, 1987; dir. adopt-a-sch. project Va. Dept. Edn., Richmond, 1988-90; developer instructional materials Va. Hwy. Dept., Richmond, 1987-90. Contbr. articles to profl. jours. Advisor Paralyzed Vets. Am., Richmond, 1988-89; vol. Am. Cancer Soc., Leukemia Soc.; writer, vol. ESL programs for schs. and communities. Recipient Meritorious Achievement award Longwood Coll.; scholar Delta Kappa Gamma, 1978; grantee Longwood Coll. Mem. ASCD, Internat. Reading Assn., New Horizons for Learning, Phi Delta Kappa, Sigma Sigma Sigma. Methodist. Home: 9603 Summercliff Ct Chesterfield VA 23832-2495 Office: Longwood Coll Wynne Blvd Farmville VA 23901

WOODBURY, LEE VERNON, health care consultant, physician; b. Florence, S.C., Dec. 18, 1949; s. George Sr. and Melvena Candice (White) W.; m. Bernardette Isabelle Freeman, Aug. 25, 1973 (div.); children: Lee Vernon II, Jenifer Candice Elizabeth. BS, Morehouse Coll., 1973; MD, Med. Univ. S.C., 1977. Diplomate Nat. Bd. Med. Examiners. Intern Richland Meml. Hosp., Columbia, S.C., 1977-80, resident in internal medicine, 1980; chief med./surg. svcs. S.C. Dept. Mental Health, Columbia, 1984-86, dir. profl. svcs., 1987-88, facility dir., CEO Tucker Ctr., 1988-92, divsn. dir., long term care, 1992-94, cons. spl. projects, 1994—; chmn. Agy. Pharmacy and Therapeutics Com., Columbia, 1988-94; emergency med. cons. Space Shuttle Landing Team, Edwards AFB, Calif., 1981-83; dir. ICU Edwards AFB Hosp., 1981-83; cons. internal medicine S.C. Dept. Mental Health, Columbia, 1986—. Chmn. bd. dirs. Profl. Health Svcs., Columbia, 1987-90; chmn. bd. trustees First N.E. Bapt. Ch., Columbia, 1988-91; chmn. advisor Am. Security Coun. Found., Washington, 1982-89; dir. med. group United Way of Midlands, 1991-92; active NAACP, 1993—, Healthy People-2000, 1992—. Maj. USAF, 1980-84. Recipient Recognition award Am. Security Coun. Found., 1983. Mem. S.C. State Employees Assn. (bd. dirs. 1988—). Office: SC Dept Mental Health Office Occupl Health/Safety 2100 Bull St Columbia SC 29202

WOODCOCK, RICHARD WESLEY, educational psychologist; b. Portland, Oreg., Jan. 29, 1928; s. Carol Wesley and Captola Winifred (Catterlin) W.; m. Annie Lee Plant, Aug. 16, 1951; children: Donna, Dianne, Judy, Wayne; m. Ana Felicia Muñoz-Sandoval, June 14, 1991. BS, U. Oreg., 1949, MEd, 1953, EdD, 1956. Diplomate of Am. Bd. of Profl. Psychol. Lt. USN, 1945-46, 50-51; elem. tchr. Arago Schs., Oreg., 1951-52; dir. spl. edn. Coos County Sch., Coquille, Oreg., 1952-54, Corvallis Pub. Schs., Coquille, 1955-57; asst. prof. psychol. Western Oreg. State Coll., 1957-61; assoc. prof. spl. edn. Univ. No. Colo., Greeley, 1961-63; prof. spl. edn., Peabody Coll. Vanderbilt Univ., 1963-68; editor, dir. rsch. Am. Guidance Svc., 1968-72; dir. Measurement Learning Cons., Tenn., Oreg., 1972—; vis. scholar Univ. of Ariz., 1985-88, Univ. So. Calif., L.A., 1988-91; rsch. prof. psychology U. Va., 1993—; cons. NCAA, 1989-94. Author: (battery tests) Mini-Battery of Achievement, 1994, Woodcock Language Proficiency Battery English and Spanish forms, 1991, 95, Woodcock-Muñoz Language Surveys, 1993, W-J Psycho-Edn. Battery, 1977, 89, Bateria Woodcock Psico-Educativa en Español, 1982, 96, Woodcock Reading Mastery Tests, 1973-87, Scales of Independent Behavior, 1984, 95, G-F-W Auditory Skills Battery, 1976, The Peabody Rebus Reading Program, 1967, The Colorado Braille Battery, 1966; contbr. numerous articles to profl. jours. Fellow Am. Acad. Sch. Psychology.

WOODFORD, DUANE HUGH, aerospace equipment manufacturing company executive, electrical engineer; b. Dunseith, N.D., Jan. 1, 1939; s. Harold George and Edna Evelyn (Lagerquist) W.; m. Grace Carol Vandal, July 18, 1962; children: Robert Kent, Kim Ann. BS in Elec. Engring., U. N.D., 1961; student Western Electric grad. engring. tng. program, 1962; Mini MBA, Coll. St. Thomas, 1977, postgrad., 1978. Sr. sales engr. Electric Machinery, Hartford, Conn., 1969-76, product mktg. mgr., Mpls., 1976-79, mgr. parts and svc., 1979-80, commercial ops. mgr., 1980-83, gen. mgr., 1983-87, v.p., gen. mgr., 1987-89; pres. PTC Aerospace, Seating Products Divsn., Litchfield, Conn., 1989-94; pres., CEO Burns Aerospace Corp., 1994-96; group v.p. B/E Aerospace Ops., Winston-Salem, 1996—; power engr. Western Electric, Chgo., 1961-63; application engr. Electric Machinery, Mpls., 1963-65, sales engr., N.Y.C., Pitts., 1965-68. Scoutmaster Boy Scouts U.S., Aurora, Ill., 1962-63; coach, Babe Ruth Baseball, Plymouth, Minn., 1978-80; treas. PTA, Wayzata (Minn.) Sch. Dist. 284, 1978-79; chmn. adv. bd. child guidance Bowman Grey Hosp., Winston-Salem, 1995—. Served with USMC, 1960-66. Mem. ASME (sec. gas turbine div. electric utility com. 1972-74), TAPPI, N.W. Conn. C. of C. (bd. dirs. 1991-95). Republican. Methodist. Home: 3101 Allerton Lake Dr Winston Salem NC 27106-4481 Office: Burns Aerospace Corp 1455 Fairchild Rd Winston Salem NC 27105-4549

WOODGER, WALTER JAMES, JR., management consultant; b. N.Y.C., Aug. 29, 1913; s. Walter James and Annie (Keast) W.; AB, Bowdoin Coll., 1935; LLB, Fordham U., 1939; m. Valerie McCormick, June 23, 1979. With internat. dept. J.P. Morgan & Co., N.Y.C., 1935-49; asst. mgr. London office Chase Manhattan Bank, 1949-55; treas. Warren Petroleum Internat. Corp. subs. Gulf Oil Corp. and mgr. gas and gas liquids Gulf Eastern Co., London, 1955-65; exec. v.p. Boyden Indsl. Svcs., Inc., N.Y.C., 1965-72; pres. Woodger Assocs., Inc., N.Y.C., 1972—. Served to capt. Judge Adv. Gen. Corps, U.S. Army, 1943-47; ETO. Decorated Reconnaissance Franç aise. Mem. Am. Bar Assn., N.Y. Bar, Judge Adv. Gen.'s Assn., Tournament Players Club. Home: 7728 Club Ln Sarasota FL 34238-5644

WOODHOUSE, JOHN FREDERICK, food distribution company executive; b. Wilmington, Del., Nov. 30, 1930; s. John Crawford and Anna (Houth) W.; m. Marilyn Ruth Morrow, June 18, 1955; children: John Crawford II, Marjorie Ann Woodhouse Purdy. BA, Wesleyan U., 1953; MBA, Harvard U., 1955. Bus. devel. officer Can. Imperial Bank of Commerce, Toronto, Ont., 1955-59; various fin. positions Ford Motor Co., Dearborn, Mich., 1959-64, Cooper Industries, Inc., Mount Vernon, Ohio, 1964-67; treas. Houston, 1967-69, Crescent-Niagara Corp., Buffalo, 1968-69; exec. v.p., chief fin. officer Sysco Corp., Houston, 1969-71, pres., chief operating officer, 1972-83, pres., chief exec. officer, 1983-85, chief exec. officer, chmn. bd., 1985—, mem. exec. and fin. coms., also bd. dirs.; bd. dirs. Shell Oil Co., Winrock Internat.; dir. Harvard Bus. Sch. Assocs., 1995—. Chmn. Mich. 16th dist. rep. Club, 1962-64; treas. Cooper Industries Found., 1967-69; trustee Wesleyan U., 1976-92, vice-chmn., 1986-92; ruling elder Presbyn. Ch.; bd. trustees Mt. Holyoke Coll., South Hadley, Mass., 1996—. Mem. Nat. Am. Wholesale Grocer's Assn. (bd. dirs. 1990—, vice chmn. 1992, chmn. 1994-96), Internat. Foodservice Distbrs. Assn. (bd. dirs. 1988—), Houston Soc. Fin. Analysts, Fin. Execs. Inst., Harvard Bus. Sch. Club (bd. dirs.), Sigma Chi. Office: Sysco Corp 1390 Enclave Pky Houston TX 77077-2025

WOODLAND, NAAMAN JOHNSON, JR., history educator; b. Alexandria, La., June 20, 1926; s. Naaman Johnson Sr. and Olive (Coe) W.; m. Mary Eugenia Baldwin, Dec. 23, 1958; children: Rebecca Coe, Philip Baldwin. BA, La. State U., 1946, BS, 1949; MA, Northwestern U., 1950. Tchr. history, English, govt. Lake Side High Sch., Hot Springs, Ark., 1949; tchr. history Lamar U., Beaumont, Tex., 1957-95, Regents prof. history, 1989—, disting. faculty lectr., 1989; emergency substitute tchr. history, govt., sociology Lyons Twp. Jr. Coll., Oak Park, Ill., 1956. Assoc. editor: With a Dome More Vast: History of First United Meth. Church, 1987. Chair Beaumont Pub Libr. Commn., 1972-94; founding mem. Beaumont Civic Opera; chmn. history and records com. 1st United Meth. Ch., Beaumont; mem. Tex. Conf. United Meth. Ch. Commn. Archives and History; bd. dirs. Spindletop/Gladys City Mus. Adv. Bd., 1992—. With U.S. Army, 1950-52. Recipient Julie and Ben Rogers Cmty. Svc. award, 1981, Outstanding Achievement by arts/humanities vol. award S.E. Tex. Arts Coun., 1992. Mem. Tex. Assn. Coll. Tchrs. (pres. Lamar chpt.), Tex. State Hist. Assn., Tex. Gulf Hist. Soc. (v.p. program chair 1992-94, pres. 1994-96, exec. coun. mem.-at-large, 1996—), East Tex. Hist. Assn. (bd. dirs. 1992-94, Ottis Lock award 1987), Southeast Tex. Genealogical and Hist. Soc. (bd. dirs., pres., program chair 1980-94), Tyrrell Hist. Libr. Assn. (bd. dirs. 1989—), Beaumont Music Commn. (first v.p., chair artists selection com. 1983—), Beaumont Heritage Soc. (bd. dirs.), Beaumont History Conf. (bd. dirs. 1991—), St. Augustine (Fla.) Hist. Soc., Tex. State Libr. Assn., Am. Studies Assn. of Tex., SW Social Sci. Assn., Beaumont Interfaith Choral Soc. Democrat. Methodist. Home: 5640 N Circuit Dr Beaumont TX 77706-4425 Office: Lamar U Dept History PO Box 10048 Beaumont TX 77710-0048

WOODMAN, WALTER JAMES, lawyer; b. Talara, Peru, Jan. 21, 1941; s. Walter James and Nora Carmen (Wensjoe) W.; m. Ruth Meyer, Dec. 19, 1970; children: Justin Meyer, Jessica Hilary. BA, U. Miami, 1964; JD, So. Meth. U., 1967. Bar: Tex. 1967, U.S. Dist. Ct. (no. dist.) Tex. 1967, U.S. Ct. Appeals (5th cir.) 1968, U.S. Supreme Ct. 1971, U.S. Dist. Ct. (we. dist.) La. 1979, La. 1980, U.S. Dist. Ct. (ea. dist.) Tex. 1983, U.S. Dist. Ct. (mid. dist.) La. 1988, U.S. Dist. Ct. (ea. dist.) La. 1989. Lawyer Dallas, 1967-72, Waxahachie, Tex., 1972-79; pvt. practice Shreveport, La., 1979—; bd. dirs. N.W. La. Legal Svcs., Shreveport, 1993-96. Author book revs. and articles. Candidate Tex. Ho. of Reps., 1972; bd. dirs. Gov.'s Pan Am. Commn., Baton Rouge, 1993-96. Mem. North La. Civil War Roundtable. Home: Nonesuch Farm 12250 Ellerbe Rd Shreveport LA 71115 Office: 9045 Ellerbe Rd Ste 102 Shreveport LA 71106-6799

WOODMANSEE, GLENN EDWARD, employee relations executive; b. Feb. 8, 1936; s. Glenn E. and Elaine (Turnquist) Harty; m. Sharon E. Horne, Sept. 5, 1959; chidlren: Lynn Ann, Thomas Edward. Student, Coe Coll., 1954-55; BS, Ariz. State U., 1960. Assoc. group mem. Prudential Ins. Co., Seattle, 1960-64; regional mgr. Blue Cross, N.Y.C., 1964-72; mgr. employee benefits McDermott Inc./Babcock & Wilcox, New Orleans, 1972-82; dir. employee relations Tidewater Inc., New Orleans, 1982-95; v.p. S&E Enterprise Co., Carriere, Miss., 1995-96. Bd. dirs. CPC Hosp., New Orleans, 1988-94; pres. Manalapan Rep. Club, Englishtown, N.J., 1977; county committeeman N.J. Rep. Party, Englishtown, 1970-77. Served to cpl. U.S. Army, 1955-57. Recipient N.Y.C. Marathon medal N.Y.C. Track Club, 1987. Mem. SAR, Am. Soc. Pers. Assocs., Bus. Coalition Health (treas. 1986-88, pres. 1988-90), Tng. and Devel. Assn. Am., Risk Ins. Mgmt. Soc. Republican. Presbyterian. Club: New Orleans Athletic, South Shore Yacht. Home: 104 Pine Burr Rd Carriere MS 39426

WOODRELL, FREDERICK DALE, health care executive; b. St. Charles, Mo., Sept. 4, 1954; s. Robert Lee and Jeananne Monique (Daily) W.; m. Brenda Kay Justice, Aug. 10, 1974; children: Sara, Grace, Evan. BS in Acctg., Emporia State U., 1976; MPA, U. Mo., 1977. Cons. Robert Brown Consulting, Kansas City, 1976-78; asst. adminstr. Lee's Summit (Mo.) Community Hosp., 1978-79; asst. adminstr. Leesburg (Fla.) Regional Med. Ctr., 1979-82, adminstr., 1982-86; pres., CEO Ctrl. Fla. Heathcare Devel., Leesburg, Fla., 1986-92; dir. U. Miss. Hosp. & Clinic, Jackson, Miss., 1992—; healthcare exec. and cons. Quorum Health Resources, Nashville, 1979—. Active Friends of Children's Hosp., Jackson, 1992—; chmn. Assn. Retarded Citizen, Lake Tavares, Fla., 1990-92. Named Lake County Citizen of Yr. by Orlando (Fla.) Sentinal, 1988. Mem. Am. Hosp. Assn., Am. Coll. Healthcare Execs., Jackson Rotary. Home: 2164 Brackenshire Cir Jackson MS 39211-5836 Office: U Hosps & Clinics U Miss Med Ctr 2500 N State St Jackson MS 39216-4500*

WOODROW, RANDALL MARK, lawyer; b. Anniston, Ala., June 17, 1956; s. Herbert Milisam and Rose (Marshall) W.; m. Carolyn Ann Jackson, Jan. 7, 1977; children: Amanda Lauren, Emily Claire, Taylor Jackson, Douglas Cockrell. BA in Polit. Sci., Jacksonville (Ala.) State U., 1978; JD, Samford U., 1981. Bar: Ala. 1981. Law clk. to judge U.S. Dist. Ct. (no. dist.) Ala., 1981-82; ptnr. Doster & Woodrow, Anniston, Ala., 1990—; asst. dist. atty. 7th Jud. Cir., Anniston, 1983; adj. prof. Jacksonville State U., 1985-86. Chmn. crusade Calhoun County Cancer Soc., Anniston, 1983; mem. adminstrv. bd. dirs. 1st United Meth. Ch., Anniston, 1984—; pres. Boys Clubs of Anniston, Inc., 1985; mem. Calhoun County Econ. Devel. Coun., 1994—; mem. Jacksonville (Ala.) Planning Commn., 1995—. Mem. ABA, Ala. Bar Assn., Calhoun County Bar Assn., Calhoun County C. of C. Home: 509 6th St NE Jacksonville AL 36265-1617 Office: Doster & Woodrow 1000 Quintard Ave Anniston AL 36201-5788

WOODRUFF, CHIVERS RICHARD, JR., physician; b. Birmingham, Ala., Aug. 11, 1944; s. Chivers Richard Sr. and Cherry (Scogin) W.; m. Julia Walls Mariani, Aug. 3, 1968; children: Chivers III, Jake James. BS in Pharm., Samford U., 1967; PhD, U. Ala., Birmingham, 1972, MD, 1974. Diplomate Am. Bd. Med. Examiners, Am. Bd. Family Practice. Pvt. practice Birmingham, 1975—; med. dir. Beverly Health Care Ctr., Birmingham, 1980—, Oak Knoll Nursing Home, Birmingham, 1984—; assoc. prof. of family practice Dept. Family Practice U. Ala., Birmingham, 1980—; intern Birmingham Bapt. Hosp., 1974-75; pres. med. staff Brookwood Hosp., Birmingham, 1989-91, chmn. dept. medicine, 1985-89. Contbr. articles to profl. jours. Recipient physician recognition award AMA, 1992; fellow Am. Found. for Pharm. Edn., 1970-72. Fellow Am. Acad. Family Physicians; mem. So. Med. Assn., Jefferson County Med. Soc., Med. Assn. Ala., Birmingham C. of C. Republican. Methodist. Home: 1206 Cheval Ln Birmingham AL 35216-2037 Office: 200 Montgomery Hwy Birmingham AL 35216-1802

WOODRUFF, DEBRA A., occupational health nurse; b. Salem, Ill., Dec. 22, 1952; d. Merle D. and Georgia Lee (Johnson) Anderson; m. Thomas E. Howarth, June 16, 1973 (div. Sept. 1979; 1 child, Michael T. Diploma in Practical Nursing, Vo-Tech Teche Area, New Iberia, La., 1972; ADN, Miss. Delta Jr. Coll., Moorhead, 1975. LPN, La.; cert. occupl. health nurse. LPN in ICU Iberia Gen. Hosp., New Iberia, 1972-73, head nurse ICU, 1979-81; charge nurse infection control Bolivar County Hosp., Cleveland, Miss., 1973-79, dir. long-term care, 1981-89; sr. indsl. nurse Baxter Healthcare Corp., Cleveland, 1989—. Mem. Am. Assn. Occupl. Health Nurses, Miss. Assn. Occupl. Health Nurses. Republican. Baptist. Office: Baxter Healthcare Corp 7511 114th Ave N Largo FL 33773

WOODRUFF, JOHN DOUGLAS, non-profit association administrator, retired air force officer; b. Bonham, Tex., Feb. 12, 1944; s. Alexander Campbell and Lois Kathryn (Turner) W.; m. Carol Lynne Thompson, June 11, 1966; children: Keith Byron, Jill Marie, David Kent. BS in Sociology/Psychology, Tex. A&M U. Commerce, 1966; grad. with distinction, AFROTC, 1966; MS in Edn., U. So. Calif., 1970; grad. with distinction, Air Command and Staff Coll., 1977; USAF exch. student, U.S. Army War Coll., 1980-81. Commd. 2d lt. USAF, 1966; advanced through grades to col. USAF Air Rescue Svc., 1990; comdr. USAF Air Rescue Svc., McClellan AFB, Calif., 1990-93; vice comdr. 314th Airlift Wing, Little Rock, 1993-95; field svc. manager ARC, Little Rock, 1995—; adj. instr. psychology Golden Gate U., Pope AFB, N.C., 1975-76; com. chmn. Sec. of Air Force's Blue Ribbon Panel on Space, Maxwell AFB, Ala., 1988. Contbr. articles to USAF mag. Mil. sponsor for civic leader program Mil. Affairs Com., Abilene, Tex., 1982-83, Logstar Civilian Hon. Comdr. Program, Sacramento, 1990-93; mem. Cmty. Coun., Jacksonville, Ark., 1993-95. Decorated Legion of Merit with 2 oak leaf clusters, Meritorious Svc. medal with 3 oak leaf clusters, Air Force Commendation medal. Mem. Air Force Assn. (Citation of Honor 1989), Airlift/Tanker Assn., Air Rescue Assn., Jolly Green Pilots Assn., Order of Daedalians. Episcopalian. Home: 7305 Yuma Ct North Little Rock AR 72116-4359 Office: Amer Red Cross 401 S Monroe Little Rock AR 72205

WOODRUFF, MARTHA JOYCE, home health agency executive; b. Unadilla, Ga., Jan. 3, 1941; d. Metz Loy and Helen (McCorvey) Woodruff. BA, Shorter Coll., 1963; MA, U. Tenn.-Knoxville, 1972. Tchr., Albany H.S. (Ga.), 1963-69; instr. U. Tenn.-Knoxville, 1970-72; asst. prof. Valdosta State Coll. (Ga.), 1972-76; coord. Staff Builders, Atlanta, 1976-78; pres., owner Med. Pers. Pool, Knoxville, 1978-93; owner, pres. Priority Healthcare Svcs, Knoxville, 1993—, Pers. Pool of Knoxville, Inc., 1985-87; mem., adviser Owners Adv. Coun., Pers. Pool of Am., Ft. Lauderdale, Fla., 1980-82; active Altzheimers Assn. Mem. Nat. Coun. on Aging, Nat. Assn. for Adult Daycare, Exec. Women Internat. (bd. dirs. Knoxville chpt. 1996), East Tenn. Women's Polit. Caucus, Tenn. Assn. Home Care, Nat. Assn. Homecare, Knoxville C. of C. (com. for cost containment 1982-85), Blount County C. of C. (retirement com. 1983, mem. indsl. rels. com. 1983). Republican. Methodist.

WOODRUFF, WANDA LEA, elementary education educator; b. Woodward, Okla., May 2, 1937; d. Milton Casper and Ruth Arlene (Bradshaw) Shuck; m. William Jennings Woodruff, Aug. 18, 1962; children: Teresa Kaye, Bruce Alan, Neal Wayne. BS, Northwestern State U., 1959; MA in Edn., Olivet Nazarene U., 1973. Cert. K-8th grade tchr. 2d grade tchr. Anthony (Kans.) Pub. Schs., 1959-60, transition class tchr., 1960-61, 1st grade tchr., 1961-62; 5th grade tchr. Versailles (Ky.) Pub. Schs., 1962-63; 1st grade tchr. Bradley (Ill.) Elem. Schs., 1968-93; presch. vol. Concern Ctr., Bartlesville, Okla., 1994—. Com. chmn. Bus. and Profl. Women, Anthony, 1959-62; sec. com. PTA, Anthony, 1959-63, Bradley (Ill.) PTA, 1968-93. Recipient grant for edn. First of Am. Bank, 1991-92, 92-93. Mem. Bartlesville Pilot Club Internat. (edn./patriotism chairperson 1994-95, dir. 1995-96, mem. com. Spl. Olympics 1995-96, pres-elect 1996—). Home: 2373 Mountain Dr Bartlesville OK 74003-6926

WOODRUFF, WILLIAM JENNINGS, theology educator; b. Vassar, Kans., Sept. 30, 1925; s. Kenneth Arthur and Carrie (Brecheisen) W.; m. Wanda Lea Shuck, Aug. 18, 1962; children: Teresa Kaye, Bruce Alan, Neal Wayne. BA, Ottawa U., 1954; MDiv, Fuller Theol. Sem., Pasadena, Calif., 1958; MRE, Asbury Theol. Sem., Wilmore, Ky., 1963, ThM, 1964; postgrad., U. Pa., 1965-68, Concordia Theol. Seminary, 1976-84, Trinity Theol. Seminary, 1993-95. Youth dir. Hyde Park EUB Ch., Wichita, 1958-59; tchr. Lenora (Kans.) Rural High Sch., 1959-60; pastor Attica (Kans.) EUB Ch., 1960-62, Jersey City EUB Ch., 1964-65, Phila. EUB Ch., 1965-68; with Olivet Nazarene U., Kankakee, Ill., 1968—, prof.; ret., 1991. Contbr. to Religious and Theol. Abstracts, 3 jours., 1968-94; contbr. articles to profl. jours. Cpl. U.S. Army, 1951-53, Republic of Korea. Mem. Evang. Theol. Soc., Evang. Tchrs. Tng. Assn., Wesleyan Theol. Soc., Near East Archaeol. Soc., Phi Delta Lambda, Theta Pi, Kappa Delta Pi. Home: 2373 Mountain Dr Bartlesville OK 74003-6926

WOODRUM, PATRICIA ANN, librarian; b. Hutchinson, Kans., Oct. 11, 1941; d. Donald Jewell and Ruby Pauline (Shuman) Hoffman; m. Clayton Eugene Woodrum, Mar. 31, 1962; 1 child, Clayton Eugene, II. BA, Kans. State Coll., Pittsburg, 1963; MLS, U. Okla., 1966. Br. libr. Tulsa City-County Libr. System, 1964-65, head brs., 1965-66, head reference dept., 1966-67, chief extension, 1967, chief pub. svc., 1967-73, asst. dir., 1973-76, exec. dir., 1976—; bd. dirs. Local Am. Bank Tulsa. Mem. editorial bd. Jour. of Library Administration. Active Friends of Tulsa Libr., Leadership Tulsa Alumni; regent UCT/RSC, Tulsa. Recipient Disting. Libr. award Okla. Libr. Assn., 1982, Leadership Tulsa Paragon award, 1987, Women in Comm. Newsmaker award, 1989, Outstanding Alumnus award U. Okla. Sch. Libr. Info. Studies, 1989, Headliner award Tulsa Press Club, 1996; inducted into Tulsa City-County Libr. Hall of Fame, 1989, Okla. Womens Hall of Fame, 1993. Mem. ALA, Pub. Libr. Assn. (pres. 1993-94), Okla. Libr. Assn. (pres. 1978-79, Disting. Libr. award 1982, Meritorious Svc. award 1996), Tulsa C. of C. Democrat. Episcopalian. Office: Tulsa City-County Libr 400 Civic Ctr Tulsa OK 74103-3857

WOODS, BARBARA A. SHELL, psychotherapist; b. Banner Elk, N.C., June 11, 1939; d. Oscar Ketron and Mamie Maruja (Perry) Shell; m. James Wesley Woods, May 7, 1966; children: Jonathan Scott, Eric Jason. BS in Bus. Mgmt., East Tenn. State U., 1961; MA in Counseling and Devel., George Mason U., 1983, postgrad., 1985-88. Cert. clin. mental health counselor, mediator, Va.; nat. cert. counselor, nat. cert. career counselor; lic. profl. counselor, Va. Office asst. vet. affairs East Tenn. State U., Johnson City, 1958-61; sec. purchasing dept. U. Tenn., Knoxville, 1961-62; social worker I and II Tenn. Welfare Dept., Knoxville, 1962-66; daycare coord. Econ. Opportunity of Atlanta, 1966-67; child welfare worker Forsyth County Dept. of Welfare, Winston Salem, N.C., 1967-68; dir., tchr. Woodland Pre-Sch., Alexandria, Va., 1975-78; pers. mgmt. Woodward & Lothrup, Tyson's Corner, Va., 1983; career coord. Nat. Bd. for Cert. Counselors, Alexandria, 1984; counselor, trainer The Women's Ctr. of Northern Va., Vienna, Va., 1985-90; counseling dir. The Women's Health Connection, Vienna, 1990-92; trainer, counselor City of Falls Ch. Youth At Risk Program, Falls Church, 1993-94; dir./owner Change & Growth Consulting, Tyson's Corner and Woodbridge, Va., 1984—. Zoning chairperson West Springfield (Va.) Civic Assn., 1980-82; citizen mem. Fairfax County Citizens Planning Task Force, Springfield, 1979-82. Scholarship Am. Legion, 1957. Mem. ACA, No. Va. Chpt. clin. Counselors (chairperson 1990-92, Appreciation award 1992), Va. Clin. Counselor (regional rep. 1990-92), Nat. EAP Assn. (sec. 1989-90), Met. Area Career/Life Planning Network (founder, Appreciation award 1985), Va. Counselors Assn. Methodist. Office: Change and Growth Cons 1334 G St Woodbridge VA 22191-1603

WOODS, BARRY ALAN, lawyer; b. N.Y.C., Nov. 21, 1942; s. Harry E. and Lillian (Breath) W.; m. Elsie Payne, Dec. 1980; children: Meredith Rose, Pamela Brett, B. Morgan, Catherine Alana. BS, N.Y. U., 1965, LLM in Taxation, 1969; JD, Bklyn. Law Sch., 1968. Bar: N.Y. 1968, U.S. Tax Ct. 1969, P.R. 1970, U.S. Dist. Ct. P.R. 1971; Ptnr. firm Baker & Woods, Santurce, P.R., 1970-76; mng. partner Woods & Woods, Hato Rey, P.R., 1976-81, Woods Rosenbaum Luckeroth & Perez-Gonzalez, 1981-96, Woods Rosenbaum & Luckeroth, 1996—; spl. cons. Tax Mgmt., Inc.; mem. Bur.

Nat. Affairs, Adv. Bd. Internat. Taxation. Mem. Am. Soc. Internat. Law, Am. Bar Assn., Colegio de Abogados de P.R. Clubs: Caribe Hilton Swimming and Tennis, AAA Gun, Bankers of P.R., NYU, Arraq Tennis. Author: United States Business Operations in Puerto Rico; Repatriation of Puerto Rico Source Earnings-Implication of Proposed Section 936; other publs. in field. Office: PO Box 1292 Hato Rey San Juan PR 00902-1292

WOODS, CHARLES REECE, JR., pediatrician, educator; b. Dothan, Ala., Dec. 11, 1958; s. Charles Reece and Jo Ann Woods; m. Mary Fern Wallace, Nov. 29, 1986; children: John Charles, Alison Marie. BS, Samford U., 1981; MD, Baylor Coll. Medicine, 1985. Intern Baylor Affiliated Hosps., Houston, 1985-86, resident in pediatrics, 1986-88, chief resident in pediatrics, 1988-89, fellow in pediatric infectious diseases, 1989-92; asst. prof. pediatrics Bowman Gray Sch. of Medicine, Winston-Salem, N.C., 1992—. Contbr. articles to profl. jours. Fellow Am. Acad. Pediatrics; mem. Infectious Diseases Soc. Am., Pediatric Infectious Diseases Soc., Am. Soc. for Microbiology, Alpha Omega Alpha. Office: Bowman Gray Sch Medicine Medical Center Blvd Winston Salem NC 27157

WOODS, DONNA SUE, education educator, reading consultant, state agency administrator; b. Springhill, La., Jan. 15, 1954; children: Klaten A., Matthew M., Laura E., Gabriele E. BA, La. Tech U., 1975; MEd, La. State U., 1983; EdD, Okla. State U., 1992. Cert. English, social studies, gifted edn. tchr., La.; cert. English, gifted edn. and reading tchr., Okla. Tchr. English, Grawood (La.) Christian Schs., 1979-80; tchr. spl. edn. Bossier Parish Sch. Bd., Benton, La., 1981-83, curriculum developer, 1990; tchr. gifted Curtis Elem. Sch., Bossier City, La., 1983-88; tchr. lang. arts Elm Grove (La.) Jr. High Sch., 1988-90; teaching asst., univ. rep. Okla. entry yr. assistance Okla. State U., Stillwater, 1990-92, co-dir., instr. 13th ann. reading workshop, 1991, instr. Coll. Vet. Medicine, 1991, developer, dir. student tchr. seminar, 1992; asst. prof. Coll. Edn. Northwestern Okla. State U., Alva, 1992-95; dir. reading and literacy Okla. State Dept. Edn., Oklahoma City, 1995—; adj. instr. Oklahoma City C.C., 1991-92, U. Okla., 1995—; dir. Okla. Nat. Young Readers' Day, 1994, 95-96; presenter in field. Tutor YWCA, Shreveport, La., 1975; supt. youth Sun. schs. 1st Presbyn. Ch., Edmond, Okla., 1991, youth choir dir., 1994—, youth handbells dir., 1995—. Named Favorite Tchr. of Yr., Bossier C. of C., 1987; Centennial scholar Okla. State U. Coll. Edn. Alumni Assn., 1992. Mem. Internat. Reading Assn. (conf. presenter 1996), Okla. Reading Assn. (conf. presenter 1993—), Okla. Early Childhood Tchrs. Assn. (conf. presenter 1991), Alpha Upsilon Alpha (faculty sponsor 1994-95), Kappa Delta Pi, Phi Delta Kappa. Republican. Home: 777 E 15th St #160 Edmond OK 73013

WOODS, HARRY ARTHUR, JR., lawyer; b. Hartford, Ark., Feb. 15, 1941; s. Harry Arthur and Viada (Young) W.; m. Carol Ann Meschter, Jan. 21, 1967; children: Harry Arthur III, Elizabeth Ann. BA in Econs., Okla. State U., 1963; JD, NYU, 1966. Bar: N.Y. 1966, Okla. 1970. Assoc. White & Case, N.Y.C., 1966-67; assoc. Crowe & Dunlevy, Oklahoma City, 1971-75, ptnr., 1975—. Councilman City of Edmond, 1975-79, mayor pro tem, 1977-79. Capt. U.S. Army, 1967-71. Mem. ABA, Okla. Bar Assn. (outstanding svc. award 1982), Oklahoma County Bar Assn. (Golden Gavel award 1983). Democrat. Methodist. Office: Crowe & Dunlevy 1800 Mid-America Tower 20 N Broadway Ave Oklahoma City OK 73102-8202

WOODS, HENRY, federal judge; b. Abbeville, Miss., Mar. 17, 1918; s. Joseph Neal and Mary Jett (Wooldridge) W.; m. Kathleen Mary McCaffrey, Jan. 1, 1943; children—Mary Sue, Thomas Henry, Eileen Anne, James Michael. B.A., U. Ark., 1938, J.D. cum laude, 1940. Bar: Ark. bar 1940. Spl. agt. FBI, 1941-46; mem. firm Alston & Woods, Texarkana, Ark., 1946-48; exec. sec. to Gov. Ark., 1949-53; mem. firm McMath, Leatherman & Woods, Little Rock, 1953-80; judge U.S. Dist. Ct. (ea. dist.) Ark., 1980—; referee in bankruptcy U.S. Dist. Ct., Texarkana, 1947-48; spl. assoc. justice Ark. Supreme Ct., 1967-74, chmn. com. model jury instrns., 1973-80; chmn. bd. Ctr. Trial and Appellate Advocacy, Hastings Coll. Law, San Francisco, 1975-76; mem. joint conf. com. ABA-AMA, 1973-78, Ark. Constl. Revision Study Commn., 1967-68. Author treatise comparative fault.; Contbr. articles to legal jours. Pres. Young Democrats Ark., 1946-48; mem. Gubernatorial Com. Study Death Penalty, 1971-73. Mem. ABA, Ark. Bar Assn. (pres. 1972-73, Outstanding Lawyer award 1975), Pulaski County Bar Assn., Assn. Trial Lawyers Am. (gov. 1965-67), Ark. Trial Lawyers Assn. (pres. 1965-67), Internat. Acad. Trial Lawyers, Internat. Soc. Barristers, Am. Coll. Trial Lawyers, Am. Bd. Trial Advocates, Phi Alpha Delta. Methodist. Home: 42 Wingate Dr Little Rock AR 72205-2556 Office: US Dist Ct PO Box 3683 Little Rock AR 72203-3683

WOODS, J. P., pharmaceutical company executive; b. Houston, June 22, 1950; s. William Oliver and Lilly Virginia (Hetherington) W. Student, Blinn Coll., Brenham, Tex., 1968-69; BA, Ft. Lewis Coll., Durango, Colo., 1971. Div. mgr. Gateway Sporting Goods, Denver, 1971-74; dist. mgr. Super X Drug, Inc., Cin., 1974-77; v.p. sales Bon Ton, Inc., Dallas, 1977-80; regional sales mgr. John O. Butler Co., Chgo., 1980-81; sales mgr. Fox Meyer, Inc., Oklahoma City, 1981-82; sales cons., trainer Rugby Labs., Inc., N.Y.C., 1982-83; nat. dir. key accounts United Rsch. Labs., Inc., Mut. Pharm., Inc., Phila., 1983-88; v.p. Western div. Barr Labs., Pomona, N.Y., 1988—; elected to Tex. State Bd. Pharmacy, 1992. Author, editor: Sales and Marketing Techniques, 1984. Mem. Rep. Presdl. Task Force, Washington, 1982—, life membership honor roll; mem. Presdl. Commn., 1988; sustaining mem. Rep. Nat. Com., Washington, 1983—, cert. recognition, 1991-92; preferred mem. Nat. Conservative Polit. Action Com., Washington, 1983—; elected mem. Rep. Campaign Coun. Com., 1992—; elected del. State Tex. Rep. Party, 1992; founding mem. CBN Founders, Virginia Beach, Va., 1986—; active Christian Coalition, 1992, Kenneth Copeland Ptnrs. Ministries, 1992. Recipient Medal of Merit, Ronald Reagan, Pres., Washington, 1985, Presdl. Commn. from Ronald Reagan, 1986, Cert. of Recognition Rep. Nat. Com., 1991-92; named to Rep. Presdl. Task Force Life Membership Honor Roll. Mem. Nat. Assn. Chain Druggists, Nat. Wholesale Drug Assn., Nat. Assn. Retail Druggists, Tex. Pharm. Assn. (com. mem. 1991-92), DAV Comdrs., U.S. Senatorial Club (founder). Mem. Full Gospel Ch.

WOODS, JAMES DUDLEY, manufacturing company executive; b. Falmouth, Ky., July 24, 1931; s. Alva L. and Mabel L. (Miller) W.; m. Darlene Mae Petersen, Nov. 8, 1962; children: Linda, Debbie, Jeffrey, Jamie. AA, Long Beach City Coll., 1958; BA, Calif. State U.-Fullerton, 1967, postgrad., 1968-70. Mgr. planning and control Baker Internat. Corp., Los Angeles, 1965-68, v.p. fin. and adminstrn. Baker div., 1968-73, corp. v.p., group fin. officer, 1973-76, corp. v.p., 1977, past exec. v.p.; pres., chief exec. officer Baker Internat. Corp., Houston; also dir. Baker Internat. Corp.; pres. Baker Packers, Houston, 1976-77, Baker Oil Tools, Orange, Calif., 1977-87; chmn. Baker Hughes Inc., Houston, 1996—. Served with USAF, 1951-55. Republican. Lutheran. Office: Baker Hughes Inc 3900 Essex Ln Houston TX 77027-5111*

WOODS, JAMES MICHAEL, history educator; b. Little Rock, Nov. 28, 1952; s. Henry and Kathleen Mary (McCaffrey) W.; m. Rebecca Ann Williams, June 23, 1979; children: Matthew Henry, Theresa Ruth, Lydia Kathleen. BA in History, U. Dallas, 1976; MA in History, Rice U., 1979; PhD in History, Tulane U., 1983. Tchr. Jesuit H.S., New Orleans, 1981-83, La. Sch., Natchitoches, La., 1986-88; prof. history Claflin Coll., Orangeburg, S.C., 1983-85, Northwestern State U. of La., Natchitoches, 1985-86, Ga. So. U., Statesboro, 1988—. Author: Rebellion and Realignment, 1987, Mission and Memory, 1993 (award 1995). Mem. Orgn. Am. Historians, So. Hist. Assn., Phi Alpha Theta (faculty advisor 1989—). Republican. Roman Catholic. Office: Ga So U History Dept LB 8054 Statesboro GA 30460

WOODS, JANIS HAMRICK, nursing administrator; b. Morganton, N.C., June 10, 1945; d. Everett Burton Teasley and Nona Gray (Baker) Hamrick; m. Gerald Anthony Woods, Jan. 2, 1977; 1 child, Sarah Elizabeth. RN, Sinai Hosp. Sch. of Nursing, Balt., 1967; BA, Loyola Coll., Balt., 1976; MBA, Katz Grad. Sch. Bus., 1988. Vis. nurse Vis. Nurse Assn., Balt., 1969-71; coord. cottage program Western Carolina Ctr., Morganton, 1971-73; unit dir. Rosewood State Hosp., Owings Mills, Md., 1973-77; staffing coord. Hubert Rutland Meml. Hosp., St. Petersburg, Fla., 1979-80; staff devel. liaison St. Francis Med. Ctr., Pitts., 1981-88; fin. planner Fin. Investment Analysts, Inc., Carnegie, Pa., 1988-89; nursing supr. Forbes Ctr. for Gerontology, Pitts., 1989-91; dir. nursing Ladies G.A.R. Home, Swissvale, Pa., 1991-92; DON Britthaven of Morganton, N.C., 1992, Brian Ctr. of Hickory East, 1992-93; nurse cons. Caldwell Meml. Hosp., 1994—; DON Grace Heights, Morganton, 1994-95; owner L'il Bit of Everything Co., 1995—. Coach Aspinwall (Pa.) Girls Softball League, 1991; mem. Pitts. Chorale East, 1991, Son Shine Quartet, 1994, Drexel Comty. Club, 1994; chairperson Drexel St. Festival, 1994; active Morganton Comty. Band, 1996. Mem. Sinai Hosp. Nurses Alumnae Assn., U. Pitts. Alumnae Assn., Burke City C. of C. Office: 211 Baxter St Drexel NC 28619

WOODS, JEFF CHANDLER, lawyer; b. Lewisburg, W.Va., Mar. 28, 1954; s. Frank William and Catherine (Brown) W.; children: Christi, Jennifer. BA in Sociology, W.Va. State Coll., 1975; postgrad., W.Va. Coll. Grad. Studies, 1976; JD, Howard U., 1979. Bar: W.Va. 1979, U.S. Dist. Ct. (so. dist.) W.Va. 1979, U.S. Ct. Appeals (4th cir.) 1980, U.S. Ct. Mil. Appeals, 1982, U.S. Supreme Ct. 1992. Law clk. W.Va. Supreme Ct. Appeals, Charleston, 1979-80; prosecutor U.S. Army, Ft. Polk, La., 1980-83; assoc. Jackson, Kelly, Holt & O'Farrell, Charleston, W.Va., 1983-87; ptnr. Jackson & Kelly, Charleston, 1988—; chmn. workers compensation com. W.Va. State Bar, 1985-89; adj. instr. W.Va. Coll. Grad. Studies, W.Va. State Coll., W.Va. Sch. Osteo. Medicine. Radio talk show host. Judge adv. W.Va. N.G., Charleston, 1983-86; bd. dirs. Mattie V. Lee Home, Charleston, 1985-88, Black Diamond coun. Girl Scouts U.S., 1988-89, Charleston Legal Aid Soc.; mem. alumni adv. bd. W.Va. State Coll., 1992—; chmn. Friends and Foremr Students of Bolling Sch., Inc., 1993—. Mem. ABA, Phi Delta Phi, Alpha Phi Alpha. Democrat. Baptist. Office: Jackson & Kelly 1600 Laidley Tower Charleston WV 25301-2138

WOODS, JOHN MERLE, mathematics educator, chairman; b. Monroe, Okla., Jan. 10, 1943; s. Harry A. and Vi Ada (Young) W.; m. Thelma Ann Farrar, Jan 24, 1964 (div. Apr. 1976); children: John M. Jr., Roxanne; m. Paula Gail Newman, Jan 23, 1982 (div. Aug. 1991); children: Benjamin, Paul. BS, Okla. State U., 1965; MA in Teaching, Harvard U., 1966; PhD, Fla. State U., 1973. Tchr. math. John Burroughs Sch., Ladue, Mo., 1966-67; prof. math. Okla. Bapt. U., Shawnee, 1967-88, math. series supr. Upward Bound, 1967-70; mathematician, computer analyst USAMERDC, Ft. Belvoir, Va., summer 1968; prof., chmn. math. dept. Southwestern Okla. State U., Weatherford, 1988—, also dir. Title II workshops, 1989—; P.I. in SWOSU-NSF Young Scholars Program, 1994—; supr. rsch. grants NSF, Shawnee, 1974-75. Active disaster relief unit Pott-Lincoln Assn., Shawnee, 1984-88; with carpentry missionary So. Bapt. Ch., Billings, Mont., 1984-86; young adult Sunday sch. tchr. Calvary Bapt. Ch., Shawnee, 1982-87; bd. dirs. Okla. Wildlife Fedn., 1992—, also conservation v.p. Danforth Found. fellow, 1970-73, Harvard U. fellow, 1965-66. Mem. AAUP, Okla Coun. Tchrs. of Math. (state v.p., bd. dirs.). Home: 517 N 4th St Thomas OK 73669-9012 Office: Southwestern Okla State U 100 Campus Dr Weatherford OK 73096-3001

WOODS, PHYLLIS MICHALIK, elementary school educator; b. New Orleans, Sept. 12, 1937; d. Philip John and Thelma Alice (Carey) Michalik; 1 child, Tara Lynn Woods. BA, Southeastern La. U., 1967. Cert. speech and English tchr., libr. sci., La. Tchr. speech, English and drama St. Charles Parish Pub. Schs., Luling, La., elem. tchr., secondary tchr. remedial reading, Chpt. I reading specialist; Wicat tchr. coord.; tchr. cons. St. Charles parish writing project La. State U. Writing Project. Author: Egbert, the Egret, Angel Without Wings; songwriter; contbr. articles and poems to River Parish Guide, St. Charles Herald. Sch. rep. United Fund, St. Charles Parish Reading Assn.; parish com. mem. Young Authors, Tchrs. Who Write; active 4-H. Mem. ASCD, Internat. Reading Assn., St. Charles Parish Reading Coun., Newspaper in Edn. (chmn., historian), La. Assn. Newspapers in Edn. (state com.).

WOODS, ROY LANDON, principal; b. Oct. 31, 1935; s. Nelson Lynn and Mary Woods; m. Coleta Mae Grice, July 27, 1953; children: Michael Landon, Rebecca Gay. BS, N.W. Okla. State U., 1970, MS, 1975; supt. cert., West Tex. A&M U., 1991. Cert. elem. and secondary tchr., mid-mgmt. supt., Tex. Letter carrier U.S. Postal Svc., Oklahoma City, 1959-67; tchr. Windsor (Colo.) Pub. Schs., 1970-71, Ponca City (Okla.) Schs., 1983-86; tchr., coach Scott County Unified Schs., Scott City, Kans., 1971-75; prin. jr. and sr. high schs. Tonkawa (Okla.) Pub. Schs., 1975-78; agt. Okla. Farm Bur., Ponca City, 1978-81, Daily Oklahoman, Ponca City, 1981-83; prin. Dalhart (Tex.) Elem. Sch., 1986—; negotiator Kans. NEA/Scott County, 1972-75. Mem. Connect Tex., Austin, 1992. With USAF, 1955-59. Named Scott County Young Educator of Yr., 1974, Outstanding Kiwanian, Tonkawa, 1979, 80; recipient Golden Cow Chip award, 1994. Mem. ASCD, Assn. Tex. Profl. Educators, Toastmasters (sgt. arms, sec., v.p., pres. 1994, publicity com. Dalhart 1991-96, Competent Toastmaster award 1992). Democrat. Nazarene. Home: PO Box 133 Dalhart TX 79022-0133 Office: Dalhart Elem Sch 1401 Tennessee Blvd Dalhart TX 79022-5137

WOODS, STEPHANIE ELISE, sales professional; b. Kansas City, Kans., July 26, 1962; d. Benoyd Myers and Lee Ann (Parks) Ellison; m. Reginald Elbert Woods; children: Erin Elise, Ryan Ellison. BA in Bus. Adminstrn., Wichita State U., 1984. Software sales specialist IBM, Houston, 1985—. Mem. NAFE, Alpha Kappa Alpha, Omicron Delta Kappa Alumni, Mortar Bd. Alumni. Democrat. Methodist. Office: IBM 2 Riverway Houston TX 77056-1912

WOODSIDE, DONNA J., nursing educator; b. Ft. Wayne, Ind., Feb. 3, 1940; d. Evan Russell and Helen Bernice (High) Owens; m. Henry W. Schroeder, Nov. 28, 1959 (dec.); children: William Schroeder, Michael Schroeder; m. Robert J. Woodside, Jan. 11, 1974; children: Chris, Tracy. BSN, U. Evansville, 1970; MSN, U. Cin., 1975, EdD, 1981. Cert. diabetes educator, gerontology nurse. Staff nurse Wahiawa (Hawaii) Community Hosp., Health Profl. Agy., Cin.; instr. Bethesda Hosp. Sch. Nursing, Cin.; assoc. prof. U. Cin., 1991; pres. Concepts R & D Inc., 1989—; field nurse Willowbrook Home Health Care, Inc., 1993—. Mem. Am. Assn. Diabetes Educators, Sigma Theta Tau. Home: 2230 Oakleaf Dr Franklin TN 37064-7413

WOODSIDE, JANE HARRIS, editor, writer, folklorist; b. Phila., Jan. 26, 1952; d. Clifford Campbell and Ann (Palczuk) Harris; m. Jack Richard Woodside, Jr., Jan. 27, 1979; children: Jessica, Nicholas, Christopher. BA, Bucknell U., 1974; MA in English, Temple U., 1977; MA in Folklore, U. N.C., 1987. Editorial asst. Bus. Week McGraw Hill, Phila., 1976-79; freelance writer Charlottesville, Va., 1979-80; rsch. asst., casewriter U. Va. Colgate Darden Bus. Sch., Charlottesville, 1980-82; folklore cons. Ctr. for Appalachian Studies, Svcs. E. Tenn. State U., Johnson City, 1987-88, rsch. assoc., 1988-90, asst. dir., 1991-95, asst. dir., editor Now and Then, 1995—; mem. Folk Arts Panel, Tenn. Arts Commn., 1991-95, Folk Arts Panel, Ky. Arts Coun., 1992. Editor: (book) Communities in Motion, 1995; assoc. editor: (monograph) A Folk Medical Lexicon of South Central Appalachia, 1990. Mem. Am. Folklore Soc., Appalachian Studies Assn., Tenn. Writers Alliance (founding bd. mem. 1991-95, chmn. 1994-95), Phi Beta Kappa. Office: Ctr for Appalachian Studies & Svcs Ea Tenn State U Box 70556 Johnson City TN 37614

WOODSIDE, NINA BENCICH, psychiatrist; b. Washington, June 1, 1931; m. Byron C. Woodside, Oct. 8, 1955; children: David B., Andrew B., Steven P., Anne N., Kevin N., Jason S. BS, George Washington U., 1953; MD cum laude, Med. Coll. Pa., 1957; MPH, Johns Hopkins U., 1963. Diplomate Am. Bd. Psychiatry and Neurology, Am. Bd. Preventive Medicine. Dir. divsn. health svcs. Dept. of Health, Fairfax, Va., 1963; chief bur. chronic disease control Dept. Pub. Health, Washington, 1964-68, assoc. dir. for planning and rsch., 1968-70; acting dep. dir. health svcs. adminstrn. Dept. Human Resources, Washington, 1969-70, acting dir., 1970; dir. office community health and program activities Met. Washington Regional Med. Program, 1970-72; assoc. clin. prof. dept. health care adminstrn. George Washington U., Washington, 1970-73; dir. ctr. for women in medicine Med. Coll. Pa., Phila., 1973-76; resident in psychiatry No. Va. Mental Health Inst., Falls Church, 1976-79; pvt. practice, 1979—; vis. assoc. prof. dept. community health and preventive medicine Med. Coll. Pa., Phila., 1973-76; assoc. prof. dept. health care adminstrn. George Washington U., 1971-73, clin. asst. prof., 1970-73, lectr. in pub. health sch. nursing, 1963-64; pres. med. staff Prince William Hosp., 1986-87, bd. dirs., 1986-89, chmn. dept. psychiatry, 1984, past pres., 1987-88; bd. dirs. PWH, Inc., 1987-89, mem. strategic planning com., 1988. Co-author: Introduction to Health Planning, 1974, 2d edit., 1979, 3d edit., 1984, Women in Medicine: A Bibliography of the Literature on Women Physicians, 1977; contbr. articles to profl. jours. and chpts. to books. Fellow Am. Psychiat. Assn., Royal Soc. Health, Am. Pub. Health Assn. (past mem. governing coun.), Am. Coll. Preventive Medicine (past sec.-treas., past mem. com. on fin.); mem. Washington Psychiat. Soc. (treas. No. Va. br. 1983-84), Prince William County Med. Soc., Med. Soc. Va., Fed. Women's Award Assn., Johns Hopkins U. Alumni Assn., Woman's Med. Coll. Alumni Assn., Zeta Phi. Office: 8712 Sudley Rd Manassas VA 22110-4405

WOODSON, AL CURTIS, software company executive, software engineer; b. Phila., May 22, 1960; s. Alfred Curtis and Evelyn Gretel Woodson; m. Lenora Vinett Dunham, Aug. 25, 1990. BS in Mktg., Hampton U., 1982. Cons. J.E.S. Search Firm Inc., Atlanta, 1986; sales rep. Inacomp Computer Ctrs., Atlanta, 1986-87, desk top pub. specialist, 1987, store mgr., 1987, Apple mktg. mgr., 1987-88, Apple bus. devel. engr., 1988-89; Apple systems engr. Datagraphic, Inc., Roswell, Ga., 1989-90, product mgr. computer networking, 1990-91, mgr. product rsch. and devel., 1991-93; pres. Questeck, Ltd., Alpharetta, Ga., 1993—; speaker in field. Officer inf. U.S. Army, 1982-85. Mem. Nat. Assn. Desktop Pubs. (futrends group), Nat. Bus. Forms Assn. (ANSI X12 standards rev. com., EDI standard revs. com., non-impact com.), Xplor Internat., Omega Psi Phi. Home: 10535 Willow Meadow Cir Alpharetta GA 30202-5710 Office: Questeck Ltd Ste 401-268 10945 State Bridge Rd Alpharetta GA 30202

WOODSON, DANNY, lawyer; b. St. Louis, June 2, 1949; s. William Melvin Woodson and Wanda Jean (Lucas) Bradford; m. Barbara Ann Cook, Aug. 7, 1971; children: Christopher Allen, Timothy Jon. BS, East Tex. State U., 1970; JD, Tex. Tech. U., 1977. Bar: Tex. 1978, U.S. Dist. Ct. (ea. dist.) Tex. 1979. Assoc. Kenley, Boyland, Hawthorne, Star and Coughlin, Longview, Tex., 1978, Florence and Florence, Hughes Springs, Tex., 1978-83; sole practitioner, Mt. Pleasant, Tex., 1983—; adv. bd. mem. Bowie-Cass Mental Health Svcs., Cass County, Tex., 1981; chmn., adv. bd. mem. Couch Phys. Therapy and Rehab. Svcs., Mt. Pleasant, 1994—. Coach Dixie League Baseball, Mt. Pleasant, 1984, 88, 89, Mt. Pleasant Soccer Assn., 1984-85; chmn. legis. com. Mt. Pleasant C. of C., 1984-85; bd. deacons Trinity Bapt. Ch., Mt. Pleasant, 1986-88. Mem. Cass County Bar Assn. (pres. 1981-82), N.E. Tex. Bar Assn., Titus County Bar Assn., Tex. Trial Lawyers Assn., Assn. Trial Lawyers of Am. Baptist. Office: PO Box 399 Mount Pleasant TX 75456-0399

WOODWARD, DAVID LUTHER, lawyer, consultant; b. Alexandria, La., Mar. 18, 1942; s. Luther Washburn and Ruby Ellen (Robertson) W.; m. Adeline Myree Peterson, July 12, 1965 (div. 1971); m. Louisette Marie Forget, Nov. 12, 1973. BA, Fla. State U., 1965, JD, 1969; LLM, U. London, 1982. Bar: Fla. 1969, Okla. 1982, Tex. 1987, U.S. Dist. Ct. (mid. and so. dists.) Fla. 1971, U.S. Dist. Ct. (no. and we. dists.) Okla. 1983, U.S. Dist. Ct. (no. dist.) Tex. 1985, U.S. Dist. Ct. (ea. dist.) Wis. 1992, U.S. Ct. of Claims 1970, U.S. Ct. Appeals (fed. and D.C. cirs.) 1970, (5th and 11th cirs.) 1981, (10th cir.) 1982, (9th cir.) 1985, U.S. Tax Ct. 1970, U.S. Ct. Mil. Appeals 1970, U.S. Supreme Ct. 1973. Trial atty. USDA, Washington, 1970; asst. atty. gen. State of Fla., Tampa, 1971-73; ptnr. Rose & Woodward, Tampa, 1973-76; pvt. practice The Law Offices of David Luther Woodward, Tampa, 1976-80; appellate pub. defender State of Okla., 1980-81; instr. U. Okla. Coll. Law, Norman, 1980-81; assoc. Jones, Gungoll, Jackson, Collins & Dodd, Enid, Okla., 1982-84, Brice & Barron, Dallas, 1985-86; pvt. practice Dallas, 1986—; of counsel Kenneth R. Guest & Assocs., Dallas, 1990-91, Sapp & Madden, Dallas and Austin, 1991, Bennett & Kurtzman, Dallas, 1991-93. Contbr. articles to profl. jours. Episcopalian. Office: 222 Turtle Creek Tower 3131 Turtle Creek Blvd Dallas TX 75219-5431

WOODWARD, HANSON MARK, English and German languages educator, minister; b. Kansas City, Mo., Oct. 23, 1947; s. Hanson E. and Daisy B. (Lyles) W.; m. Sherrylee Johnson, Apr. 11, 1971; children: Philip Gary, Benjamin Johnson, Emily Joy. BA, Harding U., 1969; MA, U. Miss., 1971; PhD, U. Tex., Dallas, 1987. Ordained to ministry Ch. of Christ, 1966. Campus min. Oxford (Miss.) Ch. of Christ, 1969-71; missionary Midtown Ch. of Christ, Ft. Worth, 1971-79; prof. Okla. Christian U., Oklahoma City, 1979—, chair lang. and lit. dept., 1994—. Author: Let's Start Talking, 1992; author, editor (lang. workbooks) Friends Speak Series (4 titles), 1984—. Coach Edmond (Okla.) Soccer Club, 1983-88; referee U.S. Soccer Assn., Colorado Springs, Colo., 1988—. Home: 2920 Gettysburg Rd Edmond OK 73013-6458 Office: Oklahoma Christian Univ PO Box 11000 Oklahoma City OK 73136-1100

WOODWARD, ISABEL AVILA, educational writer, foreign language educator; b. Key West, Fla., Mar. 14, 1906; d. Alfredo and Isabel (Lopez) Avila; student Fla. State Coll. for Women, 1925, A.B. in Edn., 1938; cert. in teaching Spanish, U. Miami, 1961; summer study U. Fla., Eckerd Coll.; postgrad. St. Lawrence U., U. Miami; m. Clyde B. Woodward, June 6, 1944 (dec.); children: Joy Avis Ball, Greer Isabel Woodward Sucke. Tchr., Key West, 1927-42, remedial reading cons., 1941-42; reading tchr., asst. reading lab. and clinic St. Lawrence U., summer 1941; Spanish translator U.S. Office of Censorship, Miami, 1943; tchr. Central Beach Elem. Sch., Miami Beach, Fla., 1943-44, Silver Bluff Elem. Sch., 1943-50, Henry West Lab. Sch., Coral Gables, Fla., 1955-57, Dade Demonstration Sch., Miami, 1957-61; author 125 sch. radio lessons for teaching Spanish, Dade County Elem. Schs., 1961; tchr. Spanish Workshop for Fla.; speaker poetry and short story writing, 1977; guest lectr. on writing the short story Fla. Inst. Tech., Jensen Beach, 1981; guest lectr. Circle Bay Yacht Club, Stuart, Fla., 1995; freelance writer; contbr. to Listen Mag., Sunshine Mag., Lookout Mag., Christian Sci. Monitor, Miami Herald, Three/Four, Child Life, Wee Wisdom, Fla. Wildlife, Young World; sponsor Port St. Lucie Jr. Woman's Club, 1983. Recipient Honoris Causa award Alpha Delta Kappa, 1972-74, award Contra Costa Times, Calif., 1985, 1st prize for short story in nat. Ark. writers conf. contest, 1992; named one of 5 Outstanding Fla. Tchrs., 1972-74. Mem. Nat. League Am. Pen Women (1st v.p. Greater Miami br. 1974-76, historian 1978—, librarian 1978—, awards for writing 1973, 74, 77, 1st and 3d place state writing awards for adult and juvenile fiction 1983, state 1st prize short story 1985), AAUW, Alpha Delta Kappa, Psi Psi Psi. Address: Apt 6-301 1950 SW Palm City Rd Stuart FL 34994

WOODWARD, JAMES HOYT, academic administrator, engineer; b. Sanford, Fla., Nov. 24, 1939; s. James Hoyt and Edith Pearl (Breeden) W.; m. Martha Ruth Hill, Oct. 13, 1956; children: Connie, Tracey, Wade. BS in Aero. Engring. with honors, Ga. Tech. Inst., 1962, MS in Aero. Engring., 1963, PhD in Engring. Mechanics, 1967; MBA, U. Ala.-Birmingham, 1973. Registered profl. engr., Ala. Asst. prof. engring. mechanics USAF Acad., Colo., 1965-67, assoc. prof., 1967-68; asst. prof. engring. mechanics N.C. State U., 1968-69; assoc. prof. engring. U. Ala., Birmingham, 1969-70, assoc. prof., 1973-77, prof. civil engring., 1977-89, asst. v.p., 1973-78, dean engring., 1978-84, acad. v.p., 1984-89; chancellor U. N.C., Charlotte, 1989—; dir. tech. devel. Rust Engring. Co., Birmingham, 1970-73; cons. in field. Contbr. articles to profl. jours. With USAF, 1965-68. Mem. ASCE, ASME, Am. Soc. Engring. Edn., Am. Mgmt. Assn., Sigma Xi. Methodist. Office: U NC Charlotte Office of Chancellor Charlotte NC 28223

WOODWARD, KENNETH EMERSON, retired mechanical engineer; b. Washington, Oct. 30, 1927; s. George Washington and Mary Josephine (Compton) W.; m. Mary Margaret Eungard, Mar. 29, 1956; children: Stephen Mark, Kristi Lynn. BME, George Washington U., 1949, M Engring. Adminstrn., 1960; MS, U. Md., 1953; PhD, Am. U., 1973. Mech. engr. Naval Rsch. Lab., Washington, 1950-54; value engring. program mgr. Harry Diamond Labs., Washington, 1955-74; sci. adviser U.S. Army Med. Bioengring. R & D Lab., Ft. Detrick, Md., 1974-75; mech. engr. Woolcot & Co., Washington, 1975-90; ret., 1990. Author: Solar Energy Applications for the Home, 1978; contbr. over 40 articles to profl. publs. With U.S. Army, 1946-47. Recipient Dept. of the Army Decoration for Exceptional Civilian Svc., Honors Achievement award Angiology Rsch. Found., Purdue Frederick Co., Engring. Alumni Achievement award George Washington U., Washington, 1987. Mem. ASME, Am. Soc. for Artificial Internal Organs. Republican. Baptist. Home: 1701 Hunts End Ct Vienna VA 22182-1833

WOODWARD, MICHAEL VAUGHAN, secondary education educator; b. Plymouth, Mass., Mar. 22, 1947; s. Barclay Jefferis Woodward and Barbara Ellen (Vaughan) Garside; m. Nancy Kay Hatch, Sept. 20, 1975; children: Natalie Kaye Hatch, Vanessa Hatch. BA, U. South Fla., 1969, MA, 1971;

PhD, U. Ga., 1982. Instr. history U. South Fla., Tampa, 1971-72; teaching fellow U. Ga., Athens, 1972-77, instr. history evening divsn., 1973-79; chair dept. history Berkeley Prep. Sch., Tampa, 1979-86; dean instr. Chatham (Va.) Hall, 1986-87; Howard H. Baker Jr. chair Am. history McCallie Sch., Chattanooga, 1987—; cons. for advanced placement Am. history Coll. Bd., Atlanta, 1987; speaker in field; adj. instr. history and polit. sci. U. Tenn.-Chattanooga, 1990—. Contbr. articles to profl. jours. Grantee NEH, 1988, Nat. Fellowship for Ind. Study in Humanities, 1989; William Robertson Coe fellow, 1991, 94. Mem. So. Hist. Assn., Orgn. Am. Historians, Ga. Hist. Assn., Am. Polit. Sci. Assn., Phi Alpha Theta. Libertarian. Home: 809 Chestnutwood Ln Chattanooga TN 37421-4502 Office: McCallie Sch 500 Dodds Ave Chattanooga TN 37404-3949

WOODWARD, WAYNE WILLIAM, librarian, minister; b. Greenburg, Ind., May 4, 1930; s. Arthur Coy and Hazel Prue (Ayres) W.; m. H. Corinne Vaughn, Jan. 17, 1956; children: Gail, Karen. AB, Taylor U., 1952; BDiv, Asbury Theol. Sem., 1955; MA, Appalachian State U. (formerly Appalachian Coll.), Boone, N.C., 1960; MLS, U. Ky., 1967. Pastor United Meth. Ch., N.C., 1955-59, 61-64; asst. to the libr. Asbury Theol. Sem., Wilmore, Ky., 1965-67; libr. Asbury Coll., Wilmore, 1967-77, reference libr., 1977-78; dir. libr. svc. Wesley Bibl. Sem., Jackson, Miss., 1978—. Office: Wesley Bibl Sem PO Box 9938 Jackson MS 39286-0938

WOODWARD, WILLIAM LEE, retired savings bank executive; b. Lexington, Ky., Jan. 12, 1926; s. Joel Henry and Ophelia Martha (Wallace) W.; A.B., U. Ky., 1950, M.A., 1952; m. Dorothy J. Dekle, Dec. 31, 1949; children—Pamela, William Lee, Martha. Tchr., Lafayette High Sch., 1950-52; asst. prin. Ft. Benning (Ga.) Children's Schs., 1952-53; asst. mgr. Lexington (Ky.) Fed. Savs. & Loan Assn., 1953-54, exec. v.p., 1954-73, pres., 1973-96. Pres. Lexington Deaf Oral Sch., 1968; trustee Midway (Ky.) Coll., 1968-80; treas. Bluegrass Found., 1967-95; dir. Ky. Housing Corp., 1979-80. Served with USN, 1944-46. Mem. Ky. Savs. and Loan League (pres. 1969). Mem. Christian Ch. Clubs: Rotary, Lafayette.

WOODWORTH, GENE BOSWELL, educational writer, educator; b. Collinwood, Tenn., Oct. 11, 1926; d. Carl and Vida (Langford) Boswell; BS, Middle Tenn. State U., 1968, MA, 1975; children: Jill, Camille, Patricia, John. Tchr. Tullahoma (Tenn.) Sch. Sys., 1968-91. Author: (musical play) Will Thomas, 1993—, (play) Murder on the Twelfth Night, 1996. Named Tchr. of Yr., Tullahoma, Tenn., 1984-85. Del. to UN 4th Internat. Congress for Women, Beijing, 1995. Mem. LWV, Ret. Tchrs. Assn., Tenn. Edn. Assn., Tullahoma Edn. Assn., Mid. Tenn. Edn. Assn., Mid. Tenn. Social Studies Assn. (pres. 1987-88), Bus. and Profl. Women Manchester (Woman of Yr. 1985-86, Lady of Distinction 1994-95), Soroptimist Internat. (v.p. 1990-94, pres., 1994-95). Democrat. Methodist. Home and Office: 704 Madison St Manchester TN 37355-1941

WOODY, CLYDE WOODROW, lawyer; b. Princeton, Tex., Oct. 3, 1920; s. James W. and Emma Mae (Heard) W.; m. Paula Fay Mullen, Aug. 23, 1969; children: Todd, Joe. BS, U. Houston, 1951, JD, 1951; postgrad. St. Mary's U., San Antonio, 1952, U. Colo., 1953. Bar: Tex. 1952, U.S. Ct. Appeals (5th cir.) 1956, U.S. Supreme Ct. 1958, U.S. Ct. Appeals (6th cir.) 1973, U.S. Ct. Appeals (11th cir.) 1981; cert. specialist in criminal law and family law Tex. Bd. Legal Specialization. Pvt. practice law Houston, 1952-66; ptnr., then sr. ptnr. Woody & Rosen, Houston, 1966-80; pvt. practice law, Houston, 1980—; city atty. Southside Pl., Houston, 1955-57; bd. dir. Unitedbank-Houston, Cen. Bank Holding Co., Miami, Fla.; lectr. Bd. dirs. Mossler Found., 1966-70; del. People to People Internat. Citizen Amb. Program, 1988, 91; sect. chmn. State Bar Tex., 1964-65; staff judge adv. N.Am. Air Def. Command, Ent ARB. Capt. U.S. Army, 1941-45, to capt. USAF, 1951-53; PTO, CBI. Mem. Am. Judicature Soc., Nat. Assn. Criminal Def. Lawyers, Tex. Trial Lawyers Assn., Assn. Trial Lawyers Am., ABA, Houston Bar Assn., Tex. Criminal Def. Lawyers Assn., Nat. Transp. Safety Bd. Bar Assn., Phi Delta Phi. Democrat. Methodist. Clubs: University, Texas, (Houston). Contbr. articles to legal jours. Home: 731 Brogden Rd Houston TX 77024-3003 Office: PO Box 19028 Houston TX 77224-9028

WOODY, MARK EDWARD, financial planner; b. Ft. Worth, July 25, 1967; s. Eulas Clyde and Linda Beth (Hanley) W.; m. Kelly Lynn Taylor, June 20, 1987; children: Cassia May, Paul Edward. BBA, U. Okla., 1989. CFP, Internat. Bd. Standards and Practice for CFP. Equipment installer LeFebure, Dallas, 1983-85; intramural sports supr. intramural dept. U. Okla., Norman, 1985-88; rsch. assoc. Distbn. Rsch. Program, Norman, 1988-89; CFP, mem. Advanced Planner Group Am. Express Fin. Advisors, Oklahoma City, 1990—; Rsch. assoc.: (exec. chart book) Wholesaling in America: An Executive Chart Book, 1989. Mem., treas. Berry Rd. Ch. of Christ, Norman, 1988—, Canterbury Choral Soc., Oklahoma City, 1992-96. Mem. Inst. CFP, Internat. Assn. Fin. Planners, Am. Assn. CLU/ChFC, Coll. Bus. Adminstrn. Alumni Coun. (exec. com.). Republican. Office: Am Express Fin Advisors Ste 900 3030 NW Expressway Oklahoma City OK 73112

WOOFTER, R. D., utilities company executive; b. Weston, Va., 1923; married. BEE, W.Va. U., 1950. With Tex.-N.Mex. Power Co. (formerly Community Pub. Service Co.), Ft. Worth, 1950—, v.p., mgr. communications, 1967-73, v.p. ops., 1973-74, exec. v.p., 1974-75, pres., chief exec. officer, from 1975, chmn., 1977—, also bd. dirs.; chmn. TNP Enterprises Inc., Ft. Worth. Served with USAF, 1940-45. *

WOOLARD, WILLIAM LEON, lawyer, electrical distributing company executive; b. Bath, N.C., Aug. 26, 1931; s. Archie Leon and Pearl Irene (Boyd) W.; m. Virginia Harris Stratton, June 17, 1961; children: William Leon Jr., Margaret Anne. AB, Duke U., 1953, LLB, JD, 1955. Bar: N.C. 1955, U.S. Dist. Ct. (we. and mid. dists.) N.C. 1960. Claims analyst Md. Casualty Co., Charlotte, N.C., 1955-56; dist. mgr. Chrysler Corp., Charlotte, 1956-60; ptnr. Jones, Hewson & Woolard, Charlotte, 1960-86, of counsel, 1986—; pres. Armature Winding Co., Inc., Charlotte, 1970—, also bd. dirs.; v.p. Power Products Mfg. Co., Charlotte, 1970—, also bd. dirs. Mem. adminstrv. bd. 1st United Meth. Ch., Charlotte, 1961-78, trustee, 1984-87; trustee Lawyers Ednl. Found., Charlotte, 1970-78; bd. dirs. Christian Rehab. Ctr., Charlotte, 1972-73, N.C. Eye and Human Tissue Bank, Winston-Salem, 1978-79. Recipient Order of Civil Merit Moran award Republic of Korea, 1990, Disting. Svc. medal Republic of China, 1990, Medal of Friendship Pope John Paul II, 1990, Humanitarian Citizen of Merit medal Republic of China, 1990, Humanitarian medal France, 1990, Outstanding Svc. medal Mayor of Paris, 1990, numerous others; Angier B. Duke scholar Duke U., 1949-53; Carnegie Found. fellow Duke U., 1951-52, Melvin Jones fellow Lions Found., 1978. Mem. ABA, N.C. Bar Assn., N.C. State Bar Assn., 26th Jud. Dist. Bar Assn., Am. Judicature Soc., Lions (pres. Charlotte Cen. club 1972-73, pres., trustee ednl. found. 1973-87, dist. gov., chmn. coun. govs. internat. orgn. 1978-79, internat. bd. dirs. 1981-85, Ambassador of Goodwill award 1983, internat. 3d v.p. 1986-87, 2d v.p. 1987-88, 1st v.p. 1988-89, internat. pres. 1989-90, immediate past pres. 1990-91, chmn. bd. trustee 1990-91), Masons, Shriners, Phi Kappa Sigma, Delta Theta Phi. Home: 638 Hempstead Pl Charlotte NC 28207-2320 Office: PO Box 32277 Charlotte NC 28232-2277

WOOLDRIDGE, THOMAS DEAN, nephrologist; b. Grenada, Miss., Feb. 25, 1946; s. Reuben Dean and Katherine (Shipp) W.; m. Luanne Lyle, Oct. 25, 1975; 1 child, Thomas D. Jr. BS, BA, Millsaps Coll., 1968; MD, U. Miss., 1972. Diplomate Am. Bd. Internal Medicine, Am. Bd. Nephrology. Med. dir. dialysis North Miss. Med. Ctr., Tupelo, 1977—. Named among best doctors in the southeast Best Doctors in Am., 1995.8. Mem. Miss. Nephrol. Soc. (pres. 1994-95). Methodist. Office: North Miss Med Ctr 104 Northwood Dr Tupelo MS 38801-1047

WOOLDRIDGE, WALTER BRUCE, quality assurance administrator; b. Waco, Tex., July 15, 1955; s. George Harold and Jessie Loucille (Hand) W.; m. Cornelia Kroell, Feb. 6, 1982; 1 child, Erik Bryant. BS, Tex. A&M U., 1977; MBA, U. Dallas, 1989. Quality assurance engr. Tex. Instruments, Inc., Dallas, 1983-84; program quality assurance engr. Tex. Instruments, Inc., Lewisville, 1984-89; mgr. process control engring. DSC Comm., Inc., Plano, Tex., 1989-90, mgr. printed circuit bd. assembly mfg. engring., 1990-91, mgr. process quality assurance, 1991—; mem., vice chmn. IPC-A-610 task group Inst. for Interconnecting and Packaging Electronic Circuits, Lincolnwood, Ill., 1990—. Capt. U.S. Army, 1977-83. Mem. Am. Soc. for Quality Control, Nat. Mgmt. Assn. Home: 4007 Pepperwood Dr Flower Mound TX 75028-1249 Office: DSC Comm Inc 1000 Coit Rd Plano TX 75075-5802

WOOLERY, RAY CHARLES, logistician, military officer; b. Dawson, Minn., Mar. 5, 1954; s. Charles Marlin and Arlene Delores (Harstad) W.; m. Pamela Derice Torres, July 28, 1952; children: Christopher, Jon. Student, S.D. State U., 1977, Chapman U., 1992. Commd. 2d lt. U.S. Army, 1977, advanced through grades to lt. col., 1996; exec. officer C troop 2/17 cav. U.S. Army, Korea, 1986-87; asst. program mgr. advanced attack helicopter U.S. Army, St. Louis, 1987-88, dep. logistics chief advanced attack helicopter, 1988-90; exec. officer 1-501st aviation bn. U.S. Army, Korea, 1990-91, force modernization officer 17th aviation brigade, 1991-92; ops. officer test and experimentation U.S. Army, Ft. Hood, Tex., 1992; owner Spuds/Sandbar Inc., Panama City, Fla., 1992-96; sr. analyst Advanced Engring. and Planning, St. Louis, 1996, sr. logistician, 1996—. Decorated Meritorious Svc. medal, 1992; recipient Security Svc. award Republic of Korea, 1991, Army Commendation award, 1985. Mem. Army Aviation Assn. (v.p. programs 1977), Assn. of U.S. Army (chpt. pres. 1976). Home: 123 Carlyle E Belleville IL 62221 Office: Advanced Engring and Planning Ste 200 4433 Woodson Rd Saint Louis MO 63134

WOOLLEN, THOMAS HAYES, insurance consultant; b. Winston-Salem, N.C., Oct. 6, 1934; s. Junius Wesley and Ruth (Millikan) W.; m. Velva Hayden Whitescarver, Oct. 21, 1960; children: Thomas Hayes Jr., John Carter, Mark Hayden, Velva Hayden. AB, Duke U., 1956. CLU; chartered fin. cons.; registered investment advisor; accredited estate planner. Regional sales mgr. John H. Harland Co., Atlanta, 1965-75; ins. cons. Planning Cons., Inc., Charlotte, N.C., 1975-81; ins. specialist Merrill Lynch Life Agy., Charlotte, 1981-85; pres. Consol. Cons., Inc., Charlotte, 1985—; mem. steering com. Estate Planners Day Queens Coll., Charlotte, 1988—; bd. dir. N.C. State Bd. CPA Examiners, Raleigh. Ruling elder Covenant Presbyn. Ch., Charlotte, 1980—. Mem. Internat. Assn. Fin. Planners, N.C. Planned Giving Coun., Charlotte Assn. Life Underwriters, Charlotte Estate Planning Coun., Am. Soc. CLU and ChFC (local bd. dirs.), Charlotte Country Club. Republican. Home: 1318 Queens Rd W Charlotte NC 28207-2142 Office: Consol Cons Inc 428 E 4th St Ste 102 Charlotte NC 28202-2434

WOOLUMS, MARGARET CARMICHAEL, thoroughbred bloodline researcher; b. Charleston, W.Va., Aug. 8, 1935; d. H. St. G.T. Jr. and Margaret Lyle (MacCorkle) Carmichael; m. Dan Dudley Gravitt (div. 1956); 1 child Margaret Lyle Gravitt; m. William Howard Woolums Jr. (dec. 1992); 1 child, Anna Hetzel Woolums Carney. BBA, U. Ky., 1960. Statistician Blood-Horse Mag., Lexington, Ky., 1954-66; adminstrv. asst., stats. bur. The Jockey Club, Lexington, 1966-69; sec., treas. Pedigree Assocs., Inc., Lexington, 1970-82, pres., 1982-96; v.p. info. Racing Corp. of Am., Inc. div. Ky. Horse Ctr., 1990-91; pres. Pedigree Prodns., Inc., Lexington, 1990—; adviser Internat. Cataloguing Stds., London, 1982—; editor, owner South Am. Thoroughbred Qtr. mag., 1990-92; divsn. dir. Ky. Racing Commn., 1992-93; prin. asst. Ky. Pub. Svc. Commn., 1993-95; coord. internal info. Jockey Club Racing Svcs., Inc., 1995—. Editor Internat. Catalog Stds., 1961—, Racing Update, Inc., 1993-95; contbr. articles to topical publs. Mem. Am. United Profl. Horsemen's Assn., Thoroughbred Club Am., Cen. Ky. Riding for Handicapped (bd. dirs. 1986-91), Va. Horse Ctr. (bd. dirs. 1985-91), Bloodstock Rsch. Informational Svcs. (bd. dirs. 1984-89). Democrat. Episcopalian. Office: Pedigree Prodns Inc 909911 N Broadway Lexington KY 40505

WOON, PAUL SAM, technical executive; b. Shanhai, China, July 1, 1942; s. Ramon L. and Rita C. (Wu) W.; m. Lin-Sun Juan, Dec. 7, 1973; children: Audrey Hui, Eric Chih. BS, U. Iowa, 1965, MS, 1968; PhD, U. Akron, 1974. Rsch. chemist clin. rsch. ctr. U. Iowa, Iowa City, 1965-68; rsch. chemist PPG Industries, Barberton, Ohio, 1968-71; instr. dept. chemistry Cuyahoga Coll., Cleve., 1972-73; staff rsch. assoc. Appleton (Wis.) Papers-NCR, 1974-76; rsch. mgr. Kimberly-Clark Corp., Neenah, Wis., 1976-81, rsch. dir., 1981-87; sr. rsch. dir. Kimberly-Clark Corp., Roswell, Ga., 1987-90, dir. nonwovens internat., 1990-95; v.p. product and materials devel. Asia-Pacific Region Kimberly Clark Corp., Bangkok, Thailand, 1995—; chmn. minority retention and recruitment com. Kimberly-Clark Corp., 1989-91. Contbr. articles to profl. jours.; patentee in field. Named Indsl. fellow U. Akron, 1971-74. Mem. Orn. Chinese-Ams. (pres. Ga. chpt. 1993). Office: Kimberly-Clark Corp PO Box 349 Neenah WI 54957-0349

WOOTAN, GERALD DON, osteopathic physician, educator; b. Oklahoma City, Nov. 19, 1944; s. Ralph George and Corrinne (Loafman) W. BA, Cen. State U., Edmond, Okla., 1970, BS, 1971; MEd, Cen. State U., 1974; MB, U. Okla., Oklahoma City, 1978; DO, Okla. State U., 1985. Dir. mfg. engring. lab. GE, Oklahoma City, 1965-70; counseling psychologist VA Hosp., Oklahoma City, 1970-76; physician asst. Thomas (Okla.) Med. Clin., 1978-81; pvt. practice, Jenks, Okla., 1986—; intern Tulsa Regional Med. Ctr., 1985-86; assoc. prof. Okla. State U. Coll. Osteo. Medicine, 1986-95, with Springer Clinic, 1995—; sec. Springer Clinic Inc., Tulsa, 1990-91; chmn. gen. practice quality assurance Tulsa Regional Med. Ctr., 1989-91; v.p. New Horizons Counseling Ctr., Clinton, Okla., 1977-81; sr. aviation med. examiner FAA, Tulsa, 1991—; pres. S.W. Diagnostics, Inc., Tulsa, 1989-91, Okla. Edn. Found. Osteo. Medicine, Tulsa, 1988-89; pres., trustee Tulsa Long Term Care Authority. Contbr. articles to profl. jours.; patentee for human restraint. Advancement chmn., chmn. Eagle bd. rev. Boy Scouts Am., Tulsa, 1987-88; trustee Tulsa Long Term Care Authority, 1988-91; trustee Tulsa Community Found. for Indigent Health Care, Inc., 1988-91. With USN, 1962-64. Named Clin. Preceptor of Yr., U. Okla., 1980, Outstanding Alumni award Okla. State U. Coll. Osteo. Medicine, 1990. Mem. Am. Osteo. Assn., Okla. Osteo. Assn., Tulsa Dist. Osteo. Soc. (pres. 1991-92), Am. Acad. Physician Assts., Am. Coll. Gen. Practitioners, Okla. Acad. Gen. Practitioners (v.p.), Am. Coll. Osteo. Family Physicians (bd. cert. 1993, pres. Okla. chpt. 1993-94), Okla. State U. Coll. Osteo. Medicine Alumni Assn. (pres. 1988-89). Home: 4320 E 100th St Tulsa OK 74137-5305 Office: Jenks Health Team 324 W Main St Jenks OK 74037-3747

WOOTEN, FRANK THOMAS, research facility executive; b. Fayetteville, N.C., Sept. 24, 1935; s. Frank Thomas and Katherine (McRae) W.; m. Linda Walker, July 14, 1962; children: Laurin Walker, Patrick Thomas, Ashley Tripp. BSEE, Duke U., 1957, PhD, 1964. Engr. Corning Glass Works, Raleigh, N.C., 1964-66; engr. Research Triangle Inst., Research Triangle Park, N.C., 1966-68, mgr. biomed. engring., 1968-75, exec. asst. to pres., 1975-80, v.p., 1980-89, pres., 1989—. Contbr. articles on semiconductors and biomed. engring. to profl. publs., 1966-83; patentee semiconductors tech. Bd. dirs. N.C. Biotech. Ctr., 1989—, MCNC, 1989-94; corp. mem. Nat. Inst. Statis. Scis., 1990—. Served to lt. (j.g.) USN, 1957-59. Shell fellow, 1961; recipient Disting. Engring. Alumnus award Duke U., 1991. Mem. IEEE, Assn. for Advancement Med. Instrumentation (chmn. com. on aerospace tech. 1971-77), Ballistic Missile Def. Orgn. (tech. application rev. panel 1990-94). Baptist. Office: Research Triangle Inst PO Box 12194 3040 W Cornwallis Rd Research Triangle Park NC 27709

WOOTEN, HOLLIS DARWIN, engineer; b. South Pittsburg, Tenn., Sept. 29, 1939; s. Lawson Wade and Lila Mae (Hill) W.; m. Elserean Phelps, June 26, 1976. BS in Engring., U. Tenn., 1975. Advanced engr. Westinghouse, Richland, Wash., 1975-79; sr. engr. Westinghouse, Oak Ridge, Tenn., 1979-84; sr. design engr. Los Alamos Tech. Assn., Oak Ridge, 1984-86; devel. assoc. Oak Ridge Gaseous Diffusion Plant, 1987-89; devel. staff mem. Oak Ridge Nat. Lab., 1989-92, devel. group leader, 1992—. Scoutmaster Boy Scouts Am., South Pittsburg, 1960; pres. McReynolds PTA, South Pittsburg, 1960; mem. South Pittsburg Aux. Police, 1967. Mem. ASHRAE, Tenn. Soc. Profl. Engrs., Order of Engr., K.C. (mem. coun.), Chattanooga Engrs. Club. Roman Catholic. Office: Martin Marietta Energy Sys Oak Rigde Nat Lab K-25 Site PO Box 2003 Oak Ridge TN 37831-7294

WOOTEN, JON CHARLES, sales executive; b. Tampa, Fla., Sept. 18, 1944; s. Albert L. and Rose B. (Reynolds) W.; m. Mary Speer, June 12, 1982; children: Shannon, Jonna. BS in Chemistry, U. N.C., Wilmington, 1965. Various J.P. Stevens & Co., Inc., Wallace, N.C., 1966-75; tech. sales Millmaster Onyx, Lyndhurst, N.J., 1976-82, Hydrolabs, Inc., Albemarle, N.C., 1982—. Home and Office: PO Box 1177 Carolina Beach NC 28428-1177

WOOTTEN, JOHN ROBERT, investor; b. Chickasha, Okla., Feb. 5, 1929; s. Henry Hughes and Ella Gayle (Ditzler) W.; BS, Colo. A&M U., 1953; m. Mary Lou Schmausser, Mar. 15, 1952 (div.); children: Pamela Jean, Robert Hughes; m. Geraldine Ann Theisen, Aug. 14, 1982. Sec., S.W. Radio & Equipment Co., Oklahoma City, 1953-55; pres. Belcaro Homes, Inc., 1955-60, Bob Wootten Ford, Yukon, Okla., 1960-68, Bus. Data Systems, 1968-72; chmn., chief exec. officer 1st Nat. Bank, Moore, Okla., 1970-72; pres. Communications Enterprises, Inc., Liberal, Kans., 1967-79, Trebor Leasing Co., 1965-87, Okla. Sch. Book Depository, Inc., Oklahoma City, 1976-80, S.W. Sch. Book Depository, Inc., Dallas, 1976-86; chmn., chief exec. officer Exchange Nat. Bank Del City (Okla.), 1976-78; dir. S.W. Bancshares Corp., Oklahoma City. Pres., Okla. chpt. Am. Cancer Soc., 1966-67, Okla. chpt. Arthritis Found., 1973-76, Lyric Theater Okla., 1976-77; chmn. bd. trustees Bone and Joint Hosp., 1976-81; bd. dirs. Okla. Theater Center, Dallas Theater Center; trustee Oklahoma City U.; pres. Last Frontier council Boy Scouts Am., 1968-70, Silver Beaver award, 1971; Republican nominee for Lt. Gov. of Okla., 1966. Mem. Ind. Bankers Assn., Am. Bankers Assn., Tex. Bookmen's Assn., Okla. Bookmen's Assn., Tex. Assn. Sch. Adminstrs., Econ. Club Okla., Navy League. Republican. Episcopalian. Club: Oklahoma City Rotary (pres. 1963-64). Home: 6760 Gato Rd El Paso TX 79932-3210

WOOTTEN, THOMAS FRANKLIN, criminal justice administrator; b. Orlando, Fla., Jan. 13, 1931; s. John Franklin and Betty (Shadburn) W.; m. Ruth Marie Raiman, Sept. 26, 1953 (div. 1978); m. Heidi Herbold, Apr. 12, 1978. AB in Clin. Psychology, Ohio State U., 1953, postgrad., 1958-59; postgrad., Nova U., 1977-82. Comdr. USN, 1949, active duty at sea and overseas, 1949-76, ret., 1976; mgmt. adminstr. Office Commonwealth Atty., Virginia Beach, Va., 1977-79; pres., CEO Inst. Applied Polygraph Sci., Virginia Beach, 1979-82; undersheriff Portsmouth (Va.) Sheriff's Office, 1982-93; co-chair Va. Polygraph Adv. Bd., Va. Dept. Commerce, 1988—. Decorated Legion of Merit (valor), Air Medal, Nat. Honor medal Republic of Vietnam. Mem. VFW, Am. Polygraph Assn. (various coms. 1976—, chair stds. and ethics 1985-86, co-chair accreditation com. 1991-92), Am. Assn. Police Polygraphists, Am. correctional Assn., Nat. Sheriff's Assn., Internat. Assn. Chiefs Police, Navy League, U.S. Power Squadron, Am. Legion, Sons Confederate Vets., U.S. Naval Inst., Pi Kappa Alpha, Psi Chi. Republican. Home: 2228 Windward Shore Dr Virginia Beach VA 23451-1728

WOOTTON, BROOKII E., investor relations professional; b. Uvalde, Tex., Mar. 4, 1965; d. Charles K. and Leona Agnus (Farley) W.; m. John J. Ferguson Jr.; 1 child, J. Grey Ferguson. BS, SW Tex. State U., 1988. Operator test floor Motorola, Austin, Tex., 1987-88; stockbroker's asst. Shearson Lehman Hutton, Austin, 1988-89; instr. office adminstrn. Devine (Tex.) Ind. Sch. Dist., 1989-91; asst. to chief exec. officer Turbeco, Inc., Houston, 1991-96, in investor rels., 1996—; rep. for Turbeco, Inc. N.W. C. of C. Active community and charitable orgns.; sponsor cheerleading and twirling; judge, contest dir. Am. Twirling Festival. Mem. NEA, NAFE, AAUW, VOTAT, Bus. Profls. Am. Club (sponsor), Tex. Tchrs. Assn., Tex. Bus. Educators Assn., Devine Educators Assn. (v.p.), N.W. Houston C. of C. (rep.). Jr. League N.W. Harris County, Tex. Computer Edn. Assn., Golden Key Nat. Alumni Soc., Order of Omega, Phi Theta Kappa, Alpha Phi, Phi Upsilon Omicron. Office: 7030 Empire Central Dr Houston TX 77040

WORDEN, ELIZABETH ANN, artist, comedy writer, singer; b. Karnes City, Tex., Nov. 8, 1954; d. Alan Walker and Mary Paralee (Long) W. BS in Comms., U. Tex., 1977. Disc jockey, newsperson KMMK Radio, McKinney, Tex., 1978, KPBC Radio, Irving, Tex., 1979-80, KDNT Radio, Denton, Tex., 1980-81, KJIM Radio, Ft. Worth, 1981-82, KPBC Radio, Irving, 1983, KRYS Radio, Corpus Christi, Tex., 1984; owner Worden Industries, Corpus Christi, Tex. Executed paintings for Am. Embassy, Bogota, Colombia; one-woman shows include Art Ctr., Corpus Christi, 1990; exhibited in group shows at Tex. A&M, corpus Christi, 1986, 92, Galeria Chapparal, Corpus Christi, 1988, New Eng. Fine Art Inst., Boston, 1993, Am. Embassy, Bogota; paintings in pvt. collections throughout the country. Mem. Art Ctr. Corpus Christi. Mem. Tex. Fine Arts Assn., Nat. Assn. Fine Artists. Home and Office: Worden Industries 3842 Brookhill Dr Corpus Christi TX 78410-4404

WORK, BRUCE ALEXANDER, JR., obstetrics and gynecology educator; b. Frankfort, Ind., Apr. 29, 1934; m. Janis Ann Silverstone; children: Paul Alexander, Kirsten Ann. MD, U. Mich., 1959. Diplomate Am. Bd. Ob-Gyn, Am. Bd. Maternal-Fetal Medicine. Intern Bronson Meth. Hosp., Kalamazoo, Mich., 1959-60; resident in ob-gyn. U. Mich., Ann Arbor, 1963-67, instr ob-gyn., 1969-73, asst. prof. ob-gyn., 1969-73, assoc. prof. ob-gyn., 1973-80; prof. ob-gyn. U. Ill., Chgo., 1980-86; prof., head ob-gyn. U. Minn., Mpls., 1986-90, prof. ob-gyn., 1990-91; prof. ob-gyn. Med. Coll. Ga., Augusta. 1991—; served on numerous hosp. and univ. coms. Contbr. chpts. to books, numerous articles to profl. jours. and abstracts to conf. procs. Flight surgeon USN, 1960-63. Mem. AMA, Am. Fertility Soc., Am. Med. Informatics Assn., Assn. Profs. Gyn.-Ob., Norman F. Miller Gynecol. Soc., Perinatal Assn. Mich. (bd. trustees 1974-80, chmn. com. 1976), Ctrl. Assn. Ob-Gyn , Soc. Perinatal Obstetricians (chmn. com. 1980-81, bd. dirs. 1980-83, v.p. 1981, pres. 1982), Chgo. Gynecol. Soc., Augusta-Ob-Gyn. Soc., Med. Assn. Ga., Ga. Perinatal Assn., Ga. Ob-Gyn. Soc., Phi Rho Sigma. Office: Med Coll of Ga Maternal-Fetal Med Sect Dept Ob-Gyn Augusta GA 30912

WORKMAN, GEORGE HENRY, engineering consultant; b. Muskegon, Mich., Sept. 18, 1939; s. Harvey Merton and Bettie Jane (Meyers) W.; Asso. Sci., Muskegon Community Coll., 1960; B.S.E., U. Mich., 1966, M.S.E., 1966, Ph.D., 1969; m. Vicki Sue Hanish, June 17, 1967; children—Mark, Larry. Prin. engr. Battelle Meml. Inst., Columbus, Ohio, 1969-76; pres. Applied Mechanics Inc., Longboat Key, Fla., 1976—; instr. dept. civil engring. Ohio State U., 1973, 82. Served with USN, 1961-64. Named Outstanding Undergrad. Student, Engring. Mechanics dept. U. Mich., 1965-66, Outstanding Grad. Student, Civil Engring. dept., 1968-69. Registered profl. engr., Ohio. Mem. Am. Acad. of Mechanics, ASME, Sigma Xi, Chi Epsilon, Phi Kappa Phi, Phi Theta Kappa. Congregationalist. Contbr. tech. papers to nat. and internat. confs. Home and Office: 3431 Bayou Ct Longboat Key FL 34228-3028

WORKMAN, MARGARET LEE, state supreme court justice; b. May 22, 1947; d. Frank Eugene and Mary Emma (Thomas) W.; m. Edward T. Gardner III; children: Lindsay Elizabeth, Christopher Workman, Edward Earnshaw. AB in Polit. Sci., W.Va. U., 1969, JD, 1974. Bar: W.Va. 1974. Asst. counsel to majority, pub. works com. U.S. Senate, Washington, 1974-75; law clk. 13th jud. cir., W.Va. Ct., Charleston, 1975-76, judge, 1981-88; pvt. practice Charleston, 1976-81; justice W.Va. Supreme Ct. Appeals, Charleston, 1989—, chief justice, 1993. Advance person for Rosalyn Carter, Carter Presdl. Campaign, Atlanta, 1976. Democrat. Episcopalian. Office: State Supreme Ct 317 State Capitol Charleston WV 25305-0001

WORKMAN, WILLIAM DOUGLAS, III, former mayor; b. Charleston S.C., July 3, 1940; s. William Douglas, Jr. and Rhea (Thomas) W.; BA, The Citadel, 1961; grad. U. S.C., 1993; m. Marcia Mae Moorhead, Apr. 23, 1966 (div. Dec. 1995); children: William Douglas IV, Frank Moorhead. Reporter, Charleston News & Courier, 1965-66, Greenville (S.C.) News, 1966-70; tchr., adminstr., dean allied health scis. Greenville Tech. Coll., 1967-75; exec. asst. to Gov. of S.C., Columbia, 1975-78; mktg. exec. Daniel Internat. Corp., Greenville, 1978-90, dir. of facilities Fluor Daniel, 1991-93; v.p. S.C. ops. Piedmont Natural Gas, 1994—; mayor City of Greenville, 1983-95. Chmn. Greenville County Rep. Conv., 1980, 82, 87, 89, 91, S.C. 4th Congl. Dist. Rep. Conv., 1980, 82, 84; chmn. S.C. Rep. Conv., 1984, 89, vice chmn., 1982, 87; Rep. nominee U.S. Congress 4th Dist. S.C., 1986; mem. S.C. Adv. Commn. on Intergovtl. Rels., 1990—; bd. dirs. S.C. Appalachian Coun. of Govts., 1991-95; mem. Mcpl. Assn. S.C. 1981-95 (bd. dirs., 1990—, pres., 1993-94); trustee Sch. Dist. Greenville County, 1969-75, also vice chmn.; bd. dirs. YMCA Camp Greenville, 1973-83, 90-95, chmn., 1975; chmn. S.C. Health Coordinating Coun., 1976-78; founder S.C. Literacy Assn., treas., 1969-73; mem. Greenville City Council, 1981-83; mem. Southern Growth Policies Bd., 1992—, S.C. Adv. Commn. on Intergovtl. Rels., 1991—. Served with AUS, 1962-64; lt. col. Res. Decorated Army Commendation medal with 2 oak leaf clusters, Legion of Merit; named Outstanding State Chmn., S.C. Jaycees 1969; Order of Palmetto, 1978. Mem. Res. Officers Assn., Assn. U.S. Army, Am. Legion, Southea. Gas Assn., Nat. Mgmt. Assn. (mgr. yr. award Greenville chpt. 1985), Newcomen Soc. (S.C. com.), S.C. Downtown

Devel. Assn. (bd. dirs.), Greenville Country Club, Greenville-Piedmont Citadel Club (past pres.), Greenville City Club (bd. dirs.), Poinsett Club, Greenville adv. bd. Nat. Bank of S.C. Home: 30 Craigwood Rd Greenville SC 29607-3652 Office: PO Box 1905 Greenville SC 29602

WORLEY, JAMES FLOYD, school system administrator, educator; b. Delight, Ark., Apr. 28, 1941; s. Henry Clell and Manie Savannah (Westbrook) W.; m. Linda Louise Graves, Nov. 23, 1962; children: Kimberley Ann Worley Huggins, Libby Toinette Worley Baker. B of Ednl. Adminstrn., U. Ark., 1962, MEd, 1965; D of Ednl. Adminstrn., Southern Ark. U., 1981. Cert. supr., elem. tchr., Tex., Ark. Tchr., elem. principal El Dorado (Ark.) Pub. Schs., 1962-64, Pine Bluff (Ark.) Pub. Schs., 1964-81; asst. supr. Springdale (Ark.) Pub. Schs., 1981-84; elem. principal, adminstrv. asst. Southwest Ind. Sch. Dist., San Antonio, 1984-90; dir. of instruction Diboll (Tex.) Ind. Sch. Dist., 1990-94; sch. supr. Apple Springs (Tex.) Ind. Sch. Dist., 1994—. Author: The Relationship Between North Central Self Study and Organizational Health, 1981. Active Diboll Cares, 1994. Mem. Assn. for Supervision and Curriculum Devel., Tex. Assn. Sch. Adminstrn., Tex. Assn. of Sch. Bds., Lions. Republican. Baptist. Home: 909 Dogwood Ridge Diboll TX 75941 Office: Apple Spring ISD PO Box 125 Apple Springs TX 75926-0125

WORLEY, KAREN BOYD, psychologist; b. Hot Springs, Ark., Apr. 23, 1952; d. Wayne Johnson and Lou (Hull) Boyd; m. Timothy Riker, Sept. 22, 1979; children: Travis, Tyler, Kaitlin, Kelsey. BA, Okla. State U., 1974; PhD, Tex. Tech. U., 1983. Lic. psychologist, Ark. Rsch. asst. Rsch. and Tng. Ctr. for Mentally Retarded Tex. Tech. U., Lubbock, 1974-77, teaching asst., 1977-78; psychology intern Kansas City (Mo.) VA Med. Ctr., 1978-79; psychologist Johnson County Mental Health Ctr., Shawnee Mission, Kans., 1979-81; pvt. practice Pleasant Valley Clinic, Little Rock, 1982—; asst. prof. dept. pediatrics U. of Ark. for Med. Scis., 1991—, dir. family treatment program, 1996—; mem. Gov.'s Task Force on Child Abuse in Arks., 1983-85, Pulaski County Child Abuse Task Force, 1985, Pulaski County Family Svcs. Rev. Com., 1986-87, Com. to Rev. Investigation Procedures Ark. Children and Family Svcs., 1986, Child Sexual Abuse Network, 1988-93; bd. dirs. Ark. Child Sexual Abuse Edn. Commn., 1985-91, Suspected Child Abuse and Neglect, 1986-92, Ark. Commn. on Child Abuse, Rape and Domestic Violence, 1991—, Victims of Crime Act Bd., 1992—; cons. Mother's Support Group, Parent Ctr., Little Rock, 1983-92. Contbr. articles to profl. publs. Mem. APA, Ark. Psychol. Assn., Nat. Register Health Svc. Providers in Psychology (coun.), Am. Profl. Soc. on Abuse of Children, Assn. for Treatment of Sexual Abusers, Phi Kappa Phi. Methodist. Office: Family Treatment Program 1120 Marshall St Little Rock AR 72202-4600 also: Pleasant Valley Clinic 12361 Hinson Rd North Little Rock AR 72113

WORLEY, NELSON, library director; b. Petersburg, Va., July 8, 1948; s. Wilbur Nelson and Nellie Ruth (Brown) W.; m. Linnie Louise Herron, May 26, 1974; children: Brian Nelson, Beth Anne, Rebecca Allison. AA, Ferrum Coll., 1968; BA, King Coll., 1970; MA, U. Southwest La., 1972; MLS, Vanderbilt U., 1974. From catalogin libr. to regional libr. dir. Appomattox Regional Libr., Hopewell, Va., 1974-96; dir. libr. devel. & networking The Libr. of Va., Richmond, 1996—. Mem. ALA, Va. Libr. Assn., Pub. Libr. Assn., Va. Pub. Libr. Assn. (pres. 1995-96), Capital Area Pub. Libr. Dirs. Assn. (pres. 1989-90, 91-92). Home: 3405 Clay St Hopewell VA 23860 Office: The Libr of Va 800 E Broad Richmond VA 23219

WORRELL, BILLY FRANK, health facility administrator; b. Columbia, Ala., Oct. 12, 1939; s. Beachum Worrell and Madeline (Scott) Wells; children: Jon, Kevin, Heather; m. Lorna Faye Jones, Nov. 26, 1991. A in Bus., Thomas Coll., Thomasville, Ga., 1978; BS magna cum laude, Albany State Coll., 1990, MBA, 1991; MS, LaSalle U., 1995, PhD, 1996. Registered respiratory therapist, respiratory care profl., arterial blood gas technician, neo-natal advanced life support technician. Electrician USN, 1957-60, Newport News (Va.) Shipbldg., 1960-63; mfg. mgr. Lockheed Aircraft, Marietta, Ga., 1963-70, Champion Homes, Thomasville, Ga., 1970-74; salesman Cadillac dealership Thomasville, 1974-76; estimator Knight-Dodson Constrn. Co., Thomasville, 1976-78; adminstr. Ga. Army Nat. Guard, Thomasville, 1978-84; ret., 1984; allied health mgr. Phoebe Putney Meml. Hosp., Albany, 1988-93; dir. cardiopulmonary dept. Mitchell County Hosp., Camilla, Ga., 1994-95; dir. cardiopulmonary contract svcs. Sumter County Hosp., Americus, Ga., 1995—. Columnist newspaper column Lee County Ledger, 1990; actor film and plays. Vol. Salvation Army, Thomasville, 1978-83, Sr. Citizens Group, Thomasville, 1980-83, Kidney Found., Thomasville, 1980-85. Mem. Nat. Bd. Respiratory Care, Ga. Respiratory Care, Toastmasters. Republican. Home: 1142 Philema Rd S Leesburg GA 31763-9314 Office: Sumter County Hospital Americus GA 31709

WORRELL, DAN L., management educator; b. Wichita Falls, Tex., June 26, 1948; s. Jones Danforth and Louise (Garrison) W.; m. Diane Featherston, Dec. 29, 1976; 1 child, James Casey. BS in Bus., La. State U., 1971, MS in Mgmt., 1974, PhD in Mgmt., 1978. Asst. prof. mgmt. dept. U. Southwestern La., Lafayette, 1977-80, Appalachin State U., Boone, N.C., 1980-82, U. N. Tex., Denton, 1983-86; prof. and mgmt. dept. chair Appalachin State U., Boone, N.C., 1986-90; prof. mgmt. dept. Appalachin State U., Boone, 1990-93; prof and mgmt. dept. chair Coll. of Bus. U. Tex., Arlington, 1993-95, prof. and assoc. dean, 1995—; cons. and expert witness. Contbr. over 40 articles to profl jours. including Acad. Mgmt. Jour., Jour. of Mgmt., Strategic Mgmt. Jour., Indsl. Rels. and others; also presentations at acad. profl. confs. include over 50 papers. 2d lt. U.S. Army, 1971. Mem. Nat. Acad. Mgmt., Strategic Mgmt. Soc., Decision Sci. Inst., Internat. Assn. for Bus. and Soc., S.W. Acad. Mgmt. Office: U Tex Arlington Coll of Bus Box 19377 Arlington TX 76019

WORSHAM, BERTRAND RAY, psychiatrist; b. Atkins, Ark., Feb. 14, 1926; s. Lewis Henry and Emma Lavada (Burris) W.; m. Margaret Ann Dickson, June 4, 1947 (div. 1960); children: Eric Dickson, Vicki Gayle; m. Lynne Ellen Reynolds, Aug. 27, 1976; children: Mary Ellen Clarice, Richard Andrew (dec.). BA, U. Ark., 1951; MD, U. Ark., Little Rock, 1955. Intern Hillcrest Med. Ctr., Tulsa, 1955-56; resident in psychiatry Menninger Sch. Psychiatry, Topeka, 1956-59; pvt. practice, 1959-78; clin. instr. U. Okla. Sch. Medicine, 1965-78; coord. drug and alcohol treatment unit Washington D.C. VA Med. Ctr., 1978-84; med. dir. Norman divsn. Okla. State Vets. Ctr., 1984-89; psychiat. cons. Comty. Counselling Ctr., Oklahoma City, 1989—; cons. Oklahoma City Vets. Hosp., 1959-72, State Dept. Pub. Health, 1960-65; dir. Cmty. Mental Health Ctr., Shawnee, Okla., 1965-72; mem. staff Coyne Campbell Hosp., 1960-78, Bapt. Med. Ctr., 1960-78, Mercy Health Ctr., 1960-78, Deaconess Hosp., 1963-78, Dr.'s Gen. Hosp., 1963-78, Presbyn. Hosp., 1962-78, U. Health Sci. Ctr., 1962-78, Children's Meml. Hosp., 1968-78, Oklahoma City VA Hosp., 1960-78, Washington D.C. Va. Hosp., 1978-84, Okla. Vets. Ctr., Norman, 1984-89. Mem. Civil Disaster Com., Oklahoma City, 1966, USN League, Okla., 1972—. With USAF, 1944-46; capt. USNR, 1957-86, ret. Fellow Menninger Found., Charles F. Menninger Found.; mem. AMA, Am. Psychiat. Assn. (Okla. dist. br. 1959-78, 84—), Assn. Mil. Surgeons of U.S., Ret. Officers Assn., World Fedn. for Mental Health, Internat. Platform Assn., Washington Psychiat. Assn., No. Va. Mental Health Assn., Masons (32 degree). Republican. Episcopalian. Home: 9915 N Kelley Ave Oklahoma City OK 73131-2022 Office: Comty Counseling Ctr 1140 N Hudson Ave Oklahoma City OK 73103-3918

WORSTELL, JONATHAN HARLAN, process chemist, research engineer; b. Indpls., Dec. 10, 1950; s. Jene Harold and Evelyn Helen (Socks) W.; m. Sinta Laksana, Aug. 19, 1977; children: Jeffrey H., John H. BS, Northwestern Univ., 1976; MS, Ball State Univ., 1978; PhD, Colo. Sch. Mines, 1980. Sr. chemist Dupont, Bay City, Tex., 1980-87; staff rsch. chemist Shell Chem. Co., Houston, 1987—; vis. instr. Colo. Sch. Mines, Golden, Colo., 1979-80. Contbr. articles to profl. jours. V-p. Lamar Little League, Richmond, Tex., 1994. With USMC. Mem. Masonic Lodge, AIChE, ACS, AAAS. Office: Shell Chem Co 3333 Hwy 6 South Houston TX 77082

WORTELL, LINDA DIANE, medical/surgical nurse; b. Balt., Mar. 8, 1962; d. Gerald William and Janet Gail (Lang) Harbaugh; m. Frank Michael Wortell, Jan. 3, 1986; children: Michael Anthony, Heidi Lynn. BSN, U. Tex., 1984; MSN, U. Ariz., 1987; PhD in Nursing, U. Miami, Fla., 1994. RN, Tex., Fla., Ariz. Staff nurse med./surg. unit Seton Med. Ctr., Austin, Tex.; clin. nurse instr. Pima C.C., Tucson; staff nurse med./surg. unit Tucson Med. Ctr., 1986-88; clin. nurse specialist med./surg. unit, sch. nurse, rschr. Bapt. Hosp., Miami, 1988—; asst. prof. Fla. Internat. U., Miami, 1993-95. Mem. ANA, Fla. Nurses Assn., Am. Assn. Legal Nurse Cons., So. Nursing Rsch. Soc., Sigma Theta Tau. Home: 9820 SW 121st St Miami FL 33176-4924

WORTH, JAMES GALLAGHER, engineer, chemist; b. Phila., Sept. 20, 1922; s. Wilmon W. and Elsie (Gallagher) W.; Assoc. Sci., Rochester Inst. Tech., 1949; BS, U. Miami, 1949-51; postgrad. U. So. Calif., 1961—; m. Esther Alberta Cring, Sept. 11, 1943 (dec. 1981); children: Nancy Jeanne, Constance Anne, James Gallagher; m. Barbara Marie Demarest, Mar. 22, 1985. Chem. technician Internat. Paper Co., 1942-43, Eastman Kodak Co., 1946-49; pres., founder, engr.-chemist Applied Rsch. Labs. Fla., Inc., Hialeah, 1949-84, chmn. bd., 1956-84; pres., chmn. bd. Ra-Chem Lab., Inc., Hialeah, 1964-66; Worth Engring., Inc., Hialeah, 1984—. Served to maj. USAAF, 1943-46; with USAFR, 1946-82. Registered profl. engr., Calif., Fla. Fellow Am. Inst. Chemists; mem. Am. Chem. Soc., Am. Soc. Testing Materials, Am. Soc. Metals, Nat. Soc. Profl. Engrs., Fla. Engring. Soc., Nat. Fire Protection Assn. Democrat. Methodist. Mason. Home: 751 Oriole Ave Miami FL 33166-3811 Office: 650 Palm Ave Hialeah FL 33010-4316

WORTH, JUDSON LEE BLACKLEY, social worker; b. Ann Arbor, Mich., May 7, 1960; s. James J.B. and Sarah (Shoemaker) W.; m. Margaret Mitchell, June 28, 1991; children: Christopher, Wayne, Michael, Katie. BS in Recreation, Calif. State U., San Jose, 1983; MS in Recreation Adminstrn., U. N.C., 1985. Lic. social worker, W.Va. Recreation therapist concurrent practicum program pediatrics N.C. Meml. Hosp., Chapel Hill, 1983-84; recreation therapist pediatric unit Duke U. Med. Ctr., Durham, N.C., 1984; recreation therapist Assn. for Retarded Citizens, Chapel Hill, 1984-85; pvt. duty recreation therapist Durham, 1984-85; recreation therapist Anne Sullivan Enterprises, Inc., Chapel Hill, 1984-86, mgmt. coord., 1985-86; owner country store Minnehaha Springs, W.Va., 1986-88; rschr. W.Va. Spl. Edn. Effectiveness Rev. System, Marlinton, 1989-90; parent coord. Pocahontas County Schs., Marlinton, 1988-93; parenting profl., case mgr., regional dir. Timberline Health Group, Marlinton, 1993—; adj. instr. spl. edn. Coll. Grad. Studies, U. W.Va., Institute, 1991-92; cons., provider seminars on child behavior and ADD (attention deficit disorder) to schs., agys. and pvt. groups, 1991—. Developer various tng. programs, including: (copyrighted) Child Behavior Management . . . A Parent's Choice, 1989, Behavior Management in the Classroom . . . A Teacher's Choice, 1991. Instr. SCUBA diving Camp Minnehaha, Minnehaha Springs, W.Va., summers; pres. Pocahontas County Child Adv. Task Force, 1990-92. Mem. Profl. Assn. Diving Instrs. (master SCUBA diver cert. 1992, SCUBA dive master cert. 1993). Democrat. Home: HC 82 Box 147 Marlinton WV 24954-9511

WORTHAM, JAMES MASON, landman; b. Ft. Worth, Nov. 21, 1954; s. John Lilburn and Mary Elizabeth (Mason) W.; m. Rhonda Dee Richards, Aug. 16, 1980 (div. 1995); children: James Mason Jr., William Charles. Student, USAF Acad., 1973-75; BBA in Stats., U. Tex., Austin, 1977; MBA in Fin., U. Houston, 1989. Teller Capital Nat. Bank, Austin, 1976-77; abstractor First Title Co., Houston, 1977-78, escrow officer, 1978-80; div. order analyst Mitchell Energy Corp., The Woodlands, Tex., 1980-81, landman I, 1981-83, landman II, 1983-89, sr. landman, 1989—. Pres. Genesis Class St. Luke's Meth., Houston, 1983. Recipient Young Texan award Ft. Worth Optimist Club, 1973, award Woodlands YMCA Marathon Competition, 1985, Multiple Sclerosis 150 Mile Bike Ride, 1995, 96, Houston-Tennaco Marathon, 1996. Mem. Am. Assn. Petroleum Landmen, Houston Assn. Petroleum Landmen (2d pl. Tennis 1983, 89), The Woodlands Lions Club (lion tamer 1990-91, 1st v.p. 1992-93, pres. 1993-94), Houston Jr. League Charity Ball, Woodlands Coun. Realtors Benefit. Republican. Methodist. Home: 10600 Six Pines Rd Apt 131 The Woodlands TX 77380-1469 Office: Mitchell Energy Corp 2001 Timberloch Pl PO Box 4000 The Woodlands TX 77387-4000

WORTHINGTON, ANNE PEPPER POOLE, English language educator, writer; b. Kinston, N.C., May 27, 1943; d. Walter Roy and Mary (Ruffin) Poole; 1 child, Dean Walter. BA, Meredith Coll., 1965; MLA, Johns Hopkins, 1969; PhD, U. Md., 1976. Cert. English tchr., N.C., Md. English tchr. Columbia (N.C.) High Sch., 1966-67, Northeast High Sch., Pasadena, Md., 1967-72; prof. English Mount Olive (N.C.) Coll., 1979—. Author: Travels with Dr. Pepper, 1990, Stand Up and Be A Voice, 1991, The Triadic Archetype in Keats' Poetry, 1992, Rights and Responsibilities, 1993; editor Mount Olive Rev., 1987-93, Mount Olive Coll. Press, 1991-93; freelancer Carteret News-Times. Home: 1600 Cambridge Dr Kinston NC 28501-2002 Office: Mount Olive Coll 634 Henderson St Mount Olive NC 28365

WORTHINGTON, (WARD) CURTIS, III, neurosurgeon; b. Charleston, S.C., Dec. 5, 1951; s. Ward Curtis Jr. and Floride Calhoun (McDermid) W.; m. Jane Leslie Tyler, Aug. 1, 1987; children: Suzanne Jane, Cecelia Calhoun, Ian Chalmers. BA in English Lit., New Coll., 1974; MD, Med. U. S.C., 1978. Diplomate Am. Bd. Neurol. Surgery, Nat. Bd. Med. Examiners, State Bd. Med. Examiners S.C.; lic. physician, N.Y. Intern in gen. surgery Med. U. Hosps./Med. U. S.C., Charleston, 1979; resident in gen. surgery and emergency svcs. Charleston County Hosp.-Med. U. S.C., Charleston, 1980; resident in neurol. surgery various hosps. McGill U., Montreal, Que., Can., 1980-85, chief resident in neurol. surgery Montreal Neurol. Hosp., 1983-84; mem. staff Roper Hosp., Charleston, 1985—, Bon Secours St. Francis Xavier Hosp., Charleston, 1985—, Trident Regional Med. Ctr., Charleston, 1985—, AMI East Cooper Hosp., Mt. Pleasant, S.C., 1985—; neurosurgeon Neurology-Neurosurgery Clinic, P.A., Charleston, 1985—, ptnr., 1988—; instr. neuroanatomy Montreal Neurol. Inst. and Hosp., 1983-84; attending physician Med. U. Hosp., Charleston, 1985—; co-dir. dynamic stereotactic radiosurgery program Roper Hosp. and Med. Univ. S.C.; S.C. del. Joint Coun. of State Neurosurg. Socs., 1992-96; clin. asst. prof. neurosurgery Med. U. S.C., 1985-92, clin. assoc. prof., 1992—, clin. assoc. prof.radiation oncology, 1993—; mem. quality assurance com. Franklin Fetter Health Ctr., Charleston, 1986-89; presenter many profl. confs., 1984—. Co-contbr. chpt. to: Stereotactic Radiosurgery Update, 1992; contbr. articles and revs. to profl. pubIs.; guest editor spl. issue on med. and surg. mgmt. of epilepsy Jour. of S.C. Med. Assn., 1991; editor: Literacy Charleston: A Lowcountry Reader. Bd. dirs. Montreal Neurol. Hosp., 1983-85, Med. U. S.C. Assn. (Wickliffe House), 1991-94; pres. Fellows Soc., Montreal Neurol. Inst., 1983-84; mem. med. adv. bd. Carolina Ctr. for Athletes, Charleston, 1991—; mem. citizens adv. com. Hollings Oncology Ctr., Med. U. S.C., 1992—; mem. coms. Preservation Soc. Charleston, 1991-93; mem. Widows and Orphans Soc., 1991—, Charleston Symphony Singers Guild, Piping and Marching Soc. of Lower Chalmers St.; lay reader Ch. of the Holy Communion. Recipient Penfield award for Neurosurgery, Montreal Neurol. Inst., 1985. Fellow ACS; mem. Am. Assn. Neurol. Surgeons, Congress of Neurol. Surgeons, Am. Soc. for Stereotactic and Functional Neurosurgery, S.C. Med. Assn., Charleston County Med. Soc. (mem. com. on nominations, policy, pub. and profl. rels. 1990-94), So. Med. Assn., Am. Epilepsy Soc., Internat. Stereotactic Radiosurgery Soc., World Soc. for Stereotactic and Functional Neurosurgery, Med. Soc. S.C., Carolina Yacht Club. Episcopalian. Home: 50 Rutledge Ave Charleston SC 29401-1702 Office: Neurology-Neurosurg Clin PA 125 Dougherty St Ste 400 Charleston SC 29403

WORTHINGTON, DONALD THOMPSON, JR., journalist; b. Rome, N.Y., Apr. 20, 1956; s. Donald Thompson and Nellie Doris (Palmer) W. BS, U. Tenn., Chattanooga, 1978; MA, The Am. U., 1982. Sports editor The No. Va. Sun, Arlington, Va., 1978-80, mng. editor, 1980-81; sports writer The Alexandria (La.) Town Talk, 1982-87; asst. sports editor Teh Alexandria (La.) Town Talk, 1987-88; sports editor The Newport (R.I.) Daily News, 1988-90; auditor Navy Fed. Credit Union, Vienna, Va., 1990-92; editor, assoc. pub. The Connection Newspapers, Reston, Va., 1992-93; writer The Winchester (Va.) Star, 1993—. Clarinetist Newport (R.I.) Cmty. Band, 1988-90, Kerrstown Meth. Ch. Ensemble, Winchester, Va., 1995—; clarinetist, saxophonist: Alexandria (Va.) Citizens Band, 1991-95, Mount Vernon Swing Band, Alexandria, 1992-95. Recipient First Place writing awards La. Sportswriters Assn., 1984, 86, 88; named Gulf Star Conf. Sportswriter of Yr., 1985-86. Mem. Soc. Profl. Journalists, Investigative Reporters and Editors, Education Writers Assn., Winchester-Fredericks County Hist. Soc. Home: 209 Peppertree Ln #31 Winchester VA 22601 Office: The Winchester Star 2 N Kent St Winchester VA 22601

WORTHINGTON, J.B., business executive. Dir. strategic planning Kerr-McGee Corp., Oklahoma City, Okla. Office: Kerr-McGee Corp PO Box 25861 Oklahoma City OK 73125

WORTHINGTON-WHITE, DIANA ALICE, research scientist; b. Cleve., Jan. 7, 1956; d. Cyril Frank and Jerroldyn Faye (Paul) Worthington-White. BS, U. Cin., 1977, MEd, 1978. Rsch. technician U. Hosp. Cleve., 1979-81; asst. instr. U. Fla., Gainesville, 1981-90, assoc. instr., 1990-95; applied rsch. lead specialist U. S.C., Columbia, 1996—. Editor: Bone Marrow Purging & Processing, 1990, Advances in Bone Marrow Purging & Processing, 1992, Advances in Bone Marrow Purging & Processing, 1994; contbr. articles to profl. jours. Treas. Alachua County CROP Walk, Gainesville, 1988-95; vol. Ronald McDonald House, Gainesville, 1984-95; fin. sec., 1st Luth. Ch., Gainesville, 1984-86, youth dir., 1986-89. Recipient NIH rsch. grant, 1992. Mem. AAAS, Internat. Soc. for Hematotherapy & Graft Engring. (founding mem., sec. 1992—), Am. Med. Writers Assn. Home: 405 Bentley Ct Columbia SC 29210 Office: Univ SC Divsn Transplantation CCTR 7 Medical Park Columbia SC 29203

WORTHY, FRED LESTER, computer science educator; b. Greeley, Colo., Mar. 8, 1936; s. William and Gladys (Walburn) W.; m. Susan Worthy, June 4, 1963; children: Michael (dec.), Nina E. BS in Math., Colo. State Coll., 1959; MA in Physics, Colo. State U., 1965; cert. computer sci., Clemson U., 1978; student Computer Tchrs. Inst., Ctrl. State U., Edmond, Okla., 1989-90. Physics tchr. Littleton (Colo.) H.S., 1959-63, King H.S., Tampa, 1963-65; prof. physics Ga. So. Coll., Statesboro, 1965-66; rschr. USAF (NASA), Tullahoma, Tenn., 1966-68; prof. physics Bapt. Coll., Charleston, S.C., 1968-78; registrar, asst. dean Bapt. Coll., Charleston, 1969-70; prof. computer sci. Charleston So. U., 1978—; bus. cons. Charleston, 1981—; dir. Developed Creative Physics Labs. for H.S. as part of Self-Paced Physics, 1962-63, Established Hands-On Computer Curriculum, 1979-86, Hands-On Teaching Labs. for Computers Across the Curriculum, 1987-93; developer new physics labs. for coll. NSF, Bapt. Coll., Charleston, 1970-72. Author: Twenty-Five Self-Paced Computer Laboratories, 1986-93. Chmn., deacon Summerville (S.C.) Bapt. Ch., 1978-85; chmn. judge com. Miss Charleston-Miss America, Charleston, 1992—; mem. Miss S.C. Judges List, 1991—. Home: 104 Three Iron Dr Summerville SC 29483-2937

WOURMS, JOHN PETER BARTON, biology educator; b. N.Y.C., Apr. 30, 1937; s. John Peter and Mary Victoria (Barton) W.; m. Deborah Ruth Deane, June 5, 1972; 1 child, Nicholas Stephen. BS in Biology, Fordham U., 1958, MS in Biology, 1960; PhD in Biol. Scis., Stanford U., 1966. Postdoctoral fellow Harvard U., Cambridge, Mass., 1966-68; asst. prof. zoology McGill U., Montreal, Que., Can., 1968-72; assoc. rsch. scientist, dir. elec.-micro lab. N.Y. Ocean Sci. Lab., Montauk, N.Y., 1972-76; assoc. prof. biol. scis. Clemson (S.C.) U., 1976-80, prof., 1980—; mem. adv. panel in developmental biology NASA, 1984. Author, editor: Genetics of Fishes I, 1976; editor: Reproduction and Development of Sharks, Skates, Rays, and Ratfishes, 1993; assoc. editor: Jour. Exptl. Zoology, 1978-84, Environ. Biology of Fishes, 1982—, Jour. Morphology, 1991—, Acta Zoologica, 1996—. Fellow USPHS-NIH, 1962-66, Am. Cancer Soc., 1966-68, NRC, 1976, Guggenheim Found., 1984-85. Fellow Explorer's Club; mem. Am. Soc. Cell Biology, Am. Soc. Zoologists (divsn. sec. 1983-85, divsn. chair 1996—), Marine Biol. Assn. U.K., Internat. Soc. Developmental Biology. Soc. for Developmental Biology, Am. Soc. Ichthyologists and Herpetologists. Office: Clemson U Dept Biol Scis Clemson SC 29634-1903

WRAY, BETTY BEASLEY, allergist, immunologist, pediatrician; b. Ga., 1935. MD, Med Coll. Ga., 1960. Diplomate Am. Bd. Allergy and Immunology, Am. Bd. Clin. Lab. Immunology. Intern Talmadge Meml. Hosp., Augusta, Ga., 1960-61, resident in pediatrics, 1962, 64-65, fellow in pediatric allergy, 1966-68; staff mem. U. Hosp., Augusta, Ga., 1974—, Eisenhower Med. Ctr., Augusta, Ga., 1978—; staff mem. Med. Coll. Ga., Augusta, Ga., 1979—, prof. pediatric medicine, chief allergy and immunology; vice-chair dept. pediats. Mem. Am. Acad. Allergy and Immunology, Am. Acad. Pediatrics, Am. Coll. Allergy and Immunology, So. Med. Assn. Office: Med Coll of Georgia Cj # 141 Augusta GA 30912

WRAY, CHARLES HERMAN, JR., nursing educator, mental health nurse; b. Leaksville, N.C., Feb. 1, 1950; s. Charles Herman Sr. and Ruby (Cruise) W.; m. Patricia Ann Hall; 1 child, Anne Marie. BSN, U. N.C., 1979; MSN, U. Va., 1985. RN, N.C. Asst. head nurse Children's Psychiat. Unit-Duke U., Durham, N.C., 1985-87; asst. to v.p., dir. nursing Duke Med. Ctr., Durham, 1987-90; course coord. mental health Piedmont C.C., Roxboro, N.C., 1990—. Recipient NIMH traineeship, 1984. Mem. ANA, MENSA, Reed Organ Soc. Episcopalian. Office: Piedmont CC PO Box 1197 Roxboro NC 27573-1197

WRAY, GERALDINE SMITHERMAN (JERRY WRAY), artist; b. Shreveport, La., Dec. 15, 1925; d. David Ewart and Mary Virginia (Hoss) Smitherman; m. George Downing Wray, June 24, 1947; children: Mary Virginia Hill, Deanie Galloway, George D. Wray III, Nancy Armistead. BFA with honors, Newcomb Art Sch., Tulane U., 1946. One woman shows include Don Batman Gallery, Kansas City, Mo., 1982, Gallery II, Baton Rouge, 1985, McNeese Coll., Lake Charles, La., 1987, Dragonfly Gallery, Shreveport, La., 1987, Barnwell Garden and Art Ctr., Shreveport, 1988, 95, Southdown Mus., Houma, La., 1989, La. State U., Shreveport, 1991, WTN Radio Station, Shreveport, 1993, The Cambridge Club, Shreveport, 1993, Centerary Coll., 1993, Northwestern State U., Natchitoches, La., 1995, Goddard Mus., Ardmore, Okla., 1996, Art Buyers Caravan, Atlanta, 1996, Lockhaven (Pa.) U., 1996, Billingsley Gallery, Pensacola, Fla., 1996; Group shows include Watercolor USA Springfield., Mo., 1988, Waddell's Gallery, Shreveport, 1988, 91, Water Works Gallery, Dallas, 1990, Southwestern Watercolor Show, 1991 (D'Arches award), Masur Mus. Exhibition (honorable mention 91, 92), , Bossier Art Ctr., Bossier City, La., 1992, ving Art Assn. (honorable mention), 1992, Leon Loard Gallery, Montgomery, Ala., 1993, Ward-Nasse Gallery, N.Y.C., 1993, Soc. Experimental Artists Internat. (1st. place, honorable mention), 1993, Palmer Gallery, Hot Springs, Ark., 1994, Art Expo, N.Y.C., 1996, Carson Gallery, Dallas, Billinglsey Gallery, Pensacola, Fla., 1996, Hummingbird Gallery, Ft. Worth, Tex., Casa D'Arte, Shreveport, La., Lock Haven U., Pa., 1996, Casa D'Arte, Shreveport, 1996, Art Buyers Caravan, Atlanta, 1996. Art chmn. Jr. League, Shreveport, 1955-60; bd. dirs. Holiday-in-Dixie Cotillion, Shreveport, 1974-76. Mem. Nat. Watercolor Soc. (signature mem. 1994, 96), Southwestern Watercolor Soc. (signature mem. 1991), La. Watercolor Soc. (signature mem. 1990), La. Artists Inc. (elected mem.), Nat. Assn. Women Artists (included in The Encyclopedia of Landscape Techniques by Sloan). Episcopalian. Home: 573 Spring Lake Dr Shreveport LA 71106-4603

WRAY, THOMAS JEFFERSON, lawyer; b. Nashville, July 17, 1949; s. William Esker and Imogene (Cushman) W.; m. Susan Elizabeth Wells, Aug. 19, 1972; children: William Clark, Caroline Kell. BA, Emory U., 1971; JD, U. Va., 1974. Bar: Tex. 1974, U.S. Dist. Ct. (so., no. and ea. dists.) Tex. 1976, U.S. Ct. Appeals (5th and 11th cirs.) 1976, U.S. Supreme Ct. 1987. Assoc. Fulbright & Jaworski, L.L.P., Houston, 1974-82; ptnr. Fulbright & Jaworski, Houston, 1982—. Mem. ABA, Houston Bar Assn., Houston Mgmt. Lawyers Forum (chmn. 1981-82), Houston Club, Briar Club, Phi Beta Kappa. Republican. Episcopalian. Home: 3662 Ella Lee Ln Houston TX 77027

WREFORD, DEBRA RENEE, communication corporation manager; b. Detroit, Feb. 11, 1955; d. Fred S. and Charmaine (Weathers) W. BA in Psychology, Oakland U., 1978. Programmer Mich. Bell Telephone, Southfield, Mich., 1979-81; depreciation engr. Mich. Bell Telephone, Detroit, 1981-83; system analyst AT&T, Parsippany, N.J., 1983-89; mgr. AT&T, Somerset, N.J., 1990-96, Maitland, Fla., 1996—. Mem. NAFE, Women Support Exch., Women of AT&T (fund raising chair '96 Nat. Conf.), Summit Bus. and Profl. Women, Women in Mgmt., Nomad.

WREN, DANIEL ALAN, business management educator; b. Columbia, Mo., Jan. 8, 1932; s. Eulon Leon and Maude (Eubank) W.; m. Karen Lynn Tower, Jan. 27, 1962 (dec. 1979); children: Jonathan Daniel, Laura Lynn, Lynda Kay. BSBA, U. Mo., 1954, MS in Mgmt., 1960; PhD in Bus., U. Ill., 1964. Prof. mgmt. Fla. State U., Tallahassee, 1963-73; David Ross Boyd prof. of mgmt. U. Okla., Norman, 1973—; McCasland Found. prof. of Am. free enterprise U. Okla., curator Harry Bass bus. history collection, 1973—.

Author: The Evolution of Management Thought, 1972, 79, 87, 94, White Collar Hobo: Whiting Williams, 1987, Management: Process and Behavior, 1984; editor: Early Management Thought, 1996. 1st lt. USAF, 1954-58. Fellow Acad. Mgmt. (Disting. Educator award 1991), So. Mgmt. Assn. (pres. 1973-74). Republican. Home: 4017 Oxford Way Norman OK 73072 Office: U Okla 307 W Brooks Norman OK 73019

WREN, ROBERT JAMES, aerospace engineering manager; b. Moline, Ill., May 12, 1935; m. Jordis Wren; children: James, Patrick, Kiley. BSCE, U. Tex., 1956; MSCE, So. Meth. U., 1962; doctoral candidate, U. Houston. Registered profl. engr. Tex. Engring. aide Ctrl. Power and Light Co., Corpus Christi, 1954; sta. clk. City of Austin (Tex.) Power Plant, 1954-55; assoc. engr., hydraulic engr. U.S. Bur. of Reclamation, Austin, 1955-57; structural test engr. Gen. Dynamics, Ft. Worth, 1957-62; sr. structural dynamics engr., mgr. vibration and acoustic test facility NASA-Manned Spacecraft Ctr., Houston, 1962-63, 63-66, head exptl. dynamics sect., 1965-70; mgr. Apollo Spacecraft 2TV-1 CSM Test Program, 1966-68, Apollo Lunar Module-2 Drop Test Program, 1968-70; mgr. structural design space sta., space base, lunar base, mars mission NASA-Manned Spacecraft Ctr., Houston, 1970-73; mgr. structural design and devel., space shuttle carrier aircraft-747 NASA Johnson Space Ctr., Houston, 1973-74, mgr. structural div. space shuttle payload systems, 1974-84; mgr. engring. directorate for space shuttle payload safety NASA-Johnson Space Ctr., Houston, 1984-94, alternate chmn. space shuttle payload safety review panel, 1990—, mgr. engring. dir. vehicle and payload flight sys. safety, 1994—. Pres. Friendswood Little League Baseball, 1980-83; bd. dirs. Bay Area YMCA, Houston, 1982—, chmn., 1983-84. Recipient Sustained Superior Performance award NASA, Personal Letter of Commendation, George Low NASA Apollo Program, Outstanding Svc. award NASA, Group Achievement awards NASA; Paul Harris fellow Rotary. Mem. Space Ctr. Rotary (dir., treas., sec., v.p. 1979-85, pres. 1985-86, Rotary dist. 5890/govt. rep. 1986-87, area coord. 1987-89, zone leader 1988-89, gov.'s aide 1989-90, chmn. dist. assembly 1989-90, 93-94, fin. com. 1989-91, Rotary Nat. award for Space Achievement Found./co-founder, bd. dirs. 1984—), Rotary World Health Found. Plastic Surgery for Children (co-founder, bd. dirs. 1985—), Rotary Space Meml. Found. (co-founder, bd. dirs. 1986—). Methodist. Home: PO Box 1466 Friendswood TX 77549-1466 Office: NASA Johnson Space Ctr Houston TX 77058

WRENN, CHRISTOPHER JAY, physician; b. Margarita, Republic of Panama, July 16, 1947; s. Earl Walton and Maxine Elizabeth (Luther) W.; m. Nancy Margaret Bowie, June 27, 1970; children: Kristina Elizabeth, Courtney Bowie. BS, Baylor U., 1969; MD, U. Nebr., 1973. Diplomate Am. Bd. Pediatrics, Am. Bd. Allergy and Immunology. Intern pediatrics Children's Med. Ctr., Dallas, 1973-74, resident pediatrics, 1974-76, chief resident pediatrics, 1976-77; staff pediatrician Los Barrios Unidos Community Clinic, Dallas, 1977-78; fellow allergy and immunology Med. Br. U. Tex., Galveston, Tex., 1978-80; practice medicine specializing in allergy Graves-Gilbert Clinic, Bowling Green, Ky., 1980-83, Wichita Clinic, 1983-84, Allergy Clinic, Tyler, Tex., 1984—; staff pediatrician Dallas County Children's Shelter, 1975-78, Dallas County Juvenile Detention Ctr., 1975-78, Buckner Bapt. Children's Home, 1977-78. Author (chpt. of book) Pediatrics by Self Instruction, 1982. Fellow Am. Acad. Pediatrics, Am. Coll. Allergists; mem. Am. Acad. Allergy and Immunology, Elks. Methodist. Office: Allergy Clinic 1128 Medical Dr Tyler TX 75701-2109

WRIGHT, ARTHUR DOTSON, telecommunications professional; b. Wilmington, N.C., Oct. 13, 1944; s. Lloyd G. and Edith (Sosebee) W.; m. Carol Elaine Floyd, Sept. 2, 1967; children: Devin, Darron, Dustin. BS in Physics, North Ga. Coll., 1966; postgrad., U. Ga., 1967. Sci. tchr. Forsyth County Bd. Edn., Cumming, Ga., 1968-69; engr. assoc. Western Electric, Atlanta, 1969-76; staff analyst Southern Bell, Atlanta, 1976—; owner Custom Security System, Cumming, 1967—. Mem., vice chmn. Forsyth County Bd. Edn., Cumming, 1981—, chmn.; 4 H advisor Ga. 4 H Club, Cumming, 1982—; bd. dirs. Ga. Sch. Bd. Assn., 1974—; elected deacon Salem Bapt. Ch., Gainesville, Ga., 1981. 1st lt. U.S. Army, 1966-68, Vietnam. Recipient Award of Excellence Ga. Sch. Bd. Assn., 1985. Mem. Masons, Silver Shoal Royal Arch (royal arch 1970—). Home: 4200 Oaktree Ln Cumming GA 30131-8800

WRIGHT, BETH SEGAL, art historian, educator; b. N.Y.C., July 23, 1949; d. Ben and Ella (Litvack) Segal; m. Woodring Erik J. Wright, Sept. 5, 1971; children: Benjamin, Joshua. AB cum laude, Brandeis U., 1970; MA, U. Calif., Berkeley, 1972, PhD, 1978. Instr. Mountain View Coll., Dallas, 1978-82; lectr. U. Tex., Dallas, 1980-81, Tex. Christian U., Ft. Worth, 1981; asst. prof. U. Tex., Arlington, 1984-88, assoc. prof., 1988—; adj. and vis. asst. prof. art history U. Tex., Arlington, 1981-84. Contbr. articles to Art Bull., Arts Mag., Nouvelles de l'Estampe, others. Kress Found. hon. traveling fellow, 1975-76; NEH Travel to Collections grantee, Paris, 1987, 93; U. Tex. Arlington Rsch. Enhancement grantee, Paris, 1990, 93, Coll. Art Assoc. Meiss grant, 1996. Mem. Société de l'Histoire de l'Art Française (contbr. articles to bull.), Am. Soc. for 18th-Century Studies, Coll. Art Assn., Midwest Art History Soc. (bd. dirs. 1990-93).

WRIGHT, BILL J., geologist; b. Lone Wolf, Okla., Aug. 4, 1931; s. William P. and Annette (Overstreet) W.; m. Dorothy Jean Dittmer, Dec. 27, 1953 (wid. Mar. 1981); children: Catherine, Douglas. BS in Geology., Okla. State U., 1953. Cert. petroleum geologist. Area geologist Champlin Oil & Refining Co., Wichita, Kans., 1955-65; dist. geologist Champlin Oil & Refining Co., Oklahoma City, 1965-68; divsn. mgr. Champlin Petroleum Co., Calgary, Alberta, Can., 1968-69; exploitation mgr. Champlin Petroleum Co., Ft. Worth, Tex., 1969-71, asst. to pres. for exploration, 1971-73; pres. Bill J. Wright Ind. Ops., Oklahoma City, 1973—, Park Ave. Pubs. Inc., Oklahoma City, 1991—; petroleum cons., 1973—; bd. dirs. West X Southwest Imports, Irving, Tex.; pres. Rio Lobo Western Co., Okla. City. Contbg. author: Oil Fields of Kansas, 1962; editor various books. Pres. Quail Creek Home Owners Assn., Oklahoma City, 1982-84, bd. dirs. 1979—. 1st lt. U.S. Army Corp Engrs., 1953-55, ETO. Recipient Outstanding Svc. award USA Track and Field, USA, 1988, Track and Field Hall of Honors, Okla. State U., Stillwater, 1983; Olympic ofcl. USA Olympic Orgn. Com., Atlanta, 1996. Mem. Am. Assn. Petroleum Geologists, Kans. Geol. Soc. (bd. dirs. 1955—), Okla. City Geol. Soc., Ft. Worth Geol. Soc., Assn. Profs. Geol. Scientists. Office: Park Ave Publ Inc PO Box 20010 Oklahoma City OK 73156

WRIGHT, BOBBIE JEAN, sociology educator; b. Oklahoma City, Apr. 3, 1933; d. Loy Conda and Lanelta (Stalcup) Knight; m. Donald K. Wright, Sept. 30, 1955 (div. 1969); children: Sheryl Ann McLaughlin, Terri Lynn Coon, Karie Kaye. BA in Sociology, Okla. State U., 1954; MRE, So. Bapt. Theol. Sem., 1957; EdD, Nova U., 1976. Dir. student nurses Highland Bapt. Hosp., Louisville, 1954-55; counselor Ormsby Village Delinquent Home, Louisville, 1955-56; asst. exec. dir., teenage dir. YWCA, Allentown, Pa., 1961-64; nat. teenage cons. nat. bd. YWCA, N.Y.C., 1964-65; nat. recruiter YWCA, Tex., 1965-68; owner Char-Burger Restaurant, Sherman, Tex., 1965-67; co-owner Manhattan Janitorial Services, Hampton, Va., 1969-77; asst. prof. sociology Cen. Va. Community Coll., Lynchburg, Va., 1967-68; prof. Thomas Nelson Community Coll., Hampton, 1968—; with rsch. and devel. United Way, Hampton, 1975-80. Co-author: Demographic Academic and Perceptual Characteristics of Reverse Transfer Students, 1973, Statistical Computation of Post-Developmental and Regular Students, 1974, Instructor's Study Guide, Sociology, 1981, 84; mem. editorial bd. Ann. Editions, Sociology, 1981—, Ann. Editions, Social Problems, 1995—. Judge sci. fairs Hampton, Newport News (Va.) Pub. Schs., 1980—; tng. leader Contact Peninsula, Hampton, Newport News, 1983-86; vol. Va. Spl. Olympics, 1984-87; Ident-I-Kid, Hampton, Newport News, 1985-86; treas. Tidemill Civic Assn., Hampton, 1986-87. Mem. Am. Sociol. Assn., Va. Sociol. Assn. (pres. 1980-81), World Populations Soc., World Futurists Soc., So. Assn. Colls. and Schs. (reaffirmation team 1991-95), Hampton Roads C. of C. (Leadership Inst., 1990, tng. com. 1989-91, bus., industry, govt. and edn. coun. 1989-91), Delta Kappa Gamma (v.p.). Baptist. Home: 213 Deerfield Blvd Hampton VA 23666-1708

WRIGHT, BRENDA CAROL, dental laboratory owner, photographer; b. Danville, Va., Sept. 2, 1952; d. Lester Mitchell and Mary Frances (Conner) W.; m. Lawrence Eisenbiegler, Apr. 11, 1986. Student, Averett Coll., 1970-73; cert. of study, J. Sargent Reynolds, 1990. Supr. denture dept. Va. Dental Lab., Norfolk, 1975-85; owner Cen. Dental Lab., Suffolk, Va., 1985—, Shooting Star Studio and Gallery, 1996—. One person shows include Bache Gallery, Norfolk, Va., 1983, Portsmouth (Va.) Mus. and Fine Arts Ctr., 1984, Old Dominion U. Gallery, Norfolk, 1984; group shows include Art in the Esplanade Invitational, Norfolk, 1980 (award of Excellence), Photography Alliance Exhbn., Norfolk, 1981 (Purchase award), Peninsula Fine Arts Ctr., Newport News, Va., 1982 (Photography award), 83, 85, 88, 89, 90, Harborfest Juried Exhbn., Norfolk, 1982 (Merit award), Ephebi Gallery, Washington, 1983, The Wilson Gallery, Norfolk, 1984, The Quarberg Gallery, Norfolk, 1990, numerous others. Member Downtown Suffolk Assn., 1990—, Chrysler Mus., 1991—. Recipient Preservation award Downtown Suffolk Assn., 1990. Mem. Peninsula Fine Arts Ctr., Nat. Assn. Dental Labs. Democrat. Baptist. Home: 439 New Jersey Ave Norfolk VA 23508-2716 Office: Cen Dental Lab 118 N Main St Suffolk VA 23434-4508

WRIGHT, CALVIN PERSINGER, businessman; b. Rochester, Pa., Dec. 17, 1928; s. Jesse A. and Clara R. (Persinger) W. m. Anne Graham Lacy, Nov. 14, 1970; children: Calvin Jr., Jacob; children by previous marriage: Cynthia Wright Kern, Sally Wright Hawkins, Lauren Wright Haynes. Pres., Wright Edsel Sales, Covington, 1957-59, Allegheny Motor Corp., 1959-81, Downtown Autowash, 1972—, Riverside Spraywash, 1975-82, Sta. WXCF, 1972-79, The Stable Wash, 1983—; Stablewash Too, 1989—; animal breeder, antique auto dealer; dir. State Bank Alleghenies. Pres. High Acres Village, Va., 1965—. Active, Alleghany Hist. Soc.; dir. Persinger Meml. Cemetery. Presbyterian. Home and Office: Merry Go Round Farm 3730 Llama Dr Covington VA 24420

WRIGHT, CAMERON HARROLD GREENE, electrical engineer; b. Quincy, Mass., Jan. 21, 1956; s. Frederick Herman Greene and Dorothy Louise (Harrold) W.; m. Robin Michele Rawlings, May 14, 1988. BSEE summa cum laude, La. Tech. U., 1983; MSEE, Purdue U., 1988; PhD, U. Tex., 1996. Registered profl. engr., Calif. Commd. 2d lt. USAF, 1983, advanced through grades to major, 1995; avionics design engr. USAF Avionics Lab., Wright-Patterson AFB, Ohio, 1983-86; divsn. chief space test range space divsn. USAF, L.A. AFB, 1988-90, dir. advanced satellite systems, 1990-91; instr. elec. engring. USAF Acad., Colorado Springs, 1991-93, asst. prof., 1996—; mem. exec. com. Nat. Aerospace and Electronics Conf., Dayton, Ohio, 1983-86. Contbr. articles to profl. jours.; reviewer profl. jours.; co-author, editor: An Introduction to Electrical Engineering, 1994. Coord. tech. career motivation Dayton Sch. Dist., 1983-86; speaker engring. careers Colorado Springs Middle Sch., 1991-93; vol. computer/network cons. Project Transitions Hospice, Austin, Tex., 1995-96. Mem. IEEE (sr., bd. dirs. Rocky Mountain Bioengring. symposium), Air Force Assn. (life, dir. L.A. Young Astronaut program 1988-91, Officer of Yr. 1991), Am. Soc. for Engring. Edn. Office: Dept Elec Engring 2354 Fairchild Dr Ste 2F6 United States Air Force Acad CO 80840

WRIGHT, CATHERINE, small business owner; b. Chauny, France, May 11, 1960; arrived in U.S., 1984; d. Roland and Jeanine (Decarsin) Guillemont; m. Steven William Wright, Apr. 11, 1986. BA, U. Sorbonne, Paris, 1983; MBA, Ga. State U., 1987. Pres., owner Rsch. Pros, Inc., Atlanta, 1987—. Mem. Am. Mktg. Assn., Ga. Coun. Internat. Visitors, Internat. Bus. Women's Network, Toastmasters. Office: Rsch Pros Inc 590 Valley Hall Dr Atlanta GA 30350-4631

WRIGHT, CATHY HESS, secondary education educator; b. Battle Creek, Mich., Oct. 28, 1958; d. Robert Jr. and Eleanore Coulter (Kelley) Hess; m. Eugene Stephen Wright III, May 29, 1993; 1 child, Cody Stephen. BFA, Fla. State U., 1980, MFA, 1982. Profl. artist-in-residence, instr. Montgomery (Ala.) Ballet, 1983-90, Ala. Dance Theatre, Montgomery, 1990-93; founding dance dept. head Carver Creative and Performing Arts Magnet H.S., Montgomery, 1983—, lead tchr., 1996—; adj. instr. Auburn U., Montgomery, 1983-89; com. mem. Gov. Folsom's subcom. on edn. reform, Montgomery, 1994; mem. dance grant selection com. Ala. State Coun. on Arts, Montgomery, 1987, 89, mem. spkr. bur., 1988-89; bd. cons. Ala. Alliance for Arts Edn., Montgomery, 1995-96. Choreographer (dance) Comic Relief, 1988, (First Prize award), Opiate, 1989 (First Prize award). Mem. steering com. Nat. High Sch. Dance Festival, 1992—. Recipient Am. Tchr. award honor in dance Walt Disney Corp., 1992; choreographic fellow Ala. State Coun. on the Arts, 1988, Artist-in-Edn. fellow Nat. Endowment for the Arts & Coun. for Basic Edn., 1995-96; named one of 1000 Outstanding Women of the Nineties, Mirabella Mag., 1994. Mem. NEA, Assn. for Supervision and Curriculum Devel., Nat. Dance Assn.-Am. Alliance for Health, Physical Edn., Recreation and Dance, Ala. Edn. Assn., Ala. State Assn. for Health, Physical Edn., Recreation and Dance (Dance Educator of Yr. 1990-91), Kappa Delta Pi. Office: Booker T Washington Magnet HS 632 S Union St Montgomery AL 36104

WRIGHT, CHARLES ALAN, law educator, author; b. Phila., Sept. 3, 1927; s. Charles Adshead and Helen (McCormack) W.; m. Mary Joan Herriott, July 8, 1950 (div. Jan. 1955); 1 child, Charles Edward; m. Eleanor Custis Broyles Clarke, Dec. 17, 1955; children: Henrietta, Cecily; stepchildren: Eleanor Custis Clarke, Margot Clarke. BA, Wesleyan U., Middletown, Conn., 1947; LL.B., Yale U., 1949; LHD (hon.), Episcopal Theol. Sem. S.W., 1992. Bar: Minn. 1951, Tex. 1959. Law clk. to Hon. Charles E. Clark, U.S. Ct. Appeals (2d cir.), New Haven, 1949-50; asst. prof. law U. Minn., Mpls., 1950-53, assoc. prof., 1953-55; assoc. prof. law U. Tex., Austin, 1955-58, prof., 1958-65, McCormick prof., 1965-80, Bates prof., 1980—; Arthur Goodhart vis. prof. legal sci. Cambridge (Eng.) U., 1990-91, Hayden W. Head regents chair, 1990-91; vis. prof. U. Pa., 1959-60, Harvard U., 1964-65, Yale U., 1968-69; vis. fellow Wolfson Coll., Cambridge U., 1984; reporter study div. of juridstiction between state and fed. cts. Am. Law Inst., 1963-69; mem. adv. com. on civil rules Jud. Conf. U.S., 1961-64, standing com. on rules of practice and proc., 1964-76, 87-93; cons., counsel for Pres., 1973-74; mem. com. on infractions NCAA, 1973-83, chmn., 1978-83, chmn. adminstrv. rev. panel, 1993-94; mem. permanent com for Oliver Wendell Holmes Devise, 1975-83; mem. Commn. on Bicentennial of U.S. Constn., 1985-92. Author: Wright's Minnesota Rules, 1954, Cases on Remedies, 1955, (with C.T. McCormick and J.H. Chadbourn) Cases on Federal Courts, 9th edit., 1992, Handbook of the Law of Federal Courts, 5th edit., 1994, (with H.M. Reasoner) Procedure-The Handmaid of Justice, 1965, Federal Practice and Procedure: Criminal, 2d edit., 1982, (with A.R. Miller) Federal Practice and Procedure: Civil, 1969-73, 2d edit. (with A.R. Miller and M.K. Kane), 1983—, (with A.R. Miller and E.H. Cooper) Federal Practice and Procedure: Jurisdiction and Related Matters, 1975-82, 2d edit., 1986—, (with K.W. Graham and V.J. Gold) Federal Practice and Procedure: Evidence, 1977—; mem. editorial bd. Supreme Ct. Hist. Soc. Yearbook, 1987-93—. Trustee St. Stephen's Episc. Sch., Austin, Tex., 1962-66, St. Andrew's Episc. Sch., Austin, 1971-74, 77-80, 81-84, chmn. bd., 1973-74, 79-80; trustee Capitol Broadcasting Assn., Austin, 1966—, chmn. bd., 1969-90; trustee Austin Symphony Orch., 1966—, mem. exec. com., 1966-70, 72-83, 86—; trustee Austin Choral Union, 1984-90, Austin Lyric Opera Soc., 1986—; bd. dirs. Am. Friends of Cambridge (Eng.) U., 1994—. Hon. fellow Wolfson Coll. Cambridge U., 1986—. Mem. ABA (commn. on standards jud. adminstrn. 1970-77), AAAS, Am. Law Inst. (coun. 1969—, 2d v.p. 1987-88, 1st v.p. 1988-92, pres. 1993—), Am. Bar Found. (Rsch. award 1989), Inst. Jud. Adminstrn., Am. Judicature Soc., Philos. Soc. Tex., Am. Friends Cambridge U. (bd. dirs. 1994—), Country Club, Tarry House Club, Headliners Club, Ridge Harbor Yacht Club, Barton Creek Lakeside Club (Austin), Century Club, Yale Club (N.Y.C.), Mid Ocean Club (Bermuda). Republican. Episcopalian. Home: 5304 Western Hills Dr Austin TX 78731-4822 Office: U Tex Sch Law 727 E 26th St Austin TX 78705-3224

WRIGHT, CHARLES ELLIOTT, county official, municipal official; b. Washington, Mar. 1, 1946; s. William James and Mildred Aleen (Priolean) W.; m. Barbara Howard, July 12, 1969; children: Charles E., Philip H.C. BA in Sociology, Howard U., 1969; postgrad., Miami Dade Coll., 1986. Dir. sales devel. Ea. Airlines, Inc., 1980-86, mgr. cruiseline sales, 1986-91, dir. spl. markets, 1989-91; chief internat. tourism divsn. tourism Fla. Dept. Commerce, Tallahassee, 1991-95; exec. dir. Leon County Tourist Devel. Coun., Tallahassee, 1995—; pres., CEO, Tallahassee Area Conv. and Visitors Bur., 1995—; del. White House Conf. on Tourism; spkr. 1st Western Hemisphere Tourism Mins. Meeting, 1994. Prodr., host Kaleidoscope, pub. affairs program Sta. WCIX-TV, CBS, 1986-88. Mem. Tallahassee Regional Airport Adv. Bd.; usher Wildwood Presbyn. Ch.; former mem. bd. dirs. Transplant Found. South Fla., U. Miami Sch. Medicine; former chmn. Miami-Dade Trade and Tourism Commn. With D.C. N.G., 1969-75. Recipient numerous cmty. svc. awards, including Golden Helm award, 1994. Mem. Nat. Assn. Black Meeting Planners (founding assoc.), Talahassee C. of C. (bd. dirs.), Capital City C. of C. (bd. dirs.), SKAL Club Tallahassee (v.p.). Office: Tallahassee Conv & Visitors Bur 200 W College Ave Tallahassee FL 32301-7710

WRIGHT, CHARLES PENZEL, JR., English language educator; b. Pickwick Dam, Tenn., Aug. 25, 1935; s. Charles Penzel and Mary Castleman (Winter) W.; m. Holly McIntire, Apr. 6, 1969; 1 child, Luke Savin Herrick. B.A., Davidson (N.C.) Coll., 1957; M.F.A., U. Iowa, 1963; postgrad., U. Rome, 1963-64. Mem. faculty U. Calif., Irvine, 1966-83; prof. English U. Calif., 1976-83; mem. faculty U. Va., Charlottesville, 1983—; Fulbright vis. prof. N.Am. lit. U. Padua, Italy, 1968-69; disting. vis. prof. U. Degli Studi, Florence, Italy, 1992. Author: The Dream Animal, 1968, The Grave of the Right Hand, 1970, The Venice Notebook, 1971, Hard Freight, 1973, Bloodlines, 1975, Colophons, 1977, China Trace, 1977, Wright: A Profile, 1979, The Southern Cross, 1981, Country Music: Selected Early Poems, 1982, The Other Side of the River, 1984, Zone Journals, 1988, Halflife, 1988, Xionia, 1990, The World of the 10,000 Things, 1990, Chickamauga, 1995, Quarter Notes, 1995; trans.: The Storm and Other Poems (Eugenio Montale), 1978, Orphic Songs (Dino Campana), 1984. Served with AUS, 1957-61. Recipient Pen Translation Prize, 1979, Nat. Book award for poetry, 1983, citation in poetry Brandeis U. Creative Arts Awards, 1987, Merit medal Am. Acad. and Inst. Arts and Letters, 1992, Ruth Lilly Poetry prize, 1993; Fulbright scholar, 1963-65; Guggenheim fellow, 1976, Ingram Merrill fellow, 1980, 93. Mem. Fellowship of So. Writers, Am. Acad. Arts and Letters. Home: 940 Locust Ave Charlottesville VA 22901-4030 Office: English Dept Univ Va Charlottesville VA 22901

WRIGHT, CHARLOTTE JEAN, accounting educator; b. Brownfield, Tex., Dec. 16, 1949; d. Jimmy Houston and Syble Daphne (Potts) Mackey; m. Sammy Joe Wright, Dec. 22, 1967; children: Steven Todd, Michael Tate. BBA in Acctg., U. Tex., Arlington, 1976, M Profl. Acctg., 1977; PhD in Bus. Adminstrn., U. North Tex., 1982. CPA, Tex., Okla. Staff acct. Atlantic Riehfield Co., Dallas, 1977-79; rsch. fellow Inst. Petroleum Acctg., Denton, Tex., 1979-82; asst. prof. acctg. Okla. State U., Stillwater, 1982-86, assoc. prof. acctg., 1986-91, prof. acctg., 1991—; pres. Wright Cons., Stillwater, 1991—. Contbr. articles to profl. jours. Grantee Okla. Ctr. for Energy Rsch., 1986, 89; recipient Nat. Lit. award Am. Women's Soc. CPAs, 1986. Mem. Am. Acct. Assn., Beta Gamma Sigma (Disting. Faculty award 1985), Beta Alpha Psi. Office: Okla State U 413 Coll of Bus Stillwater OK 74078

WRIGHT, CLARK PHILLIPS, computer systems specialist; b. Orange, Tex., Aug. 30, 1942; s. Madison Brown and Mary Elizabeth (Phillips) W.; m. Stacy Charlotte Klutz, June 5, 1965 (div. Oct. 1979); m. Cora Lou Alexandria Schelling, Oct. 31, 1979; 1 child, Isaac Schelling. BA, U. Tex., 1965. Computer programmer Lockheed Electronics Co., Houston, 1965-67; prin. analyst Control Data Corp., St. Paul, 1967-76; computer scientist DBA Systems, Inc., Lanham, Md., 1976-79; engring. specialist Ford Aerospace Corp., Houston, 1979-90, Loral Aerospace Corp., 1990—. Precinct chmn. Rep. Party of Tex., 1982-86. Mem. IEEE, Math. Assn. Am., Assn. Computing Machinery, SAR (chartered, sec., treas.), Sons Republic Tex., Info. Sys. Security Assn., Masons, Rotary. Home: 5000 Park Ave Dickinson TX 77539-7013 Office: Loral Aerospace Corp PO Box 58487 Houston TX 77258-8487

WRIGHT, CLIFFORD SIDNEY, accounting educator; b. New Orleans, Mar. 7, 1943; s. Samuel H.P. and Winifred (Vonderhaar) W.; m. Jane Eniz Truch, Aug. 2, 1969; children: Mark, Christopher, Erin. BA, BS, U. New Orleans, 1967; MBA, Loyola U., 1970; JD, Northwestern Calif. Sch. Law, 1990. CPA, La. Mgr. FNBC, New Orleans, 1967-70; prof. bus. Xavier U., New Orleans, 1970—; pvt. practice, Metairie, La., 1970—. Deacon Archdiocese of New Orleans, 1987—; bd. dirs. Hospice, Metairie, 1996, St. Vincent de Paul Soc., Metairie, 1996. Mem. AICPA, La. Soc. CPAs, Am. Acctg. Assn., Nat. Acctg. Assn., Nat. Soc. Pub. Accts., Assn. Govt. Accts. Democrat. Roman Catholic. Home: 3716 Fran St Metairie LA 70001 Office: Xavier U La 7325 Palmetto St New Orleans LA 71025

WRIGHT, CONSTANCE MOHR, elementary school educator; b. N.Y.C., Oct. 28, 1934; d. Conrad Franz Josef and Olga Maria (Kuttner) Mohr; children: Melani Mohr, Bradley Edward. B in Music Edn., Westminster Coll., 1956; MEd, Fla. Atlantic U., 1980; EdS, Nova U., 1983. Tchr. Waldwick (N.J.) Schs., 1956-58, East Orange (N.J.) Schs., 1958-59, Ramsey (N.J.) Schs., 1959-64; tchr. Palm Beach County Schs., West Palm Beach, Fla., 1978—, tchr. vocat. edn., exceptional student edn. coord., 1986—; child care cert. trainer HRS, Palm Beach County, 1986; adj. prof. Palm Beach C.C. and Nova U.; assoc. Master Tchr., Fla.; presenter Nat. Assn. for Gifted Children. Corr. sec. Greenacres (Fla.) PTA, 1986-87; deacon First Presbyn. Ch., Delray Beach, Fla.; vice chair water events SunFest. Ednl. grantee Edn. Found. Palm Beach County, 1986. Mem. Nat. Assn. for Gifted Children (presenter), Fla. Assn. for Gifted (area VII coord.), Zeta Tau Alpha, Phi Delta Kappa. Republican. Presbyterian. Home: 245 Walton Heath Dr Atlantis FL 33462-1127

WRIGHT, COREY ROBERT, secondary school educator; b. Oklahoma City, July 29, 1969; s. Richard Ronald and Terry Ann (Frye) W.; 1 child, Courtney Grace. BA in History Edn., East Ctrl. U., Ada, Okla., 1993; MA in Phys. Edn., Western Ky. U., 1995. Student athletic trainer East Ctrl. U., 1987-93; grad. asst. phys. edn. dept. Western Ky. U., Bowling Green, 1993-94; tchr. Oklahoma City schs., 1994—. Asst. scoutmaster Boy Scouts Am., 1988—. Mem. AAHPERD.

WRIGHT, DANIEL, wine specialist, consultant; b. Hull, Yorkshire, Eng., June 24, 1931 came to U.S., 1971; s. Edwin Vincent and Agnes Mary (Paden) W.; m. Agnes Macdonald Doull, July 9, 1955 (div. 1977); children: Oliver Hamish, Alistair Louis, Edwina Moira, William Joseph, Jeffrey Peter. Diploma in hotel and catering ops.-mgmt., Westminster Tech. Coll., London, 1952. Trainee, asst. mgr. wine dept. Fortes & Co., Hoteliers, London, 1952-57; tech. mgr. Asher Storey & Co., wine shippers, London, 1958; wine mgr. St. James Bonded Warehouses, London, 1958-64; gen. mgr. wine and spirits dept. Hunt Edmonds Brewery, Banbury, Oxford, Eng., 1964-68; wine and spirit contr. Vaux Brewery, Sunderland, Durham, Eng., 1968-71; corp. wine dir. Ga. Crown Distbg. Co., Atlanta, 1978-89; wine specialist, cons. Jax Beer & Wine (formerly Greens Beer & Wine Stores), Atlanta, 1990—; mem. adv. bd. Atlanta Wine Festival, 1981—, judge wine competitions, 1981—. Bd. dirs. Park North Homeowners Assn., Atlanta, 1986-88; chief judge Atlanta Wine Festival, 1991. With Brit. Army, 1949-51. Fellow Brit. Bottlers Inst.; mem. Chaine des Rotisseurs (chevalier Atlanta 1977—), Companions of Beaujolais. Home: 6709 Park Ave NE Atlanta GA 30342-2366 Office: Jax Beer & Wine 5901 Roswell Rd NE Atlanta GA 30328-4907

WRIGHT, DAVID BRIAN, systems engineering consultant; b. Evansville, Ind., July 12, 1961; s. Donald R. and Betty L. (Odom) W. BA in Math./Computer Sci., DePauw U., 1983, BA in Physics, 1983; MS in Computer Sci., U. Ill., 1989, PhD in Computer Sci., 1991. Intern physics divsn. Oak Ridge (Tenn.) Nat. Lab., 1982; teaching asst. U. Ill., Urbana, 1983-85, rsch. asst., 1985-87, 90-91; cons. Full Udder, Inc., Merced, Calif., 1988-93; software rschr. Advanced Switching Lab. NEC Am., Irving, Tex., 1992-94; sys. engr. Southwestern Bell Tech. Resources, Austin, Tex., 1994—. Eagle Scout, Boys Scouts Am. Named Nat. Merit scholar and rector scholar DePauw U. Mem. IEEE, Assn. for Computing Machinery, Phi Beta Kappa, Phi Gamma Delta (grad. advisor). Home: 8741 Wafer Ash Way Austin TX 78750 Office: Southwestern Bell Tech Resources 4505 Arboretum Blvd Austin TX 78759

WRIGHT, DAVID RAY, secondary school educator; b. Lampasas, Tex., Oct. 31, 1953; s. James Arlen and Peggy Pauline (Hail) W.; m. Marion Kay Hewitt, Nov. 9, 1989; children: Rebecca Jane, Gregory Neill. BS, S.W. Tex. State U., 1976; postgrad., Baylor U., 1989-90. Cert. tchr., Tex. Tchr./coach Copperas Cove (Tex.) I.S.D., 1976—; supt. adv. com. Copperas Cove I.S.D., 1987-89, 96-97, profl. consultation com., 1989-90; test devel. advisor TAAS Instr. Objectives for Wellness, Tex. Edn. Agy., Austin, 1993. Actor: (motion picture) Gilbert Grape, 1993; dancer/actor: (motion picture for TV) Another Pair of Aces, 1991, Seduction in Travis County, 1992, Big T, 1992; singer

Bluegrass Gospel Band; mem. First Bapt. Players Drama group. Recipient Excellence in Teaching award Killeen Daily Herald, 1987; tchr. of the Yr. award Copperas Cove Vets. of Foreign Wars, Post 8577, 1991. Mem. Nat. Dance Assn., AAHPERD, Tex. Assn. of Health, Phys. Edn., Recreation, and Dance (clinician State Convs. 1991, 93, chair Phys. Edn. Pub. Info. Com. 93-94), Tex. Clogging Coun., Lloyd Shaw Found., Country Song and Dance Found., Western Swing Hall of Fame. Baptist. Home: 1608 E Robertson Ave Copperas Cove TX 76522-3175

WRIGHT, DONALD GENE, accountant; b. Grand Junction, Tenn., June 7, 1950; s. Ernest Young and Frances Irene (Reeder) W.; children: Richard Benjamin, Jacqueline; m. Helen "Vicki" Elizabeth Holt Wright, Oct. 1, 1988; step children: Veronica Reynolds, Mindy Reynolds. A Engrng. (e-quivalent), U. Tenn., Martin, 1970; degree in Acctg., Lambeth U., 1987. Cost acctg. clk. Harman Automotive, Inc., Bolivar, Tenn., 1975-79, sr. acct., 1979-85, budget & spl. projects mgr., 1985-92, acctg., estimating mgr., 1992-95; controller Kingston-Warren Corp., Wytheville, Va., 1995—; bd. dirs. West Tenn. Chpt. NAA, Jackson, Tenn., 1987-95. Editor: VP Communications Monthly Newsletter, 1991, Director of Newsletter Monthly Newsletter, 1989. Mem. Nat. Assn. Accts. (pres. West Tenn. chpt.), Civitan Club. Baptist. Home: PO Box 602 Wytheville VA 24382 Office: Kingston-Warren Corp 1150 S Third St Wytheville VA 24382

WRIGHT, FREDERICK LEWIS, II, lawyer; b. Roanoke, Va., Sept. 17, 1951; s. Frederick Lewis and Dorothy Marie (Trent) W.; m. Margaret Suzanne Rey, Oct. 16, 1982; children: Lauren Elizabeth, Emily Trent. BA, Ga. State U., 1978; JD, U. Ga., 1981. Bar: Ga. 1982, U.S. Dist. Ct. (no. dist.) Ga. 1984, U.S. Ct. Appeals (11th and 8th cirs.) 1984, U.S. Supreme Ct. 1990. Law clk. to presiding justice U.S. Ct. Appeals, Atlanta, 1981-82; ptnr. Smith, Currie and Hancock, Atlanta, 1982—. Articles editor Ga. Law Rev., 1980-81. Mem. ABA (forum com. constrn. industry), Assn. Trial Lawyers Am., Fed. Bar Assn., Order of Coif. Methodist.

WRIGHT, HARROLD EUGENE, petroleum engineer; b. Vernon, Tex., Aug. 28, 1924; s. Jess Newton and Bess Bailey (Burroughs) W.; m. Joyce Overbay (div. 1970); m. Joy Lavon Robinson, Dec. 13, 1970; children: Marianne Wright Arnold, Elizabeth, Arthur L., Amy Wright Rosche, Bradley. BEE, Tex. Tech. U., 1944. Registered profl. engr., Tex. Resident engr. Freese & Nichols, Consulting Engrs., San Augustine, Tex., 1946-48; petroleum engr. Hiawatha Oil & Gas Co., Midland, Tex., 1948-52, San Juan Oil Co., Dallas, 1952-55; v.p. Producing Properties, Inc., Dallas, 1956-63; pres. Swift Ops., Inc., Dallas, 1963-68; pres., chief exec. officer Gene Wright, Inc., Dallas, 1968—, San Juan Exploration Co., Dallas, 1973-81; pres. San Juan Exploration Co., 1988—, Olde English Village, Inc., Tyler, Tex., 1981—; mem. U.S. Dept. Commerce Industry Adv. Com., 1983-90, chmn. 1983; chmn. liaison com. Cooperating Oil and Gas Assns., 1982-83; chmn. Petroleum Industry Security Coun., 1981-84. Chmn. Dem. Com. for Responsible Gulf, Dallas County, 1966; chmn., vice chmn. Polit. Action for Petroleum Industry, Tyler, 1978-85; bd. dirs. Drug Free Youth in Tex., 1989-90. Lt. (j.g.) USNR, 1944-46, PTO. Mem. Soc. Petroleum Engrs. (chmn. admissions com. 1961-63), Am. Assn. Petroleum Geologists, Natural Gas Supply Assn. (chmn. 1981-82), Ind. Petroleum Assn. Am. (chmn. natural gas com. 1978-81), Tex. Producers and Royalty Owners Assn. (pres., chmn. 1981-83), Dallas Petroleum Club, Southwest Energy and Commerce Coun. (chmn. 1988—), East Tex. Producers and Royalty Owners Assn. (v.p. 1988—), Tyler Area C. of C. (retail and svcs. com. chmn. 1989-90), East Tex. C. of C. (v.p. 1983-87). Home: 828 Colonial Dr Tyler TX 75701-6926 Office: Gene Wright Inc 318 E 5th St Tyler TX 75701-4225

WRIGHT, HARRY HERCULES, psychiatrist; b. Charleston, S.C., Jan. 4, 1948; s. Harry Vernon and Agnes Lucile (Simmons) W.; BS, U. S.C., 1970; MD, U. Pa., 1976, MBA, 1976. Resident in psychiatry Wm. S. Hall Psychiat. Inst., Columbia, S.C., 1977-79; adminstrv. fellow in psychiatry NIMH, Rockville, Md., 1979; fellow in child psychiatry William S. Hall Psychiat. Inst., 1979-81, teaching child psychiatrist, 1981—; instr. dept. neuropsychiatry and behavioral sci. U. S.C. Sch. Medicine, 1981-82, asst. prof., 1982-86, assoc. prof., 1986-90, prof., 1990—. Bd. dirs. Carolina Children's Home, 1992; mem. landmarks commn. City of Columbia, 1986. Falk fellow, 1977-79; Laughlin fellow, 1979; recipient Freed award Hall Psychiat. Inst., 1978, Outstanding Service award Sickle Cell Found. Mem. AAAS, Am. Acad. Child Psychiatry, World Psychiat. Assn., World Assn. Infant Mental Health, Am. Soc. Adolescent Psychiatry, Am. Pub. Health Assn., Am. Psychiat. Assn., So. Med. Assn., Riverbank Zool. Soc., Autism Soc. Am., Acad. Orgnl. and Occupl. Psychiatry, Soc. Study Psychiatry and Culture, Omicron Delta Kappa, Sigma Xi. Methodist. Contbr. articles to profl. jours. Home: PO Box 12474 Columbia SC 29211-2474 Office: PO Box 202 Columbia SC 29202-0202

WRIGHT, ISAAC WILSON, JR., quality assurance professional; b. Nashville, Oct. 22, 1948; s. Isaac Wilson and Julia Frances (Nixon) W.; m. Giovanna Finn Wright, Nov. 12, 1988. BS in Elec. Engring., U. Tenn., 1970, MBA in Indsl. Mgmt., 1973. Cert. quality engr.; cert. quality auditor. Staff asst. to prodn. mgr. disposal med. devices Baxter-Travenol Labs., Cleveland, Miss., 1974-75; quality engr. Stephens-Adamson, Inc., divsn. Allis-Chalmers Corp., Clarksdale, Miss., 1976-81, supr. quality assurance, 1981-84; mgr. quality assurance and safety Fontaine Fifth Wheel Co., Birmingham, Ala., 1985-90, dir. quality assurance, 1990-95; sr. quality assurance engr. Harley-Davidson Motor Co., Milw., 1996—. Book reviewer Quality Progress. Mem. Am. Soc. Quality Control (organizer, sect. chair Birmingham sect. 1986-88, organizer Montgomery sub-sect. 1992-93, dir. at large Birmingham sect. 1990-91, Testimonial award 1994), Singles South Civitan (newsletter editor 1986-87, dist. award 1987), Cleveland Evening Lions (pres. 1981-82, dist. publicity and info. chmn., newsletter editor 1980-81, dist. award 1981), Exchange Club (bd. dirs. 1975), U. Tenn. Alumni Assn. and Century Club, Beta Theta Pi. Methodist. Office: Quality Assurance Mgmt 11700 Capitol Dr Wauwatosa WI 53222

WRIGHT, JAMES DAVID, sociology educator, writer; b. Logansport, Ind., Nov. 6, 1947; s. James Farrell and Helen Loretta (Moon) W.; m. Christine Ellen Stewart, July 25, 1987; children: Matthew James, Derek William. BA, Purdue U., 1969; MS, U. Wis., 1970, PhD, 1973. Cert. specialist social policy and evaluation rsch. Asst. prof. sociology U. Mass., Amherst, 1973-76, assoc. prof., 1976-79, prof., 1979-88; Favrot prof. human rels. Tulane U., New Orleans, 1988—. Author/co-author: The Dissent of the Governed, 1976, Under the Gun, 1983, The State of the Masses, 1986, Homelessness and Health, 1987 (commendation Nat. Press Club 1988), Address Unknown: Homeless in America, 1989, The Greatest of Evils: Urban Poverty and the Urban Underclass, 1993, others; editor: (book series) Social Institutions and Social Change, 1984—, (jour.) Social Sci. Rsch. Jour., 1978—; contbr. numerous articles, essays, book chpts. to profl. publs. Mem. Am. Sociol. Assn., Soc. for Study Social Problems. Democrat.

WRIGHT, JANE BROOKS, university foundation professional; b. Athens, Ga., Oct. 31, 1935; d. Joseph Welchel and Sophia (Porter) Brooks; m. Fred Hamilton Wright, June 26, 1956 (div. Nov. 1969); children: Judy Anne Wright Cusick, Gary Allen (dec. Oct. 1993), Mark. BA in Edn., U. Fla., 1971, MA in Edn., 1972. Bookkeeper Paul Smith Constrn. Co., Cape Canaveral, Fla., 1956-57; owner, dir. Children's Corner Sch., Cocoa, Fla., 1964-69; sec. U. Fla. Found., Inc., Gainesville, 1972-73, staff asst., 1973-86, mgr. prospect rsch., 1986-95, part-time asst. mgr., 1995—. Jehovah's Witness. Office: U Fla Found Inc 2012 W University Ave Gainesville FL 32603-1734

WRIGHT, JOHN SPENCER, school system administrator; b. Washington, May 8, 1948; s. Clarence S. and Florence (Nagel) W.; m. Debra Kim Buck, Aug. 4, 1973; 1 child, Deanna Michelle. BA in Econs., U. Va., 1969, MEd in Secondary Adminstrn., 1971, EdD in Adminstrn. and Supervision, 1976. Cert. social studies tchr., prin., supt., fin. officer, N.C.; registered sch. bus. adminstr. Tchr. govt. and social studies Lane H.S., Charlottesville, Va., 1969-72, spl. asst. to prin., 1972-74; supr. Sch. Gen. Learning Charlottesville H.S., 1974-75; exec. dir. Va. Assn. Sch. Execs., Charlottesville, 1976-78; prin. E.C. Glass H.S., Lynchburg, Va., 1978-82; dir. bus. svcs. Lynchburg Pub. Schs., 1982-86, dir. fin. and planning svcs., 1986; asst. supt. bus. and fin. svcs. Greensboro (N.C.) Pub. Schs., 1986-90, assoc. supt. human and fin. resources, 1990-93; assoc. supt. adminstrv. svcs. Guilford County (N.C.) Schs., 1993—; investigating probation officer 8th Regional Juvenile and Domestic Rels. Ct., Charlottesville, 1970-71; grad. asst., teaching asst. Sch. Edn., U. Va., 1975-76; rsch. asst. Tayloe Murphy Inst., U. Va., 1975-76; asst. prof. Grad. Sch. Edn., U. Va., 1976-78; part time asst. prof. Grad. Sch. Edn., U. Va., 1978-80; adj. prof. U. Va., Sch. Continuing Edn., 1983, 86. Co-author: Charlottesville Change Project: Year End Report, 1974; editor: Developments in School Law, 1976-78; contbr. articles and reviews to profl. jours. Bd. dirs. Triad Sickle Cell Anemia Found.; past bd. dirs. Presbyn. Home and Family Svcs., Inc.; past v.p. deductible fund Local Govt. Ins. Funds, Greensboro, Guilford, N.C., past pres. liability fund; mem. N.C. Profl. Practices Commn., 1996—; mem. Com. 100, Greensboro Human Rels. Commn. Mem. ASCD, Am. Assn. Sch. Adminstrs., Am. Assn. Sch. Pers. Adminstrs., Assn. Sch. Bus. Officials, Southeastern Assn. Sch. Bus. Officials, N.C. Assn. Sch. Bus. Officials (legis. com., past region chmn., vice-chair and mem. state exec. com.), Nat. Orgn. on Legal Problems Edn., Sch. Edn. Found. (dean's coun. U. Va.), Distributive Edn. Clubs Am. (hon. life), Greensboro C. of C. (govtl. affairs coun., minority/women bus. devel. coun.), U. Va. Alumni Assn. (former class agt.), Va. Student Aid Found., Leadership Greensboro Alumni Assn., Greensboro Civitans (vice pres. 1993-94, bd. dirs. 1994-96), Human Resources Mgmt. Assn. Greensboro, Phi Delta Kappa (former chpt. treas.), Kappa Delta Pi, others. Presbyterian. Home: 4610 Charlottesville Rd Greensboro NC 27410-3655 Office: Guilford County Schools PO Box 880 Greensboro NC 27402-0880

WRIGHT, JOHN TIMOTHY, dentistry educator; b. Wilmington, Del., June 17, 1954; s. John Collins and Margaret Ann (Cyphers) W.; m. Sally Ann Symark, Dec. 22, 1973; children: Jonathon Keegan, Kelly Frances, Rebecca Caitlin. Student, Ft. Lewis Coll., Durango, colo., 1972-73; DDS, W.Va. U., 1978; MS, U. Ala., Birmingham, 1984. Diplomate Am. Bd. Pediatric Dentistry. Clin. instr. W.Va. U., Morgantown, 1979-80; asst. prof. dentistry U. Ala., Birmingham, 1984-87, assoc. prof., 1987-90; assoc. prof. U. N.C., Chapel Hill, 1990-95, prof., 1995—, dir. Dentist Scientist program, 1992-93. Editor: Special Patients in Dentistry, 1989; contbr. some 50 articles to profl. jours. NIDR rsch. grantee, 1986-95. Fellow Am. Acad. Pediatric Dentistry (Rsch. award 1995, Grad. Rsch. award 1984), Am. Coll. Dentistry; mem. ADA, Internat. Assn. for Dental Rsch., European Orgn. for Caries Rsch., Am. Soc. Dentistry for Chidlren, N.C. Dental Rsch. Assn. (pres. 1994-95). Home: 113 Chestnut Rd Chapel Hill NC 27514 Office: U NC Sch Dentistry CB7450 Chapel Hill NC 27599

WRIGHT, JOSEPH ROBERT, JR., corporate executive; b. Tulsa, Sept. 24, 1938; s. Joe Robert and Ann Helen (Cech) W. B.S., Colo. Sch. Mines, 1961; M.I.A., Yale U., 1964. Vice pres. Booz, Allen & Hamilton, 1965-71; dep. dir. Bur. Census, Dept. Commerce, 1971-72; dep. adminstr. Social and Econ. Statis. Adminstrn., 1972-73, acting asst. sec. econ. affairs, 1973; asst. sec. adminstr. Dept. Agr., 1973-76; pres. Citicorp Retail Inc. and Retail Consumer Services Inc., N.Y.C.; v.p. Citicorp, Inc., 1976-81; dep. sec. Dept. Commerce, Washington, 1981-82; dep. dir. Office Mgmt. and Budget, Washington, 1982-88; chmn. Pres.'s Council on Integrity and Efficiency, 1982-89; chmn. Pres.'s Coun on Mgmt. Improvement, 1984-89; dir. Office Mgmt. and Budget, 1988-89; exec. v.p., vice chmn. W.R. Grace & Co., N.Y.C., 1989-94; chmn. Grace Environ., Inc., 1989-94, Avic Group Internat., 1995—, Jefferson Ptnrs., 1995—; bd. dirs. Travelers Corp., 1990—, Harcourt, Brace, Jovanovich, Inc., 1990-91, W.R. Grace & Co., 1989-91, Canonie Environ., Inc., 1989-94, Grace Energy, Inc., 1990-94, Productora de Papeles, S.A., 1991-94, La Posta Recycling Ctr., Inc., 1992-94, Nat. Assn. Mfg.; bd. advs. Baker & Taylor, 1992—, Netmatics, 1996—, Deswell Industries, Inc., 1995—, Ardshiel, Inc., 1990-94; fed. co-chmn. Coastal Plains Regional Commn., 1981-82, Four Corners Regional Commn., 1981-82, New Eng. Regional Commn., 1981-82, Old West Regional Commn., 1981-82, Pacific N.W. REgional Commn., 1981-82, S.W. Border Regional Commn., 1981-82; ptnr. Gulfstream Capital, 1995—, Austin Trading Co., 1995—. Mem. adv. bd. Coun. for Excellence in Govt., 1988-96, The Jefferson Group, 1993—; trustee Hampton U., 1990—. 1st lt. AUS, 1963-65. Recipient Pres.'s Citizens award and medal, 1989; named Govt. Exec. of Yr., Govt. Computer News Mag., 1988, medal disting. achievement Colo. Sch. Mines, 1985. Mem. Young Pres. Orgn., Nat. Acad. Pub. Adminstrn., Colo. Sch. Mines Alumni Assn., Pres.'s Export Coun., Chief Execs. Orgn., World Bus. coun., Reagan Alumni Assn., Palm Beach (Fla.) Golf and Polo Club, Banyon Country Club (Fla.), Sky Club (N.Y.C.). Home: 2 Ocean Ln Lake Worth FL 33462-3337 Office: 2100 W Sample Rd Ste 300 Pompano Beach FL 33064 also: Jefferson Capital 1341 G St NW Washington DC 20005 also: Avic Group Internat 599 Lexington Ave New York NY 10022

WRIGHT, MARY BETH, special education educator; b. Madison, Wis., Jan. 3, 1952; d. Harry Wesley and Rita Cecelia (Schreier) W. AA, U. Wis., LaCrosse, 1972; BA, U. South Fla., 1980, MA, 1982. Subsitute tchr. Hillsborogh Pasco County Schs., Tampa and Land O'Lakes, Fla., 1980-81; tchr. specific learning disabilities Lutz (Fla.) Elem., 1981-86; tchr. specific learning disabilities, soccer coach Thomas Jefferson High Sch., Tampa, 1986-87; head tchr. Downtown Alt., Tampa, 1987-88; math and sci. tchr. Brandon (Fla.) Alt., 1988-91; specific learning disabilities tchr. King and Chamberlain High Sch., 1991—; tutor Hillsborough County Schs., 1981-91; cons. Hillsborough Cmty. Coll., Tampa, 1984-91; aerobics instr. Shapes Health Fitness, Tampa, YMCA, 1985-94. Scout leader Girl Scouts U.S.A., Tampa, 1981. Mem. Fla. Assn. for Children with Learning Disabilities, Women in Mil. Svc., Orton Dyslexic Soc. Republican. Lutheran. Home: 11822 Wildeflower Pl Tampa FL 33617-2720 Office: King High Sch 6815 N 56th St Tampa FL 33610-1921

WRIGHT, MARY JAMES, multimedia instructional designer; b. Charlottesville, Va., Aug. 20, 1946; d. Harry Beech and Virginia Allen (Root) James; m. Paul Sims Wright, July 26, 1969; children: Christopher Brennan, Keith Allen. BA summa cum laude, Mary Washington Coll., 1968; MA, Northwestern U., 1969; postgrad., Trinity Coll., 1981, Gallaudet U., 1991. Instr. drama and speech Mary Washington Coll., Fredericksburg, Va., 1969-71, Charles County Community Coll., La Plata, Md., 1973-79; arts and media coord. Charles County Arts Coun., La Plata, 1973-82, Gen. Smallwood Mid. Sch., Indian Head, Md., 1980-82, No. Va. Community Coll., Annandale, 1982-84; computer-based learning specialist USDA Grad. Sch., Washington, 1984-85, U.S. Army Engr. Sch., Ft. Belvoir, Va., 1985-87, Battelle Meml. Inst., Columbus, Ohio, 1987-88; videodisc designer Kendrick & Co., Washington, 1988-90; instrnl. design mgr. The Discovery Channel, Bethesda, Md., 1990-93; instnl. design mgr. Edunetics Corp., Arlington, Va., 1994-95; interactive multimedia designer and developer Smart House, Ltd. Partnership, Upper Marlboro, Md., 1990; project mgr., instl. designer Toby Levine Comms., Inc., 1990—. Author, dir.: Story-Theatre for Children, 1979; contbr. articles to profl. jours.; pub. videodiscs, CD-ROMS, Web sites; classroom guides for nat. media products: PBS, Discovery Channel, Nat. Geographic, Edunetics Corp. Pres. Am. Christian Television System of No. Va., Action for Women, Charles County AAUW; sign lang. interpreter Deaf Ministry. Nat. Danforth fellow 1969; recipient Achievement award Dept. of Army, 1986, Kendrick & Co., 1989; recipient Outstanding Arts Programming award Md. Dept. Parks and Recreation, 1980, Silver and Bronze Cindy awards (Cinema in Industry and Edn.), 1992, Red Ribbon Am. Film & Video Assn. Festival, Special Gold Jury award Houston Internat. Film Festival, 1992, Gold award Nebr. Interactive Media, 1993. Mem. ASCD, Internat. Interactive Courseware Soc. (Mark of Excellence award 1992), Assn. for Devel. Computer-Based Instrn. Systems (coord. spl. interest groups D.C. chpt. 1989-90), No. Va. Registry Interpreters for the Deaf, Mortar Bd., Alpha Psi Omega, Alpha Phi Sigma. Home and office: 4302 Rolling Stone Way Alexandria VA 22306-1225

WRIGHT, MICHAEL PHILLIP, health researcher, computer software developer; b. Norman, Okla., Mar. 10, 1947; s. Charles William and Nannina Bessie Wright. BA in Polit. Sci., U. Okla., 1969, MA in Sociology, 1976. Cons., rschr. Norman, 1974-83, musician, 1979-84; rsch. dir. Sci. Social Rsch., Norman, 1983—; innovator in med. informatics. Copyright computer software. Antiwar activist and community organizer, Norman, 1960's. Recipient Small Bus. Innovation Rsch. grants Nat. Cancer Inst., 1991, 93, grant Nat. Inst. Allergy and Infectious Diseases, 1991, grant Ctrs. for Disease Control, 1991. Home: PO Box 204 Norman OK 73070-0204

WRIGHT, MILDRED ANNE (MILLY WRIGHT), conservator, researcher; b. Athens, Ala., Sept. 9, 1939; d. Thomas Howard and Anne Louise (Ashworth) Speegle; m. William Paul Wright, Nov. 20, 1965; children: Paul Howard, William Neal. BS in Physics, U. Ala., Tuscaloosa, 1963. Rschr. in acoustics Wyle Labs., Huntsville, Ala., 1963-64; tchr. physics, English Huntsville H.S., 1964-67; ptnr. Flying Carpet Oriental Rugs, Florence, Ala., 1974—; adj. mem. faculty U. North Ala., Florence, 1988, lectr. Inst. for Learning in Retirement, 1991—. Columnist Times Daily, 1992—; photojournalist, writer River Views Mag., 1993—; contbr. articles to profl. jours. (1st pl. award 1986, 87). Pianist, organist Edgemont Meth. Ch., Florence, 1987-90 (Outstanding Svc. award 1990); mem. steering com. Melton Hollow Nature Ctr., Florence, 1990—, Design Ala., Florence, 1991, River Heritage Discovery Camp, 1993-95; mem. River Heritage Com., Florence, 1991—; accompanist Shoals Boy Choir, Muscle Shoals, Ala., 1992-93; bd. dirs. Heritage Preservation, Inc., 1989—, Capital award, 1992, pres., 1990-92, 96—, treas., 1995-96, Tenn. Valley Hist. Soc., pres., 1991-95, Ala. Preservation Alliance, treas., 1993-96, Florence Main Street program, 1992-94, Maud Lindsay Free Kindergarten, Frank Lloyd Wright Rosenbaum House Found., Inc., 1992—, Gen. Joseph Wheeler Home Found., 1994—, treas. 1995—, newsletter editor, 1995—; sec. Friends of the Ala. Archives, 1995—; mem. adv. coun. Human Environ. Scis. Dept.; mem. Coby Hall steering com. U. North Ala., 1992—, Kennedy-Douglas Ctr. Arts; adv. bd. Old Cahawba of Ala., 1996—; adv. bd. Waterloo Mus., 1995—, Florence Children's Mus., 1995-96. Recipient Disting. Svc. award Ala. Hist. Commn., 1991, Merit award Ala. Preservation Alliance, 1995, Southeastern Muss. Assn., 1996. Mem. Ala. Writers' Conclave (Creative Works award 1986, 87), Ala. Hist. Assn., Ala. Archeol. Soc., Natchez Trace Geneal. Soc., Colbert County Hist. Landmarks Found., Nat. Trust for Hist. Preservation, Tennessee Valley Art Assn. (exhibit chmn. 1996—), La Grange Living History Assn., Trail of Tears Assn., Firenze Club (past pres., pres. 1996—), Optimist Club, Sigma Pi Sigma. Home: PO Box 279 Florence AL 35631-0279

WRIGHT, NANCY JANE, English language educator; b. Springfield, Ill., Feb. 28, 1939; d. William Joseph and Elizabeth (Walton) Lucasey; m. Arthur Lee Wright, Aug. 21, 1960; 1 child, John Arthur. BS magna cum laude, Western Ill. U., 1961; MS summa cum laude, So. Ill. U., 1963; PhD, Tex. A&M U., 1975. Tchg. asst. So. Ill. U., Carbondale, 1961-62; instr. Ferris State Coll., Big Rapids, Mich., 1962-65, Christian Coll., Columbia, Mo., 1965-70; tchg. asst. then instr. Tex. A&M U., College Station, 1971-76; instr. lit. Blinn Coll., Bryan, Tex., 1977—; mem. Am. Disabilities Task Force, Blinn Coll., Bryan, 1994—, mem. curriculum com., 1993-94, acad. advisor coord., 1995—; workshop leader. Co-author: How to Prepare for the Tasp, 1991, 2d edit., 1994. Vol. instr. LIFT Program, Dallas, 1970-71; dir. music, pianist/accompanist First Christian Ch., Bryan. Mem. Blinn Coll. Profl. Assn. (founding pres.), Nat. Coun. Tchrs. English, Tex. Jr. Coll. Tchrs. Assn. Republican. Mem. Disciples of Christ Ch. Home: 1008 Holt St College Station TX 77840-2621

WRIGHT, OLGA, artist, aesthetician; b. Mangum, Okla., Feb. 6, 1932; m. George Wayne Polly, Jr., Aug. 21, 1956. Student, N.Y. Art Students League, 1959; BS, Arts and Industries U., Kingsville, Tex., 1962. Owner Olga Wright Aesthetics, Corpus Christi, Tex., 1937—. One-woman shows include Centenial Mus., 1978. Recipient Best of Show award Dimension Show, 1977, Best Oil of Show award, 1977, 79, All Membership Show of Art Ctrs. Artfest '96. Mem. Art Ctr. Corpus Christi, Art Assn., Art Guild, Pastel Soc., South Tex. Art League, Water Color Soc. South Tex. Home: 4238 Estate Dr Corpus Christi TX 78412-2429 Office: Olga Wright Aesthetics 4238 Estate Dr Corpus Christi TX 78412-2429

WRIGHT, PATRICIA ANN, advertising consultant; b. Texarkana, Tex., Oct. 6, 1952; d. James Harold and Frances Elizabeth (Rivers) Fagan; m. Michael J. Buckley, Mar. 9, 1974 (div. July, 1979); m. Steven Carl Wright, July 2, 1988; children: Shelby Catherine, Mackenzie Fagan. BS in English, Theatre, Edn., Tex. Christian U., 1973. From prodn. mgr. to account exec. B.E. Fichte & Assocs., Arlington, Tex., 1975-81; owner, mgr. Buckley Agy., Arlington, 1981-89; advt. adminstr. Dresser Rand Compression Svcs., Broken Arrow, Okla., 1989-94; mktg. mgr. Samson Cos., Tulsa, 1994—. Recipient Gold Addy award direct mail, 1987, Silver Addy award farm pub. Fort Worth Advt. League, 1987, Gold Tops award direct mail, 1987, Gold Tops award farm pub. Dallas Advt. League, 1987, Gold medal direct mail Nat. Advt. Fedn. 10th dist., 1987. Home: 1416 N Umbrella Ave Broken Arrow OK 74012-9152 Office: Samson Cos 2 W 2d St Tulsa OK 74103

WRIGHT, R(ALEIGH) LEWIS, neurosurgeon; b. Roanoke, Va., Apr. 16, 1931; s. Raleigh Lewis and Mary Lillian (Major) W.; m. Sarah Bird Grant, Sept. 7, 1963; 1 child, Alexander Grant. B.A., U. Richmond, 1951; M.D., Med. Coll. Va., 1955. Intern, Duke U. Hosp., 1955-56, surg. resident, 1956-57; neurosurg. resident Mass. Gen. Hosp., Boston, 1959-63; practice medicine specializing in neurosurgery, Boston, 1964-70, Richmond, Va., 1970—; mem. staff St. Mary's, Retreat, Stuart Circle hosps., ; faculty Harvard Med. Sch., Boston, 1962-70; faculty neurosurgery Med. Coll. Va., 1970—. Author: Postoperative Craniotomy Infections, 1966; Septic Complications of Neurosurgical Spinal Procedures, 1970; Artists in Virginia Before 1900, 1983. Contbr. articles to profl. jours., also author articles on early so. artists. Served with M.C., USNR, 1957-59. King Trust Fund fellow, 1963-64. Diplomate Am. Bd. Neurol. Surgery, Nat. Bd. Med. Examiners. Fellow ACS; mem. AMA, Am. Assn. Neurol. Surgeons, Congress Neurol. Surgeons, Southern Neurosurg. Soc., Med. Soc. Va., Richmond Acad. Medicine. Episcopalian. Club: Commonwealth. Home: 3505 Old Gun Rd Midlothian VA 23113-1334 Office: 4908 Monument Ave Richmond VA 23230

WRIGHT, ROBERT JOSEPH, lawyer; b. Rome, Ga., Dec. 13, 1949; s. Arthur Arley and Maude T. (Lacey) W.; m. Donna Ruth Bishop, Feb. 18, 1972; children: Cynthia Ashley, Laura Christine. BA cum laude, Ga. State U., 1979; JD cum laude, U. Ga., 1983. Bar: GA. 1983, U.S. Dist. Ct. (no. dist.) Ga. 1983, U.S. Dist. Ct. (mid. dist.) Ga. 1985. Assoc. Craig & Gainer, Covington, Ga., 1983-84, Heard, Leverett & Adams, Elberton, Ga., 1984-86; gen. counsel Group Underwriters, Inc., Elberton, 1987—. Editorial staff Ga. Jour. Internat. and Comparative Law, 1981-82. Mem. State Bar Ga. (sec. legal econs. sect. 1987-88, chmn. legal econs. sect. 1988-90), Order of the Coif, Masons, Phi Alpha Delta. Baptist. Home: 1030 E Canyon Creek Ct Watkinsville GA 30677-1500

WRIGHT, ROBERT PAYTON, lawyer; b. Beaumont, Tex., Feb. 15, 1951; s. Vernon Gerald and Huberta Read (Nunn) W.; m. Sallie Chesnutt Smith, July 16, 1977; children: Payton Cullen, Elizabeth Risher. AB, Princeton U., 1972; JD, Columbia U., 1975. Bar: Tex. 1975. Ptnr. Baker & Botts, L.L.P., Houston, 1975—. Author: The Texas Homebuyer's Manual, 1986. Mem. Am. Coll. Real Estate Lawyers, State Bar Tex. (chmn. coun. real estate, probate, trust law sect. 1994-95), Houston Bar Assn. (chmn. real estate sect. 1989-90), Tex. Coll. Real Estate Lawyers, Houston Real Estate Lawyers Coun., Houston Club (mem. com. young mems. 1987). Episcopalian. Office: Baker & Botts LLP 910 Louisiana St Houston TX 77002

WRIGHT, ROBERT ROSS, III, law educator; b. Ft. Worth, Nov. 20, 1931; m. Susan Webber; children: Robert Ross IV, John, David, Robin. BA cum laude, U. Ark., 1953, JD, 1956; MA (grad. fellow), Duke U., 1954; SJD (law fellow), U. Wis., 1967. Bar: Ark. 1956, U.S. Supreme Ct. 1968, Okla. 1970. Instr. polit. sci. U. Ark., 1955-56; mem. firm Forrest City, Ark., 1956-58; partner firm Norton, Norton & Wright, Forrest City, 1959; asst. gen. counsel, asst. sec. Crossett Co., Ark.; atty. Crossett div. Ga.-Pacific Corp., 1960-63; asst. sec. Pub. Utilities Co., Crossett, Triangle Bag Co., Covington, Ky., 1960-62; mem. faculty law sch. U. Ark., 1963-70; asst. prof., dir. continuing legal edn. and research, then asst. dean U. Ark. (Little Rock div.), 1965-66, prof. law, 1967-70; vis. prof. law U. Iowa, 1969-70; prof. U. Okla., 1970-77; dean U. Okla. (Coll. Law); dir. U. Okla. (Law Center), 1970-76; vis. prof. U. Ark., Little Rock, 1976-77; Donaghey Disting. prof. U. Ark, 1977—; Ark. commr. Nat. Conf. Commrs. Uniform State Laws, 1967-70; past chmn. Com. Uniform Eminent Domain Code; past mem. Com. Uniform Probate Code, Ark. Gov.'s Ins. Study Commn.; chmn. Gov. Commn. on Uniform Probate Code; chmn. task force joint devel. Hwy. Research Bd.; vice chmn. Okla. Jud. Council, 1970-72, chmn., 1972-75; chmn. Okla. Center Criminal Justice, 1971-76. Author: Arkansas Eminent Domain Digest, 1964, Arkansas Probate Practice System, 1965, The Law of Airspace, 1968, Emerging Concepts in the Law of Airspace, 1969, Cases and Materials on Land Use, 3d edit., 1982, supplement, 1987, 4th edit., 1991, Uniform Probate Code Practice Manual, 1972, Model Airspace Code, 1973, Land Use in a Nutshell, 1978, 2d edit., 1985, 3d edit., 1994, The Arkansas Form Book, 1979, 2d edit., 1988, Zoning Law in Arkansas: A Comparative Analysis,

1980; contbr. numerous articles to legal jours. Mem. Little Rock Planning Commn., 1978-82, chmn., 1982. Named Ark. Man of Year Kappa Sigma, 1958. Fellow Am. Law Inst., Am. Coll. Probate Counsel (acad.); mem. ABA (chmn., exec. coun. gen. practice sect., former chmn. new pubs. editl. bd., sect. officers conf.), Ark. Bar Assn. (exec. coun. 1985-88, ho. of dels., life mem., chmn. eminent domain code com., past mem. com. new bar ctr., past chmn. preceptorship com., exec. com. young laywers sect.), Okla. Bar Assn. (past vice-chmn. legal internship com., former vice-chmn. gen. practice sect.), Pulaski County Bar Assn., Ark. Bar Found., U. Wis. Alumni Assn., Duke U. Alumni Assn., U. Ark. Alumni Assn., Order of Coif, Phi Beta Kappa, Phi Alpha Delta, Omicron Delta Kappa. Episcopalian. Home: 249 Pleasant Valley Dr Little Rock AR 72212-3170 Office: U Ark Law Sch 1201 McAlmont St Little Rock AR 72202-5142

WRIGHT, SUSAN WEBBER, judge; b. Texarkana, Ark., Aug. 22, 1948; d. Thomas Edward and Betty Jane (Gary) Webber; m. Robert Ross Wright, III, May 21, 1983; 1 child, Robin Elizabeth. BA, Randolph-Macon Woman's Coll., 1970; MPA, U. Ark., 1972, JD with high honors, 1975. Bar: Ark. 1975. Law clk. U.S. Ct. Appeals 8th Circuit, 1975-76; asst. prof. law U. Ark.-Little Rock, 1976-78, assoc. prof., 1978-83, prof., 1983-90, asst. dean, 1976-78; dist. judge U.S. Dist. Ct. (ea. dist.) Ark., Little Rock, 1990—; vis. assoc. prof. Ohio State U., Columbus, 1981, La. State U., Baton Rouge, 1982-83; mem. adv. com. U.S. Ct. Appeals 8th Circuit, St. Louis, 1983-88. Author: (with R. Wright) Land Use in a Nutshell, 1978, 2d edit., 1985; editor-in-chief Ark. Law Rev., 1975; contbr. articles to profl. jours. Mem. ABA, Ark. Bar Assn., Pulaski County Bar Assn., Ark. Assn. Women Lawyers (v.p. 1977-78). Episcopalian. Office: US Courthouse 600 W Capitol Ave Ste 302 Little Rock AR 72201-3323

WRIGHT, THOMAS HENRY, bishop; b. Wilmington, N.C., Oct. 16, 1904; s. John Maffitt and Josie Young (Whitaker) W.; m. Hannah Hagans Knowlton, Dec. 1, 1937; children—Thomas Henry, Hannah K., James K., John M. A.B., U. of South, 1926, D.D., 1946; B.D., Va. Theol. Sem., Alexandria, Va., 1930, D.D., 1946; D.D., Washington and Lee U., 1940, U. N.C., 1965. Clk. Standard Oil Co. of N.J., Wilmington, 1926-27; ordained to ministry P.E. Ch., 1929, nat. acting sec. of coll. work, 1933-34; Episcopal chaplain U. of N.C., 1931-32, Va. Mil. Inst., 1934-41, Washington and Lee U., 1934-41; rector Robert E. Lee Meml. Ch., Lexington, Va., 1934-41; dean Grace Cathedral, San Francisco, 1941-43; rector St. Mark's Ch., San Antonio, Tex., 1943-45; consecrated bishop of Diocese of East Carolina, St. James Ch., Wilmington, N.C., Oct. 1945; Pres. of Province.; U.S. rep. to World Christian Student Fed. Meeting, Holland, 1932; Regional dir. Ch. Soc. for Coll. Work; asso. mem. Forward Movement Commn., P.E. Ch.; chmn. overseas dept. Nat. Council of Episcopal Ch. Contbr. to jours. Trustee U. of South. Mem. Sigma Nu (former grand chaplain), Sigma Upsilon, Alpha Phi Epsilon; hon. mem. Omicron Delta Kappa. Democrat. Address: The Bishop's House 1625 Futch Creek Rd Wilmington NC 28405-9377

WRIGHT, WAYNE KENNETH, federal agency statistician; b. Chelsea, Mass., Jan. 26, 1944; s. Wayne K. and Louise Annette (Olson) W.; m. Sharon Kay Brown, Aug. 30, 1964 (div. 1974); 1 child, Trent; m. Linda Susan Berkel, Mar. 15, 1975 (div. 1979); 1 child, Stacey; m. Bonnie Sue Oberhelman, Apr. 3, 1982; 1 child, Forrest. BS in Sociology, U. Iowa, 1971; postgrad., U. North Iowa, 1971-72; cert., Atlanta U., 1988. Survey asst. Shive-Hall-Hattery Engring., Cedar Rapids, Iowa, 1962-66; chem. lab technician Wilson Packing Plant, Cedar Rapids, 1966-71; grad. rsch. asst. U. No. Iowa, Cedar Falls, 1971-72, grad. teaching asst., 1972-73; survey statistician U.S. Bur. Census, Kansas City, Kans., 1973-74, info. specialist, 1974-83; info. specialist U.S. Bur. Census, Charlotte, N.C., 1983-90; data specialist U.S. Bur. of Census, Charlotte, N.C., 1991—. Named Ky. Col., 1987; named Hon. Citizen, City of Beloit (Wis.), 1974. Fellow Alpha Kappa Delta. Lutheran. Home: 1417 Morrocroft Trl Gastonia NC 28054-6499 Office: US Bur Census 901 Center Park Dr Ste 106 Charlotte NC 28217-2935

WRIGHT, WILLIAM KRIEGER, psychology and economics educator, consultant, musician, realtor; b. Detroit, May 18, 1944; s. Edmund William and Florence Ruth (Krieger) W.; m. Mary Follett, Dec. 26, 1976; children: Louis Hawn, Lisa Hawn Lomax. BA, U. Mich., 1966; MA, Mich. State U., 1970, postgrad., 1971-76, 89-90. Licensed realtor Mich., Fla.; life, health, variable annuities, Fla. Instr. econ., psychology Okemos (Mich.) H.S., 1967-90; instr. social sci., econ. Lansing (Mich.) C.C., 1990-92; prof. econ., psychology Edison C.C., Ft. Myers, Fla., 1992—; realtor Punta Gorda, Fla., 1994—; counselor Lansing C.C., 1971-72; counselor Mich. State U., 1974-75, instr. psychology, 1975-77; instr. psychology Edison C.C., 1988; fin. cons. tchrs. Mich., 1980-92; fin. rep. Pub. Employees Svc. Co., 1992—; mem. Joint Coun. Econ. Edn.; raltor, Port Charlotte, Fla., 1988. Piano player clubs, restaurants, Mich., Fla., 1960—. Mem. APA, Am. Econ. Assn. Home: 101 Maria Ct Punta Gorda FL 33950-5126 Office: Edison C C 3011 Coll Pky Fort Myers FL 33904

WRIGHT, WILLIAM MICHAEL, sales executive; b. Rome, Ga., July 25, 1955; s. William Howard and Clara Jane (Duffey) W.; m. Deborah Lynn Chandler, Sept. 7, 1985; children: Vanessa Michele, Lauren Victoria. BBA in Mgmt., Kennesaw State Coll., 1987. Owner, pres. Finewear Inc., Fayetteville, Ga., 1974—; v.p. sales & mktg. Textile Enterprises Inc., Whitesburg, Ga., 1978-82; exec. v.p. U.S. div. Splash Products Inc., Faringdon, England, 1982-83; v.p., gen. mgr. Trans Pak, Atlanta, 1983-91; coo/gen. mgr. Creative Products, Inc., Fairburn, Ga., 1991-92; sales mgr. Star Packaging Corp., College Park, Ga., 1992—. Eagle Scout Boy Scouts Am., 1971; mem. Exec. Round. Table, Marietta, 1985-87; sponsor Silver Fox Girls Softball Team, Whitesburg, Ga., 1981-82; pres. Breckenridge Homeowners Assn. Named to the Nat. Deans List of Colls. & Univs., Ednl. Communications, 1985-86. Mem. Kennesaw Ambassador Corps (prs. 1986-87), Kennesaw State Coll. Alumni Assn., Cobb County C. of C., Inst. Packaging Profls. Republican. Methodist. Home: 135 Breckenridge Way Fayetteville GA 30214-3244 Office: Star Packaging Corp 45385 Circle College Park GA 30349

WROBLE, ARTHUR GERARD, lawyer; b. Taylor, Pa., Jan. 21, 1948; s. Arthur S. and Sophia P. Wroble; m. Mary Ellen Sheehan, Nov. 19, 1977; children: Sophia Ann, Sarah Jean, Stacey Margaret. BSBA with honors, U. Fla., 1970, MBA, 1971, JD, 1973. Bar: Fla. 1973, U.S. Ct. Appeals (5th cir.) 1974, U.S. Ct. Appeals (11th cir.) 1981, U.S. Dist. Ct. (so. dist.) Fla. 1974, U.S. Dist. Ct. (mid. dist.) Fla. 1982, U.S. Dist. Ct. (no. dist.) Fla. 1986, U.S. Army Ct. Mil. Rev. 1989, U.S. Ct. Mil. Appeals, 1990, U.S. Supreme Ct., 1976. Ptnr. Burns, Middleton, Farrell & Faust (now Steel, Hector, Davis, Burns & Middleton), Palm Beach, Fla., 1973-82; ptnr. Wolf, Block, Schorr & Solis, Cohen, Phila. and West Palm Beach, Fla., 1982-87, Scott, Royce, Harris & Bryan, P.A., Palm Beach, 1987-89, Grantham and Wroble, P.A., Lake Worth, 1989-92; prin. Arthur G. Wroble, P.A., West Palm Beach, 1992—; mem. 15th Jud. Cir. Ct. Nominating Commn., 1979-83; mem. U. Fla. Law Ctr. Council, 1981-84, U.S. Magistrate Merit Selection Panel, So. dist. Fla., 1987; mem. adv. bd. alternative sentencing program Palm Beach County Pub. Defender's Office; adj. instr. bus. law Coll. of Boca Raton (now Lynn U.), 1988. Contbr. articles to profl. jours. Served to lt. col. JAG, USAR, 1990-91. Named Eagle Scout, Boy Scouts Am., 1962. Mem. ABA, Fla. Bar (bd. govs. young lawyers sect. 1979-83, bd. govs. 1985-89), Palm Beach County Bar Assn. (pres. young lawyers sect. 1978-79, bd. dirs. 1979-81, sec.-treas. 1981-83, pres. 1984-85), Fla. Bar Found. (bd. dirs. 1990-93), Fla. Assn. Women Lawyers, Fla. Council Bar Assn. Pres. (bd. dirs. 1986-92), Guild Cath. Lawyers Diocese Palm Beach, Inc. (pres. 1980-81, bd. dirs. 1981—, Monsignor Jeremiah P. O'Mahoney Outstanding Lawyer award 1993), Legal Aid Soc. Palm Beach County, Inc. (bd. dirs. 1981—), Univ. Fla. Alumni Assn. Palm Beach County Club (pres. 1983-84), Kiwanis (pres. 1980-81, pres. West Palm Beach found. 1989—, dir. 1981—, Citizen of Yr. 1994), KC (grand knight 1978-79). Roman Catholic. Home: 7645 Clarke Rd West Palm Beach FL 33406-8709 Office: 1615 Forum Pl West Palm Beach FL 33401-2320

WU, CHIEN-YUN (JENNIE WU), nursing educator; b. People's Republic China, Dec. 5, 1943; d. Wen-yu and Chao-yu (Cheng) Yuan; m. Chieh Wu, Dec. 4, 1966; children: Lawrence, David, James. Diploma, Taiwan Nat. Jr. Coll. Nursing, Taipei, 1964; BSN, Villanova U., 1973; MS in Nursing, George Mason U., Fairfax, Va., 1982, PhD, 1990. RN, Va.; cert. critical care nurse, in nursing edn. Dir. insvc. edn. Cherry Hill (N.J.) Med. Ctr., 1973-75; supr. Magee Rehab. Ctr., Phila., 1976; critical care nurse clinician Fair Oaks Hosp., Fairfax, 1983-91; assoc. prof. med.-surg. nursing, pathophysiology, pharm., nursing rschr. George Mason U., 1990—; rschr. in nursing ednl. program evaluation and cardiopulmonary nursing; WHO and UNDP cons. on nursing edn. and nursing practice reform in China; initiator Systematic Approach to Holistic Nursing Care-Model Units Establishment, China, 1994—. Nurse cons. nursing ednl. program in China. Recipient Outstanding Undergrad. Faculty award George Mason U. Coll. Nursing, 1990, Medallion for Disting. Contbns. to Profession Villanova U., 1994. Mem. ANA, Chinese Nurses Assn. (hon. mem.), Nightingale Soc., Sigma Theta Tau. Home: 5813 Hampton Forest Way Fairfax VA 22030-7254

WU, GARY G., petroleum engineer, consultant; b. Beijing, People's Republic of China, Oct. 28, 1960; came to U.S., 1985; s. Baoshan Wu and Fengzi Yu; m. Ding Zhu, Dec. 27, 1992; children: Woody, Andrew. BS in Petroleum, China Petroleum U., Beijing, 1982; MS in Petroleum, U. Tex., 1988, PhD in Petroleum, 1992. Registered profl. engr., Tex. Process engr. China Oil Devel. Co., Beijing, 1982-83; project mgr. China Nat. Offshore Oil Co., Beijing, 1983-85; rsch. asst. U. Tex., Austin, 1986-90; rsch. engr. Texaco Inc., Houston, 1990-91; rsch. asst. U. Tex., Austin, 1991-92; project scientist Texaco Inc., Houston, 1992—; cons. U. Tex., Austin, 1993-94. Contbr. articles to profl. jours. and procs. Mem. Soc. Petroleum Engrs. (assoc. mem., chmn. student chpt. 1988-89, author procs. 1994). Home: 19831 Emerald Springs Houston TX 77094 Office: Texaco-EPTD 3901 Briarpark Houston TX 77042

WU, GUOYAO, nutrition, physiology, and animal science educator; b. China, July 28, 1962; s. Fanjiu Wu and Meixiao Huang; m. Yan Chen, Aug. 7, 1995. BS in Animal Sci., South China Agrl. U., 1982; MS in Animal Nutrition, Beijing (People's Republic of China) Agrl. U., 1984; MS in Animal Biochemistry, U. Alberta, Can., 1986, PhD in Animal Biochemistry, 1989; postgrad. in metabolism/diabetes, McGill U., Mont., Can., 1989-91; postgrad. in biochemistry, Meml. U. Nfld., Can., 1991. Grad. teaching asst. U. Alberta, 1985-88; postdoctoral rschr. Royal Victoria Hosp., McGill U., 1989-91, Meml. U. Newfoundland, 1991; asst. prof. dept. animal sci. and faculty nutrition Tex. A&M U., College Station, 1991-96; assoc. prof. Tex. A&M U., 1996—. Reviewer Amino Acids, Am. Jour. Clin. Nutrition, Am. Jour. Physiology, Analytical Biochemistry, Can. Jour. Physiology and Pharmacology, Diabetes, Diabetologia, Jour. Animal Sci., Jour. Nutrition, Jour. Nutritional Biochemistry, Jour. Cellular Physiology, Metabolism, Poultry Sci., Can. Diabetes Assn., Med. Rsch. Coun. Can., U. Toronto Banting and Best Ctr., Can.; editl. advisor Biochem. Jour., 1993-96; contbr. articles to profl. jours. Grantee Tex. A&M U., 1992—, Ajinomoto Inc., Japan, 1992, USDA, 1992—, Houston Livestock Show and Rodeo, 1992-95, Am. Heart Assn., 1995—; nat. scholarship for grad. studies abroad Ministry Edn. China, 1984-86, grad. tchg. assistantship U. Alta., 1985-88, dissertation fellowship, 1989, Ctr. Rsch. Fund award, 1988, Andrew Stewart Grad. prize, 1989, U. Alberta, Can. Rsch. Inst. fellowship Royal Victoria Hosp., 1988, fellowship Can. Diabetes Assn., 1989, Med. Rsch. Coun. Can. fellow, 1989-91. Mem. AAAS, Am. Diabetes Assn., Am. Inst. Nutrition, Am. Physiol. Soc., Am. Soc. Animal Sci., Biochem. Soc. U.K., Can. Soc. Nutritional Scis., Juv. Diabetes Found. Internat. (grantee 1992-94). Home: 4707 Shoal Creek Dr College Station TX 77845 Office: Tex A&M Univ Dept Animal Sci College Station TX 77843

WU, WILLIAM CHIEN LIN, internist; b. Bac Lieu, Vietnam, July 24, 1955; came to U.S., 1983.; s. Ban Ngo and Hue Lien; m. Crystal Hwang, 1983; children: Albert, James. MD, Kao Hsiung (Taiwan) Med. Coll., 1982; MPH, Johns Hopkins U., 1984. Cert. in internal medicine and cardiovasc. disease. Staff physician U. Ark. for Med. Scis., Little Rock, 1990-91; clin. instr. U. Tex., San Antonio, 1995—; pvt. practice San Antonio, 1990—; cons. in cardiology. Fellow Am. Coll. Cardiology; mem. ACP. Home: 13910 Bluff Wind San Antonio TX 78216-7915 Office: Cen Cardiovascular Clin 927 McCullough Ave San Antonio TX 78215

WU, YING-CHAN FRED, electrical engineer; b. Taipei, Taiwan, Feb. 24, 1958; came to U.S., 1983; s. Tieh-Hui and Hui-Jen (HWang) W.; m. Li-Chu Wang, Dec. 27, 1986. BSEE, Tatung Inst. Tech., 1980; MSEE, Iowa State U., 1984, PhD in Computer Engring., 1988. Asst. prof. U. Miami (Fla.), 1988-96; advanced engr. Westinghouse Electric Corp., Orlando, Fla., 1996—. Contbr. papers to profl. publs. Mem. IEEE, Assn. Computing Machinery. Office: Westinghouse Electric Corp PG TD/TD Mail Code 200 4400 Alafaya Tr Orlando FL 32826-2399

WUEBBELS, THERESA ELIZABETH, visual art educator; b. Breese, Ill., Nov. 8, 1950; d. Wilson Theodore and Selma Maria (Haake) W. BA, Notre Dame Coll., St. Louis, 1972; postgrad., Boston Coll., 1976-79, Pembroke State U., 1988. Teaching nun Sch. Sisters of Notre Dame, St. Louis, 1969-80; art tchr. Cathedral Sch., Belleville, Ill., 1972-76, Sacred Heart Sch., Fort Madison, Iowa, 1976-80; missionary sister Little Sisters of Jesus, 1980-87; art tchr. Balden County Schs., Clarkton, N.C., 1989—; visual art tchrs. coord. Bladen County Schs., Elizabethtown, N.C., 1991—. Coord. Celebration of the Arts Festival for Bladen County, 1992—; task force mem. founding Clarkton Sch. Discovery, Clarkton, N.C., 1993-94. Named Tchr. of Yr. Clarkton Sch. of Discovery, 1992-93, 93-94, 94-95. Mem. N.C. Art Edn. Assn., Nat. Art Edn. Assn., Visual Art Guild. Roman Catholic. Home: 653 Poe Elkins Rd Clarkton NC 28433-7243 Office: Clarkton Sch Discovery PO Box 127 Clarkton NC 28433-0127

WUEBKER, VIRGINIA ANN, retired elementary school educator, program director; b. Waco, Tex., Oct. 29, 1928; d. Oliver Ernest and Bertha Elizabeth Blume; m. William Herbert Wuebker, Sept. 21, 1954; children: Robin Battershell, Bonnie, Cardinal. BS in Edn., Baylor U., 1951, MS in Edn., 1957. Cert. elem. tchr., Tex. Primary tchr. Connally Ind. Sch., Lacy-Lakeview, Tex., 1958-60, Midway Ind. Sch., Woodway, Tex., 1960-65; 2d, 4th grade tchr. Robinson (Tex.) Sch., 1966-89; ret. from teaching, 1989; dir. Summer Reading Inst., Waco, Tex., 1980—; dir. Univ. Interscholastic Competition, Waco, West, Whitney, Tex., 1987-89; tchr. evaluator Robinson Ind. Sch. Dist., 1982-83; supr. student tchrs. Baylor U., Waco, 1990-91. Author: You, Your Child and Reading, 1975, Mud Is Nice, 1994, The Tale of Yip, 1994, Blockhead, 1994; contbr. column to newspaper publs. Pres. C. of C., Robinson, 1970, Cemetery Assn., Robinson, 1974; founder Sr. Citizens Ctr., Robinson, 1966. Mem. NEA, Tex. State Tchrs. Assn., Robinson PTA, Tex. Reading Coun., Internat. Reading Assn., Tex. Classroom Tchrs. Assn. United Ch. of Christ. Home: 604 N Robinson Dr Waco TX 76706-5312

WUENSCHE, VERNON EDGAR, construction company executive; b. Elgin, Tex., Nov. 25, 1945; s. Harry Edwin Jacob and Emma Martha (Dube) W. BBA, U. Tex., 1967, MBA, 1968. CPA, Tex. Audit asst. Arthur Andersen & Co., Houston, 1968-70; tax cons. Peat Marwick Mitchell & Co., Houston, 1970; cost acct. Bemis Bros. Bag Co., Houston, 1970-71; asst. controller Prodn. Systems Internat., Inc., Houston, 1971-72; controller Am. Housing Guild, Inc., Houston, 1972-73; controller Wood Bros. Homes, Inc., Houston, Dallas, 1973-75, Oklahoma City, 1973-75; pres., founder, custom home builder Woodmark Homes, Inc., Houston, Dallas, Austin, Tex., 1975—. Election judge Harris County, Houston, 1978, Rep. state del., Tex., 1978, 80, 94, 96; elder Meml. Luth. Ch., Houston, 1982—; finisher marathon, Galveston, Tex., 1970, 71; founder Texans for Efficiency in Govt., 1991; dir. Houston Entrepreneurs Forum. With USAR, 1968-74. Mem. Alley Theater Guild, Tex. Wendish Heritage Soc., U. Tex. Ex-Students Assn., Rice Design Alliance, Mus. of Fine Arts, Arts Symposium of Houston, Phi Kappa Phi, Beta Gamma Sigma. Home: 14211 Swiss Hill Dr Houston TX 77077-1029

WUETIG, JOYCE LINDA, realtor; b. Little Rock, Feb. 11, 1938; d. John Clifford and Viva Emily (Summerhill) Dilbeck; m. James Russell McKinney, Aug. 30, 1958 (div. Sept. 1981); children: Melissa Ellen, James Blake; m. Frederick Lewis Wuetig, June 1, 1985. BA, Hendrix Coll., 1959; postgrad., Incarnate Word Coll., 1970-072. Cert. residential specialist; lic. real estate broker, Tex., Ark. Tchr. Little Rock Sch. Dist., 1959-62; fashion cons. Doncaster, Inc., San Antonio, 1975-83; tchr. Edgewood Ind. Sch. Dist., San Antonio, 1982-83; sales assoc. Dijon Plaza Realtors, San Antonio, 1978-83; relocation specialist HEB Grocery Co., San Antonio, 1981-82; asst. v.p. Independence Fed. Bank, Little Rock, 1984-85; sales assoc. Agar Realtors, Little Rock, 1986-89; broker assoc., cert. residential specialist McKay & Co. Residential Realtors, Little Rock, 1989—. Mem. com. Southwest Found. Forum, San Antonio, 1975-81; chmn. San Antonio Kitchen Tour, 1977-80; host mother, area activities chmn. Am. Field Svc., San Antonio, 1975-76, 77-78; life mem. Tex. PTA. Mem. AAUW, DAR, Nat. Assn. Realtors, Ark. Realtors Assn., Little Rock Realtors Assn., Little Rock Realtors Million Dollar Club (life). Methodist. Home: 20 Inverness Cir Little Rock AR 72212-2923

WUICHET, JOHN W., policy analyst; b. Atlanta, Oct. 31, 1967; s. Louis and Janet Wuichet. BA in Philosophy with honors, Oglethorpe U., 1990; MS in Environ. Pub. Policy, Ga. Inst. Tech., 1995. Rschr. Emory U., Atlanta, 1990-92, Ga. Inst. Tech., Atlanta, 1992-93; assoc. fellow Office of Asst. Sec. of Army Army Environ. Policy Inst., Atlanta, 1993—. Contbr. chpt., editor volume: Ethics on the Ark: Zoos, Animal Welfare, and Wildlife Conservation, 1995. Bd. dirs., mem. High Meadows Sch., Roswell, Ga., 1996—; bd. trustees, student rep. Oglethorpe U., Atlanta, 1989-90. Lowry Endowed scholar, 1990, Ty Cobb scholar, 1990. Mem. AAAS, Internat. Soc. for Ecosys. Health, Soc. Conservation Biology. Home: 397 Richards St NW Atlanta GA 30318 Office: US Army Environ Policy Inst 430 10th St NW Atlanta GA 30318

WUNDERLICH, GENE LEE, economist; b. Bottineau, N.D., Sept. 29, 1928; s. Arnold Arthur and Evelyn (Olson) W.; m. Gooloo Sahiar, Mar. 19, 1957; children: Karl, Roshna. BS, U. N.D., 1949; MS, Iowa State U., 1951, PhD, 1955 Economist USDA, Washington, 1955-95; advisor Bulgarian Ministry Agr., 1992, Armenian Ministry Agr., 1993, Ukrainian Ministry Agr., 1993; cons. World Bank, Moldova, 1994, cons. USAID, Ukraine, 1996. Editor Jour. Agrl. Econs. Rsch., 1987-92; author: Land Ownership and Taxation in American Agriculture, 1993, Agricultural Landownership in Transitional Economies, 1995; contbr. chpts. to books and numerous articles to profl. jours. Recipient Superior Svc. award USDA, 1976, 93, award Econ. Rsch. Svc., 1992, 93; Fulbright scholar Bombay U., 1953-54, 62-63; fellow Yale U. Law Sch., 1966-67. Mem. Am. Econ. Assn., Am. Agrl. Econs. Assn., Internat. Assn. Agrl. Econs. Home: 4704 Randolph Ct Annandale VA 22003-6216

WURTH, SUSAN WINSETT, medical/surgical nurse; b. McKenzie, Tenn., Dec. 17, 1953; d. James Edward and Betty Arnold (Winsett) Paris; m. Michael Wurth, Sept. 21, 1974; children: Jonathan Michael, Brandi Michelle. AS, Paducah (Ky.) Community Coll., 1974. Staff nurse, team leader Community Hosp., Mayfield, Ky., 1974-76; staff nurse, team leader Western Bapt. Hosp. Paducah, 1976-87, day charge nurse orthopaedic and urology unit, 1987-96, case mgr., 1996—; speaker in field; coord. Prostate Support Group, chairperson edn. com., 1992—. Developed patient care pathways for total knee, total hip and radical prostatectomy, 1994, 95. Home: 7305 Wurth Rd Paducah KY 42001

WURZ, JOHN ARNOLD, architect; b. Clarksdale, Miss., Feb. 11, 1936; s. Arnold George and Mildred (Whittle) W.; BS, Ga. Inst. Tech., 1958, BArch, 1959; children: Valli Elizabeth, Susan Priscilla, John Arnold, Corbett Ann, Charles W. Project mgr. Rich's, Inc., Atlanta, 1962-63; project mgr. Heery & Heery Architects & Engrs., Atlanta, 1963-65, assoc. architect, 1965-67, ptnr., 1967-77; v.p. Cadre Corp., 1977-80; founder, pres., chief exec. officer Wurz Wisecarver & Pruett, Inc., Architects, 1980-90, dir. aviation design Sverdrup Corp., 1991-93, v.p., gen. mgr. Batson Cook, Atlanta, 1993—. Bldg. research adv. bd. Nat. Acad. Sci., 1979-82. Bd. dirs., Coll. Architecture Ga. Inst. Tech., 1987-90. Served to capt. USAF, 1959-62, Res., 1962-72. Registered architect, 20 states and U.K. Mem. Atlanta Art Assn., Bldg. Futures Coun. (dir. 1988—), Ga. Indsl. Devel. Assn., Ga. Tech. Alumni Assn., AIA, Sigma Nu Alumni Assn. Club: Cherokee Town and Country (bd. dirs. 1984-87), Phoenix Soc. Address: 32 Paces West Pl NW Atlanta GA 30327-2730 Office: Batson Cook Co 700 Galleria Pky Atlanta GA 30339

WYANT, MICHAEL BENJAMIN, nuclear pharmacist; b. Niles, Mich., Dec. 10, 1957 s. Victor L. and Donna J. (Fraze) W.; m. Mary Ann Woerner, Sept. 10, 1988. AS, South Western Mich. Coll., 1978; BS in Pharmacy, Ferris State Coll., 1981. Pharmacy mgr. Syncor Internat. Corp., Louisville, 1982—; pres. Ky. Bd. of Pharmacy, Frankfort. Mem. Ky. Pharmacists Assn., Jefferson County Acad. Pharmacists, Kappa Psi. Office: Syncor Internat Corp 831 S 6th St Louisville KY 40203-2123

WYATT, DORIS FAY CHAPMAN, English language educator; b. Del Rio, Tex., July 12, 1935; d. Cecil Cornelius and Lola Wade (Veazey) Chapman; m. Jimmy Trueman Wyatt, June 2, 1956 (div. Nov. 1977); children: Abra Natasha Smith, Kent Colin Wyatt, Garrett Bret Wyatt. BS in Edn., S.W. Tex. State U., 1956; MA in English, U. North Tex., 1969; MA in Counseling, East Tenn. State U., 1983. Cert. profl. tchr. career ladder III, Tenn.; cert. marriage and family therapist. Elem. tchr. Clover Pk. Pub. Schs., Tacoma, 1957-58; jr. high reading tchr. Levelland (Tex.) Pub. Schs., 1964-67; tchr. English Denton (Tex.) Pub. Schs., 1967-70; tchr. reading & English Vets. Upward Bound, East Tenn. State U., Johnson City, 1981-87; tchr. English Johnson City (Tenn.) Pub. Schs., 1970—; beauty cons. Mary Kay Cosmetics, Johnson City, 1971-95; adj. faculty mem. Tusculum Coll., Greeneville, Tenn., 1993—; pine plantation owner. Area dir. People-to-People Student Ambassador Program, Washington County, Tenn., 1975-94, tchr.-leader, Johnson City, 1974-84. Named to Nat. Dean's list, 1982-83. Mem. NEA, AAUW, Johnson City Edn. Assn. (pres., bd. dirs. 1989-90), Tenn. Edn. Assn., Nat. Coun. Tchrs. English, Alpha Delta Kappa (pres. 1994-96), Phi Kappa Phi. Democrat. Methodist. Home: 1805 Sundale Rd Johnson City TN 37604-3023 Office: Johnson City Pub Schs Sci Hill High Sch John Exum Pky Johnson City TN 37604-4553

WYATT, EDWARD AVERY, V, city manager; b. Petersburg, Va., Nov. 1, 1941; s. Edward Avery and Martha Vaughan (Seabury) W.; AS in Bus. Bluefield Coll.; BS in Bus., Pub. Adminstrn., Va. Poly. Inst., 1964; M.Commerce, U. Richmond, 1969; MA in Polit. Sci., Appalachian State U., 1977; m. Regina Helen Stec, Aug. 23, 1969; children: Edward Avery VI, Stephen Alexander, Kent Seabury. Chief gen. svc., City of Petersburg, Va., 1966-67, asst. to city mgr., Petersburg, 1967-70; city mgr., Washington, N.C., 1970-73, Morganton, N.C., 1973-78, Greenville, N.C., 1978-82, Fairfax, Va., 1982-91, Wilson, N.C., 1991—; adj. lectr. George E. Mason U. Bus. Sch., 1985-86; bd. dirs. Electricities of N.C.; commr. Ea. N.C. Mcpl. Power Agy. Chmn. N.C. Code Ofcls. Qualification Bd., 1980-82; mem. adv. bd. Wilson Salvation Army, 1992—; bd. dirs. Wilson United Fund. Served with USNG and USAR, 1964-70. Paul Harris fellow Rotary Internat.; Dennis Duffey Meml. award Fairfax Police Youth Club. Mem. ASPA (ea. N.C. chpt.), Internat. City Mgmt. Assn. (endowment com., chair 1991-92, coun. mgr. Flan task force, 1993-94), Va. Local Govt. Mgmt. Assn. (pres. 1989-90), N.C. City/ County Mgmt. Assn., Ea. N.C. C. of C. (mem. exec. com., vice chair mcpl. membership), Soc. Cincinnati in Va., Descendants of Francis Epes of Va. (v.p.), Wilson Rotary (bd. dirs.). Contbr. numerous articles to profl. jours. and newsletters. Home: 1307 Waverly Rd NW Wilson NC 27896 Office: City of Wilson PO Box 10 Wilson NC 27896-0010

WYATT, FOREST KENT, university president; b. Berea, Ky., May 27, 1934; s. Forest E. and Almeda (Hymer) W.; m. Janice Collins, Mar. 4, 1956; children: Tara Janice Wyatt Mounger, Elizabeth Pharr Wyatt Mitchell. BS in Edn., Delta State U., Cleveland, Miss., 1956; MEd, U. So. Miss., 1960; EdD, U. Miss., 1970; postgrad., Harvard Inst. Ednl. Mgmt., 1975. Instr., coach Univ. Mil. Sch., Mobile, Ala., 1956-60; tchr., adminstr. Bolivar County dist. schs., Cleveland, Miss., 1960-64; alumni sec. Delta State U., 1964-69, adminstrv. asst. to pres., dir. adminstrv. services, asso. prof. edn., 1969-75, pres., 1975—; dir. Grenada Bank. Contbr. articles to profl. jours. Past bd. dirs. United Givers Fund, Cleveland Beautification Commn.; past bd. dirs., past v.p. Miss. Com. for Humanities, Delta Area coun. Boy Scouts Am. Friends of State Libr. Commn.; past chmn. Indsl. Devel. Found.; past pres. Cleveland Crosstie Arts Coun.; past trustee So. Bapt. Theol. Sem.; past bd. dirs. Miss. Econ. Coun.; past pres. Gulf South Conf.; bd. dirs. Southeastern Regional Vision for Edn. With U.S. Army, 1957-58. Recipient Kossman award for Outstanding Community Svc. C. of C., 1987. Mem. Miss. Assn. Educators, Am. Coun. on Edn. (mem. com. on govtl. rels.), Am. Coun. on Tchrs. Edn., Miss. Assn. Sch. Adminstrs., Am. Assn. State Colls. and Univs. (chmn. athletic com., com. governance, com. profl. devel. task force on athletics), NCAA (coun., past chmn. student-athlete adv. com., pres's. commn., gender equity com., exec. dir. search com., chmn. athletics cert. study com. divsn. II), Miss. Assn. Colls. (past pres.), So. Assn. Colls. and Schs. (Commn. on Colls.), Inter-Alumni Coun., Cleve. C. of C. (past pres.), Cleve. Country Club (dir.), Lions, Phi Delta Kappa, Omicron Delta Kappa, Kappa Delta Pi. Address: Delta State U Cleveland MS 38733

WYATT, JOE BILLY, academic administrator; b. Tyler, Tex., July 21, 1935; s. Joe and Fay (Pinkerton) W.; m. Faye Hocutt, July 21, 1956; children: Joseph Robert, Sandra Faye. B.A., U. Tex., 1956; M.A., Tex. Christian U., 1960. Systems engr. Gen. Dynamics Corp., 1956-65; mgr. Digital Computer Lab., 1961-65; dir. computer ctr., assoc. prof. computer sci. U. Houston, 1965-72; dir. Office Info. Tech. Harvard U., 1972-76, sr. lectr. computer sci., 1972-82, v.p. adminstrn., 1976-82; chancellor Vanderbilt U., Nashville, 1982—; mem. faculty Kennedy Sch. of Harvard U., 1976-82; bd. dirs., chmn. com. on math/sci., Am. Coun. of Edn.; bd. dirs. Reynolds Metals Co., SONAT Corp., Advanced Networking and Sys. Corp. Author (with others) Financial Planning Models for Colleges and Universities, 1979; editor-in chief: Jour. Applied Mgmt. Systems, 1983; contbr. articles to profl. jours.; patentee in field of data processing. Trustee Harvard U. Press, 1976-83, pres., 1975-76, chmn. bd., 1976-79; trustee EDUCOM, Princeton, N.J., 1973-81, Leadership Nashville, 1983-93; bd. dirs. Nashville Inst. Arts, 1982-83, Ingram Industries, 1990—; chmn. adv. com. IST, NSF, 1978-85; vice chmn. bd. Mass. Tech. Devel. Corp., Boston, 1977-83; mem. Coun. Competitiveness; fellow Gallaudet Coll., 1981-83; mem. alumni bd. dirs. Harvard Bus. Sch., 1982-92. Recipient award for exemplary leadership CAUSE, Hilton Head, S.C., 1982, Nat. Tree of Life award Jewish Nat. Fund, 1988; named Outstanding Tennessean Gov. of Tenn., 1986. Fellow AAAS; mem. IEEE, Assn. Am. Univs. (chair exec. com. 1990-91), Hosp. Corp. Am. (bd. dirs. 1984-89), Nat. Assn. Ind. Colls. and Univs. (policy bd. 1980-82), Am. Coun. edn. (chair adv. com. on tech. edn. 1980-81, bd. dirs. 1990-92), Assn. Computing Machinery (pres. Dallas and Ft. Worth chpt. 1963-65), U. Rsch. Assn. (bd. trustees 1988—), So. U. Rsch. Assn., Inc. (chmn. coun. pres. 1988-89), Bus. Higher Edn. Forum (exec. com. 1990-93), Aircraft Owners and Pilots Assn., Nashville C. of C. (bd. dirs. 1983-86, pres.-elect 1995), Experimental Aircraft Assn. (pres. adv. com.), Govt. Univ. Industry Rsch. Roundtable, Sigma Xi, Beta Gamma Sigma, Phi Beta Kappa (hon.), Harvard Club (N.Y.C.). Methodist. Office: Vanderbilt U Office of Chancellor 211 Kirkland Hall Nashville TN 37240*

WYATT, LESLIE, academic administrator; m. Jeanne Cogburn; children: Cathey, Will, Betsy. BA, Abilene Christian U.; BFA in Studio Graphic Arts, U. Tex., MFA in Mus. Edn., PhD in Edn. Assoc. dean Coll. Fine Arts U. Tex.; vice chancellor univ. advancement, dean Coll. Fine Arts U. Ark., Little Rock; vice chancellor exec. affairs U. Miss.; pres. Ark. State U., 1995—. Bd. dirs. Jonesboro Indsl. Devel. Corp., United Way of Jonesboro; chmn. St. Bernards Regional Med. Ctr. Heart Walk. Mem. Greater Jonesboro C. of C. (bd. dirs.). Office: Office of Pres PO Box 10 State University AR 72467

WYATT, MARSHA KAPNICKY, sales executive; b. Morgantown, W.Va., Oct. 7, 1956; d. Paul Nicholas and Iris Kathleen (Kelly) Kapnicky; m. Royce J. Watts, II, July 29, 1978 (div. Sept. 1981); m. A. James Wyatt, Jr., Jan. 7, 1984. BS in Journalism, W.Va. U., 1978. Sales rep., R.L. Polk Co., Richmond and Atlanta, 1978-79; sales rep. Designers Color, Inc., Atlanta, 1979-84; v.p. sales Wace The Imaging Network, Atlanta, 1984—. Mem. Atlanta Print Prodn. Assn., Nat. Assn. Female Execs., Atlanta Advt. Club (bd. dirs.), W.Va. U. Alumni Assn. Home: 3355 Floral Ct Suwanee GA 30174-2833 Office: Wace Atlanta 3135 Presidential Dr Atlanta GA 30340

WYATT, OSCAR SHERMAN, JR., energy company executive; b. Beaumont, Tex., July 11, 1924; s. Oscar Sherman Sr. and Eva (Coday) W.; m. Lynn Sakowitz; children: Carl, Steven, Douglas, Oscar Sherman III, Brad. BS in Mech. Engring., Tex. Agrl. and Mech. Coll., 1949. With Kerr-McGee Co., 1949, Reed Roller Bit Co., 1949-51; ptnr. Wymore Oil Co., 1951-55; founder Coastal Corp., Corpus Christi, Tex., 1955; now chmn. bd. Coastal Corp., Houston. Served with USAAF, World War II. Office: Coastal Corp Coastal Tower 9 Greenway Plz Houston TX 77046

WYATT, ROBERT LEE, IV, lawyer; b. Las Cruces, N.Mex., Mar. 9, 1964; s. Robert Lee III and Louise Carole (Bard) W. BS, Southeastern Okla. State U., 1986; JD, U. Okla., 1989. Bar: Okla. 1989, U.S. Dist. Ct. (we. dist.) Okla. 1990, U.S. Ct. Appeals (10th cir.) 1990, U.S. Dist. Ct. (no. dist.) Okla. 1991, U.S. Ct. Appeals (8th cir.) 1991, U.S. Supreme Ct. 1993. Intern Okla. State Bur. Investigation, Oklahoma City, 1988-89, guest lectr., 1989; dep. spl. counsel Gov. of Okla., 1995; atty. Jones, Wyatt & Roberts, Enid, Okla., 1989—. Mem. ABA (mem. criminal & litigation sects.), Okla. Bar Assn. (mem. ins., family and litigation sects.), Garfield County Bar Assn., Okla. Criminal Def. Lawyers Assn., Nat. Inst. for Trial Advocacy, Phi Delta Phi, Alpha Chi. Democrat. Baptist. Home: 2430 Sherwood Dr Enid OK 73703 Office: Jones Wyatt & Roberts 114 E Broadway Enid OK 73701

WYATT-BROWN, ANNE MARBURY, linguistics educator; b. Balt., Apr. 8, 1939; d. William Luke and Natalie Ingraham (Jewett) Marbury; m. Bertram Wyatt-Brown, June 30, 1962; children: Laura Mathews (dec.), Natalie Ingraham. AB, Radcliffe Coll., 1961; MAT, Johns Hopkins U., 1962; PhD in English, Case Western Res. U., 1972. Instr. English Cleve. Inst. Art, 1974-77, assoc. prof., 1978-83; lectr. in linguistics U. Fla., Gainesville, 1983-89, asst. in linguistics, 1989-92, asst. prof., 1992-96, assoc. prof., 1996—; part time instr. English Colo. State U., Ft. Collins, 1962-64, U. Colo., Boulder, 1964-66; adj. lectr. Cleve. State U., 1980; adj. asst. prof. Case Western Res. U., 1982-83. Author: Barbara Pym: A Critical Biography, 1992; editor: (with Janice Rossen) Aging and Gender in Literature: Studies in Creativity, 1993; editor Age Studies, Univ. Press of Va., Charlottesville, 1993—. Democrat. Episcopalian. Home: 3201 NW 18th Ave Gainesville FL 32605-3705 Office: U Fla Program in Linguistics PO Box 11545 # U Gainesville FL 32611-5454

WYCHE, BRADFORD WHEELER, lawyer; b. Greenville, S.C., Feb. 22, 1950; s. C. Thomas and Harriet Durham (Smith) W.; m. Carolyn Diane Smock, July 1, 1978; children: Charles Denby Smock, Jessica Kaye. AB in Environ. Sci., Princeton U., 1972; MS in Natural Resource Mgmt., Yale U., 1974; JD, U. Va., 1978. Bar: S.C. 1978, U.S. Dist. Ct. S.C. 1978, U.S. Ct. Appeals (4th cir.) 1978. Ptnr. Wyche, Burgess, Freeman & Parham, Greenville, 1979—. Contbr. articles to profl. jours. Mem. S.C. Gov.'s Coun. on Natural Resources, Columbia, 1983-84, Pendleton Place, Greenville, 1984-88, S.C. Coastal Coun., 1986-95; pres. Warehouse Theatre, Greenville, 1982-83, Greenville's Symphony Assn., 1989-90; chair Greenville Cmty. Found., 1994. Mem. S.C. Bar Assn. Home: 312 Raven Rd Greenville SC 29615-4248 Office: Wyche Burgess Freeman & Parham PO Box 728 44 E Camperdown Way Greenville SC 29602

WYCHE, MARGUERITE RAMAGE, realtor; b. Birmingham, Ala., May 30, 1950; d. Raymond Crawford and Marguerite Getaz (Taylor) Ramage; m. Madison Baker Wyche III, Aug. 7, 1971; children: Madison Baker IV, James Ramage. BA cum laude, Vanderbilt U., 1972. Lic. broker, S.C., also cert. real estate specialist, grad. Real Estate Inst. Real estate agt. Slappey Realty Co., Albany, Ga., 1973-76, McCutcheon Co., Greenville, S.C., 1973-76; real estate agt. Furman Co., Greenville, 1985-87, broker's assoc., 1987-95; v.p., broker in charge The Furman Co. Residential LLC, Greenville, 1995—; v.p. The Furman Co. Residential LLC, 1996. Bd. dirs. Christ Ch. Episcopal Sch., Greenville, 1979-82, 86-89, chmn. bd. visitors, 1992-93; bd. dirs., cmty. v.p. Jr. League of Greenville, 1983, state pub. affairs chair S.C. Jr. League, 1984; mem. Greenville Cmty. Planning Coun., 1983; bd. dirs., chmn. long range planning com. Meals on Wheels, Greenville, 1990-93; mem. Palmetto Soc.-United Way of Greenville, 1992—; mem. elves workshop com. Children's Hosp., Greenville, 1992-93; mem. Greenville Tech. Found. Bd., 1995—, Met. Arts Coun., 1996—, Endowment Corp. Christ Ch., 1996—, Mayor's Task Force, 1996—. Mem. Greenville Bd. Realtors, Million Dollar Club (life), Vanderbilt Alumni Assn., Christ Ch. Episcopal Sch. Alumni Assn. (pres., bd. dirs. 1980-81), Mortar Board, Delta Delta Delta. Republican. Episcopalian. Home: 134 Rockingham Rd Greenville SC 29607-3621 Office: The Furman Co 252 S Pleasantburg Dr Ste 100 Greenville SC 29607-2547

WYCHE, SAMUEL DAVID, sportscaster; b. Atlanta, GA, Jan. 5, 1945; m. Jane Wyche; children—Zak, Kerry. B.A., Furman U., 1966; Masters degree, U. S.C. Profl. football player Continental Football League, Wheeling Ironmen, 1966; profl. football player Cin. Bengals, 1968-70, Washington Redskins, 1971-73, Detroit Lions, 1974-75, St. Louis Cardinals, 1976, Buffalo Bills, 1976; owner sporting goods store, Greenville, S.C., 1974-92; asst. coach San Francisco 49ers, 1979-82; head coach Ind. U., Bloomington, 1983, Cin. Bengals, 1984-91, Tampa Bay (Fla.) Buccaneers, 1992-95; sports analyst NBC Sports, Tampa, 1996—. Named Coach of Yr. NFL, 1988, Nat. Football League, 1988. Office: Sam Wyche Inc 334 Blanca Ave Tampa FL 33606-3630

WYCKOFF, LYDIA LLOYD, art curator; b. Washington, Nov. 16, 1937; d. Edward Lester Lloyd and Martha Alethea Hall; m. David Willard Wyckoff, June 1, 1963 (div. July 1990); children: Barbara, Christopher. MFA, U. Lausanne, Switzerland, 1955; MA, Wesleyan U., 1975; MPhil, Yale U., 1980, PhD, 1985. Lectr. U. Miami, 1962-67; rsch. assoc. Mus. of Am. Indian-Heye Found., N.Y.C., 1967-79; postdoctoral fellow Yale U., New Haven, Conn., 1985-87; curator, dir. Native Am. and non-western art Philbrook Mus. Art, Tulsa, 1991—; cons. Housatonic Adolescent Hosp., Newtown, Conn., 1985; bd. dirs. Osage Tribal Mus., Pawhuska, Okla.; guest curator Yale U., 1993—; adj. assoc. prof. U. New Haven, 1967-77; vis. asst. prof. Bard Coll., 1983-84; adj. asst. prof. Fairfield (Conn.) U., 1986-90, U. Tulsa, 1990—. Author, editor: Hopis, Tewas and American Road, 1983 (Choice award 1983); author: Designs and Factions, 1990, (jours.) New Scholar, 1986, Am. Anthropology, 1991; author: editor: Visions and Voices, 1996; contbr. articles and revs. to profl. publs. Rsch. grantee Mus. of Am. Indian, 1960s, Ctr. for Inter-Am. Studies, 1960s, Yale Ctr. for Native Am. Art and Anthropology, 1979, NEA, 1993, 96.. Fellow Am. Anthropol. Assn.; mem. AAUP, Coun. for Mus. Anthropology. Home: RR 1 Barnsdall OK 74002-9801 Office: Philbrook Mus Art 2727 S Rockford Rd Tulsa OK 74114-4104

WYLIE, DON L., aviation executive; b. Flint, Mich., Nov. 5, 1939; s. Laurence Vincent and Ethel Grace (Brewer) W.; m. Marie Frances Kukla, July 2, 1960; children: Angela Marie Wylie Manka, Stephen Matthew, Melanie Lynn Wylie Ballinger. BA, Troy State U., 1974; MA, Ball State U., 1978. Officer USAF, worldwide, 1959-81; prin. Kors, Marlar, Savage, Inc., Houston, 1981-87; pres. Wylie Aviation, Inc., Houston, 1987-92; v.p. Tex. Air Aces, Spring, 1992-95, pres., 1995—. Decorated Disting. Flying Cross, Silver Star, air medals, meritorious svc. medals. Mem. Air Force Assn., Exptl. Aircraft Assn. Republican. Office: Tex Air Aces 8319 Thora A-5 Spring TX 77379

WYLLIE, ALFRED LINN, real estate broker, mortgage broker; b. Clearwater, Fla., Jan. 2, 1949; s. Alfred Charles and Winnie Marion (O'Neal) W.; m. Anne Louise McCarren, Oct. 18, 1969 (div. Feb. 1972); m. Virginia Gail Linder, Jan. 19, 1974; children: Alfred Adrian, Judy Linn. Student, St. Petersburg Jr. Coll., 1968-69; grad., Constrn. Inst., Tampa, Fla., 1972; grad. as salesman and broker, Bert Rodgers Sch. of Real Estate, Clearwater, 1977, 80. Cert. gen. contractor, Fla.; lic. real estate and mortgage broker, Fla. V.p. Alfred C. Wyllie, Inc., Clearwater, 1967-82, Linmark Corp., Clearwater, 1970-82, Wyllie Enterprises, Inc., Clearwater, 1970-82; pres. A. Linn Wyllie & Co., Inc., Clearwater, 1982—; pres. Carib-Gulf Corp., Dunedin, Fla., 1978—, A Priori Internat., Inc., Clearwater, 1985—, Clearwater Skyport Authority, Inc., 1986-92; co-founder Praxis Global Svcs., 1990; bd. dirs. Virtual Prime, Inc., 1993-95. Chmn. 1st Ann. Internat. St. Festival, Clearwater, 1985; vice sec. Downtown Clearwater Assn., 1985-86; chmn. symposium Downtown Progress Com., Clearwater, 1986; bd. dirs. Nat. Drowning Prevention Coalition, 1990; mem. Rep. Nat. Com., NRA-Inst. for Legis. Action. Mem. Nat. Assn. Home Builders, Nat. Assn. Realtors, Internat. Real Estate Fedn., Realtors Nat. Mktg. Inst. (comml. investment real estate coun.), Fla. Real Estate Exchangors, Clearwater Real Estate Exchangors (vice chmn. 1978-79), Greater Clearwater Bd. Realtors (mem. profl. stds. com. 1987-92), Greater Clearwater C. of C. (state and fed. legis. com. 1987-88), The Braintrust (founder 1985—), Aircraft Owners and Pilots Assn., PsiNet (founder 1986—), Fla. Gulfcoast Comml. Assn. Realtors. Republican. Episcopalian. Clubs: Belleview Biltmore Cabana (Clearwater). Home: One Shore Dr Dunedin FL 34698 Office: A Priori Internat Inc 2555 Enterprise Rd Ste 12 Clearwater FL 34623-1150

WYLLIE, MALCOLM ROBERT JESSE, retired oil company executive, farmer; b. Cape Town, South Africa, July 31, 1919; s. Hugh Macrae and Jeanie Katherine (Jesse) W.; m. Margaret Boyd Jones, Aug. 2, 1947; children: Ashton Robert Jesse, Peta Jean. BSc in Chem. Engring., U. Cape Town, South Africa, 1939; DPhil, Oxford U., Eng., 1943, DSc, 1958. Dep. dir. Admiralty R&D, India, 1944-45; dir. reservoir mechanics divsn. Gulf R&D Co., Pa., 1955-64, dir. exploration and prodn. dept., 1964-67, adminstrv. v.p., 1967-68, pres., 1968-70; exec. v.p. Gulf Oil Co. Eastern Hemisphere, London, 1970-73, pres., 1973-75, chmn., 1975; dir. Kuwait Oil Co., London, 1971-75, chmn., 1974; v.p. exploration and prodn. West Coast and Alaska Gulf Oil Corp., 1976-78; farmer registered Aberdeen Angus cattle farm Troy, Va., 1980—; dir. Esso-France, Paris, 1973-75. Author: Fundamentals of Well Log Interpretation, 1963; contbr. chpts. to books; patentee in field. Lt. comdr. Royal Navy, 1942-46. Rhodes scholar Rhodes Trustees, 1940, fellow by courtesy Johns Hopkins U., 1946-47. Mem. AIME (hon.), Am. Chem. Soc. (life), Soc. Profl. Well Log Analysts (hon., gold medal 1968). Home and Office: Cumber Farm Rte 1 Box 2300 Troy VA 22974

WYLLY, BARBARA BENTLEY, performing arts association administrator; b. Bala-Cynwyd, Pa., June 10, 1924; d. William Henry and Virginia (Barclay) Bentley; m. William Beck Wylly, Apr. 26, 1947; children: Virginia Wylly Johnson, Barbara L., Thomas C. II. A, Briarcliff Jr. Coll., 1943. Pres. bd. dirs. Hillside Hosp. Inc., Atlanta, 1982, mem. adv. coun., 1982—; pres. Atlanta Symphony Assocs., 1975-76, mem. adv. bd., 1976—; chmn. bd. dirs. Ctr. for Puppetry Arts, Atlanta, 1988—. Republican. Episcopalian. Home: 940 Foxcroft Rd NW Atlanta GA 30327-2622 Office: Ctr Puppetry Arts 1404 Spring St NW Atlanta GA 30309-2820

WYMAN, A. CAROL R., nurse, childbirth educator; b. Pitts., Nov. 16, 1943; d. Joseph Michael and Jean Reda (Austin) Evans; m. Bruce Dana Wyman, Oct. 22, 1966; 1 child, Bruce D. Jr. Diploma in nursing, Braddock Gen. Hosp., 1964. RN, Pa., Va.; cert. cesarean childbirth educator Cesarean Families Assn., cert. childbirth educator, ASPO/Lamaze. Staff nurse We. Psychiat. Clinic, U. Pitts., 1964-65; asst. head nurse Phipps Clinic, Johns Hopkins Hosp., Balt., 1965-66; office nurse to pvt. practice orthopedist Norfolk, Va., 1966-68; childbirth educator ARC, Seattle, 1975; ind. cons., childbirth educator Cesarean Families Assn., Reston, Va., 1975-79; childbirth educator ASPO/Lamaze Virginia Beach, Va., 1979-81; field examiner, advanced supr. PMI mgr. regional sales and exec. Equifax, Inc., McLean, Va., 1980—; sales assoc., then store mgr. J. Putnam, Inc., Fairfax, Va., 1981-83; sales assoc. The Orchard, Inc., McLean, Va., 1983-84; ind. cons., childbirth educator Burke, Va., 1981—; childbirth educator Fairfax Hosp., Falls Church, Va., 1991—, Fair Oaks (Va.) Hosp., 1995—; bd. dirs. Cesarean Families Assn., Washington, 1976-79. Contbr. articles on childbirth to topical publs. Fellow Am. Coll. Childbirth Educators; mem. No. Va. Life Underwriters Assn., No. Piedmont Assn. Life Underwriters (treas. 1988—, Vol. of Yr. 1990), ASPO/Lamaze (pres. Washington chpt. 1982-85), Rotary Internat. (treas. Burke Centre chpt. 1990-91, sec. 1991). Home: 6147 Poburn Landing Ct Burke VA 22015-2535 Office: Equifax-PMI 8180 Greensboro Dr Fl 3 Mc Lean VA 22102-3821

WYMAN, RICHARD THOMAS, information services consultant; b. Wilmington, Del., June 4, 1951; s. William Harper and Marian Kathryn (Bode) W. Pa. State U., 1969-71, Def. Language Inst., 1974-75, Control Data Inst., Dallas, 1979. Enlisted U.S. Army, 1971, served to staff sgt., 1979; data ctr. mgr. thrift svcs. div. ADP Inc., Dallas, 1979-80; support mgr. Electronic Data Systems, Inc., Dallas, 1980-85, info. modeling analyst, 1985-90; pres. Strategic InfoSource, Plano, Tex., 1991-93; sr. cons. The SABRE Group, Ft. Worth, Tex., 1993—; rep. 101st Airborne Div. Nat. Conf. Skill Maintenance, Ft. Meade, Md., 1977. Author: (Spl. course) U.S. Army Intelligence, 1978-79. Co-chmn. sub-com. City Bond Referendum Com., Plano, 1990; mem. City of Plano Historic Landmark Com., 1993—, vice chmn. 1996, chmn. 1996—. Recipient Army Commendation medal, 1978, '79, Vol. Svc. award, Office of Mayor, Plano, 1990. Home: 717 Kipling Dr Plano TX 61961 Office: The Sabre Group PO Box 619616 MD1450 Dallas TX 75261

WYNDHAM, CHRISTOPHER R.C., cardiologist; b. Melbourne, Australia, Aug. 22, 1942; came to U.S., 1973; s. Robert and Mary (Wells) W.; m. Ann Wyndham, Aug. 27, 1966; children: Jeremy, Tiffany, Natasha. MB, BS, U. Adelaide, Australia, 1966. Resident, cardiology fellow Royal Adelaide Hosp., 1967-73, clin. asst., 1968-69; instr. medicine Abraham Lincoln Sch. Medicine, Chgo., 1973-74, assoc. in medicine, 1974-75; cardiology fellow U. Ill. Hosp., Chgo., 1973-75, attending physician, cons. cardiologist, 1975-80; attending physician West Side VA Hosp., Chgo., 1975-80; dir. electrocardiology/electrophysiology The Meth. Hosp., Houston, 1980-88, Presbyn. Hosp. of Dallas, 1988—; asst. prof. medicine Abraham Lincoln Sch. Medicine, Chgo., 1975-80; assoc. prof. medicine Baylor Coll. Medicine, Houston, 1980-88; clin. prof. medicine U. Tex.-Southwestern Med. Sch., Dallas, 1988—. Recipient Gen. Practitioners prize Royal Australian Coll., 1966; Nat. Heart Found. of Australia grantee, 1973; Fulbright-Hays fellow, 1973. Fellow Royal Australasian Coll. Physicians, Am. Coll. Cardiology; mem. Tex. Med. Soc., N.Am. Soc. of Pacing and Electrophysiology, Dallas County Med. Soc., N.Tex. Electrophysiology Soc. (founding mem.), Am. Heart Assn. (coun. on basic rsch.). Office: North Texas Heart Ctr 8230 Walnut Hill Ln Ste 220 Dallas TX 75231-4469

WYNER, LAWRENCE MICHAEL, physician; b. Cleve., Apr. 16, 1957; s. Milton Howard and Adele G. (Greenberger) W. AB in Biology cum laude, Princeton U., 1979; MD, U. N.C., 1983. Diplomate Am. Bd. Urology. Resident in surgery U. Pitts. Hosps., 1983-89; transplant fellow Cleve. Clinic Found., 1989-92, assoc. staff, 1992—; W.Va. rep. Mid-Atlantic Renal Coalition, Transplant Subcom., Washington, 1994—. Contbr. articles to profl. jours. Recipient Charles M. Cannon Meml. prize in biology Princeton U., 1979. Mem. AMA, Am. Urol. Assn. (key contact 1992—), Am. Soc. Transplant Physicians. Office: Cleve Clinic Found 415 Morris Ste 403 Charleston WV 25301

WYNKOOP, RODNEY ALAN, choral music director; b. Indpls., Aug. 4, 1951; s. Raymond Clarence and Mary Gwendlyn (Holloway) W.; m. Leigh Moseley Joyner, June 25, 1988. BA, Yale U., 1973, M of Musical Arts, 1980, D of Musical Arts, 1985; MusM, U. Wis., 1975. Dir. concert choir Mt. Holyoke Coll., S. Hadley, Mass., 1976-77; dir. Battell Chapel choir Yale U., New Haven, 1977-80; instr. in choral music Yale Inst. Sacred Music, New Haven, 1977-80; dir. chapel music U. Chgo. Rockefeller Chapel, 1980-84, condr. univ. chorus, 1980-84; condr. chorale Duke U., Durham, N.C., 1984—, dir. chapel music, dir. univ. choral music, 1989—; condr. Durham Civic Choral Soc., 1986—. Named Classical Musician of Yr., The Independent, 1990. Mem. Am. Choral Dir. Assn., Coll. Music Soc., Condrs. Guild. Home: 104 Wainwright Ct Durham NC 27712-1226 Office: Duke Univ Chapel Durham NC 27708

WYNN, CHARLES MILTON, lawyer; b. Marianna, Fla., Jan. 21, 1953; s. Milton Gerard and Joanne (Wandeck) W.; m. Roberta Lyn Hovanec, Jan. 28, 1977; 1 child, Charles Philip Wynn. AA, Chipola Jr. Coll., 1972; BA, U. Fla., 1974; JD, Nova U., 1977. Bar: Fla. 1977, U.S. Dist. Ct. (no. dist.) Fla. 1978, U.S. Ct. Appeals (11th cir.) 1981, U.S. Dist. Ct. (mid. dist.) Fla. 1985. Assoc. Herman Laramore Law Offices, Marianna, 1977-78; pvt. practice, Marianna, 1978—; trustee U.S. Bankruptcy Ct., No. Dist. Fla., 1988-90; assoc. pub. defender, Marianna, 1977—; panel trustee U.S. Trustee's Office, Atlanta, 1988-90. Bd. dirs. Jackson County Guidance Clinic, Marianna, 1978-83, Dayspring Christian Acad., Inc., 1993; pres. Bright Start Learning Ctr., Inc., Marianna, 1984; co-founder New Life Family Ch.; mem. Marianna Gideon Camp, 1984—, chmn. Jackson County Freedom Coun., Marianna, 1986; mem. Full Gospel Businessmen's Fellowship, bd. dirs., 1986-87. Mem. Fla. Bar Assn., Panhandle Bar Assn. (pres. 1984), Pub. Defender's Assn., Comml. Law League of Am. (Cert. of Appreciation 1979), Marianna Jaycee's (Membership award 1979), Phi Alpha Delta (v.p. 1985—). Democrat. Home: 3086 Watson Dr Marianna FL 32446-2204 Office: PO Box 761 Marianna FL 32447-0761

WYNN, JOHN THOMAS, retired college president, farming executive, economic consultant; b. Corsicana, Tex., May 4, 1938; s. Sam Grady and Marjorie (Reese) W.; m. Sally Ruth Adams, Mar. 19, 1958 (div. 1975); children: Martha Maria, Catherine Clarissa, Lorraine Lemae; m. Myra Louise Alexander, Oct. 30, 1976; 1 child, John Thomas. AA, Wharton County Jr. Coll., 1960; BBA in Gen. Bus., Agrl. and Mech. Coll. Tex., 1962; MBA, Tex. A&M U., 1965; PhD in Higher Edn. Mgmt., U. So. Miss., 1973. Asst. registrar, then. instr. Tex. A&M U., College Station, 1962-67; exec. dean Delgado Community Coll., New Orleans, 1967-74, program dir., 1977-78; asst. exec. sec. So. Assn. Colls and Schs., Atlanta, 1974-77; pres. emeritus Williamsburg Tech. Coll., Kingstree, S.C., 1978-94; pres., CEO econ. cons. M&W Farm & Ranch, Egypt, Tex., 1994—; cons. AID, Dominican Republic, 1966; bd. govs. Coastal Edn. Consortium, Conway, S.C., 1982-90; mem. exec. com. pres.'s coun. S.C. Tech. Edn. Coll., Columbia, 1985-86. Vestryman St. Thomas Episc. Ch., College Station, 1962-67, St. George Episc. Ch., New Orleans, 1969-72. Served as sgt. USAR, 1955-62. Recipient Order of the Palmetto S.C. Gen. Assembly, 1994; named Hon. Order of Ky. Cols.; col. Aide-de-Camp, La., col. Aide-de-Camp, Ala. Mem. S.C. Tech. Edn. Assn. (bd. dirs. 1985-88), Kingstree C. of C. (bd. dirs. 1981-84), Kiwanis, Masons (32 degree), Shriners, Phi Delta Kappa, Kappa Delta Pi. Home and Office: PO Box 307 Egypt TX 77436-0307

WYNN, LINDA DELOIS THOMPSON, state agency administrator, educator, researcher; b. Nashville, July 22, 1948; D. George Edward and Frances Delois (Coleman) T.; m. Ronald Eugene Wynn, Dec. 19, 1970. BS in History, Tenn. State U., 1969, MS in History, 1971, MPA, 1980. Social worker Met. Health Dept., 1971-73; grants mgmt. officer Tenn. Hist. Commn., State of Tenn., Nashville, 1974-82, adminstv. svcs. asst. II, 1982-89, asst. dir. state programs, 1989—; adj. instr. African-Am. history Fisk U., 1991-92, 94—, lectr. Baynard Ruskin seminar; lectr. Saturday Acad. for Tchg. and Learning African-Am. History, U. Toledo, 1992; lectr. Extended Summer Tchrs. Inst., Tenn. State U.-NEH, 1981-82, cons. grant on constrn., 1986—; mem. legis task force com. on African-Am. history in Tenn. pub. schs., 1990; mem. doscementary adv. panel Electrovision/for African-Am. history in Tenn.; cons. Tenn. Dept. Edn., 1992—; mayoral appointee history com. City of Nashville. Contbr. profiles to: Notable Black American Women, 1992, book II, 1996, Epic Lives: One Hundred Women Who Made a Difference, 1993, A Bicentennial Tribute to Tennessee Women, 1796-1996; co-editor: Profiles of African-Americans in Tennessee History, 1996; contbr. to Bicentennial edit. Tenn. Hist. Quar., 1996; contbr. articles to profl. publs. Founding mem. Local Conf. on Afro-Am. Culture and History; mem. Tenn. Treasures rev. com. Tenn. State Mus., 1993; mem. adv. coun. World War II Tenn. Maneuvers Commn., 1993; copy cons. Tenn. Dept. Tourism, 1993; lectr. Cohn Adult Learning Ctr., 1993—; mem. planning com., co-chairperson Conf. on Tenn. Women's History, 1993—; panelist book festival Dyersburg State C.C., 1993; mem. documentary adv. panel Electrovision/S. Ctrl. Bell/Tennessee Valley Authority, 1993; bd. dirs. Friends of Mill Creek Graveyard, 1994—; mem. Southeastern African-Am. Regional Archives Planning Com., Rosenwald Schs. Conf. Planning Com. (MTSU Ctr. for Historic Preservation), adv. panel A Bicentennial Tribute to Tenn. Women; cons. to Sec. of State's Office for the Bicentennial Issue of the Tenn. Blue Book; apptd. to Tenn. Commemorative Woman's Sufferage Commn., Nashville's History Com. Named Outstanding Young Woman Am., 1975, 82; recipient cert. appreciation Nat. Alliance Bus., 1975, 82, plaque Spruce St. Bapt. Ch., 1975, 82. Mem. ASPA (Tenn. chpt), So. Hist. Assn., Tenn. Hist. Soc. (co-chair Mid. Tenn., vol. discussion leader Tenn. bicentennial celebration conf. 1989, adv. bd. for minority concerns 1990, lectr.), NAACP (Nashville chpt. history and tours com. Nat. Conv. 1992), Orgn. of African Am. Ch. Historians, Southern Baptist Hist. Assn., Southern Assn. for Women Historians. Office: Tenn Hist Commn 2941 Lebanon Rd Nashville TN 37214-2508

WYNN, SUSAN RUDD, physician. BS, Tex. A&M U., 1979, MD, 1981; postgrad., Mayo Grad. Sch. Medicine, 1981-84, 84-86. Diplomate Am. Bd. Pediatrics, Am. Bd. Allergy and Immunology; lic. Tex. Assoc. cons. dept. pediatrics Mayo Clinic, Rochester, Minn., 1987; pvt. practice, allergy and clin. immunology Fort Worth (Tex.) Allergy and Asthma Assocs., 1988—; instr. in pediatrics, Mayo Med. Sch., 1986-87; presenter in field. Contbr. articles to profl. jours. Bd. visitors Scott and White Clinic, 1994—; adv. bd. M. D. Anderson Physicians, 1992-94. Recipient Disting. Student award Tex. A&M U., 1975, Residents' award Northwest Pediatric Soc., 1984, Leon Unger award Am. Coll. Allergists, 1985, Geigy Fellowship Am. Coll. Allergists, 1987, travel grants; named to Outstanding Young Women of Am., 1989. Mem. AMA (chair med. student sect. 1980-81, chair com. on women in medicine 1987-89), Mayo Assn. of Fellows (treas. 1984-85), Mayo Alumni Assn. (exec. com. 1983-87, 95—), The Mayo Alumnus (adv. bd. 1983-87),

Tarrant County Med. Soc. (bd. dirs. 1990—, v.p. 1994-95, pres.-elect 1995-96, pres. 1996—), Minn. Med. Assn. (trustee 1984-85), Tex. Med. Assn. (various coms.), Am. Acad. Pediats., Am. Coll. Allergy and Immunology (bd. regents 1994—), Alpha Omega Alpha, Alpha Zeta, others. Office: 5929 Lovell Ave Fort Worth TX 76107-5029

WYNNE, CAREY HOWARD, JR. (JEAN-PIERRE SOLÔMON), history and religion educator; b. Pine Bluff, Ark., Mar. 16, 1950; s. Carey Howard and Gertie (Lamb) W. AB, Morehouse Coll., 1970; AM, U. Chgo., 1972; postgrad., 1972-73; DD (hon.), Universal Ch. Faculty assoc. U. Chgo. Div. Sch., 1972-74; assoc. religion dept. history Morehouse Coll., Atlanta, 1973—; cons. U.S. News and World Report, others; advisor Morehouse Coll.; cons. Msgr. A. Lanzoni, dept. head Secretariat of State, The Vatican, also to Pope John Paul II; Episcopal convenor Synod of Bishops, The Vatican, 1984. Exec. sec. Democratic party Fulton County; active Butler St. YMCA, Atlanta U. Ctr. Community Chorus; tenor soloist; candidate Ark. Commn. on African-Am. History, 1991—; chair Mayor's Adv. Com. on Dr. Martin Luther King, Jr. Meml., Pine Bluff, Ark., 1996; mem. Ark. Martin Luther King Jr. Commn., State of Ark., 1996—. Recipient J.J. Starks Best Man of Affairs award Morehouse Coll., 1970; Rockefeller Protestant fellow, 1970; Lyndon Baines award U. Tex.-Austin, 1970; Ford Found. fellow, 1971-75, Gov.'s award in Race Rels., 1993, Letter of Commendation from Pres. Bill Clinton, 1993. Mem. Am. Soc. Ch. History, Internat. Patristics Council, Am. Acad. Religion, Songwriters, Resources and Services (Music Union), Internat. Religious Assn., Inc., Phi Alpha Theta. Democrat. Roman Catholic (mem. Faith Community of St. Charles Lwanga). Contbr. to books, profl. jours.; author: The Tradition: Sacerdotium and Regnum and the Two Beckets, 1972; The Spiritual Significance of Pope John Paul II, San Vittorino, Italia, 1978; On the Rhythm of Soul Truth, 1982; What Are Visions and Values without God?, 1983; On Rhythms of Liberation Notes, 1984; Arius and the Castle of Misty Blue, 1985, Dr. Martin Luther King, Jr.: Who Were You?, 1993, The Arkansas "I Have A Dream" Memorial In Honor of Dr. Martin Luther King, Jr. (1929-68), 1994; host T.V. shows Dr. Wynn's Journal, 1993—, Confrontation, 1993—, The Vigil: 1995, 96; composer musical score, For Thine is the Kingdom, The Power, and the Glory, Forever, Amen, 1982; composer Obedience, 1983; God: The Almighty Power, 1984; The Love of God, 1985, The Beatitudes, 1986. Prin. works include Sculpture in Red Bronze: The Trinity, 1988, Cleopatra, 1988, Pine Bluff Bus. for the Arts Award, 1988, Abalone, 1988, Alpha and Omega Trinity Cross, 1989, The Betton Clinic, 1989, The Ark. Meml. to Dr. Martin Luther King, Jr., Philander Smith Coll., Little Rock, 1989, The Transfiguration of Christ, 1990, The Resurrection of Christ, 1990, The Quest For Justice, 1980— (semi-finalist Nat. Civil Rights Mus. 1990, Memphis Paralaxis 1990), The Revelation of Christ, 1990, Alpha and Omega Cross: Seven Spirits of God, 1989, Caduceus, 1989; semi-finalist in internat. competition art ctr. work Nat. Civil Rights Mus. Memphis, Tenn., Hyde Found. sponsor, 1990; The Resurrection of Christ, 1990, The Transfiguration of Christ, 1990, Paralaxis, 1990, The Family of God, 1990; paintings include St. Augustine, 1990, The Christ of the Resurrection , 1990, The World: He's Got the Whole World in His Hands, 1994; represented in permanent collections (Ltd. edit. Bronze medallion entitled Dr. Martin Luther King, Jr.: Drum-Major for Justice) The Ark. Sickle Cell Anemia Found., 1990, Ark.-La. Gas Co., 1990, 1993, Fla. State U., 1990, Cen. Mich. U., 1990, Southwestern Bell Corp., 1990, Morehouse Coll., 1991, The Ark. Gov.'s Mansion, 1991, Ark. Mus. Sci. and History 1992, The Dr. Martin Luther King, Jr. Altarpiece, The Dr. Martin Luther King, Jr. Internat. Meml. Chapel at Morehouse Coll., Atlanta, 1995.

WYNNE, WILLIAM JOSEPH, lawyer; b. Little Rock, July 17, 1927. Student Little Rock U., 1946-48; J.D., U. Ark., 1951. Bar: Ark. 1951, U.S. Dist. Ct. Ark. 1951, U.S. Supreme Ct. 1958; pres. Diversified Drilling Svcs., Inc., Elco Equipment Leasing Co., Inc., Columbia Pipeline Co.; v.p., gen. counsel El Dorado paper Bag Mfg. Co., Inc.; ordained to ministry Presbyterian Ch. Sr. counsel Murphy Oil Corp., El Dorado, 1951-68; ptnr. Crumpler, O'Connor & Wynne, El Dorado, 1963—; adj. prof. law U. Ark., Little Rock; gen. counsel and hearing officer Ark. Oil and Gas Commn.; pastor St. Andrew Cumberland Presbyterian Ch.; pres. Diversified Drilling Svcs., Inc., Elco Equipment Leasing Co., Inc.; v.p. and gen. counsel El Dorado Paper, Balmir Col., Inc. Mem. ABA, Ark. Bar Assn., Union County Bar Assn., Assn. Trial Lawyers Am., Ark. Trial Lawyers Assn., El Dorado C. of C. (Outstanding Young Man 1961-62). Home: 1501 W Block St El Dorado AR 71730-5301 Office: NBC Pla Ste 308 El Dorado AR 71730

WYSNEWSKI, ROY EDWARD, physicist; b. Cin., Aug. 24, 1935; m. Barbara Elaine Brennan, Sept. 19, 1957 (div. Sept. 1976); David, Donna Sue Wysnewski DeGuzman, Daniel; m. Judith Elizabeth Bates, Mar. 18, 1978. BS in Physics/Math., U. Cin., 1959. Asst. engr. GE Co., Evandale, Ohio, 1956-57, nuclear physicist, 1959-61; physicist Hercules Powder Co., Cumberland, Md., 1961-63; chief radiographer Gen. Dynamics Corp., San Diego, 1963-65; sr. tech. specialist GAF Corp., Binghamton, N.Y., 1965-80, DuPont Co., Wilmington, Del., 1980-83; tech. mgr. Fuji NDT Sys., Roselle, Ill., 1983—; instr. video: Fundamentals of Film Interpretation, 1987. Author: (copyright) Energy Level for Film Substitution, 1994. Mem. Zoning Bd. Appeals, Conklin, N.Y., 1968-72. Fellow Am. Soc. for Non-Destructive Testing; mem. ASTM (E-7 Cert. of Appreciation 1996). Democrat. Home and Office: 5785 Beaurivage Ave Sarasota FL 34243

WYSS, NORMA ROSE TOPPING, counselor, supervisor, educator, writer; b. Wautoma, Wis., Jan. 7, 1919; d. Eugene Leonard Topping and Sylvia Maude (Attoe-Dumond) Topping Schubert; m. Werner Oscar Wyss; children: Werner Oscar II (dec.), Christine Camille (dec.), Melanie Rose (dec.), Sylvia Ann (dec.). Diploma, Waushara Normal, 1939; BA in Elem. Edn., Fla. State U., 1949, MS, 1960; postgrad., U. Md., 1964; PhD in Social Change and Counselling, Walden U., 1986; grad., Inst. Children's Lit., West Redding, Conn., 1993. Cert. employment counselor and supr. Tchr. Hoeft Sch., Berlin, Wis., 1939-40, Escambia County Sch. Bd., Pensacola, Fla., 1946-66; area I counselor supr. Fla. State Dept. of Labor, Pensacola and Tallahassee, 1966-79; freelance writer N.Y.C., 1986-90; field interviewer Arbitron, Laurel, Md., 1985-88; counselor Career Mgmt. Specialists, 1994-95. Author: Core Counseling: The Christian Faith and the Helping Relationship: A Paradigm of Social Change, 1990; children's short stories. Communicant mem., usher, greeter, cantor, pre-marriage counselor, good shepherd o-chmn. Luth. Ch. of the Resurrection, Pensacola, Fla. Mem. Am. Counseling Assn., Nat. Assn. Ret. Tchrs., Escambia Educators (life), Fla. Ret. Educators (life), DAR (treas. Pensacola chpt. 1988-90, Alpha Delta Kappa (1st pres. Fla. Alpha chpt. 1953), Kappa Delta Pi. Democrat. Office: 92B-2600 W Michigan Ave Pensacola FL 32526

XANTHOPOULOS, PHILIP, SR., brokerage house executive, financial advisor; b. Pottstown, Pa., Sept. 20, 1944; s. Sopho and Beatrice Ann (Rudwolis) X.; m. Diane Mae Johnson, June 17, 1966 (div. 1976); children: Philip, Sherri Lynn; m. Iris Elana Bowden, Dec. 31, 1977. Student, Valley Forge Mil. Acad.; BA, Pa. State U., 1966. CFP. Owner several businesses Pottstown, 1967-79; account exec. Merrill Lynch Pierce Fenner & Smith, Ft. Walton Beach, Fla., 1979-83; 1st v.p., portfolio mgr. Investments Prudential Securities, Inc., Ft. Walton Beach, 1983—. Past. pres. Okaloosa Symphony Orch.; bd. dirs. Panhandle Animal Welfare Soc., Speech and Hearing Clinic. Mem. Internat. Assn. for Fin. Planning, Ft. Walton Bech Hosts Coun., Ft. Walton Beach C. of C., Ft. Walton Yacht Club, Millionaires Club, Krewe of Bowlegs, Masons, Sertoma (past pres.), Rotary (past pres.). Office: Prudential Securities 315 Mary Esther Blvd Mary Esther FL 32569-1603

XU, HUA-SHENG (HOWARD XU), surgical oncologist, researcher; b. Putian, Fujian, China, Feb. 15, 1947; came to U.S., 1983; m. Shu-Qiong Peng, June 3, 1972; children: Ruth, Jane. MD, Sun Ya-Sen U., Guangzhou, China, 1970; MD in Surg. Oncology, Guangxi Med. U., Nanning, China, 1981. Resident in surgery Fusui Hosp., Nanning, 1970-77; chief resident Guangxi Med. U., 1981-82, asst. prof., 1986-89, adj. prof., vice chmn. dept. surgery, 1992—; rsch. fellow Duke U. Med. Ctr., Durham, N.C., 1983-85; rsch. scientist Ea. Va. Med. Sch., Norfolk, 1985-86; rsch. assoc. U. Va. Health Scis. Ctr., Charlottesville, 1989—. Contbr. articles to med. jours. Mem. Chinese Med. Soc., Chinese Anti-Cancer Assn. Home: 114 Oak Forest Cir Charlottesville VA 22901-1610 Office: U Va Med Sch PO Box 181 Charlottesville VA 22908-0181

XU, LE, biophysicist, physicist; b. Guilin, Guang Xi, People's Republic of China, Dec. 30, 1941; came to U.S., 1986; s. Xuehan Xu and GuangXi Zhu; m. Qi-Yi Liu, Dec. 16, 1967; 1 child, Song Liu. Student, Nankai U., Tianjin, People's Republic of China, 1958-63, PhD equivalent, 1966. Tchr., lectr., assoc. prof. Nankai U., Tianjin, 1963-86; vis. scholar Mich. State U., East Lansing, 1980-82; vis. asst. prof. U. N.C., Chapel Hill, 1986-88, rsch. scholar, 1988-90, rsch. assoc., 1990—. Contbr. articles to IEEE, Philos. Mag. B, Jour. Electronics, Archives of Biochemistry and Biophysics, Jour. Gen. Physiol. Mem. Am. Biophys. Soc. Office: Dept Biochemistry and Biophysics Univ NC CB # 7260 Chapel Hill NC 27599-7260

XU, WENWEI, geneticist, researcher; b. Linxia City, Gansu, People's Republic of China, Sept. 13, 1962; came to U.S., 1987; s. Mingling Xu and Cungui Zhang; m. Yuping Sun, Aug. 11, 1986; children: Jia, Laura. BS in agronomy, Agrl. U. Gansu Province, People's Republic of China, 1982; MS in crop genetics and breeding, Chinese Acad. Agrl. Scis., People's Republic of China, 1985; PhD in genetics, U. Mo., 1992. Rschr. Inst. Crop Germplasm Resources, CAAS, Beijing, People's Republic of China, 1985-87; vis. scientist U. Mo., Columbia, 1987-88, grad. rsch. asst., 1988-92, postdoctoral fellow, 1992-93; postdoctoral rsch. assoc. Tex. Tech. U., Lubbock, 1993-95; rsch. scientist Tex. Tech U., Lubbock, 1995—. Contbr. articles to profl. jours. Recipient Sears-Longwell award for contbn. to genetics in agr. U. Mo., 1992, Outstanding Student award from Agrl. U. Gansu Province, 1979, 81, 82, Outstanding Mem. Youth League award Ministry of Agr., People's Republic of China, 1984. Mem. AAAS, Am. Soc. Agronomy, Crop Sci. Soc. Am., (Gerald O. Mott Meritorious Grad. Student award), Sigma Xi. Home: 5401 50th St Apt C-6 Lubbock TX 79414-1723 Office: Tex Tech U Main St Stop 2122 Lubbock TX 79401-2921

YACAVONE, DAVID WILLIAM, military officer, consultant, researcher; b. Newark, Feb. 5, 1945; s. William Michael and Rose Marie (Cerrato) Y.; m. Nancy Weissman; children: Nancy Christine, Rebecca Noel, Jason David, Briana Lynn. BA in Non-Western History, Seton Hall U., 1966, MA in Chinese History, 1968; DO, Chgo. Coll. Osteo. Medicine, 1974; MPH, Harvard U., 1986. Diplomate Am. Bd. Gen. and Preventive Medicine, Am. Bd. Aerospace Medicine. Rotating intern Chgo. Osteo. Med. Ctr., 1975; asst. prof. community medicine Mich. State U., East Lansing, 1975-76; bn. surgeon USN, Lansing, Mich., 1975-77; flight surgeon U.S. Naval Aerospace Med. Inst., Pensacola, Fla., 1977, USN, Jacksonville, Fla., 1977-79; sr. med. officer USN, USS Saratoga, 1979; resident aerospace medicine U.S. Naval Aerospace Med. Inst., Pensacola, Fla., 1986-88; capt. med. corps USN USN, USS Dwight D. Eisenhower, 1988-90, 93-96, 1993-96; head aeromed. div. Naval Safety Ctr., Norfolk, Va., 1990-93; capt. med. corps USN USS Harry S. Truman, 1996—; staff mem. Lansing (Mich.) Gen. Hosp., 1975-76, Jackson (Much.) Gen. Hosp., 1976-77, Jacksonville (Fla.) Gen. Hosp., 1977-81, Daytona Beach (Fla.) Gen. Hosp., 1979-81, Naval Hosp., Corpus Christi, Tex., 1982-85, dir. mil. medicine, 1982-84; adj. instr. W.Va. Coll. Osteo. Medicine, 1977-79; tng. instr. Flight Instr.'s Tng., 1982-85, flight surgeon's sch. Naval Aerospace Med. Inst., 1986-88, 90-93, aircraft accident investigation technique, Armed Forces Inst. Pathology, 1990—; presenter in field. Author: (with others) Aviation, Space and Environmental Medicine, 1987, edit., 1992; editor: Aeromedical News, 1990-93. ACLS instr. Tex. Heart Assn., 1983-85. Recipient Steinbaum Meml. award, Kirksville Coll. Osteo. Medicine, 1971. Fellow Aerospace Med. Assn.; mem Soc. U.S. Naval Flight Surgeons (past officer), Assn. Mil. Surgeons of U.S., numerous coms. Office: USS Dwight D Eisenhower # Cvn-69 FPO AE 09532

YACK, PATRICK ASHLEY, editor; b. Little Rock, Oct. 25, 1951; s. Leo Patrick and Sarah Ann (Dew) Y.; m. Susan Marie Courtney, June 7, 1980; children: Alexander Ryan, Kendall Elizabeth. BFA, So. Meth. U., 1974. Staff asst. U.S. Rep. Alan Steelman, Washington, 1975-76; press aide U.S. Senator Charles Percy, Chgo., 1977-78; reporter Fla. Times-Union, Jacksonville, 1979-80; regional reporter Fla. Times-Union, Atlanta, 1981-82; reporter The Denver Post, 1983-85, Washington bur. chief, 1985-87; nat. editor Atlanta Constitution, 1987-89; mng. editor The Register-Guard, Eugene, Oreg., 1989-94; editor News & Record, Greensboro, N.C., 1994—. Mem. Am. Soc. Newspaper Editors, AP Mng. Editors Assn.

YADALAM, KASHINATH GANGADHARA, psychiatrist; b. Bangalore, India, Dec. 17, 1954; came to U.S., 1980; s. Gangadhara N. and Ramarathna G. (Daglur) Y.; m. Jyothi Kashinath, Feb. 26, 1981; children: Akhila, Adithya. MD, Kasturba Med. Coll., Manipal, India, 1977. Diplomate, Am. Bd. Psychiatry and Neurology. Resident in psychiatry U. Nebr., Omaha, 1980-83; clin. fellow psychopharmacology Med. Coll. Pa., Phila., 1983-84; instr. Med. Coll. Pa., 1984-85, asst. prof., 1985-89, dir. neuropsychiatry clinic, 1987-91, assoc. prof., 1989-91; med. dir. Diagnostic and Consultation Ctr. Med. Coll. of Pa.; assoc. dir. The Neuropsychiat. Clinic of La., 1991-96, med. dir., 1996—; med. dir. Schizophrenia Diagnostic and Consultation Ctr., 1990. Author: (with others) Drug Induced Dysfunction in Psychiatry, 1992; contbr. articles to med. jours. Grantee, NIMH, 1987; recipient Young Investigator award, Internat. Congress Schizophrenia Rsch., Balt., 1987, Young Scientist award Winter Workshop on Schizophrenia, Badgastein, Austria, 1990. Mem. Am. Psychiat. Assn., Am. Coll. Clin. Pharmacology, Nat Alliance of the Mentally Ill. Hindu. Office: 2829 4th Ave Ste 150 Lake Charles LA 70601-7887

YAEGER, THEODORE EDWARD, radiation oncologist; b. Washington, Nov. 22, 1950; s. Theodore Edward III and Joyce (Brady) Y.; m. Cheri Mears, June 7, 1987. MD, Hahnemann Univ., 1981. Diplomate Am. Bd. Radiology. Intern Hahnemann Univ. Hosp., 1981-82, resident, 1982-85; v.p. Radiation Oncology Assocs., Daytona Beach, Fla., 1994—. Recipient Physician Recognition award AMA, 1995, Vol. award Volusic County Med. Soc., 1995. Mem. Halifax River Yacht Club, Am. Coll. Radiology. Office: 303 N Clyde Morris Blvd Daytona Beach FL 32114-2709

YALCINTAS, M. GÜVEN, medical physicist; b. Milas, Turkey, Apr. 11, 1946; came to U.S., 1968; s. Kazim and Samiye Yalcintas; 1 child, Banu. BS in Physics, Ankara U., 1967; MS in Health Physics, U. Rochester, 1971, PhD in Med. Physics, 1974. Dir. EGE MEd. Sch., Izmir, Turkey, 1975-76, EMI Med., Chgo., 1976-77; group leader Oak Ridge (Tenn.) Nat. Lab., 1977-88; dir. tech. transfer Lockheed Martin, Oak Ridge, 1988-93, dir. tech. transfer of environ. techs. HAZWRAP, 1993—; adj. prof. radiation biology Tenn. Tech U.; adj. prof. environ. scis. Tusculcum Coll., adv. bd. environ. sci. program. Contbr. articles to profl. jours. Lt. Turkish Army, 1975-76. Mem. Am. Nuclear Soc. chmn. 1986—, newsletter editor), East Tenn. Health Physics Assn., Health Physical Soc. Home: 208 Toqua Greens Ln Loudon TN 37774 Office: Lockheed Martin Box 2003 MS 7172 Oak Ridge TN 37831-7172

YAMAGUCHI, YUKIO, chemistry research scientist; b. Hiroshima, Japan, Feb. 22, 1941; came to U.S., 1970; s. Tameo and Miyuki (Kodama) Y.; m. Masako Iwamura, Aug. 3, 1994. BE, Kyushu U., Fukuoka, Japan, 1964, ME, 1966; PhD, U. Tex., Austin, 1978. Research assoc. Kyushu U., Fukuoka, 1966-70; postdoctoral fellow U. Tex., Austin, 1979-80; postdoctoral fellow U. Calif. and Lawrence Berkeley Lab., Berkeley, 1980-82, chemistry rsch. scientist, 1982-87; chemistry rsch. scientist U. Ga., Athens, 1987—. Author: (with Y. Osamura, J.D. Goddard and H.F. Schaefer) A New Dimension to Quantum Chemistry: Analytic Derivative Methods in Ab Initio Molecular Electronic Structure Theory; contbr. articles to profl. jours. Mem. Am. Chem. Soc., Chem. Soc. of Japan. Office: U Ga Ctr Computational Quantum Chem Athens GA 30602

YANCEY, ELEANOR GARRETT, retired crisis intervention clinician; b. Ga., Oct. 24, 1933; adopted d. Overton LaVerne Garrett; m. Robert Grady Yancey, Nov. 10, 1961 (div. Apr. 1968); children: Katherine La Verne, David Shawn. Student, High Mus. Art Inst., 1952-53, Ga. State U., 1953-55, 78; BA, La Grange Coll., 1958. Social worker, case worker Fulton County Dept. Family and Children's Svcs., Atlanta, 1957-61; asst. tchr. Atlanta (Ga.) Bd. Edn., 1973-85; mental health crisis intervention clinician Dekalb County Bd. Health, Decatur, 1985-95, acting dir. crisis intervention, 1988-90; ret., 1995. Performed summer stock, 1969-70. Performed with Rogers & Co., 1969, 70; band booster pres. Henry Grady High Sch., Atlanta, 1977-78, v.p. PTA, 1978-79; pres. PTA Morningside Elem. Sch., Atlanta, 1977; grand juror Dekalb County, Decatur, 1983; active Sesquicentennial Celebration of Ala. Statehood. Mem. Kappa Kappa Iota (Lambda chpt. state pres. 1987-88, Eta pres. local chpt. 1992—). Democrat. Home: 3425 Regalwoods Dr Doraville GA 30340-4019

YANCEY, ROBERT EARL, JR., oil company executive; b. Ashland, Ky., June 16, 1945; s. Robert E. Sr. and Estelline (Tackett) Y.; m. Nina McGee, June 16, 1962; children: Rob, Yvonne, Elizabeth. BS in Chem. Engring., Cornell U., 1967. Sr. v.p., group operating officer; supt. Catlettsburg (Ky.) Refinery, 1976-79; exec. asst. Ashland (Ky.) Petroleum Co., 1979-80, group v.p., 1980-81, sr. v.p., 1981-86, pres., 1986—; sr. v.p., group operating officer Ashland Inc., 1988—. Republican. Home: 504 Amanda Furnace Dr Ashland KY 41101-2193 Office: Ashland Petroleum Co PO Box 391 Ashland KY 41105-0391

YANCIS, RONALD ALAN, banker; b. Rochester, N.Y., Nov. 17, 1945; s. Bronislau Donald and Ann Louise (Lysko) Y.; m. Martha Ann Bryant, Feb. 14, 1969. AAS, Monroe Community Coll., 1965; BBA, U. Miss., 1967; MBA, La. State U., 1971. Asst. prof. N.W. Miss. Community Coll., Senatobia, 1969-76; assoc. examiner, comptr. currency Nat. Bank, Dallas, 1976-81; asst. mgr. loan rev. 1st Nat. Bank of Jefferson Parish, Gretna, La., 1981-82; mgr. loan rev. The Miss. Bank, Jackson, 1982-84; credit adminstr. 1st Nat. Bank, Covington, La., 1984-88; adminstr. credit Parish Nat. Bank, Covington, 1988-93; owner, cons. Ronald Yancis & Assocs., Covington, 1988-93; cons. Pickering & Assocs., New Orleans, 1994-95; v.p. loan rev. examiner Bank One of La., Baton Rouge, 1995—. Mem. Leadership Inst., Springfield, Va., 1990, CATO Inst., Washington, 1991, Coun. of Conservative Citizens, St. Louis, 1994. Recipient appreciation Credit Women Inst., 1988. Mem. Am. Bankers Assn., La. Bankers Assn., Am. Mgmt. Assn., U. Miss. Alumni Assn. (life), Ole Miss Loyalty Found., Confederate Soc. Am., KC (dep. grand knight 1992-93), Ole Miss Bus. Alumni Chpt., NRA, Figure Skating Club of New Orleans (v.p. 1980-82). Republican. Roman Catholic. Home: 3027 Golden Dr Slidell LA 70460-3905 Office: Bank One of La 451 Florida St PO Box 1511 Baton Rouge LA 70821

YANCEY, ROBERT JAMES, dean; b. Tifton, Ga., Mar. 10, 1944; s. Preston Martin and Margaret Elizabeth (Robinson) Y.; m. Dorothy Cowser, Sept. 8, 1967; 1 child, Yvonne Cowser. BA, Morehouse Coll., 1964; MBA, Atlanta U., 1966; PhD, Northwestern U., 1973. Instr. So. U., Baton Rouge, 1965-66, Albany (Ga.) State Coll., 1966-67; asst. prof. Hampton (Va.) U., 1967-69; pres., chief exec. officer ZEBRA Corp., Atlanta, 1972-82; assoc. prof. Atlanta U., 1971-82; prof. So. Poly. State U. (formerly So. Coll. Tech.), Marietta, Ga., 1983-86, dean Sch. Mgmt., 1986—; Chmn. Regents Adv. Com. on Bus. and Econs., 1986-90, Regents Adv. Com. on Grad. Work, 1989-90; chmn. bus. adminstrn. acad. rev. team Ft. Valley State Coll., 1988-89. Author: Federal Policy and Black Enterprise, 1973, Principles of Production Scheduling, 1980, Manufacturing Scheduling, 1980; co-author: Labor and Personnel Relations, 1980. Bd. dirs. Met. Atlanta Girls Clubs, 1975-78, Kennesaw chpt. March of Dimes, Atlanta, 1988—, Cobb County Urban League, 1993; chmn. membership Butler St. YMCA, Atlanta, 1976; mem. fin. com. Open Gate, Marietta, 1987-89; vestry mem. Ch. of the Incarnation. Recipient Black Georgian of Yr. award State Com. on Life and History Black Georgians, 1981, Community Svc. award in edn. Nat. Alliance Postal and Fed. Employees, 1989; scholar Morehouse Coll., 1960; fellow Ford Found., 1969-73, NASA-Am. Soc. for Engring. Edn., 1968-69. Mem. Acad. Mgmt., Soc. Internat. Bus. Fellows, Morehouse Coll. Alumni Assn., 100 Black Men of Atlanta Inc., Omega Psi Phi. Episcopalian. Office: So Poly State U 1100 S Marietta Pky Marietta GA 30060-2855

YANCY, WILLIAM SAMUEL, pediatrician; b. Pittsboro, Miss., Aug. 17, 1939; s. Lester Truman and Maxyne (Lindsay) Y.; m. Susan Elizabeth Guest, June 19, 1965; children: Amy Yancy Lee, William Samuel Jr., James Michael. BA, Duke U., 1961, MD, 1965. Resident in pediatrics Duke U. Med. Ctr., Durham, N.C., 1965-66, 67-68; resident in pediatrics, then fellow in adolescent medicine U. Rochester (N.Y.) Med. Ctr., 1966-67, 70-71; pediatrician Durham Pediatrics, 1971—; dir. adolescent medicine tng. program Duke U. Med. Ctr., 1971—, dir. behavioral pediat. tng. program, 1978-90, assoc. clin. prof. psychiatry, 1982—, clin. prof. pediatrics, 1984—; dir. pediat. tng. program Durham Regional Hosp., 1977-80, med. coun., 1980-86, chmn. dept. pediatrics, 1980-86, chmn. nursery com., 1986— ; pediatrician Duke U. Affiliated Physicians, 1995—; bd. mem. Am. Bd. Pediatrics, 1992—; chmn. Coalition for Healthy N.C. Youth, 1991-95; editl. bd. Jour. Devel. and Behavioral Pediatrics, 1984—. Bd. dirs. Child Advocacy Commn. Durham, 1973-76, 79-85, pres. 1973-74; bd. dirs. Durham Cmty. Guidance Clinic, 1974-76; coun. N.C. State Coordinating Coun., Raleigh, 1994-95; vestry St. Stephen's Episcopal Ch., Durham, 1985-87, 95—. Lt. cmdr. U.S. Navy, 1968-70. Fellow Am. Acad. Pediatrics, Soc. Adolescent Medicine (exec. sec.-treas. 1978-83, pres. 1985-86, chmn. fin. com. 1989-93); mem. AMA, Internat. Assn. Adolescent Health, Soc. Devel. & Behavioral Pediatrics (pres. 1984-85), N.C. Pediat. Soc. (chmn. com. on adolescents 1989—), Beta Omega Sigma, Omicron Delta Kappa. Home: 59 Kimberly Dr Durham NC 27707 Office: Durham Pediatrics 2609 N Duke St #801 Durham NC 27704

YANDLE, SYLVESTER ELWOOD, II, sales executive, inventor; b. Lafayette, La., Sept. 14, 1932; s. Arthur Ray and Marie (Delhomme) Y.; m. Gretchen Ehrensing, June 28, 1957; children: Gretchen Marie, Sylvester E. III, Gladys Anne, Henry Arthur. Student, Southwestern La. Inst. Well logger Core Labs., Lafayette, La., 1954-56; salesman Security Rock Bits, Lafayette, La., 1956-61, Orbit Valve, New Orleans, 1961-62, So. Engine & Pump, New Orleans, 1962-66; owner, pres. Indsl. Pump Sales, Inc., Belle Chasse, La., 1967—, Commodore Boat Stores, Belle Chasse, La., 1978—, Hydro Damp Inc., Belle Chasse, La., 1992—. Inventor: Air bag for airlines (patent 1991), Hydro Damp (patent 1989), Indicators Studs for Railroads (patent pending). Active mem. Aurora Civic Assn., La. Sgt. 1st class, M.C., USAR, 1948-59. Mem. New Orleans C.C., Airplane Owners & Pilots Assn. Republican. Roman Catholic. Home: 5883 Rhodes Ave New Orleans LA 70131-3925 Office: Indsl Pump Sales Inc 2814 Engineers Rd Belle Chasse LA 70037-3153

YANG, BAIYIN, adult education educator; b. Changshu, Jiangsu, China, Mar. 17, 1962; came to U.S., 1992; s. Zongde Yang and Fengyin Gu; m. Xiaoping Lu, Dec. 14, 1987; children: Zhuowei, Zhuoyu. BS, Nanjing U., 1982; M Continuing Edn., U. Sasktchewan, Can., 1992; PhD, U. Ga., 1996. Lectr. The Chinese Acad. Scis., Nanjing, 1982-87, coord. tng. and devel., 1987-90; computer lab. advisor U. Saskatchewan, Saskatoon, 1990-92; stat. cons. U. Ga., Athens, 1993-96; asst. prof. adult edn. Auburn (Ala.) U., 1996—; rsch. asst. U. Ga., 1992-96, tchg. asst. summer 1992; rsch. asst. U. Saskatchewan, 1990-91. Contbr. articles to profl. jours. Mem. Am. Ednl. Rsch. Assn., Am. Assn. Adult and Continuing Edn., ASTD, Kapp Delta Pi. Office: Auburn U Dept Vocat & Adult Edn Auburn AL 36849

YANG, CHAO YUH, chemistry educator; b. Pingtung, Taiwan, May 8, 1939; came to U.S., 1982; s. Shang-Sheng and Kuei-Mei (Lee) Y.; m. Manlan Lou Yang; children: Tseming, Tseliang, Thomas. BS, Tamkang U., Taipei, Taiwan, 1962; MS, Georg-August U., Goettingen, Germany, 1970, PhD, 1973. Tchr. Chiatung Agr. High Sch., Pingtung, Taiwan, 1963-64; chemist Kuantu Glass Plant, Taipei, 1964-68; postdoctoral fellow dept. molecular biology Max-Planck Inst. for Exptl. Medicine, Goettingen, 1973-75, scientist dept. immunochemistry, 1975-82; asst. prof. biochemistry Baylor Coll. Medicine, Houston, 1982-89, asst. prof. dept. medicine, 1983-86, rsch. assoc. prof. dept. medicine, 1986-90, rsch. assoc. prof. dept. biochemistry, 1989-91, rsch. prof. medicine, 1990—, 1990-95; rsch. prof. biochemistry, 1991-95, prof. medicine and biochemistry, 1995—; dir. peptide core Nat. Rsch. and Demonstration Ctr. in Arteriosclerosis, Baylor Coll. Medicine, 1984—, mem. internal adv. com., 1986—; mem. organizing com. 10th Internat. Conf. on Methods in Protein Structure Analysis, Snowbird, Utah, 1994; mem. sci. com. 7th Internat. Conf. on Methods in Protein Sequence Analysis, Berlin, 1988, 8th Internat. Conf., Sweden, 1990; reviewer grants Biomed. Rsch. rev. Com., Nat. Inst. on Drug Abuse, NSF, Washington; lectr. in field. Reviewer papers for Jour. Chromatography, Jour. Lipid Rsch., Jour. Protein Chemistry, Molecular and Cellular Biochemistry, Biochemistry, Arteriosclerosis; contbr. numerous articles to profl. jours. Pres. Taiwanese Am. Citizens League of Houston, 1988-90, Taiwanese Am. Assn. of Houston, 1985-86. Grantee NIH, 1986—, Meth. Hosp. Found., 1988-91, AHA, 1985-87, 87-90, BRSG Funds, 1982-83. Home: 4102 Levonshire Dr Houston TX 77025-3915 Office: Baylor Coll Medicine 6565 Fannin St Houston TX 77030-2704

YANG, HONG-QING, mechanical engineer; b. Chang Chun, Jilin, People's Republic China, July 9, 1961; came to U.S., 1983; s. Chang-Ken and Jian-Ming (Pan) Y.; m. Vicky Qian Zhang, June 9, 1992; 1 child, Kevin Hung Yang. BS, Shanghai Jiao Tong U., 1982; MS, U. Notre Dame, 1986, PhD, 1987. Rsch. asst. U. Notre Dame, Ind., 1983-87, postdoctoral fellow, 1987-88; project engr. CFD Rsch. Corp., Huntsville, Ala., 1988-90, sr. project engr., 1990—; cons. Miles Lab., Elkhart, Ind., 1983-87. Co-author: Numerical Application in Welding, 1985; contbr. articles to profl. jours. Mem. AIAA, ASME, Am. Phys. Soc. Office: CFD Rsch Corp 3325D Triana Blvd SW Huntsville AL 35805-4643

YANG, WEIMING, physicist, researcher; b. Hefei, Anhui, China, Aug. 16, 1965; arrived in U.S., 1994; BS, U. Sci. and Tech. of China, Anhui, 1984; PhD in Theoretical Physics, Academia Sinica, Beijing, 1991. Postdoctoral rsch. fellow Beijing Inst. of Applied Math. and Computational Physics, 1991-93; postdoctoral rsch. fellow Ctr. for Complex Sys. Fla. Atlantic U., Boca Raton, 1994—. Author: Characterizing Complex Systems, 1994. Mem. Am. Phys. Soc.

YANG, WEITAO, chemistry educator; b. Chaozhou, Guangdong, China, Mar. 31, 1961; came to U.S., 1982; m. Helen Wen Zhang, Nov. 20, 1993. BS, Peking U., China, 1982; PhD, U. N.C., 1986. Asst. prof. Duke U., 1989. Co-Author: Density Functional Theory of Atoms and Molecules, 1989. Recipient Sloan fellow, A.F. Sloan Found., 1993-95. Mem. ACS, Am. Phys. Soc., Sigma Xi. Office: Duke Univ Chemistry Dept Durham NC 27708

YANKEE, WILLIAM JOSEPH, forensic psychophysiologist, educator; b. Traverse City, Mich., Oct. 11, 1925; s. Max M. and Julia A. (DeNoyer) Y.; m. Clara Ray, Mar. 6, 1946 (div. Nov. 1946); 1 child, Linda Newhouse; m. Beverly Ann Klepac, Sept. 6, 1947; children: William Joseph Jr., Gay Ann Colby. BS in Psychology, Western Mich. U., 1954, MA in Psychology, 1957; PhD in Edn., Mich. State U., 1970. Lic. polygraph examiner, N.C., Mich. Psychiat. nurse Traverse City State Hosp., 1948-50; patrolman/detective Kalamazoo (Mich.) Police Dept., 1950-56; instr. to asst. prof. Western Mich. State U., Kalamazoo, 1956-66; dean of acad. affairs Delta Coll., University City, Mich., 1966-70, exec. v.p., 1970-73; pres. Northwestern Mich. Coll., Traverse City, 1973-81; pvt. cons., dir. polygraph tng./rsch. quality and control DoD Polygraph Inst., Fort McClellan, Ala., 1987—; cons. A. Madley Corp. and Revco Drug, Ohio and N.C., 1981-87; instr., cons. Keeler Polygraph Inst., Chgo., 1960-80, Am. Inst. Polygraph Sci., Detroit, 1973-87; mem. Mich. Polygraphy Lic. Bd., 1973-76. Editor: Polygraph jour., 1981-82, assoc. editor 1981—. With USN, 1943-46. Recipient teaching fellowship, Western Mich. U., 1956, grants Nat. Security Agy., Charlotte, 1985-87. Mem. APA (assoc., Profl. Svc. award 1986), Soc. Psychophysiol. Rsch., Am. Polygraph Assn., N.C. Assn. Polygraph Examiners, Colo. Assn. Polygraph Examiners, Mich. Assn. Polygraph Examiners (Disting. Svc. award 1988, John Reid award for Edn. and Rsch. 1988), Am. Assn. Police Polygraphists, Fraternal Order of Police. Home: 611 3rd St Apt 4 Traverse City MI 49684-2262

YANNI, JOHN MICHAEL, pharmacologist; b. St. Mary's, Pa., Nov. 3, 1952; s. John Paul and Regina (Emmert) Y.; m. Nancy Jane Reedy, Sept. 22, 1979; children: Susan Elizabeth, Jennifer Ruth, Steven Reedy. BS, Allegheny Coll., 1974; MS, Va. Commonwealth U., 1979, PhD, 1982. Biologist A.H. Robins Co., Richmond, Va., 1980-82, sr. rsch. biologist, 1982-86, rsch. assoc., 1986-88; group leader Eastman Kodak Co., Rochester, N.Y., 1988-90; asst. dir. Alcon Labs., Inc., Fort Worth, 1990-92, dir., 1992-93, sr. dir., 1993—. Contbr. articles to profl. jours. Alden scholar Allegheny Coll., 1974. Mem. Am. Soc. Pharmacology and Exptl. Therapeutics, N.Y. Acad. Sci., Assn. for Rsch. in Vision and Ophthalmology, Soc. for Leukocyte Biology. Office: Alcon Labs Inc 6201 S Freeway Fort Worth TX 76134

YAPUNDICH, ROBERT ANTHONY, physician; b. N.Y.C., Jan. 3, 1963; s. David Robert and Rose Magdelana (Jimenez) Y.; m. Linda Gayle Billips, May 18, 1991; 1 child, Morgan Taylor. BA in Chemistry magna cum laude, W.Va. U., 1985, MD, 1991. Diplomate Nat. Bd. Med. Examiners; lic. physician, Ala., N.C.; cert. basic and advanced cardiac life support. Research chemist Mylan Pharmaceuticals, Morgantown, W.Va., 1985-86; intern internal medicine U. Ala., Birmingham, 1991-92, resident neurology, 1992-95, instr., fellow dept. neurology, 1995-96, mem. computer com. Physician Info. Network, 1993-94, EMG/neuromuscular disease fellow, 1995-96; neurologist Neurology Assocs. Hickory, N.C., 1996—. Contbr. articles to profl. jours. Mem. parish coun. St. Johns Cath. Ch., Morgantown, W.Va., 1983-84. Mem. AMA, Am. Acad. Neurology, Phi Kappa Phi, Alpha Epsilon Delta. Roman Catholic. Office: Neurology Assocs Hickory 1985 Tate Blvd SE Hickory NC 28602-1498

YARBOROUGH, WILLIAM GLENN, JR., military officer, forest farmer, defense and international business executive; b. Rock Hill, S.C., June 21, 1940; s. William Glenn and Bessie (Rainsford) Y.; m. Betsy Gibson, Jan. 24, 1969; children: Bill, Clinton, Frank, Elizabeth. BS, U. S.C., 1961, MBA, 1969; postgrad. Command and Gen. Staff Coll., 1970, Naval War Coll., 1979, Colgate-Darden Grad. Bus. Sch., U. Va., 1983. Commd. to U.S. Army, advanced through grades to col., 1980; co. and troop comdr. and squadron staff officer, Vietnam, Europe, 1961-71, strategist, Washington, 1971-73, chief of assignments, Office Personnel Mgmt., Mil. Personnel Ctr., Washington, 1973-76; comdr. 1st Squadron, 1st Cavalry, Europe, 1976-78; chief of staff and spl. asst. to chief of staff 1st Armored Div., Europe, 1978; br. chief Office of Chief of Staff, Washington, 1979-80; exec. to dep. commanding gen. Material Devel. and Readiness Command, Washington, 1980-81; mil. dep. for asst. sec. for research, devel. and acquisition, Washington, 1981-85; army mktg. dir. Grumman Corp., Bethpage, N.Y., 1990-93; corp. v.p. Allied Rsch. Corp., Vienna, Va., 1993—; bd. dirs. Carleton Techs. Decorated Silver Star, Bronze Star medal with 4 oak leaf clusters and V device, Purple Heart. Mem. Assn. U.S. Army (George Washington chpt., v.p. membership), Am. Legion, Armed Forces Communications and Electronics Assn., U.S. Army Armor Assn., SAR, Am. Def. Preparedness Assn. (bd. dirs. N.Y. chpt.), Nat. Guard Assn., Res. Officer Assn., Purple Heart VFW Soc., Army-Navy Club, Army Navy Country Club, Belle-Meade Country Club, Tower Club.

YARBROUGH, EDWARD MEACHAM, lawyer; b. Nashville, Dec. 17, 1943; s. Gurley McTyeire and Miriam (Mefford) Y. BA, Rhodes Coll., 1967; JD, Vanderbilt U., 1973. Bar: Tenn. 1973. Asst. dist. atty. Davidson County, Nashville, 1973-76; ptnr. Hollins, Wagster & Yarbrough, Nashville, 1976—. Chmn. com. Crime Commn., Nashville, 1981-82; mem. task force House Judiciary Com., Nashville, 1984; chmn. Crimestoppers Inc., Nashville, 1983—; trustee United Way, Nashville, 1983—, Belmont U., 1993—; bd. dirs. Big Bros. Inc., Nashville, 1983-85. Served to 1st lt. U.S. Army, 1969-71, Vietnam. Decorated Bronze Star. Fellow Nat. Speleological Soc. (bd. dirs. 1960—); mem. ABA (bd. dirs. 1985), Tenn. Bar Assn., Nashville Bar Assn. (pres. 1983), Tenn. Criminal Def. Lawyers, Nashville Kiwanis (pres. 1992), Richland Country Club, City Club (Nashville). Democrat. Baptist. Home: 5230 Granny White Pike Nashville TN 37220-1715 Office: Hollins Wagster & Yarbrough 424 Church St Nashville TN 37219

YARBROUGH, LEILA ESTHER KEPERT, artist, graphics company owner; b. Katoomba, Australia, Mar. 23, 1932; came to U.S., 1945; d. Victor Ralph and Leila Esther Menere (Kepert) King; m. James Edgar Yarbrough III, Aug. 23, 1952 (div. June 1974); children: Suzanne Rene, James Edgar IV. Student, U. Fla., Gainesville, 1950, 52, Atlanta Sch. Art, 1963-71. Receptionist Sta. WDBO-AM, Orlando, Fla., 1950, control oper., 1950-52; traffic mgr. WRUF-AM, Gainesville, 1952-55; owner, artist Yarbrough Graphics, Atlanta, 1971—; gallery affiliates include Artists Assocs., Atlanta, 1971-90, Abstein Gallery, Atlanta, 1973-89, Gimpel Weitzenhoffer Gallery, N.Y.C., 1973-75, Windsor's Gallery, Dania, Fla., 1984—, Winn/Regency Gallery, Atlanta, 1985—, Miriam Perlman Gallery, Chgo., 1985—, Stabler Gallery, Birmingham, Ala., 1988—; pub. Ronbie Editions, Yardley, Pa., 1973-89. Creator 105 titled etchings, 1973—. Recipient Purchase award Norfolk Mus. Arts and Scis., 1971, Gt. Smoky Mountains Nat. Park, 1974, 1st prize 1st Nat. Monoprint Exhbn., 1973. Mem. Fla. Printmaking Soc. Democrat. Home: Yarbrough Graphics 4061 Arden Way NE Atlanta GA 30342

YARBROUGH, MARIANNE JUNE, auditor; b. Frankfurt, Germany, May 29, 1950; came to the U.S., 1952; d. John Ezekiel and Zofia (Mudrak) Greer; m. Billy Charles Yarbrough, July 31, 1970; 1 child, Timothy Alan. BS in Edn., North Tex. State U., 1979; BBA in Acctg., Tex. Woman's U., 1983, MBA, 1989; PhD, U. North Tex., 1994. CPA, Tex. Acctg. asst. Tex. Woman's U., Denton, 1977-83, grants acct., 1983-85, dir. internal audits, 1985—; acct. Denton Baseball, Inc., 1992-94. Author: Internal Audit Guide ... Higher Education, 1983. Scholar PTA, 1968. Mem. Assn. Coll. and Univ. Auditors, Tex. Assn. Coll. and Univ. Auditors, Tex. Woman's U. Alumnae Assn., Nat. Assn. Coll. and Univ. Bus. Officers. Democrat. Office: Tex Womans U Po Box 425587 Denton TX 76204

YARBROUGH, SONJA DIANNE, marketing and public relations professional; b. Trenton, Fla., June 6, 1948; d. George Charlie and Dorothy Mae (Carver) Y. BA in English, U. Fla., 1971; MS in Pub. Rels., Boston U., 1980. Pub. rels. asst. Digital Equipment Corp., Maynard, Mass., 1979; interim editor, rsch. asst. Rehab. Rsch. Inst., Gainesville, Fla., 1980-81; bus. mgr. Dental Specialty Practice, Atlanta, 1982-84; asst. account exec. Grizzard Advt., Atlanta, 1984-86; pub. rels. mktg. cons. Atlanta, 1987-88; account exec. Northlake Typography, Atlanta, 1988-89, TypoGraphics Atlanta, 1989-90; mktg. coord. Future Aviation Profls., Atlanta, 1990-93; pub. rels./mktg. cons. Atlanta, 1993-94; pub. rels. dir. Tech. Coll. of the Lowcountry, Beaufort, S.C., 1994—. Scholarship in Communications Boston U., 1979; recipient Bernice McCullar award Exemplary Leadership, 1990-91. Mem. Women in Communications, Inc. (co-chairperson ACE Competition 1989-90, publicity guide 1989-90, v.p. programs 1990-91, pres. 1992-93, past pres. 1993-94). Democrat. Home: 3125 W University Ave Gainesville FL 32607-2575 Office: 100 S Ribaut Rd PO Box 1288 Beaufort SC 29901

YARBROUGH, VICKIE JANE, elementary reading specialist; b. Kingsport, Tenn., Aug. 31, 1947; d. Haywood and Alberta Mae (Tate) Bowen; m. Chris Malcolm Yarbrough, June 7, 1969; 1 child, Katherine Jane. BS, East Tenn. State U., Johnson City, 1969, MA, 1976; postgrad., Western Carolina U., Cullowhee, N.C., 1988-90. Tchr. Rockbridge County, Lexington, Va., 1969-70; tchr. McDowell County, Marion, N.C., 1970-75, reading specialist, 1975-80, tchr., 1980-88, asst. prin., 1988-90, reading specialist, 1990—. Mem. planning bd. Town of Old Fort, N.C., 1995—. Named Tchr. of Yr. Old Fort Sch., 1991-92, Citizen of Yr. Kiwanis Club of Old Fort, 1994. Mem. NEA, Reading Recoevery Coun. N.Am., N.C. Assn. Educators (v.p. McDowell 1991-92), Kappa Delta Pi.26417774. Office: Old Fort Elem Sch 301 Mauney Ave Old Fort NC 28762

YASGER, TIMOTHY FRANCIS, secondary education educator; b. Robbinsdale, Minn., Aug. 18, 1961; s. Jerome Damus and Judith Ann (Myre) Y.; m. Theresa Ann Jablonski, Nov. 20. 1993. BS in Edn. magna cum laude, St. Cloud State U., 1989. Cert. English tchr., Tex. Reading tchr. Ysleta Ind. Sch. Dist., El Paso, 1990-95, San Elizario (Tex.) Ind. Sch. Dist., 1995—; doctorate rev. com. mem. U. Tex. El Paso, 1995, grad. peer review com. mem., 1995. Mem. Assn. for Supervision and Curriculum Devel., Phi Delta Kappa.

YATES, ELLA GAINES, library consultant; b. Atlanta, June 14, 1927; d. Fred Douglas and Laura (Moore) Gaines; m. Joseph L. Sydnor (dec.); 1 child, Jerri Gaines Sydnor Lee; m. Clayton R. Yates (dec.). A.B., Spelman Coll., Atlanta, 1949; M.S. in L.S, Atlanta U., 1951; J.D., Atlanta Law Sch., 1979. Asst. br. librarian Bklyn. Pub. Library, 1951-54; head children's dept. Orange (N.J.) Pub. Library, 1956-59; br. librarian E. Orange (N.J.) Pub. Library, 1960-69; med. librarian Orange Meml. Hosp., 1967-69; asst. dir. Montclair (N.J.) Pub. Library, 1970-72; asst. dir. Atlanta-Fulton Pub. Library, 1972-76, dir., 1976-81; dir. learning resource ctr. Seattle Opportunities Industrialization Ctr., 1982-84; asst. dir. adminstrn. Friendship Force, Atlanta, 1984-86; state librarian Commonwealth of Va., 1986-90; library cons. Price Waterhouse, 1991; adv. bd. Library of Congress Center for the Book, 1977-85; cons. in field; vis. lectr. U. Wash., Seattle, 1981-83; mem. Va. Records Adv. Bd., 1986-90; mem. Nagara Exec. Bd., 1987-91. Contbr. to profl. jours. Vice chmn. N.J. Women's Coun. on Human Rels., 1957-59; chmn. Friends Fulton County Jail, 1973-81; bd. dirs. United Cerebral Palsy Greater Atlanta, Inc., 1979-81 Coalition Against Censorship, Washington, 1981-84, YMCA Met. Atlanta, 1979-81, Exec. Women's Network, 1979-82, Freedom To Read Found., 1979-85, Va. Black History Mus., Richmond, 1990-91; sec., exec. dir. Va. Libr. Found. Bd., 1986-90. Recipient meritorious svc. award Atlanta U., 1977, Phoenix award City of Atlanta, 1980, Serwa award Nat. Coalition 100 Black Women, 1989, Black Caucus award, 1989, disting. svc. award Clark-Atlanta U., 1991, ednl. support svc. award Tuskegee Airmen, 1993; named profl. woman of yr. NAACP N.J., 1972, outstanding chum of yr., 1976; named outstanding alumni Spelman Coll., 1977, named to alumni hall of fame, 1995. Mem. ALA (exec. bd. 1977-83, commn. freedom of access to info.), NAACP, Southeastern Libr. Assn., Nat. Assn. Govt. Archives and Records Adminstrn. (exec. bd. 1987-91), Delta Sigma Theta. Baptist. Home and Office: 1171 Oriole Dr SW Atlanta GA 30311-2424

YATES, HELEN LOUISE, labor and delivery, critical care nurse; b. Neosho, Mo., Mar. 2, 1941; d. John Merlin and Ella Mae Pratt; children: Roger Dean, Rogenia Louise. Grad., Sch. Cosmetology, Neosho, 1974; lic. in practical nursing, Crowder Coll., 1977; ADN, Northeastern Okla. A&M Coll., 1981. RN, Calif., Tex., Ariz.; cert. in phlebotomy, intravenous therapy, chemotherapy, thermoregulation and critical care of infant, fetal heart monitoring I, II and advanced, neonatology outreach edn., critical care/emergency nursing; cert. provider ACLS, Am. Heart Assn. Team leader proarrhythmic effects of antiarrhythmic drugs Sale Hosp., Neosho, 1978-83; cons. nurse King Fahad Hosp., Riyadh, Saudi Arabia, 1983; team leader nurse N.W. Hosp., Tucson, 1984-85; labor/delivery nurse Sierra Vista (Ariz.) Hosp., 1985-88; travel nurse Judy's Nurses, Tucson, 1988—, SEAMC Hosp., Douglas, Ariz., 1988—; cons. HCA, Saudi Arabia, 1983. Author: Financial Care Plan, 1992. Cert. provider ACLS, Am. Heart Assn., 1990—. Home: 1440 S Via Viento Sierra Vista AZ 85635-4523

YATES, LARRY LAMAR, activist; b. Durham, N.C., Apr. 7, 1950; s. Warren Grice and Margaret Ann (Buchanan) Y.; m. Carol Stroebel, Sept. 4, 1993. Grad. high sch., McLean, Va., 1967. Asst. libr. Richmond (Va.) City Jail, 1980-81; exec. dir. Va. Housing Coalition, Richmond, 1981-83; planner Va. Dept. Housing & Cmty. Devel., Richmond, 1983-86; exec. dir. Richmond United Neighborhoods, 1987-88; dir. nat. anti-displacement project Nat. Low Income Housing Coalition, Washington, 1988-90, dir. field svcs., 1991-95; pres. Social Justice Connections, Arlington, Va., 1995—; pres., bd. dirs. Richmond United Neighborhoods, 1986. Editor (newsletter): Shuting The Back Door, 1988, Virginia Housing Coalition Voice, 1981-83. Coun. mem. Richmond Urban Inst., 1981-85; founder, sec. Va. Coalition for Coop., 1980; founding organizer Va. Assn. Neighborhoods Conf., Roanoke, Va., 1985. Named Mem. of Yr. Va. Assn. Neighborhoods, 1988; recipient Award for Svc. Va. Housing Coalition, 1983. Home: 2600 16th St S Apt 712 Arlington VA 22204-4949 Office: Social Justice Connections PO Box 4090 Arlington VA 22204

YATES, LINDA FAE, women's health nurse; b. Blount County, Ala., Dec. 17, 1947; d. Frank D. and Lillie Mae (Mangum) Yates; children: Lynn Sweatman, Huelet Sweatman, Preston Sweatman. Lic. in practical nursing, Wallace State Community Coll., Hanceville, Ala., 1984, ADN, 1990. Pvt. duty nurse Profl. Med. Svcs., Boaz, Ala.; charge nurse Oneonta (Ala.) Manor, Garden City (Ala.) Health Care; staff and charge nurse level II nursing, scrub nurse, orthopedic nursing Carraway Meth. Med. Ctr., Brimingham, Ala. Recipient Den Leader award Cub Scouts Am., Scout Master award. Mem. ANA, Ala. State Nurses Assn.

YATES, MARVIN CLARENCE, advertising artist, painter, illustrator; b. Jackson, Tenn., Sept. 22, 1943; s. Marvin Caleb and Mary Louise (Wright) Y.; m. Margaret Sarah Lea, Dec. 6, 1975; children: Wesley, Christen. Student Memphis Acad. Arts, 1962-65. Advt. artist, illustrator Memphis Pub. Co., 1967—. Served to 1st class petty officer USCG, 1966-72. Mem. Am. Watercolor Soc., So. Watercolor Soc. (co-founder), Tenn. Watercolor Soc. (co-founder), Memphis Watercolor Group (co-founder, pres. 1968-84). Avocations: sports, photography. Home: 1457 Hwy 304 Hernando MS 38632-8409 Office: Memphis Pub Co 495 Union Ave Memphis TN 38103-3242

YATES, NORRIS WILLIAM, JR., lawyer; b. Alamo Heights, Tex., July 6, 1926; s. Norris William and Maggie Barkley (Curry) Y.; m. Mary Hutchings Spencer, Dec. 30, 1947 (div. Aug. 1949); 1 child, William Spencer; m. Jimmie Carolyn Cook, Sept. 17, 1955; children: Victoria Carolyn Marullo, Rebecca Elizabeth Yates Bird. BA in Econs., Tex. A&M U., 1950; JD, U. Tex., 1957. Bar: U.S. Ct. of Military Appeals, 1963, U.S. Supreme Ct., 1964, Tex., 1957. Asst. to mgr. rates and tariffs Slick Airways, Inc., San Antonio, 1950; assoc. Beckmann, Stanard, Wood, Barrow & Vance, San Antonio, 1957-60; pvt. practice San Antonio, 1960-67, 83—; asst. criminal dist. atty. Bexar County Dist. Atty.'s Office, San Antonio, 1967-82, chief civil sect., 1967-82; mcpl. ct. judge City of San Antonio, 1966-67. Editor The Subpoena, 1958-59. Exec. com. Bexar County Dem. Party, San Antonio. Cpl. U.S. Army, Airborne Infantry, 1944-46; ETO; 1st lt. USAF, 1951-55, B-29 Bomber Pilot, Korea, lt. col. USAFR, ret. 1978. Decorated Bronze Star medal, combat infantry badge, Glider badge, pilot's wings, three battle stars. Mem. USAF Pilot Class 52-George Assn. (past sec., dir.), 307th Bomb Group/Wing Inc. (v.p.), Toastmasters (past pres., Disting. Dist. Gov. 1969-70, Disting. Toastmaster 1984, Presdl. citation 1992), Masons (past master, masonic lodge, 32 degree), Scottish Rite, San Antonio A&M Club (dir.). Democrat. Presbyterian. Home: 2118 Kenilworth Blvd San Antonio TX 78209

YATES, PATRICIA ENGLAND, employment company executive; b. Sparta, Tenn., Sept. 18, 1958; d. Edsel and Gladys Mary (Garland) England; m. Dennis Eugene Yates, Nov. 30, 1990. BS in Home Econs., Tenn. Tech. U., 1982. Purchasing sec. Porelon, Inc., Cookeville, Tenn., 1982-87; buyer purchasing dept. Tenn. Tech. U., Cookeville, Tenn., 1987-88; dir. pers. J & S Constrn. Co., Inc., Cookeville, 1988-93; placement coord. Holland Employment (formerly Putnam Employment Svc. Inc.), Cookeville, 1993-95; svc. specialist Hamilton-Ryker Co., Shelbyville, Tenn., 1995—; dir. projects Nat. and Internat. Issues Rsch., Sparta, Tenn., 1982—. Mem. Nat. Exch. Club, Profl. Secs. Internat., Bus. and Profl. Women's Orgn. (treas. 1990, 2d v.p. 1992, Finalist Young Careerist 1994), U.C. Soc. Resource Mgmt. (treas. 1993), Internat. Platform Assn. Office: The Hamilton-Ryker Co 100 Public Square Shelbyville TN 37160

YATES, STEVEN ALAN, writer; b. Bartlesville, Okla., Aug. 26, 1957; s. William Clyde and Alice Mae (Belles) Y. BA in Philosophy, U. Tulsa, 1980; MA in Philosophy, U. Ga., 1983, PhD in Philosophy, 1987. Instr. U. Ga., Athens, 1985-87; vis. asst. prof. Clemson (S.C.) U., 1987-88; temp. asst. prof. Auburn (Ala.) U., 1988-89, 90-93; F. Leroy Hill fellow Inst. for Humaane St., Fairfax, Va., 1989; vis. asst. prof. Wofford Coll., Spartanburg, S.C., 1990, U. S.C., Columbia, 1993-95; staff Roper Pers., Columbia, 1995-96; Bradley vis. fellow Acton Inst., Grand Rapids, Mich., summer 1996; ind. distbr. New Image Internat., Georgetown, Ky., 1996—. Author: Civil Wrongs, 1994; contbr. articles to profl. jours. Guest spkr. Ala. Libertarian Party, Montgomery, 1992. Salvatori fellow Heritage Found., 1992-94. fellow Acton Inst.; mem. Am. Philos. Assn., Southern League. Baptist.

YATES, WILLIAM JOHN, business owner, counselor; b. Wurtzburg, Fed. Republic of Germany, Mar. 15, 1959; came to U.S., 1959; s. Jack John and Georgia Ann (McFeron) Y.; m. Jacqueline Renee Wheeler, July 20, 1982 (div. July 1987). Grad., high sch., Wharton, Tex., 1977; PhD Counseling, PhD Theocentric Psy., 1995. Ordained minister, Calif. Autobody shop mgr. Don Elliot Chevrolet, Wharton, 1978-79; autobody mechanic/painter Cochran Motor Co., Wharton, 1979-80; truck driver The Orlgmud Co., Needville, Tex., 1980-81; dewatering plant operator Valero Energy Corp., Boling, Tex., 1981-83; auto parts counterperson Dependable Motor Parts, Wharton, 1983-84; automotive restoration specialist Bud's Quality Shop, Wharton, 1984-85; power plant mechanic, asst. operator, asst. boiler fireman Imperial Sugar Co., Sugarland, Tex., 1985-87; autobody repairman, painter Gary's Body Shop, Texarkana, Tex., 1987-88; autobody repairman Helfman Ford, Houston, 1988-89, Jack Roach Ford, Houston, 1989; automotive sales rep. Mac Haik Ford, Houston, 1990, Luke Johnson Ford, Houston, 1991; bus. owner Yates and Assocs., Wharton, 1991—. Mem. Hazelden Grass Roots Polit. Network, Tex., 1994; cmty. liaison counselor Area Counties Coun. on Alcoholism and Drug Abuse, Wharton, 1993-95. With USAF and Tex. Air N.G., 1977-83; sys. integrator Info. Technology Tech. VAR/VAD. Mem. N.G. Assn. Tex., Nat. Assn. of the Self-Employed Bus. Owner. Republican. Office: Yates & Assocs 1823 Stadium Rd #209 Wharton TX 77488

YAU, STEPHEN SIK-SANG, computer science and engineering educator, computer scientist, researcher; b. Wusei, Kiangsu, China, Aug. 6, 1935; came to U.S., 1958, naturalized, 1968; s. Pen-Chi and Wen-Chum (Shum) Y.; m. Vickie Liu, June 14, 1964; children: Andrew, Philip. BS in Elec. Engring, Nat. Taiwan U., China, 1958; MS in Elec. Engring, U. Ill., Urbana, 1959, PhD, 1961. Asst. prof. elec. engring. Northwestern U., Evanston, Ill., 1961-64, assoc. prof., 1964-68, prof., 1968-88, prof. computer scis., 1970-88, Walter P. Murphy prof. Elec. Engring. and Computer Sci., 1986-88, also chmn. dept. computer scis., 1972-77; chmn. dept. elec. engring. and computer sci. Northwestern U., 1977-88; prof. computer and info. sci., chmn. dept. U. Fla., Gainesville, 1988-94; prof. computer sci. and engr., chmn. Ariz. State U., 1994—; conf. chmn. IEEE Computer Conf., Chgo., 1967; symposium chmn. Symposium on feature extraction and selection in pattern recognition Argonne Nat. Lab., 1970; gen. chmn. Nat. Computer Conf., Chgo., 1974, First Internat. Computer Software and Applications Conf., Chgo., 1977; Trustee Na. Electronics Conf., Inc., 1965-68; chmn. organizing com. 11th World Computer Congress, Internat. Fedn. Info. Processing, San Francisco, 1989; gen. co-chmn. Internat. Symposium on Autonomous Decentralized Systems, Japan, 1993, gen. chmn., Phoenix, 1995. Editor-in-chief Computer mag., 1981-84; assoc. editor Jour. Info. Scis., 1983—; editor IEEE Trans. on Software Engring., 1988-91; contbr. numerous articles on software engring., distributed and parallel processing systems, computer sci., elec. engring. and related fields to profl. publs.; patentee in field. Recipient Louis E. Levy medal Franklin Inst., 1963, Golden Plate award Am. Acad. of Achievement, 1964, The Silver Core award Internat. Fedn. Info. Processing, 1989, Spl. award, 1989. Fellow IEEE (mem. governing bd. Computer Soc. 1967-76, pres. 1974-75, dir. Inst. 1976-77, chmn. awards com., 1996—; Richard E. Merwin award Computer Soc. 1981, Centennial medal 1984, Extraordinary Achievement 1985, Outstanding Contbn. award Computer Sci. Soc. 1985), AAAS, Franklin Inst.; mem. Assn. for Computing Machinery, Am. Fedn. Info.-Processing Socs. (mem. exec. com. 1974-76, 79-82, dir. 1972-82, chmn. awards com. 1979-82, v.p. 1982-84, pres. 1984-86; chmn. Nat. Computer Conf. Bd. 1982-83), Am. Soc. Engring. Edn., Sigma Xi, Tau Beta Pi, Eta Kappa Nu, Pi Mu Epsilon. Office: AZ State U PO Box 875 406 Tempe AZ 85287-5406

YAUNG, ALAN TSU-I, computer scientist; b. Taipei, Taiwan, China, Jan. 27, 1957; came to the U.S., 1982; s. Chen-Hwa and Chen (Shu) Y.; m. Fangling Chang, Dec. 23, 1983; 1 child, Stephanie Jinyu. BBA in Stats., Nat. Cheng Kung U., Tainan, Taiwan, 1979; MS in Computer Sci., U. Tex., Arlington, 1984, PhD in Computer Sci., 1988. Grad. teaching asst. dept. computer sci. and engring. U. Tex., Arlington, 1983-86; intern Microelectronics and Computer Tech. Corp., Austin, Tex., 1986; grad. rsch. asst. dept. computer sci. and engring. U. Tex., Arlington, 1986-87, asst. instr. dept computer sci. and engring., 1988; asst. prof. dept. computer sci. N.E. La. U., Monroe, La., 1988-90; adv. devel. analyst IBM Corp., Roanoke, Tex., 1990—; lectr. dept. computer sci. and engring. U. Tex. Arlington, 1992—; reviewer First Internat. Conf. on Systems Integration, Morristown, N.J., 1990, Software Engring. Program, NSF. Reviewer: IEEE Internat. Conf. on Requirements Engring., Jour. Computer Langs., IEEE Computer, IEEE Software; book reviewer Van Nostrand Reinhold; contbr. articles to profl. jours.; inventor in field. Mem. IEEE/Computer Soc., Assn. for Computing Machinery, Omega Rho (annual scholarship 1987), Upsilon Pi Epsilon, Tau Beta Pi.

YAWN, DAVID MCDONALD, journalist; b. Knoxville, Tenn., Aug. 11, 1956; s. McDonald Yawn and Eva (Taylor) Quinn; m. Cathy Whitmire, Sept. 8, 1990. BA in Print Journalism, U. Miss., 1981. Staff writer Clarksdale (Miss.) Press Register, 1982-85; sr. staff writer Memphis Bus. Jour., 1985—; cons. editor Guild Bindery Press book publs., 1993—; one of 3 Am. journalists invited to take econ. tour of Germany, 1995. Editor: In the Shadow of the Wall, The Partnering Paradigm, Sane Investing for the Non-Financial; contbg. editor internat. for Cotton Farming mag. Active Memphis Long Range Econ. Devel. Planning Com. Named one of Outstanding Young Men Am., 1984, 89; recipient Sch. Bell award Miss. Assn. Educators, 1983. Mem.

Soc. Profl. Journalists (Mid South chpt. Award of Excellence 1995), Nat. Assn. Real Estate Editors. Republican. Presbyterian. Home: 1082 Kings Park Rd Memphis TN 38117-5434 Office: Memphis Bus Jour 88 Union Ave Ste 102 Memphis TN 38103-5100

YAZ, EDWIN ENGIN, electrical engineer, educator; b. Istanbul, Turkey, May 11, 1954; s. Vahap and Husniye (Zenginer) Y.; m. Ilke Durak, Aug. 29, 1980. BSEE, Bosphorus U., Istanbul, 1976; MSEE, Bosphorus U., 1979, PhD in EE, 1982. Registered profl. engr., Ark. Researcher Marmara Research Inst. & Inst. Basic Scis., Gebze/Kocaeli, Turkey, 1982-84; research fellow U. Ill., Urbana, 1984; asst. prof. elec. engring. U. Ark., Fayetteville, 1985-87; assoc. prof. elec. engring. U. Ark., 1987-91, prof. elec. engring., 1991—; vis. prof. Purdue U., Ind., 1992. Contbr. over 180 book chpts. and articles to profl. jours. and conf. procs.; assoc. editor IEEE Transactions on Automatic Control; mem. editl. bd. IEEE Control Systems Soc. Conf. Recipient Excellence in Rsch. award Halliburton Found. Dept. Elec. Engring., 1987, 91, Outstanding Faculty award Ark. Acad. Elec. Engring., 1986, 89, Best Presentations award Am. Control Confs., 1991, 94; grantee Turkish Sci. and Tech. Rsch. Coun/NATO, 1984, Ark. Sci. and Tech. Authority, 1986-87, 90-91, 92-93, NSF, 1991-93, 94—, EPRI/Swepco, 1992-96, UN TOKTEN, 1993, 96; recipient U. Ark. Alumni Assn. Dist. Rsch. Achievement award 1996, others. Mem. IEEE (sr. mem.), AAUP (chpt. sec. 1994), Am. Soc. Engring. Edn., Tau Beta Pi, Eta Kappa Nu. Office: Elec Engring Dept Univ Ark BEC 3217 Fayetteville AR 72701

YAZIGI, RASHID A., allergist, immunologist, pediatrician; b. Syria, Jan. 15, 1941. MD, Damascus U. Diplomate Am. Bd. Allergy & Immunology, Am. Bd. Pediatrics. Intern Huron Road Hosp., Cleve., 1970-71; resident in pediatrics Wayne State U., Detroit, 1971-72, Tulane U./Charity Hosp., New Orleans, 1972-73, U. Hosp., Jacksonville, Fla., 1974; fellow in allergy & clin. immunology La. State U. Med. Ctr., New Orleans, 1976-78; with Meth. Hosp., Pendleton Meml. Meth. Hosp., Slidell Meml. Hosps., North Shore Med. Ctr., La. Fellow Am. Assn. Immunologists, Am. Acad. Allergy and Immunology; mem. AMA. Office: Allergy Asthma Clinic 5640 Read Blvd Ste 620 New Orleans LA 70127-3130

YEAGER, ANDREW MICHAEL, pediatrics educator; b. Newark, July 10, 1950; m. Marty Johnson; children: Jonathan Webster, Elizabeth Bennett. BA, Johns Hopkins U., 1972, MD, 1975. Intern dept. pediatrics The Johns Hopkins Hosp., Balt., 1975-76, asst. resident dept. pediatrics, 1976-78, chief resident outpatient dept. pediatrics, 1980-81, chief resident inpatient dept. pediatrics, 1981-82; fellow pediatric hematology and oncology The Oncology Ctr. Sch. Medicine, The Johns Hopkins U., Balt., 1978-80, asst. prof. oncology, asst. prof. pediatrics, 1982-87, assoc. prof. oncology, assoc. prof. pediatrics, 1987-93, assoc. prof. neurology, 1989-93; prof. pediatrics, medicine and neurology Sch. Medicine, Emory U., Atlanta, 1993—, prof. Winship Cancer Ctr., 1993—, dir. divsn. hematology/oncology, bone marrow transplantation, dept. pediatrics, 1993—; dir. Leukema/BMT program, dept. medicine Emory U., Altanta, 1995—; evaluator Westinghouse Nat. Sci. Talent Search, Washington, 1979—, judge, 1986—; mem. med. adv. bd. The Children's Cancer Found., 1987—; spl. rev. exptl. therapeutics-2 study sect divsn. rsch. grants NIH, 1990-91, permanent mem., 1991-95; chair ad hoc tech. rev. group contract rev. br. Nat. Cancer Inst., NIH, 1992; co-organizer 6th Internat. Autologous Bone Marrow Transplant Symposium, Houston, 1992; bd. dirs. Children's Oncology Svcs. Ga., Atlanta. Author chpts. in books; mem. editorial bd. Bone Marrow Transplantation, 1988—, Am. Jour. Pediatric Hematology/Oncology, 1989-95, Archives of Pediatrics and Adolescent Medicine, 1993—; rev. Blood, 1986—, Jour. Clin. Oncology, 1986—, Annals Internal Medicine, 1991, Cancer Chemotherapy and Pharmacology, 1991—, Cancer Rsch., 1991—, Jour. Clin. Investigation, 1992—; contbr. over 125 chpts. to books and 70 articles to profl. jours. Mem. Am. Acad. Pediatrics, Am. Soc. Pediatric Hematology-Oncology, Am. Fedn. Clin. Rsch., Am. Soc. Clin. Oncology, Am. Soc. Hematology, Am. Assn. Cancer Rsch., Internat. Soc. Experimental Hematology, Pediatric Oncology Group, European Soc. Pediatric Rsch., Ea. Soc. Pediatric Rsch., Soc. Pediatric Rsch. (co-chair abstract selection com. and hematology-oncology session 1992, 94), Phi Beta Kappa. Office: Emory U Sch Medicine Divsn Pediatric Hematology 2040 Ridgewood Dr NE Atlanta GA 30307-1028

YEAGER, CHARLES WILLIAM, lawyer, newspaper publisher; b. Frederick, Md., Sept. 18, 1921; s. Ralph A. and Ina Jane (Nuckles) Y.; m. Charlotte L. Matthews, Nov. 26, 1958; children: Gretchen A. Murphy, Kristin A. Bridge, Charles W. Yeager Jr., Matthew R. Yeager. BA, W.Va. U., 1943; LLB, U. Va., 1948. Bar: W.Va. 1948, Fla. 1969, U.S. Supreme Ct. 1968. Ptnr. Steptoe & Johnson, Charleston, W.Va., 1948-93; of counsel Rose and Atkinson, Charleston, 1993—. Pub., editor The Nicholas CHronicle. Maj. U.S. Army, 1942-46. Democrat. Office: Nicholas Chronicle 603 Church St Summersville WV 26651-1411

YEAROUT, ROBERT DEWITT, management educator, retired army officer; b. Waynesboro, Va., July 6, 1940; s. James Leon Yearout and Geniveve Brown; m. Marcia Warren Eckley, June 16, 1962; children: Robert Elliott, Gwendolyn Eckley Yearout Carrion. BSCE, Va. Mil. Inst., 1962; MS in Sys. Mgmt., U. So. Calif., 1982; MS in Indsl. Engring., Kans. State U., 1985, PhD in Indsl. Engring., 1987. Commd. 2d lt. U.S. Army, 1962, advanced through grades to lt. col., 1978, various inf. assignments, 1962-66, 70-79; comdr. spl. forces Mike Force Bat., 1966-67; detachment comdr. 5th Spl. Forces, Vietnam, 1966-67; ops. officer 38th and 9th Infs., Vietnam, 1968-69; chmn. mgmt. dept. Command and Gen. Staff Coll., Ft. Leavenworth, Kans., 1980-84; ret., 1984; assoc. prof. U. N.C., Asheville, 1987—, faculty rep. NCAA and Big South Conf., 1990—; mem. nat. governing bd., editor procs. Nat. Confs. on Undergrad. Rsch., 1990—. Contbr. articles to profl. jours. Bd. dirs. Mountain Area Residential Facility, Asheville, 1988-91, Ctr. for Jewish Studies, Asheville, 1995—. Decorated Bronze Star with V device; Vietnamese Cross of Gallantry with palm. Mem. Ergonomics and Human Factors Soc., Internat. Indsl. Ergonomic and Occupl. Health Soc., Sigma Xi, Tau Beta Pi. Baptist. Office: U NC Dept Mgmt and Acctg Owen Hall Asheville NC 28804-3299

YEATTS, COLEMAN BENNETT, JR., judge; b. Danville, Va., Dec. 28, 1942; s. Coleman Bennett and Grace Ruth (Cook) Y.; m. Caryl Elizabeth Hogg, July 6, 1968. BA in Polit. Sci., U. Richmond, 1965, MA in Polit. Sci., 1967, JD, 1972. Tchr. govt./history Hargrave Mil. Acad., Chatham, Va., 1967; tchr. govt. Danville (Va.) C.C., 1971; ptnr. Yeatts, Overbey & Yeatts, Chatham, 1973-87; judge 22d dist. Juvenile and Domestic Rels. Dist. Ct., Chatham, 1987-91, chief judge, 1991—; atty. Town of Gretna, Va., 1975-87. Bd. trustees Hargrave Mil. Acad., Chatham, 1993—, Nat. Coun. Juvenile and Family Ct. Judges; candidate for Va. State Senate, 19th Dist., 1983. Lt. col. USAR, 1967-94. Recipient Disting. Alumnus Achievement award Hargrave Mil. Acad., 1988, 96. Mem. Va. Bar Assn., Res. Officers Assn. U.S., Assn. Dist. Ct. Judges Va. (past com. chair), Nat. Coun. Juvenile and Family Ct. Judges (past com. chair), Am. Judges Assn., Hargrave Mil. Acad. Alumni Assn. (pres. 1975-77), Rotary (pres. 1978). Home: PO Box 364 Cherrystone Rd Chatham VA 24531 Office: 22nd District Court Main St PO Box 270 Chatham VA 24531

YEATTS, DOROTHY ELIZABETH FREEMAN, nurse, retired county official, educator; b. Richmond, Va., Jan. 19, 1925; d. Robert Franklin and Elizabeth Bell (Wiggins) Freeman; m. Roy Earl Yeatts, Nov. 27, 1948; children: Martha Jane Yeatts Couch, Robert Patrick. Diploma in nursing, Stuart Circle Hosp., Richmond, Va., 1947; BS in Nursing, Coll. William and Mary, 1947; cert. pub. health nursing supr., U. N.C., 1974. RN, Va., N.C. Vis. nurse Instructive Vis. Nurses Assn., Richmond, 1947-49; maternity nurse N.C. Bapt. Hosp., Winston-Salem, 1969-71; pub. health nurse I, Forsyth County Health Dept., Winston-Salem, 1971-72, pub. health nurse coord., 1972-74, pub. health nurse supr., 1974-78; instr. ARC, Winston-Salem, 1978-93; vol. Am. Red Cross, 1993—. Pres. Buckingham Park Garden Club, Richmond, 1956-58; elder Trinity Presbyn. Ch., Winston-Salem, 1978-81, Sunday sch. tchr., 1960-84, circle bible moderator, 1984—, pres. Women of Trinity Presbyn. Ch., 1963-64; Sunday sch. tchr. Tuckahoe Presbyn. Ch., 1954-57; bd. dirs. Forsyth Cancer Soc., Winston-Salem, 1980-86; vol. ARC. Republican. Home: 703 Devon Ct Winston Salem NC 27104-1269

YEATTS, MARIAN SUNNY, secondary school educator; b. Arlington, Tex., July 14, 1944; d. Bert Simpson and Maxine Jean (Acker) Smith; m. Fred Henry Yeatts, Dec. 21, 1963; 1 child, Denise Joann. BS, Tex. Woman's U., 1968, MA, 1976; English cert., U. North Tex., 1970. Cert. theater, speech, English, history, econs., geography, debate, and govt. tchr., Tex. Grad. teaching fellow Tex. Woman's U., Denton, 1968-69, 70-74; tchr. Pilot Point (Tex.) High Sch., 1969-70, Carrollton (Tex.) Farmers Br. Ind. Sch. Dist., 1974-78, Sanger (Tex.) High Sch., 1978—; artistic advisor Sanger Arts Coun., 1996—. Designer numerous sets, costumes and lights for shows, also dir. Mem. Sanger Mayor's Fine Arts Com., 1989; bd. dirs. Denton Community Theatre, 1989-92; acting cons. Denton Light Opera Co., 1990; bd. dirs., performance cons. Denton Civic Ballet, 1992—. Recipient set design award Denton Community Theater; named Tchr. of Yr., Sanger High Sch. Faculty, 1981. Mem. Tex. Ednl. Theatre Assn., Sanger Edn. Assn. (past pres.), Sanger C. of C. (sesquicentennial com. 1986, past pres. women's aux.), Internat. Thespians (advisor thespian state adv. bd.), Order Ea. Star, Zeta Phi Eta (adviser 1968-71). Democrat. Baptist. Home: 312 Cherry St Sanger TX 76266-8852 Office: Sanger High Sch PO Box 188 Sanger TX 76266-0188

YELTON, DAVID KEITH, historian, educator; b. Rutherfordton, N.C., May 23, 1960; s. Charles Ray and Frances (Womack) Y.; m. Karen Denise Baynard, June 9, 1984; 1 child, Kaitlyn Nicole. BA, Appalachian State U., 1982; MA in History, U. N.C., 1985, PhD of History, 1990. Grad. asst., instr. U. N.C., Chapel Hill, 1983-90; asst. prof. history Gardner-Webb U., Boiling Springs, N.C., 1990—. Presenter in field; contbr. articles to profl. jours. Grantee German Acad. Exch. Svc., 1988. Mem. Am. Hist. Assn., Nat. History Edn. Network, Soc. Mil. History, WWII Studies Assn., Assn. Historians N.C. Methodist. Office: Gardner-Webb Univ PO Box 204 Boiling Springs NC 28017

YENTIS, RICHARD DAVID, psychiatrist; b. Phila., June 24, 1938; s. Herbert and Mary (Susner) Y.; m. Edie Ann Tomlinson, Mar. 21, 1964; children: Amiee Killpack, Richard Jr. BA in Am. Civilization, U. Pa., 1959, MD, 1963. Diplomate Am. Bd. Psychiatry and Neurology; lic. physician Calif., Fla., Pa., Tex. Intern Mt. Sinai Hosp., Miami Beach, Fla., 1963-64; resident in psychiatry Inst. of Pa. Hosp., Phila., 1964-66; fellow in child psychiatry St. Christopher's Hosp., Phila., 1966-68; pvt. practice child and adult psychiatry Ft. Worth, Tex., 1969—; clin. instr. psychiatry U. Tex. (Southwestern Med. Sch.), Dallas, 1969; acting med. dir. and med. dir. Psychiat. Inst. Ft. Worth, through 1974, dir. adolescent svc., 1974; adj. prof. psychiatry Tex. Osteo. Med. Sch., 1974-83; lectr. in field; past med. dir. Oak Grove Resdl. Treatment Ctr., Psychiat. unit Campbell Meml. Hosp., Weatherford, Tex., 1986; dir. RESTORE, N.E. Comty. Hosp., 1989-90; expert witness Dept. Profl. Regulation, State of Fla., 1993-95; chief proctor Harris Meth. Hosp., 1993; presenter seminar Inst. Personal Growth and Achievement, 1993-95; active staff All Saints Hosp., Ft. Worth, All Saints Behavioral Health, Ft. Worth, Harris Meth. Hosp., Ft. Worth, Harris Meth. S.W., Ft. Worth, Columbia, Plaza Med. Ctr., Ft. Worth; courtesy staff All Saints Citiview, Ft. Worth, , Ft. Worth, Health South Rehab. Hosp., Ft. Worth, Huguley Meml. Hsp., Ft. Worth, others. Contbr. articles to profl. jours.; editor Interraction, 1979-80; reader for clin. psychiatry, 1978, 79, 80. Adv. bd. The Rsch. Inst., 1983; bd. dirs. Dan Dancinger Community Ctr., 1974-76, Elmwood Found., 1980; pres. Torch Club, 1980-90. With USPHS, 1964-69. Fellow Internat. Acad. Behavioral Medicine, Counseling and Psychotherapy; mem. Tex. Med. Assn., Tex. Med. Found., Tarrant County Med. Soc., Ft. Worth Pediat. Soc., Am. Psychiat. Assn., Am. Soc. Adolescent Psychiatry, Am. Acad. Child Psychiatry, Am. Acad. Clin. Psychiatry, Ft. Worth Neurosci. Soc., Am. Soc. of Addiction Medicine, Am. Bd. Med. Psychotherapists, Obsessive Compulsive Found., Nat. Anorexic Aid Soc., Internat. Transactional Analysis Assn., Am. Anorexia/Bulimia Assn. Home: 2615 Simondale Dr Fort Worth TX 76109-1245 Office: 1501 Merrimac Cir Ste 210 Fort Worth TX 76107-6568

YEOMAN, LYNN CHALMERS, cancer researcher, medical educator; b. Evanston, Ill., May 17, 1943; s. Kenneth Chalmers and Lillian (Worner) Y.; m. Carol S. Jeanes-Yeoman; children: Caroline, Christopher, Sarah. BA, DePauw U., 1965; PhD, U. Ill., 1970. Instr. Baylor Coll. of Medicine, Houston, 1972-73, asst. prof., 1975-76, assoc. prof., 1976-84, prof., 1984—; assoc. dir. Bristol-Baylor Lab, Houston, 1989-90; assoc. dir. anti-cancer drug discovery and cell and molecular biology Bristol-Myers Co., Wallingford, Conn., 1989-90; dir. curriculum database program Baylor Coll. Medicine, Houston, 1995—; cons. Litton Bionetics, Ft. Detrick, Md., 1977-78, Colon Cancer Working Group, Houston, 1985-86, Oncos, Ltd., Houston, 1985-87, Bristol-Myers Co., Wallingford, Conn., 1985-89; mem. com. revision U.S. Pharmacopeial Conv., 1985-90, 1995—. Editor: Vols. 19 and 20 of Methods in Cancer Research, 1982; author numerous articles in profl. jours. Parliamentarian, Marilyn Estates Civic Assn., Houston, 1984. NCI grantee, 1987—. Mem. Am. Chem. Soc., Am. Soc. Biochem. and Molecular Biology. Republican. Methodist. Home: 5454 Rutherglenn Dr Houston TX 77096-4032 Office: 1 Baylor Plz Houston TX 77030-4032

YEOWELL, HEATHER NINA, medical educator; b. Bristol, Eng., Feb. 22, 1940; d. Frederic Cecil and Florence Nina (Workman) Grant; m. David A. Yeowell, Nov. 7, 1964; children: Karen, Andrew, Angela. BS, U. Bristol, 1961; PhD, U. N.C., 1983. Organic rsch. chemist May and Baker Ltd., Dagenham, Essex, Eng., 1962-64; organic rsch. profl. Burroughs Wellcome Co., Tuckahoe, N.Y., 1965-68; rsch. assoc. Duke U. Med. Ctr., Durham, 1989-92, asst. rsch. prof. of medicine, 1993-96, assoc. rsch. prof. medicine, 1996—; sr. fellow Ctr. for Study of Aging and Human Devel. Duke U., 1993—; vis. fellow Nat. Inst. Environ. Health Scis., NIH, Research Triangle Park, N.C., 1984-87, vis. assoc., 1987-89. Contbr. articles to profl. jours. Grantee March of Dimes Birth Defects Found., 1993-95; Dermatology Found. Pfizer Rsch. grantee, 1996-97; recipient Ind. Rsch. Support and Transition award NIA, 1992-97, Upjohn Rsch. award 1990, NATO scholarship, 1961-62. Mem. Soc. Toxicology, Am. Soc. Biochemistry and Molecular Biology, Soc. Investigative Dermatology, Am. Soc. Human Genetics. Episcopalian. Office: Duke U Med Ctr PO Box 3135 Durham NC 27715-3135

YESLOW, ROSEMARIE, real estate professional; b. Detroit; d. Karl E. and Madeline E. (Paret) Norberg; widowed; children: Bradford (dec.), Tod, Eric (dec.), Mark. Student, U. Miami, 1947-49; AA in Journalism, Broward Jr. Coll., 1972; student, Fla. Atlantic U., 1973-75; grad., Realtor Inst., 1995. Ins. agt. Wittenstein Ins. Agy., Hollywood, Fla., 1965-75; owner, operator The Karl Motel/Apartments, Hallandale, Fla., 1980—; realtor/assoc. The Keyes Co., Hollywood, 1990-93; realtor, assoc. Ebby Halliday Real Estate, Dallas, 1993—; real estate investor, Hollywood, 1960—. Contbr. articles to profl. jours. Edn. v.p. Nat. Coun. Jewish Women, Hollywood, 1960-66; unit and dept. chmn. LWV, Ft. Lauderdale, Fla., 1960-72; edn. chmn. Dem. Exec. Com., Broward County, Fla., 1976-78; mem. planning and zoning bd. City of Hallandale, 1988-92. Recipient Sch. Bell award Fla. Edn. Assn., 1966. Mem. Nat. Assn. Realtors, Hollywood Bd. Realtors, Hallandale Adult Cmty. Ctr. (adv. com., Cert. of Appreciation 1989), Hallandale Citizens United, Hallandale C. of C. (bd. dirs. 1987-92, Small Bus. Person of Yr. award 1990), Sierra Club. Democrat. Jewish. Home: 4247 Throckmorton St Dallas TX 75219-2206 Office: Ebby Halliday Real Estate 8333 Douglas Ave Ste 100 Dallas TX 75225-5811

YETT, FOWLER REDFORD, mathematics educator; b. Johnson City, Tex., Oct. 18, 1919; s. James William, Sr. and Rebecca Jane (Stribling) Y.; BS in Chem. Engring. (Univ. scholar), U. Tex., Austin, 1943, MA in Math., 1952; PhD, Iowa State U., 1955; m. Mary Sue Lytle, June 17, 1945 (div. 1977); children: Jane Marie, Rebecca Yett Root, Mary Wester Yett Coutts. Research chemist, research chem. engr. Manhattan Project, U. Chgo., 1943-44, Richland, Wash., 1944-45, Dow Chem. Co., Freeport, Tex., 1945; owner, mgr. Camera Supplies of Houston, 1946-49; teaching fellow math. U. Tex., Austin, 1949-52, asst. prof., 1956-65; instr. math. Iowa State U., Ames, 1952-55; asst. prof. math. Long Beach (Calif.) State Coll., 1955-56; prof. math. U. So. Ala., Mobile, 1965-89, chmn. dept., 1965-68; sr. rsch. engr. N.Am. Aviation, Inc., Downey, Calif., summers 1956-57, 59; faculty rsch. assoc. Boeing Co., Seattle, summer 1958; pres. Dr. Fowler Redford Yett & Daus., Inc., Dr. Yett's Oil Co., Dr. Yett's Royal Chinese Herb Co., Solar, Inc.; founder Dr. Fowler Redford Yett's World Acad. of Faith, Health Langs. and Scis. Active all Lyndon Baines Johnson election campaigns, 1937-68. Mem. Am. Math. Soc., Tau Beta Pi, Omega Chi Epsilon, Phi Lambda Upsilon, Phi Eta Sigma, Pi Mu Epsilon. Methodist (tchr. Sunday sch. 1970-71). Home: 660 Merritt Dr Mobile AL 36609-6026

YEUNG, ALBERT TAK-CHUNG, civil engineering educator; b. Hong Kong, July 13, 1959; came to U.S., 1984; s. Siu-Hung and Pui-Chan (Lip) Y.; m. Kitman Iris Luk, Jan. 16, 1986; children: Loren Wayne, Ernest Hayes. BSc in Engring., U. Hong Kong, 1982; MS, U. Calif., Berkeley, 1985, PhD, 1990. Registered profl. engr., Tex., civil engr., Hong Kong; chartered engr., U.K. Engring. asst. T.H. Chuah & Assocs. Cons. Engrs., Singapore, 1980, Geotech. Control Office, Hong Kong, 1981; staff engr. Binnie & Ptnrs. Internat., Hong Kong, 1982-83, staff resident engr., 1984; lectr. Haking Wong Tech. Inst., Hong Kong, 1983-84; rsch. asst. U. Calif., Berkeley, 1985, 86, 87-89, grad. student instr., 1985-87; rsch. asst. Lawrence Berkeley Lab., 1989; asst. prof. civil engring. Northeastern U., Boston, 1990, Tex. A&M U., College Station, 1991—; asst. rsch. engr. Tex. Transp. Inst., College Station, 1991—; pres. Albert T. Yeung Geotech. Engr., College Station, 1992-96; faculty advisor Hong Kong Students Assn., Tex. A&M U., College Station, 1991-93, Asian Am. Assn., 1992-94; spkr. H.S. JETS Club, 1991—. Lead editor: Vertical and Horizontal Deformations of Foundations and Embankments, 2 vols., 1994; co-author: Laboratory Soil Testing for Engineers, 3rd edit., 1994; assoc. editor: Practice Periodical of Hazardous, Toxic, and Radioactive Waste Management/ASCE, 1996—; contbr. articles to profl. jours. Earth Tech. Corp. fellow, Long Beach, Calif., 1987-89; rsch. grantee Tex. Advanced Tech. Program, Tex. Higher Edn. Coord. Bd., Austin, 1992, 94, Tex. Dept. Transp. Coop. Rsch. Program, Austin, 1992, Gulf Coast Hazardous Substance Rsch. Ctr., Beaumont, Tex., 1992, Nat. Coop. Hwy. Rsch. Program, Transp. Rsch. Bd., NRC, Washington, 1993, Energy Resources Program, Tex. A&M U. Sys., 1993; recipient Rsch. Initiation award NSF, Washington, 1992, Select Young Faculty award Tex. Engring. Exptl. Sta., 1993. Fellow The Geological Soc., mem. AAUP, ASTM (mem. com. D18 on soil and rock and com. D34 on mixed waste 1993—), ASCE (editl. bd. Jour. Geotech. Engring. 1994—, publs. com. geotech. engring. divsn. 1994—, environ. geotech. com. engring. divs. 1992—, sec. Tex. sect. geotech. com. 1993-94, vice chmn. Tex. sec. geotech. com. 1994-95, chair 1995-96, groundwater com., environ. engring. divs., Arthur Casagrande Profl. Devel. award 1996, Tex. section ASCE Civil Engring. Paper award 1996), Am. Soc. Surface Mining and Reclamation (com. on containment and mitigation of toxic mine waste 1994—), Am. Soc. Engring. Edn. (Dow Outstanding New Faculty award 1994, chair environ. engring. divs. 1993-94), Internat. Soc. Soil Mechanics and Found. Engring., Hong Kong Instn. of Engrs. (prize 1981, Kumagai prize 1994), Clay Mineral Soc., Inst. of Civil Engrs. Office: Tex A&M U Dept Civil Engring College Station TX 77843-3136

YII, HUNG SIONG, computer engineer; b. Sibu Sarawak, Malaysia, May 25, 1965; came to U.S., 1986; s. Hee C. and Su C. (Lau) Y. BS in Computer Sci. Engring., U. Tex., Arlington, 1989; MSEE, St. Mary U., San Antonio, 1993. Rsch. engr. U. Tex., Arlington, 1989; computer engr. Flight Safety Internat., San Antonio, 1989-93; software engr. Spectrum Cellular Inc., Dallas, 1994-95, DSc Comms., Plano, Tex., 1995—. Co-chmn., instr. Alamo PC, San Antonio. Mem. Assn. for Computing Machinery. Home: 1608 Hearthstone Dr Plano TX 75023-7411 Office: DSc Comms MS # 121 1000 Coit Rd Plano TX 75075

YOCHMOWITZ, MICHAEL GEORGE, biostatistician, computer educator, consultant; b. Bklyn., Apr. 27, 1948; s. David and Charlotte Dorothy (Haber) Y.; m. Yolanda Maria Pearson, Apr. 1, 1978; 1 child, Samuel Alexander. BA cum laude, Union Coll., 1970, BS cum laude, 1970; MA, U. Rochester, 1972; MPH, U. Mich., 1973, PhD, 1974. Chief sci. analyst function USAF Sch. Aerospace Medicine, Brooks AFB, Tex., 1974-79, chief hazard evaluation function, 1979-85, chief statis. analysis function, 1986-87; instr. math. San Antonio Coll., 1977-85, dir. Computer Learning Ctr., 1983—, pres. Computer & Stats. Inc., 1986—; cons. dept. oncology Health Sci. Ctr., San Antonio, 1979-80; abstractor Exec. Scis. Inst., Whippany, N.J., 1979-85. Contbr. articles to profl. jours. and Ency. Statis. Scis. V.p. Council for Internat. Relations, San Antonio, 1985-86; computer contbr. San Antonio Exec., Real Estate Newsline, San Antonio; bd. dirs. One Elm Place, San Antonio. Grantee NSF, 1970-72; USPHS trainee, 1972-73; UpJohn Gen. fellow, 1973-74. Served to capt. USAF, 1974-79. Mem. Am. Statis. Assn., Am. Prodn. and Inventory Control Soc., Biometric Soc., Data Processing Mgrs. Assn., Sigma Xi. Jewish. Avocations: model railroading, reading, gardening, travel, volleyball, marine aquariums. Home: 19919 Encino Royale St San Antonio TX 78259-2307 Office: Computer Learning Ctr 11107 Wurzbach Rd # 102 San Antonio TX 78230-2553

YOCHUM, GILBERT RONALD, economics educator; b. Pitts., Mar. 17, 1947; s. Gilbert Roderick and Marion Elizabeth (Tice) Y.; 1 child, Heidi. BA, Indiana U. Pa.; PhD, W.Va. U., 1974. Prof. econs., chmn. dept. Old Dominion U., Norfolk, Va. Office: Old Dominion U Dept Econs Norfolk VA 23529

YODER, EDWIN MILTON, JR., columnist, educator, editor, writer; b. Greensboro, N.C., July 18, 1934; s. Edwin M. and Mytrice M. (Logue) Y.; m. Mary Jane Warwick, Nov. 1, 1958; children: Anne Daphne, Edwin Warwick. B.A., U. N.C., 1956; BA, MA (Rhodes scholar), Oxford (Eng.) U., 1958; D.H.L. (hon.), Grinnell Coll., 1980, Elon Coll., 1986; DLitt (hon.), U. N.C., 1993, Richmond Coll., London. Editorial writer Charlotte (N.C.) News, 1958-61; editorial writer Greensboro Daily News, 1961-64, assoc. editor, 1965-75; asst. prof. history U. N.C., Greensboro, 1964-65; editorial page editor Washington Star, 1975-81; syndicated columnist Washington Post Writers Group, 1982—; prof. journalism and humanities Washington and Lee U., 1992—. Author: Night of the Old South Ball, 1984, The Unmaking of a Whig, 1990, Joe Alsop's Cold War, 1995, The Historical Present; contbr. articles to periodicals. Recipient awards editorial writing N.C. Press Assn., 1958, 61, 66, Walker Stone award Scripps-Howard Found., 1978, Pulitzer prize editorial writing, 1979; Disting. Alumnus award U. N.C., Chapel Hill, 1980. Mem. Nat. Conf. Editorial Writers, Am. Soc. Newspaper Editors. Democrat. Episcopalian. Home: 4001 Harris Pl Alexandria VA 22304-1720

YODER, NELSON BRENT, oil company executive; b. N.Y.C., May 31, 1944; s. Nelson James and Doris Anne (Abel) Y.; m. Linda Kay Osborne, Aug. 21, 1965 (div. Oct. 1978); m. Mary Frances Byrnes, Aug. 23, 1980; 1 child, Nelson James II. BS in Zoology, Tex. Tech U., 1966, MS in Geology, 1968. Paleontologist Gulf Oil Corp., New Orleans, 1968-71; geologist Gulf Research and Devel. Co., Houston, 1971-74; pres. Integrated Exploration Services, Inc., La Porte, Tex., 1974—; cons. geologist specializing in carbonate petrography; part-time instr. geology San Jacinto Coll., 1993—. Mem. Internat. Assn. Sedimentologists, Am. Assn. Petroleum Geologists, Soc. Econ. Paleontologists and Mineralogists (treas. Gulf Coast sect. 1983-84), Houston Geol. Soc., Sigma Gamma Epsilon. Republican. Avocations: sculpture, painting, fishing, photography. Home: 1010 S Country Club Dr PO Box 1546 La Porte TX 77571 Office: Integrated Exploration Svcs Inc 3903 Spur # 501 La Porte TX 77571

YOELS, WILLIAM CHARLES, sociology educator; b. Jamaica, N.Y., Oct. 31, 1941; s. Irving and Harriet (Epstein) Y.; children: Leandra, Joanna. BA, Queens Coll., 1964; MA, U. Minn., 1967, PhD, 1971. Asst. prof. Boston Coll., Chestnut Hill, Mass., 1971-74, SUNY, Albany, 1974-76; assoc. prof. Ind. U. N.W., Gary, 1976-79, Wayne State U., Detroit, 1980-82; prof. U. Ala., Birmingham, 1983—. Co-author: Being Urban, 1977, 2d edit., 1991, Symbols, Selves and Society, 1979, Sociology in Everyday Life, 1986, 2d edit., 1993, Experiencing the Life Cycle, 1982, 2d edit., 1993; assoc. editor Symbolic Interaction, 1982-83, The Social Sci. Jour., 1993—. NSF fellow, 1966, NEH summer fellow, 1978. Mem. Soc. Study of Symbolic Interaction, Am. Sociol. Assn., Soc. Study of Social Problems. Office: Univ of Ala Dept Sociology 237 Ullman Bldg Birmingham AL 35294

YOHO, ROBERT WAYNE, company executive; b. Ardmore, Md., Jan. 26, 1936; s. Wilbert Wiley Sr. and Effie Pauline (Bowen) Y.; m. Alice Pilar Tenorio, Aug. 29, 1952; children: Robert Jr., Gary W., Dana M. BSME, Md. U., 1959; BA in Bus., Southeastern U., 1961. Lic. mech. contractor, Calif., Ga., Fla., Mich., N.C. Asst. to pres. Griffith Consumers, Washington, 1955-63; pres. Triple A Corp., College Park, Md., 1963-66; exec. v.p. Howdeshell Mech., Clearwater, Fla., 1967-71; pres. Schneider-Yoho Corp. (Fla. and Calif.), 1971-76; pres., founder Tropic-Kool Engring., Clearwater, Fla., 1977-87; pres. New Thermal Techologies, Clearwater, 1988—. Patentee roof curbs, control panels, hoods, desiccant air conditioners, others. Mem. Krew of Neptune, Treasure Island, 1992; active various civic orgns., St.

Petersburg, Fla., 1987-93. Recipient Gov.'s award State of Fla., 1993, Fla. award Fla. Dept. Commerce, 1993, Tech. award Tampa Bay Planning Coun., 1993, award Dept. of Energy. Mem. ASHRAE, Assn. Energy Engrs. (sr.), Fla. Soc. Profl. Engrs. Home: 5812 Toucan Pl Clearwater FL 34620-2380 Office: New Thermal Tech 12900 Automobile Blvd Clearwater FL 34622-4715

YOKUBAITIS, ROGER T., lawyer; b. Wharton, Tex., Jan. 9, 1945. Attended, St. Louis U.; BA, JD, U. Houston, 1969. Bar: Tex. 1969. Ptnr. Carmody & Yokubaitis, L.L.P., Houston. Mem. ABA, Houston Bar Assn., State Bar of Tex., Houston Bankruptcy Conf., Am. Bankruptcy Inst. Office: Carmody & Yokubaitis LLP 5718 Westheimer Ste 1010 Houston TX 77057-5732

YONG, LOONG KWET, nuclear engineer, consultant; b. Johor Baru, Johor, Malaysia, May 17, 1962; came to U.S., 1980; m. Janet Wagner. BS in Nuclear Engring., Iowa State U., 1984; MS in Nuclear Engring., Ga. Inst. Tech., 1985. Mgr. Atlan-Tech, Inc., Oak Ridge, Tenn., 1986-94; sr. health physicist Sci. Applications Internat. Corp., Oak Ridge, 1994-95; environ. svcs. mgr. Advanced Integrated Mgmt. Svcs., Inc., Oak Ridge, 1995—. Hon. mem. Historical Preservation Soc., Atlanta, 1987-88. Mem. Health Physics Soc., Am. Nuclear Soc. Office: Oak Ridge Nat Lab Bldg 7824 Oak Ridge TN 37831

YORK, BARBARA LEE, genealogist; b. Yoakum, Tex., Sept. 10, 1930; d. Horace Cecil and Della (Dehnisch) Wauson; m. James Arthur York Sr., Sept. 13, 1946; children: James Jr., Francis Dusek, Robert Cecil. Prof. genealogist Houston, 1983-92, Yoakum, Tex., 1992—; geneal. chmn. Carl & Mary Welhausen Libr., Yoakum, 1990—. Author: CSA Graves in Texas, 1989, 90, 91; editor: Beck Funeral Home, 1990-94, Buffington Funeral Home, 1993. V.p. Friends of Clayton Libr., Houston, 1986. Mem. DAR (registar 1986), Dau. of War of 1812 (pres. 1988), Daus. of the Colonial Wars (treas. 1990), Daus. Republic of Tex. (historian 1985), United Daus. of the Confederary (pres. 1990). Home: 111 Whitfield St Yoakum TX 77995-4153

YORK, DAVID ANTHONY, biomedical sciences researcher; b. Birmingham, Eng., Mar. 29, 1945; came to U.S., 1990; s. Horace William and Irene Gertrude (Adams) Y.; m. Barbara York, Mar. 25, 1967; children: Duncan James, Emily Elizabeth. BSc, U. Southampton, Eng., 1966, PhD, 1969. Postdoctoral fellow New Eng. Med. Ctr., Boston, 1969-70, UCLA Sch. Medicine, Torrance, 1970-71; lectr. Southampton U., 1971-82, sr. lectr., 1982-88, reader, 1988-89; chief obesity rsch. program Pennington Biomed. Rsch. Ctr., Baton Rouge, 1990—, head basic scis., 1992—; Hibernia-Schleider chair, 1995—. Rsch. grantee NICHD, 1992—, NIDDK, 1992—. Office: Pennington Biomed Rsch Ctr 6400 Perkins Rd Baton Rouge LA 70808-4124

YORK, JOHN LYNDAL, medical educator; b. Morton, Tex., Aug. 14, 1936; s. James Lee and Jewell Fern (Braden) Y.; m. Cynthia Carolyn Giles, Aug. 29, 1958; children: John Lee, Michelle Anette. BS in Chemistry and Math., Harding Coll., 1958; PhD in Physiol. Chemistry, Johns Hopkins U., 1962. NIH predoctoral rsch. fellow Johns Hopkins U., Balt., 1958-62, fellow dept. physiol. chemistry Sch. Medicine, 1962-64; biochemist Stanford Rsch. Inst., Menlo Park, Calif., 1964-65; asst. prof. dept. biochemistry Coll. Basic Med. Sci. U. Tenn., Memphis, 1965-68; assoc. prof. dept. biochemistry Coll. Medicine U. Ark., Little Rock, 1968-76, prof. dept. biochemistry, 1977—; mem. faculty-student liason com. U. Ark., 1969-70, co-chair edn. bldg. II wet lab. design com., 1973-74, computer aided instrn. com., 1972-74, rep. to univ. senate coun., 1973-74, animal care com., 1975-76, chmn. grad. com., 1976-80, rep. to pres.'s grad. adv. coun., 1976-78, subcom. on curriculum, 1976-77, program evaluation com., 1976-78, search com. for pharmacology chmn., 1976-77, chmn. biochemistry grad. student admissions, 1975-79, med. biochemistry cirriculum com., 1975-80, 89—, grad. biochemistry com., 1981-85, coll. med. appeals bd., 1980—, com. on ednl. devel. Acad. Senate, 1979-80, com. on ednl. resources, 1979-80, chmn. com. on acad. affairs., 1980-81, search com. for assoc. dean grad. sch., 1982, dir. grad. program dept. biochemistry, 1983-85, dir. seminar program dept. biochemistry, 1986-95, chmn. biochemistry faculty recruitment com., 1982-86, 90-92, exec. com. dept. biochemistry, 1982—, chmn. faculty senate, 1987, handbook com., 1988-89, com. on assessment instrn., 1991-92; vis. prof. dept. coagulation rsch. Karolinska Inst., Stockholm, 1974-75; judge biochemistry divsn. Ark. State Sci. Fair, 1985—; mem. River Mountain Park adv. com. Little Rock Parks Dept., 1991; mem. Gov's Mercury Adv. Com., 1993—. Author: The Porphyrias, 1972, (with N.S. Sloan) Review of Biochemistry, 1969, translated into German, 1972; contbr. numerous articles and abstracts to profl. and sci. jours. Grantee NIH, 1966-69, 76-78, 80-84, 89-91, 91-94, NSF, 1969-74, Swedish Med. Rsch. Coun., 1974-75, Am. Cancer Soc., 1986-88. Fellow Swedish Med. Rsch. Coun.; mem. AAAS, AAUP (Ark. conf. exec. com. 1994, co-chair Ark. Conf. conf. 1995—), Am. Chem. Soc. (vice chmn. ctrl. Ark. sect. 1971-72, chmn. 1972-73, program chmn. 33rd Southwest regional meeting 1977, 43rd Southwest regional meeting 1987, Disting. Svc. award 1989), Soc. Biol. Chemists, Johns Hopkins Med. and Surg. Assn., Sigma Xi., Alpha Chi. Home: 42 Pine Manor Dr Little Rock AR 72207-5137 Office: U Ark Med Sci Dept Biochemistry & Molecular Biology 4301 W Markham St Little Rock AR 72205-7101

YORK, VERMELLE CARDWELL, real estate broker and developer; b. Evergreen, Ala., Jan. 30, 1925; d. Frederick Lofton and Emmie Mildred (Pitts) Cardwell; m. E. Travis York, Jr., Dec. 26, 1946; children: Lisa, Travis. BS, Auburn U., 1946. Pres. Tralisa Corp., Gainesville, Fla., 1966-87, sec., treas., 1988-94; sec., treas. Caret Corp., Gainesville, Fla., 1979-86, pres., 1987—. Mem. devel. com. Harn Mus., Gainesville, Fla., 1990-96, Hospice House, Gainesville, 1992-96; co-chair March of Dimes, Gainesville, 1995, Red Ribbon Campaign, 1989, 90. Recipient President's Medallion, U. Fla., 1980; named Woman of Distinction Santa Fe C. C., 1988. Mem. The Heritage Club (mem. amb. com. 1991-96), P.E.O. (pres. 1989-90), Surfside N. Club, (dir. 1988-91), Gainesville Women's Forum (membership chair 1994-96), DAR, Phi Kappa Phi. Home: 4020 SW 78th St Gainesville FL 32608 Office: Caret Corp 4020 SW 78th St Gainesville FL 32608-3608

YORMARK, ALANNA KATHERINE, pediatrics nurse; b. Clayton, N.Y., Oct. 30, 1955; d. William Frederick and Elaine Laurena (Cantwell) Wood; m. David Louis Yormark, Aug. 6, 1983; children: Katelyn Elaine, Tyler Frederick. BSN, SUNY, Plattsburg, 1977; M in Health Mgmt., St. Thomas U., 1987. RN, N.Y. Staff and charge nurse pediatrics dept. North Broward Med. Ctr., Pompano Beach, Fla., 1978-79, staff and charge nurse med./surg. fl., 1979-80; from staff nurse to asst. head nurse neonatal ICU Broward Gen. Med. Ctr., Ft. Lauderdale, Fla., 1980-87; nurse mgr. antepartum, gyn. postpartum and nursery Broward Gen. Med. Ctr., Ft. Lauderdale, 1987—. Mem. Assn. Women's Health, Obstetric, and Neonatal Nurses. Home: 5226 NW 55th St Coconut Creek FL 33073-3744

YOSHIDA, JAMES ATSUSHI, carbon fiber marketing company executive; b. Ohmiya, Watarai-gun, Mei-ken, Japan, Sept. 6, 1932; came to U.S., 1993; s. Hideo Yoshida and Sumiko (Aya) Murata; m. Sumiko Yoshida, Nov. 23, 1957; children: Linda Emmie Yoshida Wenstrand, Juri Yoshida Kameda. BA, George Pepperdine U., L.A., 1955; MA, U. S.C., 1958. Corp. planning mgr. Mitsui Petrochem, Tokyo, 1958-63; v.p. licensing, Japan rep. Sci. Design Co./Halcon, Tokyo, 1964-70; exec. v.p. mktg. Arco-Sumika Joint Venture, Tokyo, 1971-81; mng. dir. BASF Japan, Tokyo, 1981-92; pres. Toho Carbon Fibers, Palo Alto, Calif., 1993—; mktg. cons. Toho Rayon Co., Tokyo. Home: 8 Versailles Dr Menlo Park CA 94025-4226 Office: 444 High St Palo Alto CA 94301-1620

YOST, RICHARD ALAN, chemistry educator; b. Martins Ferry, Ohio, May 31, 1953; s. Donald Errold and Jessie Lee (Hoover) Y.; m. Katherine Sarah Fitzgerald, June 16, 1979; children: Sarah Elizabeth, Michael Patrick, Matthew Jefferson. BS in Chemistry, U. Ariz., 1974; PhD in Analytical Chemistry, Mich. State U., 1979. Asst. prof. chemistry U. Fla., Gainesville, 1979-83, assoc. prof., 1983-89, prof., 1989—, head divsn. analytical chemistry, 1994—; cons. Lawrence Livermore Nat. Lab., Finnigan MAT Corp., Bristol-Myers Squibb. Patentee in field. Dist. commr. Boy Scouts Am., 1981-84. Recipient Disting. Contribution award ASMS, 1993. Fellow NSF, 1975-79, Am. Chem. Soc. Analytical Div., 1977-78. Mem. Am. Chem. Soc., Am. Soc. Mass Spectrometry, Phi Beta Kappa. Office: U Fla Chemistry Dept Gainesville FL 32611

YOSTE, CHARLES TODD, lawyer; b. Vicksburg, Miss., Nov. 11, 1948; s. Harry M. and Charlene (Todd) Y. BS, Miss. State U., 1971; JD, U. Miss., 1976. Bar: Miss. 1976, U.S. Dist. Ct. Miss. 1976, U.S. Ct. Appeals, 1982. Sole practice, Starkville, Miss., 1976—; city atty. Starkville, Miss., 1979-85, pros. atty., 1977-79, city judge, 1981-82. Candidate for Congress 2d dist. Miss., 1980. Served to capt. U.S. Army, 1971-73. Recipient Outstanding Young Man award Starkville Jaycees, 1980. Mem. ABA, Miss. Bar Assn., Am. Trial Lawyers Assn., Miss. Trial Lawyers Assn. (bd. govs. 1988—), Starkville C. of C. (pres. 1982), Am. Legion. Republican. Roman Catholic. Lodge: Rotary. Home: 902 Montgomery St Starkville MS 39759 Office: PO Box 488 Starkville MS 39760-0488

YOTHER, ANTHONY WAYNE, critical care nurse, nurse manager; b. Anniston, Ala., Jan. 30, 1964; s. Johnny Wayne and Carol Sue (Bradshaw) Y. BSN, Jacksonville State U., 1987; MSN, U. Ala., Birmingham, 1992; MS in Health Care Policy and Adminstrn., Mercer U., 1994. Cert. med.-surg. nursing, med.-surg. clin. specialist, nursing adminstrn., adult critical care nursing, pediatric adv. life support. ICU mgr. Grady Health Sys., Atlanta, 1994—. Mem. ANA (cert.), AACCN (cert.), Am. Heart Assn., Ga. Nurses Assn., Laurleen B. Wallace Coll. Nursing Alumni Assn. (v.p. 1988-90, pres. 1990-92), U. Ala.-Birmingham Alumni Assn., Mercer U. Alumni Assn., Jacksonville State U. Alumni Assn., Sigma Theta Tau Internat.

YOUMANS, WILLIAM CORY, SR., electrical engineer; b. Oneonta, N.Y., July 7, 1955; s. Charles Leroy Jr. and Phyllis Ann (Kloeti) Y.; m. Julie ann Raes Youmans; children: Jennifer Anne, William Cory Jr. AAS, Rochester Inst. Tech., 1977, BSEE, 1978; MSSM, U. So. Calif., 1982. Program mgr. U.S. Army, 1978-82; project dir. U.S. Army, Orlando, Fla., 1982-93; lead project engr. USN, Orlando, Fla., 1993—. Bd. mgmt. YMCA, Oviedo, Fla., 1992-96. Lt. col. U.S. Army Res. Mem. Assn. U.S. Army (v.p. programs 1994-96, award 1996, exec. v.p. 1996—). Republican. Roman Catholic. Home: 707 Ironwood Ct. Winter Springs FL 32708 Office: US Army STRICOM 12350 Research Pkwy Orlando FL 32826-3261

YOUNAN, NICOLAS HANNA, electrical engineering educator; b. Magdoushe, Sidon, Lebanon, Nov. 24, 1954; came to U.S., 1978; BSEE, Miss. State U., 1982, MSEE, 1984; PhD in Elec. Engring., Ohio U., 1988. Asst. prof. Miss. State U., Starkville, 1990-93, assoc. prof., 1993—, grad. program dir., 1995—; vis. asst. prof. Miss. State U., 1988-90; rsch. scientist Praxis Internat., Exton, Pa., 1989-90. Contbr. articles to profl. jours. Grantee in field. Mem. IEEE (chmn. N.E. Miss. subsect. 1993-94, vice-chmn. 1992-93, sec./treas. 1991-92), N.Y. Acad. Sci., Phi Kappa Phi, Tau Beta Pi, Eta Kappa Nu. Office: Miss State U Dept Elec/Computer Engring Box 9571 Mississippi State MS 39762

YOUNER, DAVID, insurance brokerage executive; b. N.Y.C., July 21, 1926; s. Morris I. and Hanna S. (Heifetz) Y.; m. Jeanette C. Youner, Sept. 17, 1950 (div. 1976); children: Sara A., Rebecca N., Johannah S.; m. Ellen Sinsal, Sept. 17, 1988. BA, NYU, 1949. Pres. David Youner Advt., N.Y.C., 1952-64; ins. agt. Mass. Mut. Life Ins. Co., N.Y.C., 1964-67; pres. Physicians Econ. Svcs., Inc., Sunrise, Fla., 1967—; life ins. cons. Physicians Econ. Svcs., Inc., N.Y.C., 1964-94; ins. benefits rep. Med-Care Advantage North Ridge Med. Ctr., Ft. Lauderdale, Fla., 1994—. Office: Physicians Econ Svcs Inc PO Box 450580 Sunrise FL 33345

YOUNG, ALFRED, social sciences educator; b. New Orleans, Feb. 21, 1946; s. Landry and Mattie (Rayno) Y.; m. Angela Broussard, Aug. 31, 1969; children: Tomara, Marcus, Malcolm, Miles. BA, U. New Orleans, 1970; MA, Syracuse U., 1972, PhD, 1977. African-Am. fellow Syracuse (N.Y.) U., 1970-72; asst. prof. history SUNY, Oswego, 1972-82, assoc. prof. history, 1982-89; prof. history, assoc. prof., dir. African and African-Am. studies Ga. So. U., Statesboro, 1989—; vis. prof. history and African Am. studies Syracuse U., 1995-97; faculty advisor, cons. Nat. Model Orgn. of African Unity, Howard U., Washington, 1981—; acad. coun. U. System of Ga. Regent's Global Ctr., 1992—. Editor: Education and the Black Experience, 1979; cons. editor: African Homefront; mem. editorial bd. Internat. Jour. Africana Studies; contbg. adv. editor Word: A Black Culture Jour., 1990. Bd. dirs. Blitch St. Ctr., Statesboro, 1991—; edn. com. NAACP, Statesboro, 1992—. With USN, 1965-67. African-Am. fellow Syracuse U., 1970-72; grantee N.Y. State African-Am. Inst., 1987, Dept. Edn., 1991-93. Fellow Nat. Coun. Black Studies (bd. dirs., exec. bd. 1992—); mem. Omega Psi Phi. Office: Ga So U # Lb8054 Statesboro GA 30460

YOUNG, ANDREW JACKSON, civil rights leader, clergyman, former mayor, former ambassador, former congressman; b. New Orleans, Mar. 12, 1932; s. Andrew J. and Daisy (Fuller) Y.; m. Jean Childs, June 7, 1954; children—Andrea, Lisa Dru, Paula Jean, Andrew J. III. Student, Dillard U., 1947-48; B.S., Howard U., 1951; B.D., Hartford Theol. Sem., 1955; D.D. (hon.), Wesleyan U., 1970, United Theol. Sem. Twin Cities, 1970; LL.D. (hon.), Wilberforce U., 1971, Clark Coll., 1973, Yale U., 1973, Swarthmore Coll., Atlanta U., others; numerous other hon. degrees. Ordained to ministry Congl. Ch., 1955; pastor in Thomasville, Ga., 1955-57; assoc. dir. dept. youth work Nat. Council Chs., 1957-61; mem. staff So. Christian Leadership Conf., 1961-70, adminstr. citizen edn. program, 1961-64, exec. dir., 1964-70, exec. v.p., 1967-70; now bd. dirs.; mem. 93d-95th Congresses from 5th Ga. Dist.; mem. Rules com.; U.S. ambassador to UN, 1977-79; mayor of Atlanta, 1982-89; co-chmn. Atlanta Com. for the Olympic Games, 1996. Chmn. Atlanta Community Relations Commn., 1970-72; chmn. bd. Delta Ministry of Miss.; bd. dirs. Martin Luther King, Jr. Center for Social Change, Robert F. Kennedy Meml. Found., Field Found., So. Christian Leadership Conf. Recipient Pax-Christi award St. John's U., 1970; Springarn medal.; Medal of Freedom, 1980, French Legion of Honor medal, 1982; co-recipient, Martin Luther King, Jr., Award for Public Svc. (Ebony mag.), 1990. Mem. Ams. Dem. Action. Law International: PO Box 888013 Atlanta GA 30356-0013

YOUNG, BARNEY THORNTON, lawyer; b. Chillicothe, Tex., Aug. 10, 1934; s. Bayne and Helen Irene (Thornton) Y.; m. Sarah Elizabeth Taylor, Aug. 31, 1957; children: Jay Thornton, Sarah Elizabeth, Serena Taylor. BA, Yale U., 1955; LLB, U. Tex., 1958. Bar: Tex. 1958. Assoc. Thompson, Knight, Wright & Simmons, Dallas, 1958-65; ptnr. Rain, Harrell, Emery, Young & Doke, Dallas, 1965-87; mem. firm Locke Purnell Rain Harrell (A Profl. Corp.), 1987—; bd. dirs. Jones-Blair Co. Mem. adv. coun. Dallas Cmty. Chest Trust Fund, Inc., 1964-66; bd. dirs. Mental Health Assn. Dallas County, Inc., 1969-72, Trammell Crow Family Found., 1984-87; trustee Hockaday Sch., Dallas, 1971-77, 90—, chmn., 1994-96, Dallas Zool. Soc., 1986-92, Lamplighter Sch., Dallas, 1976—, chmn., 1983-86, St. Mark's Sch., Dallas, 1970—, pres., 1976-78, The Found. for Callier Ctr. and Comm. Disorders, 1988—, Friends of Ctr. for Human Nutrition, 1988—, Shelter Ministries of Dallas Found., 1993—, Dallas Hist. Soc., 1993—; mem. Yale Devel. Bd., 1984-91. Fellow Tex. Bar Found., Dallas Bar Found.; mem. ABA, Tex. Bar Assn., Dallas Bar Assn., Am. Judicature Soc., Order of Coif, Phi Beta Kappa, Pi Sigma Alpha, Phi Gamma Delta, Phi Delta Phi, Dallas Country Club., Petroleum Club (Dallas), Yale Club (Dallas, N.Y.C.). Home: 6901 Turtle Creek Blvd Dallas TX 75205-1251 Office: Locke Purnell Rain Harrell 2200 Ross Ave Dallas TX 75201-7903

YOUNG, BILLY DEVON, communications executive; b. Foley, Ala., June 19, 1947; s. Lawerance Devon and Beauetta (James) Y.; m. Martha Ann Stocke, Sept. 2, 1972; children: Kimberly Ann, Lea Ann. AAS, Faulkner State Jr. Coll., 1972; BSBA, Troy State U., 1979. cert. engr.; cert. EMT; cert. safety profl. Engr., safety dir. Gulf Telephone Co., Inc., Foley, Ala., 1972-89; gen. mgr. Bruce (Miss.) Telephone Co., Inc., 1989—. Instr. trainer ARC, Miss., 1974—; chmn., commr. Calhoun County E911 Commn., 1990—; chmn. utilities divsn. Nat. Safety Coun.; bd. dirs. Nat. Safety Coun., Lafayette County ARC. Mem. Nat. Assn. Radio and Telecomms. Engrs., Inc. (bd. dirs.), Am. Soc. Safety Engrs., Ind. Telephone Pioneer Assn., Bruce C. of C. (pres.), Lions Club. Baptist. Home: PO Box 903 Bruce MS 38915-0903 Office: Bruce Telephone Co Inc North Side of Square Bruce MS 38915

YOUNG, DAISY ALMEDA, small business owner; b. Morgan Mill, Tex., May 16, 1932; d. Benjamin F. and Dollie Lenora (Earp) Laughlin; m. Don W. Young; 1 child, Robert L. Grad. h.s., Portland, Oreg. Owner Daisy's Employment Svc., Ft. Worth, 1969—. Patron Kimbell Art Mus., Ft. Worth; coord. tutors/adopt a sch. program All Saints Hosp./Daggett Mid. Sch., Ft. Worth, 1989-90. Mem. Bus. and Profl. Women (bd. dirs. Ft. Worth chpt. 1989—), Better Bus. Bur. (arbitrator Ft. Worth chpt. 1983—), Nat. Hist. Preservation Soc., Women's Health Forum, Ft. Worth Bot. Soc. (life), Ft. Worth Zoo Soc., Tex. Heritage (life), Thistle Hill Doscent Guild, Internat. Comm. Club (pres. Ft. Worth chpt. 1989—). Home: 1316 6th Ave Fort Worth TX 76104-4326 Office: Daisy's Employment Svc 609-5 Sinclair Bldg Fort Worth TX 76102

YOUNG, DANIEL DAVID, laser physicist, researcher; b. Toledo, July 18, 1944; s. Harold Albert and Lorraine A. (McClay) Y.; m. Sally Sue Campbell, June 17, 1967; children: Matthew David, Mark Nathan. BS, U. Toledo, 1967; MS, Air Force Inst. Tech., 1969, PhD, 1977. Commd. 2nd lt. USAF, 1967, advanced through grades to maj., 1981; sci. officer USAF, Wright-Patterson AFB, Ohio, 1967-81; program mgr. Def. Systems Mgmt. Coll., Ft. Belvoir, Va., 1981-82, Armament div. USAF, Eglin AFB, Fla., 1982-87; interferometric synthetic aperture radar bus. area. mgr. Radar Lab., Ann Arbor, 1987-96; dir. engring. OptoMechanik Inc., Palm Bay, 1996—. Recipient Tech. Achievement award USAF, 1977. Republican. Episcopalian. Home: 617 Tortoise Way Satellite Beach FL 32937 Office: OMI 2330 Commerce Park Dr NE Ste 2 Palm Bay FL 32905-7721

YOUNG, DARLENE ANN, small business owner; b. Pasadena, Calif., Nov. 2; d. James Burdick and Alice (Fussell) Slemons; m. F. Thomas Meehan, July 23, 1960 (div. 1969); children: Tamara Meehan D'Ornellas, Michael Thomas; m. John R. Young, July 10, 1970. BS in Econs., U. Calif., Davis, 1959. Owner, mgr. Royal Coach Village and Royal Coach Trails, Houston, 1978—. Past pres. Glendale (Calif.) Philharm., Child Help, Performing Arts Coun. Orange County. Mem. Rsch. Assn. U. Calif.-Irvine Coll. Medicine (hon.). Republican. Presbyterian. Office: Royal Coach Village 700 W Greens Rd Houston TX 77067-4435

YOUNG, DAVID HAYWOOD, lawyer; b. San Antonio, Feb. 6, 1943; s. Haywood V. Jr. and Mary Sue (Whitehead) Y.; m. Sharon L. Seals, Nov. 24, 1967; children: David H. Jr., Darrow F., Kelley L. BA, U. Tex., 1965, JD, 1972. Bar: Tex. 1968, U.S. Dist. Ct. (we. dist.) Tex. 1974, U.S. Ct. Appeals (5th cir.) 1976, U.S. Supreme Ct. 1977, U.S. Ct. Appeals (11th cir.) 1981, U.S. Dist. Ct. (so. dist.) Tex. 1982. Atty. Tex. Dept. Human Resources, 1968-73; chief counsel Tex. Dept. Human Resources, Austin, 1973-76; asst. atty. gen. State of Tex., Austin, 1976-81; sole practice San Antonio, 1981—; sec. San Antonio Alliance of Bus., 1985-87; pres. San Antonio Bus. Forum, 1985-86. Mem. Tex. Bar Assn., San Antonio Bar Assn., Bus. and Profl. Club San Antonio (pres. 1986). Clubs: Plaza (San Antonio), San Antonio. Home: 6506 River Hls San Antonio TX 78239-2825 Office: 111 Soledad St Ste 300 San Antonio TX 78205-2229

YOUNG, DAVID LYNN, regulatory consultant; b. Austin, Tex., Apr. 27, 1944; s. Richard Alden and Nell (Wallace) Y.; m. Rebecca Jane Vanemburg, Aug. 24, 1968 (div. Jan. 1980); children: Davy Young, Rebecca Young. BA in Math., U. Tex., 1967; MA in Biblical Studies, Dallas Theol. Sem., 1976. Campus min. Campus Crusade for Christ, San Bernardino, Calif., 1967-74; coll. instr. Dallas Bible Coll., 1975-78; major appliance sales rep. Montgomery Ward, Richardson, Tex., 1978-85; merchandiser GM Warehouse, Seagoville, Tex., 1985; regulator Tex. Dept. of Ins., Austin, 1986-93; regulatory cons. Austin, 1994—; founder, pres. Scriptural Prayer Emphasis Ministries Internat., Richardson, 1974-79. Author: Prayer God's Way, 1981. Candidate lt. gov. Dem. Primary, Tex., 1986, candidate for railroad commn., 1992, 94; Candidate U.S. Senator Rep. Primary, 1996; chorale mem., tenor Riverbend Ch., Austin, 1990-96, Sunday sch. tchr., 1986-96. Home: 1911 Hether Austin TX 78704

YOUNG, DAVID NELSON, information consultant; b. Baton Rouge, Nov. 12, 1953; s. Nelson Joseph and Agnes (LeBlanc) Young; m. Michéle Marie-Therese Bedél, May 7, 1979; children: Jason, Jessica. Student, La. State U., 1972, U. S.W. La., 1975. News editor Gonzales (La.) Weekly, 1976-77; prs. D.N. Young & Assocs., Inc., Gonzales, Washington, Moscow, 1977—; organizer Soviet/Am. Culinary Exch., 1989, Soviet/Am. High Sch. Basketball Excha., 1990; cons. in field. Bd. dirs. Ascension Cancer/Leukemia Soc., Gonzales, 1978—, Ctr. for Russian/Am. Bus., Washington, 1992; fundraiser St. Jude's Rsch. Hosp., Memphis, 1993. Recipient Best-in-Depth Reporting award La. Newspaper Assn., 1984, Appreciation award USIA, 1988, Sovincentr Medal Honor, Moscow World Trade Ctr., 1988. Mem. East Ascension Genealogical Soc. (pres. 1980-81), East Ascension Sportsman League, La./CIS C. of C. Roman Catholic. Office: DN Young and Assocs Inc 203 W Ascension St Gonzales LA 70737-2803

YOUNG, DEBRA ANN, English language educator; b. Panama City, Fla., Sept. 15, 1955; d. Lincoln G. and Adele L. Bailey; 1 child, David Edward. BS in Secondary Edn., Pensacola Christian Coll., 1977; MA in English, Westfield State Coll., 1992; postgrad., Indiana U. of Pa., 1994—. Legal sec. Updike, Kelly & Spellacy, Hartford, Conn., 1988-92; faculty mem. English dept. Pensacola (Fla.) Christian Coll., 1992—, chairperson English dept., 1995—. Mem. MLA, Nat. Coun. Tchrs. English. Republican. Baptist. Home: 7748 Coronet Dr Pensacola FL 32514 Office: Pensacola Christian Coll Box 18000 Pensacola FL 32525

YOUNG, DOUGLAS HAMILTON, lawyer, literary agency executive, novelist; b. Kitchener, Ont., Can., Apr. 1, 1938; s. Nelles Douglas and Beatrice (Hamilton) Y.; m. Barbara Jean Pereira, Dec. 11, 1964; 1 child, Jean. BA, U. Toronto, Ont.; diploma, Hague Acad. Internat. Law, Holland, 1962; JD, York U., Toronto, 1962; LLM, NYU, 1963; LLM, Harvard U., 1970. With law dept. Celanese Corp. Am., N.Y.C., 1963-64; exec. Exxon, Inc., N.Y.C., 1965-66; asst. sec. Esso Exploration, Inc., N.Y.C., 1965-66; sec. Esso Can., Inc., N.Y.C., 1965-66; sec. Esso Australia, Inc., N.Y.C., 1965-66; sec. Esso Inter-Am., N.Y.C., 1965-66; exec. asst. to sec. Creole Petroleum Corp., Caracas, Venezuela, also sec. to exec. com., 1966-68; asst. prof. law and internat. affairs Carleton U., Ottawa, Ont., 1970-71; atty. Internat. Trade and Investment, Ft. Lauderdale, Fla., 1971—; pres. Writer's Lit. Agy., Ft. Lauderdale, 1981—. Author: The Tidy Bowl Man Lives, 1982, Jiffy John, 1982, HT-HT, 1986, Don't Fence Me In, 1995; co-author: How Peace Came to the World, 1986; contbr. monographs in U.N. library. Active Christian Children's Fund. Mem. Internat. Law Soc., World Federalists, Smithsonian Instn. Club: Broward Harvard. Home: 615 NE 15th Ct Fort Lauderdale FL 33304-1130

YOUNG, EARL LAVAUGHN, minister; b. Kingstree, S.C., May 1, 1938; s. Hubert Eugene and Orie Fanny (Bingham) Y.; m. Sarah Magdalene Powell, July 23, 1960; 1 child, Joyce Ann. BS in Sacred Lit., Holmes Coll. of Bible, 1959, BS in Theology, 1972; BS in Sociology, Franics Marion Coll., 1973; MA in Counseling, Liberty U., 1991; PhD in Counseling, Atlantic Bapt. Coll. and Sem., 1993. Ordained to ministry Christian Ch., 1960; cert. tchr., profl. counseling. Pastor Life Christian Assembly, Charleston, S.C., 1989—; field promoter, Internat. Christian Ch., Daytona Beach, Fla., 1983-89, seminar tchr., Internat. Life Christ Ministries, Daytona Beach, 1983-89, v.p. Rep. princint promoter. Rockingham, N.C., 1976-78, Sumter, S.C., 1986-88. Mem. Nat. Christian Counselors Assn. (counselor). Office: Life Christian Assembly 3001 Landing Pky Charleston SC 29420

YOUNG, ERNESTINE JONES, retired postal clerk; b. Eudora, Miss., June 22, 1930; d. James Herron and Ollie (Jones) Holmes; m. Arnett Young Jr., Jan. 3, 1947; children: Davena L., Gwendolyn M., Ernestine, Thelma O., Arnett III, William O., Gloria L. Student, Internat. Acctg. Soc., Chicago, 1966-69, Owen-Lemoyne Coll., 1961-63, U. Tenn., 1963-64; BS, Liberty U., 1994. Clk., ins. and acctg. E.H. Crump Hosp., Memphis, 1963-64; clk., staff asst. U.S. Postal Svc., Memphis, 1964-77; cons. Am. Bapt., Area VI Women, Memphis, 1989—; guest facilitator Ch. Missionary Workshops, Memphis, 1992. Pres. 25th Ward Civic Club, Memphis, 1960-62; bd. dirs., co-chmn. Sch. for Illiteracy, Memphis, 1963; pres. Walker Elem. PTA, Memphis, 1961-63, Lincoln Jr. High Sch. PTA, Memphis, 1964-69; bd. dirs. March of Dimes, 1982-84, Memphis City Beautiful Commn., 1966-68; mem. com. on hypertension U. Tenn., 1978-79; vol. dir. Metro. Bapt. Ch., Memphis, 1983—; dir. Call for Action WDIA, Memphis, 1977-80; asst. to dir. So. Region Call for Action, N.Y.C., 1979-80; sch. dist. chmn. Am. Cancer Soc. & Heart Assn., Memphis, 1964-70; co-chmn. budget com. Nat. Congress of

Colored Parents & Tchrs., Memphis, 1966-70. Recipient Outstanding Sch. & Community Svc. award, Lincoln Jr. High Sch., 1969, Leadership award Call for Action, 1980, Cert. Appreciation for Valuable Contbn., 1981, Dorothy M. Lofton award for Meritorious Svc., Metro Bapt. Ch., 1991, Key to City and Cert. Appreciation for Outstanding and Meritorious Svcs. to Community, Memphis, 1991, Proclamation for Accomplishments and Contbns., Congressman Harold Ford, 1991. Mem. NAFE, (charter) NAACP, Am. Bapt. Women (sec. 1982-84, pres. area VI 1984-89, Outstanding & Dedicated Svc. award), Nat. Coun. Negro Women, YMCA, Zeta Phi Beta (dir. Storks' Nest 1981-83). Home: 4458 Whitepine Cv Memphis TN 38109-5922

YOUNG, FREDDA FLORINE, steel manufacturing manager; b. Gadsden, Ala., Feb. 11, 1937; d. Freddie Edmond and Jessie Florine (McCulley) Y.; children: Herbert Donald Watson Jr., Therone Lanier Watson. Grad. high sch., Gadsden, Ala. Material expediter Simpson Electric Co., Chgo., 1955-57; bookkeeper Am. Nat. Bank, Gadsden, 1957-60; bookkeeper, cashier Atlantic Liquor Co., Miami, Fla., 1960-70; sales sample assembler Gen. Time Co., Gadsden, 1974-76, Republic Steel Co., Gadsden, 1976; melt shop supr. Republic Steel, L.T.V. Steel, Gulf State Steel, Gadsden, 1977-92, supr. shipping dept., 1993—. Home: 115 Elsmore Blvd Gadsden AL 35904 Office: 174 S 26th St Gadsden AL 35904-1935

YOUNG, FREDDIE GILLIAM, educational administrator; b. Miami, Fla., Nov. 1, 1939; d. Thomas and Myrtle (Gibson) Gilliam. BS, Fla. A&M U., 1961; MS, Hunter Coll., 1970; postgrad., U. Ghana, 1970; EdD, Nova U., 1990; cert. Prin.'s Exec. Tng. Program, Dade County Pub. Schs. Cert. supervision and adminstrn., African studies, elem. and jr. coll. Tchr. Collier County Pub. Schs., Naples, Fla., N.Y.C. Pub. Schs., Bronx, N.Y.; tchr. Dade County Pub. Schs., Miami, prin.; adj. lead prof. Nova U.; presenter Am. Assn. Ethnic Studies Conf., Fla. Atlantic U., 1991, Assn. Carribean Studies Cairo, 1993, Georgetown, Guyana, 1994. Del. 19th congl. dist. Dem. conv., 1988; mem. Am. Jewish Com. Named Most Outstanding Black Woman, S. Fla., Women's C. of C., Educator of Yr. Zeta Phi Beta; recipient 50 outstanding svc. awards Prin. Ctr. Harvard U. Sch. Edn., 1989, Metro Dade County commendation for dedicated svc.; finalist for Adminstr. of Yr., 1991, DCAA. Mem. AAUW, ASCD, Am. Jewish Com., Nat. Alliance Black Educators, S. Fla. Exec. Educators, Leadership Miami, Miami Alliance Black Educators, Dade County Adminstrs. Assn. (chair), Fla. Reading Assn., Dade Reading Coun., Fla. A&M U. Alumni Assn. (pres. Miami-Dade chpt.), Nova U. Alumni Assn. (sec. Miami chpt.), Phi Delta Kappa. Home: 12390 SW 144th Ter Miami FL 33186-7419

YOUNG, GARY THOMAS, advertising executive; b. Syracuse, N.Y., Dec. 19, 1946; s. Forest Edwin and Arlene Katherine (Weber) Y.; children: Michele Lee, Nikki Lee. Diploma, DOD Broadcast Sch., 1966. Cert. auctioneer, Tex., Ind. Producer, dir. Sta. WNDU-TV, South Bend, Ind., 1967-69, Sta. WKJG-TV, Ft. Wayne, Ind., 1969-71; dep. auditor Allen County, Ft. Wayne, 1971-73; v.p., dir. advt. Kruse Cos., Auburn, Ind., 1973-79; dir. advt. Lowes Exec. Auction Service, South Bend, 1979-81; v.p. Charleston Auctioneers, Ft. Wayne, 1981-84; mgr. Group 400 Advt., San Antonio, 1984—; v.p., dir. Superior Auctioneers & Mktg., Inc., San Antonio, 1984—, v.p., 1991—; co-owner Reflexions Hair and Nail Salon, San Antonio, 1986-90; pub. rels. cons. Tex. Mother/Dau. Pageant, San Antonio, 1986—; bd. dirs. Thomas Daniel Prodns. Ltd., San Antonio; asst. sec., treas. Superior Oil and Gas Ops., Inc. Pres. Miss San Antonio Scholarship Pageant, 1985-92, Miss Bexar County Scholarship Pageant, San Antonio, 1986-88, Miss. Tex. State Assn. Local Franchise Holders, 1989-92; bd. dirs. Miss Tex. Pageant, 1990-91; state dir. Mrs. Tex. Pageant, 1993—. With USAF, 1964-66. Mem. Am. Mktg. Assn., Nat. Auctioneers Assn. (Best of Show award 1971-83), Am. Advt. Fedn. (Addy award 1968-85, Dist. Gold award 1974, gov. 10th dist. 1994—), Tex. Auctioneers Assn., San Antonio Advt. Fedn. (bd. dirs. 1986, pres. 1989-91, pres.'s award 1986), Comm. Arts Soc. San Antonio, Greater San Antonio C. of C. (mem. bus. inquiry com. 1986-88), North San Antonio C. of C. (mem. bus. edn. com. 1986-89). Republican. Lutheran. Office: Superior Auctioneers & Mktg Inc 12002 Huebner Rd Ste 200 San Antonio TX 78230-1213

YOUNG, HARRISON, II, software development and marketing executive; b. Bklyn., Feb. 11, 1944; s. Harrison and Bobbie Aline (King) Y.; m. Shirley Gene Stanfield, Aug. 31, 1967 (div. Sept. 21, 1992); children: Melanie Marie, Tracy Lea; m. Emelie Martha Mannweiler, Dec. 18, 1993. BBA, Pacific Western U., L.A., 1990; MBA, U. Leicester, Eng., 1993. Cert. computer profl. Sr. systems rep. Info. Systems divsn. RCA, Houston, 1967-70; sr. scientist and program mgr. Tetra Tech Inc., San Diego, 1970-74; co-founder, exec. v.p. and sr. program mgr. Atlantic Analysis Corp., Norfolk, Va., 1974-85; program mgr. Comarco Inc., Anaheim, Calif., 1985-86, v.p., divsn. gen. mgr., 1986-87; pres. Washington-based subs. Comarco Inc., 1987-88; pres., CEO, dir. Comarco Inc., Anaheim, 1985-90; pres., CEO Tetra Tech Systems Integration subsidiary Honeywell, San Diego, 1990-92; pres., COO JWK Internat. Corp., Annandale, Va., 1992-94; pres., CEO Advanced Programming Concepts, Austin, Tex., 1994—. Bd. dirs. Blue Cross Blue Shield of Va., 1976-81. With USN, 1961-67. Mem. Am. Mgmt. Assn., Armed Forces Comms. and Electronics Assn., Nat. Contract Mgmt. Assn., Data Processing Mgmt. Assn., Instrumentation Soc. Am. Home: 12633 Pony Ln Austin TX 78727 Office: Advanced Programming Concepts 7004 Bee Caves Rd Austin TX 78746-5065

YOUNG, JAMES OLIVER, dentist, communication company executive; b. Parris Island, S.C., Apr. 19, 1945; s. William Oliver and Ruth Cherokee (Risner) Y.; m. Virginia Evelyn Koontz; children: Amy Robyn, Jenny Elizabeth, Thomas William. BS, Southeast State U., Okla., 1967; DDS, Baylor U., 1972. Practice dentistry, Ardmore, Okla., 1972-93; v.p. Cherokee Telephone Co., Calera, Okla., 1963-94, pres., 1994—; v.p. Cherokee Cellular, Inc., 1989—; pres. Communication Equipment Co., Calera, 1984—, Cherokee Telephone Co., Calera, Okla., 1994. Trustee Ardmore Devel. Authority, 1980-85; bd. dirs. Ardmore Community Concerts Assn., 1980-90, Salvation Army, 1990-91; scoutmaster Boy Scouts Am., pres. Arbuckle Area coun., 1994, 95; mem. Okla. state adv. bd. Easter Seal Soc. Named one of Outstanding Young Men Am., 1981. Fellow Acad. Gen. Dentistry, Acad. of Dentistry Internat.; mem. ADA, Okla. Dental Assn., Ind. Dentists of So. Okla. (pres. 1986), Okla. C. of C. (bd. dirs. 1984-85). Republican. Episcopalian. Lodge: Masons. Avocations: skiing, sailing. Home: 2207 Ridgeway St Ardmore OK 73401-3405 Office: PO Box 445 Calera OK 74730-0445

YOUNG, JAMES VINCENT, international business consultant; b. Mount Clemons, Mich., Sept. 18, 1941; s. Ernest C. and Alta Duncan (Young) Fuller; m. Jody Elston Young, Nov. 13, 1960; children: James V., Chad Duncan, Joshua Fuller. BA in Polit. Sci., U. Okla., 1963; MA in Internat. Rels., U. S.C., 1973; grad., Army War Coll., Carlisle, Pa., 1985. Cert. Korean linguist. Officer U.S. Army, 1963-69; co. comdr. 1st Infantry Div., Vietnam, 1969-70; Army attache to Korea Am. Embassy, Seoul, Korea, 1977-80; chief of staff 1st Signal Brigade, Seoul, Korea, 1980-81; dir. joint ops. Army Staff Coll., Fort Leavenworth, Kans., 1981-85; spl. asst. to sec. of def. Pentagon, Washington, 1985-87; def. attache to Korea Am. Embassy, Seoul, Korea, 1987-90; pres. JVY Pacific Assocs., Burke, Va., 1990—; cons. Bird-Johnson Co., Walpole, Mass., 1990—, SYSCON Corp., Washington, 1990—, Foodmaker Corp., San Diego, 1991—, Eaton Corp., 1994—, United Techs., 1994—, Vrendenburg Corp. Author: On My Watch: Thirty Years of Korean Memories, 1994; contbr. articles to profl. jours. Recipient numerous military awards and medals. Mem. Am. C. of C., Assn. U.S. Army, Korea Soc., Army-Navy Country Club, Pinewild Country Club. Methodist. Home: 61 Devon Dr Pinehurst NC 28374

YOUNG, JANET CHERYL, electrical engineer; b. Roanoke, Va., Oct. 3, 1960; d. Don Gordon and Barbara Hill (Mumpower) Y. BS in Physics, U. Tenn., Chattanooga, 1982; MSEE, Va. Tech. Inst., 1991. Engr. Sci. Applications Internat. Corp., Springfield, Va., 1982-91, UTC Svc. Corp., Washington, 1991-93; LCC, LLC, Arlington, Va., 1993—. Active in World Peace Mission Foundry United Meth. Ch., Washington, 1984, Community Band, Vienna, Va., 1985; vol. Shakespeare Theatre Co., 1996—. Mem. IEEE (mem. Electromagnetic Compatibility Soc. 1987—, Comm. Soc. 1992—). Methodist. Home: 4044 Chetham Way Lake Ridge VA 22192-5079 Office: LCC LLC 2300 Clarendon Blvd Ste 800 Arlington VA 22201-3367

YOUNG, JERRY LEE, writer, critic, engineer; b. Danville, Ill., Nov. 20, 1951; s. Harold Eugene and Lois Marie Young; m. Helen Margaret Parr, May 20, 1978; 1 child, Julius Berryman. MusB in Theory/Composition, U. Tex., 1974, MusM in Theory, 1980, BSEE, 1988. Radio announcer KMFA-FM, Austin, Tex., 1976—; dance columnist Austin Am.-Statesman, Austin, Tex., 1987-90, classical music journalist, 1985—; arts writer Duende, Austin, 1986-87. Composer mus. compositions Ur-Bugle, 1977, TARTR, 1979, Why Don't You Sneeze, 1980, Let There Be Oboes, 1990, Why Do You Not Sneeze, 1994, Why Then Don't You Sneeze, 1994, Back Alley Cat Fish Cake Walk Way Back Alley Alley Cat Fish Cake Walk Way, 1994, The Paper Viceroy, 1996; author: Insider's Guide to Power PC Computing, 1994, Japanese transl., 1995, Portuguese transl., 1996. Active mem. Men's Garden Club of Am., Austin, 1983, Am. Hort. Soc., 1989, Austin Gagaku Soc., 1979—. Mem. IEEE, Soc. Tech. Comms., Eta Kappa Nu, Pi Kappa Lambda. Democrat. Home: 5700 Shoalwood Ave Austin TX 78756-1122

YOUNG, JESS WOLLETT, lawyer; b. San Antonio, Sept. 16, 1926; s. James L. and Zetta (Alonso) Y.; m. Mary Alma Keeter, Apr. 17, 1954; children—Zetta, Imogen. BA, Trinity U., San Antonio, 1957; LLB, St. Mary's U., 1958. Bar: Tex. 1957, U.S. Dist. Ct. (we. dist.) Tex. 1960, U.S. Dist. Ct. (so. dist.) Tex. 1961, U.S. Tax Ct. 1970, U.S. Ct. Appeals (5th cir.) 1981, U.S. Supreme Ct. 1981. Ptnr. Thompson, Thompson, Young & Jones, San Antonio, 1958-63, Moursund, Ball & Young, San Antonio, 1965-73; v.p., dir. Moursund, Ball & Young, Inc., San Antonio, 1973-78; pres., dir. Young & Richards, Inc., San Antonio, 1978-81, Young, Murray & Richards, Inc., San Antonio, 1981-82, Young & Murray, Inc., 1983-87, sole practice, 1987-91, 94—; staff atty., sheriff Bexar County, Tex.; county judge, Bexar County (Tex.), 1964; city atty. City of Olmos Park (Tex.), 1965-70, City of Poteet (Tex.), 1975-76; spl. county judge, Bexar County, 1967. Mem. Tex. State Dem. Exec. Com., 1970-72, Tex. State Rep. Exec. Com., 1984-92, Rep. Precinct committeeman, 1984-92; Dem. precinct committeeman, San Antonio, 1964-76. Served with USNR, 1944-46. Mem. ABA, Tex. Assn. Def. Counsel, Tex. Assn. Bank Counsel, San Antonio Bar Assn., Delta Theta Phi. Episcopalian. Clubs: San Antonio Petroleum, San Antonio Gun (dir. 1958-63, 80-82). Home: 321 Thelma Dr San Antonio TX 78212-2521 Office: 9846 Lorene Ln San Antonio TX 78216-4438

YOUNG, JOHN PAUL, lawyer, retired army officer; b. Newport, R.I., Feb. 7, 1946; s. Rapheal Juan and Catherine Rita (Murphy) Y.; m. Cathy Jo Boehm, Aug. 24; children: George, Margaret. BA in History, U. Tex., 1971; JD, Tex. Tech U., 1975; postgrad., U.S. Army JAG Sch., Charlottesville, Va., 1983. Bar: Tex., Marshall Islands, U.S. Ct. Appeals, U.S. Ct. Mil. Appeals, U.S. Army Ct. Appeals. Enlisted man U.S. Army, 1965-68, commd. capt., 1975, advanced through grades to maj., 1983; def. atty. III Corps, Ft. Hood, Tex., 1975-77; judge adv. 13th Corps Support Command, Ft. Hood, 1977-79; appellate atty. U.S. Army LSA, DAD, Washington, 1979-80; command judge adv. 10th Spl. Forces Group, 1980-82, Kwajalein Missile Range, Marshall Islands, 1983-85; sr. def. counsel 82d Airborne Divsn., Ft. Bragg, N.C., 1985-87; chief of justice Mil. Dist. Washington, 1987-89; ret., 1992; pvt. practice, San Antonio, 1992—. Home: 109 Garrapata St San Antonio TX 78232-1107 Office: PO Box 700776 San Antonio TX 78270

YOUNG, JOHN WATTS, astronaut; b. San Francisco, Sept. 24, 1930; s. William H. Y.; m. Susy Feldman; children by previous marriage: Sandra, John. BS in Aero. Engring, Ga. Inst. Tech., 1952; D Applied Sci. (hon.), Fla. Technol. U., 1970; LLD (hon.), Western State U., 1969; DSc (hon.), U. S.C., 1981, Brown U., 1983. Joined USN, 1952, advanced through grades to capt.; test pilot, program mgr. F4 weapons systems projects, 1959-62; then maintenance officer Fighter Squadron 143, Naval Air Sta., Miramar, Calif.; chief astronaut office Flight Ops. Directorate, 1975-87, spl. asst. dir. JSC for engring. ops., safety, 1987-96, comdr. 54-hour, 36-orbit 1st flight of Shuttle Space, 1981, and 10 day orbital shuttle 1st flight Space Lab., 1983, assoc. dir. tech. JSC, 1996—. Decorated DFC (3), D.S.M. (2); recipient NASA Disting. Svc. medal (3), NASA Exceptional Svc. medal (2), NASA Engring. Achievement medal, 1988, NASA Outstanding Leadership medal, 1992, NASA Outstanding Achievement medal, 1994, Congl. Space medal of honor, 1981; named Disting. Young Alumni Svc. award Ga. Tech. Acad. Disting. Engrs., 1994; named to Nat. Aviation Hall of Fame, 1988. Fellow Am. Astronautical Soc. (Flight Achievement award 1972, 81, 83, Space Flight award 1993), Soc. Exptl. Test Pilots (Iven Kincheloe award 1972, 81), AIAA (HAley Astronautics award 1973, 82, 84); mem. Sigma Chi. Office: NASA Johnson Space Ctr Houston TX 77058

YOUNG, JOSEPH RUTLEDGE, JR., lawyer; b. Charleston, S.C., Mar. 28, 1943; s. Joseph Rutledge and Elizabeth Evans (Jenkins) Y.; m. Kathleen Baldwin Kimmell, Aug. 10, 1968; children—Joseph Rutledge, Simons Waring. B.A. with distinction in History, U. Va., 1965, LL.B., 1968. Bar: S.C. 1968, U.S. Dist. Ct. (so. dist.) S.C. 1968, U.S. Ct. Appeals (4th cir.) 1972. Assoc. Young, Clement, Rivers & Tisdale, Charleston, 1970-75, ptnr. 1975—. pres. Cen. R.R. of S.C., 1988—; bd. dirs. So. Nat. Bank of S.C., 1988-95, Branek Bank and Trust Co. of S.C., 1995—. Contbr. articles to profl. jours. Mem. Charleston City Council, 1975-80; v.p. Historic Charleston Found., 1993-95, pres., 1996—; trustee Middleton Place Found., 1987—, Charleston Day Sch., 1985-91. Served to capt. U.S. Army, 1968-70, Vietnam. Decorated Bronze Star. Fellow Am. Coll. Trial Lawyers; mem. S.C. Bar Assn. (chmn. CLE 1982-84, bd. govs. 1984-88, sec. 1991, treas. 1992-93, pres.-elect 1993-94, pres. 1994-95, exec. com. bd. commrs. on grievances and discipline 1983-86), Am. Bd. Trial Advocates (diplomate), Fedn. Ins. and Corp. Counsel, St. Andrews Soc., St. George's Soc., Preservation Soc., U.S. Supreme Ct. Hist. Soc. (state chmn.), Carolina Yacht Club, Farmington Country Club, Yeamans Hall Club. Office: Young Clement Rivers & Tisdale 28 Broad St Charleston SC 29401-3004

YOUNG, LOIS CATHERINE WILLIAMS, poet, former reading specialist; b. Wakeman, Ohio, Mar. 10, 1930; d. William McKinley and Leona Catherine (Woods) Williams; m. William Walton Young; children: Ralph, Catherine, William. BS, NYU, 1957; MS, Hofstra U., 1962, profl. diploma, 1967, EdD, 1981; M Pub. Adminstrn., Fla. Internat. U., 1988. Cert. tchr., sch. supr., N.Y., pub. mgmt., Fla. Tchr. Copiague (N.Y.) Schs., 1957-59; research assoc. Columbia and Hofstra Univs., Hempstead, N.Y., 1964-69; tchr. Half Hollow Hills Pub. Schs., Dix Hills, N.Y., 1970-72; instr. Conn. Coll., New London, 1972-73; tchr., supr., reading coordinator Hempstead (N.Y.) Pub. Schs., 1975-85; cons. South African project AID Fla. Meml. Coll., Miami, Fla., 1987-88; clinician Hofstra U., Hempstead, 1962-64; tchr. trainer Amityville (N.Y.) Pub. Schs., 1965, Hofstra Univ., 1982; key speaker Internat. Reading Assn., N.Y., Calif., Caribbean Islands, 1982-86. Author numerous poems. Sec. Nassau County (N.Y.) chpt. Jack and Jill of Am., 1960-62; pres. PTA, Uniondale, N.Y., 1962-68; active Boy Scouts Am., Uniondale, N.Y., 1963-65; bd. dirs. Miami chpt. UN Assn./USA, 1987-92, 1st v.p. 1989-91, Broward Fort Lauderdale chpt., 1993—; active multilateral project, 1987-90; contbr. Procs. South African Project, 1987. Recipient Lifetime Membership award PTA, 1964, rsch. grant N.Y. State Fed. Programs, 1978, Laurel Wreath award Doctoral Assn. of N.Y. Educators, 1982, Cert. of award UN Assn./USA, 1987, 88, Outstanding Achievement award Fla. Internat. U., 1988, Golden Poet award World of Poetry, 1990, 91; fellow Fla. Internat. U., 1987. Mem. Internat. Soc. Poets (life, lifetime adv. panel 1993—, award, Nat. Libr. of Poetry award 1994, 95, Poetry Today 1996), Fla. Internat. U. Alumni Assn., NYU Alumni Assn. (bd. dirs. 1983-90, 2d v.p. 1986-87), Hofstra U. Alumni Assn., Tuskegee Airmen, Inc., Weston (Fla.) Toastmasters Club (charter), Toastmasters Internat., Kappa Delta Pi, Alpha Kappa Alpha, Theta Iota Omega (global affairs com. 1984-86), Phi Delta Kappa. Home: 7187 Crystal Lake Dr W Palm Beach FL 33411

YOUNG, MALCOLM BLACK, consulting company executive; b. Bronxville, N.Y., Dec. 18, 1940; s. Herrick Black and Charlotte Elizabeth Young; m. C. Ann Krebs, Aug. 18, 1962; children: Bethany C., Malcolm Scott, Marta M., Charlotte Tycie. BA, Wabash Coll., 1962; M of Pub. and Internat. Affairs, U. Pitts., 1964, PhD, 1972. Sr. assoc. Devel. Assocs., Inc., Arlington, Va., 1972-82, v.p., 1982—; v.p., treas. Elder-In Inc., Arlington, 1987-89; pres., chmn. Quaker Morning Svcs., Arlington, 1995—; adj. prof. George Washington U., 1974-78. Author: Politics and Planning in the Philippines, 1972. Elder Presbyn. Ch., Arlington, 1976—; chair planning com. Nat. Capital Presbytery, Washington, 1978-85; pers. dir., bd. mem. Literacy Coun. No. Va., Fairfax, 1989—; bd. mem. Welfare of the Blind, Arlington, 1992—. Mem. Am. Ednl. Rsch. Assn., Am. Evaluation Assn., Am. Soc. for Pub. Adminstrn., Kiwanis Club Arlington. Office: Devel Assocs Inc 1730 N Lynn St Arlington VA 22205

YOUNG, MARGARET ALETHA MCMULLEN (MRS. HERBERT WILSON YOUNG), social worker; b. Vossburg, Miss., June 13, 1916; d. Grady Garland and Virgie Aletha (Moore) McMullen; BA cum laude, Columbia Bible Coll., 1949; grad. Massey Bus. Coll., 1958; MSW, Fla. State U., 1965; postgrad. Jacksonville U., 1961-62, Tulane U., 1967; m. Herbert Wilson Young, Aug. 19, 1959. Dir. Christian edn. Eau Claire Presbyn. Ch., Columbia, S.C., 1946-51; tchr. Massey Bus. Coll., Jacksonville, Fla., 1954-57, office mgr., 1957-59; social worker, unit supr. Fla. div. Family Svcs., St. Petersburg, 1960-66, dist. casework supr., 1966-71; social worker, project supr., program supr. Project Playpen, Inc., 1971-81, pres. bd., 1982-83, cons., 1986-89; pvt. practice family counselor, 1982—; mem. coun. Child Devel. Ctr., 1983-89; mem. transitional housing com., Religious Community Svcs., 1984-90. Mem. Acad. Cert. Social Workers, Nat. Assn. Social Workers (pres. Tampa Bay chpt. 1973-74), Fla. Assn. for Health and Social Services (pres. chpt. 1971), Nature Conservancy, Eta Beta Rho. Democrat. Presbyn. Rotary Ann (pres. 1970-71). Home: Presbyterian Home CMR 13 201 W 9th North St Summerville SC 29483-6721

YOUNG, MICHAEL ANTHONY, lawyer; b. Lima, Ohio, Sept. 3, 1960; s. William John and Bettye Jean (Day) Y. BS magna cum laude, U. Cen. Fla., 1981; JD with honors, Fla. State U., 1984. Bar: Ga. 1984, Fla. 1985. Assoc. Kilpatrick & Cody, Atlanta, 1984-86, Stokes, Lazarus & Carmichael, Atlanta, 1986-89; pvt. practice, Atlanta, 1989—; jud. intern U.S. Dist. Ct. (no. dist.) Fla., 1984; weekend atty. Atlanta Legal Aid Soc., 1985-86. Rsch. editor Fla. State U. Law Rev., 1982-84; contbr. articles to legal jours. Dir., pres. ChildKind Found. Mem. ABA, Assn. Trial Lawyers of Am., Fla. Bar Assn., Ga. Bar Assn., Atlanta Bar Assn. Home: 1495 Highland Ave NE Atlanta GA 30306-3357 Office: Ste 440 17 Executive Park Dr NE Atlanta GA 30329-2222

YOUNG, MICHAEL WILLIAM, English language educator; b. Pitts., May 21, 1957; s. William Franklin and Frances Marie (Keating) Y. BA in Lit. and Creative Writing, Duquesne U., 1980; MA in Playwrighting and 20th Century Am. Lit., Kans. State U., 1983; PhD in Creative Writing and Lit., U. Cin., 1989. Instr. dept. English Kans. State U., 1983-85; grad. tchg. asst. dept. English U. Cin., 1985-89; vis. asst. prof. dept. English U.Nebr., Lincoln, 1989-92; asst. prof. dept. English Davis & Elkins (W.Va.) Coll., 1992-95; adj. prof. dept. comm. Robert Morris Coll., 1995—; presenter papers in field. Author poetry, fiction and articles. Recipient William Boyce award for Excellence in Teaching, U. Cin.; Tchr. Coun. Rsch. grantee U. Nebr., Lincoln, 1990-91, 91-92, Faculty Enrichment grantee Govt. of Can., 1993-94, Baldwin rsch. grantee, 1993; Univ. Grad. scholar U. Cin., 1985-89. Mem. MLA, N.E. MLA, Nat. Coun. Tchrs. English, Conf. Coll. Composition and Commn, Sigma Tau Delta, Sigma Delta Chi, U. Nebr.-Lincoln Alumni Assn., U.S. Olympic Soc. Republican. Roman Catholic.

YOUNG, MICHELLE DIANE, editor; b. Norman, Okla., Dec. 18, 1966; d. Gerald Wayne Wuest and Diane Lee (Osborn) Giddings; m. Derek Allen Young, June 3, 1990. BA in Sociology, Southwestern U., 1989; MEd in Bilingual Spl. Edn., U. Tex., 1993, postgrad., 1993—. Adminstrv. asst. J. Neill Wilkerson Atty., Georgetown, Tex., 1983-85, legal aide, libr., 1985-89; English tchr. Surat Thani Polytech., Thailand, 1990-91; rsch. dir. EBSRDI-UT, Austin, 1994-95; mng. editor QSE, Austin, 1995—; mem. dean's evaluation bd. U. Tex. Coll. of Edn., Austin, 1995—; adv. bd. mem. Grad. Adv. Com., 1994-95. Contbr. articles to profl. jours. Mem. Nat. Orgn. of Women, Austin, 1993-95; mem. Nat. Coalition of Edn. Advocates, Washington, 1993-95. Capt. Army Nat. Guard, 1986—. Univ. fellowship U. Tex. Grad. Sch., 1995-96, Alexander Caswell Ellis fellowship Coll. of Edn. U. Tex., 1995-96. Mem. Women in Edn. (chairwoman 1995), Edn. Policy Students Assn. (pres. 1995), Ednl. Adminstr. Student's Assn. (co-pres. 1994-95), Am. Ednl. Rsch. Assn. (divsn. A rep. 1993-95), Soc. for the Study of Symbolic Interactionism, Soc. for the Study of Edn., Nat. Assn. of Univ. Women, Nat. Orgn. of Women, Nat. Coalition of Edn. Advocates, Phi Kappa Phi, Kappa Delta Pi. Home: 1624 W 6th St Apt L Austin TX 78703 Office: U Tex Coll of Edn Austin TX 78712-1291

YOUNG, MIKE, design company executive. Pres. Mike Young Designs. Address: 2360 Cole Springs Rd PO Box 289 Watkinsville GA 30677

YOUNG, NERISSA ANN, journalist; b. Bluefield, W.Va., June 3, 1965; d. James Weldon and Nonree Amie (Wallace) Y. BS in edn., Concord Coll., 1987; MA in journalism, Marshall Univ., 1993. Radio personality WMTD Radio, Hinton, W.Va., 1986-88, 89-90; tchr. Monroe County Schs., Union, W.Va., 1988-89, 90-91; journalist The Register-Herald/Beckley Newspapers, Beckley, W.Va., 1993—. Contbr. articles to profl. jours. Pianist, choir mem., drama dir. Fairview Bapt. Ch., Forest Hill, W.Va., 1982—; camp counselor Summers County 4-H Camp, Hinton, 1985-89, 94-95. Recipient 1st place for crime/ct. coverage W.Va. Press Assn., 1995. Mem. Soc. Profl. Journalists (sec./treas. 1994-95, v.p. 1995-96, pres. 1996—, nat. ethics com. 1995-97). Baptist. Home and Office: 510 Greenville Rd Forest Hill WV 24935

YOUNG, RAYMOND GUINN, music educator; b. Morrilton, Ark., Dec. 21, 1932; s. Theodore T. and Vida Mae (Guinn) Y.; m. Barbara Ann Woolcox, Aug. 29, 1953 (div. Nov. 1986); children: Steven Cary, Dale, Michael, Rae Ann; m. Joan Arno, Nov. 20, 1994. MusB, U. Mich., 1955, MusM, 1956. Band dir. Trenton (Mich.) High Sch., 1956-61; asst. band dir., instr. trombone and euphonium U. So. Miss., Hattiesburg, 1961-68, dir. bands, 1968-72; dir. bands La. Tech. U., Ruston, 1972-85, head dept. mus., 1972-88, prof. music, 1988-91; dir. orch. Ruston Civic Symphony, 1975-80; condr. USA Honor Bands, Honolulu, 1975-88; soloist Tokyo Kosei Wind Orch., 1985. Dir. choir Univ. Presbyn. Ch., Ruston, 1973-85. Mem. Am. Bandmaster Assn., La. Bandmaster Assn. (Bandmaster of Yr. 1983), Nat. Band Assn., Coll. Band Dirs. Nat. Assn., Ruston Antique Car Assn. (pres. 1984, 85), Phi Beta Mu, Phi Mu Alpha Sinfonia, Kappa Kappa Psi, Sigma Alpha Iota. Lodge: Masons (illustrious master 1969, 70). Home: 149 Sherlock Herring Rd Purvis MS 39475-3150

YOUNG, ROBERT A., III, freight systems executive; b. Ft. Smith, Ark., Sept. 23, 1940; s. Robert A. and Vivian (Curtis) Y.; m. Mary Carleton McRae; children—Tracy, Christy, Robert A. IV, Stephen. BA in Econs., Washington and Lee U., 1963. Supr. terminal ops. Ark. Best Freight, Ft. Smith, 1964-65; pres. Data-Tronics Inc., Ft. Smith, 1965-67; sr. v.p. Nat. Bank of Commerce, Dallas, 1967-70; v.p. fin. Ark. Best Corp., Ft. Smith, 1970-73, exec. v.p., 1973, pres., chief operating officer, 1973-88, chief exec. officer, 1988—; pres. ABF Freight Systems, Inc., Ft. Smith, 1979-94; bd. dirs. First Nat. Bank, Ft. Smith, Mosler Corp., Hamilton, Ohio. Pres. United Way, Ft. Smith, 1981; vice chmn. bd. dirs. Sparks Regional Med. Ctr., Ft. Smith, 1995; chmn. bd. trustees Ark. Coll.; bd. dirs. ATA Found., Inc., Ft. Smith Boys Club; chmn. bd. trustees Lyon Coll. Recipient Silver Beaver award Boy Scouts Am. Mem. Am. Trucking Assn. (vice chmn.), Ark. State C. of C. (pres., bd. dirs., chmn.), Phi Delta Theta. Presbyterian. Home: Ark Best Corp P O Box 10048 Fort Smith AR 72917-0048 Office: ABF Freight Systems Inc 3801 Old Greenwood Rd Fort Smith AR 72903 Also: Ark Best Corp 3801 Old Greenwood Rd Fort Smith AR 72903

YOUNG, ROBERT LINDLEY, endocrinologist, internist, educator; b. Butte, Mont., Mar. 27, 1936; s. Charles Lindley and Margaret (Farrell) Y.; m. Adelaide Elizabeth Davenport, Feb. 25, 1976; children: Wendy, Craig, Shawn. BA in Psychology, Dartmouth Coll., 1959, MD, 1960. Lic. physician Tex., Nev., N.Mex. Commd. 2d lt. USAF, 1962, advanced through grades to col., 1978; ret., 1981; intern internal medicine, resident, fellow in endocrinology Wilford Hall USAF Med. Ctr., Lackland AFB, Tex., 1962-67, chief nuclear medicine, 1967-70, chief endocrine-metabolic svc., 1971-81; pvt. practice El Paso, Tex., 1981; advisor on internal medicine to command surgeon MACV and surgeon-gen. Vietnamese Armed Forces, 1970-71; hosp. privileges Columbia Med. Ctr. West, Providence, Sierra, Columbia-East, Columbia Behavioral Ctr., El Paso; from clin. assoc. prof. to clin. prof. medicine U. Tex. Health Sci. Ctr., San Antonio, 1971-82, clin. assoc. prof. medicine, El Paso, 1982—; regional cons. endocrinology Wilford Hall USAF Med. Ctr., 1971-75; cons. endocrinology Air Force Surgeon Gen., 1977-81; chmn. radioisotope com. Wilford Hall USAF Med. Ctr., 1971-81, dir. endocrinology fellowship program, 1971-81, mem. audit com. and resident evaluation com. divsn. medicine, 1971-81, chmn. audit com. divsn. medicine, 1979-81; chmn. med. dept. Sun Towers Hosp., 1985-87, radioisotope com. Vista Hills, 1985-86. Contbr. articles to profl. jours. Fellow ACP; mem. AMA, Endocrine Soc., Soc. Nuclear Medicine, Soc. Air Force Physicians, Am. Thyroid Assn., Am. Diabetes Assn., Am. Assn. Clin. Endocrinologists, Tex. Med. Assn. (sec. sect. nuclear medicine 1983-84, chmn. sect. nuc. medicine 1984-85, mem. radiation safety com. 1987-89), Tex. Assn. Physicians in Nuc. Medicine, El Paso County Med. Soc. Office: Bldg 7 1201 E Schuster Ave Ste 7 El Paso TX 79902-4646

YOUNG, ROBERT PAUL, state agency administrator; b. Miami, Dec. 28, 1939; s. Robert Jr. and Doreen (Reeves) Y.; m. Nancy Wilson Young, Aug. 5, 1971; 1 child, Ryan Paul. BS, Morehouse Coll., 1961; MA, U. Miami, 1972, EdD, 1982. Asst. v.p. acad. affairs U. Miami, Coral Gables, 1972-76, dir. rockefeller program, 1976-79; asst. dir. dept. of stadiums City of Miami, 1982-85, exec. dir., gen. mgr., 1985-87; dep. city mgr. City of Riviera Beach, Fla., 1988; exec. dir. CEO Primary Health Care Consortium, Miami, 1988-91; regional mgr. Fla. Dept. of Labor, Miami, 1991—; program officer of project devel. Cmty. Rels. Bd. of Dade County, Miami, 1971-72. Founding mem., bd. dirs. Coconut Grove Family Health Ctr., 1971—; vice mayor City of South Miami, 1994—, commr., 1994—; mem. Upfront Polit. Club, Miami, 1995. Rockefeller Found. fellow, 1979; recipient Outstanding Pres. award Fla. Jaycees. Mem. Fla. League of Cities, Inc., Fla. Assn. Cmty. Health Ctrs., Am. Mgmt. Assn., Internat. Assn. of Augitorium, Nat. Forum for Pub. Adminstrs. Home: 6825 Hardee Rd Miami FL 33143 Office: City of South Miami 6130 Sunset Dr Miami FL 33143

YOUNG, ROGER WILSON, accountant, lawyer, financial advisor; b. Little Rock, Oct. 3, 1949; s. German Preston and Mamie Demetrius (Rogers) Y.; children by previous marriage: Heather Sacha, Hays Wilson; m. Judith Lucile Russ, Sept. 17, 1977; 1 child, Tracy René. BA in Acctg., Memphis State U., 1972, JD, 1977. CPA, Ga. Acct. Kraft Foods, Memphis, 1969-71; staff acct. Clyde Hudson, CPA, Memphis, 1971; mng. ptnr. Hudson & Young, CPAs, Memphis, 1972-75; pres. R.W. Young & Co., PC, Memphis, 1976-80, Atlanta, 1981—. Fellow AICPA, Ga. Soc. CPAs; mem. Country Club of the South (bd. govs. 1990—). Republican. Episcopalian. Office: RW Young & Co PC 700 Old Roswell Lakes Pky Roswell GA 30076-1611

YOUNG, S. JUNE, insurance executive; b. Harrison, Ark., Nov. 26, 1937; d. Paul Loy and Mildred L. (Taylor) Turney; m. Sam A. Young, Feb. 4, 1956; children: Linda Young-Shumate, Susan A. Young Thomas, Lori Beth Young Griggs, Sammye Young Silva. Grad. profl. ednl. program, Longman R & R Newkirk, 1990. Cert. fraternal ins. counselor fellow. Bookkeeper Harrison Grocer Co., Harrison, 1955-57; traffic mgr. Sta. KHOZ Radio, Harrison, 1957-59; co-owner, mgr. The Young Store, Pyatt, Ark., 1963-86; owner, mgr. Ozarks Satelite Systems, Pyatt, 1984-86; field rep. Woodmen of World Life Ins. Soc., Omaha, Nebr., 1986-88; area mgr. Woodmen of World Life Ins. Co., Omaha, Ark., 1988—. Author poems. Mem. Marion County Indsl. Devel., Yellville, 1983-88; tchr. Sunday sch., Pyatt, 1970-96; organist Pyatt First Bapt. Ch. Mem. Nat. Assn. Life Underwriters, Ark. Fraternal Ins. Counselors, Bus. and Profl. Women's Fund, Nat. Guild Piano Players, Marion County C. of C., Rotary, Woodmen of World (pres. cabinet 1987-88, club prs. 1989-90, 91, lodge sec. 1986-96, President's Club 1987, 88, 95). Home: 1 Foster Pyatt AR 72672 Office: Woodmen of World Life Ins Soc PO Box 1237 Yellville AR 72687-1237

YOUNG, SANDRA JOYCE, nursing administrator, consultant; b. Chattanooga, Aug. 18, 1952; d. J. Franklin and Mary Nell (Junkins) Masters; m. Michael Jacob Young, May 26, 1973; children: Sandra Michele, Michael Jacob, Matthew Oliver. Diploma, Baroness Erlanger Sch. Nursing, Chattanooga, 1973; student, U. Tenn., Chattanooga. Cert. Tenn. care pre-admission mgr. Blue Cross Blue Shield Tenn. Charge nurse Suburban Hosp., Louisville; charge nurse Erlanger Med. Ctr., Chattanooga, asst. head nurse in ophthalmology; supr. nurse cons. Blue Cross/Blue Shield of Tenn., Chattanooga. Mem. Tenn. Nursing Assn. Home: 500 Shawnee Trl Chattanooga TN 37411-3001

YOUNG, STEPHEN FLINN, editor; b. Jackson, Miss., May 7, 1945; s. Robert Harold and Cary Nell (Flinn) Y.; m. Susan Elizabeth Siddall, Nov. 5, 1964 (div. Mar. 1973); 1 child, Brian Scott Young; m. Diana Cates, Nov. 25, 1982. BA, U. So. Miss., 1967, MA, 1969, postgrad., 1990-91; postgrad., Auburn (Ala.) U., 1973-74, La. State U., 1974-76. adj. faculty Honors Coll., U. So. Miss.; co-founder The Studio, Inc., Hattiesburg, Miss. Instr. Troy (Ala.) State U., 1969-73, U. West Fla., Pensacola, 1973-78; exec. dir. Quinlan Art Ctr., Gainesville, Fla., 1978-79, Living Arts and Scis. Ctr., Lexington, Ky., 1979-80; curator of exhbns. Miss. State Hist. Mus., Jackson, 1980-83; writer New Orleans, 1983-87; programs dir. Miss. Arts Commn., Jackson, 1987-89; mng. editor The So. Quar., Hattiesburg, 1989-90, editor, 1990—; writer-in-residence Chimneyville Sch. Design, Jackson, Miss., 1981-82; cons. Miss. Humanities Coun., Jackson, 1991-92; artist-in-residence Ecole Nationale de la Photographie, Arles, France, 1993; spkr. in field. Author: Life in Acadiana, 1976, North American Indian Art, 1979, Southeastern Art on Paper, 1980, Paperworks 80 Southeast, 1980, Mississippi Choctaw Crafts, 1983, Mississippi Crafts, 1983, Biloxi's Ethnic Heritage: Images of Change and Tradition, 1989, Ethnic Mississippi, 1992, Earl's Art Shop: Building Art with Earl Simmons, 1995; exhibited in group shows including Woods Gallery, U. So. Miss., 1991, S.E. Regional Conf. of the Am. Crafts Coun., 1991, Arts Coun., 1990, Miss. Mus. Art, 1983, 90, Itawamba Jr. Coll., 1982, many others. Com. chair Operation Comeback, New Orleans, 1986-87, Hattiesburg Downtown Assn., 1992—, Clinton-Gore campaign, Forrest County, Miss., 1992; v.p. Mag. St. Assn., New Orleans, 1984-87. Grantee Miss. Humanities Coun., 1993-94, 91, 90, 89, 88, Fla. Arts Coun., 1979, Lexington Arts Coun./Ky. Arts Coun., 1980, Tenn. Valley Authority, 1982, So. Arts Fedn., 1983, Nat. Endowment for the Humanities, 1983, 91, Nat. Endowment for the Humanities/Rockefeller Found., 1990, 92-93, Miss. Arts Commn., 1992, Miss. com. for the Humanities, 1983. Mem. MLA, Soc. for the Study of So. Lit. (exec. com.), Coll. Art Assn., Club Pyramid, Downtown Hattiesburg Assn., Internat. Visual Sociology Assn., Miss. Folklore Soc., Southeastern Coll. Art Assn., Soc. for the Study of So. Lit., Soc. for Scholarly Pub., Coun. of Editors of Learned Jours., Contemporary Art Ctr. of New Orleans. Home: PO Box 1584 Hattiesburg MS 39403-1584 Office: The So Quar PO Box 5078 Hattiesburg MS 39406-5078

YOUNG, TERI ANN BUTLER, pharmacist; b. Littlefield, Tex., Aug. 22, 1958; d. Doyle Wayne and Bettie May (Lair) Butler; m. James Oren Young, Aug. 1, 1981; children: Andrew Wayne, Aaron Lee. BS in Pharmacy, Southwestern Okla. State U., 1981. Staff pharmacist St. Mary of Plains Hosp., Lubbock, Tex., 1981-84; staff pharmacist West Tex. Hosp., Lubbock, 1984-85, asst. dir. pharmacy, 1985-86; pharmacist cons. for nursing homes Billy D. Davis & Assocs., Lubbock, 1986—; relief pharmacist Prescription Lab., Med. Pharmacy and Foster Infusion Care, Lubbock, 1987-89; staff pharmacist Univ. Med. Ctr., 1990—, diabetic teaching pharmacist, 1995—; relief pharmacist West Tex. Hosp., 1986-91, Highland Hosp., 1990—, Med. Infusion Technology, 1992—. Mem. Lubbock Area Soc. of Hosp. Pharmacists (sec., treas. 1982-83), Lubbock Area Pharm. Assn., West Tex. Pharm. Assn., Am. Soc. Hosp. Pharmacists, Pilot Internat., Lubbock Genealogical Soc. Republican. Baptist. Lodge: Eastern Star. Home: 7410 Toledo Ave Lubbock TX 79424-2214 Office: Univ Med Ctr 602 Indiana Ave Lubbock TX 79415-3364

YOUNG, THOMAS ELTON, librarian; b. Ft. Worth, June 12, 1950; s. Edmund Richard and Mary Elizabeth (Stevens) Y. BA in History, Okla. State U., 1972; MLS, U. Okla., 1976. Libr. asst. sci. and pub. policy program U. Okla., Norman, 1976-77; libr., asst. registrar Philbrook Mus. Art, Tulsa, 1978—. Author: (catalog) Edward Buehler Delk Architect, 1993, (catalog) Documentary Paintings from Collection of Standard Oil Co., 1996; editor: (newsletter) Art Libraries of North America-Central Plains Newsletter, 1985—. Mem. Art Librs. Soc. N.Am. (vice chmn. ctrl. plains chpt. 1984-85, chmn. ctrl. plains chpt. 1985-86). Democrat. Unitarian. Office: Philbrook Mus Art 2727 S Rockford Rd Tulsa OK 74114-4104

YOUNG, THOMAS RICHARD, sales professional; b. Winston-Salem, N.C., May 13, 1959; s. James Lawrence and Jacquolyn (Watts) Y.; m. Janet Allison Walls Young, Apr. 25, 1987. BBA, N.C. Wesleyan Coll., 1982. Mgmt. trainee Planters Nat. Bank and Trust Co., Rockymount, N.C., 1982-83; br. mgr. Planters Nat. Bank and Trust Co., Wilmington, N.C., 1983-84; sales rep. Dictaphone Corp., Atlanta, 1984-85; account rep. Glasrock Home Healthcare, Atlanta, 1985-86; sr. sales rep. Renal div. Baxter Healthcare Corp., Birmingham, Ala., 1986-90; profl. sales rep. Amgen, Inc., Birmingham, 1990—. Com. mem. Nat. Kidney Found. Polo Benefit, Mobile, Ala., 1988; exec. com. treas. March of Dimes Birth Defects Found., Wilmington, 1984, com. mem. United Way Advanced Gifts div., Rocky Mount, N.C., 1983. Recipient Spl. Merit award Greater Wilmington C. of C., 1984, Amgen Presidents Club award, 1994. Mem. Rocky Mount Area C. of C. (life, Pres. award 1983), Amgen Pres.'s Club (pres. 1994). Republican. Baptist. Home and Office: 6567 Mill Creek Cir Birmingham AL 35242-4153

YOUNG, THOMAS WADE, journalist; b. Raleigh, N.C., Jan. 16, 1962; s. Bobby Wade and Harriett Thomas (Daniel) Y.; m. Kristen Lucille Gooch, June 7, 1986. BA, U. N.C., 1983, MA, 1987. Part time announcer WCBQ Radio, Oxford, N.C., 1979-83; reporter, news anchor WDNC Radio, Durham, N.C., 1984-86; writer, prodr., editor AP, Washington, 1987—. Author of short stories and essays. Mem. Radio and TV Corr. Assn. Baptist. Home: 1524 Mount Eagle Pl Alexandria VA 22302-2120 Office: AP Broadcast Svcs 1825 K St NW Washington DC 20006-1202

YOUNG, VERA MILLER, portfolio manager; b. Galveston, Tex., Nov. 11, 1927; d. Thomas Morgan and Vera (Shaw) Miller; m. William Jackson Standley, Feb. 17, 1946 (dec. 1973); children: Weldon, Yvonne Standley Huffhines, Mansel; m. William Jackson Young, July 3, 1975 (dec. 1979). AB, Galveston Coll., 1971. Analyst Am. Nat. Ins. Co., Galveston, 1972-74, securities analyst, 1974-78, sr. securities analyst, 1978-83, asst. v.p., 1984-86, 87—; v.p., portfolio mgr. Securities Mgmt. & Rsch. Inc. and subs., Galveston, 1987—. Republican. Baptist. Office: Securities Mgmt & Rsch Inc 1 Moody Plz Galveston TX 77550-7948

YOUNG, WILLIAM DAVID, computer scientist; b. Albuquerque, Nov. 22, 1953; s. Youree Harold and Alma Catherine (Callahan) Y. BS in Math. with honors, U. Tex., 1975, BA in Philosophy with high honors, 1976, MA in Philosophy, 1976, MA in Computer Sci., 1980, PhD in Computer Sci., 1988; postgrad., U. Notre Dame, 1976-77. Rsch. engring. sci. asst., systems analyst U. Tex., Austin, 1978-87; computing rsch. sci. Computational Logic, Inc., Austin, 1987-88, sr. computing rsch. sci., 1988—, also bd. dirs.; part-time instr. Austin C.C., 1978-80, Southwest Tex. State U., San Marcos, 1980-81, 83-86; rsch. sci. Honeywell Secure Computing Tech. Ctr., St. Anthony, Minn., 1984-87; invited lectr., presenter, speaker in field; publ. chair Computer Security Workshop III, 1990, IV, 1991; chmn. panel Symposium Software Analysis, Testing and Verification, 1991, program com., 1991; organizer, chmn. panel computer security founds. Computer Security Workshop II, 1989; bd. dirs. Computational Logic, Inc. Mem. editl. bd. Jour. Computer Security; contbr. articles to profl. jours. papers in field. Mem. IEEE, Assn. Computing Machienry, Abelian Group Investment Club (pres. 1992-96), Phi Beta Kappa, Phi Eta Sigma, Pi Mu Epsilon, Upsilon Pi Epsilon. Home: 2208 Lindell Ave Austin TX 78704-5131 Office: Computational Logic Inc 1717 W 6th St Ste 290 Austin TX 78703-4777

YOUNG, WILLIAM DEAN, psychologist; b. Flushing, N.Y., June 11, 1946; s. Dean and Laura Hervey (Smith) Y.; m. Pamela Sue Williams, Mar. 23, 1968; children: Stephanie D., Matthew W. BA, U. Tulsa, 1968; MEd, U. Md., 1971; EdD, U. Tulsa, 1985. Lic. prof. counselor, Okla.; nat. cert. gerontol. counselor. Mgr. sales adminstrn. Global Internat. Forwarding, Anaheim, Calif., 1972-76; reg. sales mgr. Global Internat. Forwarding, Tulsa, 1976-78; nat. sales mgr. Allied Van Lines, Transvault div., Broadview, Ill., 1978-79; exec. v.p. Hodges Allied Van Lines, Tulsa, 1979-82; gen. mgr. Graebel Okla. Movers, Tulsa, 1982-85; pres. Career Devel. Svcs., Tulsa, 1985—; mem. staff, vocat. cons. Laureate Psychiat. Clinic and Hosp., 1990; cons. The Warren Found., Tulsa, 1986, Graebel Van Lines, 1985-87; exec. dir. Okla. Alliance for Mentally Ill, 1992-95. Author: Job Search Skills Workbook, 1988; author pamphlet: Moving with Children, 1988. Pres. Mental Health Assn., Tulsa, 1987-88; mem. Okla. Mental Health Planning Coun., Oklahoma City, 1988-94, chmn., 1990-92; mem. med. adv. coun. Okla. Health Care Authority, 1995—; Mem. Tulsa County Planning and Coordinating Bd., 1991-92, mem. Dept. Rehab. Svcs., Rehab. Adv. Coun., 1993-96; mem. med. advisory com. Okla. Healthcare Authority, 1995-96. Recipient Meritorious Svc. award Mental Health Assn. Tulsa, 1988, Commendation for community svc. Tulsa Psychiat. Ctr., 1987; named Internat. Salesman of the Yr., Allied Van Lines, Chgo., 1980. Mem. ACA, Am. Rehab. Counselors Assn., Assn. for Adult Devel. and Aging (com. chmn. 1986—, mem.-at-large bd. dirs. 1990-93), Nat. Rehab. Assn., Nat. Career Assn. Nat. Assn. Forensic Economists. Republican. Episcopalian. Office: Career Devel Svcs Inc Ste 6110 5555 E 71st St Tulsa OK 74136

YOUNG, WILLIAM EDGAR, religious organization official, educator; b. Whitesburg, Ga., July 28, 1930; s. Edgar Woodfin and Maude Alva (Duke) Y.; student Warren Wilson Coll., 1951, 54; AB, Mercer U., 1956; M.R.E., Southwestern Bapt. Theol. Sem., 1958; postgrad. George Peabody Coll. Tchrs., U. Tenn., Nashville, So. Meth. U., U. San Francisco, Lesley Coll.; m. Mary Todd Watts, Mar. 9, 1963; children: William Jefferson, Todd Woodfin. Minister of edn. and music 1st Bapt. Ch., Swainsboro, Ga., 1958-59, Sherman, Tex., 1960-64; tchr. North Cobb High Sch., Marietta, Ga., 1959-60; ch. bus. adminstrn. cons., 1964-65; dir. ch. adminstrn. field svcs. Bapt. Sunday Sch. Bd., Nashville, 1965-70, mgr. presch. children's sect. discipleship tng. dept., 1970-92, childhood edn. and family life cons., 1992—; adj. prof. Sch. Religious Edn., So. Bapt. Theol. Sem., Louisville; adj. prof. childhood edn. Golden Gate Bapt. Theol. Sem., Mill Valley, Calif., 1980, 94, Sch. Religious Edn., Southwestern Bapt. Theol. Sem., Ft. Worth, 1984, 94; guest lectr. creative writing East Tex. State U., Texarkana. Chmn. Dist. II citizens adv. coun. Metro Schs., 1975-76; pres. Stanford PTA, 1974-75, Grassland PTA, 1977-78; lectr. European Bapt. Conv.; So. Bapt. conv. rep. U.S. Dept Health and Human Svcs., Nat. Conf. on Child Abuse and Neglect; pres. Franklin High Community Assn.; parent rep. Williamson County curriculum assessment group Middle Sch. Task Force, 1979; mem. adv. council edn. dept. Belmont Coll.; bd. dirs. Tenn. Parents Anonymous. Served with USAF, Korea, 1951-54. Recipient Disting. Service award Metro Assn. Religious Edn. Dirs., 1980; Founders award Ga. Ch. Secs. Assn., 1981, Disting. Alumni award S.W. Bapt. Theological Seminary, 1993. Mem. So. Bapt. Religious Edn. Assn. (pres. 1977-78, sec.-treas., bd. dirs. 1984-90, treas., bd dirs. 1990-95, Disting. Leadership award 1996), Assn. Supervision and Curriculum Devel., Assn. Childhood Edn. Internat. (pub. affairs com., early adolescent com.), Nat. Assn. Edn. of Young Children, So. Assn. for Children Under Six, Am. Soc. Tng. and Devel., Internat. Network Children's Ministry (bd. dirs. 1994—, Excellence in Ministry to Children award 1994). Author: Moses, God's Helper, 1976; Jesus, Lord and Savior, 1984, How To Plan and Conduct A Conference, 1987, Now That I Am A Christian, 1992, Heroes of Mission, 1993; compiler, writer: Developing Your Children's Church Training Program, 1977; contbg. author: The Ministry of Childhood Education, 1985; contbr. chpts. in books; curriculum writer religious publs. Home: 605 Williamsburg Dr Franklin TN 37064-4191 Office: 605 Williamsburg Dr Franklin TN 37069-4191

YOUNGBLOOD, ELAINE MICHELE, lawyer; b. Schenectady, N.Y., Jan. 9, 1944; d. Roy W. and Mary Louise (Read) Ortoleva; m. William Gerald Youngblood, Feb. 14, 1970; children: Flagg Khristian, Megan Michele. BA, Wake Forest Coll., 1965; JD, Albany Law Sch., 1969. Bar: Tex. 1970, U.S. Dist. Ct. (no. dist.) Tex. 1971, U.S. Dist. Ct. (so. dist.) Tex. 1972, Tenn. 1978, U.S. Dist. Ct. (mid. dist.) Tenn. 1978. Assoc. Fanning & Harper, Dallas, 1969, Crocker & Murphy, Dallas, 1970-71, McClure & Burch, Houston, 1972-75, Brown, Bradshaw & Plummer, Houston, 1975-76; ptnr. Seligmann & Youngblood, Nashville, 1977-88; atty. Law Offices of Elaine M. Youngblood, Nashville, 1988-94; of counsel Ortale, Kelley Herbert & Crawford, 1994—. Mem. Com. for Women in Govt., Dallas, 1969-71, Law Day com. of Dallas Bar Assn., 1970-71. Mem. ABA, Tex. Bar Assn., Tenn. Bar Assn., Nashville Bar Assn. (fee dispute com. 1990—, vice chmn. 1996, chmn. 1997, CLE com. 1996, L.A.W. 1996—, bd. dirs. 1996, blvd. bolt com. 1996, publicity), Tenn. Trial Lawyers Assn., Nat. Assn. Women Lawyers, Phi Beta Pi, Cable Club of Nashville (charter), Davidson County Rep. Women's Club. Republican. Episcopalian. Address: PO Box 198985 200 Fourth Ave N Fl 3 Noel Pl Nashville TN 37219-8985

YOUNGBLOOD, J. CRAIG, lawyer; b. Ft. Worth, July 6, 1947; s. Angus O'Neal and Kathleen (Hill) Y.; m. Linda Gilman, Apr. 17, 1982; children: Jesica Caye, Jaclyn Cristine. Student, Rice U., 1965-66; BA in Polit. Sci. and Math, U. Tex., San Antonio, 1977; JD, U. Tex., Austin, 1980. Bar: Tex. 1982, U.S. Dist. Ct. (so. dist.) Tex. 1982, U.S. Ct. Appeals (D.C., 3rd, 5th and 11th cirs.) 1982, U.S. Ct. Appeals (10th cir.) 1983. Assoc. Vinson & Elkins, Houston, 1981-87, ptnr., 1988—; adv. bd. grad. program in energy and natural resources U. Houston Law Ctr. Mem. Tex. Law Rev.; contbr. chpt. to book; contbr. articles to profl. jours., lectr. in field. Mem. ABA, Tex. Bar Assn., Houston Bar Assn., Fed. Energy Bar Assn., Tex. Law Rev. Assn. Republican. Home: 11 Red Sable Pt The Woodlands TX 77380-2687 Office: Vinson & Elkins 2300 First City Tower 1001 Fannin St Houston TX 77002-6760

YOUNGER, PATRICIA ANN, port authority administrator; b. Houston, Oct. 10, 1947; d. Tony Joseph and Rose Marie (Eppilito) Sirvello; 1 child, Kevin Younger. BA, U. Houston, 1969. Secondary edn. tchr. Aldine Ind. Sch. Dist., Houston, 1969-71, Jenks (Okla.) Ind. Sch. Dist., 1971-74, Spring Br. Ind. Sch., Houston, 1975-79; asst. athletic dir. U. Houston, 1979-86; dir. sports mktg. Mariner Hotel Corp., Houston, 1986-88; legis. affairs mgr. Port of Houston Authority, 1988—; presdl. appointee as vice-chmn. Houston-Galveston Coast Guard Safety Adv. Coun., Houston, 1995—; mem. adv. com. Coalition to Save the Intracoastal Waterway, Houston, 1989; mem. adv. bd. Tex. Ports and Waterways Inst., Houston, 1995. Author manual: Sports Marketing, 1987. First Female Inductee to All Am. Collegiate Hall of Fame, 1995. Mem. Women Profls. in Govt., Gulf Ports Assn. (chmn. legis. com. 1991—), Tex. Ports Assn. (chmn. legis. com. 1991—, v.p., then pres. and first female officer). Office: Port of Houston Authority 111 E Loop N Houston TX 77029

YOUNGMAN, DAVID A., biology educator; b. Dundee, N.Y., Nov. 25, 1960; s. Graydon A. and Molly R. (DeBack) Y.; m. Becky J. Foxworthy, Dec. 31, 1990; 1 child, Kelsey M. BS in Biology, St. John Fisher Coll., 1983; MS in Sci. Edn., Fla. Inst. of Tech., 1985. Sci. tchr. Lake Worth (Fla.) Mid. Sch., 1985-89; rsch. asst. N.Y. State Graphic Program, Penn Yan, N.Y., 1983-84; biology instr. Atlantic H.S., Delray Beach, Fla., 1989—. Mem. AAAS, Nat. Assn. Biology Tchrs., Aircraft Owners and Pilots Assn., Classroom Tchrs. Assn. Republican. Presbyterian. Office: Atlantic High Sch 2501 Seacrest Blvd Delray Beach FL 33444-4348

YOUNGSTRUM, DAVID MANSFIELD, financial executive; b. Racine, Wis., Sept. 2, 1942; s. George Gustav and Marion E. (Lundberg) Y.; m. Dorothy M. Oldham Smedly, May 25, 1985. BS in Stats., Colo. State U., 1964; MS in Bus. Adminstrn., U. No. Colo., 1980. Cert. fin. examiner. Asst. actuary United Am. Life Ins. Co., Denver, 1964-73; asst. treas. United Am. Securities, Denver, 1973; chief actuary Colo. Div. Ins., Denver, 1973-86; chief fin. officer Metlife HealthCare Network of Colo., Golden, 1986-88; sr. actuary Ptn. Nat. Health Plans (merged with Aetna Health Plans) Irving, Tex., Champus div., 1988-90, dir, 1990, HMO Experience Rating and Ins. Svcs., 1990-91; sr. cons. ALEA Assocs., Carrollton, Tex., 1991—. Recipient award Am. Math. Assn., 1964. Fellow Life Mgmt. Inst.; mem. Am. Statis. Assn., Assn. Investment Mgmt. and Rsch., Soc. Fin. Examiners, Mensa, Nat. Eagle Scout Assn. Republican. Presbyterian. Club: Collie of Colo. Office: ALEA Assocs 2102 Antibes Dr Carrollton TX 75006-4326

YOUNT, JAMES ROBERT, physical and biological sciences educator; b. Erie, Pa., Apr. 28, 1960; s. Daniel V. and Janet (Kertis) Hedges. BS in Biology, Gannon U., 1982; MS in Environ. Sci., Fla. Inst. Tech., 1984, PhD in Sci. Edn., 1988. Teaching asst. dept. biology Gannon U., 1980-82; teaching asst. dept. environ. sci. Fla. Inst. Tech., 1982-84, rsch. asst. dept. sci. edn., 1985-87, adj. faculty dept. sci. edn., 1988-89; prof. phys. scis. Brevard C.C., Titusville, Fla., 1987—. Contbr. articles to profl. jours. Mem. Nat. Assn. Rsch. in Sci. Teaching, Fla. Assn. Sci. Tchr., Fla. Acad. Scis. Democrat. Roman Catholic. Home: 1005 Knox Mcrae Dr Apt 104 Titusville FL 32780-6102 Office: Brevard Community Coll 1311 N Us Highway 1 Titusville FL 32796-2157

YOURITZIN, VICTOR KOSHKIN, art educator; b. N.Y.C., Dec. 20, 1942; s. Basil and Tatiana (Koshkin) Y.; m. Glenda Allen Green (div. 1980); m. Cynthia Lee Kerfoot, Jan. 19, 1996. BA in Art History cum laude, Williams Coll., 1964; MA in Art History, Inst. Fine Arts, NYU, 1967; cert. in Mus. Tng., Met. Mus. Art, NYU, 1969. Instr. art history Vanderbilt U., Nashville, 1968-69, Newcomb Coll., Tulane U., New Orleans, 1969-72; asst. prof. art history U. Okla., Norman, 1972-80, assoc. prof., 1980-94, prof., 1994—; lectr. in field; v.p. Koussevitzky Rec. Soc., Inc., Boston, 1992—; panelist program art on film Met. Mus. Art and J. Paul Getty Trust, N.Y.C., 1987, NEH, 1984; trustee Mabee-Gerrer Mus. Art, Shawnee, Okla., 1995—, chmn. bd. trustees, 1996—; mem. coun. advisors Ogden Mus. So. Art, U. New Orleans, 1995—; trustee Okla. Mus. Art, Oklahoma City, 1978-84; mem. acquisitions com. Oklaloma City Art Mus., 1992—; lectr. Met. Mus. Art, Art Students League N.Y., Dallas Mus. Art, also others, including Eng., France, the Caribbean; guest lectr. Cunard Line, 1993. Author: Oklahoma Treasures, 1986, American Watercolors from the Metropolitan Museum of Art, 1991, Five Contemporary Russian Artists, 1992, Twentieth-Century Russian Art, 1994, Paintings, Drawings, and Prints from the Late 19th and Early 20th Centuries, 1996; contbr. articles to profl. jours. Ford Found. fellow Inst. Fine Arts, NYU, 1967-69, IBM and Noble fellow Columbia U., 1964-65; recipient Baldwin award Excellence in Teaching, U. Okla., 1987, Gov.'s Arts and Edn. award, Oklahoma City, 1992, Hon. citation State of Okla. House Reps., 1993. Home: 1721 Oakwood Dr Norman OK 73069-4449 Office: U Okla 520 Parrington Oval Norman OK 73019

YOUSUFF, SARAH SAFIA, physician; b. Binghampton, N.Y., Dec. 8, 1960; d. Mohamed and Razia (Sivaramasastry) Y.; m. Donald John Sudy, Aug. 7, 1993. BA in Zoology, U. Tex., Austin, 1982; MD, U. Tex., 1988. Diplomate Am. Bd. Anesthesiology, Am. Bd. Pain Medicine. Fellow in med. mgmt. U. N.C., Chapel Hill, 1992-93; resident in anesthesiology U. Wash., Seattle, 1988-92; staff anesthesiologist Krōn Med., Research Triangle Park, N.C., 1992-94; med. dir. dept. anesthesiology Southwest Hosp., Little Rock, Ark., 1994-96; pres. Southwest Anesthesia Assocs., Little Rock, 1994-95; ptnr. Pain Cons. Ark., 1995—; dir. Southwest Pain Mgmt. Clinic, Little Rock, 1995—. capt. USAR, 1990—. Mem. AMA, Am. Soc. Anesthesiology, Am. Coll. Physician Execs., Ark. Med. Soc., Pulaski County Med. Soc., Internat. Spinal Injection Soc., Internat. Assn. for Study of Pain, Am. Acad. of Pain Medicine, Am. Soc. of Regional Anesthesia. Home: 18 Edenfield Cv Little Rock AR 72212-2667 Office: Southwest Pain Mgmt Clinic 11401 Interstate 30 Little Rock AR 72209

YOZWIAK, BOBBIE, arts and science center administrator. CEO, Living Arts and Sci. Ctr., Inc., Lexington, Ky. Office: Living Arts and Sci Ctr Inc 362 Martin Luther King Blvd Lexington KY 40508

YU, AITING TOBEY, engineering executive; b. Chekiang, China, Jan. 6, 1921; came to U.S., 1945, naturalized, 1955; s. H.K. and A. (Chow) Y.; m. Natalie Kwok, Nov. 10, 1951; children: Pamela, Leonard T. BS, Nat. Cen. U., Chungking, China, 1943; SM, MIT, 1946; PhD, Lehigh U., 1949; MBA, Columbia U., 1972. Registered profl. engr., Fla. Asst. prof. engring. NYU, 1949-51; design engr. Hewitt-Robins Inc., 1951-54, chief design engr., 1955-58, engring. mgr., 1958-59; dir. systems engring. Hewitt-Robins Inc., Totowa, N.J., 1967-68, v.p. ops., 1968-71; tech. dir. West S.Am. Overseas Corp., N.Y.C., 1959-67; prin. A.T. Yu Cons. Engrs., 1971-72; co-founder, chmn. Orba Corp., Mountain Lakes, N.J., 1972—, now chmn. emeritus. Contbr. articles to profl. jours; patentee in field. Recipient nat. outstanding engring. achievement awards by ASCE, NSPE, AIME, ASME. Mem. NAE, AIME (chmn. minerals processing div., SME pres. 1986), NSPE, Nat. Acad. Forensic Engrs., Nat. Acad. Engring., Sigma Xi. Home: 962 Gullane Dr Cypress Run Tarpon Springs FL 34689 Office: Orba Corp 1250 W Sam Houston Pky S Houston TX 77042-1907

YU, JIUJIANG, research geneticist; b. Liaoning, China, Nov. 7, 1953; came to U.S., 1987; s. Zhuoqing Yu and Chunyong Liu; m. Yaney Yan Gao, Sept. 29, 1984; 1 child, Michael Miao Yu. Grad. in Agronomy, Shenyang (China) Agrl. U., 1978; MS in Plant Breeding, Northwestern U. Agr., Yangling, China, 1982; PhD in Molecular Genetics, Ariz. State U., 1992. Plant breeder Liaoning Acad. Agrl. Scis., Shenyang, 1982-87; vis. scientist SIGCO Rsch. Inc., Breckenridge, Minn., 1987; rsch. assoc. dept. Botany Ariz. State U., Tempe, 1988-90, teaching assoc. dept. Botany, 1990-92; rsch. geneticist USDA, New Orleans, 1992—. Contbr. articles to profl. jours. Office: USDA Agrl Rsch Svc 1100 Robert E Lee Blvd New Orleans LA 70124-4305

YU, ROBERT KUAN-JEN, biochemistry educator; b. Chungking, China, Jan. 27, 1938; came to U.S., 1962; s. Shin-cheng and June Chien-yu (Tsao) Y.; m. Helen Chow, July 1, 1972; children: David S., Jennifer S. BS, Tunghai U., Taiwan, 1960; PhD, U. Ill., 1967; Med.ScD. (hon.), Tokyo, 1980; MA (hon.), Yale U., 1985. Rsch. assoc., instr. Albert Einstein Coll. Medicine, Bronx, 1967-72; asst. prof. Yale U., New Haven, 1973-75, assoc. prof., 1975-82, prof., 1983-88; prof. biochemistry, chmn. dept. Va. Commonwealth U., Richmond, 1988—; mem. study sect. NIH, Washington, 1980-84; mem. Bd. Lab. Svcs., Va., 1994—. Editor: Gangioside Structure Function and Biomedical Potential, 1984, New Trends in Ganglioside Research, 1988; contbr. over 500 articles to profl. publs. Josiah Macy scholar, 1979; grantee NIH, 1975—; recipient Va. Outstanding Scientist of Yr. award, 1995, Jacob Javits award NIH, 1984-91, Alexander von Humboldt award, 1990. Mem. AAAS, Am. Soc. Cell Biology, Am. Soc. Neurochemistry (mem. coun. 1983-86, 91—), Internat. Soc. Neurochemistry, Soc. Neurosci., Am. Soc. Biochemistry and Molecular Biology, Am. Chem. Soc., N.Y. Acad. Sci. Home: 306 Cheswick Ln Richmond VA 23229-7660 Office: Va Commonwealth Univ Medical College Virginia Richmond VA 23298-0614

YUDOF, MARK G., law educator, academic administrator; b. Phila., Oct. 30, 1944; s. Jack and Eleanor (Parris) Y.; m. Judith Lynn Gomel, July 11, 1965; children: Seth Adam, Samara Lisa. BA, U. Pa., 1965, LLB, 1968. Bar: Pa. 1970, U.S. Supreme Ct. 1974, U.S. Dist. Ct. (we. dist.) Tex. 1975, U.S. Ct. Appeals (5th cir.) 1976, Tex. 1980. Law clk. to judge U.S. Ct. Appeals (5th cir.), 1968-69; assoc. gen. counsel to ABA study FTC, 1969; research assoc. Harvard Ctr. Law and Edn., 1969-70, sr. staff atty., 1970-71; lectr. Harvard Grad. Sch. Edn., 1970-71; asst. prof. law U. Tex., Austin, 1971-74, prof., 1974—, assoc. dean, 1979-84, James A. Elkins Cent. Chair in Law, 1983—, dean, 1984-94, exec. v.p., provost, 1994—, John Jeffers Rsch. Chair in Law, 1991-94; of counsel Pennzoil vs. Texaco, 1987; mem. adv. bd. Inst. for Transnat. Arbitration, 1988—, Am. Jour. Edn., 1991—; chmn. bd. contbrs. to Tex. Lawyer, 1988—; mem. nat. bd. contbrs. Am. Lawyer Newspapers Group, Inc., 1988—; mem. telecomm. infrastructure fund bd. State of Tex. Author: When Government Speaks, 1983 (Scribes Book award 1983, cert. merit ABA 1983), (with others) Educational Policy and the Law, 1992, (with others) Gender Justice, 1986. Mem. Tex. Gov.'s Task Force on Sch. Fin., 1989-90, Tex. Gov.'s Select Com. on Edn., 1988; bd. dirs. Freedom to Read Found., 1989-91; mem. adv. bd. Austin Diagnostic Clinic Cmty., 1989-95; mem. Austin Cable Commn., 1981-84, chmn., 1982; mem. nat. panel on sch. desegregation rsch. Ford Found., 1977-80; mem. state exec. com. Univ. Interscholastic League, 1983-86; mem. rsch. adv. com. Ctr. for Policy Rsch. in Edn., 1985—; bd. dirs. Jewish Children's Regional Svc., 1980-86, Austin Diagnostic Med. Ctr., 1995—; mem. Gov.'s Select Task Force on Pub. Edn., 1995—; mem. Telecomms. Infrastructure Fund Bd., State of Tex., 1995—. Recipient Teaching Excellence award, 1975, Most Meritorious Book award Scribes, 1983, Humanitarian award Austin region NCCJ, 1988, Antidefamation League Jurisprudence award, 1991; fellow Queen Mary and Westfield Coll., U. London. Fellow Tex. Bar Found., Am. Bar Found.; mem. ABA (legal edn. and admissions to bar sect. 1984—), Am. Law Inst., Tex. Bar Assn., Assn. Am. Law Schs. (chmn. law and edn. sect. 1983-84, mem. exec. com. 1988-90), Univ. Club, Headliners Club, Met. Club. Office: U Tex Exec Vice Pres/Provost MAI 201 Austin TX 78712

YUEN, BENSON BOLDEN, airline management consultant, software executive; b. Hong Kong, Nov. 20, 1960; came to U.S., 1968; s. Eugene Howard and Janet (Chan) Y. BSBA in Fin. summa cum laude, U. Cen. Fla., 1983. Mgr. market planning and automation Fla. Express, Inc., Orlando, 1983-85, dir. pricing, 1986-87; dir. customer svc. Seabrook Mktg., Inc., Houston, 1988-91, v.p. customer svc., 1992-94; v.p. consulting svcs. PROS Strategic Solutions, Inc., Houston, 1994-96, sr. v.p. mktg. and consulting svcs., 1996—; cons. airline revenue mgmt., mktg. automation, bus. mgmt., sys. devel. and bus. process engrng. to more than 50 airlines and industry-related firms world wide. Designer (software) Passenger Revenue Forecast and Optimization System, 1989, Group Revenue Optimization and Management System Version 3, 1990-94, Version 4, 1995—. Office: PROS Strategic Solutions 3223 Smith St Ste 100 Houston TX 77006

YUKISH, JOSEPH FRANCIS, education educator; b. Martin, Pa., Sept. 13, 1944; s. Joseph F. Sr. and Elizabeth M. (Vrabel) Y.; m. Frances H. Kovacic, June 6, 1970 (div. Dec. 1995); children: Matthew J., Nicholas R. BS in Elem. Edn., California (Pa.) State U., 1965, MEd in Spl. Edn., 1972; PhD in Elem. Edn./Reading, U. Akron, 1978. Cert. tchr. elem. edn./spl. edn., Pa.; cert. reading specialist, reading revovery tchr. leader, Ohio; cert. reading recovery leader trainer, S.C. Tchr. reading and English Washington (Pa.) Sch. Dist., 1965-66; tchr. spl. edn. Brownsville (Pa.) Area Sch. Dist., 1966-67; teaching prin. Ctrl. Elem. Sch., Uniontown, Pa., 1967-71, Intermediate Unit 1, Uniontown, 1971-73; assoc. prof. spl. edn. Duquesne U., Pitts., 1979-80; prof. reading recovery tchr. leader Ashland (Ohio) U., 1973-89, Clemson (S.C.) U., 1989—; profl. storyteller Nat. Storytelling Assn., Jonesboro, Tenn., 1984—; guided reading cons. The Wright Group, Bothell, Wash., 1994—. Author: (textbook) Curriculum and Methods for the Mildly Handicapped, 1982; (children's books) Fishing, My Doll, 1991, 92, I Can't Wait to Read, 1994, The Big Bad Cook, 1996, Matt Gets the Big Fish, 1996, White and Shiny Sneakers, 1997, Nick Goes Fishing, 1997. Recipient Pioneer award for excellence in tng. Southeastern Reading Recovery Coun., 1994. Mem. AAUP, ASCD, Reading Recovery Coun. N.Am. (com. chair 1993—), Internat. Reading Assn., Nat. Coun. Tchrs. English, Nat. Storytelling Assn. Home: 419 Brown Bottom Rd Anderson SC 29630 Office: Clemson U 409-C Tillman Hall Clemson SC 29634

YURKIN, JOSEPH, health consultant, small business owner; b. Jersey City, July 18, 1960; s. Joseph and June (De Mea) Y.; m. Laura Elena Antunez, Dec. 14, 1990; children: Blas, Fernando, Clementine. Fitness dir. YMCA, Boca Raton, Fla., 1980; instr.. Broward C.C., Coconut Creek, Fla., 1982-83, health cons., 1983—; fitness cons., owner Quantum Health & Fitness, Deerfield Beach, Fla., 1983—. Author: (audio book) The Disciple of Life, 1995.

ZAAS, BRIAN MARC, telecommunications and program management executive; b. Washington, Oct. 27, 1966; s. Michael Jay and Sharon Ann (Love) Z.; m. Debra Ann Wiegand, Dec. 31, 1989; children: Jenna Leigh Irma, Kayla Rose Dona. AA, Anne Arundel C.C., Arnold, Md., 1987; BA in Polit. Sci., U. Md., Balt., 1988; MA in Administrv.-Mgmt., U. Md.-Bowie State U., 1993. Cert. project mgmt. profl. Sr. legis. analyst Md. Gen. Assembly, Annapolis, 1986-88; computer analyst Md. Nat. Capital Park and Planning Commn., Riverdale, Md., 1988-89; mgr. software devel. Best Programs, Inc., Reston, Va., 1989-94; mgr. program mgmt. and planning MCI Telecomms. Inc., Arlington, Va., 1994-96; dir. profl. svcs. wireless bus. cons. and program mgmt. Bellcore, 1996—. Legis. liaison Disabled Am. Vets., 1986-88; active Glenn Dale Civic Assn., 1992-94. Mem. ASPA, Am. Mgmt. Assn., Project Mgmt. Inst. (D.C. chpt.). Democrat. Home: 5803 Sir Galahad Rd Glenn Dale MD 20769-8924 Office: MCI Telecomms Inc 601 12th St S Ste 714N Arlington VA 22202-4205

ZABEL, PATRICIA LYNN, librarian; b. Dallas, Feb. 7, 1960; d. William Albert and Dorothy Fay (Holleman) Z. BA in Biology, Austin Coll., 1982; MLS, U. North Tex., 1985. Reference libr. Libr. at INFOMART, Dallas, 1987-88; asst. dir. Ft. Smith (Ark.) Pub. Libr., 1988—. Pres. Ft. Smith Literacy Coun., 1993-94, 96-97; mem. Leadership Ft. Smith Class of 1995 and alumni assn., 1995—, Jr. League Ft. Smith, 1993—, LWV Ft. Smith, 1994—. Mem. ALA, Ark. Libr. Assn., Bus. and Profl. Women (treas. Ft. Smith chpt. 1991—, pres.-elect 1996-97, Woman of Yr. 1994), Altrusa Internat. (sec., treas. Ft. Smith chpt. 1990—). Office: Ft Smith Pub Libr 61 S 8th St Fort Smith AR 72901

ZABEL, VIVIAN ELLOUISE, secondary education educator; b. Randolph AFB, Tex., July 28, 1943; d. Raymond Louis and Dolly Veneta (Lyles) Gilbert; m. Robert Lee Zabel, Feb. 18, 1962; children: René Lynne, Robert Lee Jr., Randel Louis, Regina Louise. BA in English and Speech, Panhandle State U., 1977; postgrad., U. Ctrl. Okla., 1987-92. Cert. tchr., Okla. Tchr. English, drama, speech, debate Buffalo (Okla.) H.S., 1977-79; tchr. English, drama, speech Schulter (Okla.) H.S., 1979-80; tchr. English Morris (Okla.) H.S., 1980-81; tchr. speech, drama, debate Okla. Christian Schs., Edmond, 1981-82; tchr. English, drama, debate, speech/debate coach Braman (Okla.) H.S., 1982-83; debate coach Pawhuska (Okla.) H.S., 1983-84; tchr. English, French, drama, speech and debate coach Luther (Okla.) H.S., 1984-95; tchr. debate, forensics, yearbook, newspaper, English, competitive speech Deer Creek H.S., Edmond, Okla., 1995—; dir. drama Nazarene Youth Impace Team, Collinsville, Okla., 1979-81; tchr. h.s. Sun. sch. class Edmond Ch. of Nazarene, 1991-94; mem. cmty.-sch. rels. com. Luther Pub. Schs., 1991-92, supt.'s adv. com., 1992-94. Editor Potpourri mag., 1975-77; author poetry, short stories. Adult supr. Texas County 4-H, Adams, Okla., 1975-77; double diamond coach NFL; adjudicator and tournament dir. qualifying OSSAA Tournaments. Recipient Disting. Svc. award NFL, 1994. Mem. Nat. Debate Coaches Assn., Nat. Fedn. Interscholastic Speech and Debate Assn., Okla. Speech Theatre Communications Assn., Okla. Coun. Tchrs. Engl. Republican. Nazarene. Home: 2912 Rankin Ter Edmond OK 73013-5344 Office: Deer Creek HS Rte 1 Box 139 Edmond OK 73003

ZABLE, MARIAN MAGDELEN, physician assistant, consultant; b. Beaver Dam, Wis., Oct. 13, 1933; d. John Joseph and Agatha Mary (Eschlie) Fernbach; m. Jerome Edward Zable, July 30, 1960 (div. 1970); children: Terrence, Andrea, Michael. BS, U. Wis., 1964; Physician Asst., U. Fla., 1975. Tchr. Brown Deer (Wis.) Sch. System, 1964, Orange County (Fla.) Schs., 1965-70; curriculum devel., adminstr. So. Coll., Orlando, Fla., 1970-72; physician asst., asst. dir. Longevity Ctr., Orlando, 1977; physician asst. Pritikin Longevity Ctr., Miami, Fla., 1978-83, Cardiovascular Assocs., Kissimmee, Fla., 1984-92; pres., physician asst., cons. Physician's Svcs., Inc., Orlando, 1986—. Mem. Am. Acad. Physician Assts., Fla. Acad. Physician Assts. Home: 3407 Trentwood Blvd Orlando FL 32812-4850 Office: Tai Poinciana Clinic 2 Doverplum Ave Poinciana FL 34759-3409

ZABOSKI, MICHAEL EDWARD, operations research analyst; b. Lower Burrell, Pa., June 23, 1964; s. Edward Anthony and Constance Genevieve (Adamski) Z. BS in Elec. Engring., Pa. State U., 1986; postgrad., U. Va., Falls Church, 1993. Cert. contracting and procurement mgmt. Tech. writer Technosystems Inc., Pitts., 1987; computer analyst U. Pitts., 1988-89; ops. rsch. analyst Dept. of Navy, Crystal City, Va., 1989—. Mem. Soc. Cost Estimating and Analysis, Internat. Soc. Parametric Analysts, Pa. State Engring. Soc. (treas. 1982-83). Republican. Roman Catholic. Home: 7378 Lee Hwy Apt 201 Falls Church VA 22046-4768

ZACHARIAS, DONALD WAYNE, academic administrator; b. Salem, Ind., Sept. 28, 1935; s. William Otto and Estelle Mae (Newlon) Z.; m. Tommie Kline Dekle, Aug. 16, 1959; children: Alan, Eric, Leslie. BA, Georgetown (Ky.) Coll., 1957, LLD (hon.), 1983; MA, Ind. U., 1959, PhD, 1963. Asst. prof. communication and theatre Ind. U., 1963-69; assoc. prof. U. Tex., Austin, 1969-72; prof. U. Tex., 1972-79, asst. to pres., 1974-77; exec. asst. to chancellor U. Tex. System, 1978-79; pres. Western Ky. U., 1979-85, Miss. State U., 1985—; bd. dirs. First Fed. Savs. & Loan Assn., Bowling Green, Ky., Inst. for Tech. Devel., Sanderson Farms, Inc., Miss. econ. Coun. Author: In Pursuit of Peace: Speeches of the Sixties, 1970. Bd. dirs. Greenview Hosp.; pres. Southeastern Conf., 1989-91. With U.S. Army, 1959-60. Named Mississippian of Yr. Data Processing Mgmt. Assn.; recipient Teaching award Ind. U. Found., 1963, Cactus Teaching award U. Tex., 1971, Justin Smith Morrill award U.S. Dept. Agriculture, 1992. Mem. Inst. Tech. Devel. (bd. dirs. 1985-92), Nat. Assn. State Univs. and Land-Grant Colls. (exec. com. 1990-92), Phi Kappa Phi (pres. 1978). Democrat. Episcopalian. Office: Miss State U Office of Pres PO Box J Mississippi State MS 39762

ZACHARIAS, WILLIAM F., retired law educator; b. London, June 28, 1905; s. Christian and Lily (Pollard) Z.; m. Lenore Tortorich, Feb. 29, 1928; 1 child, Diane Manzelmann. Ph.B., U. Chgo., 1931; LLB, Chgo.-Kent Coll. Law, 1933, LLM, 1934, JSD, 1949. Bar: Ill. 1933, U.S. Supreme Ct. 1960. Instr. Chgo.-Kent Coll. Law, 1933-34, asst. prof., 1934-35, prof., 1935-70, dean, 1959-70, dean and prof. emeritus, 1970—. Chmn. editorial bd. Chgo.-Kent Law Rev., 1942-55. Mem. ABA, Ill. State Bar Assn., Chgo. Bar Assn., Am. Judicature Soc., Phi Delta Phi. Home: 2674 Winkler Ave Apt 409 Fort Myers FL 33901-9318

ZACHEM, HARRY M., oil company executive; b. Ironton, Ohio, Aug. 14, 1944; s. Charles Russell and Millie (Norris) Z.; m. Mary M. Hamilton, 1987; children: Nancy Kathryn, Mary Elizabeth. BA, U. Ky., 1968; A.M.P., Harvard U., 1985. Supr. Ky. State Govt., Frankfort, 1968-71; sales rep. Ashland Oil Inc., Balt., 1972-74; pub. relations rep. Ashland Oil Inc., Ashland, Ky., 1974-75; Washington rep. Ashland Oil Inc., 1975-81, v.p. fed. govt. relations, 1981-86; adminstrv. v.p. Ashland Oil Inc., Ashland, 1986-88; sr. v.p. external affairs Ashland, Inc., 1988—. bd. dirs. Danny Thompson Leukemia Found., Sun Valley, Idahom, 1996—; mem. global adv. coun. Thunderbirds-Am. Grad. Sch. Internat. Mgmt., Phoenix, 1996—. Mem. Nat. Assn. Mfrs. (bd. dirs. 1992—). Episcopalian. Office: Ashland Inc PO Box 391 Ashland KY 41105-0391

ZACHRY, AMY POARCH, environmental scientist; b. Birmingham, Ala., Sept. 18, 1967; d. John Carl and Margaret Nancy (Goode) Poarch; m. Jimmy Dell Zachry, June 25, 1994. BS, Livingston U., 1990. From pollution control specialist to environ. scientist II Ala. Dept. Environ. Mgmt., Montgomery, 1989—. Choir leader, children's leader First Baptist Ch., Montgomery, 1993—; weekly vol. Ala. Pub. TV, Montgomery, 1992—. Mem. Solid Waste Assn. N.Am., Capitol City Jaycees (mem.-at-large 1995, bd. dirs., mem. exec. bd.). Office: Ala Dept Environ Mgmt 1751 Dickinson Dr Montgomery AL 36130

ZADECK, DONALD JULIAN, oil and gas exploration company executive; b. St. Louis, Sept. 12, 1927; s. Sam Edward and Dorothy (Glatstein) Z.; m. Frances Katzenstein, Nov. 22, 1951; children: Donald J. Jr., Frank Kenneth, Julie. LLB, La. State U., 1950. Pres. Julie Ann Textiles, Shreveport, La., 1970-78, Zadeck Energy Group, Inc., Shreveport, 1978—. Pres. La. State U. Found., Baton Rouge, 1981; chmn. bd. dirs. Premier Med. Mgmt., Inc.; mem. La. Bd. Regents, Baton Rouge, 1981-86; chmn. Shreveport Mcpl. Fire and Police Civil Svc. Commn., 1988—; dir. La. divsn. Am. Heart Assn., 1990, Coun. Alcoholism and Drug Abuse Northwestern La., 1991—; pres. Com. 100, 1980-81; pres. B'nai Zion Congregation, 1970-72. Recipient Mr. Shreveport award, 1981. Mem. Shreveport C. of C. (pres. 1977, Bus. Leader of Yr. 1980), La. Assn. Bus. and Industry (chmn. 1978-79), Shreveport Country Club, So. Trace Country Club, Shreveport Club. Republican. Jewish. Home: 1 Walton Pl Shreveport LA 71106-1713 Office: Zadeck Energy Group Inc 504 Texas St Ste 300 Shreveport LA 71101-3526

ZAEPFEL, GLENN PETER, psychologist; b. N.Y.C., Feb. 15, 1951; s. Walter Henry and Lillian Adair (Kovach) Z.; m. Linda Carrie Grinton, June 1, 1974; children: Peter, Caroline, Christine. BA, U. S.C., 1973; MEd, Ga. State U., 1980, PhD, 1986. Milieu therapist Peachtree-Parkwood Hosp., Atlanta, 1978-80; dir. Roswell St. Counseling Ctr., Marietta, Ga., 1980-84; dir. counseling and psychol. svcs. DeKalb Pain Control and Rehab. Ctr., Decatur, Ga., 1981-85; pvt. practice psychology, Columbia, S.C., 1985—; Author: He Wins, She Wins, 1994; founder, program dir. Bapt. Med. Ctr. Pain Mgmt. Program, Columbia, 1985-87; founder, pres. Columbia Counseling Ctr., P.A., 1986—; dir. behav. health Carolina Primary Care, L.L.C., adv. bd. mem. Mem. Am. Psychol. Assn., Christian Assn. for Psychol. Studies, Am. Rehab. Counseling Assn., Am. Assn. Counseling and Devel., Am. Bd. Med. Psychotherapists. Republican. Presbyterian. Club: Sinfonia Fraternity (Columbia). Avocations: sports, music. Home: 1153 Scotts Hill Rd Chapin SC 29036-8974 Office: 900 Saint Andrews Rd Columbia SC 29210-5816 also: 601 Polo Rd Columbia SC 29223-2905 also: 122 Powell Dr Lexington SC 29072-9203

ZAGER, STEVEN MARK, lawyer; b. Memphis, Nov. 16, 1958; s. Jack and Sylvia (Bloomfield) Z. BA, Vanerbilt U., 1979, JD, 1983. Bar: Tex. 1983, U.S. Dist. Ct. (all dists.) Tex. 1983, U.S. Dist. Ct. Ariz. 1992, U.S. Ct. Appeals (5th, 6th, and 11th cirs.) 1983, D.C. 1991, U.S. Supreme Ct. 1991. Assoc. Fulbright & Jaworski, Houston, 1983-86; assoc. Weil, Gotshal & Manges, Houston, 1986-90, ptnr., 1990—, head Houston office litigation sect., 1994-96; adj. prof. U. Houston Sch. Law, 1990-95. Contbr. articles to Tex. Bar Jour., Houston Lawyer. Bd. dirs., mem. exec. com. Alley Theatre, Houston, 1988—, Tex. Accts. and Lawyers for the Arts, Houston, 1984-88. Named Oustanding Young Man in Am., U.S. Jaycees, 1983, Outstanding Young Lawyer in Houston, Houston Bar Assn., 1991; recipient Frank J. Scurlock award for State Bar Tex., 1991, Outstanding Pro Bono Svc. Mem. ATLA, ABA (litigation sect.), Tex. Bar Assn., Houston Bar Assn. (sec. 1996—, bd. dirs. 1993-96, chair law and arts com. 1994, chair adminstrn. of justice com. 1995), Fed. Bar Assn., Masons. Office: Weil Gotshal & Manges 1600 NationsBank Ctr Houston TX 77002

ZAGNOLI, ROLAND CANDIANO, management and marketing consultant, pharmacist; b. Highland Park, Ill., Nov. 6, 1931; s. Valerio Walter and Maria Adalgisa (Solignani) Z.; m. Virginia Louise Rizzo, Oct. 7, 1961; children: Roland Christopher, Lisa Louise, Regina Marie, Laurette Rene, Annia Lynn. BS in Pharmacy, U. Mich., 1955; LLB, LaSalle Extension U., 1963; MBA, Harvard U., 1957. RPh, Fla.; registered consulting pharmacist, Fla. Tech. & adminstrv. rotation trainee Abbott Labs., Inc., North Chgo., 1957-59, corp. product mgr., 1959-63; dir. product mgmt. & new mktg. devel. Ross pediatric div. Abbott Labs., Inc., Columbus, Ohio, 1963-65; dir. product mgmt. internat. div. Abbott Labs., Inc., North Chgo., 1965-67; dir. mktg. & sales diagnostics div. Abbott Labs., Inc., North Chgo. & Los Angeles, 1967-70; dual mgr. Amp-Vial project & mfg. hosp. div. Abbott Labs., Inc., North Chgo. & Rocky Mountain, N.C., 1970-73; pres., gen. mgr. Health Care Industries, Inc., Michigan City, Ind., 1973-76, pres., chmn. bd., chief exec. officer, 1976-81; pres., chief exec. officer M/PIC Cons., Deltona, Fla., 1982—, Med. Inventors Corp., Orlando, Fla., 1988—; charter mem. Pharmacy Advancement Com. U. Mich., 1976-91; mem. Cen. Fla. Inventors Coun., Orlando, 1984-89; charter mem., bd. advisors Southtech Growth Fund, Ltd., Orlando, 1988-89; advisor Internat. Med. Techs., Winter Springs, Fla., 1989-92. Inventor Dye Pharm. Chem. (tablets dye-coating stability), 1958; patentee, 1959. Charter mem. Cen. Fla. Coun. High Tech., Orlando, 1984-94; gen. chmn. Notre Dame Parish Festival, Michigan City, 1977-79; pres. Evans Scholars Alumni, 1961-62; mem., cons. Mktg. & Mgmt. Ctrl. Fla. Innovation, Corp. 1995—; fund raiser various orgns. Evans Scholar of Yr. Western Golf Assn., 1954; won 8 golf tournament weekend championships at 7 sites in 4 states; William Douglas McAdams fellow, 1955-57. Mem. Am. Pharm. Assn., Ctrl. Fla. Soc. Hosp. Pharmacists, Fla. Soc. Hosp. Pharmacists, Cen. Fla. Pharmacy Assn. (v.p. 1990-91), Fla. Pharmacy Assn., Assn. Univ. Tech. Mgrs., Walnut Hill Country Club (Columbus), Pottawattamie Country Club (Michigan City), Kiwanis, Rotary, Phi Eta Sigma, Rho Chi. Home and Office: 1936 Saxon Blvd Deltona FL 32725

ZAGORIA, RONALD JAY, radiologist, educator; b. Washington, May 10, 1957; s. Samuel David and Sylvia Beatrice (Bomse) Z.; m. Laura Kathryn Futrelle, May 21, 1983; children: David Carleton, Michael Jay. BA, Johns Hopkins U., 1979; MD, U. Md., 1983. Diplomate Am. Bd. Diagnostic Radiology and subsplty. cert. in vascular and interventional radiology. Resident in diagnostic radiology Bowman Gray Sch. Medicine, Wake Forest U., Winston-Salem, N.C., 1983-87, fellow in abdominal imaging and endourology, 1986-87, instr. dept. radiology, 1987-88, asst. prof. radiology, 1988-92, assoc. prof. radiology, 1992—; vis. prof. Ohio State U. Sch. Medicine, Columbus, 1992; examiner genitourinary radiology tract Am. Bd. Radiology, 1993, 94, 95; spkr., presenter, lectr. in field. Co-author: Radiology of the Small Bowel, 1992; assoc. editor Am. Jour. Roentgenology; reviewer Jour. Lithotripsy and Stone Disease, 1989—, Am. Jour Roentgenology, 1990; mem. editl. bd. Abstracts in Radiology, 1991—; contbr. articles to profl. publs., chpts. to books. Mem. Commn. on Alcohol Abuse and Chem. Dependency, Home Morovian Ch., Winston-Salem, 1993—. Fellow U. Md. Hosp., 1980, NIMH, 1981; grantee Merck, Sharp and Dohme Rsch. Lab., 1990-91, Mallinckrodt Med., Inc., 1992, N.C. Bapt. Hosp. Clin. Innovations in Medicine. Mem. AMA, Am. Coll. Radiology (del. 1986-87), Radiol. Soc. N.Am. (refresher course com. 1994), N.C. State Med. Assn., Forsyth County Med. Assn., Am. Roentgen Ray Soc., Assn. Univ. Radiologists (rules com. 1993, AMA alt. del. 1993), Soc. Uroradiology, Assn. Program Dirs. in Radiology (program com. 1993). Republican. Office: Bowman Gray Med Ctr Medical Center Blvd Winston Salem NC 27157

ZAGORIA, SAM D(AVID), arbitrator, author, educator; b. Somerville, N.J., Apr. 9, 1919; s. Nathan and Rebecca (Shapiro) Z.; m. Sylvia Bomse, Dec. 21, 1941; children: Paul, Marjorie Zagoria Isacks, Ronald. BL in Journalism, Rutgers U., 1941. With New Brunswick (N.J.) Daily Home News, 1940-41, N.J. Def. Coun., Trenton, 1941-42; Fed. Office Govt. Reports, Newark, 1942; reporter Washington Post, 1946-55; adminstrv. asst. to Senator Clifford P. Case, Washington, 1955-65; mem. NLRB, Washington, 1965-69; dir. Labor-Mgmt. Rels. Svc. U.S. Conf. of Mayors, Washington, 1970-78; mem. U.S. Consumer Product Safety Commn., 1978-84; ombudsman Washington Post, 1984-86; arbitrator, writer, 1986—; Fulbright lectr., Copenhagen, 1987; vis. prof. Fla. Atlantic U., Boca Raton, 1988-91; adj. prof. Wake Forest U., Winston-Salem, N.C., 1993—. Author: Public Workers, Public Unions, 1972, The Ombudsman: How Good Governments Handle Citizens' Grievances, 1988. Campaign mgr. reelection Senator Case, 1960; campaign mgr. race for gov., former Sec. of Labor James P. Mitchell, 1961. With USAAF, 1942-45. Nieman fellow Harvard, 1954. Mem. Common Cause, Nat. Consumers League, Rutgers U. Alumni Assn. Jewish. Home and Office: 2864 Wynfield Crossing Ln Winston Salem NC 27103-6597 also: 3101 S Ocean Blvd Apt 622 Highland Beach FL 33487

ZAGURSKY, GEORGE PALMER, nuclear engineer; b. N.Y.C., Dec. 14, 1943; s. George and Kathryn (Hreneczko) Z.; m. Jacquelyn Susan Hayden, Aug. 29, 1969; 1 child, Adam Hayden. BS in Nuclear Engring., Miss. State U., 1968; MBA, U. Miami, Coral Gables, Fla., 1975; Doctorate, Nova U., Ft. Lauderdale, Fla., 1982. Test engr. Fla. Power & Light, Turkey Point, 1968-71, hot functional coord., 1971-73, tech. support plant supr., 1973-75; group supr. gen. office Fla. Power & Light, 1975-82; asst. to v.p. Inst. Nuclear Power, Atlanta, 1982-85, tech. support sect. head, design engring. evaluator, 1985-87; nuclear cons. UESC and Quadrex, Atlanta, 1987—; prof., lectr. Oglethorpe U., Atlanta, 1982—, St. Leo (Fla.) Coll., 1982—, Roger Williams Coll., R.I., 1986-88. Contbr. articles on configuration mgmt. to profl. jours. Mem. AAUP, Am. Nuclear Soc. Home: 2718 Chimney Springs Dr Marietta GA 30062-6322

ZAHN, DONALD JACK, lawyer; b. Albany, N.Y., Oct. 24, 1941; s. Jerome and Clara (Zinsher) Z.; m. Laurie R. Hyman, Aug. 19, 1966; children: Lawrence, Melissa. AB, NYU, 1963; LLB, Union U., 1966; LLM in Taxation, NYU, 1967. Bar: N.Y. 1966, U.S. Dist. Ct. (no. dist.) N.Y. 1966, U.S. Tax Ct. 1969, U.S. Ct. Appeals (2d cir.) 1970, Tex. 1972, U.S. Ct. Appeals (5th and 11th cirs.). Assoc., Bond, Schoeneck and King, Syracuse, N.Y., 1967-71; ptnr. Haynes and Boone, Dallas, 1971-82, Akin, Gump, Strauss, Hauer & Feld, Dallas, 1982-92; assoc. prof. internat. taxation, fed. income taxation, bus. assns., corp. taxation Tex. Wesleyan Sch. Law , Irving, Tex., 1992—; adj. lectr. Baylor U. Sch. of Law Fed. Income Taxation, 1995; vis. prof. U. San Diego Sch. of Law Grad. Taxation Program, 1996; adj. prof. Sch. Law, So. Meth. U., Dallas, 1972-87, 90-91. Trustee, sec. mem. exec. and fin. com., nominating com. Greenhill Sch., Addison, Tex., 1980-90; trustee, chmn. budget com., mem. fin. com. Jewish Fedn. Greater Dallas, 1978-89; trustee, chmn. Found. Jewish Fedn., Dallas, 1980-89; trustee, v.p., pres. Dallas chpt. Am. Jewish Com., 1980-92; mem. Tex. World Trade Council, 1986-87, Dallas Mayor's Internat. Com. Mem. State Bar Tex. (sec. 1982-83, chmn. tax sect. 1984-85, newsletter taxation sect. editor 1980-81), Internat. Bar Assn., Internat. Comte (N. Tex. commn.), Southwestern Legal Found. (adv. bd., treas. Internat. and Comparative Law Ctr., lectr. Acad. in Internat. Law), N.Y. State Bar Assn. Jewish. Office: Tex Wesleyan U Sch of Law 2535 E Grauwyler Rd Irving TX 75061-3410

ZAHN, LOUIS JENNINGS, foreign language educator, administrator; b. Atlanta, Nov. 24, 1922; s. William Jennings and Rosina Marie (Hunerkopf) Z. AB, Emory U., 1947, MA, 1949; PhD, U. N.C., 1957. Instr. Armstrong Coll., Savannah, Ga., 1948-49, Emory U., Atlanta, 1950-57; asst. prof. Ga. Inst. Tech., Atlanta, 1957-60, assoc. prof., 1960-64, prof., 1964—, head dept. modern langs., 1976-85, acad. adminstr. intensive courses English for fgn. students, 1958-85, dir. Lang. Inst., 1985-87, prof., dir. emeritus modern langs., 1988—; cons. 1987— . Author: Vocabulario etimologico documentado del Libro de los exenplos por abc de Sanchez de Vercial, 1961; History of St. John's Lutheran Church, 1869-1969, 1969, Addendum, 1969-1996, 1996; Teoria y ejercicios sobre la fonologia y la morfologia de la lengua espanola, 1974; Juan Ruiz, Libro de buen amor, Part I, Stanzas 1-387, 1975, Part II, Stanzas 388-891 (student edits.), 1976. Vice-pres. Circulo Hispanoamericano, Atlanta, 1958-60. Fellow, Emory U. 1947, U. N.C., 1949. Mem. Tchrs. English to Speakers of Other Langs., Nat. Assn. Fgn. Student Affairs, Am. Council Teaching Fgn. Langs., Nat. Assn. Tchrs. Spanish and Portuguese (pres. Ga. chpt. 1958-62), Modern Lang. Assn. Am. (state coordinator Spanish 1958-64), S. Atlantic Modern Lang. Assn., Phi Sigma Iota.

Lutheran. Avocations: antiques, photography, travel. Home: 3131 Queens Walk NE Atlanta GA 30345-2165 Office: Ga Inst Tech Lang Inst Atlanta GA 30332

ZAHN, MARTIN DAVID, biology educator; b. Cleve., May 5, 1946; s. Glenn Martin and Adeline Marie (Scheutzow) Z.; m. Jill Marsha Miller, June 8, 1968; children: David Martin, Megan Noel. BA, Cornell Coll., Mt. Vernon, Iowa, 1968; MPhil, Yale U., 1970; MA, U. Colo., 1979. Commd. 2d lt. USAF, 1969, advanced through grades to lt. col., ret., 1993; assoc. prof. biology USAF Acad., Colorado Springs, Colo., 1975-79; asst. prof. biology Thomas Nelson C.C., Hampton, Va., 1993—. Scout master Boy Scouts Am., Eagle River, Alaska, 1986-87; vol. mental health therapist Pikes Peak Mental Health, Colorado Springs, 1977-79, Parents United and Ctr. for Children & Parents, Anchorage, 1980-81. NSF grad. fellow, 1968-69; Sloan Found. grantee, 1967, Profl. Devel. grantee Va. Cmty. Coll. Sys., 1995-96. Mem. Va. Acad. of Sci., Va. Assn. for Biol. Edn., Yale Sci. and Engring. Assn., Am. Mus. Natural History, Smithsonian Instn., Nature Conservancy (assoc.), Phi Beta Kappa. Office: Thomas Nelson CC 99 Thomas Nelson Dr Hampton VA 23670

ZAHRT, MERTON STROEBEL, investor; b. Ellington, Wis., May 8, 1910; s. Francis Henry and Anna Barbara (Maves) Z.; m. Genevieve Rosalie Kottler, Aug. 20, 1932 (div. Aug. 1952); children: Barbara Ann, Merton William (dec.), Sally Sue Zahrt-O'Leary; m. Hilda Elizabeth Bouck, Aug. 23, 1952; 1 child, Nancy Joanne Zahrt-Maxwell. MusB, Lawrence U., 1932; MusM, U. Rochester, 1943; EdD, Columbia U., 1950. Prof. music, head dept. Ft. Hays (Kans.) State Coll., 1949-50; assoc. prof. Ithaca (N.Y.) Coll., 1950-52; prof. music Chgo. Mus. Coll., 1952-58, acting chmn. music edn., 1957-58; asst. to dean of men U. Ill., Chgo., 1953-62, asst. dean of men, 1962-65; prof. music edn. U. So. Miss., Hattiesburg, 1965-71, coord. grad. studies in music edn., 1968-71; real estate salesman Hubbard Real Estate, Richmond, Va., 1971-78; profl. investor Zahrt Revocable Trust U/A, Dunedin, Fla., 1978—; trustee, 1988—; adjudicator sch. music competitions, Ark., Ill., Ind., Kans., Minn., Okla., Wis., 1940-65; conv. chmn. Ill. State Music Tchrs. Assn., Chgo., 1957; ch. choir dir. Coll. Ch., Hampden-Sydney, Va., 1978-79. Contbr. articles to profl. jours. Asst. dir. YMCA Men's Glee Club, Green Bay, Wis., 1935-36; dir. Hays (Kans.) Community Chorus, 1949-50; lay eucharistic min. Ch. Ascension, Clearwater, Fla., 1986—; music com. mem. Episcopal Ch. of the Ascension, Clearwater, 1988-91. Community music programs grantee U. So. Miss., 1967-68. Mem. Am. Assn. Retired Persons, State Univs. Annuitants Assn. (Ill.), Lawrence U. Legacy Circle, The Inst. Econometric Rsch., Phi Gamma Delta, Phi Mu Alpha Sinfonia, Kappa Kappa Psi, Kappa Delta Pi. Republican. Episcopalian.

ZAHRT, WILLIAM DIETRICH, II, lawyer; b. Dayton, Ohio, July 12, 1944; s. Kenton William and Orpha Catharine (Wagner) Z.; m. Patricia Ann Marek, June 10, 1969; children—Justin William, Alitheia Patricia. BS in Physics, Yale U., 1966, JD, 1969, M of Pub. and Pvt. Mgmt., 1990. Bar: N.Y. 1970, Ohio 1972, Tex. 1982, N.C. 1992, U.S. Ct. Appeals (Fed. cir.) 1977. Assoc. Kenyon & Kenyon, N.Y.C., 1969-71; assoc. Biebel, French & Nauman, Dayton, Ohio, 1971-80; sr. patent atty. Schlumberger Well Svcs., Houston, 1980-82; sole practice, Kingwood, Tex., 1982-85, 88-90; patent atty. Shell Oil Co., Houston, 1985-88; sr. patent counsel Raychem Corp., Fuquay-Varina, N.C., 1990—. Mem. ABA, Am. Intellectual Property Law Assn., Tex. Bar Assn., N.C. State Bar Assn., Carolina Patent, Trademark, and Copyright Law Assn., Dayton Racquet Club, Masons. Anglican. Home: 111 Sylvan Grove Dr Cary NC 27511-9607 Office: 8000 Purfoy Rd Fuquay Varina NC 27526

ZAISER, KENT AMES, lawyer; b. St. Petersburg, Fla., June 10, 1945; s. Robert Alan and Marion (Brown) Z. AB Duke U., 1967; postgrad. U. Calif.-Berkeley, 1971; JD, U. Fla., 1972. Bar: Fla. 1973, U.S. Dist. Ct. (no. dist.) Fla. 1974, U.S. Supreme Ct. 1978, U.S. Dist. Ct. (so. dist.) Fla. 1980, U.S. Dist. Ct. (mid. dist.) Fla. 1981, U.S. Ct. Appeals (11th cir.) 1981. Rsch. aide Fla. Supreme Ct., Tallahassee, 1973-75, adminstrv. asst. to chief justice, 1975-76; asst. gen. counsel Fla. Dept. Natural Resources, Tallahassee, 1976-80; asst. atty. gen. Fla. Dept. Legal Affairs, Tallahassee, 1980-85; dep. gen. counsel S.W. Fla. Water Mgmt. Dist., Brooksville, 1985-89, gen. counsel, 1989-92; ptnr. Foley and Lardner, Tallahassee, 1992-93; prin. Kent A. Zaiser, P.A., Tallahassee, 1994—; cons. Fla. State Cts. Adminstr., Tallahassee, 1975. Contbg. author: Environmental Regulation and Litigation in Florida, 1980-84. Campaign chmn. Vince Fechtel for State Rep. of Fla., Leesburg, 1972. Mem. Tallahassee Bar Assn., Jefferson County Bar Assn. Democrat. Episcopalian. Club: Governors. Home: 3286 Longleaf Rd Tallahassee FL 32310-6406 Office: PO Box 6045 Tallahassee FL 32314-6045

ZAK, ROBERT JOSEPH, lawyer; b. Steubenville, Ohio, July 29, 1946; s. Joseph and Pearl (Munyas) Z.; m. Kristy Hubbard Winkler, Sept. 13, 1980; children: Elizabeth Adele, Robert Joseph Jr., Barbara Ann. BS, W.Va. U., 1968, JD, 1975. Bar: W.Va. 1975, U.S. Dist. Ct. (so. dist.) W.Va. 1975, U.S. Dist. Ct. (no. dist.) W.Va. 1989, U.S. Ct. Appeals (4th cir.) 1990. Staff atty. Pub. Svc. Commn. of W.Va., Charleston, 1975-76; assoc. Preiser & Wilson L.C., Charleston, 1976-81, ptnr., 1981-85; sr. ptnr. Zak & Assocs., Charleston, 1985—; hearing examiner W.Va. Bd. Regents, Charleston, 1987-90; spl. asst. atty. gen. State of W.Va., Charleston, 1980-87; chmn. civil svc. commn. City of Charleston, 1987-90; mem. State of W.Va. Worker's Compensation Appeals Bd., Charleston, 1991—. With U.S. Army, 1969-71, Vietnam. Fellow Am. Acad. Matrimonial Lawyers; mem. Order of Barristers. Republican. Presbyterian. Office: Zak & Assocs 607 Ohio Ave Charleston WV 25302-2228

ZAKI, AHMED SOLIMAN, information scientist educator; b. Cairo, Egypt, Nov. 12, 1927; came to U.S., 1972; s. Soliman and Neemat (Hamdi) Z.; m. Salwa W. Omar, Oct. 2, 1960; children: Saifallah, Kareem. Neematallah. BSc, Cairo U.; MA in Ops. Mgmt., Am. U., Cairo; PhD in Ops. Rsch., U. Wash., 1977. Asst. prof. MIS and ops. rsch. Wash. State U., Pullman, 1976-80; asst. prof. MIS Coll. William and Mary, Williamsburg, Va., 1980-82, prof. MIS, 1982—; vis. assoc. prof. U. Wash., Seattle, 1982, Simon Fraser U., Vancouver, B.C., Can., 1982-83; prof. bus. adminstrn. grad. sch. bus. Simon Fraser U., Vancouver, 1984—; cons. and presenter in field. Mem. editorial bd. Jour. Mgmt. Info. Sis., Jour. Info. Tech. Mgmt.; author manuals; contbr. numerous articles to profl. jours. NASA/ASEE fellow, 1986, 87. Office: Coll William and Mary MIS Dept Williamsburg VA 23187

ZAKI, SALEH ABBAS, forensic pathologist; b. Cairo, Oct. 25, 1935; came to U.S., 1969, naturalized, 1976; s. Abbas S. and Hamida M. (Ali) Z.; m. Afaf A. Kassaby, May 18, 1960; children—Maha, Karaz. M.D., Cairo U., 1959; Ph.D., U. Birmingham (Eng.), 1964. Diplomate Am. Bd. Pathology. Rotating intern Cairo U. Teaching Hosp., 1960-61; clin. demonstrator in histopathology Assuit (Egypt) U. Med. Sch., 1961, clin. demonstrator in pathology 1965, lectr. pathology, 1965-68, supr. histopathology labs., 1966-68; research fellow, hon. research fellow dept. pathology U. Birmingham, 1961-65; tutor in pathology dept. pathology, Queen's U. Belfast (No. Ireland), 1968-69; assoc. in pathology Emory U. Sch. Medicine, Atlanta, 1969-70, sr. resident, instr. anatomic pathology dept. pathology, Atlanta, 1972, fellow in cytopathology and clin. instr., 1972, clin. asst. prof. pathology, 1975-77, clin. asst. prof. pediatrics, 1974-77; assoc. prof. div. pathology U. Calgary (Alta., Can.), 1970-71; assoc. med. examiner Fulton County, Atlanta, 1973-77, dir. residency tng. program, 1976-77; assoc. med. staff dept. pathology St. Joseph's Infirmary, Atlanta, 1975-77; assoc. prof. pathology U. Ala.-Birmingham, 1977-78; assoc. coroner/med. examiner Jefferson County, Ala., 1977-78; assoc. med. examiner Fulton County, Atlanta, 1973-77, 78-88, chief med. examiner, 1988—; assoc. pathologist Hugh Spalding Med. Ctr., Atlanta, 1982-89. Bd. dirs. Am. Arab Community Ctr., 1982-83; clin. assoc. prof. pathology Morehouse Sch. Medicine, Atlanta, 1983— . Brit. Council scholar, 1961-65. Fellow Am. Acad. Forensic Sci., Coll. Am. Pathologists; mem. Pathol. Soc. Gt. Britain and Ireland, Atlanta Soc. Pathologists, AMA, Med. Assn. Atlanta, Ga. Med. Assn., Am. Heart Assn., Nat. Assn. Med. Examiners. Republican. Moslem. Contbr. articles to profl. jours. Home: 8-A Park Pl 2660 Peachtree Rd NW Atlanta GA 30305-3673 Office: 50 Coca Cola Pl SE Atlanta GA 30303-3043

ZALESKI, ILENE, librarian; b. Worcester, Mass., Sept. 26, 1946; d. John Dominic and Emily Viola (Jarvais) Z. BS in Zoology cum laude, U. Mass., 1968; MLS, U. R.I., 1973. Biology tchr. Northampton (Mass.) Sch. for Girls, 1968-69; asst. circulation libr. U. R.I. Libr., Kingston, 1972-73, audiovisual cataloger computerized cataloging libr., 1973-75; asst. editor Deep Sea Rsch/Oceanographic Abstracts and Bibliography, Woods Hole, Mass., 1977; scientific book reviewer Small Press Rev., Vt., 1977-78; assoc. editor Oceanographic Lit. Rev., Woods Hole, 1978-83; cons. editor RP Record in Natural Resources and Environ. Mgmt., Woods Hole, 1983-84; sr. editor Woods Hole Data Base, 1983-84. Ofcl. del. Gov.'s Conf. on Librs. and Info. Svcs., 1990. Named Vol. of Yr. Learn to Read Vols. of Miami, 1989; Ilene Zaleski Day named in City of North Miami, 1991, 94. Mem. ALA, Fla. Pub. Libr. Assn. (dir.-at large 1994—, sec. 1993, Libr. Employee of Yr. 1989-90), North Miami Woman's Club (pres. 1993-95, v.p. 1991-93, treas. 1989-91), Assn. Fla. Laubach Orgns. (pres. 1990-91). Office: North Miami Pub Libr 835 NE 132nd St Miami FL 33161

ZALLEN, EUGENIA MALONE, dietitian, consultant; b. Camp Hill, Ala., July 18, 1932; d. Benjamin Floyd and Pauline Phillips (Kelly) Malone; m. Harold Zallen, Aug. 23, 1959. BS, Auburn U., 1953; MS, Purdue U., 1960; PhD, U. Tenn., 1974. Registered and lic. dietitian. Assoc. adminstr., dietitian Duke U. Med. Ctr., Durham, N.C., 1954-57; asst. chief dietitian Emory U. Hosp., Atlanta, 1957-58; from instr. to asst. prof. Auburn (Ala.) U., 1962-66; asst. prof. U. Md., College Park, 1967-72; dir., assoc. prof. U. Okla., Norman, 1974-80; dean sch. home econs. East Carolina U., Greenville, N.C., 1980-84, prof., 1980-90; exec. v.p. Malone Group Internat. Cons., Columbus, Ga., 1990—; vis. prof. U. Hawaii, Manoa, Honolulu, 1989; cons. ZTA Nat. Housing Corp., Indpls., 1992—. Co-author: Ideas Plus Dollars, 1976, 2d edit., 1980, Equipment Care and Use, 1984, Procurement and Cost Control, 1984, Quantity Food Production, 1984, Sanitation and Safety, 1984; editor: Oklahoma Diet Manual, 1979; contbr. articles to profl. jours. Vol. Am. Heart Assn., Columbus, 1991—; vol. educator Ala. Camp for Diabetic Children, Tallapoosa County, 1992; vol. cons. Ga. Bapt. Children's Emergency Shelter, Columbus, 1991-95; pres. Windsor Park Garden Club, Columbus, 1995-97. Named Ark. Traveler Gov. of Ark., 1976, Disting. Alumni Auburn U., 1981, 92; recipient Gold Alumni Achievement award Purdue U., 1990, Disting. Svc. award Ga. Dietetic Assn., 1996. Mem. Am. Dietetic Assn., Am. Home Econs. Assn. (bylaws com. 1988-90, Silver Circle award 1991), Inst. Food Tech., Phi Kappa Phi, Sigma Xi (councilor 1976-80), Kappa Omicron Nu. Baptist. Office: PO Box 8767 Columbus GA 31908-8767

ZALOKAR, ROBERT H., bank executive; b. 1927. BS, Univ. Kans., 1950. Examiner FDIC, Washington, 1950-55; asst. v.p. Old Dominion Bank, 1955-58; exec. v.p. Bank of Annadale, 1958-65; pres. Falls Ch. Bank, 1965-69; exec. v.p. First Va. Bank, 1969-74, pres., chief adminstrv. officer, 1974-78, pres., chief exec. officer, 1978—, also chmn. bd., dir., 1984—. With USN, 1945-46. Office: First Va Banks Inc 6400 Arlington Blvd Falls Church VA 22042-2336

ZAMAN, MD SARWAR, biology educator; b. Chapainawabjang, Bangladesh, Mar. 1, 1957; s. Kamruz Zaman and Gul Helena Begum; m. Fahmida Zereen, Aug. 20, 1992. BS in Zoology, U. Dhaka, Bangladesh, 1980; MS in Biology, Tex. Woman's U., 1985, MSSE in Biology, 1989, PhD in Radiation Biology, 1989. Rsch., tchg. asst. dept. biology Tex. Woman's U., Denton, 1984-89; postdoc. rsch. fellow Johns Hopkins U. Sch. Med., 1989-91; asst. prof. biology Alcorn State U., Lorman, Miss., 1991—. Contbr. articles to profl. jours. including Jour. Environ. Sci. Health, Alcohol and Drug Rsch., also others. Recipient Nat. Collegiate Nat. Science award, 1987; TWU gen. scholar, 1987-88, Ray and Bertha Lakey Competitive scholar, TWU, 1986-87, Univ. scholar, U. Dacca, 1981; ASU Institutional rsch. grantee, 1991-92, 93-94, Dept. of Energy grantee, 1995-96. Mem. Miss. Acad. Scis., Tex. Acad. Scis., Tex. Soc. for Electron Microscopy, Beta Beta Beta. Office: Alcorn State U Dept Biology Box 870 Lorman MS 39096

ZAMAN, MUSHARRAF, civil engineering educator; b. Rajshahi, Bangladesh, Mar. 8, 1952; came to U.S., 1979; s. Md. Gias Uddin and Jahanara Begum; m. Afroza Khanam, Aug. 7, 1981; children: Jessica, Ashiq. MS in Civil Engring., Carleton U., Can., 1979; PhD in Civil Engring., U. Ariz., 1982. Registered profl. engr., Okla. Lectr. civil engring. U. Engring. and Tech., Dhaka, Bangladesh, 1975-76; rsch. assoc. Asian Inst. Tech., Bangkok, 1976-77; grad. teaching asst. Carleton U., Ottawa, Can., 1977-79; rsch. asst. Va. Tech., Blacksburg, 1979-81; rsch. assoc. U. Ariz., Tucson, 1981-82; asst. prof. U. Okla., Norman, 1982-88, assoc. prof., 1988-93, prof., 1993—; faculty advisor Bangladesh Student Assn., U. Okla., Norman, 1983—, Muslim Student Assn., 1990—; summer faculty fellow Argonne (Ill.) Nat. Lab., 1986; v.p. geotech. Consortium Internat., Oklahoma City, 1992-94; co-organizer U.S.-Can. Geomechanics Workshop, 1992. Co-editor Internat. Jour. for Numerical and Analytical Methods in Geomechanics (application briefs); assoc. editor Jour. Petroleum Sci. and Engring.; contbr. articles to European Jour. Mechanics, Computer Methods in Applied Mechanics and Engring., Internat. Jour. Numerical Analytical Met. Geomech., Internat. Jour. Petroleum Sci. and Engring., Applied Math. Modelling, ASME Jour. Applied Mechanics, ASME Jour. Energy Resources Tech., Jour. Geotech. Engring. divsn. ASCE, Jour. Engring. Mechanics divsn. ASCE, Jour. Transp. Engring. divsn. ASCE, Arabian Jour. Sci. and Engring., Transp. Rsch. Record. Mem. ASCE (mem. deep found. com. 1987—), Internat. Assn. Computer Methods and Advances in Geomechanics (co-chmn. internat. conf. 1992-94, co-editor newsletter 1989—, mem. internat. adv. com. 9th conf., bd. dirs. 1996—), Am. Rock Mechanics Assn. (founding mem.). Home: 501 Starbrook Ct Norman OK 73072-4722 Office: U Okla 202 W Boyd St Rm 334 Norman OK 73019-1020

ZAMBRANO, JAIME M., foreign language educator, researcher; b. El Tigre, Anzoategui, Venezuela, Apr. 22, 1953; came to U.S., 1981; s. Jaime C. and Paula (Montoya) Z.; m. Linda Joy Spinar, Dec. 21, 1990. BS, Univ. Nacional de Colombia, Bogotá, 1979; MA, U. Mo., 1986, PhD, 1993. Asst. prof. U. Ctrl. Ark., Conway, 1991—; instr. Stephens Coll., Columbia, Mo., 1989-90; mem. scholarship com., curriculum com. U. Ctrl. Ark. Mem. MLA, Am. Assn. Tchrs. Spanish and Portuguese, Latin Am. Students Assn., Sigma Delta Pi (pres. 1987-89). Roman Catholic. Office: U Ctrl Ark Dept Fgn Langs Conway AR 72032

ZAMORANO, WANDA JEAN, secondary education educator; b. Mertzon, Tex., Aug. 11, 1947; d. A.L. and Billie Louise (Byler) Sawyer; married; 1 child, Anna. BS, Sul Ross State Univ., 1970; MEd, Tex. Tech., 1974; EdD, Nova Southeastern U., 1994. Cert. tchr., Tex. Migrant edn. tchr. Balmorhea (Tex.) ISD, 1970-72; reading tchr. Hurst-Euless Bedford (Tex.) ISD, 1972-92; owner cons. firm WZ Enterprizes; cons. Tex. Tech. U., 1980-81; demonstration tchr. Ednl. Svcs. Ctr., Austin, 1975; instr. Richland Coll., Dallas, 1982; mem. nat. faculty Turner Ednl. Svcs. Inc.; adj. prof. Tex. Woman's U.; presneter 67th annual So. N.Mex. Tech. Conf., 1994. Contbr. articles to profl. jours. Active Bedford Jr. High PTA. Named Tchr. of Yr., Bedford, 1984, Most Prominent Educators Tex., 1983, Cable Tchr. of Yr., 1991, Tchr. of Month, Bronco News, 1993; TCI Cable grantee, 1995. Mem. NEA, AAUW (Named USA Today faculty mem.), Hurst-Euless-Bedford Tex. State Tchrs. Assn. NEA (v.p. 1994-95, Internat. Reading Assn., Tex. State Tchr. Assn. (exec. bd.), The Governor's Club (charter), Kappa Delta Pi. Democrat. Home: 2403 Finley Rd Apt 1107 Irving TX 75062-3348 Office: Bedford Jr High 325 Carolyn Dr Bedford TX 76021-4111

ZAMRINI, EDWARD YOUSSEF, behavioral neurologist; b. Cairo, Apr. 27, 1958; s. Joseph Boutros and Therese Edouard Zamrini; m. Cynthia Lynn Douglass, Oct. 2, 1993; 1 child, Omar Edward. BSc, Am. U. Beirut, 1980, MD, 1984. Dir. geriatric neuropsychiatry program VA Med. Ctr., Augusta, Ga., 1990—. Contbr. articles to profl. jours. Mem. AMA, ACP, N.Y. Acad. Scis., Am. Acad. Neurology, Alzheimer's Disease and Related Disorders Assn. (bd. dirs. 1990-95, chair edn. com. 1990-92, columnist 1989-94, pres. Augusta chpt. 1993-94), Amnesty Internat. (chpt. rep. 1990). Office: VA Med Ctr 1 Freedom Way Augusta GA 30904-6258

ZANA, DONALD DOMINICK, data processing executive; b. Pitts., Oct. 9, 1942; s. Dominick Jr. and Kathryn (Turino) Z.; m. Janet Ann Kundrak, May 30, 1964; children: Christine Ann, Michael Steven, Anthony Phillip. BS in Edn., Indiana U. of Pa., 1964; M of Commerce in Mgmt., U. Richmond, Va., 1972; grad. with honors, Army Logistics Mgmt. Ctr., 1973, Army Command and Gen. Staff Coll., 1978; postgrad., Harvard U., 1993. Commd. 2nd lt. U.S. Army, 1964, advanced through grades to lt. col., 1980, ret., 1984; prin. systems analyst Teledyne Brown Engring., Huntsville, Ala., 1984-85, sr. systems analyst, 1985-86, br. mgr. software acquisition and evaluation, 1986-90, mgr. automation integration, 1990-91, dir. computing resources and tech., chief info. officer, 1991—. Mem. IEEE, Assn. for Computing Machinery, Assn. of U.S. Army, Ret. Officers Assn. Roman Catholic. Home: 7807 Springbrook Dr SE Huntsville AL 35802 Office: Teledyne Brown Engring 300 Sparkman Dr NW # 17 Huntsville AL 35805-1912

ZAND, LLOYD CRAIG, radiologist; b. N.Y.C., May 1, 1942; s. Walter Paul and Estelle Leone (Teitler) Z.; m. Mardan Jeanne Foster, June 9, 1968; children: Jason Matthew, Jory Meagan. AB, U. Ill., 1964; MD, Chgo. Med. Sch., 1968. Intern U. Minn., Mpls., 1968-69; resident in radiology U. Miami, Fla., Fla., 1969-70, 72-74; clin. instr. U. Miami, Fla., 1973-80; attending radiologist North Shore Med. Ctr., Miami, 1974—, chmn. dept. radiology, 1989—, chmn. dept. medicine, 1995—; pres. Mar-J Enterprises, Inc., Miami, 1990—; chmn. Diagnostic Network, Inc., 1993—; mem. med. adv. bd. 3M Corp., Mpls., 1988-90; chmn. Med. Resources Devel. Corp., Miami, 1985-88; bd. dirs. MTR, Inc., Atlanta. Trustee Zool. Soc. Fla., Miami, 1986—. Lt. comdr. USNR, 1970-72. Mem. AMA, Am. Coll. Radiology, Radiology Soc. of Fla., Soc. Cardiovascular and Interventional Radiology. Office: North Shore Med Ctr 1100 NW 95th St Miami FL 33150-2038

ZANES, GEORGE WILLIAM, management, marketing, human resources consultant; b. Laconia, N.H., May 13, 1926; s. Robert Lewis and Mina (Edgerly) z.; m. Anne Schuetz, Dec. 21, 1957 (div. 1970); children: Laura, David, Scott, Hugh; m. Ruth Weissman, June 17, 1970; stepchildren: Glenn, Lee. BS, U. N.H., 1952. Dir. indsl. rels., cons. I.P.C. Inc., Bristol, N.H., 1953-56; dir. spl. projects Am. Rsch. Bur. Inc., Beltsville, Md., 1957-60, Alfred Politz Rsch. Inc., N.Y.C., 1960-62; v.p. Simulmatics Corp., N.Y.C., 1962-63; group rsch. mgr. Foote Cone & Belding Inc., N.Y.C., 1963-65; v.p. Trendex Inc., N.Y.C., 1965-67; pres. Zanes & Assocs. Inc., Ft. Lee, N.J., 1967-80, chmn., chief exec. officer, 1980-88; also bd. dirs., pres. The Mktg. Rsch. Workshop Inc., Ft. Lee, N.J., 1974-88; cons. Strategic Resource Group Inc., 1988-89; cons., ceo G & R Enterprises, Tallahassee, Fla., Alpharetta, Ga., 1989—, bd. dirs. Ad Net, Inc. Mem. F. Lee Rent Leveling Bd., past pres., Jaycees, Bristol, N.H. With U.S. Army, 1944-47; ETO, capt. USAR, 1947-60. Mem. Am. Mktg. Assn. (v.p. programs Atlanta chpt. 1993-94), Greater North Fulton C. of C., Acacia.

ZANFAGNA, PHILIP EDWARD, government executive, urban planner; b. Lawrence, Mass., Dec. 5, 1936; s. Philip Edward and Edna Edith (Hill) Z.; m. Joan Elizabeth Criswell, Sept. 9, 1961; children: Deborah Carol Bass, Gary Philip. BA, Ohio Wesleyan U., 1958; MDiv, Yale U., 1961; JD, George Washington U., 1964. Certified in sr. exec. svcs., acquisition profl. Sr. negotiator USN, Washington, 1964-72; dep. dir. contracts dept. Navy USMC, Washington, 1972-80, dir. contracts, 1980-90, asst. chief of staff installations and logistics, 1990—; pres. Lewinsville Inc., McLean, Va., 1980-95. Commr., vice chmn. Fairfax (Va.) County Planning Commn., 1973-77; active Dulles Airport Planning Com., Fairfax, 1975-76, Fairfax Blue Ribbon commn., 1986-87; pres. Dranesville Dist. Coun., McLean, 1982-83; chmn. bd. dirs. McLean Citizens Assn., 1979-81; trustee McLean Found., 1980-86. Mem. Sr. Exec. Assn., Yale U. Alumni Assn., Fed. Exec. Inst. Assn., Nat. Def. U. Alumni Assn., Harvard U. Sch. Govt. Alumni Assn. Presbyterian. Office: HQMC I & L Dept Code LB 3033 Wilson Blvd # 725 Arlington VA 22201-3843

ZANGENEH, FEREYDOUN, pediatrics educator, pediatric endocrinologist; b. Tehran, Iran, July 11, 1937; came to U.S., 1962, 86; married. MD, U. Tehran, Iran, 1961. Diplomate Am. Bd. Pediatrics and Pediatric Endocrinology. Intern Washington Hosp. Ctr., 1962; resident in pediatrics U. Chgo. Hosps. & Clinics, 1963-65; fellow in pediatric endocrinology Children's Memorial Hosp., Chgo., 1965-66, U. Wash., Seattle, 1966-68; asst. prof. to prof. U. Tehran, Iran, 1968-86; assoc. prof. pediatrics Marshall U. Sch. of Medicine, Huntington, W.Va., 1986-89; assoc. prof. pediatrics W.Va. U., Charleston, 1989-95, prof. pediatrics, 1995—, dir. pediatric endocrinology, 1989—; instr. pediatrics U. Wash., Seattle, 1967-68; dir. dept. endocrinology Children's Hosp. Med. Ctr., Tehran, Iran, 1968-86; dir. pediatric endocrinology Marshall U. Sch. Medicine, Huntington, 1986-89; mem. W.Va. Adv. Com. on Newborn Metabolic Screening, W.Va. Adv. Com. on Diabetes Mellitus. Author: (with others) Pediatric Endocrinology and Metabolism; contbr. articles and abstracts to profl. jours. Bd. dirs., rsch. com., camp com. Am. Diabetes Assn., W.Va. affiliate, Charleston, active in Huntington W.Va. affiliate, 1986-89; bd. dirs. Diabetes Camp of W.Va. Capt. Iranian Army Med. Corps, 1969-71. Recipient Gharib Rsch. award, Iranian Pediatric Soc., Tehran, 1976. Fellow Am. Acad. Pediatrics, Am. Coll. Endocrinology; mem. Internat. Pediatric Assn. (adv. expert panel 1977-83), Union Mid. Ea. and Mediterranean Pediatric Socs. (exec. coun. 1979-85), Lawson Wilkins Pediatric Endocrine Soc., Endocrine Soc., Am. Assn. Clin. Endocrinologists. Office: WVa U Dept Pediatrics 830 Pennsylvania Ave Ste 104 Charleston WV 25302-3389

ZAPFFE, NINA BYROM, retired elementary education educator; b. Independence, Mo., Aug. 17, 1925; d. Richmond Douglas and Nina Belle (Howell) Byrom; m. Robert Glenn Fessler, June 25, 1946 (dec. June 1947); 1 child, Robert Glenn Fessler Zapffe; m. Fred Zapffe, July 1, 1952; children: Paul Douglas, Carl Raymond. BA, So. Meth. U., 1946. Fin. sec. Tyler St. Meth. Ch., Dallas, 1948-49; tchr. Dallas Ind. Sch. Dist., 1949-52, Norman (Okla.) Pub. Schs., 1966-74; cert. chief reader for GED Writing Skills Test Part II GED Testing Svc., Am. Coun. on Edn., Washington, 1990—; adv. com. (Learning Skills Ctr.) Moore-Norman Vocat.-Tech. Sch., 1988—. Adv. bd. Norman Salvation Army, 1978-90; organizer, historian Norman Salvation Army Womens Auxiliary, 1983—, Norman Literacy Coun., 1976—; organizing com., past pres. Norman Interfaith Coun., 1974-93; organizing com., past treas. Friends of the Norman Libr., 1979—; mem. McFarlin Meml. United Meth. Ch. (pres., historian 2-in-1 Sunday Sch. class, 1996, lay leader, 1980-81; vice chmn. Cleveland County Election Bd., 1977-79, pct. vice chmn., former pct. chmn. Named to Literacy Hall of Fame Pioneer Libr. Sys., Norman, 1995. Mem. DAR (vice regent Black Beaver chpt. 1996), Nat. Soc. Daus. 1812 (state treas. 1996), Old Regime Study Club (sec. 1996), Coterie Club (pres. 1996), Delta Delta Delta Alumnae. Republican. Home: 2717 Walnut Rd Norman OK 73072-6940

ZAPHIRIOU, GEORGE ARISTOTLE, lawyer, educator; b. Athens, Greece, July 10, 1919; came to U.S., 1973, naturalized, 1977; s. Aristotle George and Calli Constantine (Economos) Z.; m. Peaches J. Griffin, June 1, 1973; children: Ari, Marie. JD, U. Athens, 1940; LLM, U. London, 1950. Bar: Supreme Ct. Greece 1946, Eng. 1956, Ill. 1975, Va. 1983. Gen. counsel Counties Ship Mgmt. and R & K Ltd., London, 1951-61; lectr. City of London Poly., barrister, 1961-73; joint editor Jour. Bus. Law, London, 1962-73; vis. prof. Ill. Inst. Tech.-Chgo. Kent Coll. Law, 1973-76; sole practice, Northbrook, Ill., 1976-78; prof. law George Mason U. Sch. Law, 1978-94, emeritus prof. law, 1994—; prof. internat. transactions George Mason U. Internat. Inst., 1992-94; mem. Odin, Feldman & Pittelman P.C., Fairfax, Va., 1994—. Bd. editors Am. Jour. Comp. Law, 1980-94. Mem. Am. Arbitration Assn. (mem. panel arbitrators), Am. Soc. Internat. Law, S. Maritime Law Assn. U.S. (mem. com. on carriage of goods by sea), George Mason Am. Inn of Ct. Author: Transfer of Chattels in Private International Law, 1956, USA edit., 1981, European Business Law, 1970; co-author: Declining Jurisdiction In Private International Law, 1995; contbr. articles to law revs. and profl. jours. Home: 400 Green Pasture Dr Rockville MD 20852-4233 Office: 9302 Lee Hwy Ste 1100 Fairfax VA 22031-1215

ZAPOROZHETZ, LAURENE ELIZABETH, dean, librarian, educator; b. Detroit, Nov. 25, 1950; d. Peter S. and Emily M. (Pryma) Z. BA with honors, Mich. State U., 1972; MS in Librarianship, Western Mich. U., 1974; PhD, U. Oreg., 1987. Ednl. specialist Mass. Dept. Edn., Boston, 1974-76; instr. social scis. ref. libr. U. Nebr. Libr., Omaha, 1976, instr., edn. ref. specialist, 1976-78, instr., acting ref. chairperson, 1977-78; asst. prof. U. Oreg. Main Libr., Eugene, 1979-84, assoc. prof., coord. libr. instrn., 1984-85; assoc. prof., chair info. svcs. Bowling Green (Ohio) State U. Jerome Libr., 1985-87, assoc. prof., dir. info. scis., 1987-88; dir. U. South Fla. Tampa Campus Libr., 1988-90; dir., libr., assoc. prof. edn. La. State U. Noel Meml. Libr., Shreveport, 1991-92; dean, libr., assoc. prof. edn. Noel Meml. Libr., Shreveport, La., 1993—; guest lectr. in field. Contbr. articles to profl. jours. Mem. Nebr. Task Force on Women, Alchohl and Drugs, 1976-78; mem. edn. com. Mayor's Commn. on Status of Women, Omaha, 1976-77, abused women task force, 1976-77; mem. edn. com. Human Rels. Bd., Omaha, 1977, LWV, 1976; mem. Concerned Citizens for Omaha Com., 1976-77; mem. Shreveport regional arts com. Cultural Cmty. Plan, 1992-94. Ukrainian Culture Ctr. scholar, 1981-82; Assn. Coll. and Rsch. Libr. Librs. grantee, 1990; apptd. Adm. in Great Navy of State of Nebr., 1978. Mem. ALA, Am. Soc. Info. Sci., Acad. Libr. Dirs. La., Assn. Coll. and Rsch. Librs. (La. chpt. vice chair 1993, chair 1994), La. Acad. Libr. Info. Network Consortium (vice chair 1995, chair 1996), La. Libr. Assn., La. Libr. Network Commn. (commr. 1995—), No. La. Acad. Libr. Group (pres. 1992), Noel Found. Inc. (bd. dirs. 1991—, sec./treas. 1996—), Fla. Libr. Assn., Tampa Bay Libr. Consortium (bd. dirs. 1989-90, chair planning com. 1989-90), Suncoast Info. Specialists, Fla. Ctr. Libr. Automation (bd. dirs. 1989-90), Acad. Libr. Assn. Ohio, Nebr. Libr. Assn. (coll. and univ. sect. chairperson 1976-77, 77-78), Kappa Delta Pi, Phi Kappa Phi. Home: 111 Elmview Ln Haughton LA 71037-9267 Office: La State Univ Noel Meml Libr One University Pl Shreveport LA 71115-2301

ZARANKA, ALBERT J., musical director, pianist, educator; b. Manchester, Conn., July 28, 1949; s. Anthony Joseph and Lottie (Mazurek) Z.; m. Ellen Fadden, Oct. 21, 1978. B in Music, Boston Conservatory of Music, 1971. Faculty mem. Hartford (Conn.) Conservatory of Music, 1971-73, Boston Conservatory of Music, 1973-74, Bklyn. Music Sch., 1975-78; founder Studio One A, N.Y.C., 1978-86, Rivenoak Studio, Fayetteville, N.C., 1986—; instr. Meth. Coll., 1990—. Musical dir. more than 30 projects, N.Y., Pa., Va., Conn., N.C., 1973-86; musical composer The Happy Journey, N.Y., 1985; guest soloist Bach 2-Piano Concerto Lee County Orch., 1992. Bd. dirs. Arts Coun. of Fayetteville/Cumberland County, 1992—, mem. grants com. panel, 1994. Mem. Music Tchrs. Nat. Assn., N.C. Piano Tchrs. Assn., Fayetteville Piano Tchrs. Assn. (pres. 1987-91, recording sec. 1992-94, corres. sec. 1994—), Am. Fedn. Musicians, Kappa Gamma Psi. Democrat. Home and Office: 201 Rivenoak Dr Fayetteville NC 28303-4626

ZARATE, ANN GAIRING, academic administrator, lawyer; b. Oak Park, Ill., Oct. 28, 1959; d. Donald Albert and Beverly Jean (Eppink) Gairing; m. Eugene Anthony Zarate, Oct. 5, 1985; children: Anthony Michael, Melissa Ann. BA in Comm. magna cum laude, Tulane U., 1982; JD, Cleve. State U., 1985. Bar: Ohio. Atty. Seymour Gross, Assoc., Cleve., 1985; adminstr. endowment trusts Case Western Res. U., Cleve., 1986-91; dir. devel. Salvation Army, Cleve., 1991-92; exec. dir. and asst. v.p. univ. advancement U. North Ala. Found., Florence, 1992—. Mem. Jr. women's com. Cleve. Playhouse, 1989-92. Mem. AAUW, Leadership Shoals/Shoals C. of C., Florence Rotary Club, Alpha Lambda Delta. Office: Univ North Ala Found PO Box 5059 Florence AL 35630

ZARDIACKAS, LYLE DEAN, biomaterials educator, consultant; b. Topeka, Dec. 20, 1944; s. Kastantas Joseph Zardiackas and Eulalee (Zirschky) Scribner; children: Jason A., Kara Ann; m. Linda Gail Norsworthy, Oct. 14, 1982; 1 stepchild, Jason L. Williams. BS in Materials Sci., Calif. State U., San Jose, 1972; MS in Materials Sci., U. Va., 1974, PhD in Materials Sci., 1977. Rsch. engr. Stanford (Calif.) Med. Ctr., 1971-72; asst. prof., dir. dental materials Ohio State U., Columbus, 1977-79; asst. prof. Sch. of Dentistry U. Miss. Med. Ctr., Jackson, 1979-82, assoc. prof. Sch. of Dentistry, 1982-87, dir. biomaterials and orthopaedic rsch. Sch. of Dentistry, 1987—; prof. Sch. Dentistry, 1992—; asst. prof. U. Miss. Sch. Medicine, 1982-94, prof., 1994—; adj. prof. Miss. State U., 1990—; mgr. biomaterials sect. Inst. for Tech. Devel., Jackson, 1984-87; cons Synthes, Ltd., U.S.A., Paoli, Pa., 1986—. Contbr. articles to profl. jours. With USAF, 1963-67. Fellow Acad. Dental Materials (corp. liaison 1983—, bd. dirs., pres. 1992-94); mem. Internat. Assn. Dental Rsch., Am. Assn. Dental Schs., Soc. Biomaterials (chair dental biomaterials SIG 1994—). Baptist. Office: U Miss Med Ctr 2500 N State St Jackson MS 39216-4500

ZAREH, MO, engineering executive; b. Shiraz, Fars, Iran, Nov. 13, 1943; came to U.S., 1961; s. Habib and Parvin (Masah) Z.; m. Mahvash Aslani, Apr. 12, 1994; children from previous marriage: Adrian, Roya, Shadawn. BS in Engring., Portland State U., 1967, MS in Engring., 1971. Registered profl. engr., Oreg., Ga., Ala., Tenn., Miss., Maine, Va., Tex., Fla., Md., Ark. Project mgr. Swan Wooster, Portland, Oreg., 1973-78; v.p., mgr. Swan Wooster, Atlanta, 1978-86; v.p., gen. mgr. Sandwell, Inc. USA, Atlanta, 1986—, also bd. dirs.; pres. VEP Assocs. (subs. Sandwell Inc.). Mem. Cons. Engrs. Assn., Brookfield Country Club. Republican. Office: Sandwell Inc USA 2690 Cumberland Pky NW Atlanta GA 30339-3913

ZARIN, JERALD LAWRENCE, pediatrician, physician executive; b. N.Y.C., Feb. 21, 1942; s. Emanuel B. and Esther Feldman Zarin; m. Aileen Carole Singer, May 24, 1970; children: Jason, Randall, Marni. BS, Rensselaer Poly. Inst., 1962; MD, Albert Einstein Coll. Medicine, 1966; MBA, Houston Bapt. U., 1988. Diplomate Am. Bd. Pediatrics, Nat. Bd. Med. Examiners. Intern in pediatrics U. Hosps. Cleve., 1966-67, resident in pediatrics, 1967-69; pvt. practice Houston, 1971—; pres. Inwood Pediatric Assocs., Houston, 1978—; med. dir. Tex. Children's Health Plan, Houston, 1996—; asst. clin. prof. pediatrics Baylor Coll. Medicine, Houston, 1976—. Maj. USAF, 1969-71. Fellow Am. Acad. Pediatrics; mem. AMA, ACP Execs., Tex. Med. Assn., Tex. Pediatric Soc., Houston Pediatric Soc. Home: 12330 Boheme Dr Houston TX 77024-4902 Office: Tex Childrens Health Plan PO Box 301011 1919 S Braeswood Blvd Houston TX 77030

ZARZAR, NAKHLEH PACIFICO, psychiatrist; b. Bethlehem, Palestine, Jan. 21, 1932; came to U.S., 1956; s. Pacifico and Anita Zarzar; m. Doris Azzam, Sept. 22, 1957; children: Michael, Nicholas, David. BA, Am. U. Beirut, 1952, MD, 1956. Diplomate Am. Bd. Psychiatry and Neurology. Clin. dir. family sect. John Umstead Hosp., Butner, N.C., 1959-62, clin. dir., dir. tng., 1962-63, supt., 1964-68; interim supt. Dorothea Dix Hosp., Raleigh, N.C., 1966; regional commr. N.C. Dept. Mental Health, Raleigh, 1966-73, dir., 1973-77; pvt. practice Raleigh, 1971-73, 76—; adj. prof. U. N.C., Chapel Hill, 1959—; cons. NIMH, Washington, 1971-77, Vance County Mental Health, Henderson, N.C., 1977-93; lectr. Duke U., Durham, N.C., 1976—. Chmn. Commn. on Mental Health and Human Svcs., So. Regional Edn. Bd., 1977; chair sr. citizens com. Rotary Club West Raleigh, 1991-93. Recipient Spl. award N.C. Mental Health Assn., 1976, N.C. Psychiat. Assn., 1990, Christan Holloman award Raleigh Rotary Club, 1966. Fellow Am. Psychiat. Assn. (life); mem. AMA, N.C. Med. Assn., So. Psychiat. Assn. Home: 4727 Wedgewood St Raleigh NC 27612-5702 Office: Glenwood Psychiat Assn 5711 Six Forks Rd Ste 200 Raleigh NC 27609

ZAUNER, CHRISTIAN WALTER, university dean, exercise physiologist, consultant; b. Phila., July 21, 1930; s. Philip Walter and Margaret Helen (Gilmor) Z.; m. Betty Ann Schwenk, Feb. 1, 1957; children: Beth, Ward, Joe. BS, West Chester State, 1956; MS, Syracuse U., 1957; PhD, So. Ill. U., 1963. Asst. prof. Temple U., Phila., 1963-65; prof. phys. edn. and medicine U. Fla., Gainesville, 1965-84; dir. Sports Medicine Inst., Mt. Sinai Med. Ctr., Miami Beach, Fla., 1984-87; chmn. exercise sci. Oreg. State U., Corvallis, 1987-94; dean health and human performance East Carolina U., Greenville, N.C., 1994—; cons. in exercise rehab. Hosp. Corp. Am.; cons. in sports medicine State of Kuwait, Arab Gulf; cons. sport sci. curriculum Ministry Edn., Thailand. Contbr. numerous articles to various profl. jours. Served with USN, 1951-54. Grantee U. Fla., 1971, Am. Scandinavian Foun., 1971, Fla. Blue Key, 1978, Nat. Acad. Sci., 1985-86, 88, 90, 94. Fellow Am. Coll. Sports Medicine; mem. Am. Physiol. Soc., N.Y. Acad. Scis., AAHPERD, Sigma Chi. Democrat. Roman Catholic. Office: East Carolina U Sch Health & Human Performance Greenville NC 27858-4353

ZBIEGIEN, ANDREA, religious education educator, consultant, educational administrator; b. Berea, Ohio, May 12, 1944; d. Leopold and Anna Meri (Voskovich) Z. BS in Edn., St. John Coll., 1969; MS in Edn., John Carroll U., 1973; MDiv, Grad. Theol. Union, 1986, D of Ministry, 1988. Tchr. jr. high sch. Diocese of Cleve., 1964-76, instr. dept. religious edn., 1971-82, dir. religious edn., 1976-82; diocesan dir. religious edn. Diocese of Toledo, 1982-87; instr. Dept. Christian Formation Diocese of Savannah, Ga., 1987—; dir. religious edn. Diocese of Savannah, 1987—; substitute tchr., Cleve., also Brunswick, Ga., 1976—; cons. Benziger Pub. co., Ohio, 1971-78, Our Sunday Visitor Pubs., 1978-90, Silver, Burdett & Ginn, Savannah, Charleston, St. Augustine, 1988—; adj. prof. St. John U. Grad. Theol. Sem., summers 1978—. Author: RCIA: Parish Team Formation, 1987; producer, author: (videos) RCIA: Parish Team Formation, 1987; contbr. articles to profl. jours. Facilitator Bishop's Task Force Action for a Change, Cleve., 1969-72; advocate, facilitator Systematic Techniques of Effective Parenting, Huron County, Ohio, 1982-87; advocate Commn. on Children and Youth, Glynn County, Ga., 1989—; vol. Medicine for World's Poor. Recipient scholarship KC, Cleve., 1961-69. Mem. AAUW, ASCD, YWCA, Nat. Assn. of Pastoral Coords. and Dirs., Nat. Cath. Edn. Assn., Sisters for Christian Cmty., Ind. Order of Foresters, Golden Isles Fiberarts Guild. Home: 707A Newcastle St Brunswick GA 31520-8012 Office: SFX Christian Formation Ctr 1116 Richmond St Brunswick GA 31520-7545

ZEANAH, ROBERT CLYDE, principal; b. Scottsboro, Ala., Apr. 15, 1951; s. Clyde Martin and carolyn Eulaine (McCracker) Z.; m. Hope Miller Zeanah; children: John Robert, Samuel Jefferson. BS in Edn., Auburn U., 1974, EdD, 1986; M in Edn., U. West Fla., 1977. Tchr. Troop County Schs., LaGrange, Ga., 1974, Escambia County Schs., Pensacola, Fla., 1974-78, Auburn (Ala.) City Schs., 1978-79; prin. Eufaula (Ala.) City Schs., 1979-89, Gulf Shores (Ala) Elem. Sch., 1989—; cons. Auburn Ctr. for Coop. Ednl. Leadership, 1983—, Ala. Adminstrv. Incentive Pay Plan Task Force, Montgomery, 1985—, Leader 1,2,3; mem. Ala. State Dept. of Edn. Task Force for Excellence in Sch. Adminstrn., 1988—. Contbr. articles to profl. jours. Div. chmn. Eufaula United Way, 1980-83, bd. dirs. 1982-84; v.p. Gulf Coast Arts Coun. Named Tchr. of Yr. Ferry Pass (Fla.) Elem. Sch., 1979. Mem. ACA, Nat. Assn. Elem. Sch. Prins., Ala. Assn. Elem. Sch. Adminstrs. (pres. 1986-88, Disting. Prin. Dist. 8 1987), Ala. Coun. Sch. Adminstrn. and Supervision, Internat. Reading Assn., Barbour County Naturalist Club, Gulf Coast Arts Coun. (pres.), Rotary. Democrat. Methodist. Home: 404 Camelia Cir Gulf Shores AL 36542-3049 Office: Gulf Shores Elem Sch PO Box 1339 Gulf Shores AL 36547-1339

ZEDIK, ROBERT JOHN, food scientist, consultant; b. Rochester, N.Y., Aug. 27, 1960; s. Robert, Sr. and Marilyn Joy (Warner) Z. BS, U. Mass., 1982; MS, Tex. A&M U., 1985. Quality assurance mgr. Southland Corp., Dallas, 1985-86; quality control tech. Frito Lay, Inc., Dallas, 1986-87; group leader H.V. shustek, Quincy, Mass., 1987-89; dir. tech. svcs. Nat. Confectioner Assn., McLean, Va., 1989—. Mem. Inst. of Food Technologists (treas. 1993-95, chair-elect D.C. sect. 1995). Roman Catholic. Home: 1137 Roaring Springs Rd Fort Worth TX 76114

ZEEMAN, JOAN JAVITS, writer, inventor; b. N.Y.C., Aug. 17, 1928; d. Benjamin Abraham and Lily (Braxton) Javits; m. John Huibert Zeeman III, Mar. 20, 1954; children: Jonathan Huibert, Andrea Zeeman Deane, Eloise Zeeman Scharff, Phoebe Zeemon Fitch, Merrily Margaret. BA, Vassar Coll., 1949; MEd, U. Vt., 1976. Pub. relations exec. Benjamin Sonnenberg, N.Y.C., 1949-51; freelance writer, 1952—. Trustee Theatreworks (formerly Performing Arts Repertory Theatre), N.Y.C., 1953-83, Profl. Childrens Sch., N.Y.C., 1980-89, Palm Beach Sch. Arts Found., 1993—, Fla. Theatrical Assn., 1994—. Author: The Compleat Child, 1964. Lyricist musical plays: Young Abe Lincoln, 1961; Hotel Passionato, 1965; Author, lyricist: Young Columbus, 1992; song lyricist: Santa Baby, 1953. Patentee Alphacube. Mem. ASCAP, Dramatists Guild, Gilbert and Sullivan Soc., Vassar Club (sec. 1978-84, v.p. 1984-86) (Westchester, N.Y.). Home: 230 Palmo Way Palm Beach FL 33480-3135

ZEHL, OTIS GEORGE, optical physicist; b. Elizabeth, N.J., July 9, 1946; s. Otis George and Elizabeth Theresa (Blehart) Z.; m. Ellen Mayo Hummel, May 18, 1985; 1 child, Elizabeth. BA in Physics with high honors, Rutgers U., 1968; PhD in Physics, U. Md., 1978. Teaching asst. grad. physics lab. U. Md., College Park, Md., 1971-73; doctoral rsch. asst. solid state physics U. Md., Md., 1973-78; sr. scientist Amecom Litton Systems, Md., 1979-91; sr. optical physicist Sachs Freeman Assn., Landover, Md., 1991-95; cons., 1995—; dir. Planning Design Implementation, Inc., Vienna, Va., 1987-92. Contbr. articles to profl. jours. Dir. Rosslyn Children's Ctr., Arlington, Va., 1991—. With U.S. Army, 1969-71. Supporter Friends of the Libraries-Rutgers, 1991—. Home: 10113 Windy Knoll Ln Vienna VA 22182-1542

ZEIGLER, ANN DEPENDER, lawyer; b. Spokane, Wash., June 7, 1947; d. F. Norman and Dorothy (Wolter) dePender; m. Paul Stewart Zeigler, June 20, 1970; 1 child, Kate Elizabeth. BA magna cum laude, Ft. Wright Coll. Holy Names, Spokane, 1969; MFA in Creative Writing, U. Mont., 1975; JD, U. Houston, 1984. Bar: Tex. Course adminstr. legal communications U. Houston, 1982-84; assoc. Dula, Shields & Egbert, 1984-87; ind. project atty., 1987; assoc. Dow, Cogburn & Friedman, 1987-90; assoc. bankruptcy sect./avoidance litigation Hughes, Watters & Askanase, Houston, 1990—. Coeditor: Insurance Guide-Arts Nonprofits, 1993, Basic Issues in Estate Planning-Representing the Artist, 1994; contbr. articles to legal jours. Mem. publs. com., writer Tex. Accts. and Lawyers for Arts, Houston, 1988—; mem. Supreme Ct. of Tex. Unauthorized Practice of Law Com., Houston; vol. Houston Lawyers for Hunger Relief, 1988-90. Mem. ABA, State Bar Tex. (internat. law sect. profl. practice com.), Houston Bar Assn. (chair law and the arts com. 1996—), Can. Bar Assn., Phi Alpha Delta. Democrat. Home: 4038 Cheena Dr Houston TX 77025-4702 Office: Hughes Watters & Askanase 1415 Louisiana St Fl 37 Houston TX 77002-7360

ZEIGLER, JEANINE BAHRAM PATTON, guidance counselor; b. Chgo., Nov. 9, 1928; d. Lester H. and Florence (Toney) Bahram; m. Daniel J. Patton, Jr. (dec.); children: Daniel J., Deborah J., Denise J.; m. Lamar Henry Zeigler, June 19, 1971. BA, Mich. State U., 1965, MA, 1969. Lic. profl. counselor; nat. cert. counselor. Successively elem. tchr., sch. social worker, elem. sch. prin. Battle Creek (Mich.) pub. schs., 1965-77; guidance counselor So. U., New Orleans, 1977—, asst. prof., 1983—, dean jr. divsn., 1994—; chmn. bd. dirs. Bethany Day Care Ctr., New Orleans, 1978—; hon. chmn. Battle Creek Cancer Crusade, 1976; bd. dirs. Y Ctr., Battle Creek, 1974-77; role model YWCA, New Orleans, 1989, v.p., bd. dirs., Greater New Orleans, 1991, pres. bd. dirs., 1993—; mem. Friend of Odyssey House. Recipient various svc. awards. Mem. ASCD, APGA, AAUW (pres. Battle Creek br. 1974-76, membership v.p. La. divsn. 1981—, pres. New Orleans br. 1984-86, nat. membership com., pres. La. divsn. 1986), NAFE, LACADA, Nat. Acad. Advising Assn., Am. Assn. Non-White Concerns, Am. Coll. Pers. Assn., Am. Assn. Counseling and Devel., Am. Assn. Multicultural Counseling Devel. (v.p. membership divsn. 1981-83, pres. La. divsn. 1987—), La. Assn. Coll. and Univ. Student Personnel Adminstrs., La. Assn. Counseling and Devel., Urban League, Nat. Coun. Negro Women (bd. dirs.), Moneychangers Investment Club (pres. 1981—), Women in the Forefront, Crescent City Links, Inc., Nat. Smart Set Club, Internat. Y Men's Club, Delta Sigma Theta. Methodist. Office: 6400 Press Dr New Orleans LA 70126-1009

ZEILE, FRED CARL, oceanographer, meteorologist; b. Phila., Nov. 3, 1950; s. Fred Carl Jr. and Catherine Elizabeth (Wolfrum) Z.; children: Kirche Leigh, Alicia Elizabeth; m. Ingrid Elizabeth Leyrer, Dec. 17, 1988. BS in Oceanography, U.S. Naval Acad., 1973; MS in Meteorology and Oceanography, Naval Postgrad. Sch., 1979; MA in Nat. Security & Strategic Studies, Naval War Coll., 1991. Commd. ensign USN, 1973, advanced through grades to comdr., 1988; meteorologist USS Inchon, Norfolk, Va., 1979-81; oceanography instr. U.S. Naval Acad., Annapolis, Md., 1981-83; commanding officer Oceanographic Unit 4 USNS Chauvenet, Indonesia, 1984-85; dep. asst. chief staff for emerging systems Comdr. Naval Oceanography Command, Stennis Space Center, Miss., 1987-90; commanding officer Naval Oceanography Command Facility, Keflavik, Iceland, 1990-92; tactical oceanography br. head Office of Oceanographer of Navy, Washington, 1992-93; bus. area mgr. Analysis & Technology, Inc., Bay St. Louis, Miss., 1993—. Mem. VWF (life), Am. Meteorol. Soc., Marine Tech. Soc. (chmn. Gulf Coast chpt. 1994), Masons (master Mason), Sigma Xi. Republican. Lutheran. Home: 101 Brushfire Ln Slidell LA 70458-5567 Office: Analysis & Tech Inc 321 Shieldsboro Sq Bay Saint Louis MS 39520-2823

ZEISLER, DENNIS J., music educator; b. Columbus, Ga., Jan. 25, 1947; s. Kasriel and Frances (Fleishman) Z.; m. Kathleen Perrin, Sept. 7, 1974 (div. Mar. 1985); children: Nathaniel William, Jennifer Edith, Sarah Mallory, Jeffrey Daniel; m. Carol Corcoran, June 20, 1987. BM, BME, U. Mich., 1970, MM, 1971; postgrad., NYU, 1987—; pvt. study, Mozarteum, Salzburg, Austria, 1972, 76; pvt. study clarinet, Rudolf Jettel, 1972, 76; pvt. study chamber music, Antonio Janegro, 1976. Clarinet tchg. fellow U. Mich., Ann Arbor, 1969-71; tchg. asst., asst. band dir. NYU, N.Y.C., 1975-76; asst. prof., dir. bands, studio woodwinds Augusta (Ga.) Coll., 1976-77, Ft. Lewis Coll., Durango, Colo., 1977-79; assoc. prof., dir. bands, prof. clarinet/saxophone Old Dominion U., Norfolk, Va., 1979—, chmn. dept. music, 1992—, chmn. music dept. Gov.'s Magnet Sch. Arts, 1984-86; prin. clarinet tchr. Blue Lake Fine Arts Camp, Twin Lake, Mich., 1983—; vis. asst. prof., dir. bands Spring semester Coll. William and Mary, Williamsburg, Va., 1984; prin. clarient U. Mich. Symphony Band, Ann Arbor, 1965-71, Augusta Symphony, 1976-77, Animas Chamber Music Festival, Durango, Colo., 1978-80, Va. Beach Pops, 1983-91, Blue Lake Fine Arts Camp, 1983-96, Am. Chamber Orch., 1984; prin. clarinet/asst. condr. Tidewater Winds, Norfolk, Va., 1985-94; mem. The Va. Saxophone Quartet, 1987—, others; numerous solo and chamber music recitals including Old Dominion U., 1979—, Norfolk Chamber Consort, 1983, 86, 89, 91, Va. Symphony Chamber Players, 1986, 88, 93, Longwood Coll. Chamber Music Series/Va. Saxophone Quartet, 1996, numerous others; numerous wind ensemble performances Old Dominion U.; condr. Va. Symphony, Va. Symphony Pops, Va. Symphony Youth Orch., numerous others; cons./adjudicator in field; external evaluator Syracuse U., 1988, Va. Commonwealth U., 1990, Marshall U., 1995; cons. Gov.'s Magnet Sch. for the Arts, 1984-90. Recordings include: (sound track) Another Life, 1980-82, The Revelli Years, 1980-83, Band Classics, 1995, others. Mem. Va. Coalition for the Arts, 1992—; chmn. orch. com. The Va. Beach Pops, 1983-91; youth svcs. com. Va. Symphony, 1991-96; adv. bd. Young Audiences, 1992-96. Mem. Nat. Band Assn. (Va. state chair 1996—), Coll. Band Dirs. Nat. Assn. (So. Divsn. pres. 1993-95, state chair 1983-91), Internat. Clarinet Soc. (state chair 1982—), Music Educators Nat. Conf., N.Am. Saxophone Alliance, Va. Music Educators Assn. (coll. sect. pres. 1990-92), Coun. of Arts Adminstrs. in Va. Higher Edn. (sec.-treas., pres. elect 1995), Coll. Band Dirs. Nat. Assn. (exec. com. 1993-95), Phi Beta Mu, Phi Mu Alpha, Pi Kappa Lambda. Democrat. Jewish. Home: 411 Kingsley Ln Norfolk VA 23505 Office: Old Dominion University Dept Music Norfolk VA 23529

ZEISSIG, HILMAR RICHARD, oil and gas executive; b. Berlin, Germany, June 29, 1938; came to U.S., 1978; s. Richard W. and Sigrid (Von Knauer) Z.; m. Heidi Harlandt, Sept. 6, 1967 (div. Oct. 1982); m. Ria M. Lobert, Oct. 4, 1983; children: Philipp, Richard, Isabel, Alexander. Student, U. Kiel, Fed. Republic Germany, 1959-60, U. Lausaunne, Switzerland, 1961; JD, U. Bonn, Fed. Republic Germany, 1964; PhD, U. Cologne, Fed. Republic Germany, 1969. Rsch. assoc. UN Econ. Commn. for Latin Am. and the Carribean, Santiago, Chile, 1965-66; legal advisor Export Industry Assn., Hamburg, Fed. Republic Germany, 1967-69; corp. counsel Gelsenberg A.G., Essen, Fed. Republic Germany, 1970; chief negotiator Deminex Oil Co., Dusseldorf, Fed. Republic Germany, 1971-73; gen. mgr. Deminex Peru, Lima, 1973-75, Deminex Egypt, Cairo, 1976-77; pres., chief exec. officer Lingen Oil & Gas Inc., Houston, 1978-84; chmn., pres. Houston Internat. Bus. Corp., 1982—; exec. v.p., dir. Natural Res. Group, Inc., Houston, 1985-94; officer, bd. dirs. Control Ambiental Integral S.A. de C.V., Mexico City, 1992—; U.S. rep. Prakla-Seismos AG Germany, Houston, 1986-92; energy cons. Econ. Commn. for Latin Am. and Caribbean, UN, Interam. Devel. Bank, Mex. and Cen. Am., 1986—; environ. cons. to govts., Germany and Mex., 1989—. Author ann. study on C.Am. energy problems, 1986—. Bd. dirs. German-Peruvian C. of C., Lima, 1973-75; active Econ. Devel. Com., Sugar Land, Tex., 1990-93. Mem. Ibero Am. Verein Hamburg, Houston C. of C. (chmn. various coms. 1980-86), Houston World Trade Assn. (bd. dirs. 1980—), German Am. C. of C. (bd. dirs. 1979—, chmn. 1993-95), Rotary (chmn. group study exch. dist. 5890 1986—). Home: 823 Alhambra Ct Sugar Land TX 77478-4003 Office: Houston Internat Bus Corp 2825 Wilcrest Dr Ste 550 Houston TX 77042-3358

ZEKAUSKAS, SUSAN B., nursing educator; b. Cedar Falls, Iowa, July 26, 1945; d. George Ernst and Dolly Mae (Brown) Behrenfeld; children: Leslie, Suzanne, R. Andrew. BSN, U. Okla., 1968; MSN in Pediat. Nursing, Yale U., 1975, PNP, 1975. Instr., pediatric nurse practitioner Yale U., New Haven, Conn., 1975-76; pediatric endocrine nurse practitioner Children's Med. Ctr., Tulsa, 1987—; asst. prof. Tulsa Cmty. Coll. Author: Pathophysiology The Basis for Disease, 1995; (with others) Essentials of Pediatrics, 1992, 3d edit., 195, Nursing Care of Infants and Children, 5th edit., 1993; contbr. articles to profl. jours. Named Outstanding Young Women Am. Mem. Sigma Theta Tau. Home: 2121 E 25 Pl Tulsa OK 74114

ZELBY, LEON WOLF, electrical engineering educator, consulting engineer; b. Sosnowiec, Poland, Mar. 26, 1925; came to U.S., 1946, naturalized, 1951; s. Herszel and Helen (Wajnryb) Zylberberg; m. Rachel Kupfermintz, Dec. 28, 1954; children: Laurie Susan, Andrew Stephen. BSEE, Moore Sch. Elec. Engring., 1956; MS, Calif. Inst. Tech., 1957; PhD, U. Pa., 1961. Registered profl. engr., Pa., Okla. Mem. staff RCA, Hughes R & D Labs., Lincoln Lab., MIT, Sandia Corp., Argonne (Ill.) Nat. Labs., Inst. for Energy Analysis; mem. faculty U. Pa., 1959-67, assoc. prof., 1964-67; assoc. dir. plasma engring. Inst. Direct Energy Conversion, 1962-67; prof. U. Okla., Norman, 1967-95, dir. Sch. Elec. Engring., 1967-95; ret., 1995; cons. RCA, 1961-67, Moore Sch. Elec. Engring., 1967-68, also pvt. firms. Editor Tech. and Soc. mag., 1990-93; contbr. articles on energy-associated problems and issues to profl. jours. With AUS, 1946-47. Cons. Electrodynamic Corp. fellow Calif. Inst. Tech., 1957, Mpls.-Honeywell fellow U. Pa., 1957-58, Harrison fellow, 1958. Mem. IEEE, Franklin Inst., Sigma Xi, Tau Beta Pi, Eta Kappa Nu, Pi Mu Epsilon, Sigma Tau, Phi Kappa Phi. Home: 1009 Whispering Pines Dr Norman OK 73072-6912

ZELBY, RACHEL, realtor; b. Sosnowiec, Poland, May 6, 1930; came to U.S., 1955; d. Herschel Kupfermintz and Sarah Rosenblatt; m. Leon W. Zelby, Dec. 28, 1954; children: Laurie Susan, Andrew Stephen. Student, U. Pa., 1955, Realtors' Inst., Norman, Okla., 1974; grad., Realtors Inst., Oklahoma City, 1978. Lic. realtor, broker, Okla.; cert. residential specialist, Okla. Realtor, broker, ptnr. Realty World Norman Heritage, 1973-81; realtor, broker Century 21 Parker Real Estate, Norman, 1981—, residential specialist, 1986—. Mem. Jr. Svc. League, Norman, 1980—; charter mem. Assistance League Norman, 1970—; bd. dirs. Juvenile Svcs., Inc., Norman, 1975-76; bd. viss. Coll. Fine Arts U. Okla., 1992—. Mem. Nat. Assn. Realtors, Norman Bd. Realtors, Women's Coun. Realtors (treas. 1985), U. Okla. Women's Assn. (past pres.), Norman C. of C., LWV. Home: 1009 Whispering Pines Dr Norman OK 73072-6912 Office: Century 21 Parker Real Estate 319 W Main St Norman OK 73069-1312

ZELDES, ILYA MICHAEL, forensic scientist, lawyer; b. Baku, Azerbaidjan, USSR, Mar. 15, 1933; came to U.S., 1976; s. Michael B. and Pauline L. (Ainbinder) Z.; m. Emma S. Kryss, Nov. 5, 1957; 1 child, Irina Zeldes Rieser. JD, U. Azerbaidjan, Baku, 1955; PhD in Forensic Scis., U. Moscow, 1969. Expert-criminalist Med. Examiner's Bur., Baku, 1954-57; rsch. assoc. Criminalistics Lab., Moscow, 1958-62; sr. rsch. assoc. All-Union Sci. Rsch. Inst. Forensic Expertise, Moscow, 1962-75; chief forensic scientist S.D. Forensic Lab., Pierre, 1977-93; owner Forensic Scientist's Svcs., Pierre, 1977-93. Author: Physical-Technical Examination, 1968, Complex Examination, 1971, The Problems of Crime, 1981; contbr. numerous articles to profl. publs. in Australia, Austria, Bulgaria, Can., Eng., Germany, Holland, India, Ireland, Israel, Rep. of China, Taiwan, U.S. and USSR. Mem. Internat. Assn. Identification (rep. S.D. chpt. 1979-93, chmn. forensic lab. analysis subcom. 1991-97), Assn. Firearm and Tool Mark Examiners (emeritus). Home: 5735 Foxlake Dr Apt 1 Fort Myers FL 33917-5661

ZELENY, MARJORIE PFEIFFER (MRS. CHARLES ELLINGSON ZELENY), psychologist; b. Balt., Mar. 31, 1924; d. Lloyd Armitage and Mable (Willian) Pfeiffer; BA, U. Md., 1947; MS, U. Ill., 1949, postgrad., 1951-54; m. Charles Ellington Zeleny, Dec. 11, 1950 (dec.); children: Ann Douglas, Charles Timberlake. Vocational counseling psychologist VA, Balt., 1947-48; asst. U. Ill. at Urbana, 1948-50, research asso. Bur. Research, 1952-53; chief psychologist dept. neurology and psychiatry Ohio State U. Coll. Medicine, Columbus, 1950-51; research psychologist, cons., Tucson, Washington, 1954—. Mem. Am., D.C. psychol. assns., AAAS, Southeastern Psychol Assn., DAR, Nat. Soc. Daus. Colonial Wars, Nat. Soc. Colonial Dames XVII Century, Nat. Soc. Descendants of Early Quakers, Nat. Soc. Daus. of Am. Colonists, Nat. Soc. Dames of Ct. of Honor, Nat. Soc. U.S. Daus. of 1812, Mortar Bd., Delta Delta Delta, Sigma Delta Epsilon, Psi Chi, Sigma Tau Epsilon. Roman Catholic. Home: 6825 Wemberly Way Mc Lean VA 22101-1534

ZELINSKI, JOSEPH JOHN, engineering educator, consultant; b. Glen Lyon, Pa., Dec. 30, 1922; s. John Joseph and Lottie Mary (Oshinski) Z.; m. Mildred G. Sirois, July 22, 1946; children: Douglas John, Peter David. BS,

Pa. State U., 1944, PhD, 1950. Grad. fellow Pa. State U., University Park, 1946-50; project supr. applied physics lab. Johns Hopkins U., Silver Spring, Md., 1950-58; staff scientist Space Tech. Labs. (now TRW, Inc.), Redondo Beach, Calif., 1958-60; head chem. tech. div. Ops. Evaluation Group MIT, Cambridge, 1960-62; prin. rsch. scientist Avco Everett (Mass.) Rsch. Lab., 1962-64; prof. mech. engring. Northeastern U., Boston, 1964-85, prof. emeritus, 1985—; pres. World Edn. Resources, Ltd., Tampa, Fla., 1984—; cons. Avco Everett Rsch. Lab., 1964-71, Pratt & Whitney Aircraft, East Hartford, Conn., 1966-70, Modern Electric Products and Phys. Scis. Co., Inc., Boston, 1980-82, Morrison, Mahoney and Miller, Boston, 1984; vice-chmn., chmn. exec. com. Univ. Grad. Coun., Northeastern U., Boston, 1980-84, dir. mech. engring. grad. program, 1982-85; del. 4th World Conf. Continuing Engring. Edn., Beijing China People to People, Spokane, Wash., 1989. Contbr. articles to profl. jours. Prin. Confraternity Christian Doctrine, Andover, Mass., 1961-64; pres. Andover Edn. Coun., 1962-64; vice chmn. Dem. Town Com., Boxford, Mass., 1980-84. Lt. (j.g.) USNR, 1943-46, PTO. Mem. AAAS, ASME, Am. Chem. Soc., N.Y. Acad. Scis., Combustion Inst. Democrat. Roman Catholic. Home: Hunters Green 9207 Jubilee Ct Tampa FL 33647-2511

ZELLER, MICHAEL EUGENE, lawyer; b. Queens, N.Y., June 19, 1967; s. Hans Ludwig and Geri Ann (Schottenstein) Z. BA, Union Coll., 1989; JD, Temple Law Sch., 1992; LLM magna cum laude, U. Hamburg, Germany, 1994. Bar: N.Y. 1992, U.S. Dist. Ct. (so. and ea. dists.) N.Y. 1995, N.C. 1996. Fgn. intern Bryan Gonzalez Vargas y Gonzalez Baz, Mexico City, 1990; student law clerk Hon. Jane Cutler Greenspan, Phila., 1990-91; fgn. clerk DROSTE, Hamburg, 1991, fgn. assoc., translator, 1992-94; freelance translator Charlotte, N.C., 1995—; assoc. Internat. and Corp. Law Group of Moore & Van Allen PLLC, Charlotte, 1995—; vol. atty. Children's Law Ctr. Mem. Charlotte World Affairs Coun., Charlotte Mayor's Internat. Cabinet; bd. dirs. Alemannia Soc. Recipient scholarship Fedn. German/Am. Clubs, 1987. Mem. ABA, N.Y. State Bar Assn., N.C. Bar Assn., Mecklenburg County Bar Assn., Gewerblicher Rechtsschutz und Urheberrecht e.V., European Am. Bus. Forum, Am. Translators Assn. Office: 100 N Tryon St Fl 47 Charlotte NC 28202-4003

ZELLER, RONALD JOHN, lawyer; b. Phila., Jan. 28, 1940; m. Lucille Bell; children: John, Kevin, Suzanne. BSBA, LaSalle Coll., 1964; JD, Ohio State U., 1967. Bar: Mich. 1968, Fla. 1971. Ptnr. Patton & Kanner, Miami, Fla., 1973-80, of counsel, 1980-89; pres., chief exec. officer Norwegian Cruise Lines, 1980-86; pres. Twenty First Century Mgmt. Group, Inc., Coconut Grove, Fla., 1986-90, Miami Voice Corp., 1990-92; gen. counsel Splty. Mgmt. Co., Delray Beach, Fla., 1992-93, pres., 1994-96; ptnr. Zeller & Keihner, Palm Beach, Fla., 1996—; dep. chmn. Cruise Lines Internat. Assoc., N.Y.C., 1981-85, chmn., 1986. Trustee United Way of Dade County, 1981-86; pres. Cath. Charities, Archdiocese of Miami 1976-78, Broward County, 1975-76, Excalibur Devel. Ctrs., Inc., 1973-75; mem. Citizens Bd. U. Miami; mem. exec. bd. New World Sch. of Arts, 1986-87, Centennial Campaign Com. Coll. of Law Ohio State U., 1982-92, Nat. Coun. Coll. of Law Ohio State U.; mem. Coun. Pres.'s Assocs., LaSalle U., 1982-87; mem. Postsecondary Edn. Planning Commn., State of Fla., 1986-87; mem. Cmty. Assns. Inst., 1995—. Mem. ABA, Fla. Bar Assn., Maritime Law Assn. (proctor in admiralty), Pres.' Club Ohio State U. Office: Zeller & Keinher LLP First Union Bank Bldg # 200 411 South County Rd Palm Beach FL 33430

ZELNICK, RONALD STUART, surgeon; b. N.Y.C., Dec. 6, 1958. BS, George Washington U., 1980; MD, Albany Med. Coll., 1984. Diplomate Am. Bd. Surgery, Am. Bd. Colon Rectal Surgery. Resident gen. surgery L.I. Jewish Hosp., New Hyde Park, N.Y., 1984-89; private practice Palm Beach Gardens, Fla., 1988—; fellowship colon and rectal surgery Henry Ford Hosp., Detroit, 1989-90. Fellow ACS, Am. Soc. Colon Rectal Surgeons; mem. Fla. Surg. Soc., Fla. Colon Rectal Surgery Soc. Office: 3385 Burns Rd Ste 200 Palm Beach Gardens FL 33410-4328

ZELSMANN, MICHAEL JOSEPH, advertising executive; b. Chgo., Sept. 19, 1942; s. Edgar Thomas and Jeanne (Burke) Z.; m. Sandra Marie LaMountain, Nov. 1, 1975; 1 child, Michael Jr. BBA, St. Edward's U., Austin, Tex., 1964. Media buyer McCann-Erickson, Chgo., 1964-69; advt. mgr. Weber Marking Systems, Arlington Heights, Ill., 1969-79; account exec. Bloom Agy., Dallas, 1979-80; account supr. Infocom Assocs., Dallas, 1980-82; advt. mgr. oil well divsn. U.S. Steel, Dallas, 1982-83; advt. mgr. Tucker Electronics, Garland, Tex., 1983-85; account supr. Lemons Communications Group, Irving, Tex., 1985-86; advt. mgr. def. group Tex. Instruments, Dallas, 1986-94, market comms. program mgr. personal computer products, 1994-95, mgr. Mixed Signal and Analog Products, 1995—. Served to capt. U.S. Army, 1965-68. Mem. Bus. Mktg. Assn. (bd. dirs. 1975-77, 83-85, treas. 1989-90, Dallas pres. 1990-91, S.W. regional v.p. 1991-93), KC (grand knight Plano chpt. 1963-64, 81). Republican. Roman Catholic. Office: Texas Instruments Inc 8505 Forest Ln Dallas TX 75243

ZEMAN, HERBERT DAVID, medical physicist; b. N.Y.C., Mar. 17, 1944; s. Mark Waldo and Adele (Cohen) Zemansky. AB magna cum laude, Oberlin Coll., 1965; MS, Stanford U., 1966, PhD, 1972. Fellow U. Muenster, Fed. Republic Germany, 1972-74; physicist SRI Internat., Menlo Park, Calif., 1974-76; rsch. assoc. Stanford U., Calif., 1976-78, sr. rsch. assoc., 1980-87; staff scientist Xerox Med. Systems, Palo Alto, Calif., 1978-80; med. physicist Nat. Synchroton Light Source Brookhaven Nat. Labs., Upton, N.Y., 1987-90; assoc. prof. biomed. engring. and radiology U. Tenn., Memphis, 1990—. Contbr. articles to profl. jours. Chmn. Charleston Meadows Neighborhood Orgn., Palo Alto, 1977-84; founder Palo Alto Coalition for Equal Rights, 1981; steering com. mem. Palo Alto Civic League, 1983-84; sec. AIDS/KS Found., Santa Clara County, 1983-84; second tenor Memphis Symphony Chorus, 1994—. Fellow NSF, Woodrow Wilson Found., Alexander von Humboldt Found. Mem. Am. Phys. Soc., Am. Assn. Physicists in Medicine, PFP Investment Club (sec. 1983-87), Phi Beta Kappa, Sigma Xi. Democrat. Jewish. Home: 1687 Peach Ave Memphis TN 38112 Office: UTMe Biomed Engin 899 Madison Ave Memphis TN 38103-3405

ZEMEL, DAVID MICHAEL, charitable organization administrator, human services educator; b. St. Louis, Feb. 16, 1949; s. Jack and Delores Mae (Aubuchon) Z.; m. Jane Mary Sandler, Jan. 14, 1973; children: Abby Sandler, Rebecca Clare. BS in Edn., U. Mo., 1971; MSW, Washington U., St. Louis, 1975. Tchr. Title I, St. James Schs., Mo., 1971-72; social worker II Boys Town Mo., St. James, 1972-75; program dir. St. Louis County Juvenile Court, 1975-79; dir. devel. Providence Program, Inc., St. Louis, 1979-80; devel. officer United Way Greater St. Louis, 1980-82, v.p., 1982-88; exec. officer United Way Bartholomew County, Ind., 1988-94; sr. program officer Donald W. Reynolds Found., Tulsa, 1995—; assoc. prof. human services St. Louis Community Coll., 1975-88; lectr. George Warren Brown Sch. Social Work, Washington U., 1987-88; cons. in field. Author tng. manuals on fundraising & mgmt. & planning. Mem. com. alternative edn. University City Schs., 1979-85; trainer United Way Mgmt. Assistance Ctr., St. Louis, 1980-88; mem. nat. profl. adv. com. Strategic Planning and Market Research, Nat. Acad. for Volunteerism, United Way Am., 1986-87; grad. Leadership St. Louis, 1987-88; bd. dirs. Confluence St. Louis, 1983-84, Boys Town Mo., St. Louis; mem. state adv. coun. Ind. Dept. Family & Children, 1992-94; Leadership Bartholomew County, 1989-91; mem. Cmty. Svc. Coun. Greater Tulsa, 1995. Mem. Nat. Soc. Fund Raising Execs. (chmn. legis. 1982-83), Washington U. Alumni Assn. (ann. program com.), Ind. Assn. United Ways (chmn. state staff conf. 1993, chmn. exec. roundtable 1994). Jewish. Home: 5510 E 110th Pl Tulsa OK 74137-7256 Office: Donald W. Reynolds Found 7130 S Lewis Ste 900 Tulsa OK 74136

ZEMEL, MICHAEL BARRY, nutritional physiologist; b. Newark, N.J., Apr. 6, 1954; s. Sylvan and Sylvia L. (Saffer) Z.; m. Paula Carney, Dec. 29, 1976; children: Abigail, Rachel. BS, U. Wis., 1976, MS, 1978, PhD, 1980. Asst. prof. nutrition and food sci. Wayne State U., Detroit, 1980-85, assoc. prof., 1985-90, assoc. prof. endocrinology and hypertension, 1985-90; rsch. biochemist VA Med. Ctr., Allen Park, Mich., 1987-91; prof., dept. head dept. nutrition U. Tenn., Knoxville, 1990—, prof. of medicine and physiology, 1990—. Patentee calcium fortification; contbr. articles to profl. jours. Grantee Nat. Dairy Coun., 1982, 84, 85-87, 87-89, 89-91, VA, 1987-90, 89-92, Marion Labs., 1989-90, Ciba Corp., 1987-88, Lederle Labs., 1987-89, Searle Pharms., 1987-89, 87-88, Sandoz Rsch. Inst., 1988-93, Princeton Pharms., 1990-91, Glaxo Pharms., 1990-91, Am. Heart Assn., 1991-93, 93-95. Fellow Coun. on High Blood Pressure Rsch.; mem. Am. Fedn. Clin. Rsch., Am. Inst. Nutrition, Am. Soc. Clin. Nutrition, Am. Soc. Hypertension, Endocrine Soc., Inter-Am. Soc. Hypertension, N.Y. Acad. Scis., Sigma Xi. Home: 328 E Heritage Dr Knoxville TN 37922-2744 Office: U Tenn 1215 Cumberland Ave # 229 Knoxville TN 37916-3905

ZEN, E-AN, research geologist; b. Peking, China, May 31, 1928; came to U.S., 1946, naturalized, 1963; s. Hung-chun and Heng-chi'h (Chen) Z. AB, Cornell U., 1951; MA, Harvard U., 1952, PhD, 1955. Research fellow Woods Hole Oceanographic Inst., 1955-56, research asso., 1956-58; asst. prof. U. N.C., 1958-59; geologist U.S. Geol. Survey, 1959-80, rsch. geologist, 1981-89; adj. rsch. prof. geology U. Md., 1990—; vis. assoc. prof. Calif. Inst. Tech., 1962; Crosby vis. prof. MIT, 1973; Harry H. Hess sr. vis. fellow Princeton U., 1981; counselor 28th Internat. Geol. Congress. 1986-89. Contbr. articles to profl. jours. Recipient Maj. John Coke medal Geol. Soc. London, 1992, Outstanding Contbn. to Pub. Understanding of Geology award Am. Geol. Inst., 1994, Thomas Jefferson medal Va. Mus. Natural History Found., 1996. Fellow AAAS, Am. Acad. Arts and Scis., Geol. Soc. Am. (councillor 1985-88, v.p. 1991, pres. 1992, Day medal 1986), Mineral. Soc. Am. (coun. 1975-77, pres. 1975-76, Roebling medal 1991); mem. NAS, Geol. Soc. Washington (pres. 1973), Mineral. Assn. Can. Office: U Md Dept Geology College Park MD 20742

ZENANKO, CARL MICHAEL, learning center educator; b. Little Rock, Ark., June 23, 1950; s. Carl and Mary Elizabeth (Womack) Z.; m. Marsha Anne McGowan, Aug. 4, 1982; children: Alexander Michael, Natasha Anne. BA in Humanities, Hendrix Coll., 1976; MEd in Sci. Edn., Vanderbilt, 1986. Cert. tchr. Tenn., Ark., Tex., Ala. Tchr. Perryville (Ark.) H.S., 1979-80, 86-89; tchr., coach Montgomery Bell Acad., Nashville, 1980-84; tchr. Plainview (Tex.) H.S., 1988-89; coord. supervision of multimedia instrnl. labs. Jacksonville (Ala.) State U., 1989—. Chief editor Standard Tutoring Newsletter, 1992-95. Pres. Kitty Stone Elem. PTA, 1994-95. Mem. Nat. Orgn. Tutoring (organizer 1992, mem. exec. bd., editor newsletter 1996-97). Home: 907 9th Ave NE Jacksonville AL 36265-1211

ZENG, ZHAO-BANG, geneticist, educator; b. Wuhan, China, Dec. 8, 1957; came to the U.S., 1986; s. Guangming and Yulan (Ni) Z.; m. Jia Ma, Sept. 9, 1983; 1 child, Jiemin. BS, Huazhong Agrl. U., 1981; PhD, U. Edinburgh, 1986. Asst. lectr. Huazhong Agrl. U., Wuhan, 1982-83; postdoctoral rsch. assoc. N.C. State U., Raleigh, 1986-90, vis. asst. prof., 1990-91, rsch. asst. prof., 1992-94; rsch. assoc. prof., 1994—; adj. prof. Hunzhong Agrl. U., Wuhan, China, 1995—. Assoc. editor Genetics, 1994—, Theoretical Population Biology, 1995—; contbr. articles and revs. to profl. jours. Grantee NIH, 1990—, NSF, 1993—, USDA, 1994—. Mem. Am. Soc. Genetics, Soc. for Study Evolution, Biometric Soc., Phi Kappa Phi, Sigma Xi. Home: 112 Kirkfield Dr Cary NC 27511-6815 Office: NC State U Dept Statistics Box 8203 Raleigh NC 27695

ZENKER, PAUL NICOLAS, epidemiologist, pediatrician, medical director; b. San Francisco, Oct. 4, 1953; s. Nicolas and Anne Marie (Gianni) Z.; m. Bernarda Marie Mullek, June 21, 1986; children: Kate, Nicolas. BS in Biology, U. Notre Dame, 1975; MD, U. Md., 1982; MPH, TM, Tulane U., 1987. Diplomate Am. Bd. Pediat., Am. Bd. Preventive Medicine. Resident in pediat. Tulane Med. Ctr./Charity Hosp., New Orleans, 1982-85, fellow pediatric infectious disease, 1986-88; chief resident pediat. La. State U. Med. Ctr., New Orleans, 1985-86; with epidemic intelligence svc. divsn. sexually transmitted diseases Ctrs. Disease Control and Prevention, Atlanta, 1988-90; med. epidemiologist Okla. State Dept. Health, Okla. City, 1990-91, state epidemiologist, 1991-93; asst. state health officer, pediat. cons., adv. coun. sexually transmitted diseases Ala. Dept. Pub. Health, Montgomery, 1993-95; med. dir. Franklin Meml. Primary Health Ctr., Mobile, Ala., 1995—; instr. H.S., country coord. UN Devel. Program, Peace Corps, Tonga, South Pacific, 1975-77; instr. Jemicy Sch. Dyslexic Children, Balt., 1978-79; clin. asst. prof. adolescent sect. Children's Meml. Hosp., Oklahoma City, 1991-93; clin. asst. prof. internal medicine and pediat. U. South Ala., 1995—; mem. ethics com. Charity Hosp., 1985-86; lectr. in field; presenter abstracts confs., assns., meetings. Contbr. articles to profl. jours. Fellow APHA, Am. Acad. Pediat. (adolescent medicine sect., epidemiology sect.), Am. Sexually Transmitted Disease, Pediat. Infectious Disease Soc., Physicians for Nat. Health Policy, Union of Concerned Scientists. Office: Franklin Meml Prim Hlth Ctr 1555 Springhill Ave PO Box 2048 Mobile AL 36652

ZEPEDA, ENRIQUE E., V, lawyer; b. Mexico City, June 20, 1963; came to U.S., 1993; s. Enrique and Rosalba (Vazquez) Z.; m. Silvia Ceballos, Jan. 22, 1994. JD, U. Nat. Autonoma de Mex., Mexico City, 1994. Cert. lawyer Ministry Edn. Mex. Assoc. gen. dir. Bufete Zepeda Trujillo, Mexico City, 1982-93; vice consul, assoc. legal attaché Office Atty. Gen. Mex., Consulate Gen. of Mex., San Antonio, 1993—. Office: Office Atty Gen Mex 100 W Houston St Ste 1441 San Antonio TX 78205

ZERFOSS, LESTER FRANK, management consultant, educator; b. Mountaintop, Pa., Nov. 2, 1903; s. Clinton and Mabel (Wilcox) Z.; B.A. cum laude, Pa. State U., 1926, M.Ed., 1934, Ed.D., 1958; m. Harriet Mildred Cary, Dec. 21, 1928 (dec. Dec. 1978); children—Patricia Ann (Mrs. Thomas Sibben), Clinton Cary, Robert Williamson; m. Irma J. Allen, July 12, 1980. Coll. tchr., pub. sch. adminstr., Pa., 1928-41; supr. design, devel. Gen. Motors Inst., 1942-46; head supervisory devel. Detroit Edison Co., 1946-52; corporate tng. dir. Am. Enka Corp. (N.C.), 1952-59, dir. indsl. relations, mgmt. services, 1959-66, mgmt. cons. tech., mgmt. devel., 1966-73; prof. psychology, dir. mgmt. devel. programs U. N.C. at Asheville, 1966-74, prof. mgmt. and developmental psychology, chmn. dept. mgmt., 1974-76 emeritus prof. mgmt., 1976—; pres. L.F. Zerfoss Assos., Inc., Mgmt. Consultants, 1976—; cons. on mgmt. devel. State of N.C. Mem. N.C. Personnel Bd., 1966-72, Southeastern Regional Manpower Adv. Com., 1966-71, N.C. Community Coll. Adv. Council, 1966—. Trustee, exec. bd., chmn. instructional com. Brevard Coll.; trustee Mountain Manpower Corp. Recipient Disting. Prof. award U. N.C., 1976. Mem. Am. Mgmt. Assn. (lectr. mgmt. devel. pres.'s assn.), Nat. Soc. Advancement Mgmt. (profl. mgr. citation 1962), Am. Soc. Tng. and Devel., Phi Delta Kappa (Disting. Service award 1982), Kappa Phi Kappa, Iota Alpha Delta, Kappa Delta Pi, Delta Sigma Phi. Contbg. author Training and Development Handbook, 1967, Management Handbook for Plant Engineers, 1978, Psychology in Action, 1978; author: Developing Professional Personnel in Business, Industry and Government, 1968, (with Irma Zerfoss) All God's Children Got Wings, 1988; contbr. to Personnel Administration in the Collegium, 1982; contbr. articles to profl. jours. Home and Office: 100 Cardinal Ct Simpsonville SC 29681-5807

ZERNER, MICHAEL CHARLES, chemistry and physics educator, consultant, researcher; b. Boston, Jan. 31, 1940; s. Maurice Bernard and Blanche (Deutsch) Z.; m. Anna Gunilla Fojerstam, May 5, 1966; children: Erik Mark, Emma Danielle. BS, Carnegie Mellon Inst., 1961; MA, Harvard U., 1962, PhD, 1966; postdoctoral U. Uppsala, (Sweden), 1968-70. Asst. prof. U. Guelph (Ont., Can.), 1970-74, assoc. prof., 1974-80, prof., 1980-82, adj. prof., 1982-87; prof. chemistry and physics U. Fla., Gainesville, 1981—, chmn. dept. chemistry, 1988-94; cons. in theoretical chemistry; co-organizer Internat. Sanibel Symposium on Theoretical Chemistry, 1983—. Served to capt. U.S. Army, 1966-68. Recipient cert. U.S. Army Materials Command, 1975, Humboldt prize, 1991-94, Achievement award Internat. Soc. Quantum Bio., 1986; named Fulbright Disting. Prof., 1987; NIH fellow, 1968-70; Grantee NSF, Nat. Sci. and Engring. Rsch. Coun. of Can., Office Naval Rsch. Fellow AAAS, Am. Inst. Physics; mem. Am. Chem. Soc., Sigma Xi, others. Patentee in photoconduction and polymer sci.; co-editor Procs. Internat. Conf. Quantum Chemistry and Internat. Conf. Quantum Biology and Pharmacology, 1978—; Internat. Congress Quantum Chemistry, 1983—; editor Adv. Quantum Chemistry; assoc. editor Internat. Jour. Quantum Chemistry; contbr. pubs. to profl. lit. Office: U Fla Dept Of Chemistry Gainesville FL 32611

ZEVNIK-SAWATZKY, DONNA DEE, litigation coordinator; b. Tulsa, Dec. 15, 1946; d. Robert Joseph Z. and Dorothy Dee (Robertson) Zink; m. Kenneth Sawatzky, May 30, 1965; children: K. Brian, Kaira D. Student, U. Ctrl. Okla., 1977, Okla. State U., 1984. Cert. AIDS educator, State of Okla. Sec. Farmers Ins. Co., Oklahoma City, 1974-80; office mgr. S.A.F.E., Inc., Oklahoma City, 1980-83; jr. acct. Southeast Exploration Corp., Oklahoma City, 1983-84; acct. Young Bros., Inc., Oklahoma City, 1984-88, The Denman Co., Inc., Oklahoma City, 1988-89; litigation coord. ACLU Okla., Oklahoma City, 1994—; bd. dirs. ACLU Okla., treas., 1994—. Author and illustrator: That Place--Otherwhere, 1994, Something for Otherwhere, 1995; author: At Our House, 1979-83; columnist Putnam City-N.W. News, Warr Acres, Okla., 1979-83; designer stage sets Miss Warr Acres Pageant, 1971-88. Bd. dirs. Miss Warr Acres (Okla.) Pageant, 1984-88, Warr Acres C. of C., 1981-85; treas. ACLU of Okla., 1995—, bd. dirs., 1994—; child welfare advocate Okla. State Dept. Human Svcs., Oklahoma City, 1987-89; coord. AIDS clinic Triangle Assn., Oklahoma City, 1994—. Named Honorary Mayor of Warr Acres, 1971, Super Citizen, 1973, Outstanding Vol. Okla. State Dept. Human Svcs., 1988; recipient Svc. award Warr Acres C. of C., 1979, Legis. Commendation State of Okla., 1988, numerous Okla. Newspaper Column of Month awards Okla. Press Assn., Oklahoma City, 1981-82. Mem. Amnesty Internat., The Interfaith Alliance, Pflag, Human Rights Campaign, Okla. Coalition to Abolish the Death Penalty. Republican. Methodist. Office: 3012 N Lee Ste A Oklahoma City OK 73103

ZHANG, JINGWU, immunologist; b. Shanghai, Feb. 2, 1956; arrived in Belgium, 1986; s. Yuzeng and Xiochin Zhang; m. Ying Chin, Feb. 19, 1986; children: Linda, Peter. MD, Shanghai (China) Med. U., 1984; DSc, U. Brussels, 1990. Lic. MD. Rsch. fellow Dr. Willems Inst., Diepenbeek, Belgium, 1986-90, head dept., 1990—; rsch. assoc. Harvard Med. Sch., Boston, 1991-92; vis. prof. Baylor Coll. Medicine, Houston, 1993; prof. Limburgs U. Ctr., Diepenbeek, 1994—, Shanghai Med. U., 1995. Contbr. articles to profl. jours.; patentee in field. Recipient Rsch. award Am. Multiple Slcerosis Soc., 1990, Achievement award Belgian Soc. Clin. Immunology, 1993, Internat. award Assn. Malattie Rare, 1994. Mem. AAAS, N.Y. Acad. Scis., European Immunology Fedn. Office: Baylor Coll Medicine Dept Neurology Houston TX 77030

ZHANG, XIAODONG, computer science educator and researcher; b. Beijing, China, July 16, 1958; came to the U.S., 1983; s. Min and Yishan (Jiang) Z.; m. Yan Meng, July 20, 1985; 1 child, Simon. BS, Beijing (China) Poly. U., 1982; MS, U. Colo., 1985, PhD, 1989. Rsch. asst. Beijing (China) Poly. U., 1982-83, Environ. Rsch. Lab., Boulder, Colo., 1983-85, U. Colo., Boulder, 1985-89; tech. staff Toplogix Inc., Denver, 1989; asst. prof. U. Tex., San Antonio, 1989-92, assoc. prof., 1993—, chair computer sci., 1993, dir. high performance computing and software lab., 1993—; vis. scientist Rice U., 1990-91; guest prof. Wuhan U., China; adv. panelist NSF, 1995, 96; program chair 4th Internat. Workshop on Modeling, Analysis and Simulation of Computer and Telecomm. Systems; keynote spkr. 8th Internat. Conf. on Parallel and Distributed Computer Sys., 1996. Co-author: Multiprocessor Performance, 1994; editor Jour. of Parallel Computing, 1994-95; contbr. articles to profl. jours. Recipient Disting. Rsch. Achievement award U. Tex., 1993, Best Paper award 9th Internat. Conf. on Supercomputing, 1995; grantee NSF, 1990—, Southwestern Bell, 1992—, USAF, 1993—, AFOSR, 1995—, ONR, 1995—. Mem. IEEE (sr.; chmn. tech. com. on supercomputing applications, disting. visitor), Assn. Computing Machinery (nat. lectr.), Soc. Indsl. and Applied Math. Office: U Tex Computer Sci San Antonio TX 78249

ZHAO, HONG, medicophysiologist; b. Beijing, Mar. 22, 1960; came to U.S., 1989; s. Suxing Zhao and Min Lin. MD, The Capital Inst. Medicine, Beijing, 1983. Physician Beijing Erlong Hosp., Beijing, 1983-89; rsch. fellow Southwestern Med. Ctr., Dallas, 1989—; product specialist, mktg. mgr. Global Health Rsch. Ctr., Beijing, 1985-87, v.p. mktg. and sales, 1987-89. Contbr. articles to profl. jours. Mem. China Med. Assn. Home: PO Box 12004 Dallas TX 75225-0004

ZHAO, JOHN QUANSHENG, political science educator; b. China, Jan. 9, 1949; came to U.S., 1981; BA in Internat. Politics, Peking U., China, 1981; MA in Polit. Sci., U. Calif., Berkeley, 1982, PhD in Polit. Sci., 1987. Tchg. and rsch. asst. U. Calif., Berkeley, 1981-85, 86-87; asst. prof. Cleve. State U., 1987-88; rsch. fellow East-West Ctr., Honolulu, 1989-90; Pacific Basin rsch. fellow Kennedy Sch. Govt. Harvard U., 1993-94; dir. inst. Asian studies, assoc. prof. polit. sci. Old Dominion U., Norfolk, Va., 1988-96; asso. prof. internat. svc. Am. U., Washington, 1996—; sr. rsch. assoc. Oxford U., 1984; vis. rsch. fellow U. Tokyo, 1985-86; adj. prof. polit. sci. U. Hawaii, 1990-91; peace fellow U.S. Inst. Peace, 1991; adj. assoc. prof. internat. politics Tufts U. Fletcher Sch. Law and Diplomacy, 1993-94; cons. McCutchen, Doyle, Brown & Enerson, San Francisco, Mitsui Trading Co., San Francisco; vis. assoc. prof. polit. sci. Hong Kong U. Sci. and Tech., 1994-95. Author: Japanese Policymaking: The Politics Behind Politics -- Informal Mechanisms and the Making of China Policy, 1993 (Outstanding Acad. Book award Choice 1994), Interpreting Chinese Foreign Policy: The Micro-Macro Linkage Approach, 1996; author (with others), editor: (with Robert Sutter) Politics of Divided Nations: China, Korea, Germany and Vietnam, 1991; author: (with others) Teaching at Berkeley, 1985, Chinese Intellectuals on Society, Politics, and Economy, 1988, Japan, China and the Newly Industrialized Economies of East Asia, 1989, Studies of Taiwan-Mainland China Relations, 1990, Modernization of Japan and China: Prospect for the 21st Century, 1990, State of the Pacific Basin, 1990, Politics of Divided Nations: China, Korea, Germany and Vietnam, 1991, Politics of Divided Nations: China, Korea, Germany and Vietnam, 1991, Japan's Foreign Aid: Power and Policy in a New Era, 1993, Great Policies: Strategic Innovations in Asia and the Pacific Basin, 1995, China Review, 1995, The United Nations and Keeping Peace in Northeast Asia, 1995; mem. editorial adv. bd. Am. Asian Review, 1992—; contbr. numerous articles to profl. jours. V.p. Va. Consortium Asian Studies, 1992-93. Grantee Asia Found., 1991-93, U. Calif., Berkeley, 1981, 83, 86-87, U. Mich., 1988, U. Chgo., 1988, Earlhart Found., 1989, Old Dominion U., 1989, 92, 95, Harvard-Yenching Libr., Harvard U., 1991, Pacific Culture Found., 1992, Pacific Basin Acad. grantee Ohira Meml. Found., 1990; fellow Josephine de Karman Found., 1984, Japan Found., 1984, East-West Ctr., 1990, United Daily Cultural Found., 1995, Asia Found., 1996. Mem. Am. Polit. Sci. Assn. (program organizer conf. group on China studies 1992—). Office: Am Univ Sch Internat Svc Washington DC 20016-8071

ZHENG, XIAONAN SHANNON, research scientist; b. Shenyang, Liaoning, China, Aug. 9, 1966; arrived in U.S., 1989; s. Chongwei and Shuxian (Zhang) Z.; m. Lanqing Wang, Sept. 17, 1965; 1 child, Katie Julia. BS, U. Sci. and Tech. of China, Hefei, 1989; PhD, Emory U., 1993. Postdoctoral fellow Brookhaven Nat. Lab., Upton, N.Y., 1993-94; postdoctoral fellow Ga. Inst. Tech., Atlanta, 1994-95, rsch. scientist, 1995—. Contbr. articles to profl. jours. Office: Georgia Institute Tech Sch Earth and Atmos Sci Baker Bldg 107 Atlanta GA 30332

ZHOU, HUANCHUN, chemist, administrator; b. Shanghai, Oct. 1, 1939; came to U.S., 1985; s. Qingyun and Wanxian (Hu) Z.; m. Qingliang Li, Sept. 5, 1967; 1 child, Fugang. BS equivalent, Fudan U., China, 1962; MS, Shanghai U. Tech., China, 1981; PhD equivalent, U. Fla., 1990. Engr. Wuxi Oil Pump Factory, Jiangsu, China, 1962-67; laborer, analytical technician Wuxi Oil Pump Factory, 1968-76; faculty Shanghai U. Tech., 1982-84; rschr. dept. chemistry U. Fla., Gainesville, 1985-91; chemist Fla. Dept. Agr., 1991—; chem. lab. chief Wuxi Oil Pump Factory, 1963-66; chmn. sect. chem. analysis Wuxi Sci-Tech. Assn., 1963-66; lectr. to 201st Am. Chem. Soc. Meeting, 1991. Corr. editor: Jour. Chem. Analysis and Phys. Test, 1964-66; contbr. articles to profl. jours. Co-grantee Office of Naval Rsch., 1991. Home: 7517-C Pitch Pine Cir Tampa FL 33617

ZHOU, SU, economics educator, researcher; b. Shanghai, China, Aug. 5, 1956; came to U.S., 1986; d. Qing-quan Zhou and Ming Cai; m. Yongan Zhang, Aug. 3, 1985; 1 child, Susan Zhang. BS in Physics, Jiao Tong U., Shanghai, 1982; MS in Econs., Ariz. State U., 1988, PhD in Econs., 1991. Instr. Jiao Tong U., 1982-84, rsch. fellow, 1984-85; grad. asst. Ariz. State U., Tempe, 1986-90, grad. assoc., 1990-91; rsch. assoc. Inst. for Internat. Econs., Washington, 1990; asst. prof. U. Tex., San Antonio, 1991—. Contbr. rsch. papers to profl. jours. Recipient rsch. grant Coll. Bus., U. Tex., 1992, William H. Barchilon award in economics Dept. Econs, Ariz. State U., 1989. Mem. Am. Economic Assn., Assn. for Comparative Economic Studies, Chinese Economist Soc., Phi Kappa Phi, Beta Gamma Sigma. Office: Dept Econs and Finance U Tex at San Antonio 6900 N Loop 1604 West San Antonio TX 78249-0633

ZHU, JIANCHAO, computer and control scientist, engineer, educator; b. Handan, Hebei, People's Republic of China, July 12, 1952; came to U.S., 1982; s. Jiezi and Jiyun (Lu) Z.; m. Yan Ma, Sept. 16, 1986. BSEE, Beijing Polytech. U., 1976; MSEE, U. Ala., 1984, MA in Math., 1986, PhD, 1989. Tchr., mem. rsch. staff Beijing Polytech. U., 1977-82; rsch. assoc. U. Ala., Huntsville, 1989-90; asst. prof. elec. computer engring. La. State U., Baton Rouge, 1990—; rsch. faculty mem. Remote Sensing and Image Processing Lab., La. State U., Baton Rouge, 1990—; prin., co-prin. investigator on various fed. and state govt. and indsl. rsch. contracts and grants; condr./lectr. seminars to univs. and rsch. insts. in U.S., Japan, China. Contbr. articles to profl. jours. Recipient Rsch. Initiation award NSF, 1991. Mem. IEEE (sr., steering com. southeastern symposium on sys. theory 1990—, gen. chmn. 28th 1996, exec. com. Baton Rouge sect. 1991-92, vice chmn. 1992-93, newsletter editor 1993-94, vice chmn. program com. 34th conf. on decision and control 1995, tech. assoc. editor IEEE Control Sys. mag., guest editor spl. issue, assoc. editor conf. editl. bd. IEEE Control Sys. Soc.), Soc. Indsl. and Applied Math., AIAA. Office: La State U Elec Computer Engring Dept Baton Rouge LA 70803

ZHU, XUEGONG, neuroscientist; b. Taixin, Jiang Su, China, Sept. 20, 1957; came to U.S., 1988; s. Gengsheng and Sufen (Liu) Z.; m. Yin Jiang, Aug. 8, 1986. BS, Beijing U., 1982; MS, Shanghai Inst. Biochemistry, 1985; PhD, U. Tenn., 1993. Rsch. asst. Shanghai Inst. Pharm. Industry, 1985-88; grad. teaching asst. U. Tenn., Memphis, 1988-93, postdoctoral fellow, 1993—. Mem. Soc. Neurosci., Am. Peptide Soc., Am. Soc. Mass Spectrometry. Office: U Tenn 956 Court Ave Rm A-218 Memphis TN 38103-2814

ZIDOVEC, MIRTA ROSA, Spanish language professional; b. Tacanitas, Argentina, Mar. 28, 1945; d. Emilio Rodriguez Cereijo and Josefa (Mora) Rodriguez; m. Davor Felix Andres Zidovec, Dec. 30, 1969; children: Vladimir Rodrigo, Mariana Silvia, Liza Veronica. Grad., Nat. U. of La Plata, Argentina, 1974; MA in Spanish Lang. and Lit., SUNY, Buffalo, 1985, PhD in Spanish Lang. and Lit., 1991. Elem. tchr. La Plata (Argentina) Sch. Dist., 1966-70; social worker Escuela Diferencial Puerto Madryn, Argentina, 1977-80; tchr. in law Bus. High Sch., Puerto Madryn, 1976-80; tchng. asst. SUNY, Buffalo, 1983-87, rsch. asst. dept. critical langs., 1984-86; tchr. of Spanish lang. The Nichols Mid. Sch., 1985-86; tchr. of Spanish Niagara Falls (N.Y.) Sr. High Sch., 1987-88, La Salle Sr. High Sch., Niagara Falls, 1988-89; Spanish instr. Millard Fillmore Coll., Buffalo, 1984-88; adj. prof. Spanish, U. North Fla., 1990-91, Jacksonville U., 1992, Fla. C.C., Jacksonville, 1991, lang. lab. facilitator, 1995-96, prof Spanish FCCJ, 1996—; mem. Spanish grad. program admission com. SUNY, Buffalo, 1988-90; mem. local arrangements com. for III Congress of the Internat. Fedn. of Latin Am. and Caribbean Studies, Ctr. for Tomorrow, SUNY, Buffalo, 1987. Author essays in field., "Kismet", Published in Carrings in Stone, The National Library of Poetry and " Winter Leave", The Sounds of Poetry, 1996. Vol. ARC, Niagara Falls, 1981, Am. Cancer Soc., Niagara Falls, 1985, Am. Heart Assn., Jacksonville, 1994. Mem. MLA, Am. Assn. Tchrs. of Spanish and Portuguese, Instituto Literario Cultural Hispánico.

ZIEBURTZ, WILLIAM BLASIE, JR., economist; b. Miami, Fla., Mar. 11, 1959; s. William Blasie and Elgy Jean (Stiles) Z.; m. Ava Jane Kelley, July 16, 1983; children: Katherine Rose, William Edward. BBA in Econs., U. Ga., 1981, MA in Econs., 1985. Economist CH2M Hill Inc., Atlanta, 1986-95; dir. cons. svcs. Thomson Environ. Network, 1995—. Contbr. articles to profl. jours. Mem. City's Econ. Devel. Citizens Com., Snellville, Ga., 1993; com. chair Ga. Water and Pollution Control Assn. Mem. Nat. Assn. Bus. Economists, Water Environment Fedn., Am. Water Works Assn. Libertarian.

ZIEGER, ROBERT HARMAN, history educator, historian; b. Englewood, N.J., Aug. 2, 1938; s. John H. Zieger and Grace Elizabeth Harman; m. Gay Annette Pitman, June 30, 1962; 1 child, Robert E. BA, Montclair State Coll., 1960; MA, U. Wyo., 1961; PhD, U. Md., 1965. From asst. to assoc. prof. history U. Wis., Stevens Point, 1964-73; assoc. prof. history Kans. State U., Manhattan, 1973-77; prof. history Wayne State U., Detroit, 1977-86, U. Fla., Gainesville, 1986—. Author: Rebuilding the Pulp and Paper Workers' Union, 1984 (Taft award 1985), American Workers, American Unions, 1920-85, 1986, 2d rev. edit., 1994, John L. Lewis: Labor Leader, 1988, Republicans and Labor, 1919-1929, 1969, The CIO, 1925-1955, 1995; editor: Organized Labor in the 20th Century South, 1991; mem. editl. bd. Labor History, 1991. Recipient Taft award, 1996, grant NEH, 1972, 83, Faculty Enrichment Programme award Can. Govt., 1985, rsch. grant Am. Philos. Soc., 1974, 80, rsch. grant Am. Coun. Learned Soc., 1982, rsch. grant Rockefeller Archives Ctr., 1994. Mem. Am. Hist. Soc., Orgn. Am. Historians, So. Hist. Assn., Historians of Am. Communism (pres. 1990-92). Democrat. Unitarian. Home: 2025 NW 18th Ln Gainesville FL 32605-3959 Office: Univ Fla Dept History Gainesville FL 32611

ZIEGLER, DHYANA, broadcasting educator; b. N.Y.C., May 5, 1949; d. Ernest and Alberta Allie (Guy) Z. BS cum laude, CUNY, 1981; MA in Radio and TV, So. Ill. U., 1983, PhD in Higher Edn., 1985. Freelance researcher Essence Mag., N.Y.C., 1972-75; copywriter, radio producer Rosenfeld, Sirowitz & Lawson Advt. Agy., N.Y.C., 1974-75; exec. v.p. Patten & Guest Prodns., N.Y.C., 1976-79; prodn. intern Sta. WNEW TV, N.Y.C., 1979-80; upward bound counselor Seton Hall U., South Orange, N.J., 1979-81; prodn. intern Sta. WCBS TV, N.Y.C., 1980-81; asst. prof. Jackson (Miss.) State U., 1984-85; assoc. dir. Diversity Resources and Ednl. Svcs. U. Tenn., Knoxville, 1985—; bd. dirs. Knoxville Women's Ctr., 1989-92; bd. trustees East Tenn. Discovery Ctr., Knoxville, 1989-92; adv. bd. Bethel Love Kitchen, Knoxville, 1990-93. Author books; contbr. articles to profl. jours.; producer, dir. (video documentary) Single Parenting, 1988 (2d Pl. award), Rape is a Reality, 1982 (UPI Outstanding Achievement award 1982). Chmn. comms. Knoxville chpt. NAACP, 1990-91, chpt. advisor U. Tenn. student chpt., 1989—, chmn. chancellor's commn. for blacks, 1990-95, pres. faculty senate, 1995—; chmn. social action com. Delta Sigma Theta, Knoxville, 1986-89, mem. commn. on arts and letters, 1990-91; bd. dirs. East Tenn. regional Am. Heart Assn., 1990—; mem. athletics bd. U. Tenn., 1990—; regional devel. edn. coord. Delta Rsch. and Ednl. Found.; mem. allocations com. United Way, Knoxville, 1990-91. Recipient Gov.'s Outstanding Faculty Mem. of the Yr., 1987-88 and Rsch. award, 1992, Coll. of Comms., Outstanding Faculty award, Interfraternity Coun., 1992, YWCA Finalist in Edn., 1990, Consortium of Dr.'s award, 1991; inductee U. Tenn. African Am. Hall of Fame, 1994; grantee FISPE, U.S. Dept. of Edn., 1989—; Delta Rsch. & Ednl. Found., 1987, 90; fellow Poynter Inst., 1992. Mem. NAFE, Women in Comm. (pres. Knoxville chpt. 1990—), Broadcast Edn. Assn. (chair multicultural div. 1989-92, chair gender divsn. 1996—), Speech Comm. Assn., Soc. Profl. Journalists (Jane Pauley task force on mass comm. edn. 1995-96, co-author Jane Pauley Task Force Report 1996), Golden Key Nat. Honor Soc., Kappa Tau Alpha, Phi Delta Kappa, Delta Sigma Theta (Post-secondary Educators award 1992, Black Achievement award 1993). Office: U Tenn 295 Communications Bldg Knoxville TN 37996

ZIEGLER, JOHN ALAN, historian, political scientist, educator; b. Belleville, Ill., Jan. 28, 1933; s. John Wendell and Georgia Elizabeth (Reppel) Z.; B.S., So. Ill. U., Carbondale, 1955, M.S., 1956; Rotary Found. fellow, St. Andrews (Scotland) U., 1956-57; Ph.D., Syracuse U., N.Y., 1970; m. Carol Ruth Alcorn, June 15, 1963; children—Mimi, Robin. Asst. prof. polit. sci. and social sci. Calif. State U., Hayward, 1966-72; lectr. Am. civilization Calif. State Poly. U., Pomona, 1972-74; assoc. prof. polit. sci. Hendrix Coll., Conway, Ark., 1974-84, prof., 1984-91, Harold and Lucy Cabe disting. prof. history and politics, 1991—, also coord. Hendrix-Oxford program, head social sci. area, 1978-82, chmn. dept. polit. sci. and history, 1974-83; guest lectr. St. Peter's Coll., Oxford U., 1983, 90, 94, Clare Coll., Cambridge U., 1988, 89, Dundee U., 1994, Oxford U., 1994; Churchill life fellow Westminster Coll., Fulton, Mo.; participant Wilton Pk. Confs., Wiston House Internat. Conf. Ctr., Sussex, England, 1979—. Author: Experimentalism and Institutional Change. Served with AUS, 1957-60. Mem. AAUP, Friends Churchill Meml. (life), Am. Friends Wilton Park, ACLU, London Topographical Soc., Nat Trust Historic Preservation, Royal Oak Found., Friends of Canterbury Cathedral. Soc. Sussex Downsmen (life). Mem. United Ch. Christ. Club: Dundee (Scotland) Curling. Home: 14 Oakdale Dr Conway AR 72032-6137 Office: Hendrix Coll Conway AR 72032

ZIEGLER, ROBERT OLIVER, special education educator; b. Cullman, Ala., Sept. 6, 1939; s. Mary Catherine (Taylor) McDonald; adopted Edgar and Kathryn Ziegler; m. Gladys L. Friese, May 3, 1962 (div. Jan. 1970); children: Robert, Edgar, Lesha, Kathy. BS, U. Ala., Tuscaloosa, 1961, MA, 1964, PhD, 1970. Cert. spl. edn. tchr., sch. counselor, music tchr., Ga. Band dir. Phillips Jr. H.S., Mobile, Ala., 1961-62, Wiggins (Colo.) H.S., 1962-63, Eastwood Jr. H.S., Tuscaloosa, 1963-65, McAdory H.S., McCalla, Ala., 1966-70, Calera (Ala.) H.S., 1971-72; prof. music edn. Tift Coll., Forsyth, Ga., 1972-78; jr. H.S. counselor Clayton County Schs., Jonesboro, Ga., 1978-80; elem. sch. counselor Rockdale County Schs., Conyers, Ga., 1980-82; spl. edn. tchr. Henderson Jr. H.S., Jackson, Ga., 1982-87; spl. edn. tchr. Clayton County Schs., Jonesboro, Ga., 1987-92, gen. music tchr., 1996—; spl. edn. tchr. City Schs. of Decatur, Ga., 1992-96; elem. sch. music tchr. Clayton County Schs., 1996—; clarinetist Mobile (Ala.) Symphony Orch., 1961-62; vis. lectr. Stillman Coll., Tuscaloosa, Ala., 1970-71; prof. grad. sch. Mercer U., Macon, 1972-74; vis. lectr. in music Wesleyan Coll., Macon, Ga., 1975-76; acting head music dept. Tift Coll., Forsyth, Ga., 1976-77; curriculum cons. South Metro Psychoednl. Ctr., Atlanta City Schs., 1989. Contbr. articles to profl. publs. Minister of music, choir dir. United Meth. Ch., 1961-90, lay leader, 1989-94; mem. South Metro Concert Band, Morrow, Ga., 1978—, Tara Wind Band, Jonesboro, Ga., 1987-88. Recipient Cert. of Appreciation United Meth. Ch., 1990, Spl. Mission Recognition award United Meth. Women, 1983; U. Ala. grantee, 1960-61;. Mem. Profl. Assn. Ga. Educators (bldg. rep. 1994-96), Soc. for Preservation and Encouragement of Barber Shop Quartet Singing in Am. (founding, co-dir. Fayetteville chpt. 1990). Home: 2669 Jodeco Dr Jonesboro GA 30236-5311 Office: City Schs of Decatur 917 S Mcdonough St Decatur GA 30030-4930

ZIEGLER, RONALD LOUIS, association executive, former government official; b. Covington, Ky., May 12, 1939; s. Louis Daniel and Ruby (Parsons) Z.; m. Nancy Lee Plessinger, July 30, 1960; children: Cynthia Lee Charas, Laurie Michelle Albright. Student, Xavier U., 1957-58; BS, U. So. Calif., 1961; DSc (hon.), Mass. Coll. Pharmacy, 1989, L.I. U., 1993. With Procter & Gamble Distbg. Co., 1961; account rep. J. Walter Thompson Co., 1962-68; press dir. Calif. Rep. Central Com., 1961-62; press aide to Richard Nixon in Calif. gubernatorial campaign, 1962; press aide staff Richard Nixon, 1968-69; press sec. to Pres. Nixon, 1969-74, asst. to, 1973-74; mng. dir., sr. v.p. internat. services Syska and Hennessy, Inc., Washington, 1975-80; pres. Nat. Assn. Truck Stop Operators, Alexandria, Va., 1980-87; pres., chief exec. officer Nat. Assn. Chain Drug Stores, Alexandria, 1987—; mem. nat. adv. bd. U. Okla.; adv. coun. Pharm. Found. U. Tex. Bd. dirs. Nat. Coun. on Patient Info. and Edn., Nat. Conf. on Pharm. Assns., Richard Nixon Libr. and Birthplace. Mem. Am. Soc. Assn. Execs., Nat. Retail Fedn. (bd. dirs.), Pharmacists Against Drug Abuse, Assn. White House Press Secs., Nat. Orgn. Rare Disorders, Sigma Chi Alumni. Office: Nat Assn Chain Drug Stores 413 N Lee St Alexandria VA 22314

ZIENTARA, SUZANNAH DOCKSTADER, insurance company executive; b. Wichita, Kans., Oct. 1, 1945; d. Ralph Walter and Patricia Ann (Harvey) Dockstader; m. Larry Henry Zientara, Oct. 18, 1975; 1 child, Jillian Sue Zientara Cox. Student, U. Kans., 1963-64; BS in Bus. Edn., Ft. Hays State U., 1968; MEd in Secondary Guidance and Counseling, U. Mo., St. Louis, 1973. CLU. Sec. to supt. Wichita Pub. Schs., 1968-69; tchr. bus. edn. Wichita Heights High Sch., 1969-71, Lindbergh High Sch., St. Louis, 1971-72, Holman Jr. High Sch., St. Louis, 1972-75; guidance counselor Pattonville Heights Jr. High Sch., St. Louis, 1975-79; tchr. data processing Lawrence (Kans.) High Sch., 1979-85; ins. agt. State Farm Ins. Cos., Lawrence, 1985-90; agy. mgr. State Farm Ins. Cos., Tulsa, 1990-95; agy. field exec. State Farm Ins. Cos., Topeka, 1995—; mem. Regional Mgr. Coun., Tulsa, 1992-93; participant Purdue Profl. Mgmt. Inst., West Lafayette, Ind., 1993. Author: Introduction to Data Processing, 1983. Mem. Williams Edn. Fund, U. Kans. Named Outstanding Young Woman of Am., 1974. Mem. Am. Soc. CLU's and ChFC's, USTA, Am. Ski Assn., Topeka C. of C., U. Kans. Alumni Assn., PEO, Shawnee Country Club, Mortar Bd., Pi Omega Pi. Republican. Episcopalian. Home: 3637 SW Kings Forest Rd Topeka KS 66610 Office: State Farm Ins Cos 2930 Wanamaker Dr Ste 6 Topeka KS 66614

ZIENTEK, DAVID MICHAEL, cardiologist; b. Amarillo, Tex., Mar. 11, 1959; s. Ralph John and Odile Mary (Suhre) Z. BA in Biology with honors, Johns Hopkins U., 1981; MD, The John Hopkins U., 1985. Diplomate Am. Bd. Internal Medicine, 1988, Am. Bd. Internal Medicine Cardiovascular Disease, 1991; med. lic. Ill. 1991, Tex. 1992; radioactive material lic. Tex. 1992. Intern in internal medicine Vanderbilt U., Nashville, Tenn., 1985-86, resident in internal medicine, 1986-88, fellow cardiology, 1988-91; fellow interventional cardiology Rush-Presbyn-St. Luke's Med. Ctr., Chgo., 1991-92; cardiologist Austin Cardiology Cons., Austin, Tex., 1992-94, Austin Heart (merger of Austin Cardiology Cons., Austin Heart Assocs.), 1994—; instr. Vanderbilt U., 1990-91; on staff Seton Med. Ctr., 1992—, Seton N.W. Hosp., 1992—; presenter Am. Coll. Cardiology, Calif., 1993. Contbr. to profl. jours. Fellow Am. Coll. Cardiology; mem. Am. Coll. Physicians, Travis County Med. Soc., Tex. Med. Assn., Phi Beta Kappa. Office: Austin Heart 1301 W 38th St Ste 300 Austin TX 78705-1010

ZIETS, GEORGE A., consumer products company executive. V.p. R&D Maybelline, Inc. Address: 3030 Jackson Ave Memphis TN 38101

ZIMMER, DONALD WILLIAM, coach professional athletics, former professional baseball manager; b. Cin., Jan. 17, 1931; s. Harold Lesley and Lorraine Bertha (Ernst) Z.; m. Jean Carol Bauerle, Aug. 16, 1951; children: Thomas Jeffrey, Donna Jean. Student pub. schs., Cin. Baseball player Dodger Farm Clubs, 1949-54, Bklyn. Dodgers, 1954-57, Los Angeles Dodgers, 1958-59, Chgo. Cubs, 1960-61, N.Y. Mets, 1962, Cin. Reds, 1962, Los Angeles Dodgers, 1963, Washington Senators, 1963-65, Toei Flyers, Tokyo, 1966; mgr. Cin. Reds Farm Clubs, Knoxville and Buffalo, 1967, Indpls., 1968; mgr. San Diego Padre Farm Clubs, Key West, Fla., 1969, Padre Farm Club, Salt Lake City, 1970; coach Montreal Expos, Que., Can., 1971; mgr. San Diego Padres, 1972-73; coach Boston Red Sox, 1974-76, mgr., 1976-80; mgr. Tex. Rangers, 1981, 82; coach N.Y. Yankees, 1983, 86, 96, Chgo. Cubs, 1984, 85, 86, San Francisco Giants, 1987; mgr. Chgo. Cubs, 1988-91; coach Boston Red Sox, 1992, Colo. Rockies, Denver, 1993-95, N.Y. Yankees, 1996—; mem. minor league All-Star Teams, Hornell, N.Y., 1950, Elmira, N.Y., 1951, Mobile, Ala., 1952, St. Paul, 1953; player World Series teams 1955, 56, 59, coach 1975. Recipient Bill Stern award NBC, 1949; named St. Paul Rookie of Yr., 1953; mem. All Star Team, 1961, 78, 81, 90; named Nat. League Mgr. of Yr. 1989. Mem. Profl. Baseball Players Am. (life), Old Time Ball Players Wis. Office: care NY Yankees Yankee Stadium Bronx NY 10451

ZIMMER, WILLIE MAE, medical/surgical nurse; b. Knoxville, Tenn., Sept. 18, 1941; d. William Baynoise and Edith Mae (Fain) Bains; div.; children: Sharon Kay Zimmer-Wood, Clifton Leroy Zimmer Jr. Diploma, Knoxville Vocat. Sch., 1977; ASN, Walters State Community Coll., Morristown, Tenn., 1986. Cert. med.-surg. nurse. Supr. Camel Mfg. Co., Knoxville, 1965-77; staff nurse Ft. Sanders Regional Med. Ctr., Knoxville, 1977, charge nurse, 1977—, charge nurse, shift leader med.-surg. respiratory unit, 1991—; physicians asst., office nurse local surgeon, 1990-91. Mem. Beta Sigma Phi. Home: 4717 Maplehill Dr Knoxville TN 37914-2916

ZIMMERMAN, DAVID ALAN, cardiologist; b. Akron, Ohio, Sept. 22, 1962; s. Henry Edward and Betty Jane (Young) Z; m. Karlyn Marie Hooton, June 4, 1994. BS, Ohio State U., 1985; MD, Duke U., 1991. Diplomate Am. Bd. Internal Medicine. Intern Ohio State U., Columbus, 1991-92, resident, 1992-94; fellow transplantation cardiology Ochsner Med. Found., New Orleans, 1995-96; fellow in cardiology Tulane U., New Orleans, 1996—. Mem. AMA, Internat. Soc. for Heart and Lung Transplantation, Am. Soc. Transplant Physicians, Am. Coll. Cardiology.

ZIMMERMAN, JAMES ROBERT, radiologist, engineer; b. Dearborn, Mich., Dec. 26, 1960; s. Carl Edward and Mary Kathleen (Devlin) Z. B Mech. Engring., GM Engring. and Mgmt. Inst., Flint, Mich., 1984; MD, U. Miss., Jackson, 1990. Resident in surgery Roanoke (Va.) Meml. Hosps., 1990-92; resident in radiology U. Miss. Med. Ctr., 1992-96; radiologist Upson Regional Med. Ctr., Thomaston, Ga., 1996—. Contbr. articles to med. jours. Mem. Rep. Task Force, Washington, 1994. Mem. AMA, Radiol. Soc. N.Am., Am. Roentgen Ray Soc., So. Med. Assn. Roman Catholic. Home: 619 Kingston Rd Thomaston GA 30286 Office: Upson Regional Med Ctr 801 W Gordon St Thomaston GA 30286

ZIMMERMAN, RAYMOND, retail chain executive; b. Memphis, TN, 1933; married. V.p. Service Mdse. Co., Inc., Nashville, from 1959, pres., 1973-1981, chmn., 1981—, now also chief exec. officer, also bd. dirs. Office: Service Merchandise Co Inc 7100 Service Merchandise Dr Brentwood TN 37027-2927

ZIMMERMAN, S(AMUEL) MORTON (MORT ZIMMERMAN), electrical and electronics engineering executive; b. Paterson, N.J., Mar. 18, 1927; s. Solomon Zimmerman and Miriam (Feder) Glatzer; m. Marion Patricia Boque, Sept. 15, 1951 (dec. 1993); children: Judy, Suzy, Sharon, Dan; m. Evie Levine, Feb. 24, 1996. Student, Ga. Inst. Tech., 1942-44, 46-48, Oglethorpe U., 1948-51; BSEE, Pacific Internat. U., L.A., 1958. Pres. Comml. Electronics Corp., Dallas, 1954-56, Electron Corp. subs. LTV Corp., 1956-65; chmn. bd., pres. Capital Bancshares, Inc., 1965-66; chmn. bd. Capital Nat. Bank Tampa (formerly Springs Nat. Bank), Fla., 1965, Capital Nat. Bank Miami (name now Peoples Downtown Bank), Fla., 1966, Merc. Nat. Bank Miami Beach (name now Barnett Bank), Fla., 1967, Underwriters Bank & Trust Co. N.Y. (name now Banco Cen.), 1968; chmn. bd., pres. Capital Gen. Corp., 1967, Comml. Tech., Inc., 1977—, Petro Imperial Corp. and subs. DOL Resources and Tech.-Star, Dallas, 1983—; chmn. bd., pres. Tans Exchange Corp., 1965—, Electric & Gas Tech., Inc., 1985—; also chmn. 8 subs. cos.; chmn. bd. Video Sci. Tech., Inc., 1981-92; Interfed. Capital, Inc., 1990—. Patentee: TV camera video amplifier and blanking circuits, electronic thermometer, video x-ray image system and methods, video system and method for presentation and reproduction x-ray film images, electromagnetic radio frequency lighting system, laser display of electronically generated image signal; patent applied for: new tech. for electronic refrigeration system. Petty oficer USN, 1942-45. Recipient Interfaith award City of N.Y. Mem. IEEE, Brookhaven Country Club. Republican. Jewish. Home: 5901 Yardley Ct Dallas TX 75248 Office: Electric & Gas Tech Inc 13636 Neutron Rd Dallas TX 75244-4410

ZIMMERMAN, SARAH LYDIA MAYES, nursing administrator, educator; b. Akron, Ohio, June 10, 1950; d. Harold and Margie Belle (Dempsey) Mayes; m. Donald James Zimmerman, Sept. 2, 1972; children: Cathy Ann, Gary Stuart. BSN, U. Akron, 1972; MS, Kans. State U., 1976. CPR instr. Intensive care and coronary care nurse VA Hosp., Topeka; instr. med.-surg. and critical care nursing Massillon (Ohio) Community Hosp. Sch. Nursing; assoc. prof. nursing Manatee Community Coll., Bradenton, Fla.; adminstr. home health Columbia Blake Med. Ctr., Bradenton; spkr. in field. Author: Home Health Care Management and Practice, 1996; facilitator task force for book: Innovative Benchmarking: A Practical Approach to Improving Productivity, 1994. Mem. AACN (charter mem., officer Topeka chpt.), Hosp. Home Care Assn. Fla. (bd. dirs., sec. 1994-96, pres.-elect 1996—, facilitator producitivity task force). Home: 10306 Tam O'Shanter Pl Bradenton FL 34202-4020

ZIMMERMAN, SHELDON, college president, rabbi; b. Toronto, Ont., Can., Feb. 21, 1942; s. Morris and Helen Z.; m. Judith Elaine Baumgarten, Aug. 9, 1964; children: Brian, Kira, David, Micol. BA, U. Toronto, 1964, MA, 1965; BHL, Hebrew Union Coll., Jewish Inst. Religion, 1969, MAHL, 1970. Ordained rabbi, 1970. Asst. rabbi Cen. Synagogue, N.Y.C., 1970-72, sr. rabbi, 1972-85; rabbi Temple Emanu-El, Dallas, 1985-96; pres. Hebrew Union Coll.-Jewish Inst. Religion, N.Y.C., 1996—; adj. prof. religious studies So. Meth. U., Dallas, Perkins Sch. Theology; adj. faculty Auburn Theol. Sem.; lectr. liturgy and rabbinics N.Y. Sch. of Hebrew Union Coll.-Jewish Inst. Religion, bd. govs.; lectr. theology Fordham U.; instr. philosophy Hunter Coll. of CUNY; v.p., then pres. Cen. Conf. of Am. Rabbis; bd. trustees Union Am. Hebrew Congregations; mem. Nat. Rabbinic Cabinet of United Jewish Appeal; bd. dirs. World Ctr. for Jewish Unity; bd. govs. Synagogue Coun. Am.; v.p. World Union Progressive Judaism, lectr. in field. Contbr. articles to profl. jours. Bd. dirs. Vis. Nurses Assn. Tex., Children's Med. Found., Jewish Fedn. Dallas, Solomon Schechter Acad. Dallas, S.W. REgion of Am. Jewish Congress, Community Outreach Coalition.; adv. bd. CONTACT-Dallas Telephone Counseling Ctr., Downtown Dallas Family Shelter, The AIDS-ARMS Adv. Coun. Dallas, Pastoral Care Adv. Com. of Children's Med. Ctr., Women's Ctr. of Dallas, Chaplain's ADv. Bd. of So. Meth. U.; v.p. Jewish Community Rels. Coun. Dallas. Recipient Marshall Hochhauser Meml. Award, Fedn. Jewish Philanthropies, N.Y.C. Office: HUC-JIR 3101 Clifton Ave Cincinnati OH 45220

ZIMMERMAN, SOLOMON, dentist, educator; b. Munich, Apr. 21, 1948; came to U.S., 1951; s. Abraham and Helen (Suchecki) Z.; m. Lynn Carol Bracco, June 11, 1972; children: Michael Paul, Rebecca Lisa. BA, CCNY, 1970; DDS, NYU, 1975. Assoc. dentist Jerome W. Schonfeld, DDS, Portsmouth, Va., 1980-81; pvt. practice dentistry Virginia Beach, Va., 1981—; forensic odontology cons. Chief Med. Examiner Tidewater Dist., Norfolk, Va., 1984—; speaker Tidewater Dental Assts. Soc., Virginia Beach, 1986, dental advisor, 1987—; speaker Dental Health Week, Newport News, Va., 1977, Dental Health Month, Virginia Beach, 1984, 87. Advisor for merit badge Boy Scouts Am., Ft. Eustis, Va., 1976-78. Served as maj. U.S. Army, 1975-80, USAR, 1980—. Recipient Commendation medal U.S. Army, 1979, Service ribbon, U.S. Army, 1981. Mem. ADA, Va. Dental Assn., Tidewater Dental Assn., Nat. Fedn. Ind. Bus., Assn. Mil. Surgeons U.S., Alpha Omega. Jewish. Office: 4849 Shore Dr Virginia Beach VA 23455-2714

ZIMMERMANN, CHARLENE MARCELLA, primary school educator; b. Schulenburg, Tex., Oct. 30, 1938; d. Charlie Frank and Judith Anne (Veselka) Z. BS, U. Tex., Austin, 1959. Tchr. Brentwood Elem., Austin Ind. Sch. Dist., 1960—; curriculum writer Austin Ind. Sch. Dist., 1970—, career level II, 1981-86, career level III, 1987—. Mem. NEA (life), Tex. State Tchrs. Assn. (life), Tex. Edn. Execs. (life), Austin Assn. Tchrs., Tex. PTA (life), U. Tex. Ex Students (life), Delta Kappa Gamma Epsilon. Lutheran. Home: 3004 White Rock Dr Austin TX 78757-4449 Office: Brentwood Elem Sch 6700 Arroyo Seco Austin TX 78757-2506

ZIMMERMANN, G. FLOYD, III, construction company executive; b. Clearwater, Fla., Jan. 26, 1944; s. G. Floyd and Dorothy (Johns) Z.; m. Janet Lee Snow, May 15, 1965; children: Laura Kristine, Jinna S. Zimmermann Harmon. BS, Fla. So. Coll., 1965; postgrad., Emory U., 1965-66, Cen. Piedmont Coll., 1968-69; grad., Builders Inst., Realtors Inst. Cert. class A gen. contractor, Fla., cert. grad. remodeler; lic. real estate broker, Fla.; profl. designations AIBD, ASID. Counselor Ga. Dept. Labor, Atlanta, 1966-67; personnel psychologist U.S. Army Recruiting Command, Charlotte, N.C., 1967-69; v.p. G.F. Zimmermann, Inc., Lakeland, Fla., 1969-74; pres. Zimmermann Assocs., Inc., Lakeland, 1974—, KJ Futures, Inc., Lakeland, 1984-94; bd. dirs. Bentley Lumber Co., Alexandria, La., 1st Fed. Fla. Savs. & Loan, mem. exec. com.; bd. dirs. Zimmerman Lands, Inc., Alexandria, La.; adv. counselor Lakeland Regional Med. Ctr., 1996—; trustee Lakeland Pension. Bd. dirs. Lakeland Historic Preservation Bd., 1982-88, Habitat for Humanity, 1992—; mem. adv. bd. Lakeland Salvation Army, 1980—, chmn., 1984-87; mem. City of Lakeland Arbitration Bd., 1984—; adminstrv. bd. mem., trustee First United Meth. Ch., 1995—; vice chmn. civil svc. bd. City of Lakeland, 1995—; trustee and dir. Pension Bd. City of Lakeland. Named Contractor of Yr. Lakeland Historic Preservation Bd., 1994, one of Am.'s Top 250 Bldg. Profls., 1995, one of Am.'s Top 500 Remodeling Profls., 1991, 92, 95, 96; recipient Cert. of Merit Custom Builder Mag., 1995. Mem. Nat. Assn. Home Builders, Am. Inst. Bldg. Designers (profl.), Am. Soc. Interior Designers (allied), Internat. Interior Design Assn. (assoc.), So. Bldg. Code Congress Internat. (profl.), Remodelers Coun., Nat. Trust for Historic Preservation, Historic Lakeland, Polk Builders Assn., Lakeland Pres.' Roundtable, Lakeland C. of C. (charter mem. better bus. coun.), Kiwanis (v.p. 1990-92, pres. 1992-93, bd. dirs. Lakeland Found. 1990—, Kiwanis Found. bd. dirs. 1990—, pres. 1994—). Republican. Methodist. Office: Zimmermann Assocs Inc 203 Kerneywood St Lakeland FL 33803-2947

ZIMMERMANN, STEPHAN FRITZ-PETER, investment company executive; b. Leipzig, Germany, Nov. 28, 1945; came to U.S., 1956; m. Pamela Clare Dawson, Mar. 29, 1980 (div. 1984); 1 child, Helen Jennifer. BA in Polit. Sci., U. Calif., Berkeley, 1971; cert. in internat. econs., Cambridge (Eng.) U., 1975; MA in Internat. Econs., Monterey Inst., 1976. Jr. underwriter Home Ins. Co., San Francisco, 1968-70; account exec. Dean Witter & Co., Inc., Berkeley, 1971-73; mcpl. fin. analyst Bartle Wells Assocs., San

Francisco, 1973-74; sr. analyst, CEO, CFO, Zimmermann, Wilson & Co., Inc., Carmel, Calif., 1976-88; exec. v.p., CFO, Saratoga Internat., Inc., Little Rock, 1990—; instr. debate U. San Francisco, 1971-72; instr. econs. Golden Gate U., San Francisco, 1974-76, Monterey (Calif.) Peninsula Coll., 1976-80; adj. prof. econs. Monterey Inst. Internat. Studies, 1976-80; columnist Berkeley Gazette, 1969-71, Pacific Grove Tribune, 1976-80, Carmel Valley Sun, 1977-81. Author: (book and screenplay) The Sonja Factor, (screenplay) Easy Going, (book) Christmas Strike, The Almost Done Deal, 1993; also poems, song lyrics, collaborations; contbr. to month newsletter Perspectives, 1976-85; prodr. record albums Pat Duval - Old Monterey, Heartsounds. Bd. dirs. Mems. of Barre (Ballet Ark.), 1991—. With USAF, 1966-67. Recipient Dow Jones Award in Economics, 1976. Mem. Pi Kappa Delta (life). Office: Saratoga Internat Inc 124 W Capitol Ave Ste 1003 Little Rock AR 72201-3732

ZIMMET, STEVEN MICHAEL, physician; b. Washington, May 30, 1942; s. Sol L. and Min (Goldberg) Z.; m. Susan Rita Goldstein, Oct. 31, 1970; children: Amy Rebecca, Emily Beth. BA with high honors, U. Va., 1964, MD, 1968. Diplomate Am. Bd. Internal Medicine. Intern, then resident in internal medicine Georgetown U. Sch. of Medicine, 1968-70; physician Pulmonary and Med. Assocs. of No. Va., Arlington, 1974—; clin. prof. Georgetown U. Sch. Medicine, Washington, 1990—; mem. dir. ICU, Arlington Hosp., 1985—. Contbr. articles to profl. jours. Bd. dirs. Am. Lung Assn. of Va., Richmond, 1994—; pres. Am. Lung Assn. No. Va., Fairfax, 1984-86. Named Vol. of the Decate, Am. Lung Assn. No. Va. Fellow ACP; mem. Nat. Assn. for Med. Dirs. Respiratory Care (bd. dirs. 1995—), Va. Thoracic Soc. (pres. 1989-91), Va. Soc. Internal Medicine (pres. 1981-82, Disting. Internist of Yr. 1995), No. Va. Acad. Internal Medicine (pres. 1982-83). Home: 1631 Maddux Ln McLean VA 22101 Office: Pulmonary and Med Assocs of No Va Ltd 1400 S Joyce St # 126 Arlington VA 22202

ZIMNAVODA, DIANNE M., manufacturing executive; b. L.A., Sept. 8, 1949; d. Jack M. and Trysa P. (Selco) Kramer; m. Richard A. Zimnavoda, Aug. 22, 1969; children: Lena Anne, Pauline Beth, Avigail Freda, Rachel Naomi, Sara Rebecca. BA, UCLA, 1981, MBA, 1987. Exec. v.p. RCF Seals & Couplings, Oxnard, Calif., 1975-86; pres., CEO RCF Seals & Couplings, Vidalia, Ga., 1986—. Mem. NAFE, Soc. Automotive Engrs., Am. Prodn. and Inventory Control Soc. Office: RCF Seals & Couplings PO Box 642 Vidalia GA 30474-0642

ZIMOWSKA-HANDLER, GRAZYNA JOANNA, insect physiologist; b. Warsaw, Poland, Sept. 3, 1954; came to U.S., 1988; Magister, U. Warsaw, Poland, 1978, PhD in Biology, 1984. Doctoral scholar U. Warsaw, 1979-81, from rsch. teaching asst. to asst. prof., 1981-91; vis. scientist U.S. Dept. Agriculture, Gainesville, Fla., 1988—. Contbr. articles to profl. jours. V.p. Ctr. Modern Art, Gainesville, 1992—. Alexander von Humboldt fellow, Bonn, Germany, 1984-85; Brit. Consul scholar to U. Liverpool, Eng., 1988. Office: USDA/ARS 1700 SW 23rd Dr Gainesville FL 32608-1069

ZINKHAN, GEORGE MARTIN, III, marketing educator; b. Balt., Feb. 17, 1952; s. George Martin Jr. and Mary Elizabeth (Stoner) Z.; children: George M. IV, Lydia F., Sam S. BA in English Lit., Swarthmore Coll., 1974; MBA in Ops. Rsch., U. Mich., 1979, PhD in Bus. Adminstrn., 1981. Stats. lab. counselor U. Mich., Ann Arbor, 1978-79, teaching fellow, 1979-81; asst. prof. U. Houston, 1981-86, Conn prof. mktg., 1989-93; Coca-Cola prof. mktg. U. Ga., Athens, 1994—; vis. assoc. prof. U. Pitts., 1987-88; mem. exec. com. faculty Senate, U. Houston, 1991-92; cons. FTC, Washington, 1992-93, San Francisco, 1994-96. Editor: Enhancing Knowledge Developments in Marketing, 1995; editor Jour. Advt., Richmond, Va., 1991-95; book rev. editor, mem. rev. bd. Jour. of Mktg., College Station, Tex., 1991—; mem. rev. bd. Jour. Current Issues, 1991—, Jour. Bus. Rsch., 1994—. Mem. Am. Mktg. Assn. (track chair 1991-96, v.p. for rsch. 1996—), Am. Acad. Advt. (named one of Top 12 Contbrs. to Advt. 1990), Acad. Mktg. Sci. (track chair, promotion mgmt. 1994), Assn. Consumer Rsch. (session chair 1990), Soc. Computer Simulation. Democrat. United Ch. of Christ. Home: 195 S Finley St Athens GA 30605-1113 Office: Univ Ga Dept Mktg Brooks Hall Athens GA 30602-6258

ZINMAN, JACQUES, former insurance agency executive; b. Phila., Nov. 7, 1922; BS, U. Va., 1943; postgrad. U. Pa., 1945. Chmn., The Zinman Group, Ins. Agy., 1950-82. Mem. exec. com. Pa. state Rep. fin. com.; mem. Presdl. Electoral Coll. from Pa., 1972; bd. dirs. Pop Warner Nat. Football League; pres. Lake Agy. of Fla., 1990—. Ensign USNR, 1943-44. Recipient Outstanding Young Man Phila. award Jewish Nat. Fund, 1961. Mem. Variety Club, Theta Delta Chi. Lodge: Masons. Contbr. articles to profl. jours. Office: Lakes Agy of Fla 627 E Atlantic Blvd Pompano Beach FL 33060-6343

ZIPKIN, SHELDON LEE, lawyer, educator; b. Washington, June 10, 1951; s. Sol and Selma (Rumerman) Z.; m. Ellen Linda Reitman, July 1, 1973; children: Saul Moshe, Shana Chaya, Joel Mordechai, Abigail Deborah. Student, Hebrew U., Jerusalem, 1970-71; BA, U. Fla., 1973, MA, Cert. in Urban Studies, 1977; JD, Emory U., 1980. Bar: Ga. 1980, Fla. 1980, U.S. Dist. Ct. (so. dist.) Fla. 1983. Assoc. Gladstone Assocs., Miami, Fla., 1973-75; ptnr. Emory Assocs., Atlanta, 1979-80; dep. consumer adv. Metro Dade County, Miami, 1980-81; asst. pub. defender 11th Jud. Cir., Miami, 1981-83; ptnr. Roth & Zipkin, Miami, 1984-86; pvt. practice, Miami, 1986-87, 88-91; chief consumer litigation sect. Fla. Dept. Legal Affairs, Miami and Tallahassee, 1987-88; ptnr. Roth, Zipkin, Cove & Roth, Miami, 1991-95; pvt. practice law, 1995—; adj. prof. law U. Miami; pres., chmn. bd. Analytic Prognostication, Inc., Miami, 1988—. Pres., chmn. bd. dirs. Sta. WDNA-FM Pub. Radio, Miami, 1981-82; mem. consumer adv. coun. Fla. Hosp. Cost Containment Bd., Tallahassee, 1988-89. Fellow Soc. for Applied Anthropology; mem. ABA, ATLA, North Dade Bar Assn., Dade County Bar Assn., Fla. Bar Assn. (consumer protection com. 1988—), Omicron Delta Kappa. Democrat. Jewish. Office: 2020 NE 163rd St North Miami Beach FL 33162

ZIPP, RONALD DUANE, judge; b. New Braunfels, Tex., Dec. 7, 1946; s. Nolan William and Irene Alyce (Stiba) Z.; children: Robert Andrew, Kristi Nicole; m. Saundra Zipp, Mar. 5, 1989. BBA, Tex. A&M U., 1968; JD St. Mary U., San Antonio, 1971. Bar: Tex. 1971, U.S. Dist. Ct. (so. dist.) Tex. 1972, U.S. Dist. Ct. (we. dist.) Tex. 1974, U.S. Ct. Appeals (5th cir.) 1973, U.S. Supreme Ct. 1974. Assoc. Kelley, Looney, Alexander & Hiester, Edinburg, Tex., 1971-73; ptnr. Pena, McDonald, Prestia & Zipp, Edinburg, 1973-81; sole practice, New Braunfels, 1981-82, 89—; judge Comal County (Tex.) Ct.-at-Law, New Braunfels, 1983—. Bd. dirs. New Braunfels Community Services, 1992—, pres. 1981-83, sec. 1994; bd. dirs. Child Welfare, vice-chmn., 1981-82, chmn. 1982-83; active Drover-Comal County Fair Assn.; vol. H.O.S.T.S.; vice chmn. Folkfest, 1994, chmn., 1995—. Mem. ABA, Greater New Braunfels C. of C. (legislative com., resources com., heritage com.), Tex. State Jr. Bar (criminal law com. 1975-76), Tex. Criminal Def. Lawyers' Assn. (bd. dirs. 1976-77, mem. various coms.), Tex. Aggie Bar Assn. (charter), Comal County Bar Assn. (past pres.), Comal County A&M Club (pres.), Hidalgo County Bar Assn. (treas. 1972-75), Opa and Kleine Opa of Wurstfest Assn. (chmn. Folkfest), Hidalgo County A&M Club (pres.), Phi Delta Phi. Lutheran. Lodges: Elks, Kiwanis, Lions (1st and 2nd v.p.). Author local newspaper column; contbr. articles to profl. jours. Office: 384 Landa St New Braunfels TX 78130-5401

ZIPRIN, RICHARD LEWIS, microbiologist, researcher; b. N.Y.C., Feb. 25, 1943; s. Irving and Lottie Zelia Ziprin; m. Yolanda Asacio, Aug. 28, 1973; 1 child, Brian Aaron. BS in Biology, Fairleigh Dickinson U., 1964; MS in Microbiology, L.I. U., 1967; PhD in Bacteriology, Iowa State U., 1970. Teaching fellow L.I. U., Bklyn., 1964-66; teaching asst. Iowa State U., Ames, 1967-70, rsch. assoc., 1970-71, 74-75; postdoctoral fellow Ohio State U., Columbus, 1971-72; full master Conestoga Coll., Guelph, Ont., Can., 1972-73; microbiologist ARS Agrl. Rsch. Svc. USDA, College Station, Tex., 1975—; vis. asst. prof. Iowa State U., Ames, 1973-74. Author: (with others) Air Pollution: Physiological Effects, 1982; author: Foodborne Disease Handbook, 1994. Mem. Am. Soc. for Microbiology, U.S. Animal Health Assn., Soc. for Leukocyte Biology, Am. Assn. Immunologists, Poultry Sci. Assn. Jewish. Office: USDA Food Animal Protection Rsch Lab, Agrl Rsch Svc Rt 5 Box 810 College Station TX 77845

ZIRKLE, WILLIAM VERNON, philanthropist; b. Berlin, Germany, Feb. 5, 1959; (parents Am. citizens); s. Michael Neale and Nancy (Behrend) Z. AAS in Electronics, Northern Va. C.C., 1980; BA in Humanities, U. Va., 1984. Cons. designer audio system Uno's Pizzeria, Washington, 1989; cons. strategies mgmt. APC, Merrifield, Va., 1993; cons. tech. WESCO, Falls Church, Va., 1977—; proprietor Circle Enterprises, Arlington, Va., 1984—. Canvass Children's Defense Fund, Washington, 1991, 92; specializer Md. Sherriff's Youth Ranch, 1991; chair Adult Religious Edn., Falls Church, 1986. Named to Outstanding Young Men of Am., 1992, 96. Mem. Cath. Alumni Club (v.p. 1991), Cath. Young Adults Club (religion com. 1988-89, parliamentarian 1987-88), U. Va. Alumni Club. Independent. Home: 5051 7th Rd S Apt 302 Arlington VA 22204-2520

ZIRPS, FOTENA ANATOLIA, psychologist, researcher; b. Pitts., Mar. 27, 1958; d. George T. and Barbara F. (Skinner) Z. BA, U. Akron, 1983, MA, 1987; PhD, Fla. State U., 1990. Sch. psychologist Canton (Ohio) City Schs., 1985-86; sch. psychologist Leon County Schs., Tallahassee, 1986-88, program evaluator, 1988-90; cons. Evaluation Systems Design, Inc., Tallahassee, 1990-91; pres. Zirps, Vella and Assocs., Inc., Tallahassee, 1991—; dir. program evaluation Families First, Atlanta, 1991-94; assoc. prof. Fla. Mental Health Inst. U. South Fla., 1995—; Fla. mental health coord. Fla. Mental Health Inst.-U. South Fla., 1995—; coord. spl. studies for children Comprehensive Cmty. Mental Health Program-U. South Fla., 1995—; tchr. Fla. State U., Tallahassee, summers 1988-91, grant coord., 1989-90; cons. hild Welfare League Am.; coord. spl. studies Comprehensive Cmty. Mental Health Svcs. Children with Severe Emotional Disturbances. Author: Sun and Moon, 1991, Doing It Right th First Time: A Model Quality Assurance for Human Services Agencies, 1994, (with others) Computer Models of Reading, 1989; author, cartoonist: (slides show/audio tape) Human Rights, 1986; co-inventor: (games) Beauty Pageant, Alien Abduction; editor, coauthor: Quality Improvement Program and Program Evaluation in Child Welfare: Managing into the Next Century; panel standards writers Coun. on Accreditation Svcs. for Families and Children, Inc. Chmn. grad. student adv. com. Fla. State, 1986-88. Mem. Am. Psychol. Assn., Am. Evaluation Assn., Am. Ednl. Rsch. Assn. (Disting. Presenter 1991), Nat. Coun. Rsch. in Child Welfare, Fla. Ednl. Rsch. Assn. (Disting. Author 1990). Quaker. Office: U South Fla Fla Mental Health Inst 13301 Bruce B Downs Blvd Tampa FL 33612-3807

ZISKA, DAVID LEE, public relations professional; b. Belleville, Ill., Sept. 7, 1931; s. Fred Marion and Mulvina Adelle (Henderson) Z.; m. Carol Gene Dinges, Aug. 16, 1952 (div. 1977); children: Cynthia, Nancy, Jayne, Judy; m. Julie Anne Oldford, May 20, 1978; children: Kenneth, Brian. BSBA, Washington U., St. Louis, 1953; MBA, Washington U., 1956. Mktg. rep. IBM, St. Louis, 1956-65; devel. mgr. IBM, White Plains, N.Y., 1965-68; adminstrv. asst., v.p. corp. staff IBM, Armonk, N.Y., 1968-70; br. mgr. IBM, Miami, Fla., 1970-86; dir. external programs IBM, Miami, 1986-94; pres. Life's Precious Memories, Miami, 1994—; mem. bus. adv. bd., Nat. Alliance Bus., Washington, 1988-90. Vice-chmn. Met. Miami Action Plan, 1986—; bd. dirs. Bus. Vols. for Arts, 1987—; pres. Greater Miami Partnership, 1989; chmn. bd. dirs. Jr. Achievement of Greater Miami, 1983; bd. dirs. Pvt. Industry Coun. of South Fla., 1983—, chmn. bd. dirs., 1985-87; bd. dirs. Dade County Safety Coun., 1990—. Mem. Greater Miami C. of C. (trustee 1972-87). Republican. Office: IBM One Columbus Place Coral Gables FL 33134

ZISLIS, PAUL MARTIN, software engineering executive; b. Chgo., Feb. 8, 1948; s. Harold Solomon and Beatrice (Bossen) Z.; m. Sharon Margo Kaufmann, June 8, 1969; children: Daniel, Benjamin, Rachel. BS in Computer Sci., U. Ill., 1969; SM in Info. Sci., U. Chgo., 1971; PhD in Computer Sci., Purdue U., 1974. Mem. tech. staff AT&T Bell Labs., Naperville, Ill., 1969-72, 74-77; supr. data network devel. AT&T Bell Labs., Holmdel, N.J., 1977-81, dept. head data network architecture, 1981-82; dept. head advanced software tech. AT&T Bell Labs., Naperville, 1982-90; dir. software engring. Ericsson Raynet Corp., Menlo Park, Calif., 1990-93, dir. product validation, 1993-95; v.p. comm. sys. software Am. Mobile Satellite Corp., Reston, Va., 1995—. Contbr. articles to profl. jours. Grad. fellow IBM, 1973-74. Mem. IEEE, Assn. for Computing Machinery, Phi Beta Kappa. Office: Am Mobile Satellite Corp 10802 Parkridge Blvd Reston VA 22091

ZISSON, JAMES STERN, investment management consultant; b. N.Y.C., Nov. 2, 1952; s. Miles and Norma Z.; m. Anita Neiman, Oct. 16, 1988. BA in Human Studies, Brown U., 1974. Lic. investment advisor cons. Gen. mgr. A&M Records, N.Y.C., 1976-78, Los Angeles, 1976-78; prin., owner Sound & Vision Mgmt., Palm Beach, Fla., 1978-84; sr. v.p., sr. investment mgmt. cons. Smith Barney, West Palm Beach, Fla., 1987-96; mem. dir.'s coun. Shearson Lehman Bros., West Palm Beach, Fla., 1987-93, mem. president's coun., 1985; mem. dirs. adv. group Smith Barney, West Palm Beach, 1993-95; mem. dir.'s coun. Shearson Lehman Bros., West Palm Beach, 1987-91, dir.'s coun., 1986, pres.'s coun., 1985. Mem. Investment Mgmt. Cons. Assn., Beach Point, Gov.'s Club, Phi Beta Kappa. Home: 1600 N Ocean Blvd Palm Beach FL 33480-3022 Office: Smith Barney 777 S Flagler Dr Ste 800 West Palm Beach FL 33401-6161

ZLATKIS, ALBERT, chemistry educator; b. Pomorzany, Poland, Mar. 27, 1924; came to Can. 1927, U.S., 1949, naturalized, 1959; s. Louis and Zisel (Nable) Z.; m. Esther Shessel, June 15, 1947; children: Debra, Lori, Robert. B.A.Sc., U. Toronto, 1947, M.A.Sc., 1948; Ph.D., Wayne State U., 1952. Rsch. chemist Shell Oil Co., Houston, 1953-55; asst. prof. chemistry U. Houston, 1955-58, assoc. prof., 1958-63, chmn. chemistry dept., 1958-62, prof. chemistry, 1963—; adj. prof. chemistry Baylor Coll. Medicine, 1975—; tour speaker Am. Chem. Soc., 1961, 63, 66, South Africa Chem. Inst., 1971, USSR Acad. Scis., 1973, Polish Acad. Scis., 1977; chmn. Internat. Symposium on Advances in Chromatography, 1963—. Author: Practice of Gas Chromatography, 1967, Preparative Gas Chromatography, 1971, Advances in Chromatography, 25 vols., 1963-88, A Concise Introduction to Organic Chemistry, 1973, High Performance Thin-Layer Chromatography, 1977, 75 Years of Chromatography—A Historical Dialogue, 1979, Instrumental HPTLC, 1980, Electron Capture—Theory and Practice in Chromatography, 1981; contbr. articles to profl. jours.; mem. editorial bd. Jour. High Resolution Chromatography, Jour. Chromatograpic Science, Chromatographia, Jour. Chromatography. Recipient Analyst of Yr. award Dallas Soc. Analytical Chemistry, 1977, Tswett Meml. medal USSR Acad. Scis., 1980, Tswett Chromatography medal, 1983, NASA Tech. award, 1975, 80, NASA Patent award, 1978, Disting. Tex. Scientist award Tex. Acad. Sci., 1985, James L. Waters Pioneers in Devel. Analytical Instrumentation award, 1990; grantee USPHS, 1966, NASA, 1964-76, Welch Found., 1969, AEC, 1967, NSF, 1978, EPA, 1979, U.S. Army Rsch. Office, 1982, Gulf Coast Hazardous Substance Rsch. Ctr., 1989, Tex. Advanced Rsch. Program, 1991. Mem. Am. Chem. Soc. (chmn. S.E. Tex. sect. 1964, award in chromatography 1973, S.W. regional award 1988), Groupement pour l'Avancement des Méthodes Spectrographiques (France), Sigma Xi, Phi Lambda Upsilon. Home: 22 Sandalwood Dr Houston TX 77024-7122

ZLOCH, WILLIAM J., federal judge; b. 1944. Judge U.S. Dist. Ct. (so. dist.) Fla., Ft. Lauderdale, 1985—. Office: US Dist Ct 299 E Broward Blvd Fort Lauderdale FL 33301-1944

ZOCCHI, LOUIS JOSEPH, product designer, game company executive; b. Chgo., Feb. 16, 1935; s. Louis Alexander and Martha (Adams) Z.; m. Elissa Lorelei Scott, June 8, 1959 (Sept. 1976); children: David, Suzanne, LaRee, Lisa; m. Sharon Annette Olson, May 25, 1985; 1 child, Heidi Olson. Cert. air traffic controller, 1955, air traffic control instr., 1964. Commd. USAF, 1954, advanced through grades to tech. sgt.; air traffic contr. USAF, Offut AFB, Nebr., 1954, Lincoln AFB, Nebr., 1955-59, Misawa AFB, Japan, 1959-63, Holloman AFB, N.Mex., 1963-64; air traffic control instr. USAF, Keesler AFB, Miss., 1964-70; air traffic contr. USAF, Mather AFB, Calif., 1970-71, Kimpo AFB, Korea, 1971-72, George AFB, Calif., 1972-73, Biloxi, Miss., 1973-75; ret. USAF, 1975; commd. 1st lt. Miss. State Guard, 1991, advanced through grades to capt., 1993; owner Zocchi Distbrs., Victorville, Calif., 1972—; pres. Gamescience, Inc., Cedarhurst, N.Y., 1974—; cruise dir. Europa Star cruise ship, 1988; cons. Dupuy Inst., 1995. Designer (games) Battle of Britain, 1968, Star Fleet Battle Manual, 1977 (Gamesday award 1981), Basic and Advanced Fighter Combat, 1980 (H.G. Wells award 1981); inventor Zocchihedron 100 sided dice, 1985. Recipient Hobbyist award Metro Detroit Gamers, 1979, Spl. Svc. award Strategists Club, 1982, Charles Roberts Adventure Gaming Hall of Fame award, 1987, Gama Honor of Svc. award 1991. Mem. Game Mfrs. Assn. (chmn. membership com. 1978-84, v.p. 1978-84, bd. dirs. 1985), Internat. Brotherhood Magicians, Hobby Industry Assn. (pres. gaming div. 1981), Gulf Coast Jazz Soc. (pres.), Soc. Am. Magicians (pres.). Home and Office: Gamescience Inc 7604 Newton Dr North Biloxi MS 39532

ZODHIATES, PHILIP SPIROS, advertising executive; b. Hackensack, N.J., July 17, 1955; s. Spiros George and Joan Carol (Wassil) Z.; m. Kathie Lee Gentry, May 25, 1981; children: William, Victoria, Josiah. BS cum laude, Fairleigh Dickenson U., 1976. Advt. dir. AMG Internat., Ridgefield, N.J., 1974-76; mktg. dir. AMG Internat., Chattanooga, 1976-80; acting pub. Pulpit Helps, Chattanooga, 1976-80; account exec. Infomat Mktg., Palos Verdes, Calif., 1981; v.p. Internat. Christian Communications, Niagara Falls, N.Y., 1981-84, Christian Aid, Charlottesville, Va., 1984-88; pres. Response Unltd., Waynesboro, Va., 1979—. Bd. dirs. GlobaLink Ministries, 1988-94, Advancing Native Missions, 1993—. Mem. Christian Ministries Mgmt. Assn. Office: Response Unltd RR 5 Box 251 Waynesboro VA 22980-9111

ZOGHBI, WILLIAM ANTOINE, cardiologist educator; b. Beirut, Lebanon, Oct. 28, 1955; came to U.S., 1977; m. Huda El Hibri, Sept. 17, 1983; children: Roula Maya, Anthony William. BS, Am. U., Beirut, 1975; postgrad., Am. U., 1975-77; MD, Meharry Med. Coll., 1979. Diplomate Am. Bd. Internal Medicine, Cardiovascular Diseases; cert. ACLS. Intern U. Tex. Med. Br. Hosps., Galveston, 1979-80; resident Baylor Coll. Medicine, Houston, 1980-82, fellow in cardiology, 1982-85, instr., asst. prof., 1985-91, assoc. prof., 1991—; asst. dir. Meth. Hosp., Houston, 1989—. Reviewer Sci. Jours.; contbr. articles to profl. jours. Fellow Am. Coll. Cardiology, Coun. on Clin. Cardiology; mem. Am. Soc. Echocardiography (ad hoc com. on rsch. 1993-96, ad hoc writing group on stress echocardiography), Am. Heart Assn. (program com. 1991-94), Tex. Med. Assn., Harris County Med. Soc., Alpha Omega Alpha. Home: 6618 Sewanee Houston TX 77005 Office: Baylor Coll Medicine 6550 Fannin St # SM677 Houston TX 77030-2705

ZOHDI, MAGD ELDIN, engineering educator; b. Cairo, Apr. 18, 1933; came to U.S., 1964, naturalized, 1971; s. Ismail Abdella and Nemat (Rizk) Z.; diploma Cairo U., 1954, BS, 1962; MS, U. Kan., 1965; PhD, Okla. State U., 1969; m. Omnia Elmenshawy, Sept. 17, 1964; children—Tarek, Mona. With Maintenance Machinery, Cairo, 1954-60; instr. Cairo U., 1962-64; grad. tchg. asst. Okla. State U., Stillwater, 1966-69; assoc. prof. La. State U., Baton Rouge, 1969-75, prof. indsl. and mfg. sys. engring., 1977—; pres. Am. Contracting and Trading Corp., Baton Rouge, 1978, Quality Contracting Inc.; mem. U.S. Engring. Adv. Com. to State of Qatar, 1977—. Fulbright scholar, 1964; recipient Excellence in Undergrad. Tchg. award Standard Oil Found., 1971; Presdl. Honor award Okla. State U., 1968; Outstanding Educators of Am. award 1972; Disting. Faculty fellow La. State U. Sys., 1985. Mem. Soc. Mfg. Engrs., Am. Inst. Indsl. Engrs., Am. Mil. Engrs., Sigma Xi, Tau Beta Pi. Mem. editl. bd. Mech. Engrs. Handbook; contbr. articles to profl. jours., chpts. to tech. textbooks. Achievements include application of mathematical programming for optimization of air to ground gunnery design and effectiveness. Home: 5050 S Chalet Ct Baton Rouge LA 70808-4839 Office: La State U 3132 Ceba Bldg Baton Rouge LA 70803-7877

ZOHNY, A. Y., law educator, business educator, consultant, international development consultant; b. Cairo, May 13, 1946; s. Younis Zohny and Dawlat Hussein; m. Patricia Trobian, Aug. 20, 1983; 1 child, Josephine. BS, El Shorta Acad., Cairo, 1969; LLB, Ain Shams U., Cairo, 1969; MA in Polit. Sci., Bloomsburg U., 1976; PhD in Pub. and Internat. Affairs, U. Pitts., 1984. Assoc. prof. European divsn. U. Md., Heidelberg, Fed. Republic of Germany, 1987-88; assoc. prof. bus. adminstrn., dir. Inst. for Internat. Devel. & Strategic Studies Southea. U., Washington, 1988-90; prof. bus. law and bus. adminstrn. Strayer Coll., Washington, 1990—; CEO, pres. Mid East Devel. and Sci. Inst., Hanover, Md., 1992—; faculty assoc. Johns Hopkins U., Balt., 1994—; sr. advisor Ednl. Mission Embassy of Saudi Arabia, Washington, 1985-86; internat. devel. cons. World Bank, USDA. Author: (book) Politics, Economics and Dynamics of Development Administration, 1988. Recipient scholarship Bloomsburg U., 1975-76; fellow U. Pitts., 1979-84. Mem. Congress of Polit. Economists, Acad. of Mgmt. Democrat. Office: Mid East Devel and Sci Inst Inc # 144 2657 Gold Annapolis Rd Hanover MD 21076

ZOLLER, MICHAEL, otolaryngologist, educator; b. New Orleans, July 21, 1947; s. Harry and Mildred (Daitch) Z.; m. Linda Kramer, Dec. 21, 1974; children: Rebecca, Jonathan. BS, U. New Orleans, 1968; MD, Tulane U., 1972. Resident in gen. surgery Jewish Hosp., St. Louis, 1972-74, Washington U. Sch. Medicine; resident in otolaryngology Mass. Eye and Ear Infirmary, Harvard U., Boston, 1974-77; pres. Ear, Nose and Throat Assocs., Savannah, Ga., 1977—; asst. clin. prof. surgery Med. Coll. Ga., Augusta, 1982-96; assoc. clin. prof. surgery, 1996—; co-dir. otoneurology dept. St. Joseph's Hosp., Savannah, 1994—. Chmn. med. divsn. United Way, Savannah, 1990, chmn. profl. divsn., 1991, 94, 95; v.p. Am. Cancer Soc., Savannah, 1994, bd. dirs., 1993—, pres. Chatham County Unit, 1996; bd. dirs. Savannah Country Day Sch., 1993—, chmn. ann. campaign, 1995-96; pres. Savannah Jewish Fedn., 1991-93. Recipient Young Leadership award Savannah Jewish Fedn., 1985, Boss of Yr. award Savannah Jaycees, 1993, Celebrate Savannah award for outstanding contbns. to Savannah, Ga. Guardian, 1996; Harvard U. Med. Sch. fellow, 1976-77. Fellow ACS; mem. AMA, Am. Acad. Head and Neck Soc., Am. Neurotology Soc., Ga. Med. Soc. (v.p. endowment fund 1996, sec. endowment fund 1992, pres. 1992, John B. Rabun Cmty. Svc. award 1995), 1st Dist. Med. Assn. (pres. 1987-88), Med. Assn. Ga. (bd. dirs., mem. ho. dels., Ga. Cup award 1993, Ayest-Wyeth Cmty. Svc. award 1996), So. Med. Assn., Ga. Soc. Otolaryngology (sec.-treas. 1995-96), Savannah C. of C. Office: Ear Nose and Throat Assocs 5201 Frederick St Savannah GA 31405-4501

ZOMBER, BEVERLY LOUISE, medical, surgical, geriatric and psychiatric nurse, educator; b. Evergreen Park, Ill., June 24, 1945; d. Louis and Irene (Cloud) Z. BA, DePaul U., 1967; MA, Northwestern U., 1969; ADN, Fla. Keys Community Coll., 1990. RN, Fla. Ins. claims specialist R.R. Retirement Bd., Chgo., 1969-77; Medicare specialist Social Security Adminstrn., Key West, Fla., 1979-88, L.A., 1979-88; mental health technician Guidance Clinic of Middle Keys, Marathon, Fla., 1988-90; staff/charge nurse Marathon Manor Convalescent Ctr., 1990-92; med.-surg. staff nurse, team leader Mariner's Hosp., Tavernier, Fla., 1992; staff nurse/counselor Marathon Comprehensive Psychiat. Clinic, 1992—; area dir. Nursing Unlimited, Inc., Marathon, 1993; mktg. dir., mem. adj. faculty, cons. Nursing Unltd., Florida Keys, Fla., 1992; owner, pres. Forms Inc., 1992—; instr. English lit., composition and creative writing Fla. Keys C.C., Marathon, 1993—; instr. practical nursing Monroe County Sch. System, Fla. Keys, 1993—; dir. nursing Griswold Spl. Care, Fla. Keys, 1993-96. Former chmn. Inter-Agy. Coun. Monroe County, Fla. Ill. State scholar 1963-67, DePaul U. scholar, 1963-67. Mem. ANA, Fla. Nurses Assn., Marathon Bus. and Profl. Women.

ZOMLEFER, WENDY BETH, botanist, biological illustrator; b. Fitchburg, Mass., Sept. 22, 1954; d. Jack and Dorothy (Friedman) Z. BS in Botany summa cum laude, U. Vt., 1976; MS in Botany, U. Fla., 1980, PhD in Botany, 1991. Lab technician Polysar Chem. Corp., Leominster, Mass., 1971-72; rsch. asst. dept. botany U. Vt., Burlington, 1973-75, herbarium asst. Pringle Herbarium, 1976; herbarium asst., staff biol. illustrator Marie Selby Botanical Gardens, Sarasota, Fla., 1976-78; rsch. asst. FLAS Herbarium Fla. Agrl. Sta., Herbarium U. Fla., Gainesville, 1978; biol. illustrator dept. botany U. Fla., Gainesville, 1978, 79, teaching asst., graphic designer dept. botany, 1979-80, rsch. asst., biol. illustrator dept. ornamental horticulture, 1980-81, med. illustrator dept. natural scis. Fla. Mus. Natural History, 1981-94, postdoctoral assoc. botany dept., 1995—; freelance cons. Biol. Illustrations, Inc., Gainesville, 1981—; teaching asst., rsch. asst. dept. botany U. Vt., Burlington, 1974-75; teaching asst. dept. botany U. Fla., Gainesville, 1979, U. Mich. Biol. Sta., 1987; herbarium asst. Fla. Agr. Sta. Herbarium, U. Fla., 1981; substitute tchr. U. Fla., 1988, 89. Author: Common Florida Angiosperm Families, Part 1, 1983, Part 2, 1986, Flowering Plants of Florida: A Guide to Common Families, 1989, Guide to Flowering Plant Families, 1994; contbr. articles to profl. jours. Mem. Am. Soc. Plant Taxonomists, Am. Bryological and Lichenological Soc., Internat. Assn. Bryologists, Fla. Native Plant Soc., Guild of Natural Sci. Illustrators, Com. Small

Magazine Editors and Pubs., Phi Beta Kappa. Office: Biological Illustrations Inc PO Box 15292 Gainesville FL 32604-5292

ZOOK, THERESA FUETTERER, gemologist, consultant; b. Barberton, Ohio, Mar. 12, 1919; d. Charles Theodore and Ethel May (Knisely) Fuetterer; m. Donovan Quay Zook, June 21, 1941; children: Theodore Alan, Jacqueline Deborah Zook Cochran. AB, Ohio U., 1941; MA in Pub. Adminstrn., Am. U., 1946. Adminstrv. intern Nat. Inst. Pub. Affairs, Washington, 1941-42; mgmt. intern U.S. Dept. Agr., Washington, 1941-42; adminstrv. analyst Office Emergency Mgmt., Washington, 1942-43, Office Price Adminstrn., Washington, 1943-45; founder Zook and Zook Cons., Arlington, Va., 1945-47; tchr. ancient history and U.S. govt. Fairfax County (Va.) Pub. Schs., 1963-64; founder, pres. Associated Gem Consulting Lab., Alexandria, 1974—, Alpha Gate Crafts Ltd., Alexandria, 1977—; color cons. Internat. Com. on Color in Gems, Bangkok, Thailand, 1983. Author: Directory of Selected Color Resources Annotated Guide, 1982, Reunion of Descendants of David and Magdalena (Blough) Zook, 1983, Basic Machine Knitting, 1979; contbr. articles to profl. jours. Bd. dirs. Am. Embassy Com. on Edn., Montevideo, Uruguay, 1962; co-founder Workshop of Arts, Santiago, Chile, 1958; mem. Nat. Trust for Hist. Preservation, Nat. Mus. Women in Arts, Nat. Mus. Am. Indian, Am. Horticulture Soc., Textile Mus. Fellow Gemmological Assn. of Gt. Britain (diplomate); mem. AAUW, DAR, Nat. Geneal. Soc., Inter-Soc. Color Coun. (chmn. com. color in gemstones 1982-84, Appreciation cert. 1984), Accredited Gemological Assn. (co-founder, v.p.). Home: PO Box 6310 Alexandria VA 22306-0310

ZOOROB, ROGER JAMIL, physician; b. Kuwait, Educator, Aug. 2, 1960; arrived in U.S., 1989; s. Jamil K. and Aida J. (Fata) Z.; m. Grace R. Khouri, June 7, 1988; children: Andrew, Michael. BS, Am. Univ. Beirut, Beirut, Lebanon, 1981, MD, 1985, MPH, 1988. Diplomate Am. Bd. Family Practice. Residency Anderson (S.C.) Meml. Hosp., 1989-92; fellowship Univ. Ky., Lexington, 1994-95; faculty dept. family practice Am. Univ. Beirut, 1988-89; pvt. practice Brown County Hosp., Georgetown, Ohio, 1992-94; assoc. dir. grad. medical edn. dept. family practice Univ. Ky., Lexington, 1995—; vol. faculty Univ. Cin., 1992-94; family medicine cons. dept. family practice U. Bahrain, Manama, Bahrain, 1989. Author (book chpts.): Saunders Family Practice Review, 1995; contbr. articles to profl. jours. Bd. dirs. Am. Heart Assn. 1993-94. Recipient Outstanding Family Practice Resident award Am. Acad. Family Physicians, 1992. Mem. Am. Acad. Family Physicians, Soc. of Tchrs. of Family Medicine, Am. Pub. Health Assn., Ky. Acad. Family Physicians, Am. Assn. Medical Coll. United Methodist. Office: Univ Ky dept family practice Kentucky Clinic Lexington KY 40536

ZORIE, STEPHANIE MARIE, lawyer; b. Walla Walla, Wash., Mar. 18, 1951; d. Albert Robert and L. Ruth (Land) Z.; m. Francis Benedict Buda, Apr. 18, 1981 (div. 1985). BA, U. Fla., 1974, JD, 1978. Bar: N.Mex. 1991, Fla. 1978, U.S. Dist. Ct. (so. and mid. dists.) Fla. 1979, U.S. Ct. Appeals (5th cir.) 1979, U.S. Tax Ct. 1980, U.S. Ct. Customs and Patent Appeals 1980, U.S. Customs Ct. 1980, U.S. Ct. Mil. Appeals 1980, U.S. Ct. Claims 1981, U.S. Ct. Internat. Trade 1981, U.S. Ct. Appeals (11th cir.) 1981, U.S. Ct. Appeals (fed. cir.) 1982, U.S. Supreme Ct. 1988; cert. civil ct. mediator Fla. Supreme Ct., cert. cir. ct. mediator. Assoc. Richard Hardwich, Coral Gables, Fla., 1978-79, Brown, Terrell & Hogan P.A., Jacksonville, Fla., 1979-80, Dorsey, Arnold & Nichols, Jacksonville, 1980-81; sole practice Jacksonville, 1981-84; ptnr. Blakeley & Zorie P.A., Orlando, Fla., 1985-86; sole practice Orlando, Fla., 1986—, Santa Fe; owner Coyote Cody Co., 1991. Recipient Rep. Claude Pepper award, 1978. Mem. John Marshall Bar Assn., Spanish-Am. Law Students Assn., Phi Alpha Delta (local sec.-treas. 1978-79). Address: PO Box 2898 Santa Fe NM 87504-2898 also: PO Box 372118 Indian Harbor Beach FL 32937

ZORN, ROBERT EUGENE, software company executive; b. Manhasset, N.Y., July 26, 1957; s. Eugene Christian Jr. and Elizabeth (Orban) Z. AB, Duke U., 1979; MBA, U. Pa., 1981. Mktg. prin. Trammell Crow Co., Richmond, Va., 1986-90; chmn. Russell-Zorn Computing Corp., Dallas, 1991—. Author: Real Golfers Don't Take Mulligans, 1994; creator: (software products) Chief Legal Officer for Windows, 1994, Work Order Wonder for Windows, 1995. Mem. alumni bd. St. Mark's Sch. Tex., Dallas, 1993—. Mem. Northwood Golf Club. Home and Office: 4216 Hanover Ave Dallas TX 75225-6746

ZSCHAU, JULIUS JAMES, lawyer; b. Peoria, Ill., Apr. 1, 1940; s. Raymond Johann Ernst and Rosamond Lillian (Malicoat) Z.; m. Leila Joan Krueger, Aug. 7, 1971; children: Kristen Elisabeth, Kimberly Erna, Kira Jamie, Karla Johanna. BS, U. Ill., Champaign, 1964, JD, 1966; LLM, John Marshall Law Sch., 1978. Bar: Ill. 1966, Fla. 1975. Atty., Ill. Central Gulf R.R. Co., Chgo., 1966-68; assoc. Coin & Sheerin, Chgo., 1968-70, Snyder, Clarke et al, Waukegan, Ill., 1970-72; counsel Ill. Ctr. Corp., Chgo., 1972-74; v.p., gen. counsel, sec. Am. Agronomics Corp., Tampa, Fla., 1974-76; pres. Sorota & Zschau, Clearwater, Fla., 1976-90; shareholder Buynard, Harrell, Ostow & Ulrich PA, 1990-94, Johnson, Blakely, Pope, Bokor, Ruppel and Burns, Clearwater, 1994—; bd. dirs. Attys. Title Ins. Fund, Inc. (chmn. bd. dirs. 1994-95); chmn. com. on land trusts, exec. com. real property sect., vice chair grievance com., 1985-87, Fla. Bar, chair leadership conf. 1987; chmn. Jud. Nominating Commn. of 6th Jud. Dist., 1991-94; Bd. dirs. Nat. Attys. Title Assurance Fund, Attys. Title Guaranty Fund of Colo.; mem. Pinellas County Exec. Com., Tampa Regional Planning Coun., 1988-92. Served to capt. USNR, 1962-92. Fellow Am. Bar Found.; mem. ABA (chmn. land trust com.), Am. Coll. Real Estate Lawyers (chmn. condominium com.), Ill. Bar Assn., Chgo. Bar Assn., Clearwater Bar Assn. (past pres.), Fla. Coun. Bar Assn. (past pres., past chmn. vol. bar liaison com.), Fla. Bar Found. (legal aid to poor com., chair judicial nominating commn. 1991-94, chmn. judicial nominations procedures com.), Clearwater C. of C. (bd. govs., exec. com., past pres.). Republican. Lutheran. Clubs: Countryside Country (Clearwater, Fla.); Masons, Scottish Rite, Shriners. Home: 1910 Saddle Rd N Dunedin FL 34698-2437

ZUBILLAGA, JOSE GUSTAVO, education specialist; b. N.Y.C., Jan. 31, 1945. BA, U. Md., 1974; BS, Regents College SUNY, Albany, N.Y., 1994; MEd, Boston U., 1977; MPA, Brenau Coll., 1985; EdD, U. S.C., 1996. Commd. 2d lt. U.S. Army, 1970, advanced through grades to 1st lt.; procurement officer U.S. Army, Vietnam, 1971-72, Heidelberg, Fed. Republic of Germany, 1972-75; edn. svcs. officer Army Continuing Edn. System, Muenster, Fed. Republic of Germany, 1975-80, Bayreuth, Fed. Republic of Germany, 1980-82; edn. specialist U.S. Army Signal Sch., Ft. Gordon, Ga., 1982-90; tng. coord. Westinghouse Savannah River Co., Aiken, S.C., 1990-92, sr. tng. specialist, lead instr., 1992—; mgr. Hispanic employment program 7th Army Tng. Command, Bayreuth, 1980-82, U.S. Army Signal Sch., Ft. Gordon, Ga., 1983-87. Mem. NRA, Nat. Arbor Day Found., Nat. Image Inc. (founder local chpt., pres. 1987-88), Am. Legion, Internat. Platform Assn., Webb Lodge 166 (master mason), Lions Club. Republican. Roman Catholic. Home: PO Box 207 Johnston SC 29832-0207 Office: Westinghouse Savannah River PO Box 616 Aiken SC 29802-0616

ZUBIZARRETA, JOHN, English language educator; b. N.Y.C., Sept. 1, 1950; s. Juan and Consuelo (Romero) Z.; m. Margaret Elizabeth Carlisle, Aug. 2, 1980; children: Anna Ruth, Maria Elizabeth. AA, Miami-Dade Jr. Coll., 1971; BA, Fla. Internat. U., 1973; MA, U. S.C., 1975, PhD, 1983. Instr. Western Carolina U., Cullowhee, N.C., 1979-82, 85-86; tchr. Ashley Hall Upper Sch., Charleston, S.C., 1986-87; vis. asst. prof. Coll. of Charleston, 1986-88; prof. Columbia (S.C.) Coll., 1988—, dir. honors, 1989—; tchg. improvement cons., nationwide, 1992—. Contbr. articles to profl. jours., publs. Mem. S.C. Humanities Coun. Speakers Bur., 1989—, S.C. Libr. "Let's Talk About It" Program, 1990—. Recipient Outstanding Tchr. award South Atlantic MLA, 1993, Gov.'s Disting. Prof. award S.C. Commn. on Higher Edn., 1992, Exemplary Tchr. award Nat. United Meth. Bd. Higher Edn., 1992, Outstanding Faculty award Columbia Coll., 1991, Sears-Roebuk Found. Teaching Excellence and Campus Leadership award, 1991, Outstanding Faculty Citizen and Exemplary Tchr. recognition Am. Assn. for Higher Edn., 1994; named CASE U.S. Prof. of Yr. for S.C., Carnegie Found. for Advancement of Tchg., 1994. Mem. Modern Lang. Assn., Am. Lit. Assn., Nat. Collegiate Hons. Coun., Conf. on Christianity and Lit. (Michael K. Maher prize for Outstanding Essay 1990).

ZUCCO, RONDA KAY, addictions program administrator; b. Peoria, Ill., Apr. 3, 1960; d. Richard Leon Zucco. BA, So. Ill. U., 1981. Cert. addictions profl.; internat. cert. alcohol and drug counselor. Counselor Spl. Supportive Svcs., So. Ill. U., Carbondale, 1981-83; substance abuse counselor Interventions, Chgo., 1984-86; addictions counselor Parkside at BroMenn, Bloomington, Ill., 1986-89; dir. continuing care/sr. counselor Fla. Hosp. (formerly Parkside), Orlando, Fla., 1989-95, cmty. rels. rep. Ctr. for Psychiatry, 1995; addictions program mgr. Charter Behavioral Health Sys., Kissimmee, Fla., 1995—; tng. instr. for group facilitation Parkside/Fla. Hosp., 1989-95; presenter seminars in field, bd. dirs. Ill. Cert. Bd. Addiction Profls., Bloomington, 1986-89. Vol. ARC, Cardondale, 1978-81, crisis hotline Jackson County Cmty. Mental Health Ctr., Cardondale, 1981, Alliance for the Mentally Ill Greater Orlando, 1995—, Coalition for the Homeless, Orlando, 1995—; active AIDS Spkr.'s Bur., BroMenn Healthcare, Bloomington, Ill., 1986-89. State of Ill. Gen. Assembly scholar, 1977-81. Mem. Am. Mktg. Assn., Am. Assn. for Counseling and Devel., Am. Mental Health Counselors Assn., Fla. Alcohol and Drug Abuse Assn., Fla. Prevention Assn., Nat. Businesswomen's Leadership Assn., C. of C. Greater Orlando, Kappa Delta Pi, Chi Sigma Iota. Home: 10600 Bloomfield Dr Apt 311 Orlando FL 32825

ZUCCONI, DAVID G., zoo and museum director. Office: Tulsa Zool Pk 5701 E 36th St N Tulsa OK 74115-2105

ZUCKER, MARK J., art history educator; b. N.Y.C., Apr. 19, 1944; s. Abner and Florence (Newman) Z.; m. Susan Villa, Aug. 11, 1982. BA magna cum laude, Columbia U., 1964, MA, 1966, PhD, 1973. Instr. Syracuse (N.Y.) U., 1969-71; asst. prof. Fordham U., N.Y.C., 1971-76, U. Wis., Milw., 1976-81; assoc. prof. La. State U., Baton Rouge, 1981-92, prof., 1992—. Author: The Illustrated Bartsch, Early Italian Masters, Vol. 25, 1984, Vol. 24, part 1, 1993, Vol. 24, part 2, 1994; mem. editl. bd. Explorations in Renaissance Culture jour., Source: Notes in History of Art jour.; contbr. articles to profl. jours. Recipient Rsch. grant Fordham U., 1973, Rsch. grant U. Wis., 1980. Mem. Coll. Art Assn., Southeastern Coll. Art Conf., South Ctrl. Renaissance Conf., Italian Art Soc., Renaissance Soc. Am., Phi Beta Kappa. Office: La State Univ School Of Art Baton Rouge LA 70803

ZUCKERMAN, MARC JAY, gastroenterologist, medical educator; b. N.Y.C., Mar. 26, 1952; s. Jack and Estelle (Wittlin) Z. BA, U. Rochester, 1973; MD, Tufts U., 1977. Diplomate Am. Bd. Internal Medicine, Am. Bd. Gastroenterology. Intern in internal medicine Bay State Med. Ctr., Tufts U., Springfield, Mass., 1977-78, resident in internal medicine, 1978-80; gastroenterology fellow Albert Einstein Coll. Medicine, Bronx, N.Y., 1980-83; asst. prof. medicine Health Scis. Ctr., Tex. Tech U., El Paso, 1983-90, assoc. prof., 1990-96, prof., 1996—; chief divsn. gastroenterology Health Scis. Ctr., Tex. Tech U., 1983—; med. dir. endoscopy Thomason Hosp., El Paso, 1983—. Contbr. articles to profl. jours. Mem. Dallas chpt. Crohns and Colitis Found. Am., 1985. Fellow ACP, Am. Coll. Gastroenterology; mem. Am. Gastroent. Assn., Am. Soc. for Gastrointestinal Endoscopy, Am. Assn. for Study of Liver Disease. Office: Tex Tech U Health Scis Ctr 4800 Alberta Ave El Paso TX 79905-2709

ZUCKERMAN, SIDNEY, retired allergist, immunologist; b. N.Y.C., May 2, 1918; s. Max and Rose (Katz) Z.; m. Irene Elinor Cohen, Oct. 27, 1945; children: Elaine, Laurie, Jed, Amy. BA, Columbia Coll., 1939; MD, N.Y. Med. Coll., 1943. Diplomate Am. Bd. Internal Medicine, Am. Bd. Allergy and Immunology. Chief medicine 72d Sta. Hosp. US Army Med. Corps., Sendai, Japan, 1945-47; med. dir. Ford Instrument Co. divsn. Sperry Corp., N.Y.C., 1947-60; pvt. practice N.Y.C., 1947-91; med. dir. Sperry Rand Corp., Great Neck, N.Y., 1960-90. Capt. U.S. Army Med. Corps., 1945-47, Japan. Fellow ACP, Am. Coll. Allergists and Immunologists, Am. Acad. Allergy and Immunology, Am. Coll. Occupational Medicine, Am. Assn. Cert. Allergists; mem. Masons (jr. warden). Home: 4140 Bocaire Blvd Boca Raton FL 33487-1148

ZUHDI, NAZIH, surgeon; b. Beirut, May 19, 1925; came to U.S., 1950; s. Omar and Lutfiye (Atef) Z.; children by previous marriage: Omar, Nabil; m. Annette McMichael; children: Adam, Leyla, Zachariah. BA, Am. U., Beirut, 1946, MD, 1950. Diplomate Am. Bd. Surgery, Am. Bd. Thoracic Surgery. Intern St. Vincent's Hosp., S.I., N.Y., 1950-51, Presbyn.-Columbia Med. Ctr., N.Y.C., 1951-52; resident Kings County SUNY Med. Ctr., N.Y.C., 1952-56; fellow SUNY Downstate Med. Ctr., Bklyn., 1953-54; resident Univ. Hosp., Mpls., 1956; resident Univ. Hosp., Oklahoma City, 1957-58, practice surgery specializing in cardiovascular and thoracic, 1958-87, practice in heart transplantation, lung transplantation and heart-lung transplantation, 1985—; founder, dir. Transplantation Inst. Bapt. Med. Ctr., 1984—, chmn. dept. transplantation, 1994—; transplantation surgeon in chief Bapt. Hosp., Oklahoma City, 1984—; founder, chmn. Okla. Cardiovascular Inst., Oklahoma City, 1983-84, Okla. Heart Ctr., Oklahoma City, 1984-85. Contbg. author Cardiac Surgery, 1967, 2d edit., 1972; contbr. articles to profl. jours.; developer numerous med. devices, techniques, rsch. and publs. on cardiopulmonary bypass, internal hypothermia, assisted circulation, heart surgery and transplantation of thoracic organs; developer heart-lung machines; designer, use of exptl. plastic bypass hearts; originator use of banked citrated blood for cardiopulmonary bypass for open heart surgery, of clin. non-hemic primes of heart-lung machines producing intentional hemodilution, at present, the universally accepted principle of cardiopulmonary bypass for partial and total body perfusion; researcher in cardiovascular studies. Founder Islamic Ctr., Inc., Oklahoma City. Named Hon. Citizen, Brazil; inducted into Okla. Hall of Fame, 1994; Named NCCJ Humanitarian honoree, 1996. Fellow ACS; mem. AMA, NCCJ (Humanitarian award 1996), Am. Thoracic Soc., Okla. Thoracic Soc., So. Med. Assn., Okla. Med. Assn., Internat. Coll. Angiology, Am. Coll. Chest Physicians, Oklahoma City C. of C., Oklahoma County Med. Soc., Oklahoma City Clin. Soc., Okla. Surg. Assn., Oklahoma City Surg. Soc., Southwestern Surg. Congress, Am. Coll. Cardiology, Am. Soc. Artificial Internal Organs, Soc. Thoracic Surgeons (founding mem.), Am. Assn. for Thoracic Surgery, Internat. Cardiovasc. Soc., Okla. State Heart Assn., Osler Soc., So. Thoracic Surg. Assn., Lillehei Surg. Soc., Internat. Soc. Heart Transplantation, Dwight Harken's Founder's Group Cardiac Surgery, Internat. Soc. Cardiothoracic Surgery (Japan, founder), Am. Soc. Transplant Surgeons, Milestones of Cardiology of Am. Coll. Cardiology, Okla. City Golf and Country Club, Okla. Hall of Fame. Home: 7305 Lancet Ct Oklahoma City OK 73120-1430

ZUMBANO, ANTHONY RALPH, risk, claims management executive; b. Jersey City, May 11, 1947; s. Carl R. and Catherine (Guddemi) Z.; children: Carl Robert, Brian Joseph; m. Kathy E. Kenny, Oct. 7, 1989. BS, St. Peter's Coll., Jersey City, 1969; Dipl. Claims Law, Am. Ednl. Inst., Basking Ridge, N.J., 1973. Supr. Travelers Ins. Co., Morris Plains, N.J., 1969-78; v.p. Marsh & McLennan Inc., N.Y.C., 1978-84; pres., chief exec. officer AMNA Corp., Ft. Lauderdale, Fla., 1984-92; pres. PLCM Group, Inc., Ft. Lauderdale, 1993—. Contbr. articles to profl. jours. Vol. Broward County Spl. Olympics, Ft. Lauderdale, 1991—; bd. pres. Las Olas Villas, Ft. Lauderdale, 1986-88. Mem. Am. Soc. for Healthcare Risk Mgmt., Fla. Med. Malpractice Claims Coun., Tower Club. Republican. Roman Catholic. Home: Navarro Isle Fort Lauderdale FL 33301 Office: PLCM Group Inc 321 SE 18th St Fort Lauderdale FL 33316-2817

ZUNDE, PRANAS, information science educator, researcher; b. Kaunas, Lithuania, Nov. 26, 1923; came to U.S., 1960, naturalized, 1964; s. Pranas and Elzbieta (Lisajevic) Z.; m. Alge R. Bizauskas, May 29, 1945; children: Alge R., Audronis K., Aurelia R., Aidis L., Gytis J. Dipl. Ing., Hannover Inst. Tech., 1947; MS, George Washington U., 1965; PhD, Ga. Inst. Tech., 1968. Dir. project Documentation Inc., Bethesda, Md., 1961-64; mgr. mgmt. info. system Documentation Inc., Bethesda, 1964-65; sr. research scientist Ga. Inst. Tech., Atlanta, 1965-68, assoc. prof., 1968-72, prof. dept. computer sci., 1973-91, prof. emeritus, 1991—; cons. UNESCO, Caracas, Venezuela, 1970-72, Esquela Polit. Nacional, Quito, Ecuador, 1974-75, State of Ga., Atlanta, 1976-78, Royal Sch. Librarianship, Copenhagen, 1985-87, Clemson (N.C.) U., 1987—, N.Y. State Dept. Edn., 1993; vis. prof. Simon Bolivar U., Caracas, 1976, J. Kepler U., Austria, 1981; vis. scientist Riso Nat. Lab., Roskilde, Denmark, 1983, Lithuanian Acad. Scis., Vilnius, 1988-89. Author: Agriculture in Soviet Lithuania, 1962, National Science Information Systems in Eastern Europe, 1972; editor: Procs. Info. Utilities, 1974, Procs. Founds. of Info. and Software Sci., 1983-90; contbr. articles to tech. and sci. jours. Mem. senate Vitoldus Magnus U., Kaunas, Lithuania, 1990—. NSF grantee; Fulbright prof. NAS, 1975. Mem. Am. Soc. Info. Sci., Semiotic Soc. Am., Soc. Sigma Xi. Roman Catholic. Office: Ga Inst Tech Coll Computing North Ave Atlanta GA 30332

ZUNKER, SHARON JIENELL, commercial expediters company executive; b. Charleston, W.Va., July 28, 1943; d. Clifford W. and Iva A. (Neeley) Kenneway; m. Anthony F. Zunker, Sept. 19, 1980; children: Tibor Kreiter, Melissa J., Anthony F. Jr. Diploma, Sprayberry High Sch., 1963. Various clerical positions N.Y. and Ga.; mgr. Winn Dixie, Ft. Lauderdale, Fla., 1973-76; owner, operator Union 76 Svc. Sta., Manistee, Mich., 1980-82; pres., owner Am. Comml. Expediters, Pompano Beach, Fla., 1988—; sec.-treas. Atlanta Envelope Co., 1962-64. Mem. Am. Legion, Odd Fellows, Rosecrucions, Internat. Platform Assn. U.S. C. of C., Smithsonian. Republican. Home: 6250 SW 6th St Pompano Beach FL 33068-1709 Office: Am Comml Expediters 1852 NW 21st St Pompano Beach FL 33069-1306

ZUO, YUEGANG, research scientist; b. Ezhou, Hubei, China, Sept. 17, 1958; came to U.S., 1992; s. Ganbo and Fang (Peng) Z.; m. Yiwei Deng, Sept. 6, 1986; children: Ruixiao, Ruiting. BS, Wuhan (China) U., 1982; MS, Academia Sinica, Beijing, 1984; PhD, Swiss Fed. Inst. Tech., Zurich, 1992. Chemistry lectr. Huarong H.S., Echeng, Hubei, China, 1976-78; rsch. asst. Inst. Environ. Chemistry Academia Sinica, Beijing, 1984-86, rsch. assoc. Rsch. Ctr. for Eco-environ. Scis., 1986-88; rsch. asst. Swiss Fed. Inst. Environ. Sci. and Tech., Duebendorf, Switzerland, 1988-92; postdoctor Drinking Water Rsch. Ctr. Fla. Internat. U., Miami, 1992-93, rsch. scientist S.E. Environ. Rsch. Program, 1993—; cons. S.E. Environ. Rsch. Program, Miami, 1992—. Author: (with others) Aquatic and Surface Photochemistry, 1993; contbr. articles to profl. jours. Recipient Outstanding Tchr. award Ezhou, China, 1977; Presidential Found. grad. fellow, Zurich, 1988-92. Mem. AAAS, Am. Chem. Soc., Am. Geophys. Union, European Photochemistry Assn., Chinese Environ. Scis. Soc., Chinese Chem. Soc. Office: SERP Fla Internat U 107th Ave SW 8th St Miami FL 33199

ZUPANCIC, BRANDON LEE, career officer; b. Denver, Nov. 5, 1966; s. Larry Joseph and Mary Suzan (Stanton) Z.; m. Amanda Miller, Oct. 10, 1991. BA, Tulane U., 1989. Commd. U.S. Army, 1991, advanced through grades to capt., 1996; asst. logistics officer 1st bn. 37th armor U.S. Army, Vilseck, Germany, 1991-92, tank platoon leader company B 1st bn. 37th armor, 1992-93, support platoon leader 1st bn. 37th armor, 1993-94, asst. opers. officer 1st bn. 37th armor; opers. officer 2nd bn. 81st armor U.S. Army, Ft. Knox, Ky., 1995-96, commdr. co. F 2nd bn. 81st armor; assoc. 1st armor tng. BDE future opers. group, Ft. Knox, Ky., 1995-96, advanced warfighting working group, Ft. Knox, 1996. Contbr. articles to profl. jours. Mem. Assn. U.S. Army, U.S. Army Armor Assn., Hopportunity Knox Homebrewers' Club (pres. 1996).

ZURAWSKI, JEANETTE, rehabilitation services professional; b. June 30, 1951. Student, U. Wis., 1969-70, Portland C.C., 1974-78; BS in Chemistry, Portland State U., 1981; MD, Oreg. Health Scis. U., 1985. Diplomate Am. Bd. Phys. Medicine and Rehab. Resident U. Kans. Med. Ctr., Kansas City, 1985-89; med. dir. rehab. svcs. North Miss Med. Ctr., Tupelo, 1989—; pvt. practice Tupelo, Miss.; mem. adv. com. Medicare Carrier; presenter in field. Past chair pers. com. Big Brothers/Big Sisters, Lee County, Miss., mem. exec. bd., current co-chair fundraising com. Mem. AMA, Am. Acad. Phys. Medicine and Rehab. (chairperson edn. com., mem. exec. coun. resident physician sect.), Am. Med. Women's Assn., Am. Bus. Women's Assn. (chair membership com., treas.), Miss. State Med. Assn., Assn. Acad. Physiatrists, Iota Sigma Pi. Office: 502 Eason Blvd Ste E Tupelo MS 38801-5954

ZUSCHLAG, RICHARD EMERY, small business owner; b. Greenville, Pa., Mar. 28, 1948; s. Emery Eugene and Mary Janet (Knapp) Z.; m. Elaine Dupuis; children: Blair, Beth, Blaise. BSEE, Capitol Inst. Tech., 1970. Salesperson Greenville (Pa.) Broadcasting Co., 1968-70; def. training officer Westinghouse Electric Co., Balt. and Lafayette, La., 1970-71; co-owner Acadian Ambulance Service, Inc., Lafayette; bd. dirs. Bank One, Lafayette. Chmn. Lafayette Parish Comm.; bd. dirs. Acadiana Safety Assn., 1978-81; trustee U. Southwestern La. Found.; chmn. Leadership La.; v.p. Coun. for Better La.; pres., bd. dirs. S.W. La. Edn. and Referral Ctr. Named Businessman of Yr. for State of La. SBA, 1980, Marketer of Yr. Sales and Mktg. Internat. Greater Baton Rouge, 1988. Mem. Internat. Elec. Engrs., La. Hosp. Assn. (chmn. ems), La. Press Assn., La. Assn. Broadcasters, Lafayette C. of C. (bd. dirs.), La. Assn. Bus. and Industry. Democrat. Roman Catholic. Office: Acadian Ambulance Service Inc 302 Hopkins PO Box 98000 Lafayette LA 70509-8000

ZWART, STEVEN PAUL, computer programmer; b. St. Louis, Sept. 7, 1960; s. Claude Henriet and Marnis Ellen (Grothen) Z.; m. Pamela Jean Dunlap, Jan. 2, 1982; children: Eric Christopher, Allen Michael. BSBA cum laude, S.E. Mo. State U., 1982. Programmer T.G.& Y. Stores, Inc., Oklahoma City, Okla., 1982-84; systems engr. Info. Industries, Inc., Kansas City, Mo., 1984-85; adv. programmer IBM-Integrated Systems Solutions Corp., Lexington, Ky., 1985—. Scout leader Boy Scouts Am., Lexington, 1989-93. Home: 3968 Hillside Dr Lexington KY 40514-1522 Office: ISSC EUEC 200/3 455 Park Pl Lexington KY 40511-1830

ZWEIGHAFT, RONALD M., neurologist; b. Beaumont, Tex., Oct. 5, 1947; s. Albert Philip and Kay (Attra) Z.; m. Teresa Clare Richardson, Aug. 28, 1971; 1 child, Amy Lauren. BA cum laude, Rice U., 1970; MD, U. Tex. Southwestern, 1974. Intern U. N.C., Chapel Hill, 1974-75; resident Parkland Meml. Hosp., Dallas, 1978-81; assoc. Diagnostic Neurology Clinic of Houston, Tex., 1981—; pres. Diagnostic Neurology Clinic of Houston, 1985—; chief of staff Meml. City Med. Ctr. Hosp., Houston, 1993; dir. West Houston (Tex.) Physician-Hosp. Orgn., 1993-94. Asst. surgeon USPHS, 1975-78. Fellow Am. Acad. Neurology; mem. AMA, Tex. Med. Assn., Tex. Neurology Soc., Harris County Med. Soc. (Western br. v.p. 1993, pres.-elect. 1994, pres. 1995), Houston Neurol. Soc., Alpha Omega Alpha. Office: Diagnostic Neurology Clinic 909 Frostwood Dr Ste 304 Houston TX 77024-2306

ZWIGARD, BRUCE ALBERT, brokerage house executive; b. Newark, Apr. 10, 1948; s. Albert Henry and Doris Emily (Sigmund) Z.; m. Eva Crescencia Lan, June 24, 1973; children: Brian Albert, Bradley William. BA, Rider Coll., 1971; MBA, Fla. Internat. U., 1976. Tchr. physics Wardlaw Sch., Plainfield, N.J., 1971-72; tchr. physics Dade County Schs., Miami, Fla., 1972-77, tchr. gifted, 1977-79; registered rep. Investacorp Inc., Miami Lakes, Fla., 1979-80, v.p., 1980-81, pres., chmn. bd. dirs., 1981—. Office: Investacorp Inc 15450 New Barn Rd Hialeah FL 33014-2169

Professional Index

AGRICULTURE

UNITED STATES

ALABAMA

Montgomery
Frazer, Stuart Harrison, III *cotton merchant*

ARKANSAS

Humphrey
Wilson, Victoria Jane Simpson *farmer, former nurse*

Little Rock
Justus, Jack Glenn *farm organization executive, livestock farmer*

FLORIDA

Clermont
Ray, Ruth Alice Yancey *rancher, real estate developer*

Gainesville
Nair, Ramachandran P.K. *agroforestry educator, researcher*

Tallahassee
Karschau-Lowenfish, Sonja *breed association executive, publisher*

GEORGIA

Atlanta
Wright, Daniel *wine specialist, consultant*

Griffin
Lycan, Rebecca Tatum *professional dog handler*

KENTUCKY

Lexington
Goetz, Stephan Juergen *agricultural economics educator*
Woolums, Margaret Carmichael *thoroughbred bloodline researcher*

LOUISIANA

Lake Charles
Stacey, Norma Elaine *farmer, civic worker*

MISSISSIPPI

Starkville
Gregg, Billy Ray *seed industry executive*

NORTH CAROLINA

Trenton
Arthur, Guy *farming executive*

OKLAHOMA

Purcell
Coldiron, Vicki Irene *farm owner*

Vinita
Gray, Donald Lyman *orchard owner*

SOUTH CAROLINA

Dillon
Chandler, Marcia Shaw Barnard *farmer*

Greer
Gregg, Marie Byrd *retired farmer*

TEXAS

Brackettville
Belcher, William Alvis *rancher, veterinarian*

College Station
Shumway, Charles Richard *agricultural economics educator*

Devers
Boyt, Patrick Elmer *farmer, real estate executive*

Houston
Dartez, Louis Avery *rancher, typographer*

Industry
Huitt, Jimmie L. *rancher, oil, gas, real estate investor*

San Antonio
Davenport, Pamela Beaver *rancher, small business owner*

Satin
Epperson, Jean Warner *rancher*

Seymour
Danilow, Deborah Marie *rancher, musician, bondsman*

Uvalde
Stoner, Royal Clinton *rancher*

Valley View
Wallace, Donald John, III *rancher, former pest control company executive*

VIRGINIA

Blacksburg
Buss, Glenn Richard *agricultural researcher*

Charlottesville
Tice, David Allan *forester, environmental consultant*

Chesapeake
Shirley, Charles William *farm owner*

Marshall
Hardin, Mark *thoroughbred horse breeder*

Mc Lean
McIlwain, Clara Evans *agricultural economist, consultant*

ADDRESS UNPUBLISHED

Ebert, Robert Anthony *agricultural educator*
See, French Augustus *farmer, banker*
Spencer, William H. *farming executive*
Weaver, Marguerite McKinnie *plantation owner*
Wilson, Stanley Porter *retired agricultural association executive*

ARCHITECTURE AND DESIGN

UNITED STATES

ALABAMA

Montgomery
Adams, Beth Ford *interior designer*

ARKANSAS

Fayetteville
Jones, Euine Fay *architect, educator*

Little Rock
Burruss, Terry Gene *architect*
Wallace, Minor Gordon, Jr. *architect*

CALIFORNIA

San Francisco
Matas, Myra Dorothea *interior designer, kitchen and bath designer*

DISTRICT OF COLUMBIA

Washington
Flynn, Patrick *designer, programmer*

FLORIDA

Bal Harbour
Alexander, Michael C. *interior designer, business owner*

Boca Raton
Stillman, Evelyn *interior designer*
Wirtz, Michael H. *interior designer*

Bonita Springs
Trudnak, Stephen Joseph *landscape architect*

Bradenton
Keane, Gustave Robert *architect, consultant*

Coral Gables
Warburton, Ralph Joseph *architect, engineer, planner, educator*

Daytona Beach
Amick, William Walker *golf course architect*

Deltona
Clifton, George *design company executive*
Ezell, Kenneth C. *design company executive*

Dundee
McHugh-Barben, Karen Lynne *architectural resource consultant*

Fernandina Beach
Burns, Stephen Redding *golf course architect*

Fort Lauderdale
Cartaya, Mario *architect*
Stone, Edward Durell, Jr. *landscape architect and planner*

Hobe Sound
Graham, Bruce John *architect*

Jacksonville
Rumpel, Peter Loyd *architect, educator, artist*
Saylor, Michael J. *golf course architecture design company executive*
Smith, Ivan Huron *architect*

Jupiter
Fazio, Tom *design firm executive, golf course designer*

Lake Worth
Waite, Joy Elizabeth *interior decorator*

Lakeland
Garrott, Frances Carolyn *architectural technician*
Smyers, Steve *golf course architect*

Longwood
Gasperoni, Ellen Jean Lias *interior designer*

Miami
Farcus, Joseph Jay *architect, interior designer*
Feinberg, David Jay *architect*
Lapidus, Morris *retired architect, interior designer*
Patricios, Nicholas Napoleon *architectural educator, consultant*

Miami Beach
Saruski, Michael *interior designer*

Naples
Grissom, Jerry Bryan *interior designer*
Jones, Richard Wallace *interior designer*
Lewis, Gordon Gilmer *golf course architect*

Orlando
Dean, Gary Neal *artist, architect*
Ellis, James Jolly *landscape resort official*
Evans, Donald Fredrick *architect*
Vining, F(rancis) Stuart *architect, consultant*

Palm Bay
Hanna, Emma Harmon *architectural designer, business owner, official*

Ponte Vedra Beach
Larsen, Eric *golf course design company executive*
Minchew, Harrison Gray *director golf course architecture*

Sarasota
Snyder, Wesley Warren *interior space planner and designer*

Stuart
Ankrom, Charles Franklin *golf course architect, consultant*

Tallahassee
Pugh, Thomas Doering *architecture educator*

Vero Beach
McGee, Humphrey Glenn *architect*

West Palm Beach
Edge, Donald Richard *architect, planner*

GEORGIA

Athens
Ferguson, Bruce Kirkman *landscape architect, educator*

Atlanta
Bowman, Juliette Joseph *interior decorator, gourmet food consultant*
Bull, Frank James *architect*
Byrd, William C. *architect*
Crane, Jonathan Townley *architect*
Nimmons, M(ajor) Stuart, III *architect*
Rauh, Richard Paul *architect*
Rekau, Richard Robert *architect*
Robison, Richard Eugene *architect*
Wurz, John Arnold *architect*

Duluth
Burk, John Edward *architect*
Stewart, James Camp *architect*

Marietta
Stahr, Rebecca *interior designer*

Riverdale
Gibbs, Rose L. *interior designer*

Roswell
DeVictor, D. J. *landscape architect*

Saint Simons
Webb, Lamar Thaxter *architect*

Savannah
Pou, Linda Alice *interior designer, architectural designer*

KENTUCKY

Louisville
Vitiello, Eric Charles, Sr. (Ric Vitiello) *roofing consultant*

Murray
Beane, Kenneth Mark *designer, scientist, engineering researcher*

LOUISIANA

Baton Rouge
Lee, Betty Redding *architect*

Harvey
Atteberry-Luckinbill, Clara DeAnn *interior designer*

Metairie
Favrot, Henri Mortimer, Jr. *architect, real estate developer*

New Orleans
Easley, Patsy Fletcher *interior designer*
Falzarano, Jeffrey Mark *naval architecture and offshore engineering educator, researcher*
Klingman, John Philip *architect, educator*
Mathes, Edward Conrad *architect*

Shreveport
Forte, Stephen Forrest *interior designer*
Querbes, Betty-Lane Shipp *interior designer, real estate agent*

MARYLAND

Baltimore
Gentner, Paul LeFoe *architect, consultant*

Silver Spring
Ware, Thomas Earle *building consultant*

MISSISSIPPI

Biloxi
Zocchi, Louis Joseph *product designer, game company executive*

Hattiesburg
Blake, Edward Leonard, Jr. *landscape architect*

Jackson
Burns, Robert, Jr. *architect, freelance writer, artist*

NORTH CAROLINA

Charlotte
Sellers, Macklyn Rhett, Jr. *architect*

High Point
Culler, Robert Ransom *furniture designing and product development company executive*

Kinston
Baker-Gardner, Jewelle *business executive, interior designer*

Oriental
Sutter, Madeline Ann *landscape architect*

Pinehurst
Maples, Dan *golf course designer*

Raleigh
Smith, Owen Franklin *architect*

Research Triangle Park
McClure, Christopher Ewart *architect*

Winston Salem
Ernst Bogdan, Janet Lee *interior designer*

OKLAHOMA

Norman
Gruenwald, Hermann *architecture educator*
Sipes, James Lamoyne *landscape architect, educator*
Tuttle, Arthur Norman, Jr. *architect, university administrator*

Oklahoma City
Lamell, Robert Charles *architect, artist*

Tulsa
Ball, Rex Martin *urban designer, architect*
Crosby, Jim *design company executive*
Kennedy, Nancy Louise *retired draftsman*

OREGON

Beaverton
Connor, Edward Hollis, III *golf course architect*

SOUTH CAROLINA

Anderson
Pflieger, Kenneth John *architect*

Cayce
Baker, Charles Douglas, Jr. *architect*

Clemson
Halfacre, Robert Gordon *landscape architect, educator*
Kishimoto, Yuji *architect, educator*

Florence
Belissary, Karen *interior designer*

Greenville
Lawton, Joseph Benjamin, IV *commercial and residential interior designer*
Rhoads, Stephen Douglas *architect*

Hilton Head Island
Kelley, Debra Stephens *interior designer*

Spartanburg
Stroup, David Richard *architect*

Sumter
Compton, Rebecca Bailes *interior designer*

TENNESSEE

Clinton
Gorman, Charles Matthews, Jr. *landscape architect*

Greeneville
Ashworth, Denise Marchant *landscape architect*

Hendersonville
Jones, Beth Wilee *interior designer*

Knoxville
Rabun, Josette Hensley *interior design educator*

Nashville
Bramlett, Shirley Marie Wilhelm *interior decorator, artist*
Davidson, Charles *design company executive*
Kulinski, Stephen Edward *interior designer*
Onge, Page Burton *architect*
Orr, Frank Howard, III *architect*
Scalf, James Franklin, III *architect*

TEXAS

Austin
Box, John Harold *architect, educator, academic dean*

College Station
Ulrich, Roger Steffen *environmental design educator, researcher*

Dallas
Blevins, Gary Lynn *architect, real estate broker, real estate appraiser*
Brown, John Hall *architect*
Davis, Maria Teresa *architect*
Frazier, Alton Eugene *interior designer*
Graves, William *architect*
Jalonick, George Washington, IV *landscape company executive*
Lundy, Victor Alfred *architect, educator*
Rees, Frank William, Jr. *architect*
Salinas, Albert *golf course architecture company executive*
Springfield, Stephen Ray *architect*
Staffelbach, Andre *interior designer*
Tucker, John Edward *architect, consultant*
Vondracek, Betty Sue *interior designer, remodeling contractor, real estate agent*

El Paso
Carroll, Edwin Winford *architect*
Korth, Charlotte Brooks *furniture and interior design firm executive*

Flower Mound
Morrish, Thomas Jay *golf course architect*

Galveston
Brashears, Kent Baker *interior designer*

Houston
Boddeker, Edward William, III *retired architect*
Bryan, Mary Ann *interior designer*
Calhoun, Harold *architect*
Dumont, Edward Abdo *intern architect, registered interior designer*
Jackson, R. Graham *architect*
Nicholson, Franklin N. *interior designer*
Obiora, Chris Sunny *architect*
Spann, Baxter *design company executive*
Thomas, Lavon Bullock *interior designer*
Walton, Conrad Gordon, Sr. *architect*

Irving
Chris, Harry Joseph *architect, architectural company executive*
McLaren, James Kevin *architect*

Lubbock
Frazier, Eugene Richard *designer*
Leftwich, Cynthia Shelton *commercial interior designer*

Saginaw
Norman, Lena (Sutera) *drafting engineer, artist, poet*

San Antonio
Ammann, Lillian Ann Nicholson *interior landscape executive*
Davis, George Edward *industrial designer*
Graves, Kenneth Martin *architect*
Lowe, Douglas Howard *architect*
Pfanstiel Parr, Dorothea Ann *interior designer*

San Augustine
Wade, Julia Howard *interior designer*

Sugar Land
Huckaby, Edward Earl *architect*

VIRGINIA

Alexandria
Pavlick, Charles Raleigh *architect, engineer, retired air force officer*
Simonds, Marie Celeste *architect*

Arlington
Meden, Robert Paul *interior design educator*

Blacksburg
Bliznakov, Milka Tcherneva *architect*

Charlottesville
Root, James Benjamin *landscape architect*

Falls Church
Lederer, Paul Edward *landscape architect*

Fredericksburg
Keplinger, Duane *architectural executive*
Weselin, Mary Lou *interior designer*

Hampton
Vogan, David Nicholas *architect*

Leesburg
Foster, R. Pam *interior designer*

Mc Lean
Freyer, Victoria C. *fashion and interior design executive*

Mechanicsville
Bock, John Louis *architect*

Newport News
McReynolds, Charles Bertram *architect*

Oakton
Kerr, Charlotte Bowden *interior designer*

Richmond
George, Lester Lee *golf course architectural firm executive*

WEST VIRGINIA

Fairmont
Anthony, Gretchen Wilhelmina Hauser *architect*

Morgantown
Brown, Michelle Renee *interior designer*

Sistersville
Archer, Joseph Neale *industrial designer*

MILITARY ADDRESSES OF THE UNITED STATES

PACIFIC

APO
Haddix, Robert Allen *architect*

ADDRESS UNPUBLISHED

Arango, Richard Steven *architect, graphic and industrial designer*
Beahm, Emily Barclay *interior designer*
Beckemeyer, Nancy Scott *landscape architect*
Bunch, Franklin Swope *architect*
Cremer, Claudine Pfeiffer *landscape firm executive*
Diffenbaugh, John Nicholas *architect*
Douglass, Harry Robert *architect, health care consultant, educator*
Gaillard, George Siday, III *architect*
Horton, William Alan *structural designer*
James, Barbara Woodward *small business owner, interior designer, antique appraiser, consultant*
Kahn, Charles Howard *architect, educator*
Klink, Robert Michael *consulting engineer, management consultant, financial consultant, property developer*
Lewcock, Ronald Bentley *architect, educator*
Mc Pheeters, Edwin Keith *architect, educator*
Muncey, James Arthur, Jr. *architect*
Peterson, William Canova *architect*
Rabon, William James, Jr. *architect*
Rice, Richard Lee *retired architect*
Schuth, Mary McDougle *interior designer, educator*
White, Robert Frederick *landscape architect*
Wilson, William Glenn, Jr. *graphic designer*

ARTS: LITERARY. *See also* COMMUNICATIONS MEDIA.

UNITED STATES

ALABAMA

Birmingham
Cruse, Irma Belle Russell *writer*
Lide, Neoma Jewell Lawhon (Mrs. Martin James Lide, Jr.) *poet*
Stallworth, Anne Nall *writer, writing educator*

Foley
Shoenight, Pauline Aloise Souers (Aloise Tracy) *writer*

Huntsville
Hudson, Ralph Magee *writer, artist*
Luther, Susan Militzer *poet*
Sharpe, Mitchell Raymond *science writer*
Smith, Philip Wayne *writer, communications company executive*

Montgomery
Ridolphi, Lucy Elizabeth *writer, public relations professional*

Tuscaloosa
Bowman, Susan *writer*

ARIZONA

Scottsdale
Shreffler, Genevieve *author*

ARKANSAS

Bentonville
Strong, B. Jean *writer, publisher*

Camden
Wilson, Jane C. Luck *author*

Fayetteville
Williams, Miller *poet, translator*

Hot Springs National Park
Katchen, Carole Lee *writer, artist*

Jacksonville
Crane, Regina Ann *technical writer*

Little Rock
Brown, Dee Alexander *author*
D'Arezzo, Karen Williams *science writer*

North Little Rock
Roberts, Emily Burgin *writer, editor, communications consultant*

FLORIDA

Bay Harbor Islands
Klein, Roberta Phyllis *writer, editor, consultant, architect and designer*

Clearwater
Horton, Donna Alberg *technical writer*

Coconut Grove
Alschuler, Al *freelance writer, public relations counselor*

Coral Springs
Mrazik, Tina Maria *writer*

Davie
Humann, Paul Huldrich *writer, photographer*

Daytona Beach
Chesnut, Nondis Lorine *writer, consultant, former English language educator*

De Funiak Springs
Karger, Delmar William *author, consultant, investor*

Deland
Becker, Herbert Lawrence *writer, accountant*

Delray Beach
Burbank, Kershaw *writer*
Murphy, Kevin George *novelist*

Flagler Beach
Grieder, Theodore *poet, editor*

Fort Lauderdale
Maurer, Yolanda Tahar *publisher*

Gainesville
Katritzky, Linde (Agnes Juliane Dietlinde) *writer, researcher, educator*

Hallandale
Henigson, Ann Pearl *freelance writer, songwriter, lyricist*

Hollywood
Blate, Michael *author, lecturer*
Maxwell, Fredric Alan *writer, library activist*

Key West
Whitney, Thomas Porter *writer, translator*

Largo
Craft Davis, Audrey Ellen *writer, educator*

Lutz
Terrell, David LeRoy *author*

Lynn Haven
Leonard, Venelda Hall *writer*

Maitland
Kumiski, John A. *writer, photographer fly fishing guide and teacher*

Melbourne
Stone, Elaine Murray *author, composer, television producer*

Miami
Abril, Marcia *author*
Beasley, James Ronald *television, video scriptwriter, producer*
Berger, Arthur Seymour *author, vice-mayor, lawyer, cultural organization volunteer*
Cameron, Carroll Dunham *writer*
Camner, Howard *author, poet*
Levine, Paul Jacob *writer, screenwriter*
Pardo Mazorra, Angel Enrique *poet, writer*
Robinson, David Bradford *poet, scientific writer*

Miami Beach
Angel-Junguito, Antonio *writer*

Milton
Tarvin, Albert Leon *writer*

Miramar
Abbott, Paul Scott *writer, public relations executive, consultant*

Mount Dora
Hart, Valerie Gail *writer*

Naples
Thompson, Didi Castle (Mary Bennett) *writer, editor*

Orlando
Blum, Richard Arthur *writer, media educator*
Roe, Allie Jones *technical writer*

Palm Beach
Young, Lois Catherine Williams *poet, former reading specialist*
Zeeman, Joan Javits *writer, inventor*

Palm Beach Gardens
Klein, Gail Beth Marantz *freelance writer, dog breeder*

Palm City
Peter, Janet (Erica Carle) *writer, historian*

Panama City Beach
Homesley, Horace Edward (Nicholas S. Sokolnikov) *writer*

Pembroke Pines
Koch, Dott Clarke *writer*

Pensacola
Klepper, Robert Kenneth *writer, journalist*
Sargent, James O'Connor *freelance writer*

Pompano Beach
Kaskinen, Barbara Kay *author, composer, songwriter, musician, music educator*
Lis, Janet C. *visual artist, writer/illustrator*

Port Orange
Turner, Rebecca Sue *writer*

Sarasota
Davis, Maggie (Marie Hill) *writer*
Jakus, Stephanie *writer, composer, musician, instructor*
Weeks, Albert Loren *author, educator, journalist*

Stuart
Lamoureux, William Albert *poet*
Woodward, Isabel Avila *writer, foreign language educator*

Tallahassee
Bagley, James Robert *freelance writer*
Suarez, Virgil *writer*

Tampa
Foster, Joseph James, III *creative writer*
Hanford, Grail Stevenson *writer*
Shimberg, Elaine Fantle *writer*

Tequesta
Dauphin, Sue *writer, producer*

Vero Beach
Phillips, Marion Grumman *writer, civic worker*

West Palm Beach
Arnold, Bill *freelance writer*

Winter Park
Eckbert, William Fox *author, psychiatrist*

GEORGIA

Acworth
Putnam, Kimberly Ann *freelance writer, editor*

Atlanta
Austin, Judy Essary *scriptwriter*
Cashman, Paul Walker *writer, editor*
Cooley, Nicole R. *writer*
Corseri, Gary Steven *writer, educator*
Dunn, John Clinton *writer, editor*
Geigerman, Clarice Furchgott *writer, actress, consultant*

Hauke, Kathleen Armstrong *writer, editor*
Jones, Nicholas Charles *writer, editor, broadcaster*
Levison, Andrew Hugh *author, information specialist*

Decatur
Wade, James Bradley *writer*
Williams, Amanda Kyle *writer*

Dublin
Wilson, Barbara Davenport *writer, editor*

Duluth
Lazenby, Henry F. *writer, consultant*

Marietta
Pallotta, Gail Cassady *writer*

Robins AFB
Treadway, Susan Marie *technical writer*

Roswell
Christmas, Bobbie Jaye *independent editor, freelance writer*

Saint Simons
Cedel, Melinda Irene *music educator, violinist*

Savannah
Thomas, Dwight Rembert *writer*

Thomson
Wilson, Donna Owen *author, artist*

Toccoa
Losier, Andrew J. *writer, missionary*

Watkinsville
Smith, Shelley Merrifield *writer, non-profit organization administrator*

KENTUCKY

Corydon
Wood, J. Barclay *technical writer, forensic firearms consultant*

Frankfort
Hazelett, Priscilla Sue *writer*

Lexington
Johnson, Jane Penelope *freelance writer*

Louisville
Mitchell, Eddie *writer, activist, health issues educator*
Shorter, Ninette *writer*

Utica
Henry, Loretta M. *writer*

West Liberty
Engle, John David, Jr. *poet*

LOUISIANA

Baton Rouge
Houk, James Titus *writer, educator*
Madden, David *author*

Lafayette
Webb, Bernice Larson *writer, consultant, press owner, publisher*

Lake Charles
Butler, Robert Olen *writer, educator*

Mandeville
Harton, Merle Carter, Jr. *writer*

Many
Lee, James Ashley *writer, film producer*

New Orleans
Cooley, Peter John *poet, educator*

Ruston
Pankey, George Edward *researcher, former educator*

Zachary
Blevins, Donna Caton *writer*

MICHIGAN

Ann Arbor
Meador, Roy Edward *commercial writer*

MINNESOTA

Minneapolis
Olson, Ted (Charles Strong) *writer*

MISSISSIPPI

Soso
Mitchell, Malinda Jane *writer*

NEW JERSEY

Ocean Grove
Patterson, Steven-Michael *editor, literary translator*

NEW YORK

Babylon
Pearson, Sela *poet, speaker*

New York
Bourjaily, Vance *novelist*
Shomer, Enid *poet, fiction writer*

NORTH CAROLINA

Asheville
Thrasher, James Parker *writer*

Benson
Stephenson, Shelby *poet, editor, educator, singer*

Chapel Hill
Brandon, Diane Laine *personal empowerment consultant, writer*
Harmon, William Ruth *poet, English language educator*
Vick, Marsha Cook *writer, African American studies educator*

Charlotte
Kratt, Mary Norton *writer*

High Point
Dula, Bobby *writer, poet*

Mooresville
Schorb, E(dwin) M(arsh) *poet*

Murfreesboro
Burke, Marguerite Jodi Larcombe *writer, computer consultant*

New Bern
Foss, John Houston *writer, consultant, educator*

Research Triangle Park
Houston, Susan Jeannine Hudson *writer*

Wadesboro
Garris Bowman, Mary Louise *poet, singer, songwriter*

Wilmington
Lamica, George Edward, Sr. *writer, importor*

Winston Salem
Ehle, John Marsden, Jr. *writer*
Long, Nichola Y. *technical writer*

OHIO

Cleveland
Warren, Sandra Kay *writer*

OKLAHOMA

Bartlesville
Tiedemann, Ruth Elizabeth Fulton (Sunnye Tiedemann) *writer, educator*

Claremore
Carter, Joseph Henry, Sr. *writer, museum manager*

Norman
Scaperlanda, María de Lourdes Ruiz *writer, journalist*

Oklahoma City
Anderson, Kenneth Edwin *writer, educator*
Lewis, Clyde A. *author, counselor*
Mather, Ruth Elsie *writer*
Shapard, Sandra Gales *poet*

Perry
Beers, Frederick Gordon *writer, retired corporate communications official*

Skiatook
Collins, Judith Charlene (Judy Rhodes Collins) *writer, poet*

Tulsa
Mojtabai, Ann Grace *author, educator*

Yukon
Morris, Julie Ann Rose *poet, foundation executive*

SOUTH CAROLINA

Columbia
Newton, Rhonwen Leonard *writer, microcomputer consultant*
Stamps, Laura Anne *writer, artist, editor*
Swanson, Marshall Symmes *writer and editor*

Greenville
Jeansonne, Jerold James *technical communications manager*
Monroe, Robin Prince *writer, educator*

Hollywood
Hull, Edward Whaley Seabrook *freelance writer, consultant*

Little River
Ehrlich, John Gunther *writer*

Mount Pleasant
Cooper, Barbie Perkins *writer*
Côté, Richard Norman *international writer, historian, biographer*

Pacolet
Dickerson, Georgie Julian *writer, artist*

Sullivans Island
Ralston, Gilbert Alexander *writer, educator*

Summerville
Reisman, Rosemary Moody Canfield *writer, humanities educator*

TENNESSEE

Jefferson City
Marion, Jeff Daniel *poet, educator*

Johnson City
Stahl, Ray Emerson *writer*

Kingsport
Kiss, Mary Catherine Clement *writer*

Memphis
Foote, Shelby *author*
Gawehn-Frisby, Dorothy Jeanne *freelance technical writer*
Ryan, John Fergus *novelist, probation officer, educator*
Walne, Sarah West *writer, educator*

Nashville
Brown, Aletha Fern *author, poet*
Browne, Harry *writer, investment advisor*
Eng, Steve *freelance writer*
Winstead, Elisabeth Weaver *poet, writer, English language educator*

Newport
Dykeman, Wilma *writer, educator*

Oak Ridge
Calvert, Jennifer Hamilton *freelance writer, photographer*
Turov, Daniel *financial writer, investment executive*

TEXAS

Alvin
Johnson, Cheryl Elizabeth *writer, publisher, educator*

Austin
Bishop, Amelia Morton *freelance writer*
Falkstein, Jasmine Dauphine *writer*
Garner, Douglas Russell *science writer*
Person, Lawrence *writer, editor*
Phillips, Jeffrey Edward *writer, editor*
Taylor, John Renford, Jr. *writer, business consultant*

Bellaire
Leslie, Mae Sue *writer*

Canyon
Roper, Beryl Cain *writer, publisher, retired library director*

College Station
Norton, Saundra Elithe *writer*

Corpus Christi
McCoy, Dorothy Eloise *writer, educator*
Sommers, Maxine Marie Bridget *writer, educator, publisher*
Walraven, Joseph William (Bill Walraven) *writer, publisher*

Crowley
Sizemore, Deborah Lightfoot *writer, editor*

Crystal Beach
Dunn, Glennis Mae *writer, lyricist*

Dallas
Cohn, Linkie Seltzer *professional speaker, author*
Davis, Elise Miller (Mrs. Leo M. Davis) *writer*
Siegel, Jeff *writer*
Smith, William George *writer/journalist*

Denton
Reynolds, Richard Clay *writer, editor*

El Paso
Subraman, Mary Belinda (Belinda Subraman) *writer*

Fort Worth
Bean, Jack Vaughan *author, publisher*
Jones, Kathryn Ann *writer, artist*
Lale, Cissy Stewart (Lloyd Lale) *freelance writer*
Newsom, Douglas Ann Johnson *writer, journalism educator*

Galveston
Plunkett, Jack William *writer, publisher*

Groves
Nolen, Cynthia Estelle *writer, poet*

Happy
Wilhelm, Mary Evelyn *writer*

Houston
Boardman, Robert B. *author*
de Vries, Robbie Ray Parsons *author, illustrator, international consultant*
Lamb, Patricia Clare *poet*
Matthews, Harold Downs *author, consultant*
McPhail, JoAnn Winstead *writer, producer, publisher, art dealer*

Irving
Ide, Arthur Frederick *author, publisher*

Katy
Harbour, Patricia Ann Monroe *poet*

Lubbock
Bronwell, Nancy Brooker *writer*
Wilkinson, David Andy *writer*

Marquez
Korhonen, Marilyn Rice *educational grant writer*

Mineral Wells
Baker, Deborah Alysande *poet*

New Boston
Gabbard, Gregory Norman *poet*

Plano
Gallardo, Henrietta Castellanos *writer*
Lang, Darice Mouquin *technical writer*
Wisler, Gary Clifton *writer, educator*

Quinlan
Black, Sheryl Elaine Hale *author*

Richardson
Bonura, Larry Samuel *writer*
Harris, Miriam Kalman *writer, educator, consultant*

Round Top
Heap, Denise Elaine *writer, accountant*

San Antonio
Glueck, Sylvia Blumenfeld *writer*
Kerr, Rita Lee *writer, storyteller*
Milligan, Bryce *author, arts administrator*
Rogers, Frances Evelyn *author, retired educator and librarian*
Stuart, Lillian Mary *writer*
Swiggett, Harold E. *writer, photographer*

San Marcos
Payne, Emily Miller *reading educator, literacy consultant*

Spring
Kerr, Alva Rae *writer, editor, association executive, playwright*

Springtown
Marrs, James F. (Jim), Jr. *author, journalist, educator*

Waco
Bulmahn, Lynn *journalist, freelance writer*
Weems, John Edward *writer*

Wharton
Vivelo, Jacqueline Jean *author, English language educator*

VIRGINIA

Alexandria
David, Joseph Raymond, Jr. *writer, periodical editor*
Tatham, Julie Campbell *writer*
Weimer, Michael John *researcher, writer, editor*

Arlington
Constantine, Lynne Mary *writer, consultant*
Dominguez, Muriel Farley *writer, consultant, educator*
England, Robert Stowe *writer*
Greene, Harris *author, retired foreign service and intelligence officer*
Hittle, James D. *writer, business consultant*
Scott, Suzanne *writer, artist*
Stahl, O(scar) Glenn *writer, lecturer, former government official*
Turk, Paul Albert *writer, editor, consultant*

Big Stone Gap
Keuling-Stout, Frances Eileen *literature and poetics educator*

Callao
Freeman, Anne Hobson *writer, English language educator*

Charlottesville
Casey, John Dudley *writer, English language educator*
Dove, Rita Frances *poet, English language educator*

Fairfax
Bausch, Richard Carl *writer, educator*
Parrish, Florence Tucker *writer, retired government official*
Redd, Mary Allen *writer educator*

Falls Church
Leighton, Frances Spatz *writer, journalist*
Morrison, H. Robert *writer, editor, politician*

Ferrum
Horn, Geoffrey Michael *writer, editor*

Fort Belvoir
Smith, Margherita *writer, editor*

Fort Valley
Lewis, Thomas Allison *writer*

Hillsboro
Farwell, Byron Edgar *writer*

Lynchburg
Fulcher, Hugh Drummond *author*

Manassas
Holmes, Marjorie Rose *author*

Mc Kenney
Doyle, John Robert, Jr. *writer*

Mc Lean
Priem, Richard Gregory *writer, information systems executive, entertainment company executive*

Newport News
Hatton, Quindell Louise *poet*

Norfolk
Basco, Julie Ann *poet, activist*
Butler, Allen Todd *poet*

Richmond
Hemingway, Beth Rowlett *author, columnist, lecturer*
Rhodenbaugh, Suzanne Wadley *poet*

Roanoke
Walker, Gary Chitwood *author*

Springfield
Cinca, Silvia (Roberta King) *writer, producer*
Laubenthal, Sanders Anne *writer, editor*

Staunton
Lembke, Janet Nutt *writer*

Williamsburg
Mott, Michael Charles Alston *writer*

Woodbridge
Richardson, Sharon Young *writer, public relations executive*

WEST VIRGINIA

Martinsburg
Brown, John Gracen *writer*

Rippon
Kubic, Frank *author, industrial engineer*

ENGLAND

London
Poe-Borden, Audrey *writer, business educator*

ADDRESS UNPUBLISHED

Arnel, Craig Lee *poet, lyricist, musician*
Barger, Timothy Knox *writer, researcher*
Barry, Susan Brown *writer, manufacturer*
Baur, Isolde Nacke *translator, freelance writer, public speaker*
Berger, Linda Fay *writer*
Berler, Beatrice Adele *translator, author*
Bissell, Le Clair *medical researcher and writer*
Boston, Bruce Ormand *writer, editor, publications consultant*
Briscoe, Constance Yvonne *writer*
Brown, Paul Ferrell *writer*
Burns, Theresa Louise *children's books author and illustrator*
Chambliss, Lavonda Jo Eastup *writer, poet, songwriter*
Desjardins, Daniel Dee *poet, translator and playwright*
Dickerson, James L. *writer, photographer, consultant*
Donadio, Beverly Rose *writer*
Dunn, Mária Bach *writer, researcher, translator*
Ehlonan, Jeffrey D. *writer, educator*
Emerson, Russell George *writer*
Gibilisco, Stanley Philip *science writer, graphic artist*
Holleman, Gary Layne *writer*
James, Tracey Faye *screenwriter*
Johnson, Mike McAllister *writer*
Jones, Maryneal Williams *freelance writer*
Kaplan, Debra Arlene *writer, photographer, media consultant*
Kearney, Susan Hope *writer*
Kennedy, Bonnie Ruth *creative writer, instructor*
King, Cynthia Bregman *writer*
Krieg, Rebecca Jane *editor*
LyListon, William Philip *writer, poet*
Marble, Melinda Smith *writer, editor*
McCrimmon, Barbara Smith *writer, librarian*
McDonnell, Jean-Marie *writer, public relations educator*
McWilliams, Karen Joan *writer*
Mellor, Gail McGowan *author*
Muldoon, Thomas Lyman *writer*
Neal, Margaret Sherrill *writer*
Parsons, Helga Lund *writer*
Partridge, Benjamin Waring *writer*
Pike, Bonnie Haykin *playwright, lyricist*
Reno, Dawn Elaine *writer, photographer, educator*
Rhodes, Karen LeSueur Packard *writer*
Riscuta, Dorutu Honorius *writer*
Rogers, Del Marie *poet, editor*
Sallis, James *writer*
Seabolt, James Davidson *statistical writer*
Singer, Donna Lea *writer, editor, educator*
Stern, Daniel *author, executive, educator*
Stuart, Doris Todd (Dee Stuart) *writer*
Summers, Joseph Frank *author, publisher*
Tennant, Donna Kay *writer*
Thompson, Craig Owen *author*
Waller, John Henry *author, international consultant*
Yates, Steven Alan *writer*

ARTS: PERFORMING

UNITED STATES

ALABAMA

Birmingham
Dougherty, Dana Dean Lesley *television producer, educator*

Florence
Risher, Thomas Douglas, Sr. *music educator*

Mobile
Handy, Loretta Raymoré *entertainer, minister*
Jones, William John *music educator*

Montevallo
Lumby, Betty Louise *music educator, organist, composer*

Northport
Mundy, Laurie Jo *radio news director, producer*

Talladega
Lanier, Anita Suzanne *musician, piano educator*

Tuscaloosa
Castalno, Paul C. *theatre educator, author*

ARIZONA

Phoenix
Plylar, Deborah Koch *musician, music educator*

ARKANSAS

Arkadelphia
Kindall, Susan Carol *music educator*

Batesville
Counts, Michael L. *theatre educator*
Harris, Gary Marcel *theater educator*

Harrisburg
Sanders, Barbara Heeb *writer, consultant*

Little Rock
Berentsen, Kurtis George *music educator, choral conductor*
Raney, Miriam Day *actress*

Paragould
Stallings, Phyllis Ann *music educator*

State University
Spears, Gay Holmes *music educator*

CALIFORNIA

Beverly Hills
Presley, Priscilla *actress*

COLORADO

El Jebel
Rowe, Henry Theodore, Jr. (Ted Rowe) *industrial video producer, director*

Golden
Brailsford, June Evelyn *musician, educator*

DISTRICT OF COLUMBIA

Washington
Horton, John Ernest *motion picture industry consultant*
Konstantinov, Tzvetan Krumov *musician, concert pianist*

FLORIDA

Boca Raton
Gold, Catherine Anne Dower *music history educator*
Schwartz, Sergiu *concert artist*
Wallis, John James (Jimmy Wallis) *entertainer, ventriloquist, comedy writer, video production executive*

Boynton Beach
Davis, Gillian Frances *dance educator*

Clearwater
Iselin, Ellin *television producer*
Tucker, Shirley Elizabeth *music educator*

Cortez
Fowler, Arden Stephanie *music educator*

Deerfield Beach
Waldman, Alan I. (Alawana) *songwriter, composer, lyricist, computer programmer*

Deland
Sorensen, Jacki Faye *choreographer, aerobic dance company executive*

Dunedin
Flemm, Eugene William *concert pianist, educator, conductor, chamber musician*

Fort Lauderdale
LeRoy, Miss Joy *model, designer*
Rasmussen, Geraldine Dorothy *composer, artist, musician, author*

Fort Pierce
Herd, Charmian June *singer, actress*
Norton, Robert Howard *entertainer, musical arranger, author*

Gibsonton
Hall, Ward Miles *show producer, writer*

Hollywood
Manocchio, Vivienne Cinda (Vicki Lane) *vocalist, composer*
Washington, Michael O'Neal *musician*

Jacksonville
Stewart, Sandra Kay *music educator*

Key West
Mitchell, John Dietrich *theatre arts institute executive*

Largo
Fournier, Serge Raymond-Jean *orchestra conductor*

Lecanto
Max, Buddy (Boris Max Pastuch) *musician*

Madison
Bentley-Shaw, Kathleen *violist*

Miami
Allen, Charles Norman *television, film and video producer*
Catanzaro, Tony *dancer*
Gaynor, Leah *radio personality, commentator, broadcaster*
Heuer, Robert Maynard, II *opera company executive*

Odessa
Cobb, Terri R. (Ceci Cobb) *film and video producer*

Orlando
Walsh, James Anthony (Tony Walsh) *theater and film educator*

Pompano Beach
MacLaren, Neil Moorley, Jr. *musician, music educator*

Port Charlotte
Clark, Keith Collar *musician, educator*
Labousier, Susan Evelyn *choreographer, dancer*

Punta Gorda
Kavanaugh, Frank James *film producer, educator*

Sarasota
Kirschner, Kerry Groom *television personality, public policy foundation director*
Streetman, Nancy Katherine *cellist*

Shalimar
Sublette, Julia Wright *music educator, performer, adjudicator*

Sun City Center
Beu, Marjorie Janet *music director*

Surfside
Berman, Mona S. *actress, playwright, theatrical director and producer*

Tallahassee
Cramer, Bruce Eric *television news director*
Hale, Christopher Allen *music director*
Roseman, Joseph Jacob *flutist*

Tampa
Finelli, Patrick Michael *theater educator*

West Palm Beach
Hale, Marie Stoner *artistic director*
Robinson, Raymond Edwin *musician, music educator, writer*
Rosenberg, Leslie Karen *media director*

GEORGIA

Atlanta
Boehm, John Charles *music educator*
deLavallade, Michael Lyndon *videographer*
McClure, Pamella Anne *drama educator, stage director*
Patterson, James Hardy *entertainer, conductor, musician, educator, arranger, composer*
Scott, Mary Shy *music consultant*

Cartersville
Ward, Kevan Eulis *video specialist*

Clarkston
Downs, Jon Franklin *theater educator, director*

Conyers
Smith, Michael Joseph *composer, pianist, lecturer*

Dunwoody
Clark, Faye Louise *drama and speech educator*

Gainesville
Demling, Ann Marie *theatre educator*
McCord, Gloria Dawn Harmon *music educator, choral director, organist*

Mableton
Rowe, Bonnie Gordon *music company executive*

Macon
Thomas, Harold Edward *saxophonist, producer, engineer, recording artist*

Marietta
East, Nancy McKinley *private primary music educator*
Wells, Palmer Donald *performing arts executive*

Millen
Cremer, Thomas Gerhard *music educator*

Smyrna
Waters, Cynthia Winfrey *media advertising specialist*

Waleska
Lucktenberg, George Hazard *classical musician*

ILLINOIS

Chicago
Moffatt, Joyce Anne *performing arts executive*

Mount Prospect
DeVol, Skip *entertainer*

Skokie
Fletcher, Thelma *musician, performing company executive*

INDIANA

Culver
Jones, William Adrian *percussionist, education program administrator*

Knox
Weiss, Randall A. *television producer, supermarket executive*

KANSAS

Manhattan
White, (Edwin) Chappell *retired music educator*

KENTUCKY

Lexington
Pen, Ronald Allen *music educator, music critic*

Louisville
Doran, David Stephen *music educator*
Jones, Alun *artistic director*
Smillie, Thomson John *opera producer*
Tofteland, Curt L. *producer, director*

Murray
Malinauskas, Mark Jerome *communication and theatre educator*

Russellville
Carver, Hazel Oates *music educator, editor*

LOUISIANA

Baker
Carson, Albert Gus, IV *video producer*

Baton Rouge
Constantinides, Dinos Demetrios (Constantine Constantinides) *music educator, composer, conductor*
Hendricks, Aileen Alana *theatre educator, director, actress*
Mathews, Sharon Walker *artistic director, secondary school educator*
Toney, Kelly Lynne Smith *violinist, educator*

Hammond
Frederic, Cheryl Ann *theatre educator*

Lafayette
Daniel, Margaret Hagen *music and voice educator*
Schmalz, Robert Frederick, II *music educator*

Monroe
Greene, Gary Allen *musician, educator*

Natchitoches
Francis, Mark Louis *composer, educator, musician*

New Orleans
Cosenza, Arthur George *opera director*
Watkins, Stephen Lee *music educator*

Pineville
Sennett, Henry Herbert, Jr. *theatre arts educator and consultant*

Ruston
Rogers, Benjamin Kimble *music educator, composer*

Scott
Richard, Ralph Zachary *singer, songwriter, poet*

Thibodaux
Hammerli, Angela Mitchell *dance educator*
Klaus, Kenneth Sheldon *choral conductor, vocalist, music educator*

MISSISSIPPI

Clarksdale
McLeod, Lindy Gale *music educator*

Hattiesburg
Wood, Vivian Poates *mezzo soprano, voice educator*

Jackson
Holly, Ellistine Perkins *music educator*
Johnson, Barbara H. *retired opera company manager*
Lee, Lillian Aldridge *music educator*

Purvis
Young, Raymond Guinn *music educator*

NEW MEXICO

Las Cruces
Jagoe, Kevin Dean *musician*

Santa Fe
Rubenstein, Bernard *orchestra conductor*

NORTH CAROLINA

Boiling Springs
Bennett, Elizabeth Susan *music educator*

Chapel Hill
Camp, Joseph Shelton, Jr. *film producer, director, writer*

Charlotte
Carter Covington, Claudia McGinnis *literary manager, educational director*
Jacob, Karen Hite *music director*

Cullowhee
Waters, Michael Vincent *music and Spanish language educator*

Durham
Jaffe, Stephen Abram *composer, music educator*
Nakarai, Charles Frederick Toyozo *music educator, adjudicator*
Pruett, Lilian Pibernik-Benyovszky *music educator*
Wynkoop, Rodney Alan *choral music director*

Elizabeth City
Callahan, Gary Luther *music educator, researcher*

Fayetteville
Artley, Nathan Monroe *music educator*
Williams, Robert Weston *music educator*
Zaranka, Albert J. *musical director, pianist, educator*

Greensboro
Russell, Peggy Taylor *soprano, educator*

Hudson
Kincaid, Tina *entertainer, producer*

New Bern
Hale-Robinson, Lorraine Augusta *musician*

Raleigh
Elliott, Jennifer Sue *television producer*

Winston Salem
Kairoff, Peter David *music educator, concert pianist*

OHIO

Nelsonville
Caplinger, James Clair *theatrical producer*

OKLAHOMA

Clinton
Askew, Penny Sue *choreographer, artistic director, ballet instructor*

Edmond
Reiman, Sue Ellen *theatre company administrator, actress*

Lawton
Klein, Scott Richard *acting and directing educator*

Norman
Tussing, Marilee Appleby *music educator*

Oklahoma City
Albert, Phillip *filmmaker and videographer*
Pitts, Bryan *performing company executive*
Thomas, Gary Wayne *actor*
Wheeler, Ellen Jayne *music educator*

Stillwater
Foster, Gayla Catherine *musician*
Hemberger, Glen James *university band director, music educator*

Tulsa
Fender, Freddy (Baldemar Huerta) *singer*
Hawk, Samuel Silas *broadcast engineer, announcer*
Helmerich, Peggy Varnadow *actress*
Larkin, Moscelyne *retired artistic director, dancer*
Owens, Jana Jae *entertainer*

Valliant
Biard, Catherine *piano educator*

Weatherford
Chapman, Charles W. *music educator*

SOUTH CAROLINA

Anderson
Carroll, Edward Perry *instrumental music educator, conductor*

Charleston
Welsh, Wilmer Hayden *music educator, composer, organist*

Columbia
Gasque, (Allard) Harrison *radio personality, entertainer*
Panter, Richard Franklin *television documentary producer and director*

Greenville
Rogers, Kenneth R. *broadcaster, child care center owner*

Spartanburg
Feinstein, Marion Finke *artistic director, dance instructor*
White, Robert Bruce *keyboard instruments company acoustical consultant*

TENNESSEE

Auburntown
Nemeth, Bonnie Keith *dance educator, choreographer, writer, publisher*

Chattanooga
Van Cura, Barry Jack *dancer, choreographer*

Cordova
Schorman, Tedd J. *film producer*

Hendersonville
DeWolfe, Martha Rose *singer, songwriter, publisher*

Jefferson City
Measels, Donald Clark *music educator*

Johnson City
Jenrette, Thomas Shepard, Jr. *music educator, choral director*

Kingsport
Davis, Tammie Lynette *music educator, director*

Knoxville
Roberts, Esther Lois *piano educator, composer, writer*
Trevor, Kirk David Niell *orchestra conductor, cellist*

Madison
Prince, Anna Lou *composer, music publisher, construction company executive*

Memphis
Hathcock, John Edward *vocalist*
McRee, Celia *composer*

Nashville
Godwin, Paul Milton *musician, educator*
Laczko, Brian John *theater director*
Needham, Maureen *dance educator*
Speer, Joseph Enrique *videographer, editor, producer*
Wildun, Regina Duncan *songwriter, writer, singer*

Paris
Revel, Ricky Joe *producer, songwriter*

Savannah
Irons, Robert Eugene *music educator*

TEXAS

Abilene
Rathbun, James Ronald *music educator, conductor*

Amarillo
Grooms, Suzanne Simmons *music educator*

Arlington
Russell, Andrew Milo *music educator*

Aubrey
Pizzamiglio, Nancy Alice *performing company executive*

Austin
Lary, Banning Kent *video producer, publisher*
Morrow, Frank Spurgeon, Jr. *alternative views television program producer*
Mueller, Peggy Jean *dance educator, choreographer, rancher*
Sanders, John Burton *pianist*
Slavin, Alexandra Nadal *artistic director, educator*
Tschirhart, John Hipolyte *motion picture producer*

Borger
Allen, Bessie Malvina *music educator, church organist*

Buffalo Gap
Waltrip, Burroughs Allen *dance band leader, retired navy officer*

Carrollton
McGuire, Katie Elizabeth *dancer, choreographer, performing company executive*

Cedar Hill
Kilgore, Janice Kay *musician, educator*

College Station
Toler, Ray Edward *conductor, band director*

Commerce
Hanners, John *theatre educator*

Corpus Christi
Allison, Joan Kelly *music educator, pianist*
Munro, Cristina Stirling *artistic director*

Dallas
Eagar, Stephen Wade *television news anchor/ reporter*
Etgen, Ann *ballet educator*
Foutch, Michael James *actor, dancer, period dance researcher, producer*
Galt, John William *actor, writer*
Kline, George William, II *television producer*
Mandrake, Mark Wayne *actor*
Palmer, Christine (Clelia Rose Venditti) *operatic singer, performer, pianist, vocal instructor*
Pell, Jonathan Laurence *artistic administrator*
Pride, Charley *singer*
Schmidt, René R. *music educator, organist, choirmaster*
Vance, Vince *entertainer/bandleader, composer*

Denton
Collins, Michael Bruce *music educator*
Davidson, Norma Lewis *concert violinist, composer, music educator, psychologist*
Killian, Janice Kay Nelson *music educator, researcher*
McTee, Cindy *classical musician, educator*
Rodean, Richard William *musician, educator*

Fort Hood
Booker, Shirley Ruth *entertainment specialist*

Fort Worth
Colson, William Wilder *music theory and composition educator*
Giordano, John Read *conductor*
Mejia, Paul Roman *choreographer, dancer*
Rhodes, Ann L. *theatrical producer, investor*

Garland
Ferré, Susan Ingrid *musician*

Hallsville
Hutcherson, Donna Dean *music educator*

Harlingen
Godfrey, Aline Lucille *music specialist, church organist*

Houston
Boyd, Gregory *theater director*
Burt, Robert Hampton *composer, music publisher*
Filipp, Carolyn Francine *music educator, insurance agent*
Gearhart, John Wesley, III *musician, educator*
Girouard, Peggy Jo Fulcher *ballet educator*
Jacoby, Peter Fredrickson *music educator*
Jones, Florence M. *music educator*
Magnum, Wyatt D. *entertainment consulting company executive*
Marshall, Margo *artistic director*
Pino, Joseph David *sound designer*
Rigsby, Carolyn Erwin *music educator*
Stevenson, Ben *artistic director*
Troutt, Don Ray *radio executive*

Huntsville
Russell, George Haw *video production company executive*

Irving
Wahlstrom, Paul Burr *television producer*

Lubbock
Deahl, Robert Waldo *retired music educator, trombonist*

Mcallen
Guilliouma, Larry Jay, Jr. *performing arts administrator, music educator*

Mesquite
Montgomery, Marvin *musical producer*

Mission
Mohner, Carl Martin Rudolf *movie actor, artist*

Moulton
Koudelka, George John *music educator*

Munday
Bennett, Rodney Dee *music educator*

Nacogdoches
Waters, Walter Kenneth, Jr. *theatre educator*

Pampa
Cooley, Loralee Coleman *professional storyteller*

Round Top
Dick, James Cordell *concert pianist*
Royall, Richard Royster *classical music festival administrator*

San Antonio
Baker-White, Robert Elliott *drama educator*
Burns, Leslie Kaye *documentary video producer and director*
Loomis, Melinda Atkins *conductor, singer*
Powell Hill, Elizabeth T. *singer, small business owner*
Rossett, Ben Wyoming *television producer, editor*

San Marcos
Stuart, James Lester, Jr. *communications educator*

Sherman
Duhaime, Ricky Edward *music educator, woodwind specialist*

Tyler
Hatfield, James Allen *theater arts educator*
Rogers, Cheryl Lynn *music and dance educator*

Vernon
Cook, Marcella Kay *drama educator*

Victoria
Weber, Michael James *conductor*

Whitehouse
Baker, Rebecca Louise *musician, music educator, consultant*

Willis
Sinistre, Jean Paul *television producer, journalist*

VIRGINIA

Alexandria
Mathers, Daniel Eugene *musician, educator*

Fairfax
Hilbrink, William John *violinist*

Falls Church
Butler, Quincy Gasque *musician*

Keswick
Massey, Donald Wayne *microfilm consultant, small business owner*

Leesburg
McCann, Andrew Hughes *dance consultant, journalist*

Manassas
Kopczick, Ron James *communications director, editor*

Mc Lean
Drummond, Carol Cramer *voice educator, singer, artist, writer*
Rugala, Karen Francis (Karen Francis) *television producer, painter*

Newport News
Edmonds, Michael Darnell *music educator*

Norfolk
Mark, Peter *director, conductor*
Zeisler, Dennis J. *music educator*

Richmond
Baum, Alvin John, Jr. *professional clown, optometrist*
Levit, Heloise B. (Ginger Levit) *arts administrator, fine arts and media consultant*

Sterling
Jefferson, Sandra Traylor *choreographer, ballet coach*

Sweet Briar
Kershner, William Robert *theatre educator*

Vienna
Kinsolving, Sylvia Crockett *musician, educator*

Virginia Beach
Mohan, Tungesh Nath *television and film producer, film educator*

Waynesboro
Edwards, Virginia Davis *music educator, concert pianist*

Williamsburg
Hornsby, Bruce Randall *composer, musician*
Johnson, Gayle Harrison *artistic director*
Preston, Katherine Keenan *music educator*

Woodbridge
Bales, Richard Henry Horner *conductor, composer*

WEST VIRGINIA

Charleston
Conlin, Thomas (Byrd) *conductor*

Falling Waters
Schellhaas, Robert Wesley *songwriter, musician*

Inwood
Rizzetta, Carolyn Teresa *musical instrument, sound recording entrepreneur*

Mannington
Schumacher, Theresa Rose *singer, musician*

Sistersville
Anderson, Dolores May *music educator*

ADDRESS UNPUBLISHED

Allen, David Roger *theatre educator*
Allen, Marilyn Myers Pool *theater director, video producer*
Arova, Sonia *artistic director, ballet educator*
Benarroch Reinfeld, Mary *music and holistic human development educator*
Bencini, Sara Haltiwanger *concert pianist*
Berk, James Lawrence, II *entertainment executive, producer, songwriter*
Bujones, Fernando Calleiro *ballet dancer*
Cantwell, Don *artistic director*
Carine, Edwin Thomas *actor, playwright*
Clem, Elizabeth Ann Stumpf *music educator*
Coffey, Kevin T. *actor*
Coleman, Malcolm James, Jr. *band director, music educator*
Cooper, Brown *cinematographer*
Davidson, (Emily) Suzanne *performing arts association administrator*
Dufallo, Richard John *conductor*
Elgart, Larry Joseph *orchestra leader*
Ely, Richard McBrier *video/film producer, writer*
Gage, John *opera company executive*
Gallian, Virginia Anne *music educator*
Gockley, (Richard) David *opera director*
Hatfield, Joel Thane *music educator, minister*
Hill, Thomas Harry *music education educator*
James, Hugh Neal *video, record, movie producer, director*
Jennings, Waylon *country musician*
Kent, Gary Warner *film director, writer*
Lee, Katie Brooks *songwriter, entertainer*
Livingstone, Trudy Dorothy Zweig *dancer, educator*
McCachren, Jo Renee *musicologist, theorist, pianist, educator*
Morelan, Paula Kay *choreographer*
Page, Willis *conductor*
Rainey, Terry Lee *music educator, director*
Sanders, Glen Arthur *television producer*
Satz, Phyllis Robyne Sdoia *pianist, composer, conductor, educator*
Scrivner, Barbara E. *piano educator*
Smith, Lawrence Leighton *conductor*
Stahl, David *orchestra and opera conductor*
Surplus, Robert Wilbur *music educator*
Swing, Marce *producer, publisher*
Turkin, Marshall William *symphony orchestra, festival and opera administrator, arranger, composer*
Villella, Edward Joseph *ballet dancer, educator, choreographer, artistic director*

ARTS: VISUAL

UNITED STATES

ALABAMA

Birmingham
Price, Rosalie Pettus *artist*
Rankin, Don *art educator*

Huntsville
Pope, Mary Ann Irwin *graphic artist, designer*
Reeves, James Franklin *art broker*

Madison
Stewart, Robert Roy, III *art director*

Montgomery
Belt, Jean Rainer *art gallery owner*
Skurka, Kathleen *sculptor, educator*

Montrose
Kittrell, John Cabeen, Jr. *artist, writer*

Northport
Nutt, Craig Laurence *sculptor, furniture maker*

Theodore
Pate, William Earl *graphic services company executive, consultant*

Trussville
Best, Frederick Napier *artist, designer, educator*

Tuscaloosa
Brough, Richard Burrell *retired graphic design educator, artist*
Gourley, Paula Marie *art educator, artist, designer bookbinder*

ARKANSAS

Ashdown
Teague, Barbara Ann *art educator*

Fayetteville
Cockrill, Sherna *artist*
Peven, Michael *art educator, artist*

Little Rock
Cawood, Gary Kenneth *photography educator*
Cline, Ann *artist, designer*

North Little Rock
Paulsen, Darlyne Evelyn *artist, interior decorator*

State University
Mayes, Steven L. *art educator, artist*
Steele, Curtis Eugene *art educator, graphic designer, photographer*

CALIFORNIA

San Francisco
Held, John, Jr. *artist*

DISTRICT OF COLUMBIA

Washington
Moore, Stephen Timothy *artist, museum registration technician*
Scrupe, Mara A. (Mary Scrupe) *visual artist, sculptor*

FLORIDA

Alva
Colgin, Ann Barry *antique and arts dealer, appraiser, auctioneer*

Astor
Hupalo, Meredith Topliff *artist, illustrator*

Aventura
Cerri, Robert Noel *photographer*

Bal Harbour
Bernay, Betti *artist*

Boca Raton
Dorst, Mary Crowe *artist*
Mills, Agnes Eunice Karlin *artist, printmaker, sculptor*
Ortlip, Mary Krueger *artist*
Ortlip, Paul Daniel *artist*

Cape Coral
Paluszak, Naoko *artist*

Clearwater
Bansemer, Roger Lewis *artist*

Coconut Grove
Vadia, Rafael *visual artist*

Coral Gables
Bannard, Walter Darby *artist, art critic*

Coral Springs
Kroll, Lynne Francine *artist*

Dania
Abbott, Linda Joy *stained glass artisan, educator*
Smith, John Roscoe *glass artist*

Daytona Beach
Biferie, Dan *art educator, digital artist*
Knestrick, Janice Lee *art educator*

Englewood
Carmichael, Donald Ray *artist, educator*
Sisson, Robert F. *photographer, writer, lecturer, educator*
Tracy, Lois Bartlett *painter*

Fernandina Beach
D'Agnese, Helen Jean *artist*

Fort Lauderdale
Friedman, Sol *inventor, writer*
Janice, Barbara *illustrator*

Fort Myers
Dean, Jean Beverly *artist*

Fort Pierce
Cassens, Susan Forget *artist*

Gainesville
Blair, Eleanor Marie *artist, educator*
Grant, Elizabeth Jane Thurmond *graphic design educator, consultant*
Grissom, Eugene Edward *retired art educator, musician*
Murphy, Jeffrey Lawrence *digital imagemaker, photographer, educator*
Smith, Nan Shelley *art educator, sculptor*

Gulfport
Marshall, Nathalie *artist, writer, educator*

Hobe Sound
Houser, James Cowing, Jr. *painter, art educator*

Hollywood
Sadowski, Carol Johnson *artist*

Indian Harbour Beach
Traylor, Angelika *stained glass artist*

Jacksonville
Horowitz, Paul Martin *photographer, electronic technician*
Lawrence, Phenis Joseph *commercial artist*
Loomis, Jacqueline Chalmers *photographer*
Weeks, Edward Francis (Ted) *art appraiser, art critic, lecturer*

Juno Beach
Finlay, Steven Clyde *art director, electronic designer*

Key Largo
Fundora, Thomas *artist, journalist, composer*

Lake Mary
Bachmann, Bill *photographer*

Lake Park
Heaton, Janet Nichols *artist, art gallery director*

Lakeland
Rogers, James Gordon, Jr. *art educator*

Mary Esther
Simpson, Marilyn Jean *artist*

Melrose
Harley, Ruth *artist, educator*

Miami
Balás, Irene Barbara *artist*
Dalglish, Meredith Rennels *artist, educator*
Kitner, Jon David *art educator*
Martinez-Glander, Patricia Ann *artist*
Ralis, Paraskevy *art educator, artist*
Salinas, Baruj *artist, architect*
Strickland, Thomas Joseph *artist*
Tschumy, Freda Coffing *artist, educator*

Miami Beach
Gillman, Barbara Seitlin *artist, gallery owner*

Naples
Green, Jonathan *fine artist*

New Port Richey
Robichaud, Phyllis Ivy Isabel *artist, educator*

New Smyrna Beach
Leeper, Doris Marie *sculptor, painter*
Thomson, John Christian *financial analyst, portfolio manager*

Okeechobee
Chilcutt, Dorthe Margaret *art educator, artist*

Orange Park
Hunt, J(ulian) Courtenay *artist*

Orlando
Renee, Lisabeth Mary *art educator, artist, galley director*
Warren, Dean Stuart *artist*

Palm Bay
Galitello-Wolfe, Jane Maryann *artist, writer*

Palm Beach
Hibel, Edna *artist*
Myers, Eugene Ekander *art consultant*
Wenzel, Joan Ellen *artist*

Pensacola
Albrecht, Carol Heath *artist, educator*

Plant City
Holland, Gene Grigsby (Scottie Holland) *artist*

Plantation
Ballantyne, Maree Anne Canine *artist*
Oxell, Loie Gwendolyn *fashion and beauty educator, consultant, columnist*

Pompano Beach
Perkins, Lois Elaine *art educator, nurse assistant*
Roberts, Karen Barbara *art educator*

Ponte Vedra Beach
Draper, J(osiah) Everett *artist, author, educator*

Port Saint Lucie
Kamm, Dorothy Lila *art educator, artist, writer*

Royal Palm Beach
Halliwell, Leigh Frances *artist, writer*

Safety Harbor
Banks, Allan Richard *artist, art historian, researcher*

Saint Augustine
Connaway, Robert Wallace *artist, computer programmer*
Gilliland, Thomas *art gallery director*

Saint Petersburg
Bryant, Laura Militzer *artist*
Rigg, Carol Margaret Elizabeth Ruth *calligrapher, calligraphic designer, visual arts educator*

Sarasota
Bloomer, Carolyn Mitchell *cultural anthropologist*
Capes, Richard Edward *artist, publisher*
Chase, Jeanne Norman *artist, educator*
Deo, Marjoree Nee *painter*
Dowd, Jack Henry *sculptor*
Erickson, Joy Marilyn *artist, graphic designer, inventor, photographer*
Harmon, (Loren) Foster *art consultant*
Krate, Nat *artist*
Larsen, Robert Wesley *artist, educator*
Muller, Max Paul *artist, educator*

Silver Springs
Cini, Anthony Richard *bookbinding craftsman*

Tallahassee
Fichter, Robert Whitten *artist*

Tamarac
Smith, Rowena Marcus *artist, educator*

Tampa
Cardoso, Anthony Antonio *artist, educator*
de Lama, Alberto *artist*
Fosnaught, Patricia S. *art educator*
Kronsnoble, Jeffrey Michael *art educator*
Schofield, Roberta *artist, consultant, educator*
Winslow, Anne Branan *artist*

Temple Terrace
Kashdin, Gladys Shafran *painter, educator*

Vero Beach
Jonason, Pauline Marie *retired art educator*
Polan, Nancy Moore *artist*

Winter Park
Duplantier Rhea, Béatrice Marie Charlotte *international art consultant, interior decorator*
Lemon, Robert Sheldon, Jr. *art history educator*

Winter Springs
San Miguel, Manuel *painter, historian, composer, poet*

GEORGIA

Athens
Hammond, (Gale) Thomas *art educator, printmaker artist*
Kaufman, Glen Frank *art educator, artist*
Kent, Robert B. *artist, educator*
Sapp, William Rothwell *artist, educator*
Scott, Virginia R. *glass researcher, writer*

Atlanta
Alexander, Constance Joy (Connie Alexander) *stone sculptor*
Greco, Anthony Joseph *artist, educator, administrator*
Grumet, Priscilla Hecht *fashion specialist, consultant, writer*
Henry, David Eugene *artist, educator*
Johnston, W. Medford *artist, educator*
Lagerquist, Marion Stewart *art dealer, investor*
Laxson, Ruth Knight *artist*
Malone, James Hiram *graphic artist, painter, writer*
O'Donnell, Timothy Shawn *graphic artist*
Shank, Thomas Jeffrey *computer animator*
Wilmer, Mary Charles *artist*
Wyatt, Marsha Kapnicky *graphic arts consultant*
Yarbrough, Leila Esther Kepert *artist, graphics company owner*

Augusta
Claybrook, Marjorie Annette *fiber artist*
Schmidel, Judith S. *artist, writer, counselor*

Barnesville
Creecy, Herbert Lee, Jr. *artist*

Carrollton
Barr, Mary Jeanette *art educator*
Romain, Bella Mary *graphic designer*

Clarkesville
Mize, B. Dianne *artist*

Decatur
Tyndall, Randy R. *multimedia artist*

Dunwoody
Harris, William Elgie *art educator*

Gainesville
Taylor, Mary Jane *art educator, artist*

Lookout Mountain
Lynch, Mary Britten *artist, educator*

Macon
Gray, Elise Norris *sculptor*

Marietta
Mathis, Billie Fritz *artist*

Peachtree City
Robben, Mary Margaret *portrait artist*
Waterhouse, Mona Elisabeth *artist*

Powder Springs
Collins, Lisa Diane *art educator*

Rome
Staven, Leland Carroll *art educator*

Roswell
Sherman, Ron *photographer*

Savannah
Gabeler-Brooks, Jo *artist*

Statesboro
Hines, Jessica *art educator, artist*
Ragans, Rosalind Dorothy *textbook author, retired art educator*

Stone Mountain
Honea, Nance *artist, educator*

Thomaston
Greivell, Juliette Arnold *painter*

Thomasville
Powers, Donald Tyrone *artist*

Valdosta
Andersen, Stephen Perry *art educator, art gallery director*

Watkinsville
Young, Mike *design company executive*

KENTUCKY

Lexington
Sandoval, Arturo Alonzo *art educator, artist*
Snowden, Ruth O'Dell Gillespie *artist*

Louisville
Bright, Jeptha Barnard (Barney) *sculptor*
Parsley, Jacque *visual artist, art gallery director*

Murray
Sperath, Albert Frank *artist, museum director*

Richmond
Spears, Karen Lynn *art educator*

Shepherdsville
Lesch, Alma Wallace *fiber artist*

Williamsburg
Weedman, Kenneth Russell *artist, art educator*

LOUISIANA

Baton Rouge
Johns, Christopher Kalman *art educator*

Houma
Babin, Regina-Champagne *artist, consultant*

Lafayette
Ramsey, Billy Mack *design educator, design consultant, artist*
Savoy, Chyrl Lenore *artist, educator*

Mandeville
Rohrbough, Elsa Claire Hartman *artist*

Metairie
Tahir, Abe Mahmoud, Jr. *art consultant*

New Orleans
Boudreaux, Mark Michael *graphic designer*
Harris, Ronna S. *artist, educator*
Mullen, Ruth González *artist, secondary school educator*
Scott, John Tarrell *art educator, sculptor*
Simons, Dona *artist*
Wegmann, Mary Katherine *art director*

Shreveport
Wray, Geraldine Smitherman (Jerry Wray) *artist*

Thibodaux
Turner, Peggy Ann *graphic designer, visual artist*

MISSISSIPPI

Belzoni
Halbrook, Rita Robertshaw *artist, sculptor*

Cleveland
Brown, Patricia L. *art educator, artist*
Koehler, Ronald Gene *art educator, sculptor*

Hattiesburg
Du Boise, Kim Rees *artist, art educator*

Jackson
Wolfe, Mildred Nungester *artist*

Olive Branch
Douglas, Kenneth Dale *artist*

Vicksburg
Dortch, Alice Jean *supervisory visual information specialist*

NORTH CAROLINA

Albemarle
Moose, Talmadge Bowers *artist, illustrator, portrait artist*

Black Mountain
Tate, Gayle Blair *art dealer, artist*

Brevard
Murray, Timothy Douglas *art educator*

Buies Creek
Smith, Howard Breckinridge *art, design educator*

Chapel Hill
McKay, Renee *artist*
Saltzman, Marvin *art educator*
Williams, (Robert) Kent *artist*

Charlotte
Allred, Rita Reed *artist*
Shaw, Mary Todd *artist, art educator*

Clarkton
Wuebbels, Theresa Elizabeth *visual art educator*

Columbus
Smith, Virginia Warren *artist, writer, educator*

Durham
Muller, Yvonne *artist*
Williams, Barbara Elaine *design production company executive*

Fayetteville
Fields, William Coffield, III *artist*

Goldsboro
Lesak, Joanne Helen *artist*
Turlington, Patricia Renfrew *artist, educator*

Graham
Carter, Frank Guerrant, Jr. *graphic design educator*

Greensboro
Doren, Arnold Tilden *photography educator*

Greenville
Chamberlain, Charles Frank *artist, educator*
Haney, Arthur John *art educator, academic administrator*
Laing, Richard Harlow *artist, educator*
Wallin, Leland Dean *artist, educator*

Landis
Lynch, Samuel Curlee, Jr. (Sami Lynch) *painter, sculptor, writer*

Leasburg
Treacy, Sandra Joanne Pratt *art educator, artist*

Lenoir
Michaux, Henry Gaston *art educator*

Pinehurst
Craft, Larry *design company executive*

Siler City
Holt, Milo *retired printer*

Williamston
Wobbleton, Judy Karen *artist, educator*

Wilmington
Howell, Claude Flynn *artist*

Winston Salem
Dance, Robert Bartlett *artist*
Funderburk, Amy Elizabeth *artist, art educator, exhibition coordinator*
Lynch, George Cuninggim *art director*

OKLAHOMA

Chouteau
Ayres, Julia Spencer *artist, author*

Clinton
Lee, Mary Virginia *artist*

Duncan
Sloan, Nancy Marie *artist*

Midwest City
Gonzalez, Richard Theodore *photographer*

Norman
Bavinger, Eugene Allen *artist, educator*
Reedy, Mitsuno Ishii *artist, painter*
Youritzin, Victor Koshkin *art educator*

Oklahoma City
Boston, Billie *costume designer, costume history educator*
Richardson, Jean Brooks *artist, printmaker*
Weltzheimer, Marie Kash *artist*

Sapulpa
Roblyer, Bob Allen *art director, computer graphics consultant*

Tulsa
Hale, D. Curtis *commercial artist, painter, writer*
Malone, Patricia Lynn *artist*
Spencer, Winifred May *art educator*
Wincentsen, Edward Lee *artist*

Vinita
Castor, Carol Jean *artist, teacher*

SOUTH CAROLINA

Central
Smith, Elizabeth Shelton *art educator*

Charleston
Goodbred, Ray Edward *artist, educator*
McCallum, Corrie *painter, printmaker*
Ward, Joseph Marshall, Sr. *retired art educator*

Clemson
Petzel, Florence Eloise *textiles educator*

Columbia
Elkins, Toni Marcus *artist, art association administrator*
Hansen, Harold John *art educator*
Lipscomb, Guy Fleming, Jr. *artist, manufacturer, chemist, educator*
Mullen, Philip Edward *artist, educator*
O'Neil, John Joseph *artist, educator*
Thompson, Charles Otis *lighting designer*

Easley
Cheek, Ronald Edward *artist*

Greenville
Alberga, Alta Wheat *artist*
Bopp, Emery *art and design educator, artist, sculptor*
Dreskin, Jeanet Steckler *painter, medical artist, educator*
Koons, Darell J. *artist, art educator*

Hartsville
Chalmers, Kimberly *artist, educator*

Myrtle Beach
Powers, W. Alex *artist*

Orangeburg
Kozachek, Janet Lynne *artist, educator*

Pendleton
Shanahan, Elizabeth Anne *art educator*

Piedmont
Kaufman, Loretta Ana *sculptor*

Rock Hill
Freeman, David Lee *artist, educator*
Mintich, Mary R. *art educator, sculptor*

Sullivans Island
Smith, Carl Jennings *professional designer, educator*

Summerville
Vorwerk, E. Charlsie *artist*

TENNESSEE

Bristol
Kind, Mimi P. *art educator*
Mueller, Roy Clement *graphic arts company executive*

Chattanooga
Craft, David Ralph *artist, educator*
Mills, Charles G. *photography company executive*
Mills, Olan, II *photography company executive*

Cleveland
Finley, Mary Lou Guinn *artist, craft designer*

Johnson City
Slatton, Ralph David *printmaking educator*

Knoxville
Longobardi, Pamela Scott Dodgen *artist, educator*
Martin, Julie Warren *sculptor*

La Vergne
Corenflos, Lori Cooper *illustrator, graphic artist*

Memphis
Bernstein, Janna S. Bernheim *art educator*
Dávila, Maritza *artist, educator*
De Mere-Dwyer, Leona *medical artist*
Edelstein, Paul Ray *artist, art dealer*
Grauer, Eva Marie *sculptor, artist*
Yates, Marvin Clarence *advertising artist, painter, illustrator*

Mountain City
Nielsen, Ralph Martin *production designer, special effects expert, sound engineer*

Nashville
Aurbach, Michael Lawrence *art educator, sculptor*
Cundiff, Lou Willie *artist, sculptor, writer*
Fryd, Vivien Green *fine arts educator*
Havens, Jan *artist*
McKinney, Jane-Allen *artist and educator*
Murphy, Marilyn *artist, educator*
Oates, Sherry Charlene *portraitist*
Rutherford, Mary Louise Manlove *artist*

Seymour
LeFevre, Richard J. *art educator, illustrator*

Signal Mountain
Collins, Jim *artist*
Newman, Samuel Mark *animator*

TEXAS

Abilene
Kwiecinski, Chester M. *artist*

Arlington
Brouillette, Albert C. *watermedia painter, educator*
Munoz, Celia Alvarez *artist*

Austin
Bednar, Susan Marie *art director*
Daly, Stephen Jeffrey *art educator*
Debold, Cynthia Ann *sculptor*
Fearing, William Kelly *art educator, artist*
Frary, Michael *artist, educator*
Hatgil, Paul Peter *artist, sculptor, educator*
High, Timothy Griffin *artist, educator, writer*
Kostiuk, Michael Marion, Jr. *artist*
Lundberg, William Albert *artist, educator*
Marshall, Bruce *artist, writer*
Reeves, Dianne L. *artist*

Beaumont
Carron, Maudee Lilyan *painter, sculptor, writer*
Fornell, Martha Steinmetz *art educator, artist*

Belton
Christoff, Beth Graves *artist*

College Station
Moore, Marjorie W. *artist*

Coppell
Miiller, Susan Diane *artist*

Corpus Christi
Rote, Carey Clements *art educator*
Wilhelmi, William Merle *artist*
Williams, Ethel Laverna (Ethel Laverna Williams Steed) *painter*
Worden, Elizabeth Ann *artist, comedy writer, singer*
Wright, Olga *artist, aesthetician*

Dallas
Allison, David Lawrence (David Lawrence Screws) *graphic designer*
Amend, Eugene Michael *art advisor, appraiser*
Barta, Dorothy Elaine *portrait artist*
Blessen, Karen Alyce *free-lance illustrator, designer*
Gantz, Ann Cushing *artist, educator*
Hudgins, Louise Nan *art educator*
Lewis, Carl Edwin (Djinn) *artist, photographer, designer*
Marcus, Heather *artist, sculptor*
Meynig, Anita Rae *artist*
Sherwood, Rhonda Griffin *fashion and costume designer*
Smither, Edward Murray *art consultant, appraiser*

Denton
Cox, Barbara Claire *costume designer, educator*
Falsetta, Vincent Mario *artist, educator*
Gough, Georgia Belle *art educator*
McMath, Elizabeth Moore *graphic artist*
Weller, Laurie June *artist, educator*

Dilley
Avant, Tracy Wright *artist*

Dripping Springs
Pellicone, William *artist, sculptor, writer, architect*

Eagle Pass
Cullar, Carol Lee *visual arts educator*

Edinburg
Libbey, Darlene Hensley *artist, educator*
Manuella, Frank *art and design educator*

El Paso
Maguire, Blanche Joan (Maggie Maguire) *watercolorist*
Weitz, Jeanne Stewart *artist, educator*

Fort Worth
Abramson, Elaine Sandra *graphic designer, crafts artist, cartoonist*
Bush, Jill Lobdill *artist*
Conn, David Edward *art educator*
Watson, Ronald *painter, art educator*

Galveston
Paratore-Zarzana, Mary Gay *artist, art educator, lecturer*

Houston
Biles, Marilyn Marta *painter*
Bishop, Mary Lou *artist*
Christie, Richard Joel *studio executive*
Danko, Patricia St. John *visual artist, writer, educator*
Dent, Leanna Gail *art educator*
Fleming, Timothy Woodbridge *fine arts and communications educator*
Hamilton, Jacqueline *art consultant*
Hulce, Durward Philip *theatrical lighting designer*
Jackson, Susanne Leora *creative placement firm executive*
Jacobs, David Lee *art educator*
Larrey, Inge Harriette *jazz and blues freelance photographer*
Lyon, Giles A. *artist*
Reid, Katherine Louise *artist, educator, author*
Saks, Judith-Ann *artist*
Thompson, Judith Kay *realist painter*
Ward, Bethea *artist, small business owner*
Wolff, Dee Ivona *artist*

Huntsville
Ahysen, Harry Jules *artist, educator*

Hurst
Gates, Betty Russell *artist*
Saladino, Tony Joseph *artist*

Kerrville
Burt, Allen Daniel *artist*

Longview
Hearne, Carolyn Fox *art and history educator, artist*
Statman, Jan B. *artist*

Lubbock
Funk, Charlotte Marie *art educator, artist*
Howze, James Dean *art educator, artist*

Mcallen
Melton, Terry Raymond *artist*

Mission
McClendon, Maxine *artist*

Odessa
Lee, Nelda S. *art appraiser and dealer, film producer*
Price, Pamela Champion *art educator*

Richardson
Kessler, Margaret Marie *artist, writer*

San Antonio
Binks, Ronald Carl *art educator, artist*
Bristow, William Arthur *artist, educator*
Embrey, Carl Rice *artist*
Groover, Deborah Kate *artist, educator*
Lee, Amy Freeman *artist, educator*
McDougal, Ivan Ellis *artist*
Orr, Lisa Kay *potter*
Stephens, Martha Lockhart *art educator*
Willson, Robert (William) *glass sculpture and watercolor artist*

Sandia
Peters, Diane Peck *artist*

Seminole
Clark, Vicky Jo *artist*

Spring
von Hagge, Robert *design company executive*

Tyler
Pace, James Robert *art educator, painter, printmaker*

Waco
McClanahan, John D. *painting and design educator*

Wylie
Pototschnik, John Michael *artist*

VIRGINIA

Alexandria
Collum, Danny Duncan *fine arts educator*
Covey, Rosemary Feit *artist*
Kamen, Rebecca Ann *sculptor, art educator*
Keena, Janet Laybourn *artist*
Payne, Nancy Sloan *visual arts educator*

Annandale
Smith, Ralph *artist*

Brightwood
Skelton, Dorothy Geneva Simmons (Mrs. John William Skelton) *art educator*

Chantilly
Pope, Randall Patrick *art director*

Charlottesville
Priest, Hartwell Wyse *artist*

Fairfax
Hammond, Mary Sayer *art educator*

Fairfax Station
Jackson, Vaughn Lyle *artist, consultant*

Falls Church
Gawarecki, Carolyn Grossé *watercolor artist and educator*

Farmville
Springer, Homer Lee, Jr. *art educator*

Forest
Johnson, Leslie Diane Horvath *artist, graphic designer, small business owner*

Fredericksburg
Herndon, Cathy Campbell *artist, art educator*

Free Union
McCollum, Sarah *artist*

Front Royal
Miller, Bryane Katherine *artist, writer*

Hampton
Beachum, Sharon Garrison *graphic designer and educator*

Herndon
Noboa-Stanton, Patricia Lynn *corporate executive*

Lynchburg
Hudson, Walter Tiree *artist*
Massie, Anne Adams Robertson *artist*

Max Meadows
Lancaster, Kendell René Quesenberry *floral designer, business manager, administrator*

Mc Lean
Bryans, John Armond *artist, art educator*
Kipniss MacDonald, Betty Ann *artist, educator*

Newport News
Anglin, Betty Lockhart *artist, educator*

Norfolk
Frieden, Jane Heller *art educator*
Jones, Leon Herbert, Jr. (Herb Jones) *artist*
Myers, Sue Bartley *artist*
Nicholson, Myreen Moore *artist, researcher*
Rogic, George *graphic artist*

Oakton
Bealey, Laura Ann *artist, educator*

Radford
Kessler, Kendall Seay Feriozi *artist*
Salam, Halide *artist, art educator*
Shell, Robert Edward Lee *photographer, writer*

Richmond
Bumgardner, James Arliss *artist, educator*
Kevorkian, Richard *artist*
Savedge, Anne Creery *artist, photographer*
Taliaferro, Nancy Ellen Taylor *artist*

Roanoke
Dickerson, Vera M. *artist, educator*
Guerrant, Helen Orzel *artist*

Somerset
Sehring, Adolf *artist, sculptor*

Vienna
Flax, Florence Roselin P. *photographer*

Washington
Marshall, Laurie *artist, educator*

Waynesboro
Prye, Ellen Ross *graphic designer*

Williamsburg
Lorenz, Hans Ernest *photographer*
Stanley, Shirley Davis *artist*

WEST VIRGINIA

Elkins
Reed, Jesse Floyd *artist, art educator*

Fairmont
DeVito, Teresa Marie *artist*

Philippi
Lambert, Olivia Sue *commercial artist, writer*

Wheeling
Peace, Bernie Kinzel *art educator, artist*
Phillis, Marilyn Hughey *artist*

TERRITORIES OF THE UNITED STATES

PUERTO RICO

San Juan
Luna Padilla, Nitza Enid *photography educator*

ADDRESS UNPUBLISHED

Allan, Yvonne Leticia *medical illustrator, computer graphics designer*
Anderson, Violet Henson *artist, educator*
Andrews, Jean *artist, writer*
Bodnar-Balahutrak, Lydia *artist, educator*
Cima, Brooks Dement *art educator*
Conklin, Gloria Zamko *artist, marketing executive*
Conner, Ann *artist*
Covington, Harrison Wall *artist, educator*
Crozier, Richard Lewis *artist, educator*
Davenport, Ray Charles *artist, lithographer*
Farah, Cynthia Weber *photographer, publisher*
Frazer, James Nisbet, Jr. *artist, photographer*
Gerstein, Esther *sculptor*
Goldstein, Carl *art educator*
Guani, Filippo Ettore *photographer*
Halsey, William *artist, educator*
Hamblen, Karen *art educator*
Hancock, Patricia Ann *artist*
Harding, Ann Carol *painter*
Herring, William Arthur *artist*
Hopkins, B(ernice) E(lizabeth) *artist*
Hull, Margaret Ruth *artist, educator, consultant*
Jackson, Lola Hirdler *art educator*
Johnson, Linda Kaye *art educator*
Jones, Taylor Burnett *cartoonist*
Kasperbauer, Isabel Giles *art educator*
Kleinman, Sue *artist*
Knapp, Candace Louise *sculptor*
Leeber, Sharon Corgan *art consultant*
Leighton, Miriam *artist, consultant*
Lewis, Ronald Walter *artist*
Maree, Wendy *painter, sculptor*
Nash, Mary Harriet *artist, educator*
Pretlow, Carol Jocelyn *fashion and communications consultant*
Rauf, Barbara Claire *art educator*
Riverón, Enrique Pedro *artist*
Ross, Gloria Jean *artist*
Rowe, Bobby Louise *art educator*
Saseen, Sharon Louise *artist, painter, educator*
Schmidt, Frederick Lee *artist, educator*
Shaughnessy, Marie Kaneko *artist, business executive*
Shaw, Gloria Doris *art educator*
Storer, Frances Nell *artist, musician*
Tucci, Tony M. *lighting designer*
Van Vranken, Rose *sculptor*
Vester, Paula Jean *artist in textiles, educator*
Villoch, Kelly Carney *art director*
Waltman, Lynne Marie *medical illustrator*
Watkins, Lewis Boone *artist*
Wengrovitz, Judith *artist, educator*

ASSOCIATIONS AND ORGANIZATIONS. *See also* specific fields.

UNITED STATES

ALABAMA

Birmingham
Doyle, William Lynn *non-profit management specialist*
Kirkley, D. Christine (D. Christine Kirkley) *non-profit organization administrator*
Lee, Cathy Callans *nonprofit management executive*
Moran, William Madison *fundraising executive*
Newton, Don Allen *chamber of commerce executive*
Pattillo, Wesley Moody, Jr. *foundation executive*

Dothan
Morrison, Barbara Haney *educational administrator*
Wheelock, Elizabeth Shivers *trade association executive, small business owner*

Greensboro
Spain, Nettie Edwards (Mrs. Frank E. Spain) *civic worker*

Huntsville
Fries, Helen Sergeant Haynes *civic leader*
Ward, Michael Dennis *chamber of commerce executive*

Mobile
DeKay, Gary Earl *non-profit organization executive*

Montgomery
Cooper, J. Danny *state association administrator*
Jones, Charles William *association executive*

Scottsboro
Waldrop, Beverly Elizabeth *volunteer administrator*

Tuscaloosa
Summersell, Frances Sharpley *organization worker*

ARIZONA

Phoenix
Peck, Robert David *educational foundation administrator*

Sierra Vista
Morrow, Bruce William *educational administrator, business executive, consultant*

Tempe
Rockwell, Susan Lynn *educational association administrator*

ARKANSAS

Fayetteville
Stephens, Wanda Brewer *social services administrator, investor*

Hot Springs National Park
Benini, Lorraine Francis *fine arts foundation executive, writer*

Little Rock
Busfield, Roger Melvil, Jr. *retired trade association executive, educator*

Pine Bluff
Tate-Jackson, Patricia *fundraiser*

CALIFORNIA

San Francisco
Stauffer, Thomas Michael *university president*

COLORADO

Denver
Kellogg, Jack Lorenzo *fundraising executive, lawyer*

DISTRICT OF COLUMBIA

Washington
Bond, Julian *civil rights leader*
Brinkmann, Robert Joseph *association administrator, lawyer*
Evans, Dewitt Howard *foundation administrator*
Giardina, Susan Petrini *association executive*
LeBlanc, James Leo *business executive, consultant*
Magrath, C. Peter *educational association executive*
Reich, Alan Anderson *foundation administrator*

FLORIDA

Bal Harbour
Ash, Dorothy Matthews *civic worker*

Boca Raton
Apelian, Clover B. *non-profit management consultant*
Evans, Craig *foundation administrator, consultant, lobbyist*
Jessup, Jan Amis *arts volunteer, writer*
Williams, Charlotte Evelyn Forrester *civic worker*

Coral Gables
Noriega, Lamar Jernigan *political consultant*

Daytona Beach
Parker, Betty Morris *association administrator retired*

Fort Lauderdale
Calhoun, Peggy Joan *fundraising executive*
Long, Michael *foundation administrator*
McAusland, Randolph M. N. *arts administrator*
Miller, Jerome M. *civic worker*
Washington, Alice Hester *human services professional*
White, Mary Lou *fundraiser, writer, educator*

Gainesville
Gilliland, Marion Charlotte S. *volunteer*
Wright, Jane Brooks *university foundation professional*

Hialeah
Boeru, Laurentiu Marian *health association executive*

Jacksonville
Johnson, Leland "Lee" Harry *social services administrator*
Morris, Max King *foundation executive, former naval officer*
Ward, Jeanne Lawton *family counselor, consultant*

Jasper
Cone, Virgie Horne Hyman *former educator, civic worker*

Lake Wales
Williams, Eda Dunstan *civic worker*

Lakeland
Santangelo, Daniel L. *association administrator*
Spencer, Mary Miller *civic worker*

Melbourne
Dale, Cynthia Lynn Arpke *educational administrator*

Miami
Berger, Joyce Muriel *foundation executive, author, editor*
Bertels, Frank (Jim Anderson) *male rights activist, foundation administrator*
Blanco, Josefa Joan-Juana (Jossie Blanco) *social services administrator*
Fishman, Seymour *fundraising executive*
Gonzalez-Molina, Gabriel *research center executive*
Heiens, Richard Allen *education foundation executive*
Hills, Lee *foundation administrator, newspaper executive, consultant*
Kolker, Sondra G. *fund raising/special events executive*
Lengomin, Juan A. *educational administrator*
Lynch, Catherine Gores *social work administrator*
Shelton, Betty Clare *organization executive*
Tribble, Keith R. *athletic and social events executive*
Twigg, David Keith *public administrator, writer*
Wilson, Margaret Gibbons *social sciences educator*

North Palm Beach
Woodard, Wallace William, III *quality advocate*

Orlando
Ball, Joseph E. *association executive*
Ingram, Michael Alexander *operations and management consultant*
Matthews, Gerald *association administrator*
Moody, Donald Ernest *rescue mission administrator*
Porcher, Arthur Gigniliat, III *association administrator*
Thomas, Sandra Marie *training company executive*

Ormond Beach
Nasser, Joseph Yousef *public safety administrator, consultant*

Palm Beach
Hope, Margaret Lauten *civic worker*

Panama City
Morgan, George William *trade association administrator, consultant*

Pensacola
Bailey, George Thomas *real estate association executive*
Evans, Timothy Harris *non-profit organization executive*
Tamberrino, Frank Michael *professional association executive*
Walker, Peggy Jean *social work agency administrator*

Pinellas Park
West, Wallace Marion *cultural organization administrator*

Port Charlotte
Bell, Deborah Marie *social services administrator*

Port Saint Lucie
Weber, Alban *association executive, lawyer*

Sarasota
Perkins, Robert Eugene *foundation administrator*

Sebring
Maire, Barbara Jean *volunteer*

Tallahassee
Banfield, William Scott *educational fund raising executive*
Bishop, Barney Tipton, III *political consultant, lobbyist*

Tampa
Callan, Joseph Patrick *social service administrator*
Dowridge, Donald Lee, Jr. *motivational speaker*
Lowe, Peter Stephen *non-profit company executive*
Loyer-Davis, Sharon Lynn *social services administrator, author, poet*

Vero Beach
Johnson, Richard Harold *hospital foundation executive, fundraising consultant*

West Palm Beach
Atkinson, Regina Elizabeth *medical social worker*
Borchers, Karen Lily *child welfare administrator*
Moody, Cheryl Anne *social services administrator, social worker, educator*

Windermere
Russell, Robert Leonard *professional association executive*

Winter Haven
Wheeler, Irving *association executive*

GEORGIA

Atlanta
Bedford, Charles B. *higher education consortium executive*
Bell, Ronald Mack *university foundation administrator*
Birdsong, Alta Marie *volunteer*
Bonner, Phillip Ray *foundation executive*
Dorsey, Hattie *community economic development executive*
Hill, I. Kathryn *professional certification agency administrator*
Houchard, Michael Harlow *organization executive*
Jackson, Ronald Pippin *social services agency administrator*
King, Dexter Scott *foundation administrator*
King, Jennie Louise *research director*
Lehfeldt, Martin Christopher *nonprofit consulting company executive*
Lieberman, Laura Crowell *arts administrator, artist, critic*
Massell, Sam *civic organization executive*
McCarty, Jennifer Lewis *fraternal organization administrator*
Patterson, Anita Mattie *union administrator*
Perry, Lois Joy *non-profit corporation executive*
Rucker, Kenneth Lamar *public administrator, educator*
Starr, Charles Christopher *foundation executive, priest*
Stuart, Joan Martha *fund raising executive*
White, Ann Wells *community activist*
Wylly, Barbara Bentley *performing arts association administrator*
Young, Andrew Jackson *civil rights leader, clergyman, former mayor, former ambassador, former congressman*

Augusta
Davison, Frederick Corbet *foundation executive*
Grier, Leamon Forest *social services administrator*
Sykes, Frederick George (Rick Sykes) *association administrator*

Barnesville
Braswell, Randy Lee *educational administrator*

Decatur
Garrett, Gloria Susan *social services professional*
Rieder, Roland Conrad *foundation administrator*

Jonesboro
Wilder, Cecil Creighton *educational association administrator*

Norcross
Leake, Woodrow Wilson *professional society administrator*

Riverdale
Rhoden, Mary Norris *educational center director*

Rome
Bertrand, Annabel Hodges *civic worker, artist, calligrapher*

Roswell
Thibaudeaux, Mary Frances *cultural organization administrator*

Savannah
Williams, Michael E. *social services administrator*

Snellville
Williams, Jeffrey Lee *credit union association executive*

Stone Mountain
Dempsey, Frederick Gerard (Terry), Jr. *association management executive, consultant*

Summerville
Spivey, Suzan Brooks Nisbet *association administrator, medical technologist*

Tucker
McNair, Nimrod, Jr. *foundation executive, consultant*
Smith, Lois Ann (L.A.) *foundation administrator, consultant*

ILLINOIS

Chicago
Jowdy, Jeffrey William *development executive*

KENTUCKY

Cadiz
Saum, Elizabeth Pape *community volunteer*

Elizabethtown
Greenwell, Linda Branham *social services administrator*

Lexington
Lewis, Robert Kay, Jr. *fundraising executive*
Nichols, Patricia G. *association administrator*

Louisville
Bentley, James Robert *association curator, historian, genealogist*
Glass, Robert Dodds *foundation administrator*
Sanders, Kathey Golightly *child welfare organization executive*
Smith, Charles L. *personal care home administrator*
Watkins, Samuel Rayburn *association executive*
Watts, Beverly L. *civil rights executive*

Shelbyville
Moore, David Bruce *social service administrator, psychotherapist*

LOUISIANA

Baton Rouge
Conerly, Evelyn Nettles *educational consultant*
Falk, Myron *fundraising consultant*
Guerry, Leah Saye *professional society administrator*
Madden, Roberta Margaret *association program developer*

Metairie
Caplan, Merry Wassom *non-profit educational corporation executive*
Dufrechou, Carlton Francis *foundation administrator*
Heim, Charles William, Jr. *fund raising executive*

New Orleans
Benjamin, Adelaide Wisdom *community volunteer and activist*
Rathke, Dale Lawrence *community organizer and financial analyst*
Sullivan, Daniel Edmond *fundraising executive*

MARYLAND

Bethesda
Grenier, Edward Joseph, III *foundation administrator*
Walsh, William B., Jr. *foundation administrator*

Edgewater
Hammer, Jane Amelia Ross *advocate*

Germantown
Bonnarens, Joseph Keith *trade association administrator, pharmacist*

MISSISSIPPI

Clinton
Garrett, Ricki Rayner *educational administrator*

Crenshaw
Cooke, Gloria Grayson *trust fund director*

Jackson
Bates, Lura Wheeler *trade association executive*
Hendrix, Albert Randel *social services administrator*
Sullivan, John Magruder, II *government affairs administrator*

Laurel
Stennett, William Mitchell *association executive*

Long Beach
Kanagy, Steven Albert *foundation administrator*

Madison
Hays, Mary Katherine Jackson (Mrs. Donald Osborne Hays) *civic worker*

Pontotoc
Roberts, Rose Harrison *social services administrator, consultant*

MISSOURI

Columbia
Francis, Lee, III *trade association administrator*

Gladstone
Lewis, Harold E(ugene) *association executive*

NEW YORK

Poughkeepsie
Childers, Andrew Aisle *educational association administrator*

NORTH CAROLINA

Arden
Leavitt, Glenn Sheffield *retired rehabilitation administrator*

Asheville
Shepherd, Robert Edwin *public administrator*

Cary
Martin, Donnis Lynn *educational analyst*
Martin, William Royall, Jr. *association executive*

Chapel Hill
Baker, Linda Leslie *social services administrator, consultant*
Kenan, Thomas Stephen, III *philanthropist*
Wicker, Marie Peachee *civic worker*

Charlotte
Bailey, Kevin William *educational administrator*
Fitch, Toni Lynn *public relations coordinator association*
Kennedy, Joan Canfield *volunteer*
Kimmel, A. June Miller *council executive*
Lair, Judith Anne Trevvett *social services administrator, counselor*
Locke, Elizabeth Hughes *foundation administrator*
McArdle, Sally Schafer *association executive*
Sanders, Henry Walker *foundation executive*

Durham
Booth, Robert Harrison *association executive*
Hall, Robert H. *research director*

Greensboro
Slaughter, Thomas Edwin *family services agency executive*

Greenville
Bain, Daniel Albert *educational administrator*

Hendersonville
Kussrow, Nancy Esther *educational association administrator*
Moon, Doug *director of development*

Hickory
Perryman, Thomas Ruben *arts administrator, artist*

High Point
Caywood, Bud *association administrator*

Kill Devil Hills
Bishop, Sid Glenwood *union official*

Monroe
Carpenter, James Gaston *trade association administrator*

Raleigh
Brooker, Lena Epps *human relations program administrator*
Graham, Kent Hill *philanthropist, museum guide*
Holman, William Earl *lobbyist, consultant*
Knox, Betty Emmett *educational administrator*
Lilly, Nancy Cobb *civic worker*
Reevy, Anthony William *university development officer*

Smithfield
Taylor, Ellen Borden Broadhurst *civic worker*

Swannanoa
McMillan, Molly Colleen *educational association administrator*

Thomasville
Steen, John Warren, III *fundraising executive*

Wilson
McCain, Betty Landon Ray (Mrs. John Lewis McCain) *political party official*

Winston Salem
Jones, F(rancis) Whitney *fund raising executive, consultant*
LeMaster, Sherry Renee *fundraising administrator*
Moore, Markita Alberta *charitable trust program officer*

OKLAHOMA

Edmond
McLaughlin, Lisa Marie *educational administrator*

Lawton
Brooks, Leslie Gene *association executive*
Crane, Marilyn N. *homeless shelter administrator, director*

Norman
Burton, Ron D. *educational foundation executive*
Hammon, Norman Harold *fundraising counsel and development consultant*

Oklahoma City
Kirkpatrick, Eleanor Blake *civic worker*
Paque, Michel Jean *association executive director*
Tusing, James C. *retired association executive*

Stillwater
Dixon, Nancy Powell *educational research administrator*

Tulsa
Brunner, Ronald Gene *trade association administrator*
Ekdahl, Richard William *educational association executive*
Kidd, Vallee Melvina *charitable foundation manager*
Pray, Donald Eugene *foundation administrator, lawyer*
Rounds, Philard Leaon, Sr. *fundraiser*
Sutton, Mark F. *association administrator*
Zemel, David Michael *charitable organization adminstrator, human services educator*

PENNSYLVANIA

Pittsburgh
Peterson, Robert Stephen *administrator cultural organization*

SOUTH CAROLINA

Charleston
Crossley, Gary Exley *organization executive*
McClain, Kate Anne *trade association administrator*
Mesic, Harriet Lee Bey *medical support group administrator*

Columbia
Belew, Kathy D. *social services researcher*
Bjontegard, Arthur Martin, Jr. *foundation executive*
Chappell, Barbara Kelly *child welfare consultant*
Krech, Alan Starr *educational administrator*
McIlroy, Wilmer Lee *chamber of commerce executive*
Resch, Mary Louise *social services administrator*
Russell, Patricia Cooper *foundation administrator*
Shabazz, Aiysha Muslimah *social work administrator*
Shearin, Betty Spurlock *retired educational administrator*
Sheheen, Fred Roukos *education agency administrator*
Sigmon, Daniel Ray *foundation administrator*
Wolf, Anne Wilson *advocate*

Gaffney
Howe, Evelyn Freeman *cultural organization administrator*

Greenville
Hendrix, Susan Clelia Derrick *civic worker*

Hilton Head Island
Tucker, Frances Laughridge *civic worker*

Isle Of Palms
Phillips, David Gardiner, V *fundraising consultant*

Lancaster
Bundy, Charles Alan *foundation executive*

Mount Pleasant
Fulton, Jane Sleeth *family and consumer science educator*
Hughes, Michael Kent *trade association executive*

Spartanburg
Ely, Duncan Cairnes *human services executive, civic leader*
Taylor, Stephen John *scouting organization executive*

Surfside Beach
Turner, Gloria Townsend Burke *social services association executive*

Woodruff
Childers, Bob Eugene *educational association executive*

TENNESSEE

Chattanooga
Hurn, Paula Clark *social services administrator*
Matthews, Sherman Ervin, Jr. *social services administrator*
McNeill, Joan Reagin *volunteer consultant*

Cleveland
Lockhart, Madge Clements *educational organization executive*

Cordova
Amitrano, Shirley Ann *research associate*

Knoxville
Cox, Mary Joan Tucker *genealogist*
Drinnon, Janis Bolton *volunteer*
Free, Floyd Monroe *social services administrator*
Strange, Douglas Hart McKoy *civic worker*

Memphis
Boyd, Eleanor Dreher *director of community services*
Glasgow, Agnes Jackie *social welfare administrator, therapist*
Koerbel, Pamela Jean *corporation administrator*
May, William E. *association administrator*
Seanor, Timothy Craig *children's program administrator*

Nashville
Bond, Beverly Kay *fundraising executive*
Ivey, William James *foundation executive, writer, producer*
Mennell, Miles Horner *professional association executive*
Morin, Richard *professional society administrator*
Rudd, Willie *association administrator*
Tarleton, Bennett *arts administrator*
Turk, Thomas Liebig *cultural organization administrator*

Newport
Kridler, Jamie Branam *children's advocate, social psychologist*

Pigeon Forge
Herman, Jerry R. *not for profit foundation executive*

Savannah
King, Mary Smothers *association executive*

Signal Mountain
Sottong, Philipp C. *social services consultant, physician, writer, artist, publisher*

Soddy Daisy
Powell, David Thomas, Jr. *retired association administrator*

TEXAS

Abilene
Frosch, Patricia Ann *non-profit organization executive*
Kyker, Christine White (Chris Kyker) *human services administrator*
Merriman, Glen D. *fundraising executive*

Amarillo
Connery, Carol Jean *foundation director*
Utterback, Will Hay, Jr. *labor union administrator*

Angleton
Fowler, Thomas Howard *social services administrator*
Handy, Robert Truman *association administrator*

Arlington
Henry, Robert Lee *association executive*

Austin
Banks, Virginia Anne (Ginger Banks) *association administrator*
Birdwell, Nancy Leech *developer*
Blumenthal, Mark *organization administrator*
Boice, Margaret Rockwell (Peggy Boice) *charitable organization executive*
Dougherty, Molly Ireland *organization executive*
Fechek, Theresa Anne *professional society administrator*
Finstad, Guy W. *educational association executive*
Mc Kinney, Michael Whitney *trade association executive*
Mickey, Bob *association executive*
Pearson, Jim Berry, Jr. *employee resource officer*
Richardson, Barbara Kathryn *social worker*
Stahl, David Edward *trade association administrator*
West, Glenn Edward *business organization executive*

Beaumont
Kava, D. J. *labor union administrator, artist, meteorologist*

Belton
Wallace, Aliceanne *civic worker*

Boerne
Kaplan, Charles Paul *real estate development association executive, educator, geographer, consultant*

Canyon
Bryant, Patty Ann *foundation executive, public relations executive*

Carrollton
Criger, Nancy S. *professional society administrator*

Corpus Christi
Muñoz, Mario Arcadio *social services administrator*

Dallas
Anderson-Mann, Shelley N. *institutional review specialist*
Hay, Betty Jo *civic worker*
Mackey, Rosalyn Gale *organization official, consultant*
Scheel, William Preston *association executive, priest*
Waldrep, Alvis Kent, Jr. *non-profit foundation administrator*
Wassenich, Linda Pilcher *health policy analyst, fund raiser*
Wilson, Jean Marie Haley *civic worker*

El Paso
Deckert, Myrna Jean *executive director*
Goodman, Gertrude Amelia *civic worker*
Peak, James Matthew *fundraising executive*

Euless
Eisner, Jerome Allan *trade association executive*

Fort Worth
Crumb, Duane James *organization executive*
Dilley, Carol *association administrator*
Dilley, Carol Ann *association executive*
Johnson, Ronda Janice *fundraising consultant*
Miller, Travis Milton *association executive, accountant*
Nelson-Collins, Ella M. *foundation administrator, consultant*
Strasser, Jack C. *association professional*
Walsh, Mary D. Fleming *civic worker*

Galveston
Wilson, Nollie Andrew *cultural organization administrator*

Golidad
Martin, Pamela Jane *educational educator, adminisrator*

Grand Prairie
Arnold-Nobbman, Mildred Maxine Berry *association executive*
Rogers, Ragan *fundraiser*

Houston
Anderson, Helen Sharp *civic worker*
Bush, Barbara Pierce *volunteer, wife of former President of the United States*
Czarlinsky, Randall Gregg *organization executive*
Douglas Wanza, Isabel *foundation administrator*
Ellis, Raymond Clinton, Jr. *association executive*
Gordin, Barbara *foundation administrator*
Heckler, Walter Tim *association executive*
Keegan, Mary Barden *volunteer*
Knotts, Glenn R(ichard) *foundation administrator*
Kovalchuk, Lisbeth (Lee) Suzanne *association administrator*
Maple, Howard Donald *organbuilders association executive, organist*
Streibich, Ronald Leland *fundraising executive*
Teas, Andrew Parker *association executive, political science educator*

Lamesa
Smith, Wayne Cason *organization executive, educator*

Livingston
Clamon, Harleyne Dianne *retired social service supervisor*

Lubbock
Massingill, Harry Bradford, Jr. *retired association administrator*

Midland
Beck, Mary Slater *administrator*

North Richland Hills
Hinkley Thompson, Carol Joyce *philanthropy consultant, motivational speaker*

Odessa
Boyd, Claude Collins *educational specialist, consultant*

Pearland
Coppinger, Fran Donalson *civic worker*

Richardson
Bray, Carolyn Scott *educational administrator*
Smith, Jerralyn Renée *trade association executive*
Tollett, Eileen Rice *professional association administrator*

San Antonio
Dawley, William Riley *society administrator*
Hinojosa, Emilio Alfredo *community development director*
Jacobson, Helen Gugenheim (Mrs. David Jacobson) *civic worker*
Leal, Barbara Jean Peters *fundraising executive*
Stearley, Mildred Sutcliffe Volandt *foundation executive*

White, Mary Ruth Wathen *social services administrator*

San Marcos
Engel, Jonathan Clark *educational association administrator*

Sugar Land
Hosley, Marguerite Cyril *volunteer*

Texarkana
Hines, Betty Taylor *women's center administrator*

Texas City
Willcott, Earline Fay *social worker*

Victoria
Logan, Mary Calkin *volunteer director community relations*

Waco
Russell, Inez Snyder *non-profit organization executive*

Weatherford
Bergman, Anne Newberry *foundation administrator, civic activist*

VIRGINIA

Abingdon
Jones, Mary Trent *endowment fund trustee*

Alexandria
Bagwell, Steven Charles *association executive*
Bernhardt, Randy John *association executive*
Chang, Aaron Chauncey *trade association administrator*
Cline, Michael Patrick *association executive*
Emely, Charles Harry *trade association executive*
Finnell, Dallas Grant *fundraising executive*
Germroth, David Scott *trade association executive*
Greene, Sarah M. *educational administrator*
Kang, Shirley Seong-Yeon *meeting planner*
Kirk, Lisa Gail *association official*
Klimczuk, Stephen John *business executive, foundation director*
Monroe, Edward Lee *political campaign consultant*
Nork, Mariana *foundation administrator*
Pastin, Mark Joseph *executive consultant, association executive*
Paul, Andrew Robert *trade association executive*
Radewagen, Amata Coleman *government affairs advisor, advocate*
Rasmus, John Charles *trade association executive, lawyer*
Rector, John Michael *association executive, lawyer*
Sciulla, Michael Garri *foundation administrator*
Stanley, Robert Warren *association executive*
Stenzel, Thomas E. *association administrator*
Turner, Mary Jane *educational administrator*
Williams, Cathlene Ann *association executive, researcher*
Ziegler, Ronald Louis *association executive, former government official*

Annandale
Fritz, Joanne Lee (Joni Fritz) *association executive*
Perry, Robert Lee *non-profit association executive*

Arlington
Bossman, David A. *trade association administrator*
Fernandez, Henry A. *professional association administrator, lawyer*
Frenquelle, Peter Michael *legislative analyst, organization official*
Gilmore, Marjorie Havens *civic worker, lawyer*
Hamon, David William *organizations analyst*
Hendrickson, Jerome Orland *trade association executive, lawyer*
Hickman, Elizabeth Podesta *retired counselor, educator*
Jankowski, John Edward, Jr. *foundation administrator*
Kirtley, Jane Elizabeth *professional society administrator, lawyer*
Lampe, Margaret Sanger *community activist*
Langley, Patricia Ann *lobbyist*
McWethy, Patricia Joan *educational association administrator*
Payton, Tony *political consultant*
Sobczak, Patrick Michael *educational association administrator*
Vaught, Wilma L. *foundation executive, retired air force officer*
Vertiz, Virginia Castlen *educational administrator*
Yates, Larry Lamar *activist*

Bridgewater
Huffman, Glenn *genealogist*

Centreville
Terry, Linda *social services professional*

Charlottesville
Bischoff, Suzanne R. *social services administrator*
Cohen, Helen Herz *camp owner, director*
Easter, Peter *trade association administrator, lobbyist*
Jordan, Daniel Porter, Jr. *foundation administrator, history educator*

Dunn Loring
Rosenberg, Robert Mark *trade association executive*

Fairfax
Grunder, Fred Irwin *program administrator, industrial hygienist*
Jewell-Kelly, Starla Anne *educational administrator*
Madry-Taylor, Jacquelyn Yvonne *educational administrator*
Meenan, James Ronald *trade association administrator, retired foreign service officer*
Molino, Michael Anthony *trade association executive*
Price, Marilyn Jeanne *fundraising and management consultant*
Stebbins, Leroy Joseph (Lee Stebbins) *not-for-profit organization executive*

Fairfax Station
Crabbs, Raymond Douglas *educational organization executive*

Falls Church
Emely, Mary Ann *association executive*
Slonim, Gilven M. *educational foundation administrator, educator, former naval officer*

Flint Hill
Dietel, William Moore *former foundation executive*

Franktown
Holcomb, Caramine Kellam *volunteer worker*

Fredericksburg
Farmer, James *civil rights leader, former trade union official*

Front Royal
Greco, Barbara Ruth Gomez *literacy organization administrator*

Lynchburg
Myers, Karen Sands *social services administrator*

Mc Lean
Brandt, Edward William, III *nonprofit organization executive, consultant*
Gilmore, Thomas Meyer *trade association administrator, secretary*

Middleburg
Vitt, Lois A. *non-profit organization director, finance sociologist*

Montclair
Hinnant, Hilari Anne *educator, educational consultant*

Newport News
Feldt, Glenda Diane *educational administrator*
Hawkins, J. Michael *housing development administrator*

Norfolk
Filer, Emily Symington Harkins *social services administrator*
Stubbs, Frank Hunter *organization executive, lawyer*

Palmyra
Southworth, R. Morrison *development counsel*

Reston
Meyer, Patricia Hanes *psychiatric social worker*
Mogge, Harriet Morgan *educational association executive*
Roper, D'Arcy Wentworth, III *association executive*

Richmond
Boynton, Rex Powell *trade association executive*
Brown, Marilyn Branch *retired educational administrator*
Combs, Sandra Lynn *state parole board official*
Dell, Willie Jones *social services executive, educator*
Hench, Jane Gilbert *retired cultural organization administrator*
Jones, John Warren *associaton executive*
Linkonis, Suzanne Newbold *pretrial case manager, counselor*
Platt, Geoffrey, Jr. *cultural administrator*
Spurlock, Carolyn L. *educational administrator*

Salem
Born, Ethel Wolfe *church worker*

Stanardsville
Taylor, Clarence Albert, Jr. *housing coordinator, drug counselor*

Sterling
Munger, Paul David *educational administrator*
Trippler, Aaron Knowles *association executive*

Upperville
Smart, Edith Merrill *civic worker*

Verona
Grasty, Phillip Elwood *food bank administrator*

Vienna
Cartier, Brian Evans *foundation administrator*
Spiro, Robert Harry, Jr. *foundation and business executive, educator*

Virginia Beach
Bryant, Jacqueline Eola *educational consultant specialist*

Warrenton
Fox, Raymond Graham *educational administrator*
Sass, Arthur Harold *educational executive*

Williamsburg
Johnson, Philip Lewis *retired research commission executive*
Longsworth, Charles R. *foundation administrator*

WEST VIRGINIA

Burlington
Ulm, Les *social services administrator*

Cross Lanes
Buckley, Pamela Kay *academic organization administrator*

Morgantown
Friedland, Billie Louise *former human services administrator*

Parkersburg
Burdette, Jane Elizabeth *nonprofit association executive, consultant*
Hershberger, Kenneth Ernest *fundraiser, public relations and marketing*

TERRITORIES OF THE UNITED STATES

VIRGIN ISLANDS

Saint Thomas
Creque, Linda Ann *non-profit educational and research executive, former education commissioner*

SWITZERLAND

Geneva
Schweitzer, Theodore Gottlieb, III *United Nations administrator*

ADDRESS UNPUBLISHED

Amstutz, Daniel Gordon *trade association administrator, former grain dealer, government official*
Babb, Roberta J. *educational administrator*
Baehr, Theodore *religious organization administrator, communications executive*
Beitz, Alexandra Grigg *political activist*
Bianchi, Linda Lorraine *volunteer*
Burch, Jack Edward, Jr. *organization executive*
Cohn, Marianne Winter Miller *civic activist*
Cruver, Suzanne Lee *communications consultant, writer*
Davis, Russell Haden *association executive, pastoral psychotherapist*
Epperson, Margaret Farrar *civic worker*
Fabry, Paul Andrew *international association executive*
Field, Ellen *association executive*
Gereau, Mary Condon *corporate executive*
Green, Michael *foundation administrator*
Griggs, Bobbie June *civic worker*
Gunderson, Judith Keefer *golf association executive*
Hawley, Harold Patrick *educational consultant*
Johnson, Mary Murphy *social services director, writer*
Kidd, Darlene Joyce *social services administrator, nurse*
Levitas, Miriam C. Strickman *events coordinator, realtor, television producer*
Livingston, Margaret Gresham *civic leader*
Loucks, Nancy J. *association executive*
Martin, Kenneth Paul *social services administrator*
Morrison, Ian Alastair *foundation executive*
Mountcastle, Mary Babcock *social services administrator*
Northern, Jane Strauss *association executive*
Pellatt, Rose Felice *non-profit agency executive*
Pond, Jesse Earl *historical association administrator*
Pratt, Alice Reynolds *retired educational administrator*
Reed, Leon Samuel *policy analyst*
Rolfe, Paula Grace *educational administrator*
Schieffelin, George Richard *educational consultant*
Sheets, Martha Louise *civic activist*
Sheridan, Diane Frances *public policy facilitator*
Siegel, Mary Ann Garvin *volunteer*
Smith, Robert Powell *foundation executive, former ambassador*
Sollid, Faye Eising *volunteer*
Solo, Joyce R. *volunteer*
Speaks, John Thomas, Jr. *cultural consultant*
Stearns, Stewart Warren *charitable association executive*
Sutter, John Ben *political consultant*
Tannenbaum, Samuel Victor *philanthropic consultant*
Troyer, Lisa Lynn *marketing and activities director*
Turner, John Freeland *non-profit administrator, former federal agency administrator, former state senator*
Williams, Rebecca Walls *non-profit organization executive*
Wong, Elaine Dang *foundation executive*

ATHLETICS

UNITED STATES

ALABAMA

Birmingham
Huff, Sherri Lynn *physical education educator*
Salant, Nathan Nathaniel *athletic conference executive*

Cullman
Gambrill, Christoper Wayne *physical education educator*

Montgomery
Olson, Michele Scharff *kinesiology/physical education educator*

ARKANSAS

Conway
Garrison, Clifford Davis, Jr. *physical education educator*

Fayetteville
Edge, Jeff Lynn *physical education educator*
Weber, Dean Lee *athletic trainer*

Hot Springs National Park
Garner, Douglas Michael *gymnastics fitness center executive, team coach*

Strong
Nunnally, Dolores Burns *retired physical education educator*

CALIFORNIA

Inglewood
O'Neal, Shaquille Rashaun *professional basketball player*

San Francisco
Sanders, Deion Luwynn *baseball and football player*

FLORIDA

Atlantic Beach
Foster, John David *surfing instructor*

Davie
Johnson, Jimmy *professional football coach*
Kosar, Bernie Joseph, Jr. *professional football player*
Shula, Don Francis *professional football coach*

Daytona Beach
Gordon, Jeff *race car driver*
Marlin, Sterling *professional race car driver*

Fort Lauderdale
Kaplan, Philip A. *fitness professional*
King, Don *boxing promoter*
Vanbiesbrouck, John *professional hockey player*

Gainesville
Varnes, Jill Tutton *university official, health educator*

Hollywood
King, Alma Jean *former health and physical education educator*

Jacksonville
Coughlin, Tom *professional football coach*

Lady Lake
Hartzler, Genevieve Lucille *physical education educator*

Loxahatchee
Krogmann, Joan L. *horse trainer, writer*

Miami
Willis, Kevin Alvin *professional basketball player*

Opa Locka
Marino, Daniel Constantine, Jr. *professional football player*

Orlando
Grant, Horace Junior *professional basketball player*
Hardaway, Anfernee Deon (Penny Hardaway) *professional basketball player*
Rohe, Charles H. *sports association administrator*

Sarasota
Graham, Otto Everett, Jr. *retired athletic director*

Sebring
Joyner, John Franklin *athletics educator, consultant*

Tampa
Crisp, Terry Arthur *professional hockey coach*
Mattera, Tony *sporting company executive*

GEORGIA

Athens
Dooley, Vincent Joseph *college athletics administrator*

Atlanta
Aaron, Henry L. (Hank Aaron) *professional baseball team executive*
Babcock, Peter Heartz *professional sports executive*
Cox, Bobby (Robert Joe Cox) *professional baseball manager*
Glavine, Tom (Thomas Michael Glavine) *professional baseball player*
Graham, Sherrie L. *sports promotions company executive*
Justice, David Christopher *baseball player*
King, Marian Emma *health and physical education educator*
Maddux, Greg(ory Alan) *professional baseball player*
McGriff, Fred (Frederick Stanley McGriff) *baseball player*

Dahlonega
Ensley, Bill *sports association executive*

Douglasville
Watts, Christopher Lee *physical education educator*

Fort Valley
Porter, Douglas Taylor *athletic administrator*

Marietta
Devigne, Karen Cooke *retired amateur athletics executive*
Waples, David Lloyd *athletic director*

Metter
Ferry, James P. *physical education educator*

Savannah
Mason, Andrea Lee *physical education educator*

Statesboro
Simmons, Bradford Rena *university coach*

Valdosta
Monticello, Christine Darlea *health and physical education educator*

ILLINOIS

Champaign
Birmingham, Carolyn *recreation educator*

KENTUCKY

Lexington
Boucher, Larry Gene *sports association commissioner*
Williams, Eddie Kyene *martial arts team executive*

Prestonsburg
Fleming, Christopher George *physical education educator*

Richmond
Morgan, Tim Dale *physical education educator*

LOUISIANA

Alexandria
Sayers, Laura Kristine *physical education and special education educator*

Glenmora
Mealer, Lynda Ream *physical education educator*

Lafayette
Williford, Mabon Leslie, II (Beau Williford) *boxing promoter*

Ruston
Hilgenkamp, Kathryn Darline *physical education educator, health education educator*

Shreveport
Shemwell, Mary Anne *physical education educator*

MISSISSIPPI

Hattiesburg
Artemov, Vladimir Nikolaevich *gymnastics coach*
Giles, Michael Comer *physical education educator, aquatics consultant*

NEW YORK

Bronx
Zimmer, Donald William *coach professional athletics, former professional baseball manager*

NORTH CAROLINA

Asheville
Waters, Wright *sports association executive*

Chapel Hill
Smith, Dean Edwards *university basketball coach*

Charlotte
Mills, Samuel Davis, Jr. *professional football player*
Shinn, George *professional sports team executive*

Dana
Morgan, Lou Ann *physical education educator*

Durham
Krzyzewski, Mike *university athletic coach*

Greensboro
Free, Kenneth A. *athletic conference commissioner*

Raleigh
Davis, Kathryn Louise *physical educator*

Trinity
Weeks, Marie Cook *health and physical education educator*

OKLAHOMA

Oklahoma City
Hitchings, Owen Lyman *sports association executive, jewelry executive*

SOUTH CAROLINA

Mount Pleasant
Bennett, Janet Sandhoff *physical education educator*

TENNESSEE

Brentwood
Abernathy, Sue Eury *physical education educator*
Beebe, Robert Daniel (Dan) *sports association administrator*

Johnson City
Reeves, Lynda P. *physical education educator*

TEXAS

Amarillo
Downey, Dorothy Jean *health and physical education educator*

Arlington
Gonzalez, Juan (Alberto Vazquez) *professional baseball player*
Melvin, R. Douglas *professional sports team executive*
Rodriguez, Ivan *professional baseball player*
Rose, Edward W. (Rusty Rose) *professional sports team executive*

Austin
Crenshaw, Ben *professional golfer*

Carrollton
Foster, William Edwin (Bill Foster) *nonprofessional basketball coach*

College Station
Slocum, R.C. *university athletic coach*

Corpus Christi
Teas, Charles Bryant *physical education educator*

Dallas
Courtnall, Russ *professional hockey player*
Erwin, Scott *sporting company executive*
Fogle, Patricia Mahood *physical education educator*
Mashburn, Jamal *professional basketball player*

Denton
Shoffit, Richard Calvin *martial arts educator*

Houston
Anderson, James Edward *physical education educator*
Donie, Scott *Olympic athlete, platform diver*
Kile, Darryl Andrew *professional baseball player*
Kim, Pyung-Soo *martial arts educator*
Matthews, Bruce Rankin *professional football player*
McLane, Drayton, Jr. *professional baseball team executive*
Olajuwon, Hakeem Abdul *professional basketball player*
Patterson, Steve *professional hockey team executive*
Spencer, Albert Franklin *physical education and education educator*
Tomjanovich, Rudolph *professional athletic coach*
Watson, Bob *professional baseball executive*

Irving
Smith, Emmitt J., III *professional football player*

Lubbock
Weber, Robert Charles *adapted physical education educator, academic administrator*
Wilson, Margaret Eileen *retired physical education educator*

Nacogdoches
Finkenberg, Mel Edward *physical education administrator*

San Antonio
Marbut, Robert Gordon, Jr. *sports organization executive*
Robinson, David Maurice *professional basketball player*

Wichita Falls
Kaster, Jay *physical education educator*

VIRGINIA

Dublin
Clark, Shelia Roxanne *sports association executive, legislative analyst*

Ferrum
Sandidge, June Carol *physical education educator*

Norfolk
Anders, Elizabeth Rambo *physical education educator, athletic coach*

Suffolk
Gray, Marcia Lanette *health, physical education and recreation educator*

Vienna
Hill, Peter M. *sporting company executive*

Winchester
Lemoine, Sandra Marie *health and physical education educator*

ADDRESS UNPUBLISHED

Ball, Deborah Cheek *physical education educator*
Corrales, Patrick *coach, former professional baseball manager*
Lacko, J. Michelle *physical education, health and science educator*
Modano, Michael *professional hockey player*
Paul, Gabriel (Gabe Paul) *former professional baseball club executive*
Renegar, Robert Milton *golf equipment design consultant and manufacturer*
Rutherford, John Sherman, III (Johnny Rutherford) *professional race car driver*
Sasser, Warren T. *sporting services company executive*
Webb, Richmond Jewel *professional football player*
Wilkens, Leonard Randolph, Jr. (Lenny Wilkens) *professional basketball coach*

BUSINESS. *See* **FINANCE; INDUSTRY.**

COMMUNICATIONS. *See* **COMMUNICATIONS MEDIA; INDUSTRY: SERVICE.**

COMMUNICATIONS MEDIA. *See also* ARTS: LITERARY.

UNITED STATES

ALABAMA

Anniston
Waddle, Chris *editor*
Wilson, Douglas Emory *editor, retired army officer*

Auburn
Harvey, James Mathews, Jr. *instructional media producer, columnist*
Simms, Jack *journalism educator*

Birmingham
Bullard, James Jerdan *broadcast executive*
Casey, Ronald Bruce *journalist*
Crichton, Douglas Bentley *editor, writer*
Dake, Cynthia Lewis (Cindy Dake) *editor, freelance writer*
Daniel, Marilyn Jane *journalist*
Joynt, Stephen Wallace *reporter, writer*
Kennedy, Joe David, Jr. (Joey Kennedy) *editor*
Stephens, James T. *publishing executive*
Sullivan, Kevin Lawrence *broadcast executive*
Walker, Evelyn *retired television executive*

Coatopa
Taylor, Joe William *publishing executive, writer*

Fairhope
Barnhill, Suzanne Scoggins *editor, desktop publisher*

Gadsden
Smothers, Jimmy *editor, sportswriter*
Starr, Robert Russell (Rusty Starr) *newspaper executive editor*

Guntersville
Nichols, Laranda C. *newspaper reporter*

Huntsville
Barros-Smith, Deborah Lynne *publishing executive, editor*
Rasmussen, Sharon Lee *news reporter*

Madison
Powers, Clifford Blake, Jr. *communications researcher, consultant*

Montgomery
Hertenstein, Myrna Lynn *publishing executive*

Troy
Clark-Schubert, Donna Lynne *journalism educator*

Tuscaloosa
Addis, Gary Wayne *freelance writer*
Nelson, Debra Jean *journalist, public relations executive, consultant*

ARKANSAS

Cedarville
Whitaker, Ruth Reed *retired newspaper editor*

Dermott
Kinney, Abbott Ford *radio broadcasting executive*

Fayetteville
Douglas, Robert Roy *journalist educator*
Scheide, Frank Milo *communications educator*

Fort Smith
Huff, Jerome Joseph, Jr. *newspaper executive*

Little Rock
Lynch, Joseph Patrick *radio broadcaster*
Plopper, Bruce Loren *journalism educator*
Portis, Charles McColl *reporter, writer*
Starr, John Robert *retired newspaper editor, political columnist*
Wasson, Elizabeth Anne *newspaper editor*

Mountain Home
Anderson, Kenneth Norman *retired magazine editor, author*

Paragould
Nighswonger, James Todd *newspaper editor*

Pocahontas
Carroll, Ann Elizabeth *newspaper editor, retired*

Rogers
Lollar, Fred Paul *editor*

Russellville
Mumert, Tommy Lee *news bureau director*

Springdale
Martin, Becca Bacon *editor, journalist*

CALIFORNIA

Carmel
Klym, Kendall *journalist*

Los Angeles
Roberts, Charles Augustus, Jr. *journalist*
Sperry, Paul *newspaper columnist*
Thornburg, Lee Ellis *film executive, director*

COLORADO

Glenwood Springs
Musselman, Norman Burkey *retired editor*

DISTRICT OF COLUMBIA

Washington
Bennett, Carolyn L. *journalist, writer*
Boshart, Edgar David *editor, journalist, photographer*
Kotz, Nathan Kallison (Nick Kotz) *news correspondent*
Landers, James Michael (Jim Landers) *international editor*
Shanks, Judith Weil *editor*
Sharpe, Rochelle Phyllis *journalist*
Stuckey, Scott Sherwood *magazine editor*
Willis, Clayton *broadcaster, corporation executive, former government official, educator, arts consultant, photojournalist, lecturer*
Young, Thomas Wade *journalist*

FLORIDA

Bartow
Frisbie, Sayer Loyal *newspaper publisher, copyeditor*

Boca Grande
Heffernan, John William *retired journalist*

Bradenton
Crouthamel, Thomas Grover, Sr. *editor*
Godfrey, Paul *publisher*

Clearwater
Capps, Patricia *communications and psychology educator, counselor*
Presson, Gina *journalist, news and documentary production company executive*
Schultze, Lisa Jane *editor*
VanMeer, Mary Ann *publisher, writer, researcher*

Coral Gables
Hertz, Arthur Herman *business executive*
Stano, Carl Randolph (Randy Stano) *newspaper editor, art director, educator*

Daytona Beach
Davidson, Marc Leon *journalist, fine arts consultant*
Lane, Mark Robert *journalist*
Lima, Bob *broadcasting company executive, radio consultant*

Deland
Elfman, Douglas Sayre *journalist*

Delray Beach
Troelstrup, Glenn Clark *journalist*

Destin
Levi, Michael Alan *newspaper executive, publisher*

Fort Lauderdale
Bergal, Jenni *journalist*
Hunter, Diana Romaine *editor*
Perkel, Robert Simon *photojournalist, educator*

Fort Myers
Hunter, Mary Jane *journalist*

Gainesville
Barber, Charles Edward *newspaper executive, journalist*
Hollien, Harry Francis *speech and communications scientist, educator*
Maple, Marilyn Jean *educational media coordinator*
Stacy, Mitchell Paul *writer*

Hialeah
Acosta, Nahyr Mercedes *editor-in-chief*
Del Rio, Lourdes R. *journalist*

Hillsboro Beach
Gibbons, Celia Victoria Townsend (Mrs. John Sheldon) *editor, publisher*

Hollywood
McLinden, Hugh Patrick *editor, writer*
Olson, Peter John *business communication educator*

Homestead
Crouse, John Oliver, II *journalist, publisher*

Homosassa
Braun, Robert Frederick *publishing executive*
Nash, John Grover *journalist, photographer*

Islamorada
Hurley, James Donald, Jr. *computer consultant, lawyer*

Jacksonville
Kress, Mary Elizabeth *newspaper editor*
Stobbe, Michael *reporter*

Jupiter
Anderson, Thomas Jefferson *publisher, rancher, public speaker, syndicated columnist*

Key Biscayne
Smith, Harrison Harvey *journalism consultant*

Lake Mary
Strang, Stephen Edward *magazine editor, publisher*

Lakeland
Carney, Stephen Christopher *newspaper reporter*
Mueller, Michael Lee *editor*

Land O'Lakes
Martinez, Christopher Damon *journalist, novelist*

Lantana
Policy, Joseph J. *publisher, television producer*
Shea, Anne Joan *fashion editor*

Largo
Lang, Jean McKinney *editor, business educator*

Lochloosa
Hays, Holly Mary *editor, freelance photojournalist*

Longwood
Chernak, Jerald Lee *television executive*

Lowell
Thomas, Bill *photojournalist*

Madeira Beach
Beckerman, Milton Bernard *media broker*

Maitland
Jordan, Deane LeRoy *journalist, musician*

Melbourne
Jarrell, Patricia Lynn *photojournalist*
Spezzano, Vincent Edward *newspaper publisher*

Miami
Barry, Dave *columnist, author*
Fontaine, John C. *newspaper company executive, corporate lawyer*
Foster, Kathryn Warner *newspaper editor*
Gibbs, James Calvin *editor, publisher, composer, educator*
Goldberg, Bernard R. *news correspondent*
Gonzalez, Patricia *television news reporter*
Harris, Douglas Clay *newspaper executive*
Hoyt, Clark Freeland *journalist, newspaper editor*
Johnson, Charity Honoré *publishing executive*
Lawrence, David, Jr. *newspaper editor, publisher*
Leposky, George C. *editor*
Lew, Salvador *radio station executive*
Miller, Gene Edward *newspaper reporter and editor*
Muir, Helen *journalist, author*
Savage, James Francis *editor*
Shaklan, Allen Yale *broadcast executive*
Shipley, Alden Peverly *broadcaster, broadcasting executive*
Smiley, Logan Henry *journalist, public concern consultant*
Stacks, Don Winslow *communications educator*
Strouse, Charles E. *journalist*
Todd, Keith *editor and publisher*
Welsh, Judith Schenck *communications educator*

Naples
Beasley, George Garland *broadcasting executive*

Ocala
Stock, Stephen Michael *broadcast journalist*
Warren, Michael David *journalist*

Opa Locka
Randolph, Jennings, Jr. (Jay Randolph) *sportscaster*

Orlando
Berry, Stephen Joseph *reporter*
Clark, James Covington *journalist, historian*
Flammia, Madelyn Jane *communication educator*
Haile, L. John, Jr. *journalist, newspaper executive*
Rodeheffer, Jonathan Paul *editor*
Throne, Geraldine Gorny *journalist*
Wall, Arthur Edward Patrick *editor*

Oviedo
MacCuish, Donald Alexander *educational products manager*

Palatka
Girardin, Linda Jane Becker *editor*

Palm Coast
Beaudet, Peter Anthony *publishing executive*
Franco, Annemarie Woletz *editor*

Palmetto
Castleman, Tonya Kay *journalist*

Penney Farms
Meyer, Marion M. *editorial consultant*

Pensacola
Bannister, Denise H. *publishing executive*
Kaczor, William Stanley *journalist*

Saint Petersburg
Barnes, Andrew Earl *newspaper editor*
Callahan, Barbara *television journalist, consultant*
Edmonds, Richard Radcliffe *editor, writer, public policy consultant*
Haiman, Robert James *newspaper editor, journalism educator*
Jerman, William Edward *editor*
Leavell, William A. *publisher, editor*
Patterson, Eugene Corbett *retired editor, publisher*
Schuck, Marjorie Massey *publisher, editor, consultant*

Sarasota
Gehle, Janice Marie *news research manager*
Hoppes, Lowell Ellard *cartoonist*
Katzman, Anita *author*

Tallahassee
Brennan, Teresa Pruden *freelance editor, indexer, educator*
Dadisman, J. Carrol *publishing executive*
Grier, Barbara G. (Gene Damon) *editor, lecturer, writer*
Morgan, Lucy W. *journalist*
Smith, Elaine Campbell *editor, author*

Tampa
Friedlander, Edward Jay *journalism educator*
Henderson, Rexford Stephen *reporter*
Miller, George Henry *journalist*
Roberts, Edwin Albert, Jr. *newspaper editor, journalist*
Shevy, Allen Earl, Jr. *publishing executive*
White, Nancy G. *journalism educator*
Wyche, Samuel David *sportscaster*

Tarpon Springs
Leisner, Anthony Baker *publishing company executive*

West Palm Beach
Rivers, Marie Bie *broadcasting executive*

Winter Park
Park, W(illiam) B(ryan) *cartoonist, writer, artist*

GEORGIA

Albany
Stultz, Thomas Joseph *newspaper executive*
Williams, John Tolliver *media executive*

Athens
Agee, Warren Kendall *journalism educator*
Holder, Howard Randolph, Sr. *broadcasting company executive*
Middleton, Kent R. *communications educator*
O'Briant, Mary Frances Prevette *editor*

Atlanta
Allen, Edison Brent *journalist, columnist*
Behrens, William Blade *television program syndication executive*
Bentley, Tim *editor, journalist, association director*
Brady, Kimberly Ann *editorial director*
Bridgewater, Herbert Jeremiah, Jr. *radio host*
Bryant, George Othello, III *journalist*
Bynum, Richard Cary *publishing consultant, author*
Collier, Diana Gordon *publishing executive*
Cross, Joyce Annette Oscar *newscaster*
Darnell, Timothy Hoyt *journalist*
Day, Charles Roger, Jr. *editor-in-chief*
Dobson, Bridget McColl Hursley *television executive and writer*
Evans, Gail Hirschorn *television news executive*
Franz, Raymond Victor *editor, publisher*
Gregory, William Joseph *editor, writer*
Henderson, Charles William *health and medical publishing executive*
Jones, J. Kenley *journalist*
Martin, Ron *newspaper editor-in-chief*
May, Albert Louis, III *journalist*
Mills, Candy *magazine publisher*
Phillips, John D. *media company executive*
Plott, Monte Glenn *journalist*
Reeves, Alexis Scott *journalist*
Rierson, Robert Leak *broadcasting executive, television writer*
Skube, Michael *journalist, critic*
Stewart, Michael McFadden *professional speaker*
Thomas, Barbara Ann *record company executive*
Thompson, Susan Roberta *magazine publishing executive*
Tomasulo, Frank Peter *communications educator, writer*
Toner, Michael F. *journalist*
Trigony, Nicholas D. *broadcast executive*
Tullis, Bill *broadcasting company executive, sound engineer, music producer*
Turner, Ted (Robert Edward Turner) *television executive*
Ward, Janet Lynn *magazine editor, sports wire reporter*
Whitt, Richard Ernest *reporter*

Augusta
Morris, William Shivers, III *newspaper executive*

Carrollton
Williams, Mary Eleanor Nicole *writer*

Columbus
Dean, Pamela Lee *journalist*

Covington
Fuller, Susan Joan *broadcast executive*

Decatur
Hagood, Thomas Richard, Jr. *publisher*

Gainesville
Druckenmiller, John Charles *newspaper editor*
Oglesby, Theodore Nathaniel *editor*

Hiawassee
Karst-Campbell, Judy W. S. *broadcast stations owner*

Jesup
Davis, James Andrew *newspaper reporter*

Lawrenceville
Porteous, Thomas Clark *retired newspaper editor*

Macon
Dravis, Jacquelin Denise *editor*
Thomas, Richard Dale *newspaper editor*

Marietta
Bemis, Royce Edwin *publishing executive*
Hays, Robert William *communications consultant, educator, writer*
Sloan, Mary Jean *media specialist*

Mc Donough
Hiett, Chanley Joseph *publishing executive*

Newnan
Skinner, Walter Winston *journalist, minister*

Norcross
Lyne, James Coleman, Jr. *magazine editor, magazine writer*

Rome
Toles, Thomas Taylor *newspaper editor*

Roswell
Peterson, Westley DeZell *magazine editor*

Savannah
Blum, Donald Ralph *editor, publisher*

Smyrna
Boyd, Kenneth Wade *publishing company executive, consultant*

Stone Mountain
Knowles, Robert Gordon, Jr. *editor*

ILLINOIS

Chicago
Saunders, Doris Evans *editor, educator, business executive*

KENTUCKY

Ashland
Adams, Sam *newspaper journalist*

Calvert City
Stice, Dwayne Lee *broadcasting company executive*

Carlisle
Wolf, John Howell *retired publisher*

Covington
Trimble, Vance Henry *retired newspaper editor*

Flemingsburg
Plummer, Edward Ray *radio announcer, writer, reporter*

Fort Knox
Barnes, Larry Glen *journalist, editor, educator*

Frankfort
Lynn, Carolyn Hughes *editor*

La Grange
Millay-Fullenlove, Carmen (Kit Millay-Fullenlove) *newspaper editor*

Lexington
Bias, Jennifer Morrison *editor*
Boyd, Gordon Payne *television news reporter, anchor*
Embry, Michael Dale *news correspondent*
Keeling, Larry Dale *journalist*
Kelly, Timothy Michael *newspaper editor*
Kissling, Fred Ralph, Jr. *publishing executive, insurance agency executive*
Ryen, Dag *journalist*
Wagar, Charles Kightly "Kit" *journalist, educator*

Louisville
Bingham, George Barry, Jr. *publishing and broadcasting executive*
Douglas, Michele Theresa *communications executive*
Lewis, Ronald Chapman *record company executive*
Melnykovych, Andrew O. *journalist*
Reisz, Sara Noyes *publisher, lawyer*
Renau, Lynne Scholl *publisher, writer*
Tichenor, Fred Cooper, Jr. *newspaper columnist*

Mayfield
Patton, Kevin Joel *editor*

Murray
White, Henry Allen *journalism educator*

Owensboro
Mong, Robert William, Jr. *publisher*

Paducah
Landini, Elizabeth Leigh *journalist*

Pewee Valley
Gill, George Norman *newspaper publishing company executive*

Prospect
Falk, Lawrence Claster *publisher, editor, public official*

LOUISIANA

Baton Rouge
Burke, Marianne Marsh *editor*
Giles, William Elmer *journalism educator, former newspaper editor*
Hargroder, Charles Merlin *retired journalist*
Marshall, Rosalind Reneé *communications educator, television producer*
Moormann, David Lawrence *sportswriter, journalist*
Strawn, Karen Kay Immel *editor, educator*

Bogalusa
Hughes, Shelia Elizabeth Ann *newspaper editor, reporter*

Gonzales
Ferstel, Vicki Hutt *reporter*
Young, David Nelson *information consultant*

Grambling
Murray, Gaylon Eugene *mass communication educator*

Hammond
Kemp, John Randolph *journalist, author, academic administrator*

Lafayette
Kelly, Kathleen S(ue) *communications educator*

Lake Charles
Dixon-Gayle, Pamela Eve *reporter, journalist*
Stacey, Truman *journalist, consultant*

Metairie
Sandmel, Ben *journalist, musician*

Natchitoches
Foster, John Robert *communications educator, minister*

New Orleans
Barker, Larry Lee *communications educator*
Dupont, Nancy McKenzie *broadcast journalism educator*
Giangrosso, Patricia Ann *editorial consultant*
Lorenz, Alfred Lawrence *communications educator*
Phelps, Ashton, Jr. *newspaper publisher*

Ruston
Blick, Thomas Edward, Jr. *journalism educator, newspaper editor*
Heyen, Melanie Stone *newspaper editor, educator*

Shreveport
Eleuterius, David Wayne *journalist, graphic designer*
Tiner, Stanley Ray *business communications executive, former editor*

MARYLAND

Baltimore
Iglehart, Kenneth Robert *newspaper editor*
Jackson, Harold *journalist*

Silver Spring
Mooney, James Hugh *newspaper editor*

MISSISSIPPI

Clinton
Fortenberry, Jack Clifton (Cliff Fortenberry) *mass communications educator*

Greenwood
Jones, Carolyn Ellis *publisher, retired employment agency and business service company executive*

Hattiesburg
Reeves, Raymond Edward *editor*
Young, Stephen Flinn *editor*

Jackson
Downing, Margaret Mary *newspaper editor*

Leland
Ayres, Mary Jo *professional speaker*

Meadville
Webb, James David *editor, publisher*

Mississippi State
Forde, John Ellis *communication educator*

Ridgeland
Gordon, T. Duane *reporter*

Vicksburg
Briuer, Elke Moersch *editor*

MONTANA

Libby
Herrmann, John *editor, journalist*

NEVADA

Boulder City
Kidd, Hillery Gene *educational publisher*

NEW YORK

Ithaca
Swenson, Jill Dianne *journalism educator*

New York
Heloise *columnist, lecturer, broadcaster, author*
Loory, Stuart Hugh *journalist*
Sisk, Eileen Victoria *journalist*

Troy
Rubens, Philip *communications educator, technical writer*

NORTH CAROLINA

Asheboro
Penfield, Addison Pierce *broadcaster, marketing specialist*

Brevard
Ames, Alfred Campbell *journalist, educator*

Carolina Beach
Underwood, Shawn Michael *newspaper editor*

Carrboro
Patterson, Neil *science publisher*

Cary
Rossi, Robert John *retired group newspaper executive, consultant*

Chapel Hill
Bare, John Bowman *media consultant, writer*
Blanchard, Margaret Ann *journalism educator*
Giduz, Roland *journalist*

Hinshaw, Donald Gray *music publisher*
Meyer, Philip Edward *journalism educator*
Ravenel, Shannon *book publishing professional*
Walden, Ruth *communications educator, writer*

Charlotte
Barrows, Frank Clemence *newspaper editor*
Burgess, Harvey Waites *journalist*
Feeney, Francis X. *cable company executive, accountant*
Haines, Kenneth H. *television broadcasting executive*
Neill, Rolfe *newspaper executive*
Silverstein, Barry *cable company executive*
Sine, Richard *editor, writer, consultant*
Waid, Stephan Hamilton *publishing executive*
Williams, Edwin Neel *newspaper editor*

Durham
Arnow, Pat *editor*
Harrell, Benjamin Carlton *columnist, retired editor*
Rossiter, Alexander, Jr. *news service executive, editor*

Elizabeth City
Baker, Jean Mary *cable television executive*

Flat Rock
Curtis, William Roger, Jr. *media specialist*

Garner
Dobyns, Lloyd (Allen) *free-lance journalist*

Goldsboro
Price, Eugene *newspaper editor*

Greensboro
Gill, Evalyn Pierpoint *writer, editor, publisher*
Rochelle, Warren Gary *editor, educator, writer*

Hendersonville
Jameson, Victor Loyd *retired magazine editor*

High Point
Blount, Thomas Leon *newspaper editor*

Hillsborough
Bolduc, Jean Plumley *journalist, education activist*
Merron, Jeffrey L. *editor, educator*

Kenly
Stewart, Richard Douglas *newspaper publisher*

Lumberton
Lewis, Billy Mac *newspaper executive*

Pembroke
Courson, Maxwell Taylor *communication arts educator*
Patterson, Oscar, III *communications educator, university official*

Raleigh
Daniels, Frank Arthur, Jr. *newspaper publisher*
Effron, Seth Alan *journalist*
Entman, Robert Mathew *communications educator, consultant*
Henson, Glenda Maria *newspaper writer*
Kauffman, Terry *broadcast and creative arts communication educator*
Kochersberger, Robert Charles, Jr. *journalism educator*
Parker, Joseph Mayon *printing and publishing executive*

Research Triangle Park
Reid, Rosalind *magazine editor*

Salisbury
Post, Rose Zimmerman *newspaper columnist*

Southport
McKenzie, Susan Smith *business writer*

Spring Hope
Ripley, R(obert) Kenyon, Jr. *journalist*

Whiteville
Smith, Scottie Goodman *reporter*

Wilson
Tarleton, Harold Vernon *editor*

Winston Salem
Garber, Mary Ellen *retired sports reporter*

OHIO

Cleveland
Marr, David Francis *television announcer, former professional golfer, journalist*

OKLAHOMA

Ada
Greenstreet, Robert Wayne *communication educator, consultant*
Reese, Patricia Ann *retired editor, columnist*

Broken Arrow
Harrison, Thomas *television executive*
Wilson, Derek Kyle *journalist*

Chickasha
Adams, Brenda Kay *publisher, advertising/management consultant*

Clinton
Engleman, Charles Edward *newspaper editor and publisher*

Durant
Steinsaas, Harlan Stanley *journalism educator*

Edmond
Hocker-Hatchett, Nansi *investigative journalist, writer*
Jones, Christopher Jon *multimedia specialist*
Pydynkowsky, Joan Anne *journalist*

Moore
Khaleeluddin, Mansoor *broadcast executive*

Norman
Fleer, Marilyn June *editor*
Friedrich, Gustav William *communication educator*
Koch, Nicole Ann *reporter*
Morton, Linda P. *journalism educator*
Wang, Frank Yu-Heng *publishing executive, mathematician, consultant*

Oklahoma City
Gaylord, Edward Lewis *publishing company executive*
Gourley, James Leland *editor, publishing executive*
Gumm, Jay Paul *media specialist*
Hight, Joe Irvin *editor*
Mitrovgenis, James William, Jr. *journalist*
Ray, Mike Wallace *media specialist*
Wagner, Stephen Dean *editor*

Shawnee
Lehmann, Clifford Paul *media center director*
Trotter, Donald Wayne *publishing executive*

Stillwater
Catsis, John R. *communications educator*
Gragert, Steven Keith *publishing executive, researcher, writer*
Miller, Lisa Michelle *newspaper editor*

Tulsa
Bender, John Henry, Jr. (Jack Bender) *editor, cartoonist*
Dumit, Edward Salim *communications educator*
Haring, Robert Westing *newspaper editor*
Upton, Howard B., Jr. *management writer, lawyer*
Wanenmacher, Kathleen Murphy *executive producer*
Williams, Robert Joseph *energy journalist*

PENNSYLVANIA

State College
Lawrence, Ken *columnist*

SOUTH CAROLINA

Aiken
Bray, Chadwick McFall *journalist*
Patterson, Gregory Brownell *reporter*
Ryan, William Joseph *multimedia and distance education designer*

Beaufort
Cato, James Anthony *newspaper editor*

Cayce
Morris, Roy Allen *publishing executive*

Charleston
Anderson, Ivan Verner, Jr. *newspaper publisher*
French, Kenneth Wayne *radio station executive, consultant*
Schreadley, Richard Lee *writer, retired newspaper editor*
Smith, Bruce Mackenzie *journalist, writer, publisher*
Spence, Edward Lee *publisher, historian, archaeologist*

Clinton
Franklin, Larry Brock *publishing executive*

Columbia
Ashley, Perry Jonathan *journalism educator*
Cleveland, Kathleen Connor Parker (Kathleen Parker) *syndicated columnist, public relations consultant*
Crim, Reuben Sidney *newspaper publishing executive*
Johnson, Stephen Scott *journalist*
McNeely, Patricia Gantt *journalism educator*
Nichols, Padgett Singleton *publishing executive*
Osman, Mary Ella Williams *journal editor*
Thelen, Gil *newspaper editor*

Greenwood
Hawthorne, F(loyd) Donald *publishing company executive*
Husbands, Anita Rosette *desktop publisher*

Hilton Head Island
McKinney, Donald Lee *magazine editor*

Myrtle Beach
Ausband, Jerry C. *newspaper editor*
Heddinger, Frederick Martin, Sr. *publisher*

North Augusta
Middleton, David Andrew *radio announcer, printer*
Verhovsek, Mary Ann Dana *radio news anchor, reporter*

Orangeburg
Hendren, Lee Edward *journalist, publisher*

Simpsonville
Gilstrap, Leah Ann *media specialist*

TENNESSEE

Brentwood
Edwards, Joe Michael *journalist*

Bristol
Lundberg, Jon Clark *news anchor, reporter*
Macione, Joe, Jr. *television broadcasting executive*

Chattanooga
Anderson, Lee Stratton *newspaper publisher, editor*
Bornfeld, Steve Ira *journalist*
Chesney, Walter Allen *journalist, travel writer*
Sachsman, David Bernard *communications educator*

Collegedale
Sauls, Richard Lynn *journalism educator*

Crossville
Heeschen, Barbara Ann *retired music critic*

Dyersburg
Bumpus, Jamie Edward *newspaper copy editor*

Franklin
Campbell, Nancy Colene *magazine editor*

Hampshire
Delk, Fay Louise *journalist*

Johnson City
Woodside, Jane Harris *editor, writer, folklorist*

Knoxville
Ashdown, Paul George *journalist, educator*
Hooper, William Edward *broadcast journalist*
Howard, Herbert Hoover *broadcasting and communications educator*
McDavid, Marion Foy Jr. *journalist*
Miller, Edgar Hudson, Jr. *newspaper editor, journalism educator*
Rukeyser, William Simon *journalist, business executive*
Teeter, Dwight Leland, Jr. *journalism educator*
Ziegler, Dhyana *broadcasting educator*

La Follette
Smith, Larry Keith *newspaper publisher, editor, educator*

Lebanon
Howard, Lounita Cook *journalist*

Manchester
Jernigan, Verland Henry *retired newspaper writer*

Maryville
Stone, Hubert Dean *editor, journalist*

Memphis
Bedwell, Randall Jerome *publisher*
Bostick, Brian *publishing executive, book*
McAdory, Jeffrey Kent *picture editor*
McEachran, Angus *newspaper editor*
Ramirez, Michael P. *editorial cartoonist*
Teas, Charlotte Ann *editor*
Yawn, David McDonald *journalist*

Morristown
Fishman, Robert Jack *publisher*

Mountain City
Shutt, Howard Steven *journalist*

Murfreesboro
Badger, David Pierson *journalism educator*

Nashville
Atkins, Chester Burton *record company executive, guitarist, publisher*
Brock, Kerry Lynn *broadcast executive*
Clayton, Rose Marie McAfee *journalist, writer, talent agent, television producer*
Espenant, Karen E. Jeffries *journalist*
Forder, Reg Arthur *publishing executive*
Frey, Herman S. *publishing company executive*
Hollaway, Ernest Lee, III *journalist, public relations consultant*
Lowe, Harold Gladstone, Jr. *photojournalist, small business owner, farmer*
Mayhew, Aubrey *music business executive*
Pfeiffer, Andrew Harding *publication editor*
Roberts, Sandra *editor*
Rogers, Barbara Jean (B.J. Rogers) *writer, editor*
Russell, Fred McFerrin *journalist, author, lawyer*
Stahl, Gael Bernard *editor*
Stone, Lawrence Mynatt *publishing executive*
Summerville, James Melvin Smith *editor*
Toalston, Arthur Joseph, Jr. *editor*
White, Frank William *editor*
Wood, Edwin Thomas *journalist*

Oak Ridge
Smyser, Richard David *retired newspaper editor, retired secondary education educator*

Paris
Williams, William Bryant, Jr. *publisher*

Pigeon Forge
Long, Ellen Adair *publicist*

Powell
Bauch, Mary Householder *retired secondary education educator*

Sevierville
Stone, Mary Overstreet *newspaper editor*

Waynesboro
Davis, Sharon Denise (Sherry Davis) *editor*

TEXAS

Abilene
Marler, Charles Herbert *journalism educator, historian, consultant*
O'Connor, Michael Wayne *news editor*

Allen
Lahart, F. Vern *publishing executive*

Arlington
LaRocque, Paul Robert *journalist, educator, retired, consultant*
Otto, Ludwig *publisher, educator*

Austin
Armstrong, David G. *journalist*
Fischer, Norman, Jr. *media broker*
Jayson, Sharon Kay *reporter*
Kjellstrand, William Sander *newspaper editor*
Laine, Katie Myers *communications consultant*
Matthews, Jay Arlon, Jr. *publisher, editor*
McCann, William Donald *journalist, public relations specialist*
Moore, Lisa Lynne *literary critic, English educator*
Oliphant, Edward Davis (Dave Oliphant) *editor*
Saunders, Patricia Gene *textbook editor*
Sklar, Judith Rosenberg *editor, copywriter*
Spielman, Barbara Helen New *editor, consultant*
Vaidhyanathan, Siva *journalist, educator*
Young, Jerry Lee *writer, critic, engineer*
Young, Michelle Diane *editor*

Bay City
Jares, Andrea Lynn *newspaper reporter*

Baytown
Sheley, Susan Cummings *journalism educator, rancher*

Beaumont
Coone, Kelly Marie *broadcast journalist, reporter, anchorperson*
Roth, Lane *communications educator*

Bellaire
Ballanfant, Kathleen Gamber *newspaper executive, public relations company executive*

College Station
Schaefer, Richard J. *communications educator*
Starr, Douglas Perret *journalism educator*

Commerce
Stewart, Fred Ray *journalism educator*

Corpus Christi
Cook, Joe Thomas *retired newspaper publisher*
Prichard, Ella Gayle Wall *publishing company executive*
Sullivan, Stephen Wentworth *publisher*

Dallas
Allison, Stephen Galender *broadcast executive*
Aynesworth, Hugh Grant *reporter, author*
Creany, Cathleen Annette *television station executive*
Cummins, James Duane *correspondant, media executive*
Daily, Ellen Wilmoth Matthews *technical publications specialist*
Dillon, David Anthony *journalist, lecturer*
Evans, William Wilson *journalism educator, retired newspaper editor*
Fiddick, Paul William *broadcasting company executive*
Frailey, David Codori *communications consultant*
Gerlin, Andrea L. *journalist*
Glines, Carroll Vane, Jr. *magazine editor*
Gunnels, Kerry Paul *newspaper editor, educator*
Halbreich, Jeremy L. *newspaper publishing executive*
Holloway, James Glen *marketing opinon and media researcher*
Johnson, Jay D. *publishing executive*
Jordan, Karen Leigh *newspaper travel editor*
Langer, Ralph Ernest *journalist*
Long, Joann Morey *publishing company executive, editor*
Osborne, Burl *newspaper publisher, editor*
Scogin, Troy Pope *publishing company executive, accounts executive*
Stradley, William Lamar *agricultural publisher*
VanVleck, Amy Ann *editor, communications executive*
Wieland, Robert Graham *journalist, media relations consultant*
Wienandt, Christopher *newspaper desk chief*
Wilson, Anna Marie S. *magazine editor, publisher*

Del Rio
Gonzales, Diana España *journalist*

Denton
Budilovsky, Susan Andrea *journalist*
Jeffrey, Shirley Ruthann *publisher*
Shelton, James Keith *journalism educator*
Vick, Frances Brannen *publishing executive*

Diboll
Perkins, Sue Dene *journalist*

Dripping Springs
Rios, Evelyn Deerwester *columnist, musician, artist, writer*

El Paso
Brown, Naomi Yanagi *publisher, author*
Macias, Gloria Patricia *editor*
Persky, Allan Lee *educator, editor*

Fort Worth
Buckley, Betty Bob *journalist, consultant*
Caffee, Marcus Pat *publishing company executive*
Cochran, John Michael *journalist*
Eliasoph, Jeffrey Paul *television news anchor*
Haber, Marian Wynne *journalism educator, writer*
Jones, Jim Wayne *editor*
Malone, Dan F. *journalist*
Smith, Gregory Marshall *sports editor, communications executive*
Thomason, Tommy George *journalism educator*

Graham
Cornelius-Ratcliff, Cindy Lee *newspaper editor, photographer*

Houston
Barlow, Jim B. *newspaper columnist*
Beck, Robert James *editor, energy economist, author, consultant*
Blackmon, Sue Ellen *journalism educator, publications adviser*
Burns, Bebe Lyn *journalist*
Entman, Barbara Sue *broadcaster, writer, photographer*
Hawes, William Kenneth *communication educator*
Johnson, Richard James Vaughan *newspaper executive*

Lucas, Gregory Charles *sports announcer*
Maier, Anne Marie McDonald *journalist*
Mc David, George Eugene (Gene Mc David) *newspaper executive*
McGarry, Susan Hallsten *magazine editor*
Miller, John Pendleton *publishing company executive*
Morris, David Hargett *broadcast executive, rancher*
Morris, Donald R(obert) *publisher, journalist*
Newman, Mary Thomas *communications educator, management consultant*
Osgood, Christopher Mykel *radio account executive*
Pederson, Tony Weldon *newspaper editor*
Randazzo, Gary Wayne *newspaper executive*
Read, Michael Oscar *editor, consultant*
Rust, Robert Francis *publishing executive*
Villarreal, Jesus Morón *newswriter, publisher, poet, artist*
Williams, Kenneth Howard *historical editor*

Huntsville
Fensch, Thomas Charles *journalism educator, writer*

Irving
Schultz, Carmen Helen *copywriter, translator*

Kelly A F B
Stringer, Jerry Ray *magazine editor*

Kerrville
Dozier, William Everett, Jr. *newspaper editor and publisher*
Williams, William Henry, II *publisher*

Kingwood
van Wijk, Maike Hedwig Gisela *reporter*

Laguna Vista
Rasmussen, Duane Archer *retired publishing executive, consultant*

Lindale
Lewis, Charles Robert *newspaper columnist*

Littlefield
Lovvorn, Joella *newspaper editor*

Lockhart
Hosey, Victor Phillip *photojournalist*

Lubbock
Brown, William Arthur *editor-in-chief*
Watts, Elizabeth Anne *journalism educator*

Mansfield
Gravois, John Reed *editor*

Marfa
Oliver, Gary Lynn *cartoonist*

North Richland Hills
Summers, Mark Steven *publishing executive, lawyer*

Plano
Collin, Bruce Edward *publishing company executive*
Kephart, Sherrie Ann *photojournalist, graphic artist*

Richardson
Hancock, Mark Matthew *photojournalist, journalist*
Patrick, James Nicholas, Sr. *radio, television, newspaper commentator, consultant*

Round Rock
Burns, Laura Elizabeth *editor*
Koloen, John Seiver *editor*

San Antonio
Belgin, Harvey Harry *photojournalist*
Bull, Mary Maley *radio executive*
Draper, Everett T., Jr. *publishing executive, educator*
Gwathmey, Joe Neil, Jr. *broadcasting executive*
Harte, Houston Harriman *newspaper, broadcasting executive*
Jondle, Marnita Lea *journalist, desktop publisher*
Juhasz, Stephen *editor, consultant*
Kilpatrick, Charles Otis *newspaper editor, publisher*
Mammen, Sam *publishing executive, entrepreneur*
Marbut, Robert Gordon *communications and broadcast executive*
Mays, Lester Lowry *broadcast executive*
Ostmo, David Charles *broadcasting executive*

San Marcos
Green, Don J. *publisher, editor*

Spring
Jackson, Guida Myrl *writer, magazine editor*
Mohalley, Patricia JoAnn *library media specialist*

The Woodlands
Anderson, Dale *film production executive*

Tomball
Overman, Mary Reut *reporter*

Tyler
Berry, David Val *newspaper editor*
Pratt, Robert Thomas, Jr. *journalist, editor*

Waco
Foster, Bill C. *newspaper publisher*
Lindsey, Libby *editor, graphic designer*
Ranton, Jason Douglas *news writer*

Wimberley
Hall, Jerry Frank *retired journalist*

VIRGINIA

Alexandria
Abbott, Frances Elizabeth Dowdle *journalist, civic worker*
Bowman, James Vaughn *journalist*
DeBolt, Joseph Wayne, Jr. *editorial assistant*
DuVall, Jack *television executive, fund raiser, speechwriter*
Fichenberg, Robert Gordon *newspaper editor, consultant*
Hume, Ellen Hunsberger *broadcast executive, media analyst, journalist*
Mudd, Mary Mollie B. *editor*
Shosky, John Edwin *communications consultant, speechwriter*
Wright, Mary James *multimedia instructional designer*
Yoder, Edwin Milton, Jr. *columnist, educator, editor, writer*

Arlington
Athanas, Emanuel Stylianos *journalist, educator, radio program director*
Barbato, Joseph Allen *writer*
Berry, Fred Clifton, Jr. *author, magazine editor, book packager*
Curley, John J. *diversified media company executive*
Curley, Thomas *newspaper executive*
DeFrancesco, Gerry *broadcasting company executive*
Hurlburt, Sidney Hollady *newspaper editor*
Mazzarella, David *newspaper editor*
Nelson, Warren Louis *newspaper editor, writer*
Obermayer, Herman Joseph *newspaper publisher*
Palor, John *media group executive*
Quinn, John Collins *publishing executive, newspaper editor*
Seamans, Andrew Charles *editorial and public relations consultant, columnist, author*
Stuckey, Barbara Kathryn *publishing executive, trainer, consultant*
Tanzer, Lester *editor*
Walker, Cecil L. *broadcast executive*
Watson, Gary L. *newspaper executive*
White, Dale Timothy (Tim White) *television journalist*
Williams, Jeanne Marie *editor, writer*
Williams, John Clifford (Jack Williams) *journalist*

Blacksburg
Rystrom, Kenneth Fred, Jr. *communications educator*

Bridgewater
Bittel, Muriel Helene *managing editor*

Charlottesville
Crystal, Charlotte Helen *journalist*
Giles, Scott Andrew *public affairs consultant*
Mogielnicki, John Wayne *journalist*
Parrish, David Walker, Jr. *legal publishing company executive*

Chesapeake
Cooper, Elizabeth Ownley *university administrator*

Clifton
Rash, Wayne, Jr. *journalist*

Covington
Rohr, Dwight Mason *news director, radio marketing consultant*

Crozet
Crosby, James Earl *newspaper publisher*

Culpeper
Utnik, David Alan *newspaper editor, journalist*

Dunn Loring
Ferranti, Jennifer *journalist*

Fairfax Station
Abuzaakouk, Aly Ramadan *publishing executive*

Falls Church
Benton, Nicholas Frederick *publisher*
Cromley, Allan Wray *journalist*
Dupuy, Arnold Christian *publisher, military historian*
Green, Gerald *editor, consultant*
Landau, Jacob Charles *journalist*
Stone, Marvin Lawrence *journalist, government official*

Fort Belvoir
Startzman, Shirley Kayleen *editor*

Galax
Leonard, Angela Marie *editor*

Gloucester
Dragoo, Christine Worthington *editor*

Herndon
Shevis, James Murdoch *journalist*

Leesburg
Guttman, Jon Sheldon *magazine editor, historian*
Spannaus, Nancy Bradeen *political newspaper editor*

Lexington
Bland, Larry Irvin *historical documents editor*

Madison
Graham, Hantford Leroy *publishing executive, elementary education educator*

Manassas
Elliott, Edwin Powers, Jr. *magazine editor, clergyman*

Mc Lean
Jolly, Bruce Overstreet *retired newspaper executive*

Newport News
Davis, Jack Wayne, Jr. *newspaper publisher*
Kale, Wallace Wilford, Jr. *journalist, communicator, administrator*

Norfolk
Griffin, O. Daniel, Jr. *reporter, writer, photographer, audio engineer, videographer*
Keever, Rebecca Regan *copy editor*
Ruehlmann, William John *communications educator*

Oakton
Casey, Martin *newspaper editor*

Radford
Huttenstine, Marian Louise *journalism educator*
Wille, Lois Jean *retired newspaper editor*

Reston
Grubisich, Thomas James *newspaper editor and publisher*
Merrill, Cheryl Singer *editor*
Miller, Donald Lane *publishing executive*
Pyle, Thomas Alton *instructional television and motion picture executive*

Richmond
August, A. T., III *publishing executive*
Baker, Donald Parks *journalist, educator*
Bryan, John Stewart, III *newspaper publisher*
Dillon, John Ambrose *journalist*
Dunford, Junius Earle, Jr. *retired newspaper editor and journalism instructor*
Goodykoontz, Charles Alfred *newspaper editor, retired*
Nuwer, Henry Joseph (Hank Nuwer) *journalist, educator*
Owen, Rob *journalist*
Rogers, James Curtis *publisher, psychologist*
Smith, Ted Jay, III *mass communications educator*
Smith, Tucker Freeman *publishing executive*
Weatherford, Gregory Osina *journalist*

Roanoke
Feuer, A.B. Bud *retired journalist, historian, writer*
Flora, Philip Craig *magazine publisher*
Foster, Richard Donithan *journalist, freelance writr*
Garrett, Lee (Homer Simmons Holcomb) *retired broadcaster*
Rugaber, Walter Feucht, Jr. *newspaper executive*

Saint Paul
Gregory, Ann Young *editor, publisher*

Springfield
Hillis, John David *television news executive, producer, writer*
Lynch, Wayne Alan *broadcasting executive*
Rankin, Jacqueline Annette *communications expert, educator*

Stanardsville
Anns, Arlene Eiserman *publishing company executive*

Vienna
Blevins, Charles Russell *publishing executive*
Mc Arthur, George *journalist*
McKinley, Sarah Elizabeth *journalist*
Nuhn, John Marshall *editor*

Virginia Beach
Cherry, Leon Patrick *publisher*
Graves, Michael Phillip *communication educator, dean*
Walzer, Philip Samuel *journalist*
Wells, Steven Charles *media company executive*

Waynesboro
Kerby, Robert Browning *communications consultant*

Williamsburg
Winstead, Joy *journalist, consultant*

Winchester
Smith, Virginia A. *media consultant*
Worthington, Donald Thompson, Jr. *journalist*

Woodbridge
Silverberg, Howard J. (Hank Silverberg) *broadcast journalist*

WASHINGTON

Pullman
Davis, Fred *columnist, educator*

WEST VIRGINIA

Beckley
Gilham, Elizabeth Lynne *journalist*

Charleston
Bailey, James (Jack) Richard *newspaper editor*
Brown, Kathy Alice *broadcast journalist*
Grimes, Richard Stuart *editor, writer*
Haught, James Albert, Jr. *journalist, newspaper editor*
Truman, Gary Tucker *photojournalist*

Forest Hill
Young, Nerissa Ann *journalist*

Grafton
Gelhausen, Marvin Duane *newspaper editor*

Hinton
Long, Frederick Daniel *editor, publishing executive, writer*

Parkersburg
Northrup, Timothy A. *publisher*

Pineville
Maxey, Nigel Aaron *publisher*

Shepherdstown
Snyder, Joseph John *consulting editor, historian, author, lecturer, consultant*

Wheeling
Staffel, Peter L. *copy editor, writer, English educator*

ADDRESS UNPUBLISHED

Adams, Caroline Jeanette H. *writer*
Allen, Bonnie Marie *reporter*
Andrisani, John Anthony *editor, author, golf consultant*
Avery, Susan Elizabeth *journalist*
Baggett, Donnis Gene *journalist, editor*
Bixby, Robert Jay *editor, writer*
Bohle, Robert Henry *journalism educator*
Braden, Thomas Wardell *news commentator*
Castle, Vernon Charles *recording company executive*
Christiansen, Lara Irene *journalist*
Cornett, Gregg *newspaper publisher, newspaper editor, computer company executive*
Davis, Paul Milton *television news administrator*
Dracos, Theodore Michael *journalist, television producer*
Durshimer, Margo Ellen Gilbert *freelance writer*
Erwin, John Seymour *writer, editor, composer*
Erwin, Shelia Kaye *newspaper publisher*
Ferre, Antonio Luis *newspaper publisher*
Fodiman, Aaron Rosen *publishing executive*
Foster, Brad Wayne *publishing executive*
Gainer, Leila Josephine *media relations strategist, consultant*
Gordon, Richard E. *publishing executive*
Gretser, George Westfall *publisher*
Gurinsky, Sylvia *journalist*
Halfen, David *publishing executive*
Harden, Patrick Alan *journalist, news executive*
Heimbold, Margaret Byrne *publisher, marketing professional, educator*
Held, Michael Joseph *broadcasting executive*
Henkin-Bookman, Jean Patricia *editor, writer, literary agent*
Kappeler, Jana Snapp *publisher*
Killgore, Le *journalist, political columnist*
Kilpatrick, James Jackson, Jr. *columnist, author*
King, Beverly Ann *publishing executive*
Kitchen, Kristin Wilson *journalist, social worker*
Kleinberg, Howard J. *newspaper columnist*
Krebs, Elizabeth Louise *photojournalist, editor*
Lambro, Donald Joseph *columnist*
Lane, Cason Wesley *writer, editor, media specialist*
Levin, Jordan G. *journalist*
Long, Kenneth Hammond *publishing executive*
Lumpkin, Anne Craig *retired television and radio company executive*
McCorkindale, Douglas Hamilton *publishing company executive, corporate lawyer*
Michel, Daniel John *broadcast educator, writer, photographer, artist*
Millett, Ralph Linwood, Jr. *retired newspaper editor*
Millman, Barry A. *editor-in-chief*
Minnigh, Brice Martin *journalist, researcher*
Nelson, Alan Rex *editor*
Nicholas, Timothy Alan *journalist*
Parker, Richard Leo *journalist*
Pierce, Jim *recording industry producer*
Pierson, Gil *broadcast executive*
Plank, (Ethel) Faye *editor, photographer, writer*
Policinski, Eugene Francis *author, newspaper editor*
Pollock, Candace Marie *reporter*
Rao, Lawrence Michael *writer, radio producer*
Rice, Alison Maria *editor*
Ridder, Paul Anthony *newspaper executive*
Rivas, Ernesto *newspaper columnist*
Roberts, Delmar Lee *editor*
Rourke, Arlene Carol *publisher*
Schaver, Mark J. *journalist*
Scruggs, Charles G. *editor*
Singletary, Russell Pressley *journalist*
Smith, Brian C. *newscaster*
Smith, Jamesetta Delorise *author*
Sommers, Laurie Kay *folklorist, ethnomusicologist*
Squier, Thomas Keith *columnist, educator, writer, environmentalist*
Stahl, Michael Len *professional speaker, actor, educator*
Stanton, John Jeffrey *editor, broadcast journalist, government programs director, analyst*
Stiff, Robert Martin *newspaper editor*
Suarez, Roberto *retired newspaper publishing executive*
Tarpley, James Douglas *journalism educator, magazine editor*
Van Deventer, Micki Jo *magazine writer, editor*
Walls, Carmage Lee, Jr. *newspaper executive, consultant*
Wartella, Ellen Ann *communications educator, consultant*
Whitten, Bessie Emrick *editor*
Williams, Paige Ashley *reporter, writer*
Yack, Patrick Ashley *editor*

EDUCATION. For postsecondary education, *See also* specific fields.

UNITED STATES

ALABAMA

Albertville
Rogers, Tiffany Heather *special education educator*

Alexander City
Harrell, Karen Leigh Sasser *secondary school educator*

Andalusia
Windham, Susan Kay Harper *early childhood educator*

Anniston
Bailey, Charles Dennis *school system administrator*
Cline, Claude Wayne *technical and vocational educator, writer*
Smith, Judith Day *early childhood educator*

Athens
Ruth, Betty Muse *school system administrator*

Auburn
Bond, Gordon Crews *college dean*
Davis, Rebecca Annette *elementary educator*
Lishak, Lisa Anne *secondary education educator*
Muse, William Van *academic administrator*
Yang, Baiyin *adult education educator*

Bessemer
Stephens, Betsy Bain *retired elementary school educator*

Birmingham
Branham, Grady Eugene *principal*
Bruess, Clint E. *academic administrator*
Clarke, Juanita M. Waiters *education educator*
Corts, Thomas Edward *university president*
Eddowes, E(lizabeth) Anne *early childhood education specialist*
Edwards, Margaret McRae *college administrator, lawyer*
Hames, Carl Martin *educational administrator, art dealer, consultant*
Hendley, Dan Lunsford *retired university official*
Kramer, Roy Foster *school superintendent*
Marsch, Andrew Johnson, III *university dean*
Mc Callum, Charles Alexander *university official*
Stith, Cheryl Diane Adams *elementary school educator*
Talley, Bette Sue *elementary education educator*
Thompson, Dorothea Wideman *educator*
Wood, Clinton Wayne *middle school educator*

Centreville
Parker, Janice Marie *assistant principal, day camp director*

Daphne
Rosandich, Thomas James *academic administrator*
Williams, Bettie White *special education educator*

Decatur
Blalock, Carmen *education educator*
Davis, Marian Bloodworth *secondary school educator*

Eufaula
Mims, Paula Cain *secondary education educator*

Evergreen
Stinson, Donald Lee *school administrator*

Florence
Barfield, Kenny Dale *religious school administrator*
Gillaspie, Lynn Clara *education educator, director clinical experience*
Potts, Robert Leslie *academic administrator*
Zarate, Ann Gairing *academic administrator, lawyer*

Foley
Wood, Linda Sherrill *secondary education educator*

Fort Payne
Harris, Melba Iris *secondary school educator, state agency administrator*

Fruithurst
Murphy, Ricky Keith *elementary school principal*

Gulf Shores
Zeanah, Robert Clyde *principal*

Hamilton
Goggans, Roberta Daily *retired school system administrator*

Hanceville
Galin, Jerry Dean *college dean*

Hartselle
Sloan, Tina Rye *elementary school educator*
Smith, Pamela Rodgers *elementary education educator*

Highland Home
Wilson, Ginny Charlotte *guidance counselor*

Homewood
Hart, Virginia Wade *elementary education educator*
Offutt, Elizabeth Rhodes *education educator*

Hoover
Parrish, Sherry Dye *elementary school educator*
Pyles, Adrienne Maughan *elementary school educator*
Slovensky, Deborah Wilbanks *secondary education educator*

Huntsville
Black, Daniel Hugh *secondary school educator*
Franz, Frank Andrew *university president, physics educator*
Helton, Norma Jean *special education educator*
Hollowell, Jan Bennett *adult education educator*
Hoppe, Lea Ann *elementary education educator*
Johnson, Judy Sherrill *secondary school educator, educational consultant*
Morgan, Beverly Hammersley *middle school educator, artist*
Quick, Jerry Ray *academic administrator*
Vought, Barbara Baltz *secondary school educator*

Jacksonville
Austin, Dan *retired dean*
Hale, Judy Ann *education educator*
McGee, Harold Johnston *academic administrator*

Jasper
Rowland, David Jack *academic administrator*

Lester
Matthews, Linda Nell *secondary school educator*

Livingston
Green, Asa Norman *university president*

Madison
McCarty, Lisa Ann *elementary and early childhood educator*

Mobile
Baker, Amanda Sirmon *university dean, nursing educator*
Byrd, Gwendolyn Pauline *school system superintendent*
Byrd, Mary Jane *education educator*
Floyd, Cinthia Ann *secondary school educator, coach*
Lambert, Clarissa Savell *education educator*
Shank, Marilyn Sue *special education educator*
Strodl, Peter *educational administrator, educator*
Sullivan, Patricia Jackson *parochial school educator, consultant*
Whiddon, Frederick Palmer *university president*
White, James Patrick *creative writing educator, writer*

Montevallo
Hagler, Robyn L. *education educator*

Montgomery
Arnold, Frances Deupree *early childhood educator*
Bigham, Wanda Ruth *college president*
Boles, John Raymond *secondary education educator*
Brown, Joan Hall *elementary school educator*
Deaton, Cheryl Davis *school system administrator*
Harris, William Hamilton *academic administrator*
Hill, Elizabeth Reese *elementary education educator*
Kurth, Ronald James *university president, retired naval officer*
Ladner, Ann-Marie Calvo *special education educator*
Thornton, Patricia Walker *school development director*
Tracy, Patricia Ann Koop *secondary school educator*
Walker, Annette *counseling administrator*
Williams, James Orrin *university administrator, educator*
Wright, Cathy Hess *secondary education educator*

Muscle Shoals
Smith, Harry Delano *educational administrator*

Pell City
Drechsel, Charles Nicklos *private school educator, horticulturist*

Pike Road
Cox, George Stanley *principal*

Rainsville
Reece, Marilyn King *college dean*

Scottsboro
McGill, Judy Annell McGee *early childhood and elementary educator*

Selma
Moore, Jean Moore *secondary education educator*

Sumiton
Wiersma, Karen Guthrie *learning disabilities educator*

Talladega
Anderson, Sharon Rice *special education educator*
Paris, Virginia Hall (Ginger Paris) *elementary school educator*

Tallassee
Stewart, Carl Denver *principal*

Troy
Strain Bynum, Robin Michelle *academic administrator*

Tuscaloosa
Bills, Robert E(dgar) *emeritus psychology educator*
Cain, Rosemary Prince *early childhood education educator*
Fendley, William Ray, Jr. *university administrator, educator*
Hamilton, Deborah *educational administrator*
Jackson, Cynthia Williford *special education educator*
Miller, Michael T. *education educator*
Smith, Lois Colston *secondary school educator*
Strong, Thomas S. *college director*
Sutton, Kathy Ballard *middle school educator, band director*
Willard, Ann Elam *retired special education educator*

Tuskegee
Green, Elbert P. *university official*
Reder, Elizabeth Ann *elementary school educator*

Union Grove
Burgess, Margaret Louise *elementary education educator*
Hinton, Susan Frazier *elementary education educator*

Vance
Green, Kay Owen *special education educator*

Vestavia Hills
Jacobs, Delores Hamm *secondary education educator*

Wetumpka
Curlee, Robert Glen, Jr. *special education educator*

ARIZONA

Tucson
Padró, Fernando Francisco *dean of students, history educator*

ARKANSAS

Alpena
Sawyer, Anita Dawn *special education educator*

Arkadelphia
Dunn, Charles DeWitt *academic administrator*

Bella Vista
Godfrey, Garland Alonzo *retired academic administrator*

Camden
Bradshaw, Otabel *elementary school educator*
Owen, Larry Gene *dean, educator, electronic and computer integrated manufacturing consultant*

Conway
Doyle, Nell Meadows *program director*
Holmes, Barbara Deveaux *college president*
Thompson, Winfred Lee *university president, lawyer*
Witcher, Ann Elizabeth *education educator*

Eureka Springs
Harmony, Barbara Helen *educational administrator, environmental educator*
Seeligson, Molly Fulton *educational consultant*
Ward, Sharon Dee *secondary school educator*

Fayetteville
Farrell, Karolyn Kay McMillan *adult education educator*
Ferritor, Daniel E. *university official*
Henry, Ann Rainwater *education educator*
Schoppmeyer, Martin William *education educator*
Van Patten, James Jeffers *education educator*
Webb, James David *assistant principal*

Forrest City
McConnon, Lorena Anna *secondary education educator*

Fort Smith
Gooden, Benny L. *school system administrator*

Harrison
Vincent, Merle Allen *learning center administrator, educator*

Hartford
Roller Hall, Gayle Aline *gifted and talented educator*

Hot Springs National Park
Spencer, Thomas Morris *community college president*

Jacksonville
Dokes, Geneva *secondary school educator*

Little Rock
Daniels, Roy Melvin *elementary school principal*
Flemmons, Mari Robertson *secondary school educator, writer*
Hathaway, Charles E. *academic administrator*
Keaton, William Thomas *academic administrator, pastor*
Nelson, Susan Branon *coordinator comprehensive system personnel development*
Northrop, Gaylord Marvin *dean, university official*
O'Neal, Nell Self *retired principal*
Williams, Karmen Petersen *secondary school educator*

Magnolia
Gamble, Steven G. *academic administrator*

Pine Bluff
Scott, Vicki Sue *school system administrator*

Russellville
Morris, Lois Lawson *education educator*

Stamps
Moore-Berry, Norma Jean *secondary school educator*

State University
Moore, Thomas Alva *information services director*
Wyatt, Leslie *academic administrator*

Van Buren
Breeden, Betty Loneta *secondary school educator*

West Helena
Murphree, Kenneth Dewey *elementary school educator*

CALIFORNIA

Los Angeles
Watts, Judith-Ann White *academic administrator*

Placentia
Sexson, Stephen Bruce *educational writer, educator*

San Jose
Pitts, Griff D. *academic administrator*

COLORADO

Lakewood
Illade, Boris Julius *elementary school educator*
Reed, Joan-Marie *special education educator*

Littleton
Tabacchi, Patricia *elementary education educator*

CONNECTICUT

New Britain
Shumaker, John William *academic administrator*

Storrs
Austin, Philip Edward *university chancellor*

DISTRICT OF COLUMBIA

Washington
Hilburn, Andrea L. *principal*
Tlou, Josiah S. *education educator*

FLORIDA

Alachua
Thornton, J. Ronald *technology center director*

Altamonte Springs
Harner, David Paul *development administrator*
Huyett, Debra Kathleen *elementary education educator*
Poland, Phyllis Elaine *secondary school educator, consultant*
Williford, James Richard *university administrator*

Apalachicola
Burton, Shearor Fay *school system administrator, educator, computer consultant*
Kelley, Beverly Cashul *principal*

Apopka
Bergstrom, Trudy Sonderegger *elementary school educator*
Witengier, Mary Joan MacGilvray *retired special education educator, physical therapist*

Atlantis
Wright, Constance Mohr *elementary school educator*

Avon Park
Stutzman, Beth Ann *middle school educator*

Babson Park
Cloud, Linda Beal *retired secondary school educator*

Bartow
Black, B. R. *educational administrator*
Mercadante, Anthony Joseph *special education educator*

Belle Glade
Grear, Effie Carter *principal*

Belleview
Kielborn, Terrie Leigh *secondary education educator*

Boca Raton
Averett-Short, Geneva Evelyn *college administrator*
Caputi, Marie Antoinette *university official*
Catanese, Anthony James *academic administrator*
Costa, Terry Ann *educational administrator*
deHaven-Smith, Westi Jo *academic administrator*
Guglielmino, Lucy Margaret Madsen *education educator, researcher, consultant*
Hallenberg, Nancy Lee *school administrator*
Ross, Donald Edward *university administrator*

Bradenton
Clark, Sara Mott *retired home economics educator*

Brandon
Blomgren, David Kenneth *dean, pastor*
Fleetwood, Mary Annis *education association executive*

Brooksville
Manieri-Harvey, Michele Dawn *elementary school educator, musician*
Warsick-Rinzivillo, Mary Katrina *counselor, educator*

Callahan
Tippins, Susan Smith *elementary school educator, consultant*

Cape Coral
Roseberry, Richard Lee *secondary education educator, retired coast guard*

Clearwater
Baty, David F. *student services professional*
Jacobs, Marilyn Arlene Potoker *gifted education educator, consultant, author*
Mattice, Howard LeRoy *education educator*

Cocoa
Brewer, Ernest Andrew, Jr. *elementary education educator*

Coconut Creek
Coburn, Louis *library sciences educator, school librarian*
Wolf-Schein, Enid Gordon *special education researcher, educator, consultant*

Coral Gables
Nirschel, Roy Joseph *academic administrator*

Coral Springs
Colton, Susan Adams *principal*
Rubin, Joyce Linda *education educator*

Dade City
Marler, Addie Karen *elementary school educator*

Davie
Kumi-Diaka, James *college educator, researcher*

Daytona Beach
Cool, Mary L. *elementary education educator*
Richmond, Patricia Northrup *elementary art educator*

Deland
Judy, Elaine Marie *secondary school educator*
Leahy, Robert Maurice *education educator*
Lee, Howard Douglas *academic administrator*

Delray Beach
Knapp, Janis Ann *elementary school educator*
Rowland, Patricia Ann *special education educator*

Deltona
Bondinell, Stephanie *counselor, former educational administrator*
Martin, Carolyn Stewart *school system administrator, counselor*
Venuti, Ruth Louise *secondary school educator, counselor*

Dover
Brown, Margaret Mary *special education educator*

Eagle Lake
Stroupe, Cynthia Kay *secondary school counselor, educator*

Fernandina Beach
Fishbaugh, Carole Sue *secondary school educator*

Fort Lauderdale
Bivens, Constance Ann *elementary school educator*
Corll, Vivian Ann Morgan *secondary education educator, writer*
Fine, Joyce Caplan *education educator*
Fischler, Abraham Saul *academic administrator*
Ginn, Vera Walker *educational administrator*
Krauser, Janice *special education educator*
Lewis, Ovid C. *dean, law educator, lawyer*
Silfen, Roberta Dawn *school system administrator*
Trubey, Lillian Priscilla *secondary education educator, retired*
Walsh, William John *educational administrator*

Fort Myers
Carrigan, John Donley *retired secondary educator*
Hoffman, Nelson Miles, Jr. *retired academic administrator, consultant*
Warner, Elizabeth Jane Scott *exceptional education educator*

Fort Pierce
Jespersen, Susan Howell *career counselor, educator*

Fort Walton Beach
Register, Annette Rowan *reading educator*
Stevenson, Mary Eva Blue *elementary education educator*

Gainesville
App, James Leonard *dean*
Brown, Perry Edmond *academic administrator*
Chait, Andrea Melinda *special education educator*
Daleuski, Edward Joseph *principal*
Gonzalez, Gerardo Merced *university dean*
Harper, Marsha Lea *special education educator*
Lombardi, John V. *university administrator, historian*
McKinney, Susan Annette *university administrator*
Meyer, Harvey Kessler, II *retired academic administrator*
Penland, Arnold Clifford, Jr. *college dean, educator*
Phillips, Winfred Marshall *dean, mechanical engineer*
Schneider, Richard Harold *university dean, educator*

Goulds
Cooper, Kenneth Stanley *educational administrator*

Graceville
Collier, Evelyn Myrtle *elementary school educator*
Collins, Charles Jesse *college official, psychology educator*
Kinchen, Thomas Alexander *college president*

Hialeah
Behrman, Robin Leslie *primary education educator*

Hilliard
Clough, Lauren C. *special education educator*

Holiday
Gatti, Ellen Grandy *educational administrator, real estate broker*

Hollywood
Sillman, Adrienne Patiteaux *educational specialist, consultant*
Wilson, Linda Edmiston *secondary school science educator*

Homestead
Brammer, Barbara Allison *secondary school educator, consultant*

Indian Harbour Beach
Coleman, Julie Kathryn *middle school educator*
Haggis, Lewanna Strom *principal, author, consultant*

Inverness
Anderson, Barbara *elementary school educator*

Jacksonville
Alexander, Edna M. DeVeaux *elementary education educator*
Borstein, Jeanne Erwin *secondary school educator*
Carter, Paula Stanley *special education educator*
Carver, Joan Sacknitz *university dean*
Colby, Lestina Larsen *secondary education educator*
Goodwin, Elizabeth Carol *special education educator*
Herbert, Adam William, Jr. *university president*
MacDonald, Carolyn Helms *gifted education educator*
Main, Edna (June) Dewey *education educator*
Piotrowski, Sandra A. *elementary education educator*
Rogerson, Constance Jean *guidance counselor*
Russo, Louis S. *dean, neurology educator*
Spiers, William Kesler, Jr. *financial aid administrator*
Tinsman, Mary Elizabeth *special education educator*

Juno Beach
Miller, Annette Yaffey *elementary school educator*

Jupiter
Loper, Lucia Ann *retired elementary school educator*
Moseley, Karen Frances F. *school system administrator, educator*

Kissimmee
Boswell, Tommie C. *middle school educator*
Evans-O'Connor, Norma Lee *secondary school educator, consultant*
Jablon, Elaine *education consultant*
Kintner, Treva Carpenter *retired education educator*
Toothe, Karen Lee *elementary and secondary school educator*

Lake City
Munch-Keen, Mary Virginia *primary education educator*

Lake Wales
Hodapp, Shirley Jeaniene *curriculum administrator*

Lakeland
Hammond, Vernon Francis *school administrator*
Spruill, Howard Vernon *former academica administrator, minister*

Land O'Lakes
Branham, Pamela Helen *special education educator*

Largo
Brooks, Mary McLeod *retired early childhood education educator*
Hinesley, J. Howard *superintendent*
Lowry, Christine Ossenberg *elementary school educator*

Lecanto
Mathia, Mary Loyola *parochial school educator, nun*

Leesburg
Burns, Diane *gifted education educator*
Hayes, K. William *secondary school educator*
Schumacher, Cynthia Jo *secondary education educator, retired*

Lehigh Acres
Inman, Margaret E. *elementary education educator*

Longwood
Dunne, James Robert *academic administrator, management consultant, business educator*

Madison
Catron, James Otis *college counseling administrator, social science educator*

Maitland
Fernandez, Joseph Anthony *educational administrator*

Marianna
Daniels, Elrea Mae *retired elementary and special education educator*

Melbourne
Delisio, Sharon Kay *secondary school educator, school administrator*
Ryan, Ellen Marie *elementary education and gifted education educator*
Stark, Norman *secondary school educator*
Weaver, Lynn Edward *academic administrator, consultant, editor*

Merritt Island
Bickford-Wilcox, Barbara Jean *elementary education educator, canvas fabricator*
Dukes, Melinda Shaw *elementary school educator*
McClanahan, Leland *academic administrator*

Miami
Allington, Gloria Jean Ham *medical education administrator*
Alpart, Nancy Michele *special education educator*
Brenner, Esther Hannah *elementary school educator*
Castillo, Tomas Franklin *secondary school educator*
Clarke, Donald Duhaney *secondary education educator*
Conrad, Louis E. *student affairs director, educator*
Cornelius, Vicki Lynn *middle school educator*
Deling, Elaine Marie *special education educator*
Dottin, Erskine S. *education educator*
Ferguson, Madelyn Kristina *education educator*
Firestone, Sheila Meyerowitz *gifted and talented education educator*
Foote, Edward Thaddeus, II *university president, lawyer*
Geis, Tarja Pelto *educational coordinator, consultant, counselor, teacher, professor*
Henderson, William Eugene *education educator*
Jackson, Jacqueline *assistant principal*
Knisely, Debra Sue *secondary education educator*
Love, Mildred Allison *retired secondary school educator, historian, writer, volunteer*
Maidique, Modesto Alex *academic administrator*
Maldonado, Otmara Lina *university administrator*
McCabe, Robert Howard *college president*
Merves, Marlene *elementary school educator*
Morales, Carlota Eloisa *principal*
Newport, Carol Wimmler *special education educator*
Okpala, Columba Christopher *art educator*
Polster, Eleanor Bernice *management educator, university administrator*
Quigley, John Joseph *special education educator*
Rogers, Wilma Messer *retired elementary school educator*
Rossie, Carlos Enrique *computer school administrator*
Stern, Joanne Thrasher *elementary school educator*
Suarez, Celia Cristina *university official*
Warren, Emily P. *retired secondary school educator*
Young, Freddie Gilliam *educational administrator*

Miami Beach
Szlegier, Rachel Ellen *elementary school educator*

Naples
Brusco, Lynne Patricia *secondary education educator, administrator*
Loft, Bernard Irwin *education educator, consultant*

Niceville
Sandlin, Beverly Ruth *education educator*

North Miami Beach
Weinberger, Gwen Lee Schaller *academic administrator*

Oakland Park
Adams, Nancy Ann *school system administrator*

Ocala
Hodges, Elizabeth Swanson *educational consultant, tutor*
Montgomery, Mary Kathryn Keener *special education educator*
Sills, Sallie Alexander *elementary school educator*
Williams, Pauline Elizabeth *special education educator*

Okeechobee
Raulerson, Phoebe Hodges *school superintendent*

Opa Locka
Brooks, Claybourne Lenor, Jr. *adult education educator, youth pastor*
Budnik, Patricia Mc Nulty *elementary education educator*
Hopton, Janice *elementary school principal*
Reid, Joan Loraine *primary school educator*

Orange Park
Miller, Martin Eugene *school system administrator, negotiator*
Myers, Bertina Satterfield *secondary education business educator, administrator*
Oglesby, Beverly Clayton *kindergarten educator*

Orlando
Ady, Laurence Irvin *academic administrator*
Brookes, Carolyn Jessen *early childhood education educator*
Colbourn, Trevor *retired university president, historian*
Crane, Glenda Paulette *private school educator*
Hardesty, Stephen Don *secondary education educator*
Henriott, Doris Susan *technology and publications services educator*
Hitt, John Charles *university president*
Johns, Elizabeth Jane Hobbs *educational administrator*

Ormond Beach
Boyle, Susan Jean Higle *elementary school educator*

Orviedo
Mendez, Erwin Peter *elementary and secondary education educator*

Palm Bay
Colman, Charles Kingsbury *academic administrator, criminologist*
Shiley, Andrea Gail *secondary school educator*

Palm Beach
Steere, Anne Bullivant *retired student advisor*

Palm Beach Gardens
Orr, Joseph Alexander *educational administrator*

Palm Coast
Brandão, Frank Raposo *counselor*

Panama City
Alan-Moorman, Tess *special education educator*
Garrett, Louise Lin *secondary school educator*
Pate, Sharon Shamburger *secondary school educator*
Sheffield, Nancy Y. *secondary school educator*
Smith, Jani Marie *special education educator*
Smith, Sarah Estelle *elementary education educator*

Pensacola
Abercrombie, Charlotte Manning *reading specialist, supervisor*
Leach, Luann Marie *elementary school educator, beauty consultant*
Marx, Morris Leon *academic administrator*
McLeod, Stephen Glenn *education educator*
Wyss, Norma Rose Topping *counselor, supervisor, educator, writer*

Pinellas Park
Athanson, Mary Catheryne *elementary school principal*

Plant City
Morris, Jennifer Kelly *early childhood specialist*

Pompano Beach
Marged, Judith Michele *middle school educator*
Rios, Julie A. *education educator*

Port Charlotte
Gravelin, Janesy Swartz *elementary education educator*

Port Saint Lucie
Centerbar, Alberta Elaine *education educator*

Punta Gorda
McGregor, Janet Eileen *elementary school educator*
Outland, Max Lynn *school system administrator*

Riverview
Wells, Betty Calhoun *elementary education educator*

Saint Augustine
Horn, Patricia Solomon *technology curriculum facilitator*
Sullivan, Mary Jean *elementary school educator*

Saint Leo
Hale, Charles Dennis *education educator*

Saint Petersburg
Jacob, Bruce Robert *dean, academic administrator, law educator*
Sanchez, Vanessa Diane *special education educator*
Shumate, Gloria Jones *retired educational administrator*
Smith, Betty Robinson *elementary education educator*

San Mateo
Wood, Shelton Eugene *college educator, consultant, minister*

Sanford
Brown, Barbara Jean *special and secondary education educator*
Lane, Mary Frances *health, physical education curriculum specialist*
Williams, Andrew D. *secondary school educator*

Sarasota
Biegel, Alice Marie *secondary school educator*
Felker, Ouida Jeanette Weissinger *special education educator*
Lee, Ann McKeighan *secondary school educator*
Rice, Anthony Hopkins *dean, artist*
Russell, Margaret Jones (Peg Russell) *secondary school educator*
Saltonstall, Nathaniel *educational consultant*
Williams, Julia Rebecca Keys *secondary school educator*

Sebring
Murray, Eleanor F. *educator, freelance writer*

Seffner
Thie, Genevieve Ann *secondary school educator*

Seminole
Durrick, George Thomas *elementary school educator*

Spring Hill
Johnson, Henry Eugene, III *middle school educator*
Stockford, Barbara Lynn *middle school educator*
Weber, Mary Linda *preschool educator*

Stuart
Roe, Radie Lynn *secondary school educator*

Sun City Center
Andrews, Michael Frank *education educator*

Tallahassee
Barker, Jeanne Wilson *principal, computer educational consultant*
Bert, Clara Virginia *home economics educator, administrator*
Brown, Ernest Lee *education educator*
Crider, Irene Perritt *education educator, small business owner, consultant*
D'Alemberte, Talbot (Sandy D'Alemberte) *academic administrator, lawyer*
Daniels, Irish C. *principal*
Humphries, Frederick S. *university president*
Lick, Dale Wesley *academic administrator*
Mills, Belen Collantes *early childhood education educator*
Pride, Fleetwood Martin, III (Fleet Pride) *education administrator, consultant*
Reed, Charles Bass *academic administrator*
Sinclair, Carol *educational specialist*

Tampa
Boyd, Lowe Adlai *academic administrator*
Bradley, Charles Ernest *educational leadership consultant, music educator*
Cannella, Deborah Fabbri *elementary school educator*
Hammett, Theresa Clair Hoy *elementary school educator*
Henning, Dorothy Ann *special education educator*
Hoover, Betty-Bruce Howard *private school educator*
Kennelly, Michael Francis *school system administrator*
Lawson, Mary Carolyn *elementary education educator*
Luddington, Betty Walles *library media specialist*
McDermott, Robert James *academic administrator*
Miles, Bruce William *academic administrator*
Paloumpis, Andreas Athanasios *academic administrator*
Riggs, Carl Daniel *academic administrator, biologist*
Scruggs, Charles Eugene *university administrator*
Wiemken, Deborah Lynn *elementary education educator*
Wright, Mary Beth *special education educator*

Tarpon Springs
Green, May Clayman *early childhood educator and administrator*

Tavares
Harper, Jane Walker *educational administrator*

Temple Terrace
Palmer, Eddie Allen *elementary education educator*

Tierra Verde
Schmitz, Dolores Jean *primary education educator*

Titusville
Chodosh, Robert Ivan *middle school educator, coach*

Trenton
Schubert, Patricia Ann *middle school educator*

Valrico
Benjamin, Sheila Pauletta *secondary education educator*

Venice
Farrell, June Eleanor *retired middle school educator*

Vero Beach
Michaels, Agnes Isabelle *education educator*

Viera
Shelton, Patricia Cook *staff development specialist*

Wellington
McGee, Lynne Kalavsky *principal*

West Palm Beach
Corts, Paul Richard *college president*
Russell, Joyce Weber *principal*
Ward, Alice Faye *elementary education educator*

Winter Park
Albers, Edward James, Sr. *secondary school educator*

Winter Springs
Chrissos, George *retired secondary education educator*

Zephyrhills
Abercrombie, Freda A. *secondary education educator*
Johnson, Ruth Marie *educator*

GEORGIA

Adel
Darby, Marianne Talley *elementary school educator*

Albany
Keith, Carolyn Austin *secondary school counselor*

Paschal, James Alphonso counselor, educator secondary school
Pringle, Sammie, Sr. academic administrator
Stanley-Chavis, Sandra Ornecia special education educator, consultant

Alpharetta
Satterfield, Mark Edward consultant, columnist

Athens
Andrews, Grover Jene adult education educator, administrator
Coley, Linda Marie secondary school educator
Crowley, John Francis, III university dean
Crowther, Ann Rollins dean, political science educator
Hart, Laurie Ellen education educator
Landrum, Thomas Steel university administrator
Mixon, Deborah Lynn Burton elementary school educator
Wiegel, Juergen Kurt Wilhelm education educator

Atlanta
Alfred, Dewitt Clinton, Jr. university dean, psychiatrist
Arsan, Janice Holt university administrator
Bailey, Joy Hafner university program administrator, psychologist, educator
Bickerton, Jane Elizabeth university research coordinator
Bouchillon, John Ray education coordinator, real estate executive
Bronner, Sheba director private school, modeling instructor
Brunner, Kenneth August educational consultant, author
Chace, William Murdough university administrator
Chandler, Mary M. Szegedy principal
Chase, William M. academic administrator
Cranford, Donnella Bryant school system administrator
Curry, Toni Griffin counseling center executive, consultant
Ferris, James Leonard academic administrator
Flanigan, Robert Daniel, Jr. academic administrator
Frost, Susan Henson academic administrator
Gerson, Martin Lyons secondary school educator
Hershatter, Andrea Silver university official
Hogan, John Donald college dean, finance educator
Ingram, Judith Myrna university specialist
Johnson, Anne Trippe secondary school educator
Lamkin, Jane Eagar elementary school educator
Lucas-Tauchar, Margaret Frances university official
Massin, Steven Scott business education educator
Messer, Mitchel Anthony educational consultant, electrical engineer
Mock, Larry John elementary education educator
Moreland-Bey, Terri Lynn elementary school educator
Parko, Joseph Edward, Jr. academic administrator
Patton, Carl Vernon academic administrator, educator
Peebles, Lucretia Neal Drane principal
Pesch, Barbara Hasier special education educator
Rogers, Brenda Gayle educational administrator, educator, consultant
Sims, David Suthern university maintenance official
Sims, Robert McNeill retired school administrator, soccer coach
Slider, Russell Logan dean
Spence, Susan Bateman counselor
Stanton, Donald Sheldon academic administrator
Starks, Kenneth Maurice elementary school educator, poet
Sullivan, (Elsie) Lee counselor
Walker, Carolyn Smith college services administrator, counselor
Wasmer, Charlotte Carlton secondary school educator
White, Annette Jones early childhood education administrator

Augusta
Lambert, Vickie Ann dean
Levy, Maurice education educator, researcher
Puryear, James Burton college administrator
Tedesco, Francis Joseph university administrator

Austell
Carlton, Jennifer Lenore elementary education educator
Wheeler, Virginia Ann secondary school educator

Bainbridge
Smith, Margaret Dill academic administrator
Tutcher, Larry Clifford middle school educator

Bakersville
Greene, Tammy Renea early childhood educator

Bonaire
Cherry, Carol Lynn principal
Griffin, Barbara Conley kindergarten educator, antique store owner

Brunswick
Gray, Margaret Gayle secondary school educator
Harper, Janet Sutherlin Lane educational administrator, writer
Holder, Kathleen elementary education educator
Swann, Mary Olivia (Libby Swann) special education educator
Talbott, Mary Ann Britt secondary education educator

Calhoun
McKenzie, Kathleen Rose primary school educator

Carrollton
Bulach, Cletus Ralph education educator
Butler, Jody Talley gifted education educator
Harden, Gail Brooks elementary school educator
Myers, John William academic administrator
Willis, Roni May Lewis library administrator

Cartersville
Barnett, Harold Thomas school system superintendent
Wheeler, Susie Weems retired educator

Chatsworth
Haven, Martha Billie school system administrator
Witherow, Jimmie David secondary school educator

Clarkston
Clow, Elizabeth D. academic administrator

College Park
Ferguson, Wendell private school educator

Columbus
Cook, Mary Gooch elementary school educator
Duncan, Frances Murphy retired special education educator
Edmondson, Michael Herman secondary school educator
Hilt, Diane Elaine middle school educator, computer specialist
Ingersoll, Margaret Lee school principal
Jinright, Noah Franklin vocational school educator
Montgomery, Anna Frances elementary school educator
Ripple, Rochelle Poyourow educational administrator, educator

Conyers
Pearce, Sara Margaret Culbreth middle school educator

Covington
Griffey, Karen Rose special education educator

Crawford
Bower, Douglas William pastoral counselor, psychotherapist, clergyman

Cumming
Benson, Betty Jones school system administrator

Cuthbert
Swinson, Sue Whitlow secondary education educator
Treible, Kirk college president

Dacula
Reid, Ginger Meredith school counselor, educator

Dallas
Calhoun, Patricia Hanson secondary education educator
Graham, Sylvia Swords secondary school educator

Dalton
Coker, Bert L. principal
Meek, Mary Virgelia Cleveland special education administrator, psychologist

Danielsville
Bond, Joan elementary school educator

Decatur
Bland, Cynthia Zenobia elementary school educator, writer
Bryant, James Cecil, Jr. academic administrator
Cooper, Davis Alfonso, Jr. principal
Keaton, Mollie M. elementary school educator
Mabry, Cathy Darlene elementary school educator
Slaughter, Gloria Jean elementary education educator
Ziegler, Robert Oliver special education educator

Demorest
Booth, Ronnie Lee college official, educator

Douglasville
Hall, Mary Hugh secondary school educator
Landy, Lois Clouse principal, counselor

Dublin
Bonner, Annie Stuckey secondary educator
Rookey, Thomas Jerome dean

Duluth
Cooney, Patricia Ann elementary school educator, secondary school educator
Pitman, Sharon Gail middle school counselor

Evans
Bryant, Mary Roselyn Glasgow visual arts educator
Shrader, Lynne Ann secondary school educator, coach

Fayetteville
DeCotis, John Decio school administrator
Ford, Frances Annette secondary educator
Howard, Clarice Hardee special education educator
Phillips, Gary Lee principal

Forest Park
Kirkland, Russell Kermit principal

Fort Oglethorpe
Stephens, Mary June secondary school educator

Fort Valley
Kendricks, Vivian Davis education educator

Franklin
Lipham, William Patrick principal, educator

Franklin Springs
Harrison, William Timothy college administrator

Gainesville
Burd, John Stephen academic administrator, music educator
Childers, Shirley Ruth vocational education educator
Clark, Debbie Suzanne secondary school educator
Embry, Karen Thompson elementary education educator
Martin, James Harbert school administrator, retired Air Force officer

Garden City
Holmes, Robin Enyce secondary education educator

Griffin
Bolton, Elaine Hazleton gifted education educator, principal
Eady, Charlotte King elementary education educator
Jones, Sara Woods elementary education educator
Skelton, Janice Kenmore retired secondary school educator

Hawkinsville
Ragan, Carolyn Lancaster secondary school educator
Sanders, Julia Jean primary school educator
Sheffield, Gloria Carol elementary education educator

Hinesville
Welborn, Annie B. primary school educator

Hogansville
Spradlin, Charles Leonard secondary school educator

Jonesboro
Blevins, Andrea Elizabeth secondary education educator
Smith, Robyn Doyal elementary and middle school educator
Sprayberry, Roslyn Raye secondary school educator

Kennesaw
Anderegg, M. L. education educator

Lagrange
Ault, Ethyl Lorita special education educator, consultant
Smrekar, Pamela Louise secondary education educator

Lawrenceville
Adair, Lila McGahee secondary education physics educator

Lilburn
Magill, Dodie Burns early childhood education educator
Wagner, Douglas Alan secondary school educator

Lithia Springs
Craft, Janice Yvonne art educator

Locust Grove
Short, Betsy Ann elementary education educator

Lovejoy
Rich, Lee Wayne vocational education educator

Lyons
Cancer, Cathy Lynn elementary education educator

Macon
Bowen, Eva Joyce (Eva Joyce Jones) evaluation program educator, consultant
Godsey, R(aleigh) Kirby university president
Hitchcock, Cheryl Hodges former middle school educator, business owner
Mitchell, Carolyn Cochran college official
Reese, Angela Kathleen curriculum director
Smith, Constance Lewis secondary school educator
Williamson, Christine Wilder preschool specialist, educational consultant, small business owner

Manchester
McIntyre, Richard Rawlings, II elementary school educator

Marietta
Brown, Billy Charlie secondary school educator
Day, Afton J. elementary school educator, administrator
Dechman, Thomas Alexander, II gifted education educator
Douglas, Darcy special education educator
Dunbar, Georgia Lee educator
Laframboise, Joan Carol middle school educator
Matias, Patricia Trejo secondary education educator
Ramsey, Virginia Carol Marshall middle school educator
Yancy, Robert James dean

Mc Donough
Bomar, Robert Linton assistant principal

Metter
Jarvis, Suzanne Jones secondary school educator

Midway
Smith, Hazel Gwynn elementary school educator

Milledgeville
Dixon, Mary Oletta special education educator

Norcross
Burnett, Cassie Wagnon middle school educator
Holzer, Tamera Lee-Phillis middle school educator

Ocilla
Pugh, Joye Jeffries educational administrator

Peachtree City
Browning, Mary Ann Pizza reading specialist

Powder Springs
Davis, Karen Barnett special education educator

Riverdale
Lambert, Ethel Gibson Clark secondary school educator

Robins AFB
Hunnicutt, Victoria Anne Wilson school system administrator

Rome
Gibson, (Ramona) Ferne G(rimmett) assistant principal, music coordinator
Morgan, Sylvia Denise (Mrs. Harold Morgan) school administrator

Rossville
Knight, Marsha Dianne special education educator

Roswell
Hoskinson, Carol Rowe middle school educator

Savannah
Bowles, Steffanie Noreen elementary school educator
Butler, Mary Anne school principal
Chappell, Kimberly Ann elementary education educator
Coberly, Patricia Gail secondary education educator
Jarnigan-Williams, Angela Renee elementary school educator
Klein, Sally Rountree college educator
Singleton, Audrey Barnes elementary education educator
Strauser, Beverly Ann education educator
Thompson, Larry James school system administrator
Wolfe, John Thomas, Jr. university president

Scottdale
Tolbert, Vincent Tyson secondary education educator

Sharpsburg
Lyles, Martin Dale secondary school educator

Smyrna
Force, Crystal Ann school counselor

Statesboro
Buller, Jeffrey Lynn associate dean
Davenport, John Wayne education educator
Henry, Nicholas Llewellyn college president, political science educator

Stone Mountain
Allen, Cynthia Lynn elementary education educator

Suwanee
Quinn, Carolyn Anne special education educator

Swainsboro
Simmons, Frankie Wheeler primary school educator

Thomasville
Harvard, Ashley Wheeler primary school educator

Thomson
Sapough, Roy Sumner, Jr. educational administrator

Toccoa
Gardner, William Wayne academic administrator

Tyrone
Taylor, Robert John academic administrator

Valdosta
Adams, Maerita Elaine Owen early childhood educator
Williams, La Ronnia Vernon Dobson retired educator, news correspondent, educational consultant

Vidalia
Lewis, William S., Jr. educator

Villa Rica
Gordon, Barbara Elaine school counselor

Warner Robins
Madison, Miriam Frances educational administrator
Owens, Helen Dawn elementary school educator, reading consultant

Watkinsville
Kennon, Pamela Canerday secondary school educator

Waycross
Mooneyhan, Mark Earnest secondary school educator, administrator, coach
Strickland, Lynda McKay special education educator

Winder
Hutchins, Cynthia Barnes special education educator

Winterville
Anderson, David Prewitt university dean

Young Harris
Putnam, Joanne White college financial aid administrator, bookkeeper

Zebulon
Bizzell Yarbrough, Cindy Lee school counselor

HAWAII

Honolulu
Morrison, K. Jaydene education counseling firm executive

ILLINOIS

Chicago
Dye, Carl Melvyn academic administrator, educational association executive, insurance consultant

KANSAS

Liberal
Wilkerson, Rita Lynn special education educator, consultant

KENTUCKY

Beattyville
Cook, Gordon F. school system administrator, educator

Berea
Hammond, Claude Ellis university public relations administrator

Bowling Green
Briggs, Steven Ross university director
Droddy, Jesse Daryl education educator

Haynes, Robert Vaughn *retired university official, historian*
Meredith, Thomas C. *academic administrator*

Bronston
Mitchell, Steve Harold *child development specialist*

Brooksville
Kalb, Sarah Cummins *principal*
King, Sharon A. *elementary school educator*

Calvert City
Coakley, Patricia Davis Vaughn *gifted education educator*

Campbellsville
Conner, Jeanette Jones *elementary school educator*
Skaggs, Karen Gayle *elementary school educator*

Clinton
Clark, Linda Wilson *educational administrator*

Covington
Bensman, Charles J. *academic administrator*
Berg, Lorine McComis *retired guidance counselor*
Hall, Mary Beth *special education educator, writer*

Edmonton
Gibson, Mark Anthony *secondary school educator*

Elizabethtown
Lee, William Christopher *vocational school educator*

Falmouth
Mudd, Sheryl Kay *secondary school educator, guidance counselor*

Frankfort
Bennett, Ivan Stanley *school administrator*
Harris, Lee Charles *health and nursing educator*
McDaniel, Karen Jean *university library administrator*
Smith, Carson Eugene *university administrator*

Georgetown
Powell, Rebecca Gaeth *education educator*

Hazard
Hughes, George Edward *college president*

Henderson
Mattingly, L. Sharon *elementary principal*
Thurman, Susan Sommers *secondary education educator*
Wayne, Bill Tom *secondary school educator, coach*

Highland Heights
Berry, Michael Cody *educational administrator*
Boothe, Leon Estel *university president emeritus*

Hindman
Thompson, Marcia Slone *choral director, educator*

Hodgenville
Morrison, Helena Grace *guidance counselor*

Lexington
Blackburn, Vickie Carlee *vocational rehabilitation counselor*
Carr, Ben W., Jr. *academic administrator*
Chapman, James Paul *university official*
Lawson, Frances Gordon *child guidance specialist*
Peck, Claudia Jones *associate dean*
Phillips, Jane Ellen *education educator*
Walker, Retia Scott *dean, researcher, educator, consultant*
Wethington, Charles T., Jr. *academic administrator*
Williams, Carolyn Antonides *university dean*

London
Webb, Billie Jean *retired middle school educator*

Louisville
Bratton, Ida Frank *secondary school educator*
Cannon, Dannie Parker *special education educator*
Cecil, Bonnie Susan *elementary education educator*
Ford, Deborah Lynne *dean*
Highland, Martha Ellen *retired education educator, consultant*
Hoye, Robert Earl *adult education educator*
March, Wallace Eugene *dean, religious studies educator*
Martin, Janice Lynn *special education educator*
Mohler, Richard Albert, Jr. *academic administrator, theologian*
Schneider, Jayne B. *school librarian*
Swain, Donald Christie *retired university president, history educator*
Walker, Carol Ellen Burton *elementary school educator*

Madisonville
Aubrey, Sherilyn Sue *elementary school educator*
Byrd, Linda Lou Fitzgerald *elementary education educator*

Magnolia
Mather, Donna Cottrell *secondary school educator*

Maysville
Hunter, Nancy Donehoo *education educator*

Mc Kee
Carroll, Angela Christine *vocational and home economics educator*

Middlesboro
Jarvis, JoAnn Helton *counselor*

Morehead
Daulton, Marietta *education educator*

Mount Washington
Williams, Kathryn Sanders *elementary education administrator*

Murray
Bumgardner, Cloyd Jeffrey *school principal*

Herndon, Donna Ruth Grogan *educational administrator*

Newport
Clinkenbeard, James Howard *principal*

Nicholasville
Crouch, Dianne Kay *secondary school guidance counselor*

Owensboro
Hicks, Judith M. *secondary education educator*
Hooks, Vandalyn Lawrence *former elementary school educator*
Norris, Melanie Thomas *secondary education educator*

Owenton
Traylor, Shirley Kincaid *secondary school educator*

Pembroke
Brame, Tracey Anne *elementary education educator*

Radcliff
Lewis, Mary Carol *early childhood educator*

Richmond
Funderburk, H(enry) Hanly, Jr. *college president*

Saint Matthews
Bickel, Ted, Jr. *secondary school educator*

Shelbyville
Medley, Deborah Langley *elementary and secondary education educator*

Somerset
Caldwell, Donna Frances *elementary education educator*
Kincaid, Carolyn Wade *special education educator*

Tyner
Fields, Wanda Lee *special education educator*

Union
Cook, Janice Eleanor Nolan *elementary school educator*
Wiener, Kathleen Marie *elementary education educator*

Vanceburg
Phillips, Susan Diane *secondary school educator*

Wilmore
Hoag, David Alan *academic administrator, fundraising consultant*

Winchester
Dulin, Teresa Dianne *primary school educator*
Stephenson, Joseph Anderson *vocational school educator*

LOUISIANA

Arnaudville
Davis, Jessie Pavy *secondary English educator*
Prejean, Louise Marie *elementary school educator*

Baton Rouge
Bennett, Toni Zimmer *special education educator*
Branton, David Carl *secondary school educator, consultant*
Copping, Allen Anthony *university president*
Doty, Gresdna Ann *education educator*
Foley, Helen Claiborne *university administrator*
Hargrove, Gail Annette *educational administrator*
Harrelson, Clyde Lee *secondary school educator*
Jones, Mary Elizabeth *school counselor*
Kelly, Mary Joan *librarian*
Montgomery, Judy G(lass) *child care center executive*
Rabideau, Peter Wayne *university dean, chemistry educator*

Bogalusa
Barges, Daisy Teress *special education educator*

Bossier City
Darling, Shannon Ferguson *special education educator*

Chalmette
Dysart, Diana Barcelona *school system administrator*

Covington
Heinz, Dollie Wooley *secondary education educator*

Destrehan
Bruce, Rickie Joseph *secondary school educator, gifted and talented educator*
Greene, Glen Lee, Jr. *secondary school educator*

Hammond
Sellers, Beverly Burch *university administrator*
Smith, Grant Warren, II *academic administrator, physical sciences educator*

Harahan
Meisner, Jennifer Lee *secondary school educator*

Houma
Cortez, Martin Lynn *assistant principal*

Kenner
Moghis, Cherie Lynn *elementary school educator, marketing professional*
Regan, Siri Lisa Lambourne *gifted education educator*

Lafayette
Asher, Inness *college educator, author*
Authement, Ray P. *college president*
Clemons, Maggie Ruth *elementary school educator*
Cosper, Sammie Wayne *educational consultant*
Gorelick, Risa Paige *secondary education educator*

Petry, Ruth Vidrine *assistant principal*
Rieck, William Albert *secondary school educator, professor*

Lake Charles
Bradley, Judy Faye *elementary school educator*
Dronet, Virgie Mae *educational technology educator*
Fields, Anita *dean*
Hebert, Robert D. *academic administrator*

Logansport
Thomas, Jimmie Kay *secondary education educator*

Mandeville
Arrowsmith, Marian Campbell *secondary education educator*

Marrero
Cole, Louis B. *retired educator*
Love, Gayle Magalene *special education educator, adult education educator*

Metairie
Wagner, Samuel, V *secondary school English language educator*

Monroe
Burton, Joe Ella *elementary educator, dance educator*
Taylor, James Albert *university administrator*

Napoleonville
Jones, Leslie Faye *secondary mathematics education educator*

Natchitoches
Reeves, Mary Elizabeth *education educator, researcher*
Ryan, Lois Agnes *secondary mathematics educator*
Wolfe, George Cropper *private school educator, artist, author*

New Iberia
Ledbetter, Deidre Leday *special education educator*
Thornton, Don Ray *gifted education educator, poet, artist*

New Llano
Boren, Lynda Sue *gifted education educator*

New Orleans
Brazier, Mary Margaret *psychology educator, researcher*
Carter, James Clarence *university administrator*
Chambers, Thomas Edward *college president, psychologist*
Danahar, David C. *academic administrator, history educator*
Garrity, Raymond Joseph *community college administrator, consultant*
Gery, John Roy Octavius *secondary education educator*
Gipe, Joan Patricia *education educator*
Johnson, Clifford Vincent *college administrator*
Kelly, Eamon Michael *university president*
Levitt, Gregory Alan *education educator*
McCall, John Patrick *college president, educator*
Melton, Judy Pierotti *university official*
O'Brien, Gregory Michael St. Lawrence *university official*
Parikh, Arvindkumar Madhavlal *education educator, video producer*
Payton, Annie Malessia *librarian*
Ross, Brenda Marie *elementary school educator*
Ross, Kathleen *secondary school educator, author, consultant*
Vanselow, Neal Arthur *university administrator, physician*
Wetzel, Albert John *university executive, systems engineer, former air force officer, consultant*
Zeigler, Jeanine Bahram Patton *guidance counselor*

Pearl River
Pendarvis, Donna Kaye *elementary secondary school educator, adminstrator*

Port Sulphur
Riley, Alison Ducro *middle school educator*

Quitman
Davis, Ella Delores *special education educator, elementary school educator*

Ruston
Benedict, Barry Arden *dean*
Reneau, Daniel D. *university administrator*

Saint Gabriel
Knight, Diane *special education educator*

Shreveport
Driscoll, Barbara Hampton *special education educator*
Ferrell, Michael Timothy *academic administration*
Gates, Daryl Lamar *special education educator, musician*
Whitehead, Barbara Ann *secondary school educator*
Zaporozhetz, Laurene Elizabeth *dean, librarian, educator*

Slidell
Dabdoub, Paul Oscar *academic administrator*
Gatlin, Linda Sue *secondary educator*
Sanders, Georgia Elizabeth *secondary school educator*
Schofield, Barbara Curtright *school administrator*
Troxclair, Debra Ann *gifted education educator*

Welsh
Lyons, Cynthia Dianne *special education educator, lecturer*

Winnfield
Koeppen, Kevin Michael *counseling consultant*

Zachary
Mustiful, Curtis James *education educator*

MISSISSIPPI

Batesville
Carter, Gail Marie *special education educator*

Biloxi
Manners, Pamela Jeanne *middle school educator*
Simpson, Elizabeth Ann *reading and language arts educator*

Cleveland
Baker-Branton, Camille B. *counselor, educator*
Mohd Zain, A. Zaidy *academic administrator*
Wyatt, Forest Kent *university president*

Clinton
Mc Farland, Martha Ann *education educator*

Columbus
Rent, Clyda Stokes *academic administrator*

Forest
Knowles, Carolyn Sue Edwards *secondary education educator*

Gulfport
Daffron, Martha *retired education educator*
Knowles-Smith, Jaime Ann *elementary school educator*

Hattiesburg
Armstrong, Sarah Price *librarian*
Diket, Mary Read M. *academic administrator, educator*
Fleming, Horace Weldon, Jr. *higher education administrator, educator*
Lucas, Aubrey Keith *university president*
Miller, April D. *special education educator*
Phillips, Lyn Walters *secondary education educator*

Itta Bena
Sutton, William W. *university administrator, biology educator*

Jackson
Anglin, Linda McCluney *elementary school educator*
Burnham, Tom *state school system administrator*
Corry, Barbara Prather *developmental center administrator*
Everly, Jane *gifted education educator*
Imhoff, Robert Jay *educational administrator*
Jones, Mattie Saunders *secondary school educator*
Peirce, Anne Griswold *dean*
Rogers, Oscar Allan, Jr. *academic administrator*

Laurel
Malone, Carolyn DeLoris *elementary education educator*

Liberty
Filbert, Eleanor Jane *special education educator*

Long Beach
Paola, Carol Western *gifted education educator*
White, Edith Roberta Shoemake *elementary school educator*

Lorman
Waters, Rudolph Earl *university administrator*
Williams, Robert LeEdward *academic administrator, dean*

Lucedale
Rouse, Edna Frances *special education educator*

Meridian
Hoskins, Mable Rose *secondary education educator, English language educator*
Reed, Vanessa Regina *secondary education educator*

Mississippi State
Hare, Rufus Dwight *education educator*
Hughes, Patricia Newman *academic administrator*
Powe, Ralph Elward *university administrator*
Watson, James Ray, Jr. *education educator*
Zacharias, Donald Wayne *academic administrator*

Natchez
Pendergrast, Brynda Marie *elementary school educator*
Profice, Rosena Mayberry *elementary school educator*

Nettleton
Hairald, Mary Payne *vocational education educator, coordinator*

Okolona
Rupert, Daniel Leo *elementary education administrator*

Oxford
Knight, Aubrey Kevin *vocational education educator*

Pascagoula
McKee, Ronald Gene *vocational education educator*
Singh, Balwant *secondary education educator*

Starkville
Hunt, Pamela Stafford *secondary school educator*
Roberts, Willard John *secondary school educator*

Terry
Smith, Sheila *secondary education educator*

Tylertown
Alford, Linda Conerly *elementary education educator*

University
Khayat, Robert C. *chancellor*
Lindgren, Carl Edwin *educational consultant, antiquarian, photographer*
Meador, John Milward, Jr. *university dean*

Vicksburg
Ellis, Donnell *elementary school principal*
Keulegan, Emma Pauline *special education educator*

Trigg, Glyn Ray *guidance counselor, educational administrator*

Waveland
Jackson, Judith Ann *elementary education educator*

Whitfield
Whitehead, Zelma Kay *special education educator*

Yazoo City
Cartlidge, Shriley Ann Bell *school administrator*

MISSOURI

Branson
White, Raye Mitchell *educational administrator*

NEW HAMPSHIRE

Rindge
Palmer, Bruce Harrison *college director*

NEW JERSEY

Oakland
Butterfield, Charles Edward, Jr. *educational consultant*

NEW YORK

Kingston
Steller, Arthur Wayne *educational administrator*

NORTH CAROLINA

Ahoskie
Moore, Clemmie Archer *elementary school educator*

Asheville
Bryson, Paula Kay *secondary school educator*
Edmonds, Max Earl *secondary education educator*
Rains, Curtis Ray *educational administrator*
Rodman, Richard Eugene *associate dean*
Teitelbaum, Daniel Joseph *secondary education educator*

Boone
Howe, Richard Davis *academic administrator, professor, leadership in educational studies*
Roytman, Grigory *education educator*

Buies Creek
Wallace, Jerry McLain *academic administrator*
Wiggins, Norman Adrian *university administrator, legal educator*

Camden
Stone, Delores Barrow *special education educator*

Canton
Furci, Joan Gelormino *early childhood education educator*

Cary
Bat-haee, Mohammad Ali *educational administrator, consultant*
Beals, Betsy Jones *elementary school educator*

Chapel Hill
Campbell, B(obby) Jack *university official*
Carroll, Roy *academic administrator*
Clark, David Louis *education educator, author*
Cross, Dennis Wayne *academic administrator*
Cunningham, James William *literacy education educator, researcher*
Edwards, David Nesbit, Jr. *university administrator*
Fordham, Christopher Columbus, III *university dean and chancellor, medical educator*
Friday, William Clyde *university president emeritus*
Simmons, Michael Anthony *dean*
Spangler, Clemmie Dixon, Jr. *academic administrator*
Ware, William Brettel *education educator*
Weiss, Patricia Finnerty *educational consultant*

Charlotte
Adcock, Scotty Wilson *elementary education educator*
Eppley, Frances Fielden *retired secondary school educator, author*
Gulledge, Karen Stone *educational administrator*
Hardin, Elizabeth Ann *academic administrator*
Lockhart, Lillie Walker *retired primary school educator*
Middleton, Silvia Gilbert *dean, engineering educator*
Phillips, Sandra Allen *primary school educator*
Spear, Andrea Ashford *principal, educator*
Waldrep, Leigh Barnhardt *primary school educator*
Witzel, Barbara Binion *elementary education educator*
Woodward, James Hoyt *academic administrator, engineer*

China Grove
Hall, Telka Mowery Elium *educational administrator*

Clinton
Friedman, Deborah Leslie White *educational administrator*

Clyde
Rogers, Frances Nichols *assistant principal*

Cullowhee
Corbin, Renee Perry *university administrator*
Coulter, Myron Lee *retired academic administrator*
DePaolo, Rosemary *college dean*
Reed, Alfred Douglas *university director*

Davidson
Kuykendall, John Wells *academic administrator, educator*

Deep Gap
Tompkins, James Richard *special education educator*

Denver
Higbie, Patricia D. *assistant principal*

Durham
Abernathy, Margaret Denny *elementary school educator*
Bechtel-Hoopes, Brenda Jean *educator English, biology, environmental chemistry*
Chambers, Julius LeVonne *academic administrator, lawyer*
Dowell, Earl Hugh *university dean, aerospace and mechanical engineering educator*
Horner, John Edward *former college president*
Horowitz, Judith Anne *dean*
Keohane, Nannerl Overholser *university president, political scientist*
Lindsey, Lydia *education educator, researcher*
Mullikin, Kent Roberts *academic administrator*
Ringer, Catharina Win *elementary education educator*
Schmalbeck, Richard Louis *university dean, lawyer*
Steckley, Linda Goodridge *university official*

Elon College
Barner, John Charles *academic administrator*

Falcon
Forehand, Robert Jackson *education administrator*

Fayetteville
Datta, Rama D. *education educator*
Ogilvie, Margaret Pruett *former school counselor, marriage counselor*

Four Oaks
Wiggs, Shirley JoAnn *secondary school educator*

Goldsboro
Kelly, Edward John, V *counselor*

Graham
Corbett, Lenora Meade *community college educator*
Lancaster, Carolyn Hohn *secondary school educator*

Greensboro
Derosa, Donald V. *academic administrator*
Lyons, Charles Henry *academic director*
McIntosh, Michael Lorenzo *principal*
Mosier, Stephen Russell *college program director, physicist*
Prodan, James Christian *university administrator*
Rogers, William Raymond *college president emeritus, psychology educator*
Wright, John Spencer *school system administrator*

Greenville
Eakin, Richard Ronald *academic administrator, mathematics educator*
Leggett, Donald Yates *academic administrator*
Leggett, Nancy Porter *university official*
Powers, Evelyn Mae *education educator*
Zauner, Christian Walter *university dean, exercise physiologist, consultant*

Hamlet
Walker, Wanda Gail *special education educator*

Hickory
Parsons, Eileen Carlton *science education educator*
Sims, Janette Elizabeth Lowman *educational director*

High Point
Farlow, Joel Wray *school system administrator*
Koelb, Christina Holding *elementary education educator*
Martinson, Jacob Christian, Jr. *academic administrator*

Hillsborough
Buckla, Robert Joseph *college administrator, consultant*
Dula, Rosa Lucile Noell *retired secondary education educator*
Stockstill, James William *secondary school educator*

Hudson
Boham, Kenneth Arnold *academic administrator*

Huntersville
Canipe, Stephen Lee *principal*

Kannapolis
Hyatt, Cathy Beaver *elementary school educator*

Lexington
Miller, Steven Arthur *academic administrator*

Liberty
Feaster, Charlotte Josephine S. *school administrator*

Lincolnton
Saine, Betty Boston *elementary school educator*

Lowell
Davis, Frank William, Jr. *elementary and secondary school educator*

Lumberton
Harding, Barry *school system administrator, educational consultant*

Marion
Bergemann, Verna Elmyra *education educator*

Matthews
Benton, Faye Louise *child care administrator*

Mocksville
Chapman, Jennifer Boersema *elementary school educator*

Monroe
McCollum, Nancy Edwards *vocational educator*
Rorie, Nancy Katheryn *elementary and secondary school educator*

Mooresville
Neill, Rita J. *elementary school educator*

Morganton
Rader, Todd David *elementary education educator*

Mount Airy
Short, Linda Matthews *reading educator*

Mount Olive
Ostheim, Phillis Quinn *secondary education administrator*

Murfreesboro
Brett, Mauvice Winslow *retired educational administrator, consultant*
Gowler, David Brian *dean*
Whitaker, Bruce Ezell *college president*

New Bern
Hemphill, Jean Hargett *college dean*

Newton
Elliott, Anne Nixon *gifted and talented education educator*

Old Fort
Yarbrough, Vickie Jane *elementary reading specialist*

Pope AFB
Vaughan, Clyde Vernelson *program director*

Raleigh
Burris, Craven Allen *education educator*
Dornan, John Neill *public policy center professional*
Howell, Bruce Inman *academic administrator*
Hunter, Wiley Leigh *middle school educator*
Jenkins, Clauston Levi, Jr. *college president*
Keyes, Joyce Ann Hester *academic director, consultant, researcher*
Leggett, Eugenia Harris *college director*
Monteith, Larry King *university chancellor*
Parker, Wetonah Rice *education educator, consultant*
Poulton, Bruce Robert *former university chancellor*
Reeves, Terry K. Price *college administrator*
Serow, Robert Charles *education educator, writer, consultant*
Shaw, Talbert O. *university president*
Taylor, Raymond George, Jr. *educator*
Upton, Sharon Lakin *university program director*

Roaring River
Byrd, Ida Fay *college official*

Rocky Mount
Hardy, Linda Lea Sterlock *media specialist*
Jackson, Reed McSwain *educational administrator*
Sulfaro, Joyce A. *parochial school educator*
Van Kuren, Nancy Ellen *academic administrator*

Rosman
Dutton, Sharon Gail *elementary school educator*

Rutherfordton
Conley, Katherine Logan *religious studies educator*
Metcalf, Ethel Edgerton *elementary school educator*

Spruce Pine
Rensink, Jacqueline B. *secondary school educator*

Statesville
Rivers-Lucey, Amanda Hope *elementary school educator*

Taylorsville
Leonhardt, Debbie Ann *counselor, writer, minister*

Troy
Bailey, Larry Ronald *elementary school educator*

Wake Forest
Buchanan, Edward A. *education educator*

Warrenton
Spence, Faye Yvonne *elementary school educator*

Waynesville
Wangberg, Louis M. *academic administrator*

Weaverville
Boyce, Emily Stewart *retired library and information science educator*

Wendell
Ludwick, Mike John *secondary education educator*

Wilmington
Leutze, James Richard *academic administrator, television producer and host*
McAllister, Nancy Hardacre *music academy administrator*
Rorison, Margaret Lippitt *reading consultant*

Wilson
Bailey, Grace Daniel *retired secondary school educator*
Morris, Sharon Louise Stewart *former day care provider*

Winston Salem
Crowder, Lena Belle *retired special education educator*
Grogg, Sam *dean*
Harkrader, Sue Robertson *secondary school educator*
Hearn, Thomas K., Jr. *academic administrator*
Hill, Alton McKiver *university official, small business owner*
Jarrell, Iris Bonds *elementary school educator, business executive*
Mabe, Sharon Russell Applegate *academic official*
Roth, Marjory Joan Jarboe *special education educator*
Sayers, Martha McCray *retired secondary school educator*
Suttles, Donald Roland *academic administrator, business educator*
Thompson, Cleon F., Jr. *university administrator*

OHIO

Cincinnati
Zimmerman, Sheldon *college president, rabbi*

Oxford
Souder, Annette Denise *secondary education educator*

OKLAHOMA

Ada
Dennison, Ramona Pollan *special education educator*
Gray, Edna Jane *elementary education educator*
Groves, Noralene Katherine *elementary school educator*
Sukholutskaya, Mara Emmanuilovna *secondary education educator*

Altus
Hensley, Stephen Ray *academic administrator*

Bartlesville
Chambers, Imogene Klutts *school system administrator, financial consultant*
Sauter, Marsha Jeanne *elementary school educator*
Woodruff, Wanda Lea *elementary education educator*

Bethany
Crabtree, John Michael *college administrator, consultant*
Reinbold, Janice Kay *school librarian*

Broken Arrow
Roberson, Deborah Kay *secondary school educator*
Stirling, Jo Lynn *special education educator*

Broken Bow
Ivie, Brenda Karen *adult literacy educator*

Claremore
McClain, Marilyn Russell *admission and retention counselor*

Coweta
Mannon, Carolyn Sue *elementary school educator, reading specialist*

Drummond
Harris, Joyce Faye *elementary education educator*

Durant
Barnes, Sheila Kaye *educator, consultant*
Christy, David Hardacker *secondary school educator, music educator*
Decker, Barbara Cooper *education educator*
Williams, Larry Bill *academic administrator*

Edmond
Harryman, Rhonda L. *education educator*
Merriott, Vicki Ann *elementary and secondary education teacher*
Woods, Donna Sue *education educator, reading consultant, state agency administrator*
Zabel, Vivian Ellouise *secondary education educator*

Enid
Dyche, Kathie Louise *secondary school educator*
Warkentien, Paul David *electronics technology educator*

Guthrie
Dowdy, Fredella Mae *secondary school educator*

Harrah
Roberts, Gerry Rea *elementary school educator, organist*

Keota
Davis, Thomas Pinkney *secondary school educator*

Lawton
Cates, Dennis Lynn *education educator*
Mabry, Dorothy Mae *elementary school principal*
McKeown, Rebecca J. *principal*

Maramec
Blair, Marie Lenore *retired elementary school educator*

Midwest City
Saulmon, Sharon Ann *librarian*

Moore
Eaton, Timothy Walter *college dean, minister*

Muskogee
Felts, Joan April *elementary school educator*
Meyer, Billie Jean *special education educator*

Ninnekah
Wilson, Ginger *elementary education educator*

Norman
Boren, David Lyle *academic administrator*
Gertsch, William Darrell *university research administrator, consultant*
Jones, Charlotte *principal*
Stover, Curtis Sylvester *retired vocational school educator*
Van Horn, Richard Linley *academic administrator*
Zapffe, Nina Byrom *retired elementary education educator*

Oklahoma City
Bollman, Jeanette Vogt *learning disabilities educator*
Brady-Black, Wandalene *secondary school educator*
Burton, Charles *elementary school principal*

Butler, Suzanne B. *secondary education educator*
Clark, Carter Blue *university administrator*
Dooley-Hanson, Barbara Ann *special education educator*
Hansen, John Henry *secondary school teacher*
Harlin-Fischer, Gayle C. *elementary education educator*
Harper, Sandra Stecher *university administrator*
Johnson, Lonnie *special education educator*
Kraker, Deborah Schovanec *special education educator*
Noakes, Betty L. *retired elementary school educator*
Nokes, Mary Triplett *former university president, counselor, artist*
Smith, Clodus Ray *academic administrator*
Waldo, Catherine Ruth *private school educator*
Walker, Jerald Carter *university administrator, minister*
Weir, Richard Dale *elementary education educator*
Wilson, Jim V. *school system administrator*

Paden
Adams, Darlene Agnes *secondary education educator*

Picher
Scott, Rilla Rebecca *special education educator*

Piedmont
Roberts, Kathleen Mary *school system administrator*

Ponca City
Poole, Richard William, Jr. *secondary school educator*
Scott, Carol Lee *child care educator*

Prague
Stefansen, Peggy Ann *special education educator*

Sallisaw
Morris, Michele Dian *secondary education educator*

Sapulpa
Houghton, Phyllis Sue *vocational school educator*

Shawnee
Agee, Bob R. *university president, educator, minister*
Hill, Bryce Dale *school administrator*

Stillwater
Allen, Timothy Michael *secondary education educator*
Bryant, John Hulon *education educator*
Hayes, Kevin Gregory *university administrator*
Shaklee, Toni Sue *university administrator*
Webster, David Steven *education educator*

Tahlequah
Duncan, Janice Marie *education educator*
Hill, Helen Katherine *librarian, educator*
Webb, W. Roger *university president*

Tulsa
Barnes, Cynthia Lou *gifted education educator*
Buthod, Mary Clare *school administrator*
Christopher, Michael Mayer *secondary education development director*
Donaldson, Robert Herschel *university administrator, educator*
Graber, John Paul *elementary education educator*
Hamilton, Carl Hulet *academic administrator*
Kukura, Rita Anne *elementary school educator*
Rosamond, Sandra Pauline (Sandi Rosamond) *secondary education educator*
Smith, Penny *middle school educator*
Undernehr, Laura Lee *elementary education educator*
Wood, Emily Churchill *gifted and talented education educator*

Wheatland
Nance, Retha Hardison *reading specialist*

Woodward
Selman, Minnie Corene Phelps *elementary school educator*

OREGON

Portland
Leupp, Edythe Peterson *retired education educator, administrator*

PENNSYLVANIA

New Hope
Ford, Kelly Curtis *educational consultant*

Wyomissing
Moran, William Edward *academic administrator*

SOUTH CAROLINA

Aiken
Alexander, Robert Earl *university chancellor, educator*
Salter, David Wyatt *secondary school educator*
Sheppard, Deborah Cody *hearing handicapped educator, clinician*
Tully, Susan Sturgis *adult education educator*
Zubillaga, Jose Gustavo *education specialist*

Allendale
Clayton, Carl A. *university dean*

Anderson
Sayegh, Glenda Faye *elementary school educator*

Ballentine
McMahon, Dennis Owen *school superintendent*

Batesburg
Covington, Tammie Warren *elementary education educator*

Beaufort
Plyler, Chris Parnell *dean*
Sheldon, Jeffrey Andrew *college official*

Bennettsville
McLeod, Marilynn Hayes *educational administrator, farmer*

Blackville
Tobin, Shirley Ann *elementary school educator*

Cayce
McGill, Cathy Broome *gifted and talented education educator*

Central
Sinnamon, Walter Bruce *college administrator, biology educator*

Charleston
Bellack, Janis Peacock *university official*
Cleghorn, G. Dean *university official, educator*
Gay, Frances Marion Welborn *private school educator*
Greenberg, Raymond Seth *academic administrator, educator*
Gunn, Morey Walker, Jr. *secondary school educator, choir director, organist*
Joczik, Mark Tametomo *program director*
Kinard, Fredrick William *retired college dean*
Malloy, Phoebe Smalls *secondary school educator*
Mauldin, Mary Power *academic administrator*
Sanders, Tence Lee Walker *elementary education educator*
Sarasohn, Evelyn Lois Lipman *principal*
Simms, Lois Averetta *retired secondary education educator, musician*
Suggars, Candice Louise *special education educator*
Voorneveld, Richard Burke *education educator, college official*

Clemson
Hipps, Opal Shepard *dean, nursing educator*
Underwood, Sandra Jane *planning and management director*
Yukish, Joseph Francis *education educator*

Clinton
Simmons, Sharon Dianne *elementary education educator*

Columbia
Broome, Michael Cortes *college administrator*
Dixon, Albert King, II *university administrator*
Felix, Judith Joan *elementary educator*
Fields, Harriet Gardin *counselor, educator, consultant*
Goblirsch, Kurt Gustav *foreign language educator*
Hause, Edith Collins *college administrator*
King, John Ethelbert, Jr. *education educator, former academic administrator*
LeClair, Betty Jo Cogdill *special education and early childhood educator*
Lefton, Lester Alan *dean, psychology educator*
Mbuh, Rebecca Neh *university administrator*
Palms, John Michael *academic administrator, physicist*
Pruitt, Dennis Alan *educational administrator, consultant*
Vinel, Catherine Davis *elementary education educator*

Conway
Sarvis, Elaine Magann *assistant principal*
Wiseman, Dennis Gene *university dean*

Estill
Exum, Cynthia Phillips *headmaster*

Florence
Boggs, David Glenn, Jr. *early childhood educator*
Rutherford, Vicky Lynn *special education educator*

Fort Mill
Lisk, Anne Murray *daycare owner, administrator, educator*

Fountain Inn
James, Jeannie Henrietta *education educator*

Gaffney
Davis, Lynn Hambright *culinary arts educator*

Garnett
McKenzie, Melba Hughes *gifted and talented education educator*

Goose Creek
Boland, Barbara *counselor*

Greenville
Alford, Robert Wilfrid, Jr. *elementary school educator*
Donalley, Judith D. *education educator*
Hill, Grace Lucile Garrison *education educator, consultant*
Huff, Archie Vernon, Jr. *college administrator*
Jenkins, Ronald Vance *university administrator*
Jones, Robert Thaddues *principal*
Jordan, Betty Sue *retired special education educator*
Norris, Joan Clafette Hagood *elementary school educator*
Whitmire, John Lee *daycare provider*
Winstead, Philip Connor *education educator, university administrator*

Greenwood
Fullard, Daniel *business education educator, retired, financial secretary*
Williams, Sylvester Emanual, III *elementary school educator, consultant*

Hartsville
Daniels, James Douglas *academic administrator*

Hilton Head Island
Lachenauer, Robert Alvin *retired school superintendent*
Mulhollan, Paige Elliott *academic administrator emeritus*

Ladson
Cannon, Major Tom *special education educator*

Lake City
Hawkins, Linda Parrott *school system administrator*

Mullins
Reaves, Franklin C. *secondary school educator*

North Charleston
Carnell, Claude Mitchell, Jr. *academic administrator*

North Myrtle Beach
Cassidy, Dorothy Ann *special education educator*

Orangeburg
Briggman, Jessie B. *special education educator*
Creekmore, Verity Veirs *media specialist*

Pickens
Perry, Jean Peters *elementary school principal*

Ridge Spring
Puryear, Arlene Scurry *elementary school educator*

Rock Hill
Brown, Betsy Etheridge *dean*
Mitlin, Laurance Robert *university dean, educator*
Wishert, Jo Ann Chappell *elementary and secondary education educator*

Saluda
Nussbaumer, Melany Hamilton *program director*

Shaw AFB
Mingo, Joe Louis *elementary school educator*

Simpsonville
Anderson, Martha Jean *media specialist*
Dean, Virginia Agee *principal*

Society Hill
King, Amanda Arnette *elementary school educator*

Spartanburg
Moore, Charles Gerald *educational administrator*
Moore, Wanda C. *college administrator*
Todd, John Dickerson, III *special education administrator*

Sumter
Abbott, Vicky Lynn *educational administrator*
Bach, Linda Wallinga *special education educator*
Bligen, Corine Illery *elementary school educator*
Coon, William Aaron *assistant principal*

Timmonsville
McDonald, Robert Irving *secondary education mathematics and science educator*

Wagener
Gantt, Phyllis Crowley *secondary education educator*

Westminster
Duncan, Gwendolyn McCurry *elementary education educator*

Woodruff
Byrd, LaVerne *elementary school educator*

York
Clinch, Nicholas *assistant principal*

TENNESSEE

Alcoa
Widner, Nelle Ousley *retired elementary education educator*

Antioch
Wisehart, Mary Ruth *academic administrator*

Birchwood
Blankenship, Ronnelle Eaves *elementary education educator*

Blountville
Walters, Gregory Norman *college administrator*

Bluff City
Anderson, William Harvey, Jr. *secondary education educator*

Bolivar
Graham, Carolyn Jones *elementary school administrator*

Brentwood
May, Deborah Lynn *secondary school educator*

Brownsville
Scott-Wilson, Susan Rice *principal*

Camden
Allen, Wanda Ruth *secondary school educator*

Centerville
Bulison, Jerry Wayne *superintendent*

Chattanooga
Daves, Jada Ledford *secondary education educator, motivational speaker*
Evans, Philip Rodney *educator*
Fortenberry, Elizabeth Waller *private school educator*
Gough, Jessie Post (Mrs. Herbert Frederick Gough) *retired education educator*
Nunley, Malinda Vaughn *retired elementary school educator*
Obear, Frederick Woods *academic administrator*
Powell, Patricia Ann *secondary school educator*
Rende, Toni Lynn *principal, counselor*
Woodward, Michael Vaughan *secondary education educator*

Chuckey
Casteel, DiAnn Brown *elementary school educator*

Clarksville
Bowers, Carolyn Powers *business and office education educator*

Cleveland
Hixson, Doris Kennedy *secondary education educator*
Lawson, Billie Katherine *elementary school educator*
Owens, Kelly Ann *elementary education educator*

Collegedale
McClarty, Jack Lee *academic administrator*

Collinwood
Thrasher, Billie Lee *school counselor*

Columbia
Cantrell, Sharron Caulk *secondary school educator*
Loper, Linda Sue *learning resources center director*

Cookeville
Bailey, Carolyn Sue Dodson *home economics educator, apparel designer*
Porter, Wilma Jean *university director*
Volpe, Angelo Anthony *university administrator, chemistry educator*

Cordova
Atkeison, Barbara Jean Garrison *university administrator*
Kern, Angeline Frazier *educational administrator*

Denmark
Petty, Alyce Miller *elementary school educator*

Elkton
Newman, Sharon Lynn *elementary education educator*

Englewood
Jones, Vivian M. *secondary and elementary education educator*

Fayetteville
Curry, Nancy Maddox *elementary education educator*

Franklin
Awalt, Marilene Kay *principal*
Daniel, Cathy Brooks *tutor, educational consultant*

Gallatin
Glover, Nancy Elliott *elementary school administrator*
Ramer, Hal Reed *academic administrator*
Whiteside, Ann Birdsong *university public relations director*

Germantown
Seymour, Natasha Denise *secondary education educator*

Goodlettsville
Vatandoost, Nossi Malek *art school administrator*

Harrogate
Miller, Scott Douglas *college president*

Hendersonville
Leslie, Lynn Marie *secondary education educator*
Poynor, Robert Allen, Jr. *guidance counselor*

Hermitage
Wilmore, Faye C. *elementary and secondary education educator*

Humboldt
Moore, Alice Cravens *secondary school educator*

Huntingdon
Hancock, Sandra Olivia *secondary and elementary school educator*

Huntsville
Ellis, Lonnie Calvert *secondary school educator*

Jackson
Bailey, James Andrew *middle school educator*
Barefoot, Hyran Euvene *academic administrator, educator, minister*
Harris, John Robert *secondary education educator*
Headen, Carol Mary Skinner *university administrator*
Lee, Changnam *education educator*
Rahm, Nancy Lee *music education director*
Smith, Jonathan Kennon Thompson *retired academic administrator, volunteer, genealogist*
Toomey, Sheila Crawford *education educator, consultant*
Troupe, Marilyn Kay *education educator*

Jefferson City
Butler, Vickie Burkhart *college official*
Taylor, William Douglas *college administrator*

Johnson City
Nicks, Roy Sullivan *university president*
Paxton, J. Willene *retired university counseling director*
Peterson, Norma Jo *elementary school educator*
Rudder, Bobby Joel *technology educator*

Jonesborough
Broyles, Ruth Rutledge *principal*
Sisk, Zenobia Ann *secondary school educator*

Kingsport
Fuzek, Bettye Lynn *secondary education educator*
Walton, Willard Fred *principal*

Kingston
Alexander, Deborah Radford *elementary education administrator*

Knoxville
Anderson, Yasmin Lynn Mullis *educational consultant, small business owner*
Bodenheimer, Sally Nelson *reading educator*
Bryant, Gay Davis *office systems educator*
Cooke, Suzanne Gamsby *middle school educator*
Griffin, Mary Jane Ragsdale *educational consultant, writer, small business owner*
Harris, Roland Arsville, Jr. *college official*
Mays, Kate S. *primary education educator*
Moor, Anne Dell *education director*
Moran, James D., III *child development educator, university administrator*
Ratliff, Eva Rachel *elementary education educator*
Reynolds, Marjorie Lavers *secondary school educator*
Reynolds, Megan Beahm *primary and elementary education educator*
South, Stephen A. *academic administrator*
Stoneking, Jerry Edward *dean*
Stooksbury, Jayne Moyer *special education educator*

Lafayette
Flynn, David Wayne *secondary school educator*

Lebanon
Whittle, Melissa Sue *kindergarten educator*

Manchester
Woodworth, Gene Boswell *public school educator, writer*

Martin
Byford, James Lloyd *dean*
Smith, Robert Mason *university dean*

Maryville
Cate, Catherine Eleanor *college administrator, educator*

Mc Minnville
Henry, Mary Lou Smelser *elementary education educator*

Memphis
Daughdrill, James Harold, Jr. *academic administrator*
Flowers, Kathy René *elementary school educator*
Hedgeman, Lulah M. *secondary education educator*
Holmes, Frank Randall *university administrator*
House, Naomi Geraldine (Gerry House) *school system administrator*
James, Linda Green *education specialist administrator, researcher*
Osage, Frank John *university administrator*
Palinchak, Robert Stephen *academic administrator*
Phipps, Carolyn Sisk *secondary educator*
Roberson, William Ralph *dean, artist, educator*
Sigler, Lois Oliver *retired secondary school educator*
Tuggle, Gloria Harris *school system administrator*
Watson, Ada *secondary education educator*
Werle, Robert Geary *academic administrator*

Murfreesboro
Bader, Carol Hopper *developmental studies educator*
Craig, James Donald *dean*
Doyle, Delores Marie *elementary education educator*
Duggin, Nancy Youree *primary school educator*
Paraiso, Johnna Kaye *elementary education educator*
Walker, James E. *academic administrator, educator*

Nashville
Baugher, Kathryn Hester *dean*
Chambers, Carol Tobey *elementary school educator*
Hazelip, Herbert Harold *academic administrator*
Hines, Peggy Dale *middle school educator*
Longhurst, Robert Russell *retired secondary school educator*
Minardi, Raymond Anthony *librarian*
Tremper, Bobbie Jo *special education educator*
Warren, Jerry Lee *academic administrator, conductor*
Weaver, John Lawson, III *vocational education educator*
Whitaker, Evans Parker *academic administrator*
Williams, Carolyn Ruth Armstrong *university official*
Willis, Eleanor Lawson *university official*
Wyatt, Joe Billy *academic administrator*

Newport
Ball, Travis, Jr. *educational systems administrator, consultant, editor*
Runnion, Cindie J. *elementary school educator*

Oak Ridge
O'Neil, Charlotte Cooper *environmental education administrator*

Oliver Springs
Heacker, Thelma Weaks *retired elementary school educator*

Portland
Miller, Sandra Perry *middle school educator*

Sewanee
Kepple, Thomas Ray, Jr. *college administrator*
Lorenz, Anne Partee *special education educator, consultant*
Patterson, William Brown *university dean, history educator*

Shelbyville
Austin, Margaret Cully *school administrator*

Signal Mountain
Efaw, Suzanne Hall *elementary school educator*

Soddy Daisy
Hamrick, Rita Gale *elementary school educator*
Watson, James Stanley *secondary education educator*

Sparta
Langford, Jack Daniel *elementary school educator*

Unicoi
Hatcher, James Mitchell *principal*

TEXAS

Abilene
Booth, Linda Leigh *vocational educator*
Crymes, Mary Cooper *secondary school educator*
Kim, Thomas Kunhyuk *college administrator*
Merrell, David Boles *registrar*
Shimp, Robert Everett, Jr. *academic administrator, historian*
Wallace, Linda Jo *elementary education educator*

Alamo
Forina, Maria Elena *gifted education educator*

Aledo
Lindsay, John, IV *principal*

Alpine
Ortego y Gasca, Felipe de *education educator*

Alvin
Dojahn, Julie Goodman *secondary school educator*
Johnson, Dennis Burl *secondary school educator*

Amarillo
Lanier, Roger Alan *regional dean*
Sutterfield, Deborah Kay *special education educator*
Taylor, Mary Lee *college administrator*

Andrews
Scarbrough, Glenda Judith *elementary education educator*

Angleton
Hejl, James George *principal*

Apple Springs
Worley, James Floyd *school system administrator, educator*

Arlington
Gray, David A. *college educator*
Hawkins, Robert A. *college administrator*
Last, Susan Walker *curriculum developer*
Meiners, Roger Evert *university administrator, researcher*
Newby, Steven Ray *headmaster*

Atascosa
Hale, Nancy Annette *kindergarten educator*

Austin
Campbell, Grover Stollenwerck *university official*
Chapa, Jorge *university dean*
Cunningham, William Hughes *academic administrator, marketing educator*
Franklin, Billy Joe *international higher education specialist*
Grieder, Terence *art history educator, artist*
Haneke, Dianne Myers *education educator*
Hayes, Patricia Ann *university president*
Holmes, Cole E. *graduate admissions administrator*
Jackson, Charles Edward *technologist, educational consultant*
Johnson, Ray Monroe *university medical administrator, physician*
Kane, Ruth Anne *principal*
Kelley, Henry Paul *university administrator, psychology educator*
Lehmann-Carssow, Nancy Beth *secondary school educator, coach*
Lewis, Nancy Louine Lambert *school counselor*
Meier, Enge *preschool educator*
Schumaker, Karen Ann *education and literacy educator*
Schwei, Michael A. *assistant principal*
Selke-Kern, Barbara Ellen *university official, writer*
Sparks, Hugh Cullen *university official*
Warner, David Cook *public affairs educator*
Zimmermann, Charlene Marcella *primary school educator*

Bay City
Peabody, Wanda Nell *secondary school educator*

Baytown
Bigham, Cynthia Dawn *kindergarten educator*
Black, Sarah Joanna Bryan *secondary school educator*
Chudleigh, Norma Lane *adult education educator, genealogy consultant*
Culp, Barbara June *secondary school educator*
Kelling, David Henry *educational administrator, accountant*
Payne, Ruby Krabill *educational director, publisher*

Beaumont
Brentlinger, William Brock *college dean*
Buscher, Henry N. *secondary school educator*
Gilliam, Georgie Ann *primary education educator*
LeBlanc, Earline Hart *special education educator*

Bedford
Zamorano, Wanda Jean *secondary education educator*

Bedias
Williamson, Norma Beth *adult education educator*

Bellaire
Kahlden, Nancy Wargo *director of studies*
Skaggs, Arline Dotson *elementary school educator*

Belton
Andreason, George Edward *university administrator*
Ham, Clarence Edward *university administrator*
Taylor, Tom Allen Bryan *educational consulting firm executive*

Big Spring
Simmons, Lorna Womack *elementary school educator*

Borger
Meyer, Cheryl Lynn *secondary school educator*

Brownsville
Hall, Michael Dale *middle school educator, small business owner*
Lytle, Michael Allen *university administrator, consultant*
Santa-Coloma, Bernardo *secondary school educator, counselor*

Brownwood
DeHay, Jerry Marvin *business educator*
Newbury, Don *university administrator*

Bryan
Voelkel, Jane Claudette *elementary education educator, home economist*

Candelaria
Chambers, Johnnie Lois *elementary school educator, rancher*

Canyon
Long, Russell Charles *academic administrator*

Carrollton
Grimes, Mary Woodworth *special educational consultant*
Grinnell, Paula C. *educational researcher*
Restivo, Janet Di Maria *elementary school educator, education consultant*

Cibolo
Evans, Linda Marie *secondary education educator*

College Station
Adkisson, Perry Lee *university system chancellor*
Bowen, Ray Morris *academic administrator, engineering educator*
Carpenter, Delbert Stanley *educational administration educator*
Gage, E. Dean *university administrator*
Peddicord, Kenneth Lee *academic administrator*
Sadoski, Mark Christian *education educator*

Combes
De La Garza, Joel Santiago *assistant principal*

Commerce
Lutz, Frank Wenzel *education administration educator*
Morris, Jerry Dean *academic administrator*
Travis, Jon Eric *education educator*

Conroe
Corley, Donna Jean *education educator, language arts educator*
Milliff, Karen Champagne *secondary education educator*

Converse
Vontur, Ruth Poth *elementary school educator*

Coppell
Warlick, Karla Jan *school counselor*

Copperas Cove
Wright, David Ray *secondary school educator*

Corpus Christi
Farmer, Lola Kay *middle school educator*
Gentry, Cynthia Sue *childhood education executive*
Grubbs, Donald Ray *educational director, educator, welder*
Gutierrez, Elia Garza *elementary school educator*
Hamrick, Bill Allen *principal, retired*
Krepel, Thomas Leon *dean*
Pérez-Gonzalez, Esmeralda *principal, educator*
Robeau, Sally Garwood *secondary school educator*

Corsicana
Franks, Robert Yates *college administrator*
Orsak, Charlie George *community college administrator*

Cypress
Sorrell, Adrian Lloyd *education educator*

Daingerfield
Nesbitt, Jimmie A. *elementary school educator*

Dalhart
Woods, Roy Landon *principal*

Dallas
Benoit, Joyce Difford *school system administrator*
Berkeley, Betty Life *college educator*
Carmichael, John Craig, Jr. *career counselor*
Cook, Gary Raymond *university president, clergyman*
Davis, Patricia M. *literacy educator*
Dickerson, Mildred Thornhill *public school educator*
Dillard, Mary Katherine *secondary education educator*
Duckworth, Paula Oliver *secondary school educator, freelance artist, writer, photographer*
Green, Hubert Gordon *university dean, pediatrician*
Hare, Kimberly Dawn *communications director*
Hester, Linda Hunt *university dean, counselor*
Hopkins, Zora Clemons *training and development specialist*
Isom, Christina Michelle *early childhood educator*
Jaffe, Sandra Michelle *special education educator*
McLaughlin, Sharon Gail *principal, small business owner*
Olivares, Rosa Maria Guajardo *bilingual educator*
Phillips, Bettie Mae *elementary school educator*
Poindexter, Barbara Glennon *secondary school educator*
Rosato, Michael James *dean, education educator*
Turner, Gerald *academic administrator*
Turner, Robert Gerald *academic administrator*
Walsh, Sarah Feeney *elementary education educator*
Wenrich, John William *college president*
Wheeler, Alvina P. *education educator*
Wilcox, Diane Pou *guidance counselor*

De Soto
Judah, Frank Marvin *school system administrator*

Decatur
Jordan, Linda Susan Darnell *elementary school educator*

Denton
Brownell, Blaine Allison *university administrator, history educator*
Crocker, Betty Charlotte *education educator*
Garner, Dianne Graham *special education consultant, early childhood consultant*
Hurley, Alfred Francis *university administrator, historian, retired career officer*
Johnson, Stanley Webster *college educator*
McDonald-West, Sandi M. *headmaster, consultant*
Palermo, Judy Hancock *elementary school educator*
Pettigrew, Johnnie Delonia *educational diagnostician*
Pickett, Stephen Wesley *university official*
Schumacker, Randall Ernest *educational psychology educator*
Smith, Howard Wellington *education educator, dean*

Edcouch
Uresti, Ronda VeVerka *elementary bilingual education educator*

Edinburg
Avellano, George Paul *academic administrator*
Cardenas, Norma Alicia *secondary school orchestra director, violist, violinist*
Nevarez, Miguel A. *university president*

Egypt
Wynn, John Thomas *retired college president, farming executive, economic consultant*

El Paso
Clarkson, Pamela Jean *elementary school educator*
Hernandez, Roberto Reyes *secondary school educator*
Natalicio, Diana Siedhoff *academic administrator*
Peterson, Sandra Dee *elementary school educator*
Rorie, Charles David, Sr. *college official*
Schecter, Erline Dian *educational administrator*
Waller, Michael Lawrence *headmaster*
Willmarth, Roger A. *academic financial administrator*

Emory
Allen, G. Christy L. *elementary schoool educator*

Euless
Ramsay, Michael Landon *middle school educator*

Fabens
Baker, Sara Ann *vocational education educator*

Farwell
Franse, Jean Lucille *secondary school educator*

Floresville
Migl, Sandra Mitchell *secondary education educator*

Forney
Cass, Barbara Fay *elementary school educator*

Fort Worth
Alland, Lawrence Martin *pastoral counselor, marriage and family therapist*
Bickerstaff, Mina March Clark *university administrator*
Braudaway, Gary Wayne *secondary school educator*
Desha, Doris Hollingsworth *retired elementary education educator*
Diffily, Deborah Lynn *early childhood education educator*
Estes, Carolyn Ann Hull *elementary school educator*
Felán, George Daniel *elementary school educator, education advocate*
Hernandez, Daniel Arthur *elementary school educator*
Jones, Evelene Manns *principal, minister*
Killingsworth, Maxine Armatha *special education educator*
Kitchens, Larry Edwin *university administrator*
Marquez, Hope *school system worker, educator*
Mays, Glenda Sue *retired education educator*
McClure, Connie Diane *elementary school educator*
McKimmey, Martha Anne *elementary education educator*
Plummer, Robert Eugene *educational administrator*
Rainwater, Joyce Kelley *special education educator, consultant*
Ratliff, Erin Sue *elementary education educator*
Scott-Wabbington, Vera V. *elementary school educator*
Tucker, William Edward *academic administrator, minister*
Von Rosenberg, Gary Marcus, Jr. *parochial school educator*
White, Warren Travis *educational consultant firm executive*
Wilson-Webb, Nancy Lou *adult educational administrator*

Freeport
Lopez, Alfredo Saldivar *elementary school educator*

Frisco
Donahoo, Ann Rochelle *elementary education educator*

Galveston
Goodwin, Sharon Ann *academic administrator*
Hawkins, Ida Faye *elementary school educator*
Hayes, Brenda Joyce *school counselor*
Heins, Mary Frances *educational administrator, nun*
Rathburn, Carlisle Baxter, III *college administrator*

Garland
Lockhart, Mary Ann *elementary education educator*
Michaels, Cindy Whitfill (Cynthia G. Michaels) *educational consultant*
Shugart, Jill *school system administrator*
Strozeski, Michael Wayne *director research*
Warner, Douglas Wayne *education educator*

Georgetown
Mock, Marilyn Rhoads *university administrator*
Shilling, Roy Bryant, Jr. *academic administrator*

Gilmer
Brown, Karen Lynn *elementary education educator*

Gladewater
Cox-Beaird, Dian Sanders *middle school educator*

Granbury
Ketron, Carrie Sue *secondary school educator*

Grand Prairie
Craig, Larry Vernon *secondary school educator*

Grapevine
Boyd, Jane Gail *program director*
Hirsh, Cristy J. *school counselor*
Wong, Sylvia Law *preschool education educator*

Hale Center
Courtney, Carolyn Ann *school librarian*

Haltom City
Deering, Brenda Florine *secondary education educator*

Harlingen
Glasgow, Harold Glyn *military academy administrator*

Hearne
Williams, Mary Lee *elementary school educator*

Hillsboro
Auvenshine, William Robert *academic administrator*

Hondo
Sandusky, Camille Martin *special education diagnostician*

Houston
Adams, Elaine Parker *college president*
Beckingham, Kathleen Mary *education educator, researcher*
Berti, Margaret Ann *early childhood education educator*
Bourgeois, Patricia Ann *middle school educator*
Bowden, Nancy Butler *school administrator*
Boyett-Thompson, C. Christine *secondary education educator*
Carroll, Michael M. *academic dean, mechanical engineering educator*
Davis, Bruce Gordon *retired principal*
DiRosa, Linda Mary *education specialist, diagnostic company executive*
Douglass, James *academic administrator*
Doyle, Joseph Francis, III *art educator*
Ehlinger, Janet Ann Dowling *elementary school educator*
Fairbanks, James David *academic administrator*
Fertitta, Robert S. *dean*
Fisher, Janet Warner *secondary school educator*
Friedrich, Katherine Rose *educational researcher*
Fuller, Theodore, Jr. *elementary education educator*
Goerke, Glenn Allen *university administrator*
Gubitz, Stephen Page *university administrator*
Hamilton, Lorraine Rebekah *adult education consultant*
Hill, Lesley Susan *university official*
Hitchman, Cal McDonald, Sr. *secondary education educator*
Holmes, Roscette Yvonne Lewis *educational administrator, consultant*
Jimmar, D'Ann *elementary education educator, fashion merchandiser*
Johnson, Thelma Jean *secondary and elementary education educator*
Kendrick, Robert Warren *university administrator*
Kinnaird, Susan Marie *special education educator*
Lang, Gaydelle Marie *principal*
Lemons, Albert Lee *principal, musician*
Mansell, Joyce Marilyn *special education educator*
May, Beverly *elementary school educator*
Mc Fadden, Joseph Michael *academic administrator*
McNutt, D. Gayle *academic administrator*
Meddleton, Francis Charles *elementary and secondary school educator*
Moore, Teresa Ann *middle school mathematics educator*
Norris, Cynthia Jeanette *education educator*
North, Henry *education educator, consultant*
Pasternak, Joanna Murray *special education and gifted and talented educator*
Paul, Alida Ruth *secondary school educator*
Phillips, Bernice Cecile Golden *retired vocational education educator*
Pickering, James Henry, III *academic administrator*
Pinson, Artie Frances *elementary school educator*
Polhemus, Mary Ann *elementary school principal, educator*
Robertson, Earlene *elementary school educator*
Roos, Sybil Friedenthal *retired elementary school educator*
Sage, Lois Elliott *educational diagnostician*
Sayer, Coletta Keenan *gifted education educator*
Sayers, Kathleen Marie *associate dean*
Sharp, Douglas Andrew *secondary school educator*
van Cleave, Kirstin Dean (Kit van Cleave) *martial arts educator, writer, educator, publishing executive*
Wagner, Charlene Brook *middle school educator, consultant*
Walker, Sammie Lee *retired elementary education educator*
Wallace, Betty Jean *elementary school educator, lay minister*
Ward, Calvin H. *academic director, environmental science educator, federal agency administrator*
Webb, Marty Fox *principal*
Whiting, Martha Countee *retired secondary education educator*
Wilks, William Lee *educator, dean*

Huntsville
Bowers, Elliott Toulmin *university president*
Hopper, Margaret Sue *academic administrator, educational diagnostician, consultant*
Olson, Judith Elaine *education educator*
Saumell-Muñoz, Rafael E. *secondary education educator*

Irving
Bielss, Otto William, Jr. *secondary school educator*
McVay, Barbara Chaves *secondary education mathematics educator*

Jasper
Warner, James Barry *school system administrator*

Jewett
Beddingfield, Carol Anne *secondary school educator*

Killeen
Beck, Barbara Nell *elementary school educator*
Brindley, Joan Harriet *elementary educator*
Harvey, Hilda Ruth *special education educator*

Kingsville
Ibanez, Manuel Luis *university official, biological sciences educator*
Wiley, Millicent Yoder *retired secondary school educator, realtor*

Klein
Slater, Joan Elizabeth *secondary education educator*

La Grange
Weishuhn, Carolyn Ann *elementary education educator*

Lake Creek
Smith, Shirley Ann Nabors *secondary school educator*

Lake Dallas
Coleman, Brenda Forbis *gifted and talented educator*

Lake Jackson
Livingston, Patricia Dianne *secondary education educator*

Lancaster
Schlachter, Deborah Bristow *special education educator, consultant*

Laredo
Condon, Maria del Carmen *retired elementary school educator*
Fierros, Ruth Victoria *retired secondary school educator*

League City
Brandt, Mitzi Marianne *educational specialist*

Lewisville
Whiteley, Harold Lee *director*

Longview
Davis, Jimmie Mae Clayborn *elementary school educator*
Dunnavant, Betsy R. *elementary school educator*
Northcutt, Kathryn Ann *elementary school and gifted-talented educator, reading recovery educator*

Lubbock
Curl, Samuel Everett *university dean, agricultural scientist*
Haragan, Donald Robert *university administrator, geosciences educator*
Hisey, Lydia Vee *educational administrator*
Huggins, Cannie Mae Cox Hunter *retired elementary school educator*
Nelson, Toza *elementary school educator*
Rios, Juan-Ernesto *elementary education educator*
Schmidly, David J. *academic administrator, dean*

Lufkin
Ball, Margie Barber *elementary school educator*

Marshall
Dahl, Shirley Ann Wise *education educator*
Hawkins, Audrey Denise *academic administrator, educator*
Helton, Karen Johnson *college administrator*
Newman, Dorothy Anne *secondary school educator*

Mcallen
Chavez, Janie Ignacia *education educator*
Gonzalez, Rolando Noel *secondary school educator, religion educator, photographer*

Mesquite
Hughes, Selma Elizabeth *special education educator*
Patrick, Pamela Ann *secondary school educator, research analysis consultant*
Pratt, Sharon L. *secondary and elementary education educator*
Reid, Helen Veronica *dean*
Taylor, Martha Ellen *private school educator*

Midland
McClendon, Susan K. *secondary education educator*

Missouri City
Trichel, Mary Lydia *middle school educator*

Nacogdoches
Cornish, Christopher Scott *secondary education educator*
Rhodes, Kris Evon *academic program director*

Nederland
Rhodes, Cheryle Kemble *elementary school educator*

New Ulm
Whitehead, David Lynn *school counselor*

Nolan
Blair, Terri Jean *special education teacher*

Odessa
Box, Jay Keith *college administrator*
Folsom, Hyta Prine *educational grant writer, consultant*
Langham, Edward Lee *secondary education educator*
Maharg, Meredith McClintock *education director*
Rasor, Doris Lee *secondary education educator*
Watson, Kay *school system administrator, retired*

Omaha
Moos, Verna Vivian *special education educator*

Orange
Shahan, J. Michael *academic administrator*

Pampa
Anderson, Donna Elaine *elementary and secondary school educator*
Diller, Marcella Mary *middle school educator*

Pasadena
Baker, Betty Sue *elementary and secondary education educator*
Hall, Georganna Mae *elementary school educator*
Reyna, Wanda Wong *early childhood education educator*
Shaffer, Anita Mohrland *counselor*

Pecos
Busby, Shannon Nixon *special education educator*
Thomas, Beverly Irene *special education educator*

Plainview
Davis, Wallace Edmond, Jr. *university administrator, educator*
Porter, Joan Margaret *elementary education educator*

Plano
Agers, Bobby Lee *middle school educator, coach*
Fleming, Christina Samusson *special education educator*
France-Deal, Judith Jean *parochial school educator*
Johnson, Sherri Dale *educational consultant*
McWilliams, Mary Ann *school administrator*
Statman, Jackie C. *career consultant*

Port Aransas
Cook, Marilyn Jane *elementary school educator*

Port Arthur
Weber, Katie *special education educator*

Portland
Cessac, Joyce Eve LaBorde *elementary school educator*

Prairie View
Gonzalez, Antonio *academic administrator, mortgage company executive*
Jackson, Frank Donald *university director*
Trotty, Willie Francis *university dean*

Quitman
Warren, Patsy Ruth *elementary school educator*

Ravenna
Greene, Jennifer *elementary school counselor*

Richardson
Baker, Katherine June *elementary school educator, minister*
Blaydes, Winifred Jean *elementary school educator*
Weaver, Jo Nell *elementary school educator*

Rio Vista
Monk, Kathy Jo *secondary education educator*

Rockdale
Conoley, Joann Shipman *educational administrator*
Estell, Dora Lucile *retired educational administrator*

Rockwall
Williams, Jan Koret *secondary school educator*

Round Rock
Ledbetter, Sharon Faye Welch *educational consultant*

San Angelo
Davison, Elizabeth Jane Linton *education educator*
Palmer, Deborah Kay *university administrator, educator, consultant*
Person, Ruth Janssen *academic administrator*

San Antonio
Burgos-Sasscer, Ruth *college president*
Droke, Rose Mary *university administrator*
Dudley, Brooke Fitzhugh *educational consultant*
Garcia, Yolanda Vasquez *educational services manager, educator*
Garner, Jo Ann Starkey *elementary school educator*
Gutierrez, Guadalupe Salvador *elementary school educator*
Kirkpatrick, Samuel Alexander *university president, social and policy sciences educator*
Kocurek, Patricia Terrazas *elementary education educator*
Koym, Zala Cox *elementary education educator*
Kruckenberg, Dina Kirsten *elementary educator*
Logan, Linda Jo *secondary school educator*
Madrid, Olga Hilda Gonzalez *retired elementary education educator, association executive*
Malone, Virginia *educational measurement professional*
Manuel, David P. *university dean*
Massey, Patti Chryl *elemetary school educator*
Maxwell, Diana Kathleen *early childhood education educator*
McElveen-Combs, Gail Marie *middle school educator*
Menchaca, Robert *elementary education educator*
Moder, John Joseph *academic administrator, priest*
Nelson, Glenda Kay *special education educator*
Paloczy, Susan Therese *elementary school principal*
Plofchan, Thomas Kenneth *college official*
Robertson, Samuel Luther, Jr. *special education educator, therapist*
Salisbury, Margaret Mary *retired elementary school educator*
Shade, Cynthia Specia *gifted and talented education educator*
Speer, Glenda O'Bryant *middle school educator*
Sueltenfuss, Sister Elizabeth Anne *academic administrator*
Taliaferro, Cecil Raynard *college dean*
Tavel, Linda Benitez *educational facility administrator*
Terry, James Crockett *school system administrator, mediator*
Wimpee, Mary Elizabeth *elementary school educator*

San Diego
Pena, Modesta Celedonia *retired principal*

San Marcos
Busby, Mark Bayless *university administrator, educator, writer*
Clayton, Katy *elementary education educator*
Fite, Kathleen Elizabeth *education educator*
Hethcock, Wendell Harold *private school educator, principal*

Miloy, Leatha Faye *university program director*
Sánchez, Elaine Ruby *academic librarian*

Sanger
Shelton, Patricia Ann Atnip *elementary education educator*
Yeatts, Marian Sunny *secondary school educator*

Seguin
Hastings, Evelyn Grace *retired elementary school educator*
Larsen, Ethel Paulson *retired secondary school educator*

Seminole
Linthicum, James Harold *principal*

Sheridan
Gohlke, Lillian Marie *retired secondary school educator*

Sherman
Garrett, Sandra *elementary education educator*
Page, Oscar Cletice *academic administrator*

Snyder
McCabe, Helen Ann *school system administrator*

Spring
Eissler, Veda Alicia *middle school educator, musician*

Stafford
Herrera, Mary Cardenas *education educator, music minister*

Sugar Land
Finney, Patricia Ann *elementary education educator*
Ramos, Rose Mary *elementary education educator*
Thompson, Alice M. Broussard *special education administrator*

Temple
Jackson, Karen Lee *elementary school educator*
Kreitz, Helen Marie *retired elementary education educator*
Roberts, Jimmy Dan *educational administrator*
Staten, Donna Kay *elementary art educator*
Van Ness, James Samuel *academic administrator, historian*

Terrell
Rice, Albert Brockhouse *college program director*

Tomball
Bozic, William Joseph, Jr. *secondary school educator*

Tyler
Coker, Melinda Louise *counselor*
Fouse, Anna Beth *education educator*
Hamm, George Francis *university president*
Houser, Cindy L. *middle school educator, counselor*
Marsh, Owen Robert *education educator*
Scott, Dorothy Marie *retired education educator, civic worker*
Sharpe, Aubrey Dean *college administrator*
Thrash, Artie Yvonne Adams *college foundation director*
Waller, Wilma Ruth *retired secondary school educator and librarian*

Uvalde
Wilson, Benjamin Franklin, Jr. *education educator*

Valle De Oro
Miesse, Mary Elizabeth (Beth Miesse) *special education educator*

Van Horn
Hoskins, Katy Garren *secondary school educator*

Victoria
Haynes, Karen Sue *university president, social work educator*
Smith, Don Noel *academic administrator*

Waco
Dube, William John, III *dean*
Hastings, Chester Ran *education educator, director student services*
Hollingsworth, Martha Lynette *secondary school educator*
Moseley, Mary Prudence *elementary school educator*
Reynolds, Herbert Hal *academic administrator*
Wuebker, Virginia Ann *retired elementary school educator, program director*

Waxahachie
Hastings, Ronnie Jack *secondary school educator*

Weatherford
Chenault, Shirley *college educator, college administrator*

Webster
Dalke, Barbara Helen *elementary school educator*

Weslaco
Jordan, Timothy Edward *secondary education educator*

Wharton
Jenkins, Loretta Jean *retired educator*
Vivelo, Frank Robert *college administrator, anthropologist*

Whiteface
Lamb, Stacie Thompson *elementary school educator*

Whitehouse
Stansell, Aiszeleen *secondary school educator*

Wichita Falls
Harvill, Melba Sherwood *university librarian*
Leavell, Landrum Pinson, II *seminary administrator, clergyman, educator*
Rodriguez, Louis Joseph *university president, educator*

VIRGINIA

Abingdon
Gardner, Richard Calvin *retired elementary school educator, librarian*
Luker, Jean Knarr *school system administrator*

Alexandria
Anderson, Ann Davis *curriculum and staff development specialist*
Edgell, Karin Jane *reading specialist, special education educator*
Marshak, Lisa Rachel *special education educator*
Nekritz, Leah Kalish *dean, college administrator*
Richards, Ashton White *dean*

Amherst
Campbell, Catherine Lynn *elementary school educator*
Herbert, Amanda Kathryn *special education educator*
Paciocco, Thomas *middle school educator*

Annandale
Wilhelmi, Mary Charlotte *education educator, college official*

Arlington
Berg, Sister Marie Majella *university chancellor*
Davis-Imhof, Nancy Louise *elementary school educator*
Hartley, Craig Sheridan *dean, mechanical engineering educator*
Hedges, Jean Kyle *educator*
Lane, Neal Francis *university provost, physics researcher, federal administrator*
Mandanis, Alice Subley *academic official*
McCaskill, James H. *secondary education educator, consultant*
Simms, Frances Bell *elementary education educator*
Slater, James Gregory *primary education educator*

Ashburn
Brooks, Anne Lee *assistant principal, educator*
Wheedleton, Katharine Marie *elementary school educator*

Ashland
Tompkins, Edward Deal *academic administrator*

Baskerville
Simmons, Barry William *university official, consultant*

Bassett
Taylor, Marsha Lopez *secondary school educator*

Bedford
Henry, Nancy Sinclair *middle school educator*
Robertson, Sylvia Douglas *middle school educator*

Blacksburg
Campbell, Joan Virginia Loweke *secondary school educator, language educator*
Carlisle, Ervin Frederick *university provost, educator*
Carlton, Patrick William *educational administration educator*
Clowes, Darrel Austin *education educator, retired*
Lynch, Sherry Kay *counselor*
Martin, Margaret (Hill) *vocational school educator*
Tillar, Thomas Cato, Jr. *university alumni relations administrator, consultant*
Wall, Robert Thompson *secondary school educator*

Bridgewater
Geisert, Wayne Frederick *educational consultant, retired administrator*
Richardson, John MacLaren, Jr. *school superintendent*

Bristol
Hagy, Teresa Jane *elementary education educator*
Mashburn, Donald Eugene *middle school educator*

Buena Vista
Ripley, John Walter *academic administrator*

Charlottesville
Carey, Robert Munson *university dean, physician*
Casteen, John Thomas, III *university president*
DiCroce, Deborah Marie *college president*
Hine, Jonathan Trumbull, Jr. *university administrator, translator*
Keats, Patricia Hart *counselor, educator*
Mahanes, Joanne Ridob *assistant dean*
O'Neil, Robert Marchant *university administrator, law educator*
Payne, John Howard *university program director*
Selig, Camden Wood *associate athletic director*
Stauff, William James *facility director*
Verstegen, Deborah A. *education educator*
Williams, Lois Ann *secondary and elementary education educator*

Chesapeake
Clarkson, Phyllis Owens *early childhood educator*
Lewter, Helen Clark *elementary education educator*

Chester
Spindler, Judith Tarleton *elementary school educator*

Culpeper
Furgiuele, Margery Wood *vocational educator*
Smith, Lisa E. *guidance counselor*

Cumberland
Anderson, Karen Suzanne Sigmon *elementary educator*

Dahlgren
Finazzo, Kathy Jo *primary school educator*

Danville
Carter, Thomasine E. *principal, academic program administrator*
Foster, Betty Jo *academic administrator*

Dumfries
Stevens, Dianne Farria *secondary school educator*

Edinburg
Litten, Deborah Jean *elementary school educator*

Fairfax
Bader, Lawson Reece *university programs director*
Carr, Patricia Warren *adult education educator*
Graves, Dana Louise *elementary school educator*
Johnson, George William *university president*

Fairfax Station
Belefski, Michael Edward *secondary education educator, business owner*

Falls Church
Marshall, Mary Elizabeth *secondary school English educator*
Todd, Shirley Ann *school system administrator*

Farmville
Dotson, Vicky Lynn *special education educator*
Woodburn, Mary Stuart *education educator*

Fishersville
Geiman, Stephen Royer *secondary school educator, coach*

Fort Belvoir
Summers, Wilson, IV *college dean*

Fort Monroe
Robinson, Naomi Jean *educational training systems educator*

Franklin
Sprouse, Earlene Pentecost *educational diagnostician*

Fredericksburg
Jenks-Davies, Kathryn Ryburn *retired daycare provider, civic worker*
Lauer, Susan Parker *primary school educator*

Glade Hill
Wilson, Lisa Renée *special education educator*

Hampden Sydney
Wilson, Samuel V. *academic adminstrator*

Hampton
Calver, Richard Allen *college dean*
Harvey, William Robert *university president*
Hightower, John Brantley *arts administrator*
Steele, James Eugene *secondary school educator*

Harrisonburg
Carrier, Ronald Edwin *university administrator*
Slye, Carroll James *instructional supervisor*

Haysi
Deel, George Moses *elementary school educator*
Rife, Lisa June Delaney *physical education educator*

Heathsville
Sisson, Jean Cralle *middle school educator*

Irvington
Breslin, David Dunbar *elementary educator*

Lakeridge
Derrickson, Denise Ann *secondary school educator*

Lexington
Elrod, John William *university president, philosophy and religion educator*
Radulescu, Domnica Vera Maria *education educator*

Lynchburg
Bashore, Robert LeRoy *college administrator*
Guillermin, Armand Pierre *university administrator*
Schewel, Rosel Hoffberger *education educator*
Simms, Alice Jane *secondary school educator*
Sullivan, Gregory Paul *secondary education educator*
Swain, Diane Scott *principal*

Manassas
Bateman, Sandra Bizzle *primary school educator*
Shaw, Susan Kime *secondary school educator, administrator*

Mc Dowell
Harkleroad, Jo-Ann Decker *special education educator*

Mc Lean
Michalowicz, Karen Dee *secondary education educator*

Middleburg
Kaplan, (Norma) Jean Gaither *reading specialist, retired educator*

Midlothian
Leighty, Diane Carol *secondary education educator*
Smith, Alma Davis *elementary education educator*

Natural Bridge
Golden, Leah Waller *elementary education educator*

New Kent
Kirby, Mary Weeks *elementary education educator, reading specialist*

Newport News
Drummond, Neil Hiden *retired secondary school educator*
Goode, Constance Loper *elementary school assistant principal*
Kent, Nancy Lee *elementary school educator*
Levy, Robin Carole *elementary guidance counselor*
Meade, Angela Kaye *special education educator*
Santoro, Anthony Richard *academic administrator*
Wiatt, Carol Stultz *elementary education educator*

Norfolk
Arnold, Leslie Bisger *educational administrator*
Cartwright, Bonnie Reed *secondary school educator*
Koch, James Verch *academic administrator, economist*
Myers, Donald Allen *university dean*
Oberne, Sharon Brown *elementary education educator*
Proctor, Ronald Eugene *academic administrator, educator, consultant*
Ritz, John Michael *education educator*
Russell, Susan Webb *elementary and middle school education educator*
Sebren, Lucille Griggs *retired private school educator*
Seme, Phillipine Jane N. *education educator, consultant*
Shannon, Isabelle Louise *education director*
Wilson, Harrison B. *academic administrator*

Norton
Bowen, Bill Monroe *educational administrator*

Nottoway
Bradley, Douglas Oliver *school principal*

Onley
Mason, Benjamin Page *director of vocational education*

Palmyra
Robertson, John Michael *education educator*

Poquoson
Parry, Thomas Herbert, Jr. *school system administrator, educational consultant*

Port Republic
Blackwell, Chadwick Carter *elementary education educator*

Portsmouth
Dudley, Delores Ingram *secondary education educator, poet, writer*

Powhatan
Alligood, Mary Sale *special education educator*

Reston
Keefe, James Washburn *educational researcher, consultant*

Richmond
Ackell, Edmund Ferris *university president*
Batch, Mary Lou *guidance counselor, educator*
Blunde, Mary Catherine *admissions director*
Brooks, Neils Willard *vocational/adult education educator*
Cribbs, Jeffrey Scott, Sr. *educational administrator*
David, Candace Heiderich *educational consultant*
Elliott, April Lee *educational consultant*
Heilman, E. Bruce *academic administrator*
Hosey, Sheryl Lynn Miller *university health facility administrator*
Miller, Margaret Alison *chief state academic officer*
Morrill, Richard Leslie *university administrator*
Oliver, Arnold Robert *chancellor*
Pate, Donald Wayne *academic administrator, educator*
Ragland, Ines Colom *principal*
Rosenblum, John William *dean*
Sasser, Ellis A. *gifted and talented education educator*
Simmons, S. Dallas *university president*
Slonaker, Celester Lee *principal*
Tan, Dali *secondary school educator*
Torrence, Rosetta Lena *educational consultant*
Trani, Eugene Paul *academic administrator, educator*
Withers, Donald Chris *university administrator*

Roanoke
King, Stephen Emmett *educational administrator*
Nickens, Harry Carl *academic administrator*

Rustburg
Olah, Susan May *secondary school educator, respiratory therapist*

Salem
Lubbs, Gresilda Anne Tilley *secondary school educator*

Saxe
Andrews, Marie Staylor *special education educator*

Spotsylvania
Aaronson, Joyce Rosalind *elementary school educator*
Hamilton, Joyce Marie *adult education educator*

Springfield
De Nigris, Anna Maria Theresa *middle school educator*
Jones, Bonnie Damschroder *special education specialist*
Leavitt, Mary Janice Deimel *special education educator, civic worker*
Saunders, Tracie Lee *day care provider*

Staunton
Shuey, Judith Lewis *counselor*
Sproul, Loretta Ann Schroeder *elementary school educator, reading specialist*

Sterling
Rankin, Betty Hill *special education educator*

Suffolk
Graham, Evelyne Moore *retired school administrator, consultant*
Matson, Virginia Mae Freeberg (Mrs. Edward J. Matson) *retired special education educator, author*

Sweet Briar
Baldwin, Nancy Godwin *program director*
Hill, Barbara Ann *academic administrator, consultant*
Muhlenfeld, Elisabeth S. *college president, educator, author*
Shea, Brent Mack *social science educator*

Tazewell
TePoel, Donna Lee Fuller *former education educator*

Virginia Beach
Corbat, Patricia Leslie *special education educator*
Lang, Vicki Scott *primary school educator*
McKinney, Pamela Anne *elementary principal*
Selig, William George *university official*
Tully, Margie Gaines *school system administrator*

Warrenton
Haley, Jeanne Ackerman *preschool director*

Waynesboro
Lunger, James Brown *secondary school administrator*
Tynes, Theodore Archibald *educational administrator*

White Stone
Benson, Kimberly Leggett *elementary education educator*

Williamsburg
Humphreys, Homer Alexander *former principal*
Van Tassel-Baska, Joyce Lenore *education educator*
Williams, Ruth Elizabeth (Betty Williams) *retired secondary school educator*

Winchester
Davis, James Arnold *academic administrator*
Pleacher, David Henry *secondary school educator*
Smith, Harold Allen *educational administrator, researcher, educator*

Wise
Kendrick, Richard Lofton *university administrator, consultant*

Woodbridge
Lavid, Jean Stern *school director*
Packard, Mildred Ruth *middle school educator*

Yorktown
Eysmans, Debra Morrison *former university public relations executive*
Rogers, Sheila Wood *elementary and secondary school educator*
Staples, Steven Ray *school system administrator, education educator*

WEST VIRGINIA

Bethany
Cummins, Delmer Duane *academic administrator, historian*
Krug, John Carleton (Tony Krug) *college administrator, library consultant*

Bluefield
Barsi, Louis Michael *college dean*
Patsel, E. Ralph, Jr. *registrar*

Caldwell
Diem, Debra R. *elementary school educator*

Charleston
Allen, Noreen Jeanne *secondary school educator*
Hambrick, Arlene *school system administrator, minister*
Krotseng, Marsha Van Dyke *higher education administrator*
Manning, Charles W. *academic administrator*
Moore, Jeanne *arts educator and administrator*
Welch, Edwin Hugh *academic administrator*

Clarksburg
Kittle, Robert Earl *school system administrator*

Dailey
Kolsun, Bruce Alan *special education educator*

Dunbar
Davis, Billie Johnston *school counselor*

Elizabeth
Shaver, Martha Eileen *secondary school teacher*

Elkins
MacConkey, Dorothy I. *academic administrator*
Minear, Alana Wilfong *alumni affairs director*

Glen Jean
Beverly, Laura Elizabeth *special education educator*

Harpers Ferry
Blue, Kathy Jo *elementary school educator*

Huntington
Coburn, Frances Gullett *retired elementary school educator*
Cole, Patricia Ann *elementary school educator*
Gilley, James Wade *university president*
Gould, Alan Brant *academic administrator*
Morgan, Linda Rice *secondary education educator*

Institute
Batson, Stephen Wesley *university administrator, consultant*
Epps, Gregory Dean *program director*

Lahmansville
Harman, Jo Ann Snyder *secondary school educator*

Montgomery
Keenan, Mary Elizabeth *vocational education educator*

Morgantown
Bucklew, Neil S. *educator, past university president*
Drvar, Margaret Adams *vocational education educator*

Ona
Roebuck, Judith Lynn *secondary school educator*

Parkersburg
Meadows, Lois Annette *elementary education educator*

Philippi
Wilkins, Flo *elementary education educator*

Princeton
Bolen, Bettye Sue *academic administrator*

Ridgeley
Unger, Roberta Marie *special education educator*

Ripley
Riffe, Stacy Christine *secondary school educator*

Saint Albans
Carte, Suzanne Lewis *elementary school educator*
Smith, Robert Carlisle *department administrator, welding educator*

Salem
Ohl, Ronald Edward *academic administrator*

Shady Spring
Meador, Richard Lewis *school counselor*

Spencer
Parker, Theresa Ann *special education educator*

Stanaford
Wilson, Lucinda Glade Rees *elementary school educator*

Williamson
Shaw, Laurie Jo *grant project director*

WISCONSIN

Belgium
Murphy, Greta Werwath *retired academic administrator*

TERRITORIES OF THE UNITED STATES

PUERTO RICO

Aguadilla
Jaramillo, Juana Segarra *dean*

Humacao
Delgado-Rodriguez, Manuel *secondary school educator*

Rio Piedras
Ramos-Rodriguez, Isabel *education educator*

San Juan
del Toro, Ilia *retired education educator*
Gonzalez, Jose Ramón *academic administrator*
Maldonado, Norman I. *academic administrator, physician educator*

VIRGIN ISLANDS

Christiansted
Sewpershad, Lionel *principal*

Frederiksted
Petrait, Brother James Anthony *secondary education educator, clergy member*

Saint Thomas
Kean, Orville *academic administrator*

ADDRESS UNPUBLISHED

Adamson, Jane Nan *elementary school educator*
Alberto, Paul A. *special education educator*
Armacost, Mary-Linda Sorber Merriam *former college president*
Armstead, Tressa Maddux *secondary school educator*
Armstrong, Warren Bruce *university president, historian, educator*
Arnold, P. A. *special education educator*
Banter, Mary Jean McKenzie *gifted educator*
Barnett, Linda Kay Smith *vocational guidance counselor*
Barton, Kathryn Jean *elementary education educator*
Becker, Richard Charles *retired college president*
Beeth, Pamela Williams *educational diagnostician*
Beresford, Wilma *secondary school educator, gifted education educator*
Bernath, Mary Therese *special education educator*
Black, Georgia Ann *mathematics facilitator*
Black, Rhonda Stout *vocational special needs educator*
Blecke, Arthur Edward *principal*
Boli, Fred Clark *academic administrator*
Bourgeois, Priscilla Elzey *educational administrator*
Boyd, Emilie Lou *elementary school educator, consultant*
Brady, Virginia Winegar *retired school librarian*
Brewton, Dudley Cornelius, Jr. *school administrator*
Brown, Bertha Faye *early childhood and elementary school educator*
Brown, Rubye Golsby *secondary education educator, artist*
Bulcken, Carolyn Anne Brooks *retired special education educator*
Burbridge, Ann Arnold *elementary school educator*
Camp, Richard Glenn *special education educator, coach*
Carr, Bessie *retired middle school educator*
Carson, Barbara Gilbert *college educator, consultant*
Carter, Frances B. *secondary school educator*
Casler, Frederick Clair *academic administrator, law enforcement educator*
Castor, Betty *academic administrator*
Cobb, Millicent Amelia *special education educator*
Cobb, Pauline Lane *retired federal educational programs director*
Davis, Robert Aldine *academic administrator*
Delahanty, Rebecca Ann *school system administrator*
Dema, Robert John *public school system administrator*
Denham, Caroline Virginia *retired college official*
Dennis, Gordon Scott *secondary school educator*
Diem, Richard A. *college educator, educational consultant*
Doby, Janice Kay *elementary education educator*
Dubois, Nancy Q. *elementary school educator*
Duncan, Sylvia Lorena *gifted education educator*
Dunn, Sally Skeehan *school system administrator*
Eads, Albert E., Jr. *school administrator*
Eaton, Dorel *elementary school educator*
Eggemeyer, Alicia Ann *elementary education educator*
Eller, Brenda Ann *elementary school educator, recreational director*
Evans, Valerie Elaine *elementary education educator*
Falk, Marshall Allen *retired university dean, physician*
Fears, Louise Mathis *private school educator*
Felder, Pamela Theresa *child care director*
Fletcher, Patrice Tomasky *special education educator*
Fletcher, Sarah Carolyn *retired elementary education educator*
Forney, Virginia Sue *educational counselor*
Foster, Martha Tyahla *educational administrator*
Fountain, Andre Ferchaud *academic program director*
Franklin, Mary Ann Wheeler *retired administrator, educator, higher education and management consultant*
French, Earl Allan *principal*
Fuller, Maxine Compton *retired secondary school educator*
Gadson, Ronald Cedric *middle school educator*
Garcia-Mely, Rafael *retired education educator*
Godwin, Nancy Elizabeth *home economics supervisor*
Golden, Beth *community college administrator*
Grant, Miriam Rosenbloum *secondary school educator, journalist*
Green, Nancy Loughridge *higher education executive*
Greene, Carl David *academic administrator*
Guedri, Terry Tyrrell *secondary education educator, educational consultant*
Handly-Johnson, Patricia *school administrator, school psychologist, educational consultant*
Harris, Annie Rene *elementary school educator*
Harris, Delmarie Jones *elementary education educator*
Hayden, Linda C. *school librarian*
Hayden, Michael Allen *technology educator*
Hebert, Christine Anne *elementary education educator*
Heestand, Diane Elissa *educational technology educator, medical educator*
Hepp, Roberta Ann *primary education educator*
Hildenburg, Sydney Leigh *elementary education educator*
Holcomb, Mildred Geneva Comrie *elementary education educator*
Humble, Joan Marie *elementary school educator*
Hutson, Henry Critchfield *academic administrator*
Ignatonis, Sandra Carole Autry *special education educator*
Iliff, Vicki Weber *special education educator*
Inglett, Betty Lee *retired media services administrator*
Jackson, Barbara W. *school system administrator*
Jones, Barbara Archer *counselor, consultant*
Jost, Norma Lillian *secondary education educator, consultant*
Keebler, Lois Marie *elementary school educator*
Keith, Leroy, Jr. *former college president*
Kennedy, Nancy J. *education educator*
Kimberling, Charles Ronald *academic administrator*
King, Annie Roberts *elementary and secondary education educator*
King, Frances *education educator*
Kitchin, Kate Parks *retired guidance counselor and secondary English language educator*
Koeth, Leonard Alfred *counselor, educator*
Koiner, Michelle Elizabeth *elementary school educator*
Krueger, Christine Marie *vocational studies educator*
Latimer, Billie Luan *elementary education educator*
Leavitt, Maura Lynn *elementary education educator*
Looser, Donald William *academic administrator*
Lunde, Katherine LaMontagne *educational consultant*
Lynn, Mark Wayne *secondary school educator, administrator*
Mack, Sandra Lee *secondary school educator*
Martin, Judy Brackin Hereford *higher education administrator*
Martin, Marta N. *special education educator*
McCall, Patricia Alene *elementary and secondary music education educator*
McCalla, Sandra Ann *principal*
McClaron, Louisianna Clardy *retired secondary school educator*
McConnell, Albert Lynn *college educator*
McCoy, Mary Elizabeth *primary school educator*
McKnight, Patricia Marie *elementary education educator*
McNully, Lynnette Larkin *elementary education educator*
McPeak, Allan *career services director, educator, lawyer, consultant*
Meyer, Frances Margaret Anthony *elementary and secondary school educator, health education specialist*
Miner, Mary Elizabeth Hubert *secondary school educator*
Moore, Robert Paul *elementary school educator*
Morgan, Ruth Prouse *academic administrator, educator*
Morrin, Virginia White *retired education educator*
Mouton, Francis Edward, III *academic administrator*
Muntz, Charles Edward *school system administrator*
Murphy, Mary Kathleen Connors *college administrator, writer*
Naglieri, Eileen Sheridan *special education educator*
Nance, Mary Joe *secondary education educator*
Newberry, Trudell McClelland *retired dean*
Nierste, Robert Walter *secondary school educator*
Olsen, Miles Jeffrey *religious educator, minister*
Olson-Hagan, Arlene *parochial school administrator*
Osnes, Pamela Grace *special education educator*
Paxton, Juanita Willene *retired university official*
Peebles, Ruth Addelle *secondary education educator*
Phillips, Joy Eugenia *counselor, consultant*
Piper, Margarita Sherertz *retired school administrator*
Pippin, James Adrian, Jr. *middle school educator*
Posner, Gary Jay *educational consulting company executive*
Propst, Harold Dean *retired academic administrator*
Quarles, Peggy Delores *secondary school educator*
Ramirez, Maria C(oncepción) *educational administrator*
Rawdon, Cheryl Ann *elementary school educator*
Ray, Michelle Morris *secondary education educator, mediator*
Ray, Shirley Dodson *educational administrator, consultant*
Renda, Rosa A. *special education educator*
Reuschling, Thomas Lynn *academic administrator, consultant*
Reyes, Maria Elena *academic program director*
Rice, Patricia Oppenheim Levin *special education educator, consultant*
Riggs, Sonya Woicinski *elementary school educator*
Roaden, Arliss Lloyd *retired higher education executive director, former university president*
Robbins, Jane Lewis *elementary school educator*
Robertson, Wyndham Gay *university official*
Ross, Ann Dunbar *secondary school educator*
Rowe, Katherine Elaine *school counselor, therapist*
Rusk, Johanna Neppi-Marie *secondary education educator*
Sanborn, Lisa Diane *elementary education educator*
Sanger, Stephen Thomas *secondary school educator*
Schon, Sandra Diane *elementary school educator*
Scott, Loretta Claire *elementary education educator*
Scruggs, Sandra Lynn *secondary school educator, writer*
Shearer, Charles Livingston *academic administrator*
Shields, Rana Colleen *special education educator*
Slater, William Thomas *dean, communications researcher*
Slaydon, Jeanne Miller *secondary school educator*
Sloat, Robert Stuart *academic consultant*
Smith, Jearld Van *secondary education educator, realtor*
Smith, Michael *retired university chancellor*
Sockey, Felicia Willene *elementary school educator*
Southerland, Thomas Paul *retired university administrator*
Spain, Steve Randall *secondary school educator*
Spiesicke, Margrit Herma *counselor*
Spruill, Louise Elam *retired secondary educator*
Stauffer, Louise Lee *retired secondary school educator*
Stewart, John Ezell *educational and business consultant*
Stoker, Howard W. *former education educator, educational administrator, consultant*
Surber, Regina Brammell *early childhood education educator, administrator*
Surles, Carol D. *university president*
Sweetland, Annette Florence (Annie Sweetland) *special education educator*
Thomasson, John Melvin *college administrator*
Thomson, Mabel Amelia *retired elementary school educator*
Todd, Joan Abernathy *secondary school educator*
Travis, Nancy *program director*
Vanderbeek, Ann Randle *elementary education educator*
Vander Gheynst, Carol M. *coordinator of planning*
Viletto, Christina Ann *elementary education educator*
Vorous, Margaret Estelle *primary and secondary school educator*
Walker, Alice Davis *retired audio-visual specialist educator*
Walker, Nancy Ann *American studies educator, English language educator*
Wallace, Milton DeNard *school system administrator*
Walton, Ronald Elwood *retired school superintendent*
Ward, Lynda Sue Scoville *special education educator, writer*
Washington, Walter *retired academic administrator*
Watkiss, Regina (Regina Monks) *secondary school educator*
Watson, Marilyn Kaye *elementary education educator*
Watson, Merlyn Fohrell *retired public school media specialist*
West, Marsha *elementary school educator*
Wexler, Jeffrey F. *education educator, Montessori training administrator*
Wheeler, Townsend, III *academic administrator*
Whitsell, Sunny Suzanne *assistant principal*
Wiley, Elizabeth Greene Williams *secondary education educator*
Willingham, Dennis Ray *secondary education educator*
Wilson, Denise Watts *secondary school educator*
Wilson, Jeannette Solomon *retired elementary education educator*
Winokur, Mark *secondary education educator*
Witt, Judith Anne *elementary education educator*
Woltering, Margaret Mae *secondary school educational consultant*
Woods, Phyllis Michalik *elementary school educator*
Wright, Corey Robert *secondary school educator*
Yasger, Timothy Francis *secondary education educator*

ENGINEERING

UNITED STATES

ALABAMA

Auburn
Foster, Winfred Ashley, Jr. *aerospace engineering educator*
Jaeger, Richard Charles *electrical engineer, educator, science center director*

Axis
Michaels, Alan J. *safety, occupational health and security executive*

Birmingham
Adams, Alfred Bernard, Jr. *environmental engineer*
Bunt, Randolph Cedric *mechanical engineer*
Goodrich, Thomas Michael *engineering and construction executive, lawyer*
Johnson, James Hodge *retired engineering company executive*
Kader, Jac B. *design engineer*
Pitt, Robert Ervin *environmental engineer, educator*
Scott, Owen Myers, Jr. *nuclear engineer*

Daphne
van Aken, John Henry *marine surveyor, engineer, consultant*

Dozier
Grantham, Charles Edward *broadcast engineer*

Eufaula
Dixon, Giles H. *engineering manager*

Florence
Smith, James Lee *aerospace engineer, educator*

Guntersville
Brown, Wallace Lamar *design engineer*

Huntsville
Adams, Gary Lee *engineering manager*
Ashcraft, James Harold, Jr. *engineer*
Balint, David Lee *engineering company executive*
Buckelew, Robin Browne *aerospace engineer*
Buddington, Patricia Arrington *engineer*
Chassay, Roger Paul, Jr. *engineering executive, project manager*
Cotney, Carol Ann *independent researcher*
Craig, Thomas Franklin *electrical engineer*
Emerson, William Kary *engineering company executive*
Evensen, Alf John *engineer, researcher*
Frink, William David, Jr. *senior systems engineer*
Gervais, Kevin Michael *computer network engineer*
Gregory, Daniel Richard *safety and environmental engineer*
Hart, Gerry Keith *computer engineer*
Joner, Bruno *aeronautical engineer*
Katsinis, Constantine *electrical engineering educator*
Kim, Young Kil *aerospace engineer*
Lambing, Steven Jay *aerospace engineer*
LeMaster, Robert Allen *mechanical engineer*
McDaniels, David Martin *aerospace engineer, researcher*
Murray, Dale Norris *engineering scientist, researcher*
Pastrick, Harold Lee *aeronautical engineer*
Pittman, William Claude *electrical engineer*
Polites, Michael Edward *aerospace engineer*
Reddy, Thikkavarapu Ramachandra *electrical engineer*
Scales, John Richard *systems engineer*
Shuford, David Wilson *aerospace engineer*
Sims, Samuel Richard Farrell *electronic engineer*
Son, Chang Hyun *mechanical engineer*
Stermer, Jo Carol *electrical engineer*
Theisen, Russell Eugene *electrical engineer*
Vaughan, Otha H., Jr. *aerospace engineer, research scientist*
Wieland, Paul Otto *environmental control systems engineer*
Yang, Hong-Qing *mechanical engineer*

Muscle Shoals
Badger, Phillip Charles *engineer*
Barrier, John Wayne *engineer, management consultant*
Burchfield, Donald Francis *safety engineer, recreation administrator, consultant*

Normal
Saha, Pabitra Kumar *civil and structural engineering educator, consultant*

Redstone Arsenal
Grider, Kelly Vernon *engineering executive*
Smith, Troy Alvin *aerospace research engineer*

Shelby
Jackson, Jimmy Lynn *engineer, consulting spectroscopist*

Stevenson
Manaker, Arnold Martin *mechanical engineer, consultant*

Tuscaloosa
El-Keib, Abdurrahim A. *electrical engineering educator, consultant*
Moynihan, Gary Peter *industrial engineering educator*

Tuskegee
Hargrove, S. Keith *mechanical engineer, educator*

Vernon
Newell, Harold Joe *quality assurance engineer*

ARIZONA

Mesa
Jackson, Andrew Edwin *engineering educator, researcher*

Scottsdale
Richmond, Robert Paul *chemical engineer, retired*

ARKANSAS

Arkadelphia
Herbert, Jay Andrew *assembly engineering professional*

Bella Vista
Thompson, William Dennison, Jr. *aeronautical consultant*

Fayetteville
Yaz, Edwin Engin *electrical engineer, educator*

Hot Springs National Park
Ray, Arliss Dean *retired environmental consultant*

Jonesboro
Miksa, Ronald W. *mechanical engineer*

Little Rock
Hocott, Joe Bill *chemical engineer*
Logan, Stephen Bean, III *safety engineer*
Miller, Scott Andrew *geotechnical engineer*

Magazine
Abrahamson, Michael William *process engineering technician*

Osceola
Gilham, James Richard *mechanical engineer*

Russellville
Kuenke, Frederick William *electrical engineer*

CALIFORNIA

Atascadero
Stanton, Jack Pershing *chemical engineer*

Long Beach
Thorn, James Douglas *safety engineer*

Sunnyvale
Khan, Khalid Saifullah *engineering executive*

COLORADO

Longmont
Smith, Gary Lee *process and design engineer*

United States Air Force Acad
Wright, Cameron Harrold Greene *electrical engineer*

CONNECTICUT

Stamford
Lantigua, Jose Salvador *computer engineer, consultant*

DISTRICT OF COLUMBIA

Washington
Chambers, Dale *mechanical engineer*
James, Kathryn Kanarek *electrical engineer*
Sedlak, Jeffrey Michael *electrical engineer, career officer*

FLORIDA

Alachua
Dinculescu, Antonie *chemical engineer, researcher*

Atlantic Beach
Engelmann, Rudolph Herman *electronics consultant*

Boca Raton
Arockiasamy, Madasamy *engineering educator*
Doe, Patricia Louise *industrial engineer*
Grant, John Alexander, Jr. *engineering consultant*
Han, Chingping Jim *industrial engineer, educator*
Mahannah, James *engineering company executive*
Pajunen, Grazyna Anna *electrical engineer, educator*
Reynolds, George Anthony, Jr. *engineering executive*
Schnars, Jeffrey *engineering company executive*
Su, Tsung-Chow Joe *engineering educator*

Cape Canaveral
Kimmons, Kent Allen *logistics engineer*

Cape Coral
Smith, Bruce William *safety engineer*

Clearwater
Benavente, Javier Edgar *engineering company executive*
Cain, Frank *electrical engineer*

Cocoa
Byers, William Sewell *electrical engineer, educator*

Cocoa Beach
Gunn, Kenneth David *explosives safety specialist, consultant*
Skrobot, Garrett Lee *space system engineer*

Coral Gables
Novis, Roberto Augusto Passos *civil engineer*
Swift, Jill Anne *industrial engineer, educator*

Coral Springs
Tomlinson, Colin Henry *engineer*
Valasquez, Joseph Louis *industrial engineer*

Daytona Beach
Helfrick, Albert Darlington *electronics engineering educator, consultant*
Hill, Eric von Krumreig *aerospace engineer, educator*
Murphy, Arthur Ellery *safety manager*
Sliwa, Steven Mark *engineering executive, academic administrator*

Destin
Larson, Lorell Vincent *aviation consultant*

Eglin AFB
Gal, Richard John *industrial engineer*

Fort Lauderdale
Brown-Wynn, Kathy Allison *process control engineer, database administrator*
Cassidy, Terrence Patrick, Jr. *engineering consultant*
DiPaolo, Peter Thomas *engineering executive, educator*
Fishe, Gerald Raymond Aylmer *engineering executive*
Parsons, Bruce Andrew *biomedical engineer, scientist*

Fort Myers
Kareh, Ahmad Ragheb *civil engineer*

Gainesville
Abbaschian, Reza *materials science and engineering educator*
Cooper, James Ralph *engineering executive*
Delfino, Joseph John *environmental engineering sciences educator*
Dinkler, Leonard Ronald *engineering consultant*
Drucker, Daniel Charles *engineer, educator*
Proctor, Charles Lafayette, II *mechanical engineer, educator, consultant*
Sherif, S. A. *mechanical engineering educator*
Westphal, Roger Allen *electrical engineer*

Hialeah
Worth, James Gallagher *engineer, chemist*

Indialantic
Davenport, Fountain St. Clair *electronic engineer*

Jacksonville
Henderson, Kaye Neil *civil engineer, business executive*
Joyce, Edward Rowen *retired chemical engineer, educator*
Klabosh, Charles Joseph *aerospace research and development executive*
Lawrence, Christopher *engineering executive*
Robinson, Steven Earl *structural engineer*
Russell, David Emerson *mechanical engineer, consultant*
Sharp, Howard Roger Emlyn *civil engineer*

Jupiter
Elwell, Howard Andrew *safety engineer*

Kennedy Space Center
Fussell, Ronald Moi *aerospace engineer*
Scrupski, Scott Edward *environmental engineer*
Swift, Dori Hosley *environmental engineer, consultant*

Lake City
Summers, Hugh Bloomer, Jr. *chemical engineer*

Lake Placid
Rew, William Edmund *civil engineer*

Lake Worth
Davis, Paul B. *mechanical engineer, civil engineer, retired*

Lakeland
Earp, James Francy *civil engineer*
Sikora, Eugene Stanley *civil engineer*

Lighthouse Point
Farho, James Henry, Jr. *mechanical engineer, consultant*

Longboat Key
Workman, George Henry *engineer, consultant*

Longwood
Tiblier, Fernand Joseph, Jr. *municipal engineering administrator*

Maitland
Salyzyn, Mark Gregory *software and hardware design engineer*

Melbourne
Baylis, William Thomas *senior systems logistics engineer*
Denaburg, Charles Robert *metallurgical engineer, retired government official*
Garrett, John C. *electrical engineer, manufacturing executive*
Luecke, Conrad John *aerospace educator*

Miami
Attoh-Okine, Nii Otokunor *civil engineer, educator*
Barthel, William Frederick, Jr. *engineer, electronics company executive*
Daub, S. Spencer *computer engineer, consultant*
Ehrlich, Richard *electrical engineer, researcher*
Greenbaum, Steven Randall *mechanical engineer*
Jones, William Kinzy *materials engineering educator*
Polo, Richard Joseph *engineering executive*
Solares, Andres Jose *civil engineer, human rights advocate*
Solé, Pedro *chemical engineer*
Torres, Milton John *industrial engineering educator*
Ural, Oktay *civil engineering educator*

Naples
DeHart, Arnold O'Dell *engineering and design consultant*
Holloman, Harry Hunter *civil engineer*
Montone, Liber Joseph *engineering consultant*
Thampi, Mohan Varghese *environmental health and civil engineer*

New Smyrna Beach
Claridge, Richard *structural engineer*

North Palm Beach
Bible, Carl Raymond, Jr. *electrical engineer*
Mathavan, Sudershan Kumar *nuclear power engineer*
Sooy, William Ray *electrical engineer*

Orange Park
Rodgers, Billy Russell *chemical engineer, research scientist*

Orlando
Caine, Robert *electrical engineer*
Carter, Thomas Allen *engineering executive, consultant*
Casanova-Lucena, Maria Antonia *computer engineer*
Derick, Kenneth *engineering executive*
Israel, Seymour D. *engineering company executive*
Marsh, Malcolm Roy, Jr. *electronics engineer*
Massaro, Mark V. *civil engineer*
Moo Young, Cathy Rhea *industrial engineer*
Pet-Edwards, Julia Johanna Agricola *systems engineering educator, researcher*
Wu, Ying-Chan Fred *electrical engineer*
Youmans, William Cory, Sr. *electrical engineer*

Osprey
Boldt, Heinz *aerospace engineer*

Palatka
Jenab, S. Abe *civil and water resources engineer*

Palm City
Denison, Lloyd William *retired mechanical engineer*

Palm Coast
Hooper, Carl Glenn *civil engineer, software writer*

Palm Harbor
McIlveen, Walter Ronald *architectural engineer*

Panama City
Tuan, Christopher Young-Bee *structural engineer, researcher*

Pensacola
Clare, George *safety engineer, systems safety consultant*
McSwain, Richard Horace *materials engineer, consultant*

Plantation
Cutcher, Jeffrey Lee *electrical engineer*
Staple, Bruce William *acoustical engineer*

Pompano Beach
Sanchez, Javier Alberto *industrial engineer*

Port Saint John
Christian, Carl Franz *electromechanical engineer*

Port Saint Lucie
Huang, Denis Kuo Ying *chemical engineer, consultant*

Saint Augustine
Lilly, Wesley Cooper *marine engineer, surveyor*
Lund, Frederick Henry *aerospace and electrical engineer*

Saint Marks
Labitzke, Dale Russell *chemical processing engineer*

Sarasota
Griffiths, Charles Robert *electronic and ceramic engineer*
Pender, Michael Roger *engineering consultant*

Stuart
Shane, Robert Samuel *chemical engineer, consultant*

Sun City Center
Edwards, Paul Beverly *retired science and engineering educator*

Sunrise
Diaz, Gustavo Adolfo *computer integrated manufacturing engineer*

Tallahassee
Anderson, John Roy *grouting engineer*
Chen, Ching Jen *mechanical engineering educator, research scientist*
Coloney, Wayne Herndon *civil engineer*
Hall, Houghton Alexander *electrical engineering*
Ramaswamy, Jegadhabi Nachiappagoundar *environmental engineer, state agency executive*
Wekezer, Jerzy Wladyslaw *civil engineering educator*

Tampa
Aguinaldo, Jorge Tansingco *chemical engineer, water treatment consultant*
Grifel, Stuart Samuel *management engineer, consultant*
Kaw, Autar Krishen *mechanical engineer, educator*
King, Jack Howell *transportation engineering executive*
Mines, Richard Oliver, Jr. *civil and environmental engineer*
Schmaltz, Lawrence Gerard *engineer, consultant*
Stephens, Robert David *environmental engineering executive*
Wade, Thomas Edward *electrical engineering educator, university research administrator*
Zelinski, Joseph John *engineering educator, consultant*

West Palm Beach
Gillette, Frank C., Jr. *mechanical engineer*
Klein, Harvey Leon *engineering executive*
Laura, Robert Anthony *coastal engineer, consultant*

Winter Garden
Kirby, John Robert *city engineer*

Winter Park
Granberry, Edwin Phillips, Jr. *safety engineer, consultant*
Kerr, James Wilson *engineer*

GEORGIA

Adrian
McCord, James Richard, III *chemical engineer, mathematician*

Albany
Ritter, Guy Franklin *structural engineer*

Alpharetta
Barker, Michael Dean *nuclear engineer, internet engineer*

Athens
Foutz, Timothy Lee *engineering educator*
Marlar, John Thomas *environmental engineer*
Tollner, Ernest William *agricultural engineering educator, agricultural radiology consultant*

Atlanta
Armanios, Erian Abdelmessih *aerospace engineer, educator*
Bellanca, Joseph Paul *engineering/construction executive*
Beohm, Richard Thomas *senior loss control engineer*
Callahan, Leslie Griffin, Jr. *engineer educator*
Draper, Stephen Elliot *engineer, lawyer*
Eckert, Charles Alan *chemical engineering educator*
Feeney, Michael Thomas *civil engineer*
Fiegle, Francis Edwin, II *civil engineering manager*
Gentry, David Raymond *engineer*
Hojjatie, Bahram *mechanical engineer, educator, researcher*
Hurley, John Steven *electrical engineering educator, research scientist*
Jenkins, Robert Severance *concrete construction engineer, consultant*
Kim, Bruce Changshik *research engineer*
Komerath, Narayanan Menon *aerospace engineer*
Lebow, Jeffrey Albert *manufacturing engineer*
Ludovice, Peter John *chemical engineer*
Lyles-Anderson, Barbara Dunbar *civil engineer*
Lynn, David F. *transportation design engineer*
Michelson, Robert Carroll *electronics engineer, educator*
Neitzel, George Paul *engineer, educator*
O'Kon, James Alexander *engineering company executive*
Roberts, Ronnie Spencer *chemical engineering educator, researcher*
Rodenbeck, Sven E. *environmental engineer, consultant*
Rouhani, Shahrokh *civil engineering/environmental educator,*
Russell, Armistead (Ted) Goode *enviromental engineering educator, consultant*
Smith, Mary Lynn *electrical engineer*
Solymossy, Joseph Martin *nuclear engineer, military officer*
Su, Kendall Ling-Chiao *engineering educator*
Tedder, Daniel William *chemical engineering educator*
Teja, Amyn Sadrudin *chemical engineering educator, consultant*
Thompson, George Leroy *mechanical engineer*
Turkia, Kalevi Matti *engineer*
Vachon, Reginald Irenee *mechanical engineer*
White, John Austin, Jr. *engineering educator, dean, consultant*
Zareh, Mo *engineering executive*

Augusta
Tangman, Darrell Grant *computer engineer*

Baxley
Reddy, Yenemala Jaysimha *mechanical engineer*

Cumming
Burand, Stephen Harold *civil engineer*

Duluth
Cooke, Steven John *chemical engineer, consultant, scientist*

Fort Benning
Whitehead, Christopher Cleo *industrial engineer, researcher*

Griffin
Ezeike, Gabriel O.I. *agricultural engineering educator*
Hoogenboom, Gerrit *agricultural engineer*

Grovetown
Baldwin, James Edwin *civil engineer, land development executive*

Jasper
McClure, David H. *industrial engineer, utilities company manager*

Kennesaw
Shannon, Timothy Mayze *industrial designer, consultant*
Sowers, George Frederick *civil engineer*

Lawrenceville
Johnson, Paul Vernon *consulting civil engineer*

Locust Grove
Smith, Al Jackson, Jr. *environmental engineer, lawyer*

Macon
DeLoach, Robert Earl, II *civil and environmental engineer, consultant*
Porenski, Harry Stephen *material engineer*

Marietta
Donehoo, Sheila Rowan *engineering educator*
Garrett, Joseph Edward *aerospace engineer*
Jordan, George Washington, Jr. *engineering company executive*
Miles, Thomas Caswell *aerospace engineer*
Morrison, Raymond Earl, Jr. *engineering executive*
Osborne, Bartley P., Jr. *aeronautical engineer*
Pounds, Gerald Autry *aerospace engineer*
Rowe, William Jeffrey *electrical engineer*
Wineman, Clarence Edward *aerospace engineer*
Zagursky, George Palmer *nuclear engineer*

Martin
Watson, Laura Humphreys *structural engineer*

Norcross
Engleman, Dennis Eugene *electrical engineer*
Minch, Virgil Adelbert *civil engineer*
Moore, Christopher Barry *industrial engineer*
Storey, Bobby Eugene, Jr. *electrical engineer, engineering consultant*
Strickland, Michael Lee *engineering executive, school administrator*

Oxford
Johnson, Roger Warren *chemical engineer*

Robins AFB
Manley, Nancy Jane *environmental engineer*

Roswell
Sanner, George Elwood *electrical engineer*
Smith, Preston Earl *corporate executive*

Saint Simons
Hicks, Harold Eugene *chemical engineer*

Savannah
Belles, Martin Russel *manufacturing engineer*
Haywood, John William, Jr. *engineering consultant*
Herbel, LeRoy Alec, Jr. *telecommunications engineer*
Hsu, Ming-Yu *engineer, educator*
Miles, James L(arry), Jr. *environmental and safety consultant*
Nawrocki, H(enry) Franz *propulsion technology scientist*
Thomas, Michael I. *engineering executive*

Smyrna
Stevenson, Earl, Jr. *civil engineer*

Woodstock
Webb, Edsel Philip *retired textile engineer*

KANSAS

Rose Hill
Brown, Rick Dean *engineer, consultant*

Wichita
Schwartz, Bonnie Jo *electrical engineer*

KENTUCKY

Bowling Green
Bush, Arthur Joe *mining enginner, educator*

Catlettsburg
Fischer, Robert Lee *engineering executive, educator*

Cynthiana
Mobley, Paul Ray *retired engineering technician, writer*

Fort Campbell
Oakes, Thomas Wyatt *environmental engineer*

Frankfort
Nagda, Durga Shanker *environmental engineer, researcher*

Lancaster
Krimm, Martin Christian *electrical engineer, educator*

Lexington
Cremers, Clifford John *mechanical engineering educator*
Drake, David Lee *electronics engineer*
Drake, Vaughn Paris, Jr. *electrical engineer*
Grimes, Craig Alan *electrical engineering educator*
Kaiser, Robert Lee *engineer*

Louisville
Edward, David Andrew *environmental engineer*
Reinbold, Darrel William *energy engineering specialist*
Smith, Robert F., Jr. *civil engineer*
Tran, Long Trieu *industrial engineer*

LOUISIANA

Baker
Moody, Lamon Lamar, Jr. *retired civil engineer*

Baton Rouge
Bourgoyne, Adam Theodore, Jr. *petroleum engineering educator*
Corripio, Armando Benito *chemical engineering educator*
Gammon, Malcolm Ernest, Sr. *surveying and engineering executive*
Gernon, Clarke Joseph, Sr. *mechanical and forensic engineering consultant*
Ikossi-Anastasiou, Kiki *electrical and computer engineer*
Kak, Subhash Chandra *engineering educator, writer*
Moody, Gene Byron *engineering executive, small business owner*
Sajo, Erno *nuclear engineer, educator, physicist, consultant*
Valsaraj, Kalliat Thazhathuveetil *chemical engineering educator*
Zohdi, Magd Eldin *engineering educator*

Covington
Tusa, Dominic Frank *radio communications consultant*

Dubach
Straughan, William Thomas *engineering educator*

Hahnville
Harvey, Kim Lyle *chemical engineer*
Jefferies, Joseph Vincent *safety engineer*

Houma
Davis, Michael Jordan *civil engineer, natural gas company executive*

Lacombe
Mangus, Carl William *technical safety and standards consultant, engineer*

Lafayette
Liang, Qingjian Jim *petroleum engineer*
Salters, Richard Stewart *engineering company executive*

Lake Charles
Levingston, Ernest Lee *engineering executive*

Mandeville
Hruska, Francis John *marine surveyor, consultant*

Metairie
Nicoladis, Michael Frank *engineering company executive*

Monroe
Miles, Oscar Landon, III *engineering company executive*

New Orleans
Alexander, Beverly Moore *mechanical engineer*
Angelides, Demosthenes Constantinos *civil engineer*
Baratta, Richard Victor *biomedical engineer*
Hallila, Bruce Allan *welding engineer*
Logreco, Gerard Ernest *industrial engineer*
Peattie, Robert Addison *engineering educator*
Thomas, Kevin Anthony *biomedical engineer*
Trayanova, Natalia Alexandrova *biomedical engineering educator*

Plaquemine
Goodwin, Billy Wayne *chemical engineer*

Ruston
Hale, Paul Nolen, Jr. *engineering administrator, educator*

Shreveport
Ristig, Kyle Gregory *engineer*
Stansell, Robin Lowel *aeronautical engineer, pilot*

Ville Platte
LaFleur, Stephen Alan *electrical engineer, information technologist, systems intergration consultant*

MARYLAND

Gaithersburg
Williford, Robert Marion *civil engineer*

Silver Spring
Wallin, Eve Linda *engineering executive*

MASSACHUSETTS

Boston
Sittig, Dean Forrest *medical informatician and biomedical engineer*

Worcester
Parrish, Edward Alton, Jr. *electrical and computer engineering educator, academic administrator*

MICHIGAN

Dearborn
Psaris, Amy Celia *manufacturing engineer*

MISSISSIPPI

Columbus
Murphy, Ben Carroll *engineering company executive*

Jackson
Eichelberger, Jerry Wayne *computer engineer*

Lorman
Hylander, Walter Raymond, Jr. *retired civil engineer*

Mississippi State
Truax, Dennis Dale *civil engineer, educator, consultant*
Younan, Nicolas Hanna *electrical engineering educator*

Moss Point
Chapel, Theron Theodore *quality assurance engineer*

Ridgeland
Brady, Michael Jay *environmental engineer, geologist*

Starkville
McKee, Jewel Chester, Jr. *electrical engineer, educator, academic administrator*
Priest, Melville Stanton *retired consulting hydraulic engineer*

Stennis Space Center
Nail, Jasper Monroe *electrical engineer*

University
Chen, Wei-Yin *chemical engineering educator, researcher*
Sadana, Ajit *chemical engineering educator*
Uddin, Waheed *civil engineer, educator*

Vicksburg
Stafford, James Polk, Jr. *civil engineer*

Waynesboro
Brashier, Edward Martin *environmental consultant*

NEVADA

Las Vegas
Long, Cecil Leneir *engineer*

NORTH CAROLINA

Asheville
Scalise, Gary Denis *quality systems engineer*

Candler
Boggs, William Brady *quality engineering and applied statistics consultant*

Cary
Elliott, Richard Verbryck *marine engineer*
Khan, Masrur Ali *nuclear and chemical engineer, physicist*
Saracelli, Kristine Dorthie *systems engineer, consultant*

Chapel Hill
Harris, Robert Lee *environmental engineering educator*
Kusy, Robert Peter *biomedical engineering and orthodontics educator*

Charlotte
Jones, James Richard *mechanical engineer*
Keanini, Russell Guy *mechanical engineering educator, researcher*
Phibbs, Garnett Ersiel *engineer, educator, minister, religious organization administrator*
Rosser, David Pendleton *chemical engineer*
Stoy, Joseph Frank *chemical engineer, consultant*

Clayton
Amy, James Borden *mechanical engineer*
Hinton, David Owen *retired electrical engineer*

Davidson
Vincent, Thomas Estes *engineering executive*

Durham
Kapturowski, Edward James *electrical engineer*
Mobley, J. David *environmental engineer*
Petroski, Henry Joseph *engineer educator*
Plonsey, Robert *electrical and biomedical engineer*
Rasmusson, Randall Lee *biomedical engineer*
Stelling, John Henry Edward *chemical engineer*
Strohbehn, John Walter *engineering science educator*
Vatavuk, William Michael *chemical engineer, author*
Wilson, Blake Shaw *electrical engineer, researcher*

Flat Rock
Davidson, Clayton Leslie *chemical engineer*
Matteson, Thomas Dickens *aeronautical engineer, consultant*

Gastonia
Larion, Florin-George *mechanical engineer*

Greensboro
Cazel, Hugh Allen *industrial engineer, educator*
Daniels, Joseph Howard, II *broadcast engineer*
Haas, Gregory George *mechanical engineer*
Hunter, Larry Lee *electrical engineer*

Hendersonville
Schooley, Charles Earl *electrical engineer, consultant*

High Point
Huston, Fred John *retired automotive engineer*

Matthews
Toth, James Joseph *power systems engineer*

Morehead City
Baker, Edward George *retired mechanical engineer*
Williams, Winton Hugh *civil engineer*

Murphy
Kerr, Walter Belnap *retired missile instrumentation engineer, English language researcher, consultant*

Nags Head
Rogallo, Francis Melvin *mechanical, aeronautical engineer*

New Bern
Bachman, John Andrew, Jr. *retired engineer*

Raleigh
Beasley, David Beach *agricultural engineering educator, administrator*
Havner, Kerry Shuford *civil engineering and solid mechanics educator*
Kriz, George James *agricultural research administrator, educator*
Langer, Dale Robert *electrical engineer*
Mayo, Robert Michael *nuclear engineering educator, physicist*
Meier, Wilbur Leroy, Jr. *industrial engineer, educator, former university chancellor*
Murray, Raymond Le Roy *nuclear engineering educator*
Odum, Jeffery Neal *mechanical engineer*
Piver, William Crawfurd *civil engineer, consultant*
Wahls, Harvey Edward *civil engineering educator*
Williams, Hugh Alexander, Jr. *retired mechanical engineer, consultant*
Wilson, James Reed *industrial engineering educator*

Research Triangle Park
Henschel, D. Bruce *chemical engineer, environmental researcher*
Miller, Charles Gregory *biomedical researcher*
Moon, Billy G. *electrical engineer*

Sanford
Mullings, Arnold R. *engineering manager*

Supply
Webb, Thomas George *aircraft manufacturing engineer*

Swannanoa
Stuck, Roger Dean *electrical engineering educator*

Thomasville
Hinkle, William Paul *mechanical and electrical engineer, consultant*

Weaverville
Weng, Chuan *mechanical engineer*

Wilmington
Sims, David Bryson, Jr. *engineer*

Winston Salem
Henderson, Richard Martin *chemical engineer*
Tan, Ping *computer systems manager*

OHIO

Piqua
She, (Shing) Sixing *development engineer*

Ripley
McMillan, James Albert *electronics engineer, educator*

Youngstown
Stahl, Joel Sol *plastic and chemical engineer*

OKLAHOMA

Bartlesville
Clay, Harris Aubrey *chemical engineer*
Lew, Lawrence Edward *chemical engineer*
Mihm, John Clifford *chemical engineer*

Buffalo
Anthony, Jack Ramon *mechanical engineer, retired*

Chickasha
Rienne, Dozie Ignatius *structural engineer*

Duncan
Sears, Leslie Ray, III *electrical engineer*

Edmond
Carpenter, Bruce Neil *engineering executive*
Scharp, Robert Charles *mining engineer, energy company executive*

Fairfax
Funk, Gary Lloyd *control engineer*

Jenks
Leming, W(illiam) Vaughn *electronics engineer*

Miami
Vanover, Boyd Russell *engineer*

Norman
Altan, M(ustafa) Cengiz *mechanical engineering educator*
Bert, Charles Wesley *mechanical and aerospace engineer, educator*
Menzie, Donald E. *petroleum engineer, educator*
Scamehorn, John Frederick *chemical engineer*
Zaman, Musharraf *civil engineering educator*
Zelby, Leon Wolf *electrical engineering educator, consulting engineer*

Oklahoma City
Aguirre, Samuel Honorato *electrical engineer*
Allen, James Harmon, Jr. *civil engineer*
Dillon, Ray William *engineering technician*
Jones, William Hawood *electrical engineer*
Lovelace, George David, Jr. *quality engineer*
Mikkelson, Dean Harold *geological engineer*
Miller, Herbert Dell *petroleum engineer*
Thompson, Guy Thomas *safety engineer*

Oologah
Knight, Gary Charles *mechanical engineer*

Pawhuska
Barker, Newell Keith *petroleum engineer, chief branch of minerals*

Ponca City
Hardin, Donald Wayne *standards and industrial manufacturing engineer*

Stillwater
Elliott, Ronald Lee *agricultural engineer, educator*
Noyes, Ronald Tacie *agricultural engineering educator*

Tahlequah
Lindsey, James Kendall *civil engineer*

Tulsa
Chin, Alexander Foster *electronics educator*
Cobbs, James Harold *engineer, consultant*
Prayson, Alex Stephen *drafting and mechanical design educator*
Ryan, James Chris *electrical engineer*
Tubbs, David Eugene *mechanical engineer, marketing professional*

Yale
Berger, Billie David *corrosion engineer*

Yukon
Morgan, Robert Steve *mechanical engineer*

PENNSYLVANIA

New Galilee
Randza, Jason Michael *engineer*

SOUTH CAROLINA

Aiken
Cauthen, Rea Kimbrell, Jr. *engineer*
Grosso, Vincent Joseph *quality systems engineering professional*
Hayhoe, George Frederick, III *technical communication consultant*
Hootman, Harry Edward *retired nuclear engineer, consultant*
Murphy, Edward Thomas *engineering executive*
Voss, Terence J. *human factors scientist, educator*

Anderson
Bergmann, Warren Clarence *mechanical engineer*

Beaufort
Koppernaes, Christian *electrical engineer*

Charleston
Bolin, Edmund Mike *electrical engineer, franchise engineering consultant*
Reich, Michael *electronics engineer*

Clemson
Golan, Lawrence Peter *mechanical engineering educator, energy researcher*
Grady, C.P. Leslie, Jr. *engineering educator*
Taylor, Joseph Christopher *audio systems electrical and controls engineer*
von Recum, Andreas F. *bioengineer*

Columbia
Baskin, C(harles) R(ichard) *retired civil engineer, physical scientist*
Bates, William Lawrence *civil engineer*
Morehouse, Jeffrey *mechanical engineering educator*

Conway
Springer, Fred Gene *manufacturing engineer, mechanical engineer*

Fort Mill
Brooks, Jerry Claude *safety engineer, educator*

Goose Creek
Floss, Mark Thaddeus *civil engineer, computer scientist*

Greenville
Carlay, Ronald Leon *mechanical engineer*
Plumstead, William Charles *quality engineer, consultant*
Schneider, George William *retired aircraft design engineer*

Greenwood
Spearman, Lionel *mechanical engineer*

Hartsville
Terry, Stuart L(ee) *plastics engineer*

Hilton Head Island
Barrows, John Frederick *mechanical engineer*
Huckins, Harold Aaron *chemical engineer*

Jenkinsville
Loignon, Gerald Arthur, Jr. *nuclear engineer*

Laurens
Bost, John Rowan *retired manufacturing executive, engineer*

North Charleston
Howerton, Jack Thompson *manufacturing engineer, consultant*

Orangeburg
Isa, Saliman Alhaji *electrical engineering educator*

Rock Hill
Evans, Wallace Rockwell, Jr. *mechanical engineer*
Fitzpatrick, James Ward, Jr. *engineering technology educator*

Spartanburg
Jones, Neill E. *engineer, consultant*

West Union
Klutz, Anthony Aloysius, Jr. *health, safety and environmental manager*

Winnsboro
Hobbs, Ralph Lee *textile consultant*

York
Fritz, Edward William *mechanical engineer*

TENNESSEE

Arnold AFB
Chapman, Randall Allen *research engineer*

Blountville
Okes, Duke Wayne *quality engineer, management consultant*

Brentwood
Isom, Sam *engineering executive*

Brighton
McFarland, Gary Lane *fire protection engineer, consultant*

Brownsville
Stevenson, William Edward *chemical engineer*

Chattanooga
Arndt, Steven Andrew *nuclear engineer*
Duckworth, Jerrell James *electrical engineer*
McCormick, Jack Randall *environmental engineer*
McDonald, Gary Haywood *mechanical engineering educator*
Williams, Robert Carlton *electrical engineer*

Cleveland
Beeler, Warren Jennings *retired engineering consultant*

Cookeville
Sissom, Leighton Esten *engineering educator, dean, consultant*
Smaili, Ahmad *mechanical engineering educator*
Ting, Kwun-Lon *engineer, educator, consultant*

Cordova
Waters, Douglas Stuart, Jr. *engineering company consultant, civil engineer*

Goodlettsville
Krauss, William Edward *engineering executive*

Kingsport
Reasor, Roderick Jackson *industrial engineer*
Rex, David Lawrence *project manager*
Sales, James William *chemical engineer*

Knoxville
Bressler, Marcus N. *consulting engineer*
Campbell, William Buford, Jr. *materials engineer, chemist, forensic consultant*
Chou, Karen Chai Kwan *civil engineering educator*
Cliff, Steven Burris *engineering executive*
Cummings, Peter Thomas *chemical engineering educator*
Graves, Phillip James *marketing professional*
Katz, Elaine Marcia *nuclear engineering educator*
Laroussi, Mounir *electrical engineer*
Mashburn, John Walter *quality control engineer*
McGinley, Suzanne *environmental and civil engineer*
Murphy, David Frank *mechanical engineering executive*
Pearce, James Walker *electronics engineer*
Schuler, Theodore Anthony *retired civil engineer, retired city official*
Sorrells, Frank Douglas *mechanical engineer, consultant*

Loudon
Waldrop, William Rheuben *chemical engineer*

Memphis
French, Louis Bertrand *engineering educator*
Lewis, Gladius *mechanical engineer, educator*
Long, Allan Henry *electrical engineer*
Maksi, Gregory Earl *engineering educator*
Malasri, Siripong *engineering educator*
Malkin, Robert Allen *biomedical engineer*
Williams, Edward F(oster), III *environmental engineer*
Williams, Mark Mason *engineering educator, consultant*

Nashville
Davis, Paul Estill *environmental executive*
Hughes, Gayle Womack *civil engineer, educator*

Oak Ridge
Bopp, Charles Daniel *retired chemical engineer*
Brown, Robert Frederick *industrial systems engineer, technology applications, industrial systems and management systems consultant*
Fontana, Mario H. *nuclear engineer*
Kasten, Paul Rudolph *nuclear engineer, educator*
Korsah, Kofi *nuclear engineer*
Marz, Loren Carl *environmental engineer, chemist*
Moore, Marcus Lamar *environmental engineer, consultant*
Mulkey, Charles Eric *environmental engineer*
Rivera, Angel Luis *chemical engineer*
Tcherneshoff, Lyndon Mark *business development executive*
Wooten, Hollis Darwin *engineer*
Yong, Loong Kwet *nuclear engineer, consultant*

Shelbyville
White, James Claiborne *manufacturing engineer executive*

Smyrna
Justis, Lewis Craig *manufacturing engineer*

South Pittsburg
Cordell, Francis Merritt *instrument engineer, consultant*

Tullahoma
Baucum, William Emmett, Jr. *electrical research engineer*
Garrison, George Walker, Jr. *mechanical and industrial engineering educator*
Hill, Susan Sloan *safety engineer*

TEXAS

Abilene
Gray, Gordon Harris *petroleum consultant*

Allen
Dawes, Robert Leo *research company executive*

Amarillo
Blain, Richard Eugene, Jr. *manufacturing engineer*
Brown, William Larry *manufacturing engineer*
Harris, Hollis Ward *electrical engineer*
Keaton, Lawrence Cluer *safety engineer, consultant*
Von Eschen, Robert Leroy *electrical engineer, consultant*

Anahuac
Fontenot, Jackie Darrel *safety and health consultant*

Arlington
Clark, Dayle Meritt *civil engineer*
Deaver, Pete Eugene *civil and aeronautical engineer*
Imrhan, Sheik Nazir *industrial engineer, educator*
Notch, James Stephen *structural engineering executive, consultant*
Ptaszkowski, Stanley Edward, Jr. *civil engineer, structural engineer*
Rollins, Albert Williamson *civil engineer, consultant*

Austin
Akujuobi, Cajetan Maduabuchukwu *research engineer, electrical engineering educator*
Alizy, Nouri *reliability engineer*
Baker, Lee Edward *biomedical engineering educator*
Barlow, Joel William *chemical engineering educator*
Brown, Stephen Neal *computer engineer*
Carroll, Irwin Dixon *engineer*
Castaldi, Frank James *environmental engineer, consultant*
Estrada, David Robert *quality engineering consultant*
Fults, Kenneth Wyatt *civil engineer, surveyor*
Gavande, Sampat Anand *agricultural engineer, soil scientist*
Grimm, Clayford Thomas *architectural engineer, consultant*
Hixson, Elmer L. *engineering educator*
Jirsa, James Otis *civil engineering educator*
Juricic, Davor *mechanical engineering educator*
Koen, Billy Vaughn *mechanical engineering educator*
Koepsel, Wellington Wesley *electrical engineering educator*
Luedecke, William Henry *mechanical engineer, company executive*
Mautz, Karl Emerson *engineering executive*
Moon, Tessie Jo *mechanical engineering educator*
Murthy, Vanukuri Radha Krishna *civil engineer*
O'Geary, Dennis Traylor *contracting and engineering company executive*
Richards-Kortum, Rebecca Rae *biomedical engineering educator*
Sanchez, Isaac Cornelius *chemical engineer, educator*
Saunders, Jimmy Dale *aerospace engineer, physicist, naval officer*
Schmidt, Philip S. *mechanical engineering educator*
Swartzlander, Earl Eugene, Jr. *engineering educator, former electronics company executive*
Tesar, Delbert *machine systems and robotics educator, researcher, manufacturing consultant*
Wright, David Brian *systems engineering consultant*

Bangs
Whiteley, James Morris *retired aerospace engineer*

Beaumont
Williams, Curt Alan *mechanical engineer*

Bellaire
Wisch, David John *structural engineer*

Boerne
Mitchelhill, James Moffat *civil engineer*
Patti, Tony J. *retired electrical engineer*

Bulverde
Loop, Robert Kenneth *aerospace engineer*

Burnet
Gomes, Norman Vincent *retired industrial engineer*

College Station
Coble, Charlie Grover *agricultural engineering educator*
Godbey, Luther David *architectural and engineering executive*
Isdale, Charles Edwin *chemical engineer*
Lowery, Lee Leon, Jr. *civil engineer*
Lytton, Robert Leonard *civil engineer, educator*
Neff, Ray Quinn *electric power educator, consultant*
Nguyen, Cam Van *electrical engineer, researcher*
O'Neal, Dennis Lee *mechanical engineering educator*
Parlos, Alexander George *systems and control engineering educator*
Pitt, Woodrow Wilson, Jr. *engineering educator*
Reddy, Thikkavarapu Agami *mechanical engineer, educator, researcher*
Richardson, Herbert Heath *mechanical engineer, educator, institute director*
Valdes, Juan B. *engineering educator*
Wagner, John Philip *safety engineering educator, science researcher*
Wilhelm, Wilbert Edward *industrial and systems engineering educator*
Yeung, Albert Tak-Chung *civil engineering educator*

Conroe
Barron, Oscar Noel *gas engineer, consultant*

Corpus Christi
Green, William Wells *civil engineer*
Umfleet, Lloyd Truman *electrical engineering technology educator*

Corsicana
Jessup, Steven Lee *ceramics engineer*

Dallas
Brown, A.C., Jr. *electrical engineer*
Cave, Kirk Clark *engineer, computer specialist*
Chau, Hin-Fai *electrical engineer*
Chen, Walter Yi-Chen *electrical engineer*
Cruikshank, Thomas Henry *energy services and engineering executive*
Durkee, Joe Worthington, Jr. *nuclear engineer*
Fischer, Marsha Leigh *civil engineer*
Fix, Douglas Martin *electrical engineer*
Fowler, Delbert Marcom *design and construction engineer*
Giesen, Herman Mills *engineering executive, consultant, mechanical forensic engineer*
Honkanen, Jari Olavi *electrical engineer*
Huang, Yen Ti *civil engineer*
Kilby, Jack St. Clair *electrical engineer*
Le, Can *mechanical engineer, inventor, author*
Lutz, Robert Brady, Jr. *engineering executive, consultant*
McCall, Clyde Samuel, Jr. *petroleum engineer*
Melgar, Julio *retired mechanical engineer*
O'Grady, Albert Thomas *electrical engineer*
Roth, Robert William *computer field engineer*
Skaggs, Merton Melvin, Jr. *environmental engineer*
Vining, William Macon, Jr. *industrial hygienist*
Ward, Phillip Wayne *electrical engineer*
Zimmerman, S(amuel) Morton (Mort Zimmerman) *electrical and electronics engineering executive*

Deer Park
Mujica, Mary Bernadette *mechanical engineer*

Del Rio
Hayes, Vernon Holgate *retired design engineer*

Denton
Head, Gregory Alan *mechanical engineer, consultant*

El Paso
Dwight, Kenneth Harlan *metallurgical engineer*
Fahy, Michael P. *civil and environmental engineer*
Heide, John Wesley *engineering executive*
Knuteson, Knut Jeffery *computer engineer*
Obermeyer, Gerald Frederick *industrial engineer*
Quintana, Rolando *industrial engineer*
Shadaram, Mehdi *electrical engineering educator*
Wicks, Harry Oliver, III *mechanical engineer*

Flower Mound
Ross, Lesa Moore *quality assurance professional*

Fort Worth
Buckner, John Kendrick *aerospace engineer*
Friberg, Emil Edwards *mechanical engineer, consultant*
Kolesar, Edward Steven, Jr. *electrical engineering educator*
McLane, William Delano *mechanical engineer*
Olson, David Allen *engineer*
Romine, Thomas Beeson, Jr. *consulting engineering executive*
Vick, John *engineering executive*

Freeport
Frazier, Terry Francis *engineering manager*

Friendswood
Lampton, Robert Donald, Jr. *chemical engineer, consultant*
Wood, Loren Edwin *aerospace engineer, consultant*

Galveston
Otis, John James *civil engineer*
Sheppard, Louis Clarke *biomedical engineer, educator*

Garland
Brooks, Carson Eugene *electrical engineer*
Christensen, Allan Robert *electrical engineer, enrolled agent*

Granbury
Harmon, John LaFayette *retired petroleum engineer*

Greenville
White, William Dudley *safety engineer*

Houston
Allman, Mark C. *engineer, physicist*
Antalffy, Leslie Peter *mechanical engineer*
Baca, Ernesto *environmental engineer, consultant*
Beauchamp, Jeffery Oliver *mechanical engineer*
Bishop, David Nolan *electrical engineer*
Bishop, Thomas Ray *retired mechanical engineer*
Bozeman, Ross Elliot *engineering executive*
Brandl, Ernest David *civil engineer*
Brouse, Michael *petroleum engineer, management consultant*
Campbell, Hilton Earl *reliability engineer*
Chavez, Victor Manuel *process engineer*
Chen, James Chiang-Tung *environmental engineer*
Collipp, Bruce Garfield *ocean engineer, consultant*
Copeland, Robert Michael *mechanical engineer*
David, Yadin B. *biomedical engineer, health care technology consultant*
Dawn, Frederic Samuel *chemical and textile engineer*
Duerr, David *civil engineer*
Dwyer, John James *mechanical engineer*
Edwards, Lance A. *engineering executive*
Elliot, Douglas Gene *chemical engineer, engineering company executive, consultant*
Gernon, George Owen, Jr. *civil engineer*
Gilbert, David Wallace *aerospace engineer*
Haist, Charles Frederick *systems engineer*
Hale, Leonard Peter, III *instrumentation and electrical engineer*
Heit, Raymond Anthony *civil engineer*
Hinman-Sweeney, Elaine Marie *aerospace engineer*
Huddleston, Billy Pete *petroleum engineer*
Hunter, Hassell Eugene *petroleum engineer, consultant*
Iyer, R. Ravi *engineering consultant*
Judah, Janeen Sue *petroleum engineer, lawyer*
King, Robert Augustin *engineering executive*
Kirby, Sarah Ann Van Deventer *aerospace engineer*
Klotz, David Wayne *executive, civil engineer*
Kobs, Alfred W. *engineer*
Larks, Jack *forensic engineer, consultant*
Lopez-Nakazono, Benito *chemical and industrial engineer*
Machol, Frederick Bernhard *mining engineer*
Mau, Sheng Taur *engineering educator*
McEvilly, Michael James *civil engineer*
McLeod, Harry O'Neal, Jr. *petroleum engineer, consultant*
Miele, Angelo *engineering educator, researcher, consultant, author*
Miller, Charles Rickie *thermal/fluid systems analyst, engineering manager*
Montijo, Ralph Elias, Jr. *engineering executive*
Muller, Frank Mair, III *industrial engineer*
Nicastro, David Harlan *forensic engineer, consultant, author*
Nordgren, Ronald Paul *engineering educator, researcher*
Oxer, John Paul Daniell *civil engineer*
Peng, Liang-Chuan *mechanical engineer*
Reddy, Gopal Baireddy *engineering educator*
Reese, James Carl, Jr. *drilling engineer*
Remington, Will Myron *engineering executive*
Robinson, Ronald James *petroleum engineer*
Roth, Brian Andrew *project engineer*
Sandstrum, Steve D. *industry manager*
Sawyer, David Neal *petroleum industry executive*
Schulze, Arthur Edward *biomedical engineer, researcher*
Sloan, Harold David *chemical engineering consultant*
Smalley, Arthur Louis, Jr. *engineering and construction company executive*
Stamm, Robert Calvin *mechanical engineer, consultant*
Stauffer, Titus *electrical engineer, writer, publisher*
Tellez, George Henry *safety professional, consultant*
Tiller, Frank M. *chemical engineering educator*
Tiras, Herbert Gerald *engineering executive*
Tucker, Randolph Wadsworth *engineering executive*
Venditto, James Joseph *chemical engineer*
Wang, Tong *mechanical engineer, senior research scientist*
Wren, Robert James *aerospace engineering manager*
Wu, Gary G. *petroleum engineer, consultant*
Yu, Aiting Tobey *engineering executive*

Hurst
Bishara, Amin Tawadros *mechanical engineer, technical services executive*

Irving
Halter, Edmund John *mechanical engineer*
Longwell, H.J. *petroleum engineer*
McCormack, Grace Lynette *civil engineering technician*
Robinson, Charles Emanuel *systems engineer, consultant*
Wells, Jon Barrett *engineer*

Katy
Ciminieri, Ubaldo Tomas *industrial engineer*

Kerrville
Sinninger, Dwight Virgil *engineer*

Kingwood
Bowman, Stephen Wayne *quality assurance engineer, consultant*

Lake Jackson
Losier, Thomas Philip *chemical engineer*
McCutchen, Charles William *chemical engineer*

League City
Senyard, Corley Price, Jr. *engineering executive, consultant*

Lindale
Wilson, Leland Earl *petroleum engineering consultant*

Livingston
Hayes, Gordon Glenn *civil engineer*

Longview
Canfield, Glenn, Jr. *metallurgical engineer*
Lee, B. Kyun *mechanical engineer, educator*

Lubbock
Giesselmann, Michael Guenter *electrical engineer, educator, researcher*
Heath, Brent Alan *electrical engineer*
Ishihara, Osamu *electrical engineer, physicist, educator*
Neblock, Carl Scott *chemical engineering educator*

Marble Falls
Tretter, Vincent Joseph, Jr. *chemical engineer, retired*

Mesquite
Kennedy, Keith Clyde *mechanical engineer, entrepreneur, administrator*

Midland
Beard, Thomas LeRoy *chemical engineer*
Dimit, Robert Leslie *petroleum engineer*
Mody, Bharat Gangadas *engineer*
Pappas, James Marcus *petroleum engineer*
Simpson, Berry Don *petroleum engineer*

Nacogdoches
Allen, John Timothy *mechanical engineer*
O'Keefe, Joseph Kirk *systems engineer*

Nash
Hance, Douglas James, Jr. *aerospace research engineer, consultant*

North Richland Hills
Steele, Davis Tillou *mechanical engineer*

Orange
Olive, Stewart Broadwell *retired chemical engineer, management executive*

Pasadena
Cheng, Chung Ping *chemical engineer*

Pearland
Jones, Lionel Troy, Jr. *electronic engineer*

Plano
Clement, Clarence Clark, Jr. *petroleum engineer*
Hemmi, Christian Otto *electrical engineer*
Schmidt, Glenn Frederic *electronics engineer*
Seals, Ryan Brown *electronics engineer*

Port Arthur
Naizer, Kenneth C. *electrical engineer*

Richardson
Chase, Victoria Byler *mechanical engineer*
Duplantier, Chantler Wayne *telecommunications engineer*
Witherspoon, W(illiam) Tom *engineering consultant*

Rio Medina
Weiblen, Michael Don *electrical engineer*

Rockport
Herring, David M(ayo) *engineering consultant*

Rosenberg
Tourtellotte, Mills Charlton *mechanical and electrical engineer*

San Antonio
Abramson, Hyman Norman *engineering and science research executive*
Belzung, Paul Edward *engineering executive*
Brown, Ronald Kaye *civil engineer, minister*
Buster, Alan Adair *control engineer*
Chan, Kwai Shing *materials engineer, researcher*
Cutshall, Jon Tyler *aerospace engineer, researcher*
D'Arcy, Thomas Joseph *engineering consultant*
Diego, Manuel Roxas *production engineer*
Dougherty, Robert James *safety consultant*
Ong, Joo Leng *biomaterials engineering educator*
Sasscer, Donald Stuart *mechanical engineer, nuclear engineer*
Stebbins, Richard Henderson *electronics engineer, peace officer, security consultant*
Vafeades, Peter *mechanical engineering educator*
Weinbrenner, George Ryan *aeronautical engineer*

Sherman
Chaffin, Lyle Dwain *semiconductor integrated circuits executive*
Reid, William Michael *mechanical engineer*

Spring
Cross, Carole Ann *plastics engineer*
Riley, Arthur Roy *consulting engineer*
Szymczak, Edward Joseph *mechanical engineer*

Stafford
Burzynski, Tadeusz *engineering executive*

Sugar Land
Johanson, Knut Arvid, Jr. *systems engineer*
Westphal, Douglas Herbert *engineering company executive*

Temple
Patureau, Arthur Mitchell *chemical engineer, consultant*

Texas City
Lamar, James Lewis, Jr. *chemical engineer*

The Woodlands
Lanclos, Ritchie Paul *petroleum engineer*
Pillai, Raviraj Sukumar *chemical engineer, researcher*
Saikowski, Ronald Alexander *consulting engineer*

Tyler
Trent, Warren C. *mechanical engineer*
Wright, Harrold Eugene *petroleum engineer*

Universal City
Atchley, Curtis Leon *mechanical engineer*

Waco
Solomon, Charles Francis *electronics educator*
Stallings, Frank, Jr. *industrial engineer*

Webster
Epright, Charles John *aerospace engineer*
Stephens, Douglas Kimble *chemical engineer*
Terry, Reese *engineering executive*

Wichita Falls
Hinton, Troy Dean *civil engineer*
Peterson, Holger Martin *electrical engineer*

VIRGINIA

Afton
Anderson, Donald Norton, Jr. *retired electrical engineer*

Alexandria
Brackett, James Vincent *electrical engineer*
Doeppner, Thomas Walter *electrical engineer, consultant*
Ellison, Thorleif *consulting engineer*
Glynn, Ernest B. *civil engineer, environmental engineer*
Hodge, Donald Ray *systems engineer*
Karpiscak, John, III *engineer, army officer*
MacLaren, William George, Jr. *engineering executive*
Muller, Lloyd Holden *logistics and education consultant*
Murray, Russell, II *aeronautical engineer, defense analyst, consultant*
Thompson, LeRoy, Jr. *radio engineer, military reserve officer*

Annandale
Geiger, Richard Bernard *engineer, retired federal agency administrator*
Schlegelmilch, Reuben Orville *electrical engineer, consultant*

Arlington
Baughman, George Washington *aeronautical operations research scientist*
Chan, Wan-Kang Will *mechanical engineer*
Ciarula, Thomas Alan *engineer, retired navy officer*
Cohen, Eliot Dorsey *electrical engineer*
Colliver, Keith Wayne *international program analyst*
Davis, Michael *engineering company executive*
Floyd, James Burris *electrical engineer*
Gilbert, Arthur Charles *aerospace engineer, consulting engineer*
Gustafson, Richard Alexander *engineering executive*
Harrington, George Fred *aviation consultant*
Kemble, James Richard *professional engineering services executive*
Murray, Arthur Joseph *business executive, lecturer*
Reagan, Lawrence Paul, Jr. *systems engineer*
Stevens, Donald King *aeronautical engineer*
Sullivan, Patrick Gerald, Jr. *electronics engineer*
Young, Janet Cheryl *electrical engineer*

Blacksburg
Cox, David Fullen *chemical engineering educator*
Dillaha, Theo A., III *environmental engineer, educator, consultant*
Eiss, Norman Smith, Jr. *mechanical engineering educator*
Fabrycky, Wolter Joseph *engineering educator, author, industrial and systems engineer*
Gray, Festus Gail *electrical engineer, educator, researcher*
Inman, Daniel John *mechanical engineer, educator*
Jones, James Beverly *retired mechanical engineering educator, consultant*
Jovanovic, Milan Miodrag *electrical engineer, researcher*
Kirk, Robley Gordon *mechanical engineering educator*
Neu, Wayne Lawrence *ocean engineering educator*
Perumpral, John Verghese *agricultural engineer, administrator, educator*
Smith, Charles William *engineering educator*

Burke
Lynch, Charles Theodore, Sr. *materials science engineering researcher, consultant, educator*

Centreville
Bucciero, Joseph Mario, Jr. *executive engineering firm*

Chantilly
Alexander, Michael Edward *systems engineer*

Charlottesville
Adams, James Milton *biomedical engineering educator*
Bly, Charles Albert *nuclear engineer, research scientist*
Dorning, John Joseph *nuclear engineering, engineering physics and applied mathematics educator*
Hudson, John Lester *chemical engineering educator*
Lu, Yichi *materials scientist*
Matthews, George Bostert *engineering educator*
Theodoridis, George Constantin *biomedical engineering educator, researcher*
Townsend, Miles Averill *aerospace and mechanical engineering educator*
Uddin, Rizwan *engineering educator, researcher*

Chesapeake
Bockwoldt, Todd Shane *nuclear engineer*

Hillery, Robert Charles *naval engineer, management consultant*
Jaques, James Alfred, III *communications engineer*

Culpeper
Reed, Christopher Robert *civil engineer*

Fairfax
Cooper, Henry Franklyn *engineering, technology and national security affairs consultant*
Khan, Mohammad Shamim *civil engineer*
Lott, Wayne Thomas *systems engineer*
Nailor, Richard Anthony, Sr. *research company executive*
Pedersen, George J. *engineering company executive, computer support company executive*
Schilling, William Richard *aerospace engineer, research and development company executive*
Snyder, Thomas Daniel *electronics engineer, consultant*
Sumner, John Healy *systems engineer*
Thai, Van Albert *design engineer*

Fairfax Station
Coaker, James Whitfield *mechanical engineer*

Falls Church
Villarreal, Carlos Castaneda *engineering executive*

Farmville
Williams, Albert Theophilus Wadi *consulting engineer, educational guidance executive*

Fort Belvoir
Barnholdt, Terry Joseph *chemical, industrial, and general engineer*
Van Derlaske, Dennis Peter *electrical engineer*

Glen Allen
Kappatos, Konstantinos Nicholas *engineering executive*

Great Falls
Litton, Robert Clifton *marine engineer, consultant*

Hampton
Chu, Li-Chuan *aerospace engineer, consultant*
Farrukh, Usamah Omar *electrical engineering educator, researcher*
Kelly, Jeffrey Jennings *mechanical engineer*
Looges, Peter John *systems engineer, architect*
Meyers, James Frank *electronics engineer*
Sleeman, William Clifford, Jr. *aerospace technologist*
Whitesides, John Lindsey, Jr. *aerospace engineering educator, researcher*

Harrisonburg
Auckland, James Craig *mechanical engineer*

Herndon
Cheatham, Patrick Seale *engineering executive*
Kohr, Robert Leon *safety engineer*

Lynchburg
Barkley, Henry Brock, Jr. *research and development executive*
Farkas, Steven *engineering executive*
Gray, Kevin Troy *manufacturing engineer*
Latimer, Paul Jerry *non-destructive testing engineer*
Moeller, Helen Hergenroder *ceramic engineer*

Marion
Pratt, Mark Ernest *mechanical engineer*

Mc Lean
Airst, Malcolm Jeffrey *electronics engineer*
Dargan, Pamela Ann *systems/software engineer*
Gay, William Karl *systems integration program manager*
Kim, John Chan Kyu *electrical engineer*
Klopfenstein, Rex Carter *electrical engineer*
Lane, Susan Nancy *structural engineer*
Liu, Charles Chung-Cha *transportation engineer, consultant*
Schmeidler, Neal Francis *engineering executive*

Newington
Chase, Emery John, Jr. *nuclear engineer, researcher*
Foster, Eugene Lewis *engineering executive*

Newport News
Hempfling, Gregory Jay *mechanical engineer*
Pohl, John Joseph, Jr. *retired mechanical engineer*
Thompson, Mathew John *mechanical engineer*

Norfolk
Denyes, James Richard *industrial engineer*
Estes, Edward Richard, Jr. *engineering consultant, engineer, retired educator*

Portsmouth
Luther, Mark Alan *electrical deisgn engineer*

Reston
Chickinsky, Alan *computer engineer, educator*
Diaz, Rafael José *electrical engineer, communications engineer, consultant*
Ethridge, Max Michael *civil engineer*
Evans, Richard Taylor *aerospace engineer, consultant*
Trimble, Brian Edward *structural engineer*

Richmond
Atchison, Arthur Mark *industrial, research and development engineer*
Doraiswamy, Deepak *chemical engineer*
Ludden, George Clemens *metallurgical engineer*
Palik, Robert Richard *mechanical engineer*
Sallome, Sam *electrical engineer, writer*
Washington, James MacKnight *former chemical engineer*
Wist, Abund Ottokar *biomedical engineer, radiation physicist, educator*

Roanoke
Hamilton, Gordon Stokes *mechanical engineer, consultant*
Jackson, Daniel Wyer *electrical engineer*
Stadler, Donald Arthur *management engineer*
Uhm, Dan *process engineer*

Salem
Bhavsar, Sanatkumar Navinchandra *chemical engineer*
Lane, Lawrence Jubin *retired electrical engineer, consultant*
Pommerenke, Roger Lee *electronics engineer*

Springfield
Beale, David Anthony *structural engineering consultant*
Duff, William Grierson *electrical engineer*
Fowler, Ray Harland *engineering consultant*

Sterling
Fothergill, John Wesley, Jr. *systems engineer, design company executive*

Suffolk
Lewis, Robert Earl *city traffic engineer*

Verona
Smith, Rodney Wike *engineering executive*

Vienna
Dodson, Louis Raymond *computer systems engineer*
Gilkey, Herbert Talbot *engineering consultant*
Meisinger, Henry Peter *electronics engineer*
Salah, Sagid *retired nuclear engineer*
Woodward, Kenneth Emerson *retired mechanical engineer*

Virginia Beach
Glenn, Joe Davis, Jr. *retired civil engineer, consultant*

Warrenton
Frazer, Russell Theodore *general engineer*

Waynesboro
Aronson, Mark Theodore *chemical engineer*
McNair, John William, Jr. *civil engineer*

Williamsburg
Dunn, Ronald Holland *civil engineer, management executive, railway consultant*
Hughes, George Farant, Jr. *safety engineer*

Woodbridge
Medding, Walter Sherman *environmental engineer*

WASHINGTON

Renton
Saladino, Anthony Joseph *aerospace engineer*

WEST VIRGINIA

Charleston
Sterling, Donald Eugene *civil engineer*

Elkins
Armstrong, Deanna Frances *engineer*

Fairmont
Brizendine, Anthony Lewis *civil engineering educator*
Lowers, Gina Cattani *process and instrumentation engineer*

Kenova
Ornosky, Paul M. *production engineer*

Morgantown
Eck, Ronald Warren *civil engineer, educator*
Guthrie, Hugh Delmar *chemical engineer*
Prucz, Jacky Carol *mechanical and aerospace engineer, educator*
Schroder, John L., Jr. *retired mining engineer*

Ravenswood
Hamrick, Leslie Wilford, Jr. *metallurgy supervisor*

South Charleston
Nielsen, Kenneth Andrew *chemical engineer*

Washington
Pace, John Edward, III *chemical engineer*

Weirton
Adamczyk, Edmond David *metallurgical engineer*

WYOMING

Lander
Field, Francis Edward *electrical engineer, educator*

TERRITORIES OF THE UNITED STATES

PUERTO RICO

Mayaguez
Romaguera, Mariano Antonio *consulting engineer*

VIRGIN ISLANDS

Kingshill
Garde, Daniel Frederick *safety engineer*

MILITARY ADDRESSES OF THE UNITED STATES

PACIFIC

APO
Carlson, Robert Arthur *engineer*
Turner, David Lowery *safety engineer*

GERMANY

Stuttgart
Nagel, Joachim Hans *biomedical engineer, educator*

ADDRESS UNPUBLISHED

Baig, Ejaz Ahmed *environmental engineer*
Bardin, Rollin Edmond *electrical engineering executive*
Barker, Lisa Ann *aerospace engineer*
Beebe, Larry Eugene *quality engineering educator, management consultant*
Bergfield, Gene Raymond *engineering educator*
Bertolett, Craig Randolph *mechanical engineer consultant*
Black, Robert Samuel *engineering executive*
Buoy, William Edward, Jr. *electronics designer, consultant*
Caffey, James Enoch *civil engineer*
Campbell, Curtis Milton *associate engineer, technician*
Chastain, Denise Jean *process improvement engineer*
Chen, Min-Chu *mechanical engineer*
Chin, Robert Allen *engineering graphics educator*
Cooper, David Wayne *aerospace engineer*
Cormia, Frank Howard *industrial engineering administrator*
Cullingford, Hatice Sadan *chemical engineer*
Dawson, Gerald Lee *engineering company executive*
Donahoo, Melvin Lawrence *aerospace management consultant, industrial engineer*
Dunlap, Stanton Parks *risk assessment and loss control consultant*
Eissmann, Robert Fred *manufacturing engineer*
Ellis, Michael David *aerospace engineer*
Fero, Lester K. *aerospace engineer, consultant*
Geoghegan, Joseph Edward *retired electrical engineer*
Glover, Everett William, Jr. *environmental engineer*
Gordon, Michael D. *electronics engineer and nurse, air force officer*
Hamel, David Charles *health and safety engineer*
Hickox, Gary Randolph *pulp and paper engineer*
Higby, Edward Julian *safety engineer*
Iaquinto, Joseph Francis *electrical engineer*
James, Earl Eugene, Jr. *aerospace engineering executive*
Jesse, James Edward *engineering executive*
Johnson, Robert Walter *marine engineer, priest*
Jones, David Allan *electronics engineer*
Kennedy, Leo Raymond *engineering executive*
Kinsman, Frank Ellwood *engineering executive*
Kisak, Paul Francis *engineering company executive*
Kleinsorge, William Peter *metallurgical engineer*
Knott, Wiley Eugene *retired electronic engineer*
Knussmann, Willard Theodore *mechanical engineer*
Lessis, Gary Paul *engineer, sales executive*
Lindsley, John Martin *chemical engineer*
Lu, Yingzhong *nuclear engineer, educator, researcher*
Lumpkin, Alva Moore, III *electrical engineer, marketing professional*
Lyon, Martha Sue *research engineer, retired military officer*
Mason, Robert Lester *engineer, small business computer consultant*
McCorkle, Michael *electrical engineer*
Meindl, James Donald *electrical engineering educator, administrator*
Miah, Abdul Malek *electrical engineer, educator*
Moll, David Carter *civil engineer*
Moyers, Ernest Everett S. *retired missile research scientist*
Neshyba, Victor Peter *retired aerophysics engineer*
O'Reilly, John Joseph *engineer*
Plunkett, Joseph Charles *electrical engineering educator*
Priester, Gayle Boller *engineer, consultant*
Rackin, Mark Henry *electrical engineer*
Roth, James Joseph *telecommunications engineer*
Sayka, Anthony *process engineer*
Shupe, Stephen Paul *electronics engineer*
Shuster, John A. *civil engineer*
Simpson, Murray *engineer, consultant*
Smeltz, Edward J. *engineer*
Stephens, Lawrence Wesley *engineering executive*
Stonebridge, Peter William John *telecommunications engineering executive*
Underwood, Gerald Timothy *business consultant*
Walker, Matthew, III *biomedical engineer*
Wilcox, Robert Howard *mechanical engineer*
Williford, Clifford Frederick *system engineer, retired air force officer*

FINANCE: BANKING SERVICES. *See also* FINANCE: INVESTMENT SERVICES.

UNITED STATES

ALABAMA

Birmingham
Jones, D. Paul, Jr. *banker, lawyer*
Malone, Wallace D., Jr. *bank executive*
McCalley, Heather Barnhill *bank executive*
Nash, Warren Leslie *banker*
Powell, William Arnold, Jr. *retired banker*
Wilborn, Randy Charles *banker*

Huntsville
Boykin, Betty Ruth Carroll *mortgage loan officer, bank executive*

Mobile
Coker, Donald William *economic, healthcare, valuation and banking consultant*

Troy
Mims, M. Douglas *banker*

ARKANSAS

Forrest City
Stipe, John Ryburn *bank executive*

Little Rock
Bohlken, Deborah Kay *banking executive, government consultant, lobbyist*

FLORIDA

Coral Gables
Gutierrez, Jose Ramon *bank executive*

Delray Beach
Petruzzi, Anthony Joseph, Jr. *mortgage company executive*

Fort Lauderdale
Chiger, Jeffrey Stuart *banker*
De Padro Gainey, Anne Michelle *banker, accountant, trust tax officer*
Robinson, James H. *banker*
Wills, Donald *bank executive*

Jacksonville
Rice, Charles Edward *bank executive*
Stern, Steven Alan *bank executive*

Miami
Giller, Norman Myer *banker, architect, author*
Stevens, Mark *banker*
Turner, William Joseph *bank executive*

Naples
Kley, John Arthur *banker*

New Smyrna Beach
Howard, Stanley Louis *investment banker*

Orlando
Deutsch, Hunting Folger *banker*
Jasica, Andrea Lynn *mortgage banking executive*
Koehn, George Waldemar *bank executive*
Shirek, John Richard *retired savings and loan executive*

Palm Beach
Harper, Mary Sadler *banker*
Levine, Laurence Brandt *investment banker*
Lickle, William Cauffiel *banker*

Palm Harbor
Dunbar, David Wesley *bank executive*

Pensacola
Nickelsen, Eric J. *bank executive*
Timberlake, Stephen Grant *trust officer, bank officer*

Stuart
Shaw, Stephen Ragsdale *trust investment executive*

Tampa
Sink, Adelaide Alexander *banker*

Tarpon Springs
Screnock, Gregory Howard *mortgage company executive*

Tequesta
Turrell, Richard Horton, Sr. *retired banker*

West Palm Beach
O'Brien, Robert Brownell, Jr. *investment banker, consultant, yacht broker, opera company executive*

GEORGIA

Atlanta
Carlisle, Patricia Kinley *mortgage company executive, paralegal*
Chapman, Hugh McMaster *banker*
Chupp, Raymond Jeffery *mortgage banker*
Halwig, Nancy Diane *banker*
Hollis, Timothy Martin *bank executive*
Ivey, Michael Wayne *mortgage banker*
Rogers, William H., Jr. *banker, securities executive*
Schuelke, Constance Patricia *mortgage company executive*
Smith, Thomas Arthur *banker*
Spiegel, John William *banker*
Wallace, James Joseph *banking executive*
Watts, Anthony Lee *bank executive*
Williams, James Bryan *banker*
Williams, John Young *merchant banker*

Buford
Henderson, Larry Ray *banker*

Marietta
Sandell, George Norman *banking executive*

Sea Island
Bedner, Mark A. *banker*

Thomson
Knox, Boone A. *bank executive*

KENTUCKY

Frankfort
Wallace, Gary *bank executive*

Inez
Duncan, Robert Michael *banker, lawyer*

Louisa
Burton, John Lee, Sr. *banker*

Louisville
Boyd, Morton *banker*
Harreld, Michael N. *banker*
Siegel, Joy Hayes *banker, writer, educator, entrepreneur*
Stiff, Ronald David *corporate banker*

Marion
Morris, Roger Dale *bank officer, artist*

LOUISIANA

Alexandria
Bolton, Robert Harvey *banker*

Amite
Cefalu, Mary Ann *banker*

Baton Rouge
Griffin, G. Lee *banker*
Yancis, Ronald Alan *banker*

Covington
Thier, Annette *mortgage banking company executive*

MISSISSIPPI

Hattiesburg
Moore, Henderson Alfred, Jr. *retired savings and loan executive*

Jackson
McMillan, Howard Lamar, Jr. *banker*
Robinson, E. B., Jr. *bank executive*

Tupelo
Patterson, Aubrey Burns, Jr. *banker*
Ramage, Martis Donald, Jr. *banker*

NORTH CAROLINA

Charlotte
Creel, Sharon Swenson *bank adminstrator*
Crutchfield, Edward Elliott, Jr. *banking executive*
Diamond, David Arthur *manufacturing company executive*
Figge, Fredric J., II *bank executive*
Georgius, John R. *bank executive*
Hance, James Henry, Jr. *bank executive*
Krefting, Carol Lee *banker*
McColl, Hugh Leon, Jr. *bank executive*

Gastonia
Teem, Paul Lloyd, Jr. *savings and loan executive*

High Point
Burris, Betty Price *banker*
Coggins, George Miller, Jr. *strategic planning and finance educator*

Newton
Watchorn, Thomas M. *bank executive*

Pilot Mountain
Ross, Norman Alexander *retired banker*

Raleigh
Stevenson, Denise L. *business executive, banking consultant*

Rocky Mount
Greene, Janelle Langley *banker*
Mauldin, Robert Ray *banker*
Wilkerson, William Holton *banker*

Winston Salem
Baker, Leslie Mayo, Jr. *banker*
McNair, John Franklin, III *banker*
Medlin, John Grimes, Jr. *banker*
Ribeiro, Karen Lavette *bank administrator*
Williamson, Henry Gaston, Jr. *banker*

OKLAHOMA

Konawa
Rains, Mary Jo *banker*

Oklahoma City
Danforth, Louis Fremont *banker, educator*
Rainbolt, David Eugene *banker*
Rainbolt, H.E. *bank executive*

Pawhuska
Dickerson, William Joseph *bank executive*

Tulsa
Almon, Terry Michelle *banker*

Vinita
Shelton, James Lee *bank executive, rancher*

SOUTH CAROLINA

Columbia
Miller, E. Hite *banker, holding company executive*

Myrtle Beach
Kearns, Ruth Mary Schiller *bank executive*

TENNESSEE

Brentwood
Corrigan, Lynda Dyann *banker*

Cleveland
Johnson, Beverly Phillips *bank officer*

Johnson City
Surface, James Louis, Sr. *trust officer, lawyer*

Knoxville
Mikels, J(ames) Ronald *bank executive*

Maryville
Lawson, Fred Raulston *banker*

Mc Minnville
Golden, Jeffrey A. *banker, holding company executive*

Memphis
Glass, J. Kenneth *bank executive*
Montesi, John W., Jr. *mortgage banking executive*
Terry, Ronald Anderson *bank holding company executive*

Nashville
Bennett, Tanya Ulanda *bank officer*
Bottorff, Dennis C. *banker*
Cook, Charles Wilkerson, Jr. *banker, former county official*
Johnson, Albert William *mortgage banker, real estate broker*
Shell, Owen G., Jr. *banker*

TEXAS

Amarillo
Burgess, C(harles) Coney *bank executive*
Hamner, Lawrence Raeburn, Jr. *bank executive*

Austin
Carner, William John *banker*
Deal, Ernest Linwood, Jr. *banker*

Dallas
Bishop, Gene Herbert *corporate executive*
Blazin, Michael Joseph *banking executive*
Distelhorst, Craig Tipton *savings and loan executive*
Stuart, John Thomas, III *banker*

Galveston
Harris, John Woods *banker, lawyer*

Houston
Buckwalter, Alan Roland, III *banker*
Elkins, James Anderson, Jr. *banker*
Elkins, James Anderson, III *banker*
Hartman, Carol Oliver *investment banker*
Kanaly, Steven Patrick *trust company executive*
Petit, Brenda Joyce *credit bureau sales executive*
Rogers, James Tracy, Jr. *bank examiner*

Lubbock
Fulton, Joe Kirk, Jr. *banker, investor*

Pasadena
Moon, John Henry, Sr. *banker*

San Antonio
Keyser-Fanick, Christine Lynn *banker, marketing professional*
McClane, Robert Sanford *bank holding company executive*
Phillips, Alfredo O. *bank executive*

Tyler
Bell, Henry Marsh, Jr. *banking executive*
Blasingame, Donald Ray (Don Blasingame) *banker*

VIRGINIA

Alexandria
Suzuki, Gengo *banker*

Annandale
Eccles, Stephen David *retired international banker*

Arlington
Jones, Hartley M. (Lee) *bank executive*

Falls Church
Geithner, Paul Herman, Jr. *banker*
Williams, Peter John *world bank officer*
Zalokar, Robert H. *bank executive*

Mc Lean
Brendsel, Leland C. *federal mortgage company executive*
Glenn, David Wright *mortgage company executive*
Ring, James Edward Patrick *mortgage banking consulting executive*
Schools, Charles Hughlette *banker, lawyer*

Newport News
Kirkland, J. Paul *bank executive*

Norfolk
Cutchins, Clifford Armstrong, III *banker*

Richmond
Ashworth, Lawrence Nelson *bank executive*
Henley, Vernard William *banker*
McDonald, Malcolm S. *banker*
Miller, Lewis Nelson, Jr. *banker*
Ng, Pak C. *banker*
Tilghman, Richard Granville *banker*

Roanoke
Dalhouse, Warner Norris *banker*

Virginia Beach
Mann, Harvey Blount *retired banker*

WEST VIRGINIA

Charleston
Martin, Jerry Harold *bank examiner*

Huntington
Hatch, Robert Norris, Jr. *banking executive*

TERRITORIES OF THE UNITED STATES

PUERTO RICO

San Juan
Tous de Torres, Luz M. *banker*

ADDRESS UNPUBLISHED

Balderston, Thomas William *banker, corporate executive*
Burdette, William James *bank executive, lawyer*
Busch, Noel Henry *banker*
Chase, Helen Louise *banker*
Higginson, Jerry Alden, Jr. *bank executive*
Howard, John Loring *trust banker*
Newland, James LeRoy *banker*
Otto, Ingolf Helgi Elfried *banking institute fellow*
Poole, Bryan Cadenhead *banker*
Stewart, John Murray *banker*
Thurmond, John Peter, II *bank executive, rancher, archeologist*
Tipton, Mary Davison *banker*
Travis, Paul Nicholas *international banker*
Valentine, Kathryn Lois *mortgage company executive*
Wagner, Robert David, Jr. *banker*
Woodward, William Lee *retired savings bank executive*

FINANCE: FINANCIAL SERVICES

UNITED STATES

ALABAMA

Auburn
Min, Hokey *business educator*

Birmingham
Hall, Robert Alan *financial company executive*
Hardman, Daniel Clarke *accountant*
Morris, Florence Henderson *auditor*
Reed, Terry Allen *accountant*
Waligora, James *financial services consultant*

Bremen
Weathersby, Cecil Jerry *accounting and finance manager*

Deatsville
Owen, Larry Lesli *management educator, retired military officer, small business owner*

Decatur
Talley, Richard Woodrow *accountant*

Florence
Brown, Sarah Ruth *accountant, educator*
Richardson, Ruth Delene *business educator*

Foley
Bowyer, Shirley Caroline Smith *accountant*

Huntsville
Michelini, Sylvia Hamilton *auditor*
Morgan, Ethel Branman *accountant, retired electronics engineer*

Maxwell AFB
Arnold, Hollis David *financial analyst*

Mobile
Booker, Larry Frank *accountant*
Lowery, Anne Barrow *business administration dean*

Montgomery
Griffin, Tom Fleet *business & management educator*
Self, Donald Raymond *marketing educator*
Smith, Larry Steven *financial analyst, farmer, accountant*

Northport
Oliver, Clifton, Jr. *management educator*

Orange Beach
Hume, Evelyn Caldwell *accounting educator, financial consultant*

Point Clear
Salter, LaNora Jeanette *corporate financial officer*

Tuscaloosa
Gilliland, Terri Kirby *accountant*
Lee, Thomas Alexander *accountant, educator*
Miles, Minnie Caddell *retired business educator*
Stanfel, Larry Eugene *business educator*

Valley
Cook, James Herman *estate management consultant, financial advisor*

ARIZONA

Luke AFB
Stanton, John Walker *management educator, tour director, poet*

ARKANSAS

Conway
Bradley, Don Bell, III *marketing educator*
Horton, Finis Gene *management services company executive*
Moore, Herff Leo, Jr. *management educator*

Fayetteville
Cook, Doris Marie *accountant, educator*
Orr, Betsy *business education educator*

Fort Smith
Craig, David Clarke *financial advisor, instructor*

Hot Springs National Park
Mayhugh, Joel Ogden, Jr. *financial executive*

Little Rock
Adkins, Fredrick Earl, III *financial consultant, educator*
Flournoy, Jacob Wesley *internal audit director*
Scivally, Bart Murnane *accountant, auditor*

Mena
Wiles, Betty Jane *accountant*

Rogers
Phillips, L(arry) Scott *portfolio manager*

Sherwood
George, James Edward *accountant*

Siloam Springs
Hill, James Robert *accountant*

State University
Ruby, Ralph, Jr. *vocational business educator*

COLORADO

Breckenridge
Beery, Roger Lewis, II *risk management consultant*

Denver
Uliss, Barbara Turk *accountant*

DELAWARE

Wilmington
Rogoski, Patricia Diana *financial executive*

DISTRICT OF COLUMBIA

Washington
Allbritton, Joe Lewis *diversified holding company executive*
Huewitt, Kenneth Ray *auditor*
Justen, Peter Allen *financial services executive, entrepreneur*
Malek, Frederic Vincent *finance company executive*
McKinless, Kathy Jean *accountant*
Santos, Maria J. *evaluator*

FLORIDA

Altamonte Springs
Hise, Kenneth Winford *retired finance educator*

Boca Raton
DeCuir, Alfred Frederick, Jr. *financial executive*
Jessup, Joe Lee *business educator, management consultant*
Loescher, Barbara Ann *auditing executive*
Nolan, Lone Kirsten *registered investment advisor*
Schmoke, L(eroy) Joseph, III *corporate finance executive, consultant*

Boynton Beach
Bartholomew, Arthur Peck, Jr. *accountant*

Clearwater
Campolettano, Thomas Alfred *financial analyst*
Clingerman, Edgar Allen, Sr. *financial services executive*
Evans, Michael Dean *financial planner*
Jenkins, Linda Diane *accountant*
Loos, Randolph Meade *financial planner*

Cocoa Beach
Wirtschafter, Irene Nerove *tax consultant*

Coral Gables
Lampert, Wayne Morris *corporate financier*
Wainberg, Salomon *accountant*

Crestview
Scott, George Gallmann *accountant*

Crystal River
Schlumberger, Robert Ernest *accountant*

Davie
Capraro, Franz *accountant*

Daytona Beach
Swanson, James Robert *busines administration educator*

Delray Beach
Bryan, Robert Fessler *former investment analyst*
Gatewood, Robert Payne *financial planning executive*

Dunedin
Teets, Charles Edward *business consultant, lawyer*

Fort Lauderdale
Bamberg, Louis Mark *estate planning specialist*
Fuller, Steven Edward *accountant*
Gart, Alan *finance educator, consultant*
Holtzman, Gary Yale *administrative and financial executive*
Isenberg, Paul David *financial executive*
Shoemaker, William Edward *financial executive*

Fort Myers
Adams, Todd Porter *financial and investment advisor*

Fort Pierce
Garde, Susan Reutershan *accountant*

Gainesville
Davis, John Allen, Jr. (Jeff Davis) *financial planner*

Gotha
Powell, Thomas Ervin *accountant, consultant*

Gulfport
Keistler, Betty Lou *accountant, tax consultant*

Hallandale
Boyce, Henry Worth, III *portfolio manager, financial consultant*

Hialeah
Heimbuch, Joseph William *marketing educator*
Lehmann, C. Richard *financial editor*
Murphy, Ramon Birkett *financial services company executive*

Hollywood
Harkin, Daniel John *controller*

Jacksonville
Adams, Scott Leslie *accountant*
Allen, Ronald Wesley *financial executive*
Bergfeld, Rudolph Peters *financial company executive*
Edwards, Marvin Raymond *investment counselor, economic consultant*
Jenkins, Steven Marvin *controller*
Mierdierks, Kenneth A. *controller*
O'Keefe, Ruth Reneé *accountant, educator*
O'Neal, Kathleen Len *financial administrator*
Tomlinson, William Holmes *management educator, retired army officer*

Jacksonville Beach
Forrest, Allen Wright *accounting firm executive, accountant*

Jupiter
Danforth, Arthur Edwards *finance executive*
Guilarte, Pedro Manuel *holding company executive*

Lake Worth
Taylor, Mildred Juanita *accountant*

Lakeland
Ottinger, Guy Emerel *accountant*

Largo
Royak, Elizabeth *credit union executive*

Lighthouse Point
Shein, Jay Lesing *financial planner*

Longwood
Hoffberg, Alan Marshall *accountant*
Smith, Barry Merton *financial planner, consultant*

Mary Esther
Padilla, Don Diego, II *finance consultant*

Melbourne
Canfield, Constance Dale *accountant, nurse*
Fay, Robert Woods *financial executive*
Roub, Bryan R(oger) *financial executive*

Miami
Aguirre, Mirtha Guerra *accountant*
Camacho, Alfredo *accountant*
Dahlfues, Donald Michael *accountant*
Day, Kathleen Patricia *financial planner*
Dessler, Gary S. *business educator, author, consultant, administrator*
Duncanson, Harry Richard *accountant, financial executive*
Flinn, David Lynnfield *financial consultant*
Guerra, Charles Albert *financial consultant and executive*
Guerra, Emma Maria *accountant*
Hallbauer, Rosalie Carlotta *business educator*
Hendrickson, Harvey Sigbert *accounting educator*
Mouly, Eileen Louise *financial planner*
Pickering, Charles Denton *accountant*
Ramirez de la Piscina, Julian *diversified financial services company executive*
Robbins, Honey-Miam *financial executive*
Satuloff, Barth *accounting executive, dispute resolution professional*
Stone, William Samuel *financial advisor*
Svaldi, Myrthia Moore *financial advisor*
Tegnelia, Anthony G. *controller*
Torres, Hugo R. *financial analyst, international credit analyst, telecommunications analyst*
Wendel, Pamela Lois *auditor, banker*

Naples
Berry, Donald Lee *accountant*
Eastman, James Clifford *investment management consultant*

Neptune Beach
Glemann, Richard Paul *accounting executive*

North Miami
Kempa, Mark Andrew *accountant*

North Palm Beach
Frevert, James Wilmot *financial planner, investment advisor*

Ocala
Clayton, Robert Beville *insurance and financial services professional*

Ocklawaha
Silagi, Barbara Weibler *corporate administrator*

Orange Park
Glenn, Steven Claude *financial executive*

Orlando
Armacost, Robert Leo *management educator*
Gray, Anthony Rollin *capital management company executive*
Gutterson, Janet Miriam *assessor*
Kitchens, Ronald Blake *information technologies manager*
Martin, William Robert *accountant*
Neusaenger, John Michael *financial company executive*

Palm Beach
Bernard, David A. *investment advisor*
Fitilis, Theodore Nicholas *portfolio manager*

Palm Beach Gardens
Herrick, John Dennis *financial consultant, former law firm executive, retired food products executive*
Rentner, James David *financial analyst*

Pembroke Pines
Tobias, Benjamin Alan *portfolio manager, financial planner*

Pensacola
Carper, William Barclay *management educator*
McArthur, Gerald *credit union executive*
Murrell, Kenneth Lynn *management educator*

Pompano Beach
Mulvey, John Thomas, Jr. *financial consultant*

Rockledge
Layne, John Francis *accountant*

Saint Petersburg
Brock, Laura Krueger *accountant*
Macaluso, James *accountant, estate planner*
Maier, Karl George *estate and financial planner*

Santa Rosa Beach
Sprigler, Melaine Lynn *accountant, consultant*

Sarasota
Baszto, Theodore Francis, Jr. *financial planner*
Dombro, Richard *financial planner*
Pesut, Timothy S. *investment advisor, professional speaker, consultant*
Roberts, Don E. *accountant*

Spring Hill
Aldrich, David Alan *accountant*

Stuart
White, Donald Francis *financial planner, insurance agent*

Tallahassee
Giovannoni, John Michael Saffold *financial services firm executive*
Major, Don Lindbergh *management educator*
Mowell, John Byard *investment management executive, technology company executive*
TerLouw, John G. *financial analyst*

Tampa
Aidman, Barton Terry *accountant*
Becatti, Lance Norman *finance company executive*
Bradish, Warren Allen *internal auditor, operations analyst, management consultant*
Carter, James A. *finance executive*
Cotter, Gary William *financial company executive, consultant*
Hanford, Agnes Rutledge *financial adviser*
Henard, Elizabeth Ann *controller*
Hernandez, Gilberto Juan *accountant, auditor, management consultant*
Howarth, Elizabeth H. *financial advisor*
Mesco, Edward Charles Patrick *accountant, consultant*
Schine, Jerome Adrian *retired accountant*
Winoker, Diana Lee *financial consultant, educator*

Terra Ceia
Wasserman, Susan Valesky *accountant*

Vero Beach
Koontz, Alfred Joseph, Jr. *financial and operating management executive, consultant*

Wesley Chapel
Mendelsohn, Louis Benjamin *financial analyst*

West Palm Beach
Arias-Bolzmann, Leopoldo *marketing educator*
Eppley, Roland Raymond, Jr. *retired financial services executive*
Lanpher, Lucille Marlene *auditor*
Livingstone, John Leslie *accountant, management consultant, business economist, educator*

Winter Haven
Goodman, Karen Lacerte *financial services executive*

Winter Park
Therrien, Francois Xavier, Jr. *business and tax consultant*

Zephyrhills
Eckert, Charles Arthur *accountant*
Henson, John Ely *accountant*

GEORGIA

Albany
Jones, Charles Marks, Jr. *retired loan company executive*

Athens
Bamber, Linda Smith *accounting educator*
Zinkhan, George Martin, III *marketing educator*

Atlanta
Assunto, Richard Anthony *payroll executive*
Brooks, James Joe, III *accountant*
Chambers, Robert William *financial company executive*
Coulter, Lawrence P. *credit union administrator*
Craig, Anna Maynard *financial educator, consultant*
Days, Ronald Jerome *financial professional, consultant*
Dilcher, Charles F., Jr. *holding company executive*
Frank, Ronald Edward *marketing educator*
Gross, Stephen Randolph *accountant*
Haines, Helen Drake *diversified manufacturing and service company assistant controller*
Hanna, Frank Joseph *credit company executive*
Hays, William Grady, Jr. *corporate financial and bank consultant*
Hiller, George Mew *financial advisor, investment manager, lawyer*
Hites, Becky E. *financial executive*
Kimball, Curtis Rollin *investment advisor, appraiser*
Lobb, William Atkinson *financial services executive*
Mertens, David Gerhard *financial executive*
Plummer, Michael Kenneth *financial consultant*
Reid, Joseph William *accountant*
Rigdon, Edward Eugene *business educator*
Ryan, J. Bruce *health care management consulting executive*
Sikes, Ruth Cox *investment representative*
Sinanian, Loris R. *financial consultant, deacon*
Smith, Marcia Jean *accountant, tax specialist, financial consultant*
Spearman, Maxie Ann *financial analyst, administrator*
Taylor, Richard Bertrom *accountant*
Whittington, Frederick Brown, Jr. *business administration educator*
Wilder, Robert Allen *finance and leasing company executive, leasing broker, consultant*

Augusta
Bates, Rhonda Barber *financial advisor*
Jones, Thomas Watson *accountant, financial planner*

College Park
McMullan, James Franklin *financial planner*

Columbus
Huff, Lula Eleanor Lunsford *controller, accounting educator*
Newell, Silvia Anna *accountant*
Wieczorek, Robert Clayton *financial consultant*

Covington
Winn, William Moyers, Jr. *accountant*

Dalton
Winter, Larry Eugene *accountant*

Decatur
Helm, Aletha Ann *human resources specialist*
Rodgers, Richard Malcolm *management accountant*

Duluth
Rogers, William Brookins *financial consultant*

Fayetteville
Brown, L(arry) Eddie *tax practitioner, real estate broker, financial planner*

Lagrange
Cousins, Roland B. *business administration and management educator*
Turner, Fred Lamar *accountant, lawyer*

Macon
Kitchens, William Charlie *accountant*
Owens, Garland Chester *accounting educator*

Marietta
Carlin, Stewart Henry *accounting executive*
Kiger, Ronald Lee *price analyst*
North, John Adna, Jr. *accountant, real estate appraiser*
Townley, Linda Rose *financial analyst*

Milledgeville
Engerrand, Doris Dieskow *business educator*

Oakwood
Martin, Johnny Benjamin *accountant*

Peachtree City
Thompson, Claude M. *finance officer, pharmacy consultant*

Roswell
Richkin, Barry Elliott *financial services executive*
Young, Roger Wilson *accountant, lawyer, financial advisor*

Snellville
Hudgens, Kimberlyn Nan *accounting specialist*

Statesboro
Murkison, Eugene Cox *business educator*

Stone Mountain
Moulder, Wilton Arlyn *financial management consultant*

Washington
Mansfield, Norman Connie *bookkeeper*

Watkinsville
Tate, Curtis E. *management educator*

Woodstock
Aromin, Mercedes Fung *portfolio manager, investment advisor, consultant*

ILLINOIS

Chicago
Mansfield, Karla Jean *financial executive*

KENTUCKY

Frankfort
Chadwell, James Russell, Jr. *comptroller*
Hatchett, Edward Bryan, Jr. *auditor, lawyer*

Lexington
Haywood, Charles Foster *finance educator*

Louisville
Besser, Lawrence Wayne *corporate accountant*
Clark, James Gregory *financial coordinator, political consultant*
Dalton, Jennifer Faye *accountant*
Edwards, Bruce Walton, Jr. *auditor*
Hampton, Martin Justus *financial planner*
Peyron, Daniel Louis *tax specialist*

Mount Sterling
Hunt, Wanda Burton *finance executive*

Pippa Passes
Mitchell, Kossuth Mayer *business educator*

Versailles
Humes, David Walker *accountant*

LOUISIANA

Baton Rouge
Brown, Raymond Jessie *financial and insurance company executive*
Chaney, Courtland Merlyn *management educator, psychologist, consultant*
DeVille, Donald Charles *accountant*

Covington
Files, Mark Willard *business and financial consultant*

Grambling
Fields, Hall Ratcliff *finance educator*

Mandeville
Aaron, Shirley Mae *tax consultant*

Metairie
Boazman, Franklin Meador *financial consultant*
Doody, Louis Clarence, Jr. *accountant*
Thomas, Ricardo D'Wayne *financial advisor*

Monroe
Jauch, Lawrence Randall *business educator, consultant*

New Orleans
Brief, Arthur Paul *business educator*
Fisk, Raymond Paul *marketing educator*
Hansel, Stephen Arthur *holding company executive*
Jolliff, Robert Allen *treasurer*
Miller, Brian Kent *auditor*
Suber, Margaret Adele *controller*
Wall, P.Q. (Lucius John) *financial analyst, money manager*
Wright, Clifford Sidney *accounting educator*

Pineville
Beall, Grace Carter *business educator*

Prairieville
D'Souza, Alan S. *tax consultant, real estate agent, pianist, writer*

Ruston
Posey, Clyde Lee *business administration and accounting educator*

Shreveport
Lenard, Lloyd Edgar *financial consultant*
Noble, Michael Andrew *audit manager*

Thibodaux
Daigle, Sharon Roger *auditor*
Delozier, Maynard Wayne *marketing educator*

Walker
McGarr, Charles Taylor *accountant*

MARYLAND

Baltimore
Price, Alan Thomas *business and estate planner*

Columbus
Jeansonne, Angela Lynne *senior analyst*

Potomac
Gowda, Narasimhan Ramaiah *financial consultant*

MICHIGAN

Canton
Lee, Kamee Angela *financial analyst*

MISSISSIPPI

Biloxi
Askins, Arthur James *accountant, finance management and auditing executive*

Brandon
Nall, Lucia Lynn *controller*

Clarksdale
Walters, William Lee *accountant*

Diamondhead
Basanez, Edward Samuel *management educator*

Jackson
Elliott, Mitchell Lee *financial analyst*
Feller, Thomas Robert *director of special projects*

Meridian
Hubert, Scott Harold *accountant, educator*

Mississippi State
Taylor, Ronald Dean *marketing and advertising educator*

Pelahatchie
Ross, Knox Winton, Jr. *accountant*

Starkville
Duett, Edwin Harold *finance and economics educator*
George, Ernest Thornton, III *financial consultant*
Thomas, Garnett Jett *accountant*

NEVADA

Incline Village
Diederich, J(ohn) William *financial consultant*

NEW YORK

New York
Sparkes, Cheryl Flowers *accountant*

NORTH CAROLINA

Asheville
Dye, William David *pension plan administrator*
Yearout, Robert DeWitt *management educator, retired army officer*

Benson
Doyle, Sally A. *controller*

Bolivia
Horne, Lithia Brooks *finance executive*

Boone
Bowden, Elbert Victor *banking, finance and economics educator, author*
Minton, John William *management educator*

Brevard
Hansen, Erik Denslow *accountant*

Chapel Hill
Aldridge, Adrienne Yingling *accounting administrator, consultant*
Barnhill, Cynthia Diane *accountant*
Hart, Roger Louis *accounting consultant*
Morgan, Frank T. *business educator, consultant*
Roth, Aleda Vender *business educator*

Charlotte
Almond, Giles Kevin *accountant, financial planner*
Booth, Rosemary *management educator*
Branan, Carolyn Benner *accountant, lawyer*
Garner, Cindy Anne *account executive*
Gilmore, Stephen Vincent *actuary*
Knox, Havolyn Crocker *financial consultant*
Labardi, Jillian Gay *financial planner, insurance agent*
Lee, Bette Galloway *accountant*
Schulz, Walter Kurt *accountant, consultant*

Clemmons
Cawood, Merton Campbell *investment management executive*

Concord
Bradshaw, Jeffrey *company executive*

Durham
Bettman, James Ross *management educator*

Elon College
Metcalf, Corwin Moore (Mickey) *business educator, businessman, consultant*

Fayetteville
Stafford, Dan R. *small business consultant, marketing analyst*

Forest City
Allen, William Dean *financial consultant*

Graham
Hawkins, Otha Carlton *management educator, consultant*

Greensboro
Compton, John Carroll *accountant*
Hutchinson, Julius Steven *financial services company executive*
Starling, Larry Eugene *auditor*

Havelock
Lindelof, William Christian, Jr. *financial company executive*

Hendersonville
Goehring, Maude Cope *retired business educator*

Hillsborough
Pagano, Filippo Frank *financial broker, commercial loan consultant*

Manteo
Miller, Judith Ann *retired financial executive*

Mount Airy
Rotenizer, R. Eugene *financial planner, consultant and advisor*

Raleigh
Hill, Hulene Dian *accountant*
Nation, Philip David *financial planner*
Short, James Ferebee *investment advisor, financial consultant*
Ward, Edith Burnette *business educator*

Reidsville
Summerlin, Gerald Terry, Jr. *financial advisor*

Tryon
Flynn, Kirtland, Jr. *accountant*

Wilkesboro
Thomas, David Lloyd *accountant, consultant*

Wilmington
Taylor, Jerrine Steifle *retired business educator*

Winston Salem
Gallo, Vincent John *financial planner*
Middaugh, Jack Kendall, II *management educator*

OKLAHOMA

Ada
Parham, Betty Ely *credit bureau executive*

Bethany
Seyfert, Jeff Lynn *business educator*

Durant
England, Dan Benjamin *accountant*

Edmond
Hagar, Robert Montel *chief executive officer, business owner*
Wood, Charles W. *financial services company executive*

Enid
Curtis, Albert Bradley, II *financial planner, tax specialist*
Rider, John Allen, II *business educator, paralegal*

Norman
Evans, Rodney Earl *business educator*
Van Auken, Robert Danforth *business administration educator, management consultant*

Oklahoma City
Acers, Patsy Pierce *financial seminars company executive*
Cassel, John Elden *accountant*
Dozier, Russell William, Jr. *actuarial consultant, pension consultant*
Trent, Richard O(wen) *financial executive*
Woody, Mark Edward *financial planner*

Stillwater
Trennepohl, Gary Lee *finance educator*
Wright, Charlotte Jean *accounting educator*

Tulsa
Duncan, Maurice Greer *accountant, consultant*
Hart, Phillip *credit union executive*
Hoe, Richard March *insurance and securities consultant, writer*
Sachau, William Henry *auditor, consultant*
Stacey, Darla Sue *financial control consultant*

SOUTH CAROLINA

Batesburg
Drafts, James Pickens, III *financial and actuarial examiner*

Cayce
Byars, Merlene Hutto *accountant, visual artist, writer, publisher*

Charleston
Adelson, Gloria Ann *financial executive*
Franklin, Paul Deane *financial consultant, financial planner*
Hogan, Arthur James *portfolio manager*
Prewitt, William Chandler *financial executive*
Rustin, Dowse Bradwell, III *credit union executive*

Clemson
Sheriff, Jimmy Don *accounting educator, academic dean*

Columbia
Caswell, Jeffry Claxton *financial executive*
Davis, Barbara Langford *financial planner*
Denton, Robert William (Pete Denton) *financial executive*
Edwards, James Benjamin *accountant, educator*
Gasque, Diane Phillips *funding specialist*
Monahan, Thomas Paul *accountant*
Patterson, Grady Leslie, Jr. *financial advisor*
Powell, J(ohn) Key *estate planner, consultant*
Sakakibara, Yoshitaka *business educator*
Storey, Robert C. *financial planner*

Greenville
Cramer, Michael Todd *financial consultant*
Good, Stewart Earl *accountant*
Rogers, Jon Martin *financial consultant, financial company executive*

Hilton Head Island
Whitmer, William Eward *retired accountant*

Johns Island
Rhea, Marcia Chandler *accountant*

Spartanburg
Pate, John Gillis, Jr. *financial consultant, accounting educator*

Sumter
Van Bulck, Hendrikus Eugenius *accountant*

Williamston
Alewine, James William *financial executive*

TENNESSEE

Alamo
Finch, Evelyn Vorise *financial planner*

Athens
Thompson, Verdine Mae *financial planner, tax preparer*

Brentwood
Jordan, Robert Andrew *accountant*
McClary, Jim Marston *accounting executive, consultant*

Chattanooga
Russe, Conrad Thomas Campbell *accountant*
Smith, David Yarnell *financial consultant*
Swafford, Douglas Richard *corporate credit executive*

Clarksville
Pettit, John Douglas, Jr. *management educator*

Cleveland
Callais, Elaine Denise Rogers *accountant*
Geren, Brenda L. *business educator*

Cookeville
Pashley, Mary Martha *corporate finance educator*
Wood, Bob Gaines, Jr. *finance educator*

Covington
Harrington, Herbert H. *accountant*

Dayton
Lay, William Maxwell, Jr. *business educator, economics researcher*

Dyersburg
Robinson, Johnny Aubrey *controller*

Elizabethton
Taylor, Wesley Alan *accountant, consultant*

Goodlettsville
Tongate, Darrel Edwin *accountant*

Jackson
Presson, Francis Tennery *credit union official*

Johnson City
Morgan, Robert George *accounting educator, researcher*

Knoxville
Newman, Charles Judson *financial planner, employee benefits consultant*
Smallman, Joseph Dempster *financial consultant, qualified plans coordinator*

Lebanon
Hubbard, Julia Faye *accountant*

Memphis
Brandon, Elvis Denby, III *financial planner*
Johnson, Betty Zschiegner *treasurer-secretary*
Lang, Lillian Owen *accountant*
Russell, Grady *accountant, educator*
Stafford, Will Elbert *financial company executive*
Umholtz, Clyde Allan *financial analyst*

Morristown
Gerard, Alma Elizabeth *financial planner*

Mount Carmel
Arnold, Ronald Lee *financial planner*

Murfreesboro
Lee, John Thomas *finance educator, financial planner*

Nashville
Brown, Norman James *financial manager*
Christie, William Gary *finance educator*
Crawford, Donna Marie *accounting administrator*
Dykes, Archie Reece *financial services executive*
El-Shishini, Ali Salem *financial executive*
Henderson, Marcus Terrell *financial counselor*
Saunders, Ted Elliott *accountant*
Ullestad, Merwin Allan *tax services executive*

Oak Ridge
McReynolds, Pamela Kay *controller*

Sweetwater
Warren, Douglas Edgar *accountant*

Tullahoma
Hasty, Linda Hester *business educator*

Winchester
Edwards, Linda Sue *bookkeeper*
Matherley, Steve Allen *cost accountant*

TEXAS

Alvin
Nelson, William Hoyt *accountant*

Amarillo
Green, Karen Ann *accounting supervisor*

Arlington
Quant, Harold Edward *financial services company executive, rancher*
Reilly, Michael Atlee *financial company executive, venture capital investor*
Sambaluk, Nicholas Wayne *auditor*
West, John Charles *financial consultant*

Athens
Duke, Winston Wayne *auditor*

Austin
Garner, Paul Trantham *auditor*
Graydon, Frank Drake *retired accounting educator, university administrator*
Hagerty, Polly Martiel *financial analyst, construction executive*
Jennings, Ross Grant *accounting educator*
Lemens, William Vernon, Jr. *banker, finance company executive, lawyer*
Mallett, T.C. *government financial administrator, rancher*
Martin, John David *finance educator, researcher, author*
Robertson, Jack Clark *accounting educator*
Ronn, Ehud Israel *finance educator*
von Braun, Peter Carl Moore Stewart *company executive*

Beaumont
Andes, Joan Keenen *tax specialist, executive*

Bedford
Domingue, Deborah Gail *tax preparer, bookkeeper*

Bellaire
Richardson, William Wightman, III *personnel and employee benefits consultant*

Brownsville
Cohen, Barry Mendel *financial executive, educator*

Brownwood
Bell, Mary E. Beniteau *accountant*

Burkeville
Skelton, Helen Rogers *retired auditor*

Carrollton
Rodda, John Lou *finance company executive, financial consultant*
Wargetz, Georgia Lynn Rance *accountant*
Youngstrum, David Mansfield *financial executive*

College Station
Manning, Walter Scott *accountant, former educator, consultant*

Corpus Christi
Griffin-Thompson, Melanie *accounting firm executive*
Vaughan, Alice Felicie *accountant, real estate executive, tax consultant*

Dallas
Bailey, Donald Wayne *financial planner and consultant*
Brooks, Carla Jo *financial services manager*
Caldwell, Thomas Howell, Jr. *accountant, financial management consultant*
Eads, John A. *accountant*
France, Richard William *finance executive*
Harris, Lucy Brown *accountant, consultant*
Jennings, Dennis Raymond *accountant*
Johnston, Daniel *financial petroleum consultant*
Lam, Chun Hung *finance educator, consultant*
Leader, Pamela Susan *controller*
Lomax, John H. *financial service company executive*
Mahadeva, Manoranjan *financial executive*
Mc Quillan, Joseph Michael *finance company executive*
Mills, William Oliver, III *international tax accountant, consultant*
Murrell, William Ivan *accountant*
Peiser, John George *accountant, consultant*
Shimer, Daniel Lewis *corporate executive*
Smiles, Ronald *management educator*
Smith, Courtland Clement, Jr. *actuarial consultant*
Tannebaum, Samuel Hugo *accountant*
Thomas, Robert Lee *financial services company executive, consultant*
Tull, C. Thomas *investment advisor*
Walker, Mark Leslie *financial executive*

De Soto
Tabbert, Rondi Jo *accountant*

Denton
Prybutok, Victor Ronald *business educator*
Yarbrough, Marianne June *auditor*

Duncanville
Trotter, Ide Peebles *financial planner, investment manager*

El Paso
Bowen, Marcia Kay *customs house broker*
Fairall, Bonnie Jean May *pension services executive*
Hoagland, Jennifer Hope *accountant*
Morales, Pedro Allison (Pete) *accountant, consultant, writer*
Showery, Charles George, Jr. *financial services company executive, consultant*

Fort Worth
Clark, Emory Eugene *financial planning executive*
Pappas-Speairs, Nina *financial planner, educator*
Stanley, Marjorie Thines *financial educator*
Trick, Ann Louise *accountant*
Waller, Gary Wilton *administration educator, minister*

Galveston
Selig, Oury Levy *financial consultant*
Young, Vera Miller *portfolio manager*

Garland
Hughes, Arthur Hyde *accountant*
Lord, Jacqueline Ward *accountant, photographer, artist*
Threlkeld, Mary Helen *accountant*

Georgetown
Sellers, Fred Evans *accounting educator*

Greenville
Bloskas, John D. *financial executive*

Houston
Braden, John A. *accountant*
Brown, Sara Lou *accounting firm executive*
Cannon, Douglas Robert *investment executive, federal government appointee*
Coffey, Clarence W. *treasurer*
Dunn, James Randolph *chief financial officer*
Garrett, Marilyn *tax consultant*
Getz, Lowell Vernon *financial advisor*
Goldberg, William Jeffrey *accountant*
Gomez, Lucas *assistant treasurer, credit manager*
Hipple, James Blackman *financial executive*
Hlozek, Carole Diane Quast *securities company administrator*
Howard, Alex Wayne *financial consultant*
Jones, David Bentley, Jr. *auditor*
Kelly, Margaret Elizabeth *financial analyst, planner*
Mathews, Chris J. *financial executive*
Mermelstein, Isabel Mae Rosenberg *financial consultant*
Pluff, Stearns Charles, III *investment banker*
Rasbury, Julian George *financial services company executive*
Rawson, Jim Charles *accountant, executive*
Robertson, Derek Alva *finance director*
Rockwell, Elizabeth Dennis *retirement specialist, financial planner*
Roland, Melissa Montgomery *accountant*
Sims, Rebecca Gibbs *accountant, certified fraud examiner*
Starkey, Elizabeth LaRuffa *accountant*
Stephens, Joseph H., III *financial planner*
Thacker, Shannon Stephen *financial advisor*
Wells, Damon, Jr. *investment company executive*
Wilcox, Barbara Montgomery *accountant*
Wilkinson, Harry Edward *management educator and consultant*

Hurst
Sensabaugh, Mary Elizabeth *financial consultant*

Irving
Clinton, Tracy Peter, Sr. *financial executive, systems analyst*
Cook, W.B. *controller*
Geisinger, Janice Allain *accountant*
Grayson, Scott Embry *research manager*
Martin, Stacey *accountant*
Meredith, Karen Ann *accountant, financial executive*
Mobley, William Hodges *management educator, researcher*
Stevens, Dennis Max *audit director*

Kerrville
Davis, Stewart Thorpe *accountant*

Kilgore
Thurmon, Jack Jewel *financial services executive*

Kingsville
Stanford, Jane Herring *business administration educator*

Laredo
Power, Jacqueline Lou *accounting educator*

Lindale
Hale, Ford R., Jr. *retired accountant*

Livingston
Simpson, Wendell Phillips *chartered financial consultant*

Lubbock
Chavarria, Dolores Esparza *financial service executive*
Holcombe, Forrest Douglas *business administration educator, retired naval officer*
Peterson, Mark Frederick *business administration educator*
Sears, Robert Stephen *finance educator*

Marshall
Thames, Earl Glenn *accounting educator*

Mc Kinney
Brewer, Ricky Lee *investment broker, estate planner*

Midland
Groce, James Freelan *financial consultant*
Tom, James Robert *accountant*

Orange
Bates, Patricia Stamper *accountant*

Pasadena
Scott, William Floyd *accountant*

Pearland
Thomas, James Raymond *accountant*

Plainview
Duvall, Wallace Lee *management educator, consultant*

Plano
Carter, Rodney *corporate finance executive*
Checki, John Joseph, Jr. *financial services company executive*
Grant, Joseph Moorman *finance executive*
Wiese, Terry Eugene *consulting executive, financial services, telecommunications and utilities sales and marketing executive*

Richardson
Burke, Thomas William *executive benefits consulting company official*

Round Rock
Puri, Rajendra Kumar *business and tax specialist, consultant*

San Antonio
Collins, William Arthur, III *accountant*
Copeland, Kenton Leonard *personal financial advisor*
Eash, Jimmie Ruth *accountant*
Fuhrmann, Charles John, II *strategic and finance consultant*
Hannah, John Robert, Sr. *accountant*
Jensen, Teresa Elaine *financial planner*
Kimmel, Paul Robert *financial and systems director*
Little, Mark McKenna *financial management executive*
Neiheisel, Steven Richard *educator*
Neiner, A(ndrew) Joseph *corporate executive*
Newman, Betty Louise *accountant*
Reddy, Paul W. *accountant*
Rose, Chester Arthur *accountant, financial planner*
Vital, Rafael, Jr. *auditor*

Spring
Griffith Fries, Martha *controller*

Sugar Land
Farrar, Pauline Elizabeth *accountant, real estate broker*
Keefe, Carolyn Joan *tax accountant*

Temple
Harris, Bruce Eugene *financial analyst*

Texarkana
Mitcham, Julius Jerome *accountant*

Texas City
Janssens, Joe Lee *controller*

The Woodlands
West, James Odell, Jr. *finance executive*

Universal City
Smith, James Earlie, Jr. *accountant*

Waco
Harrison, Walter Thomas, Jr. *accounting educator, chair*
Miller, Carl Chet *business educator*

Wichita Falls
Silverman, Gary William *financial planner*

Wylie
Morrison, Grace Blanch Simpson *auditor, accountant, government official*

VIRGINIA

Alexandria
Brickhill, William Lee *international finance consultant*
Capps, Russell Craig *controller*
Hammad, Alam E. *international business consultant, educator*
Le, Thuy Xuan *financial control systems developer, consultant*
Price, Joanne *financial executive*

Annandale
Jones, David Charles *international financial and management consultant*

Arlington
Donnellan, Barbara McCarthy *tax specialist*
Gavian, Peter Wood *investment banker*
Kalas, Frank Joseph, Jr. *financial consultant*
Parker, Payuina Ernest *accountant, business consultant*
Thomas, Jimmy Lynn *financial executive*

Blacksburg
Brozovsky, John A. *accounting educator*
Patterson, Douglas MacLennan *finance educator*

Bridgewater
Armstrong, Martha Susan *accountant, educator*

Bristol
Creger, David L. *financial planner, insurance executive*
Watson, Kerr Francis *management educator*

Broad Run
Kube, Harold Deming *retired financial executive*

Catharpin
Fischer, John Arthur *financial analyst*

Chantilly
Schneckenburger, Karen Lynne *finance executive*

Charlottesville
Awad, Elias Michael *business educator, computer consultant*
Bodily, Samuel Edwin *business administration educator*
Carter, William Kemp *accounting educator*
Ellett, John Spears, II *retired taxation educator, accountant, lawyer*
Gwin, John Michael *marketing educator, consultant*
Horton, Madeline Mary *financial planner, consultant*
Kehoe, William Joseph *business educator*
Mallan, Francis Scott *accounting manager*
Minehart, Jean Besse *tax accountant*
Tayloe, Edward Dickinson, II *portfolio manager*
Trent, Robert Harold *business educator*
Tuttle, Donald Latham *finance executive*
Wheeler, David Wayne *accountant*

Chester
Roane, David James, Jr. *auditor*

Fairfax
Khoury, Riad Philip *corporation executive, financial consultant*
Patel, Vinod Motibhai *accountant*

Falls Church
Hahn, Thomas Joonghi *accountant*
Kaplan, Jocelyn Rae *financial planning firm executive*
McVay, Mary Frances *portfolio manager*
Pulsifer, Roy *transportation, financial and business consultant*
Purvis, Ronald Scott *financial counselor, real estate executive*
Runyon, Michael *holding company executive*

Floyd
McBroom, Diane Craun *accountant, horse trainer*

Fredericksburg
Gorman, Lawrence James *finance company executive*

Hampton
Douglass, James Frederick *business administration educator*
Siegfeldt, Denise Vanasse *management educator*
Wiedman, Timothy Gerard *management educator*

Haymarket
Phillips, Robert Benbow *financial planner*

Keswick
Pochick, Francis Edward *financial consultant*

Mc Lean
Drew, K *financial advisor, management consultant*
Maul, Kevin Jay *financial consultant*

Mechanicsville
Bowles, Betty Jones *business education educator*
Mann, Stephen Ashby *financial counselor*

Mount Vernon
Saadian, Javid *accountant, consultant*

Newport News
Le Mons, Kathleen Ann *portfolio manager, investment broker*
Malvin, Frederick Bage *accountant*

Norfolk
McKee, Timothy Carlton *taxation educator*
Paige, Vivian Jo-Ann *accountant*
Watkins, Wesley Lee *accountant*
West, Roger Seiker, III *finance executive*

Oakton
Houlihan, Patricia Powell *financial planner*

Palmyra
Sahr, Morris Gallup *financial planner*

Radford
Herring, Robert Alexander, III *management educator*

Reston
Lee, Johnson Y. *financial executive*
Polemitou, Olga Andrea *accountant*

Richmond
Cook, Angela Denise *business analyst*
Coronado, William J. *controller*
Dye, David Ray *tax accountant, financial advisor*
Hall, Dorothy J. *credit union executive*
Kaye, Jerome *accountant*
McDermott, William Thomas *accountant, lawyer*
Scott, Sidney Buford *financial services company executive*

Roanoke
Hudick, Andrew Michael, II *finance executive*
Mitchell, Sharon Stanley *supply analyst*
Ramsey, Michael Lee *financial planner*

Rosslyn
Cross, Susan Lee *consulting actuary*

Vienna
Bauer, Karen Mary *accountant, consultant*
Hackeman, Calvin Leslie *accountant*
Townsend, Irene Fogleman *accountant, tax specialist*
Vreeland, Russell Glenn *accountant, consultant*

Virginia Beach
DiCarlo, Susanne Helen *financial analyst*
Martin, William Raymond *retired financial executive*
O'Brien, Robert James *financial consultant, business owner*

Williamsburg
Tarleton, Jesse S. *business educator*

Woodbridge
Dillaber, Philip Arthur *budget and resource analyst, economist, consultant*

Wytheville
Wright, Donald Gene *accountant*

WEST VIRGINIA

Bluefield
Snead, John David *business administration educator*

Charleston
Brotherton, Ann Caskey *financial advisor*
Lamb, Patrick John *research associate, accountant*
Morton, Mark Edward *accountant, clothing store executive*

Inwood
Cloyd, Helen Mary *accountant, educator*

Morgantown
Wolfe, Michael David *management educator*

Wheeling
Hudacek, George C. *tax specialist*

TERRITORIES OF THE UNITED STATES

PUERTO RICO

Hato Rey
Vilches-O'Bourke, Octavio Augusto *accounting company executive*

San Juan
Rosso de Irizarry, Carmen (Tutty Rosso de Irizarry) *finance executive*

VENEZUELA

San Cristobel
Weatherby, Michael F. *security technology executive*

ADDRESS UNPUBLISHED

Alvarez, Jose Armando *accountant*
Barcenas, Jude R. L. *financial services company executive*
Bavis, Karen Ann *accountant*
Borum, Rodney Lee *financial business executive*
Boudreau, Diane Elaine *business educator*
Bowne, Shirlee Pearson *credit union executive, real estate executive*
Boyd, Danny Douglass *financial counselor, marriage and family counselor*
Brdlik, Carola Emilie *accountant*
Bulla, Ben F. *retired manufacturing company executive*
Caso, Philip Michael *financial services company executive, educator*
Caylor, Dee Jerlyn *accountant*
Chattin, Gilbert Marshall *financial analyst*
Clapp, Beverly Booker *accountant*
Collette, Frances Madelyn *retired tax consultant, lawyer*
Conkling, Sara Ann *management educator*
Covington, Gary Wayne *accountant*
Cunningham, Nancy Schieffelin *business educator*
Davis, Claude Harrison, II *accountant*
Eggan, Hugh Melford *accountant*
Finger, Bernard L. *financial services consultant*
Fiorio, Gianfranco R. *financial consultant*
Folea, Richard Victor, Sr. *educational business management administrator*
Forest, Philip Earle *finance consultant*
Holman, Darrell Edward *programmer/analyst, cost accountant*
Holton, Grace Holland *accountant*
Huddleston, Marilyn Anne *international financier, merchant banker, educator*
Kalishman, Reesa Joan *accountant*
Kelley, Sylvia Johnson *financial services firm executive*
Kennedy, Beverly (Kleban) B. *financial consultant, radio talk show host*
Kennedy, Thomas Patrick *financial executive*
Kessler, John Paul, Jr. *financial planner*
Lamont, Alice *accountant, consultant*
Mauldin, Jean Ann *controller*
Miller, Jane Andrews *accountant*
Moinet, Eric Emil *accountant, controller, cost accountant, inventory control and internal systems specialist, traffic safety administrator*
Moyer, Jerry Mills *financial service company executive*
Myers, Miller Franklin *finance company executive, retail executive*
Nank, Lois Rae *financial executive*
Newill, James Wagner *accounting executive*
Owens, Doris A. *controller*
Quirk, Kenneth Paul *accountant*
Reeves, Peggy Lois Zeigler *accountant*
Rodriguez, Elena Garcia *retired pension fund administrator*
Rosett, Jacqueline Berlin *financial executive*
Sefcik, John Delbert *financial services executive*
Shelet, Dawn Ardelle *financial analyst*
Shepherd, Steven Stewart *auditor, consultant*
Shoop, Glenn Powell *investment consultant*
Small, Rebecca Elaine *accountant*
Sobol-Given, Mary Valerie *hospital financial services administrator*
Swan, Joyce Ann *comptroller*
Tongue, Paul Graham *financial executive*
Treat, James J. *accountant, business executive*
Trippe, Charles White *financial and development executive*
Vaught, Darrel Mandel *accountant*
Wigley-Morrison, Karen *accountant, travel consultant, paralegal, administrative assistant*
Williams, Gaylen Eugene *accountant*
Wood, Robert Charles *financial consultant*

FINANCE: INSURANCE

UNITED STATES

ALABAMA

Birmingham
Truitt, John H. *insurance agency executive*

Decatur
Weatherford, David C. *insurance training manager*

Foley
Russell, Ralph Timothy *insurance company executive, mayor*

Mobile
Hooper, Edna Rosier *insurance company executive*

Montgomery
Owens, Doris Jerkins *insurance underwriter*
Robinson, Kenneth Larry *insurance company executive*

Sylacauga
Gann, Jean Pope *insurance agency executive, fine arts appraiser*

ARKANSAS

Carlisle
Berry, William Dale *insurance agent*

Flippin
Hawkins, Lionel Anthony *life insurance company executive*

Jonesboro
Calaway, Dennis Louis *insurance company executive, real estate broker, financial executice*

Little Rock
Scott, James Merlin *insurance company executive*

Sherwood
Keaton, Frances Marlene *sales representative*

Yellville
Young, S. June *insurance executive*

DISTRICT OF COLUMBIA

Washington
Turner, Marvin Wentz *insurance company executive*

FLORIDA

Altamonte Springs
Hull, John Doster *retired insurance company executive*

Auburndale
Tidwell, Mary Ellen *risk/insurance coordinator*

Casselberry
Kasmir, Gail Alice *insurance company official, accountant*

Cocoa Beach
Jamieson, Russell Ladeau, Jr. *insurance executive, consultant*

Coral Gables
Piélago, Ramon *insurance company executive*

Coral Springs
Tharp, Karen Ann *insurance agent*

Daytona Beach
Adams, John Carter, Jr. *insurance executive*

Englewood
Regan, Linda Anne *insurance agent*

Fort Lauderdale
Donoho, Tim Mark *insurance and publishing executive*
Lilley, Mili Della *insurance company executive, entertainment management consultant*
McIntyre, Charles Earl *insurance executive*
Zumbano, Anthony Ralph *risk, claims management executive*

Gainesville
Niblack, Nancy Lee Parham *insurance agent, financial consultant*
Robertson, James Cole *consultant*

Hollywood
Napsky, Martin Ben *insurance executive*

Jacksonville
Kitchens, Frederick Lynton, Jr. *insurance company executive*
Lyon, Wilford Charles, Jr. *insurance executive*
Ohnsman, David Robert *insurance consultant*
Skup, David Alan *insurance company executive*

Largo
Alpert, Barry Mark *insurance company and banking executive*
Eisele, William David *insurance agency executive*
Guthrie, John Craver *insurance agency owner*

Longwood
Brown, Donald James, Jr. *insurance company executive*
Lynch, Mary Patricia *insurance sales executive*

Miami
George, Stephen Carl *insurance company executive, educator, consultant*
Gindy, Benjamin Lee *insurance company executive*
Shusterman, Nathan *life underwriter, financial consultant*
Toro, Carlos Hans *insurance/financial products marketing executive*
Villalobos, Hector *insurance agent*

Milton
Hallett, Dean Allan *insurance company executive*

New Port Richey
Balkcom, Carol Ann *insurance agent*
Hanahan, James Lake *insurance executive*

Orange Park
Hudson, William Mark *insurance company executive, owner*

Orlando
Conrad, Judy L. *insurance company executive*

Ormond Beach
Burt, Wallace Joseph, Jr. *insurance company executive*

Oviedo
Brethauer, William Russell, Jr. *claim investigator*

Palatka
Ginn, John Arthur, Jr. *insurance agent*

Palm Beach
Becker, John Lionel, Jr. *insurance company executive, marketing company executive*

Plant City
Feola, Ralph Leonard *insurance agent*

Pompano Beach
Zinman, Jacques *former insurance agency executive*

Saint Petersburg
Araico, Enrique Jesus *insurance executive*
Fraser, John Wayne *insurance executive, consultant, underwriter*

Sarasota
Mills, David Reeve *insurance agent, commissioner*

Sunrise
Youner, David *insurance brokerage executive*

Tallahassee
Gabor, Jeffrey Alan *insurance and financial services executive*
Hunt, John Edwin *insurance company executive, consultant*

Tampa
Hanisee, Mark Steven *employee benefits professional*
Vanderburg, Paul Stacey *insurance executive, consultant*

Titusville
Hardister, Darrell Edward *insurance executive*

Vero Beach
Feagles, Robert West *insurance company executive*

Wellington
Cook, Gary E. *insurance agent*

West Palm Beach
Flah, Richard *life insurance executive*

GEORGIA

Atlanta
Andrews, Robert Lloyd *insurance company executive*
Dunbar, James Reginald, II *insurance agent, Baptist minister*
Fowler, Vivian Delores *insurance company executive*
Fox, Lloyd Allan *insurance company executive*
Hoke, Alexander Peabody *life underwriter, financial consultant*
Huntley, William Thomas, III *insurance agent, consultant*
Johnson, James Douglas *insurance executive*
Parker, William Thomas *insurance executive*
Smith, Dennis A. *insurance company executive*
Witty, Robert Wilkes *insurance services company executive*

Columbus
Amos, Daniel Paul *insurance executive*
Pesante, Angel Eduardo *insurance executive*

Gainesville
Clary, Ronald Gordon *insurance agency executive*

Lagrange
Hudson, Charles Daugherty *insurance executive*

Macon
Dorsey, Donna Bagley *insurance agent*

Marietta
Todd, Imo Kellam *insurance association executive*

Roswell
Fried, Lawrence Philip *insurance company executive*

Smyrna
Cressey, Douglas B. *insurance company executive*

Statesboro
Parrish, Benjamin Emmitt, II *insurance executive*

Stone Mountain
Denney, Laura Falin *insurance company executive*

Tucker
Fitchett, W(illiam) Calvin *insurance executive*

ILLINOIS

Chicago
Bartholomay, William C. *insurance brokerage company executive, professional baseball team executive*

KANSAS

Topeka
Zientara, Suzannah Dockstader *insurance company executive*

KENTUCKY

Jeremiah
Smith, Roger Keith *insurance agent*

Lexington
Davis, William Wootton, Jr. *insurance executive*
Johnson, Lizabeth Lettie *insurance agent*

Louisville
Bailey, Irving Widmer, II *insurance holding company executive*
Haddaway, James David *retired insurance company official*
Hickey, Bobby Ray *underwriting assistant*
Ouimet, James Michael *insurance company executive*
Rosky, Theodore Samuel *insurance company executive*

Murray
Rogers, Jane Hooks *insurance agent*

LOUISIANA

Baton Rouge
Jay, James Albert *insurance company executive*
Tutt, Gloria J. Rutherford *insurance company executive*

Kenner
Kuebler, David Wayne *insurance company executive*

Metairie
Milam, June Matthews *life insurance agent*

New Orleans
Jones, Marquis E. *management sales executive, insurance executive*
Kraus, Jean Elizabeth Grau *insurance agent*
Marks, Charles Dennery *insurance salesman*
Purvis, George Frank, Jr. *life insurance company executive*
Roberts, John Kenneth, Jr. *life insurance company executive*

Shreveport
Harbuck, Edwin Charles *insurance agent*

MISSISSIPPI

Meridian
Coleman, Marion Leslie *insurance company executive*

Summit
Jones, Lawrence David *insurance and medical consultant*

Tunica
Koonce, Ellis Everett *insurance agent*

NEW YORK

Hicksville
Rough, Herbert Louis *insurance company executive*

NORTH CAROLINA

Chapel Hill
Fine, J(ames) Allen *insurance company executive*

Charlotte
Bebon, Robert E. *insurance executive*
Waldon, Grace Roberta *insurance agent*
Woollen, Thomas Hayes *insurance consultant*

Durham
Fromm, Erwin Frederick *retired insurance company executive, health facility executive*

Fayetteville
McDonald, Patricia Hamilton *insurance agency administrator, real estate broker*

Greensboro
Carr, Howard Ernest *retired insurance agency executive*
Goslen, Frank Odell *insurance adjustment company executive, lawyer*
Parrish, Bobby Lee *insurance executive*

Greenville
Powell, Robert Jackson, III *insurance agent*

Hendersonville
Stokes, William Finley, Jr. *insurance executive*

Matthews
Dean, William Gromer *insurance company executive*

Whitsett
Crouch, James Bonneau, Jr. *insurance executive*

Winston Salem
Beardsley, Charles Mitchell *retired insurance company executive*

OKLAHOMA

Edmond
Graham, Carol Ethlyn *insurance company administrator*

Enid
Allen, Diana D. *insurance agent, author*

Marlow
Jackson, Ruth Robertson *insurance company executive*

Oklahoma City
Crawford, John P. *insurance commissioner*
Hamilton, Thomas Allen *insurance agent, registered representative*

Perry
Doughty, Michael Dean *insurance agent*

Tulsa
Abbott, William Thomas *claim specialist*
Bryant, Dennis Michael *insurance executive*
Livingston, Pamela Janelle *insurance company executive*

SOUTH CAROLINA

Spartanburg
Stewart, James Charles, II *insurance agent*

TENNESSEE

Chattanooga
Chandler, J. Harold *insurance company executive*
Pals, Dean Clifford *insurance company executive*

Knoxville
Gunnels, Thomas Curtis *seminar company executive*

Lookout Mountain
Hardy, Thomas Cresson *insurance company executive*

Memphis
Lowery, F(loyd) Lynn, Jr. *insurance executive*
Stern, Donna Virginia *underwriter*

Nashville
Elberry, Zainab Abdelhaliem *insurance company executive*
Gaultney, John Orton *life insurance agent, consultant*
Pentecost, William Ronald *insurance company executive*

TEXAS

Abernathy
Sanderson, David Odell *insurance broker*

Abilene
Forêt, Randy Blaise *insurance executive*

Austin
Caldwell, William McNeilly *insurance agent*
Ellis, Glen Edward, Jr. *insurance agent, financial planner*
Nolen, William Lawrence, Jr. *insurance agency owner, real estate investor*
Spielman, David Vernon *retired insurance, finance and publications consultant*
Young, David Lynn *regulatory consultant*

Beaumont
Newman, Maxine Placker *insurance consultant*

Conroe
Purdom, R. Don *insurance claims consultant*

Corpus Christi
Vargas, Joe Flores *insurance claims executive*

Crockett
Jones, Don Carlton *insurance agent*

Dallas
Beck, Luke Ferrell Wilson *insurance specialist*
Cizza, John Anthony *insurance executive*
Head, Mark D. *insurance and employee benefit broker*
Johnson, William Ray *insurance company executive*
Madden, Teresa Darleen *insurance agency owner*
Rieger, Sam Lee *insurance company executive*
Rinne, Austin Dean *insurance company executive*
Weakley, Clare George, Jr. *insurance executive, theologian, entrepreneur*
Williamson, Walker Kendrick *insurance executive*
Willis, Thomas Delena *health insurance company executive*

Del Rio
Nelson, Bernard P. *publishing executive, writer*

Fort Worth
Brannon, Treva Lee (Wood) *insurance company executive*
Faherty, John Kevin *insurance broker, consultant*
Kern, Edna Ruth *insurance executive*

Galveston
Monts, Elizabeth Rose *insurance company executive*
Moody, Robert Lee *insurance company executive*
Regini, Judith L. *insurance company professional*

Houston
Alexander, Harold Campbell *insurance consultant*
Bickel, Stephen Douglas *insurance company executive*
Clark, Edward Ernest *insurance administrator*
Dean, Robert Franklin *insurance company executive*
Delaney, Andrew *retired insurance company executive, consultant*
Farr, Walter Emil, Jr. *insurance agent*
Harris, Richard Foster, Jr. *insurance company executive*
Hook, Harold Swanson *insurance company executive*
Lyons, Phillip Michael, Sr. *insurance accounting and real estate executive*
Martin, Andrew Delleney *life and health underwriter, financial and employee benefits consultant*
Martin, Kenneth Frank *insurance company executive*
Mintz, Stuart Alan *insurance company executive, consultant*
Momoh, Paul J. *educator, insurance underwriter*
Rhodes, Lawrence *insurance executive*
Taylor, Carole Jan Hudson *insurance company administrator*
Tueff, James Rodrick *insurance company executive*
West, Thomas Lowell, Jr. *insurance company executive*

Irving
Coil, Charles Ray *managed healthcare executive*
Cooper, Alcie Lee, Jr. *insurance executive*

Lake Jackson
Elbert, James Peak *independent insurance agent, minister*

Mc Kinney
Terry, Linda Stewart *insurance agent*

Mcallen
Whisenant, B(ert) R(oy), Jr. *insurance company executive*

Nixon
Nixon, Sam A. *retired insurance company medical executive*

Palestine
Douthitt, Shirley Ann *insurance agent*

Plano
Williams, Robert Michael *insurance executive*

Richardson
Coleman, Rogers King *insurance company executive*
White, Irene *insurance complex case manager*

San Antonio
Broome, Jack Harrison *insurance executive*
Colyer, Kirk Klein *insurance executive, real estate investment executive*
Cook, John Roscoe, Jr. *insurance executive*
Herres, Robert Tralles *insurance company executive*
Mawhinney, King *insurance company executive*
McAllister, Walter Williams, III *insurance company executive*
Mc Dermott, Robert Francis *insurance company executive*
Wellberg, Edward Louis, Jr. *insurance company executive*
White, Robert Miles Ford *life insurance company executive*

Spring
Clarkson, Carole Lawrence *insurance company professional*
Templeton, Randall Keith *insurance company executive*

Temple
Gillett, Victor William, Jr. *title insurance company executive*

Tyler
Guin, Don Lester *insurance company executive*

Vidor
Slaughter, Ted David *public relations executive, health care executive*

VIRGINIA

Abingdon
Graham, Howard Lee, Sr. *corporate executive*

Charlottesville
Long, Charles Farrell *insurance company executive*
Selman, Joe B. *insurance company executive*

Chesterfield
Jacobs, James A. *insurance professional*

Harrisonburg
Price, Charles Grattan, Jr. *retired insurance agency executive*

Herndon
Downer, Richard Fenton *insurance agency executive*

Huddleston
Saunders, Dorothy Ann *insurance company executive, sales management*

Lynchburg
Dolan, Ronald Vincent *insurance company executive*

Norfolk
Dungan, William Joseph, Jr. *insurance broker, economics educator*

Richmond
Coleman, Ronald Lee *insurance claims executive*
Holt, Elbert Hilton, Jr. *insurance company executive*
Jacobs, James Paul *retired insurance executive*
Payne, William Sanford *insurance company executive*
Scott, Kenneth Pleasant, Jr. *life insurance agent*

Vienna
Palumbo, James Fredrick *insurance company executive*

Virginia Beach
Ellis, John Carroll, Jr. *life insurance sales executive*
Kantor, David Scott *insurance and tax consultant*

WASHINGTON

Bellevue
Clay, Orson C. *insurance company executive*

WEST VIRGINIA

Charleston
Bodge, Steven Alton *insurance special investigator*

Clendenin
Kerns, Stephen Rimmer *insurance executive*

Grafton
Knotts, Robert Lee *insurance executive*

TERRITORIES OF THE UNITED STATES

PUERTO RICO

Hato Rey
Baerga-Vaquer, Rafael Antonio *insurance agent*

ADDRESS UNPUBLISHED

Childress, Walter Dabney, III *insurance executive, financial planner*
DeCrescenzo, Jame Melisse *insurance company executive*
Gresso, Vernon Riddle *insurance company executive*
Hauenstein, George Carey *life insurance executive*
Hensley, Stephen Allan *insurance executive*
Hook, Cornelius Henry *insurance agency owner*
Moore, Rick Alan *insurance adjuster*
Nelson, Barbara Kay *insurance agent*
Polito, Susan Evans *insurance agency official*
Richardson, Gordon Banning *insurance company executive, estate planner*
Ryan, James *insurance company executive*
Sharick, Merle Dayton, Jr. *mortgage insurance company executive*
Smith, Margaret Brand *insurance executive, lawyer*

FINANCE: INVESTMENT SERVICES

UNITED STATES

ALABAMA

Birmingham
Camp, Ehney Addison, III *investment banking executive*
Mc Cain, Maurice Edward *investment firm executive*
Miree, Kathryn Waller *brokerage house executive*

Montgomery
Blount, Winton Malcolm, III *investment executive*
Taylor, Watson Robbins, Jr. *investment banker*

Sylacauga
Comer, Braxton Bragg, II *entrepreneur*

ARIZONA

Phoenix
Taylor, Elizabeth Jane *investment consultant, real estate and international marketing executive*
Wood, Gregory Burton, Jr. *brokerage house executive*

ARKANSAS

Little Rock
Light, Jo Knight *stockbroker*
Zimmermann, Stephan Fritz-Peter *investment company executive*

Newport
Holmes, Paul Kinloch, Jr. *private investor*

DISTRICT OF COLUMBIA

Washington
Tucker, Howard McKeldin *investment banker, consultant*

FLORIDA

Boca Raton
Barbarosh, Milton Harvey *merchant banking executive*
Cohen, Melvyn Douglas *securities company executive*
Fine, Norman David *investment management executive*
Nangle, Clint *investment company executive, writer*
Skurnick, Sam *stockbroker, investment manager*

Bradenton Beach
Nelson, Ralph Erwin *investment company executive, coin dealer*

Clearwater
Loick, Walter Julius *investment company executive*

Clermont
Turner, Justin Leroy *investor, consultant*

Coconut Grove
Saunders, Phyllis S. *business and commodities broker, off-shore investment consultant*

Coral Springs
Brown, Ted Leon, Jr. *investment company executive*
Levitz, John Blase *investment manager, consultant*

Destin
Horne, Thomas Lee, III *entrepreneur*

Fort Lauderdale
Sands, Roberta Alyse *real estate investor*

Fort Myers
Hawley, Phillip Eugene *investment banker*

Hialeah
Zwigard, Bruce Albert *brokerage house executive*

Homosassa
Nagy, Albert N. *entrepreneur, consultant*

Jupiter
Kulok, William Allan *entrepreneur, venture capitalist*
Malm, Rita H. *securities executive*

Madeira Beach
Ashton, Thomas Walsh *investment banker*

Mary Esther
Xanthopoulos, Philip, Sr. *brokerage house executive, financial advisor*

Miami
Capdevielle, Xavier O. *entrepreneur, aviation consultant*
Dorion, Robert Charles *entrepreneur, investor*
Gittlin, Arthur Sam *industrialist, banker*

Naples
Finley, Jack Dwight *investments and consultation executive*
Osias, Richard Allen *international financier, investor, real estate investment executive, corporate investor*

Ocala
Geyer, G. Nicholas *investment banker*

Odessa
Ault, Jeffrey Michael *investment banker*

Palm Beach
Andrews, Holdt *investment banker*
Halmos, Peter *investment company executive*
Lede, Richard *investment company executive*

Pompano Beach
Johnson, Donald Harry *investment company executive*
Presley, Brian *investment company executive*

Saint Petersburg
Fulp, James Alan *securities firm executive*
Godbold, Francis Stanley *investment banker, real estate executive*
Scott, Lee Hansen *retired holding company executive*

Sarasota
Balliett, John William *entrepreneur*
Cox, Houston Abraham, Jr. *futures markets consultant*
Prade, Jean Noël Cresta *entrepreneur*

Stuart
Martin, Ralph Harding *investor*

Tampa
Hackett, Edward Vincent *investment company executive*
Michaels, John Patrick, Jr. *investment banker, media broker*
Sigety, Charles Birge *investment company executive*

Tequesta
Kraft, Otto Fritz *investment adviser, artist*

West Palm Beach
Cano, Marta Mendendez *securities company executive, financial consultant*
Pincus, Laura Rhoda *investor, accountant*
Zisson, James Stern *investment management consultant*

Winter Park
Maher, William James *investment executive*

GEORGIA

Athens
Holcomb, Alice Willard Power *diversified investments executive*

Atlanta
Atchison, Michael David *financial and management consultant, investor, investment bank executive*
Averitt, Richard Garland, III *securities executive*
Barker, Sandra Mills *securities analyst*
Christy, Robert Allen *investment broker, investment advisor*
Dietz, Arthur Townsend *investment counseling company executive*
Flading, John Joseph *brokerage house executive*
Jackson, Geraldine *entrepreneur*
Jackson, Maynard *securities executive*
Keough, Donald Raymond *investment company executive*
McNabb, Dianne Leigh *investment banker, accountant*
Moran, Christa Ilse Merkel *investor, linguist, educator*
Moss, Dan, Jr. *stockbroker*
Nash, Charles D. *investment banker*
Roberts, Cassandra Fendley *investment company executive*
Roberts, Thomasene Blount *entrepreneur*
Shelton, Charles Bascom, III *investment banker*
Stern, Wayne Brian *investment company executive, management consultant*
Whitman, Homer William, Jr. *investment counseling company executive*

Cleveland
Lewis, Richard, Sr. *securities broker, consultant*

Columbus
Diaz-Verson, Salvador, Jr. *investment advisor*

Norcross
Cardin, Jackson Eugene *commodities trader*

Peachtree City
Stewart, Anthony Joseph *investment consultant*

Tucker
Royer, David Lee *investment banker*

ILLINOIS

Chicago
Reid, Donald Wayne *investment management executive, researcher*

KENTUCKY

Frankfort
Nall, Sandra Lillian *securities company official*

Morehead
Radez, David Charles *financial planning and investment company executive*

LOUISIANA

Morgan City
Dahlberg, Carl Fredrick, Jr. *entrepreneur*

New Orleans
Fischer, Ashton John, Jr. *investor*
Flower, Walter Chew, III *investment counselor*
Welch, Robert Ballinger *investment planner*

Shreveport
Boniol, Eddie Eugene *investments executive*

MISSOURI

Springfield
Looney, Ronald Lee *investment executive*

NEW YORK

New York
Rosen, Benjamin Maurice *venture capitalist, computer company executive*

NORTH CAROLINA

Asheville
Alderson, Creed Flanary, Jr. *financial service executive*

Boone
Mackorell, James Theodore, Jr. *entrepreneur, small business owner*

Charlotte
Bartee, Ted Ray *commodities trader, rancher*
Grimaldi, James Thomas *investment fund executive*
Hardin, Thomas Jefferson, II *investment counsel*
Prud'homme, Albert Fredric *securities company executive, financial planner*

Durham
Reeves, John Mercer, II *international trade finance professional*
Scott, Lee Allen, Sr. *securities company executive*

Efland
Efland, Simpson Lindsay *entrepreneur*

Fayetteville
Taylor, Sylvia Pindle *educational entrepreneur*

Greensboro
Johnson, Marshall Hardy *investment company executive*

Oriental
Blowers, Bobbie *entrepreneur*

Raleigh
Tucker, Garland Scott, III *investment banker*

Winston Salem
Cavanagh, John Joseph, Jr. (Jack Cavanagh) *investment broker, consultant*
Hall, Dwayne Allen *investment broker*
Strickland, Robert Louis *business executive*

OKLAHOMA

Oklahoma City
Hammert, Dorothy Savage *investment company executive*
Livingston, Peter Gaskill *entrepreneur, consultant*
Munhollon, Samuel Clifford *investment brokerage house executive*
Puckett, Thomas Roger *entrepreneur, minister*
Sulc, Dwight George *investment advisor*

Tulsa
Healey, David Lee *investment company executive*

PENNSYLVANIA

Pittsburgh
Mock, Lawrence Edward, Jr. *venture capitalist*

SOUTH CAROLINA

Columbia
Ader, Joseph Daniel *stockbroker*
Holloway, Thomas Edward *investor*
Lynch, Fran Jackie *investment advisory company executive*

Greenville
Oxner, Glenn Ruckman *financial executive*

Hilton Head Island
Scott, Kerrigan Davis *private investor, philanthropist*
Urato, Barbra Casale *entrepreneur*

Pawleys Island
Hudson-Young, Jane Smither *real estate investor*

Simpsonville
Hanold, R. C. Frederick, III *entrepreneur*

TENNESSEE

Chattanooga
Corey, Charles William *investment banker*

Johnson City
Wilkes, Clem Cabell, Jr. *stockbroker*

Knoxville
Penn, Dawn Tamara *entrepreneur*

Lexington
Franks, Hollis Berry *retired investment executive*

Memphis
Morgan, Allen B., Jr. *securities executive*

Nashville
Burch, John Christopher, Jr. *investment banker*
Byrd, Andrew Wayne *investment company executive*
Hanselman, Richard Wilson *entrepreneur*
Liles, Malcolm Henry *stockbroker*
Martin, Andrew Douglas *investment broker*
Oliver, William Langdon *brokerage office executive*
Wagner, Michael Grafton *investor, corporation executive, resources advisor, business consultant*

Williamsport
Cheek, Will T(ompkins) *investor*

TEXAS

Amarillo
Barfield, Bourdon Rea *investor*
Horton, Thomas Mark *futures and options trader, commodity consultant*

Austin
Arnold, Stephen Paul *investment professional*
Thornhill, Gabriel Felder, III *securities company executive*

Brownwood
Beakley, Grover Jahue, Jr. *investor*

Conroe
Adams, John White *investment company executive, engineer*

Corpus Christi
Bateman, John Roger *investment holding company executive*

Dallas
Bond, Myron Humphrey *investment executive*
Buchholz, Donald Alden *stock brokerage company executive*
Crockett, Felicia Dodee Frost *brokerage firm executive*
Fisher, Richard Welton *venture capitalist*
Fritz, Terrence Lee *investment banker, strategic consultant*
Leason, Jack Walter *investment advisor*
Lohrman, William Walter *investment company executive, consultant*
Lutes, Benjamin Franklin, Jr. *investor*
Lynch, William Wright, Jr. *investment executive, engineer*
Reed, Jesse Francis *entrepreneur, artist, inventor, theologian, business consultant*

De Soto
Harrington, Betty Byrd *entrepreneur*

Denton
Wong, Benedict Ding Chung *investor*

El Paso
Wootten, John Robert *investor*

Friendswood
Arnaud, Sandra *financial advisor*

Houston
Altman, William Carl *investment manager, consultant*
Barrere, Clem Adolph *business brokerage company executive*
Bollich, Elridge Nicholas *investment executive*
Cunningham, R. Walter *venture capitalist*
Currie, John Thornton (Jack Currie) *retired investment banker*
Dantone, W. Bryan *real estate investor, principal*
Dworsky, Clara Weiner *merchandise brokerage executive, lawyer*
Fain, Jay Lindsey *brokerage house executive, consultant*
Frischkorn, David Ephraim Keasbey, Jr. *investment banker*
Marziale, Antonio *investment company executive*
McBride, Keith L. *investment banker*
Metzger, Lewis Albert *brokerage house executive, financial consultant*
Mosher, Edward Blake *investment company executive, consultant*
Parsons, Edmund Morris *investment company executive*
Pate, A. J. *investment advisor*
Poindexter, John Bruce *entrepreneur*
Richards, Leonard Martin *investment executive, consultant*
Riesser, Gregor Hans *arbitrage investment adviser*
Taylor, James B. *securities trader, financial planner*
Vaughan, Eugene H. *investment company executive*
Williams, Edward Earl, Jr. *entrepreneur, educator*

Irving
Dyess, Jeffrey Alan *investment representative*
Siefkin, William Charles *international growth investor, consultant, publisher, writer*

Plano
Parent, David Hill *investment company executive*

Rockport
Morel, Eugene Allen *entrepreneur*

San Antonio
Lord, Dick *brokerage house executive*

Sherman
Sprowl, David Charles *brokerage house executive*

Sugar Land
Freeman, Clifford Echols, Jr. *investment banker*

Texas City
Legan, Robert William *securities analyst*

VIRGINIA

Alexandria
Hannon, Michael *investment banker*
Speck, David George *investment executive*

Annandale
Khim, Jay Wook *high technology systems integration executive*

Arlington
Gregg, David, III *investment banker*
Lampe, Henry Oscar *stockbroker*
Stambaugh, William Scott *investor, economist*

Goode
Garland, Ray Lucian *investment company executive, columnist*

Herndon
Jiang, Hubin *entrepreneur, software engineer*

Lexington
Murphy, Michael Gordon *investment consultant*

Mc Lean
Bisbee, Gerald Elftman, Jr. *investment company executive*
Herbolsheimer, Lawrence Frederick *entrepreneur*

Petersburg
Ryan, James Herbert *security and retail services company executive*
Washburn, John Rosser *entrepreneur*

Reston
Takeuchi, Hiroshi *investment company executive, consultant*

Richmond
Binns, Walter Gordon, Jr. *investment management executive*
Fields, William Jay *investment banker*
Gorr, Louis Frederick *investment consultant*
Gunter, Bradley Hunt *capital management executive*
Kienel, Frederick Edward *financial executive*
Phillips, Thomas Edworth, Jr. *investment executive, senior consultant*
Scott, George Cole, III *stockbroker*

Virginia Beach
Lawson, Beth Ann Reid *strategic planner*

Williamsburg
Gordon, Baron Jack *stockbroker*
Hargrove, Roy Belmont, III *stockbroker*
Montgomery, Joseph William *investment broker*

WEST VIRGINIA

Huntington
Riggs, Mary Lou *investment executive*

TERRITORIES OF THE UNITED STATES

PUERTO RICO

San Juan
Uribe, Javier Miguel *investment executive*

ADDRESS UNPUBLISHED

Armstrong, Michael David *investment banker*
Arp Lotter, Donna *investor, venture capitalist*
Barnes, Craig Martin *commodity trading advisor, accountant*
Bondarenko, Hesperia Aura Louis *entrepreneur*
Brown, Samuel *retired corporate executive*
Burns, Barbara Belton *investment company executive*
Conlon, Peter John, Jr. *investment advisor*
Crawford, Michael Wayne *investment company executive*
Dunlap, Albert John *venture capitalist*
Hampton, Margaret Frances *international trade and finance consultant*
Heckler, John Maguire *stockbroker, investment company executive*
Hickey, Joseph Michael *investment banker*
Hill, John Edward, Jr. *investment banker, small business owner*
Kilborne, George Briggs *investment company executive*
Kock, Robert Marshall *investment banker*
Kulesha, Kevin John *investment banker*
Logan, Dan *investment professional*
Robertson, Mark Wayne *investment specialist*
Roland, Catherine Dixon *entrepreneur*
Uchida, Prentiss Susumu *entrepreneur, management executive*
Zahrt, Merton Stroebel *investor*

FINANCE: REAL ESTATE

UNITED STATES

ALABAMA

Arab
Hammond, Ralph Charles *real estate executive*

Auburn
Cooper, Dorothy Summers *real estate agent*

Mobile
Perkins, Marie McConnell *real estate executive*

Saraland
Smith, Paul Lowell *realtor, minister*

Tuscaloosa
McFarland, James William *real estate development company executive*
Straley, John Adrian *urban planner*

ARIZONA

Scottsdale
Garling, Carol Elizabeth *real estate executive and developer*

ARKANSAS

Fayetteville
Jackson, Robert Lee *real estate agent, broker*

Hampton
Cronin, Gerard Thomas *community planner, negotiations specialist, writer*

Hot Springs National Park
Craft, Kay Stark *real estate broker*

Jonesboro
Jones, Philip Arthur *real estate developer*
Peters, Mary Helen *real estate agent*

Little Rock
McCarley, Robert Edward *real estate executive, real estate appraiser*
Shults, Robert Lee *real estate executive, airline executive*
Wuetig, Joyce Linda *realtor*

Lonoke
Knox, Charles Henry *real estate executive*

Pine Bluff
Holmes, Claire Coleman *real estate broker*

CALIFORNIA

San Francisco
Frush, James Carroll, Jr. *real estate development company executive*

COLORADO

Englewood
Ellsworth, Joseph Cordon *real estate executive, lawyer*

CONNECTICUT

New London
Langfield, Raymond Lee *real estate developer*

FLORIDA

Boca Raton
Carr-Allen, Elizabeth *real estate and mortgage broker, metaphysician*
Goray, Gerald Allen *real estate executive, lawyer*
Innes-Brown, Georgette Meyer *real estate and insurance broker*
Lagin, Neil *property management executive, landscape designer*
Lippman, Alfred Julian *retired real estate executive*
MacCurdy, John A. *real estate appraiser, consultant*
Mandor, Leonard Stewart *real estate company executive*

Bradenton
Varga, Jonalynn Ruth *real estate salesperson*

Brandon
Chesler, Doris Adelle *real estate professional*
Proctor, Mark Alan *real estate executive, television panelist, commentator*

Cape Coral
Mutters, David Ray *real estate broker*

Cedar Key
Starnes, Earl Maxwell *urban and regional planner, architect*

Clearwater
Wyllie, Alfred Linn *real estate broker, mortgage broker*

Coral Gables
Blumberg, Philip Flayderman *real estate developer*
Walsh-McGehee, Martha Bosse *conservationist*
West, Macdonald *real estate executive*

Daytona Beach
Hastings, Mary Lynn *real estate broker*

Deland
Caccamise, Alfred Edward *real estate executive*

Edgewater
Robinson, Hermon Clayton (Rob), III *real estate broker*

Fort Lauderdale
Bird, Linda W. *realtor*
Cummings, Virginia (Jeanne) *former real estate company executive*
Moraitis, Karen Karl *real estate broker*
Van Howe, Annette Evelyn *retired real estate agent*
Wietor, Michael George *real estate executive, commodity trading advisor, export purchasing agent*

Fort Myers
Van Vleck, Pamela Kay *commercial real estate broker*
Wagner, Robert Wayne *real estate executive*

Gainesville
Emerson, Donald McGeachy, Jr. *appraisal company executive*
May, Jackson Campbell *real estate developer, writer*
York, Vermelle Cardwell *real estate broker and developer*

Gulf Breeze
Jenkins, Robert Berryman *real estate developer*

Hollywood
Burton, John Jacob *retired real estate company executive appraiser*

Jacksonville
Parker, David Forster *real estate development consultant*
Pearce, Jennifer Sue *real estate appraiser*
Sibley, Richard Carl *real estate executive*

Key West
Green, Sandra Staap *mortgage broker, real estate appraiser*

Lake Park
Peller, Marci Terry *real estate executive*
Totten, Gloria Jean (Dolly Totten) *real estate executive, financial consultant*

Lantana
Weeks, Charles, Jr. *real estate executive, retired publishing company executive*

Longwood
Gasperoni, Emil, Sr. *realtor, developer*

Marco Island
Gavey, James Edward *investment and real estate brokerage company executive*
Llewellyn, Leonard Frank *real estate broker*

Melbourne
Evans, Arthur Forte *real estate developer*
Nero, Shirley Mae *real estate executive*

Miami
Adler, Michael M. *real estate developer, construction executive*
Esslinger, Anna Mae Linthicum *realtor*
Guerra, Roland *regional property manager*
Lopez-Munoz, Maria Rosa P. *land development company executive*
Ocampo, Angela Patricia *real estate broker*
Roemer, Elaine Sloane *real estate broker*
Salas, Nestor Augusto *real estate executive*
Taylor, Adam David *real estate executive*
Villalón, Silvia Durán *real estate executive*

Naples
Evans, Elizabeth Ann West *realtor*
Link, Raymond Roger *property broker, natural resource consultant*
Stratton, John Caryl *real estate executive*

North Miami
Tate, J. Kenneth *real estate executive*

Ocala
Booth, Jane Schuele *real estate broker, executive*

Orlando
DeGrilla, Robert J. *real estate executive*
Lothrop, Thomas Low *environmentalist*
Watson, Barry Lee *real estate and mortgage broker, investor, contractor, builder, developer*

Palatka
Sigua, Gilbert C. *environmental specialist*

Palm Beach
Shepherd, Charles Clinton *real estate executive*

Palm Beach Gardens
Freeman, Donald Wilford *real estate developer, horse breeder*

Palm City
Holtz, Mary Heston *realtor, retired fashion coordinator*

Palmetto
Rains, Gloria Cann *environmentalist company executive*

Panama City
Lawrence, James Huckabee *commercial realtor*

Plantation
Neff, Cecil Lewis, Jr. *real estate appraiser, author*

Pompano Beach
Epstein, Jaye Mark *city planner*

Ponte Vedra Beach
Berry, Clare Gebert *real estate broker*
Davis, Kim McAlister *real estate sales executive, real estate broker*
Palmer, Marianne Eleanor *real estate broker, educator*

Port Orange
Brown, Timothy Wayne *urban planner*

Punta Gorda
Graham, William Aubrey, Jr. *real estate broker*

Saint Petersburg
Baiman, Gail *real estate broker*
Hurley, Frank Thomas, Jr. *realtor*
Puckett, Stanley Allen *realtor, marketing and management educator, historian*
Rummel, Harold Edwin *real estate development executive*

Sarasota
Bennett, Lois *real estate broker*
Scheitlin, Constance Joy *real estate broker*
Tate, Manley Sidney *real estate broker*

Sebring
Sherrick, Daniel Noah *real estate broker*

Shalimar
Crosby, Robert Davis *property manager, consultant*

Sunrise
Cronin, Mary Haag *real estate referral agent*

Tallahassee
Lisenby, Dorrece Edenfield *realtor*
Morgan, Constance Louise *real estate executive*
Tookes, James Nelson *real estate investment company executive*

Tampa
Corbitt, Doris Orene *real estate agent, dietitian*
Finch, Susan McGuire *urban planner*
Mortenson, Thomas Carl *property and business developer*
Parrado, Peter Joseph *real estate executive*
Purcell, Henry, III *real estate developer*

Wellington
Morales-Hendry, Maria Holguin *real estate agent, poet*

Winter Garden
Tillman, Kay Heidt *real estate executive, commodity broker*

Winter Haven
Biggs, Antoinette Bailey *real estate broker*

Winter Park
Strawn, Frances Freeland *real estate executive*

GEORGIA

Athens
David, Martha Lena Huffaker *real estate agent, former educator*
Melton, Wayne Charles *real estate executive*

Atlanta
Bugg, William Adolphus, Jr. *real estate executive*
Comstock, Robert Donald, Jr. *real estate executive*
Cupp, Robert Erhard *golf course designer, land use planner*
Curtis, Philip Kerry *real estate developer*
Lebow, Laurel Mary Lavin *real estate developer, real estate asset manager*
Nash, William Wray, Jr. *retired city planning educator*
Ossewaarde, Anne Winkler *real estate developer*
Raines, Tim D. *real estate corporation executive*
Rastegar, Nader E. *real estate developer, businessman*
Searles, David Sewall, Jr. *real estate executive*
Simpson, Allan Boyd *real estate company executive*
Winchester, Jesse Gregory *real estate lending company executive*

Augusta
Mayberry, Julius Eugene *realty company owner, investor*
Price, William Anthony *real estate broker*

Folkston
Crumbley, Esther Helen Kendrick *realtor, retired secondary education educator*

Macon
Jones, John Ellis *real estate broker*

Marietta
Cline, Robert Thomas *retired land developer*

Milledgeville
Ogden, Joanne *real estate executive*

Newnan
Barron, Thomas Willis *real estate broker*

Norcross
Colgan, George Phillips *real estate analyst*

Statesboro
Neal, Frank Allen, Jr. *city planner*

Stone Mountain
Taylor, Z. Lowell *environmental company executive*

Tucker
Knox, Kenneth Joe *development consultant*

INDIANA

Greenwood
Stewart, Eileen Rose *real estate broker*

KENTUCKY

Lexington
Poynter, Melissa Venable *real estate broker*
Tyson, Rosendo Felicito, Jr. *urban planner*
Webb, Thomas Richard *environmental services administrator*

Louisville
Gott, Marjorie Eda Crosby *conservationist, former educator*
Hoeh, David Charles *urban planning consultant*
Thompson, Michael J. *environmentalist*

LOUISIANA

Baton Rouge
Marvin, Wilbur *real estate executive*
Mohr, Jeffrey Michael *real estate and insurance executive*
Siegel, Lawrence Iver *real estate development company executive*
Skillman, Ernest Edward, Jr. *real estate sales and management executive*

Harvey
Chee, Shirley *real estate broker*

Marksville
Voinche, Woody Mark *commercial property entrepreneur*

Metairie
Perrin, Roy Albert, Jr. *real estate developer*

New Orleans
Bell, Bryan *real estate and oil investment executive, educator*
Evans, Audrey Anne *environmentalist*
Lupo, Robert Edward Smith *real estate developer and investor*

Shreveport
Herrin, Joseph Richard *real estate developer*

MAINE

Rockport
Duarte, Patricia M. *real estate and insurance broker*

MARYLAND

Chevy Chase
Bracken, Marilyn Casey *environmental company executive*

MISSISSIPPI

Clarksdale
Magdovitz, Lawrence Maynard *real estate executive, lawyer*

Columbus
Hardy, Robert Baskerville *city planner*

Hattiesburg
Johnson, Ellen Randel *real estate broker*

Meridian
Church, George Millord *real estate executive*

Oxford
Davis, James Randall *real estate developer*

NORTH CAROLINA

Ararat
Marsh, Joseph Virgil *real estate and investment broker*

Asheville
Morosani, George Warrington *real estate developer, realtor*
Retskin, Bill Allan *real estate broker*

Atlantic Beach
Rike, Linda Stokes *real estate broker*

Camden
Pefley, Charles Saunders *real estate broker*

Chapel Hill
Brock, Eunice Lee Miller *realtor*
Weiss, Shirley F. *urban and regional planner, economist, educator*

Charlotte
Diemer, Arthur William *real estate executive*
Fortenberry, Carol Lomax *real estate appraiser*
Silverman, Marc H. *real estate developer, business owner*
Wiggins, Nancy Bowen *real estate broker, market research consultant*

Fayetteville
Kendrick, Mark C. *real estate executive*

Four Oaks
Johnson, Wanda Dale Jernigan *property management executive*

Greensboro
Conrad, David Paul *real estate broker, retired restaurant chain executive*
Hiatt, Mabel Strader *real estate investment executive*

Hickory
Powell, Louise Fox *real estate developer*

Kinston
Brooks, Henry Franklin *real estate company executive*

Raleigh
Stephens, George Myers *real estate market research consultant, real estate broker*
Willer, Edward Herman *real estate broker*

Southern Pines
Saunders, Susan Presley *real estate executive*

Winston Salem
Gallimore, Margaret Martin *real estate executive*

OKLAHOMA

Ada
Davison, Victoria Dillon *real estate executive*

Lawton
McKesson, Edward Lee, Jr. *association executive, small business owner*

Mcalester
Heilig, Terry Len *economic development executive*

Miami
Taylor, Vesta Fisk *real estate broker, educator*

Muskogee
Embry, Richard Henry *real estate broker*

Norman
Zelby, Rachel *realtor*

Oklahoma City
Wall, Edward Millard *environmental consulting executive*
Wheeler, Albert Lee, III *real estate appraiser, consultant, lawyer*

Stillwater
Ellis, Grace Carol *real estate executive*

Tulsa
Henderson, James Ronald *industrial real estate developer*
Hill, Josephine Carmela *realtor*
Matthews, Dane Dikeman *urban planner*
Nicholas, Jonathan David *realtor*
Vincent, Carl G., Jr. *real estate portfolio manager*

Wagoner
Semore, Mary Margie *abstractor*

SOUTH CAROLINA

Charleston
Limehouse, Harry Bancroft, Jr. *real estate developer*
Rivers, John Minott, Jr. *real estate developer*

Columbia
Duvall, David Garland *real estate company executive, accountant*
Kahn, Alan Bruce *real estate development and construction executive*

Easley
Spearman, Patsy Cordle *real estate broker*

Florence
Dupre, Judith Ann Neil *real estate agent, interior decorator*

Gilbert
Jones, William Riley, Jr. *real estate executive*

Greenville
Crawford, William David *real estate broker, developer*
Dobson, Robert Albertus, III *lawyer, investment manager, lay minister, volunteer*
Simmons, David Jeffrey *real estate executive*
Wyche, Marguerite Ramage *realtor*

Hilton Head Island
Cramer, Laura Schwarz *realtor*
Kemp, Mae Wunder *real estate broker, consultant*
Nash, Johnny Collin *real estate broker and appraiser*

Mount Pleasant
Hill, Max Lloyd, Jr. *realtor*

Myrtle Beach
Cranford, James Blease *real estate executive*

Salem
Harbeck, William James *real estate executive, lawyer, international consultant*

Union
Berry, Peter DuPre *real estate executive*

TENNESSEE

Alamo
Raines, Irene Freeze *real estate broker*

Hampton
McClendon, Fred Vernon *real estate professional, business consultant, equine and realty appraiser, financial consultant*

Knoxville
Brown, Kevin James *real estate broker*
Cossé, R. Paul *realty company executive*

Murfreesboro
Hampton, Thomas Edward *real estate appraiser*
Roberts, Candice Kay *realty association executive*

Nashville
Anderson, Janice Linn *real estate brokerage professional*
Beck, Robert Beryl *real estate executive*
Driscoll, Joseph Francis *real estate executive*
Estes, Moreau Pinckney, IV *real estate executive, lawyer*
Gernert, Irwin William (Bill Gernert) *real estate developer, industrial designer, entrepreneur*
Greer, Herschel Lynn, Jr. *real estate broker*
Harper, James Leo *real estate appraiser, consultant*

Signal Mountain
Reiff, Dovie Kate *urban planner*

TEXAS

Amarillo
Emmett, Walter Charles *business broker*

Arlington
Adams, Victoria Eleanor *retired realty company executive*

Austin
Boeker, Herbert Ralph, Jr. *urban planner*
Lancaster, Tina *real estate executive, small business owner, rancher*
Sandlin, Ann Marie *real estate broker*
Shefman, Marga R. *real estate educator*

Bay City
Aylin, Elizabeth Twist Pabst *real estate broker, developer*

Beaumont
Cater, Alice Ruth Wallace *real estate educator, broker*
Cook, William Carlyle *real estate appraiser*

Brenham
Moorman, Robert Lawson *real estate appraiser*

Canyon
Wheelock, Moira Myrl Brewer *real estate broker, educator, church musician*

College Station
Goode-Haddock, Celia Ross *title company executive*
Roeseler, Wolfgang Guenther Joachim *city planner*

Conroe
Judge, Dolores Barbara *real estate broker*

Corpus Christi
Norman, Wyatt Thomas, III *landman, consultant*

Crockett
Pennington, James Richard (Ric Pennington) *real estate appraiser*

Dallas
Cameron, Glenn Nilsson *real estate broker*
Cansler, Denise Ann *real estate executive*
Copeland, Suzanne Johnson *real estate executive*
Curran, David Bernard, Jr. *real estate executive*
Doran, Mark Richard *real estate financial executive*
Garison, Lynn Lassiter *real estate executive*
Garrett, Randy Jack *commercial real estate broker*
Gidel, Robert Hugh *real estate investor*
Golden, Leslie Black *real estate agent*
Grisham, Thomas J. *real estate professional*
Hewett, Arthur Edward *real estate developer, lawyer*
Kimbler, Larry Bernard *real estate executive, accountant*
Maier, Robert Henry *real estate executive*
Meara, James Francis, Jr. *real estate broker, land developer*
Moss, Robert Williams *real estate developer*
Netzer, Aharon *environmental consultant*
Yeslow, Rosemarie *real estate professional*

Denton
Gulrich, Silla Remmel *real estate executive*

El Paso
Karch, Robert E. *real estate company executive*
Lyle, James Arthur *real estate broker*

Elgin
Osborne, Michael James *real estate executive, energy executive*

Fort Worth
Davis, Carol Lyn *research consultant*
Underwood, Harvey Cockrell *real estate executive*

Galveston
McLeod, E. Douglas *real estate developer, lawyer*

Grand Prairie
Charbonneau, Armand Bernard *real estate developer*

Harlingen
Bonner, Donna Pace *real estate investments, consultant, volunteer*

Houston
Adams-Allen, June Evelyn *real estate broker*
Barrere, Jamie Newton *real estate executive*
Harris, Lyttleton Tazwell, IV *property management and publishing executive*
Henry, Randolph Marshall *real estate broker, company executive*
Lassiter, James Morris, Jr. *real estate investment executive*
Lestin, Eric Hugh *real estate investment banking executive*
Ling, Lily Hsu-Chiang *real estate executive, accountant*
Lusk, Charles Michael, III *real estate professional*
Nguyen, An Duc *industrial development, consultant*
Powell, Robert Burney *real estate broker*
Raia, Carl Bernard *commercial real estate executive and developer*
Rosin, Morris *real estate, land development company executive*
Shroyer, Patricia Faye *real estate agent*
Strudler, Robert Jacob *real estate development executive*
Waltrip, Robert L. *environmentalist*
Wolff, David Stephen *investments and real estate development executive*

Irving
Cowart, John Lawhon *real estate company executive*

La Marque
Gordy, Charlie Leon *real estate broker, insurance broker, consultant*

Lewisville
Plichta, Thomas Francis *real estate executive*

Lubbock
Wall, Betty Jane *real estate consultant*

Mico
Shockey, Thomas Edward *real estate executive, engineer*

Midland
Chalfant, William Arthur *petroleum landman*
Wade, Margaret Gaston *real estate property manager, educator*

Plano
Virtanen, Perttu Hannes *urban planner, consultant*
Wilke, Chet *real estate executive*

Port Arthur
Underhill, Mark Lynn *marine surveyor*

Salado
Mackie, Donald John, Jr. *real estate developer*

San Antonio
Anthony, Laura G. *real estate broker*
Emick, William John *real estate investor, retired federal executive*
Joiner, Lorell Howard *real estate development and investment executive*
Pina, Alberto Buffington *real estate company official*

Spring
Coy, Elba Boone *real estate developer*

Temple
Aldrich, C. Elbert *real estate broker*
Moore, Joanna Elizabeth *real estate professional*

Texarkana
Atkinson, Diane Lee *environmental resource planner*

The Woodlands
Harvey, Billy Dale *landman*
Wortham, James Mason *landman*

Vidor
Paradice, Sammy Irwin *real estate investor*

Waco
Rusling, Barbara N(eubert) *real estate executive, state legislator*

Weatherford
Owen, Rodney Doyle *real estate appraiser*

VIRGINIA

Alexandria
Machanic, Roger *real estate developer*
Marino, Ann Dozier *real estate agent*

Arlington
Culter, Ray Michael *conservation executive*

Chantilly
Long, Henry Arlington *real estate executive*

Charlottesville
Greenwood, Virginia Maxine McLeod *real estate executive, broker*
Harris, William McKinley, Sr. *urban planning educator, consultant*

Fairfax
Boerner, Jo M. *real estate trainer*

Falls Church
Frazier, Walter Ronald *real estate investment company executive*

Gwynn
Pickle Beattie, Katherine Hamner *real estate agent*

Haymarket
Crafton-Masterson, Adrienne *real estate executive, writer, poet*

Mc Lean
Backman, Jean Adele *real estate executive*
Nobil, James Howard, Jr. *real estate investor, developer, consultant, broker*
Wilbur, Mark *environmental executive*

Newport News
Berdensey, Harold Kenneth *real estate broker*
Goldberg, Ivan Baer *real estate executive*
Goldberg, Stanley Irwin *real estate executive*

Norfolk
DeFelice, Sofia *real estate broker, owner*

Oakton
Brauer, Gwendolyn Gail *real estate broker*

Philomont
Cooley, Hilary Elizabeth *real estate manager*

Reston
Miller, Lynne Marie *environmental company executive*

Richmond
Girone, Joan Christine Cruse *commercial real estate agent, former county official*
Moeser, John Victor *urban studies and planning educator*

Roanoke
Cutler, Malcolm Rupert *environmentalist*

Springfield
Borum, Olin Henry *realtor, former government official*

Suffolk
Cross, Hugh Ritchie *real estate broker, computer consultant*

Virginia Beach
Gallagher, Vicki Smith *real estate agent*

WEST VIRGINIA

Huntington
Davis, Donald Eugene *real estate management executive*

Morgantown
Schaeffer, Peter (Viktor) *urban and regional planning educator*

ADDRESS UNPUBLISHED

Arrington, Dorothy Anita Collins *retired real estate broker*
Aulbach, George Louis *property investment company executive*
Barrett, Linda L. *real estate executive*
Bergau, Frank Conrad *real estate, commercial and investment properties executive*
Brown, Ann Lenora *community development consultant*
Burgess, Diane Glenn *real estate broker, paralegal*
Burk, Sylvia Joan *petroleum landman, freelance writer*
Cottingham, Stephen Kent *real estate development executive, researcher*
Davis, Mary Byrd *conservationist, researcher*
Gray, Gwen Cash *real estate broker*
Gray, Robert McDonnell *consulting petroleum landman*
Kendrick, Daniel Frederick, III *real estate executive*
Kern, Constance Elizabeth *retired real estate broker*
Lamy, M(ary) Rebecca *land developer, former government official*
Ledford, Janet Marie Smalley *real estate appraiser, consultant*
Mallen, Bruce *real estate developer, educator, producer, economist, consultant*
Mandel, Marilyn *community planner, medical assistant*
Marshall, Doyle *real estate executive*
Matthews, Frances Keller *retired real estate agent, researcher*
McDonald, Barbara Jean *real estate broker*
McManus, Joseph Warn *urban planner, architect*
Meyer, Annette Cole *real estate company executive*
Millar, Dorine Marie Agnes *real estate agent, artist*
Newcomb, Robert Carl *real estate broker*
Nicholson, James Richard *real estate consultant*
Payne, Rosser Hamilton *urban planner, consultant*
Saunders, Alexander Hall *real estate executive*
Selber, Arlene Bork *environmentalist*
Sullivan, Ben Frank, Jr. *real estate broker*
Tiefel, Mark Gregory *real estate executive*
Weisinger, Ronald Jay *economic development consultant, real estate developer*
White, Charles Edwin *real estate management company executive*

GOVERNMENT: AGENCY ADMINISTRATION

UNITED STATES

ALABAMA

Athens
Wilson, Lucy Lynn Willmarth *postal service administrator*

Birmingham
Bigelow, Honey Lynn *postal employee*
Johnson, Johnny *police chief*

Cullman
Munger, James Guy *protective services executive*

Kimberly
Howell, Pamela Ann *federal agency professional*

Montgomery
Harris, Joseph Lamar *state agency administrator*
Wilson, John *protective services official*

ARKANSAS

Jonesboro
Humway, Ronald Jimmie *state agency administrator*

Little Rock
Caudell, Louie C., Jr. *police chief*
Jones, Beverly Ward *state agency administrator*
Wilhoit, Gene *state agency administrator*

CALIFORNIA

Coronado
Straley, Ruth A. Stewart *federal agency administrator, small business owner*

DISTRICT OF COLUMBIA

Washington
Erdreich, Ben Leader *federal agency executive*
Lasowski, Anne-Marie Francoise *federal agency executive*
Locke, Thomas Bernard *federal agency administrator*
Richlen, Scott Lane *federal government program administrator*
Waldron, Ronald James *protective services official*
Wilson, Larry Joseph *federal agency administrator*

FLORIDA

Bradenton
McGarry, Marcia Langston *community service coordinator*
Sheffield, Henry Lee *fire chief*

Clearwater
Patterson, Jeffrey Lynn *police officer*

Delray Beach
Bowdre, Paul Reid *protective services official, consultant*

Deltona
Knecht, Julia Ann *firefighter, paramedic*

Fort Myers
Nottingham, James (Leroy Nottingham) *retired protective services official, professional society administrator*

Fort Pierce
Boucher, Mildred Eileen *state agency administrator*

Fort Walton Beach
Adams, Lisa Ann *public administrator*
Culver, Dan Louis *federal agency administrator*

Jacksonville
Cheek, William Shields, Jr. *protective services official*
McMillian, James *protective services official*

Largo
Schobel, Gerhardt Beaven *law enforcement officer*

Lauderdale Lakes
Gay, John Marion *federal agency administrator, organization-personnel analyst*

Melbourne
Polansky, Joel Justin Jones *public administrator, information specialist*

Miami
Fern, Emma E. *state agency administrator*
Gimenez, Carlos Antonio *fire chief*
Warshaw, Donald *police chief*
Young, Robert Paul *state agency administrator*

Palm Beach
Asencio, Diego C. *state agency administrator, former federal commission administrator, consultant, business executive*

Saint Petersburg
Barca, James Joseph *fire department administrative services executive*
Callahan, James K. *fire chief*
Stephens, Darrel W. *protective services official*

Tallahassee
Bedard, Roy Raymond *law enforcement official, consultant*
Coe, Thomas R. *police chief*
Durrence, James Larry *state executive, history educator*
Ehlen, Martin Richard *state agency administrator, management analyst*
Milligan, Robert F. *state agency administrator*
Stanford, Karen Anne *state agency administrator*

Tampa
Holder, Ben R. *protective services official*

West Palm Beach
Thurber, James Cameron *law enforcement officer, consultant, author*

GEORGIA

Americus
Hill, Eula Vertner *former state agency administrator*

Atlanta
Brent, Frank Nevil *state agency administrator*
Collins, Marcus E., Sr. *state agency administrator*
Creed, Thomas Wayne *retired federal agency administrator, individual investor*
Harris, Earl Douglas *state agency administrator*
Harvard, Beverly Joyce Bailey *police chief*
Henderson, Howard Michael *federal agency administrator, mediator*
Potter, Anthony Nicholas, Jr. *hospital security executive, consultant*
Randolph, Lynwood Parker *federal space agency manager, physicist*
Solaski, Paul Edward *retired fire protection specialist*

Douglasville
Paterson, Paul Charles *private investigator, security consultant*

Marietta
Hensley, Allan Lance *security consultant, litigation support specialist*

Moultrie
Crouch, Richard W. *protective services official, management consultant*

Robins AFB
Lewis, Clinton *federal agency administrator*

Sylvania
Kile, Mike *protective services official*

Tucker
Crosa, Peter James *private investigator*

ILLINOIS

Schaumburg
Denton, Jesse Leslie, Jr. *fire protection professional*

KENTUCKY

Bowling Green
Wells, Jerry Wayne *police official*

Central City
Higgs, David Wayne *state agency administrator*

Frankfort
Evans, Helen Horlacher *state agency administrator, foundation adminstrator*
McDonald, Alice Coig *state agency administrator*
McDonald, Deborah Halcomb *state agency consultant*
Whaley, Charles E. *state agency administrator*

Hopkinsville
Watson, Roger Elton *state agency administrator*

Lexington
Bizzack, John W. *protective services official*
McComas, Gary *fire chief*
Walsh, Al E. *protective services official*

Louisville
Adams, Robert Waugh *state agency administrator, economics educator*
Hamilton, Edward Douglas *protective services official*
Sanders, Russell Edward *protective services official*

Madisonville
Veazey, Doris Anne *state agency administrator*

Nancy
Walters, Robert Ancil, II *protective services coordinator*

West Liberty
Bates, Hurl *correctional officer*

LOUISIANA

Angie
McCloud, Marvin Lynn *state agency administrator*

Baton Rouge
Franklin, Bobby Jo *state education agency administrator*
Parks, James William, II *public facilities executive, lawyer*

Bogalusa
Henke, Shauna Nicole *police dispatcher, small business owner*

New Orleans
Pennington, Richard J. *police chief*

MARYLAND

Rockville
Keston, Joan Balboul *government agency administrator*

MISSISSIPPI

Jackson
Bennett, Marshall Goodloe, Jr. *state official, lawyer*
Green, John Clancy *protective services official*
Mitchell, Jackie Williams *state agency administrator, consultant*

Mississippi State
Holder, Susan Lewis *state agency administrator*

NEW YORK

Angola
Meno, Lionel R. *state agency administrator*

NORTH CAROLINA

Asheville
Gilpin, Peter Randall *retired state government insurance regulator*
Roberts, Bill Glen *retired fire chief, investor, consultant*

Charlotte
Nowicki, Dennis *protective services official*
Wright, Wayne Kenneth *federal agency statistician*

Durham
Sarvis, Edward Earl *police official*
Shoaf, Chon Regan *federal agency health sciences administrator*

Edenton
Eure, Linda Jordan *state agency administrator*

Elizabeth City
Lewis, Tola Ethridge, Jr. *state agency administrator, martial arts instructor*

Fort Bragg
Tippy, Margaret Grinder *public affairs officer*

Greensboro
Ridgill, Marc Wayne *protective services official*

Hope Mills
Windham, Cuyler LaRue *police official*

Raleigh
Boney, Leslie Norwood, III *state agency administrator*
Brown, Mitchell W. *protective services official*
Rosefield, Herbert Aaron, Jr. *state agency administrator*

OKLAHOMA

Ada
Stewart, Steven Elton *state agency administrator*

Collinsville
Conley, Billy Dean *retired protective services offical*

Oklahoma City
Gonzales, Sam C. *police chief*
Harbour, Robert Randall *state agency administrator*
Pratt, Billy Kenton *police officer*

Tulsa
Braswell, Kern F. *protective services official*
Jones, Anne Elizabeth *motor license agent, insurance executive*
Palmer, Ronald *police chief*

Yukon
Bridges, Leroy W. *retired state agency administrator, consultant*

SOUTH CAROLINA

Charleston
Greenberg, Reuben M. *protective services official*

Columbia
Duffie, Virgil Whatley, Jr. *state agency administrator*
Knight, James Eugene *state agency administrator*
Long, Kenneth D'Vant *state agency administrator*
Thompson, William Carrington, Jr. *federal agency administrator*
Waters, Mary Baskin *state agency administrator, educator*

Manning
Jones, Carter Helm *fire department official*

North Charleston
Miller, Paula *government employee*

Swansea
Inabinet, George Walker, Jr. *retired state agency administrator*

TENNESSEE

Brighton
King, James Andrew *protective services educator and administrator*

Knoxville
Holmes, Paul Hermon (Tony Holmes) *federal agency official*
Jones, Bobby Eugene *state agency administrator, educator*
Stewart, John Gilman *government official*

Memphis
Black, Kay Freeman *public affairs administrator*
Edwards, Leonard *police officer*
Winfrey, Walter J. *police chief*

Morristown
Price, James Eldridge *police officer, emergency medical technician*

Nashville
Chandler, Sadie Arnette *state educational administrator, consultant*
Guy, Sharon Kaye *state agency executive*
Smith, Charles Edward *state agency administrator*
Wynn, Linda Delois Thompson *state agency administrator, educator, researcher*

Pickwick Dam
Casey, Beverly Ann *postmaster*

TEXAS

Amarillo
Bull, Walter Stephen *police officer*
Neal, Jerry Harold *protective services official*

Arlington
Renteria, Cheryl Christina *retired federal agency administrator*

Austin
Hammarth, Raymond Jean *state commission administrator*
Ludeke, Aaron Kim *geographic information systems manager, educator*
Martin, David Hugh *private investigator, business executive, writer*
Watson, Elizabeth Marion *protective services official*

Bryan
Owens, Harold B. *former state agency consultant*

Carrollton
Varner, Bruce H., Jr. *fire department official, educator*

Dallas
Bowers, Thomas Daniel, Jr. *policeman*
Click, Bennie R. *protective services official*
Hall, Anna Christene *federal agency administrator*
Jones, Peggy W. *postal official, poet*
Maberry, Joe Michael *federal agency administrator*
Thomas, Chester Wiley *protective services official*

Denison
Langdon, Vicki N. *public information coordinator*

Denton
Jackson, Stephen Eric *police official*

Fort Worth
Sasser, William Jack *retired federal agency administrator, consultant*
Williams, Lyle Keith *federal agency administrator*
Windham, Thomas *protective services official*

Galena Park
Price, Joe Sealy *law enforcement officer*

Garland
Mayfield, J. W. *police official*

Houston
Faison, Holly *state agency administrator*
Hacker, Anthony Wayne *private investigator*
Kaup, David Earle *law enforcement officer*
Nuchia, Samuel M. *protective services official*
Williamson, Jon Creighton *federal agency administrator*

Lockhart
Shomette, C.D. *protective services official*

Mesquite
Acker, Woodrow Louis (Lou Acker) *private investigator, security consultant*

Plano
McIntire, Wesley Kevin *private investigator*

Richardson
Garreans, Leonard Lansford *protective services official, criminal justice professional*

Stonewall
Betzer, Roy James *national park service administrator*

Taylor
Bodisch, Robert John, Sr. *state agency administrator*

Victoria
Tyng, Sharon Ann *former federal agency administrator*

VIRGINIA

Alexandria
Cowles, Roger William *federal agency administrator*
Leggett, David John *federal agency adminstrator, lawyer*

Arlington
Brodsky, Lewis Carl *federal agency administrator*
Ehrman, Madeline Elizabeth *federal agency administrator*
Secular, Sidney *federal agency administrator, procurement analyst*
Weech, William Allen *foreign service officer*

Centreville
Robbins, Christopher Lindsay *federal government official*

Danville
Dameron, John Preston *postal worker*

Falls Church
Wade, James P., Jr. *government official, industry executive*

Fort Belvoir
Gallups, Vivian Lylay Bess *federal contracting officer*

Fredericksburg
Moncure, Thomas McCarty, Jr. *state agency adminstrator*

Haymarket
Walters, Jerry Willard *retired federal agency administrator*

Lovettsville
McMillen, Robert Doane *public information government official*

Manassas
Webb, Dennis Wayne *protective services official*

Mc Lean
Mater, Maud E. *federal agency administrator, lawyer*

Newport News
Drum, Joan Marie McFarland *federal agency administrator*

Norfolk
Henson, Henry Paul *protective services official*
High, Melvin C. *police chief*
Melvin C., High *protective services official*
Wakeham, Ronald T. *protective services official*

Petersburg
Thomas, Joseph Douglas *police forensic detective*

Quantico
LeDoux, John Clarence *law enforcement official*

Reston
Wilkinson, Edward Starsmeare, Jr. *federal agency executive*

Richmond
Davies, Gordon K. *state agency administrator*
Klisz, Cynthia Ann *state agency executive*
Mitchell, Michelle B. *protective services official*
Oliver, Jerry A. *protective services official*

Ruther Glen
Bush, Mitchell Lester, Jr. *retired federal agency administrator*

Vienna
Bond, Thomas Jefferson, Jr. *former federal agency administrator*

Virginia Beach
Wootten, Thomas Franklin *criminal justice administrator*

Winchester
Brewer, William Robert, Jr. *army acquistion administrator, federal specialist*

WEST VIRGINIA

Beaver
Sherwood, Arlene Gail *federal agency administrator*

Charleston
Douglass, Gus Ruben *state agency administrator*
Marockie, Henry R. *state school system administrator*
Marshall, Fredrick L. *protective services official*

Clarksburg
Wick, Gary Allen *police officer*

Hurricane
Williams, Roger Francis *state agency administrator*

Parkersburg
Miller, Steven Douglas *federal agency executive*

Wheeling
Robbins, William David *retired police officer*

ADDRESS UNPUBLISHED

Belton, Deborah Carolyn Knox *state agency administrator, accountant*
Boysen, Thomas Cyril *state school system administrator*
Camp, Alethea Taylor *correctional program specialist*
Dealy, William Austin, Jr. *federal agency administrator, consultant*
Griffith, Carl Leslie *protective services official*
Keene, Mary Ellen *federal agency executive*
Mangino, Stephen Joseph *protective services official*
Messersmith, William Dale *retired corrections official*
Szilagyi, John Alex *federal agency administrator*
Teague, Wayne *state agency administrator*
Ward, Thomas A(ugustine), III *federal immigration officer*

GOVERNMENT: EXECUTIVE ADMINISTRATION

UNITED STATES

ALABAMA

Bessemer
Bains, Lee Edmundson *state attorney general*

Birmingham
Arrington, Richard, Jr. *mayor*
Bonfield, Barbara Goldstein *municipal agency administrator*
Dentiste, Paul George *city and regional planning executive*
Weems, Frances Elizabeth *lawyer, county official*
Wheeler, Cathy Jo *government official*

Gadsden
Hudgins, Don Franklin *city official*

Huntsville
Hettinger, Steve *mayor*

Mobile
Higginbotham, Prieur Jay *city official*
Morgan, Glenda Anderson *municipal government official, educator*

Montgomery
Baxley, Lucy *state treasurer*
Bennett, James Ronald *secretary of state*
Bridges, Edwin Clifford *state official*
Cauthen, H(arvey) E(llington), Jr. *governmental relations consultant, agriculturist*
James, Fob, Jr. (Forrest Hood James) *governor*
Sessions, Jefferson Beauregard, III *state attorney general*
Siegelman, Don Eugene *state official*
Wallace, George Corley *former governor*
Williams, Phillip Wayne *state official, securities and diversified company executive, former army officer, consultant*

ARKANSAS

Alma
Green, Jonathan Mitchell *municipal official*

Barling
Haberman, Richard Edward *city administrator*

Fayetteville
Swain, Brian Todd *municipal official*

Hot Springs National Park
McLane, Bobbie Jones *retired government executive, genealogist, publisher*

Little Rock
Bryant, Winston *state attorney general*
Fisher, Jimmie Lou *state official*
Gilleland, Diane Suitt *state official*
Huckabee, Michael Dale *governor*
Jones, Mark Perrin, III *special assistant to attorney general, editor*
Priest, Sharon Devlin *state official*

Warren
Reep, Robert Gregg, Sr. *mayor*

COLORADO

Parker
Hogan, Aden Ellsworth, Jr. *city government administrator*

DISTRICT OF COLUMBIA

Washington
Hunt, Robert Gayle *government official*
Naland, John Kiddoo *diplomat*
Romero-Barceló, Carlos Antonio *governor of Puerto Rico*
Steele, Howard Loucks *government official*
Villegoureix-Ritaud, Patrick *diplomat*
Watson, Arthur Dennis *government official*

FLORIDA

Altamonte Springs
Richter, Lawrence McCord *municipal government official*

Anna Maria
Alban, Genevieve Novicky *city official*

Brooksville
Anderson, Richard Edmund *city manager, management consultant*
Hetrick, Charles Brady *county official*

Clearwater
Berfield, Sue Ann *city commissioner, legal assistant*
Rice, Kathy Strickland *assistant city manager*

Dunedin
Kelly, Anne Catherine *retired city official*

Florida City
Casals, Rafael Gabriel *assistant city manager*

Fort Lauderdale
Garver, James Amos *municipal official*
Markham, William *county official*

Fort Myers
Flannery, Edward E. *municipal official*

Fort Pierce
Dusanek, Linda Sue *municipal housing official*

Gainesville
Stefan, Charles Gordon *retired foreign service officer and educator*

Green Cove Springs
Lee, Ruth Davidson *tax collector*

Jacksonville
Ramsey, Jettie Cecil *county official*

Kennedy Space Center
Banks, Lisa Jean *government official*
Thomas, James Arthur *government official, electrical engineer*

Melbourne
Eads, Lyle Willis *retired government inspector*

Merritt Island
Patterson, William Henry *regional planner, retired army officer*

Miami
León, Eduardo A. *diplomat, business executive*
Moorman, Rose Drunell *county administrator, systems analyst*
Redruello, Rosa Inchaustegui *municipal official*

Palm Bay
White, David Alan *municipal official*

Palm City
Henry, David Howe, II *former diplomat and international organization official*

Pensacola
Raines, Thomas Edward *county official*

Plant City
McDaniel, James Roosevelt *municipal official*

Ponte Vedra Beach
Searles, John Rumney, Jr. *retired city planner and developer*

Saint Augustine
Borchardt, Duke *federal labor relations professional*

Saint Petersburg
Habgood, John Frisbie *city administrator*
Mussett, Richard Earl *city official*
Shelton, Jammi M. *municipal official*

Sarasota
Matthews, Wade Hampton Bynum *consul, consultant*

Tallahassee
Butterworth, Robert A. *state attorney general*
Chiles, Lawton Mainor *governor, former senator*
Crawford, Bob *state commissioner*
Gunter, Karen Johnson *government official*
MacKay, Kenneth Hood (Buddy MacKay) *state official, former congressman*
Mortham, Sandra Barringer *state official*
Nelson, Bill *state official*
Nelson, William *state insurance commissioner*
Ramsey, Sally Ann Seitz *retired state official*
Wright, Charles Elliott *county official, municipal official*

Tampa
Brown, Steven Thomas *state regulatory policy director*
Freedman, Sandra Warshaw *former mayor*
Moss, Sidney Louise Gill *county official*
Proto, Paul William *government consulting company executive*

Venice
Dailey, Kathleen Marie *city official*
Williams, Justin *retired government official*

Vero Beach
White, Thomas Patrick *county official, small business owner*

West Palm Beach
Winchester, Jacqueline Canton *county government official*

Winter Haven
Cheatham, Robert Carl, Sr. *city manager*

GEORGIA

Atlanta
Bennett, Bobbie Jean *state commissioner*
Bowers, Michael Joseph *state attorney general*
Carter, Jimmy (James Earl Carter, Jr.) *former President of United States*
Durden, Robert J. *state commissioner, lawyer*
Howard, Pierre *state official*
Irvin, Thomas T. *state commissioner of agriculture*
Malone, Perrillah Atkinson (Pat Malone) *retired state official*
Massey, Lewis *state official*
Miller, Zell Bryan *governor*
Oxendine, John *state insurance commissioner, state official*
Ryles, Tim *state commissioner*
Sullivan, Louis Wade *former secretary health and human services, physician*
Wuichet, John W. *policy analyst*

Carrollton
Harrison, Earle *former county official*

Columbus
Peters, Bobby G. *mayor*

Conyers
Poynter, Randolph W. *county official*

Covington
Westlake, James Roger *retired federal program manager*

Lithia Springs
Turnbull, Terri Durrett *county and non-profit organization consultant*

Marietta
Warfel, Joseph Rosser *local government official, retired military officer*

Saint Simons
Douglas, William Ernest *retired government official*

Savannah
Rousakis, John Paul *former mayor*

Warner Robins
Alexander, Charles *housing authority executive*

KENTUCKY

Frankfort
Brown, John Y. *state official*
Codell, James C. III *state official*
Cox, Gary S. *state education official*
Gorman, Chris *state attorney general*
Hamilton, John Kennedy *state treasurer*
Henry, Stephen Lewis *state official, orthopedic surgeon, educator*
Palmore, Carol M. *state official*
Patton, Paul E. *governor*
Sonego, Ian G. *state assistant attorney general*

Hebron
Holscher, Robert F. *county official*

Lexington
Miller, Pamela Gundersen *mayor*

Louisville
Ahl, Marian Antoinette *government investigator*
Freund, Adrian Paul *county official*

Nicholasville
Short, Donald Wayne *city official*

Owensboro
Alls, Gary Lee *municipal official*

LOUISIANA

Alexandria
Miller, Charles Murphy *city official*

Baton Rouge
Blanco, Kathleen Babineaux *lieutenant governor*
Brown, James H., Jr. *state insurance commissioner, lawyer*
Duncan, Kenneth *state treasurer*
Foster, Murphy J., Jr. (Mike Foster) *governor*
Ieyoub, Richard Phillip *state attorney general*
McKeithen, Walter Fox *secretary of state*

Hahnville
Lassus, Joseph Patrick *parish official*

New Orleans
Hunter, Sue Persons *former state official*
Levell, Edward, Jr. *city official*
Ortique, Revius Oliver, Jr. *city official*
Stansbury, Harry Case *state commissioner*

Opelousas
Duplechain, Rhyn Louis *parish assessor*

Slidell
Dearing, Reinhard Josef *city official*

MISSISSIPPI

Gulfport
Dickerson, Monar Stephen *city official, newspaper reporter*

Jackson
Clark, Eric C. *state official*
Ditto, (John) Kane *mayor*
Fordice, Kirk, Jr. (Daniel Kirkwood Fordice) *governor, construction company executive, engineer*
Moore, Mike *state attorney general*
Musgrove, Ronnie *state official*
Ross, Jim Buck *state commissioner*

Madison
Hays, Donald Osborne *retired government official*

Picayune
Davis, James Carl *retired government official, government consultant*

Stennis Space Center
Blair, Ruth Reba *government official*

NEW JERSEY

Moonachie
Malley, Raymond Charles *retired foreign service officer, industrial executive*

NORTH CAROLINA

Asheville
Whitaker, C. Bruce *postal worker*

Cary
Saunders, Barry Wayne *state official*

Charlotte
Fox, Gerald G. *county manager*
Miller, Albert Leon *county official*

Greensboro
Carmany, Sandra Garrett *city council member*
Nussbaum, V. M., Jr. *former mayor*
Pate, William Patrick *city manager*
Smith, Donald Everett *city official*

Hendersonville
Niehoff, Fred Harold, Jr. *mayor*

King
Whicker, Christine Spainhour *municipal official*

Madison
Smith, Bradley Kirk *town manager*

Mount Gilead
McNeill, Maxine Currie *county official*

Raleigh
Boyles, Harlan Edward *state official*
Cella, Eugene Joseph *state official*
Easley, Michael F. *state attorney general*
Graham, James A. *state commissioner*
Hunt, James Baxter, Jr. *governor, lawyer*
Long, James E. *state commissioner*
Payne, Harry Eugene, Jr. *state labor commissioner*
Stevens, Richard Yates *county official*
Wicker, Dennis A. *state official*

Randleman
Boling, Jewell *retired government official*

Rutherfordton
Andrews, Karen Elizabeth *town manager*

Timberlake
Ashley-Canter, Christie *municipal administrator*

Wendell
Fuller, Ira Calvin *town manager*

Wilson
Wyatt, Edward Avery, V *city manager*

Windsor
Bell, Holley Mack *retired foreign service officer, writer*

Winston Salem
Wood, Martha Swain *mayor*

OKLAHOMA

Enid
Stephenson, Craig Alan *assistant city manager*

Lawton
Ellenbrook, Edward Charles *county government social services administrator*

Leonard
Barnett, Rosalea *government official*

Norman
Price, Linda Rice *community development administrator*

Oklahoma City
Butkin, Robert *state treasurer*
Cole, Tom *state official*
Edmondson, Drew *attorney general*
Edmondson, W. A. Drew *state attorney general*
Fallin, Mary Copeland *state official*
Keating, Francis Anthony, II *governor, lawyer*
Kennedy, John H., Jr. *former state official*
McKenzie, Clif Allen *Indian tribe official, accountant*
Norick, Ronald J. *mayor*

Park Hill
Mankiller, Wilma Pearl *tribal leader*

Wyandotte
Bearskin, Leaford *chief Wyandotte Nation*

SOUTH CAROLINA

Aiken
Thompson, Steven Terry *city manager*

Beaufort
Mattox, Thomas Forrest *county official*

Charleston
Moore, Carl Sanford, Sr. *management analyst local government*

Columbia
Beasley, David Muldrow *governor*
Condon, Charles Molony *state attorney general*
Miles, Jim *state official*
Morris, John Allen, Jr. *state government administrator, educator*
Peeler, Bob *state official*

Greenville
Seals, Gerald *city manager*
Watts, Aubrey Vernon, Jr. *city manager*
Workman, William Douglas, III *former mayor*

Summerville
Wilbanks, John Flanders *town administrator*

Sumter
Noonan, William Thomas *county administrator*

TENNESSEE

Athens
Hunter, Harold Ray *city official*

Elizabethton
Stahl, Charles J., IV *city manager*

Memphis
Gates, Carolyn Helm *municipal official*
Jones, Andrewnetta *county government official*

Nashville
Bredesen, Philip Norman *mayor*
Darnell, Riley Carlisle *state government executive, lawyer*
Palmer-Hass, Lisa Michelle *state official*
Sizemore, Douglas M. *state commerce and insurance commissioner*
Sundquist, Donald Kenneth (Don Sundquist) *governor, former congressman, sales corporation executive*
Wilder, John Shelton *state official, state legislator*

Sparta
Pearson, Margaret Donovan *former mayor*

Springfield
Nutting, Paul John *city official*

Waverly
Johnson, Gene Allen *retired municipal environmental administrator*

TEXAS

Amarillo
Stapleton, Claudia Ann *city official*

Arlington
Hamilton, Patrick Joseph *city official*

Austin
Ashworth, Kenneth Hayden *state educational commissioner*
Bomer, Elton *state insurance commissioner*
Buerschinger, Charles Albert *state commissioner*
Bush, George W. *governor*
Cooke, Carlton Lee, Jr. *mayor*
Jeffords, Edward Alan *former state attorney general*
Johnson, Lady Bird (Mrs. Lyndon Baines Johnson) *widow of former President of United States*
McReynolds, Mary Maureen *municipal environmental administrator, consultant*
Morales, Dan *state attorney general*
Sharp, John *treasurer*
Townsend, Richard Marvin *government insurance executive, city manager, consultant*
White, Alice Virginia *volunteer health corps administrator*
Whitehead, Martha *state official*

Beaumont
Lord, Evelyn Marlin *former mayor*

Brenham
Pipes, Paul Ray *county commissioner*

Clarendon
Chamberlain, William Rhode *county official*

Dallas
Cottingham, Jennifer Jane *city official*
Lee, Jimmy Che-Yung *city planner*
Marcotte, Michael Steven *municipal administrator*
Peterson, Richard Lee *county government official, engineering consultant*
Robertson, Karen Lee *county official*
Suhm, Mary Katherine *municipal official*

Denton
Hamilton, Marian Eloise *housing authority official*

Fort Worth
McMillen, Howard Lawrence *municipal government official*

Freeport
Stone, Gary Edward *municipal official*

Gainesville
Gray, James William *city manager, public works administrator*

Giddings
Dismukes, Carol Jaehne *county official*

Houston
Bush, George Herbert Walker *former President of the United States*
Outlaw, Thomas William *municipal agency executive*
Stall, David Keith *city manager*
Tyler-Dillard, Deborah Marie *county official, consultant*
Wenner, Michael Alfred *retired diplomat, writer*

Irving
Card, Hugh Cleveland, III *city official*
Haas, Robert Charles *municipal official*

Kingwood
Romere, Mary Elaine *public health services manager*

Laredo
Beardsley, Bruce Anthony *diplomat*
Colón, Phyllis Janet *city official*
Jones, James Robert *ambassador, former congressman, lawyer*

Leander
Place, Dale Hubert *former state commissioner*

Longview
Wade, Ronald E. *state municipal administrator*

Lubbock
Cooke, Alex "Ty", Jr. *mayor*
Stuart, Frank Adell *county official*

Mansfield
Chandler, Clayton Winthrop, III *city manager*

Mc Kinney
Paschal, Donald Eugene, Jr. *city manager*

Midland
Roomberg, Susan Kelly *city administrator*

Pampa
Chittenden, Stanley Matthew *municipal consultant*

Paris
Spencer, Anna Lou *state official*

Rowlett
Bean, Glenna Maureen *city official*

San Antonio
Wolff, Nelson W. *mayor*

Spicewood
Mathur, Rupa Ajwani *former state official, risk management consultant*

Texarkana
Hall, William David *municipal official*

Wichita Falls
Edmonson, Thomas L(ofton), Jr. *city-county health district administrator*

VIRGINIA

Alexandria
Costagliola, Francesco *former government official, macro operations analyst*
Fitton, Harvey Nelson, Jr. *former government official, publishing consultant*
McDonald, James Patrick *county official*

Amelia Court House
Wallace, John Robert *county administrator*

Annandale
Freitag, Robert Frederick *retired government official*

Arlington
Bune, Karen Louise *criminal justice official*
Covington, James Edwin *government agency administrator, psychologist*
Dworkin, Daniel Martin *government official, environmentalist*
Horner, Margo Elizabeth *municipal official*
Kaiser, Philip Mayer *diplomat*
Licalzi, Michael Charles *county official*
Smith, Myron George *former government official, consultant*

Ashland
Reynal, David Webb *municipal official*

Atkins
Evans, Mary Ann *county administrator*

Chesapeake
Ward, William E. *mayor*

Culpeper
Christie, Gary Frederick *municipal official*

Danville
Arno, Randal Eric *public administrator*

Fairfax
Johns, Michael Douglas *public policy analyst, consultant, writer, former government official*
Powers, Francis Gary, Jr. *municipal official*

Falls Church
Waska, Robert E., Sr. *retired diplomat, consultant*

Fort Belvoir
Diercks, Frederick Otto *government official*
LeBoeuf, Gibson George *government executive, engineer*

Hampton
Dean, Edwin Becton *government official*

Hanover
Casey, Joseph Patrick *county official*

Harrisonburg
Baker, Roger Dale *city administrator*

Hillsville
South, Larry Glenn *town manager*

Isle of Wight
Perry, Beryl Henry, Jr. *government official, accountant*

King George
Storke, Dwight Clifton, Jr. *government official*

Midlothian
Wantling, Brian Douglas *county official, data processor*

Norfolk
Andrews, Mason Cooke *mayor, obstetrician, gynecologist, educator*
Grabeel, Dennis Craig *federal quality specialist*

Pearisburg
Vittum, Kenneth Franklin *city manager*

Portsmouth
Webb, Gloria O. *mayor*

Reston
Staton, David Michael *government affairs consultant*

Richmond
Adiele, Nkwachukwu Moses *state official*
Allen, George Felix *governor*
Beamer, Betsy Davis *state official*
Beyer, Donald Sternoff, Jr. *state official*
Chavis, Larry Eugene *mayor*
Gilmore, James Stuart, III *state attorney general*
Martinez, Robert E. *state official*
Sgro, Beverly Huston *state official, educator*

Roanoke
Armstrong, James P. *housing administrator, policy analyst*

Williamsburg
Mouser, Grant Earl, III *retired foreign service officer*

Woodbridge
Follin, Rodney Hugh *municipal official*

WEST VIRGINIA

Bridgeport
Retton, Michael Anthony *municipal official*
Weiler, Harold Edward *municipal executive, military officer*

Charleston
Bailey, Larrie (John) *state treasurer*
Bias, Sharon G. *state commissioner*
Caperton, W. Gaston *governor*
Clark, Hanley C. *state insurance commissioner*
Drennen, William Miller, Jr. *cultural administrator, film executive, producer, director, mineral resource executive*
Hechler, Ken *state official, former congressman, political science educator, author*
Mc Graw, Darrell Vivian, Jr. *state attorney general*
Melton, G. Kemp *mayor*

Ripley
Waybright, Jeffrey Scott *county clerk*

TERRITORIES OF THE UNITED STATES

PUERTO RICO

San Juan
Díaz Saldaña, Manuel *Puerto Rican government official*
Fajardo, Victor *state commissioner*
Pierluisi, Pedro Rafael *attorney general*

MILITARY ADDRESSES OF THE UNITED STATES

EUROPE

APO
Dillen, Mark Edmund *diplomat*
Terio, Anne Dorough Linnemann *foreign service contracting officer, nurse*

ADDRESS UNPUBLISHED

Anderson, Nils, Jr. *former government official, retired business executive, industrial historian*
Bentsen, Lloyd *former government official, former senator*
Brantley, John Kenneth *government official, pilot*
Cannon, Isabella Walton *mayor*
Carr, Elizabeth Davis-Jackson *town clerk*
Carter, Rosalynn Smith *wife of former President of United States*
Clements, Jeffrey Russell *city official*
Daeschner, William Edward *retired government official*
Denny, Frank William *county clerk*
Douglass, Lee *state insurance commissioner*
Evatt, Parker *former state commissioner, former state legislator*
Griffin, Kenton Graham *city administrator*
Henderson, Geraldine Thomas *retired social security official, educator*
Laney, James Thomas *ambassador, educator*
McClinton, James Leroy *city administrator*
Rattley, Jessie Menifield *former mayor, educator*
Reed, Charles *mayor*
Rosselló, Pedro *governor*
Salmaggi, Guido Godfrey *former diplomat, opera impresario*
Sears, Ralph Westgate *mayor*
Weatherford, Catherine J. *state insurance commissioner*
Weaver, Edgar Sheldon *mayor*

GOVERNMENT: LEGISLATIVE ADMINISTRATION

UNITED STATES

ALABAMA

Birmingham
Allen, Maryon Pittman *former senator, journalist, lecturer, interior and clothing designer*

Jasper
Bevill, Tom *retired congressman, lawyer*

Mobile
Callahan, Sonny (H.L. Callahan) *congressman*
Edwards, Jack *former congressman, lawyer*

Tuscumbia
Heflin, Howell Thomas *senator, lawyer, former state supreme court chief justice*

ARKANSAS

Fayetteville
Malone, David Roy *state senator, university administrator*

Greenwood
Walters, Bill *state senator, lawyer*

DISTRICT OF COLUMBIA

Washington
Archer, William Reynolds, Jr. (Bill Reynolds) *congressman*
Barr, Robert Laurence, Jr. *congressman, lawyer*
Bateman, Herbert Harvell *congressman*
Bentsen, Kenneth E., Jr. *congressman*
Bilirakis, Michael *congressman, lawyer, business executive*
Bishop, Sanford Dixon, Jr. *congressman*
Breaux, John B. *senator, former congressman*
Browder, John Glen *congressman, educator*
Brown, Corrine *congresswoman*
Bumpers, Dale L. *senator, former governor*
Burr, Richard M. *congressman*
Canady, Charles T. *congressman, lawyer*
Clyburn, James E. *congressman*
Combest, Larry Ed *congressman*
Coverdell, Paul Douglas *senator*
Cramer, Robert E., Jr. (Bud Cramer) *congressman*
Davis, Thomas M., III *congressman*
Deal, Nathan J. *congressman, lawyer*
Diaz-Balart, Lincoln *congressman*
Doggett, Lloyd *congressman, former state supreme court justice*
Duncan, John J., Jr. *congressman*
Everett, R. Terry *congressman, farmer, newspaper executive, bank executive*
Everett, Terry *congressman*
Faircloth, Duncan McLauchlin (Lauch Faircloth) *senator, businessman, farmer*
Foley, Mark Adam *congressman*
Fowler, Tillie Kidd *congresswoman*
Frist, William H. *senator, surgeon*
Frost, Jonas Martin, III *congressman*

Funderburk, David B. *congressman, history educator, former ambassador*
Gingrich, Newt(on Leroy) *congressman*
Gonzalez, Henry Barbosa *congressman*
Goodlatte, Robert William *congressman, lawyer*
Gordon, Barton Jennings (Bart Gordon) *congressman, lawyer*
Graham, D. Robert (Bob Graham) *senator, former governor*
Graham, Lindsey O. *congressman*
Gramm, William Philip (Phil Gramm) *senator, economist*
Hall, Ralph Moody *congressman*
Hefner, W. G. (Bill Hefner) *congressman*
Heineman, Frederick K. (Fred Heineman) *congressman*
Helms, Jesse *senator*
Hilleary, Van *congressman*
Inhofe, James M. *U.S. senator*
Jackson Lee, Sheila *congresswoman*
Johnson, Eddie Bernice *congresswoman*
Johnson, Samuel (Sam Johnson) *congressman*
Johnston, John Bennett, Jr. *senator*
Jones, Walter B., Jr. *congressman*
Kingston, Jack *congressman*
Lancaster, H(arold) Martin *former congressman, former advisor to the President*
Lent, Norman Frederick, Jr. *former congressman*
Lewis, Ron *congressman*
Lincoln, Blanche Lambert *congresswoman*
Linder, John E *congressman, dentist*
Livingston, Robert Linlithgow, Jr. (Bob Livingston, Jr.) *congressman*
Lott, Trent *senator*
Lucas, Frank D. *congressman*
Mack, Connie, III (Cornelius Mack) *senator*
Mc Collum, Ira William, Jr. (Bill Mc Collum) *congressman*
McConnell, Addison Mitchell, Jr. (Mitch McConnell, Jr.) *senator, lawyer*
McCrery, James (Jim McCrery) *congressman*
McKinney, Cynthia Ann *congresswoman*
Miller, Dan *congressman*
Mollohan, Alan B. *congressman, lawyer*
Montgomery, Gillespie V. (Sonny Montgomery) *congressman*
Moran, James Patrick, Jr. *congressman, stockbroker*
Myrick, Sue *congresswoman, former mayor*
Norwood, Charles W., Jr. *congressman*
Nunn, Samuel (Sam Nunn) *senator*
Parker, Michael (Mike Parker) *congressman*
Payne, Lewis Franklin, Jr. (L.F. Payne) *congressman*
Peterson, Pete *congressman*
Pryor, David *U.S. senator*
Rahall, Nick Joe, II (Nick Rahall) *congressman*
Rockefeller, John Davison, IV (Jay Rockefeller) *senator, former governor*
Rose, Charles Grandison, III (Charlie Rose) *congressman*
Sanford, Marshall (Mark Sanford) *congressman*
Scarborough, Joe *congressman*
Shelby, Richard Craig *senator, former congressman*
Sisisky, Norman *congressman, soft drink bottler*
Spence, Floyd Davidson *congressman*
Stearns, Clifford Bundy *congressman, business executive*
Stockman, Stephen E. *congressman*
Tanner, John S. *congressman, lawyer*
Taylor, Charles H. *congressman*
Taylor, Gene *congressman*
Thompson, Fred *senator*
Thurmond, Strom *senator*
Wamp, Zach P. *congressman*
Ward, Michael Delavan *congressman, former state legislator*
Warner, John William *senator*
Watt, Melvin L. *congressman, lawyer*
Watts, J. C., Jr. *congressman*
Weldon, David Joseph, Jr. *congressman, physician*
West, Jade Christine *legislative staff*
Whitfield, Edward (Wayne Whitfield) *congressman*
Wicker, Roger F. *congressman*
Wise, Robert Ellsworth, Jr. (Bob Ellsworth) *congressman*
Wolf, Frank R. *congressman, lawyer*

FLORIDA

Jacksonville
Bennett, Charles Edward *former congressman, educator*

Miami
Fascell, Dante B. *congressman, lawyer*
Jones, Daryl Lafayette *state legislator, lawyer*

Naples
Stagg, Evelyn Wheeler *educator, state legislator*

Sarasota
Rabow, Stephen Douglas *multimedia consultant, author, publisher*

Tallahassee
Wetherell, Virginia Bacon *state legislator, state agency administrator, engineering company executive*

Tampa
Davis, Helen Gordon *former state senator*

Winter Park
Mica, John L. *congressman*

GEORGIA

Atlanta
Murphy, Thomas Bailey *state legislator*
Thomas, Robert Lindsay *former congressman*

Marietta
Sauder, Randy James *state legislator, lawyer*

HAWAII

Honolulu
Tschida, Mike J. *legislative aide*

KENTUCKY

Covington
Celella, Jan Gerding *legislative staff member*

LOUISIANA

Baton Rouge
Manning, Kim Dodd *legislative staff member*

La Place
Landry, Ronald Jude *lawyer, state senator*

Marksville
Riddle, Charles Addison, III *state legislator, lawyer*

MISSISSIPPI

Fulton
Miles, William Trice *state legislator*

NORTH CAROLINA

Fayetteville
Tyson-Autry, Carrie Eula *legislative consultant, researcher, small business owner*

High Point
Arnold, Steve *state legislator, state commissioner*

Raleigh
Cauthen, Carmen Wimberley *legislative staff member, jewelry designer*

OKLAHOMA

Oklahoma City
Garrett, Kathryn Ann (Kitty Garrett) *legislative clerk*

SOUTH CAROLINA

Greenville
Mann, James Robert *congressman*

Lancaster
Hodges, James H. *state legislator*

Spartanburg
Patterson, Elizabeth Johnston *former congresswoman*

TENNESSEE

Athens
Higdon, Linda Hampton *congressional staff*

Memphis
Jones, Tom Eugene *mayoral assistant, public affairs officer*

Nashville
Purcell, William Paxson, III *state legislator*

TEXAS

Abilene
Jones, Grant *former state senator*

Austin
Bullock, Robert D. (Bob Bullock) *state legislator, lieutenant governor, lawyer*
Denny, Mary Craver *state legislator, rancher*
Lavine, Richard Ira *legislative analyst*

Beaumont
Brooks, Jack Bascom *congressman*

Brownsville
Lucio, Eduardo Andres, Jr. *former state senator*

Fort Worth
Mowery, Anna Renshaw *state legislator*
Shannon, Larry Redding *administrative assistant*

Garland
Driver, Joe L. *state legislator, insurance agent*

Houston
Green, Gene *congressman*

Irving
Armey, Richard Keith (Dick Armey) *congressman*

Rockdale
Kubiak, Daniel J. *state legislator*

VIRGINIA

Alexandria
Shepard Towles, Stacey Ann *legislative affairs administrator*
Ticer, Patricia *state senator*

Arlington
Zanfagna, Philip Edward *government executive, urban planner*

Danville
Moorefield, Jennifer Mary *legislative staff member*

Lorton
Payne, Foster Penny, II *legislative staff member*

Mc Lean
Hirst, Nancy Hand *retired legislative staff member*
McCurdy, David Keith *former congressman, lawyer*
St. Germain, Fernand Joseph *congressman*

Norton
Kennedy, J. Jack, Jr. *law clerk, lawyer, business investor*

Richmond
Moss, Thomas Warren, Jr. *state legislator, speaker of the house*
Rest, Gregory Joel *legislative analyst*

Suffolk
Layton, Christopher James *legislative liaison*

WEST VIRGINIA

Elkins
Spears, Jae *state legislator*

ADDRESS UNPUBLISHED

Baker, Richard Hugh *congressman*
Barton, Joe Linus *congressman*
Blaschke, Renee Dhossche *alderman*
Bliley, Thomas Jerome, Jr. *congressman*
Cochran, Thad *senator*
de la Garza, Kika (Eligio de la Garza) *congressman*
Essig, Alan *legislative staff member*
Ford, Wendell Hampton *senator*
Goss, Porter J. *congressman*
Hammerschmidt, John Paul *retired congressman, lumber company executive*
Hutchison, Kay Bailey *senator*
Johnston, Harry A., II *congressman*
Kin, Leslie Schultz *legislative assistant*
Schmidt, Arthur Louis *retired state senator*
Tejeda, Frank *congressman*

HEALTHCARE: DENTISTRY

UNITED STATES

ALABAMA

Alexander City
Harrell, William Edward, Jr. *orthodontist*

Birmingham
Alling, Charles Calvin, III *oral-maxillofacial surgeon, educator, writer*
Davidson, Roy Grady, Jr. *dentist*
King, Charles Mark *dentist, educator*

Mobile
Nettles, Joseph Lee *dentist*

Tallassee
Wilbanks, Daniel Pinckney *dentist, director*

ARKANSAS

Fayetteville
Grammer, Frank Clifton *oral surgeon, researcher*

FLORIDA

Altamonte Springs
Coatoam, Gary William *periodontist*

Boca Raton
Eckelson, Robert Alan *orthodontist*
Feldstein, Stanley *dentist*
Leichter, Julian Charles *periodontist*
Lerner, Theodore Raphael *dentist*

Fort Lauderdale
Dorn, Samuel O. *endodontist*

Fort Myers
Laboda, Gerald *oral and maxillofacial surgeon*

Gainesville
Javid, Nikzad Sabet *dentist, prosthodontist educator*
Mjor, Ivar Andreas *dental educator*
Widmer, Charles Glenn *dentist, researcher*

Gulf Breeze
Shows, Clarence Oliver *dentist*

Jupiter
Nessmith, H(erbert) Alva *dentist*

Miami
Iver, Robert Drew *dentist*
Leeds, Robert *dentist*
Parnes, Edmund Ira *oral and maxillofacial surgeon*

Naples
Ruman, Margaret Ann (Peggy Ruman) *dental hygienist*

Pensacola
Dannheisser, Bertram Vivian, Jr. *dentist*

Tampa
Haller, Robert Henry *endodontist, USAF officer*
Pasetti, Louis Oscar *dentist*
Perret, Gerard Anthony, Jr. *orthodontist*
Wiest, John Andrew *dentist*

Winter Haven
Turnquist, Donald Keith *orthodontist*

GEORGIA

Acworth
Tawadros, Azmi Milad *oral surgeon*

Atlanta
Freedman, Louis Martin *dentist*

Augusta
Rogers, Michael Bruce *orthodontist*

Macon
Holliday, Peter Osborne, Jr. *dentist*
Walton, DeWitt Talmage, Jr. *dentist*

Monroe
Taylor, Steven Craig *dentist*

Moultrie
Benner, Randall Ray *dentist*

KENTUCKY

Fort Campbell
Scales, Donald Karl *dentist, army officer*

Lexington
Thomas, Mark Vincent *periodontist*

Louisville
Lee, Susan *dentist, microbiologist*

LOUISIANA

New Orleans
Misiek, Dale Joseph *oral and maxillofacial surgeon*

Shreveport
Lloyd, Cecil Rhodes *pediatric dentist*
Roberts, Gary Lynn *dentist*

MISSISSIPPI

Clinton
Allen, Frances Norman *dental association adminstrator*

Jackson
O Carroll, M. Kevin *dentist, educator, radiologist*
Serio, Francis G. *periodontist educator, researcher*

NORTH CAROLINA

Asheville
Gottfried, Beverly Jane Sickler *dental hygienist*

Chapel Hill
Whitley, John Quention, Jr. *orthodontal educator, researcher*
Wright, John Timothy *dentistry educator*

Charlotte
Freedland, Jacob Berke *dentist, endodontist*
Owen, Kenneth Dale *orthodontist*

Winston Salem
Webber, Richard Lyle *dental radiology educator*

OKLAHOMA

Broken Arrow
Lamb, Ronald James *dentist*

Calera
Young, James Oliver *dentist, communication company executive*

Durant
Craige, Danny Dwaine *dentist*

Oklahoma City
Brewer, William Wallace *dentist*
Shillingburg, Herbert Thompson, Jr. *dental educator*

Tulsa
Kelly, Vincent Michael, Jr. *orthodontist*
Sims, Fred William, Sr. *orthodontist*

SOUTH CAROLINA

Charleston
Cordova, Maria Asuncion *dentist*
Salinas, Carlos Francisco *dentist, educator*

Columbia
Witherspoon, Walter Pennington, Jr. *orthodontist*

Greenville
Mitchell, William Avery, Jr. *orthodontist*

Lake City
TruLuck, James Paul, Jr. *dentist, vintner*

TENNESSEE

Knoxville
McGuire, John Albert *dentist*

Memphis
Fields, W(ade) Thomas *dental educator*
McCullar, Bruce Hayden *oral and maxillofacial surgeon*
Spitznagel, John Keith *periodontist, researcher*

TEXAS

Big Spring
Amonett, Randall Thayne *dentist*

Dallas
Al-Hashimi, Ibtisam *oral scientist, educator*
Blanton, Patricia Louise *periodontal surgeon*
Farris, Edward Thompson *dentist, medical researcher, real estate developer and broker*
Goodwin, Joel Franklin, Sr. *dentist*
Owens, Lindsay Meggs *dentist*
Sugg, Harry Lee, Jr. *dentist*

El Paso
Torres, Israel *oral and maxillofacial surgeon*

Houston
Burroughs, Jack Eugene *dentist, management consultant*
Heath, Frank Bradford *dentist*
Masters, Ronald G. *dentist, educator*
Sweet, James Brooks *oral and maxillofacial surgeon*

Plano
Findley, John Sidney *dentist*

Rotan
Marshall, Jerry Allyn *dentist, mayor*

San Antonio
Cottone, James Anthony *dentist*
Palmer, Hubert Bernard *dentist*
Peavy, Dan Cornelius *orthodontist*

VIRGINIA

Arlington
Brown, Ronald Stephen *dental educator, clinician*

Lynchburg
Hall, Sidney Guy *retired orthodontist*

Martinsville
Renick, Fred Taylor, Jr. *dentist*

Mc Lean
Mayberry, Rodney Scott *dentist*

Pearisburg
Morse, F. D., Jr. *dentist*

Petersburg
Boyd, Herbert Reed, Jr. *dentist*

Portsmouth
Cox, William Walter *dentist*

Richmond
Butler, James Hansel *periodontist*
Laskin, Daniel M. *oral and maxillofacial surgeon, educator*

Virginia Beach
Lowe, Cameron Anderson *dentist, endodontist, educator*
Zimmerman, Solomon *dentist, educator*

ADDRESS UNPUBLISHED

Anderson-Cermin, Cheryl Kay *orthodontics educator*
Hopkins, Sharon Mattox *orthodontist*
Johnson, Dewey E(dward), Jr. *dentist*
Makins, James Edward *retired dentist, dental educator, educational administrator*
Slaughter, Freeman Cluff *retired dentist*

HEALTHCARE: HEALTH SERVICES

UNITED STATES

ALABAMA

Andalusia
Sightler, Debra H. *community health nurse*

Auburn
Banga, Ajay Kumar *pharmacy educator*
Farrell, Robert Joel, II *counselor and therapist, educator, minister*
Mansfield, Philip Douglas *veterinary medicine educator*

Birmingham
Barnard, Barbara Blackburn *dietitian*
Bennett, James Patrick *healthcare executive, accountant*
Booth, Wendy Christina *nursing educator*
Devane, Denis James *health care company executive*
Hammond, C(larke) Randolph *healthcare executive*
Holmes, Sandra Eileen Kilgore *nurse*
Holmes, Suzanne McRae *nursing supervisor*
Jones, Donna Gilbert *social worker*
Jones, Moniaree Parker *occupational health nurse*
Lofton, Kevin Eugene *medical facility administrator*
McCary, Anne Margaret *trauma nurse, medical case management service professional, nurse practitioner*
Musacchio, Marilyn Jean *nurse midwife, educator*
Owens, Sandra Nell *nurse*
Perry, Helen *educator, nurse*
Roth, William Stanley *hospital foundation executive*
Smith, Steve Allen *nursing administrator*
Taub, Edward *psychology researcher*
Williams, Marilyn *health care organization executive*

Bremen
Conley, Sheila Kay *medical/surgical nurse*

Cottondale
Neeb, Barbara Jean *women's health and geriatric nurse*

Dauphin Island
Levenson, Maria Nijole *retired medical technologist*

Demopolis
Curtis, Michaela Schmitt *emergency and maternal/fetal nurse, educator*

Dothan
Inscho, Jean Anderson *social worker*

Enterprise
Taylor, Carol *rehabilitation nurse*

Fairhope
Brumback Patterson, Cathy Jean *psychologist*

Florence
Davis, Ernestine Bady *nurse educator*

Fort Rucker
Caldwell, John Alvis, Jr. *experimental psychologist*

Fultondale
Moss, Betty Smith *social worker*

Gadsden
Cahela, Roxanne Bowden *home health nurse*

Hamilton
Vinson, Leila Terry Walker *retired gerontological social worker*

Hartselle
Penn, Hugh Franklin, Jr. *psychology educator*

Homewood
Ray, Brenda Patterson *medical-surgical nurse*

Huntsville
Cantrell, Frankie L. *retired medical and surgical nurse, educator*
Loux, Jean McCluskey *housewife, registered nurse*
Noble, Ronald Mark *sports medicine facility administrator*

Lowndesboro
Meadows, Lois *mental health nursing clinician and educator*

Mobile
Allen, Bertha Lee *social worker, family counselor*
Allen, Timothy Leland *critical care nurse*
Clark, Jack *retired hospital company executive, accountant*
Helton, Margaret Susan Young *enterostomal therapy nurse, surgical nurse*
McElhaney, Richard Franklin *quality assurance nursing coordinator*
Stevens, Gail Lavine *community health nurse, educator*
Suess, James Francis *clinical psychologist*
Vitulli, William Francis *psychology educator*

Montgomery
Felton, Norman Lee, Jr. *alcohol and drug abuse services specialistt*
Gates, Sherrie Mott *chemotherapy nurse*
Jones, Allison Bates *oncology nurse*
Laven, David Lawrence *nuclear and radiologic pharmacist, consultant*
MacMullen, Jean Alexandria Stewart *nurse, administrator*
Poundstone, Robert Emmett, III *mental health services executive*
Sparks, Asa Howard *psychotherapist, educator*

Opelika
Parker, Patsy Boyd *academic counselor, educational consultant*
Thompson, Jeffery Elders *health care administrator, minister*

Ozark
Dubose, Elizabeth *community health nurse*

Pelham
Lee, James A. *health facility finance executive*

Phenix City
Greathouse, Patricia Dodd *retired psychometrist, counselor*

Scottsboro
Sanders, Timothy Lee *therapist, writer*

Sylacauga
Bledsoe, Mary Louise *medical, surgical nurse*

Troy
Bazzell, Judy Gunnell *nursing educator*
Gilmore, Linda Louise Traywick *nursing educator*

Tuscaloosa
Davis, Mary Virginia *medical and surgical nurse*
Ford, James Henry, Jr. *hospital executive*
Neathery, Patricia Sue *dietitian, consultant*
Prigmore, Charles Samuel *social work educator*
Stover, Lynn Marie *nurse educator*

Tuscumbia
Patton, Rebecca Jones *community health nurse*

Valley
Striblin, Lori Ann *critical care nurse, medicare coordinator, nursing educator*

ARIZONA

Prescott
Samples, Martina *nursing home administrator*

Sierra Vista
Yates, Helen Louise *labor and delivery, critical care nurse*

ARKANSAS

Benton
Bonner, Mary Elaine *psychologist*

Conway
Bondy, Kathleen Nowak *nursing educator*

Corning
McKinney, Brenda Kay *nursing educator*

Enola
Brown, Lois Heffington *health facility administrator*

Fayetteville
Bolton, Brian Franklyn *psychologist, educator*
Trapp, E(dward) Philip *psychology educator*

Forrest City
Brown, Patricia Ann *child health nurse*
Creasey, Katherine Yvonne *utilization review and surgical nurse*
Spencer, Deborah Joyce *school psychologist, consultant*

Fort Smith
Banks, David Russell *health care executive*
Decker, Josephine I. *clinic administrator*
Fay, Anitra Sharane *psychologist*
Howell, James Tennyson *allergist, immunologist, pediatrician*
Marsh, Charles Clifton *pharmacist, educator*
Martin, Deborah Ann *intensive care nurse, educator*
Paskey, Monica Anne *dietitian*

Hot Springs National Park
Kirksey, Laura Elizabeth *medical, surgical nurse*

Jonesboro
Rosa, Idavonne Taylor *community health nurse*

Little Rock
Campbell, Dianne *social worker*
East, Jack Milton *rehabilitation counselor, administrator, social worker*
Edwards, Donna Reed *nurse*
Gross, Perla Dollaga *nursing administrator, medical/surgical, oncology nurse*
Lewis, Delbert O'Neal *disability consultant, former state official*
Mitchell, Jo Kathryn *hospital technical supervisor*
Nichols, Sandra B. *public health service officer*
Staggs, Michelle Denise *flight nurse*
Van Arsdale, Stephanie Kay Lorenz *cardiovascular clinical specialist, nursing educator, researcher*
Woodruff, John Douglas *non-profit association administrator, retired air force officer*
Worley, Karen Boyd *psychologist*

Lonoke
Adams, Mary Raprich *retired nursing education administrator*

Mena
Madison, Janet Elaine *geriatrics nurse*

North Little Rock
Brackmeyer, Mellody S. *oncology and emergency medicine nurse*
Tiner, Donna Townsend *nurse*

Searcy
Thompson, Linda Ruth *psychology educator, university administrator*

Springdale
Harwell, Linda Maryann *nursing educator*

CALIFORNIA

Brea
Leonard, Carole J. *community health nurse*

Emeryville
Lewis, Martha Nell *expressive arts therapist, massage therapist*

Norco
Parmer, Dan Gerald *veterinarian*

Palo Alto
Parrish, Linda Kristine *data management consultant*

COLORADO

Colorado Springs
Moore, Sheryl Stansil *medical nurse*
Smith, Dorothy Gale Batton *oncological nurse*

Denver
Owens, James M. *human services administrator, consultant, artist*

Fort Carson
Boylan, Michelle Marie Obie *medical surgical nurse*

Las Animas
Ostrander, Diane Lorraine *counselor*

Salida
Hyde, Pearl *medical/surgical and critical care nurse*

CONNECTICUT

West Haven
Patel, Tarun R. *pharmaceutical scientist*

DISTRICT OF COLUMBIA

Washington
Muth, William Henry Harrison, Jr. *medical/surgical nurse*
Ozer, Martha Ross *school psychologist*
Walder, Debby Jean *program director, quality manager, nursing service administrator, nurse, educator*

FLORIDA

Altamonte Springs
Melvin, Margaret *nurse, consultant*
Seykora, Margaret S. *psychotherapist*

Apopka
Webb, Erma Lee *nurse educator*

Aventura
McRoberts, Jeffrey Alan *nursing administrator*

Bal Harbour
Radford, Linda Robertson *psychologist*

Bay Pines
Grano, Joan Teresa *infection control practitioner*

Boca Raton
Baumgarten, Diana Virginia *gerontological nurse*
Cancalosi, Mark Francis *pharmacist*
Douglas, Andrew *rehabilitation nurse, consultant*
Greenfield-Moore, Wilma L. *social worker, educator*
Guillama-Alvarez, Noel Jesus *healthcare company executive*
Marrese, Barbara Ann *nurse, educator, program planner*
Purifoy, Judith Lynn *telemetry nurse*
Saul, Richard Steven *communication disorders educator, audiologist*

Bradenton
Aerts, Cindy Sue *nurse*
Gregory, Daniel Kevin *pharmacist*
Myette, Jeré Curry *nursing administrator*
Zimmerman, Sarah Lydia Mayes *nursing administrator, educator*

Brandon
Mussenden, Gerald *psychologist*

Charlotte
Miller, W. Denise Saunders *community health nurse*

Chipley
Cekauskas, Cynthia Danute *social worker*

Clearwater
Alexiou, Nicholas G. *health facility administrator, consultant*
Gibson, Barbara Arlene *nurse, writer*
Harrington, Joan Kathryn *counselor*
Haumschild, Mark James *pharmacist*
Kinney, Carol Stewart *dietitian*
Slone, Jim *nurse*
Sutton, Sharon Jean *surgical nurse*

Clermont
Harris, Richard Earl *pharmacist*

Coconut Creek
Yormark, Alanna Katherine *pediatrics nurse*

Coral Gables
Galindo-Ciocon, Daisy Jabrica *critical care nurse, educator*
Koita, Saida Yahya *psychoanalyst, educator*
Long, Erik L. *hospital financial executive*
Weatherford-Batman, Mary Virginia *rehabilitation counselor, educator*

Coral Springs
Wilson, Arthur Jess *psychologist, educator*

Daytona Beach
Cardwell, Harold Douglas, Sr. *rehabilitation specialist*
Newman, Thomas Walter Goldberg *therapist, consultant*
Prosser, Jean Victoria *social worker, therapist*
Salter, Leo Guilford *mental health services professional*
Wehner, Henry Otto, III *pharmacist, consultant*

Deerfield Beach
Areskog, Donald Clinton *retired chiropractor*

Deland
Lane, Patricia S. *nursing home administrator, media specialist*

Delray Beach
Erenstein, Alan *emergency room nurse, medical education consultant, aeromedical specialist*
Seelin, Judith Lee *rehabilitation specialist*

Deltona
Murphy, Wilma Louise Bryant *critical care nurse*

Destin
Bergwall, Evan Harold, Jr. *psychologist and minister*

Dunedin
Hallowell, Bruce Allen *health facility administrator*
McIntosh, Roberta Eads *retired social worker*

Englewood
Curtis, Caroline A. S. *community health and oncology nurse*

Fort Lauderdale
Cash, Ralph Eugene *psychologist*
Costa, Robin Leueen *psychologist, counselor*
Dean, Marilyn Ferwerda *nursing consultant, administrator*
Easton, Robert Morrell, Jr. *optometric physician*

Ericson, Phyllis Jane *psychologist, psychotherapist, consultant*
Forsyth, George Lionel *psychotherapist, author*
Fremont-Smith, Richard *retired federal health care executive*
Geronemus, Diann Fox *social work consultant*
Lewis, John Edward *psychologist, educator*
Lister, Mark Wayne *clinical laboratory scientist*
Maxwell, Sara Elizabeth *psychologist, educator, speech pathologist*
McBride, Wanda Lee *psychiatric nurse*
McGinnis, Patrick Bryan *mental health counselor*
McGreevy, Mary *retired psychology educator*
Phillips, Linda Darnell Elaine Fredricks *psychiatric and geriatrics nurse*
Rentoumis, Ann Mastroianni *psychotherapist*
Splaver, Sarah *psychologist*

Fort Myers
Harmer, Rose *marriage and family therapist, mental health counselor*
Newland, Jane Lou *nursing educator*
Rachman, Bradley Scott *chiropractic physician*
Rollason, Wendell Norton *social services administrator*
Wright, William Krieger *psychology and economics educator, consultant, musician, realtor*

Fort Pierce
Wohlford, James Gregory *pharmacist*

Fort Walton Beach
Villecco, Judy Diana *substance abuse, mental health counselor, director*

Fruitland Park
Ede, Joyce Kinlaw *counselor, marketing executive*

Gainesville
Balaban, Murat Omer *food science educator*
Bedinger, George Michael *psychologist*
Catasus, Jose Magin Perez *school psychologist*
Coordsen, Karen Gail *medical/surgical nurse*
Cuellar, Terrence Michael *pediatrics nurse*
Dedlow, (Edna) Rosellen *pediatric nurse practitioner*
Delafuente, Jeffrey Charles *pharmacy educator*
Dierks, Richard Ernest *veterinarian, educational administrator*
Francis-Felsen, Loretta (Loree Francis-Felsen) *nursing educator*
Hornberger, Robert Howard *psychologist*
Moore, G(eorge) Paul *speech pathologist, educator*
Piazza, Elizabeth Anne *pharmacist, educator*
Ray, Timothy Britt *social worker, lawyer, administrator*
Small, Natalie Settimelli *pediatric mental health counselor*
Sutton, Douglas Hoyt *nurse*
White, Susie Mae *school psychologist*

Greenacres
Diaz, Raul *psychologist*

Havana
Whitehead, Lucy Grace *health facility administrator*

Hawthorne
Fackler, Nancy Gray *nursing administrator, military officer*

Hialeah
Fisher, Barbara Turk *school psychologist*

High Springs
Eaton, Wayne Carl *chiropractic physician*

Holiday
Jones, Vaughn Paul *healthcare administrator*

Hollywood
Armstrong, Ivy Claudette *nursing administrator*
Weinberg, Marcy *psychologist*
Weiss, Sally Ann *nursing educator*

Homestead
Monsalve, Martha Eugenia *pharmacist*
Thomas, Dorothy Jean *counselor*
Weinstein, Eugene *pharmacist*

Hudson
Tadlock, Gerry Lee *perioperative nursing educator*

Hurlburt Field
Ingram, Shirley Jean *social worker*

Inverness
Lewis, Christina Lynn *human services administrator*
Mavros, George S. *clinical laboratory director*
Nichols, Sally Jo *geriatrics nurse*

Jacksonville
Cherry, Barbara Waterman *speech and language pathologist, physical therapist*
Fulton-Adams, Debra Ann *nurse practitioner*
Gregg, Andrea Marie *nursing administrator, educator, researcher*
Haines, Philip A. *pharmacist*
Johnson, Paul Kirk, Jr. *mental health nurse*
Leapley, Patricia Murray *dietitian*
Longino, Theresa Childers *nurse*
Mason, William Cordell, III *hospital administrator*
Monroe, Helen Leola *nurse, consultant, educator*
Pavlick, Pamela Kay *nurse, consultant*
Rubens, Linda Marcia *home health services administrator*
Russac, Randall Joseph *psychology educator*
Sanders, Leon Lloyd *nursing administrator, retired naval officer*
Sanders, Marion Yvonne *geriatrics nurse*
Shim, Eunshil *nutritionist, educator, business owner, consultant*

Jacksonville Beach
McIlmoil, L. N. *association executive*

Jensen Beach
Gamble, Raymond Wesley *marriage and family therapist, clergyman*

Jupiter
Mc Call, Charles Barnard *health facility executive, educator*

Key West
Mills, Roger Wayne *nurse administrator*
Olsen, Norman C. *critical care nurse, educator*

Kissimmee
O'Shaughnessy, Rosemarie Isabelle *clinical nutritionist*

Lake City
Vinton, William Brian *mental health nurse, educator*

Lake Helen
Hess, Janice Burdette *nursing administrator*

Lake Mary
Barry, Joyce Alice *dietitian*

Lake Wales
Rynear, Nina Cox *retired registered nurse, author, artist*

Lake Worth
Philips, Christine Ann *healthcare executive*

Lakeland
Autorino, Roberta Catherine *community health nurse*
Balish, Ruth Reitz *community health nurse, medical technologist*
Brost, Gerard Robert *mental health counselor, addictions professional, educator*
Herendeen, Carol Denise *dietitian*
LaComb-Williams, Linda Lou *community health nurse*
Moffitt, Tony Lee *emergency nurse*
Schessler, Thomas Gerard, Jr. *neonatal intensive care nurse*

Land O'Lakes
Corliss, Sandra Irene *correctional health care professional*

Largo
Beck, Donald James *veterinarian, educator*
Clutter, Gayle Ann *radiological technologist*
Collins, Gwendolyn Beth *health administrator*
Ellis, Susan Gottenberg *psychologist*
Mandelker, Lester *veterinarian*
Schwanz, Deborah Ann *psychiatric nurse*
Woodruff, Debra A. *occupational health nurse*

Lauderdale Lakes
Lancaster, Tyson Dale *pharmacist*

Lauderhill
Winters, Barbara K. *geriatrics services professional, poet*

Lehigh Acres
Brumm, Marcia Cowles *pharmacist*

Lighthouse Point
Frock, Terri Lyn *nursing educator and consultant*

Longwood
Andrews, Diane Randall *nursing administrator, critical care nurse*

Lutz
Money, Joy Ann Fuentes *healthcare administrator*

Maitland
Von Hilsheimer, George Edwin, III *neuropsychologist*

Manalapan
Price, Douglas Armstrong *chiropractor*

Mango
Spencer, Francis Montgomery James *pharmacist*

Melbourne
Gay, Sylvia France *critical care and pediatrics nurse*
Hughes, Ann Nolen *psychotherapist*
Means, Michael David *hospital administrator*
Sanders, James Norman *marriage, family, individual and group counselor*
Seifer, Ronald Leslie *psychologist*
Tatom, Kenneth Duke *pharmacist*

Miami
Albury, Charlie Powell *school psychologist*
Barkley, Marlene A. Nyhuis *nursing administrator*
Bauman, Sandra Spiegel *nurse*
Charles, John Franklyn *marriage and family therapist, clergyman*
Cherry, Andrew Lawrence, Jr. *social work educator, researcher*
Clark, Ira C. *hospital association administrator, educator*
Dann, Oliver Townsend *psychoanalyst, psychiatrist, educator*
Edic-Crawford, Darlene Marie *AIDS nurse*
Feldstein, Claire Szep *psychotherapist*
Fitzgerald, Lynne Marie Leslie *family therapist*
Frech, Kenneth Ralston, Jr. *hospital administrator*
Glaskowsky, Elizabeth Pope *nutritionist, dietitian*
Goldman, Lisa Eachus *health facility administrator*
Humphries, Joan Ropes *psychologist, educator*
Kassewitz, Ruth Eileen Blower *retired hospital executive*
Keeley, Brian E. *hospital administrator*
Kunce, Avon Estes *vocational rehabilitation counselor*
Ledo, Marlene *dialysis staff nurse*
Loewenstein, David Andrew *clinical psychologist, neuropsychologist, educator*
Lowitz, Robin Adele *nurse administrator*
Mansfield, Tobi Ellen *psychologist*
Marcus, Joy John *pharmacist, consultant*
Mezey, Judith Paul *social worker*
Milano, Cecelia Manchor *mental health nurse*
Noriega, Rudy Jorge *hospital administrator*
Perry, E. Elizabeth *social worker, real estate manager*
Price, Judith *emergency nurse, administrator*
Robie, Diane C. *nursing consultant, medical investigator*
Russell, Angela Parish Hall *health care company executive, educator*
Russell, Elbert Winslow *neuropsychologist*
Scherf, Rosalyn Feller *nurse, writer*
Schor, Olga Seemann *mental health counselor, real estate broker*
Ugwu, Martin Cornelius *pharmacist*
Wortell, Linda Diane *medical/surgical nurse*

Miami Lakes
Getz, Morton Ernest *medical facility director, gastroenterologist*

Milton
Mack, Susan Prescott *critical care nurse*

Montverde
Bloder, Lisa W. *critical care nurse, mental health nurse*

Mount Dora
Moretto, Jane Ann *nurse, public health officer, consultant*
Shyers, Larry Edward *mental health counselor, educator*

Naples
Bernhardt, Roger *psychoanalyst*
Crone, William Gerald *hospital administrator*
Eggland, Ellen Thomas *community health nurse, consultant*
Hagerson, Lawrence John *health care consultant*
Johnson, Sally A. *nursing educator*
Megee, Geraldine Hess *social worker*
Miles, Helen *oncological nurse*
Shallcross, William Charles *pharmacist*
Walker, Patricia D. *critical care nurse*

New Port Richey
Hlad, Gregory Michael *psychometrist, assessment services coordinator*

Nokomis
Collins, Kathryn Suzanne *nurse practitioner, enterostomal therapy nurse*

North Lauderdale
Miller, Barry M. *human services administrator*

Ocala
Blakeman, Carol Ann *medical/surgical nursing educator*
Houchen, Constance Elaine *nursing administrator*
Jones, Jullia Ann *nurse*
Lamon, Kathy Lynn *nursing administrator*
Layton, William G. *medical center administrator*
Moffatt-Bley, Laura L. *critical care nurse*

Ocoee
Kiehl, Ermalynn Maria *perinatal nurse*

Okeechobee
Borkosky, Bruce Glenn *psychologist*

Opa Locka
Rambana, Andrea Marie *nursing educator*

Orange Park
Bednarzyk, Michele Smith *family nurse practitioner, educator*
Brown, Linda Lockett *nutrition management executive, nutrition consultant*
Ingebrigtsen, Catherine Williams *rehabilitation consultant, health education specialist*
Reemelin, Angela Norville *dietitian consultant*

Orlando
Adkins, Rosanne Brown *speech and language pathologist, myofunctional therapist*
Bittle, Polly Ann *nephrology nurse, researcher*
Brewer, Sheryl Anne *social worker, dental hygienist*
Davidson, Debra Ann *medical and surgical, diabetes, critical care nurse*
Goldberg, Stephen Leslie *research psychologist*
Gonong, Zoila Obmana *medical/surgical nurse*
Harvill-Dickson, Clara Gean *medical facility administrator*
Hodges, Lenore Schmid *dietitian*
Jacinto, George Anthony *social worker, counselor, educator, consultant*
Kennedy, Robert Samuel *experimental psychologist, consultant*
Maynard, George Fleming, III *hospital administrator*
Meitin, Deborah Dorsky *health care executive*
Osborne-Popp, Glenna Jean *health services administrator*
Reis, Melanie Jacobs *women's health nurse, educator*
Safcsak, Karen *medical/surgical nurse*
Scott, Kathy Lynn *peri-operative nurse*
Werner, Thomas Lee *hospital administrator*
Winkler, Lorraine Toby *psychotherapist, social worker*
Witty, John Barber *health care executive*
Zucco, Ronda Kay *addictions program administrator*

Ormond Beach
Smalbein, Dorothy Ann *guidance counselor*

Palm Bay
Jones, Mary Ann *geriatrics nurse*

Palm Harbor
Centner-Conlon, Caroline Elizabeth *social worker, educator*
Ruskin, Les D. *chiropractor*

Panama City
Nelson, Edith Ellen *dietitian*

Parkland
Fink, Harold Kenneth *retired psychotherapist, technical writer*

Pembroke Pines
Mason, Mitchell Gary *emergency nurse*
Sternal, Sandra Gaunt *nutrition services administrator*

Pensacola
DeMaria, Michael Brant *psychologist*
Loesch, Mabel Lorraine *social worker*
McCann, Mary Cheri *medical technologist, horse breeder and trainer*
Peters, Douglas Alan *neurology nurse*
Shimmin, Margaret Ann *women's health nurse*
Vega, Eli Samuel *nurse anesthetist*

Pensacola Beach
Beck, Esther Ann *psychologist*

Pinellas Park
Tower, Alton G., Jr. *pharmacist*

Placida
Wood, Yvonne McMurray *nursing educator*

Plant City
Hixon, Andrea Kaye *healthcare quality specialist*

Plantation
Collins, Ronald William *psychologist, educator*
Gonshak, Isabelle Lee *nurse*

Poinciana
Zable, Marian Magdelen *physician assistant, consultant*

Pompano Beach
Astern, Laurie *psychotherapist*
Forman, Harriet *nursing publication executive*
Pigott, Melissa Ann *social psychologist*

Port Charlotte
Carroll, Joan Louise *home health and hospice nurse*
Gendzwill, Joyce Annette *retired health officer*

Port Richey
Barga, Sandra Anne Miller *medical/surgical nurse*
Mueller, Lois M. *psychologist*

Port Saint John
Lombard, Deborah Lynn *nurse midwife*

Princeton
Cottrill, Mary Elsie *family nurse practitioner*

Punta Gorda
Durham, Diana Louise *cardiovascular nurse*
Hopple, Jeanne M. *adult nurse practitioner*
O'Donnell, Mary Murphy *nurse epidemiologist, consultant*
Wood, Emma S. *nursing administrator*

Ramrod Key
Hall, Gay Patterson *nurse midwife*

Ridge Manor
Cameron, Kristen Ellen Schmidt *nurse, construction company executive, educator*

Saint Augustine
Minckley, Barbara B. *nurse, educator, retired*

Saint Petersburg
Cole, Sally Ann *critical care nurse*
Eastridge, Michael Dwayne *clinical psychologist*
Freeman, Natasha Matrina Leonidow *nursing administrator*
Galucki, Frances Jane *nursing educator, medical/surgical nurse*
Goulding, Judith Lynn *surgical technologist*
Jordan, William Reynier Van Evera, Sr. *therapist, poet*
Keyes, Benjamin B. *therapist*
Walker, Francis Roach *rehabilitation counselor*

Sanford
San Miguel, Sandra Bonilla *social worker*

Sarasota
Bailey, Cynthia Ann *neuropsychologist*
Borsos, Erika *cardiac care, medical/surgical nurse*
Byron, H. Thomas, Jr. *veterinarian, educator*
Carr, Patricia Ann *community health nurse*
Cherundolo, Mary Anne Frances *nurse*
Dearden, Robert James *retired pharmacist*
Fawks, David Robert *psychiatric nurse*
Hendon, Marvin Keith *psychologist*
Kimble, Gladys Augusta Lee *nurse, civic worker*
Markwell, Noel *psychology educator*
Middleton, Norman Graham *social worker, psychotherapist*
Mitchell, Jeffrey Thomas *health science facility administrator*
Tilbe, Linda MacLauchlan *nursing administrator*
Tucci, Steven Michael *health facility administrator, physician, recording industry executive*

Sebastian
Mauke, Leah Rachel *counselor*

Sebring
Koehler, Sharon Kay *hospice nurse*

Seffner
Fore, Carolyn Louise B. *pediatrics nurse*
Gehrke, Timothy Robert *social worker*

Seminole
Dubel, Doris Geraldine Cottrell *gerontology nurse*
Jarrard, Marilyn Mae *nursing consultant, nursing researcher*

Stuart
Fairbanks, Clifford Alan *psychologist, consultant*
Petzold, Anita Marie *psychotherapist*
Proctor, Gail Louise Borrowman *home health nurse, educator, women's health nurse*
Stevenson, Ray *health care investor*

Sunrise
Symon-Gutierrez, Patricia Paulette *dietitian*

Tallahassee
Edmiston, Marilyn *clinical psychologist*
Ford, Ann Suter *family nurse practitioner, health planner*

Green, Cecka Rose *alcohol/drug abuse adminstrator*
Hedstrom, Susan Lynne *maternal women's health nurse*
Mathews, Patricia Spaniol *outpatient services coordinator*
Rhodes, Roberta Ann *dietitian*
Rice, Nancy Marie *nursing consultant*
Tharp, David Minton *pharmacist*
Whitney, Glayde Dennis *psychologist, educator, geneticist*

Tampa
Bennett, Harriet Cook *social worker, educator*
Boutros, Linda Nelene Wiley *medical/surgical nurse*
Clark, Michael Earl *psychologist*
Coleman-Portell, Bi Bi *women's health and high risk perinatal nurse*
Einstein, Albert B., Jr. *health facility administrator, oncologist, educator*
Ferlita, Theresa Ann *clinical social worker*
Jones, David Lance *nurse*
Liller, Karen DeSafey *health education educator*
Solomon, Eldra Pearl Brod *psychologist, educator, biologist, author*
Zirps, Fotena Anatolia *psychologist, researcher*

Tarpon Springs
Georgiou, Ruth Schwab *retired social worker*

Tavernier
Fismer, Roberta D. *nursing administrator*

Titusville
Hartung, Patricia McEntee *therapist*
Lyon, Isolda Yvette *dietitian*
Roath-Algera, Kathleen Marie *massage therapist*

Venice
Ward, Jacqueline Ann Beas *nurse, healthcare administrator*

Vero Beach
Burdette, Carol Janice *gerontology nursing administrator*
Fielding, Inez Victoria Brown *community health nurse*
Whitney, J. Lee *home health care administrator*

West Palm Beach
Abernathy, Barbara Eubanks *counselor*
Ackerman, Paul Adam *pharmacist*
Bernhardt, Marcia Brenda *mental health counselor*
Bohn, Barbara Ann *laboratory director*
Clarke, Margaret Anne *maternal-child nurse*
Clemens, Nora Duenas *dietitian*
Davis, Shirley Harriet *social worker, editor*
Gilmore, Loretta Tuttle *social worker*
Glinski, Helen Elizabeth *operating room nurse*
Green, Linda Gail *international healthcare and management consultant*
Holloway, Edward Olin *human services manager*
Katz, William David *psychologist, psychoanalytic psychotherapist, educator, mental health consultant*
Klein, Harvey Allen *clinical psychologist*
Malecki, Jean Marie *public health director*
Rafaidus, David Martin *health and human services planner*
Wilson, Charles Edward *medical records administrator*

Winter Haven
Porter, Howard Leonard, III *health policy consultant*
West, Mary Elizabeth *psychiatric management professional*

Winter Park
Douglas, Kathleen Mary Harrigan *psychotherapist, educator*

GEORGIA

Albany
Chapin, Diane Louise *cardiac care nurse*
Cox, Lynetta Frances *neonatal intensive care nurse*
Gates, Roberta Pecoraro *nursing educator*

Alpharetta
Baker, Winda Louise (Wendy Baker) *social worker*
Brennan, Eileen Hughes *nurse*
Gottlieb, Sidney Alan *optometrist*
Rettig, Terry *veterinarian, wildlife consultant*
White, Carl Edward, Jr. *pharmaceutical adminstrator*

Americus
Barnes, David Benton *school psychologist*
Worrell, Billy Frank *health facility administrator*

Athens
Boudinot, Frank Douglas *pharmaceutics educator*
Cadwallader, Donald Elton *pharmacy educator*
Comer, James Anderson *veterinary parasitologist*
Hynd, George William *neuropsychology educator*
Lawson, Bonnie Hulsey *psychotherapist*
Pollack, Robert Harvey *psychology educator*
Torrance, Ellis Paul *psychologist, educator*

Atlanta
Baker, Lori Ann *physical therapist*
Banks, Bettie Sheppard *psychologist*
Bertrand, Scott Richard *chiropractic physician*
Bockwitz, Cynthia Lee *psychologist, psychology/women's studies educator*
Cannella, Kathleen Ann Silva *nursing educator, researcher*
Clance, Pauline Rose *psychology educator*
Crawford, E. Mac *health facilities executive*
Crutchfield, Carolyn Ann *physical therapy educator*
Davis, Elizabeth Emily Louise Thorpe *vision psychophysicist, psychologist and computer scientist*
Finley, Sarah Maude Merritt *social worker*
Fisk, Arthur Daniel *psychology educator*
Foerster, David Wendel, Jr. *counselor, consultant, human resources specialist*
Ganzarain, Ramon Cajiao *psychoanalyst*
Garland, LaRetta Matthews *educational psychologist, nursing educator*
Geller, Robert Jerome *pediatric toxicologist*
Gerst, Steven Richard *healthcare director, physician*
Giancola, Joyce A. *psychotherapist*
Golden, Patricia Faris *social worker*
Gordon, Helen Tate *nurse assistant*
Hardegree, Gloria Jean Fore *health services administrator*
Henry, John Dunklin *hospital administrator*
Jenkins, Helen Williams *administrative dietitian*
Johnson, Carl Frederick *marriage and family therapist*
Jolivet, Daniel N. *psychologist*
Levine, Susan Michelle *social worker*
Martin, Virve Paul *licensed professional counselor*
McCain, Lynne Annette *counselor*
McCandless, Carla Jean *rehabilitation nurse, consultant, corporate trainer*
Munoz, Steven Michael *physician associate*
Nadler, Ronald David *psychologist, educator*
Parrott, Janice Morton *medical/surgical nurse, researcher*
Robinson, Charles, Jr. *healthcare administrator*
Seifert, Alvin Ronald *psychologist*
Shepard, William Steve, Jr. *acoustics consultant*
Slavin, Hilary Bernard *psychologist, neuropsychologist*
Snarey, John Robert *psychologist, researcher, educator*
Sones, Shari Carolyn *counselor, educator*
Stempler, Benj L. *clinical social worker*
Taylor, Claudia Ann *psychotherapist, nurse*
Thaxton, Mary Lynwood *psychologist*
Thomas, Margaret Louise *rehabilitation nurse*
Tkaczuk, Nancy Anne *cardiovascular services administrator*
Wade, Thomas Edward *health and social services executive*
Walton, Carole Lorraine *clinical social worker*
Wells, Donald Eugene *hospital administrator*

Augusta
Barab, Patsy Lee *nutritionist, consultant, realtor*
Baxter, Suzanne Domel *nutrition researcher*
Belger, Peggy Coram *psychiatric clinical nurse specialist*
Hilson, Diane Niedling *nursing administrator*
Karow, Armand Monfort *medical facility executive*
Sansbury, Barbara Ann Pettigrew *nursing administrator*
Stark, Nancy Lynn *critical care nurse*
Wilson, John Frank *neonatal nurse*

Austell
Deming, Kathey S. *medical nurse*
Searcy, Laura Fischer *pediatric nurse practitioner*

Ball Ground
McGhee, Vicki Gunter *home health nurse, pediatrics psychiatry, alcohol and Drug rehabilitation*

Blue Ridge
Parrish, Ramon Olene, Jr. *gerontologist*

Bowersville
Elrod, Joy Cheek *nurse*

Brunswick
Cross, Elizabeth *nurse*
Crowe, Hal Scott *chiropractor*
Herndon, Alice Patterson Latham *public health nurse*
Shockley, Carol Frances *psychologist, psychotherapist*

Calhoun
Smith, Janice Self *family nurse practitioner*

Calvary
Jordan, Randall Warren *optometrist*

Canton
Williams, Sally Broadrick *infection control nurse and consultant*

Carrollton
Aanstoos, Christopher Michael *psychology educator*
Driver, Judy Anne *home health consultant*
Gustin, Ann Winifred *psychologist*

College Park
Hood, Ollie Ruth *health facilities executive*

Columbus
McIntosh, Joseph William *health administration consultant*
Sayers, Tracy Lamar *holding company executive*
Townsend, Heather Marie *family nurse practitioner*
Zallen, Eugenia Malone *dietitian, consultant*

Conyers
Kemp, Gina Christine *social services provider*

Dahlonega
Frank, Mary Lou Bryant *psychologist, educator*
Sanford, Cathy Elain *medical/surgical nurse administrator*

Decatur
Dade, Joann *critical care nurse, small business owner*
Dame-Brayton, Laureen Eva *nursing administrator*
Du Vall, Brenka Lynn *telemetry nurse*
Fort, Brenda Louise *critical care nurse*
Hagood, Susan Stewart Hahn *clinical dietitian*
Hawkins, Janice Edith *medical/surgical clinical nurse specialist*
Hinman, Alan Richard *health facility administrator, epidemiologist*
Peredney, Christine Booth *social worker, educator*
Pimentel, Juan Luis, Jr. *health facility administrator, medical educator*
Roman-Rodriguez, Jesse *medical center administrator, internist*
Singletary, Julie B. *home healthcare administrator, pediatrics nurse*

Demorest
Vance, Cynthia Lynn *psychology educator*

Doraville
Yancey, Eleanor Garrett *retired crisis intervention clinician*

Douglasville
Henley, Lila Jo *school social worker, consultant, retired*

Dublin
Doster, Daniel Harris *counselor, minister*
Folsom, Roger Lee *healthcare administrator*
Joyner, Jo Ann *geriatrics nurse*
Sumner, Lorene Knowles Hart *retired medical/surgical and rehabilitation nurse*

Duluth
Wolkow, Alan Edward *chiropractic physician*

Dunwoody
Bartolo, Donna Marie *hospital administrator, nurse*
Hanna, Vail Deadwyler *critical care nurse*

East Point
Fuller, Ora *nursing administrator*

Evans
Andrews, Margaret Love *nurse, educator*
Fournier, Joseph Andre Alphonse *nurse, social worker, psychotherapist*
Perry, Sarah Teresa Anderson (Teri Perry) *nurse manager, critical care nurse*

Fayetteville
Harris, Glenda Stange *medical transcriptionist, writer*

Fitzgerald
Barber, John Steven *hospital executive*

Forsyth
Johnson, Christy Lynn Rodeheaver *nurse*

Fort Gordon
Taylor, Robert Betz *healthcare administrator, military officer*

Gracewood
Whittemore, Ronald P. *hospital administrator, retired army officer, nursing educator*

Grayson
Hollinger, Charlotte Elizabeth *medical technologist, tree farmer*
Mitchell, Laura Anne Gilbert *critical care nurse*
Nease, Judith Allgood *marriage and family therapist*

Griffin
Crawford, Sally Sue *nursing educator*

Jonesboro
Frey, Bob Henry *psychotherapist, sociologist, educator, poet*

Lagrange
Naglee, Elfriede Kurz *retired medical nurse*

Lawrenceville
Carter, Dale William *psychologist*
Cranwell-Bruce, Lisa A. *mental health nurse*
Hibbitts, Marian Hayes *family nurse practitioner*
Jensen, Annette M. *mental health nurse, administrator*
Jowers, Ronnie Lee *university health sciences center executive*

Mableton
Curtis, Joycelyn *social worker*

Macon
Fickling, William Arthur, Jr. *health care manager*
Galeazzo, Constance Jane *neonatal nurse*
Landry, Sara Griffin *social worker*
Reddick, W(alker) Homer *social worker*
Watson, Beverly Ann *nurse*

Marietta
Biehle, Karen Jean *pharmacist*
Billingsley, Judith Ann Seavey *oncology nurse*
Chastain, Shirley Perkins *nursing administrator, medical/surgical nurse*
Dudley, Gary Edward *clinical psychologist*
Hawkins, Brenda L. *psychologist*
Hudson, Linda *health care executive*
Olson, Richard E(ugene), II *chiropractor, publisher, consultant*
Petit, Parker Holmes *health care corporation executive*
Pursley, Carol Cox *psychologist*
Steinberg, Eugene Barry *optician, researcher, contact lens specialist, ophthalmic technician, writer*

Milledgeville
Peterson, Dave Leonard *psychologist*
Scott, Joan *nurse educator, training program administrator*

Morganton
Whyte, Bruce MacGregor *health service executive director*

Norcross
Adams, Belinda Jeanette Spain *nursing administrator*
Andrews, John Scott, Jr. *public health administrator, educator*
Henry, Margaret Annette *activities director*
Irons, Isie Iona *retired nursing administrator*
van Reenen, Jane Smith *speech and language pathologist*

Peachtree City
Stenger, Nancy Rene *emergency room nurse*

Plainville
Mealor, Phyllis Jayne *nurse, infection control practitioner*

Quitman
McElroy, Annie Laurie *nursing educator, administrator*

Rex
Bales, Avary *nurse*

Ringgold
Hayes, Laura Joanna *psychologist*

Riverdale
Stegall, Marbury Taylor *psychiatric, mental health nurse*

Rockmart
Holley, Tammy D. Fennell *critical care nurse*

Rome
Black, Suzanne Watkins DuPuy *psychology educator*
Stone, Ann E. *health facility administrator*

Roswell
Baird, Marianne Saunorus *critical care clinical specialist*
Katoot, Karen Robbyn *critical care nurse*

Saint Simons
Edwards, Brenda Faye *counselor*

Savannah
Baker, Brinda Elizabeth Garrison *infectious disease nurse*
Barnette, Candice Lewis *speech/language pathologist*
DiClaudio, Janet Alberta *health information administrator*
Pintor, Alfonse Michael, III *community health nurse, educator*
Pittman, Bernice Nunnally *primary care nurse*
Strauser, Edward B. *psychologist, educator*
Whitaker, Von Best *nursing educator*

Shannon
Williams, Thresia Wayne Matthews *occupational health nurse*

Statesboro
Davenport, Ann Adele Mayfield *home health agency administrator*
Smith, Edward W.L. *psychology educator, psychotherapist*
Wilhoite, Laura J. *occupational health nurse*

Stone Mountain
Russell, Brenda Flannigan *critical care, medical/surgical nurse*

Thomasville
Hand, Lois Fleming *medical technologist*

Tifton
Thomas, Adrian Wesley *laboratory director*

Toccoa
Scott, Louyse Hulsey *school social worker*

Valdosta
Emmick, Patricia Anne *surgical nurse*
Horkan, Alicia M. *nursing educator*
Waldrop, Mary Louise *nursing educator*

Woodstock
Smith, Jeanne Hawkins *critical care nurse*

HAWAII

Kahului
Shaw, Virginia Ruth *clinical psychologist*

ILLINOIS

Abbott Park
Speer, Cynthia *clinical support specialist, nephrology nurse*

Chicago
Osowiec, Darlene Ann *clinical psychologist, educator, consultant*
Ramirez, Ralph Henry *nurse, corporate executive*

INDIANA

Evansville
McGuire, Brian Lyle *health science facility consultant, educator*

KANSAS

Hutchinson
Benage-Myers, Margaret Anna *pediatrics nurse*

KENTUCKY

Ashland
Ashworth, Helen Johnson *nurse educator*
Kovar, Dan Rada *pharmacist*

Beattyville
Arnold, Anita Lance *community health nurse*

Bowling Green
Hazzard, Mary Elizabeth *nurse, educator*
Lemerise, Elizabeth Ann *psychology educator*
Pierce, Verlon Lane *pharmacist, small business owner*

Calvert City
Butler, Sheila Morris *occupational health nurse*

Corbin
Johnson, Carolyn E. *medical/surgical nurse*
Mahan, Shirley Jean *nursing educator*

Covington
Gross, Joseph Wallace *hospital administrator*

Crestwood
Rose, Judy Hardin *mental health nurse*

Cynthiana
Dorton, Truda Lou *medical/surgical and geriatrics nurse*

East Bernstadt
Combs, Jeanne Maria *nurse*

Edgewood
Doherty, Colleen Ann *critical care nurse*
Sansone, Susan Mary *health facility administrator*

Florence
Krawczyk, Melinda Sue *geriatrics nurse*

Fort Mitchell
Meader, Darrell Lee *psychologist, disaster health specialist*

Frankfort
Garrison, Mark David *psychology educator, writer*

Henderson
Humbert, Melanie Lann Liles *dietitian*

Highland Heights
Littleton, Nan Elizabeth Feldkamp *mental health services professional*

Hopkinsville
Cooley, Sheila Leanne *psychologist, consultant*

Jeffersonville
Centers, Bonnie Jean *nursing administrator*

Lexington
Cobb, Ronald David *pharmacist, educator*
Dhooper, Surjit Singh *social work educator*
Dobrzyn, Janet Elaine *quality management professional*
Hines-Martin, Vicki Patricia *nursing educator*
Kimweli, David Mutua *psychologist*
Leukefeld, Carl George *researcher, educator*
McCubbin, James Allen *psychologist and researcher*
McMahon, Pamela Sue *dietitian, educator*
Partington, John Edwin *retired psychologist*
Pritchett, Lois Jane *administrator, counselor, educator*
Schmelzer, Claire Dobson *nutrition and management educator*
Seabolt, Patricia Ann *peri-operative nurse*

Louisville
Baggett, Alice Diane *critical care nurse*
Berger, Barbara Paull *social worker, marriage and family therapist*
Casey, Linda Haley *cardiopulmonary nurse*
Edgell, Stephen Edward *psychology educator, statistical consultant*
Elder, Nancy Helm *patient care attendant, author*
Grabowski, Elizabeth *healthcare administrator*
Harpring, Linda Jean *critical care nurse*
Hughes, J. Deborah *health care administrator*
Jones, David Allen *health facility executive*
Lake, Nancy Jean *nursing educator, operating room nurse*
Martin, Shirley Bogard *maternal/women's health nurse administrator*
O'Bryan, Mary Louise *nursing administrator, consultant*
Petry, Heywood Megson *psychology educator*
Snider, Ruth Atkinson *retired counselor*
Wyant, Michael Benjamin *nuclear pharmacist*

Lyndon
McElroy, Emilie Lin *mental health professional*

Maysville
Cameron, Nan *nurse*
Taylor, Gregory Eugene *optometrist*

Morehead
Johnson, Charlene Denise Logan *medical/surgical and pediatric nurse*

Mount Vernon
Nielsen, Lu Ed *retired community health nurse*

Murray
Thornton, Anna Vree *pediatrics and medical-surgical nurse*

Nicholasville
Kelley, Michael G. *critical care nurse, administrator*

Owensboro
Lott, Sheryl L. *critical care nurse*

Paducah
Cloyd, Bonita Gail Largent *rehabilitation nurse, educator*
Wurth, Susan Winsett *medical/surgical nurse*

Pikeville
Hickman, Cheryl Ann *health facility administrator, pediatric nurse*
Walters, Norman Edward *hospital administrator*

Prestonsburg
Elliott, Myra Turner *nursing educator*
Gawronski, Peggy *healthcare worker*

Russellville
Harper, Shirley Fay *nutritionist, educator, consultant*

Versailles
Rippetoe, Sandra Elaine *dietitian*

West Paducah
Clark, Sandra Faye *medical technologist*

Williamsburg
Buchanan, Jo Ann *social worker, educator*

Winchester
Farmer, Rebecca Anne *counselor*

LOUISIANA

Alexandria
Bradford, Louise Mathilde *social services administrator*
Slipman, (Samuel) Ronald *hospital administrator*

Baton Rouge
Blanchard, Laura *emergency room nurse, rehabilitation nurse*
Burtoft, John Nelson, Jr. *cardiovascular physician assistant*
Rose, Steven Raphael *social worker, educator*
Ryan, Donna Harrington *health science association administrator*
Seay, Billy Mack *psychology educator*
Speier, Karen Rinardo *psychologist*
Suhrer-Roussel, Lynda *psychology educator*
Vaeth, Agatha Min-Chun Fang *quality assurance nurse, wellness consultant, home health nurse*
Winkler, Steven Robert *hospital administrator*

Bossier City
Winham, George Keeth *retired mental health nurse*

Carville
Davis, Lila Ross *public health officer*

Covington
Priest-Mackie, Nancy Ray *nutrition consultant*

Cut Off
Adams, Laura Ann *critical care nurse*

Geismar
Thompson, Patricia Ann *nursing assistant, writer*

Gramercy
Posey, Sandra Denise *occupational health nurse*

Hall Summit
Wimberly, Evelyn Louise Russell *nursing coordinator*

Hammond
Emerson, Peter Michael *counselor*

Harahan
Ryan, Teresa Weaver *obstetrical nurse*

Haughton
Ivy, Berrynell Baker *critical care nurse*

Houma
Davis, Cheryl Suzanne *critical care nurse*
Gillespie, Betty Glover *critical care nurse*

Jeanerette
Derise, Nellie Louise *nutritionist, educator, researcher*

Jennings
Qualey, Thomas Leo, Jr. *human services administrator*

Lafayette
McCready, Dorothy Jane *post-anesthesia nurse*

Lake Charles
Briggs, Arleen Frances *mental health nurse, educator*
Cowan, Nancy Sue *nurse, hemodialysis technician*
Dilks, Sattaria S. *mental health nurse, therapist*
Middleton, George, Jr. *clinical child psychologist*

Lecompte
Clark, Mary Machen *community health nurse*

Leesville
Gutman, Lucy Toni *school social worker, educator, counselor*
Russell, Gerald Edward *social worker, retired army officer*

Mandeville
Ceips, Kathleen McCarthy *nurse consultant, healthcare manager*

Maurice
Hosey, Terry Annette *medical/surgical nurse, post critical care nurse*

Metairie
Evans, Carol Rockwell *nursing administrator*
Reynolds, Mary Elizabeth Fontaine *office administrator*
White, Olivia A. *clinical therapist*

Monroe
Devereux, Marie P. *pediatrics nurse*
McClanahan, Patsy Hitt *women's health nurse practitioner*
Stark, Elizabeth Ann *home health nurse*

Natchitoches
Egan, Shirley Anne *nursing educator, retired*
Palmer, Curtis Dwayne *cardiopulmonary practitioner, microbiologist, researcher, builder*

New Orleans
Billeter, Marianne *pharmacy educator*
Brandt, James Carl *research organization executive*
Burton, Barbara Able *psychotherapist*
Butler, Shirley Ann *social worker*
Camese, Wanda Green *nurse*
Cusimano, Cheryll Ann *nursing administrator*
Gant, Linda Ann *dietitian, consultant*
Hackman, Gwendolyn Ann *private duty nurse*
Lathrop-Skalos, Maria C. *medical social worker*
Marier, Robert L. *hospital administrator*
McGruder, Kenneth Gene *healthcare administrator*
Messer, Billy Freeman, Jr. *critical care nurse*
Mielke, Howard Walter *environmental toxicologist, educator, researcher*
Olar, Terry Thomas *health facilities administrator*
Paradise, Louis Vincent *educational psychology educator, university official*
Pickett, Stephen Alan *hospital executive*
Rodriguez, Susan Miller *geriatrics nurse*
Tchounwou, Paul Bernard *environmental health specialist*
Tynes, Susan Fournet *counselor, educator*
Washington, James Earl *healthcare administrator*

Pineville
Williams, Karen Olivia *nurse manager, maternal/child health nurse*

Raceland
Fletcher, Katherine Ann Patrick *pediatrics, emergency nurse*

Ruston
Bourgeois, Patricia McLin *women's health and pediatrics nurse, educator*

Shreveport
Carter, Louvenia McGee *nursing educator*
DeYoung, Billie Schaefer *medical clinic administrator*
Fowler, Charlotte Ann *occupational health nurse*
Heacock, Donald Dee *social worker*
Holt, Edwin Joseph *psychology educator*
Hummel, Kay Jean *physical therapist*
Launius, Beatrice Kay *critical care nurse, educator*
Marohn, Ann Elizabeth *health information professional*
Staats, Thomas Elwyn *neuropsychologist*
Vestal, Judith Carson *occupational therapist*

Terrytown
Olson, Sandra Dittman *medical and surgical nurse*

West Monroe
Cato, Sandra Ward *critical care nurse*
Houchin, John Frederick, Sr. *human services administrator*

MARYLAND

Clinton
Dudik, Rollie M. *healthcare executive*

Silver Spring
Colyer, Sheryl Lynn *psychologist*

MICHIGAN

Detroit
Wall, Jacqueline Remondet *industrial and clinical psychologist, rehabilitation counselor*

Troy
Kulich, Roman Theodore *healthcare administrator*

MINNESOTA

Baxter
McTernan, Ann Cibuzar *adult nurse practitioner*

MISSISSIPPI

Batesville
McDaniel, Gracie Swain *nursing administrator*

Bay Saint Louis
Moseley, William Latimer Tim *psychotherapist*

Biloxi
Biggers, Paula Bowers *medical/surgical nurse*
Smith, Georganne Morris *nursing administrator, nursing educator, psychiatric-mental health consultant*
Wasserman, Karen Boling *clinical psychologist, nursing consultant*

Brandon
Burch, Sharron Lee Stewart *woman's health nurse*

Carthage
Brewer, Joyce Marie *nurse midwife*

Clarksdale
Cline, Beth Marie *school psychologist*

Clinton
Sanders, Barbara Boyles *health services director*

Decatur
Usry Mabry, Tina *family nurse practitioner*

Greenville
Williamson, William Allen *optometrist*

Gulfport
Ivey, Cheryl Lynn *oncological nurse specialist*
Jones, Carol Ann *psychology educator*
Mitchell, Belinda Kaye *oncology nurse*
Perez, Jeffrey Joseph *optometrist*

Hattiesburg
Baucum, Janet Martin *nursing administrator*
Bilbo, Linda Sue Holston *home health nurse*
Hinton, Agnes Willoughby *nutritionist, university administrator*
Noblin, Charles Donald *clinical psychologist, educator*

Hazlehurst
Miller, Paulette E. *community health nurse, critical care nurse*

Horn Lake
Golliver, Cheryl Rena *nurse*

Jackson
Chadwick, Charles William *veterinarian*
Dunn, Joseph Richard *psychologist*
Goodwin, William Legree, Jr. *health care food service administrator, retired army officer*
Jones, Helene Rasberry *nursing educator*
King, Kenneth Vernon, Jr. *pharmacist*
Lilley, Evelyn Lewis *operating room nurse*
O'Bannon, Jacqueline Michele *geriatrics and mental health nurse*
Sherrill, Sabrina Rawlinson *healthcare administrator*
Wilson, Eric Lewis *medical technician*
Woodrell, Frederick Dale *health care executive*

Meridian
Lewis, Martha Anne *nurse executive*

Mississippi State
McMillen, David L. *psychology educator*
Purchase, Harvey Graham *veterinary medicine researcher*
Thorne, B. Michael *psychologist*

Natchez
Hutchins, Georgia Cameron *critical care nurse*

New Albany
Jolly, Allene R. *anesthesiology nurse*

Ocean Springs
McNulty, Matthew Francis, Jr. *health sciences and health services administrator, educator, university administrator, consultant, horse and cattle breeder*

Pass Christian
Sprague, Heather M. *oncology nurse, chart audit specialist*

Pearl
Batton, Joseph Howard *nursing educator*

Prentiss
Ross, Sadye Lee Tatman *home health geriatrics nurse*

Raleigh
Price, Tommye Jo Ensminger *community health nurse*

Senatobia
Vines, Mary Chase Austin *nursing educator*

Starkville
Collins, Robert Keith *health center administrator, physician*

Tupelo
Zurawski, Jeanette *rehabilitation services professional*

Vicksburg
Hoover, Deborah *critical care, medical and surgical nurse*

Walls
Alexander, Kathleen Denise *medical/surgical nurse*

Waynesboro
Dickerson, Marie Harvison *nurse anesthetist*

Whitfield
Little, Gregory Don *mental health services professional*

NEVADA

Las Vegas
Colvin, Gayle Ann *mental health consultant, psychotherapist, health facility administrator*
White, Betty Maynard *retired social worker*

NEW JERSEY

Basking Ridge
Manda, Joseph Alexander, III *veterinary consulting executive*

Newark
Rutan, Thomas Carl *nurse*

NEW MEXICO

Albuquerque
Brown, Olive Patricia *nursing consultant*
Carter, Craig Nash *veterinary epidemiologist, educator, researcher, software developer*

NEW YORK

Ithaca
Meilman, Philip Warren *psychologist, education educator*

NORTH CAROLINA

Aberdeen
Marcham, Timothy Victor *pharmacist*

Advance
Walser, Sandra Teresa Johnson *rehabilitation nurse, preceptor*

Ahoskie
Dacus, Edwin Curtis *mental health services professional, minister*

Arden
Adams, Pamela Jeanne *nurse, flight nurse*
Dowdell, Michael Francis *critical care and anesthesia nurse practitioner*

Asheville
Fitchett, June Wiseman *health care facility administrator*
Korb, Elizabeth Grace *nurse midwife*
Weinhagen, Susan Pouch *emergency care nurse*

Wilson, Sherry Denise *speech and language pathologist*

Ayden
Nobles, Lorraine Biddle *dietitian*

Bahama
Cooney, M(uriel) Sharon Taylor *medical/surgical nurse, educator*

Beaufort
Hardee, Luellen Carroll Hooks *school psychologist*

Boone
Alschuler, Alfred Samuel *psychology educator*
Faunce, William Dale *clinical psychologist, researcher*
Jones, Dan Lewis *psychologist*
Pollitt, Phoebe Ann *school nurse*
Singleton, Stella Wood *educator and habilitation assistant*

Burgaw
Powell, Julian Anthony *psychologist*

Burlington
Shotwell, Sheila Murray *medical/surgical nurse*

Candler
Crowder, Julian Anthony *optometrist*

Carolina Beach
Brown, Barry Stephen *research psychologist*

Chapel Hill
Brantley, Jeffrey Garland *health science facility administrator*
Evans, Billie Arnell *rehabilitation nurse, radiologic technologist*
Huff, Patsy Stoltz *pharmacist, pharmacy educator*
Konsler, Gwen Kline *oncology and pediatrics nurse*
Martikainen, A(une) Helen *retired health education specialist*
Munson, Eric Bruce *hospital administrator*
Northen, Sheila Stallings *nursing educator, consultant*
Norton, Peggy Ann Poole *nurse*
Osborne, Lauren Gardner *oncological nurse*
Williams, Suzanne *pediatric cardiovascular nursing educator*
Willingham, Emagene Emanuel *social worker*

Charlotte
Doyle, Esther Piazza *critical care nurse, educator*
Duffy, Sally M. *psychologist*
Grimsley, Douglas Lee *psychology educator, researcher*
Gross, Patricia Louise *neuropsychologist*
Kidda, Michael Lamont, Jr. *psychologist, educator*
Lowrance, Pamela Kay *medical/surgical nurse*
Martin, James Grubbs *medical research executive, former governor*
Odell, Charles Alexander *health care facility administrator, consultant, substance abuse counselor*
Philippe, Scott Louis *optometrist*
Smith, Elizabeth Hegeman *mental health therapist, hypnotherapist*
Tatsis, George Peter *research laboratory administrative director*
Thubrikar, Mano Jumdeo *medical scientist, educator*

Concord
Goodman, Darlene Earnhardt *nursing educator*

Cullowhee
Henderson, Bruce B. *psychology educator*
Koons, Eleanor (Peggy Koons) *clinical social worker*
Marx, Melvin H. *psychologist, educator*

Dobson
Atkins, Dixie Lee *critical care nurse*

Drexel
Woods, Janis Hamrick *nursing administrator*

Durham
Cotten, Catheryn Deon *medical center international advisor*
Demark-Wahnefried, Wendy *nutritionist, researcher*
Frazier, Ann Lynette *medical/surgical nurse*
Gillispie, Ronnie Stephen *health science facility administrator*
James, Nancy Caplan *pharmacist, researcher*
Johnson, Deirdre Ann *social worker*
Nevidjon, Brenda Marion *nursing administrator*
Staddon, John Eric Rayner *psychology, zoology, neurobiology educator*
Surwit, Richard Samuel *psychology educator*
Tutt, Nancy Jean *physical therapist*
Usher, Charles Lindsey *social work educator, public policy analyst*
Weber, Steven Johnson *emergency flight nurse*

Elizabeth City
Hall, Pamela Bright *school health nurse*

Fayetteville
Carter, Rebecca Gail *medical, surgical nurse*
Mayrose, Mona Pearl *critical care nurse, flight nurse, educator*
Priddy, Margaret Morgan *critical care nurse*
Shearer, Michele Slusser *acute care nurse practitioner*

Fletcher
Brown, Callie Corrinne Wrather *medical, surgical nurse, derma-technologist*

Greensboro
Byrd, Walter Raymond *court counselor*
Coltrane, Tamara Carleane *intravenous therapy nurse*
Harris-Offutt, Rosalyn Marie *counselor, therapist, nurse, anesthetist, educator, writer*
Johnson, George Andrew *veterinary medicine and food science educator*
Johnson, Willie Spoon *hospital administrator*
Joyce, Joseph Anthony *nurse anesthetist*
Rosser, Rhonda LaNae *psychotherapist*

Greenville
Crisp, Connie King *medical/surgical nurse*
Griffin, Linner Ward *social work educator*
Martoccia, Charles Thomson *psychology educator*
McKeithan, Donna Boyce *maternal/child health nurse, nursing educator*
McMahon, Maria O'Neil *social work educator*
McRae, David Carroll *hospital administrator*
Naylor, Olen Clyde, Jr. *pharmacist*
Payne, Virginia C. *nurse educator*
Stock, Margot Therese *nurse, anthropologist, consultant, educator*
Tripp, Linda Lynn *nutrition counselor*
Webster, Raymond Earl *psychology educator, psychotherapist*

Henderson
Jenkins, Clara Barnes *psychology educator*

Hendersonville
Heil, Mary Ruth *former counselor*

Hickory
Beshears, Betty Williams *nurse*
Laney, Vickie Moore *nursing administrator*

Hillsborough
Brandon, Richard Leonard *health care consultant*

Hoffman
Hill, Beatrice Zarobinski *home care services regional director*

Jacksonville
Robson, John Edward *nursing administrator*

Jamestown
Sink, Deborah J. *nursing educator*

Lenoir
Moore, Mary Ellen *community health, hospice nurse*

Lexington
Fritts, Lillian Elizabeth *retired nurse*

Lincolnton
Land, Amy N. *home health nurse, hospice nurse, nursing administrator*

Magnolia
Bass, Mary Catherine *clinical social worker, psychotherapist*

Morganton
Davis, Ann Gray *nurse, consultant*
Grady, Betty Fender *registered nurse*
Washington, Albert *health facility administrator*

Mount Airy
Carpenter, Sylvia Jo *surgical nurse*

New Bern
Smith, Larry Wayne *medical/surgical nurse*

Pfafftown
Kannry, Sybil *retired psychotherapist, consultant*

Pine Knoll Shores
Sweeny, Ruth Evans *psychotherapist*

Pinehurst
Fleming, Doris Aven *mental health nurse*
Florell, Kenneth Michael *medical dosimetrist*

Raeford
Womble, Donald Ray *public health director*

Raleigh
Berry, Joni Ingram *hospice pharmacist, educator*
Ciraulo, Stephen Joseph *nurse, anesthetist*
Corder, Billie Farmer *clinical psychologist, artist*
Drew, Nancy McLaurin Shannon *counselor, consultant*
Dubay, Stephen Newton *hospital administrator*
Eaddy, Paula Johnson *women's health nurse*
Fritz, Carol Schweinforth *nurse administrator, consultant*
Geller, Janice Grace *nurse*
Hughes, Barbara Ann *dietitian, public health administrator*
Jackson, Stephanie Ann *nurse*
Lindsay, David Michael *pharmacist*
Meelheim, Helen Diane *nursing administrator*
Morris, Theresa Louise *clinical pharmacist*
Newton-Ward, Charles Michael *public health program consultant*
Pate, David Regan *healthcare executive, financial consultant*
Rhodes-Ryan, Ginger *neonatal nurse practitioner*
Slaton, Joseph Guilford *social worker*
Taylor, Patricia Kramer *nurse*

Research Triangle Park
Batey, Sharyn Rebecca *clinical research scientist*
Goodwin, S(heila) Diane *drug information scientist*

Rockingham
Hudson, Ann Thompson *women's health nurse*

Rocky Mount
Ripley, Vickie Corbett *hospital pharmacist*

Roxboro
Broyles, Bonita Eileen *nursing educator*
Wray, Charles Herman, Jr. *nursing educator, mental health nurse*

Semora
Williams, Pauline M. *psychiatric-mental and community health nurse*

Shelby
Merck, Gerry Elizabeth *counselor*

Snow Hill
Albritton, Deborah Lynn *health administrator*

Southern Pines
Patrick, Eva Bert *nurse*

Swannanoa
Fox, Carolyn Elaine *psychiatric nurse*

Troy
Covington, Gail Lynn *nurse practitioner*

Washington
Bouillet, Sara Elizabeth *hospital administrator, marketing professional*

Weaverville
Hauschild, Douglas Carey *optometrist*

Whiteville
Gilmore, Robin Harris *emergency department nurse*

Wilmington
Pilgrim, Carol Ann *psychology educator*

Wilson
Batchelor, Ruby Stephens *retired nurse*

Winston Salem
Barber, Deborah Nunn *psychotherapist*
Hamilton, Laura Ann *social worker*
Hutcherson, Karen Fulghum *healthcare consultant*
Karnes, Lucia Rooney *psychologist*
Leonard, Susan Ruth *psychologist, consultant*
Lynch, John Ellsworth *hospital administrator*
Preslar, Len Broughton, Jr. *hospital administrator*
Restino, Maryann Susan Reynolds *pharmacist*
Yeatts, Dorothy Elizabeth Freeman *nurse, retired county official, educator*

Wrightsville Beach
McDonald, Wylene Booth *former nurse, pharmaceutical sales professional*

OKLAHOMA

Altus AFB
Thon, Patricia Frances *pediatrics nurse, medical and surgical nurse*

Antlers
Caves, Peggy *medical/surgical nurse*

Bartlesville
Tayrien, Dorothy Pauline *retired nursing educator*

Bethany
Wire, Teddy Kermit *psychotherapist*

Blackwell
Stone, Antoinette A. *outpatient coordinator*

Claremore
Cesario, Sandra Kay *women's health nurse, educator*
Marshall, Linda Lantow *pediatrics nurse*

Cushing
Cruzan, Clarah Catherine *dietitian*

Duncan
D'Spain, Suzanne Lancaster *mental health therapist*

Durant
Kennedy, Elizabeth Carol *psychologist, educator*

Edmond
Bishop, Wanda Caroline *geriatrics nurse, medical/surgical nurse*
Lewis, Gladys Sherman *nurse, educator*
Necco, E(dna) Joanne *school psychologist*
Nelson, Laurence Clyde *pastoral psychotherapist*
Oduola, Karen Ann *geriatrics nurse*
Shaver, Jenise Whitten *dietitian*
Shryock, Carmen Lawson *home health nurse, educator*

Enid
McFadden, Cheryl Ellen *health care professional*

Fort Sill
Gelsthorpe, Joanne Carini *nursing supervisor, military officer*

Frederick
Stone, Voye Lynne *women's health nurse practitioner*

Healdton
Eck, Kenneth Frank *pharmacist*

Lawton
Jurgensen, Monserrate *clinical nurse, consultant*
Mayes, Glenn *social worker*
Sparkman, Mary M. *medical, surgical and rehabilitation nurse*

Madill
Cloyde, Robert Wayne *social worker, clergyman*

Mcalester
Beggs, Syble Marie *program coordinator*

Norman
Donahue, Patricia Toothaker *retired social worker, administrator*
Gaskins-Clark, Patricia Renae *dietitian*
Hiner, Gladys Webber *psychologist*
Wright, Michael Phillip *health researcher, computer software developer*

Oklahoma City
Allbright, Karan Elizabeth *psychologist, consultant*
Applegate, J. Phillip *psychology educator, state official*
Bell, Thomas Eugene *psychologist, educational administrator*
Buckley, Stephanie Denise *health care executive*
Floyd, Kay Cirksena *medical technologist, educational association administrator*
Fountain, Linda Kathleen *health science association executive*
Hammon, Willy Ernst, III *physical therapist, educator*
Hupfeld, Stanley Francis *health care executive*
Jones, Renee Kauerauf *health care administrator*
Kalayilparampil, Thomas Itty *social worker*
Keeth, Betty Louise *geriatrics nursing director*
Kilpatrick, Billie Kay *rehabilitation nurse*
Lowell, Jeanne *nursing educator, psychiatric-mental health nurse*
Matarelli, Steven Anthony *health facility administrator*
Maxey, Wanda Jean *geriatrics nurse practitioner, consultant*
Meritt, Yvonne Edell *public health nurse*
Morgan, Catherine Marie *psychologist, writer*
Murphy, Deborah Hill *school nurse, psychotherapist*
Nixon, Sara Jo *psychologist, educator*
O'Steen, Randy A. *nursing administrator*
Ridgway White, Lurene Jane *neonatal nurse*
Rundell, Orvis Herman, Jr. *psychologist*
Sanders, Gilbert Otis *health and addictions psychologist, consultant*
Sookne, Herman Solomon (Hank Sookne) *retirement center senior executive*
Stephen, Michael *psychologist*
Wallis, Robert Joe *pharmacist, retail executive*

Owasso
Shatwell, Sherita Rhea *psychotherapist, psychiatric services director*

Perry
Frazier, Wilma Ruth *emergency nurse, clinical educator*

Piedmont
Clayton, Lawrence Otto *marriage and family therapist*

Sapulpa
Mattocks-Whisman, Frances *nursing administrator, educator*

Stillwater
Henry, Carolyn Sue *educator, family therapist*
Kincannon, Glee Talbot *dietitian*
Qualls, Charles Wayne, Jr. *veterinary pathology educator*

Tahlequah
Edmondson, Linda Louise *optometrist*
Keeley, Mark James *nutritionist*
Schopper, Sue Franks *maternal, women's health and medical/surgical nurse*
Wickham, M(arvin) Gary *optometry educator*

Tulsa
Alexander, John Robert *hospital administrator, internist*
Davis, Annalee C. *clinical social worker*
Fedrick, Johnnie Bea *psychologist*
Ginn, Connie Mardean *nurse*
Grant, Cheri Beth Hollman *obstetrical nurse, consultant*
Hill, Delinda Jean *medical/surgical nurse, enterostomal therapy nurse*
Jackson, Sandra Lee *health facility administrator*
Joice, Nora Lee *clinical dietitian*
Lambert, Carol Ann *audiologist*
Marler, Susan Ann *cardiology nurse, educator*
Muller, Patricia Ann *nursing administrator, educator*
Payne, Christine Babcock *career psychologist*
Shields, Paul Keith *psychotherapist, management consultant*
Thompson, Harold Jerome *counselor, mental retardation professional*
Young, William Dean *psychologist*
Zekauskas, Susan B. *nursing educator*

Woodward
Billings, Letha Marguerite *nurse*

PENNSYLVANIA

York
Nau, Douglas Scott *psychotherapist*

SOUTH CAROLINA

Aiken
Weed, Keri Anita *psychology educator*
Wells, Claudia Mae Ellis *nutritionist, educator*

Allendale
Solomon, Frank *retired counselor, consultant*

Anderson
Cheatham, Valerie Meador *clinical dietitian*
Harllee, Mary Beth *social worker*

Cayce
Paynter, Vesta Lucas *pharmacist*

Charleston
Bowman, Daniel Oliver *psychologist*
Buchanan, Orena Gregg *community health nurse*
Calhoun, Deborah Lynn *emergency room nurse, consultant*
Cheng, Kenneth Tat-Chiu *pharmacy educator*
Goodrich, James Alan *veterinarian, researcher*
Hall, Marcel Scott *nurse*
Keating, Thomas Patrick *health care administrator, educator*
Maree, Elizabeth Goodwin *psychiatric mental health nurse*
Purcell, Nancy Lou *alcohol/drug abuse services executive*
Robinson, Jakie Lee *human services administrator*
Sharpe, Kathryn Moye *psychologist*
Stroud, Sally Dawley *nursing educator, researcher*
Williams, Marc H. *electroencephalography technologist*

Cheraw
Williams, Morgan Lewis *pharmacist*

Clemson
Alley, Thomas Robertson *psychology educator*
Campbell, Robert Lyndsay, II *psychology educator*
Kline, Priscilla Mackenzie *nursing educator*

Columbia
Anderson, Robin Young *pharmacist*
Appel, James Barry *psychology educator*
Bland, Annie Ruth (Ann Bland) *nursing educator*
Booth, Hilda Earl Ferguson *clinical psychologist, Spanish language educator*
Furchtgott, Ernest *psychology educator*
Hinson, Donald Roy *clinical nurse specialist*
Luckes, Mary Helen B. *mental health nurse*
Madden, Arthur Allen *nuclear pharmacist, educator*
McAbee, Thomas Allen *psychologist*
Michniak-Mikolajczak, Bozena Bernadeta *pharmaceutical educator*
Ramsey, Bonnie Jeanne *mental health facility administrator, psychiatrist*
Seigler, Ruth Queen *college nursing administrator, educator, consultant, nurse*
Walters, Rebecca Russell Yarborough *medical technologist*
Woodbury, Lee Vernon *health care consultant, physician*
Zaepfel, Glenn Peter *psychologist*

Dillon
Labbe, Patrick Charles *legal nursing consultant*

Easley
Crawford, Vicky Charlene *perinatal clinical nurse specialist*
Spearman, David Hagood *veterinarian*

Florence
Coggins, Oran C(halmers) *clinical counselor, addictions specialist*
Glenn, Jeannette Charles *health facility administrator*
Harker, Helen Connie *medical/surgical nurse*
Wiseburn, Lawrence Pritchard *social worker, psychotherapist*

Georgetown
Rogers, Rynn Mobley *community health nurse*

Goose Creek
Neupert, Larry Douglas *nurse anesthetist, naval officer*

Greenville
Westrope, Martha Randolph *psychologist, consultant*

Greenwood
Baxley, Elizabeth Dawn *pharmacist*
George-Lepkowski, Sue Ann *echocardiographic technologist*

Greer
Jones, Sylvia *social worker*

Hartsville
Edson, Herbert Robbins *foundation and hospital executive*

Hilton Head Island
Kearney Nunnery, Rose *nursing administrator, educator, consultant*
Patton, Susan Oertel *clinical social worker, educator*
Stockard, Joe Lee *public health service officer, consultant*

Hopkins
Clarkson, Jocelyn Adrene *medical technologist*

Huger
Isgett, Donna Carmichael *critical care nurse, administrator*

Inman
Alwine, Linda Mae *pediatrics nurse*
Kunze, Dolores Johanna *veterinarian*

Irmo
Stewart, Alexander Constantine *medical technologist*

Johns Island
Aysse, Patricia Elaine *health facility administrator*

Lancaster
Goldsmith, J(oseph) Patrick *psychologist*

Little River
Hasiuk, Cynthia Lee *nurse practitioner, psychotherapist*

Marion
Inabinet, Lawrence Elliott *retired pharmacist*

Mauldin
Harris, Daniel Frederick *biomechanical analyst, educator*

Moncks Corner
Deavers, James Frederick *optometrist*

Mount Pleasant
Etson, Timothy Demorris *social worker, management consultant*
Krupa, Patricia Ann *nurse, consultant*

Myrtle Beach
Dail, Hilda Lee *psychotherapist*
Dunn, James Earl *psychotherapist*
Madory, James Richard *hospital administrator, former air force officer*

Orangeburg
Grimes, Tresmaine Judith Rubain *psychology educator*
Mathur, Kailash *nutritionist, educator*

Pendleton
Fehler, Polly Diane *neonatal nurse, educator*

Rock Hill
Mattison, George Chester, Jr. *health and environmental company executive, consultant*
Mazzoni, Barbara Jean *nurse*
Prus, Joseph Stanley *psychology educator, consultant*
Stewart, Lyn Varn *critical care nurse*

Saint Helena Island
Austin-Long, Jean Audrey *nurse supervisor*

Simpsonville
Hall, Marilyn M. *occupational health nurse*

Spartanburg
Armstrong, Joanne Marie *clinical and consulting psychologist, business advisor, mediator*
Day, Angela Riddle *occupational health nurse, educator*
Lynch, Karen Lee *insurance rehabilitation specialist*
Stoddard, M. Anita *psychiatric nurse*

Summerville
Benninger, Charles Olin *nurse, healthcare administrator*
Duffy, Margaret McLaughlin *nephrology nurse, educator*
Young, Margaret Aletha McMullen (Mrs. Herbert Wilson Young) *social worker*

Taylors
Hart, Fay Maria Mitchell *counselor, mediator*

Union
Sprouse, James Dean *nurse, anesthetist*

Walhalla
Watson, Jean Vaughn *critical care nurse, ambulatory surgery nurse*

West Columbia
Brown, Opal Diann *medical technologist, nurse*

TENNESSEE

Adams
Holt, Phyllis Ann *medical/surgical nurse*

Antioch
Huff, Jimmy Laurence *nurse*
Sandlin, Debbie Crowe *critical care nurse*

Arlington
Searcy, Mary Louise *private duty nursing assistant*

Bartlett
Huffman, D. C., Jr. *pharmacy executive, association administrator*

Brentwood
Gonzalez, Raquel Maria *pharmacist*
Ragsdale, Richard Elliot *healthcare management executive*

Carthage
Tongate, Scott Alan *hospital assistant administrator and controller*

Chattanooga
Arnold, Timothy Jay *therapist, educator*
Beach, Hazel Elizabeth *nurse*
Bechtel, Sherrell Jean *psychotherapist*
Duggan, Ann Cleek *medical/surgical and critical care nurse*
Pinkerton, Helen Jeanette *health care executive*
Saeger, Dixie Forester *dietitian*
Scott, Mark Alden *hospital network executive*
Stephens, Suzanne Hardy *oncology nurse*
Twitty, H. R. *hospital official*
Waring, Mary Louise *social work administrator*
Young, Sandra Joyce *nursing administrator, consultant*

Cleveland
Watson, S. Michele *home health nurse*

Clinton
Seib, Billie McGhee Rushing *nursing administrator, consultant*

Collierville
Golden, Eddie Lee *optometrist*

Cookeville
Broyles, Waymon Carroll *health facility administrator, educator*
Hedgecough, Rebecca J. *nurse*
Reynolds, Barbara C. *mental health educator, academic dean*
Richards, Melinda Lou *speech and language pathologist*

Franklin
Woodside, Donna J. *nursing educator*

Goodlettsville
Harper, Jewel Benton *pharmacist*

Greeneville
Carpenter, Judith K. *health careers educator*

Harrison
Fisher, Paul Douglas *psychologist, program director*

Harrogate
Money, Max Lee *nursing educator, medical, surgical nurse*

Hartsville
Todd, Mary Patricia *nursing administrator*

Hendersonville
Shabaaz, Ahia *family nurse practitioner*

Huntingdon
Harrington, Patsy Ann *geriatrics nurse*

Jackson
Buchholz, Angela Marie *rehabilitation nurse*
Mitchell, Elizabeth Marelle *nursing educator, medical, surgical nurse*
Smith, Geri Garrett *nurse educator*
Stutts, Gary Thomas *health facility administrator*
Tims, Ramona Faye *medical/surgical nurse*

Johnson City
Becker, Teresa Ann *neonatal nurse practitioner*
Fatherree, Laraine Caudell *hospital administrator*
Isaac, Walter Lon *psychology educator*
Kao, Race Li-Chan *medical educator*
Larkin, Donald W. *clinical psychologist*
Owens, Stephen Lee *clinical psychologist, mental health administrator*

Kingsport
Coffman, Wilma Martin *women's health nurse, educator*
Moore, Marilyn Patricia *community counselor*

Knoxville
Beckner, Diana Roberts *clinical nurse specialist*
Cloud, Gary Lynn *food and nutrition services administrator*
Earl, Dennis Charles *audiologist*
German, Ronald Stephen *health care facility administrator*
Hartsell, Michael Reed *nurse*
Lawrence, Ronald Eugene *healthcare company executive*
McGuire, Sandra Lynn *nursing educator*
McNeil, Hoyle Graham, Jr. *pharmacist, administrator, pharmacy management and consulting company executive*
Menefee-Greene, Laura S. *psychiatric nurse*
Murray, Esther Elaine *occupational health nurse*
Pierce, Martha Childress *dietitian*
Prince, Jacquelynne Bolander *nurse, consultant*
Robinette, Betsye Hunter *school psychologist*
Rothman, Richard Lee, Jr. *health facility administrator*
Swanson, Lorna Ellen *physical therapist, athletic trainer, researcher*
Zimmer, Willie Mae *medical/surgical nurse*

Lawrenceburg
Keeter, Rosemary Earlyn *home health and emergency room nurse*

Lebanon
McDonald, Lesley Scott *clinical nurse specialist*

Lexington
Swatzell, Marilyn Louise *nurse*

Loudon
Morton, Jerome Holdren *school psychologist*

Louisville
McReynolds, David Hobert *hospital administrator*

Madison
Crowell, Kenneth Wayne *hospital materials manager*

Maryville
Crisp, Polly Lenore *psychologist*

Memphis
Collins, Earline Brown *medical and surgical and nephrology nurse*
Crain, Frances Utterback *retired dietitian*
Elfervig, Lucie Theresa Savoie *ophthalmic nursing consultant*
Graham, Tina Tucker *psychiatric and pediatrics nurse*
Grant, Virginia Lee King *nutritionist, consultant*
Hodnicak, Victoria Christine *pediatric nurse*
Isom, Theresa Gillespie *nursing administrator*
Jarvis, Daphne Eloise *laboratory administrator*
Johnson, Johnny *research psychologist, consultant*
Kahane, Joel Carl *speech pathologist*
Kirksey, Terrie Lynn *multi-purpose senior center administrator, social work consultant*
Laizure, Steven Casey *pharmacy educator*
Longstreet, Hazel Lee *counselor*
McBride, Juanita Loyce *oncological nurse*
McNabb, Darcy LaFountain *medical management company executive*
Mendel, Maurice *audiologist, educator*
Nolly, Robert J. *hospital administrator, pharmaceutical science educator*
Norris-Tirrell, Dorothy Anne *public administration educator*
Roberts, H(ubert) Wilson, Jr. *counselor*
Shadish, William Raymond *psychologist, educator*
Speck, Patricia McMurry *family nurse practitioner*
Wages, Virginia Anne Sobol *pediatrics nurse*
Weston, Augustene *women's health nurse, perinatal grief counselor*

Morristown
Hardin, Melanie Anne *ophthalmic technician*
Harmon, David Eugene *optometrist, geneticist*

Mountain Home
Grant, Louise Patricia *dietitian*

Murfreesboro
Cooke, Sarah Belle *health care facility professional, farmer*

Nashville
Bach, Carole Ann *rehabilitation, nursing educator*
Castner, Nancy Miller *ambulatory services nurse*
Dale, Kathy Gail *rehabilitation rheumatology nurse*
Frist, Thomas Fearn, Jr. *hospital management company executive*
Golson, Sister Afton Almeda *health facility administrator, nun*
Graves, Rebecca O. *public health nurse, consultant*
Johnson, David *medical administrator*
Lambert, Dorothy Elizabeth *psychologist*
Land, Rebekah Ruth *marriage and family therapist*
Lynch, Patricia M. *dietitian*
McCoy, Sandra Jo *pharmacist*
Neese, Helen Duvall *healthcare practice management executive*
Pierce, Rolanda Lanetta *medical/surgical nurse*
Prince, Grace Rosene Simmons *consulting dietitian*
Raghu, Rengachari *alternative medicine, nutrition, biotechnology and chemistry consultant, agriculture consultant*
Sharp, Diana Leigh Miller *psychologist, educator*
Shousha, Annette Gentry *critical care nurse*
Sloan, Reba Faye *dietitian, consultant*
Speller-Brown, Barbara Jean *pediatric nurse practitioner*
Stringfield, Charles David *hospital administrator*
Strupp, Hans Hermann *psychologist, educator*
Urmy, Norman B. *hospital administrator*
Weiss, Judith Miriam *psychologist*
Wilson, Sheryl A. *pharmacist*

Normandy
Stockton, Kim Welch *home health nurse, administrator*

Norris
Duffley, Patricia Frances *rehabilitation counselor*

Oak Ridge
Jones, Virginia McClurkin *social worker*

Old Hickory
Davis, Fred Donald, Jr. *optometrist*

Oliver Springs
Davis, Sara Lea *pharmacist*

Pioneer
Boardman, Maureen Bell *community health nurse*

Ripley
Nunn, Jenny Wren *pharmacist*

Rockwood
Chechuck, Betty Jean *critical care nurse*

Shelbyville
Regynski, Janet Elizabeth *medical/surgical nurse, orthopedic nurse*

Trenton
McCullough, Kathryn T. Baker *social worker, utility commissioner*

Tullahoma
Scalf, Jean A. Keele *medical/surgical, geriatrics and home health nurse*

Wartburg
Freytag, Addie Lou *nurse*

Winchester
Cashion, Joe Mason *home health care administrator*

TEXAS

Abilene
Calvert, Linda Darnell *women's health nurse, educator*
Crowell, Sherry Diegel *clinical psychologist*
Hennig, Charles William *psychology educator*
Morrison, Shirley Marie *nursing educator*
Smith, Jeff Scott *trauma, critical care nurse*
Sorrels, John Paul *psychology educator*

Albany
Humphreys-Musselman, Carolyn Earl (Lyn Earl) *marriage and family counselor*

Allen
Garner, Julie Lowrey *occupational therapist*
Gilliland, Mary Margarett *healthcare consultant*
Jones, Kenneth *medical company executive*

Alvarado
Hadley, Pamela Lynn *adolescent counselor*

Alvord
King, Barbara Jean *nurse*

Amarillo
Burrows, Emily Ann *neonatal nurse*
Jones, Michael Wayne *health services administrator*
Loe, Emmett Baxter *social worker*
Polster, Joyce Schumann *nurse educator*

Aransas Pass
Moreno, Joseph Florencio *nurse*

Arlington
Adams, Phyllis Curl *nursing educator*
Bunten, Brenda Arlene *geriatrics nurse*
Estes, Josie Elizabeth *counselor*
Fortier, Robert Elve *healthcare company executive*
Glisson, Melissa Ann *dietitian*
Grzesiak, Robert Charles *therapist*
McNairn, Peggi Jean *speech pathologist, educator*
Miller, Darwin Leon *healthcare administrator*
Watkins, Ted Ross *social work educator*
Watts, Thomas Dale *social work educator*

Austin
Acker, Virginia Margaret *nursing educator*
Aida, Yukie *psychological educator, researcher*
Attal, Gene (Fred Eugene Attal) *hospital administrator and public relations executive*
Drake, Stephen Douglas *clinical psychologist, health facility administrator*
Easley, Christa Birgit *nurse, researcher*
Eldredge, Linda Gaile *psychologist*
Gardner, Joan *medical, surgical nurse*
Golden, Kimberly Kay *critical care, flight nurse*
Hall, Beverly Adele *nursing educator*
Heffley, James Dickey *nutrition counselor*
Herrington-Borre, Frances June *sign language school director*
Hurley, Laurence Harold *medicinal chemistry educator*
Hutchins, Karen Leslie *psychotherapist*
Larkam, Beverley McCosham *clinical social worker, family therapist*
LeVieux-Anglin, Lizette Louise *pediatric nurse, nursing educator*
Moore, Rebecca Ann Rucker *speech-hearing and language therapist*

Pepper, Mary Janice *educational consultant*
Richardson, Betty Kehl *nursing educator, administrator, counselor, resear*
Riggs, Deborah Kay *critical care, pediatrics nurse*
Smith, Bert Kruger *mental health services professional, consultant*
Wilczynski, Walter *psychology educator, neuroscience researcher*

Baytown
Coker, Mary Shannon *surgical nurse*

Beaumont
Mendoza, Joann Audilet *nurse*
Tucker, Gary W. *psychiatric care nurse*

Bedford
Flaherty, Carole L. *medical, surgical and mental health nurse*

Beeville
Jensen, W. Lynne *nursing educator*

Bellaire
Mayo, Clyde Calvin *organizational psychologist, educator*

Big Sandy
Walther, Richard Ernest *psychology educator, library administrator*

Bonham
Phillips, Don Lee *nursing administrator*

Brenham
Dalrymple, Christopher Guy *chiropractor*

Bridgeport
Farris, Susan Ann *nursing home administrator, dietitian*

Brownsville
French, Bertha Doris *medical, surgical and geriatrics nurse*

Bryan
Marquardt, Mary Meyers *critical care nurse, educator*
Sulik, Edwin (Pete Sulik) *health care administrator*

Burleson
Erinakes, Janet Levernie *health consulting company owner*
Gabbert, J(osephine) Ann *nurse, administrator*
Walsh Hansel, Jeanetta Lynn *home infusion nurse*

Carrollton
Withrow, Lucille Monnot *nursing home administrator*

Castroville
Strickland, Sandra Jean Heinrich *nursing educator*

Cedar Hill
Norris, Sherrie Lynn Kincaid *clinical research and surgical intensive care unit nurse*

Cedar Park
Koop, Tobey Kent *research consultant, educational psychologist*

Chillicothe
Brock, Helen Rachel McCoy *retired mental health and community health nurse*

Cibolo
Lust, Barbara Louise *nursing educator, health facility administrator*

College Station
Beaver, Bonnie Veryle *veterinarian, educator*
David, J(ames) Barry *equine veterinarian*
Honnas, Clifford M. *equine orthopedic surgeon*
Johnson, James Harvey *veterinary medical educator*
Luepnitz, Roy Robert *psychologist, consultant, small business owner, entrepreneur*
Murphy, Kathleen Jane *psychologist, educator*

Conroe
Shepherd, Elizabeth Poole *health science facility administrator*
Sowers, Amelia Barnet *speech and language pathologist*

Converse
Droneburg, Nancy Marie *geriatrics nurse*

Copperas Cove
Townsend, Linda Ladd *mental health nurse*

Corpus Christi
Baicy, Janet Karen *nursing executive*
Cipriano, Irene Pena *medical technician*
Clark, Joyce Naomi Johnson *nurse*
Clarkson, Edith West *nursing administrator*
Cutlip, Randall Brower *retired psychologist, college president emeritus*
Hamilton, Paul Martin *psychologist*
Long, Ralph Stewart *clinical psychologist*
Scheper, George H. *nursing administrator*

Crosby
Cole, Edith Fae *dietitian, consultant*

Crosbyton
Beeler, Bulah Ray *medical/surgical nurse*

Dallas
Alford, Dolores Ida M. *nursing consultant*
Anderson, Ron Joe *hospital administrator, physician, educator*
Barnett, Peter Ralph *health science facility administrator, dentist*
Bell-Tolliver, LaVerne *social worker*
Blome, Dorothy Carter *pediatrics nurse*
Collins, Lynn M. *oncology clinical nurse specialist*
Doone, Michele Marie *chiropractor*
Dykes, Virginia Chandler *occupational therapist*
Fleming, Jon Hugh *psychology educator, business executive, educational consultant*
Fritze, Julius Arnold *marriage counselor*
Goodson, Shannon Lorayn *behavioral scientist, author*
Gouge, Betty Merle *family therapist*
Haid, Stephen Donald *health facility administrator*
Haire, William J. *healthcare executive*
Hanratty, Carin Gale *pediatric nurse practitioner*
Harmon, Jane Ellen *occupational therapist, writer*
Herbelin, Karen *survey and certification specialist, dietitian*
Johnson, Murray H. *optometrist, researcher, consultant, lecturer*
Keeling, Elizabeth Burfoot *health facility administrator*
Kelly, John Price *hospital administrator*
Largent, Mildred M. *community health nurse*
Laster-Sprouse, Charline Higgins *health care facility administrator, educator, family therapist*
Lawrence, Alma Jean Kelley *research nurse*
Le Vieux, Jane Stuart *pediatrics nurse*
McGregor, Scott Duncan *optometrist, educator*
Medlock, Norman Dudley *healthcare company executive*
Metzler, Jerry Don *nursing administrator*
Miller, Jo Carolyn Dendy *family and marriage counselor, educator*
O'Bannion, Mindy Martha Martin *nurse*
Pelosof, Henri Vidal *physical medicine and rehabilitation physician, educator*
Powell, Boone, Jr. *hospital administrator*
Price, Kenneth Paul *clinical psychologist, educator*
Richardson, Wanda Louise Gibson *family practice nurse*
Schiller, Lawrence Rudolph *academic administrator*
Schultze, Maribeth Jane *psychologist*
Sims, Konstanze Olevia *social worker*
Smith, William Randolph (Randy Smith) *health care management association executive*
Stevens, Julie Ann *peri-operative nurse*
Strader, Melinda Ann Amason *nursing consultant*
Talley, Linda Jean *food scientist, dietitian*
Warshak, Richard Ades *clinical and research psychologist, author*
Watts, Sara Casey *marriage and family therapist*
Wolf, Michael Ellis *clinical psychologist*

Deer Park
Mayr, Linda Hart *internal medicine nurse*

Denton
Drapo, Peggy Jean *community health, pediatric, mental health nurse*
Ealey, Chrysta Lea *medical/surgical nurse*
Gershon, Elaine A. *medical/surgical nurse*
Mathes, Dorothy Jean Holden *occupational therapist*
Newell, Thomas David *pediatric/family nurse practitioner*
Norris, William Randal *psychologist*

Dripping Springs
Nicholas, Nickie Lee *retired industrial hygienist*

Dublin
Corta, Nancy Ruth *nurse*

Dumas
Nowell, Medora *medical/surgical nurse*

Edinburg
Wilson, Bruce Keith *men's health nurse*

El Campo
Abshire, Mary Young *dietitian, small business owner*

El Paso
Adams, Nancy R. *nurse, military officer*
Bartlett, Janet Sanford (Walz) *school nurse*
Juarez, Antonio *psychotherapist, consultant, counselor, educator*
Longnecker, Beth Anne *audiologist*
Mitchell, Paula Rae *nursing educator*
Monsivais, Diane B. *surgical nurse, writer*
Staeger, Earl *nurse*

Elsa
Garcia, Iris Escobedo *public health nurse*

Euless
Hughes, Sandra K. *nursing administrator*

Fort Hood
Shuler, George Nixon, Jr. *social worker, writer*

Fort Sam Houston
Abbott, Cynthia Allen *nurse administrator*

Fort Worth
Benepe, Virginia Lynn *medical/surgical and oncological nurse*
Brockman, Leslie Richard *social worker*
Brodale, Louise Lado *medical, post surgery and geriatrics nurse*
Byas, Teresa Ann Uranga *healthcare professional*
Cook, Peggy Jo *psychotherapist, consultant*
Dees, Sandra Kay Martin *psychologist, research consultant*
Demaree, Robert Glenn *psychologist, educator*
Enlow, Rick Lynn *chiropractor*
Ford, Kathleen Marie *home health nurse, trainer*
Hauss, Edward Earl *nurse legal consultant*
Jensen, Harlan Ellsworth *veterinarian, educator*
Manning, Walter Scott, Jr. *veterinarian*

Freeport
Baskin, William Gresham *counselor, music educator, vocalist*

Galveston
Cabanas, Elizabeth Ann *nutritionist*
Head, Elizabeth Spoor *mycology consultant*
Hoskins, Sara Lynn *pediatrics critical care nurse*
Lawrence, Kathy *medical, surgical, and radiology nurse*
Low, Jaclyn Faglie *occupational therapist*
Psencik, Penny Lynn *flight nurse*
Shannon, Mary Lou *adult health nursing educator*
Thomas, Leelamma Koshy *women's health care nurse*

Georgetown
Elder, John Blanton *psychologist, clergyman*

Graham
Campbell, Glenda Gail *medical and surgical nurse*
Ritchlin, Martha Ann *occupational therapist*

Granbury
Southern, David Lynn *healthcare facilities operating company executive, psychologist*

Grapevine
Arnott, Ellen Marie *medical case management and occupational health executive*

Greenville
Ellis, Karan Ann *health care facility administrator*

Hearne
Helpert-Nunez, Ruth Anne *clinical social worker, psychotherapist*

Henderson
Howard, Barbara Ann *obstetrical/gynecological nurse practitioner*
McDonald, Benna J. *nursing educator, critical care nurse*

Hermleigh
Barnes, Maggie Lue Shifflett (Mrs. Lawrence Barnes) *nurse*

Houston
Adams, John Wilson, Jr. *healthcare executive*
Adams, Richard Paul *healthcare management executive*
Alpher, Victor Seth *clinical psychologist, consultant*
Ambler, Joyce Anne *psychotherapist*
Armentrout, Debra Catherine *neonatal nurse practitioner*
Becker, Frederick Fenimore *cancer center administrator, pathologist*
Brucker, Janet Mary *nurse*
Burdine, John A. *hospital administrator, nuclear medicine educator*
Cadwalder, Hugh Maurice *psychology educator*
Caggins, Ruth Porter *nurse, educator*
Callender, Norma Anne *psychology educator, counselor*
Cappelle, Ann Aleace *supervisory recreation therapist*
Cheung, William Kong-Lung *nuclear medicine technologist*
Crisp, Jennifer Ann Clair *neurosurgical nurse*
Davis-Lewis, Bettye *nursing educator*
DeVilla, Lucena M. *home healthcare nurse, administrator, business owner*
Donath, Janet Sue *hospice and home health care nurse*
Dougan, Deborah Rae *neuropsychology professional*
Dybell, Elizabeth Anne Sledden *clinical psychologist*
Frenger, Paul Fred *medical computer consultant, physician*
Garnes, Delbert Franklin *clinical and consulting psychologist, educator*
Gerhart, Glenna Lee *pharmacist*
Gouti, Sammy Yasin *psychology educator, psychotherapist*
Grossett, Deborah Lou *psychologist, behavior analyst, consultant*
Gunn, Joan Marie *health care administrator*
Hempfling, Linda Lee *nurse*
Holmes, Harry Dadisman *health facility administrator*
Hoskin, Sandra Ruble *medical equipment company executive, nurse*
Hrna, Daniel Joseph *pharmacist, lawyer*
Hudson, W. Gail *social worker*
Hughes, William L. *health delivery system administrator*
Jackson, Evelyn Ardeth *nurse*
Jackson, Harper Scales, Jr. *healthcare executive*
Janes, Joseph Anthony, Jr. *optometrist*
Jhin, Michael Kontien *health care executive*
Kershaw, Carol Jean *psychologist*
Kirsner, Kenneth Mark *nurse anesthetist educator*
Knolle, Mary Anne Ericson *psychotherapist, communications consultant*
Kurzenberger, Dick *health services executive*
Lachman, Roy *research psychologist*
Le Blanc, Stacy Ann *animal science facility administrator*
Lygas, Marjorie MacGregor *critical care nurse*
Mallia, Marianne Hagar *medical writer*
Mariotto, Marco Jerome *psychology educator, researcher*
Mathis, Larry Lee *health care administrator*
Mathis, Sharon Ann *home health nurse, mental health nurse, consultant, columnist, entrepreneur*
McGuire, Dianne Marie *psychotherapist*
Miller, Janel Howell *psychologist*
Minton, Melanie Sue *neuroscience nurse*
Moore, Lois Jean *health science facility administrator*
Mortel, Karl Frederick *neuropsychologist*
Nasser, Moes Roshanali *optometrist*
Owen, Dian Grave *healthcare organization executive*
Park, Cheryl Antoinette *women's health nurse, educator*
Park, Phocion Samuel, Jr. *family and drug abuse therapist*
Pate, Patricia Ann *women's health nurse*
Phillips, Linda Lou *pharmacist*
Prather, Rita Catherine *psychology educator*
Richardson, Deborah Kaye *clinical nurse specialist, educator*
Rosin, Lindsay Zweig *clinical psychologist*
Ruppert, Susan Donna *critical care nursing educator, family adult nurse practitioner*
Schiflett, Mary Fletcher Cavender *health facility executive, researcher, educator*
Shinn, Susa Jane *medical/surgical nurse*
Smith, J. Thomas *psychotherapist*
Sollenberger, Donna Fitzpatrick *hospital and clinics executive*
Springfield, William Francis *pharmacist, consultant*
Stroud, Rebecca Ann *pediatrics nurse practitioner*
Toombs, Margaret Stutts *speech and language pathologist*
Van Fleet, Sharon Kay *psychiatric clinical nurse*
Wallace, Mark Allen *hospital executive*
Wendtland, Mona Bohlmann *dietitian, consultant*
Williams, Wright *psychologist, educator*
Windle, Pamela Evelyn *surgical nurse*
Wisecup, Barbara Jean *medical/surgical nurse*
Wolinsky, Ira *nutritionist*
Wong-Liang, Eirene Ming *psychologist*

Hughes Springs
Koelker, Gail *family nurse practitioner*

Humble
Aalund, Peggy Machell *nurse, educator*
Stevens, Elizabeth *psychotherapist, consultant*

Huntsville
Budge, Marcia Charlene *family nurse practitioner*
Vick, Marie *retired health science educator*

Hurst
Siebenthall, Curtis Alan *counselor, consultant, psychology educator*

Irving
Donnelly, Barbara Schettler *medical technologist*
Porter, James Franklin *psychologist*

Katy
Adkins, Susan Irene *pediatric orthopedic nurse*

Kaufman
New, Claudia Moss *hospice social worker*

Kemp
Sheffield, Sue *nursing educator*

Kerrville
Rhodes, James Devers *psychotherapist*

Kilgore
Wilcox, Nancy Diane *nurse, administrator*

Kingsville
Ibanez, Jane Bourquard *stress management consultant, lecturer*
Robins, James Dow *counselor*

Kingwood
Mathis, Jane Ann *nursing educator, safety and legal consultant*

Kyle
Flacy, Frank Landom *family therapist*

Lackland AFB
Burghardt, Walter Francis, Jr. *veterinarian*
Gordon, Ella Dean *women's health nurse*

Lago Vista
Kinsey, Julia Catherine *medical records coding specialist*

Lamesa
Miller, Patricia Anne *speech and language pathologist*

Lampasas
Crawford, Norma Vivian *nurse*

Laredo
Mora, David Saul *optometrist*

Lockhart
Scott, Mike *pharmacist, consultant*
Williams, Margaret Lu Wertha Hiett *nurse*

Longview
Mann, True Sandlin *psychologist, consultant*

Lubbock
Cogan, Dennis Clark *psychology educator*
Elder, Bessie Ruth *pharmacist*
Ickes, William Keith *audiology educator*
Rose, Sharon Marie *critical care nurse*
Smith, Doris Corinne Kemp *retired nurse*
Stout, Josephine Singerman *clinical psychologist*
Young, Teri Ann Butler *pharmacist*

Lufkin
Weismuller, Connie Lynn Gardner *ambulatory care nurse*

Lumberton
McDonald-Green, A. Michelle *critical care nurse*

Marshall
Weathers, Melba Rose *hospital administrator*

Mc Dade
Carson, David Costley *psychologist, health care administrator*

Mcallen
Keyes, Emmalou *nurse practitioner*

Mesquite
Williamson, Barbara Jo *community health nurse, educator*

Mexia
Chambers, Linda Dianne Thompson *social worker*

Midland
Arview, Kathleen Yvonne *geriatrics nurse*
Fredrickson, Mark Allan *health facility administrator, physician*
Sullivan, Patricia G. *maternal, child and women's health nursing educator*

Mission
Rapp, Joanna A. *retired geriatrics nurse, mental health nurse*

Montgomery
Gooch, Carol Ann *psychotherapist consultant*

Mount Vernon
Horvath, Carol Mitchell *home health administrator*

Nacogdoches
Cart-Rogers, Katherine Cooper *emergency nurse*

Migl, Donald Raymond *therapeutic optometrist, pharmacist*

New Braunfels
Hooker, Renée Michelle *postanesthesia and perinatal nurse*

Newton
Hopkins, Sallye F. *women's health nurse*

Odessa
Jackson, Dorothy Faye Greene *nursing educator*
Knox, Glenda Jane *retired health and safety specialist, educator*
Pokky, Eric Jon *pharmacist*

Pampa
Lane, Jerry Ross *alcohol and drug abuse service counselor*

Paris
Sawyer, Mary Catherine *hospital administrator*
Stallings, Nancy Roosevelt *rehabilitation nurse*

Pasadena
White, Michael James *managed care/case management consultant*

Plano
Carmicle, Linda Harper *psychotherapist*
Fay, Roberta Marie *nurse, educator*
Kincaid, Elsie Elizabeth *educational therapist*
Weiner, Robert Harold *clinical psychologist*

Ponder
Barnett, Janice Elaine *critical care nurse*

Port Arthur
Vinecour, Oneida Agnes *nurse*

Rancho Viejo
Schwab, Therese Mathes *nursing educator*

Richmond
Eversole, Sandra Joy *operating room nurse*

Roanoke
Kleinkort, Joseph Alexius *physical therapist, consultant*

Rockdale
Brown, Rubye Ellen *retired nursing administrator*

Roscoe
Richardson, Robert Alvin *pharmacist*

Rosenberg
Landers, Susan Mae *psychotherapist, professional counselor*

Round Rock
Bruce-Juhlke, Debbie *nursing consultant, social worker*
Schroer, Jane Hastings *nurse practitioner*

Rowlett
Newkirk, Trixie Darnell *critical care nurse*
Ogden, LouAnn Marie *dietitian, consultant*

Rusk
Harper, Christine Johnson *psychiatric clinical nurse, administrator*

San Angelo
Tillery-Tate, Johnnie Lea *mental health and geriatrics nurse*

San Antonio
Barnes, Betty Rae *counselor*
Brooks, Phyllis M. Britto *gerontological nurse, nursing educator*
Brown, Beth Marie *dietitian, hospital administrator*
Celmer, Virginia *psychologist*
Clark, Lady Ellen Marie *occupational health nurse, consultant*
Davis, John Wesley, III *health facility administrator*
Davis, Yolette Marie Toussaint *critical care, flight, orthopedic and surgical nurse*
Delgado, Eric Dirk *optometrist*
Eaves, Sandra Austra *social worker*
Flaherty, Sergina Maria *ophthalmic medical technologist*
Fraley, Debra Lee *critical care nurse*
Gilliland, Irene Lydia *nursing educator*
Haynes, Cheryl Ettora *healthcare industry marketing representative*
Hopper, Vanessa J. *oncological nurse*
Jackson, Brenda S. *nursing educator*
Johnson, Katherine Anne *health research administrator, lawyer*
Kossaeth, Tammy Gale *intensive care nurse*
Lau-Patterson, Mayin *psychotherapist*
Martinez Rogers, Norma Elia *nursing educator*
McCaughrin, William Cass *health management educator*
McIntosh, Dennis Keith *veterinary practitioner, consultant*
McIntosh, Ruth Lynne *maternal, pediatric nurse*
Mika, Walter Valentine *nurse, nursing administrator, quality assurance professional*
Minton, Kathy Dickerson *rehabilitation administrator*
Nisbett, Dorothea Jo *nursing educator*
Paris, Karen Marie *nurse, educator*
Parks, Madelyn N. *nurse, retired army officer, university official*
Price, Craig Gammell *medical liability management consultant, editor, publisher*
Ribble, Ronald George *psychologist, educator, writer*
Rivera, Marlyn Feliciano *medical facility administrator*
Rosenow, Doris Jane *critical care nurse, nursing consultant*
Sawyer-Morse, Mary Kaye *nutritionist, educator*
Schönhoff, Kathleen Marie *nursing educator*
Schultz, Marilyn Ann *medical/surgical nurse*
Scott, Ronald William *educator, physical therapist, lawyer, writer*
Shackelford, Alphonso Leon *pharmacist, medical writer*
Simmons, Cecelia E. *quality improvement, infection control and employee health nurse*
Skelley, Dean Sutherland *clinical laboratory administrator*
Skelton, John Goss, Jr. *psychologist*
Slate, Joanne Talbott *mental health counselor*
Swansburg, Russell Chester *medical administrator educator*
Todd, Jan Theresa *counselor*
Valdez, Maria del Rosario *perinatal nurse*
Walker, Mary Erline *critical care nurse*
Wilson, Lloyd Kenton *neuropsychologist, consultant*
Wood, Thomas Willard *health care industry executive*

San Marcos
Mooney, Robert Thurston *health care educator*
Mullins, Wayman C. *psychologist, educator, consultant*

Shamrock
Tallant, Mary Kay *school nurse*

Sheppard AFB
Rinta, Christine Evelyn *nurse, air force officer*

Smithville
Rundhaug, Joyce Elizabeth *biochemist, former nurse*

Spicewood
Doerr, Barbara Ann *health facility director*

Temple
Frost, Juanita Corbitt *hospital foundation coordinator*
Harrison, Roscoe Conklin, Jr. *special projects administrator*
Holder, Eugene Paul *clinical pharmacist, researcher*
Morrison, Gary Brent *hospital administrator*
Tobin, Margaret Ann *cardiac medical critical care nurse*

The Woodlands
Martineau, Julie Peperone *social worker*

Tomball
Henry, Patricia Ann *nutrition coordinator, dietitian*

Troup
Smith, Linda Ann *dietitian, consultant*

Tyler
Markham, Carole Pillsbury *medical-surgical nurse educator*
Smith, Janna Hogan *nursing administrator, surgical nurse*

Universal City
Lamoureux, Gloria Kathleen *nurse, air force officer*
Roehr, Kathleen Marie *nursing administrator*

Victoria
Tinney, Richard Dale, Jr. *mental health marketing administrator*

Waco
Corley, Carol Lee *school nurse*
Hynan, Linda Susan *psychology educator*
Kahn, Alan Harvey *therapist, administrator, consultant*

Waxahachie
Heatherley, Melody Ann *nursing administrator*

Weatherford
Buckner-Reitman, Joyce *psychologist, educator*

White Deer
Martin, Aloise Marie Britten *school nurse*

Wichita Falls
Cagle, Paulette Bernice *mental health administrator and psychologist*
Cleary, Thomas J. *social worker, administrator*

Winnsboro
Sparkman, Lila Gillis *healthcare facility administrator*

Yoakum
Leahy, Lawrence Marshall *health care administrator, marketing consultant*

VIRGINIA

Abingdon
Ramos-Cano, Hazel Balatero *social worker, early childhood educator, food service director, executive chef, innkeeper, caterer*
Vaughn, JoAnn Wolfe *family nurse practitioner*

Alexandria
Daniel, Dorothy Isom *nurse specialist, consultant*
Hindle, Paula Alice *nursing administrator*
Revere, Virginia Lehr *clinical psychologist*

Altavista
Taylor, Kimberly A. *geriatrics nurse*

Arlington
Adreon, Beatrice Marie Rice *pharmacist*
Chipman, Susan Elizabeth *psychologist*
Contis, George *medical services company executive*
Downing, Diane Virginia *public health nurse*
Frantz, Cecilia Aranda *psychologist*
Hassig, Susan Elizabeth *health research administrator, epidemiologist*
Morton, Janice Kenefake *nurse administrator*
Papadopoulos, Patricia Marie *healthcare professional*
Schneider, Clara Garbus *dietitian, consultant*
Seifert, Patricia Clark *cardiac surgery nurse*
Steinglass, Robert Cary *public health administrator*

Aroda
Nisly, Loretta Lynn *medical and surgical nurse, geriatrics nurse*

Berryville
White, Eugene Vaden *pharmacist*

Blacksburg
Dallman, Mark Jay *veterinarian*

Bracey
Myatt, Sue Henshaw *nursing home administrator*

Centreville
Guillett, Sharron Elaine *nursing educator*

Charlottesville
Chalam, Ann *healthcare administrator*
Cook, Lynn J. *nursing educator*
Cumming, Cathleen Mary *dietitian, nutritionist*
Halseth, Michael James *medical center administrator*
Hawkins, Deborah Craun *community health nurse*
Hinnant, Clarence Henry, III *health care executive*
Kiewra, Gustave Paul *psychologist, educator*
Killgallon, Christine Behrens *healthcare administrator*
Robinson, Karen Vajda *nutritionist*
Wilson, Melvin Nathaniel *psychology educator*

Chesapeake
Jerome-Ebel, Angela Marie *pediatrics nurse*
Martin, Angela Carter *nursing educator*
McCarthy, Mary Elizabeth *psychologist*
Sexton, Brenda Atwell *nursing educator*

Chester
Sadler, Charles Benjamin, Jr. *pharmacist, real estate associate, marketing professional*

Chesterfield
Beverly, Betty Moore *counselor*
Pinkleton, Randy Franklin *veterinarian*

Claremont
Seward, Troilen Gainey *psychologist*

Culpeper
Frazier-Petty, Esther Irene *nursing educator, registered nurse*

Danville
Carroll-Dovenmuehle, Bettye Turpin *counselor*
Dowdy, Cecelia Young *critical care and medical/surgical nurse*
Sexauer, Bradley Lester *healthcare administrator*

Deltaville
Crittenden, Katherine Lucina *nurse*

Dublin
Henderson, Nancy Carr *dietitian, medical transcriber, writer*

Duffield
Orr, Emma Jane *pharmacist, educator*

Earlysville
Ralston, Ruth Anne *women's health nurse*

Fairfax
Knee, Ruth Irelan (Mrs. Junior K. Knee) *social worker, health care consultant*
Littlefield, Danielle Joan *renal nutritionist*
Madison, Octavia Dianne *mental health services professional*
Nidiffer, Sheri Lynn *medical/surgical nurse*
O'Hare, Christine Marie *critical care nurse*
Priesman, Elinor Lee Soll *family dynamics administrator, mediator, educator*
Raiche, Bernard Marcel *psychotherapist, heath care consultant*
Taylor, Carolyn A. *women's health nurse, administrator*
Turjanica, Mary Ann *clinical nurse specialist, consultant*
Wu, Chien-yun (Jennie Wu) *nursing educator*

Fairfax Station
Johansen, Eivind Herbert *special education services executive, former army officer*

Falls Church
Dunton, James Gerald *association executive*
Fink, Charles Augustin *behavioral systems scientist*

Forest
Holland, Charlotte Sue *counselor*

Fredericksburg
Karpiscak, Linda Sue *pediatrics nurse*
Speirs, Carol Lucille *nurse, naval officer*

Gloucester Point
Podbesek, Katherine J. Woofter *critical care nurse, administrator*

Great Falls
Kagan, Constance Henderson *psychotherapist, consultant*

Hampton
Brown, Frances Anne *nurse, therapist*
Johnson, Jetsie White *nurse, consultant*
Kulp, Eileen Bodnar *social worker*

Harrisonburg
Brubaker, Beryl Mae Hartzler *administrator, educator*
Morrison, Linda Marie *dietitian*

Haymarket
Arnold, Nancy Nakamura *mental health therapist*

Herndon
Hawley, John L., Jr. *mental health facility administrator, psychologist*

Keysville
Mattox, Ronald Eugene *counselor*

Lancaster
Beane, Judith Mae *psychologist*

Leesburg
Daddio, Peter Michael *chiropractor*

Lorton
Kirby, Diana Cherne *nurse, former military officer*

Low Moor
Loudermilk, Peggy Joyce *pediatrics nurse, public health nurse*

Lynchburg
Goding, Judith Germaine *residential facility administrator, musician*
Sprinkle, Sarah Dawn *medical/surgical nurse, civic worker*
Weimar, Robert Henry *counselor, clinical hypnotherapist*
Whittemore, Linda Genevieve *clinical psychologist*

Manassas
Bass-Rubenstein, Deborah Sue *social worker, educator, consultant*
Lytton, Linda Rountree *marriage and family therapist, test consultant*
Twitchel, Nancy Lou *medical/surgical and emergency room nurse*

Max Meadows
Dillon, Janie *nurse*

Mc Gaheysville
Shortell, Annabelle Petersen *family nurse practitioner*

Mc Lean
Cuffe, Robin Jean *nursing educator*
Dean, Lydia Margaret Carter (Mrs. Halsey Albert Dean) *nutrition coordinator, author, consultant*
Gladeck, Susan Odell *social worker*
Smith, Carey Daniel *acoustician, undersea warfare technologist*
Smith, Dorothy Louise *pharmacy consultant, author*
Walsh, Marie Leclerc *nurse*
Wyman, A. Carol R. *nurse, childbirth educator*
Zeleny, Marjorie Pfeiffer (Mrs. Charles Ellingson Zeleny) *psychologist*

Midlothian
Andrako, John *health sciences educator*

Montpelier
Schloemer, Nancy Ford *retired health facility administrator*

Newport News
Coleman, James Eugene *national laboratory administrator*
Lidstrom, Peggy Ray *mental health administrator, psychotherapist*
Ludford, Geoffrey Wayne *psychotherapist, counselor, educator*
Mahlan-Ditch, Michelle T. *maternal/child home health nurse*
Phillips, Denise *critical care nurse*
Warren, Daniel Churchman *health facility administrator*

Norfolk
Harper, William Thomas, III *psychologist, educator*
Kern, Howard Paul *hospital administrator*
Knox, Richard Douglas, Jr. *healthcare executive*
Martin, Wayne A. *clinical social worker*
McDuffie, Adelina Ferraro *pediatrics nurse*
Nichols, Brenda Sue *nursing educator*
Wilson, Angela Saburn *nursing educator*

Oakton
Trifoli-Cunniff, Laura Catherine *psychologist, consultant*

Occoquah
Elliott, Sigrid Isolde *clinical social worker*

Palmyra
Chapin, Suzanne Phillips *retired psychologist*

Petersburg
Eastman, Edward Shirrell, Jr. *clinical psychologist*
Northrop, Mary Ruth *mental retardation nurse*
Parr, Rick Vincent *rehabilitation services professional*

Portsmouth
Barnes, Judith P. *nursing administrator*
Glasson, Linda *hospital security and safety official*

Powhatan
Huff, Cynthia Fae *medical and orthopedic nurse*

Purcellville
Campbell, Valerie Lynn *veterinarian*

Radford
Reed, Helen I. *medical, surgical nurse*

Reston
Kader, Nancy Stowe *nurse, consultant*

Richmond
Becker, Herman Eli *retired pharmacist*
Bovender, Jack Oliver, Jr. *health care executive*
Catarsi, Charlotte Marie *pharmacist*
Critchfield, Tami Sue *nutrition and diabetes educator*
Edloe, Leonard Levi *pharmacist*
Ferree, Patricia Ann *corporate managed care analyst, nurse*
Fischer, Carl Robert *health care facility administrator*
Freund, Emma Frances *medical technologist*
Goode, Jean-Venable R. (Kelly) *pharmacy educator*
Hardage, Page Taylor *health care administrator*
McMurray, Carol Dolber *human services administrator*
Murdoch-Kitt, Norma Hood *psychologist*
Palmer, Tekla Fredsall *retired dietitian, consultant*
Pontiflet, Addie Roberson *nurse, educator*
Saunderlin, George Raymond *nurse*
Simpson, John Noel *healthcare administrator*
Singh, Nirbhay Nand *psychology educator, researcher*
Vartanian, Isabel Sylvia *dietitian*

Weeks, Gwendolen Brannon *nurse, educator*
Whiteman, Stephanie Ann *neonatal nurse*
Winter, Joan Elizabeth *psychotherapist*

Roanoke
Duff, Doris Eileen (Shull) *critical care nurse*
Manns, Linda Greene *community health nurse coordinator*

Rockville
Smith, Lucy Anselmo *mental health nurse*

Salem
Dagenhart, Betty Jane Mahaffey *nursing educator, administrator*
Jordan, Belinda Lee *nutritionist, dietitian*

Smithfield
Lauder, Robert Scott *health education administrator*

Springfield
Rich, Irene M. *women's health nurse, administrator*

Stafford
Fahey, Sharon Anne *nurse administrator*
Woldt, Gerald D. (Jay Woldt) *nurse anesthetist*

Sterling
Finn, Gloria Inez *geriatrics nurse*
Gunberg, Edwin Woodrow, Jr. *counseling psychologist, consultant, researcher*

Vienna
Rovis, Christopher Patrick *clinical social worker*

Virginia Beach
Abbott, Regina A. *neurodiagnostic technologist, consultant, business owner*
Brookes, Kimberly Ann *perinatal/neonatal clinical nurse specialist*
Lawrence, Joyce Wagner *health facility administrator, educator*
Radford, Gloria Jane *retired medical/surgical nurse*

Warrenton
Rodgers, Lynne Saunders *women's health nurse*

Williamsburg
Austin, Sigrid Linnevold *counselor*
Rosche, Loretta G. *medical, surgical nurse*
Rosen, Ellen Freda *psychologist, educator*

Woodbridge
Flori, Anna Marie DiBlasi *nurse anesthetist, educational administrator*
Woods, Barbara A. Shell *psychotherapist*

Woodstock
Golden, Sandra Jean *nurse*

Wytheville
Huddle, Rita Kegley *medical, surgical and home health nurse, administrator*

Yorktown
Bikowski, Vera Ellen Polakas *speech pathologist*

WEST VIRGINIA

Beckley
Baker, Dreama Gail *psychologist*

Charleston
Elliott, David Patrick *pharmacist, educator*
Goodwin, Phillip Hugh *hospital administrator*
Walton, Suzanne Marie Chapman *clinical pharmacist, educator*

Clarksburg
Sherlock, Lynn *critical care, emergency nurse*

Fairmont
Roberts, Scott Boyd *psychologist*

Huntington
Engle, Jeannette Cranfill *medical technologist*
Fabry, Susan Kingsland *pediatric nurse practitioner*
Stultz, Patricia Adkins *health care risk administrator*

Hurricane
Nance, Martha McGhee *rehabilitation nurse*

Institute
Brown, Elizabeth Taylor *psychology educator*
McNamara, Paula Ruth Wagner *therapeutic recreation programs director*

Lewisburg
Byrd, Julie Anderson *nurse*

Marlinton
Worth, Judson Lee Blackley *social worker*

Morgantown
Barba, Roberta Ashburn *retired social worker*
Lattal, Kennon Andy *psychology educator*
Massey, W(ilmet) Annette *nurse, former educator*
Odom, James Vernon *research psychologist*
Ponte, Charles Dennis *pharmacist, educator*
Sarkar, Mohamadi Alibhai *pharmacy educator, researcher*
Sobong, Loreto Calibo *nursing researcher*
Westfall, Bernard G. *university hospital executive*

Moundsville
Kraft, Frederick Glenn *pharmacist*

Oak Hill
Beckelheimer, Christine Elizabeth Campbell *nurse*

Parkersburg
Bui, Quinn Van *community health promotion specialist*

Pratt
Terrell-McDaniel, Robin F. *cardiac rehabilitation and critical care nurse*

Ridgeley
Hammond, Anna Josephine *nurse practitioner*

Ronceverte
Fowler, Linda McKeever *hospital administrator, management educator*

Saint Albans
Alderson, Gloria Frances Dale *rehabilitation specialist*

South Charleston
Bleidt, Barry Anthony *pharmacy educator*

Wardensville
Vance, Dama Lee *obstetrical/gynecological nurse, ultrasound sonographer*

Wayne
Crockett, Patricia Jo Fry *psychiatric-mental health nurse*

West Liberty
Brace, Jeanette Warning *nurse educator*

Wheeling
Goddard, Thelma Taylor *critical care nurse, nursing educator*
Poland, Michelle Lind *medical/surgical and critical care nurse*
Urval, Krishna Raj *health facility administrator, educator*

TERRITORIES OF THE UNITED STATES

PUERTO RICO

Hormigueros
Acosta, Ursula *psychologist*

Rio Piedras
Davila, Norma *developmental psychologist and program evaluator*

San Juan
de Snyder, Soami Santiago *audiologist*
Díaz de Gonzalez, Ana María *psychologist, educator*
Fariña de Woodbury, Margarita *psychotherapist*
Gonzalez, Michael John *nutrition educator, nutriologist*
Rivera-Urrutia, Beatriz Dalila *psychology and rehabilitation counseling educator*

Trujillo Alto
Antoun, Mikhail *medicinal chemistry and pharmacognosy educator*

VIRGIN ISLANDS

Charlotte Amalie
Mason, Stephanie Olive *medical/surgical nurse, educator*

MILITARY ADDRESSES OF THE UNITED STATES

PACIFIC

FPO
Francis, La Francis Diana *nursing administrator, career officer*

ADDRESS UNPUBLISHED

Abernethy, Kathryn Grant *mental health nurse, rehabilitation nurse*
Adamo, Debra Orvis *nurse research specialist*
Adams, Corlyn Holbrook *nursing facility administrator*
Ahlgren, Denise Mary *nursing consultant*
Alcantara, Felicisima Garcia *dietitian, nutrition consultant*
Alexander, Elizabeth Faye Tutor *nursing educator*
Alexander, Robert Harold *clinical psychologist*
Andrau, Maya Hedda *physical therapist*
Andruzzi, Ellen Adamson *nurse, marital and family therapist*
Angst, Karen K. *mental health nurse*
Armstrong, Jennifer Jo *adult nurse practitioner*
Ashe, Betty L. *nursing educator*
Ayres, Jayne Lynn Ankrum *community health nurse*
Baker, Judith J. *nurse manager*
Baldwin, Deanna Louise *dietitian*
Bales, Roberta Kinter *critical care nurse*
Barnes, Julia Diane Walls *community health, oncology and geriatrics nurse*
Barnett, Shirley R. *nursing educator*
Barton, Nancy Shover *nursing administrator*
Beaty, Susan Ballard *nursing educator*
Bell, Karen June *critical care nurse*
Belles, Anita Louise *health care researcher, consultant*
Bennett, Michele Margulis *women's health nurse*
Berke, Sarah Ballard *geriatrics nurse, mental health nurse*
Bernfield, Lynne *psychotherapist*
Bernheim, Mary Josephine *nurse anesthetist*
Bihuniak, Jeanette Lee *medical records administrator*
Bishop, (Ina) Sue Marquis *psychiatric and mental health nurse educator, researcher, administrator*
Blackstock, Linda Mahoney *healthcare facility official, consultant*
Blanchard, Louis A. *medical/surgical nurse, educator*
Blue, Charlotte Ann *intensive care nurse*
Blumenau, Iris Warech *nursing consultant*
Boatman, Deborah Ann *hospice nurse*
Bonds, Sophia Jane Riddle *geriatrics, medical/surgical nurse*
Bourgeois, Susan K. *critical care nurse*
Bradley, Darnita Sue *community health nurse*
Bradley, Sandra Lynn *nursing administrator*
Braswell, Jackie Terry *medical, surgical nurse*
Braun, Mary Lucile Dekle (Lucy Braun) *therapist, consultant, counselor*
Braziel, Susan Lansdown *mental health/rehabilitation nurse, administrator*
Brigance, Marcelena *critical care nurse*
Brinkley, Glenda Willis *medical/surgical nurse, women's health nurse*
Britton, Patricia Ann *nursing educator, nursing administrator*
Brown, Carol Rentiers *health facility administrator*
Brown, Carolyn Brewer *family nurse practitioner*
Brown, Hardin *occupational health nurse*
Brown, Lynda Nell *nursing educator*
Burd, Shirley Farley *clinical specialist, mental health nurse*
Burton, Carol Nystrom *newborn nursery nurse*
Cain, Charles E. *manager administrator*
Calamita, Kathryn Elizabeth *nursing administrator*
Calkins, JoAnn Ruby *nursing administrator*
Camayd-Freixas, Yoel *management, strategy & planning consultant*
Camp, Virginia Ann *medical/surgical nurse*
Campbell, Claire Patricia *nurse practitioner, educator*
Carrillo, Geraldine Mary Deehan *trauma, medical/surgical and women's health nurse*
Carter, Marilyn Ray *nurse*
Casasanta, Mary Frances *medical/surgical nurse*
Cash, Sandra Kay *critical care nurse*
Caudill Housel, Judy L. *emergency nurse, administrator*
Cauthorne-Burnette, Tamera Dianne *family nurse practitioner, healthcare consultant*
Cecil, Maxine *critical care nurse*
Chadwick, Nanenia Elaine B. *mental health nurse*
Chamberlain, John Meredith *health facility executive, consultant*
Chambers, Judith Tarnpoll *speech pathologist*
Chamings, Patricia Ann *nurse, educator*
Chapman, LuRee *health care administrator*
Cleveland, Charlene S. *community health nurse*
Cloud, Marina Taylor *mental health counselor*
Clover-Lee, Shevonne Jones *geriatrics nurse*
Cole, Kimberly Alice *critical care and post-anesthesia care nurse*
Coleman, Jean Black *nurse, physician assistant*
Collins, Melissa Ann *oncological nurse*
Conner, Colin L. *nursing educator*
Cooper, Cheryl *mental health nurse*
Cotton, Laura Leigh *oncology nurse*
Cox, Carol A. *oncological nurse*
Crawford, Pamela J. *critical care nurse*
Crimm, Marcy Ware Jones *geritrics nurse, educator*
Curlee, Dorothy Sumner *social worker*
Davis, Gloria J. *gerontology clinical specialist*
Deal, Robin Sink *women's health nurse*
De Graves, Fred John *veterinarian, educator*
Deidan, Cecilia Theresa *neuropsychologist*
Delaney, Robert Anthony *clinical pharmacist, researcher*
Delgado, Gloria Eneida *medical nurse*
Denmark, Kathy Bryant *critical care and medical/surgical nurse*
DiMaria, Rose Ann *nursing educator*
Dison, Charlotte Anne *nursing administrator*
Donohue, Maureen Ann *nursing administrator, operating room nurse*
Donovan, Marion Conran *school social worker*
Dove, Lorraine Faye *gerontology nurse*
Dowd, Brian John *healthcare executive*
Dozier, Nancy Kerns *retired geriatrics nurse*
Echevarria, Alvarado Ana H. *clinical psychologist, criminologist*
Edmonds, Velma McInnis *nursing educator*
Ekery, Adriana Teresa *healthcare administrator, oncology nurse*
Emerson, Ann Parker *dietitian, educator*
English, Jujuan Bondman *women's health nurse, educator*
Evans, Jeanette Marie *operating room nurse*
Everette, Marlene Miller *nursing administrator, surgical nurse*
Fanning, Judy G. *mental health nurse*
Farrington, Bertha Louise *nursing administrator*
Finney, Carl Richard *emergency medical technician*
Fisher, Margaret Ella *medical/surgical nurse*
FitzSimons, Corinne Marie *medical/surgical nurse*
Foldesy, Lynn *mental health nurse*
Fragale, Mary Lynch *emergency nurse*
Frank-Fitzner, Fontaine Lynne *geriatrics, medical and surgical nurse*
Fulp, Estelle Marie *retired nursing administrator*
Galatas, Laureen *psychiatric nurse*
Gandy, Bonnie Sergiacomi *oncological and intravenous therapy nurse*
Gardner, Kathryn Johanna *nursing educator, community health nurse*
Garnett, Linda Kopec *nurse, researcher*
Garrett, Roberta Kampschulte *nurse*
Geary, Pamela Blalack *community health and medical/surgical nurse*
George, Susan E. Gould *health facility administrator*
Giles, Susan Michele *medical/surgical nurse*
Gilliam, Nancy D. *operating room nurse*
Gilmore, David Schneiter *administrator*
Gilmore, Louisa Ruth *retired nurse, retired firefighter*
Gomez-Souto, Joseph *hospital administrator*
Goodwyn Roseboro, Wanda *medical/surgical nurse*
Goslawski, Violet Ann *nurse, substance abuse counselor*
Graham, Brenda J. *nurse*
Grantham, Shonnette Denise *mental health nurse, care facility supervisor*
Gray, Glenn Richard *rehabilitation nurse*
Gregory, Jackie Sue *critical care nurse*
Griffin, Christopher Oakley *hospital professional*
Griffin, Eren G. *nursing educator*
Griffin, Myrna McIntosh *critical care nurse*
Grizzle, Patricia Sutton *enterostomal therapy nurse, educator*
Grogan, Debby Elaine *home health care nurse, medical/surgical nurse*
Guerrero, Lilia *school nurse*
Haber, Paul *health psychologist, educator*
Hagan, John Joseph *health care executive*
Halden, Martha Ann *pediatrics nurse, educator*
Haley, Patricia Ann *psychiatric therapist, school counselor, administrator*
Hallas, Gail *healthcare and nursing home consultant, executive*
Hamblin, J. Anthony *medical/surgical nurse*
Hamilton, Nancy Richey *critical care nurse, educator*
Hanna, Lee Ann *critical care nurse*
Hanrahan, Lawrence Martin *healthcare consultant*
Harrell, Ina Perry *maternal/women's and medical/surgical nurse*
Hartford, Shaun Alison *pediatrics nurse, educator*
Harvey, Dreama Joyce *operating room nurse*
Hayes, Judy Diane *medical/surgical and ophthalmological nurse*
Heckley, Teresa JoAnn *health facility administrator*
Hegwood, Elizabeth Z. *nurse educator and manager*
Heidler, Cecile E. *public health nurse*
Herd, Joanne May Beers *intravenous therapy nurse, educator*
Herndon, Rhonda Dianne *dietitian*
Herrin, Frances E. *critical care nurse*
Herring, Lucille M. *retired community health nurse*
Herth, Kaye Ann *nursing educator, academic administrator, hospice nurse*
Hertz, Kenneth Theodore *health care executive*
Hicks, Claude Alvis *retired children's home administrator*
Higdon, Shirley A. *medical/surgical nurse*
Hill, Lois Jane *nutritionist, dietitian*
Holden, Janell M. *geriatrics nurse*
Hollis, Mary Fern Caudill *community health nurse*
Holt, Teresa Jan *community health nurse*
Homestead, Susan E. (Susan Freedlender) *psychotherapist*
Howard, Charlene *community health nurse, administrator*
Howe, John Prentice, III *health science center executive, physician*
Huey, Margie Lou *medical, surgical and critical care nurse*
Hutzler, Lisa Ann *mental health nurse, adult clinical psychologist*
Ivey, Jan Denise *health services administrator*
Jacobs, Sister Margaret Mary *nursing administrator*
Jeannette, Joan Marie *pediatrics nurse*
Jew, Henry *pharmacist*
Johnson, Crystal Duane *psychologist*
Johnson, Naomi Bowers *nurse*
Karlson, Kevin Wade *trial, forensic, and clinical psychologist, consultant*
Kirby, Priscilla Crosby *dietitian*
Kleer, Norma Vesta *critical care nurse*
Knight, Sandra Bloomster *emergency and critical care nurse*
Koerber, Marilynn Eleanor *gerontology nursing educator, consultant, nurse*
Kolasa, Kathryn Marianne *food and nutrition educator, consultant*
Krouse, Helene June *nursing educator*
Kuerley-Schaffer, Dawn R. *medical/surgical nurse*
Lafont, Lydia Ann *nurse manager*
Lambert, E. Warren *psychologist*
Landreneau, Betty C. *nursing educator, medical/surgical nurse*
Landrum, Beverly Hollowell *nurse*
Latiolais, Minnie Fitzgerald *nurse, hospital administrator*
LaValley, Judy Tucker *cardiology critical care nurse*
Lavender, T. J. (Jody) *critical care nurse, administrator*
Lawson, Nancy Katherine *medical/surgical nurse*
Lee, Brenda B. *critical care nurse*
Lehigh, George Edward *medical group consultant, management consultant*
Leonard, Margaret Beasley *gerontology nurse*
Lewis, Russell Carl, Jr. *family nurse practitioner*
Lex, Angela Kay *oncological nurse*
Lilly, Tamara Faith *psychiatric and geriatric nurse*
Limbrick, Marjorie *critical care nurse*
Linto, Nancy *nursing case manager*
Linz, Gerhard David *psychologist*
Liverman, Lynda M. *community health nurse*
Lowman, Rodney Lewis *psychologist, author, educator*
Luton, Mary Kathryn *hospital patient relations administrator*
Lyons, Natalie Beller *family counselor*
Mace, Teresa Ann *geriatrics nurse*
Malone, David *healthcare company executive*
Maness, Diane Mease *pediatrics nurse*
Marks-DeMourelle, Karen *diabetes nurse*
Martin, Colleen E. *medical/surgical, oncological, post-anesthesia nurse, emergency room nurse*
Martin, William Collier *hospital administrator*
Masten, W. Yondell *nursing educator*
Maxwell, Cynthia Neagle *mitigation professional*
Maxwell, Daniel Gareth *psychotherapist*
McBride, Sandra Teague *critical care nurse*
McCrary, Sharon Hash *medical and surgical nurse*
McDaniel, Geraldine Howell *geriatrics rehabilitation nursing consultant*
McGarity, Ginger G. *medical/surgical nurse*
McHugh, Elizabeth Ann *infection control occupational health nurse*
McLendon, Dorothy *school psychologist*
McQueen-Gibson, Ethlyn *medical/surgical nurse*
Melton, Nancy Kerley *medical/surgical and oncological nurse*
Mendoza, Marilyn L. *nurse practitioner*
Merilh, Marietta Paula *critical care nurse*
Middleton, Charlene *retired medical and surgical nurse, educator*
Mikan, Kathleen Joyce Kehrer *medical/surgical nurse, educator*
Miller, Janice Lynne *medical/surgical nurse*
Miller, Rita Gayle *respiratory therapist, biofeedback specialist*
Miltner, Rebecca Suzanne *women's health nurse, pediatrics nurse*
Milton, Marcia E. *critical care nurse*
Mitchell, Adele Dickinson *health facility administrator*
Moak, Elizabeth *critical care and operating room nurse*
Moffitt, Susan Raye *critical care nurse*
Mogy, Catherine Waddell *nurse anesthetist, critical care nurse*
Mohamed, Donna Fahimah *counselor*
Monroe, Paula Ruth *psychologist*
Monteith, MaryAnn *critical care nurse, nursing educator*
Monzingo, Agnes Yvonne *veterinary technician*
Morandi, John Arthur, Jr. *nursing administrator, educator, nurse*
Morgan, Evelyn Buck *nursing educator*
Morgan, Wanda Busby *health care executive, educator*
Moss, Nancy Evans *nurse midwife, women's health nurse*
Muller, Frederica Daniela *psychology educator*
Munro, Cindy Louise *nursing educator*
Murphy, Mary Kathleen *nursing educator*

Nall, LaWanda Carol *nursing administrator*
Natale, Laurel A. *nursing case manager*
Nichols, Sandra Lee *community health nurse*
Obianwu-Land, Marian Marie *nurse*
O'Brien, MaryAnn Antoinette *nursing educator*
O'Neill, Donald Edmund *health science executive*
O'Quinn, Nancy Diane *nurse, educator*
Owens, Flora Concepcion *critical care nurse*
Owens, John Franklin *health care administrator, consultant, nurse*
Oxhandler, Myra *mental health nurse*
Ozbolt, Judy G. *nursing educator*
Padgett, W. Lee *critical care nurse*
Pappachristou, Joyce Flores *dietitian, educator*
Parker, Sandra Gayle *emergency room nurse*
Patrick, Brenda Jean *educational consultant*
Patterson, Evangelina G. *nursing educator*
Paul, Evelyn Rose *critical care nurse*
Pawlyshyn, William John *nurse*
Pelletier, Nancy Anne *obstetrical and gynecological nurse, educator*
Penn, William Robert *critical care nurse*
Petree, Betty Chapman *anesthetist*
Pignataro, Evelyn Dorothy *trauma clinician, operating room nurse*
Pippin, Linda Sue *pediatrics nurse, educator*
Pitasi, Judy *nurse*
Pittas, Peggy Alice *psychology educator*
Pittman, Barbara Schoonover *counselor*
Polk, Melissa Leigh *nurse*
Polucci, Ashley V. *staff nurse*
Poole, Jennifer Clark *nurse*
Porter, Betty Melissa Griffith *nursing education administrator*
Poston, Iona *nursing educator*
Price, Jeannine Alleenica *clinical psychologist, retired computer consultant*
Price, Sheryl O'Rear *pediatrics, women's health and community health nurse*
Proctor-Saufley, Diana *medical/surgical nurse, consultant*
Pursley-Crotteau, Margaret Suzanne *psychiatric nurse, substance abuse professional*
Ramirez, Ana Milagros *psychologist*
Randolph, Nancy Adele *nutritionist, consultant*
Raper, Julia Taylor *pediatric and neonatal nurse*
Rawls, Nancy Lee Stirk *nursing educator*
Ray, Marilyn Anne *nursing educator, nursing researcher*
Riggs, Suzanne Marie *critical care nurse*
Rippee, Yvette M. *nurse*
Roberts, Mary Lou *school psychologist*
Robinette, Betty Lou *occupational health and infection control nurse*
Robinson, Victoria Lee *critical care, medical/surgical nurse*
Rogers, Norma Elia Martínez *nursing educator*
Rowell, John Thomas *psychologist, consultant*
Saari, Joy Ann *family nurse practitioner, geriatrics medical and surgical nurse*
Sadler, Dolores Ann (Dee Sadler) *retired clinical social worker, psychotherapist*
Sadler, William Jacques *social worker*
Salts, Nancy Lee *critical care, emergency nurse*
Samuels, Michael Edwin *health administration educator, consultant*
Sandman, David Edward, Jr. *rehabilitation nurse*
Santos, Barbara Lynn *nurse*
Santos, Lisa Wells *critical care nurse*
Sass, Anne Michele *pediatric nurse practitioner, clinical nurse specialist*
Savage, Dixie Lee Kinney *nursing administrator*
Shaffer, Deborah *nurse*
Shanks, Kathryn Mary *health care administrator*
Shapiro, Marcia Haskel *speech and language pathologist*
Sharpe, Judith A. *mental health nurse, administrator, psychiatric clinical specialist*
Shaw, Mary Ann *psychologist*
Sheppard, Kathryn Anne *pediatrics nurse, educator*
Sibert, Luther Lewren *health services administrator*
Simpson, Jack Benjamin *medical technologist, business executive*
Singleton, LaVerna *community health nurse*
Sklencar, Mary *nurse*
Slaven, Bettye DeJon *psychotherapist*
Sloane, Arlene L. *rehabilitation nurse, specialist*
Smaistrla, Jean Ann *family therapist*
Small, Linda Juanita Bond *nursing administrator*
Smith, Deborah S. *maternal and women's health nurse*
Smith, Donna Tratnyek *flight nurse, pediatric specialist nurse*
Smith, Geraldine Field *medical/surgical nurse*
Smith, Leonard, Jr. *medical/surgical and oncology nurse*
Smolik, Debbie Bowman *consulting dietitian*
Snow, Julie Ann *maternal-child nurse*
Snyder, Kathleen Louise *community health nurse*
Soebbing, Janice Bromert *occupational health nurse*
Sojourner, Martha A. *healthcare administrator*
Sovde-Pennell, Barbara Ann *sonographer*
Spelios, Lisa Garone *nurse, educator*
Spence, Marjorie A. *medical/surgical nurse*
Spencer-Cisek, Patricia A. *oncological nurse*
Spencer-Dahlem, Anita Joyce *medical, surgical and critical care nurse*
Stagner, Shirley *oncological nurse practitioner*
Stanley, Melinda Louise *mental health nurse, oncology researcher*
Steele, Donna K. *endocrinology nurse specialist, educator*
Stein, Gordon Edward *mental health and chemical dependency nurse*
Steinberger, Emil *health facility executive, educator*
Steiner, Kenneth Keith *nursing administrator*
Stewart, Cindy Kathleen *school social worker, educator*
Stokes, Grace Hamrick *retired occupational health nurse*
Stowell, Penelope Mary *nursing administrator, community health nurse*
Struth, Raymond John, Jr. *dietitian*
Summers, Amy Elder *neonatal nurse*
Sutemeier, Anne Manchester *occupational therapist*
Tamayo, Raquel *medical/surgical nurse*
Tanner, Teresa L. *medical nurse*
Tatkon-Coker, Andrea Laura *nurse, business consultant*
Taylor, Karen Annette *mental health nurse*
Taylor, Nathalee Britton *nutritionist*
Thompson, Joanne Guimond *pediatric nurse, educator*
Thornton, Mary Elizabeth Wells *critical care nurse, educator*
Tinner, Franziska Paula *social worker, artist, designer, educator*
Tran, Henry Bang Q. *social work case manager*
Tuck, Mary Beth *nutritionist, educator*
Twitty, Myrtis Jolene *medical/surgical nurse, psychiatric nurse*
Utsman, Faye Mildred *surgical patient educator*
Uzsoy, Patricia J. *nursing educator and administrator*
Vann, Diane E. Swanson *nursing educator*
Waldrop, Enid Johnson *nurse*
Waldrop, Linda M. *medical administrator*
Walker, Donald William *home health care nurse, critical care nurse*
Walsh, Cheryl L. *women's health nurse*
Ware, Leigh Ann Carter *neonatal critical care nurse*
Warner, Heidi C. *clinical research nurse*
Washburn, Caryl Anne *occupational therapist*
Weaver, Esther Ruth *medical and surgical, geriatrics and oncology nurse*
Welch, Madeleine Lauretta *medical/surgical and occupational health nurse*
Welch, Robyn Perlman *pediatric critical care nurse*
Wen, Helen Hwa Jung *occupational health nurse*
Wenger, Dorothy Mae *retired dietitian*
Wert, Mary Cox *health facility administrator*
West, Raymond L. *nurse*
Westerman, Harriet Heaps *nurse, certified case manager*
White, Sharon LaRue *social worker, therapist*
White, Sharon Lee *critical care nurse*
Wieber, Patricia McNally *medical/surgical nurse, orthopaedics nurse*
Wiley, Myra *mental health nurse*
Williams-Maddox, Janice Helen *nurse*
Willingham, Ozella M. *medical/surgical and cardiac nurse*
Wilson, Linda Ann *renal dialysis nurse*
Wilson, Mary Elizabeth *geriatrics nurse*
Wing, Lilly Kelly Raynor *health services administrator*
Wolfe, Susan Marie *program evaluation consultant*
Wolfson, Lawrence Aaron *hospital administrator*
Wood, Deborah Christine *critical care nurse, educator*
Woodcock, Richard Wesley *educational psychologist*
Woodruff, Martha Joyce *home health agency executive*
Yates, Linda Fae *women's health nurse*
Yother, Anthony Wayne *critical care nurse, nurse manager*
Yurkin, Joseph *health consultant, small business owner*
Zomber, Beverly Louise *medical, surgical, geriatric and psychiatric nurse, educator*

HEALTHCARE: MEDICINE

UNITED STATES

ALABAMA

Alexander City
Powers, Runas, Jr. *rheumatologist*

Andalusia
Vyas, Vijay Chandrakant *nephrologist*

Anniston
Black, Clyde Edward *radiologist*

Auburn
McEldowney, Rene *health care educator, consultant*
Parsons, Daniel Lankester *pharmaceutics educator*

Birmingham
Aldrete, Joaquin Salcedo *surgeon, educator, researcher*
Allen, James Madison *family practice physician, lawyer, consultant*
Allman, Richard Mark *physician, gerontologist*
Berland, Lincoln Lewis *radiologist*
Blankson, Mary Lartey *pediatrician*
Carpenter, John Topham, Jr. *medical educator*
Cooper, Max Dale *physician, medical educator, researcher*
Diethelm, Arnold Gillespie *surgeon*
Eby, Thomas Lee *neuro-otologist, educator*
Finley, Wayne House *medical educator*
Finney, James Owen, Jr. *cardiologist*
Frenette, Luc *anesthesiologist, educator*
Glaser, Wolfram *psychiatrist*
Granger, Wesley Miles *medical educator*
Hardin, James Michael *health sciences educator, researcher*
Harrell, Lindy Ellyson *neurologist*
Hawkins, Jeffrey William *pulmonary physician*
Johnson, Bruce King *internist*
Kelly, David Reid *pathologist*
McLain, David Andrew *internist, rheumatologist, health facility administrator*
McLaughlin, Richard P. *internist, health facility administrator*
Meezan, Elias *pharmacologist, educator*
Meredith, Ruby Frances *radiation oncologist, researcher, educator*
Meythaler, Jay Merlin *physician, researcher, educator*
Michael, Max, III *internist, health facility administrator*
Nepomuceno, Cecil Santos *physician*
Nuckols, Frank Joseph *psychiatrist*
Oh, Myung-Hi Kim *pediatrician, educator*
Philips, Joseph Bond, III *medical educator*
Ranieri, William J. *medical association administrator*
Schroeder, Harry William, Jr. *physician, scientist*
Shumate, Charles Raymond *oncology and general surgeon*
Siegal, Gene Philip *pathology educator*
Sigman, Kenneth Martin *gastroenterologist, educator*
Stevenson, Edward Ward *retired physician, surgeon, otolaryngologist*
Strange, Martha *neonatologist*
Strickler, Howard Martin *physician*
Thomas, David Raymond *physician, educator*
Tieszen, Ralph Leland, Sr. *internist*
Warnock, David Gene *nephrologist*
Wilcox, William Edward *physician*
Winders, Suzan Eileen *preventive medicine educator*
Woodruff, Chivers Richard, Jr. *physician*

Daphne
Rinderknecht, Robert Eugene *internist*

Fairfield
Walters, Cynthia Voigt *internal medicine physician*

Florence
Burford, Alexander Mitchell, Jr. *physician, pathologist*
Daugherty, J(ames) Patrick *oncologist*

Gadsden
Brown, Andrew M. *otolaryngologist, allergist*
Hanson, Ronald Windell *cardiologist, lawyer, physicist*

Huntsville
Cowart, Norton E., Sr. *physician*
Huber, Donald Simon *physician*
Loux, Peter Charles *anesthesiologist*
Nuessle, William Raymond *surgeon*
Smith, Robin Gregory *radiation oncologist*
Tietke, Wilhelm *gastroenterologist*

Mobile
Agaliotis, Dimitrios Philippos *hematologist, oncologist*
Atkinson, William James, Jr. *retired cardiologist*
Barik, Sailen *biomedical scientist, educator*
Brown, Claude Lamar, Jr. *psychiatrist, educator*
Burnham, Judith F. *medical librarian*
Coker, Albert Steinhart, Jr. *infectious disease consultant, physician*
Durizch, Mary Lou *radiology educator*
Hamilton, William Joseph *osteopath*
Hanlon, Phillip Rollins *anesthesiologist*
Kemp, Stephen Frederick *physician*
McCombs, Candace Cragen *medical educator*
Raider, Louis *physician, radiologist*
Searcy, Chris Jackson *obstetrician, gynecologist*
Snow, Ruth Darr *radiologist educator*
Thomas, Joseph Paul *psychiatrist*
Zenker, Paul Nicolas *epidemiologist, pediatrician, medical director*

Montgomery
Frazer, David Hugh, Jr. *allergist*
Givhan, Edgar Gilmore *physician*
Hunker, Fred Dominic *internist, medical educator*

Northport
Mauritson, David Richard *cardiologist, flight instructor*

Phenix City
Greene, Ernest Rinaldo, Jr. *anesthesiologist, chemical engineer*

Pisgah
Ata, Muhammad Ejaz *internist*

Talladega
Bice, Jeannette Munroe *medical educator*

Tallassee
Bianchi, Thomas Deverell *gastroenterologist*

Tuscaloosa
Moody, Maxwell, Jr. *retired physician*
Nevels, Charles Thomas *psychiatrist*
Newsom, Barry Douglas *cardiovascular and thoracic surgeon*
Philp, James Ramsay *internal medicine educator*
Pieroni, Robert Edward *internist, educator*
Umakantha, Kaggal V. *physiatrist*

ARIZONA

Fort Huachuca
Silberman, Warren Steven *internist*

Phoenix
England, David P. *anesthesiologist, educator*
Kaplan, Andrew Jon *physician*

Tucson
Carter, L. Philip *neurosurgeon, consultant*
Martinez, Maria Dolores *pediatrician*

ARKANSAS

Bella Vista
Rose, Donald L. *physician, educator*

Clarksville
Pennington, Donald Harris *physician*

Conway
McCarron, Robert Frederick, II *orthopedic surgeon*

De Valls Bluff
Jones, Robert Eugene *physician*

El Dorado
Fraser, David Ben *psychiatrist*
Tommey, Charles Eldon *retired surgeon*

Fayetteville
Brown, Craig Jay *ophthalmologist*

Fort Smith
Coleman, Michael Dortch *nephrologist*
Drolshagen, Leo Francis, III *radiologist, physician*
Paris, Charles Henry, Jr. *gastroenterologist*
Still, Eugene Fontaine, II *plastic surgeon, educator*
Whiteside, Edwin *allergist, immunologist*

Jonesboro
Jones, Kenneth Bruce *surgeon*

Little Rock
Barnes, Robert Webster *medical educator*
Boop, Frederick Alan *neurosurgeon*
Doherty, James Edward, III *physician, educator*
Elbein, Alan David *medical science educator*
Feild, Charles Robert *pediatrician, educator*
Garcia-Rill, Edgar Enrique *neuroscientist*
Grissom, James Roger *hematologist, oncologist*
Hopkins, Robert Howard, Jr. *internist, pediatrician, medical educator*
Hough, Aubrey Johnston, Jr. *pathologist, physician, educator*
Jagannath, Sundar *physician, educator*
Jones, Robin Richard *pathology educator*
Kemp, Stephen Frank *pediatric endocrinologist, educator, composer*
Kramer, Thomas Andrew Moss *psychiatry educator*
Maloney, Francis Patrick *physiatrist, educator*
Mann, Edwina Walls *medical librarian*
Paslidis, Nick (Nickolaos) John *physician, scientist*
Ramaprasad, Subbaraya *medical educator*
Ronis, Martin Jorn Janis *pediatrics researcher and educator*
Schmitz, Michael Leland *pediatric anesthesiologist, pediatrician, educator*
Shah, Sudhir Vithalbhai *nephrologist, educator, researcher*
Smith, Samuel David *pediatric surgeon, educator*
Sotomora-von Ahn, Ricardo Federico *pediatrician, educator*
Stern, Harold Patrick *behavioral pediatrician*
Strode, Steven Wayne *physician*
Ward, Harry Pfeffer *physician, university chancellor*
York, John Lyndal *medical educator*
Yousuff, Sarah Safia *physician*

North Little Rock
Biondo, Raymond Vitus *dermatologist*

CALIFORNIA

Bakersfield
Rahal, Paramvir Singh *physician*

Mountain View
Whyte, John Joseph *internist*

San Francisco
Petrakis, Nicholas Louis *physician, medical researcher, educator*

COLORADO

Colorado Springs
Sayers, Michael Eugene *rheumatologist*

Denver
Shemesh, Gareth Eli *physiatrist, critical care physician*

Longmont
Beyer, Craig Franklin *ophthalmologist*

CONNECTICUT

Hartford
McKenna, Patrick Hayes *pediatric urologist, educator, naval officer*

Waterbury
Dudrick, Stanley John *surgeon, scientist, educator*

Wilton
Rogers, Mark Charles *physician, educator*

DISTRICT OF COLUMBIA

Washington
Johnson, Kurt Edward *anatomist, educator, publisher*
Richardson, LeRoy Reeves *medical researcher*
Spagnolo, Samuel Vincent *internist, pulmonary specialist, educator*
Tavassoli, Fattaneh Abbas-zadeh *pathologist, consultant*

FLORIDA

Altamonte Springs
Korpman, Michael David *family practice physician*

Aventura
Grant, Penny *pediatrics educator*

Bal Harbour
Nathan, David Aaron *retired cardiologist*

Bartow
Cobb, Brian Wayne *emergency physician*

Bay Pines
Harwood, Steven J. *nuclear medicine physician, consultant*
Wasserman, Fred, III *internist*

Belleair
Dexter, Helen Louise *dermatologist, consultant*
Lasley, Charles Haden *surgeon, consultant*

Boca Raton
Cohen, Barry Allan *psychiatrist*
Diamond, Paul Craig *family practice physician*
Friend, Harold Charles *neurologist*
Michel, Stephen Lewis *physician*
Ostreich, Leonard L. *obstetrician, gynecologist*
Zuckerman, Sidney *retired allergist, immunologist*

Bradenton
Ambrusko, John Stephen *retired surgeon, county official*
Soler, Joseph Manuel *emergency physician*
Sprenger, Thomas Robert *orthopedic surgeon*
Thomas, George *cardiologist*

Bradenton Beach
Vega, Mario *family practice physician*

Brandon
Belli, Vahit M. *cardiologist, nephrologist*

Stablein, John Joseph, III *physician*

Casselberry
Stelling, Herbert Pund *family physician*

Clearwater
Gordon, Marcia Laura *psychiatrist*
Loewenstein, George Wolfgang *retired physician, UN consultant*
Maza, Richard Kazdin *internist*
McAllister, Charles John *nephrologist, medical administrator*
Rinde, John Jacques *internist*
Shapiro, David Howard *surgeon*
Wheat, Myron William, Jr. *cardiothoracic surgeon*

Coconut Grove
Good, Raphael S. *psychiatrist, obstetrician, gynecologist*

Coral Gables
Chirino, Fernando Porfirio *medical educator*
Latta, Loren Lee *orthopaedic research educator*
Perez, Josephine *psychiatrist, educator*

Coral Springs
Andrews, George Andreas *cardiologist*

Dade City
McBath, Donald Linus *osteopathic physician*

Davie
Wong, Antonio Ham *family physician*

Daytona Beach
Ahmed, Jeffrey Jalil *neurologist*
Brown, Benjamin Thomas *urologist, educator*
Di Nicolo, Roberto *allergist*
Goldberg, Paul Bernard *gastroenterologist, clinical researcher*
Kerman, Herbert David *radiation oncologist*
Yaeger, Theodore Edward *radiation oncologist*

Deland
Hollmann, Mark William *orthopaedic surgeon*

Delray Beach
Rosenfeld, Steven Ira *ophthalmologist*
Snyder, Louis D. *cardiovascular physician*

Dunedin
Gambone, Victor Emmanuel, Jr. *physician*
McAloon, Edward Joseph *oncologist*

Fort Lauderdale
Abel, Howard Richard *oncologist, hematologist*
Adams, Kelly Lynn *emergency physician*
Copen, Mark Jay *internist*
Corteguera, Homero Joseph *psychiatrist*
Haimo, Michael Jay *colon and rectal surgeon*
Maulion, Richard Peter *psychiatrist*
Merson, Charles Samuel *anesthesiologist*
Morris, James Bruce *internist, educator*
Nguyen, Hoa Ngoc *gynecology researcher*
Nogueras, Juan Jose *surgeon*
Price, Alexander *retired osteopathic physician*
Rappa, Hugh Gregory *medical educator*
Raybeck, Michael Joseph *surgeon*
Rendon-Pellerano, Marta Ines *dermatologist*
Reyes, Ricardo Ramon *internist, infectious disease physician, immunologist*
Shechter, Oded *physician*
Smolar, Edward Nelson *physician, consultant*
Swiller, Randolph Jacob *internist*

Fort Myers
Brown, Robin Cotten *otolaryngologist*
Schultz, Robert Brown *physician*
Steier, Michael Edward *cardiac surgeon*
Zeldes, Ilya Michael *forensic scientist, lawyer*

Fort Pierce
Glaspey, Ben Lee *family practice physician*

Fort Walton Beach
Thompson, William West *allergist, immunologist, pediatrician*

Gainesville
Anderson, Richard McLemore *internist*
Cluff, Leighton Eggertsen *physician*
Gulig, Paul Anthony *medical researcher, educator*
Keller-Wood, Maureen *physiology researcher, educator*
Mills, Roger Marion *cardiologist*
Muniz, Carlos Enrique *psychiatry educator*
Palovcik, Reinhard Anton *research neurophysiologist*
Rarey, Kyle Eugene *anatomy educator, researcher*
Richards, Bruce Alfred *neurologist*
Romano, Geno Vincent *emergency medicine physician*
Scarpace, Philip James *geriatric researcher, administrator, educator*
Schatz, Desmond Arthur *pediatrician, endocrinologist*
Silverstein, Burton Victor *cardiologist*
Thomas, William Clark, Jr. *internist, medical facility administrator*
Uthman, Basim Mohammad *neurologist, epileptologist, consultant*
Vaughen, Justine L. *rehabilitation hospital medical professional*
Wingard, John Reid *medical educator*
Wingo, Charles Spurgeon *medical and physiology educator*
Winter, William Ernest *physician, educator*

Gulf Breeze
Pettyjohn, Frank Schmermund *emergency medicine educator*

Hallandale
Haspel, Arthur Carl *podiatrist, surgeon*

Hialeah
Economides, Christopher George *pathologist*
Iribar, Manuel R. *internist, health facility administrator*

Hollywood
Isaacson, Marvin Gerald *psychiatrist*
Krovetz, L. Jerome *pediatric cardiologist*
Levy, Ralph M. *cardiologist*
Roth, Stephen L. *cardiologist*
Sheffel, Donald David *neurosurgeon*
Ursetta, Terrance Thomas *anesthesiologist*

Hudson
Merkin, Donald H. *internist*

Inverness
Dodge, R(alph) Edward *family physician*
Esquibel, Edward Valdez *psychiatrist, clinical medical program developer*
Marcus, M. Jeffrey *physician*

Jacksonville
Amornmarn, Rumpa *physician*
Borger, James Andrew *pediatric surgeon*
Bosworth, William Posey *physician, physical education educator*
Boylan, Kevin Bernard *neurologist*
Burger, Charles Dwayne *physician*
Fetchero, John Anthony, Jr. *otorhinolaryngologist*
Huddleston, John Franklin *obstetrics and gynecology educator*
Irby, B(enjamin) Freeman *obstetrician, gynecologist*
Kolts, Byron Edward *gastroenterologist*
Lewis, Richard Harlow *urologist*
Lipkovic, Peter *chief medical examiner*
Ly, Raymond Hoa Binh *physician*
Mizrahi, Edward Alan *allergist*
Mollitt, Daniel Lawrence *pediatric surgeon*
Paryani, Shyam Bhojraj *radiologist*
Pineiro, Eduard Efraly *anesthetist*
Prempree, Thongbliew *oncology radiologist*
Rosenbaum, Donald Herman, Jr. *orthopaedic surgeon*
Safford, Robert Eugene *cardiologist, health facility administrator, educator*
Solberg, Lawrence Arthur, Jr. *hematologist, oncologist, medical educator*
Thorsteinsson, Gudni *physiatrist*
Tucker, N(imrod) H(olt), III *physician*
Vinsant, George O'Neal *surgery educator*

Jupiter
Otero, Elizabeth *allergist*

Key West
Stein, Michael Alan *cardiologist*

Lake City
Lindquist, Leo Anselm *surgeon*

Lake Worth
Dober, Stanley *pediatrician*
Spunberg, Jerome J. *radiation oncologist*
Stone, Ross Gluck *physician*

Lakeland
Kottke, Bruce A. *internist*
Miller, Randel Kenneth *rheumatologist*
Riker, David Lewis *medical services executive*
Spoto, Angelo Peter, Jr. *internist, allergist*
Tabb, Waller Crockett *allergist, immunologist*
Wiley, Albert Lee, Jr. *physician, engineer, educator*

Largo
Ratcliffe, David Nelson *surgeon*

Leesburg
Gelfand, Francine Losen *psychiatrist, educator*

Marianna
Galard, Maurice Jaoquim *family practice physician*

Melbourne
Broussard, William Joseph *physician, cattleman, environmentalist*
Minor, Mark William *allergist*
Weiss, Gary M. *neurologist*

Miami
Altman, Roy Davis *rheumatologist, medical educator*
Antunez de Mayolo, Jorge Carlos *hematologist, oncologist, geriatrician*
Bahadue, George Paul *general, family physician*
Barkin, Jamie Steven *gastroenterologist, educator*
Bauer, Charles Ronald *medical educator*
Beck, Morris *allergist*
Carballo, Pedro Pablo *cardiologist*
Chakko, Simon C. *cardiologist, educator*
Cohn, Lawrence Sherman *psychiatrist, educator, psychoanalyst*
Demiris, Chris H. *medical manufacturing diagnostics administrator*
Dokson, Joel Steven *neurologist*
Dominguez, Roberto Alfonso *psychiatrist*
Feldman, Israel *dermatologist, educator*
Furst, Alex Julian *thoracic and cardiovascular surgeon*
Gaylis, Norman Brian *internist, rheumatologist, educator*
Gittelson, George *physician*
Granat, Pepi *physician*
Greenman, Richard Leonard *physician*
Hotchner, Kirby Ross *osteopath*
Howell, Ralph Rodney *pediatrician, educator*
Hultquist, Karl Albert *medical educator*
Kessler, Kenneth Michael *cardiologist*
Layton, Robert Glenn *radiologist*
Levy, Elliot Gene *physician*
Lian, Eric Chun-Yet *hematologist, educator*
Livingstone, Alan Samuel *surgeon*
Macintyre, Dugald Stewart *physician, educator*
Mandri, Daniel Francisco *psychiatrist*
Margolis, James Robineau *cardiovascular physician, educator*
Marks, Jennifer Byrne *internist, endocrinologist, educator*
Martínez, Luís Osvaldo *radiologist, educator*
Mettinger, Karl Lennart *neurologist*
Mintz, Daniel Harvey *diabetologist, educator, academic administrator*
Moffat, Frederick Larkin, Jr. *surgeon, surgical oncologist*
Patarca, Roberto *immunologist, molecular biologist, physician*
Perez, Guido O. *medical educator*
Picard-Ami, Luis Alberto *plastic surgeon*
Poblete, Rita Maria Bautista *physician, educator*
Porter, Wayne Randolph *dermatologist*
Quencer, Robert Moore *neuroradiologist, researcher*
Raines, Jeff *biomedical scientist, medical research director*
Richton, Samuel M. *physician*
Ricordi, Camillo *surgeon, transplant and diabetes researcher*
Rogachefsky, Richard Alan *surgeon, educator*
Scerpella, Ernesto Guillermo *physician researcher*
Serafini, Aldo N. *radiology educator, medical educator*
Sichewski, Vernon Roger *physician*
Siddiqui, Farooq Ahmad *medical educator*
Smiddy, William Earl *ophthalmologist*
Smith, Stanley Bertram *clinical pathologist, allergist, immunologist, anatomic pathologist*
Sommer, Leonard Samuel *medical educator*
Spear, Harold Charles *physician, thoracic/ cardiovascular surgeon*
Struhl, Theodore Roosevelt *surgeon*
Suarez, George Michael *urologist*
Taylor, Andrew Lex *endocrinologist, educator*
Trapido, Edward Jay *epidemiologist*
Tse, David *ophthalmologist, surgeon*
Viamonte, Manuel *surgeon*
Weinberger, Malvin *pediatric surgeon*
Wheeler, Steve Dereal *neurologist*
Wolfson, Aaron Howard *radiation oncologist, educator*
Zand, Lloyd Craig *radiologist*

Miami Beach
Lehrman, David *orthopedic surgeon*
Sayfie, Eugene Joe *cardiologist, internist, educator*
Schotz, Sylvan Art *physician*
Simmonds, Warren L. *podiatrist*

Naples
Gahagan, Thomas Gail *obstetrician, gynecologist*
Harvey, Walter H(ayden) *hematologist, medical oncologist*

New Port Richey
Hauber, Frederick August *ophthalmologist*
Hu, Chen-Sien *surgeon*

North Miami Beach
Hutman, Burton S. *psychiatrist, educator*

North Palm Beach
Stein, Mark Rodger *allergist*

Ocala
Altenburger, Karl Marion *allergist, immunologist*
Cabrera-Mendez, Fabio *psychiatrist*
Corwin, William *psychiatrist*
Estrada, Adahli *rheumatologist*
Stewart, George Edward, II *physician*

Oldsmar
Rogers, James Virgil, Jr. *retired radiologist and educator*

Orlando
Fernandez, Guillermo J. *ophthalmologist, medical-paralegal consultant*
Garrett, Paul R., Jr. *physician*
Getting, Vlado Andrew *medical and public health educator, consultant*
Loy, Randall Alan *endocrinologist*
Marsh, Ella Jean *pediatrician*
Miller, Gary Donald *physician*
Nelson, Loren Douglas *surgeon, educator, critical care intensivist*
Norris, Franklin Gray *thoracic and cardiovascular surgeon*
Shub, Harvey Allen *surgeon*
Townes, Andrew W., Jr. *allergist, immunologist, pediatrician*
Williamson, Paul Richard *medical educator, surgeon*
Wilson, Terence Scott *osteopath*

Ormond Beach
Farmer, Harry Frank, Jr. *internist*
Raimondo, Louis John *psychiatrist*
Rubin, Mark Stephen *ophthalmic surgeon*

Oviedo
Mammino, Jere Joseph *dermatologist*

Palatka
Michaels, Michael Maged *urologist*

Palm Beach
Unger, Gere Nathan *physician, lawyer*

Palm Beach Gardens
Small, Melvin D. *physician, educator*
Warshaw, Ira Greg *family physician*
Zelnick, Ronald Stuart *surgeon*

Palm City
Saltzman, Edward Jacob *retired pediatrician*

Palm Harbor
Drapkin, Robert Louis *medical oncologist*
Kaplan, Kerry Joseph *internist, cardiologist*
McLaughlin, Timothy Thomas *physician*

Panama City
Schuler, Burton Silverman *podiatrist*
Walker, Richard, Jr. *nephrologist, internist*
Walters, George John *oral and maxillofacial surgeon*

Pensacola
Andrews, Edson James, Jr. *radiologist*
Bumagat, Ferdinand Mendoza *military physician*
Dauser, Kimberly Ann *physician assistant*
Dillard, Robert Perkins *pediatrician, educator*
Kleinman, Gary E. *obstetrician, maternal-fetal specialist, educator*
Lautier, Yves Laurent *physician*
Pickens, William Stewart *cardiologist*
Sharp, Elaine Cecile *obstetrician, gynecologist*
Terrell, Charles Oliver *anesthesiologist*
White, William Clinton *pathologist*

Plantation
Alvarado, Alfredo *surgeon*
Betancourt, Oscar *pediatrician*
Gewirtzman, Garry Bruce *dermatologist*
Nickelson, Kim René *internist*
Ramos, Manuel Antonio, Jr. *pulmonologist*

Ponte Vedra Beach
ReMine, William Hervey, Jr. *surgeon*

Port Charlotte
Tobin, Mark Stuart *internist, oncologist*

Port Saint Lucie
Sarkar, Chitto Priyo *family medicine physician, researcher*
Wertheim, Michael Stanley *oncologist*

Punta Gorda
Kalosis, John Joseph, Jr. *physician, air force officer*

Safety Harbor
Weiss, Steven Gary *physician*

Saint Petersburg
Barbosa, Jerry Levy *pediatric hematologist, oncologist*
Collins, Paul Steven *vascular surgeon*
Daicoff, George Ronald *surgeon, educator*
Jacobson, Geraldine Meerbott *radiation oncologist*
Lee, John Francis *surgeon*
Rosenblum, Martin Jerome *ophthalmologist*
Thompson, John Morgan *neurological surgeon, educator*

Sanford
Kaplan, Ted Adam *pediatrician, educator*

Sarasota
Aull, Susan *physician*
Giordano, David Alfred *internist, gastroenterologist*
Jelks, Mary Larson *retired pediatrician*
Klutzow, Friedrich Wilhelm *neuropathologist*

Seminole
Nesbitt, Robert Edward Lee, Jr. *physician, educator, scientific researcher*
Schwartzberg, Roger Kerry *osteopath, internist*

Spring Hill
Finney, Roy Pelham, Jr. *urologist, surgeon, inventor*

Stuart
Delagi, Edward Francis *physician*
Ritter, William Stanley *physician*
Thompson, Dennis Scott *psychiatrist*

Tallahassee
Brodsky, Lewis *psychiatrist, educator*
Deeb, Larry Charles *pediatric endocrinologist, epidemiologist*
Hernandez, Jose Yolando Balastas *physician, surgeon*
Maguire, Charlotte Edwards *retired physician*

Tampa
Barclay, Laurie Lynn *neurologist, consultant*
Benson, Kaaron *physician, pathology educator*
Bernal, Nancy Ellen *medical librarian*
Branch, William Terrell *urologist, educator*
Brantley, Stephen Grant *pathologist*
Bukantz, Samuel Charles *physician, educator*
Bunker-Söler, Antonio Luis *physician*
Cho, Jai Hang *internist, hematologist, educator*
Cintron, Guillermo B. *cardiologist, medical educator*
Douidar, Samir Mohamad *pediatrics educator*
Eichberg, Rodolfo David *physician, educator*
Fenske, Neil A. *dermatologist*
Fields, Karen Keyse *physician*
Fox, Roger Williams *allergist and immunologist, educator*
Gieron-Korthals, Maria Antonina *pediatrician, neurologist, medical educator*
Hadden, John Winthrop *immunopharmacology educator*
Hahn, Keith Worden *physiatrist*
Hoffman, Mitchel Scott *gynecologic oncologist*
Holfelder, Lawrence Andrew *pediatrician, allergist*
Horowitz, Susan Amy *pathologist and cytopathologist*
Hulls, James Robert *emergency physician*
Jacobs, Timothy Andrew *epidemiologist, international health consultant*
Ledford, Dennis Keith *physician*
Lockey, Richard Funk *allergist, educator*
Lyman, Gary Herbert *epidemiologist, cancer researcher, educator*
Marcadis, Abraham S. *plastic surgeon*
Martin, Robert Leslie *physician*
Mc Collough, Newton Clark, III *orthopaedic surgeon*
Murtagh, Frederick Reed *neuroradiologist, educator*
Phelps, Christopher Prine *neuroscientist*
Phuphanich, Surasak *neurologist, oncologist*
Ransohoff, Joseph *neurosurgeon*
Reintgen, Douglas Scott *surgical oncology educator, researcher*
Ridley, Marion Berton *otolaryngologist/facial plastic surgeon, medical educator*
Robinson, Lary Allen *cardiothoracic surgeon*
Ruckdeschel, John Charles *oncologist, researcher*
Sanberg, Paul Ronald *medical educator*
Schmidt, Paul Joseph *physician, educator*
Shenefelt, Philip David *dermatologist*
Shephard, Bruce Dennis *obstetrician, educator, medical writer*
Shons, Alan Rance *plastic surgeon, educator*
Silver, Archie Aaron *psychiatry educator, psychiatry director*
Skelton, William Paul, III *medical educator*
Tabibzadeh, Siamak Shokri *pathologist, educator*
Trunnell, Thomas Newton *dermatologist*
White, Melvin Jeffrey *ophthalmologist, environmental medicine physician*

Vero Beach
Geiger, Ralph Bruce *physician*

West Palm Beach
Craft, Jerome Walter *plastic surgeon, health facility administrator*
Dugan, Charles Clark *physician, surgeon*
Kapnick, S. Jason *oncologist*
Kinney, John Patrick *dermatologist*
Whitfield, Graham Frank *orthopedic surgeon*

Winter Haven
Smith, Rick Montgomery *physician, consultant*

Winter Park
Penn, John G. *plastic and reconstructive surgeon*
Pollack, Robert William *psychiatrist*
Sharfman, Marc Irwin *neurologist*
Stieg, Frank Henry, III *plastic surgeon*
Trevisani, Michael F. *surgeon*

GEORGIA

Albany
Smith, Larry R. *pediatrician, allergist, immunologist*

Alpharetta
Bauer, Joseph Gerard *plastic surgeon*
Harris, James Herman *pathologist*

Athens
Erwin, Goodloe Y. *physician, land company executive*
Gardner, Edward Clinton, Jr. *gastroenterologist*
Giberson, Thomas Paul *emergency medicine physician*
Kretzschmar, Claudia Suzanne *physician*
Newland, Hillary Reid *pathologist*
Shah, Narendra Keshavlal *radiologist*

Atlanta
Alarcon, Renato Daniel *psychiatry educator, researcher, medical facility executive*
Ambrose, Samuel Sheridan, Jr. *urologist*
Aranson, Robert *physician*
Ballard, Wiley Perry III *hematologist, oncologist*
Beasley, Ernest William, Jr. *endocrinologist*
Bliwise, Donald Linn *neurology educator*
Byrd, Larry Donald *behavioral pharmacologist*
Capone, Antonio *psychiatrist*
Cooper, Gerald Rice *clinical pathologist*
Cross, George Lee, III *orthopedic surgeon*
DiSanto, Vinson Michael *osteopath*
Dutt, Kamla *medical educator*
Fresh, Edith McCullough *behavioral medicine educator, psychologist*
Frumkin, Howard *medical educator, epidemiologist*
Ganaway, George Kenneth *psychiatrist*
Goldman, John Abner *rheumatologist, immunologist, educator*
Gonzalez, Emilio Bustamante *rheumatologist, educator*
Gordon, Robert Dana *transplant surgeon*
Hanson, Victor Arthur *surgeon*
Hirsh, Eugene Harold *gastroenterologist*
Holland, Amy Jeanette *psychiatrist*
Hord, Allen Henry *medical educator*
Inderbitzin, Lawrence Ben *psychiatry educator*
Jarvis, William Robert *epidemiologist, educator*
Jones, Mark Mitchell *plastic surgeon*
Kahn, Henry Slater *physician, epidemiologist, educator*
Kaufman, Stephen Lawrence *radiologist, educator*
Kaufmann, Robert S. *medical educator*
Keyserling, Harry L. *pediatric infectious disease physician, researcher*
Knobel, Roland Jefferson *health adminstration educator*
Lathan, Samuel Robert, Jr. *internist, educator*
Leighton, Leslie Steven *gastroenterologist*
Lindsay, Michael Kenneth *obstetrics and gynecology educator*
Lippitt, Alan Bruce *orthopedic surgeon*
Majmudar, Bhagirath *medical educator*
McKay, Marilynne *medical educator*
Medford, Russell Marshall *physician*
Meyer, George Wilbur *internist, health facility administrator*
Nahai, Foad *plastic surgery educator*
Newcom, Samuel Ralph *physician*
Neylan, John Francis, III *nephrologist, educator*
Nichols, Joseph J., Sr. *surgeon*
Perkins, James Morris *psychiatrist*
Pettitt, Barbara Jean *pediatric surgeon*
Pratt, Michael Francis *physician and surgeon, otolaryngologist*
Rodriguez, Victor M. *obstetrician, gynecologist*
Rosenstock, Joel *physician*
Short, Louise Joy *epidemiologist*
Skillan, Mark *internist*
Spangler, Dennis Lee *physician*
Sperry, Kris Lee *forensic pathologist*
Spraker, Mary Katherine *pediatric dermatologist*
Steinberg, James Paul *infectious diseases physician, hospital administrator*
Stern, Barney Joel *neurologist*
Stieber, Andrei Carol *surgeon*
Strasser, Dale Christian *physiatrist*
Strikas, Raymond Algimantas *medical epidemiologist*
Templeton, Stephen Farwell *dermatopathologist, dermatologist*
Thun, Michael John *epidemiologist, cancer researcher*
Tomer, Aaron *medical educator*
Tyler, Carl Walter, Jr. *physician, health research administrator*
Van Assendelft, Onno Willem *hematologist*
Waller, John Louis *anesthesiology educator*
Watts, Nelson Barnett *endocrinologist, medical educator*
Weed, Roger Oren *rehabilitation educator and counselor*
Willis, Isaac *dermatologist, educator*
Wilson, Frank Lyndall *surgeon*
Yeager, Andrew Michael *pediatrics educator*
Zaki, Saleh Abbas *forensic pathologist*

Augusta
Colborn, Gene Louis *anatomy educator, researcher*
Dolen, William Kennedy *allergist, immunologist, pediatrician, educator*
Goldstein, Barry David *pharmacology educator, university administrator*
Guill, Margaret Frank *pediatrics educator, medical researcher*
Hawkins, Michael Lawrence *trauma surgeon*
Haynes, Michael Steward *pulmonologist, critical care specialist*
Hooks, Vendie Hudson, III *surgeon*
House, Fredrick Crisler *allergist, immunologist*
Karp, Warren Bill *medical and dental educator, researcher*
Loomis, Earl Alfred, Jr. *psychiatrist*
Loring, David William *neuropsychologist, researcher*
Mahesh, Virendra Bhushan *endocrinologist*
McDonough, Paul Gerard *obstetrician-gynecologist, educator*
Merin, Robert Gillespie *anesthesiology educator*
Meyer, Carol Frances *pediatrician, allergist*
Pallas, Christopher William *cardiologist*
Pearson-Shaver, Anthony Lloyd *pediatrician, educator*
Perugini, Daniel Francis *physician, military officer*
Plouffe, Leo, Jr. *reproductive endocrinologist*
Prisant, L(ouis) Michael *cardiologist*
Puchtler, Holde *histochemist, pathologist, educator*
Rausch, Jeffrey Lynn *psychiatrist, psychopharmacologist*
Rivner, Michael Harvey *neurologist*
Ryan, James Walter *physician, medical researcher*
Schultz, Everett Hoyle, Jr. *radiologist, educator*
Sethi, Kapil Dev *physician*
Smith, Randolph Relihan *plastic surgeon*
Strickland, Daniel Michael *reproductive endocrinologist, obstetrician*
Stubbs, David Manning *radiology educator*
Trott, Edward Ashley *reproductive endocrinologist*
Wei, John Pin *surgery educator*
Work, Bruce Alexander, Jr. *obstetrics and gynecology educator*
Wray, Betty Beasley *allergist, immunologist, pediatrician*
Zamrini, Edward Youssef *behavioral neurologist*

Austell
Halwig, J. Michael *allergist*

Baxley
Ferrari, Thomas J. *physician*

Columbus
Leichter, Steven Bruce *endocrinologist*
Wood, Richard Elgin, Jr. *family physician*

Decatur
Ballard, David Joseph *epidemiologist, educator*
Fine, Robert M. *allergist, immunologist, dermatologist*
Morris, Elsie Coleman *allergist, immunologist, pediatrician*
Nahmias, Brigitte Buchmann *physician, radiologist*
Sessions, George Purd *physician*
Whitesides, Thomas Edward, Jr. *orthopaedic surgeon*

Dublin
Johnson, Otto Bernice, Jr. *physician*

Dunwoody
Koger, Linwood Graves, III *surgeon, educator*

East Point
Cheves, Harry Langdon, Jr. *physician*

Evans
Spirnak, Joseph Patrick *physician*

Fort Benning
Chan, Philip *dermatologist, army officer*
Vaughan, Robert E. *diagnostic radiologist, army officer*

Fort Gordon
Ramirez, Manuel Fernando *surgeon, career officer*

Fort Stewart
Byrnes, Thomas Raymond, Jr. *osteopath*

Fort Valley
Nathan, Daniel Everett *retired surgeon*
Swartwout, Joseph Rodolph *obstetrics and gynecology educator, administrator*

Gainesville
Maloney, Michael James *allergist, pediatrician*
Nish, William Anderson *allergist, pediatrician*

Georgetown
Austin, Phylis Ann *medical writer, editor*

Hapeville
Fowler, Paul Raymond *physician, lawyer, educator*

Jesup
Dede, J. Anthony *obstetrician, gynecologist*

Kingsland
Tippetts, Charles Sanford, Jr. *family practice physician, educator*

Macon
Luu, Quyen Ngoc *physician, educator*
Matragrano, Margherite Paula *medical librarian*

Marietta
Fineman, Stanley Mark *allergist, immunologist, pediatrician*
Hagood, M. Felton *surgeon*
Holtz, Noel *neurologist*
Thomas, Pamella Delores *medical director, physician, educator*
Tissue, Mike *medical educator, respiratory therapist*
Wheatley, Joseph Kevin *physician, urologist*

Milledgeville
Evans, Frank Owen, Jr. *physician*
Goodrich, Samuel Melvin *obstetrician, gynecologist*

Norcross
Shockley, Robert Kenneth *medical researcher*

Roswell
Rudert, Cynthia Sue *gastroenterologist*
Udoff, Eric Joel *diagnostic radiologist*

Saint Marys
Anderson, Donald Roger *cardiologist*

Saint Simons
Beck, Charles Edward *psychiatrist, lawyer*

Savannah
Goldkrand, John Wolf *obstetrician/gynecologist*
Jenkins, Mark Guerry *cardiologist*
Rinderknecht, Michael Anthony *physician's assistant*
Stonnington, Henry Herbert *physician, medical executive, educator*
Taylor, Roslyn Donny *family practice physician*
Zoller, Michael *otolaryngologist, educator*

Suwanee
Hecht, Alan *retired physician, insurance company executive*

Thomaston
Zimmerman, James Robert *radiologist, engineer*

Tifton
Dorminey, Henry Clayton, Jr. *allergist*
Lanier, Randall Clark *internist, chest physician*

Valdosta
Sherman, Henry Thomas *retired physician*
Von Taaffe-Rossmann, Cosima T. *physician, writer, inventor*

Warm Springs
Knowles, James Barron *rehabilitative medicine physician*
Peach, Paul E. *physician, medical facility administrator*

Warner Robins
Charkatz, Harry Marvin *psychiatrist*
Locke, Thomas J., III *physician*

Watkinsville
Johnson, Norman James *physician, lawyer*

ILLINOIS

Urbana
Austin, Jean Philippe *medical educator, radiologist*

INDIANA

Jeffersonville
Thind, Gurdarshan S. *medical educator*

IOWA

Des Moines
Timberlake, Gregory Alan *surgeon, educator*

KANSAS

Kansas City
Sciolaro, Charles Michael *cardiac surgeon*

KENTUCKY

Ashland
Roth, Oliver Ralph *radiologist*

Bellevue
Ahmed, Syed Mahtab *physician, immunologist, nutritionist*

Berea
Lamb, Irene Hendricks *medical researcher*

Bowling Green
Thamb, Indar Mohan *physician*

Elizabethtown
Rahman, Rafiq Ur *oncologist, educator*

Elkton
Manthey, Frank Anthony *physician, director*

Harlan
Morfesis, Florias Andrew *surgeon*

Hyden
Townsend, Horrell, III *obstetrician, gynecologist*

Lexington
Archer, Sanford Mitchell *otolaryngologist*
Bowman, Lynne Barnett *medical librarian*
Chatterjee, Sunil K. *cancer research scientist*
Chien, Sufan *surgeon, educator*
Hill, John Sylvester *allergist, immunologist*
Humphries, Laurie Lee *child and adolescent psychiatrist, researcher*
Hyde, Gordon Lee *surgeon, educator*
Jokl, Ernst F. *retired physician*
Jones, Janet Hall *child and adolescent psychiatrist*
Kang, Bann C. *immunologist*
Kaplan, Martin P. *allergist, immunologist, pediatrician*
Kenady, Daniel Edward *surgery educator*
Kraman, Steve Seth *physician, educator*
Markesbery, William R. *neurology and pathology educator, physician*
Mayer, Lloyd D. *allergist, immunologist, physician, medical educator*
Moody, Edward Bridges *physician, biomedical engineer*
O'Brien, John Michael *obstetrician/gynecologist*
O'Connor, William Noel *pathologist*
Pauly, Thomas Howard *neonatologist*
Ramsbottom-Lucier, Mary *physician, medical educator*
Randall, David Clark *medical educator, medical researcher*
Sandler, Nat Harold *psychiatrist*
Slevin, John Thomas *neurologist, educator*
Whayne, Thomas French, Jr. *cardiologist*
Zoorob, Roger Jamil *physician*

Louisville
Adamkin, David Howard *pediatric medicine educator*
Bhatnagar, Kunwar Prasad *medical educator*
Bhattacherjee, Parimal *pharmacologist*
Bosse, George Michael *emergency medicine physician*
Carstens, Per Henrik Becher *pathology educator*
Cummings, Norman Allen *rheumatologist, educator*
Daus, Arthur Theadore, Jr. *pain medicine physician, psychiatrist*
Elbl, Francisco *pediatrician, educator*
El-Mallakh, Rif S. *psychiatry educator, researcher*
Farman, Allan George *oral pathologist, radiologist*
Fechtner, Robert David *physician*
Galandiuk, Susan *colon and rectal surgeon, educator*
Hobson, Douglas Paul *psychiatrist*
Jacob, Robert Allen *surgeon*
Karibo, John Michael *allergist, immunologist, pediatrician*
Katz, Lowell Dean *surgeon*
La Rocca, Renato V. *oncologist, researcher*
Lewis, Blaine, Jr. *surgeon*
Moyer, Ronald Peter *allergist, immunologist, pediatrician*
O'Connor, Dennis Michael *physician*
Olson, William Henry *neurology educator, administrator*
Pence, Hobert Lee *physician*
Pietrantoni, Marcello *obstetrician-gynecologist*
Seligson, David *orthopedic surgeon, educator*
Sigdestad, Curtis Paul *radiobiology educator*
Singer, Igor *cardiologist, electrophysiologist*
Slater, A. David *surgeon, educator*
Slung, Hilton B. *surgeon*
Smith, Charles Clarence, Jr. *physician, medical educator*
Strauss, Gordon Darrow *psychiatrist, educator*
Sublett, James Lee *allergist, immunologist, pediatrician*
Syed, Ibrahim Bijli *medical educator, theologist*
Tsai, Tsu-Min *surgeon*
Uhde, George Irvin *physician*
Van Daalen, James Michael *thoracic surgeon*
Walker, Frank Alexander *pediatrician, educator*
Weisskopf, Bernard *pediatrician, child behavior, development and genetics specialist, educator*

Madisonville
Stulc, Jaroslav Peter *surgeon, educator*

Nicholasville
Parr, Eugene Quincy *retired orthopaedic surgeon*

Russellville
Hattem, Albert Worth *physician*

Salyersville
Abalo, Tomas Confesor *physician*

Warsaw
Kutnicki, Benjamin *family physician*

LOUISIANA

Alexandria
Myers, Charles Lawrence *anesthesiologist*
Naalbandian, Arsham *neurologist*

Baton Rouge
Billoups, Edd *medical administrator*
Bishop, George Albert *psychiatrist*
Estes, Jeanne Mittler *psychiatrist*
Jayasinghe, Mahinda Desilva *cardiologist*
Kidd, James Marion, III *allergist, immunologist, educator*
Krotoski, Wojciech Antoni *research physician, educator*
Parra, Pamela Ann *physician, educator*
Romero, Jorge Antonio *neurologist, educator*
Scollard, David Michael *pathologist*
York, David Anthony *biomedical sciences researcher*

Benton
Dunnihoo, Dale Russell *physician, medical educator*

Eunice
Landreneau, Rodney Edmund, Jr. *physician*

Hammond
Hejtmancik, Milton Rudolph *medical educator*

Harvey
Lamid, Sofjan *physician, educator*

Houma
Conrad, Harold Theodore *psychiatrist*
Eschete, Mary Louise *internist*

Kentwood
Carter, Mary Kathleen *pharmacologist, educator, researcher*

Lafayette
Longo, Margaret Fay *surgeon*

Lake Charles
Drez, David Jacob, Jr. *orthopedic surgeon, educator*
Gunderson, Clark Alan *orthopedic surgeon*
Mocklin, Kevin Etienne *physician, medical educator*
Rathmell, Aretta Jennings *psychiatrist*
Yadalam, Kashinath Gangadhara *psychiatrist*

Mandeville
Guillot, Jacques Louis *internist, pediatrician*
Ray, Charles Jackson *retired surgeon*

Marrero
Imseis, Manuel Yusuf *pediatrician, allergist, immunologist*

Metairie
Bower, Philip Jeffrey *cardiologist, administrator*
Conway, James Donald *internist, educator*
Harell, George S. *radiologist*
Lake, Wesley Wayne, Jr. *internist, allergist, educator*
Maumus, Craig W(alther) *psychiatrist, consultant*
Melcher, Archibald Louis, III *neurologist*
Metzner, David Mark *plastic and reconstructive surgeon*
Ochsner, Seymour Fiske *radiologist, editor*
Samuels, Bernard *obstetrician, gynecologist*
Spruiell, Vann *psychoanalyst, educator, editor, researcher*
Sugar, Max *physician, psychiatrist, medical educator*

Monroe
Blondin, Joan *nephrologist educator*

New Orleans
Abrahams, Lawrence Michael *psychiatrist*
Anderson, Russell Lee *family medicine educator*
Bautista, Abraham Parana *immunologist*
Beck, David Edward *surgeon*
Brazda, Frederick Wicks *pathologist*
Cohn, Isidore, Jr. *surgeon, educator*
Corrigan, James John, Jr. *pediatrician, dean*
Daniels, Robert Sanford *psychiatrist, administrator*
Deichmann, Richard E. *internal medicine physician*
Elkins, Thomas Edward *obstetrician-gynecologist*
England, John David *neurologist*
Ensenat, Louis Albert *surgeon*
Espinoza, Luis Rolan *rheumatologist*
Ewin, Dabney Minor *surgeon*
Fisch, Bruce Jeffrey *physician*
Fisher, William Paul, Jr. *medical educator, medical outcomes researcher*
Franklin, Rudolph Michael *ophthalmologist, medical association administrator*
Gabert, Harvey A. *obstetrician, gynecologist, educator*
Gathright, John Byron, Jr. *colon and rectal surgeon, educator*
Gatipon, Betty Becker *medical educator, consultant*
Gottlieb, Marise Suss *physician*
Greenfield, D(avid) Tyler *cardiothoracic surgery educator*
Griffin, Jeffrey Farrow *surgeon*
Howard, Richard Ralston, II *medical health advisor, researcher, financier*
Hyman, Albert Lewis *cardiologist*
Hyman, Edward Sidney *physician, researcher*
Hyslop, Newton Everett *allergist, immunologist*
Incaprera, Frank Philip *internist, medical educator, health facility administrator*
Joyce, James Joseph *cardiologist*
Kaye, Jefferson James *orthopaedic surgeon*
Kewalramani, Laxman Sunderdas *surgeon, consultant*
Krane, N. Kevin *physician*
Krogstad, Donald John *infectious diseases physician, educator*
Martin, Louis Frank *surgery and physiology educator*
Maxwell, Donald Power, Jr. *ophthalmologist, physician, educator*
McGrath, Hugh *medical educator*
McKinnon, William Mitchell Patrick *surgeon*
Montgomery, Douglas Morrison *perinatologist, obstetrician-gynecologist*
Nichols, Ronald Lee *surgeon, educator*
Olubadewo, Joseph Olanrewaju *pharmacologist, educator*
O'Quinn, April Gale *physician, educator*
Peyman, Gholam Ali *ophthalmologist*
Pfister, Richard Charles *physician, radiology educator*
Phelps, Carol Jo *neuroendocrinologist*
Plavsic, Branko Milenko *radiology educator*
Reisin, Efrain *nephrologist, researcher, educator*
Reyes, Raul Gregorio *surgeon*
Rietschel, Robert Louis *dermatologist*
Roberts, Elliott C., Sr. *public health educator*
Rodenhauser, Paul *psychiatry educator*
Rossowski, Wojciech Jozef *medical educator, research scientist*
Salatich, John Smyth *cardiologist*
Sander, Gary Edward *medical educator*
Schally, Andrew Victor *endocrinologist, researcher*
Seltzer, Benjamin *neurologist, educator*
Sizemore, Robert Carlen *immunologist, educator*
Sorensen, Ricardo Uwe *pediatrics educator*
Stewart, Gregory Wallace *physician*
Svenson, Ernest Olander *psychiatrist, psychoanalyst*
Timmcke, Alan Edward *physician and surgeon*
Udall, John Nicholas, Jr. *pediatric gastroenterologist*
Van Meter, Clifford Holly, Jr. *surgeon*
Wallstrom, Randi Ruth *rheumatologist, educator*
Weiss, Larry David *medical educator*
Wiley, Kenneth LeMoyne *physician*
Wolfe, Margaret Ann Reed *medical scientist*
Yazigi, Rashid A. *allergist, immunologist, pediatrician*

Opelousas
Pinac, André Louis, III *obstetrician, gynecologist*

Pineville
Hirsch, Joe Elbe *surgeon*
Swearingen, David Clarke *physician, musician*

Rayville
Krin, Charles Steven *osteopath*

Scott
Bergeron, Wilton Lee *physician*

Shreveport
Block, Ernest Francis Jonathan *surgeon*
Campbell, G. Douglas *medical educator*
Chesson, Andrew Long, Jr. *neurology educator*
Fort, Arthur Tomlinson, III *physician, educator*
Freeman, Arthur Merrimon, III *psychiatry educator, dean*
Griffith, Robert Charles *allergist, educator, planter*
Hogan, Daniel James *dermatologist, educator*
Huot, Rachel Irene *biomedical educator, research scientist*
Levine, Steven Neil *endocrinologist*
Levy, Harold Bernard *pediatrician*
Mancini, Mary Catherine *cardiothoracic surgeon, researcher*
McBride, William A. *psychiatrist, educator*
Mullen, Andrew Judson *physician*
Naples, Jean Marie *physician*
San Pedro, Gerardo Santos *pulmonary and critical care physician, researcher*
Sanusi, Irwan Daniel *pathology educator*
Schwalke, Michael Allen *general surgeon, surgical oncologist*
Shelby, James Stanford *cardiovascular surgeon*
Thurmon, Theodore Francis *medical educator*
Willis, Marilyn *medical librarian*

Slidell
McBurney, Elizabeth Innes *physician, educator*
Muller, Robert Joseph *gynecologist*
Romano, Esteban Oscar *urologist*
Thornton, William Earl *physician, psychiatrist, psychoanalyst*

Thibodaux
Hebert, Leo Placide *physician*

West Monroe
Scott, Eugene Benson, II *general practice and family medicine physician*

MARYLAND

Bethesda
Nelson, Stuart James *internist, health facility administrator*
Williams, Mark Leon *medical educator, researcher*

Rockville
Gilliam, Bruce Lawrence *internist*

MASSACHUSETTS

Boston
Steinsapir, Jaime *physician, researcher*

MICHIGAN

Traverse City
Yankee, William Joseph *forensic psychophysiologist, educator*

MINNESOTA

Bloomington
Lakin, James Dennis *allergist, immunologist, director*

MISSISSIPPI

Biloxi
Fontenelle, Larry Jules *cardiothoracic surgeon*
Ozolek, John Anthony *pediatrician, neonatologist*

Brandon
Nelson, Norman Crooks *surgeon, academic administrator, educator*

Gulfport
Kaufman-Derbes, Linda Ruth *physician*
Sangani, Bharat Himatlal *cardiologist*

Hattiesburg
Bellare, Nagendranath *physician*
Brinson, Ralph Alan *physician, pediatrician, neonatologist*

Jackson
Brooks, Thomas Joseph, Jr. *preventive medicine educator*
Caine, Curtis Webb *anesthesiologist*
Cruse, Julius Major, Jr. *pathologist, educator*
Das, Suman Kumar *plastic surgeon, researcher*
Didlake, Ralph Hunter, Jr. *surgeon*
Eigenbrodt, Marsha Lillian *internal medicine educator, epidemologist*
Freeland, Alan Edward *orthopedic surgery educator, physician*
Geissler, William Bennett *orthopaedic surgeon*
Haines, Duane E. *neuroscience educator, academic administrator*
Hutchinson, Richard Glenn *medical educator, researcher*
Johnson, Samuel Britton *ophthalmologist, educator*
Kermode, John Cotterill *pharmacology educator, researcher*
King, Ralph Edwin, Jr. *health care educator*
Malamud, Fernando *oncologist*
Mihas, Anastasios Athanasios *gastroenterologist*
O'Connell, John Bernard, Jr. *medical educator, chairman department of medicine*
Poole, Galen Vincent *surgeon, educator, researcher*
Russell, Robert Pritchard *ophthalmologist*
Sneed, Raphael Corcoran *physiatrist, pediatrician*
Thigpen, James Tate *physician, oncology educator*
Vance, Ralph Brooks *oncologist and educator*
Walcott, Dexter Winn *allergist*

Keesler AFB
Rone, James Kellett *endocrinologist, career officer*

Laurel
Lacey, Peeler Grayson *diagnostic radiologist*
Lindstrom, Eric Everett *ophthalmologist*

Meridian
Cook, Donald Eugene *orthopedist*

Tupelo
Wooldridge, Thomas Dean *nephrologist*

Waveland
Kendrick, Leland Ray *physician*

Whitfield
Kliesch, William Frank *physician*

MISSOURI

Jefferson City
Forks, Thomas Paul *osteopathic physician*

Joplin
Daus, Arthur Steven *neurological surgeon*

Kansas City
Geller, Robert Burns *medical educator, researcher*

NEBRASKA

Omaha
Lackner, Rudy Paul *cardiothoracic surgeon*

NEW HAMPSHIRE

Keene
Olsson, Peter Alan *psychiatrist, psychoanalyst*

NEW MEXICO

Albuquerque
Storrs, Bruce Bryson *pediatric neurosurgeon*

NEW YORK

Brooklyn
Mohaideen, A. Hassan *surgeon, healthcare executive*

New York
Rainess, Alan Edward *psychiatrist*

NORTH CAROLINA

Asheville
Astler, Vernon Benson *surgeon*
Cowan, Thomas David *emergency medical services professional*
Enriquez, Manuel Hipolito *physician*
Maloney, Sean Robert *physician, biomedical engineer*
Summerlin, Harry Holler, Jr. *family physician, educator*
Thielman, Samuel Barnett *psychiatrist*
White, Terry Edward *physician*

Banner Elk
Littlejohn, Mark Hays *radiologist*

Boone
Folts, William Edward *academic administrator, educator*

Brevard
Hendel, Robert Charles *surgeon*

Burlington
Morris, George Thomas Arnold *internist*

Cameron
Meltzer, Morton *physician*

Cary
Amtoft-Nielsen, Joan Theresa *physician, educator, researcher*
Morris, Peter Delaney *epidemiologist*

Chapel Hill
Criado-Pallares, Enrique *vascular surgeon*
De Rosa, Guy Paul *orthopedic surgery educator*
Egan, Thomas Michael *surgeon, educator*
Fine, Jo-David *dermatologist*
Freeman, David Franklin *psychoanalyst, psychiatrist*
Golden, Robert Neal *psychiatrist, researcher*
Graham, John Borden *pathologist, writer, educator*
Hall, Colin David *neurologist*
Herbst, Charles Arthur, Jr. *general surgeon, educator*
Koruda, Mark Joseph *surgeon, educator, nutrition educator*
Lee, Joseph King Tak *radiologist, medical educator*
Merten, David Fischer *radiologist, pediatrician and educator*
Mill, Michael Robert *cardiothoracic surgeon, educator*
Morrow, A. Leslie *neuropharmacology, neurobiology and toxicology educator*
Nebel, William Arthur *obstetrician, gynecologist*
Pagano, Joseph Stephen *physician, researcher, educator*
Sanders, Charles Addison *physician*
Semelka, Richard Charles *medical educator*
Shea, Thomas Charles *physician, educator*
Sobsey, Mark David *public health educator, researcher*
Thomas, Colin Gordon, Jr. *surgeon, medical educator*
Tomsick, Robert Stanley *dermatologist*
Wang, Jingsong *immunologist*
Wilcox, Benson Reid *cardiothoracic surgeon, educator*

Charlotte
Backeljauw, Philippe Ferdinand *pediatric endocrinologist, clinical researcher*
Berkowitz, Gerald Phillip *physician*
Berman, Larry F. *physician, health facility administrator*
Divish, Margaret Mary *physician*
Fulp, Sam Russell *gastroenterologist*
Hall, James Bryan *gynecological oncologist*
Hudson, Paul J. *physician*
Humphrey, John Edward *psychiatrist*
Hutcheson, J. Sterling *allergist, immunologist, physician*
Kleinmann, Richard Eckert *endocrinologist*
McCall, Marvin Mather, III *internist, educator*
Nicholson, Henry Hale, Jr. *surgeon*
Ramp, Warren Kibby *orthopedist, educator*
Saikevych, Irene A. *pathologist*
Shah, Nandlal Chimanlal *physiatrist*
Shaver, David Corydon *obstetrician, gynecologist*
Short, Earl de Grey, Jr. *psychiatrist, consultant*
Taylor, William Farnham *emergency physician*
Thompson, John Albert, Jr. *dermatologist*
Walker, William Alfred *colon and rectal surgeon*
Weinrib, David A. *infectious disease physician, consultant*

Durham
Allen, Nancy Bates *medical educator*
Amory, David William *anesthesiologist, educator*
Barboriak, Daniel Paul *radiologist*
Barry, David Walter *infectious diseases physician, researcher*
Blazer, Dan German *psychiatrist, epidemiologist*
Bohjanen, Paul Robert *internist, scientist*
Brodie, Harlow Keith Hammond *psychiatrist, educator*
Carroll, Barbara Anne *radiologist, educator*
Carson, Culley Clyde, III *urologist*
Cohen, Harvey Jay *physician, educator*
Drezner, Marc Kenneth *endocrinologist*
Gaede, Jane Taylor *pathologist*
Goldstein, Larry Bruce *neurologist, educator*
Halperin, Edward Charles *physician*
Herbert, William Norman Parke *obstetrician, gynecologist, administrator*
Hertzberg, Barbara Spector *academic radiologist*
Hoffman, Maureane Richardson *pathologist and researcher*
Howard, Thad Alan *research analyst*
Hunt, Christine Marie *gastroenterologist*
Kisslo, Joseph Andrew *cardiology, educator*
Kurtzberg, Joanne *pediatrics educator*
Langley, Ricky Lee *occupational medicine physician*
Layfield, Lester James *pathologist, educator*
Llewellyn, Charles Elroy, Jr. *psychiatrist*
Lyerly, Herbert Kim *surgical oncology educator, researcher*
Mallon, William James *orthopaedic surgeon, sports historian*
Mark, Daniel Benjamin *internist, cardiologist, medical educator*
Massey, Janice Munn *neurology educator*
Masters, David Lee *pediatrician*
Murray, William James *anesthesiology educator, clinical pharmacologist*
Navas, Luis Ramon *family physician*
Piantadosi, Claude Anthony *pulmonologist, educator*
Platt, Jeffrey Louis *surgery educator, immunology educator, pediatric nephrologist*
Ritter, Frederick Edmond *plastic surgeon, educator*
Schuch, Charles Michael *medical educator, researcher*
Serafin, Donald *plastic surgeon*
Snyderman, Ralph *medical educator, physician*
Sundy, John Sargent *physician, immunologist*
Tombaugh, Geoffrey Clarke *neurobiologist*
Varia, Indira Mahesh (Indu Varia) *psychiatry educator*
Weiner, Debra Kaye *physician, educator*
Weiner, Richard David *psychiatrist, researcher*
Weitzner, Stanley Wallace *physician, medical educator*
Winton, Robert Emmett *psychiatrist*
Yancy, William Samuel *pediatrician*
Yeowell, Heather Nina *medical educator*

Emerald Isle
Brenton, Harold L. *physician*

Fayetteville
Hurdle, Thomas Gray *urologist*
Marcotte, David Bacon *psychiatrist*

Fort Bragg
Jenkins, Pamela Ruth *medical researcher*

Gastonia
Prince, George Edward *pediatrician*

Goldsboro
Maier, Rudolph Joseph *neurologist*

Greensboro
Baird, Haynes Wallace *pathologist*
Cotter, John Burley *ophthalmologist, corneal specialist*
Curnes, John Taylor *neuroradiologist*
DeChurch, Frances Elizabeth *physician*
Robinson, Edward Norwood, Jr. *physician, educator*
Schall, Stewart Allan *pediatric cardiologist*
Stevens, Elliott Walker, Jr. *allergist, pulmonologist*
Taylor, Shahane Richardson, Jr. *ophthalmologist*
Truesdale, Gerald Lynn *plastic and reconstructive surgeon*

Greenville
Chiang, Karl Sy-Cherng *interventional radiologist*
Cunningham, Paul Raymond Goldwyn *surgery educator*
Dar, Mohammad Saeed *pharmacologist, educator*
Hoffman, Donald Richard *pathologist, educator*
Joshi, Vijay V. *pathologist, educator*
Lee, Kenneth Stuart *neurosurgeon*
Lee, Tung-Kwang *pathologist, cancer researcher*
Meggs, William Joel *internist, emergency physician, educator*
Metzger, W. James, Jr. *physician, researcher, educator*
Moskop, John Charles *bioethics educator*
Movahed, Assad *cardiologist*
Peterson, Gary Michael *neuroscientist, educator*
Poole, Max Calvin *endocrinology educator*
Pories, Walter Julius *surgeon, educator*
Volkman, Alvin *pathologist, researcher, educator*

Hampstead
Solomon, Robert Douglas *pathology educator*

Hickory
Dickey, Richard Allen *endocrinologist*
Tart, David Earl *dermatologist*
Yapundich, Robert Anthony *physician*

High Point
Bardelas, Jose Antonio *allergist*

Holly Ridge
Dieckmann, Merwin Richard *retired physician*

Kernersville
Meschan, Isadore *radiologist, educator*
Meschan, Rachel Farrer (Mrs. Isadore Meschan) *obstetrics and gynecology educator*

Lexington
Welborn, James Todd *physician*

Matthews
Hendrix, Robert Andrew *otolaryngologist*

Monroe
Smith, Jeffrey Alan *occupational medicine physician, toxicologist*

Morganton
Baden, Thomas James *dermatologist*
Tanas, Khalil Saliba *psychiatrist*

Mount Airy
Thoppil, Cecil Koshey *pediatrician, educator*

Nags Head
Crow, Harold Eugene *physician, family medicine educator*

Pinehurst
Jacobson, Peter Lars *neurologist, educator*
Storch, Samuel Jay *urologist*

Raleigh
Archie, Joseph Patrick, Jr. *vascular surgeon, educator*
Carter, Alan Bruce *psychiatrist*
Chaudhry, Abdul Ghafoor *surgeon*
Hoellerich, Vincent L. *anesthesiologist*
Levine, Ronald H. *physician, state official*
Majors, Robert Powell, Jr. *surgeon*
Martin, Philip Lee *ophthalmologist, surgeon*
McElveen, John Thomas, Jr. *physician, medical educator*
Riviere, Jim Edmond *pharmacologist, educator*
Satterfield, Benton Sapp *obstetrician, gynecologist*
Veenhuis, Philip Edward *psychiatrist, educator, administrator*
Warren, Larry Estel *internist*
Zarzar, Nakhleh Pacifico *psychiatrist*

Research Triangle Park
Davis, Cynthia Marie *medical writer*
Elion, Gertrude Belle *research scientist, pharmacology educator*
Jarrell, Donald Ray *medical technologist*
Stave, Gregg Martin *occupational health physician*

Rocky Mount
Lee, Soong Hyun *psychiatrist, educator*

Salisbury
Katzin, David Simon *physician*
Kiser, Glenn Augustus *retired pediatrician, philanthropist, investor*

Southport
Forstner, James Robert *family practice physician*

Statesville
Nicholson, John Christie *internist*

Wilmington
Calhoun, Linda Palmon (Linda C. Palmon) *cardiologist*
Gillen, Howard William *neurologist, medical historian*
Gonzalez, Jorge Jose *medical educator*
Joyner, William Lawrence *family physician, health center administrator*
Ungaro, Peter Curt *hematology and oncology educator*
Wilkins, Lucien Sanders *gastroenterologist*

Wilson
Kushner, Michael James *neurologist, consultant*

Winston Salem
Bey, Richard Doud *neurologist, electromyographer*
Bowton, David Lowell *physician*
Boyce, William Henry *former urologist, educator*
Chen, Michael Yu Men *physician*
Cheng, Che Ping *cardiologist, researcher, educator*
Crandall, Sonia Jane *medical educator*
Elster, Allen DeVaney *radiologist, educator, scientific researcher*
Fleischer, Alan Bernard, Jr. *dermatologist, educator*
Fleming, Ronald A. *clinical pharmacologist*
Georgitis, John *allergist, educator*
Hazzard, William Russell *geriatrician, educator*
Herrington, David McLeod *cardiologist, educator*
Howell, Charles Maitland *dermatologist*
Kaufman, William *internist*
Miller, Mark Steven *pharmacologist, educator*
Mueller-Heubach, Eberhard August *obstetrician gynecologist, medical researcher*
Ott, David James *diagnostic radiologist*
Podgorny, George *emergency physician*
Richards, Frederick *hematologist/oncologist*
Tobin, Joseph Raphael *medical educator*
Toole, James Francis *medical educator*
Veille, Jean-Claude *maternal-fetal medicine physician, educator*
Voytko, Mary Lou *neuroscientist*
Walker, John Samuel *retired pediatrician*
Washburn, Ronald Glenn *infectious disease physician*
Woods, Charles Reece, Jr. *pediatrician, educator*
Zagoria, Ronald Jay *radiologist, educator*

Zebulon
Sedwitz, Joseph Lee *surgeon, gynecologist*

OHIO

Cleveland
Luce, Edward Andrew *plastic surgeon*

Hudson
Gusz, John Robert *general surgeon*

Ironton
Newmark, Howard *surgeon, entrepreneur*

OKLAHOMA

Ada
Mynatt, Cecil Ferrell *psychiatrist*
Van Burkleo, Bill Ben *osteopath, emergency physician*

Altus
Stine, Earle John, Jr. *radiologist*

Ardmore
Veazey, John Hobson *internist*

Enid
Dandridge, William Shelton *orthopedic surgeon*
Tagge, James Fredrick *internist*

Eufaula
Parmar, Jitendra Ravji *internist, gastroenterologist*

Guymon
Lim, Jeffrey James *internist*

Jenks
Wootan, Gerald Don *osteopathic physician, educator*

Lawton
Riccitelli, Kevin Mark *family practice physician*

Mc Loud
Whinery, Michael Albert *physician*

Mcalester
Jumelle, Antoine Jean Michel *surgeon*
Reed, Walter George, Jr. *osteopath*

Muskogee
Kent, Bartis Milton *physician*
Wood, Charles Douglas *surgeon educator*

Norman
Lanzidelle, George Arthur *practical nurse*

Oklahoma City
Aulthouse, Amy Lynn *anatomist and educator*
Bahr, Carman Bloedow *internist*
Baltaro, Richard J. *pathologist*
Bozalis, John Russell *physician*
Bradford, Reagan Howard, Jr. *ophthalmology educator*
Brumback, Roger Alan *neuropathologist, researcher*
Claflin, James Robert *pediatrician, allergist*
Comp, Philip Cinnamon *medical researcher*
Ellis, Robert Smith *allergist, immunologist*
Farris, Bradley Kent *neuro-ophthalmologist*
Felton, Warren Locker, II *surgeon*
Filley, Warren Vernon *allergist, immunologist*
Gavaler, Judith Ann Stohr Van Thiel *bio-epidemiologist*
George, James Noel *hematologist-oncologist, educator*
Gibbs, John Patrick *physician, educator*
Haas, Gilbert George, Jr. *reproductive endocrinologist*
Hampton, James Wilburn *hematologist, medical oncologist*
Harvey, William Gipson, Jr. *physician*
Hays, Charles Wilfred *medical epidemiologist, public health educator*
Haywood, B(etty) J(ean) *anesthesiologist*
Hull, Stephen Simmons, Jr. *medical educator*
Kimerer, Neil Banard, Sr. *psychiatrist, educator*
Kinasewitz, Gary Theodore *medical educator*
King, Robert Wallace, Jr. *nephrologist*
Lee, Lela Ann *dermatology educator, researcher*
Lorentzen, James Clifford *internist*
McCarty, David Lewis *emergency physician*
Medbery, Clinton Amos, III *radiation oncologist, internist*
Oehlert, William Herbert, Jr. *cardiologist, administrator, educator*
Oommen, Kalarickal Joseph *neurologist*
Parke, David Wilkin, II *ophthalmologist, educator, healthcare executive*
Parker, John R. *physician, pathologist*
Perez-Cruet, Jorge *psychiatrist, psychopharmacologist, psychophysiologist*
Rayan, Ghazi M. *surgeon*
Rayburn, William Frazier *obstetrician, gynecologist, educator*
Reinke, Lester Allen *pharmacologist*
Robison, Clarence, Jr. *surgeon*
Troncoso, Carlos Alberto *surgeon*
Venkataraman, Tirunelveli Viswanathan *nephrologist*
Walters, Roland A, III *ophthalmologist*
Weigand, Dennis Allen *dermatologist, educator*
Worsham, Bertrand Ray *psychiatrist*
Zuhdi, Nazih *surgeon*

Okmulgee
Rico, David M. *physician, researcher*

Shawnee
Wilson, Robert Godfrey *radiologist*

Tahlequah
Stucky, Don E. *family physician*

Tulsa
Brunk, Samuel Frederick *oncologist*
Crockett-Archer, Deborah Dawn *surgeon*
Donovan, Gerard Kevin *pediatrician*
Goodman, Thomas Allen *psychiatrist, educator*
Irwin, Richard Craig *pediatrician*
Kamp, George Hamil *physician, radiology administrator*
King, Joseph Willet *child psychiatrist*
Lang, Michael John *neonatologist*
Llewellyn, Thomas Sylvester, III *radiologist, educator*
McCullough, Robert Dale, II *osteopath*
Miller, Gerald Cecil *immunologist, laboratory administrator, educator*
Nebergall, Robert William *orthopedic surgeon, educator*
Okada, Robert Dean *cardiologist*
Portman, Glenda Carolene *forensic document examiner*
Reed, Guy Dean *osteopathic physician*
Say, Burhan *physician*
Shane, John Marder *endocrinologist*
Smith, Vernon Soruix *neonatologist, pediatrician, educator*
Wehrs, Roger E. *physician*

Vinita
Neer, Charles Sumner, II *orthopedic surgeon, educator*

PENNSYLVANIA

Philadelphia
Platsoucas, Chris Dimitrios *immunologist*

RHODE ISLAND

Little Compton
Small, Wilfred Thomas *surgeon, educator*

SOUTH CAROLINA

Aiken
von Buedingen, Richard Paul *urologist*

Anderson
Jones, Frederic Gordon *family medicine educator*

Charleston
Baron, Paul Lawrence *surgical oncologist, educator*
Bissada, Nabil Kaddis *urologist, educator, researcher, author*
Carabello, Blase Anthony *cardiology educator*
Crawford, Fred Allen, Jr. *cardiothoracic surgeon, educator*
Crumbley, Arthur Jackson, III *cardiothoracic surgeon*
Cuddy, Brian Gerard *neurosurgeon*
Cunningham, John Thomas *medicine educator, gastroenterologist*
Curry, Nancy Lynne Stiles *radiologist, educator*
DeBanto, John Robert *internist*
Elliott, Bruce Michael *vascular surgeon*
Favaro, Mary Kaye Asperheim (Mrs. Biagino Philip Favaro) *pediatrician*
Friedman, Richard Joel *orthopaedic surgeon*
Halushka, Perry Victor *physician, medical educator*
Hawk, John Chrisman, III *surgeon*
Haynes, Gary R. *anesthesiologist*
Hochman, Marcelo L. J. *facial plastic surgeon*
Key, Janice Dixon *physician, medical educator*
Langdale, Emory Lawrence *physician*
Leman, Robert Burton *cardiology educator*
McCurdy, Layton *medical educator*
Mohr, Lawrence Charles *physician*
Rustin, Rudolph Byrd, III *physician*
Sahn, Steven Alan *internist, educator*
Saunders, Richard Ames *ophtholmologist, educator*
Schuman, Stanley H. *epidemiologist, educator*
Strange, Charlton Bell, III *internal medicine educator*
Stuart, Robert Kenneth *internist, oncologist, hematologist, educator*
Thiers, Bruce Harris *dermatology educator*
Turner, William Redd *urologist, educator*
Wall, Robert Thorp, Jr. *internist, hematologist, oncologist*
Worthington, (Ward) Curtis, III *neurosurgeon*

Columbia
Brannon, William Lester, Jr. *neurologist, educator*
Brenner, Eric Richard *epidemiologist*
Clare, Fountain Stewart, III *pathologist*
Flanagan, Clyde Harvey, Jr. *psychiatrist, psychoanalyst, educator*
Hollins, William Joseph, II *cardiologist, educator*
Hoppmann, Richard Anthony *physician*
Hwang, Te-Long *neurologist, educator*
Johnson, Elbert Neil, Jr. *internist*
Kaplan, Eugene Herbert *academic psychoanalyst*
Lin, Tu *endocrinologist, educator, researcher, academic administrator*
Pressley, Lucius C. *psychiatrist*
Schwarz, Ferdinand (Fred Schwarz) *ophthalmologist, ophthalmic plastic surgeon*
Sheppe, Joseph Andrew *surgeon*
Wilson, Marlene Ann *neuroscientist, educator*
Wright, Harry Hercules *psychiatrist*

Florence
Harley, Al Boyce, Jr. *psychiatrist*
Imbeau, Stephen Alan *allergist*
Windham, Nancy Quintero *obstetrician, gynecologist*

Gaffney
Wheeler, William Earl *general surgeon*

Greenville
Anderson, Mark Wendell *gastroenterologist*
Anglea, Joy Sharon *family practice physician*
Bessinger, Colonel Donivan, Jr. *surgeon, writer*
Brundage, Stephanie Carol *physician*
Croskery, Richard W. *internist*
Ferlauto, Jerry Joseph *neonatologist*
Henderson, Joseph H. *cardiologist*
Hoffman, Michael Robert *physician*
Kilgore, Donald Gibson, Jr. *pathologist*
Raunikar, Robert Austin *cardiology and pediatrics educator*
Riddle, Charles Daniel (Dan Riddle) *biomedical educator*
Robson, William Lane McKenzie *pediatrician, medical educator*
Walls, Jay David *hematologist, oncologist*
Weathers, William Travis *pediatrician, educator*

Greenwood
Abercrombie, Stoney Alton *family physician*

Greer
Grubbs, Raymond Van *surgeon*

Johns Island
Semmens, James Pike *obstetrician, gynecologist, educator*

Lumberton
Carter, David Lucion *medical services administrator*

Mc Bee
Whitaker, Halford Snyder *physician*

North Augusta
McRee, John Browning, Jr. *physician*

North Charleston
Moscatello, Salvatore Anthony *gastroenterologist*

Rock Hill
Hull, William Martin, Jr. *ophthalmologist*
Lehman, William Louis, Jr. *orthopaedic surgeon*

Saint Helena Island
Dunn, Adolphus William *orthopedic surgeon*

Seneca
Uden, David Elliott *cardiologist, educator*

Spartanburg
Baughman, Otis Lee, III *family physician*
Guthrie, John Robert *physician, writer*
Sovenyhazy, Gabor Ferenc *surgeon*

Summerville
Orvin, George Henry *psychiatrist*

Taylors
Anderson, Albert Severin *allergist, nutritionist*

West Columbia
Arora, Sri Nath *internist, hematologist*
Carter, Saralee Lessman *immunologist, microbiologist*

TENNESSEE

Athens
Wallace, Jeffrey Leigh *surgeon*

Bolivar
Morson, Philip Hull, III *psychiatrist, osteopath*

Brentwood
Himmelfarb, Elliott Harvey *radiologist*
McCord, J. William *anesthesiologist*

Bristol
Patel, Ashvin Ambalal *psychiatrist*

Chattanooga
Bond, Rae Young *medical society administrator*
Eberle, David Eugene *gastroenterologist*
Franklin, Donald Benjamin, Jr. *nephrologist*
Kaplan, Hyman M. *internist*
Shuck, Edwin Haywood, III *surgeon*
Thow, George Bruce *surgeon*

Cordova
Lieberman, Phillip Louis *allergist, educator*

Franklin
Moessner, Harold Frederic *allergist*

Goodlettsville
Jenkins, James Sherwood, Jr. *pharmacologist*

Jackson
Carlton, Bradley Joseph *medical educator*
Ibach, Michael Brett *physician, educator*

Jefferson City
Muncy, Estle Pershing *physician*

Johnson City
Carbone, Robert James *family practice physician*
Fukuda, Aisaku Isaac *reproductive endocrinologist*
Hamdy, Ronald Charles *geriatrician*
Joyce, Larry Wayne *physician*
Konikiewicz, Leonard Wieslaw *biomedical communications educator*
Kostrzewa, Richard Michael *pharmacology educator*
Laird, Kimberly Jeanne *medical librarian, educator*
Mehta, Ashok Vallavdas *pediatric cardiologist*
Mehta, Jayant B. *internist, health facility administrator*
Merrick, Raymond Daniel *internist, educator*
Miyamoto, Michael Dwight *neuroscience educator, researcher*
Olive, Kenneth Everett *internist, health facility administrator*
Olsen, Martin E. *obstetrician/gynecologist*
Peiris, Alan Nilrathan *medical educator*
Shurbaji, M. Salah *pathologist*
Trivett, Martha Stover *medical librarian*

Knoxville
Adams, Linas Jonas *gastroenterologist*
Bukovsky, Antonin Vaclav *physician, obstetrician, gynecologist, educator*
Cook, Nedra Johnson *medical librarian*
Davidson, Evelyne Monique *internist*
DePersio, Richard John *otolaryngologist, plastic surgeon*
Martin, Robert O. *cardiologist*
Pool, Michael Lee *psychiatrist*
Richmond, Robert Southwick *pathologist*
Schneider, William James *plastic and reconstructive surgeon*
Trofatter, Kenneth Frank *obstetrician, gynecologist*

La Follette
Farris, James Clarence *internal medicine physician*

Maryville
Lucas, Melinda Ann *pediatrician, educator*

Memphis
Abell, Thomas Lyman *physician*
Bada, Henrietta Salvilla *medical educator*
Chesney, Thomas McColl *pathologist*
Christopher, Robert Paul *physician*
Cicala, Roger Stephen *physician, educator*
Dempsey, Buckley Kinard *cardiologist*
Eby, Patricia Lynn *plastic surgeon*
Economides, Nicholas George *plastic surgeon*
Gavant, Morris Leonard *radiologist*
Godsey, William Cole *physician*
Grum, Daniel Frank *anesthesiologist, educator, medical administrator*
Hall, Johnnie Cameron *pathologist*
Heimberg, Murray *pharmacologist, biochemist, physician, educator*
Hughes, James G. *pediatrics educator*
Hurwitz, Julia Lea *immunologist*
Jacewicz, Michael *neurologist, educator*
Jackson, Robert Lewis *dermatologist*
Kreth, Timothy Kerwin *cardiologist*
Lazar, Rande Harris *otolaryngologist*
Lew, D(ukhee) Betty *physician*
Lewis, Myron *physician*
Martin, Daniel C. *surgeon, educator*
Morreim, E. Haavi *medical ethics educator*
Pourmotabbed, Ghassem *medical educator*
Pratt, Charles Benton *pediatric oncologist*

Rose, Susan Rogers *endocrinologist, researcher*
Samuels, Alan Daniel *internist, gastroenterologist*
Shokouh-Amiri, M. Hosein *transplant surgeon, educator*
Shulman, Lee Philip *medical educator*
Siegel, Jerome Seymour *cardiologist*
Simmons, Bryan Paul *physician, researcher*
Skinner, Edward Folland *retired thoracic surgeon*
Stewart, Marcus J(efferson) *retired orthopedic surgeon, consultant, educator*
Summitt, Robert Layman *pediatrician, educator*
Thomas, Michael Chumley *surgeon*
Tutko, Robert Joseph *radiology administrator, educator*
Watson, Donald Charles *cardiothoracic surgeon, educator*
Weaver, Charles H. *internist, oncologist*
Witte, Michael Myron *molecular biologist, educator*
Zhu, Xuegong *neuroscientist*

Mountain Home
Swartz, Conrad Melton *psychiatrist*

Murfreesboro
Eubanks, Marie Harris *medical librarian*

Nashville
Bernard, Louis Joseph *surgeon, educator*
Boothby, Mark R. *immunologist*
Brackin, Henry Bryan, Jr. *psychiatrist*
Butler, Merlin Gene *physician, medical geneticist, educator*
Byron, Joseph Winston *pharmacologist*
Clinton, Mary Ellen *neurologist*
Crabtree, Yvette Guislain *internist*
Edeki, Timi Imoafije *medical educator*
Edwards, William Hawkins *surgeon, educator*
Fenner, Catherine Munro *medical association administrator*
Fields, James Perry *dermatologist, dermatopathologist, allergist*
Fischell, Tim Alexander *cardiologist*
Frederiksen, Rand Terrell *cardiologist*
Grossman, Laurence Abraham *cardiologist*
Horowitz, David Harvey *dermatologist*
Horton, Frederick Tyron, Jr. *child psychiatrist*
Houston, Marcus Clarence *physician*
Jackson, C. Gary *otologist*
Jennings, Henry Smith, III *cardiologist*
Kenner, William Davis, III *psychiatrist*
Lavin, Patrick James *neurologist*
Leftwich, Russell Bryant *allergist, immunologist, consultant*
Marney, Samuel Rowe *physician, educator*
McLeod, Alexander Canaday *physician*
Meador, Clifton Kirkpatrick *internist, health facility administrator, educator*
Morrow, Jason Drew *medical and pharmacology educator*
Mozdab, Laila *osteopath*
Petrie, William Marshall *psychiatrist*
Pinson, Charles Wright *transplant surgeon*
Potts, James Lafayette *internist, cardiologist, health facility administrator*
Pribor, Hugo Casimer *physician*
Quinn, Robert William *physician, educator*
Robertson, David *pharmacologist, clinical investigator, educator*
Rosenblum, Sol A. *medical educator*
Sharp, Vernon Hibbett *psychiatrist*
Smith, William Barney *allergist*
Snyder, Stanley Owen *vascular surgeon*
Whitlock, James Alan *pediatrics educator*
Wood, Alastair James Johnston *physician, educator*

Oak Ridge
Miller, Kenneth Turner, Jr. *surgeon*
Spray, Paul E. *surgeon*

Paris
Whitby, Rodney Scott *internist, pediatrician*

Tullahoma
Cowan, Richard Howard *pediatrician*

Williamsport
Dysinger, Paul William *physician, educator, health consultant*

TEXAS

Abilene
Richert, Harvey Miller, II *ophthalmologist*
Russell, Byron Edward *physical therapy educator*

Amarillo
Archer, Grace Emily *obstetrician, gynecologist*
Berry, Rita Kay *medical technologist*
Marupudi, Sambasiva Rao *surgeon, educator*
Meyers, Charles Louis *occupational physician, consultant*
Nelson, Scott Russell *osteopath*
Norrid, Henry Gail *osteopath, surgeon, researcher*
Parker, Gerald M. *physician, researcher*
Perman, Phillip *physician, photographer*
Pratt, Donald George *physician*
Saadeh, Constantine Khalil *internist, health facility administrator, educator*

Arlington
Algilani, Kamran Cameron *physician, surgeon, researcher*
Carsia, Gene Vincent *physician*
Gates, Steven Leon *physician*
Keller, Ben Robert, Jr. *gynecologist*
Kline, Ronald Steven *colon and rectal surgeon*

Austin
Austin, John Riley *surgeon, educator*
Brender, Jean Diane *epidemiologist, nurse*
Coghe, David William *child psychiatrist*
Elequin, Cleto, Jr. *retired physician*
Fulmer, Robert Irwin *gynecologist*
Glass, Gary *psychiatrist*
Goodman, Louis Joel *medical society executive*
Hibbert, William Andrew, Jr. *surgeon*
Huang, Philip P. *physician*
Kreisle, James Edwin *physician internal medicine*
Le Maistre, Charles Aubrey *internist, epidemiologist, educator*
Moskow, John Bruce *emergency physician*
Painter, Theophilus Shickel, Jr. *physician*
Race, George William Daryl *psychiatrist*
Reid, William Howard *psychiatrist, educator*
Sutton, Beverly Jewell *psychiatrist*
Zientek, David Michael *cardiologist*

Beaumont
Lee, Shung-Man *nephrologist*
Lozano, Jose *nephrologist*
Phan, Tâm Thanh *medical educator, psychotherapist, consultant, researcher*
Remirez, Antonio *physician*
Sooudi, Matthew M. *surgeon*

Bedford
Rousch, Bernard Lawrence *psychiatrist*

Bellaire
Canales, Luis I. *gastroenterologist*
Pokorny, Alex Daniel *psychiatrist*

Bellville
Neely, Robert Allen *ophthalmologist*

Brenham
Charlesworth, Ernest Neal *allergist, dermatologist, immunologist, educator*

Camp Wood
Triplett, William Carryl *physician, researcher*

Cibolo
Jensen, Andrew Oden *obstetrician, gynecologist*

College Station
Rohack, John James *cardiologist*
Ufema, John William *radiologist, educator*

Colleyville
Jones, Mitchell Mark *medical researcher*

Conroe
Shepherd, Donald Ray *pathologist*

Corpus Christi
Appel, Truman Frank *surgeon*
Cook, Kenneth Ray *radiologist*
Everett, Orel Michael *family physician*
Lim, Alexander Rufasta *neurologist, clinical investigator, educator, writer*
Norstrom, Craig Wilbur *retired neurological surgeon*
Sisley, Nina Mae *physician, public health officer*
Wiggins, Robert Allan *physician*

Corsicana
LeMay, Sonley Robert, Jr. *otolaryngologist*

Dallas
Bashour, Fouad Anis *cardiology educator*
Baum, Michel Gerard *pediatrician, educator*
Berbary, Maurice Shehadeh *physician, military officer, hospital administrator, educator*
Boswell, George Marion, Jr. *orthopedist, health care facility administrator*
Brown, Orval Eric *otolaryngologist*
Cheatham, David Alan *internist*
Collins, Robert Howard, Jr. *oncologist, internist*
Coln, Dale *pediatric surgeon, educator*
Dees, Tom Moore *internist*
Dott, Gregory Alan *physician*
Edlin, John Charles *pediatrician*
Edwards, W.L. Jack *retired physician*
Einspruch, Burton Cyril *psychiatrist*
Ericson, Ruth Ann *psychiatrist*
Fierro-Carrion, Gustavo Adolfo *internist*
Fleckenstein, James Lawrence *radiologist*
Fleischmann, Roy Mitchell *rheumatologist, educator, researcher*
Gaulden, Mary Esther *medical/science educator*
Giesecke, Adolph Hartung *anesthesiologist, educator*
Gilman, Alfred Goodman *pharmacologist, educator*
Goldstein, Joseph Leonard *physician, medical educator, molecular genetics scientist*
Goldstein, Robert Michael *transplant surgeon*
Gonwa, Thomas Arthur *nephrologist, transplant physician*
Gray, Kevin Franklin *neuropsychiatrist*
Gross, Gary Neil *allergist, physician*
Guy, L(eona) Ruth *medical educator*
Guzzetta, Philip Conte, Jr. *pediatric surgeon, educator*
Hall, William Lloyd *surgeon*
Harrington, John Norris *ophthalmic plastic and reconstructive surgeon, educator*
Harris, Robert Alan, Jr. *physician*
Hughes, Waunell McDonald (Mrs. Delbert E. Hughes) *retired psychiatrist*
Hurd, Eric Ray *rheumatologist, internist, educator*
Jessen, Michael Erik *surgeon, educator*
Johnson, Robert Lee, Jr. *physician, educator, researcher*
Kaufmann, Margaret C. *psychiatrist, educator*
Kollmeyer, Kenneth Robert *surgeon*
Korngut, Irwin Steven *physician*
Landschulz, William Harras *endocrinologist*
Leib, Luis *physician*
Levi, Moshe *nephrologist, medical educator, researcher*
Lumry, William Raymond *physician, allergist*
Mabry, Richard Lee *otolaryngologist*
Margolin, Solomon Begelfor *pharmacologist*
Marynick, Samuel Philip *physician, educator*
McClain, Joni Lynn *medical examiner*
McConnell, John Dowling *urologist, educator*
McCracken, Alexander Walker *pathologist*
Menter, M(artin) Alan *dermatologist*
Mickey, Bruce Edward *neurosurgeon*
Miller, Edward Godfrey, Jr. *biomedical sciences educator, researcher*
Mitchell, Teddy Lee *physician*
Moore, William Thomas *psychiatrist, educator*
Munford, Robert Sims, III *internist, researcher, educator*
Nachimson, Harold Irwin *physician, mediator*
Odom, Floyd Clark *surgeon*
Olinger, Sheff Daniel *neurologist, educator*
Page, Richard Leighton *cardiologist, medical educator, researcher*
Pakes, Steven P. *medical school administrator*
Parkey, Robert Wayne *radiology and nuclear medicine educator, research radiologist*
Petty, Kevin Joseph *medical scientist, educator*
Pollock, Harlan *plastic surgeon, educator*
Purdue, Gary Frederick *surgeon, educator*
Quinn, Charles Treman *pediatrician*
Race, George Justice *pathology educator*
Roberts, Lynne Jeanine *physician*
Robertson, K. Joy *pulmonary/critical care educator*
Rogers, Lon Edmond *physician*
Rogers, Zora Rowena Nereid Esther *pediatrician*
Rohrich, Rodney James *plastic surgeon, educator*
Roland, Peter Sargent *otolaryngologist*
Rousseau, Wyatt Easterling *pulmonologist, internist*
Rush, Augustus John *psychiatrist, educator*
Salyer, Kenneth E. *surgeon*
Sánchez, Pablo J. *pediatrician, educator*
Schneider, Nancy Reynolds *pathologist*
Simon, Theodore Ronald *physician, medical educator*
Sklaver, Neal Lawrence *internist*
Smiley, James Donald *rheumatology educator*
Smith, Barry Samuel *physiatrist*
Sowell, David S., III *internist, insurance company executive*
Sperry, David Bartow *pediatric neurologist, physician*
Stewart, Rege Szuts *psychiatrist, educator*
Stone, Marvin Jules *physician, educator*
Talmadge, John Mills *physician*
Telford, Van Quincy *pathologist*
Tong, Alex Waiming *immunologist*
Valentine, Rawson James *surgeon, educator*
Wasserman, Richard Lawrence *pediatrician, educator*
Weiner, Myron Frederick *psychiatrist, educator, clinical investigator*
Wheeler, Clarence Joseph, Jr. *physician*
Whitfield, Jonathan Martin *pediatrician*
Wildenthal, C(laud) Kern *physician, educator*
Wyndham, Christopher R.C. *cardiologist*

El Campo
Goelzer, Ronald Eric *surgeon*

El Paso
Crossen, John Jacob *radiologist, educator*
De Vargas, Cecilia Cordoba *psychiatrist*
Hand, William Lee *physician*
Levine, Johanan Sidney *neurologist*
Mrochek, Michael J. *physician*
Pazmiño, Patricio Augusto *physician, scientist, consultant*
Unger, Albert Howard *allergist, immunologist*
Wilcox, James Allen *psychiatrist*
Young, Robert Lindley *endocrinologist, internist, educator*
Zuckerman, Marc Jay *gastroenterologist, medical educator*

Fort Hood
Pfanner, Timothy Paul *gastroenterologist*

Fort Sam Houston
O'Hara, Mary Ann *pediatric ophthalmologists*
O'Rourke, Timothy John *internist, hematologist, health facility administrator, educator*

Fort Worth
Ahmed, M. Basheer *psychiatrist, educator*
Atkinson, Barbara Ann *internist*
Black, Timothy Lee *physician*
Bowling, John Robert *osteopathic physician, educator*
Brooks, Ann *medical librarian*
Brooks, Lloyd William, Jr. *osteopath, interventional cardiologist, educator*
de Sousa, Byron Nagib *physician, anesthesiologist, clinical pharmacologist, educator*
Elam, Craig Stephen *medical librarian*
Joe, George Washington *clinical researcher, quantitative methodologist*
Kelly, Robert Hart *physician, internist*
Mandell, Harold Lance *internist, hematologist*
McCartney, Mitchell David *electron microscopist, anatomist*
Prud'homme, Eck Gabriel, Jr. *physician, consultant*
Rubin, Bernard Ross *osteopathic medicine educator*
Schussler, Irwin *psychiatrist, educator*
Smith, Thomas Hunter *ophthalmologist, ophthalmic plastic and orbital surgeon*
Suba, Steven Antonio *obstetrician, gynecologist*
Van Deventer, Jon Nelson *physiatrist*
Wynn, Susan Rudd *physician*
Yanni, John Michael *pharmacologist*
Yentis, Richard David *psychiatrist*

Fredericksburg
Johnson, Marilyn *obstetrician, gynecologist*

Galveston
Bello-Reuss, Elsa Noemi *physician, educator*
Bissell, Michael Gilbert *pathologist*
Boisaubin, Eugene V. *internist*
Burns, Chester Ray *medical history educator*
Chonmaitree, Tasnee *pediatrician, educator, infectious disease specialist*
Dawson, Earl Bliss *obstetrician/gynecologist, educator*
Desai, Manubhai Haribhai *surgeon*
Garfield, Robert Edward *medical educator*
Gohil, Mahendra Nandlal *radiologist, educator*
Gold, Daniel Howard *ophthalmologist, educator*
Goodrum, Linda Ann *physician*
Gugliuzza, Kristene Koontz *transplant and general surgery educator*
Heggers, John Paul *surgery, immunology, microbiology educator*
Hirschfeld, Robert M.A. *psychiatrist*
Holland, Owen Bryan *medical educator*
Jahadi, Mohammad Reza *surgeon*
Koeppe, Patsy Poduska *internist, educator*
Levin, William Cohn *hematologist, former university president*
Luthra, Gurinder Kumar *osteopath*
Nusynowitz, Martin Lawrence *nuclear medicine physician*
Pearl, William Richard Emden *pediatric cardiologist*
Sparks, Sherman Paul *osteopathic physician*
Suzuki, Fujio *immunologist, educator, researcher*
White, Robert Brown *medical educator*

Garland
Duren, Michael *cardiologist*
Hockett, Sheri Lynn *radiologist*

Georgetown
Schofield, James Roy *medical consultant, educator*

Harlingen
Dahm, Lawrence John *pathologist*

Hillsboro
Cason, Dick Kendall *physician*

Houston
Able, Luke William *retired pediatric surgeon, consultant*
Alpert, Jack Nathaniel *neurologist*
Aslam, Muhammed Javed *physician*
Assouad, Mario *internist, nephrologist*
Baldwin, John Charles *surgeon, researcher*
Ballantyne, Christie Mitchell *medical educator*
Barrett, Bernard Morris, Jr. *plastic surgeon*
Bast, Robert Clinton, Jr. *medical researcher, medical educator*
Batsakis, John George *pathology educator*
Bean, Samuel Franklin *dermatologist*
Bhandari, Arvind *oncologist*
Blacklock, Jerry Bob *neurosurgeon*
Blanco, Jorge Desiderio *physician, medical educator, researcher*
Bodey, Gerald Paul *medical educator, physician*
Booser, Daniel James *physician, oncologist*
Brown, Frank Reginald, III *pediatrician, educator*
Burns, Sally Ann *medical association administrator*
Burzynski, Stanislaw Rajmund *internist*
Buster, John Edmond *gynecologist, medical researcher*
Carpenter, Robert James, Jr. *medical educator*
Casscells, Samuel Ward, III *cardiologist, educator*
Chakrabarty, Subhas *medical educator*
Chan, Ka Wah *physician*
Clark, Gary D. *medical educator, researcher*
Clifton, Guy L. *neurosurgeon, educator*
Cooley, Denton Arthur *surgeon, educator*
Cooper, Sharon P. *epidemiologist, educator*
Daily, Louis *ophthalmologist*
DeBakey, Michael Ellis *cardiovascular surgeon, educator, scientist*
Decker, Norman *psychiatrist, educator*
de la Torre, Jorge *psychiatrist, psychoanalyst, educator, physician*
Doubleday, Charles William *dermatologist, educator*
Dreyer, William Jeffrey *pediatrician, researcher*
Dunbar, Burdett Sheridan *anesthesiologist, pediatrician, educator*
Elwood, William Norelli *medical researcher*
Engelhardt, Hugo Tristram, Jr. *physician, educator*
Estrov, Zeev *medical educator*
Eton, Omar *oncologist*
Evans, Harry Launius *pathology educator*
Feldman, Zeev Tuvia *neurosurgeon*
Frates, Ralph Coryell, Jr. *pediatrician, educator*
Frishman, Laura Jean *visual physiologist*
Fritsch, Derek Adrian *nurse anesthetist*
Fuller, Lillian Mary *radiation oncologist, educator*
Galati, Joseph Stephen *hepatologist*
George, Julie Berny *epidemiologist*
Gershenson, Davis Marc *oncology educator, university administrator*
Gilger, Mark Alan *pediatrician, educator*
Gillard, Baiba Kurins *medical educator, research scientist*
Glassman, Armand Barry *physician, pathologist, scientist, educator, administrator*
Gonzales, Edmond Tassin *pediatric urologist*
Graham, William Robert *medical educator*
Gruber, Nelson Peter *physician, psychiatrist*
Gupta, Kaushal Kumar *internist*
Hamberger, Arthur Donald *radiation oncologist*
Hawash, Ralph R. *obstetrician, gynecologist*
Haywood, Theodore Joseph *physician, educator*
Higgs, J. Jeffrey *retired physician and medical director*
Hohn, David *physician*
Huge, Donald Sehrt *physician*
Hurwitz, Richard Louis *medical sciences educator*
Ibrahim, Nuhad Khalil *oncologist*
Jackson, Gilchrist L. *surgeon*
Janjan, Nora Anita *radiation oncologist*
Jenkins, Daniel Edwards, Jr. *physician, educator*
Jones, Clyde Michael *hematologist*
Jones, James Wilson *physician, cell biologist*
Katrana, David John *plastic and reconstructive surgeon*
Kellaway, Peter *neurophysiologist, researcher*
Khan-Dawood, Firyal Sultana *obstetrics/gynecology educator*
Kim, E. Edmund *radiology educator*
Kirkland, Rebecca Trent *pediatric endocrinologist*
Kline, Allen Haber *pediatrician*
Kline, Mark Wendel *pediatric medicine educator*
Kutka, Nicholas *nuclear medicine physician*
Lee, Jeffrey Edwin *surgeon*
Lee, Jin Soo *oncologist, educator*
Letsou, George Vasilios *cardiothoracic surgeon*
Levine, Aaron M. *physiatrist*
Lippman, Scott Michael *oncologist*
Low, Morton David *physician, educator*
Macdonald, Eleanor Josephine *epidemiology educator, cancer epidemiology consultant*
Maillard, Albert Achilles Joseph *head and neck surgeon, educator*
Malseed, Lynn Marie *child and adolescent psychiatrist*
Manso, Gilbert *physician*
Marrack, David *pathologist*
Marshall, Gailen Daugherty, Jr. *physician, scientist, educator*
Max, Ernest *surgeon*
McCullough, Laurence Bernard *medical educator, consultant*
McCutcheon, Ian Earle *neurosurgeon*
McGovern, John Phillip *physician, educator*
McKechnie, John Charles *gastroenterologist, educator*
McMillan, Mae Frances *child psychiatrist*
Meyer, John Stirling *neurologist, educator*
Mizrahi, Eli M. *neurologist, pediatrician, educator*
Munk, Zev Moshe *allergist, researcher*
Nader, Shahla *endocrinologist educator*
Newmark, Michael Ede *neurologist*
Nosé, Yukihiko *surgeon, educator*
Ordonez, Nelson Gonzalo *pathologist*
Ott, David Alan *cardiac surgeon*
Owen, William Reagan *cardiologist*
Palacios, Ronald *immunologist*
Patt, Richard Bernard *anesthesiologist*
Pearson, Robert Edwin *psychiatrist*
Phung, Nguyen Dinh *medical educator*
Raijman, Isaac *gastroenterologist, endoscopist, educator*
Ramsey, David Jed *medical researcher, computer consultant*
Ramzy, Ibrahim *pathologist, educator*

Raymer, Warren Joseph *retired allergist*
Redmon, Agile Hugh, Jr. *allergist*
Reyes, Guillermo Antonio *cardiologist*
Riley, William J. *pediatrician, educator*
Roberts, W. Mark *pediatric hematologist/oncologist*
Romaguera, Jorge Enrique *internist, educator*
Ross, Patti Jayne *obstetrics and gynecology educator*
Roth, Dover *psychiatrist*
Rudolph, Andrew Henry *dermatologist, educator*
Sanderson, Mary Louise *medical association administrator*
Santos, Lisa Diane *plastic surgeon*
Schachtel, Barbara Harriet Levin *epidemiologist, educator*
Scheuerle, Angela Elizabeth *pediatrician*
Schwartz, Mary Rebecca *pathologist*
Selke, Oscar O., Jr. *physiatrist, educator*
Sell, Stewart *pathologist, immunologist, educator*
Sellin, Joseph Henry *gastroenterologist*
Shearer, William Thomas *pediatrician, educator*
Sljivich, Milan *allergist*
Speer, Michael Emery *neonatologist, educator*
Steinkuller, Joan Sommers *physician, educator*
Taffet, George Efrem *geriatrician*
Tanous, Helene Mary *physician*
Thomas, Orville C. *physician*
Tomasovic, Stephen Peter *oncologist*
Tornos, Carmen *surgical pathologist*
Towbin, Jeffrey Allen *pediatric cardiologist, educator*
Trick, Otho Lee *psychiatrist*
Tuel, Stephen Michael *medical educator*
Valadka, Alex Bruno *neurosurgeon, educator*
Van Horn, Gage, III *neurologist, educator*
Woehler, Thomas Richard *allergist, immunologist*
Wolinsky, Jerry Saul *neurology educator*
Yeoman, Lynn Chalmers *cancer researcher, medical educator*
Zarin, Jerald Lawrence *pediatrician, physician executive*
Zhang, Jingwu *immunologist*
Zoghbi, William Antoine *cardiologist educator*
Zweighaft, Ronald M. *neurologist*

Humble
Schappel, Arthur Walter *neuropsychiatrist*
Trowbridge, John Parks *physician*

Irving
Garcia, Raymond Lloyd *dermatologist*
Schwartz, Joyce Gensberg *pathologist*

Jacksonville
Boston, John Armistead *psychiatrist, educator*

Killeen
Vancura, Stephen Joseph *radiologist*

Kingwood
Shickman, Barry Louis *physician, obstetrician, gynecologist*

La Porte
Butler, Donald B. *surgery educator, mediator*

Lackland AFB
Cheu, Henry Wong *physician pediatric surgery*
Farmer, Joseph Christopher *physician*
Karulf, Richard E. *surgeon, department chairman*
Snyder, Russell Robert *obstetrician, gynecologist, educator, pathologist*

Laredo
Keene, Gladys Cronfel *allergist, immunologist, pediatrician*

League City
Moore, Walter D., Jr. *pathologist*

Longview
Frase, Larry Lynn *internist, medical association administrator*

Lubbock
Beck, George Preston *anesthesiologist, educator*
Epstein, Anne Carol *physician*
Heavner, James E. *anesthesiology educator, pharmacologist*
Jackson, Francis Charles *physician, surgeon*
Keung, Yi-Kong *oncologist, hematologist*
Kimbrough, Robert Cooke, III *infectious diseases physician*
Kurtzman, Neil A. *medical educator*
Mailliard, Mark E. *medical educator*
Martinelli, Lawrence Phillip *infectious diseases physician*
McMahon, Terry Calvin *psychiatrist, medical educator*
Rapini, Ronald Peter *dermatology educator*
Sabatini, Sandra *physician*
Selby, John Horace *surgeon*
Shaw, R. Preston *physician, psychiatrist, educator*
Shires, George Thomas *surgeon, educator*
Winter, Mark Lee *physician*

Lufkin
Perry, Lewis Charles *emergency medicine physician, osteopath*

Marshall
Sudhivoraseth, Niphon *pediatrician, allergist, immunologist*

Mexia
Holder, Timothy Wayne *physician*

Midland
Rebik, James Michael *otolaryngologist*
Van de Water, Susan D. *physiatrist*

Odessa
Lane, Daniel McNeel *pediatric hematologist, lipidologist*

Paris
Stewart, David Lawrence *gastroenterologist*

Pasadena
D'Andrea, Mark *radiation oncologist*
Harkins, Anna Marie, Jr. *cardiologist, preventive medicine physician*
Shapiro, Edward Muray *dermatologist*

Pearland
Cochran, Gloria Grimes *pediatrician, retired*

Plainview
Troedel, Lowell Jean *anesthesiologist, nurse*

Plano
Kantipong, Vara P. *allergist, immunologist, pediatrician*

Porter
Rubio, Pedro A. *surgeon*

Raymondville
Montgomery-Davis, Joseph *osteopathic physician*

Richardson
Ponsonby, David Pemberton *sports medicine researcher*
Ross, Colin Andrew *psychiatrist*

Richmond
Hay, Richard Carman *retired anesthesiologist*

Salado
Wilmer, Harry Aron *psychiatrist*

San Angelo
Bridges, Robert Goltra *obstetrics-gynecologist*
Cornell, Jess Michael *vascular surgeon, physician, medical educator*
Darby, John Preston *internist*
Dunham, Gregory Mark *obstetrician, gynecologist*

San Antonio
Bentch, H(erman) Leonard *internist, gastroenterologist*
Bragan, John Frederick *emergency physician*
Brown, Frederick William, III *psychiatrist*
Brown, Willis Ellsworth, Jr. *neurosurgeon, educator*
Chanh, Tran Cong *immunologist*
Cohen, Melvin Lee *pediatrician, psychiatrist, educator*
Comeaux, Elizabeth Anne *medical librarian*
Dwyer, Mary Jo *medical librarian*
Gillean, William Otho, Jr. *physician, psychiatrist*
Glickman, Randolph David *ophthalmology educator, researcher*
Gong, Alice Kim *neonatologist, educator, researcher*
Hale, Albert Spencer, Jr. *radiologist*
Hecker, Richard Bernard *osteopathic physician, anesthesiologist*
Hernandez, Linda Luree Welch *physician*
Holshouser, Claire K. *anesthesiologist*
Horton, Granville Eugene *nuclear medicine physician, retired air force officer*
James, Vernon Lester *pediatrician, educator*
Jorgensen, James H. *pathologist, educator, microbiologist*
Kamada-Cole, Mika M. *allergist, immunologist, medical educator*
Kaye, Celia Ilene *pediatrics educator*
Lee, Wen-Hwa *medical educator*
Lyons, Roger Michael *physician*
Marlin, Arthur Edward *pediatric neurosurgeon, educator*
Martin, Bryan Leslie *allergist, immunologist*
Martinez, Joe Louis, Jr. *neurobiologist*
Matthews, Ed C. *internist*
McAnelly, Robert D. *physiatrist, researcher*
Mira, Joaquin Gomez, Jr. *oncologist, educator*
Morales, Carlos F. *physician, military officer*
New, Pamela Zyman *neurologist*
Olsson, James Edward *otologist, neurotologist*
Ramos, Raul *surgeon*
Rawls, Henry Ralph *biomedical educator*
Romero, Emilio Felipe *psychiatry educator, psychotherapist, hospital administrator*
Root, Harlan David *surgery educator*
Rothenberg, Mace Lawrence *physician, medical educator*
Russell, I. Jon *medical educator*
Sarabia, Fermin *psychiatrist*
Schneider, Frank David *family physician*
Sertich, Anthony Patrick, Jr. *otorhinolaryngologist, facial/plastic surgeon*
Shanfield, Stephen B. *medical educator, physician*
Smith, John Marvin, III *surgeon, educator*
Strodel, William Edward *surgeon, medical educator*
Townsend, Frank Marion *pathology educator*
Wei, Ming *epidemiology researcher*
Widman, Lawrence Edward *cardiology and computer science educator*
Williams, Thomas Eugene *pharmaceutica consultant*
Wu, William Chien Lin *internist*

Santa Fe
Wilkinson, Gregg Stuart *epidemiologist*

Seminole
Gremmel, Gilbert Carl *family physician*

Sherman
Essin, Emmett Mohammed, Jr. *obstetrician, gynecologist*

Sugar Land
Olmo, Jaime Alberto *physician*
Rumbaut, Rubén Dario *psychiatrist, educator*
Shaw-Rice, Judi *internist, health facility administrator*

Temple
Brasher, George Walter *physician*
Coffield, King Scott *urologist, educator*
Holleman, Vernon Daughty *physician, internist*
Wadenberg, Marie-Louise Gertrud *psychopharmacologist, researcher*
Wajimi, Takeshi *hematologist, medical oncologist, researcher*

Texarkana
Fournier, Donald Charles *allergist, immunologist*
Harrison, James Wilburn *gynecologist*

Texas City
Korndorffer, William Earl *forensic pathologist*

Tyler
Azghani, Ali Owsat *biomedical researcher*
Pinkenburg, Ronald Joseph *ophthalmologist*
Wrenn, Christopher Jay *physician*

Waco
Gray, James Edward *gastroenterologist*
Richie, Rodney Charles *critical care and pulmonary medicine physician*

Webster
Farnam, Jafar *allergist, immunologist, pediatrician*
Rappaport, Martin Paul *internist, nephrologist, educator*

Wharton
Khalil, A. Arif *cardiologist*

Wichita Falls
Fontenot, James Nolan, Jr. *orthopedist*
Harvey, Peter Marshall *podiatrist*

UTAH

Salt Lake City
Saltz, Renato *plastic surgeon*

VIRGINIA

Alexandria
Buhain, Wilfrido Javier *medical educator*
Carty, Brian Clifford *family practice physician*
Emich, Charles Henry *orthopedist, retired navy officer*
Highsmith, Wanda Law *retired association executive*
Kao, Tzu-Min *physiatrist*
Moschella, Ralph *physician*
Pritchett, Anne McDonald *medical association administrator*

Annandale
French, James Harold, Jr. *plastic surgeon*
Robert, Nicholas James *hematolgist, oncologist*

Arlington
Amedeo, Ralph Michael *physician*
Butler, Thomas Parke *internist, oncologist*
Delta, Basil George *physician*
Katona, Ildy Margaret *allergist, immunologist, pediatrician*
Nguyen-Dinh, Thanh *internist, geriatrician*
Sheridan, Andrew James, III *ophthalmologist*
Sloand, Elaine Marie *hematologist*
Zimmet, Steven Michael *physician*

Blackstone
Walton, G. Clifford *family practice physician*

Charlottesville
Bruns, David Eugene *medical educator, researcher*
Chan, Donald Pin-Kwan *orthopaedic surgeon, educator*
Clarke, William Linus *pediatrics educator*
DeSilvey, Dennis Lee *cardiologist, educator, university administrator*
Durieux, Marcel Eloy *anesthesiology educator, researcher*
Epstein, Robert Marvin *anesthesiologist, educator*
Ferguson, James Edward, II *obstetrician, gynecologist, maternal-fetal medicine specialist*
Finney, Marcia Day *medical educator, academic administrator*
Gay, Spencer Bradley *radiologist, educator*
Gillenwater, Jay Young *urologist, educator*
Haley, Elliott Clarke, Jr. *neurologist, educator*
Howards, Stuart S. *physician, educator*
Jenkins, Alan Deloss *urologic surgeon, educator*
Keats, Theodore Eliot *physician, radiology educator*
Kesler, Richard William *pediatrician, educator*
Langenburg, Scott Edward *surgeon*
Levine, Paul Albert *head and neck surgeon*
Marohn, Mary Lynn *anesthesiologist*
Mintz, Paul David *pathologist*
Petri, William Arthur, Jr. *medical educator, researcher*
Philbrick, John Tracy *medical educator*
Shaffer, Hubert Adams, Jr. *radiologist*
Stoler, Mark Howard *pathologist, educator*
Thorup, Oscar Andreas, Jr. *internist, educator, researcher, administrator*
Wilkins, Paul Cole *psychiatrist*
Winston, David Charles *pathologist*
Xu, Hua-Sheng (Howard Xu) *surgical oncologist, researcher*

Chesapeake
Kovalcik, Paul Jerome *surgeon*

Courtland
Brown, René Lillian *medical librarian*

Danville
Nevin, James Edmonson, III *surgeon*

Fairfax
Schulman, Joseph Daniel *physician, medical geneticist, executive, reproductive biologist, educator*
Vilasi, Vincent John *anesthesiologist*

Falls Church
Harrison, Virginia Florence *retired anatomist and educator, philanthropist*
Ho, Hien Van *pediatrician*
Sawchuk, William Samuel *dermatologist*

Fredericksburg
Roseberry, Elizabeth Ann *neonatologist*

Great Falls
Rosenthal, Richard Raphael *allergist, researcher*

Hampton
Green, Stephen Lloyd *epidemiologist*
Sale, Thomas Wirt, Jr. *surgeon, educator*

Herndon
Payne, Fred J. *physician, educator*

Kilmarnock
Williams, Richard Kennon *ophthalmologist*

Lancaster
Duer, Ellen Ann Dagon *anesthesiologist*

Leesburg
McDow, Russell Edward, Jr. *surgeon*
Mitchell, Russell Harry *dermatologist*

Lynchburg
Cooper, Alan Michael *psychiatrist*
Cresson, David Homer, Jr. *pathologist*
Glenn, Robert Lee *internist*

Manassas
Woodside, Nina Bencich *psychiatrist*

Marion
Angliker, Colin C.J. *forensic psychiatrist*

Mc Lean
LeNard, Peter Dennis *general surgeon*
Sacks, Charles Bernard *physician, educator*

Newport News
Forbes, Sarah Elizabeth *gynecologist, real estate corporation officer*
Mann, William Joseph, Jr. *gynecologic oncologist*

Norfolk
Baker, Jay Milton *obstetrician/gynecologist*
Ciccone, Alvin Jacob *physician*
Dandalides, Steven Michael *gastroenterologist, educator*
de Veciana, Margarita *obstetrician, gynecologist*
Harris, Richard John *medical librarian*
Karlson, Karl Henrik, Jr. *pediatrician, educator*
Oelberg, David George *neonatologist, biomedical researcher*
Parker, John Patrick *cardiologist*
Redding, Marshall Simms *ophthalmologist*
Robinson, Adam Mayfield, Jr. *surgeon*
Rohn, Reuben David *pediatric educator and administrator*
van Wolkenten, Raymond Vincent *medical educator*
Whitmore, William Harvey *retired physician, securities dealer*

North Garden
Moses, Hamilton, III *neurology educator, hospital executive, management consultant*

Norton
Vest, Steven Lee *gastroenterologist, hepatologist, internist*

Portsmouth
Wolf, Jeffrey Stephen *physician*

Radford
Kishore, Anand *physician*

Reston
Sager, Dennis Wayne *internist, engineer*

Richlands
Peralta, Antonio Martinez *family physician*

Richmond
Arnold, Gayle Gardner *pediatrician*
Atwill, William Henry *physician*
Bates, Hampton Robert, Jr. *pathologist*
Blumberg, Michael Zangwill *allergist*
Caravati, Charles Martin *dermatologist*
Carmichael, Miriam Willena *neurologist, educator, consultant*
Clore, John Newton *endocrinologist, educator*
Harris, Louis Selig *pharmacologist, researcher*
Hurt, W. Glenn *obstetrics and gynecology educator*
Jacobson, Eric Sheldon *internist, infectious diseases physician*
Kendig, Edwin Lawrence, Jr. *physician, educator*
Kitces, Edward Nathan *dermatologist, physician*
Kuzel, Anton John *physician*
Leichnetz, George Robert *anatomy educator*
Lofland, Gary Kenneth *cardiac surgeon*
Marshall, Wayne Keith *anesthesiology educator*
Megson, Mary Norfleet *pediatrician, educator, medical facility administrator*
Minisi, Anthony Joseph *cardiologist, educator*
Mitchell, Robert Edgar, Jr. *gastroenterologist*
Mollen, Edward Leigh *pediatrician, allergist and immunologist*
Orenstein, Robert *physician*
Pellock, John Michael *child neurologist*
Schieken, Richard Merrill *physician*
Schmitt, James Kenneth *internist, health facility administrator, educator*
Seibel, Hugo Rudolf *anatomist, university dean*
Smith, Wade Kilgore *physician, educator, researcher*
Sugerman, Harvey Jay *surgery educator*
Towne, Alan Raymond *neurologist, educator*
Vieweg, Walter Victor Rudolph *psychiatrist, educator*
Wolf, James Stuart *surgeon, administrator*
Wolking, Fred Louis *retired health physicist*
Wright, R(aleigh) Lewis *neurosurgeon*

Roanoke
Enright, Michael Joseph *radiologist*

Salem
Lewis, Verna Mae *physiatrist*
Perkins, Marvin Earl *psychiatrist, educator*
Schleupner, Charles John *internist, educator, health facility administrator*

Shawsville
Smith, George Robert, Jr. *family physician*

Staunton
Klein, David Stephen *anesthesiologist*
Ryan, Eileen Patricia *psychiatrist, educator*

Vienna
Penrose, Cynthia C. *health plan administrator, consultant*

Virginia Beach
Cooper, William Robert *pulmonary physician, health facility administrator*
Fischer, Daniel Edward *psychiatrist*
Kornylak, Harold John *osteopathic physician*

Malixi, Edwin Camacho *family physician, navy officer*
Mallenbaum, Sidney *neurologist*
Wallace, Duncan Saron *psychiatrist, educator*

Woodbridge
Vachher, Prehlad Singh *psychiatrist*

Wytheville
McConnell, James Joseph *internist*

WEST VIRGINIA

Albright
Moyers, Sylvia Dean *retired medical record librarian*

Beckley
Johnson, Eugene Franklin, Jr. *emergency room physician, osteopath*

Bluefield
Blaydes, James Elliott *ophthalmologist*

Charleston
AbuRahma, Ali F. *surgeon, educator*
Bates, Mark C. *cardiologist*
Tully, Christopher Carl *retired physician, hospital administrator*
Wyner, Lawrence Michael *physician*
Zangeneh, Fereydoun *pediatrics educator, pediatric endocrinologist*

Huntington
Edwards, Roy Alvin *physician, psychiatrist, educator*
Leppla, David Charles *pathology educator*
Tolley, Gary Maurice *radiologist*

Lewisburg
Houts, Larry Lee *osteopathic medicine educator*
Steele, Karen Mason *medical educator*
Willard, Ralph Lawrence *surgery educator, physician, former college president*

Man
Bofill, Rano Solidum *physician*

Martinsburg
Malin, Howard Gerald *podiatrist*

Morgantown
Albrink, Margaret Joralemon *medical educator*
Arbid, Elias Joseph *vascular surgeon, researcher, medical educator*
Fintor, Louis John *epidemiologist, researcher, writer*
Friedline, John Allen *pathologist*
Hill, Ronald Charles *surgeon, educator*
Kirk, Ralph Gary *anatomy educator*
Mansmann, Paris Taylor *medical educator*
Nugent, George Robert *neurosurgeon*
Pearson, R. John C. *epidemiologist, educator*
Vallyathan, Val *pathologist and educator*

Princeton
de la Piedra, Jorge *orthopedic surgeon*

Wheeling
Bontos, George Emmanuel *physician*
Feder, Arlene Stern *endocrinology educator*

WISCONSIN

Madison
Spear, Scott Jay *physician*

Milwaukee
Vesole, David H. *physician*

TERRITORIES OF THE UNITED STATES

PUERTO RICO

Ponce
Alcala, Jose Ramon *anatomy educator*

Rio Piedras
Altieri, Pablo Ivan *cardiologist*

San Juan
Ghaly, Evone Shehata *pharmaceutics and industrial pharmacy educator*
Rodriguez Arroyo, Jesus *gynecologic oncologist*
Rosario-Guardiola, Reinaldo *dermatologist*
Sahai, Hardeo *medical statistics educator*

Santurce
Fernandez-Martinez, Jose *physician*

MILITARY ADDRESSES OF THE UNITED STATES

EUROPE

APO
Bernstein, Stephen Adam *physician, career officer*
Migala, Alexandre Frederyk *physician, osteopath*

SOUTH AFRICA

Johannesburg
Rodenberg, Howard David *emergency medicine educator*

SWITZERLAND

Geneva
Rio, Francesco A. *tropical medicine and public health specialist*

ADDRESS UNPUBLISHED

Balconis, Andrea Jo *physician*
Barat, Lawrence M. *epidemiologist*
Barber, D.A. *pharmacology educator*
Barlascini, Cornelius Ottavio, Jr. *physician*
Beavers, William Robert *psychiatrist, educator*
Benavides, Jaime Miguel *orthopedist*
Bergquist, Sandra Lee *medical and legal consultant, nurse*
Bernstein, David Eric *gastroenterologist, educator*
Boone, O. Riley *retired surgeon*
Bowman, Laura Catherine *pediatric oncologist*
Brohammer, Richard Frederic *psychiatrist*
Butcher, Carmen Julie-Ann Ortiz *medicine and nephrology educator*
Bynes, Frank Howard, Jr. *physician*
Cain, Darren Lee *internist*
Cohen, Irvin Myron *psychiatrist*
Cohen, Joy Esther *medical educator*
Cornell, Paul James *physician, consultant*
Crowell, Edward Browning, Jr. *medical educator*
DeVault, William Leonard *orthopaedic surgeon*
Durant, John Ridgeway *physician*
Enarson, Cam Edwin *medical educator*
Ferguson, Emmet Fewell, Jr. *surgeon*
Ferraz, Francisco Marconi *neurosurgeon*
Fillman, Stephen Douglas *physician*
Frank, Michael M. *physician*
Gangarosa, Raymond Eugene *epidemiologist, engineer*
Garrett, William E. *general surgeon*
Gibney, Pamela *physician*
Glass, Dorothea Daniels *physiatrist, educator*
Gleaton, Harriet E. *retired anesthesiologist*
Gonzalez, Jose L. *pediatrician, educator*
Guffee, Guy Keel *surgeon*
Guinee, Vincent F. *medical epidemiologist*
Gusdon, John Paul, Jr. *obstetrics and gynecology educator, physician*
Hamilton, Thomas Percy *preventive medicine physician, military officer*
Hancock, John C. *pharmacologist*
Hardy, Kenneth James *rheumatologist, educator*
Harshman, Edward Jay *physician, author*
Herrera, Guillermo Antonio *pathologist*
Hines, Jonathan S. *internist*
Huber, Douglas Crawford *pathologist*
Hunt, Oliver Raymond, Jr. *thoracic and cardiovascular surgeon*
Hunter, Richard Grant, Jr. *neurologist, executive*
Jefferies, William McKendree *internist, educator*
Jones, Walton Linton *internist, former government official*
Keil, Julian Eugene *epidemiology educator and researcher*
Keim, Robert John *otolaryngologist, educator*
Kelley, Scott Streater *orthopaedic surgeon*
Kerwin, Joseph Peter *physician, former astronaut*
Kidd, Thornton Lenoir, Jr. *allergist*
Kiesnowski, Brian *surgeon*
Krapin, Lee Coleman *neurologist*
Lam, Tukien Michael *internist*
Lanska, Douglas John *neurologist*
Larson, Richard Smith *pathologist, researcher*
Lauterbach, Edward Charles *psychiatric educator*
Lohmann, George Young, Jr. *neurosurgeon, hospital executive*
Long, Charles William *child and adolescent psychiatrist*
Luxenberg, Steven Neuwahl *physician*
MacDuffee, Robert Colton *family physician, pathologist*
Malik, Rajeev *physician*
Markoe, Arnold Michael *radiation oncologist*
Marshall, Kenneth Alan *anesthesiologist, consultant*
Mathias, John Robert *gastroenterologist*
Matthews, James Gordon, Jr. *obstetrician, gynecologist*
Miller, Margaret Ann *physician, military officer*
Minocha, Anil *physician, educator, researcher*
Montgomery, Hubert Theron, Jr. *physician, health care administrator*
Montgomery, Philip O'Bryan, Jr. *pathologist*
Morse, Martin A. *surgeon*
Mountain, Clifton Fletcher *surgeon, educator*
Nicholls, Richard Aurelius *obstetrician, gynecologist*
Nishioka, Kenji *cancer researcher, educator, consultant*
Pace, Harry Richard *retired obstetrician, gynecologist*
Palmer, J.D. Keith *rehabilitative medicine physician*
Parker, Edward Frost *retired surgeon*
Pesola, Gene Raymond *physician, educator*
Pharo, Wayne Joseph *cardiologist*
Poster, Don Steven *internist, hematologist, oncologist*
Ramsay, James Gordon *anesthesiologist, educator*
Ranney, Robert John *medical consultant*
Robson, Gordon MacDonald *anesthesiologist*
Roehm, Dan Christian *physician, nutritionist*
Sanchez, Juan Antonio *cardiovascular surgeon, educator*
Schneider, Sanford *physician, educator*
Sessions, Roger Carl *emergency physician*
Shandles, Ira David *podiatrist*
Skinner, Michael Haven *pharmacologist, educator*
Smith, Jack Wayne *family practice physician*
Spiers, Alexander Stewart D. *medical educator*
Spinner, Robert Jay *orthopedic surgeon*
Stiles, Charles Merrill *physician*
Taylor, Lesli Ann *pediatric surgery educator*
Thompson, Bobby Joe *family physician*
Thorne, George Clifford *pediatrician, educator*
Trehan, Rajeev R. *psychiatrist, neurologist*
Tulanon, Paitoon *surgeon*
Wajsman, Zev *urologist educator*
Watne, Alvin L. *surgeon, educator*
Way, Wilson Spencer *retired osteopathic physician and surgeon*
Wechsler, Arnold *osteopathic obstetrician, gynecologist*
Weinberg, Joseph Arnold *pediatrician, educator*
White-Sims, Susanne Tropez *pediatrician, educator*
Wojciechowski, Frank Andrew *urologist*
Zimmerman, David Alan *cardiologist*

HUMANITIES: LIBERAL STUDIES

UNITED STATES

ALABAMA

Auburn
Andelson, Robert Vernon *social philosopher, educator*
Guernsey, Julia Carolyn *English language educator*

Birmingham
Dobbins, Austin C. *retired English language educator*
Lasseter, Janice Milner *English language educator*
Morton, Marilyn Miller *genealogy and history educator, lecturer, researcher, travel executive, director*
Weaver, Jeanne Moore *retired history educator*

Dothan
Albano, Robert A. *English language educator*

Florence
Gartman, Max Dillon *language educator*
Minor, Lisa Graves *English language educator*

Huntsville
Bounds, Sarah Etheline *historian*
Buksa, Irena *language and literature educator*
Gooding, Lela Moore *language educator, department chairman*
Mebane, John Spencer *language and literature educator, dean*

Jacksonville
Zenanko, Carl Michael *learning center educator*

Mobile
Eckart, Gabriele Ruth *German language educator*
Harrison, Patricia Greenwood *historian*
Murillo, José-Luis *Spanish language educator*
Neal, Patricia Anne *English language educator*
Rountree, Virginia Ward *English language educator*
Whyde, Janet Marciel *literature educator, editor*

Montevallo
Hughes, Elaine Wood *literature educator*
Lott, John Bertrand *English language educator, university dean*

Montgomery
Barmettler, Robert Stephen *speech educator, writer*
Futrell, Robert Frank *military historian, consultant*
Rosen, Philip Terry *history educator*
Sumner, Gordon Heyward *foreign language educator*
Whitt, Mary F. *reading specialist, educator*

Normal
Gilbert, Virginia Lee *English language educator, poet, photographer*

Ramer
Napier, John Hawkins, III *historian*

Troy
McPherson, Milton Monroe *history educator*

Tuscaloosa
Fox, Thomas Charles *foreign language educator*
Marvin, Roberta Montemorra *musicologist*
Robel, Ronald Ray *history educator*
Terry, Edward Davis *Latin-American studies and literature educator*

ARKANSAS

Arkadelphia
Bass, Carol Ann (Mitzi) *English language educator*
Graves, John William *historian*

Conway
Bailey, Phillip Douglas *foreign language educator*
Schmidt, Lawrence Kennedy *philosophy educator*
Zambrano, Jaime M. *foreign language educator, researcher*
Ziegler, John Alan *historian, political scientist, educator*

De Queen
Sarna, Jan Christopher *history educator*

El Dorado
Boulden, Dorathy Ann *genealogist*

Fayetteville
Bell, Steven Michael *foreign language educator*
Gatewood, Willard Badgett, Jr. *historian*
Montgomery, Lyna Lee *English language educator*
Stephens, Dorothy Anne *English language educator*

Hughes
Pemberton, Lisa Suzanne *English language and oral communications educator*

Little Rock
Murphy, Russell Elliott *literature educator*

Magnolia
Davis, Elizabeth Hawk *English language educator*

Mountain Home
Easley, June Ellen Price *genealogist*

Mountain View
McNeil, William K. *folklorist*

Springdale
Cordell, Beulah Faye *English language educator*

State University
Schichler, Robert Lawrence *English language educator*

DISTRICT OF COLUMBIA

Washington
Iudicello, Kathleen Ann *English language educator*
Raines, Edgar Frank, Jr. *historian*
Thompson, Wayne Wray *historian*

FLORIDA

Altamonte Springs
Davis, Donna Jo *English language educator*

Beverly Hills
Larsen, Erik *art history educator*

Boca Raton
Collins, Robert Arnold *English language educator*
Embree, Lester Eugene *philosophy educator*

Bonita Springs
Payne, Alma Jeanette *English language educator, author*

Bradenton
Stewart, Priscilla Ann Mabie *art historian, educator*

Cape Coral
Martin, Thomas Sherwood *history and political science educator*

Coral Gables
Benstock, Shari *English language educator*
Chabrow, Sheila Sue *English language educator*
Goldman, Alan H. *philosophy educator*
Levine, Robert Martin *historian*
McCarthy, Patrick A. *English language educator*
Speiller-Morris, Joyce *English composition educator*

Davie
Helguero, Grace (Graciela Helguero) *language educator*

Daytona Beach
Glassman, Steve *humanities educator*
Williams, Reginald Anthony *educator, author, artist, actor*

Deerfield Beach
O'Connell, Richard (James) *English literature educator, poet*

Deland
Johnston, Sidney Philip *historian*
Kaivola, Karen Lennea *educator in English*

Edgewater
Mason, Aimee Hunnicutt Romberger *retired philosophy and humanities educator*

Fort Lauderdale
Grish, Marilyn Kay *speech educator*
Mendell, Jay Stanley *humanities educator*
Van Alstyne, Judith Sturges *English language educator, writer*

Fort Myers
Rumberger, Regina *retired English language educator*

Gainesville
Bullivant, Keith *modern German literature educator*
Geggus, David Patrick *history educator*
Holland, Norman Norwood *English language educator*
Jimenez, Reynaldo Luis *foreign language educator*
Johnson, Edward Joe, Jr. *foreign language educator*
McKnight, Stephen Alen *history educator*
Schutte, Ofelia M. *philosophy educator*
Scott, John Fredrik *art history educator, consultant*
Smocovitis, Vassiliki Betty *history educator*
Snodgrass, Chris *English literature educator*
Sussman, Lewis Arthur *classics educator*
Wyatt-Brown, Anne Marbury *linguistics educator*
Zieger, Robert Harman *history educator, historian*

Interlachen
Wilson, Jeanne Irene *language educator*

Jacksonville
Bizot, Richard Byron *English language educator*
Crooks, James Benedict *history educator*
Harmon, Gary Lee *English language educator*
Lloyd, Jacqueline *English language educator*
Stanton, Robert John, Jr. *English language educator*
Striar, Brian *literature educator*

Lake Worth
Wilson, William J. *English language educator*

Lakeland
Becker, Magdalene Neuenschwander *English language educator*
Fadley, Ann Miller *English language and literature educator, writer*

Largo
Williams, Trudy Anne *English language educator, college administrator*

Lighthouse Point
Hampares, Katherine James *retired foreign language educator*

Miami
Berger, Fran Blake *speech professional*
Johnson-Cousin, Danielle *French literature educator*
Martinez, Maria Leonor *translator, counselor, educator*
Mendez, Jesus *history educator, education administrator*
Palacios, Conny *Spanish language educator, literary critic*

Pau-Llosa, Ricardo Manuel *English language educator, poet, art critic, curator*
Shivel, Gail Lauren *English language educator*
Treadgold, Warren Templeton *history and literature educator*

Naples
Griffin, Linda Louise *English language and speech educator*
McLean, Albert Forbes *retired literature educator*
Wemple-Kinder, Suzanne Fonay *history educator*

New Port Richey
Morgan, Lona Scaggs *speech professional educator*

North Miami
Dufresne, John Louis *English language educator*

Opa Locka
Fitz Gerald-Bush, Frank Shepard *historian, poet*

Orlando
Haber, Jennifer Rieben *English language educator*
Jones, Daniel Richard *English language educator, consultant*
Leckie, Shirley Anne *historian, educator*

Oviedo
Verkler, Karen Wolz *foreign language educator*

Penney Farms
Shuman, Marjorie D. (Gould) Murphy *retired English language educator*

Pensacola
Coker, William Sidney *historian, educator*
Dews, Carlos Lee *English language educator, writer*
Maddock, Lawrence Hill *language educator, writer*
Stolhanske, Linda Louise *English language educator*
Young, Debra Ann *English language educator*

Port Saint Lucie
Wedzicha, Walter *foreign language educator*

Saint Augustine
Horner, Carl Stuart *English language educator*

Saint Petersburg
McGinn, Donald Joseph *English language educator*
Walker, Brigitte Maria *translator, linguistic consultant*

Sanford
Stokes, Lisa Odham *humanities educator*

Sarasota
Doenecke, Justus Drew *history educator*
Ebitz, David MacKinnon *art historian, museum director*
Gerlovich, Karen J. *historian, musicologist*
Strong, Leah Audrey *humanities educator*

Tallahassee
Bartlett, Richard Adams *American history educator, history consultant*
Bucher, François *art history educator*
Cunningham, Karen Jean *humanities educator*
Dillingham, Marjorie Carter *foreign language educator*
Gruender, Carl David *philosophy educator*
Hawkins, Hunt *English language educator*
Jumonville, Neil Talbot *history educator*
Laird, Doris Anne Marley *humanities educator, musician*
McCaskey, Nancy Ann *English language educator*
Mock, David Benjamin *history educator*
Ortiz-Taylor, Sheila *English language educator*
Walters, Lori J. *medieval literature and language educator*

Tampa
Adderley, Christopher Mark *English educator*
Linnehan, Paul Joseph *English language educator*
Mitchell, Mozella Gordon *English language educator, minister*
Moss, Stephanie Ellen *drama educator, actress, theater manager*
Olson, Gary Andrew *English language educator*
Perry, James Frederic *philosophy educator, author*
Preto-Rodas, Richard A. *foreign language educator*
Schuh, Sandra Anderson *ethics educator*
Snyder, Robert Edward *American studies educator*
Weatherford, Roy Carter *philosophy educator, academic unionist*
Welsh, Sachiko Ann *Japanese language educator, librarian*

Temple Terrace
Thayer, Mary Norene *English language educator*

Tierra Verde
Diomede, Matthew *English language educator, author*

Winter Park
Benedict, Dorothy Jones *genealogist, researcher*
Papay, Twila Yates *English language educator*

GEORGIA

Albany
Formwalt, Lee William *history educator*

Americus
Isaacs, Harold *history educator*

Athens
Anderson, James L. *history educator, business developer*
Broussard, Ray F. *history educator*
Chick, Nancy Leigh *English language educator*
Coleman, Joel Lee *literature educator*
Covington, Michael Aaron *linguist*
Fallows, Noel *foreign language educator*
Ferré, Frederick Pond *philosophy, religion, technology and ethics educator*
García-Castañón, Santiago *Spanish educator, researcher, translator, poet*
Halper, Edward Charles *philosophy educator*
Hellerstein, Nina Salant *French literature and language educator*
López-Calvo, Ignacio *foreign language educator*
McCaskill, Barbara Ann *African American literature educator*
McGregor, James Harvey Spence *comparative literature educator*
Miller, Ronald Baxter *English language educator, author*
Moore, Margaret Bear *American literature educator*
Nagel, James Edward *English literature educator*
Peterson, David James *English language educator, librarian, archivist*
Shoaf, Kristin Elizabeth *foreign language educator*
Whigham, Thomas Lyle *historian, educator*
Williams, Anne *English studies educator*

Atlanta
Adamson, Walter Luiz *history educator*
Brownley, Martine Watson *English language educator*
Chafee, Ingrid Roberta Hoover Coleman *French language educator*
Ditmann, Laurent *French language educator*
Erickson, Wayne Kenneth *English language educator*
Garrett, Franklin Miller *historian*
Gold, Hazel *Spanish language educator*
Gruber, William Edmund *English language educator*
Levenduski, Cristine Marie *American literature and culture educator*
Long, Richard Alexander *English language educator*
Mafico, Temba Levi Jackson *Old Testament and Semitic languages educator, clergy*
Neu, Joyce *linguist educator*
Puckett, James Manuel, Jr. *genealogist*
Renick, Timothy Mark *philosophy and religious studies educator*
Richtarik, Marilynn Josephine *English language educator*
Robins, Rosemary Gay *Egyptologist*
Rothacker, Kenneth Charles *linguist*
Rubin, Larry Jerome *literature educator*
Sizemore, Christine Wick *English language educator*
Stone-Miller, Rebecca Rollins *art historian, educator, curator*
Williams, Emily Allen *English language educator*
Zahn, Louis Jennings *foreign language professional educator, administrator*

Augusta
Caldwell, Lee Ann *history educator*
Puryear, Joan Copeland *English language educator*

Austell
Robinson, Maisah B. *language educator*

Carrollton
Brown, Amy Benson *English language and literature educator*
Mims, Nancy Griffin *English language educator*

Cochran
Hines, Susan Carol *English language educator*

Columbus
Ross, Daniel W. *English language educator*

Dalton
Beesley, Bernard Franklin *English language educator*

Decatur
DuBose, Dorothy *educator, publishing consultant*
Khwaja, Waqas Ahmad *English language educator, writer*

Demorest
Greene, David Louis *language professional educator, genealogist*
Whited, Stephen Rex *English literature and language educator*

Dublin
Claxton, Harriett Maroy Jones *retired English language educator*

Fort Gordon
Dyer, James Harold, Jr. *English language educator*

Griffin
Canup, Sherrie Margaret *foreign languages educator*

Jonesboro
Valeri-Gold, Maria *reading educator*

Kennesaw
Corley, Florence Fleming *history educator*

Lagrange
Slay, Jack, Jr. *English language educator*

Lawrenceville
Preston, Deborah Elaine *English language educator*

Lilburn
Jackson, Marsha Louise *French language educator*

Macon
Hennecy, Bobbie Bobo *English language educator*
Huffman, Joan Brewer *history educator*

Milledgeville
Noel, Roger Arthur *French and German language educator*

Moody AFB
Kennedy, Kimberly Kaye *history educator, bookkeeper*

Mount Berry
Smith, Michael Bradley *French language educator, translator*

Mount Vernon
Dobbin, Marjorie Wilcox *English language educator*

Robins AFB
Head, William Pace *historian, educator*

Statesboro
Joiner, George Hewett *historian, educator*
Robinson, David Wayne *English language educator, researcher*
Woods, James Michael *history educator*

Tucker
Twining, Henrietta Stover *retired English language educator*

Valdosta
Adler, Brian Ungar *English language educator, program director*
McClain, Benjamin Richard *music educator, educational administrator*

Waycross
Daane, Mary Constance *English language educator*

INDIANA

Terre Haute
Montañez, Carmen Lydia *Spanish language educator, literature researcher, lawyer*

KENTUCKY

Alvaton
Porterfield, Nolan *English language educator, writer*

Berea
Schneider, Robert James *languages educator*

Bowling Green
Goldfarb, Nancy Dena *English literature educator*
Hardin, John Arthur *history educator*
Harrison, Lowell Hayes *historian, educator*
Johnson, Ellen *linguist, educator*
Klein, Michael Eugene *art history educator*
Minter, Patricia Hagler *history educator*
Trutty-Coohill, Patricia *art historian, educator*

Campbellsville
Stafford, Sarah Jane *English language educator*

Elizabethtown
Cantrell, Douglas Eugene *history educator, author*

Falmouth
Reid, Carolyn Kay *language educator*

Florence
Miller, Sammy Joe *historian, writer, editor*

Georgetown
Cooper, Patricia Unterspan *Spanish language educator*
Kruschwitz, Robert Bruce *philosophy educator*

Hardinsburg
Potter, Harold Claude *philosopher*

Highland Heights
Klaw, Barbara Anne *language educator*
Paradis, Philip *English language educator*

Lexington
Schatzki, Theodore Richard *philosopher*
Stanton, Edward F. *Spanish language educator*
Wolfgang, James Stephen *history educator, minister*

London
Cunningham, Don Rodger *English language educator, researcher*

Louisville
Adams, Mary Elissa *English language educator, consultant*
Ford, Gordon Buell, Jr. *English language, linguistics, and medieval studies educator, author, retired hospital industry financial management executive*
Freibert, Lucy Marie *humanities educator*
Hornback, Bert Gerald *English language educator, writer*
Kearney, Anna Rose *history educator*
Mackey, Thomas Clyde *historian*
Richardson, Harold Edward *literature educator, author*

Morehead
Battaglia, Rosemarie Angela *English language educator*

Murray
Bryant, Keri Lynn *German language educator*

Owensboro
Combs, John Raymond *English literature educator*
Searles, Paul David *historian*
West, William Robert *history educator*

Pikeville
Riley, James Alan *English language educator*

Pippa Passes
Harty, John, III *humanities educator*

Radcliff
Cranston, John Welch *historian, educator*

Richmond
Allameh, Elinor Joy *English language educator*
Shearon, Forrest Bedford *humanities educator*
Sutton, Dorothy Moseley *poet, literature educator*

Williamsburg
Faught, Jolly Kay *English language educator*
Fish, Thomas Edward *English language educator*
Wake, Eric L. *history educator*

Wilmore
Kuhn, Anne Naomi Wicker (Mrs. Harold B. Kuhn) *foreign language educator*
McKinley, Edward Harvey *history educator, author*

LOUISIANA

Baton Rouge
Fogel, Daniel Mark *English language educator, author*
Joseph, Mary J. *English educator*
Owen, Thomas Charles *history educator*
Ricapito, Joseph Virgil (Giuseppe) *Spanish and comparative literature educator*
Roberts, Josephine Anastasia *English literature educator*
Sasek, Gloria Burns *English language and literature educator*
Tarver, John Reed *historian*
Zucker, Mark J. *art history educator*

Bossier City
Labor, Gayle Johnson *English language educator*

Hammond
Dowie, William John, Jr. *English language educator*
Harrison, Lucia Guzzi *foreign languages educator*
Thorburn, James Alexander *humanities educator*

Lafayette
Brasseaux, Carl Anthony *historian*
Gentry, Judith Anne Fenner *history educator*
Heckenbach, Ida Eve *modern languages educator*
James, Randy Ray *English language educator*
Nicassio, Susan Vandiver *history and humanities educator*
Noble, Michael Jay *English language educator, poet*
Scott, Ann Martin *English language educator*

Lake Charles
Schwerin, Alan Kenneth *philosophy educator*

Metairie
Baisier, Maria Davis *English language educator, theater director*

Monroe
Sloan, LaRue Love *English language and literature educator*

Natchitoches
McCorkle, James Lorenzo, Jr. *history educator*
Sanchez, Maria Felisa *foreign language professional*
Snowden, Fraser *philosophy educator*

New Orleans
Altman, Ida *history educator*
Anderson, Nancy Fix *history educator*
Bourgeois, Patrick Lyall *philosophy educator*
Brumfield, William Craft *Slavic studies educator*
Charles, Anne M. *English language educator*
Gimenez, Raphael Antoine *French and Spanish languages educator, writer*
Hallock, Ann Hayes *Italian language and literature educator*
Hazlett, John Downton *English language educator*
Kukla, Jon (Keith) *historian, museum director*
Luza, Radomir Vaclav *historian, educator*
McClay, Wilfred Mark *history educator, writer*
Pindle, Arthur Jackson, Jr. *philosopher, researcher*
Pollock, Linda Anne *history educator*
Qian, Zhaoming *translator, critic, literature educator*
Rambuss, Richard *English language educator*
Sturges, Robert Stuart *English language educator*

Pineville
Howell, Thomas *history educator*
Tapley, Philip Allen *English language and literature educator*

Shreveport
Leitz, Robert Charles, III *English language educator*
Shepherd, Samuel Claude, Jr. *history educator*

Thibodaux
Swetman, Glenn Robert *English language educator, poet*

MASSACHUSETTS

Roslindale
Koepke, Wulf *retired humanities educator*

MICHIGAN

Macatawa
Evans, Robert Owen *English language educator, educational administrator*

MISSISSIPPI

Biloxi
Duncan, Elaine Hermoine *reading educator*

Clinton
Fant, Gene Clinton, Jr. *English language educator*

Crystal Springs
Brewer, Pamela Sue Didlake *English and Latin languages educator*

Goodman
Jones, Rita Ann *speech, theater educator*

Hamilton
Lancaster, Jane Cleo *historian, writer*

Hattiesburg
Kolin, Philip Charles *English language educator*
McDaniel, Linda Elkins *English language and literature educator*

Hurley
Morgan, Phillis Pierce *English language educator*

Jackson
Curtis, Verna P. *reading educator*
Palmer, Dora Deen Pope *English and French language educator*

Smith, Steven Garry *philosopher, religious studies educator*
Tashiro, Paul Yukio *Assyriology educator*

Long Beach
Krystek, Dennis John *liberal arts educator*

Magnolia
Coney, Elaine Marie *English and foreign languages educator*

Mississippi State
Belatèche, Lydia *language educator*
Crowell, Lorenzo Mayo *historian, educator*
Smith, Jonathan Richardson *English language educator*

Oxford
Baskett, Franz Keith *creative writing educator*
Coles, Felice Anne *foreign language educator*
Northart, Debra Lynne *history educator, social activist*

Summit
Ginn, B(arbara) Merrielyn *history educator*

Tougaloo
Horvath, John, Jr. *English language educator*

University
Kiger, Joseph Charles *history educator*

NORTH CAROLINA

Asheville
Hubbell, Elizabeth Wolfe *English language educator*
Mills, Sophie Jane Victoria *classics educator*

Boiling Springs
Binfield, Kevin Scott *English language educator*

Boone
Barth, Melissa Ellen *English language and women's studies educator*
Buchanan, Harriette Cuttino *humanities educator*
Goff, James Rudolph, Jr. *history educator*
McEntee, Grace Elizabeth *language educator*
Stolberg, Mary Margaret *historian*

Buies Creek
Peterman, Gina Diane *English language educator*
Shelley, Bryan Keith *English language educator*

Cary
Mata, Elizabeth Adams *language educator, land investor*

Chapel Hill
Bister-Broosen, Helga *German linguistics educator*
Craven, Roberta Jill *literature educator*
Dessen, Alan Charles *English language educator*
Dominguez, Frank A. *language educator*
Dunstan, William Edward *historian*
Durand, Alain-Philippe *French language educator*
Headley, John Miles *history educator*
Jackson, Blyden *English language educator*
McVaugh, Michael Rogers *historian, educator*
Mews, Siegfried *German language educator*
Mews, Siegfried Ernst *language educator*
Reed, Mark Lafayette, III *English literature educator*
Rivero-Potter, Alicia *Spanish language educator*
Stanberry, Dosi Elaine *English literature educator, writer*
Stephens, Laurence David, Jr. *linguist, financial executive*
Vance, Robert Dale *philosophy educator, sculptor*
West, Janet L. *German language educator*

Charlotte
Miller, Martha LaFollette *foreign languages and literature educator*
Thiede, Ralf *English linguistics educator*

Davidson
Levering, Ralph Brooks *history educator*
McCarthy, Margaret R. *German language and literature educator*
Williams, Robert Chadwell *history educator*

Durham
Beasley-Murray, Jon *English language educator*
Burian, Peter Hart *literature and classics educator, translator*
Capwell, Richard Leonard *English language educator*
Clay, Diskin *classical studies educator*
Humphreys, Margaret Ellen *historian, educator, physician*
Murrell, Carlos Devonne *poet, Spanish language educator, translator*
Richardson, Lawrence, Jr. *Latin language educator, archeologist*
Smith, Barbara Herrnstein *English language and literature educator, writer*
Thomas, Jean-Jacques Robert *Romance languages educator*
Wheeler, Everett Lynn *historian, editor*
Williams, Jocelyn Jones *reading educator*

Elon College
Crowe, David M. *history educator*

Fayetteville
Eddy, Robert *English language educator, author*
McMillan, Bettie Barney *English language educator*

Greensboro
Almeida, José Agustín *romance languages educator*
Benson, Brian Joseph *English language educator, author*
Darnell, Donald Gene *English language professional*
Dawson, James Doyne *historian, educator*
Gaines, Sarah Fore *retired foreign language educator*
Garren, Samuel Baity *English language educator*
Link, William Allen *history educator*
Penninger, Frieda Elaine *retired English language educator*
Rosenblum, Joseph *English language educator*

Stoesen, Alexander Rudolph *history educator*

Greenville
Arias, Judith Hepler *Spanish language educator*
Kopelman, Loretta Mary *philosophy educator*
Palumbo, Donald Emanuel *English language educator, department chair*
Ryan, Cynthia Ann *English language educator*
Shields, Edgar Thomson, Jr. *American literature educator*
Steelman, Joseph Flake *history educator*
Williams, Jeffrey James *English language educator*

High Point
Patton, Tamara J. *foreign language educator*
Sellers, Georgeanna *English language educator*
Wilson, Paul Eddy *philosophy educator*

Hillsborough
Idol, John Lane, Jr. *English language educator, writer, editor*

Kannapolis
Hyner, Karen Elaine *language educator, writer*

Laurinburg
Bayes, Ronald Homer *English language educator*

Lexington
Burkhart, Dorthea Davenport *language educator*

Louisburg
Davis, Sarah Irwin *retired English language educator*

Mars Hill
Clemons, Gregory Alan *foreign language educator*

Matthews
Black, Albert George *English language educator*

Mount Olive
Worthington, Anne Pepper Poole *English language educator, writer*

Murfreesboro
Davis, John Howard *English language educator*

New Bern
Brack, Jacques *language educator, linguistics researcher, author*
Fegely, Eugene Leroy *retired humanities educator*

Pembroke
Brown, Monika Christiane Bargmann *English language educator*
Rundus, Raymond Joe *English language educator*

Pope AFB
Conley, Raymond Leslie *English language educator*

Raleigh
Adcock, Betty S. *poet, humanities educator*
Edwards, Vivian *retired humanities educator*
Fountain, Anne Owen *Spanish language educator*
Hambourger, Robert Michael *philosophy educator*
Jones, Frederick Claudius *English language and linguistics educator*
Pettis, Joyce *English language educator*
Thomas, Erik Robert *linguistics educator*

Shelby
Bolich, Gregory Gordon *humanities educator*

Weldon
Lewter, Alice Jenkins *history and political science educator*

Wilmington
Gould, Christopher *English language educator*

Winston Salem
Caron, Simone Marie *history educator*
Hans, James S. *English language educator*

NORTH DAKOTA

Jamestown
Heizer, Ruth Bradfute *philosophy educator*

OHIO

Cincinnati
Miller, Danny Lester *English language educator*

New Concord
Williamson, Richard Joseph *English language educator*

Springfield
Mintz, Susannah Beth *English language educator*

OKLAHOMA

Ada
Daniel, Arlie Verl *speech education educator*

Bartlesville
Austerman, Donna Lynne *Spanish language educator*

Chickasha
Meredith, Howard Lynn *American Indian studies educator*

Edmond
Sevier, Elisabeth *French language educator, writer*

El Reno
Rupp, Kelly S. *English language educator*

Goodwell
Bender, Joyce Jackson *university English educator*

Norman
Dharwadker, Aparna *English studies educator*
Fears, Jesse Rufus *historian, educator, academic dean*
Hobbs, Catherine Lynn *English language and literature educator*
Lason, Sandra Woolman *linguistics, ESL, and gifted educator*
Liesenfeld, Vincent Joseph *English language educator*
Mitman, Gregg Alden *history of science educator*
Norwood, Stephen Harlan *history educator*
Palmer, Allison Lee *art history educator*
Rapf, Joanna E. *English literature and film educator*
Sellars, Nigel Anthony *historian, writer*
Skeeters, Martha C. *historian, educator*

Oklahoma City
Lestina, Roger Henry *English language educator*
Todd, Joe Lee *historian*
Woodward, Hanson Mark *English and German languages educator, minister*

Shawnee
Agee, Nelle Hulme *art history educator*

Stillwater
Fischer, LeRoy Henry *historian, educator*
Glover, Kyle Stephen *English language educator*
Heflin, Ruth Janelle *English language educator*
Olson, Nadine Faye *foreign language educator, consultant*

Tahlequah
Corbett, William Paul *history educator, historian, consultant*

Tinker AFB
Allin, Lawrence Carroll *historian, educator*

Tulsa
Capaldi, Nicholas *philosophy educator*

Weatherford
Hayden, John Kelly *historian*
Pettijohn, Viki Ann *English and Spanish languages educator*

PENNSYLVANIA

Media
Markley, Arnold Albert, IV *English language educator*

SOUTH CAROLINA

Aiken
Hochel, Sandra Stroope *speech communication educator, researcher*
Rich, John Stanley *English language educator*

Beaufort
Pazant, Rosalie Frazier *retired English language educator*
Villena-Alvarez, Juanita I. *language educator, consultant*

Central
Black, Laura Neath *language professional*

Charleston
Cox, Victoria Kathleen *humanities educator*
Crout, Robert Rhodes *historian, educator*
Drago, Edmund Leon *history educator*
Dulaney, William Marvin *history educator, curator*
Lesses, Glenn *philosophy educator*

Cheraw
Thornton, Robert Donald *emeritus English language educator*

Clemson
Chapman, Wayne Kenneth *English language educator*
Cranston, Philip Edward *foreign language professional*
Dettmar, Kevin John Hoffmann *English language educator*
Heusinkveld, Paula Rae *foreign language educator, writer*
Howard, Tharon Wayne *English literature educator*
Johnston, Carol Elizabeth *English language educator*
Kuehn, Thomas *history educator*
Kuehnel, Jean *humanities educator*

Clinton
Skinner, James Lister, III *English language educator*

Columbia
Aviram, Amittai F. *English and comparative literature educator*
Edmiston, William F. *foreign language educator*
Gardiol, Rita Mazzetti *foreign language educator*
Gatlin, Eugene S., Jr. *retired English language educator, consultant*
Goodwin-Davey, Alice Anne *English language educator*
Joiner, Elizabeth Garner *French language educator*
Khushf, George Peter *bioethicist*
Mathisen, Ralph Whitney *ancient history educator*
Rivers, William Elbert *English language educator*
Scott, Patrick Greig *language educator, librarian*
Sellers, Cleveland Louis, Jr. *history educator*
Synnott, Marcia Graham *history educator*

Conway
Michie, Joseph Allen *English language educator*
Purcell, Sarah C. (Sally) *English language educator*
Talbert, Roy, Jr. *history educator*

Denmark
Di Medio, Gregory Lawrence *English language educator, writer*
Lebby, Gloria C. *history educator*
McCord, Betty J. *reading specialist*

Gaffney
Fincher, Hugh McCommon, III *foreign language educator*

Greenville
Allen, Gilbert Bruce *English language educator, poet*
Prior, Richard Edmon *classics educator*

Greenwood
Figueira, Robert Charles *history educator*
Smith, Sara Elizabeth Cushing *English language educator, writer*

Hilton Head Island
Chase, Jean Cox *retired English language educator*

Isle Of Palms
Soltow, James Harold *historian, researcher*

Newberry
O'Shea, Michael Joseph *humanities educator*

Orangeburg
Wallace, Nathaniel Owen *English language educator*

Pendleton
Roper, Donna Kaye *historian*

Rock Hill
Cormier, Raymond *humanities educator, author*
Friedman, Donald Flanell *foreign language educator*
Haynes, Edward Sheldon *history educator*
Pettus, Mildred Louise *retired history educator, writer*
Viault, Birdsall Scrymser *history educator*
Webb, Ross Allan *historian, educator*

Spartanburg
Clark, Elizabeth Adams (Liz Clark) *genealogy educator*
Deku, Afrikadzata *African language educator, consultant*
Epps, Edwin Carlyle *English language educator*
Packer, Mark Neil *philosophy educator*

York
Lee, Joseph Edward *history educator*

TENNESSEE

Chattanooga
Townsend, Gavin Edward *art history educator*

Clarksville
Muir, Malcolm, Jr. *history educator*

Cookeville
Kharif, Wali Rashash *history educator*
Reagan, Patrick Dennis *history educator*
Schrader, William Christian, III *history educator*
Slotkin, Alan R. *English language educator*

Dayton
Legg, Raymond Elliott, Jr. *English language educator*

Harrogate
Ferris, Kathleen Richard *English language educator and professional*

Jackson
Carls, Stephen Douglas *history educator*
Grose, Janet Lynne *English language educator*
Gundersen, Lawrence Garfield, Jr. *historian, educator*

Johnson City
Greninger, Edwin Thomas *history educator*
Ray, Rickey Joe *philosophy educator, minister*
Riley, Esther Powell *English language educator, editor*
Wyatt, Doris Fay Chapman *English language educator*

Kingsport
Egan, Martha Avaleen *history educator, archivist*
Wing, Linda King *English language educator*

Knoxville
Breslaw, Elaine Gellis *history educator*
Craig, Christopher Patrick *classicist, educator*
Handelsman, Michael *Hispanic studies educator*
Klein, Milton Martin *history educator*
Miller, Helen *history educator*
Peretti, Burton William *history educator*
Smith, Arthur *English language educator*
Wampler, Andrew Todd *English language educator*

Martin
Effiong, Philip U. *English language educator*

Maryville
Overstreet, Samuel A. *English language educator*

Memphis
Crouse, Maurice Alfred *history educator*
Jolly, William Thomas *foreign language educator*
Jones, Marguerite Jackson *English language educator*
Maitland, Carla Love *history educator, program coordinator*
Shaheen, Naseeb *English literature educator*
Stagg, Louis Charles *English language and literature educator*
Strong, Carson McCarty *medical ethics educator*
Vest, James Murray *foreign language and literature educator*
Vinson, Mark Alan *English language and literature educator*
Watanabe, Albert Tohru *classical studies educator*

Murfreesboro
Brantley, William Oliver, Jr. *English language educator*
Brewer, Gay *poet, English language and literature educator*
Brookshire, Jerry Hardman *historian, educator*
Curtis, Mary Ann Carter *English language educator*
Ferris, Norman Bernard *history educator*

Rupprecht, Nancy Ellen *historian, educator*

Nashville
Bost, Suzanne Michelle *humanities educator*
Compton, John Joseph *philosophy educator*
Doody, Margaret Anne *English language educator*
Freedman, Paul Harris *history educator*
Goodman, Lenn Evan *philosopher*
Hassel, Rudolph Christopher *English language educator*
Kelton, William Jackson *English language and social science educator*
Leach, Douglas Edward *history educator, writer*
Lovett, Bobby Lee *history educator, university dean*
Mueller, Agnes C. *German language educator*
Pfanner, Helmut Franz *German language educator*
Phillips, Philip Edward *lecturer in English*
Ransom, Nancy Alderman *sociology and women's studies educator, university administrator*
Sallis, John Cleveland *philosophy educator*
Sevin, Dieter Hermann *language and literature professional, educator*
Tichi, Cecelia *English language educator*

Sewanee
Chitty, (Mary) Elizabeth Nickinson *university historian*
Goldberg, Harold Joel *history educator*
Mills, Kathryn Oliver *French language educator*
Williamson, Samuel Ruthven, Jr. *historian, university administrator*

Shiloh
Hawke, Paul Henry *historian*

Trezevant
Blanks, Naomi Mai *retired English language educator*

Tullahoma
Copeland, Dawn G. *English language educator*

TEXAS

Abilene
Hamner, Robert Daniel *English language educator, writer, literary critic*
Miller, Doris Anne *English language educator*

Alpine
Champion, Laurie *English literature educator*
Dillard, Betty Lynn *English language educator*

Amarillo
Morey, Mark Howard *museum educator*

Arlington
Herring, Susan Catherine *linguistics educator*
Reeder, Harry Paul *philosophy educator*
Richmond, Douglas Wertz *history educator*
Silva, David James *linguistics educator*

Austin
Abzug, Robert Henry *historian, educator*
Arens, Katherine Marie *language educator*
Benavides, Adan, Jr. *historian*
Bowman, Shearer Davis *historian, educator*
Braybrooke, David *philosopher, educator*
Campbell, Kermit Ernest *assistant professor*
Crunden, Robert Morse *history educator*
Green, Peter Morris *classics educator, writer, translator*
Gutmann, Myron Peter *history educator*
Harris, Elizabeth Hall *writer, English language educator*
Justus, Carol Faith *linguistics educator*
Kent, David L. *genealogist, publisher*
Louis, William Roger *historian, educator, editor*
Moeller, Hans-Bernhard *Germanic languages, literature and film educator*
Reed, Cory Arthur *Spanish literature educator*
Schulz-Behrend, George *German language educator*
Seaholm, Megan *history educator, historian*
Sledd, James Hinton *English language educator*
Smith, Wendell Patrick *language educator, writer*

Beaumont
Fritze, Ronald Harold *historian, educator*
Woodland, Naaman Johnson, Jr. *history educator*

Bellaire
Pass, Susan Jeanette *American history educator*

Brownwood
Murphy, Justin Duane *history educator*

Buffalo
Oakes, Helen Miller *language educator*

Burleson
Robin, Clara Nell (Claire Robin) *English language educator*

Canyon
Furnish, Shearle Lee *English and modern languages educator*

College Station
Billingsley, Nadine Young *genealogist*
Dunsford, Deborah Williams *English language, journalism educator*
Hoagwood, Terence Allan *English language and literature educator*
Ives, Maura Carey *English language educator*
Myers, David Gershom *English language educator, writer*
Parrish, Paul Austin *English language educator*
Portales, Marco Antonio *English language educator, executive assistant*
Saatkamp, Herman Joseph *philosophy educator*
Stout, Janis Pitts *English language educator*
Wright, Nancy Jane *English language educator*

Commerce
Jonz, Jon Graham *linguistics educator*
Linck, Charles Edward *English language educator*
Perry, Thomas Amherst *English literature and language educator*
Reid, Robin Anne *English language educator, writer*
Sengupta, Gunja *historian, educator*

Corpus Christi
Williams, Mary Elmore *English language and history educator, educational administrator*

Dallas
Bradley, Charles Henry *linguistic anthropologist*
Britton, Wesley Alan *English language educator*
Countryman, Edward Francis *historian, educator*
Crusius, Timothy Wood *English language educator*
Davis, Daisy Sidney *history educator*
Longacre, Robert Edmondson *linguist, educator*
Lutz, Gretchen Kay *English language educator*
Martin, Carol Jacquelyn *educator, artist*
Ndimba, Cornelius Ghane *language educator*
Rutledge, Mary Elizabeth *English language educator*

Denton
Campbell, Randolph Bluford *historian, educator*
Chipman, Donald Eugene *history educator*
Green, Suzanne Disheroon *language and literature educator, researcher*
Langston, Camille Anne *rhetoric educator*
Longoria, Francisco Anselmo *English and Spanish language educator*
Palmer, Joyce Arline Cornette *English language educator*
Palmer, Leslie Howard *literature educator*
Polizzi, Allessandria Elizabeth *English language educator*
Rektorik-Sprinkle, Patricia Jean *Latin language educator*
Shockley, Martin Staples *retired English studies educator, writer*
Snapp, Harry Franklin *historian*
Tanner, William E. *English language educator*
Wilson, William H. *history educator*

Edinburg
Barrera, Eduardo *Spanish language and literature educator*
McCurdy, Pamela Paris *linguistics educator*
Vassberg, Liliane Mangold *foreign language educator*
von Ende, Frederick (Ted) *English language educator, university director*

El Paso
Bledsoe, Robert Terrell *English language educator*
Clymer, Kenton James *history educator*
Haddox, John Herbert *philosophy educator*
Louden, David Bruce *classical literature and languages educator*
Lujan, Rosa Emma *bilingual specialist, trainer, consultant*
Righter, Robert Willms *history educator*
Torok, George Dennis *history educator*

Fort Worth
Blakeney, Rae *art historian, artist, writer, arts editor*
Durham, Carolyn Richardson *foreign language and literature educator*
Estep, William Roscoe, Jr. *church history educator, minister*
Henry, Floreen Barger *foreign language educator*
Kilborne, William Skinner *English language educator, playwright, lyricist, writer*
Patoski, Margaret Nancy *historian, educator*
Stevens, Kenneth R. *history educator*
Thistlethwaite, Mark Edward *art history educator*

Galveston
Ryan, James Gilbert *historian, educator, writer*

Garland
Rushing, Dorothy Marie *retired historian, educator*

Georgetown
Proctor, Claude Oliver *Russian language educator*

Grapevine
Cuellar, Virginia Adrien *art historian and consultant*

Harlingen
Martin, Leland Morris (Pappy Martin) *history educator*

Houston
Athy, Lawrence Ferdinand, Jr. *historian*
Chance, Jane *English literature educator*
Cortina, Rodolfo José *Spanish language educator, researcher, consultant*
Folk, Katherine Pinkston *English language educator, writer, journalist*
Hyman, Harold M. *history educator, consultant*
Kanellos, Nicolás *foreign language and liberal studies educator, publisher*
Kemmer, Suzanne Elizabeth *linguistics researcher, educator*
Lamb, Sydney MacDonald *linguistics and cognitive science educator*
Martin, James Kirby *historian, educator*
McBride, Sharan Schmidt *English language educator*
Melosi, Martin Victor *history educator, researcher, writer*
Patten, Robert Lowry *English language educator*
Pryor, William Daniel Lee *humanities educator*
Shi, Ming Zheng *history educator*
Smith, Richard Joseph *history educator*
Urbina, Manuel, II *legal research historian, history educator*
Wintz, Cary Decordova *history educator*

Huntsville
Raymond, Kay E(ngelmann) *Spanish language educator, consultant*
Ruffin, Paul Dean *English language educator*
Schwetman, John William *English language professional educator*

Hurst
Pate, J'Nell Laverne *history and government educator*

Irving
Sepper, Dennis Lee *philosophy educator*
Sullivan, Charles Robert *history educator*

Kerrville
Breeden, David Marion *English language educator, writer*
Freeman, Walden Shanklin *retired history educator, college administrator*

Jones, Barbara Christine *educator, linguist, creative arts designer*
Tran, Qui-Phiet *English language educator*

Kingsville
Clatanoff, Doris Ann *English language educator*
Smith, Julia Amelia *English language educator*

Lancaster
Christman, Calvin Lee *history educator*

Levelland
Sears, Edward L. *English language educator*

Lubbock
George, Edward Vincent *classical languages educator*
Ketner, Kenneth Laine *philosopher, educator*
McCloud, Nedra *English language educator*
Miller, Paul Allen *literature educator*
Tate, Carolyn E. *art historian*

Manchaca
Hall, James Granville, Jr. *history educator*

Midland
Simmons, Charles Edward Phillip *history educator*

Nacogdoches
Abernethy, Francis Edward *English educator*
Gaston, Edwin Willmer, Jr. *retired English language educator*

Orange
Preslar, Andrew Basil *English language educator*

Ranger
Jones, Roger Walton *English language educator, writer*

Richardson
Akmakjian, Alan Paul *English language, literature and creative writing educator*
Butler, Steven Ray *history educator, historian, genealogist*
Chandler, Joan Mary *humanities educator*
Clements, Brian N. *English language educator*
Graff, Harvey J. *history and humanities educator*
Kratz, Dennis Merle *language educator, college dean*

Round Top
Lentz, Edwin Lamar *art historian*

San Antonio
Baird, Scott James *English language educator*
Craven, Alan Elliott *English language educator, university dean*
Himelblau, Jack Joseph *Latin-American literature and culture educator*
Igo, John *English language educator*
McCusker, John J. *history educator, economist*
Oleszkiewicz, Malgorzata *Latin American literature and culture educator*
Schott, Linda Kay *historian, educator*
Sillars, Stuart John *English literature educator, writer*
Stroud, Matthew David *foreign languages educator*
Weinberg, Florence May *modern language and literature educator*
Wells, Colin Michael *Roman history educator, archaeologist*
Wickham, Christopher John *foreign language educator*

San Diego
Valdez, Ana Maria Briones *English language educator*

San Marcos
Brown, Ronald Conklin *history educator*
de la Teja, Jesús Francisco *historian, educator*
Skerpan, Elizabeth Penley *English language educator*

Seguin
Hsu, Patrick Kuo-Heng *languages educator, librarian*

Sherman
Lincecum, Jerry Bryan *English language educator*

Snyder
Barkowsky, Edward Richard *English language educator*

Stafford
Sigmar, Lucia Anne Stretcher *English language educator, administrator*

Stephenville
Power, Sherry Decker *English language educator*

Sugar Land
Dvoretzky, Edward *German language educator*

Tomball
Norwood, William D., Jr. *English language educator*

Uvalde
Wood, James Albert *foreign language educator*

Victoria
Janda, Paul L. *historian, educator*

Waco
Hankins, Barry Gene *historian, university institute director*
Kramer, Denny B. *English language educator*
Norden, Ernest Elwood *foreign language educator*
Sharpless, Mary Rebecca *historian*
Smith, Evelyn Elaine *language educator*

Wichita Falls
Bourland, D(elphus) David, Jr. *linguist*
Campbell, Jefferson Holland *English language educator*
Kindig, Everett William *history educator*
Smith, Evans Lansing *English language educator*

Yoakum
York, Barbara Lee *genealogist*

VIRGINIA

Abingdon
Brown, Dick Erie *genealogist, archivist*

Alexandria
DeZarn, Guy David *English language educator*
Hixson, Stanley G. *computer technology, speech, language educator*

Annandale
Hutcheon, Wallace Schoonmaker *history educator*

Arlington
Mahoney, Kevin A. *historian, consultant*
Mills, Elizabeth Shown *genealogical editor*
Strelau, Renate *historical researcher, artist*
Wierich, Jochen *American studies educator*

Batesville
Ryder, Frank Glessner *German literature educator, researcher*

Blacksburg
Hardcastle, Valerie Gray *philosophy educator*
Heilker, Paul *English language educator*
Shumsky, Neil Larry *historian, educator*
Snoke, Judith Houtz *English language educator*
Soniat, Katherine *English language educator*
Tucker, Edward Llewellyn *English language educator*
Wallenstein, Peter *historian, educator*

Bridgewater
McQuilkin, David Karl *history educator*

Charlottesville
Courtney, Edward *classics educator*
Felski, Rita *language educator*
Garrett, George Palmer, Jr. *creative writing and English language educator, writer*
Jost, Walter Paul, III *English language educator*
Kezar, Dennis Dean *English language educator*
Kolb, Harold Hutchinson, Jr. *English language educator*
Kraehe, Enno Edward *history educator*
Langbaum, Robert Woodrow *English language educator, author*
McClymonds, Marita Petzoldt *musicologist*
Megill, Allan D. *historian, educator*
Nohrnberg, James Carson *English language educator*
Rubin, David Lee *French literature educator, critic, editor, publisher*
Scarlett, Elizabeth Ann *foreign language educator*
Stocker, Arthur Frederick *classics educator*
Wright, Charles Penzel, Jr. *English language educator*

Chester
Tompkins, Patrick *English language educator, writer*

Culpeper
Fergus, Patricia Marguerita *English language educator emeritus, writer, editor*

Danville
Hayes, Jack Irby *historian*
Trakas, William Samuel *history educator*

Fairfax
Garson, Helen Sylvia *English language educator, writer*
Hodges, Devon Leigh *English language educator*
Nadeau, Robert Lee *English language educator, inventor, entrepreneur*
Orens, John Richard *historian, educator*

Farmville
Etheridge, Elizabeth Williams *history educator*
Hevener, Fillmer, Jr. *English language educator, writer, portrait artist*
Orth, Geoffrey Charles *modern languages educator*
Reynolds, John Francis *foreign language educator*

Fort Lee
Sims, Lynn Lee *historian, educator*

Fort Monroe
Stensvaag, James Thomas *public historian, educator*

Fredericksburg
Fallon, Paul Dennis *linguistics educator*
Funk, Ella Frances *genealogist, author*
Koos, Leonard Robert *French educator*
Wasson, John Marvin *English language educator*
Wellington, Marie Annette *French language educator*

Hampton
Bell, Margaret Shearin *English language educator*
Henney, Frederic Allison *English language educator*
Johnson, Vernon Eugene *history educator, educational administrator*
Khawaja, Mabel Masuda *English language educator*
Thompson, Victor Harold *English language educator*

Harrisonburg
Arndt, John Christopher *history educator*
Bertolet, Craig Eugene *English language educator*
Flage, Daniel Ervin *philosophy educator*
LePera, Darla Craft *English language educator*

Herndon
Kaufman, Janice Horner *foreign language educator*

Hollins
Moore, John Rees *retired language educator, editor*

Lexington
Brooke, George Mercer, Jr. *historian, educator*
Wells, Anne Sharp *historian, researcher*

Lynchburg
Shoemaker, M. Wesley *history educator*
Tiner, Elza Cheryl *English language educator*

Manassas
Larrieu, Duane Paul *translator, educator*

Mc Lean
García-Godoy, Cristián *historian, educator*

Mechanicsville
Pollock, Michael Elwood *historian, genealogist*

Newport News
Kleber, Brooks Edward *military historian*
Mazzarella, Mario Domenic *history educator*

Norfolk
Boyd, Carl *history educator*
Greene, Douglas George *humanities educator, author, publisher*
Martin, Mary Coates *genealogist, writer, volunteer*
McColley, Beverly Alice *English language educator*
Moreno, Susan Elizabeth *Spanish language educator*
Pope, Stephanie Marie *classicist, educator*
Rutyna, Richard Albert *history educator*

Petersburg
Smith, Paul Edmund, Jr. *philosophy and religion educator*

Poquoson
French, James Thomas *historian, educator*

Portsmouth
Williams, Lena Harding *English language educator*

Quantico
Gudmundsson, Bruce I. *military historian*

Radford
Acereda, Alberto *Spanish language and literature educator*
Arbury, Andrew Stephen, III *art historian*
Hensley, Susan Eleanore *communications and language educator*
McClellan, Charles Wayne *history educator, researcher*
Small, Robert Coleman, Jr. *English language educator*

Richmond
Anderson, Frederick Jarrard *historian*
Gentry, Daphne Sue *historian*
Gray, Clarence Jones *foreign language educator, dean emeritus*
Kirkpatrick, Peter Steven *foreign language educator*
McLees, Ainslie Armstrong *French language educator*
Moore, James Tice *history educator*
Perry, Patricia H. *English language educator*
Phillips, Richard England *foreign language specialist, art history educator*
Robert, Joseph Clarke *historian, consultant*
Salmon, Emily Jones *historian, editor*
Strohm, Robert Frank *historian*

Roanoke
Tappert, Tara Leigh *art historian, archivist, researcher*
Trethewey, Eric Peter *English language educator*

Rocky Mount
Guthrie, Donna Morter *English language and journalism educator*

Sweet Briar
Piepho, (Edward) Lee *humanities educator*
Richards, Michael Dulany *history educator*

Topping
Willett, Albert James, Jr. *family historian*

University Of Richmond
Terry, Robert Meredith *foreign language educator*

Vienna
Frenze, Karin M.E. Alexis *art historian*

Williamsburg
Fraser, Howard Michael *foreign language educator, editor*
Hoffman, Ronald *historical institute administrator, educator*
MacGowan, Christopher John *literature educator*
Matthews, J. Rosser *historian, educator*
Pierce, Catherine Maynard *history educator*
Potkay, Adam Stanley *English language educator*
Scancarelli, Janine Laura *linguistics educator, researcher*

Willis
Smith, Michael William *English language educator*

Woodbridge
Gates, Sheree Hunt *elementary education educator, writer*

Yorktown
Carpenter, Nan Cooke *English language educator*

WEST VIRGINIA

Beckley
Holloway, Brian Ray *English language educator*

Charles Town
Na, (Terry) Tsung Shun *Chinese studies educator, writer*

Huntington
Bailey, Louise Slagle *English language educator*

Kenna
Withrow, Dolly Mae *English language educator*

Morgantown
Carr, Mike *English language educator*
Drange, Theodore Michael *philosophy educator*
McNamara, Gregory Vaughn *English language educator*
Schlunk, Jurgen Eckart *German language educator*
Singer, Armand Edwards *foreign language educator*

Salem
Leland, John Lowell *humanities educator*

Wheeling
Laker, Joseph Alphonse *history educator*

TERRITORIES OF THE UNITED STATES

PUERTO RICO

Rio Piedras
Marcano, Conchita Soltero *Spanish language educator*

San Juan
Ocasio-Melendez, Marcial Enrique *history educator*

ADDRESS UNPUBLISHED

Ahl, Janyce Barnwell *historian, writer, speaker, retired educator*
Arnett, Traci Wendell *English language educator*
Bassett, Lisa Jane *English language educator, author*
Benz, Todd David *English Latin and history educator*
Botwinick, Rita Steinhardt *history educator*
Bree, Germaine *French literature educator*
Carman, Patricia Dobbs *language educator*
Cartwright, Talula Elizabeth *writing and career development educator, communication and leadership consultant*
Clarke, John Robert *art history educator, art critic*
Clubbe, John Louis Edwin *humanities educator*
Cobb, John Cecil, Jr. (Jack Cobb) *Latin America area specialist, communications specialist and executive*
Comabella, Luis Fernando *Spanish language educator*
Demenchonok, Edward Vasilevich *philosopher, linguist, researcher, educator*
Edwards, Barry Michael *English language educator*
Fackler, Naomi Paula *librarian*
Fisher, Anita Jeanne *English language educator*
Franklin, John Hope *historian, educator, author*
Gerlach, Jeanne Elaine *English language educator*
Gleaton, Martha McCalman *English language educator*
Gonzalez-Vales, Luis Ernesto *historian, educational administrator*
Graham, John Marshall *French language educator*
Hansen, Elisa Marie *art historian*
Harper, Paula *art history educator, writer*
Hartsock, Pamela Ann *English language educator*
Holien, Kim Bernard *historian*
Hood, Ronald Chalmers, III *historian, writer*
Johnson, Alex Claudius *English language educator*
Johnson, Carolyn W. (Carrie Johnson) *historian, author*
Johnson, Clifton Herman *historian, archivist, former research center director*
Jones, Suejette Albritton *basic skills educator*
Jones, Susan Emily *English language educator*
Kulstad, Mark Alan *philosophy educator*
Lambert, Edythe Rutherford *retired language educator, civic volunteer*
Lawson Donadio, Carolina Anna *foreign language educator, translator*
Lightburn, Faye Marie *genealogist*
Lindley, Lester Gale *legal and constitutional historian*
Mayo, Marti *art historian, curator*
McBride, William Michael *historian, educator*
McNally, James Joseph, Jr. *English language educator*
Monas, Sidney *retired history educator*
Montenyohl, Eric Lawrence *English language educator, folklorist*
Norman, Rosella *English language educator*
Olsan, Lea S. Thompson *English and foreign language educator*
Ortega, Rafael Clemente *English and Romance language educator*
Premo, Mary Katharyn (Cassie) *English language and women's studies educator*
Rickard, Ruth David *retired history and political science educator*
Sabat-Rivers, Georgina *Latin American literature educator*
Sarbo, Linda Diane *English language educator*
Selch, Andrea Helen *English and American literature educator, writer*
Smith, R. Mark *English language educator*
Smith, Rebecca Godwin *English language educator*
Surguy, Maria Teresa *language educator*
Thomas, Mark Ellis *English language educator*
Williams, Patrice Dale *linguist, educator*
Winter, Marsha Terry *French language educator*
Wolfard, Lorrie Elaine *English language educator*
Wright, Beth Segal *art historian, educator*
Wynne, Carey Howard, Jr. (Jean-Pierre Solòmon) *history and religion educator*
Young, Michael William *English language educator*
Zidovec, Mirta Rosa *Spanish language professional*
Zubizarreta, John *English language educator*

HUMANITIES: LIBRARIES

UNITED STATES

ALABAMA

Aliceville
Potts, Ethelda Oaks *library director*

Auburn
Straiton, T(homas) Harmon, Jr. *librarian*

Birmingham
Bulow, Jack Faye *library director*
Murrell, Susan DeBrecht *librarian*
Stewart, George Ray *librarian*

Brewton
Biggs-Williams, Evelyn Ann *librarian*

Cullman
Myrick, John Paul *librarian, library building consultant*

Florence
Meagher, Elizabeth Strapp *librarian*

Huntsville
Mathews, Fred Leroy *librarian*
Miller, Carol Lynn *librarian*

Jacksonville
Hubbard, William James *library director*

Maxwell AFB
Stewart, Martha Mitchell *librarian*

Mobile
Peplowski, Celia Ceslawa *librarian*

Montevallo
Scales, Diann Roylette *librarian*

Montgomery
Breedlove, Michael Alan *archivist*
Harris, Patricia Lea *librarian*
Medina, Sue O'Neal *librarian*
Singleton, Patricia Moore *librarian*

Tuscaloosa
Malinconico, S. Michael *librarian, educator*

ARKANSAS

Arkadelphia
Petty, Jenny Beth *librarian, educator*

Camden
Cook, Juanita Kimbell *library director, educator*

Fayetteville
Boyd, Molly Denise *librarian, English educator*

Fort Smith
Larson, Larry *librarian*
Zabel, Patricia Lynn *librarian*

Little Rock
Berry, Janet Claire *librarian*
Mulkey, Jack Clarendon *library director*

Lonoke
Ross, Philip Rowland *library director*

Magnolia
Tornquist, Kristi Malinda *librarian*

North Little Rock
Curol, Helen Ruth *librarian, English language educator*
McKinney, Barbara Jean *librarian*

State University
Bailey, Jeffrey Randolph *librarian*

DISTRICT OF COLUMBIA

Washington
Stallings, Elizabeth Arundell *governmental library management analyst*

FLORIDA

Atlantis
Gough, Carolyn Harley *library director*

Boca Raton
Golian, Linda Marie *librarian*
Hermann, Naomi Basel *librarian, interior decorator*

Boynton Beach
Farace, Virginia Kapes *librarian*
Romo, Jose León *library educator*

Clearwater
Ritz, Paul Stephen *library manager*
Werner, Elizabeth Helen *librarian, Spanish language educator*

Coleman
Crenshaw, Tena Lula *librarian*

Davie
McNulty, Mary Pat *library administrator*

Daytona Beach
Valk, Judy P. *librarian*

Deland
Caccamise, Genevra Louise Ball (Mrs. Alfred E. Caccamise) *retired librarian*
Everett, David Dean *librarian*
Ryan, Susan Magness *librarian, educator*

Florida City
Valdes, Rolando Hector *library director, law librarian*

Fort Lauderdale
Hershenson, Miriam Hannah *librarian*
Simons-Oparah, Tanya *library administrator*

Fort Myers
Hoeth, Kathleen Ann *librarian*
Rose, Susan A. Schultz *retired theological librarian*

Fort Pierce
Profeta, Patricia Catherine *librarian*

Gainesville
Greenberg, Mark I. *historian*
Harrer, Gustave Adolphus *librarian, educator*
Jenkins, Dolores Christina *librarian, consultant*

Graceville
Murrell, Irvin Henry, Jr. *librarian, minister*

Jacksonville
Marion, Gail Elaine *reference librarian*
Mullen, Corazon Alip *librarian*
Williams, Judith L. *library administrator*

Key West
Jensen, Karen Marie *librarian*

Lakeland
Reich, David Lee *library director*

Lighthouse Point
Gauthier, Doreen Ann *librarian*

Madison
Hiss, Sheila Mary *librarian*

Maitland
Potter, Karen *library director*

Melbourne
Helmstetter, Wendy Lee *librarian*
Regis, Nina *librarian, educator*

Miami
Friedman, Sylvia *librarian*
Lehman, Douglas Kent *librarian*
Mead-Donaldson, Susan Lee *librarian, administrator*
Santiago, Raymond *library administrator, educator*
Zaleski, Ilene *librarian*

Naples
Hainsworth, Melody May *information professional, researcher*
Johnson, Gerald Bertram *newspaper librarian, writer*

Oakland Park
Kilpatrick, Clifton Wayne *book dealer*
Rosenthal, Susan Barbara *retired librarian*

Orlando
Martindale, Carla Joy *librarian*
Mead, Harriet Council *librarian, author*

Palm Bay
Hoefer, Margaret J. *librarian*

Palm Harbor
Jones, Winona Nigels *retired library media specialist*

Pensacola
Johnson, Theresa Peruit *librarian*
Toifel, Ronald Charles *librarian*

Saint Augustine
Bishop, Claire DeArment *engineering librarian*

Saint Leo
Kosuda, Kathleen L. *library director*

Saint Petersburg
Henry, Deborah Boran *librarian*
Neville, Tina Marie *associate university librarian*
Schell, Joan Bruning *information specialist, business science librarian*

Sanibel
Allen, Patricia J. *library director*

Sarasota
Clopine, Marjorie Showers *librarian*
Hummel, Dana D. Mallett *librarian*
Julien, Dorothy Cox *librarian*

Sebastian
Walsh, Lynn Renee *library director*

Tallahassee
Trezza, Alphonse Fiore *librarian, educator*
Wilkins, (George) Barratt *librarian*

Tampa
Campbell, Margaret Georgeson *retired librarian*
Cardina, Claire Armstrong *archivist, records manager*
Gregory, Vicki L. *library and information scienc educator*
Harkness, Mary Lou *librarian*
Kemp, Thomas Jay *librarian*
Koon, Wiley Emmett, Jr. *librarian*
Schweibinz, Carl Joseph *learning resources manager*
Tabor, Curtis Harold, Jr. *library director*

West Palm Beach
Storch, Barbara Jean Cohen *librarian*
Terwillegar, Jane Cusack *librarian, educator*

Winter Park
Bloodworth, Velda Jean *librarian, educator*
Rogers, Rutherford David *librarian*

GEORGIA

Athens
Baker, Barry Boyd *librarian*
Hurst, Anne Shirley *reference librarian*
Wald, Marlena Malmstedt *librarian*

Atlanta
Budlong, Thomas Francis, Jr. *library administrator*
Cann, Sharon Lee *health science librarian*
Flagg Davis, Vivian Annette *librarian, researcher, public policy consultant*
McDavid, Sara June *librarian*
Robison, Carolyn Love *librarian*
Tope, Diana Ray *library administrator*
Yates, Ella Gaines *library consultant*

Augusta
Nelson, William Neal *librarian, Latin American culture specialist*
Rowland, Arthur Ray *librarian*

Bainbridge
Maggio, Theresa Griffin *librarian*

Barnesville
Anderson, Nancy Dixon *librarian*

Cairo
Kaye, Alan Leslie *library director*

Carrollton
Goodson, Carol Faye *librarian*

Dalton
Cody, Sara Elizabeth *librarian*
Jones-Glaze, Barbara Ann *library media specialist*
Orsee, Joe Brown *library director*

Decatur
Landram, Christina Louella *librarian*
Lassiter, Dorothy Tate *library director*

Lagrange
Becham, Gerald Charles *library director*

Marietta
Blomeley, Sherry Lynn *librarian*
Kendall, Susan Gardes *librarian*

Oxford
McNeill, Mary Kathryn Morgan *librarian*

Rome
Owen, Wiley C. *librarian, consultant, retired*

Smarr
Evans, Rosemary King (Mrs. Howell Dexter Evans) *librarian, educator*

Valdosta
Gaumond, George Raymond *librarian*

Vidalia
Gres, Dusty Beverly Snipes *librarian*

Washington
Harber, Patty Sue *librarian*

Woodbine
Christian, John H. *librarian*

Young Harris
Richardson, Robert Janecek *library director*

INDIANA

Franklin
Jacobs, Betty Carla *library director*

IOWA

Dubuque
McCracken, John Robert *library science educator*

KENTUCKY

Bowling Green
Alexander, Linda Baldwin *library skills educator*

Burlington
Crouch, Arline Parks *librarian*

Covington
Averdick, Michael Robert *librarian*

Frankfort
Levstik, Frank Richard *archivist*

Grayson
Waite, Lemuel Warren *library director*

Hartford
Leavy, Rebecca Shrewsbury *librarian*

Lexington
Mason, Ellsworth Goodwin *librarian*
Schabel, Donald Jacob *library director*
Willis, Paul Allen *librarian*

Louisville
Coalter, Milton J., Jr. *library director, educator*
Henderson, Harriet *librarian*
Poston, Janice Lynn *librarian*

Morehead
Hall, Juanita Justice *librarian*
Nutter, Carol Angell *academic librarian*

Newport
Winner, Marian Carol *library director, educator*

Owensboro
UmBayemake, Linda *librarian*

Summer Shade
Smith, Ruby Lucille *librarian*

Williamsburg
Burch, John Russell *technical services librarian*

Wilmore
Butler, Douglas James *academic librarian*

LOUISIANA

Baton Rouge
Allen, Dorothy Jean *librarian*
Bingham, Elizabeth Elliott *librarian*
Cretini, Blanche Myers *librarian*
Hoover, Jimmie Hartman *librarian, educator*
Johnson, Kathryn Weisner *librarian*
Lane, Margaret Beynon Taylor *librarian*
Shiflett, Orvin Lee *librarian, educator*

Chalmette
Wheeler, Genevieve Stutes *library administrator, educator*

Luling
Strother, Garland *public library director*

Monroe
Smith, Donald Raymond *librarian*

New Orleans
Craft, Carol Ann *librarian*
Nolan, Charles Edward *archivist, educator*
Robinson, Cummie Adams *librarian*
Shields, Theodosia T. *librarian*
Square, Brenda Billips *archivist, librarian*
Wilson, C. Daniel, Jr. *library director*

Paradis
Shiflett, Mary Ellen *library media specialist*

Plaquemine
Mc Cray, Evelina Williams *librarian, researcher*

Schriever
Shaffer, Margaret Minor *retired library director*

Shreveport
Craig, James Pat *medical library director, consultant*
Green, Rachael Paulette *librarian*
Pelton, James Rodger *librarian*

Slidell
Taylor, Rebecca Anne *librarian*

Zachary
Lusk, Glenna Rae Knight (Mrs. Edwin Bruce Lusk) *librarian*

MARYLAND

Lanham Seabrook
Banks, William Ashton *librarian*

MISSISSIPPI

Bay Saint Louis
Plauché, Prima *library director*

Clarksdale
Stanford, Yvonne McClinton *librarian*

Cleveland
Latour, Terry Stephen *archivist, librarian*

Columbia
Gonzalez, Rosemary Massey *library media specialist*

Hattiesburg
Boyd, William Douglas, Jr. *library science educator, clergyman*

Indianola
Powell, Anice Carpenter *librarian*

Keesler AFB
Province, William Robert *librarian*

Macon
Koostra, Margaret Elizabeth *library director*

Moss Point
Holmes, Julia Faye *librarian*

Natchez
McLemore, Joan Meadows *librarian, consultant*

Pascagoula
Smith, Janet *librarian*

Philadelphia
Hughes, Leslie Ivan *librarian*

Picayune
Megehee, Josephine Zeller *library administrator*

West Point
Price, Marty G. *librarian*

NORTH CAROLINA

Albemarle
Ingram-Tinsley, Dorothy Catherine *library automation specialist, horse stables owner*

Boiling Springs
Yelton, David Keith *historian, educator*

Cary
Fracker, Robert Granger *retired librarian, consultant*

Chapel Hill
Holley, Edward Gailon *library science educator, former university dean*
Kilgour, Frederick Gridley *librarian, educator*
Mullin, Patrick Joseph *librarian*
Tibbo, Helen Ruth *information and library science educator*
Tuttle, Marcia Lee *librarian*

Charlotte
Cannon, Robert Eugene *librarian, public administrator, fund raiser*
Welch, Jeanie Maxine *librarian*

Clinton
Buckrham, Gail Williams *children's librarian*

Cove City
Hawkins, Elinor Dixon (Mrs. Carroll Woodard Hawkins) *retired librarian*

Dallas
Reinhardt, Carol Kent *library supervisor*

Durham
Berger, Kenneth Walter *librarian*
Carrington, Bessie Meek *librarian*
Jaskot, Pamela E. *librarian*
Shearer, Kenneth Decker, Jr. *library science educator*

Eden
Williams, Sue Darden *library director*

Gastonia
Burton, Melvin Keith *librarian*

Greensboro
Catlett, James Stephen *archivist, librarian*
Fogarty, Nancy Clark *librarian*

Hillsborough
Stephens, Brenda Wilson *librarian*

Kings Mountain
Turner, Marguerite Rose Cowles *library administrator*

Morehead City
Lynk, Deena Hancock *public information professional*

New Bern
Jones, Vance Harper *librarian, musician*

Pembroke
Sexton, Jean Elizabeth *librarian*
Toomer, Clarence *library administrator*

Raleigh
Davis, Jinnie Yeh *librarian*
Littleton, Isaac Thomas, III *retired university library administrator, consultant*

Wilmington
Oakley, Carolyn Cobb *library director, academic administrator*

Wingate
Wetherbee, James Milton *librarian*

Winston Salem
Montle, Vicki Lemp *library director*
Snow, Sharon Elizabeth *rare books curator*

NORTH DAKOTA

Fargo
Joseph, Lura Ellen *librarian, geologist*

OKLAHOMA

Bartlesville
Funk, Vicki Jane *librarian*

Clinton
Ray, Dee Ann *library director*

Hodgen
Brower, Janice Kathleen *library technician*

Norman
Cook, Peggy Kristine *librarian*
Hodges, Thompson Gene *librarian*
Kemp, Betty Ruth *librarian*
Kidd, Claren Marie *librarian*
Patterson, Lotsee Frances *library and information studies educator*
Sherman, Mary Angus *public library administrator*

Oklahoma City
Campbell, Carol Ann *newspaper library manager*
King, Barbara Sue *librarian*
Shoemaker, Edward Connie *librarian*
Simpson, Jerome Dean *librarian*
Slemmons, David Robert *librarian*
Welge, William D. *archivist*

Okmulgee
Doan, Patricia Nan *librarian*

Taft
Varner, Joyce Ehrhardt *librarian*

Tulsa
Fisk, Francine Joan *librarian*
Parker, Richard Melvin *librarian*
Williams, Michael Burl *librarian*
Woodrum, Patricia Ann *librarian*
Young, Thomas Elton *librarian*

Woodward
Connell, Karen Sue *librarian technician*

SOUTH CAROLINA

Aiken
McAulay, Louise Salzman *library administrator*
Sutherland, C(arl) Tom *librarian*

Charleston
Beagle, Donald Robert *library director*
Causey, Enid Rutherforth *library director, educator*
Proctor, Martha Jane *library manager*

Clemson
Boykin, Joseph Floyd, Jr. *librarian*
Holley, Edward Jens *librarian*

Columbia
Callaham, Betty Elgin *librarian*
Duggan, Carol Cook *library director*
Griffin, Mary Frances *retired library media consultant*
Hamilton, Nanette Louise *librarian*
Helsley, Alexia Jones *archivist*
Toombs, Kenneth Eldridge *librarian*

Greenwood
Cleland, Abby Hatch *library administrator*
Townsend, Catherine Anne Morgan *information specialist*

Orangeburg
Caldwell, Rossie Juanita Brower *retired library service educator*
Thompson, Marguerite Myrtle Graming (Mrs. Ralph B. Thompson) *librarian*

Saint Matthews
Huff, Margaret Joan Farris *librarian*

Summerville
O'Brien, Doris J. *librarian*

Sumter
Geddings, Charles McIjor, III *librarian*

Walhalla
Andrus, Susan Joyce *librarian*

TENNESSEE

Brownsville
Stevenson, Ramona Shrum *library director*

Chattanooga
Clapp, David Foster *library administrator*
Pack, Nancy Clara *librarian*

Clarksville
Humble, Linda Faye *librarian, educator*

Cleveland
Nicol, Jessie Thompson *librarian*

Dresden
Powell, Wanda Garner *librarian*

Hermitage
Blevins, Melissa Frances *library media specialist*

Jackson
Baker, Michael Lee *librarian*

Johnson City
Frizzell, Lucille Bridgers *retired librarian*
Irwin, Ned L. *archivist, historian, writer*

Knoxville
Cottrell, Jeannette Elizabeth *retired librarian*
Lowe, Carolyn Elizabeth *librarian*

La Follette
Green, Nancy Joyce *librarian*

Memphis
Burnett, Rosa Scott *librarian*
Drescher, Judith Altman *library director*
Evans, Catherine Gulley *librarian*
Pourciau, Lester John *librarian*
Verble, Frances Helen *librarian*
Wallis, Carlton Lamar *librarian*

Nashville
Gleaves, Edwin Sheffield *librarian*
Hester, Bruce Edward *library media specialist, lay worker*
Jones, Randolph Sutton *archivist*
Letson, Ruth Stafford *librarian*
Lyle, Virginia Reavis *retired archivist, genealogist*
Perry, Glenda Lee *health science librarian*
Stewart, David Marshall *librarian*
Ward, James Everett *library director*
Wilson, Carolyn Taylor *librarian*

Sewanee
Camp, Thomas Edward *retired librarian*
Dunkly, James Warren *theological librarian*

Spencer
Grove, Nora Imogene *librarian*

TEXAS

Alamo
McKelvy, Nicole Andrée *librarian*

Alpine
Gardner, Kerry Ann *librarian*

Arlington
Burson, Betsy Lee *librarian*

Austin
Billings, Harold Wayne *librarian, editor*
Ebbers, Frances Ann *librarian*
Felsted, Carla Martindell *librarian, travel writer*
Flores-Manges, Irma *library administrator*
Fox, Beth Wheeler *library director*
Howard, Carol Spencer *librarian, journalist*
Jackson, Eugene Bernard *librarian*
Lincoln, Timothy Dwight *library director*
Smith, Dorothy Brand *retired librarian*
Warren, Karen Cohen *librarian*

Beaumont
Montgomery, David Emerson *library director*

Bellaire
Mote, Marie Therese *reference librarian*

Belton
Giles, Audrey Elizabeth *reference librarian*

Brownsville
Nutter, Daniel Lyon *librarian*

Cedar Park
Lam, Pauline Poha *library director*

College Station
Hoadley, Irene Braden (Mrs. Edward Hoadley) *librarian*

Conroe
Doolittle, Beth D. *librarian*

Corpus Christi
Whitton-Henley, Lynda Jean *librarian*

Corsicana
Roberts, Nancy Mize *retired librarian, composer, pianist*

Dallas
Bellavance, Maria Isabel *librarian*
Bockstruck, Lloyd DeWitt *librarian*
Holleman, Curt Paul *librarian*
Howell, Bradley Sue *librarian*
Moore, William Carey *librarian, editor, writer*
Murphy, Kristine Lynn *librarian*
Pastine, Maureen Diane *librarian*
Salazar, Ramiro S. *library administrator*
Silcox, Tinsley Edward *fine arts library director, choral conductor*
Willett, Holly Geneva *librarian, educator*

Deer Park
Hill, Kathryn Viereck *library administrator*

Denton
Hepner, John Carson *librarian*
Lavender, Kenneth *rare book librarian, educator*
Snapp, Elizabeth *librarian, educator*
Wilkes, Adeline Wood *library science educator*

El Paso
Caballero, Cesar *librarian*
Freeman, Mary Anna *librarian*
Phillips, Patricia Alwood Rich *librarian*
Ramsey, Donna Elaine *librarian*
Strait, Viola Edwina Washington *librarian*

Fort Worth
Allmand, Linda F(aith) *library director*
Bastien, Carol Langford *librarian*
Heyer, Anna Harriet *retired music librarian*
Hughston, Milan Ross *librarian*
Lefever, Alan Jeffrey *archivist*
Potter, Cynthia Jean *library director*

Galveston
Watson, Diane B. *librarian*

Georgetown
Fountain, Joanna F. *library consultant, business owner*

Gilmer
Green, Douglas Alvin *retired library director*

Hawkins
Heath, Cheryl Delores *librarian*
Hudson, Shirley Spencer *librarian*

Houston
Boyd, Barbara Jean *librarian*
Harris, Anne Ruth *volunteer services administrator*
Henington, David Mead *library director*
Newbold, Benjamin Millard, Jr. *library manager, education consultant*
Porter, Exa Lynn *librarian*
Russell, John Francis *retired librarian*
Tong, Louis Lik-Fu *information scientist*

Huntsville
Hoffmann, Frank William *library science educator, writer*

Irving
Ayres, Edwin Michael *librarian*
Chamberlain, Enrique King *library director*
Cochran, Carolyn *library director*

Kilgore
Pipkin, Wade Lemual, Jr. *reference librarian*

Laredo
Hastings, John Paris *librarian*

Liberty
Schaadt, Robert Lee, Jr. *library director, archivist*

Lubbock
Murrah, David J. *archivist, historian*
Rippel, Jeffrey Alan *library director*

Mc Camey
Farley, Gail Conley *retired librarian*

Mcallen
Kadhim, Estelle Beverly *librarian, educator*

Mesquite
Spinks, John Lynn *librarian*

Midland
Dawkins, Diantha Dee *librarian*
Miranda, Cecilia *librarian, consultant*
Tillman, Barbara Nyleve *librarian*

Odessa
Marcum, James Walton *library director, educator*
Rocha, Osbelia Maria Juarez *librarian*

Palestine
Williams, Franklin Cadmus, Jr. *bibliographer*

Pharr
Liu, David T. *librarian, writer*

Plano
Thompson, Mary Ann *library assistant, publisher*

Port Arthur
Stockinger, Jill Faith *librarian*

Port Isabel
Smith, Mary Lou *librarian*

Progreso
Fernández, Yolanda Garza *librarian*

San Antonio
Brewster, Olive Nesbitt *retired librarian*
Kozuch, Julianna Bernadette *librarian, educator*
Lussky, Warren Alfred *librarian, educator, consultant*
Maroscher, Betty Jean *librarian*
Nance, Betty Love *librarian*
Sylvia, Margaret Joost *librarian*
Wallace, James Oldham *librarian*

Seminole
Molinar, Lupe Rodriquez *librarian, library director*

Smithville
Allen, Marjorie Joan *librarian*

Tyler
Cleveland, Mary Louise *librarian, media specialist*

Vernon
Strickland, Jimmy Ray *librarian*

Waco
Berecka, Alan Michael *librarian*
Rogers, James Benjamin *archivist, clergyman*

VIRGINIA

Alexandria
Cross, Dorothy Abigail *retired librarian*
Eilers, Marlene Anna Louise *librarian, gealogist*
O'Brien, Patrick Michael *library administrator*
Pierce, Linda Radcliffe *librarian*

Blacksburg
Ward, Robert Carl *library director, consultant*

Bristol
Muller, William Albert, III *library director*

Charlottesville
Berkeley, Francis Lewis, Jr. *retired archivist*
Granitz, Adrienne Diana *librarian*
Hassan, Khan Mamnoon *librarian*
Jordan, Ervin Leon, Jr. *archivist, historian*

Chesapeake
Forehand Stillman, Margaret P. *library director*
Reid, Kendall Martin *librarian*

Dumfries
Gaudet, Jean Ann *librarian, educator*

Ferrum
Dillon, Cyrus Irvine *librarian*
Nelson, Wesley Joseph *librarian*

Fort Story
Smail, Leslie Anne *librarian*

Fredericksburg
Farr, Patricia Hudak *librarian*

Hampton
Winters, Sharon Ann *librarian, library educator*

Harrisonburg
Gill, Gerald Lawson *librarian*
Lehman, James Orten *library director*
Ramsey, Inez Linn *librarian, educator*

Hopewell
Koutnik, Chuck John *librarian*

Lexington
Stanley, Clyde Vaughan, III *librarian*

Lynchburg
Hostetler, Theodore Jan *library director*
Seibert, Barbara Ann Welch *school librarian*

Newport News
Keeling, Mary Odell *librarian*
Trask, Benjamin Harrison *librarian*

Norfolk
Drye, Jerry Lipe, Sr. *librarian*

Richmond
Costa, Robert Nicholas *library director*
Gwin, James Ellsworth *librarian*
Hall, Bonlyn Goodwin *librarian*
Shelton, Ronald Alphonso *librarian, archivist*
Walsh, Robert Raymond *librarian, consultant*
Worley, Nelson *library director*

Roanoke
Harris, Belinda Jean *librarian*
Henn, Shirley Emily *retired librarian*

South Boston
Johnson, Kenneth Paul *librarian, writer*

Williamsburg
Hansel, Patsy J. *library director*
Marshall, Nancy Haig *library administrator*
Parham, Annette Relaford *librarian*

Winchester
Hughes, Donna Jean *librarian*

Wytheville
Mattis, George Evans, Jr. *librarian*

WEST VIRGINIA

Bradley
Chesley, Eddie A. *librarian, educator*

Charleston
Glazer, Frederic Jay *librarian*

Fairmont
Burke, John Jeffrey *librarian*

Glenville
Tubesing, Richard Lee *library director*

Institute
Wiley, Ronald Ross *librarian*

Morgantown
Bender, Nathan Edward *librarian, archivist*

ADDRESS UNPUBLISHED

Bowden, Ann *bibliographer, educator*
Coy, Howard Louis, Jr. *librarian*
Driver, Lottie Elizabeth *librarian*
Hughes, Sue Margaret *retired librarian*
Kerby, Ramona Anne *librarian*
Leather, Victoria Potts *college librarian*
Levin-Wixman, Irene Staub *librarian*
Miller, Charles Edmond *library administrator*
Ortego, Gilda Baeza *librarian, information professional*
Patterson, Karen Kay *reference librarian*
Patterson, Robert Hudson *library director*
Reynolds, Cynthia Michelle *librarian, writer*
Roberts, Judith Marie *librarian, educator*
Rouse, Roscoe, Jr. *librarian, educator*
Smith, Dentye M. *library media specialist*
Sparkman, Glenda Kathleen *librarian, educator*
Stallworth-Barron, Doris A. Carter *librarian, educator*

HUMANITIES: MUSEUMS

UNITED STATES

ALABAMA

Anniston
Quick, Edward Raymond *museum director, educator*

Birmingham
Brooks, Daniel F. *historic site director*
Nordan, Antoinette Spanos *curator*

Florence
Wright, Mildred Anne (Milly Wright) *conservator, researcher*

Mobile
Schenk, Joseph Bernard *museum director*
Taylor, Barbara E. *museum director*

Montgomery
Johnson, Mark Matthew *museum administrator*

ARKANSAS

Little Rock
Bradshaw, William C. *museum director*
Wolfe, Townsend Durant, III *art museum director, curator*

DISTRICT OF COLUMBIA

Washington
Sharrer, George Terry *museum curator*

FLORIDA

Daytona Beach
Libby, Gary Russell *museum director*

Delray Beach
Shute, Melodie Ann *museum director*

Fort Lauderdale
Bolge, George Stephen *museum director, exhibition design consultant*
Moffett, Kenworth W. *art museum director*
Walker, F. K. *executive*

Gainesville
Bishop, Budd Harris *museum administrator*
Milbrath, Susan *museum curator, art historian*
Valdés, Karen W. *art gallery director, educator*

Hobe Sound
Payson, John Whitney *art dealer*

Jacksonville
Dundon, Margo Elaine *museum director*

Key West
Burnside, Madeleine Hilding *museum director, educator*

Lakeland
Stetson, Daniel Everett *museum director*

Miami
Dursum, Brian A. *museum curator, art educator*
Morgan, Dahlia *museum director*

Orlando
Lowrie, Walter *science museum administrator*
Morrisey, Marena Grant *art museum administrator*

Panama City
Odle, Wesley Paul, Jr. *museum director, pastor*

Saint Petersburg
Rousseau, T(hurl) Marshall *museum director*

Sarasota
Weinberg, Bella Rebecca *art gallery director, writer*

Tampa
Kass, Emily *art museum administrator*

Tequesta
Messersmith, Harry Lee *museum director, sculptor*

Valparaiso
LaRoche, Christian Simons *museum director*

West Palm Beach
Orr-Cahall, Christina *art gallery director, art historian*

Winter Park
Ruggiero, Laurence Joseph *museum director*

GEORGIA

Albany
Close, Timothy *art museum administrator*

Athens
Laerm, Joshua *museum director, zoologist*
Phagan, Patricia Elaine *museum curator*

Atlanta
Bibb, Daniel Roland *antique painting restorer and conservator*
Elliot, J. H. *museum director*
Hiers, Mary A. *museum director*
Larson, Judy L. *curator*
Oliver, Ann Breeding *fine arts education curator*

Augusta
Claussen, Louise Keith *art museum director*

Columbus
Butler, Charles Thomas *museum director, curator*
Lawson, Karol Ann *art museum curator*

Macon
Anderson, Nancy *musuem administrator*
Johnson, Walker P. *museum administrator*
Oliver, Katherine C. *museum director*

Saint Simons
Brown, Brad *museum administrator*

Savannah
Smith, Anne P. *historical society director*

Statesboro
Presley, Delma Eugene *museum director, educator*

KENTUCKY

Lexington
Fowler, Harriet Whittemore *art museum director*
Powell, Mary Lucas *museum director*
Yozwiak, Bobbie *arts and science center administrator*

Louisville
Cloudman, Ruth Howard *museum curator*
Holmberg, James John *curator*

Owensboro
Hood, Mary Bryan *museum director, painter*

LOUISIANA

Baton Rouge
Bacot, Henry Parrott *museum administrator, art historian, consultant*
Gikas, Carol Sommerfeldt *museum director*

New Orleans
Bullard, Edgar John, III *museum director*
Casellas, Joachim *art gallery executive*
Glasgow, Vaughn Leslie *museum curator and administrator*
Sefcik, James Francis *museum director*
Weaver, Virginia Dove *museum executive*

Shreveport
Norton, Richard W., Jr. *art gallery director*

MISSISSIPPI

Madison
Hiatt, Jane Crater *arts agency administrator*

NEW MEXICO

Ruidoso Downs
Eldredge, Bruce Beard *museum director*

NEW YORK

Brooklyn
Madigan, Richard Allen *museum director*

NORTH CAROLINA

Asheville
Cecil, William A. V., Sr. *landmark director*
Thomson, Frank Ehrlich, III *curator*

Chapel Hill
Bolas, Gerald Douglas *art museum administrator, art history educator*

Charlotte
Evans, Bruce Haselton *art museum director*
Nicholson, Freda H. *museum administrator*
Wolf, Sara Hevia *art librarian*

Dallas
Waufle, Alan Duane *museum director, consultant*

Durham
Krakauer, Thomas Henry *museum director*

Gastonia
Stout, Richard Alan *museum director*

Greensboro
Jones, Fred T. *museum administrator*

Highlands
Boggs, Willene Graythen *art director, oil and gas broker, consultant*

Raleigh
Kuhler, Renaldo Gillet *museum official, scientific illustrator*
Wheeler, Lawrence J. *art museum administrator*
Wolk, Robert George *museum administrator, biologist*

Winston Salem
Gray, Thomas Alexander *museum trustee*
Rauschenberg, Bradford Lee *museum research director*

OHIO

Dayton
Ruffer, David Gray *museum director, former college president*

OKLAHOMA

Anadarko
Ellison, Rosemary *curator*

Lawton
Wilson, Steve *museum director*

Norman
Toperzer, Thomas Raymond *art museum director*

Oklahoma City
Pitts, Bill *museum director*
Price, B. Byron *museum director*
Shorney, Margo Kay *art gallery owner*

Tulsa
Manhart, Marcia Y(ockey) *art museum director*
Wyckoff, Lydia Lloyd *art curator*

PENNSYLVANIA

State College
Muhlert, Jan Keene *art museum director*

SOUTH CAROLINA

Charleston
Brumgardt, John Raymond *museum administrator*
McDaniel, George William *historic site administrator, historian, educator*

Columbia
Cilella, Salvatore George, Jr. *museum director*

Greenville
Davis, Joan Carroll *museum director*
Hodge, Dorothy Wilson (Scottie Hodge) *gallery executive*

Pawleys Island
Tarbox, Gurdon Lucius, Jr. *retired museum executive*

TENNESSEE

Chattanooga
Scarbrough, Cleve Knox, Jr. *museum director*

Columbia
Holtzapple, John Croft *museum director*

Knoxville
Chapman, Jefferson *museum director*

Memphis
Carmean, E. A., Jr. *art museum director, art historian*
Luebbers, Leslie Laird *museum director*
Noble, Douglas Ross *museum administrator*

Nashville
Riggins-Ezzell, Lois *museum administrator*

TEXAS

Austin
Bennett, Valerie Welch *museum curator*
Crain, William Henry *retired curator*
Ellis, Bianca J. *conservator*
Hite, Jessie Otto *art museum director*

Dallas
Meadows, Patricia Blachly *art curator, civic worker*

El Paso
Shannon, Mary Kay *museum administrator*

Fort Worth
Otto, Donald R. *museum director*
Pillsbury, Edmund Pennington *museum director*
Sullivan, Ruth Wilkins *museum curator, author*

Gun Barrel City
Smith, Thelma Tina Harriette *gallery owner, artist*

Houston
Baldridge, Melissa Anne *curator, editor*
Marzio, Peter Cort *museum director*

San Antonio
Chiego, William J. *museum director*

VIRGINIA

Arlington
Clyne, Maureen Ann *fine arts consultant, artist*
Ewers, John Canfield *museum administrator*
McCutcheon, Mary Shaw *museum consultant*

Fairfax
Cargo, Russell Allen *art executive*

Fredericksburg
McGill, Forrest *art museum director, art historian*

Martinsville
Sutton, Donald MacLear, Jr. *museum executive*

Mount Vernon
Rees, James Conway, IV *historic site administrator*

Radford
Fariello, Mary Anna *museum director, art educator*

Richmond
Callahan, Colleen Ruth *museum curator, educator, consultant*
Cormack, Malcolm *museum curator*

Waynesboro
Rippe, Peter Marquart *museum administrator*

Williamsburg
Garrison, George Hartranft Haley *curator*
Houghland, Sarah Roberts *museum administrator*

WISCONSIN

Milwaukee
Rosen, Barry Howard *museum director, history educator*

ADDRESS UNPUBLISHED

Blumenthal, Arthur Richard *art museum director, art educator*
English, Bruce Vaughan *museum director and executive, environmental consultant*
Lutts, Ralph Herbert *museum administrator, scholar, educator*
Malt, Carol Nora *art museum director*
Mezzatesta, Michael Philip *art museum director*
Moore, William Jason *museum director*
Perret, Donna C. *art gallery director*
Rifkin, Ned *museum director*
Robert, Henry Flood, Jr. *museum official*
Shannon, George Ward, Jr. *museum director, anthropologist, archaeologist*
Shapiro, Michael Edward *museum administrator, curator, art historian*
Vroom, Steven Michael *director university gallery*

INDUSTRY: MANUFACTURING. *See also* FINANCE: FINANCIAL SERVICES.

UNITED STATES

ALABAMA

Andalusia
Taylor, James Marion, II *automotive wholesale executive*

Birmingham
Bolton, William J. *food products executive*
Campbell, Charles Alton *manufacturing corporate executive*
Edwards, Thomas Henry, Jr. *retired construction company executive*
Goldberg, Edward Jay *general contractor*
Holton, J(erry) Thomas *concrete company executive*
Richey, V. L. *steel company executive*
Sklenar, Herbert Anthony *industrial products manufacturing company executive*

Bon Secour
Nelson, Chris *fisheries company executive*

Clanton
Folsom, Wynelle Stough *retired wood products manufacturing executive*

Decatur
Horton, Francis Knapp *manufacturing executive, industrial engineer*

Fairfield
Hanna, Pete M. *executive steel company*
Jones, William K. *executive steel company*

Florence
Morris, Howard Eugene *construction company executive*

Gadsden
Young, Fredda Florine *steel manufacturing manager*

Huntsville
King, Olin B. *electronics systems company executive*
Sapp, A. Eugene, Jr. *electronics executive*

Leeds
Ritchey, James Salem *office furniture manufacturing company executive*

Montgomery
McDaniel, Benny Joe *automotive executive*
Root, Raymond Francis *food broker account executive*

Opelika
Jenkins, Richard Lee *manufacturing company executive*

Theodore
Mc Coy, Lee Berard *paint company executive*

ARKANSAS

Conway
Morgan, Charles Donald, Jr. *manufacturing executive*
Rogers, Earl F., Sr. *automotive supply company executive*

El Dorado
Aaron, Donnie Ray *carpenter, poet*

Fort Smith
Boreham, Roland Stanford, Jr. *electric motor company executive*
Qualls, Robert L. *manufacturing executive, banker, former state official, educator*

Helena
Foster, Mike *food products executive*
Frazler, Rod *agricultural products executive*

Little Rock
McCoy, Stuart Sherman *manufacturing executive*

North Little Rock
Harrison, Stephen Earle *manufacturing executive*

Springdale
Tyson, Donald John *food company executive*

Stuttgart
Hillman, Tommy *food products company executive*

Waldo
Dennis, Barry Lee *timber company executive*

Waldron
Bentley, William Antero *manufacturing company executive*

CALIFORNIA

Carmichael
Rich, Albert Clark *solar energy manufacturing executive*

Palo Alto
Jones, Roger Lee *pharmaceutical executive*

CONNECTICUT

Darien
Bowling, James Chandler *retired executive, farmer, philanthropist*

Greenwich
Mead, Dana George *diversified industrial manufacturing company executive*

Somers
Siver, Chester Asa *manufacturing executive*

Stamford
Hood, Edward Exum, Jr. *retired electrical manufacturing company executive*

DELAWARE

Seaford
Slater, Charles James *construction company executive*
Slater, Kristie *construction company executive*

Wilmington
Sganga, John B. *furniture holding company executive*

DISTRICT OF COLUMBIA

Washington
Park, Frances Mihei *food products executive, author*

FLORIDA

Belle Glade
Alvarez, Jose Florencio *food products executive, mechanical engineer*
Knight, Samuel, Jr. *citrus and cattle company executive*

Boca Raton
Brand, Frank Amery *retired electronics company executive*
Breslauer, Charles S. *chemical company executive*
Costello, Albert Joseph *chemicals executive*
O'Donnell, Joseph Michael *electronics executive*
Perez, Jorge Luis *manufacturing executive*
Rabinowitz, Wilbur Melvin *container company executive, consultant*

Bonita Springs
Sargent, Charles Lee *manufacturing company executive*

Boynton Beach
Force, Elizabeth Elma *retired pharmaceutical executive, consultant*

Clearwater
Bomstein, Alan Charles *construction company executive*
Douglas, John Harold *manufacturing executive*
Hoel, Robert Fredrick, Jr. *construction executive, civil engineer*
Raymond, Steven A. *computer equipment company executive*
Repetto, Allison W. *agricultural company executive*
Yoho, Robert Wayne *company executive*

Cocoa
Anderson, Ronald Earl *precision machining company executive*

Coral Gables
Sherman, Beatrice Ettinger *business executive*

Daytona Beach
Fly, James Lawrence, Jr. *construction executive*
Frank, Harvey *foodservice distributing company executive*
Perschmann, Lutz Ingo *shoe company executive, real estate consultant*

Delray Beach
Fuente, D. I. *office supply manufacturing executive*

Fort Lauderdale
Carter, James Thomas *contractor*
Mason, Ray *company executive*

Fort Myers
Bumpous, Earle Thomas, III *concrete products company executive*
Kelley, Michael James *medical services executive, author*

Fort Pierce
Osteen, Paul Allen *construction executive*
Viamontes, Ralph *agricultural services executive*

Groveland
Sallin, Michael *agricultural company executive*

Gulf Breeze
Sponheimer, Jon M. *food products executive*
Strength, Robert Samuel *manufacturing company executive*

Gulf Stream
Stone, Franz Theodore *retired fabricated metal products manufacturing executive*

Haines City
Abbit, Ben *food products executive*

Hialeah
Gomez, Luis Carlos *manufacturing executive*

Hollywood
Holland, Michael James *financial executive*

Holmes Beach
Rose, Dennis Norman *manufacturing company executive*

Homestead
Brooks, Neal *agricultural services executive*
Willner, Eugene Burton *food and liquor company executive*

Homosassa
De Rosa, Thom Vincent *acoustical engineer, musician*

Jacksonville
Belin, Jacob Chapman *paper company executive*
Devine, Michael Joseph *construction executive*
McGehee, Thomas Rives *paper company executive*
Rogers, Betty Gravitt *research company executive*
Saltzman, Irene Cameron *perfume manufacturing executive, art gallery owner*

Lake Mary
Scott, Gary LeRoy *photographic manufacturing executive, photographer*
Uhler, Bruce Dean *medical company executive*

Lake Monroe
Hayes, David Vaughn *construction equipment company executive*

Lake Placid
Grigsby, Ronald *food products executive*

Lakeland
Zimmermann, G. Floyd, III *construction company executive*

Largo
Newman, Francis A. *executive medical device company*

Leesburg
Talley, William Giles, Jr. *container manufacturing company executive*

Lighthouse Point
Friedrichs, Arthur Martin *manufacturing company executive, retired*

Loxahatchee
Jones, Gaston C(arlisle) *adminstrative executive*

Maitland
Nelson, Michael James *distribution executive*
Taylor, James Daniel *beverage and chemical companies executive*

Miami
Anscher, Bernard *manufacturing executive, investor, management consultant*
Arkin, Stanley Herbert *construction executive*
Borkan, William Noah *biomedical electronics company executive*
Campello, Valeria Vandelli *fashion designer and importer, publisher*
Frigo, James Peter Paul *industrial hardware company executive*
Garcia, Antonio de Jesus *manufacturing executive*
Gregory, Gus *food products executive*
Spencer, Richard Thomas, III *healthcare industry executive*
Thompson, Allen Joseph *construction executive, civil engineer*

Miami Beach
Schmid, Henry Frederick *construction executive*

Naples
Coppens, Thomas Adriaan *retired pharmaceutical manufacturing executive*
Forbis, Melvin Richard *construction executive*
Kapnick, Harvey Edward, Jr. *retired corporate executive*
von Arx, Dolph William *food products executive*

New Port Richey
Oosten, Roger Lester *medical manufacturing executive*
Sebring, Marjorie Marie Allison *former home furnishings company executive*

Oldsmar
Beverland, Wanda Lou *textile executive, consultant*

Orlando
Ashington-Pickett, Michael Derek *construction company executive, journalist*
Cates, Harold Thomas *aircraft and electronics company executive*
Cawthon, Frank H. *retired construction company executive*
Grogan, Bette Lowery *steel fastener distribution executive*
Harris, Richard Leonard *automotive executive, entrepreneur*
Hughes, David Henry *manufacturing company executive*
Jones, Constance Irene *medical products executive*
Pierce, Jerry Earl *business executive*

Ormond Beach
Connors, Michele Perrott *wholesale beverage company executive*

Palm Beach
Roberts, Margot Markels *business executive*
Rumbough, Stanley Maddox, Jr. *industrialist*

Palm Harbor
McCalister, Michael Eugene *pharmaceutical and medical product sales executive*

Paxton
Kearns, John William (Bill Kearns) *electronics inventor and executive*

Pompano Beach
Fritsch, Billy Dale, Jr. *construction company executive*
Grigsby-Stephens, Klaron *corporate executive*

Ponte Vedra Beach
Fry, Russell Jackson *plastics company executive*

Punta Gorda
DePlonty, Duane Earl *builder, real estate developer*
Norris, John C. *food products executive*
Uze, Irving *automotive executive*

Quincy
Maxwell, William *food products executive*
Williams, Paul E. *agricultural company executive*

Reddick
Corwin, Joyce Elizabeth Stedman *construction company executive*

Safety Harbor
Dohnal, William Edward *retired steel company executive, consultant, accountant*

Saint Petersburg
Barbieri, Joseph James *food company executive*
Joyce, Walter Joseph *retired electronics company executive*

Sarasota
Miranda, Carlos Sa *food products company executive*
Morris, Gordon James *company executive, financial consultant*

Stuart
DeRita, Thomas, Jr. *automobile company executive*
Jaffe, Jeff Hugh *retired food products executive*

Tallahassee
Jones, Bob *fisheries association executive*
Leeper, Zane H. *automotive company executive, consultant*
Skagfield, Hilmar Sigurdsson *business executive*
Thorpe, Betsy Tucker *contracting company official*

Tamarac
Auletta, Joan Miglorisi *construction company executive, mortgage and insurance broker*

Tampa
Cohen, Frank Burton *wholesale novelty company executive*
Creed, Thomas G. *steel company executive*
Flom, Edward Leonard *retired steel company executive*
Funk, Smith Adam *construction executive*
Genter, John Robert *winery executive*
Sada, Federico G. *glass manufacturing executive*
Wieland, William Dean *health care consulting executive*

Tarpon Springs
Jackel, Simon Samuel *food products company executive, technical marketing and business consultant*

Umatilla
Corbett, James Otho *industrial instrumentation company executive*

Vero Beach
Furrer, John Rudolf *retired manufacturing business executive*
Walker, Harry Webster, II *food products executive*

West Palm Beach
Oppenheim, Justin Sable *business executive*
Saraf, Shevach *company executive*

Windermere
Alexander, Judd Harris *retired paper company executive*

Winter Garden
Gorman, Robert W. *food products executive*

Winter Haven
Roe, Willard E. *agricultural company executive*

Winter Park
Jones, Joseph Wayne *food and beverage company executive, entrepreneur*

GEORGIA

Ashburn
Harvey, J. Ernest, Jr. *agricultural company executive*

Atlanta
Aftuck, Rodney D. *food products executive*
Biggers, William Joseph *retired manufacturing company executive*
Cantrell, Wesley Eugene, Sr. *office equipment company executive*
Cassell, Robert Bernard *council executive*
Correll, Alston Dayton, Jr. *forest products company executive*
Creekmore, William Brown *construction company executive*
Davis, Marvin Arnold *manufacturing company executive*
DeLashmet, Gordon Bartlett *newsprint executive*
DeLucca, Gregory James *wine industry executive*
Dickson, John J. *soft drink company executive*
Festa, Edward J. *company executive*
French, Michael Bruce *beverage company executive*
Frendahl, Dennis Michael *beverage company executive*
Friedman, Harold Bertrand *retired chemical company executive*
Fuqua, James Franklin *pharmaceutical executive*
Goizueta, Roberto Crispulo *food and beverage company executive*
Hahn, Thomas Marshall, Jr. *forest products corporation executive*
Hudson, Frank Parker *retired company executive*
Hunter, Douglas Lee *elevator company executive*
Johnson, Frederick Ross *international management advisory company executive*
Johnston, Summerfield K., Jr. *food products executive*
Kuse, James Russell *chemical company executive*
Liebmann, Seymour W. *construction consultant*
Marcus, James Elbert *manufacturing company executive*
McQueen, Rebecca Hodges *health care executive, consultant*
Millikan, James Rolens *cleaning service executive, musician, composer*
Mitchell, Stephen Milton *manufacturing executive*
Petersen-Frey, Roland *manufacturing executive*
Prince, Larry L. *automotive parts and supplies company executive*
Pruett, Clayton Dunklin *biotechnical company executive*
Sands, Don William *agricultural products company executive retired*
Schimberg, Henry Aaron *soft drink company executive*
Seydel, Scott O'Sullivan *chemical company executive*
Stevens, James M. *food processing executive*
Ware, Carl *bottling company executive*
Watson, Denise Sander *medical products sales executive*

Augusta
Barton, Raymond Oscar, III *concrete company executive*
Carter, Ed *construction company executive*
McKnight, Mason, III *construction company executive*

Brunswick
Iannicelli, Joseph *chemical company executive, consultant*

Buford
Dwyer, Dennis Grant *food broker executive*

Carrollton
North, Alexa Bryans *business educator*

Columbus
Carmack, Comer Aston, Jr. *steel company executive*

Conyers
Burman, Marsha Linkwald *lighting manufacturing executive, marketing development professional*
Mc Clung, Jim Hill *light manufacturing company executive*
Morse, Richard Van Tuyl *manufacturing executive, consultant*

Cumming
Garrett, Ronald Doyle *electronics company executive*

Dalton
Shaw, Julius C., Sr. *carpet manufacturing company executive*
Shaw, Robert E. *carpeting company executive*

Decatur
Morris, John Scott *textile company executive*

Dry Branch
Hein, Jerry Marvin *manufacturing company executive*

Duluth
Love, Mary Angelean *company executive*

Dunwoody
Murthy, Kris *computer services executive*

Fitzgerald
Hazy, Jeffrey Lee *metal products executive*

Franklin
Rogers, Denney H. *building contractor*

Gainesville
Pilgrim, James Rollins *retail furniture company executive*

Hinesville
Baer, William Harold *business executive*

Lawrenceville
McGinnis, Robert William *electronics company executive*

Loganville
Arnold, Susan Bird *safety education training consulting and products company executive*

Marietta
Albani, Thomas J. *manufacturing company executive*
Lewis, William Headley, Jr. *manufacturing company executive*
Madren, Don Athron *pharmaceutical executive, researcher*
Randall, Carolyn Mayo *chemical company executive*
Riggs, Lawrence Wilson *electronics executive*

Milledgeville
Williamson, John Thomas, Sr. *minerals company executive*

Morganton
Alderman, Eugene Wayne *metal products executive, mathematics educator*

Morrow
Fahy, Nancy Lee *food products marketing executive*

Moultrie
Ansley, Campbell Wallace, Jr. *retired veterinary drug distributor*

Norcross
Holyoak, William Harding *machine tool company executive*
Thomas, Robert L. *manufacturing company executive*

Oakwood
Smith, David Claiborne *construction company executive*

Roswell
Brands, James Edwin *medical products executive*

Saint Simons
Shetty, Shankara Rama *packaging technologist, food packaging consultant*

Savannah
Chang, Kunya *food products executive*
Sprague, William Wallace, Jr. *retired food company executive*

Smyrna
Lubker, John William, II *manufacturing executive, civil engineer*

Thomasville
Flowers, William Howard, Jr. *food company executive*
Mc Mullian, Amos Ryals *food company executive*

Tifton
Grist, Robert *agricultural products executive*

Union Point
Redding, John Arthur, Jr. *textile manufacturing executive*

Vidalia
Zimnavoda, Dianne M. *manufacturing executive*

Villa Rica
Matthews, Jeanne Pearson *logistic support analyst company executive*

ILLINOIS

Chicago
Fiscus, Donna Rau *chemical company executive*
Kelly, Gerald Wayne *chemical coatings company executive*

KENTUCKY

Ashland
D'Antoni, David J. *chemicals executive*

Bowling Green
Holland, John Ben *clothing manufacturing company executive*
Walters, Sue Fox *business executive, accountant*

Brandenburg
Jackson, Charles Wayne *food products executive, former telecommunications industry executive*

Clinton
Latimer, W. H. (Bill Latimer) *agricultural company executive*
Ward, Kenny *food products executive*

Georgetown
Moffat, MaryBeth *automotive company executive*

Henderson
Maple, Timothy Michael *chemical company executive*

Lexington
Murray, Alan L. *construction executive*

Louisville
Clayton, Marvin Courtland *engineering, manufacturing sourcing and health wellness consultant*
Colclazier, John Warren *food company executive*
Mateus, Lois *manufacturing executive*
Mountz, Wade *retired health service management executive*
Myers, Mark Eden *chemical sales executive*
Rapp, Christian Ferree *textile home furnishings company executive*
Sutton, John Schuhmann, Jr. *company executive*
Vogel, Werner Paul *retired machine company executive*

Morehead
Huber, John Michael *lumber executive*

Paducah
Frankel, Andrew Joel *manufacturing company executive*

LOUISIANA

Baton Rouge
Paulsen, Susan Carol *health company executive*
Penton, Harold Roy, Jr. *chemical company executive, researcher*
Schulz, Michael Anthony, Jr. *construction company executive, real estate developer*

Houma
Bourgeois, Roger Robert *fire protection systems company executive*

Lacombe
Bellingham, Paul Hasty, II *manufacturers' representative*

Lafayette
Mallet, Alexis, Jr. *construction company executive*

Lake Charles
Heiserman, Russell Lee *electronics educator*

Mandeville
Napier, William James, Jr. *marine oil and gas construction consultant*

Many
Byles, Robert Valmore *manufacturing company executive*

New Orleans
Bordeaux, Pierre William Harriston (Peter Bordeaux) *beverage alcohol company executive*
Collins, Harry David *construction consultant, forensic engineering specialist, mechanical and nuclear engineer, retired army officer*
Cospolich, James Donald *electrical engineering executive, consultant*
Deasy, William John *construction, marine dredging, engineering and mining company executive*
Gaubert, Lloyd Francis *shipboard and industrial cable distribution executive*
Hebert, Leonard Bernard, Jr. *contractor*
Howson, Robert E. *construction company executive*
Robinson, Harold Ivens *lumber company executive*
Rubba, Rose Ann *electronics technician*

Saint Rose
Lennox, Edward Newman *holding company executive*

MAINE

Madawaska
Vollmann, John Jacob, Jr. *cosmetic packaging executive*

MICHIGAN

Detroit
Kalman, Andrew *manufacturing company executive*

MISSISSIPPI

Biloxi
Crapo, Gregory Kempton *furniture industry executive*

Corinth
O'Rear, Jack *company executive*

Gulfport
Fleming, Randolph Ingersoll *food products executive*
Raj, Anil *shipbuilding executive*

Hattiesburg
Chain, Bobby Lee *electrical contractor, former mayor*

Houlka
Washington, Gerald *manufacturing executive*

Iuka
Vaniman, Jean Ann *manufacturing executive*

Jackson
Adkison, Ronnie Darrell *metal company executive, sales executive*
Williams, James Kelley *diversified resources company executive*

Meridian
Balliet, James Lee *manufacturing company executive*

Ocean Springs
Sims, Thomas Auburn *retired shipbuilding company executive*

Pontotoc
Hansberger, William Lyle *manufacturing executive*

Scott
Malkin, Roger D. *agricultural products executive*
Robinson, Frederic Murry *agricultural products company executive*

MISSOURI

Saint Louis
Priestley, G. T. Eric *manufacturing company executive*

NEW JERSEY

Morristown
Slocum, Donald Hillman *product development executive*

NEW MEXICO

Albuquerque
Abbott, Cris Pye *apparel executive*

NEW YORK

New York
Greenberg, Frank S. *textile company executive*
Levin, Jerry Wayne *cosmetics executive*

NORTH CAROLINA

Asheboro
Klaussner, Hans *manufacturing executive*

Burlington
Flagg, Raymond Osbourn *biology executive*

Cary
Dennehy, Leisa Jeanotta *company executive*

Chapel Hill
Morgan, G. Kenneth *association executive*

Charlotte
Belk, Thomas Milburn *apparel executive*
Bowden, James Alvin *construction company financial executive*
Dalton, Robert Issac, Jr. *textile executive, consultant, researcher*
Darlington, Frank *industrial engraving company executive*
Diamond, Harvey Jerome *machinery manufacturing company executive*
Dickson, Rush Stuart *holding company executive*
Goryn, Sara *textiles executive, real estate developer, psychologist*
Harrison, J. Frank, Jr. *soft drink company executive*
Kelley, Robert C. *retired construction industry executive*
Rinaldi, Richard A. *manufacturing company executive*
Squires, James Ralph *development company executive*

Durham
Althaus, David Steven *chemicals executive, controller*
Burton, Richard Max *management and healthcare educator*

Elon College
Powell, William Council, Sr. *service company executive*

Fayetteville
Richardson, Emilie White *manufacturing company executive, investment company executive, lecturer*

Fremont
Smith, Mark Eugene *architectural engineering service company executive*

Gastonia
Lawson, William David, III *retired cotton company executive*

Greensboro
Brecht, Blaine Richard *manufacturing company executive*
Mebane, George Allen IV *corporate executive, rancher*
Peterson, John Edgar, Jr. *retired agricultural executive, textile company executive*

Hendersonville
Stepkoski, Robert John *automobile dealership executive*

Hickory
Shuford, Harley Ferguson, Jr. *furniture manufacturing executive*

Madison
Millner, Thomas *manufacturing and holding company executive*

Morven
Jones, Sheila McLendon *construction company executive*

Murphy
Boyer, William Edward *manufacturing professional*

New Bern
Rivenbark, Rembert Reginald *shipbuilding executive*

North Wilkesboro
Matthews, John Carroll *manufacturing executive*

Oriental
Sutter, John Richard *manufacturer, investor*

Raleigh
Copulsky, William *chemical company executive*
Key, Karen Letisha *pharmaceutical executive*
Lindenmuth, Richard Alan *electronics company executive*
Prior, William Allen *electronics company executive*
Reese, Marc Charles *operations administrator*
Stone, Minnie Strange *retired automotive service company executive*
Wahlbrink, James Roy *construction executive*

Research Triangle Park
Maar, Rosina *medical organization executive*
Williams, James Lawrence *pharmaceutical executive*

Rocky Mount
Simpson, Dennis Arden *lighting contracting company executive*

Sanford
Kilmartin, Joseph Francis, Jr. *business executive, consultant*

Sapphire
Arbib, John A. *home builder, developer*

Southern Pines
Baxter, Barbara Morgan *plastics manufacturing company executive, educator*
Lipton, Clifford Carwood *retired glass company executive*

Statesville
Stelzner, Paul Burke *textile company executive*
Walters, Robert P. *manufacturing executive*

Tarboro
Finkelday, Karen Lynn *manufacturing executive*

Thomasville
Starr, Frederick Brown *furniture manufacturing executive*

Wilson
Kehaya, Ery W. *tobacco holding company executive*
Murray, J. Alec G. *manufacturing executive*

Winston Salem
Fordham, Sharon Ann *food company executive*
Sticht, J. Paul *retired food products and tobacco company executive*
Turner, Robert Carlton *manufacturing company executive*
Wallace, Roanne *hosiery company executive*
Woodford, Duane Hugh *aerospace equipment manufacturing company executive, electrical engineer*

OKLAHOMA

Bixby
Garrett, James Lowell *contractor*

Enid
Berry, Robert Bass *construction executive*

Goodwell
Morton, Luis Jac-Remelg M. *manufacturing executive, educator*

Guthrie
Williams, Thomas E. *pharmaceuticals executive*

Oklahoma City
Bentley, Earl Wilson, Jr. *construction executive*
Bradford, Dennis Doyle *textiles executive, real estate broker*
Clonts, George Gary *packaging company executive*
Colbert-Beavers, Annette Darcia *silver company executive*
Dearmon, Thomas Alfred *automotive industry financial executive, life insurance executive*
Hennigan, George R. *chemicals executive*
Kilbourne, Lewis Buckner *food service company executive*
Mc Pherson, Frank Alfred *manufacturing corporate executive*
Morgan, Ralph Rexford *manufacturing company executive*

Sand Springs
Ray, Eddye Robert *occupational safety and health professional*

Sulphur
Prather, Gary Benton *manufacturing company executive*

Tulsa
Bump, Larry J. *international engineering and construction company executive*
Primeaux, Henry, III *automotive executive, author, speaker*
Riggs, David Lynn *company executive*
Sprague, Christopher Bentley *manufacturing executive*
Tomer, Mark John *manufacturing/research and development executive*
Williams, Joseph Hill *retired diversified industry executive*

PENNSYLVANIA

Derry
Walker, Gary Linn *materials and logistics executive, consultant*

SOUTH CAROLINA

Aiken
Houston, Robert Lee *defense systems manufacturing company executive*

Bowman
Weathers, Lawrence Martin *agricultural executive*

Catawba
Malenick, Donald H. *metals manufacturing company executive*

Charleston
Geentiens, Gaston Petrus, Jr. *former construction management consultant company executive*
Kent, Harry Ross *construction executive, lay worker*

Columbia
Lawler, James Patrick *manufacturing executive*
Robinson, Robert Earl *chemical company executive*
Sumwalt, Robert Llewellyn, Jr. *construction company executive*
Synnett, Robert John *construction company executive*

Easley
Chandler, Marlene Merritt *construction executive*

Florence
Swink, James *food products executive*

Fort Mill
Elisha, Walter Y. *textile manufacturing company executive*

Georgetown
Harvey, Herschel Ambrose, Jr. *glass company executive*

Greenville
Dobson, Robert Albertus, IV *corporate executive*
Maguire, D.E. *electronics executive*
Varin, Roger Robert *textile executive*

Greer
Lane, James Garland, Jr. *diversified industry executive*

Hartsville
Browning, Peter Crane *packaging company executive*
Coker, Charles Westfield *diversified manufacturing company executive*

Hilton Head Island
Ranney, Maurice William *chemical company executive*
Stoll, Richard Edmund *retired manufacturing executive*

Kingstree
McCrea, Michael Andrea *manufacturing company executive*

North Charleston
Perkins, Robert Edgeworth *retired automotive executive*

Piedmont
Hodges, Allen Arthur *plastics film company executive*

Spartanburg
Mahanes, Michael Wayne *audio-visual electronics company executive*
Milliken, Roger *textile company executive*

Sunset
Ryan, Daniel Luciole *company executive*

Swansea
Mc Farland, Terry Lynn *construction company executive*

Travelers Rest
Theisen, George I. *manufacturing executive*

TENNESSEE

Arlington
Dillingham, Johnny Roy *materials manager*

Brentwood
Cline, Judy Butler *human resources executive*

Chattanooga
Gregg, Roy Dennis *manufacturing company executive*
Lee, Leslie W. *truck parts manufacturing company executive*

Clarksville
Rice, David A. *metals company executive*
Wall, Jim *metals company executive*

Cookeville
Villa, Edmond Roland *corporate executive*

Cordova
Bellantoni, Maureen Blanchfield *manufacturing executive*
Mann, Mel *food products company executive*

Ducktown
Hopkins, David Lee *medical manufacturing executive*

Gallatin
Crutcher, Dimetrec Artez *electronics technician*

Greeneville
Renner, Glenn Delmar *agricultural products executive*

Henderson
Herndon, Robert Edward *construction executive*

Humboldt
Jackson, Robert Keith *manufacturing company executive*

Johnson City
Schooley, Kenneth Ralph *manufacturing company executive*

Kingsport
Bradford, James Warren, Jr. *manufacturing executive*
Deavenport, Earnest W., Jr. *chemical executive*
Head, William Iverson, Sr. *retired chemical company executive*

Knoxville
Faires, Ross N. *manufacturing company executive*
Klingerman, Robert Harvey *manufacturing company executive*
Lynch, Mildred Virginia *lead company executive*
Macfarlane, Alastair Iain Robert *business executive*
McClain, Larry French *lumber company executive*
Murphy, James J. *electronics executive*
Wesley, Stephen Harrison *pharmaceutical company executive*

Memphis
Ballou, Howard Burgess *commercial plumbing designer*
Duke, Gary James *electronics executive*
Dunnigan, T. Kevin *electrical and electronics manufacturing company executive*
Mantey, Elmer Martin *food company executive*
McMinn, William A. *chemicals company executive*
Weaver, Charles *company executive*

Nashville
Hass, Joseph Monroe *automotive executive*
Hofstead, James Warner *laundry machinery company executive, lawyer*
Hummell, Burton Howard *food distribution company executive*
McGee, Thomas Lee *industrial automation specialist, engineer*
Mizell, Andrew Hooper, III *concrete company executive*
Scott, Richard L. *health and medical products company executive*

Newport
Gray, Sylvia Inez *pallet manufacturing executive*

Pulaski
Walker, Paul Dean *manufacturing executive*

Union City
Graham, R(ichard) Newell *soft drink bottling company executive*

TEXAS

Amarillo
Attebury, William Hugh *construction company executive*
Brashears, Wilford Session, Jr. *retired metals company executive, priest*

Angleton
Cohen, Robert *medical device manufacturing-marketing executive*

Arlington
Hodges, Edwin Clair *company executive*
Kemp, Thomas Joseph *electronics company administrator*

Austin
Alich, John Arthur, Jr. *manufacturing company executive*
Argo, William Frank *automotive executive*

Culp, Joe C(arl) *electronics executive*
Dell, Michael S. *manufacturing executive*
Jenkins, Marie Hooper *manufacturing company executive, engineer*
Juve, Arthur James *aerospace electronics executive*
McBee, Frank Wilkins, Jr. *industrial manufacturing executive*
Nagel, LeRoy F. *manufacturing and supply company executive*
Sullivan, Jerry Stephen *electronics company executive*

Barker
Atchley, Daniel Gene *business executive*

Beaumont
Ware, John David *valve and hydrant company executive*

Bellaire
Lancaster, Carroll Townes, Jr. *corporate executive*

Carrollton
Heath, Jinger L. *cosmetics executive*

College Station
Kubacak, Lawrence Don *energy efficient design and construction company executive*

Coppell
Fowler, William Dix *construction company executive*
Minyard, Liz *food products executive*
Williams, Gretchen Minyard *food store executive*

Corpus Christi
Turner, Elizabeth Adams Noble (Betty Turner) *healthcare executive, former mayor*

Corsicana
Martin, George M. *food products executive*

Dallas
Ash, Mary Kay *cosmetics company executive*
Balfanz, Robert Don *automotive executive, investment counselor*
Bartos, Jerry Garland *corporate executive, mechanical engineer*
Bradford, William Edward *oil field equipment manufacturing company executive*
Bucy, J. Fred, Jr. *retired electronics company executive*
Chupik, Eugene Jerry *business executive, financial consultant*
Contreras, Israel *manufacturing executive*
Davis, Craig Carlton *aerospace company executive*
Dorris, Carlos Eugene *chemicals executive*
Geyer, Frederick Francis *chemical company executive*
Gielisse, Victor A.L. *food company executive*
Gillilan, William J, III *construction company executive*
Gray, James Larry *metals company executive*
Heiberg, William Lytle *defense industry executive*
Hirsch, Laurence Eliot *construction executive, mortgage banker*
Hirsh, Bernard *supply company executive, consultant*
Hunter, Robert Charles *food company executive*
Kortschak, Sepp August *cosmetics company executive*
Kostas, Evans *manufacturing executive*
Martin, David D. *electronics executive*
McCally, Charles Richard *construction company executive*
Miller, Clint *technology company executive*
Miller, Erica T(illinghast) *aesthetician, skincare and cosmetics company executive, writer*
Murphy, John Joseph *manufacturing company executive*
Prengaman, R. David *company executive*
Quinn, David W. *building company executive*
Rochon, John Philip *cosmetics company executive*
Rogers, Ralph B. *industrial business executive*
St. John, Bill Dean *diversified equipment and services company executive*
Tew, E. James, Jr. *electronics company executive*
Wallace, William Ray *fabricated steel manufacturing company executive*
Watts, Marie Elizabeth (Mitzi Watts) *mining and heavy construction executive, art consultant*
Weber, William P. *electronics company executive*
White, Tom Willingham *wholesale beer/beverage distributor executive*
Wilson, Lawrence Alexander *construction company executive*

Diboll
Grum, Clifford J. *manufacturing company executive*
Harbordt, Charles Michael *forest products executive*

El Campo
Rotholz, Max B. *agricultural products executive*

El Paso
Peinado, Arnold Benicio, Jr. *consulting engineer*

Fort Mc Kavett
Stokes, Charles Eugene, Jr. *retired wool merchant*

Fort Worth
Barber, Larry Lee *manufacturing executive*
Brachman, Leon Harold *chemical company executive*
Bradshaw, James Edward *automotive company executive, consultant*
Cummings, Patrick Henry *manufacturing executive*
Pearce, Betty McMurray *retired manufacturing company executive*
Roland, Billy Ray *electronics company executive*

Georgetown
Embree, James Ray *construction company executive, director*

Grand Prairie
Mansen, Steven Robert *manufacturing company executive*
Robertson, Michael Wayne *automation company executive*

Houston
Bayliss, Geoffrey S. *chemical company executive*
Boren, William Meredith *manufacturing executive*
Bryan, Gloria Elaine *beauty and fashion consultant*
Cizik, Robert *manufacturing company executive*
Cotros, Charles H. *food products company executive*
De Wree, Eugene Ernest *manufacturing company executive*
Dye, Ken *chemical company executive*
Farnsworth, Cherrill Kay *corporate executive*
Fechik, Lloyd (Buck Fechik) *medical products company executive*
Godchaux, Frank Area, III *food company executive*
Hafner, Joseph A., Jr. *food company executive*
Harrop, George Bert *construction executive*
Heimbinder, Isaac *construction company executive, lawyer*
Helland, George Archibald, Jr. *manufacturing company executive, former government official, management consultant*
Hurwitz, Charles Edwin *manufacturing company executive*
Irelan, Robert Withers *metal products executive*
Jacobson, Charles Allen *aerospace company executive*
Johnson, Frederick Dean *former food company executive*
Keepers, Charles Joseph *building supply company executive*
King, Carl B. *tool company executive*
Klausmeyer, David Michael *scientific instruments manufacturing company executive*
Kornbleet, Lynda Mae *insulation, fireproofing and acoustical contractor*
La Duc, John *manufacturing executive*
Mangapit, Conrado, Jr. *manufacturing company executive*
Martin, J. Landis *manufacturing company executive, lawyer*
Menscher, Barnet Gary *steel company executive*
Pognonec, Yves Maurice *steel products executive*
Ryan, Frank J. *construction executive*
Sebastian, Michael James *retired manufacturing company executive*
Shaw, Michael Joseph *automotive executive*
Sims, Gregory Evans *electronics distribution company executive*
Smith, Michael William *construction and consulting company executive*
Snowden, Bernice Rives *former construction company executive*
Tatum, John Allen, Jr. *manufacturing company executive*
Taylor, Edward Reginald *food and beverage industry executive*
Temple, Robert Winfield *chemical company executive*
Waggoner, James Virgil *chemicals company executive*
White, David Alan, Jr. *manufacturing company executive*
Wilson, Carl Weldon, Jr. *construction company executive, civil engineer*
Wnuk, Wade Joseph *manufacturing and service company executive*
Woods, James Dudley *manufacturing company executive*
Wuensche, Vernon Edgar *construction company executive*

Irving
Craig, Nadine Karamarkovich *pharmaceutical executive*
Lott, William Ronald *contracting company owner*
Spies, Jacob John *health care executive*

Kilgore
Turner, Lisa Joyce *paint manufacturing company executive*

Longview
Mann, Jack Matthewson *bottling company executive*

Lubbock
Hester, Ross Wyatt *business forms manufacturing company executive*

Magnolia
Broadrick, Steven Mark *manufacturing executive*

Marshall
Poindexter, Kenneth Wayne *automobile executive*

Midlothian
Adams, Harold Dale *food company executive*

Pasadena
Stephens, Sidney Dee *chemical manufacturing company executive*

Plano
Bauge, Cynthia Wise *distributing company executive*
Errickson, Barbara Bauer *electronic equipment company executive*
Gibson, Ernest L., III *healthcare consultant*

Pleasanton
Warnken, Byron *food products executive*

Port Lavaca
Fisher, (Mary) Jewel Tanner *retired construction company executive*

Richardson
Bolin, Roger Kenneth *electronics executive*
Richards, Frederick Francis, Jr. *manufacturing company executive*

Round Rock
Whitlock, Darrell Dean *manufacturing company executive*

San Angelo
Henry, William Charles *manufacturing company administrator*

San Antonio
Chen, Shih-Fong *pharmaceutical executive*
Cloud, Bruce Benjamin, Sr. *construction company executive*
Martinez, Pete R. *beverage company executive*
Myer, Jerry O'Brien *manufacturing technologist, computer programmer*
Scott, Martha Sue *food company executive*
Smith, Pat Everett *chemical company executive*

Santa Fe
Lambert, Willie Lee Bell *mobile equipment company owner, educator*

Stafford
Hinojosa, Alma Alicia *pharmaceuticals executive*
Selecman, Charles Edward *business executive*

Sugar Land
Kempner, Isaac Herbert, III *sugar company executive*
Kjos, Otto Dennis *construction industry executive*

Texas City
Chen, Yuan James *chemical company executive*

Tyler
Smith, Howard Thompson *business executive*

VIRGINIA

Altavista
Tyler, K. Scott, Jr. *manufacturing company executive*

Arlington
Danjczek, David William *manufacturing company executive*
Pollock, Neal Jay *electronics executive*

Ashburn
Cuteri, Frank R., Jr. *automotive executive*

Bassett
Spilman, Robert Henkel *furniture company executive*

Blacksburg
Kincade, Doris Helsing *apparel marketing educator*
Pickering, Timothy Lee *chemical research center administrator*

Bristol
Shean, Timothy Joseph *manufacturing company executive*

Broadway
Keeler, James Leonard *food products company executive*

Covington
Wright, Calvin Persinger *business executive*

Edinburg
Rhodes, Stephen Michael *poultry company executive*

Fairfax
Guirguis, Raouf Albert *health science executive*
Sowder, Donald Dillard *chemicals executive*

Falls Church
Mellor, James Robb *electronics executive*
Salvatori, Vincent Louis *corporate executive*

Glen Allen
Fife, William Franklin *retired drug company executive*
Smook, John T. *manufacturing company executive*

Herndon
Harris, Shelley Follansbee *contracts administrator*

Hopewell
Leake, Preston Hildebrand *tobacco research executive*

Independence
McAllister, William Alexander, Jr. *manufacturing company executive*

Kilmarnock
Moore, William Black, Jr. *retired aluminum company executive*

Manassas
Buchko, Michael Scott *construction executive*

Mc Lean
Graf, Dorothy Ann *business executive*
Levy, Michael Howard *environmental management professional*
Perry, Stephen Clayton *manufacturing executive*
Schar, Dwight C. *construction company executive*

New Market
Howell, Leo A. *metals manufacturing executive*

Newport News
Fricks, William Peavy *shipbuilding company executive*

Portsmouth
Mintz, Susan Ashinoff *menswear manufacturing comapany executive*

Richmond
Bourke, William Oliver *retired metal company executive*
Bunzl, Rudolph Hans *retired diversified manufacturing company executive*
Gottwald, Bruce Cobb *chemical company executive*
Gottwald, Floyd Dewey, Jr. *chemical company executive*
Halsey, Brenton Shaw *paper company executive*
Holder, Richard Gibson *metal products executive*
Jackson, Richard Brinkley *metal company executive*
Jordan, Henry Preston, Jr. *manufacturering executive*
Marsh, Miles L. *textile company executive*
Martin, Norma Anne Holmes *electronic technician*
Minor, George Gilmer, III *drug and hospital supply company executive*
Pastore, Peter Nicholas, Jr. *metal processing company executive*
Pauley, Stanley Frank *manufacturing company executive*
Rogers, James Edward *paper company executive*
Totten, Arthur Irving, Jr. *retired metals company executive, consultant*
Walker, Charles B. *chemicals company executive*
Watts, Robert Glenn *retired pharmaceutical company executive*
Whelan, Karen Mae Leppo *manufacturing executive*

Springfield
Cicolani, Angelo George *research company executive, operating engineer*

Vienna
Bajpai, Sanjay Kumar *pharmaceutical executive, consultant*

Virginia Beach
Toth, Stephen Michael *electronics specialist*

Williamsburg
Merritt, William Dorris *electronics company executive*

Winchester
Murtagh, John Edward *alcohol production consultant*

WEST VIRGINIA

Charleston
Gunnoe, Nancy Lavenia *food executive, artist*

Davisville
Duckworth, Joseph Clyde *manufacturing technician, writer*

Morgantown
Raese, John R. *steel company executive*

New Haven
Wolfe, Michael Patrick *metal products executive*

Weirton
Elish, Herbert *retired manufacturing company executive*

Wheeling
Clarke, S. Bruce *paper company executive*
Wareham, James Lyman *steel company executive*

WISCONSIN

Larsen
Stern, Douglas Donald *retired foundry company executive*

Milwaukee
Borleis, Herbert William *pharmaceutical company executive*

Neenah
Woon, Paul Sam *technical executive*

TERRITORIES OF THE UNITED STATES

PUERTO RICO

Dorado
Spector, Michael Joseph *agribusiness executive*

San Juan
Abella, Marisela Carlota *business executive*

ADDRESS UNPUBLISHED

Allen, Eugene R. *construction executive*
Alm, John Richard *beverage company executive*
Andrews, William Frederick *manufacturing executive*
Aronowitz, Jack Leon *biotechnology and diagnostic manufacturing company executive, consultant*
Baumgardner, Karen Thornton *retired newspaper executive*
Bennett, Jay Brett *medical equipment company executive*
Bossier, Albert Louis, Jr. *shipbuilding company executive*
Bratton, William Edward *electronics executive, management consultant*
Brown, Jerry Milford *medical company executive*
Carmody, Thomas Roswell *business products company executive*
Chmielinski, Edward Alexander *electronics company executive*
Clawson, Harry Quintard Moore *business executive*
Correnti, John David *steel company executive*
Curry, Edward Thomas, Jr. *tire dealership executive*
De Raad, Bernard Ruth *food and ingredient broker, researcher, consultant*
Doyle, Irene Elizabeth *electronic sales executive, nurse*
Dozier, Glenn Joseph *medical, surgical products distribution executive*
Durham, G. Robert *diversified manufacturing company executive*
Fiehn, George Roger *home building company executive, consultant*
Franco, Alexander *construction company executive*
Fullerton, Jymie Luie *pharmaceutical company executive, consultant*
Harrell, Henry Howze *tobacco company executive*
Hauptli, Barbara Beatrice *environmental specialist*
Hodge, Mary Gretchen Farnam *manufacturing company distributor, manager and executive*
Holland, Charles Edward *medical products corporate executive*
Joyce, William Robert *textile machinery company executive*
Jubran, Raja Jubran *engineering and general contracting executive*
Junkin, Jerry R. *manufacturing company executive*
Keith, Brian Thomas *automobile executive*
Kellgren, George Lars *manufacturing company executive*
Killhour, William Gherky *paper company executive*

Laughlin, Christine Nelson *manufacturing company executive*
Lennon, A. Max *food products company executive*
Leonard, Guy Meyers, Jr. *international holding company executive*
Lorinsky, Larry *international trade executive and consultant*
Martin, Paul Lee *building contractor, consultant*
Mason, Frank Henry, III *automobile company executive, leasing company executive*
Mauro, George Theodore *corporate executive*
May, Kenneth Nathaniel *food industry consultant*
Messmore, David William *construction executive, former psychologist*
Mitchell, Guy Patrick *manufacturing executive*
Monk, Richard Hunley, Jr. *textile company executive*
Morin, Thomas H. *food distribution executive*
Mukamal, David Samier *sign manufacturing company executive*
Newman, Tillman Eugene, Jr. *food company executive*
Novak, Alan Lee *retired pharmaceutical company executive*
Nowak, Stephen Francis *medical equipment company sales executive*
O'Connor, Terence James *roofing company executive*
Osborne, Gayle Ann *manufacturing executive*
Picard, Thomas Joseph, Jr. *aerospace company executive*
Prillaman, Bob Maurice *paper corporation executive*
Raley, William L. *agricultural executive*
Roline, Eric Alfred *manufacturing company executive*
Roper, John Lonsdale, III *shipyard executive*
Rose, Neal Nicholas *maintenance and construction company executive*
Rosen, Ana Beatriz *electronics executive*
Sanders, Wayne R. *manufacturing executive*
Schoonover, Hugh James *roofing company executive*
Shirley, George Milton, Jr. *chemicals executive*
Silver, George *metal trading and processing company executive*
Stewart, Joe J. *manufacturing executive*
Strohm, Raymond William *laboratory equipment manufacturing company executive*
Tucker, Charles Ray *metalworking company executive, sales and service engineer*
Walter, James W. *diversified manufacturing executive*
Watts, Wendy Hazel *wine consultant*
Weisinger, Charles *produce executive, consultant*
Woods, J. P. *pharmaceutical company executive*

INDUSTRY: SERVICE

UNITED STATES

ALABAMA

Alexander City
Dunn Arnoff, Rebecca Diane *human resources specialist*

Birmingham
Axel, Bernard *restaurant owner*
Bloom, Charles Robert *public relations professional*
Bruno, Ronald G. *food service executive*
Carter, Carl Douglas *public relations executive*
Clemmons, Barry Wayne *marketing operations executive*
Etterer, Sepp *industrial relations consultant*
Griffin, Glen J. *company executive*
Martin, Billy C. *advertising executive*
Martin, David C. *advertising exective*
Metz, Robert Edward *quality assurance executive*
Pendleton, Janice Bishop *company executive*
Spahn, James Francis *marketing professional*
Stuart, Juanita Ryan *recreation facility executive*
Young, Thomas Richard *sales professional*

Brewton
Last, Sondra Carole *public relations consultant, writer, teacher*

Eufaula
Dixon, Giles *company executive*

Florence
Fischer, Alvin Eugene, Jr. *marketing executive*

Gadsden
Tawpash, William Robert *public relations executive*

Heflin
Brady, Jennie M. *wholesale and retail sales professional*

Hope Hull
Stites, Darl Kay *marketing professional*

Huntsville
Barnes, Ben Blair *company executive, electrical engineer*
Bendickson, Marcus J. *company executive*
Burns, Pat Ackerman Gonia *information systems specialist, software engineer*
Childs, Rand Hampton *data processing executive*
Collazo, Francisco J. *company executive*
Dayton, Deane Kraybill *computer company executive*
Gray, Ronald W. *business executive*
Little, Jon Warren *materials executive*
Lynch, James Charles *security consultant*
McIntyre-Ivy, Joan Carol *data processing executive*
Meadlock, James W. *computer graphics company executive*
Richter, William, Jr. *technical management consulting executive*
Shafer, Roberta W. Crow *human resources executive, career marketing consultant, venture capital consultant*
Solley, Michael William *computer executive, educator*
Zana, Donald Dominick *data processing executive*

Hurtsboro
Bouilliant-Linet, Francis Jacques *global management consultant*

Jacksonville
Carmode, Ralph E. *communications educator*
Fairleigh, Marlane Paxson *retired business consultant, educator*

Madison
Clark, Stephen Michael *information systems analyst*

Mc Calla
Walker, Victor Louis *computer company executive*

Mobile
Bowersox, Christina A. *public relations executive*
Tunnell, William Newton, Jr. *tourism executive*

Montgomery
Alfred, Bob *business executive*
Murkett, Philip Tillotson *human resource executive*
Robinson, Peter Clark *general management executive*

Normal
Scott, Stanley VanAken *administrator, educator, consultant*

Ohatchee
Ellis, Bernice Allred *personnel executive*

Pennington
Hazard, Sherrill John, III *business team leader*

Perdue Hill
Pitts, Jacqueline Ione *secretary, poet*

Point Clear
Williams, Willie John, II *marketing consultant*

Tuscaloosa
Patterson, Coleman E.P. *management educator*
Plumley, Joseph Pinkney, Jr. *public relations educator, consultant*

Webb
Barley, Doris Faye *sales executive*

ARIZONA

Tucson
Beaty, Gilbert R. *private investigator*
Wedow, David Walter *marketing analyst*

ARKANSAS

Bauxite
Miller, Cleve Arthur *auctioneer*

Bella Vista
Greene, Eliot Bruce *public relations executive, historic conservator*

Bentonville
Hacker, Mark Gregory *training and development executive*

Clarksville
Mooney, Robbi Gail *operations officer*

Fayetteville
Burton, Scot *marketing educator*
Combs, Linda Jones *management company executive, researcher*
Edmark, David Stanley *communications director*

Fort Smith
Ellis, June B. *human resource consultant*
Pendergrass, Ewell Dean *communications executive*
Stubblefield, David Edward *marketing executive*
Sullivan, Nell Inklebarger *administrative secretary, counselor assistant*

Hot Springs National Park
Short, Edgar Dean *sales executive, environmental scientist*

Jonesboro
Tims, Robert Austin *data processing official, pilot*

Leachville
Adams, Charles *company executive*
Adams, Eddie *company executive*

Little Rock
Adams, Rose Ann *management consultant*
Babin, Claude Hunter, Jr. *marketing executive*
Bolton, Jan E. *business executive*
Brown, Brent Burris *data processing executive*
Clark, Ouida Ouijella *public relations executive, educator*
Dillard, Alex *executive*
Dillard, Mike *executive*
Freeman, James I. *executive*
Hawkins, John *department store executive*
Russell, Jerry Lewis *public relations counselor, political consultant*
Stebbins, L. Kay *communications executive*
Walker, Sarah Frances *marketing, public relations consultant*
Wilson, Amy Louise *public relations executive*

Magnolia
Kimbell, Richard Lee *professional computer consultant*

Monticello
Smith, John Holmes, IV *trucking terminal manager, sales representative*

Siloam Springs
Barnes, Anthony *business executive*

Springdale
Brooks, Steve *business executive*
Smith, Danny Leon *sales executive*

West Memphis
Arledge, David A. *business executive*

CALIFORNIA

Altadena
Willans, Richard James *religious organization executive, human resources management consultant*

Laguna Beach
Smith, Patricia Jacquline *marketing executive*

Palo Alto
Yoshida, James Atsushi *carbon fiber marketing company executive*

San Diego
Barr, Robert Edward *computer company executive*

CONNECTICUT

Danielson
May, John M. *sales and marketing executive, consultant*

Kent
Gutelius, Edward Warner *marketing professional*

DISTRICT OF COLUMBIA

Washington
Brunson, James McDuffie, Sr. *management consultant*
Hilburg, Alan Jay *crisis management consultant*
Lambert, Deborah Ketchum *public relations executive*
Lombard, Judith Marie *human resource policy specialist*
Salino, Jeffrey Alan *leasing executive*

FLORIDA

Altamonte Springs
Weintraub, Abner Edward *information services executive*

Atlantic Beach
Filips, Nicholas Joseph *management consultant*

Aventura
Mucciano, Stephanie Lyons *hospitality, marketing and association management executive*

Bartow
Bruwelheide, Dale A. *business executive*
Mooney, Eugene C. *food company executive*

Boca Raton
Albrecht, Arthur John *advertising agency executive*
Allen, Barry Morgan *corporate communications consultant*
Atchley, Roger Kent *marketing and management consultant*
Bracken, Louis Everett *retired sales executive, health services executive*
D'Egidio, Connie Sue *contracts specialist*
Finegold, Ronald *computer service executive*
Flynn, Sharon Ann *marketing executive, educator*
Frank, William Edward, Jr. *executive recruitment company executive*
Guirado, Burt *restaurant management*
Kewley, Sharon Lynn *systems analyst, consultant*
Langbort, Polly *retired advertising executive*
Turner, Lisa Phillips *human resources executive*

Boynton Beach
Ashley, James MacGregor *management consultant*
Geltner Schwartz, Sharon *communications executive*
Grinnell, Lawrence Jeffrey *systems administrator*
Koteen, Jack *management consultant, writer*
Shachnow, Douglas Allen *travel industry educator, writer*

Bradenton
Womack, A. Barton *business educator*

Cape Canaveral
Jackson, Jonathan Jene *quality assurance professional*

Cape Coral
Andert-Schmidt, Darlene *management consultant and trainer*
Brevoort, Richard William *public relations executive*
Cheek, Arthur Lee *marketing professional*

Clearwater
Brenner, Rena Claudy *communications executive*
Chisholm, William DeWayne *retired contract executive*
Corcoran-Cramb, Elizabeth Hecht *marketing and market research company executive*
Donahue, Katherine Mary *sales executive*
Roberson, Richard W. *company executive*
Taylor, J(ames) Bennett *management consultant*
VanNahmen, Ava Marie *public relations executive*
White, Mary Louise *management consultant*

Cocoa Beach
Pearson, Patricia Kelley *marketing representative*

Coconut Creek
Brent, Hal Preston *sales executive*

Coconut Grove
Amos, Betty Giles *restaurant company executive, accountant*

Coral Gables
Hammes, Therese Marie *advertising, public relations and marketing executive*
La Forge, Raymond Bernard, Jr. *marketing and sales consultant*
Ziska, David Lee *public relations professional*

Coral Springs
Bosted, Dorothy Stack *public relations executive*
Charles, Joel *forensic audio and video tape analyst, voice identification consultant*

Davie
Saltz, Ivan K(enneth) *data processing executive*
Todd, Robert Edward, Jr. *purchasing manager*

Daytona Beach
Furstman, Shirley Elsie Daddow *advertising executive*
Jaffe, Richard Paul *corporate executive, lawyer*

Debary
Fortmueller, Heinz William Erich *quality assurance professional*
Schaeffer, Barbara Hamilton *retired rental leasing company executive, writer*

Delray Beach
Corbin, Arnold *marketing educator, management consultant*
Corbin, Claire (Mrs. Arnold Corbin) *marketing educator*
Sondak, Arthur *management consultant*

Deltona
Zagnoli, Roland Candiano *management and marketing consultant, pharmacist*

Dunedin
Metcalf, Robert John Elmer *industrial consultant*

Englewood
Kleinlein, Kathy Lynn *training and development executive*

Fernandina Beach
D'Agnese, John Joseph *sanitation and pest management consultant*
Mather, Hal Frederick *management consultant*

Floral City
Wise, Lawrence George *human resources executive*

Fort Lauderdale
Bimstein, Benjamin William *caterer, chef*
Coolman, C. Douglas *company executive*
Danzig, Sheila Ring *marketing and direct mail executive*
Danzig, William Harold *marketing executive*
Dejean, Betty L. *county administrator*
Fitzgerald, Carol *administrative assistant*
Flynn, Donald F. *entertainment company executive*
Harris, Stanley Louis, Jr. *advertising executive*
Honahan, H(enry) Robert *motion picture theatre executive*
Horn, Lewis Martin *business analyst*
Motes, Joseph Mark *cruise and convention promotion company executive*
Olen, Milton William, Jr. *marketing executive*
Page, Earl Michael *management specialist*
Paul, Joseph B. *customer service administrator, desktop publisher*
Seegers, Gerald E. *recreation facility executive*
Smith, Scott Clybourn *media company executive*
Thompson, Richard Victor, Jr. *service executive*
Weinstein, Art Ted *marketing professional, educator*

Fort Myers
Garside, Marlene Elizabeth *advertising executive*
Ryan, William Joseph *communications company executive*
Waites, William Ernest *advertising executive*

Fort Myers Beach
Caracciolo, Francis Samuel *management consultant*

Fort Pierce
Hurley, William Joseph *retired information systems executive*
Thoma, Richard William *chemical safety and waste management consultant*

Fort Walton Beach
Brown, Gary Allen *defense analysis company executive*
Fallin, Barbara Moore *human resources director*

Gainesville
Shugan, Steven Mark *marketing educator*
Southworth, David Leslie *company financial executive*

Gulf Breeze
MacKenzie, Malcolm Robert *personnel management consultant*

Heathrow
Graziani, N. Jane *communications executive, publisher*

Hollywood
Angstrom, Wayne Raymond *communications executive*
Ladin, Eugene *communications company executive*
Lurier, Peter Bruce *marketing professional*

Homestead
Brooks, Pal *business executive*

Hudson
Miller, Mary Jeannette *office management specialist*

Hurlburt Field
Bunting, Gary Glenn *operations research analyst, educator*

Immokalee
Nobles, Lewis J., Jr. *executive*

Indian Harbour Beach
Koenig, Harold Paul *management consultant, ecologist, author*

Indian Rocks Beach
Sullivan, Paul William *communications specialist*

Jacksonville
Balog, Richard Thomas *management consultant, educator*
Bodkin, Ruby Pate *corporate executive, real estate broker, educator*
Brodeur, Thomas J. *information systems specialist*
Constantini, JoAnn M. *information management consultant*
Craft, Mary Faye *public relations consultant, television producer*
Davis, A. Dano *grocery store chain executive*
Davis, T. Wayne *executive of golf course management company*
deLaFountaine, Charles Randall *security company official*
Gniech, Thomas Anthony *public relations executive, consultant*
Hatch, Donald James (Jim Hatch) *business leadership and planning executive*
Hopkins, William B. *golf course management group executive*
Humm, Charles Allen *sales and marketing professional*
Lestinger, Alan *company executive*
McSweeney, William Patrick *public relations practitioner*
Motsett, Charles Bourke *sales and marketing executive*
Murphy, Patrick Francis *printing company executive*
Rinehart, Harry Elmer *retired sales executive*
Schiffers, Peggy Espy *management consultant*
Shoup, James Raymond *computer systems consultant*
Welsh, Timothy John *human resources specialist*

Jacksonville Beach
Jones, Herman Otto, Jr. *corporate professional*

Jupiter
Merritt, Jean *consulting firm executive*
Taylor, Claude J. *sales executive, consultant*

Key Colony Beach
Siegel, Robert James *communications executive*

Labelle
Berry, Jack, Jr. *business executive*

Lake Buena Vista
Brightwell, Rebecca Lynn *marketing professional*
Nunis, Richard A. *amusement parks executive*
Parke, Robert Leon *communications executive*

Lake Park
Anderson, Mark Stephen *recovery company executive*

Lake Wales
Oakley, Ronald E. *business executive*
Oakley, Thomas E. *company executive*
Updike, Samuel D. *business executive*

Lake Worth
Bell, Melvin *management consultant*
Bertino, Sheila Elaine *college relations and marketing director*
Stevens, William John *management consultant, former association executive*

Lakeland
Fox, Kenneth Ian *company manager*
Huggins, Richard Leonard *development director*
Jenkins, Howard M. *supermarket executive*
Siedle, Robert Douglas *management consultant*
Summers, Richard Lyle *safety executive, consultant*
Wiggs, Robert Howard *advertising agency executive*

Largo
Atkins, Candi *management consultant, small business owner*
Chambers, Ray Wayne *security and loss control consultant*
Gould, Glenn Hunting *marketing professional, consultant*
Martin, Leslie Earl, III *marketing executive*

Lecanto
Leek, Jay Wilbur *management consultant*

Leesburg
Nobles, Robert L. *business executive*

Lighthouse Point
Price, Gail Elizabeth *research firm executive*

Longboat Key
Cook, James Winfield Clinton *sales and marketing company executive*
Holcomb, Constance L. *sales and marketing management executive*

Longwood
Manjura, Bonnie Doreen *marketing and advertising executive, educator*
Walters, Philip Raymond *foundation executive*

Macdill AFB
Grubb, Todd C. *human resources educator*

Marathon
Coldren, Sharon Louise *strategic and corporate planner*

Melbourne
Costa, Manuel Antone *recreational facility manager*
Farmer, Phillip W. *company executive*
Herro, John Joseph *software specialist*
Hughes, Edwin Lawson *retired management consultant*
Jenkins, Marshall Whitfield *communications consultant, entrepreneur*
Kvasnok, Joseph Douglas *quality assurance professional*
Vilardebo, Angie Marie *management consultant, parochial school educator*

Miami
Anders, Walter Charles *human resources administrator*
Argibay, Jorge Luis *information systems firm executive and founder*
Arison, Micky *cruise line company executive*
Bonilla, James Joseph *international marketing director*
Calienes, Armando Luis, Sr. *information technology executive*
Carter, Harriet Vanessa *public relations specialist, congressional aide*
Cohen, Ted Ellis *public relations executive, publishing executive*
Collins, Susan Ford *leadership consultant*
Daoud, Abraham Joseph, IV *funeral director, former police officer*
Denny, Dwight D. *rental company executive*
Fernandez, Isabel Lidia *human resources specialist*
Fine, Joel Ted *marketing and management consultant*
Fromkin, Ava Lynda *management consultant, healthcare risk management services*
Frost, Philip *company executive*
Henson, John Denver *international management consulting firm executive*
Howard, Elsie Sterling *marketing executive*
Knight, Kenneth Vincent *leisure company executive, entrepreneurventure capitalists*
McFarland, William Chandler *advertising executive*
McKinnon, Thomas E. *human resources executive*
Mestepey, John Thomas *executive search consultant*
Nadeau, Joseph Eugene *health care management consultant, information systems consultant*
Newman, Terrie Lynne *advertising and marketing executive*
O'Day, Sharon *marketing professional*
Ortiz, Loida A. *communications executive*
Paz, Lucio R. *management consultant*
Perez, Alfredo *business executive*
Polen-Dorn, Linda Frances *communications executive*
Prussin, Jeffrey A. *management consultant*
Rakow, B.J. *management consultant*
Ross, Robert Clark *public relations executive*
Roth, Robert *advertising executive*
Schwartz, Gerald *public relations and fundraising agency executive*
Strong, Charles Robert *waste management administrator*
Strul, Gene M. *communications executive*
Whittington, Robert Wallace *business executive*

Miami Beach
D'Gabriel, Carlos Leonardo *travel executive*

Miami Lakes
Perez de la Mesa, Manuel Jose *company executive*

Miami Shores
Halpern, Peter Jay *marketing professional*

Naples
Censits, Richard John *business consultant*
Legue, Laura Elizabeth *resort and recreational facility executive*
Mathias, Alyce Ann *advertising and graphic design executive*
Mehaffey, John Allen *marketing, newspaper management and advertising executive*
Schmidt, Richard Alan *management company executive*

Navarre
Wesley, Stephen Burton *training professional*

North Miami
Roslow, Sydney *marketing educator*

North Palm Beach
McCarthy, Michael Fitzmichael *business executive*
Robertson, Randall Ball *marketing professional, sporting events promoter*

North Port
Berking, Max *retired advertising company executive*

Ocala
Kaplan, Judith Helene *corporate professional*
Strout, Steven Brian *media executive, infosystems specialist*

Okeechobee
Hedges, Bobette Lynn *business administrator*

Oldsmar
MacLeod, Donald Martin *corporate professional*

Opa Locka
Nelsen, Martin Claude *management services professional*

Orange Park
Critchlow, Susan Melissa *public relations executive, advertising and printing consultant*
Murphy, Jimmy Dean *consulting company executive*

Orlando
Brooks, Fred *executive recreational facility*
Buckley, Linda Tibbetts *public relations executive*
Connolly, Joseph Francis, II *defense company executive*
Guetzloe, Douglas M. *public relations executive*
Hall, Lawrie Platt *consumer products executive, public, community and government relations executive, consultant*
Hipscher, Jerome Jay *educator, writer, actor*
Macbeth, Hugh James *data processing executive*
Neiman, Norman *aerospace business and marketing executive*
Renard, Meredith Anne *marketing and advertising professional*
Williams, Tom *recreational facility executive*

Ormond Beach
Coke, C(hauncey) Eugene *consulting company executive, scientist, educator, author*
McGee, James Edward *sales executive*
Shepard, Janie Ray (J. R. Shepard) *software development executive*
Stogner, William Louis *pharmaceutical company sales executive*

Palm Bay
Bigda, Rudolph A. *business and financial consultant*

Palm Beach
Bennett, Paul Henry *business consultant*

Palm Beach Gardens
Denney, Robert Blake *public relations specialist*
Wackenhut, Richard Russell *security company executive*

Palm Coast
Silverstein, Victoria *retired sales executive*

Palm Harbor
McDonald, Peggy Ann Stimmel *retired automobile company official*
Schafer, Edward Albert, Jr. *data processing executive*

Pensacola
Fisher, Rosalind Anita *personnel executive*

Plant City
McDaniel, David Glenn *business owner, author*

Pompano Beach
Danziger, Terry Leblang *public relations and marketing consultant*
Donnelly, Michael Joseph *management consultant*
Freimark, Jeffrey Philip *retail supermarket executive*
Zunker, Sharon Jienell *commercial expediters company executive*

Port Saint Lucie
Donohue, Edith M. *human resources specialist, educator*

Punta Gorda
Coleman, H. Robert *food company executive*
Jacobson, Robert Arthur *management consulting executive*

Safety Harbor
Hutchinson, David Robert, IV *sales executive*

Saint Augustine
Fliegel, Robert Aalbu *park administrator*
Preysz, Louis Robert Fonss, III *management consultant, educator*
Rowsey, Nora Kathleen *management consultant*
Tuseo, Norbert Joseph John *marketing executive, consultant*

Saint Petersburg
Butcher-Towzey, David *public relations executive*
Greer, Tommy D. *marketing executive*
Richardson, Joseph H. *company executive*

Sanford
Westerfield, Francis Clark *quality assurance professional*

Sanibel
Sheldon, Nancy Way *environmental management consultant*

Sarasota
Bloom, Stephen Edward *marketing professional, consultant*
Campbell, Donna Marie *telecommunications executive*
Fendrick, Alan Burton *retired advertising executive*
Honner Sutherland, B. Joan *advertising executive*
Huff, Russell Joseph *public relations and publishing executive*
Kelly, John Love *public relations executive*
Kindred, George Charles *lithography executive*
La Marre, Mildred Holtz *business executive*
Minette, Dennis Jerome *financial computing consultant*
Neeley, Delmar George *human resources consultant*
Woodger, Walter James, Jr. *management consultant*

Seminole
Payne, David Gordon *marketing professional*

Spring Hill
Kraatz, Karen Lucille *office manager*

Stuart
DeRubertis, Patricia Sandra *software company executive*

Sunrise
Stufano, Thomas Joseph *investigative firm executive*

Tallahassee
Layne, Margaret Edith *environmental services administrator*
Meyer, Linda Corrine Smith *employment and training operations executive*
Williams, Lawrence Carroll *data processing executive*

Tampa
Arango, Anthony Glenn *sales executive*
Bellas, Marc Andrew *sales and marketing specialist*
Brackin, Phyllis Jean *recruiting professional*
Butler, John Paul *sales executive*
Caro, Charles Crawford *microcomputer company executive, international consultant*
Gamble, Mary G(race) *marketing and quality professional*
Grossman, Paul Leslie *sales and marketing executive*
Hatch, William G. (Bill) *management consultant*
Heuer, Martin *temporary services executive*
Hevner, Alan Raymond *educator, consultant*
Highsmith, Jasper Habersham *sales executive*
Johnson, Tesla Francis *data processing executive, educator*
Kessen, George William *employment agency manager*
Mangiapane, Joseph Arthur *consulting company executive, applied mechanics consultant*
McGibbon, Donald Bruce *public relations executive*
McKeown, Frank Edward *consumer services executive*
Meriwether, William Crawford *personnel executive*
Miller, Bonnie Sewell *marketing professional*
Ortinau, David Joseph *marketing specialist, educator*
Silver, Paul Robert *marketing executive, consultant*
Sinkhorn, Mary Jean *real estate executive*
Smith, Robin Albertson *public relations executive*
Stephens, Patricia Ann *marketing professional*
Taylor, Austin Randall *sales executive*
Townsend, David Lee *public relations executive*
West, Benjamin B. *advertising executive*
Wizner, Linda Jean *communications executive*

Tequesta
Gregory, Thomas Raymond *management consultant*

Treasure Island
Foote, Frances Catherine *association executive, living trust consultant*

Valrico
Foster, Michael Paul *sales and marketing representative*
Harber, Loretta Michele *retired corporate executive*
Morris, John Charles *sales executive*

Venice
Christy, Audrey Meyer *public relations consultant*

Vero Beach
Calevas, Harry Powell *management consultant*
Luther, John M. *business executive*

West Palm Beach
Bowers, Patricia Newsome *communications executive*
Gorman-Gordley, Marcie Sothern *personal care industry franchise executive*
Heinz, Toni Sue *irrigation company executive*
Ronan, William John *management consultant*
Sardanopoli, Bruno Sardi *retired television station sales official*

Winter Haven
Cover, Norman Bernard *electronic data processing administrator*
De Nitto, John Francis *human resources administrator, medical researcher*

Winter Springs
Cook, Joan Torrieri *marketing professional, business coach*
Kaalstad, Oscar William *management consultant*
Whitfield, David *company executive*

GEORGIA

Acworth
Paul, Jo Ann *management consultant*

Ailey
Windsor, James Thomas, Jr. *printing company executive, newspaper publisher*

Albany
Ezeamii, Hyacinth Chinedum *public administration educator*

Alpharetta
Bobo, Genelle Tant (Nell Bobo) *office administrator*
Demerau, Scott *business executive*
Eubanks, Omer Lafayette *data communications specialist*
Mills, Stephen Nathaniel *computer software company executive*
West, Delouris Jeanne *project management company executive*
Woodson, Al Curtis *software company executive, software engineer*

Andersonville
Hall, Paul V. *company executive*
McCarthy, Timothy J. *company executive*

Athens
Golembiewski, Robert Thomas *public and business administration educator, consultant*
Hofer, Charles Warren *strategic management, entrepreneurship educator, consultant*
Jackson, Thomas Harold, Jr. *public relations administrator*
Lane, Walter Ronald, Jr. *advertising executive, educator*
McNiven, Malcolm Albert *marketing educator*
Whiteside, Jerry Eugene *human resources administrator, consultant*

Atlanta
Allio, Robert John *management consultant, educator*
Ashley, John Bryan *software executive, management consultant*
Barnett, Elizabeth Hale *organizational consultant*
Barrios, Roger *software company executive*
Bennett, Catherine June *data processing manager, educator, consultant*
Bergonzi, Al *company executive*
Bernhard, Harry Barnett *management consultant, educator*
Biggins, Paul Alexandre *marketing professional*
Brooks, Jeffrey Martin *marketing and sales executive*
Buoch, William Thomas *corporate executive*
Carter, Eric Vincent *marketing educator*
Clark, Edwin Green, Jr. *advertising agency executive*
Coady, William Francis *information services executive, consultant*
Coley, Barbara Yvonne *computer software consultant*
Cone, Frances McFadden *data processing consultant*
Conner, Patricia Ann *public relations executive*
Conrad, Edward Charles *trade shows producer*
Cornell, Jennifer A. *software company executive*
Delahanty, Edward Lawrence *management consultant*
Dysart, Benjamin Clay, III *consultant, conservationist, engineer*
Ehrlich, Jeffrey *data processing company executive*
Flammer, Carol Morgan *public relations specialist*
Fuqua, John Brooks *retired consumer products and services company executive*
Giarrano, Thomas *marketing executive*
Goldstein, Burton Benjamin, Jr. *communications executive*
Hall, J(ohn) Daniel, II *asset management consultant*
Hast-Lansdell, Joan Eileen *cellular communications manager*
Hessamfar, Elahe *communications executive*

Hoffman, Fred L. *human resources professional*
Holmes, Barry Trevor *business and cross cultural development consultant*
Hyle, Charles Thomas *marketing specialist*
Invester, M. Douglas *consumer products company executive*
Johnston, Wesley James *marketing educator, consultant*
Jolles, Scott Alan *advertising executive*
Jones, Walter Edward *management consultant*
Jorgensen, Alfred H. *computer software and data communications executive*
Kelly, Carol White *company executive*
Kent, Philip *communications executive*
Kingery, Terry Hall *sales professional*
Knapp, John Charles *public relations executive*
Laubscher, Robert James *consumer products company executive*
Leisy, William Bernard *management consultant*
Lian, Karl *corporate educator*
Marks, Marilyn *company executive*
Mashburn, Guerry Leonard *marketing professional*
Mashburn, Sylvia Anita Smith *public relations specialist*
McAteer, Deborah Grace *travel executive*
Miles, Robert Henry *management consultant, educator*
Mitchum, Donald C. *advertising executive*
Moore, Linda Kathleen *personnel agency executive*
Mullenix, Kathy Ann *relocation company executive*
Nelson, Linda Carol *corporate chief executive*
Pace, Wayne H. *communications executive*
Parr, Sandra Hardy *government affairs administrator*
Powers, Esther Safir *organization design consultant*
Reasoner, Elizabeth Diane *public relations executive*
Reed, Diane Gray *business information service company executive*
Resnik, Kim *communications executive*
Rink, Christopher Lee *information technology consultant, photographer*
Rogers, C. B., Jr. *information services executive*
Rollins, Gary Wayne *service company executive*
Rosenberg, George A. *public relations company executive*
Salay, Cindy Rolston *technical specialist, nurse*
Shelton, Robert Warren *marketing executive*
Sherrington, Paul William *marketing communications executive*
Siegel, Randy *public relations executive*
Smith, David Doyle *international management consultant, consulting engineer*
Summerlin, Glenn Wood *advertising executive*
Tomaszewski, Richard Paul *market representation specialist*
Toyne, Marguerite Castles *management consultant, business executive*
Treco-Jones, Sheryl Lynn *public relations professional*
Troop, Paul Melvin *public relations executive, journalist*
Vissicchio, Andrew John, Jr. *linen service company executive*
Wemmers, Frederick Richard, Jr. *advertising executive*
Wesley, James Wyatt, Jr. *communications company executive*
White, Jeff V. *information services company executive*
White, Norman Lee *marketing professional*
White, Ronald Leon *financial management consultant*
Wittenstein, Michael David *management consultant*
Wood, Andy *business executive*
Zunde, Pranas *information science educator, researcher*

Augusta
Duncan, Douglas Ronald, Jr. *golf company executive*
Mayfield, William Cary *personnel executive*

Blakely
Beaty, Thomas A. *business executive*
Bowen, John W. *business executive*

Buena Vista
Harris, Michelle Kaye *advertising executive, publishing executive*

Calhoun
Anderson, Amy Kinsey *sales executive, bridal consultant*
Ryberg, Thomas Carl *quality assurance professional*

College Park
Wright, William Michael *sales executive*

Columbus
Cartee, Marvin Lewis *corporate senior security officer*

Conyers
Dorsett, Patricia Jean Poole *business consultant*
Smith, William Lester *sales executive*

Cumming
Hodgson, Reginald Hutchins, Jr. *corporate executive*

Dalton
Anderson, Janice Gwendolyn *quality control professional*
Ashworth, Robert Vincent *data processing executive*

Darien
Akins, Kenneth Mauney *historic park manager*

Decatur
Becker, Robert Stephen *digital multimedia producer*
Berry, Charles Ross *sales/marketing executive*

Duluth
Johnson, Ralph Ronald *manufacturer's representative*
Masterson Raines, Judith Amanda *marketing executive*
Milaski, John Joseph *business transformation industry consultant*
Tate, Richard Albert *marketing research consultant*

Dunwoody
Kynerd, Marybeth *sales executive*

East Point
Dinwoodie, Roxan Emmert *marketing consultant*

Fairburn
Hankinson, Harriette Foster *amusement company executive*

Forest Park
JarAllah, Tajuddin Mufarridun Oluwatoyin *food service executive, chef*

Fort Benning
Alles, Rodney Neal, Sr. *information management executive*
Richardson, Eleanor Elizabeth *marketing professional*

Gainesville
Davis, Connie Waters *public relations and marketing executive*

Griffin
Marshall, Allen Wright, III *communications executive, financial consultant*

Hazlehurst
Welsh, Michael L. *business executive*

Hiram
Koopmann, Reta Collene *sales executive*

Jackson
Brookins, James Robert *customer service professional*

Kennesaw
Durkee, Karen Marie *marketing professional*

La Fayette
Thompson, Arthur Raymond *marketing professional*

Lawrenceville
Knight, Lila Cucksee *executive secretary, poet, school bus driver*

Mableton
Stalker, Suzy Wooster *human resources executive*

Macon
Gurley, Steven Harrison *sales executive*

Marietta
Bradshaw, Rod Eric *personnel consultant*
Condron, Gary *company executive*
Curtiss, Jeffery Steven *management consultant*
Gamblin, James E. *quality assurance specialist*
McNamara-Raisch, M. Eileen *marketing professional*
Needel, Stephen Paul *marketing research executive*
Reisner, Robert F. *software executive*
Rogers, Glenda Mae *quality assurance manager*
Smith, Beverly Ann Evans *performance management consultant*
Smith, Jeffrey Eugene *public relations executive*
Spann, Laura Nason *data processing executive*
Stone, Mary Alice *sales executive*

Mineral Bluff
Alexander, Patricia Ross *administrative assistant*

Mount Berry
Evans, Thomas Passmore *business and product licensing consultant*

Norcross
Emanuele, R.M. *business executive*
Flynn, Paul Arthur *marketing professional*
Jondahl, Terri Elise *importing and distribution company executive*
Mak, Kai-Kwong *hazardous waste company executive, engineer*
Mitchell, Ruth Ellen (Bunny Mitchell) *advertising executive*
Rogers, Richard Hilton *hotel company executive*
Sherwood, Kenneth Wesley *information systems executive, consultant*
Vitello, Robert Blair *sales executive*

Ocilla
Ross, Kenneth S. *business executive*

Oxford
Stamps, George Moreland *communications consultant, facsimile pioneer*

Peachtree City
Price, Caroline Leona *personnel consulting company executive*

Riverdale
Lane, Linda Lee *landscape company executive*

Robins AFB
Corley, Rose Ann McAfee *customer service representative*

Roswell
Dudley, Perry, Jr. *business executive*
Guiness, Steven *sales executive*
Holder, Susan McCaskill *computer company executive, small business owner*
Jaric, Robert Ronald *business executive*
Myrmo, Erik *computer company executive*
Wells, Rona Lee *consumer products company executive*

Saint Simons
Clay, Ryburn Glover, Jr. *resort executive*
Dressner, Paul Robert *outside sales and customer service representative*

Savannah
Highsmith, Anna Bizzell *executive secretary*
Lindqvist, Gunnar Jan *management consultant, international trade consultant*
Priester, Horace Richard, Jr. *quality assurance professional*
Salgueiro, Alex *restaurant executive*
Vantrease, Alice Twiggs *marketing executive*

Statesboro
Rompf, Paul Douglas *hotel and restaurant administration educator*

Stockbridge
Williams, Kristina (Michelle Spurrier) *executive secretary*

Stone Mountain
Dalton, James Carroll *market research professional*
Knight, Delos Lavern, Jr. *public relations executive*

Sugar Hill
Jordan, Henry Hellmut, Jr. *management consultant*

Tifton
Hill, La Joyce Carmichael *marketing professional*

Tucker
Broucek, William Samuel *printing plant executive*
Manley, Lance Filson *data processing consultant*
Wiseman, Rose Freschman *public relations executive*

Union City
Graham, John Hamilton, II *customer service specialist*

ILLINOIS

Chicago
Brandt, William Arthur, Jr. *consulting executive*

INDIANA

Princeton
Jenkins, Robert Lee *information system specialist*

IOWA

Davenport
Johnson, Frank William *marketing professional*

KENTUCKY

Albany
Smith, Eugenia Sewell *funeral home executive*

Anchorage
Martin, Mary Evelyn *advertising, marketing and business writing consultant*

Ashland
Carter, David Edward *communications executive*

Bardstown
Willett, A. L. Thompson *public relations executive, consultant*

Campbellsville
Whitt, Marcus Calvin *public relations and marketing executive*

Covington
Surber, David Francis *public affairs consultant, journalist, television producer*

Danville
Votaw, Donald Gene *quality assurance professional*

Elizabethtown
Polis, Sheri Helene *marketing and education professional*

Flatwoods
Willis, Dwayne David *information systems consultant*

Florence
Maxfield, Anne M. *sales executive*

Fort Thomas
Korotkin, Audrey Rhona *communications executive*
Patton, L(ewis) K(ay) *advertising agency executive, educator*

Franklin
Herndon, Wallace Eugene, Jr. *human resources manager*

Hopkinsville
Neville, Thomas Lee *food service company executive*

Lexington
Blanchard, Richard Emile, Sr. *management services executive, consultant*
Cashman, John A. *business executive*
Clark, Joseph H. *executive*
Dorio, Martin Matthew *material handling company executive*
Fugazzi, Paul Anthony *sales executive*
Kuvzinske, Richard *company executive*
Millard, James Kemper *marketing executive*
Nichols, Rick *business executive*
Preston, Thomas Lyter *public relations executive, crisis management, anti-terrorism consultant*
Scharlatt, Harold *management company executive*

Louisville
Bergwerk, Jack Edward *retired sales executive consultant*
Charley, Nancy Jean *communications professional*
Cranor, John *food service executive*
Everett, Elbert Kyle *marketing executive, consultant*
Lega, Nicholas Robert *information systems specialist*
Louden, Victoria Anhalt *public relations professional*
Osborn, Rita Deisenroth *public relations executive*
Wilson, Dewey Errol *sales and marketing executive*

Mammoth Cave
Smith, Margaret Gretel *park ranger*

Murray
Jackson, Robert L. *skincare products company executive*
Olson, Donald George *computer services administrator*

New Hope
Stearns, Joseph T. *printing company supervisor*

Nicholasville
Fain, Howard Douglas *mortician*

Richmond
Chamberlin, Shelia Diane *office administrator*

LOUISIANA

Alexandria
Glass, Vicky Lynn Rhame *office manager*
Richmond, Angie Anna Alice Murray *administrative assistant*
Turner, R(alph) Chip *public relations and telecommunications executive, religious studies educator*

Baton Rouge
Brent, Allan Rudolph *advertising agency executive*
Crusemann, F(rederick) Ross *advertising agency official*
East, Charles E., Jr. *advertising and public relations executive*
Friedman, George *business intelligence executive*
Morris, Susan Steers *service executive*
Stalder, Richard L. *executive secretary*
Williams-Daly, Angelia Evette *marketing executive, small business owner*

Belle Chasse
Yandle, Sylvester Elwood, II *sales executive, inventor*

Chauvin
Dagg, Mike *business executive*

Crowley
Martin, Edythe Louviere *business educator*

Gretna
Norton, Robert Dillard, Jr. *marketing professional*

Kaplan
Frederick, Myrna Sue LaBry *sales executive, beauty consultant*

Kenner
Marullo, Michael Anthony *marketing consultant*

Lafayette
Baudoin, Peter *family business consultant*
Love, Frances Taylor *public relations consultant*

Lake Charles
Sasser, Patricia Jane *sales executive*

Metairie
Allen, Peggy Graffignia *data processing consultant*
Doody, Barbara Pettett *computer specialist*
Gereighty, Andrea Saunders *polling company executive, poet*
Goss, Donald Davis *consultant, author, lecturer*
Klein, Bernard J. *management specialist*
Smith, Arthur Morgan *public relations executive*

New Orleans
Allerton, William, III *public relations executive*
Bacot, Marie *management consultant, researcher*
Barden, Janice Kindler *personnel company executive*
Feran, Russell G. *sales executive*
Fertel, Ruth U. *restaurant owner*
Fosberg, Barry L. *research consultant*
Johnson, Arnold Ray *public relations executive*
Kirtley, Michelle Diane *training and development company executive*
Silva, Donna Steedle *coffee service company official*
Tahir, Mary Elizabeth *retail marketing and management consultant*

Shreveport
Buckman, Mary Warner *promotions and public relations executive*
Sorrels, James Robert *computer company executive*
Stewart, Lynn Beard *public relations executive*
Trusty, Gregg Kenneth, Sr. *public information director, magazine editor*

Slidell
Blackburn, Traci Michelle *public relations assistant*

Thibodaux
Hoffmann, Mary Anne *music company executive, consultant*

MAINE

Augusta
Jacobson, James Lamma, Jr. *data processing company executive*

MARYLAND

Annapolis
Hagood, Wesley Olan *management consultant*

Baltimore
Weger, William John *public relations executive*

Bethesda
Estrin, Melvyn J. *computer products company executive*
Kelly, Thomas Joseph *information systems specialist*

Hyattsville
Bisher, Jamie Furman *intelligence and security analyst, writer*

Seabrook
Macfarlane, David Gordon *defense systems design and development executive*

MASSACHUSETTS

Waltham
Kasputys, Joseph Edward *corporate executive, economist*

MICHIGAN

Grosse Pointe
LaNier-Gesell, Mary Catherine (Kitty LaNier) *public relations, advertising and marketing executive*

MISSISSIPPI

Bay Saint Louis
Kokessch, Allen J. *entertaiment industry executive*
Torguson, Marlin F. *entertainment company executive*
Winchester, Sam Allen *computer systems specialist*

Biloxi
Ernst, James E. *company executive*
Noland, Anginette Roberts *retired sales executive*

Booneville
Jackson, Bobby Charles *consumer products company executive*

Bruce
Young, Billy Devon *communications executive*

Carriere
Woodmansee, Glenn Edward *employee relations executive*

Clarksdale
Flowers, Judith Ann *marketing and public relations director*

Columbus
Holt, Robert Ezel *data processing executive*

Gautier
Farrior, Charles Warrick *adminstrative contracting officer*

Greenwood
Ricks, John Paul *management consultant*

Hattiesburg
Schoell, William Frederick, III *marketing educator*
Watkins, Cathy Collins *corporate purchasing agent*

Jackson
Berry, Linda Tomlinson *international communications corporation executive*
Gunn, Frank Michael *direct marketing professional*
McCreery, James Allan *business services company executive*
Skelton, Gordon William *data processing executive, educator*

Meridian
Cole, James Mariner, Jr. *warehouse executive*

Olive Branch
Frischenmeyer, Michael Leo *sales executive*

Philadelphia
Molpus, Dick H. *resource management company executive*

Southaven
Thompson-Stafford, Betty *secretary*

Stennis Space Center
Sprouse, Susan Rae Moore *human resources specialist*

Tupelo
Jones, Bobbye Franks *state public works administrator*

Vicksburg
Neilsen, Craig H. *business executive*

MISSOURI

Saint Louis
Moseley, Marc Robards *sales executive*

NEVADA

Las Vegas
Cronk, Denis Steven *human resources educator, researcher, writer*

NEW JERSEY

Marlboro
Frank, William Fielding *computer systems design executive, consultant*

NEW MEXICO

Albuquerque
Geary, David Leslie *communications executive, educator, consultant*

NEW YORK

New York
Hardin, James Edmond *executive recruiter*
McNally, Jay Michael *computer company executive, consultant*

Pittsford
Schramek, Lynn Beth Gottlieb *communications executive*

NORTH CAROLINA

Asheville
Myer, John Daniel, II *restaurant executive*
Turcot, Marguerite Hogan *innkeeper, medical researcher*

Boone
Goddard, Robert DeForest, III *management administrator, consultant*
Palmer, Sherry Regina Lee *human resource specialist*
Parker, William Dale *management consultant, political adviser*
Patton, Wesley Ennis, III *marketing educator*

Burlington
Eddins, James William, Jr. *marketing executive*

Canton
Dixon, Shirley Juanita *restaurant owner*

Carolina Beach
Wooten, Jon Charles *sales executive*

Cary
Wait, George William *sales executive*

Chapel Hill
Hill, Robert Folwell, Jr. *information systems specialist*
Swanson, Michael Alan *sales and marketing executive*
Williams, John Trent *public policy company executive*

Charlotte
Coffin, H(arris) Alexander *public relations executive, educator*
Counts, Connie Brown *executive secretary*
Harris, Ernest Clay, Sr. *marketing consultant, engineer*
Hudgins, Catherine Harding *business executive*
Kallman, Kathleen Barbara *marketing and business development professional*
Kopatich, William Edward *computer company executive*
Loeffler, William George, Jr. *advertising executive*
Lyerly, Elaine Myrick *advertising executive*
Mascavage, Joseph Peter *sales executive*
Perkowitz, Robert Michael *management executive, consultant*
Perlmutter, Barry Arthur *marketing and sales engineering executive*
Sanford, James Kenneth *public relations executive*
Scarborough, Frances Songer *marketing executive, consultant, public speaker*
Simpson, Jerry Howard, Jr. *travel company executive*
Suter, George August *management and marketing consultant*
Walker, Robert Bernard *sports executive*
Williams, M. Jane *marketing and sales executive*
Wilson, Barnett Ronald *sales specialist, writer*

Clayton
Williams, David Loren *employment interviewer*

Clemmons
Mabe, R. Keith *marketing executive*

Clinton
Fetterman, Annabelle *packing company executive*

Cullowhee
Kane, William Duncan, Jr. *management educator*

Durham
Ladd, Marcia Lee *medical equipment and supplies company executive*
Lieberman, Rochelle Phyllis *relocation company executive*
St. Wecker, Peter Grant Reeves *pharmaceutical clinical research executive*
Taylor, James Francis *marketing professional*
Tsang, William Xue-Ting *computer company executive*

Edenton
Rossman, Robert Harris *management consultant*

Elkin
Walker, R. Tracy *personnel director*

Fletcher
Sherman, Malcolm Charles *business consultant*
Summey, Steven Michael *advertising company executive*

Garner
Barbour, Charlene *management firm executive*

Gastonia
Eads, Ronald Preston *management consultant*
Eddings, James Dean *data processing executive*
Wood, Larry Wayne *human resources executive, city manager*

Goldsboro
Barkley, Monika Johanna *quality control professional*

Greensboro
Andrews, Jo Boney *corporate communications manager*
Charles, Howard Clifton, Jr. *public warehousing executive*
Kerley, Janice Johnson *personnel executive*
Sanders, William Eugene *marketing executive*
Sullivan, John James, Jr. *sales executive*

Greenville
Finkelday, John Paul *retail sales executive*
Guest, Donald Britnor *marketing educator*
Robinson, Robert Arthur *telecommunications marketing administrator*

Hickory
Davis, Tom Ivey, II *management executive*
Hilton, Deanie Herman *human resources executive, telecommunications manager*

High Point
Winn, Walter Garnett, Jr. *marketing strategist, advertising executive*

Jefferson
Van Arnam, Mark Stephen *sales executive*

Matthews
Allen, Robert English *business development executive, consultant*

Morrisville
Wallace, Richard Lea *marketing professional*

North Wilkesboro
Herring, Leonard Gray *marketing company executive*

Pine Knoll Shores
Griffin, Thomas Lee, Jr. *industrial and federal government specialist*

Pinehurst
Grantham, Joseph Michael, Jr. *hotel executive, management and marketing consultant*
Young, James Vincent *international business consultant*

Pisgah Forest
Powers, Jack W. *development executive*
Pulliam, Steve Cameron *sales executive*

Raleigh
Butler, Carol King *advertising executive*
Cook, Norma Baker *consulting company executive*
Copulsky, Lewis *marketing professional*
Doherty, Robert Cunningham *advertising executive*
Grigereit, Hugh Reeves, Jr. *industrial relations executive*
Hatcher, Bruce Alderman *entertainment event company executive*
Holt, J. Darrin *corporate executive*
Hutchison, Humphrey Gray *retired compensation and benefits consulting company executive*
Larsen, Eric Lyle *data processing executive, author, consultant*
Lewis, Richard Jay *marketing educator, university dean*
Mowrey, Timothy James *management and financial consultant*
Nelson, Cynthia Kaye *training professional*
Oakley, Wanda Faye *management consultant, educator*
Poole, George William *human resources specialist, consultant*
Reynolds, Sidney Rae *marketing communications executive*
Robinson, Keith *sales and marketing executive*
Roisler, Glenn Harvey *quality assurance professional*
Waugaman, Paul Gray *management consultant*

Reidsville
Hutchens, Ruby R. *executive secretary*

Research Triangle Park
Clark, Kevin Anthony *communications executive*
Hamner, Charles *company executive*
Hart, Frank *company executive*
Sumney, Larry W. *research company executive*
Tracy, Philip R. *computer company executive*

Rocky Mount
Polk, Ronald Thomas *marketing executive*

Rural Hall
Wager, Michael *company executive*

Sanford
Schneider, Steven L. *company executive*

Skyland
Miller, Joseph Alfred *printing executive*

Statesville
Grogan, David R. *company executive*

Trenton
Brown, Clifton *business executive*

Welcome
Walters, Sylvia Annette *public relations and communications executive*

Wilmington
Flohr, Daniel P. *company executive*
Lees, Anthony Philip *business consultant*
Norako, Vincent Walter, Sr. *marketing executive*

Wilson
Dean, Tad *research laboratory executive*
Mulkey, Carrole Anne *marketing communications professional*

Winston Salem
Cartee, Thomas Edward, Jr. *financial consultant*
Griswold, George *marketing, advertising and public relations executive*
Guin, Debra Mauriece *sales executive*
Hamlin, Edwin Cliburn *account executive*
Jackson, Mae Boger *executive adminstrative assistant, secretary*
Johnston, James Wesley *retired tobacco company executive*
Walker, Wendy K. *marketing executive*
Wolfe, Nancy Beals *public relations executive, educator*

OHIO

Cleveland
Burmester, Joseph Kirk *information technology executive, consultant*

Dayton
Dreckshage, Brian Jeffrey *materials manager*

OKLAHOMA

Ada
Mildren, Jack *legal services company executive, former state official*

Altus
Wilcoxen, Joan Heeren *fitness company executive*

Broken Arrow
Everett, Carl Nicholas *management consulting executive*

Cheyenne
Kahoa, Linda Lou *public relations consultant*

Edmond
Ackerman, Bruce Ainslie *public relations professional*
Boyd, Bill Gerald *business executive*
Keckel, Peter J. *advertising executive*

Maysville
Robinson, Richard Duane *oil and gas leasor*

Miami
Dicharry, James Paul *company official, retired air force officer*

Midwest City
Taylor, Woodrow Manning *computer company executive, military officer*

Mustang
Laurent, J(erry) Suzanna *technical communications specialist*

Norman
Carver, Charles Ray *retired information systems company executive*
Smith, Micah Pearce, Jr. *advertising executive*
Wren, Daniel Alan *business management educator*

Oklahoma City
Adams, Warren Lynn *publisher, business consultant*
Bailey, Clark Trammell, II *public relations/public affairs professional*
Blackwell, John Adrian, Jr. *computer company executive*
Burke, Kieran E. *business executive*
Burns, Marion G. *management consultant, retired council executive*
Crow, Charles Delmar *human resources manager, consultant*
Dang, James Bac *business planner, educator*
Dozier, L(awrence) Dow *public relations executive*
Grupe, Robert Charles *corporate training consultant*
Heuser, Oscar Edward *marketing professional*
Hollander, Luella Jean *public relations executive, educator*
Huff, Dennis Lyle *marketing professional*
Jones, Brenda Kaye *public relations executive*
Peters, John *sales executive*
Ruhrup, Clifton Brown *sales executive*
Smith, Debra Ann *advertising executive*
Stauth, Robert E. *food service executive*
Story, Gary *business executive*
Stricklin, James Thomas, II *sales executive*
Webb, Randy *business executive*
Worthington, J.B. *business executive*

Perkins
Sasser, William David *advertising company executive*

Perry
Shaffer, David Ellsworth *marketing executive*

Tulsa
Davis, Lourie Irene Bell *computer education and systems specialist*
Geen, Tim Dow *restaurant executive*
Goldsmith, H. Randall *management consultant*
Naumann, William Carl *consumer products company executive*
Parks, Andrea Marrotte *public relations executive*
Robertson, Vicki Dawn *adminstrative secretary, writer*
Sellers, Joanne Grant *community relations executive*
Shaft, Teresa Marie *data processing educator*
Stirling, Douglas Bleecker, Jr. *human resources specialist*
Wright, Patricia Ann *advertising consultant*

PENNSYLVANIA

Reading
Lane, James Hamilton *quality assurance executive*

SOUTH CAROLINA

Aiken
Howell, Jennifer Chandler *human resources representative*

Anderson
Alexander, Arthur Frank *sales executive*
Rivers, Otis Thomas *sales executive*
Vaughan, Dennis J. *business executive*

Beaufort
Yarbrough, Sonja Dianne *marketing and public relations professional*

Camden
Davis, Paul Michael *sales executive*

Fowler, Sharmila Mathur *marketing and planning executive*

Charleston
Dowell, Richard Patrick *computer company executive*
Hassell, John Fleming, III *business consulting company executive*
Milkereit, John Eugene *public relations and marketing executive, consultant*
Perry, Evelyn Reis *communications company executive*

Clemson
LaForge, Mary Cecile *marketing educator*
Moore, Emma Sims *executive secretary*

Columbia
Duggan, Kevin *information systems specialist*
Ferillo, Charles Traynor, Jr. *public relations executive*
Floyd, Frank Albert, Jr. *management executive*
Fort, Claire Caudill *business development executive*
Goble, Robert Thomas *planning consultant*
Gore, David Curtiss *software company executive, consultant*
Grimball, Caroline Gordon *sales professional*
Hayes, Rebecca Anne *communications professional*
Jaco, Thomas Wright *hazardous materials administrator*
Meehan, Mark William *college executive assistant*
Owen, Dorothy *company executive*
Quinn, Michael William *public affairs specialist*
Reynolds, Nancy F. *public relations counselor, registered nurse*
Sears, Gordon Mortimer *public relations consultant*

Elloree
Dantzler, J.A. *business executive*

Florence
Bethea, Edward Evans *public relations executive*

Greenville
Carlson, Bruce Herbert *interim personnel company executive*
Cribb, Deborah Ann *public relations executive*
Finch, Roger Dean *labor activist, legislative administrator*
Gerretsen, Gilbert Wynand (Gil Gerretsen) *marketing and management consultant*
Leahy, Robert David *communications executive*
Meade, Rex Lee *consulting firm executive, counselor*
Morton, James Carnes, Jr. *public relations executive*

Greer
Dawkins, David Michael *data processing executive*

Hartsville
Cecil, Allan *corporate communications executive*
Gruene, Peter Hans *environmental services administrator*

Hilton Head Island
Butler, Howard Edward *quality assurance professional*
Coble, Paul Ishler *advertising agency executive*
Haley, Cain Calmes *computer consultant*
McDowell, Theodore Noyes *public relations consultant*
Winkler, H. Donald *public relations executive*

Irmo
Carder, Larry William *display and exhibit executive*

Lake City
TruLuck, John M. *business executive*

Lake Wylie
Buggie, Frederick Denman *management consultant*

Lexington
Bruce, Samuel Byrd *management consultant*

Lugoff
Clow, Thomas James *quality professional*

Mauldin
Frank, Myra Linden *consultant*

Mount Pleasant
Hill, Larkin Payne *real estate company data processing executive*

Myrtle Beach
Brittain, Clay D. *golf club executive*
Hale, W. Thomas *golf club executive*

Ridgeland
Gardner, James *recreational management executive, personal care industry executive*

Simpsonville
Zerfoss, Lester Frank *management consultant, educator*

Spartanburg
Adamson, James B. *business executive*
King, David Steven *quality control executive*

York
White, Bruce Emerson, Jr. *restaurant chain executive*

TENNESSEE

Brentwood
Hall, Lucinda Genevieve Long *public relations executive, writer*
McMahon, Donna Marie *travel agency executive*
Mitchell, Kimberly Jean *human resources director*
Power, Elizabeth Henry *consultant*
Regel, Terry Lynn *quality systems administrator*

Chattanooga
De Riemer, Daniel Louis *leasing company executive*
Goodman, Michael Frederick *advertising executive*
Rinehart, James Forrest *sales executive*
Whitt, John *company executive*

Cleveland
Priaulx, David Lloyd *marketing executive*

Collierville
Shepard, Raymond Guy *purchasing executive*

Cordova
McKinney, William Douthitt, Jr. *sales and engineering company executive*

Crossville
Roe, Michael Henry *computer specialist, business manager*

Dandridge
Cagle, John B. *marketing educator*

Dyersburg
Baker, Kerry Allen *executive business recruiter*

Erwin
Baer, Thomas Strickland *environmental company executive*

Franklin
Berkowitz, Ralph Steven *business executive*

Gallatin
Bradley, Nolen Eugene, Jr. *personnel executive, educator*

Gatlinburg
Flanagan, Judith Ann *marketing and entertainment specialist*

Germantown
Mehaffey, Robert Anderson *company executive, sales consultant*
Pruitt, Gary Wayne *human resources professional*

Hermitage
Amiot, David Bruce *information officer*

Jackson
Cunningham, Brenton Jon *marketing educator*
Slaughter, Phillip Howard *computer company executive*

Kingsport
McKinley, John Henry *sales executive*

Knoxville
Alexander, Burt Edward *quality improvement consultant, management consultant*
Bissonette, William Theadore, Sr. *executive recruiter*
Castleberry Roberts, Sharon Elaine *business consultant*
Drennen, Jean Cobble *retired public relations executive, linguist*
Herndon, Anne Harkness *sales executive*
Siler, Susan Reeder *communications educator*
Toedte, Sharon Lynn Simon *marketing professional*

Maryville
Davis, William (Walter) *recruiter, trainer*

Memphis
Boerschmann, James F. *hotel executive*
Burgess, Robert Ronald *human resources executive*
Driscoll, James Joseph, Jr. *advertising executive*
Dunn, David John *human resources executive*
Hogan, Cecil Everett *security company executive*
Krieger, Robert Lee, Jr. *management consultant, educator, writer, political analyst*
Linder, Ann Laura *marketing administrator*
Mann, Donald Cameron *marketing company executive*
Pulido, Miguel Lazaro *marketing professional*
Shands, Jack L. *human resource executive, lawyer*
Weatherford, Keith Anderson *information system specialist*
Webb, Lynne McGovern *communication educator, consultant*
Young, Ernestine Jones *retired postal clerk*
Ziets, George A. *consumer products company executive*

Millington
O'Connor, Dennis *business executive*

Moscow
Kaler, Gervis Wilton *quality assurance professional*

Murfreesboro
Mitchell, Jerry Calvin *environmental company executive*

Nashville
Ambrose, Charles Stuart *sales executive*
Caldwell, Donald Wilson *communications executive*
Chism, Mark Thomas *computer company project leader*
Claughton, Hugh Dawson, Sr. *cruise company executive, veterinarian*
Cristina, Francis McDermott (Frank Cristina) *corporate security company executive*
Dobbs, George Albert *funeral director, embalmer*
Dorland, John Howard *international management consultant*
Fields, Billy Wayne *executive assistant*
Hepker, Robert Eugene *environmental executive*
Jackson, Lady Loyd Appleby *personnel executive*
James, Kay Louise *management consultant, healthcare executive*
Jones, Regi Wilson *data processing executive*
Lee, Robert Justin *information systems programmer and analyst*
Lightner, A. LeRoy, Jr. *advertising agency executive*
Meredith, Owen Nichols *public relations executive, genealogist*
Moore, William Grover, Jr. *management consultant, former air freight executive, former air force officer*
Patterson, James Thurston *marketing executive, consultant*
Phipps, Tony Randell *advertising production consultant, singer, record producer*
Short, Sallie Lee *physical plant service worker*
Stewart, Jenise Dorene *sales executive*
Stockell, Albert W., III *information systems analyst, accountant*

Wendell, Earl W. *entertainment company executive*

Oak Ridge
Creech, Donna Lothel *public relations executive*
Kuhaida, Andrew Jerome, Jr. *environmental manager*
O'Hara, Frederick M., Jr. *technical communications consultant, information specialist*

Shelbyville
Yates, Patricia England *employment company executive*

Soddy Daisy
Dall, Peter Andrew *management and organizational consultant*

Watauga
Fair, Steve Edward *pharmaceutical marketing executive*

TEXAS

Allen
Williams, Marvin *management consultant*

Amarillo
Borchardt, Paul Douglas *recreational executive*
Dunn, Jim Edward *sales executive*
Mize, Johnny Edwin *risk management information systems company executive*

Argyle
Erwin, Val L. *business executive*
Merritt, Joe Frank *industrial supply executive*

Arlington
Farci, Andre *business executive*
Harris, Vera Evelyn *personnel recruiting and search firm executive*
Henderson, Arvis Burl *data processing executive, biochemist*
Rainey, Robert Edward *human resources management consultant*
Wiig, Karl Martin *knowledge management expert and consultant*
Worrell, Dan L. *management educator*

Austin
Braasch, Steven Mark *advertising executive*
Buchanan, Randal Thomas *supplier relations director*
Casey, James Francis *management consultant*
Cloutier, Madison Joseph *software company executive*
Collier, Steven Edward *management consultant*
Coore, Bill *company executive*
Curle, Robin Lea *computer software industry executive*
Dabbs, Jeanne McCluer Kernodle *retired public relations executive*
Devenport, John Thomas, Jr. *public relations professional*
Duplantier, Dawn Elizabeth *communications director*
Friedman, Susan Lynn Bell *community relations specialist*
Howard, Dean Allen *purchasing agent*
Ludeman, Kate *human resources consultant*
Lundgren, Clara Eloise *public affairs administrator, journalist*
Maguire, Kevin *travel management consultant*
McCann, James Todd *marketing professional*
Morgante, John-Paul *state government training administrator*
Muenzler, Kendell Dean *purchasing manager, city government administrator*
Palmer, Daisy Ann *marketing coordinator*
Pate, Jacqueline Hail *retired data processing company executive*
Rector, Clark Ellsworth *advertising executive*
Reynolds, Don William, Jr. *computer software company executive, financial analyst*
Shaw, James *computer systems analyst*
Shipley, George Corless *political consultant*
Skaggs, James B. *executive*
Smith, Barry Alan *hotel executive*
Talbot, Alfred Wayne, Jr. *human resources executive*
Vandel, Diana Geis *management consultant*
Walls, Carl Edward, Jr. *communications company official*
Young, Harrison, II *software development and marketing executive*

Beaumont
Harrison, Thomas W. *company executive*

Bedford
Purdon, Kevin Eric *food service executive*

Bellaire
Nunnelee, John Roger *pharmaceutical marketing professional*

Big Sandy
Delamater, Thomas Robert *public relations and fundraising executive*

Brownsville
Boze, Betsy Vogel *marketing educator, dean*

Bryan
Gulledge, Richard D. (Dick Gulledge) *security firm executive, consultant*
Pearce, Stephen Lamar *management consultant*

Canyon
Carpenter, Bette Joan *business educator*

Carrollton
Graham, Richard Douglas *computer company executive, consultant*
Saur, Ronald Garlin *personal and organizational development specialist*

Carthage
Ivey, Sharon Elizabeth Thurman *sales executive*

Cleveland
Rice, J. Andrew *management consultant, tree farmer*

College Station
Evans, Carol Ann Butler *administrative assistant*
Hitchens, Duncan *company executive*
Leigh, James Henry *marketing educator*
Szymanski, David Mark *marketing specialist, educator*
Varadarajan, Poondi Rajan *marketing educator*

Colleyville
Compo, Lawrence Judd *sales and marketing executive*
Thompson, James Richard *human resources management consultant*

Comfort
DeFoore, John Norris *management consultant*

Coppell
Rehm, Bobby Lee *marketing executive*

Corpus Christi
Fox, Ruth Ellen *personal care industry executive*

Cypress
Laird, William David *manufacturing executive*

Dallas
Aars, Rallin James *management and marketing communications executive*
Baxter, Gregory Wayne *human resources consultant*
Benn, Douglas Frank *information technology, computer science executive*
Bennett, Verna Green *employee relations executive*
Bolton, Kevin Michael *human resources executive*
Bowman, James Robert *communications and public relations executive*
Buccino, Marguerite *management consultant, free lance writer*
Caffee, Virginia Maureen *secretary*
Caldwell, Paula Day *telecommunications executive*
Carl, Robert E. *retired marketing company executive*
Cave, Skip *company executive*
Conrad, Suzanne Lane *marketing professional, organization administrator*
Curry, Richard Gilbert, Jr. *information systems specialist*
Cyran, William John *marketing professional*
Dalton, Harry Jirou, Jr. *public relations executive*
Dodson, George W. *computer company executive, consultant*
Drury, John E. *retired waste management company executive*
Elam, Andrew Gregory, II *convention and visitors bureau executive*
Eyerman, David John *computer company administrator*
Filbin, Charles Everett *loss control representative*
Flores, Marion Thomas *advertising executive*
Frerichs, Edwin Nathan *retail planning consultant*
Fullingim, John Powers *consulting firm executive*
Gardner, Stanley Dwain *communications company executive*
Gossen, Emmett Joseph, Jr. *motel chain executive, lawyer*
Graber, Harris David *sales executive*
Grote, Richard Charles *management consultant, educator, radio commentator*
Gruer, William E. *management consultant*
Halpin, James F. *business executive*
Harkness, R. Kenneth *restaurant chain executive*
Hayes, Michael Bernard *sales executive*
Hennelly, Kay Elizabeth *travel agency executive*
Heydrick, Linda Carol *consulting company executive, editor*
Hopkins, Patricia Anne (Tracy) *advertising agency executive*
Hopson, Mary Louise Carstens *marketing consultant*
Jeffreys, Charles Wayne *advertising executive*
Jones, Rosemarie Frieda *service executive*
Keath, (Martin) Travis *business valuation consultant*
Keith, Camille Tigert *airline marketing executive*
Leigh-Manuell, Robert Allen *training executive, educator*
Lersch, DeLynden Rife *computer engineering executive*
Lombard, Mitchell Monte *marketing professional*
Loveless, Kathy Lynne *client services executive*
Lucier, James Alfred *advertising executive*
Luna, Cherry Martin *marketing professional*
Madden, Marie Frances *marketing professional*
McCabe, Tom *advertising executive*
McPherson, Gail *advertising and real estate executive*
Meek, Charles Ronald, II *human resources professional*
Morrison-Carbone, Dawn Elizabeth *communications director*
Murphy, Randall Kent *training consultant*
Osborn, Jacqueline Elizabeth *water treatment systems company executive*
Pace, Carolina Jolliff *communications executive, commercial real estate investor*
Pacheco, Margaret Mary *marketing executive*
Papermaster, Barry A. *marketing and sales executive*
Parmerlee, Mark S. *food service executive*
Pratt, Jack E., Sr. *hotel executive*
Pratt, Jack E., Jr. *hotel and casino executive*
Pruzzo, Judith Josephine *office manager*
Rose, Charles David *consulting company executive*
Rosene, Linda Roberts *organizational consultant, researcher*
Routman, Daniel Glenn *marketing professional, lawyer*
Salerno, Philip Adams *information systems specialist*
Saville, R. Allen *management consultant*
Scragg, George Henry, Jr. *marketing executive*
Smith, Jerry Don *food service executive*
Solomon, Risa Greenberg *video software industry executive*
Sozio, Marquita Lynelle *travel manager, educator*
Spaeth, David Hollingsworth *corporate planner, consultant*
Staber, Dorothee Beatrice *administrative assistant*
Tate, Sharon Sue *special events and catering executive*
Thomas, Robert Ray *management consultant*
Van Horn, Trenda R. *retail marketing management executive, consultant*
Walenta, Ronald James *risk management consultant*
Walter, Gary Steven *hotel manager*
Walton, Chester Lee, Jr. *management consultant*
Waters, Rollie Odell *management consultant*

Webb, James Robert *strategic management consultant*
Wyman, Richard Thomas *information services consultant*
Zelsmann, Michael Joseph *advertising executive*
Zorn, Robert Eugene *software company executive*

Denton
Welch, Joe Lloyd *marketing educator*

Diboll
Huber, Herbert Eugene *human resource development consultant*

Dyess AFB
Lawson, Melanie Kay *management administrator, early childhood consultant*

Eastland
Quinn, Janita Sue *city secretary*

Edinburg
De Los Santos, Gilberto *marketing educator*

El Paso
Gillis, Richard Paul *management consultant*
Straughan, Carol Annette *human resource director*
Stuart, Alexander James, Jr. *executive*

Euless
Self, Mark Edward *communications consultant*

Farmers Branch
Barley, Stephen W. *company executive*
Somereve, Margaret Mary *administrative assistant, political campaigner*

Fort Worth
Anderson, Joan Wellin Freed *communications executive, consultant, freelance journalist, writer*
Baine, Burton H. *company executive*
Brooks, Mark D. *company executive*
Brown, Janet McNalley *retirement plan consultant*
Butcher, Harry William *security and investigation company executive*
Dagnon, James Bernard *human resources executive*
Lanier, James Newton *marketing executive*
Livengood, Charlotte Louise *employee development specialist*
McHenry, William Irvin *marketing executive*
Michalski, Jeanne Ann *human resources professional*
Owens, Merle Wayne *executive search consultant*
Park, Beth Guenzel *public relation professional*
Poole, Anita Joyce *marketing and publishing company executive*
Rudolph, Deborah Ann *materials management executive*
Spears, Georgann Wimbish *marketing executive*

Galena Park
Joseph, Gerald Wayne *director parks and recreation, consultant*

Galveston
May, Joy Elaine *recreational facility executive*

Garland
Freeman-Landgraf, Dolores J. *administrative assistant*
Reimer, Keith Brian *sales executive, marketing professional*
Sims, Judy *software company executive*

Grand Prairie
Cunningham, Thomas Craig *human resources professional*
Sallee, Bill *business consultant*
Vanbebber, Michael Craig *public relations executive*

Grapevine
Holley, Cyrus Helmer *management consulting service executive*
Micklow, Craig Woodward *marketing and financial executive*

Greenville
Brown, Harley Mitchell *retired computer company executive, writer*

Hereford
Griffin, A. T. *advertising and agricultural products executive*

Hillsboro
Stovall, Steven Austin *human resources administrator*

Houston
Ables, Nancy Bumstead *sales executive*
Adams, C. Lee *marketing executive*
Barnhill, Stephen Fuller *advertising executive*
Berchelmann, D. Kevin *management consultant*
Bergman, Andrew James *quality control consultant*
Billick, L. Larkin *marketing executive*
Bodner, Emanuel *industrial recycling company executive*
Bostic, Jacqueline Whiting *management consultant, retired postmaster, association executive*
Bullock, Jerry D. *company executive*
Burnett, Susan Walk *personnel service company owner*
Croxall, Mark Y., II *advertising executive*
Crystal, Jonathan Andrew *executive recruiter*
Dobbs, Rita Marie *travel company executive*
Eckhardt, Robert Fuess *safety and environmental director*
Finch, Diane Shields *retail sales administrator*
Flato, William Roeder, Jr. *software development company executive*
Halter, Kyle William *marketing professional*
Hodge, Ann F. *environmental company executive*
Hughes, William Joseph *management consultant*
Hux, Robert C. *company executive*
Jenkin, Douglas Alan *computer consultant*
Jones, Sonia Josephine *advertising agency executive*
Kaye, Howard *business executive*
King, Carl Edward *employee screening executive*
King, James A. *executive*
Koby, William A. *company executive, lawyer*
Kramm, Deborah Ann *data processing executive*
Krueger, Artur W. G. *international business consultant*
Landureth, Lewis James (Jim Landureth) *communications executive*
Leighton, Kim Gregory *information systems specialist*
Lewis, Philip C. *company executive*
Mauck, William M., Jr. *executive recruiter, small business owner*
Metcalf, Margaret Louise Faber *infosystems specialist, small business owner, consultant*
Mills, Carol Elaine *sales representative*
Myers, Norman Allan *marketing professional*
Neidigk, Dianne *management consultant*
Nesbitt, Vance Gordon *computer software company executive*
Nevins, Janice Ruth *management consultant*
Ng, Lily Ka-Po *hotel hospitality consultant*
O'Brient, David Warren *sales executive, consultant*
Orr, Joseph Newton *recreational guide, outdoor educator*
Osborn, David Guy *sales executive*
Pfeiffer, Eckhard *computer company executive*
Riley, Harold John, Jr. *business executive*
Saunders, William Arthur *management consultant*
Scheffler, Steve John *communications executive*
Shoenfelt, Catherine Ruth *marketing executive*
Sill, Gerald de Schrenck *hotel executive*
Slack, Karen Kershner *advertising agency executive*
Sperber, Matthew Arnold *direct marketing company executive*
Springer, Wayne Gilbert *computer leasing executive*
Stanley, James Gordon *retired engineering marketing executive, writer*
Tesarek, Dennis George *business consultant, writer, educator*
Todd, William H., Jr. *company executive*
Untermeyer, Charles Graves (Chase) *computer company executive*
Welch, Kathy Jane *information technology executive*
Whiddon, Thomas Gayle *retired marketing executive*
Wiginton, Jay Spencer *sales executive*
Wike, Andrew *data processing executive*
Willmann, Donnie Glenn *safety executive*
Woods, Stephanie Elise *sales professional*
Wootton, Brookii E. *investor relations professional*
Yuen, Benson Bolden *airline management consultant, software executive*

Humble
Hahne, C. E. (Gene Hahne) *computer services executive*
Vermylen, Debra Mae Singleton *sales executive*

Huntsville
Stowe, Charles Robinson Beecher *management consultant, educator, lawyer*

Hurst
Buford, Evelyn Claudene Shilling *jewelry specialist, merchandising professional*
Owen, Cynthia Carol *sales executive*

Irving
Boultinghouse, (Dannie) Carol *business development specialist*
Forman, Peter Gerald *marketing professional*
Gretzinger, Ralph Edwin, III *management consultant*
Judge, Stephen *advertising executive*
Neal, Mark Lee *quality assurance manager*
Rosene, Ralph Walfred *consulting company executive*
Schneider, Cheryl *human resources professional*
Temerlin, Liener *advertising agency executive*
Thomas, Philip Robinson *management consulting company executive*
Tucker, Phyllis Anita *sales representative, guidance counselor*
White, Brian Douglas *public relations executive*
Wilbanks, Darrel Jay *automation applications executive*

Joshua
Hoggard, William Zack, Jr. *amusement park executive*

Junction
Evans, Jo Burt *communications executive*

Killeen
Baker, Samuel Garrard *advertising agency executive*

Lewisville
Mebane, Barbara Margot *service company executive, studio owner*
Richardson, K. Scott *sales executive*

Lubbock
French, Kari Lyn *sales representative*
Miller, Stephen Laurence *responsive services executive*

Luling
Hanson, Henry Oran *computer company executive, consultant*

Manvel
Barbour, Jack Robert *security and loss prevention generalist, forensic consultant*

Mc Kinney
Nanda, Chitta Ranjan *industrial hygienist, metallurgical engineer*

Midland
Kuhn, John Mark *computer company executive, educator*
Roberts, David Glen *marketing director*

Missouri City
Norton, Charnette *foodservice management advisory company executive*

Montgomery
Snider, Robert Larry *management consultant*

Normangee
Parry, James Thomas *management consultant*

North Richland Hills
Kunkle, Danielle Lynn *staffing industry administrator, journalist*

Onalaska
Dutton, Frank Elroy *data processing executive*

Pasadena
McClay, Harvey Curtis *data processing executive*

Plano
Alberthal, Lester M., Jr. *information processing services executive*
Anderson, Gerald M(ichel) *electronics marketing executive*
Cancino, Enrique Alberto *management consulting company executive*
Collumb, Peter John *communications company executive*
Dougherty, F(rancis) Kelly *data processing executive*
Forray, Gabe *information systems executive*
Fuller, William Harrison *technology company executive*
Gerhardt, Glenn Rodney *sales executive*
Hahn, Cathy Ann Clifford *sales executive*
Hammond, Karen Smith *marketing professional, paralegal*
Hollocker, Charles Peter *computer company executive*
James, Michael Thames *information technology executive, consultant*
Kriegler, Arnold Matthew *management consultant*
Rees, Lane Charles *industrial relations consultant*
Ryan, John Michael *municipal employee*
Wooldridge, Walter Bruce *quality assurance administrator*

Randolph AFB
Blankenbeker, Joan Winifred *communications/ information management executive*

Richardson
Anderson, John Kerby *communications executive, radio talk show host*
Bearden, Fred B(urnette), Jr. *marketing executive*
Bick, David Greer *health care marketing executive*
Epling, Gerald Arthur *consulting company executive*
Fahrlander, Henry William, Jr. *management consultant*
Harrison, James Richard *business management educator*
Ido, Yoshimitsu *computer company program executive*
Li, Shu *business executive*
Natarajan, T. Raj *communications executive, electrical engineer*
Scrantom, John Gardner *retired company executive*
Tiller, Kathleen Blanche (Kay) *public relations consultant, photojournalist*

Rockwall
Wiorkowski, Gabrielle Kay *senior data base consultant*

Rosenberg
Jaunal, Bridget Kennedy *energy and environmental company executive, consultant*

Round Rock
Troxell, Richard Harold *retired data processing company executive*
Wahl, William Bryan *marketing professional, real estate officer*

San Antonio
Bruff, Beverly Olive *public relations consultant*
Cooper, Ralph *environmental management consultant*
Dubois, Jules Edward *security firm executive, consultant*
English, Ruth Ann Cowder *personnel consultant*
Eskin, Jim *public affairs professional*
Gary, Roger Vanstrom *marketing executive*
Giles, Katharine Emily (J. K. Piper) *administrative assistant, writer*
Hargrave, Robert Warren *hair styling salon chain executive*
Hyman-Sprute, Betty Harpole *technical equipment consultant*
Jeffries, Carol J(ean) *information systems educator*
LeMahieu, James Joseph *business consultant*
Martinez, Ernesto, III *sales professional*
Montemayor, Carlos R. *advertising executive*
Sauder, Michael Hockensmith *travel agency executive*
Strezishar, Anthony Michael *corporate executive*
Ullmer, (R.) John *computer company executive, retired educator*
Weatherston, George Douglas, Jr. *food service executive*
Wickstrom, Jon Alan *telecommunications executive, consultant*
Young, Gary Thomas *advertising executive*

Sherman
Bumgarner, Edward Scott *quality assurance professional*

Southlake
Farquhar, Karen Lee *commercial printing company executive, consultant*
Friedman, Barry *financial marketing consultant*

Spring
Cooley, Andrew Lyman *corporation executive, former army officer*
Maxfield, Mary Constance *management consultant*
Pavel, Elmer Lewis *corporate executive, consultant*

Stafford
Brown, Chris *telecommunications company executive*
Brown, Ronald Chris *telecommunications executive*
Mendoza, Sharon Ruth *customer service manager*

Sugar Land
Kelly, Linda Sue *personnel specialist*
Moss, David Neal *administrative assistant*
Weatherall, William Bailey *human resources administrator*

Temple
Mathis, Marsha Debra *software company executive*
Mauk, Amy Margaret *purchasing agent*

Trophy Club
Haerer, Deane Norman *marketing and public relations executive*

Tyler
Stacey, Patrick *account executive*

Waco
Burke, Tom Clifton *marketing executive*
Chesser, Barbara Russell *human resources executive, writer*

Weatherford
McMahon, Robert Lee, Jr. (Bob McMahon) *information systems executive*

Winnie
Cone, Thomas Conrad *communications executive*

Winona
Harris, Maxine *administrative assistant*

VIRGINIA

Alexandria
Bailey, Steven Scott *operations research analyst*
Burns, Martha A. *association management company executive*
Bussler, Robert Bruce *management consultant*
Costley, Shawn Eric *sales specialist*
Davis, Ruth Margaret (Mrs. Benjamin Franklin Lohr) *technology management executive*
Del Fosse, Claude Marie *aerospace software executive*
Feist-Fite, Bernadette *international education consultant*
Formo, Brenda Terrell *travel company executive*
Gallagher, Matthew Philip, Jr. *advertising agency executive*
Garvey, Sheila *office administrator*
Harrison, James Harvey, Jr. *information systems specialist*
Harvey, James E. *graphic communications executive*
Hazard, Christopher Wedvik *international business executive*
Kemp, Bernard Walter, Jr. *marketing executive*
Kenner, Mary Ellen *marketing and communications executive*
Lord, Leslie Bain *management specialist, marketing professional*
Loving, William Rush, Jr. *public relations company executive, consultant*
Mayo, Louis Allen *corporation executive*
McFarland, Janet Chapin *consulting company executive*
Peeler, Alexandra Ann *public relations executive*
Puerling, Joanne Renee *information specialist*
Reid, Ralph Waldo Emerson *management consultant*
Skeen, David Ray *computer systems administrator*
Souser, Gerard Allen, Jr. *marketing professional*
Tyrrell, Tamara Joan *public affairs executive*

Annandale
Jarvis, Elbert, II (Jay Jarvis) *employee benefits specialist*
Osborn, Len *business executive*

Arlington
Anderson, Steven Hunter *media relations professional*
Blankinship, Henry Massie *data processing executive*
Cetron, Marvin Jerome *management executive*
Cevasco, Francis Michael *international business consultant*
Christy, James Thomas *public affairs executive, lawyer*
Cocolis, Peter Konstantine *business development executive*
Floyd, Julie A. *management analyst*
Gehron, Michael McDermott *information technology company executive*
Gemma, Peter Benedict, Jr. *political, public relations and fund raising consultant*
Gennin, George Stratford *defense company executive, aviation consultant*
Gormley, Dennis Michael *consulting company executive*
Groeber, Sara Virginia *human resources executive*
Haymore, Curtis Joe *environmental consultant*
Infosino, Iara Ciurria *management consultant*
Jewell, Charles Linwood, Jr. *information systems specialist, programmer*
Johnson, Rosemary Wrucke *personnel management specialist*
Kanter, L. Erick *public relations executive*
London, J. Phillip *information technology company executive*
Mellon, William Daniel *communications executive*
Metzfield, William *supply company executive*
Morgan, Michael John *international consultant*
Murray, Tom Reed, II *program manager, engineer*
Naide, Adam Michael *sales executive*
Oleson, Ray Jerome *computer service company executive*
Shaker, William H. *marketing professional, public policy reformer*
Silva, Alan Augustine *retired international ecomonic development*
Smith, Mary Howard Harding *business consultant*
Young, Malcolm Black *consulting company executive*
Zirkle, William Vernon *philanthropist*

Blacksburg
Smith, Robert Lee *marketing researcher*

Boissevain
Tabor, William Eugene *employment relations specialist, writer, poet*

Broadway
Price, Gail Elizabeth *corporate communications specialist, writer, educator*

Burke
Ansley, Darlene H. *communications executive*
Carr, Robert Kimbrel *technology consultant*
Glacel, Barbara Pate *management consultant*

Centreville
Hanson, Lowell Knute *seminar developer and leader, information systems consultant*
Roberts, William Dan *data processing executive*
Weir, Julia Marie *psychic readings company executive*

Charlottesville
Ruggieri, Elaine *public relations administrator*
Wiley, Jerold Wayne *environmental services executive, retired air force officer*

Chesapeake
Garrett, Larry Carlton *sales executive*
Porter, Allen Wayne *bail bondsman*

Chesterfield
Hoffman, Mitchell Wade *corporate executive*

Elkton
Hicks, Robin Kline *marketing research professional*

Fairfax
Abbott, Gayle Elizabeth *human resources consultant*
Baker, Daniel Richard *computer company executive, consultant*
Bluitt, Karen *technical manager, software engineer*
Dame, William Karl *technical training professional*
Ethier, Donald Noel *professional association executive*
Gross, Patrick Walter *business executive, management consultant*
Levy-Myers, Eric *management consultant*
Mendelsohn, Stuart *management consultant, environmental engineer, lawyer*
Palmer, James Daniel *information technology educator*
Pan, Elizabeth Lim *information systems company executive*
Saverot, P.M. *business executive*
Varley, Robert Christopher Gough *management consultant, economist*

Falls Church
Bonzagni, Vincent Francis *program administrator, analyst, researcher*
Carwise, Edward Roland *information systems specialist*
Ehrlich, Geraldine Elizabeth *food service management consultant*
Garner, John Kenneth *lithography company executive*
Glass, Lawrence *business executive*
Gray, Christopher Michael *management and public policy consultant, writer*
Ibañez, Alvaro *patent design company executive, artist*
Nashman, Alvin Eli *computer company executive*
Orkand, Donald Saul *management consultant*
Werner, Stuart Lloyd *computer services company executive*

Farnham
Durham, James Michael, Sr. *marketing consultant*

Floyd
Wilson, Gregory Glenn *funeral home official*

Franklin
Marks, B. E., Jr. *company executive*

Fredericksburg
Geary, Patrick Joseph *naval security administrator*
Hickman, Margaret Capellini *advertising executive*
Hickman, Richard Lonnie *advertising executive*
Jacocks, Henry Miller *sales executive*
McElgunn, Peggy *management executive*

Front Royal
Sneath, William Emmet *development professional, retired naval officer*

Great Falls
Harris, Jack Howard, II *consulting firm executive*

Hampton
Brown, Martin Adin *job search consultant*
Morgan, Michael Joseph *consultant*
Schauer, Catharine Guberman *public affairs specialist*
Schauer, Irwin Jay *quality and productivity officer*

Haymarket
Douglas, Clarence James, Jr. *corporation executive, management consultant*

Herndon
Beery, Donald Thomas *business development executive*

Independence
Selzer, Michael David *sales executive*

King George
James, L. Eldon, Jr. *development consultant*

Lynchburg
George, John David, Jr. *management educator*
Shircliff, James Vanderburgh *communications executive*

Lyndhurst
Sidebottom, William George *communications executive*

Manassas
Ulvila, Jacob Walter *management consultant*

Matoaca
Chrzan-Seelig, Patricia Ann *corporate professional*

Mc Lean
Garnes, Ronald Vincent *marketing executive, finance broker, consultant*
Hershberger, Carrie Lee *program developer*
Kolombatovic, Vadja Vadim *management consulting company executive*
Mason, John *research and consulting company executive, mayor*
McNichols, Gerald Robert *consulting company executive*
Miller, Christine Marie *marketing executive*
Mintz, Daniel Gordon *technical company executive*
Reppert, Jeffrey Roy *procurement analyst, systems administrator*
Richardson, Fredrick Glenn *consulting company executive*
Steventon, Robert Wesley *marketing executive*
Watson, Jerry Carroll *advertising executive*

Merrifield
Nelson, Ruth Naomi *marketing professional*
Pascoe, Charles Thomas, Jr. *computer systems company executive*

Middleburg
King, Robert Bennett *technical marketing specialist*

Midlothian
Doumlele, Ruth Hailey *communications company executive, broadcast accounting consultant*

Newport News
Fisher, Denise Butterfield *marketing executive*
Turner, Mary Louise *computer specialist*
Weber, Patricia *speaker, human resources training executive*

Norfolk
Bland, Gilbert Tyrone *foodservice executive*
Elliott, Ritta Faye *administrative assistant*
Haug, James Charles *business and management educator*
Valentine, Herman Edward *computer company executive*

Penn Laird
Ratner, Peter John *computer graphics educator*

Radford
Spillman, Robert Daniel *information systems educator*

Reston
Blaemire, Robert Aaron *computer services executive*
Blanchard, Townsend Eugene *service companies executive*
Brooker, Susan Gay *employment consulting firm executive*
Dawson, Gary John *defense firm analyst*
Deane, Silas Edward, II *marketing executive*
Easton, Glenn Hanson, Jr. *management and insur: nce consultant, federal official, naval officer*
Flynn, Daniel Clarke *human resources executive, educator*
Salisbury, Alan Blanchard *information systems executive*
Schropp, Mary Lou *public relations executive*
Showalter-Keefe, Jean *data processing executive*
Sullivan, Penelope Dietz *computer consulting and software development company executive*
Sweeney, Robert Francis *marketing professional*
Vesely, Paul T. *imaging software development firm executive, consultant*

Richmond
Bohannon, Sarah Virginia *personnel operations technician*
Campbell, James Albert Barton *marketing executive*
Cothran, Phyllis L. *personal care industry executive*
Gross, Paul Allan *health service executive*
Hanzak, Gary A. John *credit and leasing executive*
Jacobs, Harry Milburn, Jr. *advertising executive*
Jochim, Michael Eugene *food service executive*
Kennedy, Susan Estabrook *historian, educator, dean*
King, Allen B. *company executive*
Moyne, Yves M. *water treatment executive*
Nabhan, Lou Anne Jones *public relations executive*
Roper, Hartwell H. *tobacco company executive*
Stapleton, James Edward *sales executive*
Steger, Martha Wessells *public relations executive*
Taylor, William L. *executive*
Toler, Ann Patrick *public relations executive*
Tuszynski, Daniel J., Jr. *sales, management and marketing consultant*
Weinberg, Roger David *communications executive*
Weistroffer, Heinz Roland *information systems professional, educator*
Williams, Robert C. *company executive*

Roanoke
Bear, Joseph Wolfe, III *personnel administrator*
Johnson, Boreham Boyd *printing company executive, consultant, accountant*
Sentell, Jackie Roberta Ratliff *secretary*

Rosslyn
James, Louis Meredith *personnel executive*

Seaford
Jenkins, Margaret Bunting *human resources executive*

Springfield
Fedewa, Lawrence John *information technology company executive*
Stout, Gary *company executive*

Stafford
Brown, Janet Louise *continuing education specialist*
Kline, Denny Lee *hazardous devices and explosives consultant*

Sterling
Bennett, William Leo, Jr. *management consultant*

Sweet Briar
Mays, Cathy Cash *development officer*

Vienna
Brandel, Ralph Edward *management consultant*
Feld, Kenneth J. *entertainment executive*
Gallagher, Anne Porter *business executive*
Hale, Thomas Morgan *professional services executive*
Hubbell, Katherine Jean *marketing consultant*
Jandreau, James Lawrence *program manager*
Rothery, Chet *business executive*
Smith, Charles E. *company executive*
Unger, Paul Temple *search firm executive, consultant*
Veasey, Byron Keith *information systems consultant*

Vinton
Nester, George Walter *management consultant*

Virginia Beach
Allen, Elizabeth Maresca *marketing executive*
Burgess, Marvin Franklin *human resources specialist, consultant*
Byler, Jennifer Curtis *marketing consultant, publisher, editor*
Colgan, Catherine Carpenter *communications company executive*
Dixon, John Spencer *international executive*
Ede, Fred Okotchy *marketing educator*
Goffigan, Christopher Wayne *research associate*
Goodwin, Robert *human resources specialist*
McDermott, Victoria Ann Elizabeth *sales executive*
Ritzel, Frederick Howard *marketing manager*

Warrenton
Molloy, Michael John *public relations professional*

Waynesboro
Zodhiates, Philip Spiros *advertising executive*

Williamsburg
Aaron, Bertram Donald *corporation executive*
Coffman, Orene Burton *hotel executive*
Springmann, Douglas Mandel, Jr. *sales and marketing executive, fund raising consultant*

Winchester
Vaughan, Stephanie Ruth *water aerobics business owner, consultant*

Woodbridge
Cosner, David Dale *plastics industry executive, marketing executive*
Douglass, Wilford David *corporate executive*
Krimmer, Linda K. *business educator, accountant*

Wytheville
Hansen, B(obby) J. *management consultant, real estate investor and developer*

Yorktown
Behlmar, Cindy Lee *business manager, consultant*

WASHINGTON

Kirkland
Dixon, Judy E(arlene) *management and marketing executive, consultant*

Seattle
Ruckelshaus, William Doyle *waste disposal services company executive*

WEST VIRGINIA

Clarksburg
Huber, Clayton Lloyd *marketing professional, engineer*

Great Cacapon
Chapple, Abby *consumer comunications consultant*

Huntington
Markun, Frank O. *food services executive*
McSorley, Danny Eugene *sales executive*
Underwood, Cecil H. *company executive, past governor of West Virginia*

New Martinsville
Slider, Gary Jay *computer technician*

Parkersburg
Crooks, Dorena May (Dee Crooks) *administrative assistant, social worker*
Fahlgren, H(erbert) Smoot *advertising agency executive*

South Charleston
Berchtold, Gladys *business executive*

Sylvester
Mace, Mary Alice *coal company administrator*

Triadelphia
Mc Cullough, John Phillip *management consultant, educator*

Vienna
Guckert, Janice Elaine *office manager*

Wellsburg
Wellman, Gerald Edwin, Jr. *safety and fire inspector*

White Sulphur Springs
Kappa, Margaret McCaffrey *resort hotel consultant*

WISCONSIN

Pewaukee
Hyland, Brian Christopher *sales executive*

Wauwatosa
Wright, Isaac Wilson, Jr. *quality assurance professional*

TERRITORIES OF THE UNITED STATES

PUERTO RICO

Guayama
Flores-Nazario, Margarita *human resources director*

VIRGIN ISLANDS

Christiansted
Baar, James A. *public relations and corporate communications executive, author, consultant, software developer*

Cruz Bay
Blitz, Peggy Sanderfur *corporate travel management company official*

CANADA

ONTARIO

Guelph
Osen, Gregory Alan *water conditioning company executive*

SINGAPORE

Tung Li
Mathews, Geoffrey Kevin *advertising executive*

ADDRESS UNPUBLISHED

Alston, Eugene Benson *communications company executive*
Barager, Wendy Ayrian *communications executive*
Bassford, Daniel Joseph *marketing and business planning executive*
Battle, Emery Alford, Jr. *sales executive*
Berry, Jack M. *business executive*
Blackburn, Sadie Gwin Allen *executive*
Boatwright, Charlotte Jeanne *hospital marketing and public relations executive*
Bohannan, Jules Kirby *printing company executive*
Boone, Alicia Kay Lanier *marketing communications consultant, writer*
Brown, Robert Howard *customer support specialist*
Burgess, Lester Phillips *quality assurance manager*
Burnham, J. V. *sales executive*
Burris, Frances White *personnel director*
Caldwell, Judy Carol *advertising executive, public relations executive*
Cameron, Daniel Forrest *communications executive*
Carmony, Janet Carolyn (Janet Carolyn Kopf) *sales and marketing executive, consultant*
Carpenter-Mason, Beverly Nadine *health care/ quality assurance nurse consultant*
Chriscoe, Christine Faust *industrial trainer*
Cittone, Henry Aron *hotel and restaurant management educator*
Clark, Jeanette McLain *advertising agency executive, author*
Coenson Crook, Barbara *marketing professional*
Crawford, William Walsh *retired consumer products company executive*
Cromwell, Virginia Pace *communication professional*
Crouse, Joseph John *marketing researcher, retired journalist*
Davis, Barbara Jean Siemens *service company executive*
De Marco, Natalie Anne *sales and marketing executive*
Dennis-Hollis, Robbie Smagula *marketing communications executive*
De Sofi, Oliver Julius *data processing executive*
DeVore, Kimberly K. *sales executive*
Dickey, Patrice Jane *public relations executive, sales educator*
Donovan, Lowava Denise *data processing administrator*
Dudley, Elizabeth Hymer *retired security executive*
Eggleston, G(eorge) Dudley *management consultant, publisher*
Farmer, Deborah Kiriluk *marketing professional*
Fellman, Barry L. *computer systems company executive*
Fernández, Alberto Antonio *security professional*
Fielder, Barbara Lee *management, leadership and communications trainer*
Flickinger, Joe Arden *telecommunications educator*
Franey, Eric D. *advertising agency executive*
Gambrell, Luck Flanders *corporate executive*
Gee, Kent Leong *management consultant*
George, Carole Schroeder *computer company executive*
Gerwin, Leslie Ellen *public affairs and community relations executive, lawyer*
Gilbreath, Robert Dean *management consultant, author*
Gillice, Sondra Jupin (Mrs. Gardner Russell Brown) *sales and marketing executive*
Gordon, Felton Hays *public relations executive*
Gossett, Danette Estelle *marketing professional*
Gravely, Jane Candace *computer company executive*
Green, William A. *sales executive, consultant*
Griffiths, Dale Lee *marketing executive*
Griggs, Emma *management executive*
Grundlehner, Conrad Ernest *information company executive, economic consultant*
Guerra, Armando J. *corporate professional*
Gulledge, Sandra Smith *publicist*
Haemmerlein, Bob *company executive*
Hall, Dennis Sanford *sales executive*
Hammond, Nicolas John *computer executive*
Heil, Holly Ann *public relations practitioner, consultant*
Hendrickson, William George *business executive*
Hensel, John Eric *sales executive, educator*
Hickman, Terrie Taylor *administrator*
Hines, Ruth E. *retired postal worker*
Hinton, Barbara Lorraine *corporate tax assistant*
Hitchcock, Denise Thornburg *public relations executive*
Holmes, Robert Wayne *service executive, consultant, biological historian*
Houghtaling, Pamela Ann *public relations executive*
Houx, Shirley Ann *personal and business services company executive, consultant, researcher*
Hyde, James A. *service executive*
Infante-Ogbac, Daisy Inocentes *sales and real estate executive, marketing executive*
Irvine, William Burriss *management consultant*
Irwin, Linda Belmore *marketing consultant*
Jackson, Glenn Richard *information services executive*
Jacobs, John, IV *marketing professional*

Jankus, Alfred Peter *international management and marketing consultant*
Jaquish, Michael Paul *human resources administrator*
Johnson, Dianne Jean *human resources executive*
Kaufman, Charlotte S. *communications executive*
Kennedy, Jerrie Ann Preston *public relations executive*
Klein, Irma Molligan *career development educator, consultant*
Knight, Dan Phillip *marketing executive*
Koh, Christa M. *technical translator, realtor, physical therapist*
Korgaonkar, Pradeep Kashinath *marketing educator*
Lamalie, Robert Eugene *retired executive search company executive*
Landers, Linda Ann *public relations and fundraising executive*
Lindsey, Dottye Jean *marketing executive*
Lipman, Ira Ackerman *security service company executive*
Lokmer, Stephanie Ann *public relations counselor*
Love, Mildred Lois (Jan Love) *public relations executive*
Lowrie, Walter Olin *management consultant*
Luna, Patricia Adele *marketing executive*
Lynn, Sheilah Ann *service executive, consultant*
Manuti, Annabelle Theresa *advertising executive*
Marcus, Lee Evan *business consultant*
Marlar, Janet Cummings *public relations officer*
Massey, William Walter, Jr. *sales executive*
Mathay, Mary Frances *marketing executive*
McCormick, Robert *hospital food service administrator, dietitian consultant*
McCullough, R. Michael *management consultant*
McGervey, Teresa Ann *technology information specialist*
Medina, Thomas Julian *information management consultant, educator*
Metzger, Marian *retired management consultant*
Milligan, John Michael *visual communication educator*
Miracle, James Franklin *hospitality company executive*
Moltzau, Hughitt Gregory *retired management training specialist*
Moore, George Elliott *management consultant*
Moradi, Ahmad F. *software company executive, consultant*
Moran, Samuel Joseph *public relations executive*
Morgan, Marianne *corporate professional*
Moses, Jeffrey Michael *customer services executive*
Naquin, Patricia Elizabeth *employee assistance consultant*
O'Connor, John Joseph *operations executive*
Olivarius-Imlah, MaryPat *sales, advertising and marketing executive*
Olsen, John Richard *education consultant*
O'Shea, Catherine Large *marketing and public relations consultant*
Pang, Kau Chai *marketing professional*
Payne, Timothy E. *management consultant*
Penaloza, Betty Raquel *international affairs consultant*
Perry, Donny Ray *electrician*
Phillips, John David *communications executive*
Powers, Eldon Nathaniel *computer mapping executive*
Raftery, William A. *management consultant*
Richardson, Roy *management consultant*
Richter, Carol Dean *sales representative*
Ridlen, Lillian May Heigle *public relations, sales and marketing executive, writer, inventor*
Rittelmeyer, John Mosal, Jr. *manufacturer representative, paper company executive, financial consultant, investor*
Robinson, Barbara Olivia *food service specialist*
Rockwell, Sherman Ralph, Jr. *sales executive, packaging consultant*
Rolof, Marcia Christine *sales executive*
Royston, Lloyd Leonard *educational marketing consultant*
Rutherford, Samuel Kenneth, Jr. *marketing executive*
Satre, Philip Glen *casino entertainment executive, lawyer*
Sawyer, Raymond Lee, Jr. *motel chain executive*
Schwartz, Stephen Blair *retired information industry executive*
Scutt, Cheryl Lynn *communications executive*
Shalhoup, Judy Lynn *marketing communications executive*
Shumick, Diana Lynn *computer executive*
Sims, Albert Maurice *marketing professional*
Soper, Howard Kent *printing company executive*
Stephens, C. Michael *service executive*
Stevens, Hal *food service manager*
Stover, Brian Allan *advertising executive, marketing consultant*
Strupp, Jacqueline Virginia *small business specialist*
Sturgeon, Charles Edwin *management consultant*
Sullivan, Patrick Raney *labor management consultant*
Sutherland, Sam S(helton), III *marketing and technical communications specialist*
Thorn, Brian Earl *retail company executive*
Toole, Linda Jernigan *quality control technician, cosmetics company admininstrator*
Townsend, Jerrie Lynne *environmental services administrator*
Ulosevich, Steven Nils *management consultant, educator*
Viscelli, Therese Rauth *materials management consultant*
Walker, Gloria Lee *service company executive*
Wallace, Carolyn Marie *administrative assistant*
Warren, Richard Ernest *advertising executive*
Warwick, John Benjamin *marketing professional*
Watkins, Nancy Hobgood *sales executive*
Weaver, Carrie Etta *sales executive*
Wheeler, William Bryan, III *systems company executive*
Whitaker, Shirley Ann *telecommunications company marketing executive*
Whittaker, Mary Frances *educational and industrial company official*
Wilkinson, Rebecca Elaine *human resources systems analyst*
Williams, Alfred Blythe *business communication educator*
Williams, Cheryl *service company executive*
Wilson, Charles Thomas *technology company executive, corporate restructuring consultant*
Wilson, Jeanette Ouren *office manager*
Wise, Susan Tamsberg *management and communications consultant, speaker*
Womack, Samuel Edward *computer company executive*
Wreford, Debra Renee *communication corporation manager*
Zanes, George William *management, marketing, human resources consultant*

INDUSTRY: TRADE

UNITED STATES

ALABAMA

Birmingham
Garrison, Paul F. *retail executive*
George, Frank Wade *small business owner, antiquarian book dealer*
Swope, William Richards *retail executive, lawyer*

Dothan
Koach, Stephen Francis *distribution executive, retired army officer*

Hartselle
Penn, Hugh Franklin *small business owner*

Huntsville
Dobbs, Elwyn Harold *food service executive*

Montgomery
Grewelle, Larry Allan *travel agency owner*

Pelham
Wabler, Robert Charles, II *retail and distribution executive*

Selma
Franklin, Rita Sims *retail executive*

ARIZONA

Scottsdale
McGaw, Kenneth Roy *wholesale distribution executive*

ARKANSAS

Bentonville
Glass, David D. *department store company executive, professional baseball team executive*
White, Nicholas J. *retail company executive*

Jonesboro
Russell, Phillip Ray *retail executive*

Little Rock
Dillard, William, II *department store chain executive*
Kemp, Edgar Ray, Jr. *retail executive*
Stephenson, G. Warren *wholesale distribution executive*

Pine Bluff
Kirby, Jackie *business owner*

FLORIDA

Bradenton
Blankenship, Dwight David *business owner*
Corey, Kay Janis *business owner, designer, nurse*
Simpson, Bill Kempton, Jr. *retail executive*

Brandon
Pomeroy, Wyman Burdette *business owner, consultant*

Clearwater
Bernstein, Michael Joel *retail corporation executive*

Coral Gables
Currier, Susan Anne *computer software company executive*
Groover, Sandra Mae *retail executive*

Dania
Altshuler, Lanny Stephen *retail executive*

Daytona Beach
Auer, Rudolph Gerhart *small business owner*
Stinson, Robert Wayne *meat company executive*

Deerfield Beach
Moran, Patricia Genevieve *corporate executive*

Deland
Tetor, Carol Lynn *business owner*

Fort Lauderdale
Loos, John Thompson *business owner*
Wojcik, Cass *decorative supply company executive, former city official*

Fort Myers
Anthony, Susan Mae *entrepreneur*
Colgate, Doris Eleanor *retailer, sailing school owner and administrator*

Gainesville
Hollien, Patricia Ann *small business owner, scientist*
McClellan, Richard Augustus *small business owner*
Steadham, Charles Victor, Jr. *entertainment agent, producer, software developer*

Heathrow
Deyo, Steve *small business owner, professional speaker*

Holiday
Mercandino, Sharon Ann *small business owner*

Jacksonville
Jelsma, Denny Gene *water company executive*
Kufeldt, James *retail grocery store executive*
McGehee, Thomas Rives, Jr. *wholesale distribution company executive*
Samiian, Barazandeh *business owner, educator*
Trenkler, Michael *small business owner*

Lake Worth
Kinser, Dianne Lee *typography service executive*

Lakeland
Luther, George Albert *truck brokerage executive*

Marco Island
Jahn, Steve Curtis *small business owner*

Melbourne
Smith, Willis Ballard (Milton Smith) *business owner*

Merritt Island
Smith, David Edward *business executive*

Miami
Morris, Anna Rochelle *retail and wholesale executive*
Thompson, Gerard Maurice *import-export company executive, merchant banker*
Tuttle, Toni Brodax *swimming pool company executive*

Miami Beach
Katzenstein, Thea *retail executive, jewelry designer*

Mount Dora
Edgerton, Richard *restaurant and hotel owner*

Naples
Caperton, Richard Walton *automobile repair company executive*
Simmons, Warren Hathaway, Jr. *retired retail executive*

Orlando
Feitsma, Laurinda Dawn *business owner*
Hall-Kelly, Kathy B. *small business owner, columnist, speaker*
Warner, Richard Allen *small business owner*

Palm Harbor
Stettner, Jerald W. *retail drugs stores executive*

Pompano Beach
Santanna, Ricardo Pereira *trade company executive*
Schmidt, Thomas *small business owner, writer*

Riverview
Crowder, Bonnie Walton *small business owner, composer*

Sanibel
Perkinson, Diana Agnes Zouzelka *import company executive*

Sarasota
Broth, Ray *retail executive*
Burrell, Nancy Bradbury *retail executive*
Meyer, B. Fred *small business executive, home designer and builder, product designer*

Sebastian
Becker, Jim *small business owner*

Sebring
Blackman, James Timothy *automobile dealer*

Tampa
Gregorio, Peter Anthony *retail grocer, artist*
Torretta-Guagliardo, Joann *small business owner, image consultant, lecturer*

Venice
Cool, Kim Patmore *retail executive, needlework consultant*

GEORGIA

Alpharetta
Watts, William David *corporate executive, business owner*

Atlanta
Cabey, Alfred Arthur, Jr. *business owner, publisher*
Farmer, Mary Bauder *small business owner*
Marcus, Bernard *retail executive*
Moore, Faye Halford *jewelry manufacturer*
Smith, Marilyn Lynne *small business owner*
Wright, Catherine *small business owner*

Augusta
Doyle, Michael O'Brien *retail executive*

Buford
Radford, Edward W. *small business owner, retired military officer*

Covington
Penland, John Thomas *import and export and development companies executive*

Decatur
Wiedenkeller, Barry Arnold *bookseller, art director*

Duluth
Raines, Stephen Samuel *franchising, consulting and development firm executive, lawyer*

Kennesaw
Haygood, David Louis *pet care professional, entrepreneur*

Macon
Jones, Carolyn Evans *small business owner*

Newnan
Scroggin, David Fred *small business owner*

Statesboro
Bacon, Martha Brantley *small business owner*

Valdosta
Halter, H(enry) James, Jr. (Diamond Jim Halter) *retail executive*

Vidalia
Fortner, Billie Jean *small business owner*

KENTUCKY

Florence
Stallings, Michael Dean *retail executive*

Lancaster
Arnold, Cecil Benjamin *former small business owner*

Lexington
Stockdale, Gayle Sue *wholesale florist*

Louisville
Smith, Donald Ray *magazine dealer*

Midway
Jones, Brereton C. *small business owner, former governor*

Morehead
Rose, Melissa Eva Anderson *small business owner*

Paducah
Simmons, Gary M. *small business owner, writer*

Winchester
Book, John Kenneth (Kenny Book) *retail store owner*

LOUISIANA

Alexandria
Allen, Frank *retail executive, entrepreneur, writer*

Baton Rouge
Fabre, Fred Ruffin *small business owner*
Samuels, Rosemarie *small business owner, consultant*

Houma
Rhodes, Gene Paul *small business owner*

Lafayette
Guidry, Rodney-Lee Joseph *small business owner*
Zuschlag, Richard Emery *small business owner*

Metairie
Asher, Kathleen Ann *small business owner*

New Orleans
Giglio, David Thomas *small business owner*
Maselli, Joseph *distribution company executive*
McCaffrey, Kevin John *small business owner*

Shreveport
Dickson, Markham Allen *wholesale distribution executive*

Slidell
Stanton, Sylvia Doucet *small business owner*

MISSISSIPPI

Indianola
Crouse, Ted *grocery company executive*

Meridian
Anderson, Ethel Avara *retired retail executive*

Ridgeland
Davis, Robert Lee *small business owner*

NORTH CAROLINA

Asheville
Keleher, Michael Cassat *cabinet maker*
Pine, Charles *retail executive*

Charlotte
Graham, Sylvia Angelenia *wholesale distributor, retail buyer*
Griffing, Clayton Allen *retail executive*
Webber, Wendy Elizabeth *association management company executive*

Davidson
Gardner, Gwendolyn Smith *retail executive*

Gastonia
Taylor, Thomas Hudson, Jr. *import company executive*

Greensboro
Kiser, Mose, III *small business owner*

Hendersonville
Heltman, Robert Fairchild *distribution executive*

Hickory
Lynn, Tony Lee *import company executive*

Highlands
Shaffner, Randolph Preston *shop owner, educator, writer*

Huntersville
Evans, Trellany Victoria Thomas *entrepreneur*

Leicester
Stewart, Claudette Suzanne *small business owner, author*

Matthews
Burns, Thomas David *small business owner*

Monroe
Melton, Elaine Wallace *small business owner*

North Wilkesboro
Wessling, Gregory Jay *retail executive*

Rutherfordton
Howard, Bill Osborne *small business owner*

Shelby
Arey, Robert Jackson, Jr. *small business owner*

Statesville
Lawson, Willard Francis, Jr. *paper company owner, sales executive*

Troy
Morgan, Virginia Deapo *business owner*

OKLAHOMA

Bartlesville
Hollis, Paul Richard, Jr. *wholesale/retail business owner*

Bixby
Brown, James Roy *retail executive*

Oklahoma City
Barnes, Bernard Ellis *small business executive*
Werries, E. Dean *food distribution company executive*

Tulsa
Brown, Connie Yates *business owner*

SOUTH CAROLINA

Charleston
Ilderton, Jane Wallace *small business owner*
McDaniel, Lynn *small business owner*

North Charleston
Peters, Randolph William *small business owner*

Summerville
Mertz, Susan Jeanne *small business owner, writer*

Yemassee
Olendorf, William Carr, Jr. *small business owner*

TENNESSEE

Brentwood
Zimmerman, Raymond *retail chain executive*

Bristol
Cauthen, Charles Edward, Jr. *retail executive, business consultant*

Jackson
Richards, Jerry Cecil *store owner, writer*

Johnson City
Sell, Joan Isobel *mobile home company owner*

Kingsport
Hamilton, Bobby Wayne *small business owner*
Ice, Billie Oberta *retail executive*

Knoxville
Harris, Charles Edgar *retired wholesale distribution company executive*
Jenkins, Frances Owens *retired small business owner*
Tweel, Phillip Cory *import-export company executive*

Madison
Cross, Betty Felt *small business owner*

Maryville
Hendren, Jo Ann *small business owner*

Memphis
Clarkson, Andrew MacBeth *retail executive*
Johnson, Robert Lewis, Jr. *retail company executive*
Levitch, Harry Herman *retail executive*
Schaefgen, Philip P. *business owner, consultant, accountant*
Smith, Forrest Allen *business owner, graphic artist*

Moscow
Rowlett, Bobby N. *executive of fitness equipment company*
Timms, Richard M. *executive of fitness equipment company*

Nashville
Carpenter, Susan *modeling and talent agency owner*
Reid, Donna Joyce *small business owner*

Oak Ridge
Beeler, B. Diane *executive, writer*

TEXAS

Anton
Harrell, Wanda Faye *retail executive*

Arlington
Burnett, Paul David *small business owner*

Athens
Geddie, Thomas Edwin *retired small business owner*

Austin
Beaman, Margarine Gaynell *scrap metal broker*
Lenoir, Gloria Cisneros *small business owner, business executive*

Beaumont
Alter, Nelson Tobias *jewelry retailer and wholesaler*
Everett, John Howard *diving business owner, paramedic*

Bellaire
Teas, John Frederick *small business owner*

Boerne
Morton, Michael Ray *retail company executive*

Bryan
Smith, Elouise Beard *restaurant owner*

Carrollton
Butler, Abbey J. *pharmaceutical distribution company executive*

Carthage
Cooke, Walta Pippen *automobile dealership owner*

Corpus Christi
DuVall, Lorraine *recreation center owner*
Finley, George Alvin, III *wholesale executive*
Salem, Joseph John *jeweler, real estate developer*

Dallas
Augur, Marilyn Hussman *distribution executive*
Callahan, Rickey Don *business owner*
Collum, W(illiam) Harold *small business owner*
Matthews, Clark J(io), II *retail executive, lawyer*
Shapiro, Robert Alan *retail executive*
Smith, Elizabeth Hull *small business owner*

El Paso
Harden, Doyle Benjamin *import-export company executive*
Simmons, Randall Allen *small business owner, consultant*

Fort Worth
Deats, James Lawton *retail executive*
Provasek, Emil Frank, Jr. *small business owner*
Roach, John Vinson, II *retail company executive*
Sitterly, Connie Sue *management training specialist, author, consultant, speaker*
Swords, Henry Logan, II *retail executive*
Winn, Herschel Clyde *retail electronics company executive*
Young, Daisy Almeda *small business owner*

Garland
Bowman, Richard Andrew *business owner*

Georgetown
Logan, Gordon Baker *small business owner*

Hitchcock
Shaffer, Richard Paul *business owner, retired career military officer*

Houston
Barrett, Lyle Eugene *retail buyer, designer, artist*
Baysal, Fatih Dogan *trading company executive*
Hughes, James Baker, Jr. *retail executive, consultant*
Isbell, Garnett Knowlten, II *retail executive*
Lindig, Bill M. *food distribution company executive*
Moursund, Kenneth Carroll *grocery chain executive*
Naderi, Jamie Benedict *hazardous waste services brokerage executive*
Nesbitt, DeEtte DuPree *small business owner, investor*
Swiff, Kelly *small business owner, civic volunteer, author*
Wike, D. Elaine *business executive*
Woodhouse, John Frederick *food distribution company executive*
Young, Darlene Ann *small business owner*

Irving
Skinner, John Vernon *retail credit executive*

Lewisville
Roberts, Janis Elaine *small business owner, adjuster, nurse*

Longview
Mc Kinley, Jimmie Joe *business executive*
Sonnier, David Joseph *wholesale distributing executive*

Lubbock
Willingham, Mary Maxine *retail store executive*

Marble Falls
Simpson, H. Richard (Dick Simpson) *retailer*

Mc Kinney
Fairman, Jarrett Sylvester *retail company executive*

Nacogdoches
Chumley, Donnie Ann *business owner, consultant*

Odessa
Brumelle, Kenneth Coy *retail store owner*

Plainview
Brown, Robert William *small business owner, musician*

Plano
Oesterreicher, James E. *department stores executive*
Samford, Karen Elaine *small business owner, consultant*
Walker, Walter Wayne *retail management executive*

San Antonio
Hutson, Herbert Don *wholesale distribution executive*

Seabrook
Spears, James Grady *small business owner*

Spring
Green, Sharon Jordan *interior decorator*

Sulphur Springs
Kinsey, John Paul *consultant*
McKenzie, Michael K. *wholesale executive*

Terrell
Wolfe, Tracey Dianne *distributing company executive*

Tyler
Edwards, D. M. *retail, wholesale distribution and commercial real estate investment executive*

Victoria
Donoghue, William Thomas *antiquary, jeweler, gemologist*

Wharton
Yates, William John *business owner, counselor*

VIRGINIA

Alexandria
Peterson, Scott Lee *music retailer*
Williams, Emma Crawford *business owner*

Arlington
Walker, Walter Gray, Jr. *small business owner, program statistician*

Charlottesville
Lupton, Mary Hosmer *retired small business owner*

Fairfax
Rogers, William Fenna, Jr. *supermarket executive, management consultant*

Herndon
Edwards, Phillip Milton *import-export company executive*
Houston, Brian Christopher Michael *small business owner*

Manassas
Gage, David Floyd *business owner, entrepreneur*

Mc Lean
Hagar, James Thomas *retail executive*

Richmond
Coker, Donna Sue *retail executive, nurse*
Gresham, Ann Elizabeth *retailer, horticulturist executive, consultant*
Mayo, Robert Bowers *art company owner*
Sharp, Richard L. *retail company executive*
Tomaszewski, Carole Louise *small business owner*

Sterling
Moulton, James Roger *small business owner*

Suffolk
Wright, Brenda Carol *dental laboratory owner, photographer*

Vienna
Bond, Wilma McCrary *antique silver dealer, retired educator*
Gardner, Joel Sylvanus *tempest products company executive*
Miller, J. Douglas *business owner*

Virginia Beach
DeVenny, Lillian Nickell *trophy company executive*

WEST VIRGINIA

Charleston
Lipton, Allen David *retail executive*

Granville
Rogers, Thomas Paul *retail chain executive*

North Parkersburg
Treharne, George David *small business owner*

MEXICO

Mexico City
Burgos, Hector Hugo *trading company executive*
Kim, Earnest Jae-Hyun *import and export company executive*

ADDRESS UNPUBLISHED

Bice, Michael David *retail and wholesale executive*
Birne, Cindy Frank *business owner*
Booker, Monroe James *small business owner*
Farrigan, Julia Ann *small business owner, educator*
Gilley, W. Kay *small business owner, consultant, writer*
Goulder, Gerald Polster *retail executive*
Haas, Edward Lee *business executive, consultant*
Johnson, Barbara Anne Umberger *business owner, editor, publisher*
Kimmel, Charity Allen *small business owner, writer*
Lively, H(oward) Randolph, Jr. *retail company executive*
Nicholas, Lawrence Bruce *import company executive*
Norton, Larry Allan *retailer*
Polichino, Joseph Anthony, Jr. *wholesale company executive*
Ruland, Midlred Ardelia *retail executive, retail buyer*
Smith, Shelly Gerald, Jr. *small business owner, author*
Trinh, Victor *small business owner*
Wentworth, Malinda Ann Nachman *former small business owner, real estate broker*

INDUSTRY: TRANSPORTATION

UNITED STATES

ALABAMA

Birmingham
Brough, James A. *airport terminal executive*
Bryant, Perrin Cranford *pilot*

Daleville
Rendzio, Robert Joseph *safety director, aviation accident investigator*

Dothan
Coggins, Charles E. *transportation company executive*

Huntsville
Heidish, Louise Oridge-Schwallie *transportation specialist, marketing professional*

Meridianville
Oberhausen, Joyce Ann Wynn *aircraft company executive, artist*

Mobile
Nix, Joseph Hanson, Jr. *aviation instructor*

ARKANSAS

Fort Smith
Young, Robert A., III *freight systems executive*

Hindsville
Pogue, William Reid *former astronaut, foundation executive, business and aerospace consultant*

Huntsville
Carr, Gerald Paul *former astronaut, business executive, former marine officer*

Norfork
Price, George Dwight *airline repair specialist*

COLORADO

Breckenridge
Stewart, Sally Beal *pilot*

DISTRICT OF COLUMBIA

Washington
Scheer, Frank Reeder *corporate freight traffic administrator, library curator, information specialist*

FLORIDA

Boynton Beach
Crane, L(eo) Stanley *retired railroad executive*

Coral Springs
Stow, Weston Loghry *shipping company executive*

Jacksonville
Anderson, John Quentin *rail transportation executive*
Godfrey, Herb *air transportation executive*
Goodwin, Paul Richard *transportation company executive*
Hamilton, Susan Owens *transportation company executive, lawyer*
Hardrick, Charles M. *airport executive*

Lake Mary
Curboy, Robert Edward *aviation safety consultant*

Merritt Island
Sasseen, George Thiery *retired aerospace engineering executive*

Miami
Burns, Mitchel Anthony *transportation services company executive*
Dellapa, Gary J. *airport terminal executive*
Huston, Edwin Allen *transportation company executive*
Pubillones, Jorge *transit adminstration administrator*
Romeo, Anthony C. *air transportation services executive*
Sapp, Neil Carleton *air transportation executive, consultant*
Shugrue, Martin Roger, Jr. *airline executive*
Wilklow, Charles Manfred *air transportation executive, pilot*

Naples
Bush, John William *federal transportation official*
Reitz, Douglas John Frank *airline captain, computer consultant*
Schmidt, Gene *air transportation executive*

Orange City
Williams, Sandra Wheeler *commercial pilot*

Orlando
Bullock, Robert B. *air transportation executive*
Davis, H. Alan *retired airline captain, consultant*

Pompano Beach
Brookes, David Alexander *pilot, educator, computer consultant, entrepreneur*
Wright, Joseph Robert, Jr. *corporate executive*

Ponte Vedra Beach
Fiorentino, Thomas Martin *transportation executive, lawyer*

Tampa
Bean, George J. *airport executive*
Thomas, Roger Nelson *pilot*

Tarpon Springs
Timpany, Robert Daniel *railroad executive*

Winter Park
Cerbin, Carolyn McAtee *transportation executive, writer*

GEORGIA

Atlanta
Gittens, Angela *airport executive*
Jordan, Lewis H. *airline executive*
Matthews, Herbert R. *transportation company executive*
Thakker, Ashok *aerospace engineering company executive*

Dunwoody
Ferguson, Erik Tillman *transportation consultant*

Macon
Hails, Robert Emmet *aerospace consultant, business executive, former air force officer*

Marietta
Kelleher, Daniel Michael *trucking company executive*
Williams, Paul Leland *transportation executive*

Roswell
Belyew, Philip A. *holding company executive*
Dolan, Dennis Joseph *airline pilot, lawyer*

KENTUCKY

Frankfort
Robey, John Dudley *transportation executive*

Louisville
Dunman, Leonard Joe, III *trucking company executive*

LOUISIANA

Broussard
Busbice, Bill A., Jr. *transportation company executive*
Lagneaux, Bob *transportation company executive*

New Orleans
Amoss, W. James, Jr. *shipping company executive*
Cazayoux, Charles *airport executive*
Johnsen, Erik Frithjof *transportation executive*
Johnson, Peter Forbes *transportation executive, business owner*

Shreveport
Fish, Howard Math *aerospace industry executive*

MISSISSIPPI

Jackson
Caraway, George Michael *transportation executive*

NORTH CAROLINA

Cary
Harrington, Thomas Kevin *transportation planner*

Charlotte
Hutchinson, Olin Fulmer, Jr. *transportation executive, data processing consultant*
Murray, Peter William *airline executive, educator, college administrator*
Orr, T(homas) J(erome) (Jerry Orr) *airport terminal executive*

Cherryville
Huffstetler, Palmer Eugene *transportation executive, retired lawyer*
Mayhew, Kenneth Edwin, Jr. *transportation company executive*

Fayetteville
Whitaker, Frederick Stamey *pilot*

Winston Salem
Miller, James Alfred Locke, Jr. *aircraft maintenance technician*

OKLAHOMA

Broken Arrow
Moody, George Walter *aviation executive*

Oklahoma City
Trent, Luther E. *airport executive, state agency executive*

Tulsa
Blankenship, David Lee *aerospace executive*
Kitchen, Brent A. *airport executive*
Whitney, Edwin Joseph *airlines executive*

SOUTH CAROLINA

Charleston
Chapin, Fred *airport executive*
Hoerter, Sam Spalding *transportation executive*

TENNESSEE

Arnold AFB
Nelson, Clara Singleton *aerospace company executive*

Knoxville
Igoe, Terence B. *airport terminal executive*

Memphis
Broadhead, Joseph James *airline company executive*
Bruns, Michael *transportation company executive*
Cox, Larry D. *airport terminal executive*
Haas, Robert Donnell *flight instructor, airline transport pilot, lawyer*
Martin, Bob *airport executive*
McGehee, James E. *air transportation executive*
Smith, Frederick Wallace *transportation company executive*

Millington
Lecuyer, Robert Raymond *aviation maintenance administrator*

Nashville
Campbell, Timothy Lee *airport executive*

TEXAS

Amarillo
Smith, Robert Francis *transportation executive*

Arlington
Boyer, Vincent Lee *aerospace executive*

Bedford
Krick, Patrick Joseph *transportation consultant, economist*

Bridge City
Smith, Phillip Carl *marine and ship pilot, rancher*

Dallas
Baker, Robert Woodward *airline executive*
Barrett, Colleen Crotty *airline executive*
Barron, Gary A. *airline executive*
Bates, Carolyn R. *air transportation executive*
Cleveland, Linda Joyce *delivery service executive*
Denison, John G. *airline executive*
Gillan, Allan Wayne *airline captain, consultant*
Keck, Philip Walter *transportation executive*
Kelleher, Herbert David *airline executive, lawyer*
Kelly, Robert Vincent, III *transportation executive*
Miller, William Q. *airlines executive*
Oelrich, Paul Raymond *airline executive*
Parsons, Wayne Douglas *air transportation risk specialist*

Denison
Williams, Henry Rudolph *retired railroad executive*

Dickinson
Bush, Robert Thomas *shipping company executive*

Euless
Tunnell, Clida Diane *air transportation specialist*

Fort Worth
Crandall, Robert Lloyd *airline executive*
Shoemaker, Sandra Kaye *aerospace executive*

Harlingen
Farris, Robert Gene *transportation company executive*

Houston
Bethune, Gordon *airline executive*
Gaines, Paul B. *airport executive*
Kenley, Elizabeth Sue *commerce and transportation executive*
Reeves, Micheal Aaron *aerospace corporation executive*
Thagard, Norman E. *astronaut, physician, engineer*
Young, John Watts *astronaut*
Younger, Patricia Ann *port authority administrator*

Lindale
Carter, Thomas Smith, Jr. *retired railroad executive*

Lufkin
Perkins, David Mark *railroad executive, forest resource consultant*

Mcallen
Mc Creery, James F. *air transportation executive*
McCreery, Robert J. *air transportation executive*

Port Lavaca
Fisher, King *marine contracting company executive*

Roanoke
Steward, Jerry Wayne *air transportation executive, consultant*

San Antonio
Gonzalez, Efren *airport executive*
Kutchins, Michael Joseph *airport executive*

Southlake
Brandt, William Paul *pilot*

Spring
Wylie, Don L. *aviation executive*

Waco
Wingate, David Arthur *aircraft mechanic*

VIRGINIA

Alexandria
Carpenter, Stanley Hammack *retired military aviation organization executive*
Litzsinger, Orville Jack *aerospace technology executive*
Lund, Rita Pollard *aerospace consultant*

Arlington
Kirk, Robert L. *aerospace and transportation company executive*
Parker, Robert Curtis *railway executive*
Shortal, Terence Michael *systems company executive*

Haymarket
Hanscom, Fred Robert, III *transportation executive*

Mc Lean
Halstead, Warren Wayne *aviation consultant*

Newport News
Cooper, William James *transportation executive*

Norfolk
Goode, David Ronald *transportation company executive*
McKinnon, Arnold Borden *transportation company executive*
Scott, Kenneth R. *transportation executive*

Reston
Crawford, Lawrence Robert *aviation and aerospace consultant*
Nicoson, Patricia McLaughlin *transportation planner*

Richmond
Aron, Mark G. *transportation executive, lawyer*
Ermer, James *transportation company executive*
Hintz, Robert Louis *transportation company executive*
Owen, David Dalrymple *transportation company executive*
Sheahan, Melody Ann *transportation executive*
Watkins, Hays Thomas *retired railroad executive*

WISCONSIN

Milwaukee
Laemmrich, Gregory A. *airline pilot*

TURKEY

Ankara
Andrews, Steven James *aerospace company executive*

ADDRESS UNPUBLISHED

Ayer, John Butler *transportation executive*
Barber, Theodore Francis *aircraft mechanics professional*
Burkett, Ben Vern, Sr. *aircraft support company executive*
Cooper, John Byrne, Jr. *airline pilot*
Di Girolamo, Michael *airport executive*
Goldstein, Bernard *transportation and casino gaming company executive*
Heitz, Edward Fred *freight traffic consultant*
Kiefer, Roy William *aerospace company executive*
LaGreca, John S. *transportation executive*
Phillips, William Ray, Jr. *retired shipbuilding executive*
Rose, James Turner *aerospace consultant*
Snow, John William *railroad executive*
Swanson, Ralph William *aerospace executive, consultant, engineer*
Vieweg, Christian Seitz *airline pilot*

INDUSTRY: UTILITIES, ENERGY, RESOURCES

UNITED STATES

ALABAMA

Birmingham
Kuehn, Ronald L., Jr. *natural resources company executive*

Citronelle
Stechmann, Richard Henry *oil company executive*

Daphne
Jeffreys, Margaret Villar (Peggi Jeffreys) *oil company executive*

Foley
St. John, Henry Sewell, Jr. *utility company executive*

ARKANSAS

El Dorado
McNutt, Jack Wray *oil company executive*

Fayetteville
Scharlau, Charles Edward, III *natural gas company executive*

Hot Springs National Park
Counts, Mary Lou *retired telephone company executive*

Little Rock
Ford, Joe Thomas *telephone company executive, former state senator*
Maulden, Jerry L. *utility company executive*

Russellville
Cooper, Robert Michael *nuclear energy industry specialist*

CALIFORNIA

Torrance
Schanzer, Mark Joseph *petroleum company executive*

COLORADO

Golden
Olexa, George Ronald *cellular telecommunication executive*

FLORIDA

Bonifay
Quattlebaum, Walter Emmett, Jr. *telephone company executive*

Boynton Beach
Babler, Wayne E. *retired telephone company executive, lawyer*

Davie
Kaplan, Laura Garcia *emergency and disaster preparedness consultant*

Deerfield Beach
Laser, Charles, Jr. *oil company executive*

Gainesville
Ganskopp, William Fredrick *oil company executive*

Jacksonville
Clemons, Julie Payne *telephone company manager*
Stanley, David Wayne *utilities executive*

Juno Beach
Broadhead, James Lowell *electrical power industry executive*

Lake Worth
Wildschuetz, Harvey Frederick *electric industry executive*

Leesburg
Brown, Paula Kinney *heating and air conditioning contractor*

Miami
Driscoll, Garrett Bates *telecommunications executive*

Pensacola
Drain, Evelyn Louise *telecommunications specialist*

Quincy
Laughlin, William Eugene *electric power industry executive*

Saint Petersburg
Campbell, George Leroy *utilities executive*
Critchfield, Jack Barron *utilities company executive*

Tampa
Griffin, Gregg Russell *utilities supervisor*

West Palm Beach
Smith, Betsy Keiser *telecommunications company executive*

GEORGIA

Atlanta
Brinkley, Donald R. *oil industry executive*
Chipka, Stephen Thomas *telecommunications company executive*
Clendenin, John L. *telecommunications company executive*
Dahlberg, Alfred William *electric company executive*
Gilman, Joseph Michael *telecommunications executive*
McCoy, William O. *retired telecommunications executive*
Shaver, Edwards Boone *telephone company executive*
Stein, Ronald Marc *telecommunications executive*
Tigh, Mark Stephen *telecommunications executive, engineering consultant*

Baxley
Belcher, Ronald Anthony *nuclear energy educator*

Conyers
Kilkelly, Brian Holten *lighting company executive*

Cumming
Wright, Arthur Dotson *telecommunications professional*

Jackson
Anderson, Henry Warren *petroleum company executive*

Lithonia
Keyes, David Taylor *telecommunications company administrator*

Marietta
Kagan, Jeffrey Allen *telecommunications analyst, consultant, cilumni author, columnist*

Newnan
McBroom, Thomas William, Sr. *utility manager*

Norcross
Born, Allen *mining executive*
Sharon, Thomas E. *science company executive*

Tucker
Hall, Joyce Turner *utility company administrator*

KENTUCKY

Ashland
Boyd, James Robert *oil company executive*
Brothers, John Alfred *oil company executive*
Chellgren, Paul Wilbur *petroleum company executive*
Hartl, William Parker *oil company executive*
Luellen, Charles J. *retired oil company executive*
Newman, John Wilburn *oil company executive*
Quin, Joseph Marvin *oil company executive*
Yancey, Robert Earl, Jr. *oil company executive*
Zachem, Harry M. *oil company executive*

Central City
Cardwell, Sue Poole *reclamation services company executive*

Georgetown
Shropshire, Grover Craig *oil company executive*

Glasgow
Duvo, Mechelle Louise *oil company executive, consultant*

Owensboro
Vickery, Robert Bruce *oil industry executive, consultant*

LOUISIANA

Baton Rouge
Strahan, Howard Lawson *oil field exploration executive, retired*

Monroe
Burgess, Robert Lester, Jr. *telephone company executive*
Fouts, James Fremont *mining company executive*

New Orleans
Bachmann, Richard Arthur *oil company executive*
Moffett, James Robert *oil and gas company executive*
Rondeau, Clement Robert *gas industry executive, petroleum geologist*

Plain Dealing
Davis, Wayne T. *oil company and insurance agency executive*

Shreveport
Grigsby, Chester Poole, Jr. *oil and investments company executive*
Zadeck, Donald Julian *oil and gas exploration company executive*

MARYLAND

Easton
Boutte, David Gray *oil industry executive, lawyer*

Gibson Island
Kiddoo, Richard Clyde *retired oil company executive*

MICHIGAN

Detroit
Cordes, James F. *gas transmission company executive*

MISSISSIPPI

Hattiesburg
Ware, James T. *electric company executive*

NEW YORK

Aurora
Slocum, George Sigman *energy company executive*

New York
Murray, Allen Edward *retired oil company executive*

NORTH CAROLINA

Black Mountain
Cody, Hiram Sedgwick, Jr. *retired telephone company executive*

Charlotte
Grigg, William Humphrey *utility executive*
Osborne, Richard Jay *electric utility company executive*

Durham
Ferguson, David Robert *energy research manager*

Greensboro
Griffin, Haynes Glenn *telecommunications industry executive*

Raleigh
Barham, Charles Dewey, Jr. *electric utility executive, lawyer*
Clapp, Allen Linville *electric supply and communications utility consultant, mediator/arbitrator*
Racine, Brian Stanley *telecommunications executive*
Smith, Sherwood Hubbard, Jr. *utilities executive*
Starkey, Russell Bruce, Jr. *utilities executive*

OKLAHOMA

Ada
Surgnier, David Heral *gas company executive*

Bartlesville
Allen, W. Wayne *oil industry executive*
Cox, Glenn Andrew, Jr. *petroleum company executive*
Silas, Cecil Jesse *retired petroleum company executive*

Enid
Dolezal, Leo Thomas *telecommunications executive*
Ward, Llewellyn O(rcutt), III *oil company executive*

Jennings
Nixon, Arlie James *gas and oil company executive*

Oklahoma City
Estes, Stuart Hardison *oil industry executive*
Fitkin, Barbara Weldon *oil company executive*
Hefner, William Johnson, Jr. (W. John Hefner, Jr.) *oil and gas industry executive*
Lyons, Frank Daniel *retired oil company executive*
O'Keeffe, Hugh Williams *oil industry executive*
Pollock, Eks Wye, III *oil company executive*
Schader, Billy Wayne *oil company executive*
Wilkerson, Matha Ann *oil company executive*

Stroud
Lackey, Robert Dean *oil company executive, consultant*

Tulsa
Bailey, Keith E. *petroleum pipeline company executive*
Barnes, James E. *energy company executive*
Berlin, Steven Ritt *oil company financial official*
Chaback, Joseph John *oil industry researcher*
Fadem, Lloyd Robert *oil production executive*
Hall, Ronald E. *retired oil company executive*
Neas, John Theodore *petroleum company executive*
Nyberg, Donald Arvid *oil company executive*
Randall, Bill Verl *retired oil company executive*
Repasky, Mark Edward *oil and gas company executive*
Steinke, Jeffrey Jay *oil and gas company executive, lawyer*
Walters, Wilfred Nelson, Jr. *resource management company executive, engineering and economics educator*
Warren, W. K., Jr. *oil industry executive*
Wheeler, Ed *natural gas company executive*

Waynoka
Olson, Rex Melton *oil and gas company executive*

Wetumka
Hughes, Steven Bryan *gas measurement company executive*

Yukon
Willis, Donna Rose *oil company executive*

SOUTH CAROLINA

Columbia
Gressette, Lawrence M., Jr. *utilities executive*

Eastover
Sullivan, Neil Maxwell *oil and gas company executive*

Jenkinsville
Hipp, Leslie Carol *nuclear energy industry executive*

North Myrtle Beach
Atkinson, Harold Witherspoon *utilities consultant, real estate broker*

TENNESSEE

Antioch
Williams, Dolores Louise *retired telecommunications executive*

Knoxville
Eldridge, Robert Coulter *retired telephone company executive*

Morristown
Johnson, John Robert *petroleum company executive*

Nashville
Denny, J(ames) William *utility company executive*
Goodwin, William Dean *oil and gas company executive*

Smithville
Enoch, Leslie Blythe, II *gas industry executive, lawyer*

TEXAS

Abilene
Tindell, William Norman *oil company executive, petroleum geologist*

Amarillo
Dufur, Bill *utility field supervisor*
Schulte, James Michael *gas industry executive*

Arlington
Radley, Mary Ann *oil company executive*

Austin
Larkam, Peter Howard *electric utility executive, entrepreneur*
Manson, Lewis Auman *energy research executive*

Beaumont
Long, Alfred B. *retired oil company executive, consultant*

Carrollton
Rump, Ronnie Beth *oil and gas company executive*

Chandler
Sanders, Sharon Raye (Sharri Sanders) *telecommunications executive, educator*

Crane
Dohlman, Dennis Raye *oil company executive*

Cypress
Day, Robert Michael *oil company executive*

Dallas
Allen, Denny *energy company executive*
Blessing, Edward Warfield *petroleum company executive*
Brachman, Malcolm K. *oil company executive*
Brooks, E. R. (Dick Brooks) *utility company executive*
Carson, Virginia Hill *oil and gas executive*
Farrington, Jerry S. *utility holding company executive*
Gratton, Patrick John Francis *oil company executive*
Griffitts, Keith Loyd *oil industry executive*
Hacker, Shelley Gordon *oil and chemical company manager*
Haddock, Ronald Wayne *oil company executive*
Harbin, John Pickens *oil well company executive*
Hunt, Ray L. *petroleum company executive*
Jones, Dale P. *oil service company executive*
Jones, Everett Riley, Jr. *oil company executive*
Killam, Jill Minervini *oil and gas company executive*
McCormick, J. Philip *natural gas company executive*
Meek, Paul Derald *oil and chemical company executive*
Nye, Erle Allen *utilities executive, lawyer*
Rugg, Peter *oil company executive*
Smith, R. J., Jr. *oil company executive*
Stevens, Cheryl B. *utility company executive*

Duncanville
Bilhartz, James Rohn, Jr. *independent oil producer*

El Paso
Wise, William Allan *oil company executive, lawyer*

Fort Worth
Armiger, Gene Gibbon *telecommunications executive, consultant*
Bass, Perry Richardson *oil company executive*
Johnson, Dennis Ray *utility supply executive*
Munn, John William *telecommunications executive*
ONeal, Patricia Jeanne *oil company executive*
Walsh, F. Howard *oil producer, rancher*

Friendswood
Durham, Bill George *safety consultant company executive*

Granbury
Carder, Thomas Allen *nuclear energy industry emergency planner, educator*

Houston
Barracano, Henry Ralph *retired oil company executive, consultant*
Barrow, Thomas Davies *oil and mining company executive*
Bartling, Phyllis McGinness *oil company executive*
Billings, Roger Lewis *oil company executive*
Bradley, Robert Edward Lee, Jr. *energy economist, public policy professional*
Campbell, Carl David *oil industry executive, landman*
Carter, James Sumter *oil company executive, tree farmer*
Chimène, Calvin Alphonse *oil company executive, geology consultant, writer*
Condray, A. L. *oil industry executive*
Cox, Frank D. (Buddy Cox) *oil company executive, exploration consultant*
Danburg, Jerome Samuel *oil company executive*
DeVault, John Lee *oil company executive, geophysicist*
Dice, Bruce Burton *retired exploration company executive*
Dodd, Anita Adreon *oil company executive*
Evans, Bob *research director*
Freund, Alan Eugene *petrochemical company executive*
Frost, John Elliott *minerals company executive*
Gower, Bob G. *gas and oil industry executive*
Harrington, Mark Garland *oil company executive, venture capitalist*
Harrison, Otto R. *oil industry executive*
Hendrix, Dennis Ralph *energy company executive*
Hesse, Nancy Jane *gas company executive*
Honea, T. Milton *gas industry executive*
Jackson, Terrence J. *coal company executive*
Jayroe, William Gordon *oilfield service company executive*
Jones, Larry Leroy *oil company executive*
Jordan, Don D. *electric company executive*
Jordan, John William *former oil company executive and chemist*
Jorden, James Roy *retired oil company engineering executive*
Kinder, Richard Dan *natural gas pipeline, oil and gas company executive*
Kuntz, Hal Goggan *petroleum exploration company executive*
Lackey, S. Allen *petroleum company executive, corporate lawyer*
Lay, Kenneth Lee *diversified energy company executive*
Mazanec, George L. *natural gas company executive*
Morgan, Alan H. *oil company executive*
Nestvold, Elwood Olaf *telecommunications industry executive*
Nicandros, Constantine Stavros *business consultant, retired oil company executive*
Norton, Henry W., Jr. *gas industry executive*
Oshlo, Eric Lee *oil company executive*
Pate, James Leonard *oil company executive*
Patin, Michael James *oil company executive*
Payton, Christopher Charles *oil service company executive*
Reynolds, John Terrence *oil industry executive*
Richardson, Frank H. *retired oil industry executive*
Robbins, Earl L. *oil operator*
Saizan, Paula Theresa *oil company executive*
Schaefer, George Peter *utility company executive*
Sharp, John Lewis *oil industry executive, geologist*
Smith, David Kingman *retired oil company executive, consultant*
Spencer, W. E. *oil company executive*
Spincic, Wesley James *oil company executive, consultant*
Stewart, Charles Henry, Jr. *oil company executive*
Strake, George William, Jr. *oil and gas industry executive*
Tchoryk, Robert Charles *oil company administrator*
Thrash, John Curtis, Jr. *petroleum engineer, executive*
Van Dyke, Gene *oil company executive*
Watson, C. L. (Chuck Watson) *gas industry executive*
Wilkinson, G. Thomas *gas and oil industry executive*
Williams, Robert Henry *oil company executive*
Wilson, Guilford James, Jr. *oil company executive*
Wyatt, Oscar Sherman, Jr. *energy company executive*
Zeissig, Hilmar Richard *oil and gas executive*

Irving
Bayne, James Elwood *oil company executive*
Hess, Edwin John *oil company executive*
Plummer, Paul James *telephone company executive*

Kaufman
Baxter, Turner Butler *independent oil operator*

Kingwood
Ramsey, William Dale, Jr. *petroleum consultant, inventor*

La Porte
Yoder, Nelson Brent *oil company executive*

Mc Kinney
Hoffmann, Manfred Walter *consulting company executive*

Mesquite
Schlegel, Rob Allen *utilities executive*

Midland
Bitting, George Capen *oil company executive*
Franklin, Robert Drury *oil company executive*
Grover, Rosalind Redfern *oil and gas company executive*
Roper, Eddie Joe *energy company executive*
Thomas, Carroll Morgan *petroleum consultant, business developer*
Vinson, Morty (Conrad) *oil company executive, rancher*

Montgomery
Falkingham, Donald Herbert *oil company executive*
Farmer, Joe Sam *petroleum company executive*

Plano
Mackenzie, John *retired oil industry executive*

Richardson
Jones, Malinda Thiessen *telecommunications company executive*
Sullivan, Timothy Patrick *telecommunications company executive*

San Antonio
Benninger, Edward C., Jr. *petroleum and natural gas company executive*
Garcia, Henry Frank *finance and administration executive*
Greehey, William Eugene *energy company executive*
Hemminghaus, Roger Roy *energy company executive, chemical engineer*
Marmor, Robert Ruben *drilling contracting executive, petroleum engineer*
McCoy, Reagan Scott *oil company executive, lawyer*
Pope, Robert Glynn *telecommunications executive*
Shipman, Ross Lovelace *petroleum executive*
Whitacre, Edward E., Jr. *telecommunications executive*

Spearman
Archer, Carl Marion *oil and gas company executive*

The Woodlands
Ritter, Dennis Daniel, Jr. *oil industry executive*
Thompson, John Kenton *energy company executive, natural gas engineer*

Waco
Hamilton, Peter Scott *management consultant*

Winnsboro
Fairchild, Raymond Eugene *oil company executive*

VIRGINIA

Abingdon
Reid, William James *mining machinery executive*

Arlington
Zaas, Brian Marc *telecommunications and program management executive*

Centreville
Tyler, Michael Augustus *telecommunication industry consultant*

Chantilly
Willner, Larry Elliott *telecommunications company executive, consultant*

Fairfax
Noto, Lucio R. *gas and oil industry executive*

Floyd
Newell, James Robert *telephone company executive*

Reston
Van Meter, Kenneth Don *telecommunications company executive*

Richmond
Berry, William Willis *retired utility executive*
Capps, Thomas Edward *utilities company executive, lawyer*

Troy
Wyllie, Malcolm Robert Jesse *retired oil company executive, farmer*

Vienna
Thomas, Clayton Allen, Jr. *telecommunications executive*

WEST VIRGINIA

Charleston
Ray, James Allen *oil company executive, petroleum engineer*

Elkview
Banonis, Edward Joseph *gas industry executive*
Kozera, Gregory Allen *oil and gas company executive, engineer*

Mabscott
Gangopadhyay, Nirmal Kanti *mining company executive*

Morgantown
Ludwig, Ora Lee Kirk *coal company executive*

ADDRESS UNPUBLISHED

Anderson, Paul Milton *steel company executive*
Carson, Margaret Marie *gas industry executive, marketing professional*
Clarke, Kenneth Le Roy *telecommunications executive*
Dickens, Charles Allen *petroleum company executive*
Estes, Jack Charles *oil service company executive, scientist*
Herron, Edwin Hunter, Jr. *energy consultant*
Jernigan, Joseph Michael *public utilities administrator*
Kousparis, Dimitrios *oil consulting company executive*
Le Van, Daniel Hayden *gas industry executive*
Lortie, John William *solar research company executive*
Lowry, Leo Elmo *former petroleum executive*
Lupberger, Edwin Adolph *utility executive*
Macdonald, Sheila de Marillac *transaction management company executive*
Martens, John Dale *telecommunications company executive*
Murphy, Charles Haywood, Jr. *retired petroleum company executive*
Perkins, Frederick Myers *retired oil company executive*
Quillen, Lloyd Douglas *oil and gas executive*
Raymond, Lee R. *oil company executive*
Rogers, Joe O'Neal *international mangement consultant*
Sama, Meg E. *telecommunications executive*
Sledge, C. Linden *oil company executive*
Smith, John Kenneth *oil company executive, retired*
Turner, Thomas Marshall *telecommunications executive, consultant*
Vincent, Bruce Havird *investment banker, oil and gas company executive*
Watson, David L(ee) *nuclear energy training specialist, educator*
Westheimer, Jerome Max, Sr. *petroleum executive, geologist*
Woofter, R. D. *utilities company executive*

LAW: JUDICIAL ADMINISTRATION

UNITED STATES

ALABAMA

Birmingham
Acker, William Marsh, Jr. *federal judge*
Clemon, U. W. *federal judge*
Goldstein, Debra Holly *judge*
Guin, Junius Foy, Jr. *federal judge*
Nelson, Edwin L. *federal judge*
Pointer, Sam Clyde, Jr. *federal judge*

Florence
Haltom, Elbert Bertram, Jr. *federal judge*

Huntsville
Battle, Joseph Laurie *circuit court judge*

Mobile
Butler, Charles Randolph, Jr. *federal judge*
Cox, Emmett Ripley *federal judge*
Hand, William Brevard *federal judge*
Howard, Alex T., Jr. *federal judge*
Kahn, Gordon Barry *federal bankruptcy judge*
McCall, Daniel Thompson, Jr. *retired judge*
Pittman, Virgil *federal judge*
Thomas, Daniel Holcombe *federal judge*

Montgomery
Albritton, William Harold, III *federal judge*
Almon, Reneau Pearson *state supreme court justice*
Black, Robert Coleman *judge, lawyer*
Butts, Terry Lucas *state supreme court justice*
Cook, Ralph D. *judge*
De Ment, Ira *judge*
Dubina, Joel Fredrick *federal judge*
Godbold, John Cooper *federal judge*
Hooper, Perry Ollie *judge*
Hornsby, (E.C.) Sonny *judge*
Houston, James Gorman, Jr. *state supreme court justice*
Ingram, Kenneth Frank *state supreme court justice*
Johnson, Frank Minis, Jr. *federal judge*
Kennedy, (Henry) Mark *judge*
Maddox, Alva Hugh *state supreme court justice*
Maddox, Hugh *state supreme court justice*
Shores, Janie Ledlow *state supreme court justice*
Steele, Rodney Redfearn *judge*
Torbert, Clement Clay, Jr. *state supreme court justice*
Varner, Robert Edward *federal judge*

Selma
Jackson, Michael Wayne *judge, lawyer*

ARKANSAS

Conway
Hays, Steele *state supreme court judge*

El Dorado
Barnes, Harry F. *federal judge*

Fayetteville
Waters, H. Franklin *federal judge*

Fort Smith
Hendren, Jimm Larry *federal judge*

Harrison
Henley, J. Smith *federal judge*

Little Rock
Arnold, Morris Sheppard *federal judge*
Corbin, Dib *state supreme court justice*
Eisele, Garnett Thomas *federal judge*
Glaze, Thomas A. *state supreme court justice*
Harris, Oren *retired federal judge*
Holt, Jack Wilson, Jr. *state supreme court chief justice*
Howard, George, Jr. *federal judge*
Newbern, David *state supreme court justice*
Newbern, William David *state supreme court justice*
Roy, Elsijane Trimble *federal judge*
Shelton, Gary Richard *administrative law judge*
Stroud, John Fred, Jr. *state supreme court justice*
Wilson, William R., Jr. *judge*
Woods, Henry *federal judge*
Wright, Susan Webber *judge*

DISTRICT OF COLUMBIA

Washington
Robinson, Wilkes Coleman *federal judge*
Scott, Irene Feagin *federal judge*
Simpson, Charles Reagan *retired judge*

FLORIDA

Fort Lauderdale
Gonzalez, Jose Alejandro, Jr. *federal judge*
Zloch, William J. *federal judge*

Gainesville
Coleman, Mary Stallings *retired chief justice*

Jacksonville
Fryefield, Peter Jay *judge*
Hill, James Clinkscales *federal judge*
Melton, Howell Webster, Sr. *federal judge*
Moore, John Henry, II *federal judge*
Schlesinger, Harvey Erwin *judge*

Lakeland
Schoonover, Jack Ronald *judge*

Merritt Island
Johnson, Clarence Traylor, Jr. *circuit court judge*

Miami
Atkins, C(arl) Clyde *federal judge*
Davis, Edward Bertrand *federal judge*
Dyer, David William *federal judge*
Fay, Peter Thorp *federal judge*
Fletcher, John Greenwood II *state judge*
Gold, Alan Stephen *judge, lawyer, educator*
Graham, Donald Lynn *federal judge*
Highsmith, Shelby *federal judge*
Kehoe, James W. *federal judge*
King, James Lawrence *federal judge*
Marcus, Stanley *federal judge*
Moore, Kevin Michael *federal judge*
Moreno, Federico Antonio *federal judge*
Nesbitt, Lenore Carrero *federal judge*
Rosinek, Jeffrey *judge*
Ungaro-Benages, Ursula Mancusi *federal judge*

Panama City
Smith, Larry Glenn *retired state judge*

Pensacola
Vinson, C. Roger *federal judge*

Saint Petersburg
Carrere, Charles Scott *judge*
Grube, Karl Bertram *judge*
Roney, Paul H(itch) *federal judge*

Tallahassee
Anstead, Harry Lee *judge*
Grimes, Stephen Henry *state supreme court chief justice*
Harding, Major Best *state supreme court justice*
Hatchett, Joseph Woodrow *federal judge*
Kogan, Gerald *state supreme court justice*
Mc Cord, Guyte Pierce, Jr. *retired judge*
Overton, Benjamin Frederick *state supreme court justice*
Shaw, Leander Jerry, Jr. *state supreme court justice*
Stafford, William Henry, Jr. *federal judge*
Webster, Peter David *judge*
Wells, Charles Talley *judge*

Tampa
Bucklew, Susan Cawthon *federal judge*
Kovachevich, Elizabeth Anne *federal judge*
Merryday, Steven D. *federal judge*
Nimmons, Ralph Wilson, Jr. *federal judge*

West Palm Beach
Eschbach, Jesse Ernest *federal judge*
Paine, James Carriger *federal judge*
Ryskamp, Kenneth Lee *federal judge*

GEORGIA

Albany
Sands, Willie Louis *federal judge*

Americus
Smith, R. Rucker *superior court judge*

Athens
Brackett, Colquitt Prater, Jr. *judge*

Atlanta
Benham, Robert *state supreme court justice*
Camp, Jack Tarpley, Jr. *federal judge*
Carnes, Julie E. *federal judge*
Evans, Orinda D. *federal judge*
Fletcher, Norman S. *state supreme court justice*
Henderson, Albert John *federal judge*
Hunstein, Carol *judge*
Kravitch, Phyllis A. *federal judge*
Nichols, Horace Elmo *state justice*
O'Kelley, William Clark *federal judge*
Thompson, Hugh P *justice*
Ward, Horace Taliaferro *federal judge*

Augusta
Bowen, Dudley Hollingsworth, Jr. *federal judge*

Brunswick
Alaimo, Anthony A. *federal judge*

Cleveland
Barrett, David Eugene *judge*

Columbus
Elliott, James Robert *federal judge*

Lawrenceville
Reeves, Gene *judge*

Macon
Owens, Wilbur Dawson, Jr. *federal judge*

Marietta
Smith, George Thornewell *retired state supreme court justice*

Rome
Murphy, Harold Loyd *federal judge*
Vining, Robert Luke, Jr. *federal judge*

KENTUCKY

Ashland
Wilhoit, Henry Rupert, Jr. *federal judge*

Bowling Green
Huddleston, Joseph Russell *judge*

Danville
Lively, Pierce *federal judge*

Fort Thomas
Pendery, Edward Stuart *deputy county judge*

Frankfort
Stephens, Robert F. *state supreme court chief justice*
Stumbo, Janet L. *judge*
Wintersheimer, Donald Carl *state supreme court justice*

Lexington
Forester, Karl S. *federal judge*

London
Siler, Eugene Edward, Jr. *federal judge*
Unthank, G. Wix *federal judge*

Louisville
Allen, Charles Mengel *federal judge*
Boggs, Danny Julian *federal judge*
Heyburn, John Gilpin, II *federal judge*
Martin, Boyce Ficklen, Jr. *federal judge*
Mather, Roland Donald *administrative law judge*
Simpson, Charles R., III *judge*

Mount Vernon
Lambert, Joseph Earl *state supreme court justice*

Paducah
Johnstone, Edward Huggins *federal judge*

Wickliffe
Shadoan, William Lewis *judge*

LOUISIANA

Baton Rouge
Cole, Luther Francis *former state supreme court associate justice*
Parker, John Victor *federal judge*
Polozola, Frank Joseph *federal judge*

Crowley
Harrington, Thomas Barrett *judge*

Denham Springs
Kuhn, James E. *judge*

Gretna
Wicker, Thomas Carey, Jr. *judge*

Lafayette
Davis, William Eugene *federal judge*
Doherty, Rebecca Feeney *federal judge*
Duhe, John Malcolm, Jr. *federal judge*
Haik, Richard T., Sr. *federal judge*
Melançon, Tucker Lee *judge*

Lake Charles
Hunter, Edwin Ford, Jr. *federal judge*
McLeod, William Lasater, Jr. *judge, former state legislator*
Trimble, James T., Jr. *federal judge*

New Orleans
Alarcon, Terry Quentin *judge*
Beer, Peter Hill *federal judge*
Berrigan, Helen Ginger *federal judge*
Calogero, Pascal Frank, Jr. *state supreme court chief justice*
Clement, Edith Brown *federal judge*
Duplantier, Adrian Guy *federal judge*
Marcus, Walter F., Jr. *state supreme court justice*
McNamara, A. J. *federal judge*
Mentz, Henry Alvan, Jr. *federal judge*
Mitchell, Lansing Leroy *federal judge*
Schwartz, Charles, Jr. *federal judge*
Sear, Morey Leonard *federal judge, educator*
Wisdom, John Minor *federal judge*

Norco
Marino, Ruche Joseph *district court judge*

Shreveport
Politz, Henry Anthony *federal judge*
Stagg, Tom *federal judge*
Stewart, Carl E. *federal judge*
Walter, Donald Ellsworth *federal judge*
Wiener, Jacques Loeb, Jr. *federal judge*

MISSISSIPPI

Aberdeen
Davidson, Glen Harris *federal judge*
Senter, Lyonel Thomas, Jr. *federal judge*

Biloxi
Gex, Walter Joseph, III *federal judge*

Bruce
Crocker, Ottis Brazel, Jr. *municipal judge*

Gulfport
Russell, Dan M., Jr. *federal judge*

Hattiesburg
Pickering, Charles W. *federal judge*

Jackson
Banks, Fred Lee, Jr. *state supreme court judge*
Barbour, William H., Jr. *federal judge*
Barksdale, Rhesa Hawkins *federal judge*
Lee, Tom Stewart *judge*
McRae, Charles R. *state supreme court justice*
Payne, Mary Libby *judge*
Prather, Lenore Loving *state supreme court presiding justice*
Roberts, James L., Jr. *state supreme court justice*
Smith, James W., Jr. *judge*
Sugg, Robert Perkins *former state supreme court justice*
Sullivan, Michael David *state supreme court justice*
Wingate, Henry Travillion *federal judge*

Oxford
Biggers, Neal Brooks, Jr. *federal judge*

NORTH CAROLINA

Charlotte
Mullen, Graham C. *federal judge*
Potter, Robert Daniel *federal judge*
Voorhees, Richard Lesley *chief federal judge*

Greensboro
Bullock, Frank William, Jr. *federal judge*
Gordon, Eugene Andrew *judge*

Morganton
Ervin, Samuel James, III *federal judge*

Raleigh
Britt, W. Earl *federal judge*
Frye, Henry E. *state supreme court justice*
Lake, I. Beverly, Jr. *state supreme court justice*
Martin, John Charles *judge*
Mitchell, Burley Bayard, Jr. *state supreme court chief justice*
Orr, Robert F. *justice*
Webb, John *state supreme court justice*
Whichard, Willis Padgett *state supreme court justice*

Wilmington
Fox, James Carroll *federal judge*

Winston Salem
Erwin, Richard Cannon *federal judge*
Ward, Hiram Hamilton *federal judge*

OKLAHOMA

Atoka
Gabbard, (James) Douglas, II *judge*

Oklahoma City
Alley, Wayne Edward *federal judge, retired army officer*
Bohanon, Luther L. *federal judge*
Echols, M. Eileen *judge*
Hargrave, Rudolph *justice*
Henry, Robert H. *federal judge, former attorney general*
Hodges, Ralph B. *state supreme court justice*
Holloway, William Judson, Jr. *federal judge*
Lavender, Robert Eugene *state supreme court justice*
Leonard, Timothy Dwight *judge*
Opala, Marian P(eter) *state supreme court justice*
Russell, David L. *federal judge*
Salyer, Jerry L(ee) *judge*
Simms, Robert D. *state supreme court justice*
Thompson, Ralph Gordon *federal judge*
Watt, Joseph Michael *state supreme court justice*
West, Lee Roy *federal judge*
Wilson, Alma *state supreme court justice*

Tulsa
Brett, Thomas Rutherford *federal judge*
Brightmire, Paul William *retired judge*
Cook, Harold Dale *federal judge*

Waurika
Staton, Jon Tom *judge*

SOUTH CAROLINA

Aiken
Simons, Charles Earl, Jr. *federal judge*

Anderson
Anderson, George Ross, Jr. *federal judge*

Charleston
Blatt, Solomon, Jr. *federal judge*
Hawkins, Falcon Black, Jr. *federal judge*
Norton, David C. *federal judge*

Columbia
Bristow, Walter James, Jr. *retired judge*
Burnettt, E. C., III *state supreme court justice*
Chapman, Robert Foster *federal judge*
Hamilton, Clyde Henry *federal judge*
Toal, Jean Hoefer *state supreme court justice, lawyer*

Florence
Currie, Cameron McGowan *judge*

Greenville
Smith, Willie Tesreau, Jr. *retired judge, lawyer*
Traxler, William Byrd, Jr. *federal judge*
Wilkins, William Walter, Jr. *federal judge*

Greenwood
Moore, James E. *state supreme court justice*

Marion
Waller, John Henry *judge*

Myrtle Beach
Harwell, David Walker *retired state supreme court chief justice*

Orangeburg
Williams, Karen Johnson *federal judge*

Spartanburg
Russell, Donald Stuart *federal judge*

Sumter
Finney, Ernest Adolphus, Jr. *state supreme court chief justice*

TENNESSEE

Chattanooga
Edgar, R(obert) Allan *federal judge*
Franks, Herschel Pickens *judge*
Milburn, Herbert Theodore *federal judge*
Summitt, Robert Murray *circuit judge*

Greeneville
Hull, Thomas Gray *federal judge*

Jackson
Todd, James Dale *federal judge*

Johnson City
Kiener, John Leslie *judge*

Knoxville
Anderson, Edward Riley *state supreme court justice*
Jarvis, James Howard, II *judge*
Jordan, Robert Leon *federal judge*

Memphis
Allen, James Henry *magistrate*
Brown, Bailey *federal judge*
Gibbons, Julia Smith *federal judge*
Horton, Odell *federal judge*
McCalla, Jon P. *federal judge*
Turner, Jerome *federal judge*
Wellford, Harry Walker *federal judge*

Nashville
Birch, Adolpho A., Jr. *judge*
Daughtrey, Martha Craig *federal judge*
Drowota, Frank F., III *state supreme court justice*
Echols, Robert L. *federal judge*
Merritt, Gilbert Stroud *federal judge*
Nixon, John Trice *judge*
Reid, Lyle *judge*
Wall, Marion Pryor *judge*
Wiseman, Thomas Anderton, Jr. *federal judge*

Newport
Porter, James Kenneth *retired judge*

Signal Mountain
Cooper, Robert Elbert *state supreme court justice*

TEXAS

Amarillo
Robinson, Mary Lou *federal judge*

Austin
Baker, James A. *justice*
Benavides, Fortunato Pedro (Pete Benavides) *federal judge*
Cornyn, John *state supreme court justice*
Coronado, Santiago Sybert (Jim Coronado) *judge*
Derounian, Steven Boghos *lawyer, retired judge*
Enoch, Craig Trively *state supreme court justice*
Garwood, William Lockhart *federal judge*
Gonzalez, Raul A. *state supreme court justice*
Hecht, Nathan Lincoln *state supreme court justice*
Nowlin, James Robertson *federal judge*
Phillips, Thomas Royal *judge*
Pope, Andrew Jackson, Jr. (Jack Pope) *retired judge*
Ray, Cread L., Jr. *retired state supreme court justice*
Reavley, Thomas Morrow *federal judge*
Sparks, Sam *federal judge*

Beaumont
Cobb, Howell *federal judge*
Fisher, Joseph Jefferson *federal judge*

Brownsville
Vela, Filemon B. *federal judge*

Corpus Christi
Jack, Janis Graham *judge*

Dallas
Buchmeyer, Jerry *federal judge*
Chae, Don B. *judge, educator*
Higginbotham, Patrick Errol *federal judge*
Kendall, Joe *federal judge*
Luce, Thomas Warren, III *former chief justice, lawyer*
Maloney, Robert B. *federal judge*
Meier, Gerry Holden *judge*
Moyé, Eric Vaughn *district court judge, lawyer*
Robertson, Ted Zanderson *judge*
Sanders, Harold Barefoot, Jr. *federal judge*

Denton
Stewart, Wesley Holmgreen *judge, lawyer*

Edinburg
Hinojosa, Federico Gustavo, Jr. *judge*

El Paso
Dinsmoor, Robert Davidson *judge*
Hudspeth, Harry Lee *federal judge*

Fort Worth
Belew, David Owen, Jr. *judge*
King, Steve Mason *judge, lawyer*
Mahon, Eldon Brooks *federal judge*
McBryde, John Henry *federal judge*
Means, Terry Robert *federal judge*
Wallace, Steven Charles *judge*

Galveston
Kent, Samuel B. *federal judge*

Hillsboro
McGregor, Frank Bobbitt, Jr. *district judge*

Houston
Black, Norman William *federal judge*
DeAnda, James *retired federal judge*
Harmon, Melinda Furche *federal judge*
Hittner, David *federal judge*
Hughes, Lynn Nettleton *federal judge*
Jones, Edith Hollan *federal judge*
King, Carolyn Dineen *federal judge*
Lake, Simeon Timothy, III *federal judge*
Rosenthal, Lee H. *federal judge*
Schwarz, Paul Winston *judge, lawyer, business company executive*
Singleton, John Virgil, Jr. *retired federal judge, lawyer*
Smith, Jerry Edwin *federal judge*
Sondock, Ruby Kless *retired judge*
Steen, Wesley Wilson *former judge, lawyer*
Werlein, Ewing, Jr. *federal judge, lawyer*

Laredo
Kazen, George Philip *federal judge*

Mcallen
Hinojosa, Ricardo H. *federal judge*

New Braunfels
Zipp, Ronald Duane *judge*

Pampa
Cain, Donald Ezell *judge*
Peet, Richard Dwayne *county judge*

Pottsboro
Karau, Jon Olin *judge*

Richmond
Elliott, Brady Gifford *judge*

Rusk
Hassell, Morris William *judge*

San Angelo
Sutton, John Ewing *judge*

San Antonio
Clark, Leif Michael *federal judge*
Garza, Emilio M(iller) *federal judge*

Sherman
Brown, Paul Neeley *federal judge*

Temple
Skelton, Byron George *federal judge*

Tyler
Hannah, John Henry, Jr. *judge*
Justice, William Wayne *federal judge*
Parker, Robert M. *federal judge*
Steger, William Merritt *federal judge*

Waco
Smith, Walter S., Jr. *federal judge*

VIRGINIA

Abingdon
Widener, Hiram Emory, Jr. *federal judge*
Williams, Glen Morgan *federal judge*
Wilson, Samuel Grayson *federal judge*

Alexandria
Ellis, Thomas Selby, III *federal judge*
Hilton, Claude Meredith *federal judge*

Charlottesville
Michael, James Harry, Jr. *federal judge*
Wilkinson, James Harvie, III *federal judge*

Chatham
Yeatts, Coleman Bennett, Jr. *judge*

Clifton
Gales, Robert Robinson *judge*

Danville
Kiser, Jackson L. *federal judge*

Fairfax
Williams, Marcus Doyle *judge*

Falls Church
Barton, Robert L., Jr. *judge, educator*
Spector, Louis *retired federal judge, lawyer, arbitrator, consultant*

King George
Revercomb, Horace Austin, III *judge*

Mc Lean
Luttig, J. Michael *federal judge*

Norfolk
Adams, David Huntington *judge*
Clarke, J. Calvitt, Jr. *federal judge*
Doumar, Robert George *judge*
Jackson, Raymond A. *federal judge*
Kellam, Richard B. *judge*
Morgan, Henry Coke, Jr. *judge*
Smith, Rebecca Beach *federal judge*

Richmond
Carrico, Harry Lee *state supreme court chief justice*
Compton, Asbury Christian *state supreme court justice*
Hassell, Leroy Rountree, Sr. *state supreme court justice*
Keenan, Barbara Milano *judge*
Lacy, Elizabeth Bermingham *state supreme court justice*
Merhige, Robert Reynold, Jr. *federal judge*
Payne, Robert E. *federal judge*
Poff, Richard Harding *state supreme court justice*
Spencer, James R. *federal judge*
Stephenson, Roscoe Bolar, Jr. *state supreme court justice*
Williams, Richard Leroy *federal judge*

Roanoke
Turk, James Clinton *federal judge*

Salem
Koontz, Lawrence L., Jr. *judge*

Winchester
Whiting, Henry H. *state supreme court justice*

WEST VIRGINIA

Beckley
Hallanan, Elizabeth V. *federal judge*

Bluefield
Faber, David Alan *federal judge*

Charleston
Albright, Joseph P. *judge*
Brewer, Lewis Gordon *judge, lawyer, educator*
Cleckley, Franklin D. *judge*
Haden, Charles H., II *federal judge*
Hall, Kenneth Keller *federal judge*
Knapp, Dennis Raymond *federal judge*
Marland, Melissa Kaye *judge*
McHugh, Thomas Edward *state supreme court justice*
Workman, Margaret Lee *state supreme court justice*

Clarksburg
Keeley, Irene Patricia Murphy *federal judge*

Elkins
Maxwell, Robert Earl *federal judge*

Union
Sprouse, James Marshall *retired federal judge*

TERRITORIES OF THE UNITED STATES

PUERTO RICO

Hato Rey
Acosta, Raymond Luis *federal judge*

San Juan
Fusté, José Antonio *federal judge*
Laffitte, Hector Manuel *federal judge*

VIRGIN ISLANDS

Charlotte Amalie
Moore, Thomas Kail *chief judge*

Christiansted
Finch, Raymond Lawrence *judge*

ADDRESS UNPUBLISHED

Bertelsman, William Odis *federal judge*
Bootle, William Augustus *retired federal judge*
Box, Dwain D. *former judge*
Brown, Robert Laidlaw *state supreme court justice*
Bunton, Lucius Desha, III *federal judge*
Butzner, John Decker, Jr. *federal judge*
Castagna, William John *federal judge*
Ceci, Louis J. *former state supreme court justice*
Daugherty, Frederick Alvin *federal judge*
Davis, Marguerite Herr *judge*
Eaton, Joe Oscar *federal judge*
Foster, Robert Lawson *retired judge, deacon*
Hancock, James Hughes *federal judge*
Harris, Ed Jerome *retired judge*
Hightower, Jack English *former state supreme court justice and congressman*
Kauger, Yvonne *state supreme court justice*
Lee, Dan M. *state supreme court justice*
Meyer, Louis B. *superior court judge, retired state supreme court justice*
Michael, M. Blane *federal judge*
Negron-Garcia, Antonio S. *state supreme court justice*
Nesbit, Phyllis Schneider *judge*
Phillips, James Dickson, Jr. *federal judge*
Spain, Thomas B. *retired state supreme court justice*
Staker, Robert Jackson *senior federal judge*
Stamp, Frederick Pfarr, Jr. *federal judge*
Steagall, Henry Bascom, II *retired state supreme court justice*
Tillman, Massie Monroe *federal judge*
Vollmer, Richard Wade *federal judge*
Watson, Jack Crozier *retired state supreme court justice*

LAW: LAW PRACTICE AND ADMINISTRATION

UNITED STATES

ALABAMA

Anniston
Thomas, Cleophus, Jr. *lawyer*
Woodrow, Randall Mark *lawyer*

Birmingham
Akers, Ottie Clay *lawyer, publisher*
Alexander, James Patrick *lawyer*
Beasley-Carlisle, Lois René *lawyer, educator, nurse*
Boardman, Mark Seymour *lawyer*
Braswell, Walter E. *U.S. attorney*
Christ, Chris Steve *lawyer*
Cornelius, Walter Felix *lawyer*
Cullen, William Zachary *lawyer*
Farley, Joseph McConnell *lawyer*
Floyd, John Malcom *lawyer*
Foster, Arthur Key, Jr. *lawyer*
Fox, Anthony N. *lawyer*
Friedman, Linda Anne *lawyer*
Furman, Howard *mediator, lawyer*
Givhan, Robert Marcus *lawyer*
Harris, George Bryan *lawyer*
Hilley, Joseph Henry *lawyer*
Howell, William Ashley, III *lawyer*
Irons, William Lee *lawyer*
Kracke, Robert Russell *lawyer*
Langum, David John *law educator, historian*
Max, Rodney Andrew *lawyer, mediator*
Mays, Joseph Barber, Jr. *lawyer*
Mc Millan, George Duncan Hastie, Jr. *lawyer, former state official*
Newton, Alexander Worthy *lawyer*
Palmer, Robert Leslie *lawyer*
Phillips, John William, II *law librarian*
Privett, Caryl Penney *lawyer*
Robin, Theodore Tydings, Jr. *lawyer, engineer, consultant*
Savage, Kay Webb *lawyer, health center administrator, accountant*
Scherf, John George, IV *lawyer*
Sinclair, Julie Moores Williams *consulting law librarian*
Stewart, Joseph Grier *lawyer*
Trimmier, Charles Stephen, Jr. *lawyer*
Weaver, David Christopher *lawyer*
Whiteside, David Powers, Jr. *lawyer*
Whitmire, Bryant Andrew, Jr. *lawyer*
Wilson, James Charles, Jr. *lawyer*

Clanton
Jackson, John Hollis, Jr. *lawyer*

Clayton
Jackson, Lynn Robertson *lawyer*

Cullman
Poston, Beverly Paschal *lawyer*

Dadeville
Oliver, John Percy, II *lawyer*

Decatur
Blackburn, John Gilmer *lawyer*

Demopolis
Dinning, Woodford Wyndham, Jr. *lawyer*

Fultondale
Blanton, Fred, Jr. *lawyer*

Hoover
Cole, Charles DuBose, II *law educator*

Huntsville
Potter, Ernest Luther *lawyer*
Stephens, (Holman) Harold *lawyer*

Mobile
Brock, Paul Warrington *lawyer*
Holberg, Ralph Gans, Jr. *lawyer*
Holland, Lyman Faith, Jr. *lawyer*
Huff, William Jennings *lawyer, educator*
Johnston, Neil Chunn *lawyer*
Kimbrough, William Adams, Jr. *lawyer*
Murchison, David Roderick *lawyer*
Oldweiler, Thomas Patrick *lawyer*
Peebles, E(mory) B(ush), III *lawyer*
Pierce, Donald Fay *lawyer*
Reeves, William Boyd *lawyer*

Montgomery
Ashworth, Edward *lawyer, legal association administrator*
Borg, Joseph Philip *lawyer*
Chancellor, Joann *lawyer, legal association adminstrator*
Dees, Morris S. *lawyer*
Eubanks, Ronald W. *lawyer, broadcaster*
Gooden, Pamela Joyce *lawyer*
Graddick, Charles Allen *lawyer*
Howell, Allen Windsor *lawyer*
Kloess, Lawrence Herman, Jr. *lawyer*
Laurie, Robin Garrett *lawyer*
Lewis, Joseph Brady (Jay Lewis) *lawyer*
McFadden, Frank Hampton *lawyer, business executive, former judge*
Proctor, David Ray *lawyer*

Smith, Maury Drane *lawyer*
Wood, James Jerry *lawyer*

Moulton
Dutton, Mark Anthony *lawyer*

Orange Beach
Adams, Daniel Fenton *law educator*

Tuscaloosa
Christopher, Thomas Weldon *legal educator, administrator*
Hoff, Timothy *law educator, priest*
Martin, Sheree (Tamela Martin) *lawyer*
Stewart, Sandra Marie *juvenile court administrator*
Williams, Roger Courtland *lawyer*

ARIZONA

Scottsdale
Peshkin, Samuel David *lawyer*

ARKANSAS

Blytheville
Fendler, Oscar *lawyer*

Crossett
Hubbell, Billy James *lawyer*

El Dorado
Wynne, William Joseph *lawyer*

Fayetteville
Copeland, John Dewayne *law educator*
Gitelman, Morton *law educator, dean, publisher*
Niblock, Walter Raymond *lawyer*
Pearson, Charles Thomas, Jr. *lawyer*

Forrest City
Lewis, Anna *legal secretary, writer*

Little Rock
Boe, Myron Timothy *lawyer*
Bohannon, Charles Tad *lawyer*
Campbell, George Emerson *lawyer*
Cherry, Sandra Wilson *lawyer*
Creasman, William Paul *lawyer*
Darr, James Earl, Jr. *lawyer*
Dillahunty, Wilbur Harris *lawyer*
Dumeny, Marcel Jacque *lawyer*
Eubanks, Gary Leroy, Sr. *lawyer*
Hall, John Wesley, Jr. *lawyer*
Hoover, Paul Williams, Jr. *lawyer*
Jones, Stephen Witsell *lawyer*
Julian, Jim Lee *lawyer*
Lipe, Linda Bon *lawyer*
Roe, Ramona Jeraldean *lawyer, state official*
Warner, Cecil Randolph, Jr. *lawyer*
Wright, Robert Ross, III *law educator*

Mena
Thrailkill, Daniel B. *lawyer*

Pine Bluff
Jones, John Harris *lawyer, banker*
Strode, Joseph Arlin *lawyer*

Rogers
Myers, Dane Jacob *lawyer, podiatrist*

Texarkana
Whitefield, Carolyn Lee *lawyer*

Van Buren
Gant, Horace Zed *lawyer*

DISTRICT OF COLUMBIA

Washington
Fleit, Martin *lawyer*
Frazer, Victor Olanzo *lawyer*
Horahan, Edward Bernard, III *lawyer*
Huge, Harry *lawyer*
Kiko, Philip George *lawyer*
Konselman, Douglas Derek *lawyer*
Ma, Michael John *legal assistant*
Martin, David Alan *law educator, government official*
Melton, Michael Eric *lawyer, engineer*
Mostoff, Allan Samuel *lawyer, consultant*
Muir, J. Dapray *lawyer*
Munsell, Elsie Louise *lawyer*
Nolan, David Brian *lawyer*
O'Toole, Francis J. *lawyer*
Piorkowski, Joseph D., Jr. *lawyer, military officer, educator, physician*
Richardson, Elliot Lee *lawyer*
Roberts, James Harold, III *lawyer*
Robinson, Douglas George *lawyer*
Rose, Jonathan Chapman *lawyer*
Ross, Douglas *lawyer, legal academic administrator*
Sagawa, Shirley Sachi *lawyer*
Salemi, Dominick John *lawyer, publisher, writer*
Shenefield, John Hale *lawyer*
Stinger, Kenneth Frank *lawyer, professional association executive*
Uehlein, E(dward) Carl, Jr. *lawyer*
Ward, Joe Henry, Jr. *lawyer*
Watson, Jack H., Jr. *lawyer*
Webster, James Kelsey, IV *legal assistant*
Weiss, Rhett Louis *lawyer*

FLORIDA

Altamonte Springs
Heindl, Phares Matthews *lawyer*
Hoogland, Robert Frederics *lawyer*

Bartow
Evans, William Earl, Jr. *lawyer*

Boca Raton
Beber, Robert H. *lawyer, financial services executive*
Bovarnick, Bennett *lawyer, management consultant*
Brett-Major, Lin *lawyer, mediator, arbitrator, lecturer*
Dudley, Everett Haskell, Jr. *lawyer*
Erdman, Joseph *lawyer*
Haight, Carol Barbara *lawyer*
Jacobs, Joseph James *lawyer, communications company executive*
Kitzes, William Fredric *lawyer, safety analyst, consultant*
Schechterman, Lawrence *securities arbitration executive*
Sigety, Charles Edward *lawyer, family business consultant*
Silver, Barry Morris *lawyer, lay preacher*

Bonita Springs
Olander, Ray Gunnar *retired lawyer*

Boynton Beach
Armstrong, Jack Gilliland *lawyer*

Bradenton
Lopacki, Edward Joseph, Jr. *lawyer*
Stewart, Thomas Wilson *lawyer*

Brandon
Tittsworth, Clayton (Magness) *lawyer*

Cape Coral
Lusk, Lisa Marie *lawyer*

Clearwater
Bairstow, Frances Kanevsky *labor arbitrator, mediator, educator*
Falkner, William Carroll *lawyer*
Gassman, Alan Scott *lawyer*
Hopkins, Edward John *lawyer*
Peters, Robert Timothy *circuit judge*
Weidemeyer, Carleton Lloyd *lawyer*

Coconut Grove
Arboleya, Carlos Joaquin *lawyer, broker*
Joffe, David Jonathon *lawyer*
McAmis, Edwin Earl *lawyer*

Coral Gables
Aran, Fernando Santiago *lawyer*
Chonin, Neil Harvey *lawyer*
Hoffman, Carl H(enry) *lawyer*
Kniskern, Joseph Warren *lawyer*
Sacasas, Rene *lawyer*
Telepas, George Peter *lawyer*

Coral Springs
Blyler, William Edward *lawyer*
Just, Chester A. *lawyer*

Daytona Beach
Dunagan, Walter Benton *lawyer, educator*
Neitzke, Eric Karl *lawyer*

Delray Beach
Larry, R. Heath *lawyer*
Ugelow, Seymour Joseph *retired lawyer*

Dunedin
Zschau, Julius James *lawyer*

Fernandina Beach
Manson, Keith Alan Michael *lawyer*

Floral City
Williams, Nelson Garrett *lawyer, mediator, arbitrator*

Fort Lauderdale
Adams, Salvatore Charles *lawyer, speaker, financial consultant, radio and television commentator*
Anastasiou, Van E. *lawyer*
Barnard, George Smith *lawyer, former federal agency official*
Bass, Daniel Barry *lawyer*
Brawer, Marc Harris *lawyer*
Bunnell, George Eli *lawyer*
Burris, Johnny Clark *law educator*
Bustamante, Nestor *lawyer*
Clark, Desmond Laverne *immigration legal secretary, editor, minister*
Colsky, Andrew Evan *lawyer, mediator, arbitrator*
Cooney, David Francis *lawyer*
Cubit, William Aloysius *lawyer*
Dressler, Robert A. *lawyer*
Friedman, Linda Joy *senior litigation paralegal, journalist*
Goldberg, Alan Joel *lawyer*
Golden, E(dward) Scott *lawyer*
Haddad, Fred *lawyer*
Haliczer, James Solomon *lawyer*
Heidgerd, Frederick Cay *lawyer*
Hess, George Franklin, II *lawyer*
Hirsch, Jeffrey Allan *lawyer*
Hoines, David Alan *lawyer*
Jarvis, Robert Mark *law educator*
Kramish, Marc Eric *lawyer*
Krathen, David Howard *lawyer*
Kreizinger, Loreen I. *lawyer, nurse*
Magrino, Peter Frank *lawyer*
Meeks, William Herman, III *lawyer*
Mintz, Joel Alan *law educator*
Moss, Stephen B. *lawyer*
Nussbaum, Howard Jay *lawyer*
Rose, Norman *lawyer*
Roselli, Richard Joseph *lawyer*
Schneider, Laz Levkoff *lawyer*
Schreiber, Alan Hickman *lawyer*
Sherman, Richard Allen *lawyer*
Shulmister, M(orris) Ross *lawyer*
Spann, Ronald Thomas *lawyer*
Stankee, Glen Allen *lawyer*
Stapleton, John Owen *lawyer*
Tripp, Norman Densmore *lawyer*
Turner, Hugh Joseph, Jr. *lawyer*
Walton, Rodney Earl *lawyer*
Wich, Donald Anthony, Jr. *lawyer*
Young, Douglas Hamilton *lawyer, literary agency executive, novelist*

Fort Myers
Dalton, Anne *lawyer*
Epperson, Joel Rodman *lawyer*
McNeil, Kenneth Eugene *law firm administrator*
Zacharias, William F. *retired law educator*

Fort Myers Beach
Cotter, Richard Timothy *lawyer*

Gainesville
Boyes, Patrice Flinchbaugh *lawyer, environmental executive*
Freeland, James M. Jackson *lawyer, educator*
Huszar, Arlene Celia *lawyer, mediator*
Maurer, Virginia Gallaher *law educator*
Moffat, Robert Charles Lincoln *law educator*
Wagner, William Robert *lawyer*
Weyrauch, Walter Otto *law educator*

Hialeah
Dominik, Jack Edward *lawyer*

Hollywood
Fischler, Shirley Balter *lawyer*

Inverness
Stepp, Kenneth Stephenson *lawyer*

Jacksonville
Braddock, Donald Layton, Sr. *lawyer, accountant*
Callender, John Francis *lawyer*
Christian, Gary Irvin *lawyer*
Drew, Horace Rainsford, Jr. *lawyer*
Fawbush, Andrew Jackson *lawyer*
Gabel, George DeSaussure, Jr. *lawyer*
Grizzard, Richelle Allene *legal assistant*
Horne, Mark J. *lawyer*
Houser, John Edward *lawyer*
Kendrick, Darryl D. *lawyer*
Korn, Michael Jeffrey *lawyer*
Legler, Mitchell Wooten *lawyer*
Link, Robert James *lawyer, educator*
McBurney, Charles Walker, Jr. *lawyer*
Mc Carthy, Edward, Jr. *lawyer*
Moseley, James Francis *lawyer*
Oberdier, Ronald Ray *lawyer*
Pillans, Charles Palmer, III *lawyer*
Sadler, Luther Fuller, Jr. *lawyer*
Still, Lisa Stotsbery *lawyer*
Thomas, Archibald Johns, III *lawyer*
White, Edward Alfred *lawyer*

Jasper
McCormick, John Hoyle *lawyer*

Jupiter
Brophy, Gilbert Thomas *lawyer*
Click, David Forrest *lawyer*
del Russo, Alessandra Luini *law educator*
King, Regina Ann *lawyer*

Key Largo
Mattson, James Stewart *lawyer, environmental scientist, educator*

Key West
Eden, Nathan E. *lawyer*

Lake City
Ellis, Herbert Wayne *lawyer*

Lakeland
Artigliere, Ralph *lawyer, educator*
Henry, William Oscar Eugene *lawyer*
Schott, Clifford Joseph *lawyer*

Largo
Fine, A(rthur) Kenneth *lawyer*
Greef, Thomas Edward *arbitrator, mediator*

Leesburg
Austin, Robert Eugene, Jr. *lawyer*

Longwood
Dicks, Jack William *lawyer*
Tomasulo, Virginia Merrills *retired lawyer*

Margate
Shooster, Frank Mallory *lawyer*

Marianna
Wynn, Charles Milton *lawyer*

Melbourne
Ballantyne, Richard Lee *lawyer*
Gougelman, Paul Reina *lawyer*
Trachtman, Jerry H. *lawyer*

Miami
Abrams, Brenda M. *lawyer*
Alonso, Antonio Enrique *lawyer*
Amber, Laurie Kaufman *lawyer*
Armstrong, James Louden, III *lawyer*
Bartel, Jeffrey Scott *lawyer*
Baumberger, Charles Henry *lawyer*
Berger, Steven R. *lawyer*
Berman, Bruce Judson *lawyer*
Blackburn, Roger Lloyd *lawyer*
Blumberg, Edward Robert *lawyer*
Bronis, Stephen J. *lawyer*
Cano, Mario Stephen *lawyer*
Castillo, Angel, Jr. *lawyer*
Chabrow, Penn Benjamin *lawyer*
Cheleotis, Tassos George *lawyer*
Citron, Beatrice Sally *law librarian, lawyer, educator*
Clarke, Mercer Kaye *lawyer*
Claughton, Edward Napoleon, Jr. *lawyer*
Cohen, Jeffrey Michael *lawyer*
Connor, Terence Gregory *lawyer*
de Leon, John Louis *lawyer*
DuFresne, Elizabeth Jamison *lawyer*
England, Arthur Jay, Jr. *lawyer, former state justice*
Ferrell, Milton Morgan, Jr. *lawyer*
Fishman, Barry Stuart *lawyer*
Fishman, Lewis Warren *lawyer, educator*
Fitzgerald, Joseph Michael, Jr. *lawyer*
Fleming, Joseph Z. *lawyer*
Fontes, J. Mario F., Jr. *lawyer*
Freeman, Gill Sherryl *lawyer*
Garber, Harold Michael *lawyer*
Goldstein, Thomas *lawyer*
Gonzalez-Pita, J. Alberto *lawyer*
Gragg, Karl Lawrence *lawyer*
Greenleaf, Walter Franklin *lawyer*
Gross, Leslie Jay *lawyer*
Hall, Miles Lewis, Jr. *lawyer*
Hartman, Douglas Cole *lawyer*
Herron, James Michael *lawyer*
Hickey, John Heyward *lawyer*
Hirsch, Milton Charles *lawyer*
Hoffman, Larry J. *lawyer*
Hudson, Robert Franklin, Jr. *lawyer*
Klein, Peter William *lawyer, corporate officer, investment company executive*
Kleinfeld, Denis A. *lawyer*
Kline, Charles C. *lawyer*
Lipcon, Charles Roy *lawyer*
Maher, Stephen Trivett *lawyer, educator*
Mank, Rodney Layton *lawyer*
Marx, Richard Benjamin *lawyer*
Mc Laughlin, (Edward) Bruce *lawyer, actor*
Metz, Larry Edward *lawyer*
Miller, Raymond Vincent, Jr. *lawyer*
Moore, Michael T. *lawyer*
Mudd, John Philip *lawyer*
Murai, Rene Vicente *lawyer*
Myers, Kenneth M. *lawyer*
Nachwalter, Michael *lawyer*
Nagin, Stephen E. *lawyer, educator*
Nelson, Richard M. *lawyer*
Pallot, Joseph Wedeles *lawyer*
Payne, R.W., Jr. *lawyer*
Quentel, Albert Drew *lawyer*
Quirantes, Albert M. *lawyer*
Reeves, Mark Thomas *lawyer, architect*
Rosen, Howard Robert *lawyer*
Rothman, David Bill *lawyer*
Ruffner, Charles Louis *lawyer*
Saldana, Alfonso Manuel *lawyer*
Sargent, Joanne Elaine *lawyer*
Sarnoff, Marc David *lawyer*
Schleifer, Nancy Faye *lawyer, writer*
Sharpstein, Richard Alan *lawyer*
Skolnick, S. Harold *lawyer*
Sparks, Meredith Pleasant (Mrs. William J. Sparks) *lawyer*
Spencer, W(alter) Thomas *lawyer*
Stansell, Leland Edwin, Jr. *lawyer, educator*
Starr, Ivar Miles *lawyer*
Stein, Allan Mark *lawyer*
Stokes, Paul Mason *lawyer*
Touby, Kathleen Anita *lawyer*
Traurig, Robert Henry *lawyer*
Weiner, Jeffrey Stuart *lawyer*
Weiner, Lawrence *lawyer*
Weinger, Steven Murray *lawyer*
Werth, Susan *lawyer*
Wheeler, Harold Austin, Sr. *lawyer, former educational administrator*
Whisenand, James Dudley *lawyer*
Wiseheart, Malcolm Boyd, Jr. *lawyer*
Wolfe, Bardie Clinton, Jr. *law librarian, educator*

Miami Lakes
Sharett, Alan Richard *lawyer, environmental litigator, mediator and arbitrator, law educator*

Naples
Budd, David Glenn *lawyer*
Cimino, Richard Dennis *lawyer*
Crehan, Joseph Edward *lawyer*
Dutton, Clarence Benjamin *lawyer*
Emerson, John Williams, II *lawyer*
Grimm, William Thomas *lawyer*
Humphreville, John David *lawyer*
Mac'Kie, Pamela S. *lawyer*
McMackin, F. Joseph, III *lawyer*
Sparkman, Richard Dale *lawyer, author*

North Miami
Bonham-Yeaman, Doria *law educator*

North Miami Beach
Snihur, William Joseph, Jr. *lawyer*
Zipkin, Sheldon Lee *lawyer, educator*

North Palm Beach
Boyden, Christopher Wayne *lawyer, divorce mediator*
O'Flarity, James P. *lawyer*
Williams, Paul Whitcomb *lawyer*

Ocala
Thompson, Raymond Edward *lawyer*

Okeechobee
Selmi, William, Jr. *lawyer*

Orlando
Allen, William Riley *lawyer*
Bailey, Michael Keith *lawyer*
Baumgardner, Theodore Rogers *lawyer*
Baxter, Richard David *lawyer, minister*
Blackwell, Bruce Beuford *lawyer*
Boyles, William Archer *lawyer*
Conti, Louis Thomas Moore *lawyer*
Dempsey, Bernard Hayden, Jr. *lawyer*
Dietz, Robert Lee *lawyer*
Durie, Jack Frederick, Jr. *lawyer*
Eagan, William Leon *lawyer*
Feuvrel, Sidney Leo, Jr. *lawyer, educator*
Genzman, Robert Wayne *lawyer*
Gold, I. Randall *lawyer*
Gray, J. Charles *lawyer, cattle rancher*
Handley, Leon Hunter *lawyer*
Hedrick, David Warrington *lawyer*
Hendry, Robert Ryon *lawyer*
Ioppolo, Frank S., Jr. *lawyer*
Kelaher, James Peirce *lawyer*
Lang, Thomas Frederick *lawyer*
Lord, John Stanley, Jr. *lawyer*
Losey, Ralph Colby *lawyer*
Lowndes, John Foy *lawyer*
Martinez, Melquiades R. (Mel Martinez) *lawyer*
Mock, Frank Mackenzie *lawyer*
Nants, Bruce Arlington *lawyer*
Nelson, Frederick Herbert *lawyer*
Nichols, Jack Britt *lawyer*
Reed, John Alton *lawyer*
Rosenthal, Paul Edmond *lawyer*
Sheaffer, William Jay *lawyer*
Skambis, Christopher Charles, Jr. *lawyer*
Snively, Stephen Wayne *lawyer*
Spoonhour, James Michael *lawyer*
Wagner, Lynn Edward *lawyer*

Ormond Beach
Barker, Robert Osborne (Bob Barker) *mediator, property management and public relations executive*

Logan, Sharon Brooks *lawyer*

Palm Beach
Crawford, Sandra Kay *lawyer*
Snedeker, Sedgwick *lawyer*
Zeller, Ronald John *lawyer*

Palm Beach Gardens
Golis, Paul Robert *lawyer*
Hayes, Neil John *lawyer*
Kahn, David Miller *lawyer*
Koffler, Warren William *lawyer*
Olson, Carl Eric *lawyer*
Pumphrey, Gerald Robert *lawyer*

Palm Harbor
Murphy, Lester F(uller) *lawyer*

Panama City
Patterson, Christopher Nida *lawyer*

Pembroke Pines
Slivka, Michael Andrew *lawyer*

Pensacola
Geeker, Nicholas Peter *lawyer, judge*
Levin, David Harold *lawyer*
Marsh, William Douglas *lawyer*
McKenzie, James Franklin *lawyer*
Windham, John Franklin *lawyer*

Plant City
Buchman, Kenneth William *lawyer*

Ponte Vedra Beach
Kuhn, Bowie K. *lawyer, former professional baseball commissioner, consultant*

Port Richey
Richardson, Richard Lewis *lawyer*

Saint Petersburg
Allen, John Thomas, Jr. *lawyer*
Brown, Jacqueline Ley White *lawyer*
Elson, Charles Myer *law educator*
Escarraz, Enrique, III *lawyer*
Henniger, David Thomas *lawyer*
Ross, Howard Philip *lawyer*

Sanford
Smith, Vicki Lynn *lawyer*

Sarasota
Christopher, William Garth *lawyer*
Davis, Louis Poisson, Jr. *lawyer, consultant*
Dillon, Rodney Lee *lawyer*
Fetterman, James C. *lawyer*
Friar, George Edward *lawyer, state official*
Garland, Richard Roger *lawyer*
Herb, F(rank) Steven *lawyer*
Janney, Oliver James *lawyer, plastics and chemical company executive*
Phillips, Elvin Willis *lawyer*
Rossi, William Matthew *lawyer*
Salomone, William Gerald *lawyer*
Schofield, John Marcus *retired lawyer, writer*
Shults, Thomas Daniel *lawyer*

Sebring
McCollum, James Fountain *lawyer*

Stuart
George, Anthony Dale *lawyer*
Watson, Robert James *lawyer*

Tallahassee
Barley, John Alvin *lawyer*
Barnett, Martha Walters *lawyer*
Davis, William Howard *lawyer*
Ehrhardt, Charles Winton *law educator*
Fonvielle, Charles David *lawyer*
France, Belinda Takach *lawyer, business owner*
Green, William H. *lawyer, scientist*
Herskovitz, S(am) Marc *lawyer*
Holcomb, Lyle Donald, Jr. *retired lawyer*
Kerns, David Vincent *lawyer*
Manley, Walter Wilson, II *lawyer*
Marshall, Marilyn Josephine *lawyer*
Minnick, Bruce Alexander *lawyer*
Norman, James William, Jr. *lawyer*
Peacock, Valerie Lynn *paralegal*
Quattlebaum, William Franklin *lawyer*
Roland, Raymond William *lawyer*
Thiele, Herbert William Albert *lawyer*
Whitney, Enoch Jonathan *lawyer*
Zaiser, Kent Ames *lawyer*

Tampa
Aitken, Thomas Dean *lawyer*
Anton, S. David *lawyer*
Barker, Chris A(llen) *lawyer*
Collins, Peter Barton *international law officer*
England, Lynne Lipton *lawyer, speech pathologist, audiologist*
Gardner, J. Stephen *lawyer*
Gifford, Donald Arthur *lawyer*
Gillen, William Albert *lawyer*
Gonzalez, Alan Francis *lawyer*
Gonzalez, Joe Manuel *lawyer*
Hapner, Elizabeth Lynn *lawyer, writer*
Hughes, Linda Renate *lawyer, arbitrator, mediator*
Jones, John Arthur *lawyer*
Kiernan, William Joseph, Jr. *lawyer, real estate investor*
LeFevre, David E. *lawyer, professional sports team executive*
MacDonald, Thomas Cook, Jr. *lawyer*
McQuigg, John Dolph *lawyer*
Oehler, Richard Dale *lawyer*
Olson, John Karl *lawyer*
Pacheco, Felipe Ramon *lawyer*
Rosen, Stephen Leslie *lawyer*
Soble, James Barry *lawyer*
Somers, Clifford Louis *lawyer*
Stagg, Clyde Lawrence *lawyer*
Steiner, Geoffrey Blake *lawyer*
Stephens, Steven Scott *lawyer, educator*
Stiles, Mary Ann *lawyer*
Sweet, Charles G. *paralegal school administrator, dean*
Vessel, Robert Leslie *lawyer*
Watson, Roberta Casper *lawyer*
Whatley, Jacqueline Beltram *lawyer*
Winkles, Dewey Frank *lawyer*

West Palm Beach
Baker, Bernard Robert, II *lawyer*
Barnhart, Forrest Gregory *lawyer*
Beall, Kenneth Sutter, Jr. *lawyer*
Bertles, James Billet *lawyer*
Conrad, John Regis *lawyer*
Gildan, Phillip Clarke *lawyer*
Herring, Grover Cleveland *lawyer*
James, Keith Alan *lawyer*
Kiely, Dan Ray *lawyer, banking and real estate development executive*
Ladwig, Patti Heidler *lawyer*
Lampert, Michael Allen *lawyer*
Layman, David Michael *lawyer*
McHale, Michael John *lawyer*
Montgomery, Robert Morel, Jr. *lawyer*
Spillias, Kenneth George *lawyer*
Tanzer, Jed Samuel *lawyer, financial consultant*
Wroble, Arthur Gerard *lawyer*

Winter Park
Brooten, Kenneth Edward, Jr. *lawyer*
Goldsmith, Karen Lee *lawyer*
Hadley, Ralph Vincent, III *lawyer*
Salzman, Gary Scott *lawyer*

GEORGIA

Alpharetta
Linder, Harvey Ronald *lawyer, arbitrator, mediator*

Athens
Davis, Claude-Leonard *lawyer, educational administrator*
Elkins, Robert Neal *lawyer*
Green, James Larry *legal administrator*
Huszagh, Fredrick Wickett *lawyer, educator, information management company executive*
Tolley, Edward Donald *lawyer*

Atlanta
Anderson, Peter Joseph *lawyer*
Apolinsky, Stephen Douglas *lawyer*
Ashbourne, William H. *lawyer*
Baker, Anita Diane *lawyer*
Barker, Clayton Robert, III *lawyer*
Barkoff, Rupert Mitchell *lawyer*
Baum, Stanley M. *lawyer*
Beckman, Gail McKnight *law educator*
Billington, Barry E. *lawyer*
Bird, Wendell Raleigh *lawyer*
Blank, A(ndrew) Russell *lawyer*
Block, Mitchell Stern *lawyer*
Booth, Gordon Dean, Jr. *lawyer*
Boynton, Frederick George *lawyer*
Branch, Thomas Broughton, III *lawyer*
Brown, (William) Theodore, Jr. *lawyer, writer*
Byrne, Granville Bland, III *lawyer*
Cahoon, Susan Alice *lawyer*
Calhoun, Scott Douglas *lawyer*
Callner, Bruce Warren *lawyer*
Campbell, Pollyann S. *lawyer*
Carpenter, David Allan *lawyer*
Cataland, Louis S. *lawyer*
Chilivis, Nickolas Peter *lawyer*
Chisholm, Tommy *lawyer, utility company executive*
Cobb, Charles Kenche *lawyer, real estate broker*
Cooper, Lawrence Allen *lawyer*
Davis, Frank Tradewell, Jr. *lawyer*
Denham, Vernon Robert, Jr. *lawyer*
Duffey, William Simon, Jr. *lawyer*
Duncan, Martha Grace *law educator*
Eckl, William Wray *lawyer*
Egan, Michael Joseph *lawyer*
England, John Melvin *lawyer, clergyman*
Epstein, David Gustav *lawyer*
Etheridge, Jack Paul *arbitrator, mediator, former judge*
Fiorentino, Carmine *lawyer*
Foreman, Edward Rawson *lawyer*
Fox, Susan E. *legal assistant*
Gladden, Joseph Rhea, Jr. *lawyer*
González, Carlos A. *lawyer*
Gray, Herbert Harold, III *lawyer*
Grove, Russell Sinclair, Jr. *lawyer*
Harkey, Robert Shelton *lawyer*
Harness, William Walter *lawyer*
Harper, James Roland, Jr. *lawyer*
Harrison, Bryan Guy *lawyer*
Hawks, Barrett Kingsbury *lawyer*
Henson, Howard Kirk *lawyer*
Hoff, Gerhardt Michael *lawyer, insurance company executive*
Hoffman, Michael William *lawyer, accountant*
Holmes, Sherie Bell Shortridge *lawyer*
Hopkins, George Mathews Marks *lawyer, business executive*
Howell, Arthur *lawyer*
Humphries, James Donald, III *lawyer*
Jester, Carroll Gladstone *lawyer*
Johnson, Weyman Thompson, Jr. *lawyer*
Jones, Glower Whitehead *lawyer*
Kaufman, Mark David *lawyer*
Kelley, Jeffrey Wendell *lawyer*
Killorin, Edward Wylly *lawyer, tree farmer*
Killorin, Robert Ware *lawyer*
Klamon, Lawrence Paine *lawyer*
Kolber, Daniel Hackner *lawyer*
Landau, Michael B. *law educator, musician*
Leach, James Glover *lawyer*
Leonard, David Morse *lawyer*
Lipshutz, Robert Jerome *lawyer, former government official*
Marshall, John Treutlen *lawyer*
Marvin, Charles Arthur *law educator*
Maycock, William W. *lawyer*
Mobley, John Homer, II *lawyer*
Moss, Sandra Hughes *law firm administrator*
Murphy, Richard Patrick *lawyer*
Murty, Komanduri Srinivasa *criminal justice educator*
Newman, Stuart *lawyer*
Ortiz, Jay Richard Gentry *lawyer*
Padgett, Douglas Ralph Xavier *lawyer*
Paquin, Jeffrey Dean *lawyer*
Parker, John Garrett *lawyer*
Persons, W. Ray *lawyer, educator*
Pilcher, James Brownie *lawyer*
Pless, Laurance Davidson *lawyer*
Podgor, Ellen Sue *lawyer, educator*
Pryor, Shepherd Green, III *lawyer*
Reed, Glen Alfred *lawyer*
Ridley, Clarence Haverty *lawyer*
Rogers, C. B. *lawyer*
Rusher, Derwood H., II *lawyer*
Schaudies, Jesse P., Jr. *lawyer*
Schroder, Jack Spalding, Jr. *lawyer*
Sibley, James Malcolm *retired lawyer*
Smith, Gregory Stuart *lawyer*
Somers, Fred Leonard, Jr. *lawyer*
Stahl, Ruthanne *legal administrator*
Stamps, Thomas Paty *lawyer, consultant*
Stanhope, William Henry *lawyer*
Stewart, Jeffrey Bayrd *lawyer, commodity trading advisor*
Stokes, Arch Yow *lawyer, writer*
Stone, Matthew Peter *lawyer*
Swan, George Steven *law educator*
Sweeney, Neal James *lawyer*
Togut, Torin Dana *lawyer*
Varner, Chilton Davis *lawyer*
Veal, Rex R. *lawyer*
Volentine, Richard J., Jr. *lawyer*
Weathersby, James Roy *lawyer*
Weisz, Peter R. *lawyer*
Wellon, Robert G. *lawyer*
West, Ruth Tinsley *lawyer*
Williams, David Howard *lawyer*
Winkler, Allen Warren *lawyer*
Young, Michael Anthony *lawyer*

Augusta
Cooney, William J. *lawyer*
Hall, James Randal *lawyer*

Cartersville
Pope, Robert Daniel *lawyer*

Clayton
Slowen, Warren Thomas *lawyer*

Columbus
Brinkley, Jack Thomas *lawyer, former congressman*
Harp, John Anderson *lawyer*
Johnson, Walter Frank, Jr. *lawyer*
McGlamry, Max Reginald *lawyer*
Patrick, James Duvall, Jr. *lawyer*
Shelnutt, John Mark *lawyer*

Duluth
Cardin, Charles Edward *lawyer*

Fayetteville
Johnson, Donald Wayne *lawyer*

Gainesville
Schuder, Raymond Francis *lawyer*

Griffin
Watson, Forrest Albert *lawyer, bank executive*

Hamilton
Byrd, Gary Ellis *lawyer*

Jasper
Marger, Edwin *lawyer*

Lawrenceville
Harrison, Samuel Hughel *lawyer*

Macon
Cole, John Prince *lawyer*
Kalish, Katherine McAulay *lawyer, mediator*
Robinson, W. Lee *lawyer*

Marietta
Ahlstrom, Michael Joseph *lawyer*
Bentley, Fred Douglas, Sr. *lawyer*
Ingram, George Conley *lawyer*
Nowland, James Ferrell *lawyer*

Metter
Doremus, Ogden *lawyer*

Milledgeville
Buice, Bonnie Carl *lawyer, priest*

Norcross
Anderson, Albert Sydney, III *lawyer*
Hahn, Stanley Robert, Jr. *lawyer, financial executive*
Head, William Carl *lawyer, author*
Sloan, Donnie Robert, Jr. *lawyer*

Perry
Geiger, James Norman *lawyer*

Savannah
Bowman, Catherine McKenzie *lawyer*
Dickey, David Herschel *lawyer, accountant*
Forbes, Morton Gerald *lawyer*
Kenrich, John Lewis *lawyer*
Miller, Jack Everett *retired lawyer*
Snyder, Charles William *lawyer*

Snellville
Giallanza, Charles Philip *lawyer*

Stone Mountain
Allgood, John Franklin *lawyer*

Tucker
Armstrong, Edwin Alan *lawyer*

Valdosta
Bright, Joseph Converse *lawyer*

Watkinsville
Wright, Robert Joseph *lawyer*

ILLINOIS

Glenview
Martin, Wayne Mallott *lawyer*

KENTUCKY

Ashland
Compton, Robert H. *lawyer*
Feazell, Thomas Lee *lawyer, oil company executive*

Bowling Green
Rudloff, William Joseph *lawyer*

Covington
Wolnitzek, Stephen Dale *lawyer*

Crestwood
Ray, Ronald Dudley *lawyer*

Eddyville
Story, James Eddleman *lawyer*

Elkton
Boone, George Street *retired lawyer*

Florence
Bogucki, Raymond Spencer *lawyer*

Fort Thomas
Whalen, Paul Lewellin *lawyer*

Frankfort
Chadwick, Robert *lawyer, judge*
Chandler, Ben *attorney general*
Palmore, John Stanley, Jr. *retired lawyer*
Wilborn, Woody Stephen *lawyer*

Glasgow
Dickinson, Temple *lawyer*

Harlan
Lawson, Susan Coleman *lawyer*

Harrods Creek
Hendricks, James W. *lawyer, real estate executive*

Hickory
Bell, Craig Steven *lawyer*

Lexington
Bagby, William Rardin *lawyer*
Beshear, Steven L. *lawyer*
Breckinridge, Scott Dudley, Jr. *retired law educator*
Garmer, William Robert *lawyer*
Lewis, Thomas Proctor *law educator*
Michael, Douglas Charles *law educator*
Oberst, Paul *law educator*
Rogers, Lon B(rown) *lawyer*
Turley, Robert Joe *lawyer*
Vimont, Richard Elgin *lawyer*
Vish, Donald H. *lawyer*

London
Keller, John Warren *lawyer*

Louisville
Aberson, Leslie Donald *lawyer*
Barr, James Houston, III *lawyer*
Bias, Dana G. *lawyer*
Bishop, Robert Whitsitt *lawyer*
Brown, Bonnie Maryetta *lawyer*
Buckaway, William Allen, Jr. *lawyer*
Cowan, Frederic Joseph *lawyer*
Dolt, Frederick Corrance *lawyer*
Dudley, George Ellsworth *lawyer*
Elliott, James V. *corporate lawyer*
Fuchs, Olivia Anne Morris *lawyer*
Gilman, Sheldon Glenn *lawyer*
Guethlein, William O. *lawyer*
Hectus, Charles Thomas *lawyer*
Keeney, Steven Harris *lawyer*
Lay, Norvie Lee *law educator*
Maggiolo, Allison Joseph *lawyer*
Manly, Samuel *lawyer*
Meuter, Maria Coolman *lawyer*
Morreau, James Earl, Jr. *lawyer, entrepreneur*
Noe, Randolph *lawyer*
Shaikun, Michael Gary *lawyer*
Volz, Marlin Milton *law educator*
Welsh, Alfred John *lawyer, consultant*

Madisonville
Monhollon, Leland *lawyer*

Newport
Jones, William Rex *law educator*
Siverd, Robert Joseph *lawyer*

Owensboro
Miller, James Monroe *lawyer*

Pikeville
Stalnaker, Phil A. *lawyer*

Richmond
Martin, James Neal *lawyer*

Scottsville
Secrest, James Seaton, Sr. *lawyer*

Somerset
Prather, John Gideon *lawyer*

LOUISIANA

Baton Rouge
Bybee, Jay Scott *lawyer, educator*
Dixon, Jerome Wayne *lawyer*
Giglio, Steven Rene *lawyer*
Johnson, Joseph Clayton, Jr. *lawyer*
Karns, Barry Wayne *lawyer*
Lamar, Charles Wilbur, III *lawyer*
Lamonica, P(aul) Raymond *lawyer, academic administrator, educator*
LeClere, David Anthony *lawyer*
Leonard, Paul Haralson *retired lawyer*
Mc Clendon, William Hutchinson, III *lawyer*
Price, Donald Wayne *lawyer*
Ray, Betty Jean G. *lawyer*
Richards, Marta Alison *lawyer*
Schroeder, Leila Obier *retired law educator*

Unglesby, Lewis O. *lawyer*
Walsh, Milton O'Neal *lawyer*

Covington
Reynolds, Richard Louis *lawyer*

Franklin
McClelland, James Ray *lawyer*

Jefferson
Conino, Joseph Aloysius *lawyer*

Kenner
DeMartini, Edward John *lawyer, real estate investor*

La Place
Cicet, Donald James *lawyer*

Lafayette
Breaux, Paul Joseph *lawyer, pharmacist*
Durio, William Henry *lawyer*
Judice, Marc Wayne *lawyer*
Mansfield, James Norman, III *lawyer*
Myers, Stephen Hawley *lawyer*
Pate, James Lavert *lawyer*
Saloom, Kaliste Joseph, Jr. *lawyer, retired judge*
Simien, Clyde Ray *lawyer*
Swift, John Goulding *lawyer*

Lake Charles
Davidson, Van Michael, Jr. *lawyer*
Parkerson, Hardy Martell *lawyer*
Veron, J. Michael *lawyer*

Metairie
Butcher, Bruce Cameron *lawyer*
Derbes, Albert Joseph, III *lawyer, accountant*
Ford, Robert David *lawyer*
Hardy, Ashton Richard *lawyer*
McMahon, Robert Albert, Jr. *lawyer*
Olivier, Jason Thomas *lawyer*
Quidd, David Andrew *paralegal*
Weaver, Marshall Gueringer *lawyer*

Natchitoches
Brittain, Jack Oliver *lawyer*

New Orleans
Abaunza, Donald Richard *lawyer*
Acomb, Robert Bailey, Jr. *lawyer, educator*
Barry, Francis Julian, Jr. *lawyer*
Beck, William Harold, Jr. *lawyer*
Benjamin, Edward Bernard, Jr. *lawyer*
Bernstein, Joseph *lawyer*
Bordelon, Alvin Joseph, Jr. *lawyer*
Brian, A(lexis) Morgan, Jr. *lawyer*
Bronfin, Fred *lawyer*
Burr, Timothy Fuller *lawyer*
Cassibry, Fred James *lawyer, retired federal court judge*
Coleman, James Julian, Jr. *lawyer, industrialist, real estate executive*
David, Robert Jefferson *lawyer*
Dwyer, Ralph Daniel, Jr. *lawyer*
Eustis, Richmond Minor *lawyer*
Fierke, Thomas Garner *lawyer*
Friedman, Joel William *law educator*
Goins, Richard Anthony *lawyer, educator*
Grundmeyer, Douglas Lanaux *lawyer, editor*
Hammond, Margaret *lawyer*
Hearn, Sharon Sklamba *lawyer*
Johnson, Beth Exum *lawyer*
Judell, Harold Benn *lawyer*
Kelly, William James, III *lawyer*
Leake, Robert Edward, Jr. *lawyer*
Lovett, William Anthony *law and economics educator*
Lowe, Robert Charles *lawyer*
McDougal, Luther Love, III *law educator*
McMillan, Lee Richards, II *lawyer*
Molony, Michael Janssens, Jr. *lawyer*
Moore, Lawrence William *law educator*
Pearce, John Y. *lawyer*
Perez, Luis Alberto *lawyer*
Ponoroff, Lawrence *law educator, legal consultant*
Schoemann, Rudolph Robert *lawyer*
Schumacher, Carl Joseph, Jr. *lawyer, educator*
Sher, Leopold Zangwill *lawyer*
Simon, H(uey) Paul *lawyer*
Steeg, Moise S., Jr. *lawyer*
Stone, Saul *lawyer*
Thomas, Joseph Winand *lawyer*
Thomas, Lee Daniel *lawyer*
Vance, Robert Patrick *lawyer*
Wax, George Louis *lawyer*
Willems, Constance Charles *lawyer*

Plaquemine
Politz, Nyle Anthony *lawyer*

Shreveport
Cox, John Thomas, Jr. *lawyer*
Hall, Pike, Jr. *lawyer*
Hetherwick, Gilbert Lewis *lawyer*
Jeter, Katherine Leslie Brash *lawyer*
Ratcliff, John Garrett *lawyer*
Rigby, Kenneth *lawyer*
Roberts, Robert, III *lawyer*
Smith, Brian David *lawyer, educator*
Woodman, Walter James *lawyer*

Slidell
Shamis, Edward Anthony, Jr. *lawyer*
Singletary, Alvin D. *lawyer*

Sulphur
Sumpter, Dennis Ray *lawyer, construction company executive*

MARYLAND

Hanover
Zohny, A. Y. *law educator, business educator, consultant, international development consultant*

MISSISSIPPI

Batesville
Cook, William Leslie, Jr. *lawyer*

Biloxi
O'Barr, Bobby Gene, Sr. *lawyer*

Clarksdale
Merkel, Charles Michael *lawyer*
Twiford, H. Hunter, III *lawyer*

Cleveland
Howorth, Lucy Somerville *lawyer*

Columbus
Geeslin, Gary Lloyd *lawyer*
Gholson, Hunter Maurice *lawyer*
Pounds, Billy Dean *law educator*

Greenville
Martin, Andrew Ayers *lawyer, physician, educator*

Gulfport
Harral, John Menteith *lawyer*

Hernando
Brown, William A. *lawyer*

Jackson
Black, D(eWitt) Carl(isle), Jr. *lawyer*
Byrd, Isaac K., Jr. *lawyer*
Carmody, Victor Wallace, Jr. *lawyer*
Chinn, Mark Allan *lawyer*
Fuselier, Louis Alfred *lawyer*
Hauberg, Robert Engelbrecht, Jr. *lawyer*
Henegan, John Clark *lawyer*
Holbrook, Frank Malvin *lawyer*
Hughes, Byron William *lawyer, oil exploration company executive*
Hurt, Joseph Richard *law educator*
Keyes, Samuel Wayne, Jr. *lawyer*
Phillips, George Landon *prosecutor*
Ray, H. M. *lawyer*
Van Slyke, Leonard DuBose, Jr. *lawyer*
West, Carol Catherine *law educator*
Wilson, William Roberts, Jr. (Bob Wilson) *lawyer, apparel executive*

Lumberton
Tonry, Richard Alvin *lawyer, pecan farmer*

Meridian
Eppes, Walter W., Jr. *lawyer*

Oxford
Lewis, Ronald Wayne *lawyer*

Pascagoula
Baggett Boozer, Linda Dianne *lawyer*
Krebs, Robert Preston *lawyer*
Lawson-Jowett, M. Juliet *lawyer*

Ridgeland
Dye, Bradford Johnson, Jr. *lawyer, former state official*

Starkville
Yoste, Charles Todd *lawyer*

Tupelo
Moffett, T(errill) K(ay) *lawyer*

Tylertown
Mord, Irving Conrad, II *lawyer*

Vicksburg
James, Ceola *lawyer, judge*

West Point
Morrison, Harvey Lee, Jr. *lawyer*

NEVADA

Las Vegas
Goodwin, John Robert *law educator, author*

NEW MEXICO

Santa Fe
Zorie, Stephanie Marie *lawyer*

NEW YORK

Long Island City
Barnholdt, Terry Joseph, Jr. *lawyer, real estate executive*

New York
Mills, Edward Warren *lawyer, corporate executive*

NORTH CAROLINA

Asheville
Cogburn, Max Oliver *lawyer*
Dillard, John Robert *lawyer*
Hamilton, Jackson Douglas *lawyer*
Lavelle, Brian Francis David *lawyer*

Beaufort
Tilghman, Carl Lewis *lawyer*

Boone
Brown, Wade Edward *lawyer*
McGee, Linda Mace *lawyer*

Buies Creek
Davis, Ferd Leary, Jr. *law educator, lawyer, consultant*

Burnsville
Peterson, Allen Jay *lawyer, educator*

Cary
Glass, Fred Stephen *lawyer*

Chapel Hill
Brower, David John *lawyer, urban planner, educator*
Crassweller, Robert Doell *retired lawyer, writer*
Haskell, Paul Gershon *law educator*
Herman-Giddens, Gregory *lawyer*
Martin, Harry Corpening *lawyer, retired state supreme court justice*
Wegner, Judith Welch *law educator, dean*

Charlotte
Bragg, Ellis Meredith, Jr. *lawyer*
Buckley, Charles Robinson, III *lawyer*
Campbell, Clair Gilliland *lawyer*
Coffey, Larry B(ruce) *lawyer*
Gage, Gaston Hemphill *lawyer*
Gordon, David Stott *lawyer*
Harris, Richard Foster, III *lawyer*
McGill, John Knox *lawyer*
Murchison, Bradley Duncan *lawyer*
Newitt, John Garwood, Jr. *lawyer*
Penn, Philip Julian *lawyer*
Pollard, John Oliver *lawyer*
Thigpen, Richard Elton, Jr. *lawyer*
Van Alstyne, Vance Brownell *arbitration management consultant*
Walker, Clarence Wesley *lawyer*
Woolard, William Leon *lawyer, electrical distributing company executive*
Zeller, Michael Eugene *lawyer*

Cullowhee
Wilson, LeVon Edward *law educator, lawyer*

Durham
Burrows, Virginia Moore *paralegal*
Carpenter, Charles Francis *lawyer*
Carrington, Paul DeWitt *lawyer, educator*
Cox, James D. *law educator*
Danner, Richard Allen *law educator, dean*
Demott, Deborah Ann *lawyer, educator*
Gann, Pamela Brooks *law educator*
Graham, William Thomas *lawyer*
Lange, David L. *law educator*
McMahon, John Alexander *law educator*
Sloan, Maceo Kennedy *lawyer, investment executive*
Van Alstyne, William Warner *law educator*

Elkin
Gillespie, James Davis *lawyer*

Fairview
Rhynedance, Harold Dexter, Jr. *lawyer, consultant*

Fayetteville
Mitchell, Ronnie Monroe *lawyer*
Ruppe, Arthur Maxwell *lawyer*
Townsend, William Jackson *lawyer*

Fuquay Varina
Zahrt, William Dietrich, II *lawyer*

Graham
Walker, Daniel Joshua, Jr. *lawyer*

Greensboro
Clark, David M. *lawyer*
Davis, Herbert Owen *lawyer*
Donaldson, Arthur Joseph *lawyer*
Gabriel, Richard Weisner *lawyer*
Turner, James R. *lawyer*

Greenville
Burti, Christopher Louis *lawyer*
Clark, John Graham, III *lawyer*
Hopf, James Fredrik *lawyer*

Hickory
Smith, Young Merritt, Jr. *lawyer*

Lenoir
Flaherty, David Thomas, Jr. *lawyer*

Lumberton
McIntyre, Douglas Carmichael, II *lawyer*

Morganton
Simpson, Daniel Reid *lawyer*

Murphy
Bata, Rudolph Andrew, Jr. *lawyer*

New Bern
Kellum, Norman Bryant, Jr. *lawyer*
Stoller, David Allen *lawyer*

Oxford
Burnette, James Thomas *lawyer*

Raleigh
Borden, William Henry *lawyer*
Case, Charles Dixon *lawyer*
Collins, G. Bryan, Jr. *lawyer*
Cummings, Anthony William *lawyer, educator*
Davis, Thomas Hill, Jr. *lawyer*
Dixon, Daniel Roberts, Jr. *tax lawyer*
Edwards, Charles Archibald *lawyer*
Foley, Peter Michael *lawyer*
Hall, John Thomas *lawyer*
Huggard, John Parker *lawyer*
Hunter, Richard Samford, Jr. *lawyer*
Jordan, John Richard, Jr. *lawyer*
Joyner, Walton Kitchin *lawyer*
Miller, Robert James *lawyer*
Parker, John Hill *lawyer*
Pinnix, John Lawrence *lawyer*
Poyner, James Marion *retired lawyer*
Ragsdale, George Robinson *lawyer*
Sanford, Terry *lawyer, educator, former United States Senator, former governor, former university president*
Sasser, Jonathan Drew *lawyer*
Schwab, Carol Ann *law educator*
Trott, William Macnider *lawyer*
Verdon, Jane Kathryn *lawyer*

Smithfield
Schulz, Bradley Nicholas *lawyer*

Southern Pines
Caliri, David Joseph *retired lawyer, insurance agent*

Tryon
Stinson, George Arthur *lawyer, former steel company executive*

Washington
Rader, Steven Palmer *lawyer*

Waynesville
Cole, James Yeager *legal sentencing advocate, consultant*

Wilmington
McCauley, Cleyburn Lycurgus *lawyer*

Winston Salem
Adams, Alfred Gray *lawyer*
Blynn, Guy Marc *lawyer*
Durham, Richard Monroe *lawyer*
Gunter, Michael Donwell *lawyer*
Hopkins, Muriel-Beth Norbrey *lawyer*
Loughridge, John Halsted, Jr. *lawyer*
Maready, William Frank *lawyer*
Motsinger, John Kings *lawyer*
Osborn, Malcolm Everett *lawyer*
Steele, Thomas McKnight *law librarian, law educator*
Strayhorn, Ralph Nichols, Jr. *lawyer*
Walker, George Kontz *law educator*
Zagoria, Sam D(avid) *arbitrator, author, educator*

OHIO

Cleveland
Canary, Nancy Halliday *lawyer*

OKLAHOMA

Bartlesville
Hitchcock, Bion Earl *lawyer*

Broken Arrow
Stewart, Murray Baker *lawyer*

Claremore
Steidley, Juan Dwayne *lawyer, legislator*

Cushing
Draughon, Scott Wilson *lawyer, social worker*

Del City
Wood, Paula Davidson *lawyer*

Durant
McPheron, Alan Beaumont *lawyer*

Edmond
Loving, Susan B. *lawyer, former state official*

El Reno
Grantham, Robert Edward *lawyer, educator*

Enid
Jones, Stephen *lawyer*
Martin, Michael Rex *lawyer*
McNaughton, Alexander Bryant *lawyer*
Wyatt, Robert Lee, IV *lawyer*

Jones
Dean, Bill Verlin, Jr. *lawyer*

Kingfisher
Baker, Thomas Edward *lawyer, accountant*

Lawton
Stabler, Jeffrey Calvin *lawyer, accountant*

Miami
Breaune, Joseph George *retired lawyer, judge*

Muskogee
Robinson, Adelbert Carl *lawyer, judge*
Williams, Betty Outhier *lawyer*

Norman
Fairbanks, Robert Alvin *lawyer*
Geyer, Bill R. *lawyer*
Hemingway, Richard William *law educator*
Huchteman, Ralph Douglas *lawyer*
Miley, Nina M. *law librarian*
Scaperlanda, Michael Anthony *law educator*
Talley, Richard Bates *lawyer*

Oklahoma City
Allen, Robert Dee *lawyer*
Almond, David R. *lawyer*
Angel, Steven Michael *lawyer*
Beech, Johnny Gale *lawyer*
Boston, William Clayton *lawyer*
Bryant, Ira Houston, III *lawyer*
Chubbuck, Gary Mitchell *lawyer*
Coats, Andrew Montgomery *lawyer, former mayor*
Decker, Michael Lynn *lawyer, judge*
Denton, Michael David, Jr. *lawyer*
Derrick, Gary Wayne *lawyer*
Elder, James Carl *lawyer*
Enis, Thomas Joseph *lawyer*
Featherly, Henry Frederick *lawyer*
Fitch, Mark Keith *lawyer*
Frizzell, Gregory Kent *lawyer*
Gatewood, Tela Lynne *lawyer*
Grennan, Jim *lawyer*
Hanna, Terry Ross *lawyer, small business owner*
Hastie, John Douglas *lawyer*
Hill, Carolyn Gregg *lawyer*
Kaufman, James Mark *lawyer*
Kline, David Adam *lawyer, educator, writer*
Kline, Timothy Deal *lawyer*
Lambird, Mona Salyer *lawyer*
Manning, Nancy Anne *law librarian*
McBride, Kenneth Eugene *lawyer, title company executive*
Parrott, Nancy Sharon *lawyer*
Pfefferbaum, Betty Jane *law educator, psychiatry educator*
Schwabe, George Blaine, III *lawyer*
Smith, Carl Michael *lawyer*
Sowers, Wesley Hoyt *lawyer, management consultant*

Strickland, Rennard James *law educator, dean*
Stump, T(ommy) Douglas *lawyer, educator*
Taliaferro, Henry Beauford, Jr. *lawyer*
Tompkins, Raymond Edgar *lawyer*
Towery, Curtis Kent *lawyer*
Turpen, Michael Craig *lawyer*
Tytanic, Christopher Alan *lawyer*
White, Joe E., Jr. *lawyer*
Woods, Harry Arthur, Jr. *lawyer*
Zevnik-Sawatzky, Donna Dee *litigation coordinator*

Sapulpa
Lane, Tom Cornelius *lawyer*

Shawnee
Chumley, Phillip Lee *prosecutor*

Stillwater
Severe, John Thomas *lawyer*

Tulsa
Abrahamson, A. Craig *lawyer*
Abramowitz, Jerrold *lawyer*
Atkinson, Michael Pearce *lawyer*
Belsky, Martin Henry *law educator, lawyer*
Brewster, Clark Otto *lawyer*
Cooper, Richard Casey *lawyer*
Craft, Joseph W., III *lawyer*
Davenport, Gerald Bruce *lawyer*
Davis, G. Reuben *lawyer*
Dexter, Deirdre O'Neil Elizabeth *lawyer*
Eagan, Claire Veronica *lawyer*
Eldridge, Richard Mark *lawyer*
Hatfield, Jack Kenton *lawyer, accountant*
Hood, William Wayne, Jr. *lawyer*
Howard, Gene Claude *lawyer, former state senator*
Huffman, Robert Allen, Jr. *lawyer*
Imel, John Michael *lawyer*
Kihle, Donald Arthur *lawyer*
La Sorsa, William George *lawyer, educator*
Matthies, Mary Constance T. *lawyer*
McGonigle, Richard Thomas *lawyer*
Nemec, Michael Lee *lawyer*
Schwartz, Bernard *law educator*
Slicker, Frederick Kent *lawyer*
Steltzlen, Janelle Hicks *lawyer*
Strecker, David Eugene *lawyer*

Westville
Lawbaugh, Emanuel Sylvester, IV *lawyer, educator*

PENNSYLVANIA

Philadelphia
Lowery, William Herbert *lawyer*
Weinstein, David *lawyer, educator*

RHODE ISLAND

Providence
Juchatz, Wayne Warren *lawyer*

SOUTH CAROLINA

Beaufort
Scott, Vernell Izora *lawyer*

Charleston
Bigler, Rose Johnson *criminal justice educator*
Cannon, Hugh *lawyer*
Clement, Robert Lebby, Jr. *lawyer*
Darling, Stephen Edward *lawyer*
Farr, Charles Sims *lawyer*
Hood, Robert Holmes *lawyer*
Kahn, Ellis Irvin *lawyer*
Laddaga, Lawrence Alexander *lawyer*
Mulholland, Angela Broadway *lawyer*
Robinson, Neil Cibley, Jr. *lawyer*
Spitz, Hugo Max *lawyer*
Warren, John Hertz, III *lawyer*
Young, Joseph Rutledge, Jr. *lawyer*

Columbia
Austin, Charles Perry *law enforcement administrator*
Babcock, Keith Moss *lawyer*
Blanton, Hoover Clarence *lawyer*
Carpenter, Charles Elford, Jr. *lawyer*
Day, Richard Earl *lawyer*
Dunbar, James V., Jr. *lawyer, educator, real estate broker, broadcaster, business consultant*
Gibbes, William Holman *lawyer*
Handel, Richard Craig *lawyer*
Jedziniak, Lee Peter *lawyer, educator, state insurance administrator*
McCormick, Nancy Campbell *lawyer*
Rouse, LeGrand Ariail, II *retired lawyer, educator*
Sheftman, Howard Stephen *lawyer*
Swerling, Jack Bruce *lawyer*

Conway
Martin, Gregory Keith *lawyer*

Gaffney
Rhoden, William Gary *lawyer*

Greenville
Edwards, Harry LaFoy *lawyer*
Foulke, Edwin Gerhart, Jr. *lawyer*
Mauldin, John Inglis *lawyer*
Phillips, Joseph Brantley, Jr. *lawyer*
Simmons, Charles Bedford, Jr. *lawyer*
Smith, Barney Oveyette, Jr. *lawyer*
Wyche, Bradford Wheeler *lawyer*

Hartsville
DeLoach, Harris E(ugene), Jr. *lawyer, manufacturing company executive*

Hilton Head Island
Carter, Stephen Edward *lawyer*
McKay, John Judson, Jr. *lawyer*
Scarminach, Charles Anthony *lawyer*

Langley
Bell, Robert Morrall *lawyer*

Lexington
Kelehear, Carole Marchbanks Spann *legal administrator*
Wilkins, Robert Pearce *lawyer*

Myrtle Beach
Breen, David Hart *lawyer*
Lawrimore, Eugene Salmon Napier *lawyer*
Ray, Michael Robert *legal assistant*

Pawleys Island
Daniel, J. Reese *lawyer*

Spartanburg
Adams, Samuel Franklin *lawyer*

Summerville
Mortimer, Rory Dixon *lawyer*

Sumter
Reynolds, William MacKenzie, Jr. *lawyer*

Walterboro
Boensch, Arthur Cranwell *lawyer*

TENNESSEE

Chattanooga
Akers, Samuel Lee *lawyer*
Cooper, Gary Allan *lawyer*
Durham, J(oseph) Porter, Jr. *lawyer, educator*
Eason, Marcia Jean *lawyer*
Moore, Hugh Jacob, Jr. *lawyer*
Newton, Michael David *lawyer*
Parks, Jane deLoach *law librarian, legal assistant*
Phillips, John Bomar *lawyer*
Stophel, John Carroll *lawyer, accountant*

Church Hill
Faulk, Michael Anthony *lawyer*

Cookeville
Acuff, John Edgar *lawyer*
Day, David Owen *lawyer*

Crossville
Marlow, James Allen *lawyer*

Fayetteville
Dickey, John Harwell *lawyer, public defender*

Germantown
Sisson, Jerry Allan *lawyer*

Hendersonville
McCaleb, Joe Wallace *lawyer*

Johnson City
Epps, James Haws, III *lawyer*
Jenkins, Ronald Wayne *lawyer*

Knoxville
Ailor, Earl Starnes *lawyer*
Bailey, Bridget *lawyer*
Bly, Robert Maurice *lawyer*
Creekmore, David Dickason *lawyer*
Cremins, William Carroll *lawyer*
Hess, Amy Morris *law educator*
Lloyd, Francis Leon, Jr. *lawyer*
London, James Harry *lawyer*
Lucas, John Allen *lawyer*
Lynch, Carole Yard Worthington *lawyer*
Midkiff, Kimberly Ann *paralegal*
Murphree, Sharon Ann *lawyer*
Murphy, Deborah June *lawyer*
Oberman, Steven *lawyer*
Roach, Jon Gilbert *lawyer*
Routh, John William *lawyer*
Sanger, Herbert Shelton, Jr. *lawyer, former government official*
Schmidt, Benno Charles, Jr. *lawyer, educator*
Skaggs, Kathy Cheryl *lawyer*
Trant, Douglas Allen *lawyer*
Vogel, Howard H. *lawyer*
White, Edward Gibson, II *lawyer*

Mc Minnville
Potter, Clement Dale *public defender*

Memphis
Babaoglu, Rehim *lawyer*
Bland, James Theodore, Jr. *lawyer*
Burch, Lucius Edward, Jr. *lawyer*
Carr, Oscar Clark, III *lawyer*
Clark, Ross Bert, II *lawyer*
Cook, August Joseph *lawyer, accountant*
Davis, Frederick Benjamin *law educator*
DeWitt, Charles Benjamin, III *lawyer, educator*
Friedman, Robert Michael *lawyer*
Gentry, Gavin Miller *lawyer*
Gilman, Ronald Lee *lawyer*
Harpster, James Erving *lawyer*
Hon, Ralph Clifford *retired arbitrator, educator*
LaCasse, James Phillip *lawyer*
Ledbetter, Paul Mark *lawyer, writer*
Mc Carty, Raymond M. *lawyer, poet*
McLean, Robert Alexander *lawyer*
Newman, Charles Forrest *lawyer*
Pickard, Howard Brevard *law educator, consultant*
Rice, George Lawrence, III (Larry Rice) *lawyer*
Rutledge, Roger Keith *lawyer*
Simonton, Gail Maureen *lawyer*
Smith, Joseph Philip *lawyer*
Sossaman, William Lynwood *lawyer*
Spore, Richard Roland, III *lawyer, educator*
Summers, James Branson *lawyer*
Tate, Stonewall Shepherd *lawyer*
Terry, Joseph Ray, Jr. *lawyer*
Waddell, Phillip Dean *lawyer*
Walsh, Thomas James, Jr. *lawyer*
Wilder, James Sampson, III *lawyer, judge*

Murfreesboro
Lane, William Arthur *lawyer*

Nashville
Alexander, Andrew Lamar (Lamar Alexander) *lawyer, former secretary of education, former governor*
Anderson, Charles Hill *lawyer*
Blumstein, James Franklin *legal educator, lawyer, consultant*
Bostick, Charles Dent *lawyer, educator*
Bramlett, Paul Kent *lawyer*
Cantrell, Luther E., Jr. *lawyer*
Cooney, Charles Hayes *lawyer*
Farris, Frank Mitchell, Jr. *lawyer*
Freeman, James Atticus, III *lawyer, insurance and business consultant*
Gannon, John Sexton *lawyer, management consultant*
Hardin, Hal D. *lawyer, former U.S. attorney, former judge*
Harris, James Harold, III *lawyer, educator*
Hildebrand, Donald Dean *lawyer*
Lyon, Philip K(irkland) *lawyer*
Madu, Leonard Ekwugha *lawyer, human rights officer, newspaper columnist*
May, Joseph Leserman (Jack) *lawyer*
Oldfield, Russell Miller *lawyer*
Parker, Mary Ann *lawyer*
Penny, William Lewis *lawyer*
Phillips, Bruce Harold *lawyer*
Shepherd, Robert Patrick *lawyer*
Soderquist, Larry Dean *lawyer, educator*
Torrey, Claudia Olivia *lawyer*
Weeks, Kent McCuskey *lawyer*
White, Bruce David *law and ethics educator*
Winstead, George Alvis *law librarian, biochemist, educator, consultant*
Yarbrough, Edward Meacham *lawyer*
Youngblood, Elaine Michele *lawyer*

Newport
Bell, John Alton *lawyer*

Powell
Hyman, Roger David *lawyer*

Ripley
Walker, Joseph Hillary, Jr. *lawyer*

Signal Mountain
Leitner, Gregory Marc *lawyer*

Springfield
Wilks, Larry Dean *lawyer*

Trenton
Harrell, Limmie Lee, Jr. *lawyer*

Union City
Graham, Hardy Moore *lawyer*

White House
Ruth, Bryce Clinton, Jr. *lawyer*

TEXAS

Abilene
Boone, Celia Trimble *lawyer*
Grisham, Robert Douglas *lawyer*
Suttle, Stephen Hungate *lawyer*
Whitten, C. G. *lawyer*

Allen
Johnson, Staci Sharp *lawyer*

Alvin
Hewitt, Otto D., III *lawyer*

Amarillo
White, Sharon Elizabeth *lawyer*

Arlington
Moore, Tresi Lea *lawyer*
Rosenberry, William Kenneth *lawyer, educator*

Austin
Allday, Martin Lewis *lawyer*
Bartlett, Roger Alan *attorney*
Binder, Bob *lawyer*
Budka, James D. *lawyer, educator*
Byrd, Linward Tonnett *lawyer, rancher*
Cantilo, Patrick Herrera *lawyer*
Churgin, Michael Jay *law educator*
Cunningham, Jack Wayne *lawyer*
Cunningham, Judy Marie *lawyer*
Davis, Creswell Dean *lawyer, consultant*
Denius, Franklin Wofford *lawyer*
Dougherty, John Chrysostom, III *lawyer*
Gammage, Robert Alton (Bob Gammage) *lawyer*
Gibbins, Bob *lawyer*
Gibson, William Willard, Jr. *law educator*
Graham, Seldon Bain, Jr. *lawyer, engineer*
Greene, John Joseph *lawyer*
Hamilton, Dagmar Strandberg *lawyer, educator*
Hamilton, Robert Woodruff *law educator*
Hampton, Charles Edwin *lawyer, mathematician, computer programmer*
Hardin, Dale Wayne *retired law educator*
Harrington, James Charles *lawyer*
Harrison, Richard Wayne *lawyer*
Helburn, Isadore B. *arbitrator, mediator, educator*
Henderson, George Ervin *lawyer*
Hughes, Lin Gearing *lawyer*
Ikard, Frank Neville, Jr. *lawyer*
Jentz, Gaylord Adair *law educator*
Johnson, Corwin Waggoner *law educator*
Kenyon, Terry Frazier *lawyer*
Kulhavy, Joseph Bannister *lawyer, educator*
Mauzy, Oscar Holcombe *lawyer, retired state supreme court justice*
McCullough, Frank Witcher, III *lawyer*
Miller, John Eddie *lawyer*
Moss, Bill Ralph *lawyer, publisher*
Nattier, Frank Emile, Jr. *lawyer, educator*
Patman, Philip Franklin *lawyer*
Pearl, Roberta Louise (Roberta Getman) *lawyer, arbitrator, mediator*
Pena, Richard *lawyer*
Ray, Hal Roberts, Jr. *lawyer*
Roan, Forrest Calvin, Jr. *lawyer*
Saltmarsh, Sara Elizabeth *lawyer*
Schulze, Eric William *lawyer, legal publications editor, publisher*
Schwartz, Leonard Jay *lawyer*
Shapiro, David L. *lawyer*
Sherman, Edward Francis *law educator*
Strauser, Robert Wayne *lawyer*
Sudduth, Albert Scott, Jr. *lawyer*
Sullivan, Teresa Ann *law and sociology educator, academic administrator*
Tigar, Michael Edward *lawyer, educator*
Tottenham, Terry Oliver *lawyer*
Wagner, William Bradley *lawyer*
Weinberg, Louise *law educator, author*
Westbrook, Jay Lawrence *law educator*
White, Michael Lee *lawyer*
Wiseman, J(ames) Patrick *lawyer*
Wright, Charles Alan *law educator, author*
Yudof, Mark G. *law educator, academic administrator*

Bangs
McDonald, Charles Eugene *lawyer*

Bastrop
Van Gilder, Derek Robert *lawyer, engineer*

Bay City
Peden, Robert F., Jr. *retired lawyer*

Baytown
Vickery, Glenn Wheeler *lawyer*

Beaumont
Hambright, Robert John *lawyer*
Oxford, Hubert, III *lawyer*
Scofield, Louis M., Jr. *lawyer*

Bellaire
Chappell, Danny Michael *lawyer*
Eckman, David Walter *lawyer*

Belton
Miller, Richard Joseph *lawyer*

Big Spring
Morrison, Walton Stephen *lawyer*

Bonham
Peeler, Ray Doss, Jr. *lawyer*

Borger
Edmonds, Thomas Leon *lawyer, management consultant*

Brownsville
Ray, Mary Louise Ryan *lawyer*
Weisfeld, Sheldon *lawyer*

Brownwood
Bell, William Woodward *lawyer*

Bryan
Miller, Thomas Eugene *lawyer, writer*
Smith, Steven Lee *lawyer, judge*
Steelman, Frank (Sitley) *lawyer*

Burleson
Johnstone, Deborah Blackmon *lawyer*

Canton
White, Jeffery Howell *lawyer*

Cleveland
Campbell, Selaura Joy *lawyer*

Coppell
Rooney, Michael James *lawyer, educator*

Corpus Christi
Alberts, Harold *lawyer*
Bucklin, Leonard Herbert *lawyer*
Carnahan, Robert Narvell *lawyer*
Cartwright, Charles Nelson *lawyer*
Duncan, Ernest Louis, Jr. *lawyer*
Fancher, Rick *lawyer*
Gregory, Wanda Jean *paralegal, court reporter, singer, musician, writer*
Hall, Ralph Carr *lawyer, real estate consultant*
Harrison, William Oliver, Jr. *lawyer, small business owner*
Laws, Gordon Derby *lawyer*
Locke, William Henry *lawyer*
Nesbitt, Frank Wilbur *lawyer*
Porter, Charles Raleigh, Jr. *lawyer*
Wallace, Robert Barnes, Jr. *lawyer*

Dallas
Anglin, Michael Williams *lawyer*
Austin, Ann Sheree *lawyer*
Beuttenmuller, Rudolf William *lawyer*
Blount, Charles William, III *lawyer*
Bonesio, Woodrow Michael *lawyer*
Boyd, Dan Stewart *lawyer*
Brister, Bill H. *lawyer, former judge*
Bromberg, Alan Robert *law educator*
Burke, William Temple, Jr. *lawyer*
Burns, Sandra *lawyer, educator*
Carpenter, Gordon Russell *lawyer, banker*
Case, Thomas Louis *lawyer*
Clark, Robert M., Jr. *lawyer*
Coleman, Lester L. *corporate lawyer*
Copley, Edward Alvin *lawyer*
Corman, Jack Bernard *lawyer, investment manager*
Courtney, Constance E. *lawyer*
Cowling, David Edward *lawyer*
Crain, Christina Melton *lawyer*
Crowley, James Worthington *retired lawyer, business consultant, investor*
Davis, Clarice McDonald *lawyer*
Davis, M. G. *lawyer*
Dean, David Allen *lawyer*
Demarest, Sylvia M. *lawyer*
Dicus, Brian George *lawyer*
Douglass, Frank Russell *lawyer*
Dowben, Carla Lurie *lawyer, educator*
Drake, Edward Junius *lawyer*
Eaton, Michael William *lawyer, educator*
Ellis, Alfred Wright (Al Ellis) *lawyer*
Emery, Herschell Gene *lawyer*
Farquhar, Robert Michael *lawyer*
Figari, Ernest Emil, Jr. *lawyer*
Flegle, Jim L. *lawyer*
Flood, Joan Moore *paralegal*
Freytag, Sharon Nelson *lawyer*
Gerberding Cowart, Greta Elaine *lawyer*
Girards, James Edward *lawyer*
Goodrich, Alan Owens *lawyer*

Gores, Christopher Merrel *lawyer*
Govett, Brett Christopher *lawyer*
Goyne, Roderick A. *lawyer*
Grayson, Walton George, III *retired lawyer*
Hamilton, Robert Brooks *lawyer*
Hartnett, Thomas Robert, III *lawyer*
Hartt, Grover, III *lawyer*
Hawkins, Scott Alexis *lawyer*
Henderson, David Allen *lawyer*
Hinshaw, Chester John *lawyer*
Howie, John Robert *lawyer*
Hughes, Vester Thomas, Jr. *lawyer*
Hyden, Joe Bailey *lawyer*
Johnson, Alonzo Bismark *legal assistant, court administrator*
Johnson, James Harold *lawyer*
Jordan, Robert W. *lawyer*
Kearney, Douglas Charles *lawyer, journalist*
Keithley, Bradford Gene *lawyer*
Kinser, Katherine Anne *lawyer*
Kirby, Le Grand Carney, III *lawyer, accountant*
Kneipper, Richard Keith *lawyer*
Kobdish, George Charles *lawyer*
Kohl, Kathleen Allison Barnhart *lawyer*
Lacy, John Ford *lawyer*
Lafving, Brian Douglas *lawyer*
Langenheim, Roger Allen *lawyer*
Leeper, Harold Harris *arbitrator*
Lenox, Roger Shawn *lawyer*
Levin, Hervey Phillip *lawyer*
Levin, Richard C. *lawyer*
Levine, Harold *lawyer*
Malorzo, Thomas Vincent *lawyer*
Malouf, Edward Wayne *lawyer*
Maris, Stephen S. *lawyer, educator*
Marquardt, Robert Richard *lawyer*
Martin, Richard Kelley *lawyer*
Marvel, Kenneth Robert *lawyer, corporate executive*
McColloch, Murray Michael *lawyer*
McCurley, Carl Michael *lawyer*
Mc Elhaney, John Hess *lawyer*
McGarry, Charles William *lawyer*
McLean, Susan Ralston *lawyer, federal government*
McNamara, Martin Burr *lawyer, oil and gas company executive*
McWhorter, Kathy Marie *legal secretary*
Mills, Jerry Woodrow *lawyer*
Moore, Stanley Ray *lawyer*
Morgan, Timi Sue *lawyer*
Moss, Joe Albaugh *lawyer*
Murray, John William, Jr. *legal investigator, writer*
Nordlund, William Chalmers *lawyer*
O'Bannon, Don Tella, Jr. *lawyer*
Owens, Rodney Joe *lawyer*
Parr, Richard Arnold, II *lawyer*
Portman, Glenn Arthur *lawyer*
Portman, Susan Newell *lawyer*
Powell, Michael Vance *lawyer*
Pratt, Donald Oliver *lawyer*
Purnell, Charles Giles *lawyer*
Scott, John Roland *lawyer, oil company executive*
Scuro, Joseph E., Jr. *lawyer*
Siegel, Mark Jordan *lawyer*
Sloman, Marvin Sherk *lawyer*
Spears, Robert Fields *lawyer*
Swanson, Wallace Martin *lawyer*
Tubb, James Clarence *lawyer*
Udashen, Robert N. *lawyer*
Veach, Robert Raymond, Jr. *lawyer*
Walkowiak, Vincent Steven *lawyer*
Watson, Jim Albert *lawyer*
Webb, Brian Lockwood *lawyer*
Weiland, Stephen Cass *lawyer*
Whitlow, James Adams *lawyer*
Wileman, George Robert *lawyer*
Wilkins, Jerry L. *lawyer, clergyman*
Winship, Peter *law educator*
Wolf, Linda Joyce *legal assistant*
Woodward, David Luther *lawyer, consultant*
Young, Barney Thornton *lawyer*

Denton
Biles, David Wallace *lawyer*
Waage, Mervin Bernard *lawyer*

El Paso
Ainsa, Francis Swinburne *lawyer*
McDonald, Charles Edward *lawyer*
Olivas, Valerie Segura *legal assistant*
Rosenthal, Richard *law librarian*
Smith, Tad Randolph *lawyer*

Eldorado
Kosub, James Albert *lawyer*

Fort Worth
Andrews, Christina *lawyer*
Blair, Sloan Blackmon *lawyer*
Carr, Thomas Eldridge *lawyer*
Chalk, John Allen, Sr. *lawyer*
Collins, Whitfield James *lawyer*
Cooke, Michael Thomas *lawyer*
Crumley, John Walter *lawyer*
Curry, Donald Robert *lawyer, oil company executive*
Dean, Beale *lawyer*
Dent, Edward Dwain *lawyer*
Emerson, Douglas Theodore *lawyer*
Griffith, Richard Lattimore *lawyer*
Law, Thomas Hart *lawyer*
Light, Russell Jeffers *lawyer*
Mullanax, Milton Greg *lawyer*
Phillips, Robert James, Jr. *corporate executive*
Randolph, Robert McGehee *lawyer*
Sartain, James Edward *lawyer*
Shannon, Joe, Jr. *lawyer*
Sharpe, James Shelby *lawyer*
Tilley, Rice M(atthews), Jr. *lawyer*
Tracy, Barbara Marie *lawyer*
Tracy, J. David *lawyer, educator*
Wagner, James Peyton *lawyer*
Watson, Robert Francis *lawyer*

Galveston
Neves, Kerry Lane *lawyer*
Roy, Richard James *lawyer, engineer, consultant*
Sullivan, Thomas Patrick *lawyer*

Garland
Irby, Holt *lawyer*

Georgetown
Baker, Mark Bruce *lawyer, educator*
Wilkerson, James Neill *lawyer*

Granbury
Fletcher, Riley Eugene *lawyer*

Grand Prairie
Avery, Reigh Kessen *legal assistant*

Hallettsville
Baber, Wilbur H., Jr. *lawyer*

Harlingen
Pope, William L. *lawyer, judge*
Wise, Miguel David *lawyer*

Houston
Aarons-Holder, Charmaine Michele *lawyer*
Abbott, Greg Wayne *lawyer*
Abercia, Ralph *lawyer, financial advisor*
Addison, Linda Leuchter *lawyer*
Agraz, Francisco Javier *lawyer, public affairs representative*
Aldrich, Lovell W(eld) *lawyer*
Allender, John Roland *lawyer*
Allison, William B. *lawyer*
Anderson, Eric Severin *lawyer*
Attermeier, Fredric Joseph *lawyer*
Banks, John Robert, Jr. *lawyer*
Bargfrede, James Allen *lawyer*
Barnett, Don Marvin *lawyer*
Becher, Andrew Clifford *lawyer*
Beirne, Martin Douglas *lawyer*
Berry, Thomas Eugene *lawyer*
Bircher, Edgar Allen *lawyer*
Blackmon, Willie Edward Boney *lawyer*
Bliss, Ronald Glenn *lawyer*
Bluestein, Edwin A., Jr. *lawyer*
Boettcher, Armin Schlick *lawyer, banker*
Boswell, John Howard *lawyer*
Bradie, Peter Richard *lawyer, engineer*
Brann, Richard Roland *lawyer*
Bridges, David Manning *lawyer*
Brinson, Gay Creswell, Jr. *lawyer*
Brunson, John Soles *lawyer*
Carr, Edward A. *lawyer*
Carter, Daniel Roland *lawyer*
Caudill, William Howard *lawyer*
Chavez, J. Anthony *lawyer*
Clarke, Robert Logan *lawyer*
Cline, Vivian Melinda *lawyer*
Clore, Lawrence H. *lawyer*
Cook, Eugene Augustus *lawyer*
Dack, Christopher Edward Hughes *lawyer*
Dampier, Harold Dean, Jr. *lawyer*
Davis, Martha Algenita Scott *lawyer*
Denny, Otway B., Jr. *lawyer*
Diaz-Arrastia, George Ravelo *lawyer*
Dimitry, Theodore George *lawyer*
Dinkins, Carol Eggert *lawyer*
Dykes, Osborne Jefferson, III *lawyer*
Edwards, Blaine Douglass *lawyer*
Eiland, Gary Wayne *lawyer*
Ekwem, Robertson M. *lawyer*
England, Rudy Alan *lawyer*
Essmyer, Michael Martin *lawyer*
Farenthold, Frances Tarlton *lawyer*
Farnsworth, T. Brooke *lawyer*
Feldcamp, Larry Bernard *lawyer*
Finch, Michael Paul *lawyer*
Fladung, Richard Denis *lawyer*
Fleming, Michael Paul *lawyer*
Forbes, Arthur Lee, III *lawyer*
Foster, Charles Crawford *lawyer, educator*
Frois, Theodore Michael *lawyer*
Gardner, Dale Ray *lawyer*
Gissel, L. Henry, Jr. *lawyer*
Goldman, Nathan Carliner *lawyer, educator*
Gonynor, Francis James *lawyer*
Gover, Alan Shore *lawyer*
Graham, Michael Paul *lawyer*
Graving, Richard John *law educator*
Gray, Archibald Duncan, Jr. *lawyer*
Hamel, Lee *lawyer*
Harrington, Bruce Michael *lawyer, investor*
Harris, Warren Wayne *lawyer*
Heggen, Ivar Nelson *lawyer*
Heinrich, Randall Wayne *lawyer, investment banker*
Henderson, Archibald, III *lawyer*
Hollyfield, John Scoggins *lawyer*
Houston, Shirley Mae (Mrs. Thomas H. Houston) *court reporter*
Huck, Lewis Francis *lawyer, real estate consultant and developer*
Jewell, George Hiram *lawyer*
Jones, Frank Griffith *lawyer*
Jordan, Charles Milton *lawyer*
Kaplan, Lee Landa *lawyer*
Katz, M. Marvin *lawyer*
Kelly, William Franklin, Jr. *lawyer*
Ketchand, Robert Lee *lawyer*
Kirk, John Robert, Jr. *lawyer*
Kline, Allen Haber, Jr. *lawyer*
Knull, William H., III *lawyer*
Krieger, Paul Edward *lawyer*
Lavenant, Rene Paul, Jr. *lawyer*
Lawson, Ben F. *lawyer, international legal consultant*
Long, Thomas *lawyer*
Looper, Donald Ray *lawyer*
Lopez, David Tiburcio *lawyer, educator, arbitrator, mediator*
Louck, Lisa Ann *lawyer*
Luck, Gregory Matthew *lawyer*
Maloney, James Edward *lawyer*
Marlow, Orval Lee, II *lawyer*
Marsel, Robert Steven *law educator, mediator, arbitrator*
Marston, Edgar Jean, III *lawyer*
Martin, Neil *lawyer*
Martin, Paul Edward *lawyer*
Massad, Stephen Albert *lawyer*
Masters, Claude Bivin *lawyer*
McClure, Daniel M. *lawyer*
McEvily, Daniel Vincent Sean *lawyer, author*
McGreevy, Terrence Gerard *lawyer*
McKinney, Carolyn Jean *lawyer*
McQuarrie, Claude Monroe, III *lawyer*
Melamed, Richard *lawyer*
Michaels, Kevin Richard *lawyer*
Monck, Harry Nelson, IV *lawyer*
Moroney, Linda L. S. *lawyer, educator*
Moya, Olga Lydia *law educator*
Myers, Franklin *lawyer, oil service company executive*
Nacol, Mae *lawyer*
Nolen, Roy Lemuel *lawyer*
O'Donnell, Lawrence, III *lawyer*
Oldham, Darius Dudley *lawyer*
Pate, Stephen Patrick *lawyer*
Paul, Thomas Daniel *lawyer*
Paulsen, James Walter *law educator*
Pettiette, Alison Yvonne *lawyer*
Pilko, Robert Michael *lawyer*
Pitts, Gary Benjamin *lawyer*
Pravel, Bernarr Roe *lawyer*
Prestridge, Pamela Adair *lawyer*
Ransom, Clifton Louis, Jr. *lawyer, real estate investor*
Reasoner, Barrett Hodges *lawyer*
Reasoner, Harry Max *lawyer*
Rider, Roger Alan *lawyer*
Riley, Timothy Dennis *lawyer*
Roberts, Cecil Kenneth *lawyer*
Rogers, Arthur Hamilton, III *lawyer*
Ryan, Thomas William *lawyer*
Sales, James Bohus *lawyer*
Schechter, Arthur Louis *lawyer*
Schroeder, Walter Allen *lawyer, banker*
Selke, Charles Richard *lawyer, mediator, real estate professional*
Seymour, Barbara Laverne *lawyer*
Sheinfeld, Myron M. *lawyer, educator*
Shurn, Peter Joseph, III *lawyer*
Sing, William Bender *lawyer*
Smith, Brooke Ellen *lawyer*
Sorrels, Randall Owen *lawyer*
Stewart, Pamela L. *lawyer*
Stinemetz, Steven Douglas *lawyer*
Storey, JoAnn *lawyer*
Stradley, William Jackson *lawyer*
Stuart, Walter Bynum, IV *lawyer*
Susman, Karen Hyman *lawyer*
Susman, Morton Lee *lawyer*
Swanson, Roy Joel *lawyer*
Szalkowski, Charles Conrad *lawyer*
Tartt, Blake *lawyer*
Terrell, G. Irvin *lawyer*
Toth, Justin Tyler *lawyer*
Touchy, Deborah K. P. *lawyer, accountant*
Tran, Bao Quoc *lawyer*
Tripp, Karen Bryant *lawyer*
Wakefield, Stephen Alan *lawyer*
Wall, Kenneth E., Jr. *lawyer*
Wallingford, John Rufus *lawyer*
Wallis, Olney Gray *lawyer*
Warnock, Curtlon Lee *lawyer*
Waska, Ronald Jerome *lawyer*
Watson, John Allen *lawyer*
Weber, Fredric Alan *lawyer*
Weberpal, Michael Andrew *lawyer*
Wells, Benjamin Gladney *lawyer*
Westby, Timothy Scott *lawyer*
Wheelan, R(ichelieu) E(dward) *lawyer*
Wickliffe, Jerry L. *lawyer*
Williams, Percy Don *lawyer*
Winton, James C. *lawyer*
Wood, Ivan, Jr. *lawyer*
Woody, Clyde Woodrow *lawyer*
Wray, Thomas Jefferson *lawyer*
Wright, Robert Payton *lawyer*
Yokubaitis, Roger T. *lawyer*
Youngblood, J. Craig *lawyer*
Zager, Steven Mark *lawyer*
Zeigler, Ann dePender *lawyer*

Humble
Ellis, Jeffrey L. *lawyer*

Hurst
Casey, David Robert *lawyer*

Irving
Auerbach, Ernest Sigmund *lawyer, company executive, writer*
Cooper, Steven Mark *law educator*
Kisselburgh, Robert McKirdy *lawyer*
Zahn, Donald Jack *lawyer*

Jourdanton
Ellison, Alton Lynn, Jr. *lawyer*

Kaufman
Legg, Reagan Houston *lawyer*

Kerrville
Parmley, Robert James *lawyer, consultant*
Tomlin, Linton *court reporter*

Killeen
Pittman, Natalie Anne *paralegal*

Lampasas
Harvey, Leigh Kathryn *lawyer*

Lancaster
Fewel, Harriett *lawyer*
Pratt, John Edward *law educator*

Laredo
Herrera, Catherine Maria *lawyer, documentary film maker, photographer*

Liberty
Wheat, John Nixon *lawyer*

Longview
Welge, Jack Herman, Jr. *lawyer*

Lubbock
Davis, Jimmy Frank *lawyer*
Johnson, Philip Wayne *lawyer*
Skillern, Frank Fletcher *law educator*
Smith, James Bonner *lawyer*

Lufkin
Garrison, Pitser Hardeman *lawyer, mayor emeritus*

Mc Kinney
Roessler, P. Dee *lawyer, former judge, educator*

Mcallen
Carrera, Victor Manuel *lawyer*
Connors, Joseph Aloysius, III *lawyer*

Midland
Chappell, Clovis Gillham, Jr. *lawyer*
Frost, Wayne N. *lawyer*
Morrow, William Clarence *lawyer, mediator, investor*
Prothro, Jerry Robert *lawyer*

Missouri City
Hodges, Jot Holiver, Jr. *lawyer, business executive*

Monahans
Ratliff, Janice Kay *legal administrator*

Mount Pleasant
Woodson, Danny *lawyer*

New Braunfels
Engelhardt, John Hugo *lawyer, banker*

Palestine
Hanks, Jackson Rayburn *lawyer*

Pecos
Weinacht, John William *lawyer*

Pottsboro
Thomas, Ann Van Wynen *law educator*

Richardson
Conkel, Robert Dale *lawyer, pension consultant*
Douglas, John Paul *lawyer, mediator, arbitrator*
Neely, Vicki Adele *legal assistant, poet*
Olson, Dennis Oliver *lawyer*
Standel, Richard Reynold, Jr. *lawyer, communications executive*

Roanoke
Hunt, David Ford *lawyer*

Round Mountain
Moursund, Albert Wadel, III *lawyer, rancher*

Rusk
Phifer, Forrest Keith *lawyer*

San Antonio
Aldave, Barbara Bader *law educator, lawyer*
Avila, William Thaddeus *lawyer, economist*
Barton, James Cary *lawyer*
Berscheidt, Joanne Marie *lawyer*
Biery, Evelyn Hudson *lawyer*
Bramble, Ronald Lee *lawyer, business and legal consultant*
Cruse, Rex Beach, Jr. *lawyer*
Davison, Paul Sioussa *lawyer*
Hardy, Harvey Louchard *lawyer*
Henry, Peter York *lawyer, mediator*
Hollin, Shelby W. *lawyer*
Johnson, Edward Michael *lawyer*
Kaplan, Edward David *lawyer*
Kelly, Mary Quella *lawyer*
Labay, Eugene Benedict *lawyer*
Lenk, Christa C. *lawyer*
Lutter, Charles William, Jr. *lawyer*
Lyons, Clem V. *lawyer*
Macon, Jane Haun *lawyer*
Matthews, Dan Gus *lawyer*
McCormick, Clyde Reece, II *lawyer, educator*
Montgomery, James Edward, Jr. *lawyer*
Morrison, Edgar Carroll (Jed), Jr. *lawyer*
Moyé, Linda Everett *mediator*
Moynihan, John Bignell *lawyer*
Owens, William Councilman, Jr. *lawyer, accountant*
Parker, George Priestley, Jr. *lawyer*
Pfeiffer, Fred Nelson *lawyer*
Philbin, Donald R., Jr. *lawyer*
Pipkin, Marvin Grady *lawyer*
Putman, (James) Michael *lawyer*
Ross, James Ulric *lawyer, accountant, educator*
Sakai, Peter A. *lawyer*
Scalise, Celeste *lawyer*
Schlueter, David Arnold *law educator*
Schuk, Linda Lee *legal assistant, business educator*
Spears, Carleton Blaise *lawyer*
Vazquez, Gilbert Falcon *lawyer*
Wachsmuth, Robert William *lawyer*
Wallis, Ben Alton, Jr. *lawyer*
Welmaker, Forrest Nolan *lawyer*
Yates, Norris William, Jr. *lawyer*
Young, David Haywood *lawyer*
Young, Jess Wollett *lawyer*
Young, John Paul *lawyer, retired army officer*
Zepeda, Enrique E., V *lawyer*

Spearman
Jarvis, Billy Britt *lawyer*

Spring
Hearn-Haynes, Theresa *lawyer*
Hendricks, Randal Arlan *lawyer*
Norris, Kenneth Michael *lawyer*

Sweetwater
Jones, Charles Eric, Jr. *lawyer*

The Woodlands
Schlacks, Stephen Mark *lawyer, educator*

Tyler
Ellis, Donald Lee *lawyer*
Lake, David Alan *investments lawyer*
Patterson, Donald Ross *lawyer*

Uvalde
Kincaid, Eugene D., III *lawyer*

Victoria
Chapman, J. Milton *lawyer*

Waco
Davis, Derek Hamilton *law educator*
Page, Jack Randall *lawyer*
Ressler, Parke E(dward) *lawyer, accountant*

Weslaco
Pomerantz, Jerald Michael *lawyer*

Wichita Falls
Altman, William Kean *lawyer*
Todd, Richard D. R. *lawyer*

UTAH

Salt Lake City
Ersek, Gregory Joseph Mark *lawyer, business administrator*

VIRGINIA

Abingdon
Johnson, Janet Droke *legal secretary*

Alexandria
Apperson, Bernard James *lawyer*
Beach, Barbara Purse *lawyer*
Campbell, Thomas Douglas *lawyer, consultant*
Carlson, J(ohn) Philip *lawyer*
Carter, Richard Dennis *lawyer, educator*
Costello, Daniel Brian *lawyer, consultant*
Crane, Angus Edgar *lawyer*
Green, James Francis *lawyer, consultant*
Hussey, Ward MacLean *lawyer, former government official*
Kiyonaga, John Cady *lawyer*
Klewans, Samuel N. *lawyer*
McClure, Roger John *lawyer*
O'Connor, Raymond Vincent, Jr. *lawyer*
Paturis, E(mmanuel) Michael *lawyer*
Peyton, Gordon Pickett *lawyer*
Rubin, Burton Jay *lawyer, editor*
Schmidt, Dale Russell *lawyer*
Schroeder, James White *lawyer*
Sherk, George William *lawyer*
Spiegel, H. Jay *lawyer*
Toothman, John William *lawyer*
Van Cleve, Ruth Gill *retired lawyer, government official*
Walkup, Charlotte Lloyd *lawyer*
Watson, George William *lawyer, legal consultant*
Wendel, Charles Allen *lawyer*
Wieder, Bruce Terrill *lawyer, electrical engineer*
Wilner, Morton Harrison *retired lawyer*

Annandale
Cruz, Nestor Enrique *lawyer*
Gaberman, Harry *lawyer, economic analyst*
McGuire, Edward David, Jr. *lawyer*

Arlington
Anthony, Robert Armstrong *law educator*
Brenner, Edgar H. *legal administrator*
Goans, Judy Winegar *lawyer*
Greigg, Ronald Edwin *lawyer*
Hansen, Kenneth D. *lawyer, ophthalmologist*
Jackson, William Paul, Jr. *lawyer*
Johnson, Charles Owen *retired lawyer*
Kenworthy, James Lawrence *lawyer, government affairs and international trade consultant*
Kosarin, Jonathan Henry *lawyer*
Malone, William Grady *lawyer*
Monroe, Carl Dean, III *lawyer*
Royce, E. Scott *legal researcher, writer*
Shapiro, Nelson Hirsh *lawyer*
Shearer, Ross Sterling *consultant, retired government official*
Smith, John Michael *lawyer*
Van Landingham, Leander Shelton, Jr. *lawyer*
Walker, Woodrow Wilson *lawyer, cattle and timber farmer*

Boydton
White-Hurst, John Marshall *lawyer*

Charlottesville
Chandler, Lawrence Bradford, Jr. *lawyer*
Edwards, James Edwin *lawyer*
Elliott, Harold Wayne *lawyer, retired army officer*
Howard, Angela Kay *lawyer, accountant*
Kudravetz, David Waller *lawyer*
Meador, Daniel John *law educator*
Menefee, Samuel Pyeatt *lawyer, anthropologist*
Merrill, Richard Austin *lawyer*
Monahan, John T. *law educator, psychologist*
Musselman, Robert Metcalfe *lawyer*
O'Connell, Jeffrey *law educator*
Rutherglen, George A. *law educator*
Scott, Robert Edwin *law educator*
Slaughter, Edward Ratliff, Jr. *lawyer*
Turner, Robert Foster *law educator, former government official, writer*
White, George Edward *law educator, lawyer*
Whitehead, John Wayne *law educator, organization administrator, author*

Chesapeake
Brown, John Wayne *lawyer*
Fashbaugh, Howard Dilts, Jr. *lawyer, management educator*
Jones, John Lou *arbitrator, retired railroad executive*

Chester
Connelly, Colin Charles *lawyer*
Gray, Charles Robert *lawyer*

Danville
Goodman, Lewis Elton, Jr. *lawyer*

Fairfax
Baird, Charles Bruce *lawyer, consultant*
Elmore, Pauline R. *legal association administrator*
Hagberg, Viola Wilgus *lawyer*
Kauffman, Thomas Richard *lawyer, consultant*
Kear, Maria Martha Ruscitella *lawyer*
Newsome, George Marvin *lawyer*
Procopio, Joseph Guydon *lawyer*
Stearns, Frank Warren *lawyer*
Zaphiriou, George Aristotle *lawyer, educator*

Fairfax Station
Bishop, Alfred Chilton, Jr. *lawyer*

Falls Church
Becker, James Richard *lawyer*
Brady, Rupert Joseph *lawyer*
Kirk, Dennis Dean *lawyer*
Kondracki, Edward John *lawyer*
Nunes, Morris A. *lawyer*
Redmond, Robert *lawyer, educator*
Schmidt, Paul Wickham *lawyer*
Swartz, Christian LeFevre *lawyer*
Van Oeveren, Edward Lanier *lawyer, biologist, physician*
Winzer, P.J. *lawyer*

Franklin
Minor, Edward Colquitt *lawyer*

Fredericksburg
Savage, Thomas Yates *lawyer*
Sheffield, Walter Jervis *lawyer*
Smith, John Drake, Jr. *lawyer*

Front Royal
Napier, Douglas William *lawyer*

Great Falls
Neidich, George Arthur *lawyer*
Preston, Charles George *lawyer*
Railton, William Scott *lawyer*
Rath, Francis Steven *lawyer*

Hampton
McNider, James Small, III *lawyer*
Schon, Alan Wallace *lawyer, actor*

Harrisonburg
Wallinger, M(elvin) Bruce *lawyer*

Leesburg
Flannery, John Philip, II *lawyer*
Minchew, John Randall *lawyer*

Lexington
Kirgis, Frederic Lee, Jr. *law educator*
Massie, Ann MacLean *law educator*

Lunenburg
Marshall, Grace Thompson *court clerk*

Lynchburg
Elliott, James Ward *lawyer*
Light, William Randall *lawyer*
Packert, G. Beth *lawyer*

Madison
Coates, Frederick Ross *lawyer*

Manassas
Hammond, Patricia Flood *lawyer*
Weimer, Peter Dwight *mediator, lawyer, corporate executive*

Marshall
Matthews, Suzette *lawyer*

Martinsville
Smith, Fred Dempsey, Jr. *lawyer*
Smith, James Randolph, Jr. *lawyer*

Mc Lean
Blair, Richard Eugene *lawyer*
Church, Randolph Warner, Jr. *lawyer*
Daniels, Michael Alan *lawyer*
Duncan, Stephen Mack *lawyer*
Goolrick, Robert Mason *lawyer, consultant*
Hicks, C. Thomas, III *lawyer*
Hoffman, Ira Eliot *lawyer*
Kennedy, Cornelius Bryant *lawyer*
LeSourd, Nancy Susan Oliver *lawyer, writer*
Marino, Michael Frank *lawyer*
Morris, James Malachy *lawyer*
Olson, William Jeffrey *lawyer*
Partoyan, Garo Arakel *lawyer*
Rau, Lee Arthur *lawyer*
Stewart, James Kevin *judicial administrator, management technology consultant*
Walton, Edmund Lewis, Jr. *lawyer*

Midlothian
Bell, Mildred Bailey *retired lawyer, educator*
MacIlroy, John Whittington *lawyer*

Moneta
Moore, Harry Russell *retired lawyer, consultant*

Newport News
Hatten, Robert Randolph *lawyer*
Kamp, Arthur Joseph, Jr. *lawyer*
Segall, James Arnold *lawyer*

Norfolk
Achampong, Francis Kofi *law educator, consultant*
Bishop, Bruce Taylor *lawyer*
Boyd, Robert Friend *lawyer*
Clark, Morton Hutchinson *lawyer*
Cooper, Charles Neilson *lawyer*
Harrell, Charles Lydon, Jr. *lawyer*
Parker, Richard Wilson *lawyer*
Ryan, John M. *lawyer*
Sutton, Paul Eugene, II *lawyer*
Swope, Richard McAllister *lawyer*

Norton
Shortridge, Judy Beth *lawyer*

Palmyra
Perrin, Sarah Ann *lawyer*

Petersburg
Baskervill, Charles Thornton *lawyer*
Burns, Cassandra Stroud *prosecutor*
Everitt, Alice Lubin *arbitrator*
Shell, Louis Calvin *lawyer*
Spero, Morton Bertram *lawyer*

Portsmouth
Blachman, Michael Joel *lawyer*
Moody, Willard James, Sr. *lawyer*

Providence Forge
Richardson, William Winfree, III *lawyer*

Radford
Davis, Richard Waters *lawyer*
Showalter, Josiah Thomas, Jr. *lawyer*
Turk, James Clinton, Jr. *lawyer*

Reston
Bredehoft, Elaine Charlson *lawyer*
Bredehoft, John Michael *lawyer*
Parker, Donald Samuel *lawyer*

Richmond
Allen, Jeffrey Rodgers *lawyer*
Bagley, Philip Joseph, III *lawyer*
Billingsley, Robert Thaine *lawyer*
Booker, Lewis Thomas *lawyer*
Boyd, B(everley) Randolph *lawyer*
Brooks, Robert Franklin, Sr. *lawyer*
Buford, Robert Pegram *lawyer*
Bush, Thomas Norman *lawyer*
Carrell, Daniel Allan *lawyer*
Carter, Joseph Carlyle, Jr. *lawyer*
Clinard, Robert Noel *lawyer*
Ellis, Andrew Jackson, Jr. *lawyer*
Epps, Augustus Charles *lawyer*
Flannagan, Benjamin Collins, IV *lawyer*
Gary, Richard David *lawyer*
Hackney, Virginia Howitz *lawyer*
Harp, Reno Sheffer, III *lawyer*
Hettrick, George Harrison *lawyer*
Hill, Oliver White, Sr. *lawyer, consultant*
Jones, Reginald Nash *lawyer*
Kearfott, Joseph Conrad *lawyer*
Levit, Jay J(oseph) *lawyer*
McClard, Jack Edward *lawyer*
McFarlane, Walter Alexander *lawyer, educator*
Moore, Thurston Roach *lawyer*
Morris, Dewey Blanton *lawyer*
Pasco, Hansell Merrill *retired lawyer*
Patterson, Robert Hobson, Jr. *lawyer*
Peters, David Frankman *lawyer*
Pope, Robert Dean *lawyer*
Powell, Lewis Franklin, III *lawyer*
Rainey, Gordon Fryer, Jr. *lawyer*
Reveley, Walter Taylor, III *lawyer*
Rigsby, Linda Flory *lawyer*
Roach, Edgar Mayo, Jr. *lawyer*
Rolfe, Robert Martin *lawyer*
Rudlin, David Alan *lawyer*
Slater, Thomas Glascock, Jr. *lawyer*
Spain, Jack Holland, Jr. *lawyer*
Thomas, John Charles *lawyer, former state supreme court justice*
Thompson, Paul Michael *lawyer*
Totten, Randolph Fowler *lawyer*
Waddell, William Robert *lawyer*
Walsh, William Arthur, Jr. *lawyer*
Weis, Laura Visser *lawyer*
White, James M., III *lawyer*
Witt, Walter Francis, Jr. *lawyer*

Roanoke
Barnhill, David Stan *lawyer*
Bates, Harold Martin *lawyer*
Densmore, Douglas Warren *lawyer*
Edwards, John Saul *lawyer*
Hale, Lance Mitchell *lawyer*
Hammond, Glenn Barry, Sr. *lawyer*
Harris, Bayard Easter *lawyer*
Lemon, William Jacob *lawyer*
Mundy, Gardner Marshall *lawyer*
Perkinson, Diana Munsey *lawyer*
Skolrood, Robert Kenneth *lawyer*
Tegenkamp, Gary Elton *lawyer*
Wilson, Douglas Downes *lawyer*

Springfield
Chappell, Milton Leroy *lawyer*

Vienna
Breslin, Elvira Madden *lawyer, educator*
Howard, Daggett Horton *lawyer*
McCabe, Thomas Edward *lawyer*

Vinton
Cranwell, C. Richard *lawyer*

Virginia Beach
Hajek, Francis Paul *lawyer*
Layton, Garland Mason *lawyer*
North, Kenneth E(arl) *lawyer, educator*
Spitzli, Donald Hawkes, Jr. *lawyer*

Warm Springs
Deeds, Robert Creigh *lawyer, state legislator*

Williamsburg
Geddy, Vernon Meredith, Jr. *lawyer*
Miller, William Frederick *lawyer*
Sullivan, Timothy Jackson *law educator, academic administrator*
Wilson, Paul Lowell *lawyer*

Wytheville
Baird, Thomas Bryan, Jr. *lawyer*

WASHINGTON

Bellevue
Treacy, Gerald Bernard *lawyer*

WEST VIRGINIA

Bluefield
Kantor, Isaac Norris *lawyer*

Buckhannon
McCauley, David W. *lawyer, educator*

Charleston
Cline, Michael Robert *lawyer*
Cowan, John Joseph *lawyer*
Dues, Theodore Roosevelt, Jr. *lawyer*
Michelson, Gail Ida *lawyer*
Neely, Richard *lawyer*
Teare, John Richard, Jr. *lawyer*
Woods, Jeff Chandler *lawyer*
Zak, Robert Joseph *lawyer*

Clarksburg
Jarvis, John Cecil *lawyer*

Fairmont
Cohen, Richard Paul *lawyer*
Stanton, George Patrick, Jr. *lawyer*

Fairview
Bunner, Patricia Andrea *lawyer*
Bunner, William Keck *lawyer*

Hurricane
Cecil, John David *lawyer*

Mac Arthur
Rhoades, Marye Frances *paralegal*

Parkersburg
Powell, Eric Karlton *lawyer, researcher*

Summersville
Yeager, Charles William *lawyer, newspaper publisher*

Weirton
Hill, Barry Morton *lawyer*

Wellsburg
Viderman, Linda Jean *paralegal, corporate executive*

Wheeling
Riley, Arch Wilson, Jr. *lawyer*

WISCONSIN

Hudson
Lombard, Richard Spencer *lawyer*

TERRITORIES OF THE UNITED STATES

PUERTO RICO

San Juan
Rodriguez-Diaz, Juan E. *lawyer*
Rua, Milton Francisco *retired lawyer*
Vallone, Ralph, Jr. *lawyer*
Woods, Barry Alan *lawyer*

VIRGIN ISLANDS

Christiansted
Hart, Thomas Hughson, III *lawyer*

MILITARY ADDRESSES OF THE UNITED STATES

PACIFIC

FPO
Collins, William Joseph, Jr. *lawyer, officer of marines*

ADDRESS UNPUBLISHED

Adams, David Gray *lawyer*
Adams, Frances Grant, II *lawyer*
Adkins, Barbara L. *mediator*
Aikman, Albert Edward *lawyer*
Ansley, Shepard Bryan *lawyer*
Bain, William Donald, Jr. *lawyer, chemical company executive*
Batson, David Warren *lawyer*
Bechtold, Susan Hatfield *legal assistant*
Berman, Richard Bruce *lawyer*
Blackburn, Catherine Elaine *lawyer, pharmacist*
Blume, James Donald *lawyer, consultant*
Boggs, Judith Susan *lawyer, health policy expert*
Boone, Richard Winston, Sr. *lawyer*
Bryant, Cecil Farris *lawyer, retired insurance company executive*
Burcham, Randall Parks *lawyer, farmer*
Bush, Robert G., III *lawyer, state legislator*
Caldwell, Claud Reid *lawyer*
Cambrice, Robert Louis *lawyer*
Capps, James Leigh, II *lawyer, military career officer*
Carr, Jesse Metteau, III *lawyer, engineering executive*
Cazalas, Mary Rebecca Williams *lawyer, nurse*
Claycomb, Hugh Murray *lawyer, author*
Clelland, Robert Theodore *lawyer*
Condra, Allen Lee *lawyer*
Crown, Nancy Elizabeth *lawyer*
D'Agusto, Karen Rose *lawyer*
Davis, Mark Warden *lawyer*
DeFoor, J. Allison, II *lawyer*
Dewberry, Betty Bauman *retired law librarian*
Dewey, Anne Elizabeth Marie *lawyer*
Dilworth, Hal Conn, Jr. *lawyer, military educator*
Donlon, William James *lawyer*
Dowd, William Timothy *lawyer, energy association executive*
Durgin, Diane *lawyer*
Easterling, Charles Armo *lawyer*
Engle, William Thomas, Jr. *lawyer*
Feazell, Vic *lawyer*
Fink, Norman Stiles *lawyer, educational administrator, fundraising consultant*
Fischer, David Jon *lawyer*
Fryburger, Lawrence Bruce *lawyer, mediator, writer*
Glober, George Edward, Jr. *lawyer*
Green, Michael Pruette *lawyer*
Greer, Raymond White *lawyer*
Griffith, Steven Franklin, Sr. *lawyer, real estate title insurance agent and investor*
Grogan, Alice Washington *lawyer*
Grogan, Robert Harris *lawyer*
Guste, William Joseph, Jr. *attorney general*
Gutman, Richard Edward *lawyer*
Hardin, Paul, III *law educator*
Hausman, Bruce *lawyer*
Haynie, Tony Wayne *corporate lawyer*
Hill, Harold Nelson, Jr. *lawyer*
Horn, Andrew Warren *lawyer*
Horsburgh, Beverly *law educator*
Jack-Moore, Phyllis *work/family strategist, educational consultant*
Jacobs, Alan *lawyer*
Jamieson, Michael Lawrence *lawyer*
Johnson, Leonard Hjalma *lawyer*
Jolly, Charles Nelson *lawyer, pharmaceutical company executive*
Keaty, Robert Burke *lawyer*

Klein, Linda Ann *lawyer*
Landy, Lisa Anne *lawyer*
Lee, Clifford Leon, II *lawyer*
Leibowitt, Sol David *lawyer*
Leithead, R. James *lawyer*
Locke, John Howard *lawyer*
Marinis, Thomas Paul, Jr. *lawyer*
Martin, James William *lawyer*
McClure, Ann Crawford *lawyer*
McCormick, David Arthur *lawyer*
Metzger, Jeffrey Paul *lawyer*
Meyerson, Stanley Phillip *lawyer*
Mitchell, Allan Edwin *lawyer*
Newcomb, Marguerite E. *paralegal, educator*
Norman, Albert George, Jr. *lawyer*
O'Brien, Charles H. *lawyer, retired state supreme court chief justice*
O'Connor, Edward Vincent, Jr. *lawyer*
O'Dell, Joan Elizabeth *lawyer, business executive*
Ordover, Abraham Philip *lawyer, mediator*
Otis, Lee Liberman *lawyer, educator*
Pullen, Richard Owen *lawyer, communications company executive*
Pustilnik, David Daniel *lawyer*
Rasmussen, Wayne Roger *law educator, consultant*
Rawls, Frank Macklin *lawyer*
Reynolds, H. Gerald *lawyer*
Reynolds, William Bradford *lawyer*
Richeson, Hugh Anthony, Jr. *lawyer*
Rivera, Oscar R. *lawyer, corporate executive*
Rodriguez-Orellana, Manuel *law educator*
Roff, Alan Lee *lawyer, consultant*
Sandefer, G(eorge) Larry *lawyer*
Saxon, John David *lawyer, policy analyst, educator*
Scafetta, Joseph, Jr. *lawyer*
Schlueter, Linda Lee *law educator*
Siemont, Kathleen O. *lawyer*
Smith, Ronald Ehlbert *lawyer, referral-based distributor*
Solkoff, Jerome Ira *lawyer, consultant, lecturer*
Speaker, Susan Jane *lawyer*
Stack, Beatriz de Greiff *lawyer*
Strand, Mary Ruth *paralegal assistant*
Swacker, Frank Warren *lawyer*
Thomas, Ella Cooper *lawyer*
Thornton, John W., Sr. *lawyer*
Trachtenberg, David *lawyer*
Vinroot, Richard Allen *lawyer, mayor*
Walton, John Wayne *lawyer*
Williams, Thomas Arthur *lawyer*
Wilson, Rhys Thaddeus *lawyer*
Wright, Frederick Lewis, II *lawyer*

MEDICINE. *See* HEALTHCARE: MEDICINE.

MILITARY

UNITED STATES

ALABAMA

Bessemer
Bacon, John Lee *marine officer*

Enterprise
Mabel, Scott Edward *military officer*

Foley
Kingston, George Willis *retired naval officer, small business owner*

Fort McClellan
Sienkiewicz, Raymond Jerome *army officer*

Fort Rucker
Crowder, Henry Alvin *military officer*
Glushko, Gail M. *military officer, physician*

Huntsville
McClendon, Dennis Edward *retired military officer*
Watts, William Park *naval officer*

Jacksonville
Clarke, Mary Elizabeth *retired army officer*

Maxwell AFB
Quilliam, James David *air force officer*

Montgomery
Boston, Hollis Buford, Jr. *retired military officer*
Heck, Joel Christopher *career officer*
Pickett, George Bibb, Jr. *retired military officer*
Udouj, Ronald Eric *army reserve officer*

Union Springs
Fayne, Gwendolyn Davis *air force officer, English educator*

ARIZONA

Yuma
Callahan, Richard Dean *career officer*

ARKANSAS

Beebe
Smith, Don Edward, Jr. *army officer, pilot*

Blytheville
Slowik, Richard Andrew *air force officer, writer*

Harrison
Smith, Leland Wrightman *retired military officer*

CALIFORNIA

Oceanside
Keisler, Joshua Allen *career officer*

San Francisco
Patton, Warren Andre *non-commissioned officer, journalist*

DELAWARE

Seaford
Policastro, Anthony Michael *retired military officer, pediatrician*

DISTRICT OF COLUMBIA

Washington
Kearns, Darien Lee *marine officer*
Loftus, Jill Vines *civilian military employee*
Raiford, Robert Charles *army officer*
Tussing, Bert Bud *military officer*
Webb, Schuyler Cleveland *naval officer*

FLORIDA

Cocoa
Hayton, Richard Neil *retired military officer, writer, publisher*

Davie
Pierce, Edward Martin *administrator*

Eglin AFB
Simmons, Jesse Donald, Jr. *government acquisition manager*
Stewart, J. Daniel *air force development and test center administrator*

Gainesville
Parker, Harry Lee *retired military officer, counselor*

Jacksonville
Beeson, Virginia Reed *naval officer, nurse*

Kissimmee
Dean, James Wendell *military officer, nurse*

Largo
Renshaw, Daryl Curtis *retired army officer, management consultant*

Miami
Mossbarger, David Lee *career officer*

Orange Park
Stevens, David Michael *retired naval officer*

Orlando
Laning, Richard Boyer *naval officer, writer, retired*
Smetheram, Herbert Edwin *government official*

Pensacola
De Lisser, Robert Medcalfe *naval officer*
Johnson, Alfred Carl, Jr. *former navy officer*

Port Orange
Leeks, Arnold Bernard *military executive*

Saint Augustine
Forrester, Ken *retired military officer*

Saint Petersburg
Smith, John Herbert *career officer*

Sarasota
Heiser, Rolland Valentine *former army officer, foundation executive*

Tampa
Matheny, Charles Woodburn, Jr. *retired army officer, retired civil engineer, former city official*

Valrico
Eden, Noble Keith *career officer*

GEORGIA

Atlanta
Malcom, Joseph Adams *military officer*
McGuinn, Michael Edward, III *retired army officer*

Duluth
Holutiak-Hallick, Stephen Peter, Jr. *retired military officer*

Fort McPherson
Champion, Charles Howell, Jr. *army officer*

Peachtree City
Harris, Nicholas Robert *army officer*

Richmond Hill
Iwanski, Lawrence Matthew *career officer*

Robins AFB
Rodefer, Joanne Marie *military officer*
Saville, Michael J. *air force officer*

Saint Marys
Jordan, Neil Robert *government telecommunications consultant*

Warner Robins
Coleman, Carl *air force noncommissioned officer*
Rider, Richard Walter *career officer*

HAWAII

Honolulu
Radzykewycz, Dan Theodore *retired Air Force officer, educator*

KANSAS

Fort Leavenworth
Thompson, Larry M. *career officer*

KENTUCKY

Ashland
Robinette, Anthony Edward *military officer*

Louisville
Septer, Glenn A. *army officer*

LOUISIANA

Abbeville
Breaux, David Lee *retired military officer*

Baton Rouge
Bain, Dale Wade *marine officer*

New Orleans
Block, Oliver J. *marine corps officer*

MARYLAND

Aberdeen Proving Ground
Orton, Robert Dell *military officer*

Annapolis
Brittain, Jerry Lee *naval officer, neuropsychologist*

Bethesda
Wishart, Leonard Plumer, III *army officer*

MISSISSIPPI

Keesler AFB
Rigdon, David Tedrick *air force officer, geneticist, director*

Newton
Gilmore, Kenny B. *career officer*

Pascagoula
Batiste, Robert Joseph *military non-commissioned officer, educator*

NEBRASKA

Omaha
Dickey, Lorraine Arlene *air force officer, neonatologist*

NEW JERSEY

Trenton
Ross, James Patrick *army officer*

NEW MEXICO

Kirtland AFB
Thompson, Erik *naval officer*

NORTH CAROLINA

Boone
Parker, Jacquelyn Susan *military officer*

Camp Lejeune
Greene, Stephen Joseph *marine corps officer*
Rueger, Brian Lee *marine corps officer*

Cherry Point
Laviolette, Bruce Edward *maintenance administrator*

Fayetteville
Harms, Blaire Michele *army officer*
Kilgore, Joe Everett, Jr. *army officer*
Larson, Gregory Paul *army officer*

Fort Bragg
Whittaker, Christopher James *army officer*

Jacksonville
Anderson, Kenneth Leverne *military officer*
Poudrier, Joel Philip *marine corps officer*

Matthews
Hixson, Nathan Hanks *retired military officer*

Southern Pines
Van Arsdale, Lee Arnold *career military officer*

Swansboro
Juhl, Harold Alexander *military officer*

OHIO

Evendale
Ante, Richard Louis *civilian military employee*

Wright Patterson AFB
Klimack, William Klaeve *army officer*

OKLAHOMA

Oklahoma City
Siewert, Edgar Allen *retired military non-commissioned officer*
Vaughn, James Eldon *retired military officer, civic volunteer*

Tinker AFB
Goodman, Ernest Monroe *air force officer*
Kennedy, John Joseph, Jr. *military officer*
Puckett, Mary Christine *logistics management specialist*

PENNSYLVANIA

Devon
Miller, George William, III *career officer, financial banking executive*

SOUTH CAROLINA

Charleston
Hathaway, Amos Townsend *retired naval officer, educator*
Turner, Gerald Rufus *government contracting official*
Watts, Claudius Elmer, III *retired air force officer*

Columbia
Lapp, Derrick Edward *army officer*

Edgefield
Leonard, Richard Douglas *army officer*

Hilton Head Island
Weis, Arthur John *naval officer*

Spartanburg
Davis, Dempsie Augustus *former air force officer, educator*

TENNESSEE

Clarksville
Lowder, Ned Edward, Jr. *army officer*
Scott, Richard Kevin *army officer*

Memphis
Cunningham, David Coleman *career officer*

TEXAS

Arlington
Delgado, Jose Antonio *retired air force officer, history educator*

Austin
Amoscato, Guy Thomas *retired air force officer, information analyst*
Council, Terry Ray *military officer*

Dyess AFB
Sandstrom, Dirk William *air force officer, hospital administrator*
Vatt, Richard Douglas *medical corps officer*

El Paso
Shapiro, Stephen Richard *retired air force officer, physician*
Simcic, Kenneth Joseph *career officer, endocrinologist*

Fort Bliss
Owens, Bobby *noncommissioned officer*

Fort Hood
Burke, Charles Michael *military officer*
Fretwell, Lincoln Darwin *career officer, dentist, consultant*
Hamontree, George Samuel, III *military officer*
Sprabary, Larry Drew *military analyst*

Frankston
Metcalf, Lynnette Carol *retired naval officer, journalist, educator, gemologist*

Garland
Stimpson, Ritchie Ples *retired air force officer*

Grand Prairie
Loo, Maritta Louise *military officer, nurse*

Lackland AFB
Davis, Cindy Ann *military officer, nursing educator*

Lubbock
Vordermark, Jonathan Sawyer *retired military officer, pediatric urologist*

Randolph AFB
Winney, David Lee *career officer*

San Antonio
Hill, William Victor, II *retired army officer, secondary school educator*
Jones, David Randolph *retired air force officer, aerospace psychiatrist*
Marsh, Nelson Leroy *military officer*
Nolan, Gerald *career officer*
Reneau, Marvin Bryan *military officer, business educator*
Ryder, Gene Ed *retired United States Air Force training administrator*

San Marcos
Bullock, Jerry McKee *retired military officer, consultant, educator*

Victoria
Voge-Black, Victoria Mae *retired military officer, physician*

Waco
Mitchell, William Allen *air force officer, political geography educator*

VIRGINIA

Alexandria
Dunn, Bernard Daniel *former naval officer, consultant*
Hughes, Harley Arnold *career officer, retired, corporation consultant*
Minor, Mary Ellen *civilian military employee*
Petzrick, Paul Arthur, Jr. *army officer*
Stafford, Thomas Patten *retired military officer, former astronaut*
Strunz, Kim Carol *military officer*
Wilson, Charles H(arrison) *retired air force officer, financial planner, human resource development professional*

Annandale
Watts, Helena Roselle *military analyst*

Arlington
Clanton, John Charles *army officer*
Cogliano, Gerard Raymond *army officer*
Davison, Michael Shannon *retired military officer*
Forrester, Eugene Priest *former army officer, management marketing consultant*
Hansen, Robert Carl, Jr. *naval officer*
Marini, Elizabeth Ann *civilian military executive*
McGinley, Edward Stillman, II *naval officer*
Peterson, David Glenn *retired career officer*
Quiterio, Manuel Lawrence, III *army officer*
Singstock, David John *military officer*
Suycott, Mark Leland *naval flight officer*
Taylor, Thomas *retired air force officer, security policy analyst*
Thompson, Jonathan Sims *army officer*

Blacksburg
Cheek, Sidney Michael *retired military officer*

Charlottesville
Crowll, John Lee *intelligence research specialist*

Fairfax
Daugherty, William James *military officer, intelligence officer, educator*

Falls Church
Gillard, James Henry *naval officer, ocean engineer*
Gray, D'Wayne *retired marine corps officer*

Fort Belvoir
Francis, Clifford Larry *retired career officer, management analyst*
Hoppe, William Charles *military officer*

Fort McNair
Andrews, Aaron R. *army officer*

Fort Myer
Hart, Herbert Michael *military officer*

Langley AFB
Robbe, Adrian Donald *military officer*

Mc Lean
Manitsas, Nikitas Constantin *career officer, automotive executive*
Sullivan, Kenneth Joseph *strategic and intelligence programs analyst*

Newington
Miggins, Michael Denis *retired career officer, arms control analyst*

Newport News
Dawson, Sylvia Etora *government employee, vocalist, writer*

Norfolk
Geisendorff, Tyson Baine *marine corps officer*
Gerhardt, William Paul *army officer, university administrator*
Guth, James Donald *commanding officer*
Heinze, Marvin H. *naval officer*
Kanellis, Anthony Nick *army officer, pilot*
Krantz, Kenneth Allan *military officer, judge*
Luttrell, William Ernest *naval officer,industrial hygienist, toxicologist*
Rendin, Robert Winter *environmental health officer*

Quantico
Bradunas, John Joseph *marine corps officer*
McLaughlin, William Preston *military officer, educator*
Perry, Steven Elliott *marine corps officer*
Sklenka, Stephen Douglas *marine corps officer*
White, Kevin Lee *officer of marines*
Wilson, Jeffery Brad *career officer*

Staunton
Dindinger, Jack Wilson *military officer*

Vienna
Robison, Kenneth Gerald *former naval officer, national security consultant, historian*

Virginia Beach
Price, Lester Lee *naval aviator*
Tazewell, Calvert Walke (William Stone Dawson) *retired military officer, publisher, author, historian, webmaster*

Warrenton
Ashton, Ronald Irving *army officer*

Woodbridge
Sullivan, John Francis *military officer*

WASHINGTON

Tacoma
Kangas, David Martin *army officer*

MILITARY ADDRESSES OF THE UNITED STATES

ATLANTIC

FPO
Sass, James Allen *navy officer*

EUROPE

APO
Charlip, Ralph Blair *career officer*
Moloff, Alan Lawrence *army officer, physician*
Stringer, David Lawrence *air force officer*

FPO
Griffin, Paul, Jr. *navy officer, engineer, educator*
Yacavone, David William *military officer, consultant, researcher*

KOREA

APO
Moloney, Michael Charles *career officer, pilot*

ADDRESS UNPUBLISHED

Bryson, Marion Ritchie *army scientist*
Campbell, Brian Scott *army officer*
Christovich, Daniel Joseph *coast guard officer*
Crippen, Robert Laurel *former naval officer and astronaut*
Daso, Dik Alan *military officer, history educator*
Delano, Kenneth James, Jr. *air force officer*
Evans, Lawrence Eric *military officer, systems analyst*
Evans, Roxanne Romack *retired military officer, hospital administrator*
Gilbert, James Riley, II *career officer*
Jermyn, Helen Williams *air force officer, environmental engineer*
Kelley, Larry Dale *retired army officer*
Kerwin, Walter Thomas, Jr. *career officer, consultant*
Linnstaedt, John Byron *retired military officer, operations researcher*
Marshall, Gilly Anthony *air force officer*
Neff, Diane Irene *naval officer*
Nulk, Raymond Howard *army officer*
Russell, Timothy Jerome *career officer*
Sagan, Stanley Daniel *career officer, retired*
Swentkofske, Mark Francis *air force officer*
Yarborough, William Glenn, Jr. *military officer, forest farmer, defense and international business executive*
Zupancic, Brandon Lee *career officer*

RELIGION

UNITED STATES

ALABAMA

Andalusia
Patterson, Edwin *minister*

Birmingham
Day, Janeth Norfleete *religious studies educator*
Garrett, Linda Oaks *theology educator*
Hull, William Edward *theology educator*
Jenkins, Edwin Fred *minister*
Miller, Robert Oran *bishop*
Morrison, Gregg Scott *minister*
Threadcraft, Hal Law, III *pastor, counselor*

Decatur
Ragland, Wylheme Harold *minister, health facility administrator*

Hartselle
Adams, Thurman Leon, Jr. *minister*

Huntsville
Chandler, Gordon Harold *minister*
Lewis, Robert Henry *lay worker*

Jemison
Otts, James Mitchell *minister*

Mobile
Lipscomb, Oscar Hugh *archbishop*

Monroeville
Adkisson, Randall Lynn *minister*

Montgomery
Bullard, Mary Ellen *retired religious study center administrator*

Sylacauga
Bailey, Robert Leslie *minister*

ARKANSAS

Ashdown
Copley, Stephen Jean *minister*

Conway
Harris, Marjorie Jane *religious studies educator*

Gravette
Hawkins, Phillip Lee *Christian Science practitioner*

Little Rock
Caldwell, Happy *religious organization executive*
Dyer, David Harrison *clergyman*
Mc Donald, Andrew J. *bishop*
Trulove, Harry David *religious organization administrator*
Truscott, Judith Farren *church education administrator*
Wilke, Richard B. *bishop*

Mount Holly
Mabson, Robert Langley *clergyman, librarian*

North Little Rock
Fitzpatrick, Joe Allen *music minister*

Pine Bluff
Adair, Toby Warren, Jr. *minister*

Russellville
Thompson, Robert Jaye *minister*

Smackover
Parsley, Robert Charles *minister*

DELAWARE

Rehoboth Beach
Johnson, Kermit Douglas *minister, retired military officer*

FLORIDA

Boca Raton
Eisenberg, Robin Ledgin *religious education administrator*
Singer, Merle Elliot *rabbi*

Boynton Beach
Gill, Milton Randall *minister*

Bradenton
Birney, Leroy *minister*
McGrew, Michael Bruce *music minister*
Platman, Robert Henry *religious educator*

Bushnell
Brown, Ashmun N. *priest*

Clearwater
Hilton, James Arthur *clergy member*

Englewood
Seeley, David William *minister*

Eustis
Klann, Richard *theology and religious studies educator*
Pinkston, Isabel Hay *minister, writer, educator, therapist*

Fort Lauderdale
Eynon, Steven Scott *minister*
Harr, Sheldon Jay *rabbi*
Mallory-Young, Shirley *religion educator*

Fort Myers
Snelling, Lonie Eugene, Jr. *minister*

Fort Pierce
Westman, Steven Ronald *rabbi*

Gainesville
Mueller, James R. *religious studies educator*

Jacksonville
Afflick, Clive Henry *minister, guidance counselor*
Holliday, Patricia Ruth McKenzie *evangelist*
MacNutt, Francis Scott *religious organization administrator*
Reed, Loy Wayne *minister, ministry director*
Vines, Charles Jerry *minister*

Lakeland
Bagwell, Gerald E. *minister*

Largo
Williams, Harry George *minister*

Maitland
Nicole, Roger *theology educator*

Melbourne
Walker, Harriette Katherine *religious administrator*

Miami
Beatty, Robert Clinton *religious studies educator*
Fitzgerald, John Thomas, Jr. *religious studies educator*
Hoy, William Ivan *minister, religion educator*
Kofink, Wayne Alan *minister*
Patterson, Rickey Lee *clergyman*
Schofield, Calvin Onderdonk, Jr. *bishop*
Weeks, Marta Joan *priest*

Miami Beach
Rubin, Menachem M. *rabbi, author*

Naples
Caruthers, J. C. *religious association executive*

New Port Richey
Sorensen, John Frederick *retired minister*

New Smyrna Beach
Hollis, Reginald *archbishop*

Opa Locka
Reid, Audley George *religion and philosophy educator*

Orlando
Grady, Thomas J. *bishop*
Pelli, Moshe *Judaic studies educator*
Ponder, James Alton *clergyman, evangelist*

Pace
Peaden, Glennis Faye *minister*
Sumrall, Kenneth Irvin *religious organization administrator*

Palm Beach
Feldman, Leonid Ariel *rabbi*

Palm Harbor
Morgan, George Pidcock *minister*

Panama City
Bailey, Earl Eugene *religion educator*

Penney Farms
Bronkema, Frederick Hollander *retired minister and church official*

Port Orange
Newton, Howard Edwin *retired minister*

Saint Augustine
McCarty, Doran Chester *religious organization administrator*
Patterson, John Bernard *lay worker, writer*

Saint Leo
McKay, Joel Gardner *Benedictine monk, musician*

Saint Petersburg
Doddridge, Rock Edward *pastor, educator*
Harris, Rogers S. *bishop*
Henderson, Robb Alan *minister*

Sarasota
Beal, Winona Roark *retired church administrator*
Castle-Hasan, Elizabeth E. *religious organization administrator*
Hamel, Joseph Donat *minister*
Kerr, Donald Craig *retired minister*

Tallahassee
Gregory, Terence Van Buren *clergyman*

Tampa
Justice, Eunice McGhee *missionary, evangelist*
Pope, Jesse Curtis *theology and religious studies educator*
Powell, Steven Loyd *minister*
Reeher, James Irwin *minister*
Rives, Thomas Nelson *minister*
Smith, Elton Edward *clergyman, religious studies educator*

West Palm Beach
Nolan, Richard Thomas *clergyman, educator*

Winter Haven
Gage, Robert Clifford *minister*

Winter Park
Armstrong, (Arthur) James *minister, religion educator, religious organization executive, consultant*
Johnson, Constance Ann Trillich *minister, librarian, educator, internet service provider, small business owner, writer, researcher, lecturer*

Zellwood
Wallcraft, Mary Jane Louise *religious organization executive, songwriter, author*

GEORGIA

Alpharetta
Dawson, Lewis Edward *minister, retired military officer*
Mills, Robert Theo *denominational executive minister*

Athens
Segars, John Kelvin *minister*

Atlanta
Barker, Carolyn Sims *diaconal minister*
Collins, James Lee *pastor*
Cooper, Jeffery Bernard *minister, university administrator*
Culpepper, Richard Alan *religious studies educator*
Ellingsen, Mark *history of Christian thought educator*
Ficken, Carl Frederick Wilhelm *theology educator*
Knox, James Lloyd *bishop*
Morris, Robert Renly *minister, clinical pastoral education supervisor*
Patrick, James Cary *religious organization administrator*
Runyon, Theodore Hubert, Jr. *religion educator, minister*
Skillrud, Harold Clayton *minister*
Stokes, Mack (Marion) Boyd *bishop*

Augusta
Oliver, John William Posegate *minister*

Blue Ridge
Morgan, Victor Hall *clergyman*

Brooks
Buzzard, Sir Anthony Farquhar *religion educator*

Brunswick
Zbiegien, Andrea *religious education educator, consultant, educational administrator*

Cumming
Begaye, Helen Christine *editor, religious organization official*

Decatur
Gary, Ethel *minister*
Gary, Julia Thomas *minister*

Hudnut-Beumler, James David *theology educator*
Larson, D(avid) Miles *music minister, vocal soloist, concert artist*

Eatonton
Adams, Carolyn Betha *minister*

Garfield
Fountain, Edwin Byrd *minister, educator, librarian, poet*

Lilburn
Webb, James Calvin *minister*

Lithonia
Kinnebrew, James Melvin *biblical theologian, educator, entrepreneur*

Lookout Mountain
Beisner, Ernest Calvin *theology and social ethics educator*

Macon
Doster, June Marken *minister*
Franklin, Roosevelt *minister*
Staton, Cecil Pope, Jr. *religious publisher*

Metter
Guido, Michael Anthony *evangelist*

Monroe
Johnson, Robert Hoyt *minister*

Norcross
Kyle, John Emery *mission executive*

Peachtree City
Dillard, George Stewart, III *minister*
Epps, William David *minister*

Riverdale
Waters, John W. *minister, educator*

Roswell
Winokur, Harvey Jay *rabbi*

Savannah
Lessard, Raymond W. *bishop*

Suwanee
Schmidt, June Laurel *minister*

Sylvania
Martin, Charles Wade *pastor*

Tifton
Cravey, Charles Edward *minister, publisher, poet*

Toccoa
Evearitt, Daniel Joseph *religion educator*
Sprinkle, Joe Melvin *religious studies educator*

Tucker
Ramey, Robert Homer, Jr. *theological seminary educator*

Valdosta
Robertson, Dale Wayne *minister*

Washington
Via, John Albert *priest*

INDIANA

Yorktown
Jaggers, Steven Bryan *minister*

KENTUCKY

Beaver Dam
Birkhead, Thomas Larry *minister*

Covington
Hughes, William Anthony *bishop*

Denniston
Ferrell, J(ames) Glenn *minister*

Fort Mitchell
Cave, John David *religious studies educator, researcher*

Frankfort
Hestand, Joel Dwight *minister, evangelist*

Harrodsburg
DeFoor, William Robert *minister*

Lexington
Davison, Lisa Michele *religious educator*
Emmert, Emery Myers *religious counselor*
Harrison, Mary *religious organization executive*
Williams, James Kendrick *bishop*

Louisville
Blaising, Craig Alan *religious studies educator*
Brown, Glenn Edward *minister, tennis educator*
Dale, Judy Ries *religious organization administrator*
Kelly, Thomas Cajetan *archbishop*
Miller, John Ulman *minister, author*
Rapport, Joe Rooks *rabbi*
Reed, David Benson *bishop*

Nortonville
Pate, Gary Ray *minister*

Owensboro
McRaith, John Jeremiah *bishop*

Union
Adams, Mendle Eugene *minister*

Vine Grove
McNamara, Patricia Rae *religious organization administrator, school system administrator*

Wilmore
Kalas, J(ohn) Ellsworth *religious educator, minister*

Winchester
Hall, Bennett Freeman *minister*

LOUISIANA

Baton Rouge
Hughes, Alfred Clifton *bishop*
Witcher, Robert Campbell *bishop*

Bossier City
Tice, William Fleet, Jr. *pastor*

Donaldsonville
Watson, Stanley Ellis *clergyman, financial company executive*

Foley
Horn, Joseph Robert, IV *priest*

Greenwood
Scudder, Robert *minister, youth home administrator*

Gretna
Lee, Hien Quang *religious organization executive*

Homer
Anglin, Walter Michael *evangelist, minister, law enforcement professional*

Lafayette
Hermes, Mother Theresa Margaret *prioress*
O'Donnell, Edward Joseph *bishop, former editor*

Meraux
Broome, Randall *evangelist*

New Orleans
Brown, James Barrow *bishop*
Clancy, Thomas Hanley *seminary administrator*
Green, Charles Edward *minister*
Johnson, Audrey Jackson *minister*
Mathis, Robert Rex *church administrator, educator*
Schulte, Francis B. *archbishop*
Stovall, Gerald Thomas *religious organization administrator*
Warren, William Frampton, Jr. *religion educator*

Opelousas
McKnight, A. J. *religious organization executive*

Ragley
Magee, Thomas Eston, Jr. *minister*

Saint Bernard
Lee, Melvin Joseph *minister*

Shreveport
Fisher, Jacob Alexander Shultz *clergyman*
Friend, William Benedict *bishop*

West Monroe
Edmondson, Jerry Hollis *clergyman*

MICHIGAN

Livonia
Quigley, John Francis *clergy member, minister*

MISSISSIPPI

Clinton
Hensley, John Clark *religious organization administrator, minister*

Gulfport
Freret, René Joseph *minister*

Hattiesburg
Taylor, David Neil *minister*

Indianola
Matthews, David *clergyman*

Jackson
Allin, John Maury *bishop*
Arrington, Teresa Ross *religion educator, language educator*
Elliott, Charles Mark *Greek Orthodox priest*
McKnight, William Edwin *minister*
Woodward, Wayne William *librarian, minister*

Kosciusko
Kearley, F. Furman *minister, religious educator, magazine editor*

Long Beach
Horton, Jerry Smith *minister*

Meridian
Lindstrom, Donald Fredrick, Jr. *priest*

Myrtle
Pirkle, Estus Washington *minister*

Thaxton
McCutcheon, Elwyn Donovan *minister*

Vicksburg
Sansing, Gordon H. *minister*

MISSOURI

Bolivar
Jackson, Gregory Allen *minister*

Monett
Block, Michael David *minister*

NEW JERSEY

Princeton
Neely, Alan Preston *religious studies educator*

NEW MEXICO

Albuquerque
Sheehan, Michael Jarboe *archbishop*

NEW YORK

New York
Harris, Lyndon F. *priest*

NORTH CAROLINA

Black Mountain
Blaisdell, Russell Carter *minister, religious organization administrator*

Boiling Springs
Arnold, Ernest Woodrow *minister*

Cary
Harvey, Daniel Richard *minister*

Chapel Hill
Ernst, Carl William *religious studies educator, researcher*

Charlotte
DiPianti, Robert *religious association executive*
Freeman, Sidney Lee *minister, educator*
Grigg, Eddie Garman *minister*
Lash, André Duane *minister of music*
Michael, Caroline Marshall *religious organization administrator*
Prosser, Bruce Reginal, Jr. (Bo Prosser) *minister, consultant*
Samuel, James Ray *minister, dean*
Walker, Jewett Lynius *clergyman, church official*
Wilson, Edward Cox *minister*

Clyde
Rogers, Garry Lee *minister, medical technician*

Concord
Sloop, Gregory Todd *clergyman*

Dunn
Sauls, Don *religious organization administrator, clergyman*

Durham
Brill, Earl Hubert *clergyman, educator*
Efird, James Michael *theology educator*
Goranson, Stephen Craft *history of religions educator, researcher*
Green, Mary Hester *evangelist*
King, Arnold Kimsey, Jr. *retired clergyman, nursing home executive, statistician*
Langford, Thomas Anderson *theology educator, academic administrator*
Meyers, Carol Lyons *religion, history and archaeology educator*
Meyers, Eric Mark *religion educator*

Ellenboro
Burgin, Max Edward *minister, military officer*

Fairmount
Kisseih, Libby Malloy *minister*

Fairview
Eck, David Wilson *minister*

Fayetteville
Hatcher, William Wayne *retired clergyman and church executive*
Tyson, Anne Elizabeth Dodge *theologian*

Gastonia
Owens, Robin Shane *clergyman*

Graham
Weckerly, William Clarence *minister*

Greensboro
Hull, James Ernest *religion and philosophy educator*
Lolley, William Randall *minister*
Rights, Graham Henry *minister*
Willis, C. Paul *minister*

Greenville
Thompson, Emerson McLean, Jr. *retired clergyman*
Wood, Gerald David *religious organization administrator*

Harrisburg
Helton, Max Edward *minister, consultant, religious organization executive*

Haw River
Poindexter, Richard Grover *minister*

Hendersonville
Sims, Bennett Jones *minister, educator*

Hickory
McDaniel, Michael Conway Dixon *bishop, theology educator*

Jamesville
Weaver, James Paul *minister*

Lake Junaluska
Goodgame, Gordon Clifton *minister*
Tullis, Edward Lewis *retired bishop*

Manteo
Miller, William Lee, Jr. *minister*

Marshville
Steagald, Thomas Ray *minister*

Mill Spring
Osborn, Christopher Raymoln, Jr. *minister*

Morganton
MacLeod, John Daniel, Jr. *religious organization administrator*

Mount Olive
Boyd, Julia Margaret (Mrs. Shelton B. Boyd) *lay church worker*

Newton
Foster, Daniel George *minister of music, organist, choirmaster*
Groth, John Henry Christopher *pastor, author*

North Wilkesboro
Laney, Howard Elimuel *clergyman*

Pfafftown
Dellinger, Charles Wade *minister*

Pinehurst
Black, Bobby C. *chaplain*

Raleigh
Dempsey, Joseph Page *retired minister, counselor*
Ennis, Ralph Colwell *religious organization administrator, educator*
Gossman, Francis Joseph *bishop*
Huffman, David Curtis *minister*
Miller, Jerry Elkin, Jr. *minister*

Reidsville
Hart, Richard Wesley *religious organization administrator, pastor*

Robbins
Mac Kenzie, James Donald *clergyman*

Rocky Mount
Smith, Preston *minister*

Saint Pauls
Alvis, Joel Lawrence, Jr. *minister*

Shelby
Cagle, Terry Dee *clergyman*
Watterson, Gene Lee *clergyman*

Southern Pines
Hughes, Lisa Lynn *lay church worker*

Southport
Harrelson, Walter Joseph *minister, religion educator emeritus*

Wake Forest
Blackmore, James Herrall *clergyman, educator, author*
Lanier, David Emory *religion educator*

Wallace
Johnson, James Wilson *pastor*

Willow Springs
Mathers, Norman Wayne *minister*

Wilmington
Wright, Thomas Henry *bishop*

Winston Salem
Fitzgerald, Ernest Abner *retired bishop*
Marsden, Keith Lynn *minister, counselor*
Pollard, Alton Brooks, III *religion educator, minister*

OKLAHOMA

Bartlesville
Woodruff, William Jennings *theology educator*

Bethany
Johnson, John Randall, Sr. *religious organization administrator*
Moore, Ronald Quentin *minister*
Shelton, Muriel Moore *religious education administrator*

Cordell
Finley, T.J. *evangelist, songwriter, poet, writer*

Del City
Abernathy, Jerry Don *clergy member, educator*

Enid
Lowery, Richard Harlin *religious studies educator*

Mcalester
Sledge, Terry Lynn *minister*

Oklahoma City
Hampton, Carol McDonald *religious organization administrator, educator, historian*
Hardy, William McDonald, Jr. *clergyman, physician assistant*
Jones, Charles Edwin *chaplain, historian, bibliographer*
Keenen, Howard Gregory *minister*
MacManamy, Gary Allan *minister*
Ridley, Betty Ann *educator, church worker*
Sheldon, Eli Howard *minister*
Shelton, Malcolm Wendell *biblical studies educator*

Underwood, Bernard Edward *religious organization administrator*
White, James Robert *minister*

Tulsa
Cox, William Jackson *bishop*
Hatfield, William Keith *minister*
Mosier, Edward Bert *minister*
Osborn, La Donna Carol *clergywoman*
Rex, Lonnie Royce *religious organization administrator*
Roberts, (Granville) Oral *clergyman*
Slattery, Edward J. *bishop*
Tillman, Kevin Lamar *minister*

Vici
McCoy, Carroll Pierce *retired minister*

PENNSYLVANIA

Bryn Mawr
Ledwith, Sister Margaret Christine *nun, counselor*

Warrington
Walker, Edwin Stuart, III *retired missionary organization executive*

SOUTH CAROLINA

Anderson
Wisler, Darla Lee *pastor*

Charleston
Salmon, Edward Lloyd, Jr. *bishop*
Thompson, David B. *bishop*
Young, Earl LaVaughn *minister*

Columbia
Aull, James Stroud *retired bishop*
Jackson, Charles Benjamin *minister*
McCrory, Sarah Graydon *church lay leader, retired lawyer*
Moore, Edward Raymond, Jr. *pastor, chaplain, campaign consultant*

Due West
Farley, Benjamin Wirt *religious studies educator, writer*

Florence
Baroody, Albert Joseph, Jr. *pastoral counselor*

Gaffney
Harrison, Richard Dean *minister, counselor*

Georgetown
Allison, Christopher FitzSimons *bishop*

Greenville
Kowalski, Paul Randolph *minister*
Miller, Russell Edmund *lay worker, energy investment banker*
Waters, Curtis Jefferson *retired minister, evangelist*

Greenwood
Morton, Theodore Roosevelt, Jr. *clergyman*

Heath Springs
Feagin, Eugene Lloyd *pastor*

Hilton Head Island
Kinney, William Lee *minister, religious writer*

Inman
Williams, Mark Anthony *minister*

Lexington
Borgkvist, Joseph, Jr. *minister*

Newberry
Arp, Robert Kelley *clergyman*
Martell, Denise Mills *lay worker*

North Myrtle Beach
Kantner, Helen Johnson *church education administrator*

Pelzer
Blackmon, Michael Eugene *minister*

Spartanburg
Bullard, John Moore *religion educator, church musician*
Ely, Elizabeth Wickenberg *priest*

Summerville
Holler, Adlai Cornwell, Jr. *minister*

Taylors
Vaughn, John Carroll *minister, educator*

Warrenville
Fallaw, Carol Freeman *religious organization administrator*

Winnsboro
McCants, Clyde Taft *minister*

TENNESSEE

Antioch
Messer, Trymon *religious organization executive*
Waddell, R. Eugene *minister*

Bristol
Hill, Kenneth Clyde *clergyman*

Chattanooga
Hughes, Michael Randolph *evangelist*
Maloney, J. Patrick *minister, educator, seminary administrator*
Mohney, Nell Webb *religion educator, speaker, author*

Cleveland
Hughes, Ray Harrison *minister, church official*
Jackson, Joseph Essard *religious organization administrator*
Land, Steven Jack *minister, theology educator*
Reyes, Jose Antonio, Sr. *minister*
Taylor, William Al *church administrator*

Collierville
Ratzlaff, David Edward *minister*

East Ridge
Hodge, Raymond Douglas *minister*

Elizabethton
Ingram, Osmond Carraway, Jr. *minister*

Franklin
Young, William Edgar *religious organization official*

Jackson
Duduit, J(ames) Michael *clergyman, public relations executive, university official*

Jamestown
Walker, Dana Eugene *evangelist*

Johnson City
Bradford, Michael Lee *religious organization administrator, clergyman*
Phillips, Dorothy Alease *lay church worker, educator, freelance writer*
Shaw, Angus Robertson, III *minister*

Kingsport
Robelot, Milton Paul *deacon, architect*

Knoxville
Kitts, Elbert Walker *minister*
O'Connell, Anthony J. *bishop*
Stooksbury, William Claude *minister*

La Follette
Eads, Ora Wilbert *clergyman, church official*

Livingston
Harrison, Jim Rush, Jr. *minister of music*

Mc Minnville
Gammon, James Edwin, Sr. *clergyman*

Memphis
Brown, Lee R. *minister*
Broyles, J(ohn) Allen *clergyman*
Hamilton, David Eugene *minister, educator*
Hester, James Herbert, Jr. *minister*
Meredith, Donald Lloyd *librarian*
Steib, James Terry *bishop*
Todd, Virgil Holcomb *clergyman, religion educator*

Milligan College
Walker, Dorothy Keister *minister*

Milton
Coaker, George Mack *minister*

Nashville
Abstein, William Robert, II *minister*
Bass, George Harold *religious organization administrator*
Beeman, Bob Joe *minister*
Boone, John Lewis *religious organization administrator*
Criscoe, Arthur Hugh *religious organization administrator, educator*
Dockery, David Samuel *theology educator, editor*
Forlines, Franklin Leroy *minister, educator*
Hampton, Ralph Clayton, Jr. *pastoral studies educator, clergyman*
Kmiec, Edward Urban *bishop*
Land, Richard Dale *minister, religious organization administrator*
McInteer, Jim Bill *minister, publishing executive, farmer*
Pursell, Cleo Wilburn *church official*
TeSelle, Eugene Arthur, Jr. *religion educator*
Walker, Arthur Lonzo *religious organization administrator*

Newport
Starks, Charles Wiley *minister*

Sewanee
Hughes, Robert Davis, III *theological educator*
Patten, William Thomas *priest, consultant*

Sneedville
Hodges, James Stephen *community development missionary*

Sweetwater
Johnson, Charlie James *minister*

TEXAS

Abilene
Baird, Larry Don *minister, nurse*
Smith, Ronald Aubrey *theology educator*

Aledo
Barton, Charles David *religious studies educator, author, researcher, historian*

Alice
Tetlie, Harold *priest*

Amarillo
Klein, Jerry Lee *religion educator, minister*
Matthiesen, Leroy Theodore *bishop*
Meenan, Alan John *clergyman, theological educator*

Arlington
Cadwallader, Chester Samuel, Jr. *missions educator*
Lee, Sara Nell *lay worker, small business owner*
Lingerfelt, B. Eugene, Jr. *minister*

Austin
Denham, William Ernest, Jr. *minister*
Ellwanger, John P(aul) *minister*
Gardner, Dan Nobles *deacon, church official*
Hale, Arnold Wayne *religious studies educator, army officer, clergyman, psychotherapist*
Johnson, Jennie *chaplain, social worker*
Mc Carthy, John Edward *bishop*
Middendorf, Michael Paul *clergyman educator*
Muck, Terry Charles *religious publisher and educator*
Puffe, Paul *minister*

Bay City
Boren, Edward Daniel *priest*

Baytown
Gossett, Mark Valton *minister*

Beaumont
Creasong, Johnny Joe *minister*

Brownsville
Fitzpatrick, John J. *bishop*
Pena, Raymundo Joseph *bishop*

Brownwood
Chapman, Dan G. *minister*

Colleyville
Maddox, Roger Wayne *minister*

Conroe
Fitts, R. Lewis *minister, business administrator*

Corpus Christi
Kenna, John Thomas *priest*
Lowe, Joe Allen *minister*
McDonagh, Kathleen *theology educator, researcher*

Crockett
Hillman, Pearl Elizabeth *minister*

Dallas
Barnhouse, Ruth Tiffany *priest, psychiatrist*
Choun, Robert Joseph, Jr. *religious studies educator*
Closser, Patrick Denton *radio evangelist, artist*
Gross, Harriet P. Marcus *religious studies and writing educator*
Habito, Ruben Leodegario Flores *religion educator*
Harrell, Roy Harrison, Jr. *minister*
Heidt, John Harrison *priest*
Herbener, Mark Basil *bishop*
Holleman, Sandy Lee *religious organization administrator*
Kirby, James Edmund, Jr. *theology educator*
Latus, Timothy Dexter *psychic consultant*
Morgan, Larry Ronald *minister*
Oden, William Bryant *bishop, educator*
Pedraja, Luis Gregorio *theology educator*
Spencer, Stephen Robert *theology educator*
Spooner, Bernard Myrick *religious organization administrator*
Tyson, Joseph Blake *religion educator*
Wood, Charles Monroe *theology educator*

De Soto
Jackson, Johnny W. *minister*

Deer Park
Deutsch, Lawrence Ira *minister*

Devine
Markham, Meeler *retired minister*

East Bernard
Dunn, Margaret Ann *religious studies educator, administrator, minister*

El Paso
Bryan, Jesse Dwain *minister, missionary*

Fort Worth
Ballard, Ronald Doyle *theologian, educator*
Boeglin, Timothy Ray *minister*
Brister, Commodore Webster, Jr. *religion educator*
Cranford, Lorin Lee *clergyman, educator*
Edwards, Samuel Lee *religious organization executive*
Eldridge, Daryl Roger *religious educator, dean*
Elliott, John Franklin *clergyman*
Garrett, James Leo, Jr. *theology educator*
Hall, William *minister*
Huey, F. B., Jr. *minister, theology educator*
Lawson, Carole Jean *religious educator, author, poet*
Putt, B. Keith *religion educator*
Rogers, Charles Ray *minister, religious organization administrator*
Teegarden, Kenneth Leroy *clergyman*
Toulouse, Mark Gene *religion educator*
Wawee, Robert William *priest*

Frisco
Wicker, James Robert *minister*

Galveston
Millikan, Charles Reagan *pastor*
Wells, Robert Louis *priest*

Garrison
Herrington, Dale Elizabeth *lay worker*

Houston
Arnold, James Phillip *religious studies educator, history educator*
Barrett, Michael Joseph *priest*
Brown, Virgil Jackson *minister*
Bui, Long Van *church custodian, translator*
Capes, David Bryan *theology educator*
Hipps, Larry Clay *clergyman, evangelistic association executive*
Kaliszewski, Charles Stanley *clergyman, international evangelist*
Karff, Samuel Egal *rabbi*
Prescott, William Bruce *minister*
Stephens, Carson Wade *minister*

Ingleside
Sumner, Robert Leslie *minister*

Irving
Evans, Michael David *clergyman, author*
Norris, John Martin *theology educator*

Jacksonville
Pruitt, William Charles, Jr. *minister, educator*

Kingwood
Barkley, Bronson Lee *minister*

League City
Ellis, Walter Leon *minister*

Liberty
Hughes, Paul Anthony *minister, musician, songwriter, author, publisher*

Lubbock
Bowyer, Charles Lester *chaplain*

Mexia
Johnson, Clarence Ray *minister*

Orange
Delarue, Louis C(harles) *priest*

Pecan Gap
Williams, Jessie Willmon *church worker, retired librarian*

Quitman
Sutton, Jesse Noel *minister*

Ranger
Brooks, Shelly Ann *minister, osteopath*

Richardson
Barrus, Paul Wells *priest*
Conrad, Flavius Leslie, Jr. *minister*

San Angelo
Mathews, James Harold *minister*

San Antonio
Cruz, David Ramirez *priest*
Culver, John Blaine *minister*
Ellos, William Joseph *priest, educator*
Flores, Patrick F. *archbishop*
Fogg, Ernest Leslie *minister, retired*
Knox, Robert Burns *religious organization administrator*
Mc Allister, Gerald Nicholas *retired bishop, clergyman*
Nix, Robert Lynn *minister*
Teran, Sister Mary Inez *nun, educator*
Walker, William Oliver, Jr. *educator, university dean*

San Marcos
Price, John Randall *theology educator, researcher*

Spring
Hunt, T(homas) W(ebb) *retired religion educator*

Sugar Land
McDonald, Jeffery Blake *youth ministries administrator, educator*

Texarkana
Tucker, Bobby Glenn *minister*

Tyler
Carmody, Edmond *bishop*
Webb, John Weber, Jr. *minister*

Van Alstyne
Daves, Don Michael *minister*

Waco
O'Brien, James Randall *minister*
Wood, James E., Jr. *religion educator, author*

VIRGINIA

Accomac
Plonk, William McGuire *retired minister*

Arlington
Bailey, Amos Purnell *clergyman, syndicated columnist*
Moshier, David Irwin *church administrator*

Ashland
Stinnette, Timothy Earl *minister*

Berryville
Delery, Alfred Albert *priest, physician*

Big Island
Buchanan, Ray Allen *clergyman*
Horne, Kenneth Chester *minister*

Blackstone
Phillips, Zolton Julius, III *minister*

Bluefield
Crawford, Timothy Gray *Old Testament and Hebrew language educator*

Charlottesville
Finley, Robert Van Eaton *minister*
Lindner, John M. *publisher, editor, minister*
Scott, Nathan Alexander, Jr. *minister, educator, literary critic*

Chesapeake
Stafford, Kenneth Victor, Sr. *minister*

Colonial Beach
McClain, Gregory David *minister*

Dillwyn
Davenport, James Guython *minister*

Fairfax
Anders, Camille Shephard *director of adult and family ministries*
Southern, Lonnie Steven *minister*

Falls Church
Timm, Jeffrey Thomas *chaplain, air force officer*

Front Royal
Skeris, Robert Alexander *theology educator*

Glen Allen
Collier, Roger Malcolm *minister*

Hampton
Henderson, Salathiel James *minister, clergy*
Landis, Homer Warren *minister*

Harrisonburg
Goodman, Katheryne Lockridge (Kay Goodman) *church administrator, elder*

Jetersville
Gibson, Charles Walter *minister*

Lynchburg
Nelson, Joseph Lee, Jr. *religion educator*

Manassas
Gustavson, Brandt *religious association executive*

Martinsville
McCann, Thomas Ryland, Jr. *minister*
Shackleford, William Alton, Sr. *minister*

Mc Lean
Lotz, Denton *minister, church official*
Topping, Eva Catafygiotu *writer, lecturer, educator*

Middletown
Ibach, Douglas Theodore *minister*

Midlothian
Lee, Jerome Odell *minister*

Montross
Helm, Gary Stewart *minister*

Mount Crawford
Creswell, Norman Bruce *minister*

Norfolk
Hays, Franklin Ernest *minister, chaplain*
Vest, Frank Harris, Jr. *bishop*

North Tazewell
Oldham, William Edward *minister, accountant, educator*

Palmyra
Brown, Nan Marie *clergywoman*

Patrick Springs
Torrence, Billy Hubert *minister*

Reedville
Westbrook, Walter Winfield *minister*

Reston
Coutu, Charles Arthur *deacon*

Richmond
Aigner, Emily Burke *lay worker*
Bagby, Daniel Gordon *religious studies educator, clergyman*
Barton, Jonathan Miller *clergyman*
Deekens, Elizabeth Tupman *writer*
Dorsey, Richard Neal *minister*
Laha, Robert Randall, Jr. *minister*
Lee, Peter James *bishop*
Moore, John Sterling, Jr. *minister*
Richerson, Stephen Wayne *minister*
Sapp, William David *minister*
Simms, Albert Egerton *minister, retirement communities consultant*
Spence, Jeffrey Bennett *minister, religious association administrator*
Turner, James Wesley *minister, former church administrator*

Roanoke
Harding, Margaret Tyree *minister*
Light, Arthur Heath *bishop*
Marmion, William Henry *retired bishop*
Matheny, Paul Duane *minister, theological researcher*

Salem
Bansemer, Richard Frederick *bishop*

Springfield
Cates, Marian Ward *Christian Science practitioner*

Staunton
Kopp, George Philip, Jr. *minister*

Sterling
Piper, Thomas Samuel *minister, consultant*

Virginia Beach
Jackson, Jesse Luther, III *pastor*
Smith, Ashton Carpenter *minister*

Williamsburg
Hindman, David Meredith *minister*

Winchester
Christianson, Conrad Johan, Jr. *retired minister, church official*
Kohl, Harold *missionary, educator*

Woodbridge
Townsend, Kenneth Ross *retired priest*

WEST VIRGINIA

Barboursville
Vance, Charles Randall *minister*

Beckley
Rehbein, Edward Andrew *minister, geologist, consultant*

Charleston
Leasor, Jane *religion and philosophy educator, musician*
Prichard, John David *minister*

Fairmont
Stevens, Earl Patrick *minister*

Hamlin
Barrett, Brian Lee *minister, evangelist*

Hinton
Glaser, Robert Harvey, Sr. *pastor*

Morgantown
Cayton, Mary Evelyn *clergyman*

Sharples
Perry, Sharon Lynn York *religious organization administrator, educator*

Williamstown
Simmons, Robert Daniel *clergyman, machinist*

TERRITORIES OF THE UNITED STATES

PUERTO RICO

Ponce
Torres Oliver, Juan Fremiot *bishop*

MILITARY ADDRESSES OF THE UNITED STATES

ATLANTIC

FPO
Girardin, David Walter *chaplain, military officer*

MEXICO

Mexico City
Corripio Ahumada, Ernesto Cardinal *retired archbishop*

ADDRESS UNPUBLISHED

Charlton, Gordon Taliaferro, Jr. *retired bishop*
Chinula, Donald McLean *religious studies educator*
Dixon, Ernest Thomas, Jr. *retired bishop*
Ette, Ezekiel *minister, mental health counselor*
Farrar, Martha Ann *lay worker, retired gift shop owner*
Fisher, Robert Bruce *priest*
Gonzalez, Maria Elena, Sr. *religious organization executive*
Grahmann, Charles V. *bishop*
Gutmann, Reinhart Bruno *clergyman, social worker*
Haberer, John Henry, Jr. *minister*
Handy, William Talbot, Jr. *bishop*
Hinkle, Jeffrey Wayne *religious writer, speaker*
Kendall, Jonathan Philo *rabbi*
King, Charles Benjamin *minister*
MacPhail, Deborah *mission service volunteer, educator*
McClinton, Wendell C. *religious organization administrator*
Mc Kay, Samuel Leroy *clergyman*
McKee, Adele Dieckmann *retired church music director, educator*
Moreton, Thomas Hugh *minister*
Netterville, George Bronson *minister*
Osborne, James Alfred *religious organization administrator*
Patterson, Donis Dean *bishop*
Pearson, Anthony Alan *minister*
Reed, Cynthia Kay *minister*
Scherch, Richard Otto *minister, consultant*
Seale, James Millard *religious organization administrator, clergyman*
Smith, Ann Hamill *retired religion educator*
Stevens, John Flournoy *priest*
Stone, Kurt Franklin *rabbi*
Sullivan, James Lenox *clergyman*
Taylor, Lewis Jerome, Jr. *priest*
Wallace, Mark Harris *minister*
Weinhauer, William Gillette *retired bishop*

SCIENCE: LIFE SCIENCE

UNITED STATES

ALABAMA

Auburn
Bowen, Kira L. *plant pathologist*
Daniell, Henry *molecular genetics educator*
Huffman, Dale L. *food science educator*
Lovell, Richard Thomas *aquaculture researcher*
Oli, Madan Kumar *wildlife ecologist*

Birmingham
Dooley, Thomas Patrick *molecular biologist*
Elgavish, Ada *molecular, cellular biologist*
Finley, Sara Crews *medical geneticist, educator*
Gerlach, Gary G. *botanical garden director, columnist*
Morrison, Richard Pearce *microbiologist*
Rouse, John Wilson, Jr. *research institute administrator*
Tang, De-chu *molecular biologist, gene therapist, researcher*
Van Groen, Thomas *neurobiologist*
Wallace, Carl Jerry *zoo director*

Dauphin Island
Cowan, James Howard, Jr. *fishery scientist, biological oceanographer*

Huntsville
Reddy, Chandrasekhara K. *agronomy educator*
Thornton, Beretha *plant biotechnologist*

Mobile
Bhatnagar, Yogendra Mohan *biology educator*
Fitzpatrick, J(oseph) F(erris), Jr. *biology educator, consultant*
French, Elizabeth Irene *biology educator, violinist*
Spector, Michael Phillip *biomedical scientist, microbiologist*
Taylor, Aubrey Elmo *physiologist, educator*

Normal
Bishnoi, Udai Ram *agronomy and seed technology educator*
Coleman, Tommy Lee *soil science educator, researcher, laboratory director*
Green, Thomas Harris *forestry educator*
Mays, David Arthur *agronomy educator, small business owner*
Sohni, Youvraj Rooplal *microbiology educator, research scientist*

Redstone Arsenal
Rhoades, Richard Gardner *government research executive*

Tuscaloosa
Wetzel, Robert George *botany educator*

Tuskegee
Childs, Theodore Francis *biologist, retired educator*
Smith, Edward Jude *biologist*

ARIZONA

Rio Rico
Le, Ton Da *horticulturist, researcher*

Tucson
McCusker, J. Stephen *zoo director*

ARKANSAS

Conway
Choinski, John Stanley, Jr. *biology educator, botanist*

Fayetteville
Riggs, Robert Dale *plant pathology/nematology educator, researcher*
Templeton, George Earl, II *plant pathologist*

Jefferson
Lu, Ming-Hsiung *research biologist*

Little Rock
Hardin, Hilliard Frances *microbiologist*
Lindley, Barry Drew *medical educator*

Magnolia
Tollett, James Terrell *agriculture educator, department chair*

Monticello
Cain, Michael Dean *research forester*

State University
Bednarz, James C. *wildlife ecologist educator*

CALIFORNIA

Oakland
Wilson, Thomas Woodrow, III *research scientist, consultant*

Sunnyvale
Lim, Hwa Aun *research geneticist, bioinformaticist, consultant*

COLORADO

Pagosa Springs
Preston, Rodney Leroy *animal science educator*

DISTRICT OF COLUMBIA

Washington
Chamot, Dennis *research organization executive*
Greenberg, Frank *clinical geneticist, educator, academic administrator*

FLORIDA

Argyledria
Rafey, Larry Dean *microbiologist, clinician*

Clearwater
Whedon, George Donald *medical administrator, researcher*

Coconut Creek
Rault, Jules *food technologist, consultant*

Coral Gables
Savage, Jay Mathers *biology educator*

Delray Beach
Youngman, David A. *biology educator*

Fort Lauderdale
Su, Nan-Yao *entomology educator*

Fort Pierce
Jaramillo, Juan Camilo *marine biologist*
Rice, Mary Esther *biologist*

Gainesville
Cantliffe, Daniel James *horticulture educator*
Childers, Norman Franklin *horticulture educator*
Christie, Richard Gary *plant pathologist*
Curtis, Lisa Margaret *biological scientist*
Gelband, Craig Harris *physiologist*
Greiner, Ellis Charles *zoology educator*
Hansen, Peter James *reproductive physiologist, researcher*
Jaeger, Marc Julius *physiology educator, researcher*
Jeyaprakash, Ayyamperumal *biologist, researcher*
Jones, David Alwyn *geneticist, botany educator*
Mayer, Marion Sidney *research entomologist*
McSorley, Robert *nematology researcher, educator*
Mead, Frank Waldreth *taxonomic entomologist*
Olila, Oscar Gesta *soil and water scientist*
Ott, Edgar Alton *animal nutrition educator*
Schelske, Claire L. *limnologist, educator*
Seale, James Lawrence, Jr. *agricultural economics educator, international trade researcher*
Shirk, Paul David *research physiologist*
Ward, Daniel Bertram *botanist, educator*
Webb, Roger Stuart *forestry educator*
Wei, Cheng-I *toxicologist, microbiologist*
Wilcox, Charles Julian *geneticist, educator*
Zimowska-Handler, Grazyna Joanna *insect physiologist*
Zomlefer, Wendy Beth *botanist, biological illustrator*

Homestead
Revuelta, René Sergio *marine scientist, educator*

Jacksonville
Allen, Ted Tipton *biology educator*
Martin, David Lance *botanist*
Tardona, Daniel Richard *ethologist, naturalist, writer, park ranger, educator*

Jay
Brecke, Barry John *weed scientist, researcher, educator*

Lake Alfred
Rouseff, Russell Lee *food chemistry educator, researcher*

Lakeland
Niswonger, Jeanne Du Chateau *biologist, writer*

Live Oak
Tramontana, Eileen Mary *environmental educator, agricultural producer*

Melbourne
Dhople, Arvind Madhav *microbiologist*

Miami
Baumbach, Lisa Lorraine *research scientist*
Boucher, George *aquarium administrator*
Bunge, Richard Paul *cell biologist, educator*
Cook, Clark *administrator science museum*
Correll, Helen Butts *botanist, researcher*
Dezfulian, Manoucher *microbiology educator*
Dong, Quan *ecologist, educator*
Fontana, Al *director of Miami Metropolitan Zoo*
Muench, Karl H. *clinical geneticist*
Sanborn, Allen Francis *biologist, educator*
Zuo, Yuegang *research scientist*

Orlando
McKently, Alexandra H. *agricultural biotechnologist, researcher, educator*
Quinn, Sondra *science center executive*
Smith, Paul Frederick *plant physiologist, consultant*
White, Albert Cornelius *entomologist, researcher*

Palm Beach
Hopper, Arthur Frederick *biological science educator*

Palm Harbor
Heifetz, Carl Louis *microbiologist*

Panama City
Cilek, James Edwin *medical and veterinary entomologist*
Olson, Jean Kathryn *chemistry educator*

Pensacola
Foster, Virginia *retired botany educator*
Garrison, Wanda Brown *environmental consultant*

Pompano Beach
Franks, Allen *research institute executive, educator*

Punta Gorda
Beever, James William, III *biologist*

Saint Petersburg
Kellogg, Christina Anne *marine microbiologist*
Kormilev, Nicholas Alexander *retired entomologist*
Mueller, O. Thomas *molecular geneticist, pediatrics educator*

Sarasota
Bierner, Mark William *botanist, botanical garden director*
Pierce, Richard Harry *research director for laboratory*

Silver Springs
Wheeler, Jeanette Norris *entomologist*

Tallahassee
Brennan, Leonard Alfred *research scientist, administrator*
Feng, Jinan *plant and soil science researcher*

James, Frances Crews *zoology educator*
Lamikanra, Olusola *food scientist*

Tampa
Hickman, Hugh Vernon *science educator, researcher*
Jove, Richard *molecular biologist*
Kousseff, Boris Georgiev *geneticist, pediatrician*
McLean, Mark Philip *physiologist, educator*
Rao, Papineni Seethapathi *physiologist, educator, researcher*
Snow, Thomas Russell *technical writer*

Tavernier
Grove, Jack Stein *naturalist, marine biologist*

Vero Beach
Watanabe, Wade Osamu *marine biologist*

West Palm Beach
Schuette, James *biologist*

Winter Haven
Price, Mary Ann *plant virologist*

Winter Park
Fluno, John Arthur *entomologist, consultant*

GEORGIA

Athens
Atwater, Mary Monroe *science educator*
Barb, Claude Richard *research physiologist, research scientist*
Hildebrand, Don *science foundation executive*
Huang, Yao-wen *food science educator, researcher*
Joshi, Balawant Shankar *research scientist*
Marks, Henry Lewis *poultry scientist*
Porter, James Watson *ecology and marine science educator*
Shimkets, Lawrence Joseph, Jr. *microbiology educator*

Atlanta
Cavallaro, Joseph John *microbiologist*
Circeo, Louis Joseph, Jr. *research center director, civil engineer*
Grissom, Raymond Earl, Jr. *toxicologist*
Hilenski, Lula Lail *research scientist*
Joiner, Ronald Luther *toxicologist*
Lu, Qun *cell biologist, educator*
Lubin, Ira Martin *molecular biologist, biochemist*
Matthews, Hewitt William *science educator*
Mirsky, Jeffrey *science foundation administrator*
Morse, Stephen Allen *microbiologist, researcher*
Nadijcka Hanson, Mary Diane *biologist, consultant*
Schwartz, Miriam Catherine *biology educator*
Warren, Stephen Theodore *human geneticist, educator*
Watt, Charles *research scientist*
Williams, Robert Larry *environmental toxicologist*
Zheng, Xiaonan Shannon *research scientist*

Columbus
Riggsby, Ernest Duward *science educator, educational development executive*

Dublin
Falk, Russell Louis *forestry consultant*

Forest Park
Werner, David Francis *forensic serologist*

Griffin
Doyle, Michael Patrick *food microbiologist, educator, administrator*

Kennesaw
Waller, William Kenneth *health physicist*

Lawrenceville
Maestripieri, Dario *research scientist*

Macon
Adkison, Linda Russell *geneticist, consultant*
Harrison, James Ostelle *ecologist*

Marietta
Lain, David Cornelius *health scientist, researcher*

Newton
Walton, William Robert *academic administrator*

Norcross
McDonald, James *science foundation executive*

Sapelo Island
Newell, Steven Young *research microbial ecologist*

Statesboro
Parrish, John Wesley, Jr. *biology educator*

Thomasville
Winter, Calvin Arnold, Jr. *agricultural and horticultural resource specialist*

Valdosta
Gerber, Brian Lynn *science educator, consultant*

Waycross
Hatfield, Margaret Clark *biology educator*

ILLINOIS

Chicago
Kolchinsky, Alexander *geneticist educator*

IOWA

Ames
DiLorenzo, Carrie Lucas *research scientist, medical illustrator*

KANSAS

Manhattan
Huang, Bingru *plant physiologist*

KENTUCKY

Frankfort
Martin, William Haywood *ecologist, scientist*
Williams, Tim *administrator wild life sanctuary*

Lexington
Diana, John Nicholas *physiologist*
Hennig, Bernhard *nutritional science educator*
Knapp, Fred William *entomologist, educator*
Mangena, Venkata S. Murty *microbiologist, researcher*
Nothnick, Warren Ben *reproductive physiologist*
Rajagopalan, Melappalayam Srinivasan *microbiologist*
Rangnekar, Vivek Mangesh *molecular biologist, researcher*
Rodriguez, Lorraine Ditzler *biologist, consultant*

Louisville
Heinicke, Ralph Martin *biotechnology company executive*

Prestonsburg
Pridham, Thomas Grenville *retired research microbiologist*

LOUISIANA

Baton Rouge
Burns, Paul Yoder *forester, educator*
Hansel, William *biology educator*
Head, Jonathan Frederick *cell biologist*
Holcomb, Gordon Ernest *plant pathology educator*
Jones, Jack Earl *plant breeding and genetics specialist, agronomist, researcher, consultant*
Kang, Manjit Singh *genticist, plant breeder*
Levy, H. Nathan, III *science foundation executive*
Louviere, James Peter *science foundation administrator, writer, inventor*
Murai, Norimoto *plant molecular biologist, educator*
Squadrito, Giuseppe Luciano *research scientist, chemist, educator*
Storz, Johannes *veterinary microbiologist, educator*
Sundberg, Marshall David *biology educator*
Tedford, Bruce Leroy *physiologist, researcher*

Chauvin
Sammarco, Paul *marine science educator*

Covington
Harrison, Richard Miller *physiologist, researcher, educator*

Haughton
De Ment, James Alderson *soil scientist*

Homer
Boddie, Richard Lee *agriculturalist, researcher*
DeRouen, Sidney Marc *animal sciences researcher*
Owens, William Edward *microbiologist*

Lafayette
McTigue, Teresa Ann *biologist*

Metairie
Newfield, Nancy Lang *naturalist, writer*
Westerman, Albert Barry *marine surveyor*

Monroe
Baum, Lawrence Stephen *biologist, educator*
Mehendale, Harihara Mahadeva *toxicologist, educator*
Swaffar, Diane Shomin *research scientist, pharmacology educator*
Thomas, R. Dale *biologist, curator*

New Orleans
Bennett, Joan Wennstrom *biology educator*
Brown, Robert Lawrence *research plant pathologist*
Dickinson, Catherine Schatz *retired microbiologist*
Inscho, Edward William *physiology educator*
Klich, Maren Alice *mycologist*
Levitzky, Michael Gordon *physiology educator*
Rossowska, Magdalena Joanna *physiology educator, research scientist*
Shapira, Emmanuel *clinical geneticist, biochemical geneticist, educator*
Superneau, Duane William *geneticist, physician*
Tetlow, Louis Mulry *clinical psycholgist*
Yu, Jiujiang *research geneticist*

Ruston
Bissic, David Wayne *biologist, educator*

MISSISSIPPI

Biloxi
Deegen, Uwe Frederick *marine biologist*

Forest
Washington, Aaron Anthony *biologist*

Greenville
Duke, Stephen Oscar *physiologist, researcher*

Hattiesburg
Larsen, James Bouton *biological scientist, educator*
Tornow, Joanne Susan *molecular biologist, educator*

Jackson
Boyll, Jamie Frances *ecologist*
Zardiackas, Lyle Dean *biomaterials educator, consultant*

Lorman
Zaman, Md Sarwar *biology educator*

Meridian
Blackwell, Cecil *science association executive*

Mississippi State
Jackson, Jerome Alan *biological scientist, educator, researcher*
Jenkins, Johnie Norton *research geneticist, research administrator*
May, James D. *physiologist*
Triplett, Glover Brown *agronomist, educator*
Vilella, Francisco José *wildlife research biologist*

Ocean Springs
Gunter, Gordon *zoologist*

Ridgeland
Evans, Wayne Edward *environmental microbiologist, researcher*

Springs
Overstreet, Robin Miles *parasitologist, researcher, educator*

Starkville
Rudis, Victor Augustine *research forester, ecologist*
Sellers, Terry, Jr. *wood science and technology scientist, educator*

Stoneville
Wilson, Alphus Dan *plant pathologist, researcher*

West Point
Vicks, JoAnn *biology educator*

Wiggins
Bryan, James Edwin, Jr. *forester, consultant*

NEVADA

Las Vegas
Spangelo, Bryan Lee *biochemist, chemistry educator*

Reno
Qualls, Robert Gerald *ecologist*

NORTH CAROLINA

Archdale
Riddick, Douglas Smith *horticultural industrialist, industrial designer*

Beaufort
Forward, Richard Blair, Jr. *marine biology educator*
Rittschof, Daniel *biology educator*

Burlington
Turanchik, Michael *research and development director*

Chapel Hill
Andersen, Melvin Ernest *toxicologist, consultant*
Bott, Kenneth Francis, Jr. *microbiology educator*
Chen, Zibin *physiologist, educator*
Farber, Rosann Alexander *geneticist, educator*
Froehner, Stanley C. *neurobiology educator*
Huang, Eng-Shang *virology educator, biomedical engineer*
Judd, Burke Haycock *geneticist*
Marks, Bonita L. *physiologist, researcher, educator*
Shapiro, Lee Tobey *planetarium administrator, astronomer*

Charlotte
Hudson, Michael Carl *biology educator*

Durham
Abdel-Rahman, Mohamed *agribusiness consultant*
Blum, Jacob Joseph *physiologist, educator*
Covey, Ellen *neurobiologist, researcher*
Dougherty, David Edward *agricultural research scientist*
Gross, Samson Richard *geneticist, biochemist, educator*
He, Chaoying *molecular biologist, researcher*
Kahler, Stephen G. *clinical biological geneticist, pediatrician*
Reller, L. Barth *medical microbiologist, physician, educator*
Richardson, Stephen Giles *biotechnology company executive*
Sassaman, Anne Phillips *science administrator*
Smialowicz, Ralph Joseph *immunotoxicologist*
Swaim, Mark Wendell *molecular biologist, gastroenterologist*
Wilbur, Robert Lynch *botanist, educator*

Emerald Isle
Hardy, Sally Maria *retired biological sciences educator*

Franklinton
Lange, Niels Erik Krebs *biotechnology company executive*

Greensboro
Kirchoff, Bruce Kenneth *plant scientist, educator*
Leise, Esther Marcia *biology educator*
Maynard, Michael Scott *toxicologist*
O'Hara, Robert James *evolutionary biologist*

Greenville
Boklage, Charles Edward *medical educator*
Fulghum, Robert Schmidt *microbiologist, educator*
Pederson, Nels E. *molecular virologist, educator*
Rulifson, Roger Allen *fisheries and marine science researcher, educator*
Wiley, John Edwin *cytogeneticist*

Old Fort
Dries, Alice Emerita *horticulturist, educator*

Oxford
Witherell, Peter Charles *regulatory entomologist*

Pinehurst
Burris, Kenneth Wayne *biologist, educator*

Raleigh
Allen, Nina Strömgren *biology educator*
Blum, Udo *botany educator*
Burns, Joseph Charles *plant physiologist and educator*
Hardin, James W. *botanist, herbarium curator, educator*
Hassan, Hosni Moustafa *microbiologist, biochemist, toxicologist and food science educator*
Heatwole, Harold Franklin *ecologist*
Johnson, William Lawrence *animal scientist, educator*
Lytle, Charles Franklin *biology educator*
Moreland, Donald Edwin *plant physiologist*
Timothy, David Harry *biology educator*
Zeng, Zhao-Bang *geneticist, educator*

Research Triangle Park
Bond, James Anthony *toxicologist*
Folinsbee, Lawrence John *physiologist, researcher*
Mason, James Michael *geneticist, researcher*
McClellan, Roger Orville *toxicologist*
Mumford, Stephen Douglas *population growth control research scientist*
Reinhard, John Frederick, Jr. *scientist, educator*
Wooten, Frank Thomas *research facility executive*

Washington
Thomson, Stuart McGuire, Jr. *science educator*

Wilmington
Bolen, Eric George *biology educator*

Winston Salem
Ganz, Charles *laboratory executive*
Hammarback, James Arvid *molecular biologist*
Kucera, Louis Stephen *virology educator*
Laxminarayana, Dama *geneticist, researcher*

Wrightsville Beach
Phull, B. S. *scientist*

OKLAHOMA

Ada
Sinclair, James Lewis *research microbiologist*

Ardmore
Dixon, Richard Arthur *botany educator, researcher*

Durant
Williams, Judy Ann *biological scientist*

Edmond
Bidlack, James Enderby *plant physiologist, plant anatomist*

Langston
Mallik, Muhammad Abdul-Bari *soil microbiologist*

Norman
Braun, Janet K. *biologist*
McInerney, Michael Joseph *microbiology educator*
Russell, Scott Daniel *botany educator, electron microscopist*
Schindler, Charles Alvin *microbiologist, educator*

Ochelata
Hitzman, Donald Oliver *microbiologist*

Oklahoma City
Branch, John Curtis *biology educator, lawyer*
D'Cruz, Osmond Jerome *research scientist, educator*
Fechter, Laurence David *toxicology educator, researcher*
Frank, Mark Barton *immunogeneticist, molecular biologist*
Shimasaki, Craig David *research scientist*

Ponca City
Bolene, Margaret Rosalie Steele *bacteriologist, civic worker*

Stillwater
Banks, Donald Jack *plant geneticist, plant biologist*
Campbell, John Roy *animal scientist educator, academic administrator*
Grischkowsky, Daniel Richard *research scientist, educator*
Huang, Yinghua *plant molecular biology researcher, educator*
Welsh, Ronald Dean *veterinary microbiologist*
Whitcomb, Carl Ervin *horticulturist, researcher*

Tulsa
Zucconi, David G. *zoo and museum director*

Weatherford
Grant, Peter Michael *biologist, educator*

PENNSYLVANIA

Horsham
Parker, Robert Michael *toxicologist, anatomy educator*

West Point
Caskey, Charles Thomas *biology and genetics educator*
Palker, Thomas Joseph *biologist, researcher*

SOUTH CAROLINA

Aiken
Attardo, Lewis Charles *business and technology development consultant*

Charleston
Burrell, Victor Gregory, Jr. *marine scientist*
Ross, Philippe Edward *biology educator, environmental toxicology researcher*

Clemson
Dean, Ralph Adrian *plant pathologist, educator*

Gangemi, J(oseph) David *microbiology educator, biomedical researcher, research administrator, hospital administrator*
Powell, Gary L. *biochemistry educator*
Skelley, George Calvin *animal science educator*
Wourms, John Peter Barton *biology educator*

Columbia
Abel, Francis Lee *physiology educator*
Best, Robert Glen *geneticist*
Mishra, Nawin Chandra *genetics educator*
Mousseau, Timothy Alexander *biology educator*
Peters, Kenneth Earl *educator*
von Kap-Herr, Christopher Gerhart *cytogeneticist*
Worthington-White, Diana Alice *research scientist*

Gaffney
Jones, Nancy Gale *retired biology educator*

Greenville
Cureton, Claudette Hazel Chapman *biology educator*

Orangeburg
Scott, David G. *geneticist*

Rock Hill
Mitlin, Norman *physiologist, consultant*

Sumter
Salthouse, Thomas Newton *cell biologist, biomaterial researcher*

Yemassee
Izard, Mary Kathryn *reproductive biologist*

TENNESSEE

Brentwood
Hansard, William Ney *environmental scientist, consultant*

Brighton
Payne, Linda Carol *physiologist*

Bristol
Dunbar, Jacob Ross, III *toxicologist*

Clinton
Tyndall, Richard Lawrence *microbiologist, researcher*

Gallatin
Morris, Nancy Garnett *biology educator, administrator*

Johnson City
Joyner, William Lyman *physiology educator*
Thatcher, Samuel Selden *reproductive biologist, physician*

Knoxville
Carroll, Roger Clinton *medical biology educator*
Chen, James Pai-fun *biology educator, researcher*
Draughon, Frances Ann *microbiology educator*
Zemel, Michael Barry *nutritional physiologist*

Mc Kenzie
Nelson, John Peter, Jr. *biology educator*

Memphis
Broughton, Helen Reed *science educator*
Davis, Kenneth Bruce, Jr. *biologist*
Johnson, Leonard Roy *physiologist, educator*
Vines, Angela *molecular biologist*

Nashville
Altman, David Wayne *geneticist*
Mokha, Sukhbir Singh *physiology educator, researcher*
Phillips, John A(tlas), III *geneticist, educator*
Spiller, Hart *microbiologist*
Trenary, Carlos Francisco *systems analyst, network manager*

Oak Ridge
Clauberg, Martin *research scientist*
Norby, Richard James *plant physiologist*
Olins, Ada Levy *cell biologist*
Sharples, Frances Ellen *zoologist, researcher*
Van Berkel, Gary Joseph *research scientist*
Wiesehuegel, Richard Erwin *science, engineering and mathematics educator*

Sewanee
Berner, Nancy Jane *biology educator and researcher*

TEXAS

Abilene
Pilcher, Benjamin Lee *biology educator*

Alvarado
Evans, Garen Lee *laboratory director, regulatory compliance officer*

Amarillo
Laird, Hugh Edward, II *pharmacologist, toxicologist*
Myers, Terry Lewis *clinical geneticist, educator*

Austin
Albin, Leslie Owens *biology educator*
Biesele, John Julius *biologist, educator*
Blumenfeld, Joshua Charles *plant ecologist, editor, writer*
Bronson, Franklin H. *zoology educator*
Drummond Borg, Lesley Margaret *clinical geneticist*
Earhart, Charles Franklin, Jr. *microbiology educator*
Hillis, David Mark *zoology educator*
Northington, David Knight, III *research center director, botanist, educator*
Reeder, William Glase *zoologist, museum administrator*
Turner, Billie Lee *botanist, educator*
Tuttle, Merlin D. *zoologist*

Brownsville
Farst, Don David *zoo director, veterinarian*

Bryan
Miller, Frederick Robert *sorghum breeder, agronomist*

Canyon
Killebrew, Flavius Charles *biology educator, academic administrator*

College Station
Armstrong, Robert Beall *physiologist*
Borlaug, Norman Ernest *agricultural scientist*
Burson, Byron Lynn *geneticist*
Feagin, Clarence Elmer, Jr. *microbiologist*
Frederiksen, Richard Allan *plant pathology educator*
Granger, Harris Joseph *physiologist, educator*
Grimes, James Edward *microbiologist*
Honeycutt, Rodney Lee *biologist, educator*
Klemm, William Robert *scientist, educator*
Kunkel, Harriott Orren *life science educator*
McCallum, Roderick Eugene *microbiologist*
Petrikovics, Ilona *toxicologist*
Tesh, Vernon Lewis *biomedical researcher*
Turner, Nancy Delane *animal nutritionist*
Wu, Guoyao *nutrition, physiology, and animal science educator*
Ziprin, Richard Lewis *microbiologist, researcher*

Corpus Christi
Berkebile, Charles Alan *geology educator, hydrogeology researcher*

Crockett
Burns, Gary Allen *forester, consultant, appraiser*

Dallas
Brown, Michael Stuart *geneticist, educator, administrator*
Denur, Jack Boaz *scientific researcher, scientific consultant*
Johnson, Gifford Kenneth *testing laboratory executive*
Legg, Larry Barnard *biology educator*
Mitchell, Jere Holloway *physiologist, researcher, medical educator*
Morris, Terry Lee *ergonomist, management educator*
Reinert, James A. *entomologist, educator*
Siegel, Charles Eric *curator of birds*
Sinton, Christopher Michael *neurophysiologist, educator*
Soble, Frieda *research center administrator*
Zhao, Hong *medicophysiologist*

Edinburg
Judd, Frank Wayne *population ecologist, physiological ecologist*

El Paso
Johnson, Jerry Douglas *biology educator*
Pillai, Suresh Divakaran *environmental microbiologist, researcher*

Fort Davis
Williams, Mary Margaret Lahiff *park ranger*

Fort Worth
Romeo, Tony *microbiology educator*
Shi, Xiangrong *physiologist*
Sohmer, Seymour Hans *botanist*
Szal, Grace Rowan *research scientist*
Zedik, Robert John *food scientist, consultant*

Galveston
Baskaran, Mahalingam *marine science educator*
Boldogh, Istvan *scientist, microbiology educator*
Chopra, Ashok Kumar *microbiologist, educator*
Sharma, Rashmi *toxicologist, researcher*
Srinivasan, Ganesan *molecular biologist, educator*
Thompson, Edward Ivins Brad *biological chemistry and genetics educator, molecular endocrinologist, department chairman*

Houston
Baughn, Robert Elroy *microbiology educator*
Bellen, Hugo Josef *genetics educator*
DeBakey, Lois *science communications educator, writer, editor*
DeBakey, Selma *science communications educator, writer, editor, lecturer*
Hung, Mien-Chie *cancer biologist*
Kimbrell, Deborah Ann *geneticist, educator*
Marriott, Susan *virology educator*
Oka, Kazuhiro *cell biologist, biochemist*
O'Malley, Bert William *cell biologist, educator, physician*
Ouellette, Jane Lee Young *biology educator*
Patterson, Donald Eugene *research scientist*
Riggs, Penny Kaye *cytogeneticist*
Sass, Ronald Lewis *biology and chemistry educator*
Schull, William J. *geneticist, educator*
Thompson, Timothy Charles *research scientist*

Irving
Fukui, George Masaaki *microbiology consultant*
Hopkins, Karen Martin *cytologist, educator*
Hoy, Eric Stuart *clinical microbiologist*

Kemah
McClure, John Edward *research biomedical scientist, virologist*

Kerrville
Kunz, Sidney *entomologist*

Longview
Martin, Ulrike Balk *laboratory analyst*

Lubbock
Allen, Vivien Gore *agronomist, researcher*
Hentges, David John *microbiology educator*
Jackson, Raymond Carl *cytogeneticist*
McGlone, John James *biologist*
Pence, Danny B. *parasitology educator, researcher*
Xu, Wenwei *geneticist, researcher*

Magnolia
Ramsey, Kathleen Sommer *toxicologist*

Portland
Hopkins, Sidney Wayne *agriculturist*

Richardson
Rutford, Robert Hoxie *geoscience educator*
Sun, Ji *research scientist*

Round Rock
Schneider, Dennis Ray *microbiology educator*

San Antonio
Blystone, Robert Vernon *developmental cell biologist, educator, textbook consultant*
Corrigan, Helen González *cytologist*
Deviney, Marvin Lee, Jr. *research institute scientist, program manager*
Doane, Thomas Roy *environmental toxicologist*
Donaldson, Willis Lyle *research institute administrator*
Goland, Martin *research institute executive*
Lanford, Robert Eldon *microbiologist, educator*
Mery, Laura Rose Bashard *microbiologist, educator*
Sears, William John *physiologist*
Spannagel, Alan Wayne *physiologist*

Snyder
Hefner, Terry Thomas *soil conservationist*

Stephenville
Rosiere, Randy Eugene *range scientist, educator*

Waco
Jackson, Janis Lynn *biology educator*

Weslaco
Amador, Jose Manuel *plant pathologist, research center administrator*
Legaspi, Jesusa Crisostomo *agricultural scientist, entomologist*

UTAH

Cedar City
Veigel, Jon Michael *science administrator*

VIRGINIA

Alexandria
Funk Orsini, Paula Ann *health economist*

Annandale
Eckerlin, Ralph Peter *biology educator*

Arlington
Adams, Donald Edward *biotechnology patent examiner*
Basu, Sunanda *scientific administrator, researcher in space physics*
Corell, Robert Walden *science administration educator*
Duryee, William Rankin *retired cell physiology educator, consultant*
Furlow, Edward Pennington *consulting forester*
Knipling, Edward Fred *retired research entomologist, agricultural administrator*
Morse, M. Patricia *biology educator*
Myers, Charles Edwin *science foundation administrator*
Porter, Leah LeEarle *biological researcher*
Senti, Frederic Raymond *food safety consultant*
Williams, Luther Steward *science foundation administrator*

Big Stone Gap
Ogbonnaya, Chuks Alfred *entomologist, agronomist, environmentalist*

Blacksburg
Alley, Marcus M. *agronomy educator*
Chen, Jiann-Shin *biochemistry and microbiology educator*
De Datta, Surajit Kumar *soil scientist, agronomist, educator*
Gwazdauskas, Francis Charles *animal science educator, dairy scientist*
Inzana, Thomas Joseph *microbiologist, educator*
Kosztarab, Michael *entomologist*
Smeal, Paul Lester *retired horticulture educator*

Charlottesville
Elder, John Fletcher, IV *science educator, researcher*
Fox, Jay William *microbiology educator*
Garrett, Reginald Hooker *biology educator, researcher*
Hamilton, Howard Laverne *zoology educator*
Kelly, Thaddeus Elliott *medical geneticist*
Murray, Joseph James, Jr. *zoologist*
Somlyo, Andrew Paul *physiology, biophysics and cardiology educator*

Clifton
Lunsford, Richard Early *biology educator*

Covington
Walton, Harry A., Jr. *retired dairy manager*

Dahlgren
Westbrook, Susan Elizabeth *horticulturist*

Dillwyn
Moseley, John Marshall *nurseryman*

Fairfax
Howard-Peebles, Patricia N. *clinical cytogeneticist*
Peters, Esther Caroline *aquatic toxicologist, pathobiologist, consultant*

Falls Church
Gorges, Heinz August *research engineer*
Simpson, John Arol *retired government executive, physicist*

Franklin
Malm, Richard Lewis *forester*

Fredericksburg
Moorman, William Jacob *agronomist, consultant*
Wieland, Werner *biology educator*

Gloucester Point
Patterson, Mark Robert *marine biology educator*

Hampton
Owens, Vivian Ann *plant science educator, researcher*
Zahn, Martin David *biology educator*

Isle of Wight
Vick, Mary Postell *biology educator*

Leesburg
Mokhtarzadeh, Ahmad Agha *agronomist, consultant*

Lorton
Koschny, Theresa Mary *environmental biologist*

Mc Lean
Cardwell, Thomas Augusta, III *scientist, retired career officer, executive*
Layson, William McIntyre *research consulting company executive*

Monterey
Barton, Alexander James *retired ecologist, educator, naval officer*

Newport News
Grau, Harold James *biology educator*

Norfolk
Spangenberg, Dorothy Breslin *biology educator*

Petersburg
Ezekwe, Michael Obi *reseach scientist*
Noakes, David Ronald *research scientist, educator*

Richmond
Ching, Melvin Chung-Hing *retired physiologist, anatomy educator, researcher*
Gregory, Jean Winfrey *ecologist, educator*
Loria, Roger Moshe *microbiology, virology and immunology educator*
Peters, Gerald Alan *biology educator*
Witorsch, Raphael Jay *physiologist, educator*
Wolf, Barry *genetics, pediatric educator*
Yu, Robert Kuan-jen *biochemistry educator*

Virginia Beach
Munday, John Clingman, Jr. *science policy educator, remote sensing researcher*

Wallops Island
Ailes, Marilyn Carol *ecologist*

Williamsburg
Griffith, Melvin Eugene *entomologist, public health official*
Manos, Dennis Michael *science educator*
Ware, Stewart Alexander *biologist, educator*

WEST VIRGINIA

Falling Waters
Schellhaas, Linda Jean *toxicologist, consultant*

Franklin
Pratt, Dorothy Jane *environmental executive*

Great Cacapon
Belton, William *ornithologist, retired foreign service officer*

Morgantown
Cochrane, Robert Lowe *biologist*
Gladfelter, Wilbert Eugene *physiology educator*
Good, Gregory Alan *science history educator*
Inskeep, Emmett Keith *physiology educator, researcher*

South Charleston
Britton, Laurence George *research scientist*

TERRITORIES OF THE UNITED STATES

VIRGIN ISLANDS

Kingshill
Crossman, Stafford Mac Arthur *agronomist, researcher*

CANADA

BRITISH COLUMBIA

Vancouver
Suttle, Curtis *science educator*

ADDRESS UNPUBLISHED

Barnard, Donald Roy *entomologist*
Champlin, William Glen *clinical microbiologist-immunologist*
Cockerham, Lorris G. *radiation toxicologist*
Coleman, Richard Walter *biology educator*
Curtin, Richard Brendan *research institute executive*
Evans, Charles Wayne, II *biologist, researcher*
Giordano, James Joseph *neuroscientist, educator*
Hardin, Clyde Durham *federal senior executive scientist*
Izlar, Robert Lee *forester*
Johnson, Barry Lee *public health research administrator*
Knuckles, Joseph Lewis *biology educator*

Mathew, Porunelloor Abraham *molecular biologist, educator*
McFarland, Victor Alan *toxicologist*
Melnick, Joseph L. *virologist, educator*
Newbern, Laura Lynn *forestry association executive, editor*
Phillips, Fred Young *technology management educator, researcher*
Pujol, Thomas Joseph *exercise and applied physiology educator*
Redding, G.A. *researcher*
Smeltzer, Debra Jean *botanist*
Smith, George Louis *research scientist*
Sullivan, Harry Truman *research scientist*
Szaniszlo, Paul Joseph *microbiology educator, fungal biologist*
Tomlinson, Charles Edwin *forestry consultant, writer*
Wang, Yang *science researcher*
Wilkinson, Carol Lynn *mycologist*
Wood, Dolores Funai *horticultural lecturer, writer*

SCIENCE: MATHEMATICS AND COMPUTER SCIENCE

UNITED STATES

ALABAMA

Auburn
Johnson, Peter Dexter, Jr. *mathematics educator*

Bay Minette
Lake, Charles Donald *computer science educator, administrator*

Birmingham
Bryant, Barrett Richard *computer and information sciences educator*
Kinzey, Ouida Blackerby *retired mathematics educator, photographer, photojournalist*
Usher, Tommy *computer software engineer, consultant*

Decatur
Whigham, Mark Anthony *computer scientist*

Florence
Alexander, Paulette S. *computer information systems educator*
Foote, Avon Edward *webmaster, communications educator*

Huntsville
Freas, George Wilson, II *computer consultant*
Green, Linda Lou *systems analyst*
Lucas, Carolyn Holden *procurement analyst*
McAuley, Van Alfon *aerospace mathematician*
Pruitt, Alice Fay *mathematician, engineer*

Mobile
Taylor, Washington Theophilus *mathematics educator*
Yett, Fowler Redford *mathematics educator*

Pelham
Turner, Malcolm Elijah *biomathematician, educator*

Robertsdale
Goulart, Paul A. *computers educator, electronics educator*

Smiths
Przybyzewski, Leslie Camille *mathematics educator*

Spanish Fort
Copper, Michael Steven *computer scientist, educator*

ARIZONA

Phoenix
Hamilton, Scott Eric *computer software engineer, communications executive*

Tempe
Yau, Stephen Sik-sang *computer science and engineering educator, computer scientist, researcher*

ARKANSAS

Fayetteville
Berghel, Hal L. *computer science educator, columnist, author*

Fort Smith
Smith-Leins, Terri L. *mathematics educator*

Little Rock
McDermott, Cecil Wade *mathematics educator, educational program director*
Mills, Bruce Randall *infosystems and micro computer specialist*
Roberson, Paula Karen *biostatistician*
Townsend, James Willis *computer scientist*

CALIFORNIA

San Jose
Manganaris, Stefanos *computer scientist*

San Juan Capistrano
Botway, Lloyd Frederick *computer scientist, consultant*

Santa Maria
Evans, Gary Wayne *computer engineer*

DISTRICT OF COLUMBIA

Washington
Ryan, David Alan *computer specialist*

FLORIDA

Alachua
Neubauer, Hugo Duane, Jr. *software engineer*

Boca Raton
Brewer, James William *mathematics educator*
Grosse, Edward Ralph *systems analyst*

Cape Canaveral
Field, Thomas Harold *software engineer*

Cassadaga
Boland, Lois Walker *retired mathematician and computer systems analyst*

Clearwater
Klingbiel, Paul Herman *information science consultant*
White, June Miller *mathematics educator, education consultant*

Cocoa Beach
Gillette, Halbert George *mathematics educator*

Coral Gables
Howard, Bernard Eufinger *computer science and mathematics educator*

Coral Springs
Sanders, Marc Andrew *computer technical consultant*

Davie
Olmstead, Phyllis Melody *computer specialist*

Delray Beach
Hegstrom, William Jean *mathematics educator*

Fort Lauderdale
De Alvaré, Ana Maria *systems engineer*

Fort Walton Beach
Babineau, Alphee Adam *systems analyst, educator*

Gainesville
Agresti, Alan *statistics educator*
Chakravarthy, Upen Sharma *computer science educator*
Fu, Limin *biomedical and computer science educator*
Fujimoto, Ichiro *mathematics educator, researcher*

Green Cove Springs
Boatright, Joanna Morson *computer programmer, analyst*

Jacksonville
Hazen, Charles Melville *mathematics educator*
Klein, John Sharpless *retired mathematics educator*
Price, Daniel O'Haver *retired mathematics educator, statistician*
Roth, Robert Allen *systems consultant*

Kennedy Space Center
Evenson, Michael Donald *software engineer*

Maitland
Routhenstein, Lawrence Richard Green *software engineer*

Miami
Green, Willie Harold *mathematician, physicist*
Johnson, Gervais Collins, Jr. *computer scientist*
Newlin, Kimrey Dayton *personal computer analyst*
Stein, Lotte C. *mathematics educator*
Van Dyk, Michael Anthony *software designer*

Milton
McKinney, George Harris, Jr. *training systems analyst*

Naples
Ciano, James Francis *computer systems analyst*
Wheeling, Robert Franklin *computer consultant*

Navarre
Johnson, Vicky K. *beauty and computer consultant*

Ocala
Johnson, Winston Conrad *mathematics educator*

Orlando
Denton, Carol Forsberg *training systems designer*
Grecsek, Matthew Thomas *software developer*
Hua, Kien Anh *computer science educator*

Palm Bay
Bellstedt, Olaf *senior software engineer*
Olejar, Paul Duncan *former information science administrator*

Plantation
Polansky-Joseph, Isa *information management director, consultant*

Port Charlotte
Soben, Robert Sidney *computer scientist*

Port Saint Lucie
Byrd, Sandra Judith *information scientist*

Punta Gorda
Smith, Charles Edwin *computer science educator, consultant*

Saint Petersburg
Fishman, Mark Brian *computer scientist, educator*
Shi, Feng Sheng *mathematician*

Sarasota
Petrie, George Whitefield, III *retired mathematics educator*

Tallahassee
Leavell, Michael Ray *computer programmer, analyst*
Nichols, Eugene Douglas *mathematics educator*
Presmeg, Norma Christine *mathematics educator, researcher*
Stino, Farid K.R. *biostatistician, educator, researcher, consultant*
Stinson, Stanley Thomas *computer consultant*
Traphan, Bernard Richard *computer scientist, educator*

Tampa
Bryant, Herbert McCoy, Jr. (Herbie DeLaney) *statistician*
Couturier, Gordon Wayne *computer information systems educator, consultant*
Harriman, Malcolm Bruce *software developer, healthcare consultant*
Nielsen, Marco Kjaer *computer programmer*
Saff, Edward Barry *mathematics educator*
Thompson, Denisse R. *mathematics educator*
Williams, Thomas Arthur *biomedical computing consultant, psychiatrist*

Wellington
Stang, Louis George *computer scientist*

GEORGIA

Athens
Huberty, Carl J *statistician/methodologist, educator*
Rumely, Robert S. *mathematician*

Atlanta
Cotecson, Allan Bruce *systems analyst*
Duncan, Ralph V., Jr. *computer scientist, consultant*
Ehrlich, Margaret Isabella Gorley *systems engineer, mathematics educator, consultant*
Elofson, Gregg Steven *computer information systems educator, consultant*
Goforth, Daniel Reid *computer scientist, consultant*
Kerven, David Scott *computer science educator, consultant*
King, K(imberly) N(elson) *computer science educator*
Onukwuli, Francis Osita *computer scientist, mathematics educator*
Stiller, Lisa Ann *biostatistician*

Augusta
Craig, Cynthia Mae *mathematics educator*
Lawless, William Frere *mathematics and psychology educator*
Luoma, Keith Elliott *mathematics educator*

Blythe
Kitchin, Christopher H. *computer scientist, consultant*

College Park
Brantley, Jerry Lee, Jr. *systems programmer*

Duluth
Millikan, Marshall Robert *software engineer*

East Point
Pierre, Charles Bernard *mathematician, statistician, educator*

Glynco
Mihal, Sandra Powell *computer systems educator*

Marietta
Bramlett, Joyce Fielder *mathematics educator*
Kanter, Donald Richard *statistician, pharmaceutical and psychobiology researcher*
Rutherford, Rebecca Hudson *computer science educator*
Tanrikorur, Tulu M. *computer programmer, systems analyst*

Powder Springs
Hodges, Mitchell *computer executive*

Smyrna
Chandler, Ira Ansel *computer technician*

Valdosta
Meghabghab, George Victor *computer scientist, educator*

Waynesboro
Moody, Charles Emory *information systems analyst*

KENTUCKY

Hebron
Neufelder, Ann Marie *software consulting company executive, consultant*

Lexington
Holsapple, Clyde Warren *decision and information systems educator*
Lewis, Forbes Downer *computer scientist, educator*
Vickers, George Lewis *computer consultant*
Zwart, Steven Paul *computer programmer*

Louisville
Fiedler, Hans Karl *communications analyst, consultant*
Graham, James Henry *computer science and engineering educator, consultant*
Greaver, Joanne Hutchins *mathematics educator, author*
Kibiloski, Floyd Terry *business and computer consultant, editor, educator*
Schneider, Arthur *computer graphics specialist*
Srinivasan, S. *computer science educator, consultant*

Morehead
Mann, James Darwin *mathematics educator*

Murray
Lyle, William Frederick, III *computer science educator*

LOUISIANA

Baton Rouge
Delzell, Charles Neal *mathematics educator*
Mayers, Hans Joseph *systems programmer*
Oxley, James Grieve *mathematics educator*
Zhu, Jianchao *computer and control scientist, engineer, educator*

Harvey
Garrison, Patricia A. *mathematics educator*

Lafayette
Pissinou, Niki *computer studies educator*

Lake Charles
Denny, William Francis *computer science educator*

Ruston
Dorsett, Charles Irvin *mathematics educator*

Shreveport
Weiler, James G. *computer scientist*

MARYLAND

Bethesda
Clema, Joe Kotouc *computer scientist*

Oxon Hill
Shaffer, Sheila Weekes *mathematics educator*

Towson
Wissinger, Robert Alan *biomedical software engineer*

MISSISSIPPI

Bay Saint Louis
Landry, Debby Ann *computer programmer*

Cleveland
Strahan, Jimmie Rose *mathematics educator*

Madison
Phillips, Linda Graves *computer educator, legal secretary*

Natchez
Smith, Robert Ervin *mathematics and computer science educator*

University
Roach, David Giles *computing and information systems manager*

MISSOURI

Columbia
Musser, Dale Roy *software engineer, instructional designer, educator*

Saint Louis
Woolery, Ray Charles *logistician, military officer*

NEVADA

Las Vegas
Huey, George Irving, Jr. *computer senior systems consultant*

NORTH CAROLINA

Asheville
Pate-Fuller, Denise *mathematics educator*

Cary
Ford, Marcyanne Rose *computer consultant*
Rauf, Robert Charles *systems specialist*

Chapel Hill
Coulter, Elizabeth Jackson *biostatistician, educator*

Charlotte
Burger, André Eric *computing system project manager*
Gardner, Robert Charles *systems analyst, administrator*
McLuskie, William Dean *computer scientist*

Clyde
Codd, Richard Trent, Jr. *computer scientist, educator*

Cullowhee
Willis, Ralph Houston *mathematics educator*

Dudley
Howell, Lindsey Raiford *mathematics educator*

Durants Neck
Sutton, Louise Nixon *retired mathematics educator*

Durham
Anderson, Margery Lawrence *computer programmer, consultant*
Hodel, Richard Earl *mathematics educator*
Keepler, Manuel *mathematics educator, researcher*
Reif, John Henry *computer science educator*

Fayetteville
Chan, Tat Wing *computer science educator*

Greensboro
Blanchet-Sadri, Francine *mathematician*
Casterlow, Gilbert, Jr. *mathematics educator*
Kurepa, Alexandra *mathematician*
Wang, Jie *computer science educator*

Morrisville
Walker, James Robert *software products developer*

Mount Holly
Carter, Donald Lee *computer services executive*

Murfreesboro
McLawhorn, Rebecca Lawrence *mathematics educator*

Raleigh
Dwyer, Rex Allen *computer scientist*
Fabrizio, Louis Michael *computer educator, consultant*
Kiser, Anita Hope *project team leader, technical writer*
Lester, James Curtis *computer scientist*
McAllister, David Franklin *computer science educator*
McPherson, Samuel Dace, III *computer scientist, instructor, consultant*
Welsh, James John *computer consultant*
Wetsch, John Robert *information systems specialist*

Research Triangle Park
Board, Rebecca Ruth Batchelor *software engineer*
Haseman, Joseph Kyd *biostatistician, researcher*
James, Peter Robert *computer programmer*
Martinez, Richard Daniel *computer programmer*

Swansboro
Mullikin, Thomas Wilson *mathematics educator*

Wilmington
Cheek, Gorrell Paul *computer engineer*
Schell, George Powell *information systems educator*

Winston Salem
Lu, Dan *systems analyst, mathematician, consultant*
Mangan, Patricia Ann Pritchett *research statistician*
Wiles, Jerri Fulp *microcomputer educator, accountant, consultant*

OKLAHOMA

Ada
McGrew, John Gilbert *computer science educator*

Bartlesville
Malley, Marjorie Caroline *science and mathematics educator, historian*

Jones
Jones, Jeffery Lynn *software engineer*

Lawton
McKellips, Terral Lane *mathematics educator, university administrator*
McMasters, Bobby Lowell *statistician*

Norman
Bright, Jerlene Ann *information systems program administrator*
Kim, Changwook *computer science educator*
Lakshmivarahan, Sivaramakrishnan *computer science educator*
MacFarland, Miriam Katherine *computer science consultant, writer*
Magid, Andy Roy *mathematics educator*
Watts, Gerald Dale *software engineer, researcher*

Oklahoma City
Palkovich, David Allan *mathematics educator*
Philipp, Anita Marie *computer sciences educator*
Samadzadeh, Farideh Ansari *computer science educator*
Tang, Irving Che-hong *mathematician, educator*

Stillwater
Provine, Lorraine *mathematics educator*

Tulsa
Thompson, Carla Jo Horn *mathematics educator*

Weatherford
Woods, John Merle *mathematics educator, chairman*

SOUTH CAROLINA

Aiken
Bodie, Carol Hoover *computer services professional*

Bamberg
Gwaltney, Javy Rudolph, III *computer operations consultant*

Clemson
Hare, Eleanor O'Meara *computer science educator*
Jamison, Robert Edward *mathematics educator*

Columbia
Bayrak, Coskun *computer scientist, researcher, educator*
Eastman, Caroline Merriam *computer science educator*
Moland, Kathryn Johnetta *computer scientist, software engineer*
Watt, (Arthur) Dwight, Jr. *computer programming and microcomputer specialist*

Florence
Whitaker, Wilma Neuman *mathematics instructor*

Greenwood
Marino, Louis John *mathematics educator*

Orangeburg
Clark, Paul Buddy *management information systems educator, consultant*

Saint Helena Island
Dickert, Linda Going *computer science educator*

Spartanburg
Hilton, Theodore Craig *computer scientist, computer executive*

Summerville
Worthy, Fred Lester *computer science educator*

TENNESSEE

Chattanooga
Ebiefung, Aniekan Asukwo *mathematics educator and researcher*

Cleveland
Laws, Charles George *mathematics educator, quality engineer*

Dickson
Peterson, Bonnie Lu *mathematics educator*

Gallatin
Evans, Robert Byron *software engineer, educator*

Johnson City
Huang, (Margaret) Janice Fernald *mathematics educator*
Pumariega, JoAnne Buttacavoli *mathematics educator*

Knoxville
Berry, Michael Waitsel *computer science educator*
Borden, Eugene Owen *software engineer*
Coleman-Bird, Vicky *computer contractor*
Rosinski, Jan *mathematics educator*
Walker, Jackson Venus *systems analyst, consultant*

Martin
Austin, Bill Ray *mathematician, mathematics educator*

Memphis
Cutter, Portia Lynette *mathematics educator*
Hawk, Charles Silas *computer programmer, analyst*
McMahon, Anthony Hugh, Sr. *computer program manager, systems integrator*

Murfreesboro
Thweatt, Joe Mack *computer science educator*

Nashville
Comer, Jimmy M. *systems analyst*
Williams, Marsha Rhea *computer scientist, educator, researcher, consultant*

Oak Ridge
Bugg, Keith Edward *computer software developer, software company executive*
Kliewer, Kenneth Lee *computational scientist, research administrator*
Reister, David Bryan *systems analyst*

Tullahoma
Arman, Sandra Ann *mathematics educator*

TEXAS

Amarillo
Hinds, Ann M. *programmer, systems analyst*

Arlington
Flaming, Wade A. *software engineer*
Raisinghani, Mahesh (Mike) Sukhdev *software consultant*
Springston, Raymond Leroy *computer science educator*
Umbaugh, Lloyd David *computer science educator*

Austin
Crane, Gary Wade *mathematician, physicist*
Eskew, Russell Clark *programmer*
Fox, Marian Cavender *mathematics educator*
Huang, Yee-Wei *strategic analyst, chemical engineering educator*
Isensee, Scott Harlan *computer scientist*
Jones, William Richard *open systems product support representative*
Lam, Simon Shin-Sing *computer science educator*
Lorentz, George *mathematics educator*
McDilda, Wayne Allen *systems programmer*
Mills, Andy Ray *computer programmer*
Misra, Jayadev *computer science educator*
Moyers, Robert Charles *systems analyst, state official, microcomputer consultant*
Rentz, Tamara Holmes *software consultant*
Russinoff, David Michael *computer scientist*
Sadun, Lorenzo Adlai *mathematician*
Sturdevant, Wayne Alan *computer scientist, instructor*
Taber, Patrick E. *computer programmer*
Turney, James Edward *computer scientist*
Williamson, Hugh Jackson *statistician*
Young, William David *computer scientist*

Belton
Bumpus, Floyd David, Jr. *microcomputer analyst*

Carrollton
Dossin, Steven Charles *statistician, consultant, educator*

College Station
Hicks, David Lane *computer systems analyst*
Massoud, Samia Lamie *mathematics educator, computer systems analyst*
Vinzé, Ajay S. *information systems educator*

Dallas
Barr, Richard Stuart *computer science and engineering management science educator*
Collichio, Steven *software engineer*
Conger, Sue Ann *computer information systems educator*
Gensheimer, Elizabeth Lucille *software specialist*
Hecht, Karl Eugene *bank software company specialist*
Ho, Min-Chung *computer scientist*
Hough, Donald Lee *computer consultant*
Lockley, Jeanette Elaine *mathematics educator, statistics educator*
Matelan, Mathew Nicholas *software engineer*
Sepulvado, Joseph Michael *computer information scientist*
Thompson, Craig Warren *computer scientist, researcher*
Touma, Walid Rachid *computer consultant*
Welsh, Leonard Woodrow, Jr. *computer programmer*

De Soto
Ball, Millicent Joan (Penny Ball) *multimedia developer*

Denton
Das, Sajal Kumar *computer science educator, researcher*

El Paso
Gianelli, Victor F. *mathematics and physics educator*
Quevedo, Hector Adolf *operations research analyst, environmental scientist*

Fort Worth
Ponder, Blair Arlan *computer programmer*

Garland
Harris, Samuella Rosalyn *mathematics educator*

Grand Prairie
Chapura, John Robert *computer scientist*

Grapevine
Gibbons, Michael Lawrence *software engineer*

Houston
Auchmuty, Giles *applied mathematics educator*
Austin, Joe Dan *mathematics educator, researcher*
Brown, Sharon Elizabeth *software engineer*
Davis, Barry Robert *biostatistician, physician*
Fenn, Sandra Ann *programmer, analyst*
Fisher, Glenn Edward *computing specialist, researcher, retired*
Gamble, Wesley *information technology consultant*
Goodson, Carole Edith McKissock *mathematics technology educator*
Hoang, Hung Manh *information systems analyst, consultant*
Hodgess, Erin Marie *statistics educator*
Huang, Jung-chang *computer science educator*
Johnson, Gordon Gustav *mathematician, educator*
Kimmel, Marek *biomathematician, educator*
Leiss, Ernst Ludwig *computer science educator*
Moore, Fay Linda *software quality engineer*
Sauerzopf, Michael Alfred *software development consultant*
Tolle, Donald MacDavid *computer scientist*
Vardi, Moshe Ya'akov *computer science researcher*
Vijayaraghavan, Vasu *systems consultant*
Ward, Jo Alice *computer consultant, educator*
Wendelin, Marian *computer systems analyst*
Willis, Jerry Weldon *computer systems educator, writer*
Woo, Walter *computer systems consultant*
Wright, Clark Phillips *computer systems specialist*

Huntsville
Middaugh, Richard *information systems analyst, researcher*

Irving
Anastasi, Richard Joseph *computer software consultant*
Anderson, Michael Curtis *computer industry analyst*
Savage, Richard Mark *systems analyst*

Killeen
LaGrone, John Martin *computer scientist, educator*

Kingsville
Morey, Philip Stockton, Jr. *mathematics educator*

Kingwood
Burghduff, John Brian *mathematics educator*
Clevenson, Aaron Ben *artificial intelligence consultant*

Lancaster
Seay, Charles Frank, III *educator, systems analyst*

Laredo
Mendiola, Anna Maria G. *mathematics educator*

Lewisville
Ferguson, R. Neil *computer systems consultant*

Longview
Anderson, Larry Arnold *mathematician, educator*

Lubbock
Hennessey, Audrey Kathleen *computer researcher, educator*
Li, Hua Harry *computer scientist*
Milnes, Harold Willis *mathematician, physicist*
Pratt, Robert Wayne *computer maintenance executive*

Mc Kinney
Hanson, David Alan *software engineer*

Mcallen
Cox, George Sherwood *computer science educator*

Mesquite
Shultz, Ronald Eugene *computer specialist*

Plano
Conrad, Philip Jefferson *software development engineer*
Hinton, Norman Wayne *information services executive*
Yii, Hung Siong *computer engineer*

Richardson
Aranas, Noel Bautista *systems analyst, consultant*
Marple, Mary Lynn *software engineer, environmental scientist*
McCord, Tim James *telecommunications software engineer*
Wiorkowski, John James *mathematics educator*

San Antonio
Bennett, Gerard Paul *computer scientist*
Blaylock, Neil Wingfield, Jr. *applied statistics educator*
Estep, Myrna Lynne *systems analyst, philosophy educator*
Hall, Douglas Lee *computer science educator*
Tucker, Roy Nelson *mathematics educator, minister*
Yochmowitz, Michael George *biostatistician, computer educator, consutltant*
Zhang, Xiaodong *computer science educator and researcher*

Snyder
Anderson, Elsie Miners *mathematics educator*

Tyler
Edmonds, Graydon Preston *mathematics educator*
Kulkarni, Arun Digambar *computer science educator*

Venus
Mathison, James Anthony (Tony Mathison) *mathematics educator*

Waco
Trower, Jonathan K. *management information systems educator*

VIRGINIA

Alexandria
Awtry, Thomas Harold *mathematician*
Engler, Brian David *systems operations executive*
Perchik, Benjamin Ivan *operations research analyst*

Annandale
Santi, Ellyn E. *mathematics educator*

Arlington
Brown, Ronald Ellsworth, Sr. *software engineer, consultant*
Edwards, Don Raymond *computer programmer*
Huffman, Patricia Elizabeth *software engineer*
Tomlinson, Ian *software engineer*

Blacksburg
Hinkelmann, Klaus Heinrich *statistician, educator*
Olin, Robert Floyd *mathematics educator and reseacher*

Chantilly
Eldreth, John Paul *systems analyst*

Charlottesville
English, James William *software engineer*
Pang, Maybeline Miusze (Chan) *software and systems engineer, analyst*

Clifton
Hoffman, Karla Leigh *mathematician*

Fairfax
Croog, Roslyn Deborah *computer systems analyst*
Hungate, Joseph Irvin, III *computer scientist*
Mulvaney, Mary Frederica *systems analyst*
Pullen, J(ohn) Mark *computer science and engineering educator*
Sage, Andrew Patrick, Jr. *systems information and software engineering educator*
Santore, Carrie-Beth *computer management professional*
Sapery, David L. *systems analyst*
Tucker, Dewey Duane *systems analyst*
Wnek, Janusz *artificial intelligence research scientist*

Falls Church
Flory, Robert Mikesell *computer systems analyst, personnel management specialist*
Zaboski, Michael Edward *operations research analyst*

Fort Belvoir
Juul, Larry Christian *strategic planner*
Raymond, George Edward, Jr. (Chip Raymond) *operations research analyst*

Fort Lee
Johnson, Harry Watkins *defense analyst*

Fredericksburg
Violette, Peter Raymond *logistician*

Hampton
Keyes, David Elliot *scientific computing educator, researcher*

Herndon
Gullace, Marlene Frances *systems analyst, programmer, consultant*
Hermansen, John Christian *computational linguist*
Rathore, Bajrang Singh *software engineer, consultant*
Stewart, William Bartley *software developer*
Wade, Suzanne *computer software company consultant*

Lexington
Tierney, Michael John *mathematics and computer science educator*

Lynchburg
Moorman, Steve Thomas *systems analyst*

Manassas
Smith, Todd Lawrence *computer scientist*

Mc Lean
Garner, David Paul *defense analyst*
Houston, Kelli Anne *software engineering specialist*
Ketchum, Harry Wilbur, Jr. *software engineer*
Schneck, Paul Bennett *computer scientist*
Seykowski, Rosemary Teresa *operations research, management scientist*

Melfa
Fluharty, Jerry Kenneth, Jr. *mathematics educator*

Newport News
Bradie, Brian David *mathematics educator*

Norfolk
Saur, Joseph Michael *software engineer*

Radford
Carter, Edith Houston *statistician, educator*

Reston
Maslov, Vadim (Yuryevich) *computer scientist*
Zislis, Paul Martin *software engineering executive*

Richmond
Crisci, Steven *computer programmer*
Goyal, Amita *information systems educator, consultant*
Hamlett, Robert Barksdale *systems engineer*

Stafford
Davis, Ralph Paul *software developer*

Sterling
Bergeman, George William *mathematics educator, software author*

Sweet Briar
Wassell, Stephen Robert *mathematics educator, researcher*

Vienna
de Planque, Emile, III *computer consultant*
Garvin, Patrick Patillo *internet systems architect, computer security*
Nauta, Frans *operations research analyst*
O'Brien, William James *software engineer*

Virginia Beach
Cheng, Richard Tien-ren *computer scientist, educator*

Williamsburg
Zaki, Ahmed Soliman *information scientist educator*

Yorktown
Risden, Nancy Dika *mathematics educator*

WEST VIRGINIA

Charleston
Smith, Robert Keith *information technology analyst*

Elkins
Reed, Elizabeth May Millard *mathematics and computer science educator, publisher*

Morgantown
Kankanahalli, Srinivas *computer scientist, educator*

Shenandoah Junction
Sorensen, Jill Ann *computer scientist*

Shepherdstown
Hendricks, Ida Elizabeth *mathematics educator*

ADDRESS UNPUBLISHED

Ballengee, Bruce Van *software developing company executive*
Baum, Susan Diane *mathematics educator*
Bockman, Linda Ann *computer design analyst*
Carroll, John Millar *computer science and psychology educator*
Caudill, Samuel Patton *statistician*
Covin, Carol Louise *computer consultant*
Everhart, Kenneth Albert, III *information services administrator*
Ezell, Margaret Prather *information systems executive*
Gammon, Jack Albert *computer scientist*
Gotsopoulos, Barbara Lynn *computer consultant*
Guillott, Barbara Faye *computer science and mathematics educator*
Horton, Wilfred Henry *mathematics educator*
House, Stephen Eugene *information systems consultant*
Jodoin, Jeffrey Charles *software engineer*
Johnson, Deborah Crosland Wright *mathematics educator*
Kelley, Mary Elizabeth (LaGrone) *computer specialist*
Kellogg, Michael Stubbs *computer specialist*
Kent, Jack Thurston *retired mathematics educator*
Knight, Thomas Jefferson, Jr. *computer consultant, trainer*
Lamm, Harriet A. *mathematics educator*
Larson, Janice Talley *computer science educator*
Low, Emmet Francis, Jr. *mathematics educator*
Mahoney, Linda Kay *mathematics educator*
Malone, David Clay *computer specialist, retired police officer*
McCormick, Roscoe *mathematician, educator, career officer, retired*
McKinnon, Kathleen Ann *software engineer*
McLauglin, Robert Bruce *software designer*
Messier, William Paul *computer science educator, software developer*
Moores, Anita Jean Young *computer consultant*
Ogando, Roger Marlon *software engineer*
Patterson, Patricia Lynn *applied mathematician, geophysicist, inventor*
Pattison, Jon Allen *computer scientist, consultant*
Pendleton, Richard F. *logistics systems analyst*
Piegorsch, Walter William *statistics educator, statistician*
Porter, Hayden Samuel *computer science educator*
Reese, Edward James, Jr. *computer scientist*
Roberts, Marie Dyer *computer systems specialist*
Rollins, Grey James *computer operator, author*
Rouhani, Behnaz *mathematics educator*
Seidman, Stephen Benjamin *computer science educator*
Somes, Grant William *statistician, biomedical researcher*
Stabler, Mason Wesley *mathematics educator*
Urban, Gary Ross *computer and information processing consultant*
Warren, Lloyd Van *software engineer, conceptual designer*
Willis, Russell Earl *consultant*
Yaung, Alan Tsu-I *computer scientist*

SCIENCE: PHYSICAL SCIENCE

UNITED STATES

ALABAMA

Auburn
Bozack, Michael James *physicist*
King, David Thompson, Jr. *geology educator*
McKee, Michael Leland *computational chemist*
Paxton, Ralph *biochemist*
Vodyanoy, Vitaly Jacob *biophysicist, educator*

Birmingham
Cheung, Herbert Chiu-ching *biophysicist, educator*
Elgavish, Gabriel Andreas *physical biochemistry educator*
Krishna, N(epalli) Rama *biochemist*
Meng, Qing Cheng *chemistry educator*
Shealy, Y. Fulmer *biochemist*

Decatur
Kuehnert, Harold Adolph *retired petroleum geologist*

Huntsville
Cuntz, Manfred Adolf *astrophysicist, researcher*
Gillani, Noor Velshi *atmospheric scientist, researcher, educator*
Jaenisch, Holger Marcel *physicist*
McCaul, Eugene Williamson, Jr. *meteorologist*
McCollough, Michael Leon *astronomer*
Montgomery, Willard Wayne *physicist*
Musielak, Zdzislaw Edward *physicist, educator*
Nuotio-Antar, Vappu Sinikka *physicist*
Perkins, James Francis *physicist*
Roberts, Thomas George *retired physicist*
Smith, Robert Earl *space scientist*
Stewart, Dorathy Anne *retired meteorologist*
Witherow, William Kenneth *physicist*

Mobile
Moore, Robert Blaine *biochemistry and cell biology educator, researcher*
Perry, Nelson Allen *radiation physicist, radiological consultant*

Montgomery
Lieberman, Robert *radio chemist*
Tan, Boen Hie *biochemist*
Zachry, Amy Poarch *environmental scientist*

Normal
Caulfield, Henry John *physics educator*

Redstone Arsenal
Miller, Walter Edward *physical scientist, researcher*

Selma
Collins, Eugene Boyd *chemist, molecular pathologist, consultant*

Sheffield
Sheridan, Richard Collins *chemist, educator, historian*

Tuscaloosa
Byrd, Gene Gilbert *astronomer, educator*
LaMoreaux, Philip Elmer *geologist, hydrogeologist, consultant*
Rindsberg, Andrew Kinney *geologist, educator*
Visscher, Pieter Bernard *physicist, educator*

ARKANSAS

Fayetteville
Benoit, Paul Harland *geologist*
Lacy, Claud H. Sandberg *astronomer*

Little Rock
Wold, Donald Clarence *physicist*

Marianna
Carroll, Stephen Douglas *chemist, research specialist*

Pine Bluff
Walker, Richard Brian *chemistry educator*

State University
Reeve, Scott Wayne *chemical physics educator*

CALIFORNIA

West Covina
Gong, Jeh-Tween *physicist, philosopher*

COLORADO

Denver
Quinn, John Michael *physicist, geophysicist*

DISTRICT OF COLUMBIA

Washington
Friedman, Herbert *physicist*
Mao, Ho-kwang *geophysicist, educator*
Wallace, Jane House *geologist*

FLORIDA

Bell
Evans, James Giles *former chemistry and computer educator*

Boca Raton
Kerr, Russell Greig *chemistry educator*
Párkányi, Cyril *chemistry educator*
Ross, Fred Michael *organic chemist*

Clearwater
Roberson, Ronald William *industrial hygienist*

Cocoa
Hutton, Michael Thomas *planetarium and observatory administrator*

Dania
Burney, Curtis Michael *oceanographer, educator*

Daytona Beach
Ekpo, Efremfon Frank *physicist, educator*

Deland
Liberman, Michael *metallurgist, researcher*

Delray Beach
Drimmer, Bernard E. *research physicist*
March, Jacqueline Front *retired chemist*
Shang, Charles Yulin *medical physicist*

Fort Pierce
Parsons, Robert William, Jr. *forensic chemist, consultant*

Gainesville
Adair, James Hansell *materials science and engineering educator*
Ernsberger, Fred Martin *retired materials scientist*
Green, Alex Edward Samuel *physicist, mechanical engineering educator*
Harrison, Willard W. *chemist, educator*
Hope, George Marion *vision scientist*
Katritzky, Alan Roy *chemistry educator, consultant*
Klauder, John Rider *physics educator*
Mao, Jintong *physicist*
Merdinger, Emanuel *retired chemistry educator*
Pop, Emil *research chemist*
Randazzo, Anthony Frank *geology educator*
Sikivie, Pierre *physics educator*
Simon, Charles G. *chemist*
Sullivan, Neil Samuel *physicist, researcher, educator*
Szczepanski, Jan *chemistry and physics educator, researcher*
Trickey, Samuel Baldwin *physics educator, researcher*
Vala, Martin Thorvald *chemistry educator, researcher*
Yost, Richard Alan *chemistry educator*
Zerner, Michael Charles *chemistry and physics educator, consultant, researcher*

Hialeah
Stewart, Burch Byron *chemist, physicist*

Hollywood
Robins, William Lewis *medical physicist*

Jacksonville
Enns, John Benjamin *polymer scientist*
Nguyen, Duy Thai *research scientist*

Jupiter
Jacobson, Jerry Irving *biophysicist, theoretical physicist*
McGinnes, Paul R. *environmental chemist*

Longboat Key
Brown, Henry *chemist*

Longwood
Koppenhoefer, Robert Mack *chemist*

Marco Island
Hyde, James Franklin *chemist, consultant*

Melbourne
Nelson, Gordon Leigh *chemist, educator*
von Ohain, Hans Joachim P. *aerospace scientist*

Miami
Carter, James Harrison *chemist, research director*
Dammann, William Paul *oceanographer*
Millero, Frank Joseph, Jr. *marine and physical chemistry educator*
Mooers, Christopher Northrup Kennard *physical oceanographer, educator*
Precht, William Frederick *environmental specialist*
Rotenberg, Don Harris *chemist*

Mount Dora
Foote, Nathan Maxted *retired physical science educator*

Naples
Long, James Alvin *exploration geophysicist*
Stewart, Harris Bates, Jr. *oceanographer*

North Palm Beach
Bonifazi, Stephen *chemist*

Orlando
Barlow, Nadine Gail *planetary geoscientist*
Head, Clarence McMahon *environmental scientist*
Ting, Robert Yen-ying *physicist*
Weishampel, John Frederick *environmental scientist*

Ormond Beach
Cyr, Ellie R. *retired geologist, educator*

Palm Bay
Young, Daniel David *laser physicist, researcher*

Palm Harbor
Santilli, Ruggero M. *physicist*

Panama City
Rackers, Thomas William *physicist*

Saint Augustine
Li, Chung-Li Jason *scientist*

Saint Petersburg
Rester, Alfred Carl, Jr. *physicist*
Rydstrom, Carlton Lionel *chemist, paint and coating consultant*
Tolley, Stephen Gregory *oceanographer*

Sarasota
Liu, Suyi *biophysicist*
Wysnewski, Roy Edward *physicist*

Tallahassee
Ablordeppey, Seth Y. *medicinal chemistry educator*
Berg, Bernd Albert *physics educator*
DeHan, Rodney Samuel *environmental scientist, researcher*
Elsner, James Brian *meteorologist, educator*
Linder, Bruno *chemist, educator*
Saltiel, Jack *chemistry educator*
Schmidt, Walter *geologist*
Schrieffer, John Robert *physics educator, science administrator*
Winchester, John Widmer *oceanography educator*
Winters, Stephen Samuel *geology educator*

Tampa
Binford, Jesse Stone, Jr. *chemistry educator*
Johnson, Anthony O'Leary (Andy Johnson) *meteorologist, consultant*
Maybury, P(aul) Calvin *chemistry educator*
Russell, Daniel N. *physicist*
Zhou, Huanchun *chemist, administrator*

Titusville
McCord, Scott Anthony *chemistry educator*
Yount, James Robert *physical and biological sciences educator*

Winter Park
Ihndris, Raymond Will *chemist*

GEORGIA

Albany
McManus, James William *chemist, researcher*

Athens
DerVartanian, Daniel Vartan *biochemistry educator*
Dudley, Gary Alton *exercise science educator*
Railsback, Loren Bruce *geologist*
Yamaguchi, Yukio *chemistry research scientist*

Atlanta
Abraham, John Edward *environmental health scientist*
Bosah, Francis N. *molecular biochemist, educator*
Gist, Ginger Lee *environmental scientist*
Gokhale, Arun Mahadeo *materials science and engineering educator*
Harmer, Don Stutler *physics and nuclear engineering educator*
Hentschel, Hilary George *physicist, educator*
Hicks, Heraline Elaine *environmental health scientist, educator*
Iacobucci, Guillermo Arturo *chemist*
Kaufman, Myron Jay *chemistry educator*
Lin, Ming-Chang *physical chemistry educator, researcher*
Melhuish, Kirk Thomas *meteorologist, journalist*
Mueller, Patricia Westbrook *research chemist*
Smith, David Carr *organic chemist*
Stafford, Patrick Morgan *biophysicist*
Strekowski, Lucjan *chemistry educator*
Wiita, Paul Joseph *astrophysicist*

Augusta
Banick, Cyril Joseph *chemist*
Graboff, Paul *chemist, consultant*
Leibach, Frederick Hartmut *biochemist, educator*
Stone, John Austin *nuclear chemist*
Swamy-Mruthinti, Satyanarayana *biochemist, molecular biologist*

Cumming
Shaffer, Peter Thomas Barnum *consultant*

Dahlonega
Prior, Richard Marion *physics educator*

Decatur
Sadun, Alberto Carlo *astrophysicist, physics educator*

Duluth
Gregg, Lawrence Terrell *geologist*

Marietta
Gerhardt, Rosario Alejandrina *materials scientist*

Savannah
Ananthanarayanan, Venkataraman *physics educator*
Froelicher, Franz *chemist, geologist, environmental consultant*
Loganathan, Bommanna Gounder *environmental chemist, biologist, researcher, educator*
Simonaitis, Richard Ambrose *chemist*

Statesboro
Boxer, Robert Jacob *chemist, educator, science writer*

Tucker
Lundin, Ann Frances *chemist, medical technologist*

Warner Robins
Lavdas, Leonidas G. *meteorologist, religion educator*

ILLINOIS

Hinsdale
Kaminsky, Manfred Stephan *physicist*

INDIANA

Mount Vernon
Sastri, Vinod Ram *polymer chemist, educator*

KENTUCKY

Ashland
Rigsby, Lee Scott *chemist, consultant*
Wombles, Robert Huston *chemist, petroleum company executive*

Carrollton
Tatera, James Frank *chemist, process analysis specialist*

Danville
Muzyka, Jennifer Louise *chemist, educator*

Lexington
Chen, Linda Li-Yueh Huang *nutritional biochemistry educator, program director*
Drahovzal, James Alan *geologist*
Hamilton-Kemp, Thomas Rogers *organic chemist, educator*
Lodder, Robert Andrew *chemistry and pharmaceutics educator*
Ng, Kwok-Wai *physics educator*
Weil, Jesse Leo *physicist, educator*

Louisville
Peterson, Mark Lee *research chemist*

Mount Vernon
Fritsch, Albert Joseph *director environmental demonstration center*

Murray
Volp, Robert Francis *chemistry educator*

Richmond
Kepferle, Roy Clark *geology educator, consultant*

Sturgis
Thornsberry, Willis Lee, Jr. *chemist*

LOUISIANA

Alexandria
Rogers, James Edwin *geology and hydrology consultant*

Baton Rouge
Bouma, Arnold Heiko *geology educator, consultant*
Hamilton, William Oliver *physics educator, researcher*
Landolt, Arlo Udell *astronomer, educator*
Lorenzo, Juan Manuel *geophysics educator*
Omoike, Isaac Irabor *chemist, publisher, author*
Stockbauer, Roger Lewis *physicist, educator*
Strongin, Robert Michael *organic chemist*
Suleiman, Ahmad Abdul-Fattah *chemistry educator*
Sygula, Andrzej *chemist, researcher*
West, Philip William *chemistry educator*

Kenner
deMonsabert, Winston Russel *chemist*

Lafayette
Moncrief, James E. *petroleum geologist*

Metairie
Hartman, James Austin *retired geologist*
Horkowitz, Sylvester Peter *chemist*

New Orleans
Andrews, Bethlehem Kottes *research chemist*
O'Neal, Edwin A. *geologist, geophysicist, petroleum engineer*
Radhakrisnamurthy, Bhandaru *biochemistry educator*
Seab, Charles Gregory *astrophysicist*
Stowell, John Charles *chemistry educator*
Sumrell, Gene *research chemist*

Shreveport
Goorley, John Theodore *consulting chemist*
Grimes, Sidney Ray, Jr. *research biochemist*

Slidell
Breeding, J. Ernest, Jr. *physicist, travel consultant, photographer*

MARYLAND

College Park
Zen, E-an *research geologist*

Hanover
Nieporent, Richard Joel *physicist, consultant, educator*

Silver Spring
White, Herbert Laverne *meterologist, federal agency administrator*

MINNESOTA

Lakeville
Phinney, William Charles *retired geologist*

MISSISSIPPI

Bay Saint Louis
Durham, Donald Lee *oceanographer*
Frazier, Claude Clinton, III *dermatologist, chemistry consultant*
Zeile, Fred Carl *oceanographer, meteorologist*

Carriere
Megehee, Louis Dan *meteorologist*

Hattiesburg
Bedenbaugh, Angela Lea Owen *chemistry educator, researcher*
Dunn, Dean Alan *oceanographer, geologist, educator*

Jackson
Leszczynski, Jerzy Ryszard *chemistry educator, researcher*

Picayune
Lowrie, Allen *geologist, oceanographer*

Stennis Space Center
Hurlburt, Harley Ernest *oceanographer*
Lewando, Alfred Gerard, Jr. *oceanographer*
Sprague, Vance Glover, Jr. *oceanography executive, naval reserve officer*

Tougaloo
McGinnis, Richard Provis *chemical educator*

University
Panetta, Charles Anthony *chemistry educator*

MISSOURI

Saint Louis
Gokel, George William *organic chemist, educator*
Profeta, Salvatore, Jr. *chemist*

NORTH CAROLINA

Asheville
Deitch, D. Gregory *meteorologist*
Haggard, William Henry *meteorologist*

Black Mountain
Lathrop, Gertrude Adams *chemist, consultant*

Cary
Maroney, John Edward *environmental scientist*

Chapel Hill
Crimmins, Michael Thomas *chemistry educator*
Johnson, Charles Sidney, Jr. *chemistry educator*
Jorgenson, James Wallace *chromatographer, educator*
Merzbacher, Eugen *physicist, educator*
Neumann, Andrew Conrad *geological oceanography educator*
Superfine, Richard *physicist*
Wolfenden, Richard Vance *biochemistry educator*
Xu, Le *biophysicist, physicist*

Charlotte
Hurley, Jeffrey Scott *research chemist*
Monroe, Frederick Leroy *chemist*
Mueller, Werner Heinrich *organic chemist, technology administrator*
Spitzer, Jan Josef *chemist*
Walker, Stanley Maurice *nuclear physicist*

Davidson
Cain, Laurence Sutherland *physics educator, researcher*
Schuh, Merlyn Duane *chemist, educator*

Durham
Brine, Dolores Randolph *chemist*
Jaszczak, Ronald Jack *physicist, researcher, consultant*
Kelce, William Reed *biochemist, toxicologist*
Kim, Chong Soong *aerosol technology and environmental health researcher, engineer*
Kohn, Michael Charles *theoretical biochemistry professional*
Opara, Emmanuel Chukwuemeka *biochemistry educator*
Pirrung, Michael Craig *chemistry educator, consultant*
Schlesinger, William H. *biochemist, educator*
Shaw, Robert Wilson *chemist*
Smith, Peter *chemist, educator, consultant*
Yang, Weitao *chemistry educator*

Elizabeth City
Choudhury, Abdul Latif *physics educator*

Fayetteville
Higgins, Robert Hall *chemistry educator*

Gastonia
Wedinger, Robert Scott *research chemist, business manager*

Greensboro
Banegas, Estevan Brown *environmental biotechnology executive*

Kitty Hawk
Majewski, Theodore Eugene *chemist*

Laurinburg
Dotson, Allen Clark *physics and mathematics educator*

Linwood
Barnes, Melver Raymond *retired chemist*

Morrisville
Goehl, Thomas Joseph *chemist*

New Hill
Weber, Michael Howard *senior nuclear control operator*

Raleigh
Arya, Satya Pal *meteorology educator*
Comins, Daniel Lee *chemistry educator, consultant*
Droessler, Earl George *geophysicist educator*
Ebisuzaki, Yukiko *chemistry educator*
Leidy, Ross Bennett *research scientist, educator*
Owens, Tyler Benjamin *chemist*
Risley, John Stetler *physics scientist, educator*
Sykes, Alston Leroy *analytical chemist, musician*
Won, Ihn-Jae *geophysicist*

Research Triangle Park
Chao, James Lee *chemist*
Rodbell, Martin *biochemist*
Wani, Mansukhlal Chhaganlal *chemist*

Rockingham
Aiken, Walter Jeff, III *chemical company executive*

Spring Hope
Lavatelli, Leo Silvio *retired physicist, educator*

Thomasville
Gray, Bowman *chemist*

Wendell
Price, Howard Charles *chemist*

Wilmington
Bissette, Samuel Delk *astronomer, artist, financial executive*
Humphreys, Charles Raymond, Jr. *retired research chemist*

Winston Salem
Dobbins, James Talmage, Jr. *analytical chemist, researcher*
Sorci-Thomas, Mary Gay *biomedical researcher, educator*
Townsend, Alan Jerome *biochemistry educator, pharmacology researcher*

OHIO

Dayton
Won, Deanna Cerise *physicist*

OKLAHOMA

Bartlesville
Dwiggins, Claudius William, Jr. *chemist*

Edmond
Troutman, George William *geologist, geological consulting firm executive*

Fort Towson
Pike, Thomas Harrison *plant chemist*

Lawton
Nalley, Elizabeth Ann *chemistry educator*

Norman
Brown, Rodger Alan *meteorologist, researcher*
Eilts, Michael Dean *research meteorologist, manager*
Maddox, Robert Alan *atmospheric scientist*
Pigott, John Dowling *geologist, geophysicist, geochemist, educator, consultant*
Richman, Michael B. *meteorologist*
Roberts, Raymond Url *geologist*

Oklahoma City
Aclin, Keith Andrew *radar meteorologist*
Alaupovic, Petar *biochemist, educator*
Broyles, Robert Herman *biochemistry and molecular biology educator*
Collins, Gary Allen *environmental specialist*
England, Gary Alan *television meteorologist*
Jackson, Gaines Bradford *environmental science educator*
May, John Andrew *petrophysicist, geologist*
Smith, Paul Winston *petroleum geologist*
Thompson, Richard Arlen *environmental scientist*
Weigel, Paul Henry *biochemistry educator, researcher, consultant*
Wright, Bill J. *geologist*

Stillwater
Eisenbraun, Edmund Julius *chemist educator*
Focht, William Jarrell *geology educator*
Spivey, Howard Olin *biochemistry and physical chemistry educator*
Tong, Penger *physicist*

Tulsa
Anderson, David Walter *physics educator, consultant*
Bennison, Allan Parnell *geological consultant*
Vogt, C. O. *geophysical research company executive*
Wagner, Fred John, Jr. *petroleum geologist*

SOUTH CAROLINA

Aiken
Inhaber, Herbert *physicist*
Miller, Phillip Edward *environmental scientist*

Anderson
Apinis, John *chemist*
Molz, Fred John, III *hydrologist, educator*

Awendaw
Nelson, George Humphry *biochemist, physician, researcher*

Charleston
Berlinghieri, Joel Carl *physicist, educator, consultant*
Fenn, Jimmy O'Neil *physicist*
Mabrouk, Suzanne Theresa *chemistry educator*
McAfee, Lyle Vernon *chemistry educator*

Clemson
Krause, Lois Ruth Breur *chemistry educator*

Columbia
Anandan, Jeeva Satchith *physics educator*
Cohen, Arthur David *geological and marine science educator*
Gandy, James Thomas *meteorologist*
Safko, John Loren *physics and astronomy educator*
Schuette, Oswald Francis *physics educator*
Shafer, John Milton *hydrologist, consultant, software developer*
Tour, James Mitchell *chemistry and biochemistry educator*

Conway
Skinner, Samuel Ballou, III *physics educator, researcher*

Hilton Head Island
Ballantine, Todd H. *environmental scientist*

TENNESSEE

Chattanooga
Howe, Lyman Harold, III *chemist*
Orofino, Thomas Allan *chemistry educator*

Clarksville
Bhatia, D.M.S. *geologist, educator*

Cookeville
Kumar, Krishna *physics educator*
Swartling, Daniel Joseph *chemistry educator, researcher*
Wells, John Calhoun *physics educator*

Jackson
Wade, Malcolm Smith *chemist, chemical engineer*

Jefferson City
Bahner, Carl Tabb *retired chemistry educator, researcher*

Kingsport
Fuzek, John Frank *chemical consultant*
Germinario, Louis Thomas *materials scientist*
Gose, William Christopher *chemist*
Sharma, Mahendra Kumar *chemist*

Knoxville
Alexandratos, Spiro Dionisios *chemistry educator*
Cook, Kelsey Donald *chemistry educator, consultant*
Hatcher, Robert Dean *research scientist, geology educator*
Renshaw, Amanda Frances *retired physicist, nuclear engineer*
Schweitzer, George Keene *chemistry educator*
Steinhauff, David Mark *geologist, environmental consultant*

Memphis
Cohen, Kenneth Allan *chemist*
Desiderio, Dominic Morse, Jr. *chemistry and neurochemistry educator*
Franceschetti, Donald R. *physicist, educator*
Jarrett, Harry Wellington, III *biochemistry educator*
Kress, Albert Otto, Jr. *polymer chemist*
Lasslo, Andrew *medicinal chemist, educator*
Lin, Jack Eyih *chemist*
Wescott, Lyle DuMond, Jr. *chemistry educator*
Zeman, Herbert David *medical physicist*

Morristown
Culvern, Julian Brewer *retired chemist, educator*

Nashville
Bartelt, John Eric *physics researcher and educator*
Cohen, Stanley *biochemistry educator*
Ernst, David John *physicist, educator*
Moses, Henry Archie *biochemistry educator*
Smith, Howard Edward *chemistry educator*

Oak Ridge
Baldocchi, Dennis David *micrometeorologist*
Bicehouse, Henry James *health physicist*
Carlsmith, Roger Snedden *chemistry and energy conservation researcher*
Cawley, Charles Nash *enviromental scientist*
Darden, Edgar Bascomb, Jr. *consultant, retired biophysicist*
Dickens, Justin Kirk *nuclear physicist*
Grimes, James Gordon *geologist*
Hingerty, Brian Edward *biophysicist, researcher*
Hunt, Rodney Dale *chemist, researcher*
Larson, Bennett Charles *solid state physicist, researcher*
Marshall, William Leitch *chemist*
Pinnaduwage, Lal Ariyaritna *physicist, educator*
Postma, Herman *physicist, consultant*
Read, Kenneth Francis, Jr. *physics educator, researcher*
Stabin, Michael Gregory *health physicist*
Stoller, Roger Earl *materials scientist, researcher*
Trivelpiece, Alvin William *physicist, corporate executive*
Vo-Dinh, Tuan *physical chemist, researcher*
Watson, Evelyn Egner *radiation scientist*
Whealton, John H. *physicist, educator*
Wong, Cheuk-Yin *physicist*
Yalcintas, M. Güven *medical physicist*

Tullahoma
Dahotre, Narendra Bapurao *materials scientist, researcher, educator*

TEXAS

Abilene
Pickens, Jimmy Burton *earth and life science educator, military officer*

Alpine
Whitford-Stark, James Leslie *geologist, educator*

Amarillo
Chisum, Matthew Eual *senior project scientist*

Arlington
Damuth, John Erwin *marine geologist*
Ellwood, Brooks Beresford *geophysicist, educator*

Austin
Bard, Allen Joseph *chemist, educator*
Clark, Roy Thomas, Jr. *chemistry educator, administrator*
Cranberg, Lawrence *physicist, consultant*
Curran, Dian Beard *physicist, consultant*

Gilbert, John Carl *chemistry educator*
Hilburn, John Charles *geologist, geophysicist*
Hill, David Wayne *geologist*
Kimmel, Troy Max, Jr. *meteorologist*
Krishna, J. Hari *hydrologist, engineer*
Nguyen, Truc Chinh *analytical chemist*
Oakes, Melvin Ervin Louis *physics educator*
Posey, Daniel Earl *analytical chemist*
Schwitters, Roy Frederick *physicist, educator*
Sharp, John Malcolm, Jr. *geology educator*

Beaumont
Westgate, James William *geologist*

Brownsville
Tijerina, Raul Martin *physics and mathematics educator*

Canyon
Cepeda, Joseph Cherubini *geology educator*

Carrollton
Ali, Odeh Said *petroleum geologist*
Wang, Peter Zhenming *physicist*

College Station
Allen, Roland Emery *physicist*
Anderson, Duwayne Marlo *earth and polar scientist, university administrator*
Berg, Robert Raymond *geologist, educator*
Cotton, Frank Albert *chemist, educator*
Duff, Michael James *physicist*
Fitzpatrick, Paul Frederick *biochemist*
Gangi, Anthony Frank *geophysics educator*
Goodman, David Wayne *research chemist*
Gunn, John Martyn *biochemistry educator*
Hall, Michael Bishop *chemistry educator*
Horvat, Vladimir *physicist, research scientist*
Jaric, Marko Vukobrat *physicist, educator, researcher*
King, Lauriston Rackliffe *science research administrator, marine educator*
Martell, Arthur Earl *chemistry educator*
McIntyre, John Armin *physics educator*
Meyer, Edgar F. *crystallographer*
Mouchaty, Georges *accelerator physicist*
Nachman, Ronald James *research chemist*
Pandey, Raghvendra Kumar *physicist, educator*
Rumpho-Kennedy, Mary Ellen *plant biochemistry educator*
Stewart, Robert Henry *oceanographer, educator*
Stipanovic, Robert Douglas *chemist, researcher*

Corpus Christi
Gordon, Ian Robert *geophysicist, geologist*

Crosby
Griffin, John Joseph, Jr. *chemist, video producer*

Dallas
Benge, Raymond Doyle, Jr. *astronomy educator*
Fisher, Charles William *biochemist*
Gibbs, James Alanson *geologist*
Hosmane, Narayan Sadashiv *chemistry educator*
Kokkinakis, Demetrius Michael *biochemist, researcher*
Marshall, John Harris, Jr. *geologist, oil company executive*
Ray, Bradley Stephen *petroleum geologist*
Ries, Edward Richard *petroleum geologist, consultant*
Robertson, Herbert Chapman, Jr. *geoscience consulting company executive*
Sharp, William Wheeler *geologist*
Wheeler, Edward Norwood *chemical consultant*

Deer Park
VanArsdale, William Eugene *chemist, researcher*

Denton
Freeman, Bruce L., Jr. *physicist, researcher*

Edinburg
Newton, Clarence Jonathan *physicist*

El Paso
Wang, Paul Weily *materials science and physics educator*

Fort Worth
Barker, Heather Ann *earth and environmental scientist*
Caldwell, Billy Ray *geologist*
Conrow, Raymond Eugene *organic chemist*
Hlavay, Jay Alan *geologist, analyst*
Koger, David Gordon *satellite image analyst, photogeology consultant*
Lang, John Calvin *physical chemist*
Wilson, Ronald James *geologist*

Freeport
Mercer, William Edward, II *chemical research technician*
Metzger, Marie Cruz *chemist*

Galveston
LaGrone, Lavenia Whiddon *chemist, real estate broker*
Liu, Danxia *neurochemistry educator, biophysicist*
Mc Adoo, David John *neurochemist*
Mills, Gordon Candee *biochemist educator*
Schoenbucher, Bruce *health physicist*

Houston
Ahmad, Salahuddin *nuclear scientist*
Black, David Charles *astrophysicist*
Brandt, I. Marvin *chemist, engineer*
Brotzen, Franz Richard *materials science educator*
Cameron, William Duncan *plastics company executive*
Cantwell, Thomas *geophysicist, electrical engineer*
Davids, Robert Norman *petroleum exploration geologist*
De Bremaecker, Jean-Claude *geophysics educator*
Downs, Hartley H., III *chemist*
Goloby, George William, Jr. *environmental scientist, ornithologist, aviculturist*
Herke, Robert, Sr. *chemist, researcher*
Hubig, Stephan Maria *chemistry educator*
Hussain, Moinuddin Syed *geologist, reservoir engineer, consultant*
Jones, Thomas Allen *geologist, researcher*
Kalmaz, Errol Ekrem *environmental scientist*
Kasi, Leela Peshkar *pharmaceutical chemist*
Kiefer, Walter Scott *geophysicist, educator*
Kochi, Jay Kazuo *chemist, educator*
Ledley, Tamara Shapiro *earth system scientist, climatologist*
Leon, Bruce Frederick *environmental scientist*
Liao, Warren Shau-Ling *biochemistry and molecular biology educator*
Lopez, Jorge Luis *physicist, educator*
Mack, Mark Philip *chemical company executive*
Mateker, Emil Joseph, Jr. *geophysicist*
Mathew, Joy *biochemist, educator*
Meindl, Max J., III *environmental consultant, professional inspector*
Middleditch, Brian Stanley *biochemistry educator*
Miller, John Harris, Jr. *physics educator*
Moss, Simon Charles *physics educator*
Reso, Anthony *geologist, earth resources economist*
Ronzio, Robert Anthony *biochemist, educator*
Semple, Thomas Carl *physical-organic chemist*
Soileau, Kerry Michael *aerospace technologist, researcher*
Tatham, Robert Haines *geophysicist*
Trocki, Linda Katherine *geoscientist, natural resource economist*
Tung, Shih-Ming Samuel *medical physicist*
Weisman, R(obert) Bruce *physical chemist, educator*
Wilson, Thomas Leon *physicist*
Winzeler, Ted J. *geologist*
Worstell, Jonathan Harlan *process chemist, research engineer*
Yang, Chao Yuh *chemistry educator*
Zlatkis, Albert *chemistry educator*

Irving
Holdar, Robert Martin *chemist*

Kingsville
Loden, Ronald Lynn *physicist*

Klein
Frnka, Jerome Victor *chemistry educator*

Lubbock
Bartsch, Richard Allen *chemist, educator*
Chatterjee, Sankar *geology educator*
Headley, Allan Dave *chemistry educator*
Laing, Malcolm Brian *geologist, consultant*
Marx, John Norbert *chemistry educator*

Marathon
Kurie, Andrew Edmunds *mining geologist*

Midland
Shaw, Stephen Lynn *geoscientist*

New Braunfels
Wilson, James Lee *retired geology educator, consultant*

Pasadena
Kolodziej, Eric William *chemist*
Root, M. Belinda *chemist*

Plano
Moore, Christopher Robertson Kinley *petroleum geologist*

Richardson
Parr, Christopher Alan *chemistry educator, university dean*
Stern, Robert James *geologist, educator*
Urquhart, Sally Ann *environmental scientist, chemist*

Rockport
Jones, Lawrence Ryman *retired research chemist*
Mulle, George Ernest *petroleum geologist*

San Antonio
Bhandari, Basant *biochemist, molecular biologist, chemical engineer, food technologist, chemist*
Duncan-Simon, Jo Dee *chemist, research and development specialist*
Greenberg, Marvin Keith *chemist*
Jones, James Ogden *geologist, educator*
Krakower, Terri Jan *biochemist, researcher*
Lyle, Robert Edward *chemist*
Markwell, Dick R(obert) *retired chemist*
Masters, Bettie Sue Siler *biochemist, educator*
Rodgers, Robert Aubrey *physicist*
Sablik, Martin John *research physicist*
Tsin, Andrew Tsang Cheung *biochemistry educator*

Seguin
Scheie, Paul Olaf *physics educator*

Sugar Land
Mata, Zoila *chemist*

Temple
Coulter, John Breitling, III *biochemist, educator*
Gaa, Peter Charles *organic chemist, researcher*

Texas City
Fuchs, Owen George *chemist*

The Woodlands
Mulvey, Dennis Michael *chemist*
Westmoreland, Thomas Delbert, Jr. *chemist*

Tyler
Black, Shaun Dennis *biochemist, educator, software developer*
Rao, Vijay Mohan *biochemist*
Walsh, Kenneth Albert *chemist*

Vernon
Roberson, Mark Allen *physicist, educator*

Wichita Falls
Gilbert, Jerry Lon *petroleum geologist*

VIRGINIA

Abingdon
Taylor, Alfred Raleigh *geologist*

Alexandria
Baker, George Harold, III *physicist*
Shapiro, Maurice Mandel *astrophysicist*
Zook, Theresa Fuetterer *gemologist, consultant*

Annandale
Matuszko, Anthony Joseph *research chemist, administrator*
Said, Rushdi *geologist*

Arlington
Addison, Randolph *biochemistry educator*
Cruger, Thomas Wayne *chemistry educator*
Erb, Karl Albert *physicist, government official*
Lawrence, Ray Vance *chemist*
Mooney, John Bradford, Jr. *oceanographer, engineer, consultant*
Rosner, Anthony Leopold *chemist, biochemist*
van der Vink, Gregory Evans *geologist, educator*
Wayland, Russell Gibson, Jr. *retired geology consultant, government official*

Bedford
Lew, Edwin Wayne *chemist*

Blacksburg
Hudlicky, Milos *former chemistry educator*

Charlottesville
Dukes, Edmond Craig *physicist, educator*
Garstang, Michael *atmospheric sciences educator, consultant*
Kellermann, Kenneth Irwin *astronomer*
Marshall, James Arthur *chemistry educator*
Sundberg, Richard Jay *chemistry educator*

Crewe
Hardin, James Oran *retired biochemist*

Dahlgren
Cronce, Donald Thomas *research chemist*
Knowles, Stephen Howard *space scientist*

Falls Church
Berg, Lillian Douglas *retired chemistry educator*
Spindel, William *chemist, consultant*

Fredericksburg
Burns, Grover Preston *retired physicist*

Gainesville
Steger, Edward Herman *chemist*

Galax
Sense, Karl August *physicist, educator*

Hampden Sydney
Kniffen, Donald Avery *astrophysicist, educator, researcher*
Sipe, Herbert James, Jr. *chemistry educator*

Hampton
Deepak, Adarsh *meteorologist, aerospace engineer, atmospheric scientist*
Egalon, Claudio Oliveira *physicist, researcher*
Wang, Liang-guo *research scientist*

Lexington
Goller, Edwin John *chemsitry educator*
Spencer, Edgar Winston *geology educator*

Lynchburg
Morgan, Evan *chemist*

Manassas
Button, James David, II *physics educator*

Mc Lean
Waesche, R(ichard) H(enley) Woodward *combustion research scientist*
Watt, William Stewart *physical chemist*

Norfolk
Vušković, Leposava *physicist, educator*

Petersburg
Stronach, Carey Elliott *physicist, educator*

Reston
Cohen, Philip *retired hydrogeologist*
Eaton, Gordon Pryor *geologist, research director*

Richmond
Gowdy, Robert Henry *physics educator, researcher*
Lilly, Arnys Clifton, Jr. *physicist*
Myers, Clifford Alexander *chemist*
Suleymanian, Mirik *biophysicist*
Tiedemann, Albert William, Jr. *chemist*

Vienna
Zehl, Otis George *optical physicist*

Warm Springs
Orem, Henry Philip *retired chemist, chemical engineer, consultant*

Williamsburg
Muller, Julius Frederick *chemist, business administrator*

WEST VIRGINIA

Buckhannon
Withey, Paul Andrew *physics educator*

Charleston
Bryant, George Macon *chemist*
Meschke, Debra JoAnn *polymer chemist*

Institute
Garber, Eric A.E. *chemistry educator, researcher*

Logan
Galya, Thomas Andrew *geologist*

Morgantown
Das, Kamalendu *chemist*
Douglass, Kenneth Harmon *physicist*
McDowell, Ronald Russell *geologist*
Wallace, William Edward *research physicist*
Wells, John Gaulden *technology education educator*

New Martinsville
Carter, Russell Paul, Jr. *chemist*

South Charleston
Harrison, Arnold Myron *chemist*

TERRITORIES OF THE UNITED STATES

PUERTO RICO

San Juan
Pabon-Perez, Heidi *physicist*

ADDRESS UNPUBLISHED

Albrecht, Urs Emanuel *biochemist*
Alexander, Steven Albert *physics researcher*
Almond, Joan *retired chemist*
Barnes, Norman Patrick *laser scientist*
Boyes, Stephen Richard *hydrogeologic consultant*
Brown, Barbara S. *environmental scientist*
Buis, Patricia Frances *geology educator, researcher*
Deisenhofer, Johann *biochemistry educator, researcher*
Hassan, Sayed Mohammed *analytical chemist*
Jiang, Bai-Chuan *optical educator*
Jung, Hilda Ziifle *physicist*
Kendall, David Nelson *chemist*
Kirsch, Thomas Gerhard Werner *biochemist*
Kisvarsanyi, Eva Bognar *retired geologist*
Kravitz, Rubin *chemist*
Lee, Terrence Allan *analytical chemist, chemistry educator, researcher*
Lurix, Paul Leslie, Jr. *chemist*
Miller, W. Schuyler *chemistry*
Moody, Evelyn Wilie *consulting geologist, educator, artist*
Parreira, Helio Correa *physical chemist*
Reagan, Theodore John *geologist, exploration consultant, oil and gas mineral investment evaluator*
Reynolds, Don William *geologist*
Richardson, Jasper Edgar *nuclear physicist*
Rideout, Janet Litster *chemist*
Ridgway, Helen Jane *chemist, consultant*
Robinson, Bruce Butler *physicist*
Salzer, Louis William *chemist*
Shahied, Ishak I. *biochemistry educator*
Stevenson, Paul Michael *physics educator, researcher*
Synek, M. *physics consultant, researcher*
Teal, Edwin Earl *retired engineering physicist, consultant*
Temple, Carroll Glenn, Jr. *medicinal chemist*
Weinberg, Steven *physics educator*
Weller, Richard Irwin *physics educator*
Wells, Robert Hartley *chemistry professional*
Wilson, Leonard Richard *geologist, consultant*
Yang, Weiming *physicist, researcher*

SOCIAL SCIENCE

UNITED STATES

ALABAMA

Arab
Hall, Atlee Burpee *researcher*

Auburn
Dunkelberger, John Edward *sociology educator*
Johnson, Paul Marshall *political science educator, consultant*
Laband, David Neil *economics educator*
Thompson, Henry Lelon, Jr. *economist, educator*
Thornton, Mark Christopher *economist*
Whitten, David Owen *economics educator*

Birmingham
Drewry, Lyman Aubrey *economics educator*
Garrett, John Charles *economist*
Lee, Seung-Dong Leigh *economics and statistics educator*
McCarl, Henry N. *economics and geology educator*
Morrisey, Michael A. *health economics educator*
Nicassio, Anthony Robert *economist, lecturer, consultant*
Ohsfeldt, Robert Lee *health economist, educator*
Powell, Lane Holland *family sociology educator*
Sloan, John Joseph, III *sociology educator*
Yoels, William Charles *sociology educator*

Collinsville
Beasley, Mary Catherine *home economics educator, administrator, researcher*

Florence
Butler, Michael Ward *economics educator*

Huntsville
Kestle, Wendell Russell *cost and economic analyst, consultant*

Livingston
Griffith, Mark F. *political science educator*

Mobile
Kressley, Konrad Martin *political science educator*

Montgomery
Jehle, Kathryn Elizabeth *criminal justice educator, lawyer*
Nathan, James A. *political science educator*
Sollars, David Lindsey *economics educator*

Tuscaloosa
Hollingsworth, J. Selwyn *sociology educator*
Oneal, John Robert *political science educator*
Oths, Kathryn Sue *anthropology educator*

ARIZONA

Tucson
Rogers, John Alvin *retired technical educator, writer, publisher*

ARKANSAS

Arkadelphia
Bass, Harold Franklin, Jr. *political science educator*

Batesville
Lankford, George Emerson, III *social sciences educator*

Conway
Hamblin, Daniel Morgan *economist*
Kordsmeier, William Frank *economics educator*

Fayetteville
Ahrendsen, Bruce Louis *economist, educator*
Cramer, Gail Latimer *economist*
Savage, Robert L. *political science educator*

Little Rock
Ledbetter, Cal R. *political scientist, educator*
Metzger, James Edward *economics consultant, educator*

Pine Bluff
Tai, Chong-Soo Stephen *political scientist, educator*

Russellville
Rogers, Kenneth Allan *social sciences educator*

DISTRICT OF COLUMBIA

Washington
Kerns, Wilmer Lee *social science researcher*
Lee, Daniel Kuhn *economist*
Lindsey, Lawrence Benjamin *economist, federal official*
Rozell, Mark James *political scientist, educator*
Zhao, John Quansheng *political science educator*

FLORIDA

Alva
Maxwell, Steven Robert *social studies educator*

Boca Raton
Hartwig, Robert Paul *economist*
McNulty, James Ergler *finance educator*

Bonita Springs
McDonald, Jacquelyn Milligan *parent and family studies educator*

Boynton Beach
Mittel, John J. *economist, corporate executive*

Coral Gables
De Alessi, Louis *economist, educator*

Fernandina Beach
Wilson, Albert John Endsley, III *social gerontologist, administrator*

Fort Lauderdale
Bartelstone, Rona Sue *gerontologist*
Oliver, Eloise Dolores (Kitty) *ethnic diversity consultant, writer*
Sayeed, Khalid Bin *political scientist, educator*

Fort Myers
Wahlberg, Katherine Eleanor *anthropologist*

Gainesville
Austin, Roger Quarles, III *political consultant, lawyer*
Conway, Mary Margaret *political science educator*
Crumbley, Deidre Helen *anthropology educator*
Du Toit, Brian Murray *anthropology educator*
Golant, Stephen Myles *geographer, gerontologist, educator*
Harris, Marvin *anthropology educator*
Kenny, Lawrence Wagner *economist*
Langham, Max Raymond *economist, educator*
Smith, Karen Cole *sociologist, educator*
Strain, James Robert *agricultural economist*
Streib, Gordon Franklin *sociology educator*
Taylor, Timothy Gordon *economics educator*
von Mering, Otto Oswald *anthropology educator*

Hollywood
Foreman, Edwin Francis *economist, real estate broker*

Jacksonville
Brady, James Joseph *economics educator*
Ejimofor, Cornelius Ogu *political scientist, educator*
Lockett, Cornelius Randolph, Jr. *social science educator*
Seroka, James Henry *social sciences educator, university administrator*

Kissimmee
Williams, Clynn Worthington *social studies educator*

Lakeland
Johnson, Marson Harry *criminologist*

Macdill AFB
Schwendinger, Charles Joseph *public administration educator, researcher*

Miami
Callaghan, Karen Ann *sociology educator*
Duchatelet, Martine *economics educator*
Stinchcomb, James Delwin *criminologist, training consultant, educator, administrator*

Naples
Halvorson, William Arthur *economic research consultant*

Palm Harbor
Evans, William Robert, III (Butch Evans) *anthropologist*

Pensacola
Killian, Lewis Martin *sociology educator*
Long, H. Owen *retired economics educator, fiction writer*

Pompano Beach
Gilchrist, William Risque, Jr. *economist*

Saint Petersburg
Austin, Robert James *archaeologist*
Serrie, Hendrick *anthropology and international business educator*

Sarasota
Almy, Marion Marable *archaeologist*
Andrews, Anthony Parshall *anthropology educator, archaeologist*
Furbay, Walter M. *economist*
Greenwald, Douglas *economist*
Pierce, Rhonda Yvette *criminologist*
Stevens, Dana Nelson *economist*

Tallahassee
Cockrell, Wilburn Allen *archaeologist*
Kleck, Gary David *criminologist, educator*
Parker, Glenn Richard *political science educator*
Thompson, Gregory Lee *social sciences educator*
Williams, James Howard *sociologist, research agency executive*
Wisenbaker, James Michael *archaeologist, writer*

Tampa
Aruffo, Henry Anthony *geographer, educator*
Dembo, Richard *criminology educator*
James, Arthur Pettus *economist, educator*
Kushner, Gilbert *anthropology educator*
Mellish, Gordon Hartley *economist, educator*
Piper, John Richard *political science educator*
Stone, John Vincent *applied anthropologist, researcher*
Thomas, Carole Dolores *gerontologist*
Wienker, Curtis Wakefield *physical anthropologist, educator*

GEORGIA

Albany
Kooti, John G. *economist, educator*

Athens
Allsbrook, Ogden Olmstead, Jr. *economics educator*
Atkinson, Scott Estes *economics educator*
Dunn, Delmer Delano *political science educator*
Knapp, Charles Boynton *economist, educator, academic administrator*
Morris, Kenneth Earl *sociology educator, writer*
Timberlake, Richard Henry, Jr. *retired economics educator*
Turner, Steven Cornell *agricultural economics educator*

Atlanta
Curran, Christopher *economics educator*
Endicott, John Edgar *international relations educator*
Ferriss, Abbott Lamoyne *sociology educator emeritus*
Fox, Mary Frank *sociology educator and researcher*
Freedman, Jonathan Andrew *clinical sociologist*
Kennedy, Robert *international affairs educator*
Knippenberg, Joseph Michael *political science educator*
Levy, Daniel *economics educator*
McCrackin, Bobbie Humenny *economist*
Orme, John David *political science educator*
Richardson, William Donald *political science educator, consultant*
Rubin, Paul Harold *economist*
Thomas, John Clayton *public administration educator, academic official*
Wald, Michael Leonard *economist*
Watson, William Downing, Jr. *economist, educator*

Augusta
Chukwuma, Godwin Nwabisi *sociology educator*
Leightner, Jonathan Edward *economist, educator*
Scarboro, Allen *sociologist, educator*

Carrollton
Clark, Janet Eileen *political scientist, educator*
Sanders, Robert Mark *political science educator*

Duluth
Scoular, Marion Ethel *embroidery educator*

Kennesaw
Fein, Melvyn Leonard *sociologist, educator*

Lilburn
Neumann, Thomas William *archaeologist*

Marietta
Murray, Barry Wayne *economics educator*

Milledgeville
Bouley, Eugene Edward, Jr. *criminal justice and sociology educator*
Moffitt, Derrick L. *political science educator*

Oxford
Cody, William Bermond *political science educator*

Rome
Spruce, Kenneth Lawrence *political scientist, educator*

Statesboro
Young, Alfred *social sciences educator*

Valdosta
Higgs, Elizabeth Wayne *anthropology educator*

ILLINOIS

Champaign
Brandis, Royall *economist, educator*

KENTUCKY

Danville
Weston, William Joseph (Beau Weston) *sociologist, educator*

Highland Heights
Trundle, Robert Christner, Jr. *social sciences educator*

Lexington
Alam, Mohammed Badrul *history and political science educator*
Hochstrasser, Donald Lee *cultural anthropologist, community health and public administration educator*
Jennings, Edward Theodore, Jr. *public administration educator*
Schmitt, Frederick Adrian *gerontologist, neuropsychologist*
Stempel, John Dallas *international studies educator*

Louisville
DiBlasi, Philip James *archaeologist*
Izyumov, Alexei *political economy educator*
Jones, W. Landis *political science educator*
Krukones, Michael George *political science educator*
Segal, Edwin S. *anthropology educator*
Tewksbury, Richard Allan *sociologist, educator*

Prestonsburg
Mc Aninch, Robert Danford *philosophy and government affairs educator*

Richmond
Minor, Kevin Isaac *criminology educator*

LOUISIANA

Baton Rouge
Archambeault, William George *criminologist, educator, researcher*
Gasiorowski, Mark Joseph *political scientist, educator*
Kamo, Yoshinori *sociology educator, writer*
Mathewson, Kent, II *geography educator*

Hammond
Hsing, Yu *economics educator*

Lake Charles
Sirgo, Henry Barbier *political science educator*

Monroe
Kogut, Carl Andrew *economics educator*
Weirick, William Newton *economics educator, university administrator*

New Orleans
Balée, William L. *anthropology educator*
Bricker, Harvey Miller *anthropology educator*
Efesoa-Mokosso, Henry (Teddy) *social sciences educator*
Hadley, Charles David, Jr. *political science educator, researcher*
Lee, Silas, III *sociologist, public opinion research consultant*
Maveety, Nancy Lois *political science educator*
Miller, Edward McCarthy *economics educator*
Robins, Robert Sidwar *political science educator, administrator*
Shull, Steven A. *political science educator, researcher, author*
Theobald, Robert *futurist, writer, consultant*

MISSISSIPPI

Biloxi
Cox, Albert Harrington, Jr. *economist*

Hattiesburg
Davis, Charles Raymond *political scientist, educator*
Wheat, Edward McKinley *political science educator, researcher*

Itta Bena
Ero, Morgan Zan *political scientist, educator*

Jackson
Chao, Ching Yuan *economics educator*

Mississippi State
Meyer-Arendt, Klaus John *geography educator*
Wall, Diane Eve *political science educator*

Starkville
Loftin, Marion Theo *sociologist, educator*

University
Bomba, Anne Killingsworth *family relations and child development educator*
Womer, Norman Keith *economist, educator*

MISSOURI

Marshall
De Graw, Darrel Garvin *criminal justice educator*

NEW MEXICO

Edgewood
Stewart, Joseph, Jr. *political science educator, researcher*

Las Cruces
Reese, Catherine Caroline *political scientist, educator*

Santa Fe
Petersen, Eric Charles *archaeologist*

NORTH CAROLINA

Asheville
Dickens, Charles Henderson *retired social scientist, consultant*

Cary
Gunter, Linda Faith *social studies educator, state senator*

Chapel Hill
Blau, Judith Rae *sociology educator, researcher*
Butler, David Ray *geography educator*
Giddens, Lynn Neal *adoption educator*
Larsen, Clark Spencer *anthropology educator*
Lunde, Anders Steen *demographer*
Meade, Melinda Sue *geographer, educator*
Nonini, Donald Macon *anthropologist, educator*
Pfouts, Ralph William *economist, consultant*

Charlotte
Pyle, Gerald Fredric *medical geographer, educator*
Webster, Murray Alexander, Jr. *sociologist*

Cullowhee
Jarrell, Stephen Brooks *economics educator*

Davidson
Ratliff, Charles Edward, Jr. *economics educator*

Dillsboro
Lefler, Lisa Jane *anthropologist and social sciences educator*

Durham
Budd, Isabelle Amelia *research economist*
Gold, Deborah T. *gerontology and sociology educator*
Land, Kenneth Carl *sociology educator, demographer, statistician, consultant*
O'Barr, Jean Fox *political science and women's studies educator*
Salinger, Marion Casting *international studies educator, poet, consultant*
Simons, Elwyn LaVerne *physical anthropologist, primatologist, paleontologist, educator*
Tiryakian, Edward Ashod *sociology educator*

Elon College
Lilly, Gregory Alan *economics educator, researcher*

Fayetteville
Johnson, Lillian Beatrice *sociologist, educator, counselor*

Greensboro
Carroll, William Alexander *political scientist, educator*
Ruhm, Christopher John *economics educator*

Greenville
Scavo, Carmine Peter Francis *political science educator*
Tollinger, Melissa Lee *geographer*

High Point
McCully, Michael John *economics educator*

Hillsborough
Goodwin, Craufurd David *economics educator*

Raleigh
Daley, Dennis Michael *political science educator*
Fearn, Robert Morcom *economics and business educator, consultant*
Gibran, Daniel Kahlil *international relations educator, researcher*
Girgis, Maurice A. *economist, consultant*
Hayes, Charles Austin *economist, consultant*
Johnson, Thomas *economics educator*
Pasour, Ernest Caleb, Jr. *economics educator*
Wimberley, Ronald C. *sociology educator, researcher*

Salisbury
Tseng, Howard Shih Chang *business and economics educator, investment company executive*

Stony Point
Miller, Mildred Jenkins *local historian, genealogist*

Wilmington
Landy, David *anthropologist, educator*

Winston Salem
Pubantz, Jerry James *political science educator*
Whaples, Robert MacDonald *economic history educator*

OKLAHOMA

Altus
Newman, Bruce Allan *political science educator*

Edmond
Smock, Donald Joe *governmental liaison, political consultant*

Norman
Bilas, Richard A. *economist*
Dauffenbach, Robert C. *economic and management administrator, educator*
Frankland, Erich Gene *political science educator, researcher*

Holloway, Harry Albert *political science educator*

Oklahoma City
Craig, George Dennis *economics educator, consultant*

Stillwater
Johnson, Margaret Anne *sociologist*
Poole, Richard William *economics educator*
Wikle, Thomas Adams *geography educator, researcher*

Tulsa
Dugger, William Mayfield *economics educator*
Nixon, James Gregory *economic development consultant*
Loziglia, Carla Miller *forensic scientist*
Odell, George Hamley *archaeology educator*

PENNSYLVANIA

Pittsburgh
Larsen, Elizabeth Anne *sociologist*

SOUTH CAROLINA

Beaufort
McCaslin, F. Catherine *consulting sociologist*

Charleston
Davis, Edward Braxton, III *political science educator*
Simmons, Susan Annette *production management and statistics educator*

Clemson
Curry, Linda Jean *social studies educator*

Columbia
Kegley, Charles William, Jr. *political science educator, author*
Marshall, Donald Bruce *political science educator*
Martin, Robert William *econometrician*
Thomas, Ralph Upton *economic developer*

Georgetown
Hopkins, Linda Ann *school psychologist*

Greenville
Fraser, Cleveland Robert *political science educator*
Guth, James Lee *political science educator*
McNamara, Robert Paul *sociology educator*

Newberry
Fritz, Kathlyn Ann *sociology educator*

Pendleton
Gosnell, Candace Shealy *industrial sociologist, educator*

TENNESSEE

Chattanooga
Clark, Jeff Ray *economist*
Efaw, Fritz *economics educator*
Rabin, Alan Abraham *economics educator*
Wilson, Richard Lee *political science educator*

Church Hill
Taylor, Teresa Brooks *sociologist, educator*

Clinton
Scarbrough-Luther, Patsy Wurth *geographic information systems specialist*

Cookeville
Haynes, Ada Faye *sociology educator*
Williams, Steven Dale *political science educator*

Knoxville
Bowlby, Roger Louis *economist, educator, researcher*
Davidson, Paul *political economics educator, consultant*
Neale, Walter Castle *retired economics educator*
Schuman, Bernard Thomas *political science educator*
Smith, Lisa White *sociologist*
Stephens, Otis Hammond, Jr. *political science educator*
Welborn, David Morris *political science educator*

Memphis
Daniel, Coldwell, III *economist, educator*
Kamery, Rob Herlong *economics educator, management consultant*
Kamrava, Mehran *political scientist, educator*
McNutt, Charles Harrison *archaeologist, educator*

Murfreesboro
Carroll, Carole Makeig *sociology educator, researcher*
Van Dervort, Thomas Raymond *political science educator*
Vile, John Ralph *political science educator*

Nashville
Blasi, Anthony Joseph *sociology educator, writer*
Broad, David Benjamin *sociologist*
Jamison, Connie Joyce *sociology educator*
Jensen, Gary Franklin *sociology educator*
Klein, Christopher Carnahan *economist*
Russell, Clifford Springer *economics and public policy educator*
Shadden, Marie Christine *criminal justice research professional*
Smith, Dani Allred *sociologist, educator*

Oak Ridge
Colston, Freddie Charles *political science educator*

Watauga
Davison, E. Holly O. *home economics educator*

TEXAS

Abilene
Wallace, Robert W. *sociologist, educator*

Arlington
Waller, David Vincent *sociology educator*

Austin
Arnold, J(ames) Barto, III *marine archaeologist*
Craft, James Pressley, Jr. *retired political science educator, financial consultant*
Davis-Floyd, Robbie Elizabeth *anthropologist, educator*
Kumbhakar, Subal Chandra *economics educator*
Lintz, Christopher Ray *archaeologist*
Lopreato, Joseph *sociology educator, author*
Nwachie, Judy Flakes *government educator, consultant*
Phelps, Gerry Charlotte *economist, minister*
Pingree, Dianne *sociologist, educator, mediator*
Smith, Todd Malcolm *political consultant*
Thore, Sten Anders *economics and aerospace engineering educator*
Tolo, Kenneth William *public affairs educator, university administrator*
Tulis, Jeffrey Kent *political scientist*
Wilson, Robert Hines *urban policy educator*

Bryan
Branson, Robert Earl *marketing economist*

Canyon
Duman, Barry Lance *economics educator*

College Station
Bass, George Fletcher *archaeology educator*
Bond, Jon Roy *political science educator*
Burk, James Steven *sociologist, trust company officer*
Edwards, George Charles, III *political science educator, writer*
Hall, Billy Ray, Jr. *political scientist*
Johnson, Charles Andrew *political scientist, educator*
Portis, Edward Bryan *political science educator*
Saving, Thomas Robert *economics educator, consultant*
Tian, Guoqiang *economics educator*
Wachsmann, Shelley A.Z. *archaeology educator*

Dallas
Betts, Dianne Connally *economist, educator*
Brettell, Caroline B. *anthropology educator*
Duca, John Vincent *economist, researcher*
Free, Mary Moore *anthropologist*
Kemper, Robert Van *anthropologist, educator*
Maasoumi, Esfandiar *economics educator*
Murphy, John Carter *economics educator*

Denison
Mullins, Don Elroy *economics educator*

Denton
Belfiglio, Valentine John *political science educator, pharmacist*
Koelln, Kenneth *economics educator*
Nieswiadomy, Michael Louis *economics educator*
Sadri, Mohmoud *sociology educator*

El Paso
Blevins, Leon Wilford *political science educator, minister*
Fullerton, Thomas Mankin, Jr. *economist*

Fort Worth
Baldon, Suzanne Brown *anthropologist*
Becker, Charles McVey *economics and finance educator*
Fleshman, Linda Eilene Scalf *private investigator, writer, columnist, consultant, communications and marketing executive*
Newman, Jay Richard *archaeologist*

Frisco
Lewis, Ted Adam *political science educator*

Georgetown
Camp, Thomas Harley *economist*

Houston
Ahmed, Syed Z. *anthropologist*
Cloninger, Dale Owen *finance and economics educator*
Condit, Linda Faulkner *economist*
Davenport, Christian *political scientist, educator*
Davidson, Chandler *sociologist, educator*
Ewoh, Andrew Ikeh Emmanuel *political science educator*
Faubion, James Daniel *anthropologist, educator*
Foster, Dale Warren *political scientist, educator, management consultant, real estate*
Franklin, Mark Newman *political science educator*
Islam, Anisul Mohammed *economist*
Kohlhase, Janet Ellen *economics educator*
Mills, Bobby Eugene *sociologist, educator*
Mote, Victor Lee *political science educator*
Pelaez, Rolando Federico *economics educator, consultant*
Rosenau, Pauline Vaillancourt (Pauline Marie Vaillancourt-Rosenau) *public health educator*
Sharp, John Erbin *criminal justice educator*
Strassmann, Diana Louise *economist*
Tesarek, William Paul *business consultant, writer, financial executive*
Wlezien, Christopher Brian *political science educator*

Huntsville
Harris, Mary B. *home economics educator*

Irving
Thomas, Cynthia Gail *public policy research executive*

Kingsville
Hartwig, Richard Eric *political science educator*

Lubbock
Havens, Murray Clark *political scientist, educator*

Olney
Timmons, Gordon David *economics educator*

Prairie View
Server, Ronald Douglas *criminologist, political scientist, lawyer, educator*

Richardson
Andrews, Melinda Wilson *human development researcher*
Vijverberg, Wim Petrus Maria *economics educator*

San Antonio
Firestone, Juanita Marlies *sociology educator*
Halbardier, Sheryl Linette *social studies educator, counselor*
Hazuda, Helen Pauline *sociologist, educator*
Martin, Harry W. *sociologist, educator*
Quinn-Musgrove, Sandra Lavern *political science educator*
Vivekananda, Franklin Chinna *economics educator*
Wagener, James Wilbur *social science educator*
Whittington, Floyd Leon *economist, business consultant, retired oil company executive, foreign service officer*
Zhou, Su *economics educator, researcher*

San Marcos
Balanoff, Howard Richard *social sciences educator*
Boehm, Richard Glennon *geography and planning educator, writer*

Texas City
Ginsberg, Alan Harvey *social sciences educator*

Tomball
Kral, Nancy Bolin *political science educator*

Tyler
Dolan, Timothy Emmett *political scientist, educator*
Ramirez, Enrique Rene *social sciences educator*

Waco
April, John James *sociology educator, clergyman*
Gardner, Harold Stephen *economics educator, researcher*
Maki-Wallace, Susan *anthropology educator*
Sharp, Ronald Arvell *sociology educator*

VIRGINIA

Alexandria
Cymrot, Donald Jay *economist, researcher*
Kollander, Mel *social scientist, statistician*
Lee, Armistead Mason *economics consultant*
Quester, Aline Olson *research director, economist*
Victor, James Stuart, III *political consultant*

Annandale
Wood, John Thurston *cartographer, jazz musician*
Wunderlich, Gene Lee *economist*

Arlington
Brana-Shute, Gary *anthropology educator, educational director*
Sayers, Chera Lee *economics educator*

Berryville
Kobetz, Richard William *criminologist, consultant*

Blacksburg
Hult, Karen Marie *political science educator*
Hyde, William Frederick *economics and forestry educator, researcher, consultant*
Luciak, Ilja Alexander *political science educator*
Mandelstamm, Allan Beryle *economics educator, consultant*
Morgan, George Emir, III *financial economics educator*
Walcott, Charles Eliot *political science educator*

Burke
Uwujaren, Gilbert Patrick *economist, consultant, realtor*

Centreville
Reinhard, Andrew *archaeologist*

Chantilly
Dowdy, Dorothy Williams *political science educator*

Charlotte Court House
Prophett, Andrew Lee *political science educator*

Charlottesville
Elzinga, Kenneth Gerald *economics educator*
Gottesman, Irving Isadore *psychology educator*
Lynch, Allen Charles *political science researcher*
O'Brien, William Joseph *political scientist*
Stern, Steven Neal *economics educator*
Wagner, Roy *anthropology educator, researcher*

Emory
Cumbo, Lawrence James, Jr. *economics and business educator, consultant*

Fairfax
Avruch, Kevin *anthropologist*
Buchanan, James McGill *economist, educator*
Kolker, Aliza *sociology educator*
Lipset, Seymour Martin *sociologist, political scientist, educator*
Rowley, Charles Kershaw *economics educator*
Thorbecke, Willem Hendrik *economics educator*
Williams, Thomas Rhys *anthropologist, educator*

Falls Church
Gable, Karen Lynn *social worker*
Green, James Wyche *sociologist, anthropologist, psychotherapist*
Shriner, Robert Dale *economist, management consultant*

Hampton
Jirran, Raymond Joseph *social studies educator*
Wright, Bobbie Jean *sociology educator*

Harrisonburg
Blake, Charles Henry, II *political science educator*
Rosser, John Barkley, Jr. *economics educator*

Herndon
Altalib, Omar Hisham *sociologist*
Spragens, William Clark *public policy educator, consultant*

Lynchburg
Abell, John Davis *economics educator*
Duff, Ernest Arthur *political scientist, educator*

Mc Lean
Nothaft, Frank Emile *economist*
Robock, Leonard Irving *foreign policy consultant*

Norfolk
Lopez, Thomas Samuel *sociology educator*
Rountree, Helen Clark *anthropology educator*
Yochum, Gilbert Ronald *economics educator*

Reston
Attanasi, Emil Donald *economist, municipal official*

Richmond
Baretski, Charles Allan *political scientist, librarian, educator, historian, municipal official*
Geary, David Patrick *criminal justice educator, consultant, author*
Heiss, Frederick William *political science educator, public administrator, policy researcher*
Parham, Iris Ann *gerontology educator*
Peterson, Steven P. *economics educator, consultant*

Springfield
Whitener, Lawrence Bruce *political consultant, consumer advocate, educator*

Staunton
Chester, Francis *political science educator, lawyer*

Suffolk
Tritten, James John *national security educator*

Sweet Briar
Perry, Barbara Ann *political science educator*

Vienna
Schneider, Peter Raymond *political scientist*

Williamsburg
Feldman, David Hall *economics educator*
Gilmour, John Brayton *political science educator*
McGlennon, John Joseph *political science educator*

WASHINGTON

Friday Harbor
Olson, Oscar Julius *international economist*

WEST VIRGINIA

Fairmont
Fulda, Michael *political science educator, space policy researcher*

Morgantown
Dilger, Robert Jay *political scientist*
Dougherty, Michael John *social sciences educator*
Labys, Walter Carl *economics educator*
Mooney, Christopher Zimmer *political science educator*

Saint Albans
Richards, John Dale *sociology and philosophy educator, counselor*

Salem
Frasure, Carl Maynard *political science educator*

ADDRESS UNPUBLISHED

Auchter, Edmund Louis *economist, consultant*
Beckman, James Wallace Bim *economist, marketing executive*
Beyle, Thad Lewis *political science educator*
Bredfeldt, John Creighton *economist, financial analyst, retired air force officer*
Cash, Carol Vivian *sociologist*
Christophersen, Dale Bjørn *political science educator*
Clark, Caleb Morgan *political scientist, educator*
Clites, Roger Myron *economics educator*
Dwyer, Gerald Paul, Jr. *economics educator, consultant*
Grow, Robert Theodore *economist, association executive*
Gyimah-Brempong, Kwabena *economics educator*
Hady, Thomas Frank *economist, retired government administrator*
Hage, George Campbell *social studies educator, minister, and counselor*
Hiler, Monica Jean *sociology and reading educator*
Howell, Benita Jankle *anthropologist*
Laughlin, Louis Gene *economic analyst, consultant*
Ludden, John Franklin *retired financial economist*
Miernyk, William Henry *economics educator*
Obligacion, Freddie Rabelas *sociology educator, researcher*
Ononye, Daniel Chuka *social scientist*
Patterson, Patrick O'Brian *criminology educator*
Price, Gregory N. *economist, educator*
Schultz, David Andrew *political science educator*
Siddayao, Corazón Morales *economist, educator, energy consultant*
Smith, Vme (Verna Mae Edom Smith) *sociology educator, freelance writer, photographer*
Solomon, Shirl G. *handwriting expert, researcher*
Sonstegaard, Miles Harry *economics educator*
Turk, David Scott *intelligence research specialist*
Udick, Robert Alan *political science and media educator*
Vedlik, Csaba Sandor, Jr. *political science educator*
Wright, James David *sociology educator, writer*
Zieburtz, William Blasie, Jr. *economist*